AHA Guide® to the Health Care Field

2025 Edition

AHA Item Number 010025
Telephone ORDERS 1–800–AHA–2626

ISBN: 55648–498–4
ISBN–13: 978-1-55648-514-5

Copyright © 1986–1996 American Hospital Association
Copyright © 1997–2025 Health Forum LLC, an affiliate of the American Hospital Association

All rights reserved. No portion of the AHA Guide may be duplicated or reproduced without prior written consent of Health Forum LLC.
Printed in the U.S.A.

Contents

Section

	v	Acknowledgements and Advisements
	vi	Introduction
	ix	AHA Offices, Officers, and Historical Data

A Hospitals Institutional and Associate Members

A1	Contents of Section A
2	AHA Guide Hospital Listing Requirements
3	Explanation of Hospital Listings
6	Annual Survey
15	Hospitals in the United States, by State
730	Hospitals in Areas Associated with the United States, by Area
737	U.S. Government Hospitals Outside the United States, by Area
738	Index of Hospitals
783	Index of Health Care Professionals
1015	AHA Membership Categories
1016	Other Institutional Members
1021	Associate Members

B Networks, Health Care Systems and Alliances

B1	Contents of Section B
2	Introduction
3	Statistics for Multihospital Health Care Systems and their Hospitals
4	Health Care Systems and their Hospitals
155	Headquarters of Health Care Systems, Geographically
164	Networks and their Hospitals
179	Alliances

© 2025 AHA Guide

Section

 Indexes   C1 Abbreviations Used in the AHA Guide
                        2 Index

Acknowledgements and Advisements

Acknowledgements

The AHA Guide® to the Health Care Field is published annually by Health Forum LLC, an affiliate of the American Hospital Association. Contributions are made by Information Systems and Technology, Field Engagement, Office of the President, Office of the Secretary, Printing Services Group, AHA Resource Center and the following participants:

Andy Chao
Dianna Doyle
DeAnn Ellis
Terrence Fields
Deanna Frazier
Evan Gagnon
Konstadena Giannakopoulos
Jennifer Gillespie
Veronica Houle
Clisby Jackson
Danny Jackson
Nicholas Kirwen
Mary Krzywicki
Ellen Nixon
Juan Reyes
Susan Sheffey
Elaine Singh

Health Forum LLC acknowledges the cooperation given by many professional groups and government agencies in the health care field, particularly the following: American College of Surgeons; American Medical Association; Council of Teaching Hospitals of the Association of American Medical Colleges; The Joint Commission; DNV Healthcare Inc.; Center for Improvement in Healthcare Quality; Commission on Accreditation of Rehabilitation Facilities; American Osteopathic Association, Centers for Medicare & Medicaid Services; and various offices within the U.S. Department of Health and Human Services.

Advisements

The data published here should be used with the following advisements: The data is based on replies to an annual survey that seeks a variety of information, not all of which is published in this book. Therefore, the data does not reflect an exhaustive list of all services offered by all hospitals. Additionally, Health Forum LLC supplements this publication with information from internal systems that are not self-reported by hospitals. For information on the availability of additional data visit www.ahadata.com.

Health Forum LLC does not assume responsibility for the accuracy of information voluntarily reported by the individual institutions surveyed.

The purpose of this publication is to provide basic data reflecting the delivery of health care in the United States and associated areas and is not to serve as an official and complete list of all services offered by individual hospitals. The information reflected is based on data collected as of September 27, 2024.

Introduction

An Introduction to AHA Guide

Welcome, and thank you for purchasing the 2025 edition of *AHA Guide®*. This section is designed to aid you in using the book. While the primary focus of *AHA Guide* is on hospitals, it also contains information on other areas of the health care field, divided across its two major sections:

- A. Hospitals
- B. Health care systems, networks, and alliances

The information contained within this publication was compiled using AHA membership, and the AHA Annual Survey of Hospitals. *AHA Guide* is the leading hospital directory and represents hospitals with or without AHA membership.

Additional information contained in the front of AHA Guide includes:

- A section by section table of contents
- Recognition of the source of data in the *Acknowledgements and Advisements* section
- Information on AHA's history as well as a listing of our awards in *AHA Offices, Officers, Historical Data, and Awards*

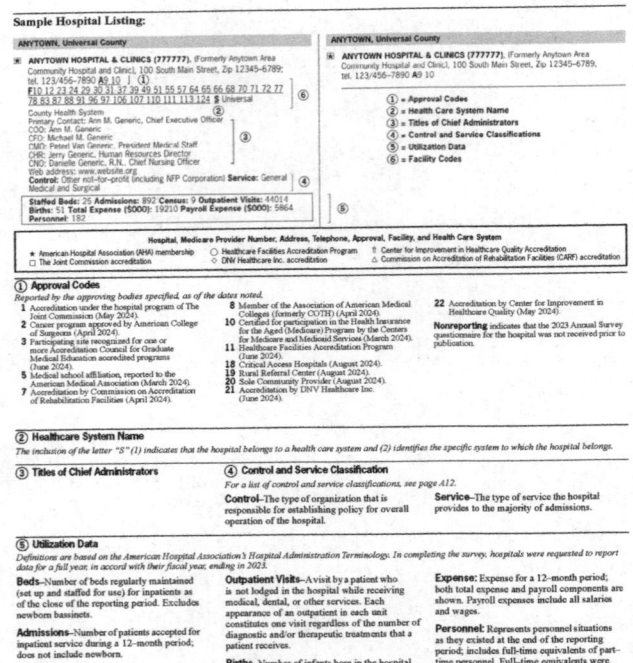

Open the front cover and *AHA Guide* begins with the *2025 AHA Guide Code Chart*. This two page section (front and back) explains how to find and understand the most important elements of each hospital's listing.

The *Code Chart* is a very useful tool to have when reading. It allows new users to become familiar with the data, and it aids returning users in understanding the new design and layout of *AHA Guide*. At the top of the chart, there is a sample listing. If you have used this publication before, you will notice the new columnar listing of all hospital entries by city. The city and county names are highlighted in gray, and all hospitals within the city follow. After the hospital name, you will find the address, telephone number, approval, facility and service codes, and health care systems to which the hospital belongs. Following this are the chief administrators and classifications for the hospital.

Utilization data for the hospital is found in the box at the bottom of each hospital's entry in *AHA Guide*.

The chart further demonstrates how to understand these important elements:

1. **Approval codes** refer to certifications held by a hospital; they represent information supplied by various national approving and reporting bodies. For example, code A–3 indicates accreditation under one of the programs of the Accreditation Council for Graduate Medical Education, evidence that the hospital has been approved for participation in residency training.

2. **Health Care System names** reference specific health care system headquarters to which the hospital belongs. The presence of a system name indicates that the hospital is a member. If no names are listed, the hospital does not belong to a system.

3. **Titles of Chief Administrators** including the Chief Executive Officer and, when available, other C-Suite officers such as the Chief Financial Officer, Chief Information Officer, Chief Medical Officer, Chief Operating Officer, Chief Human Resources Officer, and Chief Nursing Officer.

4. **Classification** refers to two items in *AHA Guide*. **Control** classification indicates the organization that operates the hospital, and **Service** classification refers to the type of service the hospital offers. Previously, this section utilized numerical codes corresponding with a literal value, but the new design of *AHA Guide* bypasses the codes and

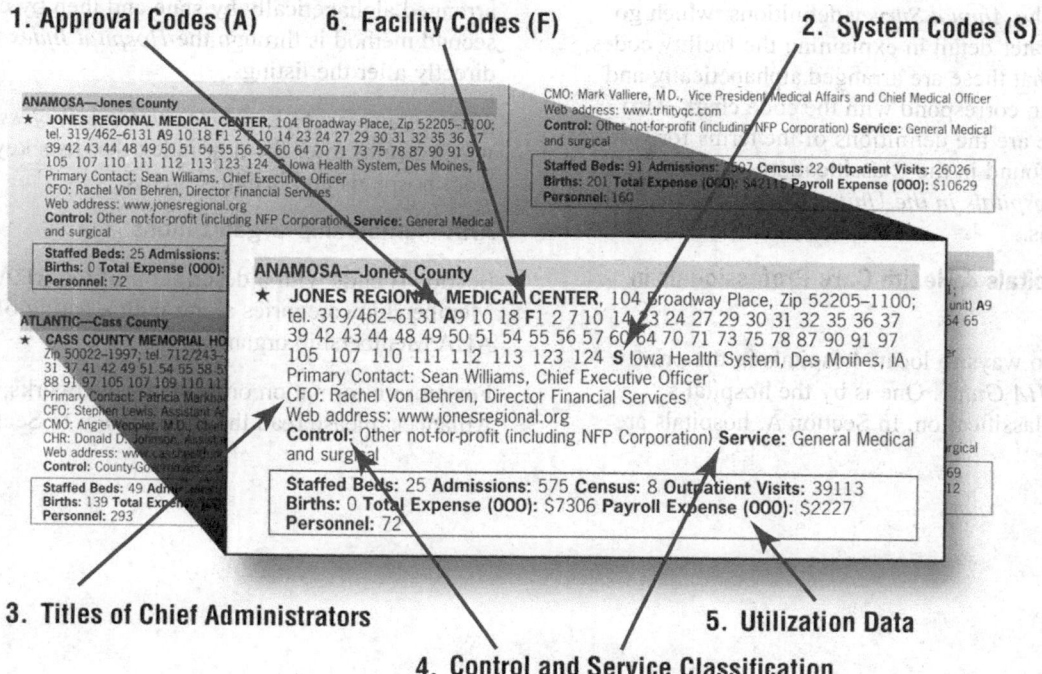

1. Approval Codes (A)
2. System Codes (S)
3. Titles of Chief Administrators
4. Control and Service Classification
5. Utilization Data
6. Facility Codes (F)

instead displays the literal classifications for control and service.
- **Control:** In this section, organizations are divided among nonfederal government hospitals, nongovernment not-for-profit hospitals, investor owned for-profit hospitals, and federal government hospitals.
- **Service:** This section displays the primary type of service that a hospital offers. The most common value is general hospital. Among the other services listed in this section are specialties such as psychiatric hospitals or children's hospitals.
5. **Utilization Data** contains the statistics related to the day-to-day and cumulative operation of the hospital. The information included in this section consists of:
- **Beds:** Number of beds regularly maintained.
- **Admissions:** Amount of patients accepted for inpatient services over a 12-month period.
- **Census:** Average number of patients receiving care each day.
- **Outpatient Visits:** Amount of visits by patients not lodged in the hospital while receiving care.
- **Births:** Number of infants born in the hospital and accepted for service in a newborn infant bassinet.
- **Expense:** Includes all expenses (including payroll) that the hospital had over the 12- month period.
- **Personnel:** Represents personnel situations as they existed at the end of the reporting period. In this area, full time equivalency is calculated on the basis that two part-time persons equal one full-time person.
6. **Facility codes** provide a description of the specific services offered by a hospital. Code F-14, for instance, indicates that the hospital contains a Blood Donor Center.

How To Use This Book

Section A begins with the *AHA Guide Hospital Listing Requirements*. This explains the requisite accreditations or characteristics a hospital must meet to be included in *AHA Guide*.

After this there is *An Explanation of the Hospital Listings*. These two pages review the information included in the Code Chart and are a vital resource in identifying the information, symbols, and codes for each hospital's listing.

© 2025 AHA Guide

Next up are the *Annual Survey* definitions, which go into even greater detail in explaining the facility codes. Please note that these are arranged alphabetically and numerically to correspond with the code chart. Also included here are the definitions of the terms for Control and Service found in the Classification section. The listings of *Hospitals in the United States, by State* follow the definitions.

Finding Hospitals & Health Care Professionals in Section A

There are two ways to locate hospitals in the print version of *AHA Guide*. One is by the hospital's geographic classification. In Section A, hospitals are arranged alphabetically by state and then by city. The second method is through the *Hospital Index* that appears directly after the listings.

There is also an *Index of Health Care Professionals* which begins after the first index that lists key people from hospitals and health systems.

AHA Membership Organizations

Section A ends with a description of the AHA Membership categories along with a listing of various AHA Membership organizations.

For more information on Systems, Networks, and Alliances, please read the introduction to Section B.

AHA Offices, Officers, and Historical Data

Chicago: 155 N. Wacker Drive, Chicago, IL 60606; tel. 312/422-3000

Chair of the Board of Trustees: Joanne M. Conroy, M.D., CEO and President, Dartmouth Health, One Medical Center Drive, Lebanon, NH 03756-0001
Chair-Elect of the Board of Trustees: Christina (Tina) Freese Decker, MHA, MSIE, FACHE, President and CEO, Corewell Health, 100 Michigan Street NE (MC060), Grand Rapids, MI 49503-2551

Washington: 800 10th Street, N.W., Two CityCenter, Suite 400, Washington, DC 20001; tel. 202/638-1100

Immediate Past Chair: John M. Haupert, FACHE, President and CEO, Grady Health System, 80 Jesse Hill Jr. Drive Atlanta, GA 30303
President & CEO: Richard J. Pollack, 800 10th Street, NW, Two CityCenter, Suite 400, Washington, DC 20001
General Counsel and Secretary: Chad Golder, 155 N. Wacker Drive, Chicago, IL 60606

Senior Vice President, Association Services and Chief Financial Officer: James (Jay) Tyler, Jr., 155 N. Wacker Drive, Chicago, IL 60606
Executive Vice President and Chief Operating Officer: M. Michelle Hood, 155 N. Wacker Drive, Chicago, IL 60606

Past Presidents/Chairs†

Year	Name	Year	Name	Year	Name
1899	★James S. Knowles	1941	★B. W. Black, M.D.	1983	★Elbert E. Gilbertson
1900	★James S. Knowles	1942	★Basil C. MacLean, M.D.	1984	Thomas R. Matherlee
1901	★Charles S. Howell	1943	★James A. Hamilton	1985	★Jack A. Skarupa
1902	★J. T. Duryea	1944	★Frank J. Walter	1986	Scott S. Parker
1903	★John Fehrenbatch	1945	★Donald C. Smelzer, M.D.	1987	Donald C. Wegmiller
1904	★Daniel D. Test	1946	★Peter D. Ward, M.D.	1988	★Eugene W. Arnett
1905	★George H. M. Rowe, M.D.	1947	★John H. Hayes	1989	★Edward J. Connors
1906	★George P. Ludlam	1948	★Graham L. Davis	1990	David A. Reed
1907	★Renwick R. Ross, M.D.	1949	★Joseph G. Norby	1991	C. Thomas Smith
1908	★Sigismund S. Goldwater, M.D.	1950	★John N. Hatfield	1992	★D. Kirk Oglesby, Jr.
1909	★John M. Peters, M.D.	1951	★Charles F. Wilinsky, M.D.	1993	Larry L. Mathis
1910	★H. B. Howard, M.D.	1952	★Anthony J. J. Rourke, M.D.	1994	Carolyn C. Roberts
1911	★W. L. Babcock, M.D.	1953	★Edwin L. Crosby, M.D.	1995	Gail L. Warden
1912	★Henry M. Hurd, M.D.	1954	★Ritz E. Heerman	1996	Gordon M. Sprenger
1913	★F. A. Washburn, M.D.	1955	★Frank R. Bradley	1997	Reginald M. Ballantyne III
1914	★Thomas Howell, M.D.	1956	★Ray E. Brown	1998	John G. King
1915	★William O. Mann, M.D.	1957	★Albert W. Snoke, M.D.	1999	Fred L. Brown
1916	★Winford H. Smith, M.D.	1958	★Tol Terrell	2000	★Carolyn Boone Lewis
1917	★Robert J. Wilson, M.D.	1959	★Ray Amberg	2001	Gary A. Mecklenburg
1918	★A. B. Ancker, M.D.	1960	★Russell A. Nelson, M.D.	2002	★Sr. Mary Roch Rocklage, RSM
1919	★A. R. Warner, M.D.	1961	★Frank S. Groner	2003	★Dennis R. Barry
1920	★Joseph B. Howland, M.D.	1962	★Jack Masur, M.D.	2004	David L. Bernd
1921	★Louis B. Baldwin, M.D.	1963	★T. Stewart Hamilton, M.D.	2005	George F. Lynn
1922	★George O'Hanlon, M.D.	1964	★Stanley A. Ferguson	January–April 2006	Richard J. Umbdenstock
1923	★Asa S. Bacon	1965	★Clarence E. Wonnacott	April–December 2006	George F. Lynn
1924	★Malcolm T. MacEachern, M.D.	1966	★Philip D. Bonnet, M.D.	2007	Kevin E. Lofton
1925	★E. S. Gilmore	1967	★George E. Cartmill	2008	William D. Petasnick
1926	★Arthur C. Bachmeyer, M.D.	1968	★David B. Wilson, M.D.	2009	Thomas M. Priselac
1927	★R. G. Brodrick, M.D.	1969	★George William Graham, M.D.	2010	Richard P. de Filippi
1928	★Joseph C. Doane, M.D.	1970	★Mark Berke	2011	John W. Bluford
1929	★Louis H. Burlingham, M.D.	1971	★Jack A. L. Hahn	2012	Teri G. Fontenot
1930	★Christopher G. Parnall, M.D.	1972	★Stephen M. Morris	2013	Benjamin K. Chu, M.D.
1931	★Lewis A. Sexton, M.D.	1973	★John W. Kauffman	2014	James H. Hinton
1932	★Paul H. Fesler	1974	★Horace M. Cardwell	2015	Jonathan B. Perlin, M.D., Ph.D.
1933	★George F. Stephens, M.D.	1975	★Wade Mountz	2016	Jim Skogsbergh
1934	★Nathaniel W. Faxon, M.D.	1976	★H. Robert Cathcart	2017	Eugene A. Woods
1935	★Robert Jolly	1977	★John M. Stagl	2018	Nancy Howell Agee
1936	★Robin C. Buerki, M.D.	1978	★Samuel J. Tibbitts	2019	Brian Gragnolati
1937	★Claude W. Munger, M.D.	1979	★W. Daniel Barker	2020	Melinda L. Estes, M.D.
1938	★Robert E. Neff	1980	★Sister Irene Kraus	2021	Rodney F. Hochman, M.D.
1939	★G. Harvey Agnew, M.D.	1981	★Bernard J. Lachner	2022	Wright Lassiter
1940	★Fred G. Carter, M.D.	1982	★Stanley R. Nelson	2023	Richard J. Pollack

Chief Executive Officers

Years	Name	Years	Name	Years	Name
1917–18	★William H. Walsh, M.D.	1954–72	★Edwin L. Crosby, M.D.	1991–2007	★Richard J. Davidson
1919–24	★Andrew Robert Warner, M.D.	1972	★Madison B. Brown, M.D. (acting)	2007–2015	Richard J. Umbdenstock
1925–27	★William H. Walsh, M.D.	1972–86	★J. Alexander McMahon	2015	Richard J. Pollack (current)
1928–42	★Bert W. Caldwell, M.D.	1986–91	Carol M. McCarthy, Ph.D., J.D.		
1943–54	★George Bugbee	1991	★Jack W. Owen (acting)		

★Deceased

Distinguished Service Award

The award recognizes significant lifetime contributions and service to health care institutions and associations.

Year	Name	Year	Name	Year	Name
1934	Matthew O. Foley	1963	Ray E. Brown	1988	Elbert E. Gilbertson
1939	Malcolm T. MacEachern, M.D.	1964	Russell A. Nelson, M.D.	1989	Donald G. Shropshire
1940	Sigismund S. Goldwater, M.D.	1965	Albert W. Snoke, M.D.	1990	John W. Colloton
1941	Frederic A. Washburn, M.D.	1966	Frank S. Groner	1991	Carol M. McCarthy, Ph.D., J.D.
1942	Winford H. Smith, M.D.	1967	Rev. John J. Flanagan, S.J.	1992	David H. Hitt
1943	Arthur C. Bachmeyer, M.D.	1968	Stanley W. Martin	1993	Edward J. Connors
1944	Rt. Rev. Msgr. Maurice F. Griffin, LL.D.	1969	T. Stewart Hamilton, M.D.		Jack W. Owen
1945	Asa S. Bacon	1970	Charles Patteson Cardwell, Jr.	1994	George Adams
1946	George F. Stephens, M.D.	1971	Mark Berke	1995	Scott S. Parker
1947	Robin C. Buerki, M.D.	1972	Stanley A. Ferguson	1996	John A. Russell
1948	James A. Hamilton	1973	Jack A. L. Hahn	1997	D. Kirk Oglesby, Jr.
1949	Claude W. Munger, M.D.	1974	George William Graham, M.D.	1998	Henry B. Betts, M.D.
1950	Nathaniel W. Faxon, M.D.	1975	George E. Cartmill	1999	Mitchell T. Rabkin, M.D.
1951	Bert W. Caldwell, M.D.	1976	D. O. McClusky, Jr.	2000	Gail L. Warden
1952	Fred G. Carter, M.D.	1977	Boone Powell	2001	Gordon M. Sprenger
1953	Basil C. MacLean, M.D.	1978	Richard J. Stull	2002	Carolyn Boone Lewis
1954	George Bugbee	1979	Horace M. Cardwell	2003	C. Thomas Smith
1955	Joseph G. Norby	1980	Donald W. Cordes	2004	Michael C. Waters
1956	Charles F. Wilinsky, M.D.	1981	Sister Mary Brigh Cassidy	2005	John G. King
1957	John H. Hayes	1982	R. Zach Thomas, Jr.	2006	Gary A. Mecklenburg
1958	John N. Hatfield	1983	H. Robert Cathcart		Sr. Mary Roch Rocklage, RSM
1959	Edwin L. Crosby, M.D.	1984	Matthew F. McNulty, Jr., Sc.D.	2007	Richard J. Davidson
1960	Oliver G. Pratt	1985	J. Alexander McMahon	2008	Fred L. Brown
1961	E. M. Bluestone, M.D.	1986	Sister Irene Kraus	2009	George F. Lynn
1962	Mother Loretto Bernard, S.C., R.N.	1987	W. Daniel Barker	2010	James J. Mongan, M.D.

†On June 3, 1972, the House of Delegates changed the title of the chief elected officer to chairman of the Board of Trustees, and the title of president was conferred on the chief executive officer of the Association.

© 2025 AHA Guide

2011	Thomas C. Royer, M.D.	2016	William Petasnick	2021	Kevin E. Lofton
2012	Karen Davis, Ph.D.	2017	Richard J. Umbdenstock	2022	Jim Skogsbergh
2013	Thomas C. Dolan, Ph.D., FACHE	2018	C. Duane Dauner	2023	Jim Skogsbergh
2014	Thomas M. Priselac	2019	Ralph W. Muller	2024	Nancy Howell, Agee Brian Gragnolati
2015	Richard P. de Filippi	2020	Teri Fontenot		

Award of Honor

Awarded to individuals, organizations, or groups to recognize an exemplary contribution to the health and well being of the people through leadership on a major health policy or social initiative.

1966	Senator Lister Hill	1999	Joseph Cardinal Bernardin, Literacy Volunteers of America	2013	George C. Halvorson Reach Out and Read
1967	Emory W. Morris, D.D.S.	2000	Institute for Safe Medication Practices	2014	Rhonda Anderson, R.N. Ohio Hospital Association
1971	Special Committee on Provision of Health Services (staff also)	2001	Dennis R. Barry		
1982	Walter J. McNerney	2002	Donald M. Berwick, M.D.	2015	Spencer C. Johnson Robert Wood Johnson Foundation
1989	Ruth M. Rothstein	2003	Steven A. Schroeder, M.D.	2016	Henry J. Kaiser Family Foundation
1990	Joyce C. Clifford, R.N.		Dan S. Wilford	2017	Joel T. Allison
1991	Haynes Rice	2004	Ron J. Anderson, M.D. Johnson & Johnson		Doug Leonard
1992	Donald W. Dunn	2005	Sr. Mary Jean Ryan	2018	Ronald R. Peterson Sister Carol Keehan
	Ira M. Lane, Jr.	2006	Jordan C. Cohen, M.D.	2019	Darrell G. Kirch, M.D.
1993	Elliott C. Roberts, Sr. William A. Spencer, M.D.		James W. Varnum		John Bluford
1994	Robert A. Derzon	2007	Edward A. Eckenhoff	2020	March of Dimes
1995	Russell G. Mawby, Ph.D. John K. Springer		Stanley F. Hupfeld	2021	American Medical Association
1996	Stephen J. Hegarty	2008	Regina M. Benjamin, M.D., MBA Alfred G. Stubblefield		American Nurses Association
	Mothers Against Drunk Driving (MADD)	2009	The Center to Advance Palliative Care Paul B. Hofmann, Dr.PH		Anthony S. Fauci, M.D.
1997	Paul B. Batalden, M.D. Habitat for Humanity International	2010	Jack Bovender	2022	University Hospitals
1998	John E. Curley, Jr. National Civic League	2011	Cary Medical Center, Caribou, ME	2023	Speaker Emerita Nancy Pelosi
		2012	Ronald McDonald House Charities The Schwartz Center for Compassionate Healthcare	2024	Ken Kaufman

Justin Ford Kimball Innovators Award

Recognition to individuals or organizations that have made outstanding, innovative contributions to health care financing and/or delivery that improves access or coordination of care.

1958	E. A. van Steenwyk	1976	J. Ed McConnell	1998	Montana Health Research and Education Foundation
1959	George A. Newbury	1978	Edwin R. Werner	1999	Kenneth W. Kizer, M.D.
1960	C. Rufus Rorem, Ph.D.	1979	Robert M. Cunningham, Jr.	2002	David M. Lawrence, M.D.
1961	James E. Stuart	1981	Maurice J. Norby	2003	Lowell C. Kruse
1962	Frank Van Dyk	1982	Robert E. Rinehimer	2006	Spencer Foreman, M.D.
1963	William S. McNary	1983	John B. Morgan, Jr.	2009	On Lok
1964	Frank S. Groner	1984	Joseph F. Duplinsky	2012	Thomas S. Nesbitt, M.D.
1965	J. Douglas Colman	1985	David W. Stewart	2015	Glenn D. Steele, Jr., M.D.
1967	Walter J. McNemey	1988	Ernest W. Saward, M.D.	2016	Dan Wolterman
1968	John W. Paynter	1990	James A. Vohs	2017	James N. Weinstein, DO
1970	Edwin L. Crosby, M.D.	1993	John C. Lewin, M.D.	2018	Nicholas Wolter, M.D.
1971	H. Charles Abbott	1994	Donald A. Brennan	2020	Bernard Tyson (posthumous)
1972	John R. Mannix	1995	E. George Middleton, Jr. Glenn R. Mitchell	2021	Spectrum Health
1973	Herman M. Somers	1997	Harvey Pettry	2022	Jim Hinton
1974	William H. Ford, Ph.D.		D. David Sniff		
1975	Earl H. Kammer				

Board of Trustees Award

Individuals or groups who have made substantial and noteworthy contributions to the work of the American Hospital Association.

1959	Joseph V. Friel John H. Hayes	1984	Jack W. Owen Howard J. Berman	2004	Richard L. Clarke Thelma Traut
1960	Duncan D. Sutphen, Jr.		O. Ray Hurst	2005	Merrill Gappmayer Leo Greenawalt
1963	Eleanor C. Lambertsen, R.N., Ed.D.		James R. Neely		
1964	John R. Mannix	1985	James E. Ferguson	2006	Robert L. Harman
1965	Albert G. Hahn		Cleveland Rodgers		Kenneth G. Stella
	Maurice J. Norby	1986	Rex N. Olsen	2007	Deborah Freund, Ph.D.
1966	Madison B. Brown, M.D.	1987	Michael Lesparre		Michael D. Stephens
	Kenneth Williamson	1988	Barbara A. Donaho, R.N.	2008	James R. Castle
1967	Alanson W. Wilcox	1989	Walter H. MacDonald	2009	Richard M. Knapp, Ph.D.
1968	E. Dwight Barnett, M.D.		Donald R. Newkirk	2010	Fred Hessler
1969	Vane M. Hoge, M.D.	1990	William T. Robinson		John G. O'Brien
	Joseph P. McNinch, M.D.	1992	Jack C. Bills	2011	Carolyn F. Scanlan
1972	David F. Drake, Ph.D.		Anne Hall Davis		Charlotte S. Yeh, M.D.
	Paul W. Earle	1993	Theodore C. Eickhoff, M.D.	2012	Larry S. Gage
	Michael Lesparre		Stephen W. Gamble		Larry McAndrews
	Andrew Pattullo		Yoshi Honkawa	2013	Jeffrey D. Selberg
1973	Tilden Cummings	1994	Roger M. Busfield, Jr., Ph.D.	2014	Russell D. Harrington, Jr.
	Edmond J. Lanigan	1995	Stephen E. Dorn		Daniel Sisto
1974	James E. Hague		William L. Yates	2015	Todd C. Linden
	Sister Marybelle	1996	Leigh E. Morris		R. Timothy Rice
1975	Helen T. Yast		John Quigley	2016	Sandra Bennett Bruce
1976	Boynton P. Livingston	1998	John D. Leech		Michael G. Rock, M.D.
	James Ludlam	1999	Sister Carol Keehan	2017	Kris A. Doody, R.N.
	Helen McGuire		C. Edward McCauley		Daniel L. Gross, R.N.
1979	Newton J. Jacobson		Stephen Rogness	2018	Ian Morrison
	Edward W. Weimer	2000	Dennis May	2019	Jeanette Clough, Bruce Bailey
1980	Robert B. Hunter, M.D.	2001	Spencer C. Johnson	2020	Nicholas R. Tejeda
	Samuel J. Tibbitts		Michael M. Mitchel		Ninfa Saunders
1981	Vernon A. Knutson	2002	Victor L. Campbell	2021	Scott Malaney, Thomas F. Zenty III
	John E. Sullivan		Joseph A. Parker	2023	Marna Borgstrom, Andy W. Carter
1982	John Bigelow	2003	J. Richard Gaintner, M.D.	2024	Christina Campos, Steven Summer
	Robert W. O'Leary		Donald A. Wilson		

Citation for Meritorious Service

1968	F. R. Knautz Sister Conrad Mary, R.N.	1973	Madison B. Brown, M.D. Samuel J. Tibbitts	1976	Chaiker Abbis Susan Jenkins
1971	Hospital Council of Southern California	1975	Kenneth B. Babcock, M.D.		Gordon McLachlan
1972	College of Misericordia, Dallas, PA		Sister Mary Maurita Sengelaube	1977	Theodore Cooper, M.D.

This citation is no longer awarded

1979	Norman D. Burkett John L. Quigley William M. Whelan	1981	Richard Davi Pearl S. Fryar	1985	John A. D. Cooper, M.D. Imperial Council of the Ancient Arabic Order of the Nobles of the Mystic Shrine for North America
1980	Sister Grace Marie Hiltz Leo J. Gehrig, M.D.	1982 1983 1984	Jorge Brull Nater David M. Kinzer Donald L. Custis, M.D.	1986 1987	Howard F. Cook David H. Hitt Lucile Packard

Dick Davidson NOVA Award

This award honors effective, collaborative programs focused on improving community health status.

1994

Health Partners of Philadelphia (PA): Albert Einstein Medical Center, Episcopal Hospital, Frankford Hospital, Medical College of Pennsylvania Hospital, St. Christopher's Hospital for Children, Temple University Hospital

Decker Family Development Center: Children's Hospital Medical Center of Akron (OH)
Denver (CO) School–Based Clinics: The Children's Hospital

Basic Health Plan: Dominican Network; Mount Carmel Hospital, Colville, WA; St. Joseph's Hospital, Chewelah, WA; and Holy Family Hospital, Spokane, WA
HealthLink: Lakes Region General Hospital, Laconia, NH

1995

Bladen Community Care Network: Bladen County Hospital, Elizabethtown, NC
Building a Healthier Community: Community–Kimball Health Care System, Toms River, NJ

Injury Prevention Program: Harlem Hospital Center, New York City, NY
The Community Ministries & Outreach Program: Reaching Out to Our Vickery/Meadow Neighborhood: Presbyterian Healthcare System, Dallas, TX

"CHOICES": Shriners Hospitals for Crippled Children, Tampa, FL

1996

Lincoln and Sunnyslope: John C. Lincoln Hospital and Health Center, Sunnyslope, AZ
Growing into Life Task Force: Aiken (SC) Regional Medical Centers

People Caring for People: Beatrice (NE) Community Hospital and Health Center
Injury Prevention Center of the Greater Dayton (OH) Area: The Children's Medical Center, Good Samaritan Hospital and Health Center, Grandview Hospital, Kettering Memorial Hospital, Miami Valley Hospital, and St. Elizabeth Medical Center

Family Road: Hutzel Hospital, Detroit, MI

1997

Health Promotion Schools of Excellence Program: Alliant Health System and Kosair Children's Hospital, Louisville, KY
Health, Outreach, Prevention, and Education (HOPE): Health First Holmes Regional Medical Center, Melbourne, FL

Healthy Community Initiative: Roper Care Alliance, Charleston, SC
Obstetrical Care and Prenatal Counseling Program: St. Alexius Medical Center, Bismarck, ND

HIV/AIDS Neighborhood Service Program: Yale–New Haven Hospital, New Haven, CT

1998

Partners for a Healthier Community: Evergreen Community Health Care, Group Health Cooperative of Puget Sound, Overlake Hospital Medical Center, Providence Health System/Medalia HealthCare, Seattle, WA
Glenwood–Lyndale Community Clinic: Hennepin County Medical Center, Minneapolis, MN

Greater Dallas (TX) Injury Prevention Center: Parkland Health & Hospital System, Children's Medical Center of Dallas, Baylor Health Care System, Methodist Hospitals of Dallas, and Presbyterian Healthcare System
Network of Trust: Phoebe Putney Memorial Hospital, Albany, GA

The Lauderdale Court: A Community Partnership: St. Joseph Hospital and Health Centers, Memphis, TN

1999

Making a Case for Community Health: Middletown (OH) Regional Hospital
The Family Resource Center: Mount Carmel Medical Center, Pittsburgh, KS

The Health Neighborhood Project: St. Patrick Hospital, Missoula, MT
Kids for Health: Washington Regional Medical Center, Fayetteville, AR

Children's Village: Yakima Memorial Hospital, Yakima, WA

2000

Community Healthcare Network: Columbus (GA) Regional Healthcare System
Pasadena County Asthma Project: Huntington Memorial Hospital, Pasadena, CA

Ashe County Health Council "Health Carolinias Task Force": Ashe Memorial Hospital, Jefferson, NC
Caritas–Connection Project: St. Mary's Hospital, Passaic, NJ

Correctional Health Care Program: Baystate Health System, Springfield, MA

2001

J.C. Lewis Health Center: Memorial Health and St. Joseph's Candler Health System, Savannah, GA
Project C.A.R.E.: Mercy Medical Center, Canton, OH

TeenHealthFX.com: Atlantic Health System, Florham Park, NJ
Vista ElderCARE: Vista Health, Waukegan, IL

Western Village Enterprise School: INTEGRIS Health, Oklahoma City, OK

2002

Chester Community Connections: Crozer–Keystone Health System, Springfield, PA
The Hope Street Family Center: California Hospital Medical Center, Los Angeles, CA

Mobile Health Outreach Ministry: St. Vincent's Health System, Jacksonville, FL
Operation Access: Kaiser Foundation Hospitals, Oakland; Sutter Health, Sacramento; San Francisco General Hospital, San Francisco; St. Rose Hospital, Hayward; and Santa Rosa Memorial Hospital, Santa Rosa, CA
Wilmington Health Access for Teens: New Hanover Health Network, Wilmington, NC

2003

C.O.A.C.H. for Kids: Cedars–Sinai Medical Center, Los Angeles, CA
Community Action Network: Trinity Regional Medical Center, Fort Dodge, IA

Hearts N' Health: Glendale Adventist Medical Center, Glendale, CA
Saint Joseph Health Center: Saint Joseph Regional Medical Center, South Bend, IN

St. Mary Medical Center Bensalem Ministries: St. Mary Medical Center, Langhorne, PA

2004

Better Beginnings: Brockton Hospital, Brockton, MA
Buffalo County Community Health Partners: Good Samaritan Health Systems, Kearney, NE

Quad City Health Initiative: Genesis Health System, Davenport, IA and Trinity Regional Health System, Rock Island, IL
Quality of Life in the Truckee Meadows: Washoe Health System, Reno, NV

Solano Coalition for Better Health, Inc.: NorthBay Healthcare Group, Fairfield, CA; Sutter Solano Medical Center, Vallejo, CA; and Kaiser Permanente, Martinez, CA

2005

Children's Health Connection: McKay-Dee Hospital Center, Ogden, UT
Palmetto Health's Vision Health Initiative: Palmetto Health, Columbia, SC

Project Dulce, Whittier Institute for Diabetes: Scripps Health, San Diego, CA
Toledo/Lucas County CareNet: Mercy Health Partners, ProMedica Health System, and Medical University of Ohio, all of Toledo, OH and St. Luke's Hospital, Maumee, OH

Volunteer Health Advisor (VHA) Program: Cambridge Health Alliance, Cambridge, MA

2006

Healthy Learners, Columbia, SC: Allendale County Hospital, Fairfax, SC; McLeod Medical Center–Dillon, Dillon, SC; Sisters of Charity Providence Hospitals, Columbia, SC; and Self Regional Healthcare, Greenwood, SC

Primary Care Access Network (PCAN): Health Central, Ocoee, FL; Florida Hospital, Winter Park, FL; and Orlando Regional Healthcare, Orlando, FL **ProHealth Care Community Health Outreach Initiative:** ProHealth Care, Waukesha, WI

St. Joseph Mobile Health Services: Saint Joseph HealthCare Inc., Lexington, KY
Yonkers Childhood Health Initiative: St. John's Riverside, Yonkers, NY

2007
Medical-Legal Partnership for Children: Boston Medical Center, Boston, MA
NOW (Nutritional Options for Wellness) Program: Spectrum Health, Grand Rapids, MI
Richland Care: Palmetto Health, Columbia, SC

Trauma Nurses Talk Tough: Legacy Health System, Portland, OR
UMass Memorial Medical Center Healthy Youth Development Initiative: UMass Memorial Health Care, Worcester, MA

Youth Health Partnership-Patee Market Youth Dental Clinic: Heartland Health, St. Joseph, MO

2008
Partnership for Community Health: California Pacific Medical Center, San Francisco, CA
Every Child Succeeds: Cincinnati Children's Hospital Medical Center, Cincinnati, OH

Memorial Hermann Health Centers for Schools: Memorial Hermann, Houston, TX
Nutrition Center of Maine: Saint Mary's Health System, Lewiston, ME

***ENERGIZE!* Pediatric Diabetes Intervention Program:** WakeMed Health & Hospitals, Raleigh, NC

2009
Lighten Up 4 Life: Mission Health System, Asheville, NC
Project BRIEF: Jacobi Medical Center and North Central Bronx Hospital, Bronx, NY

Really Awesome Health (RAH) and Wholesome Routines: Duke Raleigh Hospital, Raleigh, NC

Student Success Jobs Program: Brigham and Women's Hospital, Boston, MA
Taos First Steps Program: Holy Cross Hospital, Taos, NM

2010
Community-Based Alternatives to the Emergency Room: Lee Memorial Health System, Fort Meyers, FL
Health-e-Access Telemedicine: University of Rochester Medical Center, Rochester, NY

Healthy Futures: Munson Healthcare System, Traverse City, MI
Healthy San Francisco: San Francisco General Hospital, University of California Medical Center, Chinese Hospital, California Pacific Medical Center, Saint Francis Memorial Hospital, St. Mary's Medical Center, and Kaiser Permanente, San Francisco, CA
Pediatric Asthma Program: Sinai Health System, Chicago, IL

2011
Emergency Department Consistent Care Program: Providence St. Peter Hospital, Olympia, WA
Integrated Community Nursing Program at Parkview Health: Parkview Health, Fort Wayne, IN

Milwaukee Health Care Partnership: Aurora Health Care, Children's Hospital & Health System, Inc., Columbia St. Mary's, and Froedtert Health, all of Milwaukee, WI, and Wheaton Franciscan Healthcare, Glendale, WI

The Diabetes Collaborative: Northwestern Memorial Hospital, Chicago, IL
Rochester Youth Violence Partnership: University of Rochester Medical Center and Rochester General Health System, Rochester, NY

2012
The Beth Embraces Wellness: An Integrated Approach to Prevention in the Community: Newark Beth Israel Medical Center and Children's Hospital of New Jersey, Newark, NJ

CARE Network: St. Joseph Health Queen of the Valley Medical Center, Napa, CA
Fitness in the City: Boston Children's Hospital, Boston, MA
Puff City: Henry Ford Health System, Detroit, MI

Rural Health Initiative: Shawano Medical Center of ThedaCare, Shawano, WI

2013
Bangor Beacon Community: EMHS, Brewer, ME and St. Joseph Healthcare, Bangor, ME
Chippewa Health Improvement Partnership (CHIP): St. Joseph's Hospital, Chippewa Falls, WI

Core Health Program of Healthier Communities: Spectrum Health, Grand Rapids, MI
Free Preventive Screenings Program: Good Samaritan Hospital, Vincennes, IN

Hope Clinic and Pharmacy: Ephraim McDowell Health, Danville, KY

2014
FirstReach: FirstHealth of the Carolinas, Pinehurst, NC
Children's Hospital Center for Pediatric Medicine Asthma Action Team: Greenville Health System, Greenville, SC

Let's Go!: The Barbara Bush Children's Hospital at Maine Medical Center, Portland, ME
Hearts Beat Back: The Heart of New Ulm (HONU) Project: New Ulm Medical Center, part of Allina Health, New Ulm, MN

Finney County Community Health Coalition: St. Catherine Hospital, Garden City, KS

2015
Activate Whittier: PIH Health, Whittier, Calif. And Kaiser Permanente Downey Medical Center, Downey, CA
Bithlo Transformation Effort: Florida Hospital, Orlando, FL

Blood Pressure Advocate Program: University of Rochester Medical Center, Rochester, NY
Community Health: Healthy Eating: Presbyterian Healthcare Services, Albuquerque, NM

Mayor's Healthy City Initiative (Healthy BR): Baton Rouge General Medical Center, Ochsner Medical Center-Baton Rouge, Our Lady of the Lake Regional Medical Center and Woman's Hospital, Baton Rouge, LA

2016
Baylor Scott & White Health's Diabetes Health and Wellness Initiative at the Juanita J. Craft Recreation Center: Baylor Scott & White Health, Dallas, TX

Building a Healthy Community Initiative, East Ocean View: Bon Secours Hampton Roads Health System, Norfolk, VA
Memorial Hermann Mobile Dental Program: Memorial Hermann Health System, Houston, TX

Spectrum Health Healthier Communities – Strong Beginnings: Spectrum Health, Grand Rapids, MI
Get Healthy, Live Well: Tanner Health System, Carrollton, GA

2017
Morrison County Community-Based Care Coordination: CHI St. Gabriel's Health, Little Falls, MN
The Health and Wellness Alliance Asthma Collaboration: Children's Health, Dallas, TX

Healthy Youth Transitions: Memorial Healthcare System, Hollywood, FL
Pediatric Care-A-Van: Norwegian American Hospital, Chicago, IL

Palmetto Health Dental Health Initiative: Palmetto Health, Columbia, SC

2018
Unity Center for Behavioral Health: Adventist Health, Kaiser Permanente, Legacy Health, Oregon Health & Science University, Portland, OR
Annapolis Community Health Partnership: Anne Arundel Medical Center, Annapolis, MD

Enos Park Access to Care Collaborative: HSHS St. John's Hospital and Memorial Medical Center, Springfield, IL
Kids Teaching Kids: Medical City Healthcare, Dallas, TX

Healthy Kids Express: St. Louis Children's Hospital, St. Louis, MO

2019
Stark County Toward Health Resiliency for Infant Vitality and Equality (THRIVE): Aultman Hospital and Canton City Public Health, Canton, OH

Project Ujima: Children's Hospital of Wisconsin, Milwaukee, WI
Women-Inspired Neighborhood Network: Henry Ford Health System, Detroit, MI

House of Mercy Homeless Center: Mercyhealth, Janesville, WI
Transforming Communities Initiative: Trinity Health, Livonia, MI

2020
Eagle Valley Behavioral Health: Vail Health, Vail, Colo.
Hackensack Meridian School of Medicine at Seton Hall University: Edison, N.J.

Supportive Housing for the Homeless: Baltimore City Hospitals, Baltimore, Md.
Healthy Roanoke Valley: Carilion Clinic, Roanoke, Va.

Mothers in Recovery, Memorial Healthcare System, Hollywood, Fla.

2021
Connected Community Network and Homeless Health Initiative: CommonSpirit Health, San Francisco, CA
COVID-19 Community Prevention Program: Luminis Health, Annapolis, MD

Memorial ALLIES [Adults Living Life Independently, Educated & Safe] Program: Memorial Healthcare System, Hollywood, FL
Better Outcomes Thru Bridges (BOB): Providence Health & Services, Portland, OR

Blue Zones Project Fort Worth: Texas Health Resources, Fort Worth, TX

2022
Continuous Care Program, Children's Diagnostic & Treatment Center: Broward Health, Fort Lauderdale, Fla.
The Doorway: Cheshire Medical Center, Keene, N.H.
Community Connect: Children's Minnesota, Minneapolis/St. Paul

Monterey County Diabetes Collaborative: Salinas Valley Memorial Healthcare System, Salinas, Calif. Montage Health, Monterey, Calif.

School Blue Envelope Suicide Prevention Program: Spectrum Health West Michigan, Grand Rapids, Mich.

2024
Resourceful program, Essentia Health, Duluth, Minn.
Beyond Violence, John Muir Health, Walnut Creek, Calif.

UH Food for Life Markets®, University Hospitals, Cleveland, Ohio.
TC Street Medicine, Munson Healthcare, Traverse City, Mich.

Forensic Health and Trauma Recovery Center Services, Palomar Health, Escondido, Calif.

The Carolyn Boone Lewis Living the Vision Award

Organizations and individuals living AHA's vision of a society of healthy communities where all individuals reach their highest potential for health.

1998 Memorial Healthcare System, Hollywood, FL Baptist Health System, Montgomery, AL	**2003** Franklin Memorial Hospital, Farmington, ME	**2013** St. Joseph's Hospital Health Center, Syracuse, NY Cheshire Medical Center/Dartmouth–Hitchcock Keene, Keene, NH
1999 Robert A. DeVries, Battle Creek, MI Memorial Health System, South Bend, IN	**2004** Jamaica Hospital Medical Center, Jamaica, NY	
2000 Rockingham Memorial Hospital, Harrisonburg, VA	**2005** Fairbanks Memorial Hospital, Fairbanks, AK Boston Medical Center, Boston, MA	**2014** TPR Collaborative, MD
2001 Salina Regional Health Center, Salina, KS	**2010** Lehigh Valley Health Network, Allentown, PA	**2016** Saint Elizabeth's Medical Center, Wabasha, MN
2002 Health Improvement Collaborative of Greater Cincinnati, Cincinnati, OH	**2011** Alaska Native Tribal Health Consortium, Anchorage, AK	

This citation is no longer awarded

Circle of Life Award

This award celebrates innovation in palliative and end-of-life care.

2000
Improving Care through the End of Life, Franciscan Health System, Gig Harbor, WA

The Hospice of The Florida Suncoast, Largo, FL

Louisiana State Penitentiary Hospice Program, Angola, LA

2001
Department of Pain Medicine and Palliative Care, Beth Israel Medical Center, New York, NY

Palliative CareCenter & Hospice of the North Shore, Evanston, IL

St. Joseph's Manor, Trumbull, CT

2002
Children's Program of San Diego Hospice and Children's Hospital and Health Center of San Diego, San Diego, CA
Hospice of the Bluegrass, Lexington, KY

Project Safe Conduct, Hospice of the Western Reserve and Ireland Cancer Center, Cleveland, OH

Special Circle of Life Award Population-based Palliative Care Research Network (PoPCRN), Denver, CO

2003
Hospice & Palliative CareCenter, Winston-Salem, NC

Providence Health System, Portland, OR

University of California Davis Health System, Sacramento, CA

2004
Hope Hospice and Palliative Care, Fort Myers, FL
St. Mary's Healthcare System for Children, Bayside, NY

University of Texas M.D. Anderson Cancer Center Palliative Care, Houston, TX

2005
High Point Regional Health System, High Point, NC

Palliative and End-of-life Care Program, Hoag Memorial Hospital Presbyterian, Newport Beach, CA

Thomas Palliative Care Unit, VCU Massey Cancer Center, Richmond, VA

2006
Continuum Hospice Care, New York, NY

Mercy Supportive Care, St. Joseph Mercy Oakland, Pontiac, MI

Transitions and Life Choices, Fairview Health Services, Minneapolis, MN

2007
UCSF Palliative Care Program, San Francisco, CA
Covenant Hospice, Pensacola, FL

Woodwell: A Program of Presbyterian SeniorCare and Family Hospice and Palliative Care, Oakmont, PA

2008
Children's Hospitals and Clinics of Minnesota, Pain and Palliative Care Program, Minneapolis, MN

Haven Hospice, Gainesville, FL

The Pediatric Advanced Care Team, The Children's Hospital of Philadelphia, Philadelphia, PA

2009
Four Seasons, Flat Rock, NC

Oregon Health and Science University Palliative Medicine & Comfort Care Program, Portland, OR

Wishard Health Services Palliative Care Program, Indianapolis, IN

2010
Department of Veteran Affairs, VA New York/New Jersey Healthcare Network, Brooklyn, NY

Kansas City Hospice & Palliative Care, Kansas City, MO
Snohomish Palliative Partnership, Everett, WA

2011
The Center for Hospice & Palliative Care, Cheektowaga, NY

Gilchrist Hospice Care, Hunt Valley, MD

St. John Providence Health System, Detroit, MI

2012
Haslinger Family Pediatric Palliative Care Center, Akron Children's Hospital, Akron, OH

Calvary Hospital, Bronx, NY
Sharp HealthCare, San Diego, CA

2013		
The Denver Hospice and Optio Health Services, Denver, CO	Hertzberg Palliative Care Institute at the Mount Sinai Medical Center, New York, NY	UnityPoint Health, Iowa and Illinois

2014		
OACIS/Palliative Medicine, Lehigh Valley Health Network, Allentown, PA	Supportive & Palliative Care, Baylor Health Care System, Dallas, TX	Yakima Valley Memorial Hospital, Yakima, WA

2015
Care Dimensions, Danvers, MA

2016		
Bon Secours Palliative Medicine, Richmond, VA	Cambia Palliative Care Center of Excellence at UW Medicine, Seattle, WA	Susquehanna Health Hospice and Palliative Care, Williamsport, PA

2017	
Bluegrass Care Navigators, formerly Hospice of the Bluegrass, Lexington, KY	Providence TrinityCare Hospice, Providence Little Company of Mary Medical Center Torrance and Providence Institute for Human Caring, Torrance, CA

2018		
Hospice of the Valley, Phoenix, AZ	Western Connecticut Health Network, Danbury, CT	Penn Wissahickon Hospice and Caring Way, Philadelphia, PA

2019		
Western Reserve Navigator, Hospice of the Western Reserve, Cleveland, OH	Palliative Care Services, UCHealth University of Colorado Hospital, Aurora, CO	University Health System Palliative Care Team, San Antonio, TX

2020	
Caring Circle, Spectrum Health Lakeland, St. Joseph, MI	Choices and Champions, Novant Health, Winston-Salem, NC

2023		
Center for Hospice Care, Mishawaka, IN	Johns Hopkins Bayview, Baltimore, MD	Optum, Eden Prairie, MN

The American Hospital Association Quest for Quality Prize*
Honoring Leadership and Innovation in Patient Care Quality, Safety, and Commitment

2002		
Missouri Baptist Medical Center, St. Louis, MO	**Finalist:** Fairview Hospital, Greater, Barrington, MA	**Finalist:** Minnesota Children's Hospital and Clinics, Minneapolis, MN

2003		
Abington Memorial Hospital, Abington, PA	**Finalist:** Beaumont Hospitals, Royal Oak, MI	**Finalist:** University of Wisconsin Hospital and Clinics, Madison, WI

2004		
Sentara Norfolk General Hospital, Norfolk, VA	**Finalist:** The Johns Hopkins Hospital, Baltimore, MD	**Finalist:** Mary Lanning Memorial Hospital, Hastings, NE

2005		
North Mississippi Medical Center, Tupelo, MS	**Finalist:** El Camino Hospital, Mountain View, CA	**Finalist:** NewYork-Presbyterian Hospital, New York, NY

2006
Cincinnati Children's Hospital Medical Center, Cincinnati, OH

2007		
Columbus Regional Hospital, Columbus, IN	**Finalist:** Cedars-Sinai Medical Center, Los Angeles, CA	**Finalist:** INTEGRIS Baptist Medical Center, Oklahoma City, OK

2008	
Munson Medical Center, Traverse City, MI	**Finalist:** University of Michigan Hospitals & Health Centers, Ann Arbor, MI

2009	
Bronson Methodist Hospital, Kalamazoo, MI	**Finalist:** Beth Israel Deaconess Medical Center, Boston, MA

2010	
McLeod Regional Medical Center, Florence, SC	**Finalist:** Henry Ford Hospital, Detroit, MI

2011		
Memorial Regional Hospital, Hollywood, FL	**Finalist:** AtlantiCare Regional Medical Center, Atlantic City, NJ	**Finalist:** Northwestern Memorial Hospital, Chicago, IL

2012		
University Hospitals Case Medical Center, Cleveland, OH	**Finalist:** Lincoln Medical and Mental Health Center, Bronx, NY	**Finalist:** University of North Carolina Hospitals, Chapel Hill, NC and Life Choices, Fairview Health Services, Minneapolis, MN

2013	
Beth Israel Deaconess Medical Center, Boston, MA	**Finalist:** Franklin Woods Community Hospital, Johnson City, TN

2014	
VCU Medical Center, Richmond, VA	**Finalist:** Carolinas Medical Center-Northeast, Concord, NC

2015	
Children's Hospital Colorado in Aurora, CO	**Finalist:** Duke University Hospital, Durham, NC

2016
Memorial Medical Center, Springfield, IL **Finalist:** Memorial Hermann Greater Heights, Houston, TX

2018
Northwell Health, New Hyde Park, NY **Finalist:** Anne Arundel Medical Center, Annapolis, MD **Finalist:** Aurora Health Care, Milwaukee, WI

2019
Carolinas Rehabilitation, Charlotte, NC **Finalist:** Finalist: Mission Health, Asheville, NC

2021
Yale New Haven Health, New Haven, CT **Finalist:** Memorial Healthcare System, Hollywood, FL **Finalist:** Yuma Regional Medical Center, Yuma, AZ

2022
University Hospitals, Cleveland, OH **Finalist:** Ochsner Medical Center, New Orleans, LA **Finalist:** WellSpan Health, York, Pa.

2023
Main Line Health System, Bryn Mawr, PA **Finalist:** Atlantic Health System, Morristown, NJ **Finalist:** University of Chicago cMedicine, Chicago, IL

2024
WellSpan Health York, Pa. **Finalist:** Carilion Clinic Roanoke, Va. Jefferson Health, Philadelphia **Finalist:** MUSC Health Charleston, SC

(*This award was sponsored from 2001-2016 by McKesson. RLDatix sponsored this award from 2018-2021.)

Foster G. McGaw Prize
Honors health delivery organizations that have demonstrated exceptional commitment to community service.

1986	Lutheran Medical Center, Brooklyn, NY	1997	Bladen County Hospital Rural Health Network, Elizabethtown, NC	2010	Allegiance Health, Jackson, MI
1987	Copley Hospital, Morrisville, VT Mount Sinai Hospital, Hartford, CT			2011	Mt. Ascutney Hospital and Health Center, Windsor, VT
		1998	Allina Health System, Minneapolis, MN	2012	St. Joseph's/Candler Health System, Savannah, GA
1988	MetroHealth System, Cleveland, OH	1999	LAC+USC Healthcare Network, Los Angeles, CA	2013	Crozer-Keystone Health System, Delaware County, PA
1989	Greater Southeast Healthcare System, Washington, DC	2000	Kaweah Delta Health Care District, Visalia, CA	2014	Palmetto Health, Columbia, SC
1990	Mount Zion Medical Center of The University of California-San Francisco, San Francisco, CA	2001	Memorial Hospital of South Bend, South Bend, IN	2015	Massachusetts General Hospital, Boston
		2002	John C. Lincoln Health Network, Phoenix, AZ	2016	Spectrum Health, Grand Rapids, MI
1991	Franklin Regional Hospital, Franklin, NH	2003	Phoebe Putney Memorial Hospital, Albany, GA	2017	Yale New Haven Hospital, New Haven, CT
1992	Mount Sinai Hospital Medical Center of Chicago, Chicago, IL	2004	Henry Ford Health System, Detroit, MI	2018	Penn Medicine Lancaster General Health, Lancaster County, PA
		2005	Venice Family Clinic, Venice, CA		
1993	The Cambridge Hospital, Cambridge, MA	2006	Memorial Healthcare System, Hollywood, FL	2021	ProMedica, Toledo, OH
1994	Parkland Memorial Hospital, Dallas, TX	2007	Harborview Medical Center, Seattle, WA	2022	Texas Health Resources, Arlington, Texas
1995	Our Lady of Lourdes Medical Center, Camden, NJ	2008	St. Mary's Health System, Lewiston, ME	2023	Memorial Hermann Health System, Houston, TX
1996	St. Mary's Hospital, Rochester, NY	2009	Heartland Health, St. Joseph, MO	2024	Boston Medical Center, Boston, MA

Dick Davidson Quality Milestone Award for Allied Association Leadership
The award recognizes state, regional or metropolitan hospital association leadership in improving health care quality.

2011	Michigan Health & Hospital Association		Tennessee Hospital Association	2017	California's Hospital Quality Institute
	South Carolina Hospital Association	2014	Connecticut Hospital Association	2018	Missouri Hospital Association
2012	Iowa Hospital Association		Wisconsin Hospital Association		
	Washington State Hospital Association	2015	Minnesota Hospital Association		
2013	Florida Hospital Association	2016	Maryland Hospital Association		

This citation is no longer awarded

Carolyn Boone Lewis Equity of Care Award
The award is presented to hospitals or care systems that are noteworthy leaders and examples to the field in the area of equitable care.

2014	Massachusetts General Hospital, Boston, MA
2015	Henry Ford Health System, Detroit, MI
	Robert Wood Johnson University Hospital, New Brunswick, NJ
2016	Cleveland Clinic, Cleveland, OH
2017	Kaiser Permanente, Oakland, CA
2018	Navicent Health, Macon, GA
2019	Anne Arundel Medical Center, Annapolis, MD
2020	Cone Health - Greensboro, N.C.
2021	Atrium Health - Charlotte, N.C.
2022	
2023	Mount Sinai Health System, New York City, NY

Hospitals, Institutional and Associate Members

A2	AHA Guide Hospital Listing Requirements
3	Explanation of Hospital Listings
6	Annual Survey
15	Hospitals in the United States, by State
730	Hospitals in Areas Associated with the United States, by Area
737	U.S. Government Hospitals Outside the United States, by Area
738	Index of Hospitals
783	Index of Health Care Professionals
1015	AHA Membership Categories
1016	Other Institutional Members
1016	*Institutional Member Hospitals*
1017	*Associated University Programs in Health Administration*
1018	*Hospital Schools of Nursing*
1019	*Nonhospital Preacute and Postacute Care Facilities*
1020	*Provisional Hospitals*
1021	Associate Members
1021	*Ambulatory Centers and Home Care Agencies*
1021	*Blue Cross Plans*
1022	*Other Associate Members*

AHA Guide
Hospital Listing Requirements

An institution is considered a hospital by the American Hospital Association if it is licensed as general or specialty hospital by the appropriate state agency, and accredited as a hospital by one of the following organizations: The Joint Commission; Accreditation Commission for Health Care, Inc. (ACHC); accreditation by DNV GL Healthcare; Center for Improvement in Healthcare Quality accreditation; or Medicare certified as a provider of acute service under Title 18 of the Social Security Act.

Types of Hospitals

Hospitals are listed as one of four types of hospitals: general, special, rehabilitation and chronic disease, or psychiatric. The following definitions of function by type of hospital and special requirements are:

General

The primary function of the institution is to provide patient services, diagnostic and therapeutic, for a variety of medical conditions. A general hospital also shall provide:

- diagnostic x–ray services with facilities and staff for a variety of procedures
- clinical laboratory service with facilities and staff for a variety of procedures and with anatomical pathology services regularly and conveniently available
- operating room service with facilities and staff.

Special

The primary function of the institution is to provide diagnostic and treatment services for patients who have specified medical conditions, both surgical and nonsurgical. A special hospital also shall provide:

- such diagnostic and treatment services as may be determined by the Executive Committee of the Board of Trustees of the American Hospital Association to be appropriate for the specified medical conditions for which medical services are provided shall be maintained in the institution with suitable facilities and staff. If such conditions do not normally require diagnostic x–ray service, laboratory service, or operating room service, and if any such services are therefore not maintained in the institution, there shall be written arrangements to make them available to patients requiring them.
- clinical laboratory services capable of providing tissue diagnosis when offering pregancy termination services.

Rehabilitation and Chronic Disease

The primary function of the institution is to provide diagnostic and treatment services to handicapped or disabled individuals requiring restorative and adjustive services. A rehabilitation and chronic disease hospital also shall provide:

- arrangements for diagnostic x–ray services, as required, on a regular and conveniently available basis
- arrangements for clinical laboratory service, as required on a regular and conveniently available basis
- arrangements for operating room service, as required, on a regular and conveniently available basis
- a physical therapy service with suitable facilities and staff in the institution
- an occupational therapy service with suitable facilities and staff in the institution
- arrangements for psychological and social work services on a regular and conveniently available basis
- arrangements for educational and vocational services on a regular and conveniently available basis
- written arrangements with a general hospital for the transfer of patients who require medical, obstetrical, or surgical services not available in the institution.

Psychiatric

The primary function of the institution is to provide diagnostic and treatment services for patients who have psychiatric–related illnesses. A psychiatric hospital also shall provide:

- arrangements for clinical laboratory service, as required, on a regular and conveniently available basis
- arrangements for diagnostic x–ray services, as required on a regular and conveniently available basis
- psychiatric, psychological, and social work service with facilities and staff in the institution
- arrangements for electroencephalograph services, as required, on a regular and conveniently available basis
- written arrangements with a general hospital for the transfer of patients who require medical, obstetrical, or surgical services not available in the institution

The American Hospital Association may, at the sole discretion of the Executive Committee of the Board of Trustees, grant, deny, or withdraw the listing of an institution.

---

* Physician—Term used to describe an individual with an M.D. or D.O. degree who is fully licensed to practice medicine in all its phases.

‡ The completed records in general shall contain at least the following: the patient's identifying data and consent forms, medical history, record of physical examination, physicians' progress notes, operative notes, nurses' notes, routine x–ray and laboratory reports, doctors' orders, and final diagnosis.

Explanation of Hospital Listings

Sample Hospital Listing:

ANYTOWN, Universal County

✠ **ANYTOWN HOSPITAL & CLINICS (777777)**, (Formerly Anytown Area Community Hospital and Clinic), 100 South Main Street, Zip 12345–6789; tel. 123/456–7890 **A**9 10] ①
F10 12 23 24 29 30 31 37 39 49 51 55 57 64 65 66 68 70 71 72 77 78 83 87 88 91 96 97 106 107 110 111 113 124 **S** Universal ⑥
County Health System ②
Primary Contact: Ann M. Generic, Chief Executive Officer
COO: Ann M. Generic
CFO: Michael M. Generic ③
CMO: Peterl Van Generic, President Medical Staff
CHR: Jerry Generic, Human Resources Director
CNO: Danielle Generic, R.N., Chief Nursing Officer
Web address: www.website.org
Control: Other not–for–profit (including NFP Corporation) **Service:** General Medical and Surgical ④

Staffed Beds: 25 **Admissions:** 892 **Census:** 9 **Outpatient Visits:** 44014
Births: 51 **Total Expense ($000):** 19210 **Payroll Expense ($000):** 5864
Personnel: 182 ⑤

ANYTOWN, Universal County

✠ **ANYTOWN HOSPITAL & CLINICS (777777)**, (Formerly Anytown Area Community Hospital and Clinic), 100 South Main Street, Zip 12345–6789; tel. 123/456–7890 **A**9 10

① = Approval Codes
② = Health Care System Name
③ = Titles of Chief Administrators
④ = Control and Service Classifications
⑤ = Utilization Data
⑥ = Facility Codes

Hospital, Medicare Provider Number, Address, Telephone, Approval, Facility, and Health Care System

★ American Hospital Association (AHA) membership
□ The Joint Commission accreditation
○ Healthcare Facilities Accreditation Program
◇ DNV Healthcare Inc. accreditation
⇑ Center for Improvement in Healthcare Quality Accreditation
△ Commission on Accreditation of Rehabilitation Facilities (CARF) accreditation

① Approval Codes

Reported by the approving bodies specified, as of the dates noted.

1 Accreditation under the hospital program of The Joint Commission (May 2024).
2 Cancer program approved by American College of Surgeons (April 2024).
3 Participating site recognized for one or more Accreditation Council for Graduate Medical Education accredited programs (June 2024).
5 Medical school affiliation, reported to the American Medical Association (March 2024).
7 Accreditation by Commission on Accreditation of Rehabilitation Facilities (April 2024).
8 Member of the Association of American Medical Colleges (formerly COTH) (April 2024).
10 Certified for participation in the Health Insurance for the Aged (Medicare) Program by the Centers for Medicare and Medicaid Services (March 2024).
11 Healthcare Facilities Accreditation Program (June 2024).
18 Critical Access Hospitals (August 2024).
19 Rural Referral Center (August 2024).
20 Sole Community Provider (August 2024).
21 Accreditation by DNV Healthcare Inc. (June 2024).
22 Accreditation by Center for Improvement in Healthcare Quality (May 2024).

Nonreporting indicates that the 2023 Annual Survey questionnaire for the hospital was not received prior to publication.

② Healthcare System Name

The inclusion of the letter "S" (1) indicates that the hospital belongs to a health care system and (2) identifies the specific system to which the hospital belongs.

③ Titles of Chief Administrators

④ Control and Service Classification

For a list of control and service classifications, see page A12.

Control–The type of organization that is responsible for establishing policy for overall operation of the hospital.

Service–The type of service the hospital provides to the majority of admissions.

⑤ Utilization Data

Definitions are based on the American Hospital Association's Hospital Administration Terminology. In completing the survey, hospitals were requested to report data for a full year, in accord with their fiscal year, ending in 2023.

Beds–Number of beds regularly maintained (set up and staffed for use) for inpatients as of the close of the reporting period. Excludes newborn bassinets.

Admissions–Number of patients accepted for inpatient service during a 12–month period; does not include newborn.

Census–Average number of inpatients receiving care each day during the 12–month reporting period; does not include newborn.

Outpatient Visits–A visit by a patient who is not lodged in the hospital while receiving medical, dental, or other services. Each appearance of an outpatient in each unit constitutes one visit regardless of the number of diagnostic and/or therapeutic treatments that a patient receives.

Births–Number of infants born in the hospital and accepted for service in a newborn infant bassinet during a 12–month period; excludes stillbirths.

Expense: Expense for a 12–month period; both total expense and payroll components are shown. Payroll expenses include all salaries and wages.

Personnel: Represents personnel situations as they existed at the end of the reporting period; includes full-time equivalents of part–time personnel. Full–time equivalents were calculated on the basis that two part–time persons equal one full–time person.

Explanation of Hospital Listings

Sample Hospital Listing:

ANYTOWN, Universal County

▣ **ANYTOWN HOSPITAL & CLINICS (777777)**, (Formerly Anytown Area Community Hospital and Clinic), 100 South Main Street, Zip 12345–6789; tel. 123/456–7890 **A**9 10 ①
F10 12 23 24 29 30 31 37 39 49 51 55 57 64 65 66 68 70 71 72 77 78 83 87 88 91 96 97 106 107 110 111 113 124 **S** Universal County Health System ②
Primary Contact: Ann M. Generic, Chief Executive Officer
COO: Ann M. Generic
CFO: Michael M. Generic ③
CMO: Peterl Van Generic, President Medical Staff
CHR: Jerry Generic, Human Resources Director
CNO: Danielle Generic, R.N., Chief Nursing Officer
Web address: www.website.org
Control: Other not-for-profit (including NFP Corporation) **Service:** General Medical and Surgical ④
Staffed Beds: 25 **Admissions:** 892 **Census:** 9 **Outpatient Visits:** 44014
Births: 51 **Total Expense ($000):** 19210 **Payroll Expense ($000):** 5864
Personnel: 182 ⑤

ANYTOWN, Universal County

▣ **ANYTOWN HOSPITAL & CLINICS (777777)**, (Formerly Anytown Area Community Hospital and Clinic), 100 South Main Street, Zip 12345–6789; tel. 123/456–7890 **A**9 10

- ① = Approval Codes
- ② = Health Care System Name
- ③ = Titles of Chief Administrators
- ④ = Control and Service Classifications
- ⑤ = Utilization Data
- ⑥ = Facility Codes

Hospital, Medicare Provider Number, Address, Telephone, Approval, Facility, and Health Care System

- ★ American Hospital Association (AHA) membership
- ☐ The Joint Commission accreditation
- ○ Healthcare Facilities Accreditation Program
- ◇ DNV Healthcare Inc. accreditation
- ⇑ Center for Improvement in Healthcare Quality Accreditation
- △ Commission on Accreditation of Rehabilitation Facilities (CARF) accreditation

---

⑥ Facility Codes

Provided directly by the hospital; for definitions, see page A6.

(Numerical Order)

1. Acute long-term care
2. Adult day care program
3. Airborne infection isolation room
4. Alcoholism-drug abuse or dependency inpatient services
5. Alcoholism-drug abuse or dependency outpatient services
6. Alzheimer center
7. Ambulance services
8. Ambulatory surgery center
9. Arthritis treatment center
10. Assisted living
11. Auxiliary
12. Bariatric/weight control services
13. Birthing room-LDR room-LDRP room
14. Blood donor center
15. Breast cancer screening/mammograms
16. Burn care services
17. Cardiac intensive care
18. Adult cardiology services
19. Pediatric cardiology services
20. Adult diagnostic catheterization
21. Pediatric diagnostic catheterization
22. Adult interventional cardiac catheterization
23. Pediatric interventional cardiac catheterization
24. Adult cardiac surgery
25. Pediatric cardiac surgery
26. Adult cardiac electrophysiology
27. Pediatric cardiac electrophysiology
28. Cardiac rehabilitation
29. Case management
30. Chaplaincy/pastoral care services
31. Chemotherapy
32. Children's wellness program
33. Chiropractic services
34. Community health education
35. Community outreach
36. Complementary and alternative medicine services
37. Computer assisted orthopedic surgery (CAOS)
38. Crisis prevention
39. Dental services
40. On-campus emergency department
41. Pediatric emergency department
42. Off-campus emergency department
43. Trauma center (certified)
44. Enabling services
45. Optical colonoscopy
46. Endoscopic ultrasound
47. Ablation of Barrett's esophagus
48. Esophageal impedance study
49. Endoscopic retrograde cholangiopancreatography (ERCP)
50. Enrollment assistance services
51. Extracorporeal shock wave lithotripter (ESWL)
52. Fertility clinic
53. Fitness center
54. Freestanding outpatient care center
55. Genetic testing/counseling
56. Geriatric services
57. Health fair
58. Health research
59. Health screenings
60. Hemodialysis
61. HIV-AIDS services
62. Home health services
63. Hospice program
64. Hospital-based outpatient care center services
65. Immunization program
66. Indigent care clinic
67. Intermediate nursing care
68. Linguistic/translation services
69. Meal delivery services
70. Medical surgical intensive care services
71. Mobile health services
72. Neonatal intensive care
73. Neonatal intermediate care
74. Neurological services
75. Nutrition programs
76. Obstetrics
77. Occupational health services
78. Oncology services
79. Orthopedic services
80. Other special care
81. Outpatient surgery
82. Pain management program
83. Inpatient palliative care unit
84. Palliative care program
85. Patient controlled analgesia (PCA)
86. Patient education center
87. Patient representative services
88. Pediatric intensive care services
89. Pediatric medical-surgical care
90. Physical rehabilitation inpatient services
91. Assistive technology center
92. Electrodiagnostic services
93. Physical rehabilitation outpatient services
94. Prosthetic and orthotic services
95. Robot-assisted walking therapy
96. Simulated rehabilitation environment
97. Primary care department
98. Psychiatric care
99. Psychiatric pediatric care
100. Psychiatric consultation-liaison services
101. Psychiatric education services
102. Psychiatric emergency services
103. Psychiatric geriatric services
104. Psychiatric outpatient services
105. Psychiatric partial hospitalization services
106. Psychiatric residential treatment
107. CT scanner
108. Diagnostic radioisotope facility
109. Electron beam computed tomography (EBCT)
110. Full-field digital mammography (FFDM)
111. Magnetic resonance imaging (MRI)
112. Intraoperative magnetic resonance imaging
113. Magnetoencephalography (MEG)
114. Multi-slice spiral computed tomography (MSCT) (<64 slice CT)
115. Multi-slice spiral computed tomography (64 + slice CT)
116. Positron emission tomography (PET)
117. Positron emission tomography/CT (PET/CT)
118. Single photon emission computerized tomography (SPECT)
119. Ultrasound
120. Image-guided radiation therapy (IGRT)
121. Intensity-modulated radiation therapy (IMRT)
122. Proton beam therapy
123. Shaped beam radiation therapy
124. Stereotactic radiosurgery
125. Retirement housing
126. Robotic surgery
127. Rural health clinic
128. Skilled nursing care
129. Sleep center
130. Social work services
131. Sports medicine
132. Support groups
133. Swing bed services
134. Teen outreach services
135. Tobacco treatment/cessation program
136. Bone marrow transplant services
137. Heart transplant
138. Kidney transplant
139. Liver transplant
140. Lung transplant
141. Tissue transplant
142. Other transplant
143. Transportation to health services
144. Urgent care center
145. Virtual colonoscopy
146. Volunteer services department
147. Women's health center/services
148. Wound management services
149. Violence prevention programs for the workplace
150. Violence prevention programs for the community
151. Alcoholism-chemical dependency pediatric services
152. Alcoholism-chemical dependency partial hospitalization services

A4 Hospital Listings   © 2025 AHA Guide

Explanation of Hospital Listings

153 Psychiatric intensive outpatient services
154 Telehealth
155 Air ambulance services
156 Diabetes prevention program
157 Employment support services
158 Supportive housing services
160 Medication assisted treatment for Opioid Use Disorder
161 Medication assisted treatment for other substance use disorders
162 Prenatal and postpartum psychiatric services
163 Forensic psychiatric services
164 Suicide prevention services
165 Social and community psychiatry
166 Biocontainment patient care unit
167 Basic interventional radiology
168 Hospital at home program
169 Prenatal and postpartum services

© 2025 AHA Guide

Hospital Listings **A5**

Annual Survey

Each year, an annual survey of hospitals is conducted by the American Hospital Association through its Health Forum affiliate.

The facilities and services found below are provided by the hospital. For data products reflecting the services provided by a hospital through its health care system, or network or through a formal arrangement with another provider contact Health Forum at 800/821-2039, or visit www.healthforum.com.

The AHA Guide to the Health Care Field does not include all data collected from the 2023 Annual Survey. Requests for purchasing other Annual Survey data should be directed to Health Forum LLC, an affiliate of the American Hospital Association, 155 N. Wacker Drive, Chicago, IL 60606, 800/821-2039.

Definitions of Facility Codes

1. **Acute long-term care.** Provides specialized acute hospital care to medically complex patients who are critically ill, have multisystem complications and/or failure, and require hospitalization averaging 25 days, in a facility offering specialized treatment programs and therapeutic intervention on a 24-hour/7 day a week basis.

2. **Adult day care program.** Program providing supervision, medical and psychological care, and social activities for older adults who live at home or in another family setting, but cannot be alone or prefer to be with others during the day. May include intake assessment, health monitoring, occupational therapy, personal care, noon meal, and transportation services.

3. **Airborne infection isolation room.** A single-occupancy room for patient care where environmental factors are controlled in an effort to minimize the transmission of those infectious agents, usually spread person to person by droplet nuclei associated with coughing and inhalation. Such rooms typically have specific ventilation requirements for controlled ventilation, air pressure and filtration.

4. **Alcoholism-drug abuse or dependency inpatient unit.** Provides diagnosis and therapeutic services to patients with alcoholism or other drug dependencies. Includes care for inpatient/residential treatment for patients whose course of treatment involves more intensive care than provided in an outpatient setting or where patient requires supervised withdrawal.

5. **Alcoholism-drug abuse or dependency outpatient unit.** Organized hospital services that provide medical care and/or rehabilitative treatment services to outpatients for whom the primary diagnosis is alcoholism or other chemical dependency.

6. **Alzheimer center.** Facility that offers care to persons with Alzheimer's disease and their families through an integrated program of clinical services, research, and education.

7. **Ambulance services.** Provision of ambulance services to the ill and injured who require medical attention on a scheduled or unscheduled basis.

8. **Ambulatory surgery center.** Facility that provides care to patients requiring surgery who are admitted and discharged on the same day. Ambulatory surgery centers are distinct from same day surgical units within the hospital outpatient departments for purposes of Medicare payments.

9. **Arthritis treatment center.** Specifically equipped and staffed center for the diagnosis and treatment of arthritis and other joint disorders.

10. **Assisted living.** A special combination of housing, supportive services, personalized assistance and health care designed to respond to the individual needs of those who need help in activities of daily living and instrumental activities of daily living. Supportive services are available, 24 hours a day, to meet scheduled and unscheduled needs, in a way that promotes maximum independence and dignity for each resident and encourages the involvement of a resident's family, neighbor and friends.

11. **Auxiliary.** A volunteer community organization formed to assist the hospital in carrying out its purpose and to serve as a link between the institution and the community.

12. **Bariatric/weight control services.** Bariatrics is the medical practice of weight reduction.

13. **Birthing room-LDR room-LDRP room.** A single room-type of maternity care with a more homelike setting for families than the traditional three-room unit (labor/delivery/recovery) with a separate postpartum area. A birthing room combines labor and delivery in one room. An LDR room accommodates three stages in the birthing process—labor, delivery, and recovery. An LDRP room accommodates all four stages of the birth process—labor, delivery, recovery and postpartum.

14. **Blood donor center.** A facility that performs, or is responsible for the collection, processing, testing or distribution of blood and components.

15. **Breast cancer screening/mammograms.** Mammography screening-the use of breast x-ray to detect unsuspected breast cancer in asymptomatic women. Diagnostic mammography-the x-ray imaging of breast tissue in symptomatic women who are considered to have a substantial likelihood of having breast cancer already.

16. **Burn care services.** Provides care to severely burned patients. Severely burned patients are those with any of the following: 1. Second-degree burns of more than 25% total body surface area for adults or 20% total body surface area for children; 2. Third-degree burns of more than 10% total body surface area; 3. Any severe burns of the hands, face, eyes, ears or feet or; 4. All inhalation injuries, electrical burns, complicated burn injuries involving fractures and other major traumas, and all other poor risk factors.

17. **Cardiac intensive care.** Provides patient care of a more specialized nature than the usual medical and surgical care, on the basis of

physicians' orders and approved nursing care plans. The unit is staffed with specially trained nursing personnel and contains monitoring and specialized support or treatment equipment for patients who, because of heart seizure, one-heart surgery, or other life-threatening conditions, require intensified, comprehensive observation and care. May include myocardial infarction, pulmonary care, and heart transplant units.

18. **Adult cardiology services.** An organized clinical service offering diagnostic and interventional procedures to manage the full range of adult heart conditions.

19. **Pediatric cardiology services.**

20. **Adult diagnostic catheterization.** (also called coronary angiography or coronary arteriography) is used to assist in diagnosing complex heart conditions. Cardiac angiography involves the insertion of a tiny catheter up into the artery in the groin then carefully threading the catheter up into the aorta where the coronary arteries originate. Once the catheter is in place, a dye is injected which allows the cardiologist to see the size, shape and distribution of the coronary arteries. These images are used to diagnose heart disease and to determine, among other things, whether or not surgery is indicated.

21. **Pediatric diagnostic catheterization.** (also called coronary angiography or coronary arteriography) is used to assist in diagnosing complex heart conditions. Cardiac angiography involves the insertion of a tiny catheter up into the artery in the groin then carefully threading the catheter up into the aorta where the coronary arteries originate. Once the catheter is in place, a dye is injected which allows the cardiologist to see the size, shape and distribution of the coronary arteries. These images are used to diagnose heart disease and to determine, among other things, whether or not surgery is indicated.

22. **Adult interventional cardiac catheterization.** Nonsurgical procedure that utilizes the same basic principles as diagnostic cathereterization and then uses advanced the techniques to improve the heart's function. It can be less invasive alternative to heart surgery.

23. **Pediatric diagnostic catheterization.** Nonsurgical procedure that utilizes the same basic principles as diagnostic cathereterization and then uses advanced the techniques to improve the heart's function. It can be less invasive alternative to heart surgery.

24. **Adult cardiac surgery.** Includes minimally invasive procedures that include surgery done with only a small incision or no incision at all, such as through a laparoscope or an endoscope and more invasive major surgical procedures that include open chest and open heart surgery.

25. **Pediatric cardiac surgery.** Includes minimally invasive procedures that include surgery done with only a small incision or no incision at all, such as through a laparoscope or an endoscope and more invasive major surgical procedures that include open chest and open heart surgery defibrillator implantation and follow- up.

26. **Adult cardiac electrophysiology.** Evaluation and management of patients with complex rhythm or conduction abnormalities, including diagnostic testing, treatment of arrhythmias by catheter ablation or drug therapy, and pacemaker/ defibrillator implantation and follow- up.

27. **Pediatric cardiac electrophysiology.**

28. **Cardiac rehabilitation.** A medically supervised program to help heart patients recover quickly and improve their overall physical and mental functioning. The goal is to reduce risk of another cardiac event or to keep an already present heart condition from getting worse. Cardiac rehabilitation programs include: counseling to patients, an exercise program, helping patients modify risk factors such as smoking and high blood pressure, providing vocational guidance to enable the patient to return to work, supplying information on physical limitations and lending emotional support.

29. **Case management.** A system of assessment, treatment planning, referral and follow–up that ensures the provision of comprehensive and continuous services and the coordination of payment and reimbursement for care.

30. **Chaplaincy/pastoral care services.** A service ministering religious activities and providing pastoral counseling to patients, their families, and staff of a health care organization.

31. **Chemotherapy.** An organized program for the treatment of cancer by the use of drugs or chemicals.

32. **Children's wellness program.** A program that encourages improved health status and a healthful lifestyle of children through health education, exercise, nutrition and health promotion.

33. **Chiropractic services.** An organized clinical service including spinal manipulation or adjustment and related diagnostic and therapeutic services.

34. **Community health education.** Education that provides health information to individuals and populations as well as support for personal, family and community health decisions with the objective of improving health status.

35. **Community outreach.** A program that systematically interacts with the community to identify those in need of services, alerting persons and their families to the availability of services, locating needed services, and enabling persons to enter the service delivery system.

36. **Complementary and alternative medicine services.** Organized hospital services or formal arrangements to providers that provide care or treatment not based solely on traditional western allopathic medical teachings as instructed in most U.S. medical schools. Includes any of the following; acupuncture, chiropractic, homeopathy, osteopathy, diet and lifestyle changes, herbal medicine, massage therapy, etc.

37. **Computer assisted orthopedic surgery (CAOS).** Orthopedic surgery using computer technology, enabling three–dimensional graphic models to visualize a patient's anatomy.

38. **Crisis prevention.** Services provided in order to promote physical and mental well being and the early identification of disease and ill health prior to the onset and recognition of symptoms so as to permit early treatment.

39. **Dental services.** An organized dental service, not necessarily involving special facilities, that provides dental or oral services to inpatients or outpatients.

40. **On-campus emergency department.** Hospital facilities for the provision of unscheduled outpatient services to patients whose conditions require immediate care. Must be staffed 24 hours a day.

Annual Survey

41. **Pediatric emergency department.** Hospital facilities for the provision of unscheduled outpatient services to patients whose conditions require immediate care.

42. **Off-campus emergency department.** A facility owned and operated by the hospital but physically separate from the hospital for the provision of unscheduled outpatient services to patients whose conditions require immediate care. A freestanding ED is not physically connected to a hospital but has all the necessary emergency staffing and equipment on site.

43. **Trauma center (certified).** A facility certified to provide emergency and specialized intensive care to critically ill and injured patients.

44. **Enabling services.** A program that is designed to help the patient access health care services by offering any of the following linguistic services, transportation services, and/or referrals to local social services agencies.

45. **Optical colonoscopy.** An examination of the interior of the colon using a long, flexible, lighted tube with a small built-in camera.

46. **Endoscopic ultrasound.** Specially designed endoscope that incorporates an ultrasound transducer used to obtain detailed images of organs in the chest and abdomen. The endoscope can be passed through the mouth or the anus. When combined with needle biopsy the procedure can assist in diagnosis and staging of cancer.

47. **Ablation of Barrett's esophagus.** Premalignant condition that can lead to adenocarcinoma of the esophagus. The non surgical ablation of the premalignant tissue in Barrett's esophagus by the application of thermal energy or light through an endoscope passed from the mouth into the esophagus.

48. **Esophageal impedance study.** A test in which a catheter is placed through the nose into the esophagus to measure whether gas or liquids are passing from the stomach into the esophagus and causing symptoms.

49. **Endoscopic retrograde cholangiopancreatography (ERCP).** A procedure in which a catheter is introduced through an endoscope into the bile ducts and pancreatic ducts. Injection of contrast materials permits detailed x-ray of these structures. The procedure is used diagnostically as well as therapeutically to relieve obstruction or remove stones

50. **Enrollment assistance services.** A program that provides enrollment assistance for patients who are potentially eligible for public health insurance programs such as Medicaid, State Children's Health Insurance, or local/state indigent care programs. The specific services offered could include explanation of benefits, assist applicants in completing the application and locating all relevant documents, conduct eligibilty interviews, and/or forward applications and documentation to state/local social service or health agency.

51. **Extracorporeal shock wave lithotripter (ESWL).** A medical device used for treating stones in the kidney or urethra. The device disintegrates kidney stones noninvasively through the transmission of acoustic shock waves directed at the stones.

52. **Fertility clinic.** A specialized program set in an infertility center that provides counseling and education as well as advanced reproductive techniques such as: injectable therapy, reproductive surgeries, treatment for endometriosis, male factor infertility, tubal reversals, in vitro fertilization (IVF), donor eggs, and other such services to help patients achieve successful pregnancies.

53. **Fitness center.** Provides exercise, testing, or evaluation programs and fitness activities to the community and hospital employees.

54. **Freestanding outpatient care center.** A facility owned and operated by the hospital, but physically separate from the hospital, that provides various medical treatments on an outpatient basis only. In addition to treating minor illnesses or injuries, the center will stabilize seriously ill or injured patients before transporting them to a hospital. Laboratory and radiology services are usually available.

55. **Genetic testing/counseling.** A service equipped with adequate laboratory facilities and directed by a qualified physician to advise parents and prospective parents on potential problems in cases of genetic defects. A genetic test is the analysis of human DNA, RNA, chromosomes, proteins, and certain metabolites in order to detect heritable disease–related genotypes, mutations, phenotypes, or karyotypes for clinical purposes. Genetic tests can have diverse purposes, including the diagnosis of genetic diseases in newborns, children, and adults; the identification of future health risks; the prediction of drug responses; and the assessment of risks to future children.

56. **Geriatric services.** The branch of medicine dealing with the physiology of aging and the diagnosis and treatment of disease affecting the aged. Services could include: Adult day care program; Alzheimer's diagnostic–assessment services; Comprehensive geriatric assessment; Emergency response system; Geriatric acute care unit; and/or Geriatric clinics.

57. **Health fair.** Community health education events that focus on the prevention of disease and promotion of health through such activities as audiovisual exhibits and free diagnostic services.

58. **Health research.** Organized hospital research program in any of the following areas: basic research, clinical research, community health research, and/or research on innovative health care delivery.

59. **Health screenings.** A preliminary procedure, such as a test or examination to detect the most characteristic sign or signs of a disorder that may require further investigation.

60. **Hemodialysis.** Provision of equipment and personnel for the treatment of renal insufficiency on an inpatient or outpatient basis.

61. **HIV–AIDS services.** Services may include one or more of the following: HIV–AIDS unit (special unit or team designated and equipped specifically for diagnosis, treatment, continuing care planning, and counseling services for HIV–AIDS patients and their families.) General inpatient care for HIV–AIDS (inpatient diagnosis and treatment for human immunodeficiency virus and acquired immunodeficiency syndrome patients, but dedicated unit is not available.) Specialized outpatient program for HIV–AIDS (special outpatient program providing diagnostic, treatment, continuing care planning, and counseling

for HIV–AIDS patients and their families.)

62. **Home health services.** Service providing nursing, therapy, and health–related homemaker or social services in the patient's home.

63. **Hospice program.** A program providing palliative care, chiefly medical relief of pain and supportive services, addressing the emotional, social, financial, and legal needs of terminally ill patients and their families. Care can be provided in a variety of settings, both inpatient and at home.

64. **Hospital–based outpatient care center services.** Organized hospital health care services offered by appointment on an ambulatory basis. Services may include outpatient surgery, examination, diagnosis, and treatment of a variety of medical conditions on a nonemergency basis, and laboratory and other diagnostic testing as ordered by staff or outside physician referral.

65. **Immunization program.** Program that plans, coordinates and conducts immunization services in the community.

66. **Indigent care clinic.** Health care services for uninsured and underinsured persons where care is free of charge or charged on a sliding scale. This would include "free clinics" staffed by volunteer practitioners, but could also be staffed by employees with sponsoring health care organizations subsidizing the cost of service.

67. **Intermediate nursing care.** Provides health–related services (skilled nursing care and social services) to residents with a variety of physical conditions or functional disabilities. These residents do not require the care provided by a hospital or skilled nursing facility, but do need supervision and support services.

68. **Linguistic/translation services.** Services provided by the hospital designed to make health care more accessible to non–English speaking patients and their physicians.

69. **Meal delivery services.** A hospital sponsored program which delivers meals to people, usually the elderly, who are unable to prepare their own meals. Low cost, nutritional meals are delivered to individuals' homes on a regular basis.

70. **Medical surgical intensive care services.** Provides patient care of a more intensive nature than the usual medical and surgical care, on the basis of physicians' orders and approved nursing care plans. These units are staffed with specially trained nursing personnel and contain monitoring and specialized support equipment of patients who, because of shock, trauma, or other life–threatening conditions, require intensified, comprehensive observation and care. Includes mixed intensive care units.

71. **Mobile health services.** Vans and other vehicles used to deliver primary care services.

72. **Neonatal intensive care.** A unit that must be separate from the newborn nursery providing intensive care to all sick infants including those with the very lowest birth weights (less that 1500 grams). NICU has potential for providing mechanical ventilation, neonatal surgery, and special care for the sickest infants born in the hospital or transferred from another institution. A full–time neonatologist serves as director of the NICU.

73. **Neonatal intermediate care.** A unit that must be separate from the normal newborn nursery and that provides intermediate and/or recovery care and some specialized services, including immediate resuscitation, intravenous therapy, and capacity for prolonged oxygen therapy and monitoring.

74. **Neurological services.** Services provided by the hospital dealing with the operative and nonoperative management of disorders of the central, peripheral, and autonomic nervous system.

75. **Nutrition programs.** Those services within a health care facility which are designed to provide inexpensive, nutritionally sound meals to patients.

76. **Obstetrics.** Levels should be designated: (1) unit provides services for uncomplicated maternity and newborn cases; (2) unit provides services for uncomplicated cases, the majority of complicated problems, and special neonatal services; and (3) unit provides services for all serious illnesses and abnormalities and is supervised by a full–time maternal/fetal specialist.

77. **Occupational health services.** Includes services designed to protect the safety of employees from hazards in the work environment.

78. **Oncology services.** Inpatient and outpatient services for patients with cancer, including comprehensive care, support and guidance in addition to patient education and preventiion, chemotherapy, counseling, and other treatment methods.

79. **Orthopedic services.** Services provided for the prevention or correction of injuries or disorders of the skeletal system and associated muscles, joints, and ligaments.

80. **Other special care.** Provides care to patients requiring care more intensive than that provided in the acute area, yet not sufficiently intensive to require admission to an intensive care unit. Patients admitted to the area are usually transferred here from an intensive care unit once their condition has improved. These units are sometimes referred to as definitive observation, step–down, or progressive care units.

81. **Outpatient surgery.** Scheduled surgical services provided to patients who do not remain in the hospital overnight. The surgery may be performed in operating suites also used for inpatient surgery, specially designated surgical suites for outpatient surgery, or procedure rooms within an outpatient care facility.

82. **Pain management program.** A hospital wide formalized program that includes staff education for the management of chronic and acute pain based on guidelines and protocols like those developed by the agency for Health Care Policy Research, etc.

83. **Inpatient palliative care unit.** An inpatient palliative care ward is a physically discreet, inpatient nursing unit where the focus is palliative care. The patient care focus is on symptom relief for complex patients who may be continuing to undergo primary treatment. Care is delivered by palliative medicine specialists.

84. **Palliative care program.** An organized program providing specialized medical care, drugs or therapies for the management of acute or chronic pain and/or the control of symptoms adminstered by specially trained physicians and

other clinicians; and supportive care services, such as counseling on advanced directives, spiritual care, and social services, to patients with advanced disease and their families.

85. **Patient controlled analgesia (PCA).** Patient Controlled Analgesia (PCA) is intravenously administered pain medicine under the patient's control. The patient has a button on the end of a cord than can be pushed at will, whenever more pain medicine is desired. This button will only deliver more pain medicine at pre-determined intervals, as programmed by the doctor's order.

86. **Patient education center.** Written goals and objectives for the patient and/or family related to therapeutic regimens, medical procedures, and self care.

87. **Patient representative services.** Organized hospital services providing personnel through whom patients and staff can seek solutions to institutional problems affecting the delivery of high–quality care and services.

88. **Pediatric intensive care services.** Provides care to pediatric patients that is of a more intensive nature than that usually provided to pediatric patients. The unit is staffed with specially trained personnel and contains monitoring and specialized support equipment for treatment of patients who, because of shock, trauma, or other life–threatening conditions, require intensified, comprehensive observation and care.

89. **Pediatric medical–surgical care.** Provides acute care to pediatric settings) or in a traditional setting (gymnasium) using motor learning principles.

90. **Physical rehabilitation inpatient services.** Provides care encompassing a comprehensive array of restoration services for the disabled and all support services necessary to help patients attain their maximum functional capacity.

91. **Assistive technology center.** A program providing access to specialized hardware and software with adaptations allowing individuals greater independence with mobility, dexterity, or increased communication options.

92. **Electrodiagnostic services.** Diagnostic testing services for nerve and muscle function including services such as nerve conduction studies and needle electromyography.

93. **Physical rehabilitation outpatient services.** Outpatient program providing medical, health–related, therapy, social, and/or vocational services to help disabled persons attain or retain their maximum functional capacity.

94. **Prosthetic and orthotic services.** Services providing comprehensive prosthetic and orthotic evaluation, fitting, and training.

95. **Robot-assisted walking therapy.** A form of physical therapy that uses a courts, public health nurses, welfare agencies, clergy and so forth. The purpose is to expand the mental health knowledge and competence of personnel not working in the mental health field and to promote good mental health through improved understanding, attitudes, and behavioral patterns.

96. **Simulated rehabilitation environment.** Rehabilitation focused on retraining functional skills in a contextually appropriate environment (simulated home and community settings) or in a traditional setting (gymnasium) using motor learning principles.

97. **Primary care department.** A unit or clinic within the hospital that provides primary care services (e.g. general pediatric care, general internal medicine, family practice and gynecology) through hospital–salaried medical and or nursing staff, focusing on evaluating and diagnosing medical problems and providing medical treatment on an outpatient basis.

98. **Psychiatric care.** Provides acute or long–term care to emotionally disturbed patients, including patients admitted for diagnosis and those admitted for treatment of psychiatric problems, on the basis of physicians' orders and approved nursing care plans. Long–term care may include intervention, and assistance to persons suffering acute emotional or mental distress.

99. **Psychiatric pediatric care.** The branch of medicine focused on the diagnosis, treatment, and prevention of mental, emotional, and behavioral disorders in pediatric patients.

100. **Psychiatric consultation–liaison services.** Provides organized psychiatric consultation/liaison services to nonpsychiatric hospital staff and/or department on psychological aspects of medical care that may be generic or specific to individual patients.

101. **Psychiatric education services.** Provides psychiatric educational services to community agencies and workers such as schools, police, courts, public health nurses, welfare agencies, clergy and so forth. The purpose is to expand the mental health knowledge and competence of personnel not working in the mental health field and to promote good mental health through improved understanding, attitudes, and behavioral patterns.

102. **Psychiatric emergency services.** Services or facilities available on a 24–hour basis to provide immediate unscheduled outpatient care, diagnosis, evaluation, crisis intervention, and assistance to persons suffering acute emotional or mental distress.

103. **Psychiatric geriatric services.** Provides care to emotionally disturbed elderly patients, including those admitted for diagnosis and those admitted for treatment.

104. **Psychiatric outpatient services.** Provides medical care, including diagnosis and treatment of psychiatric outpatients.

105. **Psychiatric partial hospitalization services.** Organized hospital services of intensive day/evening outpatient services of three hours or more duration, distinguished from other outpatient visits of one hour.

106. **Psychiatric residential treatment.**

107. **CT scanner.** Computed tomographic scanner for head and whole body scans.

108. **Diagnostic radioisotope facility.** The use of radioactive isotopes (Radiopharmaceutical) as tracers or indicators to detect an abnormal condition or disease.

109. **Electron beam computed tomography (EBCT).** A high tech computed tomography scan used to detect coronary artery disease by measuring coronary calcifications. This imaging procedure uses electron beams which are magnetically steered to produce a visual of the coronary artery and the images are produced faster than conventional CT scans.

110. **Full–field digital mammography (FFDM).** Combines the x–ray generators and tubes used in analog screen–film mammography (SFM) with a detector plate that converts the x–rays into a digital signal.

111. **Magnetic resonance imaging (MRI).** The use of a uniform magnetic field and radio frequencies to study tissue and structure of the body. This procedure enables the visualization of biochemical activity of the cell in vivo without the use of ionizing radiation, radioisotopic substances, or high–frequency sound.

112. **Intraoperative magnetic resonance imaging.** An integrated surgery system which provides an MRI system in an operating room. The system allows for immediate evaluation of the degree to tumor resection while the patient is undergoing a surgical resection. Intraoperative MRI exists when a MRI (low–field or high–field) is placed in the operating theater and is used during surgical resection without moving the patient from the operating room to the diagnostic imaging suite.

113. **Magnetoencephalography (MEG).** A noninvasive neurophysiological measurement tool used to study magnetic fields generated by neuronal activity of the brain. MEG provides direct information about the dynamics of evoked and spontaneous neural activity and the location of their sources in the brain. The primary uses of MEG include assisting surgeons in localizing the source of epilepsy, sensory mapping and the study of brain function. When it is combined with structural imaging, it is known as magnetic source imaging (MSI).

114. **Multi–slice spiral computed tomography (MSCT) (<64 slice CT).** A specialized computed tomography cycles per second to visualize internal body structures.

115. **Multi–slice spiral computed tomography (64 + slice CT).** Involves the acquisition of volumetric tomographic x–ray absorption data expressed in Hounsfield units using multiple rows of detectors. 64+ systems reconstruct the equivalent of 64 or greater slices to cover the imaged volume.

116. **Positron emission tomography (PET).** A nuclear medicine imaging technology which uses radioactive (positron emitting) isotopes created in a cyclotron or generator and computers to produce composite pictures of the brain and heart at work. PET scanning produces sectional images depicting metabolic activity or blood flow rather than anatomy.

117. **Positron emission tomography/CT (PET/CT).** Provides metabolic functional information for the monitoring of chemotherapy, radiotherapy and surgical planning.

118. **Single photon emission computerized tomography (SPECT).** A nuclear medicine imaging technology that combines existing technology of gamma camera imaging with computed tomographic imaging technology to provide a more precise and clear image.

119. **Ultrasound.** The use of acoustic waves above the range of 20,000 cycles per second to visualize internal body structures.

120. **Image-guided radiation therapy (IGRT).** Automated system for image– guided radiation therapy that enables clinicians to obtain high–resolution x– ray images to pinpoint tumor sites, adjust patient positioning when necessary, and complete a treatment, all within the standard treatment time slot, allowing for more effective cancer treatments.

121. **Intensity–modulated radiation Therapy (IMRT).** A type of three–dimensional radiation therapy, which improves the targeting of treatment delivery in a way that is likely to decrease damage to normal tissues and allows varying intensities diagnosis of genetic diseases in newborns, children, and adults; the identification of future health risks; arrange for acute and long term care through affiliated institutions.

122. **Proton beam therapy.** A form of radiation therapy which administers proton beams. While producing the same biologic effects as x–ray beams, the energy distribution of protons differs from conventional x–ray beams in that they can be more precisely focused in tissue volumes in a three–dimensional pattern resulting in less surrounding tissue damage than conventional radiation therapy permitting administration of higher doses.

123. **Shaped beam radiation therapy.** A precise, non–invasive treatment that involves targeting beams of radiation that mirror the exact size and shape of a tumor at a specific area of a tumor to shrink or destroy cancerous cells. This procedure delivers a therapeutic dose of radiation that conforms precisely to the shape of the tumor, thus minimizing the risk to nearby tissues.

124. **Stereotactic radiosurgery.** Stereotactic radiosurgery (SRS) is a radiotherapy modality that delivers a high dosage of radiation to a discrete treatment area in as few as one treatment session. Includes gamma knife, cyberknife, etc.

125. **Retirement housing.** A facility which provides social activities to senior citizens, usually retired persons, who do not require health care but some short–term skilled nursing care may be provided. A retirement center may furnish housing and may also have acute hospital and long–term care facilities, or it may arrange for acute and long term care through affiliated institutions.

126. **Robotic surgery.** The use of mechanical guidance devices to remotely manipulate surgical instrumentation.

127. **Rural health clinic.** A clinic located in a rural, medically under-served area in the United States that has a separate reimbursement structure from the standard medical office under the Medicare and Medicaid programs.

128. **Skilled nursing care.** Provides non–acute medical and skilled nursing care services, therapy, and social services under the supervision of a licensed registered nurse on a 24–hour basis.

129. **Sleep center.** Specially equipped and staffed center for the diagnosis and treatment of sleep disorders.

130. **Social work services.** Services may include one or more of the following: Organized social work services (services that are properly directed and sufficiently staffed by qualified individuals who provide assistance and counseling to patients and their families in dealing with social, emotional, and environmental problems associated with illness or disability, often in the context of financial or discharge planning coordination.) Outpatient social work services (social work services provided in ambulatory care areas.) Emergency department social work services (social work services provided to emergency department patients by social workers dedicated to the emergency department or on call.)

131. **Sports medicine.** Provision of diagnostic screening and assessment and clinical and rehabilitation services for the prevention and treatment of sports–related injuries.

132. **Support groups.** A hospital sponsored program which allows a group of individuals with the same or similar problems who meet periodically to share experiences, problems, and solutions, in order to support each other.

133. **Swing bed services.** A hospital bed that can be used to provide either acute or long–term care depending on community or patients needs. To be eligible a hospital must have a Medicare provider agreement in place, have fewer than 100 beds, be located in a rural area, not have a 24 hour nursing service waiver in effect, have not been terminated from the program in the prior two years, and meet various service conditions.

134. **Teen outreach services**. A program focusing on the teenager which encourages an improved health status and a healthful lifestyle including physical, emotional, mental, social, spiritual and economic health through education, exercise, nutrition and health promotion.

135. **Tobacco treatment/cessation program.** Organized hospital services with the purpose of ending tobacco–use habits of patients addicted to tobacco/nicotine.

136.–142. **Transplant services.** The branch of medicine that transfers an organ or tissue from one person to another or from one body part to another to replace a diseased structure or to restore function or to change appearance. Services could include: Bone marrow transplant program (136. Bone marrow); heart (137. Heart transplant), kidney (138. Kidney transplant), liver (139. Liver transplant) lung (140. Lung transplant), tissue (141. Tissue transplant). Please include heart/lung or other multi- transplant surgeries inn other (142. Other Transplant).

143. **Transportation to health services.** A long–term care support service designed to assist the mobility of the elderly. Some programs offer improved financial access by offering reduced rates and barrier–free buses or vans with ramps and lifts to assist the elderly or handicapped; others offer subsidies for public transport systems or operate mini–bus services

144. **Urgent care center.** A facility that provides care and treatment for problems that are not life–threatening but require attention over the short term. These units function like emergency rooms but are separate from hospitals with which they may have backup affiliation arrangements.

145. **Virtual colonoscopy.** Noninvasive screening procedure used to visualize, analyze and detect cancerous or potentially cancerous polyps in the colon.

146. **Volunteer services department.** An organized hospital department responsible for coordinating the services of volunteers working within the institution.

147. **Women's center.** An area set aside for coordinated education and treatment services specifically for and promoted by women as provided by this special unit. Services may or may not include obstetrics but include a range of services other than OB.

148. **Wound management services.** Services for patients with chronic wounds and non–healing wounds often resulting from diabetes, poor circulation, improper seating and immunocompromising conditions. The goals are to progress chronic wounds through stages of healing, reduce and eliminate infections, increase physical function to minimize complications from current wounds and prevent future chronic wounds. Wound management services are provided on an inpatient or outpatient basis, depending on the intensity of service needed.

149. **Violence prevention programs for the workplace.** A violence prevention program with goals and objectives for preventing workplace violence against staff and patients.

150. **Violence prevention programs for the community.** An organized program that attempts to make a positive impact on the type(s) of violence a community is experiencing. For example, it can assist victims of violent crimes, e.g., rape, or incidents, e.g., bullying, to hospital or to community services to prevent further victimization or retaliation. A program that targets the underlying circumstances that contribute to violence such as poor housing, insufficient job training, and/or substance abuse through means such as direct involvement and support, education, mentoring, anger management, crisis intervention and training programs would also qualify.

151. **Alcoholism-chemical dependency pediatric services.** Provides diagnosis and therapeutic services to pediatric patients with alcoholism or other drug dependencies. Includes care for inpatient/residential treatment for patients whose course of treatment involves more intensive care than provided in an outpatient setting or where patient requires supervised withdrawal.

152. **Alcoholism-chemical dependency partial hospitalization services.** Organized hospital services providing intensive day/evening outpatient services of three hour or more duration, distinguished from other outpatient visits of one hour.

153. **Psychiatric intensive outpatient services.** A prescribed course of treatment in which the patient receives outpatient care no less than three times a week (which might include more than one service/day).

154. **Telehealth.** A broad variety of technologies and tactics to deliver virtual medical, public health, health education delivery, and support services using telecommunications technologies. Telehealth is used more commonly as it describes the wide range of diagnosis and management, education, and other related fields of health care. This includes, but are not limited to: dentistry, counseling, physical and occupational therapy, home health, chronic disease monitoring and management, disaster management, and consumer and professional education, and remote patient monitoring.

155. **Air ambulance services.** Aircraft and especially a helicopter equipped for transporting the injured or sick. Most air ambulances carry critically ill or injured patients, whose condition could rapidly change for the worse.

156. **Diabetes prevention program.** Program to prevent or delay the onset of type 2 diabetes by offering evidence-based lifestyle changes based on research studies, which showed modest behavior changes helped individuals with prediabetes reduce their risk of developing type 2 diabetes.

157. **Employment support services.** Services designed to support individuals with significant disabilities to seek and maintain employment.

158. **Supportive housing services.** A hospital program that provides decent, safe, affordable, community-based housing with flexible support services designed to help the individual or family stay housed and live a more productive life in the community.

160. Medication assisted treatment for Opioid Use Disorder. Medication assisted treatment (MAT) is the use of medications, in combination with counseling and behavioral therapies, to provide a "whole-patient" approach to the treatment of substance use disorders. Medications used in MAT are approved by the Food and Drug Administration (FDA) and MAT programs are clinically driven and tailed to meet each patient's needs.

161. Medication assisted treatment for other substance use disorders. Medication assisted treatment (MAT) is the use of medications, in combination with counseling and behavioral therapies, to provide a "whole-patient" approach to the treatment of substance use disorders. Medications used in MAT are approved by the Food and Drug Administration (FDA) and MAT programs are clinically driven and tailed to meet each patient's needs.

162. Prenatal and postpartum psychiatric services. Psychiatric care during and post-pregnancy. Includes perinatal depression and postpartum depression.

163. Forensic psychiatric services. A medical subspecialty that includes research and clinical practice in many areas in which psychiatric is applied to legal issues.

164. Suicide prevention services. A collection of efforts to reduce the risk of suicide. These efforts may occur at the individual, relationship, community and society levels.

165. Social and community psychiatry. Social psychiatry deals with social factors associated with psychiatric morbidity, social effects of mental illness, psycho-social disorders and social approaches to psychiatric care. Community psychiatry focuses on detection, prevention, early treatment and rehabilitation of emotional and behavioral disorders as they develop in a community.

166. Biocontainment patient care unit. A permanent unit that provides the first line of treatment for people affected by bio-terrorism or highly hazardous communicable diseases. The unit is equipped to safely care for anyone exposed to a highly contagious and dangerous disease. Please do not report temporary COVID-19 units on this line (report COVID units as other special care.)

167. Basic interventional radiology. Therapies include embolization, angioplasty, stent placement, thrombus management, drainage and ablation among others. Facilities providing interventional radiology should have a radiologist with additional certification and training in diagnostic radiology, interventional radiology, or radiation oncology.

168. Hospital at home program. Hospital-at-home enable some patients who need acute-level care to receive care in their homes, rather than in a hospital.

169. Prenatal and postpartum services. Pregnancy care consists of prenatal (before birth) and postpartum (after birth) healthcare for expectant mothers. It involves treatments and trainings to ensure a healthy pre-pregnancy, pregnancy, labor and delivery.

Control and Service Classifications

Control

Government, nonfederal
State
County
City
City–county
Hospital district or authority

Nongovernment not–for–profit
Church operated
Other

Investor–owned (for–profit)
Individual
Partnership
Corporation

Department of Defense, Government, federal*
Public Health Service other than 47
Veterans Affairs

Osteopathic
Church operated Other not–for–profit
Other
Individual for–profit
Partnership for–profit
Corporation for–profit

Service

General medical and surgical
Hospital unit of an institution (prison hospital, college infirmary, etc.)
Hospital unit within a facility for persons with intellectual disabilities
Surgical
Psychiatric
Tuberculosis and other respiratory diseases
Cancer
Heart
Obstetrics and gynecology
Eye, ear, nose, and throat
Rehabilitation
Orthopedic
Chronic disease
Other specialty
Children's general
Children's hospital unit of an institution
Children's psychiatric
Children's tuberculosis and other respiratory diseases
Children's eye, ear, nose, and throat
Children's rehabilitation
Children's orthopedic
Children's chronic disease
Children's other specialty
Intellectual disabilities
Long–Term Acute Care
Alcoholism and other chemical dependency
Children's Long–Term Acute Care
Children's Cancer
Children's Heart
Rural Emergency Hospital

---

* Starting with the 2018 Annual Survey, Air Force, Army, and Navy are now rolled up into the Department of Defense.

Hospitals in the United States, by State

AL

ALABAMA

ALABASTER—Shelby County

☐ **NOLAND HOSPITAL SHELBY (012013)**, 1000 First Street North, 3rd Floor, Zip 35007–8703; tel. 205/620–8641, (Nonreporting) **A**1 10 **S** Noland Health Services, Inc., Birmingham, AL
Primary Contact: Laura S. Wills, Administrator
Web address: www.nolandhospitals.com
Control: Other not–for–profit (including NFP Corporation) **Service:** Acute long–term care hospital

Staffed Beds: 52

☒ **SHELBY BAPTIST MEDICAL CENTER (010016)**, 1000 First Street North, Zip 35007–8703; tel. 205/620–8100, (Nonreporting) **A**1 10 **S** TENET Healthcare Corporation, Dallas, TX
Primary Contact: Holly Dean, Chief Executive Officer
COO: Megan Drake, Chief Operating Officer
CFO: Jennifer Pittman, Chief Financial Officer
CMO: Jade Brice Roshell, M.D., Chief Medical Officer
CIO: Mike Nighman, Facility Coordinator Information Systems
CHR: Cindy Nicholson, Director Human Resources
CNO: Susan Bria, Chief Nursing Officer
Web address: https://www.shelbybaptistmedicalcenter.com/
Control: Church operated, Nongovernment, not–for–profit **Service:** General medical and surgical

Staffed Beds: 231

ALEXANDER CITY—Tallapoosa County

☐ **RUSSELL MEDICAL (010065)**, 3316 Highway 280, Zip 35010–3369, Mailing Address: P.O. Box 939, Zip 35011–0939; tel. 256/329–7100, **A**1 3 10 19 **F**3 15 18 20 22 28 29 30 31 34 35 40 43 45 50 51 53 56 57 59 60 67 75 76 77 78 79 80 81 85 89 93 102 107 108 110 111 115 116 119 121 123 126 127 129 131 133 143 144 146 148 149 154 167 169
Primary Contact: Lother E. Peace III, President and Chief Executive Officer
CFO: J. Matthew Fisher, Chief Financial Officer
CMO: Michele Goldhagen, M.D., Chief Medical Officer
CIO: Donna Carter, Chief Information Officer and Security Officer
CHR: Holly Williams, Human Resources Director
Web address: www.russellmedcenter.com
Control: Other not–for–profit (including NFP Corporation) **Service:** General medical and surgical

Staffed Beds: 69 **Admissions:** 1604 **Census:** 13 **Outpatient Visits:** 96355 **Births:** 238 **Total Expense ($000):** 89566 **Payroll Expense ($000):** 33504 **Personnel:** 497

ANDALUSIA—Covington County

☒ **ANDALUSIA HEALTH (010036)**, 849 South Three Notch Street, Zip 36420–5325, Mailing Address: P.O. Box 760, Zip 36420–1214; tel. 334/222–8466, (Nonreporting) **A**1 10 **S** ScionHealth, Louisville, KY
Primary Contact: Vickie Demers, Chief Executive Officer
CFO: Shirley M Smith, Chief Financial Officer
CIO: Matthew Perry, Director Information Systems
CHR: Brian Woods, Human Resources Director
CNO: Pam Aud, Chief Clinical Officer
Web address: www.andalusiahealth.com
Control: Corporation, Investor–owned (for–profit) **Service:** General medical and surgical

Staffed Beds: 78

ANNISTON—Calhoun County

☐ **NOLAND HOSPITAL ANNISTON (012011)**, 400 East 10th Street, 4th Fl, Zip 36207–4716; tel. 256/741–6141, (Nonreporting) **A**1 10 **S** Noland Health Services, Inc., Birmingham, AL
Primary Contact: Trina Woods, Administrator
Web address: www.nolandhealth.com
Control: Other not–for–profit (including NFP Corporation) **Service:** Acute long–term care hospital

Staffed Beds: 38

☒ **RMC ANNISTON (010078)**, 400 East Tenth Street, Zip 36207–4716, Mailing Address: P.O. Box 2208, Zip 36202–2208; tel. 256/235–5121, (Nonreporting) **A**1 2 10 19
Primary Contact: Louis A. Bass, Chief Executive Officer
COO: Tripp Johnson, Assistant Vice President Operations
CFO: Mark D. North, Chief Financial Officer
CMO: David Zinn, M.D., Vice President Medical Affairs
CIO: Pete Furlow, Chief Information Officer
CHR: Doug Scott, Vice President Human Resources
CNO: Elaine Davis, Chief Nursing Officer and Vice President Patient Services
Web address: www.rmccares.org
Control: Hospital district or authority, Government, Nonfederal **Service:** General medical and surgical

Staffed Beds: 216

ASHLAND—Clay County

CLAY COUNTY HOSPITAL (010073), 83825 Highway 9, Zip 36251–7981, Mailing Address: P.O. Box 1270, Zip 36251–1270; tel. 256/354–2131, (Nonreporting) **A**10
Primary Contact: Stephen Young, Chief Executive Officer
CFO: Kerry W Tomlin, Associate Administrator
CMO: David Hensleigh, Director Medical Staff
CIO: Patrick Smith, Director Information Technology
CHR: Linda T Smith, Director Human Resources
CNO: Charles Griffin, Director of Nursing
Web address: www.claycountyhospital.com
Control: County, Government, Nonfederal **Service:** General medical and surgical

Staffed Beds: 129

ATHENS—Limestone County

☐ **ATHENS–LIMESTONE HOSPITAL (010079)**, 700 West Market Street, Zip 35611–2457, Mailing Address: P.O. Box 999, Zip 35612–0999; tel. 256/233–9292, (Nonreporting) **A**1 5 10 **S** Huntsville Hospital Health System, Huntsville, AL
Primary Contact: Traci Collins, President
COO: Randy Comer, Chief Operating Officer
CFO: Randy Comer, Chief Financial Officer
CMO: Jon Bignault, M.D., Chief of Staff
CIO: Kim Hoback, Supervisor Information Systems
CHR: Rachel Frey, Director Human Resources
CNO: Traci Collins, Chief Nursing Officer
Web address: www.athenslimestonehospital.com
Control: Hospital district or authority, Government, Nonfederal **Service:** General medical and surgical

Staffed Beds: 71

NORTH ALABAMA SPECIALTY HOSPITAL (012014), 700 West Market Street, 2 South, Zip 35611–2457; tel. 256/262–6767, (Nonreporting) **A**10 22
Primary Contact: Gene Smith, Chief Executive Officer
Web address: www.amgnash.com
Control: Corporation, Investor–owned (for–profit) **Service:** Acute long–term care hospital

Staffed Beds: 31

ATMORE—Escambia County

ATMORE COMMUNITY HOSPITAL (010169), 401 Medical Park Drive, Zip 36502–3091; tel. 251/368–2500, (Nonreporting) **A**10
Primary Contact: Brad Lowery, Chief Executive Officer
COO: Brad Lowery, Director of Operations
CFO: Keith Strickling, Chief Financial Officer
CHR: Linda Lowrey, Human Resources Officer
CNO: Suzanne McGill, Director of Nursing
Web address: www.atmorehealth.org/
Control: Other not–for–profit (including NFP Corporation) **Service:** General medical and surgical

Staffed Beds: 33

Hospital, Medicare Provider Number, Address, Telephone, Approval, Facility, and Physician Codes, Health Care System

★ American Hospital Association (AHA) membership ○ Healthcare Facilities Accreditation Program ⇧ Center for Improvement in Healthcare Quality Accreditation
☐ The Joint Commission accreditation ◇ DNV Healthcare Inc. accreditation △ Commission on Accreditation of Rehabilitation Facilities (CARF) accreditation

© 2025 AHA Guide

Hospitals **A15**

Hospitals, U.S. / ALABAMA

BAY MINETTE—Baldwin County

NORTH BALDWIN INFIRMARY (010129), 1815 Hand Avenue, Zip 36507–4110, Mailing Address: P.O. Box 1409, Zip 36507–1409; tel. 251/937–5521, **A**3 10 **F**3 13 18 28 29 30 31 34 35 40 41 43 45 50 53 55 56 57 59 64 65 68 74 75 76 77 78 79 81 85 87 93 98 103 107 108 111 114 118 119 130 132 135 145 146 149 154 156 157 169 **P**4 7 **S** Infirmary Health System, Mobile, AL
Primary Contact: Kenny Breal, President
CFO: J Patrick Murphy, Chief Financial Officer
Web address: https://www.infirmaryhealth.org/locations/north-baldwin-infirmary/
Control: Other not–for–profit (including NFP Corporation) **Service**: General medical and surgical

Staffed Beds: 113 **Admissions**: 2494 **Census**: 33 **Outpatient Visits**: 34808 **Births**: 174 **Total Expense ($000)**: 57992 **Payroll Expense ($000)**: 17832 **Personnel**: 342

BESSEMER—Jefferson County

MEDICAL WEST (010114), 995 Ninth Avenue SW, Zip 35022–4527; tel. 205/481–7000, **A**1 3 10 **F**3 11 13 15 18 20 28 29 30 31 33 34 40 42 43 45 49 50 53 54 57 59 60 64 68 70 74 75 76 77 78 79 81 85 86 90 92 93 94 96 98 100 101 102 103 104 107 108 110 111 114 115 118 119 129 130 132 146 147 148 149 154 167 **P**6 **S** UAB Health System, Birmingham, AL
Primary Contact: Brian Keith. Pennington, President and Chief Executive Officer
CFO: Brandon H Slocum, Senior Vice President and Chief Financial Officer
CMO: Conrad De Los Santos, President Medical Staff
CIO: Bob Duckworth, Director Information Systems
CHR: Gannon Davis, Director Human Resources
CNO: Pamela Spencer Autrey, R.N., Ph.D., MSN, Chief Nursing Officer
Web address: www.medicalwesthospital.org
Control: Hospital district or authority, Government, Nonfederal **Service**: General medical and surgical

Staffed Beds: 236 **Admissions**: 6578 **Census**: 116 **Outpatient Visits**: 258897 **Births**: 318 **Total Expense ($000)**: 165032 **Payroll Expense ($000)**: 63249 **Personnel**: 1088

BIRMINGHAM—Jefferson County

ASCENSION ST. VINCENT'S BIRMINGHAM (010056), 810 St Vincent's Drive, Zip 35205–1695, Mailing Address: P.O. Box 12407, Zip 35202–2407; tel. 205/939–7000, (Nonreporting) **A**1 2 3 5 10 **S** Ascension Healthcare, Saint Louis, MO
Primary Contact: Tim Puthoff, President
COO: Andy Davis, Chief Operating Officer
CFO: Wilma Newton, Executive Vice President and Chief Financial Officer
CMO: Wesley Smith, M.D., FACS, Chief Medical Officer and Physician Advisor
CIO: Timothy Stettheimer, Vice President and Chief Information Officer
CHR: Michelle Galipeau, Director Human Resources
Web address: https://healthcare.ascension.org/locations/alabama/albir/birmingham-ascension-st-vincents-birmingham
Control: Other not–for–profit (including NFP Corporation) **Service**: General medical and surgical

Staffed Beds: 387

ASCENSION ST. VINCENT'S EAST (010011), 50 Medical Park East Drive, Zip 35235–9987; tel. 205/838–3000, **A**1 2 3 5 10 **F**3 11 12 17 18 20 22 24 26 28 29 30 31 35 37 40 43 44 45 46 49 50 51 53 57 59 70 74 77 78 79 81 84 85 86 87 90 93 98 100 102 103 107 108 111 114 118 119 120 121 123 124 126 129 130 132 135 146 147 149 154 167 **S** Ascension Healthcare, Saint Louis, MO
Primary Contact: Suzannah Campbell, President
CFO: Jan DiCesare, Vice President Financial Operations
CMO: Frank Malensek, M.D., Chief Medical Officer
CIO: Beverly Golightly, Director Information Technology
CHR: Carol Maietta, Vice President Human Resources and Chief Learning Officer
CNO: Amy Shelton, Chief Nursing Officer
Web address: https://healthcare.ascension.org/locations/alabama/albir/birmingham-ascension-st-vincents-east
Control: Other not–for–profit (including NFP Corporation) **Service**: General medical and surgical

Staffed Beds: 308 **Admissions**: 13982 **Census**: 239 **Outpatient Visits**: 43514 **Births**: 0 **Total Expense ($000)**: 221475 **Payroll Expense ($000)**: 87933

BIRMINGHAM VA MEDICAL CENTER, 700 South 19th Street, Zip 35233–1927; tel. 205/933–8101, **A**1 2 3 5 7 8 **F**3 5 15 17 18 24 26 28 29 30 31 33 34 35 36 37 38 39 40 45 46 47 48 49 54 56 57 58 59 60 62 63 64 70 74 75 77 78 79 80 81 82 83 84 85 86 87 91 92 93 94 95 96 97 100 101 102 104 107 108 109 110 111 112 113 114 115 116 117 118 119 120 126 127 129 130 132 133 135 138 143 144 147 148 149 153 154 156 157 164 165 167 **S** Department of Veterans Affairs, Washington, DC
Primary Contact: Oladipo A. Kukoyi, M.D., Executive Director, Chief Executive Officer
COO: Phyllis J. Smith, Associate Director
CFO: Mary S Mitchell, Chief Resource Management Services
CMO: William F Harper, M.D., Chief of Staff
CIO: Antonia Mohamed, Acting Chief Information Officer
CHR: Jacqueline Caron, Chief Human Resources
CNO: Cynthia Cleveland, Ph.D., R.N., Associate Director for Patient Care Services and Nurse Executive
Web address: www.birmingham.va.gov/
Control: Veterans Affairs, Government, federal **Service**: General medical and surgical

Staffed Beds: 141 **Admissions**: 6377 **Census**: 71 **Outpatient Visits**: 848170 **Births**: 0 **Total Expense ($000)**: 992040 **Payroll Expense ($000)**: 419225 **Personnel**: 2860

BIRMINGHAM VAMC See Birmingham VA Medical Center

BROOKWOOD BAPTIST MEDICAL CENTER (010139), 2010 Brookwood Medical Center Drive, Zip 35209–6875; tel. 205/877–1000, (Nonreporting) **A**1 3 5 7 10 **S** TENET Healthcare Corporation, Dallas, TX
Primary Contact: Jeremy L. Clark, Chief Executive Officer
CMO: Vish Sachdev, M.D., Chief Medical Officer
CIO: Manuel Price, Director Information Systems
CHR: Ronnelle Stewart, Chief Human Resources Officer
CNO: Jacquelyn Martinek, R.N., Group Chief Nursing Officer
Web address: https://www.brookwoodbaptisthealth.com/
Control: Corporation, Investor–owned (for–profit) **Service**: General medical and surgical

Staffed Beds: 595

CHILDREN'S OF ALABAMA (013300), 1600 Seventh Avenue South, Zip 35233–1785; tel. 205/638–9100, (Nonreporting) **A**1 3 5 8 10
Primary Contact: Tom Shufflebarger, President and Chief Executive Officer
COO: Andrew Loehr, Senior Vice President and Chief Operating Officer
CFO: Dawn Walton, Chief Financial Officer
CMO: Crayton A Fargason, M.D., Medical Director
CIO: Robert Sarnecki, Interim Chief Information Officer
CHR: Douglas B Dean, Chief Human Resources Officer
CNO: Delicia Y Mason, Vice President of Nursing Operations
Web address: www.childrensal.org
Control: Other not–for–profit (including NFP Corporation) **Service**: Children's general medical and surgical

Staffed Beds: 351

ENCOMPASS HEALTH LAKESHORE REHABILITATION HOSPITAL (013025), 3800 Ridgeway Drive, Zip 35209–5599; tel. 205/868–2000, (Nonreporting) **A**1 10 **S** Encompass Health Corporation, Birmingham, AL
Primary Contact: Michael Bartell, Chief Executive Officer
CFO: Kimberly Thrasher, Controller
CMO: Michael Rosemore, M.D., Medical Director
CHR: Julie Smith, Director Human Resources
CNO: April Cobb, Chief Nursing Officer
Web address: www.encompasshealth.com/lakeshorerehab
Control: Corporation, Investor–owned (for–profit) **Service**: Rehabilitation

Staffed Beds: 100

GRANDVIEW MEDICAL CENTER (010104), 3690 Grandview Parkway, Zip 35243–3326; tel. 205/971–1000, (Nonreporting) **A**1 3 5 10 **S** Community Health Systems, Inc., Franklin, TN
Primary Contact: Daniel McKinney, Chief Executive Officer
CFO: Michael Cotton, Chief Financial Officer
CMO: David Wynne, President Medical Staff
CIO: Tim Townes, Director Information Systems
CHR: Jeri Wink, Director Human Resources
CNO: Sherry Cole, Chief Nursing Officer
Web address: www.grandviewhealth.com
Control: Corporation, Investor–owned (for–profit) **Service**: General medical and surgical

Staffed Beds: 434

HEALTHSOUTH MEDICAL CENTER See UAB Highlands

Hospitals, U.S. / ALABAMA

☐ **HILL CREST BEHAVIORAL HEALTH SERVICES (014000)**, 6869 Fifth Avenue South, Zip 35212–1866; tel. 205/833–9000, **A**1 10 **F**29 30 32 35 38 50 59 65 68 75 98 99 100 102 106 122 130 135 149 156 163 164 **S** Universal Health Services, Inc., King of Prussia, PA
Primary Contact: Ballard Sheppard, Ph.D., Chief Executive Officer
CFO: Mark Teske, Chief Financial Officer
Web address: www.hillcrestbhs.com
Control: Partnership, Investor–owned (for-profit) **Service:** Psychiatric

Staffed Beds: 170 **Admissions:** 724 **Census:** 130 **Outpatient Visits:** 0 **Births:** 0 **Total Expense ($000):** 25400 **Payroll Expense ($000):** 14566 **Personnel:** 234

☐ **NOLAND HOSPITAL BIRMINGHAM (012009)**, 50 Medical Park East Drive, 8th Floor, Zip 35235; tel. 205/838–5100, (Nonreporting) **A**1 10 **S** Noland Health Services, Inc., Birmingham, AL
Primary Contact: Laura S. Wills, Administrator
COO: Sharon Engle, Director Clinical Services
CMO: Mark Middlebrooks, M.D., Medical Director
CHR: Ashley Clark, Coordinator Human Resources
CNO: Rachel Chapman, Nurse Manager
Web address: www.nolandhealth.com
Control: Other not–for–profit (including NFP Corporation) **Service:** Acute long–term care hospital

Staffed Beds: 45

✠ **PRINCETON BAPTIST MEDICAL CENTER (010103)**, 701 Princeton Avenue SW, Zip 35211–1303; tel. 205/783–3000, (Nonreporting) **A**1 3 5 10 **S** TENET Healthcare Corporation, Dallas, TX
Primary Contact: Daniel Listi, Chief Executive Officer
CFO: Amanda Dyle, Chief Financial Officer
CMO: Alan Craig, M.D., Chief Medical Officer
CHR: Jason Hatter, Chief Human Resource Officer
CNO: Van McGrue, R.N., MSN, Chief Nursing Officer
Web address: www.bhsala.com
Control: Church operated, Nongovernment, not–for–profit **Service:** General medical and surgical

Staffed Beds: 315

✠ **SELECT SPECIALTY HOSPITAL-BIRMINGHAM (012008)**, 2010 Brookwood Medical Center Drive, 3rd Floor, Zip 35209–6804; tel. 205/599–4600, (Nonreporting) **A**1 10 **S** Select Medical Corporation, Mechanicsburg, PA
Primary Contact: Andrew Howard, Chief Executive Officer
CMO: Allan Goldstein, M.D., Medical Director and Chief of Staff
Web address: www.birmingham.selectspecialtyhospitals.com
Control: Corporation, Investor–owned (for-profit) **Service:** Acute long–term care hospital

Staffed Beds: 38

ST. VINCENT'S BIRMINGHAM See Ascension St. Vincent's Birmingham

ST. VINCENT'S EAST See Ascension St. Vincent's East

UAB HIGHLANDS See University of Alabama Hospital, Birmingham

✠ **UNIVERSITY OF ALABAMA HOSPITAL (010033)**, 619 19th Street South, Zip 35249–1900; tel. 205/934–4011, (Includes UAB HIGHLANDS, 1201 11th Avenue South, Birmingham, Alabama, Zip 35205–5299, tel. 205/930–7000; Frank Sortino, Administrator) **A**1 2 3 5 8 10 **F**3 4 5 6 7 9 11 12 13 15 16 17 18 20 22 24 26 28 29 30 31 34 35 36 37 38 39 40 41 42 43 44 45 46 47 48 49 50 51 52 53 54 55 56 57 58 59 60 61 62 64 65 66 68 70 71 72 73 74 75 76 77 78 79 81 82 83 84 85 86 87 90 91 92 93 94 96 97 98 99 100 101 102 103 104 105 107 108 110 111 112 113 114 115 116 117 118 119 120 121 123 124 126 127 129 130 131 132 135 136 137 138 139 140 141 142 143 144 145 146 147 148 149 150 152 153 154 155 156 157 160 161 162 164 165 167 169 **S** UAB Health System, Birmingham, AL
Primary Contact: Brenda H. Carlisle, R.N., Chief Executive Officer
CMO: Loring Rue, M.D., Senior Vice President, Quality Patient Safety and Clinical Effectiveness
CIO: Joan Hicks, Chief Information Officer
CHR: Alesia Jones, Chief Human Resources Officer
CNO: Terri Lyn Poe, Chief Nursing Officer
Web address: www.uabmedicine.org
Control: State, Government, Nonfederal **Service:** General medical and surgical

Staffed Beds: 1304 **Admissions:** 53252 **Census:** 1165 **Outpatient Visits:** 979178 **Births:** 4108 **Total Expense ($000):** 2879740 **Payroll Expense ($000):** 1015757 **Personnel:** 13090

BOAZ—Marshall County

☐ **MARSHALL MEDICAL CENTER SOUTH (010005)**, US Highway 431 North, Zip 35957–0999, Mailing Address: P.O. Box 758, Zip 35957–0758; tel. 256/593–8310, (Nonreporting) **A**1 10 19 **S** Marshall Health System, Guntersville, AL
Primary Contact: Christopher Rush, President
CFO: Taylor Walker, Chief Financial Officer
Web address: www.mmcenters.com//index.php/facilities/marshall_south
Control: Hospital district or authority, Government, Nonfederal **Service:** General medical and surgical

Staffed Beds: 107

BREWTON—Escambia County

☐ **D. W. MCMILLAN MEMORIAL HOSPITAL (010099)**, 1301 Belleville Avenue, Zip 36426–1306, Mailing Address: P.O. Box 908, Zip 36427–0908; tel. 251/867–8061, (Nonreporting) **A**1 10
Primary Contact: Stacy Hines, Administrator
CIO: Ian Vickery, Director Information Technology
CHR: Autherine Davis, Director Human Resources
CNO: LeAnne Rowell, Director of Nursing
Web address: www.dwmmh.org
Control: Hospital district or authority, Government, Nonfederal **Service:** General medical and surgical

Staffed Beds: 49

BUTLER—Choctaw County

CHOCTAW GENERAL HOSPITAL See Ochsner Choctaw General

★ **OCHSNER CHOCTAW GENERAL (011304)**, 401 Vanity Fair Avenue, Zip 36904–3032; tel. 205/459–9100, (Nonreporting) **A**10 18 **S** Ochsner Health, New Orleans, LA
Primary Contact: Kawanda Johnson, Ph.D., MSN, Administrator
Web address: www.choctawgeneral.com/cgh/
Control: Other not–for–profit (including NFP Corporation) **Service:** General medical and surgical

Staffed Beds: 25

CENTRE—Cherokee County

☐ **ATRIUM HEALTH FLOYD CHEROKEE MEDICAL CENTER (010022)**, 400 Northwood Drive, Zip 35960–1023; tel. 256/927–5531, (Nonreporting) **A**1 10 **S** Atrium Health, Inc., Charlotte, NC
Primary Contact: Tifani Kinard, Chief Executive Officer
CFO: Philip Wheeler, Chief Financial Officer
CHR: Marlene Benefield, Director Human Resources
CNO: Tifani Kinard, Chief Nursing Officer
Web address: www.cherokeemedicalcenter.com
Control: Other not–for–profit (including NFP Corporation) **Service:** General medical and surgical

Staffed Beds: 45

CENTREVILLE—Bibb County

☐ **BIBB MEDICAL CENTER (010058)**, 208 Pierson Avenue, Zip 35042–2918; tel. 205/926–4881, (Nonreporting) **A**3 5 10 13
Primary Contact: Joseph Marchant, Administrator
CFO: Heather Desmond, Chief Financial Officer
CMO: John Meigs, M.D., Jr, Chief of Staff
CHR: Karen Daniel, Director Human Resources
Web address: www.bibbmedicalcenter.com
Control: County, Government, Nonfederal **Service:** General medical and surgical

Staffed Beds: 166

CHATOM—Washington County

WASHINGTON COUNTY HOSPITAL (011300), 14600 St Stephens Avenue, Zip 36518–9998, Mailing Address: P.O. Box 1299, Zip 36518–1299; tel. 251/847–2223, (Nonreporting) **A**10 18
Primary Contact: Teresa G. Grimes, Chief Executive Officer
CMO: Steve Donald, M.D., Chief of Staff
CIO: Brady Wright, Information Technology Network Administrator
CHR: Linda Randolph, Director Personnel Services
CNO: Michelle Alford, R.N., MSN, Director of Nursing
Web address: www.wchnh.org
Control: County, Government, Nonfederal **Service:** General medical and surgical

Staffed Beds: 20

Hospital, Medicare Provider Number, Address, Telephone, Approval, Facility, and Physician Codes, Health Care System

★ American Hospital Association (AHA) membership   ○ Healthcare Facilities Accreditation Program   ⇧ Center for Improvement in Healthcare Quality Accreditation
☐ The Joint Commission accreditation   ◇ DNV Healthcare Inc. accreditation   △ Commission on Accreditation of Rehabilitation Facilities (CARF) accreditation

© 2025 AHA Guide

Hospitals, U.S. / ALABAMA

CLANTON—Chilton County

ASCENSION ST. VINCENT'S CHILTON (010173), 2030 Lay Dam Road, Zip 35045; tel. 205/258-4400, (Nonreporting) **A**1 10 **S** Ascension Healthcare, Saint Louis, MO
Primary Contact: Shanon Hamilton, Administrator
Web address: https://www.stvhs.com/chilton/
Control: Church operated, Nongovernment, not-for-profit **Service**: General medical and surgical

Staffed Beds: 36

VINCENT'S CHILTON HOSPITAL See Ascension st. Vincent's Chilton

CULLMAN—Cullman County

CULLMAN REGIONAL MEDICAL CENTER (010035), 1912 Alabama Highway 157, Zip 35055, Mailing Address: P.O. Box 1108, Zip 35056-1108; tel. 256/737-2000, (Nonreporting) **A**1 10
Primary Contact: James Clements, Chief Executive Officer
COO: Nesha Donaldson, Chief Operating Officer
CMO: William E. Smith, M.D., Chief Medical Officer
CIO: Nancy Zavatchen, Director Information Technology
CHR: Toni Geddings, Director Human Resources
CNO: Charna Brown, Chief Nursing Officer
Web address: www.crmhospital.com
Control: Other not-for-profit (including NFP Corporation) **Service**: General medical and surgical

Staffed Beds: 145

DADEVILLE—Tallapoosa County

LAKE MARTIN COMMUNITY HOSPITAL (010052), 201 Mariarden Road, Zip 36853-6251, Mailing Address: P.O. Box 629, Zip 36853-0629; tel. 256/825-7821, (Nonreporting) **A**10
Primary Contact: Michael Bruce, Chief Executive Officer
CHR: Karen Treadwell, Director Human Resources
Web address: www.lakemartincommunityhospital.com
Control: Partnership, Investor-owned (for-profit) **Service**: General medical and surgical

Staffed Beds: 25

DAPHNE—Baldwin County

★ **EASTPOINTE HOSPITAL (014017)**, 7400 Roper Lane, Zip 36526-5274; tel. 251/378-6500, (Nonreporting) **A**3 10 **S** AltaPointe Health Systems, Mobile, AL
Primary Contact: Jarett Crum, Chief Hospital Officer
CFO: Kevin Markham, Chief Financial Officer
CMO: Sandra K Parker, M.D., Chief Medical Officer
CIO: Steve Dolan, Chief Information Officer
CHR: Alicia Donoghue, Director Human Resources
Web address: https://altapointe.org/eastpointe-hospital/
Control: Other not-for-profit (including NFP Corporation) **Service**: Psychiatric

Staffed Beds: 66

DECATUR—Morgan County

DECATUR GENERAL HOSPITAL-WEST See Decatur Morgan Hospital-West

☐ **DECATUR MORGAN HOSPITAL (010085)**, 1201 Seventh Street SE, Zip 35601-3303, Mailing Address: P.O. Box 2239, Zip 35609-2239; tel. 256/341-2000, (Includes DECATUR MORGAN HOSPITAL PARKWAY CAMPUS, 1874 Beltline Road SW, Decatur, Alabama, Zip 35601-5509, P O Box 2239, Zip 35609-2239, tel. 256/350-2211; DECATUR MORGAN HOSPITAL-WEST, 2205 Beltline Road SW, Decatur, Alabama, Zip 35601-3687, P O Box 2240, Zip 35609-2240, tel. 256/306-4000) (Nonreporting) **A**1 3 5 10 19 **S** Huntsville Hospital Health System, Huntsville, AL
Primary Contact: Kelli Powers, President
CFO: Danny Crowe, Chief Financial Officer
CMO: Allen J Schmidt, M.D., President, Medical Staff
CIO: Mark Megehee, Vice President and Chief Information Officer
CNO: Anita Walden, Vice President and Chief Nursing Officer
Web address: www.decaturgeneral.org
Control: Hospital district or authority, Government, Nonfederal **Service**: General medical and surgical

Staffed Beds: 110

DECATUR MORGAN HOSPITAL See Decatur Morgan Hospital Parkway Campus

DEMOPOLIS—Marengo County

BRYAN W. WHITFIELD MEMORIAL HOSPITAL See Whitfield Regional Hospital

WHITFIELD REGIONAL HOSPITAL (010112), 105 US Highway 80 East, Zip 36732-3616, Mailing Address: P.O. Box 890, Zip 36732-0890; tel. 334/289-4000, (Nonreporting) **A**3 5 10 20 **S** UAB Health System, Birmingham, AL
Primary Contact: Douglas L. Brewer, Chief Executive Officer
COO: Dereck Morrison, Assistant Administrator
CFO: Doug A. Brooker, Chief Financial Officer
CMO: John G. Kahler, M.D., Radiologist
Web address: www.bwwmh.com
Control: Hospital district or authority, Government, Nonfederal **Service**: General medical and surgical

Staffed Beds: 47

DOTHAN—Houston County

ENCOMPASS HEALTH REHABILITATION HOSPITAL OF DOTHAN (013030), 1736 East Main Street, Zip 36301-3040, Mailing Address: P.O. Box 6708, Zip 36302-6708; tel. 334/712-6333, (Nonreporting) **A**1 10 **S** Encompass Health Corporation, Birmingham, AL
Primary Contact: Margaret A. Futch, Chief Executive Officer
CFO: Heath Watson, Controller
CHR: Lydia Christion, Director Human Resources
Web address: www.encompasshealth.com/dothanrehab
Control: Corporation, Investor-owned (for-profit) **Service**: Rehabilitation

Staffed Beds: 51

FLOWERS HOSPITAL (010055), 4370 West Main Street, Zip 36305-4000, Mailing Address: P.O. Box 6907, Zip 36302-6907; tel. 334/793-5000, **A**3 5 10 19 **F**3 12 13 15 17 18 20 22 24 26 28 29 30 34 35 40 43 45 46 47 49 50 51 57 59 60 63 64 65 68 70 72 74 75 76 77 79 81 82 92 97 100 102 107 108 110 111 114 115 116 117 119 126 129 130 132 144 146 147 148 149 154 156 167 **P**6 **S** Community Health Systems, Inc., Franklin, TN
Primary Contact: Jeffrey M. Brannon, Chief Executive Officer
COO: Matthew H Blevins, Chief Operating Officer
CFO: Phillip Childree, Chief Financial Officer
CIO: Matthew Garrett, Director Information Systems
CHR: Jennifer Odom, Interim Director Human Resources
CNO: Dan L Cumbie, Chief Nursing Officer
Web address: www.flowershospital.com
Control: Corporation, Investor-owned (for-profit) **Service**: General medical and surgical

Staffed Beds: 203 Admissions: 12823 Census: 161 Outpatient Visits: 134581 Births: 1464 Total Expense ($000): 201890 Payroll Expense ($000): 66056 Personnel: 1210

LAUREL OAKS BEHAVIORAL HEALTH CENTER (014013), 700 East Cottonwood Road, Zip 36301-3644; tel. 334/794-7373, (Nonreporting) **A**1 10 **S** Universal Health Services, Inc., King of Prussia, PA
Primary Contact: Jeanette Jackson, Chief Executive Officer
CMO: Nelson Handol, M.D., Medical Director
CHR: Lorrie Evans, Director Human Resources
Web address: www.laureloaksbhc.com
Control: Corporation, Investor-owned (for-profit) **Service**: Children's hospital psychiatric

Staffed Beds: 118

☐ **NOLAND HOSPITAL DOTHAN (012010)**, 1108 Ross Clark Circle, 4th Floor, Zip 36301-3022; tel. 334/699-4300, (Nonreporting) **A**1 10 **S** Noland Health Services, Inc., Birmingham, AL
Primary Contact: Dennis W. Stewart, Administrator
Web address: www.nolandhealth.com
Control: Other not-for-profit (including NFP Corporation) **Service**: Acute long-term care hospital

Staffed Beds: 38

⇧ **SOUTHEAST ALABAMA MEDICAL CENTER (010001)**, 1108 Ross Clark Circle, Zip 36301-3024, Mailing Address: P.O. Box 6987, Zip 36302-6987; tel. 334/793-8111, (Nonreporting) **A**3 5 10 19 21
Primary Contact: Richard O. Sutton, FACHE, Chief Executive Officer
COO: Charles C Brannen, Senior Vice President and Chief Operating Officer
CFO: Derek Miller, Senior Vice President and Chief Financial Officer
CMO: Charles Harkness, D.O., Vice President Medical Affairs
CIO: Eric Allen Daffron, Division Director, Information Systems
CHR: Tony Welch, Vice President Human Resources
CNO: Diane Buntyn, MSN, R.N., Vice President Patient Care Services
Web address: www.samc.org
Control: Hospital district or authority, Government, Nonfederal **Service**: General medical and surgical

Staffed Beds: 387

Hospitals, U.S. / ALABAMA   AL

ENTERPRISE—Coffee County

☒ **MEDICAL CENTER ENTERPRISE (010049)**, 400 North Edwards Street, Zip 36330–2510; tel. 334/347–0584, **A**1 10 **F**3 11 13 15 18 26 29 30 34 35 40 45 50 57 59 60 68 70 74 76 77 79 80 81 82 85 87 93 107 108 110 111 115 118 119 129 133 135 146 147 148 154 169 **S** Community Health Systems, Inc., Franklin, TN
Primary Contact: Joey Hester, Chief Executive Officer
CFO: Greg McGilvray, Chief Financial Officer
CMO: Patrick Lett, M.D., Medical Doctor
CIO: Stephen Smothers, Director Information Systems
CHR: Toni Kaminski, Director Human Resources
CNO: Barry Eads, R.N., Chief Nursing Officer
Web address: www.mcehospital.com
Control: Corporation, Investor–owned (for–profit) **Service:** General medical and surgical

Staffed Beds: 99 **Admissions:** 3824 **Census:** 37 **Outpatient Visits:** 63626 **Births:** 846 **Total Expense ($000):** 55232 **Payroll Expense ($000):** 21964 **Personnel:** 370

EUFAULA—Barbour County

MEDICAL CENTER BARBOUR (010069), 820 West Washington Street, Zip 36027–1899; tel. 334/688–7000, (Nonreporting) **A**10 20
Primary Contact: Janet Kinney, Interim Chief Executive Officer
CFO: Vann Windham, Chief Financial Officer
CHR: Cindy Griffin, Director Human Resources
CNO: Missy Thomas, Chief Nursing Officer
Web address: www.medctrbarbour.org
Control: Hospital district or authority, Government, Nonfederal **Service:** General medical and surgical

Staffed Beds: 47

EUTAW—Greene County

GREENE COUNTY HEALTH SYSTEM (010051), 509 Wilson Avenue, Zip 35462–1099; tel. 205/372–3388, (Nonreporting) **A**10
Primary Contact: Marcia Pugh, Chief Executive Officer
CFO: Beverly Averette, Chief Financial Officer
Web address: www.gcheutaw.com
Control: County, Government, Nonfederal **Service:** General medical and surgical

Staffed Beds: 92

EVERGREEN—Conecuh County

EVERGREEN MEDICAL CENTER (010148), 101 Crestview Avenue, Zip 36401–3333, Mailing Address: P.O. Box 706, Zip 36401–0706; tel. 251/578–2480, (Nonreporting) **A**10 **S** Gilliard Health Services, Evergreen, AL
Primary Contact: Tom McLendon, President and Chief Executive Officer
CFO: Sharon Jones, Chief Financial Officer
CMO: William Farmer, M.D., Chief of Staff
CHR: Tracey Rhodes, Coordinator Human Resources
CNO: Angie Hendrix, Director of Nursing
Web address: www.evergreenmedical.org
Control: Partnership, Investor–owned (for–profit) **Service:** General medical and surgical

Staffed Beds: 44

FAIRHOPE—Baldwin County

☐ △ **THOMAS HOSPITAL (010100)**, 750 Morphy Avenue, Zip 36532–1812, Mailing Address: P.O. Box 929, Zip 36533–0929; tel. 251/928–2375, **A**1 2 3 5 7 10 19 **F**3 8 11 13 15 18 20 22 24 26 28 29 30 31 34 35 37 40 41 42 43 45 46 49 50 53 54 55 57 58 59 64 65 66 68 70 74 75 76 77 78 79 81 82 84 85 87 89 104 105 107 108 110 111 114 115 116 117 118 119 120 121 126 129 130 131 132 135 146 148 149 153 156 164 167 169 **P**4 7 **S** Infirmary Health System, Mobile, AL
Primary Contact: Ormand P. Thompson, President
COO: Douglas Garner, Vice President
CMO: Michael McBrearty, M.D., Vice President Medical Affairs
CNO: Julie Rowell, R.N., Chief Nursing Officer
Web address: www.thomashospital.com
Control: Other not–for–profit (including NFP Corporation) **Service:** General medical and surgical

Staffed Beds: 255 **Admissions:** 11978 **Census:** 150 **Outpatient Visits:** 146297 **Births:** 1481 **Total Expense ($000):** 229437 **Payroll Expense ($000):** 79694 **Personnel:** 1297

FAYETTE—Fayette County

☐ **FAYETTE MEDICAL CENTER (010045)**, 1653 Temple Avenue North, Zip 35555–1314, Mailing Address: P O Drawer 710, Zip 35555–0710; tel. 205/932–5966, (Nonreporting) **A**1 10 **S** DCH Health System, Tuscaloosa, AL
Primary Contact: Donald J. Jones, FACHE, Administrator
CFO: Jeff Huff, Assistant Administrator Finance
CHR: Felicia Solomon–Owens, Director Human Resources
Web address: www.dchsystem.com
Control: Hospital district or authority, Government, Nonfederal **Service:** General medical and surgical

Staffed Beds: 167

FLORENCE—Lauderdale County

☒ **NORTH ALABAMA MEDICAL CENTER (010006)**, 1701 Veterans Drive, Zip 35630–6033; tel. 256/629–1000, (Nonreporting) **A**1 3 5 10 19 **S** Lifepoint Health, Brentwood, TN
Primary Contact: Russell Pigg, Chief Executive Officer
COO: Mike Howard, Chief Operating Officer
CFO: Steve E. Hobbs, Chief Financial Officer
CMO: Oliver Matthews, M.D., Chief Medical Officer
CIO: Raul Velez, Information Technology Director
CHR: Cheryl Lee, Human Resources Director
Web address: https://namccares.com/
Control: Corporation, Investor–owned (for–profit) **Service:** General medical and surgical

Staffed Beds: 239

FOLEY—Baldwin County

☒ **SOUTH BALDWIN REGIONAL MEDICAL CENTER (010083)**, 1613 North McKenzie Street, Zip 36535–2299; tel. 251/949–3400, (Nonreporting) **A**1 3 5 10 19 **S** Community Health Systems, Inc., Franklin, TN
Primary Contact: Margaret Roley, Chief Executive Officer
CFO: Brad Hardcastle, Chief Financial Officer
CMO: Lee Eslava, Chief Medical Officer
CHR: Pamela J Brunson, Director Human Resources
CNO: Margaret Roley, Chief Nursing Officer
Web address: www.southbaldwinrmc.com
Control: Corporation, Investor–owned (for–profit) **Service:** General medical and surgical

Staffed Beds: 112

FORT PAYNE—Dekalb County

☐ **DEKALB REGIONAL MEDICAL CENTER (010012)**, 200 Medical Center Drive, Zip 35968–3458, Mailing Address: P.O. Box 680778, Zip 35968–1608; tel. 256/845–3150, (Nonreporting) **A**1 10 20 **S** Huntsville Hospital Health System, Huntsville, AL
Primary Contact: Darrell Blaylock, Chief Executive Officer
CFO: Phillip Fouts, Chief Financial Officer
CMO: Anthony Sims, M.D., Chief of Staff
CIO: Joseph Helms, Director Information Systems
CHR: Kim Reed, Director Human Resources
CNO: Angela Bennett, Chief Nursing Officer
Web address: www.dekalbregional.com
Control: Corporation, Investor–owned (for–profit) **Service:** General medical and surgical

Staffed Beds: 115

GADSDEN—Etowah County

☒ **ENCOMPASS HEALTH REHABILITATION HOSPITAL OF GADSDEN (013032)**, 801 Goodyear Avenue, Zip 35903–1133; tel. 256/439–5000, (Nonreporting) **A**1 10 **S** Encompass Health Corporation, Birmingham, AL
Primary Contact: Al Rayburn, Chief Executive Officer
CFO: Lori Norman, Chief Financial Officer
CMO: Vladimir Slutsker, Medical Director
CIO: Lori Norman, Chief Financial Officer
CHR: Rhonda Young, Human Resource Director
CNO: Barry Eads, R.N., Chief Nursing Officer
Web address: www.encompasshealth.com/gadsdenrehab
Control: Corporation, Investor–owned (for–profit) **Service:** Rehabilitation

Staffed Beds: 44

Hospital, Medicare Provider Number, Address, Telephone, Approval, Facility, and Physician Codes, Health Care System

★ American Hospital Association (AHA) membership
☐ The Joint Commission accreditation
○ Healthcare Facilities Accreditation Program
◇ DNV Healthcare Inc. accreditation
⇑ Center for Improvement in Healthcare Quality Accreditation
△ Commission on Accreditation of Rehabilitation Facilities (CARF) accreditation

© 2025 AHA Guide   Hospitals   A19

Hospitals, U.S. / ALABAMA

GADSDEN REGIONAL MEDICAL CENTER (010040), 1007 Goodyear Avenue, Zip 35903–1195; tel. 256/494–4000, (Nonreporting) **A**1 3 10 19 **S** Community Health Systems, Inc., Franklin, TN
Primary Contact: Mark Dooley, Chief Executive Officer
COO: Josh Hester, Chief Operating Officer
CFO: Kandi Garmany, Interim Chief Financial Officer
CMO: John Pirani, M.D., Chief Medical Officer
CIO: Glenn Phillips, Director Information Systems
CHR: Allison Casey, Director
CNO: Martha Seahorn, Chief Nursing Officer
Web address: www.gadsdenregional.com
Control: Corporation, Investor–owned (for–profit) **Service**: General medical and surgical

Staffed Beds: 272

MOUNTAIN VIEW HOSPITAL (014006), 3001 Scenic Highway, Zip 35904–3047, Mailing Address: P.O. Box 8406, Zip 35902–8406; tel. 256/546–9265, (Nonreporting) **A**1 10
Primary Contact: Renae Strickler, Chief Executive Officer
CFO: Mary Jensen, Controller
CMO: G Michael Shehi, M.D., Medical Director
CHR: Dave Jensen, Director Human Resources, Performance Improvement and Risk Management
Web address: www.mtnviewhospital.com
Control: Corporation, Investor–owned (for–profit) **Service**: Psychiatric

Staffed Beds: 68

RIVERVIEW REGIONAL MEDICAL CENTER (010046), 600 South Third Street, Zip 35901–5399; tel. 256/543–5200, (Nonreporting) **A**1 10 19 **S** Prime Healthcare, Ontario, CA
Primary Contact: John Langlois, Chief Executive Officer
CIO: Jay Terrell, Manager Management Information Systems
CHR: Leslie Morton, Manager Human Resources
Web address: www.riverviewregional.com
Control: Corporation, Investor–owned (for–profit) **Service**: General medical and surgical

Staffed Beds: 280

GENEVA—Geneva County

WIREGRASS MEDICAL CENTER (010062), 1200 West Maple Avenue, Zip 36340–1694; tel. 334/684–3655, (Nonreporting) **A**10
Primary Contact: Janet Smith, Chief Executive Officer
CHR: Tim Tidwell, Human Resources Director
CNO: Ashley Tanner, Director of Nursing
Web address: www.wiregrassmedicalcenter.org
Control: Hospital district or authority, Government, Nonfederal **Service**: General medical and surgical

Staffed Beds: 147

GREENSBORO—Hale County

HALE COUNTY HOSPITAL (010095), 508 Green Street, Zip 36744–2316; tel. 334/624–3024, (Nonreporting) **A**10
Primary Contact: Shay Cherry, Administrator
Web address: www.halecountyhospital.com
Control: Hospital district or authority, Government, Nonfederal **Service**: General medical and surgical

Staffed Beds: 20

GREENVILLE—Butler County

REGIONAL MEDICAL CENTER OF CENTRAL ALABAMA (010150), 29 L V Stabler Drive, Zip 36037–3800; tel. 334/382–2671, (Nonreporting) **A**1 3 5 10 20
Primary Contact: Patrick Trammell, Chief Executive Officer
CFO: David Wilcox, Chief Financial Officer
CMO: Norman F McGowin, M.D., III, Chief of Staff
CIO: Doug Burkett, Manager Information Technology
CHR: Robert Foster, Director Human Resources
CNO: Kimberli Weaver, Chief Nursing Officer
Web address: www.rmcca.org/
Control: City, Government, Nonfederal **Service**: General medical and surgical

Staffed Beds: 61

GROVE HILL—Clarke County

GROVE HILL MEMORIAL HOSPITAL (010091), 295 South Jackson Street, Zip 36451–3231, Mailing Address: P.O. Box 935, Zip 36451–0935; tel. 251/275–3191, (Nonreporting) **A**10
Primary Contact: Allen Jordan, Interim Chief Executive Officer
CFO: Alyson Overstreet, Chief Financial Officer
CMO: Eniola Fagbongbe, M.D., Chief Medical Staff
CIO: Aaron Harrell, Director
CHR: Aubrey Sheffield, Administrative Assistant Human Resources and Public Relations
CNO: Karen Coleman, Director of Nursing
Web address: https://gh-health.org/
Control: City, Government, Nonfederal **Service**: General medical and surgical

Staffed Beds: 34

GUNTERSVILLE—Marshall County

MARSHALL MEDICAL CENTER NORTH (010010), 8000 Alabama Highway 69, Zip 35976; tel. 256/571–8000, (Nonreporting) **A**1 5 10 **S** Marshall Health System, Guntersville, AL
Primary Contact: Christopher Rush, President
CFO: Taylor Walker, Chief Financial Officer
CMO: Victor Sparks, M.D., Chief of Staff
CIO: David Mize, Director of Information Technology
CHR: Sabrina Weaver, Director of Human Resources
CNO: Kathy Woodruff, R.N., MSN, Chief Nursing Officer
Web address: www.mmcenters.com
Control: Hospital district or authority, Government, Nonfederal **Service**: General medical and surgical

Staffed Beds: 76

HALEYVILLE—Winston County

LAKELAND COMMUNITY HOSPITAL (010125), Highway 195 East, Zip 35565–9536, Mailing Address: P.O. Box 780, Zip 35565–0780; tel. 205/486–5213, (Nonreporting) **A**1 10
Primary Contact: Jennifer Young, Chief Executive Officer
CFO: Kimberly Albright, Chief Financial Officer
Web address: https://lakelandcommunityhospital.com
Control: Hospital district or authority, Government, Nonfederal **Service**: General medical and surgical

Staffed Beds: 59

HAMILTON—Marion County

NORTH MISSISSIPPI MEDICAL CENTER–HAMILTON (010044), 1256 Military Street South, Zip 35570–5003; tel. 205/921–6200, (Nonreporting) **A**10 21 **S** North Mississippi Health Services, Inc., Tupelo, MS
Primary Contact: Robin Mixon, Administrator
CMO: Jarred Sartain, M.D., President Medical Staff
CHR: Anne Lawler, Director Human Resources
CNO: Jennifer Cagle, Director of Nursing
Web address: www.nmhs.net
Control: Other not-for-profit (including NFP Corporation) **Service**: General medical and surgical

Staffed Beds: 15

HUNTSVILLE—Madison County

CRESTWOOD MEDICAL CENTER (010131), 1 Hospital Drive, Zip 35801–3403; tel. 256/429–4000, (Nonreporting) **A**1 3 5 10 **S** Community Health Systems, Inc., Franklin, TN
Primary Contact: Matthew Banks, Chief Executive Officer
CFO: Sherry J Jones, Chief Financial Officer
CHR: David A Brown, Human Resources Director
CNO: Martha Delaney Walls, R.N., MSN, Chief Nursing Officer
Web address: www.crestwoodmedcenter.com
Control: Corporation, Investor–owned (for–profit) **Service**: General medical and surgical

Staffed Beds: 180

ENCOMPASS HEALTH REHABILITATION HOSPITAL OF NORTH ALABAMA (013029), 107 Governors Drive SW, Zip 35801–4326; tel. 256/535–2300, (Nonreporting) **A**1 10 **S** Encompass Health Corporation, Birmingham, AL
Primary Contact: Brent Mills, Chief Executive Officer
Web address: www.encompasshealth.com/huntsvillerehab
Control: Corporation, Investor–owned (for–profit) **Service**: Rehabilitation

Staffed Beds: 70

Hospitals, U.S. / ALABAMA

☐ **HUNTSVILLE HOSPITAL (010039)**, 101 Sivley Road SW, Zip 35801-4470; tel. 256/265-1000, (Includes HUNTSVILLE HOSPITAL FOR WOMEN AND CHILDREN, 911 Big Cove Road SE, Huntsville, Alabama, Zip 35801-3784, tel. 256/265-1000; MADISON HOSPITAL, 8375 Highway 72 West, Madison, Alabama, Zip 35758-9573, tel. 256/265-2012; Mary Lynne Wright, R.N., President) **A**1 2 3 5 10 19 **F**3 7 8 12 13 14 15 16 17 18 19 20 22 24 26 28 29 30 31 35 37 38 40 41 43 45 46 47 48 49 50 51 53 54 56 57 59 60 63 64 68 70 71 72 73 74 75 76 78 79 80 81 82 84 85 86 87 88 89 93 98 100 102 103 107 108 109 110 111 114 115 116 117 119 120 121 123 124 126 129 130 131 135 145 146 147 148 149 154 156 157 164 167 169 **P**6 **S** Huntsville Hospital Health System, Huntsville, AL
Primary Contact: Jeff Samz, Chief Executive Officer
CFO: Kelli Powers, Chief Financial Officer
CMO: Robert Chappell, M.D., Chief Medical Officer and Chief Quality Officer
CIO: Rick Corn, Chief Information Officer
CHR: Andrea P Rosler, Vice President Human Resources
CNO: Karol Jones, Chief Nursing Officer
Web address: www.huntsvillehospital.org
Control: Hospital district or authority, Government, Nonfederal **Service**: General medical and surgical

Staffed Beds: 942 **Admissions**: 48966 **Census**: 730 **Outpatient Visits**: 1005462 **Births**: 5944 **Total Expense ($000)**: 1266816 **Payroll Expense ($000)**: 553691 **Personnel**: 8586

HUNTSVILLE HOSPITAL EAST See Huntsville Hospital for Women and Children

UNITY PSYCHIATRIC CARE-HUNTSVILLE (014018), 5315 Millennium Drive NW, Zip 35806-2458; tel. 256/964-6700, (Nonreporting) **A**10 **S** Tennessee Health Management, Parsons, TN
Primary Contact: Kyle Smith, Administrator
Web address: https://www.unitypsych.com/huntsville
Control: Corporation, Investor-owned (for-profit) **Service**: Psychiatric

Staffed Beds: 20

JACKSON—Clarke County

JACKSON MEDICAL CENTER (010128), 220 Hospital Drive, Zip 36545-2459, Mailing Address: P.O. Box 428, Zip 36545-0428; tel. 251/246-9021, (Nonreporting) **A**10 **S** Gilliard Health Services, Evergreen, AL
Primary Contact: Jennifer M. Ryland, R.N., Chief Executive Officer
COO: Jennifer M Ryland, R.N., Chief Administrative Officer
CHR: Kathy Jones, Director Human Resources
Web address: www.jacksonmedicalcenter.org
Control: Partnership, Investor-owned (for-profit) **Service**: General medical and surgical

Staffed Beds: 26

JASPER—Walker County

✣ **WALKER BAPTIST MEDICAL CENTER (010089)**, 3400 Highway 78 East, Zip 35501-8907, Mailing Address: P.O. Box 3547, Zip 35502-3547; tel. 205/387-4000, (Nonreporting) **A**1 10 20 **S** TENET Healthcare Corporation, Dallas, TX
Primary Contact: Sean Johnson, Chief Executive Officer
CFO: Amanda Dyle, Chief Financial Officer
CIO: Kenny Horton, Director Information Systems
CHR: Pat Morrow, Director Human Resources
Web address: www.bhsala.com
Control: Church operated, Nongovernment, not-for-profit **Service**: General medical and surgical

Staffed Beds: 178

LUVERNE—Crenshaw County

☐ **BEACON BEHAVIORAL HOSPITAL (014015)**, 150 Hospital Drive, Zip 36049; tel. 334/335-5040, (Nonreporting) **A**1 10
Primary Contact: Shannon Hudson, Chief Executive Officer
Web address: www.beaconchildrenshospital.com
Control: Other not-for-profit (including NFP Corporation) **Service**: Children's hospital psychiatric

Staffed Beds: 28

BEACON CHILDREN'S HOSPITAL See Beacon Behavioral Hospital

CRENSHAW COMMUNITY HOSPITAL (010008), 101 Hospital Circle, Zip 36049-7344; tel. 334/335-3374, (Nonreporting) **A**10
Primary Contact: David L. Hughes, Administrator
COO: Victoria Lawrenson, Chief Operating Officer
CMO: Charles Tompkins, M.D., Chief of Staff
CHR: Patricia Jarry, Manager Human Resources
Web address: www.crenshawcommunityhospital.com
Control: Corporation, Investor-owned (for-profit) **Service**: General medical and surgical

Staffed Beds: 65

MADISON—Madison County

BRADFORD HEALTH SERVICES AT HUNTSVILLE, 1600 Browns Ferry Road, Zip 35758-9601, Mailing Address: P.O. Box 1488, Zip 35758-0176; tel. 256/461-7272, (Nonreporting) **S** Bradford Health Services, Birmingham, AL
Primary Contact: Bob Hinds, Executive Director
Web address: www.bradfordhealth.com
Control: Corporation, Investor-owned (for-profit) **Service**: Substance Use Disorder

Staffed Beds: 84

MOBILE—Mobile County

★ **BAYPOINTE BEHAVIORAL HEALTH (014014)**, 5800 Southland Drive, Zip 36693-3313; tel. 251/661-0153, **A**3 10 **F**50 98 99 101 102 106 122 130 154 164 **S** AltaPointe Health Systems, Mobile, AL
Primary Contact: Jarett Crum, Hospital Director
Web address: www.altapointe.org
Control: Other not-for-profit (including NFP Corporation) **Service**: Psychiatric

Staffed Beds: 60 **Admissions**: 1409 **Census**: 41 **Births**: 0 **Personnel**: 197

☐ **INFIRMARY LONG TERM ACUTE CARE HOSPITAL (012006)**, 5 Mobile Infirmary Circle, Zip 36607-3513, Mailing Address: P.O. Box 2226, Zip 36652-2226; tel. 251/660-5239, (Nonreporting) **A**1 10 **S** Infirmary Health System, Mobile, AL
Primary Contact: Susanne Marmande, Administrator
Web address: www.theinfirmary.com/
Control: Other not-for-profit (including NFP Corporation) **Service**: Acute long-term care hospital

Staffed Beds: 38

☐ △ **MOBILE INFIRMARY MEDICAL CENTER (010113)**, 5 Mobile Infirmary Drive North, Zip 36607-3513, Mailing Address: P.O. Box 2144, Zip 36652-2144; tel. 251/435-2400, (Includes ROTARY REHABILITATION HOSPITAL, 5 Mobile Infirmary Circle, Mobile, Alabama, Zip 36607, P O Box 2144, Zip 36652, tel. 251/435-3400) **A**1 2 3 5 7 10 19 **F**3 8 11 12 14 15 16 17 18 19 20 22 24 26 28 29 30 31 34 35 37 40 41 42 43 44 45 46 47 48 49 50 51 53 54 55 56 57 58 59 64 65 68 70 71 74 76 77 78 79 81 82 84 85 87 89 98 102 103 107 108 110 111 114 115 116 117 118 119 120 121 124 126 129 130 132 145 146 148 149 154 157 164 167 169 **P**4 7 **S** Infirmary Health System, Mobile, AL
Primary Contact: Susan E. Boudreau, President
CFO: Joe Denton, Executive Vice President and Chief Financial Officer
CMO: John Dixon, Chief Medical Officer
CIO: Eddy Stephens, Vice President Information Technology
CHR: Sheila Young, Vice President Human Resources
Web address: www.infirmaryhealth.org
Control: Other not-for-profit (including NFP Corporation) **Service**: General medical and surgical

Staffed Beds: 538 **Admissions**: 22813 **Census**: 418 **Outpatient Visits**: 180423 **Births**: 812 **Total Expense ($000)**: 521405 **Payroll Expense ($000)**: 168897 **Personnel**: 2294

PROVIDENCE HOSPITAL See USA Health Providence Hospital

ROTARY REHABILITATION HOSPITAL See Mobile Infirmary Medical Center, Mobile

---

Hospital, Medicare Provider Number, Address, Telephone, Approval, Facility, and Physician Codes, Health Care System

★ American Hospital Association (AHA) membership
☐ The Joint Commission accreditation
○ Healthcare Facilities Accreditation Program
◇ DNV Healthcare Inc. accreditation
⇑ Center for Improvement in Healthcare Quality Accreditation
△ Commission on Accreditation of Rehabilitation Facilities (CARF) accreditation

Hospitals, U.S. / ALABAMA

☐ △ **SPRINGHILL MEDICAL CENTER (010144)**, 3719 Dauphin Street, Zip 36608-1798, Mailing Address: P.O. Box 8246, Zip 36689-0246; tel. 251/344-9630, (Nonreporting) **A**1 3 5 7 10
Primary Contact: Jeffery M. St Clair, President and Chief Executive Officer
COO: Rene Areaux, Vice President and Chief Operating Officer
CFO: Jan Grigsby, Vice President and Chief Financial Officer
CMO: Liston Jones, M.D., Medical Director
CIO: Mark Kilborn, Director Information Systems
CHR: Daniela Batchelor, Director Human Resources
CNO: Paul Read, R.N., MSN, Vice President and Chief Nursing Officer
Web address: www.springhillmedicalcenter.com
Control: Corporation, Investor-owned (for-profit) **Service**: General medical and surgical

Staffed Beds: 219

SPRINGHILL MEMORIAL HOSPITAL See Springhill Medical Center

⊞ **USA HEALTH CHILDREN'S & WOMEN'S HOSPITAL (013301)**, 1700 Center Street, Zip 36604-3301; tel. 251/415-1000, **A**1 3 5 10 **F**3 7 11 13 15 19 21 27 29 30 31 34 35 40 41 48 49 52 55 58 59 64 68 72 73 74 75 76 77 78 79 80 81 84 85 86 87 88 89 93 108 111 114 115 119 120 121 124 126 130 131 132 146 147 149 154 157 164 167 **S** USA Health, Mobile, AL
Primary Contact: Deborah Browning, MSN, R.N., Chief Executive Officer
CFO: Traci Jones, Chief Financial Officer
CMO: Michael Chang, M.D., Chief Medical Officer
CIO: Dan Howard, Chief Information Officer
CHR: Janice Rehm, Manager Human Resources
Web address: www.usahealthsystem.com/usacwh
Control: State, Government, Nonfederal **Service**: Other specialty treatment

Staffed Beds: 174 **Admissions**: 9773 **Census**: 163 **Outpatient Visits**: 232869 **Births**: 2872 **Total Expense ($000)**: 259393 **Payroll Expense ($000)**: 85772 **Personnel**: 1275

⊞ **USA HEALTH PROVIDENCE HOSPITAL (010090)**, 6801 Airport Boulevard, Zip 36608-3785, Mailing Address: P.O. Box 850429, Zip 36685-0429; tel. 251/633-1000, (Nonreporting) **A**1 2 3 5 10 **S** USA Health, Mobile, AL
Primary Contact: Richard Metzger, Interim Chief Executive Officer
COO: C Susan Cornejo, Chief Operating Officer
CMO: William M Lightfoot, M.D., Vice President Medical Services
CHR: Christopher Cockrell, Executive Director Human Resources
CNO: Peter Lindquist, Vice President and Chief Nursing Officer
Web address: https://healthcare.ascension.org/locations/alabama/almob/mobile-providence-hospital
Control: Church operated, Nongovernment, not-for-profit **Service**: General medical and surgical

Staffed Beds: 305

⊞ **USA HEALTH UNIVERSITY HOSPITAL (010087)**, 2451 University Hospital Drive, Zip 36617-2293; tel. 251/471-7000, **A**1 2 3 5 8 10 19 **F**3 7 16 18 20 22 24 26 29 31 34 40 43 45 46 47 48 49 50 51 54 57 58 59 61 64 65 67 70 74 77 78 79 80 81 85 87 107 108 111 114 115 119 120 121 124 126 130 131 132 145 146 148 149 154 155 157 167 **S** USA Health, Mobile, AL
Primary Contact: Josh Snow, Chief Executive Officer
CFO: Traci Jones, Chief Financial Officer
CIO: Mark Lauteren, Chief Information Officer
CHR: Anita Shirah, Director Human Resources
CNO: Lisa Mestas, Associate Administrator and System Chief Nursing Officer
Web address: www.usahealthsystem.com/usamc
Control: State, Government, Nonfederal **Service**: General medical and surgical

Staffed Beds: 240 **Admissions**: 13507 **Census**: 258 **Outpatient Visits**: 157803 **Births**: 0 **Total Expense ($000)**: 390281 **Payroll Expense ($000)**: 158385 **Personnel**: 2766

MONROEVILLE—Monroe County

★ **MONROE COUNTY HOSPITAL (010120)**, 2016 South Alabama Avenue, Zip 36460-3044, Mailing Address: P.O. Box 886, Zip 36461-0886; tel. 251/575-3111, (Nonreporting) **A**10 20
Primary Contact: Elizabeth Kirby, Chief Executive Officer
CFO: Wes Nall, Chief Financial Officer
CMO: David Stallworth, M.D., Chief of Staff
CIO: Jody Falkenberry, Director Information Systems
CHR: Tara Nowling, Director Human Resources
CNO: Barbara Harned, R.N., MSN, Chief Nursing Officer
Web address: www.mchcare.com
Control: Hospital district or authority, Government, Nonfederal **Service**: General medical and surgical

Staffed Beds: 44

MONTGOMERY—Montgomery County

☐ **BAPTIST MEDICAL CENTER EAST (010149)**, 400 Taylor Road, Zip 36117-3512, Mailing Address: P.O. Box 241267, Zip 36124-1267; tel. 334/747-8330, **A**1 3 5 10 **F**3 11 13 15 18 19 29 30 34 35 40 44 45 47 50 57 60 63 70 72 74 75 76 77 79 81 82 85 86 87 89 93 94 107 108 111 114 115 119 126 129 130 132 135 146 147 148 154 167 169 **S** Baptist Health, Montgomery, AL
Primary Contact: Jeff G. Rains, Chief Executive Officer
CFO: Christine Bruton, Chief Financial Officer
CHR: Kay R Bennett, Vice President Human Resources
Web address: www.baptistfirst.org
Control: Hospital district or authority, Government, Nonfederal **Service**: General medical and surgical

Staffed Beds: 176 **Admissions**: 10599 **Census**: 156 **Outpatient Visits**: 141525 **Births**: 3832 **Total Expense ($000)**: 185199 **Payroll Expense ($000)**: 85456 **Personnel**: 839

☐ **BAPTIST MEDICAL CENTER SOUTH (010023)**, 2105 East South Boulevard, Zip 36116-2409, Mailing Address: Box 11010, Zip 36111-0010; tel. 334/288-2100, **A**1 2 3 5 10 **F**3 5 11 13 15 17 18 20 22 24 26 28 29 30 31 34 35 37 40 43 44 45 46 47 49 50 56 57 58 59 60 63 64 65 68 70 72 74 75 76 77 78 79 81 82 83 84 85 86 87 93 94 98 99 100 101 102 104 107 108 110 111 114 115 116 117 118 119 126 129 130 131 132 135 146 147 148 153 167 169 **S** Baptist Health, Montgomery, AL
Primary Contact: J Peter. Selman, FACHE, Chief Executive Officer
CFO: Melissa Johnson, Chief Financial Officer
CMO: Donovan Kendrick, M.D., Chief Medical Officer
CIO: Steve Miller, Director Information Systems
CHR: Kay R Bennett, System Director Human Resources
CNO: Karen McCaa, R.N., Vice President Patient Care Services and Chief Nursing Officer
Web address: www.baptistfirst.org
Control: Hospital district or authority, Government, Nonfederal **Service**: General medical and surgical

Staffed Beds: 456 **Admissions**: 15191 **Census**: 293 **Outpatient Visits**: 377353 **Births**: 657 **Total Expense ($000)**: 620518 **Payroll Expense ($000)**: 187966 **Personnel**: 1641

CENTRAL ALABAMA HCS See Central Alabama VA Medical Center–Montgomery

CENTRAL ALABAMA VA HEALTH CARE SYSTEM–MONTGOMERY DIVISION See Montgomery Division

⊞ **CENTRAL ALABAMA VA MEDICAL CENTER–MONTGOMERY**, 215 Perry Hill Road, Zip 36109-3798; tel. 334/272-4670, (Includes MONTGOMERY DIVISION, 215 Perry Hill Road, Montgomery, Alabama, Zip 36109-3798, tel. 334/272-4670; TUSKEGEE DIVISION, 2400 Hospital Road, Tuskegee, Alabama, Zip 36083-5001, tel. 334/727-0550) (Nonreporting) **A**1 3 5 **S** Department of Veterans Affairs, Washington, DC
Primary Contact: Valerie Russell, Interim Medical Center Director
CFO: Debra Nicholson, Manager Finance
CMO: Randall Weaver, M.D., Acting Chief of Staff
CIO: Rhoda Tyson, Chief Information Officer
CHR: Janice Hardy, Chief Human Resource Management Service
Web address: www.centralalabama.va.gov/
Control: Veterans Affairs, Government, federal **Service**: General medical and surgical

Staffed Beds: 258

⊞ **ENCOMPASS HEALTH REHABILITATION HOSPITAL OF MONTGOMERY (013028)**, 4465 Narrow Lane Road, Zip 36116-2900; tel. 334/284-7700, (Nonreporting) **A**1 10 **S** Encompass Health Corporation, Birmingham, AL
Primary Contact: Erin Collier, Chief Executive Officer
CFO: Heath Watson, Controller
CMO: Jeffrey Eng, M.D., Medical Director
CIO: Anidra Billingslea, Health Insurance Management
CHR: Kim McDaniel, Director Human Resources
CNO: Gretchen Vercher, Chief Nursing Officer
Web address: www.encompasshealth.com/montgomeryrehab
Control: Corporation, Investor-owned (for-profit) **Service**: Rehabilitation

Staffed Beds: 75

⊞ **JACKSON HOSPITAL AND CLINIC (010024)**, 1725 Pine Street, Zip 36106-1117; tel. 334/293-8000, (Nonreporting) **A**1 3 5 10 19
Primary Contact: Joe B. Riley, FACHE, President and Chief Executive Officer
COO: Michael James, Chief Operations Officer
CFO: Paul Peiffer, Chief Financial Officer and Vice President
CHR: Gilbert Darrington, Director Human Resources
Web address: www.jackson.org
Control: Other not-for-profit (including NFP Corporation) **Service**: General medical and surgical

Staffed Beds: 262

MONTGOMERY DIVISION See Central Alabama VA Medical Center–Montgomery, Montgomery

☐ **NOLAND HOSPITAL MONTGOMERY (012007)**, 1725 Pine Street, 5 North, Zip 36106–1109; tel. 334/240–0532, (Nonreporting) **A**1 10 **S** Noland Health Services, Inc., Birmingham, AL
Primary Contact: William Elsesser, Administrator
Web address: www.nolandhealth.com
Control: Other not–for–profit (including NFP Corporation) **Service**: Acute long–term care hospital

Staffed Beds: 65

MOULTON—Lawrence County

☐ **LAWRENCE MEDICAL CENTER (010059)**, 202 Hospital Street, Zip 35650–1218, Mailing Address: P.O. Box 39, Zip 35650–0039; tel. 256/974–2200, (Nonreporting) **A**1 10 **S** Huntsville Hospital Health System, Huntsville, AL
Primary Contact: Kim Roberson, Interim Chief Executive Officer
CFO: Jim Crawford, Chief Financial Officer
CIO: Jeremy Duncan, Director Information Systems
CHR: Diane K Secor, Director Human Resources
Web address: www.lawrencemedicalcenter.com
Control: County, Government, Nonfederal **Service**: General medical and surgical

Staffed Beds: 43

MUSCLE SHOALS—Colbert County

✠ **NORTH ALABAMA SHOALS HOSPITAL (010157)**, 201 Avalon Avenue, Zip 35661–2805, Mailing Address: P.O. Box 3359, Zip 35662–3359; tel. 256/386–1600, (Nonreporting) **A**1 3 10 **S** Lifepoint Health, Brentwood, TN
Primary Contact: Russell Pigg, Chief Executive Officer
CFO: Steve E. Hobbs, Chief Financial Officer
CMO: Terry true, M.D., Chief of Staff
CIO: William Johnson, Director Information Systems
CHR: Nancy Bowling, Director Human Resources
Web address: www.shoalshospital.com
Control: Hospital district or authority, Government, Nonfederal **Service**: General medical and surgical

Staffed Beds: 137

SHOALS HOSPITAL See North Alabama Shoals Hospital

NORTHPORT—Tuscaloosa County

NORTHPORT HOSPITAL–DCH See Northport Medical Center

ONEONTA—Blount County

✠ **ASCENSION ST. VINCENT'S BLOUNT (011305)**, 150 Gilbreath, Zip 35121–2827, Mailing Address: P.O. Box 1000, Zip 35121–0013; tel. 205/274–3000, (Nonreporting) **A**1 10 18 **S** Ascension Healthcare, Saint Louis, MO
Primary Contact: Greg Brown, President
CFO: Jennifer Kingry, Chief Financial Officer
CMO: David R Wilson, M.D., Chief of Staff
CIO: John Laliberte, Chief Information Officer
CHR: Kristin L. Costanzo, Direct–In–Market Lead Human Relations Partner
CNO: Kira Schnittker, Director of Nursing
Web address: https://healthcare.ascension.org/locations/alabama/albir/oneonta-ascension-st-vincents-blount
Control: Other not–for–profit (including NFP Corporation) **Service**: General medical and surgical

Staffed Beds: 25

ST. VINCENT'S BLOUNT See Ascension St. Vincent's Blount

OPELIKA—Lee County

✠ **EAST ALABAMA MEDICAL CENTER (010029)**, 2000 Pepperell Parkway, Zip 36801–5452; tel. 334/749–3411, (Includes EAST ALABAMA MEDICAL CENTER–LANIER, 4800 48th Street, Valley, Alabama, Zip 36854–3666, tel. 334/756–9180; Greg Nichols, Chief Executive Officer) (Nonreporting) **A**1 2 3 10
Primary Contact: Laura D. Grill, R.N., Chief Executive Officer
COO: Sarah Nunnelly, Executive Vice President and Chief Operating Officer
CFO: Sam Price, Executive Vice President Finance/Chief Financial Officer
CMO: William Golden, M.D., Chief Medical Officer
CIO: Sarah Gray, Vice President Information Services
CHR: Susan Johnston, Vice President Human Resources
CNO: Jane Fullum, Vice President Patient Care Services
Web address: www.eamc.org
Control: Hospital district or authority, Government, Nonfederal **Service**: General medical and surgical

Staffed Beds: 544

OPP—Covington County

MIZELL MEMORIAL HOSPITAL (010007), 702 Main Street, Zip 36467–1626, Mailing Address: P.O. Box 1010, Zip 36467–1010; tel. 334/493–3541, (Nonreporting) **A**10
Primary Contact: Lori Stanfield, Interim Chief Executive Officer
CFO: Amy Bess, Chief Financial Officer
CIO: Elizabeth Cook, Chief Information Officer
CHR: Dianne Morrison, Director Human Resources
CNO: Steven Skeen, R.N., Chief Nursing Officer
Web address: www.mizellmh.com
Control: Other not–for–profit (including NFP Corporation) **Service**: General medical and surgical

Staffed Beds: 59

OZARK—Dale County

DALE MEDICAL CENTER (010021), 126 Hospital Avenue, Zip 36360–2080; tel. 334/774–2601, (Nonreporting) **A**10
Primary Contact: Vernon Johnson, Chief Executive Officer
CFO: Brad Hull, Chief Financial Officer
CMO: Steve Brandt, M.D., Chief of Staff
CHR: Sheila Dunn, Assistant Administrator Human Resources
Web address: www.dalemedical.org
Control: County, Government, Nonfederal **Service**: General medical and surgical

Staffed Beds: 69

PELHAM—Shelby County

✠ **ENCOMPASS HEALTH REHABILITATION HOSPITAL OF SHELBY COUNTY (013031)**, 900 Oak Mountain Commons Lane, Zip 35124; tel. 205/216–7600, (Nonreporting) **A**1 10 **S** Encompass Health Corporation, Birmingham, AL
Primary Contact: Michael Bartell, Chief Executive Officer
Web address: www.encompasshealth.com/shelbycountyrehab
Control: Corporation, Investor–owned (for–profit) **Service**: Rehabilitation

Staffed Beds: 34

PELL CITY—St. Clair County

✠ **ASCENSION ST. VINCENT'S ST. CLAIR (010130)**, 7063 Veterans Parkway, Zip 35125–1499; tel. 205/814–2105, (Nonreporting) **A**1 10 **S** Ascension Healthcare, Saint Louis, MO
Primary Contact: Lisa Nichols, President
CFO: Isaac Plunkett, Chief Financial Officer
Web address: https://healthcare.ascension.org/locations/alabama/albir/pell-city-ascension-st-vincents-st-clair
Control: Other not–for–profit (including NFP Corporation) **Service**: General medical and surgical

Staffed Beds: 40

ST. VINCENT'S ST. CLAIR See Ascension St. Vincent's St. Clair

Hospitals, U.S. / ALABAMA

PHENIX CITY—Russell County

☐ **JACK HUGHSTON MEMORIAL HOSPITAL (010168)**, 4401 Riverchase Drive, Zip 36867-7483; tel. 334/732-3000, **A**1 3 5 10 13 **F**29 40 70 79 81 107 111 119 122 126 131 167
Primary Contact: Mark A. Baker, Chief Executive Officer
COO: Rachel H. Crenshaw, Chief Operating Officer
CFO: Angela Shelton, Chief Financial Officer
CMO: James F. Zumstein, M.D., Chief of Medicine
CHR: Lana Thomas-Folds, System Director Human Resources
CNO: Sylvia Thomas, Chief Nursing Officer
Web address: www.hughston.com
Control: Corporation, Investor-owned (for-profit) **Service:** General medical and surgical

Staffed Beds: 34 **Admissions:** 2092 **Census:** 14 **Outpatient Visits:** 23242 **Births:** 0 **Total Expense ($000):** 75953 **Payroll Expense ($000):** 19705 **Personnel:** 346

✠ **REGIONAL REHABILITATION HOSPITAL (013033)**, 3715 Highway 280/431 North, Zip 36867; tel. 334/732-2200, **A**1 10 **F**3 9 28 29 34 35 56 57 59 65 74 75 77 79 86 90 91 95 96 97 130 132 148 149 **S** Encompass Health Corporation, Birmingham, AL
Primary Contact: Lora Davis, FACHE, Chief Executive Officer
CFO: Bobby Edmondson, Controller
CMO: Nitin Desei, M.D., Medical Director
CIO: Jacki Cuevas, Director Health Information Services
CHR: Cindy Glynn, Director Human Resources
CNO: Wendy Lee, Chief Nursing Officer
Web address: www.regionalrehabhospital.com
Control: Corporation, Investor-owned (for-profit) **Service:** Rehabilitation

Staffed Beds: 58 **Admissions:** 1659 **Census:** 56 **Outpatient Visits:** 0 **Births:** 0 **Total Expense ($000):** 27360 **Payroll Expense ($000):** 12255 **Personnel:** 174

PRATTVILLE—Autauga County

✠ **PRATTVILLE BAPTIST HOSPITAL (010108)**, 124 South Memorial Drive, Zip 36067-3619, Mailing Address: P.O. Box 681630, Zip 36068-1638; tel. 334/365-0651, **A**1 10 **F**3 11 15 18 29 30 34 35 40 44 45 50 56 57 59 60 63 64 68 70 74 75 77 81 84 85 86 87 98 100 103 107 111 115 119 129 132 146 149 154 157 **S** Baptist Health, Montgomery, AL
Primary Contact: Eric Morgan, Chief Executive Officer
CFO: LaDonna McDaniel, Financial Manager
CIO: B Blaine Brown, Vice President and General Counsel
CHR: Kymberli Skipper, Manager Human Resources
Web address: www.baptistfirst.org/facilities/prattville-baptist-hospital/default.aspx
Control: Hospital district or authority, Government, Nonfederal **Service:** General medical and surgical

Staffed Beds: 71 **Admissions:** 3159 **Census:** 53 **Outpatient Visits:** 97551 **Births:** 0 **Total Expense ($000):** 61850 **Payroll Expense ($000):** 26809 **Personnel:** 263

RED BAY—Franklin County

★ **RED BAY HOSPITAL (011302)**, 211 Hospital Road, Zip 35582-3858, Mailing Address: P.O. Box 490, Zip 35582-0490; tel. 256/356-9532, **A**5 10 18 **F**7 11 15 29 34 35 40 53 57 59 68 77 85 87 93 97 107 110 114 119 127 130 131 133 157 **S** Huntsville Hospital Health System, Huntsville, AL
Primary Contact: Sherry Jolley, Administrator
CFO: Penny Westmoreland, Chief Financial Officer
CMO: Kristy Crandall, M.D., Medical Staff President
CHR: Amy Leigh Bishop, Director Human Resources
CNO: Margaret Thorn, Interim Director of Nursing
Web address: www.redbayhospital.com
Control: Hospital district or authority, Government, Nonfederal **Service:** General medical and surgical

Staffed Beds: 22 **Admissions:** 312 **Census:** 7 **Outpatient Visits:** 7642 **Births:** 0 **Total Expense ($000):** 11355 **Payroll Expense ($000):** 4896 **Personnel:** 103

RUSSELLVILLE—Franklin County

☐ **RUSSELLVILLE HOSPITAL (010158)**, 15155 Highway 43, Zip 35653-1975, Mailing Address: P.O. Box 1089, Zip 35653-1089; tel. 256/332-1611, (Nonreporting) **A**1 10 **S** Curae Health, Clinton, TN
Primary Contact: Chris Ware, Chief Executive Officer
CHR: Stephen Proctor, Director of Human Resources/Risk
CNO: Belinda Johnson, R.N., Chief Nursing Officer/Chief Clinical Officer
Web address: www.russellvillehospital.com
Control: Partnership, Investor-owned (for-profit) **Service:** General medical and surgical

Staffed Beds: 92

SCOTTSBORO—Jackson County

☐ **HIGHLANDS MEDICAL CENTER (010061)**, 380 Woods Cove Road, Zip 35768-2428, Mailing Address: P.O. Box 1050, Zip 35768-1050; tel. 256/259-4444, (Nonreporting) **A**1 5 10 20
Primary Contact: Ashley Pool, President
CFO: Dan Newell, Chief Financial Officer
CIO: Doug Newby, Chief Information Officer
CHR: Susanna S Sivley, Chief Personnel Officer
Web address: www.highlandsmedcenter.com
Control: Hospital district or authority, Government, Nonfederal **Service:** General medical and surgical

Staffed Beds: 92

SELMA—Dallas County

✠ **VAUGHAN REGIONAL MEDICAL CENTER (010118)**, 1015 Medical Center Parkway, Zip 36701-6352; tel. 334/418-4100, (Nonreporting) **A**1 3 5 10 **S** ScionHealth, Louisville, KY
Primary Contact: J. David. McCormack, Chief Executive Officer
CFO: Tyler Adkins, Chief Financial Officer
CMO: Walid Freij, M.D., Chief of Staff
CIO: Matthew McHugh, Director Information Services
CHR: Dionne Williams, Director Human Resources
CNO: Patricia Hannon, Chief Nursing Officer
Web address: www.vaughanregional.com
Control: Corporation, Investor-owned (for-profit) **Service:** General medical and surgical

Staffed Beds: 149

SHEFFIELD—Colbert County

☐ **HELEN KELLER HOSPITAL (010019)**, 1300 South Montgomery Avenue, Zip 35660-6334, Mailing Address: P.O. Box 610, Zip 35660-0610; tel. 256/386-4196, **A**1 5 10 **F**3 7 8 11 13 15 18 20 21 28 29 30 31 34 35 37 40 45 47 49 50 51 53 57 59 60 64 65 68 70 74 75 76 77 78 79 80 81 82 83 84 85 86 87 89 91 92 93 94 107 108 110 111 114 115 117 118 119 126 129 130 131 132 135 145 146 147 148 149 154 157 167 169 **S** Huntsville Hospital Health System, Huntsville, AL
Primary Contact: Kyle Buchanan, President
CFO: Morris S Strickland, Chief Financial Officer
CHR: Pam Bryant, Director Human Resources
Web address: www.helenkeller.com
Control: Hospital district or authority, Government, Nonfederal **Service:** General medical and surgical

Staffed Beds: 147 **Admissions:** 5688 **Census:** 75 **Outpatient Visits:** 98460 **Births:** 841 **Total Expense ($000):** 137315 **Payroll Expense ($000):** 58978 **Personnel:** 948

SYLACAUGA—Talladega County

☐ **COOSA VALLEY MEDICAL CENTER (010164)**, 315 West Hickory Street, Zip 35150-2996; tel. 256/401-4000, (Nonreporting) **A**1 10
Primary Contact: Glenn C. Sisk, President
CFO: Janice Brown, Chief Financial Officer
CIO: Sandra Murchison, Director Medical Records
CHR: Christy Knowles, Chief Human Resources Officer
Web address: www.cvhealth.net
Control: Other not-for-profit (including NFP Corporation) **Service:** General medical and surgical

Staffed Beds: 101

TALLADEGA—Talladega County

✠ **CITIZENS BAPTIST MEDICAL CENTER (010101)**, 604 Stone Avenue, Zip 35160-2217, Mailing Address: P.O. Box 978, Zip 35161-0978; tel. 256/362-8111, (Nonreporting) **A**1 10 19 **S** TENET Healthcare Corporation, Dallas, TX
Primary Contact: Frank D. Thomas, Chief Executive Officer
CFO: Zach Abercrombie, Chief Financial Officer
CHR: Sandra Willis, Director of Human Resources
CNO: Ann McEntire, MSN, R.N., Chief Nursing Officer
Web address: www.brookwoodbaptisthealth.org
Control: Church operated, Nongovernment, not-for-profit **Service:** General medical and surgical

Staffed Beds: 72

Hospitals, U.S. / ALABAMA

TALLASSEE—Elmore County

COMMUNITY HOSPITAL (010034), 805 Friendship Road, Zip 36078–1234; tel. 334/283–6541, (Nonreporting) **A**10
Primary Contact: Jennie R. Rhinehart, Administrator and Chief Executive Officer
Web address: www.chal.org
Control: Other not–for–profit (including NFP Corporation) **Service**: General medical and surgical

Staffed Beds: 47

THOMASVILLE—Clarke County

THOMASVILLE REGIONAL MEDICAL CENTER (010174), 300 Medical Park Drive, Zip 36784; tel. 334/636–2525, (Nonreporting) **F**3 11 15 29 30 34 35 40 45 46 50 57 59 64 65 68 75 77 81 86 87 97 107 110 111 115 119 132 133 146 148 154 156 157 **P**6
Primary Contact: Curtis James, FACHE, Chief Executive Officer
Web address: https://trmc-al.com/
Control: Corporation, Investor–owned (for–profit) **Service**: General medical and surgical

Staffed Beds: 29

TROY—Pike County

☐ **TROY REGIONAL MEDICAL CENTER (010126)**, 1330 Highway 231 South, Zip 36081–3058; tel. 334/670–5000, (Nonreporting) **A**1 10
Primary Contact: Rick Smith, Chief Executive Officer
CMO: Paul Dulaney, M.D., Chief of Staff
CIO: Michael Moore, Director Information Systems
CHR: Beth Nissen, Director Human Resources
CNO: Amy Minor, Chief Nursing Officer
Web address: www.troymedicalcenter.com
Control: City, Government, Nonfederal **Service**: General medical and surgical

Staffed Beds: 43

TUSCALOOSA—Tuscaloosa County

☐ **BRYCE HOSPITAL (014007)**, 200 University Boulevard, Zip 35401–1294; tel. 205/507–8299, (Nonreporting) **A**1 10
Primary Contact: Audrey McShan, Facility Director
CFO: Wendell Summerville, Chief Financial Officer
CMO: Cynthia Moore Sledge, M.D., Medical Director
CIO: Ronene Howell, Director Health Information Management
CHR: Jim Elliott, Director Human Resources
Web address: www.mh.alabama.gov/
Control: State, Government, Nonfederal **Service**: Psychiatric

Staffed Beds: 820

☐ **DCH REGIONAL MEDICAL CENTER (010092)**, 809 University Boulevard East, Zip 35401–2029; tel. 205/759–7111, (Includes NORTHPORT MEDICAL CENTER, 2700 Hospital Drive, Northport, Alabama, Zip 35476–3360, tel. 205/333–4500; Luke Standeffer, Administrator) **A**1 2 3 5 10 **F**3 5 11 12 13 15 17 18 22 24 26 28 29 30 31 35 40 43 44 45 46 48 49 50 51 56 57 58 59 60 61 62 64 68 70 72 74 75 76 77 78 79 81 82 83 84 86 87 89 90 91 92 93 95 96 98 100 101 102 103 107 108 110 111 114 115 117 118 119 120 121 124 126 130 132 146 149 156 162 164 167 169 **S** DCH Health System, Tuscaloosa, AL
Primary Contact: Luke Standeffer, Chief Executive Officer
CMO: Kenneth Aldridge, M.D., Vice President Medical Affairs
CIO: Kim Ligon, Director Information Services
CHR: Peggy Sease, Vice President Human Resources
CNO: Lorraine Yehlen, R.N., Vice President Patient Care Services
Web address: https://www.dchsystem.com/locations/dch-regional-medical-center/
Control: Hospital district or authority, Government, Nonfederal **Service**: General medical and surgical

Staffed Beds: 577 **Admissions**: 22758 **Census**: 410 **Outpatient Visits**: 434661 **Births**: 2895 **Total Expense ($000)**: 632541 **Payroll Expense ($000)**: 254936 **Personnel**: 3767

☐ **MARY'S HARPER GERIATRIC PSYCHIATRY CENTER (014012)**, 200 University Boulevard, Zip 35401–1250; tel. 205/366–3010, (Nonreporting) **A**1 10
Primary Contact: Christine Rembert, MSN, R.N., Facility Director
CFO: Sarah Mitchell, Director Finance
CMO: Robin Barton Lariscy, M.D., Medical Director
CIO: Sarah Mitchell, Director Finance
CHR: Jim Elliott, Director Human Resources
Web address: www.mh.alabama.gov
Control: Corporation, Investor–owned (for–profit) **Service**: Psychiatric

Staffed Beds: 96

☐ **NOLAND HOSPITAL TUSCALOOSA (012012)**, 809 University Blvd E, 4th Fl, Zip 35401–2029; tel. 205/759–7241, (Nonreporting) **A**1 10 **S** Noland Health Services, Inc., Birmingham, AL
Primary Contact: Jack Gibson, Administrator
Web address: www.nolandhealth.com
Control: Other not–for–profit (including NFP Corporation) **Service**: Acute long–term care hospital

Staffed Beds: 32

☐ **TAYLOR HARDIN SECURE MEDICAL FACILITY (014011)**, 1301 Jack Warner Parkway, Zip 35404–1060; tel. 205/556–7060, (Nonreporting) **A**1 10
Primary Contact: Kimberly McAlpine, Facility Director
Web address: www.mh.alabama.gov/
Control: Corporation, Investor–owned (for–profit) **Service**: Psychiatric

Staffed Beds: 114

✠ **TUSCALOOSA VA MEDICAL CENTER**, 3701 Loop Road East, Zip 35404–5015; tel. 205/554–2000, (Total facility includes 150 beds in nursing home-type unit) **A**1 **F**4 5 6 11 29 30 33 34 35 36 38 39 44 50 53 54 56 57 58 59 61 63 65 71 74 75 77 78 82 83 84 86 87 90 91 93 94 96 97 98 100 101 102 103 104 105 106 107 108 109 115 119 127 128 130 132 135 144 146 147 148 149 150 152 153 154 156 157 158 160 164 165 **S** Department of Veterans Affairs, Washington, DC
Primary Contact: John F. Merkle, Medical Center Director
COO: Gary D Trende, FACHE, Associate Director
CFO: Angelia Stevenson, Manager Finance
CMO: Carlos E. Berry, M.D., Acting Chief of Staff
Web address: www.tuscaloosa.va.gov
Control: Veterans Affairs, Government, federal **Service**: General medical and surgical

Staffed Beds: 335 **Admissions**: 1193 **Census**: 219 **Outpatient Visits**: 160214 **Births**: 0 **Total Expense ($000)**: 309489 **Payroll Expense ($000)**: 137897 **Personnel**: 1276

TUSCALOOSA VAMC See Tuscaloosa VA Medical Center

TUSKEGEE—Macon County

CENTRAL ALABAMA VETERANS AFFAIRS HEALTH CARE SYSTEM– TUSKEGEE DIVISION See Tuskegee Division

TUSKEGEE DIVISION See Central Alabama VA Medical Center–Montgomery, Montgomery

UNION SPRINGS—Bullock County

☐ **BULLOCK COUNTY HOSPITAL (010110)**, 102 West Conecuh Avenue, Zip 36089–1303; tel. 334/738–2140, (Nonreporting) **A**3 10 20
Primary Contact: Amanda Trawick, Chief Executive Officer
COO: Victoria Lawrenson, Chief Operating Officer
CMO: Maria Bernardo, M.D., Chief of Staff
CNO: Robbin Pumphrey, Chief Nursing Officer
Web address: www.bullockcountyhospital.com/
Control: Corporation, Investor–owned (for–profit) **Service**: General medical and surgical

Staffed Beds: 54

VALLEY—Chambers County

LANIER HEALTH SERVICES See East Alabama Medical Center–Lanier

---

Hospital, Medicare Provider Number, Address, Telephone, Approval, Facility, and Physician Codes, Health Care System

★ American Hospital Association (AHA) membership
☐ The Joint Commission accreditation
○ Healthcare Facilities Accreditation Program
◇ DNV Healthcare Inc. accreditation
⇑ Center for Improvement in Healthcare Quality Accreditation
△ Commission on Accreditation of Rehabilitation Facilities (CARF) accreditation

© 2025 AHA Guide

Hospitals, U.S. / ALABAMA

WARRIOR—Jefferson County

BRADFORD HEALTH SERVICES AT WARRIOR LODGE, 1189 Allbritt Road, Zip 35180, Mailing Address: P.O. Box 129, Zip 35180–0129; tel. 205/647–1945, (Nonreporting) **S** Bradford Health Services, Birmingham, AL
Primary Contact: Roy M. Ramsey, Executive Director
Web address: www.bradfordhealth.com
Control: Corporation, Investor–owned (for–profit) **Service**: Substance Use Disorder

Staffed Beds: 100

WEDOWEE—Randolph County

★ **TANNER MEDICAL CENTER/EAST ALABAMA (011306)**, 1032 South Main Street, Zip 36278–7428; tel. 256/357–2111, (Nonreporting) **A**10 18 **S** Tanner Health System, Carrollton, GA
Primary Contact: Heather Stitcher, Administrator
Web address: www.tanner.org/eastalabama
Control: Other not–for–profit (including NFP Corporation) **Service**: General medical and surgical

Staffed Beds: 15

WETUMPKA—Elmore County

ELMORE COMMUNITY HOSPITAL (010097), 500 Hospital Drive, Zip 36092–1625, Mailing Address: P.O. Box 130, Zip 36092–0003; tel. 334/567–4311, (Nonreporting) **A**10
Primary Contact: Michael Bruce, Chief Executive Officer
CFO: Michael Bruce, Chief Financial Officer
CHR: Cindy Futral, Director Human Resources
Web address: www.ivycreekhealth.com/hospital/elmore-community-hospital/
Control: Partnership, Investor–owned (for–profit) **Service**: General medical and surgical

Staffed Beds: 49

WINFIELD—Marion County

☐ **NORTHWEST MEDICAL CENTER (010086)**, 1530 US Highway 43, Zip 35594–5056; tel. 205/487–7000, (Nonreporting) **A**1 10 **S** Curae Health, Clinton, TN
Primary Contact: Cathy Mitchell, Chief Eecutive Officer
CFO: Glenda Reyes, Chief Financial Officer
CMO: David Corbett, M.D., Chief of Staff
Web address: https://northwestmedcenter.net/
Control: Corporation, Investor–owned (for–profit) **Service**: General medical and surgical

Staffed Beds: 56

YORK—Sumter County

HILL HOSPITAL OF SUMTER COUNTY (010138), 751 Derby Drive, Zip 36925–2121; tel. 205/392–5263, (Nonreporting) **A**10
Primary Contact: Loretta Wilson, Chief Executive Officer/Administrator
CFO: Joyce Wedgeworth, Financial Clerk
CMO: Gary Walton, M.D., Chief Medical Officer
CNO: Cynthia Brown, Director of Nursing
Control: Other not–for–profit (including NFP Corporation) **Service**: General medical and surgical

Staffed Beds: 33

ALASKA

ANCHORAGE—Anchorage County

☒ **ALASKA NATIVE MEDICAL CENTER (020026)**, 4315 Diplomacy Drive, Zip 99508-5926; tel. 907/563-2662, (Nonreporting) **A**1 3 5 10
Primary Contact: Alan Vierling, R.N., Acting Hospital Administrator
CMO: Paul Franke, M.D., Chief Medical Officer
CHR: Sonya Conant, Senior Director Human Resources
Web address: https://anmc.org/
Control: Other not-for-profit (including NFP Corporation) **Service:** General medical and surgical

Staffed Beds: 173

☐ **ALASKA PSYCHIATRIC INSTITUTE (024002)**, 3700 Piper Street, Zip 99508-4677; tel. 907/269-7100, (Nonreporting) **A**1 10
Primary Contact: Scott York, Chief Executive Officer
COO: Gavin H Carmichael, FACHE, Chief Operating Officer
CFO: Gavin H Carmichael, FACHE, Chief Operating Officer
CMO: Claudette A. Zarema, M.D., Medical Officer
CIO: Stephen Schneider, Manager Information Services
CHR: Katie E. Gratrix, Administrative Assistant III
CNO: Sharon Bergstedt, Director of Nursing
Web address: www.hss.state.ak.us/dbh/API/
Control: State, Government, Nonfederal **Service:** Psychiatric

Staffed Beds: 80

☒ **ALASKA REGIONAL HOSPITAL (020017)**, 2801 Debarr Road, Zip 99508-2997; tel. 907/264-1754, (Nonreporting) **A**1 2 10 **S** HCA Healthcare, Nashville, TN
Primary Contact: Jennifer Opsut, Chief Executive Officer
COO: Victor Rosenbaum, Chief Operating Officer
CMO: David Cadogan, Chief Medical Officer
CIO: Gene Kaplanis, Director Information Technology
CNO: Linda Doughty, Chief Nursing Officer
Web address: www.alaskaregional.com
Control: Corporation, Investor-owned (for-profit) **Service:** General medical and surgical

Staffed Beds: 250

☒ **NORTH STAR BEHAVIORAL HEALTH SYSTEM (024001)**, 2530 DeBarr Circle, Zip 99508-2948; tel. 907/258-7575, (Includes NORTH STAR BEHAVIORAL HEALTH, 1650 South Bragaw, Anchorage, Alaska, Zip 99508, tel. 907/258-7575) (Nonreporting) **A**1 5 10 **S** Universal Health Services, Inc., King of Prussia, PA
Primary Contact: William Newcombe, Chief Executive Officer and Managing Director
CFO: Alan Barnes, Chief Financial Officer
CMO: Ruth Dukoff, M.D., Medical Director
CIO: Brian O'Connell, Director Information Services
CHR: Sabrina Ben, Director Human Resources
CNO: Brandy Proctor, Director of Nursing
Web address: www.northstarbehavioral.com
Control: Corporation, Investor-owned (for-profit) **Service:** Psychiatric

Staffed Beds: 200

NORTH STAR HLTH SYST See North Star Behavioral Health

☒ **PROVIDENCE ALASKA MEDICAL CENTER (020001)**, 3200 Providence Drive, Zip 99508-4615, Mailing Address: P.O. Box 196604, Zip 99519-6604; tel. 907/562-2211, (Includes CHILDREN'S HOSPITAL AT PROVIDENCE, 3200 Providence DR, Anchorage, Alaska, Zip 99508-4615, 3200 Providence Drive, Zip 99508, tel. 907/212-3130) **A**1 2 3 5 10 13 **F**3 4 5 8 13 17 18 19 20 21 22 23 24 26 27 28 29 30 31 35 40 43 45 46 48 49 50 51 53 55 58 59 60 67 68 70 72 74 75 76 77 78 79 80 81 82 84 85 87 88 89 91 93 96 98 99 100 102 104 105 106 107 108 109 110 111 112 113 114 115 116 117 118 119 120 121 123 124 126 130 146 148 149 151 152 153 154 157 160 161 162 167 169 **S** Providence, Renton, WA
Primary Contact: Ella M. Goss, MSN, R.N., Chief Executive Officer
CFO: Anthony Dorsch, Chief Financial Officer
CMO: Roy Davis, M.D., Chief Medical Officer
CIO: Stephanie Morton, Chief Information Officer
CHR: Scott Jungwirth, Chief Human Resources Officer
CNO: James Reineke, Chief Nurse Executive
Web address: www.alaska.providence.org/locations/p/pamc
Control: Other not-for-profit (including NFP Corporation) **Service:** General medical and surgical

Staffed Beds: 401 **Admissions:** 15085 **Census:** 301 **Outpatient Visits:** 323679 **Births:** 2026 **Total Expense ($000):** 736710 **Payroll Expense ($000):** 269048 **Personnel:** 2539

☒ **PROVIDENCE ST. ELIAS SPECIALTY HOSPITAL (022001)**, 4800 Cordova Street, Zip 99503-7218; tel. 907/561-3333, **A**1 3 10 **F**1 3 29 30 50 59 60 68 75 77 84 90 91 96 107 114 119 130 148 149 154 157 **S** Providence, Renton, WA
Primary Contact: Jessica Oswald, Chief Executive Officer
CFO: Andrew Fitch, Chief Financial Officer
Web address: www.st-eliashospital.com
Control: Other not-for-profit (including NFP Corporation) **Service:** Acute long-term care hospital

Staffed Beds: 56 **Admissions:** 672 **Census:** 39 **Outpatient Visits:** 0 **Births:** 0 **Total Expense ($000):** 40652 **Payroll Expense ($000):** 23397 **Personnel:** 235

ST. ELIAS SPECIALTY HOSPITAL See Providence St. Elias Specialty Hospital

THE CHILDREN'S HOSPITAL AT PROVIDENCE See Children's Hospital at Providence

BARROW—North Slope County

☒ **SAMUEL SIMMONDS MEMORIAL HOSPITAL (021312)**, 7000 Uulu Street, Zip 99723, Mailing Address: P.O. Box 29, Zip 99723-0029; tel. 907/852-4611, (Nonreporting) **A**1 10 18
Primary Contact: Richard Hall, Chief Executive Officer
CMO: Devon Allen, M.D., Chief of Medical Staff
Web address: www.arcticslope.org
Control: Other not-for-profit (including NFP Corporation) **Service:** General medical and surgical

Staffed Beds: 14

BETHEL—Bethel County

☒ **YUKON–KUSKOKWIM DELTA REGIONAL HOSPITAL (020018)**, 700 Chief Eddie Hoffman Highway, Zip 99559-3000, Mailing Address: P.O. Box 528, Zip 99559-0528; tel. 907/543-6300, (Nonreporting) **A**1 3 5 10
Primary Contact: Dan Winkelman, President and Chief Executive Officer
CFO: Tommy Tompkins, Vice President, Finance and Chief Financial Officer
CIO: William Pearch, Chief Information Officer
Web address: www.ykhc.org
Control: Other not-for-profit (including NFP Corporation) **Service:** General medical and surgical

Staffed Beds: 82

Hospitals, U.S. / ALASKA

CORDOVA—Valdez–Cordova County

★ **CORDOVA COMMUNITY MEDICAL CENTER (021307)**, 602 Chase Avenue, Zip 99574, Mailing Address: P.O. Box 160, Zip 99574–0160; tel. 907/424–8000, (Total facility includes 10 beds in nursing home–type unit) **A**10 18 **F**1 3 5 29 34 35 38 40 50 57 59 64 66 68 69 75 77 82 93 97 100 107 119 132 133 134 135 146 147 148 149 152 153 154 160 164 165 **P**6
Primary Contact: Hannah Sanders, M.D., Chief Executive Officer
CFO: Eric Price, Chief Financial Officer
CMO: Hannah Sanders, M.D., Medical Director
CHR: Kim Wilson, Human Resources Coordinator
CNO: Kelly Kedzierski, R.N., BSN, RN, Director of Quality
Web address: www.cdvcmc.com
Control: Hospital district or authority, Government, Nonfederal **Service:** General medical and surgical

| Staffed Beds: 23 Admissions: 41 Census: 11 Births: 0 Total Expense ($000): 15694 Payroll Expense ($000): 6472 Personnel: 74 |

DILLINGHAM—Dillingham County

BRISTOL BAY AREA HEALTH CORPORATION (021309), 6000 Kanakanak Road, Zip 99576, Mailing Address: P.O. Box 130, Zip 99576–0130; tel. 907/842–5201, (Nonreporting) **A**1 3 10 18
Primary Contact: Robert J. Clark, President and Chief Executive Officer
COO: Lucrecia Scotford, Executive Vice President and Chief Operations Officer
CFO: David Morgan, Vice President and Chief Financial Officer
CMO: Arnold Loera, M.D., Clinical Director
CIO: Bill Wilcox, Chief Information Technology Officer
CHR: John Davis, Chief Human Resources Officer
CNO: Starla Fox, Director of Nursing
Web address: www.bbahc.org
Control: Other not–for–profit (including NFP Corporation) **Service:** General medical and surgical

| Staffed Beds: 16 |

ELMENDORF AFB—Anchorage County

U. S. AIR FORCE REGIONAL HOSPITAL, 5955 Zeamer Avenue, Zip 99506–3702; tel. 907/580–2778, (Nonreporting) **A**1 **S** Department of the Air Force, Washington, DC
Primary Contact: Major Mark Lamey, Commander
COO: Colonel Rebecca Seese, Chief Operating Officer
CFO: Major Felicia Burks, Chief Financial Officer
CMO: Colonel Marriner Oldham, M.D., Chief Medical Officer
CIO: Major Phillip Oliphant, Chief Information Officer
CHR: Mark Clark, Human Resources Liaison
Web address: https://elmendorfrichardson.tricare.mil/
Control: Air Force, Government, federal **Service:** General medical and surgical

| Staffed Beds: 64 |

FAIRBANKS—Fairbanks North Star County

FAIRBANKS MEMORIAL HOSPITAL (020012), 1650 Cowles Street, Zip 99701–5998; tel. 907/452–8181, (Nonreporting) **A**1 2 3 5 10
Primary Contact: Shelley Ebenal, Chief Executive Officer
COO: Clint Brooks, Chief Operating Officer
CFO: Steve Leslie, Chief Financial Officer
CIO: Johnathan Free, Information Security Officer
CHR: Nicole Welch, Chief Human Resources Officer
CNO: Karen Justin-Tanner, R.N., Chief Nursing Officer
Web address: https://www.foundationhealth.org/fmh
Control: Other not–for–profit (including NFP Corporation) **Service:** General medical and surgical

| Staffed Beds: 217 |

FORT WAINWRIGHT—Fairbanks North Star County

BASSETT ARMY COMMUNITY HOSPITAL, 1060 Gaffney Road, Box 7400, Zip 99703–5001, Mailing Address: 1060 Gaffney Road, Box 7440, Zip 99703–5001; tel. 907/361–4000, (Nonreporting) **A**1 3 **S** Department of the Army, Office of the Surgeon General, Falls Church, VA
Primary Contact: Colonel Eli Lozano, Commander
CMO: Colonel Leo Bennett, M.D., Deputy Commander Clinical Services
CHR: Terri Morefield, Deputy Chief Human Resources Division
Web address: https://bassett-wainwright.tricare.mil/
Control: Army, Government, federal **Service:** General medical and surgical

| Staffed Beds: 21 |

HOMER—Kenai Peninsula County

★ **SOUTH PENINSULA HOSPITAL (021313)**, 4300 Bartlett Street, Zip 99603–7000; tel. 907/235–8101, (Total facility includes 28 beds in nursing home–type unit) **A**10 18 **F**3 11 13 15 29 31 32 34 35 40 46 50 54 57 59 62 64 65 67 70 75 76 77 79 81 93 97 100 104 107 110 111 115 119 129 130 133 147 148 149 154 156 160 169 **P**6
Primary Contact: Ryan K. Smith, Chief Executive Officer
CMO: Sarah Spencer, M.D., Chief of Staff
CIO: Jim Bartilson, Manager Information Systems
CNO: Rachael Kincaid, Chief Nursing Officer
Web address: www.sphosp.org
Control: Other not–for–profit (including NFP Corporation) **Service:** General medical and surgical

| Staffed Beds: 50 Admissions: 680 Census: 32 Outpatient Visits: 92627 Births: 124 Total Expense ($000): 110624 Payroll Expense ($000): 51628 Personnel: 548 |

JUNEAU—Juneau County

BARTLETT REGIONAL HOSPITAL (020008), 3260 Hospital Drive, Zip 99801–7808; tel. 907/796–8900, **A**1 10 20 **F**3 4 5 13 15 28 29 31 32 34 35 37 38 40 44 45 46 47 50 57 59 62 63 64 65 70 76 78 79 81 85 86 93 96 98 100 102 104 106 107 108 110 111 115 116 119 126 129 130 131 132 148 149 154 160 161 162 164 165 169
Primary Contact: Ian Worden, Interim Chief Executive Officer
COO: Kim McDowell, Chief Nursing Officer and Chief Operating Officer
CFO: Joe Wanner, Chief Financial Officer
CMO: Sharon Fisher, M.D., Chief of Staff
CIO: Martha Palicka, Manager Information Systems
CHR: Dallas Hargrave, Human Resources Director
CNO: Kim McDowell, Chief Nursing Officer and Chief Operating Officer
Web address: www.bartletthospital.org
Control: City, Government, Nonfederal **Service:** General medical and surgical

| Staffed Beds: 57 Admissions: 1713 Census: 24 Births: 266 |

KETCHIKAN—Ketchikan Gateway County

★ **PEACEHEALTH KETCHIKAN MEDICAL CENTER (021311)**, 3100 Tongass Avenue, Zip 99901–5746; tel. 907/225–5171, (Total facility includes 25 beds in nursing home–type unit) **A**5 10 18 21 **F**3 13 15 29 30 40 43 45 50 62 63 64 65 70 75 76 77 78 79 81 84 85 86 87 91 93 96 97 100 102 107 108 110 111 115 119 128 130 131 133 147 149 154 156 157 167 169 **S** PeaceHealth, Vancouver, WA
Primary Contact: Dori Stevens, Chief Administrative Officer
CFO: Ken Tonjes, Chief Financial Officer
CMO: Peter Rice, M.D., Medical Director
CIO: Tim Walker, Manager Information Services
CHR: Lanetta Lundberg, Vice President Culture and People
Web address: https://www.peacehealth.org/hospitals/ketchikan-medical-center
Control: Other not–for–profit (including NFP Corporation) **Service:** General medical and surgical

| Staffed Beds: 54 Admissions: 1152 Census: 45 Outpatient Visits: 46977 Births: 125 Total Expense ($000): 75090 Payroll Expense ($000): 34598 Personnel: 345 |

KODIAK—Kodiak Island County

PROVIDENCE KODIAK ISLAND MEDICAL CENTER (021306), 1915 East Rezanof Drive, Zip 99615–6602; tel. 907/486–3281, **A**1 10 18 **F**3 15 29 30 35 40 42 45 48 50 56 68 70 75 76 77 78 81 82 84 85 91 93 96 97 98 100 102 103 107 111 119 127 130 133 146 147 148 149 152 154 165 167 169 **S** Providence, Renton, WA
Primary Contact: Karl Edward. Hertz, Administrator
COO: Brenda Zawacki, Chief Operating Manager
CFO: Timothy Hocum, Chief Financial Officer
CMO: Steve Smith, M.D., Chief of Staff
CIO: David Johnson, Manager Information Services
CNO: LeeAnn Horn, Chief Nurse Executive
Web address: www.providence.org
Control: Other not–for–profit (including NFP Corporation) **Service:** General medical and surgical

| Staffed Beds: 21 Admissions: 545 Census: 6 Outpatient Visits: 34687 Births: 83 Total Expense ($000): 47299 Payroll Expense ($000): 28805 Personnel: 171 |

Hospitals, U.S. / ALASKA

KOTZEBUE—Northwest Arctic County

☒ **MANIILAQ HEALTH CENTER (021310)**, 436 5th Avenue, Zip 99752–0043, Mailing Address: P.O. Box 43, Zip 99752–0043; tel. 907/442–7344, (Nonreporting) **A**1 10 18
Primary Contact: Tim J. Gilbert, President and Administrator
COO: Timothy Schuerch, President and Chief Executive Officer
CFO: Lucy Nelson, Director Finance, Vice President
CMO: Robert Onders, M.D., JD, Medical Director
CIO: Eugene Smith, Chief Information Officer
CHR: Gerty Gallahorn, Director Human Resources
CNO: Commander Donna K Biagioni, R.N., MSN, Director of Nursing
Web address: www.maniilaq.org
Control: PHS, Indian Service, Government, federal **Service**: General medical and surgical

Staffed Beds: 34

NOME—Nome County

☒ **NORTON SOUND REGIONAL HOSPITAL (021308)**, Bering Straits, Zip 99762, Mailing Address: P.O. Box 966, Zip 99762–0966; tel. 907/443–4519, (Nonreporting) **A**1 10 18
Primary Contact: Angela Gorn, Vice President
COO: Roy Agloinga, Chief Administrative Officer
CMO: David Head, M.D., Chief Medical Staff
CIO: Dan Bailey, Director Information Systems
CHR: Tiffany Martinson, Director Human Resources
Web address: www.nortonsoundhealth.org
Control: Other not–for–profit (including NFP Corporation) **Service**: General medical and surgical

Staffed Beds: 36

PALMER—Matanuska–Susitna County

☒ **MAT–SU REGIONAL MEDICAL CENTER (020006)**, 2500 South Woodworth Loop, Zip 99645–8984, Mailing Address: P.O. Box 1687, Zip 99645–1687; tel. 907/861–6000, (Nonreporting) **A**1 10 **S** Community Health Systems, Inc., Franklin, TN
Primary Contact: David Wallace, Chief Executive Officer
CMO: Christopher Sahlstrom, M.D., Chief of Staff
CIO: Bryan Meurer, Director Information Systems
CHR: Cathy Babuscio, Director Human Resources
CNO: Emily Stevens, Chief Nursing Officer
Web address: www.matsuregional.com
Control: Partnership, Investor–owned (for–profit) **Service**: General medical and surgical

Staffed Beds: 125

PETERSBURG—Petersburg County

★ **PETERSBURG MEDICAL CENTER (021304)**, 103 Fram Street, Zip 99833, Mailing Address: Box 589, Zip 99833–0589; tel. 907/772–4291, (Nonreporting) **A**10 18
Primary Contact: Phil A. Hofstetter, Chief Executive Officer
CFO: Doran Hammett, Chief Financial Officer
CHR: Cynthia Newman, Manager Human Resources
CNO: Jennifer Bryner, Director Nursing
Web address: www.pmcak.org
Control: City, Government, Nonfederal **Service**: General medical and surgical

Staffed Beds: 27

SEWARD—Kenai Peninsula County

★ **PROVIDENCE SEWARD MEDICAL CENTER (021302)**, 417 First Avenue, Zip 99664, Mailing Address: P.O. Box 365, Zip 99664–0365; tel. 907/224–5205, **A**10 18 **F**3 15 29 30 40 43 68 75 79 93 94 107 110 114 119 128 130 133 148 149 **P**6 **S** Providence, Renton, WA
Primary Contact: Helena Maria. Jagielski, Administrator
CMO: Amy Bukac, M.D., Medical Director
CNO: Heather McKean, Director of Patient Care Services
Web address: https://www.providence.org/locations/ak/seward-medical-center
Control: Other not–for–profit (including NFP Corporation) **Service**: General medical and surgical

Staffed Beds: 46 **Admissions**: 69 **Census**: 1 **Births**: 0 **Total Expense ($000)**: 25123 **Payroll Expense ($000)**: 15925 **Personnel**: 119

SITKA—Sitka County

☒ **SEARHC MT. EDGECUMBE HOSPITAL (021314)**, 222 Tongass Drive, Zip 99835–9416; tel. 907/966–2411, (Nonreporting) **A**1 5 10 18
Primary Contact: Charles Clement, Chief Executive Officer
COO: Daniel P Neumeister, Senior Vice President and Chief Operating Officer
CFO: Barbara Searls, Chief Financial Officer
CMO: David Vastola, Medical Director
CIO: Bob Cita, Chief Information Officer
CHR: Peggy Bernhardt–Kadlec, Chief Human Resources Officer
CNO: Patricia L Giampa, Chief Nursing Officer
Web address: www.searhc.org
Control: Other not–for–profit (including NFP Corporation) **Service**: General medical and surgical

Staffed Beds: 25

SOLDOTNA—Kenai Peninsula County

☒ **CENTRAL PENINSULA HOSPITAL (020024)**, 250 Hospital Place, Zip 99669–6999; tel. 907/714–4404, (Total facility includes 60 beds in nursing home–type unit) **A**1 3 10 20 **F**3 4 5 11 13 15 28 29 30 31 32 34 35 36 37 38 40 43 45 46 47 48 49 50 51 54 57 59 64 65 68 70 74 75 76 77 78 79 81 82 84 85 86 87 93 97 100 102 104 105 106 107 108 110 111 114 115 118 119 126 128 129 130 131 132 133 135 144 146 147 148 149 152 153 154 156 160 167 169 **P**6
Primary Contact: Shaun Patrick. Keef, Chief Executive Officer
CMO: Gregg Motonaga, M.D., Chief of Staff
CIO: Bryan Downs, Director Information Systems
CHR: John Dodd, Vice President Human Resources
Web address: www.cpgh.org
Control: Other not–for–profit (including NFP Corporation) **Service**: General medical and surgical

Staffed Beds: 119 **Admissions**: 2693 **Census**: 90 **Outpatient Visits**: 178343 **Births**: 340 **Total Expense ($000)**: 223607 **Payroll Expense ($000)**: 97916 **Personnel**: 908

VALDEZ—Valdez–Cordova County

★ **PROVIDENCE VALDEZ MEDICAL CENTER (021301)**, 911 Meals Avenue, Zip 99686–0550, Mailing Address: P.O. Box 550, Zip 99686–0550; tel. 907/835–2249, **A**5 10 18 **F**3 5 13 29 30 32 34 35 38 40 43 44 45 50 53 56 57 59 64 65 67 68 75 76 77 81 85 86 93 94 97 101 102 104 107 111 114 119 128 130 132 133 134 135 147 148 149 150 153 154 156 157 160 161 162 164 165 169 **P**6 **S** Providence, Renton, WA
Primary Contact: Melanee Tiura, Administrator
CMO: John Cullen, M.D., Chief of Staff and Medical Director Long Term Care
CHR: Maureen Radotich, Director Human Resources
Web address: https://www.providence.org/locations/ak/valdez-medical-center
Control: Other not–for–profit (including NFP Corporation) **Service**: General medical and surgical

Staffed Beds: 21 **Admissions**: 111 **Census**: 2 **Outpatient Visits**: 10611 **Births**: 17 **Total Expense ($000)**: 19640 **Payroll Expense ($000)**: 10778 **Personnel**: 90

WRANGELL—Wrangell County

☒ **WRANGELL MEDICAL CENTER (021305)**, First Avenue & Bennett Street, Zip 99929, Mailing Address: P.O. Box 1081, Zip 99929–1081; tel. 907/874–7000, (Nonreporting) **A**1 10 18
Primary Contact: Carly Allen, Hospital Administrator
CIO: Cathy Gross, Director Health Information Management Systems
CNO: Sherri Austin, MSN, R.N., Chief Nursing Officer
Web address: https://searhc.org/location/wrangell-medical-center/
Control: City, Government, Nonfederal **Service**: General medical and surgical

Staffed Beds: 22

Hospital, Medicare Provider Number, Address, Telephone, Approval, Facility, and Physician Codes, Health Care System

★ American Hospital Association (AHA) membership   ○ Healthcare Facilities Accreditation Program   ⇑ Center for Improvement in Healthcare Quality Accreditation
☐ The Joint Commission accreditation   ◇ DNV Healthcare Inc. accreditation   △ Commission on Accreditation of Rehabilitation Facilities (CARF) accreditation

Hospitals, U.S. / ARIZONA

ARIZONA

APACHE JUNCTION—Pinal County

✠ **BANNER GOLDFIELD MEDICAL CENTER (030134)**, 2050 West Southern Avenue, Zip 85120–7305; tel. 480/733–3300, **A**1 10 **F**3 18 29 30 34 35 40 45 67 68 75 79 81 82 85 87 100 107 115 119 130 131 135 146 148 149 154 156 167 **S** Banner Health, Phoenix, AZ
Primary Contact: Brian Kellar, Chief Executive Officer
CFO: Tracy French, Chief Financial Officer
CMO: Jason Brown, M.D., Chief Medical Officer
CHR: Rebecca McLaughlin, Chief Human Resource Officer
CNO: Terresa Ann Paulus, Chief Nursing Officer
Web address: www.bannerhealth.com/Locations/Arizona/Banner+Goldfield+Medical+Center/_Welcome+to+Banner+Goldfield.htm
Control: Other not–for–profit (including NFP Corporation) **Service:** General medical and surgical

| Staffed Beds: 20 Admissions: 765 Census: 5 Outpatient Visits: 18468
Births: 0 Total Expense ($000): 24524 Payroll Expense ($000): 8765
Personnel: 88 |

AVONDALE—Maricopa County

☐ **COPPER SPRINGS HOSPITAL (034032)**, 10550 West McDowell Road, Zip 85392–4864; tel. 602/314–7800, (Includes COPPER SPRINGS EAST, 3755 S Rome ST, Gilbert, Arizona, Zip 85297–7361, 3755 Rome Street, Zip 85295, tel. 480/667–5500) (Nonreporting) **A**1 10 **S** Springstone, Louisville, KY
Primary Contact: Jessica Black, Market Chief Executive Officer
Web address: https://coppersprings.com/
Control: Corporation, Investor–owned (for–profit) **Service:** Psychiatric

| Staffed Beds: 144 |

BENSON—Cochise County

★ **BENSON HOSPITAL (031301)**, 450 South Ocotillo Street, Zip 85602–6403; tel. 520/586–2261, (Nonreporting) **A**10 18
Primary Contact: Gary Kartchner, R.N., MSN, Chief Executive Officer
COO: Teresa Vincifora, Chief Operating Officer
CFO: Ken Goranson, Chief Financial Officer
CMO: Barbara Hartley, Chief Medical Officer
CIO: Rob Roberts, Director Information Technology
CHR: Ashley Dickey, Director Human Resources
Web address: www.bensonhospital.org
Control: Other not–for–profit (including NFP Corporation) **Service:** General medical and surgical

| Staffed Beds: 22 |

BISBEE—Cochise County

★ **COPPER QUEEN COMMUNITY HOSPITAL (031312)**, 101 Cole Avenue, Zip 85603–1399; tel. 520/432–5383, (Nonreporting) **A**3 10 18
Primary Contact: Robert L. Seamon, Chief Executive Officer
CFO: James Ehasz, Chief Financial Officer
CIO: David Chmura, Chief Information Officer
CHR: Virginia Martinez, Director Human Resources
CNO: Sadie Maestas, Interim Chief Nursing Officer
Web address: https://cqch.org/
Control: Other not–for–profit (including NFP Corporation) **Service:** General medical and surgical

| Staffed Beds: 14 |

BULLHEAD CITY—Mohave County

✠ **WESTERN ARIZONA REGIONAL MEDICAL CENTER (030101)**, 2735 Silver Creek Road, Zip 86442–8303; tel. 928/763–2273, **A**1 10 19 **F**3 8 11 13 15 18 20 22 28 29 34 35 37 40 43 45 50 54 56 57 59 64 65 68 69 70 75 76 77 79 80 81 82 85 87 93 97 102 107 108 110 111 114 115 116 119 130 131 144 146 147 148 149 154 156 157 **S** Community Health Systems, Inc., Franklin, TN
Primary Contact: Brent Parsons, Chief Executive Officer
CFO: Christopher Frysztak, CPA, Chief Financial Officer
CNO: Heidi Greenman, Interim Chief Executive Officer
Web address: www.warmc.com
Control: Corporation, Investor–owned (for–profit) **Service:** General medical and surgical

| Staffed Beds: 106 Admissions: 4592 Census: 54 |

CASA GRANDE—Pinal County

✠ **BANNER CASA GRANDE MEDICAL CENTER (030016)**, 1800 East Florence Boulevard, Zip 85122–5399; tel. 520/381–6300, **A**1 3 10 **F**3 13 15 18 20 22 26 29 30 34 38 40 41 43 45 46 47 48 53 56 57 60 64 68 70 73 74 75 76 77 79 80 81 85 87 93 102 107 108 111 114 115 116 119 126 129 130 135 141 146 147 148 149 152 154 164 167 169 **S** Banner Health, Phoenix, AZ
Primary Contact: John Scherpf, Chief Executive Officer
CMO: Devin Minior, M.D., Chief Medical Officer
CHR: Carol D'Souza, Chief Human Resources Officer
CNO: Audra Valentino, Chief Nursing Officer
Web address: https://www.bannerhealth.com/locations/casa-grande/banner-casa-grande-medical-center
Control: Other not–for–profit (including NFP Corporation) **Service:** General medical and surgical

| Staffed Beds: 141 Admissions: 5739 Census: 69 Outpatient Visits: 48202
Births: 721 Total Expense ($000): 154249 Payroll Expense ($000): 58098
Personnel: 684 |

CHANDLER—Maricopa County

☐ **ARIZONA ORTHOPEDIC SURGICAL HOSPITAL (030112)**, 2905 West Warner Road, Suite 1, Zip 85224–1674; tel. 480/603–9000, (Nonreporting) **A**1 10 **S** United Surgical Partners International, Addison, TX
Primary Contact: Patricia K. Alice, Chief Executive Officer
CMO: Randall Hardison, M.D., Chief Medical Officer
CIO: John Langenfeld, Medical Records Coordinator
CNO: Caroline Herpfer, Chief Nursing Officer
Web address: www.azosh.com
Control: Corporation, Investor–owned (for–profit) **Service:** Surgical

| Staffed Beds: 24 |

✠ **BANNER OCOTILLO MEDICAL CENTER (030147)**, 1405 South Alma School Road, Zip 85286; tel. 480/256–7000, **A**1 **F**3 13 18 20 22 29 30 34 40 41 44 45 46 48 49 50 51 64 68 70 73 74 75 76 79 81 84 85 87 96 100 102 107 108 111 115 119 126 130 135 146 147 148 149 154 164 167 **S** Banner Health, Phoenix, AZ
Primary Contact: Laura Robertson, R.N., Chief Executive Officer
COO: Nate Shinagawa, Chief Operating Officer
Web address: www.bannerhealth.com
Control: Other not–for–profit (including NFP Corporation) **Service:** General medical and surgical

| Staffed Beds: 94 Admissions: 3840 Census: 41 Outpatient Visits: 24497
Births: 762 Total Expense ($000): 102095 Payroll Expense ($000): 32622
Personnel: 394 |

✠ **CHANDLER REGIONAL MEDICAL CENTER (030036)**, 1955 West Frye Road, Zip 85224–6282; tel. 480/728–3000, **A**1 3 5 10 19 **F**3 8 11 12 13 17 18 20 22 24 26 28 29 30 31 32 34 35 37 40 41 42 43 44 45 46 47 48 49 50 51 54 57 58 59 60 64 65 66 68 70 71 72 73 74 75 76 77 78 79 81 82 83 84 85 86 87 93 96 107 108 111 114 115 119 126 130 131 132 135 143 144 146 148 156 167 **S** CommonSpirit Health, Chicago, IL
Primary Contact: Mark F. Slyter, FACHE, President and Chief Operating Officer
COO: Mark F. Slyter, FACHE, President and Chief Operating Officer
CFO: Mark Kem, Vice President Finance and Chief Financial Officer
CMO: Terry J Happel, M.D., Vice President and Chief Medical Officer
CHR: Renea Brunke, Vice President Human Resources
CNO: Peg Smith, Vice President and Chief Nursing Officer
Web address: www.chandlerregional.com
Control: Other not–for–profit (including NFP Corporation) **Service:** General medical and surgical

| Staffed Beds: 429 Admissions: 28730 Census: 350 |

DIGNITY HEALTH EAST VALLEY REHABILITATION HOSPITAL (033040), 1515 West Chandler Boulevard, Zip 85224–6141; tel. 602/594–5400, **A**3 10 22 **F**3 29 90 91 95 96 148 **S** Kindred Healthcare, Chicago, IL
Primary Contact: Greg Blackburn, Chief Executive Officer
Web address: www.dignityhealthevrehab.com
Control: Corporation, Investor–owned (for–profit) **Service:** Rehabilitation

| Staffed Beds: 50 Admissions: 1404 Census: 46 Outpatient Visits: 0
Births: 0 Total Expense ($000): 23051 Payroll Expense ($000): 13890 |

Hospitals, U.S. / ARIZONA

☐ **OASIS BEHAVIORAL HEALTH – CHANDLER (034029)**, 2190 North Grace Boulevard, Zip 85225–3416; tel. 480/917–9301, (Nonreporting) **A**1 10 **S** Acadia Healthcare Company, Inc., Franklin, TN
Primary Contact: Jennifer Nunez, Chief Executive Officer
CFO: Dino Quarante, CPA, Chief Financial Officer
CHR: Barbara Mitchell, Director Human Resources
CNO: Charissa Davis, Chief Nursing Officer and Director of Nursing
Web address: www.obhhospital.com/about/location
Control: Corporation, Investor–owned (for-profit) **Service**: Psychiatric

Staffed Beds: 146

CHINLE—Apache County

✠ **CHINLE COMPREHENSIVE HEALTH CARE FACILITY (030084)**, Highway 191, Zip 86503, Mailing Address: Highway 191 Hospital Drive, Zip 86503–8000; tel. 928/674–7001, (Nonreporting) **A**1 10 **S** U. S. Indian Health Service, Rockville, MD
Primary Contact: Darlene Chee, Acting Chief Executive Officer
CFO: Philene Tyler, Chief Finance Officer
CMO: Eric Ritchie, M.D., Clinical Director
CIO: Perry Francis, Supervisory Information Technology Specialist
CHR: Lorraine Begaye, Supervisory Human Resource Specialist
Web address: www.ihs.gov
Control: PHS, Indian Service, Government, federal **Service**: General medical and surgical

Staffed Beds: 60

COTTONWOOD—Yavapai County

✠ **VERDE VALLEY MEDICAL CENTER (030007)**, 269 South Candy Lane, Zip 86326–4170; tel. 928/639–6000, **A**1 3 5 10 13 20 **F**3 13 15 18 20 22 26 28 29 30 31 37 40 42 44 45 48 49 50 51 55 58 60 61 64 65 68 70 74 75 76 77 78 79 81 82 84 85 86 87 93 94 102 107 108 111 115 119 120 124 130 131 146 147 148 149 154 156 167 169 **S** Northern Arizona Healthcare, Flagstaff, AZ
Primary Contact: Ronald Haase, Chief Administrative Officer
CFO: Jeffrey Treasure, Chief Financial Officer, Northern Arizona Healthcare
CMO: Leon Pontikes, M.D., Chief Medical Officer
CIO: Marilynn Black, Chief Information Officer, Northern Arizona Healthcare
CNO: Lori A Stevens, MSN, R.N., Interim Chief Nursing Officer
Web address: https://nahealth.com/
Control: Other not-for-profit (including NFP Corporation) **Service**: General medical and surgical

Staffed Beds: 87 **Admissions**: 4393 **Census**: 32 **Outpatient Visits**: 33546 **Births**: 409 **Total Expense ($000)**: 165031 **Payroll Expense ($000)**: 47549 **Personnel**: 715

FLAGSTAFF—Coconino County

✠ **FLAGSTAFF MEDICAL CENTER (030023)**, 1200 North Beaver Street, Zip 86001–3118; tel. 928/779–3366, **A**1 3 5 10 **F**3 5 7 12 13 17 18 19 20 22 24 26 29 30 31 37 40 43 44 45 46 47 48 49 50 51 55 57 58 60 61 64 65 68 70 72 74 75 76 77 78 79 81 82 84 85 86 87 88 89 93 94 98 100 102 104 107 108 111 114 115 118 119 120 124 126 130 131 135 143 146 147 148 149 154 155 156 164 167 169 **S** Northern Arizona Healthcare, Flagstaff, AZ
Primary Contact: David Cheney, President and Chief Executive Officer
CFO: Jeffrey Treasure, Chief Financial Officer, Northern Arizona Healthcare
CMO: Derek Feuquay, M.D., Chief Medical Officer
CIO: Marilynn Black, Chief Information Officer, Northern Arizona Healthcare
Web address: www.nahealth.com
Control: Other not-for-profit (including NFP Corporation) **Service**: General medical and surgical

Staffed Beds: 268 **Admissions**: 10972 **Census**: 145 **Outpatient Visits**: 49634 **Births**: 1030 **Total Expense ($000)**: 481918 **Payroll Expense ($000)**: 134550 **Personnel**: 1878

☐ **GUIDANCE CENTER (034023)**, 2187 North Vickey Street, Zip 86004–6121; tel. 928/527–1899, (Nonreporting) **A**1 10
Primary Contact: Devon Forrest, Chief Executive Officer
CFO: Steve Finch, Chief Financial Officer
CMO: Chris Linskey, M.D., Acting Chief Medical Officer
CIO: John Crockett, Chief Information Officer
Web address: www.tgcaz.org
Control: Other not-for-profit (including NFP Corporation) **Service**: Psychiatric

Staffed Beds: 16

☐ **REHABILITATION HOSPITAL OF NORTHERN ARIZONA (033041)**, 1851 North Gemini Drive, Zip 86001–1607; tel. 928/774–7070, (Nonreporting) **A**1 3 10 **S** Ernest Health, Inc., Albuquerque, NM
Primary Contact: Jon Cook, Chief Executive Officer
Web address: www.ernesthealth.com/gallery-item/rehabilitation-hospital-of-northern-arizona/
Control: Corporation, Investor–owned (for-profit) **Service**: Rehabilitation

Staffed Beds: 40

FORT DEFIANCE—Apache County

★ **TSEHOOTSOOI MEDICAL CENTER (030071)**, Highway 12 & Bonito Drive, Zip 86504, Mailing Address: P.O. Box 649, Zip 86504–0649; tel. 928/729–8000, (Nonreporting) **A**5 10
Primary Contact: Robbie Whitehair, Chief Executive Officer
COO: Valonia Hardy, Chief Healthy Living Officer
CFO: Rachel Sorrell, Chief Financial Officer
CMO: Michael Tutt, M.D., Chief Medical Officer
CIO: Virgil Chavez, Director Information Technology
CHR: Vivian Santistevan, Chief Human Resources
CNO: Tori Davidson, R.N., Chief Nursing Officer
Web address: www.fdihb.org
Control: Public Health Service other than 47, Government, federal **Service**: General medical and surgical

Staffed Beds: 39

FORT MOHAVE—Mohave County

✠ **VALLEY VIEW MEDICAL CENTER (030117)**, 5330 South Highway 95, Zip 86426–9225; tel. 928/788–2273, **A**1 10 **F**3 8 11 13 15 18 20 22 29 45 50 51 56 59 64 70 76 77 81 85 87 90 93 107 108 111 114 115 116 117 119 135 144 149 154 **S** Lifepoint Health, Brentwood, TN
Primary Contact: Jeff Bourgeois, FACHE, Interim Chief Executive Officer
CFO: Emma Canlas, Chief Financial Officer
CIO: Monique Murphy–Mijares, Chief Information Officer
CHR: Bonnie Guerrero, Director Human Resources
CNO: Teresa Reynolds, Chief Nursing Officer
Web address: www.valleyviewmedicalcenter.net
Control: Corporation, Investor–owned (for-profit) **Service**: General medical and surgical

Staffed Beds: 84 **Admissions**: 1421 **Census**: 16

GANADO—Apache County

✠ **NAVAJO HEALTH FOUNDATION – SAGE MEMORIAL HOSPITAL (031309)**, Highway 264, Zip 86505, Mailing Address: P.O. Box 457, Zip 86505–0457; tel. 928/755–4500, **A**1 10 18 **F**3 5 18 29 30 32 34 35 36 38 57 59 60 61 64 65 67 70 80 90 101 102 104 132 133 135 144 146 148 149 154 160 164 165 **S** U. S. Indian Health Service, Rockville, MD
Primary Contact: Melinda White, R.N., Chief Executive Officer
COO: Netrisha Dalgai, Director of Operations
CHR: Gary Pahe, Manager Human Resources
CNO: Ernasha McIntosh, Interim Director of Nursing
Web address: www.sagememorial.com
Control: PHS, Indian Service, Government, federal **Service**: General medical and surgical

Staffed Beds: 43 **Admissions**: 282 **Census**: 3 **Outpatient Visits**: 9261 **Births**: 0

GILBERT—Maricopa County

✠ **BANNER GATEWAY MEDICAL CENTER (030122)**, 1900 North Higley Road, Zip 85234–1604; tel. 480/543–2000, **A**1 3 10 19 **F**3 8 12 13 15 18 29 30 31 34 35 36 40 44 45 46 47 48 49 50 51 55 57 58 59 60 60 68 70 72 73 74 75 76 77 78 81 85 87 90 93 102 107 108 110 111 114 115 116 117 118 119 120 121 123 124 126 130 132 135 136 141 146 147 148 149 154 167 168 169 **S** Banner Health, Phoenix, AZ
Primary Contact: Michael Herring, R.N., Chief Executive Officer
COO: Darren McCollem, Chief Operating Officer
CFO: Cody Ziemer, Chief Financial Officer
CMO: George Figueroa, M.D., Chief Medical Officer
CHR: Brittany Hviding, Senior Human Resources Director
CNO: Kelley Kieffer, Chief Nursing Officer
Web address: www.bannerhealth.com/Locations/Arizona/Banner+Gateway+Medical+Center/
Control: Other not-for-profit (including NFP Corporation) **Service**: General medical and surgical

Staffed Beds: 286 **Admissions**: 12361 **Census**: 163 **Outpatient Visits**: 140167 **Births**: 3368 **Total Expense ($000)**: 654265 **Payroll Expense ($000)**: 162261 **Personnel**: 1413

Hospital, Medicare Provider Number, Address, Telephone, Approval, Facility, and Physician Codes, Health Care System
★ American Hospital Association (AHA) membership ◯ Healthcare Facilities Accreditation Program ⇈ Center for Improvement in Healthcare Quality Accreditation
☐ The Joint Commission accreditation ◇ DNV Healthcare Inc. accreditation △ Commission on Accreditation of Rehabilitation Facilities (CARF) accreditation

Hospitals, U.S. / ARIZONA

DIGNITY HEALTH EAST VALLEY REHABILITATION HOSPITAL – GILBERT (033044), 1850 South San Tan Village Parkway, Zip 85295–6245; tel. 623/269–6000, (Nonreporting)
Primary Contact: Samantha Caldwell, Chief Executive Officer
Web address: https://www.dignityhealthevrehabgilbert.com/
Control: Church operated, Nongovernment, not–for–profit **Service:** Rehabilitation

Staffed Beds: 40

MERCY GILBERT MEDICAL CENTER (030119), 3555 South Val Vista Road, Zip 85297–7323; tel. 480/728–8000, (Nonreporting) **A**1 3 10 19 **S** CommonSpirit Health, Chicago, IL
Primary Contact: Mark F. Slyter, FACHE, President and Chief Operating Officer
COO: Mark F. Slyter, FACHE, President and Chief Operating Officer
CFO: Chuck Sowers, Vice President Finance and Chief Financial Officer
CIO: Larissa Spraker, Vice President Business Development and Chief Strategy Officer
CHR: Anita Harger, Director Human Resources
Web address: www.mercygilbert.org
Control: Church operated, Nongovernment, not–for–profit **Service:** General medical and surgical

Staffed Beds: 197

GLENDALE—Maricopa County

ABRAZO ARROWHEAD CAMPUS (030094), 18701 North 67th Avenue, Zip 85308–7100; tel. 623/561–1000, (Includes ABRAZO ARIZONA HEART HOSPITAL, 1930 East Thomas Road, Phoenix, Arizona, Zip 85016, tel. 602/532–1000; Stephen Garner, Chief Executive Officer) (Nonreporting) **A**1 3 5 10 19 **S** TENET Healthcare Corporation, Dallas, TX
Primary Contact: Stephen Garner, Chief Executive Officer
COO: Matt Sartorius, Chief Operating Officer
CFO: Robert Oertel, Chief Financial Officer
CMO: Patrick Smith, M.D., Chief Medical Officer
CHR: Sarah Hastings, Chief Human Resources Officer
Web address: www.arrowheadhospital.com
Control: Corporation, Investor–owned (for–profit) **Service:** General medical and surgical

Staffed Beds: 217

AURORA BEHAVIORAL HEALTH SYSTEM WEST (034024), 6015 West Peoria Avenue, Zip 85302–1213; tel. 623/344–4400, (Nonreporting) **A**1 10 **S** Signature Healthcare Services, Corona, CA
Primary Contact: Bruce Waldo, Chief Executive Officer
CFO: Rebekah Francis, JD, Chief Financial Officer
CHR: Vicki Thomsen, Director Human Resources
CNO: Lori Milus, R.N., MSN, Director of Nursing
Web address: www.aurorabehavioral.com
Control: Corporation, Investor–owned (for–profit) **Service:** Psychiatric

Staffed Beds: 100

BANNER THUNDERBIRD MEDICAL CENTER (030089), 5555 West Thunderbird Road, Zip 85306–4696; tel. 602/865–5555, (Includes BANNER BEHAVIORAL HEALTH CENTER–THUNDERBIRD CAMPUS, 5555 West Thunderbird Road, Glendale, Arizona, Zip 85306, tel. 602/588–5555) **A**1 3 5 10 **F**3 5 13 17 18 19 20 22 24 26 28 29 30 31 32 34 35 38 40 41 43 45 46 47 48 49 50 51 59 60 61 64 65 68 70 72 74 75 76 77 78 79 81 84 85 87 88 89 98 99 100 101 102 104 107 108 109 111 114 115 116 117 119 120 121 122 123 124 126 129 130 132 135 145 146 148 149 153 154 157 167 **S** Banner Health, Phoenix, AZ
Primary Contact: Debbie Flores, Chief Executive Officer
COO: Amy Shlossman, Chief Operating Officer
CMO: Kathryn Perkins, M.D., Chief Medical Officer
CHR: Laura Witt, Administrator Human Resources
Web address: https://www.bannerhealth.com/locations/glendale/banner-thunderbird-medical-center
Control: Other not–for–profit (including NFP Corporation) **Service:** General medical and surgical

Staffed Beds: 595 **Admissions:** 28232 **Census:** 411 **Outpatient Visits:** 120166 **Births:** 4410 **Total Expense ($000):** 658993 **Payroll Expense ($000):** 235832 **Personnel:** 2330

ENCOMPASS HEALTH VALLEY OF THE SUN REHABILITATION HOSPITAL (033032), 13460 North 67th Avenue, Zip 85304–1042; tel. 623/878–8800, **A**1 10 **F**29 62 64 75 90 93 132 **S** Encompass Health Corporation, Birmingham, AL
Primary Contact: Mark A. Roth, Chief Executive Officer
CFO: Kathryn Haney, Controller
CMO: Michael Kravetz, M.D., Medical Director
CHR: Danette Garcia, Director Human Resources
CNO: Stephanie Palmer, Chief Nursing Officer
Web address: https://www.encompasshealth.com/valleyofthesunrehab
Control: Corporation, Investor–owned (for–profit) **Service:** Rehabilitation

Staffed Beds: 75 **Admissions:** 1209 **Census:** 43 **Births:** 0

SAMARITAN BEHAVIORAL HLTH CTR See Banner Behavioral Health Center–Thunderbird Campus

GLOBE—Gila County

★ **COBRE VALLEY REGIONAL MEDICAL CENTER (031314)**, 5880 South Hospital Drive, Zip 85501–9454; tel. 928/425–3261, (Nonreporting) **A**10 18 **S** HealthTech Management Services, Plano, TX
Primary Contact: Neal Jensen, Chief Executive Officer
COO: Preston Pollock, Chief Operating Officer
CFO: Harold Dupper, Chief Financial Officer
CIO: Sharon Bennett, Manager Information Systems
CHR: Rita Murphy, Director Human Resources
Web address: www.cvrmc.org
Control: Other not–for–profit (including NFP Corporation) **Service:** General medical and surgical

Staffed Beds: 36

GOODYEAR—Maricopa County

ABRAZO WEST CAMPUS (030110), 13677 West McDowell Road, Zip 85395–2635; tel. 623/882–1500, (Nonreporting) **A**1 3 5 10 **S** TENET Healthcare Corporation, Dallas, TX
Primary Contact: Hans Driessnack, Chief Executive Officer
COO: Willie Payton Jr, Chief Operating Officer
CFO: Jennifer Orona, Chief Financial Officer
CHR: Michelle Wilkerson, Chief Human Resources Officer
CNO: Ashley Holmstrom, Chief Nursing Officer
Web address: www.abrazohealth.com
Control: Corporation, Investor–owned (for–profit) **Service:** General medical and surgical

Staffed Beds: 188

CITY OF HOPE PHOENIX (030138), 14200 West Celebrate Life way, Zip 85338–3005; tel. 623/207–3000, (Nonreporting) **A**1 2 3 10 **S** City of Hope, Schaumburg, IL
Primary Contact: Kevin Tulipana, Executive Vice President, Arizona Market
Web address: www.cancercenter.com/western-hospital.cfm
Control: Corporation, Investor–owned (for–profit) **Service:** Cancer

Staffed Beds: 14

KEAMS CANYON—Navajo County

HOPI HEALTH CARE CENTER (031305), Highway 264 Mile Marker 388, Zip 86042, Mailing Address: P.O. Box 4000, Polacca, Zip 86042–4000; tel. 928/737–6000, (Nonreporting) **A**1 3 5 10 18 **S** U. S. Indian Health Service, Rockville, MD
Primary Contact: Amanda Lea. Hicks, R.N., Chief Executive Officer
COO: Alysia Cardona, Chief Operating Officer
CFO: Dorothy Sulu, Budget Analyst
CHR: Trudy Begay, Human Resources Specialist
Web address: https://www.ihs.gov/phoenix/healthcarefacilities/hopi/
Control: PHS, Indian Service, Government, federal **Service:** General medical and surgical

Staffed Beds: 15

KINGMAN—Mohave County

★ ⇧ **KINGMAN REGIONAL MEDICAL CENTER (030055)**, 3269 North Stockton Hill Road, Zip 86409–3691; tel. 928/757–2101, (Nonreporting) **A**2 3 5 10 13 21
Primary Contact: Heath Evans, President and Chief Executive Officer
COO: Ryan Kennedy, Chief Operating Officer
CFO: Timothy D Blanchard, Chief Financial Officer
CMO: Thomas Gaughan, M.D., Chief Medical Officer
CIO: Arek Shennar, Chief Information Officer
CHR: Anita Harger, Chief Human Resource Officer
CNO: James Wells, R.N., Chief Nursing Officer
Web address: www.azkrmc.com
Control: Hospital district or authority, Government, Nonfederal **Service:** General medical and surgical

Staffed Beds: 160

LAKE HAVASU CITY—Mohave County

HAVASU REGIONAL MEDICAL CENTER (030069), 101 Civic Center Lane, Zip 86403–5683; tel. 928/855–8185, (Nonreporting) **A**1 10 **S** Lifepoint Health, Brentwood, TN
Primary Contact: Philip Fitzgerald, Chief Executive Officer
CFO: Alan Phelps, Market Chief Financial Officer
CMO: Michael Rosen, M.D., Chief Medical Officer
CIO: Linda Toy, Director Information Systems
CNO: Suzanne Delboccio, Chief Nursing Officer
Web address: www.havasuregional.com
Control: Corporation, Investor–owned (for–profit) **Service:** General medical and surgical

Staffed Beds: 162

Hospitals, U.S. / ARIZONA

LAKESIDE—Navajo County

CCC AT PINEVIEW HOSPITAL (034027), 1920 West Commerce Drive, Zip 85929; tel. 928/368–4110, (Nonreporting) **A** 10
Primary Contact: Rosemary Anderson, Administrator
Web address: www.ccc-az.org
Control: Other not–for–profit (including NFP Corporation) **Service:** Psychiatric

Staffed Beds: 16

LAVEEN—Maricopa County

✠ **DIGNITY HEALTH ARIZONA GENERAL HOSPITAL (030136)**, 7171 South 51st Avenue, Zip 85339–2923; tel. 623/584–5100, (Nonreporting) **A**1 10 **S** CommonSpirit Health, Chicago, IL
Primary Contact: Jane E. Hanson, R.N., Chief Executive Officer
CFO: Anthony Cirocco, Chief Financial Officer
CMO: Aaron Mickelson, M.D., Chief Medical Officer
CNO: Cynthia Rosenberg, Vice President, Chief Nursing Officer
Web address: www.dignityhealth.org/arizonageneral/
Control: Other not–for–profit (including NFP Corporation) **Service:** Acute long–term care hospital

Staffed Beds: 16

MARICOPA—Pinal County

☐ **EXCEPTIONAL COMMUNITY HOSPITAL MARICOPA (030152)**, 19060 North John Wayne Parkway, Zip 85139–2923; tel. 520/534–0700, (Nonreporting) **A**1 10
Primary Contact: Bruce W. McVeigh, Chief Operating Officer
Web address: www.ehc24.com
Control: Corporation, Investor–owned (for–profit) **Service:** Other specialty treatment

Staffed Beds: 9

MESA—Maricopa County

☐ **ARIZONA SPINE AND JOINT HOSPITAL (030107)**, 4620 East Baseline Road, Zip 85206–4624; tel. 480/832–4770, **A**1 10 **F**29 34 77 79 81 **S** National Surgical Healthcare, Chicago, IL
Primary Contact: Elizabeth Kearney, R.N., Chief Executive Officer
CHR: Diane Hearne, Director Human Resources
CNO: Stacy Hayes, R.N., Chief Nursing Officer
Web address: www.azspineandjoint.com
Control: Corporation, Investor–owned (for–profit) **Service:** Orthopedic

Staffed Beds: 23 **Admissions:** 776 **Census:** 3 **Births:** 0

✠ **BANNER BAYWOOD MEDICAL CENTER (030088)**, 6644 East Baywood Avenue, Zip 85206–1797; tel. 480/321–2000, **A**1 10 19 **F**3 15 18 29 30 31 34 35 36 37 40 43 44 45 46 47 48 49 50 51 56 57 58 59 60 61 63 64 65 68 70 74 75 77 78 79 81 84 85 86 87 90 92 97 100 102 107 108 110 111 115 118 119 126 130 135 146 147 148 149 154 156 167 **S** Banner Health, Phoenix, AZ
Primary Contact: Brian Kellar, Chief Executive Officer
CFO: Derek Lythgoe, Chief Financial Officer
CMO: Michael P O'Connor, M.D., Chief Medical Officer
CIO: Lori Matthews, Vice President Information Technology System
CHR: Tiffany Werner, Senior Human Resource Business Partner
CNO: Kelley Kieffer, Chief Nursing Officer
Web address: www.bannerhealth.com/locations/Arizona/banner+baywood+medical+center
Control: Other not–for–profit (including NFP Corporation) **Service:** General medical and surgical

Staffed Beds: 337 **Admissions:** 12233 **Census:** 178 **Outpatient Visits:** 73291 **Births:** 0 **Total Expense ($000):** 294251 **Payroll Expense ($000):** 107596 **Personnel:** 1242

BANNER CHILDREN'S HOSPITAL See Cardon Children's Medical Center

✠ **BANNER DESERT MEDICAL CENTER (030065)**, 1400 South Dobson Road, Zip 85202–4707; tel. 480/412–3000, (Includes CARDON CHILDREN'S MEDICAL CENTER, 1400 South Dobson Road, Mesa, Arizona, Zip 85202–4707, tel. 480/412–3000; Justin Bradshaw, Chief Executive Officer; SAMARITAN BEHAVIORAL HEALTH CENTER–DESERT SAMARITAN MEDICAL CENTER, 2225 West Southern Avenue, Mesa, Arizona, Zip 85202, tel. 602/464–4000) **A**1 3 5 10 **F**3 11 13 17 18 19 20 21 22 23 24 25 26 27 28 29 30 31 32 34 35 37 40 41 43 44 45 46 47 48 49 50 51 56 58 59 60 61 63 64 68 70 72 73 74 75 76 77 78 79 80 81 84 85 86 87 88 89 91 92 96 100 105 107 108 111 114 115 118 119 120 121 123 124 126 129 130 135 146 147 148 149 154 164 167 169 **S** Banner Health, Phoenix, AZ
Primary Contact: Laura Robertson, R.N., Chief Executive Officer
COO: Cristal Mackay, Chief Operating Officer
CFO: Scott Leckey, Chief Financial Officer
CMO: Tanya Kne, M.D., Chief Medical Officer
CIO: Stacey Hinkle, Director Information Technology
CHR: Kevin McVeigh, Chief Human Resources Officer
Web address: https://www.bannerhealth.com/locations/mesa/banner-desert-medical-cente
Control: Other not–for–profit (including NFP Corporation) **Service:** General medical and surgical

Staffed Beds: 763 **Admissions:** 32221 **Census:** 483 **Outpatient Visits:** 131629 **Births:** 3131 **Total Expense ($000):** 802519 **Payroll Expense ($000):** 287652 **Personnel:** 3010

✠ **BANNER HEART HOSPITAL (030105)**, 6750 East Baywood Avenue, Zip 85206–1749; tel. 480/854–5000, **A**1 3 10 19 **F**3 17 18 20 22 24 26 28 29 30 34 35 36 44 50 57 58 59 60 68 75 81 84 85 86 87 119 130 132 146 148 149 154 156 **S** Banner Health, Phoenix, AZ
Primary Contact: Brian Kellar, Chief Executive Officer
CFO: Derek Lythgoe, Chief Financial Officer
CMO: Paul Hurst, M.D., Chief Medical Officer
CHR: Tiffany Werner, Senior Human Resource Business Partner
CNO: Kelley Kieffer, Chief Nursing Officer
Web address: https://www.bannerhealth.com/locations/mesa/banner-heart-hospital
Control: Other not–for–profit (including NFP Corporation) **Service:** Heart

Staffed Beds: 111 **Admissions:** 4843 **Census:** 57 **Outpatient Visits:** 7916 **Births:** 0 **Total Expense ($000):** 140923 **Payroll Expense ($000):** 35310 **Personnel:** 365

CARDON CHILDREN'S MEDICAL CENTER See Banner Desert Medical Center, Mesa

✠ **DIGNITY HEALTH ARIZONA GENERAL HOSPITAL MESA, LLC (030139)**, 9130 East Elliot Road, Zip 85212–9675; tel. 480/410–4500, (Nonreporting) **A**1 10 **S** CommonSpirit Health, Chicago, IL
Primary Contact: Jane E. Hanson, R.N., President and Chief Executive Officer
CFO: John Bauer, Vice President, Chief Financial Officer
CMO: Aaron Mickelson, M.D., Chief Medical Officer
CIO: Bradley Pristelski, Division Vice President, Chief Information Officer
CHR: Maureen Sterbach, Vice President, Human Resource Service Area
CNO: Cynthia Rosenberg, Vice President, Chief Nursing Officer
Web address: https://locations.dignityhealth.org/
Control: City–county, Government, Nonfederal **Service:** General medical and surgical

Staffed Beds: 50

✠ **ENCOMPASS HEALTH REHABILITATION HOSPITAL OF EAST VALLEY (033037)**, 5652 East Baseline Road, Zip 85206–4713; tel. 480/567–0350, (Nonreporting) **A**1 10 **S** Encompass Health Corporation, Birmingham, AL
Primary Contact: Vidhya Kannan, Chief Executive Officer
CMO: Martin Yee, M.D., Medical Director
CHR: Nancy Pickler, Director of Human Resources
CNO: Hope Dunn, Chief Nursing Officer
Web address: https://www.encompasshealth.com/eastvalleyrehab
Control: Corporation, Investor–owned (for–profit) **Service:** Rehabilitation

Staffed Beds: 59

Hospital, Medicare Provider Number, Address, Telephone, Approval, Facility, and Physician Codes, Health Care System

★ American Hospital Association (AHA) membership ○ Healthcare Facilities Accreditation Program ⇧ Center for Improvement in Healthcare Quality Accreditation
☐ The Joint Commission accreditation ◇ DNV Healthcare Inc. accreditation △ Commission on Accreditation of Rehabilitation Facilities (CARF) accreditation

Hospitals, U.S. / ARIZONA

KPC PROMISE HOSPITAL OF PHOENIX (032006), 433 East 6th Street, Zip 85203-7104; tel. 480/427-3000, (Nonreporting) **A**10 **S** KPC Healthcare, Inc., Santa Ana, CA
Primary Contact: Larry Niemann, Chief Executive Officer
COO: Wendy Larson, Chief Clinical Officer
CFO: Theo Clark, Director Financial Services
CMO: Syed Shahryar, M.D., Medical Director
CHR: Christie Brea, Manager Human Resources
Web address: www.phoenix.kpcph.com/
Control: Corporation, Investor-owned (for-profit) **Service**: Acute long-term care hospital

Staffed Beds: 40

⇑ **MOUNTAIN VISTA MEDICAL CENTER (030121)**, 1301 South Crismon Road, Zip 85209-3767; tel. 480/358-6100, (Includes FLORENCE HOSPITAL, A CAMPUS OF MOUNTAIN VISTA MEDICAL CENTER, 4545 North Hunt Highway, Florence, Arizona, Zip 85132-6937, 1301 South Crismon Road, Mesa, Zip 85209-3767, tel. 520/868-3333; Damon Brown, President) (Nonreporting) **A**3 5 10 13 19 21 **S** Steward Health Care System, LLC, Dallas, TX
Primary Contact: William J. Comer, President
CHR: Kathleen Cartwright, Director Human Resources
Web address: https://www.mvmedicalcenter.org/
Control: Corporation, Investor-owned (for-profit) **Service**: General medical and surgical

Staffed Beds: 178

SAMARITAN BEHAVELBACK HOSPITAL See Samaritan Behavioral Health Center-Desert Samaritan Medical Center

SAMARITAN BEHAVIORAL HEALTH CENTER-DESERT SAMARITAN MEDICAL CENTER See Banner Desert Medical Center, Mesa

NOGALES—Santa Cruz County

✠ **CARONDELET HOLY CROSS HOSPITAL (031313)**, 1171 West Target Range Road, Zip 85621-2415; tel. 520/285-3000, (Nonreporting) **A**1 10 18 **S** TENET Healthcare Corporation, Dallas, TX
Primary Contact: Dina Rojas-Sanchez, Chief Executive Officer
CFO: Alan Strauss, Chief Financial Officer
CMO: Roy Farrell, M.D., Chief Medical Officer
Web address: https://www.carondelet.org/locations/detail/holy-cross-hospital
Control: Other not-for-profit (including NFP Corporation) **Service**: General medical and surgical

Staffed Beds: 25

ORO VALLEY—Pima County

✠ **ORO VALLEY HOSPITAL (030114)**, 1551 East Tangerine Road, Zip 85755-6213; tel. 520/901-3500, (Nonreporting) **A**1 3 10 **S** Community Health Systems, Inc., Franklin, TN
Primary Contact: Cody Barnhart, Chief Administrative Officer
CFO: Maurene Polashek, Chief Financial Officer
CNO: Julie Hunt, R.N., MS, Chief Nursing Officer
Web address: www.orovalleyhospital.com
Control: Corporation, Investor-owned (for-profit) **Service**: General medical and surgical

Staffed Beds: 146

PAGE—Coconino County

✠ **PAGE HOSPITAL (031304)**, 501 North Navajo Drive, Zip 86040, Mailing Address: P.O. Box 1447, Zip 86040-1447; tel. 928/645-2424, **A**1 10 18 **F**3 13 15 29 34 40 43 57 63 76 80 81 84 85 89 93 97 107 108 115 127 133 146 148 169 **S** Banner Health, Phoenix, AZ
Primary Contact: Ralph Parker, Chief Executive Officer and Chief Nursing Officer
CFO: Matt King, Senior Finance Director
CMO: Aaron Knudson, Chief Medical Officer
CIO: Paul Caldwell, Facility Coordinator Information Technology Customer Relations
CHR: Ed Franklin, Chief Human Resources Officer
CNO: Ralph Parker, Chief Executive Officer and Chief Nursing Officer
Web address: https://www.bannerhealth.com/locations/page/page-hospital?y_source=1_MTE5MDczNTQtNzE1LWxvY2F0aW9uLmdvb2dsZV93ZWJzaXRlX292ZXJyaWRl
Control: Other not-for-profit (including NFP Corporation) **Service**: General medical and surgical

Staffed Beds: 25 **Admissions**: 292 **Census**: 2 **Outpatient Visits**: 14282 **Births**: 99 **Total Expense ($000)**: 23269 **Payroll Expense ($000)**: 11777 **Personnel**: 87

PARKER—La Paz County

○ **LA PAZ REGIONAL HOSPITAL (031317)**, 1200 West Mohave Road, Zip 85344-6349; tel. 928/669-9201, (Nonreporting) **A**10 11 18
Primary Contact: Zafer L. Genc, Chief Executive Officer
CFO: Brant Truman, PharmD, Chief Financial Officer
CMO: Jack Dunn, M.D., Chief of Staff
CHR: Regina M Martinez, Director Human Resources
CNO: Maria Martinez, Chief Nursing Officer
Web address: www.lapazhospital.org
Control: Other not-for-profit (including NFP Corporation) **Service**: General medical and surgical

Staffed Beds: 25

✠ **U. S. PUBLIC HEALTH SERVICE INDIAN HOSPITAL (031307)**, 12033 Agency Road, Zip 85344-7718; tel. 928/669-2137, (Nonreporting) **A**1 10 18 **S** U. S. Indian Health Service, Rockville, MD
Primary Contact: Barbara Asher, Chief Executive Officer
CFO: Robin Tahbo, Financial Management Officer
CMO: Laurence Norick, M.D., Clinical Director
CIO: JayLynn Saavedra, Chief Information Officer
Web address: www.ihs.gov
Control: PHS, Indian Service, Government, federal **Service**: General medical and surgical

Staffed Beds: 20

PAYSON—Gila County

✠ **BANNER PAYSON MEDICAL CENTER (031318)**, 807 South Ponderosa Street, Zip 85541-5599; tel. 928/474-3222, **A**1 3 5 10 18 **F**3 13 15 18 26 28 29 30 31 35 38 40 43 45 50 51 53 54 56 59 64 68 70 74 75 76 77 78 79 81 82 85 86 87 89 96 100 102 107 108 110 111 115 119 127 129 130 133 146 148 149 153 154 164 167 169 **S** Banner Health, Phoenix, AZ
Primary Contact: Hoyt Skabelund, President
CFO: Matt King, Senior Director of Finance
CMO: Cynthia Booth, Chief Medical Officer
CIO: Nick Vandermeer, Director Information Systems
CHR: Shawn M. Thomas, Director Human Resources
CNO: Lura Ryden, Chief Nursing Officer
Web address: https://www.bannerhealth.com/locations/payson/banner-payson-medical-center
Control: Other not-for-profit (including NFP Corporation) **Service**: General medical and surgical

Staffed Beds: 25 **Admissions**: 1261 **Census**: 11 **Outpatient Visits**: 35498 **Births**: 114 **Total Expense ($000)**: 54214 **Payroll Expense ($000)**: 20097 **Personnel**: 162

PEORIA—Maricopa County

KINDRED HOSPITAL ARIZONA-NORTHWEST PHOENIX See Curahealth Phoenix

REUNION REHABILITATION HOSPITAL PEORIA (033045), 13451 North 94th Drive, Zip 85381-5056; tel. 623/303-7101, (Nonreporting) **A**22 **S** Nobis Rehabilitation Partners, Allen, TX
Primary Contact: Shawn McCallum, Chief Executive Officer
Web address: https://reunionrehabhospital.com/locations/peoria/
Control: Corporation, Investor-owned (for-profit) **Service**: Rehabilitation

Staffed Beds: 40

PERIDOT—Gila County

✠ **SAN CARLOS APACHE HEALTHCARE CORPORATION (031320)**, 103 Medicine Way Road, Zip 85542; tel. 928/475-1400, (Nonreporting) **A**1 10 18 **S** U. S. Indian Health Service, Rockville, MD
Primary Contact: Victoria D. Began, R.N., MS, President and Chief Executive Officer
CFO: Vivie Hosteenez, Chief Financial Officer
CMO: Douglas Brinkerhoff, M.D., Clinical Director
CIO: Nimmy Mathews, Acting Director Quality Management
CHR: Shirley M Boni, Administrative Officer
Web address: www.ihs.gov
Control: PHS, Indian Service, Government, federal **Service**: General medical and surgical

Staffed Beds: 12

Hospitals, U.S. / ARIZONA

PHOENIX—Maricopa County

ABRAZO CENTRAL CAMPUS (030030), 2000 West Bethany Home Road, Zip 85015–2443; tel. 602/249–0212, (Includes ABRAZO MESA HOSPITAL, 5750 E Baseline RD, Mesa, Arizona, Zip 85206–4806, tel. 602/833–6900) (Nonreporting) **A**1 3 5 10 19 **S** TENET Healthcare Corporation, Dallas, TX
Primary Contact: Gregory Pearson, Chief Executive Officer
COO: Michelle L. Beverly, Chief Operating Officer
CFO: Keslie Blackwell, Chief Financial Officer
CHR: Tim Howard, Chief Human Resources Officer
CNO: Michelle Henderson, Chief Nursing Officer
Web address: www.abrazohealth.com
Control: Corporation, Investor–owned (for–profit) **Service**: General medical and surgical

Staffed Beds: 206

ABRAZO SCOTTSDALE CAMPUS (030083), 3929 East Bell Road, Zip 85032–2196; tel. 602/923–5000, (Nonreporting) **A**1 10 **S** TENET Healthcare Corporation, Dallas, TX
Primary Contact: Ruben Castro, Chief Executive Officer
CFO: Nathan Esparza, Chief Financial Officer
CIO: Erin Gonzalez, Chief Human Resources Officer
Web address: www.abrazoscottsdale.com
Control: Corporation, Investor–owned (for–profit) **Service**: General medical and surgical

Staffed Beds: 136

ARIZONA CHILDREN'S CENTER MARICOPA MEDICAL CENTER See Arizona Children's Center

ARIZONA HEART HOSPITAL See Abrazo Arizona Heart Hospital

ARIZONA STATE HOSPITAL (034021), 2500 East Van Buren Street, Zip 85008–6079; tel. 602/244–1331, (Nonreporting) **A**1 3 5 10
Primary Contact: Aaron Bowen, Chief Executive Officer
CHR: Christine Jeanine Decker, Manager Human Resources
Web address: https://www.azdhs.gov/az-state-hospital/index.php
Control: State, Government, Nonfederal **Service**: Psychiatric

Staffed Beds: 261

BANNER – UNIVERSITY MEDICAL CENTER PHOENIX (030002), 1111 East McDowell Road, Zip 85006–2666, Mailing Address: P.O. Box 2989, Zip 85062–2989; tel. 602/239–2000, **A**1 3 5 8 10 19 **F**3 6 9 11 12 13 15 16 17 18 20 22 24 26 28 29 30 31 34 35 36 37 38 40 43 44 45 46 47 48 49 50 51 54 55 56 57 58 59 60 61 64 65 66 68 70 72 73 74 75 76 77 78 79 81 82 84 85 86 87 88 89 90 91 92 93 94 97 98 100 101 102 104 107 108 109 110 111 114 115 116 117 118 119 120 121 123 124 126 128 129 130 131 132 135 137 138 139 141 146 147 148 149 150 153 154 156 160 167 **S** Banner Health, Phoenix, AZ
Primary Contact: Daniel Post, Chief Executive Officer
COO: Amy Shlossman, Chief Operating Officer
CFO: Kathy Kotin, Chief Financial Officer
CMO: Paul Stander, M.D., Chief Medical Officer
CIO: Michael S Warden, Senior Vice President Information Technology
CHR: Michael Fleming, Chief People Officer
CNO: Charlotte Ciudad, R.N., Associate Chief Nursing Officer
Web address: https://www.bannerhealth.com/locations/phoenix/banner-university-medical-center-phoenix
Control: Other not–for–profit (including NFP Corporation) **Service**: General medical and surgical

Staffed Beds: 625 **Admissions**: 34416 **Census**: 600 **Outpatient Visits**: 133901 **Births**: 6790 **Total Expense ($000)**: 1273267 **Payroll Expense ($000)**: 399171 **Personnel**: 5087

BANNER ESTRELLA MEDICAL CENTER (030115), 9201 West Thomas Road, Zip 85037–3332; tel. 623/327–4000, **A**1 3 5 10 **F**3 11 12 13 18 20 22 24 28 29 30 31 34 35 36 37 38 40 41 43 44 45 46 49 50 51 57 58 59 60 61 63 64 68 70 72 74 75 76 77 78 79 81 82 83 84 85 86 87 96 102 107 108 111 114 115 119 126 130 131 132 135 145 146 147 148 149 154 157 167 169 **S** Banner Health, Phoenix, AZ
Primary Contact: Courtney Ophaug, FACHE, Chief Executive Officer
COO: Gary Foster, R.N., Associate Administrator
CFO: Dean Shepardson, Chief Financial Officer
CHR: Wendy Labadie, Chief Human Resource Officer
CNO: Wendi Sears, Chief Nursing Officer
Web address: https://www.bannerhealth.com/locations/phoenix/banner-estrella-medical-center
Control: Other not–for–profit (including NFP Corporation) **Service**: General medical and surgical

Staffed Beds: 317 **Admissions**: 18283 **Census**: 219 **Outpatient Visits**: 85708 **Births**: 5493 **Total Expense ($000)**: 391606 **Payroll Expense ($000)**: 148454 **Personnel**: 1564

BANNER REHABILITATION HOSPITAL PHOENIX (033042), 775 East Willetta Street, Zip 85006–2723; tel. 480/581–3900, (Includes BANNER REHABILITATION HOSPITAL WEST, 12740 North Plaza Del Rio Boulevard, Peoria, Arizona, Zip 85381–8100, tel. 480/581–3600; Sharon Almeida, Chief Executive Officer) **A**1 3 10 **F**3 29 44 68 77 86 87 90 91 95 96 130 132 148 149 157 **S** Select Medical Corporation, Mechanicsburg, PA
Primary Contact: Thomas Rufrano, Chief Executive Officer
Web address: https://www.bannerhealth.com/locations/phoenix/banner-rehabilitation-hospital-phoenix
Control: Partnership, Investor–owned (for–profit) **Service**: Rehabilitation

Staffed Beds: 168 **Admissions**: 3675 **Census**: 137 **Outpatient Visits**: 0 **Births**: 0 **Personnel**: 634

CARL T. HAYDEN VETERANS' ADMINISTRATION MEDICAL CENTER, 650 East Indian School Road, Zip 85012–1892; tel. 602/277–5551, (Nonreporting) **A**1 3 5 **S** Department of Veterans Affairs, Washington, DC
Primary Contact: Bryan C. Matthews, Medical Center Director
CFO: Christine Hollingsworth, Chief Financial Officer
CMO: Maureen McCarthy, M.D., Chief of Staff
Web address: www.phoenix.va.gov/
Control: Veterans Affairs, Government, federal **Service**: General medical and surgical

Staffed Beds: 175

CHILDREN'S HEALTH CENTER ST. JOSEPH'S HOSPITAL AND MEDICAL CENTER See Children's Health Center

HAVEN BEHAVIORAL HOSPITAL OF PHOENIX (034020), 1201 South 7th Avenue, Suite 200, Zip 85007–4076; tel. 623/236–2000, (Nonreporting) **A**10 **S** Haven Behavioral Healthcare, Nashville, TN
Primary Contact: Luis Gonzalez, FACHE, Chief Executive Officer
CHR: Erin McEldowney, Manager Human Resources
CNO: Debbie Swiers, Director of Nursing
Web address: https://www.havenofphoenix.com/
Control: Corporation, Investor–owned (for–profit) **Service**: Psychiatric

Staffed Beds: 45

★ ⇑ **HONORHEALTH DEER VALLEY MEDICAL CENTER (030092)**, 19829 North 27th Avenue, Zip 85027–4002; tel. 623/879–6100, **A**3 5 10 19 21 **F**3 11 15 18 20 22 24 26 28 29 30 34 35 37 38 40 43 44 45 46 49 50 54 57 58 59 60 64 65 68 70 74 75 77 78 79 81 82 84 85 87 92 102 107 108 110 111 112 114 115 119 126 130 132 146 148 149 154 156 157 164 167 **S** HonorHealth, Scottsdale, AZ
Primary Contact: Kimberly Post, R.N., Chief Operating Officer
COO: Kimberly Post, R.N., Chief Operating Officer
CMO: Mary Ann Turley, D.O., Medical Director
CHR: Frank L Cummins, Vice President Human Resources
Web address: www.jcl.com
Control: Other not–for–profit (including NFP Corporation) **Service**: General medical and surgical

Staffed Beds: 204 **Admissions**: 14022 **Census**: 166 **Outpatient Visits**: 89937 **Births**: 0 **Total Expense ($000)**: 285381 **Payroll Expense ($000)**: 111761 **Personnel**: 1345

Hospital, Medicare Provider Number, Address, Telephone, Approval, Facility, and Physician Codes, Health Care System

★ American Hospital Association (AHA) membership
☐ The Joint Commission accreditation
○ Healthcare Facilities Accreditation Program
◇ DNV Healthcare Inc. accreditation
⇑ Center for Improvement in Healthcare Quality Accreditation
△ Commission on Accreditation of Rehabilitation Facilities (CARF) accreditation

Hospitals, U.S. / ARIZONA

★ ⍦ **HONORHEALTH JOHN C. LINCOLN MEDICAL CENTER (030014)**, 250 East Dunlap Avenue, Zip 85020–2825; tel. 602/943–2381, **A**3 5 10 19 21 **F**3 8 11 12 15 17 18 20 22 26 28 29 30 34 35 37 38 40 43 44 45 46 47 49 50 53 54 56 57 58 59 60 64 68 70 74 75 77 78 79 81 84 85 87 102 107 108 111 114 119 126 130 132 146 147 148 149 154 156 157 167 **S** HonorHealth, Scottsdale, AZ
Primary Contact: Kimberly Post, R.N., Chief Operating Officer
COO: Kimberly Post, R.N., Chief Operating Officer
CMO: Christopher Shearer, M.D., Chief Medical Officer
Web address: www.jcl.com
Control: Other not–for–profit (including NFP Corporation) **Service**: General medical and surgical

Staffed Beds: 239 **Admissions**: 12393 **Census**: 159 **Births**: 0
Total Expense ($000): 585138 **Payroll Expense ($000)**: 137939
Personnel: 1686

★ ⍦ **HONORHEALTH SONORAN CROSSING MEDICAL CENTER (030146)**, 33400 North 32nd Avenue, Zip 85085–8876; tel. 623/683–5000, **A**10 21 **F**3 11 13 18 26 29 30 35 37 38 40 41 44 45 46 47 48 50 51 57 58 59 60 64 65 68 70 73 74 75 76 78 79 81 82 84 85 87 102 107 108 111 115 119 126 130 135 146 147 148 149 154 157 167 **S** HonorHealth, Scottsdale, AZ
Primary Contact: Kimberly Post, R.N., Chief Operating Officer
COO: Kimberly Post, R.N., Chief Operating Officer
CMO: Kevan Pickrel, M.D., Chief Medical Officer
CNO: Kathy Stinson, Vice President, Chief Nursing Officer and Chief Operating Officer
Web address: www.honorhealth.com
Control: Other not–for–profit (including NFP Corporation) **Service**: General medical and surgical

Staffed Beds: 79 **Admissions**: 3561 **Census**: 33 **Outpatient Visits**: 38280 **Births**: 841 **Total Expense ($000)**: 90682 **Payroll Expense ($000)**: 33321 **Personnel**: 406

✠ **MAYO CLINIC HOSPITAL IN ARIZONA (030103)**, 5777 East Mayo Boulevard, Zip 85054–4502; tel. 480/342–2000, **A**1 2 3 5 8 10 19 **F**3 5 6 8 9 11 12 14 15 17 18 20 22 24 26 28 29 30 31 33 34 35 36 37 40 44 45 46 47 48 49 50 51 52 53 54 55 56 57 58 59 60 61 64 65 66 68 70 74 75 77 78 79 80 81 82 83 84 85 86 87 92 93 96 97 100 104 107 108 110 111 112 114 115 116 117 118 119 120 121 122 123 124 126 129 130 131 132 135 136 137 138 139 141 142 145 146 147 148 149 150 154 156 157 160 161 164 167 168 **S** Mayo Clinic, Rochester, MN
Primary Contact: Richard Gray, M.D., Vice President Operations
CFO: Jeffrey R Froisland, Chief Financial Officer
CMO: Alyssa B Chapital, M.D., Medical Director, Mayo Clinic Hospital
CIO: Paul Lenko, Section Head Information Technology
CHR: Nichelle A Baker, Chair Human Resources
CNO: Teresa Connolly, R.N., Chief Nursing Officer
Web address: www.mayoclinic.org/arizona/
Control: Other not–for–profit (including NFP Corporation) **Service**: General medical and surgical

Staffed Beds: 338 **Admissions**: 18797 **Census**: 280 **Outpatient Visits**: 80732 **Births**: 0

☐ **OASIS HOSPITAL (030131)**, 750 North 40th Street, Zip 85008–6486; tel. 602/797–7700, (Nonreporting) **A**1 3 5 10
Primary Contact: Tim Bogardus, Chief Executive Officer
Web address: www.oasishospital.com
Control: Partnership, Investor–owned (for–profit) **Service**: Orthopedic

Staffed Beds: 64

★ △ ⍦ **PHOENIX CHILDREN'S (033302)**, 1919 East Thomas Road, Zip 85016–7710; tel. 602/933–1000, (Nonreporting) **A**3 5 7 10 21
Primary Contact: Robert L. Meyer, President and Chief Executive Officer
COO: Tamra Kaplan, PharmD, Senior Vice President, Operations
CFO: Michelle Bruhn, Executive Vice President, Chief Financial Officer
CMO: Jared Muenzer, M.D., Chief Physician Executive
CIO: Brian Meyer, Senior Vice President and Chief Administrative Officer
CHR: Steve Schuster, Interim Senior Vice President, Human Resources
CNO: Rhonda Thompson, R.N., Chief Nursing Officer and Senior Vice President, Patient Care Services
Web address: www.phoenixchildrens.com
Control: Other not–for–profit (including NFP Corporation) **Service**: Children's general medical and surgical

Staffed Beds: 373

PHOENIX HCS See Carl T. Hayden Veterans' Administration Medical Center

⍦ **PHOENIX MEDICAL PSYCHIATRIC HOSPITAL (034038)**, 1346 East McDowell Road, Zip 85006; tel. 623/600–2730, (Nonreporting) **A**10 21 **S** NeuroPsychiatric Hospitals, Mishawaka, IN
Primary Contact: Steven Scott, Chief Executive Officer
COO: Christy Gilbert, President and Chief Operating Officer
CFO: Carlos Missagia, Chief Financial Officer
CHR: Becky Holloway, Vice President, Human Resources
Web address: https://www.neuropsychiatrichospitals.net/
Control: Individual, Investor–owned (for–profit) **Service**: Psychiatric

Staffed Beds: 96

☐ **QUAIL RUN BEHAVIORAL HEALTH (034031)**, 2545 West Quail Avenue, Zip 85027–2418; tel. 602/455–5700, (Nonreporting) **A**1 3 10
Primary Contact: Chris Ruble, Chief Executive Officer
Web address: www.quailrunbehavioral.com/
Control: Other not–for–profit (including NFP Corporation) **Service**: Psychiatric

Staffed Beds: 102

REUNION REHABILITATION HOSPITAL PHOENIX (033043), 1675 East Villa Street, Zip 85006–4435; tel. 480/801–6700, (Nonreporting) **A**10 **S** Nobis Rehabilitation Partners, Allen, TX
Primary Contact: Eric Mueller, Market Chief Executive Officer Phoenix Metro
Web address: https://reunionrehabhospital.com/locations/phoenix/
Control: Corporation, Investor–owned (for–profit) **Service**: Rehabilitation

Staffed Beds: 48

✠ **SELECT SPECIALTY HOSPITAL–PHOENIX (032001)**, 350 West Thomas Road, 3rd Floor Main, Zip 85013–4409; tel. 602/406–6810, (Nonreporting) **A**1 10 **S** Select Medical Corporation, Mechanicsburg, PA
Primary Contact: Karen Cawley, Chief Executive Officer
Web address: https://phoenix.selectspecialtyhospitals.com
Control: Corporation, Investor–owned (for–profit) **Service**: Acute long–term care hospital

Staffed Beds: 48

✠ **SELECT SPECIALTY HOSPITAL–PHOENIX DOWNTOWN (032005)**, 1111 East McDowell Road, 11th Floor, Zip 85006–2612; tel. 602/839–6550, (Nonreporting) **A**1 10 **S** Select Medical Corporation, Mechanicsburg, PA
Primary Contact: Raymond Ramos, FACHE, Chief Executive Officer
Web address: www.selectmedicalcorp.com
Control: Corporation, Investor–owned (for–profit) **Service**: Acute long–term care hospital

Staffed Beds: 32

✠ △ **ST. JOSEPH'S HOSPITAL AND MEDICAL CENTER (030024)**, 350 West Thomas Road, Zip 85013–4496, Mailing Address: P.O. Box 2071, Zip 85001–2071; tel. 602/406–3000, (Includes CHILDREN'S HEALTH CENTER, 350 West Thomas Road, Phoenix, Arizona, Zip 85013–4409, tel. 480/581–3600; ST. JOSEPH'S WESTGATE MEDICAL CENTER, 7300 North 99th Avenue, Glendale, Arizona, Zip 85307–3003, tel. 602/406–0000; Mary Ragsdale, Interim President and Chief Executive Officer) **A**1 3 5 7 10 19 **F**2 3 6 7 10 11 12 13 15 17 18 20 22 24 26 28 29 30 31 32 34 35 36 37 38 40 41 42 43 44 45 46 47 48 49 50 51 53 54 55 56 57 58 59 60 61 62 64 65 66 68 70 71 72 74 75 76 77 78 79 80 81 82 84 85 86 87 90 91 92 93 94 95 96 97 100 101 102 104 107 108 110 111 112 113 114 115 117 118 119 120 121 123 124 126 127 130 131 132 134 135 138 139 140 141 142 143 144 145 146 147 148 149 150 153 154 156 157 158 162 164 165 167 169 **P**6 **S** CommonSpirit Health, Chicago, IL
Primary Contact: Mary Ragsdale, Interim President and Chief Executive Officer
COO: Mary Ragsdale, Chief Operating Officer
CMO: Edward Donahue, M.D., Chief Medical Officer
CNO: Julie Ward, MSN, R.N., Chief Nursing Officer
Web address: www.stjosephs-phx.org
Control: Other not–for–profit (including NFP Corporation) **Service**: General medical and surgical

Staffed Beds: 594 **Admissions**: 30910 **Census**: 475 **Outpatient Visits**: 760371 **Births**: 3961 **Total Expense ($000)**: 1686953 **Payroll Expense ($000)**: 643797 **Personnel**: 5718

⍦ **ST. LUKE'S BEHAVIORAL HEALTH CENTER (034013)**, 1800 East Van Buren, Zip 85006–3742; tel. 602/251–8546, (Nonreporting) **A**10 21 **S** Steward Health Care System, LLC, Dallas, TX
Primary Contact: Gregory L. Jahn, R.N., Chief Executive Officer
CFO: Ruby Majhail, Chief Financial Officer
CHR: Amy M Howell, Director Human Resources
Web address: https://www.stlukesbehavioralhealth.org/
Control: Corporation, Investor–owned (for–profit) **Service**: Psychiatric

Staffed Beds: 85

Hospitals, U.S. / ARIZONA

☐ **THE CORE INSTITUTE SPECIALTY HOSPITAL (030108)**, 6501 North 19th Avenue, Zip 85015–1646; tel. 602/795–6020, (Nonreporting) **A**1 3 10
Primary Contact: Eric Tomlon, Chief Executive Officer
CFO: Barbara Chacon, Chief Financial Officer
CMO: Christopher A. Yeung, M.D., Chief of Staff
CHR: Sherrie A Wagner, Manager Human Resources
CNO: Deborah Roberts, R.N., Chief Nursing Officer
Web address: www.thecoreinstitutehospital.com/
Control: Corporation, Investor–owned (for–profit) **Service:** Surgical

Staffed Beds: 33

⊞ **U. S. PUBLIC HEALTH SERVICE PHOENIX INDIAN MEDICAL CENTER (030078)**, 4212 North 16th Street, Zip 85016–5389; tel. 602/263–1200, (Nonreporting) **A**1 3 5 10 **S** U. S. Indian Health Service, Rockville, MD
Primary Contact: Debra Ward Lund, Chief Executive Officer
CFO: Geraldine Harney, Chief Financial Officer
CMO: Dave Civic, M.D., Associate Director Clinical Services
CIO: Vina Montour, Director Information Technology
CHR: Betty Weston, Chief Human Resources Officer
Web address: www.ihs.gov
Control: PHS, Indian Service, Government, federal **Service:** General medical and surgical

Staffed Beds: 127

☐ **VALLEY HOSPITAL PHOENIX (034026)**, 3550 East Pinchot Avenue, Zip 85018–7434; tel. 602/957–4000, (Nonreporting) **A**1 5 10 **S** Universal Health Services, Inc., King of Prussia, PA
Primary Contact: Julie Miller, Chief Executive Officer
Web address: www.valleyhospital-phoenix.com
Control: Corporation, Investor–owned (for–profit) **Service:** Psychiatric

Staffed Beds: 122

★ ⇧ **VALLEYWISE HEALTH (030022)**, 2601 East Roosevelt Street, Zip 85008–4956; tel. 602/344–5011, (Includes ARIZONA CHILDREN'S CENTER, 2601 East Roosevelt Street, Phoenix, Arizona, Zip 85008–4973, tel. 602/344–5051) **A**3 5 8 10 19 21 **F**3 13 15 16 18 20 22 29 30 31 34 35 38 39 40 41 42 43 45 46 47 48 49 50 51 52 53 54 58 59 60 61 64 65 66 68 70 72 74 75 76 78 79 81 82 85 86 87 88 89 93 97 98 100 101 103 104 107 108 110 111 114 115 118 119 126 130 131 132 135 146 147 148 149 153 154 156 164 167 169
Primary Contact: Stephen A. Purves, FACHE, President and Chief Executive Officer
CFO: Claire Agnew, Chief Financial Officer
CMO: Michael White, M.D., Executive Vice President and Chief Clinical Officer
CIO: Kelly Summers, Senior Vice President, Information Technology and Chief Information Officer
CHR: Susan Lara Willars, Senior Vice President and Chief Human Resource Officer
CNO: Sherry Stotler, R.N., MSN, Chief Nursing Officer
Web address: https://valleywisehealth.org/
Control: Hospital district or authority, Government, Nonfederal **Service:** General medical and surgical

Staffed Beds: 758 **Admissions:** 16816 **Census:** 452 **Outpatient Visits:** 566200 **Births:** 2365 **Total Expense ($000):** 878467 **Payroll Expense ($000):** 383614 **Personnel:** 3843

PRESCOTT—Yavapai County

⊞ **BOB STUMP DEPARTMENT OF VETERANS AFFAIRS MEDICAL CENTER**, 500 Highway 89 North, Zip 86313–5000; tel. 928/445–4860, **A**1 **F**1 3 4 12 16 17 18 29 30 31 34 35 36 38 39 40 44 45 50 53 54 56 57 58 59 62 63 64 65 66 67 68 70 71 72 73 74 75 77 78 79 80 82 83 84 85 86 87 88 89 90 91 93 94 95 97 98 100 101 102 104 107 111 115 119 128 130 131 135 143 146 147 148 149 152 153 154 156 157 158 160 161 164 165 166 **S** Department of Veterans Affairs, Washington, DC
Primary Contact: Steven Sample, Medical Center Director
CFO: Ame Callahan, Acting Manager Resource Management Service
CMO: A Panneer Selvam, M.D., Chief of Staff
CIO: Scott McCrimmon, Manager Information Technology
CHR: Jane Lewerke, Manager Human Resources
Web address: www.prescott.va.gov/
Control: Veterans Affairs, Government, federal **Service:** General medical and surgical

Staffed Beds: 220 **Admissions:** 1512 **Census:** 109 **Outpatient Visits:** 286050 **Births:** 0 **Total Expense ($000):** 441534 **Payroll Expense ($000):** 126722 **Personnel:** 1669

★ **DIGNITY HEALTH YAVAPAI REGIONAL MEDICAL CENTER (030012)**, 1003 Willow Creek Road, Zip 86301–1668; tel. 928/445–2700, (Includes YAVAPAI REGIONAL MEDICAL CENTER – EAST, 7700 East Florentine Road, Prescott Valley, Arizona, Zip 86314–2245, tel. 928/445–2700) (Nonreporting) **A**5 10 **S** CommonSpirit Health, Chicago, IL
Primary Contact: Anthony Torres, M.D., President and Chief Executive Officer
COO: Larry P Burns Jr, Chief Operating Officer
CFO: Lee Livin, Chief Financial Officer
CMO: Anthony Torres, M.D., Chief Medical Officer
CHR: Mark Timm, Executive Director Human Resources
CNO: Diane Drexler, R.N., Chief Nursing Officer
Web address: www.yrmc.org
Control: Other not–for–profit (including NFP Corporation) **Service:** General medical and surgical

Staffed Beds: 218

MEDICAL BEHAVIORAL HOSPITAL OF NORTHERN ARIZONA (034036), 181 Whipple Street, Zip 86301–1705; tel. 928/227–3424, (Nonreporting) **A**10 **S** NeuroPsychiatric Hospitals, Mishawaka, IN
Primary Contact: LeAnne Aragon, Chief Executive Officer
COO: Christy Gilbert, President and Chief Operating Officer
CFO: Carlos Missagia, Chief Financial Officer
CHR: Becky Holloway, Vice President, Human Resources
Control: Individual, Investor–owned (for–profit) **Service:** Psychiatric

Staffed Beds: 24

NORTHERN ARIZONA HCS See Bob Stump Department of Veterans Affairs Medical Center

YAVAPAI REGIONAL MEDICAL CENTER See Dignity Health Yavapai Regional Medical Center

PRESCOTT VALLEY—Yavapai County

☐ **MOUNTAIN VALLEY REGIONAL REHABILITATION HOSPITAL (033036)**, 3700 North Windsong Drive, Zip 86314–1253; tel. 928/759–8800, (Nonreporting) **A**1 10 **S** Ernest Health, Inc., Albuquerque, NM
Primary Contact: Josh Davis, R.N., Chief Executive Officer
CFO: Mark A. Roth, Chief Financial Officer
CMO: Alan S. Berman, M.D., Medical Director
CHR: Troy Eagar, Director Human Resources
CNO: Leah Walters, R.N., Director of Nursing
Web address: https://ernesthealth.com/portfolio-item/mountain-valley-regional-rehabilitation-hospital/
Control: Corporation, Investor–owned (for–profit) **Service:** Rehabilitation

Staffed Beds: 16

★ **POLARA HEALTH (034025)**, 3347 North Windsong Drive, Zip 86314–2283, Mailing Address: 3343 North Windsong Drive, Zip 86314–1213; tel. 928/445–5211, (Nonreporting) **A**10
Primary Contact: Tamara Player, Chief Executive Officer
COO: Pamela Pierce, Deputy Chief Executive Officer
CFO: Doug Oliver, Chief Financial Officer
CMO: Shane Russell-Jenkins, M.D., Medical Director
CIO: Laura Norman, Chief Development and Information Officer
CHR: Pamela Pierce, Deputy Chief Executive Officer
CNO: Esther Grear, Director Hospital Social Work and Assistant Hospital Administrator
Web address: www.wygc.org
Control: Other not–for–profit (including NFP Corporation) **Service:** Psychiatric

Staffed Beds: 16

WINDHAVEN PSYCHIATRIC HOSPITAL See Polara Health

SACATON—Pinal County

☐ **HUHUKAM MEMORIAL HOSPITAL (031308)**, 483 West Seed Farm Road, Zip 85147, Mailing Address: P.O. Box 38, Zip 85147–0001; tel. 602/528–1200, (Nonreporting) **A**1 3 5 10 18
Primary Contact: Anthony J. Santiago, M.D., Chief Executive Officers
COO: Pamela Thompson, Chief Operations Officer
CMO: Noel Habib, M.D., Chief Medical Officer
CHR: Michael Freeman, Director Human Resources
Web address: www.grhc.org
Control: Other not–for–profit (including NFP Corporation) **Service:** General medical and surgical

Staffed Beds: 15

Hospital, Medicare Provider Number, Address, Telephone, Approval, Facility, and Physician Codes, Health Care System

★ American Hospital Association (AHA) membership ○ Healthcare Facilities Accreditation Program ⇧ Center for Improvement in Healthcare Quality Accreditation
☐ The Joint Commission accreditation ◇ DNV Healthcare Inc. accreditation △ Commission on Accreditation of Rehabilitation Facilities (CARF) accreditation

© 2025 AHA Guide

Hospitals, U.S. / ARIZONA

SAFFORD—Graham County

★ **MT. GRAHAM REGIONAL MEDICAL CENTER (031319)**, 1600 South 20th Avenue, Zip 85546–4097; tel. 928/348–4000, **A**3 5 10 18 **F**3 11 13 15 19 29 34 35 40 41 45 47 48 49 50 54 57 70 76 77 79 81 82 97 104 107 108 110 111 114 115 117 118 119 127 129 133 146 147 148 154 156 167 169
Primary Contact: Roland Knox, Chief Executive Officer
CFO: Keith Bryce, Vice President Finance and Chief Financial Officer
CIO: Anthon Ellsworth, Director Information Technology
CHR: Irvan Wick Lewis, Vice President Human Resources
CNO: Lori Burress, Vice President Patient Services and Chief Nursing Officer
Web address: www.mtgraham.org
Control: Other not–for–profit (including NFP Corporation) **Service**: General medical and surgical

Staffed Beds: 25 **Admissions**: 979 **Census**: 8 **Outpatient Visits**: 117691 **Births**: 482 **Total Expense ($000)**: 83682 **Payroll Expense ($000)**: 38086 **Personnel**: 492

SAHUARITA—Pima County

NORTHWEST MEDICAL CENTER SAHUARITA (030148), 16260 South Rancho Sahuarita Boulevard, Zip 85629–0047; tel. 520/416–7100, (Includes NORTHWEST MEDICAL CENTER HOUGHTON, 2200 South Houghton Road, Tucson, Arizona, Zip 85748–7632, tel. 520/543–6100; Brett Lee, Chief Executive Officer) (Nonreporting) **A**1 **S** Community Health Systems, Inc., Franklin, TN
Primary Contact: Brett Lee, Chief Administrative Officer
CFO: Joshua Custer, Chief Financial Officer
CIO: Brad Booth, Market Director, Information Services
CHR: Tiffany Rivera, Market Director, Human Resources
Web address: www.healthiertucson.com
Control: Corporation, Investor–owned (for–profit) **Service**: General medical and surgical

Staffed Beds: 18

SAN TAN VALLEY—Pinal County

BANNER IRONWOOD MEDICAL CENTER (030130), 37000 North Gantzel Road, Zip 85140–7303; tel. 480/394–4000, **A**1 3 10 **F**3 13 18 29 30 35 40 45 49 50 53 60 67 68 70 73 75 76 79 81 82 85 87 89 96 100 107 111 115 119 126 130 131 135 146 148 149 154 156 167 **P**8 **S** Banner Health, Phoenix, AZ
Primary Contact: Brian Kellar, Chief Executive Officer
CFO: Tracy French, Chief Financial Officer
CMO: Darren West, M.D., Interim Chief Medical Officer
CHR: Janine Polito, Chief Human Resources Officer
CNO: Terresa Ann Paulus, Chief Nursing Officer
Web address: www.bannerhealth.com/Locations/Arizona/Banner+Ironwood/
Control: Other not–for–profit (including NFP Corporation) **Service**: General medical and surgical

Staffed Beds: 89 **Admissions**: 4852 **Census**: 50 **Outpatient Visits**: 37700 **Births**: 1283 **Total Expense ($000)**: 115387 **Payroll Expense ($000)**: 39774 **Personnel**: 483

SCOTTSDALE—Maricopa County

BANNER BEHAVIORAL HEALTH HOSPITAL – SCOTTSDALE (034004), 7575 East Earll Drive, Zip 85251–6915; tel. 480/941–7500, **A**1 3 10 **F**4 5 29 30 34 35 38 44 50 57 68 75 86 87 98 99 100 101 102 104 130 132 134 135 146 149 153 154 160 164 **S** Banner Health, Phoenix, AZ
Primary Contact: Debbie Flores, Chief Executive Officer
CFO: Michael A. Cimino Jr, Chief Financial Officer
CMO: Gagandeep Singh, M.D., Chief Medical Officer Behavioral Health
CHR: Zsaber Gere, Chief Human Resource Officer
CNO: Cherri Anderson, Chief Nursing Officer
Web address: https://www.bannerhealth.com/locations/scottsdale/banner-behavioral-health-hospital
Control: Other not–for–profit (including NFP Corporation) **Service**: Psychiatric

Staffed Beds: 128 **Admissions**: 5512 **Census**: 101 **Outpatient Visits**: 834 **Births**: 0 **Total Expense ($000)**: 53822 **Payroll Expense ($000)**: 25648 **Personnel**: 318

ENCOMPASS HEALTH REHABILITATION HOSPITAL OF SCOTTSDALE (033025), 9630 East Shea Boulevard, Zip 85260–6267; tel. 480/551–5400, (Nonreporting) **A**1 10 **S** Encompass Health Corporation, Birmingham, AL
Primary Contact: Lisa Barrick, Chief Executive Officer
CMO: Keith W Cunningham, M.D., Medical Director
CHR: Mary Beth Giczi, Director Human Resources
CNO: Diane M Caruso, MSN, Chief Nursing Officer
Web address: https://www.encompasshealth.com/locations/scottsdalerehab
Control: Corporation, Investor–owned (for–profit) **Service**: Rehabilitation

Staffed Beds: 60

△ **HONORHEALTH REHABILITATION HOSPITAL (033038)**, 8850 East Pima Center Parkway, Zip 85258–4619; tel. 480/800–3900, **A**1 3 5 7 10 **F**3 10 28 29 34 35 38 44 50 56 57 59 60 65 70 74 75 77 79 82 84 86 87 90 91 92 93 94 95 96 100 101 119 130 132 143 148 149 156 157 164 **S** Select Medical Corporation, Mechanicsburg, PA
Primary Contact: Ashlie Decker, Chief Executive Officer
Web address: www.scottsdale-rehab.com/
Control: Partnership, Investor–owned (for–profit) **Service**: Rehabilitation

Staffed Beds: 50 **Admissions**: 1205 **Census**: 43 **Outpatient Visits**: 0 **Births**: 0 **Personnel**: 242

★ ⇑ **HONORHEALTH SCOTTSDALE OSBORN MEDICAL CENTER (030038)**, 7400 East Osborn Road, Zip 85251–6403; tel. 480/882–4000, **A**3 5 8 10 19 21 **F**3 6 8 9 11 18 20 22 26 29 30 34 35 36 37 38 39 40 41 43 44 45 46 47 48 49 50 51 53 54 55 56 57 58 59 60 62 64 65 68 70 74 75 77 78 79 81 82 83 84 85 86 87 90 91 92 93 96 97 100 102 107 108 111 114 115 119 124 126 129 130 131 132 145 146 147 148 149 154 156 157 160 164 167 **S** HonorHealth, Scottsdale, AZ
Primary Contact: Kimberly Post, R.N., Chief Operating Officer
COO: Kimberly Post, R.N., Chief Executive Officer
CMO: James Burke, M.D., Senior Vice President and Chief Medical Officer
CIO: James R Cramer, Vice President and Chief Information Officer
Web address: https://www.honorhealth.com/locations/hospitals/scottsdale-osborn-medical-center
Control: Other not–for–profit (including NFP Corporation) **Service**: General medical and surgical

Staffed Beds: 303 **Admissions**: 15009 **Census**: 170 **Outpatient Visits**: 98914 **Births**: 302 **Total Expense ($000)**: 333182 **Payroll Expense ($000)**: 130685 **Personnel**: 1565

★ ⇑ **HONORHEALTH SCOTTSDALE SHEA MEDICAL CENTER (030087)**, 9003 East Shea Boulevard, Zip 85260–6771; tel. 480/323–3000, **A**3 5 10 19 21 **F**3 8 9 11 12 13 15 17 18 20 22 24 26 28 29 30 31 34 35 36 37 38 40 41 44 45 46 47 48 49 50 52 53 54 55 56 57 58 59 60 61 64 65 68 70 72 73 74 75 76 77 78 79 81 82 84 85 86 87 88 89 93 100 107 108 110 111 112 114 115 119 126 130 132 136 145 146 147 148 149 154 157 167 **S** HonorHealth, Scottsdale, AZ
Primary Contact: Kimberly Post, R.N., Chief Operating Officer
COO: Kimberly Post, R.N., Chief Operating Officer
CMO: James Burke, M.D., Senior Vice President and Chief Medical Officer
CIO: James R Cramer, Vice President and Chief Information Officer
Web address: https://www.honorhealth.com/locations/hospitals/scottsdale-shea-medical-center
Control: Other not–for–profit (including NFP Corporation) **Service**: General medical and surgical

Staffed Beds: 427 **Admissions**: 21623 **Census**: 272 **Outpatient Visits**: 145373 **Births**: 5935 **Total Expense ($000)**: 468396 **Payroll Expense ($000)**: 174392 **Personnel**: 2338

★ ⇑ **HONORHEALTH SCOTTSDALE THOMPSON PEAK MEDICAL CENTER (030123)**, 7400 East Thompson Peak Parkway, Zip 85255–4109; tel. 480/324–7000, **A**3 5 10 21 **F**3 11 18 20 22 26 29 30 35 37 38 40 44 45 49 56 57 58 59 60 64 65 68 70 75 77 79 82 84 85 87 107 108 111 115 119 126 130 146 148 149 167 **S** HonorHealth, Scottsdale, AZ
Primary Contact: Kimberly Post, R.N., Chief Operating Officer
COO: Kimberly Post, R.N., Chief Operating Officer
CFO: Alice H Pope, Chief Financial Officer
CMO: Stephanie L Jackson, M.D., Vice President and Chief Medical Officer
CHR: Wendy Crawford, Chief Human Resource Officer
Web address: www.shc.org
Control: Other not–for–profit (including NFP Corporation) **Service**: General medical and surgical

Staffed Beds: 120 **Admissions**: 6311 **Census**: 68 **Outpatient Visits**: 53966 **Births**: 0 **Total Expense ($000)**: 152475 **Payroll Expense ($000)**: 59638 **Personnel**: 705

SELLS—Pima County

U. S. PUBLIC HEALTH SERVICE INDIAN HOSPITAL-SELLS (030074), Highway 86 & Topawa Road, Zip 85634, Mailing Address: P.O. Box 548, Zip 85634–0548; tel. 520/383–7251, (Nonreporting) **A**1 10 **S** U. S. Indian Health Service, Rockville, MD
Primary Contact: Veronica Geronimo, Administrator and Chief Executive Officer
COO: Diane Shanley, Deputy Service Unit Director
CFO: Vivian Draper, Chief Financial Officer
CNO: Donna Hobbs, Nurse Executive
Web address: www.ihs.gov
Control: PHS, Indian Service, Government, federal **Service**: General medical and surgical

Staffed Beds: 12

Hospitals, U.S. / ARIZONA

SHOW LOW—Navajo County

★ **SUMMIT HEALTHCARE REGIONAL MEDICAL CENTER (030062)**, 2200 East Show Low Lake Road, Zip 85901–7800; tel. 928/537–4375, (Nonreporting) **A**3 5 10 20
Primary Contact: Jeff Comer, PsyD, Chief Executive Officer
COO: Jon Felton, Chief Operations Officer
CFO: David Rothenberger, Chief Financial Officer
CIO: Jay Larson, Chief Information Officer
CNO: William Gardner, MSN, Chief Clinical Officer
Web address: www.summithealthcare.net
Control: Other not–for–profit (including NFP Corporation) **Service:** General medical and surgical

Staffed Beds: 101

SIERRA VISTA—Cochise County

⊞ **CANYON VISTA MEDICAL CENTER (030043)**, 5700 East Highway 90, Zip 85635–9110; tel. 520/263–2000, (Nonreporting) **A**1 3 5 10 13 20 **S** Lifepoint Health, Brentwood, TN
Primary Contact: Shaun Phillips, PharmD, Chief Executive Officer
COO: William Kiefer, Chief Operations Officer
CFO: Lynn Kennington, Chief Financial Officer
CIO: Ray Baker, Director Information Technology Operations
CHR: Sonni Burrell, Director Human Resources
CNO: Karen Reed, R.N., MSN, Chief Nursing Officer
Web address: www.canyonvistamedicalcenter.com/
Control: Corporation, Investor–owned (for–profit) **Service:** General medical and surgical

Staffed Beds: 100

SPRINGERVILLE—Apache County

WHITE MOUNTAIN REGIONAL MEDICAL CENTER (031315), 118 South Mountain Avenue, Zip 85938–5104; tel. 928/333–4368, (Nonreporting) **A**10 18
Primary Contact: Wesley Babers, Chief Executive Officer
CFO: Ashley Jaramillo, Chief Financial Officer
CMO: Scott Hamblin, M.D., President Medical Staff
Web address: www.wmrmc.com
Control: Other not–for–profit (including NFP Corporation) **Service:** General medical and surgical

Staffed Beds: 20

SUN CITY—Maricopa County

⊞ **BANNER BOSWELL MEDICAL CENTER (030061)**, 10401 West Thunderbird Boulevard, Zip 85351–3004; tel. 623/832–4000, **A**1 3 5 10 19 **F**3 17 18 20 22 24 26 28 29 30 31 34 35 36 37 40 43 44 45 46 47 48 49 50 51 53 56 58 59 60 61 64 65 70 74 75 77 78 79 81 84 85 86 107 108 111 114 115 117 119 120 121 124 126 130 132 135 146 147 148 149 154 157 167 **S** Banner Health, Phoenix, AZ
Primary Contact: Stan Holm, FACHE, Chief Executive Officer
CFO: Jeremy Williams, Chief Financial Officer
CMO: Kathryn Perkins, M.D., Chief Medical Officer
CHR: Brenda Dietrich, Chief Human Resources Officer
Web address: www.bannerhealth.com/locations/sun-city/banner-boswell-medical-center
Control: Other not–for–profit (including NFP Corporation) **Service:** General medical and surgical

Staffed Beds: 410 **Admissions:** 16097 **Census:** 226 **Outpatient Visits:** 57969 **Births:** 0 **Total Expense ($000):** 400456 **Payroll Expense ($000):** 141585 **Personnel:** 1339

SUN CITY WEST—Maricopa County

⊞ **BANNER DEL E. WEBB MEDICAL CENTER (030093)**, 14502 West Meeker Boulevard, Zip 85375–5299; tel. 623/524–4000, **A**1 3 10 19 **F**3 5 11 13 15 18 20 22 28 29 30 31 34 35 36 37 40 41 43 44 45 46 47 49 50 51 53 55 56 58 59 60 61 64 65 70 74 75 76 77 78 79 80 81 84 85 86 87 91 92 93 98 100 101 102 103 104 107 108 110 111 114 115 118 119 126 130 131 132 135 141 145 146 148 149 152 153 154 157 160 164 167 **S** Banner Health, Phoenix, AZ
Primary Contact: Stan Holm, FACHE, Chief Executive Officer
COO: Nathan Shinagawa, Chief Operating Officer
CFO: Dan Stimpson, Chief Financial Officer
CMO: Scott Anderson, Chief Medical Officer
CHR: Carole Smith, Senior Human Resource Business Partner
CNO: Nancy Adamson, Chief Nursing Officer
Web address: www.bannerhealth.com/Locations/Arizona/Banner+Del+Webb+Medical+Center/
Control: Other not–for–profit (including NFP Corporation) **Service:** General medical and surgical

Staffed Beds: 391 **Admissions:** 18438 **Census:** 245 **Outpatient Visits:** 76388 **Births:** 1915 **Total Expense ($000):** 359680 **Payroll Expense ($000):** 131684 **Personnel:** 1394

SURPRISE—Maricopa County

☐ **AVENIR BEHAVIORAL HEALTH CENTER (034035)**, 16561 North Parkview Place, Zip 85374–7499; tel. 602/730–7614, (Nonreporting) **A**1 10
Primary Contact: Nicole Zuccaro, Interim Director
Web address: https://www.avenirseniorliving.com/
Control: Partnership, Investor–owned (for–profit) **Service:** Psychiatric

Staffed Beds: 32

★ **PAM HEALTH REHABILITATION HOSPITAL OF SURPRISE (033039)**, 13060 West Bell Road, Zip 85378–1200; tel. 623/499–9100, **A**10 22 **F**29 50 53 60 64 68 75 77 86 87 90 91 93 94 95 96 97 100 130 135 148 149 164 **S** PAM Health, Enola, PA
Primary Contact: Sharon Noe, Chief Executive Officer
Web address: https://pamhealth.com/index.php/facilities/find-facility/rehabilitation-hospitals/pam-health-rehabilitation-hospital-surprise
Control: Corporation, Investor–owned (for–profit) **Service:** Rehabilitation

Staffed Beds: 40 **Admissions:** 882 **Census:** 28 **Outpatient Visits:** 3072 **Births:** 0 **Total Expense ($000):** 16803 **Payroll Expense ($000):** 7685 **Personnel:** 134

TEMPE—Maricopa County

⊞ **AURORA BEHAVIORAL HEALTH SYSTEM EAST (034028)**, 6350 South Maple Street, Zip 85283–2857; tel. 480/345–5400, (Nonreporting) **A**1 3 5 10 **S** Signature Healthcare Services, Corona, CA
Primary Contact: Chelsea Vickers, Chief Executive Officer and Administrator
CFO: Rebekah Francis, JD, Chief Financial Officer
CMO: Tariq Ghafoor, Medical Director
CHR: Vicki Thomsen, Director Human Resources
CNO: Dawn Whitmore Esq, Director of Nursing
Web address: www.auroraarizona.com
Control: Corporation, Investor–owned (for–profit) **Service:** Psychiatric

Staffed Beds: 118

⇑ **TEMPE ST. LUKE'S HOSPITAL (030037)**, 1500 South Mill Avenue, Zip 85281–6699; tel. 480/784–5510, (Nonreporting) **A**3 10 19 21 **S** Steward Health Care System, LLC, Dallas, TX
Primary Contact: Jenifer Midgett, President and Chief Executive Officer
Web address: www.tempestlukeshospital.org
Control: Corporation, Investor–owned (for–profit) **Service:** General medical and surgical

Staffed Beds: 110

Hospital, Medicare Provider Number, Address, Telephone, Approval, Facility, and Physician Codes, Health Care System

★ American Hospital Association (AHA) membership   ○ Healthcare Facilities Accreditation Program   ⇑ Center for Improvement in Healthcare Quality Accreditation
☐ The Joint Commission accreditation   ◇ DNV Healthcare Inc. accreditation   △ Commission on Accreditation of Rehabilitation Facilities (CARF) accreditation

Hospitals, U.S. / ARIZONA

TUBA CITY—Coconino County

TUBA CITY REGIONAL HEALTH CARE CORPORATION (030073), 167 Main Street, Zip 86045-0611, Mailing Address: P.O. Box 600, Zip 86045-0600; tel. 928/283-2501, (Nonreporting) **A**1 3 10
Primary Contact: Joette Walters, Chief Executive Officer
CFO: Christine Keyonnie, CPA, Chief Financial Officer
CMO: Holly Van Dyk, M.D., Interim Chief Medical Officer
CIO: Shawn Davis, Chief Information Officer
CHR: George Hunter, Interim Chief Human Resources Officer
CNO: Alvina Rosales, R.N., Chief Nursing Officer
Web address: www.tchealth.org
Control: Other not-for-profit (including NFP Corporation) **Service:** General medical and surgical

Staffed Beds: 53

TUCSON—Pima County

BANNER – UNIVERSITY MEDICAL CENTER SOUTH (030111), 2800 East Ajo Way, Zip 85713-6289; tel. 520/874-2000, **A**1 3 5 10 **F**3 5 18 20 22 26 29 30 34 35 36 37 40 44 45 50 51 54 55 56 57 58 59 60 61 64 65 66 68 69 70 71 74 75 79 81 82 84 85 86 87 97 98 100 101 103 104 107 108 109 111 114 115 118 119 126 127 130 131 132 135 146 148 149 153 154 156 157 160 162 163 164 165 **S** Banner Health, Phoenix, AZ
Primary Contact: Sarah Frost, Chief Executive Officer
CFO: Jeff Buehrle, Chief Financial Officer
CMO: David Sheinbein, Chief Medical Officer
CIO: Ryan K Smith, Senior Vice President Information Technology
CHR: Jennifer L Sherwood, Division, Human Resource Business Partner
CNO: Cathy Townsend, Chief Nursing Officer
Web address: www.bannerhealth.com
Control: Other not-for-profit (including NFP Corporation) **Service:** General medical and surgical

Staffed Beds: 163 **Admissions:** 7063 **Census:** 127 **Outpatient Visits:** 53302 **Births:** 0 **Total Expense ($000):** 239619 **Payroll Expense ($000):** 73135 **Personnel:** 1935

BANNER – UNIVERSITY MEDICAL CENTER TUCSON (030064), 1501 North Campbell Avenue, Zip 85719; tel. 520/694-0111, (Includes DIAMOND CHILDREN'S HOSPITAL, 1501 North Campbell Avenue, Tucson, Arizona, Zip 85724-0001, tel. 520/694-0111) **A**1 2 3 5 8 10 19 **F**3 11 12 13 15 16 17 18 19 20 21 22 23 24 25 26 27 28 29 30 31 32 34 35 36 37 40 41 43 44 45 46 47 48 49 50 51 52 53 54 55 56 57 58 59 60 61 62 63 64 65 67 68 69 70 71 72 73 74 75 76 78 79 81 82 83 84 85 86 87 88 89 92 97 100 107 108 109 110 111 112 114 115 116 117 118 119 120 121 123 124 126 129 130 131 132 135 136 138 139 140 141 142 145 146 147 148 149 154 156 157 167 169 **S** Banner Health, Phoenix, AZ
Primary Contact: Sarah Frost, Chief Executive Officer
CFO: Bradley Hipp, Chief Financial Officer
CMO: Andreas Theodorou, Chief Medical Officer
CIO: Dan Critchley, Chief Information Officer
Web address: https://www.bannerhealth.com/locations/tucson/banner-university-medical-center-tucson
Control: Other not-for-profit (including NFP Corporation) **Service:** General medical and surgical

Staffed Beds: 589 **Admissions:** 25858 **Census:** 459 **Outpatient Visits:** 167408 **Births:** 2746 **Total Expense ($000):** 1177410 **Payroll Expense ($000):** 348342 **Personnel:** 5730

CARONDELET ST. JOSEPH'S HOSPITAL (030011), 350 North Wilmot Road, Zip 85711-2678; tel. 520/873-3000, (Nonreporting) **A**1 3 5 10 19 **S** TENET Healthcare Corporation, Dallas, TX
Primary Contact: Monica Vargas-Mahar, FACHE, Market Chief Executive Officer
CFO: Alan Strauss, Chief Financial Officer
CMO: Donald Denmark, M.D., Chief Medical Officer
CIO: Sally Zambrello, Chief Information Officer
CHR: Igor Shegolev, Vice President Human Resources
CNO: Dan Shearn, R.N., MSN, Chief Nursing Officer
Web address: www.carondelet.org
Control: Church operated, Nongovernment, not-for-profit **Service:** General medical and surgical

Staffed Beds: 486

CARONDELET ST. MARY'S HOSPITAL (030010), 1601 West St Mary's Road, Zip 85745-2682; tel. 520/872-3000, (Nonreporting) **A**1 10 19 **S** TENET Healthcare Corporation, Dallas, TX
Primary Contact: David Ziolkowski, Chief Executive Officer
COO: Ryan Harper, Chief Operating Officer
CMO: William Ellert, M.D., Medical Director
CHR: Ricky Russell, Chief Human Resource Officer
CNO: Jennifer Roy, R.N., Chief Nursing Officer
Web address: www.carondelet.org
Control: Other not-for-profit (including NFP Corporation) **Service:** General medical and surgical

Staffed Beds: 400

CORNERSTONE SPECIALTY HOSPITALS TUCSON (032004), 7220 East Rosewood Drive, Zip 85710-1350; tel. 520/546-4595, (Nonreporting) **A**10 22 **S** ScionHealth, Louisville, KY
Primary Contact: Debora Bornmann, Chief Executive Officer
CFO: Kurt Schultz, Group Chief Financial Officer
CMO: Sassan Momtazbakhsh, M.D., Medical Director
CHR: Deborah Darcy, Human Resources
CNO: Ritche Berdal, Chief Nursing Officer
Web address: www.chghospitals.com
Control: Corporation, Investor-owned (for-profit) **Service:** Acute long-term care hospital

Staffed Beds: 34

CURAHEALTH TUCSON See Select Specialty Hospital – Tucson

ENCOMPASS HEALTH REHABILITATION HOSPITAL OF NORTHWEST TUCSON (033029), 1921 West Hospital Drive, Zip 85704-7806; tel. 520/742-2800, (Nonreporting) **A**1 10 **S** Encompass Health Corporation, Birmingham, AL
Primary Contact: Jeff Christensen, Chief Executive Officer
CFO: Kaleigh Hotchkiss, Controller
CMO: Susan R. Bulen, M.D., Medical Director
CHR: Neil Cullen, Director Human Resources
CNO: Virginia Ragonese-Green, Chief Nursing Officer
Web address: https://www.encompasshealth.com/northwesttucsonrehab
Control: Corporation, Investor-owned (for-profit) **Service:** Rehabilitation

Staffed Beds: 60

ENCOMPASS HEALTH REHABILITATION INSTITUTE OF TUCSON (033028), 2650 North Wyatt Drive, Zip 85712-6108; tel. 520/325-1300, (Nonreporting) **A**1 5 10 **S** Encompass Health Corporation, Birmingham, AL
Primary Contact: Jeff Christensen, Chief Executive Officer
CFO: Mary Donovan, Controller
CMO: Jon Larson, M.D., Medical Director
CHR: Dawn Mosier, Director Human Resources
Web address: https://www.encompasshealth.com/rehabinstituteoftucson
Control: Corporation, Investor-owned (for-profit) **Service:** Rehabilitation

Staffed Beds: 80

NORTHWEST MEDICAL CENTER (030085), 6200 North La Cholla Boulevard, Zip 85741-3599; tel. 520/742-9000, (Nonreporting) **A**1 3 5 10 19 **S** Community Health Systems, Inc., Franklin, TN
Primary Contact: Brian Sinotte, Market Chief Executive officer and Interim Chief Executive Officer
CFO: Ronald Patrick, Chief Financial Officer
CIO: David Bullock, Director Information Services
CNO: Kay Stubbs, Chief Nursing Officer
Web address: www.northwestmedicalcenter.com
Control: Corporation, Investor-owned (for-profit) **Service:** General medical and surgical

Staffed Beds: 258

PALO VERDE BEHAVIORAL HEALTH (034030), 2695 North Craycroft Road, Zip 85712-2244; tel. 520/322-2888, (Nonreporting) **A**1 10 **S** Universal Health Services, Inc., King of Prussia, PA
Primary Contact: Jennifer Stokes, Chief Executive Officer
CFO: Richard N England, Chief Financial Officer
CHR: Michelle Carrasco, Director Human Resources
Web address: www.paloverdebh.com/
Control: Other not-for-profit (including NFP Corporation) **Service:** Psychiatric

Staffed Beds: 48

Hospitals, U.S. / ARIZONA

✈ **SELECT SPECIALTY HOSPITAL – TUCSON (032002)**, 2025 West Orange Grove Road, Zip 85704-1118; tel. 520/584-4500, (Includes SELECT SPECIALTY HOSPITAL – TUCSON EAST, 5301 East Grant Road, Tucson, Arizona, Zip 85712-2805, tel. 520/640-1200; Dawn M. Tschabrun, R.N., Chief Executive Officer) (Nonreporting) **A**1 10 **S** Select Medical Corporation, Mechanicsburg, PA
Primary Contact: Mark Powell, Chief Executive Officer
CFO: Lynn Sadler, Regional Director, Finance
Web address: www.selectspecialtyhospitals.com/tucson/
Control: Corporation, Investor-owned (for-profit) **Service**: Rehabilitation

Staffed Beds: 30

☐ **SONORA BEHAVIORAL HEALTH HOSPITAL (034022)**, 6050 North Corona Road, #3, Zip 85704-1096; tel. 520/469-8700, (Nonreporting) **A**1 10 **S** Acadia Healthcare Company, Inc., Franklin, TN
Primary Contact: Greer Foister, Chief Executive Officer
CMO: Steven Bupp, M.D., Medical Director
CHR: Ciria Soto, Director Human Resources
CNO: Angel Payne, Clinical Director, Director of Nursing
Control: Corporation, Investor-owned (for-profit) **Service**: Psychiatric

Staffed Beds: 106

SOUTHERN ARIZONA VETERANS AFFAIRS HEALTH CARE SYSTEM See Tucson VA Medical Center

TMC FOR CHILDREN See TMC Health, Tucson

✈ **TMC HEALTH (030006)**, 5301 East Grant Road, Zip 85712-2874; tel. 520/324-5461, (Includes TMC FOR CHILDREN, 5301 East Grant Road, Tucson, Arizona, Zip 85712-2805, tel. 520/327-5461; Judy F. Rich, MSN, R.N., President and Chief Executive Officer) (Nonreporting) **A**1 3 5 10 19
Primary Contact: Jennifer Mendrzycki, Chief Executive Officer
COO: Mimi Coomler, R.N., Senior Vice President and Chief Operating Officer
CFO: Stephen Bush, Chief Financial Officer
CMO: Rick Anderson, M.D., Senior Vice President and Chief Medical Officer
CIO: Frank Marini, Senior Vice President and Chief Information Officer
CHR: Alex Horvath, Vice President and Chief Human Resources Officer
CNO: Joy Upshaw, Vice President and Chief Nursing Officer
Web address: www.tmcaz.com
Control: Other not-for-profit (including NFP Corporation) **Service**: General medical and surgical

Staffed Beds: 598

✈ △ **TUCSON VA MEDICAL CENTER**, 3601 Sout 6th Avenue, Zip 85723-0002, Mailing Address: 3601 South 6th Avenue, Zip 85723-0002; tel. 520/792-1450, **A**1 3 5 7 8 **F**3 4 5 15 18 20 22 24 26 28 29 30 31 33 34 35 36 39 40 44 45 46 49 52 53 54 56 57 58 59 60 61 63 64 65 66 70 71 74 75 77 78 79 80 81 82 83 84 85 86 87 90 91 92 93 94 96 97 98 100 101 102 103 104 105 106 107 108 110 111 112 115 116 117 118 119 126 127 128 129 130 132 135 143 146 147 148 149 150 152 153 154 156 157 158 160 164 167 169 **S** Department of Veterans Affairs, Washington, DC
Primary Contact: Jennifer S. Gutowski, FACHE, Director
CMO: Jayendra H Shah, M.D., Chief Medical Officer
CIO: John Walston, Chief Information Officer
CHR: Patrice Craig, Manager Human Resources
Web address: www.tucson.va.gov
Control: Veterans Affairs, Government, federal **Service**: General medical and surgical

Staffed Beds: 328 **Admissions**: 9628 **Census**: 177 **Outpatient Visits**: 793708 **Births**: 0 **Personnel**: 3652

TUCSON—Pinal County

SIERRA TUCSON, 39580 South Lago Del Oro Parkway, Zip 85739-1091; tel. 520/624-4000, (Nonreporting) **A**3 **S** Acadia Healthcare Company, Inc., Franklin, TN
Primary Contact: Derek Price, Chief Executive Officer
COO: Stephen P Fahey, Executive Director
CFO: Amy Fritton, Controller
CMO: Jerome Lerner, M.D., Medical Director
CHR: Betty Dickens, Director Human Resources
CNO: Sue Menzie, R.N., Director Patient Care
Web address: www.sierratucson.com
Control: Corporation, Investor-owned (for-profit) **Service**: Substance Use Disorder

Staffed Beds: 139

WHITERIVER—Navajo County

✈ **U. S. PUBLIC HEALTH SERVICE INDIAN HOSPITAL-WHITERIVER (030113)**, 200 West Hospital Drive, Zip 85941-0860, Mailing Address: State Route 73, Box 860, Zip 85941-0860; tel. 928/338-4911, (Nonreporting) **A**1 3 5 10 **S** U. S. Indian Health Service, Rockville, MD
Primary Contact: Michelle Martinez, Chief Executive Officer
COO: Brian Campbell, Director Professional Services
CFO: Desdemona Leslie, Finance Officer
CMO: John Umhau, M.D., Clinical Director
CIO: Russell Barker, Information Officer
CHR: Lena Fasthorse, Supervisor Human Resource
CNO: Jana Towne, Nurse Executive
Web address: www.ihs.gov
Control: PHS, Indian Service, Government, federal **Service**: General medical and surgical

Staffed Beds: 35

WICKENBURG—Maricopa County

★ **WICKENBURG COMMUNITY HOSPITAL (031300)**, 520 Rose Lane, Zip 85390-1447; tel. 928/684-5421, (Nonreporting) **A**10 18
Primary Contact: Jackie Lundblad, President and Chief Executive Officer
COO: Peter Stachowicz, Interim Chief Operating Officer
CFO: Patti Clavette, Interim Chief Financial Officer
CMO: Todd Kravetz, Chief of Staff
CIO: Blue Beckham, Interim Chief Information Officer
CHR: Dede Schmallen, Chief Human Resources Officer
CNO: Linda Rankin, Chief Nursing Officer
Web address: www.wickhosp.com
Control: Other not-for-profit (including NFP Corporation) **Service**: General medical and surgical

Staffed Beds: 19

WILLCOX—Cochise County

★ **NORTHERN COCHISE COMMUNITY HOSPITAL (031302)**, 901 West Rex Allen Drive, Zip 85643-1009; tel. 520/384-3541, (Nonreporting) **A**10 18
Primary Contact: Monica Sheldon, Chief Executive Officer
COO: Bill Hopkins, Director of Operations
CFO: Carol Holden, Chief Financial Officer
CMO: Dawn Walker, D.O., Chief of Staff
CHR: Jennifer Cochran, Director Human Relations
CNO: C. Renae Dineen, Chief Nursing Officer
Web address: www.ncch.com
Control: Hospital district or authority, Government, Nonfederal **Service**: General medical and surgical

Staffed Beds: 24

WINSLOW—Navajo County

LITTLE COLORADO MEDICAL CENTER (031311), 1501 Williamson Avenue, Zip 86047-2797; tel. 928/289-4691, (Nonreporting) **A**10 18
Primary Contact: John J. Dempsey, Chief Executive Officer
CFO: Gina Reffner, Chief Financial Officer
CMO: Perry Mitchell, M.D., Chief of Staff
CIO: Jacob Garcia, Chief Information Officer
CHR: Nina L Ferguson, Director Human Resources
Web address: www.lcmcwmh.com
Control: Other not-for-profit (including NFP Corporation) **Service**: General medical and surgical

Staffed Beds: 25

YUMA—Yuma County

☐ **EXCEPTIONAL COMMUNITY HOSPITAL YUMA (030154)**, 2648 South Araby Road, Zip 85365-7236; tel. 928/877-0400, (Nonreporting) **A**1 10
Primary Contact: Bruce W. McVeigh, Chief Operating Officer
Web address: www.ehc24.com
Control: Corporation, Investor-owned (for-profit) **Service**: Other specialty treatment

Staffed Beds: 9

Hospital, Medicare Provider Number, Address, Telephone, Approval, Facility, and Physician Codes, Health Care System

★ American Hospital Association (AHA) membership ◯ Healthcare Facilities Accreditation Program ⇑ Center for Improvement in Healthcare Quality Accreditation
☐ The Joint Commission accreditation ◇ DNV Healthcare Inc. accreditation △ Commission on Accreditation of Rehabilitation Facilities (CARF) accreditation

Hospitals, U.S. / ARIZONA

AZ

★ ⇧ **YUMA REGIONAL MEDICAL CENTER (030013)**, 2400 South Avenue 'A', Zip 85364–7170; tel. 928/344–2000, (Nonreporting) **A**3 5 10 21
Primary Contact: Robert Trenschel, D.O., FACHE, M.P.H., President and Chief Executive Officer
CFO: David Willie, Chief Financial Officer
CMO: Bharat Magu, M.D., Chief Medical Officer
CIO: Fred Peet, Chief Information Officer
CHR: Randal M. Etzler, Chief Human Resources Officer
CNO: Deb Aders, MS, R.N., Vice President Patient Care Services, Chief Nursing Officer
Web address: www.yumaregional.org
Control: Other not–for–profit (including NFP Corporation) **Service**: General medical and surgical

Staffed Beds: 406

✣ **YUMA REHABILITATION HOSPITAL, AN AFFILIATION OF ENCOMPASS HEALTH AND YUMA REGIONAL MEDICAL CENTER (033034)**, 901 West 24th Street, Zip 85364–6384; tel. 928/726–5000, **A**1 10 **F**3 29 90 91 **S** Encompass Health Corporation, Birmingham, AL
Primary Contact: Kristin Parra, Chief Executive Officer
CMO: Bapu Aluri, M.D., Chief Medical Officer
CHR: Linda Woen, Director Human Resources
CNO: Carissa Dawn–Noelle Augustyn, Chief Nursing Officer
Web address: https://www.encompasshealth.com/yumarehab
Control: Corporation, Investor–owned (for–profit) **Service**: Rehabilitation

Staffed Beds: 37 **Admissions**: 1416 **Census**: 44 **Outpatient Visits**: 0 **Births**: 0 **Total Expense ($000)**: 21053 **Payroll Expense ($000)**: 11335

ARKANSAS

ARKADELPHIA—Clark County

★ **BAPTIST HEALTH MEDICAL CENTER–ARKADELPHIA (041321)**, 3050 Twin Rivers Drive, Zip 71923–4299; tel. 870/245–2622, **A**10 18 **F**3 11 13 15 29 30 34 35 40 41 43 45 46 50 57 59 64 65 68 69 70 75 76 79 81 85 87 93 97 102 107 110 111 114 119 127 129 130 133 135 146 154 156 **P**8 **S** Baptist Health, Little Rock, AR
Primary Contact: Jay Quebedeaux, FACHE, President
CFO: Robert C Roberts, Vice President and Chief Financial Officer
CIO: David House, Vice President and Chief Information Officer
CHR: Anthony Kendall, Vice President Human Resources
Web address: www.baptist-health.com/locations/accesspoint.aspx?accessPointID=187
Control: Other not–for–profit (including NFP Corporation) **Service**: General medical and surgical

Staffed Beds: 25 **Admissions:** 805 **Census:** 7 **Outpatient Visits:** 44108
Births: 122 **Total Expense ($000):** 31087 **Payroll Expense ($000):** 12555
Personnel: 188

ASHDOWN—Little River County

★ **LITTLE RIVER MEDICAL CENTER, INC. (041320)**, 451 West Locke Street, Zip 71822–3325; tel. 870/898–5011, **A**10 18 **F**3 29 40 56 59 62 65 77 93 97 107 110 115 119 133 154 167
Primary Contact: James Dowell, Chief Executive Officer
CFO: Jackie Rainey, Chief Financial Officer
CIO: Mitchell Jones, Director Information Technology
CHR: Vicki Keener, Administrative Assistant and Director Human Resources
CNO: Cynthia Metzger, Chief Nursing and Operations Officer
Web address: https://lrmh.org/
Control: Other not–for–profit (including NFP Corporation) **Service**: General medical and surgical

Staffed Beds: 25 **Admissions:** 69 **Census:** 1 **Outpatient Visits:** 10488
Births: 0 **Total Expense ($000):** 11812 **Payroll Expense ($000):** 7160
Personnel: 125

LITTLE RIVER MEMORIAL HOSPITAL See Little River Medical Center, Inc.

BARLING—Sebastian County

☐ **VALLEY BEHAVIORAL HEALTH SYSTEM (044006)**, 10301 Mayo Drive, Zip 72923–1660; tel. 479/494–5700, (Nonreporting) **A**1 10 **S** Acadia Healthcare Company, Inc., Franklin, TN
Primary Contact: Andrea Wilson, Chief Executive Officer
CMO: Richard Livingston, M.D., Medical Director
CHR: Patricia J Moore, Director Human Resource
CNO: Landon Horton, Director of Nursing
Web address: www.valleybehavioral.com
Control: Corporation, Investor–owned (for–profit) **Service**: Psychiatric

Staffed Beds: 114

BATESVILLE—Independence County

★ **WHITE RIVER HEALTH (040119)**, 1710 Harrison Street, Zip 72501–7303, Mailing Address: P.O. Box 2197, Zip 72503–2197; tel. 870/262–1200, (Nonreporting) **A**3 5 10 **S** White River Health System, Batesville, AR
Primary Contact: Chris Steel, Interim Chief Executive Officer
CFO: Shawna Ives, CPA, Chief Financial Officer
CMO: Doug Bernard, M.D., Chief Medical Officer
CIO: Jeff Reifsteck, Assistant Vice President Chief Information Officer
CHR: Lindsey Castelberry, Vice President Human Resources and General Counsel
CNO: Terri Bunch, MSN, R.N., MSN, Chief Nursing Officer
Web address: www.whiteriverhealthsystem.com
Control: Other not–for–profit (including NFP Corporation) **Service**: General medical and surgical

Staffed Beds: 226

WHITE RIVER MEDICAL CENTER See White River Health

BENTON—Saline County

☐ **RIVENDELL BEHAVIORAL HEALTH SERVICES (044007)**, 100 Rivendell Drive, Zip 72019–9100; tel. 501/316–1255, (Nonreporting) **A**1 10 **S** Universal Health Services, Inc., King of Prussia, PA
Primary Contact: Fred Knox, Chief Executive Officer
CFO: Mike Rainbolt, Chief Financial Officer
Web address: www.rivendellofarkansas.com
Control: Corporation, Investor–owned (for–profit) **Service**: Children's hospital psychiatric

Staffed Beds: 80

△ **SALINE MEMORIAL HOSPITAL (040084)**, 1 Medical Park Drive, Zip 72015–3354; tel. 501/776–6000, (Nonreporting) **A**1 5 7 10 **S** Lifepoint Health, Brentwood, TN
Primary Contact: Jeff Bourgeois, FACHE, Chief Executive Officer
COO: Carla Robertson, Chief Operating Officer and Chief Financial Officer
CFO: Carla Robertson, Chief Operating Officer and Chief Financial Officer
CIO: Andy Dick, Director Information Services
CHR: Carol Matthews, Director Human Resources
Web address: www.salinememorial.org
Control: Other not–for–profit (including NFP Corporation) **Service**: General medical and surgical

Staffed Beds: 140

BENTONVILLE—Benton County

BATES MEDICAL CENTER See Northwest Medical Center – Bentonville

BERRYVILLE—Carroll County

MERCY HOSPITAL BERRYVILLE (041329), 214 Carter Street, Zip 72616–4303; tel. 870/423–3355, **A**1 3 10 18 **F**3 11 15 28 29 30 34 35 40 45 50 64 75 81 85 93 107 108 110 115 119 129 130 132 133 146 148 156 **S** Mercy, Chesterfield, MO
Primary Contact: Darren Caldwell, Chief Executive Officer
CFO: Sherry Clouse Day, Vice President Finance
CHR: Taya James, Director
CNO: VonDa Moore, Director of Nursing
Web address: https://www.mercy.net/practice/mercy-hospital-berryville/
Control: Church operated, Nongovernment, not–for–profit **Service**: General medical and surgical

Staffed Beds: 25 **Admissions:** 315 **Census:** 3 **Outpatient Visits:** 31060
Births: 0 **Total Expense ($000):** 19008 **Payroll Expense ($000):** 10886
Personnel: 99

BLYTHEVILLE—Mississippi County

GREAT RIVER MEDICAL CENTER (040069), 1520 North Division Street, Zip 72315–1448, Mailing Address: P.O. Box 108, Zip 72316–0108; tel. 870/838–7300, (Nonreporting) **A**1 10 **S** Mississippi County Hospital System, Blytheville, AR
Primary Contact: Bryan Hargis, CPA, FACHE, Chief Executive Officer
COO: Paul Pieffer, Chief Operating Officer
CFO: Randy Nichols, Chief Financial Officer
CIO: Tammy Bratcher, Director System Information Technology
CHR: Cheri Blurton, Director Human Resources, HIPAA Privacy Officer
CNO: Felicia Pierce, R.N., Chief Nursing Officer
Web address: www.mchsys.org
Control: County, Government, Nonfederal **Service**: General medical and surgical

Staffed Beds: 73

Hospitals, U.S. / ARKANSAS

BOONEVILLE—Logan County

★ **MERCY HOSPITAL BOONEVILLE (041318)**, 880 West Main Street, Zip 72927–3443; tel. 479/675–2800, **A**10 18 **F**3 11 15 35 40 43 45 57 59 62 64 65 68 81 85 93 107 119 127 129 133 149 **S** Mercy, Chesterfield, MO
Primary Contact: Julianne Stec, Vice President, Patient Services
CMO: Michael Miranda, Chief of Staff
CHR: Doris Whitaker, Vice President and Manager
CNO: Kimberly Russell, Chief Nursing Officer
Web address: https://www.mercy.net/practice/mercy-hospital-booneville/our-locations/
Control: Church operated, Nongovernment, not–for–profit **Service**: General medical and surgical

Staffed Beds: 25 **Admissions**: 465 **Census**: 6 **Outpatient Visits**: 16346 **Births**: 0 **Total Expense ($000)**: 14827 **Payroll Expense ($000)**: 7827 **Personnel**: 66

CALICO ROCK—Izard County

IZARD COUNTY MEDICAL CENTER (041306), 61 Grasse Street, Zip 72519–7013, Mailing Address: P.O. Box 438, Zip 72519–0438; tel. 870/297–3726, (Nonreporting) **A**10 18
Primary Contact: Harley Smith, Chief Executive Officer
COO: Cathy Franks RN, Chief Operating Officer
CMO: Bethany Knight, M.D., Chief of Staff
CIO: Quentin Wildhagen, Systems Administrator
CHR: Crystal R Moody, Director Human Resources
CNO: Dana Hicks, Director of Nursing
Web address: www.cmcofic.org
Control: Other not–for–profit (including NFP Corporation) **Service**: General medical and surgical

Staffed Beds: 25

CAMDEN—Ouachita County

★ **OUACHITA COUNTY MEDICAL CENTER (040050)**, 638 California Avenue SW, Zip 71701–4699, Mailing Address: P.O. Box 797, Zip 71711–0797; tel. 870/836–1000, **A**10 20 **F**3 4 5 7 8 11 13 15 20 22 26 29 34 35 40 41 43 45 50 57 59 62 63 64 69 70 75 76 79 81 85 87 89 102 107 110 111 114 115 119 130 132 133 135 146 147 148 149 150 152 154 167 168 169
Primary Contact: Peggy L. Abbott, President and Chief Executive Officer
CFO: Robert Anders, Chief Financial Officer
CIO: Kenny Frachiseur, Chief Information Officer
CHR: Mary Bridges, Director Human Resources
CNO: Diane Isaacs, Director of Nursing
Web address: www.ouachitamedcenter.com
Control: Other not–for–profit (including NFP Corporation) **Service**: General medical and surgical

Staffed Beds: 67 **Admissions**: 1009 **Census**: 10 **Outpatient Visits**: 33891 **Births**: 162 **Total Expense ($000)**: 34305 **Payroll Expense ($000)**: 15891 **Personnel**: 321

CLARKSVILLE—Johnson County

★ **JOHNSON REGIONAL MEDICAL CENTER (040002)**, 1100 East Poplar Street, Zip 72830–4419, Mailing Address: P.O. Box 738, Zip 72830–0738; tel. 479/754–5454, **A**10 **F**3 7 11 13 15 29 34 35 40 43 45 50 57 59 62 64 68 70 75 76 77 79 81 82 85 87 90 91 93 96 98 103 104 107 108 110 111 115 119 129 130 131 132 135 143 146 147 148 153 154 167 169
Primary Contact: Tommy Hobbs, Chief Executive Officer
CFO: Whitney Campbell, Chief Financial Officer
CIO: Andy Altenburger, Chief Information Officer
CHR: Amy Powell, Director Human Resources
CNO: Nancy Hill, R.N., Chief Nursing Officer
Web address: www.jrmc.com
Control: Other not–for–profit (including NFP Corporation) **Service**: General medical and surgical

Staffed Beds: 90 **Admissions**: 2000 **Census**: 27 **Outpatient Visits**: 50453 **Births**: 319 **Total Expense ($000)**: 42300 **Payroll Expense ($000)**: 20894 **Personnel**: 334

CLINTON—Van Buren County

OZARK HEALTH MEDICAL CENTER (041313), Highway 65 South, Zip 72031–9045, Mailing Address: P.O. Box 206, Zip 72031–0206; tel. 501/745–7000, (Total facility includes 118 beds in nursing home–type unit) **A**10 18 **F**3 11 15 28 29 34 35 40 43 45 57 59 62 64 65 75 79 81 82 93 107 110 111 114 119 128 129 130 132 133 146 148
Primary Contact: David Deaton, FACHE, Chief Executive Officer
CFO: Mike Deaton, Chief Financial Officer
CMO: Steve Schoettle, M.D., Chief Medical Staff
CHR: Sally D Cassell, Manager Human Resources
CNO: Edna Prosser, Chief Nursing Officer
Web address: www.ozarkhealthinc.com
Control: Other not–for–profit (including NFP Corporation) **Service**: General medical and surgical

Staffed Beds: 143 **Admissions**: 447 **Census**: 69 **Outpatient Visits**: 18033 **Births**: 0 **Total Expense ($000)**: 33848 **Payroll Expense ($000)**: 15780 **Personnel**: 267

CONWAY—Faulkner County

⊞ **BAPTIST HEALTH MEDICAL CENTER – CONWAY (040154)**, 1555 Exchange Avenue, Zip 72032–7824; tel. 501/585–2000, **A**1 3 5 10 **F**3 13 15 18 20 22 28 29 30 34 35 40 43 45 46 51 54 59 64 70 74 76 77 79 80 81 85 86 87 90 91 92 93 96 100 107 108 110 111 115 118 119 126 130 135 146 147 149 156 164 167 169 **S** Baptist Health, Little Rock, AR
Primary Contact: April Bennett, President
CNO: Trenda Ray, Ph.D., Chief Nursing Officer
Web address: www.baptist-health.com/location/baptist-health-medical-center-conway-conway
Control: Other not–for–profit (including NFP Corporation) **Service**: General medical and surgical

Staffed Beds: 81 **Admissions**: 3867 **Census**: 52 **Outpatient Visits**: 61603 **Births**: 465 **Total Expense ($000)**: 107992 **Payroll Expense ($000)**: 29569 **Personnel**: 393

☐ **CONWAY BEHAVIORAL HEALTH (044022)**, 2255 Sturgis Road, Zip 72034–8029; tel. 855/808–5990, (Nonreporting) **A**1 3 10 **S** Acadia Healthcare Company, Inc., Franklin, TN
Primary Contact: Stefanie Magalon, Interim Chief Executive Officer
CFO: Kimberly Hibschman, Chief Financial Officer
CMO: Thomas Stinnett, M.D., Chief Medical Officer
CHR: Levi J. King, Director Human Resources
CNO: Beth Williams, R.N., Chief Nursing Officer
Web address: www.conwaybh.com
Control: Corporation, Investor–owned (for–profit) **Service**: Psychiatric

Staffed Beds: 80

⊞ **CONWAY REGIONAL HEALTH SYSTEM (040029)**, 2302 College Avenue, Zip 72034–6297; tel. 501/329–3831, **A**1 3 5 10 **F**3 11 12 13 15 17 18 20 22 24 26 28 29 30 31 34 35 37 40 43 45 46 49 50 51 53 56 57 59 61 62 64 70 74 75 76 77 78 79 81 82 85 87 89 97 98 104 107 108 110 111 115 118 119 126 127 129 130 131 135 144 146 147 148 149 154 156 157 167
Primary Contact: Matthew Troup, FACHE, President and Chief Executive Officer
COO: Alan Finley, Chief Operating Officer
CFO: Troy Brooks, Chief Financial Officer
CMO: James France, M.D., Chief of Staff
CHR: Richard Tyler, Chief Human Resource Officer
Web address: www.conwayregional.org
Control: Other not–for–profit (including NFP Corporation) **Service**: General medical and surgical

Staffed Beds: 180 **Admissions**: 8453 **Census**: 92 **Outpatient Visits**: 141166 **Births**: 1743 **Total Expense ($000)**: 260942 **Payroll Expense ($000)**: 117151 **Personnel**: 1472

CONWAY REGIONAL REHABILITATION HOSPITAL (043033), 2210 Robinson Avenue, Zip 72034–4943; tel. 501/932–3500, **A**10 **F**3 29 90 91 96 130 132 143 149 154 156 **P**8
Primary Contact: Alicia Kunert, MS, R.N., Executive Director
COO: Christy Scroggin, Director Operations and Human Resources
CMO: Roy Denton, M.D., Chief Medical Officer
CNO: Darrallyn Webb, R.N., Chief Nursing Officer
Web address: www.conwayregional.org
Control: Partnership, Investor–owned (for–profit) **Service**: Rehabilitation

Staffed Beds: 26 **Admissions**: 359 **Census**: 12 **Outpatient Visits**: 0 **Births**: 0 **Total Expense ($000)**: 5795 **Payroll Expense ($000)**: 1736 **Personnel**: 32

Hospitals, U.S. / ARKANSAS

CROSSETT—Ashley County

★ **ASHLEY COUNTY MEDICAL CENTER (041323)**, 1015 Unity Road, Zip 71635–9443, Mailing Address: P.O. Box 400, Zip 71635–0400; tel. 870/364–4111, **A**3 10 18 **F**3 11 13 15 18 29 31 34 35 40 41 43 45 50 53 56 57 59 64 65 68 70 75 76 77 78 79 81 85 91 93 100 107 108 110 111 115 119 127 130 132 133 148 154 156 167
Primary Contact: Phillip K. Gilmore, Ph.D., FACHE, Chief Executive Officer
CFO: Bill Couch, Chief Financial Officer
CMO: Brad Walsh, M.D., Chief of Staff
CIO: Dan Austin, Manager Data Processing
CHR: Shirley White, Director Human Resources
CNO: Emily Bendinelli, Director of Nurses
Web address: www.acmconline.org
Control: Other not–for–profit (including NFP Corporation) **Service**: General medical and surgical

Staffed Beds: 25 **Admissions**: 696 **Census**: 11 **Outpatient Visits**: 112646
Births: 146 **Total Expense ($000)**: 41688 **Payroll Expense ($000)**: 20432
Personnel: 265

DANVILLE—Yell County

CHAMBERS MEMORIAL HOSPITAL (040011), 719 Detroit Avenue, Zip 72833–9607, Mailing Address: P.O. Box 639, Zip 72833–0639; tel. 479/495–2241, **A**10 20 **F**3 11 15 29 34 35 40 43 45 57 59 62 68 75 77 81 87 93 96 97 98 103 107 110 114 119 128 130 133 154 **P**6
Primary Contact: Scott Peek, FACHE, Chief Executive Officer
CMO: Philip Tippin, M.D., Chief Medical Officer
CIO: Ken Masters, Director Information Technology
CNO: Michele Shoptaw, Director of Nursing
Web address: www.chambershospital.com
Control: Other not–for–profit (including NFP Corporation) **Service**: General medical and surgical

Staffed Beds: 42 **Admissions**: 1677 **Census**: 20 **Outpatient Visits**: 29291
Births: 0 **Total Expense ($000)**: 22979 **Payroll Expense ($000)**: 11089
Personnel: 207

DARDANELLE—Yell County

DARDANELLE REGIONAL MEDICAL CENTER (041302), 200 North Third Street, Zip 72834–3802, Mailing Address: P.O. Box 578, Zip 72834–0578; tel. 479/229–4677, **A**3 10 18 **F**3 29 34 40 45 56 57 59 64 65 68 75 77 81 82 91 93 97 98 100 103 107 114 115 119 128 129 130 133 135 153 154 156 166
Primary Contact: Alan Finley, President
CMO: William P Scott, M.D., Chief of Staff
CHR: Kathy Hastin–Hulsey, Administrative Assistant Human Resources
Web address: https://www.dardanelleregional.org
Control: Other not–for–profit (including NFP Corporation) **Service**: General medical and surgical

Staffed Beds: 35 **Admissions**: 575 **Census**: 14 **Outpatient Visits**: 18794
Births: 0 **Total Expense ($000)**: 19292 **Payroll Expense ($000)**: 9042
Personnel: 131

DE QUEEN—Sevier County

⇧ **SEVIER COUNTY MEDICAL CENTER (040162)**, 960 Highway 71 North, Zip 71832–9415, Mailing Address: UNDER CONSTRUCTION PO Box 960, Zip 71832–0960; tel. 870/642–6420, (Nonreporting) **A**21
Primary Contact: Stacy Dowdy, R.N., Administrator, Chief Nursing Officer
CFO: Laura Gillenwater, Chief Financial Officer
CIO: Martis Tipton, Chief Information Officer
CHR: Trey Frachiseur, Chief Human Resources Officer
CNO: Stacy Dowdy, R.N., Chief Nursing Officer
Web address: www.seviercountymedical.com
Control: County, Government, Nonfederal **Service**: General medical and surgical

Staffed Beds: 15

DEWITT—Arkansas County

DEWITT HOSPITAL See Dewitt Hospital & Nursing Home

★ **DEWITT HOSPITAL & NURSING HOME (041314)**, 1641 South Whitehead Drive, Zip 72042–9481, Mailing Address: P.O. Box 32, Zip 72042–0032; tel. 870/946–3571, (Total facility includes 35 beds in nursing home–type unit) **A**10 **F**3 11 29 34 35 40 43 57 59 64 75 77 107 109 111 114 115 119 127 128 129 133 154
Primary Contact: Brian F. Miller, Chief Executive Officer
CFO: Brandon Cotten, Chief Financial Officer
CMO: Stan Burleson, M.D., Chief Medical Staff
CIO: Brian Brooks, Information Manager
CHR: Alisa Brown, Administrative Assistant
CNO: Jerrilyn Horton, R.N., Chief Nursing Officer
Web address: www.dhnh.org
Control: Other not–for–profit (including NFP Corporation) **Service**: General medical and surgical

Staffed Beds: 65 **Admissions**: 112 **Census**: 29 **Outpatient Visits**: 10131
Births: 0 **Total Expense ($000)**: 12878 **Payroll Expense ($000)**: 5959
Personnel: 112

DUMAS—Desha County

★ **DELTA HEALTH SYSTEM (041326)**, 811 South Highway 65, Zip 71639–3006, Mailing Address: P.O. Box 887, Zip 71639–0887; tel. 870/382–4303, **A**10 18 **F**1 3 4 5 11 13 15 16 17 29 30 32 34 35 40 45 50 55 57 59 61 62 64 65 66 67 68 70 72 73 75 76 77 80 81 82 88 89 90 93 97 98 100 103 104 107 108 110 114 119 127 128 130 133 135 146 147 148 151 152 154 156 160 161 164 165 166 169 **P**6
Primary Contact: Jeremy Capps, Chief Executive Officer
CMO: Thomas Lewellen, D.O., Chief of Staff
CIO: Chris McTigrit, Manager Information Technology
CHR: Doris Fortenberry, Coordinator Human Resources
CNO: Dana Miles, Chief Nursing Officer and Chief Clinical Officer
Web address: www.deltamem.org
Control: Other not–for–profit (including NFP Corporation) **Service**: General medical and surgical

Staffed Beds: 25 **Admissions**: 591 **Census**: 9 **Outpatient Visits**: 39325
Births: 70 **Total Expense ($000)**: 19555 **Payroll Expense ($000)**: 10573
Personnel: 201

DELTA MEMORIAL HOSPITAL See Delta Health System

EL DORADO—Union County

MEDICAL CENTER OF SOUTH ARKANSAS See South Arkansas Regional Hospital

✣ **SOUTH ARKANSAS REGIONAL HOSPITAL (040088)**, 700 West Grove Street, Zip 71730–4416; tel. 870/863–2000, **A**1 10 **F**3 11 13 15 18 20 22 29 30 31 34 35 39 40 43 45 46 50 57 59 64 65 67 70 73 76 78 79 81 82 90 93 98 102 107 108 110 111 115 119 126 130 133 146 147 149 169 **S** Ovation Healthcare, Brentwood, TN
Primary Contact: Danna Taylor, Interim President
CFO: Dale Maddox, Chief Financial Officer
CMO: Misty Kneeland, Chief Medical Staff
CIO: Rob Robison, Director Information Technology
CHR: LaKeitha Davis, Director Human Resources
CNO: Kathy Degenstein Gartman, Chief Nursing Officer
Web address: https://sarhcare.org/
Control: Other not–for–profit (including NFP Corporation) **Service**: General medical and surgical

Staffed Beds: 65 **Admissions**: 3460 **Census**: 43 **Outpatient Visits**: 50930
Births: 629

EUREKA SPRINGS—Carroll County

EUREKA SPRINGS HOSPITAL (040780), 24 Norris Street, Zip 72632–3541; tel. 479/253–7400, **A**10 **F**3 29 34 35 40 43 47 64 75 81 86 93 115 119 154 **S** Allegiance Health Management, Shreveport, LA
Primary Contact: Angie Shaw, Chief Executive Officer
CFO: Taylor Smith, Chief Financial Officer
CMO: John House, M.D., Chief of Staff
CIO: Drew Wood, Director Information Technology
CHR: Jodi Smith, Administrative Assistant Human Resources
Web address: www.eurekaspringshospital.com
Control: City, Government, Nonfederal

Staffed Beds: 7 **Admissions**: 59 **Census**: 1 **Outpatient Visits**: 4399
Births: 0 **Total Expense ($000)**: 8335 **Payroll Expense ($000)**: 3705
Personnel: 54

Hospital, Medicare Provider Number, Address, Telephone, Approval, Facility, and Physician Codes, Health Care System

★ American Hospital Association (AHA) membership ○ Healthcare Facilities Accreditation Program ⇧ Center for Improvement in Healthcare Quality Accreditation
☐ The Joint Commission accreditation ◇ DNV Healthcare Inc. accreditation △ Commission on Accreditation of Rehabilitation Facilities (CARF) accreditation

Hospitals, U.S. / ARKANSAS

FAYETTEVILLE—Washington County

- **ENCOMPASS HEALTH REHABILITATION HOSPITAL, A PARTNER OF WASHINGTON REGIONAL (043032)**, 153 East Monte Painter Drive, Zip 72703-4002; tel. 479/444-2200, **A**1 10 **F**29 34 35 56 60 74 77 79 82 86 90 94 96 154 **S** Encompass Health Corporation, Birmingham, AL
Primary Contact: Sonja Buchanan, Chief Executive Officer
CFO: Corey Thomason, Controller
CMO: Borian Matinchev, M.D., Medical Director
CNO: Miriam Irvin, CNO
Web address: https://www.encompasshealth.com/fayettevillerehab
Control: Corporation, Investor-owned (for-profit) **Service**: Rehabilitation

    Staffed Beds: 80 **Admissions**: 1791 **Census**: 61 **Outpatient Visits**: 0 **Total Expense ($000)**: 26496 **Payroll Expense ($000)**: 14841 **Personnel**: 276

- **NORTHWEST HEALTH PHYSICIANS' SPECIALTY HOSPITAL (040152)**, 3873 North Parkview Drive, Zip 72703-6286; tel. 479/571-7070, **A**1 3 10 **F**3 12 29 40 45 68 79 81 82 85 86 107 111 114 119 126 131 135 **S** Community Health Systems, Inc., Franklin, TN
Primary Contact: Juli McWhorter, R.N., MSN, Chief Executive Officer
CFO: Jermaine Bucknor, Chief Financial Officer
CNO: Tim Kimball, Chief Nursing Officer
Web address: www.pshfay.com
Control: Corporation, Investor-owned (for-profit) **Service**: Surgical

    Staffed Beds: 20 **Admissions**: 982 **Census**: 4 **Outpatient Visits**: 11240 **Births**: 0 **Total Expense ($000)**: 3642 **Payroll Expense ($000)**: 695 **Personnel**: 92

- **SPRINGWOODS BEHAVIORAL HEALTH HOSPITAL (044019)**, 1955 West Truckers Drive, Zip 72704-5637; tel. 479/973-6000, **A**1 5 10 **F**3 29 34 35 38 57 98 99 100 105 130 132 134 135 143 144 147 149 150 152 153 157 160 162 164 165 **S** Universal Health Services, Inc., King of Prussia, PA
Primary Contact: Jordon Babcock, Chief Executive Officer
Web address: www.springwoodsbehavioral.com
Control: Corporation, Investor-owned (for-profit) **Service**: Psychiatric

    Staffed Beds: 80 **Admissions**: 2151 **Census**: 38 **Outpatient Visits**: 2555 **Births**: 0 **Total Expense ($000)**: 17112 **Payroll Expense ($000)**: 8430 **Personnel**: 179

- **VANTAGE POINT OF NORTHWEST ARKANSAS (044004)**, 4253 North Crossover Road, Zip 72703-4596; tel. 479/521-5731, **A**1 10 **F**4 29 35 38 56 64 98 99 103 105 106 130 149 151 153 160 164 **S** Acadia Healthcare Company, Inc., Franklin, TN
Primary Contact: Megan Wedgworth, Chief Executive Officer
CFO: Ben Winbery, Chief Financial Officer
CMO: Norman Snyder, M.D., Medical Director
CIO: Margaret Brown, Director Medical Records
CHR: Kathy Vickers, Director Human Resources
CNO: Suzette Branscum, Director of Nursing
Web address: www.vantagepointnwa.com
Control: Corporation, Investor-owned (for-profit) **Service**: Psychiatric

    Staffed Beds: 114 **Admissions**: 3275 **Census**: 86 **Outpatient Visits**: 2431 **Births**: 0 **Total Expense ($000)**: 21583 **Payroll Expense ($000)**: 12874 **Personnel**: 190

- **VETERANS HEALTH CARE SYSTEM OF THE OZARKS**, 1100 North College Avenue, Zip 72703-1944; tel. 479/443-4301, (Nonreporting) **A**1 3 5 **S** Department of Veterans Affairs, Washington, DC
Primary Contact: George Velez, FACHE, Medical Center Director
COO: Edward L. Woody, FACHE, Associate Medical Center Director
CMO: Bonnie Baker, M.D., Chief Medical Services
CHR: Kathryn L Barker, Chief Human Resources Management
Web address: www.fayettevillear.va.gov
Control: Veterans Affairs, Government, federal **Service**: General medical and surgical

    Staffed Beds: 81

WASHINGTON REGIONAL MEDICAL CENTER See Washington Regional Medical System

- **WASHINGTON REGIONAL MEDICAL SYSTEM (040004)**, 3215 North Hills Boulevard, Zip 72703-4424; tel. 479/463-1000, **A**1 3 5 10 19 **F**3 6 11 13 17 18 20 22 24 26 28 29 30 31 34 35 37 40 43 45 48 49 50 56 57 58 60 62 63 64 70 72 74 75 76 77 78 79 80 81 84 85 86 87 92 96 100 107 108 111 115 118 119 126 129 130 132 135 141 146 147 148 149 154 157 167 169 **P**8
Primary Contact: J. Larry. Shackelford, CPA, President and Chief Executive Officer
COO: Birch G. Wright, Chief Operating Officer and Administrator
CFO: Dan Eckels, Chief Financial Officer
CMO: David Ratcliff, M.D., Chief Medical Affairs
CIO: Becky Magee, Chief Information Officer
CHR: Laurie Morrow, Executive Director Human Resources
CNO: Meredith Green, Senior Vice President and Chief Nursing Officer
Web address: www.wregional.com
Control: Other not-for-profit (including NFP Corporation) **Service**: General medical and surgical

    Staffed Beds: 366 **Admissions**: 15697 **Census**: 183 **Outpatient Visits**: 136572 **Births**: 2579 **Total Expense ($000)**: 379920 **Payroll Expense ($000)**: 146501 **Personnel**: 3012

FORDYCE—Dallas County

- ★ **DALLAS COUNTY MEDICAL CENTER (041317)**, 201 Clifton Street, Zip 71742-3099; tel. 870/352-6300, **A**10 18 **F**3 11 29 34 35 40 43 56 57 59 68 77 93 97 100 107 115 119 127 128 133 135 146 148 149 154
Primary Contact: David Mantz, President and Chief Executive Officer
CFO: Billie Launius, Director Business Finance
CMO: Michael Payne, M.D., Chief of Staff
CHR: Audrey Allen, Coordinator Benefits
CNO: Hollie Raney, Director of Nursing
Web address: www.dallascountymedicalcenter.com
Control: County, Government, Nonfederal **Service**: General medical and surgical

    Staffed Beds: 25 **Admissions**: 148 **Census**: 2 **Outpatient Visits**: 14750 **Births**: 0 **Total Expense ($000)**: 13021 **Payroll Expense ($000)**: 6030 **Personnel**: 121

FORREST CITY—St. Francis County

- **FORREST CITY MEDICAL CENTER (040019)**, 1601 Newcastle Road, Zip 72335-2218; tel. 870/261-0000, **A**1 10 20 **F**3 7 13 15 29 30 34 40 43 45 50 57 70 76 79 81 82 85 87 92 107 108 109 110 111 112 114 119 129 130 145 146 147 148 **S** Quorum Health, Brentwood, TN
Primary Contact: Robert Rupp, Chief Executive Officer
CFO: Misty Gates, Chief Financial Officer
CMO: James DeRossitt, M.D., Chief of Staff
CIO: David Shaw, Director Information Technology
CHR: Sherry McLaughlin, Director Human Resources
CNO: Leslie Harris, MSN, R.N., Chief Nursing Officer
Web address: www.forrestcitymedicalcenter.com
Control: Corporation, Investor-owned (for-profit) **Service**: General medical and surgical

    Staffed Beds: 42 **Admissions**: 1434 **Census**: 10 **Outpatient Visits**: 35065 **Births**: 725 **Total Expense ($000)**: 34771 **Payroll Expense ($000)**: 10960 **Personnel**: 156

FORT SMITH—Sebastian County

- **BAPTIST HEALTH–FORT SMITH (040055)**, 1001 Towson Avenue, Zip 72901-4921, Mailing Address: P.O. Box 2406, Zip 72917-7006; tel. 479/441-4000, **A**1 3 5 10 19 **F**3 8 12 13 15 17 18 20 22 24 28 29 30 31 34 35 40 43 45 46 47 48 49 50 51 53 54 56 59 60 64 67 68 70 72 74 75 76 77 78 79 81 82 85 86 87 89 93 97 98 101 103 107 108 109 110 111 113 114 115 116 117 118 119 120 121 126 129 130 131 132 133 146 147 148 149 154 156 164 167 169 **S** Baptist Health, Little Rock, AR
Primary Contact: Jeffrey Carrier, President, Baptist Health Western Region
COO: Christian Gross, Vice President, Operations
CMO: Shane Jennings, Chief Medical Officer
CIO: Tom Sallis, Director Information Systems
CHR: Robert Freeman, Director Human Resources
CNO: Stephanie C Whitaker, Chief Nursing Officer
Web address: https://www.baptist-health.com/location/baptist-health-fort-smith/
Control: Other not-for-profit (including NFP Corporation) **Service**: General medical and surgical

    Staffed Beds: 337 **Admissions**: 12243 **Census**: 166 **Outpatient Visits**: 208181 **Births**: 496 **Total Expense ($000)**: 327189 **Payroll Expense ($000)**: 86756 **Personnel**: 1184

- **CHRISTUS DUBUIS HOSPITAL OF FORT SMITH (042008)**, 7301 Rogers Avenue, 4th Floor, Zip 72903-4100; tel. 479/314-4900, **A**1 3 10 **F**1 3 29 87 **S** LHC Group, Lafayette, LA
Primary Contact: Nancy Owens, Administrator
Web address: www.christusdubuis.org/fortsmith
Control: Corporation, Investor-owned (for-profit) **Service**: Acute long-term care hospital

    Staffed Beds: 25 **Admissions**: 335 **Census**: 17 **Outpatient Visits**: 0 **Births**: 0 **Total Expense ($000)**: 7791 **Payroll Expense ($000)**: 3927 **Personnel**: 104

Hospitals, U.S. / ARKANSAS

ENCOMPASSS HEALTH REHABILITATION HOSPITAL OF FORT SMITH (043028), 1401 South 'J' Street, Zip 72901–5155; tel. 479/785–3300, **A**1 3 10 **F**29 34 60 77 90 91 94 95 96 130 132 148 149 154 157 **S** Encompass Health Corporation, Birmingham, AL
Primary Contact: Dawn Watts, Chief Executive Officer
CFO: Brenda Forbes, Controller
CMO: Cygnet Schroeder, D.O., Medical Director
CHR: S Janette Daniels, Director Human Resources
Web address: www.healthsouthfortsmith.com
Control: Corporation, Investor–owned (for–profit) **Service**: Rehabilitation

Staffed Beds: 65 Admissions: 1607 Census: 52 Outpatient Visits: 0
Births: 0 Total Expense ($000): 21620 Payroll Expense ($000): 12448
Personnel: 135

MERCY HOSPITAL FORT SMITH (040062), 7301 Rogers Avenue, Zip 72903–4189, Mailing Address: P.O. Box 17000, Zip 72917–7000; tel. 479/314–6000, (Includes MERCY ORTHOPEDIC HOSPITAL FORT SMITH, 3601 South 79th Street, Fort Smith, Arkansas, Zip 72903–6255, tel. 479/709–8500; Ryan T. Gehrig, FACHE, President) **A**1 2 3 5 10 13 19 **F**3 8 12 13 15 18 20 22 24 28 29 30 31 32 34 35 36 38 39 40 42 43 44 45 48 49 50 53 54 56 57 58 59 60 61 62 63 64 65 66 68 70 71 72 74 75 76 77 78 79 81 82 83 84 85 86 87 89 93 96 97 104 107 108 109 110 111 114 115 116 117 119 120 121 123 124 126 127 129 131 143 146 147 148 149 154 156 157 160 164 167 **S** Mercy, Chesterfield, MO
Primary Contact: Ryan T. Gehrig, FACHE, President
COO: Jason Demke, Chief Operator Officer
CFO: Greta Wilcher, Senior Vice President and Chief Financial Officer
CMO: David Hunton, M.D., Chief Medical Officer
CHR: Bryan Brown, Executive Director
CNO: Marianne Rataj, Chief Nursing Officer
Web address: www.mercy.net/fortsmithar
Control: Church operated, Nongovernment, not–for–profit **Service**: General medical and surgical

Staffed Beds: 361 Admissions: 17446 Census: 187 Outpatient Visits: 325355 Births: 2707 Total Expense ($000): 385364 Payroll Expense ($000): 147242 Personnel: 1722

MERCY REHABILITATION HOSPITAL FORT SMITH (043037), 6700 Chad Colley Boulevard, Zip 72916–6120; tel. 479/974–5700, **A**1 3 10 **F**29 34 68 74 75 87 90 91 95 96 149 157 **S** Kindred Healthcare, Chesterfield, MO
Primary Contact: Cory VanMeter, Chief Executive Officer
CFO: H. Curtis Westlake, Controller
CMO: Mako Chen, M.D., Medical Director
CHR: Ricky Hernandez, Director Human Resources
CNO: Megan Sullivan, R.N., Chief Nursing Officer
Web address: https://www.mercy.net/practice/mercy-rehabilitation-hospital-fort-smith/
Control: Partnership, Investor–owned (for–profit) **Service**: Rehabilitation

Staffed Beds: 34 Admissions: 1042 Census: 30 Outpatient Visits: 0
Births: 0 Total Expense ($000): 12738 Payroll Expense ($000): 7560
Personnel: 113

SELECT SPECIALTY HOSPITAL–FORT SMITH (042006), 1001 Towson Avenue, 6 Central, Zip 72901–4921; tel. 479/441–3960, (Nonreporting) **A**1 3 10 **S** Select Medical Corporation, Mechanicsburg, PA
Primary Contact: Shannon Grams, Chief Executive Officer
Web address: https://fortsmith.selectspecialtyhospitals.com/
Control: Corporation, Investor–owned (for–profit) **Service**: Acute long–term care hospital

Staffed Beds: 34

GRAVETTE—Benton County

OZARKS COMMUNITY HOSPITAL (041331), 1101 Jackson Street Sw, Zip 72736–9121; tel. 479/787–5291, **A**10 18 **F**3 29 34 35 36 40 44 45 50 56 57 59 64 65 74 75 77 79 81 82 85 87 91 93 96 97 100 104 107 111 115 119 127 129 130 131 133 143 148 153 154 157
Primary Contact: Paul Taylor, Chief Executive Officer
Web address: www.ochonline.com/
Control: Other not–for–profit (including NFP Corporation) **Service**: General medical and surgical

Staffed Beds: 25 Admissions: 414 Census: 12 Outpatient Visits: 38733
Births: 0 Total Expense ($000): 72215 Payroll Expense ($000): 25767
Personnel: 270

HARRISON—Boone County

★ **NORTH ARKANSAS REGIONAL MEDICAL CENTER (040017)**, 620 North Main Street, Zip 72601–2911; tel. 870/414–4000, **A**5 10 **F**3 7 11 13 15 17 18 28 29 30 31 32 34 35 39 40 41 43 45 50 53 56 57 59 62 63 64 65 68 70 73 75 76 77 78 79 81 85 86 87 89 93 97 98 102 103 107 108 110 111 114 115 118 119 120 121 127 129 130 131 132 135 144 146 147 148 149 154 156 157 167 169 **P**8
Primary Contact: Sammie Roberson, MSN, President and Chief Executive Officer
CFO: Deana Thomas, Vice President Finance and Chief Financial Officer
CIO: William J Bogle, Director Information Systems
CNO: Donna Boehm, MSN, M.P.H., R.N., Chief Nursing Officer
Web address: www.narmc.com
Control: Other not–for–profit (including NFP Corporation) **Service**: General medical and surgical

Staffed Beds: 113 Admissions: 2166 Census: 23 Outpatient Visits: 122230 Births: 401 Total Expense ($000): 100584 Payroll Expense ($000): 45510 Personnel: 721

HEBER SPRINGS—Cleburne County

★ **BAPTIST HEALTH MEDICAL CENTER–HEBER SPRINGS (041312)**, 1800 Bypass Road, Zip 72543–9135; tel. 501/887–3000, **A**10 18 **F**3 8 11 15 28 29 34 35 37 40 45 48 50 54 57 59 64 68 75 77 78 79 81 85 93 97 102 107 110 111 115 118 119 126 127 129 131 133 146 149 154 156 157 **S** Baptist Health, Little Rock, AR
Primary Contact: Kevin L. Storey, President
Web address: www.baptist-health.com/maps-directions/bhmc-heber-springs
Control: Other not–for–profit (including NFP Corporation) **Service**: General medical and surgical

Staffed Beds: 25 Admissions: 433 Census: 4 Outpatient Visits: 49087
Births: 0 Total Expense ($000): 26998 Payroll Expense ($000): 9277
Personnel: 114

HELENA—Phillips County

HELENA REGIONAL MEDICAL CENTER (040781), 1801 Martin Luther King Drive, Zip 72342, Mailing Address: P.O. Box 788, Zip 72342–0788; tel. 870/338–5800, (Nonreporting) **A**1 10 **S** Quorum Health, Brentwood, TN
Primary Contact: Quentin Whitwell, Chief Executive Officer
CIO: Christopher Hunt, Director, Information Technologies, FISO
CHR: Juril Fonzie, Director Human Resources
CNO: Steven W. Brackeen, Chief Nursing Officer
Web address: www.helenarmc.com
Control: Corporation, Investor–owned (for–profit)

Staffed Beds: 12

HOPE—Hempstead County

⇑ **WADLEY REGIONAL MEDICAL CENTER AT HOPE (040153)**, 2001 South Main Street, Zip 71801–8194; tel. 870/722–3800, **A**10 21 **F**3 15 29 34 35 40 50 59 64 70 86 93 98 103 107 110 111 114 119 127 130 154 **S** Steward Health Care System, LLC, Dallas, TX
Primary Contact: Thomas D. Gilbert, FACHE, Chief Executive Officer
CFO: Bonny Sorensen, Chief Financial Officer
CIO: Matt Kesterson, Director Information Services
CHR: Debby Butler, Director Human Resources
CNO: Shelly Strayhorn, R.N., Chief Nursing Officer
Web address: https://www.wadleyhealthathope.org/
Control: Corporation, Investor–owned (for–profit) **Service**: General medical and surgical

Staffed Beds: 48 Admissions: 474 Census: 10 Outpatient Visits: 20961
Births: 0 Total Expense ($000): 16311 Payroll Expense ($000): 6820
Personnel: 98

Hospital, Medicare Provider Number, Address, Telephone, Approval, Facility, and Physician Codes, Health Care System

★ American Hospital Association (AHA) membership   ○ Healthcare Facilities Accreditation Program   ⇑ Center for Improvement in Healthcare Quality Accreditation
☐ The Joint Commission accreditation   ◇ DNV Healthcare Inc. accreditation   △ Commission on Accreditation of Rehabilitation Facilities (CARF) accreditation

© 2025 AHA Guide

Hospitals, U.S. / ARKANSAS

HOT SPRINGS—Garland County

☒ **CHI ST. VINCENT HOT SPRINGS (040026)**, 300 Werner Street, Zip 71913–6406; tel. 501/622–1000, **A**1 2 3 5 10 19 **F**3 11 12 13 15 18 20 22 24 26 28 29 30 31 34 35 37 38 40 43 45 46 47 49 50 53 56 57 59 64 66 68 69 70 71 73 74 75 76 77 78 79 81 82 84 85 87 89 93 97 98 102 107 108 110 111 114 115 116 117 118 119 120 121 123 124 126 130 146 147 148 149 154 156 157 167 169 **P**6 7 **S** CommonSpirit Health, Chicago, IL
Primary Contact: Douglas B. Ross, M.D., President and Chief Medical Officer
CFO: Shawn Barnett, Senior Vice President and Chief Financial Officer
CMO: Douglas B. Ross, M.D., President and Chief Medical Officer
CIO: Tracy Kirby, Assistant Vice President Business Relationship Management
Web address: www.chistvincent.com/Hospitals/st-vincent-hot-springs
Control: Church operated, Nongovernment, not–for–profit **Service**: General medical and surgical

Staffed Beds: 214 Admissions: 13880 Census: 160 Outpatient Visits: 154473 Births: 981 Total Expense ($000): 241408 Payroll Expense ($000): 84274 Personnel: 892

☒ **CHI ST. VINCENT HOT SPRINGS REHABILITATION HOSPITAL, A PARTNER OF ENCOMPASS HEALTH (043035)**, 1636 Higdon Ferry Road, Zip 71913–6912; tel. 501/651–2000, **A**1 10 **F**3 28 29 35 60 75 77 90 91 95 96 143 148 149 **S** Encompass Health Corporation, Birmingham, AL
Primary Contact: Lesalee Chilcote, Chief Executive Officer
Web address: https://www.encompasshealth.com
Control: Partnership, Investor–owned (for–profit) **Service**: Rehabilitation

Staffed Beds: 48 Admissions: 1336 Census: 43 Outpatient Visits: 0 Births: 0 Total Expense ($000): 18016 Payroll Expense ($000): 11143 Personnel: 124

☒ △ **NATIONAL PARK MEDICAL CENTER (040078)**, 1910 Malvern Avenue, Zip 71901–7799; tel. 501/321–1000, (Nonreporting) **A**1 7 10 19 **S** Lifepoint Health, Brentwood, TN
Primary Contact: Scott Bailey, Chief Executive Officer
COO: Brian Bell, Associate Administrator and Chief Operating Officer
CFO: Mike Long, Chief Financial Officer
CMO: Robert Breving, M.D., Chief of Staff
CIO: Brian Coffman, Director Information System
CHR: Tina Albright, Director Human Resources
CNO: Patsy Sue Crumpton, R.N., Chief Nursing Officer
Web address: www.nationalparkmedical.com
Control: Corporation, Investor–owned (for–profit) **Service**: General medical and surgical

Staffed Beds: 163

HOT SPRINGS NATIONAL PARK—Garland County

☐ **CHRISTUS DUBUIS HOSPITAL OF HOT SPRINGS (042004)**, 300 Werner Street, 3rd Floor East, Zip 71913–6406; tel. 501/609–4300, (Nonreporting) **A**1 10 **S** LHC Group, Lafayette, LA
Primary Contact: Kathy DeVore, R.N., Administrator
CIO: David Cook, Manager Information Systems
Web address: https://lhcgroup.com/locations/christus-dubuis-hospital-of-hot-springs/
Control: Partnership, Investor–owned (for–profit) **Service**: Acute long–term care hospital

Staffed Beds: 25

★ **LEVI HOSPITAL (040132)**, 300 Prospect Avenue, Zip 71901–4097; tel. 501/624–1281, **A**10 **F**3 34 40 50 57 59 64 68 93 98 100 102 104 107 130 132 149 154 162 164
Primary Contact: Zane Jeffers, President and Chief Executive Officer
CMO: P Ross Bandy, M.D., Chief Medical Officer and Chief of Staff
CHR: Susan Kramer, Director of Human Resources
CNO: Steven Boyd, R.N., Nurse Executive
Web address: www.levihospital.com
Control: Other not–for–profit (including NFP Corporation) **Service**: General medical and surgical

Staffed Beds: 45 Admissions: 1211 Census: 20 Outpatient Visits: 13631 Births: 0 Total Expense ($000): 8415 Payroll Expense ($000): 4996 Personnel: 93

JACKSONVILLE—Pulaski County

☒ **UNITY HEALTH – JACKSONVILLE (040164)**, 1400 Braden Street, Zip 72076–3721; tel. 501/453–5000, (Data for 199 days) **A**22 **F**3 15 29 30 34 35 40 44 50 57 59 94 98 101 102 107 110 111 115 119 135 146 149 157
Primary Contact: Kevin Burton, Administrator
CFO: Stuart Hill, Vice President and Treasurer
CHR: Randy T. Bosch, Associate Vice President Human Resources
CNO: Karen Y. Labonte, Chief Nursing Officer
Web address: www.unity-health.org/Jacksonville
Control: Other not–for–profit (including NFP Corporation) **Service**: General medical and surgical

Staffed Beds: 19 Admissions: 308 Census: 7 Outpatient Visits: 7369 Births: 0 Total Expense ($000): 15007 Payroll Expense ($000): 6676 Personnel: 160

JONESBORO—Craighead County

ARKANSAS CONTINUED CARE HOSPITAL See Arkansas Continued Care Hospital of Jonesboro

ARKANSAS CONTINUED CARE HOSPITAL OF JONESBORO (042013), 3024 Red Wolf Boulevard, Zip 72401–7415; tel. 870/819–4040, **A**10 22 **F**1 3 29 119 133 148 **P**4
Primary Contact: James Cox, Chief Executive Officer
Web address: https://arkansascontinuedcarehospital.com/
Control: Corporation, Investor–owned (for–profit) **Service**: Acute long–term care hospital

Staffed Beds: 45 Admissions: 508 Census: 33 Outpatient Visits: 0 Births: 0 Total Expense ($000): 20077 Payroll Expense ($000): 7618 Personnel: 90

☒ **ENCOMPASS HEALTH REHABILITATION HOSPITAL OF JONESBORO (043029)**, 1201 Fleming Avenue, Zip 72401–4311, Mailing Address: P.O. Box 1680, Zip 72403–1680; tel. 870/932–0440, (Nonreporting) **A**1 10 **S** Encompass Health Corporation, Birmingham, AL
Primary Contact: Kevin Spears, Chief Executive Officer
CFO: Allan Jones, Controller
CMO: Virendar Verma, M.D., Medical Director
CHR: Tammy Barley, Director, Human Resources
CNO: Becky Kimble, R.N., Chief Nursing Officer
Web address: https://www.encompasshealth.com/jonesbororehab
Control: Corporation, Investor–owned (for–profit) **Service**: Rehabilitation

Staffed Beds: 67

☒ **NEA BAPTIST MEMORIAL HOSPITAL (040118)**, 4800 East Johnson Avenue, Zip 72401–8413; tel. 870/936–1000, **A**1 2 3 5 10 19 **F**3 11 12 13 15 17 18 20 22 24 26 28 29 30 31 34 39 40 43 45 46 48 49 57 58 59 60 74 75 76 77 78 79 81 82 84 85 86 87 90 93 96 97 107 108 110 111 115 119 120 121 123 124 126 129 130 135 146 148 167 **S** Baptist Memorial Health Care Corporation, Memphis, TN
Primary Contact: Samuel Lynd, Chief Executive Officer and Administrator
COO: Melanie Edens, Chief Operating Officer
CFO: Kyle Sanders, Chief Financial Officer
CMO: Stephen Woodruff, M.D., Chief Medical Officer
CIO: Terry Crider, Information Technology Site Manager
CHR: James Keller, Director Human Resources
CNO: Paula Grimes, R.N., MSN, Chief Nursing Officer
Web address: https://www.baptistonline.org/locations/nea
Control: Other not–for–profit (including NFP Corporation) **Service**: General medical and surgical

Staffed Beds: 228 Admissions: 11645 Census: 140 Outpatient Visits: 135045 Births: 916 Total Expense ($000): 248697 Payroll Expense ($000): 82315 Personnel: 1088

☒ **ST. BERNARDS MEDICAL CENTER (040020)**, 225 East Washington Avenue, Zip 72401–3111; tel. 870/207–4100, **A**1 2 3 5 10 13 19 **F**3 5 11 12 13 15 17 18 19 20 22 24 26 27 28 29 30 31 32 34 35 37 38 39 40 43 44 45 46 48 49 50 51 53 54 55 56 57 58 59 60 61 62 63 64 66 68 70 71 72 74 75 76 77 78 79 81 82 83 84 85 86 87 89 91 92 93 96 97 98 100 101 102 103 104 107 108 109 110 111 112 114 115 116 117 118 119 120 121 123 124 126 129 130 131 132 134 135 141 145 146 147 148 149 153 154 156 157 160 162 164 166 167 168 169 **S** St. Bernards Healthcare, Jonesboro, AR
Primary Contact: Michael K. Givens, FACHE, Administrator
CFO: Ben Barylske, Chief Financial Officer
CMO: Kasey Holder, M.D., Vice President Medical Affairs
CIO: Josh Melton, Chief Information Officer
CHR: Lori J. Smith, Vice President Human Resources
CNO: Angie B. Smith, Chief Nursing Officer
Web address: www.stbernards.info
Control: Church operated, Nongovernment, not–for–profit **Service**: General medical and surgical

Staffed Beds: 411 Admissions: 20989 Census: 289 Outpatient Visits: 457766 Births: 1702 Total Expense ($000): 530875

Hospitals, U.S. / ARKANSAS

LAKE VILLAGE—Chicot County

★ **CHICOT MEMORIAL MEDICAL CENTER (041328)**, 2729 Highway 65 and 82 South, Zip 71653; tel. 870/265–5351, **A**10 18 **F**3 11 15 29 35 39 40 45 53 57 59 62 64 77 81 93 100 107 110 111 115 119 129 130 133 135 148 153 154 164 **P**6
Primary Contact: John E. Heard, Chief Executive Officer
CFO: Vicki Allen, Chief Financial Officer
CMO: Michael Bradley Mayfield, M.D., Chief of Staff
CIO: David Andrews, Manager Information Systems
CNO: Eric Selby, R.N., Chief Nursing Officer
Web address: www.chicotmemorial.com
Control: Other not–for–profit (including NFP Corporation) **Service**: General medical and surgical

Staffed Beds: 25 **Admissions:** 418 **Census:** 5 **Outpatient Visits:** 12018
Births: 0 **Total Expense ($000):** 19047 **Payroll Expense ($000):** 7667
Personnel: 158

SOUTHEAST REHABILITATION HOSPITAL (043034), 905 Borgognoni Road, Zip 71653, Mailing Address: P.O. Box 743, Zip 71653; tel. 870/265–4333, **A**10 **F**3 29 34 35 56 57 59 64 65 90 91 127 148 154 156 **P**5
Primary Contact: Catherine M. Waldrop, Administrator
CNO: Michael Vaughn, Director of Nursing
Web address: www.southeastrehab.com
Control: Partnership, Investor–owned (for–profit) **Service**: Rehabilitation

Staffed Beds: 10 **Admissions:** 148 **Census:** 5 **Outpatient Visits:** 5250
Births: 0 **Total Expense ($000):** 4737 **Payroll Expense ($000):** 3543

LITTLE ROCK—Pulaski County

✠ **ARKANSAS CHILDREN'S HOSPITAL (043300)**, 1 Childrens Way, Slot 301, Zip 72202–3500; tel. 501/364–1100, **A**1 3 5 10 **F**3 7 12 16 17 19 21 23 25 27 29 30 31 32 34 35 37 38 39 40 41 43 44 45 48 49 50 53 54 55 56 59 60 61 64 65 68 72 74 75 77 78 79 80 81 82 84 85 86 87 88 89 90 91 92 93 94 95 96 97 98 107 108 111 113 114 115 116 117 119 126 129 130 131 132 134 135 136 137 138 146 148 149 150 154 155 156 164 167 **P**8
Primary Contact: Marcella Doderer, FACHE, President and Chief Executive Officer
COO: Jamie L. Wiggins, R.N., MS, Executive Vice President and Chief Operating Officer
CFO: Gena Wingfield, Senior Vice President and Chief Financial Officer
CMO: Greg Sharp, M.D., Senior Vice President and Chief Medical Officer
CIO: Erin Parker, Senior Vice President and Chief Information Officer
CHR: Jimmy Duncan, Senior Vice President and Chief People Officer
Web address: www.archildrens.org
Control: Other not–for–profit (including NFP Corporation) **Service**: Children's general medical and surgical

Staffed Beds: 326 **Admissions:** 15637 **Census:** 244 **Outpatient Visits:** 341976 **Births:** 0 **Total Expense ($000):** 694514 **Payroll Expense ($000):** 287095 **Personnel:** 3399

☐ **ARKANSAS HEART HOSPITAL (040134)**, 1701 South Shackleford Road, Zip 72211–4335; tel. 501/219–7000, **A**1 3 5 10 **F**3 11 12 17 18 20 22 24 26 28 29 30 34 35 40 45 46 50 53 54 57 59 64 68 75 81 87 107 108 111 115 117 119 127 130 135 148 154 156 **P**4
Primary Contact: Bruce Murphy, M.D., President and Chief Executive Officer
Web address: https://www.arheart.com/location/arkansas-heart-hospital/
Control: Partnership, Investor–owned (for–profit) **Service**: Heart

Staffed Beds: 110 **Admissions:** 4852 **Census:** 55 **Outpatient Visits:** 187778 **Births:** 0 **Total Expense ($000):** 212626 **Payroll Expense ($000):** 62339 **Personnel:** 949

☐ **ARKANSAS STATE HOSPITAL (044011)**, 305 South Palm Street, Zip 72205–5432; tel. 501/686–9000, **A**1 3 5 10 **F**11 29 30 50 59 65 75 86 87 97 98 99 101 102 130 132 135 143 146 149 154 163 **P**6
Primary Contact: James Scoggins, Chief Executive Officer
CFO: Gary W Hollis, Comptroller
CMO: Steven Domon, M.D., Medical Director
CIO: Tina Grissom, Chief Information Technology Officer
CHR: Donna Sadler, Director Human Resources
CNO: James Scoggins, Director of Nursing
Web address: https://humanservices.arkansas.gov/about-dhs/dbhs/arkansas-state-hospital
Control: State, Government, Nonfederal **Service**: Psychiatric

Staffed Beds: 222 **Admissions:** 256 **Census:** 202 **Outpatient Visits:** 0
Births: 0 **Total Expense ($000):** 57046 **Payroll Expense ($000):** 27421
Personnel: 493

★ **BAPTIST HEALTH EXTENDED CARE HOSPITAL (042012)**, 9601 Baptist Health Drive, Zip 72205–7202; tel. 501/202–1070, **A**10 **F**1 3 29 31 77 85 87 130 148 158 **S** Baptist Health, Little Rock, AR
Primary Contact: Greg Stubblefield, President
CFO: Brent Beaulieu, Chief Financial Officer
CMO: Alexander Orsini, M.D., Medical Director
CIO: David House, Vice President
CHR: Cathy C. Dickinson, Chief Human Resources
CNO: Christopher Cox, Chief Nursing Officer
Web address: https://www.baptist-health.com/location/baptist-health-extended-care-hospital/
Control: Other not–for–profit (including NFP Corporation) **Service**: Acute long–term care hospital

Staffed Beds: 36 **Admissions:** 169 **Census:** 16 **Outpatient Visits:** 0
Births: 0 **Total Expense ($000):** 12529 **Payroll Expense ($000):** 6172
Personnel: 73

✠ △ **BAPTIST HEALTH MEDICAL CENTER–LITTLE ROCK (040114)**, 9601 Baptist Health Drive, Zip 72205–7299; tel. 501/202–2000, **A**1 3 5 7 10 **F**1 3 4 8 10 11 12 13 15 17 18 20 22 24 26 28 29 30 34 37 40 43 44 45 46 49 50 51 53 54 56 57 59 60 67 70 72 73 76 80 81 88 89 90 92 98 100 103 107 110 111 115 117 118 119 126 129 130 131 137 146 147 148 149 154 166 167 **S** Baptist Health, Little Rock, AR
Primary Contact: Mike Perkins, President
COO: Mackenzie Clyburn, Vice President, Operations
CFO: Robert C Roberts, Senior Vice President Financial Services
CMO: Anthony Bennett, M.D., Chief Clinical Affairs
CIO: David House, Vice President and Chief Information Officer
CHR: Anthony Kendall, Vice President Human Resources
CNO: Michele Diedrich, R.N., Chief Nursing Officer, Vice President Patient Care
Web address: https://www.baptist-health.com/location/baptist-health-medical-center-little-rock/
Control: Other not–for–profit (including NFP Corporation) **Service**: General medical and surgical

Staffed Beds: 633 **Admissions:** 27847 **Census:** 470 **Outpatient Visits:** 189325 **Births:** 2928 **Total Expense ($000):** 714122 **Payroll Expense ($000):** 225520 **Personnel:** 2455

★ **BAPTIST HEALTH REHABILITATION INSTITUTE (043026)**, 9501 Baptist Health Drive, Zip 72205–6225; tel. 501/202–7000, **A**3 5 10 **F**29 34 35 38 44 50 64 68 75 86 87 90 91 93 95 96 130 131 132 135 148 149 **S** Baptist Health, Little Rock, AR
Primary Contact: Kourtney Matlock, President
CFO: Robert C Roberts, Senior Vice President
CIO: David House, Vice President and Chief Information Officer
CHR: Anthony Kendall, Vice President Human Resources
Web address: www.baptist-health.com/locations/accesspoint.aspx?accessPointID=202
Control: Other not–for–profit (including NFP Corporation) **Service**: Rehabilitation

Staffed Beds: 60 **Admissions:** 1450 **Census:** 50 **Outpatient Visits:** 96629 **Births:** 0 **Total Expense ($000):** 37347 **Payroll Expense ($000):** 19432 **Personnel:** 244

CENTRAL ARKANSAS VETERANS HEALTHCARE SYSTEM See John L. Mcclellan Memorial Veterans' Hospital

✠ **CHI ST. VINCENT INFIRMARY (040007)**, 2 Saint Vincent Circle, Zip 72205–5499; tel. 501/552–3000, **A**1 3 5 10 **F**3 4 5 10 **F**1 3 4 5 11 12 15 17 18 20 22 24 26 28 29 30 31 34 35 37 39 40 43 44 45 46 47 48 49 50 51 53 54 56 57 59 60 61 62 64 68 70 74 75 77 78 79 80 81 82 84 85 86 87 91 93 97 98 100 102 103 104 107 108 109 110 111 114 115 116 117 118 119 126 129 130 132 135 143 144 146 147 148 149 152 153 154 156 157 160 161 164 165 167 **P**6 7 **S** CommonSpirit Health, Chicago, IL
Primary Contact: William G. Jones, M.D., President and Chief Medical Officer
CMO: William G. Jones, M.D., President and Chief Medical Officer
CIO: Tracy Kirby, Assistant Vice President Business Relationship Management
CNO: Kathy E. Neely, R.N., Interim Vice President Patient Care Services
Web address: www.chistvincent.com/
Control: Church operated, Nongovernment, not–for–profit **Service**: General medical and surgical

Staffed Beds: 413 **Admissions:** 13941 **Census:** 257 **Outpatient Visits:** 122228 **Births:** 0 **Total Expense ($000):** 457599 **Payroll Expense ($000):** 145578 **Personnel:** 1691

Hospital, Medicare Provider Number, Address, Telephone, Approval, Facility, and Physician Codes, Health Care System

★ American Hospital Association (AHA) membership ◇ Healthcare Facilities Accreditation Program ⇑ Center for Improvement in Healthcare Quality Accreditation
☐ The Joint Commission accreditation ◇ DNV Healthcare Inc. accreditation △ Commission on Accreditation of Rehabilitation Facilities (CARF) accreditation

Hospitals, U.S. / ARKANSAS

★ **CORNERSTONE SPECIALTY HOSPITALS LITTLE ROCK (042010)**, 2 Saint Vincent Circle, 6th Floor, Zip 72205-5423; tel. 501/265-0600, (Nonreporting) **A**10 22 **S** ScionHealth, Louisville, KY
Primary Contact: Kiacie Andrews, Chief Executive Officer
Web address: www.chghospitals.com/littlerock/
Control: Corporation, Investor-owned (for-profit) **Service:** Acute long-term care hospital

Staffed Beds: 30

△ **JOHN L. MCCLELLAN MEMORIAL VETERANS' HOSPITAL**, 4300 West Seventh Street, Zip 72205-5446; tel. 501/257-1000, (Includes NORTH LITTLE ROCK DIVISION, 2200 Fort Roots Drive, North Little Rock, Arkansas, Zip 72114-1706, tel. 501/661-1202) (Total facility includes 119 beds in nursing home-type unit) **A**1 2 3 5 7 **F**2 3 5 8 12 15 17 18 20 22 24 26 28 29 30 31 33 34 35 36 38 39 40 44 45 46 47 49 50 51 52 53 54 55 56 57 58 59 60 61 62 63 64 65 66 68 70 71 74 75 77 78 79 81 82 83 84 85 86 87 90 91 92 93 94 95 96 97 98 100 101 102 103 104 105 106 107 108 109 110 111 114 115 119 120 126 127 128 129 130 132 133 135 143 144 145 146 147 148 149 150 152 153 154 156 157 158 160 164 167 **S** Department of Veterans Affairs, Washington, DC
Primary Contact: Margie A. Scott, M.D., Medical Center Director
CFO: Colonel Nate Todd, Chief Financial Officer
CIO: Jim Hall, Acting Chief Information Officer
CHR: Richard Nelson, Chief of Human Resources Management Services
Web address: www.littlerock.va.gov/
Control: Veterans Affairs, Government, federal **Service:** General medical and surgical

Staffed Beds: 505 **Admissions:** 7665 **Census:** 300 **Outpatient Visits:** 905435 **Births:** 0 **Total Expense ($000):** 1059325 **Payroll Expense ($000):** 378222 **Personnel:** 4110

PINNACLE POINTE BEHAVIORAL HEALTHCARE SYSTEM (044013), 11501 Financial Center Parkway, Zip 72211-3715; tel. 501/223-3322, **A**1 10 **F**29 34 35 38 50 75 87 98 99 101 102 106 130 134 143 154 164 **S** Universal Health Services, Inc., King of Prussia, PA
Primary Contact: Courtney Bishop. Carney, Chief Executive Officer
CFO: Gina Dailey, Chief Financial Officer
CMO: Ben Nimmo, M.D., Medical Director
CIO: James L Howe, Director Human Resources
CHR: James L Howe, Director Human Resources
CNO: Bobby Alexander, R.N., Chief Nursing Officer
Web address: www.pinnaclepointehospital.com
Control: Corporation, Investor-owned (for-profit) **Service:** Children's hospital psychiatric

Staffed Beds: 127 **Admissions:** 3118 **Census:** 106 **Outpatient Visits:** 0 **Births:** 0 **Total Expense ($000):** 24823 **Payroll Expense ($000):** 15154 **Personnel:** 198

UAMS MEDICAL CENTER (040016), 4301 West Markham Street, Zip 72205-7101; tel. 501/686-7000, **A**1 3 5 8 10 19 **F**3 5 6 9 11 13 15 17 18 20 22 24 26 29 30 31 34 37 38 40 43 44 45 46 47 48 49 50 51 53 54 55 56 57 58 59 60 61 64 65 66 68 70 71 72 73 74 75 76 77 78 79 80 81 82 84 85 86 87 91 92 93 94 96 97 98 99 100 101 102 104 105 106 107 108 110 111 114 115 116 117 118 119 120 121 123 124 126 127 129 130 131 132 135 136 138 139 141 142 146 147 148 149 153 154 156 160 162 163 164 165 167 169 **P**6
Primary Contact: Michelle Krause, M.D., Senior Vice Chancellor, UAMS Health and Chief Executive Officer
COO: Timothy Hill, Chief Operating Officer
CFO: William Bowes, Chief Financial Officer
CMO: Nicholas P Lang, M.D., Chief Medical Officer
CHR: Jeff Risinger, Director Human Resources
Web address: www.uams.edu/medcenter
Control: State, Government, Nonfederal **Service:** General medical and surgical

Staffed Beds: 535 **Admissions:** 21580 **Census:** 399 **Outpatient Visits:** 708908 **Births:** 3454 **Total Expense ($000):** 1442850 **Payroll Expense ($000):** 377771 **Personnel:** 6266

MAGNOLIA—Columbia County

★ **MAGNOLIA REGIONAL MEDICAL CENTER (040067)**, 101 Hospital Drive, Zip 71753-2415, Mailing Address: P.O. Box 629, Zip 71754-0629; tel. 870/235-3000, **A**10 20 **F**3 11 15 29 35 40 43 45 50 59 62 64 70 79 81 87 93 97 107 108 110 111 115 119 126 127 129 130 146 154
Primary Contact: Brett Kinman, Chief Executive Officer
CFO: Roxane Stewart, Chief Financial Officer
CMO: James W Chambliss, Chief of Staff
CHR: Laura Akkub, Director Human Resources
CNO: Stephanie Schmittou, MSN, R.N., Chief Nursing Officer
Web address: www.magnoliarmc.org
Control: Other not-for-profit (including NFP Corporation) **Service:** General medical and surgical

Staffed Beds: 35 **Admissions:** 751 **Census:** 8 **Outpatient Visits:** 17502 **Births:** 0 **Total Expense ($000):** 31502 **Payroll Expense ($000):** 13536 **Personnel:** 185

MALVERN—Hot Spring County

★ **BAPTIST HEALTH MEDICAL CENTER–HOT SPRING COUNTY (040076)**, 1001 Schneider Drive, Zip 72104-4811; tel. 501/332-1000, **A**10 **F**3 11 15 29 30 34 35 40 43 64 70 75 93 98 102 107 110 111 115 119 127 129 130 135 146 149 154 **S** Baptist Health, Little Rock, AR
Primary Contact: Jay Quebedeaux, FACHE, President
CMO: Allen Gerber, M.D., Chief of Staff
CHR: Kelli Hopkins, Director Human Resources
CNO: Dee Schall, R.N., Chief Nursing Officer
Web address: https://www.baptist-health.com/location/baptist-health-medical-center-hot-spring-county-hot-spring-county
Control: Other not-for-profit (including NFP Corporation) **Service:** General medical and surgical

Staffed Beds: 69 **Admissions:** 1297 **Census:** 15 **Outpatient Visits:** 26649 **Births:** 0 **Total Expense ($000):** 23608 **Payroll Expense ($000):** 9268 **Personnel:** 127

MAUMELLE—Pulaski County

METHODIST BEHAVIORAL HOSPITAL (044017), 1601 Murphy Drive, Zip 72113-6187; tel. 501/803-3388, **A**1 10 **F**98 99 104 153 154 164 165 **P**5
Primary Contact: Andy Altom, President and Chief Executive Officer
Web address: https://www.methodistfamily.org/
Control: Other not-for-profit (including NFP Corporation) **Service:** Children's hospital psychiatric

Staffed Beds: 60 **Admissions:** 1575 **Census:** 45 **Outpatient Visits:** 64005 **Births:** 0 **Total Expense ($000):** 19490 **Payroll Expense ($000):** 8132 **Personnel:** 181

MCGEHEE—Desha County

★ **MCGEHEE HOSPITAL (041308)**, 900 South Third, Zip 71654-2562, Mailing Address: P.O. Box 351, Zip 71654-0351; tel. 870/222-5600, **A**10 18 **F**3 11 29 34 40 57 59 64 68 93 107 114 119 127 129 130 133 146 148 154 **P**7
Primary Contact: Terry Lee. Amstutz, FACHE, Chief Executive Officer
CFO: Teresa Morgan, Chief Financial Officer
CMO: James Young, M.D., Chief of Staff
CIO: Shaun Perry, Chief Information Officer
CNO: Sarah Calvert, Chief Nursing Officer
Web address: www.mymcgeheehospital.org/
Control: Other not-for-profit (including NFP Corporation) **Service:** General medical and surgical

Staffed Beds: 25 **Admissions:** 111 **Census:** 1 **Outpatient Visits:** 14033 **Births:** 0 **Total Expense ($000):** 14600 **Payroll Expense ($000):** 7009 **Personnel:** 122

MENA—Polk County

★ **MENA REGIONAL HEALTH SYSTEM (040015)**, 311 North Morrow Street, Zip 71953-2516; tel. 479/394-6100, **A**5 10 20 **F**3 4 11 13 15 29 30 34 35 40 43 45 56 57 59 64 68 70 75 76 77 79 81 86 87 90 91 93 96 98 100 101 103 104 107 108 110 111 115 119 127 129 130 131 144 147 149 152 154 160 169
Primary Contact: Michael Wood, Chief Executive Officer
CFO: Paul D. Ervin, Interim Chief Financial Officer
CMO: Richard Lochala, Chief of Staff
CIO: Nicholas Dunn, Director Information Systems
CHR: Chandler Cox, Director Human Resources
CNO: Teresa Wise, R.N., Chief Nursing Officer
Web address: www.menaregional.com
Control: City, Government, Nonfederal **Service:** General medical and surgical

Staffed Beds: 65 **Admissions:** 1357 **Census:** 18 **Outpatient Visits:** 79247 **Births:** 201 **Total Expense ($000):** 35649 **Payroll Expense ($000):** 17799 **Personnel:** 271

MONTICELLO—Drew County

★ **BAPTIST HEALTH MEDICAL CENTER – DREW COUNTY (040051)**, 778 Scogin Drive, Zip 71655-5729; tel. 870/367-2411, **A**5 10 20 **F**11 13 15 18 29 30 31 34 35 45 46 50 57 59 62 66 70 75 76 77 78 79 81 87 93 98 101 102 103 104 107 108 110 111 115 119 128 129 130 132 133 135 147 148 153 154 156 165 169 **P**6 **S** Baptist Health, Little Rock, AR
Primary Contact: Scott G. Barrilleaux, FACHE, Chief Executive Officer
COO: Wade Smith, Chief Operating Officer
CFO: Melodie Colwell, Chief Financial Officer
CMO: Julia Nichoson, M.D., Chief Medical Officer
CIO: Rusty Bryant, Director Information Technology
CHR: Seth Givens, Chief Human Resource Officer
CNO: Jonathan Schell, Chief Nursing Officer
Web address: www.drewmemorial.org
Control: Other not-for-profit (including NFP Corporation) **Service:** General medical and surgical

Staffed Beds: 60 **Admissions:** 1774 **Census:** 21 **Outpatient Visits:** 45654 **Births:** 233 **Total Expense ($000):** 31301 **Payroll Expense ($000):** 18476 **Personnel:** 248

Hospitals, U.S. / ARKANSAS

MORRILTON—Conway County

★ **CHI ST. VINCENT MORRILTON (041324)**, 4 Hospital Drive, Zip 72110–4510; tel. 501/977–2300, **A**10 18 **F**3 8 11 15 29 30 34 35 40 43 44 45 53 56 57 59 62 63 64 68 77 80 81 85 93 97 104 107 110 111 114 119 127 129 130 133 143 145 146 148 149 154 165 **P**6 7 **S** CommonSpirit Health, Chicago, IL
CFO: Shawn Barnett, Senior Vice President and Chief Financial Officer
CIO: Tracy Kirby, Assistant Vice President Business Relationship Management
CNO: Kathy E. Neely, R.N., Interim Vice President Patient Care Services
Web address: www.chistvincent.com/Hospitals/st-vincent-morrilton
Control: Church operated, Nongovernment, not–for–profit **Service**: General medical and surgical

Staffed Beds: 25 **Admissions**: 385 **Census**: 6 **Outpatient Visits**: 18257 **Births**: 0 **Total Expense ($000)**: 19871 **Payroll Expense ($000)**: 8444 **Personnel**: 88

MOUNTAIN HOME—Baxter County

★ **BAXTER HEALTH (040027)**, 624 Hospital Drive, Zip 72653–2955; tel. 870/508–1000, **A**10 **F**3 7 8 11 13 15 18 20 22 24 26 28 29 30 31 32 34 35 37 38 39 40 43 44 45 47 48 49 50 51 53 54 56 57 58 59 60 61 62 63 64 68 70 71 75 76 77 78 79 81 82 84 85 86 87 90 92 93 96 97 98 102 103 104 107 108 110 111 115 119 126 127 129 130 131 135 146 147 148 149 154 156 157 160 161 164 167 169 **P**6 8
Primary Contact: Ron Peterson, FACHE, President and Chief Executive Officer
CFO: Debbie Henry, Vice President and Chief Financial Officer
CHR: Karen Adams, Vice President Human Resources
Web address: www.baxterregional.org
Control: Other not–for–profit (including NFP Corporation) **Service**: General medical and surgical

Staffed Beds: 191 **Admissions**: 10777 **Census**: 127 **Outpatient Visits**: 186887 **Births**: 692 **Total Expense ($000)**: 293267 **Payroll Expense ($000)**: 125417 **Personnel**: 1830

BAXTER REGIONAL MEDICAL CENTER See Baxter Health

MOUNTAIN VIEW—Stone County

★ **STONE COUNTY MEDICAL CENTER (041310)**, 2106 East Main Street, Zip 72560–6439, Mailing Address: P.O. Box 510, Zip 72560–0510; tel. 870/269–4361, **A**10 18 **F**3 11 15 28 29 34 40 45 57 59 64 79 81 82 85 93 107 110 111 114 119 126 128 129 133 135 146 147 148 154 **S** White River Health System, Batesville, AR
Primary Contact: Kathy Thomas, MSN, R.N., Vice President/Chief Operating Officer
COO: Kathy Thomas, MSN, R.N., Chief Operating Officer
CFO: Phillip Hacker, Chief Financial Officer
CHR: Gary McDonald, Associate Administrator Human Resources
CNO: Terri Bunch, MSN, R.N., Chief Nursing Officer
Web address: https://www.whiteriverhealthsystem.com/scmc
Control: Other not–for–profit (including NFP Corporation) **Service**: General medical and surgical

Staffed Beds: 25 **Admissions**: 345 **Census**: 4 **Outpatient Visits**: 31241 **Births**: 0 **Total Expense ($000)**: 18468 **Payroll Expense ($000)**: 7690 **Personnel**: 125

NASHVILLE—Howard County

★ **HOWARD MEMORIAL HOSPITAL (041311)**, 130 Medical Circle, Zip 71852–8606; tel. 870/845–4400, **A**10 18 **F**3 11 15 28 29 30 34 35 40 45 50 53 57 64 65 70 77 81 85 87 93 97 107 108 110 115 119 126 132 133 143 146 156 **P**6
Primary Contact: John Hearnsberger, M.D., Interim Chief Executive Officer
COO: Stacy Harberson, Chief Operating Officer
CFO: William J. Craig, CPA, Chief Financial Officer
CMO: John Hearnsberger, M.D., Chief of Staff
CHR: Gayla Lacefield, Director Human Resources
CNO: Alesha Danielle Collins, MSN, R.N., Chief Nursing Officer
Web address: www.howardmemorial.com
Control: Other not–for–profit (including NFP Corporation) **Service**: General medical and surgical

Staffed Beds: 20 **Admissions**: 475 **Census**: 6 **Outpatient Visits**: 37846 **Births**: 0 **Total Expense ($000)**: 31224 **Payroll Expense ($000)**: 13436 **Personnel**: 198

NEWPORT—Jackson County

⇧ **UNITY HEALTH – NEWPORT (041332)**, 1205 McLain Street, Zip 72112–3533; tel. 870/523–8911, **A**3 10 18 21 **F**3 29 30 40 44 45 50 59 69 76 81 98 101 102 103 104 107 108 110 111 114 119 130 135 146 147 148 154 157 **P**6
Primary Contact: LaDonna Johnston, Administrator
Web address: https://www.unity-health.org/locations/unity-health-newport/
Control: State, Government, Nonfederal **Service**: General medical and surgical

Staffed Beds: 25 **Admissions**: 1626 **Census**: 18 **Outpatient Visits**: 18438 **Births**: 180 **Total Expense ($000)**: 33479 **Payroll Expense ($000)**: 16567 **Personnel**: 231

⇧ **UNITY HEALTH MIDPOINT** See Unity Health – Newport

NORTH LITTLE ROCK—Pulaski County

ARKANSAS SURGICAL HOSPITAL (040147), 5201 North Shore Drive, Zip 72118–5312; tel. 501/748–8000, **A**10 22 **F**3 29 30 34 35 37 38 40 57 59 64 74 75 78 79 81 82 85 86 87 107 111 114 119 126 130 131 149
Primary Contact: Brian Fowler, Chief Executive Officer
CFO: Charles Powell, Chief Financial Officer
CMO: Kenneth A Martin, M.D., Chief of Staff
CIO: Scott Davis, Manager Information Technology
CNO: Judy Jones, Chief Clinical Officer
Web address: www.ArkSurgicalHospital.com
Control: Corporation, Investor–owned (for–profit) **Service**: Surgical

Staffed Beds: 47 **Admissions**: 1605 **Census**: 9 **Outpatient Visits**: 24289 **Births**: 0 **Total Expense ($000)**: 74195 **Payroll Expense ($000)**: 17371 **Personnel**: 297

✠ **BAPTIST HEALTH MEDICAL CENTER – NORTH LITTLE ROCK (040036)**, 3333 Springhill Drive, Zip 72117–2922; tel. 501/202–3000, **A**1 3 5 10 **F**3 8 11 13 15 17 18 20 22 24 26 28 29 30 31 37 38 40 41 43 45 46 47 48 49 50 51 53 54 56 59 60 64 70 74 75 76 77 78 79 81 84 85 86 87 89 90 93 94 98 107 108 110 111 114 115 118 119 124 126 130 131 135 144 146 147 148 149 154 167 **S** Baptist Health, Little Rock, AR
Primary Contact: Cody Walker, President
COO: Doug Weeks, FACHE, Executive Vice President and Chief Operations Officer
CFO: Robert C Roberts, Senior Vice President Financial Services
CIO: David House, Vice President and Chief Information Officer
CHR: Cathy C. Dickinson, Vice President Human Resources
CNO: Kelley Hamby, Vice President Patient Care
Web address: https://www.baptist-health.com/location/baptist-health-medical-center-north-little-rock-north-little-rock
Control: Other not–for–profit (including NFP Corporation) **Service**: General medical and surgical

Staffed Beds: 255 **Admissions**: 13185 **Census**: 167 **Outpatient Visits**: 142119 **Births**: 1339 **Total Expense ($000)**: 286545 **Payroll Expense ($000)**: 97244 **Personnel**: 1167

CENTRAL ARKANSAS VETERANS AFFAIRS HEALTHCARE SYSTEM, EUGENE TOWBIN HEALTHCARE CENTER See North Little Rock Division

NORTH LITTLE ROCK DIVISION See John L. Mcclellan Memorial Veterans' Hospital, Little Rock

☐ **THE BRIDGEWAY (044005)**, 21 Bridgeway Road, Zip 72113–9516; tel. 501/771–1500, **A**1 10 **F**4 5 64 98 99 100 103 104 105 106 130 132 135 147 152 153 154 160 161 164 165 **P**5 6 **S** Universal Health Services, Inc., King of Prussia, PA
Primary Contact: Megan Miller, Chief Executive Officer
CFO: Fred Woods, Chief Financial Officer
CMO: Philip L Mizell, M.D., Medical Director
CHR: Neely Robison, Director Human Resources
Web address: www.thebridgeway.com
Control: Corporation, Investor–owned (for–profit) **Service**: Psychiatric

Staffed Beds: 127 **Admissions**: 2695 **Census**: 54 **Outpatient Visits**: 3756 **Births**: 0 **Total Expense ($000)**: 17630 **Payroll Expense ($000)**: 9611 **Personnel**: 255

Hospital, Medicare Provider Number, Address, Telephone, Approval, Facility, and Physician Codes, Health Care System

★ American Hospital Association (AHA) membership ○ Healthcare Facilities Accreditation Program ⇧ Center for Improvement in Healthcare Quality Accreditation
☐ The Joint Commission accreditation ◇ DNV Healthcare Inc. accreditation △ Commission on Accreditation of Rehabilitation Facilities (CARF) accreditation

Hospitals, U.S. / ARKANSAS

OSCEOLA—Mississippi County

✠ **SMC REGIONAL MEDICAL CENTER (040782)**, 611 West Lee Avenue, Zip 72370–3001, Mailing Address: P.O. Box 108, Blytheville, Zip 72316–0108; tel. 870/563–7000, **A**1 10 **F**3 11 29 34 40 43 45 57 68 81 90 93 107 114 119 133 135 146 149 154 156 **S** Ovation Healthcare, Brentwood, TN
Primary Contact: Bryan Hargis, CPA, FACHE, Chief Executive Officer
COO: Paul Pieffer, Chief Operating Officer
CFO: Randy Nichols, Chief Financial Officer
CMO: Pratapji Thakor, M.D., Chief of Staff
CIO: Tammy Bratcher, Director Information Technology
CHR: Cheri Blurton, Director Human Resources
CNO: Felicia Pierce, R.N., Chief Nursing Officer
Web address: www.mchsys.org
Control: County, Government, Nonfederal **Service**: General medical and surgical

Staffed Beds: 25 Admissions: 169 Census: 2 Outpatient Visits: 10734 Births: 0 Total Expense ($000): 10952 Payroll Expense ($000): 3599 Personnel: 54

SOUTH MISSISSIPPI COUNTY REGIONAL MEDICAL CENTER See SMC Regional Medical Center

OZARK—Franklin County

★ **MERCY HOSPITAL OZARK (041303)**, 801 West River Street, Zip 72949–3023; tel. 479/667–4138, **A**10 18 **F**3 15 35 40 43 45 57 59 64 65 68 81 85 93 107 119 133 149 **S** Mercy, Chesterfield, MO
Primary Contact: Julianne Stec, Vice President, Patient Services
CMO: John Lachowsky, M.D., Chief Medical Officer
CIO: Tiana Bolduc, Chief Information Officer
Web address: https://www.mercy.net/practice/mercy-hospital-ozark/
Control: Church operated, Nongovernment, not–for–profit **Service**: General medical and surgical

Staffed Beds: 25 Admissions: 405 Census: 6 Outpatient Visits: 14234 Births: 0 Total Expense ($000): 10443 Payroll Expense ($000): 5789 Personnel: 44

PARAGOULD—Greene County

✠ △ **ARKANSAS METHODIST MEDICAL CENTER (040039)**, 900 West Kingshighway, Zip 72450–5942, Mailing Address: P.O. Box 339, Zip 72451–0339; tel. 870/239–7000, **A**1 3 5 7 10 19 **F**3 7 10 11 13 15 18 20 22 28 29 32 34 35 40 43 45 49 50 51 53 54 57 59 62 64 68 70 75 76 79 81 85 86 87 89 90 93 97 107 108 110 111 114 115 119 124 125 129 130 131 132 133 135 144 146 147 148 154 156 169
Primary Contact: Brad Bloemer, President and Chief Executive Officer
COO: Jason Masingale, Chief Operating Officer
CFO: Brad Bloemer, Chief Financial Officer
CMO: Joel Epperson, M.D., Chief of Staff
CIO: Dan Austin, Director Information Technology
CHR: Kevin Thielemier, Director Human Resources
CNO: Lana R Williams, Chief Nursing Officer
Web address: www.arkansasmethodist.org
Control: Other not–for–profit (including NFP Corporation) **Service**: General medical and surgical

Staffed Beds: 70 Admissions: 2994 Census: 38 Outpatient Visits: 127456 Births: 405 Total Expense ($000): 80489 Payroll Expense ($000): 37482 Personnel: 570

PARIS—Logan County

★ **MERCY HOSPITAL PARIS (041300)**, 500 East Academy, Zip 72855–4040; tel. 479/963–6101, **A**10 18 **F**3 15 35 40 43 45 57 59 64 65 68 81 85 93 107 119 127 133 149 **S** Mercy, Chesterfield, MO
Primary Contact: Julianne Stec, Vice President, Patient Services
Web address: https://www.mercy.net/practice/mercy-hospital-paris/
Control: Church operated, Nongovernment, not–for–profit **Service**: General medical and surgical

Staffed Beds: 13 Admissions: 457 Census: 7 Outpatient Visits: 26780 Births: 0 Total Expense ($000): 11634 Payroll Expense ($000): 7031 Personnel: 57

PIGGOTT—Clay County

PIGGOTT COMMUNITY HOSPITAL See Piggott Health System

★ **PIGGOTT HEALTH SYSTEM (041330)**, 1206 Gordon Duckworth Drive, Zip 72454–3881, **A**10 18 **F**3 7 8 29 30 33 38 45 47 55 59 62 64 65 66 68 81 82 84 93 107 114 119 127 129 130 133 143 148 153 154 **P**8
Primary Contact: James L. Magee, Executive Director
CFO: Linda Ort, Chief Financial Officer
Web address: https://piggotthealthsystem.com/
Control: City, Government, Nonfederal **Service**: General medical and surgical

Staffed Beds: 25 Admissions: 804 Census: 8 Outpatient Visits: 35971 Births: 0 Total Expense ($000): 29053 Payroll Expense ($000): 13824 Personnel: 247

PINE BLUFF—Jefferson County

★ △ **JEFFERSON REGIONAL (040071)**, 1600 West 40th Avenue, Zip 71603–6301; tel. 870/541–7100, **A**3 5 7 10 20 **F**3 11 13 15 17 18 20 22 28 29 31 34 35 37 38 40 43 45 46 48 49 50 51 53 54 57 59 60 61 64 65 70 72 73 74 75 76 77 78 79 81 85 86 87 89 90 93 94 96 97 98 100 101 102 107 108 110 111 114 115 116 117 118 119 120 121 123 124 126 127 129 130 131 132 135 143 144 146 147 148 149 154 156 157 160 162 164 167 169 **P**6
Primary Contact: Brian N. Thomas, President and Chief Executive Officer
CFO: Jeremy Jeffery, Regional Chief Financial Officer
CMO: Reid Pierce, M.D., Chief Medical Officer
CNO: Michelle Powell, Chief Nursing Officer
Web address: www.jrmc.org
Control: Other not–for–profit (including NFP Corporation) **Service**: General medical and surgical

Staffed Beds: 258 Admissions: 7949 Census: 116 Outpatient Visits: 264515 Births: 534 Total Expense ($000): 241657 Payroll Expense ($000): 97629 Personnel: 1345

POCAHONTAS—Randolph County

★ **ST. BERNARDS FIVE RIVERS (040779)**, 2801 Medical Center Drive, Zip 72455–9436; tel. 870/892–6000, **A**10 **F**3 11 29 30 34 38 40 43 45 50 57 59 62 68 70 77 82 85 87 93 97 98 103 104 107 111 115 119 127 133 146 148 154 157 **S** St. Bernards Healthcare, Jonesboro, AR
Primary Contact: Randall Barymon, Chief Executive Officer
CFO: Matt Nichols, Chief Financial Officer
CHR: Anita Dickson, Director Human Resources
CNO: Paula Lewis, Interim Chief Nursing Officer
Web address: https://www.stbernards.info/
Control: Other not–for–profit (including NFP Corporation) **Service**: General medical and surgical

Staffed Beds: 37 Admissions: 544 Census: 8 Outpatient Visits: 25166 Births: 2 Total Expense ($000): 21277 Payroll Expense ($000): 11737 Personnel: 150

ROGERS—Benton County

EVEREST REHABILITATION HOSPITAL OF ROGERS (043036), 4313 South Pleasant Crossing Boulevard, Zip 72758–1347; tel. 479/341–4003, **A**22 **F**3 90 92 94 95 96 119 **S** Everest Rehabilitation Hospitals, LLC, Dallas, TX
Primary Contact: Wendy Yates, Chief Executive Officer
Web address: https://everestrehab.com/hospitals/rogers-ar/
Control: Partnership, Investor–owned (for–profit) **Service**: Rehabilitation

Staffed Beds: 36 Admissions: 963 Census: 35 Outpatient Visits: 0 Births: 0 Total Expense ($000): 14000 Payroll Expense ($000): 5477 Personnel: 95

✠ **MERCY HOSPITAL NORTHWEST ARKANSAS (040010)**, 2710 Rife Medical Lane, Zip 72758–1452; tel. 479/338–8000, **A**1 3 5 10 **F**3 5 7 8 11 12 13 14 15 17 18 20 22 28 29 30 31 34 35 38 40 42 43 44 45 48 49 50 51 54 55 56 57 58 59 60 61 62 63 64 65 66 68 70 72 74 75 76 77 78 79 81 82 84 85 86 87 89 90 93 97 100 102 104 107 108 110 111 114 115 118 119 124 126 129 130 131 132 135 143 144 146 147 148 149 153 154 155 156 157 162 164 165 167 169 **S** Mercy, Chesterfield, MO
Primary Contact: Ryan T. Gehrig, FACHE, President
COO: Mike Mudd, Chief Operating Officer
CFO: Benny Stover, Vice President Finance
CMO: Chris Johnson, M.D., Chief of Staff
CHR: Rick Barclay, Vice President Support Services
Web address: https://www.mercy.net/practice/mercy-hospital-northwest-arkansas/
Control: Church operated, Nongovernment, not–for–profit **Service**: General medical and surgical

Staffed Beds: 262 Admissions: 15170 Census: 168 Outpatient Visits: 316356 Births: 1940 Total Expense ($000): 340146 Payroll Expense ($000): 134363 Personnel: 1382

Hospitals, U.S. / ARKANSAS

RUSSELLVILLE—Pope County

☒ **SAINT MARY'S REGIONAL MEDICAL CENTER (040041)**, 1808 West Main Street, Zip 72801–2724; tel. 479/968–2841, (Nonreporting) **A**1 10 19 **S** Lifepoint Health, Brentwood, TN
Primary Contact: Casey Willis, Chief Executive Officer
COO: Scott Bailey, Chief Operating Officer
CFO: Wendell VanEs, Chief Financial Officer
CMO: Vickie Henderson, M.D., Chief Medical Officer
CHR: Connie Gragg, Director Human Resources
CNO: Carol Gore, MSN, R.N., Chief Nursing Officer
Web address: www.saintmarysregional.com
Control: Corporation, Investor–owned (for–profit) **Service:** General medical and surgical

Staffed Beds: 129

SALEM—Fulton County

FULTON COUNTY HOSPITAL (041322), 679 North Main Street, Zip 72576–9451, Mailing Address: P.O. Box 517, Zip 72576–0517; tel. 870/895–2691, (Nonreporting) **A**10 18
Primary Contact: Anthony Reed, MSN, R.N., Interim Administrator
Web address: www.fultoncountyhospital.org
Control: County, Government, Nonfederal **Service:** General medical and surgical

Staffed Beds: 25

SEARCY—White County

ADVANCED CARE HOSPITAL OF WHITE COUNTY (042011), 1200 South Main Street, Zip 72143–7321; tel. 501/278–3155, **A**10 **F**1 3 29 130 148 **P**5
Primary Contact: Loren J. Miller, Administrator
CMO: Miguel Aguinaga, M.D., FACS, Medical Director
CNO: Mistie Vannatter, Chief Nursing Officer
Web address: https://unity-health.org/advanced-care
Control: Other not–for–profit (including NFP Corporation) **Service:** Acute long–term care hospital

Staffed Beds: 20 **Admissions:** 176 **Census:** 11 **Outpatient Visits:** 0
Births: 0 **Total Expense ($000):** 7220 **Payroll Expense ($000):** 3759
Personnel: 52

★ **UNITY HEALTH (040014)**, 3214 East Race Avenue, Zip 72143–4810; tel. 501/268–6121, (Includes UNITY HEALTH SPECIALTY CARE, 1200 South Main Street, Searcy, Arkansas, Zip 72143–7397, tel. 501/278–3100; LaDonna Johnston, Interim President and Chief Executive Officer) **A**3 5 10 **F**3 5 8 9 11 13 15 17 18 20 22 28 29 30 31 32 34 35 38 40 43 45 50 51 57 59 60 64 65 66 68 70 74 75 76 77 78 79 81 85 87 89 90 91 92 93 95 96 98 99 100 101 102 103 104 107 108 110 111 114 115 116 119 126 129 130 131 132 134 135 146 147 148 154 156 157 164 165 167 169
Primary Contact: LaDonna Johnston, Interim President and Chief Executive Officer
CFO: Stuart Hill, Vice President and Treasurer
CIO: Phil Miller, Chief Information Officer
CHR: Pamela G Williams, Director Human Resources
CNO: Peggy Turner, Assistant Vice President and Director of Nursing
Web address: www.unity-health.org
Control: Other not–for–profit (including NFP Corporation) **Service:** General medical and surgical

Staffed Beds: 218 **Admissions:** 12281 **Census:** 144 **Outpatient Visits:** 87543 **Births:** 789 **Total Expense ($000):** 313625 **Payroll Expense ($000):** 133445 **Personnel:** 2558

WHITE COUNTY MEDICAL CENTER – SOUTH CAMPUS See Unity Health Specialty Care

SHERWOOD—Pulaski County

★ **CHI ST. VINCENT NORTH (040137)**, 2215 Wildwood Avenue, Zip 72120–5089; tel. 501/552–7100, **A**10 **F**3 11 15 18 20 22 26 29 30 34 35 40 43 45 50 53 57 58 64 68 74 79 80 81 85 87 107 108 110 111 112 114 115 118 119 129 130 135 146 149 150 167 **P**6 7 **S** CommonSpirit Health, Chicago, IL
Primary Contact: Megan Bonney, President
CFO: Shawn Barnett, Senior Vice President and Chief Financial Officer
Web address: www.stvincenthealth.com
Control: Church operated, Nongovernment, not–for–profit **Service:** General medical and surgical

Staffed Beds: 67 **Admissions:** 3473 **Census:** 49 **Outpatient Visits:** 32747
Births: 0 **Total Expense ($000):** 85567 **Payroll Expense ($000):** 34585
Personnel: 248

☒ **CHI ST. VINCENT SHERWOOD REHABILITATION HOSPITAL, A PARTNER OF ENCOMPASS HEALTH (043031)**, 2201 Wildwood Avenue, Zip 72120–5074; tel. 501/834–1800, **A**1 10 **F**3 29 50 60 75 86 87 90 91 94 95 96 130 135 143 149 154 157 **S** Encompass Health Corporation, Birmingham, AL
Primary Contact: Brian Cherry, Chief Executive Officer
CFO: Stacy Shilling, Controller
CMO: Kevin J. Collins, M.D., Medical Director
CNO: Carolynn Whitley, Chief Nursing Officer
Web address: www.stvincentrehabhospital.com/
Control: Corporation, Investor–owned (for–profit) **Service:** Rehabilitation

Staffed Beds: 83 **Admissions:** 2033 **Census:** 70 **Outpatient Visits:** 0
Births: 0 **Total Expense ($000):** 28514 **Payroll Expense ($000):** 17240
Personnel: 246

SILOAM SPRINGS—Benton County

☒ **SILOAM SPRINGS REGIONAL HOSPITAL (040001)**, 603 North Progress Avenue, Zip 72761–4352; tel. 479/215–3000, (Nonreporting) **A**1 5 10 **S** Community Health Systems, Inc., Franklin, TN
Primary Contact: Christopher Blair, Chief Administrative Officer
CFO: Todd Williams, Chief Financial Officer
CMO: Ashish Mathur, M.D., Chief of Staff
CHR: Cindy Ruffing, Director Human Resources
CNO: Maria Wleklinski, Chief Nursing Officer
Web address: www.ssrh.net
Control: Corporation, Investor–owned (for–profit) **Service:** General medical and surgical

Staffed Beds: 46

SPRINGDALE—Washington County

☒ **ARKANSAS CHILDREN'S NORTHWEST (043301)**, 2601 Gene George Boulevard, Zip 72762; tel. 479/725–6800, **A**1 10 **F**3 19 29 30 31 34 35 38 39 40 41 43 44 50 53 55 59 64 65 68 74 75 77 78 79 81 85 86 87 89 93 97 107 111 115 119 130 131 132 146 148 149 154 164 **P**8
Primary Contact: Marcella Doderer, FACHE, Chief Executive Officer
Web address: https://www.archildrens.org/locations/arkansas-childrens-nw
Control: Other not–for–profit (including NFP Corporation) **Service:** Children's general medical and surgical

Staffed Beds: 24 **Admissions:** 4035 **Census:** 21 **Outpatient Visits:** 129862
Births: 0 **Total Expense ($000):** 106680 **Payroll Expense ($000):** 41993
Personnel: 533

☒ **NORTHWEST MEDICAL CENTER – SPRINGDALE (040022)**, 609 West Maple Avenue, Zip 72764–5394, Mailing Address: P.O. Box 47, Zip 72765–0047; tel. 479/751–5711, (Includes NORTHWEST MEDICAL CENTER – BENTONVILLE, 3000 Medical Center Parkway, Bentonville, Arkansas, Zip 72712, UNIT3000 Medical Center Parkway, Zip 72712–3217, tel. 479/553–1000; Christopher Blair, Chief Executive Officer; WILLOW CREEK WOMEN'S HOSPITAL, 4301 Greathouse Springs Road, Johnson, Arkansas, Zip 72741–0544, UNITPO Box 544, Zip 72741–0544, tel. 479/684–3000) (Nonreporting) **A**1 3 5 10 19 **S** Community Health Systems, Inc., Franklin, TN
Primary Contact: Rick R. Naegler, Market Chief Executive Officer
COO: Tom Sledge, Chief Operating Officer
CMO: James Tanner, M.D., Chief Medical Officer
CIO: Mark Bokon, Chief Information Officer
Web address: https://www.northwesthealth.com/nmc-springdale
Control: Corporation, Investor–owned (for–profit) **Service:** General medical and surgical

Staffed Beds: 366

☒ **REGENCY HOSPITAL OF NORTHWEST ARKANSAS – SPRINGDALE (042009)**, 609 West Maple Avenue, 6th Fl, Zip 72764; tel. 479/757–2600, (Nonreporting) **A**1 10 **S** Select Medical Corporation, Mechanicsburg, PA
Primary Contact: Lisa Muskrat, Chief Executive Officer
COO: Ruth Jones, Chief Clinical Officer
CMO: Gary Templeton, M.D., Medical Director
CHR: Melissa Ross–Cole, Director Human Resources
Web address: www.regencyhospital.com
Control: Corporation, Investor–owned (for–profit) **Service:** Acute long–term care hospital

Staffed Beds: 25

Hospital, Medicare Provider Number, Address, Telephone, Approval, Facility, and Physician Codes, Health Care System

★ American Hospital Association (AHA) membership ○ Healthcare Facilities Accreditation Program ⇧ Center for Improvement in Healthcare Quality Accreditation
□ The Joint Commission accreditation ◇ DNV Healthcare Inc. accreditation △ Commission on Accreditation of Rehabilitation Facilities (CARF) accreditation

© 2025 AHA Guide

Hospitals, U.S. / ARKANSAS

STUTTGART—Arkansas County

★ **BAPTIST HEALTH MEDICAL CENTER–STUTTGART (040072)**, 1703 North Buerkle Road, Zip 72160–1905, Mailing Address: P.O. Box 1905, Zip 72160–1905; tel. 870/673–3511, **A**10 20 **F**3 11 13 15 18 29 34 35 40 43 45 46 57 59 64 68 75 76 78 79 81 82 85 87 93 97 107 110 111 115 119 127 129 130 131 132 133 135 146 147 148 154 156 157 164 169 **S** Baptist Health, Little Rock, AR
Primary Contact: Kevin L. Storey, President
CMO: Michael Oltmann, M.D., Chief Medical Officer
CIO: Warren Horton, Information Technologist
CNO: Lauren Reynolds, Associate Director of Nursing
Web address: https://www.baptist-health.com/location/baptist-health-medical-center-stuttgart-stuttgart
Control: Church operated, Nongovernment, not–for–profit **Service:** General medical and surgical

Staffed Beds: 49 **Admissions:** 411 **Census:** 4 **Outpatient Visits:** 41041 **Births:** 31 **Total Expense ($000):** 31110 **Payroll Expense ($000):** 10908 **Personnel:** 144

TEXARKANA—Miller County

☐ **RIVERVIEW BEHAVIORAL HEALTH (044020)**, 701 Arkansas Boulevard, Zip 71854–2105; tel. 870/772–5028, **A**1 10 **F**75 98 99 100 101 103 106 130 143 149 150 153 154 160 164 **S** Acadia Healthcare Company, Inc., Franklin, TN
Primary Contact: Colleen Vicari, Chief Executive Officer
CFO: Kimberly Hibschman, Chief Financial Officer
CIO: Jim Cruson, Chief Information Officer
CHR: Roberta Bachman, Director Human Resources
CNO: Carrie Gray, Director of Nursing
Web address: www.riverviewbehavioralhealth.com
Control: Corporation, Investor–owned (for–profit) **Service:** Psychiatric

Staffed Beds: 62 **Admissions:** 1385 **Census:** 46 **Outpatient Visits:** 1023 **Births:** 0 **Total Expense ($000):** 13327 **Payroll Expense ($000):** 7552 **Personnel:** 118

VAN BUREN—Crawford County

⊞ **BAPTIST HEALTH – VAN BUREN (040018)**, 211 Crawford Memorial Drive, Zip 72956–5322, Mailing Address: P.O. Box 409, Zip 72957–0409; tel. 479/474–3401, **A**1 10 **F**3 29 30 40 43 68 70 107 119 146 **S** Baptist Health, Little Rock, AR
Primary Contact: Jeffrey Carrier, President, Baptist Health Western Region
COO: Christian Gross, Chief Operating Officer
CHR: James Ford, Director Human Resources
Web address: https://www.sparkshealth.com/
Control: Other not–for–profit (including NFP Corporation) **Service:** General medical and surgical

Staffed Beds: 74 **Admissions:** 183 **Census:** 2 **Outpatient Visits:** 24347 **Births:** 0 **Total Expense ($000):** 12927 **Payroll Expense ($000):** 3849 **Personnel:** 43

WALDRON—Scott County

★ **MERCY HOSPITAL WALDRON (041305)**, 1341 West 6th Street, Zip 72958–7642; tel. 479/637–4135, **A**10 18 **F**3 15 35 40 43 45 57 59 64 65 68 85 93 107 119 127 133 149 **S** Mercy, Chesterfield, MO
Primary Contact: Steve Gebhart, Vice President, Patient Services
CFO: Greta Wilcher, Senior Vice President and Chief Financial Officer
CNO: Nick Hunt, Interim Director of Nursing
Web address: https://www.mercy.net/practice/mercy-hospital-waldron/
Control: Church operated, Nongovernment, not–for–profit **Service:** General medical and surgical

Staffed Beds: 24 **Admissions:** 379 **Census:** 4 **Outpatient Visits:** 11375 **Births:** 0 **Total Expense ($000):** 10155 **Payroll Expense ($000):** 6172 **Personnel:** 63

WALNUT RIDGE—Lawrence County

⊞ **LAWRENCE MEMORIAL HOSPITAL (041309)**, 1309 West Main, Zip 72476–1430, Mailing Address: P.O. Box 839, Zip 72476–0839; tel. 870/886–1200, (Total facility includes 125 beds in nursing home–type unit) **A**1 10 18 **F**3 15 29 32 34 35 40 57 59 65 84 85 87 97 107 110 111 114 119 127 128 129 130 133 135 146 149 154 164 167
Primary Contact: Aaron Hilton, President
COO: Junior Briner, Chief Operating Officer
CFO: Vanessa Wagner, Chief Financial Officer
CMO: Kevin M. Diamond, M.D., Chief Medical Officer
CIO: Josh Wise, Director Information Technology
CHR: Charles Walker, Director Human Resource
CNO: Rosalind C Casillas, Chief Nursing Officer
Web address: https://www.lawrencememorial.info/
Control: Other not–for–profit (including NFP Corporation) **Service:** General medical and surgical

Staffed Beds: 150 **Admissions:** 317 **Census:** 101 **Outpatient Visits:** 20380 **Births:** 0 **Total Expense ($000):** 28951 **Payroll Expense ($000):** 12703 **Personnel:** 285

WARREN—Bradley County

★ **BRADLEY COUNTY MEDICAL CENTER (041327)**, 404 South Bradley Street, Zip 71671–3493; tel. 870/226–3731, **A**10 18 **F**3 11 13 15 29 30 34 35 40 42 45 49 50 56 57 59 62 76 81 87 98 103 104 107 108 110 111 118 119 127 132 133 146 147 153 154 160 169 **P**6
Primary Contact: Leslie Huitt, Chief Executive Officer
CMO: Joe H Wharton, M.D., Chief of Staff
CHR: Brooke Hatch, Director Human Resource
CNO: Jamie Wolfe, Chief Financial Officer
Web address: www.bradleycountymedicalcenter.com
Control: Other not–for–profit (including NFP Corporation) **Service:** General medical and surgical

Staffed Beds: 33 **Admissions:** 399 **Census:** 3 **Outpatient Visits:** 21157 **Births:** 77 **Total Expense ($000):** 25905 **Payroll Expense ($000):** 10644 **Personnel:** 197

WEST MEMPHIS—Crittenden County

⊞ **BAPTIST MEMORIAL HOSPITAL–CRITTENDEN (040156)**, 2100 North 7th Street, Zip 72301–2017; tel. 870/394–7800, (Nonreporting) **A**1 2 10 **S** Baptist Memorial Health Care Corporation, Memphis, TN
Primary Contact: Samuel Pieh, Chief Executive Officer and Administrator
Web address: www.baptistonline.org
Control: Other not–for–profit (including NFP Corporation) **Service:** General medical and surgical

Staffed Beds: 11

☐ **PERIMETER BEHAVIORAL HOSPITAL OF WEST MEMPHIS (044021)**, 600 North Seventh Street, Zip 72301–3235; tel. 870/394–7100, (Nonreporting) **A**1 10 **S** Perimeter Healthcare, Alpharetta, GA
Primary Contact: Art Hickman, Chief Executive Officer
Web address: https://www.perimeterhealthcare.com
Control: Corporation, Investor–owned (for–profit) **Service:** Psychiatric

Staffed Beds: 24

WYNNE—Cross County

⊞ **CROSSRIDGE COMMUNITY HOSPITAL (041307)**, 310 South Falls Boulevard, Zip 72396–3013, Mailing Address: P.O. Box 590, Zip 72396–0590; tel. 870/238–3300, **A**1 10 18 **F**3 11 15 28 34 35 40 57 59 62 64 68 69 81 89 93 107 110 111 114 119 130 133 146 148 **S** St. Bernards Healthcare, Jonesboro, AR
Primary Contact: Gary R. Sparks, Administrator
COO: Bryan Mattes, Associate Administrator
CFO: Janice Morris, Accountant
CIO: Gail Copeland, Director Management Information Systems
CHR: Bertha Ragle, Director Personnel
CNO: Amelia Davis, Director of Nursing
Web address: https://www.stbernards.info
Control: Church operated, Nongovernment, not–for–profit **Service:** General medical and surgical

Staffed Beds: 15 **Admissions:** 507 **Census:** 7 **Outpatient Visits:** 19008 **Births:** 0 **Total Expense ($000):** 19485 **Payroll Expense ($000):** 8035 **Personnel:** 158

Hospitals, U.S. / CALIFORNIA

CALIFORNIA

ALAMEDA—Alameda County

☒ **ALAMEDA HOSPITAL (050211)**, 2070 Clinton Avenue, Zip 94501–4397; tel. 510/522–3700, (Total facility includes 181 beds in nursing home–type unit) **A**1 3 5 10 **F**3 11 15 18 29 31 34 35 36 39 40 43 46 50 57 58 59 70 77 78 79 81 82 84 85 93 97 107 108 110 114 118 119 128 130 132 144 146 147 148 154 **P**6 **S** Alameda Health System, San Leandro, CA
Primary Contact: James E.T. Jackson, M.P.H., Chief Executive Officer
CFO: Robert C Anderson, Interim Chief Financial Officer
CMO: Aika Sharma, M.D., President Medical Staff
CIO: Robert Lundy–Paine, Director Information Systems
Web address: www.alamedahealthsystem.org
Control: Hospital district or authority, Government, Nonfederal **Service**: General medical and surgical

Staffed Beds: 247 **Admissions**: 2718 **Census**: 180 **Outpatient Visits**: 30948 **Births**: 0 **Total Expense ($000)**: 135174 **Payroll Expense ($000)**: 62238 **Personnel**: 520

ALHAMBRA—Los Angeles County

☐ **ALHAMBRA HOSPITAL MEDICAL CENTER (050281)**, 100 South Raymond Avenue, Zip 91801–3199, Mailing Address: P.O. Box 510, Zip 91802–2510; tel. 626/570–1606, (Nonreporting) **A**1 10 **S** AHMC Healthcare, Alhambra, CA
Primary Contact: Evelyn Ku, R.N., MSN, Chief Executive Officer
CFO: Linda Marsh, Vice President Financial Services and Chief Financial Officer
CMO: Stephen Chen, M.D., Chief Medicare
CIO: Johnson Legaspi, Director Information Systems
CHR: Elizabeth Sabandit, Director Human Resources
CNO: Eleanor Martinez, Chief Nursing Officer
Web address: www.alhambrahospital.com
Control: Partnership, Investor–owned (for–profit) **Service**: General medical and surgical

Staffed Beds: 144

ALTURAS—Modoc County

★ **MODOC MEDICAL CENTER (051330)**, 1111 North Nagle Street, Zip 96101–3840; tel. 530/233–5131, (Nonreporting) **A**10 18
Primary Contact: Kevin Kramer, Chief Executive Officer
CMO: Ed Richert, M.D., Chief of Staff
CHR: Diane Hagelthorn, Human Resources Generalist
Web address: www.modocmedicalcenter.org
Control: County, Government, Nonfederal **Service**: General medical and surgical

Staffed Beds: 87

ANAHEIM—Orange County

☐ **AHMC ANAHEIM REGIONAL MEDICAL CENTER (050226)**, 1111 West La Palma Avenue, Zip 92801–2881; tel. 714/774–1450, (Nonreporting) **A**1 10 **S** AHMC Healthcare, Alhambra, CA
Primary Contact: Lisa Hahn, R.N., Chief Executive Officer
COO: Mary Anne Monje, Chief Operations Officer
CFO: Mary Anne Monje, Chief Financial Officer
CMO: Amitabh Prakash, M.D., Chief Medical Officer
CIO: Jeff DesRoches, Director Information Systems
CHR: Jason Jaquez, Human Resource Director
Web address: www.anaheimregionalmc.com
Control: Other not–for–profit (including NFP Corporation) **Service**: General medical and surgical

Staffed Beds: 223

☐ **ANAHEIM GLOBAL MEDICAL CENTER (050744)**, 1025 South Anaheim Boulevard, Zip 92805–5806; tel. 714/533–6220, (Nonreporting) **A**1 10 **S** KPC Healthcare, Inc., Santa Ana, CA
Primary Contact: Kevan Metcalfe, FACHE, Chief Executive Officer
CFO: John Collins, Chief Financial Officer
CMO: Beena Shah, M.D., Chief of Staff and Chief Medical Officer
CNO: Bonita Wells Veal, Chief Nursing Officer
Web address: https://anaheimglobalmedicalcenter.com/
Control: Corporation, Investor–owned (for–profit) **Service**: General medical and surgical

Staffed Beds: 188

☒ **KAISER PERMANENTE ORANGE COUNTY ANAHEIM MEDICAL CENTER (050609)**, 3440 East La Palma Avenue, Zip 92806–2020; tel. 714/644–2000, (Includes ORANGE COUNTY IRVINE MEDICAL CENTER, 6640 Alton Parkway, Irvine, California, Zip 92618, tel. 949/932–5000; Mark E Costa, Executive Director) **A**1 3 10 19 **F**3 7 8 13 15 18 19 20 22 26 28 29 30 31 35 36 37 38 40 44 45 46 47 48 49 50 51 53 55 56 57 59 60 61 62 63 64 65 66 68 70 72 74 75 76 77 78 79 81 82 84 85 86 87 89 97 100 101 102 107 108 110 111 114 115 116 117 119 126 130 131 135 146 148 149 150 154 155 156 157 160 162 164 166 167 169 **S** Kaiser Foundation Hospitals, Oakland, CA
Primary Contact: Payman Roshan, Senior Vice President and Area Manager, Orange County
COO: Margie Harrier, MSN, R.N., Medical Center Chief Operations Officer
CFO: Marcus Hoffman, Area Chief Financial Officer
CMO: Nancy Gin, M.D., Area Associate Medical Director
CIO: James Brady, Area Information Officer
CHR: Jocelyn A. Herrera, Director Human Resources
CNO: Martha Dispoto, R.N., I, Chief Nurse Executive, Anaheim Medical Center
Web address: www.kp.org
Control: Other not–for–profit (including NFP Corporation) **Service**: General medical and surgical

Staffed Beds: 526 **Admissions**: 26070 **Census**: 304 **Outpatient Visits**: 295288 **Births**: 6317 **Personnel**: 3931

☐ **WEST ANAHEIM MEDICAL CENTER (050426)**, 3033 West Orange Avenue, Zip 92804–3183; tel. 714/827–3000, (Nonreporting) **A**1 3 5 10 13 **S** Prime Healthcare, Ontario, CA
Primary Contact: Ayman Mousa, R.N., Chief Executive Officer
CFO: Kora Guoyavatin, Chief Financial Officer
CMO: Hassan Alkhouli, M.D., Chief Medical Officer
CIO: Vic Mahan, Director Information Technology
CHR: Stephanie Sioson, Director Human Resources
Web address: www.westanaheimmedctr.com
Control: Partnership, Investor–owned (for–profit) **Service**: General medical and surgical

Staffed Beds: 219

ANTIOCH—Contra Costa County

☒ **KAISER PERMANENTE ANTIOCH MEDICAL CENTER (050760)**, 4501 Sand Creek Road, Zip 94531–8687; tel. 925/813–6500, **A**1 2 10 **F**3 11 13 15 18 26 30 31 37 39 40 41 45 49 56 60 64 68 70 73 74 75 76 78 79 80 81 84 85 87 100 107 108 110 111 114 115 118 119 120 121 123 126 130 135 146 148 149 154 167 169 **P**6 **S** Kaiser Foundation Hospitals, Oakland, CA
Primary Contact: Pamela Galley, Senior Vice President/Area Manager, Diablo Service Area
CFO: Kerry Easthope, Area Finance Officer
CMO: Dale Poppert, M.D., Chief of Staff
CIO: Mical Cayton, Area Information Officer
CHR: Davida Lindsay–Bell, Area Human Resources Leader
CNO: Janet Jule, Chief Nurse Executive
Web address: https://health.kaiserpermanente.org/wps/portal/facility/100382
Control: Other not–for–profit (including NFP Corporation) **Service**: General medical and surgical

Staffed Beds: 109 **Admissions**: 9268 **Census**: 98 **Outpatient Visits**: 156928 **Births**: 1727 **Personnel**: 1050

☒ **SUTTER DELTA MEDICAL CENTER (050523)**, 3901 Lone Tree Way, Zip 94509–6253; tel. 925/779–7200, **A**1 10 **F**3 8 11 13 15 18 20 22 26 29 30 31 34 35 40 47 49 50 51 59 60 64 65 66 68 70 74 75 76 77 78 79 81 82 85 86 87 93 94 96 107 108 110 111 114 115 119 130 131 135 146 147 148 149 154 164 167 169 **S** Sutter Health, Sacramento, CA
Primary Contact: Trevor Brand, Chief Executive Officer
CFO: Julie Peterson, Chief Financial Officer
CMO: Anupam Mapara, M.D., Chief of Staff
CIO: Kathy Frederickson, Information Systems Site Lead
CHR: Noemi Whitehead, Administrative Director Human Resources
Web address: www.sutterdelta.org
Control: Other not–for–profit (including NFP Corporation) **Service**: General medical and surgical

Staffed Beds: 141 **Admissions**: 5412 **Census**: 62 **Outpatient Visits**: 76217 **Births**: 421 **Total Expense ($000)**: 230641 **Payroll Expense ($000)**: 81633 **Personnel**: 771

Hospital, Medicare Provider Number, Address, Telephone, Approval, Facility, and Physician Codes, Health Care System

★ American Hospital Association (AHA) membership ◯ Healthcare Facilities Accreditation Program ⇧ Center for Improvement in Healthcare Quality Accreditation
☐ The Joint Commission accreditation ◇ DNV Healthcare Inc. accreditation △ Commission on Accreditation of Rehabilitation Facilities (CARF) accreditation

Hospitals, U.S. / CALIFORNIA

APPLE VALLEY—San Bernardino County

☒ **PROVIDENCE ST. MARY MEDICAL CENTER (050300)**, 18300 Highway 18, Zip 92307-2206, Mailing Address: P.O. Box 7025, Zip 92307-0725; tel. 760/242-2311, **A**1 5 10 **F**3 8 11 13 17 18 20 22 24 26 28 29 30 34 35 40 45 46 49 50 51 57 63 65 68 70 72 75 76 77 79 81 82 84 85 86 87 89 93 100 102 107 108 111 115 119 126 130 132 135 146 148 149 154 157 160 161 164 167 169 **P**3 5 **S** Providence, Renton, WA
Primary Contact: Randall Castillo, Chief Executive Officer
CMO: Riad Z. Abdelkarim, M.D., Vice President and Chief Medical Officer
CIO: Doug Kleine, IT Director
CHR: Jean Holtman, Vice President, Human Resources
CNO: Marilyn Drone, R.N., MSN, Vice President, CNO
Web address: www.stmaryapplevalley.com/
Control: Other not-for-profit (including NFP Corporation) **Service**: General medical and surgical

Staffed Beds: 213 **Admissions**: 12641 **Census**: 167 **Outpatient Visits**: 268494 **Births**: 1612 **Total Expense ($000)**: 282448 **Payroll Expense ($000)**: 160160 **Personnel**: 1617

ST. MARY MEDICAL CENTER See Providence St. Mary Medical Center

ARCADIA—Los Angeles County

☒ **USC ARCADIA HOSPITAL (050238)**, 300 West Huntington Drive, Zip 91007-3473, Mailing Address: P.O. Box 60016, Zip 91066-6016; tel. 626/898-8000, **A**1 2 3 10 **F**3 11 12 13 17 18 20 22 24 26 29 30 31 34 35 38 40 41 46 47 49 50 51 55 57 58 59 64 65 68 70 72 74 75 76 77 78 79 81 83 85 86 87 90 92 93 94 96 107 108 111 114 115 119 126 130 132 135 146 147 148 149 154 156 157 160 167 169 **S** Keck Medicine of USC, Los Angeles, CA
Primary Contact: Ikenna Mmeje, President and Chief Executive Officer
COO: Steven A. Sisto, Senior Vice President and Chief Operating Officer
CFO: William E. Grigg, Senior Vice President and Chief Financial Officer
CIO: Alen Oganesyan, Chief Information Officer
CHR: Gwen Chambers, Executive Director Human Resources
Web address: https://www.uscarcadiahospital.org/
Control: Other not-for-profit (including NFP Corporation) **Service**: General medical and surgical

Staffed Beds: 269 **Admissions**: 11824 **Census**: 182 **Outpatient Visits**: 70858 **Births**: 1182 **Total Expense ($000)**: 343667 **Payroll Expense ($000)**: 161453 **Personnel**: 1227

ARCATA—Humboldt County

○ **MAD RIVER COMMUNITY HOSPITAL (050028)**, 3800 Janes Road, Zip 95521-4788, Mailing Address: P.O. Box 1115, Zip 95518-1115; tel. 707/822-3621, (Nonreporting) **A**10 11
Primary Contact: Douglas A. Shaw, Chief Executive Officer
CFO: Michael Young, Chief Financial Officer
CMO: Bonnie MacEvoy, Chief of Staff
CIO: Jedd Rudd, Director of Ancillary Services and Safety
CNO: Sara Isaacson, Chief Nursing Officer
Web address: www.madriverhospital.com
Control: Corporation, Investor-owned (for-profit) **Service**: General medical and surgical

Staffed Beds: 42

ARROYO GRANDE—San Luis Obispo County

AMI ARROYO GRANDE COMM HOSP See Arroyo Grande Community Hospital

ATASCADERO—San Luis Obispo County

☐ **ATASCADERO STATE HOSPITAL**, 10333 El Camino Real, Zip 93422-5808, Mailing Address: P.O. Box 7001, Zip 93423-7001; tel. 805/468-2000, (Nonreporting) **A**1 3
Primary Contact: Melvin Hunter, Hospital Administrator
COO: David Landrum, Chief Police Services
CFO: Janie Pagnini, Administrator Accounting
CMO: David Fennell, M.D., Acting Medical Director
CIO: James Grover, Manager Data Processing
CHR: Elizabeth Andres, Director Human Resources
CNO: Liz Souza, Coordinator Nursing Services
Web address: www.dmh.ca.gov/statehospitals/atascadero
Control: State, Government, Nonfederal **Service**: Psychiatric

Staffed Beds: 1184

AUBURN—Placer County

☒ **SUTTER AUBURN FAITH HOSPITAL (050498)**, 11815 Education Street, Zip 95602-2410; tel. 530/888-4500, **A**1 2 5 10 **F**3 8 11 12 15 17 18 20 28 29 30 31 34 35 37 39 40 44 47 49 50 57 58 59 62 63 64 68 70 74 75 78 79 81 85 86 87 93 107 108 110 111 114 115 117 119 120 121 123 124 126 130 131 132 135 146 147 148 149 154 164 **S** Sutter Health, Sacramento, CA
Primary Contact: Shanthi Margoschis, MSN, R.N., Chief Executive Officer
CFO: Gary Hubschman, Administrative Director Finance
CMO: John Mesic, M.D., Chief Medical Officer
CIO: Tom Ream, Regional Chief Information Officer
CHR: Yvette Martinez, Director Human Resources
CNO: Katrina Holmes, Chief Nursing Officer
Web address: www.sutterhealth.org
Control: Other not-for-profit (including NFP Corporation) **Service**: General medical and surgical

Staffed Beds: 64 **Admissions**: 3378 **Census**: 35 **Outpatient Visits**: 63341 **Births**: 0 **Total Expense ($000)**: 173242 **Payroll Expense ($000)**: 55634 **Personnel**: 464

AVALON—Los Angeles County

★ **CATALINA ISLAND MEDICAL CENTER (051307)**, 100 Falls Canyon Road, Zip 90704, Mailing Address: P.O. Box 1563, Zip 90704-1563; tel. 310/510-0700, (Nonreporting) **A**10 18
Primary Contact: Jason Paret, Chief Executive Officer
COO: Stacie Amarantos, Chief Operating Officer
CFO: John Lovrich, Chief Financial Officer
CMO: Laura Ulibarri, M.D., Chief of Staff
CIO: Leah Keeline, Clinical Informatics Specialist
CHR: Lilly Hernandez, Human Resources Director
CNO: Stacie Amarantos, Chief Operating Officer
Web address: www.catalinaislandmedicalcenter.org
Control: Other not-for-profit (including NFP Corporation) **Service**: General medical and surgical

Staffed Beds: 12

BAKERSFIELD—Kern County

☒ **ADVENTIST HEALTH BAKERSFIELD (050455)**, 2615 Chester Avenue, Zip 93301-2014, Mailing Address: P.O. Box 2615, Zip 93303-2615; tel. 661/395-3000, (Includes ADVENTIST HEALTH SPECIALTY BAKERSFIELD, 3001 Sillect Avenue, Bakersfield, California, Zip 93308-6337, tel. 661/316-6000; Jason Wells, FACHE, President, Central California Network, Adventist Health) (Nonreporting) **A**1 2 3 10 **S** Adventist Health, Roseville, CA
Primary Contact: Jason Wells, FACHE, President, Central California Network, Adventist Health
CFO: Brent Soper, Chief Financial Officer
CHR: Marlene Kreidler, Executive Director Human Resources
Web address: https://www.adventisthealth.org/bakersfield/
Control: Church operated, Nongovernment, not-for-profit **Service**: General medical and surgical

Staffed Beds: 254

☐ **BAKERSFIELD BEHAVIORAL HEALTHCARE HOSPITAL (054155)**, 5201 White Lane, Zip 93309; tel. 877/755-4907, (Nonreporting) **A**1 10 **S** Signature Healthcare Services, Corona, CA
Primary Contact: Maureen Womack, Chief Executive Officer
Web address: https://www.bakersfieldbehavioral.com/
Control: Corporation, Investor-owned (for-profit) **Service**: Psychiatric

Staffed Beds: 60

BAKERSFIELD HEART HOSPITAL See Adventist Health Specialty Bakersfield

☒ **BAKERSFIELD MEMORIAL HOSPITAL (050036)**, 420 34th Street, Zip 93301-2237; tel. 661/327-1792, **A**1 3 5 10 13 **F**3 11 13 15 16 17 18 20 22 24 26 28 29 30 31 37 40 45 50 58 60 68 70 72 74 75 76 77 78 79 81 84 85 86 88 89 93 107 108 109 111 114 115 119 120 124 126 130 146 147 148 149 152 156 160 **S** CommonSpirit Health, Chicago, IL
Primary Contact: Ken Keller, President/Chief Executive Officer
CMO: Rodney Mark Root, D.O., Vice President Medical Affairs
CHR: Sheri Comaianni, Vice President Human Resources
Web address: www.bakersfieldmemorial.org
Control: Other not-for-profit (including NFP Corporation) **Service**: General medical and surgical

Staffed Beds: 385 **Admissions**: 16306 **Census**: 199 **Outpatient Visits**: 130816 **Births**: 3351 **Total Expense ($000)**: 570125 **Payroll Expense ($000)**: 216466 **Personnel**: 1683

Hospitals, U.S. / CALIFORNIA

☐ **BAKERSFIELD REHABILITATION HOSPITAL (053044)**, 4400 Kirkcaldy Drive, Zip 93306–5542; tel. 661/374–7105, (Nonreporting) **A**1 10 **S** Ernest Health, Inc., Albuquerque, NM
Primary Contact: Shayne Perkovich, Chief Executive Officer
CMO: Adam Klang, M.D., Chief Medical Officer
CNO: Yolanda Rodriguez, Chief Nursing Officer
Web address: https://bakersfieldrehab.com/
Control: Corporation, Investor–owned (for–profit) **Service:** Rehabilitation

Staffed Beds: 50

✠ **ENCOMPASS HEALTH REHABILITATION HOSPITAL OF BAKERSFIELD (053031)**, 5001 Commerce Drive, Zip 93309–0689; tel. 661/323–5500, (Nonreporting) **A**1 10 **S** Encompass Health Corporation, Birmingham, AL
Primary Contact: Martha Samora Esq, R.N., FACHE, Chief Executive Officer
CFO: Robert Mosesian, Controller
CMO: Chris Yoon, M.D., Medical Director
CHR: Lori Brackett, Director Human Resources
CNO: Kathleen Szura, R.N., Chief Nursing Officer
Web address: www.healthsouthbakersfield.com
Control: Corporation, Investor–owned (for–profit) **Service:** Rehabilitation

Staffed Beds: 70

☐ **GOOD SAMARITAN HOSPITAL (050257)**, 901 Olive Drive, Zip 93308–4144, Mailing Address: P.O. Box 85002, Zip 93380–5002; tel. 661/215–7500, **A**1 3 10 **F**3 5 45 46 47 48 49 60 64 65 75 81 82 85 87 98 100 103 107 114 115 118 119 127 130 135 146 147 148 149 152 154 160 164 **P**1
Primary Contact: Minty Dillon, Chief Executive Officer
CFO: Gerrie Halbrook, Chief Financial Officer
CMO: Matab Singh, Chief of Staff
CNO: Toby Davis, Chief Nursing Officer
Web address: www.goodsamhospital.com
Control: Partnership, Investor–owned (for–profit) **Service:** General medical and surgical

Staffed Beds: 60 **Admissions:** 3008 **Census:** 32 **Outpatient Visits:** 15622 **Births:** 0 **Total Expense ($000):** 38929 **Payroll Expense ($000):** 17801 **Personnel:** 314

☐ **KERN MEDICAL (050315)**, 1700 Mount Vernon Avenue, Zip 93306–4018; tel. 661/326–2000, (Nonreporting) **A**1 2 3 5 10
Primary Contact: Scott Thygerson, Chief Executive Officer
COO: Jared Leavitt, Chief Operating Officer
CFO: Andrew Cantu, Chief Financial Officer
CMO: Glenn Goldis, Chief Medical Officer
CHR: Lisa K. Hockersmith, Vice President Human Resources
CNO: Toni Smith, Chief Nursing Officer
Web address: www.kernmedical.com
Control: County, Government, Nonfederal **Service:** General medical and surgical

Staffed Beds: 188

✠ **MERCY HOSPITAL DOWNTOWN (050295)**, 2215 Truxtun Avenue, Zip 93301–3698, Mailing Address: P.O. Box 119, Zip 93302–0119; tel. 661/632–5000, (Includes MERCY SOUTHWEST HOSPITAL, 400 Old River Road, Bakersfield, California, Zip 93311, tel. 661/663–6000) **A**1 3 10 **F**3 11 12 13 15 26 29 30 31 34 35 36 40 44 45 46 47 48 51 54 57 59 62 64 65 68 69 70 71 72 74 75 76 77 78 79 81 84 85 86 87 92 97 100 101 102 107 108 110 111 112 113 114 115 116 117 118 119 120 121 122 124 126 130 131 132 135 146 147 148 149 154 167 168 **S** CommonSpirit Health, Chicago, IL
Primary Contact: BJ Predum, FACHE, President/Chief Executive Officer
CIO: Jeff Vague, Regional Manager Information Systems
CHR: Jay King, Vice President Human Resources
Web address: www.mercybakersfield.org
Control: Other not–for–profit (including NFP Corporation) **Service:** General medical and surgical

Staffed Beds: 229 **Admissions:** 11145 **Census:** 123 **Outpatient Visits:** 83089 **Births:** 2407 **Total Expense ($000):** 383669 **Payroll Expense ($000):** 145303 **Personnel:** 1287

MERCY HOSPITALS OF BAKERSFIELD See Mercy Hospital Downtown

BALDWIN PARK—Los Angeles County

✠ **KAISER PERMANENTE BALDWIN PARK MEDICAL CENTER (050723)**, 1011 Baldwin Park Boulevard, Zip 91706–5806; tel. 626/851–1011, **A**1 3 5 10 **F**3 5 7 8 13 15 18 29 30 31 34 35 36 38 40 44 45 46 47 49 50 51 54 55 56 57 58 59 60 61 62 63 64 65 66 68 70 72 74 75 76 77 78 79 81 82 83 84 85 86 87 91 94 97 101 102 104 107 108 110 111 113 114 117 119 121 129 130 132 134 135 143 144 146 147 148 149 150 154 156 157 160 161 162 164 165 166 167 168 169 **P**6 **S** Kaiser Foundation Hospitals, Oakland, CA
Primary Contact: Eugene Cho, Senior Vice President/Area Manager, Baldwin Park
COO: Jagdip Kaur Gill, Chief Operating Officer
CMO: Vu Thuy Nguyen, M.D., Medical Director
CIO: William Sawtell, Information Technology Leader
CNO: Leila Ibushi–Thompson, MSN, R.N., Chief Nurse Executive
Web address: www.kp.org
Control: Other not–for–profit (including NFP Corporation) **Service:** General medical and surgical

Staffed Beds: 271 **Admissions:** 10781 **Census:** 127 **Outpatient Visits:** 394309 **Births:** 3276 **Personnel:** 2358

✠ **KINDRED HOSPITAL–BALDWIN PARK (052045)**, 14148 Francisquito Avenue, Zip 91706–6120; tel. 626/388–2700, (Nonreporting) **A**1 3 10 **S** ScionHealth, Louisville, KY
Primary Contact: Kevin Chavez, Central District Chief Executive Officer
COO: Dina Garrow, Chief Nursing Officer and Chief Operating Officer
CFO: Christine Saltonstall, Chief Financial Officer
CMO: Anil Gupta, M.D., Chief of Staff
CHR: Antoinette Bibal, Director Human Resources
CNO: Dina Garrow, Chief Nursing Officer and Chief Operating Officer
Web address: www.khbaldwinpark.com
Control: Corporation, Investor–owned (for–profit) **Service:** Acute long–term care hospital

Staffed Beds: 91

BANNING—Riverside County

★ **SAN GORGONIO MEMORIAL HOSPITAL (050054)**, 600 North Highland Springs Avenue, Zip 92220–3046; tel. 951/845–1121, (Nonreporting) **A**3 10 22
Primary Contact: Steven R. Barron Esq, Chief Executive Officer
CFO: David Recupero, Chief Financial Officer
CIO: Duane Cicchelli, Director, Information Technology Services
CHR: Annah Karam, Chief Human Resources Officer
CNO: Pat Brown, R.N., Chief Nursing Officer
Web address: www.sgmh.org
Control: Hospital district or authority, Government, Nonfederal **Service:** General medical and surgical

Staffed Beds: 79

BARSTOW—San Bernardino County

☐ **BARSTOW COMMUNITY HOSPITAL (050298)**, 820 East Mountain View Street, Zip 92311–3004; tel. 760/256–1761, (Nonreporting) **A**1 10 20 **S** Quorum Health, Brentwood, TN
Primary Contact: Adam Loris, Chief Executive Officer
CFO: Shawn Curtis, Chief Financial Officer
CIO: Scott Bullock, Director Information Systems
CNO: Donna M Smith, Chief Nursing Officer
Web address: www.barstowhospital.com
Control: Corporation, Investor–owned (for–profit) **Service:** General medical and surgical

Staffed Beds: 34

BERKELEY—Alameda County

✠ **ALTA BATES SUMMIT MEDICAL CENTER–ALTA BATES CAMPUS (050305)**, 2450 Ashby Avenue, Zip 94705–2067; tel. 510/204–4444, (Includes ALTA BATES MEDICAL CENTER–HERRICK CAMPUS, 2001 Dwight Way, Berkeley, California, Zip 94704, tel. 510/204–4444) **A**1 3 5 10 **F**3 8 11 13 15 17 18 28 29 30 31 34 35 36 37 40 46 47 49 51 55 56 57 58 59 60 61 64 70 71 72 73 74 75 76 77 78 79 81 82 84 85 86 89 93 95 98 99 100 101 102 103 104 105 107 108 109 110 111 114 116 117 118 119 120 121 123 124 126 130 131 132 135 136 141 146 147 148 149 154 156 164 167 169 **S** Sutter Health, Sacramento, CA
Primary Contact: David D. Clark, FACHE, Area Chief Executive Officer, Sutter East Bay Hospitals
CFO: Robert Petrina, Chief Financial Officer
CMO: John Gentile, M.D., Vice President Medical Affairs
Web address: www.altabatessummit.org/
Control: Other not–for–profit (including NFP Corporation) **Service:** General medical and surgical

Staffed Beds: 403 **Admissions:** 13131 **Census:** 202 **Outpatient Visits:** 184571 **Births:** 4065 **Total Expense ($000):** 799991 **Payroll Expense ($000):** 236690 **Personnel:** 1269

Hospital, Medicare Provider Number, Address, Telephone, Approval, Facility, and Physician Codes, Health Care System

★ American Hospital Association (AHA) membership ○ Healthcare Facilities Accreditation Program ⇑ Center for Improvement in Healthcare Quality Accreditation
☐ The Joint Commission accreditation ◇ DNV Healthcare Inc. accreditation △ Commission on Accreditation of Rehabilitation Facilities (CARF) accreditation

© 2025 AHA Guide   Hospitals **A57**

Hospitals, U.S. / CALIFORNIA

HERRICK HOSPITAL & HLTH CENTER See Alta Bates Medical Center–Herrick Campus

BIG BEAR LAKE—San Bernardino County

★ **BEAR VALLEY COMMUNITY HOSPITAL (051335)**, 41870 Garstin Drive, Zip 92315, Mailing Address: P.O. Box 1649, Zip 92315–1649; tel. 909/866–6501, (Nonreporting) **A**10 18 **S** Ovation Healthcare, Brentwood, TN
Primary Contact: Evan J. Rayner, Chief Executive Officer
CFO: Garth Hamblin, Chief Financial Officer
CMO: Steven Knapik, M.D., Chief of Staff
CHR: Erin Wilson, Human Resource Director
CNO: Kerri Jex, R.N., Chief Nursing Officer
Web address: www.bvchd.com
Control: Hospital district or authority, Government, Nonfederal **Service:** General medical and surgical

Staffed Beds: 30

BISHOP—Inyo County

✠ **NORTHERN INYO HOSPITAL (051324)**, 150 Pioneer Lane, Zip 93514–2599; tel. 760/873–5811, **A**1 5 10 18 **F**3 11 13 15 31 34 40 44 45 46 47 54 64 68 70 76 77 79 81 85 89 93 104 107 108 110 111 115 118 119 126 127 130 133 145 147 148 149 154 160 167 169
Primary Contact: Stephen DelRossi, Chief Executive Officer
COO: Kelli Huntsinger, Chief Operating Officer
CMO: William Timbers, M.D., Interim Chief Medical Officer
CIO: Adam Taylor, Manager Information Technology
CHR: Georgan L. Stottlemyre, Chief Human Relations Officer
CNO: Tracy Aspel, Chief Nursing Officer
Web address: www.nih.org
Control: Hospital district or authority, Government, Nonfederal **Service:** General medical and surgical

Staffed Beds: 25 **Admissions:** 820 **Census:** 6 **Outpatient Visits:** 95956 **Births:** 202 **Total Expense ($000):** 121008 **Payroll Expense ($000):** 69866

BLYTHE—Riverside County

✠ **PALO VERDE HOSPITAL (050423)**, 250 North First Street, Zip 92225–1702; tel. 760/922–4115, (Nonreporting) **A**10 21
Primary Contact: Sandra J. Anaya, R.N., Chief Executive Officer
CFO: Christa Ronde, Assistant Chief Financial Officer
CMO: Hossain Sahlolbei, M.D., Chief of Staff
CIO: Jerome Learson, Manager Information Technology and Chief Security Officer
CHR: Myrna Davis, Manager Human Resources
CNO: Nena Foreman, Chief Nursing Officer
Web address: www.paloverdehospital.org
Control: Hospital district or authority, Government, Nonfederal **Service:** General medical and surgical

Staffed Beds: 51

BRAWLEY—Imperial County

✠ **PIONEERS MEMORIAL HEALTHCARE DISTRICT (050342)**, 207 West Legion Road, Zip 92227–7780; tel. 760/351–3333, (Nonreporting) **A**3 10 21
Primary Contact: Carly Loper, Acting Chief Executive Officer
COO: Stephen J Campbell, Chief Operating Officer
CFO: Carly Loper, Chief Financial Officer
CMO: Kestutis V Kuraitis, M.D., Chief of Staff
CIO: Kathleen S. McKernan, Director Information Systems
CHR: Julie Cunningham, Associate Administrator and Chief Human Resources Officer
CNO: Robyn Atadero, R.N., Chief Nursing Officer
Web address: www.pmhd.org
Control: Hospital district or authority, Government, Nonfederal **Service:** General medical and surgical

Staffed Beds: 107

BREA—Orange County

✠ **KINDRED HOSPITAL–BREA (052039)**, 875 North Brea Boulevard, Zip 92821–2699; tel. 714/529–6842, (Nonreporting) **A**1 10 **S** ScionHealth, Louisville, KY
Primary Contact: Kevin Chavez, Central District Chief Executive Officer
COO: Denise Jenkins, Chief Clinical Officer
CFO: John Browne, Assistant Administrator Finance
CMO: Jyotika Wali, M.D., Chief of Staff
Web address: www.kindredhospitalbrea.com/
Control: Corporation, Investor–owned (for-profit) **Service:** Acute long-term care hospital

Staffed Beds: 48

BURBANK—Los Angeles County

✠ △ **PROVIDENCE SAINT JOSEPH MEDICAL CENTER (050235)**, 501 South Buena Vista Street, Zip 91505–4866; tel. 818/843–5111, **A**1 2 3 5 7 10 19 **F**3 11 12 13 15 17 18 20 22 24 26 29 30 31 34 35 36 37 39 40 41 44 45 46 47 48 49 50 51 53 54 55 56 57 58 59 63 64 65 70 72 74 75 76 77 78 79 80 81 82 83 84 85 86 87 88 90 92 93 101 102 107 108 110 111 115 116 117 118 119 120 121 124 126 130 131 132 145 146 147 148 149 154 156 162 164 167 **P**3 5 **S** Providence, Renton, WA
Primary Contact: Karl Keeler, Chief Executive, Los Angeles Valley Service Area
CFO: Glenn Bales, Chief Financial Officer
CMO: Nick Testa, M.D., Chief Medical Officer
CIO: Anne Marie Brody, Director Information Systems Customer Service
CHR: LaDonna Najieb, Service Area Director Human Resources
CNO: Elizabeth Hart, R.N., MSN, Chief Nursing Officer
Web address: www.providence.org
Control: Church operated, Nongovernment, not-for-profit **Service:** General medical and surgical

Staffed Beds: 385 **Admissions:** 15825 **Census:** 196 **Outpatient Visits:** 289056 **Births:** 2173 **Total Expense ($000):** 410332 **Payroll Expense ($000):** 202295 **Personnel:** 1969

BURLINGAME—San Mateo County

MILLS–PENINSULA HEALTH SERVICES See Mills–Peninsula Medical Center

✠ **MILLS–PENINSULA MEDICAL CENTER (050007)**, 1501 Trousdale Drive, Zip 94010–3282; tel. 650/696–5400, (Includes MILLS HEALTH CENTER, 100 South San Mateo Drive, San Mateo, California, Zip 94401, tel. 650/696–4400; Darian Harris, Chief Executive Officer; MILLS-PENINSULA MEDICAL CENTER, 1501 Trousdale DR, Burlingame, California, Zip 94010–4506, 1501 Trousdale Drive, Zip 94010–3205, tel. 650/696–5400; Darian Harris, Chief Executive Officer) **A**1 2 3 10 **F**3 5 8 11 12 13 15 18 20 22 28 29 30 31 34 35 36 37 40 44 45 46 47 48 49 50 51 54 55 57 58 59 61 64 65 70 72 73 74 75 76 77 78 79 81 84 85 86 87 91 93 96 98 99 100 101 102 104 105 107 110 111 114 115 116 117 118 119 120 121 123 124 130 131 132 145 146 147 148 149 153 154 156 164 165 167 169 **S** Sutter Health, Sacramento, CA
Primary Contact: Darian Harris, Chief Executive Officer
COO: Dolores S. Gomez, R.N., Chief Operating Officer
CFO: Catherine Messman, Chief Financial Officer
CIO: Michael Reandeau, Chief Information Officer
CHR: Claudia Christensen, Director, Human Resources
CNO: Vicki White, R.N., MS, Chief Nurse Executive
Web address: www.mills-peninsula.org
Control: Other not-for-profit (including NFP Corporation) **Service:** General medical and surgical

Staffed Beds: 240 **Admissions:** 12810 **Census:** 169 **Outpatient Visits:** 354234 **Births:** 1422 **Total Expense ($000):** 742329 **Payroll Expense ($000):** 190541 **Personnel:** 1439

PENINSULA HOSPITAL See Mills–Peninsula Medical Center

CAMP PENDLETON—San Diego County

✠ **NAVAL HOSPITAL CAMP PENDLETON**, 200 Mercy Circle, Zip 92055–5191, Mailing Address: P.O. Box 555191, Zip 92055–5191; tel. 760/725–1304, (Nonreporting) **A**1 3 5 **S** Bureau of Medicine and Surgery, Department of the Navy, Falls Church, VA
Primary Contact: Jenny S. Burkett, USN, Director
CFO: Commander Gordon Blighton, Director Resource Management
CIO: Gabe Vallido, Chief Information Officer
CHR: Lieutenant Jet Ramos, Head Staff Administration
Web address: https://camp-pendleton.tricare.mil/
Control: Navy, Government, federal **Service:** General medical and surgical

Staffed Beds: 72

CANOGA PARK—Los Angeles County, See Los Angeles

CARMICHAEL—Sacramento County

✠ **MERCY SAN JUAN MEDICAL CENTER (050516)**, 6501 Coyle Avenue, Zip 95608–0306; tel. 916/537–5000, **A**1 2 3 5 10 **F**3 8 11 12 13 17 18 20 22 24 26 29 30 31 34 35 36 37 40 43 44 45 46 47 48 49 55 59 62 63 64 65 68 70 72 76 89 100 101 102 104 130 160 162 164 **S** CommonSpirit Health, Chicago, IL
Primary Contact: Michael Korpiel, President
COO: Paul R Luehrs, Chief Operating Officer
CFO: Robert Pascuzzi, Chief Financial Officer
CMO: Mark Owens, M.D., Vice President Medical Affairs
CHR: Donna Utley, Vice President Human Resources
Web address: www.mercysanjuan.org
Control: Church operated, Nongovernment, not-for-profit **Service:** General medical and surgical

Staffed Beds: 384 **Admissions:** 20074 **Census:** 274 **Outpatient Visits:** 90232 **Births:** 1509 **Total Expense ($000):** 756277 **Payroll Expense ($000):** 304666 **Personnel:** 1848

Hospitals, U.S. / CALIFORNIA

CASTRO VALLEY—Alameda County

☒ **EDEN MEDICAL CENTER (050488)**, 20103 Lake Chabot Road, Zip 94546–5305; tel. 510/537–1234, **A**1 2 3 5 10 **F**3 11 13 15 18 29 30 31 34 35 38 40 43 45 46 47 49 50 51 54 57 58 59 64 65 70 74 75 76 77 78 79 81 84 85 86 87 107 108 110 111 115 117 118 119 120 121 123 124 126 130 131 132 135 144 146 148 149 154 158 164 167 169 **S** Sutter Health, Sacramento, CA
Primary Contact: Shannon Thomas, Chief Executive Officer
Web address: www.edenmedcenter.org
Control: Other not–for–profit (including NFP Corporation) **Service:** General medical and surgical

Staffed Beds: 130 **Admissions:** 8654 **Census:** 117 **Outpatient Visits:** 72462 **Births:** 1134 **Total Expense ($000):** 409120 **Payroll Expense ($000):** 134754 **Personnel:** 1123

CEDARVILLE—Modoc County

★ **SURPRISE VALLEY HEALTH CARE DISTRICT (051308)**, 741 North Main Street, Zip 96104, Mailing Address: P.O. Box 246, Zip 96104–0246; tel. 530/279–6111, (Nonreporting) **A**10 18
Primary Contact: Frances Hannah, Administrator/Financial Manager/CPT/AMB Operator
CFO: Renae Sweet, Chief Financial Officer
CMO: Chuck Colas, M.D., Medical Director
CHR: William Bostic, Administrative Assistant Human Resources
Web address: https://sites.google.com/view/s-v-health-care-district/home
Control: Hospital district or authority, Government, Nonfederal **Service:** General medical and surgical

Staffed Beds: 26

CERRITOS—Los Angeles County

☐ **COLLEGE HOSPITAL CERRITOS (054055)**, 10802 College Place, Zip 90703–1579; tel. 562/924–9581, (Nonreporting) **A**1 10 **S** College Health Enterprises, Santa Fe Springs, CA
Primary Contact: Stephen Witt, Chief Executive Officer
CFO: Roderick Bell, Chief Financial Officer
CHR: Holly Risha, Administrative Director Human Resources
Web address: www.collegehospitals.com
Control: Corporation, Investor–owned (for–profit) **Service:** Psychiatric

Staffed Beds: 187

CHESTER—Plumas County

★ **SENECA HEALTHCARE DISTRICT (051327)**, 130 Brentwood Drive, Zip 96020–0737, Mailing Address: P.O. Box 737, Zip 96020–0737; tel. 530/258–2151, (Nonreporting) **A**10 18
Primary Contact: Shawn McKenzie, Chief Executive Officer
CFO: Steve Boline, Chief Financial Officer
CMO: Dana Ware, M.D., Chief of Staff
CIO: Elizabeth Steffen, Director Information Technology
CHR: James Kooyman, Human Resources Manager
CNO: Karen Turner, Chief Nursing Officer
Web address: www.senecahospital.org
Control: Hospital district or authority, Government, Nonfederal **Service:** General medical and surgical

Staffed Beds: 26

CHICO—Butte County

CHICO COMMUNITY HOSPITAL See Enloe Medical Center–Cohasset

☒ **ENLOE HEALTH (050039)**, 1531 Esplanade, Zip 95926–3386; tel. 530/332–7300, (Includes ENLOE MEDICAL CENTER–COHASSET, 560 Cohasset Road, Chico, California, Zip 95926, tel. 530/332–7300) **A**1 2 3 10 **F**3 7 8 11 12 13 15 17 18 19 20 22 24 26 28 29 30 31 33 34 35 36 38 39 40 43 44 45 46 49 50 51 54 55 57 59 62 63 64 65 68 69 70 73 74 75 76 77 78 79 80 81 82 83 84 85 87 89 90 91 92 93 94 96 97 98 100 102 107 108 109 111 114 115 116 117 118 119 120 121 123 124 126 130 131 132 143 144 146 147 148 149 154 155 156 157 164 167 169
Primary Contact: Mike C. Wiltermood, President and Chief Executive Officer
CMO: Forrest Olson, M.D., Chief Medical Officer
CHR: Carol Linscheid, Vice President Human Resources
Web address: www.enloe.org
Control: Other not–for–profit (including NFP Corporation) **Service:** General medical and surgical

Staffed Beds: 255 **Admissions:** 17990 **Census:** 223 **Outpatient Visits:** 409601 **Births:** 1848 **Total Expense ($000):** 842665 **Payroll Expense ($000):** 269287 **Personnel:** 3298

ENLOE MEDICAL CENTER See Enloe Health

CHINO—San Bernardino County

☒ **CANYON RIDGE HOSPITAL (054111)**, 5353 'G' Street, Zip 91710–5250; tel. 909/590–3700, (Nonreporting) **A**1 3 10 **S** Universal Health Services, Inc., King of Prussia, PA
Primary Contact: Stephanie Bernier, Chief Executive Officer
CFO: Burt Harris, Chief Financial Officer
CMO: Mir Ali–Khan, M.D., Medical Director
CIO: Maria Patterson, Manager Health Information Management
CHR: Ericca Lopez, Director Human Resources
Web address: www.canyonridgehospital.com
Control: Corporation, Investor–owned (for–profit) **Service:** Psychiatric

Staffed Beds: 157

○ **CHINO VALLEY MEDICAL CENTER (050586)**, 5451 Walnut Avenue, Zip 91710–2672; tel. 909/464–8600, **A**3 5 10 11 12 13 **F**3 18 20 22 29 30 35 40 45 46 49 50 68 70 79 81 84 85 97 107 108 110 111 114 115 119 120 130 146 148 149 154 167 **S** Prime Healthcare, Ontario, CA
Primary Contact: Gail Aviado, MSN, R.N., Chief Executive Officer/Interim CEO of Chino Valley Medical Center
CIO: Vic Mahan, Chief Information Officer
Web address: www.cvmc.com
Control: Corporation, Investor–owned (for–profit) **Service:** General medical and surgical

Staffed Beds: 112 **Admissions:** 4028 **Census:** 39 **Outpatient Visits:** 42290 **Births:** 0 **Total Expense ($000):** 81133 **Payroll Expense ($000):** 33514 **Personnel:** 481

CHOWCHILLA—Madera County

CHOWCHILLA DISTRICT MEMORIAL HOSPITAL See Chowchilla Skilled Nursing and Rehabilitation Facillity

CHULA VISTA—San Diego County

BAYVIEW HOSP & MENTAL SYSTEM See Bayview Behavioral Health Campus

SCRIPPS MEMORIAL HOSPITAL See Scripps Mercy Hospital Chula Vista

SCRIPPS MERCY HOSPITAL CHULA VISTA See Scripps Mercy Hospital, San Diego

☒ **SHARP CHULA VISTA MEDICAL CENTER (050222)**, 751 Medical Center Court, Zip 91911–6699; tel. 619/502–5800, (Total facility includes 100 beds in nursing home–type unit) **A**1 2 10 **F**3 8 11 13 17 18 20 22 24 26 28 29 30 31 34 35 37 40 45 46 47 48 49 51 57 59 60 65 68 70 72 74 75 76 77 78 79 81 82 84 85 86 87 93 100 102 107 114 119 120 121 124 126 128 130 143 146 147 148 149 154 156 157 167 **S** Sharp HealthCare, San Diego, CA
Primary Contact: Scott Evans, PharmD, Senior Vice President/Market Chief Executive Officer, Sharp HealthCare Regional Hospitals
CMO: Lynn Welling, M.D., Chief Medical Officer
CHR: Zoe Gardner, Manager Human Resources
Web address: www.sharp.com
Control: Other not–for–profit (including NFP Corporation) **Service:** General medical and surgical

Staffed Beds: 449 **Admissions:** 18716 **Census:** 324 **Outpatient Visits:** 169303 **Births:** 2606 **Total Expense ($000):** 606129 **Payroll Expense ($000):** 254688 **Personnel:** 2394

CLEARLAKE—Lake County

☒ **ADVENTIST HEALTH CLEAR LAKE (051317)**, 15630 18th Avenue, Zip 95422–9336, Mailing Address: P.O. Box 6710, Zip 95422; tel. 707/994–6486, (Nonreporting) **A**1 10 18 **S** Adventist Health, Roseville, CA
Primary Contact: Eric Stevens, Interim President
CFO: Carlton Jacobson, Vice President of Finance
CMO: Marc Shapiro, M.D., Chief Medical Officer
CIO: Cambria Wheeler, Communications and Marketing
CHR: Audrey Barrall, Director Human Resources
Web address: www.adventisthealth.org
Control: Church operated, Nongovernment, not–for–profit **Service:** General medical and surgical

Staffed Beds: 25

Hospital, Medicare Provider Number, Address, Telephone, Approval, Facility, and Physician Codes, Health Care System

★ American Hospital Association (AHA) membership ○ Healthcare Facilities Accreditation Program ⇧ Center for Improvement in Healthcare Quality Accreditation
☐ The Joint Commission accreditation ◇ DNV Healthcare Inc. accreditation △ Commission on Accreditation of Rehabilitation Facilities (CARF) accreditation

Hospitals, U.S. / CALIFORNIA

CLOVIS—Fresno County

☐ **CLOVIS COMMUNITY MEDICAL CENTER (050492)**, 2755 Herndon Avenue, Zip 93611–6801; tel. 559/324–4000, **A**1 2 3 10 **F**3 12 13 15 17 18 20 22 24 26 29 30 31 34 35 36 37 38 40 41 44 45 46 47 49 50 51 55 57 58 59 60 64 65 68 70 73 74 75 76 77 78 79 81 84 85 86 87 93 96 97 100 102 104 107 108 110 111 115 116 117 118 119 120 121 123 124 126 130 131 132 141 146 148 149 154 167 169 **S** Community Medical Centers, Fresno, CA
Primary Contact: Craig S. Castro, President and Chief Executive Officer, Community Health Systems
CFO: Tracy Kiritani, Vice President and Chief Financial Officer
CIO: George Vasquez, Chief Technology Officer
CHR: Ginny Burdick, Senior Vice President and Chief Human Resources Officer
Web address: www.communitymedical.org
Control: Other not–for–profit (including NFP Corporation) **Service**: General medical and surgical

Staffed Beds: 352 **Admissions**: 19058 **Census**: 265 **Outpatient Visits**: 122770 **Births**: 4395 **Total Expense ($000)**: 724856 **Payroll Expense ($000)**: 243638 **Personnel**: 2320

COLTON—San Bernardino County

✠ **ARROWHEAD REGIONAL MEDICAL CENTER (050245)**, 400 North Pepper Avenue, Zip 92324–1819; tel. 909/580–1000, **A**1 3 5 10 13 19 **F**3 5 8 15 16 18 20 22 28 29 30 31 32 34 35 36 39 40 43 45 47 49 50 51 52 54 55 56 57 60 64 66 68 70 71 72 74 75 76 77 78 79 81 82 84 85 86 87 89 91 92 93 97 98 100 101 102 107 108 110 111 114 115 116 118 119 120 121 130 132 135 146 147 148 149 150 154 160 **P**5
Primary Contact: Andrew Goldfrach, Chief Executive Officer
CFO: Arvind Oswal, Chief Financial Officer
CMO: Sam Hessami, M.D., Chief Medical Officer
CIO: Adam McCartney, Chief Information Officer
CHR: Rudy Rodriguez, Human Resources Director
CNO: Nanette Buenavidez, Chief Nursing Officer
Web address: https://www.arrowheadregional.org/
Control: County, Government, Nonfederal **Service**: General medical and surgical

Staffed Beds: 456 **Admissions**: 20510 **Census**: 366 **Outpatient Visits**: 286927 **Births**: 2142 **Total Expense ($000)**: 940476 **Payroll Expense ($000)**: 302657 **Personnel**: 3705

CONCORD—Contra Costa County

✠ **JOHN MUIR BEHAVIORAL HEALTH CENTER (054131)**, 2740 Grant Street, Zip 94520–2265; tel. 925/674–4100, **A**1 10 **F**2 4 5 29 30 35 38 50 54 64 68 75 98 99 100 102 103 104 105 119 130 132 143 146 149 151 152 153 154 160 162 164 **S** John Muir Health, Walnut Creek, CA
COO: Arman Danielyan, M.D., Chief of Staff
CFO: Christian Pass, Senior Vice President and Chief Financial Officer
CMO: O B Towery, M.D., Chief of Staff
CIO: Jim Wesley, Senior Vice President and Chief Information Officer
CHR: Lisa Foust, Senior Vice President Human Resources
CNO: Cindy Bolter, Chief Nursing and Operations Officer
Web address: www.johnmuirhealth.com
Control: Other not–for–profit (including NFP Corporation) **Service**: Psychiatric

Staffed Beds: 73 **Admissions**: 3128 **Census**: 27 **Outpatient Visits**: 6427 **Births**: 0

✠ **JOHN MUIR HEALTH, CONCORD MEDICAL CENTER (050496)**, 2540 East Street, Zip 94520–1906; tel. 925/682–8200, **A**1 2 3 5 10 **F**3 12 15 17 18 20 22 24 26 28 29 30 31 34 37 39 40 41 44 45 46 47 48 49 50 55 56 57 58 59 60 61 64 68 70 74 75 77 78 79 80 81 82 83 84 85 86 87 93 100 102 107 108 110 115 118 119 120 121 123 126 130 132 141 145 146 148 149 156 157 160 161 167 **P**7 **S** John Muir Health, Walnut Creek, CA
Primary Contact: Michael S. Thomas, President and Chief Executive Officer, John Muir Health
CFO: Christian Pass, Interim Chief Financial Officer
CMO: John Merson, M.D., Chief of Staff
CIO: Jon Russell, Senior Vice President and Chief Information Officer
CHR: Lisa Foust, Senior Vice President Human Resources
CNO: Donna Brackley, R.N., MSN, Senior Vice President Patient Care Services
Web address: www.johnmuirhealth.com
Control: Other not–for–profit (including NFP Corporation) **Service**: General medical and surgical

Staffed Beds: 256 **Admissions**: 11493 **Census**: 160 **Outpatient Visits**: 136069 **Births**: 0 **Total Expense ($000)**: 607807 **Payroll Expense ($000)**: 228921 **Personnel**: 1204

CORONA—Riverside County

CIRCLE CITY MEDICAL CENTER See Corona Regional Medical Center–Rehabilitation

☐ **CORONA REGIONAL MEDICAL CENTER (050329)**, 800 South Main Street, Zip 92882–3400; tel. 951/737–4343, (Includes CORONA REGIONAL MEDICAL CENTER–REHABILITATION, 730 Magnolia Avenue, Corona, California, Zip 92879, tel. 951/736–7200; Sam Itani, Chief Executive Officer) (Nonreporting) **A**1 3 10 **S** Universal Health Services, Inc., King of Prussia, PA
Primary Contact: Alistair M. Machoka, Chief Executive Officer
COO: Morgan Topper, Chief Operating Officer
CMO: Paul Niu, Chief Medical Officer
CIO: De'Niro Pankey, Director Information Systems
CHR: Dale Cole, Director, Human Resources
CNO: Phyllis Snyder, Chief Nursing Officer
Web address: www.coronaregional.com
Control: Corporation, Investor–owned (for–profit) **Service**: General medical and surgical

Staffed Beds: 238

CORONADO—San Diego County

✠ **SHARP CORONADO HOSPITAL (050234)**, 250 Prospect Place, Zip 92118–1999; tel. 619/522–3600, (Total facility includes 105 beds in nursing home-type unit) **A**1 5 10 **F**3 8 11 12 15 18 29 30 34 35 36 37 40 44 45 46 47 49 50 53 56 57 60 64 65 68 70 74 75 77 79 81 82 85 87 93 107 108 111 119 126 128 130 143 146 148 149 154 167 **S** Sharp HealthCare, San Diego, CA
Primary Contact: Scott Evans, PharmD, Senior Vice President/Market Chief Executive Officer, Sharp HealthCare Regional Hospitals
CFO: Victoria Day, Chief Financial Officer and Vice President of Ancillary Services
CHR: Rachel Davis, Director
CNO: Christopher Walker, Chief Nursing Officer and Operating Officer
Web address: https://www.sharp.com/hospitals/coronado/
Control: Other not–for–profit (including NFP Corporation) **Service**: General medical and surgical

Staffed Beds: 155 **Admissions**: 3141 **Census**: 110 **Outpatient Visits**: 93383 **Births**: 0 **Total Expense ($000)**: 154400 **Payroll Expense ($000)**: 68897 **Personnel**: 525

SHARP CORONADO HOSPITAL AND HEALTHCARE CENTER See Sharp Coronado Hospital

COSTA MESA—Orange County

☐ **COLLEGE HOSPITAL COSTA MESA (050543)**, 301 Victoria Street, Zip 92627–7131; tel. 949/642–2734, **A**1 3 10 **F**4 29 35 38 50 54 56 68 81 89 98 99 100 101 102 104 105 107 111 114 119 130 132 134 135 143 144 148 149 153 154 160 162 163 164 165 **S** College Health Enterprises, Santa Fe Springs, CA
Primary Contact: Warren Bradley, Chief Executive Officer
CFO: Dale Bracy, Chief Financial Officer
CMO: Michael Schwartz, M.D., Chief of Staff
CIO: Eladio Aldana, Manager Information Systems
CHR: Sharon DuBruyne, Director Human Resources
Web address: www.collegehospitals.com/cosHome
Control: Individual, Investor–owned (for–profit) **Service**: Psychiatric

Staffed Beds: 157 **Admissions**: 4237 **Census**: 113 **Outpatient Visits**: 12675 **Births**: 0

COVINA—Los Angeles County

☐ **AURORA CHARTER OAK HOSPITAL (054069)**, 1161 East Covina Boulevard, Zip 91724–1599; tel. 626/966–1632, (Nonreporting) **A**1 10 **S** Signature Healthcare Services, Corona, CA
Primary Contact: John Meier, Chief Executive Officer
COO: Sheila Cordova, Director Clinical Services and Chief Operating Officer
CMO: Adib Bitar, M.D., Medical Director
CHR: Christine de la Paz, Director Human Resources
CNO: Sheila Cordova, Chief Operating Officer and Chief Nursing Officer
Web address: www.charteroakhospital.com
Control: Corporation, Investor–owned (for–profit) **Service**: Psychiatric

Staffed Beds: 146

CITRUS VALLEY MEDICAL CENTER–INTER–COMMUNITY CAMPUS See Emanate Health–Inter–Community Hospital

Hospitals, U.S. / CALIFORNIA

☒ △ **EMANATE HEALTH INTER–COMMUNITY HOSPITAL (050382)**, 210 West San Bernadino Road, Zip 91723–1515, Mailing Address: P.O. Box 6108, Zip 91722–5108; tel. 626/331-7331, (Includes EMANATE HEALTH QUEEN OF THE VALLEY HOSPITAL, 1115 South Sunset Avenue, West Covina, California, Zip 91790–3940, P O Box 1980, Zip 91793–1980, tel. 626/962-4011; EMANATE HEALTH–INTER–COMMUNITY HOSPITAL, 210 West San Bernardino Road, Covina, California, Zip 91723-1515, P O Box 6108, Zip 91722–5108, tel. 626/331-7331) **A**1 3 5 7 10 **F**3 11 17 18 22 24 30 40 70 72 76 77 81 89 90 98 99 100 107 108 111 119 120 128 143 146 153 154 **S** Emanate Health, Covina, CA
Primary Contact: Roger Sharma, President/Chief Executive Officer
CIO: Daniel J Nash, Chief Information Officer
CHR: Ryan Burke Esq, Vice President, Human Resources
CNO: Melissa Howard, Chief Nurse Executive, ICH & FPH
Web address: https://www.emanatehealth.org/locations/emanate-health-inter-community-hospital/
Control: Other not–for–profit (including NFP Corporation) **Service**: General medical and surgical

Staffed Beds: 298 **Admissions**: 19823 **Census**: 298 **Outpatient Visits**: 223466 **Births**: 3197 **Total Expense ($000)**: 483512 **Payroll Expense ($000)**: 182896 **Personnel**: 2093

CRESCENT CITY—Del Norte County

☒ **SUTTER COAST HOSPITAL (050417)**, 800 East Washington Boulevard, Zip 95531–8359; tel. 707/464-8511, **A**1 10 20 **F**3 8 11 15 18 29 30 31 34 35 40 43 44 46 47 48 50 54 57 59 62 64 65 68 70 75 76 77 78 79 81 82 84 85 86 87 93 97 107 108 110 111 115 119 127 130 131 132 144 146 147 148 149 154 164 169 **S** Sutter Health, Sacramento, CA
Primary Contact: Michael Lane, Chief Executive Officer
CNO: Rose Corcoran, R.N., Chief Nursing Executive
Web address: www.sutterhealth.org
Control: Other not–for–profit (including NFP Corporation) **Service**: General medical and surgical

Staffed Beds: 49 **Admissions**: 2023 **Census**: 24 **Outpatient Visits**: 97868 **Births**: 205 **Total Expense ($000)**: 106818 **Payroll Expense ($000)**: 32137 **Personnel**: 346

CULVER CITY—Los Angeles County

SOUTHERN CALIFORNIA HOSPITAL AT CULVER CITY (050752), 3828 Delmas Terrace, Zip 90232–6806; tel. 310/836-7000, (Nonreporting) **A**10 **S** Prospect Medical Holdings, Los Angeles, CA
Primary Contact: Omar Ramirez, Chief Operating Officer, California Hospitals
CFO: Vincent Rubin, Chief Financial Officer
CMO: Martha Sonnenberg, M.D., Chief of Staff
CIO: Carrie Bonar, Chief Information Officer
CHR: Betty J Harris, Director Human Resources
Web address: www.sch-culvercity.com
Control: Corporation, Investor–owned (for–profit) **Service**: General medical and surgical

Staffed Beds: 239

DALY CITY—San Mateo County

☐ **AHMC SETON MEDICAL CENTER (050289)**, 1900 Sullivan Avenue, Zip 94015–2229; tel. 650/992-4000, (Nonreporting) **A**1 3 10
Primary Contact: Sarkis Vartanian, Interim Chief Executive Officer
COO: Stephanie Mearns, Vice President Patient Care Services and Chief Nurse Executive
CFO: Richard Wood, Chief Financial Officer
CMO: Timothy Ranney, M.D., Chief Medical Officer
CHR: Patricia White, Vice President Human Resources
CNO: Mark R Brown, Chief Nursing Officer
Web address: https://setonmedicalcenter.com/
Control: Church operated, Nongovernment, not–for–profit **Service**: General medical and surgical

Staffed Beds: 446

SETON MEDICAL CENTER See AHMC Seton Medical Center

DAVIS—Yolo County

☒ **SUTTER DAVIS HOSPITAL (050537)**, 2000 Sutter Place, Zip 95616–6201; tel. 530/756-6440, **A**1 3 5 10 **F**3 8 11 13 15 18 28 29 30 31 34 39 40 45 46 49 51 57 59 64 65 70 74 75 76 78 79 81 84 85 86 87 93 107 108 111 115 119 124 126 130 131 141 142 145 146 147 148 149 154 164 167 169 **S** Sutter Health, Sacramento, CA
Primary Contact: Michael Cureton, FACHE, Chief Executive Officer, Sutter Amador Hospital and Sutter Davis Hospital
CFO: Patti Pilgrim, Chief Financial Officer
CMO: Deven Merchant, M.D., Chief Medical Executive
CHR: Don Hartman, Director Human Resources
CNO: Tamara Davis, R.N., Chief Nurse Executive Officer
Web address: www.sutterhealth.org
Control: Other not–for–profit (including NFP Corporation) **Service**: General medical and surgical

Staffed Beds: 57 **Admissions**: 4064 **Census**: 36 **Outpatient Visits**: 50324 **Births**: 1248 **Total Expense ($000)**: 164501 **Payroll Expense ($000)**: 57668 **Personnel**: 495

DELANO—Kern County

★ ○ **ADVENTIST HEALTH DELANO (050608)**, 1401 Garces Highway, Zip 93215–3690, Mailing Address: P.O. Box 460, Zip 93216–0460; tel. 661/725-4800, (Nonreporting) **A**10 11 **S** Adventist Health, Roseville, CA
Primary Contact: Jason Wells, FACHE, President, Central California Network, Adventist Health
CFO: Bahram Ghaffari, President
CIO: Sandy Bakich, Director Information Management
CHR: Del Garbanzos, Director Human Resources
CNO: Amy Scroggs, Chief Nursing Officer
Web address: www.drmc.com
Control: Other not–for–profit (including NFP Corporation) **Service**: General medical and surgical

Staffed Beds: 100

DOWNEY—Los Angeles County

☒ **KAISER PERMANENTE DOWNEY MEDICAL CENTER (050139)**, 9333 Imperial Highway, Zip 90242–2812; tel. 562/657-9000, **A**1 3 5 10 19 **F**2 3 11 12 14 15 29 30 31 32 33 34 38 39 40 41 44 45 46 47 48 49 50 51 52 53 54 55 56 57 58 59 60 61 62 63 64 65 66 68 70 71 72 74 75 76 77 78 79 81 82 83 84 85 86 87 88 89 93 94 96 97 100 102 104 107 108 110 111 114 115 119 126 129 130 131 132 134 135 141 144 146 147 148 149 150 153 154 156 162 164 165 167 **P**1 6 **S** Kaiser Foundation Hospitals, Oakland, CA
Primary Contact: Mitchell Winnik, FACHE, Senior Vice President, Area Manager, Downey
Web address: www.kaiserpermanente.org
Control: Other not–for–profit (including NFP Corporation) **Service**: General medical and surgical

Staffed Beds: 424 **Admissions**: 18383 **Census**: 232 **Outpatient Visits**: 256031 **Births**: 3762 **Personnel**: 3620

★ **PIH HEALTH DOWNEY HOSPITAL (050393)**, 11500 Brookshire Avenue, Zip 90241–4917; tel. 562/904-5000, **A**3 5 10 12 13 22 **F**3 8 11 15 17 18 20 22 24 29 30 37 38 40 41 45 49 50 51 54 59 60 64 65 68 70 77 79 81 85 87 91 93 94 97 107 108 110 111 115 119 130 131 135 146 148 149 154 157 164 167 **S** PIH Health, Whittier, CA
Primary Contact: James R. West, President and Chief Executive Officer
CFO: Greg Williams, Chief Financial Officer
CIO: Jason Fischer, Chief Information Officer
CHR: Sherri Hollingsworth, Chief Human Resources Officer
Web address: www.PIHHealth.org
Control: Other not–for–profit (including NFP Corporation) **Service**: General medical and surgical

Staffed Beds: 95 **Admissions**: 8565 **Census**: 88 **Outpatient Visits**: 109096 **Births**: 0 **Total Expense ($000)**: 190148 **Payroll Expense ($000)**: 81848 **Personnel**: 1075

PIH HEALTH HOSPITAL – DOWNEY See PIH Health Downey Hospital

Hospital, Medicare Provider Number, Address, Telephone, Approval, Facility, and Physician Codes, Health Care System

★ American Hospital Association (AHA) membership   ○ Healthcare Facilities Accreditation Program   ⇑ Center for Improvement in Healthcare Quality Accreditation
☐ The Joint Commission accreditation   ◇ DNV Healthcare Inc. accreditation   △ Commission on Accreditation of Rehabilitation Facilities (CARF) accreditation

Hospitals, U.S. / CALIFORNIA

☐ △ **RANCHO LOS AMIGOS NATIONAL REHABILITATION CENTER (050717)**, 7601 East Imperial Highway, Zip 90242-3496; tel. 562/401-7111, **A**1 3 5 7 10 **F**3 6 8 9 12 18 20 26 28 29 30 32 34 35 36 37 38 39 44 45 50 51 53 54 56 57 58 59 64 65 66 68 70 71 74 75 77 79 81 82 84 85 86 87 90 91 92 93 94 95 96 97 100 107 108 111 113 114 115 118 119 130 132 135 143 146 147 148 149 150 154 156 157 160 164 167 **P**6 **S** Los Angeles County–Department of Health Services, Los Angeles, CA
Primary Contact: Aries J. Limbaga, R.N., Chief Executive Officer, Rancho Los Amigos National Rehabilitation Center/System Chief Nursing Offic
COO: Benjamin Ovando, Chief Operations Officer
CFO: Robin Bayus, Chief Financial Officer
CMO: Mindy Aisen, M.D., Chief Medical Officer
CIO: Francis Tang, Chief Information Officer
CHR: Elizabeth Jacobi, Associate Director Human Resources
Web address: www.rancho.org
Control: County, Government, Nonfederal **Service**: Rehabilitation

Staffed Beds: 108 **Admissions**: 2578 **Census**: 105 **Outpatient Visits**: 52867 **Births**: 0 **Total Expense ($000)**: 613653 **Payroll Expense ($000)**: 141459 **Personnel**: 1367

DUARTE—Los Angeles County

✠ **CITY OF HOPE'S HELFORD CLINICAL RESEARCH HOSPITAL (050146)**, 1500 East Duarte Road, Zip 91010-3012; tel. 626/256-4673, **A**1 2 3 5 8 10 **F**3 8 11 14 15 18 19 29 30 31 34 35 36 38 39 44 45 46 47 49 50 54 55 56 57 58 59 61 64 68 70 74 75 77 78 79 80 81 82 83 84 85 86 87 88 89 91 92 93 94 96 100 101 104 107 108 110 111 115 116 117 118 119 120 121 123 124 126 130 132 135 136 142 145 146 147 148 149 154 156 158 166 167 **S** City of Hope, Schaumburg, IL
Primary Contact: Robert Stone, JD, President/Chief Executive Officer
COO: Jeff E. Walker, Chief Operating Officer
CFO: Jennifer Parkhurst, Chief Financial Officer
CMO: William D. Boswell, M.D., Jr, Chief Medical Officer
CIO: Mark Hulse, MSN, Chief Digital Officer
CHR: Stephanie Neuvirth, Chief Human Resource and Diversity Officer
CNO: Cynthia Ann Powers, VP, ACNO
Web address: www.cityofhope.org
Control: Other not-for-profit (including NFP Corporation) **Service**: Cancer

Staffed Beds: 232 **Admissions**: 8636 **Census**: 214 **Outpatient Visits**: 413389 **Births**: 0 **Total Expense ($000)**: 2380328 **Payroll Expense ($000)**: 725555 **Personnel**: 6330

EL CENTRO—Imperial County

✠ **EL CENTRO REGIONAL MEDICAL CENTER (050045)**, 1415 Ross Avenue, Zip 92243-4398; tel. 760/339-7100, (Nonreporting) **A**1 3 10
Primary Contact: Pablo Velez, R.N., Ph.D., Chief Executive Officer
COO: Tomas Virgen, R.N., MSN, Chief Operating Officer
CHR: Bill Moore, Chief Human Resources
Web address: www.ecrmc.org
Control: City, Government, Nonfederal **Service**: General medical and surgical

Staffed Beds: 161

ELDRIDGE—Sonoma County

SONOMA DEVELOPMENTAL CENTER (050547), 15000 Arnold Drive, Zip 95431-8900, Mailing Address: P.O. Box 1493, Zip 95431-1493; tel. 707/938-6000, (Nonreporting) **A**10
Primary Contact: Aleana Carreon, Executive Director
COO: Karen Clark, Director Administrative Services
CMO: Carol Castillo, Medical Director
CHR: Brenda Dukes, Director Human Resources
Web address: www.dds.ca.gov/sonoma
Control: State, Government, Nonfederal **Service**: Intellectual disabilities

Staffed Beds: 546

ENCINITAS—San Diego County

✠ **SCRIPPS MEMORIAL HOSPITAL–ENCINITAS (050503)**, 354 Santa Fe Drive, Zip 92024-5182, Mailing Address: P.O. Box 230817, Zip 92023-0817; tel. 760/633-6501, **A**1 10 **F**3 8 11 13 14 15 18 20 22 26 29 30 31 34 35 37 40 44 45 46 50 51 54 56 58 59 64 65 68 70 74 75 76 77 78 79 80 81 82 84 85 86 87 91 92 93 94 95 100 102 107 108 110 111 114 115 118 119 126 130 131 132 141 146 148 149 154 156 157 167 169 **S** Scripps Health, San Diego, CA
Primary Contact: Chris D. Van Gorder, FACHE, President, Chief Executive Officer
COO: Steve Miller, Vice President, Chief Operations Executive
CHR: Steve Rust, Director, Human Resources
Web address: www.scripps.org
Control: Other not-for-profit (including NFP Corporation) **Service**: General medical and surgical

Staffed Beds: 187 **Admissions**: 13687 **Census**: 153 **Outpatient Visits**: 91373 **Births**: 1927 **Total Expense ($000)**: 374048 **Payroll Expense ($000)**: 151088 **Personnel**: 1921

SCRIPPS OCEANVIEW CONV HOSP See Evergreen Encinitas Health Care Center

ENCINO—Los Angeles County

☐ **ENCINO HOSPITAL MEDICAL CENTER (050158)**, 16237 Ventura Boulevard, Zip 91436-2272; tel. 818/995-5000, (Total facility includes 27 beds in nursing home–type unit) **A**1 10 **F**3 29 45 46 49 50 56 57 70 81 90 98 101 102 103 107 108 114 115 119 128 130 149 154 157 **S** Prime Healthcare, Ontario, CA
Primary Contact: EM Vitug. Garcia, Ph.D., Chief Executive Officer
CFO: Kanner Tillman, Chief Financial Officer
CMO: Muhammad Anwar, M.D., Chief Medical Officer
CIO: Edward Barrera, Director Communications
CHR: Barbara Back, Manager Human Resources
CNO: Vilma L Dinham, R.N., Chief Nursing Officer
Web address: www.encinomed.com
Control: Other not-for-profit (including NFP Corporation) **Service**: General medical and surgical

Staffed Beds: 74 **Admissions**: 2014 **Census**: 79 **Outpatient Visits**: 10060 **Births**: 0 **Total Expense ($000)**: 55493 **Payroll Expense ($000)**: 25898 **Personnel**: 313

ESCONDIDO—San Diego County

☐ **PALOMAR HEALTH REHABILITATION INSTITUTE (053043)**, 2181 Citracado Parkway, Zip 92029; tel. 442/277-6100, (Nonreporting) **A**1 10 **S** Kindred Healthcare, Ontario, CA
Primary Contact: Jennifer Anne. Whitney, FACHE, FACHE, Chief Executive Officer
CMO: Angel Chang, M.D., Medical Director
CHR: Beth Froschauer, Director, Human Resources
CNO: Andrea Godinez, Chief Nursing Officer
Web address: www.palomarhealthrehabinstitute.com
Control: Partnership, Investor-owned (for-profit) **Service**: Rehabilitation

Staffed Beds: 52

✠ **PALOMAR MEDICAL CENTER ESCONDIDO (050115)**, 2185 Citracado Parkway, Zip 92029-4159; tel. 760/739-3000, **A**1 3 10 **F**3 13 15 17 18 20 22 24 26 28 29 30 31 35 37 38 39 40 43 45 46 47 48 49 50 51 54 56 57 64 68 70 72 74 75 76 77 78 79 81 82 83 84 85 86 87 92 93 96 97 100 107 108 110 111 112 114 115 119 120 121 123 124 126 130 131 135 146 147 148 149 154 156 162 164 167 **S** Palomar Health, Escondido, CA
Primary Contact: Diane Hansen, President and Chief Executive Officer
CMO: Duane Buringrud, M.D., Chief Medical and Quality Officer
CIO: Prudence August, Chief Information Officer
CHR: Brenda C Turner, Chief Human Resources Officer
CNO: Melvin Bruce Russell Jr, Chief Nursing Officer
Web address: www.palomarhealth.org
Control: Hospital district or authority, Government, Nonfederal **Service**: General medical and surgical

Staffed Beds: 292 **Admissions**: 19076 **Census**: 236 **Outpatient Visits**: 161631 **Total Expense ($000)**: 570306 **Payroll Expense ($000)**: 189097 **Personnel**: 2094

EUREKA—Humboldt County

HUMBOLDT COUNTY MENTAL HEALTH (054124), 720 Wood Street, Zip 95501-4413; tel. 707/268-2900, (Nonreporting) **A**10
Primary Contact: Paul Bugnaki, Adminstrator
CMO: Harpreet Duggal, M.D., Medical Director, Department of Health and Human Services
CNO: Sherry Gallagher, Director Nursing, Department of Health and Human Services
Web address: https://co.humboldt.ca.us/hhs/mhb/
Control: County, Government, Nonfederal **Service**: Psychiatric

Staffed Beds: 16

✠ **PROVIDENCE ST. JOSEPH HOSPITAL EUREKA (050006)**, 2700 Dolbeer Street, Zip 95501-4799; tel. 707/445-8121, (Includes GENERAL HOSPITAL, 2200 Harrison Avenue, Eureka, California, Zip 95501-3299, tel. 707/445-5111) **A**1 2 3 10 19 **F**3 10 11 15 17 18 20 22 24 26 28 29 30 31 34 35 39 40 43 44 45 46 47 49 50 51 53 57 58 59 62 63 64 65 66 70 72 73 74 75 76 77 78 79 81 82 84 85 86 87 90 92 93 94 102 107 108 110 111 115 116 117 118 119 120 121 123 124 125 129 130 146 147 148 149 154 158 164 167 **S** Providence, Renton, WA
Primary Contact: Michael Keleman, Chief Executive Officer
CFO: Michel Riccioni, Chief Financial Officer
CMO: Mathew Miller, M.D., Vice President and Chief Medical Officer
CIO: Wendy Thorpe, Area Director Information Systems
CHR: Linda Cook, Vice President Human Resources
CNO: Carol Reeder, R.N., Chief Nursing Officer
Web address: www.stjosepheureka.org
Control: Other not-for-profit (including NFP Corporation) **Service**: General medical and surgical

Staffed Beds: 153 **Admissions**: 6573 **Census**: 101 **Outpatient Visits**: 216359 **Births**: 668 **Total Expense ($000)**: 296152 **Payroll Expense ($000)**: 132889 **Personnel**: 1125

Hospitals, U.S. / CALIFORNIA

ST. JOSEPH HOSPITAL EUREKA See Providence St. Joseph Hospital Eureka

FAIRFIELD—Solano County

NORTHBAY MEDICAL CENTER (050367), 1200 B. Gale Wilson Boulevard, Zip 94533-3587; tel. 707/646-5000, (Includes NORTHBAY VACAVALLEY HOSPITAL, 1000 Nut Tree Road, Vacaville, California, Zip 95687-4100, tel. 707/624-7000) **A**1 2 5 10 **F**3 8 11 13 17 18 20 22 24 28 29 30 31 34 35 36 40 41 43 44 45 46 49 50 51 53 54 55 56 57 59 63 64 65 70 72 74 75 76 77 78 79 80 81 82 84 85 87 89 92 93 94 97 102 107 114 115 117 118 119 120 121 123 124 126 130 131 132 144 146 147 148 149 154 156 157 167 169
Primary Contact: Mark Behl, President and Chief Executive Officer
CFO: Michele Bouit, Vice President of Finance, Chief Financial Officer
CMO: Seth Kaufman, M.D., Chief Medical Officer
CIO: Christopher Timbers, Vice President and Chief Information Officer
CNO: Traci A Duncan, R.N., Vice President, Chief Nursing Officer
Web address: www.northbay.org
Control: Other not-for-profit (including NFP Corporation) **Service**: General medical and surgical

Staffed Beds: 177 **Admissions**: 10130 **Census**: 134 **Outpatient Visits**: 346780 **Births**: 1356 **Total Expense ($000)**: 753452 **Payroll Expense ($000)**: 275798 **Personnel**: 1612

FALL RIVER MILLS—Shasta County

★ ○ **MAYERS MEMORIAL HOSPITAL DISTRICT (051305)**, 43563 Highway 299 East, Zip 96028-0459, Mailing Address: P.O. Box 459, Zip 96028-0459; tel. 530/336-5511, (Total facility includes 87 beds in nursing home–type unit) **A**10 11 18 **F**3 6 7 11 28 29 30 32 34 35 40 45 54 56 57 59 63 64 65 68 71 75 81 93 97 107 114 115 119 127 128 130 133 135 146 148 149 154 **P**6
Primary Contact: Ryan Harris, Chief Executive Officer
CFO: Travis Lakey, Chief Financial Officer
CMO: Thomas Watson, M.D., Chief of Staff
CIO: Chris Broadway, Manager Information Technology
CHR: Julie Thompson, Manager Personnel and Payroll
CNO: Sherry Wilson, R.N., Chief Nursing Officer
Web address: www.mayersmemorial.com
Control: Hospital district or authority, Government, Nonfederal **Service**: General medical and surgical

Staffed Beds: 115 **Admissions**: 314 **Census**: 85 **Outpatient Visits**: 18197 **Births**: 1 **Personnel**: 213

FOLSOM—Sacramento County

MERCY HOSPITAL OF FOLSOM (050414), 1650 Creekside Drive, Zip 95630-3400; tel. 916/983-7400, **A**1 5 10 **F**3 8 11 12 13 29 30 34 35 36 37 39 40 49 57 59 60 64 66 68 70 74 75 76 77 79 81 82 84 85 86 93 107 108 111 114 115 118 119 126 130 132 146 147 148 154 164 167 **P**5 **S** CommonSpirit Health, Chicago, IL
Primary Contact: Lisa Hausmann, President and Chief Executive Officer
CMO: Robert Allen, M.D., Chief Medical Officer
CHR: Anthony Robinson, Manager, Human Resources
CNO: Josh Freilich, Vice President and Chief Nurse Executive
Web address: www.mercyfolsom.org
Control: Church operated, Nongovernment, not-for-profit **Service**: General medical and surgical

Staffed Beds: 106 **Admissions**: 7322 **Census**: 78 **Outpatient Visits**: 54902 **Births**: 695 **Total Expense ($000)**: 238757 **Payroll Expense ($000)**: 99768 **Personnel**: 693

VIBRA HOSPITAL OF SACRAMENTO (052033), 330 Montrose Drive, Zip 95630-2720; tel. 916/351-9151, (Nonreporting) **A**1 10 **S** Vibra Healthcare, Mechanicsburg, PA
Primary Contact: Varun Chauhan, Chief Executive Officer
CFO: Todd Scott, Chief Financial Officer
CMO: S. Kwon Lee, M.D., Chief of Staff
CHR: Glenda Franco, Director, Human Resources
Web address: www.vhsacramento.com
Control: Corporation, Investor-owned (for-profit) **Service**: Acute long-term care hospital

Staffed Beds: 58

FONTANA—San Bernardino County

KAISER PERMANENTE FONTANA MEDICAL CENTER (050140), 9961 Sierra Avenue, Zip 92335-6794; tel. 909/427-5000, (Includes KAISER PERMANENTE ONTARIO MEDICAL CENTER, 2295 South Vineyard Avenue, Ontario, California, Zip 91761-7925, tel. 909/724-5000; Georgina R. Garcia, R.N., Chief Executive Officer) **A**1 3 5 10 19 **F**3 8 11 12 13 15 17 18 20 22 24 26 29 30 31 34 35 36 40 41 44 45 46 48 49 50 51 53 56 57 58 59 60 61 62 63 64 65 68 70 72 73 74 75 76 77 78 79 81 82 84 85 86 87 88 89 92 97 100 102 107 108 110 111 114 115 116 117 118 119 124 126 130 131 132 135 136 137 146 148 149 150 154 160 161 162 164 165 166 167 168 169 **S** Kaiser Foundation Hospitals, Oakland, CA
Primary Contact: Georgina R. Garcia, R.N., Senior Vice President, Area Manager for San Bernardino County
COO: Ken Rivers, Chief Operating Officer, Fontana Medical Center
CFO: Trish Lopez, Area Chief Financial Officer
CMO: Timothy Jenkins, M.D., Area Medical Director and Chief of Staff
CIO: Heather Raymond, Area Public Relations Director
CHR: Irene Ruiz, Area Human Resources Director
CNO: Raye M. Burkhardt, Area Nurse Executive
Web address: www.kaiserpermanente.org
Control: Other not-for-profit (including NFP Corporation) **Service**: General medical and surgical

Staffed Beds: 530 **Admissions**: 31452 **Census**: 384 **Outpatient Visits**: 345158 **Births**: 6960 **Personnel**: 5044

FORT BRAGG—Mendocino County

ADVENTIST HEALTH MENDOCINO COAST (051325), 700 River Drive, Zip 95437-5495; tel. 707/961-1234, **A**1 10 18 **F**7 8 11 15 29 30 31 34 40 43 50 59 62 63 64 70 75 77 78 79 81 82 85 87 97 107 108 111 119 127 128 133 146 149 154 **S** Adventist Health, Roseville, CA
Primary Contact: Eric Stevens, Interim President
CFO: Warren Tetz, Chief Financial Officer
CMO: John Kermen, D.O., Chief Medical Staff
CIO: Jeff Edwards, Manager Information Services
CNO: Bonnie Kittner, R.N., Chief Nursing Officer
Web address: www.mcdh.org
Control: Church operated, Nongovernment, not-for-profit **Service**: General medical and surgical

Staffed Beds: 25 **Admissions**: 892 **Census**: 14 **Outpatient Visits**: 94466 **Births**: 0 **Total Expense ($000)**: 89155 **Payroll Expense ($000)**: 25009

FORT IRWIN—San Bernardino County

WEED ARMY COMMUNITY HOSPITAL, 390 North Loop Road, Zip 92310, Mailing Address: P.O. Box 105109, Zip 92310-5109; tel. 760/383-5155, (Nonreporting) **A**1 **S** Department of the Army, Office of the Surgeon General, Falls Church, VA
Primary Contact: Colonel F Cameron. Jackson, Hospital Commander
CIO: Michael Haenelt, Chief Information Management
Web address: https://weed-irwin.tricare.mil/
Control: Army, Government, federal **Service**: General medical and surgical

Staffed Beds: 27

FORTUNA—Humboldt County

PROVIDENCE REDWOOD MEMORIAL HOSPITAL (051318), 3300 Renner Drive, Zip 95540-3198; tel. 707/725-3361, **A**1 10 18 **F**3 11 15 16 17 29 30 34 35 40 45 46 49 50 59 64 70 75 77 79 81 82 84 85 86 87 90 93 97 107 108 109 110 111 119 127 130 133 146 147 148 149 164 167 **P**3 **S** Providence, Renton, WA
Primary Contact: Michael Keleman, Chief Executive Officer
COO: Joseph J Rogers, Vice President and Chief Operating Officer
CMO: Ranjit Hundal, M.D., Senior Vice President and Chief Medical Officer
CHR: Bob Sampson, Vice President Human Resources
Web address: https://www.providence.org/locations/norcal/redwood-memorial
Control: Other not-for-profit (including NFP Corporation) **Service**: General medical and surgical

Staffed Beds: 25 **Admissions**: 773 **Census**: 11 **Outpatient Visits**: 68224 **Births**: 0 **Total Expense ($000)**: 40025 **Payroll Expense ($000)**: 22474 **Personnel**: 180

REDWOOD MEMORIAL HOSPITAL See Providence Redwood Memorial Hospital

---

Hospital, Medicare Provider Number, Address, Telephone, Approval, Facility, and Physician Codes, Health Care System

★ American Hospital Association (AHA) membership
□ The Joint Commission accreditation
○ Healthcare Facilities Accreditation Program
◇ DNV Healthcare Inc. accreditation
⇑ Center for Improvement in Healthcare Quality Accreditation
△ Commission on Accreditation of Rehabilitation Facilities (CARF) accreditation

Hospitals, U.S. / CALIFORNIA

FOUNTAIN VALLEY—Orange County

FOUNTAIN VALLEY REGIONAL HOSPITAL AND MEDICAL CENTER (050570), 17100 Euclid Street, Zip 92708-4043; tel. 714/966-7200, (Nonreporting) **A** 5 10 **S** University of California Systemwide Administration, Oakland, CA
Primary Contact: Randy Rogers, FACHE, Chief Executive Officer
COO: Andrew Pete, Chief Operating Officer
CFO: Richard Wang, Chief Financial Officer
CMO: Daniel Hilton, M.D., Chief of Staff
CIO: Freddie Sanchez, Director Information Systems
CHR: Connie Worden, Chief Human Resources Officer
Web address: www.fountainvalleyhospital.com
Control: Corporation, Investor-owned (for-profit) **Service:** General medical and surgical

Staffed Beds: 380

ORANGE COAST MEDICAL CENTER (050678), 9920 Talbert Avenue, Zip 92708-5115, Mailing Address: 18111 Brookhurst Street, Zip 92708-5115; tel. 714/378-7000, **A**1 2 10 **F**3 8 11 12 13 15 17 18 20 22 24 26 28 29 30 31 34 35 37 38 40 44 45 46 47 48 49 50 51 53 55 56 57 58 59 60 64 65 68 70 72 74 75 76 77 78 79 81 82 84 85 86 87 93 100 102 107 108 110 111 114 115 116 117 118 119 124 126 130 131 132 135 143 145 146 147 149 154 157 160 167 169 **S** MemorialCare, Fountain Valley, CA
Primary Contact: Marcia Manker, Chief Executive Officer, Executive Vice President, Memorial Care Orange County Region
COO: Emily Randle, Vice President Operations
CFO: Steve McNamara, Chief Financial Officer
CIO: Scott Raymond, Director Information Systems
CHR: Michelle Gutierrez, Executive Director Human Resources
CNO: Shela Kaneshiro, Chief Nursing Officer
Web address: https://www.memorialcare.org/locations/orange-coast-medical-center
Control: Other not-for-profit (including NFP Corporation) **Service:** General medical and surgical

Staffed Beds: 221 **Admissions:** 12074 **Census:** 150 **Outpatient Visits:** 129038 **Births:** 1733 **Total Expense ($000):** 435719 **Payroll Expense ($000):** 124687 **Personnel:** 1386

FREMONT—Alameda County

FREMONT HOSPITAL (054110), 39001 Sundale Drive, Zip 94538-2005; tel. 510/796-1100, (Nonreporting) **A**1 10 **S** Universal Health Services, Inc., King of Prussia, PA
Primary Contact: Patricia Williams, Chief Executive Officer
CMO: Vikas Duvvuri, M.D., Medical Director
CHR: Tom Piz, Director Human Resources
Web address: www.fremonthospital.com
Control: Corporation, Investor-owned (for-profit) **Service:** Psychiatric

Staffed Beds: 148

KAISER PERMANENTE FREMONT MEDICAL CENTER (050512), 39400 Paseo Padre Parkway, Zip 94538-2310; tel. 510/248-3000, **A**1 2 3 5 10 **F**3 4 11 12 15 18 20 26 30 31 37 39 40 41 45 49 56 60 64 68 70 74 75 78 79 80 81 84 85 87 98 100 103 107 108 110 111 114 115 118 119 130 135 146 148 149 154 160 161 167 **S** Kaiser Foundation Hospitals, Oakland, CA
Primary Contact: Debra A. Flores, R.N., FACHE, Senior Vice President and Area Manager
Web address: www.kp.org
Control: Other not-for-profit (including NFP Corporation) **Service:** General medical and surgical

Staffed Beds: 100 **Admissions:** 4570 **Census:** 63 **Outpatient Visits:** 242490 **Births:** 21 **Personnel:** 791

WASHINGTON HOSPITAL HEALTHCARE SYSTEM (050195), 2000 Mowry Avenue, Zip 94538-1746; tel. 510/797-1111, **A**1 2 3 10 19 **F**13 15 18 20 22 24 28 29 30 31 34 35 38 40 41 43 45 46 49 50 54 55 57 58 59 60 64 65 67 68 70 72 74 75 76 77 78 79 84 85 86 87 89 91 93 96 100 102 107 108 110 111 112 114 115 116 119 120 121 123 130 132 135 143 146 147 148 149 154 156 157 160 162 167 169 **P**3
Primary Contact: Kimberly Hartz, Chief Executive Officer
COO: Edward J Fayen, Associate Administrator Operations and Support
CFO: Chris Henry, Associate Administrator and Chief Financial Officer
CMO: Albert Brooks, M.D., Chief Medical Staff Services
CIO: Robert Thorwald, Chief Information Officer
CHR: Bryant Welch, Chief Human Resources
CNO: Terri Lynn Hunter, R.N., Vice President and Chief Nursing Officer
Web address: www.whhs.com
Control: Hospital district or authority, Government, Nonfederal **Service:** General medical and surgical

Staffed Beds: 282 **Admissions:** 10603 **Census:** 158 **Outpatient Visits:** 328370 **Births:** 1508

FRENCH CAMP—San Joaquin County

SAN JOAQUIN GENERAL HOSPITAL (050167), 500 West Hospital Road, Zip 95231-9693, Mailing Address: P.O. Box 1020, Stockton, Zip 95201-3120; tel. 209/468-6000, (Nonreporting) **A**1 3 5 10
Primary Contact: Richard Castro, Chief Executive Officer
CFO: Ron Kreutner, Chief Financial Officer
CMO: Sheela Kapre, M.D., Chief Medical Officer
CIO: Don Johnston, Chief Information Officer
CHR: Lisa M Lopez, Director Human Resources
CNO: Erlinda Bolor, R.N., Chief Nursing Officer
Web address: www.sjgh.org
Control: County, Government, Nonfederal **Service:** General medical and surgical

Staffed Beds: 110

FRESNO—Fresno County

CENTRAL CALIFORNIA HCS See VA Central California Health Care System

COMMUNITY BEHAVIORAL HEALTH CENTER (054091), 7171 North Cedar Avenue, Zip 93720-3311; tel. 559/449-8000, (Nonreporting) **A**10 **S** Community Medical Centers, Fresno, CA
Primary Contact: Craig S. Castro, President and Chief Executive Officer, Community Health Systems
CFO: Stephen Walter, Senior Vice President and Chief Financial Officer
CMO: Tom Utecht, M.D., Senior Vice President and Chief Quality Officer
CIO: George Vasquez, Senior Vice President Information Services
CHR: Ginny Burdick, Vice President Human Resources
CNO: Karen L Buckley, R.N., Regional Chief Nurse Executive
Web address: www.communitymedical.org
Control: Corporation, Investor-owned (for-profit) **Service:** Psychiatric

Staffed Beds: 61

COMMUNITY REGIONAL MEDICAL CENTER (050060), 2823 Fresno Street, Zip 93721-1324, Mailing Address: P.O. Box 1232, Zip 93715-1232; tel. 559/459-6000, (Total facility includes 106 beds in nursing home-type unit) **A**1 3 8 10 **F**3 12 13 15 16 17 18 19 20 22 24 26 29 30 31 32 34 35 36 37 38 39 40 41 43 44 45 46 47 48 49 50 51 53 55 56 57 58 59 60 61 64 65 68 70 72 73 74 75 76 77 78 79 81 83 84 85 86 87 88 89 90 91 92 93 96 97 98 99 100 101 102 103 104 105 107 108 110 111 115 118 119 126 128 130 131 132 141 146 147 148 149 154 156 164 167 169 **S** Community Medical Centers, Fresno, CA
Primary Contact: Craig S. Castro, President and Chief Executive Officer, Community Health Systems
CFO: Stephen Walter, Senior Vice President and Chief Financial Officer
CMO: Tom Utecht, M.D., Chief Medical Officer
CIO: Craig S. Castro, Chief Information Officer
CHR: Ginny Burdick, Vice President Human Resources
Web address: www.communitymedical.org
Control: Other not-for-profit (including NFP Corporation) **Service:** General medical and surgical

Staffed Beds: 934 **Admissions:** 38939 **Census:** 711 **Outpatient Visits:** 267431 **Births:** 3699 **Total Expense ($000):** 1587826 **Payroll Expense ($000):** 525805 **Personnel:** 5088

FRESNO HEART AND SURGICAL HOSPITAL (050732), 15 East Audubon Drive, Zip 93720-1542; tel. 559/433-8000, (Nonreporting) **A**3 10 **S** Community Medical Centers, Fresno, CA
Primary Contact: Craig S. Castro, President and Chief Executive Officer, Community Health Systems
CFO: Ben Armfield, Chief Financial Officer
CMO: Tom Utecht, M.D., Corporate Chief Quality Officer
CIO: George Vasquez, Corporate Chief Information Officer
CHR: Julie Adair, Interim Corporate Chief Human Resources Officer
CNO: Heather Rodriguez, Chief Nursing Officer
Web address: www.fresnoheartandsurgical.org
Control: Corporation, Investor-owned (for-profit) **Service:** Heart

Staffed Beds: 60

FRESNO SURGICAL HOSPITAL (050708), 6125 North Fresno Street, Zip 93710-5207; tel. 559/431-8000, (Nonreporting) **A**1 10
Primary Contact: Jeff W. Comer, Chief Executive Officer
CFO: Bruce Cecil, Chief Financial Officer
CMO: Bruce Witmer, M.D., Medical Director
CHR: Laura Patillo, Manager Human Resources
Web address: www.fresnosurgicalhospital.com
Control: Partnership, Investor-owned (for-profit) **Service:** Surgical

Staffed Beds: 16

Hospitals, U.S. / CALIFORNIA

KAISER PERMANENTE FRESNO MEDICAL CENTER (050710), 7300 North Fresno Street, Zip 93720-2942; tel. 559/448-4500, **A**1 3 5 10 **F**3 11 12 13 15 18 26 30 31 37 39 40 41 45 49 56 60 64 68 70 72 73 74 75 76 78 79 80 81 84 85 87 100 107 108 110 111 114 115 118 119 130 135 146 148 149 154 167 169 **S** Kaiser Foundation Hospitals, Oakland, CA
Primary Contact: Tyler Hedden, Senior Vice President/Area Manager
CFO: Paula Armstrong, Chief Financial Officer
CMO: Smita Rouillard, M.D., Physician in Chief
CIO: Patty Thompson, Area Compliance Officer
CHR: Mike Silveira, Director Human Resources Business Partners
CNO: Karen S Strauman, R.N., Chief Nurse Executive
Web address: https://healthy.kaiserpermanente.org/northern-california/facilities/Fresno-Medical-Center-100363
Control: Other not-for-profit (including NFP Corporation) **Service**: General medical and surgical

Staffed Beds: 169 **Admissions**: 8631 **Census**: 88 **Outpatient Visits**: 283609 **Births**: 1655 **Personnel**: 1073

SAINT AGNES MEDICAL CENTER (050093), 1303 East Herndon Avenue, Zip 93720-3397; tel. 559/450-3000, (Nonreporting) **A**1 2 3 5 10 **S** Trinity Health, Livonia, MI
Primary Contact: Gurvinder Kaur, President and Market Leader
COO: Mark T Bateman, Interim Chief Operating Officer
CFO: Phil Robinson, Chief Financial Officer
CMO: Stephen Soldo, M.D., Chief Medical Officer
CIO: Irfan Ali, Director Information Services
Web address: www.samc.com
Control: Church operated, Nongovernment, not-for-profit **Service**: General medical and surgical

Staffed Beds: 382

△ **SAN JOAQUIN VALLEY REHABILITATION HOSPITAL (053032)**, 7173 North Sharon Avenue, Zip 93720-3329; tel. 559/436-3600, (Nonreporting) **A**1 7 10 **S** Vibra Healthcare, Mechanicsburg, PA
Primary Contact: Chase Taylor, Chief Executive Officer
CFO: Margaret Casarez, Chief Financial Officer
CMO: Michael Azevedo, M.D., Medical Director
CIO: Christi Rolff, Director Business Development
CHR: Jennifer Morrow, Director Human Resources
Web address: www.sanjoaquinrehab.com
Control: Corporation, Investor-owned (for-profit) **Service**: Rehabilitation

Staffed Beds: 62

VA CENTRAL CALIFORNIA HEALTH CARE SYSTEM, 2615 East Clinton Avenue, Zip 93703-2223; tel. 559/225-6100, (Nonreporting) **A**1 3 5 **S** Department of Veterans Affairs, Washington, DC
Primary Contact: Maisha Moore, R.N., Interim Medical Center Director
CMO: Wessel H. Meyer, M.D., Chief of Staff
CHR: Sandra Stein, Chief Human Resources Management
Web address: www.fresno.va.gov
Control: Veterans Affairs, Government, federal **Service**: General medical and surgical

Staffed Beds: 133

FULLERTON—Orange County

△ **PROVIDENCE ST. JUDE MEDICAL CENTER (050168)**, 101 East Valencia Mesa Drive, Zip 92835-3875; tel. 714/992-3000, **A**1 2 5 7 10 19 **F**3 5 8 9 11 13 15 17 18 20 22 24 26 28 29 30 31 34 35 36 37 38 39 40 44 45 46 47 48 49 50 51 53 54 55 56 57 58 59 60 61 62 63 64 65 66 67 68 70 71 72 73 74 75 76 77 78 79 80 81 82 83 84 85 86 87 90 91 92 93 94 95 96 100 101 102 107 108 109 110 111 112 114 115 116 117 118 119 120 121 123 124 126 129 130 131 132 134 135 145 146 147 148 149 150 154 156 157 164 166 167 169 **P**5 **S** Providence, Renton, WA
Primary Contact: Laura Ramos, R.N., MSN, Chief Executive Officer
CFO: Ed Salvador, Chief Financial Officer
CMO: Eugene P. Kim, M.D., Chief Medical Officer
CHR: Mark Jablonski, Vice President Mission Integration
CNO: Linda Jenkins, R.N., Vice President Patient Care Services
Web address: www.stjudemedicalcenter.org
Control: Other not-for-profit (including NFP Corporation) **Service**: General medical and surgical

Staffed Beds: 290 **Admissions**: 15758 **Census**: 226 **Outpatient Visits**: 661489 **Births**: 2200 **Total Expense ($000)**: 700378 **Payroll Expense ($000)**: 269904 **Personnel**: 2491

ST. JUDE MEDICAL CENTER See Providence St. Jude Medical Center

GARBERVILLE—Humboldt County

★ **JEROLD PHELPS COMMUNITY HOSPITAL (051309)**, 733 Cedar Street, Zip 95542-3292; tel. 707/923-3921, (Nonreporting) **A**10 18
Primary Contact: Matthew Rees, Chief Executive Officer, Administrator
COO: Kent Scown, Director Operations and Information Services
CFO: Harry Jasper, Chief Financial Officer
CMO: Marcin Matuszkiewicz, M.D., Chief of Staff and Medical Director
CIO: Kent Scown, Director Operations and Information Systems
CHR: Dee Way, Director Human Resources
CNO: Sarah Beach, Director of Nursing
Web address: www.shchd.org
Control: Hospital district or authority, Government, Nonfederal **Service**: General medical and surgical

Staffed Beds: 17

GARDEN GROVE—Orange County

☐ **GARDEN GROVE HOSPITAL AND MEDICAL CENTER (050230)**, 12601 Garden Grove Boulevard, Zip 92843-1959; tel. 714/537-5160, (Nonreporting) **A**1 10 **S** Prime Healthcare, Ontario, CA
Primary Contact: Daniel J. Brothman, Chief Executive Officer
CFO: Kora Guoyavatin, Chief Financial Officer
CMO: Hassan Alkhouli, M.D., Chief Medical Officer
CIO: Vic Mahan, Director Information Systems
CHR: Stephanie Sioson, Director Human Resources
CNO: Wanda Ruben, R.N., Chief Nursing Officer
Web address: www.gardengrovehospital.com
Control: Corporation, Investor-owned (for-profit) **Service**: General medical and surgical

Staffed Beds: 167

GARDENA—Los Angeles County

KINDRED HOSPITAL SOUTH BAY (052050), 1246 West 155th Street, Zip 90247-4062; tel. 310/323-5330, (Nonreporting) **A**1 10 **S** ScionHealth, Louisville, KY
Primary Contact: Mark Apodaca, Chief Executive Officer
CHR: Michelle Parra, Director Human Resources
Web address: www.khsouthbay.com/
Control: Corporation, Investor-owned (for-profit) **Service**: Acute long-term care hospital

Staffed Beds: 84

MEMORIAL HOSPITAL OF GARDENA (050468), 1145 West Redondo Beach Boulevard, Zip 90247-3528; tel. 310/532-4200, (Nonreporting) **A**1 10 **S** Pipeline Health, El Segundo, CA
Primary Contact: Victor Carrasco, Chief Executive Officer
COO: Gregory C. Monette, Chief Operating Officer
CHR: Matthew Kempiak, Director Human Resources and Administrative Services
CNO: Kathryn McLaughlin, Chief Nursing Officer
Web address: https://www.memorialhospitalgardena.com/
Control: Corporation, Investor-owned (for-profit) **Service**: General medical and surgical

Staffed Beds: 172

GILROY—Santa Clara County

☐ **ST. LOUISE REGIONAL HOSPITAL (050688)**, 9400 No Name Uno, Zip 95020-3528; tel. 408/848-2000, **A**1 3 10 **F**3 8 11 13 14 15 17 18 29 30 31 34 35 40 45 49 50 56 59 60 64 70 75 76 77 78 79 80 81 85 87 93 97 107 108 110 111 114 119 130 132 135 144 146 147 148 149 154 167
Primary Contact: Maria Gloria Dela Merced, Hospital Executive
CHR: Lin Velasquez, Vice President Human Resources
Web address: https://slrh.sccgov.org/Pages/home.aspx
Control: County, Government, Nonfederal **Service**: General medical and surgical

Staffed Beds: 78 **Admissions**: 3427 **Census**: 51 **Outpatient Visits**: 53473 **Births**: 279 **Total Expense ($000)**: 195195 **Payroll Expense ($000)**: 82839 **Personnel**: 445

Hospital, Medicare Provider Number, Address, Telephone, Approval, Facility, and Physician Codes, Health Care System

★ American Hospital Association (AHA) membership   ○ Healthcare Facilities Accreditation Program   ⇑ Center for Improvement in Healthcare Quality Accreditation
☐ The Joint Commission accreditation   ◇ DNV Healthcare Inc. accreditation   △ Commission on Accreditation of Rehabilitation Facilities (CARF) accreditation

Hospitals, U.S. / CALIFORNIA

GLENDALE—Los Angeles County

ADVENTIST HEALTH GLENDALE (050239), 1509 Wilson Terrace, Zip 91206-4007; tel. 818/409-8000, (Nonreporting) **A**1 2 3 5 10 19 **S** Adventist Health, Roseville, CA
Primary Contact: Alice H. Issai, President
COO: Liz Cochran, Operations Executive
CFO: Eric Krueger, Finance Officer
CIO: Sharon Correa, Chief Information Officer
CNO: Jinhee Nguyen, Patient Care Executive
Web address: https://www.adventisthealth.org/glendale/
Control: Church operated, Nongovernment, not-for-profit **Service**: General medical and surgical

Staffed Beds: 502

GLENDALE MEMORIAL HOSPITAL AND HEALTH CENTER (050058), 1420 South Central Avenue, Zip 91204-2594; tel. 818/502-1900, (Nonreporting) **A**1 10 19 **S** CommonSpirit Health, Chicago, IL
Primary Contact: Betsy Hart, Chief Executive Officer
COO: Brad Grote, Chief Operating Officer
CFO: Rebecca Cheng, Chief Financial Officer
CIO: Brian Gregor, Manager Information Technology Operations
CHR: Nga Nguyen, Manager Human Resources and Organizational Development
CNO: Jason Black Esq, Vice President and Chief Nursing Officer
Web address: www.glendalememorial.com
Control: Other not-for-profit (including NFP Corporation) **Service**: General medical and surgical

Staffed Beds: 126

★ ⇧ **USC VERDUGO HILLS HOSPITAL (050124)**, 1812 Verdugo Boulevard, Zip 91208-1409; tel. 818/790-7100, **A**3 10 21 **F**3 11 13 15 17 18 20 26 28 29 30 34 35 36 37 38 39 40 41 44 45 46 47 48 49 50 51 53 54 56 57 59 64 65 68 70 73 74 75 76 77 79 81 85 86 87 91 93 94 96 98 100 101 102 103 104 107 108 110 111 115 119 126 128 130 131 132 135 145 146 147 148 149 153 154 156 164 167 **S** Keck Medicine of USC, Los Angeles, CA
Primary Contact: Armand Dorian, M.D., FACHE, Chief Executive Officer
CMO: Stephanie Hall, M.D., Chief Medical Officer
CHR: Eva Herberger, Administrator Human Resources
CNO: Theresa Murphy, Chief Nursing Officer
Web address: www.uscvhh.org
Control: Other not-for-profit (including NFP Corporation) **Service**: General medical and surgical

Staffed Beds: 122 **Admissions**: 5439 **Census**: 83 **Outpatient Visits**: 73943 **Births**: 668 **Total Expense ($000)**: 191537 **Payroll Expense ($000)**: 94401 **Personnel**: 857

GLENDORA—Los Angeles County

EMANATE HEALTH FOOTHILL PRESBYTERIAN HOSPITAL (050597), 250 South Grand Avenue, Zip 91741-4218; tel. 626/963-8411, **A**1 3 10 **F**3 7 11 15 17 18 29 30 31 34 35 40 41 44 45 49 50 51 60 64 68 70 74 75 77 78 79 81 85 86 87 107 108 114 119 130 131 143 146 154 **S** Emanate Health, Covina, CA
Primary Contact: Roger Sharma, President and Chief Executive Officer
COO: Elvia Foulke, Executive Vice President and Chief Operating Officer
CMO: John DiMare, M.D., Medical Director
CIO: David McCobb, Chief Information Officer
Web address: https://www.emanatehealth.org/locations/emanate-health-foothill-presbyterian-hospital/
Control: Other not-for-profit (including NFP Corporation) **Service**: General medical and surgical

Staffed Beds: 72 **Admissions**: 4798 **Census**: 69 **Outpatient Visits**: 56081 **Births**: 0 **Total Expense ($000)**: 108040 **Payroll Expense ($000)**: 43814 **Personnel**: 485

☐ **GLENDORA HOSPITAL (054157)**, 150 West Route 66, Zip 91740-6207; tel. 626/852-5000, (Nonreporting) **A**1 3 10
Primary Contact: Anthony Quintero, Interim Administrator
CFO: Robert Bonner, Chief Financial Officer
CMO: Oliver Solomon, M.D., Chief Medical Officer
CIO: Jeffrey Cox, Chief Information Officer
CHR: Diana Cancel, Director Human Resources
CNO: Mary Ann Bennett, Chief Nursing Officer
Web address: https://www.glendorahospital.com/
Control: Other not-for-profit (including NFP Corporation) **Service**: Psychiatric

Staffed Beds: 63

GLENDORA OAKS BEHAVIORAL HEALTH HOSPITAL See Glendora Hospital

GRANADA HILLS—Los Angeles County, See Los Angeles

GRASS VALLEY—Nevada County

SIERRA NEVADA MEMORIAL HOSPITAL (050150), 155 Glasson Way, Zip 95945-5723, Mailing Address: P.O. Box 1029, Zip 95945-1029; tel. 530/274-6000, **A**1 2 3 10 19 **F**3 7 11 13 15 18 28 29 31 34 35 40 41 44 45 49 50 54 57 59 62 64 68 70 76 78 79 81 84 87 93 107 108 110 111 115 119 120 121 130 143 146 148 149 154 160 167 **S** CommonSpirit Health, Chicago, IL
Primary Contact: Scott Neeley, M.D., President and Chief Executive Officer
CFO: David Hall, Chief Financial Officer
CMO: Tyler Hill, D.O., Chief Medical Officer
CHR: Terri Labriola, Human Resources Officer
CNO: Julie Ostrom, Chief Nursing Officer
Web address: https://locations.dignityhealth.org/sierra-nevada-memorial-hospital
Control: Other not-for-profit (including NFP Corporation) **Service**: General medical and surgical

Staffed Beds: 104 **Admissions**: 4305 **Census**: 48 **Outpatient Visits**: 99037 **Births**: 342 **Total Expense ($000)**: 188491 **Payroll Expense ($000)**: 81228 **Personnel**: 611

GREENBRAE—Marin County

MARINHEALTH MEDICAL CENTER (050360), 250 Bon Air Road, Zip 94904-1784, Mailing Address: P.O. Box 8010, San Rafael, Zip 94912-8010; tel. 415/925-7000, **A**1 2 10 **F**3 9 11 13 18 20 22 24 26 29 30 31 34 36 37 40 43 44 49 57 58 64 70 72 74 75 76 78 79 80 81 82 84 85 87 89 93 98 100 102 104 105 107 108 110 111 114 115 119 120 121 123 124 126 130 146 148 149 153 154 156 160 164 167 **P**6
Primary Contact: David G. Klein, M.D., Chief Executive Officer
CFO: Eric Brettner, Chief Financial Officer
CMO: Karin Shavelson, M.D., Chief Medical Officer
CIO: Russell Peckenpaugh, Vice President Information Systems Administration
CHR: Eugene Lewis, Chief Human Resources Officer
CNO: Karin Reese, R.N., MS, Chief Nursing Officer and Chief Administrative Officer
Web address: https://www.mymarinhealth.org/
Control: Other not-for-profit (including NFP Corporation) **Service**: General medical and surgical

Staffed Beds: 231 **Admissions**: 9200 **Census**: 138 **Outpatient Visits**: 47334 **Births**: 1474 **Total Expense ($000)**: 584485 **Payroll Expense ($000)**: 240499 **Personnel**: 1568

GRIDLEY—Butte County

★ ⇧ **ORCHARD HOSPITAL (051311)**, 240 Spruce Street, Zip 95948-2216, Mailing Address: P.O. Box 97, Zip 95948-0097; tel. 530/846-5671, (Nonreporting) **A**10 18 21
COO: Tracy Atkins, Chief Operating and Nursing Officer
CFO: Kristina Sanke, Chief Financial Officer
CMO: Henry Starkes, M.D., Medical Director
CIO: John Helvey, Chief Information Officer
CNO: Tracy Atkins, Chief Operating and Nursing Officer
Web address: www.orchardhospital.com
Control: Other not-for-profit (including NFP Corporation) **Service**: General medical and surgical

Staffed Beds: 45

HANFORD—Kings County

ADVENTIST HEALTH HANFORD (050121), 115 Mall Drive, Zip 93230-3513; tel. 559/582-9000, (Includes ADVENTIST MEDICAL CENTER-SELMA, 1141 Rose Avenue, Selma, California, Zip 93662-3241, tel. 559/891-1000; Richard L Rawson, President and Chief Executive Officer; CENTRAL VALLEY GENERAL HOSPITAL, 1025 North Douty Street, Hanford, California, Zip 93230-3722, P O Box 480, Zip 93232-2113, tel. 559/583-2100; Wayne Ferch, President and Chief Executive Officer) (Nonreporting) **A**1 3 5 10 **S** Adventist Health, Roseville, CA
Primary Contact: Jason Wells, FACHE, President, Central California Network, Adventist Health
CIO: Michael Aubry, Director Information Systems
Web address: www.adventisthealthcv.com/hospital_newhanfordhospital.aspx
Control: Church operated, Nongovernment, not-for-profit **Service**: General medical and surgical

Staffed Beds: 173

SACRED HEART HOSP & CNTR See Central Valley General Hospital

Hospitals, U.S. / CALIFORNIA

HARBOR CITY—Los Angeles County, See Los Angeles

HAYWARD—Alameda County

☐ **ST. ROSE HOSPITAL (050002)**, 27200 Calaroga Avenue, Zip 94545-4383; tel. 510/264-4000, (Nonreporting) **A**1 10 **S** Alecto Healthcare, Irvine, CA
Primary Contact: Lex Reddy, President and Chief Executive Officer
CFO: Michael Taylor, Vice President Financial Services and Chief Financial Officer
CMO: Charles S Feldstein, M.D., Vice President Medical Affairs
CHR: John Davini, Vice President
Web address: www.srhca.org
Control: Church operated, Nongovernment, not-for-profit **Service**: General medical and surgical

Staffed Beds: 150

HEALDSBURG—Sonoma County

HEALDSBURG DISTRICT HOSPITAL See Healdsburg Hospital

✠ **HEALDSBURG HOSPITAL (051321)**, 1375 University Avenue, Zip 95448-3382; tel. 707/431-6500, **A**1 10 18 **F**3 15 29 30 39 40 45 46 64 68 70 76 81 82 84 85 87 93 107 111 115 119 128 130 132 133 146 147 148 149 154 **S** Providence, Renton, WA
Primary Contact: Michelle Oxford, Chief Administrative Officer
COO: Regina Novello, R.N., Chief Operating Officer
CFO: John S Parigi II, Interim Chief Financial Officer
CMO: Judy Widger, M.D., Chief of Staff
CIO: Steven Hansen, Director Information Technology
CHR: Kristina Holloway, Chief Human Resources Officer
Web address: https://www.providence.org/locations/norcal/healdsburg-district-hospital
Control: Other not-for-profit (including NFP Corporation) **Service**: General medical and surgical

Staffed Beds: 43 **Admissions**: 523 **Census**: 6 **Outpatient Visits**: 50617 **Births**: 0 **Total Expense ($000)**: 57741 **Payroll Expense ($000)**: 30691 **Personnel**: 249

HEMET—Riverside County

☐ **HEMET GLOBAL MEDICAL CENTER (050390)**, 1117 East Devonshire Avenue, Zip 92543-3083; tel. 951/652-2811, **A**1 3 5 10 12 13 **F**3 4 8 11 13 17 18 20 26 29 30 40 47 60 63 68 70 74 76 79 81 83 85 107 108 111 114 119 126 130 154 167 **S** Physicians for Healthy Hospitals, Hemet, CA
Primary Contact: Peter R. Baranoff, Corporate Chief Executive Officer, Managing Director
CFO: John R Collins, Chief Financial Officer
CMO: Sumanta Chaudhuri, M.D., Chief Medical Officer
CHR: Michele Bird, Chief Human Resources Officer
CNO: Kathryn McLaughlin, Chief Nursing Officer
Web address: https://www.hemetglobalmedcenter.com/
Control: Individual, Investor-owned (for-profit) **Service**: General medical and surgical

Staffed Beds: 454 **Admissions**: 7197 **Census**: 88 **Outpatient Visits**: 50597 **Births**: 256

HOLLISTER—San Benito County

☐ **HAZEL HAWKINS MEMORIAL HOSPITAL (051337)**, 911 Sunset Drive, Zip 95023-5695; tel. 831/637-5711, (Includes WILLIAM AND INEZ MABIE SKILLED NURSING FACILITY, 911 Sunset Drive, Hollister, California, Zip 95023, tel. 408/637-5711) (Nonreporting) **A**1 10 18
Primary Contact: Mary Casillas, Chief Executive Officer
COO: Mary Casillas, Chief Operating Officer
CFO: Mark Robinson, Associate Administrator and Chief Financial Officer
CIO: Julio Gil, Manager Information Services
CHR: Ysidro Gallardo, Associate Administrator Human Resources
Web address: www.hazelhawkins.com
Control: Hospital district or authority, Government, Nonfederal **Service**: General medical and surgical

Staffed Beds: 181

HAZEL HAWKINS MEMORIAL HOSPITAL See William and Inez Mabie Skilled Nursing Facility

HOLLYWOOD—Los Angeles County, See Los Angeles

HUNTINGTON BEACH—Orange County

☐ **HUNTINGTON BEACH HOSPITAL (050526)**, 17772 Beach Boulevard, Zip 92647-6896; tel. 714/843-5000, (Nonreporting) **A**1 10 **S** Prime Healthcare, Ontario, CA
Primary Contact: Daniel J. Brothman, Chief Executive Officer
CFO: Alan H Smith, Chief Financial Officer
CMO: Hassan Alkhouli, M.D., Medical Director
CIO: Adam Morquecho, Director Information Technology
CHR: Stephanie Sioson, Director Human Resources
Web address: www.hbhospital.com
Control: Other not-for-profit (including NFP Corporation) **Service**: General medical and surgical

Staffed Beds: 102

HUNTINGTON PARK—Los Angeles County

○ **COMMUNITY HOSPITAL OF HUNTINGTON PARK (050091)**, 2623 East Slauson Avenue, Zip 90255-2926; tel. 323/583-1931, (Nonreporting) **A**10 11 **S** Pipeline Health, El Segundo, CA
Primary Contact: Matthew A. Whaley, Chief Executive Officer
CNO: Guadalupe Ojeda, R.N., Chief Nursing Officer
Web address: https://www.communityhospitalhp.com/
Control: Corporation, Investor-owned (for-profit) **Service**: General medical and surgical

Staffed Beds: 81

INDIO—Riverside County

✠ **JFK MEMORIAL HOSPITAL (050534)**, 47111 Monroe Street, Zip 92201-6799; tel. 760/347-6191, (Nonreporting) **A**1 10 **S** TENET Healthcare Corporation, Dallas, TX
Primary Contact: Karen Faulis, Chief Executive Officer
CFO: Mike King, Chief Financial Officer and Chief Operating Officer
CHR: Raymond Konieczek, Chief Human Resources Officer
CNO: Heather Adams, Chief Nursing Officer
Web address: www.jfkmemorialhosp.com
Control: Corporation, Investor-owned (for-profit) **Service**: General medical and surgical

Staffed Beds: 145

INGLEWOOD—Los Angeles County

☐ **CENTINELA HOSPITAL MEDICAL CENTER (050739)**, 555 East Hardy Street, Zip 90301-4011; tel. 310/673-4660, (Nonreporting) **A**1 3 10 **S** Prime Healthcare, Ontario, CA
Primary Contact: Mohammad Naser, R.N., MSN, Chief Executive Officer
CFO: Paul Sennett, Chief Financial Officer
CMO: Paryus Patel, M.D., Chief Medical Officer
CIO: Martin Cordova, Director Information Services
CHR: George Akopyan, Director Human Resources
CNO: Karen Price-Gharzeddine, R.N., MS, Chief Nursing Officer and Administrator
Web address: www.centinelamed.com
Control: Corporation, Investor-owned (for-profit) **Service**: General medical and surgical

Staffed Beds: 369

IRVINE—Orange County

⇧ **HOAG ORTHOPEDIC INSTITUTE (050769)**, 16250 Sand Canyon Avenue, Zip 92618-3714; tel. 949/517-3149, (Nonreporting) **A**3 10 21
Primary Contact: Kim Mikes, Chief Executive Officer
CMO: Robert Gorab, M.D., Chief Medical Officer
Web address: https://www.orthopedichospital.com/
Control: Other not-for-profit (including NFP Corporation) **Service**: Orthopedic

Staffed Beds: 70

KAISER FOUNDATION HOSPITAL – ORANGE COUNTY See Orange County Irvine Medical Center

ORANGE COUNTY IRVINE MEDICAL CENTER See Kaiser Permanente Orange County Anaheim Medical Center, Anaheim

---

Hospital, Medicare Provider Number, Address, Telephone, Approval, Facility, and Physician Codes, Health Care System

★ American Hospital Association (AHA) membership
☐ The Joint Commission accreditation
○ Healthcare Facilities Accreditation Program
◇ DNV Healthcare Inc. accreditation
⇧ Center for Improvement in Healthcare Quality Accreditation
△ Commission on Accreditation of Rehabilitation Facilities (CARF) accreditation

Hospitals, U.S. / CALIFORNIA

JACKSON—Amador County

SUTTER AMADOR HOSPITAL (050014), 200 Mission Boulevard, Zip 95642-2564; tel. 209/223-7500, **A**1 3 5 10 20 **F**3 11 13 15 29 31 34 35 40 45 46 47 59 64 65 68 70 74 75 76 77 79 81 85 86 87 93 107 108 110 111 115 119 126 129 130 131 132 146 148 149 154 164 169 **S** Sutter Health, Sacramento, CA
Primary Contact: Michael Cureton, FACHE, Chief Executive Officer, Sutter Amador Hospital and Sutter Davis Hospital
CFO: Brett Moore, CPA, Assistant Administrator Finance
CMO: Ron Hood, M.D., Chief of Staff
CIO: Joy Bailey, Director Information Technology
CHR: Beverly Revels, Director Human Resources
CNO: Nikki Allen, Patient Care Executive
Web address: www.sutteramador.org
Control: Other not-for-profit (including NFP Corporation) **Service**: General medical and surgical

Staffed Beds: 48 **Admissions**: 2331 **Census**: 26 **Outpatient Visits**: 50418 **Births**: 225 **Total Expense ($000)**: 103767 **Payroll Expense ($000)**: 40031 **Personnel**: 363

JOSHUA TREE—San Bernardino County

HI-DESERT MEDICAL CENTER (050279), 6601 White Feather Road, Zip 92284; tel. 760/366-3711, (Nonreporting) **A**1 3 10 20 **S** TENET Healthcare Corporation, Dallas, TX
Primary Contact: Karen Faulis, Chief Executive Officer
COO: David Cooke, R.N., Chief Operating Officer
CMO: Jeffrey Seip, M.D., Chief Medical Staff
CIO: Darrell Goodman, Chief Information Officer
CHR: Nicole Smith, Director Human Resources
CNO: David Cooke, R.N., Chief Operating Officer
Web address: www.hdmc.org
Control: Corporation, Investor-owned (for-profit) **Service**: General medical and surgical

Staffed Beds: 59

KENTFIELD—Marin County

KENTFIELD HOSPITAL (052043), 1125 Sir Francis Drake Boulevard, Zip 94904-1455; tel. 415/456-9680, (Nonreporting) **A**1 10
Primary Contact: Ann Gors, Division President and Chief Executive Officer Kentfield Hospital, Kentfield Hospital San Francisco
CFO: Stephanie Lawrence, Chief Financial Officer
CMO: Curtis Roebken, M.D., Chief Medical Staff
CHR: Julene English, Director Human Resources
Web address: https://kentfieldhospital.com/
Control: Corporation, Investor-owned (for-profit) **Service**: Acute long-term care hospital

Staffed Beds: 60

KING CITY—Monterey County

GEORGE L. MEE MEMORIAL HOSPITAL (051336), 300 Canal Street, Zip 93930-3431; tel. 831/385-6000, (Total facility includes 48 beds in nursing home-type unit) **A**1 5 10 18 **F**3 15 29 32 40 44 45 55 59 60 65 68 69 70 75 77 79 81 82 89 91 93 97 107 110 111 114 115 119 127 128 130 131 133 146 147 148 154 169
Primary Contact: Rena Salamacha, Chief Executive Officer
CFO: Gary L Wangsmo, Chief Financial Officer
CMO: Schindelheim Roy, M.D., Chief of Staff
CIO: Mike McNamara, Chief Information Officer
CHR: Karen Wong, Chief Human Resources Officer
Web address: www.meememorial.com
Control: Other not-for-profit (including NFP Corporation) **Service**: General medical and surgical

Staffed Beds: 73 **Admissions**: 454 **Census**: 39 **Outpatient Visits**: 115768 **Births**: 0 **Total Expense ($000)**: 68314 **Payroll Expense ($000)**: 22989 **Personnel**: 309

LA JOLLA—San Diego County

SCRIPPS GREEN HOSPITAL (050424), 10666 North Torrey Pines Road, Zip 92037-1093; tel. 858/455-9100, **A**1 3 5 8 10 19 **F**3 8 11 12 14 15 17 18 20 22 26 29 30 31 34 35 36 37 44 45 46 47 49 50 51 54 58 59 61 64 65 68 70 74 75 77 78 79 80 81 82 84 85 86 87 93 107 108 110 111 115 118 119 120 121 123 124 126 130 131 132 136 138 139 141 146 148 156 157 167 **P**3 **S** Scripps Health, San Diego, CA
Primary Contact: Chris D. Van Gorder, FACHE, President and Chief Executive Officer
COO: Timothy Collins, Vice President, Chief Operations Executive
CFO: Richard Rothberger, Corporate Executive Vice President and Chief Financial Officer
CMO: James LaBelle, M.D., Chief Medical Officer
Web address: www.scrippshealth.org
Control: Other not-for-profit (including NFP Corporation) **Service**: General medical and surgical

Staffed Beds: 150 **Admissions**: 7335 **Census**: 94 **Outpatient Visits**: 94227 **Total Expense ($000)**: 377781 **Payroll Expense ($000)**: 129349 **Personnel**: 1117

SCRIPPS MEMORIAL HOSPITAL-LA JOLLA (050324), 9888 Genesee Avenue, Zip 92037-1200, Mailing Address: P.O. Box 28, Zip 92038-0028; tel. 858/626-4123, **A**1 3 5 10 **F**3 8 11 12 13 14 15 17 18 20 22 24 26 28 29 30 31 34 35 40 43 44 45 46 48 49 50 51 53 54 55 56 58 59 64 65 68 70 74 75 76 77 78 79 81 82 84 85 86 87 92 93 100 101 102 107 108 110 111 114 115 116 117 119 124 126 130 132 141 145 146 147 148 149 154 156 157 167 169 **P**3 5 7 **S** Scripps Health, San Diego, CA
Primary Contact: Carl J. Etter, Chief Executive Officer
COO: Cindy Steckel, Ph.D., R.N., Vice President, Chief Operations Executive
CFO: Alan Mandal, Vice President Financial Operations
CMO: James LaBelle, M.D., Chief Medical Officer
CHR: Shelly Blazakis, Director Human Resources Services
CNO: Cindy Steckel, Ph.D., R.N., Vice President Chief Nurse and Operations Executive
Web address: www.scripps.org/locations/hospitals__scripps-memorial-hospital-la-jolla
Control: Other not-for-profit (including NFP Corporation) **Service**: General medical and surgical

Staffed Beds: 426 **Admissions**: 22288 **Census**: 299 **Outpatient Visits**: 103744 **Births**: 3628 **Total Expense ($000)**: 812530 **Payroll Expense ($000)**: 304282 **Personnel**: 1251

SCRIPPS TORREY PINES CONV HOSP See Evergreen of La Jolla

UC SAN DIEGO SHILEY EYE CENTER See UC San Diego Shiley Eye Institute

LA MESA—San Diego County

ALVARADO PARKWAY INSTITUTE BEHAVIORAL HEALTH SYSTEM (054075), 7050 Parkway Drive, Zip 91942-1535; tel. 619/465-4411, (Nonreporting) **A**1 10
Primary Contact: Patrick C. Ziemer, Chief Executive Officer
CFO: Chad Engbrecht, Chief Financial Officer
CMO: R. Bradley Sanders, D.O., Executive Medical Director
CNO: Bonnie Asada, Chief Nursing Officer
Web address: www.apibhs.com
Control: Partnership, Investor-owned (for-profit) **Service**: Psychiatric

Staffed Beds: 66

△ **SHARP GROSSMONT HOSPITAL (050026)**, 5555 Grossmont Center Drive, Zip 91942-3019, Mailing Address: PO Box 158, Zip 91944-0158; tel. 619/740-6000, (Total facility includes 19 beds in nursing home-type unit) **A**1 2 3 7 10 **F**3 5 8 11 12 13 15 17 18 20 22 24 26 28 29 30 31 34 35 37 38 40 44 45 46 47 48 49 50 51 54 55 56 57 58 59 60 61 62 63 64 65 68 70 72 73 74 75 76 77 78 79 80 81 82 84 85 87 90 91 92 93 94 96 98 100 101 102 103 104 106 107 108 111 115 117 118 119 120 121 123 124 126 128 129 130 132 135 143 145 146 147 148 149 153 154 156 162 165 167 169 **S** Sharp HealthCare, San Diego, CA
Primary Contact: Scott Evans, PharmD, Senior Vice President and Market Chief Executive Officer, Sharp HealthCare Regional Hospitals
COO: Maryann Cone, Chief Operating Officer
CMO: Michael Murphy, M.D., JD, Chief Medical Officer
CIO: Kenneth Lawonn, Senior Vice President and Chief Information Officer
Web address: www.sharp.com
Control: Other not-for-profit (including NFP Corporation) **Service**: General medical and surgical

Staffed Beds: 514 **Admissions**: 28262 **Census**: 397 **Outpatient Visits**: 487862 **Births**: 2661 **Total Expense ($000)**: 956506 **Payroll Expense ($000)**: 416148 **Personnel**: 3427

LA MIRADA—Los Angeles County

KINDRED HOSPITAL-LA MIRADA (052038), 14900 East Imperial Highway, Zip 90638-2172; tel. 562/944-1900, (Includes KINDRED HOSPITAL SAN GABRIEL VALLEY, 845 North Lark Ellen Avenue, West Covina, California, Zip 91791-1069, tel. 626/339-5451; David Kowalski, Chief Executive Officer; KINDRED HOSPITAL SANTA ANA, 1901 North College Avenue, Santa Ana, California, Zip 92706-2334, tel. 714/564-7800; Rick Rufino, Chief Executive Officer) (Nonreporting) **A**1 3 10 **S** ScionHealth, Louisville, KY
Primary Contact: Phillip H. Wolfe, Market Chief Executive Officer
CFO: Rishab Punjabi, Chief Financial Officer
CMO: Prakash Chandra Patel, M.D., Chief of Staff
CHR: Susan Bergquist, Human Resources Generalist
CNO: Esperanza Sanchez, Chief Clinical Officer
Web address: https://www.kindredhospitals.com/locations/ltac/kindred-hospital-la-mirada
Control: Corporation, Investor-owned (for-profit) **Service**: Acute long-term care hospital

Staffed Beds: 118

Hospitals, U.S. / CALIFORNIA

LA PALMA—Orange County

☐ **LA PALMA INTERCOMMUNITY HOSPITAL (050580)**, 7901 Walker Street, Zip 90623-1764; tel. 714/670-7400, (Nonreporting) **A**1 10 **S** Prime Healthcare, Ontario, CA
Primary Contact: Ayman Mousa, R.N., Chief Executive Officer
CFO: Alan H Smith, Chief Financial Officer
CMO: Sami Shoukair, M.D., Chief Medical Officer
CIO: Vic Mahan, Director Information Technology
CHR: Stephanie Sioson, Director Human Resources
CNO: Hilda Manzo-Luna, Chief Nursing Officer
Web address: www.lapalmaintercommunityhospital.com
Control: Other not-for-profit (including NFP Corporation) **Service**: General medical and surgical

Staffed Beds: 140

LAGUNA BEACH—Orange County

SOUTH COAST MEDICAL CENTER See Mission Hospital Laguna Beach

LAGUNA HILLS—Orange County

✠ **SADDLEBACK MEDICAL CENTER (050603)**, 24451 Health Center Drive, Zip 92653-3689; tel. 949/837-4500, **A**1 10 **F**3 11 13 14 15 17 19 20 22 24 26 28 29 30 31 34 35 36 38 40 44 45 46 47 48 49 50 51 53 54 55 56 57 58 59 62 63 64 65 68 70 72 74 75 76 77 78 79 81 84 85 86 87 93 94 107 108 110 111 115 116 117 118 119 120 121 123 124 126 130 132 135 141 142 143 145 146 147 148 149 154 157 160 167 169 **S** MemorialCare, Fountain Valley, CA
Primary Contact: Marcia Manker, Chief Executive Officer/Executive Vice President, MemorialCare Orange County Region
COO: Ryan Olsen, Chief Operating Officer
CFO: Aaron Coley, Chief Financial Officer, Orange County
CMO: Kathleen Sullivan, M.D., Chief of Staff
CIO: J Scott Joslyn, Senior Vice President and Chief Information Officer
CHR: Michelle Gutierrez, Executive Director Human Resources, Orange County
CNO: Brandi Cassingham, R.N., Chief Nursing Officer
Web address: www.memorialcare.org
Control: Other not-for-profit (including NFP Corporation) **Service**: General medical and surgical

Staffed Beds: 248 **Admissions**: 11080 **Census**: 124 **Outpatient Visits**: 282428 **Births**: 1765 **Total Expense ($000)**: 420643 **Payroll Expense ($000)**: 124440 **Personnel**: 1388

LAKE ARROWHEAD—San Bernardino County

✠ **SAN BERNARDINO MOUNTAINS COMMUNITY HOSPITAL (051312)**, 29101 Hospital Road, Zip 92352-9706, Mailing Address: P.O. Box 70, Zip 92352-0070; tel. 909/336-3651, (Total facility includes 20 beds in nursing home-type unit) **A**1 10 18 **F**11 15 29 32 34 35 39 40 45 50 57 59 64 65 68 79 81 82 85 86 87 93 97 107 110 115 119 127 128 130 133 146 149 154
Primary Contact: Mark Turner, Chief Executive Officer
COO: Terry Pena, Chief Operating Officer and Chief Nursing Officer
CFO: Yvonne Waggener, Chief Financial Officer
CMO: Walter M. Maier, Chief of Staff
CIO: Patrick Miller, Technology Coordinator
CHR: Julie Atwood, Director Human Resources
CNO: Terry Pena, Chief Operating Officer and Chief Nursing Officer
Web address: www.mchcares.com
Control: Hospital district or authority, Government, Nonfederal **Service**: General medical and surgical

Staffed Beds: 37 **Admissions**: 229 **Census**: 20 **Outpatient Visits**: 35000 **Births**: 0 **Total Expense ($000)**: 34232 **Payroll Expense ($000)**: 17410 **Personnel**: 202

LAKE ISABELLA—Kern County

KERN VALLEY HEALTHCARE DISTRICT (051314), 6412 Laurel Avenue, Zip 93240-9529, Mailing Address: P.O. Box 1628, Zip 93240-1628; tel. 760/379-2681, **A**10 18 **F**3 11 29 34 40 50 57 70 71 91 93 97 107 115 119 127 128 130 133 149 154
Primary Contact: Timothy McGlew, Chief Executive Officer
CFO: Chester Beedle, Chief Financial Officer
CMO: Gary A Finstad, M.D., Chief of Staff
CIO: Paul Quinn, Information Systems Manager
CHR: Debra Hoffman, Human Resources Manager
CNO: Mark Gordon, Chief Nursing Officer
Web address: www.kvhd.org
Control: Hospital district or authority, Government, Nonfederal **Service**: General medical and surgical

Staffed Beds: 101 **Admissions**: 325 **Census**: 48 **Outpatient Visits**: 11172 **Births**: 0 **Total Expense ($000)**: 37392 **Payroll Expense ($000)**: 17546 **Personnel**: 213

LAKEPORT—Lake County

✠ **SUTTER LAKESIDE HOSPITAL (051329)**, 5176 Hill Road East, Zip 95453-6300; tel. 707/262-5000, **A**1 10 18 **F**3 8 11 13 15 18 29 30 34 35 38 40 43 44 45 51 53 54 56 57 64 65 66 68 70 74 75 76 79 81 82 85 87 91 93 97 107 108 110 111 114 115 118 127 130 131 133 135 146 147 148 149 154 164 167 169 **S** Sutter Health, Sacramento, CA
Primary Contact: Timothy Stephens, Chief Administrative Officer
CFO: Linnea Humble, Director of Finance
CMO: Diane Pege, M.D., Vice President Medical Affairs
CIO: Jack Buell, Director Information Services
CHR: Brenda DeRamus, Manager Human Resources
CNO: Teresa Campbell, R.N., Chief Nursing Executive
Web address: www.sutterlakeside.org
Control: Other not-for-profit (including NFP Corporation) **Service**: General medical and surgical

Staffed Beds: 25 **Admissions**: 1574 **Census**: 19 **Outpatient Visits**: 100498 **Births**: 199 **Total Expense ($000)**: 110458 **Payroll Expense ($000)**: 33922 **Personnel**: 350

LAKEWOOD—Los Angeles County

✠ **LAKEWOOD REGIONAL MEDICAL CENTER (050581)**, 3700 East South Street, Zip 90712-1498, Mailing Address: P.O. Box 6070, Zip 90712; tel. 562/531-2550, (Nonreporting) **A**1 10 **S** University of California Systemwide Administration, Oakland, CA
Primary Contact: Virgis Narbutas, Chief Executive Officer
COO: Michael Paul Amos, Chief Operating Officer
CFO: Eric Delgado, Chief Financial Officer
CIO: Pat Pierce, Director Information Systems
CHR: Mary Okuhara, Chief Human Resource Officer
CNO: Terri Newton, Chief Nursing Officer
Web address: www.lakewoodregional.com
Control: Corporation, Investor-owned (for-profit) **Service**: General medical and surgical

Staffed Beds: 111

LANCASTER—Los Angeles County

✠ **ANTELOPE VALLEY MEDICAL CENTER (050056)**, 1600 West Avenue 'J', Zip 93534-2894; tel. 661/949-5000, (Nonreporting) **A**1 2 3 5 10
Primary Contact: Edward Mirzabegian, Chief Executive Officer
COO: Colette Menzel, Ph.D., Chief Operating Officer and Chief Financial Officer
CFO: Colette Menzel, Ph.D., Chief Operating Officer and Chief Financial Officer
CMO: Radha Krishnan, M.D., Chief Medical Officer
CIO: Dale Lepper, Chief Information Officer
CHR: George Leisher Jr, Chief Human Resources Officer
CNO: Jack J Burke, MS, R.N., Chief Operating Officer and Chief Nursing Officer
Web address: www.avhospital.org
Control: Hospital district or authority, Government, Nonfederal **Service**: General medical and surgical

Staffed Beds: 420

LIVERMORE—Alameda County

VA PALO ALTO HEALTH CARE SYSTEM–LIVERMORE DIVISION See Veterans Affairs Palo Alto Health Care System, Livermore Division

VALLEY MEMORIAL See Stanford Health Care Tri-Valley, Pleasanton

---

Hospital, Medicare Provider Number, Address, Telephone, Approval, Facility, and Physician Codes, Health Care System

★ American Hospital Association (AHA) membership   ○ Healthcare Facilities Accreditation Program   ⇑ Center for Improvement in Healthcare Quality Accreditation
☐ The Joint Commission accreditation   ◇ DNV Healthcare Inc. accreditation   △ Commission on Accreditation of Rehabilitation Facilities (CARF) accreditation

© 2025 AHA Guide

Hospitals, U.S. / CALIFORNIA

VALLEYCARE MEDICAL CENTER See Valley Memorial

VETERANS AFFAIRS PALO ALTO HEALTH CARE SYSTEM, LIVERMORE DIVISION See VA Palo Alto Heath Care System, Palo Alto

LODI—San Joaquin County

ADVENTIST HEALTH LODI MEMORIAL (050336), 975 South Fairmont Avenue, Zip 95240–5118, Mailing Address: P.O. Box 3004, Zip 95241–1908; tel. 209/334–3411, (Includes LODI MEMORIAL HOSPITAL WEST, 800 South Lower Sacramento Road, Lodi, California, Zip 95242, tel. 209/333–0211) (Nonreporting) **A**1 5 10 **S** Adventist Health, Roseville, CA
Primary Contact: Brooke McCollough, President
CFO: Terry Deak, Chief Financial Officer
CHR: Mark T Wallace, Director Human Resources
CNO: Debbie Moreno, R.N., Patient Care Executive
Web address: https://www.adventisthealth.org/lodi-memorial/
Control: Other not–for–profit (including NFP Corporation) **Service**: General medical and surgical

Staffed Beds: 194

DOCTORS HOSPITAL OF LODI See Lodi Memorial Hospital West

LOMA LINDA—San Bernardino County

CALIFORNIA HEART AND SURGICAL HOSPITAL See Loma Linda University Heart & Surgical Hospital

JERRY L. PETTIS MEMORIAL VETERANS' HOSPITAL, 11201 Benton Street, Zip 92357–1000; tel. 909/825–7084, (Nonreporting) **A**1 2 3 5 7 **S** Department of Veterans Affairs, Washington, DC
Primary Contact: Karandeep Sraon, FACHE, Medical Center Director
COO: Shane Elliott, Associate Director Administration
CFO: Eric C Sorenson, Chief Financial Officer
CMO: Dwight Evans, M.D., Chief of Staff
CIO: Doug Wirthgen, Facility Chief Information Officer
CHR: Eugene Wylie, Chief Human Resources Officer
CNO: Anne Gillespie, R.N., Associate Director Patient Care and Nursing Services
Web address: www.lomalinda.va.gov
Control: Veterans Affairs, Government, federal **Service**: General medical and surgical

Staffed Beds: 263

LOMA LINDA UNIV COMM MED CTR See Loma Linda University East Campus Hospital

LOMA LINDA UNIVERSITY CHILDREN'S HOSPITAL (050778), 11234 Anderson Street, Zip 92354–2804; tel. 909/558–8000, **A**1 3 5 10 **F**3 11 13 17 19 21 23 25 27 29 30 31 32 34 35 38 39 40 41 43 44 45 46 49 50 52 54 55 57 58 59 60 61 64 65 68 72 74 75 76 77 78 79 81 82 84 85 86 87 88 89 100 102 119 126 130 131 132 134 136 137 138 141 146 147 148 149 150 154 156 164 169 **S** Loma Linda University Adventist Health Sciences Center, Loma Linda, CA
Primary Contact: Trevor G. Wright, Chief Executive Officer
COO: Lyndon C. Edwards, Chief Operating Officer
CFO: Angela Lalas, CPA, Chief Financial Officer
CMO: Richard Chinnock, Chief Medical Officer, LLUCH
CIO: Mark Zirkelbach, Chief Information Officer
CHR: Lizette O Norton, Vice President, Human Resources
CNO: Sherry Nolfe, MS, Chief Nursing Officer
Web address: https://lluch.org/
Control: Other not–for–profit (including NFP Corporation) **Service**: General medical and surgical

Staffed Beds: 364 **Admissions:** 17272 **Census:** 245 **Outpatient Visits:** 159431 **Births:** 3906 **Total Expense ($000):** 619015 **Payroll Expense ($000):** 219948 **Personnel:** 2058

LOMA LINDA UNIVERSITY HEART & SURGICAL HOSPITAL See Loma Linda University Medical Center, Loma Linda

LOMA LINDA UNIVERSITY MEDICAL CENTER (050327), 11234 Anderson Street, Zip 92354–2804; tel. 909/558–4000, (Includes LOMA LINDA UNIVERSITY BEHAVIORAL MEDICINE CENTER, 1710 Barton Road, Redlands, California, Zip 92373–5304, tel. 909/558–9200; Trevor G. Wright, Chief Executive Officer; LOMA LINDA UNIVERSITY EAST CAMPUS HOSPITAL, 25333 Barton Road, Loma Linda, California, Zip 92354–3053, tel. 909/558–6000; LOMA LINDA UNIVERSITY HEART & SURGICAL HOSPITAL, 26780 Barton Road, Loma Linda, California, Zip 92354, tel. 909/583–2900) **A**1 2 3 5 7 8 10 19 **F**2 3 11 12 15 17 18 20 22 24 26 28 29 30 31 34 35 37 38 39 40 43 44 45 46 47 48 49 50 51 54 56 57 58 59 60 61 64 65 68 70 74 75 77 78 79 81 82 84 85 86 87 90 91 92 93 94 95 96 100 101 102 107 108 110 111 114 115 117 118 119 120 121 122 123 124 126 129 130 132 137 138 139 141 142 143 144 146 147 148 149 150 154 156 157 164 167 **S** Loma Linda University Adventist Health Sciences Center, Loma Linda, CA
Primary Contact: Trevor G. Wright, Chief Executive Officer
COO: Lyndon C. Edwards, Chief Operating Officer
CFO: Angela Lalas, CPA, Chief Financial Officer
CMO: H Roger Hadley, M.D., Vice President, Medical Affairs
CIO: Mark Zirkelbach, Chief Information Officer
CNO: Helen Staples–Evans, MS, Chief Nursing Officer
Web address: www.llumc.edu
Control: Other not–for–profit (including NFP Corporation) **Service**: General medical and surgical

Staffed Beds: 482 **Admissions:** 26199 **Census:** 455 **Outpatient Visits:** 691518 **Births:** 0 **Total Expense ($000):** 1742166 **Payroll Expense ($000):** 487763 **Personnel:** 6167

TOTALLY KIDS REHABILITATION HOSPITAL (053038), 1720 Mountain View Avenue, Zip 92354–1727; tel. 909/796–6915, (Nonreporting) **A**1 10
Primary Contact: Doug Padgett, President/Chief Executive Officer/Chairman of the Board
Web address: https://totallykids.com/
Control: Corporation, Investor–owned (for–profit) **Service**: Rehabilitation

Staffed Beds: 81

LOMPOC—Santa Barbara County

★ **LOMPOC VALLEY MEDICAL CENTER (050110)**, 1515 East Ocean Avenue, Zip 93436–7092, Mailing Address: P.O. Box 1058, Zip 93438–1058; tel. 805/737–3300, (Nonreporting) **A**10 22
Primary Contact: Stephen Popkin, Chief Executive Officer
COO: Naishadh Buch, Chief Operating Officer
CFO: Robert M Baden, Chief Financial Officer
CMO: Randall Michel, M.D., Chief of Staff
CIO: Jim White, Chief Information Officer
CHR: Edwin R Braxton, Director Human Resources
CNO: Yvette Renee Cope, Chief Nurse Executive
Web address: www.lompocvmc.com
Control: Hospital district or authority, Government, Nonfederal **Service**: General medical and surgical

Staffed Beds: 170

LONE PINE—Inyo County

SOUTHERN INYO HEALTHCARE DISTRICT (051302), 501 East Locust Street, Zip 93545–1009, Mailing Address: P.O. Box 1009, Zip 93545–1009; tel. 760/876–5501, (Nonreporting) **A**10 18
Primary Contact: Peter Spiers, Chief Executive Officer
COO: Peter Spiers, Chief Operating Officer
CFO: Marise Andrade, Controller
CIO: Phyllis Gregory, Registered Health Information Administrator
CHR: Nancy Erickson, Human Resource Director
CNO: Colleen Wilson, Chief Nursing Officer
Web address: www.sihd.org
Control: Hospital district or authority, Government, Nonfederal **Service**: General medical and surgical

Staffed Beds: 4

LONG BEACH—Los Angeles County

COLLEGE MEDICAL CENTER (050776), 2776 Pacific Avenue, Zip 90806–2613; tel. 562/595–1911, (Nonreporting) **A**3 5 10 12 13 22
Primary Contact: Joseph Avelino, Chief Executive Officer
COO: Jennifer Ensminger, Chief Operating Officer
CFO: Jim Canedo, Chief Financial Officer
CMO: Luke Watson, M.D., Chief of Staff
CIO: Rohan Corea, Director Healthcare Information Technology
CHR: Ann Mattia Schiller, Vice President Human Resources
Web address: www.collegemedicalcenter.com/
Control: Other not–for–profit (including NFP Corporation) **Service**: General medical and surgical

Staffed Beds: 221

Hospitals, U.S. / CALIFORNIA

✦ △ **LONG BEACH MEDICAL CENTER (050485)**, 2801 Atlantic Avenue, Zip 90806–1701, Mailing Address: P.O. Box 1428, Zip 90801–1428; tel. 562/933–2000, **A**1 2 3 5 7 8 10 **F**3 8 9 11 12 14 15 17 18 20 22 24 26 28 29 30 31 34 35 36 37 38 39 40 43 44 45 46 47 48 49 50 52 53 54 55 56 57 58 59 61 63 64 65 68 70 74 75 77 78 79 81 82 84 85 86 87 90 93 96 97 100 102 107 108 110 111 114 115 116 117 118 119 120 121 123 124 126 128 129 130 131 132 135 141 142 143 144 146 147 148 149 150 154 156 157 160 164 167 **S** MemorialCare, Fountain Valley, CA
Primary Contact: Blair M. Kent, Executive Vice President/Chief Executive Officer, Long Beach Medical Center
COO: Helen Macfie, Chief Operating Officer
CFO: Yair Katz, Chief Financial Officer
CMO: Fombe Ndiforchu, Chief Medical Officer
CIO: Danny Asaoka, Executive Director Information Systems
CHR: Marcie Atchison, Vice President Human Resources
CNO: Antonio M Garcia, Chief Nursing Officer
Web address: www.memorialcare.org/LongBeach
Control: Other not–for–profit (including NFP Corporation) **Service:** General medical and surgical

Staffed Beds: 412 **Admissions:** 15743 **Census:** 283 **Outpatient Visits:** 239170 **Births:** 0 **Total Expense ($000):** 722050 **Payroll Expense ($000):** 237130 **Personnel:** 3027

☐ **MILLER CHILDREN'S & WOMEN'S HOSPITAL LONG BEACH (053309)**, 2801 Atlantic Avenue, Zip 90806–1701; tel. 562/933–5437, **A**1 2 3 5 10 **F**3 19 21 23 25 27 29 30 31 32 35 36 37 38 40 41 43 44 45 47 48 49 50 52 53 54 61 64 65 66 68 72 74 75 76 77 78 79 81 82 84 85 86 87 88 89 93 96 97 100 102 107 108 111 114 115 116 117 118 119 120 121 123 124 126 129 130 132 134 135 141 142 143 144 146 147 148 149 154 156 157 164 167 169 **S** MemorialCare, Fountain Valley, CA
Primary Contact: Blair M. Kent, Executive Vice President/Chief Executive Officer, Long Beach Medical Center
COO: Helen Macfie, Chief Operating Officer
CFO: Yair Katz, Chief Financial Officer
CMO: Graham Tse, M.D., Chief Medical Officer
CIO: Danny Asaoka, Executive Director Information Systems
CHR: Marcie Atchison, Vice President Human Resources
CNO: Antonio M Garcia, Chief Nursing Officer
Web address: https://www.memorialcare.org/locations/miller-childrens-womens-hospital-long-beach
Control: Other not–for–profit (including NFP Corporation) **Service:** Children's general medical and surgical

Staffed Beds: 371 **Admissions:** 13459 **Census:** 167 **Outpatient Visits:** 115728 **Births:** 5354 **Total Expense ($000):** 539729 **Payroll Expense ($000):** 173067 **Personnel:** 1437

✦ **ST. MARY MEDICAL CENTER LONG BEACH (050191)**, 1050 Linden Avenue, Zip 90813–3321, Mailing Address: P.O. Box 887, Zip 90801–0887; tel. 562/491–9000, **A**1 3 5 10 **F**3 12 13 15 18 19 20 22 24 25 26 28 29 30 31 32 34 35 38 39 40 41 43 44 45 46 47 48 49 50 54 55 56 57 59 61 64 65 66 68 70 71 72 74 75 76 77 78 79 80 81 82 84 85 86 87 89 93 96 97 100 104 107 108 110 111 115 118 119 120 121 122 123 130 131 143 145 146 147 153 156 167 169 **S** CommonSpirit Health, Chicago, IL
Primary Contact: Carolyn P. Caldwell, FACHE, President and Chief Executive Officer
COO: Ardel Avelino, Vice President and Chief Operating Officer
CIO: David Ung, Site Director
CHR: Denise Livingston, Director Human Resources
CNO: Gloria Carter, Chief Nurse Executive Officer
Web address: www.stmarymedicalcenter.org
Control: Other not–for–profit (including NFP Corporation) **Service:** General medical and surgical

Staffed Beds: 307 **Admissions:** 10221 **Census:** 184 **Outpatient Visits:** 87809 **Births:** 1368 **Total Expense ($000):** 436832 **Payroll Expense ($000):** 164444 **Personnel:** 1371

✦ △ **TIBOR RUBIN VA MEDICAL CENTER**, 5901 East 7th Street, Zip 90822–5201; tel. 562/826–8000, **A**1 3 5 7 8 **F**2 3 5 8 9 10 12 15 18 20 22 26 28 29 30 31 33 34 35 36 38 39 40 44 45 46 47 48 49 50 51 53 54 56 57 58 59 60 61 63 64 65 66 68 69 70 74 75 77 78 79 81 82 83 84 85 86 87 90 91 92 93 94 95 96 97 98 100 101 102 103 104 105 107 108 110 111 114 115 116 117 119 120 121 122 123 124 125 127 128 129 130 131 132 135 144 146 147 148 149 150 152 154 156 157 158 160 162 163 164 167 **S** Department of Veterans Affairs, Washington, DC
Primary Contact: Walt C. Dannenberg, FACHE, Medical Center Director
COO: Anthony DeFrancesco, Associate Director
CFO: Michael J Rupert, Chief Financial Officer
CMO: Sandor Szabo, M.D., Ph.D., M.P.H., Chief of Staff
CIO: Rodney Sagmit, Chief Information Management
CHR: Mary E McCartan, Manager Human Resources
Web address: www.longbeach.va.gov/
Control: Veterans Affairs, Government, federal **Service:** General medical and surgical

Staffed Beds: 276 **Admissions:** 8393 **Census:** 216 **Outpatient Visits:** 1445140 **Births:** 0 **Total Expense ($000):** 911101 **Payroll Expense ($000):** 595722 **Personnel:** 4411

LOS ALAMITOS—Orange County

LOS ALAMITOS MEDICAL CENTER See UCI Health – Los Alamitos

✦ **UCI HEALTH – LOS ALAMITOS (050551)**, 3751 Katella Avenue, Zip 90720–3164; tel. 562/598–1311, (Nonreporting) **A**1 10 **S** University of California Systemwide Administration, Oakland, CA
Primary Contact: Kent G. Clayton, Chief Executive Officer
CFO: Dave Vickers, Chief Financial Officer
CMO: Nirav Patel, M.D., Chief of Staff
CIO: Sally Andrada, Chief Information Officer
CHR: Mark Fisher, Chief Human Resources Officer
Web address: www.losalamitosmedctr.com
Control: Corporation, Investor–owned (for–profit) **Service:** General medical and surgical

Staffed Beds: 120

LOS ANGELES—Los Angeles County

(Mailing Addresses – Canoga Park, Encino, Granada Hills, Harbor City, Hollywood, Mission Hills, North Hollywood, Northridge, Panorama City, San Pedro, Sepulveda, Sherman Oaks, Sun Valley, Sylmar, Tarzana, Van Nuys, West Hills, West Los Angeles, Woodland Hills)

✦ **ADVENTIST HEALTH WHITE MEMORIAL (050103)**, 1720 East Cesar E. Chavez Avenue, Zip 90033–2414; tel. 323/268–5000, (Nonreporting) **A**1 2 3 5 10 19 **S** Adventist Health, Roseville, CA
Primary Contact: John Raffoul, FACHE, President
CIO: Ralf Weissenberger, Director Information Systems
CHR: Natasha Milatovich, Association Vice President Human Resources
CNO: Patricia Stone, R.N., MSN, Senior Vice President Operations and Chief Nursing Officer
Web address: www.whitememorial.com
Control: Church operated, Nongovernment, not–for–profit **Service:** General medical and surgical

Staffed Beds: 353

✦ **BARLOW RESPIRATORY HOSPITAL (052031)**, 2000 Stadium Way, Zip 90026–2696; tel. 213/250–4200, (Nonreporting) **A**1 10
Primary Contact: Amit Mohan, Ph.D., FACHE, President and Chief Executive Officer
CFO: Edward Engesser, Chief Financial Officer and Chief Information Officer
CMO: David Nelson, M.D., Medical Director
CIO: Edward Engesser, Chief Financial Officer and Chief Information Officer
CHR: Rashawn Woods, Vice President Human Resources
CNO: Gladys D'Souza, Chief Nursing Officer
Web address: https://www.barlowhospital.org/
Control: Other not–for–profit (including NFP Corporation) **Service:** Acute long–term care hospital

Staffed Beds: 105

Hospital, Medicare Provider Number, Address, Telephone, Approval, Facility, and Physician Codes, Health Care System

★ American Hospital Association (AHA) membership
☐ The Joint Commission accreditation
○ Healthcare Facilities Accreditation Program
◇ DNV Healthcare Inc. accreditation
⇑ Center for Improvement in Healthcare Quality Accreditation
△ Commission on Accreditation of Rehabilitation Facilities (CARF) accreditation

© 2025 AHA Guide

Hospitals, U.S. / CALIFORNIA

✵ **CALIFORNIA HOSPITAL MEDICAL CENTER (050149)**, 1401 South Grand Avenue, Zip 90015–3010; tel. 213/748–2411, **A**1 3 5 10 19 **F**3 8 13 15 17 18 20 22 24 26 28 29 30 31 34 35 40 41 43 49 50 57 59 64 68 70 72 74 75 76 77 78 79 80 81 83 84 87 89 100 107 110 111 114 115 119 126 130 146 147 148 149 154 156 164 167 169 **P**5 7 **S** CommonSpirit Health, Chicago, IL
Primary Contact: Alina Moran, FACHE, FABC, President
COO: Nat'e Guyton, R.N., MSN, Chief Operating Officer
CFO: Rebecca Cheng, Chief Financial Officer
CMO: Debi Siljander, M.D., Chief Medical Officer
CIO: David Ung, Director, Information Technology
CHR: Kristin Anderson, Director, Human Resources
Web address: www.chmcla.org
Control: Other not–for–profit (including NFP Corporation) **Service**: General medical and surgical

Staffed Beds: 278 **Admissions**: 14737 **Census**: 214 **Outpatient Visits**: 82896 **Births**: 2506 **Total Expense ($000)**: 576325 **Payroll Expense ($000)**: 206225 **Personnel**: 1691

✵ △ **CALIFORNIA REHABILITATION INSTITUTE (053039)**, 2070 Century Park East, Zip 90067–1907; tel. 424/363–1000, **A**1 3 5 7 10 **F**3 29 30 31 34 35 37 44 50 58 60 64 68 74 75 77 79 82 85 86 87 90 91 92 93 94 95 96 100 101 119 130 132 148 149 154 157 164 **S** Select Medical Corporation, Mechanicsburg, PA
Primary Contact: Geoffrey Hall, Chief Executive Officer
Web address: www.californiarehabinstitute.com/
Control: Corporation, Investor–owned (for–profit) **Service**: Rehabilitation

Staffed Beds: 138 **Admissions**: 3345 **Census**: 131 **Outpatient Visits**: 8416 **Births**: 0 **Personnel**: 560

✵ **CEDARS–SINAI MEDICAL CENTER (050625)**, 8700 Beverly Boulevard, Zip 90048–1865; tel. 310/423–5000, **A**1 2 3 5 8 10 19 **F**3 6 8 9 11 12 13 14 15 17 18 19 20 21 22 23 24 25 26 27 28 29 30 31 32 34 35 36 37 38 39 40 41 43 44 45 46 47 49 50 51 52 54 55 56 57 58 59 60 61 64 65 66 68 69 70 71 72 74 75 76 77 78 79 81 82 83 84 85 86 87 88 89 91 92 93 96 97 100 102 107 108 110 111 112 113 114 115 116 117 118 119 120 121 123 124 126 130 131 132 134 135 136 137 138 139 140 141 142 143 145 146 147 148 149 150 154 157 166 167 169 **P**3 5 6 **S** Cedars–Sinai Health System, West Hollywood, CA
Primary Contact: Thomas M. Priselac, President and Chief Executive Officer
COO: Bryan Croft, Executive Vice President and Chief Operating Officer
CFO: Edward M Prunchunas, Executive Vice President and Chief Financial Officer
CMO: Richard V. Riggs, M.D., Senior Vice President Medical Affairs and Chief Medical Officer
CHR: Andrew Ortiz, Senior Vice President, Human Resources and Organization Development
CNO: David R Marshall, R.N., Ph.D., Senior Vice President, Chief Nursing Executive
Web address: www.cedars-sinai.edu
Control: Other not–for–profit (including NFP Corporation) **Service**: General medical and surgical

Staffed Beds: 915 **Admissions**: 45439 **Census**: 818 **Outpatient Visits**: 1021235 **Births**: 6177 **Total Expense ($000)**: 4142362 **Payroll Expense ($000)**: 1605292 **Personnel**: 16031

✵ **CHA HOLLYWOOD PRESBYTERIAN MEDICAL CENTER (050063)**, 1300 North Vermont Avenue, Zip 90027–6306; tel. 213/413–3000, (Nonreporting) **A**1 3 10 19
Primary Contact: Jamie Yoo, Chief Executive Officer
COO: Wontae Cha, Chief Operating Officer
CIO: Steve Giles, Chief Information Officer
CHR: George Leisher Jr, Vice President Human Resources
CNO: Farideh Ara, Interim Chief Nursing Officer
Web address: www.hollywoodpresbyterian.com
Control: Partnership, Investor–owned (for–profit) **Service**: General medical and surgical

Staffed Beds: 434

★ △ ⇑ **CHILDREN'S HOSPITAL LOS ANGELES (053302)**, 4650 West Sunset Boulevard, Zip 90027–6062, Mailing Address: 4650 West Sunset Boulevard, MS #95, Zip 90027–6062; tel. 323/660–2450, **A**3 5 7 8 10 21 **F**3 7 8 9 11 14 15 17 19 21 23 25 27 28 29 30 31 32 34 35 36 37 38 39 40 41 43 44 45 46 47 48 49 50 54 55 57 58 59 60 61 64 65 68 70 72 73 74 75 77 78 79 80 81 82 83 84 86 87 88 89 90 91 92 93 94 95 107 111 115 116 117 118 119 120 121 122 124 126 129 130 131 132 134 136 137 138 139 140 141 146 148 154 155 156 157 167
Primary Contact: Paul S. Viviano, President and Chief Executive Officer
COO: Lara Khouri, Executive Vice President and Chief Operating Officer
CFO: Lannie Tonnu, Senior Vice President and Chief Financial Officer
CMO: Brent Polk, M.D., Chair Department of Pediatrics and Vice President Academic Affairs
CIO: TJ Malseed, Vice President and Chief Information Officer
CHR: Myra Gregorian, Vice President and Chief Human Resources Officer
CNO: Kelly Johnson, Senior Vice President, Chief Nursing Officer
Web address: www.chla.org
Control: Other not–for–profit (including NFP Corporation) **Service**: Children's general medical and surgical

Staffed Beds: 413 **Admissions**: 17010 **Census**: 313 **Outpatient Visits**: 371726 **Births**: 0 **Total Expense ($000)**: 1652947 **Payroll Expense ($000)**: 660322 **Personnel**: 6385

DOCS SURGICAL HOSPITAL (050785), 6000 San Vicente Boulevard, Zip 90036–4404; tel. 323/930–1040, (Nonreporting) **A**10
Primary Contact: Khawar Siddique, Co–Chief Executive Officer
Web address: www.docsspineortho.com
Control: Partnership, Investor–owned (for–profit) **Service**: General medical and surgical

Staffed Beds: 17

☐ **EAST LOS ANGELES DOCTORS HOSPITAL (050641)**, 4060 Whittier Boulevard, Zip 90023–2526; tel. 323/268–5514, (Nonreporting) **A**1 10 **S** Pipeline Health, El Segundo, CA
Primary Contact: Rick Rufino, Chief Executive Officer
CNO: Wafa El Musselmani, R.N., Chief Nursing Officer
Web address: https://www.eladoctorshospital.com/
Control: Corporation, Investor–owned (for–profit) **Service**: General medical and surgical

Staffed Beds: 127

○ **GATEWAYS HOSPITAL AND MENTAL HEALTH CENTER (054028)**, 1891 Effie Street, Zip 90026–1793; tel. 323/644–2000, (Nonreporting) **A**3 10 11
Primary Contact: Philip Wong, PsyD, Chief Executive Officer
COO: Philip Wong, PsyD, Chief Operating Officer
CMO: Imani Walker, M.D., Medical Director
CIO: Rozelle DeVera, Director of Information Systems
CHR: Vahan Demlakian, Director of Human Resources
Web address: www.gatewayshospital.org
Control: Other not–for–profit (including NFP Corporation) **Service**: Psychiatric

Staffed Beds: 55

✵ △ **GREATER LOS ANGELES HCS**, 11301 Wilshire Boulevard, Zip 90073–1003; tel. 310/478–3711, (Nonreporting) **A**1 3 5 7 8 **S** Department of Veterans Affairs, Washington, DC
Primary Contact: Robert Merchant, Interim Medical Center Director & Executive Director, Ambulatory Care Services
COO: Susan Shyshka, Associate Director
CFO: Joseph Schmitt, Chief Financial Officer
CIO: Eugene Archey, Chief Information Technology
CHR: Brenda Cabunoc, Chief Human Resources
Web address: https://www.va.gov/greater-los-angeles-health-care/
Control: Veterans Affairs, Government, federal **Service**: General medical and surgical

Staffed Beds: 422

HOLLYWOOD COMMUNITY HOSPITAL OF VAN NUYS See Southern California Hospital At Van Nuys

HOLLYWOOD PRESBYTERIAN MEDICAL CENTER See Cha Hollywood Presbyterian Medical Center

KAISER FOUNDATION MENTAL HEALTH CENTER See Kaiser Permanente Los Angeles Medical Center, Los Angeles

Hospitals, U.S. / CALIFORNIA

☒ **KAISER PERMANENTE LOS ANGELES MEDICAL CENTER (050138)**, 4867 West Sunset Boulevard, Zip 90027–5961; tel. 323/783–4011, (Includes KAISER FOUNDATION MENTAL HEALTH CENTER, 765 West College Street, Los Angeles, California, Zip 90012, tel. 213/580–7200) **A**1 3 5 8 10 19 **F**3 7 8 13 15 17 18 19 20 21 22 23 24 26 29 30 31 34 35 36 38 40 44 45 46 47 49 50 51 52 54 55 56 57 58 59 60 61 62 63 64 65 66 68 70 72 74 75 76 77 78 79 81 82 83 84 85 86 87 88 89 92 93 97 98 101 102 104 105 107 108 109 110 111 113 114 115 116 117 118 119 120 121 122 123 124 126 129 130 131 132 135 144 146 147 148 149 150 153 154 156 157 162 164 165 167 168 169 **P**6 **S** Kaiser Foundation Hospitals, Oakland, CA
Primary Contact: Robert M. Luterbach, Interim Senior Vice President/Area Manager, Los Angeles/Chief Operating Officer
COO: Robert M Luterbach, Chief Operating Officer
CFO: Brad Malsed, Area Chief Financial Officer
CMO: Michael Tome, M.D., Medical Director
CIO: David Strickland, Area Information Officer
CHR: Paul J Martin, Director Human Resources
Web address: https://healthy.kaiserpermanente.org/southern-california/facilities/los-angeles-medical-center-100099
Control: Other not–for–profit (including NFP Corporation) **Service**: General medical and surgical

Staffed Beds: 560 Admissions: 21540 Census: 339 Outpatient Visits: 130558 Births: 2400 Personnel: 3667

☒ **KAISER PERMANENTE PANORAMA CITY MEDICAL CENTER (050137)**, 13651 Willard Street, Zip 91402; tel. 818/375–2000, **A**1 3 5 10 19 **F**3 7 11 13 15 18 29 30 31 34 35 37 38 40 41 44 45 46 48 49 50 51 54 55 56 57 58 59 60 61 62 63 64 65 66 68 70 72 74 75 76 77 78 79 81 82 84 85 86 87 92 97 101 102 104 107 108 110 111 114 115 116 117 118 119 124 126 129 130 131 132 135 141 143 144 146 147 148 149 154 156 157 166 167 169 **P**6 **S** Kaiser Foundation Hospitals, Oakland, CA
Primary Contact: Camille Applin–Jones, Senior Vice President and Area Manager
COO: Laura Gallardo, Chief Operating Officer
CFO: Karla Valle, Area Chief Financial Officer
CMO: James Lau, M.D., Area Medical Director
CIO: Earle Johnson, Area Information Officer
CHR: Carole L Erken, Human Resources Leader
Web address: www.kaiserpermanente.org
Control: Other not–for–profit (including NFP Corporation) **Service**: General medical and surgical

Staffed Beds: 218 Admissions: 11142 Census: 111 Outpatient Visits: 184478 Births: 2251 Personnel: 1310

☒ **KAISER PERMANENTE SOUTH BAY MEDICAL CENTER (050411)**, 25825 Vermont Avenue, Zip 90710–3599; tel. 310/325–5111, **A**1 3 5 10 **F**3 5 8 9 11 12 13 15 24 26 28 29 30 31 32 34 35 36 40 41 44 45 46 47 48 49 50 51 53 54 55 56 57 58 59 60 61 63 64 65 66 68 70 72 74 75 76 77 78 79 81 82 83 85 86 87 91 92 93 94 96 97 100 105 107 108 110 111 114 115 116 117 118 119 126 130 131 132 134 135 144 146 147 148 149 150 154 156 157 160 162 164 165 166 167 168 169 **S** Kaiser Foundation Hospitals, Oakland, CA
Primary Contact: Margie Harrier, MSN, R.N., Senior Vice President/Area Manager, South Bay
Web address: www.kaiserpermanente.org
Control: Other not–for–profit (including NFP Corporation) **Service**: General medical and surgical

Staffed Beds: 257 Admissions: 12883 Census: 153 Outpatient Visits: 196834 Births: 2199 Personnel: 1612

☒ **KAISER PERMANENTE WEST LOS ANGELES MEDICAL CENTER (050561)**, 6041 Cadillac Avenue, Zip 90034–1700; tel. 323/857–2201, **A**1 3 5 10 19 **F**3 5 6 11 12 13 15 29 30 31 34 35 37 40 41 44 45 46 47 48 49 50 55 56 57 58 59 60 61 63 64 65 68 70 72 73 74 75 76 77 78 79 81 82 84 85 87 92 93 100 102 107 108 109 110 111 114 115 116 117 118 119 126 130 135 146 148 149 152 154 160 161 162 164 166 167 169 **S** Kaiser Foundation Hospitals, Oakland, CA
Primary Contact: Lilit Sarah. Zibari, Senior Vice President, Area Manager/West Los Angeles
CMO: Fred Alexander, M.D., Medical Director
CIO: Gregory M Sincock, Information Technology Leader
Web address: www.kaiserpermanente.org
Control: Other not–for–profit (including NFP Corporation) **Service**: General medical and surgical

Staffed Beds: 124 Admissions: 10095 Census: 124 Outpatient Visits: 330978 Births: 1727 Personnel: 1433

☒ **KAISER PERMANENTE WOODLAND HILLS MEDICAL CENTER (050677)**, 5601 DeSoto Avenue, Zip 91367–6798; tel. 818/719–2000, **A**1 3 5 10 19 **F**3 6 8 9 11 12 13 15 18 28 29 30 31 32 34 35 38 40 41 44 45 46 48 49 50 51 52 53 54 55 56 57 58 59 60 61 63 64 65 66 68 70 73 74 75 76 77 78 79 80 81 82 84 85 86 87 90 92 93 97 100 102 104 107 108 110 111 114 115 116 117 119 124 129 130 131 132 134 135 141 144 145 146 147 148 149 150 153 154 156 157 162 164 165 167 169 **P**6 **S** Kaiser Foundation Hospitals, Oakland, CA
Primary Contact: Murtaza Sanwari, Senior Vice President/Area Manager, Woodland Hills
CFO: Marilou Cheung, Assistant Administrator Finance
CMO: Gregory Kelman, M.D., Area Medical Director
CIO: Earle Johnson, Area Information Officer
CHR: Cathy Cousineau, Director Human Resources
CNO: Nancy Tankel, R.N., Chief Nurse Executive
Web address: www.kaiserpermanente.org
Control: Other not–for–profit (including NFP Corporation) **Service**: General medical and surgical

Staffed Beds: 204 Admissions: 9910 Census: 109 Outpatient Visits: 181662 Births: 1818 Personnel: 1557

☒ **KECK HOSPITAL OF USC (050696)**, 1500 San Pablo Street, Zip 90033–5313; tel. 323/442–8500, **A**1 3 5 8 10 19 **F**3 6 8 9 11 12 15 17 18 20 22 24 26 29 30 31 33 34 35 36 37 38 39 44 45 46 47 48 49 50 51 52 53 54 55 56 57 58 59 60 61 64 65 66 68 70 71 74 75 77 78 79 81 82 84 85 86 87 90 91 92 93 94 95 96 97 100 101 104 107 108 109 110 111 112 113 114 115 116 117 118 119 124 126 129 130 131 132 135 137 138 139 140 141 142 145 146 147 148 149 150 154 156 157 160 161 163 164 165 167 **P**6 **S** Keck Medicine of USC, Los Angeles, CA
Primary Contact: William Martin. Sargeant, Chief Executive Officer/Interim Chief, Office of Performance & Transformation
CMO: Stephanie Hall, M.D., Chief Medical Officer
CIO: Timothy James Malseed, Chief Information Officer
CHR: Matthew McElrath, Chief Human Resources Officer
CNO: Ceonne Houston–Raasikh, Chief Nursing Officer
Web address: https://www.keckmedicine.org/
Control: Other not–for–profit (including NFP Corporation) **Service**: General medical and surgical

Staffed Beds: 401 Admissions: 11669 Census: 240 Outpatient Visits: 377379 Births: 0 Total Expense ($000): 1414793 Payroll Expense ($000): 464465 Personnel: 3144

KEDREN COMMUNITY HEALTH CENTER (054083), 4211 South Avalon Boulevard, Zip 90011–5699; tel. 323/233–0425, (Nonreporting) **A**3 5 10
Primary Contact: Gregory Polk, Chief Executive Officer
COO: Madeline Valencerina, Chief Operating Officer
CFO: Rizwan A. Uraizee, Chief Financial Officer
CMO: Frank L. Williams, Executive Vice President/Medical Director
CNO: Essie Adams, Director of Nursing
Web address: www.kedren.org/
Control: Other not–for–profit (including NFP Corporation) **Service**: Psychiatric

Staffed Beds: 72

KEDREN COMMUNITY MENTAL HEALTH CENTER See Kedren Community Health Center

☒ **KINDRED HOSPITAL–LOS ANGELES (052032)**, 5525 West Slauson Avenue, Zip 90056–1067; tel. 310/642–0325, (Nonreporting) **A**1 10 **S** ScionHealth, Louisville, KY
Primary Contact: Mark Apodaca, Chief Executive Officer
CFO: Charles Natcher, Chief Financial Officer
Web address: www.kindredhospitalla.com/
Control: Corporation, Investor–owned (for–profit) **Service**: Acute long–term care hospital

Staffed Beds: 81

☒ **LA DOWNTOWN MEDICAL CENTER, LLC (050763)**, 1711 West Temple Street, Zip 90026–5421; tel. 213/989–6100, (Includes LA DOWNTOWN MEDICAL CENTER, LLC –INGLESIDE CAMPUS, 7500 East Hellman Avenue, Rosemead, California, Zip 91770, tel. 626/288–1160) (Nonreporting) **A**1 10
Primary Contact: Vicki Rollins, President
CFO: John Cowles, Chief Financial Officer
CMO: Louis Acosta, M.D., Chief of Staff
CIO: Scott Musack, Chief Information Officer
CHR: Sylvia Cloud, Director Human Resources
Web address: https://ladowntownmc.com/
Control: Corporation, Investor–owned (for–profit) **Service**: General medical and surgical

Staffed Beds: 211

Hospital, Medicare Provider Number, Address, Telephone, Approval, Facility, and Physician Codes, Health Care System

★ American Hospital Association (AHA) membership
□ The Joint Commission accreditation
○ Healthcare Facilities Accreditation Program
◇ DNV Healthcare Inc. accreditation
⇑ Center for Improvement in Healthcare Quality Accreditation
△ Commission on Accreditation of Rehabilitation Facilities (CARF) accreditation

Hospitals, U.S. / CALIFORNIA

LAC–OLIVE VIEW–UCLA MEDICAL CENTER See Olive View–Ucla Medical Center

LAC+USC MEDICAL CENTER See Los Angeles General Medical Center

☐ **LOS ANGELES COMMUNITY HOSPITAL AT LOS ANGELES (050663)**, 4081 East Olympic Boulevard, Zip 90023–3330; tel. 323/267–0477, (Includes LOS ANGELES COMMUNITY HOSPITAL OF NORWALK, 13222 Bloomfield Avenue, Norwalk, California, Zip 90650, tel. 562/863–4763) (Nonreporting) **A**1 10 **S** Prospect Medical Holdings, Los Angeles, CA
Primary Contact: Hector Hernandez, Chief Executive Officer
CFO: Johnnette Chong, Chief Financial Officer
Web address: www.altacorp.com/altacorp/our-hospitals/lach-menu.html
Control: Corporation, Investor–owned (for–profit) **Service**: General medical and surgical

Staffed Beds: 212

LOS ANGELES COUNTY CENTRAL JAIL HOSPITAL, 441 Bauchet Street, Zip 90012–2906; tel. 213/473–6100, (Nonreporting)
Primary Contact: Tom Flaherty, Assistant Administrator
Control: County, Government, Nonfederal **Service**: Hospital unit of an institution (prison hospital, college infirmary, etc.)

Staffed Beds: 190

LOS ANGELES GENERAL MEDICAL CENTER (050373), 2051 Marengo Street, Zip 90033–1352; tel. 323/409–1000, (Includes GENERAL HOSPITAL, 1200 North State Street, Los Angeles, California, Zip 90033, tel. 562/863–4763; WOMEN'S AND CHILDREN'S HOSPITAL, 1240 North Mission Road, Los Angeles, California, Zip 90033, tel. 562/863–4763) (Nonreporting) **A**2 3 5 10 **S** Los Angeles County–Department of Health Services, Los Angeles, CA
Primary Contact: Jorge Orozco, Chief Executive Officer
COO: Henry Ornelas, Chief Operating Officer
CFO: Mark Corbet, Interim Chief Financial Officer
CMO: Brad Spellberg, M.D., Chief Medical Officer
CIO: Oscar Autelli, Chief Information Officer
CHR: Elizabeth Jacobi, Human Resources Director
CNO: Isabel Milan, R.N., Chief Nursing Officer
Web address: www.lacusc.org
Control: County, Government, Nonfederal **Service**: General medical and surgical

Staffed Beds: 538

MARTIN LUTHER KING, JR. COMMUNITY HOSPITAL See MLK Community Healthcare

✣ **MISSION COMMUNITY HOSPITAL (050704)**, 14850 Roscoe Boulevard, Zip 91402–4677; tel. 818/787–2222, (Nonreporting) **A**1 3 5 10
Primary Contact: James Theiring, Chief Executive Officer
CFO: Mihi Lee, Chief Financial Officer
CMO: Glenn Marshak, M.D., Chief of Staff
CIO: Eric Rivers, Chief Information Officer
CHR: Carolyn Fish, Director Human Resources
CNO: Gwendolyn Dianne Wagner, R.N., MSN, Chief Nursing Officer
Web address: www.mchonline.org
Control: Other not–for–profit (including NFP Corporation) **Service**: General medical and surgical

Staffed Beds: 145

✣ **MLK COMMUNITY HEALTHCARE (050779)**, 1680 East 120th Street, Zip 90059–3026; tel. 424/338–8000, (Nonreporting) **A**1 3 5 10
Primary Contact: Elaine Batchlor, M.D., M.P.H., Chief Executive Officer
COO: Myrna Allen, R.N., MS, Chief Operating and Nursing Officer
CMO: John Fisher, M.D., Chief Medical Officer
CIO: Sajid Ahmed, Chief Information and Innovation Officer
CHR: Susan M Burrows, Vice President Human Resources
CNO: Myrna Allen, R.N., MS, Chief Operating and Nursing Officer
Web address: www.mlkcommunityhospital.org/
Control: Other not–for–profit (including NFP Corporation) **Service**: General medical and surgical

Staffed Beds: 185

MOTION PICTURE AND TELEVISION FUND HOSPITAL AND RESIDENTIAL SERVICES See MPTF/Motion Picture & Television Fund

☐ **MPTF/MOTION PICTURE & TELEVISION FUND (050552)**, 23388 Mulholland Drive, Zip 91364–2792; tel. 818/876–1888, (Nonreporting) **A**1 10
Primary Contact: Robert Beitcher, President/Chief Executive Officer
COO: David Asplund, Chief Operating Officer
CFO: Frank Guarrera, Executive Vice President and Chief Financial Officer
CHR: Nancy Rubin, Vice President Human Resources
Web address: https://mptf.org/
Control: Other not–for–profit (including NFP Corporation) **Service**: General medical and surgical

Staffed Beds: 20

☐ △ **NORTHRIDGE HOSPITAL MEDICAL CENTER (050116)**, 18300 Roscoe Boulevard, Zip 91328–4167; tel. 818/885–8500, **A**1 3 5 7 10 **F**3 11 13 15 17 18 20 22 24 26 28 29 30 31 34 35 37 38 40 41 43 45 46 49 57 59 60 61 64 68 70 72 74 75 76 77 78 79 81 82 84 85 87 89 90 93 95 97 98 102 103 104 105 107 108 110 111 114 115 119 120 121 123 124 126 130 146 147 148 153 167 169 **S** CommonSpirit Health, Chicago, IL
Primary Contact: Jeremy Zoch, President and Chief Executive Officer
CFO: Douglas Brown, Chief Financial Officer
CMO: Mark Dumais, M.D., Chief Medical Officer
CHR: Susan Paulsen, Director Human Resources
CNO: Resha T Holman, Chief Nurse Executive Officer
Web address: www.northridgehospital.org
Control: Other not–for–profit (including NFP Corporation) **Service**: General medical and surgical

Staffed Beds: 394 **Admissions**: 14363 **Census**: 212 **Outpatient Visits**: 94402 **Births**: 867 **Total Expense ($000)**: 490843 **Payroll Expense ($000)**: 203728 **Personnel**: 1753

☐ **OLIVE VIEW–UCLA MEDICAL CENTER (050040)**, 14445 Olive View Drive, Zip 91342–1438; tel. 818/364–1555, (Nonreporting) **A**1 3 5 10 **S** Los Angeles County–Department of Health Services, Los Angeles, CA
Primary Contact: Konita Wilks, Chief Executive Officer
COO: Niloo Shahi, Chief Operating Officer
CFO: Anthony Gray, Chief Financial Officer
CMO: Shannon Thyne, Chief Medical Officer
CIO: Susan Aintablian, Chief Information Officer
CHR: Thomas Beggane, Manager Human Resources
CNO: Dellone Pascascio, Chief Nursing Officer
Web address: www.dhs.lacounty.gov/wps/portal/dhs/oliveview
Control: County, Government, Nonfederal **Service**: General medical and surgical

Staffed Beds: 202

☐ **PACIFICA HOSPITAL OF THE VALLEY (050378)**, 9449 San Fernando Road, Zip 91352–1489; tel. 818/767–3310, (Nonreporting) **A**1 10
Primary Contact: Precious Velvet. Mayes, President and Chief Executive Officer
COO: Daniel Santos, Director Ancillary Services
CFO: Eileen Fisler, Chief Financial Officer
CMO: Joseph Eipe, M.D., Chief Medical Officer
CIO: Mubashir Hashmi, Chief Information Officer
CHR: Patti Alonzo, Manager Human Resources
CNO: Janet B. Latto, Chief Nursing Officer and Disaster Officer
Web address: www.pacificahospital.com
Control: Corporation, Investor–owned (for–profit) **Service**: General medical and surgical

Staffed Beds: 158

★ **PIH HEALTH GOOD SAMARITAN HOSPITAL (050471)**, 1225 Wilshire Boulevard, Zip 90017–2395; tel. 213/977–2121, **A**3 5 10 19 22 **F**3 8 13 15 17 18 20 22 24 26 29 30 31 35 40 45 46 49 53 58 60 62 68 70 72 74 75 76 77 78 79 80 81 82 84 85 87 92 93 97 107 108 111 114 115 119 120 121 123 124 130 146 147 148 149 154 167 **S** PIH Health, Whittier, CA
Primary Contact: James R. West, President and Chief Executive Officer
COO: Phillip Wolfe, Vice President of Professional Operations
CFO: Alan Ino, Chief Financial Officer
CMO: Margaret Bates, Chief of Staff
CIO: Dean Campbell, Vice President Information Services and Chief Information Officer
CHR: Lexie Schuster, Vice President Human Resources
CNO: Margaret Pfeiffer, R.N., MSN, Vice President Patient Care Services
Web address: www.goodsam.org
Control: Other not–for–profit (including NFP Corporation) **Service**: General medical and surgical

Staffed Beds: 346 **Admissions**: 12515 **Census**: 163 **Outpatient Visits**: 69309 **Births**: 1471 **Total Expense ($000)**: 394164 **Payroll Expense ($000)**: 138868 **Personnel**: 1260

✣ **PROVIDENCE CEDARS–SINAI TARZANA MEDICAL CENTER (050761)**, 18321 Clark Street, Zip 91356–3521; tel. 818/881–0800, **A**1 2 10 19 **F**3 13 17 18 20 22 24 26 28 29 30 31 34 35 37 40 41 44 45 46 49 50 51 54 56 57 58 59 63 64 65 70 72 74 75 76 77 78 79 80 81 82 84 85 86 87 89 100 102 107 108 111 114 115 118 119 126 130 131 132 146 147 148 149 154 162 164 167 169 **P**3 5 **S** Providence, Renton, WA
Primary Contact: Nick Lymberopoulos, Chief Executive Officer
COO: Phyllis Bushart, R.N., Chief Operating Officer
CMO: Howard Z Davis, M.D., Chief Medical Officer
CIO: Alex Nury, Chief Information Officer
CHR: Beverly Murray, Director of Human Resources
CNO: Deborah Carver, Chief Nursing Officer
Web address: www.providence.org/tarzana
Control: Other not–for–profit (including NFP Corporation) **Service**: General medical and surgical

Staffed Beds: 204 **Admissions**: 12569 **Census**: 125 **Outpatient Visits**: 160040 **Births**: 2412 **Total Expense ($000)**: 300144 **Payroll Expense ($000)**: 140904 **Personnel**: 1331

Hospitals, U.S. / CALIFORNIA

✠ △ **PROVIDENCE HOLY CROSS MEDICAL CENTER (050278)**, 15031 Rinaldi Street, Zip 91345–1207; tel. 818/365–8051, (Total facility includes 48 beds in nursing home–type unit) **A1** 2 7 10 19 **F3** 11 13 15 17 18 20 22 24 26 28 29 30 31 34 35 36 37 40 41 43 44 45 46 47 48 49 50 51 54 55 56 57 58 59 60 63 64 65 70 72 74 75 76 77 78 79 80 81 82 83 84 85 86 87 90 91 96 100 102 107 108 110 111 114 115 116 117 119 120 121 123 124 126 128 131 132 145 146 147 148 149 150 154 156 162 164 167 **P3** 5 **S** Providence, Renton, WA
Primary Contact: Bernard Klein, M.D., Chief Executive
CMO: Rex Hoffman, M.D., Chief Medical Officer
CHR: Pam Stahl, Regional Chief Human Resources Officer
CNO: Jodi Hein, Chief Nursing Officer
Web address: https://california.providence.org/holy-cross/Pages/default.aspx
Control: Other not–for–profit (including NFP Corporation) **Service**: General medical and surgical

Staffed Beds: 378 **Admissions**: 16354 **Census**: 267 **Outpatient Visits**: 322114 **Births**: 2492 **Total Expense ($000)**: 456994 **Payroll Expense ($000)**: 219872 **Personnel**: 1995

✠ △ **PROVIDENCE LITTLE COMPANY OF MARY MEDICAL CENTER SAN PEDRO (050078)**, 1300 West Seventh Street, Zip 90732–3505; tel. 310/832–3311, (Total facility includes 125 beds in nursing home–type unit) **A1** 7 10 **F3** 4 5 11 12 13 15 18 29 30 34 35 40 41 44 49 50 51 54 56 57 59 60 62 63 64 65 70 71 74 75 77 78 79 81 82 83 84 85 86 87 90 91 92 93 95 96 98 100 101 102 103 104 107 110 111 114 119 120 123 126 128 130 131 132 145 146 147 148 149 150 153 154 156 162 164 167 **P3** 5 **S** Providence, Renton, WA
Primary Contact: Michael Ricks, Chief Executive, Los Angeles Coastal Service Area
CFO: Elizabeth Zuanich, Chief Financial Officer
CMO: Richard Glimp, M.D., Chief Medical Officer
CIO: Kim Brant–Lucich, Director, Information Systems
CHR: Melissa Baker, Director, Human Resources
Web address: https://california.providence.org/san-pedro
Control: Other not–for–profit (including NFP Corporation) **Service**: General medical and surgical

Staffed Beds: 334 **Admissions**: 5728 **Census**: 198 **Outpatient Visits**: 121419 **Births**: 0 **Total Expense ($000)**: 183194 **Payroll Expense ($000)**: 107251 **Personnel**: 759

PROVIDENCE TARZANA MEDICAL CENTER See Providence Cedars–Sinai Tarzana Medical Center

✠ **RONALD REAGAN UCLA MEDICAL CENTER (050262)**, 757 Westwood Plaza, Zip 90095–8358; tel. 310/825–9111, (Includes MATTEL CHILDREN'S HOSPITAL, 757 Westwood Plz, Los Angeles, California, Zip 90095–8358, 757 Westwood Plaza, Zip 90095, tel. 310/825–9111) **A1** 3 5 8 10 19 **F3** 6 7 8 9 11 12 13 14 15 17 18 19 20 21 22 23 24 25 26 27 28 29 30 31 32 34 35 36 37 39 41 43 44 45 46 47 48 49 50 51 52 54 55 56 57 58 59 61 62 64 65 66 68 70 71 72 74 75 76 77 78 79 81 82 84 85 87 88 89 91 92 93 94 96 97 102 107 108 110 111 112 113 114 115 116 117 118 119 120 121 123 124 126 129 130 131 132 135 136 137 138 139 140 141 142 143 145 146 147 148 149 154 156 167 169 **P6 S** University of California Systemwide Administration, Oakland, CA
Primary Contact: Johnese Spisso, President, UCLA Health/Chief Executive Officer, UCLA Hospital System
COO: Richard Azar, Chief Operation Officer
CFO: Paul Staton, Chief Financial Officer
CMO: Robert Cherry, M.D., Chief Medical and Quality Officer
CHR: Susi Takeuchi, Chief Human Resources and Organization Development Officer
CNO: Karen A Grimley, Chief Nursing Executive
Web address: www.uclahealth.org
Control: State, Government, Nonfederal **Service**: General medical and surgical

Staffed Beds: 445 **Admissions**: 22267 **Census**: 480 **Outpatient Visits**: 639050 **Births**: 1749 **Total Expense ($000)**: 2798799 **Payroll Expense ($000)**: 1059463 **Personnel**: 8520

☐ **SHERMAN OAKS HOSPITAL (050755)**, 4929 Van Nuys Boulevard, Zip 91403–1777; tel. 818/981–7111, (Total facility includes 17 beds in nursing home–type unit) **A1** 5 10 **F18** 20 22 29 33 34 38 40 41 45 46 49 50 56 57 59 60 64 70 75 77 81 87 98 100 103 107 108 114 115 119 128 130 135 148 149 154 157 164 **S** Prime Healthcare, Ontario, CA
Primary Contact: EM Vitug. Garcia, Ph.D., Chief Executive Officer
CFO: Daniel Leon, Chief Financial Officer
CMO: Michael Malamed, M.D., Chief of Staff
Web address: www.shermanoakshospital.com
Control: Other not–for–profit (including NFP Corporation) **Service**: General medical and surgical

Staffed Beds: 88 **Admissions**: 4417 **Census**: 82 **Outpatient Visits**: 29605 **Births**: 0 **Total Expense ($000)**: 93342 **Payroll Expense ($000)**: 44792 **Personnel**: 569

☐ **SOUTHERN CALIFORNIA HOSPITAL AT HOLLYWOOD (050135)**, 6245 De Longpre Avenue, Zip 90028–9001; tel. 323/462–2271, (Includes SOUTHERN CALIFORNIA HOSPITAL AT VAN NUYS, 14433 Emelita Street, Van Nuys, California, Zip 91401, tel. 818/787–1511) (Nonreporting) **A1** 10 **S** Prospect Medical Holdings, Los Angeles, CA
Primary Contact: Omar Ramirez, Chief Operating Officer, California Hospitals
Web address: www.hollywoodcommunityhospital.org/
Control: Corporation, Investor–owned (for–profit) **Service**: General medical and surgical

Staffed Beds: 45

SOUTHERN CALIFORNIA HOSPITAL AT VAN NUYS See Southern California Hospital At Hollywood, Los Angeles

ST. ELIZABETH TOLUCA LAKE CONVALESCENT HOSPITAL See Providence St. Elizabeth Care Center

✠ **STEWART & LYNDA RESNICK NEUROPSYCHIATRIC HOSPITAL AT UCLA (054009)**, 150 UCLA Medical Plaza, Zip 90095–8353; tel. 310/825–9989, (Nonreporting) **A1** 3 5 10 **S** University of California Systemwide Administration, Oakland, CA
Primary Contact: Johnese Spisso, President, UCLA Health/Chief Executive Officer, UCLA Hospital System
COO: Richard Azar, Chief Operating Officer
CFO: Ronald Anthony Davis, Chief Financial Officer – UCLA Hospital System
CMO: Thomas Strouse, M.D., Medical Director and Professor of Clinical Psych
CHR: Susi Takeuchi, Chief Human Resources and Organization Development Officer
CNO: Patricia Matos, Chief Nursing Officer
Web address: www.semel.ucla.edu/resnick
Control: State, Government, Nonfederal **Service**: Psychiatric

Staffed Beds: 74

✠ **UCLA WEST VALLEY MEDICAL CENTER (050481)**, 7300 Medical Center Drive, Zip 91307–1900; tel. 818/676–4000, (Nonreporting) **A1** 10 **S** University of California Systemwide Administration, Oakland, CA
Primary Contact: Johnese Spisso, President, UCLA Health and Chief Executive Officer, UCLA Hospital System
CFO: David Cantrell, CPA, Vice President and Chief Financial Officer
CMO: Yale D. Podnos, M.D., Chief Medical Officer
CHR: Diana Steel, Vice President Human Resources
CNO: Kelli Wray, Chief Nursing Officer
Web address: https://www.uclahealth.org/hospitals/west-valley
Control: Corporation, Investor–owned (for–profit) **Service**: General medical and surgical

Staffed Beds: 260

✠ **USC NORRIS COMPREHENSIVE CANCER CENTER AND HOSPITAL (050660)**, 1441 Eastlake Avenue, Zip 90089–0112; tel. 323/865–3000, **A1** 2 3 5 8 10 **F3** 11 15 18 29 30 31 34 35 36 38 39 44 45 46 47 48 49 50 51 54 55 56 57 58 59 60 61 64 65 68 70 74 75 77 78 79 81 82 84 85 86 87 92 93 94 97 100 101 104 107 108 109 110 111 115 118 119 120 121 123 124 126 130 132 134 135 136 145 146 147 148 149 150 154 157 160 163 164 165 167 **P6** Keck Medicine of USC, Los Angeles, CA
Primary Contact: William Martin. Sargeant, Chief Executive Officer/Interim Chief, Office of Performance & Transformation
CMO: Stephanie Hall, M.D., Medical Director
CHR: Matthew McElrath, Chief Human Resources Officer
CNO: Annette Sy, Chief Nursing Officer
Web address: www.uscnorriscancerhospital.org
Control: Other not–for–profit (including NFP Corporation) **Service**: Cancer

Staffed Beds: 60 **Admissions**: 1460 **Census**: 38 **Outpatient Visits**: 225629 **Births**: 0 **Total Expense ($000)**: 424388 **Payroll Expense ($000)**: 89633 **Personnel**: 546

★ △ ⇑ **VALLEY PRESBYTERIAN HOSPITAL (050126)**, 15107 Vanowen Street, Zip 91405–4597; tel. 818/782–6600, **A7** 10 21 **F3** 13 18 20 22 24 29 31 34 35 37 40 41 44 45 46 49 50 55 57 59 64 65 70 72 75 76 77 78 79 80 81 85 86 87 88 89 90 96 107 108 114 115 118 119 130 146 147 148 149 169
Primary Contact: Gustavo A. Valdespino, President/Chief Executive Officer
CFO: Janice Klostermeier, Senior Vice President and Chief Financial Officer
CMO: Clyde Wesp, M.D., Chief Medical Officer
CIO: Jeff Allport, Vice President, Chief Information Officer
CHR: Deborah Gac, Vice President Human Resources
CNO: Lori Burnell, R.N., Ph.D., Senior Vice President and Chief Nursing Officer
Web address: www.valleypres.org
Control: Other not–for–profit (including NFP Corporation) **Service**: General medical and surgical

Staffed Beds: 323 **Admissions**: 13877 **Census**: 194 **Outpatient Visits**: 92154 **Births**: 2148 **Total Expense ($000)**: 316639 **Payroll Expense ($000)**: 151033

Hospital, Medicare Provider Number, Address, Telephone, Approval, Facility, and Physician Codes, Health Care System

★ American Hospital Association (AHA) membership ○ Healthcare Facilities Accreditation Program ⇑ Center for Improvement in Healthcare Quality Accreditation
☐ The Joint Commission accreditation ◇ DNV Healthcare Inc. accreditation △ Commission on Accreditation of Rehabilitation Facilities (CARF) accreditation

© 2025 AHA Guide

Hospitals, U.S. / CALIFORNIA

WEST HILLS HOSPITAL AND MEDICAL CENTER See Ucla West Valley Medical Center

WOMEN'S HOSPITAL See Women's and Children's Hospital

LOS BANOS—Merced County

MEMORIAL HOSPITAL LOS BANOS (050528), 520 West 'I' Street, Zip 93635–3498; tel. 209/826–0591, **A**1 10 20 **F**3 8 11 13 15 18 29 34 35 40 44 45 46 50 54 57 59 60 61 64 65 68 70 74 75 76 77 79 81 82 85 86 87 107 110 111 115 119 127 130 131 135 146 148 149 154 156 164 169 **S** Sutter Health, Sacramento, CA
Primary Contact: Kristie Lorraine. Marion, Chief Executive Officer and Chief Nurse Executive
CHR: Shawn Garcia, Manager Human Resources
CNO: Kristie Lorraine Marion, Chief Executive Officer and Chief Nurse Executive
Web address: www.memoriallosbanos.org/
Control: Other not–for–profit (including NFP Corporation) **Service**: General medical and surgical

Staffed Beds: 38 Admissions: 1817 Census: 14 Outpatient Visits: 90958 Births: 537 Total Expense ($000): 83127 Payroll Expense ($000): 28516 Personnel: 318

LOS GATOS—Santa Clara County

COMMUNITY HOSPITAL OF LOS GATOS See El Camino Hospital Los Gatos

LYNWOOD—Los Angeles County

ST. FRANCIS MEDICAL CENTER (050104), 3630 East Imperial Highway, Zip 90262–2636; tel. 310/900–8900, (Nonreporting) **A**1 3 10 **S** Prime Healthcare, Ontario, CA
Primary Contact: Clay Farell, Chief Executive Officer
CFO: Anil Jain, Chief Financial Officer
CMO: Rahul Dhawan, M.D., Chief Medical Officer
CIO: Judi Binderman, Chief Information Technology Officer and Chief Medical Informatics Officer
CHR: Laura Kato, Vice President Human Resources
Web address: https://stfrancismedicalcenter.com/
Control: Church operated, Nongovernment, not–for–profit **Service**: General medical and surgical

Staffed Beds: 323

MADERA—Madera County

VALLEY CHILDREN'S HEALTHCARE (053300), 9300 Valley Children's Place, Zip 93636–8761; tel. 559/353–3000, (Nonreporting) **A**1 3 5 7 8 10
Primary Contact: Todd A. Suntrapak, President/Chief Executive Officer
COO: David Hodge Jr, Chief Operating Officer
CFO: Tina Mycroft, Chief Financial Officer
CMO: David Christensen, M.D., Senior Vice President and Chief Medical Officer
CIO: Joseph Egan, Vice President and Chief Informational Officer
CHR: Nat Ponticello, Vice President Human Resources
CNO: Beverly P. Hayden–Pugh, R.N., Senior Vice President and Chief Nursing Officer
Web address: www.valleychildrens.org
Control: Other not–for–profit (including NFP Corporation) **Service**: Children's general medical and surgical

Staffed Beds: 209

MAMMOTH LAKES—Mono County

MAMMOTH HOSPITAL (051303), 85 Sierra Park Road, Zip 93546–2073, Mailing Address: P.O. Box 660, Zip 93546–0660; tel. 760/934–3311, (Nonreporting) **A**3 5 10 18 21
Primary Contact: Tom Parker, Chief Executive Officer
CFO: Melanie Van Winkle, Chief Financial Officer
CMO: Yuri Parisky, M.D., Chief of Staff
CIO: Mark Lind, Chief Information Officer
CHR: Sarah Vigilante, Administrative Services Director
CNO: Kathleen Alo, Chief Nursing Officer
Web address: www.mammothhospital.com
Control: Hospital district or authority, Government, Nonfederal **Service**: General medical and surgical

Staffed Beds: 17

MANTECA—San Joaquin County

DOCTORS HOSPITAL OF MANTECA (050118), 1205 East North Street, Zip 95336–4900; tel. 209/823–3111, (Nonreporting) **A**1 10 **S** TENET Healthcare Corporation, Dallas, TX
Primary Contact: Tina Burch, Chief Executive Officer and Chief Nursing Officer
CFO: Ryan Marshall, Chief Financial Officer
CHR: Traci Holzer, Chief Human Resources Officer
CNO: Tina Burch, Chief Executive Officer and Chief Nursing Officer
Web address: www.doctorsmanteca.com
Control: Corporation, Investor–owned (for–profit) **Service**: General medical and surgical

Staffed Beds: 56

KAISER PERMANENTE MANTECA MEDICAL CENTER (050748), 1777 West Yosemite Avenue, Zip 95337–5187; tel. 209/825–3700, (Includes MODESTO MEDICAL CENTER, 4601 Dale Road, Modesto, California, Zip 95356–9718, tel. 209/735–5000) **A**1 2 3 5 10 19 **F**3 11 13 15 18 20 22 26 30 31 37 39 40 41 45 49 56 60 64 68 70 72 73 74 75 76 78 79 80 81 84 85 87 100 107 108 110 111 114 115 118 119 126 128 130 135 146 148 149 154 167 169 **S** Kaiser Foundation Hospitals, Oakland, CA
Primary Contact: Aphriekah Duhaney–West, Senior Vice President, Area Manager, Central Valley
CFO: Debra L Brown, Area Financial Officer
CMO: Moses D Elam, M.D., Physician–in–Chief
CIO: Tom J Osteen, Director Area Technology
CHR: Pat McKeldin, Human Resource Business Partner
Web address: www.kaiserpermanente.org
Control: Other not–for–profit (including NFP Corporation) **Service**: General medical and surgical

Staffed Beds: 275 Admissions: 14409 Census: 151 Outpatient Visits: 226739 Births: 3821 Personnel: 1825

MARINA DEL REY—Los Angeles County

CEDARS–SINAI MARINA DEL REY HOSPITAL (050740), 4650 Lincoln Boulevard, Zip 90292–6306; tel. 310/823–8911, **A**1 3 10 **F**3 11 12 15 18 26 28 29 30 34 35 37 40 41 45 46 47 48 49 50 56 57 59 60 64 65 68 70 74 75 77 79 81 82 84 86 87 91 93 107 108 110 111 115 119 126 130 131 146 148 149 150 154 167 **S** Cedars–Sinai Health System, West Hollywood, CA
Primary Contact: Bryan Croft, Executive Vice President, Hospital Operations & Chief Operating Officer
COO: Joanne Laguna–Kennedy, Vice President and Chief Operating Officer
CFO: Stephen A Hargett, Senior Vice President and Chief Financial Officer
Web address: www.marinahospital.com
Control: Other not–for–profit (including NFP Corporation) **Service**: General medical and surgical

Staffed Beds: 103 Admissions: 4961 Census: 63 Outpatient Visits: 54513 Births: 0 Total Expense ($000): 171481 Payroll Expense ($000): 58952 Personnel: 618

MARIPOSA—Mariposa County

JOHN C. FREMONT HEALTHCARE DISTRICT (051304), 5189 Hospital Road, Zip 95338–9524, Mailing Address: P.O. Box 216, Zip 95338–0216; tel. 209/966–3631, (Nonreporting) **A**10 18
Primary Contact: Patricia Ryan, Interim Chief Executive Officer
COO: Lynn Buskill, Chief Operations Officer
CMO: Kenneth P Smith, Chief Medical Officer
CHR: Martha Robichaux, Chief Human Resources Officer
CNO: Lisa Hoyle, R.N., Chief Nursing Officer
Web address: www.jcf-hospital.com
Control: Hospital district or authority, Government, Nonfederal **Service**: General medical and surgical

Staffed Beds: 33

MARTINEZ—Contra Costa County

CONTRA COSTA REGIONAL MEDICAL CENTER (050276), 2500 Alhambra Avenue, Zip 94553–3156; tel. 925/370–5000, **A**1 2 3 5 10 **F**3 11 13 15 18 30 31 35 36 39 40 45 49 50 54 56 59 60 61 62 64 65 66 68 70 71 72 73 74 75 76 77 78 79 81 82 84 85 86 87 93 97 98 100 102 104 107 108 111 115 119 130 132 143 146 147 148 149 154 156 162 169 **P**6
Primary Contact: Samir Shah, M.D., Chief Executive Officer and Chief Medical Officer
COO: Timothy Thompson–Cook, Chief Operating Officer
CFO: Patrick Godley, Chief Financial Officer
CMO: David Goldstein, M.D., Chief Medical Officer
CNO: Jaspreet Benepal, Chief Nursing Officer
Web address: www.cchealth.org/medical_center/
Control: County, Government, Nonfederal **Service**: General medical and surgical

Staffed Beds: 166 Admissions: 6527 Census: 118 Outpatient Visits: 511395 Births: 1777 Total Expense ($000): 769149 Payroll Expense ($000): 267963 Personnel: 2837

Hospitals, U.S. / CALIFORNIA

KAISER FOUNDATION HOSPITAL See Kaiser Permanente Walnut Creek Medical Center, Walnut Creek

KAISER PERMANENTE MEDICAL CNTR See Kaiser Foundation Hospital

MARYSVILLE—Yuba County

☒ **ADVENTIST HEALTH AND RIDEOUT (050133)**, 726 Fourth Street, Zip 95901–5600; tel. 530/749–4300, (Includes FREMONT MEDICAL CENTER, 970 Plumas Street, Yuba City, California, Zip 95991–4087, tel. 530/751–4000) (Nonreporting) **A**1 2 10 20 **S** Adventist Health, Roseville, CA
Primary Contact: Chris Champlin, President
COO: Cyndy Gordon, Chief Operating Officer
CFO: Diane Moon, Chief Financial Officer
CMO: Azad Sheikh, Chief Medical Officer
CIO: Daniel Chibaya, Chief Information Officer
CHR: Bart R Minsky, Interim Vice President Human Resources
Web address: www.adventisthealth.org/rideout/
Control: Other not-for-profit (including NFP Corporation) **Service:** General medical and surgical

Staffed Beds: 219

MERCED—Merced County

☒ **MERCY MEDICAL CENTER MERCED (050444)**, 333 Mercy Avenue, Zip 95340–8319; tel. 209/564–5000, **A**1 2 3 5 10 19 **F**3 8 13 15 18 20 22 28 29 30 32 34 35 40 44 45 46 48 49 50 54 57 59 62 64 65 70 74 75 76 77 79 81 85 86 87 92 93 96 97 107 108 110 111 115 119 126 127 130 132 135 146 148 149 154 156 **P**3 **S** CommonSpirit Health, Chicago, IL
Primary Contact: Dale Johns, FACHE, Chief Executive Officer
CFO: Michael Strasser, Vice President and Chief Financial Officer
CMO: Robert Streeter, M.D., Vice President Medical Affairs
CIO: Daniel Andresen, Chief information Officer
CHR: Julie Rocha, Vice President Human Resources
CNO: Greg Rouleau, Vice President Nursing
Web address: www.mercymercedcares.org
Control: Other not-for-profit (including NFP Corporation) **Service:** General medical and surgical

Staffed Beds: 186 **Admissions:** 10662 **Census:** 127 **Outpatient Visits:** 175212 **Births:** 2296 **Total Expense ($000):** 369859 **Payroll Expense ($000):** 147478 **Personnel:** 1260

MISSION HILLS—Los Angeles County, See Los Angeles

MISSION VIEJO—Orange County

☐ **CHOC CHILDREN'S AT MISSION HOSPITAL (053306)**, 27700 Medical Center Road, Zip 92691–6426; tel. 949/347–8400, (Nonreporting) **A**1 10
Primary Contact: Kimberly C. Cripe, President/CEO
COO: Matthew S Gerlach, Chief Operating Officer
CFO: Kerri Ruppert Schiller, Senior Vice President and Chief Financial Officer
CMO: Maria Minon, M.D., Vice President Medical Affairs and Chief Medical Officer
CIO: John Henderson, Chief Information Officer
CHR: Thomas Capizzi, Vice President Human Resources
Web address: www.choc.org
Control: Other not-for-profit (including NFP Corporation) **Service:** Children's general medical and surgical

Staffed Beds: 54

MISSION HOSPITAL MISSION VIEJO See Providence Mission Hospital Mission Viejo

☒ △ **PROVIDENCE MISSION HOSPITAL MISSION VIEJO (050567)**, 27700 Medical Center Road, Zip 92691–6474; tel. 949/364–1400, (Includes MISSION HOSPITAL LAGUNA BEACH, 31872 Coast Highway, Laguna Beach, California, Zip 92651–6775, tel. 949/499–1311; Seth R. Teigen, Chief Executive Officer) **A**1 2 3 5 7 10 19 **F**3 8 11 12 13 15 17 18 19 20 22 24 26 28 29 30 31 32 34 35 36 37 38 39 40 41 43 44 45 46 47 48 49 50 51 53 54 55 57 58 59 60 62 63 64 65 66 68 70 72 74 75 76 77 78 79 80 81 82 84 85 86 87 88 89 90 91 92 93 96 98 99 100 101 102 104 105 107 108 110 111 114 115 116 117 118 119 120 121 123 124 126 129 130 131 132 134 135 141 142 143 145 146 147 148 149 150 153 154 156 157 160 161 162 164 165 167 169 **P**5 **S** Providence, Renton, WA
Primary Contact: Seth R. Teigen, Chief Executive
CFO: Eileen Haubl, Senior Vice President and Chief Financial Officer
CMO: Linda Sieglen, M.D., Chief Medical Officer
CIO: Bill Russell, Senior Chief Information Officer
CHR: Terri Covert, Vice President Human Resources
CNO: Jennifer Cord, R.N., Chief Nursing Officer
Web address: https://www.providence.org/locations/mission-hospital-mission-viejo
Control: Other not-for-profit (including NFP Corporation) **Service:** General medical and surgical

Staffed Beds: 269 **Admissions:** 16880 **Census:** 218 **Outpatient Visits:** 467525 **Births:** 2016 **Total Expense ($000):** 653293 **Payroll Expense ($000):** 266714 **Personnel:** 1815

MODESTO—Stanislaus County

⇧ **CENTRAL VALLEY SPECIALTY HOSPITAL (052055)**, 730 17th Street, Zip 95354–1209; tel. 209/248–7700, (Nonreporting) **A**10 21
Primary Contact: Dupinder Sidhu, Chief Executive Officer and Chief Nursing Officer
CNO: Dupinder Sidhu, Chief Executive Officer and Chief Nursing Officer
Web address: www.centralvalleyspecialty.org/CVSH/
Control: Partnership, Investor-owned (for-profit) **Service:** Acute long-term care hospital

Staffed Beds: 36

☒ **DOCTORS MEDICAL CENTER OF MODESTO (050464)**, 1441 Florida Avenue, Zip 95350–4418, Mailing Address: P.O. Box 4138, Zip 95352–4138; tel. 209/578–1211, (Nonreporting) **A**1 2 3 10 19 **S** TENET Healthcare Corporation, Dallas, TX
Primary Contact: Jaikumar Krishnaswamy, Chief Executive Officer
CFO: Greg Berry, Chief Financial Officer
CMO: Gabrielle Gaspar, M.D., Chief Medical Officer
CHR: Michele Bava, Director Human Resources
CNO: Cheryl Harless, Chief Nursing Officer
Web address: www.dmc-modesto.com
Control: Corporation, Investor-owned (for-profit) **Service:** General medical and surgical

Staffed Beds: 461

☒ **ENCOMPASS HEALTH REHABILITATION HOSPITAL OF MODESTO (053040)**, 1303 Mable Avenue, Zip 95355; tel. 209/857–3400, (Nonreporting) **A**1 10 **S** Encompass Health Corporation, Birmingham, AL
Primary Contact: Sukhraj Dhami, Interim Chief Executive Officer
CFO: Sukhraj Dhami, Chief Financial Officer
CMO: Greg A. Vigna, M.D., Medical Director
CHR: Tina Reed, Director of Human Resources
CNO: Mark Dinardo, Chief Nursing Officer
Web address: www.healthsouthmodesto.com/
Control: Corporation, Investor-owned (for-profit) **Service:** Rehabilitation

Staffed Beds: 50

KAISER FOUNDATION HOSPITAL See Modesto Medical Center

Hospital, Medicare Provider Number, Address, Telephone, Approval, Facility, and Physician Codes, Health Care System

★ American Hospital Association (AHA) membership ○ Healthcare Facilities Accreditation Program ⇧ Center for Improvement in Healthcare Quality Accreditation
☐ The Joint Commission accreditation ◇ DNV Healthcare Inc. accreditation △ Commission on Accreditation of Rehabilitation Facilities (CARF) accreditation

© 2025 AHA Guide

Hospitals, U.S. / CALIFORNIA

☒ **MEMORIAL MEDICAL CENTER (050557)**, 1700 Coffee Road, Zip 95355–2869, Mailing Address: P.O. Box 942, Zip 95353–0942; tel. 209/526–4500, (Includes MEMORIAL MEDICAL CENTER, 1700 Coffee Road, Modesto, California, Zip 95355, Box 942, Zip 95353, tel. 209/526–4500) **A**1 2 10 **F**3 8 11 12 13 18 20 22 24 26 28 29 30 31 34 35 36 37 39 40 43 44 45 46 47 48 49 50 51 53 55 57 58 59 60 64 65 68 70 72 73 74 75 76 77 78 79 81 82 84 85 86 87 100 107 108 111 114 115 119 120 121 122 123 124 126 130 131 132 146 147 148 149 154 164 167 169 **S** Sutter Health, Sacramento, CA
Primary Contact: Tracy Roman, Chief Executive Officer
COO: Steve Mitchell, Chief Operating Officer
CHR: Paula Rafala, Director, Human Resources
CNO: Sandra Proctor, R.N., MS, Chief Nurse Executive
Web address: www.memorialmedicalcenter.org
Control: Other not–for–profit (including NFP Corporation) **Service:** General medical and surgical

Staffed Beds: 419 **Admissions:** 19874 **Census:** 273 **Outpatient Visits:** 147687 **Births:** 1451 **Total Expense ($000):** 768842 **Payroll Expense ($000):** 233684 **Personnel:** 2411

MODESTO MEDICAL CENTER See Kaiser Permanente Manteca Medical Center, Manteca

MONROVIA—Los Angeles County

○ **MONROVIA MEMORIAL HOSPITAL (052054)**, 323 South Heliotrope Avenue, Zip 91016–2914; tel. 626/408–9800, (Nonreporting) **A**10 11
Primary Contact: Kathy Wojno, R.N., MSN, Chief Executive Officer
Web address: www.monroviamemorial.com
Control: Partnership, Investor–owned (for–profit) **Service:** Acute long–term care hospital

Staffed Beds: 49

MONTCLAIR—San Bernardino County

☐ **MONTCLAIR HOSPITAL MEDICAL CENTER (050758)**, 5000 San Bernardino Street, Zip 91763–2326; tel. 909/625–5411, **A**1 3 5 10 12 13 **F**13 29 40 70 76 81 93 107 115 119 130 160 **S** Prime Healthcare, Ontario, CA
Primary Contact: Gail Aviado, MSN, R.N., Chief Executive Officer
CFO: Harold Way, Chief Financial Officer
CMO: Joseph Hourany, Chief Medical Officer
CNO: Gail Aviado, MSN, R.N., Chief Nursing Officer
Web address: https://www.montclair-hospital.org/
Control: Other not–for–profit (including NFP Corporation) **Service:** General medical and surgical

Staffed Beds: 106 **Admissions:** 2771 **Census:** 27 **Outpatient Visits:** 26709 **Births:** 206 **Total Expense ($000):** 54889 **Payroll Expense ($000):** 23237 **Personnel:** 390

MONTEBELLO—Los Angeles County

ADVENTIST HEALTH WHITE MEMORIAL MONTEBELLO (050350), 309 West Beverly Boulevard, Zip 90640–4308; tel. 323/726–1222, (Nonreporting) **A**10
Primary Contact: John Raffoul, FACHE, President
CFO: Larry Pugh, Vice President and Chief Financial Officer
CMO: Kenneth L. Cohen, M.D., Chief Medical Officer
CIO: James Jaworski, Chief Information Officer
CHR: George Holtz, Adminstrative Director Human Resources
Web address: https://www.adventisthealth.org/montebello/
Control: Other not–for–profit (including NFP Corporation) **Service:** General medical and surgical

Staffed Beds: 192

MONTEREY—Monterey County

☒ △ **COMMUNITY HOSPITAL OF THE MONTEREY PENINSULA (050145)**, 23625 Holman Highway, Zip 93940–5902, Mailing Address: Box 'HH', Zip 93942–6032; tel. 831/624–5311, (Total facility includes 28 beds in nursing home–type unit) **A**1 2 7 10 19 **F**1 3 4 5 11 12 13 15 16 17 18 20 22 24 26 28 29 30 31 34 35 37 40 44 45 46 47 48 49 50 51 53 54 55 57 58 59 60 61 63 64 67 68 70 71 72 73 74 75 76 77 78 79 81 82 83 84 85 86 87 88 89 90 91 92 93 94 96 98 99 100 101 102 103 104 105 107 110 111 114 115 116 117 118 119 120 121 123 124 126 128 129 130 131 132 134 135 145 146 148 149 150 153 154 156 160 162 164 165 166 167 169
Primary Contact: Steven J. Packer, M.D., President and Chief Executive Officer, Montage Health
CFO: Laura Zehm, Vice President and Chief Financial Officer
CMO: Anthony D Chavis, M.D., Vice President Enterprise Medical Officer, Community Hospital Foundation
Web address: www.chomp.org
Control: Other not–for–profit (including NFP Corporation) **Service:** General medical and surgical

Staffed Beds: 250 **Admissions:** 15086 **Census:** 209 **Outpatient Visits:** 490526 **Births:** 1012 **Total Expense ($000):** 809927 **Payroll Expense ($000):** 306248 **Personnel:** 2420

MONTEREY PARK—Los Angeles County

☐ **GARFIELD MEDICAL CENTER (050737)**, 525 North Garfield Avenue, Zip 91754–1205; tel. 626/573–2222, **A**1 10 **F**3 13 17 18 20 22 24 26 28 29 31 40 49 70 72 74 75 76 77 78 85 90 93 126 **S** AHMC Healthcare, Alhambra, CA
Primary Contact: Herbert Villafuerte, R.N., Chief Executive Officer
CFO: Steve Maekawa, Chief Financial Officer
CMO: Thomas Lam, Chief Medical Officer
CIO: Angelica Ching, Director Information Systems
CHR: Darcy Castro, Director Human Resources
Web address: www.garfieldmedicalcenter.com
Control: Partnership, Investor–owned (for–profit) **Service:** General medical and surgical

Staffed Beds: 210 **Admissions:** 9062 **Census:** 128 **Outpatient Visits:** 27538 **Births:** 1723 **Total Expense ($000):** 326030 **Payroll Expense ($000):** 94162 **Personnel:** 1021

☐ **MONTEREY PARK HOSPITAL (050736)**, 900 South Atlantic Boulevard, Zip 91754–4780; tel. 626/570–9000, **A**1 10 **F**3 29 40 45 46 49 51 60 64 68 70 71 74 75 77 78 79 81 85 86 87 89 92 107 108 111 115 119 130 146 148 149 167 **S** AHMC Healthcare, Alhambra, CA
Primary Contact: Philip A. Cohen, Chief Executive Officer
COO: Ericka Smith, Chief Operating Officer
CFO: Daniel Song, Chief Financial Officer
CMO: Ruben Ramirez, M.D., Chief of Staff
CIO: Angelica Ching, Director Information Systems
CHR: Gretchen Lindeman, Director of Human Resources
CNO: Shirley Tang, R.N., Chief Nursing Officer
Web address: www.montereyparkhosp.com
Control: Corporation, Investor–owned (for–profit) **Service:** General medical and surgical

Staffed Beds: 85 **Admissions:** 2929 **Census:** 41 **Outpatient Visits:** 20508 **Births:** 0 **Personnel:** 318

MORENO VALLEY—Riverside County

☒ **KAISER PERMANENTE MORENO VALLEY MEDICAL CENTER (050765)**, 27300 Iris Avenue, Zip 92555–4800; tel. 951/243–0811, **A**1 3 10 **F**3 13 15 29 30 31 35 40 44 45 46 49 50 57 59 60 64 65 68 70 71 72 74 75 76 77 78 79 81 82 84 85 87 97 100 107 110 111 114 115 119 126 130 135 144 146 148 149 154 156 157 164 167 169 **S** Kaiser Foundation Hospitals, Oakland, CA
Primary Contact: Sammy R. Totah, PharmD, Senior Vice President, Area Manager Riverside & Moreno Valley, Kaiser Foundation Health Plans and Ho
COO: Nanette Vergara, Chief Operatianig Officer
CFO: JiJi Abraham, Area Chief Financial Officer
CMO: Frank M. Flowers, M.D., Area Medical Director
CIO: Alfred.T Velasquez, Area Information Officer
CHR: Cheryl M Witt, Human Resources Director
Control: Partnership, Investor–owned (for–profit) **Service:** General medical and surgical

Staffed Beds: 100 **Admissions:** 5063 **Census:** 47 **Outpatient Visits:** 84868 **Births:** 1375 **Personnel:** 503

☒ **RIVERSIDE UNIVERSITY HEALTH SYSTEM–MEDICAL CENTER (050292)**, 26520 Cactus Avenue, Zip 92555–3911; tel. 951/486–4000, **A**1 2 3 5 10 12 13 19 **F**3 8 11 13 15 17 20 22 26 29 30 31 35 40 43 45 46 48 49 50 54 56 58 67 68 70 71 72 74 76 78 79 81 82 83 84 85 87 88 89 92 93 96 97 98 100 102 104 107 108 110 111 115 117 118 119 120 126 130 135 144 146 148 149 154 156 160 164 167
Primary Contact: Jennifer Cruikshank, R.N., Chief Executive Officer
COO: Jonelle Morris, R.N., Chief Operating Officer, Medical Center & Clinics
CFO: Joe Zamora, Chief Financial Officer
CMO: Arnold Tabuenca, M.D., Medical Director
CIO: Tura Morice, Chief Information Officer
CNO: Leah Ann Patterson, R.N., Chief Nursing Officer
Web address: www.ruhealth.org/en-us
Control: County, Government, Nonfederal **Service:** General medical and surgical

Staffed Beds: 439 **Admissions:** 16716 **Census:** 344 **Outpatient Visits:** 199488 **Births:** 1696 **Total Expense ($000):** 1011631 **Payroll Expense ($000):** 372293

MOSS BEACH—San Mateo County

SETON MEDICAL CENTER COASTSIDE See AHMC Seton Medical Center Coastside

Hospitals, U.S. / CALIFORNIA

MOUNT SHASTA—Siskiyou County

✠ **MERCY MEDICAL CENTER MOUNT SHASTA (051319)**, 914 Pine Street, Zip 96067-2143; tel. 530/926-6111, **A**1 10 18 **F**5 11 13 15 28 29 30 32 33 34 35 38 40 43 44 45 54 59 62 63 64 65 66 68 70 75 76 77 79 81 82 86 87 90 96 97 102 107 108 110 111 114 115 118 119 127 130 131 132 133 135 146 148 149 154 156 157 160 164 167 169 **S** CommonSpirit Health, Chicago, IL
Primary Contact: Rodger Page, President
CMO: David Holst, M.D., Chief of Staff
CHR: Michelle Michl, Director Human Resources
CNO: Lisa Hubbard, Vice President and Chief Nursing Executive
Web address: www.mercymtshasta.org
Control: Other not-for-profit (including NFP Corporation) **Service**: General medical and surgical

Staffed Beds: 25 **Admissions**: 771 **Census**: 7 **Outpatient Visits**: 74905 **Births**: 117 **Total Expense ($000)**: 71478 **Payroll Expense ($000)**: 31614 **Personnel**: 192

MOUNTAIN VIEW—Santa Clara County

✠ △ **EL CAMINO HEALTH (050308)**, 2500 Grant Road, Zip 94040-4302, Mailing Address: P.O. Box 7025, Zip 94039-7025; tel. 650/940-7000, (Includes EL CAMINO HOSPITAL LOS GATOS, 815 Pollard Road, Los Gatos, California, Zip 95032-1438, tel. 408/378-6131) (Nonreporting) **A**1 2 3 7 10
Primary Contact: Dan Woods, Chief Executive Officer
COO: Meenesh Bhimani, M.D., Chief Operating Officer
CFO: Iftikhar Hussain, Chief Financial Officer
CMO: Mark C. Adams, M.D., Chief Medical Officer
CIO: Deborah Muro, Chief Information Officer
CHR: Kathryn M Fisk, Chief Human Resources Officer
CNO: Cheryl Reinking, DN, R.N., MS, Chief Nursing Officer
Web address: https://www.elcaminohealth.org/
Control: Hospital district or authority, Government, Nonfederal **Service**: General medical and surgical

Staffed Beds: 420

EL CAMINO HOSPITAL See El Camino Health

MURRIETA—Riverside County

✠ **ENCOMPASS HEALTH REHABILITATION HOSPITAL OF MURRIETA (053042)**, 35470 Whitewood Road, Zip 92563-2415; tel. 951/246-6500, **A**1 10 **F**3 29 60 90 91 96 149 154 **S** Encompass Health Corporation, Birmingham, AL
Primary Contact: Perry Ebeltoft, Chief Executive Officer
Web address: www.encompasshealth.com/murrietarehab
Control: Corporation, Investor-owned (for-profit) **Service**: Rehabilitation

Staffed Beds: 50 **Admissions**: 1070 **Census**: 38 **Outpatient Visits**: 0 **Births**: 0 **Total Expense ($000)**: 27322 **Payroll Expense ($000)**: 14970

✠ **LOMA LINDA UNIVERSITY MEDICAL CENTER–MURRIETA (050770)**, 28062 Baxter Road, Zip 92563-1401; tel. 951/290-4000, **A**1 2 3 5 10 **F**3 11 13 15 18 20 22 24 26 28 29 30 34 35 40 44 45 46 47 48 49 50 54 57 58 59 61 64 65 68 70 72 74 75 76 77 78 79 81 82 85 86 87 91 92 93 107 108 110 111 114 115 117 118 119 120 121 123 126 130 132 146 147 148 149 154 157 167 169 **S** Loma Linda University Adventist Health Sciences Center, Loma Linda, CA
Primary Contact: Trevor G. Wright, Chief Executive Officer
COO: Lyndon C. Edwards, Chief Operating Officer
CFO: Angela Lalas, CPA, Chief Financial Officer
CMO: Jeff Conner, M.D., Chief Medical Staff
CIO: Mark Zirkelbach, Chief Information Officer
CNO: Denise M. Robinson, M.P.H., R.N., Chief Nursing Officer
Web address: https://murrieta.lluh.org/
Control: Other not-for-profit (including NFP Corporation) **Service**: General medical and surgical

Staffed Beds: 136 **Admissions**: 11734 **Census**: 140 **Outpatient Visits**: 176066 **Births**: 1521 **Total Expense ($000)**: 332882 **Payroll Expense ($000)**: 123217 **Personnel**: 1246

SHARP HEALTHCARE MURRIETA See Rancho Springs Medical Center

✠ **SOUTHWEST HEALTHCARE SYSTEM (050701)**, 25500 Medical Center Drive, Zip 92562-5965; tel. 951/696-6000, (Includes INLAND VALLEY MEDICAL CENTER, 36485 Inland Valley Drive, Wildomar, California, Zip 92595-9700, tel. 951/677-1111; Jared Giles, FACHE, Chief Executive Officer; RANCHO SPRINGS MEDICAL CENTER, 25500 Medical Center Drive, Murrieta, California, Zip 92562-5965; tel. 951/696-6000; Jared Giles, FACHE, Chief Executive Officer) (Nonreporting) **A**1 3 10 **S** Universal Health Services, Inc., King of Prussia, PA
Primary Contact: Jared Giles, FACHE, Chief Executive Officer
CFO: Jon Zilkow, Chief Financial Officer
CMO: Reza Vaezazizi, M.D., Chief of Staff
CIO: Jeffrey Upcraft, Director Information Services
CHR: Della G Stange, Director Human Resources
CNO: Kristen Johnson, Chief Nursing Officer
Web address: https://www.southwesthealthcare.com/
Control: Corporation, Investor-owned (for-profit) **Service**: General medical and surgical

Staffed Beds: 240

NAPA—Napa County

☐ **NAPA STATE HOSPITAL (054122)**, 2100 Napa-Vallejo Highway, Zip 94558-6293; tel. 707/253-5000, **A**1 3 5 10 **F**30 39 53 56 59 61 67 68 77 86 98 128 130 132 135 146 149 154 163 164 **P**6
Primary Contact: Jennie Clay, Executive Director
COO: Dolly Matteucci, Executive Director
Web address: www.dmh.ca.gov
Control: State, Government, Nonfederal **Service**: Psychiatric

Staffed Beds: 1284 **Admissions**: 930 **Census**: 1077 **Outpatient Visits**: 0 **Births**: 0 **Total Expense ($000)**: 422688 **Payroll Expense ($000)**: 238158 **Personnel**: 2242

✠ **PROVIDENCE QUEEN OF THE VALLEY MEDICAL CENTER (050009)**, 1000 Trancas Street, Zip 94558-2906, Mailing Address: P.O. Box 2340, Zip 94558-0688; tel. 707/252-4411, **A**1 2 10 19 **F**3 11 12 13 15 17 18 20 22 24 26 29 30 31 34 35 37 39 40 43 44 45 46 47 49 50 51 53 57 59 64 68 70 73 74 75 76 77 78 79 81 82 85 86 87 90 92 93 94 96 107 108 110 111 115 117 118 119 120 121 123 124 126 130 132 144 146 147 149 154 156 164 167 169 **S** Providence, Renton, WA
Primary Contact: Garry M. Olney, Chief Executive, Northern California
CFO: Michel Riccioni, Vice President and Chief Financial Officer, Northern California Region
CMO: Amy Herold, M.D., Chief Medical Officer
CHR: Robert A Eisen, Vice President Human Resources, Northern California Region
Web address: www.thequeen.org
Control: Other not-for-profit (including NFP Corporation) **Service**: General medical and surgical

Staffed Beds: 136 **Admissions**: 6093 **Census**: 65 **Outpatient Visits**: 226642 **Births**: 799 **Total Expense ($000)**: 262681 **Payroll Expense ($000)**: 123857 **Personnel**: 985

QUEEN OF THE VALLEY MEDICAL CENTER See Providence Queen of The Valley Medical Center

NATIONAL CITY—San Diego County

☐ △ **PARADISE VALLEY HOSPITAL (050024)**, 2400 East Fourth Street, Zip 91950-2099; tel. 619/470-4321, (Includes BAYVIEW BEHAVIORAL HEALTH CAMPUS, 330 Moss Street, Chula Vista, California, Zip 91911-2005, tel. 619/470-4321; Neerav Jadeja, Administrator) (Nonreporting) **A**1 7 10 **S** Prime Healthcare, Ontario, CA
Primary Contact: Neerav Jadeja, Chief Executive Officer
CFO: Becky Levy, Chief Financial Officer
CMO: Rosemarie Lim, M.D., Chief Medical Officer
CIO: Allan Tojino, Director, Information Systems
CHR: Lorraine Villegas, Manager Human Resources
CNO: Gemma Rama-Banaag, R.N., MSN, Chief Nursing Officer
Web address: www.paradisevalleyhospital.org
Control: Corporation, Investor-owned (for-profit) **Service**: General medical and surgical

Staffed Beds: 256

Hospital, Medicare Provider Number, Address, Telephone, Approval, Facility, and Physician Codes, Health Care System

★ American Hospital Association (AHA) membership ○ Healthcare Facilities Accreditation Program ⇑ Center for Improvement in Healthcare Quality Accreditation
☐ The Joint Commission accreditation ◇ DNV Healthcare Inc. accreditation △ Commission on Accreditation of Rehabilitation Facilities (CARF) accreditation

Hospitals, U.S. / CALIFORNIA

NEEDLES—San Bernardino County

COLORADO RIVER MEDICAL CENTER (051323), 1401 Bailey Avenue, Zip 92363-3198; tel. 760/326-7100, (Nonreporting) **A**10 18
Primary Contact: Bing Lum, PharmD, Executive Vice President
COO: Knaya Tabora, Chief Operating Officer and Chief Nursing Officer
CMO: Robert Strecker, M.D., Chief of Staff
CIO: Ron Chieffo, Chief Information Officer
CHR: Pam Barrett, Human Resources Director
CNO: Knaya Tabora, Chief Operating Officer and Chief Nursing Officer
Web address: www.crmccares.com
Control: City, Government, Nonfederal **Service**: General medical and surgical

Staffed Beds: 25

NEWPORT BEACH—Orange County

★ ⇑ **HOAG MEMORIAL HOSPITAL PRESBYTERIAN (050224)**, 1 Hoag Drive, Zip 92663-4162, Mailing Address: P.O. Box 6100, Zip 92658-6100; tel. 949/764-4624, (Includes HOAG HOSPITAL IRVINE, 16200 Sand Canyon Avenue, Irvine, California, Zip 92618-3714, tel. 949/764-8240) **A**3 5 10 21 **F**3 4 5 8 9 11 12 13 14 15 17 18 20 22 24 26 28 29 30 31 32 34 35 36 37 38 40 44 45 46 47 48 49 50 51 52 53 54 55 56 57 58 59 61 62 63 64 65 66 68 70 72 73 74 75 76 77 78 79 80 81 82 84 85 86 87 90 92 93 94 96 97 100 101 102 104 107 108 109 110 111 112 113 114 115 116 117 118 119 120 121 123 124 125 126 129 130 131 132 134 135 141 143 144 145 146 147 148 149 150 152 153 154 156 160 161 162 163 164 165 167 168 **P**5 7
Primary Contact: Robert Braithwaite, President and Chief Executive Officer
COO: Marcy Brown, Senior Vice President and Chief Operating Officer
CFO: Andrew Guarni, Chief Financial Officer
CIO: Carmella Cassetta, Chief Information Officer
CHR: Jan L Blue, Vice President Human Resources
CNO: Richard Martin, MSN, R.N., Senior Vice President and Chief Nursing Officer
Web address: www.hoaghospital.org
Control: Other not-for-profit (including NFP Corporation) **Service**: General medical and surgical

Staffed Beds: 590 **Admissions**: 37257 **Census**: 426 **Outpatient Visits**: 643418 **Births**: 7938 **Total Expense ($000)**: 1783889 **Payroll Expense ($000)**: 677867 **Personnel**: 7364

NORTH HOLLYWOOD—Los Angeles County, See Los Angeles

NORTHRIDGE—Los Angeles County, See Los Angeles

NORWALK—Los Angeles County

☐ **COAST PLAZA HOSPITAL (050771)**, 13100 Studebaker Road, Zip 90650-2500; tel. 562/868-3751, (Nonreporting) **A**1 10 **S** Pipeline Health, El Segundo, CA
Primary Contact: Patrick W. Rafferty, Chief Operating Officer, Pipeline Los Angeles/ Chief Executive Officer, Coast Plaza Hospital
CNO: Downapha Britton, Chief Nursing Officer
Web address: https://www.coastplazahospital.com/
Control: Corporation, Investor-owned (for-profit) **Service**: General medical and surgical

Staffed Beds: 117

☐ **DSH METROPOLITAN (054133)**, 11401 Bloomfield Avenue, Zip 90650-2015; tel. 562/863-7011, (Nonreporting) **A**1 10
Primary Contact: Michael Barsom, M.D., Executive Director
CFO: Maybelle Manlagnit, Senior Accounting Officer
CIO: Paul Mello, Manager Data Processing
CHR: Jorge Banuedos, Director Human Resources
Web address: www.dmh.ca.gov
Control: State, Government, Nonfederal **Service**: Psychiatric

Staffed Beds: 657

LOS ANGELES COMMUNITY HOSPITAL OF NORWALK See Los Angeles Community Hospital At Los Angeles, Los Angeles

NORWALK COMMUNITY HOSPITAL See Los Angeles Community Hospital of Norwalk

NOVATO—Marin County

✠ **NOVATO COMMUNITY HOSPITAL (050131)**, 180 Rowland Way, Zip 94945-5009; tel. 415/209-1300, **A**1 10 **F**3 15 18 29 30 34 36 37 40 50 51 54 56 59 60 64 68 70 74 75 77 79 81 84 85 86 87 93 107 108 111 115 119 130 131 132 143 144 146 148 149 154 164 167 **S** Sutter Health, Sacramento, CA
Primary Contact: Lisa Gammon, Chief Executive Officer
CMO: Barbara Nylund, M.D., Chief of Staff
CIO: Kathryn Graham, Director Communications and Community Relations
CHR: Diana G Johnson, Acting Chief Human Resources Officer
CNO: Lisa Gammon, Chief Nursing Executive
Web address: www.novatocommunity.sutterhealth.org
Control: Other not-for-profit (including NFP Corporation) **Service**: General medical and surgical

Staffed Beds: 40 **Admissions**: 1972 **Census**: 18 **Outpatient Visits**: 64101 **Births**: 0 **Total Expense ($000)**: 102197 **Payroll Expense ($000)**: 32309 **Personnel**: 256

OAKDALE—Stanislaus County

✠ **OAK VALLEY HOSPITAL (050067)**, 350 South Oak Avenue, Zip 95361-3581; tel. 209/847-3011, (Nonreporting) **A**1 10
Primary Contact: Matthew M. Heyn, Chief Executive Officer
CMO: Blackhart Bruce, M.D., Chief of Staff
CIO: Sherry Peral, Director Information Systems
CHR: Brian Beck, Vice President Human Resources
CNO: Joann L. Saporito, R.N., Vice President Nursing Services
Web address: www.oakvalleycares.org
Control: Hospital district or authority, Government, Nonfederal **Service**: General medical and surgical

Staffed Beds: 150

OAKLAND—Alameda County

✠ △ **ALTA BATES SUMMIT MEDICAL CENTER - SUMMIT CAMPUS (050043)**, 350 Hawthorne Avenue, Zip 94609-3100; tel. 510/655-4000, (Includes PROVIDENCE HOSPITAL, 3100 Summit Street, Oakland, California, Zip 94609-3410, Box 23020, Zip 94623-2302, tel. 510/835-4500) **A**1 2 3 7 10 **F**3 4 8 11 12 15 17 18 20 22 24 26 29 30 31 34 35 36 37 40 46 47 49 51 56 57 58 59 60 61 64 68 70 71 74 75 77 78 79 81 82 84 85 86 87 90 91 95 96 97 100 107 108 110 111 114 115 116 117 118 119 120 123 124 126 130 131 132 135 146 148 149 154 156 164 167 **S** Sutter Health, Sacramento, CA
Primary Contact: David D. Clark, FACHE, Area Chief Executive Officer – Sutter East Bay Hospitals
CMO: John Gentile, M.D., Vice President Medical Affairs
CHR: Mark Beiting, Area Chief Executive Officer – Sutter East Bay Hospitals
Web address: www.altabatessummit.com
Control: Other not-for-profit (including NFP Corporation) **Service**: General medical and surgical

Staffed Beds: 309 **Admissions**: 11958 **Census**: 195 **Outpatient Visits**: 107975 **Births**: 0 **Total Expense ($000)**: 529940 **Payroll Expense ($000)**: 186041 **Personnel**: 1444

✠ **HIGHLAND HOSPITAL (050320)**, 1411 East 31st Street, Zip 94602-1018; tel. 510/437-4800, (Includes FAIRMONT HOSPITAL, 15400 Foothill Boulevard, San Leandro, California, Zip 94578-1009, tel. 510/895-4200; Richard Espinoza, Chief Administrative Officer; JOHN GEORGE PSYCHIATRIC HOSPITAL, 2060 Fairmont Drive, San Leandro, California, Zip 94578-1001, tel. 510/346-1300; Guy C Qvistgaard, Chief Executive Officer; SAN LEANDRO HOSPITAL, 13855 East 14th Street, San Leandro, California, Zip 94578-2600, tel. 510/357-6500; James E.T. Jackson, M.P.H., Interim Chief Executive Officer) (Total facility includes 109 beds in nursing home-type unit) **A**1 3 5 10 **F**3 11 13 15 18 20 22 28 29 30 31 35 36 38 39 70 72 76 90 98 128 **S** Alameda Health System, San Leandro, CA
Primary Contact: James E.T. Jackson, M.P.H., Chief Executive Officer
CFO: Marion Schales, Chief Financial Officer
CMO: Sang-ick Chang, M.D., M.P.H., Chief Medical Officer
CHR: Jeanette L Louden Corbett, Chief Human Resources Officer
Web address: www.alamedahealthsystem.org
Control: Hospital district or authority, Government, Nonfederal **Service**: General medical and surgical

Staffed Beds: 438 **Admissions**: 15645 **Census**: 396 **Outpatient Visits**: 454196 **Births**: 1399 **Total Expense ($000)**: 1279003 **Payroll Expense ($000)**: 615261 **Personnel**: 4025

Hospitals, U.S. / CALIFORNIA

✯ **KAISER PERMANENTE OAKLAND MEDICAL CENTER (050075)**, 3600 Broadway, Zip 94611–5693; tel. 510/752–1000; (Includes KAISER PERMANENTE RICHMOND MEDICAL CENTER, 901 Nevin Avenue, Richmond, California, Zip 94801–2555, tel. 510/307–1500; Dante' Green, FACHE, Interim Senior Vice President & Area Manager, East Bay Area) **A**1 3 5 8 10 19 **F**3 11 12 13 15 18 19 20 21 22 23 25 26 27 30 31 37 39 40 41 45 47 48 49 51 56 60 64 68 70 72 73 74 75 76 78 79 80 81 84 85 87 88 89 100 107 108 110 111 112 114 115 117 118 119 120 121 123 126 130 135 146 148 149 154 167 169 **S** Kaiser Foundation Hospitals, Oakland, CA
Primary Contact: Dante' Green, FACHE, Interim Senior Vice President & Area Manager, East Bay Area
COO: Dante' Green, FACHE, Chief Operating Officer
CFO: Dennis Morris, Area Finance Officer
CMO: John Loftus, M.D., Chief of Staff
CIO: Johnny Law, Area Information Officer
CHR: Rick Mead, Human Resources Leader
CNO: Charlene Boyer, Chief Nursing Officer
Web address: www.kaiserpermanente.org
Control: Other not–for–profit (including NFP Corporation) **Service**: General medical and surgical

Staffed Beds: 365 **Admissions**: 21908 **Census**: 281 **Outpatient Visits**: 375265 **Births**: 2466 **Personnel**: 3166

SUMMIT MEDICAL CENTER See Providence Hospital

☐ **TELECARE HERITAGE PSYCHIATRIC HEALTH CENTER (054146)**, 2633 East 27th Street, Zip 94601–1912; tel. 510/535–5115, (Nonreporting) **A**1 10
Primary Contact: Anne L. Bakar, President and Chief Executive Officer
Web address: www.tbhcare.com/
Control: Partnership, Investor–owned (for–profit) **Service**: Psychiatric

Staffed Beds: 26

☐ **UCSF BENIOFF CHILDREN'S HOSPITAL OAKLAND (053301)**, 747 52nd Street, Zip 94609–1859; tel. 510/428–3000, **A**1 3 5 10 **F**3 8 18 19 20 21 22 23 24 25 26 27 29 30 31 32 34 35 36 37 41 43 50 54 55 57 58 59 61 64 65 68 71 72 74 75 77 78 79 81 82 83 84 85 86 87 88 89 90 91 92 93 95 96 97 99 100 101 102 104 107 108 111 114 116 117 118 119 129 130 131 134 136 144 146 147 148 149 150 151 154 157 158 160 161 164 165 167 **P**4 **S** University of California Systemwide Administration, Oakland, CA
Primary Contact: Nicholas M. Holmes, M.D., President, UCSF Benioff Children's Hospitals, SVP Children's Services UCSF Health
COO: Jamie Phillips, Chief Operating Officer
CFO: Ted Wang, Chief Financial Officer
CMO: Joan Zoltanski, Chief Medical Officer
CIO: Don Livsey, Vice President and Chief Information Officer
CHR: Phyllis Weiss, Vice President, Human Resources
Web address: www.childrenshospitaloakland.org
Control: Other not–for–profit (including NFP Corporation) **Service**: Children's general medical and surgical

Staffed Beds: 216 **Admissions**: 7558 **Census**: 117 **Outpatient Visits**: 222172 **Births**: 0 **Total Expense ($000)**: 783134 **Payroll Expense ($000)**: 332480 **Personnel**: 2187

OCEANSIDE—San Diego County

✯ **TRI–CITY MEDICAL CENTER (050128)**, 4002 Vista Way, Zip 92056–4593; tel. 760/724–8411, (Nonreporting) **A**1 3 5 10
Primary Contact: Gene Ma, M.D., President and Chief Executive Officer
CIO: Kim Cook, Interim Clinical Applications Services Manager
CHR: Esther Beverly, Vice President Human Resources
CNO: Sharon A Schultz, Chief Nurse Executive and Vice President
Web address: www.tricitymed.org
Control: Hospital district or authority, Government, Nonfederal **Service**: General medical and surgical

Staffed Beds: 330

OJAI—Ventura County

⇧ **OJAI VALLEY COMMUNITY HOSPITAL (051334)**, 1306 Maricopa Highway, Zip 93023–3163; tel. 805/646–1401, (Nonreporting) **A**10 18 21 **S** Community Memorial Health System, Ventura, CA
Primary Contact: Mick Zdeblick, President/Chief Executive Officer
CFO: David Glyer, Vice President Finance
CIO: Mark Turner, Manager Information Technology
CHR: Deborah Gallagher, Manager Human Resources
Web address: www.cmhshealth.org/locations/ojai-valley-community-hospital/
Control: Other not–for–profit (including NFP Corporation) **Service**: General medical and surgical

Staffed Beds: 69

ONTARIO—San Bernardino County

✯ **KINDRED HOSPITAL–ONTARIO (052037)**, 550 North Monterey Avenue, Zip 91764–3399; tel. 909/391–0333, (Nonreporting) **A**1 10 **S** ScionHealth, Louisville, KY
Primary Contact: Julie Myers, Market Chief Executive Officer
CFO: Omar Oregel, Controller
CMO: Marc Lynch, D.O., Chief of Staff
CNO: Holly Ramos, R.N., Chief Clinical Officer
Web address: www.khontario.com/
Control: Corporation, Investor–owned (for–profit) **Service**: Acute long–term care hospital

Staffed Beds: 81

ONTARIO MEDICAL CENTER See Kaiser Permanente Ontario Medical Center

ORANGE—Orange County

☐ **CHAPMAN GLOBAL MEDICAL CENTER (050745)**, 2601 East Chapman Avenue, Zip 92869–3296; tel. 714/633–0011, (Nonreporting) **A**1 10 **S** KPC Healthcare, Inc., Santa Ana, CA
Primary Contact: Theresa Catherine. Berton, Interim Chief Executive Officer
COO: Theresa Catherine Berton, Chief Operating Officer and Chief Nursing Supervisor
CFO: John Collins, Corporate Chief Financial Officer
CMO: Gary Bennett, M.D., Chief of Medical Staff
CHR: Cynthia Garren–Oster, Human Resources Manager
CNO: Theresa Catherine Berton, Interim Chief Executive Officer/Chief Nursing Officer
Web address: www.Chapmanglobalmedicalcenter.com
Control: Corporation, Investor–owned (for–profit) **Service**: General medical and surgical

Staffed Beds: 100

☐ **CHILDREN'S HOSPITAL OF ORANGE COUNTY (053304)**, 1201 West La Veta Avenue, Zip 92868–4203, Mailing Address: PO Box 5700, Zip 92863–5700; tel. 714/997–3000, (Nonreporting) **A**1 3 5 10
Primary Contact: Kimberly C. Cripe, President and Chief Executive Officer
COO: Matthew S Gerlach, Chief Operating Officer
CFO: Kerri Ruppert Schiller, Senior Vice President and Chief Financial Officer
CMO: Maria Minon, M.D., Vice President Medical Affairs and Chief Medical Officer
CIO: John Henderson, Vice President and Chief Information Officer
CHR: Mamoon Syed, Vice President Human Resources
CNO: Melanie Patterson, R.N., Vice President Patient Care Services and Chief Nursing Officer
Web address: www.choc.org
Control: Other not–for–profit (including NFP Corporation) **Service**: Children's general medical and surgical

Staffed Beds: 334

⇧ **HEALTHBRIDGE CHILDREN'S HOSPITAL (053308)**, 393 South Tustin Street, Zip 92866–2501; tel. 714/289–2400, (Nonreporting) **A**10 21 **S** Nexus Health Systems, Houston, TX
Primary Contact: Roberta Consolver, Chief Executive Officer/Chief Clinical Officer
CIO: Roberta Consolver, Chief Information Officer
Web address: www.HealthBridgeOrange.com
Control: Partnership, Investor–owned (for–profit) **Service**: Rehabilitation

Staffed Beds: 27

✯ **PROVIDENCE ST. JOSEPH HOSPITAL ORANGE (050069)**, 1100 West Stewart Drive, Zip 92868–3849, Mailing Address: P.O. Box 5600, Zip 92863–5600; tel. 714/633–9111, **A**1 2 3 5 10 **F**3 4 5 8 12 13 15 17 18 19 20 22 24 26 28 29 30 31 34 35 37 38 39 40 41 44 45 46 47 48 49 50 51 53 54 55 56 57 58 59 60 61 63 64 65 68 70 74 75 76 77 78 79 80 81 82 83 84 85 86 87 90 91 92 93 94 98 100 101 102 104 105 107 108 109 110 111 113 114 115 116 117 118 119 120 121 123 124 126 129 130 132 135 138 145 146 147 148 149 152 153 154 156 157 158 160 161 162 164 165 167 169 **P**5 **S** Providence, Renton, WA
Primary Contact: Brian Helleland, Chief Executive, Orange County High Desert Service Area
CFO: Kristi Liberatore, Vice President and Chief Financial Officer
CMO: Scott Rusk, M.D., Chief Medical Officer
CHR: Mary P Leahy, Regional Vice President, Chief Human Resources Officer
CNO: Katie Skelton, MSN, R.N., Vice President Nursing and Chief Nursing Officer
Web address: www.sjo.org
Control: Other not–for–profit (including NFP Corporation) **Service**: General medical and surgical

Staffed Beds: 461 **Admissions**: 20967 **Census**: 244 **Outpatient Visits**: 497364 **Births**: 4340 **Total Expense ($000)**: 755921 **Payroll Expense ($000)**: 278510 **Personnel**: 2476

Hospital, Medicare Provider Number, Address, Telephone, Approval, Facility, and Physician Codes, Health Care System

★ American Hospital Association (AHA) membership
☐ The Joint Commission accreditation
○ Healthcare Facilities Accreditation Program
◇ DNV Healthcare Inc. accreditation
⇧ Center for Improvement in Healthcare Quality Accreditation
△ Commission on Accreditation of Rehabilitation Facilities (CARF) accreditation

Hospitals, U.S. / CALIFORNIA

ST. JOSEPH HOSPITAL ORANGE See Providence St. Joseph Hospital Orange

☒ **UCI HEALTH (050348)**, 101 The City Drive South, Zip 92868–3298; tel. 714/456–6011, **A**1 2 3 5 8 10 19 **F**3 4 6 8 9 11 12 13 14 15 16 17 18 19 20 22 24 26 27 28 29 30 31 32 34 35 36 37 38 39 40 41 43 44 45 46 47 48 49 50 51 52 53 54 55 56 57 58 59 61 64 65 66 68 70 71 72 73 74 75 76 77 78 79 80 81 82 84 85 86 87 88 89 90 91 92 93 96 97 98 99 100 102 103 104 105 107 108 110 111 114 115 116 117 118 119 120 121 123 124 126 130 131 132 134 135 136 138 141 142 144 145 146 147 148 149 153 154 156 160 161 164 167 168 169 **S** University of California Systemwide Administration, Oakland, CA
Primary Contact: Chad T. Lefteris, Chief Executive Officer
COO: Chad T. Lefteris, Chief Operating Officer
CFO: Ajay Sial, Chief Financial Officer, UC Irvine Health
CMO: William Wilson, M.D., Chief Medical Officer
CIO: Charles H Podesta, Chief Information Officer
CHR: Ramona Agrela, Associate Chancellor & Chief Human Resources Executive
CNO: Sonia Lane, Interim Chief Nursing Officer
Web address: www.ucirvinehealth.org
Control: State, Government, Nonfederal **Service**: General medical and surgical

Staffed Beds: 459 **Admissions**: 22609 **Census**: 411 **Outpatient Visits**: 1155587 **Births**: 1768 **Total Expense ($000)**: 1926810 **Payroll Expense ($000)**: 730192 **Personnel**: 10994

UCI MEDICAL CENTER See UCI Health

OROVILLE—Butte County

OROVILLE HOSPITAL (050030), 2767 Olive Highway, Zip 95966–6118; tel. 530/533–8500, (Nonreporting) **A**5 10
Primary Contact: Robert J. Wentz, President and Chief Executive Officer
COO: Scott Chapple, Chief Operating Officer
CFO: Ashok Khanchandani, Chief Financial Officer
CMO: Mathew N. Fine, M.D., Chief Medical Officer
CIO: Denise LeFevre, Chief Information Officer
CHR: Scott Chapple, Chief Operating Officer
CNO: Carol Speer-Smith, R.N., Chief Nursing Officer
Web address: www.orovillehospital.com
Control: Other not–for–profit (including NFP Corporation) **Service**: General medical and surgical

Staffed Beds: 279

OXNARD—Ventura County

☒ **ST. JOHN'S REGIONAL MEDICAL CENTER (050082)**, 1600 North Rose Avenue, Zip 93030–3723; tel. 805/988–2500, (Includes ST. JOHN'S HOSPITAL CAMARILLO, 2309 Antonio Avenue, Camarillo, California, Zip 93010–1414, tel. 805/389–5800; Patrick Caster, President and Chief Executive Officer) (Nonreporting) **A**1 2 5 10 **S** CommonSpirit Health, Chicago, IL
Primary Contact: Patrick Caster, President and Chief Executive Officer
CFO: Donald P Bernard, Chief Financial Officer
CMO: Lynn Jeffers, Chief Medical Officer St. John's Regional Medical Center and St. John's Hospital Camarillo
CIO: Jeff Perry, Director Information Technology
CHR: Ed Gonzales, Vice President Human Resources
Web address: www.stjohnshealth.org
Control: Other not–for–profit (including NFP Corporation) **Service**: General medical and surgical

Staffed Beds: 266

PALM SPRINGS—Riverside County

☒ **DESERT REGIONAL MEDICAL CENTER (050243)**, 1150 North Indian Canyon Drive, Zip 92262–4872; tel. 760/323–6511, (Nonreporting) **A**1 2 3 5 10 13 **S** TENET Healthcare Corporation, Dallas, TX
Primary Contact: Michele Finney, Chief Executive Officer, Desert Regional Medical Center
COO: James Santucci, Chief Operating Officer
CFO: Judi Stimson, Chief Financial Officer
CMO: Charles Anderson, M.D., Chief Medical Officer
CIO: Robert Klingseis, Director Information Systems
CHR: James Kelley, Chief Human Resources Officer
CNO: Beverly Fick, Chief Nursing Officer
Web address: www.desertregional.com
Control: Individual, Investor–owned (for–profit) **Service**: General medical and surgical

Staffed Beds: 337

PALMDALE—Los Angeles County

☐ **PALMDALE REGIONAL MEDICAL CENTER (050204)**, 38600 Medical Center Drive, Zip 93551–4483; tel. 661/382–5000, (Nonreporting) **A**1 3 10 **S** Universal Health Services, Inc., King of Prussia, PA
Primary Contact: Nana Deeb, Chief Executive Officer
COO: Ryan Moon, Chief Operating Officer
CFO: Marc Nakagawa, Chief Financial Officer
CHR: Lilly Fernandez, Director Human Resources
CNO: Dana L. Dalton, Chief Nursing Officer
Web address: www.palmdaleregional.com
Control: Corporation, Investor–owned (for–profit) **Service**: General medical and surgical

Staffed Beds: 184

PALO ALTO—Santa Clara County

☒ **LUCILE PACKARD CHILDREN'S HOSPITAL STANFORD (053305)**, 725 Welch Road, Zip 94304–1614; tel. 650/497–8000, (Nonreporting) **A**1 3 5 10
Primary Contact: Paul King, President/Chief Executive Officer
COO: Rick Majzun, FACHE, Chief Operating Officer
CMO: Dennis Lund, M.D., Chief Medical Officer
CIO: Kim Roberts, Chief Strategy Officer
CHR: Greg Souza, Vice President Human Resources
Web address: www.stanfordchildrens.org
Control: Other not–for–profit (including NFP Corporation) **Service**: Children's general medical and surgical

Staffed Beds: 334

☒ **STANFORD HEALTH CARE (050441)**, 300 Pasteur Drive, Zip 94305–2200; tel. 650/723–4000, **A**1 3 5 8 10 19 **F**3 5 6 8 9 12 15 17 18 20 22 24 26 28 29 30 31 34 35 36 37 38 39 40 41 43 44 45 46 47 48 49 52 54 55 56 57 58 59 60 61 64 65 68 70 74 75 77 78 79 81 82 84 85 86 87 92 93 95 96 97 98 100 102 103 104 107 108 110 111 112 114 115 117 118 119 120 121 123 124 126 129 130 131 132 135 136 137 138 139 140 141 142 145 146 147 148 149 154 155 156 157 160 161 167 **P**3 5 **S** Stanford Health Care, Palo Alto, CA
Primary Contact: David Entwistle, President and Chief Executive Officer
COO: Quinn McKenna, Chief Operating Officer
CFO: Daniel Morrissette, Chief Financial Officer
CMO: Norman Rizk, M.D., Chief Medical Officer
CIO: Pravene Nath, Chief Information Officer
CHR: Kety Duron, Vice President Human Resources
CNO: Nancy Lee, R.N., MSN, Vice President Patient Care Services and Chief Nursing Officer
Web address: www.stanfordhealthcare.org
Control: Other not–for–profit (including NFP Corporation) **Service**: General medical and surgical

Staffed Beds: 649 **Admissions**: 22673 **Census**: 665 **Outpatient Visits**: 1311046 **Births**: 0 **Total Expense ($000)**: 6512934 **Payroll Expense ($000)**: 2002487 **Personnel**: 18052

VA PALO ALTO HEALTH CARE SYSTEM See VA Palo Alto Heath Care System

☒ △ **VA PALO ALTO HEATH CARE SYSTEM**, 3801 Miranda Avenue, Zip 94304–1207, Mailing Address: 3801 Miranda Avenue Bldg 6, Zip 94304–1207; tel. 650/493–5000, (Includes PALO ALTO DIVISION, 3801 Miranda Avenue, Palo Alto, California, Zip 94304–1207, tel. 650/493–5000; VETERANS AFFAIRS PALO ALTO HEALTH CARE SYSTEM, LIVERMORE DIVISION, 4951 Arroyo RD, Livermore, California, Zip 94550–9650, 4951 Arroyo Road, Zip 94550, tel. 510/447–2560) (Nonreporting) **A**1 2 3 5 7 **S** Department of Veterans Affairs, Washington, DC
Primary Contact: Jean J. Gurga, Executive Medical Center Director, VA Palo Alto Health Care System
CFO: Mel Niese, Chief Fiscal Service
CMO: Lawrence Leung, M.D., Chief of Staff
CIO: Doug Wirthgen, Chief Information Officer
CHR: Lori Peery, Chief Human Resource Management Services
Web address: www.paloalto.va.gov/
Control: Veterans Affairs, Government, federal **Service**: General medical and surgical

Staffed Beds: 768

VETERANS AFFAIRS MED CENTER See Palo Alto Division

PANORAMA CITY—Los Angeles County, See Los Angeles

PARAMOUNT—Los Angeles County

☒ **KINDRED HOSPITAL PARAMOUNT (052046)**, 16453 South Colorado Avenue, Zip 90723–5011; tel. 562/531–3110, (Nonreporting) **A**1 10 **S** ScionHealth, Louisville, KY
Primary Contact: Mark Apodaca, Chief Executive Officer
Web address: www.promiseeastla.com
Control: Corporation, Investor–owned (for–profit) **Service**: Acute long–term care hospital

Staffed Beds: 177

Hospitals, U.S. / CALIFORNIA

PASADENA—Los Angeles County

HUNTINGTON HEALTH (050438), 100 West California Boulevard, Zip 91105–3097, Mailing Address: P.O. Box 7013, Zip 91109–7013; tel. 626/397–5000, **A**1 2 3 5 8 10 19 **F**3 8 13 14 15 18 20 22 24 26 28 29 30 31 34 35 36 37 38 39 40 41 43 44 45 46 47 48 49 50 51 53 55 56 57 58 59 60 61 63 64 65 66 68 70 72 74 75 76 77 78 79 81 82 84 85 86 87 89 90 93 95 97 98 100 101 102 103 104 105 107 108 111 114 115 118 119 121 126 130 131 144 145 146 147 148 149 150 153 154 156 157 162 164 167 169 **P**3 **S** Cedars–Sinai Health System, West Hollywood, CA
Primary Contact: Lori J. Morgan, M.D., President/Chief Executive Officer, Huntington Health
CFO: Steven Mohr, Senior Vice President and Chief Financial Officer
CMO: Paula Verrette, M.D., Senior Vice President Quality and Physician Services and Chief Medical Officer
CIO: Debbie Tafoya, Vice President and Chief Information Officer
CHR: Debbie Ortega, Chief Human Resource Officer and Vice President Administrative Services
CNO: Gloria Sanchez-Rico, Chief Nursing Officer and Vice President
Web address: www.huntingtonhospital.com
Control: Other not–for–profit (including NFP Corporation) **Service**: General medical and surgical

Staffed Beds: 366 **Admissions**: 24319 **Census**: 344 **Outpatient Visits**: 178014 **Births**: 2888 **Total Expense ($000)**: 799760 **Payroll Expense ($000)**: 285728 **Personnel**: 3194

HUNTINGTON HOSPITAL See Huntington Health

LAS ENCINAS HOSPITAL (054078), 2900 East Del Mar Boulevard, Zip 91107–4399; tel. 626/795–9901, (Nonreporting) **A**1 10 **S** Signature Healthcare Services, Corona, CA
Primary Contact: Trevor Asmus, Chief Executive Officer
CMO: Daniel Suzuki, M.D., Medical Director
CIO: Eric Kim, Chief Information Officer
CHR: Veronica Herrera, Director Human Resources
Web address: www.lasencinashospital.com
Control: Corporation, Investor–owned (for–profit) **Service**: Psychiatric

Staffed Beds: 118

PATTON—San Bernardino County

DSH PATTON, 3102 East Highland Avenue, Zip 92369–7813; tel. 909/425–7000, (Nonreporting) **A**1 3 5
Primary Contact: Harry Oreol, Acting Chief Executive Officer
CFO: Kathleen Gamble, Fiscal Officer
CMO: George Christison, M.D., Medical Director
CIO: Cindy Barrett, Administrative Assistant
CHR: Nancy Varela, Director Human Resources
Web address: www.dmh.cahwnet.gov/statehospitals/patton
Control: State, Government, Nonfederal **Service**: Psychiatric

Staffed Beds: 1527

PERRIS—Riverside County

KINDRED HOSPITAL RIVERSIDE (052052), 2224 Medical Center Drive, Zip 92571–2638; tel. 951/436–3535, (Nonreporting) **A**1 10 **S** ScionHealth, Louisville, KY
Primary Contact: Julie Myers, Market Chief Executive Officer
COO: Guay Khim Fugate, Chief Operations Officer
CFO: John Browne, Senior Chief Financial Officer
CHR: Tom Wright, Director Human Resources
Web address: www.khriverside.com
Control: Corporation, Investor–owned (for–profit) **Service**: Acute long–term care hospital

Staffed Beds: 40

PETALUMA—Sonoma County

PETALUMA VALLEY HOSPITAL (050136), 400 North McDowell Boulevard, Zip 94954–2366; tel. 707/778–1111, **A**1 10 **F**3 8 11 15 29 30 34 35 40 44 45 46 50 58 59 64 70 74 75 76 77 79 81 84 85 86 87 93 102 107 108 110 111 119 126 130 146 147 148 149 154 **S** Providence, Renton, WA
Primary Contact: Michelle Oxford, Chief Administrative Officer
CFO: Michel Riccioni, Chief Financial Officer
CIO: Patrick Wylie, Director Information Systems
Web address: https://www.providence.org/locations/norcal/petaluma-valley-hospital
Control: Other not–for–profit (including NFP Corporation) **Service**: General medical and surgical

Staffed Beds: 80 **Admissions**: 1690 **Census**: 20 **Outpatient Visits**: 76518 **Births**: 113 **Total Expense ($000)**: 74701 **Payroll Expense ($000)**: 38332 **Personnel**: 268

PLACENTIA—Orange County

PLACENTIA–LINDA HOSPITAL See UCI Health – Placentia Linda

UCI HEALTH – PLACENTIA LINDA (050589), 1301 North Rose Drive, Zip 92870–3899; tel. 714/993–2000, (Nonreporting) **A**1 10 **S** University of California Systemwide Administration, Oakland, CA
Primary Contact: Fred Valtairo, R.N., Chief Executive Officer
CFO: Kelsie Blackwell, Chief Financial Officer
CIO: Eleanor Laneaux, Director Information Systems
CHR: Michelle Miller, Chief Human Resources
CNO: Rhonda Sausedo, Chief Nursing Officer
Web address: www.placentialinda.com
Control: Corporation, Investor–owned (for–profit) **Service**: General medical and surgical

Staffed Beds: 74

PLACERVILLE—El Dorado County

MARSHALL MEDICAL CENTER (050254), 1100 Marshall Way, Zip 95667–5722; tel. 530/622–1441, **A**1 2 5 10 **F**3 5 8 11 12 13 15 18 20 26 28 29 30 31 34 35 40 43 45 46 49 50 51 54 56 57 59 62 64 65 70 75 76 77 78 79 81 84 85 87 93 97 100 104 107 108 110 111 115 116 117 119 126 127 130 131 135 145 146 147 148 149 154 156 160 **P**3
Primary Contact: Siri Nelson, Chief Executive Officer
COO: Shannon Truesdell, Chief Operating Officer
CFO: Laurie Eldridge, Chief Financial Officer
CMO: Rajiv Pathak, Chief of Staff
CIO: Mike Jones, Executive Director
CHR: Scott M Comer, Vice President Human Resources
CNO: Kathy Blair Krejci, Chief Nursing Officer
Web address: www.marshallmedical.org
Control: Other not–for–profit (including NFP Corporation) **Service**: General medical and surgical

Staffed Beds: 111 **Admissions**: 4344 **Census**: 46 **Outpatient Visits**: 380066 **Births**: 332 **Total Expense ($000)**: 316479 **Payroll Expense ($000)**: 104364 **Personnel**: 1180

PLEASANTON—Alameda County

STANFORD HEALTH CARE – VALLEYCARE See Stanford Health Care Tri-Valley

STANFORD HEALTH CARE TRI–VALLEY (050283), 5555 West Las Positas Boulevard, Zip 94588–4000; tel. 925/847–3000, (Includes VALLEY MEMORIAL, 1111 East Stanley Boulevard, Livermore, California, Zip 94550–4115, tel. 925/447–7000) **A**1 2 3 10 19 **F**3 8 11 12 13 15 17 18 20 22 24 26 28 29 31 34 35 40 45 46 49 50 54 57 59 60 64 68 70 72 73 74 75 76 77 78 79 81 82 85 89 93 107 108 110 111 114 115 116 117 118 119 126 130 131 132 144 146 147 148 154 155 156 157 167 **S** Stanford Health Care, Palo Alto, CA
Primary Contact: Richard Shumway, President and Chief Executive Officer
COO: Tracey Lewis-Taylor, Chief Operating Officer
CMO: David Svec, M.D., Chief Medical Officer
CIO: Bob Woods, Chief Information Officer
CHR: Chris Faber, Human Resources Analyst
Web address: https://stanfordhealthcare.org/tri-valley
Control: Other not–for–profit (including NFP Corporation) **Service**: General medical and surgical

Staffed Beds: 177 **Admissions**: 7607 **Census**: 97 **Outpatient Visits**: 292709 **Births**: 1375 **Total Expense ($000)**: 491269 **Payroll Expense ($000)**: 207428 **Personnel**: 1053

Hospital, Medicare Provider Number, Address, Telephone, Approval, Facility, and Physician Codes, Health Care System

★ American Hospital Association (AHA) membership
☐ The Joint Commission accreditation
○ Healthcare Facilities Accreditation Program
◇ DNV Healthcare Inc. accreditation
⇑ Center for Improvement in Healthcare Quality Accreditation
△ Commission on Accreditation of Rehabilitation Facilities (CARF) accreditation

Hospitals, U.S. / CALIFORNIA

POMONA—Los Angeles County

CASA COLINA HOSPITAL AND CENTERS FOR HEALTHCARE (050782), 255 East Bonita Avenue, Zip 91767–1923, Mailing Address: P.O. Box 6001, Zip 91769–6001; tel. 909/596–7733, **A**1 3 5 7 10 13 **F**3 15 18 29 30 34 35 37 45 46 48 49 50 53 54 56 57 58 59 64 65 66 68 70 74 75 79 81 85 86 87 90 91 92 93 95 96 97 104 107 110 111 115 119 126 130 131 132 134 145 146 148 149 154 158 167
Primary Contact: Kelly Linden, President and Chief Executive Officer
CFO: David Morony, Chief Financial Officer
CMO: Christopher Chalian, M.D., Medical Director
CIO: Ross Lesins, Chief Information Officer
CHR: Karen Du Pont, Chief Human Resource Officer
CNO: Kathryn Johnson, Chief Nursing Officer
Web address: www.casacolina.org
Control: Other not–for–profit (including NFP Corporation) **Service**: General medical and surgical

Staffed Beds: 99 **Admissions**: 2070 **Census**: 71 **Outpatient Visits**: 169791 **Births**: 0 **Total Expense ($000)**: 101854 **Payroll Expense ($000)**: 47058 **Personnel**: 608

POMONA VALLEY HOSPITAL MEDICAL CENTER (050231), 1798 North Garey Avenue, Zip 91767–2918; tel. 909/865–9500, **A**1 2 3 5 10 **F**3 8 11 13 15 17 18 20 22 24 26 28 29 30 31 34 35 40 41 43 45 46 47 49 50 51 53 54 55 57 58 59 60 61 63 64 68 69 70 72 74 75 76 77 78 79 81 84 85 87 89 92 93 107 108 110 111 114 115 116 117 118 119 120 121 123 124 126 129 130 131 132 135 145 146 147 148 149 154 156 167 169
Primary Contact: Richard E. Yochum, FACHE, President and Chief Executive Officer
CFO: Michael Nelson, Executive Vice President and Chief Financial Officer
CMO: Kenneth Nakamoto, M.D., Vice President Medical Affairs
CIO: Kent Hoyos, Chief Information Officer
CHR: Ray Inge, Vice President Human Resources
CNO: Darlene Scafiddi, R.N., MSN, Vice President Nursing and Patient Care Services
Web address: www.pvhmc.org
Control: Other not–for–profit (including NFP Corporation) **Service**: General medical and surgical

Staffed Beds: 412 **Admissions**: 20794 **Census**: 267 **Outpatient Visits**: 351344 **Births**: 4304 **Total Expense ($000)**: 820481 **Payroll Expense ($000)**: 370564 **Personnel**: 3530

PORTERVILLE—Tulare County

PORTERVILLE DEVELOPMENTAL CENTER (050546), 26501 Avenue 140, Zip 93257–9109, Mailing Address: P.O. Box 2000, Zip 93258–2000; tel. 559/782–2222, (Nonreporting) **A**10
Primary Contact: Theresa Billeci, Executive Director
COO: Betty Davis, Director Administrative Services
CFO: Karen Warren, Fiscal Officer
CMO: Joseph Mendoza, M.D., Medical Director
CIO: Vincent Chandler, Director Information Services
CHR: Shawna Gregg, Director Human Resources
CNO: Tom Shelton, Coordinator of Nursing Services
Web address: www.pdc.dds.ca.gov
Control: State, Government, Nonfederal **Service**: Intellectual disabilities

Staffed Beds: 484

SIERRA VIEW MEDICAL CENTER (050261), 465 West Putnam Avenue, Zip 93257–3320; tel. 559/784–1110, (Total facility includes 35 beds in nursing home–type unit) **A**1 3 5 10 **F**3 13 15 20 22 29 30 31 34 35 40 45 49 54 57 59 60 65 68 70 72 75 76 78 79 81 83 84 85 87 89 93 107 108 110 111 114 115 118 119 120 121 123 124 127 130 132 135 147 148 149 156 167
Primary Contact: Donna J. Hefner, R.N., President and Chief Executive Officer
CIO: Traci Follett, Director Clinical Informatics
CHR: Sharon Brown, Vice President Human Resources
Web address: www.sierra-view.com
Control: Hospital district or authority, Government, Nonfederal **Service**: General medical and surgical

Staffed Beds: 158 **Admissions**: 5378 **Census**: 90 **Outpatient Visits**: 156885 **Births**: 1310 **Total Expense ($000)**: 172506 **Payroll Expense ($000)**: 63052 **Personnel**: 808

PORTOLA—Plumas County

EASTERN PLUMAS HEALTH CARE (051300), 500 First Avenue, Zip 96122–9406; tel. 530/832–6500, (Nonreporting) **A**10 18
Primary Contact: Doug McCoy, Chief Executive Officer
CFO: Katherine Pairish, Chief Financial Officer
CMO: Eric Bugna, M.D., Chief of Staff
CHR: Cathy Conant, Chief Human Resources and Personnel
Web address: www.ephc.org
Control: Hospital district or authority, Government, Nonfederal **Service**: General medical and surgical

Staffed Beds: 75

POWAY—San Diego County

PALOMAR MEDICAL CENTER POWAY (050636), 15615 Pomerado Road, Zip 92064–2460; tel. 858/613–4000, (Total facility includes 129 beds in nursing home–type unit) **A**1 10 **F**3 11 12 15 29 30 31 35 37 38 39 40 44 49 50 54 56 64 65 68 70 72 74 75 76 77 79 81 82 85 86 87 91 93 94 97 98 100 101 102 107 108 111 114 119 120 124 128 130 131 135 146 147 149 154 164 167 169 **P**3 **S** Palomar Health, Escondido, CA
Primary Contact: Diane Hansen, President and Chief Executive Officer
CIO: David Pape, Vice President, Information Technology
CHR: Brenda C Turner, Chief Human Resources Officer
CNO: Joyce Volsch, Chief Nursing Officer
Web address: https://www.palomarhealth.org/facilities/palomar-poway-outpatient/
Control: Hospital district or authority, Government, Nonfederal **Service**: General medical and surgical

Staffed Beds: 233 **Admissions**: 5811 **Census**: 165 **Outpatient Visits**: 61878 **Births**: 663 **Total Expense ($000)**: 273114 **Payroll Expense ($000)**: 66637 **Personnel**: 562

QUINCY—Plumas County

PLUMAS DISTRICT HOSPITAL (051326), 1065 Bucks Lake Road, Zip 95971–9599; tel. 530/283–2121, (Nonreporting) **A**1 5 10 18
Primary Contact: JoDee Read, Chief Executive Officer
CFO: Caleb Johnson, Chief Financial Officer
CMO: Vincent Frantz, M.D., Chief of Staff
CIO: Brenda Compton, Manager Information Technology
CHR: Denise Harding, Director Human Resources
Web address: www.pdh.org
Control: Hospital district or authority, Government, Nonfederal **Service**: General medical and surgical

Staffed Beds: 16

RANCHO CUCAMONGA—San Bernardino County

KINDRED HOSPITAL RANCHO (052049), 10841 White Oak Avenue, Zip 91730–3811; tel. 909/581–6400, (Nonreporting) **A**1 10 **S** ScionHealth, Louisville, KY
Primary Contact: Julie Myers, Market Chief Executive Officer
COO: Jody Knox, Chief Operating Officer
Web address: www.khrancho.com
Control: Corporation, Investor–owned (for–profit) **Service**: Acute long–term care hospital

Staffed Beds: 55

RANCHO MIRAGE—Riverside County

EISENHOWER HEALTH (050573), 39000 Bob Hope Drive, Zip 92270–3221; tel. 760/340–3911, **A**1 2 3 5 8 10 19 **F**2 3 5 9 11 12 13 15 17 18 20 22 24 26 28 29 30 31 34 35 37 40 41 43 45 46 47 49 50 53 54 56 57 58 59 60 61 64 65 68 70 72 74 75 76 77 78 79 81 82 84 85 86 87 89 93 96 97 100 101 102 104 107 108 109 110 111 112 114 115 118 119 120 121 123 124 126 129 130 131 132 135 143 144 145 146 147 148 149 154 156 160 161 164 167 169 **P**3 5
Primary Contact: Martin J. Massiello, President/Chief Executive Officer
COO: Martin J. Massiello, Executive Vice President and Chief Operating Officer
CFO: Ken Wheat, Senior Vice President and Chief Financial Officer
CMO: Alan Williamson, M.D., Vice President, Medical Affairs and Chief Medical Officer
CIO: David Perez, Vice President, Chief Information Officer
CHR: David Kowalczyk, Vice President Human Resources
CNO: Benjamin Farber, R.N., Vice President, Patient Care and Chief Nursing Officer
Web address: https://eisenhowerhealth.org/
Control: Other not–for–profit (including NFP Corporation) **Service**: General medical and surgical

Staffed Beds: 324 **Admissions**: 22688 **Census**: 229 **Outpatient Visits**: 1164334 **Births**: 1155 **Total Expense ($000)**: 1125299 **Payroll Expense ($000)**: 425454 **Personnel**: 3767

REHABILITATION HOSPITAL OF SOUTHERN CALIFORNIA (053041), 70077 Ramon Road, Zip 92270–5201; tel. 760/671–3425, (Nonreporting) **A**1 10 **S** Ernest Health, Inc., Albuquerque, NM
Primary Contact: Rachelle Spencer, Chief Executive Officer
Web address: https://ernesthealth.com/portfolio-item/rehabilitation-hospital-of-southern-california/
Control: Corporation, Investor–owned (for–profit) **Service**: Rehabilitation

Staffed Beds: 50

VIBRA REHABILITATION HOSPITAL RANCHO MIRAGE See Rehabilitation Hospital of Southern California

Hospitals, U.S. / CALIFORNIA

RED BLUFF—Tehama County

✠ **ST. ELIZABETH COMMUNITY HOSPITAL (050042)**, 2550 Sister Mary Columba Drive, Zip 96080–4397; tel. 530/529–8000, **A**1 10 20 **F**3 7 8 11 13 15 29 30 31 34 35 38 40 43 44 45 54 59 62 64 65 66 70 75 76 79 81 85 86 87 89 94 102 107 108 110 111 114 115 116 118 119 127 130 131 135 144 146 147 148 149 154 156 157 160 161 164 167 169 **S** CommonSpirit Health, Chicago, IL
Primary Contact: Rodger Page, Market President, North State
CFO: Kim Miranda, Chief Financial Officer
CMO: James DeSoto, M.D., Vice President Medical Affairs
CIO: Henry Niessink, Senior Manager Information Technology Systems
CHR: Denise Little, Director Human Resources
Web address: www.mercy.org
Control: Other not–for–profit (including NFP Corporation) **Service:** General medical and surgical

Staffed Beds: 76 **Admissions:** 2893 **Census:** 27 **Outpatient Visits:** 203908 **Births:** 545 **Total Expense ($000):** 153496 **Payroll Expense ($000):** 57975 **Personnel:** 540

REDDING—Shasta County

✠ **MERCY MEDICAL CENTER REDDING (050280)**, 2175 Rosaline Avenue, Zip 96001–2549, Mailing Address: P.O. Box 496009, Zip 96049–6009; tel. 530/225–6000, **A**1 2 3 5 10 **F**2 3 7 8 11 13 17 18 20 22 24 26 28 29 30 31 34 35 37 40 43 44 45 46 48 49 54 56 59 60 63 64 69 70 72 74 75 76 77 78 79 80 81 84 85 87 89 92 93 107 108 111 115 119 126 130 132 143 146 148 149 154 167 169 **P**6 **S** CommonSpirit Health, Chicago, IL
Primary Contact: G. Todd. Smith, President
COO: Patrick Varga, Chief Operating Officer
CFO: Joseph D'Angina, Chief Financial Officer
CMO: James DeSoto, M.D., Vice President Medical Affairs
CIO: Henry Niessink, Regional Director Information Technology Services
Web address: www.mercy.org
Control: Church operated, Nongovernment, not–for–profit **Service:** General medical and surgical

Staffed Beds: 266 **Admissions:** 13038 **Census:** 182 **Outpatient Visits:** 159064 **Births:** 1698 **Total Expense ($000):** 568351 **Payroll Expense ($000):** 215421 **Personnel:** 1733

○ **PATIENTS' HOSPITAL OF REDDING (050697)**, 2900 Eureka Way, Zip 96001–0220; tel. 530/225–8700, (Nonreporting) **A**10 11
Primary Contact: Shari Lejsek, Administrator
CFO: Kim Needles, Manager Business Office
CMO: James Tate, M.D., Chief of Staff
CIO: Kim Cameron, Manager Health Information Services
CHR: Brenda Meline, Manager Human Resources
CNO: Diane Rieke, Director Patient Care Services
Web address: www.patientshospital.com
Control: Individual, Investor–owned (for–profit) **Service:** Surgical

Staffed Beds: 10

☐ **SHASTA REGIONAL MEDICAL CENTER (050764)**, 1100 Butte Street, Zip 96001–0853, Mailing Address: P.O. Box 496072, Zip 96049–6072; tel. 530/244–5400, (Nonreporting) **A**1 3 5 10 **S** Prime Healthcare, Ontario, CA
Primary Contact: Casey Fatch, Chief Executive Officer
COO: Becky Levy, Chief Operating Officer
CFO: Becky Levy, Chief Financial Officer
CMO: Marcia McCampbell, M.D., Chief Medical Officer
CIO: Tony VanBoekel, Director Information Systems
CHR: Andrew Torge, Director Human Resources
Web address: www.shastaregional.com
Control: Corporation, Investor–owned (for–profit) **Service:** General medical and surgical

Staffed Beds: 100

✠ **VIBRA HOSPITAL OF NORTHERN CALIFORNIA (052047)**, 2801 Eureka Way, Zip 96001–0222; tel. 530/246–9000, (Nonreporting) **A**1 10 **S** Vibra Healthcare, Mechanicsburg, PA
Primary Contact: Emily DeFillipo, Chief Executive Officer
COO: Sheba Saelee, Chief Clinical Office and Chief Operating Officer
CFO: Rebecca Andrews, Chief Financial Officer
CMO: Nanda Kumar, M.D., Chief of Staff
CIO: Mark Cardenas, Director Plant Operations
Web address: www.norcalrehab.com
Control: Corporation, Investor–owned (for–profit) **Service:** Acute long–term care hospital

Staffed Beds: 56

REDLANDS—San Bernardino County

✠ **REDLANDS COMMUNITY HOSPITAL (050272)**, 350 Terracina Boulevard, Zip 92373–0742, Mailing Address: P.O. Box 3391, Zip 92373–0742; tel. 909/335–5500, (Total facility includes 16 beds in nursing home–type unit) **A**1 10 **F**3 13 15 18 20 28 29 30 31 34 35 40 46 49 50 57 62 63 65 70 72 74 75 76 77 78 79 81 82 83 84 93 98 107 108 110 111 114 115 117 119 121 126 128 130 146 148 149 154 167 169 **P**5
Primary Contact: Jim R. Holmes, President/Chief Executive Officer
CFO: Michelle Mok, Chief Financial Officer
CHR: Lisa Guzman, Human Resource Vice President
CNO: Lauren Spilsbury, R.N., MSN, Vice President for Patient Care Services
Web address: www.redlandshospital.org
Control: Other not–for–profit (including NFP Corporation) **Service:** General medical and surgical

Staffed Beds: 213 **Admissions:** 10336 **Census:** 134 **Outpatient Visits:** 59393 **Births:** 1658 **Total Expense ($000):** 401251 **Payroll Expense ($000):** 143428 **Personnel:** 1444

REDWOOD CITY—San Mateo County

✠ **KAISER PERMANENTE REDWOOD CITY MEDICAL CENTER (050541)**, 1100 Veterans Boulevard, Zip 94063–2087; tel. 650/299–2000, **A**1 2 3 5 10 **F**3 11 13 15 18 20 26 30 31 37 39 40 41 45 49 56 60 64 68 70 72 73 74 75 76 78 79 80 81 84 85 87 100 107 108 110 111 114 115 118 119 130 135 146 148 149 154 167 169 **S** Kaiser Foundation Hospitals, Oakland, CA
COO: Sheila Gilson, R.N., Chief Operating Officer
CFO: Doug Reynolds, Area Finance Officer
CMO: William Firtch, M.D., Physician In Chief
CHR: Kimberly A Seitz, Area Human Resources Leader
Web address: www.kaiserpermanente.org
Control: Other not–for–profit (including NFP Corporation) **Service:** General medical and surgical

Staffed Beds: 153 **Admissions:** 7882 **Census:** 76 **Outpatient Visits:** 57007 **Births:** 1922 **Personnel:** 877

✠ **SEQUOIA HOSPITAL (050197)**, 170 Alameda De Las Pulgas, Zip 94062–2799; tel. 650/369–5811, **A**1 10 **F**11 12 13 15 18 20 22 24 26 28 29 30 31 32 34 35 37 40 45 46 49 50 53 57 59 60 64 68 70 74 75 76 77 78 79 81 84 86 87 92 93 94 107 108 110 111 115 118 119 120 121 123 124 126 130 132 135 146 147 149 154 156 167 169 **S** CommonSpirit Health, Chicago, IL
Primary Contact: Bill Graham, President
CFO: Kim Osborn, Chief Financial Officer
CMO: Anita Chandrasena, M.D., Vice President Medical Affairs
CIO: Ian Vallely, Information Technology Site Leader
CHR: Linde Cheema, Vice President Human Resources
Web address: www.sequoiahospital.org
Control: Other not–for–profit (including NFP Corporation) **Service:** General medical and surgical

Staffed Beds: 111 **Admissions:** 4514 **Census:** 47 **Births:** 1109 **Total Expense ($000):** 320415 **Payroll Expense ($000):** 105725 **Personnel:** 566

REEDLEY—Fresno County

✠ **ADVENTIST HEALTH REEDLEY (050192)**, 372 West Cypress Avenue, Zip 93654–2199; tel. 559/638–8155, (Nonreporting) **A**1 3 10 **S** Adventist Health, Roseville, CA
Primary Contact: Jason Wells, FACHE, President
CFO: Teresa Jacques, Interim Chief Financial Officer
CMO: Todd Spencer, M.D., Chief Medical Staff
CIO: Valerie Alvarez, Executive Assistant
CHR: Ramona Alvarado, Interim Manager Human Resources
Web address: https://www.adventisthealth.org/reedley/
Control: Other not–for–profit (including NFP Corporation) **Service:** General medical and surgical

Staffed Beds: 49

RESEDA—Los Angeles County

☐ **JOYCE EISENBERG–KEEFER MEDICAL CENTER (054147)**, 7150 Tampa Avenue, Zip 91335–3700; tel. 818/774–3000, (Nonreporting) **A**1 10
Primary Contact: Ilana Springer, Chief Executive Officer, Administrator, Safety Officer
CNO: Haya Berci, Executive Director of Nursing
Web address: https://healthy.kaiserpermanente.org/southern-california/facilities/joyce-eisenberg-keefer-medical-center-429457
Control: Other not–for–profit (including NFP Corporation) **Service:** Psychiatric

Staffed Beds: 249

Hospital, Medicare Provider Number, Address, Telephone, Approval, Facility, and Physician Codes, Health Care System

★ American Hospital Association (AHA) membership
☐ The Joint Commission accreditation
○ Healthcare Facilities Accreditation Program
◇ DNV Healthcare Inc. accreditation
⇧ Center for Improvement in Healthcare Quality Accreditation
△ Commission on Accreditation of Rehabilitation Facilities (CARF) accreditation

© 2025 AHA Guide

Hospitals, U.S. / CALIFORNIA

RICHMOND—Contra Costa County

KAISER PERMANENTE RICHMOND MEDICAL CENTER See Kaiser Permanente Oakland Medical Center, Oakland

RICHMOND MEDICAL CENTER See Kaiser Permanente Richmond Medical Center

RIDGECREST—Kern County

★ ⇑ **RIDGECREST REGIONAL HOSPITAL (051333)**, 1081 North China Lake Boulevard, Zip 93555–3130; tel. 760/446–3551, (Total facility includes 125 beds in nursing home–type unit) **A**10 18 21 **F**7 8 15 18 19 28 29 30 32 33 34 35 39 40 43 45 46 50 57 59 60 62 63 64 65 68 69 70 71 74 75 76 77 79 81 82 84 86 87 89 93 94 97 104 107 108 109 110 111 112 113 114 115 116 117 118 119 127 128 129 130 132 133 135 143 144 146 147 148 149 154 156 169
Primary Contact: James A. Suver, FACHE, Chief Executive Officer
CHR: Michelle Lemke, Administrator Human Resources and Support Services
Web address: www.rrh.org
Control: Other not–for–profit (including NFP Corporation) **Service**: General medical and surgical

Staffed Beds: 197 **Admissions**: 1613 **Census**: 73 **Outpatient Visits**: 127561 **Births**: 389 **Total Expense ($000)**: 156921 **Payroll Expense ($000)**: 60267 **Personnel**: 764

RIVERSIDE—Riverside County

✠ **KAISER PERMANENTE RIVERSIDE MEDICAL CENTER (050686)**, 10800 Magnolia Avenue, Zip 92505–3000; tel. 951/353–2000, **A**1 3 5 10 19 **F**3 13 15 17 28 29 30 31 34 35 40 44 45 46 48 49 50 51 53 59 60 62 63 64 65 68 70 71 72 74 75 76 77 78 79 81 82 83 84 85 86 87 92 93 97 100 102 107 108 109 110 111 114 115 116 117 118 119 130 131 132 135 143 144 146 147 148 149 150 154 156 157 162 167 169 **S** Kaiser Foundation Hospitals, Oakland, CA
Primary Contact: Sammy R. Totah, PharmD, Senior Vice President, Area Manager Riverside & Moreno Valley, Kaiser Foundation Health Plans and Ho
COO: Robin D. Mackenroth, Chief Operating Officer
CFO: JiJi Abraham, Chief Financial Officer
CMO: Frank M. Flowers, M.D., Area Medical Director
CIO: Alfred T Velasquez, Area Information Officer
CHR: Michelle Skipper, Director Human Resources
CNO: Rosemary M Butler, R.N., MSN, Chief Nurse Executive
Web address: www.kaiserpermanente.org
Control: Other not–for–profit (including NFP Corporation) **Service**: General medical and surgical

Staffed Beds: 225 **Admissions**: 10282 **Census**: 126 **Outpatient Visits**: 333198 **Births**: 2982 **Personnel**: 2048

☐ **PACIFIC GROVE HOSPITAL (054130)**, 5900 Brockton Avenue, Zip 92506–1862; tel. 951/275–8400, (Nonreporting) **A**1 3 5 10 **S** Acadia Healthcare Company, Inc., Franklin, TN
Primary Contact: Steven M. Hytry, PsyD, Chief Executive Officer
Web address: www.pacificgrovehospital.com
Control: Corporation, Investor–owned (for–profit) **Service**: Psychiatric

Staffed Beds: 68

☐ **PARKVIEW COMMUNITY HOSPITAL MEDICAL CENTER (050102)**, 3865 Jackson Street, Zip 92503–3998; tel. 951/688–2211, **A**1 3 10 **F**3 8 12 13 15 18 20 29 30 34 35 40 44 45 46 47 48 49 68 70 72 74 75 76 77 79 81 82 84 85 89 91 92 94 97 102 107 108 109 110 111 114 115 116 117 118 119 164 **S** AHMC Healthcare, Alhambra, CA
Primary Contact: David J. Batista, Chief Executive Officer, Doctors Hospital of Riverside/Executive Vice President, AHMC Healthcare, In
COO: Robert Brown, Chief Operating Officer
CFO: Nancy Wilson, Chief Financial Officer
CMO: Serafin Salazar, M.D., Chief of Staff
CIO: John Ciccarelli, Director Information Technology
CHR: Ilyssa DeCasperis, Director of Human Resources
Web address: www.pchmc.org
Control: Individual, Investor–owned (for–profit) **Service**: General medical and surgical

Staffed Beds: 182 **Admissions**: 5587 **Census**: 67 **Outpatient Visits**: 60874 **Births**: 1029 **Personnel**: 793

✠ **RIVERSIDE COMMUNITY HOSPITAL (050022)**, 4445 Magnolia Avenue, Zip 92501–4199; tel. 951/788–3000, (Nonreporting) **A**1 2 3 5 10 **S** HCA Healthcare, Nashville, TN
Primary Contact: Peter Hemstead, Chief Executive Officer
COO: Daniel Bowers, Chief Operating Officer
CFO: Todd LaCaze, Chief Financial Officer
CMO: David Tito, M.D., President Medical Staff
CIO: Cae Swanger, Chief Information Officer
CNO: Annette June Greenwood, Chief Nursing Officer
Web address: www.riversidecommunityhospital.com
Control: Corporation, Investor–owned (for–profit) **Service**: General medical and surgical

Staffed Beds: 478

ROSEMEAD—Los Angeles County

☐ **BHC ALHAMBRA HOSPITAL (054032)**, 4619 North Rosemead Boulevard, Zip 91770–1478, Mailing Address: P.O. Box 369, Zip 91770–0369; tel. 626/286–1191, (Nonreporting) **A**1 3 10 **S** Universal Health Services, Inc., King of Prussia, PA
Primary Contact: Peggy Minnick, R.N., Chief Executive Officer
CFO: Craig Corley, Chief Financial Officer
CMO: Wakelin McNeel, M.D., Medical Director
CIO: Debbie Irvin, Director Health Information Management
CHR: Venus Taylor, Director Human Resources
Web address: www.bhcalhambra.com
Control: Corporation, Investor–owned (for–profit) **Service**: Psychiatric

Staffed Beds: 97

SILVER LAKE MEDICAL CENTER–INGLESIDE HOSPITAL See La Downtown Medical Center, Llc –Ingleside Campus

ROSEVILLE—Placer County

✠ **KAISER PERMANENTE ROSEVILLE MEDICAL CENTER (050772)**, 1600 Eureka Road, Zip 95661–3027; tel. 916/784–4000, **A**1 2 3 5 10 **F**3 11 13 15 18 19 20 22 26 27 30 31 37 39 40 41 49 56 60 64 68 70 72 73 74 75 76 78 79 80 81 84 85 87 88 89 100 107 108 110 111 114 115 117 118 119 120 121 123 124 130 135 146 148 149 154 167 169 **S** Kaiser Foundation Hospitals, Oakland, CA
Primary Contact: Kimberly Menzel, Senior Vice President and Area Manager
Web address: www.kp.org
Control: Other not–for–profit (including NFP Corporation) **Service**: General medical and surgical

Staffed Beds: 352 **Admissions**: 24089 **Census**: 293 **Outpatient Visits**: 201936 **Births**: 6635 **Personnel**: 2538

✠ △ **SUTTER ROSEVILLE MEDICAL CENTER (050309)**, 1 Medical Plaza Drive, Zip 95661–3037; tel. 916/781–1000, **A**1 2 3 5 7 10 **F**3 8 12 13 15 17 18 20 22 26 28 29 30 31 34 35 37 43 44 49 50 55 56 58 59 60 63 64 65 68 70 72 73 74 75 76 78 79 81 82 84 85 86 87 89 90 91 93 95 96 100 101 102 104 107 108 109 111 114 116 119 120 121 123 124 126 130 131 132 141 146 147 148 149 154 164 165 167 169 **S** Sutter Health, Sacramento, CA
Primary Contact: Tamara Powers, R.N., Chief Executive Officer
COO: Dionne Miller, Chief Operating Officer
CFO: Gary Hubschman, Administrative Director Finance
CMO: Stuart Bostrom, M.D., Director Medical Affairs
CIO: Nancy Turner, Director Communications
CHR: Lynda Dasaro, Director Human Resources
CNO: Barbara J Nelson, Ph.D., R.N., Chief Nursing Executive
Web address: www.sutterroseville.org
Control: Other not–for–profit (including NFP Corporation) **Service**: General medical and surgical

Staffed Beds: 382 **Admissions**: 27112 **Census**: 348 **Outpatient Visits**: 177152 **Births**: 2507 **Total Expense ($000)**: 978711 **Payroll Expense ($000)**: 343135 **Personnel**: 2671

SACRAMENTO—Sacramento County

☐ **HERITAGE OAKS HOSPITAL (054104)**, 4250 Auburn Boulevard, Zip 95841–4164; tel. 916/489–3336, (Nonreporting) **A**1 5 10 **S** Universal Health Services, Inc., King of Prussia, PA
Primary Contact: Yannis Angouras, Chief Executive Officer
CFO: Art Wong, Chief Financial Officer
CMO: Joseph Sison, M.D., Medical Director
CHR: Lisa Myers, Director Human Resources
Web address: www.heritageoakshospital.com
Control: Corporation, Investor–owned (for–profit) **Service**: Psychiatric

Staffed Beds: 125

✠ **KAISER PERMANENTE SACRAMENTO MEDICAL CENTER (050425)**, 2025 Morse Avenue, Zip 95825–2100; tel. 916/973–5000, **A**1 2 3 5 10 19 **F**3 11 15 17 18 20 26 30 31 37 39 40 41 45 46 47 49 56 60 64 68 70 74 75 78 79 80 81 84 85 87 100 107 108 110 111 114 115 118 119 120 121 123 130 135 146 148 149 154 167 **S** Kaiser Foundation Hospitals, Oakland, CA
Primary Contact: James L. Robinson III, PsyD, Senior Vice President/Area Manager, Sacramento and South Sacramento
CFO: Jim Eldridge, Area Financial Officer
CMO: Chris Palkowski, M.D., Physician in Chief
CIO: Philip Fasano, Chief Information Officer
CHR: Gay Westfall, Senior Vice President Human Resources
Web address: www.kp.org
Control: Other not–for–profit (including NFP Corporation) **Service**: General medical and surgical

Staffed Beds: 287 **Admissions**: 13269 **Census**: 171 **Outpatient Visits**: 250294 **Births**: 4 **Personnel**: 1903

Hospitals, U.S. / CALIFORNIA

✚ **KAISER PERMANENTE SOUTH SACRAMENTO MEDICAL CENTER (050674)**, 6600 Bruceville Road, Zip 95823–4691; tel. 916/688–2430, **A**1 2 3 5 10 19 **F**3 11 12 13 15 18 20 22 26 30 31 37 39 40 41 43 45 49 56 60 64 68 70 73 74 75 76 78 79 81 84 85 87 100 107 108 110 111 114 115 118 119 126 130 135 144 146 148 149 154 167 169 **P**6 **S** Kaiser Foundation Hospitals, Oakland, CA
Primary Contact: James L. Robinson III, PsyD, Senior Vice President/Area Manager, Sacramento and South Sacramento
CFO: Kevin L Smith, Area Finance Officer
CIO: Michelle Odell, Director of Public Affairs
CHR: James Kevin Peterson, Human Resources Leader
CNO: Terri Owensby, R.N., Chief Nursing Executive
Web address: www.kp.org
Control: Other not-for-profit (including NFP Corporation) **Service**: General medical and surgical

Staffed Beds: 241 **Admissions**: 15763 **Census**: 193 **Outpatient Visits**: 195119 **Births**: 2539 **Personnel**: 1461

✚ △ **MERCY GENERAL HOSPITAL (050017)**, 4001 'J' Street, Zip 95819–3600; tel. 916/453–4545, **A**1 2 3 5 7 10 **F**3 8 11 13 17 18 20 22 24 26 28 29 30 31 34 35 36 37 38 40 44 45 46 47 48 49 50 51 53 54 56 57 58 59 61 62 63 64 65 67 68 70 74 75 76 77 78 79 81 82 84 85 86 87 90 91 92 93 94 96 100 102 107 108 111 115 118 119 126 130 131 132 135 141 142 143 145 146 148 149 154 157 160 164 166 167 **P**3 5 **S** CommonSpirit Health, Chicago, IL
Primary Contact: Christina Johnson, M.D., Sacramento Market President
COO: Clare Lee, Chief Operating Officer
CFO: Bonnie Jenkins, Chief Financial Officer
CHR: Cyndi Kirch, Vice President Human Resources
CNO: allison cotterill MSN, RN, Chief Nursing Officer
Web address: www.mercygeneral.org
Control: Other not-for-profit (including NFP Corporation) **Service**: General medical and surgical

Staffed Beds: 313 **Admissions**: 13910 **Census**: 188 **Outpatient Visits**: 115891 **Births**: 791 **Total Expense ($000)**: 648037 **Payroll Expense ($000)**: 243210 **Personnel**: 1719

✚ **METHODIST HOSPITAL OF SACRAMENTO (050590)**, 7500 Hospital Drive, Zip 95823–5477; tel. 916/423–3000, (Total facility includes 171 beds in nursing home–type unit) **A**1 3 5 10 **F**3 8 12 13 17 29 30 34 35 37 40 44 45 48 49 50 51 60 64 66 70 72 74 75 76 77 79 81 85 87 91 92 93 96 97 100 107 111 114 115 119 126 128 130 132 146 147 148 149 154 167 **S** CommonSpirit Health, Chicago, IL
Primary Contact: Phyllis Baltz, Hospital President
COO: Anita J Kennedy, Vice President Operations
CFO: Bonnie Jenkins, Chief Financial Officer
CMO: Amir Sweha, M.D., Vice President Medical Administration
CHR: Cyndi Kirch, Vice President Human Resources
CNO: Martina Evans–Harrison, R.N., MSN, Chief Nurse Executive
Web address: www.methodistsacramento.org
Control: Other not-for-profit (including NFP Corporation) **Service**: General medical and surgical

Staffed Beds: 329 **Admissions**: 10221 **Census**: 256 **Outpatient Visits**: 74587 **Births**: 1319 **Total Expense ($000)**: 356267 **Payroll Expense ($000)**: 149730 **Personnel**: 1130

SACRAMENTO REHABILITATION HOSPITAL, LLC (053045), 10 Advantage Court, Zip 95834–2123; tel. 916/628–8301, (Nonreporting) **S** Ernest Health, Inc., Albuquerque, NM
Primary Contact: Joseph G. Hugar, Chief Executive Officer
Web address: https://sacramentorehab.com/
Control: Corporation, Investor–owned (for–profit) **Service**: Rehabilitation

Staffed Beds: 50

☐ **SHRINERS CHILDREN'S – NORTHERN CALIFORNIA (053311)**, 2425 Stockton Boulevard, Zip 95817–2215; tel. 916/453–2000, (Nonreporting) **A**1 3 5 10 **S** Shriners Hospitals for Children, Tampa, FL
Primary Contact: Kenny Pawlek, Administrator/Chief Executive Officer
CFO: William Dalby, Director Fiscal Services
CIO: John Bevel, Manager Information Systems
CHR: Deborah Rubens, Director Human Resources
Web address: www.shrinershospitalsforchildren.org/Hospitals/Locations/NorthernCalifornia.aspx
Control: Other not-for-profit (including NFP Corporation) **Service**: Children's general medical and surgical

Staffed Beds: 60

SHRINERS HOSPITALS FOR CHILDREN–NORTHERN CALIFORNIA See Shriners Children's – Northern California

☐ **SIERRA VISTA HOSPITAL (054087)**, 8001 Bruceville Road, Zip 95823–2329; tel. 916/288–0300, (Nonreporting) **A**1 5 10 **S** Universal Health Services, Inc., King of Prussia, PA
Primary Contact: Mike Zauner, Chief Executive Officer/Regional Vice President
COO: Ixel Morell, Chief Operating Officer
CFO: Nicole Samuel, Chief Financial Officer
CMO: Alok Banga, M.D., Medical Director
CNO: Gwen Hubbard, Chief Nursing Officer
Web address: www.sierravistahospital.com
Control: Corporation, Investor–owned (for–profit) **Service**: Psychiatric

Staffed Beds: 171

✚ **SUTTER CENTER FOR PSYCHIATRY (054096)**, 7700 Folsom Boulevard, Zip 95826–2608, Mailing Address: 7919 Folsom Boulevard, Zip 95826–2608; tel. 916/386–3000, **A**1 3 5 10 **F**3 29 30 34 35 44 68 86 87 98 99 100 101 102 104 105 130 132 134 143 149 151 153 154 164 165 **S** Sutter Health, Sacramento, CA
Primary Contact: Dan Peterson, Chief Executive Officer
CFO: Pamela Ansley, Director Finance
CMO: Cindy Thygeson, M.D., Director Medical Affairs
CHR: Kristin Daniels, Manager Human Resources
Web address: https://www.sutterhealth.org/find-location/facility/sutter-center-for-psychiatry
Control: Other not-for-profit (including NFP Corporation) **Service**: Psychiatric

Staffed Beds: 73 **Admissions**: 2675 **Census**: 55 **Outpatient Visits**: 14132 **Births**: 0 **Total Expense ($000)**: 50561 **Payroll Expense ($000)**: 22787 **Personnel**: 239

✚ **SUTTER MEDICAL CENTER, SACRAMENTO (050108)**, 2825 Capitol Avenue, Zip 95816–6039; tel. 916/454–3333, (Includes SUTTER CHILDREN'S CENTER, 5151 F Street, Sacramento, California, Zip 95819–3223, tel. 800/478–8837; SUTTER GENERAL HOSPITAL, 2801 L ST, Sacramento, California, Zip 95816–5615, 2801 'L' Street, Zip 95816, tel. 916/454–2222) **A**1 2 3 5 10 19 **F**3 8 11 12 13 15 17 18 19 20 21 22 23 24 25 26 27 28 29 30 31 32 34 35 36 37 39 40 41 46 48 49 55 56 58 59 61 63 64 68 70 72 73 74 75 76 77 78 79 80 81 82 84 85 86 87 88 89 93 100 101 102 104 107 108 111 114 115 118 119 120 121 123 124 126 129 130 131 132 136 137 146 147 148 149 150 154 156 164 165 167 169 **S** Sutter Health, Sacramento, CA
Primary Contact: Hollie Seeley, President and Chief Executive Officer
CFO: Richard SooHoo, Chief Financial Officer
CMO: Muhammed Afzal, M.D., Chief of Staff
CIO: Jim Mills, Regional Director Information Technology
CHR: Colleen Peschel, Director Human Resources
CNO: Marchelle M McGriff, Chief Nursing Executive
Web address: www.sutterhealth.org
Control: Other not-for-profit (including NFP Corporation) **Service**: General medical and surgical

Staffed Beds: 523 **Admissions**: 30076 **Census**: 407 **Outpatient Visits**: 252731 **Births**: 5666 **Total Expense ($000)**: 1543202 **Payroll Expense ($000)**: 474798 **Personnel**: 4268

✚ **UC DAVIS MEDICAL CENTER (050599)**, 2315 Stockton Boulevard, Zip 95817–2282; tel. 916/734–2011, (Includes UNIVERSITY OF CALIFORNIA DAVIS CHILDREN'S HOSPITAL, 2315 Stockton Boulevard, Sacramento, California, Zip 95817–2201, tel. 800/282–3284) **A**1 2 3 5 8 10 19 **F**3 5 6 8 9 11 12 13 15 16 17 18 19 20 21 22 23 24 25 26 27 28 29 30 31 32 34 35 36 37 38 39 40 41 43 44 45 46 47 48 49 50 51 52 53 55 56 57 58 59 60 61 62 63 64 65 66 68 70 71 72 73 74 75 76 77 78 79 81 82 83 84 85 86 87 88 89 90 91 92 93 94 95 96 97 99 100 101 102 103 104 107 108 110 111 114 115 116 117 118 119 120 121 123 124 126 129 130 131 132 133 134 135 136 138 141 145 146 147 148 149 150 153 154 156 160 162 163 164 165 167 169 **P**6 **S** University of California Systemwide Administration, Oakland, CA
Primary Contact: Michael Condrin, Chief Administrator/System Chief Operating Officer
CFO: Timothy Maurice, Chief Financial Officer
CMO: J. Douglas Kirk, M.D., Chief Medical Officer
CIO: John Cook, Interim Chief Information Officer
CHR: Stephen Chilcott, Associate Director Human Resources
CNO: Toby Marsh, MSN, R.N., Interim Chief Patient Care Services Officer
Web address: www.ucdmc.ucdavis.edu
Control: Other not-for-profit (including NFP Corporation) **Service**: General medical and surgical

Staffed Beds: 632 **Admissions**: 33123 **Census**: 620 **Outpatient Visits**: 1034377 **Births**: 1913 **Total Expense ($000)**: 3557670 **Payroll Expense ($000)**: 1491541 **Personnel**: 13945

Hospital, Medicare Provider Number, Address, Telephone, Approval, Facility, and Physician Codes, Health Care System

★ American Hospital Association (AHA) membership ○ Healthcare Facilities Accreditation Program ⇧ Center for Improvement in Healthcare Quality Accreditation
☐ The Joint Commission accreditation ◇ DNV Healthcare Inc. accreditation △ Commission on Accreditation of Rehabilitation Facilities (CARF) accreditation

Hospitals, U.S. / CALIFORNIA

UC DAVIS REHABILITATION HOSPITAL (053046), 4875 Broadway, Zip 95820-1500; tel. 279/224-6000, (Nonreporting) **A**10 22 **S** Lifepoint Health, Brentwood, TN
Primary Contact: Dennis Sindelar, Chief Executive Officer
Web address: www.ucdavisrehabhospital.com
Control: Corporation, Investor-owned (for-profit) **Service**: Rehabilitation

Staffed Beds: 52

UNIVERSITY OF CALIFORNIA, DAVIS MEDICAL CENTER See UC Davis Medical Center

SAINT HELENA—Napa County

ADVENTIST HEALTH ST. HELENA (050013), 10 Woodland Road, Zip 94574-9554; tel. 707/963-3611, (Nonreporting) **A**1 2 10 **S** Adventist Health, Roseville, CA
Primary Contact: Steven C. Herber, M.D., FACS, President
COO: Hal Chilton, Senior Vice President and Chief Operating Officer
CIO: David Noll, Director
CHR: Audrey Barrall, Director Human Resources
CNO: Nia Lendaris, MS, R.N., Regional Vice President Patient Care
Web address: www.sthelenahospital.org
Control: Church operated, Nongovernment, not-for-profit **Service**: General medical and surgical

Staffed Beds: 82

SALINAS—Monterey County

△ **NATIVIDAD (050248)**, 1441 Constitution Boulevard, Zip 93906-3100, Mailing Address: P.O. Box 81611, Zip 93912-1611; tel. 831/647-7611, **A**1 3 5 7 10 **F**3 11 12 13 15 18 19 29 30 34 35 38 40 43 45 46 49 50 57 59 60 61 64 65 66 68 70 73 74 75 76 77 79 81 83 84 85 89 90 92 93 98 100 102 107 108 111 115 118 119 130 131 132 135 146 147 149 150 154 156 157 167 169
Primary Contact: Charles Harris, Chief Executive Officer
CMO: Craig Walls, M.D., Ph.D., Chief Medical Officer
CIO: Ari Entin, Chief Information Officer
CHR: Lawanda Janine Bouyea, Director Human Resources
Web address: www.natividad.com
Control: County, Government, Nonfederal **Service**: General medical and surgical

Staffed Beds: 172 **Admissions:** 9407 **Census:** 130 **Outpatient Visits:** 81116 **Births:** 2381 **Total Expense ($000):** 420075 **Payroll Expense ($000):** 160300 **Personnel:** 1207

NATIVIDAD MEDICAL CENTER See Natividad

SALINAS VALLEY HEALTH (050334), 450 East Romie Lane, Zip 93901-4098; tel. 831/757-4333, **A**1 2 10 19 **F**3 8 12 13 15 16 17 18 20 22 24 26 28 29 30 31 34 35 37 39 40 44 45 46 49 50 51 54 55 57 58 59 63 64 65 68 70 72 73 74 75 76 77 78 79 80 81 84 85 86 87 88 89 93 96 102 107 108 110 111 114 115 116 117 118 119 124 126 127 129 130 132 135 146 148 149 154 156 160 167 169
Primary Contact: Allen Radner, M.D., President and Chief Executive Officer
COO: Henry Ornelas, Chief Operating Officer
CFO: Augustine Lopez, Chief Financial Officer
CIO: Audrey Parks, Chief Information Officer
CHR: Michelle Childs, Chief Human Resources Officer
CNO: Christie McGuire, R.N., Chief Nursing Officer
Web address: www.svmh.com
Control: Hospital district or authority, Government, Nonfederal **Service**: General medical and surgical

Staffed Beds: 214 **Admissions:** 11808 **Census:** 130 **Outpatient Visits:** 136436 **Births:** 1462 **Total Expense ($000):** 578374 **Payroll Expense ($000):** 200797 **Personnel:** 1769

SALINAS VALLEY MEMORIAL HEALTHCARE SYSTEM See Salinas Valley Health

SAN ANDREAS—Calaveras County

MARK TWAIN MEDICAL CENTER (051332), 768 Mountain Ranch Road, Zip 95249-9998; tel. 209/754-3521, (Nonreporting) **A**1 10 18 **S** CommonSpirit Health, Chicago, IL
Primary Contact: Doug Archer, President and Chief Executive Officer
CFO: Jacob Lewis, Chief Financial Officer
CHR: Nancy Vargas, Director Human Resources
Web address: www.marktwainhospital.com
Control: Other not-for-profit (including NFP Corporation) **Service**: General medical and surgical

Staffed Beds: 25

SAN BERNARDINO—San Bernardino County

△ **BALLARD REHABILITATION HOSPITAL (053037)**, 1760 West 16th Street, Zip 92411-1160; tel. 909/473-1200, (Nonreporting) **A**1 7 10 **S** Vibra Healthcare, Mechanicsburg, PA
Primary Contact: Natalie Merckens, Chief Executive Officer
CMO: Van Chen, M.D., Medical Director
CNO: Chris Bauman, Director of Nursing
Web address: www.ballardrehab.com
Control: Corporation, Investor-owned (for-profit) **Service**: Rehabilitation

Staffed Beds: 60

COMMUNITY HOSPITAL OF SAN BERNARDINO (050089), 1805 Medical Center Drive, Zip 92411-1214; tel. 909/887-6333, **A**1 10 **F**3 8 13 15 17 18 20 22 26 29 30 31 34 35 38 40 45 46 47 48 49 50 53 57 58 59 60 69 70 72 74 75 76 77 78 79 81 84 85 86 89 97 98 100 102 104 107 108 110 111 115 119 128 129 130 146 148 154 156 157 167 **S** CommonSpirit Health, Chicago, IL
Primary Contact: June M. Collison, President
COO: Victoria Selby MHA, BSN, Vice President, Ancillary and Support Services
CFO: Dave Evans, Chief Financial Officer
CMO: Andrew Fragen, M.D., Chief Medical Officer
CIO: James Borrenpohl, Market Site Director
CHR: Deena Marano, Human Resources Director
CNO: Roz Nolan, Chief Nursing Executive Officer
Web address: www.dignityhealth.org/san-bernardino
Control: State, Government, Nonfederal **Service**: General medical and surgical

Staffed Beds: 486 **Admissions:** 10239 **Census:** 247 **Outpatient Visits:** 78602 **Births:** 1591 **Total Expense ($000):** 304169 **Payroll Expense ($000):** 128412 **Personnel:** 727

ST. BERNARDINE MEDICAL CENTER (050129), 2101 North Waterman Avenue, Zip 92404-4855; tel. 909/883-8711, (Nonreporting) **A**1 3 5 10 19 **S** CommonSpirit Health, Chicago, IL
Primary Contact: Douglas V. Kleam, President
CFO: Paul Steinke, Chief Financial Officer
CMO: Betty Daniels, M.D., Chief of Staff
CIO: James Croker, Director Information Systems
CHR: Dee Webb, Vice President Human Resources
CNO: Erin Keefe, Ed.D., R.N., Chief Nursing Executive Officer
Web address: www.stbernardinemedicalcenter.com
Control: Other not-for-profit (including NFP Corporation) **Service**: General medical and surgical

Staffed Beds: 342

SAN DIEGO—San Diego County

AURORA BEHAVIORAL HEALTHCARE SAN DIEGO (054095), 11878 Avenue of Industry, Zip 92128-3490; tel. 858/487-3200, (Nonreporting) **A**1 10 **S** Signature Healthcare Services, Corona, CA
Primary Contact: Alain Azcona, Chief Executive Officer
COO: Barbara Kennison, Director Clinical Services
CFO: Gene Fantano, Chief Financial Officer
CMO: Thomas Flanagan, M.D., Medical Director
CIO: Alain Azcona, Director Business Development
CHR: Susan Haas, Director Human Resources
Web address: www.sandiego.aurorabehavioral.com/
Control: Corporation, Investor-owned (for-profit) **Service**: Psychiatric

Staffed Beds: 80

△ **JENNIFER MORENO DEPARTMENT OF VETERANS AFFAIRS MEDICAL CENTER**, 3350 LaJolla Village Drive, Zip 92161-0002; tel. 858/552-8585, **A**1 3 5 7 **F**2 4 5 8 9 10 11 12 15 18 20 22 24 26 29 30 31 34 35 38 39 40 44 45 46 47 48 49 50 52 53 54 56 57 58 59 60 61 62 63 64 65 66 67 68 70 71 74 75 77 78 79 81 82 83 84 85 86 87 91 92 93 94 95 96 97 98 100 101 102 103 104 106 107 108 110 111 114 115 116 117 118 119 126 128 129 130 131 132 133 135 143 146 147 148 149 153 154 156 157 160 162 164 165 167 168 169 **S** Department of Veterans Affairs, Washington, DC
Primary Contact: Frank P. Pearson, Director
COO: Cynthia Abair, Associate Director
CFO: Ronald Larson, Chief Financial Officer
CIO: Ruey Keller, Acting Chief Information Officer
CHR: Stephanie Wright, Director Human Resources Management
Web address: www.sandiego.va.gov
Control: Veterans Affairs, Government, federal **Service**: General medical and surgical

Staffed Beds: 257 **Admissions:** 6323 **Census:** 188 **Outpatient Visits:** 1060932 **Births:** 0 **Total Expense ($000):** 987998 **Payroll Expense ($000):** 455207 **Personnel:** 3894

Hospitals, U.S. / CALIFORNIA

KAISER PERMANENTE ZION MEDICAL CENTER (050515), 4647 Zion Avenue, Zip 92120–2507; tel. 619/528–5100, (Includes KAISER PERMANENTE SAN DIEGO MEDICAL CENTER, 9455 Clairemont Mesa Boulevard, San Diego, California, Zip 92123–1297, tel. 858/266–5000; Elizabeth Jane Finley, Senior Vice President and Area Manager) **A**1 3 10 19 **F**3 4 6 8 9 10 11 13 15 18 19 26 28 29 30 31 32 34 35 37 38 40 41 45 46 47 48 49 50 51 54 56 57 60 61 64 65 68 70 72 74 75 76 77 78 79 81 82 84 85 86 87 89 94 97 100 102 104 107 108 110 111 114 115 116 117 118 119 126 130 131 143 146 148 149 154 156 157 162 164 165 166 167 169 **P**6 **S** Kaiser Foundation Hospitals, Oakland, CA
Primary Contact: Elizabeth Jane. Finley, Senior Vice President and Area Manager
COO: Kerry Forde, Chief Operating Officer
CFO: Lynette Seid, Area Chief Financial Officer
CIO: Laura Sullivant, Area Chief Information Officer
CHR: Jocelyn A. Herrera, Human Resources Director
Web address: www.kaiserpermanente.org
Control: Other not–for–profit (including NFP Corporation) **Service**: General medical and surgical

Staffed Beds: 412 Admissions: 24522 Census: 293 Outpatient Visits: 272393 Births: 4573 Personnel: 3736

KINDRED HOSPITAL–SAN DIEGO (052036), 1940 El Cajon Boulevard, Zip 92104–1096; tel. 619/543–4500, (Nonreporting) **A**1 10 **S** ScionHealth, Louisville, KY
Primary Contact: Robin Gomez, R.N., MSN, Chief Executive Officer
CMO: Davies Wong, M.D., Medical Director
CHR: Jody Dewen Moore, District Director Human Resources
CNO: Maureen Bodine, Chief Clinical Officer
Web address: www.kindredsandiego.com
Control: Corporation, Investor–owned (for–profit) **Service**: Acute long–term care hospital

Staffed Beds: 58

NAVAL MEDICAL CENTER SAN DIEGO, 34800 Bob Wilson Drive, Zip 92134–5000; tel. 619/532–6400, (Nonreporting) **A**1 2 3 5 **S** Bureau of Medicine and Surgery, Department of the Navy, Falls Church, VA
Primary Contact: Elizabeth M. Adriano, MC, USN, Director
CFO: Commander Thomas J. Piner, Director for Resources Management
CIO: Lieutenant Commander Ryan Jarmer, Chief Information Officer
Web address: https://sandiego.tricare.mil/
Control: Navy, Government, federal **Service**: General medical and surgical

Staffed Beds: 285

RADY CHILDREN'S HOSPITAL – SAN DIEGO (053303), 3020 Childrens Way, Zip 92123–4223, Mailing Address: 3020 Children's Way, Zip 92123–4282; tel. 858/576–1700, (Total facility includes 33 beds in nursing home–type unit) **A**1 3 5 10 **F**1 3 7 8 11 17 18 19 20 21 22 23 24 25 26 27 28 29 30 31 34 35 36 38 39 40 41 43 45 46 47 48 49 50 51 52 53 54 55 57 58 59 60 61 62 63 64 65 67 68 72 74 75 77 78 79 80 81 82 83 84 85 86 87 88 89 90 91 92 93 94 98 99 100 101 102 104 107 108 111 112 114 115 118 119 121 128 129 130 131 132 133 134 136 137 138 139 143 144 145 146 147 148 149 150 153 154 155 156 164 165 166 167
Primary Contact: Patricio A. Frias, M.D., President and Chief Executive Officer
COO: Meg Norton, Executive Vice President and Chief Administrative Officer
CFO: Roger Roux, Chief Financial Officer
CMO: Irvin A Kaufman, M.D., Chief Medical Officer
CIO: Albert Oriol, Vice President Information Management and Chief Information Officer
CHR: Mamoon Syed, Vice President Human Resources
CNO: Mary Fagan, MSN, R.N., Chief Nursing Officer
Web address: www.rchsd.org
Control: Other not–for–profit (including NFP Corporation) **Service**: Children's general medical and surgical

Staffed Beds: 342 Admissions: 19932 Census: 313 Outpatient Visits: 580867 Births: 0 Total Expense ($000): 1672648 Payroll Expense ($000): 529655 Personnel: 4827

SAN DIEGO COUNTY PSYCHIATRIC HOSPITAL (054114), 3853 Rosecrans Street, Zip 92110–3115, Mailing Address: P.O. Box 85524, Zip 92186–5524; tel. 619/692–8211, (Nonreporting) **A**1 10
Primary Contact: Angela Warneke, Deputy Director and Hospital Administrator
CFO: Raul J Loyo–Rodriguez, Administrative Analyst III
CMO: Michael Krelstein, M.D., Medical Director
CIO: Linda Cannon, Chief Medical Records Services
CHR: Francisco Puentes, Human Resource Officer
Web address: www.sdcounty.ca.gov
Control: County, Government, Nonfederal **Service**: Psychiatric

Staffed Beds: 357

SAN DIEGO HCS See Jennifer Moreno Department of Veterans Affairs Medical Center

SCRIPPS MERCY HOSPITAL (050077), 4077 Fifth Avenue, Zip 92103–2105; tel. 619/294–8111, (Includes SCRIPPS MERCY HOSPITAL CHULA VISTA, 435 H ST, Chula Vista, California, Zip 91910–4307, P O Box 1537, Zip 91910–1537, tel. 619/691–7000; Thomas A Gammiere, Chief Executive Officer) **A**1 3 5 10 19 **F**3 8 11 12 13 14 15 17 18 20 22 24 26 28 29 30 31 32 34 35 39 40 43 44 45 46 49 50 51 54 56 58 59 61 64 65 66 68 70 74 75 76 77 78 79 81 82 84 85 86 87 92 93 97 98 100 101 102 107 108 110 111 114 115 119 126 130 132 134 135 141 146 147 148 149 154 156 157 167 169 **S** Scripps Health, San Diego, CA
Primary Contact: Chris D. Van Gorder, FACHE, President and Chief Executive Officer
COO: Debra McQuillen, Vice President, Chief Operations Executive
CFO: Edward Turk, Vice President Finance
CMO: Davis Cracroft, M.D., Senior Director Medical Affairs
Web address: www.scrippshealth.org
Control: Other not–for–profit (including NFP Corporation) **Service**: General medical and surgical

Staffed Beds: 559 Admissions: 29732 Census: 437 Outpatient Visits: 202083 Births: 3857 Total Expense ($000): 1059530 Payroll Expense ($000): 434359 Personnel: 3725

SELECT SPECIALTY HOSPITAL – SAN DIEGO (052044), 555 Washington Street, Zip 92103–2294; tel. 619/260–8300, (Nonreporting) **A**1 10 **S** Select Medical Corporation, Mechanicsburg, PA
Primary Contact: Tuan Le, Chief Executive Officer
CFO: Mike Gonzales, Chief Financial Officer
CMO: John Fox, M.D., Medical Director
CHR: Tania Khalique, Director Human Resources
Web address: https://www.selectspecialtyhospitals.com/locations-and-tours/ca/san-diego/san-diego/?utm_source=gmb&utm_medium=organic
Control: Corporation, Investor–owned (for–profit) **Service**: Acute long–term care hospital

Staffed Beds: 80

SHARP MARY BIRCH HOSPITAL FOR WOMEN AND NEWBORNS (050722), 3003 Health Center Drive, Zip 92123–2700; tel. 858/939–3400, **A**1 10 **F**3 11 13 29 30 31 34 36 44 50 58 59 64 65 68 72 73 75 76 77 80 81 85 86 87 119 126 130 132 146 147 148 149 164 **S** Sharp HealthCare, San Diego, CA
Primary Contact: Trisha Khaleghi, MSN, R.N., Senior Vice President and Market Chief Executive Officer, Sharp HealthCare Metropolitan Hospitals
CMO: Colleen McNally, M.D., Chief Medical Officer
CHR: Connie Duquette, Director Human Resources
CNO: Maria Carmen Colombo, R.N., Chief Nursing Officer
Web address: www.sharp.com
Control: Other not–for–profit (including NFP Corporation) **Service**: General medical and surgical

Staffed Beds: 206 Admissions: 8668 Census: 115 Outpatient Visits: 17010 Births: 6751 Total Expense ($000): 229680 Payroll Expense ($000): 99857 Personnel: 788

△ **SHARP MEMORIAL HOSPITAL (050100)**, 7901 Frost Street, Zip 92123–2701; tel. 858/939–3400, **A**1 2 7 10 **F**3 11 12 15 17 18 20 22 24 26 28 29 30 31 34 35 36 39 40 43 44 45 46 49 50 51 54 55 56 57 58 59 60 64 65 68 70 74 75 77 78 79 80 81 82 84 85 86 87 90 93 94 96 107 108 109 110 111 114 115 116 117 118 119 120 121 124 126 130 131 132 137 138 142 143 145 146 148 149 154 164 167 **S** Sharp HealthCare, San Diego, CA
Primary Contact: Trisha Khaleghi, MSN, R.N., Senior Vice President and Market Chief Executive Officer, Sharp HealthCare Metropolitan Hospitals
COO: Janie Kramer, Chief Operating Officer
CMO: Geoffrey Stiles, M.D., Chief Medical Officer
CIO: Kenneth Lawonn, Senior Vice President and Chief Information Officer
CHR: Connie Duquette, Director Human Resources
CNO: Pamela Wells, R.N., MSN, Chief Nursing Officer
Web address: www.sharp.com
Control: Other not–for–profit (including NFP Corporation) **Service**: General medical and surgical

Staffed Beds: 459 Admissions: 22979 Census: 317 Outpatient Visits: 244858 Births: 0 Total Expense ($000): 996141 Payroll Expense ($000): 390112 Personnel: 2782

Hospital, Medicare Provider Number, Address, Telephone, Approval, Facility, and Physician Codes, Health Care System

★ American Hospital Association (AHA) membership ○ Healthcare Facilities Accreditation Program ⇧ Center for Improvement in Healthcare Quality Accreditation
☐ The Joint Commission accreditation ◇ DNV Healthcare Inc. accreditation △ Commission on Accreditation of Rehabilitation Facilities (CARF) accreditation

© 2025 AHA Guide

Hospitals, U.S. / CALIFORNIA

☒ **SHARP MESA VISTA HOSPITAL (054145)**, 7850 Vista Hill Avenue, Zip 92123–2717; tel. 858/278–4110; (Includes SHARP MCDONALD CENTER, 7989 Linda Vista Road, San Diego, California, Zip 92111–5106, tel. 858/637–6920; Trisha Khaleghi, MSN, R.N., Senior Vice President and Market Chief Executive Officer, Sharp HealthCare Metropolitan Hospitals) **A**1 3 5 10 **F**3 4 5 11 29 30 34 35 36 44 50 56 58 65 68 75 87 98 99 100 101 103 104 105 130 132 143 146 149 150 152 153 160 164 **P**5 **S** Sharp HealthCare, San Diego, CA
Primary Contact: Trisha Khaleghi, MSN, R.N., Senior Vice President and Market Chief Executive Officer, Sharp HealthCare Metropolitan Hospitals
COO: Christopher Walker, Chief Operating Officer
CFO: Tony Guerra, Chief Financial Officer
CMO: Fadi Nicolas, M.D., Chief Medical Officer
CIO: Kenneth Lawonn, Senior Vice President Information Systems
CHR: Katie Beardsley, Chief Human Resources Officer
CNO: Maria Carmen Colombo, R.N., Chief Nursing Officer
Web address: www.sharp.com
Control: Other not–for–profit (including NFP Corporation) **Service**: Psychiatric

> **Staffed Beds**: 164 **Admissions**: 4176 **Census**: 102 **Outpatient Visits**: 68555 **Births**: 0 **Total Expense ($000)**: 102134 **Payroll Expense ($000)**: 57067 **Personnel**: 480

☐ **UC SAN DIEGO HEALTH – EAST CAMPUS (050757)**, 6655 Alvarado Road, Zip 92120–5208; tel. 619/287–3270, (Nonreporting) **A**1 10 **S** University of California Systemwide Administration, Oakland, CA
Primary Contact: Kenneth D. McFarland, Chief Executive Officer
CMO: Larry Emdur, D.O., Chief Medical Officer
CIO: Wayne Bartlett, Director Information Systems
CHR: Sara Turner, Director Human Resources
CNO: Peggy Jezsu, Chief Nursing Officer
Web address: www.alvaradohospital.com
Control: Corporation, Investor–owned (for–profit) **Service**: General medical and surgical

> **Staffed Beds**: 137

☒ **UC SAN DIEGO MEDICAL CENTER – HILLCREST (050025)**, 200 West Arbor Drive, Zip 92103–9000; tel. 619/543–6222, (Includes THORNTON HOSPITAL, 9300 Campus Point Drive, La Jolla, California, Zip 92037–1300, tel. 858/657–7000; UC SAN DIEGO SHILEY EYE INSTITUTE, 9415 Campus Point Drive, Room 2411 Dept Of, Department of Ophthalmology, Mail Code 0946, La Jolla, California, Zip 92093–0946, 9415 Campus Point Drive, Zip 92093–0946, tel. 858/534–6290; Karen Anisko Ryan, Director Business Development and Communications) **A**1 2 3 5 8 10 19 **F**3 5 6 9 11 12 13 15 16 17 18 20 22 24 26 28 29 30 31 32 34 35 36 37 38 40 43 44 45 46 47 48 49 50 51 52 54 55 56 57 58 59 60 61 64 65 66 68 70 71 72 73 74 75 76 77 78 79 80 81 82 83 84 85 86 87 92 93 94 97 98 100 101 102 103 104 105 107 108 109 110 111 112 114 115 116 117 118 119 120 121 123 124 126 129 130 131 132 135 136 137 138 139 140 141 142 144 145 146 147 148 149 153 154 156 157 158 160 162 164 165 167 168 169 **P**8 **S** University of California Systemwide Administration, Oakland, CA
Primary Contact: Patty Maysent, M.P.H., Chief Executive Officer
COO: Margarita Baggett, MSN, R.N., Interim Chief Operating Officer
CFO: Lori Donaldson, Chief Financial Officer
CIO: Ed Babakanian, Chief Information Officer
CHR: William J Murin, Chief Human Resources Officer
CNO: Margarita Baggett, MSN, R.N., Chief Nursing Officer
Web address: https://health.ucsd.edu
Control: State, Government, Nonfederal **Service**: General medical and surgical

> **Staffed Beds**: 747 **Admissions**: 36156 **Census**: 671 **Outpatient Visits**: 1375804 **Births**: 4911 **Total Expense ($000)**: 3288584 **Payroll Expense ($000)**: 1057441 **Personnel**: 9705

SAN DIMAS—Los Angeles County

☐ **SAN DIMAS COMMUNITY HOSPITAL (050588)**, 1350 West Covina Boulevard, Zip 91773–3219; tel. 909/599–6811, **A**1 3 10 **F**3 13 15 29 30 40 45 46 49 50 56 70 74 76 79 81 85 107 108 110 114 119 126 130 146 148 149 160 **S** Prime Healthcare, Ontario, CA
Primary Contact: Parrish Scarboro, Chief Executive Officer
CFO: Edward Matthews, Chief Financial Officer
CMO: Rajnish Jandial, M.D., Chief Medical Officer
CIO: Jeffrey Cox, Director Information Technology
CHR: Kristina Mack, Manager, Human Resources
CNO: Holly Nagatoshi, R.N., Chief Nursing Officer
Web address: www.sandimashospital.com/
Control: Corporation, Investor–owned (for–profit) **Service**: General medical and surgical

> **Staffed Beds**: 101 **Admissions**: 3127 **Census**: 38 **Outpatient Visits**: 17169 **Births**: 167 **Total Expense ($000)**: 65048 **Payroll Expense ($000)**: 27932 **Personnel**: 273

SAN FRANCISCO—San Francisco County

CALIFORNIA PACIFIC MEDICAL CENTER See California Pacific Medical Center–Van Ness Campus

☒ **CALIFORNIA PACIFIC MEDICAL CENTER–DAVIES CAMPUS (050008)**, 45 Castro Street, Zip 94114–1010; tel. 415/600–6000, **A**1 3 5 10 **F**3 4 6 18 29 30 34 37 40 55 59 60 63 64 65 68 70 74 75 77 78 79 81 84 85 86 87 90 91 93 98 100 101 102 104 107 111 119 128 130 131 143 146 148 149 154 164 165 **S** Sutter Health, Sacramento, CA
Primary Contact: Hamila Kownacki, R.N., Chief Executive Officer
Web address: www.cpmc.org
Control: Other not–for–profit (including NFP Corporation) **Service**: General medical and surgical

> **Staffed Beds**: 209 **Admissions**: 5014 **Census**: 111 **Outpatient Visits**: 142057 **Total Expense ($000)**: 213787 **Payroll Expense ($000)**: 93219 **Personnel**: 592

☒ **CALIFORNIA PACIFIC MEDICAL CENTER–MISSION BERNAL CAMPUS (050055)**, 3555 Cesar Chavez Street, Zip 94110–4403; tel. 415/600–6000, **A**1 3 10 **F**3 13 15 18 28 29 30 34 35 39 40 44 45 55 56 57 59 60 63 64 65 68 70 74 75 79 81 85 86 87 93 100 107 111 114 118 119 126 130 131 143 146 148 149 154 164 **S** Sutter Health, Sacramento, CA
Primary Contact: Hamila Kownacki, R.N., Chief Executive Officer
CFO: Henry Yu, Vice President Finance and Chief Financial Officer
CMO: Vernon Giang, M.D., Chief Medical Executive
CIO: Ann Barr, Chief Information Officer – Bay Area
CHR: Edward Battista, Vice President Human Resources
CNO: Diana M. Karner, R.N., MSN, Chief Nursing Executive
Web address: www.stlukes-sf.org
Control: Other not–for–profit (including NFP Corporation) **Service**: General medical and surgical

> **Staffed Beds**: 98 **Admissions**: 4972 **Census**: 66 **Outpatient Visits**: 60176 **Births**: 0 **Total Expense ($000)**: 232547 **Payroll Expense ($000)**: 60568 **Personnel**: 511

CALIFORNIA PACIFIC MEDICAL CENTER–ST. LUKE'S CAMPUS See California Pacific Medical Center–Mission Bernal Campus

☒ △ **CALIFORNIA PACIFIC MEDICAL CENTER–VAN NESS CAMPUS (050047)**, 1101 Van Ness Avenue, Zip 94109–6919, Mailing Address: P.O. Box 7999, Zip 94120–7999; tel. 415/600–6000, (Includes CHILDREN'S HOSPITAL OF SAN FRANCISCO, 3700 California Street, San Francisco, California, Zip 94118, Box 3805, Zip 94119–3805, tel. 415/387–8700) **A**1 2 3 5 7 8 10 **F**3 12 13 15 17 18 20 22 24 26 29 30 33 34 35 39 40 41 45 46 47 48 49 50 54 55 59 60 63 64 65 68 70 72 73 74 75 76 78 79 81 84 85 86 87 88 89 93 100 107 108 110 111 116 117 118 119 120 121 122 123 124 126 130 131 137 138 139 141 142 143 144 146 147 148 149 154 164 167 169 **S** Sutter Health, Sacramento, CA
Primary Contact: Hamila Kownacki, R.N., Chief Executive Officer
CFO: Henry Yu, Vice President Finance and Chief Financial Officer
CMO: Vernon Giang, M.D., Chief Medical Executive
CIO: Ann Barr, Chief Information Officer – Bay Area
CHR: Edward Battista, Vice President Human Resources
CNO: Diana M. Karner, R.N., MSN, Chief Nursing Officer
Web address: www.cpmc.org
Control: Other not–for–profit (including NFP Corporation) **Service**: General medical and surgical

> **Staffed Beds**: 274 **Admissions**: 15223 **Census**: 228 **Outpatient Visits**: 307947 **Births**: 3381 **Total Expense ($000)**: 1247080 **Payroll Expense ($000)**: 345898 **Personnel**: 2102

CHILDREN'S HOSP OF SF See Children's Hospital of San Francisco

☒ **CHINESE HOSPITAL (050407)**, 845 Jackson Street, Zip 94133–4899; tel. 415/982–2400, (Nonreporting) **A**1 10
Primary Contact: Jian Q. Zhang, MS, Chief Executive Officer
CFO: Paul Ziegele, Chief Financial Officer
CMO: William Chung, M.D., Chief of Staff
CIO: Keith Minard, Chief Information Officer
CHR: Lydia Mahr-Chan, Director of Human Resources
CNO: Antonia Lendaris, Chief Nursing Operations Officer
Web address: www.chinesehospital-sf.org
Control: Other not–for–profit (including NFP Corporation) **Service**: General medical and surgical

> **Staffed Beds**: 65

JEWISH HOME OF SAN FRANCISCO See San Francisco Campus For Jewish Living

Hospitals, U.S. / CALIFORNIA

KAISER PERMANENTE SAN FRANCISCO MEDICAL CENTER (050076), 2425 Geary Boulevard, Zip 94115–3358; tel. 415/833–2000, **A**1 2 3 5 10 19 **F**3 11 13 15 17 18 20 22 24 26 30 31 37 39 40 41 45 46 49 56 60 64 68 70 72 73 74 75 76 78 79 80 81 84 85 87 89 100 107 108 110 111 114 115 118 119 126 130 135 146 148 149 154 167 169 **S** Kaiser Foundation Hospitals, Oakland, CA
Primary Contact: Tarek Salaway, Senior Vice President and Area Manager, Golden Gate Service Area
COO: Helen Archer–Duste, Chief Operating Officer
CFO: Alex Khoo, Interim Area Finance Officer
CIO: Peti Arunamata, Interim Area Director Information Technology
CHR: Diane J Easterwood, Human Resources Business Partner
Web address: www.kaiserpermanente.org
Control: Other not–for–profit (including NFP Corporation) **Service**: General medical and surgical

Staffed Beds: 239 **Admissions**: 12375 **Census**: 172 **Outpatient Visits**: 70179 **Births**: 2317 **Personnel**: 1730

★ **LAGUNA HONDA HOSPITAL AND REHABILITATION CENTER (050668)**, 375 Laguna Honda Boulevard, Zip 94116–1499; tel. 415/759–2300, (Nonreporting) **A**10
Primary Contact: Sandra Simon, Chief Executive Officer and Nursing Home Administrator
COO: Michael R Llewellyn, Chief Operating Officer
CFO: Tess Navarro, Chief Financial Officer
CMO: Colleen Riley, M.D., Medical Director
CIO: Pat Skala, Chief Information Officer
CHR: Willie Ramirez, Manager Labor Relations
Web address: www.lagunahonda.org/
Control: City–county, Government, Nonfederal **Service**: Rehabilitation

Staffed Beds: 780

SAN FRANCISCO CAMPUS FOR JEWISH LIVING (054089), 302 Silver Avenue, Zip 94112–1510; tel. 415/334–2500, (Total facility includes 362 beds in nursing home–type unit) **A**3 5 10 **F**10 29 30 56 65 75 84 98 100 103 128 130 146 148 149 **P**6
Primary Contact: Adrienne Green, M.D., President and Chief Executive Officer
COO: Kevin Ward, Chief Operating Officer
CFO: Mary Connick, Chief Financial Officer
CNO: Edwin Cabigao, Chief Nursing Officer
Web address: https://sfcjl.org/
Control: Other not–for–profit (including NFP Corporation) **Service**: Psychiatric

Staffed Beds: 375 **Admissions**: 1456 **Census**: 350 **Outpatient Visits**: 0 **Births**: 0 **Total Expense ($000)**: 98420 **Payroll Expense ($000)**: 44330 **Personnel**: 702

△ **SAN FRANCISCO VA HEALTH CARE SYSTEM**, 4150 Clement Street, Zip 94121–1545; tel. 415/221–4810, (Nonreporting) **A**1 3 5 7 **S** Department of Veterans Affairs, Washington, DC
Primary Contact: Jia F. Li, FACHE, Health Care System Director
CFO: Brian Kelly, Acting Chief Fiscal Service
CMO: C. Diana Nicoll, M.D., Ph.D., Chief of Staff
CIO: Ryan Chun, Information Resources Management
CHR: Jerry Mills, Chief Human Resources Management Services
CNO: Shirley Pikula, MSN, Associate Director Patient Center Care
Web address: www.sanfrancisco.va.gov/
Control: Veterans Affairs, Government, federal **Service**: General medical and surgical

Staffed Beds: 232

UCSF CHILDREN'S HOSPITAL See UCSF Benioff Children's Hospital

UCSF HEALTH SAINT FRANCIS HOSPITAL (050152), 900 Hyde Street, Zip 94109–4899, Mailing Address: P.O. Box 7726, Zip 94120–7726; tel. 415/353–6000, (Nonreporting) **A**1 3 5 10 **S** University of California Systemwide Administration, Oakland, CA
Primary Contact: Daryn J. Kumar, President
COO: Tiffany Caster, Chief Operating Officer
CFO: Alan Fox, Chief Financial Officer
CHR: Richard Mead, Senior Director Human Resources
Web address: www.saintfrancismemorial.org
Control: Other not–for–profit (including NFP Corporation) **Service**: General medical and surgical

Staffed Beds: 239

UCSF HEALTH ST. MARY'S HOSPITAL (050457), 450 Stanyan Street, Zip 94117–1079; tel. 415/668–1000, (Nonreporting) **A**1 3 5 10 **S** University of California Systemwide Administration, Oakland, CA
Primary Contact: Daryn J. Kumar, President
COO: Tiffany Caster, Chief Operating Officer
CMO: Francis Charlton, M.D., Jr, Chief Medical Staff
CHR: Barbara Morrissett, Vice President Human Resources
Web address: https://www.dignityhealth.org/bayarea/locations/stmarys
Control: Other not–for–profit (including NFP Corporation) **Service**: General medical and surgical

Staffed Beds: 232

UCSF MEDICAL CENTER (050454), 505 Parnassus Ave, Zip 94143–2204, Mailing Address: 500 Parnassus Avenue, Box 0296, Zip 94143–0296; tel. 415/476–1000, (Includes UCSF BENIOFF CHILDREN'S HOSPITAL, 1975 4th Street, San Francisco, California, Zip 94143–2351, tel. 888/689–8273; Nicholas M. Holmes, M.D., President, UCSF Benioff Children's Hospitals, SVP Children's Services UCSF Health; UCSF MEDICAL CENTER MISSION BAY, 1975 4th Street, San Francisco, California, Zip 94158–2351, tel. 415/353–3000) **A**1 2 3 5 8 10 19 **F**3 5 6 7 8 9 10 11 12 13 14 15 16 17 18 19 20 21 22 23 24 25 26 27 29 30 31 32 33 34 35 36 37 38 39 40 41 44 45 46 47 48 49 50 51 52 53 54 55 56 57 58 59 60 61 63 64 65 66 68 70 72 74 75 76 77 78 79 81 82 83 84 85 86 87 88 89 91 92 93 94 95 96 97 98 99 100 101 102 103 104 105 107 108 109 110 111 112 113 114 115 116 117 118 119 120 121 123 124 126 129 130 131 132 133 134 135 136 137 138 139 140 141 142 143 144 145 146 147 148 149 150 153 154 155 156 160 161 162 163 164 165 167 169 **S** University of California Systemwide Administration, Oakland, CA
Primary Contact: Suresh Gunasekaran, President and Chief Executive Officer
COO: Ken M Jones, Chief Operating Officer
CFO: Raju Iyer, Senior Vice President and Chief Financial Officer
CMO: Josh Adler, M.D., Chief Medical Officer
CIO: Joe Bergfort, Chief Information Officer
CHR: David Odato, Chief Administrative and Chief Human Resources Officer
CNO: Sheila Antrum, R.N., President
Web address: www.ucsfhealth.org
Control: Other not–for–profit (including NFP Corporation) **Service**: General medical and surgical

Staffed Beds: 910 **Admissions**: 36737 **Census**: 764 **Outpatient Visits**: 1866031 **Births**: 2516 **Total Expense ($000)**: 6305920 **Payroll Expense ($000)**: 2172734 **Personnel**: 18069

ZUCKERBERG SAN FRANCISCO GENERAL HOSPITAL AND TRAUMA CENTER (050228), 1001 Potrero Avenue, Zip 94110–3518; tel. 628/206–8000, (Total facility includes 28 beds in nursing home–type unit) **A**1 2 3 5 10 **F**3 5 13 15 18 20 22 29 30 31 32 34 35 36 38 39 40 41 43 44 45 46 47 48 49 50 55 57 58 59 60 61 64 65 66 68 70 71 72 74 75 76 77 78 79 81 82 83 84 85 86 87 89 92 93 94 97 98 100 101 102 104 107 108 110 111 115 119 128 129 130 131 132 135 144 146 147 148 149 150 151 152 154 156 157 160 162 163 167 169
Primary Contact: Susan P. Ehrlich, M.D., Chief Executive Officer
COO: Tosan O. Boyo, Chief Operating Officer
CFO: Valerie Inouye, Chief Financial Officer
CMO: Todd May, M.D., Chief Medical Officer
CIO: Winona Windolovich, Associate Chief Information Officer
CHR: Karen Hill, Departmental Personnel Officer
CNO: Terry Dentoni, Chief Nursing Officer
Web address: www.zuckerbergsanfranciscogeneral.org/
Control: City–county, Government, Nonfederal **Service**: General medical and surgical

Staffed Beds: 308 **Admissions**: 15028 **Census**: 317 **Outpatient Visits**: 756123 **Births**: 1223 **Total Expense ($000)**: 1207666 **Payroll Expense ($000)**: 486167 **Personnel**: 2807

SAN GABRIEL—Los Angeles County

SAN GABRIEL VALLEY MEDICAL CENTER (050132), 438 West Las Tunas Drive, Zip 91776–1216, Mailing Address: P.O. Box 1507, Zip 91778–1507; tel. 626/289–5454, (Nonreporting) **A**1 3 10 **S** AHMC Healthcare, Alhambra, CA
Primary Contact: Anthony Nguyen, Chief Executive Officer
CFO: Andrew Grim, Chief Financial Officer
CIO: Bernie Sauer, Director Information Technology
CHR: Victor Voisard, Director Human Resources
CNO: Gail Freeman, Chief Nursing Officer
Web address: www.sgvmc.org
Control: Partnership, Investor–owned (for–profit) **Service**: General medical and surgical

Staffed Beds: 273

Hospital, Medicare Provider Number, Address, Telephone, Approval, Facility, and Physician Codes, Health Care System

★ American Hospital Association (AHA) membership ○ Healthcare Facilities Accreditation Program ⇑ Center for Improvement in Healthcare Quality Accreditation
☐ The Joint Commission accreditation ◇ DNV Healthcare Inc. accreditation △ Commission on Accreditation of Rehabilitation Facilities (CARF) accreditation

Hospitals, U.S. / CALIFORNIA

SAN JOSE—Santa Clara County

GOOD SAMARITAN HOSPITAL – SAN JOSE (050380), 2425 Samaritan Drive, Zip 95124–3997, Mailing Address: P.O. Box 240002, Zip 95154–2402; tel. 408/559–2011, (Nonreporting) **A**1 2 10 **S** HCA Healthcare, Nashville, TN
Primary Contact: Patrick Rohan, FACHE, Chief Executive Officer
CFO: Lana Arad, Chief Financial Officer
CMO: Bruce Wilbur, M.D., Chief Medical Officer
CIO: Darrell O'Dell, Director Information Services
CHR: Edward Battista, Vice President Human Resources
CNO: Darina Kavanagh, R.N., MSN, Chief Nursing Officer
Web address: www.goodsamsanjose.com
Control: Corporation, Investor–owned (for–profit) **Service**: General medical and surgical

Staffed Beds: 474

KAISER PERMANENTE SAN JOSE MEDICAL CENTER (050604), 250 Hospital Parkway, Zip 95119–1199; tel. 408/972–7000, **A**1 2 3 5 10 **F**3 9 11 13 15 18 20 22 26 30 31 37 39 40 41 45 46 49 56 60 64 68 70 73 74 75 76 78 79 80 81 84 85 87 97 100 107 108 110 111 114 115 118 119 126 130 135 146 148 149 154 167 **S** Kaiser Foundation Hospitals, Oakland, CA
Primary Contact: Eric Henry, Senior Vice President/Area Manager, Greater San Jose Service Area
COO: Shanthi Margoschis, MSN, R.N., Chief Operating Officer
CFO: Stephen L Kalsman, Area Finance Officer
CMO: Efren Rosas, M.D., Physician in Chief
CIO: Greg Tuck, Area Information Officer
CHR: Lina Slack, Human Resources Leader
CNO: Elaine LePage Ware, R.N., Chief Nurse Executive
Web address: https://healthy.kaiserpermanente.org/northern-california/facilities/San-Jose-Medical-Center-100322
Control: Other not–for–profit (including NFP Corporation) **Service**: General medical and surgical

Staffed Beds: 247 **Admissions**: 11924 **Census**: 136 **Outpatient Visits**: 154832 **Births**: 2163 **Personnel**: 1359

O'CONNOR HOSPITAL (050153), 2105 Forest Avenue, Zip 95128–1471; tel. 408/947–2500, **A**1 2 3 5 10 **F**3 12 13 14 17 18 19 20 22 24 26 28 29 30 32 34 40 45 46 47 48 49 50 56 58 59 60 61 62 63 64 68 70 72 74 75 76 77 78 79 80 81 82 83 84 85 97 100 107 108 110 111 114 115 116 117 118 119 126 128 130 131 132 135 144 146 147 148 149 154 157 160 167 169
Primary Contact: Paul E. Lorenz, Chief Executive Officer, Santa Clara Valley Healthcare
CHR: Julie Hatcher, Vice President Human Resources
Web address: https://och.sccgov.org/Pages/home.aspx
Control: County, Government, Nonfederal **Service**: General medical and surgical

Staffed Beds: 277 **Admissions**: 10723 **Census**: 181 **Outpatient Visits**: 93738 **Births**: 1019 **Total Expense ($000)**: 580767 **Payroll Expense ($000)**: 230927 **Personnel**: 1241

REGIONAL MEDICAL CENTER OF SAN JOSE (050125), 225 North Jackson Avenue, Zip 95116–1603; tel. 408/259–5000, (Nonreporting) **A**1 10 **S** HCA Healthcare, Nashville, TN
Primary Contact: Matthew Cova, Chief Executive Officer
COO: Brian J Knecht, Chief Operating Officer
CFO: Fred Ashworth, Chief Financial Officer
CMO: William Scott, M.D., Vice President Medical Affairs
CIO: Shirley Joyal, Director Information Systems
CHR: Nancy Clark, Vice President Human Resources
Web address: www.regionalmedicalsanjose.com
Control: Partnership, Investor–owned (for–profit) **Service**: General medical and surgical

Staffed Beds: 264

SAN JOSE BEHAVORIAL HEALTH (054154), 455 Silicon Valley Boulevard, Zip 95138–1858; tel. 888/210–2484, (Nonreporting) **A**1 3 10 **S** Acadia Healthcare Company, Inc., Franklin, TN
Primary Contact: Steve Vanderpoel, Chief Executive Officer
Web address: www.sanjosebh.com
Control: Corporation, Investor–owned (for–profit) **Service**: Psychiatric

Staffed Beds: 80

SANTA CLARA VALLEY MEDICAL CENTER (050038), 751 South Bascom Avenue, Zip 95128–2699; tel. 408/885–5000, **A**1 2 3 5 7 10 **F**3 4 9 11 15 16 17 18 19 20 22 24 26 28 29 30 31 32 34 35 36 39 40 41 43 44 45 46 49 50 51 54 55 56 58 59 60 61 64 65 66 68 70 71 72 73 74 75 76 77 78 79 80 81 82 84 85 86 87 88 89 90 91 92 93 95 96 97 98 100 101 102 104 107 108 110 111 114 115 117 118 119 120 121 123 124 126 129 130 131 132 134 135 144 146 147 148 149 151 152 154 156 160 163 165 167 169
Primary Contact: Paul E. Lorenz, Chief Executive Officer, Santa Clara Valley Healthcare
COO: Curtis Ohashi, Ph.D., Chief Operating Officer
CMO: Phuong Hoang Nguyen, M.D., Chief Medical Officer
CIO: Khalid Turk, Chief Healthcare Technology Officer
CHR: David Manson, Manager Human Resources
CNO: Andrea Brollini, MSN, R.N., Chief Nursing Officer
Web address: https://www.scvmc.org/Pages/home.aspx
Control: County, Government, Nonfederal **Service**: General medical and surgical

Staffed Beds: 544 **Admissions**: 20026 **Census**: 398 **Outpatient Visits**: 813813 **Births**: 3178 **Total Expense ($000)**: 2539120 **Payroll Expense ($000)**: 1104442 **Personnel**: 5897

SAN LEANDRO—Alameda County

ALAMEDA COUNTY MEDICAL CENTER–FAIRMONT CAMPUS See Fairmont Hospital

FAIRMONT HOSPITAL See Highland Hospital, Oakland

KAISER PERMANENTE SAN LEANDRO MEDICAL CENTER (050777), 2500 Merced Street, Zip 94577–4201; tel. 510/454–1000, **A**1 2 3 10 **F**3 11 13 15 18 26 30 31 37 39 40 41 45 49 56 60 64 68 70 72 74 75 76 78 79 80 81 84 85 87 100 107 108 110 111 114 115 117 118 119 126 130 135 146 148 149 154 167 169 **S** Kaiser Foundation Hospitals, Oakland, CA
Primary Contact: Debra A. Flores, R.N., FACHE, Senior Vice President and Area Manager
Web address: www.kaiserpermanente.org
Control: Other not–for–profit (including NFP Corporation) **Service**: General medical and surgical

Staffed Beds: 216 **Admissions**: 11597 **Census**: 126 **Outpatient Visits**: 159604 **Births**: 3529 **Personnel**: 1445

KINDRED HOSPITAL–SAN FRANCISCO BAY AREA (052034), 2800 Benedict Drive, Zip 94577–6840; tel. 510/357–8300, (Nonreporting) **A**1 10 **S** ScionHealth, Louisville, KY
Primary Contact: Larry Foster, R.N., MSN, Chief Executive Officer
CFO: Ziba Aflak, Chief Financial Officer
CHR: Erin Greene, Coordinator Human Resources
CNO: Emily Gard, Chief Clinical Officer
Web address: www.kindredhospitalsfba.com
Control: Corporation, Investor–owned (for–profit) **Service**: Acute long–term care hospital

Staffed Beds: 99

WILLOW ROCK CENTER (054149), 2050 Fairmont Drive, Zip 94578–1001; tel. 510/895–5502, (Nonreporting) **A**1 10
Primary Contact: Anne L. Bakar, President and Chief Executive Officer
Web address: www.tbhcare.com
Control: County, Government, Nonfederal **Service**: Psychiatric

Staffed Beds: 16

SAN LUIS OBISPO—San Luis Obispo County

CALIFORNIA MENS COLONY CORRECTIONAL TREATMENT CENTER, Highway 1, Zip 93409–8101, Mailing Address: P.O. Box 8101, Zip 93403–8101; tel. 805/547–7913, (Nonreporting)
Primary Contact: Teresa Macias, Administrator
CFO: William Cook, Associate Warden Business Service
CIO: Terry Knight, Public Information Officer and Administrative Assistant
Web address: www.yaca.ca.gov/visitors/fac_prison_cmc.html
Control: State, Government, Nonfederal **Service**: Hospital unit of an institution (prison hospital, college infirmary, etc.)

Staffed Beds: 39

Hospitals, U.S. / CALIFORNIA

☒ **FRENCH HOSPITAL MEDICAL CENTER (050232)**, 1911 Johnson Avenue, Zip 93401–4197; tel. 805/543–5353, (Nonreporting) **A**1 2 3 10 **S** CommonSpirit Health, Chicago, IL
Primary Contact: Sue Anderson, President and Chief Executive Officer
COO: Julia Fogelson, R.N., Chief Operating Officer and Chief Nursing Executive
CFO: Debbie Wettlaufer, Chief Financial Officer
CMO: Andrea Tackett, Chief of Staff
CIO: Cyndi Lang, Director Information Services
CHR: Clara Ramirez, Manager
CNO: Julia Fogelson, R.N., Chief Operating Officer and Chief Nursing Executive
Web address: www.frenchmedicalcenter.org
Control: Other not–for–profit (including NFP Corporation) **Service**: General medical and surgical

Staffed Beds: 72

☒ **SIERRA VISTA REGIONAL MEDICAL CENTER (050506)**, 1010 Murray Avenue, Zip 93405–1806, Mailing Address: P.O. Box 1367, Zip 93405; tel. 805/546–7600, (Nonreporting) **A**1 2 10 19 **S** Adventist Health, Roseville, CA
Primary Contact: Ryan Ashlock, President
COO: Eleze Armstrong, Chief Operating Officer
CFO: Scott Wartelle, Chief Financial Officer
CIO: Robert Leonard, Director Information Services
CHR: Kristin Flynn, Chief Human Resources Officer
CNO: Nicki E Edwards, Ph.D., R.N., Interim Chief Nursing Officer
Web address: www.sierravistaregional.com
Control: Corporation, Investor–owned (for–profit) **Service**: General medical and surgical

Staffed Beds: 163

SAN MARCOS—San Diego County

★ **KAISER FOUNDATION HOSPITAL – SAN MARCOS (050855)**, 360 Rush Drive, Zip 92078–7901; tel. 442/385–7000, (Nonreporting) **S** Kaiser Foundation Hospitals, Oakland, CA
Primary Contact: Elizabeth Jane. Finley, Senior Vice President and Area Manager
COO: Max Villalobos, Chief Operating Officer
CFO: Rick King, Chief Financial Officer
CMO: Michael Lalich, M.D., Area Medical Director
CIO: Laura Sullivant, Area Information Officer
CHR: Victor Voisard, Senior Director Human Resources
CNO: Ernesto Perez–Mir, Chief Nursing Executive
Web address: www.kp.org
Control: Other not–for–profit (including NFP Corporation) **Service**: General medical and surgical

Staffed Beds: 168

SAN MATEO—San Mateo County

MILLS HEALTH CENTER See Mills–Peninsula Medical Center, Burlingame

MILLS HOSPITAL See Mills Health Center

☐ **SAN MATEO MEDICAL CENTER (050113)**, 222 West 39th Avenue, Zip 94403–4398; tel. 650/573–2222, (Total facility includes 28 beds in nursing home–type unit) **A**1 3 5 10 **F**3 15 18 19 26 29 30 31 32 36 39 40 44 45 47 49 51 53 54 55 56 57 58 59 61 64 65 66 68 70 71 74 75 77 78 79 81 82 84 85 87 90 92 93 97 98 100 101 102 107 110 111 115 119 128 130 132 134 144 146 147 148 149 154 156 160 161 167 169
Primary Contact: Chester Kunnappilly, M.D., Chief Executive Officer
COO: John Thomas, Chief Operating Officer
CFO: David S McGrew, Chief Financial Officer
CMO: Susan Fernyak, M.D., Interim Chief Medical Officer & Chief Quality Officer
CIO: Michael Aratow, M.D., Chief Information Officer
CHR: Angela Gonzales, Manager Human Resources
CNO: Joan G Spicer, R.N., Chief Nursing Officer
Web address: www.sanmateomedicalcenter.org
Control: County, Government, Nonfederal **Service**: General medical and surgical

Staffed Beds: 78 **Admissions**: 2483 **Census**: 78 **Outpatient Visits**: 497703 **Births**: 0 **Total Expense ($000)**: 431937 **Payroll Expense ($000)**: 122243 **Personnel**: 1144

SAN PEDRO—Los Angeles County, See Los Angeles

SAN RAFAEL—Marin County

☒ **KAISER PERMANENTE SAN RAFAEL MEDICAL CENTER (050510)**, 99 Montecillo Road, Zip 94903–3397; tel. 415/444–2000, **A**1 2 10 **F**3 11 15 18 20 26 30 31 37 39 40 41 45 49 56 60 64 68 70 74 75 78 79 80 81 84 85 87 100 107 108 110 111 114 115 118 119 130 135 146 148 149 154 167 169 **S** Kaiser Foundation Hospitals, Oakland, CA
Primary Contact: Tarek Salaway, Senior Vice President/Area Manager, Golden Gate Service Area
COO: Kimberly Ann Colonnelli, Chief Operating Officer and Chief Nurse Executive
CFO: Diane Hernandez, Area Finance Officer
CMO: Naveen Kumar, M.D., Physician–in–Chief
CIO: Stanley Dobrawa, Area Information Officer
CNO: Kimberly Ann Colonnelli, Chief Operating Officer and Chief Nurse Executive
Web address: www.kaiserpermanente.org
Control: Other not–for–profit (including NFP Corporation) **Service**: General medical and surgical

Staffed Beds: 116 **Admissions**: 4350 **Census**: 53 **Outpatient Visits**: 85803 **Births**: 3 **Personnel**: 732

SAN RAMON—Contra Costa County

☒ **SAN RAMON REGIONAL MEDICAL CENTER (050689)**, 6001 Norris Canyon Road, Zip 94583–5400; tel. 925/275–9200, (Nonreporting) **A**1 5 10 **S** TENET Healthcare Corporation, Dallas, TX
Primary Contact: Beenu Chadha, Interim Chief Executive Officer and Chief Financial Officer
CFO: Beenu Chadha, Chief Financial Officer
CIO: Anthony Abbate, Director of Information Services
CHR: Dennis Mills, Chief Human Resources Officer
CNO: Wendy Sirivar, Chief Nurse Officer
Web address: www.sanramonmedctr.com
Control: Corporation, Investor–owned (for–profit) **Service**: General medical and surgical

Staffed Beds: 123

SANTA ANA—Orange County

☐ **ORANGE COUNTY GLOBAL MEDICAL CENTER, INC. (050746)**, 1001 North Tustin Avenue, Zip 92705–3577; tel. 714/953–3500, (Nonreporting) **A**1 5 10 **S** KPC Healthcare, Inc., Santa Ana, CA
Primary Contact: Derek Scott. Drake, Chief Executive Officer
CFO: John Collins, Chief Financial Officer
CMO: Steven Bui, M.D., Chief of Staff
CIO: Charles Flack, Interim Chief Information Officer
CHR: Terry Bohn, Director, Human Resources
CNO: Sandra Moreno, Chief Nursing Officer
Web address: https://www.orangecountyglobalmedicalcenter.com/
Control: Corporation, Investor–owned (for–profit) **Service**: General medical and surgical

Staffed Beds: 282

☐ **SOUTH COAST GLOBAL MEDICAL CENTER (050747)**, 2701 South Bristol Street, Zip 92704–6278; tel. 714/754–5454, (Nonreporting) **A**1 10 **S** KPC Healthcare, Inc., Santa Ana, CA
Primary Contact: Kevan Metcalfe, FACHE, Chief Executive Officer
CFO: John Collins, Chief Financial Officer
CHR: Cynthia Garren–Oster, Human Resource Manager
Web address: www.SouthCoast-GMC.com
Control: Corporation, Investor–owned (for–profit) **Service**: General medical and surgical

Staffed Beds: 178

SPECIALTY HOSP OF SANTA ANA See Kindred Hospital Santa Ana

SANTA BARBARA—Santa Barbara County

COTTAGE REHABILITATION HOSPITAL See Santa Barbara Cottage Hospital, Santa Barbara

Hospitals, U.S. / CALIFORNIA

✠ **GOLETA VALLEY COTTAGE HOSPITAL (050357)**, 351 South Patterson Avenue, Zip 93111–2496, Mailing Address: PO Box 689, Zip 93102–0689; tel. 805/967–3411, **A**1 10 **F**3 8 11 12 15 40 65 68 70 75 79 81 107 110 114 119 124 130 133 146 147 148 149 160 **S** Cottage Health, Santa Barbara, CA
Primary Contact: Ronald C. Werft, President and Chief Executive Officer
COO: Steven A Fellows, Executive Vice President and Chief Operating Officer
CMO: Edmund Wroblewski, M.D., Vice President Medical Affairs and Chief Medical Officer
CIO: Alberto Kywi, Chief Information Officer
CHR: Patrice Ryan, Vice President Human Resources
Web address: www.sbch.org
Control: Other not–for–profit (including NFP Corporation) **Service**: General medical and surgical

Staffed Beds: 24 **Admissions**: 1031 **Census**: 7 **Outpatient Visits**: 63737 **Births**: 0 **Total Expense ($000)**: 100013 **Payroll Expense ($000)**: 38587 **Personnel**: 303

REHAB INST AT SANTA BARBARA See Cottage Rehabilitation Hospital

✠ △ **SANTA BARBARA COTTAGE HOSPITAL (050396)**, 400 West Pueblo Street, Zip 93105–4390, Mailing Address: P.O. Box 689, Zip 93102–0689; tel. 805/682–7111, (Includes COTTAGE CHILDREN'S HOSPITAL, 400 West Pueblo Street, Santa Barbara, California, Zip 93105–4353, tel. 877/247–3260; COTTAGE REHABILITATION HOSPITAL, 2415 De la Vina Street, Santa Barbara, California, Zip 93105–3819, tel. 805/687–7444; Melinda Staveley, President and Chief Executive Officer) **A**1 2 3 5 7 10 **F**3 4 5 8 11 12 13 15 17 18 19 20 22 24 26 28 29 30 31 34 35 40 43 45 46 50 53 54 57 58 59 60 63 64 65 68 70 72 74 75 76 77 78 79 81 84 86 88 89 90 91 92 93 96 98 100 102 104 106 107 110 111 114 115 117 119 126 130 132 135 146 148 149 151 152 153 154 155 156 160 164 167 169 **P**4 **S** Cottage Health, Santa Barbara, CA
Primary Contact: Ronald C. Werft, President and Chief Executive Officer
COO: Steven A Fellows, Executive Vice President and Chief Operating Officer
CMO: Edmund Wroblewski, M.D., Vice President Medical Affairs and Chief Medical Officer
CIO: Alberto Kywi, Chief Information Officer
CHR: Patrice Ryan, Vice President Human Resources
CNO: Herb J Geary, Vice President Patient Care Services and Chief Nursing Officer
Web address: www.cottagehealthsystem.org
Control: Other not–for–profit (including NFP Corporation) **Service**: General medical and surgical

Staffed Beds: 416 **Admissions**: 17979 **Census**: 260 **Outpatient Visits**: 139246 **Births**: 1884 **Total Expense ($000)**: 878926 **Payroll Expense ($000)**: 343000 **Personnel**: 2294

SANTA BARBARA COUNTY PSYCHIATRIC HEALTH FACILITY (054125), 315 Camino Del Remedio, Zip 93110–1332; tel. 805/681–5244, (Nonreporting) **A**10
Primary Contact: Ole Behrendtsen, M.D., Interim Director
CFO: Michael C. Evans, Chief Executive Officer and Deputy Director of Finance and Administration
CMO: Ole Behrendtsen, M.D., Medical Director
CIO: Dana Fahey, Manager Management Information Systems
CHR: Elena Molelus, Manager Human Resources
Web address: www.countyofsb.org
Control: County, Government, Nonfederal **Service**: Psychiatric

Staffed Beds: 16

SANTA CLARA—Santa Clara County

✠ **KAISER PERMANENTE SANTA CLARA MEDICAL CENTER (054150)**, 700 Lawrence Expressway, Zip 95051–5173; tel. 408/851–1000, **A**1 2 3 5 10 **F**3 8 11 13 15 17 18 19 20 22 24 26 27 30 31 37 39 40 41 45 49 56 60 64 68 70 72 73 74 75 76 78 79 80 81 84 85 87 88 89 100 107 108 110 111 114 115 117 118 119 120 121 123 126 130 135 146 148 149 154 167 168 169 **S** Kaiser Foundation Hospitals, Oakland, CA
Primary Contact: Eric Williams, Senior Vice President and Area Manager Santa Clara
CFO: Tim O'Connor, Area Finance Officer
CMO: Susan Smarr, M.D., Physician–in–Chief
CIO: Scott May, Area Director Technology
CHR: Robert Hyde, Human Resources Business Partner
Web address: www.kaiserpermanente.org
Control: Other not–for–profit (including NFP Corporation) **Service**: General medical and surgical

Staffed Beds: 343 **Admissions**: 17774 **Census**: 264 **Outpatient Visits**: 212934 **Births**: 4211 **Personnel**: 2099

SANTA CRUZ—Santa Cruz County

✠ △ **DOMINICAN HOSPITAL (050242)**, 1555 Soquel Drive, Zip 95065–1794; tel. 831/462–7700, **A**1 2 3 7 8 10 **F**3 12 13 17 18 20 22 24 28 29 30 31 34 35 40 45 46 49 50 51 55 57 58 59 60 62 64 65 68 70 71 72 74 75 76 78 79 81 84 85 86 87 89 90 92 95 96 100 107 108 111 114 115 119 120 126 130 132 135 146 147 148 149 154 156 164 167 **S** CommonSpirit Health, Chicago, IL
Primary Contact: Nanette Mickiewicz, M.D., President
COO: Chris Wernke, Chief Operating Officer
CFO: Rick Harron, Chief Financial Officer
CMO: Freddie Weinstein, M.D., Chief Medical Officer
CIO: Lee Vanderpool, Vice President
CHR: Vicki Miranda, Vice President Human Resources
Web address: www.dominicanhospital.org
Control: Church operated, Nongovernment, not–for–profit **Service**: General medical and surgical

Staffed Beds: 191 **Admissions**: 10147 **Census**: 147 **Births**: 840 **Total Expense ($000)**: 484735 **Payroll Expense ($000)**: 190450 **Personnel**: 915

☐ **SANTA CRUZ COUNTY PSYCHIATRIC HEALTH FACILITY (054152)**, 2250 Soquel Avenue, Zip 95062–1402; tel. 831/600–2801, (Nonreporting) **A**1 10
Primary Contact: Leslie Conner, M.P.H., Chief Executive Officer
Web address: https://www.telecarecorp.com/santa-cruz-psychiatric-health-facility
Control: Corporation, Investor–owned (for–profit) **Service**: Psychiatric

Staffed Beds: 16

✠ **SUTTER MATERNITY AND SURGERY CENTER OF SANTA CRUZ (050714)**, 2900 Chanticleer Avenue, Zip 95065–1816; tel. 831/477–2200, **A**1 10 **F**3 8 13 29 34 35 36 45 46 50 57 59 64 65 68 75 76 77 79 81 85 86 87 93 119 124 126 130 131 132 135 141 146 147 149 154 164 169 **S** Sutter Health, Sacramento, CA
Primary Contact: Stephanie Connor Kent, Chief Executive Officer and Interim Chief Nursing Officer
COO: Stephen Gray, Chief Administration Officer
CFO: Bonnie Liang, Divisional Finance Officer
CMO: Joseph Fabry, D.O., Chief of Staff
CIO: Ann Barr, Chief Information Officer, Sutter Health Bay Area
CHR: Maynard Jenkins, Regional Vice President Human Resources
CNO: Stephanie Connor Kent, Chief Executive Officer and Interim Chief Nursing Officer
Web address: www.suttersantacruz.org
Control: Other not–for–profit (including NFP Corporation) **Service**: Other specialty treatment

Staffed Beds: 28 **Admissions**: 847 **Census**: 6 **Outpatient Visits**: 12596 **Births**: 628 **Total Expense ($000)**: 85552 **Payroll Expense ($000)**: 28661 **Personnel**: 206

SANTA MARIA—Santa Barbara County

✠ △ **MARIAN REGIONAL MEDICAL CENTER (050107)**, 1400 East Church Street, Zip 93454–5906; tel. 805/739–3000, (Includes ARROYO GRANDE COMMUNITY HOSPITAL, 345 South Halcyon Road, Arroyo Grande, California, Zip 93420–3896, tel. 805/489–4261; Sue Andersen, Chief Executive Officer) (Nonreporting) **A**1 2 3 5 7 10 **S** CommonSpirit Health, Chicago, IL
Primary Contact: Sue Andersen, Chief Executive Officer
COO: Mark Allen, Chief Operating Officer
CFO: Sue Andersen, Vice President and Service Area and Chief Financial Officer
CMO: Chuck Merrill, M.D., Vice President Medical Affairs
CIO: Patricia Haase, Director Information Technology and Communications
CHR: Ed Gonzales, Vice President Human Resources
CNO: Candice Monge, R.N., Chief Nurse Executive Officer
Web address: www.marianmedicalcenter.org
Control: Church operated, Nongovernment, not–for–profit **Service**: General medical and surgical

Staffed Beds: 339

Hospitals, U.S. / CALIFORNIA

SANTA MONICA—Los Angeles County

☩ **PROVIDENCE SAINT JOHN'S HEALTH CENTER (050290)**, 2121 Santa Monica Boulevard, Zip 90404–2091; tel. 310/829–5511, **A**1 2 3 10 19 **F**3 5 8 11 12 13 15 17 18 20 22 24 26 29 30 31 32 34 35 36 37 38 39 40 41 44 45 46 47 48 49 50 51 53 54 55 56 57 58 59 60 63 64 65 70 72 73 74 75 76 77 78 79 80 81 82 84 85 86 87 92 93 96 100 102 107 108 110 111 114 115 118 119 120 121 123 124 126 130 131 132 135 141 146 147 148 149 154 156 157 162 164 165 167 169 **P**3 5 **S** Providence, Renton, WA
Primary Contact: Michael Ricks, Chief Executive, Los Angeles Coastal Service Area
CMO: Donald Larsen, M.D., Chief Medical Officer
CIO: Martha Ponce, Director Information Technologies and Telecommunications
CHR: Laura Morton Rowe, Director of Human Resources
CNO: Dawna Hendel, R.N., Chief Nursing Officer and Vice President Patient Care Services
Web address: www.providence.org/saintjohns
Control: Other not–for–profit (including NFP Corporation) **Service**: General medical and surgical

Staffed Beds: 211 **Admissions:** 11376 **Census:** 129 **Outpatient Visits:** 346942 **Births:** 1926 **Total Expense ($000):** 409232 **Payroll Expense ($000):** 179857 **Personnel:** 1627

☩ **UCLA MEDICAL CENTER–SANTA MONICA (050112)**, 1250 16th Street, Zip 90404–1249; tel. 310/319–4000, **A**1 3 5 10 19 **F**3 8 9 11 12 13 15 18 20 22 24 26 29 30 31 34 35 36 37 39 40 41 44 45 46 47 48 49 50 51 52 54 55 56 57 58 59 62 64 65 68 70 72 74 75 76 78 79 81 82 83 84 85 86 87 88 89 93 94 96 97 102 107 108 110 111 115 116 117 118 119 120 121 123 124 126 130 131 143 145 146 147 149 154 156 167 169 **P**6 **S** University of California Systemwide Administration, Oakland, CA
Primary Contact: Johnese Spisso, President, UCLA Health and Chief Executive Officer, UCLA Hospital System
CFO: Paul Staton, Chief Financial Officer
CMO: James Atkinson, M.D., Medical Director
CIO: Virginia McFerran, Chief Information Officer
CHR: Mark Speare, Senior Associate Director Patient Relations and Human Resources
Web address: www.healthcare.ucla.edu
Control: State, Government, Nonfederal **Service**: General medical and surgical

Staffed Beds: 281 **Admissions:** 14367 **Census:** 236 **Outpatient Visits:** 214084 **Births:** 1366 **Total Expense ($000):** 812225 **Payroll Expense ($000):** 292424 **Personnel:** 1942

SANTA ROSA—Sonoma County

AURORA SANTA ROSA HOSPITAL See Santa Rosa Behavioral Healthcare Hospital

☩ **KAISER PERMANENTE SANTA ROSA MEDICAL CENTER (050690)**, 401 Bicentennial Way, Zip 95403–2192; tel. 707/571–4000, **A**1 2 3 5 10 **F**3 8 11 13 15 16 17 18 26 30 31 35 37 39 40 41 45 49 56 60 64 68 70 72 73 74 75 76 78 79 80 81 84 85 87 88 89 100 102 107 108 110 111 114 115 118 119 126 130 135 146 148 149 154 167 169 **S** Kaiser Foundation Hospitals, Oakland, CA
Primary Contact: Abhishek Dosi, Senior Vice President and Area Manager, Santa Rose Service Area
COO: Vicky Locey, R.N., MSN, Chief Operating Officer and Chief Nursing Executive
CFO: Diane Hernandez, Area Finance Officer
CMO: Michael Shulman, Pysician–in–Chief
CIO: Stanley Dobrawa, Area Information Officer
CHR: Anna Krajna–Matherly, Human Resources Leader
CNO: Vicky Locey, R.N., MSN, Chief Operating Officer and Chief Nursing Executive
Web address: www.kaiserpermanente.org
Control: Other not–for–profit (including NFP Corporation) **Service**: General medical and surgical

Staffed Beds: 172 **Admissions:** 10191 **Census:** 113 **Outpatient Visits:** 130810 **Births:** 2008 **Personnel:** 1129

☩ **PROVIDENCE SANTA ROSA MEMORIAL HOSPITAL (050174)**, 1165 Montgomery Drive, Zip 95405; tel. 707/522–4304, **A**1 2 3 10 19 **F**3 5 8 11 15 17 18 20 22 24 26 29 30 31 32 34 35 41 43 44 45 46 47 48 49 50 54 58 59 62 63 64 65 66 68 70 71 72 73 74 75 76 77 78 79 81 82 83 84 85 86 87 89 90 93 94 96 100 102 104 105 107 108 110 111 114 115 116 117 118 119 120 123 124 126 129 130 132 144 146 148 149 150 152 153 154 160 161 164 165 167 **S** Providence, Renton, WA
Primary Contact: Donovan Taylor, Chief Administrative Officer
CFO: John Peters, Interim Chief Financial Officer
CMO: Chad Krilich, M.D., Chief Medical Officer
CIO: Greg Summers, Regional Director, Field Technical Services
CHR: Jamie Welsh, Interim Chief Human Resources Officer
CNO: Vicki White, Chief Nursing Officer
Web address: https://www.providence.org/locations/norcal/santa-rosa-memorial-hospital
Control: Other not–for–profit (including NFP Corporation) **Service**: General medical and surgical

Staffed Beds: 283 **Admissions:** 11391 **Census:** 171 **Outpatient Visits:** 377422 **Births:** 779 **Total Expense ($000):** 568794 **Payroll Expense ($000):** 253531 **Personnel:** 1689

☐ **SANTA ROSA BEHAVIORAL HEALTHCARE HOSPITAL (054151)**, 1287 Fulton Road, Zip 95401–4923; tel. 707/800–7700, (Nonreporting) **A**1 10 **S** Signature Healthcare Services, Corona, CA
Primary Contact: Tristan Ivy, Chief Executive Officer
Web address: www.aurorasantarosa.com
Control: Corporation, Investor–owned (for–profit) **Service**: Rehabilitation

Staffed Beds: 95

SANTA ROSA MEMORIAL HOSPITAL See Providence Santa Rosa Memorial Hospital

☩ **SUTTER SANTA ROSA REGIONAL HOSPITAL (050291)**, 30 Mark West Springs Road, Zip 95403; tel. 707/576–4000, (Includes WARRACK CAMPUS, 2449 Summerfield Road, Santa Rosa, California, Zip 95405–7815, tel. 707/576–4200) **A**1 2 3 5 10 **F**3 11 12 13 15 18 20 22 29 30 31 34 35 36 37 40 45 46 47 48 49 50 51 55 56 59 60 64 65 68 70 72 74 75 76 77 78 79 81 84 85 86 87 93 107 108 111 114 119 126 130 131 146 148 149 154 164 167 169 **S** Sutter Health, Sacramento, CA
Primary Contact: Megan Gillespie, R.N., FACHE, Chief Executive Officer
CMO: William Carroll, M.D., Chief Medical Executive
CNO: Peggy Clark, Chief Nurse Executive
Web address: www.sutterhealth.org
Control: Other not–for–profit (including NFP Corporation) **Service**: General medical and surgical

Staffed Beds: 124 **Admissions:** 8334 **Census:** 96 **Outpatient Visits:** 78398 **Births:** 1472 **Total Expense ($000):** 446362 **Payroll Expense ($000):** 117291 **Personnel:** 856

WARRACK HOSPITAL CAMPUS See Warrack Campus

SEBASTOPOL—Sonoma County

⇑ **SONOMA SPECIALTY HOSPITAL (052057)**, 501 Petaluma Avenue, Zip 95472–4215; tel. 707/823–8511, (Nonreporting) **A**10 21
Primary Contact: Ricardo Bautista, Chief Executive Officer
CFO: Robert Heinemeier, Interim Chief Financial Officer
Web address: https://sonomaspecialtyhospital.org/
Control: Hospital district or authority, Government, Nonfederal **Service**: Acute long–term care hospital

Staffed Beds: 37

⇑ **SONOMA WEST MEDICAL CENTER** See Sonoma Specialty Hospital

SELMA—Fresno County

SELMA COMMUNITY HOSPITAL See Adventist Medical Center–Selma

Hospitals, U.S. / CALIFORNIA

SEPULVEDA—Los Angeles County, See Los Angeles

SHERMAN OAKS—Los Angeles County, See Los Angeles

SIMI VALLEY—Ventura County

ADVENTIST HEALTH SIMI VALLEY (050236), 2975 North Sycamore Drive, Zip 93065–1277; tel. 805/955–6000, (Nonreporting) **A**1 10 **S** Adventist Health, Roseville, CA
Primary Contact: Alice H. Issai, President
COO: Caroline Esparza, R.N., Sr. VP, COO & CNO
CFO: Brian Anderson, Chief Financial Officer
CMO: John Dingilian, M.D., Chief Medical Officer
CIO: Bridget Nakamura, Director Information Systems
CHR: Susan Crabtree, Director Human Resources
CNO: Caroline Esparza, R.N., Senior Vice President, Chief Operating Officer and Chief Nurse Officer
Web address: www.simivalleyhospital.com
Control: Church operated, Nongovernment, not-for-profit **Service**: General medical and surgical

Staffed Beds: 144

SOLVANG—Santa Barbara County

SANTA YNEZ VALLEY COTTAGE HOSPITAL (051331), 2050 Viborg Road, Zip 93463–2295, Mailing Address: PO Box 689, Santa Barbara, Zip 93102–0689; tel. 805/688–6431, **A**1 10 18 **F**3 11 15 18 28 34 40 45 57 68 75 85 97 107 111 114 119 143 146 149 **P**6 **S** Cottage Health, Santa Barbara, CA
Primary Contact: Ronald C. Werft, President and Chief Executive Officer
COO: Steven A Fellows, Executive Vice President and Chief Operating Officer
CFO: Brett Tande, Chief Financial Officer
CMO: Edmund Wroblewski, M.D., Vice President Medical Affairs and Chief Medical Officer
CHR: Patrice Ryan, Vice President Human Resources
CNO: Herb J Geary, Chief Nursing Officer
Web address: www.cottagehealthsystem.org
Control: Other not-for-profit (including NFP Corporation) **Service**: General medical and surgical

Staffed Beds: 11 **Admissions**: 203 **Census**: 1 **Outpatient Visits**: 31085 **Births**: 0 **Total Expense ($000)**: 26422 **Payroll Expense ($000)**: 12672 **Personnel**: 97

SONOMA—Sonoma County

SONOMA VALLEY HOSPITAL (050090), 347 Andrieux Street, Zip 95476–6811, Mailing Address: P.O. Box 600, Zip 95476–0600; tel. 707/935–5000, (Nonreporting) **A**10 22
Primary Contact: John Hennelly, President and Chief Executive Officer
CFO: Jeanette Tarver, Director of Finance
CIO: Fe Sendaydiego, Director Information Systems
CHR: Paula M Davis, Chief Human Resources Officer
CNO: Jessica L. Winkler, Chief Nursing Officer
Web address: https://www.sonomavalleyhospital.org/
Control: Hospital district or authority, Government, Nonfederal **Service**: General medical and surgical

Staffed Beds: 51

SONORA—Tuolumne County

ADVENTIST HEALTH SONORA (050335), 1000 Greenley Road, Zip 95370–4819; tel. 209/536–5000, (Nonreporting) **A**1 3 10 **S** Adventist Health, Roseville, CA
Primary Contact: Greg McCulloch, CPA, President
CMO: Ed Clinite, D.O., Chief of Staff
CIO: Manty Drews, Chief Information Officer
CNO: Julie Kline, R.N., Senior Vice President Patient Services
Web address: www.sonoramedicalcenter.org/
Control: Church operated, Nongovernment, not-for-profit **Service**: General medical and surgical

Staffed Beds: 152

SOUTH EL MONTE—Los Angeles County

GREATER EL MONTE COMMUNITY HOSPITAL (050738), 1701 Santa Anita Avenue, Zip 91733–3411; tel. 626/579–7777, (Total facility includes 11 beds in nursing home–type unit) **A**1 10 **F**3 17 19 29 40 41 45 47 49 50 70 76 81 85 87 89 97 107 108 114 119 128 130 148 149 154 167 169 **S** AHMC Healthcare, Alhambra, CA
Primary Contact: Stanley Toy Jr, M.D., Chief Executive Officer
COO: Jose Ortega, Chief Operating Officer
CFO: Michael Chung, Chief Financial Officer
CMO: Dilip Patel, M.D., Chief of Staff
CIO: Jay Geldhof, Director Information Systems
CHR: Jason Jaquez, Director Human Resources
CNO: Evelyn Calubaquib, Chief Nursing Officer
Web address: www.greaterelmonte.com
Control: Corporation, Investor-owned (for-profit) **Service**: General medical and surgical

Staffed Beds: 115 **Admissions**: 2067 **Census**: 30 **Outpatient Visits**: 25308 **Births**: 0

SOUTH LAKE TAHOE—El Dorado County

BARTON MEMORIAL HOSPITAL (050352), 2170 South Avenue, Zip 96150–7026, Mailing Address: P.O. Box 9578, Zip 96158–9578; tel. 530/541–3420, (Total facility includes 48 beds in nursing home–type unit) **A**1 3 5 10 20 **F**3 4 8 11 13 15 18 29 30 32 34 35 38 40 43 45 46 47 48 49 50 53 54 57 59 62 63 64 65 66 68 70 75 76 77 79 81 82 84 85 86 87 89 90 92 93 94 97 100 104 107 108 110 111 112 114 115 118 119 121 122 123 124 126 127 128 129 130 131 132 135 144 146 147 148 149 154 160 167 169
Primary Contact: Clint Purvance, M.D., President and Chief Executive Officer
CFO: Kelly Neiger, Chief Financial Officer
CMO: Matthew Wonnacott, M.D., Chief Medical Officer
CIO: Jason Roberts, Director of Information Services
CHR: Elizabeth Stork, Chief Human Resources Officer
CNO: Julie B Clayton, Chief Nursing Officer
Web address: www.bartonhealth.org
Control: Other not-for-profit (including NFP Corporation) **Service**: General medical and surgical

Staffed Beds: 111 **Admissions**: 1650 **Census**: 59 **Outpatient Visits**: 265003 **Births**: 284 **Total Expense ($000)**: 171975 **Payroll Expense ($000)**: 72089 **Personnel**: 928

SOUTH SAN FRANCISCO—San Mateo County

KAISER PERMANENTE SOUTH SAN FRANCISCO MEDICAL CENTER (050070), 1200 El Camino Real, Zip 94080–3208; tel. 650/742–2000, **A**1 2 3 5 10 **F**3 11 12 15 18 26 30 31 37 39 40 41 45 49 56 60 64 68 70 74 75 78 79 80 81 84 85 87 100 107 108 110 111 114 115 118 119 120 121 123 124 130 135 146 148 149 154 167 169 **S** Kaiser Foundation Hospitals, Oakland, CA
Primary Contact: Shasta Addessi, Interim Senior Vice President and Area Manager
CMO: Michelle Caughey, M.D., Physician In Chief
CIO: Angel Shew, Director Area Technology
CHR: Sharon Barncord, Human Resource Business Partner
Web address: www.kaiserpermanente.org
Control: Other not-for-profit (including NFP Corporation) **Service**: General medical and surgical

Staffed Beds: 120 **Admissions**: 5909 **Census**: 73 **Outpatient Visits**: 99310 **Births**: 1 **Personnel**: 801

STOCKTON—San Joaquin County

DAMERON HOSPITAL (050122), 525 West Acacia Street, Zip 95203–2484; tel. 209/944–5550, (Nonreporting) **A**1 5 10 **S** Adventist Health, Roseville, CA
Primary Contact: Douglas Long, President
COO: Michael Glasberg, Senior Vice President, Chief Operating Officer
CFO: Elizabeth R Propp, Vice President Finance and Chief Financial Officer
CMO: Bradley Reinke, M.D., Vice President Medical Affairs and Chief Medical Officer
CIO: David Kerrins, Vice President Information Services and Chief Information Officer
CNO: Denise J. Hair, Vice President of Nursing Services and Chief Nursing Officer
Web address: www.dameronhospital.org
Control: Other not-for-profit (including NFP Corporation) **Service**: General medical and surgical

Staffed Beds: 170

Hospitals, U.S. / CALIFORNIA

☒ **ST. JOSEPH'S BEHAVIORAL HEALTH CENTER (054123)**, 2510 North California Street, Zip 95204–5568; tel. 209/461–2000, (Nonreporting) **A**1 3 10 **S** CommonSpirit Health, Chicago, IL
Primary Contact: Paul Rains, R.N., MSN, President
CFO: Doreen Hartmann, Chief Financial Officer
CMO: David Robinson, D.O., Medical Director
CHR: Nancy Vargas, Chief Human Resources
CNO: Benny Lee Lucas Jr, Chief Nursing Executive
Web address: www.stjosephscanhelp.org
Control: Church operated, Nongovernment, not–for–profit **Service**: Psychiatric

Staffed Beds: 35

☒ **ST. JOSEPH'S MEDICAL CENTER (050084)**, 1800 North California Street, Zip 95204–6019, Mailing Address: P.O. Box 213008, Zip 95213–9008; tel. 209/943–2000, (Nonreporting) **A**1 2 3 5 10 19 **S** CommonSpirit Health, Chicago, IL
Primary Contact: Donald J. Wiley, President and Chief Executive Officer
COO: Michaell Rose, Chief Operating Officer
CFO: Nikki Ochoa, Interim Chief Financial Officer
CIO: Randall Gamino, Director Perot Site
CHR: Nancy Vargas, Vice President Human Resources
Web address: www.stjosephsCARES.org
Control: Church operated, Nongovernment, not–for–profit **Service**: General medical and surgical

Staffed Beds: 279

STOCKTON REGIONAL REHABILITATION HOSPITAL (053047), 607 East Magnolia Street, Zip 95202–1846; tel. 209/687–5490, (Nonreporting) **S** Ernest Health, Inc., Albuquerque, NM
Primary Contact: Richard Trogman, FACHE, Chief Executive Officer
Web address: https://stocktonrehab.com/
Control: Corporation, Investor–owned (for–profit) **Service**: Rehabilitation

Staffed Beds: 50

SUN CITY—Riverside County

☐ **MENIFEE GLOBAL MEDICAL CENTER (050684)**, 28400 McCall Boulevard, Zip 92585–9537; tel. 951/679–8888, **A**1 3 10 **F**3 17 18 29 30 40 47 60 68 70 79 85 107 114 119 130 146 149 160 161 **S** Physicians for Healthy Hospitals, Hemet, CA
Primary Contact: Peter R. Baranoff, Corporate Chief Executive Officer, Managing Director
CMO: Sumanta Chaudhuri, M.D., Chief Medical Officer
CHR: Michele Bird, Chief Human Resources Officer
Web address: https://www.menifeeglobalmedicalcenter.com/
Control: Individual, Investor–owned (for–profit) **Service**: General medical and surgical

Staffed Beds: 94 **Admissions**: 2747 **Census**: 38 **Outpatient Visits**: 18554 **Births**: 0

MENIFEE VALLEY MEDICAL CENTER See Menifee Global Medical Center

SUN VALLEY—Los Angeles County, See Los Angeles

SUSANVILLE—Lassen County

☒ **BANNER LASSEN MEDICAL CENTER (051320)**, 1800 Spring Ridge Drive, Zip 96130–6100; tel. 530/252–2000, **A**1 5 10 18 **F**3 13 15 29 34 40 41 45 46 48 50 59 68 76 79 81 85 87 89 93 107 108 110 111 115 118 119 129 130 133 149 157 **S** Banner Health, Phoenix, AZ
Primary Contact: Sandy Dugger, Chief Executive Officer
CFO: Steve Fraker, Chief Financial Officer
CMO: Brent Aikin, D.O., Chief Medical Officer
CIO: Randy Moore, Chief Information Officer
CHR: Ruth Smith, Division Human Resources Business Partner
CNO: Aileen Chandler, Chief Nursing Officer
Web address: https://www.bannerhealth.com/locations/susanville/banner-lassen-medical-center
Control: Other not–for–profit (including NFP Corporation) **Service**: General medical and surgical

Staffed Beds: 25 **Admissions**: 798 **Census**: 8 **Outpatient Visits**: 32728 **Births**: 196 **Total Expense ($000)**: 47883 **Payroll Expense ($000)**: 19731 **Personnel**: 145

SYLMAR—Los Angeles County, See Los Angeles

TARZANA—Los Angeles County, See Los Angeles

TEHACHAPI—Kern County

☒ **ADVENTIST HEALTH TEHACHAPI VALLEY (051301)**, 115 West 'E' Street, Zip 93561–1607, Mailing Address: P.O. Box 1900, Zip 93581–1900; tel. 661/823–3000, (Nonreporting) **A**1 10 18 **S** Adventist Health, Roseville, CA
Primary Contact: Jason Wells, FACHE, President, Central California Network, Adventist Health
CFO: Chester Beedle, Interim Chief Financial Officer
CMO: Susan Cribbs, D.O., Chief of Staff
CIO: Dusty Colvard, Manager Information Technology
CHR: Susan Nelson-Jones, Director Human Resources
CNO: Juliana Kay Kirby, R.N., MSN, Chief Nursing Officer
Web address: www.tvhd.org
Control: Hospital district or authority, Government, Nonfederal **Service**: General medical and surgical

Staffed Beds: 24

TEMECULA—Riverside County

☒ **TEMECULA VALLEY HOSPITAL (050775)**, 31700 Temecula Parkway, Zip 92592–5896; tel. 951/331–2216, **A**1 3 10 **F**3 11 17 18 20 22 24 26 29 30 34 40 45 46 49 50 51 56 57 58 59 70 74 75 77 78 79 81 85 87 107 108 111 114 115 119 126 130 131 132 135 146 154 157 167 **S** Universal Health Services, Inc., King of Prussia, PA
Primary Contact: Darlene Wetton, R.N., Group Vice President and Chief Executive Officer
CNO: Janet L Ruffin, R.N., Chief Nursing Officer
Web address: www.temeculavalleyhospital.com
Control: Corporation, Investor–owned (for–profit) **Service**: General medical and surgical

Staffed Beds: 140 **Admissions**: 9318 **Census**: 121 **Outpatient Visits**: 51379 **Births**: 0 **Total Expense ($000)**: 212689 **Payroll Expense ($000)**: 92614 **Personnel**: 1203

TEMPLETON—San Luis Obispo County

☒ **TWIN CITIES COMMUNITY HOSPITAL (050633)**, 1100 Las Tablas Road, Zip 93465–9796; tel. 805/434–3500, (Nonreporting) **A**1 10 **S** Adventist Health, Roseville, CA
Primary Contact: Eleze Armstrong, President
COO: Mike Lane, Chief Operating Officer
CFO: Scott Wartelle, Chief Financial Officer
CHR: Diane M McCluskey, Chief Human Resources Officer
CNO: Robert Cook, Chief Nursing Officer
Web address: www.twincitieshospital.com
Control: Corporation, Investor–owned (for–profit) **Service**: General medical and surgical

Staffed Beds: 49

THOUSAND OAKS—Ventura County

☒ **LOS ROBLES HEALTH SYSTEM (050549)**, 215 West Janss Road, Zip 91360–1899; tel. 805/370–4421, (Includes THOUSAND OAKS SURGICAL HOSPITAL, 401 Rolling Oaks Drive, Thousand Oaks, California, Zip 91361–1050, tel. 805/497–2727; Natalie Mussi, President and Chief Executive Officer) (Nonreporting) **A**1 2 3 5 10 **S** HCA Healthcare, Nashville, TN
Primary Contact: Phil Buttell, Chief Executive Officer
COO: Austin Manning, Chief Operating Officer
CMO: Hannah Grossman, M.D., Chief Medical Officer
CIO: Alex Bryer, Director Information Management
CHR: Geoff Washburn, Vice President Human Resources
Web address: www.losrobleshospital.com
Control: Corporation, Investor–owned (for–profit) **Service**: General medical and surgical

Staffed Beds: 382

LOS ROBLES HOSPITAL AND MEDICAL CENTER See Los Robles Health System

Hospitals, U.S. / CALIFORNIA

TORRANCE—Los Angeles County

☐ **DEL AMO BEHAVIORAL HEALTH SYSTEM (054053)**, 23700 Camino Del Sol, Zip 90505–5000; tel. 310/530–1151, (Nonreporting) **A**1 10 **S** Universal Health Services, Inc., King of Prussia, PA
Primary Contact: Mariko Yamada, Chief Executive Officer
CFO: Norma Hudson, Chief Financial Officer
Web address: www.delamohospital.com
Control: Corporation, Investor–owned (for–profit) **Service**: Psychiatric

Staffed Beds: 70

DEL AMO HOSPITAL See Del Amo Behavioral Health System

☐ **HARBOR–UCLA MEDICAL CENTER (050376)**, 1000 West Carson Street, Zip 90502–2059; tel. 310/222–2345, (Nonreporting) **A**1 2 3 5 10 **S** Los Angeles County–Department of Health Services, Los Angeles, CA
Primary Contact: Andrea Turner, JD, Chief Executive Officer
CFO: Jody Nakasuji, Chief Financial Officer
CMO: Timothy Van Natta, M.D., Chief Medical Officer
CIO: Sandy Mungovan, Chief Information Officer
CHR: Karyl Smith, Director Human Resources
Web address: www.harbor–ucla.org
Control: County, Government, Nonfederal **Service**: General medical and surgical

Staffed Beds: 373

⊞ **PROVIDENCE LITTLE COMPANY OF MARY MEDICAL CENTER – TORRANCE (050353)**, 4101 Torrance Boulevard, Zip 90503–4664; tel. 310/540–7676, (Total facility includes 77 beds in nursing home–type unit) **A**1 2 10 **F**3 11 12 13 15 17 18 20 22 24 26 28 29 30 31 34 35 37 39 40 41 44 45 46 47 48 49 50 51 54 55 56 57 58 59 60 63 64 65 70 72 74 75 76 77 78 79 81 82 83 84 85 86 87 89 92 93 100 102 107 108 110 111 114 115 116 117 118 119 120 121 123 126 128 130 131 132 145 146 147 148 149 150 154 156 162 164 167 169 **P**3 5 **S** Providence, Renton, WA
Primary Contact: Michael Ricks, Chief Executive, Los Angeles Coastal Service Area
CFO: Elizabeth Zuanich, Chief Financial Officer
CMO: Richard Glimp, M.D., Chief Medical Officer
CIO: Andrea Flores, Director, Information Systems
CHR: Melissa Baker, Director, Human Resources
CNO: Michael Jongsma, R.N., Chief Nursing Officer
Web address: https://www.providence.org/locations/socal/plcm-torrance
Control: Other not–for–profit (including NFP Corporation) **Service**: General medical and surgical

Staffed Beds: 419 **Admissions**: 16951 **Census**: 264 **Outpatient Visits**: 268638 **Births**: 2645 **Total Expense ($000)**: 435342 **Payroll Expense ($000)**: 215054 **Personnel**: 1902

⊞ **TORRANCE MEMORIAL MEDICAL CENTER (050351)**, 3330 Lomita Boulevard, Zip 90505–5073; tel. 310/325–9110, (Total facility includes 40 beds in nursing home–type unit) **A**1 2 10 **F**3 5 8 9 11 12 13 14 15 16 17 18 19 20 22 24 26 28 29 30 31 32 34 35 36 37 39 40 41 44 45 46 47 48 49 50 51 54 55 56 57 58 59 60 61 62 63 64 65 68 70 72 74 75 76 77 78 79 81 82 83 84 85 86 87 89 91 92 93 96 100 107 108 109 110 111 114 115 116 117 118 119 120 121 123 124 126 128 129 130 131 132 134 135 141 144 145 146 147 148 149 154 156 157 164 167 169 **S** Cedars–Sinai Health System, West Hollywood, CA
Primary Contact: Keith Hobbs, FACHE, President and Chief Executive Officer
CFO: Bill Larson, Vice President Finance and Chief Financial Officer
CMO: John McNamara, M.D., Senior Vice President, Chief Medical Officer
CIO: Bernadette Reid, Vice President, Information Technology and Chief Information Officer
CHR: Linda Dobie, R.N., JD, Vice President, Legal Affairs
CNO: Mary Wright, Senior Vice President, Patient Services
Web address: www.torrancememorial.org
Control: Other not–for–profit (including NFP Corporation) **Service**: General medical and surgical

Staffed Beds: 435 **Admissions**: 25969 **Census**: 344 **Outpatient Visits**: 504256 **Births**: 2220 **Total Expense ($000)**: 789946 **Payroll Expense ($000)**: 347706 **Personnel**: 3550

TRACY—San Joaquin County

⊞ **SUTTER TRACY COMMUNITY HOSPITAL (050313)**, 1420 North Tracy Boulevard, Zip 95376–3497; tel. 209/835–1500, **A**1 10 **F**3 11 12 13 15 18 29 30 31 34 35 40 44 46 49 50 54 57 59 60 64 65 68 70 74 75 76 77 78 79 81 82 84 85 86 87 93 107 108 110 111 115 117 119 124 126 130 131 132 143 146 148 149 154 164 167 169 **S** Sutter Health, Sacramento, CA
Primary Contact: Scott Knight, Chief Executive Officer
CIO: Catherine M Larsen, Director Marketing
CHR: Melanie Wallace, Manager Human Resources
Web address: www.suttertracy.org
Control: Other not–for–profit (including NFP Corporation) **Service**: General medical and surgical

Staffed Beds: 77 **Admissions**: 3421 **Census**: 32 **Outpatient Visits**: 84138 **Births**: 376 **Total Expense ($000)**: 155841 **Payroll Expense ($000)**: 53235 **Personnel**: 516

TRAVIS AIR FORCE BASE—Solano County

⊞ **DAVID GRANT USAF MEDICAL CENTER**, 101 Bodin Circle, Building 777, Zip 94535–1809; tel. 707/423–7300, (Nonreporting) **A**1 3 5 **S** Department of the Air Force, Washington, DC
Primary Contact: Colonel Kristin Beals, Commander
CFO: Major Jonathan Richards, Chief Financial Officer
CMO: Colonel Chris Scharenbrock, M.D., Chief Medical Staff
Web address: https://travis.tricare.mil/
Control: Air Force, Government, federal **Service**: General medical and surgical

Staffed Beds: 116

TRUCKEE—Nevada County

★ ○ **TAHOE FOREST HOSPITAL DISTRICT (051328)**, 10121 Pine Avenue, Zip 96161–4856, Mailing Address: P.O. Box 759, Zip 96160–0759; tel. 530/587–6011, (Total facility includes 37 beds in nursing home–type unit) **A**2 3 5 10 11 18 **F**40 43 70 76 81 89 128 **S** Tahoe Forest Health System, Truckee, CA
Primary Contact: Louis James. Ward, Acting Chief Executive Officer
CFO: Crystal Betts, Chief Financial Officer
CMO: Shawni Coll, D.O., Chief Medical Officer
CIO: Jake Dorst, Chief Information Officer
CHR: Alex MacLennan, Chief Human Resources Officer
CNO: Karen Baffone, R.N., Chief Nursing Officer
Web address: www.tfhd.com
Control: Hospital district or authority, Government, Nonfederal **Service**: General medical and surgical

Staffed Beds: 66 **Admissions**: 1513 **Census**: 39 **Outpatient Visits**: 444379 **Births**: 425 **Total Expense ($000)**: 295588 **Payroll Expense ($000)**: 122244 **Personnel**: 1119

TULARE—Tulare County

★ ⇧ **ADVENTIST HEALTH – TULARE (050784)**, 869 North Cherry Street, Zip 93274–2287; tel. 559/688–0821, (Nonreporting) **A**3 5 10 21 **S** Adventist Health, Roseville, CA
Primary Contact: Jason Wells, FACHE, President, Central California Network, Adventist Health
COO: Alan Germany, Chief Operating Officer
CFO: Michael Bernstein, Chief Financial Officer
CMO: Pradeep Kamboj, M.D., Chief Medical Staff
CIO: Jim Peelgren, Chief Information Officer
CHR: John Barbadian, Vice President Human Resources
CNO: Patricia Mathewson, Chief Nursing Officer
Web address: https://www.adventisthealth.org/tulare/
Control: Other not–for–profit (including NFP Corporation) **Service**: General medical and surgical

Staffed Beds: 108

TURLOCK—Stanislaus County

⊞ **EMANUEL MEDICAL CENTER (050179)**, 825 Delbon Avenue, Zip 95382–2016; tel. 209/667–4200, (Nonreporting) **A**1 10 **S** TENET Healthcare Corporation, Dallas, TX
Primary Contact: Murali Naidu, M.D., FACS, Chief Executive Officer
CFO: Anil Jain, Interim Chief Financial Officer
CIO: Beth Walker, Director, Information Technology
CHR: Dianna Romo, Director, Human Resources
CNO: Sharon Perry, Chief Nursing Officer
Web address: www.emanuelmedicalcenter.org
Control: Church operated, Nongovernment, not–for–profit **Service**: General medical and surgical

Staffed Beds: 209

Hospitals, U.S. / CALIFORNIA

TUSTIN—Orange County

ENCOMPASS HEALTH REHABILITATION HOSPITAL OF TUSTIN (053034), 15120 Kensington Park Drive, Zip 92782–1801; tel. 714/832–9200, (Nonreporting) **A**1 5 10 **S** Encompass Health Corporation, Birmingham, AL
Primary Contact: Paula Redmond, Chief Executive Officer
CMO: Ann Vasile, M.D., Medical Director
CHR: JoAnn Roiz, Director Human Resources
CNO: LaDonna Butler Esq, Chief Nursing Officer
Web address: www.tustinrehab.com
Control: Corporation, Investor–owned (for–profit) **Service**: Rehabilitation

Staffed Beds: 48

FOOTHILL REGIONAL MEDICAL CENTER (050780), 14662 Newport Avenue, Zip 92780–6064; tel. 714/838–9600, (Nonreporting) **A**1 10 **S** Prospect Medical Holdings, Los Angeles, CA
Primary Contact: Araceli Lonergan, Chief Executive Officer
COO: Kara Bourne, R.N., MSN, Chief Nursing Officer and Chief Operating Officer
CIO: Darla Kennedy, Chief Information Officer
CHR: Aprille Major, Director Human Resources
Web address: www.hfcis.cdph.ca.gov/longtermcare/Facility.aspx?fac=060000013
Control: Corporation, Investor–owned (for–profit) **Service**: General medical and surgical

Staffed Beds: 127

TWENTYNINE PALMS—San Bernardino County

ROBERT E. BUSH NAVAL HOSPITAL, 1145 Sturgis Road, Zip 92278, Mailing Address: Box 788250, MCAGCC, Zip 92278–8250; tel. 760/830–2190, (Nonreporting) **A**1 **S** Bureau of Medicine and Surgery, Department of the Navy, Falls Church, VA
CHR: Virginia Ward, Human Resources Officer
CNO: Captain Sandra Mason, MSN, R.N., Director Nursing Services and Senior Nurse Executive
Web address: https://twentynine-palms.tricare.mil/
Control: Navy, Government, federal **Service**: General medical and surgical

Staffed Beds: 29

UKIAH—Mendocino County

ADVENTIST HEALTH UKIAH VALLEY (050301), 275 Hospital Drive, Zip 95482–4531; tel. 707/462–3111, (Nonreporting) **A**1 3 5 10 **S** Adventist Health, Roseville, CA
Primary Contact: Eric Stevens, President, Northern California Network
CFO: Warren Tetz, Chief Financial Officer
CHR: Rebecca Ryan, Interim Director Human Resources and Employee Health
Web address: www.adventisthealth.org
Control: Church operated, Nongovernment, not–for–profit **Service**: General medical and surgical

Staffed Beds: 50

UPLAND—San Bernardino County

SAN ANTONIO REGIONAL HOSPITAL (050099), 999 San Bernardino Road, Zip 91786–4920; tel. 909/985–2811, (Nonreporting) **A**1 2 3 5 10
Primary Contact: John T. Chapman, President and Chief Executive Officer
COO: John T. Chapman, Chief Operative Officer
CFO: Wah Chung Hsu, Senior Vice President Finance
CMO: Edward DiGiamarino, M.D., President of Medical Staff
CIO: Kamel Pandya, Director Information Services
CHR: La Donna Najieb, Vice President, Human Resources
CNO: Gudrun Moll, R.N., MSN, Chief Nursing Officer
Web address: www.sarh.org
Control: Other not–for–profit (including NFP Corporation) **Service**: General medical and surgical

Staffed Beds: 363

VACAVILLE—Solano County

CALIFORNIA MEDICAL FACILITY, 1600 California Drive, Zip 95687; tel. 707/448–6841, (Nonreporting)
Primary Contact: Lori Green, Chief Executive
CMO: Raymond Andreasen, M.D., Chief Medical Officer–Inpatient
Web address: www.cya.ca.gov/visitors/fac_prison_cmf.html
Control: State, Government, Nonfederal **Service**: Hospital unit of an institution (prison hospital, college infirmary, etc.)

Staffed Beds: 215

KAISER PERMANENTE VACAVILLE MEDICAL CENTER (050767), 1 Quality Drive, Zip 95688–9494; tel. 707/624–4000, **A**1 2 3 5 10 **F**3 11 13 15 18 26 30 31 37 39 40 41 43 45 49 56 60 64 68 70 73 74 75 76 78 79 80 81 84 85 87 100 107 108 110 111 114 115 118 119 130 135 146 148 149 154 167 **P**6 **S** Kaiser Foundation Hospitals, Oakland, CA
Primary Contact: Darryl B. Curry, Senior Vice President, Area Manager, Napa–Solano Area
Web address: www.kp.org
Control: Other not–for–profit (including NFP Corporation) **Service**: General medical and surgical

Staffed Beds: 150 **Admissions**: 6295 **Census**: 79 **Outpatient Visits**: 144110 **Births**: 1455 **Personnel**: 1083

NORTHBAY VACAVALLEY HOSPITAL See Northbay Vacavalley Hospital

NORTHBAY VACAVALLEY HOSPITAL See Northbay Medical Center, Fairfield

VALENCIA—Los Angeles County

★ ⇧ **HENRY MAYO NEWHALL HOSPITAL (050624)**, 23845 McBean Parkway, Zip 91355–2083; tel. 661/200–2000, **A**10 21 **F**3 8 11 13 15 17 18 20 22 24 26 28 29 30 31 34 35 38 40 41 43 45 49 50 55 57 59 60 64 70 72 74 75 76 77 78 79 81 82 84 85 86 87 90 93 98 100 102 107 108 110 115 119 126 130 132 135 146 147 148 154
Primary Contact: Kevin A. Klockenga, President/Chief Executive Officer
COO: John V Schleif, Senior Vice President and Chief Operating Officer
CFO: Ted D. Sirotta, Senior Vice President and Chief Financial Officer
CMO: Kingman Ho, M.D., Senior Vice President, Chief Medical and Care Innovation Officer
CIO: Ray Moss, Vice President and Chief Information Officer
CHR: Mark Puleo, Vice President and Chief Human Resources Officer
CNO: Jennifer Castaldo, R.N., Vice President, Patient Care and Chief Nursing Officer
Web address: www.henrymayo.com
Control: Other not–for–profit (including NFP Corporation) **Service**: General medical and surgical

Staffed Beds: 357 **Admissions**: 11768 **Census**: 163 **Outpatient Visits**: 132834 **Births**: 1494 **Total Expense ($000)**: 403840 **Payroll Expense ($000)**: 151542 **Personnel**: 1857

VALLEJO—Solano County

ADVENTIST HEALTH VALLEJO (054074), 525 Oregon Street, Zip 94590–3201; tel. 707/648–2200, (Nonreporting) **A**1 5 10 **S** Adventist Health, Roseville, CA
Primary Contact: Steven C. Herber, M.D., FACS, President
CFO: Edward A McDonald, Chief Financial Officer
Web address: www.sthelenahospitals.org/location/center-for-behavioral-health
Control: Church operated, Nongovernment, not–for–profit **Service**: Psychiatric

Staffed Beds: 61

ADVENTIST HEALTH VALLEJO – CENTER FOR BEHAVIORAL HEALTH See Adventist Health Vallejo

△ **KAISER PERMANENTE VALLEJO MEDICAL CENTER (050073)**, 975 Sereno Drive, Zip 94589–2441; tel. 707/651–1000, **A**1 2 3 5 7 10 **F**3 11 13 15 18 20 22 26 30 31 37 39 40 41 45 48 49 56 60 64 68 70 73 74 75 76 78 79 80 81 84 85 87 90 93 100 107 108 110 111 114 115 118 119 126 130 135 146 148 149 154 167 **P**6 **S** Kaiser Foundation Hospitals, Oakland, CA
Primary Contact: Darryl B. Curry, Senior Vice President, Area Manager, Napa–Solano Area
COO: Karen Grisnak, R.N., Chief Operating Officer and Assistant Administrator Quality Services
CMO: Steven Stricker, M.D., Physician in Chief
CIO: Gale Austin–Moore, Director Area Technology
CHR: Sherri Stegge, Director Human Resources
Web address: www.kaiserpermanente.org
Control: Other not–for–profit (including NFP Corporation) **Service**: General medical and surgical

Staffed Beds: 253 **Admissions**: 8502 **Census**: 144 **Outpatient Visits**: 173058 **Births**: 1419 **Personnel**: 1492

Hospital, Medicare Provider Number, Address, Telephone, Approval, Facility, and Physician Codes, Health Care System

★ American Hospital Association (AHA) membership ○ Healthcare Facilities Accreditation Program ⇧ Center for Improvement in Healthcare Quality Accreditation
□ The Joint Commission accreditation ◇ DNV Healthcare Inc. accreditation △ Commission on Accreditation of Rehabilitation Facilities (CARF) accreditation

Hospitals, U.S. / CALIFORNIA

☒ **SUTTER SOLANO MEDICAL CENTER (050101)**, 300 Hospital Drive, Zip 94589–2574; tel. 707/554–4444, **A**1 2 10 **F**3 8 11 15 18 29 30 31 34 35 40 46 49 50 51 55 57 58 59 60 64 68 70 74 75 77 78 79 81 84 85 86 87 100 107 108 110 111 114 118 119 120 121 123 124 130 131 132 146 148 149 154 164 167 **S** Sutter Health, Sacramento, CA
Primary Contact: Kelley Jaeger-Jackson, Chief Executive Officer
CHR: Jean Willhite, Director Human Resources
Web address: www.suttersolano.org
Control: Other not–for–profit (including NFP Corporation) **Service**: General medical and surgical

> **Staffed Beds:** 106 **Admissions:** 3561 **Census:** 52 **Outpatient Visits:** 55128 **Births:** 0 **Total Expense ($000):** 175416 **Payroll Expense ($000):** 65133 **Personnel:** 483

VAN NUYS—Los Angeles County, See Los Angeles

VENTURA—Ventura County

★ ⓘ **COMMUNITY MEMORIAL HOSPITAL – VENTURA (050394)**, 147 North Brent Street, Zip 93003–2809; tel. 805/652–5011, (Includes COMMUNITY MEMORIAL HOSPITAL, 147 North Brent Street, Ventura, California, Zip 93003–2854, tel. 805/652–5011) (Nonreporting) **A**2 3 5 10 13 21 **S** Community Memorial Health System, Ventura, CA
Primary Contact: Mick Zdeblick, President/Chief Executive Officer
COO: Adam Thunell, Chief Operating Officer and Vice President Operations
CFO: David Glyer, Vice President Finance
CMO: Stanley Frochtzwajg, M.D., Chief Medical Officer
CIO: Ron Sandifer, Chief Information Officer
CHR: Diany Klein, Vice President Human Resources
Web address: www.cmhshealth.org
Control: Other not–for–profit (including NFP Corporation) **Service**: General medical and surgical

> **Staffed Beds:** 154

☒ **VENTURA COUNTY MEDICAL CENTER (050159)**, 300 Hillmont Avenue, Zip 93003–3099; tel. 805/652–6000, (Includes SANTA PAULA HOSPITAL, 825 North 10th Street, Santa Paula, California, Zip 93060–1309, tel. 805/933–8632; John Fankhauser, M.D., Chief Executive Officer) (Nonreporting) **A**1 2 3 5 10
Primary Contact: John Fankhauser, M.D., Chief Executive Officer
COO: Diana Zenner, R.N., Chief Operating Officer
CMO: Bryan Wong, M.D., Medical Director
CIO: Terry Theobald, Chief Information Officer
CHR: Tim Rhyne, Personnel Officer
CNO: Danielle Gabele, R.N., Chief Nursing Executive
Web address: www.vchca.org
Control: County, Government, Nonfederal **Service**: General medical and surgical

> **Staffed Beds:** 145

☐ **VISTA DEL MAR HOSPITAL (054077)**, 801 Seneca Street, Zip 93001–1411; tel. 805/653–6434, **A**1 **F**30 38 98 99 100 104 105 130 132 143 153 154 **S** Signature Healthcare Services, Corona, CA
Primary Contact: Colton Reed, Chief Executive Officer
CFO: Kurt Broten, Chief Financial Officer
CMO: Steve Ruths, M.D., Chief Medical Officer
Web address: www.vistadelmarhospital.com
Control: Corporation, Investor–owned (for–profit) **Service**: Psychiatric

> **Staffed Beds:** 87 **Admissions:** 2032 **Census:** 35 **Total Expense ($000):** 16212 **Payroll Expense ($000):** 7139 **Personnel:** 100

VICTORVILLE—San Bernardino County

☐ **DESERT VALLEY HOSPITAL (050709)**, 16850 Bear Valley Road, Zip 92395–5795; tel. 760/241–8000, (Nonreporting) **A**3 10 11 **S** Prime Healthcare, Ontario, CA
Primary Contact: Dana Roesler, R.N., Chief Executive Officer
COO: Luis Leon, Chief Operating Officer
CFO: Martin Mansukhani, Chief Financial Officer
CIO: Sreekant Gotti, Director Information Systems
Web address: www.dvmc.com
Control: Corporation, Investor–owned (for–profit) **Service**: General medical and surgical

> **Staffed Beds:** 110

☐ **VICTOR VALLEY GLOBAL MEDICAL CENTER (050517)**, 15248 Eleventh Street, Zip 92395–3704; tel. 760/245–8691, (Nonreporting) **A**1 10
Primary Contact: Marilyn Drone, R.N., MSN, Chief Executive Officer
COO: Doreen Dann, R.N., Chief Operating Officer
CIO: Joe Archer, Chief Information Officer
CHR: Cesar Lugo, Director Human Resources
Web address: https://victorvalleyglobalmedicalcenter.com/
Control: Other not–for–profit (including NFP Corporation) **Service**: General medical and surgical

> **Staffed Beds:** 101

VISALIA—Tulare County

☒ △ **KAWEAH HEALTH MEDICAL CENTER (050057)**, 400 West Mineral King Avenue, Zip 93291–6263; tel. 559/624–2000, (Includes SOUTH CAMPUS, 1633 South Court Street, Visalia, California, Zip 93277, tel. 559/624–6090) (Nonreporting) **A**1 3 5 7 10
Primary Contact: Gary K. Herbst, Chief Executive Officer
COO: Thomas J Rayner, Senior Vice President and Chief Operating Officer
CFO: Malinda Tupper, Vice President and Chief Financial Officer
CIO: Doug Leeper, Chief Information Officer
CHR: Dianne E Cox, Vice President of Human Resources
CNO: Regina Sawyer, Vice President Chief Nursing Officer
Web address: https://www.kaweahhealth.org/
Control: Hospital district or authority, Government, Nonfederal **Service**: General medical and surgical

> **Staffed Beds:** 639

VISALIA COMMUNITY HOSPITAL See South Campus

WALNUT CREEK—Contra Costa County

☒ △ **JOHN MUIR MEDICAL CENTER, WALNUT CREEK (050180)**, 1601 Ygnacio Valley Road, Zip 94598–3194; tel. 925/939–3000, **A**1 2 3 5 7 10 **F**3 11 13 15 18 19 20 22 24 26 28 29 30 31 32 34 35 37 39 40 41 43 44 45 46 47 48 49 50 54 55 56 57 58 59 60 61 64 65 68 70 72 74 75 76 77 78 79 80 81 82 84 85 86 87 88 89 90 91 93 95 96 100 102 107 108 110 118 119 120 121 123 124 126 130 131 132 141 145 146 147 148 149 150 154 156 157 160 167 169 **P**7 **S** John Muir Health, Walnut Creek, CA
Primary Contact: Michael S. Thomas, President and Chief Executive Officer
COO: Raymond Nassief, Senior Vice President, Hospital Operations and Support Services
CFO: Christian Pass, Senior Vice President & Chief Financial Officer
CMO: Irving Pike, M.D., Senior Vice President and Chief Medical Officer
CIO: Jon Russell, Senior Vice President & Chief Information Officer
CHR: Lisa Foust, Senior Vice President, Human Resources
Web address: https://www.johnmuirhealth.com/
Control: Other not–for–profit (including NFP Corporation) **Service**: General medical and surgical

> **Staffed Beds:** 422 **Admissions:** 19693 **Census:** 296 **Outpatient Visits:** 329125 **Births:** 2925 **Total Expense ($000):** 1085990 **Payroll Expense ($000):** 416542 **Personnel:** 2084

☒ **KAISER PERMANENTE WALNUT CREEK MEDICAL CENTER (050072)**, 1425 South Main Street, Zip 94596–5300; tel. 925/295–4000, (Includes KAISER FOUNDATION HOSPITAL, 200 Muir Road, Martinez, California, Zip 94553–4696, tel. 510/372–1000) **A**1 2 3 5 10 **F**3 11 13 15 18 20 22 26 30 31 37 39 40 41 45 49 56 60 64 68 70 72 73 74 75 76 78 79 80 81 84 85 87 89 100 107 108 110 111 114 115 118 119 120 121 123 124 130 135 146 148 149 154 167 169 **P**6 **S** Kaiser Foundation Hospitals, Oakland, CA
Primary Contact: Pamela Galley, Senior Vice President and Area Manager, Diablo Service Area
CFO: Yakesun Wing, Business Strategy and Finance Leader
Web address: www.kaiserpermanente.org
Control: Other not–for–profit (including NFP Corporation) **Service**: General medical and surgical

> **Staffed Beds:** 196 **Admissions:** 12529 **Census:** 150 **Outpatient Visits:** 133247 **Births:** 3044 **Personnel:** 1869

WATSONVILLE—Santa Cruz County

☐ **WATSONVILLE COMMUNITY HOSPITAL (050194)**, 75 Nielson Street, Zip 95076–2468; tel. 831/724–4741, (Nonreporting) **A**1 3 10
Primary Contact: Stephen Gray, Chief Executive Officer
COO: Matko Vranjes, Chief Operating Officer
CFO: Rachel Jones, Chief Financial Officer
CIO: Sergio Nell, Director Information Systems
CNO: Donna Salvi, Chief Nursing Officer
Web address: www.watsonvillehospital.com
Control: Other not–for–profit (including NFP Corporation) **Service**: General medical and surgical

> **Staffed Beds:** 106

Hospitals, U.S. / CALIFORNIA

WEAVERVILLE—Trinity County

TRINITY HOSPITAL (051315), 60 Easter Avenue, Zip 96093, Mailing Address: P.O. Box 1229, Zip 96093-1229; tel. 530/623-2687, (Nonreporting) **A**10 18
Primary Contact: Aaron Rogers, Chief Executive Officer
CFO: Jennifer Van Matre, Chief Financial Officer
CMO: Daniel Harwood, M.D., Chief of Staff
CIO: Jake Odom, Chief Information Officer
CHR: Elizabeth Reeder, Director Human Resources
CNO: Belen Manybanseng, R.N., Chief Nursing Officer
Web address: www.mcmedical.org
Control: Hospital district or authority, Government, Nonfederal **Service**: General medical and surgical

Staffed Beds: 47

WEST COVINA—Los Angeles County

CITRUS VALLEY MEDICAL CENTER-QUEEN OF THE VALLEY CAMPUS See Emanate Health Queen of The Valley Hospital

SPECIALTY HOSPITAL See Kindred Hospital San Gabriel Valley

☐ **WEST COVINA MEDICAL CENTER (050096)**, 725 South Orange Avenue, Zip 91790-2614; tel. 626/338-8481, (Nonreporting) **A**1 10
Primary Contact: Bill Nelson, Chief Executive Officer and Chair, Governing Board
CFO: Kami Horvat, Chief Financial Officer
CMO: Erich Pollak, M.D., Chief of Staff
CHR: Lourdes Meza, Coordinator Human Resources
Web address: https://www.westcovinamc.com/
Control: Corporation, Investor-owned (for-profit) **Service**: General medical and surgical

Staffed Beds: 46

WEST HILLS—Los Angeles County, See Los Angeles

WEST LOS ANGELES—Los Angeles County, See Los Angeles

WESTMINSTER—Orange County

✠ **KINDRED HOSPITAL-WESTMINSTER (052035)**, 200 Hospital Circle, Zip 92683-3910; tel. 714/893-4541, (Nonreporting) **A**1 10 **S** ScionHealth, Louisville, KY
Primary Contact: Phillip H. Wolfe, Market Chief Executive Officer
CFO: Dale Wagner, Chief Financial Officer
Web address: www.khwestminster.com/
Control: Corporation, Investor-owned (for-profit) **Service**: Acute long-term care hospital

Staffed Beds: 109

WHITTIER—Los Angeles County

PIH HEALTH HOSPITAL - WHITTIER See PIH Health Whittier Hospital

✠ **PIH HEALTH WHITTIER HOSPITAL (050169)**, 12401 Washington Boulevard, Zip 90602-1099; tel. 562/698-0811, (Total facility includes 28 beds in nursing home-type unit) **A**1 2 3 5 10 22 **F**3 8 11 12 13 15 18 20 22 24 26 28 29 30 31 34 37 40 41 44 46 48 49 50 51 54 55 56 57 58 59 60 62 63 64 65 68 70 72 74 75 76 77 78 79 81 82 84 85 86 87 90 93 94 96 97 100 107 110 111 115 116 117 118 119 120 121 123 124 126 128 130 131 132 135 142 143 146 147 148 149 154 156 157 160 161 164 167 169 **S** PIH Health, Whittier, CA
Primary Contact: James R. West, President/Chief Executive Officer
CFO: Greg Williams, Chief Financial Officer
CMO: Rosalio J Lopez, M.D., Senior Vice President and Chief Medical Officer
CIO: Jason Fischer, Chief Information Officer
CNO: Ramona Pratt, Chief Nursing Officer
Web address: www.PIHHealth.org
Control: Other not-for-profit (including NFP Corporation) **Service**: General medical and surgical

Staffed Beds: 307 **Admissions**: 21562 **Census**: 299 **Outpatient Visits**: 465834 **Births**: 2042 **Total Expense ($000)**: 821304 **Payroll Expense ($000)**: 290365 **Personnel**: 3553

☐ **WHITTIER HOSPITAL MEDICAL CENTER (050735)**, 9080 Colima Road, Zip 90605-1600; tel. 562/945-3561, (Total facility includes 22 beds in nursing home-type unit) **A**1 10 **F**3 11 13 29 31 34 35 40 41 46 49 50 57 59 60 61 64 65 68 70 74 75 76 77 78 79 81 85 91 93 94 100 107 108 111 119 128 130 146 154 157 167 169 **P**6 **S** AHMC Healthcare, Alhambra, CA
Primary Contact: Mary Anne. Monje, Chief Executive Officer/Chief Financial Officer
COO: Mary Anne Monje, Chief Executive Officer, Chief Financial Officer
CFO: Mary Anne Monje, Chief Executive Officer, Chief Financial Officer
CIO: Jay Geldhof, Director Information Systems
CHR: Terry Jaqua, Human Resources Director
CNO: Sarkis Vartanian, Chief Nursing Officer
Web address: www.whittierhospital.com
Control: Corporation, Investor-owned (for-profit) **Service**: General medical and surgical

Staffed Beds: 178 **Admissions**: 5504 **Census**: 82 **Outpatient Visits**: 61215 **Births**: 1080 **Total Expense ($000)**: 121856 **Payroll Expense ($000)**: 53191 **Personnel**: 475

WILDOMAR—Riverside County

INLAND VALLEY REG MEDICAL CTR See Inland Valley Medical Center

WILLITS—Mendocino County

✠ **ADVENTIST HEALTH HOWARD MEMORIAL (051310)**, 1 Marcela Drive, Zip 95490-5769; tel. 707/459-6801, **A**1 10 18 **F**11 15 29 30 34 35 40 57 59 68 70 75 79 81 93 97 107 110 111 115 119 127 131 132 133 135 146 147 148 154 160 **S** Adventist Health, Roseville, CA
Primary Contact: Eric Stevens, President, Northern California Network
CFO: Warren Tetz, Chief Financial Officer
CMO: Kimberly Faucher, M.D., Chief Medical Officer
CIO: Cecilia Winiger, Community Outreach and Communication Manager
CHR: Darcy De Leon, Executive Director, Human Resources
CNO: Karen M Scott, Vice President Patient Care
Web address: https://www.adventisthealth.org/howard-memorial/
Control: Church operated, Nongovernment, not-for-profit **Service**: General medical and surgical

Staffed Beds: 25 **Admissions**: 1510 **Census**: 17 **Outpatient Visits**: 69486 **Total Expense ($000)**: 91639 **Payroll Expense ($000)**: 31756 **Personnel**: 264

WILLOWS—Glenn County

⇧ **GLENN MEDICAL CENTER (051306)**, 1133 West Sycamore Street, Zip 95988-2745; tel. 530/934-1800, (Nonreporting) **A**10 18 21
Primary Contact: Sam Singh, Chief Executive Officer
CFO: John Lovrich, Chief Financial Officer
CHR: Deborah McMillan, Director Human Resources
CNO: Timothy Speek I, Director of Nursing
Web address: www.glennmed.org
Control: Other not-for-profit (including NFP Corporation) **Service**: General medical and surgical

Staffed Beds: 15

WOODLAND—Yolo County

WOODLAND HEALTHCARE See Woodland Memorial Hospital

✠ **WOODLAND MEMORIAL HOSPITAL (050127)**, 1325 Cottonwood Street, Zip 95695-5199; tel. 530/662-3961, **A**1 2 10 **F**2 3 11 13 18 20 28 29 30 31 34 35 40 44 45 47 49 50 51 56 57 59 60 62 64 68 70 72 74 75 76 77 78 79 81 82 84 85 87 89 98 100 102 103 107 108 111 114 115 116 117 119 129 130 131 132 135 146 147 149 154 164 167 169 **S** CommonSpirit Health, Chicago, IL
Primary Contact: Gena Bravo, President/Chief Executive Officer
CMO: Sarada Mylavarapu, M.D., Chief Medical Officer
Web address: https://www.dignityhealth.org/sacramento/locations/woodland-memorial-hospital
Control: Church operated, Nongovernment, not-for-profit **Service**: General medical and surgical

Staffed Beds: 105 **Admissions**: 4535 **Census**: 61 **Outpatient Visits**: 64892 **Births**: 503 **Total Expense ($000)**: 224526 **Payroll Expense ($000)**: 78665 **Personnel**: 613

Hospital, Medicare Provider Number, Address, Telephone, Approval, Facility, and Physician Codes, Health Care System

★ American Hospital Association (AHA) membership
☐ The Joint Commission accreditation
○ Healthcare Facilities Accreditation Program
◇ DNV Healthcare Inc. accreditation
⇧ Center for Improvement in Healthcare Quality Accreditation
△ Commission on Accreditation of Rehabilitation Facilities (CARF) accreditation

Hospitals, U.S. / CALIFORNIA

WOODLAND HILLS—Los Angeles County, See Los Ange

YREKA—Siskiyou County

☒ **FAIRCHILD MEDICAL CENTER (051316)**, 444 Bruce Street, Zip 96097–3450;
tel. 530/842–4121, (Nonreporting) **A**1 10 18
Primary Contact: Jonathon Andrus, President/Chief Executive Officer
CFO: Kelly Martin, Chief Financial Officer
CMO: Moudy Youssef, M.D., Chief Medical Officer
CIO: Randy Ferguson, Information Systems Manager
CHR: Joann Sarmento, Manager Human Resources
CNO: Susan Westphal, Assistant Administrator, Patient Care Services
Web address: www.fairchildmed.org
Control: Other not–for–profit (including NFP Corporation) **Service**: General medical and surgical

Staffed Beds: 25

YUBA CITY—Sutter County

FREMONT MEDICAL CENTER See Adventist Health and Rideout, Marysville

☐ **SUTTER SURGICAL HOSPITAL – NORTH VALLEY (050766)**, 455 Plumas Boulevard, Zip 95991–5074; tel. 530/749–5700, **A**1 10 **F**3 29 30 37 64 68 79 81 82 85 87 90 126 131 146 149 164 **S** Sutter Health, Sacramento, CA
Primary Contact: Shawndra Simpson, Interim Chief Executive Officer
CHR: Michelle Guina, Manager Human Resources
CNO: David Cooke, R.N., Chief Nursing Officer
Web address: www.sshnv.org
Control: Other not–for–profit (including NFP Corporation) **Service**: General medical and surgical

Staffed Beds: 14 **Admissions:** 61 **Census:** 2 **Outpatient Visits:** 2736
Births: 0 **Total Expense ($000):** 34304 **Payroll Expense ($000):** 115
Personnel: 80

Hospitals, U.S. / COLORADO

COLORADO

ALAMOSA—Alamosa County

★ **SAN LUIS VALLEY HEALTH (060008)**, 106 Blanca Avenue, Zip 81101–2393; tel. 719/589–2511, **A**3 10 20 **F**3 7 8 13 14 15 18 28 29 30 31 32 33 34 35 36 40 43 45 46 48 49 50 59 70 75 76 77 78 79 81 82 85 87 93 97 107 108 110 111 115 119 127 129 130 131 132 133 146 147 148 154 156 157 169 **P**6 **S** San Luis Valley Health, Alamosa, CO
Primary Contact: Konnie Martin, Chief Executive Officer
COO: Patti Thompson, Chief Operating Officer
CFO: Shane Mortensen, Chief Financial Officer
CMO: Carmelo Hernandez, M.D., Chief Medical Officer
CIO: Chuck Laufle, Director of Information Services
CHR: Mandy Lee Crockett, Director Human Resources
Web address: www.sanluisvalleyhealth.org
Control: Other not–for–profit (including NFP Corporation) **Service**: General medical and surgical

Staffed Beds: 44 **Admissions**: 1539 **Census**: 14 **Outpatient Visits**: 85003 **Births**: 415 **Total Expense ($000)**: 112774 **Payroll Expense ($000)**: 41600 **Personnel**: 672

ASPEN—Pitkin County

ASPEN VALLEY HOSPITAL (061324), 0401 Castle Creek Road, Zip 81611–1159, Mailing Address: 401 Castle Creek Rd, Zip 81611–1159; tel. 970/925–1120, **A**1 10 18 **F**3 7 8 10 11 13 15 18 28 29 31 34 35 36 37 40 43 45 46 48 50 53 54 57 59 64 68 70 75 76 77 78 79 81 82 85 86 87 89 93 96 97 107 108 110 111 115 118 119 126 130 131 132 133 135 144 146 147 148 149 154 156 157 169 **P**6
Primary Contact: David Ressler, Chief Executive Officer
CFO: Ginette Sebenaler, Associate Chief Financial Officer
CMO: J Christopher Beck, D.O., President Medical Staff
CIO: Ginny Dyche, Director Community Relations
CHR: Alicia Miller, Director Human Resources
CNO: Elaine Gerson, Chief Clinical Officer and General Counsel
Web address: www.avhaspen.org
Control: Hospital district or authority, Government, Nonfederal **Service**: General medical and surgical

Staffed Beds: 25 **Admissions**: 669 **Census**: 6 **Outpatient Visits**: 71687 **Births**: 133 **Total Expense ($000)**: 158564 **Payroll Expense ($000)**: 59770 **Personnel**: 498

AURORA—Adams County

△ **CHILDREN'S HOSPITAL COLORADO (063301)**, 13123 East 16th Avenue, Zip 80045–7106; tel. 720/777–1234, (Includes CHILDREN'S HOSPITAL OF COLORADO AT MEMORIAL, 1400 East Boulder Street, Colorado Springs, Colorado, Zip 80909–5533, tel. 719/365–5000; Greg Raymond, Southern Region President) (Nonreporting) **A**1 3 5 7 8 10 **S** Children's Hospital Colorado, Aurora, CO
Primary Contact: Jena Hausmann, President and Chief Executive Officer
CFO: Jeff Harrington, Senior Vice President, Chief Financial Officer
CMO: Joan Bothner, M.D., Chief Medical Officer
CIO: Dana Moore, Chief Information Officer
CNO: Patricia Givens, R.N., Chief Nursing Officer
Web address: www.thechildrenshospital.org
Control: Other not–for–profit (including NFP Corporation) **Service**: Children's general medical and surgical

Staffed Beds: 545

COLUMBIA PRESBYTERIAN MED CTR See Medical Center of Aurora North

SPALDING REHABILITATION HOSPITAL (063027), 900 Potomac Steet, Zip 80011–6716; tel. 303/367–1166, (Nonreporting) **A**1 10 **S** HCA Healthcare, Nashville, TN
Primary Contact: Scott Rausch, Chief Executive Officer
COO: Debbie Petersen, R.N., Chief Operating Officer and Chief Nursing Officer
CFO: Joyce Webber, Chief Financial Officer
CHR: Donna Greeley, Director Human Resources
CNO: John Roque, MSN, R.N., Chief Nursing Officer
Web address: https://healthonecares.com/locations/spalding-rehabilitation-hospital/
Control: Partnership, Investor–owned (for–profit) **Service**: Rehabilitation

Staffed Beds: 100

UNIVERSITY OF COLORADO HOSPITAL (060024), 12401 East 17th Avenue, MS F417, Zip 80045–2545; tel. 720/848–0000, **A**1 2 3 5 8 10 19 **F**3 4 5 6 7 9 11 12 13 14 15 16 17 18 20 22 24 26 28 29 30 31 33 34 35 36 37 38 39 40 42 43 44 45 46 47 48 49 50 53 54 55 56 57 58 59 60 61 63 64 65 68 70 71 72 74 75 76 77 78 79 81 82 84 85 86 87 90 91 92 93 96 97 98 100 101 102 104 105 106 107 108 109 110 111 112 113 114 115 116 117 118 119 120 121 123 124 126 129 130 131 132 134 135 136 137 138 139 140 141 142 145 146 147 148 149 150 152 153 154 156 157 160 161 162 163 164 165 166 167 169 **S** UCHealth, Aurora, CO
Primary Contact: Thomas Gronow, President and Chief Executive Officer
CFO: Barbara Carveth, Chief Financial Officer
CMO: Jean Kutner, M.D., Chief Medical Officer
CIO: Steve Hess, Vice President Information Services and Chief Information Officer
Web address: www.uchealth.org
Control: Other not–for–profit (including NFP Corporation) **Service**: General medical and surgical

Staffed Beds: 831 **Admissions**: 34151 **Census**: 627 **Outpatient Visits**: 2115507 **Births**: 3714 **Total Expense ($000)**: 2612589 **Payroll Expense ($000)**: 747943 **Personnel**: 8324

AURORA—Arapahoe County

AURORA REGIONAL MEDICAL CENTER See South Campus

KINDRED HOSPITAL–AURORA (062013), 700 Potomac Street 2nd Floor, Zip 80011–6844; tel. 720/857–8333, (Nonreporting) **A**1 10 **S** ScionHealth, Louisville, KY
Primary Contact: Kevin Zachary, R.N., Chief Executive Officer
CMO: Eric Yeager, M.D., Chief Medical Officer
CHR: Becky Small, Chief Human Resources Officer
CNO: Paul Green, Chief Clinical Officer
Web address: www.khaurora.com/
Control: Corporation, Investor–owned (for–profit) **Service**: Acute long–term care hospital

Staffed Beds: 23

MEDICAL CENTER OF AURORA (060100), 1501 South Potomac Street, Zip 80012–5411; tel. 303/695–2600, (Includes CENTENNIAL HOSPITAL, 14200 East Arapahoe Road, Centennial, Colorado, Zip 80112–4065, tel. 303/699–3000; Tyler Hood, Chief Administrative Officer; MEDICAL CENTER OF AURORA NORTH, 700 Potomac Street, Aurora, Colorado, Zip 80011–6792, tel. 303/363–7200; MEDICAL CENTER OF AURORA, 700 Potomac ST, Aurora, Colorado, Zip 80011–6844, 700 Potomac Street, Zip 80011, tel. 303/360–3030; SOUTH CAMPUS, 1501 South Potomac, Aurora, Colorado, Zip 80012, tel. 303/695–2600) (Nonreporting) **A**1 2 3 5 10 19 **S** HCA Healthcare, Nashville, TN
Primary Contact: Scott Rausch, President and Chief Executive Officer
CFO: Bryce DeHaven, Chief Financial Officer
CMO: Dianne McCallister, M.D., Chief Medical Officer
CNO: John Roque, MSN, R.N., Chief Nursing Officer
Web address: www.auroramed.com
Control: Corporation, Investor–owned (for–profit) **Service**: General medical and surgical

Staffed Beds: 432

AURORA—Denver County

EASTERN COLORADO HCS See Rocky Mountain Regional VA Medical Center

ROCKY MOUNTAIN REGIONAL VA MEDICAL CENTER, 1700 North Wheeling Street, Zip 80045; tel. 303/399–8020, (Nonreporting) **A**1 3 5 **S** Department of Veterans Affairs, Washington, DC
Primary Contact: Michael Moore, Interim Director
CMO: Ellen Mangione, M.D., Chief of Staff
CIO: Don Huckaby, Chief Information Management Service
CHR: Lorene Connel, Chief Human Resources Management Service
Web address: www.denver.va.gov/
Control: Veterans Affairs, Government, federal **Service**: General medical and surgical

Staffed Beds: 271

Hospital, Medicare Provider Number, Address, Telephone, Approval, Facility, and Physician Codes, Health Care System

★ American Hospital Association (AHA) membership ○ Healthcare Facilities Accreditation Program ⇧ Center for Improvement in Healthcare Quality Accreditation
☐ The Joint Commission accreditation ◇ DNV Healthcare Inc. accreditation △ Commission on Accreditation of Rehabilitation Facilities (CARF) accreditation

Hospitals, U.S. / COLORADO

BOULDER—Boulder County

✠ **BOULDER COMMUNITY HEALTH (060027)**, 4747 Arapahoe Ave, Zip 80303–1133, Mailing Address: P.O. Box 9019, Zip 80301–9019; tel. 303/415–7000, (Includes BOULDER COMMUNITY FOOTHILLS HOSPITAL, 4747 Arapahoe Avenue, Boulder, Colorado, Zip 80303–1133, P O Box 9047, Zip 80301–9047, tel. 720/854–7000; Robert Vissers, M.D., President and Chief Executive Officer) **A**1 2 3 5 10 **F**3 5 11 13 15 18 20 22 24 26 28 30 31 35 36 37 40 41 42 43 49 50 53 54 56 59 61 64 65 68 70 73 74 75 76 77 78 79 81 84 85 87 93 94 98 100 101 102 104 105 107 108 109 110 111 114 115 118 119 126 130 132 141 144 146 147 148 149 153 154 160 164 165 167 169 **P**6
Primary Contact: Robert Vissers, M.D., President and Chief Executive Officer
COO: Jacqueline M Attlesey–Pries, MS, R.N., Chief Nursing Officer/Chief Operating Officer
CMO: Ben Keidan, CMO/Senior Physician Executive
CNO: Jacqueline M Attlesey–Pries, MS, R.N., Chief Nursing Officer & Chief Operating Officer
Web address: www.bch.org
Control: Other not–for–profit (including NFP Corporation) **Service**: General medical and surgical

Staffed Beds: 181 **Admissions**: 8986 **Census**: 100 **Outpatient Visits**: 430590 **Births**: 911 **Total Expense ($000)**: 446433 **Payroll Expense ($000)**: 183291 **Personnel**: 1525

BRIGHTON—Adams County

✠ **INTERMOUNTAIN HEALTH PLATTE VALLEY HOSPITAL (060004)**, 1600 Prairie Center Parkway, Zip 80601–4006; tel. 303/498–1600, **A**1 10 **F**3 7 13 15 18 20 22 26 28 29 30 31 34 35 40 41 43 45 49 55 59 65 68 70 73 74 75 76 77 78 79 81 85 87 90 92 93 107 108 110 111 115 119 129 130 132 135 146 147 148 149 154 167 169 **S** Intermountain Health, Salt Lake City, UT
Primary Contact: Jaime Campbell, President and Chief Executive Officer
COO: Kurt G Gensert, FACHE, R.N., Vice President Operations
CMO: Kirk Quackenbush, M.D., Chief of Staff
CIO: Timothy Brannigan, Director Information Services
CHR: Jackie J. Dunkin, Director Human Resources
Web address: www.pvmc.org
Control: Other not–for–profit (including NFP Corporation) **Service**: General medical and surgical

Staffed Beds: 98 **Admissions**: 3699 **Census**: 36 **Outpatient Visits**: 113013 **Births**: 876 **Total Expense ($000)**: 191935 **Payroll Expense ($000)**: 65413 **Personnel**: 651

BROOMFIELD—Denver County

☐ **UCHEALTH BROOMFIELD HOSPITAL (060129)**, 11820 Destination Drive, Zip 80021; tel. 303/460–6000, **A**1 3 10 **F**3 7 9 14 15 29 30 34 35 40 43 50 56 59 64 68 74 75 77 79 81 85 87 90 96 100 102 107 115 119 130 131 146 148 149 154 164 **S** UCHealth, Aurora, CO
Primary Contact: Ryan Rohman, MSN, R.N., President
Web address: www.uchealth.org/pages/OHAM/OrgUnitDetails.aspx?
Control: Other not–for–profit (including NFP Corporation) **Service**: General medical and surgical

Staffed Beds: 38 **Admissions**: 1088 **Census**: 23 **Outpatient Visits**: 45120 **Births**: 0 **Total Expense ($000)**: 74804 **Payroll Expense ($000)**: 23734 **Personnel**: 257

BRUSH—Morgan County

✠ **EAST MORGAN COUNTY HOSPITAL (061303)**, 2400 West Edison Street, Zip 80723–1640; tel. 970/842–6200, **A**1 10 18 **F**3 13 15 28 29 34 35 36 40 41 43 45 50 53 56 57 59 65 67 68 76 77 79 80 81 85 87 89 93 96 97 107 108 110 111 114 115 119 127 130 131 132 133 141 146 148 149 154 155 156 164 167 169 **S** Banner Health, Phoenix, AZ
Primary Contact: Linda Thorpe, Chief Executive Officer
CFO: Dena Klockman, Chief Financial Officer
CMO: Jeff Bacon, D.O., Chief Medical Officer
CHR: Cynthia Wentworth, Chief Human Resource Officer
CNO: Linda Lyn Roan, Chief Nursing Officer
Web address: www.emchbrush.com
Control: Other not–for–profit (including NFP Corporation) **Service**: General medical and surgical

Staffed Beds: 19 **Admissions**: 503 **Census**: 5 **Outpatient Visits**: 30424 **Births**: 146 **Total Expense ($000)**: 39657 **Payroll Expense ($000)**: 16759 **Personnel**: 139

BURLINGTON—Kit Carson County

KIT CARSON COUNTY HEALTH SERVICE DISTRICT See Kit Carson County Memorial Hospital

★ **KIT CARSON COUNTY MEMORIAL HOSPITAL (061313)**, 286 16th Street, Zip 80807–1697; tel. 719/346–5311, (Nonreporting) **A**10 18
Primary Contact: Bryan Bogle, Chief Executive Officer
CMO: Bong Pham, Chief Medical Officer
CIO: Paul Velasco, IT Manager
CHR: Robin Konecne, Manager Human Resources
CNO: Elizabeth Hampton, MS, R.N., Chief Nursing Officer
Web address: www.kcchsd.org
Control: Hospital district or authority, Government, Nonfederal **Service**: General medical and surgical

Staffed Beds: 19

CANON CITY—Fremont County

✠ **ST. THOMAS MORE HOSPITAL (061344)**, 1338 Phay Avenue, Zip 81212–2302; tel. 719/285–2000, **A**1 10 18 **F**3 12 13 15 28 29 30 34 35 40 43 45 53 57 59 64 65 70 75 76 77 79 81 85 87 89 93 107 108 110 111 115 119 129 130 131 133 146 147 148 149 154 157 160 164 **P**6 **S** CommonSpirit Health, Chicago, IL
Primary Contact: Michael Cafasso, Chief Executive Officer
COO: Dennis Bruens, Vice President Operations
CFO: Gwenyth Howard, Vice President Finance
CMO: Kern Low, M.D., Chief Medical Officer
CIO: Jillian Maes, Director Marketing and Public Relations
CHR: Janet Reedy, Manager Human Resources
CNO: James Woodard, Chief Nursing Officer
Web address: www.stmhospital.org
Control: Church operated, Nongovernment, not–for–profit **Service**: General medical and surgical

Staffed Beds: 25 **Admissions**: 1651 **Census**: 15 **Outpatient Visits**: 50667 **Births**: 251 **Total Expense ($000)**: 54698 **Payroll Expense ($000)**: 22919 **Personnel**: 249

CASTLE ROCK—Douglas County

✠ **ADVENTHEALTH CASTLE ROCK (060125)**, 2350 Meadows Boulevard, Zip 80109–8405; tel. 720/455–5000, **A**1 3 10 **F**3 11 13 15 18 20 22 29 30 32 34 35 37 38 40 41 43 44 45 48 49 50 53 57 59 60 62 64 65 68 70 72 74 75 76 77 79 81 85 86 87 91 93 101 102 107 108 110 111 114 115 118 119 126 129 130 131 135 146 147 148 154 156 169 **P**6 **S** AdventHealth, Altamonte Springs, FL
Primary Contact: Michelle Fuentes, Chief Executive Officer and President
Web address: www.castlerockhospital.org
Control: Church operated, Nongovernment, not–for–profit **Service**: General medical and surgical

Staffed Beds: 90 **Admissions**: 4535 **Census**: 43 **Outpatient Visits**: 60932 **Births**: 1059 **Total Expense ($000)**: 117378 **Payroll Expense ($000)**: 47102 **Personnel**: 578

CASTLE ROCK ADVENTIST HOSPITAL See Adventhealth Castle Rock

CHEYENNE WELLS—Cheyenne County

★ **KEEFE MEMORIAL HOSPITAL (061343)**, 602 North 6th Street West, Zip 80810, Mailing Address: P.O. Box 578, Zip 80810–0578; tel. 719/767–5661, (Nonreporting) **A**10 18
Primary Contact: Claressa Millsap, Chief Executive Officer
CMO: Christine Connolly, M.D., Chief of Staff
CIO: Jeanne Moffat, Manager Information Technology
CHR: Carrie Rico, Chief Human Resource Officer
CNO: Jesse Smith, Director of Nursing
Web address: www.keefememorial.com
Control: County, Government, Nonfederal **Service**: General medical and surgical

Staffed Beds: 11

COLORADO SPRINGS—El Paso County

☐ **CEDAR SPRINGS HOSPITAL (064009)**, 2135 Southgate Road, Zip 80906–2693; tel. 719/633–4114, (Nonreporting) **A**1 10 **S** Universal Health Services, Inc., King of Prussia, PA
Primary Contact: Daniel Zarecky, Chief Executive Officer
CFO: Cynthia D Deboer, Chief Financial Officer
CMO: Larry Shores, M.D., Executive Medical Director
CHR: Jessica McCoy, Director Human Resources
CNO: Jodi Mattson, Director of Nursing
Web address: www.cedarspringsbhs.com
Control: Corporation, Investor–owned (for–profit) **Service**: Psychiatric

Staffed Beds: 110

Hospitals, U.S. / COLORADO

CHILDREN'S HOSPITAL COLORADO – COLORADO SPRINGS (063303), 4090 Briargate Parkway, Zip 80920–7815; tel. 719/305–1234, (Nonreporting) **S** Children's Hospital Colorado, Aurora, CO
Primary Contact: Greg Raymond, President, Southern Colorado Care System
COO: Kathleen Seerup, R.N., Senior Vice President, Chief Nursing and Operations Officer
CFO: Jeff Harrington, Senior Vice President, Chief Financial Officer
CMO: Mike DiStefano, Chief Medical Officer
CIO: Amy Feaster, Senior Vice President, Chief Digital Information Officer
CHR: Linda Michael, Vice President, Chief Compliance Officer
CNO: Kathleen Seerup, R.N., Senior Vice President, Chief Nursing and Operations Officer
Web address: https://www.childrenscolorado.org/locations/colorado-springs-hospital/
Control: Other not-for-profit (including NFP Corporation) **Service:** Children's general medical and surgical

Staffed Beds: 115

ENCOMPASS HEALTH REHABILITATION HOSPITAL OF COLORADO SPRINGS (063030), 325 Parkside Drive, Zip 80910–3134; tel. 719/630–8000, (Nonreporting) **A**1 10 **S** Encompass Health Corporation, Birmingham, AL
Primary Contact: Nathan Kliniske, Chief Executive Officer
CFO: Stephanie Davis, Controller
CHR: Diana Crepeau, Director Human Resources
CNO: Cindy Nordell, Chief Nursing Officer
Web address: www.healthsouthcoloradosprings.com
Control: Corporation, Investor-owned (for-profit) **Service:** Rehabilitation

Staffed Beds: 62

MEMORIAL HOSPITAL FOR CHILDREN See Children's Hospital of Colorado At Memorial

MEMORIAL HOSPITAL NORTH See Uchealth Memorial Hospital North

PEAK VIEW BEHAVIORAL HEALTH (064026), 7353 Sisters Grove, Zip 80923–2615; tel. 719/444–8484, (Nonreporting) **A**1 10 **S** Strategic Behavioral Health, LLC, Memphis, TN
Primary Contact: Ty Meredith, Chief Executive Officer
Web address: www.strategicbh.com/peakview.html
Control: Corporation, Investor-owned (for-profit) **Service:** Psychiatric

Staffed Beds: 112

PENROSE HOSPITALS See Penrose Hospital

△ **PENROSE–ST. FRANCIS HEALTH SERVICES (060031)**, 2222 North Nevada Avenue, Zip 80907–6799; tel. 719/776–5000, (Includes PENROSE HOSPITAL, 2222 North Nevada Avenue, Colorado Springs, Zip 80907, tel. 719/776–5000; ST. FRANCIS MEDICAL CENTER, 6001 East Woodmen Road, Colorado Springs, Colorado, Zip 80923–2601, tel. 719/776–5000; Tadd M Richert, Chief Executive Officer) **A**1 2 3 5 7 10 19 **F**3 5 7 10 19 22 24 26 28 29 30 31 34 35 36 37 38 40 43 44 45 46 47 48 49 50 52 53 54 55 56 57 58 59 61 62 64 65 68 70 71 72 74 75 76 77 78 79 81 82 84 85 86 87 90 91 92 93 94 96 97 100 101 102 107 108 110 114 115 117 118 119 120 121 123 124 126 129 130 131 132 144 146 147 148 149 150 154 167 169 **S** CommonSpirit Health, Chicago, IL
Primary Contact: Kristi Olson, Chief Executive Officer
CFO: Danny Reeves, Chief Financial Officer
CMO: David Dull, M.D., Chief Medical Officer
CHR: James Humphrey, Vice President Talent Resources and Human Resources for South Side Operating Group
CNO: Cynthia Latney, Chief Nursing Officer
Web address: www.penrosestfrancis.org
Control: Church operated, Nongovernment, not-for-profit **Service:** General medical and surgical

Staffed Beds: 573 **Admissions:** 24885 **Census:** 333 **Outpatient Visits:** 172141 **Births:** 3035 **Total Expense ($000):** 645521 **Payroll Expense ($000):** 220002 **Personnel:** 1913

ST FRANCIS HEALTH CENTER See St. Francis Medical Center

UCHEALTH GRANDVIEW HOSPITAL (060130), 5623 Pulpit Peak View, Zip 80918; tel. 719/272–3600, **A**1 10 **F**3 29 30 34 35 37 38 40 43 44 50 57 59 64 65 68 75 77 79 81 82 84 85 87 92 93 96 100 102 107 110 115 119 126 130 131 135 146 149 154 156 157 164 **S** UCHealth, Aurora, CO
Primary Contact: Ron Fitch, President/UCHealth Pikes Peak Regional Hospital/Grandview Hospital/Operations and Military Affairs/U
Web address: https://www.uchealth.org/Pages/OHAM/OrgUnitDetails.aspx?OrganizationalUnitId=514
Control: Other not-for-profit (including NFP Corporation) **Service:** General medical and surgical

Staffed Beds: 22 **Admissions:** 517 **Census:** 3 **Outpatient Visits:** 50337 **Births:** 0 **Total Expense ($000):** 55005 **Payroll Expense ($000):** 14685 **Personnel:** 150

UCHEALTH MEMORIAL HOSPITAL (060022), 1400 East Boulder Street, Zip 80909–5599; tel. 719/365–5000, (Includes UCHEALTH MEMORIAL HOSPITAL NORTH, 4050 Briargate Pkwy, Colorado Springs, Colorado, Zip 80920–7815, 1400 East Boulder Street, Zip 80909, tel. 719/365–5000; Lonnie Cramer, President and Chief Executive Officer) **A**1 2 3 10 **F**3 7 9 11 12 13 14 15 17 18 20 22 24 26 28 29 30 31 34 35 37 38 40 43 44 45 46 47 48 49 50 54 55 56 57 58 59 60 61 63 64 65 68 70 72 74 75 76 77 78 79 81 82 84 85 86 87 90 92 93 96 97 100 102 107 108 110 111 115 116 117 118 119 120 121 123 124 126 129 130 131 132 135 144 146 147 148 149 154 156 157 164 167 169 **S** UCHealth, Aurora, CO
Primary Contact: Lonnie Cramer, President and Chief Executive Officer
COO: Cherie Gorby, Chief Operations Officer
CFO: Dan Rieber, Chief Financial Officer
CMO: Jose Melendez, M.D., Chief Medical Officer
CNO: Kay J Miller, R.N., MSN, Chief Nursing Officer
Web address: www.uchealth.org/southerncolorado
Control: Other not-for-profit (including NFP Corporation) **Service:** General medical and surgical

Staffed Beds: 511 **Admissions:** 29040 **Census:** 380 **Outpatient Visits:** 992222 **Births:** 4926 **Total Expense ($000):** 1185683 **Payroll Expense ($000):** 392312 **Personnel:** 4497

CORTEZ—Montezuma County

★ ⇈ **SOUTHWEST HEALTH SYSTEM (061327)**, 1311 North Mildred Road, Zip 81321–2299; tel. 970/565–6666, **A**10 18 21 **F**3 5 7 13 15 29 31 32 34 35 40 41 43 45 47 48 50 59 64 65 66 68 70 75 76 77 79 81 82 85 89 93 97 107 110 111 115 119 127 129 132 133 134 143 144 148 149 154 156 160 169
Primary Contact: Joseph Theine, Chief Executive Officer
CFO: Rick Schrader, Chief Financial Officer
CIO: Charles Krupa, Chief Information Officer and Public Information Officer
CHR: Travis Parker, Director Human Resources
CNO: Lisa Gates, Chief Nursing Officer
Web address: www.swhealth.org
Control: Other not-for-profit (including NFP Corporation) **Service:** General medical and surgical

Staffed Beds: 20 **Admissions:** 919 **Census:** 11 **Outpatient Visits:** 96796 **Births:** 131 **Total Expense ($000):** 79049 **Payroll Expense ($000):** 31309 **Personnel:** 344

CRAIG—Moffat County

★ ⇈ **MEMORIAL REGIONAL HEALTH (061314)**, 750 Hospital Loop, Zip 81625–8750; tel. 970/824–9411, **A**10 18 21 **F**3 7 8 10 15 29 30 31 34 35 36 38 40 43 44 45 46 47 48 50 57 59 62 64 67 68 70 75 77 79 81 82 83 84 87 90 93 97 105 107 108 110 111 112 115 119 127 129 130 131 133 135 147 148 149 **P**6
Primary Contact: Jennifer Riley, Chief Executive Officer
COO: Jennifer Riley, Vice President Operations
CFO: Kelsea Henry, Chief Financial Officer
CMO: Scott Ellis, D.O., Chief Medical Officer
CIO: Bryan Curtis, Chief Information Officer
CNO: Amy Peck, R.N., Chief Nursing Officer
Web address: https://memorialregionalhealth.com/
Control: County, Government, Nonfederal **Service:** General medical and surgical

Staffed Beds: 25 **Admissions:** 381 **Census:** 4 **Outpatient Visits:** 39712 **Births:** 0 **Total Expense ($000):** 69731 **Payroll Expense ($000):** 24226 **Personnel:** 350

Hospital, Medicare Provider Number, Address, Telephone, Approval, Facility, and Physician Codes, Health Care System

★ American Hospital Association (AHA) membership ○ Healthcare Facilities Accreditation Program ⇈ Center for Improvement in Healthcare Quality Accreditation
□ The Joint Commission accreditation ◇ DNV Healthcare Inc. accreditation △ Commission on Accreditation of Rehabilitation Facilities (CARF) accreditation

Hospitals, U.S. / COLORADO

DEL NORTE—Rio Grande County

★ **RIO GRANDE HOSPITAL (061301)**, 310 County Road 14, Zip 81132–8719; tel. 719/657–2510, (Nonreporting) **A**10 18
Primary Contact: Arlene Harms, Chief Executive Officer
CFO: Greg Porter, Chief Financial Officer
CMO: Heidi E Helgeson, M.D., Chief Medical Officer
CIO: Denise Fietek, Information Technology
CHR: Paula Warner-Pacheco, Chief Human Resources
CNO: Candice Allen, Director of Nursing
Web address: www.rio-grande-hospital.org/
Control: Other not–for–profit (including NFP Corporation) **Service**: General medical and surgical

Staffed Beds: 17

DELTA—Delta County

⇑ **DELTA COUNTY MEMORIAL HOSPITAL** See Delta Health

★ ⇑ **DELTA HEALTH (060071)**, 1501 East 3rd Street, Zip 81416–2815, Mailing Address: P.O. Box 10100, Zip 81416–0008; tel. 970/874–7681, (Nonreporting) **A**10 20 21
Primary Contact: Jonathan Cohee, Chief Executive Officer
CFO: Kelly Johnston, Interim Chief Financial Officer
CMO: John P Knutson, M.D., Chief Medical Staff
CIO: Mitch Van Scoyk, Manager Information Systems
CHR: Rhonda L Katzdorn, Executive Director, Human Resources
CNO: Melissa Palmer, Executive Director of Nursing
Web address: www.deltahospital.org
Control: Hospital district or authority, Government, Nonfederal **Service**: General medical and surgical

Staffed Beds: 49

DENVER—Denver, Adams and Arapaho Coun County

⊞ **ADVENTHEALTH PORTER (060064)**, 2525 South Downing Street, Zip 80210–5876; tel. 303/778–1955, **A**1 3 5 10 19 **F**3 4 5 6 8 11. 15 17 18 20 22 24 26 28 29 30 31 34 35 36 37 38 39 40 42 43 44 45 46 47 48 49 50 54 55 56 58 59 60 63 64 65 68 70 74 75 77 78 79 81 82 83 84 85 86 87 90 91 92 93 94 96 97 98 100 102 103 104 107 108 109 110 111 112 114 115 116 117 118 119 120 121 122 123 124 125 126 130 131 132 135 138 139 144 146 147 148 149 152 153 155 156 160 164 167 P6 **S** AdventHealth, Altamonte Springs, FL
Primary Contact: Todd Folkenberg, Chief Executive Officer
COO: David Dookeeram, Chief Operating Officer
CHR: Oz Muller, Director Human Resources
Web address: www.porterhospital.org/poh/home/
Control: Church operated, Nongovernment, not–for–profit **Service**: General medical and surgical

Staffed Beds: 227 **Admissions**: 7997 **Census**: 119 **Outpatient Visits**: 59873 **Births**: 0 **Total Expense ($000)**: 268802 **Payroll Expense ($000)**: 94129 **Personnel**: 797

☐ **COLORADO MENTAL HEALTH INSTITUTE AT FORT LOGAN (064003)**, 3520 West Oxford Avenue, Zip 80236–3197; tel. 303/866–7066, (Nonreporting) **A**1 3 5 10
Primary Contact: David M. Polunas, Director
CFO: Sabina Genesio, Finance Officer for Institutes
CMO: Bruce Leonard, M.D., Medical Director and Chief of Psychiatry
CNO: Nancy Kehiayan, Director of Nursing
Web address: www.cdhs.state.co.us/cmhifl
Control: State, Government, Nonfederal **Service**: Psychiatric

Staffed Beds: 297

⊞ **DENVER HEALTH (060011)**, 777 Bannock Street, Zip 80204–4507; tel. 303/436–6000, **A**1 3 5 8 10 19 **F**3 5 7 8 11 12 13 15 18 19 20 22 26 28 29 30 31 32 34 35 36 37 38 39 40 41 42 43 44 45 46 49 50 52 53 54 55 56 57 58 59 60 61 64 65 66 68 70 71 72 74 75 76 77 78 79 80 81 82 84 85 86 87 88 89 92 93 94 96 97 98 99 100 101 102 103 104 107 108 110 111 114 115 116 119 127 129 130 131 132 133 134 135 143 144 146 147 148 149 152 153 154 156 160 162 163 164 165 167 169 **P**6
Primary Contact: Donna Lynne, Chief Executive Officer
COO: Kris Gaw, Chief Operating Officer
CFO: Faraz Khan, Chief Financial Officer
CMO: Connie Price, M.D., Chief Medical Officer
CIO: Charles Scully, Chief Information Officer
CHR: Michelle Fournier Johnson, Chief Human Resource Officer
CNO: Kathy Boyle, R.N., Ph.D., Chief Nursing Officer
Web address: www.denverhealth.org
Control: Hospital district or authority, Government, Nonfederal **Service**: General medical and surgical

Staffed Beds: 451 **Admissions**: 22335 **Census**: 368 **Outpatient Visits**: 1110048 **Births**: 3837 **Total Expense ($000)**: 1418517 **Payroll Expense ($000)**: 672205 **Personnel**: 7440

⊞ **INTERMOUNTAIN HEALTH SAINT JOSEPH HOSPITAL (060028)**, 1375 East 19th Avenue, Zip 80218–1126; tel. 303/837–7111, **A**1 2 3 5 8 10 19 **F**3 11 12 13 15 17 18 20 22 24 26 28 29 30 31 34 35 36 37 40 41 42 43 44 45 46 49 50. 53 55 58 59 60 61 64 66 68 70 71 72 74 75 76 77 78 79 80 81 82 84 85 87 93 96 100 102 107 108 110 111 112 114 115 116 117 118 119 120 121 123 124 126 130 135 145 146 147 148 149 154 156 157 158 160 162 164 167 169 **S** Intermountain Health, Salt Lake City, UT
Primary Contact: Scott Peek, Front Range Market President
COO: David Biggerstaff, Vice President, Chief Operating Officer
CFO: Alice W. Rigdon, Vice President Finance
CMO: Shawn Dufford, M.D., Vice President Medical Affairs and Chief Medical Officer
CHR: William R Gould, Vice President Human Resources
Web address: www.saintjosephdenver.org/
Control: Other not–for–profit (including NFP Corporation) **Service**: General medical and surgical

Staffed Beds: 347 **Admissions**: 16599 **Census**: 222 **Outpatient Visits**: 165292 **Births**: 3755 **Total Expense ($000)**: 688245 **Payroll Expense ($000)**: 219843 **Personnel**: 3602

⊞ **KINDRED HOSPITAL–DENVER (062009)**, 1920 High Street, Zip 80218–1213; tel. 303/320–5871, (Nonreporting) **A**1 10 **S** ScionHealth, Louisville, KY
Primary Contact: Kevin Zachary, R.N., Market Chief Executive Officer
CFO: Tim Stecker, Chief Financial Officer
CMO: Eric Yeager, M.D., Medical Director
Web address: www.kh-denver.com
Control: Corporation, Investor–owned (for–profit) **Service**: Acute long–term care hospital

Staffed Beds: 68

⊞ **NATIONAL JEWISH HEALTH (060107)**, 1400 Jackson Street, Zip 80206–2762; tel. 303/388–4461, **A**1 3 5 8 10 **F**3 9 11 12 18 26 28 29 30 31 32 34 35 36 42 45 46 48 50 53 54 55 57 58 59 64 65 66 68 74 75 77 78 84 86 87 89 90 93 96 99 100 101 104 107 108 109 111 114 115 116 117 118 119 129 130 131 132 134 135 143 144 146 149 154 156 164 167 **P**6
Primary Contact: Michael Salem, M.D., President and Chief Executive Officer
COO: Ron Berge, Executive Vice President and Chief Operating Officer
CFO: Christine Forkner, Executive Vice President and Chief Financial Officer
CMO: Gary Cott, M.D., Executive Vice President Medical and Clinical Services
CIO: Lots Pook, Chief Information Officer
CHR: Sarah Taylor, Chief Human Resources
CNO: Jeff Downing, R.N., MS, Chief Nursing Officer
Web address: www.njhealth.org
Control: Other not–for–profit (including NFP Corporation) **Service**: Tuberculosis and other respiratory diseases

Staffed Beds: 46 **Admissions**: 69 **Census**: 1 **Outpatient Visits**: 116671 **Births**: 0 **Personnel**: 1558

⊞ **PAM HEALTH SPECIALTY HOSPITAL OF DENVER (062012)**, 1690 Meade Street, Zip 80204–1552, Mailing Address: 1690 North Meade Street, Zip 80204–1552; tel. 303/264–6900, **A**1 10 **F**1 3 29 60 69 75 80 82 83 87 107 130 146 148 149 154 **S** PAM Health, Enola, PA
Primary Contact: Steph Laviolette, Chief Executive Officer
Web address: https://postacutemedical.com/facilities/find-facility/specialty-hospitals/PAM-Specialty-Hospital-of-Denver
Control: Corporation, Investor–owned (for–profit) **Service**: Acute long–term care hospital

Staffed Beds: 63 **Admissions**: 173 **Census**: 56 **Outpatient Visits**: 401 **Births**: 0 **Total Expense ($000)**: 38239 **Payroll Expense ($000)**: 18582 **Personnel**: 198

PORTER ADVENTIST HOSPITAL See Adventhealth Porter

⊞ **PRESBYTERIAN/ST. LUKE'S MEDICAL CENTER (060014)**, 1719 East 19th Avenue, Zip 80218–1281; tel. 720/754–6000, (Includes ROCKY MOUNTAIN HOSPITAL FOR CHILDREN, 1719 East 19th Avenue, Denver, Colorado, Zip 80218–1235, tel. 720/754–1000; Maureen Tarrant-Fitzgerald, President and Chief Executive Officer) **A**1 2 3 5 8 10 19 **F**3 11 13 14 18 19 20 21 22 23 25 26 27 29 30 31 34 35 36 37 40 41 43 44 45 46 47 48 49 50 53 55 56 59 61 64 68 70 71 72 73 74 75 76 77 78 79 81 82 84 85 87 88 89 92 93 102 107 111 114 115 117 118 119 120 121 123 126 130 136 138 139 146 147 148 149 156 162 164 167 169 **S** HCA Healthcare, Nashville, TN
Primary Contact: David Donaldson, President and Chief Executive Assistant
CFO: Phillip Sensing, Chief Financial Officer
CMO: Andrew Weinfield, Chief Medical Officer
CIO: Ley Samson, Chief Information Officer
CHR: Keri Moore, Vice President Human Resources and Support Services
CNO: John Goerke, Chief Nursing Officer
Web address: https://www.healthonecares.com/locations/presbyterian-st-lukes-medical-center
Control: Corporation, Investor–owned (for–profit) **Service**: General medical and surgical

Staffed Beds: 381 **Admissions**: 10051 **Census**: 221 **Outpatient Visits**: 102739 **Births**: 1287 **Personnel**: 1147

Hospitals, U.S. / COLORADO

REUNION REHABILITATION HOSPITAL DENVER (063036), 4650 Central Park Boulevard, Zip 80238; tel. 720/734-3500, (Nonreporting) **A**10 22 **S** Nobis Rehabilitation Partners, Allen, TX
Primary Contact: Erika Kaye, Chief Executive Officer
CFO: Jerry Huggler, Chief, Finance
CMO: Reza Esfahani, M.D., Medical Director
CIO: Kyle Johnson, Corporate Director, Information Technology
CHR: Michelle Clopton, Director, Human Resources
CNO: Laura Dechant, Chief Nursing Officer
Web address: https://reunionrehabhospital.com/locations/denver/
Control: Partnership, Investor-owned (for-profit) **Service**: Rehabilitation

Staffed Beds: 40

ROSE MEDICAL CENTER (060032), 4567 East Ninth Avenue, Zip 80220-3941; tel. 303/320-2121, (Nonreporting) **A**1 2 3 5 10 19 **S** HCA Healthcare, Nashville, TN
Primary Contact: Casey Guber, President and Chief Executive Officer
CFO: Jac Connelly, Chief Financial Officer
CMO: Andrew Ziller, M.D., Chief Medical Officer
CIO: Dave Trevathan, Director Information Systems
CHR: Clarence McDavid, Vice President Human Resources
CNO: Laura Thornley, MSN, R.N., Chief Nursing Officer
Web address: www.rosebabies.com
Control: Corporation, Investor-owned (for-profit) **Service**: General medical and surgical

Staffed Beds: 247

DURANGO—La Plata County

ANIMAS SURGICAL HOSPITAL (060117), 575 Rivergate Lane, Zip 81301-7487; tel. 970/247-3537, (Nonreporting) **A**10
Primary Contact: Meggin Roberts, Chief Executive Officer
Web address: www.animassurgical.com/
Control: Corporation, Investor-owned (for-profit) **Service**: Surgical

Staffed Beds: 12

COMMONSPIRIT – MERCY HOSPITAL (060013), 1010 Three Springs Boulevard, Zip 81301-8296; tel. 970/247-4311, **A**1 2 10 20 **F**3 11 13 15 18 20 22 24 26 27 28 29 30 31 35 36 40 43 45 49 50 55 59 60 61 70 74 75 76 78 79 81 83 84 85 87 93 94 96 97 107 108 111 115 119 120 126 127 129 130 131 132 133 135 144 146 147 148 149 150 154 155 156 167 169 **S** CommonSpirit Health, Chicago, IL
Primary Contact: Josh Neff, Chief Executive Officer
CFO: Jane Strobel, Vice President and Chief Financial Officer
CMO: William Plauth, M.D., Vice President Operations and Chief Medical Officer
CIO: Neil Stock, Director Technology and Facilities
CHR: Cathy Roberts, Vice President Mission Integration and Human Resources
CNO: Nancy Gerilyn Hoyt, R.N., Vice President Operations, Clinical and Chief Nursing Officer
Web address: www.mercydurango.org
Control: Church operated, Nongovernment, not-for-profit **Service**: General medical and surgical

Staffed Beds: 82 Admissions: 4644 Census: 48 Outpatient Visits: 136108 Births: 793 Total Expense ($000): 183591 Payroll Expense ($000): 55796

EADS—Kiowa County

★ **WEISBROD MEMORIAL COUNTY HOSPITAL (061300)**, 1208 Luther Street, Zip 81036, Mailing Address: P.O. Box 817, Zip 81036-0817; tel. 719/438-5401, (Nonreporting) **A**10 18
Primary Contact: Beth Bell, Chief Executive Officer
CFO: Shannon Dixon, Chief Financial Officer
CMO: Jeff Waggoner, M.D., Chief of Staff
CHR: Shannon Dixon, Chief Financial Officer
CNO: Wendy McDowell, R.N., Director of Nursing
Web address: www.kchd.org
Control: County, Government, Nonfederal **Service**: General medical and surgical

Staffed Beds: 25

ENGLEWOOD—Arapahoe County

CRAIG HOSPITAL (062011), 3425 South Clarkson Street, Zip 80113-2899; tel. 303/789-8000, **A**1 3 5 10 **F**3 29 30 34 35 44 50 53 57 58 59 64 74 75 77 81 86 87 90 91 93 95 96 130 132 135 146 148 149 154 157 164
Primary Contact: Jandel Allen-Davis, M.D., President and Chief Executive Officer
CFO: Daniel Frank, Chief Financial Officer
CMO: Thomas E Balazy, M.D., Medical Director
CHR: Stacy L Abel, Vice President People and Culture
CNO: Diane Reinhard, R.N., Vice President of Patient Care Services
Web address: www.craighospital.org
Control: Other not-for-profit (including NFP Corporation) **Service**: Rehabilitation

Staffed Beds: 88 Admissions: 476 Census: 80 Births: 0 Total Expense ($000): 145669 Payroll Expense ($000): 79098 Personnel: 918

☐ **DENVER SPRINGS (064028)**, 8835 American Way, Zip 80112-7056; tel. 720/643-4300, (Nonreporting) **A**1 10 **S** Springstone, Louisville, KY
Primary Contact: Scott Acus, Chief Executive Officer
Web address: www.denversprings.com/
Control: Other not-for-profit (including NFP Corporation) **Service**: Psychiatric

Staffed Beds: 96

SWEDISH MEDICAL CENTER (060034), 501 East Hampden Avenue, Zip 80113-2702; tel. 303/788-5000, (Nonreporting) **A**1 2 3 5 10 19 **S** HCA Healthcare, Nashville, TN
Primary Contact: Scott Davis, President/Chief Executive Officer
CFO: Kathy Ashenfelter, Chief Financial Officer
CIO: Jeff Schnoor, Director Information Systems
CHR: Lisa Morris, Vice President Human Resources
CNO: Shari Chavez, Chief Nursing Officer
Web address: www.swedishhospital.com
Control: Partnership, Investor-owned (for-profit) **Service**: General medical and surgical

Staffed Beds: 371

ENGLEWOOD—Douglas County

REUNION REHABILITATION HOSPITAL INVERNESS (063038), 372 Inverness Drive South, Zip 80112-5899; tel. 720/741-8800, (Nonreporting) **A**10 **S** Nobis Rehabilitation Partners, Allen, TX
Primary Contact: Lonnie Martinez, Chief Executive Officer
Web address: https://reunionrehabhospital.com/locations/inverness/
Control: Corporation, Investor-owned (for-profit) **Service**: Rehabilitation

Staffed Beds: 40

ESTES PARK—Larimer County

⇑ **ESTES PARK HEALTH (061312)**, 555 Prospect Avenue, Zip 80517-6312, Mailing Address: P.O. Box 2740, Zip 80517-2740; tel. 970/586-2317, (Nonreporting) **A**10 18 21
Primary Contact: Vern Carda, Chief Executive Officer
CFO: Tim Cashman, Chief Financial Officer
CMO: Paul Fonken, M.D., Chief of Staff
CHR: Randy Brigham, Chief Human Resource Officer
Web address: www.epmedcenter.com
Control: Hospital district or authority, Government, Nonfederal **Service**: General medical and surgical

Staffed Beds: 79

⇑ **ESTES PARK MEDICAL CENTER** See Estes Park Health

FORT CARSON—El Paso County

EVANS U. S. ARMY COMMUNITY HOSPITAL, 1650 Cochrane Circle, Building 7500, Zip 80913-4613; tel. 719/526-7200, (Nonreporting) **A**1 3 **S** Department of the Army, Office of the Surgeon General, Falls Church, VA
Primary Contact: Colonel Kevin R. Bass, Commander
CFO: Major Bradley Robinson, Chief Financial Officer
CHR: Lieutenant Colonel Lory Gurr, Chief Human Resources Division
Web address: https://evans.tricare.mil/
Control: Army, Government, federal **Service**: General medical and surgical

Staffed Beds: 68

Hospital, Medicare Provider Number, Address, Telephone, Approval, Facility, and Physician Codes, Health Care System

★ American Hospital Association (AHA) membership
☐ The Joint Commission accreditation
○ Healthcare Facilities Accreditation Program
◇ DNV Healthcare Inc. accreditation
⇑ Center for Improvement in Healthcare Quality Accreditation
△ Commission on Accreditation of Rehabilitation Facilities (CARF) accreditation

Hospitals, U.S. / COLORADO

FORT COLLINS—Larimer County

BANNER FORT COLLINS MEDICAL CENTER (060126), 4700 Lady Moon Drive, Zip 80528–4426; tel. 970/821–4000, **A**1 10 57 **F**3 11 12 13 15 18 20 22 26 29 30 34 40 43 44 45 50 53 54 57 59 60 63 65 68 70 74 76 77 78 79 81 84 85 86 87 89 97 100 102 107 108 110 111 114 115 119 124 126 130 144 146 147 148 149 154 157 167 169 **S** Banner Health, Phoenix, AZ
Primary Contact: Alan Qualls, Chief Executive Officer
COO: Chris Kerrigan, Interim Chief Operating Officer
CMO: Steven Loecke, M.D., Chief Medical Officer
CHR: Kelly Hurt, Chief Human Resources Officer Northern Colorado and Western Region
CNO: Julia Gentry, Chief Nursing Officer, Northern Colorado
Web address: https://www.bannerhealth.com/locations/fort-collins/banner-fort-collins-medical-center
Control: Other not–for–profit (including NFP Corporation) **Service**: General medical and surgical

Staffed Beds: 29 **Admissions**: 1393 **Census**: 11 **Outpatient Visits**: 19549 **Births**: 598 **Total Expense ($000)**: 56577 **Payroll Expense ($000)**: 15752 **Personnel**: 141

UCHEALTH POUDRE VALLEY HOSPITAL (060010), 1024 South Lemay Avenue, Zip 80524–3998, Mailing Address: 2315 East Harmony Road, Suite 200, Zip 80528; tel. 970/495–7000, (Includes MOUNTAIN CREST HOSPITAL, 4601 Corbett Drive, Fort Collins, Colorado, Zip 80525, tel. 970/270–4800) **A**1 2 3 5 10 19 **F**3 4 5 7 9 11 12 13 14 15 18 20 22 26 28 29 30 31 32 34 35 36 38 39 40 42 43 45 46 47 49 50 51 54 55 56 58 59 61 63 64 65 66 68 69 70 72 74 75 76 77 78 79 81 82 84 85 87 90 93 96 97 98 99 100 101 102 103 104 105 107 108 110 111 114 115 118 119 120 121 123 124 126 129 130 131 132 135 143 146 147 148 149 150 151 152 153 154 156 157 160 161 163 164 165 167 169 **S** UCHealth, Aurora, CO
Primary Contact: Kevin L. Unger, Ph.D., FACHE, President and Chief Executive Officer
COO: Ryan Rohman, MSN, R.N., Chief Operating Officer
CFO: Stephanie Doughty, Chief Financial Officer
CIO: Fernando Pedroza, Vice President Information Technology
Web address: www.uchealth.org
Control: Other not–for–profit (including NFP Corporation) **Service**: General medical and surgical

Staffed Beds: 263 **Admissions**: 12975 **Census**: 177 **Outpatient Visits**: 751054 **Births**: 1713 **Total Expense ($000)**: 705886 **Payroll Expense ($000)**: 253930 **Personnel**: 2881

FORT MORGAN—Morgan County

COLORADO PLAINS MEDICAL CENTER See Common Spirit St. Elizabeth Hospital

COMMON SPIRIT ST. ELIZABETH HOSPITAL (060044), 1000 Lincoln Street, Zip 80701–3298; tel. 970/867–3391, **A**1 3 10 20 **F**3 15 29 30 31 34 35 40 43 45 50 53 54 56 57 59 65 68 70 76 77 81 91 93 97 100 107 108 111 112 115 119 120 146 147 148 154 169 **S** CommonSpirit Health, Chicago, IL
Primary Contact: John Swanhorst, Interim Chief Executive Officer
CHR: Janet Brinkman, Director Human Resources
Web address: https://www.centura.org/location/st-elizabeth-hospital
Control: Other not–for–profit (including NFP Corporation) **Service**: General medical and surgical

Staffed Beds: 34 **Admissions**: 782 **Census**: 7 **Outpatient Visits**: 31833 **Births**: 212 **Total Expense ($000)**: 33979 **Payroll Expense ($000)**: 12146 **Personnel**: 127

FRISCO—Summit County

COMMONSPIRIT - ST. ANTHONY SUMMIT MEDICAL CENTER (060118), 340 Peak One Drive, Zip 80443, Mailing Address: P.O. Box 738, Zip 80443–0738; tel. 970/668–3300, **A**1 10 20 **F**3 13 15 29 30 34 35 40 43 45 57 59 66 68 70 75 76 77 79 81 82 84 85 97 107 110 111 119 130 132 133 146 147 169 **S** CommonSpirit Health, Chicago, IL
Primary Contact: Trixie VanderSchaaff, Chief Executive Officer
CNO: Trixie VanderSchaaff, Chief Nursing Officer
Web address: www.summitmedicalcenter.org
Control: Church operated, Nongovernment, not–for–profit **Service**: General medical and surgical

Staffed Beds: 34 **Admissions**: 1346 **Census**: 9 **Outpatient Visits**: 29084 **Births**: 404 **Total Expense ($000)**: 69382 **Payroll Expense ($000)**: 25421 **Personnel**: 206

FRUITA—Mesa County

COLORADO CANYONS HOSPITAL AND MEDICAL CENTER See Family Health West

★ **FAMILY HEALTH WEST (061302)**, 300 West Ottley Avenue, Zip 81521–2118, Mailing Address: P.O. Box 130, Zip 81521–0130; tel. 970/858–9871, **A**10 18 **F**3 9 10 15 29 30 32 34 35 36 40 41 43 44 45 50 53 54 56 57 59 64 65 67 68 71 74 75 77 79 81 82 85 86 87 90 91 93 96 97 107 110 111 115 119 124 128 130 131 133 143 146 148 149 154 156 160 167 **P**6
Primary Contact: Korrey Klein, M.D., President and Chief Executive Offricer
COO: Lori Randall, R.N., Executive Vice President, Chief Nursing Officer, Chief Operating Officer and Hospital Administrator
CFO: Theresa Tabor, Vice President of Finance and Chief Financial Officer
CMO: Christopher Taggart, M.D., Chief Medical Officer
CIO: Derrick Diddle, Director of Information Technology
CHR: Kimber Barnes, Director of Human Resources
CNO: Lori Randall, R.N., Executive Vice President, Chief Nursing Officer, Chief Operating Officer and Hospital Administrator
Web address: www.fhw.org
Control: Other not–for–profit (including NFP Corporation) **Service**: General medical and surgical

Staffed Beds: 25 **Admissions**: 460 **Census**: 15 **Outpatient Visits**: 49078 **Births**: 0 **Total Expense ($000)**: 80395 **Payroll Expense ($000)**: 40565 **Personnel**: 385

GLENWOOD SPRINGS—Garfield County

VALLEY VIEW HOSPITAL (060075), 1906 Blake Avenue, Zip 81601–4259; tel. 970/945–6535, (Nonreporting) **A**1 2 10 20
Primary Contact: Brian Murphy, M.D., Chief Executive Officer
COO: Daniel Biggs, Chief Operating Officer
CFO: Charles Crevling, Chief Financial Officer
CMO: David Brooks, M.D., Chief Medical Officer
CNO: Dawn Sculco, Chief Nursing Officer
Web address: www.vvh.org
Control: Other not–for–profit (including NFP Corporation) **Service**: General medical and surgical

Staffed Beds: 49

GRAND JUNCTION—Mesa County

COMMUNITY HOSPITAL (060054), 2351 G Road, Zip 81505; tel. 970/242–0920, (Nonreporting) **A**1 2 10 **S** Ovation Healthcare, Brentwood, TN
Primary Contact: Chris Thomas, FACHE, President and Chief Executive Officer
COO: Joe Gerardi, R.N., Chief Operating Officer, Chief Nursing Officer
CFO: Pete Young, Interim Chief Financial Officer
CMO: Thomas Tobin, Chief Medical Officer
CIO: Bart Butzine, Director Information Technology
CHR: Amy Jordan, Chief Human Resources Officer
CNO: Joe Gerardi, R.N., Chief Operating Officer, Chief Nursing Officer
Web address: www.yourcommunityhospital.com
Control: Other not–for–profit (including NFP Corporation) **Service**: General medical and surgical

Staffed Beds: 44

GRAND JUNCTION VA MEDICAL CENTER, 2121 North Avenue, Zip 81501–6428; tel. 970/242–0731, (Nonreporting) **A**1 **S** Department of Veterans Affairs, Washington, DC
Primary Contact: Richard W. Salgueiro, Medical Center Director
COO: Patricia A Hitt, Associate Director
CFO: Laquita Gruver, Fiscal Officer
CMO: William R Berryman, M.D., Chief of Staff
CIO: Craig Frerichs, Chief Information Technology Service
CHR: William Chester, Manager Human Resources
Web address: www.grandjunction.va.gov/
Control: Veterans Affairs, Government, federal **Service**: General medical and surgical

Staffed Beds: 20

Hospitals, U.S. / COLORADO

☒ **INTERMOUNTAIN HEALTH ST. MARY'S REGIONAL HOSPITAL (060023)**, 2635 North 7th Street, Zip 81501–8209, Mailing Address: P.O. Box 1628, Zip 81502–1628; tel. 970/298–2273, **A**1 2 3 5 10 **F**3 5 7 11 12 13 15 17 18 19 20 22 24 26 28 29 30 31 34 35 37 40 41 43 45 46 48 49 50 51 54 55 58 59 60 61 64 65 68 69 70 72 74 75 76 77 78 79 81 82 84 85 86 87 89 90 91 92 93 96 97 107 108 109 110 111 113 114 115 116 117 119 120 121 122 123 124 126 129 130 132 135 143 145 146 147 148 149 154 156 167 169 **S** Intermountain Health, Salt Lake City, UT
Primary Contact: Bryan L. Johnson, President
COO: Reza Kaleel, Executive Vice President and Chief Operating Officer
CFO: Terri Chinn, Vice President Finance
CMO: Michele Arnold, M.D., Vice President and Chief Medical Officer
CIO: John Bullard, Director Information Technology
CHR: Judy White House, FACHE, Vice President Human Resources
CNO: Shelley Peterson, R.N., Vice President Patient Services and Chief Nursing Officer
Web address: www.stmarygj.com
Control: Other not–for–profit (including NFP Corporation) **Service**: General medical and surgical

Staffed Beds: 334 **Admissions**: 11665 **Census**: 163 **Outpatient Visits**: 213021 **Births**: 1241 **Total Expense ($000)**: 576739 **Payroll Expense ($000)**: 168346 **Personnel**: 2827

WEST SPRINGS HOSPITAL (064023), 515 28 3/4 Road, Zip 81501–5016; tel. 970/263–4918, (Nonreporting) **A**10
Primary Contact: John Sheehan, Chief Executive Officer
COO: Brandi Kroese, Director Operations
CFO: John Rattle, Chief Financial Officer
CMO: Jules Rosen, M.D., Chief Medical Officer
CIO: Charles Andrews, Director Information Technology
CHR: Karen Birmingham, Director Human Resources
CNO: Deborah Sharpe, R.N., Director of Nursing
Web address: www.WestSpringsHospital.org
Control: Other not–for–profit (including NFP Corporation) **Service**: Psychiatric

Staffed Beds: 32

GREELEY—Weld County

☒ **BANNER NORTH COLORADO MEDICAL CENTERNORTH COLORADO MEDICAL CENTER (060001)**, 1801 16th Street, Zip 80631–5154; tel. 970/352–4121, **A**1 2 3 5 10 **F**3 8 11 13 15 17 18 20 22 24 26 28 29 30 31 34 35 40 42 43 44 45 46 47 48 49 50 51 53 54 55 57 58 59 60 61 63 64 65 67 70 72 73 74 75 76 77 78 79 81 84 85 86 87 89 93 100 102 107 108 110 111 114 115 118 119 120 121 123 124 126 129 130 131 132 135 146 148 149 154 156 160 164 167 **S** Banner Health, Phoenix, AZ
Primary Contact: Alan Qualls, Chief Executive Officer
COO: Chris Kerrigan, Interim Chief Operating Officer
CMO: Angela Mills, Chief Medical Officer
CHR: Jeannie Gallagher, Chief Human Resource Officer
CNO: Julia Gentry, Chief Nursing Officer, Northern Colorado
Web address: www.ncmcgreeley.com
Control: Other not–for–profit (including NFP Corporation) **Service**: General medical and surgical

Staffed Beds: 266 **Admissions**: 8202 **Census**: 108 **Outpatient Visits**: 89047 **Births**: 1325 **Total Expense ($000)**: 352695 **Payroll Expense ($000)**: 102377 **Personnel**: 1060

☒ **UCHEALTH GREELEY HOSPITAL (060131)**, 6767 29th Street, Zip 80634–5474; tel. 970/652–2000, **A**1 2 10 **F**3 11 13 15 18 20 22 29 30 31 34 35 40 43 45 49 50 51 54 59 64 65 68 70 74 75 76 77 78 79 81 84 85 87 96 102 107 110 111 114 115 119 126 130 143 146 148 149 154 160 161 164 167 169 **S** UCHealth, Aurora, CO
Primary Contact: Marilyn Schock, President
CNO: Kay J Miller, R.N., MSN, Chief Nursing Officer
Web address: https://www.uchealth.org/locations/uchealth-greeley-medical-clinic/
Control: Other not–for–profit (including NFP Corporation) **Service**: General medical and surgical

Staffed Beds: 91 **Admissions**: 3952 **Census**: 44 **Outpatient Visits**: 193192 **Births**: 817 **Total Expense ($000)**: 196650 **Payroll Expense ($000)**: 61758 **Personnel**: 780

GUNNISON—Gunnison County

☒ **GUNNISON VALLEY HEALTH (061320)**, 711 North Taylor Street, Zip 81230–2296; tel. 970/641–1456, (Nonreporting) **A**1 10 18
Primary Contact: Jason Amrich, Chief Executive Officer
CFO: Mark L. VanderVeer, Chief Financial Officer
CIO: Trevor Smith, Chief Management Information Services
CHR: Christina Lovelace, Director Human Resources
Web address: https://www.gunnisonvalleyhealth.org/
Control: County, Government, Nonfederal **Service**: General medical and surgical

Staffed Beds: 24

GUNNISON VALLEY HOSPITAL See Gunnison Valley Health

HAXTUN—Phillips County

★ **HAXTUN HOSPITAL DISTRICT (061304)**, 235 West Fletcher Street, Zip 80731–2737; tel. 970/774–6123, (Nonreporting) **A**10 18
Primary Contact: Dewane Pace, Chief Executive Officer
CFO: Rick Lee Nader, Chief Financial Officer
CMO: Colby Jolley, D.O., Acting Chief of Staff
CIO: Andrea Evers, Director Information Technology
CNO: Gail Phelps, R.N., Chief Nursing Officer
Web address: www.haxtunhealth.org
Control: Hospital district or authority, Government, Nonfederal **Service**: General medical and surgical

Staffed Beds: 25

HIGHLANDS RANCH—Douglas County

☐ **UCHEALTH HIGHLANDS RANCH HOSPITAL (060132)**, 1500 Park Central Drive, Zip 80129–6688; tel. 720/848–0000, **A**1 2 10 **F**3 11 13 14 15 18 20 22 26 29 30 31 34 35 37 38 40 43 46 47 49 50 56 59 61 64 65 68 70 72 74 75 76 77 78 79 81 82 84 85 86 87 92 102 107 108 109 110 111 115 116 117 118 119 126 130 131 132 135 146 147 148 149 154 156 164 167 **S** UCHealth, Aurora, CO
Primary Contact: Merle Taylor, President
CMO: Tom Purcell, Chief Medical Officer
Web address: https://www.uchealth.org/locations/uchealth-highlands-ranch-hospital/
Control: Other not–for–profit (including NFP Corporation) **Service**: General medical and surgical

Staffed Beds: 93 **Admissions**: 6085 **Census**: 71 **Outpatient Visits**: 137792 **Births**: 1148 **Total Expense ($000)**: 267975 **Payroll Expense ($000)**: 80695 **Personnel**: 878

HOLYOKE—Phillips County

★ **MELISSA MEMORIAL HOSPITAL (061305)**, 1001 East Johnson Street, Zip 80734–1854; tel. 970/854–2241, (Nonreporting) **A**10 18
Primary Contact: Michael Hassell, Chief Executive Officer
CFO: Jason McCormick, Interim Chief Financial Officer
CMO: Dennis Jelden, M.D., Chief of Staff
CIO: David Bickford, Chief Information Officer
CHR: Sharon Greenman, Director Human Resources
CNO: Pat Notter, R.N., Chief Nursing Officer and Director Quality
Web address: www.melissamemorial.org
Control: Hospital district or authority, Government, Nonfederal **Service**: General medical and surgical

Staffed Beds: 15

HUGO—Lincoln County

⇑ **LINCOLN COMMUNITY HOSPITAL AND NURSING HOME** See Lincoln Health

Hospitals, U.S. / COLORADO

★ ⇧ **LINCOLN HEALTH (061306)**, 111 6th Street, Zip 80821–0248, Mailing Address: P.O. Box 248, Zip 80821–0248; tel. 719/743–2421, (Total facility includes 22 beds in nursing home–type unit) **A**10 18 21 **F**5 7 8 10 13 15 28 29 31 34 35 38 40 43 45 50 56 59 62 63 64 67 71 75 77 78 79 81 82 87 89 93 97 102 107 111 114 119 128 130 133 135 154 160 164 169
Primary Contact: Kevin M. Stansbury, Chief Executive Officer
CFO: Darcy Howard, Interim Chief Financial Officer
CMO: Mark Olson, M.D., Chief of Staff
CIO: Michael Gaskins, Director Information Technology
CHR: Susan Petersen, Human Resources
CNO: Dan Walker, Chief Nursing Officer
Web address: www.lincolncommunityhospital.com
Control: County, Government, Nonfederal **Service**: General medical and surgical

Staffed Beds: 37 **Admissions**: 207 **Census**: 18 **Outpatient Visits**: 20175 **Births**: 0 **Total Expense ($000)**: 30926 **Payroll Expense ($000)**: 11545 **Personnel**: 141

JOHNSTOWN—Larimer County

☐ **NORTHERN COLORADO LONG TERM ACUTE HOSPITAL (062017)**, 4401 Union Street, Zip 80534; tel. 970/619–3663, (Nonreporting) **A**1 10 **S** Ernest Health, Inc., Albuquerque, NM
Primary Contact: Christina Lea. Salas, Chief Executive Officer
Web address: www.ncltah.ernesthealth.com/
Control: Partnership, Investor–owned (for–profit) **Service**: Acute long–term care hospital

Staffed Beds: 40

☐ **NORTHERN COLORADO REHABILITATION HOSPITAL (063033)**, 4401 Union Street, Zip 80534–2800; tel. 970/619–3400, (Nonreporting) **A**1 10 **S** Ernest Health, Inc., Albuquerque, NM
Primary Contact: Christina Lea. Salas, Chief Executive Officer
CFO: Bonnie Cushman, Chief Financial Officer
CMO: Revelyn Arrogante, M.D., Medical Director
CHR: Amy Lauridsen, Director Human Resources
CNO: Mark Smith, Director Nursing Operations
Web address: www.ncrh.ernesthealth.com
Control: Corporation, Investor–owned (for–profit) **Service**: Rehabilitation

Staffed Beds: 40

JULESBURG—Sedgwick County

SEDGWICK COUNTY HEALTH CENTER (061310), 900 Cedar Street, Zip 80737–1199; tel. 970/474–3323, (Nonreporting) **A**10 18
Primary Contact: Aidan Hettler, Chief Executive Officer
CFO: Karla Dunker, Chief Financial Officer
CMO: Donald Regier, M.D., Chief Medical Officer
CHR: Sonja Bell, Coordinator Human Resources
Web address: www.schealth.org/
Control: County, Government, Nonfederal **Service**: General medical and surgical

Staffed Beds: 67

KREMMLING—Grand County

★ **MIDDLE PARK HEALTH–KREMMLING (061318)**, 214 South Fourth Street, Zip 80459, Mailing Address: P.O. Box 399, Zip 80459–0399; tel. 970/724–3442, (Includes MIDDLE PARK MEDICAL CENTER – GRANBY, 1000 Granby Park Drive South, Granby, Colorado, Zip 80446, P.O. Box 399, Kremmling, Zip 80446, tel. 970/887–5800; Jason Cleckler, Chief Executive Officer) (Nonreporting) **A**10 18
Primary Contact: Jason Cleckler, Chief Executive Officer
CMO: Thomas C. Coburn, M.D., Chief Medical Officer
CHR: Jason Bryan, Director Human Resources
CNO: Debra Plemmons, Chief Nursing Officer
Web address: www.mpmc.org
Control: Hospital district or authority, Government, Nonfederal **Service**: General medical and surgical

Staffed Beds: 10

LA JARA—Conejos County

★ **SAN LUIS VALLEY HEALTH CONEJOS COUNTY HOSPITAL (061308)**, 19021 US Highway 285, Zip 81140–0639, Mailing Address: P.O. Box 639, Zip 81140–0639; tel. 719/274–5121, (Nonreporting) **A**10 18 **S** San Luis Valley Health, Alamosa, CO
Primary Contact: Konnie Martin, President and Chief Executive Officer
CFO: Shane Mortensen, Chief Financial Officer
CIO: Kathy Rogers, Vice President Marketing
CHR: Mandy Lee Crockett, Director Human Resources
CNO: Tandra Dunn, Director of Nursing
Web address: www.sanluisvalleyhealth.org/locations/conejos-county-hospital
Control: Other not–for–profit (including NFP Corporation) **Service**: General medical and surgical

Staffed Beds: 17

LA JUNTA—Otero County

⊞ **ARKANSAS VALLEY REGIONAL MEDICAL CENTER (061336)**, 1100 Carson Avenue, Zip 81050–2799; tel. 719/469–2292, (Nonreporting) **A**1 10 18
Primary Contact: David Andrew. Flemer Jr, Chief Executive Officer
CMO: Kent E. Gay, M.D., Chief of Medical Staff
CIO: Heidi Gearhart, Director Information Systems
CHR: Kelsey B. Herman, Director Human Resources
CNO: Carrie Cutrell, Chief Nursing Officer
Web address: www.avrmc.org
Control: Other not–for–profit (including NFP Corporation) **Service**: General medical and surgical

Staffed Beds: 106

LAFAYETTE—Boulder County

⊞ **GOOD SAMARITAN MEDICAL CENTER (060116)**, 200 Exempla Circle, Zip 80026–3370; tel. 303/689–4000, **A**1 2 10 **F**3 4 11 13 15 18 20 22 26 28 29 30 31 32 34 35 37 40 41 43 45 46 47 49 50 51 59 60 64 68 70 72 74 75 76 77 78 79 80 81 84 85 86 87 90 91 92 93 98 100 102 107 108 110 111 114 115 117 118 119 120 121 123 124 126 130 146 147 148 149 150 154 156 162 167 169 **S** Intermountain Health, Salt Lake City, UT
COO: Steven D. Hankins, Chief Operating Officer
CFO: Troy Stoehr, Vice President and Chief Financial Officer
CMO: Toni Green–Cheatwood, M.D., Vice President and Chief Medical Officer
CNO: Ann M. Gantzer, Ph.D., R.N., Chief Nursing Officer
Web address: https://www.sclhealth.org/locations/good-samaritan-medical-center/
Control: Other not–for–profit (including NFP Corporation) **Service**: General medical and surgical

Staffed Beds: 185 **Admissions**: 10555 **Census**: 128 **Outpatient Visits**: 85234 **Births**: 1325 **Total Expense ($000)**: 361464 **Payroll Expense ($000)**: 114662 **Personnel**: 972

LAKEWOOD—Jefferson County

⊞ **ORTHOCOLORADO HOSPITAL (060124)**, 11650 West 2nd Place, Zip 80228–1527; tel. 720/321–5000, **A**1 10 **F**79 81 107 111 119 126 **S** CommonSpirit Health, Chicago, IL
Primary Contact: Jude Torchia, Chief Executive Officer
Web address: www.orthocolorado.org
Control: Church operated, Nongovernment, not–for–profit **Service**: Orthopedic

Staffed Beds: 48 **Admissions**: 822 **Census**: 6 **Outpatient Visits**: 4470 **Births**: 0 **Total Expense ($000)**: 72299 **Payroll Expense ($000)**: 17175 **Personnel**: 139

⊞ **ST. ANTHONY HOSPITAL (060015)**, 11600 West Second Place, Zip 80228–1527; tel. 720/321–0000, **A**1 2 3 5 10 19 **F**3 11 15 17 18 20 22 24 26 28 29 30 31 34 35 36 38 39 40 42 43 45 46 47 48 49 50 55 56 57 59 63 64 65 68 70 74 75 77 78 79 80 81 82 84 85 87 90 92 93 96 102 107 108 110 111 114 115 116 117 118 119 126 130 131 132 135 144 146 147 148 149 155 156 164 167 **P**6 **S** CommonSpirit Health, Chicago, IL
Primary Contact: Kevin Cullinan, Chief Executive Officer
CHR: Michelle Fornier–Johnson, Group Vice President Human Resources
Web address: www.stanthonyhosp.org
Control: Church operated, Nongovernment, not–for–profit **Service**: General medical and surgical

Staffed Beds: 237 **Admissions**: 13049 **Census**: 195 **Outpatient Visits**: 89523 **Births**: 0 **Total Expense ($000)**: 391409 **Payroll Expense ($000)**: 142615 **Personnel**: 1109

Hospitals, U.S. / COLORADO

LAMAR—Prowers County

★ ⇧ **PROWERS MEDICAL CENTER (061323)**, 401 Kendall Drive, Zip 81052–3993; tel. 719/336–4343, (Nonreporting) **A**10 18 21 **S** Ovation Healthcare, Brentwood, TN
Primary Contact: Karen L. Bryant, Chief Executive Officer
CFO: Steve Gilgen, Chief Financial Officer
CMO: Barry Portner, M.D., Chief of Staff
CIO: Jason Spano, Director of Information Technology
Web address: www.prowersmedical.com
Control: Hospital district or authority, Government, Nonfederal **Service:** General medical and surgical

Staffed Beds: 25

LAS ANIMAS—Bent County

VETERANS AFFAIRS MED CENTER See Southern Colorado Healthcare System

LEADVILLE—Lake County

★ **ST. VINCENT HEALTH (061319)**, 822 West 4th Street, Zip 80461–3897; tel. 719/486–0230, (Nonreporting) **A**10 18
Primary Contact: Andy Dreesen, Chief Executive Officer
CMO: Gary Petry, M.D., Chief of Staff
CHR: Cheryl Snider, Director Human Resources
CNO: Von Kilpatrick, Chief Nursing Officer
Web address: www.svghd.org
Control: Hospital district or authority, Government, Nonfederal **Service:** General medical and surgical

Staffed Beds: 8

LITTLETON—Arapahoe County

⊞ **ADVENTHEALTH LITTLETON (060113)**, 7700 South Broadway Street, Zip 80122–2628; tel. 303/730–8900, **A**1 3 5 10 **F**3 11 13 15 18 20 22 26 29 30 31 34 35 36 39 40 41 42 43 44 45 46 47 48 49 50 53 54 55 57 58 59 60 64 68 70 72 74 75 76 77 78 79 81 82 83 84 85 86 87 89 91 92 93 97 107 108 110 111 114 115 116 117 118 119 120 121 126 130 131 132 135 146 147 148 156 167 169 **P**6 **S** AdventHealth, Altamonte Springs, FL
Primary Contact: Rick Dodds, Chief Executive Officer
COO: Chase Aalborg, Chief Operating Officer
CMO: Matthew Mendenhall, M.D., Chief Medical Officer
CHR: Rita K Arthur, Director Human Resources
CNO: Kelley Kovar, R.N., Chief Nursing Officer
Web address: https://www.adventhealth.com/hospital/adventhealth-littleton
Control: Church operated, Nongovernment, not-for-profit **Service:** General medical and surgical

Staffed Beds: 221 **Admissions:** 9350 **Census:** 113 **Outpatient Visits:** 63182 **Births:** 1743 **Total Expense ($000):** 238583 **Payroll Expense ($000):** 88909 **Personnel:** 972

⊞ **ENCOMPASS HEALTH REHABILITATION HOSPITAL OF LITTLETON (063034)**, 1001 West Mineral Avenue, Zip 80120–4507; tel. 303/334–1100, (Nonreporting) **A**1 10 **S** Encompass Health Corporation, Birmingham, AL
Primary Contact: Noomi Hirsch, Chief Executive Officer
CMO: Jill Castro, M.D., Medical Director
CHR: Sarah Thomas, Director of Human Resources
Web address: www.healthsouthdenver.com
Control: Corporation, Investor-owned (for-profit) **Service:** Rehabilitation

Staffed Beds: 48

LITTLETON ADVENTIST HOSPITAL See Adventhealth Littleton

LITTLETON—Douglas County

☐ **HIGHLANDS BEHAVIORAL HEALTH SYSTEM (064024)**, 8565 South Poplar Way, Zip 80130–3602; tel. 720/348–2800, (Nonreporting) **A**1 10 **S** Universal Health Services, Inc., King of Prussia, PA
Primary Contact: Kelly Ulreich, Executive Director
Web address: www.highlandsbhs.com
Control: Corporation, Investor-owned (for-profit) **Service:** Psychiatric

Staffed Beds: 86

LITTLETON—Jefferson County

FEDERAL CORRECTIONAL INSTITUTE HOSPITAL, 9595 West Quincy Street, Zip 80123–1159; tel. 303/985–1566, (Nonreporting)
Primary Contact: Mike Hudson, Administrator
Web address: https://www.bop.gov/locations/institutions/eng/
Control: Department of Justice, Government, federal **Service:** Hospital unit of an institution (prison hospital, college infirmary, etc.)

Staffed Beds: 6

LONE TREE—Douglas County

⊞ **SKY RIDGE MEDICAL CENTER (060112)**, 10101 Ridge Gate Parkway, Zip 80124–5522; tel. 720/225–1000, (Nonreporting) **A**1 2 3 5 10 12 13 **S** HCA Healthcare, Nashville, TN
Primary Contact: Eric Evans, Chief Executive Officer
CFO: Craig Sammons, Chief Financial Officer
CMO: David Markenson, M.D., Chief Medical Officer
CIO: Evan Tice, Director Information Technology and Systems
CHR: Jim Ritchey, Director Human Resources
Web address: www.skyridgemedcenter.com
Control: Corporation, Investor-owned (for-profit) **Service:** General medical and surgical

Staffed Beds: 274

LONGMONT—Boulder County

⊞ **LONGMONT UNITED HOSPITAL (060003)**, 1950 Mountain View Avenue, Zip 80501–3162; tel. 303/651–5111, **A**1 2 10 **F**3 11 13 15 18 20 22 26 28 29 30 31 34 35 36 37 38 40 42 43 44 45 47 48 49 50 53 54 56 57 59 61 64 65 68 70 73 74 75 76 77 78 79 81 82 84 85 86 87 92 93 100 102 107 108 110 111 114 115 118 119 121 123 126 130 131 144 146 147 148 149 150 154 156 167 169 **P**6 **S** CommonSpirit Health, Chicago, IL
Primary Contact: Deb Mohesky, Chief Executive Officer
COO: Andrew Ritz, Chief Operatiang Officer
CHR: Warren Laughlin, Vice President Human Resources
CNO: Mary Hillard, MSN, R.N., Chief Nursing Officer
Web address: https://www.centura.org/location/longmont-united-hospital
Control: Other not-for-profit (including NFP Corporation) **Service:** General medical and surgical

Staffed Beds: 131 **Admissions:** 2410 **Census:** 23 **Outpatient Visits:** 33134 **Births:** 276 **Total Expense ($000):** 107252 **Payroll Expense ($000):** 39032 **Personnel:** 223

LONGMONT—Weld County

☐ **UCHEALTH LONGS PEAK HOSPITAL (060128)**, 1750 East Ken Pratt Boulevard, Zip 80504–5311; tel. 970/237–7850, **A**1 2 10 **F**3 7 8 9 11 12 13 14 15 18 20 22 29 30 34 35 38 40 43 45 46 49 50 56 59 63 64 65 68 70 74 75 76 77 79 81 85 86 87 93 100 102 107 108 111 115 117 118 119 126 129 130 131 135 146 147 148 149 154 164 165 167 169 **S** UCHealth, Aurora, CO
Primary Contact: Ryan Rohman, MSN, R.N., President
Web address: https://www.uchealth.org/locations/uchealth-longs-peak-hospital/
Control: Other not-for-profit (including NFP Corporation) **Service:** General medical and surgical

Staffed Beds: 83 **Admissions:** 4859 **Census:** 51 **Outpatient Visits:** 136254 **Births:** 890 **Total Expense ($000):** 209114 **Payroll Expense ($000):** 67434 **Personnel:** 797

LOUISVILLE—Boulder County

⊞ **ADVENTHEALTH AVISTA (060103)**, 100 Health Park Drive, Zip 80027–9583; tel. 303/673–1000, **A**1 10 **F**3 8 11 13 15 17 18 20 22 28 29 30 31 34 40 43 44 45 47 48 49 50 56 59 60 63 64 65 68 70 72 74 75 76 77 78 79 81 82 84 85 86 87 100 107 108 111 114 115 119 126 130 131 135 146 147 154 157 167 169 **P**6 **S** AdventHealth, Altamonte Springs, FL
Primary Contact: Mark T. Smith, JD, CPA, President and Chief Executive Officer
CFO: Carol Travis, Chief Financial Officer
CMO: Lief Sorensen, M.D., Chief Medical Officer
CHR: Becky Ortega, Manager Human Resources
CNO: Paul Heskin, Chief Nursing Officer
Web address: https://www.centura.org/location/avista-adventist-hospital
Control: Church operated, Nongovernment, not-for-profit **Service:** General medical and surgical

Staffed Beds: 108 **Admissions:** 4333 **Census:** 39 **Outpatient Visits:** 45225 **Births:** 2244 **Total Expense ($000):** 118922 **Payroll Expense ($000):** 47102 **Personnel:** 370

Hospital, Medicare Provider Number, Address, Telephone, Approval, Facility, and Physician Codes, Health Care System

★ American Hospital Association (AHA) membership
☐ The Joint Commission accreditation
○ Healthcare Facilities Accreditation Program
◇ DNV Healthcare Inc. accreditation
⇧ Center for Improvement in Healthcare Quality Accreditation
△ Commission on Accreditation of Rehabilitation Facilities (CARF) accreditation

© 2025 AHA Guide

Hospitals, U.S. / COLORADO

AVISTA ADVENTIST HOSPITAL See Adventhealth Avista

☐ **CENTENNIAL PEAKS HOSPITAL (064007)**, 2255 South 88th Street, Zip 80027-9716; tel. 303/673-9990, (Nonreporting) **A**1 10 **S** Universal Health Services, Inc., King of Prussia, PA
Primary Contact: Scott Snodgrass, Chief Executive Officer
COO: Lisa Strub, Chief Operating Officer
CFO: Tim Ryan, Chief Financial Officer
CMO: Konoy Mandal, M.D., Medical Director
CHR: Suzanne Martinez, Director Human Resources
CNO: Donia L Andersen, Director of Nursing
Web address: www.centennialpeaks.com
Control: Other not-for-profit (including NFP Corporation) **Service**: Psychiatric

Staffed Beds: 104

LOVELAND—Larimer County

✠ **BANNER MCKEE MEDICAL CENTER (060030)**, 2000 Boise Avenue, Zip 80538-4281; tel. 970/669-4640, **A**1 2 10 **F**3 15 18 20 22 26 28 29 30 34 35 38 40 43 44 45 47 50 53 54 55 56 57 58 59 60 62 65 68 70 74 75 77 78 79 81 84 85 87 93 94 97 98 100 101 102 103 104 105 107 108 110 111 114 115 119 120 121 123 124 126 130 132 146 148 149 153 154 164 167 **S** Banner Health, Phoenix, AZ
Primary Contact: Alan Qualls, Chief Executive Officer
COO: Chris Kerrigan, Interim Chief Operating Officer
CMO: Steven Loecke, M.D., Chief Medical Officer
CIO: Steve Rains, Director Information Services
CHR: Jeannie Gallagher
CNO: Julia Gentry, Chief Nursing Officer, Northern Colorado
Web address: https://www.bannerhealth.com/locations/loveland/mckee-medical-center
Control: Other not-for-profit (including NFP Corporation) **Service**: General medical and surgical

Staffed Beds: 89 **Admissions**: 2446 **Census**: 34 **Outpatient Visits**: 39746 **Births**: 0 **Total Expense ($000)**: 118705 **Payroll Expense ($000)**: 35736 **Personnel**: 349

MCKEE MEDICAL CENTER See Banner Mckee Medical Center

✠ **UCHEALTH MEDICAL CENTER OF THE ROCKIES (060119)**, 2500 Rocky Mountain Avenue, Zip 80538-9004; tel. 970/624-2500, **A**1 2 3 5 10 **F**3 9 11 13 14 15 17 18 20 22 24 26 28 29 30 31 34 35 38 40 42 43 45 46 50 51 58 59 61 63 64 65 68 70 71 74 75 76 77 78 79 81 82 84 85 87 93 100 102 107 110 111 114 115 119 126 129 130 132 135 143 146 147 148 149 154 156 157 160 161 164 167 169 **S** UCHealth, Aurora, CO
Primary Contact: Kevin L. Unger, Ph.D., FACHE, President and Chief Executive Officer
COO: Ryan Rohman, MSN, R.N., Chief Operating Officer
CFO: Stephanie Doughty, Chief Financial Officer
CMO: William Neff, M.D., Chief Medical Officer
CIO: Steve Hess, Vice President Information Services and Chief Information Officer
Web address: www.medctrrockies.org
Control: Other not-for-profit (including NFP Corporation) **Service**: General medical and surgical

Staffed Beds: 191 **Admissions**: 10696 **Census**: 146 **Outpatient Visits**: 297800 **Births**: 1470 **Total Expense ($000)**: 550748 **Payroll Expense ($000)**: 167438 **Personnel**: 1714

MEEKER—Rio Blanco County

★ **PIONEERS MEDICAL CENTER (061325)**, 100 Pioneers Medical Center Drive, Zip 81641-3181; tel. 970/878-5047, (Nonreporting) **A**10 18 **S** Ovation Healthcare, Brentwood, TN
Primary Contact: Liz Sellers, R.N., MSN, Chief Executive Officer
COO: Karen Iacuone, Chief Nursing Officer and Chief Operating Officer
CFO: James W Worrell, Chief Financial Officer
CMO: Christopher Williams, M.D., Chief of Staff
CIO: Curtis Cooper, Manager Information Systems
CHR: Twyla Jensen, Director Human Resources
CNO: Karen Iacuone, Chief Nursing Officer
Web address: www.pioneershospital.org
Control: Hospital district or authority, Government, Nonfederal **Service**: General medical and surgical

Staffed Beds: 16

MONTROSE—Montrose County

MONTROSE MEMORIAL HOSPITAL See Montrose Regional Health

✠ **MONTROSE REGIONAL HEALTH (060006)**, 800 South Third Street, Zip 81401-4212; tel. 970/249-2211, **A**1 10 20 **F**3 13 15 18 20 22 28 29 30 31 34 35 40 43 44 45 46 50 51 57 59 64 68 70 72 74 75 76 77 78 79 81 82 85 89 90 92 93 96 107 108 110 111 115 117 118 119 126 129 130 132 135 146 147 148 149 154 167 169 **P**5 8
Primary Contact: Jeff Mengenhausen, Chief Executive Officer
COO: Mary E Snyder, Chief Operations Officer
CFO: Stephan A Wilson, Chief Financial Officer
CMO: Richard Shannon, M.D., Chief of Staff
CIO: Carlos Lovera, Director Information Systems
CHR: Kathy McKie, Director Human Resources
Web address: www.montrosehospital.com
Control: Other not-for-profit (including NFP Corporation) **Service**: General medical and surgical

Staffed Beds: 62 **Admissions**: 2415 **Census**: 22 **Outpatient Visits**: 137731 **Births**: 368 **Total Expense ($000)**: 161795 **Payroll Expense ($000)**: 56974 **Personnel**: 826

PAGOSA SPRINGS—Archuleta County

PAGOSA SPRINGS MEDICAL CENTER (061328), 95 South Pagosa Boulevard, Zip 81147-8329; tel. 970/731-3700, (Nonreporting) **A**10 18
Primary Contact: Rhonda Webb, M.D., Chief Executive Officer, Chief Medical Officer
CMO: Rhonda Webb, M.D., Chief Executive Officer and Chief Medical Officer
Web address: www.pagosaspringsmedicalcenter.org/
Control: Hospital district or authority, Government, Nonfederal **Service**: General medical and surgical

Staffed Beds: 5

PARKER—Douglas County

✠ **ADVENTHEALTH PARKER (060114)**, 9395 Crown Crest Boulevard, Zip 80138-8573; tel. 303/269-4000, **A**1 3 5 10 **F**3 11 12 13 18 20 22 29 30 31 34 35 36 37 38 40 42 43 45 46 47 48 49 50 54 55 57 59 64 65 69 70 72 73 74 75 76 77 78 79 81 82 83 84 85 86 87 92 93 96 97 102 107 108 110 111 114 115 116 117 118 119 120 121 123 126 130 131 132 135 144 146 147 148 149 156 164 167 169 **P**6 **S** AdventHealth, Altamonte Springs, FL
Primary Contact: Michael Goebel, Chief Executive Officer
COO: Leanne Naso, Chief Operating Officer
CFO: Jonathan Fisher, Chief Financial Officer
CMO: Devin Bateman, M.D., Chief Medical Officer
CNO: Andrea Narvaez, R.N., Chief Nursing Officer
Web address: www.parkerhospital.org
Control: Church operated, Nongovernment, not-for-profit **Service**: General medical and surgical

Staffed Beds: 162 **Admissions**: 8563 **Census**: 96 **Outpatient Visits**: 89858 **Births**: 1249 **Total Expense ($000)**: 229494 **Payroll Expense ($000)**: 86202 **Personnel**: 1008

PARKER ADVENTIST HOSPITAL See Adventhealth Parker

PUEBLO—Pueblo County

☐ **COLORADO MENTAL HEALTH INSTITUTE AT PUEBLO (060115)**, 1600 West 24th Street, Zip 81003-1499; tel. 719/546-4000, (Nonreporting) **A**1 3 5 10
Primary Contact: Joe Marshall, Chief Executive Officer
CFO: Jim Duff, Chief Financial Officer
CMO: Al Singleton, M.D., Chief Psychiatry and Chief Medical Staff
CIO: Eunice Wolther, Public Information Officer
CHR: Mary Young, Director Human Resources
Web address: https://cdhs.colorado.gov/CMHHIP
Control: State, Government, Nonfederal **Service**: Psychiatric

Staffed Beds: 514

✠ **COMMONSPIRIT - ST. MARY-CORWIN HOSPITAL (060012)**, 1008 Minnequa Avenue, Zip 81004-3798; tel. 719/557-4000, **A**1 2 3 5 10 13 **F**3 15 18 29 30 31 34 35 40 43 45 47 48 49 50 53 55 57 59 64 68 70 75 78 79 81 85 86 87 100 107 108 109 110 111 114 115 116 117 118 119 120 121 122 123 124 126 130 131 132 135 146 148 149 154 167 **P**6 **S** CommonSpirit Health, Chicago, IL
Primary Contact: Michael Cafasso, Chief Executive Officer
CFO: Janiece McNichols, Chief Financial Officer
CMO: Kern Low, M.D., Chief Medical Officer
Web address: https://www.mountain.commonspirit.org/location/st-mary-corwin-hospital
Control: Church operated, Nongovernment, not-for-profit **Service**: General medical and surgical

Staffed Beds: 42 **Admissions**: 1701 **Census**: 21 **Outpatient Visits**: 78867 **Births**: 0 **Total Expense ($000)**: 113795 **Payroll Expense ($000)**: 37668 **Personnel**: 428

Hospitals, U.S. / COLORADO

ST. MARY–CORWIN MEDICAL CENTER See Commonspirit – St. Mary–Corwin Hospital

☒ **UCHEALTH PARKVIEW MEDICAL CENTER (060020)**, 400 West 16th Street, Zip 81003–2781; tel. 719/584–4000, **A**1 3 5 10 13 **F**2 3 11 12 13 14 15 17 18 20 22 24 26 28 29 30 31 34 35 37 38 40 42 43 44 45 46 48 49 50 51 53 54 56 57 58 59 61 62 64 65 66 70 71 72 74 75 76 77 78 79 81 82 84 85 86 87 89 90 92 93 94 96 97 100 101 102 104 107 108 110 111 114 115 119 120 121 123 124 126 129 130 131 135 146 147 148 149 154 156 157 164 167 169 **S** UCHealth, Aurora, CO
Primary Contact: Darrin Smith, President and Chief Executive Officer
CMO: Steve Nafziger, M.D., Vice President Medical Affairs
CIO: Steve Shirley, Chief Information Officer
CNO: Linda Flores, R.N., MSN, Vice President Nursing Services
Web address: www.parkviewmc.org
Control: Other not–for–profit (including NFP Corporation) **Service**: General medical and surgical

Staffed Beds: 292 Admissions: 13747 Census: 191 Outpatient Visits: 278114 Births: 702 Total Expense ($000): 437943 Payroll Expense ($000): 177845 Personnel: 2150

RANGELY—Rio Blanco County

★ **RANGELY DISTRICT HOSPITAL (061307)**, 225 Eagle Crest Drive, Zip 81648–2104; tel. 970/675–5011, (Nonreporting) **A**10 18
Primary Contact: Kyle Wren, Chief Executive Officer
COO: Bernard Rice, Chief Compliance Officer
CFO: Jim Dillon, Chief Financial Officer
CMO: Abigail R. Urish, M.D., Chief of Staff
CHR: Cynthia S. Stults, Executive Assistant and Human Resources Director
CNO: Sharma Vaughn Esq, Chief Nursing Officer
Web address: www.rangelyhospital.com
Control: Hospital district or authority, Government, Nonfederal **Service**: General medical and surgical

Staffed Beds: 14

RIFLE—Garfield County

★ **GRAND RIVER HOSPITAL DISTRICT (061317)**, 501 Airport Road, Zip 81650–8510, Mailing Address: P.O. Box 912, Zip 81650–0912; tel. 970/625–1510, (Nonreporting) **A**10 18
Primary Contact: James Coombs, Chief Executive Officer
COO: Bill Noel, Chief Operating Officer
CFO: Cris Bolin, Chief Financial Officer
CMO: Kevin Coleman, M.D., Chief Medical Officer
CIO: Diana Murray, Director Information Systems
CHR: Dawn Hodges, Director Human Resources
CNO: Stacy Pemberton, Chief Nursing Officer
Web address: www.grhd.org
Control: Hospital district or authority, Government, Nonfederal **Service**: General medical and surgical

Staffed Beds: 69

SALIDA—Chaffee County

☒ **HEART OF THE ROCKIES REGIONAL MEDICAL CENTER (061322)**, 1000 Rush Drive, Zip 81201–9627, Mailing Address: P.O. Box 429, Zip 81201–0429; tel. 719/530–2200, **A**1 10 18 **F**3 5 11 13 15 28 29 31 34 35 40 43 45 50 53 54 57 59 64 68 70 74 75 76 77 78 79 81 82 85 87 91 92 93 97 102 104 107 110 111 115 119 127 129 130 131 132 133 135 146 147 148 154 156 167 **P**5
Primary Contact: Robert A. Morasko, Chief Executive Officer
CFO: Lesley Fagerberg, Vice President Fiscal Services
CMO: Daniel Wardrop, M.D., Medical Director
CIO: Andy Waldbart, Department Manager
CHR: Barbara Lutz, Vice President Human Resources
CNO: Linda Johnson, R.N., Vice President, Patient Services Risk Management and Chief Nursing Officer
Web address: www.hrrmc.com
Control: Hospital district or authority, Government, Nonfederal **Service**: General medical and surgical

Staffed Beds: 25 Admissions: 821 Census: 9 Outpatient Visits: 185172 Births: 122 Total Expense ($000): 125120 Payroll Expense ($000): 58506 Personnel: 544

SPRINGFIELD—Baca County

★ **SOUTHEAST COLORADO HOSPITAL DISTRICT (061311)**, 373 East Tenth Avenue, Zip 81073–1699; tel. 719/523–4501, (Total facility includes 56 beds in nursing home–type unit) **A**10 18 **F**3 6 7 11 29 40 45 50 57 62 63 66 67 68 81 91 97 107 115 119 127 130 133 135 148 154 **P**6 **S** Ovation Healthcare, Brentwood, TN
Primary Contact: Jeff Egbert, Interim Chief Executive Officer
CFO: Dorothy Burke, Chief Financial Officer
CMO: Andrea Wismann, M.D., Chief of Staff
CIO: Chris Westphal, Chief Information Technology Officer
CHR: Sherrilyn Turner, Director Human Resources
CNO: Cecelia Deen Esq, Chief Nursing Officer
Web address: www.sechosp.org
Control: Hospital district or authority, Government, Nonfederal **Service**: General medical and surgical

Staffed Beds: 79 Admissions: 208 Census: 18 Outpatient Visits: 30924 Births: 0 Total Expense ($000): 23228 Payroll Expense ($000): 9050 Personnel: 144

STEAMBOAT SPRINGS—Routt County

☒ **UCHEALTH YAMPA VALLEY MEDICAL CENTER (060049)**, 1024 Central Park Drive, Zip 80487–8813; tel. 970/879–1322, **A**1 2 10 20 **F**3 9 11 13 15 18 28 29 31 34 35 36 37 38 40 43 45 46 48 50 51 54 55 57 59 61 64 65 68 70 74 75 76 77 78 79 81 82 84 85 86 87 93 97 102 107 110 111 115 119 126 129 130 131 133 135 144 146 147 148 149 154 156 160 164 167 169 **S** UCHealth, Aurora, CO
Primary Contact: Soniya Fidler, MS, President
CMO: Laura Sehnert, M.D., Chief Medical Officer
CHR: Dallis Howard–Crow, Chief Human Resources Officer
CNO: Kelly Gallegos, Chief Nursing Officer
Web address: https://www.uchealth.org/locations/uchealth-yampa-valley-medical-center/
Control: Other not–for–profit (including NFP Corporation) **Service**: General medical and surgical

Staffed Beds: 34 Admissions: 1090 Census: 8 Outpatient Visits: 144192 Births: 325 Total Expense ($000): 124648 Payroll Expense ($000): 51276 Personnel: 515

STERLING—Logan County

☒ **STERLING REGIONAL MEDCENTER (060076)**, 615 Fairhurst Street, Zip 80751–4523; tel. 970/522–0122, **A**1 3 10 20 **F**3 8 13 15 29 31 40 41 43 45 46 64 70 76 77 78 79 81 85 87 93 97 107 108 110 111 112 114 115 116 117 119 121 122 123 124 127 131 146 148 149 154 160 167 169 **S** Banner Health, Phoenix, AZ
Primary Contact: Ned Resch, Chief Executive Officer
CFO: Nathan Nichols, Director of Finance
CMO: Jeff Bacon, D.O., Chief Medical Officer
Web address: https://www.bannerhealth.com/locations/sterling/sterling-regional-medcenter
Control: Other not–for–profit (including NFP Corporation) **Service**: General medical and surgical

Staffed Beds: 25 Admissions: 900 Census: 7 Outpatient Visits: 30832 Births: 189 Total Expense ($000): 57762 Payroll Expense ($000): 19486 Personnel: 215

THORNTON—Adams County

☐ **DENVER REGIONAL REHABILITATION HOSPITAL (063035)**, 8451 Pearl Street, Suite 101, Zip 80229–4803; tel. 303/301–8700, (Nonreporting) **A**1 10 **S** Ernest Health, Inc., Albuquerque, NM
Primary Contact: Christine Duron, Interim Chief Executive Officer
Web address: https://drrh.ernesthealth.com/
Control: Corporation, Investor–owned (for–profit) **Service**: Rehabilitation

Staffed Beds: 31

☒ **NORTH SUBURBAN MEDICAL CENTER (060065)**, 9191 Grant Street, Zip 80229–4341; tel. 303/451–7800, (Nonreporting) **A**1 2 3 5 10 **S** HCA Healthcare, Nashville, TN
Primary Contact: Ryan Thornton, President and Chief Executive Officer
CIO: Marty Hoesch, Director Information Systems
CHR: Dena Schmaedecke, Vice President Human Resources
Web address: www.northsuburban.com
Control: Corporation, Investor–owned (for–profit) **Service**: General medical and surgical

Staffed Beds: 147

Hospital, Medicare Provider Number, Address, Telephone, Approval, Facility, and Physician Codes, Health Care System

★ American Hospital Association (AHA) membership
☐ The Joint Commission accreditation
◯ Healthcare Facilities Accreditation Program
◇ DNV Healthcare Inc. accreditation
⇑ Center for Improvement in Healthcare Quality Accreditation
△ Commission on Accreditation of Rehabilitation Facilities (CARF) accreditation

Hospitals, U.S. / COLORADO

* **VIBRA HOSPITAL OF DENVER (062014)**, 8451 Pearl Street, Zip 80229–4804; tel. 303/288–3000, (Nonreporting) **A**1 10 **S** Vibra Healthcare, Mechanicsburg, PA
Primary Contact: Lamar McBride, Chief Executive Officer
CMO: John Buckley, M.D., President Medical Staff
Web address: www.vhdenver.com
Control: Corporation, Investor–owned (for–profit) **Service**: Acute long–term care hospital

   Staffed Beds: 71

TRINIDAD—Las Animas County

★ ⇑ **MT. SAN RAFAEL HOSPITAL (061321)**, 410 Benedicta Avenue, Zip 81082–2093; tel. 719/846–9213, (Nonreporting) **A**10 18 21
Primary Contact: Kim Lucero, Interim Chief Executive Officer
CFO: Calvin Carey, Chief Financial Officer
CIO: Michael Archuleta, Chief Information Technology Officer
CHR: Tammy Rogers, Director Human Resources
CNO: Mandy Shaiffer, Chief Nursing Officer
Web address: www.msrhc.org
Control: Other not–for–profit (including NFP Corporation) **Service**: General medical and surgical

   Staffed Beds: 25

VAIL—Eagle County

* **VAIL HEALTH (060096)**, 181 West Meadow Drive, Zip 81657–5242, Mailing Address: P.O. Box 40000, Zip 81658–7520; tel. 970/476–2451, **A**1 2 3 10 20 **F**3 5 11 13 15 17 18 20 22 26 28 29 30 31 34 35 37 40 42 43 45 46 50 51 54 55 57 59 64 65 68 70 71 73 74 75 76 77 78 79 81 82 85 86 87 89 91 92 93 94 101 102 104 107 108 109 110 111 115 116 117 119 120 121 123 126 129 130 131 132 134 135 141 142 143 145 146 147 148 149 153 154 156 160 161 164 165 **P**6
Primary Contact: William Cook, President and Chief Executive Officer
CFO: Ted D. Sirotta, Chief Financial Officer
CMO: Barry Hammaker, M.D., Chief Medical Officer and Chief Clinical Officer
CHR: Rick Smith, Senior Vice President Human Resources and Chief Administrative Officer
CNO: Sheila Sherman, Vice President Patient Care Services
Web address: www.vvmc.com
Control: Other not–for–profit (including NFP Corporation) **Service**: General medical and surgical

   Staffed Beds: 56 **Admissions**: 1487 **Census**: 12 **Outpatient Visits**: 87832 **Births**: 345 **Total Expense ($000)**: 303156 **Payroll Expense ($000)**: 61880 **Personnel**: 1560

WALSENBURG—Huerfano County

★ **SPANISH PEAKS REGIONAL HEALTH CENTER AND VETERANS COMMUNITY LIVING CENTER (061316)**, 23500 US Highway 160, Zip 81089–9524; tel. 719/738–5100, (Nonreporting) **A**10 18
Primary Contact: Kay L. Whitley, President and Chief Executive Officer
CMO: Michael A. Moll, M.D., Chief Medical Officer and Chief of Staff
CHR: Tony Marostica, Chief Compliance and Human Resource Officer
CNO: Mary Cope, R.N., Chief Clinical Officer
Web address: www.sprhc.org
Control: Hospital district or authority, Government, Nonfederal **Service**: General medical and surgical

   Staffed Beds: 20

WESTMINSTER—Adams County

ST. ANTHONY NORTH HEALTH CAMPUS See St. Anthony North Hospital

* **ST. ANTHONY NORTH HOSPITAL (060104)**, 14300 Orchard Parkway, Zip 80023–9206; tel. 720/627–0000, **A**1 2 3 5 10 **F**3 11 13 15 18 20 22 26 28 29 30 34 35 36 40 42 43 49 50 51 54 57 59 60 64 65 68 70 72 74 75 76 77 78 79 81 82 84 85 87 91 92 93 97 102 107 108 110 111 114 115 119 126 130 131 132 135 146 147 148 149 150 167 169 **P**6 **S** CommonSpirit Health, Chicago, IL
Primary Contact: Constance Schmidt, FACHE, R.N., Chief Executive Officer
CFO: Carol Travis, Chief Financial Officer
CHR: Robert Archibold, Director, Human Resources
CNO: Carol A Butler, R.N., MSN, VP Patient Care Services & Operations
Web address: https://www.centura.org/location/st-anthony-north-hospital
Control: Church operated, Nongovernment, not–for–profit **Service**: General medical and surgical

   Staffed Beds: 113 **Admissions**: 7631 **Census**: 73 **Outpatient Visits**: 77808 **Births**: 1055 **Total Expense ($000)**: 187257 **Payroll Expense ($000)**: 73106 **Personnel**: 610

WESTMINSTER—Jefferson County

★ **PAM HEALTH REHABILITATION HOSPITAL OF WESTMINSTER (063037)**, 6500 West 104th Avenue, Zip 80020–4189; tel. 720/653–3440, **A**22 **F**3 29 34 44 60 62 64 74 77 79 82 86 87 90 91 93 96 130 131 **S** PAM Health, Enola, PA
Primary Contact: Cory Warner, Chief Executive Officer
CHR: Carly Kraft, Human Resources Director
Web address: www.pamhealth.com
Control: Individual, Investor–owned (for–profit) **Service**: Rehabilitation

   Staffed Beds: 36 **Admissions**: 924 **Census**: 32 **Outpatient Visits**: 1200 **Births**: 0 **Total Expense ($000)**: 20230 **Payroll Expense ($000)**: 9985 **Personnel**: 147

WHEAT RIDGE—Jefferson County

* **LUTHERAN MEDICAL CENTER (060009)**, 8300 West 38th Avenue, Zip 80033–6005; tel. 303/425–4500, (Includes EXEMPLA WEST PINES, 3400 Lutheran Parkway, Wheat Ridge, Colorado, Zip 80033, tel. 303/467–4000) **A**1 2 3 10 **F**3 4 5 11 12 13 15 18 20 22 24 26 28 29 30 31 35 36 40 41 43 45 46 47 48 49 50 55 56 58 59 60 61 63 64 68 70 71 72 74 75 76 77 78 79 81 83 84 85 86 87 94 98 100 101 102 103 104 105 106 107 110 111 114 115 118 119 120 121 123 124 126 127 128 129 130 132 146 147 148 149 152 153 154 157 160 161 162 164 165 167 **S** Intermountain Health, Salt Lake City, UT
Primary Contact: Andrea Burch, MS, R.N., President
CFO: Karen Scremin, Vice President Finance
CHR: Scott Day, Vice President Human Resources
CNO: Ann M. Gantzer, Ph.D., R.N., Interim Chief Nursing Officer
Web address: https://www.sclhealth.org/locations/lutheran-medical-center/
Control: Other not–for–profit (including NFP Corporation) **Service**: General medical and surgical

   Staffed Beds: 336 **Admissions**: 16997 **Census**: 230 **Outpatient Visits**: 119549 **Births**: 1580 **Total Expense ($000)**: 508739 **Payroll Expense ($000)**: 155991 **Personnel**: 1223

WEST PINES AT LUTHERAN MED CTR See Exempla West Pines

WOODLAND PARK—Teller County

□ **UCHEALTH PIKES PEAK REGIONAL HOSPITAL (061326)**, 16420 West Highway 24, Zip 80863; tel. 719/687–9999, **A**1 10 18 **F**3 28 29 30 31 34 35 38 40 43 44 45 50 57 59 64 65 68 75 77 78 79 81 82 84 85 87 92 93 96 100 102 107 110 111 115 119 129 130 133 135 146 148 149 154 156 157 164 **S** UCHealth, Aurora, CO
Primary Contact: Ron Fitch, President/UCHealth Pikes Peak Regional Hospital/Grandview Hospital/Operations and Military Affairs/U
CFO: Robin Ruff, Chief Financial Officer
CMO: Richard Malyszek, M.D., Chief of Staff
CHR: Arianne Randolph, Director Human Resources
Web address: https://www.uchealth.org/locations/uchealth-pikes-peak-regional-hospital/
Control: Other not–for–profit (including NFP Corporation) **Service**: General medical and surgical

   Staffed Beds: 13 **Admissions**: 271 **Census**: 2 **Outpatient Visits**: 57247 **Births**: 0 **Total Expense ($000)**: 28749 **Payroll Expense ($000)**: 11084 **Personnel**: 106

WRAY—Yuma County

★ **WRAY COMMUNITY DISTRICT HOSPITAL (061309)**, 1017 West 7th Street, Zip 80758–1420; tel. 970/332–4811, (Nonreporting) **A**3 10 18
Primary Contact: John Hart, Chief Executive Officer
CMO: Monte Uyemura, M.D., Chief of Staff
Web address: www.wraycommunitydistricthospital.com/
Control: Hospital district or authority, Government, Nonfederal **Service**: General medical and surgical

   Staffed Beds: 84

YUMA—Yuma County

★ **YUMA DISTRICT HOSPITAL (061315)**, 1000 West 8th Avenue, Zip 80759–2641; tel. 970/848–5405, (Nonreporting) **A**10 18
Primary Contact: Anne Kreutzer, Chief Executive Officer
CFO: Rick Korf, Chief Financial Officer
CMO: John Wolz, M.D., Chief Medical Staff
CIO: Jason Hawley, Director of Information Services and Security
CHR: Gini Adams, Director Employee and Public Relations
Web address: www.yumahospital.org
Control: Hospital district or authority, Government, Nonfederal **Service**: General medical and surgical

   Staffed Beds: 12

CONNECTICUT

BRANFORD—New Haven County

☐ **THE CONNECTICUT HOSPICE (070038)**, 100 Double Beach Road, Zip 06405–4909; tel. 203/315–7500, (Nonreporting) **A**1 3 5 10
Primary Contact: Barbara Pearce, Interim Chief Executive Officer
Web address: www.hospice.com
Control: Other not–for–profit (including NFP Corporation) **Service**: Other specialty treatment

Staffed Beds: 52

BRIDGEPORT—Fairfield County

✠ **BRIDGEPORT HOSPITAL (070010)**, 267 Grant Street, Zip 06610–2805, Mailing Address: P.O. Box 5000, Zip 06610–0120; tel. 203/384–3000, (Includes MILFORD HOSPITAL, 300 Seaside Avenue, Milford, Connecticut, Zip 06460–4603, tel. 203/876–4000; Lloyd Friedman, M.D., Interim President and Chief Operating Officer) **A**1 2 3 5 8 10 19 **F**3 5 6 8 11 12 13 14 15 16 17 18 20 22 24 26 28 29 30 31 32 34 35 36 37 38 39 40 41 42 43 44 45 46 47 48 49 50 51 52 54 55 56 57 58 59 61 62 64 65 66 68 70 74 75 76 78 79 80 81 82 84 85 86 87 93 96 97 98 101 102 103 104 107 108 110 111 114 115 116 117 118 119 120 121 123 124 126 129 130 131 132 134 144 145 146 147 148 149 153 154 156 161 162 164 165 167 168 169 **S** Yale New Haven Health, New Haven, CT
Primary Contact: Anne Diamond, JD, President
CFO: Patrick McCabe, Senior Vice President Finance and Chief Financial Officer
CMO: Michael Ivy, M.D., Senior Vice President for Medical Affairs and Chief Medical Officer
CHR: Melissa Turner, Senior Vice President Human Resources
Web address: www.bridgeporthospital.org
Control: Other not–for–profit (including NFP Corporation) **Service**: General medical and surgical

Staffed Beds: 470 **Admissions**: 23341 **Census**: 368 **Outpatient Visits**: 521528 **Births**: 2493 **Total Expense ($000)**: 902986 **Payroll Expense ($000)**: 283298 **Personnel**: 3037

☐ **SOUTHWEST CONNECTICUT MENTAL HEALTH SYSTEM (074012)**, 1635 Central Avenue, Zip 06610–2717; tel. 203/551–7400, (Nonreporting) **A**1 10 **S** Connecticut Department of Mental Health and Addiction Services, Hartford, CT
Primary Contact: Francis Giannini, Interim Chief Executive Officer
COO: Francis Giannini, Associate Director
CMO: Robert Berger, M.D., Medical Director
CIO: Paula Zwally, Director Quality Improvement Services and Compliance
CHR: Irena Baj-Wright, Director Human Resources
Web address: www.ct.gov/dmhas/cwp/view.asp?a=2946&q=378639
Control: State, Government, Nonfederal **Service**: Psychiatric

Staffed Beds: 62

✠ **ST. VINCENT'S MEDICAL CENTER (070028)**, 2800 Main Street, Zip 06606–4292; tel. 203/576–6000, (Includes ST. VINCENT'S BEHAVIORAL HEALTH, 47 Long Lots Road, Westport, Connecticut, Zip 06880–3800, tel. 203/221–8813) **A**1 2 3 5 10 19 **F**2 3 5 6 8 9 10 11 12 13 15 18 20 22 24 26 28 29 30 31 34 35 36 37 38 39 40 43 44 45 46 47 48 49 50 51 52 53 54 55 56 57 58 59 60 61 63 64 65 66 68 70 71 72 74 75 76 77 78 79 80 81 82 83 84 85 86 87 90 91 92 93 94 95 96 97 98 99 100 101 102 103 104 105 106 107 108 110 111 112 114 115 116 117 118 119 120 121 123 124 125 126 129 130 131 132 133 134 135 144 145 146 147 148 149 150 152 153 154 156 157 160 162 163 164 165 167 169 **P**6 **S** Hartford HealthCare, Hartford, CT
Primary Contact: William Jennings, President, Fairfield Region
COO: Brooke Karlsen, MSN, R.N., Regional Vice President, Operations
CFO: Christopher Given, Regional Vice President, Finance
CMO: Dan Gottschall, Vice President, Medical Officer
CNO: Dale Danowski, R.N., Vice President, Patient Care Services
Web address: www.stvincents.org
Control: Other not–for–profit (including NFP Corporation) **Service**: General medical and surgical

Staffed Beds: 337 **Admissions**: 13095 **Census**: 260 **Outpatient Visits**: 253530 **Births**: 1259 **Total Expense ($000)**: 607953 **Payroll Expense ($000)**: 161669 **Personnel**: 1890

BRISTOL—Hartford County

✠ **BRISTOL HEALTH (070029)**, 41 Brewster Road, Zip 06010–5161, Mailing Address: P.O. Box 977, Zip 06011–0977; tel. 860/585–3000, (Total facility includes 126 beds in nursing home–type unit) **A**1 5 10 **F**3 5 7 13 15 18 24 26 28 29 30 31 34 35 37 38 40 44 45 46 47 49 50 51 54 56 57 58 59 60 61 62 63 64 65 68 70 72 74 75 76 77 78 79 81 82 84 85 87 92 93 96 97 98 100 101 102 103 104 105 106 107 108 110 111 114 115 116 117 119 121 126 128 129 130 131 132 135 143 144 146 147 148 149 150 152 153 154 155 156 157 160 161 162 164 165 167
Primary Contact: Kurt A. Barwis, FACHE, President and Chief Executive Officer
COO: Chris Ann Meaney, Senior Vice President, Chief Operating Officer and Chief Nursing Officer
CFO: Richard Braam, Vice President, Operations and Chief Financial Officer
CHR: Christine Laprise, Vice President of Human Resources
CNO: Chris Ann Meaney, Senior Vice President, Chief Operating Officer and Chief Nursing Officer
Web address: https://www.bristolhealth.org/
Control: Other not–for–profit (including NFP Corporation) **Service**: General medical and surgical

Staffed Beds: 264 **Admissions**: 5998 **Census**: 156 **Outpatient Visits**: 34669 **Births**: 526 **Total Expense ($000)**: 160698 **Payroll Expense ($000)**: 68317

DANBURY—Fairfield County

✠ **DANBURY HOSPITAL (070033)**, 24 Hospital Avenue, Zip 06810–6099; tel. 203/739–7000, (Includes NEW MILFORD HOSPITAL, 21 Elm Street, New Milford, Connecticut, Zip 06776–2993, tel. 860/355–2611; John M. Murphy, M.D., President and Chief Executive Officer, Western Connecticut Health Network) **A**1 3 5 10 19 **F**3 5 7 8 12 13 14 15 18 20 22 24 26 28 29 30 31 32 34 35 36 37 38 39 40 41 43 44 45 46 47 48 49 50 51 53 54 55 56 57 58 59 64 65 66 68 70 71 72 74 75 76 77 78 79 81 82 84 85 86 87 89 90 93 96 98 100 101 102 104 105 107 108 110 111 114 115 116 117 119 120 121 124 126 130 131 132 134 135 141 143 145 146 147 148 149 150 153 154 155 156 157 160 161 162 164 165 167 169 **S** Nuvance Health, Danbury, CT
Primary Contact: Sharon Adams, President
CFO: Steven Rosenberg, Chief Financial Officer
CMO: Patricia Tietjen, M.D., Vice President, Medical Affairs
CIO: Kathleen DeMatteo, Chief Information Officer
CHR: Cathy Frierson, Chief Human Resource Officer
Web address: www.danburyhospital.org
Control: Other not–for–profit (including NFP Corporation) **Service**: General medical and surgical

Staffed Beds: 293 **Admissions**: 19116 **Census**: 247 **Outpatient Visits**: 514308 **Births**: 2067 **Total Expense ($000)**: 787692 **Payroll Expense ($000)**: 231236 **Personnel**: 2363

DERBY—New Haven County

✠ **GRIFFIN HEALTH (070031)**, 130 Division Street, Zip 06418–1326; tel. 203/735–7421, (Nonreporting) **A**1 2 3 5 10 19
Primary Contact: Patrick Charmel, President and Chief Executive Officer
CMO: Kenneth V Schwartz, M.D., Medical Director
CIO: George Tomas, Director Information Services
CHR: Steve Mordecai, Director Human Resources
CNO: Barbara J Stumpo, R.N., Vice President Patient Care Services
Web address: www.griffinhealth.org
Control: Other not–for–profit (including NFP Corporation) **Service**: General medical and surgical

Staffed Beds: 111

Hospital, Medicare Provider Number, Address, Telephone, Approval, Facility, and Physician Codes, Health Care System

★ American Hospital Association (AHA) membership
☐ The Joint Commission accreditation
○ Healthcare Facilities Accreditation Program
◇ DNV Healthcare Inc. accreditation
⇑ Center for Improvement in Healthcare Quality Accreditation
△ Commission on Accreditation of Rehabilitation Facilities (CARF) accreditation

Hospitals, U.S. / CONNECTICUT

FARMINGTON—Hartford County

- **UCONN, JOHN DEMPSEY HOSPITAL (070036)**, 263 Farmington Avenue, Zip 06032–1941; tel. 860/679–2000, (Nonreporting) **A**1 2 3 5 8 10 12 13 19
  Primary Contact: Andrew Agwunobi, M.D., Chief Executive Officer
  COO: Kevin Larsen, Associate Vice President, Business and Ancillary Services
  CFO: Jeffrey Geoghegan, Chief Financial Officer
  CMO: Richard Simon, M.D., Chief of Staff
  CIO: Jonathan Carroll, Chief Information Officer
  CHR: Carolle Andrews, Vice President, Interim Human Resources Officer
  CNO: Ann Marie Capo, R.N., Chief Nursing Officer, Vice President, Quality and Patient Services
  Web address: www.uchc.edu
  Control: State, Government, Nonfederal **Service:** General medical and surgical

  Staffed Beds: 219

GREENWICH—Fairfield County

- **GREENWICH HOSPITAL (070018)**, 5 Perryridge Road, Zip 06830–4697; tel. 203/863–3000, **A**1 2 3 5 8 10 19 **F**3 5 8 11 12 13 15 18 20 22 26 28 29 30 31 32 34 35 36 37 38 39 40 41 44 45 46 47 48 49 50 51 52 54 55 56 57 58 59 61 64 65 66 68 70 72 74 75 76 77 78 79 80 81 82 84 85 86 87 89 91 93 97 100 101 102 104 107 108 110 111 114 115 116 117 118 119 120 121 123 124 126 129 130 131 132 134 135 146 147 148 149 154 156 157 160 161 167 169 **S** Yale New Haven Health, New Haven, CT
  Primary Contact: Diane P. Kelly, R.N., President
  CMO: A Michael Marino, M.D., Senior Vice President Medical Administration
  Web address: https://www.greenwichhospital.org/
  Control: Other not–for–profit (including NFP Corporation) **Service:** General medical and surgical

  Staffed Beds: 206 **Admissions:** 13099 **Census:** 154 **Outpatient Visits:** 322492 **Births:** 2848 **Total Expense ($000):** 531300 **Payroll Expense ($000):** 165182 **Personnel:** 1612

HARTFORD—Hartford County

- **CONNECTICUT CHILDREN'S (073300)**, 282 Washington Street, Zip 06106–3322; tel. 860/545–9000, (Nonreporting) **A**1 3 5 10
  Primary Contact: James E. Shmerling, President and Chief Executive Officer
  CFO: Bridgett Feagin, Senior Vice President and Chief Financial Officer
  CMO: Paul Dworkin, M.D., Physician–in–Chief
  CIO: Jung Park, Interim Chief Information Officer
  CHR: Elizabeth Rudden, Vice President Human Resources
  Web address: www.connecticutchildrens.org/
  Control: Other not–for–profit (including NFP Corporation) **Service:** Children's general medical and surgical

  Staffed Beds: 185

- **HARTFORD HOSPITAL (070025)**, 80 Seymour Street, Zip 06102–8000, Mailing Address: P.O. Box 5037, Zip 06102–5037; tel. 860/545–5000, (Includes INSTITUTE OF LIVING, 400 Washington Street, Hartford, Connecticut, Zip 06106–3392, tel. 860/545–7000) (Total facility includes 104 beds in nursing home–type unit) **A**1 2 3 5 8 10 19 **F**2 3 5 6 7 8 9 10 11 12 13 15 17 18 20 22 24 26 28 29 30 31 34 35 36 37 38 39 40 43 44 45 46 47 48 49 50 51 52 53 54 55 56 57 58 59 60 61 63 64 65 66 68 70 71 74 75 76 77 78 79 80 81 82 83 84 85 86 87 90 91 92 93 94 95 96 97 98 99 100 101 102 103 104 105 106 107 108 110 111 112 114 115 116 117 118 119 120 121 123 124 125 126 128 129 130 131 132 133 134 135 137 138 139 141 143 145 146 147 148 149 150 152 153 154 155 156 157 160 162 163 164 165 166 167 169 **P**6 **S** Hartford HealthCare, Hartford, CT
  Primary Contact: Cheryl A. Ficara, R.N., MS, President
  CMO: Stuart Markowitz, M.D., Chief Medical Officer
  CIO: Stephan O'Neill, Vice President Information Services
  CHR: Richard McAloon, Vice President Human Resources
  Web address: www.harthosp.org
  Control: Other not–for–profit (including NFP Corporation) **Service:** General medical and surgical

  Staffed Beds: 906 **Admissions:** 42483 **Census:** 861 **Outpatient Visits:** 587943 **Births:** 3847 **Total Expense ($000):** 2288417 **Payroll Expense ($000):** 744070 **Personnel:** 6307

- **MOUNT SINAI REHABILITATION HOSPITAL (073025)**, 490 Blue Hills Avenue, Zip 06112–1513; tel. 860/714–3500, (Nonreporting) **A**1 7 10 **S** Trinity Health, Livonia, MI
  Primary Contact: Robert J. Krug, M.D., President and Executive Medical Director
  CFO: David Bittner, Chief Financial Officer
  Web address: https://www.trinityhealthofne.org/about-us/our-hospitals/mount-sinai-rehabilitation-center
  Control: Other not–for–profit (including NFP Corporation) **Service:** Rehabilitation

  Staffed Beds: 38

- **SAINT FRANCIS HOSPITAL (070002)**, 114 Woodland Street, Zip 06105–1208; tel. 860/714–4000, (Nonreporting) **A**1 2 3 5 8 10 19 **S** Trinity Health, Livonia, MI
  Primary Contact: Valerie L. Powell–Stafford, President
  CFO: Jennifer S. Schneider, Vice President of Finance
  CMO: Michael Grey, M.D., Interim Chief Medical Officer
  CIO: Linda L. Shanley, Vice President, Chief Information Officer
  CHR: Dennis W. Sparks, Vice President of Human Resources
  Web address: https://www.trinityhealthofne.org/location/saint-francis-hospital
  Control: Church operated, Nongovernment, not–for–profit **Service:** General medical and surgical

  Staffed Beds: 412

MANCHESTER—Hartford County

- **MANCHESTER MEMORIAL HOSPITAL (070027)**, 71 Haynes Street, Zip 06040–4188; tel. 860/646–1222, (Nonreporting) **A**1 2 3 5 10 12 13 **S** Prospect Medical Holdings, Los Angeles, CA
  Primary Contact: Deborah K. Weymouth, FACHE, President and Chief Executive Officer
  CFO: Michael D. Veillette, Senior Vice President and Chief Financial Officer
  CMO: Joel R Reich, M.D., Senior Vice President Medical Affairs
  CIO: Richard Daigle, Chief Information Officer
  CHR: Natalie Cook, Administrative Director of Human Resources
  CNO: Mary Powers, R.N., MSN, Senior Vice President and Chief Nursing Officer
  Web address: www.echn.org
  Control: Other not–for–profit (including NFP Corporation) **Service:** General medical and surgical

  Staffed Beds: 156

MANSFIELD CENTER—Tolland County

- **NATCHAUG HOSPITAL (074008)**, 189 Storrs Road, Zip 06250–1683; tel. 860/456–1311, **A**1 10 **F**4 5 29 34 44 50 56 75 77 87 98 99 100 101 103 104 105 129 130 132 149 151 152 153 154 160 161 164 **P**6 **S** Hartford HealthCare, Hartford, CT
  Primary Contact: James O'Dea, Chief Executive Officer
  COO: Thomas King, Vice President, Operations
  CFO: Paul V Maloney, Vice President Finance, Behavioral Health Network
  CMO: Carla Schnitzlein, D.O., Medical Director
  CIO: Mark Olson, Interim Chief Information Officer, Behavioral Health Network
  CHR: Laurie Clinton, Chief Human Resources Officer
  CNO: Justin Sleeper, Vice President Clinical Operations, Behavioral Health Network
  Web address: www.natchaug.org
  Control: Other not–for–profit (including NFP Corporation) **Service:** Psychiatric

  Staffed Beds: 59 **Admissions:** 1366 **Census:** 48 **Outpatient Visits:** 52357 **Births:** 0 **Total Expense ($000):** 53831 **Payroll Expense ($000):** 31509 **Personnel:** 311

MERIDEN—New Haven County

- **MIDSTATE MEDICAL CENTER (070017)**, 435 Lewis Avenue, Zip 06451–2101; tel. 203/694–8200, **A**1 2 10 19 **F**3 7 8 9 11 12 13 15 18 26 28 29 30 31 34 35 36 37 38 39 40 44 45 46 47 48 49 50 51 53 54 56 57 59 61 63 64 68 70 71 74 75 76 78 79 81 82 84 85 86 87 93 97 102 107 108 110 111 114 115 117 118 119 120 121 123 124 126 129 130 131 132 143 145 146 147 148 149 154 155 157 160 167 169 **P**6 **S** Hartford HealthCare, Hartford, CT
  Primary Contact: Gina Calder, M.P.H., FACHE, President
  CMO: Kenneth R Kurz, M.D., Chief of Staff
  CIO: Jennifer Comerford, Manager Information Services
  CHR: Kenneth W Cesca, Vice President Human Resources
  Web address: www.midstatemedical.org
  Control: Other not–for–profit (including NFP Corporation) **Service:** General medical and surgical

  Staffed Beds: 126 **Admissions:** 9448 **Census:** 116 **Outpatient Visits:** 162402 **Births:** 794 **Total Expense ($000):** 446184 **Payroll Expense ($000):** 127282 **Personnel:** 1240

MIDDLETOWN—Middlesex County

- **ALBERT J. SOLNIT CHILDREN'S CENTER (074015)**, 915 River Road, Zip 06457–3921, Mailing Address: P.O. Box 2792, Zip 06457–9292; tel. 860/704–4000, (Nonreporting) **A**1 3 5 10
  Primary Contact: Heidi Pugliese, Chief Executive Officer and Superintendent
  CFO: Connie Tessarzik, Business Manager
  CMO: Lesley Siegel, M.D., Medical Director
  CIO: Andrew J A Kass, M.D., Assistant Superintendent
  Web address: www.ct.gov
  Control: State, Government, Nonfederal **Service:** Children's hospital psychiatric

  Staffed Beds: 50

Hospitals, U.S. / CONNECTICUT

☐ **CONNECTICUT VALLEY HOSPITAL (074003)**, 1000 Silver Street, Zip 06457–3947; tel. 860/262–5000, (Includes WHITING FORENSIC HOSPITAL, 70 Obrien Drive, Middletown, Connecticut, Zip 06457, Box 70, Zip 06457–3942, tel. 860/262–5400; Michael A Norko, M.D., Acting Chief Executive Officer) (Nonreporting) **A**1 3 5 10 **S** Connecticut Department of Mental Health and Addiction Services, Hartford, CT
Primary Contact: Lakisha Hyatt, Chief Executive Officer
COO: John D'Eramo, Chief Operating Officer
CFO: Cindy Butterfield, Director, Fiscal and Administrative Services
CMO: Thomas Pisano, M.D., Chief Professional Services
CIO: Kathryn Connelly, Manager Information Technology
CHR: Cheryl Thompson, Facility Director Human Resources
Web address: https://portal.ct.gov/DMHAS/CVH/Agency-Files/CVH–Home-Page
Control: State, Government, Nonfederal **Service**: Psychiatric

Staffed Beds: 361

✠ **MIDDLESEX HEALTH (070020)**, 28 Crescent Street, Zip 06457–3650; tel. 860/358–6000, **A**1 2 3 5 10 19 **F**3 7 8 12 13 15 18 20 28 29 30 31 32 34 35 36 37 38 40 42 45 46 47 48 49 50 51 55 57 58 59 60 61 62 63 64 65 68 70 74 75 76 77 78 79 81 82 83 84 85 86 87 89 92 93 94 97 98 100 101 102 104 107 108 110 111 114 115 117 118 119 120 121 123 124 126 129 130 131 132 134 135 143 145 146 147 148 149 153 154 157 162 164 165 167 169 **P**6
Primary Contact: Vincent G. Capece Jr, President and Chief Executive Officer
CFO: Susan Martin, Chief Financial Officer and Vice President, Finance
CMO: Jesse Wagner, M.D., Chief Medical Officer and Vice President, Quality and Patient Safety
CIO: Evan Jackson, Chief Information Officer and Vice President, Planning and Business Development
CHR: Donna Stroneski, Vice President, Human Resources
CNO: Jacquelyn Calamari, MSN, MS, Chief Nursing Officer and Vice President, Patient Care Services
Web address: www.middlesexhealth.org
Control: Other not–for–profit (including NFP Corporation) **Service**: General medical and surgical

Staffed Beds: 221 **Admissions**: 10445 **Census**: 137 **Outpatient Visits**: 634712 **Births**: 836 **Total Expense ($000)**: 485732 **Payroll Expense ($000)**: 229570 **Personnel**: 2253

MIDDLESEX HOSPITAL See Middlesex Health

WHITING FORENSIC DIVISION OF CONNECTICUT VALLEY HOSPITAL See Whiting Forensic Hospital

WHITING FORENSIC HOSPITAL See Connecticut Valley Hospital, Middletown

NEW BRITAIN—Hartford County

✠ **HOSPITAL FOR SPECIAL CARE (072004)**, 2150 Corbin Avenue, Zip 06053–2298; tel. 860/223–2761, (Nonreporting) **A**1 3 5 10
Primary Contact: Lynn Ricci, President and Chief Executive Officer
CFO: Laurie A Whelan, Senior Vice President Finance and Chief Financial Officer
CMO: J. Kevin Shushtari, M.D., Chief Medical Officer
CIO: Stan Jankowski, Vice President and Chief Information Officer
CHR: Nancy M Martone, Vice President and Chief Human Resources Officer
Web address: www.hfsc.org
Control: Other not–for–profit (including NFP Corporation) **Service**: Acute long–term care hospital

Staffed Beds: 228

NEW BRITAIN GENERAL HOSPITAL See New Britain General

✠ **THE HOSPITAL OF CENTRAL CONNECTICUT (070035)**, 100 Grand Street, Zip 06052–2017, Mailing Address: P.O. Box 100, Zip 06052–2017; tel. 860/224–5011, (Includes BRADLEY MEMORIAL, 81 Meriden Avenue, Southington, Connecticut, Zip 06489–3297, tel. 860/276–5000; NEW BRITAIN GENERAL, 100 Grand Street, New Britain, Connecticut, Zip 06052–2017, P O Box 100, Zip 06050–0100, tel. 860/224–5011) **A**1 2 3 5 10 19 **F**3 7 8 11 12 13 15 18 20 22 26 28 29 30 31 34 35 37 38 40 43 44 45 49 50 51 53 54 57 58 59 60 61 64 65 66 68 70 72 74 75 76 77 78 79 81 84 85 86 87 93 97 98 100 101 102 104 105 107 108 110 111 114 115 117 118 119 120 121 123 124 126 129 130 132 135 146 147 148 149 153 154 156 157 160 162 164 165 167 **P**6 **S** Hartford HealthCare, Hartford, CT
Primary Contact: Gina Calder, M.P.H., FACHE, President
CFO: Brian Rogoz, Vice President Finance and Treasurer
CIO: Frank Pinto, Chief Information Officer
CHR: Elizabeth A Lynch, Vice President Human Resources
Web address: www.thocc.org
Control: Other not–for–profit (including NFP Corporation) **Service**: General medical and surgical

Staffed Beds: 231 **Admissions**: 13678 **Census**: 221 **Outpatient Visits**: 394064 **Births**: 1475 **Total Expense ($000)**: 654746 **Payroll Expense ($000)**: 249408 **Personnel**: 2197

NEW CANAAN—Fairfield County

☐ **SILVER HILL HOSPITAL (074014)**, 208 Valley Road, Zip 06840–3899; tel. 203/966–3561, **A**1 10 **F**4 5 29 34 35 58 64 87 98 101 104 106 130 132 146 149 153 154 160 164 **P**6
Primary Contact: Andrew J. Gerber, M.D., Ph.D., President and Chief Executive Officer
COO: Elizabeth Moore, Chief Operating Officer
CFO: Ruurd Leegstra, Chief Financial Officer
CMO: Andrew J. Gerber, M.D., Ph.D., President and Medical Director
CIO: Maria Klinga, Director Management Information Systems
CHR: Rich Juliana, Director Human Resources
Web address: www.silverhillhospital.org
Control: Other not–for–profit (including NFP Corporation) **Service**: Psychiatric

Staffed Beds: 114 **Admissions**: 1592 **Census**: 71 **Outpatient Visits**: 9990 **Births**: 0 **Total Expense ($000)**: 65873 **Payroll Expense ($000)**: 37277 **Personnel**: 405

NEW HAVEN—New Haven County

☐ **CONNECTICUT MENTAL HEALTH CENTER (074011)**, 34 Park Street, Zip 06519–1109, Mailing Address: P.O. Box 1842, Zip 06508–1842; tel. 203/974–7144, (Nonreporting) **A**1 3 5 10 **S** Connecticut Department of Mental Health and Addiction Services, Hartford, CT
Primary Contact: Michael Sernyak, M.D., Director
COO: Robert Cole, Chief Operating Officer
CFO: Robert Cole, Chief Operating Officer
CMO: Jeanne Steines, D.O., Medical Director
CIO: Paul Moore, Chief Information Officer
CHR: Carolyn Wallace, Director Human Resources
Web address: www.ct.gov/dmhas/cwp/view.asp?a=2906&q=334596
Control: State, Government, Nonfederal **Service**: Psychiatric

Staffed Beds: 32

HOSPITAL OF SAINT RAPHAEL See Yale–New Haven Hospital–Saint Raphael Campus

---

Hospital, Medicare Provider Number, Address, Telephone, Approval, Facility, and Physician Codes, Health Care System

★ American Hospital Association (AHA) membership   ○ Healthcare Facilities Accreditation Program   ⇑ Center for Improvement in Healthcare Quality Accreditation
☐ The Joint Commission accreditation   ◇ DNV Healthcare Inc. accreditation   △ Commission on Accreditation of Rehabilitation Facilities (CARF) accreditation

© 2025 AHA Guide

Hospitals, U.S. / CONNECTICUT

✠ **YALE NEW HAVEN HOSPITAL (070022)**, 20 York Street, Zip 06510–3202; tel. 203/688–4242, (Includes YALE–NEW HAVEN CHILDREN'S HOSPITAL, 1 Park Street, New Haven, Connecticut, Zip 06504–8901, tel. 203/688–4242; Cynthia Sparer, Senior Vice President and Executive Director Women's & Children; YALE–NEW HAVEN HOSPITAL–SAINT RAPHAEL CAMPUS, 1450 Chapel Street, New Haven, Connecticut, Zip 06511–4405, tel. 203/789–3000; Richard D'Aquila, President; YALE–NEW HAVEN PSYCHIATRIC HOSPITAL, 184 Liberty Street, New Haven, Connecticut, Zip 06519–1625, tel. 203/688–9704; Mark Sevilla, R.N., Executive Director) **A**1 2 3 5 8 10 19 **F**3 5 6 9 11 12 13 14 15 17 18 19 20 21 22 23 24 25 26 27 28 29 30 31 32 34 35 36 37 38 39 40 41 42 43 44 45 46 47 48 49 50 51 52 53 54 55 56 57 58 59 61 64 65 66 68 70 72 74 75 76 77 78 79 80 81 82 84 85 86 87 88 89 90 91 92 93 94 96 97 98 99 100 101 102 103 104 105 107 108 109 110 111 112 114 115 116 117 118 119 120 121 123 124 126 129 130 131 132 134 135 136 137 138 139 141 142 143 144 145 146 147 148 149 152 153 154 156 160 162 167 168 169 **S** Yale New Haven Health, New Haven, CT
Primary Contact: Katherine Heilpern, M.D., President
CMO: Thomas Balcezak, M.D., Senior Vice President Medical Affairs and Chief Medical Officer
CIO: Lisa Stump, Interim Chief Information Officer
CNO: Patricia Sue Fitzsimons, R.N., Ph.D., Senior Vice President Patient Services
Web address: www.ynhh.org
Control: Other not–for–profit (including NFP Corporation) **Service**: General medical and surgical

Staffed Beds: 1481 **Admissions:** 68898 **Census:** 1370 **Outpatient Visits:** 1726827 **Births:** 5486 **Total Expense ($000):** 4094111 **Payroll Expense ($000):** 1273475 **Personnel:** 14408

YALE PSYCHIATRIC INSTITUTE See Yale–New Haven Psychiatric Hospital

NEW LONDON—New London County

✠ **LAWRENCE + MEMORIAL HOSPITAL (070007)**, 365 Montauk Avenue, Zip 06320–4769; tel. 860/442–0711, **A**1 2 3 5 10 19 **F**3 5 7 11 12 13 15 17 18 19 20 22 26 28 29 30 31 34 35 38 40 41 42 44 45 49 50 51 54 55 56 57 58 59 60 62 63 64 65 68 70 72 74 75 76 77 78 79 81 82 84 85 86 87 89 90 91 92 93 96 97 98 100 101 102 104 107 108 110 111 114 115 116 117 118 119 120 121 123 126 129 131 132 135 146 147 148 149 153 154 160 164 165 167 169 **S** Yale New Haven Health, New Haven, CT
Primary Contact: Richard Lisitano, President
CMO: Oliver Mayorga, M.D., Chief Medical Officer
CHR: Donna Epps, Vice President and Chief Human Resources Officer
Web address: www.lmhospital.org
Control: Other not–for–profit (including NFP Corporation) **Service**: General medical and surgical

Staffed Beds: 252 **Admissions:** 12550 **Census:** 197 **Outpatient Visits:** 352286 **Births:** 1239 **Total Expense ($000):** 468963 **Payroll Expense ($000):** 172952 **Personnel:** 2131

NORWALK—Fairfield County

✠ **NORWALK HOSPITAL (070034)**, 34 Maple Street, Zip 06850–3894; tel. 203/852–2000, **A**1 3 5 10 19 **F**3 5 7 11 12 13 15 18 20 22 26 28 29 30 31 34 35 36 37 38 39 40 43 44 45 46 47 48 49 54 55 56 57 58 59 64 68 70 72 74 75 76 77 78 79 81 82 84 85 86 87 92 93 96 98 100 101 102 104 107 108 109 110 111 115 116 117 118 119 120 121 124 126 129 130 131 132 135 141 143 145 146 147 148 149 150 153 154 156 157 160 161 162 164 165 167 169 **S** Nuvance Health, Danbury, CT
Primary Contact: Peter Cordeau, President
CFO: Michael Kruzick, Acting Chief Financial Officer
CMO: Michael Marks, M.D., Chief of Staff
CHR: Anthony Aceto, Vice President Human Resources
Web address: www.norwalkhospital.org
Control: Other not–for–profit (including NFP Corporation) **Service**: General medical and surgical

Staffed Beds: 139 **Admissions:** 8740 **Census:** 116 **Outpatient Visits:** 167093 **Births:** 812 **Total Expense ($000):** 413672 **Payroll Expense ($000):** 122413 **Personnel:** 1289

NORWICH—New London County

✠ **THE WILLIAM W. BACKUS HOSPITAL (070024)**, 326 Washington Street, Zip 06360–2740; tel. 860/889–8331, **A**1 2 5 10 19 **F**3 7 8 9 11 12 13 15 18 20 26 28 29 30 31 34 35 36 37 40 42 43 45 46 47 49 50 51 54 57 58 59 61 63 64 65 68 70 71 74 75 76 78 79 80 81 82 84 85 86 87 92 93 97 98 100 101 102 104 105 107 108 110 111 114 115 116 117 118 119 120 121 126 130 132 134 135 145 146 148 149 153 154 157 164 165 167 **P**6 **S** Hartford HealthCare, Hartford, CT
Primary Contact: Donna Handley, President
COO: Carolyn Trantalis, R.N., MSN, Regional Vice President, Clinical Services and Operations
CFO: Anthony Mastroianni, Regional Vice President Finance
CMO: Robert Sidman, M.D., Regional Vice President, Medical Affairs
CIO: Angie Mathieu, System Director Information Technology and Regional Chief Information Officer
CHR: Karen James, Regional Director, Human Resources
CNO: Carolyn Trantalis, R.N., MSN, Regional Vice President, Clinical Services and Operations
Web address: www.backushospital.org
Control: Other not–for–profit (including NFP Corporation) **Service**: General medical and surgical

Staffed Beds: 196 **Admissions:** 10753 **Census:** 146 **Outpatient Visits:** 457989 **Births:** 908 **Total Expense ($000):** 472761 **Payroll Expense ($000):** 160909 **Personnel:** 1420

PUTNAM—Windham County

☐ **DAY KIMBALL HOSPITAL (070003)**, 320 Pomfret Street, Zip 06260–1836; tel. 860/928–6541, (Nonreporting) **A**1 2 5 10
Primary Contact: Kyle Kramer, Chief Executive Officer
CFO: Paul Beaudoin, Chief Financial Officer
CMO: John Graham, M.D., Vice President Medical Affairs
CIO: Odile Romanick, Chief information Officer
CHR: Jeffrey T. Corrigan, Vice President Human Resources
CNO: John O'Keefe, Chief Nursing Officer
Web address: www.daykimball.org
Control: Other not–for–profit (including NFP Corporation) **Service**: General medical and surgical

Staffed Beds: 62

ROCKY HILL—Hartford County

★ **CONNECTICUT VETERANS HOME AND HOSPITAL (072006)**, 287 West Street, Zip 06067–3501; tel. 860/616–3606, (Nonreporting) **A**10 **S** Department of Veterans Affairs, Washington, DC
Primary Contact: Thomas J. Saadi, Commissioner
CFO: Michael Clark, Fiscal Administrative Manager
CMO: Vamseedhar Alla, M.D., Director Medical Staff
CIO: Sheri DeVaux, Information Technology Manager
CHR: Noreen Sinclair, Human Resources Administrator
CNO: Jeff Lord, Director of Nursing
Web address: www.ct.gov/ctva
Control: State, Government, Nonfederal **Service**: Acute long–term care hospital

Staffed Beds: 125

SHARON—Litchfield County

✠ **SHARON HOSPITAL (070004)**, 50 Hospital Hill Road, Zip 06069–2096, Mailing Address: P.O. Box 789, Zip 06069–0789; tel. 860/364–4000, **A**1 3 10 20 **F**3 8 9 11 13 15 18 28 29 30 34 35 36 38 40 44 45 46 47 48 49 50 51 53 56 57 59 65 68 70 74 75 76 77 78 79 81 84 85 86 87 93 96 98 100 101 102 103 105 107 108 110 111 115 118 119 130 131 132 135 141 143 146 147 148 149 154 157 160 161 162 164 165 167 169 **S** Nuvance Health, Danbury, CT
Primary Contact: Christina McCulloch, President
CMO: Michael Parker, M.D., Chief of Staff
CHR: Kathleen Berlinghoff, Director Human Resources
Web address: www.sharonhospital.com
Control: Other not–for–profit (including NFP Corporation) **Service**: General medical and surgical

Staffed Beds: 28 **Admissions:** 1436 **Census:** 22 **Outpatient Visits:** 54682 **Births:** 145 **Total Expense ($000):** 73698 **Payroll Expense ($000):** 26978 **Personnel:** 229

SOMERS—Tolland County

CONNECTICUT DEPARTMENT OF CORRECTION'S HOSPITAL, 100 Bilton Road, Zip 06071–1059, Mailing Address: 24 Wolcott Hill Road, Wethersfield, Zip 06109–1152; tel. 860/692–7780, (Nonreporting)
Primary Contact: Robert Richeson, Chief Operating Officer
Web address: https://portal.ct.gov/DOC
Control: State, Government, Nonfederal **Service**: Hospital unit of an institution (prison hospital, college infirmary, etc.)

Staffed Beds: 29

Hospitals, U.S. / CONNECTICUT

SOUTHINGTON—Hartford County

BRADLEY MEMORIAL See The Hospital of Central Connecticut, New Britain

BRADLEY MEMORIAL HOSPITAL AND HEALTH CENTER See Bradley Memorial

STAFFORD SPRINGS—Tolland County

JOHNSON MEMORIAL HOSPITAL (070008), 201 Chestnut Hill Road, Zip 06076–4005; tel. 860/684–4251, (Nonreporting) **A**1 10 **S** Trinity Health, Livonia, MI
Primary Contact: Robert Roose, M.D., Chief Executive Officer
CFO: John Grish, Chief Financial Officer
CMO: Ian Tucker, M.D., Vice President Medical Affairs
CHR: Donna M Megliola, Assistant Vice President
CNO: Patricia Jagoe, Assistant Vice President Patient Care
Web address: www.jmmc.com
Control: Other not–for–profit (including NFP Corporation) **Service**: General medical and surgical

Staffed Beds: 78

STAMFORD—Fairfield County

STAMFORD HEALTH (070006), 1 Hospital Plaza, Zip 06902, Mailing Address: P.O. Box 9317, Zip 06904–9317; tel. 203/276–1000, **A**1 2 3 5 10 19 **F**3 8 12 13 15 18 19 20 22 24 26 28 29 30 31 32 34 35 36 37 38 40 41 43 44 45 46 47 48 49 50 52 53 54 55 56 57 58 59 60 61 64 65 66 67 70 72 74 75 76 77 78 79 81 82 84 85 86 87 89 90 91 92 93 95 96 97 98 100 102 104 107 108 110 111 114 115 116 117 118 119 120 121 123 124 126 129 130 131 132 135 142 144 145 146 147 148 149 150 154 157 160 162 164 167 169 **P**7
Primary Contact: Kathleen A. Silard, R.N., MS, FACHE, President and Chief Executive Officer
COO: Jonathan T Bailey, Chief Operating Officer
CFO: Kevin Gage, Chief Financial Officer
CMO: Sharon Kiely, M.D., Senior Vice President Medical Affairs and Chief Medical Officer
CIO: Steven Sakovits, Vice President Information Systems and Chief Information Officer
CHR: Elaine Guglielmo, Vice President Human Resources and Organizational Development
CNO: Ellen M Komar, R.N., Senior Vice President Patient Care Services and Chief Nursing Officer
Web address: www.stamhealth.org
Control: Other not–for–profit (including NFP Corporation) **Service**: General medical and surgical

Staffed Beds: 305 Admissions: 13337 Census: 205 Outpatient Visits: 536637 Births: 2461 Total Expense ($000): 809819 Payroll Expense ($000): 269960 Personnel: 3371

STAMFORD HOSPITAL See Stamford Health

TORRINGTON—Litchfield County

CHARLOTTE HUNGERFORD HOSPITAL (070011), 540 Litchfield Street, Zip 06790–6679, Mailing Address: P.O. Box 988, Zip 06790–0988; tel. 860/496–6666, **A**1 2 3 5 10 19 **F**2 3 5 6 8 9 10 11 12 13 15 18 28 29 30 31 33 34 35 36 37 38 39 40 41 42 44 45 46 47 48 49 50 51 52 53 54 55 56 57 58 59 61 63 64 65 66 68 70 71 74 75 76 77 78 79 81 82 83 84 85 86 87 91 92 93 94 95 96 97 98 100 101 102 104 105 106 107 108 110 111 112 114 115 116 117 118 119 120 121 123 124 125 126 129 130 131 132 133 134 135 137 138 139 141 143 145 146 147 148 149 150 152 153 154 157 158 160 162 163 164 165 167 **P**6 **S** Hartford HealthCare, Hartford, CT
Primary Contact: Bimal Patel, President, Hartford and Northwest Regions
CFO: Susan Schapp, Vice President Finance and Treasurer
CMO: Mark Prete, M.D., Vice President Medical Affairs
CHR: R James Elliott, Vice President Human Resources
Web address: www.charlottehungerford.org
Control: Other not–for–profit (including NFP Corporation) **Service**: General medical and surgical

Staffed Beds: 109 Admissions: 5662 Census: 73 Outpatient Visits: 240583 Births: 447 Total Expense ($000): 189763 Payroll Expense ($000): 93918 Personnel: 797

VERNON—Tolland County

ROCKVILLE GENERAL HOSPITAL (070012), 31 Union Street, Zip 06066–3160; tel. 860/872–0501, (Nonreporting) **A**1 5 10 **S** Prospect Medical Holdings, Los Angeles, CA
Primary Contact: Deborah K. Weymouth, FACHE, Chief Executive Officer
CFO: Michael D. Veillette, Senior Vice President and Chief Financial Officer
CMO: Joel R Reich, M.D., Senior Vice President Medical Affairs
CIO: Richard Daigle, Chief Information Officer
CHR: Natalie Cook, Administrative Director, Human Resources
CNO: Mary Powers, R.N., MSN, Senior Vice President and Chief Nursing Officer
Web address: www.echn.org
Control: Other not–for–profit (including NFP Corporation) **Service**: General medical and surgical

Staffed Beds: 47

WALLINGFORD—New Haven County

GAYLORD SPECIALTY HEALTHCARE (072003), 50 Gaylord Farm Road, Zip 06492–7048, Mailing Address: P.O. Box 400, Zip 06492–7048; tel. 203/284–2800, (Nonreporting) **A**1 3 5 7 10
Primary Contact: Sonja LaBarbera, President and Chief Executive Officer
CFO: Art Tedesco, Interim Chief Financial Officer
CMO: Stephen Holland, M.D., Vice President Chief Medical Officer and Medical Director
CIO: Gerry Maroney, Chief Information Officer and Security Officer
CHR: Wally G Harper, Vice President Human Resources
CNO: Lisa Kalafus, MSN, R.N., Chief Nursing Officer
Web address: www.gaylord.org
Control: Other not–for–profit (including NFP Corporation) **Service**: Acute long–term care hospital

Staffed Beds: 122

MASONICARE HEALTH CENTER (074016), 22 Masonic Avenue, Zip 06492–3048, Mailing Address: P.O. Box 70, Zip 06492–7001; tel. 203/679–5900, (Nonreporting) **A**5 10
Primary Contact: Jon–Paul Venoit, President and Chief Executive Officer
COO: Jon–Paul Venoit, Chief Operating Officer
CFO: Raymond Scott Thelen, Vice President and Chief Financial Officer
CMO: Ronald Schwartz, M.D., Medical Director
CHR: Edward Dooling, Vice President, Human Resources
CNO: Patti Russell, Vice President Nursing
Web address: www.masonicare.org
Control: Other not–for–profit (including NFP Corporation) **Service**: Other specialty treatment

Staffed Beds: 65

WATERBURY—New Haven County

SAINT MARY'S HOSPITAL (070016), 56 Franklin Street, Zip 06706–1281; tel. 203/709–6000, (Nonreporting) **A**1 2 3 5 10 **S** Trinity Health, Livonia, MI
Primary Contact: Kimberly Kalajainen, FACHE, Chief Administrative Officer
COO: Charles Flinn, Vice President, Chief Operating Officer
CFO: Ralph W Becker, Vice President, Chief Financial Officer
CIO: Michael Novak, Vice President, Operations and Chief Information Officer
CHR: M Clark Kearney, Vice President Human Resources
CNO: Elizabeth Bozzuto, R.N., Chief Nursing Officer and Vice President
Web address: www.trinityhealthofne.org
Control: Church operated, Nongovernment, not–for–profit **Service**: General medical and surgical

Staffed Beds: 237

WATERBURY HOSPITAL (070005), 64 Robbins Street, Zip 06708–2600; tel. 203/573–6000, (Nonreporting) **A**1 3 5 10 **S** Prospect Medical Holdings, Los Angeles, CA
Primary Contact: Deborah K. Weymouth, FACHE, President and Chief Executive Officer
CFO: Colleen M Scott, Vice President Finance
CMO: David Puzzuto, M.D., Vice President Medical Affairs and Chief Medical Officer
CIO: Michael J Cemeno, Chief Information Officer
CNO: Sandra Ladarola, Chief Nursing Officer
Web address: www.waterburyhospital.org
Control: Corporation, Investor–owned (for–profit) **Service**: General medical and surgical

Staffed Beds: 173

Hospital, Medicare Provider Number, Address, Telephone, Approval, Facility, and Physician Codes, Health Care System

★ American Hospital Association (AHA) membership
☐ The Joint Commission accreditation
○ Healthcare Facilities Accreditation Program
◇ DNV Healthcare Inc. accreditation
⇑ Center for Improvement in Healthcare Quality Accreditation
△ Commission on Accreditation of Rehabilitation Facilities (CARF) accreditation

© 2025 AHA Guide

Hospitals, U.S. / CONNECTICUT

WEST HARTFORD—Hartford County

THE HOSPITAL AT HEBREW SENIOR CARE (070040), 1 Abrahms Boulevard, Zip 06117-1525; tel. 860/523-3800, (Nonreporting) **A**10
Primary Contact: Denise Peterson, R.N., FACHE, President and Chief Executive Officer
COO: Marcia H Hickey, Senior Vice President Operations
CFO: David Houle, Executive Vice President and Chief Financial Officer
CMO: Ava Pannullo, M.D., Vice President Medical Services and Physician in Chief
CHR: Sam Vogt, Manager Human Resources
Web address: www.hebrewhealthcare.org
Control: Other not–for–profit (including NFP Corporation) **Service**: Other specialty treatment

Staffed Beds: 45

WEST HAVEN—New Haven County

VETERANS AFFAIRS CONNECTICUT HEALTHCARE SYSTEM, 950 Campbell Avenue, Zip 06516-2770; tel. 203/932-5711, (Includes WEST HAVEN DIVISION, 950 Campbell Avenue, West Haven, Connecticut, Zip 06516-2700, tel. 203/932-5711) (Nonreporting) **A**1 2 3 5 8 **S** Department of Veterans Affairs, Washington, DC
Primary Contact: Becky Rhoads, Executive Director
CFO: Joseph LaMadeleine, Chief Financial Officer
CMO: Huned Patwa, Chief of Staff
CIO: Joseph Erdos, M.D., Chief Information Officer
CHR: Mark Bain, Chief Human Resources
CNO: Bernadette Yap Jao, Chief Nursing Executive, Associate Director Patient and Nursing Services
Web address: www.connecticut.va.gov
Control: Veterans Affairs, Government, federal **Service**: General medical and surgical

Staffed Beds: 177

VETERANS AFFAIRS MEDICAL CENTER See West Haven Division

WESTPORT—Fairfield County

HALL–BROOKE HOSPITAL, A DIVISION OF HALL–BROOKE BEHAVIORAL HEALTH SERVICES See St. Vincent's Behavioral Health

ST. VINCENT'S BEHAVIORAL HEALTH See St. Vincent's Medical Center, Bridgeport

WILLIMANTIC—Windham County

WINDHAM HOSPITAL (070021), 112 Mansfield Avenue, Zip 06226-2040; tel. 860/456-9116, **A**1 2 5 10 19 **F**3 5 6 8 9 11 12 15 18 28 29 30 31 34 35 36 37 38 40 44 45 46 50 51 53 54 56 57 58 59 60 63 64 65 68 71 72 73 74 75 76 77 78 79 81 82 83 84 85 86 87 90 91 92 93 94 95 96 97 100 101 102 104 105 106 107 108 110 111 112 114 115 118 119 120 121 123 124 126 129 130 131 132 133 134 135 145 146 147 148 149 150 152 153 154 156 157 160 163 164 165 167 169 **P**6 **S** Hartford HealthCare, Hartford, CT
Primary Contact: Donna Handley, President
COO: Carolyn Trantalis, R.N., MSN, Chief Operating Officer, East Region
CFO: Daniel E Lohr, Regional Vice President Finance
CMO: Nadia Nashid, M.D., Chief of Staff
CHR: Theresa L Buss, Regional Vice President Human Resources
Web address: www.windhamhospital.org
Control: Other not–for–profit (including NFP Corporation) **Service**: General medical and surgical

Staffed Beds: 58 **Admissions:** 2141 **Census:** 21 **Outpatient Visits:** 171468 **Births:** 0 **Total Expense ($000):** 124122 **Payroll Expense ($000):** 42924 **Personnel:** 431

DELAWARE

DOVER—Kent County

☒ △ **BAYHEALTH (080004)**, 640 South State Street, Zip 19901-3530; tel. 302/674-4700, (Includes BAYHEALTH MEDICAL CENTER AT KENT GENERAL, 640 South State Street, Dover, Delaware, Zip 19901-3597, tel. 203/932-5711; BAYHEALTH MEDICAL CENTER, MILFORD MEMORIAL HOSPITAL, 21 West Clarke Avenue, Milford, Delaware, Zip 19963-1840, P O Box 199, Zip 19963-0199, tel. 302/430-5738; Michael Ashton, Administrator) **A**1 2 3 5 7 8 10 **F**3 8 12 13 15 17 18 20 22 24 26 28 29 30 31 32 34 35 38 40 41 42 43 44 45 47 48 49 50 51 54 55 57 58 59 60 61 64 67 68 70 72 73 74 75 76 77 78 79 81 82 84 85 86 87 88 89 90 93 94 98 99 100 101 102 103 104 107 108 110 111 114 115 117 118 119 120 121 123 124 126 129 130 131 132 134 135 144 146 147 148 149 169
Primary Contact: Terry Murphy, FACHE, President and Chief Executive Officer
COO: Deborah Watson, Senior Vice President and Chief Operating Officer
CFO: Mike Tretina, Senior Vice President and Chief Financial Officer
CMO: Gary M Siegelman, M.D., MSC, Senior Vice President and Chief Medical Officer
CIO: Richard Mohnk, Vice President Corporate Services
CHR: Shana Ross, Vice President Human Resources
CNO: Brenda Blain, MSN, Senior Vice President and Chief Nursing Executive
Web address: www.bayhealth.org
Control: Other not-for-profit (including NFP Corporation) **Service**: General medical and surgical

Staffed Beds: 429 **Admissions**: 18022 **Census**: 316 **Outpatient Visits**: 664145 **Births**: 2541 **Total Expense ($000)**: 941120 **Payroll Expense ($000)**: 472823 **Personnel**: 4208

BAYHEALTH MEDICAL CENTER See Bayhealth

☐ **DOVER BEHAVIORAL HEALTH SYSTEM (084004)**, 725 Horsepond Road, Zip 19901-7232; tel. 302/741-0140, (Nonreporting) **A**1 10 **S** Universal Health Services, Inc., King of Prussia, PA
Primary Contact: Jean-Charles Constant, Administrator
Web address: www.doverbehavioral.com
Control: Partnership, Investor-owned (for-profit) **Service**: Psychiatric

Staffed Beds: 104

KENT GENERAL HOSPITAL See Bayhealth Medical Center At Kent General

☒ **PAM REHABILITATION HOSPITAL OF DOVER (083027)**, 1240 Mckee Road, Zip 19904-1381; tel. 302/672-5800, **A**1 10 **F**3 28 29 54 64 77 87 90 91 93 96 135 143 146 148 **S** PAM Health, Enola, PA
Primary Contact: Ted Werner, Chief Executive Officer
Web address: https://postacutemedical.com/facilities/find-facility/rehabilitation-hospitals/pam-rehabilitation-hospital-dover
Control: Corporation, Investor-owned (for-profit) **Service**: Rehabilitation

Staffed Beds: 34 **Admissions**: 1236 **Census**: 33 **Outpatient Visits**: 11282 **Births**: 0 **Total Expense ($000)**: 20760 **Payroll Expense ($000)**: 11095 **Personnel**: 188

GEORGETOWN—Sussex County

★ **PAM HEALTH REHABILITATION HOSPITAL OF GEORGETOWN (083028)**, 22303 Dupont Boulevard, Zip 19947-2153; tel. 302/440-4866, **F**3 29 34 35 50 60 68 74 75 86 87 90 91 93 96 132 148 149 154 **P**5 6 **S** PAM Health, Enola, PA
Primary Contact: George Del Farno, Chief Executive Officer
CNO: Hannah Goss, Chief Nursing Officer
Web address: https://pamhealth.com/
Control: Corporation, Investor-owned (for-profit) **Service**: Rehabilitation

Staffed Beds: 34 **Admissions**: 1029 **Census**: 26 **Outpatient Visits**: 3165 **Births**: 0 **Total Expense ($000)**: 18011 **Payroll Expense ($000)**: 9219 **Personnel**: 156

☐ **SUN BEHAVIORAL DELAWARE (084005)**, 21655 Biden Avenue, Zip 19947-4573; tel. 302/604-5600, (Nonreporting) **A**1 10
Primary Contact: Ann Wayne, Chief Executive Officer
Web address: https://sunbehavioral.com/delaware/
Control: Corporation, Investor-owned (for-profit) **Service**: Psychiatric

Staffed Beds: 90

LEWES—Sussex County

☒ **BEEBE HEALTHCARE (080007)**, 424 Savannah Road, Zip 19958-1462; tel. 302/645-3300, **A**1 2 3 5 10 19 **F**3 8 11 12 13 15 17 18 20 22 24 26 28 29 30 31 34 35 36 37 38 39 40 41 42 43 44 45 46 47 48 49 50 51 53 57 58 59 60 61 62 63 64 65 66 67 68 70 71 74 75 76 77 78 79 81 82 84 85 86 87 89 93 96 97 100 102 107 108 109 110 111 114 115 116 117 118 119 120 121 122 123 124 126 130 131 135 144 145 146 147 148 149 154 156 157 160 161 164 167 168 169 **P**6
Primary Contact: David A. Tam, M.D., FACHE, President and Chief Executive Officer
CFO: Paul Pernice, Vice President Finance
CMO: Jeffrey Hawtof, M.D., Vice President Medical Operations and Informatics
CIO: Michael Maksymow, Vice President Information Systems
CHR: Catherine Halen, Vice President Human Resources
Web address: www.beebemed.org
Control: Other not-for-profit (including NFP Corporation) **Service**: General medical and surgical

Staffed Beds: 210 **Admissions**: 10687 **Census**: 140 **Outpatient Visits**: 739601 **Births**: 721 **Total Expense ($000)**: 554499 **Payroll Expense ($000)**: 185877 **Personnel**: 2618

MIDDLETOWN—New Castle County

☒ **ENCOMPASS HEALTH REHABILITATION HOSPITAL OF MIDDLETOWN (083026)**, 250 East Hampden Road, Zip 19709-5303; tel. 302/464-3400, **A**1 10 **F**3 29 90 95 96 132 148 149 **S** Encompass Health Corporation, Birmingham, AL
Primary Contact: Dustin McFarland, Interim Chief Executive Officer
CFO: Lisa Trimble, Controller
CMO: Ashish Khandelwal, M.D., Medical Director
CHR: Anitra Jones, Director Human Resources
CNO: Rebecca Boney, R.N., Chief Nursing Officer
Web address: www.encompasshealth.com/middletownrehab
Control: Corporation, Investor-owned (for-profit) **Service**: Rehabilitation

Staffed Beds: 40 **Admissions**: 1299 **Census**: 39 **Outpatient Visits**: 0 **Births**: 0 **Total Expense ($000)**: 21882 **Payroll Expense ($000)**: 10417 **Personnel**: 119

MILFORD—Sussex County

BAYHEALTH MEDICAL CENTER, MILFORD MEMORIAL HOSPITAL See Bayhealth, Dover

MILFORD MEMORIAL HOSPITAL See Bayhealth Medical Center, Milford Memorial Hospital

NEW CASTLE—New Castle County

☐ **DELAWARE PSYCHIATRIC CENTER (084001)**, 1901 North Dupont Highway, Zip 19720-1199; tel. 302/255-2700, (Nonreporting) **A**1 3 5 10
Primary Contact: Norman Vetter, Chief Executive Officer, Division of Substance Abuse and Mental Health
CIO: James Nau, Manager Computer and Applications Support
Web address: www.dhss.delaware.gov
Control: State, Government, Nonfederal **Service**: Psychiatric

Staffed Beds: 166

Hospitals, U.S. / DELAWARE

☐ **MEADOW WOOD BEHAVIORAL HEALTH SYSTEM (084003)**, 575 South Dupont Highway, Zip 19720–4606; tel. 302/328–3330, (Nonreporting) **A**1 10 **S** Acadia Healthcare Company, Inc., Franklin, TN
Primary Contact: Jennifer Shalk, Chief Executive Officer
CFO: Maria Valdenegro, Chief Financial Officer
Web address: www.meadowwoodhospital.com
Control: Corporation, Investor–owned (for–profit) **Service**: Psychiatric

Staffed Beds: 53

NEWARK—New Castle County

⊞ **CHRISTIANACARE (080001)**, 4755 Ogletown–Stanton Road, Zip 19718–0002, Mailing Address: P.O. Box 6001, Zip 19718; tel. 302/733–1000, **A**1 2 3 5 8 10 **F**3 5 6 7 8 11 12 13 15 17 18 20 22 24 26 28 29 30 31 32 34 35 36 37 38 39 40 41 42 43 44 45 46 47 48 49 50 53 54 55 56 57 58 59 60 61 62 64 65 66 68 70 71 72 74 75 76 77 78 79 80 81 82 84 85 86 87 89 90 92 93 94 96 97 98 100 101 102 104 107 108 110 111 114 115 117 118 119 120 121 123 124 126 129 130 131 132 134 135 136 138 143 144 145 146 147 148 149 150 154 155 156 157 160 162 164 165 167 168 169 **P**6 **S** ChristianaCare, Wilmington, DE
Primary Contact: Janice E. Nevin, M.D., M.P.H., President and Chief Executive Officer
CFO: Rob McMurray, Chief Financial Officer
CMO: Kenneth L Silverstein, M.D., Chief Clinical Officer
CIO: Randall Gaboriault, Chief Information Officer
CHR: Christopher Cowan, Senior Vice President and Chief Human Resources Officer
Web address: www.christianacare.org
Control: Other not–for–profit (including NFP Corporation) **Service**: General medical and surgical

Staffed Beds: 1318 **Admissions**: 55080 **Census**: 1093 **Outpatient Visits**: 571798 **Births**: 6325 **Total Expense ($000)**: 2592120 **Payroll Expense ($000)**: 1244950 **Personnel**: 11792

☐ **ROCKFORD CENTER (084002)**, 100 Rockford Drive, Zip 19713–2121; tel. 302/996–5480, (Nonreporting) **A**1 10 **S** Universal Health Services, Inc., King of Prussia, PA
Primary Contact: William Mason, Chief Executive Officer and Managing Director
CFO: Kumar Purohit, Chief Financial Officer
CMO: Saurabh Gupta, Chief Medical Officer
CHR: Jessi Stewart, Director Human Resources
CNO: Michelle Singletary–Twyman, Chief Nursing Officer
Web address: www.rockfordcenter.com
Control: Corporation, Investor–owned (for–profit) **Service**: Psychiatric

Staffed Beds: 138

SEAFORD—Sussex County

⊞ **TIDALHEALTH NANTICOKE (080006)**, 801 Middleford Road, Zip 19973–3636; tel. 302/629–6611, **A**1 2 3 10 19 **F**3 12 13 14 15 18 20 22 24 28 29 30 31 32 34 35 37 40 43 44 45 46 47 48 49 50 54 57 59 60 61 64 65 66 68 70 74 75 76 77 78 79 81 84 85 86 87 89 93 97 107 110 111 114 115 118 119 120 121 123 126 129 130 132 135 144 146 147 148 149 154 156 167 169 **S** TidalHealth, Salisbury, MD
Primary Contact: Penny Short, R.N., President
CFO: Denise Jester, Chief Financial Officer
CMO: Harry C. Anthony, M.D., Chief Medical Officer
CIO: Charles Palmer, Director Information Technology
Web address: www.nanticoke.org
Control: Other not–for–profit (including NFP Corporation) **Service**: General medical and surgical

Staffed Beds: 99 **Admissions**: 4465 **Census**: 52 **Outpatient Visits**: 150992 **Births**: 612 **Total Expense ($000)**: 155739 **Payroll Expense ($000)**: 55494 **Personnel**: 869

WILMINGTON—New Castle County

ALFRED I. DUPONT HOSPITAL FOR CHILDREN See Nemours Children's Hospital, Delaware

⊞ △ **NEMOURS CHILDREN'S HOSPITAL, DELAWARE (083300)**, 1600 Rockland Road, Zip 19803–3616, Mailing Address: Box 269, Zip 19899–0269; tel. 302/651–4000, (Nonreporting) **A**1 2 3 5 7 10 **S** Nemours Children Health, Jacksonville, FL
Primary Contact: Mark R. Marcantano, Enterprise Vice President, President, Chief Executive, Delaware Valley Operations
CFO: William N Britton, Associate Administrator Finance
CMO: Brent R King, Chief Medical Officer and Chief Physician
Web address: www.nemours.org
Control: Other not–for–profit (including NFP Corporation) **Service**: Children's general medical and surgical

Staffed Beds: 210

⊞ **SELECT SPECIALTY HOSPITAL–WILMINGTON (082000)**, 701 North Clayton Street, 5th Floor, Zip 19805–3948, Mailing Address: 501 West 14th Street, 9th Floor, Zip 19805–3948; tel. 302/421–4545, (Nonreporting) **A**1 10 **S** Select Medical Corporation, Mechanicsburg, PA
Primary Contact: Jordan McClure, Chief Executive Officer
CFO: David Huffman, Vice President and Controller
CMO: Hummayun Ismail, M.D., Medical Director
CHR: Barbara A Foster, Regional Human Resources Director
Web address: www.wilmington.selectspecialtyhospitals.com
Control: Corporation, Investor–owned (for–profit) **Service**: Acute long–term care hospital

Staffed Beds: 35

⊞ **ST. FRANCIS HOSPITAL (080003)**, 701 North Clayton Street, Zip 19805, Mailing Address: P.O. Box 2500, Zip 19805–0500; tel. 302/421–4100, **A**1 3 5 10 **F**3 7 12 13 14 15 18 20 22 24 26 28 29 30 31 34 35 38 40 43 44 45 46 47 48 49 50 51 54 55 56 57 58 59 60 61 62 63 64 65 66 68 69 70 71 72 74 75 76 77 78 79 81 82 84 85 86 87 91 92 93 94 96 97 107 108 109 110 111 112 113 114 115 116 117 118 119 126 129 130 131 135 145 146 147 148 149 154 156 157 164 167 169 **S** Trinity Health, Livonia, MI
Primary Contact: Marlow Levy, President
CIO: Paul W Rowe, Director Information Technology
CHR: Charlene J Wilson, Vice President Human Resources
Web address: www.stfrancishealthcare.org
Control: Other not–for–profit (including NFP Corporation) **Service**: General medical and surgical

Staffed Beds: 127 **Admissions**: 3937 **Census**: 45 **Outpatient Visits**: 68955 **Births**: 589 **Total Expense ($000)**: 122042 **Payroll Expense ($000)**: 46102 **Personnel**: 520

⊞ **WILMINGTON VETERANS AFFAIRS MEDICAL CENTER**, 1601 Kirkwood Highway, Zip 19805–4989; tel. 302/994–2511, (Nonreporting) **A**1 3 5 **S** Department of Veterans Affairs, Washington, DC
Primary Contact: Vamsee Potluri, Director
CFO: Mary Ann Kozel, Chief Fiscal
CMO: Enrique Guttin, M.D., FACS, Chief of Staff
CIO: Scott Vlars, Chief Information Technology Services
CHR: Louis McCloskey, Chief Human Resources
Web address: www.va.gov/wilmington
Control: Veterans Affairs, Government, federal **Service**: General medical and surgical

Staffed Beds: 60

Hospitals, U.S. / DISTRICT OF COLUMBIA

DISTRICT OF COLUMBIA

WASHINGTON—District of Columbia County

BRIDGEPOINT CONTINUING CARE HOSPITAL – CAPITOL HILL (092002), 223 7th Street, NE, Zip 20002–7045; tel. 202/546–5700, (Nonreporting) **A**10 22 **S** BridgePoint Healthcare, Washington, DC
Primary Contact: Ryan Zumalt, Chief Executive Officer
COO: Michelle Mullen, Chief Clinical Officer
CFO: Michael Grubb, Senior Chief Financial Officer
CMO: Harminder Sandhu, M.D., Chief of Staff
CHR: Toni Wright, Director Human Resources
CNO: Adedayo Ekundayo, Ph.D., Director of Nursing
Web address: www.bridgepointhealthcare.com/
Control: Corporation, Investor–owned (for–profit) **Service**: Acute long–term care hospital

Staffed Beds: 177

BRIDGEPOINT CONTINUING CARE HOSPITAL – NATIONAL HARBORSIDE (092003), 4601 Martin Luther King Jr Avenue, SW, Zip 20032–1131; tel. 202/574–5700, (Nonreporting) **A**10 22 **S** BridgePoint Healthcare, Washington, DC
Primary Contact: Reginald Lee, Chief Executive Officer
COO: Swenda Moreh, Vice President and Chief Operating Officer
CFO: Michael Grubb, Chief Financial Officer
CMO: Khosrow Davachi, Chief Medical Officer
CHR: Antoninette Saldivar, Vice President, Human Resources
CNO: Diane White, Chief Clinical Officer and Chief Nursing Officer
Web address: www.bridgepointhealthcare.com/
Control: Corporation, Investor–owned (for–profit) **Service**: Acute long–term care hospital

Staffed Beds: 177

BRIDGEPOINT HOSPITAL CAPITOL HILL See Bridgepoint Continuing Care Hospital – Capitol Hill

CHILDREN'S NATIONAL HOSPITAL (093300), 111 Michigan Avenue NW, Zip 20010–2916, Mailing Address: P.O. Box 1370, Bowie, MD, Zip 20718; tel. 202/476–5000, **A**1 3 5 8 10 **F**3 5 7 8 11 12 14 17 18 19 21 23 25 27 29 30 31 32 34 35 36 38 39 40 41 42 43 44 46 48 49 50 51 54 55 57 58 59 60 61 64 65 66 68 71 72 74 75 77 78 79 81 82 83 84 85 86 87 88 89 91 92 93 94 96 97 98 99 100 102 104 105 106 107 111 112 114 115 116 117 118 119 126 129 130 131 132 134 136 137 138 141 142 146 148 154 155 156 157 167 **P**2
Primary Contact: Michelle Riley–Brown, President and Chief Executive Officer
CMO: Mark L Batshaw, M.D., Physician–in–Chief, Executive Vice President and Chief Academic Officer
CIO: Brian Jacobs, M.D., Vice President Chief Information Officer and Chief Medical Information Officer
CHR: Darryl Varnado, Executive Vice President and Chief People Officer
CNO: Linda Talley, MS, R.N., Vice President and Chief Nursing Officer
Web address: www.childrensnational.org
Control: Other not–for–profit (including NFP Corporation) **Service**: Children's general medical and surgical

Staffed Beds: 323 **Admissions:** 14450 **Census:** 289 **Outpatient Visits:** 618855 **Births:** 0 **Total Expense ($000):** 1475065 **Payroll Expense ($000):** 777148 **Personnel:** 6736

△ **GEORGE WASHINGTON UNIVERSITY HOSPITAL (090001)**, 900 23rd Street NW, Zip 20037–2342; tel. 202/715–4000, **A**1 2 3 5 7 8 10 **F**3 8 11 12 13 15 17 18 20 22 24 26 29 30 31 34 35 37 38 40 43 44 45 46 47 48 49 51 53 54 55 56 57 58 59 60 61 63 64 65 68 70 72 74 75 76 77 78 79 80 81 82 84 85 86 87 90 91 92 93 94 95 96 98 100 102 107 108 110 111 112 114 115 116 117 118 119 120 121 123 124 126 129 130 131 132 134 135 136 138 139 141 144 146 147 148 149 150 154 156 160 164 166 167 169 **S** Universal Health Services, Inc., King of Prussia, PA
Primary Contact: Kimberly Russo, MS, Chief Executive Officer and Managing Director
CFO: Richard Davis, Chief Financial Officer
CMO: Bruno Petinaux, M.D., Chief Medical Officer
CIO: Louis Duhe, Senior Director Information Technology
CHR: Erin Fagan, Manager Human Resources
Web address: www.gwhospital.com
Control: Partnership, Investor–owned (for–profit) **Service**: General medical and surgical

Staffed Beds: 395 **Admissions:** 16907 **Census:** 286 **Outpatient Visits:** 162224 **Births:** 1781 **Personnel:** 2082

HOWARD UNIVERSITY HOSPITAL (090003), 2041 Georgia Avenue NW, Zip 20060–0002; tel. 202/865–6100, (Nonreporting) **A**1 3 5 8 10 **S** Adventist HealthCare, Gaithersburg, MD
Primary Contact: Roger A. Mitchell Jr, M.D., President
CFO: Joe Perry, Chief Financial Officer
CMO: Shelly McDonald–Pinkett, Chief Medical Officer
CIO: Kevin Dawson, Chief Information Officer
CHR: Maurice Roche, Chief Human Resources Officer
CNO: India Medley, Chief Nursing Officer
Web address: www.huhealthcare.com
Control: Other not–for–profit (including NFP Corporation) **Service**: General medical and surgical

Staffed Beds: 239

MEDSTAR GEORGETOWN UNIVERSITY HOSPITAL (090004), 3800 Reservoir Road NW, Zip 20007–2197; tel. 202/444–2000, **A**1 2 3 5 8 10 **F**3 6 9 11 13 15 17 18 20 26 29 30 31 32 34 35 36 37 38 40 44 45 46 47 48 49 50 51 54 55 56 57 58 59 60 61 64 65 66 68 70 71 72 74 75 76 77 78 79 80 81 82 84 85 86 87 88 89 92 93 97 98 100 101 102 103 104 105 107 108 110 111 114 115 116 117 118 119 120 121 122 123 124 126 130 131 132 134 135 136 138 139 141 142 145 146 147 148 149 150 153 154 156 157 162 164 165 167 169 **P**6 **S** MedStar Health, Columbia, MD
Primary Contact: Lisa Boyle, M.D., President
CMO: Lisa Boyle, M.D., Vice President Medical Affairs and Medical Director
CIO: John Rasmussen, Vice President for Information Technology
CHR: Mary Jo Schweickhardt, Vice President Human Resources
CNO: Eileen Brennan Ferrell, MS, R.N., Vice President and Chief Nursing Officer
Web address: www.georgetownuniversityhospital.org
Control: Other not–for–profit (including NFP Corporation) **Service**: General medical and surgical

Staffed Beds: 425 **Admissions:** 14068 **Census:** 315 **Outpatient Visits:** 290318 **Births:** 989 **Total Expense ($000):** 1036542 **Payroll Expense ($000):** 401338 **Personnel:** 3810

△ **MEDSTAR NATIONAL REHABILITATION HOSPITAL (093025)**, 102 Irving Street NW, Zip 20010–2949; tel. 202/877–1000, **A**1 3 5 7 10 **F**3 9 28 29 30 32 33 34 35 36 44 50 53 54 56 57 58 59 64 65 68 71 74 75 77 78 79 82 86 87 90 91 92 93 94 95 96 100 119 130 131 132 134 135 146 148 149 154 157 164 **P**6 **S** MedStar Health, Columbia, MD
Primary Contact: John D. Rockwood, President
CFO: Michael Boemmel, Vice President and Chief Financial Officer
CMO: Michael R Yochelson, M.D., Vice President and Medical Director
CHR: Pamela Ashby, Vice President Human Resources
CNO: Rosemary C Welch, R.N., Vice President and Chief Nursing Officer
Web address: www.medstarnrh.org
Control: Other not–for–profit (including NFP Corporation) **Service**: Rehabilitation

Staffed Beds: 137 **Admissions:** 1858 **Census:** 93 **Outpatient Visits:** 534516 **Births:** 0 **Total Expense ($000):** 175898 **Payroll Expense ($000):** 103426 **Personnel:** 1628

Hospital, Medicare Provider Number, Address, Telephone, Approval, Facility, and Physician Codes, Health Care System

★ American Hospital Association (AHA) membership
□ The Joint Commission accreditation
○ Healthcare Facilities Accreditation Program
◇ DNV Healthcare Inc. accreditation
⇑ Center for Improvement in Healthcare Quality Accreditation
△ Commission on Accreditation of Rehabilitation Facilities (CARF) accreditation

Hospitals, U.S. / DISTRICT OF COLUMBIA

MEDSTAR WASHINGTON HOSPITAL CENTER (090011), 110 Irving Street NW, Zip 20010–3017; tel. 202/877–7000, **A**1 2 3 5 8 10 **F**3 5 12 13 15 16 17 18 20 22 24 26 28 29 30 31 34 35 37 38 39 40 43 44 45 46 48 49 50 51 54 55 56 57 58 59 61 64 65 66 68 70 71 72 73 74 75 76 77 78 79 80 81 82 84 85 86 87 92 97 98 100 101 102 104 105 107 108 110 111 114 115 116 117 118 119 120 121 123 124 126 130 131 132 134 137 141 146 147 148 149 150 153 154 156 157 160 161 162 164 165 166 167 169 **P**1 6 **S** MedStar Health, Columbia, MD
Primary Contact: Gregory J. Argyros, M.D., President
COO: Robert Ross, Chief Operating Officer
CFO: William Gayne, Chief Financial Officer
CIO: Joe Brothman, Assistant Vice President, Information Systems
CHR: James P Hill, Senior Vice President Administrative Services
CNO: Ariam Gebrehiwot Yitbarek, Chief Nursing Officer
Web address: www.whcenter.org
Control: Other not–for–profit (including NFP Corporation) **Service**: General medical and surgical

Staffed Beds: 782 **Admissions**: 29216 **Census**: 628 **Outpatient Visits**: 405188 **Births**: 3606 **Total Expense ($000)**: 1549742 **Payroll Expense ($000)**: 584718 **Personnel**: 6090

PSYCHIATRIC INSTITUTE OF WASHINGTON (094004), 4228 Wisconsin Avenue NW, Zip 20016–2138; tel. 202/885–5600, (Nonreporting) **A**1 3 5 10
Primary Contact: Eric Amoh, Chief Executive Officer
COO: Carol Desjeunes, Vice President and Chief Operating Officer
CFO: Michael Silver, Chief Financial Officer
CMO: Howard Hoffman, M.D., Medical Director
CIO: Ray Santina, Director Information Systems
CHR: Dawn Hatterer–Hoag, Director Human Resources
Web address: www.psychinstitute.com
Control: Corporation, Investor–owned (for–profit) **Service**: Psychiatric

Staffed Beds: 175

★ **SAINT ELIZABETHS HOSPITAL (094001)**, 1100 Alabama Avenue SE, Zip 20032–4540; tel. 202/299–5000, (Nonreporting) **A**3 5 10
Primary Contact: Mark J. Chastang, M.P.H., Chief Executive Officer
COO: K. Singh Taneja, Chief Operating Officer
CFO: Steward Beckham, Director, Chief Operating Officer
CMO: Phillip Candilis, M.D., Director, Medical Affairs
CIO: Mark Larkins, Interim Chief Information Officer
CHR: Cynthia Hawkins, Chief Human Resources Officer
CNO: Lori Ann Yerrell–Garrett, Interim Chief Nursing Executive
Web address: www.dmh.dc.gov/
Control: City, Government, Nonfederal **Service**: Psychiatric

Staffed Beds: 292

SIBLEY MEMORIAL HOSPITAL (090005), 5255 Loughboro Road NW, Zip 20016–2633; tel. 202/537–4000, **A**1 2 3 5 10 **F**3 6 8 10 12 13 15 20 28 29 30 31 34 35 36 37 38 40 44 45 46 47 48 49 50 53 55 56 57 58 59 60 64 68 70 73 74 75 76 77 78 79 81 82 84 85 86 87 91 92 93 96 97 98 100 101 102 104 107 108 110 111 114 115 116 117 118 119 120 121 122 123 126 128 129 130 132 135 146 147 148 149 154 156 157 162 164 167 **S** Johns Hopkins Health System, Baltimore, MD
Primary Contact: Hasan A. Zia, President and Chief Executive Officer
COO: Sanjay K Saha, Chief Operating Officer
CFO: Marty Basso, Chief Financial Officer
CMO: Hasan A. Zia, Vice President of Medical Affairs and Chief Medical Officer
CIO: Christopher T Timbers, Chief Information Officer
CHR: Queenie C. Plater, Vice President, Human Resources National Capital Region Johns Hopkins Medicine
CNO: Lynn Meuer, Interim Chief Nursing Officer
Web address: www.sibley.org
Control: Other not–for–profit (including NFP Corporation) **Service**: General medical and surgical

Staffed Beds: 297 **Admissions**: 11447 **Census**: 154 **Outpatient Visits**: 164871 **Births**: 3729 **Total Expense ($000)**: 521531 **Payroll Expense ($000)**: 164551 **Personnel**: 1831

THE HSC PEDIATRIC CENTER, 1731 Bunker Hill Road NE, Zip 20017–3096; tel. 202/832–4400, (Total facility includes 16 beds in nursing home–type unit) **A**1 3 7 **F**3 7 29 30 54 65 71 75 80 84 86 91 93 94 100 104 128 130 143 146 148 149 154
Primary Contact: Debbie C. Holson, R.N., MSN, Chief Operating Officer
COO: Debbie C Holson, R.N., MSN, Chief Operating Officer
CFO: Ray Vicks, Senior Vice President, Finance and Chief Financial Officer
CMO: Andrew Metinko, M.D., Chief Medical Officer
CIO: Khalil Bouharoun, Chief Information Officer
CHR: Lynne Hostetter, Vice President Human Resources
Web address: www.hscpediatriccenter.org/
Control: Other not–for–profit (including NFP Corporation) **Service**: Children's chronic disease

Staffed Beds: 40 **Admissions**: 167 **Census**: 20 **Outpatient Visits**: 14275 **Births**: 0 **Total Expense ($000)**: 40047 **Payroll Expense ($000)**: 19681 **Personnel**: 171

UNITED MEDICAL CENTER (090008), 1310 Southern Avenue SE, Zip 20032–4623; tel. 202/574–6000, (Nonreporting) **A**1 5 10
Primary Contact: Colonel Jacqueline Payne–Borden, Chief Executive Officer
COO: Marcela Maamari, Chief Operating Officer
CFO: Lilian Chukwuma, Chief Financial Officer
CMO: Eric Li, M.D., Chief Medical Officer
CIO: Alan Johnson, Interim Chief Information Officer
CHR: Eric M. Johnson, Director
Web address: www.united-medicalcenter.com
Control: Other not–for–profit (including NFP Corporation) **Service**: General medical and surgical

Staffed Beds: 354

WASHINGTON DC VETERANS AFFAIRS MEDICAL CENTER, 50 Irving Street NW, Zip 20422–0002; tel. 202/745–8000, (Nonreporting) **A**1 2 3 5 7 **S** Department of Veterans Affairs, Washington, DC
Primary Contact: Colonel Michael S. Heimall, Medical Center Director
CFO: Frank Filosa, Fiscal Manager
CIO: Amanda Graves, Chief Information Systems
CNO: Denise Boehm, Chief Nurse Executive
Web address: www.washingtondc.va.gov/
Control: Veterans Affairs, Government, federal **Service**: General medical and surgical

Staffed Beds: 291

Hospitals, U.S. / FLORIDA

FLORIDA

ALTAMONTE SPRINGS—Seminole County

ADVENTHEALTH ALTAMONTE SPRINGS See Adventhealth Orlando, Orlando

☒ **ENCOMPASS HEALTH REHABILITATION HOSPITAL OF ALTAMONTE SPRINGS (103045)**, 831 South State Road 434, Zip 32714-3502; tel. 407/587-8600, **A**1 10 **F**3 29 74 75 79 82 86 90 91 96 130 132 148 149 **S** Encompass Health Corporation, Birmingham, AL
Primary Contact: Michael Thomas, Chief Executive Officer
Web address: www.healthsouthaltamontesprings.com
Control: Corporation, Investor-owned (for-profit) **Service**: Rehabilitation

> **Staffed Beds:** 70 **Admissions:** 1932 **Census:** 66 **Total Expense ($000):** 27996 **Payroll Expense ($000):** 14776 **Personnel:** 201

FLORIDA HOSPITAL–ALTAMONTE See Adventhealth Altamonte Springs

ORLANDO REHABILITATION HOSPITAL, 980 Gateway Drive, Zip 32714-4807; tel. 321/989-3104, (Nonreporting) **A**22 **S** Nobis Rehabilitation Partners, Allen, TX
Web address: https://www.orlando-rehabhospital.com/
Control: Partnership, Investor-owned (for-profit) **Service**: Rehabilitation

> **Staffed Beds:** 60

APALACHICOLA—Franklin County

★ **GEORGE E. WEEMS MEMORIAL HOSPITAL (101305)**, 135 Avenue G, Zip 32320-1613, Mailing Address: P.O. Box 580, Zip 32329-0580; tel. 850/653-8853, (Nonreporting) **A**10 18
Primary Contact: David Walker, Interim Chief Executive Officer
CHR: Ginny Griner, Director Human Resources
Web address: www.weemsmemorial.com
Control: County, Government, Nonfederal **Service**: General medical and surgical

> **Staffed Beds:** 25

APOPKA—Orange County

ADVENTHEALTH APOPKA See Adventhealth Orlando, Orlando

FLORIDA HOSPITAL–APOPKA See Adventhealth Apopka

ARCADIA—Desoto County

☒ **DESOTO MEMORIAL HOSPITAL (100175)**, 900 North Robert Avenue, Zip 34266-8712, Mailing Address: P.O. Box 2180, Zip 34265-2180; tel. 863/494-3535, **A**1 10 20 **F**3 5 11 15 28 29 34 35 40 45 46 54 55 57 59 60 62 64 65 68 70 74 75 77 78 79 81 82 85 87 93 100 101 103 104 105 107 108 110 111 114 119 120 130 132 135 146 148 149 152 153 154 167 **P**6
Primary Contact: Vincent A. Sica, President and Chief Executive Officer
CFO: Kellie J. Henwood, Interim Chief Financial Officer
CMO: Sam Altajar, M.D., Chief of Staff
CIO: Sarah Hipp, Director of Marketing
CHR: Lois Hilton, Director Human Resources
CNO: Tracy Winslow, Interim Chief Nursing Officer
Web address: www.dmh.org
Control: Hospital district or authority, Government, Nonfederal **Service**: General medical and surgical

> **Staffed Beds:** 49 **Admissions:** 891 **Census:** 9 **Total Expense ($000):** 47897 **Payroll Expense ($000):** 18551 **Personnel:** 253

ATLANTIS—Palm Beach County

☒ **HCA FLORIDA JFK HOSPITAL (100080)**, 5301 South Congress Avenue, Zip 33462-1197; tel. 561/965-7300, (Includes HCA FLORIDA JFK NORTH HOSPITAL, 2201 45th Street, West Palm Beach, Florida, Zip 33407-2047; tel. 561/842-6141; Ashley Vertuno, Chief Executive Officer) (Nonreporting) **A**1 2 3 5 10 19 **S** HCA Healthcare, Nashville, TN
Primary Contact: Kenneth West, Chief Executive Officer
COO: Damon Barrett, Chief Operating Officer
CFO: Jim Leamon, Chief Financial Officer
CMO: Alejandro Paya, D.O., Chief Medical Officer
CIO: Jane Stewart, Director Information Services
CHR: Trudy Bromley, Vice President Human Resources
Web address: https://www.hcafloridahealthcare.com/locations/jfk-hospital
Control: Corporation, Investor-owned (for-profit) **Service**: General medical and surgical

> **Staffed Beds:** 803

JFK MEDICAL CENTER See HCA Florida JFK Hospital

AVENTURA—Miami-Dade County

AVENTURA HOSPITAL AND MEDICAL CENTER See HCA Florida Aventura Hospital

☒ **HCA FLORIDA AVENTURA HOSPITAL (100131)**, 20900 Biscayne Boulevard, Zip 33180-1407; tel. 305/682-7000, (Nonreporting) **A**1 2 3 5 10 **S** HCA Healthcare, Nashville, TN
Primary Contact: David LeMonte, Chief Executive Officer
COO: David Was, Chief Operating Officer
CFO: Onel Rodriguez, Chief Financial Officer
CHR: April Radden, Vice President of Human Resources
CNO: Jesse Gabuat, Chief Nursing Officer
Web address: https://www.hcafloridahealthcare.com/locations/aventura-hospital
Control: Corporation, Investor-owned (for-profit) **Service**: General medical and surgical

> **Staffed Beds:** 407

BARTOW—Polk County

☒ **BARTOW REGIONAL MEDICAL CENTER (100121)**, 2200 Osprey Boulevard, Zip 33830-3308; tel. 863/533-8111, **A**1 10 **F**3 11 18 20 22 29 30 34 35 40 44 45 46 49 50 51 57 58 59 60 63 64 68 70 74 75 77 78 79 81 82 85 86 87 93 107 108 111 114 115 118 119 126 130 131 135 145 146 148 149 154 156 164 167 **S** BayCare Health System, Clearwater, FL
Primary Contact: Karen Kerr, R.N., President
CMO: Stuart Patterson, M.D., Chief of Staff
CIO: Vilakon Champavannarath, Director Information Systems
CHR: Marie Horton, Director Associate Relations
Web address: www.bartowregional.com
Control: Other not-for-profit (including NFP Corporation) **Service**: General medical and surgical

> **Staffed Beds:** 72 **Admissions:** 3296 **Census:** 35 **Outpatient Visits:** 47314 **Births:** 0 **Total Expense ($000):** 87803 **Payroll Expense ($000):** 34768 **Personnel:** 359

BAY PINES—Pinellas County

☒ △ **BAY PINES VETERANS AFFAIRS HEALTHCARE SYSTEM**, 10000 Bay Pines Boulevard, Zip 33744-8200, Mailing Address: P.O. Box 5005, Zip 33744-5005; tel. 727/398-6661, (Nonreporting) **A**1 2 3 5 7 **S** Department of Veterans Affairs, Washington, DC
Primary Contact: Paul M. Russo, FACHE, Director
COO: Kris Brown, Associate Director
CFO: Jeanine Ergle, Chief Financial Officer
CMO: George F Van Buskirk, M.D., Chief of Staff
CIO: John Williams, Chief Information Officer
CHR: Paula Buchele, Chief Human Resources
Web address: www.baypines.va.gov/
Control: Veterans Affairs, Government, federal **Service**: General medical and surgical

> **Staffed Beds:** 168

BELLE GLADE—Palm Beach County

☒ **LAKESIDE MEDICAL CENTER (100130)**, 39200 Hooker Highway, Zip 33430-5368; tel. 561/996-6571, (Nonreporting) **A**1 3 5 10 13
Primary Contact: Janet D. Moreland, Hospital Administrator
COO: Darcy Davis, Chief Financial Officer
CFO: Darcy Davis, Chief Financial Officer
CMO: Belma Andric, Vice President and Chief Medical Officer
Web address: www.lakesidemedical.org
Control: Hospital district or authority, Government, Nonfederal **Service**: General medical and surgical

> **Staffed Beds:** 70

BELLEAIR—Pinellas County

MORTON PLANT REHAB & NRSG CNTR See Madonna Ptak Morton Plant Rehabilitation Center

Hospitals, U.S. / FLORIDA

BLOUNTSTOWN—Calhoun County

CALHOUN LIBERTY HOSPITAL (101304), 20370 NE Burns Avenue, Zip 32424–1045, Mailing Address: P.O. Box 419, Zip 32424–0419; tel. 850/674–5411, (Nonreporting) **A**10 18 **S** Alliant Management Services, Louisville, KY
Primary Contact: Christinia Jepsen, R.N., Chief Executive Officer
CFO: Nathan Ebersole, Controller
CIO: Michael Flowers, Director Information Management
CHR: Lynn Pitts, Director Human Resources
CNO: Debra Summers, Chief Nursing Officer
Web address: www.calhounlibertyhospital.com
Control: Other not–for–profit (including NFP Corporation) **Service**: General medical and surgical

Staffed Beds: 25

BOCA RATON—Palm Beach County

BOCA RATON REGIONAL HOSPITAL (100168), 800 Meadows Road, Zip 33486–2368; tel. 561/955–7100, **A**1 2 3 5 10 **F**3 8 11 13 15 17 18 20 22 24 26 28 29 30 31 34 35 36 37 39 40 44 45 46 47 48 49 50 51 53 54 55 56 57 58 59 60 61 64 66 68 70 71 72 73 74 75 76 77 78 79 80 81 82 84 85 86 87 92 93 96 97 100 102 107 108 110 111 112 114 115 116 117 118 119 120 121 123 124 126 130 131 132 135 141 145 146 147 148 149 154 156 164 167 169 **S** Baptist Health South Florida, Coral Gables, FL
Primary Contact: Lincoln S. Mendez, Chief Executive Officer
COO: Mindy Shikiar, MSN, Chief Operating Officer
CFO: Dawn Javersack, Vice President and Chief Financial Officer
CIO: Robin Hildwein, Chief Information Officer
CHR: Mindy Raymond, Vice President Human Resources
CNO: Melissa Ann Durbin, R.N., MSN, Chief Nursing Officer
Web address: www.brrh.com
Control: Other not–for–profit (including NFP Corporation) **Service**: General medical and surgical

Staffed Beds: 392 **Admissions:** 17735 **Census:** 226 **Outpatient Visits:** 264172 **Births:** 2903 **Total Expense ($000):** 690104 **Payroll Expense ($000):** 210825 **Personnel:** 2463

WEST BOCA MEDICAL CENTER (100268), 21644 State Road 7, Zip 33428–1899; tel. 561/488–8000, (Nonreporting) **A**1 3 5 10 **S** TENET Healthcare Corporation, Dallas, TX
Primary Contact: Jerad Hanlon, Chief Executive Officer
CFO: Brook Thomas, Chief Financial Officer
CMO: Jack L Harari, M.D., Chief Medical Officer
CIO: Lauren Spagna, Marketing Director
CHR: Stephanie Sherman, Chief Human Resources Officer
Web address: www.westbocamedctr.com
Control: Corporation, Investor–owned (for–profit) **Service**: General medical and surgical

Staffed Beds: 195

BONIFAY—Holmes County

DOCTORS MEMORIAL HOSPITAL (101307), 2600 Hospital Drive, Zip 32425–4264, Mailing Address: P.O. Box 188, Zip 32425–0188; tel. 850/547–8000, **A**1 10 18 **F**3 11 15 29 30 40 45 50 57 59 64 70 77 81 90 93 107 110 114 119 131 133 146 148
Primary Contact: Huy Nguyen, M.D., Chief Executive Officer
CFO: Celia F Ward, Controller and Chief Financial Officer
CMO: Leisa Bailey, M.D., Chief of Staff
CIO: Rohan Anderson, Chief Information Officer
CHR: Christy Booth, Chief Human Resources Officer
CNO: Karla Rockwell, Director of Nursing
Web address: www.doctorsmemorial.org
Control: Hospital district or authority, Government, Nonfederal **Service**: General medical and surgical

Staffed Beds: 20 **Admissions:** 412 **Census:** 6 **Total Expense ($000):** 21065 **Payroll Expense ($000):** 9420 **Personnel:** 146

BOYNTON BEACH—Palm Beach County

BETHESDA HOSPITAL EAST (100002), 2815 South Seacrest Boulevard, Zip 33435–7995; tel. 561/737–7733, (Includes BETHESDA HOSPITAL WEST, 9655 West Boynton Beach Boulevard, Boynton Beach, Florida, Zip 33472–4421, tel. 561/336–7000; Jared M. Smith, Chief Executive Officer) **A**1 3 5 7 10 **F**3 12 13 17 18 19 20 22 24 26 28 29 30 31 34 35 40 41 44 45 46 47 48 49 50 51 54 56 57 59 60 61 64 68 70 72 74 75 76 77 78 79 81 82 84 85 87 90 92 93 96 107 108 110 111 114 115 118 119 120 121 124 126 129 130 131 132 135 141 146 147 148 149 154 164 167 169 **S** Baptist Health South Florida, Coral Gables, FL
Primary Contact: Jared M. Smith, Chief Executive Officer
COO: Joanne Aquilia, Vice President Operations
CFO: Donna Seymour, Assistant Vice President, Finance (Controller)
CMO: Daniel Goldman, M.D., Chief Medical Officer
Web address: https://baptisthealth.net/locations/hospitals/bethesda-hospital-east
Control: Other not–for–profit (including NFP Corporation) **Service**: General medical and surgical

Staffed Beds: 376 **Admissions:** 17319 **Census:** 235 **Outpatient Visits:** 127298 **Births:** 2560 **Total Expense ($000):** 463724 **Payroll Expense ($000):** 165682 **Personnel:** 2089

BRADENTON—Manatee County

BLAKE MEDICAL CENTER See HCA Florida Blake Hospital

CENTERSTONE HOSPITAL (104040), 2020 26th Avenue East, Zip 34208–7753, Mailing Address: P.O. Box 9478, Zip 34206–9478; tel. 941/782–4600, **A**3 5 10 13 **F**4 29 35 38 98 100 102 105 106 143 146 151 152 154
Primary Contact: Melissa Larkin-Skinner, Chief Executive Officer
CFO: Sean Gingras, CPA, Chief Financial Officer
CMO: Ranjay Halder, M.D., Chief Medical Director
CIO: Heidi L Blair, Vice President Administration
CHR: Colleen O'Connor, Director Human Resources
Web address: www.manateeglens.org
Control: Other not–for–profit (including NFP Corporation) **Service**: Psychiatric

Staffed Beds: 41 **Admissions:** 1723 **Census:** 24 **Total Expense ($000):** 8538 **Payroll Expense ($000):** 4723 **Personnel:** 80

HCA FLORIDA BLAKE HOSPITAL (100213), 2020 59th Street West, Zip 34209–4669; tel. 941/792–6611, **A**1 2 3 5 7 10 **F**3 11 15 16 17 18 20 22 24 26 28 29 30 31 34 35 40 43 48 49 50 53 57 58 59 64 68 70 74 75 77 78 79 80 81 85 87 90 91 92 93 94 96 100 107 108 110 111 114 115 118 119 126 129 130 131 132 141 146 147 148 149 150 154 **S** HCA Healthcare, Nashville, TN
Primary Contact: Steve W. Young, Chief Executive Officer
COO: Paige Laughlin, Chief Operating Officer
CFO: Andrew Smith, Chief Financial Officer
CMO: R. Lee Biggs, D.O., Chief Medical Officer
CIO: Shannon Piatkowski, Director Information Technology
CHR: Veronica Lequeux, Vice President Human Resources
CNO: Todd Haner, R.N., Chief Nursing Officer
Web address: https://www.hcafloridahealthcare.com/locations/blake-hospital
Control: Corporation, Investor–owned (for–profit) **Service**: General medical and surgical

Staffed Beds: 322 **Admissions:** 12547 **Census:** 187 **Total Expense ($000):** 287433 **Payroll Expense ($000):** 73393 **Personnel:** 933

LAKEWOOD RANCH MEDICAL CENTER (100299), 8330 Lakewood Ranch Boulevard, Zip 34202–5174; tel. 941/782–2100, (Nonreporting) **A**1 10 **S** Universal Health Services, Inc., King of Prussia, PA
Primary Contact: Andrew Guz, Chief Executive Officer
COO: Linda S Widra, FACHE, Ph.D., R.N., Chief Operating Officer
CFO: Gerald Christine, Chief Financial Officer
CHR: Trish Morales, Director Human Resources
Web address: www.lakewoodranchmedicalcenter.com
Control: Corporation, Investor–owned (for–profit) **Service**: General medical and surgical

Staffed Beds: 120

MANATEE MEMORIAL HOSPITAL (100035), 206 Second Street East, Zip 34208–1000; tel. 941/746–5111, (Nonreporting) **A**1 2 3 5 10 12 13 **S** Universal Health Services, Inc., King of Prussia, PA
Primary Contact: Tom R. McDougal Jr, FACHE, Chief Executive Officer
COO: Camie Patterson, Chief Operating Officer
CFO: Mark A Tierney, Chief Financial Officer
CIO: Troy Beaubien, Director Information Services
CHR: Sheree Threewits, Director Human Resources
Web address: www.manateememorial.com
Control: Partnership, Investor–owned (for–profit) **Service**: General medical and surgical

Staffed Beds: 319

Hospitals, U.S. / FLORIDA

SUNCOAST BEHAVIORAL HEALTH CENTER (104078), 4480 51st Street West, Zip 34210–2855; tel. 941/251–5000, **A**10 **F**4 29 34 50 64 98 99 100 101 102 103 105 149 **S** Universal Health Services, Inc., King of Prussia, PA
Primary Contact: Brandy Hamilton, Chief Executive Officer
CFO: Clifford Nelson, Chief Financial Officer
CMO: Randolph Hemsath, M.D., Medical Director
CNO: Janey Sweeney, Chief Nursing Officer
Web address: www.suncoastbhc.com
Control: Corporation, Investor–owned (for–profit) **Service**: Psychiatric

Staffed Beds: 60 Admissions: 923 Census: 37 Total Expense ($000): 13554 Payroll Expense ($000): 5888 Personnel: 92

BRANDON—Hillsborough County

HCA FLORIDA BRANDON HOSPITAL (100243), 119 Oakfield Drive, Zip 33511–5779; tel. 813/681–5551, (Nonreporting) **A**1 3 5 10 19 **S** HCA Healthcare, Nashville, TN
Primary Contact: Tripp Owings, Chief Executive Officer
COO: Kelly Lindsay, Chief Operating Officer
CFO: Gary Searls, Chief Financial Officer
CMO: Alan Harmatz, M.D., Chief Medical Officer
CIO: Eric Young, Chief Information Officer
CHR: Carole Hoffman, Vice President Human Resources
CNO: William Kyle Thrift, Chief Nursing Officer
Web address: www.brandonhospital.com
Control: Corporation, Investor–owned (for–profit) **Service**: General medical and surgical

Staffed Beds: 422

BROOKSVILLE—Hernando County

BAYFRONT HEALTH BROOKSVILLE See Tampa General Hospital Brooksville

ENCOMPASS HEALTH REHABILITATION HOSPITAL OF SPRING HILL (103042), 12440 Cortez Boulevard, Zip 34613–2628; tel. 352/592–4250, (Nonreporting) **A**1 3 10 **S** Encompass Health Corporation, Birmingham, AL
Primary Contact: Michael Thomas, Chief Executive Officer
CMO: Mira Zelin, D.O., Medical Director
CIO: Myra Merillo, Supervisor Health Information Management
CHR: Mary Salamanca, Director Human Resources
Web address: www.healthsouthspringhill.com
Control: Corporation, Investor–owned (for–profit) **Service**: Rehabilitation

Staffed Beds: 80

HCA FLORIDA OAK HILL HOSPITAL (100264), 11375 Cortez Boulevard, Zip 34613–5409; tel. 352/596–6632, **A**1 2 3 5 10 13 **F**3 11 15 18 20 22 24 26 29 30 31 34 35 40 41 45 46 48 49 50 51 56 57 59 64 70 74 75 76 77 78 79 81 85 87 89 93 107 108 110 111 114 115 118 119 126 130 131 132 146 147 148 **S** HCA Healthcare, Nashville, TN
Primary Contact: Kenneth R. Wicker, FACHE, Chief Executive Officer
COO: Leanne Salazar, Chief Operating Officer
CFO: Matt Romero, Chief Financial Officer
CMO: Ed Nast, M.D., Chief Medical Officer
CHR: Charles Snider, Vice President Human Resources
CNO: Sheila Sanders, Chief Nursing Officer
Web address: www.oakhillhospital.com
Control: Corporation, Investor–owned (for–profit) **Service**: General medical and surgical

Staffed Beds: 361 Admissions: 21242 Census: 272 Total Expense ($000): 308080 Payroll Expense ($000): 93804 Personnel: 1314

OAK HILL HOSPITAL See HCA Florida Oak Hill Hospital

SPRINGBROOK HOSPITAL (104057), 7007 Grove Road, Zip 34609–8610; tel. 352/596–4306, (Nonreporting) **A**1 3 10 **S** Oglethorpe Recovery and Behavioral Hospitals, Tampa, FL
Primary Contact: Samuel Bennett, Chief Executive Officer
Web address: www.springbrookhospital.org/
Control: Other not–for–profit (including NFP Corporation) **Service**: Psychiatric

Staffed Beds: 66

TAMPA GENERAL HOSPITAL BROOKSVILLE (100071), 17240 Cortez Boulevard, Zip 34601–8921, Mailing Address: P.O. Box 37, Zip 34605–0037; tel. 352/796–5111, (Includes TAMPA GENERAL HOSPITAL SPRING HILL, 10461 Quality Drive, Spring Hill, Florida, Zip 34609–9634, tel. 352/688–8200; Bobby Ginn, Chief Executive Officer) **A**1 10 **F**3 11 15 18 20 22 29 30 40 45 70 77 79 81 91 93 102 107 108 110 111 115 119 146 167
Primary Contact: Bobby Ginn, Chief Executive Officer
COO: Scott Hartsell, Chief Operating Officer
CFO: Matthew Seagroves, Chief Financial Officer
CMO: Mohammad A Joud, M.D., Chief of Staff
CIO: Lee Burch, Director Management Information Systems
CHR: Claudia L Jack, Director Associate Relations
Web address: https://www.tghnorth.org/locations/tampa-general-hospital-brooksville
Control: Corporation, Investor–owned (for–profit) **Service**: General medical and surgical

Staffed Beds: 254 Admissions: 10070 Census: 96 Total Expense ($000): 57952 Payroll Expense ($000): 43213 Personnel: 596

CAPE CORAL—Lee County

★ ⇑ **CAPE CORAL HOSPITAL (100244)**, 636 Del Prado Boulevard, Zip 33990–2695; tel. 239/424–2000, **A**3 10 21 **F**3 11 13 14 18 28 29 30 34 35 40 45 46 48 49 50 51 53 56 57 59 60 66 68 70 74 75 76 77 79 81 82 84 85 86 87 93 94 102 107 108 111 114 119 129 130 132 135 146 147 148 156 **S** Lee Health, Fort Myers, FL
Primary Contact: Iahn Gonsenhauser, Chief Medical Officer
CFO: Ben Spence, Chief Financial Officer
CIO: Mike Smith, Chief Information Officer
CHR: Jon C Cecil, Chief Human Resource Officer
CNO: Lisa Sgarlata, MSN, Chief Patient Care Officer
Web address: www.leememorial.org
Control: Hospital district or authority, Government, Nonfederal **Service**: General medical and surgical

Staffed Beds: 291 Admissions: 16840 Census: 230 Total Expense ($000): 332625 Payroll Expense ($000): 160161 Personnel: 1662

ENCOMPASS HEALTH REHABILITATION HOSPITAL OF CAPE CORAL (103053), 1730 North East Pine Island Road, Zip 33909–1734; tel. 239/599–3600, (Nonreporting) **A**1 **S** Encompass Health Corporation, Birmingham, AL
Primary Contact: Michelle Fitzgerald, R.N., Chief Executive Officer
Web address: https://encompasshealth.com/capecoralrehab
Control: Corporation, Investor–owned (for–profit) **Service**: Rehabilitation

Staffed Beds: 40

CELEBRATION—Osceola County

ADVENTHEALTH CELEBRATION See Adventhealth Orlando, Orlando

FLORIDA HOSPITAL CELEBRATION HEALTH See Adventhealth Celebration

CHATTAHOOCHEE—Gadsden County

FLORIDA STATE HOSPITAL (100298), US Highway 90 East, Zip 32324–1000, Mailing Address: P.O. Box 1000, Zip 32324–1000; tel. 850/663–7536, (Nonreporting) **A**10
Primary Contact: Stephen B. Lewallen, Hospital Administrator
CFO: Bill Jones, Chief Financial Officer
CMO: Josefina Balulga, M.D., Clinical Director
CIO: Wesley Pelham
CHR: Keri Bassett, Human Resources Business Partner
Web address: https://www.myflfamilies.com/service-programs/mental-health/fsh/
Control: State, Government, Nonfederal **Service**: Psychiatric

Staffed Beds: 987

Hospital, Medicare Provider Number, Address, Telephone, Approval, Facility, and Physician Codes, Health Care System

★ American Hospital Association (AHA) membership
☐ The Joint Commission accreditation
○ Healthcare Facilities Accreditation Program
◇ DNV Healthcare Inc. accreditation
⇑ Center for Improvement in Healthcare Quality Accreditation
△ Commission on Accreditation of Rehabilitation Facilities (CARF) accreditation

Hospitals, U.S. / FLORIDA

CHIPLEY—Washington County

☐ **NORTHWEST FLORIDA COMMUNITY HOSPITAL (101308)**, 1360 Brickyard Road, Zip 32428–6303, Mailing Address: P.O. Box 889, Zip 32428–0889; tel. 850/638–1610, (Total facility includes 34 beds in nursing home–type unit) **A**1 10 18 **F**3 15 18 28 29 30 34 35 40 45 57 59 65 81 85 93 107 108 111 115 119 127 128 130 131 132 133 135 148 153 154 **S** Alliant Management Services, Louisville, KY
Primary Contact: Michael A. Kozar, Chief Executive Officer
CFO: Marcey Black, Chief Financial Officer
CHR: Shelia Schiefelbein, Coordinator Human Resources
CNO: Joan Beard, Chief Nursing Officer
Web address: www.nfch.org
Control: Corporation, Investor–owned (for–profit) **Service**: General medical and surgical

Staffed Beds: 59 **Admissions**: 782 **Census**: 46 **Outpatient Visits**: 138460 **Births**: 0 **Total Expense ($000)**: 38840 **Payroll Expense ($000)**: 16702 **Personnel**: 234

CLEARWATER—Pinellas County

⊞ **MORTON PLANT HOSPITAL (100127)**, 300 Pinellas Street, Zip 33756–3804; tel. 727/462–7000, (Total facility includes 126 beds in nursing home–type unit) **A**1 2 3 5 10 19 **F**3 6 11 13 15 17 18 20 22 24 26 28 29 30 31 34 35 37 38 40 42 44 45 46 47 48 49 50 51 53 54 55 56 57 58 59 60 61 63 64 65 66 68 70 72 74 75 76 77 78 79 80 81 82 84 85 86 87 89 91 92 93 98 100 101 102 107 108 110 111 112 114 115 116 117 118 119 120 121 123 124 126 128 129 130 131 132 135 143 145 146 147 148 149 154 156 157 164 167 168 169 **S** BayCare Health System, Clearwater, FL
Primary Contact: Matthew Novak, President
CFO: Carl Tremonti, Chief Financial Officer
CMO: Jeff Jensen, D.O., Vice President, Medical Affairs
CIO: Timothy Thompson, Senior Vice President and Chief Information Officer
CHR: Angel Brown, Director Human Resources
CNO: Thomas Doria, Vice President Patient Services – West
Web address: https://baycare.org/locations/hospitals/morton-plant-hospital/patients-and-visitors
Control: Other not–for–profit (including NFP Corporation) **Service**: General medical and surgical

Staffed Beds: 715 **Admissions**: 25528 **Census**: 425 **Outpatient Visits**: 397363 **Births**: 2087 **Total Expense ($000)**: 747070 **Payroll Expense ($000)**: 244005 **Personnel**: 2824

☐ **WINDMOOR HEALTHCARE OF CLEARWATER (104017)**, 11300 US 19 North, Zip 33764; tel. 727/541–2646, (Nonreporting) **A**1 10 **S** Universal Health Services, Inc., King of Prussia, PA
Primary Contact: Joshua Rodriguez, Chief Executive Officer
Web address: www.windmoor.com
Control: Corporation, Investor–owned (for–profit) **Service**: Psychiatric

Staffed Beds: 144

CLERMONT—Lake County

ENCOMPASS HEALTH REHABILITATION HOSPITAL OF CLERMONT (103055), 2901 State Road 50, Zip 34711–6037; tel. 689/946–1000, (Nonreporting) **S** Encompass Health Corporation, Birmingham, AL
Primary Contact: Glenda Carius, R.N., MSN, Chief Executive Officer
Control: Corporation, Investor–owned (for–profit) **Service**: Rehabilitation

Staffed Beds: 50

☐ **ORLANDO HEALTH SOUTH LAKE HOSPITAL (100051)**, 1900 Don Wickham Drive, Zip 34711–1979; tel. 352/394–4071, (Total facility includes 26 beds in nursing home–type unit) **A**1 3 10 **F**3 11 13 15 18 20 22 24 26 28 29 30 31 34 35 40 42 45 46 47 48 49 50 51 53 54 57 59 64 68 70 74 75 76 77 78 79 80 81 82 85 86 87 92 93 107 108 110 111 114 115 116 117 118 119 120 121 124 126 128 129 130 132 135 142 147 148 149 150 154 156 167 **S** Orlando Health, Orlando, FL
Primary Contact: Lance Sewell, President and Chief Executive Officer
COO: Paul Johns, Chief Operating Officer
CFO: Lance Sewell, Chief Financial Officer
CHR: Stephanie Stapelfeldt, Director, Human Resources
CNO: Bonnie Onofre, Chief Nursing Officer
Web address: www.southlakehospital.com
Control: Other not–for–profit (including NFP Corporation) **Service**: General medical and surgical

Staffed Beds: 183 **Admissions**: 16321 **Census**: 169 **Outpatient Visits**: 158601 **Births**: 850 **Total Expense ($000)**: 336224 **Payroll Expense ($000)**: 114952 **Personnel**: 1363

CLEWISTON—Hendry County

⊞ **HENDRY REGIONAL MEDICAL CENTER (101309)**, 524 West Sagamore Avenue, Zip 33440–3514; tel. 863/902–3000, **A**1 10 18 **F**3 11 15 29 34 35 40 45 50 57 59 64 65 68 75 77 81 82 85 91 93 97 107 110 111 114 119 127 133 135 146 **S** Ovation Healthcare, Brentwood, TN
Primary Contact: R.D. Williams, Chief Executive Officer
CFO: John Beltz, Chief Financial Officer
CMO: Leonard Carroll, M.D., Chief of Staff
CIO: Harrington Fuller, Information Technology Director
CHR: Lisa Miller, Director Human Resources
CNO: Rebecca Springer, MSN, R.N., Chief Nursing Officer
Web address: www.hendryregional.org
Control: Hospital district or authority, Government, Nonfederal **Service**: General medical and surgical

Staffed Beds: 25 **Admissions**: 345 **Census**: 5 **Total Expense ($000)**: 43263 **Payroll Expense ($000)**: 11379 **Personnel**: 161

COCOA BEACH—Brevard County

⊞ **HEALTH FIRST CAPE CANAVERAL HOSPITAL (100177)**, 701 West Cocoa Beach Causeway, Zip 32931–5595, Mailing Address: P.O. Box 320069, Zip 32932–0069; tel. 321/799–7111, **A**1 10 **F**3 13 15 18 20 22 26 29 30 31 34 40 41 45 46 49 50 59 60 62 63 64 68 70 74 75 76 77 78 79 80 81 84 85 86 87 93 100 102 107 108 110 111 115 118 119 120 126 129 130 132 141 146 147 148 149 157 167 168 **S** Health First, Inc., Rockledge, FL
Primary Contact: Brett A. Esrock, President
COO: Deborah Angerami, Chief Operating Officer, Health First Community Hospitals
CFO: Joseph G Felkner, Senior Vice President Finance and Chief Financial Officer
CMO: Lee Scheinbart, M.D., Vice President Medical Affairs, Health First Community Hospitals
CIO: Alex Popowycz, Senior Vice President and Chief Information Officer
CHR: Paula Just, Chief Human Resources Officer
CNO: Connie Bradley, R.N., MSN, FACHE, Chief Nursing Officer
Web address: https://hf.org/healthcare-home/location-directory/cape-canaveral-hospital
Control: Other not–for–profit (including NFP Corporation) **Service**: General medical and surgical

Staffed Beds: 150 **Admissions**: 6705 **Census**: 71 **Outpatient Visits**: 107000 **Births**: 814 **Total Expense ($000)**: 185251 **Payroll Expense ($000)**: 62049 **Personnel**: 561

CORAL GABLES—Miami–Dade County

⊞ **BAPTIST HEALTH SOUTH FLORIDA, DOCTORS HOSPITAL (100296)**, 5000 University Drive, Zip 33146–2094; tel. 786/308–3000, **A**1 3 5 10 **F**3 8 18 19 29 30 31 34 35 37 38 40 44 45 47 49 50 51 53 57 58 59 60 64 68 70 74 75 77 79 80 81 82 84 86 87 93 100 102 107 108 111 115 119 126 130 131 132 134 135 141 146 148 149 154 156 157 164 167 **S** Baptist Health South Florida, Coral Gables, FL
Primary Contact: Javier Hernandez–Lichtl, Chief Executive Officer
CFO: Macia Andres, Assistant Vice President Finance (Controller)
CMO: Jack Cooper, M.D., Chief Medical Officer
Web address: www.baptisthealth.net
Control: Other not–for–profit (including NFP Corporation) **Service**: General medical and surgical

Staffed Beds: 134 **Admissions**: 4702 **Census**: 54 **Outpatient Visits**: 88207 **Births**: 0 **Total Expense ($000)**: 252508 **Payroll Expense ($000)**: 76904 **Personnel**: 922

☐ **CORAL GABLES HOSPITAL (100183)**, 3100 Douglas Road, Zip 33134–6914; tel. 305/445–8461, (Nonreporting) **A**1 10 **S** Steward Health Care System, LLC, Dallas, TX
Primary Contact: Jose Molliner, Interim Chief Executive Officer
COO: Jose Molliner, Chief Operating Officer
CFO: Henry Capote, Interim Chief Financial Officer
CMO: Pedro Friarte, Director of Physician Services
CIO: Mercy Hermosa, Director of Information System
CHR: Ana Paguaga, Director of Human Resources
Web address: www.coralgableshospital.com
Control: Corporation, Investor–owned (for–profit) **Service**: General medical and surgical

Staffed Beds: 256

VENCOR HOSPITAL–CORAL GABLES See Kindred Hospital South Florida–Coral Gables

Hospitals, U.S. / FLORIDA

CORAL SPRINGS—Broward County

☒ **BROWARD HEALTH CORAL SPRINGS (100276)**, 3000 Coral Hills Drive, Zip 33065-4108; tel. 954/344-3000, **A**1 3 10 **F**3 11 12 13 15 17 18 19 20 22 26 29 30 31 32 34 35 36 40 41 44 45 47 48 49 50 51 53 57 58 59 61 64 65 70 72 74 75 76 77 78 79 80 81 82 84 85 86 87 88 89 93 96 100 107 108 110 111 115 118 119 126 129 130 131 132 134 135 141 145 146 147 148 149 154 157 162 164 167 **S** Broward Health, Fort Lauderdale, FL
Primary Contact: Kristin Bowman, Chief Executive Officer
COO: Michael Leopold, Chief Operating Officer
CFO: Onel Rodriguez, Chief Financial Officer
CMO: Kutty Chandran, M.D., Regional Medical Officer
CNO: Carolyn Lizann Carter, Chief Nursing Officer
Web address: www.browardhealth.org
Control: Hospital district or authority, Government, Nonfederal **Service**: General medical and surgical

Staffed Beds: 250 **Admissions**: 10920 **Census**: 139 **Outpatient Visits**: 122041 **Births**: 1580 **Total Expense ($000)**: 227074 **Payroll Expense ($000)**: 88372 **Personnel**: 1361

CRESTVIEW—Okaloosa County

☒ **NORTH OKALOOSA MEDICAL CENTER (100122)**, 151 Redstone Avenue SE, Zip 32539-6026; tel. 850/689-8100, **A**1 10 **F**3 8 11 13 15 18 20 22 28 29 30 34 35 40 45 49 50 51 54 59 60 64 70 75 76 79 81 85 86 87 89 90 107 108 110 111 114 115 116 117 118 119 126 127 129 130 131 132 146 147 148 149 150 154 156 157 167 **S** Community Health Systems, Inc., Franklin, TN
Primary Contact: Michael Nordness, Chief Executive Officer
CFO: Gary S. Davis, Chief Financial Officer
CMO: Michael Foley, M.D., Chief Medical Officer
CIO: Jenny Zeitler, Network Administrator
CHR: Melody M Miller-Collette, Director Human Resources
CNO: Nina Perez, R.N., MSN, Chief Nursing Officer
Web address: www.northokaloosa.com
Control: Corporation, Investor-owned (for-profit) **Service**: General medical and surgical

Staffed Beds: 110 **Admissions**: 6022 **Census**: 64 **Outpatient Visits**: 80159 **Births**: 667 **Total Expense ($000)**: 136499 **Payroll Expense ($000)**: 36804 **Personnel**: 550

CRYSTAL RIVER—Citrus County

BAYFRONT HEALTH SEVEN RIVERS See Tampa General Hospital Crystal River

☒ **TAMPA GENERAL HOSPITAL CRYSTAL RIVER (100249)**, 6201 North Suncoast Boulevard, Zip 34428-6712; tel. 352/795-6560, (Nonreporting) **A**1 10 19
Primary Contact: Linda Stockton, Chief Executive Officer
CFO: Vickie Magurean, Chief Financial Officer
CHR: Joann Mramor, Director Human Resources
CNO: Cynthia Heitzman, R.N., Chief Nursing Officer
Web address: https://www.tghnorth.org/locations/tampa-general-hospital-crystal-river
Control: Corporation, Investor-owned (for-profit) **Service**: General medical and surgical

Staffed Beds: 128

CUTLER BAY—Miami-Dade County

☒ **ENCOMPASS HEALTH REHABILITATION HOSPITAL OF MIAMI (103038)**, 20601 Old Cutler Road, Zip 33189-2400; tel. 305/251-3800, (Nonreporting) **A**1 3 10 **S** Encompass Health Corporation, Birmingham, AL
Primary Contact: Zaynah Camp-Fry, Chief Executive Officer
CIO: Miguel Cruz, Medical Staff Credentialing Coordinator
CHR: Susan Riley, Director Human Resources
CNO: Ellen Romanowski, Chief Nursing Officer
Web address: https://encompasshealth.com/locations/miamirehab
Control: Corporation, Investor-owned (for-profit) **Service**: Rehabilitation

Staffed Beds: 60

DADE CITY—Pasco County

☒ **ADVENTHEALTH DADE CITY (100211)**, 13100 Fort King Road, Zip 33525-5294; tel. 352/521-1100, (Nonreporting) **A**1 10 **S** AdventHealth, Altamonte Springs, FL
Primary Contact: Michael Murrill, President and Chief Executive Officer
CFO: Ann Barr, Interim Chief Financial Officer
CMO: Petros Tsambiras, M.D., Chief of Staff
CIO: Cheryl Kaufman, Director Health Information Management
CHR: Tabatha Wallace, Director Human Resources
Web address: www.floridahospital.com/dade-city
Control: Church operated, Nongovernment, not-for-profit **Service**: General medical and surgical

Staffed Beds: 75

DAVENPORT—Polk County

★ ⇧ **ADVENTHEALTH HEART OF FLORIDA (100137)**, 40100 Highway 27, Zip 33837-5906; tel. 863/422-4971, **A**10 19 21 **F**3 12 13 15 18 20 22 26 28 29 30 34 35 37 40 42 45 46 49 50 51 57 59 60 64 68 70 74 75 76 77 79 81 82 85 86 87 92 93 96 100 107 110 111 114 115 119 126 130 131 135 146 147 148 149 154 156 167 **S** AdventHealth, Altamonte Springs, FL
Primary Contact: Tim Clark, Chief Executive Officer, Acute Care Services
CMO: Claudio Manubens, M.D., Chief of Staff
CIO: Louis Jones, Director Management Information Systems
CHR: Joan Allard, Director Human Resources
CNO: Dottie Mileto, Chief Nursing Officer
Web address: www.heartofflorida.com
Control: Other not-for-profit (including NFP Corporation) **Service**: General medical and surgical

Staffed Beds: 212 **Admissions**: 9490 **Census**: 116 **Total Expense ($000)**: 240495 **Payroll Expense ($000)**: 81766 **Personnel**: 920

DAVIE—Broward County

☒ **HCA FLORIDA UNIVERSITY HOSPITAL (100360)**, 3476 South University Drive, Zip 33328-2000; tel. 954/475-4311, (Nonreporting) **A**1 10 **S** HCA Healthcare, Nashville, TN
Primary Contact: Madeline Nava, Chief Executive Officer
COO: Madison Workman, Chief Operating Officer
CFO: Matt Hughes, Chief Financial Officer
CNO: Neva Spencer, MSN, Chief Nursing Officer
Web address: https://www.hcafloridahealthcare.com/locations/university-hospital
Control: Corporation, Investor-owned (for-profit) **Service**: General medical and surgical

Staffed Beds: 165

DAYTONA BEACH—Volusia County

☒ △ **ADVENTHEALTH DAYTONA BEACH (100068)**, 301 Memorial Medical Parkway, Zip 32117-5167; tel. 386/231-6000, **A**1 2 7 10 19 **F**3 8 12 13 15 17 18 20 22 24 26 28 29 30 31 32 34 35 40 41 42 45 46 47 49 50 51 53 55 57 58 59 60 64 70 72 74 75 76 78 79 80 81 84 85 86 87 89 90 93 97 107 108 110 111 115 116 117 118 119 120 121 123 124 126 130 131 132 146 147 148 149 154 156 157 169 **S** AdventHealth, Altamonte Springs, FL
Primary Contact: David Weis, President and Chief Executive Officer
COO: Darlinda Copeland, Chief Operating Officer
CFO: Debora Thomas, Chief Financial Officer
CMO: Kris David Gray, Chief Medical Officer
CHR: Opal R Howard, Executive Director Human Resources
CNO: Michele Goeb-Burkett, R.N., MSN, Chief Nursing Officer
Web address: https://www.adventhealth.com/hospital/adventhealth-daytona-beach
Control: Church operated, Nongovernment, not-for-profit **Service**: General medical and surgical

Staffed Beds: 362 **Admissions**: 21765 **Census**: 326 **Outpatient Visits**: 209593 **Births**: 1519 **Total Expense ($000)**: 725160 **Payroll Expense ($000)**: 190527 **Personnel**: 2994

HALIFAX BEHAVIORAL CENTER See Halifax Behavioral Services

Hospital, Medicare Provider Number, Address, Telephone, Approval, Facility, and Physician Codes, Health Care System

★ American Hospital Association (AHA) membership ○ Healthcare Facilities Accreditation Program ⇧ Center for Improvement in Healthcare Quality Accreditation
☐ The Joint Commission accreditation ◇ DNV Healthcare Inc. accreditation △ Commission on Accreditation of Rehabilitation Facilities (CARF) accreditation

Hospitals, U.S. / FLORIDA

☐ △ **HALIFAX HEALTH MEDICAL CENTER OF DAYTONA BEACH (100017),** 303 North Clyde Morris Boulevard, Zip 32114-2700; tel. 386/425-4000, (Includes HALIFAX BEHAVIORAL SERVICES, 841 Jimmy Ann Drive, Daytona Beach, Florida, Zip 32117-4599, tel. 386/425-3900; HALIFAX HEALTH MEDICAL CENTER OF PORT ORANGE, 1041 Dunlawton Avenue, Port Orange, Florida, Zip 32127, tel. 386/425-4700; Jeff Feasel, President and Chief Executive Officer) **A**1 3 5 7 10 19 **F**3 8 12 13 14 17 18 19 20 22 24 26 28 29 30 31 32 34 35 37 39 40 41 43 45 46 47 48 49 50 51 53 55 56 57 58 59 60 64 65 66 70 72 74 75 76 77 78 79 81 82 85 86 87 88 89 90 91 92 93 94 96 97 98 99 100 101 102 104 105 107 108 111 114 115 118 119 120 121 123 124 126 131 132 134 135 138 143 145 146 147 148 149 153 154 156 157 164 167 **P**6
Primary Contact: Jeff Feasel, President and Chief Executive Officer
COO: Mark Billings, Chief Operating Officer
CFO: Eric Peburn, Chief Financial Officer
CMO: Margaret Crossman, M.D., Chief Medical Officer
CIO: Tom Stafford, Chief Information Officer
CHR: Kimberly Fulcher, Chief Human Resources Officer
Web address: www.halifaxhealth.org
Control: Hospital district or authority, Government, Nonfederal **Service:** General medical and surgical

Staffed Beds: 703 **Admissions:** 25795 **Census:** 416 **Total Expense ($000):** 733671 **Payroll Expense ($000):** 276069 **Personnel:** 3166

☒ **SELECT SPECIALTY HOSPITAL DAYTONA BEACH (102030),** 301 Memorial Medical Parkway, 11th Floor, Zip 32117-5167; tel. 386/231-3436, (Nonreporting) **A**1 10 **S** Select Medical Corporation, Mechanicsburg, PA
Primary Contact: Robert E. Mallicoat, Chief Executive Officer
Web address: www.daytonabeach.selectspecialtyhospitals.com
Control: Corporation, Investor-owned (for-profit) **Service:** Acute long-term care hospital

Staffed Beds: 34

DEERFIELD BEACH—Broward County

☒ △ **BROWARD HEALTH NORTH (100086),** 201 East Sample Road, Zip 33064-3502; tel. 954/941-8300, **A**1 3 7 10 19 **F**3 6 11 15 16 17 18 20 22 26 29 30 31 34 35 36 37 40 43 44 45 46 47 48 49 50 51 54 56 57 58 59 61 64 65 66 70 72 73 74 75 76 77 78 79 80 81 82 84 85 86 87 88 89 90 91 92 93 96 98 105 107 108 110 111 114 115 119 120 121 126 130 131 132 135 145 146 147 148 149 150 154 157 164 166 167 **S** Broward Health, Fort Lauderdale, FL
Primary Contact: Matthew Garner, Chief Executive Officer
COO: Susan Newton, Chief Operating Officer
CFO: Joshua Szostek, Chief Financial Officer
CMO: Jerry Capote, M.D., Chief Medical Officer
CHR: Carl McDonald, Chief Human Resources Officer
CNO: Eileen Manniste, MSN, Chief Nursing Officer
Web address: https://www.browardhealth.org/locations/broward-health-north
Control: Hospital district or authority, Government, Nonfederal **Service:** General medical and surgical

Staffed Beds: 310 **Admissions:** 10935 **Census:** 183 **Outpatient Visits:** 86836 **Births:** 0 **Total Expense ($000):** 290990 **Payroll Expense ($000):** 100011 **Personnel:** 1348

DELAND—Volusia County

☒ **ADVENTHEALTH DELAND (100045),** 701 West Plymouth Avenue, Zip 32720-3236; tel. 386/943-4522, (Total facility includes 18 beds in nursing home-type unit) **A**1 2 10 19 **F**3 4 11 15 18 20 22 28 29 30 31 34 35 40 44 45 46 47 48 49 54 55 57 59 60 62 66 70 74 75 77 78 79 80 81 84 85 86 87 92 93 96 98 100 102 105 107 108 110 111 115 117 119 120 121 123 124 129 130 131 135 146 148 149 154 156 164 167 **S** AdventHealth, Altamonte Springs, FL
Primary Contact: Eric E. Lunde, President and Chief Executive Officer
COO: Samuel Aguero, Chief Operating Officer
CFO: Kyle Glass, Chief Financial Officer
CMO: Samuel Edwards, M.D., Chief of Staff
CIO: Kevin Piper, Director Information Systems
CNO: Patricia Ann Stark, R.N., CNO
Web address: https://www.adventhealth.com/hospital/adventhealth-deland
Control: Church operated, Nongovernment, not-for-profit **Service:** General medical and surgical

Staffed Beds: 152 **Admissions:** 9686 **Census:** 114 **Outpatient Visits:** 396436 **Births:** 0 **Total Expense ($000):** 205119 **Payroll Expense ($000):** 73057 **Personnel:** 776

DELRAY BEACH—Palm Beach County

☒ △ **DELRAY MEDICAL CENTER (100258),** 5352 Linton Boulevard, Zip 33484-6580; tel. 561/498-4440, (Includes FAIR OAKS PAVILION, 5440 Linton Boulevard, Delray Beach, Florida, Zip 33484-6578, tel. 561/495-1000; PINECREST REHABILITATION HOSPITAL, 5360 Linton Boulevard, Delray Beach, Florida, Zip 33484-6538, tel. 561/495-0400) **A**1 3 5 7 10 **F**3 4 11 12 15 17 18 20 22 24 26 28 29 30 31 34 35 37 38 40 42 43 45 46 49 50 51 56 57 58 59 60 64 65 71 74 75 77 78 79 80 81 82 83 84 85 87 90 91 92 93 94 96 97 98 100 101 102 103 104 107 108 111 114 115 118 119 126 129 130 131 132 135 143 146 148 149 151 154 157 **S** TENET Healthcare Corporation, Dallas, TX
Primary Contact: Heather Havericak, Chief Executive Officer
CMO: Anthony Dardano, M.D., Chief Medical Officer
CIO: Robens Rosena, Director Information Systems
CHR: Shannon Wills, Director Human Resources
Web address: www.delraymedicalctr.com
Control: Corporation, Investor-owned (for-profit) **Service:** General medical and surgical

Staffed Beds: 520 **Admissions:** 20476 **Census:** 305 **Total Expense ($000):** 421097 **Payroll Expense ($000):** 134932 **Personnel:** 1482

FAIR OAKS HOSPITAL See Fair Oaks Pavilion

DELTONA—Volusia County

☐ **HALIFAX HEALTH/UF HEALTH MEDICAL CENTER OF DELTONA (100330),** 3400 East Halifax Crossing Boulevard, Zip 32725-2914; tel. 386/425-6000, **A**1 10 **F**3 12 18 19 22 29 34 40 45 49 50 54 57 59 60 64 65 70 74 75 77 78 79 81 82 85 86 87 91 92 93 94 107 108 111 114 115 118 119 130 131 143 145 146 149 154 157 **P**6
Primary Contact: Jeff Feasel, Chief Executive Officer
COO: Alberto Tineo, Chief Operating Officer
CFO: Eric Peburn, Chief Financial Officer
CMO: Margaret Crossman, M.D., Chief Medical Officer
CIO: Michael Marques, Vice President and Chief Information Officer Information Technology
CHR: Kimberly Fulcher, Senior Vice President and Chief Human Resources Officer
CNO: Maryjo Allen, Chief Nursing Officer
Web address: https://halifaxhealth.org/
Control: Hospital district or authority, Government, Nonfederal **Service:** General medical and surgical

Staffed Beds: 43 **Admissions:** 2006 **Census:** 19 **Total Expense ($000):** 64267 **Payroll Expense ($000):** 17604 **Personnel:** 209

DUNEDIN—Pinellas County

☒ **BAYCARE ALLIANT HOSPITAL (102021),** 601 Main Street, Zip 34698-5848; tel. 727/736-9991, **A**1 10 **F**1 3 28 29 34 35 36 100 130 148 154 **S** BayCare Health System, Clearwater, FL
Primary Contact: Maya Perez, President
CFO: John Proni, CPA, Manager Finance and Operations
CMO: Leonard Dunn, M.D., Chief Medical Officer
CHR: Darlene Shelton, Coordinator Team Resources
Web address: www.baycare.org
Control: Other not-for-profit (including NFP Corporation) **Service:** Acute long-term care hospital

Staffed Beds: 34 **Admissions:** 382 **Census:** 30 **Outpatient Visits:** 0 **Births:** 0 **Total Expense ($000):** 21273 **Payroll Expense ($000):** 11035 **Personnel:** 89

☒ **MEASE DUNEDIN HOSPITAL (100043),** 601 Main Street, Zip 34698-5891; tel. 727/733-1111, **A**1 10 **F**3 11 12 15 18 29 30 31 34 35 37 38 40 44 45 49 50 56 57 59 60 64 68 70 74 75 77 78 79 81 84 85 86 87 98 99 100 101 102 103 107 108 110 111 114 115 118 119 126 130 132 135 143 145 146 148 149 154 156 164 167 **S** BayCare Health System, Clearwater, FL
Primary Contact: Kelly Enriquez, President, Mease Hospitals
CFO: Carl Tremonti, Chief Financial Officer
CMO: Tony Schuster, M.D., Vice President, Chief Medical Officer
CIO: Tim Thompson, Senior Vice President, Information Services and Chief Information Officer
CHR: Kyle J Barr, Senior Vice President, Chief Team Resources Officer
CNO: Thomas Doria, Vice President, Patient Services and Chief Nursing Officer
Web address: https://baycare.org/locations/hospitals/mease-dunedin-hospital/patients-and-visitors
Control: Other not-for-profit (including NFP Corporation) **Service:** General medical and surgical

Staffed Beds: 120 **Admissions:** 5844 **Census:** 78 **Outpatient Visits:** 40506 **Births:** 0 **Total Expense ($000):** 126459 **Payroll Expense ($000):** 50466 **Personnel:** 572

Hospitals, U.S. / FLORIDA

EGLIN AFB—Okaloosa County

☒ **U. S. AIR FORCE REGIONAL HOSPITAL,** 307 Boatner Road, Suite 114, Zip 32542–1282; tel. 850/883–8221, (Nonreporting) **A**1 3 5 **S** Department of the Air Force, Washington, DC
Primary Contact: Colonel Gregory Coleman, Commanding Officer
Web address: https://eglin.tricare.mil/
Control: Air Force, Government, federal **Service:** General medical and surgical

Staffed Beds: 57

ENGLEWOOD—Sarasota County

ENGLEWOOD COMMUNITY HOSPITAL See HCA Florida Englewood Hospital

☒ **HCA FLORIDA ENGLEWOOD HOSPITAL (100267),** 700 Medical Boulevard, Zip 34223–3978; tel. 941/475–6571, (Nonreporting) **A**1 10 **S** HCA Healthcare, Nashville, TN
Primary Contact: Joe Rudisill, Chief Executive Officer
COO: Alex Chang, Chief Operating Officer
CFO: Vickie Magurean, Chief Financial Officer
CMO: L. Craig McAskill, M.D., Chief Medical Officer
CNO: Kathleen Pace, MSN, R.N., Chief Nursing Officer
Web address: www.englewoodcommunityhospital.com
Control: Corporation, Investor–owned (for–profit) **Service:** General medical and surgical

Staffed Beds: 100

FERNANDINA BEACH—Nassau County

☒ **BAPTIST MEDICAL CENTER NASSAU (100140),** 1250 South 18th Street, Zip 32034–3098; tel. 904/321–3500, **A**1 10 **F**3 11 18 28 29 30 34 35 40 45 46 47 48 49 51 57 59 64 69 70 74 75 76 77 79 81 82 87 93 102 107 108 110 111 114 115 119 124 130 132 134 135 146 147 148 149 156 **P**5 **S** Baptist Health, Jacksonville, FL
Primary Contact: Tara Beth. Anderson, President
CFO: Patricia K Hausauer, Director Finance
CHR: Erin Jackson, Human Resources Specialist
Web address: www.baptistjax.com/locations/baptist-medical-center-nassau
Control: Other not–for–profit (including NFP Corporation) **Service:** General medical and surgical

Staffed Beds: 54 **Admissions:** 3163 **Census:** 29 **Outpatient Visits:** 71436 **Births:** 0 **Total Expense ($000):** 82920 **Payroll Expense ($000):** 24581 **Personnel:** 356

FORT LAUDERDALE—Broward County

☒ **BROWARD HEALTH IMPERIAL POINT (100200),** 6401 North Federal Highway, Zip 33308–1495; tel. 954/776–8500, **A**1 3 10 **F**3 11 12 15 18 20 22 26 29 30 31 34 35 36 40 41 44 45 49 50 51 53 56 57 58 59 61 64 65 70 74 75 77 78 79 80 81 82 85 86 87 93 98 100 102 103 107 108 110 111 114 115 126 130 131 132 135 141 146 147 148 149 154 157 164 167 **S** Broward Health, Fort Lauderdale, FL
Primary Contact: Calvin E. Glidewell Jr, Interim Chief Executive Officer
COO: Netonua Reyes, MSN, Chief Operating Officer and Chief Nursing Officer
CFO: Joseph Paul, Chief Financial Officer
CMO: Jerry Capote, M.D., Chief Medical Officer
CHR: Deven Silverman, Chief Human Resouce Officer
CNO: Netonua Reyes, MSN, Chief Operating Officer and Chief Nursing Officer
Web address: https://www.browardhealth.org/locations/broward-health-imperial-point
Control: Hospital district or authority, Government, Nonfederal **Service:** General medical and surgical

Staffed Beds: 193 **Admissions:** 6661 **Census:** 80 **Outpatient Visits:** 64143 **Births:** 0 **Total Expense ($000):** 135855 **Payroll Expense ($000):** 51604 **Personnel:** 5923

☒ **BROWARD HEALTH MEDICAL CENTER (100039),** 1600 South Andrews Avenue, Zip 33316–2510; tel. 954/355–4400, (Includes CHRIS EVERT CHILDRENS HOSPITAL, 1600 South Andrews Avenue, Fort Lauderdale, Florida, Zip 33316–2510, tel. 954/355–4400; Calvin E Glidewell Jr, Chief Executive Officer) **A**1 2 3 5 10 13 **F**3 4 5 11 12 13 15 17 18 19 20 22 24 26 28 29 30 31 32 34 35 38 39 40 41 43 44 45 46 47 48 49 50 53 54 55 56 57 58 59 61 64 65 66 70 72 73 74 75 76 77 78 79 80 81 82 83 84 85 86 87 88 89 92 93 97 98 100 101 102 107 108 109 110 111 113 115 116 117 118 119 120 121 126 129 130 131 132 133 134 135 146 147 148 149 150 153 154 156 157 160 162 164 167 **S** Broward Health, Fort Lauderdale, FL
Primary Contact: Manuel Linares, Chief Executive Officer
COO: Natassia Orr, Chief Operating Officer
CFO: Laura Thomas, Chief Financial Officer
CMO: James Roach, D.O., Chief Medical Officer
CHR: Dionne Wong, Vice President and Chief Human Resources Officer
CNO: Robyn Farrington, Chief Nursing Officer
Web address: www.browardhealth.org
Control: Hospital district or authority, Government, Nonfederal **Service:** General medical and surgical

Staffed Beds: 622 **Admissions:** 23709 **Census:** 416 **Outpatient Visits:** 190652 **Births:** 3824 **Total Expense ($000):** 621944 **Payroll Expense ($000):** 212358 **Personnel:** 2259

☒ **HOLY CROSS HOSPITAL (100073),** 4725 North Federal Highway, Zip 33308–4668, Mailing Address: P.O. Box 23460, Zip 33307–3460; tel. 954/771–8000, **A**1 2 3 5 10 **F**3 8 11 12 13 15 17 18 22 24 26 28 29 30 31 34 35 36 37 40 44 45 46 47 48 49 50 51 53 54 55 56 57 58 59 61 62 64 65 66 67 70 72 74 75 76 77 78 79 81 82 84 85 87 90 91 92 93 95 96 97 100 107 108 109 110 111 115 117 118 119 120 121 123 124 126 130 131 132 134 135 145 146 147 149 154 156 157 **S** Trinity Health, Livonia, MI
Primary Contact: Mark Doyle, President and Chief Executive Officer
CFO: Ronald Brandenburg, Vice President and Chief Financial Officer
CMO: Eduardo Locatelli, M.D., Interim Chief Medical Officer
CNO: Taren Ruggiero, R.N., MSN, Vice President and Chief Nursing Officer
Web address: www.holy-cross.com
Control: Other not–for–profit (including NFP Corporation) **Service:** General medical and surgical

Staffed Beds: 557 **Admissions:** 14812 **Census:** 215 **Total Expense ($000):** 573155 **Payroll Expense ($000):** 144145 **Personnel:** 2541

☒ **KINDRED HOSPITAL SOUTH FLORIDA–FORT LAUDERDALE (102010),** 1516 East Las Olas Boulevard, Zip 33301–2399; tel. 954/764–8900, (Includes KINDRED HOSPITAL SOUTH FLORIDA–CORAL GABLES, 5190 SW Eighth Street, Coral Gables, Florida, Zip 33134–2495, tel. 305/445–1364; Al Molina, Chief Executive Officer; KINDRED HOSPITAL SOUTH FLORIDA–HOLLYWOOD, 1859 Van Buren Street, Hollywood, Florida, Zip 33020–5127, tel. 954/920–9000; Roberta Moss, Chief Executive Officer) **A**1 10 **F**1 3 29 60 61 63 70 77 82 84 90 91 95 100 107 119 148 **S** ScionHealth, Louisville, KY
Primary Contact: Cindy Jackson, Market Chief Executive Officer
CFO: Dean Card, Chief Financial Officer
Web address: www.khfortlauderdale.com/
Control: Individual, Investor–owned (for–profit) **Service:** Acute long–term care hospital

Staffed Beds: 64 **Admissions:** 616 **Census:** 45 **Total Expense ($000):** 34770 **Payroll Expense ($000):** 13130 **Personnel:** 166

NORTH SHORE MEDICAL CENTER, FLORIDA MEDICAL CENTER CAMPUS See Florida Medical Center – A Campus of North Shore

FORT MYERS—Lee County

CHILDREN'S HOSPITAL OF SOUTHWEST FLORIDA See Golisano Children's Hospital of Southwest Florida

GOLISANO CHILDREN'S HOSPITAL OF SOUTHWEST FLORIDA See Lee Memorial Hospital, Fort Myers

★ ⇑ **GULF COAST MEDICAL CENTER (100220),** 13681 Doctor's Way, Zip 33912–4300; tel. 239/343–1000, **A**10 21 **F**3 11 13 14 20 28 29 40 45 46 49 51 60 70 74 77 79 81 84 85 86 87 93 102 107 108 111 114 115 118 119 128 130 146 154 156 167 **S** Lee Health, Fort Myers, FL
Primary Contact: Lawrence Antonucci, M.D., President/Chief Executive Officer
CFO: Ben Spence, Chief Financial Officer
CMO: Mark Greenberg, M.D., Medical Director
CIO: Mike Smith, Chief Information Officer
CHR: Jon C Cecil, Chief Human Resource Officer
CNO: Jennifer Sue Higgins, R.N., Vice President, Operations and Chief Nurse Executive
Web address: www.leememorial.org
Control: Hospital district or authority, Government, Nonfederal **Service:** General medical and surgical

Staffed Beds: 624 **Admissions:** 27953 **Census:** 472 **Total Expense ($000):** 687603 **Payroll Expense ($000):** 326373 **Personnel:** 2957

Hospital, Medicare Provider Number, Address, Telephone, Approval, Facility, and Physician Codes, Health Care System

★ American Hospital Association (AHA) membership
☐ The Joint Commission accreditation
○ Healthcare Facilities Accreditation Program
◇ DNV Healthcare Inc. accreditation
⇑ Center for Improvement in Healthcare Quality Accreditation
△ Commission on Accreditation of Rehabilitation Facilities (CARF) accreditation

© 2025 AHA Guide

Hospitals, U.S. / FLORIDA

★ △ ⚕ **LEE MEMORIAL HOSPITAL (100012)**, 2776 Cleveland Avenue, Zip 33901–5855, Mailing Address: P.O. Box 2218, Zip 33902–2218; tel. 239/343–2000, (Includes GOLISANO CHILDREN'S HOSPITAL OF SOUTHWEST FLORIDA, 9981 South HealthPark Drive, Fort Myers, Florida, Zip 33908, tel. 239/343–5437; Lawrence Antonucci, M.D., President/Chief Executive Officer; HEALTHPARK MEDICAL CENTER, 9981 South HealthPark Drive, Fort Myers, Florida, Zip 33908, tel. 239/433–7799; Armando Llechu, Chief Administrative Officer; THE REHABILITATION HOSPITAL, 2776 Cleveland Avenue, Fort Myers, Florida, Zip 33901, tel. 239/343–3900) **A**2 3 5 7 10 21 **F**3 11 12 13 14 15 17 18 19 20 21 22 24 26 28 29 30 31 32 34 40 41 43 45 46 48 49 51 53 54 55 56 57 58 59 60 68 70 72 74 75 76 77 78 79 81 82 84 85 86 87 88 89 90 93 94 100 102 104 107 108 110 111 114 115 116 117 119 126 128 129 130 131 132 135 136 146 147 148 156 167 **S** Lee Health, Fort Myers, FL
Primary Contact: Iahn Gonsenhauser, Chief Medical Officer
CFO: Ben Spence, Chief Financial Officer
CHR: Jon C Cecil, Chief Human Resource Officer
CNO: Julia Liebscher, Vice President Operations and Chief Nurse Executive
Web address: www.leememorial.org
Control: Hospital district or authority, Government, Nonfederal **Service**: General medical and surgical

Staffed Beds: 911 **Admissions**: 37425 **Census**: 559 **Total Expense ($000)**: 1282563 **Payroll Expense ($000)**: 445714 **Personnel**: 4955

☐ **PARK ROYAL HOSPITAL (104074)**, 9241 Park Royal Drive, Zip 33908–9204; tel. 239/985–2700, **A**1 10 **F**4 98 100 103 104 105 152 153 154 **S** Acadia Healthcare Company, Inc., Franklin, TN
Primary Contact: Amber Hentz, Chief Executive Officer
CFO: Sherilene De Leon, Chief Financial Officer
CHR: Robert Raynor, Human Resources Director
Web address: www.ParkRoyalHospital.com
Control: Corporation, Investor–owned (for–profit) **Service**: Psychiatric

Staffed Beds: 108 **Admissions**: 4988 **Census**: 106 **Total Expense ($000)**: 26341 **Payroll Expense ($000)**: 12937 **Personnel**: 218

✠ **SELECT SPECIALTY HOSPITAL–FORT MYERS (102029)**, 3050 Champion Ring Road, Zip 33905–5599; tel. 239/313–2900, **A**1 10 **F**1 3 29 107 122 130 148 149 **S** Select Medical Corporation, Mechanicsburg, PA
Primary Contact: Corey Cooper, Chief Executive Officer
Web address: https://fortmyers.selectspecialtyhospitals.com/
Control: Corporation, Investor–owned (for–profit) **Service**: Acute long–term care hospital

Staffed Beds: 60 **Admissions**: 517 **Census**: 38 **Outpatient Visits**: 0 **Births**: 0 **Personnel**: 256

FORT PIERCE—St. Lucie County

HARBOUR SHORES OF LAWNWOOD See Lawnwood Pavilion

✠ △ **HCA FLORIDA LAWNWOOD HOSPITAL (100246)**, 1700 South 23rd Street, Zip 34950–4803; tel. 772/461–4000, (Includes LAWNWOOD PAVILION, 1860 North Lawnwood Circle, Fort Pierce, Florida, Zip 34950, P O Box 1540, Zip 34954–1540, tel. 361/466–1500) (Nonreporting) **A**1 3 5 7 10 **S** HCA Healthcare, Nashville, TN
Primary Contact: Eric Goldman, Chief Executive Officer
COO: Alex Masmela, Chief Operating Officer
CFO: Renee Cross, Chief Financial Officer
CMO: Michael Bakerman, M.D., Chief Medical Officer
CIO: Eric Castle, Director Information Services
CHR: Pam Burchell, Director Human Resources
CNO: Cheryl Nail, Chief Nursing Officer
Web address: https://www.hcafloridahealthcare.com/locations/lawnwood-hospital
Control: Corporation, Investor–owned (for–profit) **Service**: General medical and surgical

Staffed Beds: 392

FORT WALTON BEACH—Okaloosa County

✠ △ **HCA FLORIDA FORT WALTON–DESTIN HOSPITAL (100223)**, 1000 Mar-Walt Drive, Zip 32547–6795; tel. 850/862–1111, (Nonreporting) **A**1 2 3 7 10 **S** HCA Healthcare, Nashville, TN
Primary Contact: Zachary McCluskey, Chief Executive Officer
COO: Caroline F. Burris, Chief Operating Officer
CFO: Matt King, Chief Financial Officer
CMO: Eric Schuck, M.D., Chief Medical Officer
CIO: Amy Caldeira, Director Information Technology and Systems
CHR: Julia Truman, Vice President Human Resources
CNO: Caroline Stewart, Chief Nursing Officer
Web address: https://www.hcafloridahealthcare.com/locations/fort-walton-destin-hospital
Control: Corporation, Investor–owned (for–profit) **Service**: General medical and surgical

Staffed Beds: 267

HCA FORT WALTON–DESTIN HOSPITAL See HCA Florida Fort Walton–Destin Hospital

GAINESVILLE—Alachua County

✠ **HCA FLORIDA NORTH FLORIDA HOSPITAL (100204)**, 6500 Newberry Road, Zip 32605–4392, Mailing Address: P.O. Box 147006, Zip 32614–7006; tel. 352/333–4000, **A**1 2 3 5 10 **F**3 7 12 13 15 17 18 20 22 24 26 28 29 30 31 34 35 37 40 42 45 46 48 49 50 51 56 57 58 59 60 64 70 72 74 75 76 77 78 79 80 81 84 85 86 87 89 98 107 108 109 110 111 113 114 115 116 117 118 119 120 121 123 124 126 129 130 132 135 145 146 147 148 149 167 **S** HCA Healthcare, Nashville, TN
Primary Contact: Eric Lawson, Chief Executive Officer
CFO: Stewart Whitmore, Chief Financial Officer
CMO: Sherrie Somers, D.O., Chief Medical Officer
CIO: Eric Strand, Director Information Services
CHR: Jane Fuller, Vice President Human Resources
Web address: https://www.hcafloridahealthcare.com/locations/north-florida-hospital
Control: Corporation, Investor–owned (for–profit) **Service**: General medical and surgical

Staffed Beds: 548 **Admissions**: 31865 **Census**: 414 **Total Expense ($000)**: 538136 **Payroll Expense ($000)**: 135743 **Personnel**: 1804

MALCOM RANDALL VETERANS AFFAIRS MEDICAL CENTER See Gainesville Veterans Affairs Medical Center

✠ **NORTH FLORIDA/SOUTH GEORGIA VETERAN'S HEALTH SYSTEM**, 1601 SW Archer Road, Zip 32608–1135; tel. 352/376–1611, (Includes GAINESVILLE VETERANS AFFAIRS MEDICAL CENTER, 1601 SW Archer Road, Gainesville, Florida, Zip 32608–1197, tel. 352/376–1611; LAKE CITY VETERANS AFFAIRS MEDICAL CENTER, 619 South Marion Avenue, Lake City, Florida, Zip 32025–5898, tel. 386/755–3016; Thomas Wisnieski, FACHE, Director) (Nonreporting) **A**1 3 5 **S** Department of Veterans Affairs, Washington, DC
Primary Contact: Wende Dottor, Medical Center Director
COO: Thomas Sutton, Associate Director
CFO: Jim Taylor, Chief Business Office
CMO: Brad Bender, M.D., Chief of Staff
CIO: Deborah Michel-Ogborn, Chief Information Resource Management
CHR: Michelle Manderino, Chief Human Resources
Web address: www.northflorida.va.gov
Control: Veterans Affairs, Government, federal **Service**: General medical and surgical

Staffed Beds: 545

✠ **SELECT SPECIALTY HOSPITAL–GAINESVILLE (102022)**, 1600 SW Archer Road, 5th Floor, Zip 32610; tel. 352/337–3240, (Nonreporting) **A**1 3 10 **S** Select Medical Corporation, Mechanicsburg, PA
Primary Contact: Rhonda Sherrod, Chief Executive Officer
Web address: www.gainesville.selectspecialtyhospitals.com/
Control: Corporation, Investor–owned (for–profit) **Service**: Acute long–term care hospital

Staffed Beds: 44

SHANDS AT VISTA See Uf Health Shands Psychiatric Hospital

SHANDS CHILDRENS HOSPITAL See Uf Health Shands Children's Hospital

✠ △ **UF HEALTH REHAB HOSPITAL (103046)**, 2708 Southwest Archer Road, Zip 32608–1316; tel. 352/265–5499, **A**1 7 10 **F**28 29 35 58 75 87 90 91 95 96 130 132 148 149 156 157 **S** Select Medical Corporation, Mechanicsburg, PA
Primary Contact: Anne Roper, Chief Executive Officer
Web address: https://ufhealth.org/uf-health-shands-rehab-hospital
Control: Corporation, Investor–owned (for–profit) **Service**: Rehabilitation

Staffed Beds: 60 **Admissions**: 1422 **Census**: 50 **Outpatient Visits**: 0 **Births**: 0 **Personnel**: 208

Hospitals, U.S. / FLORIDA

☒ **UF HEALTH SHANDS HOSPITAL (100113)**, 1600 SW Archer Road, Zip 32610-3003, Mailing Address: PO Box 100326, Zip 32610-0326; tel. 352/265-0111, (Includes UF HEALTH SHANDS CANCER HOSPITAL, 1515 SW Archer Road, Gainesville, Florida, Zip 32608-1134, PO Box 100326, Zip 32610-0326, tel. 352/265-0111; James J. Kelly Jr, Interim Chief Executive Officer; UF HEALTH SHANDS CHILDREN'S HOSPITAL, 1600 SW Archer Road, Gainesville, Florida, Zip 32610-3003, PO Box 100326, Zip 32610-0326, tel. 352/265-0111; James J. Kelly Jr, Interim Chief Executive Officer; UF HEALTH SHANDS PSYCHIATRIC HOSPITAL, 4101 NW 89th Blvd, Gainesville, Florida, Zip 32606-3813, 4101 NW 89th Boulevard, Zip 32606-3813, tel. 352/265-5481; Roxane Harcourt, Interim Administrator) **A**1 2 3 5 8 10 19 **F**2 3 4 5 6 7 9 11 12 13 15 16 17 18 19 20 21 22 23 24 25 26 27 28 29 30 31 32 34 35 36 37 38 39 40 41 42 43 44 45 46 47 48 49 50 51 52 53 54 55 56 57 58 59 60 61 62 63 64 65 66 68 69 70 71 72 73 74 75 76 77 78 79 80 81 82 83 84 85 86 87 88 89 91 92 93 94 96 97 98 99 100 101 102 103 104 107 108 109 110 111 112 113 114 115 116 117 118 119 120 121 122 123 124 126 129 130 131 132 134 135 136 137 138 139 140 141 142 143 144 145 146 147 148 149 150 152 154 155 156 157 160 161 162 163 164 165 167 169 **P**6 **S** UF Health Shands, Gainesville, FL
Primary Contact: James J. Kelly Jr, Interim Chief Executive Officer
CFO: James J. Kelly Jr, Senior Vice President and Chief Financial Officer
CMO: Parker Gibbs, M.D., Chief Medical Officer
CHR: Janet L. Christie, Senior Vice President Human Resources
Web address: https://ufhealth.org/
Control: Other not-for-profit (including NFP Corporation) **Service**: General medical and surgical

Staffed Beds: 1091 **Admissions**: 49045 **Census**: 910 **Outpatient Visits**: 1255787 **Births**: 3128 **Total Expense ($000)**: 2216956 **Payroll Expense ($000)**: 766875 **Personnel**: 9787

GREEN COVE SPRINGS—Clay County

☒ **KINDRED HOSPITAL NORTH FLORIDA (102015)**, 801 Oak Street, Zip 32043-4317; tel. 904/284-9230, (Nonreporting) **A**1 10 **S** ScionHealth, Louisville, KY
Primary Contact: Robbi Hudson, Chief Executive Officer
CFO: Rickie Simmons, Controller
CMO: Uriel Nazario, M.D., Chief of Medical Staff
CIO: Rick Chapman, Chief Information Officer
CNO: Ashley McRae, Chief Clinical Officer
Web address: www.khnorthflorida.com
Control: Corporation, Investor-owned (for-profit) **Service**: Acute long-term care hospital

Staffed Beds: 80

GULF BREEZE—Santa Rosa County

★ ⇧ **GULF BREEZE HOSPITAL (100266)**, 1110 Gulf Breeze Parkway, Zip 32561-4884; tel. 850/934-2000, **A**3 10 21 **F**3 11 15 18 26 29 30 34 35 40 45 46 47 49 50 56 57 59 70 75 78 79 81 82 84 85 86 87 90 93 94 107 108 110 111 114 115 119 120 121 123 130 131 132 143 146 147 149 156 167 **S** Baptist Health Care Corporation, Pensacola, FL
Primary Contact: Brett Aldridge, President
CFO: Kerry Vermillion, Senior Vice President Finance and Chief Financial Officer
Web address: www.ebaptisthealthcare.org/GulfBreezeHospital/
Control: Other not-for-profit (including NFP Corporation) **Service**: General medical and surgical

Staffed Beds: 65 **Admissions**: 3145 **Census**: 33 **Outpatient Visits**: 125677 **Births**: 0 **Total Expense ($000)**: 110216 **Payroll Expense ($000)**: 32081 **Personnel**: 387

HIALEAH—Dade County

SOUTHERN WINDS HOSPITAL See Keralty Hospital Miami, Miami

HIALEAH—Miami-Dade County

☒ **HIALEAH HOSPITAL (100053)**, 651 East 25th Street, Zip 33013-3878; tel. 305/693-6100, (Nonreporting) **A**1 3 5 10 **S** Steward Health Care System, LLC, Dallas, TX
Primary Contact: Luis R. Allende-Ruiz, Chief Executive Officer
COO: Lourdes Camps, Chief Operating Officer
CMO: Orlando Garcia, M.D., Chief Medical Officer
CHR: Yamila Herrera, Director Human Resources
Web address: www.hialeahhosp.com
Control: Corporation, Investor-owned (for-profit) **Service**: General medical and surgical

Staffed Beds: 191

☐ **LARKIN COMMUNITY HOSPITAL–PALM SPRINGS CAMPUS (100050)**, 1475 West 49th Street, Zip 33012-3275, Mailing Address: P.O. Box 2804, Zip 33012-2804; tel. 305/558-2500, (Nonreporting) **A**1 3 5 10 12 13
Primary Contact: Katherine Panesso, Chief Executive Officer
CFO: Tony Milian, Chief Financial Officer
CHR: Lourdes Anton, Director Human Resources
Web address: www.larkinhospital.com
Control: Corporation, Investor-owned (for-profit) **Service**: General medical and surgical

Staffed Beds: 261

☒ **PALMETTO GENERAL HOSPITAL (100187)**, 2001 West 68th Street, Zip 33016-1898; tel. 305/823-5000, (Nonreporting) **A**1 3 5 10 13 19 **S** Steward Health Care System, LLC, Dallas, TX
Primary Contact: Alex Contreras-Soto, President
COO: Michele Thoman, Chief Operating Officer
CFO: Oscar Vicente, Chief Financial Officer
CMO: Anais Cortes, Chief of Staff
CHR: Elizabeth Camarena, Chief Human Resource Officer
CNO: Kathleen Guido, Chief Nursing Officer
Web address: https://www.palmettogeneral.org/
Control: Corporation, Investor-owned (for-profit) **Service**: General medical and surgical

Staffed Beds: 360

HOLLYWOOD—Broward County

HOLLYWOOD MEDICAL CENTER See Memorial Regional Hospital South

KINDRED HOSPITAL–HOLLYWOOD See Kindred Hospital South Florida–Hollywood

☐ **LARKIN COMMUNITY HOSPITAL BEHAVIORAL HEALTH SERVICES (104079)**, 1201 North 37th Avenue, Zip 33021-5498; tel. 954/962-1355, **A**1 3 10 **F**98 100 101 103 105 106
Primary Contact: Yoely Hernandez, Chief Executive Officer
COO: Christopher Gabel, Chief Operating Officer
CFO: Rocky Davidson, Chief Financial Officer
CHR: Len Alpert, Director Human Resources
Web address: www.larkinbehavioral.com/
Control: Corporation, Investor-owned (for-profit) **Service**: Psychiatric

Staffed Beds: 50 **Admissions**: 1352 **Census**: 39 **Total Expense ($000)**: 8876 **Payroll Expense ($000)**: 4803 **Personnel**: 76

☒ △ **MEMORIAL REGIONAL HOSPITAL (100038)**, 3501 Johnson Street, Zip 33021-5421; tel. 954/987-2000, (Includes JOE DIMAGGIO CHILDREN'S HOSPITAL, 1005 Joe DiMaggio Drive, Hollywood, Florida, Zip 33021-5426, tel. 954/987-2000; Caitlin Beck Stella, Chief Executive Officer; MEMORIAL REGIONAL HOSPITAL SOUTH, 3600 Washington Street, Hollywood, Florida, Zip 33021-8216, tel. 954/966-4500; Philoron A. Wright II, FACHE, Chief Executive Officer) **A**1 2 3 5 7 10 **F**3 4 5 11 12 13 15 16 17 18 19 20 21 22 23 24 25 26 27 28 29 30 31 32 34 37 38 39 40 41 43 44 45 46 47 49 50 55 56 57 58 59 60 61 64 65 66 67 70 71 72 73 74 75 76 77 78 79 80 81 82 85 87 88 89 90 91 93 95 96 97 98 99 100 101 102 103 104 107 108 110 111 114 115 118 119 120 121 123 124 126 129 130 131 132 134 135 137 138 141 146 147 148 149 150 151 153 154 160 161 162 164 165 167 169 **S** Memorial Healthcare System, Hollywood, FL
Primary Contact: Philoron A. Wright II, FACHE, Chief Executive Officer
CFO: Walter Bussell, Chief Financial Officer
CMO: Donald Kim, M.D., Chief Medical Officer
CIO: Jeffrey S. Sturman, Senior Vice President and Chief Information Officer
CHR: Margie Vargas, Chief Human Resources Officer
CNO: Leslie Pollart, R.N., Chief Nursing Officer
Web address: www.mhs.net
Control: Hospital district or authority, Government, Nonfederal **Service**: General medical and surgical

Staffed Beds: 1079 **Admissions**: 37108 **Census**: 744 **Outpatient Visits**: 514000 **Births**: 5127 **Total Expense ($000)**: 1370252 **Payroll Expense ($000)**: 685259 **Personnel**: 5466

☐ **SOUTH FLORIDA STATE HOSPITAL (104001)**, 800 East Cypress Drive, Zip 33025-4543; tel. 954/392-3000, (Nonreporting) **A**1 10
Primary Contact: Lee Packer, Administrator
Web address: www.geocarellc.com/Locations/SouthFloridaStateHospital
Control: State, Government, Nonfederal **Service**: Psychiatric

Staffed Beds: 355

Hospital, Medicare Provider Number, Address, Telephone, Approval, Facility, and Physician Codes, Health Care System

★ American Hospital Association (AHA) membership
☐ The Joint Commission accreditation
○ Healthcare Facilities Accreditation Program
◇ DNV Healthcare Inc. accreditation
⇧ Center for Improvement in Healthcare Quality Accreditation
△ Commission on Accreditation of Rehabilitation Facilities (CARF) accreditation

© 2025 AHA Guide

Hospitals, U.S. / FLORIDA

HOMESTEAD—Miami-Dade County

BAPTIST HEALTH SOUTH FLORIDA, HOMESTEAD HOSPITAL (100125), 975 Baptist Way, Zip 33033-7600; tel. 786/243-8000, **A**1 7 10 **F**3 13 15 18 19 26 29 30 34 35 39 40 41 44 45 47 49 50 51 53 57 58 59 60 61 64 68 70 74 75 76 77 78 79 80 81 82 84 85 86 87 90 91 93 95 96 100 102 107 108 110 111 114 115 118 119 126 127 129 130 131 132 134 135 141 146 148 149 154 156 160 161 164 169 **S** Baptist Health South Florida, Coral Gables, FL
Primary Contact: Kenneth R. Spell, Chief Executive Officer
CFO: Patti Boylan, Assistant Vice President Finance
CMO: Charles A. Augustus, M.D., Chief Medical Officer
CNO: Ana Cabrera, Vice President, Chief Nursing Officer
Web address: www.baptisthealth.net
Control: Other not–for–profit (including NFP Corporation) **Service**: General medical and surgical

Staffed Beds: 147 **Admissions**: 7023 **Census**: 93 **Outpatient Visits**: 107432 **Births**: 1100 **Total Expense ($000)**: 298669 **Payroll Expense ($000)**: 109815 **Personnel**: 1246

HUDSON—Pasco County

HCA FLORIDA BAYONET POINT HOSPITAL (100256), 14000 Fivay Road, Zip 34667-7199; tel. 727/869-5400, **A**1 2 3 5 10 12 13 **F**3 17 18 20 22 24 26 28 29 30 31 34 35 40 41 43 45 46 48 49 50 51 56 57 58 59 60 64 70 74 75 77 78 79 81 84 85 86 87 91 94 100 107 108 109 111 114 115 118 119 129 130 132 135 141 143 146 148 **S** HCA Healthcare, Nashville, TN
Primary Contact: Sally Seymour, Chief Executive Officer
CFO: Thomas Lawhorne, Chief Financial Officer
CIO: Mike Wilms, Director Information Systems
CHR: Geoffrey A. Washburn, Vice President
CNO: Melanie Wetmore, MSN, R.N., Chief Nursing Officer
Web address: https://www.hcafloridahealthcare.com/locations/bayonet-point-hospital
Control: Corporation, Investor–owned (for–profit) **Service**: General medical and surgical

Staffed Beds: 392 **Admissions**: 16371 **Census**: 228 **Total Expense ($000)**: 325250 **Payroll Expense ($000)**: 85867 **Personnel**: 1155

REGIONAL MEDICAL CENTER BAYONET POINT See HCA Florida Bayonet Point Hospital

INVERNESS—Citrus County

CITRUS MEMORIAL HEALTH SYSTEM See HCA Florida Citrus Hospital

HCA FLORIDA CITRUS HOSPITAL (100023), 502 West Highland Boulevard, Zip 34452-4754; tel. 352/726-1551, **A**1 3 10 19 **F**1 5 7 16 17 18 19 28 29 30 31 34 35 40 45 46 49 57 59 64 65 70 75 76 78 79 81 82 84 85 86 87 93 94 102 105 107 108 111 114 115 119 124 132 135 146 147 148 149 **S** HCA Healthcare, Nashville, TN
Primary Contact: Lisa Nummi, MSN, R.N., Chief Executive Officer
COO: Hiram Jacob, Chief Operating Officer
CFO: Christopher Green, Chief Financial Officer
CMO: Raylene Platel, M.D., Chief Medical Officer
CIO: Nick Brooks, Director of Information Systems
CHR: Deborah Kamlot-Wright, Vice President, Human Resources
CNO: Holly L. Weber-Johnson, MSN, R.N., Chief Nursing Officer
Web address: https://www.hcafloridahealthcare.com/locations/citrus-hospital
Control: Corporation, Investor–owned (for–profit) **Service**: General medical and surgical

Staffed Beds: 216 **Admissions**: 11659 **Census**: 136 **Total Expense ($000)**: 223598 **Payroll Expense ($000)**: 57596 **Personnel**: 782

JACKSONVILLE—Duval County

ASCENSION ST. VINCENT'S RIVERSIDE (100040), 1 Shircliff Way, Zip 32204-4748, Mailing Address: P.O. Box 2982, Zip 32203-2982; tel. 904/308-7300, **A**1 2 3 5 10 **F**3 5 12 15 17 18 20 22 24 28 29 30 31 34 37 40 42 44 45 46 47 48 49 53 55 57 58 61 64 65 70 74 78 79 81 85 86 87 91 92 93 107 108 110 111 114 115 116 119 120 121 123 124 126 130 131 132 146 147 149 154 156 167 **S** Ascension Healthcare, Saint Louis, MO
Primary Contact: Scott Kashman, President
CIO: Ann Carey, Vice President and Chief Information Officer
Web address: https://healthcare.ascension.org/locations/florida/fljac/jacksonville-ascension-st-vincents-riverside
Control: Church operated, Nongovernment, not–for–profit **Service**: General medical and surgical

Staffed Beds: 281 **Admissions**: 16459 **Census**: 214 **Outpatient Visits**: 215668 **Births**: 743 **Total Expense ($000)**: 472092 **Payroll Expense ($000)**: 127363 **Personnel**: 1429

ASCENSION ST. VINCENT'S SOUTHSIDE (100307), 4201 Belfort Road, Zip 32216-1431; tel. 904/296-3700, **A**1 3 5 10 19 **F**3 12 13 15 17 18 20 22 26 29 30 31 34 40 42 44 46 49 50 56 57 60 61 64 65 70 72 74 75 76 77 78 79 81 82 85 86 87 90 95 102 107 108 110 111 114 115 119 126 130 131 135 146 147 149 154 156 160 164 167 169 **S** Ascension Healthcare, Saint Louis, MO
Primary Contact: Kevin Rinks, Chief Executive Officer
CIO: Ann Carey, Chief Information Officer
CHR: Kaye W Lunsford, System Director Human Resources
CNO: Kathy Hester, Chief Nursing Officer
Web address: www.jaxhealth.com
Control: Church operated, Nongovernment, not–for–profit **Service**: General medical and surgical

Staffed Beds: 234 **Admissions**: 10291 **Census**: 120 **Outpatient Visits**: 113499 **Births**: 2346 **Total Expense ($000)**: 240855 **Payroll Expense ($000)**: 73421 **Personnel**: 810

BAPTIST MEDICAL CENTER JACKSONVILLE (100088), 800 Prudential Drive, Zip 32207-8202; tel. 904/202-2000, (Includes BAPTIST MEDICAL CENTER CLAY, 1771 Baptist Clay Drive, Fleming Island, Florida, Zip 32003-8501, tel. 904/516-1000; Edward T Hubel, FACHE, President; BAPTIST MEDICAL CENTER SOUTH, 14550 Old Saint Augustine RD, Jacksonville, Florida, Zip 32258-2460, 14550 St Augustine Road, Zip 32258-2160, tel. 904/821-6000; Kyle Dorsey, FACHE, President; WOLFSON CHILDREN'S HOSPITAL, 800 Prudential Drive, Jacksonville, Florida, Zip 32207, tel. 904/202-8000; Allegra Jaros, President) **A**1 2 3 5 10 19 **F**3 5 6 8 11 12 13 15 17 18 19 20 21 22 23 24 25 26 27 28 29 30 31 33 34 35 36 37 38 39 40 41 42 45 46 47 48 49 50 51 53 54 55 56 57 58 59 60 61 62 64 68 70 72 73 74 75 76 77 78 79 81 82 85 86 87 88 89 92 93 94 98 99 100 101 102 103 104 105 107 108 109 110 111 112 113 114 115 116 117 118 119 120 121 123 124 126 129 130 132 134 135 136 145 146 147 148 149 153 154 155 156 157 162 164 165 167 **S** Baptist Health, Jacksonville, FL
Primary Contact: Nicole B. Thomas, President
CMO: Keith L Stein, M.D., Senior Vice President Medical Affairs and Chief Medical Officer
CIO: Roland Garcia, Senior Vice President and Chief Information Officer
CHR: M. Beth Mehaffey, Senior Vice President Human Resources
Web address: www.e-baptisthealth.com
Control: Other not–for–profit (including NFP Corporation) **Service**: General medical and surgical

Staffed Beds: 1147 **Admissions**: 60708 **Census**: 879 **Outpatient Visits**: 952903 **Births**: 6446 **Total Expense ($000)**: 1922615 **Payroll Expense ($000)**: 541621 **Personnel**: 7653

BROOKS REHABILITATION HOSPITAL (103039), 3599 University Boulevard South, Zip 32216-4252; tel. 904/345-7600, **A**1 3 5 7 10 **F**3 28 29 30 38 44 50 64 66 74 75 77 78 79 82 85 86 87 90 91 93 94 95 96 129 130 132 146 148 149 154 164
Primary Contact: Douglas M. Baer, Chief Executive Officer
CMO: Trevor Paris, M.D., Medical Director
CIO: Karen Green, Chief Information Officer
CHR: Karen Gallagher, Vice President Human Resources and Learning
CNO: Joanne Hoertz, Vice President of Nursing
Web address: www.brookshealth.org
Control: Other not–for–profit (including NFP Corporation) **Service**: Rehabilitation

Staffed Beds: 200 **Admissions**: 4095 **Census**: 188 **Outpatient Visits**: 243452 **Births**: 0 **Total Expense ($000)**: 125251 **Payroll Expense ($000)**: 48975 **Personnel**: 607

ENCOMPASS HEALTH REHABILITATION HOSPITAL OF JACKSONVILLE (103052), 11595 Burnt Mill Road, Zip 32256-3096; tel. 904/596-5000, (Nonreporting) **S** Encompass Health Corporation, Birmingham, AL
Primary Contact: Brian Soares, Chief Executive Officer
Web address: https://encompasshealth.com/locations/jacksonvillerehab
Control: Corporation, Investor–owned (for–profit) **Service**: Rehabilitation

Staffed Beds: 50

HCA FLORIDA MEMORIAL HOSPITAL (100179), 3625 University Boulevard South, Zip 32216-4207; tel. 904/702-6111, **A**1 2 3 5 10 19 **F**3 8 11 12 13 15 17 18 20 22 24 26 28 29 30 31 34 35 37 38 40 41 42 43 45 46 47 48 49 51 53 54 56 58 59 60 64 70 72 74 75 76 78 79 81 85 87 98 100 102 103 104 105 107 108 110 111 114 115 118 119 126 130 146 147 148 153 167 **S** HCA Healthcare, Nashville, TN
Primary Contact: Reed Hammond, Chief Executive Officer
CFO: Kevin McKeown, Chief Financial Officer
CMO: Albert E. Holt, M.D., IV, Chief Medical Officer
CIO: Patrick Adesso, Director Information Technology and Systems
CHR: Stuart Thompson, Vice President Human Resources
Web address: https://www.hcafloridahealthcare.com/locations/memorial-hospital
Control: Corporation, Investor–owned (for–profit) **Service**: General medical and surgical

Staffed Beds: 461 **Admissions**: 21068 **Census**: 284 **Total Expense ($000)**: 432361 **Payroll Expense ($000)**: 117473 **Personnel**: 1558

Hospitals, U.S. / FLORIDA

✚ **MAYO CLINIC HOSPITAL IN FLORIDA (100151)**, 4500 San Pablo Road South, Zip 32224–1865; tel. 904/953-2000, **A**1 2 3 5 8 10 11 **F**3 6 7 8 9 11 12 14 15 17 18 20 22 24 26 28 29 30 31 33 34 35 36 37 38 40 44 45 46 47 48 49 50 51 53 54 55 56 57 58 59 60 61 64 65 66 68 70 74 75 77 78 79 80 81 82 84 85 86 87 92 93 96 97 100 102 104 107 108 109 110 111 112 114 115 116 117 118 119 120 121 123 124 126 129 130 131 132 135 136 137 138 139 140 141 142 143 145 146 147 148 149 150 154 156 157 160 164 167 168 **S** Mayo Clinic, Rochester, MN
Primary Contact: Kent R. Thielen, M.D., Chief Executive Officer
COO: Ajani N. Dunn, M.D., Chief Administrative Officer
CFO: Kevin Lockett, Interim Chief Financial Officer
CMO: David Thiel, M.D., Medical Director
CIO: John Crooks, Chair Information Services
CHR: Rosemary McMullan, Chief Human Resources
CNO: Ryannon Frederick, Chief Nursing Officer
Web address: www.mayoclinic.org/jacksonville/
Control: Other not–for–profit (including NFP Corporation) **Service**: General medical and surgical

Staffed Beds: 307 **Admissions**: 18397 **Census**: 278 **Outpatient Visits**: 75001 **Births**: 0

MEMORIAL HOSPITAL JACKSONVILLE See HCA Florida Memorial Hospital

✚ **NAVAL HOSPITAL JACKSONVILLE**, 2080 Child Street, Zip 32214–5000; tel. 904/542-7300, (Nonreporting) **A**1 3 5 **S** Bureau of Medicine and Surgery, Department of the Navy, Falls Church, VA
Primary Contact: Captain Teresa M. Allen, Commanding Officer
CFO: Lieutenant Commander Michael Gregonis, Comptroller
CMO: Captain Christopher Quarles, M.D., Director Medical Services
CIO: Mike Haytaian, Head Director Information Resources Management
CHR: Captain Ruby Tennyson, Director Administration
Web address: https://jacksonville.tricare.mil/
Control: Navy, Government, federal **Service**: General medical and surgical

Staffed Beds: 64

★ **PAM HEALTH SPECIALTY HOSPITAL OF JACKSONVILLE (102012)**, 4901 Richard Street, Zip 32207–7328; tel. 904/425–0500, **A**10 22 **F**1 3 18 60 77 82 148 154 **P**5 **S** PAM Health, Enola, PA
Primary Contact: James Whitacre, Chief Executive Officer
CFO: Joshua Szostek, Chief Financial Officer
CMO: Wendell H Williams, M.D., Jr, Medical Director
CIO: Patrick Adesso, Director Information Technology and Systems
CHR: Lisa Ayala, R.N., Director Human Resources
Web address: https://pamhealth.com/index.php/facilities/find-facility/specialty-hospitals/pam-health-specialty-hospital-jacksonville
Control: Corporation, Investor–owned (for–profit) **Service**: Acute long–term care hospital

Staffed Beds: 40 **Admissions**: 413 **Census**: 29 **Outpatient Visits**: 143 **Births**: 0 **Total Expense ($000)**: 19066 **Payroll Expense ($000)**: 9363 **Personnel**: 128

☐ **RIVER POINT BEHAVIORAL HEALTH (104016)**, 6300 Beach Boulevard, Zip 32216–2782; tel. 904/724–9202, (Nonreporting) **A**1 10 **S** Universal Health Services, Inc., King of Prussia, PA
Primary Contact: Donna Smith, Ph.D., Chief Executive Officer
CFO: Jenni Stackhouse, Chief Financial Officer
CIO: Bill Willis, Director Information Technology
CHR: Cathy Calhoun, Director Human Resources
Web address: www.riverpointbehavioral.com
Control: Corporation, Investor–owned (for–profit) **Service**: Psychiatric

Staffed Beds: 92

✚ **UF HEALTH JACKSONVILLE (100001)**, 655 West Eighth Street, Zip 32209–6595; tel. 904/244–0411, (Total facility includes 56 beds in nursing home–type unit) **A**1 2 3 5 8 10 19 **F**3 5 6 7 8 9 11 13 15 17 18 20 22 24 26 28 29 30 31 32 34 35 36 37 38 40 41 42 43 44 45 46 47 49 50 51 52 53 54 55 56 57 58 59 60 61 62 64 65 66 70 71 72 73 74 75 76 77 78 79 80 81 82 84 85 86 87 88 91 92 93 94 96 97 98 100 101 102 103 104 107 108 109 110 111 114 115 116 117 118 119 120 121 123 124 126 127 128 129 130 131 132 134 135 141 144 145 146 147 148 149 150 154 156 157 160 162 164 165 167 169 **S** UF Health Shands, Gainesville, FL
Primary Contact: Patrick Green, FACHE, Chief Executive Officer
CFO: Dean Cocchi, Chief Financial Officer
CMO: David Vukich, M.D., Senior Vice President, Chief Medical Officer and Chief Quality Officer
CIO: Kari Cassel, Senior Vice President and Chief Information Officer
CHR: Lesli Ward, Vice President Human Resources
CNO: Patrice Jones, R.N., MSN, DNP, RN, Vice President and Chief Nursing Officer
Web address: www.ufhealthjax.org/
Control: Other not–for–profit (including NFP Corporation) **Service**: General medical and surgical

Staffed Beds: 644 **Admissions**: 25268 **Census**: 496 **Outpatient Visits**: 560924 **Births**: 3915 **Total Expense ($000)**: 1088470 **Payroll Expense ($000)**: 358984 **Personnel**: 4692

☐ **WEKIVA SPRINGS (104069)**, 3947 Salisbury Road, Zip 32216–6115; tel. 904/296–3533, (Nonreporting) **A**1 3 10 **S** Universal Health Services, Inc., King of Prussia, PA
Primary Contact: Sheila Carr, Chief Executive Officer
Web address: www.wekivacenter.com
Control: Other not–for–profit (including NFP Corporation) **Service**: Psychiatric

Staffed Beds: 60

JACKSONVILLE BEACH—Duval County

✚ **BAPTIST MEDICAL CENTER BEACHES (100117)**, 1350 13th Avenue South, Zip 32250–3205; tel. 904/627–2900, **A**1 10 **F**3 8 11 13 15 18 20 28 29 30 34 35 36 40 45 49 50 53 54 56 57 59 61 64 74 75 76 77 78 79 80 81 82 85 86 93 107 108 110 111 114 115 116 118 119 126 129 130 146 147 148 155 156 157 **S** Baptist Health, Jacksonville, FL
Primary Contact: Jarret Dreicer, FACHE, President
CMO: Keith L Stein, M.D., Chief Medical Officer
CIO: Roland Garcia, Senior Vice President and Chief Information Officer
Web address: https://www.baptistjax.com/locations/baptist-medical-center-beaches
Control: Other not–for–profit (including NFP Corporation) **Service**: General medical and surgical

Staffed Beds: 135 **Admissions**: 8029 **Census**: 93 **Outpatient Visits**: 112964 **Total Expense ($000)**: 175964 **Payroll Expense ($000)**: 49847 **Personnel**: 705

JAY—Santa Rosa County

★ **JAY HOSPITAL (100048)**, 14114 Alabama Street, Zip 32565–1219; tel. 850/675–8000, **A**10 **F**11 15 29 30 35 40 45 48 50 64 75 81 85 90 93 97 107 110 115 119 127 128 130 133 148 **S** Baptist Health Care Corporation, Pensacola, FL
Primary Contact: Cyd Cadena, Vice President
CFO: Keith Strickling, Chief Accountant
CMO: C David Smith, M.D., Chief Medical Officer
CHR: Heather Suggs, Manager Human Resources
CNO: Patsy Jackson, Director of Nursing
Web address: www.bhcpns.org/jayhospital/
Control: Other not–for–profit (including NFP Corporation) **Service**: General medical and surgical

Staffed Beds: 19 **Admissions**: 494 **Census**: 8 **Outpatient Visits**: 32788 **Births**: 0 **Total Expense ($000)**: 16798 **Payroll Expense ($000)**: 7672 **Personnel**: 111

Hospital, Medicare Provider Number, Address, Telephone, Approval, Facility, and Physician Codes, Health Care System

★ American Hospital Association (AHA) membership
☐ The Joint Commission accreditation
○ Healthcare Facilities Accreditation Program
◇ DNV Healthcare Inc. accreditation
⇑ Center for Improvement in Healthcare Quality Accreditation
△ Commission on Accreditation of Rehabilitation Facilities (CARF) accreditation

Hospitals, U.S. / FLORIDA

JUPITER—Palm Beach County

JUPITER MEDICAL CENTER (100253), 1210 South Old Dixie Highway, Zip 33458-7299; tel. 561/263-2234, **A1** 2 10 **F3** 8 11 13 15 17 18 20 22 24 26 28 29 30 31 34 35 37 40 41 44 45 46 47 48 49 50 53 54 55 57 58 59 60 64 65 70 72 74 75 76 77 78 79 81 82 85 86 87 89 91 93 96 97 100 107 108 109 110 111 114 115 116 117 118 119 120 121 123 126 129 130 131 132 135 141 144 145 146 147 148 149 154 156 157 167 **P6**
Primary Contact: Amit Rastogi, M.D., Chief Executive
COO: Steven Seeley, Vice President, Chief Operating Officer, Chief Nursing Officer
CFO: Dale E Hocking, Chief Financial Officer
CIO: Thomas Schoenig, Chief Information Officer
CNO: Steven Seeley, Vice President, Chief Operating Officer, Chief Nursing Officer
Web address: www.jupitermed.com
Control: Other not-for-profit (including NFP Corporation) **Service:** General medical and surgical

Staffed Beds: 256 **Admissions:** 14694 **Census:** 187 **Total Expense ($000):** 425925 **Payroll Expense ($000):** 131844 **Personnel:** 1624

PAM REHABILITATION HOSPITAL OF JUPITER (103057), 5075 Innovation Way, Zip 33458-6101; tel. 561/935-3002, (Data for 222 days) **A1 F3** 29 60 64 90 91 93 95 96 132 **S** PAM Health, Enola, PA
Primary Contact: Nikki McCartin, Chief Executive Officer
CNO: Scott Eberhardt, MSN, R.N., Chief Nursing Officer
Web address: https://pamhealth.com/facilities/find-facility/rehabilitation-hospitals/pam-health-rehabilitation-hospital-jupiter
Control: Corporation, Investor-owned (for-profit) **Service:** Rehabilitation

Staffed Beds: 42 **Admissions:** 486 **Census:** 22 **Outpatient Visits:** 545 **Births:** 0 **Total Expense ($000):** 12715 **Payroll Expense ($000):** 5840 **Personnel:** 214

KEY WEST—Monroe County

LOWER KEYS MEDICAL CENTER (100150), 5900 College Road, Zip 33040-4396, Mailing Address: P.O. Box 9107, Zip 33041-9107; tel. 305/294-5531, (Includes DE POO HOSPITAL, 1200 Kennedy Drive, Key West, Florida, Zip 33041, tel. 305/294-4692) (Nonreporting) **A1** 10 **S** Community Health Systems, Inc., Franklin, TN
Primary Contact: David Clay, Chief Executive Officer
CFO: Maureen Henslee, Chief Financial Officer
CMO: Jerome Covington, M.D., Chief Medical Officer
Web address: www.lkmc.com
Control: Corporation, Investor-owned (for-profit) **Service:** General medical and surgical

Staffed Beds: 167

KISSIMMEE—Osceola County

ADVENTHEALTH KISSIMMEE See Adventhealth Orlando, Orlando

FLORIDA HOSPITAL KISSIMMEE See Adventhealth Kissimmee

HCA FLORIDA OSCEOLA HOSPITAL (100110), 700 West Oak Street, Zip 34741-4996; tel. 407/846-2266, **A1** 2 3 5 8 10 **F3** 8 11 12 13 15 17 18 19 20 22 24 26 28 29 34 35 37 40 41 42 43 44 45 46 47 49 50 54 56 57 58 60 64 65 68 70 72 73 74 75 76 77 78 79 80 81 82 85 87 90 92 93 95 96 97 98 100 101 102 104 105 107 110 111 114 115 118 119 126 130 131 132 135 145 146 147 148 149 153 154 156 157 164 165 167 **S** HCA Healthcare, Nashville, TN
Primary Contact: David Shimp, Chief Executive Officer
COO: Jason Cunningham, Chief Operating Officer
CFO: Carrie Biggar, Chief Financial Officer
CIO: Carrie Biggar, Chief Financial Officer
CHR: Sylvia Lollis, Director Human Resources
CNO: Michelle Farris, Chief Nursing Officer
Web address: https://www.hcafloridahealthcare.com/locations/osceola-hospital
Control: Corporation, Investor-owned (for-profit) **Service:** General medical and surgical

Staffed Beds: 441 **Admissions:** 21836 **Census:** 295 **Total Expense ($000):** 420017 **Payroll Expense ($000):** 110657 **Personnel:** 1305

HCA FLORIDA POINCIANA HOSPITAL (100320), 325 Cypress Parkway, Zip 34758; tel. 407/530-2000, (Nonreporting) **A1** 10 **S** HCA Healthcare, Nashville, TN
Primary Contact: Cullen Brown, Chief Executive Officer
CFO: Chris Conn, Chief Financial Officer
CNO: Sharon Dillard, Chief Nursing Officer
Web address: www.poincianamedicalcenter.com
Control: Corporation, Investor-owned (for-profit) **Service:** General medical and surgical

Staffed Beds: 76

LAKE BUTLER—Union County

LAKE BUTLER HOSPITAL (101303), 850 East Main Street, Zip 32054-1353, Mailing Address: P.O. Box 748, Zip 32054-0748; tel. 386/496-2323, **A10** 18 **F3** 29 34 40 57 59 64 75 77 91 93 107 115 119 127 130 133 135 143 148 154
Primary Contact: Paula G. Webb, Chief Executive Officer
COO: Jennifer Thomas, Chief Operating Officer and Director of Public Relations
CMO: Cynthia Larimer, M.D., Chief of Staff
CIO: Diane Cason, Chief Information Officer, Controller and Director Human Resources
CNO: Mandy Dicks, Director of Nursing
Web address: www.lakebutlerhospital.com
Control: Corporation, Investor-owned (for-profit) **Service:** General medical and surgical

Staffed Beds: 25 **Admissions:** 198 **Census:** 8 **Total Expense ($000):** 12497 **Payroll Expense ($000):** 7170 **Personnel:** 105

RECEPTION AND MEDICAL CENTER, State Road 231 South, Zip 32054, Mailing Address: P.O. Box 628, Zip 32054-0628; tel. 386/496-6000, (Nonreporting)
Primary Contact: Priscilla Roberts, Chief Executive Officer
Web address: www.dc.state.fl.us
Control: State, Government, Nonfederal **Service:** Hospital unit of an institution (prison hospital, college infirmary, etc.)

Staffed Beds: 120

LAKE CITY—Columbia County

HCA FLORIDA LAKE CITY HOSPITAL (100156), 340 NW Commerce Drive, Zip 32055-4709; tel. 386/719-9000, (Nonreporting) **A1** 10 20 **S** HCA Healthcare, Nashville, TN
Primary Contact: Jill B. Adams, Interim Chief Executive Officer
COO: Jill B. Adams, Chief Operating Officer and Chief Financial Officer
CFO: Kerri Pintozzi, Chief Financial Officer
CMO: Miguel Tepedino, M.D., Chief Medicine
CIO: Taylor Dickerson, Chief Information Officer
CHR: Steve Gordon, Director Human Resources
Web address: https://www.hcafloridahealthcare.com/locations/lake-city-hospital
Control: Corporation, Investor-owned (for-profit) **Service:** General medical and surgical

Staffed Beds: 91

LAKE CITY MEDICAL CENTER See HCA Florida Lake City Hospital

VETERANS AFFAIRS MEDICAL CENTER See Lake City Veterans Affairs Medical Center

LAKE WALES—Polk County

★ **ADVENTHEALTH LAKE WALES (100099)**, 410 South 11th Street, Zip 33853-4256; tel. 863/676-1433, (Nonreporting) **A10** 21 **S** AdventHealth, Altamonte Springs, FL
Primary Contact: Royce Brown, Chief Executive Officer
COO: Rebecca Brewer, FACHE, Chief Operating Officer
CMO: Sunil Nihalani, M.D., Chief Medical Staff
CIO: Erwin Jaropillo, Director Information Systems
CHR: Renee Latterner, Director Human Resources
CNO: Jennifer Huston, Chief Nursing Officer
Web address: https://www.adventhealth.com/hospital/adventhealth-lake-wales
Control: Church operated, Nongovernment, not-for-profit **Service:** General medical and surgical

Staffed Beds: 150

LAKE WORTH—Palm Beach County

SELECT SPECIALTY HOSPITAL-PALM BEACH (102023), 3060 Melaleuca Lane, Zip 33461-5174; tel. 561/357-7200, (Nonreporting) **A1** 10 **S** Select Medical Corporation, Mechanicsburg, PA
Primary Contact: Larry Melby, Chief Executive Officer
Web address: www.selectspecialtyhospitals.com/company/locations/palmbeach.aspx
Control: Corporation, Investor-owned (for-profit) **Service:** Acute long-term care hospital

Staffed Beds: 60

LAKELAND—Polk County

ENCOMPASS HEALTH REHABILITATION HOSPITAL OF LAKELAND (103050), 1201 Oakbridge Parkway, Zip 33803-5945; tel. 863/279-1600, (Nonreporting) **S** Encompass Health Corporation, Birmingham, AL
Primary Contact: Sharon Hayes, Chief Executive Officer
Web address: https://encompasshealth.com/locations/lakelandrehab
Control: Corporation, Investor-owned (for-profit) **Service:** Rehabilitation

Staffed Beds: 50

Hospitals, U.S. / FLORIDA

☒ △ **LAKELAND REGIONAL HEALTH MEDICAL CENTER (100157)**, 1324 Lakeland Hills Blvd, Zip 33805–4543, Mailing Address: P.O. Box 95448, Zip 33804–5448; tel. 863/687–1100, **A**1 2 3 5 7 10 19 **F**3 4 12 13 18 20 22 24 26 28 29 30 31 34 37 38 40 41 43 44 45 46 47 49 51 56 57 58 59 60 61 64 65 66 70 72 74 75 76 77 78 79 81 82 83 84 85 86 87 88 89 90 93 95 96 98 99 100 101 102 103 107 108 109 110 111 114 115 118 119 120 121 123 124 126 130 131 132 135 143 146 147 148 149 154 156 160 164 165 167 169
Primary Contact: Danielle Drummond, MS, FACHE, President and Chief Executive Officer
COO: Sarah Bhagat, Chief Operating Officer and Vice President of Organizational Effectiveness
CFO: Lance Green, Chief Financial Officer
CMO: Timothy Regan, M.D., President and Chief Medical Officer
CIO: Stacy Bolton, Chief Technology Officer
CHR: Scott Dimmick, Senior Vice President and Chief Human Resources Officer
CNO: April Novotny, MSN, R.N., Chief Nurse Executive
Web address: www.mylrh.org
Control: Other not–for–profit (including NFP Corporation) **Service**: General medical and surgical

Staffed Beds: 892 **Admissions**: 45392 **Census**: 669 **Outpatient Visits**: 332294 **Births**: 4354 **Total Expense ($000)**: 942050 **Payroll Expense ($000)**: 385311 **Personnel**: 5906

LAND O'LAKES—Pasco County

☒ **ADVENTHEALTH CONNERTON (102026)**, 9441 Health Center Drive, Zip 34637–5837; tel. 813/903–3701, **A**1 10 **F**1 3 29 30 50 71 74 75 91 107 119 146 148 157 **S** AdventHealth, Altamonte Springs, FL
Primary Contact: Michael Murrill, President and Chief Executive Officer
COO: Debora Martoccio, R.N., Chief Operating Officer
CMO: Sharad Patel, M.D., Medical Director
Web address: https://www.adventhealth.com/hospital/adventhealth-connerton
Control: Church operated, Nongovernment, not–for–profit **Service**: Acute long-term care hospital

Staffed Beds: 77 **Admissions**: 748 **Census**: 70 **Total Expense ($000)**: 49700 **Payroll Expense ($000)**: 25336 **Personnel**: 292

LARGO—Pinellas County

☒ **ENCOMPASS HEALTH REHABILITATION HOSPITAL OF LARGO (103037)**, 901 North Clearwater–Largo Road, Zip 33770–4126; tel. 727/586–2999, (Nonreporting) **A**1 10 **S** Encompass Health Corporation, Birmingham, AL
Primary Contact: Molly Arau, Chief Executive Officer
CFO: Judith Johnson, Controller
CMO: Richard A Liles, M.D., Medical Director
CHR: Jackie Chalk, Director Human Resources
CNO: Pattie Brenner, R.N., Chief Nursing Officer
Web address: https://www.encompasshealth.com/largorehab
Control: Corporation, Investor–owned (for–profit) **Service**: Rehabilitation

Staffed Beds: 70

☒ **HCA FLORIDA LARGO HOSPITAL (100248)**, 201 14th Street SW, Zip 33770–3133; tel. 727/588–5200, (Includes LARGO MEDICAL CENTER – INDIAN ROCKS, 2025 Indian Rocks Road, Largo, Florida, Zip 33774–1096, P O Box 2025, Zip 33779–2025, tel. 727/581–9474) (Nonreporting) **A**1 2 3 5 10 12 13 19 **S** HCA Healthcare, Nashville, TN
Primary Contact: Sebastian Strom, Chief Executive Officer
COO: Wyatt Chocklett, Chief Operating Officer
CFO: Glenn Romig, Chief Financial Officer
CMO: David Weiland, M.D., Chief Medical Officer
CIO: David Saly, Director, Information Services
CNO: Brenda Simpson, R.N., Chief Nursing Officer
Web address: www.largomedical.com
Control: Corporation, Investor–owned (for–profit) **Service**: General medical and surgical

Staffed Beds: 455

SUN COAST HOSPITAL See Largo Medical Center – Indian Rocks

LAUDERDALE LAKES—Broward County

ST. ANTHONY'S REHABILITATION HOSPITAL (103027), 3485 NW 30th Street, Zip 33311–1890; tel. 954/739–6233, (Nonreporting) **A**10 **S** Catholic Health Services, Lauderdale Lakes, FL
Primary Contact: Joseph M. Catania, Chief Executive Officer
COO: James Ball, Chief Operating Officer, Executive
CFO: David D'Amico
CMO: Mark Reiner, Chief Medical Office, Executive
CIO: Dario Achury, Director of Information Management
CHR: Barbara Griffith, Vice President Human Resources
Web address: www.catholichealthservices.org
Control: Church operated, Nongovernment, not–for–profit **Service**: Rehabilitation

Staffed Beds: 26

LEESBURG—Lake County

☒ **LEESBURG REGIONAL MEDICAL CENTER (100084)**, 600 East Dixie Avenue, Zip 34748–5999; tel. 352/323–5762, **A**1 2 10 **F**3 11 13 15 17 18 20 22 24 26 28 29 30 31 34 35 40 45 47 48 49 54 57 59 64 68 70 74 75 76 77 78 79 81 82 84 85 87 93 96 100 103 106 107 108 110 111 114 115 116 119 130 132 135 144 146 147 149 154 156 167 **P**1 **S** UF Health Shands, Gainesville, FL
Primary Contact: Heather Long, R.N., Chief Executive Officer
COO: David Berger, M.D., Senior Vice President and Chief Operating Officer
CFO: Diane P Harden, Chief Financial Officer
CIO: David Steele, Vice President Chief Information Officer
CHR: Amie A. Richason, Vice President Human Resources
CNO: Joshua Fleming, Vice President Chief Clinical Officer
Web address: www.centralfloridahealth.org
Control: Other not–for–profit (including NFP Corporation) **Service**: General medical and surgical

Staffed Beds: 344 **Admissions**: 12685 **Census**: 210 **Total Expense ($000)**: 271707 **Payroll Expense ($000)**: 113650 **Personnel**: 1261

LIFESTREAM BEHAVIORAL CENTER (104018), 2020 Tally Road, Zip 34748–3426, Mailing Address: P.O. Box 491000, Zip 34749–1000; tel. 352/315–7500, (Nonreporting) **A**10
Primary Contact: Jonathan M. Cherry, President and Chief Executive Officer
COO: David Braughton, Chief Operating Officer
CFO: Carol Dozier, Chief Financial Officer
CMO: T. J. Valente, M.D., Medical Director
CIO: Chad Heim, Management Information System Director
CHR: Ben Hargrove, Human Resources Director
Web address: www.lsbc.net
Control: Other not–for–profit (including NFP Corporation) **Service**: Psychiatric

Staffed Beds: 46

LEHIGH ACRES—Lee County

☐ **LEHIGH REGIONAL MEDICAL CENTER (100107)**, 1500 Lee Boulevard, Zip 33936–4835; tel. 239/369–2101, (Nonreporting) **A**1 10 **S** Prime Healthcare, Ontario, CA
Primary Contact: Cheryl McIntire, Chief Executive Officer and Chief Financial Officer
CFO: Osman Gruhonjic, Chief Financial Officer
CMO: Joe Lemmons, D.O., Chief of Staff
CIO: Jeff Hampton, Director Information Systems
CHR: Mary Gray, Director Human Resources
CNO: Julie G Banker, R.N., MSN, Chief Nursing Officer
Web address: www.lehighregional.com
Control: Corporation, Investor–owned (for–profit) **Service**: General medical and surgical

Staffed Beds: 53

LONGWOOD—Seminole County

ORLANDO REGIONAL SOUTH SEMINOLE HOSPITAL See Orlando Health South Seminole Hospital

---

Hospital, Medicare Provider Number, Address, Telephone, Approval, Facility, and Physician Codes, Health Care System

★ American Hospital Association (AHA) membership ○ Healthcare Facilities Accreditation Program ⇧ Center for Improvement in Healthcare Quality Accreditation
☐ The Joint Commission accreditation ◇ DNV Healthcare Inc. accreditation △ Commission on Accreditation of Rehabilitation Facilities (CARF) accreditation

Hospitals, U.S. / FLORIDA

LOXAHATCHEE—Palm Beach County

☒ **HCA FLORIDA PALMS WEST HOSPITAL (100269)**, 13001 Southern Boulevard, Zip 33470-9203; tel. 561/798-3300, **A**1 3 5 10 **F**3 8 13 15 18 19 20 22 29 30 31 34 35 39 40 41 45 46 49 50 51 56 57 58 60 61 64 68 70 74 75 76 77 78 79 80 81 82 84 85 86 87 88 89 93 107 108 110 111 114 115 119 124 126 130 131 141 146 147 148 149 **S** HCA Healthcare, Nashville, TN
Primary Contact: Jason L. Kimbrell, Chief Executive Officer
COO: Lorna Kernivan, Chief Operating Officer
CIO: Martha Stinson, Director of Information Technology
CHR: Marcy Mills-Mathews, Director Human Resources
CNO: Cheryl Jean Wild, Chief Nursing Officer
Web address: https://www.hcafloridahealthcare.com/locations/palms-west-hospital
Control: Corporation, Investor-owned (for-profit) **Service**: General medical and surgical

Staffed Beds: 222 **Admissions**: 14087 **Census**: 159 **Total Expense ($000)**: 210192 **Payroll Expense ($000)**: 67860 **Personnel**: 811

PALMS WEST HOSPITAL See HCA Florida Palms West Hospital

LUTZ—Hillsborough County

☒ **ENCOMPASS HEALTH REHABILITATION HOSPITAL OF NORTH TAMPA (103047)**, 3840 Atmore Grove Drive, Zip 33548-7903; tel. 813/607-3600, (Nonreporting) **A**1 10 **S** Encompass Health Corporation, Birmingham, AL
Primary Contact: Tarif TC Chowdhury, Chief Executive Officer
CFO: Kimberly Lunt, Controller
CMO: Kadir Carruthers, M.D., Medical Officer
CHR: Jennifer Alexander, Director, Human Resources
CNO: Amy Christine Hayes, Chief Nursing Officer
Web address: www.encompasshealth.com
Control: Corporation, Investor-owned (for-profit) **Service**: Rehabilitation

Staffed Beds: 50

JOSEPH'S HOSPITAL-NORTH See St. Joseph's Hospital - North

MACCLENNY—Baker County

ED FRASER MEMORIAL HOSPITAL (100134), 159 North Third Street, Zip 32063-2103, Mailing Address: P.O. Box 484, Zip 32063-0484; tel. 904/259-3151, (Nonreporting) **A**10 20
Primary Contact: Tiffany G. Varnadoe, Chief Executive Officer
CFO: W. Steve Dudley, CPA, Chief Financial Officer
CMO: Mark Hardin, M.D., Medical Director
CIO: Ernie Waller, Director Information Technology
CHR: Stacey Conner, Human Resources Director
CNO: Valerie Markos, Chief Nursing Officer
Web address: www.bcmedsvcs.com
Control: Other not-for-profit (including NFP Corporation) **Service**: General medical and surgical

Staffed Beds: 25

NORTHEAST FLORIDA STATE HOSPITAL (104007), Highway 121, Zip 32063; tel. 904/259-6211, (Nonreporting) **A**3
Primary Contact: Linda G. Williams, Administrator
Web address: https://www.myflfamilies.com/service-programs/mental-health/nefsh/
Control: State, Government, Nonfederal **Service**: Psychiatric

Staffed Beds: 1138

MADISON—Madison County

MADISON COUNTY MEMORIAL HOSPITAL (101311), 224 NW Crane Avenue, Zip 32340-2561; tel. 850/973-2271, (Nonreporting) **A**10 18
Primary Contact: Tammy Stevens, Chief Executive Officer
CMO: Brett Perkins, M.D., Chief Medical Staff
CIO: Patrick Stiff, Coordinator Information Technology
CHR: Cindi Burnett, Chief Human Resources Officer
Web address: www.mcmh.us/
Control: Hospital district or authority, Government, Nonfederal **Service**: General medical and surgical

Staffed Beds: 25

MARATHON—Monroe County

☒ **FISHERMEN'S HOSPITAL (101312)**, 3301 Overseas Highway, Zip 33050-2329; tel. 305/743-5533, **A**1 10 18 **F**3 29 30 31 34 35 40 44 45 50 64 68 75 77 79 81 84 85 87 93 102 107 114 119 130 131 135 149 154 164 **S** Baptist Health South Florida, Coral Gables, FL
Primary Contact: Drew Grossman, Chief Executive Officer
CFO: Patti Boylan, Assistant Vice President, Finance (Controller)
CMO: Brian Magrane, M.D., Chief Medical Officer
CNO: Cheryl Cottrell, R.N., Vice President and Chief Nursing Officer
Web address: www.fishermenshospital.org
Control: Other not-for-profit (including NFP Corporation) **Service**: General medical and surgical

Staffed Beds: 4 **Admissions**: 55 **Census**: 1 **Outpatient Visits**: 21770 **Births**: 0 **Total Expense ($000)**: 36496 **Payroll Expense ($000)**: 9776 **Personnel**: 96

MARGATE—Broward County

☒ **HCA FLORIDA NORTHWEST HOSPITAL (100189)**, 2801 North State Road 7, Zip 33063-5727; tel. 954/974-0400, **A**1 3 5 10 **F**3 8 11 12 13 15 17 18 22 24 26 29 31 34 35 40 41 44 45 47 50 50 53 56 57 59 60 61 63 64 65 68 70 73 74 75 76 77 78 79 80 81 82 83 85 86 87 89 93 107 108 110 111 114 115 117 118 119 126 129 130 131 132 135 146 147 148 149 **S** HCA Healthcare, Nashville, TN
Primary Contact: Kenneth Jones, Chief Executive Officer
CFO: David Paniry, Chief Financial Officer
CMO: Jose Martinez, M.D., Chief Medical Officer
CIO: David Irizarri, Director Information Technology
CHR: Lynda Bryan, Vice President Human Resources
CNO: Rana Hall, Chief Nursing Officer
Web address: www.northwestmed.com
Control: Corporation, Investor-owned (for-profit) **Service**: General medical and surgical

Staffed Beds: 303 **Admissions**: 13360 **Census**: 159 **Total Expense ($000)**: 255577 **Payroll Expense ($000)**: 71245 **Personnel**: 884

NORTHWEST MEDICAL CENTER See HCA Florida Northwest Hospital

MARIANNA—Jackson County

☒ **JACKSON HOSPITAL (100142)**, 4250 Hospital Drive, Zip 32446-1917, Mailing Address: P.O. Box 1608, Zip 32447-5608; tel. 850/526-2200, **A**1 10 20 **F**3 11 13 15 20 29 30 31 34 35 40 45 50 53 54 57 59 70 75 76 78 79 81 85 86 87 89 97 107 108 110 111 114 115 119 127 129 130 132 133 146 147 148 154 167 169 **P**6 **S** Ovation Healthcare, Brentwood, TN
Primary Contact: Brooke G. Donaldson, Chief Executive Officer
CFO: Kevin Rovito, Chief Financial Officer
CMO: Steven Walter Spence, M.D., Chief Medical Officer
CIO: Jamie Hussey, Chief Information Officer
CNO: Jesse Roberts, Acting Chief Nursing Officer
Web address: www.jacksonhosp.com
Control: Hospital district or authority, Government, Nonfederal **Service**: General medical and surgical

Staffed Beds: 68 **Admissions**: 2219 **Census**: 32 **Outpatient Visits**: 183789 **Births**: 345 **Total Expense ($000)**: 82647 **Payroll Expense ($000)**: 32483 **Personnel**: 577

MELBOURNE—Brevard County

☐ **CIRCLES OF CARE (104024)**, 400 East Sheridan Road, Zip 32901-3184; tel. 321/722-5200, (Nonreporting) **A**1 10
Primary Contact: David L. Feldman, President and Chief Executive Officer
CFO: David L. Feldman, Executive Vice President and Treasurer
CMO: Jose Alvarez, M.D., Chief Medical Staff
CHR: Linda Brannon, Vice President Human Resources
Web address: www.circlesofcare.org
Control: Other not-for-profit (including NFP Corporation) **Service**: Psychiatric

Staffed Beds: 134

DEVEREUX HOSPITAL AND CHILDREN'S CENTER OF FLORIDA, 8000 Devereux Drive, Zip 32940-7907; tel. 321/242-9100, (Nonreporting) **S** Devereux, Villanova, PA
Primary Contact: Michelle Llorens, Executive Director
COO: Eva Horner, Assistant Executive Director Operations
CFO: Kelly Messer, Director of Finance
CMO: Manal Durgin, Network Medical Director
CIO: Diana Deitrick, Director Information Services
CHR: Tim Dillion, Vice President of Human Resources
Web address: www.devereux.org
Control: Other not-for-profit (including NFP Corporation) **Service**: Children's hospital psychiatric

Staffed Beds: 100

Hospitals, U.S. / FLORIDA

✠ **HEALTH FIRST HOLMES REGIONAL MEDICAL CENTER (100019)**, 1350 South Hickory Street, Zip 32901-3224; tel. 321/434-7000, **A**1 10 **F**3 13 17 18 20 22 24 26 28 29 30 31 34 39 40 41 43 45 46 49 50 59 60 64 70 72 74 75 76 77 78 79 80 81 84 85 86 87 89 92 93 100 102 107 108 111 115 118 119 120 126 130 132 141 146 148 149 154 155 157 167 168 **S** Health First, Inc., Rockledge, FL
Primary Contact: Brett A. Esrock, Chief Executive Officer
CMO: Michael McLaughlin, M.D., Chief Medical Officer
CIO: William Walders, Chief Information Officer
CHR: Paula Just, Chief Human Resources Officer
CNO: Cheyana Deane Fischer, Chief Nursing Officer
Web address: https://hf.org/healthcare-home/location-directory/holmes-regional-medical-center
Control: Other not-for-profit (including NFP Corporation) **Service**: General medical and surgical

Staffed Beds: 539 **Admissions**: 27163 **Census**: 383 **Outpatient Visits**: 216678 **Births**: 2930 **Total Expense ($000)**: 641002 **Payroll Expense ($000)**: 206296 **Personnel**: 2310

☐ **HEALTH FIRST VIERA HOSPITAL (100315)**, 8745 North Wickham Road, Zip 32940-5997; tel. 321/434-9164, **A**1 10 **F**3 11 12 15 16 17 18 28 29 30 34 39 40 44 45 46 47 48 49 50 51 53 54 57 59 60 62 63 64 65 68 70 72 73 74 75 77 78 79 80 81 82 84 85 86 87 88 89 92 93 96 100 102 107 108 110 111 115 116 117 118 119 120 126 129 130 131 132 141 146 148 149 154 156 157 167 168 169 **S** Health First, Inc., Rockledge, FL
Primary Contact: Brett A. Esrock, President
COO: Deborah Angerami, Chief Operating Officer
CFO: Joseph G Felkner, Chief Financial Officer
CMO: Scott Gettings, M.D., Senior Vice President and Chief Medical Officer
CIO: Alex Popowycz, Chief Information Officer
CHR: Paula Just, Chief Human Resources Officer
CNO: Connie Bradley, R.N., MSN, FACHE, Senior Vice President and Chief Nursing Officer
Web address: https://hf.org/healthcare-home/location-directory/viera-hospital
Control: Other not-for-profit (including NFP Corporation) **Service**: General medical and surgical

Staffed Beds: 84 **Admissions**: 6360 **Census**: 62 **Outpatient Visits**: 102336 **Births**: 0 **Total Expense ($000)**: 147914 **Payroll Expense ($000)**: 46487 **Personnel**: 523

✠ **KINDRED HOSPITAL MELBOURNE (102027)**, 765 West Nasa Boulevard, Zip 32901-1815; tel. 321/733-5725, **A**1 10 **F**1 3 18 29 30 34 56 60 70 74 75 77 79 82 84 85 86 87 101 107 114 149 **S** ScionHealth, Louisville, KY
Primary Contact: Pamela R. Reed, Chief Executive Officer
Web address: www.khmelbourne.com
Control: Corporation, Investor-owned (for-profit) **Service**: Acute long-term care hospital

Staffed Beds: 58 **Admissions**: 837 **Census**: 48 **Total Expense ($000)**: 31305 **Payroll Expense ($000)**: 12513 **Personnel**: 157

☐ **MELBOURNE REGIONAL MEDICAL CENTER (100291)**, 250 North Wickham Road, Zip 32935-8625; tel. 321/752-1200, (Nonreporting) **A**1 10 **S** Steward Health Care System, LLC, Dallas, TX
Primary Contact: Ron Gicca, Chief Executive Officer
CFO: Dale Armour, Chief Financial Officer
Web address: www.wuesthoff.com/locations/wuesthoff-medical-center-melbourne
Control: Corporation, Investor-owned (for-profit) **Service**: General medical and surgical

Staffed Beds: 119

✠ **SEA PINES REHABILITATION HOSPITAL, AN AFFILIATE OF ENCOMPASS HEALTH (103034)**, 101 East Florida Avenue, Zip 32901-8301; tel. 321/984-4600, **A**1 10 **F**90 91 92 94 95 96 148 **S** Encompass Health Corporation, Birmingham, AL
Primary Contact: Mark Racicot, Chief Executive Officer
CMO: Juan Lebron, M.D., Medical Director
CHR: James L Henry, Director Human Resources
CNO: Lisa Truman, Chief Nursing Officer
Web address: www.healthsouthseapines.com
Control: Corporation, Investor-owned (for-profit) **Service**: Rehabilitation

Staffed Beds: 90 **Admissions**: 2148 **Census**: 71 **Total Expense ($000)**: 30456 **Payroll Expense ($000)**: 15841 **Personnel**: 217

MIAMI—Miami-Dade County

✠ △ **BAPTIST HEALTH SOUTH FLORIDA, BAPTIST HOSPITAL OF MIAMI (100008)**, 8900 North Kendall Drive, Zip 33176-2197; tel. 786/596-1960, (Includes BAPTIST CHILDREN'S HOSPITAL, 8900 North Kendall Drive, Miami, Florida, Zip 33176-2118, tel. 786/596-1960; Albert Leon Boulenger, R.N., Chief Executive Officer) **A**1 2 3 5 7 10 **F**3 9 13 15 17 18 19 20 22 24 26 28 29 30 31 32 34 35 36 38 39 40 41 44 45 46 47 48 49 50 51 53 54 55 56 57 58 59 60 61 64 68 70 72 74 75 76 77 78 79 80 81 82 84 85 86 87 91 92 93 94 96 100 102 107 108 110 111 112 115 116 117 118 119 120 121 122 123 124 126 130 132 135 136 141 144 145 146 147 148 149 150 154 156 157 164 167 169 **S** Baptist Health South Florida, Coral Gables, FL
Primary Contact: William G. Ulbricht, Chief Executive Officer
COO: Nate Ortiz, Vice President and Chief Operating Officer
CFO: Macia Andres, Director of Finance
CMO: Sergio Segarra, M.D., Chief Medical Officer
CNO: Harold Girado, Vice President, Chief Nursing Officer
Web address: www.baptisthealth.net
Control: Other not-for-profit (including NFP Corporation) **Service**: General medical and surgical

Staffed Beds: 789 **Admissions**: 27807 **Census**: 510 **Outpatient Visits**: 601995 **Births**: 3007 **Total Expense ($000)**: 1606122 **Payroll Expense ($000)**: 430947 **Personnel**: 4388

✠ **BAPTIST HEALTH SOUTH FLORIDA, SOUTH MIAMI HOSPITAL (100154)**, 6200 SW 73rd Street, Zip 33143-4679; tel. 786/662-4000, **A**1 2 3 10 **F**3 12 13 15 17 18 19 20 22 24 26 27 29 30 31 34 35 36 40 44 45 46 48 49 50 51 52 53 54 56 57 58 59 60 61 64 68 70 72 74 75 76 77 78 79 80 81 82 84 85 86 87 93 94 102 107 108 110 111 115 118 119 126 130 132 135 141 144 146 147 148 149 154 156 157 160 161 164 167 169 **S** Baptist Health South Florida, Coral Gables, FL
Primary Contact: William M. Duquette, Chief Executive Officer
COO: Jeanette Stone, Vice President Operations
CFO: Reyna Hernandez, Assistant Vice President, Finance (Controller)
CMO: Yvonne Johnson, M.D., Chief Medical Offficer
CNO: Paul Mungo, Vice President, Chief Nursing Officer
Web address: www.baptisthealth.net
Control: Other not-for-profit (including NFP Corporation) **Service**: General medical and surgical

Staffed Beds: 350 **Admissions**: 14468 **Census**: 197 **Outpatient Visits**: 353751 **Births**: 3042 **Total Expense ($000)**: 618952 **Payroll Expense ($000)**: 207453 **Personnel**: 2061

✠ **BAPTIST HEALTH SOUTH FLORIDA, WEST KENDALL BAPTIST HOSPITAL (100314)**, 9555 SW 162nd Avenue, Zip 33196-6408; tel. 786/467-2000, **A**1 3 10 **F**3 13 18 19 20 22 26 29 30 31 32 34 35 38 40 42 44 45 49 50 51 53 57 58 59 60 61 64 68 70 71 74 75 76 77 78 79 80 81 82 84 85 86 87 93 97 100 102 107 108 111 114 115 119 126 130 131 132 135 145 146 147 148 149 150 154 164 167 169 **S** Baptist Health South Florida, Coral Gables, FL
Primary Contact: Lourdes Boue, Chief Executive Officer
CFO: Patti Boylan, Assistant Vice President, Finance (Controller)
CMO: Zulma Berrios, M.D., Chief Medical Officer
CHR: Hilde Zamora de Aguero, Human Resources Site Director
CNO: Sandra McLean MSN, RN, Vice President and Chief Nursing Officer
Web address: www.baptisthealth.net/en/facilities/West-Kendall-Baptist-Hospital/Pages/default.aspx
Control: Other not-for-profit (including NFP Corporation) **Service**: General medical and surgical

Staffed Beds: 186 **Admissions**: 9782 **Census**: 109 **Outpatient Visits**: 152551 **Births**: 1234 **Total Expense ($000)**: 322950 **Payroll Expense ($000)**: 114957 **Personnel**: 1176

CEDARS MEDICAL CENTER See University of Miami Hospital

✠ **HCA FLORIDA KENDALL HOSPITAL (100209)**, 11750 Bird Road, Zip 33175-3530; tel. 305/223-3000, (Nonreporting) **A**1 3 5 10 **S** HCA Healthcare, Nashville, TN
Primary Contact: Ben Harris, Chief Executive Officer
COO: Joe Britner, Chief Operating Officer
CIO: Matt Hernandez, Director of Information Technology and System
CHR: Knicole S White, Vice-President, Human Resources
CNO: Maria Villa, Interim Chief Nursing Officer
Web address: https://www.hcafloridahealthcare.com/locations/kendall-hospital
Control: Partnership, Investor-owned (for-profit) **Service**: General medical and surgical

Staffed Beds: 417

Hospital, Medicare Provider Number, Address, Telephone, Approval, Facility, and Physician Codes, Health Care System

★ American Hospital Association (AHA) membership ○ Healthcare Facilities Accreditation Program ⇧ Center for Improvement in Healthcare Quality Accreditation
☐ The Joint Commission accreditation ◇ DNV Healthcare Inc. accreditation △ Commission on Accreditation of Rehabilitation Facilities (CARF) accreditation

© 2025 AHA Guide

Hospitals, U.S. / FLORIDA

☒ △ **HCA FLORIDA MERCY HOSPITAL (100167)**, 3663 South Miami Avenue, Zip 33133–4237; tel. 305/854–4400, (Nonreporting) **A**1 3 5 7 10 19 **S** HCA Healthcare, Nashville, TN
Primary Contact: David Donaldson, Chief Executive Officer
CFO: Jerry Mashburn, Senior Vice President and Chief Financial Officer
CIO: Camille Rivera, Interim Chief Information Officer
CHR: Eduard Rundle, Vice President Human Resources
CNO: Ben Warner, R.N., Chief Nursing Officer
Web address: https://www.hcafloridahealthcare.com/locations/mercy-hospital
Control: Corporation, Investor–owned (for–profit) **Service**: General medical and surgical

Staffed Beds: 473

HIGHLAND PARK HOSPITAL See Jackson Behavioral Health Hospital

HOLTZ CHILDREN'S HOSPITAL JACKSON MEMORIAL HOSPITAL See Holtz Children's Hospital

JACKSON BEHAVIORAL HEALTH HOSPITAL See Jackson Health System, Miami

☒ △ **JACKSON HEALTH SYSTEM (100022)**, 1611 NW 12th Avenue, Zip 33136–1005; tel. 305/585–1111, (Includes HOLTZ CHILDREN'S HOSPITAL, 1611 NW 12th Avenue, Miami, Florida, Zip 33136–1005, tel. 305/585–5437; Joanne Ruggiero, Chief Exectuve Officer; JACKSON BEHAVIORAL HEALTH HOSPITAL, 1695 NW 9th Ave, Miami, Florida, Zip 33136–1409, 1695 NW Ninth Avenue, Zip 33136, tel. 305/324–4357; Vicky Sabharwal, Vice President and Chief Executive Officer, Jackson Behavioral Health Hospital; JACKSON HEALTH SYSTEM–MIAMI LYNN REHABILITATION CENTER, 1611 NW 12th Avenue, Miami, Florida, Zip 33136–1005, 1611 NW 12th Avenue, 5th Floor Administration Office, Zip 33136–1005, tel. 305/585–9463; Brenda Cain, Vice President and Chief Executive Officer; JACKSON MEMORIAL HOSPITAL, 1611 NW 12th Avenue, Miami, Florida, Zip 33136, tel. 305/585–1111; David Zambrana, Ph.D., R.N., Executive Vice President Hospital Operations; JACKSON NORTH MEDICAL CENTER, 160 NW 170th Street, North Miami Beach, Florida, Zip 33169–5576, tel. 305/651–1100; Sandra Severe, Senior Vice President, Chief Executive Officer; JACKSON SOUTH MEDICAL CENTER, 9333 SW 152nd Street, Miami, Florida, Zip 33157–1780, tel. 305/251–2500; Edward Borrego, Chief Exectuve Officer; JACKSON WEST MEDICAL CENTER, 2801 NW 79th Avenue, Doral, Florida, Zip 33122–1174, tel. 786/466–1000) (Total facility includes 343 beds in nursing home–type unit) **A**1 3 5 7 8 10 19 **F**3 4 5 12 13 15 16 17 18 19 20 21 22 23 24 25 26 27 28 29 30 31 32 34 35 38 39 40 41 43 45 46 47 48 49 50 51 54 55 56 58 60 61 64 65 66 68 69 70 72 73 74 75 76 77 78 79 80 81 82 83 84 85 86 87 88 89 90 91 92 93 94 95 96 97 98 99 100 101 102 103 104 107 108 110 111 115 117 118 119 120 121 123 124 126 127 128 129 130 131 132 134 135 136 137 138 139 140 142 144 147 148 149 157 160 161 163 164 169
Primary Contact: Carlos A. Migoya, President and Chief Executive Officer
COO: David Zambrana, Ph.D., R.N., Chief Operating Officer – JHS
CFO: Mark T Knight, Executive Vice President and Chief Financial Officer
CMO: Chris A. Ghaemmaghami, M.D., Executive Vice President, Chief Physician Executive and Chief Clinical Officer
CIO: Michael A. Garcia, Vice President and Chief Information Officer
CHR: Julie Staub, Vice President, Chief Human Resources Officer
CNO: Carol Cassandra Biggs, Chief Nursing Executive
Web address: www.jacksonhealth.org
Control: County, Government, Nonfederal **Service**: General medical and surgical

Staffed Beds: 2242 **Admissions:** 67556 **Census:** 1302 **Outpatient Visits:** 489696 **Births:** 7002 **Total Expense ($000):** 2845276 **Payroll Expense ($000):** 1386529 **Personnel:** 13511

JACKSON SOUTH COMMUNITY HOSPITAL See Jackson South Medical Center

JACKSON SOUTH MEDICAL CENTER See Jackson Health System, Miami

JAMES M JACKSON MEMORIAL HOSP See Jackson Memorial Hospital

KENDALL REGIONAL MEDICAL CENTER See HCA Florida Kendall Hospital

☐ ○ **KERALTY HOSPITAL MIAMI (100284)**, 2500 SW 75th Avenue, Zip 33155–2805; tel. 305/264–5252, (Includes SOUTHERN WINDS HOSPITAL, 4225 West 20th Street, Hialeah, Florida, Zip 33012–5835, tel. 305/558–9700) (Nonreporting) **A**1 3 5 10 11 13
Primary Contact: Carlos Cruz, Interim Chief Executive Officer
CFO: Joel Snook, Chief Financial Officer
CMO: Rogelio Zaldivar, M.D., Medical Director
CHR: Jennifer Ricardo, Director of Human Resources
Web address: www.westchesterhospital.com
Control: Corporation, Investor–owned (for–profit) **Service**: General medical and surgical

Staffed Beds: 125

MERCY HOSPITAL See HCA Florida Mercy Hospital

☐ **MIAMI JEWISH HEALTH (100277)**, 5200 NE Second Avenue, Zip 33137–2706; tel. 305/751–8626, (Nonreporting) **A**1 5 10
Primary Contact: Jeffrey P. Freimark, Chief Executive Officer
COO: Steven Hess, Chief Operating Officer
CFO: Michael Durr, CPA, Chief Financial Officer
CMO: Shaun Corbett, M.D., Chief Medical Officer
CIO: Bernardo Larralde II, Chief Information Officer
CHR: Elisa Hernandez, Chief Human Resource Officer
CNO: Nicole Dieudonne, R.N., MSN, Director of Nursing, DGH
Web address: www.miamijewishhealth.org
Control: Other not–for–profit (including NFP Corporation) **Service**: General medical and surgical

Staffed Beds: 32

☒ △ **MIAMI VETERANS AFFAIRS HEALTHCARE SYSTEM**, 1201 NW 16th Street, Zip 33125–1624; tel. 305/575–7000, (Nonreporting) **A**1 3 5 7 **S** Department of Veterans Affairs, Washington, DC
Primary Contact: Kalautie JangDhari, Medical Center Director
COO: Lance Davis, PharmD, Associate Director
CFO: Albert Tucker, Chief Financial Officer
CMO: Vincent DeGennaro, M.D., Chief of Staff
CIO: Anthony Brooks, Chief Information Officer
CHR: Loyman Marin, Chief Human Resources
Web address: www.miami.va.gov/
Control: Veterans Affairs, Government, federal **Service**: General medical and surgical

Staffed Beds: 262

★ ⇧ **NICKLAUS CHILDREN'S HOSPITAL (103301)**, 3100 SW 62nd Avenue, Zip 33155–3009; tel. 305/666–6511, **A**2 3 5 8 10 21 **F**3 7 17 18 19 20 21 22 23 24 25 26 27 29 30 31 32 34 35 36 37 38 39 40 41 43 44 45 46 47 48 49 50 53 54 55 57 58 59 60 61 64 65 68 71 72 74 75 77 78 79 80 81 82 84 85 86 87 88 89 91 92 93 94 96 97 98 99 100 101 102 104 105 107 108 109 111 112 115 116 117 118 119 126 129 130 131 132 136 143 144 145 146 148 149 153 154 155 156 157 164 165 167
Primary Contact: Matthew Love, Chief Executive Officer
COO: Martha McGill, Executive Vice President and Chief Operating Officer
CFO: Arianna Urquia, Chief Financial Officer
CMO: Deise Granado–Villar, M.D., Chief Medical Officer and Senior Vice President Medical Affairs
CIO: Edward Martinez, Chief Information Officer
CHR: Michael S. Kushner, Senior Vice President and Chief Talent Officer
CNO: Jacqueline Lytle Gonzalez, Senior Vice President and Chief Nursing Officer
Web address: www.mch.com
Control: Other not–for–profit (including NFP Corporation) **Service**: Children's general medical and surgical

Staffed Beds: 278 **Admissions:** 10486 **Census:** 182 **Total Expense ($000):** 874301 **Payroll Expense ($000):** 248604 **Personnel:** 2638

☐ **NORTH SHORE MEDICAL CENTER (100029)**, 1100 NW 95th Street, Zip 33150–2098; tel. 305/835–6000, (Includes FLORIDA MEDICAL CENTER – A CAMPUS OF NORTH SHORE, 5000 West Oakland Park Boulevard, Fort Lauderdale, Florida, Zip 33313–1585, tel. 954/735–6000; Michael J. Bell, President) (Nonreporting) **A**1 3 10 **S** Steward Health Care System, LLC, Dallas, TX
Primary Contact: Thomas Dunning, President
CMO: Michael Zaplin, M.D., Physician Advisor
CIO: Billy Patino, Chief Information Officer
CHR: Esther Morris, Chief Human Resource Officer
CNO: Maribel Torres, Chief Nursing Officer
Web address: https://www.northshoremc.org/
Control: Corporation, Investor–owned (for–profit) **Service**: General medical and surgical

Staffed Beds: 258

☒ **SELECT SPECIALTY HOSPITAL–MIAMI (102001)**, 955 NW 3rd Street, Zip 33128–1274; tel. 305/416–5700, (Nonreporting) **A**1 10 **S** Select Medical Corporation, Mechanicsburg, PA
Primary Contact: Monica Madrigal, Interim Chief Executive Officer
Web address: https://www.selectspecialtyhospitals.com/locations-and-tours/fl/miami/miami/
Control: Corporation, Investor–owned (for–profit) **Service**: Acute long–term care hospital

Staffed Beds: 47

Hospitals, U.S. / FLORIDA

☒ **UMHC–SYLVESTER COMPREHENSIVE CANCER CENTER (100079)**, 1475 NW 12th Avenue, Zip 33136–1002; tel. 305/689–5511, (Includes BASCOM PALMER EYE INSTITUTE–ANNE BATES LEACH EYE HOSPITAL, 900 NW 17th Street, Miami, Florida, Zip 33136–1199, Box 016880, Zip 33101–6880, tel. 305/326–6000; Michael B Gittelman, Administrator; UNIVERSITY OF MIAMI HOSPITAL, 1400 NW 12th Avenue, Miami, Florida, Zip 33136–1003, tel. 305/325–5511; Michael B Gittelman, Chief Executive Officer) **A**1 2 3 8 10 **F**3 6 8 9 11 12 15 17 18 20 22 24 26 28 29 30 31 34 35 36 37 38 39 40 42 44 45 46 47 48 49 50 51 52 53 54 55 56 57 58 59 60 61 63 64 65 66 68 70 71 74 75 77 78 79 80 81 82 83 84 85 86 87 93 94 96 97 100 101 107 108 110 111 112 113 114 115 116 117 118 119 120 121 122 123 124 125 126 129 130 131 132 134 135 136 141 142 144 146 147 148 149 154 156 157 164 167 **P**6
Primary Contact: Kymberlee Jean. Manni, Chief Executive Officer
COO: Kymberlee Jean Manni, Chief Operating Officer
CFO: Harry Rohrer, Chief Financial Officer
CMO: W Jarrad Goodwin, M.D., Director
CIO: David Reis, Ph.D., Interim Chief Information Officer
Web address: https://umiamihealth.org/
Control: Other not–for–profit (including NFP Corporation) Service: Cancer

Staffed Beds: 586 **Admissions:** 17908 **Census:** 382 **Outpatient Visits:** 1163765 **Total Expense ($000):** 2341284 **Payroll Expense ($000):** 393071 **Personnel:** 11836

☒ △ **WEST GABLES REHABILITATION HOSPITAL (103036)**, 2525 SW 75th Avenue, Zip 33155–2800; tel. 305/262–6800, **A**1 3 7 10 **F**29 34 44 58 62 75 77 82 86 87 90 91 93 94 95 96 130 131 132 135 148 149 150 154 157 **S** Select Medical Corporation, Mechanicsburg, PA
Primary Contact: Walter Concepcion, Chief Executive Officer
CFO: Sara Reohr, Regional Controller
CMO: Jose L Vargas, M.D., Medical Director
CHR: Barbara Etchason, HR Manager
CNO: Lucia Benjamin, Chief Nursing Officer
Web address: www.westgablesrehabhospital.com/
Control: Corporation, Investor–owned (for–profit) Service: Rehabilitation

Staffed Beds: 90 **Admissions:** 1858 **Census:** 82 **Outpatient Visits:** 2460 **Births:** 0 **Personnel:** 372

MIAMI BEACH—Dade County

MIAMI HEART CAMPUS AT MOUNT SINAI MEDICAL CENTER See Mount Sinai Medical Center, Miami Beach

MIAMI HEART INST & MED CTR See Miami Heart Campus At Mount Sinai Medical Center

MIAMI BEACH—Miami–Dade County

☐ △ **MOUNT SINAI MEDICAL CENTER (100034)**, 4300 Alton Road, Zip 33140–2948; tel. 305/674–2121, (Includes MIAMI HEART CAMPUS AT MOUNT SINAI MEDICAL CENTER, 4701 North Meridian Avenue, Miami Beach, Florida, Zip 33140–2910, tel. 305/672–1111; Gino R. Santorio, President and Chief Executive Officer) **A**1 2 3 5 7 8 10 19 **F**1 2 3 4 6 8 9 12 13 14 15 16 17 18 19 20 22 24 26 28 29 30 31 34 35 36 37 38 39 40 41 42 44 45 46 47 48 49 50 51 54 55 56 57 58 59 60 61 62 63 64 65 66 67 68 70 71 72 73 74 75 76 77 78 79 80 81 82 84 85 86 87 88 89 90 91 92 93 96 97 98 100 101 102 103 104 105 107 108 110 111 114 115 118 119 120 121 123 124 126 128 129 130 131 132 135 141 143 145 146 147 149 152 154 155 156 157 158 160 162 164 165 166 167 **P**6
Primary Contact: Gino R. Santorio, President and Chief Executive Officer
COO: Angel Pallin, Senior Vice President of Operations
CFO: Alex A Mendez, Executive Vice President and Chief Financial Officer
CMO: Robert Goldszer, M.D., Senior Vice President and Chief Medical Officer
CIO: Tom Gillette, Senior Vice President and Chief Information Officer
CHR: Georgia McLean, Director Human Resources
CNO: Karen W Moyer, R.N., Senior Vice President and Chief Nursing Officer
Web address: www.msmc.com
Control: Other not–for–profit (including NFP Corporation) Service: General medical and surgical

Staffed Beds: 633 **Admissions:** 25632 **Census:** 382 **Outpatient Visits:** 275472 **Births:** 2373 **Total Expense ($000):** 875285 **Payroll Expense ($000):** 409914 **Personnel:** 4552

MIAMI LAKES—Miami–Dade County

☒ **SELECT SPECIALTY HOSPITAL–MIAMI LAKES (102031)**, 14001 NW 82nd Avenue, Zip 33016–1561; tel. 786/609–9200, (Nonreporting) **A**1 10 **S** Select Medical Corporation, Mechanicsburg, PA
Primary Contact: Monica Madrigal, Chief Executive Officer
Web address: www.promise-miami.com/
Control: Corporation, Investor–owned (for–profit) Service: Acute long–term care hospital

Staffed Beds: 60

MIDDLEBURG—Clay County

☒ **ASCENSION ST. VINCENT'S CLAY COUNTY (100321)**, 1670 St. Vincent's Way, Zip 32068–8427, Mailing Address: 1670 St. Vincents Way, Zip 32068–8447; tel. 904/602–1000, **A**1 10 **F**3 13 15 18 20 22 29 30 37 40 44 46 50 51 56 59 60 61 64 65 68 70 74 75 76 77 79 81 82 84 85 86 87 105 107 108 110 111 114 115 118 119 126 129 130 133 146 149 152 154 157 164 167 **S** Ascension Healthcare, Saint Louis, MO
Primary Contact: Bryan Walrath, President
Web address: www.jaxhealth.com/
Control: Church operated, Nongovernment, not–for–profit Service: General medical and surgical

Staffed Beds: 134 **Admissions:** 7368 **Census:** 85 **Outpatient Visits:** 77173 **Births:** 1074 **Total Expense ($000):** 140396 **Payroll Expense ($000):** 47747 **Personnel:** 501

MILTON—Santa Rosa County

☒ **SANTA ROSA MEDICAL CENTER (100124)**, 6002 Berryhill Road, Zip 32570–5062; tel. 850/626–7762, **A**1 10 **F**3 11 13 15 18 20 29 30 34 35 40 45 49 54 57 64 65 74 75 76 77 79 80 81 85 87 97 107 108 111 115 119 126 129 130 132 135 144 146 147 148 149 **S** Community Health Systems, Inc., Franklin, TN
Primary Contact: Justin Serrano, Chief Executive Officer
CFO: Jared Whipkey, Chief Financial Officer
CIO: Rick Payne, Director Information Systems
CHR: Christopher Foreman, Director Human Resources
CNO: Stephanie Jones, R.N., Chief Nursing Officer
Web address: https://www.srmcfl.com/
Control: Corporation, Investor–owned (for–profit) Service: General medical and surgical

Staffed Beds: 91 **Admissions:** 4121 **Census:** 42 **Total Expense ($000):** 83563 **Payroll Expense ($000):** 29786 **Personnel:** 391

MIRAMAR—Broward County

☒ **MEMORIAL HOSPITAL MIRAMAR (100285)**, 1901 SW 172nd Avenue, Zip 33029–5592; tel. 954/538–5000, **A**1 10 **F**3 11 13 15 29 30 34 40 41 44 45 49 50 51 55 57 59 64 68 70 72 74 75 76 77 79 81 82 85 87 93 97 107 108 110 111 114 115 119 126 129 130 132 135 145 146 147 149 154 167 169 **S** Memorial Healthcare System, Hollywood, FL
Primary Contact: Stephen Demers, Chief Executive Officer
CFO: Judy Sada, Chief Financial Officer
CIO: Forest Blanton, Senior VP and Chief Information Officer
CHR: Ray Kendrick, Chief Human Resources Officer
CNO: Denise Reynolds, Chief Nursing Officer
Web address: https://www.mhs.net/locations/memorial-miramar
Control: Hospital district or authority, Government, Nonfederal Service: General medical and surgical

Staffed Beds: 160 **Admissions:** 10283 **Census:** 113 **Outpatient Visits:** 160077 **Births:** 4152 **Total Expense ($000):** 232300 **Payroll Expense ($000):** 114151 **Personnel:** 1010

MIRAMAR BEACH—Walton County

☒ **ASCENSION SACRED HEART EMERALD COAST (100292)**, 7800 Highway 98 West, Zip 32550; tel. 850/278–3000, **A**1 3 10 19 **F**3 13 15 18 20 22 24 26 28 29 30 31 34 35 37 40 44 45 46 50 51 59 60 64 68 70 72 74 75 76 77 78 79 80 81 84 85 87 91 92 93 96 107 108 110 111 114 115 116 117 118 119 124 126 130 131 146 147 148 149 154 156 157 167 169 **S** Ascension Healthcare, Saint Louis, MO
Primary Contact: Trey Abshier, Chief Executive Officer
CMO: Gary M. Pablo, M.D., Chief Medical Officer
CNO: Barbara Fontaine, Vice President, Nursing
Web address: https://healthcare.ascension.org/locations/florida/flpen/miramar-beach-ascension-sacred-heart-emerald-coast
Control: Church operated, Nongovernment, not–for–profit Service: General medical and surgical

Staffed Beds: 86 **Admissions:** 5766 **Census:** 53 **Outpatient Visits:** 108235 **Births:** 1326 **Total Expense ($000):** 157568 **Payroll Expense ($000):** 42956 **Personnel:** 531

NAPLES—Collier County

LANDMARK HOSPITAL OF SOUTHWEST FLORIDA (102032), 1285 Creekside Boulevard East, Zip 34108; tel. 239/529–1800, (Nonreporting) **A**10 22 **S** Landmark Hospitals, Cape Girardeau, MO
Primary Contact: Daniel C. Dunmyer, Chief Executive Officer
Web address: https://www.landmarkhospitals.com/critical-care-hospital-system/critical-care-hospital-southwest-florida/
Control: Partnership, Investor–owned (for–profit) Service: Acute long–term care hospital

Staffed Beds: 50

Hospital, Medicare Provider Number, Address, Telephone, Approval, Facility, and Physician Codes, Health Care System

★ American Hospital Association (AHA) membership
☐ The Joint Commission accreditation
○ Healthcare Facilities Accreditation Program
◇ DNV Healthcare Inc. accreditation
⇧ Center for Improvement in Healthcare Quality Accreditation
△ Commission on Accreditation of Rehabilitation Facilities (CARF) accreditation

© 2025 AHA Guide

Hospitals, U.S. / FLORIDA

* △ **NCH BAKER HOSPITAL (100018)**, 350 Seventh Street North, Zip 34102–5754, Mailing Address: P.O. Box 413029, Zip 34101–3029; tel. 239/624–4000, (Includes NCH NORTH NAPLES HOSPITAL, 11190 Health Park Blvd, Naples, Florida, Zip 34110–5729, 11190 Health Park Boulevard, Zip 34110–5729, tel. 239/552–7000; Paul C Hiltz, FACHE, Chief Executive Officer) **A**1 3 5 7 8 10 19 **F**3 8 9 11 12 13 14 17 18 19 20 22 24 26 28 29 30 31 32 34 35 37 40 41 42 44 45 46 47 48 49 50 53 56 57 59 64 68 70 72 74 75 76 77 78 79 81 84 85 86 87 88 89 91 93 96 102 107 108 111 115 119 126 131 135 145 146 147 148 149 156 167 169 **P**6
Primary Contact: Paul C. Hiltz, FACHE, Chief Executive Officer
CFO: Chrissie Erdmann, Executive Vice President Finance, Chief Financial Officer
CMO: Doug Ardion, M.D., Chief Medical Officer
CHR: John McGirl, Chief Human Resources Officer
CNO: Michele Thoman, Chief Nursing Officer
Web address: www.nchmd.org
Control: Other not–for–profit (including NFP Corporation) **Service:** General medical and surgical

Staffed Beds: 676 **Admissions:** 30232 **Census:** 358 **Outpatient Visits:** 368061 **Births:** 3644 **Total Expense ($000):** 727472 **Payroll Expense ($000):** 249223 **Personnel:** 3657

* **PHYSICIANS REGIONAL – PINE RIDGE (100286)**, 6101 Pine Ridge Road, Zip 34119–3900; tel. 239/348–4000, (Includes PHYSICIANS REGIONAL, 8300 Collier Boulevard, Naples, Florida, Zip 34114, tel. 239/354–6000; C Scott Campbell, Market Chief Executive Officer) (Nonreporting) **A**1 10 **S** Community Health Systems, Inc., Franklin, TN
Primary Contact: Scott Lowe, Market Chief Executive Officer
COO: Susan Takacs, Market Chief Operating Officer
CFO: Ken Warriner, Market Chief Financial Officer
CHR: Jill Gaffoli, Director Human Resources
Web address: www.physiciansregional.com
Control: Corporation, Investor–owned (for–profit) **Service:** General medical and surgical

Staffed Beds: 175

PHYSICIANS REGIONAL MEDICAL CENTER See Physicians Regional

* □ **REHABILITATION HOSPITAL OF NAPLES (103054)**, 14305 Collier Boulevard, Zip 34119–9589; tel. 239/383–6000, (Nonreporting) **A**1 **S** Encompass Health Corporation, Birmingham, AL
Primary Contact: Enid Y. Gonzalez, Chief Executive Officer
Web address: https://encompasshealth.com/locations/naplesrehab
Control: Corporation, Investor–owned (for–profit) **Service:** Rehabilitation

Staffed Beds: 50

* □ **THE WILLOUGH AT NAPLES (104063)**, 9001 Tamiami Trail East, Zip 34113–3304; tel. 239/775–4500, (Nonreporting) **A**1 10
Primary Contact: Richard Bennett, Administrator
CFO: Steve Baldwin, Vice President Finance
Web address: www.thewilloughatnaples.com/
Control: Corporation, Investor–owned (for–profit) **Service:** Psychiatric

Staffed Beds: 80

NEW PORT RICHEY—Pasco County

* **MORTON PLANT NORTH BAY HOSPITAL (100063)**, 6600 Madison Street, Zip 34652–1900; tel. 727/842–8468, **A**1 3 10 **F**3 11 15 18 20 22 28 29 30 31 34 35 37 40 44 45 49 50 57 59 60 63 64 68 70 74 75 77 78 79 81 84 85 86 87 93 94 96 98 99 100 101 102 107 108 110 111 114 115 118 119 126 130 131 132 135 143 145 146 147 149 154 156 164 167 **S** BayCare Health System, Clearwater, FL
Primary Contact: Brandon May, President
CFO: Carl Tremonti, Chief Financial Officer
CMO: Jeff Jensen, D.O., Vice President, Medical Affairs
CIO: Timothy Thompson, Senior Vice President and Chief Information Officer
CHR: Kyle J Barr, Senior Vice President, Chief Team Resources Officer
CNO: Thomas Doria, Vice President and Patient Services – West
Web address: https://baycare.org/locations/hospitals/morton-plant-north-bay-hospital/patients-and-visitors
Control: Other not–for–profit (including NFP Corporation) **Service:** General medical and surgical

Staffed Beds: 222 **Admissions:** 11811 **Census:** 157 **Outpatient Visits:** 51447 **Births:** 0 **Total Expense ($000):** 196090 **Payroll Expense ($000):** 78772 **Personnel:** 965

NEW SMYRNA BEACH—Volusia County

* **ADVENTHEALTH NEW SMYRNA BEACH (100014)**, 401 Palmetto Street, Zip 32168–7399; tel. 386/424–5000, **A**1 10 19 **F**3 8 11 15 18 20 22 28 29 30 31 34 35 40 44 46 55 57 58 59 60 62 63 64 70 75 77 78 80 81 85 86 87 93 96 105 107 108 109 110 111 115 118 119 120 121 123 130 131 132 135 146 148 149 154 156 164 167 **S** AdventHealth, Altamonte Springs, FL
Primary Contact: David Weis, President and Chief Executive Officer
COO: Steven W Harrell, FACHE, Chief Operating Officer
CFO: Al W Allred, Chief Financial Officer
CMO: Dennis Hernandez, M.D., Chief Medical Officer
CIO: Calvin Patrick II, Director Information Services
CHR: Nancy K Evolga, Director Human Resources
CNO: Linda G Breum, R.N., MSN, Chief Nursing Officer
Web address: https://www.floridahospital.com/new-smyrna
Control: Church operated, Nongovernment, not–for–profit **Service:** General medical and surgical

Staffed Beds: 109 **Admissions:** 6840 **Census:** 83 **Outpatient Visits:** 97173 **Births:** 0 **Total Expense ($000):** 169762 **Payroll Expense ($000):** 56067 **Personnel:** 754

NICEVILLE—Okaloosa County

* **HCA FLORIDA TWIN CITIES HOSPITAL (100054)**, 2190 Highway 85 North, Zip 32578–1045; tel. 850/678–4131, **A**1 10 **F**3 29 34 35 45 50 59 70 75 79 81 82 85 93 107 108 110 111 115 119 124 147 149 **S** HCA Healthcare, Nashville, TN
Primary Contact: Todd Jackson, Chief Executive Officer
CFO: Mark Day, Chief Financial Officer
CMO: Eric Schuck, M.D., Chief Medical Officer
CHR: Cyndi Ronca, Director Human Resources
Web address: www.tchealthcare.com
Control: Corporation, Investor–owned (for–profit) **Service:** General medical and surgical

Staffed Beds: 65 **Admissions:** 2295 **Census:** 21 **Total Expense ($000):** 56197 **Payroll Expense ($000):** 15934 **Personnel:** 194

NORTH MIAMI—Miami–Dade County

* □ **ST. CATHERINE'S REHABILITATION HOSPITAL (103026)**, 1050 NE 125th Street, Zip 33161–5881; tel. 305/357–1735, (Nonreporting) **A**1 10 **S** Catholic Health Services, Lauderdale Lakes, FL
Primary Contact: Jaime Gonzalez, Administrator
COO: Jim Ball, Chief Operating Officer
CFO: Mary Jo Frick, Director Finance
CMO: Miriam Feliz, M.D., Medical Director
Web address: www.catholichealthservices.org
Control: Other not–for–profit (including NFP Corporation) **Service:** Rehabilitation

Staffed Beds: 22

NORTH MIAMI BEACH—Miami–Dade County

JACKSON NORTH MEDICAL CENTER See Jackson Health System, Miami

PARKWAY REGIONAL MED CENTER See Jackson North Medical Center

NORTH VENICE—Sarasota County

* **SARASOTA MEMORIAL HOSPITAL – VENICE (103062)**, 2600 Laurel Road East, Zip 34275–3226; tel. 941/261–2797, **F**3 13 15 18 20 22 26 29 31 34 35 36 40 45 46 47 48 49 50 55 56 57 58 59 60 61 64 65 68 70 74 75 76 77 78 79 81 82 84 85 86 87 92 97 98 100 102 107 108 110 111 115 118 119 126 130 131 132 135 144 145 146 147 148 149 154 160 167 169 **S** Sarasota Memorial Health Care System, Sarasota, FL
Primary Contact: David Verinder, Chief Executive Officer
COO: Jeffrey Wesner, Chief Operating Officer
CFO: Steven Miglietta, Chief Financial Officer
CMO: James Fiorica, M.D., Chief Medical Officer
CIO: Pam Ramhofer, Chief Information Officer
CHR: Laurie Bennett, Vice President, Human Resources
CNO: Julie Polaszek, R.N., MSN
Web address: www.smh.com
Control: Hospital district or authority, Government, Nonfederal **Service:** General medical and surgical

Staffed Beds: 110 **Admissions:** 10783 **Census:** 116 **Outpatient Visits:** 110579 **Births:** 347 **Total Expense ($000):** 225543 **Payroll Expense ($000):** 82165 **Personnel:** 1370

Hospitals, U.S. / FLORIDA

OAKLAND PARK—Broward County

☐ **FORT LAUDERDALE BEHAVIORAL HEALTH CENTER (104026)**, 5757 North Dixie Highway, Zip 33301-2393; tel. 954/734-2000, (Nonreporting) **A**1 10 **S** Universal Health Services, Inc., King of Prussia, PA
Primary Contact: Manuel R. Llano, Chief Executive Officer
CFO: Burt Harris, Chief Financial Officer
CMO: Jared Gaines, M.D., Chief Medical Officer
CHR: Carlos A Gato, Director of Human Resources
CNO: Jillian Wirzman, Cheif Nursing Officer
Web address: www.ftlauderdalebehavioral.com
Control: Corporation, Investor-owned (for-profit) **Service**: Psychiatric

Staffed Beds: 182

OCALA—Marion County

☒ **ADVENTHEALTH OCALA (100062)**, 1500 SW 1st Avenue, Zip 34471-6504, Mailing Address: P.O. Box 6000, Zip 34478-6000; tel. 352/351-7200, **A**1 5 10 19 **F**3 7 11 12 17 18 20 22 24 26 28 29 30 34 35 37 40 41 42 45 46 49 51 53 54 57 59 60 62 64 70 72 74 76 77 79 81 87 89 92 93 107 108 111 114 115 119 126 130 131 143 144 146 148 149 154 155 157 167 169 **S** AdventHealth, Altamonte Springs, FL
Primary Contact: Erika Skula, Chief Executive Officer
COO: Adam Johnson, Chief Operating Officer
CFO: Frances H Crunk, Chief Financial Officer
CMO: Rodrigo Torres, M.D., Chief Medical Officer
CIO: Carl Candullo, Chief Information Officer
CNO: Patricia Price, MSN, R.N., Chief Nursing Officer
Web address: https://www.adventhealth.com/hospital/adventhealth-ocala
Control: Other not-for-profit (including NFP Corporation) **Service**: General medical and surgical

Staffed Beds: 334 **Admissions**: 18711 **Census**: 196 **Outpatient Visits**: 126822 **Births**: 2079 **Total Expense ($000)**: 208631 **Payroll Expense ($000)**: 106074 **Personnel**: 1759

☒ **ENCOMPASS HEALTH REHABILITATION HOSPITAL OF OCALA (103043)**, 2275 SW 22nd Lane, Zip 34471-7710; tel. 352/282-4000, **A**1 10 **F**29 64 75 90 93 96 100 148 **S** Encompass Health Corporation, Birmingham, AL
Primary Contact: Michael A. Franklin, FACHE, Chief Executive Officer
CFO: Sammy King, Controller
CMO: Amy Clunn, M.D., Medical Director
CHR: Tracy Sapp, Director Human Resources
CNO: Wendy Milam, Chief Nursing Officer
Web address: www.healthsouthocala.com
Control: Corporation, Investor-owned (for-profit) **Service**: Rehabilitation

Staffed Beds: 80 **Admissions**: 1579 **Census**: 54 **Total Expense ($000)**: 25831 **Payroll Expense ($000)**: 13137 **Personnel**: 181

☒ **HCA FLORIDA OCALA HOSPITAL (100212)**, 1431 SW First Avenue, Zip 34471-6500, Mailing Address: P.O. Box 2200, Zip 34478-2200; tel. 352/401-1000, (Includes HCA FLORIDA WEST MARION HOSPITAL, 4600 SW 46th Court, Ocala, Florida, Zip 34474, tel. 352/291-3000; Alan Keesee, Chief Executive Officer) (Nonreporting) **A**1 2 3 5 10 13 19 **S** HCA Healthcare, Nashville, TN
Primary Contact: Alan Keesee, Chief Executive Officer
COO: Isaiah Zirkle, Chief Operating Officer
CMO: Kevin Klauer, D.O., Chief Medical Officer
CIO: Brandon Holbert, Director, Information Services
CHR: Wayne Nielsen, Director Human Resources
Web address: https://www.hcafloridahealthcare.com/locations/ocala-hospital
Control: Corporation, Investor-owned (for-profit) **Service**: General medical and surgical

Staffed Beds: 430

☒ **KINDRED HOSPITAL OCALA (102019)**, 1500 SW 1st Avenue, Zip 34471-6504; tel. 352/369-0513, (Nonreporting) **A**1 10 **S** ScionHealth, Louisville, KY
Primary Contact: Merlene Bhoorasingh, Administrator
Web address: www.kindredocala.com/
Control: Corporation, Investor-owned (for-profit) **Service**: Acute long-term care hospital

Staffed Beds: 31

OCALA REGIONAL MEDICAL CENTER See HCA Florida Ocala Hospital

☐ **THE VINES (104071)**, 3130 SW 27th Avenue, Zip 34471-4306; tel. 352/671-3130, **A**1 10 **F**98 **S** Universal Health Services, Inc., King of Prussia, PA
Primary Contact: Mike Tacke, Chief Executive Officer
Web address: www.thevineshospital.com
Control: Corporation, Investor-owned (for-profit) **Service**: Psychiatric

Staffed Beds: 76 **Admissions**: 2998 **Census**: 54 **Total Expense ($000)**: 20717 **Payroll Expense ($000)**: 8799 **Personnel**: 148

WEST MARION COMMUNITY HOSPITAL See HCA Florida West Marion Hospital

OCOEE—Orange County

☒ **ORLANDO HEALTH – HEALTH CENTRAL HOSPITAL (100030)**, 10000 West Colonial Drive, Zip 34761-3499; tel. 407/296-1000, (Includes ORLANDO HEALTH HORIZON WEST HOSPITAL, 17000 Porter RD, Winter Garden, Florida, Zip 34787-8915, tel. 407/407-0000; Margaret (Maggie) Bonko, Chief Executive Officer) **A**1 3 10 **F**3 8 11 12 15 18 20 22 26 28 29 30 34 35 36 37 40 42 44 45 46 47 48 49 50 51 57 59 60 64 65 68 70 74 75 79 80 81 82 85 86 87 93 107 108 110 111 115 118 119 126 130 131 132 135 146 147 148 149 150 154 155 157 167 **S** Orlando Health, Orlando, FL
Primary Contact: Philip Koovakada, President
COO: Rick Smith, Chief Operating Officer
CFO: Howard Brown, Chief Financial Officer
CMO: Antonio Velardi, M.D., Chief Quality Officer
CIO: John T Sills, Chief Information Officer
CHR: Karen Frenier, Chief Human Resources Officer
CNO: Christina Marie McGuirk, R.N., Chief Nursing Officer
Web address: www.orlandohealth.com/facilities/health-central-hospital
Control: Other not-for-profit (including NFP Corporation) **Service**: General medical and surgical

Staffed Beds: 172 **Admissions**: 16542 **Census**: 161 **Outpatient Visits**: 132438 **Births**: 0 **Total Expense ($000)**: 363028 **Payroll Expense ($000)**: 131156 **Personnel**: 1408

OKEECHOBEE—Okeechobee County

☒ **HCA FLORIDA RAULERSON HOSPITAL (100252)**, 1796 Highway 441 North, Zip 34972-1918, Mailing Address: P.O. Box 1307, Zip 34973-1307; tel. 863/763-2151, (Nonreporting) **A**1 10 20 **S** HCA Healthcare, Nashville, TN
Primary Contact: Brian Melear, Chief Executive Officer
CFO: Terry L Brown, Chief Financial Officer
CMO: Arif Shakoor, Chief of Staff
CIO: Tim Hearing, Associate Information Technology Director
CHR: Cynthia Jackson, Vice President Human Resources
CNO: Adam Kless, Chief Nursing Officer
Web address: www.raulersonhospital.com
Control: Corporation, Investor-owned (for-profit) **Service**: General medical and surgical

Staffed Beds: 100

ORANGE CITY—Volusia County

☒ **ADVENTHEALTH FISH MEMORIAL (100072)**, 1055 Saxon Boulevard, Zip 32763-8468; tel. 386/917-5000, **A**1 2 10 19 **F**3 11 13 15 18 20 22 24 26 28 29 30 31 34 35 37 40 42 44 45 46 47 48 49 50 53 54 55 57 59 60 64 70 74 75 76 77 78 79 80 81 82 84 85 86 87 91 92 93 96 100 102 107 108 110 111 115 118 119 120 121 126 129 130 135 146 148 149 154 164 167 169 **S** AdventHealth, Altamonte Springs, FL
Primary Contact: Lorenzo Brown, Chief Executive Officer West Volusia Market
COO: Danielle Johnson, Chief Operating Officer
CFO: Eric Osterly, Chief Financial Officer
CMO: Stephen Knych, M.D., Chief Medical Officer
CHR: Jannina Garcia, Director of Human Resources
CNO: Jennifer Shull, R.N., Chief Nursing Officer
Web address: www.fhfishmemorial.org
Control: Church operated, Nongovernment, not-for-profit **Service**: General medical and surgical

Staffed Beds: 228 **Admissions**: 11109 **Census**: 141 **Outpatient Visits**: 120890 **Births**: 765 **Total Expense ($000)**: 250394 **Payroll Expense ($000)**: 82761 **Personnel**: 1015

Hospital, Medicare Provider Number, Address, Telephone, Approval, Facility, and Physician Codes, Health Care System

★ American Hospital Association (AHA) membership ○ Healthcare Facilities Accreditation Program ⇑ Center for Improvement in Healthcare Quality Accreditation
☐ The Joint Commission accreditation ◇ DNV Healthcare Inc. accreditation △ Commission on Accreditation of Rehabilitation Facilities (CARF) accreditation

© 2025 AHA Guide

Hospitals, U.S. / FLORIDA

ORANGE PARK—Clay County

☒ **HCA FLORIDA ORANGE PARK HOSPITAL (100226)**, 2001 Kingsley Avenue, Zip 32073–5156; tel. 904/639–8500, **A**1 3 5 10 **F**3 12 13 15 17 18 20 22 24 26 29 30 31 32 34 35 37 38 40 42 43 45 46 47 48 49 50 56 57 58 60 61 68 70 72 74 75 76 77 78 79 80 81 82 84 85 88 89 90 93 98 100 102 104 105 107 108 110 111 114 115 119 126 130 132 135 146 147 153 154 167 **S** HCA Healthcare, Nashville, TN
Primary Contact: Jeff Taylor, Chief Executive Officer
CFO: Chris Glenn, Chief Financial Officer
CMO: Bradley Shumaker, Chief Medical Officer
CHR: Brad Coburn, Vice President, Human Resources
CNO: Kathy Hester, Chief Nursing Officer
Web address: https://www.hcafloridahealthcare.com/locations/orange-park-hospital
Control: Corporation, Investor–owned (for-profit) **Service**: General medical and surgical

Staffed Beds: 389 **Admissions**: 19163 **Census**: 271 **Total Expense ($000)**: 370242 **Payroll Expense ($000)**: 116876 **Personnel**: 1493

ORANGE PARK MEDICAL CENTER See HCA Florida Orange Park Hospital

ORLANDO—Orange County

★ △ ⇈ **ADVENTHEALTH ORLANDO (100007)**, 601 East Rollins Street, Zip 32803–1248; tel. 407/303–6611, (Includes ADVENTHEALTH ALTAMONTE SPRINGS, 601 East Altamonte Drive, Altamonte Springs, Florida, Zip 32701, tel. 407/830–4321; Jeffrey D Villanueva, Chief Executive Officer; ADVENTHEALTH APOPKA, 201 North Park Avenue, Apopka, Florida, Zip 32703, tel. 407/889–1000; Parker Pridgen, Chief Executive Officer; ADVENTHEALTH CELEBRATION, 400 Celebration Place, Celebration, Florida, Zip 34747, tel. 407/303–4000; Amanda Maggard, President and Chief Executive Officer; ADVENTHEALTH EAST ORLANDO, 7727 Lake Underhill Drive, Orlando, Florida, Zip 32822, tel. 407/277–8110; Chase Tikker, Chief Executive Officer; ADVENTHEALTH FOR CHILDREN, 601 East Rollins Street, Orlando, Florida, Zip 32803–1248, tel. 407/303–9732; Lars D Houmann, President; ADVENTHEALTH KISSIMMEE, 2269 Santa Lucia ST, Kissimmee, Florida, Zip 34743–3308, 2450 North Orange Blossom Trai, Zip 34741, tel. 407/846–4343; Sheila Rankin, Chief Executive Officer; ADVENTHEALTH WINTER PARK, 200 North Lakemont Avenue, Winter Park, Florida, Zip 32792–3273, tel. 407/646–7000; Justin Birmele, Chief Executive Officer) **A**2 3 5 7 8 10 19 21 **F**3 6 7 8 9 11 12 13 15 17 18 19 20 21 22 23 24 25 26 27 28 29 30 31 32 34 35 36 37 38 40 41 42 44 45 46 47 48 49 50 51 53 54 55 56 57 58 59 60 61 62 63 64 65 66 68 70 71 72 73 74 75 76 77 78 79 80 81 82 84 85 86 87 88 89 90 91 92 93 95 96 98 100 101 102 104 107 108 109 110 111 112 113 114 115 116 117 118 119 120 121 123 124 126 129 130 131 132 134 135 136 137 138 139 140 141 142 143 144 146 147 148 149 154 155 157 160 162 164 165 167 168 169 **S** AdventHealth, Altamonte Springs, FL
Primary Contact: Robert Craig. Deininger, President and Chief Executive Officer
COO: Brian Paradis, Chief Operating Officer
CFO: Eddie Soler, Chief Financial Officer
CMO: David Moorhead, M.D., Chief Medical Officer
CHR: Sheryl Dodds, Chief Clinical Officer
Web address: www.floridahospital.com/orlando
Control: Other not–for–profit (including NFP Corporation) **Service**: General medical and surgical

Staffed Beds: 2919 **Admissions**: 165023 **Census**: 2375 **Outpatient Visits**: 2006291 **Births**: 13697 **Total Expense ($000)**: 5558554 **Payroll Expense ($000)**: 1856527 **Personnel**: 24513

ARNOLD PALMER CHILDREN'S HOSPITAL See Arnold Palmer Hospital For Children

ARNOLD PALMER HOSPITAL FOR CHILDREN See Orlando Health Orlando Regional Medical Center, Orlando

ASPIRE HEALTH PARTNERS (104067), 1800 Mercy Drive, Zip 32808–5646; tel. 407/875–3700, (Nonreporting) **A**10
Primary Contact: Babette Hankey, President and Chief Executive Officer
Web address: www.lakesidecares.org
Control: Other not–for–profit (including NFP Corporation) **Service**: Psychiatric

Staffed Beds: 90

☐ **CENTRAL FLORIDA BEHAVIORAL HOSPITAL (104072)**, 6601 Central Florida Parkway, Zip 32821–8064; tel. 407/370–0111, (Nonreporting) **A**1 3 10 **S** Universal Health Services, Inc., King of Prussia, PA
Primary Contact: Vickie Lewis, Chief Executive Officer
CFO: Marsha Burick, Chief Financial Officer
Web address: www.centralfloridabehavioral.com
Control: Other not–for–profit (including NFP Corporation) **Service**: Psychiatric

Staffed Beds: 126

FLORIDA HOSPITAL EAST ORLANDO See Adventhealth East Orlando

FLORIDA HOSPITAL FOR CHILDREN–WALT DISNEY PAVILION See Adventhealth For Children

☒ **NEMOURS CHILDREN'S HOSPITAL (103304)**, 13535 Nemours Parkway, Zip 32827–7402; tel. 407/567–4000, (Nonreporting) **A**1 3 5 8 10 **S** Nemours Children Health, Jacksonville, FL
Primary Contact: Martha McGill, President, Central Florida
COO: Randall W Hartley, Chief Operating Officer
CFO: Rodney McKendree, Senior Vice President and Chief Financial Officer
CMO: Andre Hebra, M.D., Chief Medical Officer
CIO: Bernard Rice, Chief Information Officer
CHR: Theresa M. Young, Senior Vice President Human Resources
Web address: www.nemours.org
Control: Other not–for–profit (including NFP Corporation) **Service**: Children's general medical and surgical

Staffed Beds: 108

☒ △ **ORLANDO HEALTH ORLANDO REGIONAL MEDICAL CENTER (100006)**, 52 West Underwood Street, Zip 32806; tel. 407/841–5111, (Includes ARNOLD PALMER HOSPITAL FOR CHILDREN, 92 West Miller Street, Orlando, Florida, Zip 32806, tel. 407/649–6900; Cary D'Ortona, President; ORLANDO HEALTH DR. P. PHILLIPS HOSPITAL, 9400 Turkey Lake Road, Orlando, Florida, Zip 32819, tel. 407/351–8500; Thibaut van Marcke, President; ORLANDO HEALTH SOUTH SEMINOLE HOSPITAL, 555 West State Road 434, Longwood, Florida, Zip 32750–4999, tel. 407/767–1200; Shawn Molsberger, President; WINNIE PALMER HOSPITAL FOR WOMEN AND BABIES, 83 West Miller Street, Orlando, Florida, Zip 32806, tel. 321/843–9792; Suzanne A Worthington, President) **A**1 2 3 5 7 10 19 **F**3 5 7 8 9 11 12 13 15 16 17 18 19 20 21 22 23 24 25 26 27 29 30 31 34 35 36 37 40 41 42 43 44 45 46 47 49 50 51 54 55 57 58 59 60 61 62 64 68 70 71 72 73 74 75 76 77 78 79 80 81 82 84 85 86 87 88 89 90 91 92 93 94 95 96 98 99 100 101 102 103 104 107 108 110 111 114 115 116 117 118 119 120 121 122 123 124 126 127 129 130 131 132 134 135 136 141 143 145 146 147 148 149 150 152 154 155 156 157 160 161 162 164 167 168 169 **S** Orlando Health, Orlando, FL
Primary Contact: Kelly Nierstedt, President
COO: Carlos Carrasco, Chief Operating Officer
CFO: John E. Miller, Vice President, Finance
CMO: Charles Heard, M.D., Chief of Staff
CHR: Greg Thompson, Corporate Director, Human Resources
Web address: www.orlandohealth.com/facilities/orlando-regional-medical-center
Control: Other not–for–profit (including NFP Corporation) **Service**: General medical and surgical

Staffed Beds: 1387 **Admissions**: 96142 **Census**: 1316 **Outpatient Visits**: 702277 **Births**: 14960 **Total Expense ($000)**: 3143799 **Payroll Expense ($000)**: 1015353 **Personnel**: 10210

ORLANDO REG SAND LAKE HOSP See Orlando Health Dr. P. Phillips Hospital

☐ **ORLANDO VA MEDICAL CENTER**, 13800 Veterans Way, Zip 32827–7403; tel. 407/631–1000, (Nonreporting) **A**1 3 5 **S** Department of Veterans Affairs, Washington, DC
Primary Contact: Timothy J. Cooke, Medical Center Director and Chief Executive Officer
Web address: www.orlando.va.gov
Control: Veterans Affairs, Government, federal **Service**: General medical and surgical

Staffed Beds: 370

SELECT SPECIALTY HOSPITAL–ORLANDO See Select Specialty Hospital–Orlando North

☒ **SELECT SPECIALTY HOSPITAL–ORLANDO NORTH (102003)**, 2250 Bedford Road, Zip 32803–1443; tel. 407/303–7869, (Includes SELECT SPECIALTY HOSPITAL–ORLANDO SOUTH, 5579 South Orange Avenue, Orlando, Florida, Zip 32809–3493, tel. 407/241–4800; Marinella Castroman, Chief Execuitve Officer) (Nonreporting) **A**1 10 **S** Select Medical Corporation, Mechanicsburg, PA
Primary Contact: Kelvin L. Parks, Chief Executive Officer
Web address: https://www.selectspecialtyhospitals.com/locations-and-tours/fl/orlando/orlando-north/
Control: Corporation, Investor–owned (for–profit) **Service**: Acute long–term care hospital

Staffed Beds: 75

☒ **UCF LAKE NONA MEDICAL CENTER (100350)**, 6700 Lake Nona Boulevard, Zip 32827–7729; tel. 689/216–8000, (Nonreporting) **A**1 5 **S** HCA Healthcare, Nashville, TN
Primary Contact: Wendy H. Brandon, Chief Executive Officer
CFO: Maria Garvin, Chief Financial Officer
CHR: Joseph Myszkowski, Vice President, Human Resources
Web address: www.UCFLakeNonaMedicalCenter.com
Control: Corporation, Investor–owned (for–profit) **Service**: General medical and surgical

Staffed Beds: 64

Hospitals, U.S. / FLORIDA

WINNIE PALMER HOSPITAL FOR WOMEN AND BABIES See Orlando Health Orlando Regional Medical Center, Orlando

OVIEDO—Seminole County

☒ **OVIEDO MEDICAL CENTER (100329)**, 8300 Red Bug Lake Road, Zip 32765–6801; tel. 407/890–2273, (Nonreporting) **A**1 3 10 **S** HCA Healthcare, Nashville, TN
Primary Contact: Kenneth C. Donahey, Chief Executive Officer
CFO: Jay Pettus, Chief Financial Officer
Web address: www.oviedomedicalcenter.com
Control: Other not–for–profit (including NFP Corporation) **Service:** General medical and surgical

Staffed Beds: 64

OXFORD—Sumter County

☒ **SELECT SPECIALTY HOSPITAL–THE VILLAGES (102028)**, 5050 County Road 472, Zip 34484; tel. 352/689–6400, **A**1 10 **F**1 29 75 77 82 84 90 98 107 119 **S** Select Medical Corporation, Mechanicsburg, PA
Primary Contact: Dennis Bencomo, JD, MSN, R.N., Chief Executive Officer
CNO: Janice M McCoy, MS, R.N., Chief Clinical Officer
Web address: https://thevillages.selectspecialtyhospitals.com/
Control: Corporation, Investor–owned (for–profit) **Service:** Acute long–term care hospital

Staffed Beds: 40 **Admissions:** 409 **Census:** 35 **Total Expense ($000):** 24393 **Payroll Expense ($000):** 9736 **Personnel:** 122

PALATKA—Putnam County

☒ **HCA FLORIDA PUTNAM HOSPITAL (100232)**, 611 Zeagler Drive, Zip 32177–3810; tel. 386/328–5711, **A**1 10 19 **F**3 11 13 15 18 20 22 29 30 34 35 40 45 49 50 51 54 57 59 60 64 68 70 74 75 76 77 79 81 85 87 93 107 108 110 111 114 115 119 129 130 133 135 146 147 148 149 **S** HCA Healthcare, Nashville, TN
Primary Contact: Brian Nunn, R.N., Chief Executive Officer
CFO: Stewart Whitmore, Chief Financial Officer
CIO: Yvette A Jones, Health Information Management Director
CHR: John Schneider, Human Resources Director
CNO: Kari Bolin, Chief Nursing Officer
Web address: www.pcmcfl.com
Control: Corporation, Investor–owned (for–profit) **Service:** General medical and surgical

Staffed Beds: 99 **Admissions:** 4724 **Census:** 52 **Total Expense ($000):** 75447 **Payroll Expense ($000):** 25370 **Personnel:** 341

PUTNAM COMMUNITY MEDICAL CENTER See HCA Florida Putnam Hospital

PALM BAY—Brevard County

☒ **HEALTH FIRST PALM BAY HOSPITAL (100316)**, 1425 Malabar Road NE, Zip 32907–2506; tel. 321/434–8000, **A**1 10 **F**3 15 18 20 22 29 30 34 37 39 40 41 45 46 47 48 50 51 59 60 64 68 70 74 75 77 79 80 81 84 85 86 87 97 100 102 107 108 110 111 115 118 119 126 130 132 141 146 148 149 153 154 167 168 169 **S** Health First, Inc., Rockledge, FL
Primary Contact: Brett A. Esrock, President
COO: Deborah Angerami, Chief Operating Officer, Health First Community Hospitals
CFO: Joseph G Felkner, Executive Vice President and Chief Financial Officer
CMO: Lee Scheinbart, M.D., Vice President Medical Affairs, Health First Community Hospitals
CIO: Alex Popowycz, Senior Vice President and Chief Information Officer
CHR: Paula Just, Chief Human Resources Officer
CNO: Connie Bradley, R.N., MSN, FACHE, Chief Nursing Officer
Web address: https://hf.org/healthcare–home/location–directory/palm–bay–hospital
Control: Other not–for–profit (including NFP Corporation) **Service:** General medical and surgical

Staffed Beds: 120 **Admissions:** 8423 **Census:** 93 **Outpatient Visits:** 80436 **Births:** 0 **Total Expense ($000):** 154246 **Payroll Expense ($000):** 55258 **Personnel:** 606

PALM BEACH GARDENS—Palm Beach County

☒ **PALM BEACH GARDENS MEDICAL CENTER (100176)**, 3360 Burns Road, Zip 33410–4323; tel. 561/622–1411, **A**1 5 10 **F**3 11 15 17 18 20 22 24 26 28 29 34 35 37 40 45 49 50 57 58 59 64 67 70 74 77 79 81 85 87 92 93 94 96 107 108 110 111 115 118 119 126 130 131 132 135 146 148 149 167 **S** TENET Healthcare Corporation, Dallas, TX
Primary Contact: Teresa C. Urquhart, Chief Executive Officer
CFO: Judi Stimson, Chief Financial Officer
CIO: James Vega, Director Information Systems
CHR: Kevin Caracciolo, Chief Human Resources Officer
CNO: Patricia A Rosenberg, R.N., MSN, Chief Nursing Officer
Web address: www.pbgmc.com
Control: Corporation, Investor–owned (for–profit) **Service:** General medical and surgical

Staffed Beds: 199 **Admissions:** 9411 **Census:** 133 **Total Expense ($000):** 218380 **Payroll Expense ($000):** 60697 **Personnel:** 714

PALM COAST—Flagler County

☒ **ADVENTHEALTH PALM COAST (100118)**, 60 Memorial Medical Parkway, Zip 32164–5980; tel. 386/586–2000, **A**1 2 10 **F**3 8 11 15 18 20 22 28 29 30 34 35 36 37 40 45 46 47 48 49 50 51 54 55 57 59 60 62 63 64 65 67 68 70 74 75 77 79 80 81 84 85 86 87 91 92 93 96 97 107 108 109 110 111 114 115 116 117 119 120 121 123 124 126 130 131 132 135 146 147 148 149 150 154 156 167 **S** AdventHealth, Altamonte Springs, FL
Primary Contact: Denyse Bales–Chubb, Chief Executive Officer
COO: JoAnne King, Chief Operating Officer
CFO: Cory Domayer, Chief Financial Officer
CMO: Ron Thomas, M.D., Chief Medical Officer
CHR: Joshua I Champion, Director
CNO: Robert Davis, Chief Nursing Officer
Web address: www.floridahospitalflagler.com/
Control: Church operated, Nongovernment, not–for–profit **Service:** General medical and surgical

Staffed Beds: 99 **Admissions:** 9007 **Census:** 119 **Outpatient Visits:** 571699 **Births:** 0 **Total Expense ($000):** 293908 **Payroll Expense ($000):** 89983 **Personnel:** 1233

★ **ADVENTHEALTH PALM COAST PARKWAY (100363)**, 1 AdventHealth Way, Zip 32137; tel. 386/302–1800, (Nonreporting) **S** AdventHealth, Altamonte Springs, FL
Primary Contact: Walmir Wally De Aquino, Chief Executive Officer
Web address: https://www.adventhealth.com/hospital/adventhealth-palm-coast-parkway/adventhealth-palm-coast-parkway-leadership
Control: Church operated, Nongovernment, not–for–profit **Service:** General medical and surgical

Staffed Beds: 100

PANAMA CITY—Bay County

☒ **ASCENSION SACRED HEART BAY (100026)**, 615 North Bonita Avenue, Zip 32401–3600; tel. 850/769–1511, **A**1 10 **F**3 15 17 18 20 22 24 26 28 29 30 37 40 41 42 43 45 46 49 51 64 68 70 74 77 79 81 82 84 85 87 92 93 107 115 119 126 130 135 146 147 148 149 154 167 **S** Ascension Healthcare, Saint Louis, MO
Primary Contact: Robin M. Godwin, MSN, Administrator
CHR: Donna Baird, Vice President Corporate Services
CNO: Jan Thornton, Chief Nursing Officer
Web address: https://healthcare.ascension.org/Locations/Florida/FLPEN/Panama-City-Ascension-Sacred-Heart-Bay
Control: Church operated, Nongovernment, not–for–profit **Service:** General medical and surgical

Staffed Beds: 201 **Admissions:** 7271 **Census:** 103 **Outpatient Visits:** 91730 **Births:** 0 **Total Expense ($000):** 204505 **Payroll Expense ($000):** 58538 **Personnel:** 767

☐ **EMERALD COAST BEHAVIORAL HOSPITAL (104073)**, 1940 Harrison Avenue, Zip 32405–4542; tel. 850/763–0017, (Nonreporting) **A**1 10 **S** Universal Health Services, Inc., King of Prussia, PA
Primary Contact: Tim Bedford, Chief Executive Officer
CFO: Michael J Zenone, Chief Financial Officer
CMO: Roy Deal, Chief Medical Officer
CNO: Michael B Barbour, Chief Nursing Officer
Web address: www.emeraldcoastbehavioral.com
Control: Corporation, Investor–owned (for–profit) **Service:** Psychiatric

Staffed Beds: 86

Hospitals, U.S. / FLORIDA

✠ **ENCOMPASS HEALTH REHABILITATION HOSPITAL OF PANAMA CITY (103040)**, 1847 Florida Avenue, Zip 32405-4640; tel. 850/914-8600, (Nonreporting) **A**1 10 **S** Encompass Health Corporation, Birmingham, AL
Primary Contact: Tony N. Bennett, Chief Executive Officer
CFO: Bradley Tilghman, Controller
CMO: Michael Hennigan, M.D., Medical Director
CHR: Traci Powell, Director Human Resources
CNO: Sharon Hamilton, Chief Nursing Officer
Web address: www.healthsouthpanamacity.com
Control: Corporation, Investor-owned (for-profit) **Service**: Rehabilitation

Staffed Beds: 75

GULF COAST REGIONAL MEDICAL CENTER See HCA Florida Gulf Coast Hospital

✠ **HCA FLORIDA GULF COAST HOSPITAL (100242)**, 449 West 23rd Street, Zip 32405-4593, Mailing Address: P.O. Box 15309, Zip 32406-5309; tel. 850/769-8341, **A**1 2 10 **F**3 8 12 13 15 20 22 26 29 30 31 34 35 37 39 40 41 46 47 48 49 51 54 56 57 59 60 64 68 70 72 74 75 76 77 78 79 80 81 85 86 87 89 93 107 108 109 111 114 116 117 118 119 126 130 131 132 135 144 146 147 148 149 **S** HCA Healthcare, Nashville, TN
Primary Contact: Chase Christianson, Chief Executive Officer
COO: Holly Jackson, Chief Operating Officer
CFO: Laurie Haynes, Chief Financial Officer
CHR: Tracy McGlon, Director Human Resources
CNO: Brian Pinelle, R.N., Chief Nursing Officer
Web address: https://www.hcafloridahealthcare.com/locations/gulf-coast-hospital
Control: Corporation, Investor-owned (for-profit) **Service**: General medical and surgical

Staffed Beds: 297 **Admissions**: 16301 **Census**: 207 **Total Expense ($000)**: 272929 **Payroll Expense ($000)**: 76742 **Personnel**: 987

✠ **SELECT SPECIALTY HOSPITAL–PANAMA CITY (102017)**, 615 North Bonita Avenue, 3rd Floor, Zip 32401-3623; tel. 850/767-3180, (Nonreporting) **A**1 10 **S** Select Medical Corporation, Mechanicsburg, PA
Primary Contact: Matthew Presley, Chief Executive Officer
CMO: Amir Manzoor, M.D., Medical Director
Web address: https://www.selectspecialtyhospitals.com/locations-and-tours/fl/panama-city/panama-city/
Control: Corporation, Investor-owned (for-profit) **Service**: Acute long-term care hospital

Staffed Beds: 30

PEMBROKE PINES—Broward County

✠ **MEMORIAL HOSPITAL PEMBROKE (100230)**, 7800 Sheridan Street, Zip 33024-2536; tel. 954/883-8482, **A**1 5 10 **F**3 12 29 30 34 40 42 44 45 46 47 48 49 50 51 59 64 65 66 70 74 75 77 79 81 82 85 86 87 107 108 111 115 119 126 130 132 141 144 146 148 149 154 160 167 **S** Memorial Healthcare System, Hollywood, FL
Primary Contact: Felicia Turnley, Chief Executive Officer
CIO: Forest Blanton, Chief Information Officer
Web address: www.memorialpembroke.com/
Control: Hospital district or authority, Government, Nonfederal **Service**: General medical and surgical

Staffed Beds: 191 **Admissions**: 7018 **Census**: 100 **Outpatient Visits**: 130405 **Births**: 0 **Total Expense ($000)**: 202139 **Payroll Expense ($000)**: 100284 **Personnel**: 770

✠ **MEMORIAL HOSPITAL WEST (100281)**, 703 North Flamingo Road, Zip 33028-1014; tel. 954/436-5000, **A**1 2 3 10 19 **F**3 11 12 13 15 17 18 20 22 26 28 29 30 31 34 40 41 44 45 47 49 50 55 56 57 58 64 70 72 74 75 76 77 78 79 81 82 85 87 91 93 96 97 107 108 110 111 114 115 119 120 121 123 124 126 130 131 132 136 145 146 147 148 149 154 167 169 **S** Memorial Healthcare System, Hollywood, FL
Primary Contact: Joseph Stuczynski, Chief Executive Officer
CFO: Walter Bussell, Chief Financial Officer
CMO: Eric Freling, M.D., Director Medical Staff Affairs
CIO: Forest Blanton, Chief Information Officer
CHR: Maria Naranjo, Director Human Resources
Web address: www.mhs.net
Control: Hospital district or authority, Government, Nonfederal **Service**: General medical and surgical

Staffed Beds: 486 **Admissions**: 23073 **Census**: 367 **Outpatient Visits**: 301040 **Births**: 3318 **Total Expense ($000)**: 710419 **Payroll Expense ($000)**: 329835 **Personnel**: 2684

PENSACOLA—Escambia County

✠ **ASCENSION SACRED HEART PENSACOLA (100025)**, 5151 North Ninth Avenue, Zip 32504-8795, Mailing Address: P.O. Box 2700, Zip 32513-2700; tel. 850/416-7000, **A**1 2 3 5 10 19 **F**3 8 11 12 13 15 17 18 19 20 21 22 24 26 29 30 31 34 35 37 38 40 41 42 43 44 45 46 47 48 49 50 54 55 57 58 59 60 61 65 68 70 72 73 74 75 76 77 78 79 81 82 84 85 87 88 89 91 92 93 96 107 108 110 111 112 114 116 117 119 120 124 126 129 130 131 132 135 138 146 147 148 149 154 156 167 169 **S** Ascension Healthcare, Saint Louis, MO
Primary Contact: William Condon, President
COO: Terri Smith, Chief Operating Officer
CFO: C Susan Cornejo, Chief Financial Officer
CMO: Peter Jennings, M.D., Chief Medical Officer
Web address: https://healthcare.ascension.org/Locations/Florida/FLPEN/Pensacola-Sacred-Heart-Hospital-Pensacola
Control: Church operated, Nongovernment, not-for-profit **Service**: General medical and surgical

Staffed Beds: 465 **Admissions**: 26890 **Census**: 378 **Outpatient Visits**: 785146 **Births**: 5911 **Total Expense ($000)**: 849990 **Payroll Expense ($000)**: 223189 **Personnel**: 2762

★ ⇧ **BAPTIST HOSPITAL (100093)**, 1000 West Moreno Street, Zip 32501-2316, Mailing Address: 123 Baptist Way Suite 6A, Zip 32503-2254; tel. 850/434-4011, **A**2 3 10 21 **F**3 8 11 12 13 15 17 18 20 22 24 26 28 29 30 31 34 35 40 42 43 45 46 47 48 49 50 51 54 55 56 57 58 59 60 61 64 70 74 75 76 77 78 79 80 81 82 84 85 86 87 91 92 93 96 97 98 99 103 107 108 110 111 114 115 116 117 118 119 120 121 123 126 130 131 132 146 147 148 149 154 167 169 **S** Baptist Health Care Corporation, Pensacola, FL
Primary Contact: Beau Pollard, Vice President and Baptist Hospital Administrator
CFO: Sharon Nobles, Interim Chief Financial Officer
CMO: Mike Oleksyk, M.D., Vice President and Chief Medical Officer
CIO: Steven Sarros, Vice President and Chief Information Officer
CHR: Darlene Stone, Vice President Human Resources
CNO: Cynthia Gamache, R.N., Vice President and Chief Nursing Officer
Web address: www.ebaptisthealthcare.org
Control: Other not-for-profit (including NFP Corporation) **Service**: General medical and surgical

Staffed Beds: 340 **Admissions**: 17144 **Census**: 227 **Outpatient Visits**: 571367 **Births**: 546 **Total Expense ($000)**: 561244 **Payroll Expense ($000)**: 157755 **Personnel**: 2351

✠ **ENCOMPASS HEALTH REHABILITATION HOSPITAL OF PENSACOLA (103048)**, 1101 Office Woods Drive, Zip 32504; tel. 850/805-2000, **A**1 10 **F**9 28 29 60 74 75 77 78 79 82 90 91 96 148 **S** Encompass Health Corporation, Birmingham, AL
Primary Contact: Kayla Feazell, Chief Executive Officer
CFO: Derek Hensel MHL, BNS, Controller
CMO: Arthur Kalman, M.D., Medical Director
CHR: Kimberly Franklin, Director, Human Resource
CNO: Jessica Vinson, Chief Nursing Officer
Web address: https://encompasshealth.com/pensacolarehab
Control: Corporation, Investor-owned (for-profit) **Service**: Rehabilitation

Staffed Beds: 40 **Admissions**: 1073 **Census**: 33 **Outpatient Visits**: 0 **Births**: 0 **Total Expense ($000)**: 16044 **Payroll Expense ($000)**: 8958 **Personnel**: 138

✠ △ **HCA FLORIDA WEST HOSPITAL (100231)**, 8383 North Davis Highway, Zip 32514-6088; tel. 850/494-4000, (Includes THE PAVILION, 8383 N Davis Hwy, Pensacola, Florida, Zip 32514-6039, P O Box 18900, Zip 32523, tel. 904/494-5000; WEST FLORIDA REHABILITATION INSTITUTE, 8383 North Davis Highway, Pensacola, Florida, Zip 32514, P O Box 18900, Zip 32523, tel. 850/494-6000) (Nonreporting) **A**1 2 3 5 7 10 19 **S** HCA Healthcare, Nashville, TN
Primary Contact: Guy Bullaro, Chief Executive Officer
CFO: Randy Butler, Chief Financial Officer
CMO: Terry Stallings, M.D., Chief Medical Officer
CIO: Jeff Amerson, Director Information System
CHR: Wanda Salley, Vice President Human Resources
CNO: Karen White-Trevino, Chief Nursing Officer
Web address: www.westfloridahospital.com
Control: Corporation, Investor-owned (for-profit) **Service**: General medical and surgical

Staffed Beds: 515

★ **NAVAL HOSPITAL PENSACOLA**, 6000 West Highway 98, Zip 32512-0003; tel. 850/505-6601, (Nonreporting) **A**3 5 **S** Bureau of Medicine and Surgery, Department of the Navy, Falls Church, VA
Primary Contact: Captain Alan Christian, Commanding Officer
CMO: Commander Carolyn Rice, M.D., Director Medical Services
CIO: Lieutenant Commander William Berg, Chief Information Officer
CNO: Captain Amy Tarbay, Director Nursing Services
Web address: https://www.med.navy.mil/sites/pcola
Control: Navy, Government, federal **Service**: General medical and surgical

Staffed Beds: 28

Hospitals, U.S. / FLORIDA

REHABILITATION INSTITUTE OF WEST FLORIDA See West Florida Rehabilitation Institute

☒ **SELECT SPECIALTY HOSPITAL–PENSACOLA (102024)**, 7000 Cobble Creek Drive, Zip 32504–8638; tel. 850/473–4800, (Nonreporting) **A**1 10 **S** Select Medical Corporation, Mechanicsburg, PA
Primary Contact: Randall C. Lambert, Chief Executive Officer
CMO: John Bray, M.D., Medical Director
Web address: https://www.selectspecialtyhospitals.com/locations-and-tours/fl/pensacola/pensacola/?utm_source=gmb&utm_medium=organic
Control: Corporation, Investor–owned (for-profit) **Service**: Acute long–term care hospital

Staffed Beds: 75

WEST FLORIDA HOSPITAL See HCA Florida West Hospital

WEST FLORIDA REHABILITATION INSTITUTE See HCA Florida West Hospital, Pensacola

PERRY—Taylor County

DOCTORS' MEMORIAL HOSPITAL (101314), 333 North Byron Butler Parkway, Zip 32347–2300; tel. 850/584–0800, **A**10 18 **F**3 11 15 29 34 35 40 45 50 57 59 68 70 77 81 85 86 87 93 97 107 108 110 111 115 119 127 133 146 149 154 **P**6
Primary Contact: Lauren Faison–Clark, Chief Executive Officer
CIO: Kyle Wright, Management Information System Director
CHR: Sherry Blanton, Human Resource Director
CNO: Ashley Beagle, Director of Nursing
Web address: https://www.doctorsmemorial.com/
Control: Other not–for–profit (including NFP Corporation) **Service**: General medical and surgical

Staffed Beds: 48 **Admissions**: 372 **Census**: 3 **Total Expense ($000)**: 22972 **Payroll Expense ($000)**: 7905 **Personnel**: 179

PLANT CITY—Hillsborough County

☒ **SOUTH FLORIDA BAPTIST HOSPITAL (100132)**, 301 North Alexander Street, Zip 33563–4303; tel. 813/757–1200, **A**1 10 **F**3 11 12 13 15 18 20 22 28 29 30 31 34 35 37 40 44 45 47 48 49 50 51 57 59 60 64 68 70 71 74 75 76 77 78 79 80 81 83 84 85 86 87 89 93 100 107 108 110 111 114 115 118 119 124 126 130 131 132 135 145 146 147 148 154 156 167 **S** BayCare Health System, Clearwater, FL
Primary Contact: Karen Kerr, R.N., President
COO: Beth Tancredo, Director Operations
CFO: Carl Tremonti, Chief Financial Officer
CMO: Mark Vaaler, M.D., Chief Medical Officer
CIO: Tim Thompson, Senior Vice President, Chief Information Officer
CHR: Pat Lipton, Director Team Resources
CNO: Teresa Colletti, Director Patient Services
Web address: https://baycare.org/sfbh
Control: Other not–for–profit (including NFP Corporation) **Service**: General medical and surgical

Staffed Beds: 141 **Admissions**: 5910 **Census**: 71 **Outpatient Visits**: 55227 **Births**: 435 **Total Expense ($000)**: 161492 **Payroll Expense ($000)**: 61953 **Personnel**: 708

PLANTATION—Broward County

☒ **HCA FLORIDA WESTSIDE HOSPITAL (100228)**, 8201 West Broward Boulevard, Zip 33324–2701; tel. 954/473–6600, **A**1 3 5 10 **F**3 8 11 15 17 18 20 22 24 26 29 30 31 34 35 40 44 45 48 49 50 57 59 60 68 70 74 75 77 78 79 80 81 82 85 86 87 93 107 108 110 111 114 115 117 119 126 129 130 131 132 145 146 148 **S** HCA Healthcare, Nashville, TN
Primary Contact: Drew Tyrer, Chief Executive Officer
COO: Shana Sappington–Crittenden, Chief Operating Officer
CFO: Kevin Corcoran, Chief Financial Officer
CMO: Brian Weinstein, M.D., Chief of Staff
CIO: Andres Blanco, Director Management Information Systems
CHR: Maria Rivera, Director Human Resources
Web address: www.westsideregional.com
Control: Corporation, Investor–owned (for-profit) **Service**: General medical and surgical

Staffed Beds: 250 **Admissions**: 14012 **Census**: 174 **Total Expense ($000)**: 283185 **Payroll Expense ($000)**: 77998 **Personnel**: 1008

PORT CHARLOTTE—Charlotte County

FAWCETT MEMORIAL HOSPITAL See HCA Florida Fawcett Hospital

☒ **HCA FLORIDA FAWCETT HOSPITAL (100236)**, 21298 Olean Boulevard, Zip 33952–6765; tel. 941/629–1181, **A**1 2 10 19 **F**3 8 15 18 20 22 26 29 30 31 34 35 40 45 46 47 48 49 51 57 59 64 70 74 75 77 78 79 81 85 86 87 90 91 93 96 107 108 110 111 114 119 131 132 146 147 148 **S** HCA Healthcare, Nashville, TN
Primary Contact: Michael Ehrat, Chief Executive Officer
COO: Lisa Tzanakis, Chief Operating Officer
CFO: Vickie Magurean, Chief Financial Officer
CMO: Mark Callman, M.D., Chief Medical Officer
CHR: Linda Bryan, Vice President Human Resources
CNO: Brandy Hershberger, Chief Nursing Officer
Web address: https://www.hcafloridahealthcare.com/locations/fawcett-hospital
Control: Corporation, Investor–owned (for-profit) **Service**: General medical and surgical

Staffed Beds: 253 **Admissions**: 11537 **Census**: 157 **Total Expense ($000)**: 238050 **Payroll Expense ($000)**: 62001 **Personnel**: 762

☒ **SHOREPOINT HEALTH PORT CHARLOTTE (100077)**, 2500 Harbor Boulevard, Zip 33952–5000; tel. 941/766–4122, (Nonreporting) **A**1 10 19 **S** Community Health Systems, Inc., Franklin, TN
Primary Contact: Andrew Romine, R.N., Chief Executive Officer
COO: Eric Kaplan, Chief Operating Officer
CFO: Jeffrey Mullis, Interim Chief Financial Officer
CMO: Thomas Noone, M.D., Chief Medical Officer
CHR: Karen Gardiner, Human Resources Director
CNO: Debra Clark, Chief Nursing Officer
Web address: https://www.shorepointhealthcharlotte.com/port-charlotte
Control: Corporation, Investor–owned (for-profit) **Service**: General medical and surgical

Staffed Beds: 254

PORT ORANGE—Volusia County

HALIFAX HOSPITAL PORT ORANGE See Halifax Health Medical Center of Port Orange

PORT ST JOE—Gulf County

☒ **ASCENSION SACRED HEART GULF (100313)**, 3801 East Highway 98, Zip 32456–5318; tel. 850/229–5600, **A**1 3 10 20 **F**3 18 29 30 35 40 45 64 71 77 79 81 85 87 93 107 108 110 111 114 119 127 130 133 146 154 156 157 167 **S** Ascension Healthcare, Saint Louis, MO
Primary Contact: Henry Stovall, Regional President
CMO: Gary M. Pablo, M.D., Chief Medical Officer
CNO: Robin M. Godwin, MSN, Vice President of Nursing
Web address: www.sacred-heart.org/gulf/
Control: Church operated, Nongovernment, not–for–profit **Service**: General medical and surgical

Staffed Beds: 19 **Admissions**: 418 **Census**: 4 **Outpatient Visits**: 51849 **Births**: 0 **Total Expense ($000)**: 26211 **Payroll Expense ($000)**: 9045 **Personnel**: 79

PORT ST LUCIE—St. Lucie County

☒ **HCA FLORIDA ST. LUCIE HOSPITAL (100260)**, 1800 SE Tiffany Avenue, Zip 34952–7521; tel. 772/335–4000, (Nonreporting) **A**1 3 5 10 **S** HCA Healthcare, Nashville, TN
Primary Contact: Corey Lovelace, Chief Executive Officer
CNO: Jodi LoDolce, Chief Nursing Officer
Web address: https://www.hcafloridahealthcare.com/locations/st-lucie-hospital
Control: Corporation, Investor–owned (for-profit) **Service**: General medical and surgical

Staffed Beds: 229

☐ **PORT ST. LUCIE HOSPITAL (104070)**, 2550 SE Walton Road, Zip 34952–7168; tel. 772/335–0400, (Nonreporting) **A**1 10 **S** Oglethorpe Recovery and Behavioral Hospitals, Tampa, FL
Primary Contact: Julia C. Fortune, Acting Administrator/Risk Manager
Web address: www.portstluciehospitalinc.com
Control: Corporation, Investor–owned (for-profit) **Service**: Psychiatric

Staffed Beds: 75

TRADITION MEDICAL CENTER See Cleveland Clinic Tradition Hospital

---

Hospital, Medicare Provider Number, Address, Telephone, Approval, Facility, and Physician Codes, Health Care System

★ American Hospital Association (AHA) membership ◯ Healthcare Facilities Accreditation Program ⇧ Center for Improvement in Healthcare Quality Accreditation
☐ The Joint Commission accreditation ◇ DNV Healthcare Inc. accreditation △ Commission on Accreditation of Rehabilitation Facilities (CARF) accreditation

© 2025 AHA Guide

Hospitals, U.S. / FLORIDA

PUNTA GORDA—Charlotte County

☒ **SHOREPOINT HEALTH PUNTA GORDA (100047)**, 809 East Marion Avenue, Zip 33950–3819, Mailing Address: P.O. Box 51–1328, Zip 33951–1328; tel. 941/639–3131, **A**1 10 **F**3 15 18 28 29 30 31 34 35 36 38 39 40 44 45 50 53 54 56 57 59 60 64 68 70 74 75 77 78 79 81 82 85 86 87 91 93 94 96 98 100 101 102 103 104 107 108 110 111 115 118 119 130 131 132 135 146 148 149 154 **S** Community Health Systems, Inc., Franklin, TN
Primary Contact: Andrew Romine, R.N., Chief Executive Officer
CNO: Russell Schroeder, Chief Nursing Officer
Web address: https://www.shorepointhealthcharlotte.com/punta-gorda
Control: Corporation, Investor–owned (for–profit) **Service**: General medical and surgical

Staffed Beds: 133 **Admissions**: 4270 **Census**: 58 **Total Expense ($000)**: 65528 **Payroll Expense ($000)**: 22881 **Personnel**: 294

RIVERVIEW—Hillsborough County

JOSEPH'S HOSPITAL SOUTH See St. Joseph's Hospital–South

RIVIERA BEACH—Palm Beach County

☒ **KINDRED HOSPITAL THE PALM BEACHES (102025)**, 5555 West Blue Heron Boulevard, Zip 33418–7813; tel. 561/840–0754, **A**1 10 **F**1 3 18 29 30 45 48 70 74 75 77 79 82 84 91 97 100 107 148 **S** ScionHealth, Louisville, KY
Primary Contact: Elayne Honerlaw, Chief Executive Officer
CFO: Dean Card, Chief Financial Officer
CNO: Elayne Honerlaw, Chief Clinical Officer
Web address: www.khthepalmbeaches.com/
Control: Corporation, Investor–owned (for–profit) **Service**: Acute long–term care hospital

Staffed Beds: 68 **Admissions**: 497 **Census**: 47 **Total Expense ($000)**: 30891 **Payroll Expense ($000)**: 13772 **Personnel**: 164

ROCKLEDGE—Brevard County

☐ **ROCKLEDGE REGIONAL MEDICAL CENTER (100092)**, 110 Longwood Avenue, Zip 32955–2887, Mailing Address: P.O. Box 565002, Mail Stop 1, Zip 32956–5002; tel. 321/636–2211, (Nonreporting) **A**1 10 **S** Steward Health Care System, LLC, Dallas, TX
Primary Contact: Thomas Bowden, President
CFO: Jonathan R Immordino, Chief Financial Officer
CMO: Vinay Mehindru, M.D., Medical Director
CIO: David Barnhart, Director Information Systems
CHR: Marchita H Marino, Vice President Human Resources
CNO: Mary Sue Zinsmeister, Chief Nursing Officer
Web address: https://www.rockledgeregional.org/
Control: Corporation, Investor–owned (for–profit) **Service**: General medical and surgical

Staffed Beds: 215

SAFETY HARBOR—Pinellas County

☒ **MEASE COUNTRYSIDE HOSPITAL (100265)**, 3231 McMullen Booth Road, Zip 34695–6607; tel. 727/725–6111, **A**1 2 10 19 **F**3 11 12 13 15 17 18 20 22 26 28 29 30 31 32 34 35 37 38 40 41 44 45 46 49 50 51 56 57 59 60 63 64 68 70 72 74 75 76 77 78 79 81 84 85 86 87 89 92 93 100 107 108 110 111 114 115 118 119 126 127 129 130 131 132 143 145 146 147 148 149 154 156 164 167 169 **S** BayCare Health System, Clearwater, FL
Primary Contact: Kelly Enriquez, President, Mease Hospitals
CFO: Carl Tremonti, Chief Financial Officer
CMO: Tony Schuster, M.D., Vice President, Chief Medical Officer
CIO: Tim Thompson, Senior Vice President, Informant Services and Chief Information Officer
CHR: Kyle J Barr, Senior Vice President, Chief Team Resources Officer
CNO: Thomas Doria, Vice President, Patient Services and Chief Nursing Officer
Web address: https://baycare.org/locations/hospitals/mease-countryside-hospital/patients-and-visitors
Control: Other not–for–profit (including NFP Corporation) **Service**: General medical and surgical

Staffed Beds: 387 **Admissions**: 17449 **Census**: 211 **Outpatient Visits**: 94152 **Births**: 1859 **Total Expense ($000)**: 388376 **Payroll Expense ($000)**: 136405 **Personnel**: 1604

SAINT AUGUSTINE—St. Johns County

☒ **UF HEALTH ST. JOHN'S (100090)**, 400 Health Park Boulevard, Zip 32086–5784; tel. 904/819–5155, (Nonreporting) **A**1 2 10 **S** UF Health Shands, Gainesville, FL
Primary Contact: Kerry Watson, Interim Chief Executive Officer
CFO: Lynda I Kirker, Chief Financial Officer
CMO: Douglas Dew, M.D., President Medical Staff
CIO: Bill Rieger, Chief Information Officer
CHR: Jeff Hurley, Vice President Human Resources
Web address: www.flaglerhospital.org
Control: Other not–for–profit (including NFP Corporation) **Service**: General medical and surgical

Staffed Beds: 204

SAINT CLOUD—Osceola County

☒ **ORLANDO HEALTH ST. CLOUD HOSPITAL (100302)**, 2906 17th Street, Zip 34769–6099; tel. 407/892–2135, **A**1 10 **F**3 15 18 20 22 29 30 34 35 40 44 45 46 49 57 59 68 70 74 75 77 78 79 80 81 82 85 86 87 91 93 94 96 107 108 110 111 114 115 118 119 130 146 150 154 **S** Orlando Health, Orlando, FL
Primary Contact: Brian A. Wetzel, President
COO: Marc Lillis, Chief Operating Officer
CFO: Michael E. Mueller, Chief Financial Officer
CIO: James Devlin, Director Information Systems
CHR: Jennifer Harmon, Director of Human Resources
CNO: Perry Horne, Chief Nursing Officer
Web address: www.stcloudregional.com
Control: Other not–for–profit (including NFP Corporation) **Service**: General medical and surgical

Staffed Beds: 63 **Admissions**: 5793 **Census**: 56 **Outpatient Visits**: 50888 **Births**: 0 **Total Expense ($000)**: 110242 **Payroll Expense ($000)**: 39365 **Personnel**: 476

☐ **THE BLACKBERRY CENTER (104081)**, 91 Beehive Circle, Zip 34769–1432, Mailing Address: St. Cloud, tel. 321/805–5090, (Nonreporting) **A**1 10 **S** Oglethorpe Recovery and Behavioral Hospitals, Tampa, FL
Primary Contact: Rick Bennett, Director
Web address: www.blackberrycenter.com
Control: Corporation, Investor–owned (for–profit) **Service**: Psychiatric

Staffed Beds: 64

SAINT JOHNS—St. Johns County

☐ **ASCENSION ST. VINCENT's ST. JOHNS COUNTY (100361)**, 205 Trinity Way, Zip 32259–1155; tel. 904/691–1000, (Data for 360 days) **A**1 **F**3 15 18 20 29 30 34 35 37 40 45 46 47 48 49 50 57 59 60 64 65 67 68 69 70 74 75 77 78 79 81 85 87 102 107 108 110 111 115 118 119 126 130 131 146 148 149 154 156 164 167 **S** Ascension Healthcare, Saint Louis, MO
Primary Contact: Cory Darling, Chief Executive Officer
COO: Sean Mcafee, Chief Operating Officer
Web address: https://ascension.org/stjohnsfl
Control: Church operated, Nongovernment, not–for–profit **Service**: General medical and surgical

Staffed Beds: 56 **Admissions**: 1521 **Census**: 15 **Outpatient Visits**: 17591 **Births**: 0 **Total Expense ($000)**: 44841 **Payroll Expense ($000)**: 17471 **Personnel**: 202

SAINT PETERSBURG—Pinellas County

☒ **BAYFRONT HEALTH ST. PETERSBURG (100032)**, 701 Sixth Street South, Zip 33701–4891; tel. 727/823–1234, **A**1 3 5 10 19 **F**3 13 15 17 18 20 22 24 26 29 30 34 35 40 41 42 43 45 46 49 54 57 58 59 64 65 68 70 74 76 77 79 80 81 85 90 92 93 96 97 107 108 110 111 114 115 118 119 126 129 130 144 154 167 169 **S** Orlando Health, Orlando, FL
Primary Contact: John A. Moore, FACHE, President
COO: Sarah Gilbert, Chief Operating Officer and Assistant Vice President
CFO: LaTasha Barnes, Chief Financial Officer
CMO: Trina Espinola, M.D., Chief Medical Officer
CIO: Omar Gonzalez, Corporate Director Information Technology Clinical Engineering
CHR: Jim Reames, Director Human Resources
CNO: Lorraine Parker, MSN, R.N., Chief Nursing Officer and Assistant Vice President
Web address: www.bayfrontstpete.com
Control: Other not–for–profit (including NFP Corporation) **Service**: General medical and surgical

Staffed Beds: 214 **Admissions**: 15077 **Census**: 189 **Outpatient Visits**: 81577 **Births**: 3577 **Total Expense ($000)**: 341803 **Payroll Expense ($000)**: 120650 **Personnel**: 1509

Hospitals, U.S. / FLORIDA

✠ **HCA FLORIDA NORTHSIDE HOSPITAL (100238)**, 6000 49th Street North, Zip 33709–2145; tel. 727/521–4411, **A**1 3 5 10 13 19 **F**3 11 17 18 20 22 24 26 28 29 30 34 40 45 49 50 51 53 56 57 58 59 63 65 68 70 74 75 77 79 81 85 87 92 93 100 107 108 111 114 115 119 126 135 146 148 **S** HCA Healthcare, Nashville, TN
Primary Contact: Philip Marchesini, Chief Executive Officer
COO: Peter Kennedy, Chief Operating Officer
CFO: Peggy Gatliff, Chief Financial Officer
CMO: Ira Siegman, M.D., Chief Medical Officer
CIO: Kirk Hendrick, Director Information Systems
CHR: Maggie Miklos, Director Human Resources
CNO: John Polisknowski, Chief Nursing Officer
Web address: www.northsidehospital.com
Control: Corporation, Investor–owned (for–profit) **Service**: General medical and surgical

Staffed Beds: 288 **Admissions**: 10357 **Census**: 128 **Total Expense ($000)**: 182348 **Payroll Expense ($000)**: 44655 **Personnel**: 581

✠ **HCA FLORIDA PASADENA HOSPITAL (100126)**, 1501 Pasadena Avenue South, Zip 33707–3798; tel. 727/381–1000, **A**1 10 **F**3 15 18 20 22 24 28 29 34 35 40 45 50 57 58 59 60 63 64 65 68 70 74 75 77 79 81 82 84 85 86 87 90 93 96 97 107 108 110 111 115 118 119 126 130 135 146 147 148 149 154 157 167 **S** HCA Healthcare, Nashville, TN
Primary Contact: Brent Burish, Chief Executive Officer
COO: Raynard Ware, Vice President of Opeartions
CFO: Maria Caruso, Chief Financial Officer
CMO: Ron Rasmussen, M.D., Chief Medical Officer
CIO: Danny Waters, Director, Information Services
CHR: Megan Joy Whalen, Vice President, Human Resources
CNO: Susan Laber, R.N., Chief Nursing Officer
Web address: https://www.hcafloridahealthcare.com/locations/pasadena-hospital
Control: Corporation, Investor–owned (for–profit) **Service**: General medical and surgical

Staffed Beds: 307 **Admissions**: 3837 **Census**: 51 **Total Expense ($000)**: 105116 **Payroll Expense ($000)**: 27772 **Personnel**: 335

✠ **HCA FLORIDA ST. PETERSBURG HOSPITAL (100180)**, 6500 38th Avenue North, Zip 33710–1629; tel. 727/384–1414, (Nonreporting) **A**1 2 3 5 10 12 13 **S** HCA Healthcare, Nashville, TN
Primary Contact: Brent Burish, Chief Executive Officer
COO: Amrit Dhillon, Chief Operating Officer
CFO: Shawn Gregory, Chief Financial Officer
CMO: Mitchell Rubinstein, M.D., Chief Medical Officer
CHR: Jennifer B Robinson, Vice President Human Resources
CNO: JoAnne Cattell, Chief Nursing Officer
Web address: www.stpetegeneral.com
Control: Corporation, Investor–owned (for–profit) **Service**: General medical and surgical

Staffed Beds: 215

✠ **JOHNS HOPKINS ALL CHILDREN'S HOSPITAL (103300)**, 501 6th Avenue South, Zip 33701–4634; tel. 727/898–7451, **A**1 3 5 8 10 **F**3 11 12 17 18 19 20 21 22 23 24 25 26 27 29 32 34 35 36 37 40 41 43 44 45 46 47 48 49 50 54 55 57 58 59 60 61 64 65 68 72 73 74 75 77 78 79 81 82 84 85 86 87 88 89 90 92 93 96 97 100 101 102 107 108 111 114 115 116 117 118 119 126 129 130 131 132 134 135 136 137 141 142 143 146 147 148 149 154 166 167 169 **S** Johns Hopkins Health System, Baltimore, MD
Primary Contact: K. Alicia. Schulhof, President
COO: Justin Olsen, JD, FACHE, Vice President and Chief Operating Officer
CFO: Sherron Rogers, Chief Financial Officer
CMO: Michael Epstein, M.D., Senior Vice President Medical Affairs
CIO: John McLendon, Vice President and Chief Information Officer
CHR: Jay Kuhns, Vice President Human Resources
CNO: Melissa Macogay, Vice President and Chief Nursing Officer
Web address: www.allkids.org
Control: Other not–for–profit (including NFP Corporation) **Service**: Children's general medical and surgical

Staffed Beds: 259 **Admissions**: 6750 **Census**: 173 **Outpatient Visits**: 361130 **Births**: 0 **Total Expense ($000)**: 624178 **Payroll Expense ($000)**: 211417 **Personnel**: 3344

KINDRED HOSPITAL BAY AREA See Kindred Hospital–Bay Area St. Petersburg

PALMS OF PASADENA HOSPITAL See HCA Florida Pasadena Hospital

✠ **ST. ANTHONY'S HOSPITAL (100067)**, 1200 7th Ave North, Zip 33705–1388, Mailing Address: P.O. Box 12588, Zip 33733–2588; tel. 727/825–1100, **A**1 2 3 5 10 19 **F**3 6 8 9 11 12 15 17 18 20 22 26 28 29 30 31 34 35 37 40 44 45 46 47 48 49 50 51 55 57 58 59 60 64 68 70 74 75 77 78 79 81 84 85 87 93 98 100 101 102 103 107 108 110 111 115 117 118 119 121 123 124 126 130 131 132 134 135 146 148 149 154 156 157 164 167 **S** BayCare Health System, Clearwater, FL
Primary Contact: M. Scott Smith, President
CFO: Carl Tremonti, Chief Financial Officer
CMO: John Haffner, M.D., Chief Medical Officer
CIO: Tim Thompson, Senior Vice President and Chief Informatics Officer
CHR: Kristen A Betts, Director Team Resources
CNO: Thomas Doria, Vice President and Patient Services West
Web address: www.stanthonys.com/
Control: Other not–for–profit (including NFP Corporation) **Service**: General medical and surgical

Staffed Beds: 448 **Admissions**: 18881 **Census**: 248 **Outpatient Visits**: 114697 **Births**: 0 **Total Expense ($000)**: 472979 **Payroll Expense ($000)**: 166798 **Personnel**: 1898

ST. PETERSBURG GENERAL HOSPITAL See HCA Florida St. Petersburg Hospital

SANFORD—Seminole County

CENTRAL FLORIDA REGIONAL HOSPITAL See HCA Florida Lake Monroe Hospital

✠ △ **HCA FLORIDA LAKE MONROE HOSPITAL (100161)**, 1401 West Seminole Boulevard, Zip 32771–6764; tel. 407/321–4500, (Nonreporting) **A**1 3 7 10 **S** HCA Healthcare, Nashville, TN
Primary Contact: John Gerhold, Chief Executive Officer
CFO: Richard Read, Chief Financial Officer
CIO: Jerry Ballard, Director Information Systems
CHR: Linda V Smith, Vice President Human Resources
CNO: Maria Calloway, R.N., MSN, Chief Nursing Officer
Web address: https://www.hcafloridahealthcare.com/locations/lake-monroe-hospital
Control: Corporation, Investor–owned (for–profit) **Service**: General medical and surgical

Staffed Beds: 221

SARASOTA—Sarasota County

DOCTORS HOSPITAL OF SARASOTA See HCA Florida Sarasota Doctors Hospital

✠ △ **ENCOMPASS HEALTH REHABILITATION HOSPITAL OF SARASOTA (103031)**, 6400 Edgelake Drive, Zip 34240–8813; tel. 941/921–8600, (Nonreporting) **A**1 7 10 **S** Encompass Health Corporation, Birmingham, AL
Primary Contact: Marcus Braz, Chief Executive Officer
CFO: Barbara Bierut, Chief Financial Officer
CMO: Alexander De Jesus, M.D., Medical Director
CHR: Brenda Benner, Director Human Resources
Web address: www.healthsouthsarasota.com
Control: Corporation, Investor–owned (for–profit) **Service**: Rehabilitation

Staffed Beds: 96

✠ **HCA FLORIDA SARASOTA DOCTORS HOSPITAL (100166)**, 5731 Bee Ridge Road, Zip 34233–5056; tel. 941/342–1100, (Nonreporting) **A**1 3 10 **S** HCA Healthcare, Nashville, TN
Primary Contact: Robert C. Meade, Chief Executive Officer
CFO: Charles Schwaner III, Chief Financial Officer
CMO: Jennifer Bocker, M.D., Chief Medical Officer
CHR: Theresa Levering, Director Human Resources
CNO: Kathy Mitchell, R.N., Chief Nursing Officer
Web address: www.doctorsofsarasota.com
Control: Corporation, Investor–owned (for–profit) **Service**: General medical and surgical

Staffed Beds: 155

Hospital, Medicare Provider Number, Address, Telephone, Approval, Facility, and Physician Codes, Health Care System

★ American Hospital Association (AHA) membership
☐ The Joint Commission accreditation
○ Healthcare Facilities Accreditation Program
◇ DNV Healthcare Inc. accreditation
⇑ Center for Improvement in Healthcare Quality Accreditation
△ Commission on Accreditation of Rehabilitation Facilities (CARF) accreditation

Hospitals, U.S. / FLORIDA

☐ **PAM SPECIALTY HOSPITAL OF SARASOTA (102018)**, 6150 Edgelake Drive, Zip 34240–8803; tel. 941/342–3000, **A**1 10 **F**1 3 29 60 74 75 77 85 91 97 100 107 115 130 148 **S** PAM Health, Enola, PA
Primary Contact: Jacob McGuirt, Chief Executive Officer
Web address: www.lifecare-hospitals.com/hospital.php?id=23
Control: Corporation, Investor–owned (for–profit) **Service**: Acute long–term care hospital

> Staffed Beds: 40 Admissions: 516 Census: 34 Outpatient Visits: 0
> Births: 0 Total Expense ($000): 22117 Payroll Expense ($000): 9600
> Personnel: 136

SARASOTA MEMORIAL HOSPITAL See Sarasota Memorial Hospital – Sarasota

☐ △ **SARASOTA MEMORIAL HOSPITAL – SARASOTA (100087)**, 1700 South Tamiami Trail, Zip 34239–3555; tel. 941/917–9000, **A**1 2 3 5 7 8 10 **F**3 6 8 11 12 13 15 17 18 20 22 24 26 28 29 30 31 32 34 35 36 37 38 39 40 42 43 44 45 46 47 48 49 50 51 53 54 55 56 57 58 59 60 61 64 65 66 68 70 72 73 74 75 76 77 78 79 80 81 82 83 84 85 86 87 89 90 91 92 93 95 96 97 98 99 100 101 102 103 104 105 107 108 110 111 114 115 116 117 118 119 120 121 123 124 126 130 131 132 135 143 144 146 147 148 149 150 153 154 156 157 160 164 167 168 169 **S** Sarasota Memorial Health Care System, Sarasota, FL
Primary Contact: David Verinder, President & Chief Executive Officer
CFO: Bill Woeltjen, Chief Financial Officer
CMO: James Fiorica, M.D., Chief Medical Officer
CIO: Denis Baker, Chief Information Officer
CHR: Laurie Bennett, Director Human Resources
CNO: Connie Andersen, R.N., MS, Chief Nursing Officer
Web address: www.smh.com
Control: Hospital district or authority, Government, Nonfederal **Service**: General medical and surgical

> Staffed Beds: 901 Admissions: 50455 Census: 713 Outpatient Visits: 691646 Births: 4279 Total Expense ($000): 1138733 Payroll Expense ($000): 421434 Personnel: 7424

SEBASTIAN—Indian River County

☐ **SEBASTIAN RIVER MEDICAL CENTER (100217)**, 13695 North US Hwy 1, Zip 32958–3230, Mailing Address: Box 780838, Zip 32978–0838; tel. 772/589–3186, (Nonreporting) **A**1 10 19 **S** Steward Health Care System, LLC, Dallas, TX
Primary Contact: Ronald L. Bierman, President
CFO: David Callum, Chief Financial Officer
CMO: Eric Deppert, M.D., Chief Medical Officer
CHR: Kam Storey, Director Human Resources
CNO: Rebecca Wilson, Chief Nursing Officer
Web address: https://www.sebastianrivermedical.org/
Control: Corporation, Investor-owned (for-profit) **Service**: General medical and surgical

> Staffed Beds: 145

SEBRING—Highlands County

☐ **ADVENTHEALTH SEBRING (100109)**, 4200 Sun'n Lake Boulevard, Zip 33872–1986, Mailing Address: P.O. Box 9400, Zip 33871–9400; tel. 863/314–4466, (Includes ADVENTHEALTH LAKE PLACID, 1210 US 27 North, Lake Placid, Florida, Zip 33852–7948, tel. 863/465–3777; Jason Dunkel, Chief Executive Officer) **A**1 3 10 19 **F**3 11 12 13 15 17 18 20 22 24 26 28 29 30 34 35 37 40 45 46 49 50 53 54 57 58 59 60 62 64 70 75 76 78 79 81 86 87 89 107 108 110 111 114 115 116 117 118 119 120 121 123 124 126 129 130 131 132 146 147 148 149 154 156 167 169 **S** AdventHealth, Altamonte Springs, FL
Primary Contact: Jason Dunkel, Chief Executive Officer
CNO: Stacy Kreil, Chief Nursing Officer
Web address: https://www.adventhealth.com/hospital/adventhealth-sebring
Control: Church operated, Nongovernment, not–for–profit **Service**: General medical and surgical

> Staffed Beds: 204 Admissions: 12066 Census: 154 Outpatient Visits: 245031 Births: 1082 Total Expense ($000): 307979 Payroll Expense ($000): 128719 Personnel: 1455

☐ **HCA FLORIDA HIGHLANDS HOSPITAL (100049)**, 3600 South Highlands Avenue, Zip 33870–5495, Mailing Address: Drawer 2066, Zip 33871–2066; tel. 863/385–6101, **A**1 10 19 **F**3 11 12 13 15 18 20 22 24 26 28 29 34 40 45 49 50 51 57 59 64 70 76 79 81 85 87 93 97 107 108 110 114 119 124 129 135 146 **S** HCA Healthcare, Nashville, TN
Primary Contact: Joe Gleason, Chief Executive Officer
CFO: Paul Damron, Chief Financial Officer
CIO: Nate Johnson, Chief Information Officer
CHR: Brenda Dane, Director, Human Resources
CNO: Adam Kless, Chief Nursing Officer
Web address: www.highlandsregional.com
Control: Corporation, Investor-owned (for-profit) **Service**: General medical and surgical

> Staffed Beds: 126 Admissions: 3991 Census: 45 Total Expense ($000): 86315 Payroll Expense ($000): 26556 Personnel: 324

SOUTH MIAMI—Miami–Dade County

☐ **LARKIN COMMUNITY HOSPITAL–SOUTH MIAMI CAMPUS (100181)**, 7031 SW 62nd Avenue, Zip 33143–4781; tel. 305/284–7500, **A**1 3 5 10 12 13 **F**18 26 29 30 31 34 35 40 45 46 47 48 49 50 54 56 57 58 62 68 70 74 75 77 78 79 81 82 84 85 87 91 93 98 99 100 101 102 103 104 105 107 111 115 116 117 118 119 124 126 130 135 143 148 149 153 154 157 163 164 165 167
Primary Contact: Nicholas Torres, Chief Executive Officer
COO: George J Michel, Chief Operating Officer
CFO: Edgar Castillo, Chief Financial Officer
CMO: Mario Almeida–Suarez, M.D., Chief of Staff
CIO: Orlando Suarez, Director Information Technology
CHR: Carolina Pena, Assistant Director Administrator
CNO: Mercedes Perez, Vice President Nursing
Web address: www.larkinhospital.com
Control: Individual, Investor-owned (for-profit) **Service**: General medical and surgical

> Staffed Beds: 146 Admissions: 7147 Census: 76 Outpatient Visits: 10145 Births: 0 Total Expense ($000): 105364 Payroll Expense ($000): 51744
> Personnel: 959

SPRING HILL—Hernando County

BAYFRONT HEALTH SPRING HILL See Tampa General Hospital Spring Hill

ST AUGUSTINE—St. Johns County

☐ **ENCOMPASS HEALTH REHABILITATION HOSPITAL OF ST. AUGUSTINE (103049)**, 65 Silver Lane, Zip 32084–3922; tel. 904/640–2000, (Nonreporting) **A**1 **S** Encompass Health Corporation, Birmingham, AL
Primary Contact: Thomas Laughlin, Chief Executive Officer
Web address: https://encompasshealth.com/locations/staugustinerehab
Control: Corporation, Investor-owned (for-profit) **Service**: Rehabilitation

> Staffed Beds: 40

STUART—Martin County

☒ **CLEVELAND CLINIC MARTIN NORTH HOSPITAL (100044)**, 200 SE Hospital Avenue, Zip 34994–2346, Mailing Address: P.O. Box 9010, Zip 34995–9010; tel. 772/287–5200, (Includes CLEVELAND CLINIC MARTIN SOUTH HOSPITAL, 2100 SE Salerno Road, Stuart, Florida, Zip 34997, tel. 772/223–2300; Mark E Robitaille, FACHE, President and Chief Executive Officer; CLEVELAND CLINIC TRADITION HOSPITAL, 10000 SW Innovation Way, Port St Lucie, Florida, Zip 34987–2111, tel. 772/345–8100; Mark E Robitaille, FACHE, President and Chief Executive Officer) **A**1 2 10 **F**3 7 8 12 13 15 17 18 20 22 24 26 28 29 30 31 32 34 35 36 37 40 42 45 46 47 48 49 50 51 53 54 55 57 58 59 60 64 65 70 72 74 75 76 77 78 79 81 82 84 85 86 87 89 91 92 93 97 107 108 109 110 111 114 115 116 117 118 119 120 121 123 124 126 129 130 131 132 135 143 144 146 147 148 149 154 156 157 167 169 **S** Cleveland Clinic Health System, Cleveland, OH
Primary Contact: Rishi Singh, President
CFO: Chuck Cleaver, Vice President and Chief Financial Officer
CIO: Edmund Collins, Chief Information Officer
CHR: Angie L Metcalf, Vice President and Chief Human Resource Officer
CNO: Mary Elizabeth Flippo, R.N., MSN, Vice President and Chief Nursing Officer
Web address: https://my.clevelandclinic.org/florida/locations/martin-north-hospital
Control: Other not-for-profit (including NFP Corporation) **Service**: General medical and surgical

> Staffed Beds: 500 Admissions: 33508 Census: 415 Outpatient Visits: 155899 Births: 2181 Total Expense ($000): 669465 Payroll Expense ($000): 266983 Personnel: 4525

☒ **ENCOMPASS HEALTH REHABILITATION HOSPITAL, AN AFFILIATE OF MARTIN HEALTH (103044)**, 5850 SE Community Drive, Zip 34997–6420; tel. 772/324–3500, (Nonreporting) **A**1 10 **S** Encompass Health Corporation, Birmingham, AL
Primary Contact: Ivette Miranda, Chief Executive Officer
CFO: Dawn Salas, Controller
CMO: Stephen L Chastain, M.D., Chief Medical Officer
CHR: Donna Holder–Hooper, Chief Human Resource Officer
CNO: Charmaine Blanchard, Chief Nursing Officer
Web address: www.healthsouthmartin.com
Control: Corporation, Investor-owned (for-profit) **Service**: Rehabilitation

> Staffed Beds: 34

MARTIN MEMORIAL HOSPITAL SOUTH See Cleveland Clinic Martin South Hospital

Hospitals, U.S. / FLORIDA

SUN CITY CENTER—Hillsborough County

HCA FLORIDA SOUTH SHORE HOSPITAL (100259), 4016 Sun City Center Blvd, Zip 33573–5298; tel. 813/634–3301, **A**1 10 **F**3 15 18 20 24 29 30 31 34 35 37 40 45 49 50 57 59 64 68 70 74 75 77 78 79 81 82 85 86 87 93 107 108 110 111 118 119 132 146 148 149 **S** HCA Healthcare, Nashville, TN
Primary Contact: Cathy Edmisten, R.N., FACHE, Chief Executive Officer
CFO: Warren Pate, Chief Financial Officer
CHR: Stacie Novosel, Vice President, Human Resources
CNO: Marcy Frisina, Chief Nursing Officer
Web address: https://www.hcafloridahealthcare.com/locations/south-shore-hospital
Control: Corporation, Investor–owned (for–profit) **Service**: General medical and surgical

Staffed Beds: 138 **Admissions**: 6221 **Census**: 73 **Total Expense ($000)**: 95788 **Payroll Expense ($000)**: 29267 **Personnel**: 370

SOUTH BAY HOSPITAL See HCA Florida South Shore Hospital

SUNRISE—Broward County

ENCOMPASS HEALTH REHABILITATION HOSPITAL OF SUNRISE (103028), 4399 North Nob Hill Road, Zip 33351–5899; tel. 954/749–0300, **A**1 3 10 **F**3 29 90 **S** Encompass Health Corporation, Birmingham, AL
Primary Contact: Randy Gross, Chief Executive Officer
CFO: Ruth Goodstein, Controller
CMO: Scott Tannenbaum, M.D., Medical Director
CIO: Angela Manning, Director Health Information Services
CHR: Barbara Dunkiel, Director Human Resources
CNO: Omaira D. Riano, Chief Nursing Officer
Web address: https://encompasshealth.com/locations/sunriserehab
Control: Corporation, Investor–owned (for–profit) **Service**: Rehabilitation

Staffed Beds: 126 **Admissions**: 2407 **Census**: 86 **Total Expense ($000)**: 41493 **Payroll Expense ($000)**: 21152 **Personnel**: 295

TALLAHASSEE—Leon County

CAPITAL REGIONAL MEDICAL CENTER See HCA Florida Capital Hospital

EASTSIDE PSYCHIATRIC HOSPITAL (104059), 2634 Capital Circle NE, Zip 32308–4106; tel. 850/523–3333, (Nonreporting) **A**10
Primary Contact: Jay A. Reeve, Ph.D., President and Chief Executive Officer
COO: Sue Conger, Chief Operating Officer
CFO: Virginia Kelly, Chief Financial Officer
CMO: Ludmila de Faria, M.D., Chief Medical Officer
CIO: Thad Moorer, Chief Information Officer
CHR: Candy Landry, Chief Human Resource Officer
CNO: Judy Goreau, R.N., Director of Nursing
Web address: www.apalacheecenter.org
Control: Other not–for–profit (including NFP Corporation) **Service**: Psychiatric

Staffed Beds: 24

ENCOMPASS HEALTH REHABILITATION HOSPITAL OF TALLAHASSEE (103033), 1675 Riggins Road, Zip 32308–5315; tel. 850/656–4800, (Nonreporting) **A**1 10 **S** Encompass Health Corporation, Birmingham, AL
Primary Contact: William D. Heath, Chief Executive Officer
CFO: Jennifer Spooner, Controller
CMO: Robert Rowland, M.D., Medical Director
CIO: Michael Spangler, Health Information Management Services Supervisor
CHR: Carol Bugayong, Human Resources Director
CNO: Elizabeth Squires, R.N., Chief Nursing Officer
Web address: www.healthsouthtallahassee.com
Control: Corporation, Investor–owned (for–profit) **Service**: Rehabilitation

Staffed Beds: 76

HCA FLORIDA CAPITAL HOSPITAL (100254), 2626 Capital Medical Boulevard, Zip 32308–4499; tel. 850/325–5000, (Nonreporting) **A**1 2 3 10 **S** HCA Healthcare, Nashville, TN
Primary Contact: J. Christopher. Mosley, Chief Executive Officer
CFO: Francisca Thai, Chief Financial Officer
CMO: Steve West, M.D., Chief Medical Officer
CIO: Robert A Steed, Director Information Systems
CHR: Louise Truitt, Vice President Human Resources
Web address: https://www.hcafloridahealthcare.com/locations/capital-hospital
Control: Individual, Investor–owned (for–profit) **Service**: General medical and surgical

Staffed Beds: 270

SELECT SPECIALTY HOSPITAL–TALLAHASSEE (102020), 1554 Surgeons Drive, Zip 32308–4631; tel. 850/219–6950, (Nonreporting) **A**1 10 **S** Select Medical Corporation, Mechanicsburg, PA
Primary Contact: Shawn Dilmore, Chief Executive Officer
Web address: www.tallahassee.selectspecialtyhospitals.com/
Control: Corporation, Investor–owned (for–profit) **Service**: Acute long–term care hospital

Staffed Beds: 29

TALLAHASSEE MEMORIAL HEALTHCARE (100135), 1300 Miccosukee Road, Zip 32308–5054; tel. 850/431–1155, (Total facility includes 42 beds in nursing home-type unit) **A**1 2 3 5 10 **F**3 5 8 11 12 15 17 18 19 20 22 24 26 28 29 30 31 34 35 37 40 42 43 46 47 48 49 50 51 53 54 55 56 57 58 59 60 61 62 64 65 68 70 72 73 74 75 76 77 78 79 80 81 82 84 85 86 87 88 89 91 93 96 97 98 99 100 102 103 104 107 108 110 113 114 115 117 118 119 120 121 123 124 126 127 128 129 130 131 132 135 143 144 146 147 148 149 154 155 156 164 167
Primary Contact: G. Mark. O'Bryant, President and Chief Executive Officer
COO: Jason H Moore, Vice President and Chief Operating Officer
CFO: William A Giudice, Vice President and Chief Financial Officer
CMO: Dean Watson, M.D., Chief Medical Officer
CIO: Don Lindsey, Vice President and Chief Information Officer
CHR: Steven W Adriaanse, Vice President and Chief Human Resources Officer
Web address: www.tmh.org
Control: Other not–for–profit (including NFP Corporation) **Service**: General medical and surgical

Staffed Beds: 495 **Admissions**: 29260 **Census**: 416 **Outpatient Visits**: 982564 **Births**: 3081 **Total Expense ($000)**: 975511 **Payroll Expense ($000)**: 380589 **Personnel**: 7472

TAMARAC—Broward County

HCA FLORIDA WOODMONT HOSPITAL (100224), 7201 North University Drive, Zip 33321–2996; tel. 954/721–2200, (Includes UNIVERSITY PAVILION, 7425 North University Drive, Tamarac, Florida, Zip 33328, tel. 305/722–9933) (Nonreporting) **A**1 3 5 10 **S** HCA Healthcare, Nashville, TN
CFO: Aurelio Gonzalez, Chief Financial Officer
CMO: Ran Abrahamy, M.D., Chief of Staff
CIO: Tom Scharff, Director Information Services
Web address: https://www.hcafloridahealthcare.com/locations/woodmont-hospital
Control: Corporation, Investor–owned (for–profit) **Service**: General medical and surgical

Staffed Beds: 317

UNIVERSITY HOSPITAL AND MEDICAL CENTER See HCA Florida Woodmont Hospital

TAMPA—Hillsborough County

ADVENTHEALTH CARROLLWOOD (100069), 7171 North Dale Mabry Highway, Zip 33614–2665; tel. 813/932–2222, **A**1 3 10 **F**3 12 15 18 20 22 26 29 30 34 35 40 41 42 44 45 46 47 48 49 50 51 57 58 59 60 65 68 70 71 74 75 79 81 82 87 107 108 110 111 115 119 126 130 133 143 145 146 147 148 149 154 157 167 **S** AdventHealth, Altamonte Springs, FL
Primary Contact: Joe Johnson, FACHE, President and Chief Executive Officer
COO: Mary C Whillock, R.N., MS, Associate Nursing Officer and Chief Operating Officer
CFO: Chris Sauder, Vice President and Chief Financial Officer
CNO: Deborah W Kumar, MSN, Chief Nursing Officer
Web address: https://www.adventhealth.com/hospital/adventhealth-carrollwood
Control: Church operated, Nongovernment, not–for–profit **Service**: General medical and surgical

Staffed Beds: 114 **Admissions**: 7330 **Census**: 80 **Outpatient Visits**: 75443 **Births**: 0 **Total Expense ($000)**: 215619 **Payroll Expense ($000)**: 76654 **Personnel**: 845

Hospital, Medicare Provider Number, Address, Telephone, Approval, Facility, and Physician Codes, Health Care System

★ American Hospital Association (AHA) membership
□ The Joint Commission accreditation
○ Healthcare Facilities Accreditation Program
◇ DNV Healthcare Inc. accreditation
⇑ Center for Improvement in Healthcare Quality Accreditation
△ Commission on Accreditation of Rehabilitation Facilities (CARF) accreditation

Hospitals, U.S. / FLORIDA

★ △ ⇧ **ADVENTHEALTH TAMPA (100173)**, 3100 East Fletcher Avenue, Zip 33613–4688; tel. 813/971–6000, **A**2 3 5 7 10 21 **F**3 11 12 13 15 17 18 19 20 21 22 23 24 25 26 27 28 29 30 31 33 34 35 37 40 41 42 44 45 46 47 48 49 50 54 57 58 59 60 63 64 65 68 70 71 72 74 75 76 77 78 79 80 81 82 83 84 85 86 87 88 89 90 91 92 93 96 107 108 109 110 111 112 114 115 116 117 118 119 120 121 122 123 124 125 129 130 132 135 143 144 146 147 148 149 152 154 156 164 167 169 **S** AdventHealth, Altamonte Springs, FL
Primary Contact: Bruce Bergherm, Chief Executive Officer
COO: Dick Tibbits, Vice President and Chief Operating Officer
CFO: Tyson Davis, Chief Financial Officer
CMO: Brad Bjornstad, M.D., Vice President and Chief Medical Officer
CHR: Dick Tibbits, Vice President and Chief Operating Officer
Web address: www.floridahospital.com/tampa
Control: Other not–for–profit (including NFP Corporation) **Service:** General medical and surgical

Staffed Beds: 626 **Admissions:** 26881 **Census:** 394 **Outpatient Visits:** 261072 **Births:** 2227 **Total Expense ($000):** 819954 **Payroll Expense ($000):** 252944 **Personnel:** 3223

H. LEE MOFFITT CANCER CENTER AND RESEARCH INSTITUTE (100271), 12902 Magnolia Drive, Zip 33612–9497; tel. 813/745–4673, **A**1 2 3 5 10 **F**3 8 15 26 29 30 31 34 35 36 37 38 44 45 46 47 49 50 54 55 56 57 58 59 64 68 70 71 74 75 77 78 79 80 81 82 84 85 86 87 91 92 93 94 96 97 100 101 104 107 108 110 111 114 115 116 117 118 119 120 121 123 124 126 130 132 134 135 136 143 144 145 146 147 148 149 154 164 167 **P**6
Primary Contact: Patrick Hwu, M.D., President and Chief Executive Officer
COO: Sabi Singh, Executive Vice President and Chief Operating Officer
CFO: Yvette Tremonti, Chief Financial Officer
CMO: Bob Keenan, Chief Medical Officer
CIO: Dave Summitt, Chief Information Security Officer
CNO: Jane Fusilero, Vice President Chief Nursing Officer
Web address: www.moffitt.org
Control: Other not–for–profit (including NFP Corporation) **Service:** Cancer

Staffed Beds: 217 **Admissions:** 10962 **Census:** 188 **Outpatient Visits:** 618616 **Births:** 0 **Total Expense ($000):** 2195017 **Payroll Expense ($000):** 819402 **Personnel:** 9187

HCA FLORIDA WEST TAMPA HOSPITAL (100206), 2901 Swann Avenue, Zip 33609–4057; tel. 813/873–6400, (Includes TAMPA COMMUNITY HOSPITAL, 6001 Webb Road, Tampa, Florida, Zip 33615–3291, tel. 813/888–7060) (Nonreporting) **A**1 5 10 **S** HCA Healthcare, Nashville, TN
Primary Contact: Sonia I. Wellman, Chief Executive Officer
CFO: Shelley V Kolseth, Chief Financial Officer
CMO: Christos Politis, M.D., Chief Medical Officer
CIO: John Riton, Director Information Services
Web address: www.memorialhospitaltampa.com
Control: Corporation, Investor–owned (for–profit) **Service:** General medical and surgical

Staffed Beds: 384

△ **JAMES A. HALEY VETERANS' HOSPITAL–TAMPA**, 13000 Bruce B Downs Boulevard, Zip 33612–4745; tel. 813/972–2000, (Total facility includes 64 beds in nursing home–type unit) **A**1 3 5 7 8 **F**3 5 9 12 15 17 18 20 22 24 26 28 29 30 31 33 34 35 36 38 39 40 45 46 47 48 49 50 51 53 54 55 56 57 58 59 60 61 62 63 64 65 70 71 74 75 77 78 79 80 81 82 83 86 87 90 91 92 93 94 95 96 97 98 100 101 102 104 105 107 108 109 110 111 113 114 115 116 117 118 119 120 121 123 126 127 128 129 130 131 132 135 143 144 146 147 148 149 152 153 154 156 157 158 164 167 168 169 **S** Department of Veterans Affairs, Washington, DC
Primary Contact: David K. Dunning, Medical Center Director
CFO: Robert Konkel, Manager Finance
CMO: Edward Cutolo, M.D., Jr, Chief of Staff
CIO: Jose Seymour, Chief Information Resource Management
CHR: Andrew Sutton, Chief, Human Resources Management Service
CNO: Laureen Doloresco, R.N., Associate Director for Patient Care and Nursing Services
Web address: www.tampa.va.gov/
Control: Veterans Affairs, Government, federal **Service:** General medical and surgical

Staffed Beds: 493 **Admissions:** 10203 **Census:** 330 **Outpatient Visits:** 1647655 **Births:** 0

KINDRED HOSPITAL BAY AREA–TAMPA (102009), 4555 South Manhattan Avenue, Zip 33611–2397; tel. 813/839–6341, (Includes KINDRED HOSPITAL–BAY AREA ST. PETERSBURG, 3030 Sixth Street South, Saint Petersburg, Florida, Zip 33705–3720, tel. 727/894–8719; Paul Schrank, Chief Executive Officer) **A**1 10 **F**1 3 18 28 29 30 34 56 57 59 68 74 75 82 84 85 87 100 119 **S** ScionHealth, Louisville, KY
Primary Contact: Jeffrey Harrison, Market Chief Executive Officer
CFO: Frank Billy, Chief Financial Officer
CHR: Deborah Basria, Human Resources Payroll Administrator
Web address: www.khtampa.com/
Control: Corporation, Investor–owned (for–profit) **Service:** Acute long–term care hospital

Staffed Beds: 73 **Admissions:** 324 **Census:** 40 **Total Expense ($000):** 33048 **Payroll Expense ($000):** 11469 **Personnel:** 141

KINDRED HOSPITAL CENTRAL TAMPA (102013), 4801 North Howard Avenue, Zip 33603–1411; tel. 813/874–7575, **A**1 10 **F**1 3 29 60 65 67 68 70 75 77 82 84 86 87 90 91 94 96 97 100 107 114 119 128 130 143 148 149 154 164 **P**5 **S** ScionHealth, Louisville, KY
Primary Contact: Amy Kendall, Chief Executive Officer
CFO: John Miner, Chief Financial Officer
Web address: www.kindredcentraltampa.com/
Control: Corporation, Investor–owned (for–profit) **Service:** Acute long–term care hospital

Staffed Beds: 102 **Admissions:** 538 **Census:** 51 **Total Expense ($000):** 41620 **Payroll Expense ($000):** 15601 **Personnel:** 186

ST. JOSEPH'S CHILDREN'S HOSPITAL OF TAMPA See St. Joseph's Children's Hospital

ST. JOSEPH'S HOSPITAL (100075), 3001 West Martin Luther King Jr. Boulevard, Zip 33607–6387, Mailing Address: P.O. Box 4227, Zip 33677–4227; tel. 813/870–4000, (Includes ST. JOSEPH'S CHILDREN'S HOSPITAL, 3001 Dr Martin Luther King Jr Boulevard, Tampa, Florida, Zip 33607, tel. 813/554–8500; Sarah Naumowich, President; ST. JOSEPH'S HOSPITAL – NORTH, 4211 Van Dyke Road, Lutz, Florida, Zip 33558–8005, tel. 813/443–7000; Paula McGinnis, Chief Executive Officer; ST. JOSEPH'S HOSPITAL BEHAVIORAL HEALTH CENTER, 4918 North Habana Avenue, Tampa, Florida, Zip 33614–6815, tel. 813/870–4300; Kimberly Guy, President; ST. JOSEPH'S HOSPITAL–SOUTH, 6901 Simmons Loop, Riverview, Florida, Zip 33578–9498, tel. 813/302–8000; Patrick Downes, President; ST. JOSEPH'S WOMEN'S HOSPITAL, 3030 West Dr Martin L King Boulevard, Tampa, Florida, Zip 33607–6394, tel. 813/872–2950; Sarah Naumowich, President) **A**1 2 3 5 10 19 **F**3 7 11 12 13 15 17 18 19 20 21 22 23 24 25 26 27 28 29 30 31 32 33 34 35 36 37 40 41 43 44 45 46 48 49 50 51 57 58 59 60 61 64 65 66 68 70 71 72 73 74 75 76 77 78 79 81 82 84 85 86 87 88 89 92 93 94 98 99 100 101 102 103 107 108 110 111 112 114 115 116 117 118 119 120 121 122 124 126 127 129 130 131 132 134 135 143 145 146 147 148 149 150 154 156 157 160 161 164 165 167 169 **S** BayCare Health System, Clearwater, FL
Primary Contact: Philip Minden, President
CFO: Ron Beamon, Chief Financial Officer
CMO: Peter Charvat, M.D., Chief Medical Officer
CIO: Tim Thompson, Senior Vice President and Chief Information Officer
CHR: Kristen A Betts, Director Team Resources
CNO: Joanne Mayer
Web address: www.sjbhealth.org
Control: Other not–for–profit (including NFP Corporation) **Service:** General medical and surgical

Staffed Beds: 1367 **Admissions:** 54802 **Census:** 756 **Outpatient Visits:** 628240 **Births:** 6835 **Total Expense ($000):** 1498018 **Payroll Expense ($000):** 533626 **Personnel:** 6126

ST. JOSEPH'S WOMEN'S HOSPITAL – TAMPA See St. Joseph's Women's Hospital

△ **TAMPA GENERAL HOSPITAL (100128)**, 1 Tampa General Circle, Zip 33606–3571, Mailing Address: P.O. Box 1289, Zip 33601–1289; tel. 813/844–7000, (Includes MUMA CHILDREN'S HOSPITAL AT TGH, 1 Tampa General Circle, Tampa, Florida, Zip 33606–3571, tel. 813/844–7000) **A**1 2 3 5 7 8 10 19 **F**3 4 7 8 9 11 12 13 15 16 17 18 19 20 22 24 26 28 29 30 31 32 34 35 36 37 38 39 40 41 42 43 44 45 46 47 48 49 50 52 53 54 55 56 57 58 59 60 61 62 63 64 65 66 68 69 70 71 72 73 74 75 76 77 78 79 80 81 82 83 84 85 86 87 88 89 90 91 92 93 94 95 96 97 99 100 101 102 103 107 108 109 110 111 112 114 115 116 117 118 119 120 121 123 124 126 129 130 132 134 135 136 137 138 139 140 141 142 143 144 145 146 147 148 149 150 154 155 156 157 160 162 163 164 165 167 168 169
Primary Contact: John D. Couris, Chief Executive Officer
COO: Kelly Cullen, R.N., Executive Vice President and Chief Operating Officer
CFO: Mark A Runyon, Chief Financial Officer
CMO: Peggy M. Duggan, M.D., Executive Vice President and Chief Medical Officer
CIO: Scott Arnold, Senior Vice President Information Systems
CHR: Qualenta Forrest, Executive Vice President, Chief People and Talent Officer
CNO: Annmarie Chavarria, Senior Vice President and Chief Nursing Officer
Web address: www.tgh.org
Control: Other not–for–profit (including NFP Corporation) **Service:** General medical and surgical

Staffed Beds: 1041 **Admissions:** 58426 **Census:** 868 **Outpatient Visits:** 750667 **Births:** 7274 **Total Expense ($000):** 2524343 **Payroll Expense ($000):** 823935 **Personnel:** 13161

TAMPA GENERAL HOSPITAL CHILDREN'S MEDICAL CENTER See Muma Children's Hospital At Tgh

TOWN AND COUNTRY HOSPITAL See Tampa Community Hospital

Hospitals, U.S. / FLORIDA

TARPON SPRINGS—Pinellas County

✠ **ADVENTHEALTH NORTH PINELLAS (100055)**, 1395 South Pinellas Avenue, Zip 34689–3790; tel. 727/942–5000, **A**1 5 10 **F**3 11 15 17 18 20 22 26 28 29 30 31 34 35 37 38 40 42 45 46 49 50 51 54 56 57 59 64 65 68 70 74 75 78 79 81 85 87 91 97 107 108 110 111 114 115 119 126 128 130 132 146 149 154 167 **S** AdventHealth, Altamonte Springs, FL
Primary Contact: Ryan Quattlebaum, President and Chief Executive Officer
CFO: Caleb Heinrich, Chief Financial Officer
CMO: Michael Longley, M.D., Chief Medical Officer
CIO: Brett Peterson, Director of Information Services
CHR: Vernon Elarbee, Director of Human Resources
CNO: Jennifer Segur, DNP, Chief Nursing Officer and Chief Clinical Officer
Web address: www.fhnorthpinellas.com/
Control: Church operated, Nongovernment, not–for–profit **Service:** General medical and surgical

Staffed Beds: 168 **Admissions:** 6790 **Census:** 99 **Total Expense ($000):** 170404 **Payroll Expense ($000):** 59941 **Personnel:** 777

TAVARES—Lake County

✠ **ADVENTHEALTH WATERMAN (100057)**, 1000 Waterman Way, Zip 32778–5266; tel. 352/253–3333, **A**1 2 10 **F**3 11 13 15 17 18 20 22 24 26 28 29 30 31 32 34 35 37 40 41 45 46 47 49 50 54 57 59 62 64 66 70 74 75 76 77 78 79 81 84 85 86 87 89 90 93 96 107 108 110 111 115 116 117 118 119 120 121 123 124 126 129 130 132 143 146 147 148 149 154 156 157 167 169 **P**8 **S** AdventHealth, Altamonte Springs, FL
Primary Contact: Abel Biri, Chief Executive Officer
COO: Anita Young, Chief Operating Officer
CFO: Terri Warren, Chief Financial Officer
CMO: Vinay Mehindru, M.D., Vice President/Chief Medical Officer
CHR: Madge Springer, Director Human Resources
CNO: Michael Stimson, Chief Nursing Officer
Web address: www.fhwat.org
Control: Church operated, Nongovernment, not–for–profit **Service:** General medical and surgical

Staffed Beds: 300 **Admissions:** 17996 **Census:** 231 **Outpatient Visits:** 142171 **Births:** 600 **Total Expense ($000):** 390058 **Payroll Expense ($000):** 139365 **Personnel:** 1914

✠ **PAM REHABILITATION HOSPITAL OF TAVARES (103056)**, 1730 Mayo Drive, Zip 32778–4308; tel. 352/525–3001, (Data for 320 days) **A**1 10 **F**3 18 28 29 60 64 79 82 90 93 148 154 **S** PAM Health, Enola, PA
Primary Contact: Jacob McGuirt, Chief Executive Officer
CMO: Kareen Velez, M.D., Medical Director
CHR: Stephanie Fuchsel, Human Resources Director
CNO: Denise Mayer, MSN, R.N., Chief Nursing Officer
Web address: https://pamhealth.com/facilities/find-facility/rehabilitation-hospitals/pam-health-rehabilitation-hospital-tavares
Control: Individual, Investor–owned (for–profit) **Service:** Rehabilitation

Staffed Beds: 42 **Admissions:** 502 **Census:** 19 **Outpatient Visits:** 731 **Births:** 0 **Total Expense ($000):** 14082 **Payroll Expense ($000):** 6076 **Personnel:** 119

TAVERNIER—Monroe County

✠ **BAPTIST HEALTH SOUTH FLORIDA, MARINERS HOSPITAL (101313)**, 91500 Overseas Highway, Zip 33070–2547; tel. 305/434–3000, **A**1 10 18 **F**3 15 18 28 29 30 31 34 35 40 44 45 50 51 53 59 64 68 70 74 75 77 78 79 81 84 85 87 93 102 107 108 110 111 114 115 119 129 130 131 132 133 135 141 145 146 148 149 154 156 164 **S** Baptist Health South Florida, Coral Gables, FL
Primary Contact: Drew Grossman, Chief Executive Officer
CFO: Patti Boylan, Assistant Vice President, Finance (Controller)
CMO: Brian Magrane, M.D., Chief Medical Officer
CNO: Cheryl Cottrell, R.N., Vice President and Chief Nursing Officer
Web address: www.baptisthealth.net/en/facilities/mariners-hospital/Pages/default.aspx
Control: Other not–for–profit (including NFP Corporation) **Service:** General medical and surgical

Staffed Beds: 25 **Admissions:** 438 **Census:** 4 **Outpatient Visits:** 33302 **Births:** 0 **Total Expense ($000):** 62835 **Payroll Expense ($000):** 21139 **Personnel:** 224

THE VILLAGES—Sumter County

✠ △ **UF HEALTH THE VILLAGES HOSPITAL (100290)**, 1451 El Camino Real, Zip 32159–0041; tel. 352/751–8000, **A**1 2 7 10 **F**3 11 15 18 20 22 24 26 28 29 30 31 34 35 40 42 45 49 51 57 59 64 68 70 74 75 77 78 79 81 84 85 87 90 92 93 96 97 107 108 111 114 115 119 125 126 130 132 135 146 147 149 150 154 156 167 **P**1 **S** UF Health Shands, Gainesville, FL
Primary Contact: Heather Long, R.N., Senior Vice President and Chief Operating Officer
CFO: Diane P Harden, Senior Vice President and Chief Financial Officer
CHR: Amie A. Richason, Vice President Human Resources
CNO: Mary Jane Curry–Pelyak, R.N., Vice President and Chief Clinical Officer
Web address: www.cfhalliance.org
Control: Other not–for–profit (including NFP Corporation) **Service:** General medical and surgical

Staffed Beds: 307 **Admissions:** 12504 **Census:** 206 **Total Expense ($000):** 214194 **Payroll Expense ($000):** 96044 **Personnel:** 1029

TITUSVILLE—Brevard County

☐ **PALM POINT BEHAVIORAL HEALTH (104082)**, 2355 Truman Scarborough Way, Zip 32796–1310; tel. 321/603–6550, (Nonreporting) **A**1 10
Primary Contact: Thomas J. Mahle, Chief Executive Officer
Web address: www.palmpointbehavioral.com
Control: Corporation, Investor–owned (for–profit) **Service:** Psychiatric

Staffed Beds: 74

☐ **PARRISH MEDICAL CENTER (100028)**, 951 North Washington Avenue, Zip 32796–2163; tel. 321/268–6111, **A**1 2 5 10 **F**11 13 15 18 20 22 24 26 28 29 30 34 35 37 40 45 46 50 51 53 56 57 58 59 60 62 68 70 74 75 77 78 79 81 82 86 87 92 93 97 107 110 111 112 114 115 116 117 119 120 126 129 131 143 146 147 148 149 154 156 157 169
Primary Contact: George Mikitarian Jr, FACHE, President and Chief Executive Officer
CMO: Lisa Alexanda, M.D., Vice President Medical Affairs
CIO: William Moore, Chief Information Officer
Web address: www.parrishmed.com
Control: Hospital district or authority, Government, Nonfederal **Service:** General medical and surgical

Staffed Beds: 208 **Admissions:** 4426 **Census:** 59 **Outpatient Visits:** 34007 **Births:** 519 **Total Expense ($000):** 145981 **Payroll Expense ($000):** 50123 **Personnel:** 863

TRINITY—Pasco County

✠ **HCA FLORIDA TRINITY HOSPITAL (100191)**, 9330 State Road 54, Zip 34655–1808; tel. 727/834–4900, **A**1 2 3 5 10 **F**8 11 13 15 18 20 22 26 29 30 31 34 35 38 40 45 46 47 48 49 57 59 60 67 68 70 74 75 76 77 78 79 80 81 82 84 85 86 87 93 94 98 102 103 107 108 110 111 119 126 130 132 135 146 147 148 **S** HCA Healthcare, Nashville, TN
Primary Contact: Michael Irvin, Chief Executive Officer
COO: Matthew Johnston, Chief Operating Officer
CFO: Michael Wyers, Chief Financial Officer
CMO: Corbi Milligan, M.D., Chief Medical Officer
CIO: Kurt Hornung, Director
CHR: Christena Miano, Vice President, Human Resources
CNO: Jelinda Doris Gose, MSN, R.N., Chief Nursing Officer
Web address: https://www.hcafloridahealthcare.com/locations/trinity-hospital
Control: Corporation, Investor–owned (for–profit) **Service:** General medical and surgical

Staffed Beds: 288 **Admissions:** 15626 **Census:** 167 **Total Expense ($000):** 281594 **Payroll Expense ($000):** 85451 **Personnel:** 1128

MEDICAL CENTER OF TRINITY See HCA Florida Trinity Hospital, Trinity

---

Hospital, Medicare Provider Number, Address, Telephone, Approval, Facility, and Physician Codes, Health Care System

★ American Hospital Association (AHA) membership ○ Healthcare Facilities Accreditation Program ⇧ Center for Improvement in Healthcare Quality Accreditation
☐ The Joint Commission accreditation ◇ DNV Healthcare Inc. accreditation △ Commission on Accreditation of Rehabilitation Facilities (CARF) accreditation

Hospitals, U.S. / FLORIDA

VERO BEACH—Indian River County

☒ **CLEVELAND CLINIC INDIAN RIVER HOSPITAL (100105)**, 1000 36th Street, Zip 32960-6592; tel. 772/567-4311, (Includes BEHAVIORAL HEALTH CENTER, 1190 37th Street, Vero Beach, Florida, Zip 32960-6507, tel. 772/563-4666; Jeffrey L Susi, President and Chief Executive Officer) **A**1 2 10 19 **F**3 11 12 13 15 17 18 20 22 24 26 28 29 30 31 34 35 37 40 44 45 46 47 48 49 50 51 55 57 58 59 60 61 64 70 74 75 76 77 78 79 80 81 82 84 85 87 89 91 92 93 96 97 98 99 100 101 102 103 104 107 108 110 111 114 115 116 117 118 119 120 121 124 126 129 130 131 132 135 144 146 147 148 153 154 167 168 169 **S** Cleveland Clinic Health System, Cleveland, OH
Primary Contact: David J. Peter, M.D., Interim President and Chief Medical Officer
CFO: Greg Gardner, Senior Vice President and Chief Financial Officer
CMO: David J. Peter, M.D., Vice President and Chief Medical Officer
CIO: William Neil, Vice President and Chief Information Officer
Web address: https://my.clevelandclinic.org/florida/locations/indian-river-hospital
Control: Other not-for-profit (including NFP Corporation) **Service**: General medical and surgical

Staffed Beds: 223 **Admissions**: 16750 **Census**: 213 **Outpatient Visits**: 276060 **Births**: 829 **Total Expense ($000)**: 457796 **Payroll Expense ($000)**: 227362 **Personnel**: 1954

☒ **ENCOMPASS HEALTH REHABILITATION HOSPITAL OF TREASURE COAST (103032)**, 1600 37th Street, Zip 32960-4863; tel. 772/778-2100, (Nonreporting) **A**1 10 **S** Encompass Health Corporation, Birmingham, AL
Primary Contact: Michael Morrical, Chief Executive Officer
CFO: Kevin Hardy, Chief Financial Officer
CMO: Jimmy Wayne Lockhart, M.D., Medical Director
CHR: Linda Rinehart, Director Human Resources
Web address: https://www.encompasshealth.com/treasurecoastrehab
Control: Corporation, Investor-owned (for-profit) **Service**: Rehabilitation

Staffed Beds: 80

WAUCHULA—Hardee County

☒ **ADVENTHEALTH WAUCHULA (101300)**, 735 South 5th Avenue, Zip 33873-3158; tel. 863/773-3101, **A**1 3 10 18 **F**3 29 30 34 40 53 57 58 59 107 110 111 119 127 130 131 133 149 156 **P**6 **S** AdventHealth, Altamonte Springs, FL
Primary Contact: Jason Dunkel, Chief Executive Officer
CFO: Rosalie Oliver, Senior Vice President and Chief Financial Officer
CMO: Jorge F. Gonzalez, M.D., Vice President and Chief Nursing Officer
CIO: Jeff McDonald, Information Technology Manager
CHR: Michelle F. Myers, Director Human Resources
CNO: Stacy Kreil, Chief Nursing Officer
Web address: https://www.adventhealth.com/hospital/adventhealth-wauchula
Control: Church operated, Nongovernment, not-for-profit **Service**: General medical and surgical

Staffed Beds: 25 **Admissions**: 595 **Census**: 22 **Outpatient Visits**: 27970 **Births**: 0 **Total Expense ($000)**: 32560 **Payroll Expense ($000)**: 12856 **Personnel**: 151

WELLINGTON—Palm Beach County

☐ **WELLINGTON REGIONAL MEDICAL CENTER (100275)**, 10101 Forest Hill Boulevard, Zip 33414-6199; tel. 561/798-8500, **A**1 3 5 10 13 **F**3 7 8 11 12 13 15 17 18 20 22 29 31 34 35 36 40 41 42 44 45 46 49 50 51 53 54 57 58 59 61 64 67 68 72 73 74 75 76 77 78 79 81 82 85 86 87 90 91 92 93 94 96 97 107 108 110 111 114 115 119 126 130 131 132 135 146 147 148 149 154 164 167 **S** Universal Health Services, Inc., King of Prussia, PA
Primary Contact: Pamela S. Tahan, Chief Executive Officer
CFO: Tonja Mosley, Chief Financial Officer
CMO: Richard Hays, M.D., Chief Medical Officer
CIO: Pierre Bergeron, Information Services Director
CHR: Mary Jo Caracciolo, Human Resource Director
CNO: Tracy Edelstein, MSN, R.N., Chief Nursing Officer
Web address: www.wellingtonregional.com
Control: Corporation, Investor-owned (for-profit) **Service**: General medical and surgical

Staffed Beds: 262 **Admissions**: 15330 **Census**: 193 **Total Expense ($000)**: 258019 **Payroll Expense ($000)**: 84525 **Personnel**: 1038

WESLEY CHAPEL—Pasco County

★ ⇑ **ADVENTHEALTH WESLEY CHAPEL (100319)**, 2600 Bruce B Downs Bouelvard, Zip 33544-9207; tel. 813/929-5000, (Nonreporting) **A**3 5 10 21 **S** AdventHealth, Altamonte Springs, FL
Primary Contact: Erik Wangsness, Chief Executive Officer
Web address: https://www.floridahospital.com/wesley-chapel
Control: Other not-for-profit (including NFP Corporation) **Service**: General medical and surgical

Staffed Beds: 145

★ **BAYCARE HOSPITAL WESLEY CHAPEL (100362)**, 4501 Bruce B Downs Boulevard, Zip 33544-9216; tel. 813/914-1000, (Data for 299 days) **A**10 **F**3 18 20 29 30 34 35 40 44 45 46 48 49 50 51 57 59 60 68 70 74 75 77 78 79 81 84 85 86 87 107 108 111 115 119 126 130 146 154 156 157 167 **S** BayCare Health System, Clearwater, FL
Primary Contact: Becky Schulkowski, President
Web address: www.BayCare.org
Control: Other not-for-profit (including NFP Corporation) **Service**: General medical and surgical

Staffed Beds: 86 **Admissions**: 1330 **Census**: 15 **Outpatient Visits**: 12648 **Births**: 0 **Total Expense ($000)**: 64541 **Payroll Expense ($000)**: 21685 **Personnel**: 282

☐ **NORTH TAMPA BEHAVIORAL HEALTH (104075)**, 29910 State Road 56, Zip 33543-8800; tel. 813/922-3300, **A**1 10 **F**4 5 98 100 101 102 103 104 105 106 143 153 **S** Acadia Healthcare Company, Inc., Franklin, TN
Primary Contact: Clint Hauger, Chief Executive Officer
Web address: www.northtampabehavioralhealth.com
Control: Corporation, Investor-owned (for-profit) **Service**: Psychiatric

Staffed Beds: 124 **Admissions**: 5181 **Census**: 90 **Total Expense ($000)**: 24319 **Payroll Expense ($000)**: 11923 **Personnel**: 185

WEST PALM BEACH—Palm Beach County

CHILDREN'S HOSPITAL AT ST. MARY'S MEDICAL CENTER See Palm Beach Children's Hospital

☒ **GOOD SAMARITAN MEDICAL CENTER (100287)**, 1309 North Flagler Drive, Zip 33401-3499; tel. 561/655-5511, **A**1 2 10 **F**3 12 13 15 18 20 22 26 29 30 31 34 35 40 42 45 46 49 50 51 54 55 56 57 58 59 60 68 70 72 74 75 77 78 79 81 82 84 85 86 87 93 107 108 110 111 114 115 119 126 129 130 131 132 146 147 154 157 167 **S** TENET Healthcare Corporation, Dallas, TX
Primary Contact: Sheri Montgomery, Acting Chief Executive Officer
COO: Tony Bajak, Chief Operating Officer
CFO: Taylor Guittap, Chief Financial Officer
CIO: James Dailey, Director Information Services
CNO: Joe Lopez-Cepero, Chief Nursing Officer
Web address: www.goodsamaritanmc.com
Control: Corporation, Investor-owned (for-profit) **Service**: General medical and surgical

Staffed Beds: 348 **Admissions**: 9916 **Census**: 125 **Total Expense ($000)**: 238504 **Payroll Expense ($000)**: 71368 **Personnel**: 795

JFK MEDICAL CENTER NORTH CAMPUS See HCA Florida JFK North Hospital

☒ **ST. MARY'S MEDICAL CENTER (100288)**, 901 45th Street, Zip 33407-2495; tel. 561/844-6300, (Includes PALM BEACH CHILDREN'S HOSPITAL, 901 45th Street, West Palm Beach, Florida, Zip 33407, tel. 561/844-6300) (Nonreporting) **A**1 3 10 **S** TENET Healthcare Corporation, Dallas, TX
Primary Contact: Cynthia McCauley, Chief Executive Officer
CFO: Tarek Naser, Chief Financial Officer
CNO: Ruth Schwarzkopf, Chief Nursing Officer
Web address: www.stmarysmc.com
Control: Corporation, Investor-owned (for-profit) **Service**: General medical and surgical

Staffed Beds: 460

SUNVIEW MEDICAL CENTER (104008), 1041 45th Street, Zip 33407-2494; tel. 561/383-8000, (Nonreporting) **A**10
Primary Contact: Linda De Piano, Ph.D., Chief Executive Officer
CFO: America Cordoves, Controller
CMO: Suresh Rajpara, M.D., Chief Medical Officer
CIO: Iris Garcia, Director, Information Services
CHR: Nadine Wilson, Manager, Human Resources
CNO: Holly Horvath, Director of Nursing
Web address: https://sunviewmedical.com/
Control: Other not-for-profit (including NFP Corporation) **Service**: Psychiatric

Staffed Beds: 44

Hospitals, U.S. / FLORIDA

☒ **WEST PALM BEACH VETERANS AFFAIRS MEDICAL CENTER**, 7305 North Military Trail, Zip 33410–6400; tel. 561/422–8262, **A**1 3 5 **F**1 3 5 8 9 10 11 12 15 18 20 22 24 26 29 30 31 33 34 35 36 38 39 40 43 45 46 47 48 49 53 54 55 56 57 58 59 60 61 62 63 64 65 67 68 69 70 74 75 77 78 79 81 82 83 84 85 86 87 91 92 93 94 97 98 100 101 102 104 106 107 108 109 110 111 112 113 114 115 116 117 118 119 120 121 122 123 124 126 128 130 132 133 135 136 137 138 139 140 141 142 143 146 147 148 149 150 152 153 154 156 157 158 160 164 167 **S** Department of Veterans Affairs, Washington, DC
Primary Contact: Cory P. Price, FACHE, Medical Center Director and Chief Executive Officer
CFO: Lori Hancock, Chief Business Officer
CMO: Deepak Mandi, M.D., Chief of Staff
CIO: Karen Gabaldon, Chief Management Information Systems
CHR: David Green, Chief Human Resources
Web address: www.westpalmbeach.va.gov/
Control: Veterans Affairs, Government, federal **Service**: General medical and surgical

Staffed Beds: 260 **Admissions**: 4927 **Census**: 180 **Outpatient Visits**: 967311 **Births**: 0 **Total Expense ($000)**: 808105 **Payroll Expense ($000)**: 284087 **Personnel**: 2837

WESTON—Broward County

☒ **CLEVELAND CLINIC FLORIDA (100289)**, 2950 Cleveland Clinic Boulevard, Zip 33331–3602; tel. 954/659–5000, **A**1 2 3 5 10 19 **F**3 8 9 11 12 15 17 18 20 22 24 26 28 29 30 31 34 35 36 37 39 40 41 44 45 46 47 48 49 50 51 54 55 56 57 58 59 60 61 63 64 65 68 70 74 75 77 78 79 80 81 82 84 85 86 87 91 92 93 96 97 100 102 107 108 109 110 111 114 115 116 117 118 119 120 121 123 124 126 129 130 131 133 135 137 138 139 141 145 146 147 148 149 154 156 157 164 167 **P**6 **S** Cleveland Clinic Health System, Cleveland, OH
Primary Contact: Conor P. Delaney, M.D., Ph.D., Chief Executive Officer and President
CMO: Raul Rosenthal, M.D., Interim Chief of Staff
CIO: John Santangelo, Director Information Technology
CNO: Kerry Major, R.N., MSN, Chief Nursing Officer
Web address: www.clevelandclinic.org/florida
Control: Other not–for–profit (including NFP Corporation) **Service**: General medical and surgical

Staffed Beds: 236 **Admissions**: 14143 **Census**: 215 **Outpatient Visits**: 1185684 **Births**: 0 **Total Expense ($000)**: 549946 **Payroll Expense ($000)**: 163775 **Personnel**: 4064

WINTER HAVEN—Polk County

☒ **WINTER HAVEN HOSPITAL (100052)**, 200 Avenue F NE, Zip 33881–4193; tel. 863/293–1121, (Includes WINTER HAVEN WOMEN'S HOSPITAL, 101 Avenue O SE, Winter Haven, Florida, Zip 33880–4333, tel. 863/294–7010; Tom Garthwaite, President) **A**1 3 10 19 **F**3 11 13 14 15 17 18 20 22 24 26 28 29 30 31 34 37 40 45 47 48 49 57 58 59 60 64 68 70 72 74 75 76 77 78 79 81 82 84 85 86 87 93 94 98 100 101 102 103 104 107 108 109 110 111 114 115 118 119 120 121 122 123 126 130 132 135 144 146 147 148 154 156 157 164 165 **S** BayCare Health System, Clearwater, FL
Primary Contact: Tom Garthwaite, President
COO: Diane Gibbs, Director, Operations
CFO: Ron Beamon, Vice President, Chief Financial Officer
CMO: John M. Davidyock, M.D., Vice President and Chief Medical Officer
CIO: Walter C. Barrionuevo, Director Information Services
CHR: Kristen A Betts, Director Team Resources
Web address: https://baycare.org/hospitals/winter-haven-hospital/patients-and-visitors
Control: Other not–for–profit (including NFP Corporation) **Service**: General medical and surgical

Staffed Beds: 455 **Admissions**: 18235 **Census**: 236 **Outpatient Visits**: 149564 **Births**: 1645 **Total Expense ($000)**: 457358 **Payroll Expense ($000)**: 177758 **Personnel**: 1975

WINTER PARK—Orange County

ADVENTHEALTH WINTER PARK See Adventhealth Orlando, Orlando

WINTER PARK MEMORIAL HOSPITAL See Adventhealth Winter Park

ZEPHYRHILLS—Pasco County

☒ **ADVENTHEALTH ZEPHYRHILLS (100046)**, 7050 Gall Boulevard, Zip 33541–1399; tel. 813/788–0411, **A**1 3 5 10 **F**13 15 18 20 22 26 29 40 45 50 53 64 70 74 76 79 81 82 84 107 108 111 112 115 116 117 119 126 146 147 148 154 167 **S** AdventHealth, Altamonte Springs, FL
Primary Contact: Michael Murrill, Chief Executive Officer
COO: Donald E Welch, Chief Operating Officer
CFO: Bill Heinrich, Chief Financial Officer
CMO: Hugar McNamee, D.O., Chief Medical Officer
CIO: Kelley Sasser, Director Information Systems
CHR: Laura Asaftei, Administrative Director
CNO: Gwen Alonso, Chief Nursing Officer
Web address: https://www.adventhealth.com/hospital/adventhealth-zephyrhills
Control: Church operated, Nongovernment, not–for–profit **Service**: General medical and surgical

Staffed Beds: 161 **Admissions**: 11137 **Census**: 124 **Total Expense ($000)**: 220508 **Payroll Expense ($000)**: 83609 **Personnel**: 1018

Hospital, Medicare Provider Number, Address, Telephone, Approval, Facility, and Physician Codes, Health Care System

★ American Hospital Association (AHA) membership
☐ The Joint Commission accreditation
○ Healthcare Facilities Accreditation Program
◇ DNV Healthcare Inc. accreditation
⇧ Center for Improvement in Healthcare Quality Accreditation
△ Commission on Accreditation of Rehabilitation Facilities (CARF) accreditation

GEORGIA

ADEL—Cook County

SOUTHWELL MEDICAL (110101), 260 MJ Taylor Road, Zip 31620–3485; tel. 229/896–8000, (Total facility includes 95 beds in nursing home–type unit) **A**1 10 **F**11 15 18 29 30 34 35 45 56 57 59 63 64 65 68 75 77 81 84 85 86 87 93 97 98 100 101 103 104 107 108 110 111 114 119 126 127 129 130 133 135 144 146 147 148 149 154 156 **P**6 **S** Tift Regional Health System, Tifton, GA
Primary Contact: Christopher Dorman, Chief Executive Officer
COO: Kim Wills, Chief Operating Officer
CIO: Barry Medley, Director Information Systems
CHR: Shirley Padgett, Director Human Resources
Web address: www.cookmedicalcenter.com
Control: Other not–for–profit (including NFP Corporation) **Service**: General medical and surgical

Staffed Beds: 115 Admissions: 542 Census: 85 Outpatient Visits: 22286 Births: 0 Total Expense ($000): 64849 Payroll Expense ($000): 33922 Personnel: 410

ALBANY—Dougherty County

PALMYRA MEDICAL CENTERS See Phoebe North

PHOEBE PUTNEY MEMORIAL HOSPITAL (110007), 417 West Third Avenue, Zip 31701–1943; tel. 229/312–4100, (Includes PHOEBE NORTH, 2000 Palmyra Road, Albany, Georgia, Zip 31701–1528, P O Box 1908, Zip 31702–1908, tel. 229/434–2000) (Nonreporting) **A**2 3 5 10 21 **S** Phoebe Putney Health System, Albany, GA
Primary Contact: Deborah Angerami, Chief Executive Officer
COO: Jane Gray, Interim Chief Operating Officer
CFO: Brian Church, Senior Vice President and Chief Financial Officer
CIO: Jesse Diaz, Chief Information Officer
CHR: Tony Welch, Senior Vice President and Chief Human Resources Officer
Web address: www.phoebeputney.com
Control: Other not–for–profit (including NFP Corporation) **Service**: General medical and surgical

Staffed Beds: 430

ALMA—Bacon County

BACON COUNTY HOSPITAL AND HEALTH SYSTEM (111327), 302 South Wayne Street, Zip 31510–2922, Mailing Address: P O Drawer 1987, Zip 31510–0987; tel. 912/632–8961, (Nonreporting) **A**1 3 10 18
Primary Contact: Cindy R. Turner, Chief Executive Officer
COO: Cindy R Turner, Chief Executive Officer
CFO: Kyle Kimmel, Chief Financial Officer
CMO: Lou Ellen Hutcheson, M.D., Chief of Staff
CIO: Neil O'Steen, Director Information Technology
CHR: Kerry Hancock, Director Human Resources
CNO: Deanna Hoff, R.N., Director of Nursing
Web address: www.baconcountyhospital.com
Control: Other not–for–profit (including NFP Corporation) **Service**: General medical and surgical

Staffed Beds: 113

AMERICUS—Sumter County

PHOEBE SUMTER MEDICAL CENTER (110044), 126 Highway, 280 West, Zip 31719, Mailing Address: 126 Highway 280 West, Zip 31719; tel. 229/924–6011, (Nonreporting) **A**3 10 21 **S** Phoebe Putney Health System, Albany, GA
Primary Contact: Carlyle L E. Walton, FACHE, Chief Executive Officer
CHR: Cassandra Haynes Aldridge, Chief Human Resources Officer
CNO: Susan Bruns, Chief Nursing Officer
Web address: www.phoebesumter.org
Control: Other not–for–profit (including NFP Corporation) **Service**: General medical and surgical

Staffed Beds: 54

ATHENS—Clarke County

LANDMARK HOSPITAL OF ATHENS (112017), 775 Sunset Drive, Zip 30606–2211; tel. 762/356–0759, (Nonreporting) **A**10 22 **S** Landmark Hospitals, Cape Girardeau, MO
Primary Contact: Marie Saylor, Chief Executive Officer
Web address: https://www.landmarkhospitals.com/critical-care-hospital-system/athens-ga/
Control: Individual, Investor–owned (for–profit) **Service**: Acute long–term care hospital

Staffed Beds: 42

PIEDMONT ATHENS REGIONAL MEDICAL CENTER (110074), 1199 Prince Avenue, Zip 30606–2797; tel. 706/475–7000, (Nonreporting) **A**2 3 5 10 21 **S** Piedmont Healthcare, Roswell, GA
Primary Contact: Michael Burnett, Chief Executive Officer
COO: Jason Smith, Chief Operating Officer
CFO: Wendy J. Cook, Chief Financial Officer
CMO: Geoffrey Marx, M.D., Chief Medical Officer
CIO: Louis H. Duhe, Executor Director, Information Services
CHR: Robert D. Finch, Director, Human Resources
CNO: Jeremiah Bame, R.N., Chief Nursing Officer
Web address: https://www.piedmont.org/locations/piedmont-athens
Control: Other not–for–profit (including NFP Corporation) **Service**: General medical and surgical

Staffed Beds: 366

ST. MARY'S HEALTH CARE SYSTEM (110006), 1230 Baxter Street, Zip 30606–3791; tel. 706/389–3000, **A**1 3 5 7 10 19 **F**6 10 11 12 13 14 15 18 20 22 26 28 29 30 34 35 37 40 45 46 47 48 49 50 51 53 54 55 56 57 59 60 62 63 64 65 67 68 70 72 74 75 76 77 78 79 81 83 84 85 86 87 89 90 92 93 97 107 110 111 112 114 115 118 119 122 125 126 130 132 133 135 146 147 148 154 156 157 158 165 167 168 **S** Trinity Health, Livonia, MI
Primary Contact: Stonish Pierce, FACHE, President and Chief Executive Officer
CFO: Marty Hutson, Chief Financial Officer
CMO: Bruce Middendorf, M.D., Chief Medical Officer
CIO: Kerry Vaughn, Chief Information Officer
CHR: Jeff English, Vice President Human Resources
CNO: Candice Frix, Vice President and Chief Nursing Officer
Web address: www.stmarysathens.com
Control: Corporation, Investor–owned (for–profit) **Service**: General medical and surgical

Staffed Beds: 277 Admissions: 12470 Census: 150 Outpatient Visits: 197561 Births: 1457 Personnel: 2322

ATLANTA—Fulton and De Kalb County

ANCHOR HOSPITAL (114032), 5454 Yorktowne Drive, Zip 30349–5317; tel. 770/991–6044, **A**1 10 **F**5 98 100 103 104 105 132 134 135 152 153 154 160 164 165 **S** Universal Health Services, Inc., King of Prussia, PA
Primary Contact: Gran Shinwar, Chief Executive Officer
CFO: John Kim, Chief Financial Officer
CMO: Shailesh Patel, M.D., Medical Director
CIO: Chris Hill, Information Technology
CHR: Danna Nordin, Director Human Resources
CNO: Angelica Jackson, Director of Nursing
Web address: www.anchorhospital.com
Control: Corporation, Investor–owned (for–profit) **Service**: Psychiatric

Staffed Beds: 122 Admissions: 4028 Census: 93 Outpatient Visits: 5608 Births: 0 Total Expense ($000): 26999 Payroll Expense ($000): 13739 Personnel: 158

Hospitals, U.S. / GEORGIA

☐ △ **CHILDREN'S HEALTHCARE OF ATLANTA (113300)**, 1575 Northeast Expressway NE, Zip 30329-2401; tel. 404/785-5437, (Includes CHILDREN'S HEALTHCARE OF ATLANTA AT EGLESTON, 1600 Tullie Circle, Atlanta, Georgia, Zip 30329, tel. 404/325-6000; CHILDREN'S HEALTHCARE OF ATLANTA AT HUGHES SPALDING, 35 Jesse Hill Jr Drive, SE, Atlanta, Georgia, Zip 30303-3032, tel. 404/785-9500; CHILDREN'S HEALTHCARE OF ATLANTA AT SCOTTISH RITE, 1001 Johnson Ferry Road NE, Atlanta, Georgia, Zip 30342-1600, tel. 404/256-5252) (Nonreporting) **A**1 3 5 7 8 10
Primary Contact: Donna W. Hyland, President and Chief Executive Officer
COO: Carolyn Kenny, Executive Vice President Clinical Care
CFO: Ruth Fowler, Senior Vice President and Chief Financial Officer
CMO: Daniel Salinas, M.D., Senior Vice President and Chief Medical Officer
CIO: Allana Cummings, Chief Information Officer
CHR: Linda Matzigkeit, Senior Vice President Human Resources
Web address: www.choa.org
Control: Other not-for-profit (including NFP Corporation) **Service:** Children's general medical and surgical

Staffed Beds: 496

EGLESTON CHILDREN'S HOSPITAL See Children's Healthcare of Atlanta At Egleston

☒ △ **EMORY REHABILITATION HOSPITAL (113031)**, 1441 Clifton Road NE, Zip 30322-1004; tel. 404/712-5512, **A**1 7 10 **F**11 29 30 34 35 36 50 56 58 64 68 74 75 79 86 87 90 93 94 95 96 130 132 146 148 149 **S** Emory Healthcare, Atlanta, GA
Primary Contact: Renee Hinson, Chief Executive Officer
CMO: S. Byron Milton, M.D., Medical Director
CHR: Janine Diaz, Human Resources Manager
CNO: Deborah Almauhy, R.N., Chief Nursing Officer
Web address: www.emoryhealthcare.org/rehabilitation
Control: Partnership, Investor-owned (for-profit) **Service:** Rehabilitation

Staffed Beds: 46 **Admissions:** 1026 **Census:** 43 **Outpatient Visits:** 15168 **Births:** 0 **Total Expense ($000):** 29420 **Payroll Expense ($000):** 17847 **Personnel:** 181

☒ **EMORY SAINT JOSEPH'S HOSPITAL (110082)**, 5665 Peachtree Dunwoody Road NE, Zip 30342-1701; tel. 678/843-7001, **A**1 2 3 5 10 **F**3 11 12 15 17 18 20 22 24 26 28 29 30 31 34 35 37 40 44 45 46 47 49 50 51 53 54 55 57 58 59 60 64 68 70 74 75 77 78 79 81 82 84 85 87 90 100 102 107 108 110 111 115 117 118 119 120 121 123 124 126 130 132 135 145 146 147 148 149 154 156 167 **S** Emory Healthcare, Atlanta, GA
Primary Contact: Kevin Andrews, Chief Operating Officer
CFO: JoAnn Manning, Chief Financial Officer
CMO: Thomas P. McGahan, M.D., Chief Medical Officer
CHR: Jeanne Landry, Vice President Human Resources
Web address: www.emoryhealthcare.org/locations/hospitals/emory-saint-josephs-hospital/
Control: Other not-for-profit (including NFP Corporation) **Service:** General medical and surgical

Staffed Beds: 314 **Admissions:** 16817 **Census:** 265 **Outpatient Visits:** 120591 **Births:** 0 **Total Expense ($000):** 538463 **Payroll Expense ($000):** 210004 **Personnel:** 1790

☒ **EMORY UNIVERSITY HOSPITAL (110010)**, 1364 Clifton Road NE, Zip 30322; tel. 404/712-2000, (Includes EMORY UNIVERSITY ORTHOPAEDIC AND SPINE HOSPITAL, 1455 Montreal Road, Tucker, Georgia, Zip 30084, tel. 404/251-3600; June Conner, R.N., Chief Operating Officer; EMORY WESLEY WOODS GERIATRIC HOSPITAL, 1821 Clifton Road NE, Atlanta, Georgia, Zip 30329-4021, tel. 404/728-6200; Matt Wain, Chief Executive Officer) **A**1 2 3 5 10 **F**3 5 11 14 15 17 18 20 22 24 26 29 30 31 34 35 36 38 40 44 45 46 47 48 49 50 55 56 57 58 59 60 61 63 64 68 70 74 75 77 78 79 80 81 82 84 85 86 87 90 92 93 98 100 101 102 103 104 105 107 108 110 111 114 115 116 117 118 119 120 121 123 124 126 129 130 131 132 135 136 137 138 139 140 141 142 145 146 147 148 149 151 153 154 156 157 160 161 164 165 166 167 **S** Emory Healthcare, Atlanta, GA
Primary Contact: Catherine Maloney, Chief Operating Officer
CFO: Carla Chandler, Vice President and Chief Financial Officer
CMO: Chad W.M. Ritenour, M.D., Chief Medical Officer
CIO: Sheila M Sanders, Chief Information Officer
CHR: Melanie DeGennaro, Vice President of Human Resources
CNO: Nancye R. Feistritzer, Chief Nursing Officer
Web address: https://www.emoryhealthcare.org/locations/hospitals/emory-university-hospital/index.html
Control: Other not-for-profit (including NFP Corporation) **Service:** General medical and surgical

Staffed Beds: 683 **Admissions:** 26071 **Census:** 562 **Outpatient Visits:** 224378 **Total Expense ($000):** 1346716 **Payroll Expense ($000):** 461832 **Personnel:** 4123

☒ **EMORY UNIVERSITY HOSPITAL MIDTOWN (110078)**, 550 Peachtree Street NE, Zip 30308-2247; tel. 404/686-4411, **A**1 2 3 5 8 10 **F**3 11 12 13 14 15 17 18 20 22 24 26 29 30 31 34 35 36 38 40 44 45 46 47 48 49 50 51 52 55 57 58 59 60 61 63 64 68 70 72 73 74 75 76 77 78 79 81 82 84 85 86 87 92 93 100 101 102 107 108 110 111 114 115 116 117 118 119 120 121 123 124 126 130 131 132 135 146 147 148 149 154 156 157 167 169 **S** Emory Healthcare, Atlanta, GA
Primary Contact: Adam Webb, Chief Operating Officer
CMO: James P Steinberg, M.D., Chief Medical Officer
CHR: Dallis Howard-Crow, Chief Human Resources Officer
Web address: www.emoryhealthcare.org
Control: Other not-for-profit (including NFP Corporation) **Service:** General medical and surgical

Staffed Beds: 548 **Admissions:** 25744 **Census:** 447 **Outpatient Visits:** 403884 **Births:** 4870 **Total Expense ($000):** 1580087 **Payroll Expense ($000):** 412662 **Personnel:** 3670

☒ **GRADY HEALTH SYSTEM (110079)**, 80 Jesse Hill Jr Drive SE, Zip 30303-3031, Mailing Address: P.O. Box 26189, Zip 31329-0386; tel. 404/616-1000, (Total facility includes 284 beds in nursing home-type unit) **A**1 2 3 5 8 10 **F**3 5 7 13 15 16 17 18 20 22 24 26 29 30 31 34 35 38 39 40 43 45 46 47 49 50 51 53 54 55 56 57 58 59 60 61 64 65 66 68 70 72 73 74 75 76 77 78 79 81 82 84 85 86 87 93 94 97 98 100 101 102 103 104 106 107 108 109 110 111 112 113 114 115 116 117 118 119 120 121 126 128 130 143 144 146 147 148 153 154 155 156 157 160 161 164 167 169
Primary Contact: John M. Haupert, FACHE, President and Chief Executive Officer
CFO: Anthony J Saul, Executive Vice President, Chief Financial Officer
CMO: Robert Jansen, M.D., Chief Medical Officer
CIO: Ben McKeeby, Senior Vice President and Chief Information Officer
CHR: Larry A. Callahan, Senior Vice President Human Resources
Web address: www.gradyhealthsystem.org
Control: Other not-for-profit (including NFP Corporation) **Service:** General medical and surgical

Staffed Beds: 1034 **Admissions:** 35380 **Census:** 948 **Outpatient Visits:** 652918 **Births:** 3106 **Total Expense ($000):** 1805079 **Payroll Expense ($000):** 674628 **Personnel:** 7216

GRADY MEMORIAL HOSPITAL See Grady Health System

☒ **NORTHSIDE HOSPITAL (110161)**, 1000 Johnson Ferry Road Northeast, Zip 30342-1606, Mailing Address: 1001 Summit Blvd, Zip 30319; tel. 404/851-8000, **A**1 2 3 10 **F**3 5 8 9 11 12 13 15 17 18 20 22 26 28 29 30 31 34 35 37 38 40 41 44 45 46 47 48 49 50 54 55 57 58 59 64 68 70 71 72 73 74 75 76 77 78 79 80 81 82 84 85 86 87 93 102 104 107 108 110 111 114 115 117 118 119 120 121 123 124 126 129 130 131 132 135 136 144 146 147 148 149 153 154 156 164 165 167 169 **S** Northside Healthcare System, Atlanta, GA
Primary Contact: Deidre Dixon, Chief Executive Officer
CFO: Shannon A. Banna, Chief Financial Officer
CIO: Tina Wakim, Vice President Information
Web address: https://www.northside.com/locations/northside-hospital-atlanta
Control: Other not-for-profit (including NFP Corporation) **Service:** General medical and surgical

Staffed Beds: 660 **Admissions:** 33859 **Census:** 430 **Outpatient Visits:** 2179846 **Births:** 15820 **Total Expense ($000):** 3042378 **Payroll Expense ($000):** 1044938 **Personnel:** 11793

☐ **PEACHFORD BEHAVIORAL HEALTH SYSTEM (114010)**, 2151 Peachford Road, Zip 30338-6599; tel. 770/455-3200, (Nonreporting) **A**1 10 **S** Universal Health Services, Inc., King of Prussia, PA
Primary Contact: Matthew Crouch, Chief Executive Officer and Managing Director
COO: Sharon Stackhouse, Assistant Administrator and Director Risk Management
CFO: April Hughes, Chief Financial Officer
CMO: Asaf Aleem, M.D., Medical Director
CHR: Clay Boyles, Director Human Resources
Web address: www.peachfordhospital.com
Control: Corporation, Investor-owned (for-profit) **Service:** Psychiatric

Staffed Beds: 246

Hospital, Medicare Provider Number, Address, Telephone, Approval, Facility, and Physician Codes, Health Care System

★ American Hospital Association (AHA) membership
☐ The Joint Commission accreditation
○ Healthcare Facilities Accreditation Program
◇ DNV Healthcare Inc. accreditation
⇑ Center for Improvement in Healthcare Quality Accreditation
△ Commission on Accreditation of Rehabilitation Facilities (CARF) accreditation

© 2025 AHA Guide

Hospitals, U.S. / GEORGIA

⇧ **PIEDMONT ATLANTA HOSPITAL (110083)**, 1968 Peachtree Road NW, Zip 30309–1281; tel. 404/605–5000, (Nonreporting) **A**2 3 5 10 21 **S** Piedmont Healthcare, Roswell, GA
Primary Contact: Patrick M. Battey, FACS, M.D., Chief Executive Officer
CFO: Sheryl Klink, Chief Financial Officer
CMO: Mark Cohen, M.D., Chief Medical Officer
CHR: Vicki A Cansler, Chief Human Resource Officer
CNO: Kelly Hulsey, MSN, R.N., Chief Nursing Officer
Web address: www.piedmont.org
Control: Other not–for–profit (including NFP Corporation) **Service**: General medical and surgical

Staffed Beds: 534

⇧ **PIEDMONT HOSPITAL** See Piedmont Atlanta Hospital

SCOTTISH RITE CHILDREN'S CTR See Children's Healthcare of Atlanta At Scottish Rite

✚ **SELECT SPECIALTY HOSPITAL MIDTOWN ATLANTA (112004)**, 705 Juniper Street NE, Zip 30308–1307; tel. 404/873–2871, (Nonreporting) **A**1 10 **S** Select Medical Corporation, Mechanicsburg, PA
Primary Contact: Karan Patel, Interim Chief Executive Officer
CFO: Michael Nelson, Chief Financial Officer
CMO: David N. DeRuyter, M.D., President Medical Staff
CHR: Armetria Gibson, Human Resources Generalist
CNO: Annette Harrilson, Chief Clinical Officer
Web address: https://www.selectspecialtyhospitals.com/locations-and-tours/ga/atlanta/midtown-atlanta/
Control: Partnership, Investor–owned (for–profit) **Service**: Acute long–term care hospital

Staffed Beds: 72

☐ △ **SHEPHERD CENTER (112003)**, 2020 Peachtree Road NW, Zip 30309–1465; tel. 404/352–2020, **A**1 3 5 7 10 **F**3 5 10 11 29 30 31 32 34 35 36 44 50 53 54 57 58 59 64 65 68 70 74 75 77 82 86 87 90 91 92 93 94 95 96 97 107 111 114 119 130 132 134 146 148 149 154 157 164 **P**3 6
Primary Contact: Jamie Shepherd, Chief Executive Officer
CFO: Stephen B Holleman, Chief Financial Officer
CMO: Donald P Leslie, M.D., Medical Director
CIO: Brian Barnette, Chief Information Officer
CHR: Lorie Hutcheson, Vice President of Human Resources
CNO: Tamara King, R.N., MSN, Chief Nurse Executive
Web address: https://www.shepherd.org
Control: Other not–for–profit (including NFP Corporation) **Service**: Rehabilitation

Staffed Beds: 151 **Admissions**: 888 **Census**: 129 **Outpatient Visits**: 137820 **Births**: 0 **Total Expense ($000)**: 297235 **Payroll Expense ($000)**: 131616 **Personnel**: 1533

WESLEY WOODS CENTER See Wesley Woods Health Center

WESLEY WOODS GERIATRIC HOSPITAL OF EMORY UNIVERSITY See Emory Wesley Woods Geriatric Hospital

AUGUSTA—Richmond County

✚ △ **CHARLIE NORWOOD VETERANS AFFAIRS MEDICAL CENTER**, 1 Freedom Way, Zip 30904–6285; tel. 706/733–0188, (Nonreporting) **A**1 3 5 7 8 **S** Department of Veterans Affairs, Washington, DC
Primary Contact: Robin E. Jackson, Ph.D., Chief Executive Officer
COO: John D Stenger, Acting Associate Director
CFO: Earline Corder, Chief Fiscal
CIO: Sandy Williford, Chief Health Information Management and Revenue Administration
CHR: Roger W Buterbaugh, Chief Human Resources Officer
Web address: www.augusta.va.gov/
Control: Veterans Affairs, Government, federal **Service**: General medical and surgical

Staffed Beds: 133

✚ **DOCTORS HOSPITAL (110177)**, 3651 Wheeler Road, Zip 30909–6426; tel. 706/651–3232, (Nonreporting) **A**1 2 3 5 10 **S** HCA Healthcare, Nashville, TN
Primary Contact: Joanna J. Conley, FACHE, Chief Executive Officer
CIO: Dona Hornung, Director Information and Technology Services
Web address: www.doctors-hospital.net
Control: Corporation, Investor–owned (for–profit) **Service**: General medical and surgical

Staffed Beds: 288

☐ **EAST CENTRAL REGIONAL HOSPITAL (114029)**, 3405 Mike Padgett Highway, Zip 30906–3897; tel. 706/790–2011, (Includes EAST CENTRAL REGIONAL HOSPITAL, 100 Myrtle Boulevard, Gracewood, Georgia, Zip 30812–1299, tel. 706/790–2011) (Nonreporting) **A**1 3 5 10
Primary Contact: Tammi Brown, Regional Hospital Administrator
CFO: Candace Walker, Chief Financial Officer
Web address: www.dbhdd.ga.gov
Control: State, Government, Nonfederal **Service**: Psychiatric

Staffed Beds: 253

MCG CHILDREN'S MEDICAL CENTER See Children's Hospital of Georgia

⇧ **PIEDMONT AUGUSTA (110028)**, 1350 Walton Way, Zip 30901–2629; tel. 706/722–9011, (Includes PIEDMONT AUGUSTA SUMMERVILLE CAMPUS, 2260 Wrightsboro Road, Augusta, Georgia, Zip 30904–4726, tel. 706/481–7000) (Nonreporting) **A**2 3 5 10 21 **S** Piedmont Healthcare, Roswell, GA
Primary Contact: Lily Henson, M.D., President and Chief Executive Officer
CFO: David Belkoski, Senior Vice President and Chief Financial Officer
CMO: William L Farr, M.D., Chief Medical Officer
CIO: Shirley Gabriel, Vice President and Chief Information Officer
CHR: Laurie Ott, Vice President Human Resources and President University Health Care Foundation
Web address: https://www.universityhealth.org/our-locations/university-hospital/
Control: Other not–for–profit (including NFP Corporation) **Service**: General medical and surgical

Staffed Beds: 474

✚ **SELECT SPECIALTY HOSPITAL–AUGUSTA (112013)**, 1537 Walton Way, Zip 30904–3764; tel. 706/731–1200, (Nonreporting) **A**1 10 **S** Select Medical Corporation, Mechanicsburg, PA
Primary Contact: Cynthia Greene, Chief Executive Officer
CHR: Terrie Richardson, Coordinator Human Resources
CNO: Kim Pippin, Chief Nursing Officer
Web address: www.augusta.selectspecialtyhospitals.com
Control: Corporation, Investor–owned (for-profit) **Service**: Acute long–term care hospital

Staffed Beds: 80

⇧ **UNIVERSITY HOSPITAL** See Piedmont Augusta

UNIVERSITY HOSPITAL SUMMERVILLE See Piedmont Augusta Summerville Campus

✚ **WALTON REHABILITATION HOSPITAL, AN AFFILIATE OF ENCOMPASS HEALTH (113030)**, 1355 Independence Drive, Zip 30901–1037; tel. 706/724–7746, (Nonreporting) **A**1 10 **S** Encompass Health Corporation, Birmingham, AL
Primary Contact: Eric Crossan, Chief Executive Officer
CMO: Pamela Salazar, M.D., Chief of Staff
CIO: Ann Keller, Supervisor Health Information Management
CHR: Volante Henderson, Director Human Resources
CNO: Lynn Beaulieu, Chief Nursing Officer
Web address: www.healthsouthwalton.com/
Control: Corporation, Investor–owned (for–profit) **Service**: Rehabilitation

Staffed Beds: 58

✚ **WELLSTAR MCG HEALTH (110034)**, 1120 15th Street, Zip 30912–0004; tel. 706/721–0211, (Includes CHILDREN'S HOSPITAL OF GEORGIA, 1446 Harper Street, Augusta, Georgia, Zip 30912–0012, tel. 706/721–5437; Brooks Keel, M.D., President, Augusta University) **A**1 2 3 8 10 **F**3 6 9 11 12 13 14 15 17 18 19 20 21 22 23 24 25 26 27 28 29 30 31 32 34 35 36 38 40 41 43 44 45 46 47 48 49 50 51 54 55 56 58 59 60 61 64 65 66 68 70 72 73 74 75 76 77 78 79 81 82 84 85 86 87 88 89 92 93 97 99 100 101 102 103 104 107 108 111 112 113 115 116 117 118 119 120 121 123 124 126 127 129 130 131 132 134 135 136 138 141 142 143 147 148 154 155 156 160 163 164 167 169 **S** WellStar Health System, Marietta, GA
Primary Contact: Ralph Turner, President
COO: Timothy Gaillard, Chief Operating Officer
CFO: Waite Popejoy, Interim Chief Financial Officer
CMO: Phillip Coule, M.D., Chief Medical Officer
CIO: Michael Casdorph, Ph.D., Chief Information Officer
CHR: Susan Norton, Vice President Human Resources
Web address: https://www.augustahealth.org/
Control: Other not–for–profit (including NFP Corporation) **Service**: General medical and surgical

Staffed Beds: 486 **Admissions**: 20961 **Census**: 398 **Outpatient Visits**: 672651 **Births**: 1845 **Personnel**: 4386

Hospitals, U.S. / GEORGIA

AUSTELL—Cobb County

✠ △ **WELLSTAR COBB HOSPITAL (110143)**, 3950 Austell Road, Zip 30106-1121; tel. 470/732-4000, **A**1 2 3 7 10 **F**3 4 5 8 11 12 13 15 16 17 18 20 22 24 26 28 29 30 31 33 34 35 38 40 41 43 44 45 46 48 50 51 53 54 58 59 60 61 64 65 68 70 72 73 74 75 76 77 78 79 81 82 84 85 86 87 90 92 93 94 96 97 98 100 101 102 104 107 108 109 110 111 115 116 119 121 122 123 124 126 129 130 131 132 135 141 144 146 147 148 149 150 153 154 156 160 162 164 167 169 **S** WellStar Health System, Marietta, GA
Primary Contact: Eliese Bernard, President
CFO: Darold Etheridge, Vice President and Chief Financial Officer
CMO: Thomas McNamara, D.O., Vice President Medical Affairs
CHR: Danyale Ziglor, Vice President
CNO: Kay Kennedy V, Chief Nurse Executive
Web address: https://www.wellstar.org/locations/hospital/cobb-hospital
Control: Other not-for-profit (including NFP Corporation) **Service**: General medical and surgical

Staffed Beds: 405 **Admissions:** 19745 **Census:** 273 **Outpatient Visits:** 385235 **Births:** 2768 **Personnel:** 2611

BAINBRIDGE—Decatur County

⇑ **MEMORIAL HOSPITAL AND MANOR (110132)**, 1500 East Shotwell Street, Zip 39819-4256; tel. 229/246-3500, (Nonreporting) **A**10 21
Primary Contact: James M. Lambert, FACHE, Chief Executive Officer
COO: Lee Harris, Assistant Administrator Support Services
CFO: David Paugh, Chief Financial Officer
CMO: Shawn Surratt, M.D., Chief of Staff
CIO: Nelda Moore, Director Data Processing
CHR: Angel Sykes, Director Human Resources
CNO: Cynthia Vickers, R.N., Assistant Administrator, Nursing Services
Web address: www.mh-m.org
Control: Hospital district or authority, Government, Nonfederal **Service**: General medical and surgical

Staffed Beds: 80

BAXLEY—Appling County

★ ⇑ **APPLING HEALTHCARE SYSTEM (110071)**, 163 East Tollison Street, Zip 31513-0120; tel. 912/367-9841, (Total facility includes 101 beds in nursing home-type unit) **A**10 20 21 **F**7 45 46 54 56 57 70 92 98 100 103 104 107 111 119 122 127 128 133 154
Primary Contact: Andrea Pierce Graham, Chief Executive Officer
COO: Judy M Long, R.N., MS, Chief Nursing Officer and Chief Operating Officer
CFO: Raymond J. Leadbetter Jr, Revenue Cycle Consultant
CMO: Garland Martin, M.D., Chief of Staff
CIO: Gary Gower, Chief Information Officer
CHR: Carla McLendon, Director Human Resources
CNO: Judy M Long, R.N., MS, Chief Nursing Officer and Chief Operating Officer
Web address: www.appling-hospital.org
Control: Hospital district or authority, Government, Nonfederal **Service**: General medical and surgical

Staffed Beds: 164 **Admissions:** 1397 **Census:** 101 **Outpatient Visits:** 23458 **Births:** 0 **Total Expense ($000):** 33924 **Payroll Expense ($000):** 14606 **Personnel:** 252

BLAIRSVILLE—Union County

★ ⇑ **UNION GENERAL HOSPITAL (110051)**, 35 Hospital Road, Zip 30512-3139; tel. 706/745-2111, (Total facility includes 150 beds in nursing home-type unit) **A**10 20 21 **F**3 7 11 13 15 28 29 30 34 35 40 45 46 47 48 49 50 53 57 59 64 70 76 77 79 81 82 85 86 87 93 96 107 108 110 111 114 115 119 120 127 131 132 135 143 146 147 148 149 157 **P**1 **S** Union General Hospital, Inc., Blairsville, GA
Primary Contact: Kevin Bierschenk, Chief Executive Officer
COO: Lewis Kelley, Chief Operating Officer
CFO: Stephanie L Fletcher, CPA, Chief Financial Officer
CMO: Andre Schaeffer, M.D., Chief of Staff
CIO: Mike Johnston, Director Facilities Operations
CHR: Kathy Hood, Administrative Assistant Human Resources
CNO: Julia Barnett, Chief Nursing Officer
Web address: www.uniongeneralhospital.com
Control: Other not-for-profit (including NFP Corporation) **Service**: General medical and surgical

Staffed Beds: 195 **Admissions:** 2432 **Census:** 118 **Outpatient Visits:** 90880 **Births:** 405 **Total Expense ($000):** 110875 **Payroll Expense ($000):** 51637 **Personnel:** 808

BLAKELY—Early County

⇑ **EARLY MEDICAL CENTER (111314)**, 11740 Columbia Street, Zip 39823-2574; tel. 229/723-4241, (Nonreporting) **A**10 18 21 **S** LifeBrite Hospital Group, LLC, Lilburn, GA
Primary Contact: Jeanette Filpi, Chief Executive Officer
Web address: www.pchearly.com
Control: Other not-for-profit (including NFP Corporation) **Service**: General medical and surgical

Staffed Beds: 152

BLUE RIDGE—Fannin County

BLUE RIDGE MEDICAL CENTER See Fannin Regional Hospital

FANNIN REGIONAL HOSPITAL (110780), 2855 Old Highway 5, Zip 30513-6248; tel. 706/632-3711, (Nonreporting) **A**10 **S** Quorum Health, Brentwood, TN
Primary Contact: William Henry, Chief Executive Officer
CFO: Phillip Fouts, Chief Financial Officer
CMO: Dillon D Miller, M.D., Chief Medical Officer
CIO: Timothy Snider, Manager Information Systems
CHR: Terrasina Ensley, Director Human Resources
Web address: www.fanninregionalhospital.com
Control: Corporation, Investor-owned (for-profit)

Staffed Beds: 50

BREMEN—Haralson County

✠ **HIGGINS GENERAL HOSPITAL (111320)**, 200 Allen Memorial Drive, Zip 30110-2012; tel. 770/824-2000, (Nonreporting) **A**1 10 18 **S** Tanner Health System, Carrollton, GA
Primary Contact: Jerry Morris, Administrator
CFO: Carol Crews, Chief Financial Officer
CMO: Bill Waters, M.D., Chief Medical Officer
CIO: Terri Lee, Chief Information Officer
CHR: Shari W Gainey, Human Resource Director
CNO: B. J. Brock, Nursing Director
Web address: www.tanner.org/Main/HigginsGeneralHospitalBremen.aspx
Control: Other not-for-profit (including NFP Corporation) **Service**: General medical and surgical

Staffed Beds: 23

BRUNSWICK—Glynn County

✠ **SOUTHEAST GEORGIA HEALTH SYSTEM BRUNSWICK CAMPUS (110025)**, 2415 Parkwood Drive, Zip 31520-4722, Mailing Address: P.O. Box 1518, Zip 31521-1518; tel. 912/466-7000, (Nonreporting) **A**1 2 3 10 **S** Southeast Georgia Health System, Brunswick, GA
Primary Contact: Scott Raynes, President and Chief Executive Officer
COO: Christy D Jordan, R.N., JD, Chief Operating Officer/Legal Counsel
CFO: John A Miliazzo, Vice President and Chief Financial Officer
CHR: Kelli Ann Reale, Vice President Human Resources
CNO: Judith Henson, Vice President Patient Care Services
Web address: www.sghs.org
Control: Other not-for-profit (including NFP Corporation) **Service**: General medical and surgical

Staffed Beds: 564

BUENA VISTA—Marion County

MARION MEMORIAL HOSPITAL See Marion Memorial Nursing Home

CAIRO—Grady County

✠ **ARCHBOLD GRADY (110121)**, 1155 Fifth Street SE, Zip 39828-3142, Mailing Address: P.O. Box 360, Zip 39828-0360; tel. 229/377-1150, **A**1 10 **F**3 11 13 15 29 30 39 40 45 57 59 68 76 77 79 81 85 93 107 111 119 128 133 154 **S** Archbold Medical Center, Thomasville, GA
Primary Contact: Crystal Wells, Administrator
COO: Jim Carter, Chief Operating Officer
CFO: Skip Hightower, Chief Financial Officer
CIO: Tracy Gray, Chief Information Officer
CHR: Michelle Pledger, Coordinator Human Resources
Web address: www.archbold.org
Control: Other not-for-profit (including NFP Corporation) **Service**: General medical and surgical

Staffed Beds: 47 **Admissions:** 819 **Census:** 11 **Outpatient Visits:** 61938 **Births:** 278 **Total Expense ($000):** 30064 **Payroll Expense ($000):** 12452 **Personnel:** 141

Hospital, Medicare Provider Number, Address, Telephone, Approval, Facility, and Physician Codes, Health Care System

★ American Hospital Association (AHA) membership ◯ Healthcare Facilities Accreditation Program ⇑ Center for Improvement in Healthcare Quality Accreditation
☐ The Joint Commission accreditation ◇ DNV Healthcare Inc. accreditation △ Commission on Accreditation of Rehabilitation Facilities (CARF) accreditation

Hospitals, U.S. / GEORGIA

CALHOUN—Gordon County

✠ **ADVENTHEALTH GORDON (110023)**, 1035 Red Bud Road, Zip 30701–2082, Mailing Address: P.O. Box 12938, Zip 30703–7013; tel. 706/629–2895, (Nonreporting) **A**1 2 10 19 **S** AdventHealth, Altamonte Springs, FL
Primary Contact: Chris Self, Chief Executive Officer
CFO: Steve Gottshall, Chief Financial Officer
CMO: Will Theus, M.D., Chief of Staff
CHR: Jeni Hasselbrack, Director Human Resources
CNO: Karen Bell, Chief Nursing Officer
Web address: www.gordonhospital.com
Control: Church operated, Nongovernment, not–for–profit **Service**: General medical and surgical

Staffed Beds: 83

CAMILLA—Mitchell County

✠ **ARCHBOLD MITCHELL (111331)**, 90 East Stephens Street, Zip 31730–1836, Mailing Address: P.O. Box 639, Zip 31730–0639; tel. 229/336–5284, (Total facility includes 156 beds in nursing home–type unit) **A**1 10 18 **F**3 15 29 30 35 40 41 50 54 57 58 59 68 93 100 102 107 110 111 114 119 127 128 133 135 154 **S** Archbold Medical Center, Thomasville, GA
Primary Contact: Carla Beasley, R.N., MSN, Administrator
CFO: Skip Hightower, Senior Vice President and Chief Financial Officer
CIO: Tracy Gray, Chief Information Officer
CHR: Vickie County–Teemer, Coordinator Human Resources
CNO: Carla Beasley, R.N., MSN, Director of Nursing
Web address: www.archbold.org
Control: Other not–for–profit (including NFP Corporation) **Service**: General medical and surgical

Staffed Beds: 181 **Admissions**: 422 **Census**: 157 **Outpatient Visits**: 28421 **Births**: 0 **Total Expense ($000)**: 37320 **Payroll Expense ($000)**: 19856 **Personnel**: 148

CANTON—Cherokee County

✠ **NORTHSIDE HOSPITAL CHEROKEE (110008)**, 450 Northside Cherokee Boulevard, Zip 30115–8015; tel. 770/720–5100, **A**1 2 10 **F**3 8 9 11 12 13 15 18 20 22 26 28 29 30 31 34 35 37 38 40 41 44 45 49 50 54 55 57 58 59 64 68 70 72 73 74 75 76 77 78 79 80 81 82 84 85 86 87 93 100 102 107 108 110 111 114 115 117 118 119 120 121 123 124 126 129 130 131 132 135 144 146 147 148 149 154 156 164 167 169 **S** Northside Healthcare System, Atlanta, GA
Primary Contact: William M. Hayes, Chief Executive Officer
COO: Mike Patterson, Director of Operations
CFO: Brian Jennette, Chief Financial Officer
CMO: Alexander Kessler, M.D., Chief of Staff
CIO: Bill Dunford, Manager
CHR: Roslyn Roberts, Manager
Web address: www.northside.com
Control: Other not–for–profit (including NFP Corporation) **Service**: General medical and surgical

Staffed Beds: 206 **Admissions**: 15752 **Census**: 230 **Outpatient Visits**: 532861 **Births**: 2730 **Total Expense ($000)**: 700131 **Payroll Expense ($000)**: 306105 **Personnel**: 3417

CARROLLTON—Carroll County

✠ **TANNER MEDICAL CENTER–CARROLLTON (110011)**, 705 Dixie Street, Zip 30117–3818; tel. 770/836–9666, (Nonreporting) **A**1 2 10 **S** Tanner Health System, Carrollton, GA
Primary Contact: Loy M. Howard, Chief Operating Officer
CFO: Carol Crews, Chief Financial Officer
CMO: William Waters, M.D., IV, Chief Medical Officer
CNO: Deborah Matthews, Chief Nursing Officer
Web address: www.tanner.org
Control: Other not–for–profit (including NFP Corporation) **Service**: General medical and surgical

Staffed Beds: 176

CARTERSVILLE—Bartow County

⇑ **CARTERSVILLE MEDICAL CENTER** See Piedmont Cartersville

★ ⇑ **PIEDMONT CARTERSVILLE (110030)**, 960 Joe Frank Harris Parkway, Zip 30120–2129; tel. 470/490–1000, (Nonreporting) **A**5 10 21 **S** Piedmont Healthcare, Roswell, GA
Primary Contact: Lori Rakes, R.N., Chief Executive Officer
CNO: Jan Tidwell, Chief Nursing Officer
Web address: https://www.piedmont.org/locations/piedmont-cartersville/
Control: Corporation, Investor–owned (for–profit) **Service**: General medical and surgical

Staffed Beds: 119

CEDARTOWN—Polk County

✠ **ATRIUM HEALTH FLOYD POLK MEDICAL CENTER (111330)**, 2360 Rockmart Highway, Zip 30125–6029; tel. 770/748–2500, **A**1 10 18 **F**3 15 28 29 30 34 35 40 43 44 50 56 57 59 64 68 75 77 86 87 93 107 108 110 114 119 130 133 135 143 144 146 148 149 154 156 **S** Atrium Health, Inc., Charlotte, NC
Primary Contact: Tifani Kinard, Vice President of Rural Health in SAM
CFO: Philip Wheeler, Chief Financial Officer
CNO: Tifani Kinard, Vice President of Rural Health in SAM
Web address: https://www.floyd.org/find-a-location/Pages/polkmedicalcenter.aspx
Control: Hospital district or authority, Government, Nonfederal **Service**: General medical and surgical

Staffed Beds: 25 **Admissions**: 660 **Census**: 22 **Outpatient Visits**: 53854 **Births**: 0 **Total Expense ($000)**: 23914 **Payroll Expense ($000)**: 12990 **Personnel**: 144

POLK MEDICAL CENTER See Atrium Health Floyd Polk Medical Center

CHATSWORTH—Murray County

✠ **ADVENTHEALTH MURRAY (110050)**, 707 Old Dalton Ellijay Road, Zip 30705–2060, Mailing Address: P.O. Box 1406, Zip 30705–1406; tel. 706/695–4564, (Nonreporting) **A**1 10 **S** AdventHealth, Altamonte Springs, FL
Primary Contact: Chris Self, Chief Executive Officer
CFO: Steve Gottshall, Chief Financial Officer
CMO: Blaine Minor, M.D., Chief of Staff
CIO: Jose C Rios, Director Information Services
CHR: Brandy Rymer, Coordinator Human Resources
CNO: Karen Bell, Chief Nursing Officer
Web address: https://www.adventhealth.com/hospital/adventhealth-murray
Control: Church operated, Nongovernment, not–for–profit **Service**: General medical and surgical

Staffed Beds: 16

CLAXTON—Evans County

⇑ **EVANS MEMORIAL HOSPITAL (110142)**, 200 North River Street, Zip 30417–1659, Mailing Address: P.O. Box 518, Zip 30417–0518; tel. 912/739–2611, (Nonreporting) **A**10 21
Primary Contact: William H. Lee, Chief Executive Officer
CFO: John Wiggins, Chief Financial Officer
CMO: Kyle Parks, M.D., Chief of Staff
CIO: Steve Schmidt, Director Information Systems
CHR: Gina Waters, Director Human Resources
CNO: Nikki NeSmith, Chief Nursing Officer
Web address: www.evansmemorialhospital.org/
Control: Hospital district or authority, Government, Nonfederal **Service**: General medical and surgical

Staffed Beds: 10

CLAYTON—Rabun County

MOUNTAIN LAKES MEDICAL CENTER (111336), 162 Legacy Point, Zip 30525–5354; tel. 706/782–3100, (Nonreporting) **A**10 18
Primary Contact: Kristy Hall, Chief Executive Officer
CFO: Jimmy Norman, Chief Financial Officer
CHR: Charles Harbaugh, Director Human Resources
Web address: www.mountainlakesmedicalcenter.com
Control: Hospital district or authority, Government, Nonfederal **Service**: General medical and surgical

Staffed Beds: 16

COCHRAN—Bleckley County

⇑ **BLECKLEY MEMORIAL HOSPITAL (111302)**, 145 East Peacock Street, Zip 31014–7846, Mailing Address: P.O. Box 536, Zip 31014–0536; tel. 478/934–6211, (Nonreporting) **A**10 18 21
Primary Contact: Jon Green, R.N., Chief Executive Officer
COO: John Roland, R.N., Chief Operating Officer and Chief Nursing Officer
CFO: Sandra Herndon, CPA, Chief Financial Officer
CIO: Scott Wynne, Chief Information Officer Director
CHR: Jean Allen, Human Resources Director
CNO: John Roland, R.N., Chief Operating Officer and Chief Nursing Officer
Web address: www.bleckleymemorial.com
Control: Hospital district or authority, Government, Nonfederal **Service**: General medical and surgical

Staffed Beds: 25

Hospitals, U.S. / GEORGIA

COLQUITT—Miller County

⇧ **MILLER COUNTY HOSPITAL (111305)**, 209 North Cuthbert Street, Zip 39837-3518, Mailing Address: P.O. Box 7, Zip 39837-0007; tel. 229/758-3385, (Total facility includes 217 beds in nursing home–type unit) **A**10 18 21 **F**3 15 29 32 34 35 40 44 45 50 56 57 59 62 66 68 71 75 81 83 84 85 86 87 89 97 107 110 111 115 119 127 128 130 132 133 135 148 149 154 156 158
Primary Contact: Robin Rau, Chief Executive Officer
CFO: Jill Brown, Chief Financial Officer
CMO: William Swofford, M.D., Chief of Staff
CIO: Keith Lovering, Information Technician
CHR: Karie Spence, Director Human Resources
CNO: Shawn Whittaker, Chief Nursing Officer
Web address: www.millercountyhospital.com
Control: Hospital district or authority, Government, Nonfederal **Service**: General medical and surgical

Staffed Beds: 242 **Admissions**: 736 **Census**: 230 **Outpatient Visits**: 41617 **Births**: 0 **Total Expense ($000)**: 82524 **Payroll Expense ($000)**: 40088 **Personnel**: 654

COLUMBUS—Muscogee County

BRADLEY CENTER See Bradley Center of St. Francis

BRADLEY CENTER OF ST. FRANCIS See St. Francis – Emory Healthcare, Columbus

COLUMBUS SPECIALTY HOSPITAL (112012), 616 19th Street, Zip 31901-1528, Mailing Address: P.O. Box 910, Zip 31902-0910; tel. 706/494-4075, (Nonreporting) **A**10
Primary Contact: William Eckstein, Chief Executive Officer and Chief Financial Officer
CFO: William Eckstein, Chief Executive Officer and Chief Financial Officer
CHR: Myra Whitley, Vice President, Human Resources
Web address: www.columbusspecialtyhospital.net
Control: Other not-for-profit (including NFP Corporation) **Service**: Acute long-term care hospital

Staffed Beds: 33

DOCTORS SPECIALTY HOSPITAL See Midtown Medical Center West

⇧ **PIEDMONT COLUMBUS REGIONAL MIDTOWN (110064)**, 710 Center Street, Zip 31901-1527, Mailing Address: P.O. Box 951, Zip 31902-0951; tel. 706/571-1000, (Includes MIDTOWN MEDICAL CENTER WEST, 616 19th Street, Columbus, Georgia, Zip 31901-1528, P O Box 2188, Zip 31902-2188, tel. 706/494-4262; Ryan Chandler, Chief Executive Officer) (Nonreporting) **A**2 3 5 10 13 19 21 **S** Piedmont Healthcare, Roswell, GA
Primary Contact: M. Scott. Hill, President and Chief Executive Officer
COO: Bill Tustin, Chief Operating Officer
CMO: Chris Edwards, M.D., Chief Medical Officer
Web address: www.columbusregional.com
Control: Other not-for-profit (including NFP Corporation) **Service**: General medical and surgical

Staffed Beds: 510

⇧ **PIEDMONT COLUMBUS REGIONAL NORTHSIDE (110200)**, 100 Frist Court, Zip 31909-3578, Mailing Address: P.O. Box 7188, Zip 31908-7188; tel. 706/494-2100, (Nonreporting) **A**5 10 21 **S** Piedmont Healthcare, Roswell, GA
Primary Contact: M. Scott. Hill, President and Chief Executive Officer
COO: Laura Drew, Chief Operating Officer
CFO: Roland Thacker, Chief Financial Officer
CMO: Chris Edwards, M.D., Chief Medical Officer
CIO: Douglas Colburn, Chief Information Officer
CHR: Becky Augustyniak, Director Human Resources
Web address: www.columbusregional.com
Control: Other not-for-profit (including NFP Corporation) **Service**: Orthopedic

Staffed Beds: 100

⊞ **ST. FRANCIS – EMORY HEALTHCARE (110129)**, 2122 Manchester Expressway, Zip 31904-6878, Mailing Address: P.O. Box 7000, Zip 31908-7000; tel. 706/596-4000, (Includes BRADLEY CENTER OF ST. FRANCIS, 2000 16th Avenue, Columbus, Georgia, Zip 31906-0308, tel. 706/320-3700) (Nonreporting) **A**1 3 5 10 **S** ScionHealth, Louisville, KY
Primary Contact: Melody Trimble, Chief Executive Officer
COO: Alan E George, Chief Operating Officer
CFO: Greg Hembree, Senior Vice President and Chief Financial Officer
CMO: Bobbi Farber, M.D., Chief Medical Officer
CIO: Jonathon R Jager, Chief Information Officer
CNO: Elizabeth B. Later, R.N., Chief Nursing Officer
Web address: www.mystfrancis.com
Control: Other not-for-profit (including NFP Corporation) **Service**: General medical and surgical

Staffed Beds: 331

ST. FRANCIS HOSPITAL See St. Francis – Emory Healthcare

☐ **WEST CENTRAL GEORGIA REGIONAL HOSPITAL (114013)**, 3000 Schatulga Road, Zip 31907-3117, Mailing Address: P.O. Box 12435, Zip 31917-2435; tel. 706/568-5000, (Nonreporting) **A**1 3 10
Primary Contact: Marcia Capshaw, Administrator
COO: Marcia Capshaw, Chief Operating Officer
CFO: John Frederick, Chief Financial Officer
CMO: David Morton, M.D., Clinical Director
CIO: Karen Fisher-Ford, Director of Health Information Management
CHR: Peri Johnson, Human Resources Director
CNO: Nicolise Claassens, Nurse Executive
Web address: www.dbhdd.georgia.gov/west-central-georgia-regional-hospital-columbus
Control: State, Government, Nonfederal **Service**: Psychiatric

Staffed Beds: 194

CONYERS—Rockdale County

PIEDMONT ROCKDALE HOSPITAL (110091), 1412 Milstead Avenue NE, Zip 30012-3877; tel. 770/918-3000, (Nonreporting) **A**5 10 **S** Piedmont Healthcare, Roswell, GA
Primary Contact: Monica A. Hum, Chief Executive Officer
CFO: Diane Roth, Chief Financial Officer
CMO: Lisa Gillespie, M.D., Chief Medical Officer
CIO: Gail Waldo, Director Information Technology
CHR: Marianne Freeman, Vice President Human Resources
CNO: Eleanor Post, R.N., Chief Nursing Officer
Web address: https://www.piedmont.org/locations/piedmont-rockdale
Control: Other not-for-profit (including NFP Corporation) **Service**: General medical and surgical

Staffed Beds: 158

CORDELE—Crisp County

⊞ **CRISP REGIONAL HOSPITAL (110104)**, 902 North Seventh Street, Zip 31015-3234; tel. 229/276-3100, (Total facility includes 243 beds in nursing home–type unit) **A**1 3 5 10 20 **F**3 11 13 15 29 30 31 34 35 40 43 44 45 48 49 50 51 54 56 57 58 59 60 61 62 63 64 65 69 70 71 73 75 76 77 78 79 81 84 85 86 87 93 96 97 107 108 110 111 114 115 117 118 125 126 127 128 129 130 132 133 135 144 146 147 148 149 154 156 167 169
Primary Contact: Steven Gautney, FACHE, President and Chief Executive Officer
COO: Mary Jim Montgomery, R.N., MSN, FACHE, Chief Operating Officer
CFO: Jessica Y Carter, Chief Financial Officer
CMO: David Kavtaradze, M.D., Chief of Staff
CHR: George M Laurin, Interim Director Human Resources
CNO: Marsha L. Mulderig, R.N., MSN, Chief Nursing Officer
Web address: www.crispregional.org
Control: Other not-for-profit (including NFP Corporation) **Service**: General medical and surgical

Staffed Beds: 316 **Admissions**: 2844 **Census**: 157 **Outpatient Visits**: 79070 **Births**: 248 **Personnel**: 425

Hospital, Medicare Provider Number, Address, Telephone, Approval, Facility, and Physician Codes, Health Care System

★ American Hospital Association (AHA) membership
☐ The Joint Commission accreditation
○ Healthcare Facilities Accreditation Program
◇ DNV Healthcare Inc. accreditation
⇧ Center for Improvement in Healthcare Quality Accreditation
△ Commission on Accreditation of Rehabilitation Facilities (CARF) accreditation

Hospitals, U.S. / GEORGIA

COVINGTON—Newton County

⇑ **PIEDMONT NEWTON HOSPITAL (110018)**, 5126 Hospital Drive, Zip 30014–2567; tel. 770/786–7053, (Nonreporting) **A**10 21 **S** Piedmont Healthcare, Roswell, GA
Primary Contact: Lindsey Petrini, Chief Executive Officer
CFO: Justin Roberts, Chief Financial Officer
CMO: B. Carter Rogers, Chief of Staff
CIO: Brad Collier, Director
CHR: Greg H Richardson, Assistant Administrator Human Resources
CNO: Elizabeth Timberlake BSN, RNC–, Chief Nursing Officer
Web address: https://www.piedmont.org/locations/piedmont-newton/
Control: Other not–for–profit (including NFP Corporation) **Service:** General medical and surgical

Staffed Beds: 103

CUMMING—Forsyth County

⊞ **ENCOMPASS HEALTH REHABILITATION HOSPITAL OF CUMMING (113034)**, 1165 Sanders Road, Zip 30041–5965; tel. 470/533–4200, (Nonreporting) **A**1 10 **S** Encompass Health Corporation, Birmingham, AL
Primary Contact: E. Rick. Lowe, Chief Executive Officer
COO: Jeff Leitner, Director, Facilities Management
CFO: Michael Boscia, Controller
CMO: Gregg Soifer, M.D., Medical Director
CHR: Ashley Usry, Director, Human Resources
CNO: Lynn Whelan, Chief Nursing Officer
Web address: https://encompasshealth.com/cummingrehab
Control: Corporation, Investor–owned (for–profit) **Service:** Rehabilitation

Staffed Beds: 50

⊞ **NORTHSIDE HOSPITAL FORSYTH (110005)**, 1200 Northside Forsyth Drive, Zip 30041–7659; tel. 770/844–3200, **A**1 2 10 **F**3 8 9 11 12 13 15 18 20 22 26 28 29 30 31 34 35 37 38 40 41 44 45 49 50 54 55 57 58 59 64 68 70 72 73 74 75 76 77 78 79 80 81 82 84 85 86 87 93 100 102 107 108 110 111 114 115 117 118 119 120 121 123 124 126 127 129 130 131 132 135 144 146 147 148 149 154 156 164 167 169 **S** Northside Healthcare System, Atlanta, GA
Primary Contact: Lynn Jackson, Chief Executive Officer
CFO: Eric Caldwell, Director Finance
CNO: Carolyn Booker, R.N., Chief Nursing Officer
Web address: www.northside.com
Control: Other not–for–profit (including NFP Corporation) **Service:** General medical and surgical

Staffed Beds: 384 **Admissions:** 17485 **Census:** 276 **Outpatient Visits:** 580609 **Births:** 3802 **Total Expense ($000):** 750531 **Payroll Expense ($000):** 337389 **Personnel:** 3559

DAHLONEGA—Lumpkin County

★ ⇑ **NORTHEAST GEORGIA MEDICAL CENTER LUMPKIN (110237)**, 495 Highway 400, Zip 30533–6823; tel. 770/219–9000, **A**10 21 **F**3 11 29 30 34 35 40 57 59 61 63 64 75 84 86 87 107 115 119 149 166 **S** Northeast Georgia Health System, Gainesville, GA
Primary Contact: Carol H. Burrell, Chief Executive Officer
Web address: https://www.nghs.com/locations/lumpkin/
Control: Other not–for–profit (including NFP Corporation) **Service:** General medical and surgical

Staffed Beds: 23 **Admissions:** 789 **Census:** 8 **Outpatient Visits:** 19295 **Births:** 0 **Personnel:** 112

DALTON—Whitfield County

⊞ **HAMILTON MEDICAL CENTER (110001)**, 1200 Memorial Drive, Zip 30720–2529, Mailing Address: P.O. Box 1168, Zip 30722–1168; tel. 706/272–6000, **A**1 2 5 10 19 **F**3 8 12 13 15 17 18 20 22 24 26 28 29 30 31 34 35 37 40 43 44 45 46 47 48 49 50 51 53 54 55 57 58 59 60 62 63 64 68 70 72 73 74 75 76 78 79 81 82 85 86 87 89 92 93 97 100 101 102 104 107 108 109 110 111 114 115 116 117 118 119 120 121 123 124 126 129 130 131 132 135 146 147 148 149 150 154 156 164 167 169
Primary Contact: Sandra D. McKenzie, President and Chief Executive Officer
CFO: Gary L Howard, Senior Vice President and Chief Financial Officer
CMO: Andrew C. Bland, M.D., Vice President and Chief Medical Officer
CIO: John M Forrester, Director Information Services
CHR: Jason Hopkins, Director, Human Resources
Web address: www.hamiltonhealth.com
Control: Other not–for–profit (including NFP Corporation) **Service:** General medical and surgical

Staffed Beds: 230 **Admissions:** 8718 **Census:** 109 **Outpatient Visits:** 202011 **Births:** 1596

DECATUR—Dekalb County

⊞ **ATLANTA VETERANS AFFAIRS MEDICAL CENTER**, 1670 Clairmont Road, Zip 30033–4004; tel. 404/321–6111, (Nonreporting) **A**1 3 5 **S** Department of Veterans Affairs, Washington, DC
Primary Contact: Annette Walker, Medical Center Director
CFO: Pamela Watkins, Chief Financial Officer
CMO: David Bower, M.D., Chief of Staff
CIO: William Brock, Chief Information Officer
CHR: Zeta Ferguson, Chief Human Resources
Web address: www.atlanta.va.gov/
Control: Veterans Affairs, Government, federal **Service:** General medical and surgical

Staffed Beds: 285

⊞ **EMORY DECATUR HOSPITAL (110076)**, 2701 North Decatur Road, Zip 30033–5995; tel. 404/501–1000, **A**1 2 3 5 10 **F**3 11 12 13 15 18 20 22 26 28 29 30 31 34 35 38 40 44 46 48 49 50 51 53 55 57 58 59 60 68 70 72 73 74 75 76 77 78 79 81 82 84 85 86 87 90 93 96 98 100 102 107 108 110 111 114 115 116 117 119 120 121 123 124 126 129 130 131 132 146 147 148 149 154 156 167 169 **S** Emory Healthcare, Atlanta, GA
Primary Contact: Jennifer Schuck, Chief Executive Officer
CFO: Robin Nichols, Interim Chief Financial Officer
CIO: Beth Patino, Chief Information Officer
CHR: LeRoy Walker, Vice President Human Resources
CNO: Susan Breslin, R.N., MSN, Vice President Patient Care Services and Chief Nursing Officer
Web address: https://www.emoryhealthcare.org/dekalbmedical/
Control: Other not–for–profit (including NFP Corporation) **Service:** General medical and surgical

Staffed Beds: 415 **Admissions:** 16672 **Census:** 276 **Outpatient Visits:** 148205 **Births:** 3100 **Total Expense ($000):** 471497 **Payroll Expense ($000):** 203460 **Personnel:** 1977

☐ **EMORY LONG–TERM ACUTE CARE (112006)**, 450 North Candler Street, Zip 30030–2671; tel. 404/501–6700, **A**1 10 **F**1 18 29 30 45 48 50 60 68 74 75 77 78 84 85 91 94 100 119 130 135 148 149 **S** Emory Healthcare, Atlanta, GA
Primary Contact: Jennifer Schuck, Chief Executive Officer
CMO: David Snyder, M.D., Chief of Staff
CHR: Tom Crawford, Vice President Human Resources
Web address: https://www.emoryhealthcare.org
Control: Other not–for–profit (including NFP Corporation) **Service:** Acute long–term care hospital

Staffed Beds: 50 **Admissions:** 324 **Census:** 38 **Outpatient Visits:** 0 **Births:** 0 **Total Expense ($000):** 32907 **Payroll Expense ($000):** 18008 **Personnel:** 171

☐ **GEORGIA REGIONAL HOSPITAL AT ATLANTA (114019)**, 3073 Panthersville Road, Zip 30034–3828; tel. 404/243–2100, (Total facility includes 20 beds in nursing home–type unit) **A**1 3 5 10 **F**39 98 101 102 128 163
Primary Contact: Charles Li, M.D., Administrator
COO: Sonny Slate, Chief Operating Officer
CFO: Reginald Jones, Business Manager
CMO: Emile Risby, M.D., Clinical Director
CIO: Elfie Early, Manager Data Services
CHR: Lorraine Farr, Manager Human Resources
Web address: www.atlantareg.dhr.state.ga.us
Control: State, Government, Nonfederal **Service:** Psychiatric

Staffed Beds: 260 **Admissions:** 1442 **Census:** 221 **Outpatient Visits:** 0 **Births:** 0

DEMOREST—Habersham County

★ ⇑ **NORTHEAST GEORGIA MEDICAL CENTER HABERSHAM (110041)**, 541 Historic Highway 441, Zip 30535–3118, Mailing Address: P.O. Box 37, Zip 30535–0037; tel. 706/754–2161, (Total facility includes 84 beds in nursing home–type unit) **A**10 21 **F**3 11 29 30 34 35 40 57 59 61 68 75 76 79 81 82 84 86 87 107 111 115 119 128 149 154 169 **S** Northeast Georgia Health System, Gainesville, GA
Primary Contact: Kevin Matson, Interim Chief Executive Officer
COO: Michael Gay, Chief Operating Officer
CFO: Barbara Duncan, Chief Financial Officer
CMO: Josh Garrett, Chief of Staff
CHR: Ryan Snow, Director Human Resources
Web address: www.habershammedical.com/
Control: Other not–for–profit (including NFP Corporation) **Service:** General medical and surgical

Staffed Beds: 121 **Admissions:** 1233 **Census:** 81 **Births:** 432 **Personnel:** 237

Hospitals, U.S. / GEORGIA

DONALSONVILLE—Seminole County

⇧ **DONALSONVILLE HOSPITAL (110194)**, 102 Hospital Circle, Zip 39845-1199; tel. 229/524-5217, (Nonreporting) **A**10 21
Primary Contact: James Moody, Administrator
CFO: James Moody, Chief Financial Officer
CMO: C O Walker, M.D., Chief of Staff
CHR: Jo Adams, Director Human Resources
Control: Other not-for-profit (including NFP Corporation) **Service**: General medical and surgical

Staffed Beds: 140

DOUGLAS—Coffee County

★ ⇧ **COFFEE REGIONAL MEDICAL CENTER (110089)**, 1101 Ocilla Road, Zip 31533-2207; tel. 912/384-1900, **A**2 10 20 21 **F**3 7 11 12 13 15 18 20 22 26 28 29 30 31 34 35 40 41 44 45 47 48 50 51 53 54 56 57 59 60 61 64 65 66 68 70 71 74 75 76 77 78 79 81 82 85 86 87 89 92 93 97 107 108 110 111 114 115 119 124 127 130 131 132 135 143 146 147 148 149 154 156 169 **P**8
Primary Contact: Vicki Lewis, FACHE, President and Chief Executive Officer
CFO: Lavonda Cravey, Chief Financial Officer
CHR: Laura Bloom, Director Human Resources
Web address: www.coffeeregional.org
Control: Other not-for-profit (including NFP Corporation) **Service**: General medical and surgical

Staffed Beds: 88 **Admissions:** 3950 **Census:** 41 **Outpatient Visits:** 93082 **Births:** 724 **Total Expense ($000):** 132222 **Payroll Expense ($000):** 50775 **Personnel:** 671

DOUGLASVILLE—Douglas County

✠ **WELLSTAR DOUGLAS HOSPITAL (110184)**, 8954 Hospital Drive, Zip 30134-2282; tel. 470/644-6000, **A**1 2 3 10 **F**3 11 13 15 18 20 22 28 29 30 31 37 38 40 41 44 45 48 49 50 51 53 54 59 60 61 64 68 70 72 74 75 76 77 78 79 81 82 84 85 86 87 93 94 100 102 107 108 110 111 114 115 116 117 118 119 126 129 130 132 135 144 146 147 148 154 156 167 169 **S** WellStar Health System, Marietta, GA
Primary Contact: Heath King, President
CFO: Bradley Greene, Chief Financial Officer
CMO: Noel Holtz, M.D., Chief Medical Officer
CHR: Danyale Ziglor, Vice President
Web address: https://www.wellstar.org/locations/hospital/douglas-hospital
Control: Other not-for-profit (including NFP Corporation) **Service**: General medical and surgical

Staffed Beds: 108 **Admissions:** 7293 **Census:** 92 **Outpatient Visits:** 136009 **Births:** 602 **Personnel:** 944

YOUTH VILLAGES INNER HARBOUR CAMPUS, 4685 Dorsett Shoals Road, Zip 30135-4999; tel. 770/942-2391, (Nonreporting)
Primary Contact: Patrick Lawler, Chief Executive Officer
CFO: J Steve Lewis, Director Finance
CIO: Laura Sellers, Director Information Systems
CHR: Sherry Kollmeyer, Vice President Human Resources
Web address: www.innerharbour.org
Control: Other not-for-profit (including NFP Corporation) **Service**: Children's hospital psychiatric

Staffed Beds: 190

DUBLIN—Laurens County

✠ **CARL VINSON VETERANS AFFAIRS MEDICAL CENTER**, 1826 Veterans Boulevard, Zip 31021-3620, Mailing Address: 1326 Veterans Boulevard, Zip 31021-3620; tel. 478/272-1210, (Nonreporting) **A**1 3 **S** Department of Veterans Affairs, Washington, DC
Primary Contact: David Reesman, Acting Director
COO: Gerald M DeWorth, Associate Director
CFO: Kimberly Johnson-Miller, Chief Financial Officer
CMO: Christopher Blasy, D.O., Chief of Staff
CIO: Mark Cowart, Facility Chief Information Officer
CHR: Kurt Oster, Human Resources Officer
Web address: www.dublin.va.gov/
Control: Veterans Affairs, Government, federal **Service**: General medical and surgical

Staffed Beds: 21

FAIRVIEW PARK HOSPITAL

✠ **FAIRVIEW PARK HOSPITAL (110125)**, 200 Industrial Boulevard, Zip 31021-2997, Mailing Address: P.O. Box 1408, Zip 31040-1408; tel. 478/275-2000, (Nonreporting) **A**1 3 10 19 **S** HCA Healthcare, Nashville, TN
Primary Contact: Donald R. Avery, FACHE, President and Chief Executive Officer
CFO: Ted Short, Chief Financial Officer
CMO: George E. Harrison, M.D., Chief Medical Officer
CIO: Marsha Morris, Manager Information Services
CHR: Jeff Bruton, Director Human Resources
CNO: Donna Trickey, R.N., Chief Nursing Officer
Web address: www.fairviewparkhospital.com
Control: Corporation, Investor-owned (for-profit) **Service**: General medical and surgical

Staffed Beds: 138

DULUTH—De Kalb County

GWINNETT MEDICAL CENTER-DULUTH See Northside Hospital – Duluth

NORTHSIDE HOSPITAL – DULUTH See Northside Hospital Gwinnett/Duluth, Lawrenceville

DUNWOODY—Dekalb County

VERITAS COLLABORATIVE, 41 Perimeter Center East Suite 250, Zip 30346-1902; tel. 770/871-3730, (Nonreporting) **A**3
Primary Contact: David Willcutts, Chief Executive Officer
Web address: https://veritascollaborative.com
Control: Partnership, Investor-owned (for-profit) **Service**: Psychiatric

Staffed Beds: 50

EASTMAN—Dodge County

⇧ **DODGE COUNTY HOSPITAL (110092)**, 901 Griffin Avenue, Zip 31023-6720, Mailing Address: PO BOX 4309, Zip 31023-4309; tel. 478/448-4000, (Nonreporting) **A**10 21
Primary Contact: LaDon Toole, Chief Executive Officer
CFO: Jan Hamrick, Chief Financial Officer
CIO: Victor Woodard, Manager Information Technology
CHR: Wendy Selph, Director Human Resources
CNO: Sandra M. Campbell, R.N., Chief Nursing Officer
Web address: www.dodgecountyhospital.com
Control: Hospital district or authority, Government, Nonfederal **Service**: General medical and surgical

Staffed Beds: 31

EATONTON—Putnam County

☐ **PUTNAM GENERAL HOSPITAL (111313)**, 101 Lake Oconee Parkway, Zip 31024-6054; tel. 706/485-2711, **A**1 10 18 **F**3 11 15 28 29 30 34 35 40 45 50 51 57 59 64 67 75 81 86 93 107 108 110 111 114 119 129 133 146 154
Primary Contact: Alan Horton, Chief Executive Officer
CFO: Judy Ware, Chief Financial Officer
CMO: Omar Akhras, M.D., Chief of Staff
CIO: Marcel Lundy, Chief Information Officer
CHR: Jeanine Martinez, Director Human Resources
CNO: Pam Douglas, Chief Nursing Officer
Web address: www.putnamgeneral.com
Control: Hospital district or authority, Government, Nonfederal **Service**: General medical and surgical

Staffed Beds: 25 **Admissions:** 394 **Census:** 10 **Outpatient Visits:** 19276 **Births:** 0 **Total Expense ($000):** 22374 **Payroll Expense ($000):** 6765 **Personnel:** 138

ELBERTON—Elbert County

☐ **ELBERT MEMORIAL HOSPITAL (111337)**, 4 Medical Drive, Zip 30635-1897; tel. 706/283-3151, **A**1 10 18 **F**7 11 15 29 34 35 40 45 50 53 57 59 64 77 79 81 90 91 93 107 110 111 115 119 133 146 148 149 154 **P**3 6
Primary Contact: J. Tyler. Taylor, FACHE, Chief Executive Officer
COO: Tammy Harlow, Chief Operating Officer
CIO: Greg Fields, Director Information Technology
CHR: Georgian Walton, Director Human Resources
Web address: www.emhcare.net
Control: Hospital district or authority, Government, Nonfederal **Service**: General medical and surgical

Staffed Beds: 25 **Admissions:** 227 **Census:** 2 **Outpatient Visits:** 9967 **Births:** 0 **Total Expense ($000):** 12960

Hospital, Medicare Provider Number, Address, Telephone, Approval, Facility, and Physician Codes, Health Care System

★ American Hospital Association (AHA) membership   ○ Healthcare Facilities Accreditation Program   ⇧ Center for Improvement in Healthcare Quality Accreditation
☐ The Joint Commission accreditation   ◇ DNV Healthcare Inc. accreditation   △ Commission on Accreditation of Rehabilitation Facilities (CARF) accreditation

Hospitals, U.S. / GEORGIA

FAYETTEVILLE—Fayette County

PIEDMONT FAYETTE HOSPITAL (110215), 1255 Highway 54 West, Zip 30214-4526; tel. 770/719-7000, (Nonreporting) **A**2 3 10 21 **S** Piedmont Healthcare, Roswell, GA
Primary Contact: Stephen D. Porter, Chief Executive Officer
COO: Nathan Nipper, Chief Operating Officer
CFO: Scott A. Wolfe, Chief Financial Officer
CMO: Angela Swayne, M.D., Chief Medical Officer
CIO: Geoffrey Brown, Chief Information Officer
CHR: Holly Sawyer, Director and Human Resources Business Partner
CNO: Merry Heath, Chief Nursing Officer
Web address: www.piedmont.org
Control: Other not-for-profit (including NFP Corporation) **Service**: General medical and surgical

Staffed Beds: 221

FITZGERALD—Ben Hill County

DORMINY MEDICAL CENTER (110073), 200 Perry House Road, Zip 31750-8857, Mailing Address: P.O. Box 1447, Zip 31750-1447; tel. 229/424-7100, (Nonreporting) **A**10 21
Primary Contact: Paige Wynn, Chief Executive Officer
CFO: Paige Wynn, Chief Financial Officer
CMO: Davey Herring, M.D., Chief Medical Officer
CIO: Chris Ward, Director Management Information Systems
CHR: Denise Steverson, Director Human Resources
Web address: www.dorminymedical.org
Control: Hospital district or authority, Government, Nonfederal **Service**: General medical and surgical

Staffed Beds: 58

FORSYTH—Monroe County

MONROE COUNTY HOSPITAL (111318), 88 Martin Luther King Jr Drive, Zip 31029-1682, Mailing Address: P.O. Box 1068, Zip 31029-1068; tel. 478/994-2521, (Nonreporting) **A**3 10 18 21
Primary Contact: Kerry A. Trapnell, Interim Chief Executive Officer
CFO: Judy King Ware, Chief Financial Officer
CMO: Jeremy Goodwin, M.D., President, Medical Staff
CIO: Tiffany Purmont, Supervisor Medical Records
CHR: Deborah Flowers, Director Human Resources
CNO: Casey Fleckenstein, Nurse Manager
Web address: www.monroehospital.org
Control: Hospital district or authority, Government, Nonfederal **Service**: General medical and surgical

Staffed Beds: 25

FORT BENNING—Muscogee County

BENNING MARTIN ARMY COMMUNITY HOSPITAL, 6600 Van Aalst Boulevard, Zip 31905-2102; tel. 706/544-2516, (Nonreporting) **A**1 3 5 **S** Department of the Army, Office of the Surgeon General, Falls Church, VA
Primary Contact: Colonel Kevin M. Kelly, Commander
CHR: Major Bernita Hightower, Chief Human Resources
Web address: https://martin.tricare.mil/
Control: Army, Government, federal **Service**: General medical and surgical

Staffed Beds: 57

MARTIN ARMY COMMUNITY HOSPITAL See Benning Martin Army Community Hospital

FORT GORDON—Richmond County

DWIGHT DAVID EISENHOWER ARMY MEDICAL CENTER, 300 West Hospital Road, Zip 30905-5741; tel. 706/787-5811, (Nonreporting) **A**1 3 5 **S** Department of the Army, Office of the Surgeon General, Falls Church, VA
Primary Contact: Colonel James G. Pairmore, Commander
CMO: Colonel James M Baunchalk, Deputy Chief Clinical Services
CIO: Major Joseph A Ponce, Chief Information Management
CHR: Elizabeth Shelt, Civilian Personnel Officer
Web address: https://eisenhower.tricare.mil
Control: Army, Government, federal **Service**: General medical and surgical

Staffed Beds: 107

FORT OGLETHORPE—Catoosa County

★ **CHI MEMORIAL HOSPITAL – GEORGIA (110236)**, 100 Gross Crescent Circle, Zip 30742-3669; tel. 706/858-2000, **A**10 22 **F**3 7 15 29 30 34 35 40 44 45 46 48 57 64 78 81 87 100 102 107 108 110 111 114 115 119 121 129 130 143 146 147 149 154 **P**3 6 7 8 **S** CommonSpirit Health, Chicago, IL
Primary Contact: Angela Stiggins, Market Vice President of Operations/Administrator
COO: Kevin Hopkins, Vice President of Operations
CFO: Farrell Hayes, Chief Financial Officer
CMO: John Erdman, M.D., Chief of Staff
CIO: Ruth Wright-Whitaker, Director Information Services
CHR: Cathy Hulsey, Manager of Human Resources
CNO: Sandra Siniard, Vice President of Patient Care Services
Web address: www.memorial.org/chi-memorial-hospital-georgia
Control: Church operated, Nongovernment, not-for-profit **Service**: General medical and surgical

Staffed Beds: 35 **Admissions**: 537 **Census**: 4 **Outpatient Visits**: 34911 **Births**: 0 **Total Expense ($000)**: 26920 **Payroll Expense ($000)**: 10159 **Personnel**: 102

GAINESVILLE—Hall County

★ △ **NORTHEAST GEORGIA MEDICAL CENTER (110029)**, 743 Spring Street NE, Zip 30501-3899; tel. 770/219-3553, (Includes NORTHEAST GEORGIA MEDICAL CENTER BRASELTON, 1400 River Place, Braselton, Georgia, Zip 30517-5600, tel. 770/219-9000; Carol H Burrell, Chief Executive Officer) (Total facility includes 244 beds in nursing home–type unit) **A**2 3 5 7 10 19 21 **F**3 4 7 11 12 13 15 17 18 20 22 24 26 28 29 30 31 34 35 38 40 43 44 45 46 47 48 49 50 51 54 56 57 58 59 60 61 63 64 66 68 70 72 73 74 75 76 77 78 79 81 82 83 84 85 86 87 89 90 93 98 99 100 101 104 105 107 110 111 114 115 116 117 118 119 120 121 123 124 126 128 129 130 131 132 143 144 146 147 148 149 151 152 153 154 156 160 162 165 166 167 169 **S** Northeast Georgia Health System, Gainesville, GA
Primary Contact: John Kueven, President
COO: Michael H. Covert, FACHE, President and Chief Operating Officer
CFO: Brian D Steines, Chief Financial Officer
CMO: Sam Johnson, M.D., Chief Medical Officer
CIO: Chris Paravate, Chief Information Officer
CHR: Deborah Weber, Chief Human Resource Officer
Web address: www.nghs.com
Control: Other not-for-profit (including NFP Corporation) **Service**: General medical and surgical

Staffed Beds: 937 **Admissions**: 39931 **Census**: 787 **Outpatient Visits**: 524709 **Births**: 5161 **Personnel**: 6564

GRACEWOOD—Richmond County

EAST CENTRAL REGIONAL HOSPITAL See East Central Regional Hospital, Augusta

GREENSBORO—Greene County

ST. MARY'S GOOD SAMARITAN HOSPITAL (111329), 5401 Lake Oconee Parkway, Zip 30642-4232; tel. 706/453-7331, (Nonreporting) **A**1 3 10 18 **S** Trinity Health, Livonia, MI
Primary Contact: Stonish Pierce, FACHE, President and Chief Executive Officer
CMO: Dave Ringer, M.D., Chief of Staff
CNO: Kimberly Tyler, Director of Nursing
Web address: www.stmarysgoodsam.org
Control: Church operated, Nongovernment, not-for-profit **Service**: General medical and surgical

Staffed Beds: 25

GRIFFIN—Spalding County

WELLSTAR SPALDING REGIONAL HOSPITAL (110031), 601 South Eighth Street, Zip 30224-4294, Mailing Address: P O Drawer 'V', Zip 30224-1168; tel. 770/228-2721, **A**1 3 10 **F**3 7 11 13 15 18 20 22 29 30 31 34 35 40 43 44 45 50 53 54 57 59 64 70 73 74 75 76 77 78 79 80 81 85 86 87 89 93 107 108 110 111 115 119 126 129 130 141 143 146 147 148 154 167 169 **S** WellStar Health System, Marietta, GA
Primary Contact: Tamara Ison, Senior Vice President and President
COO: Tamara Ison, Chief Operating Officer
CMO: Philip Osehobo, M.D., Chief Medical Officer
CIO: Steve Brown, Director Information Systems
CHR: Amanda Remington, Director Human Resources
CNO: Wadra McCullough, Chief Nursing Officer
Web address: www.spaldingregional.com
Control: Other not-for-profit (including NFP Corporation) **Service**: General medical and surgical

Staffed Beds: 144 **Admissions**: 7415 **Census**: 100 **Outpatient Visits**: 90436 **Births**: 913 **Personnel**: 741

Hospitals, U.S. / GEORGIA

HAWKINSVILLE—Pulaski County

⇑ **TAYLOR REGIONAL HOSPITAL (110781)**, 222 Macon Highway, Zip 31036, Mailing Address: 222 Perry Highway, Zip 31036-7297; tel. 478/783-0200, (Nonreporting) **A**10 21
Primary Contact: Jon Green, R.N., Chief Executive Officer
CFO: Lisa Halliday, Director Accounting Services
CMO: Al Baggett, M.D., Interim Chief of Staff
CIO: Dawn Warnock, Director Medical Records
Web address: www.taylorregional.org
Control: Other not-for-profit (including NFP Corporation)

Staffed Beds: 57

HAZLEHURST—Jeff Davis County

⇑ **JEFF DAVIS HOSPITAL (111333)**, 163 South Tallahassee Street, Zip 31539-2921, Mailing Address: P.O. Box 1690, Zip 31539-1690; tel. 912/375-7781, **A**10 18 21 **F**3 11 15 28 29 34 35 40 45 50 56 57 59 60 65 68 70 77 81 85 97 98 100 102 103 107 110 111 115 119 127 133 135 143 148 149 153 154
Primary Contact: Barry Bloom, Chief Executive Officer
CFO: Cathy Cason, Chief Financial Officer
CIO: Brian Fowler, Information Technology Director
CHR: Brenda McEachin, Human Resources Director
CNO: Allen Crawford, Chief Nursing Officer
Web address: www.jeffdavishospital.org
Control: Hospital district or authority, Government, Nonfederal **Service**: General medical and surgical

Staffed Beds: 33 **Admissions:** 452 **Census:** 4 **Outpatient Visits:** 30417
Births: 0 **Total Expense ($000):** 25641 **Payroll Expense ($000):** 10827
Personnel: 218

HIAWASSEE—Towns County

⇑ **CHATUGE REGIONAL HOSPITAL AND NURSING HOME (111324)**, 110 Main Street, Zip 30546-3408, Mailing Address: P.O. Box 509, Zip 30546-0509; tel. 706/896-2222, (Total facility includes 112 beds in nursing home-type unit) **A**10 18 21 **F**3 11 29 34 35 40 50 53 57 59 64 70 77 79 82 93 98 101 102 103 107 111 114 119 128 143 146 149 154 157 **S** Union General Hospital, Inc., Blairsville, GA
Primary Contact: Ryan Snow, Chief Executive Officer
CFO: Tim Henry, Accountant
CMO: Robert F Stahlkuppe, M.D., Chief of Staff
CIO: Walt Stafford, Director Information Technology
CHR: Rita Bradshaw, Director Human Resources
Web address: www.chatugeregionalhospital.org
Control: Hospital district or authority, Government, Nonfederal **Service**: General medical and surgical

Staffed Beds: 150 **Admissions:** 725 **Census:** 95 **Outpatient Visits:** 24305
Births: 0 **Total Expense ($000):** 30210 **Payroll Expense ($000):** 14612
Personnel: 246

HINESVILLE—Liberty County

⇑ **LIBERTY REGIONAL MEDICAL CENTER (111335)**, 462 Elma G Miles Parkway, Zip 31313-4000, Mailing Address: P.O. Box 919, Zip 31310-0919; tel. 912/369-9400, (Nonreporting) **A**10 18 21
Primary Contact: Tammy Mims, Chief Executive Officer
CFO: Derek Rozier, Chief Financial Officer
CNO: Donna R. Cochrane, Chief Nursing Officer
Web address: www.libertyregional.org
Control: Hospital district or authority, Government, Nonfederal **Service**: General medical and surgical

Staffed Beds: 100

✠ **WINN ARMY COMMUNITY HOSPITAL**, 1061 Harmon Avenue, Zip 31314-5641, Mailing Address: 1061 Harmon Avenue, Suite 2311B, Zip 31314-5641; tel. 912/435-6965, (Nonreporting) **A**1 5 **S** Department of the Army, Office of the Surgeon General, Falls Church, VA
Primary Contact: Colonel Julie Freeman, Commander
CIO: Arthur N Kirshner, Chief Information Management
CHR: Major Yvette McCrea, Chief Human Resources
CNO: Colonel Sharon Brown, Deputy Commander Nursing
Web address: https://winn.tricare.mil/
Control: Army, Government, federal **Service**: General medical and surgical

Staffed Beds: 37

HIRAM—Paulding County

✠ **WELLSTAR PAULDING HOSPITAL (110042)**, 2518 Jimmy Lee Smith Parkway, Zip 30141; tel. 470/644-7000, (Total facility includes 148 beds in nursing home-type unit) **A**1 2 10 **F**3 11 15 18 20 22 26 28 29 30 31 34 38 40 41 43 44 45 49 50 51 54 55 59 61 64 68 70 75 77 78 79 81 82 84 85 86 87 93 107 108 110 111 115 118 119 120 121 123 124 126 128 129 130 132 135 146 148 154 156 167 169 **S** WellStar Health System, Marietta, GA
Primary Contact: Ralph Turner, President
COO: Lindsay Rehn, Executive Director of Financial Operations
CFO: Lindsay Rehn, Executive Director of Financial Operations
CMO: Guillermo Pierluisi, Vice President of Medical Affairs
CHR: Jessica Bedsole, Director, Human Resources
CNO: Vicky Hogue, R.N., Vice President Patient Services and Chief Nursing Officer
Web address: www.wellstar.org
Control: Other not-for-profit (including NFP Corporation) **Service**: General medical and surgical

Staffed Beds: 294 **Admissions:** 10004 **Census:** 244 **Outpatient Visits:** 148297 **Births:** 0 **Personnel:** 1280

HOMERVILLE—Clinch County

★ ⇑ **CLINCH MEMORIAL HOSPITAL (111308)**, 1050 Valdosta Highway, Zip 31634-9701, Mailing Address: P.O. Box 516, Zip 31634-0516; tel. 912/487-5211, (Nonreporting) **A**10 18 21
Primary Contact: Angela Ammons, Administrator and Chief Executive Officer
COO: Wallace D Mincey, Chief Executive Officer
CFO: Teressia Shook, Chief Financial Officer
CMO: Samuel Cobarrubias, M.D., Chief of Staff
CIO: Philip Dowd, IT Director
CHR: Shelly Studebaker, Human Resources Assistant
CNO: Kellie Register, Director of Nursing
Web address: www.clinchmh.org
Control: County, Government, Nonfederal **Service**: General medical and surgical

Staffed Beds: 18

JACKSON—Butts County

★ **WELLSTAR SYLVAN GROVE HOSPITAL (111319)**, 1050 McDonough Road, Zip 30233-1599; tel. 770/775-7861, **A**3 10 18 **F**3 11 29 30 34 35 40 50 53 57 59 64 68 77 90 93 107 115 119 133 146 148 149 154 169 **S** WellStar Health System, Marietta, GA
Primary Contact: Tamara Ison, Senior Vice President and President
CFO: Tamara Ison, Chief Financial Officer
CIO: Steve Brown, Chief Information Officer
CHR: Amanda Remington, Director Human Resources
Web address: www.sylvangrovehospital.com
Control: Other not-for-profit (including NFP Corporation) **Service**: General medical and surgical

Staffed Beds: 19 **Admissions:** 317 **Census:** 12 **Outpatient Visits:** 20916 **Births:** 0 **Personnel:** 88

JASPER—Pickens County

⇑ **PIEDMONT MOUNTAINSIDE HOSPITAL (110225)**, 1266 Highway 515 South, Zip 30143-4872; tel. 706/692-2441, (Nonreporting) **A**10 21 **S** Piedmont Healthcare, Roswell, GA
Primary Contact: Denise Ray, Chief Executive Officer
CMO: Moiz Master, M.D., Medical Director of Quality
CIO: Geoffrey Brown, Chief Information Officer
CHR: Frank Leist, Human Resources Manager
CNO: Michelle Breitfelder, Chief Nursing Officer
Web address: https://www.piedmont.org
Control: Other not-for-profit (including NFP Corporation) **Service**: General medical and surgical

Staffed Beds: 52

JESUP—Wayne County

☐ **WAYNE MEMORIAL HOSPITAL (110124)**, 865 South First Street, Zip 31545-0210, Mailing Address: P.O. Box 410, Zip 31598-0410; tel. 912/427-6811, (Nonreporting) **A**1 10 20
Primary Contact: Joseph P. Ierardi, Chief Executive Officer
CFO: Greg Jones, Chief Financial Officer
CMO: Dan Collipp, M.D., Chief of Staff
CIO: Deborah Six, Coordinator Data Processing
CHR: John McIwain, Director Human Resources
Web address: www.wmhweb.com
Control: County, Government, Nonfederal **Service**: General medical and surgical

Staffed Beds: 84

Hospital, Medicare Provider Number, Address, Telephone, Approval, Facility, and Physician Codes, Health Care System

★ American Hospital Association (AHA) membership   ○ Healthcare Facilities Accreditation Program   ⇑ Center for Improvement in Healthcare Quality Accreditation
☐ The Joint Commission accreditation   ◇ DNV Healthcare Inc. accreditation   △ Commission on Accreditation of Rehabilitation Facilities (CARF) accreditation

Hospitals, U.S. / GEORGIA

JOHNS CREEK—Fulton County

EMORY JOHNS CREEK HOSPITAL (110230), 6325 Hospital Parkway, Zip 30097-5775; tel. 678/474-7000, **A**1 2 3 5 10 **F**3 11 12 13 15 18 20 22 26 29 30 31 34 35 36 40 45 49 50 53 54 55 57 58 59 60 63 64 68 70 72 73 74 75 76 77 78 79 81 82 84 85 86 87 93 100 101 102 107 108 110 111 115 116 117 119 126 129 130 131 132 146 147 148 149 154 156 167 169 **S** Emory Healthcare, Atlanta, GA
Primary Contact: Heather Redrick, Chief Operating Officer
COO: Laurie Hansen, Vice President of Operations
CFO: JoAnn Manning, Chief Financial Officer
CMO: Adedapo Odetoyinbo, M.D., Chief Medical Office
CHR: Hannah Henry, Interim Vice President of Human Resources
CNO: Heather Redrick, Chief Nursing Officer
Web address: www.emoryjohnscreek.com
Control: Other not-for-profit (including NFP Corporation) **Service**: General medical and surgical

Staffed Beds: 154 **Admissions**: 9782 **Census**: 129 **Outpatient Visits**: 96642 **Births**: 1537 **Total Expense ($000)**: 265676 **Payroll Expense ($000)**: 102371 **Personnel**: 1032

KENNESAW—Cobb County

DEVEREUX ADVANCED BEHAVIORAL HEALTH GEORGIA, 1291 Stanley Road NW, Zip 30152-4359; tel. 770/427-0147, (Nonreporting) **A**3 **S** Devereux, Villanova, PA
Primary Contact: Kathy Goggin, Director, Finance & Support Services
COO: Mary H Esposito, Assistant Executive Director
CFO: Kathy Goggin, Director of Finance
CMO: Yolanda Graham, M.D., Medical Director
CIO: Sam Maguta, Coordinator Information Systems
CHR: Rudie Delien, Director of Human Resources
CNO: Debra Sharpton, Director of Nursing
Web address: www.devereuxga.org
Control: Other not-for-profit (including NFP Corporation) **Service**: Children's hospital psychiatric

Staffed Beds: 110

LAGRANGE—Troup County

WELLSTAR WEST GEORGIA MEDICAL CENTER (110016), 1514 Vernon Road, Zip 30240-4131; tel. 706/882-1411, (Total facility includes 261 beds in nursing home-type unit) **A**1 2 10 19 **F**3 11 12 13 15 18 20 22 26 28 29 30 31 34 35 40 43 44 47 48 49 50 55 56 57 58 59 62 63 64 68 70 73 74 75 76 77 78 79 80 81 82 84 85 86 87 89 92 93 96 107 108 110 111 114 115 119 120 121 123 124 126 128 129 130 132 135 146 147 148 149 154 167 169 **S** WellStar Health System, Marietta, GA
Primary Contact: Coleman Foss, Senior Vice President and Hospital President
COO: Charis L Acree, Vice President and Chief Operating Officer
CFO: Paul R Perrotti, CPA, Chief Financial Officer
CIO: Alan Whitehouse, Chief Information Officer
CHR: Tommy Britt, Vice President of Human Resources
CNO: Tracy Gynther, R.N., Vice President and Chief Nursing Officer
Web address: https://www.wellstar.org/locations/hospital/west-georgia-medical-center
Control: Other not-for-profit (including NFP Corporation) **Service**: General medical and surgical

Staffed Beds: 386 **Admissions**: 8851 **Census**: 294 **Outpatient Visits**: 134713 **Births**: 836 **Personnel**: 1356

LAKELAND—Lanier County

SOUTH GEORGIA MEDICAL CENTER LANIER CAMPUS (111326), 116 West Thigpen Avenue, Zip 31635-1011; tel. 229/433-8440, (Nonreporting) **A**10 18 21 **S** South Georgia Medical Center, Valdosta, GA
Primary Contact: Geoff Hardy, Administrator
CFO: Libby Flemming, Controller and Chief Information Officer
CMO: Bruce Herrington, M.D., Chief Medical Officer
CIO: Libby Flemming, Controller and Chief Information Officer
CHR: Vicki Dinkins, Director Human Resources
Web address: www.sgmc.org
Control: Hospital district or authority, Government, Nonfederal **Service**: Other specialty treatment

Staffed Beds: 24

LAVONIA—Franklin County

ST. MARY'S SACRED HEART HOSPITAL (110027), 367 Clear Creek Parkway, Zip 30553-4173; tel. 706/356-7800, (Nonreporting) **A**1 10 **S** Trinity Health, Livonia, MI
Primary Contact: Stonish Pierce, FACHE, President and Chief Executive Officer
CIO: Tim Vickery, Chief Information Officer
CHR: Lauren Papka, Chief Administrative Officer
CNO: Evelyn Murphy, Chief Nursing Officer
Web address: www.stmaryssacredheart.org/
Control: Other not-for-profit (including NFP Corporation) **Service**: General medical and surgical

Staffed Beds: 48

LAWRENCEVILLE—Gwinnett County

NORTHSIDE HOSPITAL GWINNETT/DULUTH (110087), 1000 Medical Center Boulevard, Zip 30046-7694, Mailing Address: 1000 Medical Center Blvd, Zip 30046; tel. 678/312-1000, (Includes GWINNETT MEDICAL CENTER, 1000 Medical Center Boulevard, Lawrenceville, Georgia, Zip 30245, Box 348, Zip 30246, tel. 678/312-1000; Debbie Bilbro, President and Chief Executive Officer; NORTHSIDE HOSPITAL - DULUTH, 3620 Howell Ferry Road, Duluth, Georgia, Zip 30096, tel. 678/312-6800; Debbie Bilbro, President and Chief Executive Officer) **A**1 2 3 5 10 **F**3 8 9 11 12 13 15 17 18 20 22 24 26 28 29 30 31 34 35 36 37 38 40 41 43 44 45 46 47 48 49 50 54 55 56 57 58 59 64 68 70 71 72 73 74 75 76 77 78 79 80 81 82 84 85 86 87 90 93 95 96 100 102 107 108 110 111 114 115 117 118 119 126 129 130 131 132 134 135 146 147 148 149 154 156 164 167 169 **S** Northside Healthcare System, Atlanta, GA
Primary Contact: Debbie Bilbro, Chief Executive Officer
COO: Mary Shepherd, Chief Operating Officer
CFO: Shannon A. Banna, Chief Financial Officer
CIO: Ashley Petit, Chief Information Officer
CHR: Bridget Green, Chief Human Resources Officer
CNO: Pamela Garland, R.N., Chief Nursing Officer
Web address: www.gwinnettmedicalcenter.org
Control: Other not-for-profit (including NFP Corporation) **Service**: General medical and surgical

Staffed Beds: 577 **Admissions**: 30827 **Census**: 534 **Outpatient Visits**: 1305571 **Births**: 3903 **Total Expense ($000)**: 1478237 **Payroll Expense ($000)**: 627866 **Personnel**: 6250

SUMMITRIDGE HOSPITAL (114004), 250 Scenic Highway, Zip 30046-5675; tel. 678/442-5800, (Nonreporting) **A**1 10
Primary Contact: Vernell Nunn, Chief Executive Officer
Web address: www.summitridgehospital.net
Control: Other not-for-profit (including NFP Corporation) **Service**: Psychiatric

Staffed Beds: 106

LITHONIA—Dekalb County

EMORY HILLANDALE HOSPITAL (110226), 2801 DeKalb Medical Parkway, Zip 30058-4996; tel. 404/501-8000, **A**1 10 **F**3 15 18 20 22 26 28 29 30 34 35 38 40 44 49 50 51 57 59 60 61 68 70 74 75 77 78 79 81 82 84 85 86 87 93 96 100 107 111 121 129 130 131 132 148 149 156 167 **S** Emory Healthcare, Atlanta, GA
Primary Contact: Jennifer Schuck, Chief Executive Officer
CMO: Duane Barclay, D.O., Chief Medical Officer
CIO: Mark Trocino, Chief Information Officer
CHR: Tom Crawford, Vice President Human Resources
Web address: www.dekalbmedical.org
Control: Other not-for-profit (including NFP Corporation) **Service**: General medical and surgical

Staffed Beds: 99 **Admissions**: 5008 **Census**: 67 **Outpatient Visits**: 84391 **Births**: 0 **Total Expense ($000)**: 116184 **Payroll Expense ($000)**: 61428 **Personnel**: 553

LOUISVILLE—Jefferson County

JEFFERSON HOSPITAL (110100), 1067 Peachtree Street, Zip 30434-1599; tel. 478/625-7000, (Nonreporting) **A**10 20 21
Primary Contact: Wendy Martin, Chief Executive Officer
CFO: Lieutenant John Graham, Chief Financial Officer
CMO: James Polhill, M.D., Chief Medical Officer
CHR: Catherine Hall, Manager Human Resources
CNO: Stacey Smith, R.N., Director of Nursing
Web address: www.jeffersonhosp.com
Control: City-county, Government, Nonfederal **Service**: General medical and surgical

Staffed Beds: 37

Hospitals, U.S. / GEORGIA

MACON—Bibb County

★ ⇧ **ATRIUM HEALTH NAVICENT PEACH (111310)**, 777 Hemlock Street, Zip 31201-2102; tel. 478/654-2000, **A**10 18 21 **F**15 29 34 35 38 40 45 57 59 68 77 81 93 102 107 108 114 115 119 127 133 146 149 150 164 **S** Atrium Health, Inc., Charlotte, NC
Primary Contact: Laura Gentry, Chief Executive Officer
CFO: Lisa Urbistondo, Chief Financial Officer
CMO: Crystal Brown, M.D., Medical Director
CNO: Brenda Goodman, Chief Nursing Officer
Web address: www.navicenthealth.org
Control: Other not-for-profit (including NFP Corporation) **Service**: General medical and surgical

Staffed Beds: 25 **Admissions**: 1358 **Census**: 16 **Outpatient Visits**: 55184
Births: 0 **Total Expense ($000)**: 24448 **Payroll Expense ($000)**: 10017
Personnel: 170

★ ⇧ **ATRIUM HEALTH NAVICENT REHABILITATION HOSPITAL (113029)**, 3351 Northside Drive, Zip 31210-2587; tel. 478/201-6500, **A**3 10 21 **F**29 30 34 35 36 38 44 48 50 56 57 59 60 61 64 65 68 74 75 77 78 79 82 84 86 87 90 91 92 93 94 95 96 100 119 130 131 132 135 143 146 147 148 149 154 156 164 **S** Atrium Health, Inc., Charlotte, NC
Primary Contact: Gina Tipton, Hospital Administrator
COO: Darren Pearce, Executive Director
CFO: Beverly Owens, Controller
CMO: Allison Scheetz, M.D., Medical Director
Web address: www.navicenthealth.org/service-center/rehabilitation-hospital-navicent-health
Control: Other not-for-profit (including NFP Corporation) **Service**: Rehabilitation

Staffed Beds: 58 **Admissions**: 1161 **Census**: 46 **Outpatient Visits**: 25616
Births: 0 **Total Expense ($000)**: 25638 **Payroll Expense ($000)**: 17051
Personnel: 133

★ ⇧ **ATRIUM HEALTH NAVICENT THE MEDICAL CENTER (110107)**, 777 Hemlock Street, Zip 31201-2155; tel. 478/633-1000, (Includes CHILDREN'S HOSPITAL, NAVICENT HEALTH, 888 Pine Street, Macon, Georgia, Zip 31201-2155, tel. 478/633-1000) **A**2 3 5 8 10 19 21 **F**3 7 8 12 13 14 15 17 18 20 22 24 26 28 29 30 31 32 34 35 36 37 38 39 40 41 42 43 45 46 47 48 49 50 51 53 56 57 58 59 60 61 62 63 64 65 66 68 70 71 72 73 74 75 76 77 78 79 80 81 82 83 84 85 86 87 88 89 92 93 94 97 98 100 101 102 103 107 108 110 111 114 115 119 126 130 132 135 143 144 146 147 148 149 150 154 156 164 167 169 **S** Atrium Health, Inc., Charlotte, NC
Primary Contact: Delvecchio Finley, FACHE, President and Chief Executive Officer
COO: Susan Harris, R.N., Chief Operating Officer
CFO: Rhonda S. Perry, Chief Financial Officer
CMO: Christopher Hendry, M.D., Chief Medical Officer
CIO: Ed Brown, Chief Information Officer
CHR: Bernard J Price, Chief Human Resources Officer
CNO: Tracey Blalock, MSN, R.N., Chief Nurse Executive
Web address: https://www.navicenthealth.org/
Control: Other not-for-profit (including NFP Corporation) **Service**: General medical and surgical

Staffed Beds: 577 **Admissions**: 30118 **Census**: 534 **Outpatient Visits**: 391960 **Births**: 2990 **Total Expense ($000)**: 817782 **Payroll Expense ($000)**: 292829 **Personnel**: 3680

CHILDREN'S HOSPITAL See Children's Hospital, Navicent Health

⇧ **COLISEUM MEDICAL CENTERS** See Piedmont Macon

4 **COLISEUM NORTHSIDE HOSPITAL** See Piedmont Macon North

COLISEUM PSYCHIATRIC CENTER See Coliseum Center For Behavioral Health

⇧ **MEDICAL CENTER OF PEACH COUNTY, NAVICENT HEALTH** See Atrium Health Navicent Peach

⇧ **PIEDMONT MACON (110164)**, 350 Hospital Drive, Zip 31217-3871; tel. 478/765-7000, (Includes COLISEUM CENTER FOR BEHAVIORAL HEALTH, 340 Hospital Drive, Macon, Georgia, Zip 31217-3838, tel. 478/741-1355; Stephen J. Daugherty, Interim Chief Executive Officer) (Nonreporting) **A**2 3 5 10 21 **S** Piedmont Healthcare, Roswell, GA
Primary Contact: Stephen J. Daugherty, Chief Executive Officer
CFO: Scott Anderton, Chief Financial Officer
CIO: Joan Morstad, Director Information Systems
CHR: Laura Booras, Vice President Human Resources
Web address: www.coliseumhealthsystem.com
Control: Corporation, Investor-owned (for-profit) **Service**: General medical and surgical

Staffed Beds: 310

PIEDMONT MACON NORTH (110201), 400 Charter Boulevard, Zip 31210-4853, Mailing Address: P.O. Box 4627, Zip 31208-4627; tel. 478/757-8200, (Nonreporting) **A**3 10 **S** Piedmont Healthcare, Roswell, GA
Primary Contact: Stephen J. Daugherty, Chief Executive Officer
CHR: Louise Truitt, Human Resource Director
CNO: Patricia Derrico, FACHE, R.N., Chief Nursing Officer
Web address: www.coliseumhealthsystem.com
Control: Corporation, Investor-owned (for-profit) **Service**: General medical and surgical

Staffed Beds: 103

⊞ **REGENCY HOSPITAL – MACON (112016)**, 535 Coliseum Drive, Zip 31217-0104; tel. 478/803-7300, (Nonreporting) **A**1 10 **S** Select Medical Corporation, Mechanicsburg, PA
Primary Contact: Lorraine Smith, Chief Executive Officer
Web address: https://www.regencyhospital.com/locations-and-tours/ga/macon/
Control: Corporation, Investor-owned (for-profit) **Service**: Acute long-term care hospital

Staffed Beds: 60

REGENCY HOSPITAL OF CENTRAL GEORGIA See Regency Hospital – Macon

⇧ **REHABILITATION HOSPITAL, NAVICENT HEALTH** See Atrium Health Navicent Rehabilitation Hospital

MADISON—Morgan County

☐ **MORGAN MEDICAL CENTER (111304)**, 1740 Lions Club Road, Zip 30650-4762, Mailing Address: P.O. Box 860, Zip 30650-0860; tel. 706/342-1667, (Nonreporting) **A**1 10 18
Primary Contact: Ralph A. Castillo, CPA, Chief Executive Officer
CFO: Kyle Wilkinson, Chief Financial Officer
CMO: Dan Zant, M.D., Chief of Staff
CIO: Patrick Cook, Vice President Support Services
CHR: Sarah Phillips, Manager Human Resources
CNO: Beth O'Neill, Chief Nursing Officer
Web address: www.mmh.org
Control: Hospital district or authority, Government, Nonfederal **Service**: General medical and surgical

Staffed Beds: 25

MORGAN MEMORIAL HOSPITAL See Morgan Medical Center

MARIETTA—Cobb County

⊞ △ **WELLSTAR KENNESTONE HOSPITAL (110035)**, 677 Church Street, Zip 30060-1148; tel. 770/793-5000, **A**1 2 3 5 7 10 **F**3 8 10 11 12 13 15 17 18 20 22 24 26 28 29 30 31 34 36 37 38 40 41 43 44 45 46 47 48 49 50 53 54 55 58 59 60 61 64 66 68 70 72 73 74 75 76 77 78 79 80 81 82 84 85 86 87 89 90 93 94 96 97 100 102 107 108 110 111 114 115 116 117 119 120 121 123 124 125 126 129 130 132 141 146 147 148 154 156 167 169 **S** WellStar Health System, Marietta, GA
Primary Contact: Lorrie Liang, Senior Vice President and President of WellStar Kennestone and WellStar Windy Hill
COO: Constance Bradley, FACHE, R.N., Vice President and Chief Operating Officer
CFO: Anthony James (Jim) Budzinski, R.N., II, Executive Vice President and Chief Financial Officer
CMO: Vikrum Reddy, M.D., Vice President and Chief Medical Officer
CIO: Shalima Pannikode, Senior Vice President and Chief Information and Digital Officer
CHR: David A Jones, JD, Executive Vice President of Human Resources and Organizational Learning
Web address: https://www.wellstar.org/locations/hospital/kennestone-regional-medical-center
Control: Other not-for-profit (including NFP Corporation) **Service**: General medical and surgical

Staffed Beds: 544 **Admissions**: 41943 **Census**: 605 **Outpatient Visits**: 425107 **Births**: 6074 **Personnel**: 4843

Hospital, Medicare Provider Number, Address, Telephone, Approval, Facility, and Physician Codes, Health Care System

★ American Hospital Association (AHA) membership ○ Healthcare Facilities Accreditation Program ⇧ Center for Improvement in Healthcare Quality Accreditation
☐ The Joint Commission accreditation ◇ DNV Healthcare Inc. accreditation △ Commission on Accreditation of Rehabilitation Facilities (CARF) accreditation

© 2025 AHA Guide

Hospitals, U.S. / GEORGIA

☒ **WELLSTAR WINDY HILL HOSPITAL (112007)**, 2540 Windy Hill Road, Zip 30067–8632; tel. 770/644–1000, **A**1 10 **F**1 3 8 11 15 28 29 30 34 44 45 50 54 60 64 68 75 77 79 81 82 85 86 87 92 93 100 107 108 110 111 115 118 119 129 130 131 141 146 147 148 149 154 167 169 **S** WellStar Health System, Marietta, GA
Primary Contact: Lorrie Liang, Senior Vice President and President of WellStar Kennestone and WellStar Windy Hill
CFO: Marsha Burke, Senior Vice President and Chief Financial Officer
CMO: Larry Haldeman, M.D., Executive Vice President and Chief Medical Officer
CIO: Leigh Cox, Chief Information Officer
CNO: Betsy Brakovich, R.N., MSN, Vice President and Chief Nursing Officer
Web address: www.wellstar.org
Control: Other not–for–profit (including NFP Corporation) **Service**: Acute long–term care hospital

Staffed Beds: 39 **Admissions**: 256 **Census**: 23 **Outpatient Visits**: 162081
Births: 0 **Personnel**: 397

MCDONOUGH—Henry County

☒ **REHABILITATION HOSPITAL OF HENRY (113035)**, 2200 Patrick Henry Parkway, Zip 30253–4207; tel. 470/713–2000, (Nonreporting) **A**1 10 **S** Encompass Health Corporation, Birmingham, AL
Primary Contact: Amber Hester, Area Chief Executive Officer
CFO: Jenny Paul, CPA, Area Controller
CMO: Ene Ojile, M.D., Medical Director
CHR: Victoria Mounsey, Director Human Resources
CNO: Merlinda Pauleon, Chief Nursing Officer
Web address: https://encompasshealth.com/locations/henryrehab
Control: Corporation, Investor–owned (for–profit) **Service**: Rehabilitation

Staffed Beds: 50

METTER—Candler County

★ ⇧ **CANDLER COUNTY HOSPITAL (111334)**, 400 Cedar Street, Zip 30439–3338, Mailing Address: P.O. Box 597, Zip 30439–0597; tel. 912/685–5741, (Nonreporting) **A**10 18 21
Primary Contact: Michael Purvis, Chief Executive Officer
CFO: Will Bennett, Chief Financial Officer
CNO: Linda G. Coleman, Chief Nursing Officer
Web address: www.candlercountyhospital.com
Control: Hospital district or authority, Government, Nonfederal **Service**: General medical and surgical

Staffed Beds: 25

MILLEDGEVILLE—Baldwin County

★ ⇧ **ATRIUM HEALTH NAVICENT BALDWIN (110150)**, 821 North Cobb Street, Zip 31061–2351, Mailing Address: P.O. Box 690, Zip 31059–0690; tel. 478/454–3505, (Total facility includes 15 beds in nursing home–type unit) **A**10 19 21 **F**3 11 13 15 28 29 30 31 34 35 40 45 51 57 60 68 70 76 77 78 79 81 93 100 102 107 108 110 111 114 115 119 120 121 128 129 146 148 149 **S** Atrium Health, Inc., Charlotte, NC
Primary Contact: Delvecchio Finley, FACHE, Interim Chief Executive Officer
CFO: Brenda Qualls, Chief Financial Officer
Web address: www.navicenthealth.org/nhb/home
Control: Other not–for–profit (including NFP Corporation) **Service**: General medical and surgical

Staffed Beds: 91 **Admissions**: 3153 **Census**: 40 **Outpatient Visits**: 80315
Births: 486 **Total Expense ($000)**: 68724 **Payroll Expense ($000)**: 27786
Personnel: 348

☐ **CENTRAL STATE HOSPITAL**, 2450 Vinson Highway, Zip 31062–0001; tel. 478/445–4128, **A**1 3 **F**39 77 98 149 163
Primary Contact: Stephanie Stokes–Little
COO: Terry McGee, Chief Operations Officer
CMO: Scott VanSant, M.D., Chief Medical Officer
CIO: Betsy Bradley, Coordinator Performance Improvement
CHR: Myra Holloway, Director Human Resources Management
Web address: https://dbhdd.georgia.gov/be-caring/central-state-hospital-csh-milledgeville-ga
Control: State, Government, Nonfederal **Service**: Psychiatric

Staffed Beds: 184 **Admissions**: 121 **Census**: 179 **Outpatient Visits**: 0
Births: 0 **Total Expense ($000)**: 56235 **Payroll Expense ($000)**: 22118
Personnel: 559

MILLEN—Jenkins County

JENKINS COUNTY MEDICAL CENTER (111311), 931 East Winthrope Avenue, Zip 30442–1839; tel. 478/982–4221, **A**10 18 **F**3 29 40 64 68 80 93 94 98 102 103 107 115 119 122 128 133 156
Primary Contact: Antoine Poythress, Chief Executive Officer
COO: Pam Mixon, Chief Operating Officer
CFO: Cindy Bierschenk, Director of Financial Services
CIO: Christian Rekowski, Information Technology Director
CHR: Natalie Tambon, Director of Human Resources
Web address: https://jenkinsmedicalcenter.com/
Control: Hospital district or authority, Government, Nonfederal **Service**: General medical and surgical

Staffed Beds: 25 **Admissions**: 324 **Census**: 2 **Outpatient Visits**: 11043
Births: 0 **Total Expense ($000)**: 8136 **Payroll Expense ($000)**: 5353
Personnel: 94

MONROE—Walton County

⇧ **PIEDMONT WALTON HOSPITAL (110046)**, 2151 West Spring Street, Zip 30655–3115, Mailing Address: PO BOX 1346, Zip 30655–1346; tel. 770/267–8461, (Nonreporting) **A**10 21 **S** Piedmont Healthcare, Roswell, GA
Primary Contact: Blake Watts, FACHE, Chief Executive Officer
CFO: Jeffrey Mullis, Interim Chief Financial Officer
CMO: Steven Durocher, M.D., Chief Medical Officer
CIO: Cory Crayton, Director of Information Systems
CHR: Michele Monsrud, Director Human Resources
CNO: Stevanie Reynolds, Chief Nursing Officer
Web address: https://www.piedmont.org/locations/piedmont-walton/home
Control: Other not–for–profit (including NFP Corporation) **Service**: General medical and surgical

Staffed Beds: 77

☐ **RIDGEVIEW INSTITUTE – MONROE (114037)**, 709 Breedlove Drive, Zip 30655–2055; tel. 844/350–8800, (Nonreporting) **A**1 10
Primary Contact: Angie Scott, Chief Executive Officer
Web address: https://ridgeviewinstitute.com/
Control: Other not–for–profit (including NFP Corporation) **Service**: Psychiatric

Staffed Beds: 88

MONTEZUMA—Macon County

⇧ **FLINT RIVER HOSPITAL (110190)**, 509 Sumter Street, Zip 31063–1733, Mailing Address: P.O. Box 770, Zip 31063–2502; tel. 478/472–3100, (Nonreporting) **A**10 21
Primary Contact: Michael C. Patterson, Chief Executive Officer
CFO: Michael C. Patterson, Chief Financial Officer
CMO: Quincy Jordan, M.D., Chief of Staff
CHR: Vicki Stotts, Coordinator Human Resources
CNO: Lee Hughes, R.N., Chief Nursing Officer
Web address: www.flintriverhospital.com/
Control: Corporation, Investor–owned (for–profit) **Service**: General medical and surgical

Staffed Beds: 49

MONTICELLO—Jasper County

⇧ **JASPER MEMORIAL HOSPITAL (111303)**, 898 College Street, Zip 31064–1258; tel. 706/468–6411, (Total facility includes 55 beds in nursing home–type unit) **A**10 18 21 **F**11 15 18 29 34 40 57 59 65 77 90 93 97 107 110 115 119 128 133 146 148 154 167 **P**6
Primary Contact: Robert Cumbie, Administrator
CFO: Stuart Abney, Controller
CHR: Laura E Hudgins, Assistant Administrator
CNO: Robin Carey, Director of Nursing
Web address: www.jaspermemorialhospital.org
Control: Other not–for–profit (including NFP Corporation) **Service**: General medical and surgical

Staffed Beds: 67 **Admissions**: 89 **Census**: 48 **Outpatient Visits**: 7352
Births: 0 **Total Expense ($000)**: 14942 **Payroll Expense ($000)**: 8105
Personnel: 127

Hospitals, U.S. / GEORGIA

MOULTRIE—Colquitt County

✚ **COLQUITT REGIONAL MEDICAL CENTER (110105)**, 3131 South Main Street, Zip 31768–6925, Mailing Address: P.O. Box 40, Zip 31776–0040; tel. 229/985–3420, (Total facility includes 59 beds in nursing home–type unit) **A**1 3 5 10 13 **F**3 7 11 12 13 15 17 18 20 29 30 31 34 35 37 40 45 46 47 48 49 51 53 56 57 59 60 61 62 63 65 68 70 74 75 76 77 78 79 81 82 85 86 89 91 93 97 98 100 103 104 107 108 110 111 112 115 117 119 120 121 123 126 127 128 129 130 131 132 133 135 143 146 147 148 149 154 167
Primary Contact: James L. Matney, President and Chief Executive Officer
COO: Greg K Johnson, Chief Operating Officer
CFO: Shamb Purohit, Chief Financial Officer
CMO: Andy Wills, M.D., Medical Director
CIO: Bill Bishop, Chief Information Officer
CHR: Dawn Johns, Director Human Resources
CNO: Dena Zinker, MSN, R.N., Vice President Patient Services
Web address: www.colquittregional.com
Control: Hospital district or authority, Government, Nonfederal **Service**: General medical and surgical

Staffed Beds: 158 **Admissions**: 6471 **Census**: 123 **Outpatient Visits**: 188370 **Births**: 661 **Total Expense ($000)**: 194006 **Payroll Expense ($000)**: 76270 **Personnel**: 1412

TURNING POINT HOSPITAL (110209), 3015 Veterans Parkway South, Zip 31788–6705, Mailing Address: P.O. Box 1177, Zip 31776–1177; tel. 229/985–4815, (Nonreporting) **A**3 10 **S** Universal Health Services, Inc., King of Prussia, PA
Primary Contact: Judy H. Payne, Chief Executive Officer
COO: Michael James, Chief Operating Officer
CFO: Edwin Bennett, Controller
CMO: Muhammad M Alam, M.D., Medical Director
CHR: Michelle Hamilton, Human Resource Manager
CNO: Heather Hightower, Director of Nursing
Web address: www.turningpointcare.com
Control: Corporation, Investor–owned (for–profit) **Service**: Substance Use Disorder

Staffed Beds: 69

NASHVILLE—Berrien County

⇑ **SOUTH GEORGIA MEDICAL CENTER BERRIEN CAMPUS (110234)**, 1221 East McPherson Avenue, Zip 31639–2326; tel. 229/433–8600, (Nonreporting) **A**10 21 **S** South Georgia Medical Center, Valdosta, GA
Primary Contact: Kevin Moore, R.N., Hospital Administrator
Web address: www.sgmc.org/
Control: Hospital district or authority, Government, Nonfederal **Service**: General medical and surgical

Staffed Beds: 39

NEWNAN—Coweta County

☐ **CITY OF HOPE ATLANTA (110233)**, 600 Celebrate Life Parkway, Zip 30265–8000; tel. 770/400–6000, (Nonreporting) **A**1 2 3 10 **S** City of Hope, Schaumburg, IL
Primary Contact: Jonathan E. Watkins, President and Chief Executive Officer
CFO: Andrew Caldwell, Chief Financial Officer
Web address: www.cancercenter.com/southeastern-hospital.cfm
Control: Corporation, Investor–owned (for–profit) **Service**: Cancer

Staffed Beds: 50

✚ **ENCOMPASS HEALTH REHABILITATION HOSPITAL OF NEWNAN (113032)**, 2101 East Newnan Crossing Boulevard, Zip 30265–2406; tel. 678/552–6200, (Nonreporting) **A**1 10 **S** Encompass Health Corporation, Birmingham, AL
Primary Contact: Stan Hickson, Chief Executive Officer
Web address: https://encompasshealth.com/locations/newnanrehab/
Control: Corporation, Investor–owned (for–profit) **Service**: Rehabilitation

Staffed Beds: 50

⇑ **PIEDMONT NEWNAN HOSPITAL (110229)**, 745 Poplar Road, Zip 30265–1618; tel. 770/400–1000, (Nonreporting) **A**2 10 21 **S** Piedmont Healthcare, Roswell, GA
Primary Contact: Michael Robertson, Chief Executive Officer
COO: Nathan Nipper, Vice President and Chief Operating Officer
CFO: John Miles, Chief Financial Officer
CMO: Jeffrey R Folk, M.D., Vice President Medical Affairs and Chief Medical Officer
CIO: Henry Scott, Executive Director, Technical Services
CHR: Clay Boyles, Executive Director, Human Resources
CNO: Jennifer Key, Chief Nursing Officer
Web address: www.piedmont.org/locations/piedmont-newnan/pnh-home
Control: Other not-for-profit (including NFP Corporation) **Service**: General medical and surgical

Staffed Beds: 146

SOUTHEASTERN REGIONAL MEDICAL CENTER See City of Hope Atlanta

NORCROSS—Gwinnett County

LAKEVIEW BEHAVIORAL HEALTH, 1 Technology Parkway South, Zip 30092–2928; tel. 678/713–2600, (Nonreporting) **S** Acadia Healthcare Company, Inc., Franklin, TN
Primary Contact: Deagan Watson, Chief Executive Officer
Web address: www.lakeviewbehavioralhealth.com
Control: Corporation, Investor-owned (for-profit) **Service**: Psychiatric

Staffed Beds: 70

OCILLA—Irwin County

IRWIN COUNTY HOSPITAL (110779), 710 North Irwin Avenue, Zip 31774–5011; tel. 229/468–3800, (Nonreporting) **A**10
Primary Contact: Quentin Whitwell, Chief Executive Officer
CFO: Tami Gray, Chief Financial Officer
CMO: Ashfaq Saiyed, M.D., Medical Director
CHR: Becky Edwards, Manager Human Resources
Web address: www.irwincntyhospital.com
Control: County, Government, Nonfederal

Staffed Beds: 64

QUITMAN—Brooks County

✚ **ARCHBOLD BROOKS (111332)**, 903 North Court Street, Zip 31643–1315, Mailing Address: P.O. Box 5000, Zip 31643–5000; tel. 229/263–4171, **A**1 10 18 **F**15 29 30 34 40 87 93 107 110 119 133 146 149 154 **S** Archbold Medical Center, Thomasville, GA
Primary Contact: James Womack, Interim Administrator
CFO: Skip Hightower, Chief Financial Officer
CMO: Michael Sopt, M.D., Chief of Staff
CHR: Janet Eldridge, Director Human Resources and Personnel
Web address: www.archbold.org
Control: Other not-for-profit (including NFP Corporation) **Service**: General medical and surgical

Staffed Beds: 25 **Admissions**: 195 **Census**: 9 **Outpatient Visits**: 17488 **Births**: 0 **Total Expense ($000)**: 12093 **Payroll Expense ($000)**: 6272 **Personnel**: 94

REIDSVILLE—Tattnall County

⇑ **OPTIM MEDICAL CENTER – TATTNALL (111323)**, 247 South Main Street, Zip 30453–4605; tel. 912/557–1000, (Nonreporting) **A**10 18 21 **S** National Surgical Healthcare, Chicago, IL
Primary Contact: David Flanders, Chief Executive Officer
CNO: Lora Duncan, Chief Nursing Officer
Web address: www.optimmedicalcenter.com
Control: Corporation, Investor–owned (for–profit) **Service**: Orthopedic

Staffed Beds: 25

Hospital, Medicare Provider Number, Address, Telephone, Approval, Facility, and Physician Codes, Health Care System

★ American Hospital Association (AHA) membership   ○ Healthcare Facilities Accreditation Program   ⇑ Center for Improvement in Healthcare Quality Accreditation
☐ The Joint Commission accreditation   ◇ DNV Healthcare Inc. accreditation   △ Commission on Accreditation of Rehabilitation Facilities (CARF) accreditation

Hospitals, U.S. / GEORGIA

RIVERDALE—Clayton County

☐ **RIVERWOODS BEHAVIORAL HEALTH SYSTEM (114035)**, 233 Medical Center Drive, Zip 30274-2640; tel. 770/991-8500, (Nonreporting) **A**1 10 **S** Acadia Healthcare Company, Inc., Franklin, TN
Primary Contact: Angela Harris, Chief Executive Officer
COO: Jenifer Harcourt, Chief Operating Officer
CIO: Hema Patel, Director Medical Records
CHR: Tareka Beasley, Director Human Resources
Web address: www.riverwoodsbehavioral.com
Control: Corporation, Investor-owned (for-profit) **Service**: Psychiatric

Staffed Beds: 75

☐ **SOUTHERN REGIONAL MEDICAL CENTER (110165)**, 11 Upper Riverdale Road SW, Zip 30274-2615; tel. 770/991-8000, (Nonreporting) **A**1 3 10 **S** Prime Healthcare, Ontario, CA
Primary Contact: Ela C. Lena, President and Chief Executive Officer
COO: Therese O Sucher, Senior Vice President Operations
CFO: Richard G Stovall, Senior Vice President Fiscal Services and Chief Financial Officer
CMO: Willie Cochran, M.D., Jr, Chief of Staff
CIO: Karen Moore, Vice President Information Technology and Chief Information Officer
CHR: Norma Adams, Director Human Resources
Web address: www.southernregional.org
Control: Other not-for-profit (including NFP Corporation) **Service**: General medical and surgical

Staffed Beds: 331

ROME—Floyd County

⊞ **ADVENTHEALTH REDMOND (110168)**, 501 Redmond Road, Zip 30165-1415, Mailing Address: P.O. Box 107001, Zip 30164-7001; tel. 706/291-0291, (Nonreporting) **A**1 2 3 5 10 13 19 **S** AdventHealth, Altamonte Springs, FL
Primary Contact: Isaac Sendros, President and Chief Executive Officer
COO: Karen Steely, Chief Operating Officer
CFO: Kenneth Metteauer, Chief Financial Officer
CIO: Brad Treglown, Director Information Systems
CHR: Patsy Adams, Vice President Human Resources
Web address: https://www.adventhealth.com/hospital/redmond-regional-medical-center/our-location
Control: Corporation, Investor-owned (for-profit) **Service**: General medical and surgical

Staffed Beds: 230

⊞ **ATRIUM HEALTH FLOYD MEDICAL CENTER (110054)**, 304 Turner McCall Boulevard, Zip 30165-5621, Mailing Address: PO Box 32861, Charlotte, NC, Zip 28232-2861; tel. 706/509-5000, **A**1 2 3 5 10 19 **F**3 4 5 7 8 9 11 12 13 15 17 18 20 22 26 28 29 30 31 32 34 35 36 37 38 39 40 43 44 45 46 48 49 50 51 53 54 55 56 57 58 59 61 63 64 65 66 68 70 71 72 73 74 75 76 77 78 79 80 81 82 84 85 86 87 89 90 93 96 97 98 100 101 102 103 104 105 107 108 110 111 114 115 118 119 126 127 129 130 131 132 135 143 144 146 147 148 149 152 153 154 156 160 162 164 165 167 169 **S** Atrium Health, Inc., Charlotte, NC
Primary Contact: Kurt Stuenkel, FACHE, President and Chief Executive Officer
COO: Warren Alston Rigas, Executive Vice President and Chief Operating Officer
CFO: Philip Wheeler, Chief Financial Officer
CMO: Joseph Biuso, M.D., Vice President and Chief of Medical Affairs
CIO: Jeff Buda, Chief Information Officer
CHR: Beth Bradford, Director Human Resources
CNO: Sheila Bennett, R.N., Vice President & Chief Nursing Officer
Web address: www.floyd.org
Control: Other not-for-profit (including NFP Corporation) **Service**: General medical and surgical

Staffed Beds: 354 **Admissions**: 18290 **Census**: 260 **Outpatient Visits**: 274011 **Births**: 2184 **Total Expense ($000)**: 613391 **Payroll Expense ($000)**: 279468 **Personnel**: 2775

FLOYD MEDICAL CENTER See Atrium Health Floyd Medical Center

REDMOND REGIONAL MEDICAL CENTER See Adventhealth Redmond

ROSWELL—Fulton County

⊞ △ **WELLSTAR NORTH FULTON HOSPITAL (110198)**, 3000 Hospital Boulevard, Zip 30076-3899; tel. 770/751-2500, **A**1 2 3 7 10 13 **F**3 8 11 13 15 18 20 22 26 28 29 30 31 34 35 37 38 40 43 44 45 48 49 50 51 53 54 55 57 59 63 64 68 70 73 74 75 76 77 78 79 81 82 84 85 86 87 90 91 92 93 96 107 108 110 111 115 118 119 126 129 130 131 132 133 141 146 147 148 167 169 **S** WellStar Health System, Marietta, GA
Primary Contact: Jon-Paul Croom, President
COO: Lindsey Petrini, Chief Operating Officer
CFO: Felix Sotoizaguirre, Chief Financial Officer
CMO: Karim Godamunne, M.D., Chief Medical Officer
CHR: Susan Brown, Chief Human Resources Officer
CNO: Nancy Melcher, Chief Nursing Officer
Web address: https://www.wellstar.org/locations/hospital/north-fulton-hospital
Control: Other not-for-profit (including NFP Corporation) **Service**: General medical and surgical

Staffed Beds: 155 **Admissions**: 9934 **Census**: 157 **Outpatient Visits**: 107556 **Births**: 1334 **Personnel**: 1084

SAINT MARYS—Camden County

⊞ **SOUTHEAST GEORGIA HEALTH SYSTEM CAMDEN CAMPUS (110146)**, 2000 Dan Proctor Drive, Zip 31558-3810; tel. 912/576-6200, **A**1 10 20 **F**70 76 89 122 **S** Southeast Georgia Health System, Brunswick, GA
Primary Contact: Glenn Gann, Vice President and Administrator
CFO: John Milazzo, Chief Financial Officer
CMO: Robert Bernasek, M.D., Chief Medical Officer
CNO: Judith Henson, Vice President, Patient Care Services
Web address: www.sghs.org
Control: Hospital district or authority, Government, Nonfederal **Service**: General medical and surgical

Staffed Beds: 40 **Admissions**: 2519 **Census**: 15 **Outpatient Visits**: 171480 **Births**: 569 **Total Expense ($000)**: 76245 **Payroll Expense ($000)**: 23198 **Personnel**: 317

SAINT SIMONS ISLAND—Glynn County

☐ **SAINT SIMONS BY-THE-SEA HOSPITAL (114016)**, 2927 Demere Road, Zip 31522-1620; tel. 912/638-1999, (Nonreporting) **A**1 10 **S** Universal Health Services, Inc., King of Prussia, PA
Primary Contact: Marie Renner, Chief Executive Officer
CMO: Kim Masters, M.D., Medical Director
CIO: Chisty Mosely, Director Information Management
Web address: www.ssbythesea.com
Control: Corporation, Investor-owned (for-profit) **Service**: Psychiatric

Staffed Beds: 101

SANDERSVILLE—Washington County

☐ **WASHINGTON COUNTY REGIONAL MEDICAL CENTER (110086)**, 610 Sparta Road, Zip 31082-1860, Mailing Address: P.O. Box 636, Zip 31082-0636; tel. 478/240-2000, (Nonreporting) **A**1 10 20
Primary Contact: Pamela Stewart, Chief Executive Officer
CMO: Rob Gatliff, Chief of Medical Staff
CHR: Misty Ivey, Human Resources Manager
CNO: Pamela Stewart, Director of Nursing
Web address: www.wcrmc.com
Control: Hospital district or authority, Government, Nonfederal **Service**: General medical and surgical

Staffed Beds: 60

SAVANNAH—Chatham County

⊞ △ **CANDLER HOSPITAL-SAVANNAH (110024)**, 5353 Reynolds Street, Zip 31405-6015; tel. 912/819-6000, (Nonreporting) **A**1 2 7 10
Primary Contact: Paul P. Hinchey, President and Chief Executive Officer
CFO: Allen R Butcher, Chief Financial Officer
CMO: James Scott, M.D., Vice President Medical Affairs
CIO: George Evans, Vice President and Chief Information Officer
CHR: Don Stubbs, Vice President Human Resources
CNO: Sherry Danello, MSN, R.N., Vice President and Chief Nursing Officer
Web address: www.sjchs.org
Control: Church operated, Nongovernment, not-for-profit **Service**: General medical and surgical

Staffed Beds: 271

Hospitals, U.S. / GEORGIA

☐ **COASTAL HARBOR TREATMENT CENTER (114008)**, 1150 Cornell Avenue, Zip 31406–2702; tel. 912/354–3911, (Nonreporting) **A**1 3 10 **S** Universal Health Services, Inc., King of Prussia, PA
Primary Contact: Sneha Patel, Chief Executive Officer
COO: Ray Heckerman, Chief Executive Officer and Managing Director
CFO: Brad Lavoie, Chief Financial Officer
CMO: Reemon Bishara, M.D., Medical Director
CHR: Kellie Carlson, Director Human Resources
CNO: Jillisa Thornton, Director of Nursing
Web address: www.coastalharbor.com
Control: Corporation, Investor–owned (for–profit) **Service:** Psychiatric

Staffed Beds: 175

⊞ **ENCOMPASS HEALTH REHABILITATION HOSPITAL OF SAVANNAH (113033)**, 6510 Seawright DR, Zip 31406–2752; tel. 912/235–6000, (Nonreporting) **A**1 10 **S** Encompass Health Corporation, Birmingham, AL
Primary Contact: Randal S. Hamilton, Chief Executive Officer
CFO: Dana Edwards, Controller
CNO: Carla James, Chief Nursing Officer
Web address: www.rehabilitationhospitalsavannah.com
Control: Corporation, Investor–owned (for–profit) **Service:** Rehabilitation

Staffed Beds: 50

GEORGE AND MARIE BACKUS CHILDREN'S HOSPITAL See Memorial Children's Hospital

☐ **GEORGIA REGIONAL HOSPITAL AT SAVANNAH (114028)**, 1915 Eisenhower Drive, Zip 31406–5098; tel. 912/356–2011, **A**1 3 10 **F**39 59 69 75 77 98 100 101 102 130 146 149 154 163 164
Primary Contact: Beth Jones, Regional Administrator
COO: Thomas F Kurtz Jr, Chief Operating Officer
CFO: Janet Edenfield, Director Financial Services
CMO: Donald Manning, M.D., Clinical Director
CHR: Jamekia Powers, Assistant Director Human Resources
Web address: www.dbhdd.georgia.gov/georgia-regional-hospital-savannah
Control: State, Government, Nonfederal **Service:** Psychiatric

Staffed Beds: 179 **Admissions:** 281 **Census:** 162 **Births:** 0

LANDMARK HOSPITAL OF SAVANNAH (112018), 800 East 68th Street, Zip 31405–4710; tel. 912/298–1000, (Nonreporting) **A**10 22 **S** Landmark Hospitals, Cape Girardeau, MO
Primary Contact: Denise Wayne, Chief Executive Officer
Web address: www.landmarkhospitals.com/savannah
Control: Partnership, Investor–owned (for–profit) **Service:** Acute long–term care hospital

Staffed Beds: 50

MEMORIAL HEALTH See Memorial Health University Medical Center

⊞ **MEMORIAL HEALTH UNIVERSITY MEDICAL CENTER (110036)**, 4700 Waters Avenue, Zip 31404–6283, Mailing Address: P.O. Box 23089, Zip 31403–3089; tel. 912/350–8000, (Includes MEMORIAL CHILDREN'S HOSPITAL, 4700 Waters Avenue, Savannah, Georgia, Zip 31404–6220, PO Box 23089, Zip 31403–3089; tel. 912/350–7337) (Nonreporting) **A**1 2 3 10 19 **S** HCA Healthcare, Nashville, TN
Primary Contact: Bradley S. Talbert, FACHE, Chief Executive Officer
CFO: Laura Dow, Chief Financial Officer
CMO: Ramon V Meguiar, M.D., Chief Medical Officer
CIO: Kathryn McClellan, Chief Information Officer
CHR: Alisa R Griner, Director, Human Resources
CNO: Todd Isbell, R.N., MSN, Chief Nursing Officer
Web address: www.memorialhealth.com
Control: Other not–for–profit (including NFP Corporation) **Service:** General medical and surgical

Staffed Beds: 564

⊞ **SELECT SPECIALTY HOSPITAL–SAVANNAH (112011)**, 5353 Reynolds Street, 4 South, Zip 31405–6015; tel. 912/819–7982, (Nonreporting) **A**1 10 **S** Select Medical Corporation, Mechanicsburg, PA
Primary Contact: Stacey Craig, Chief Executive Officer
Web address: https://www.selectspecialtyhospitals.com/locations-and-tours/ga/savannah/savannah/
Control: Corporation, Investor–owned (for–profit) **Service:** Acute long–term care hospital

Staffed Beds: 40

☐ **ST. JOSEPH'S HOSPITAL (110043)**, 11705 Mercy Boulevard, Zip 31419–1791; tel. 912/819–4100, (Nonreporting) **A**1 2 10
Primary Contact: Paul P. Hinchey, President and Chief Executive Officer
COO: Kyle McCann, Chief Operating Officer
CFO: Allen R Butcher, Chief Financial Officer
CMO: James Scott, M.D., Vice President Medical Affairs
CIO: Nolan Henessee, Vice President and Chief Information Officer
CHR: Steve Pound, Vice President Human Resources
CNO: Sherry Danello, MSN, R.N., Vice President and Chief Nursing Officer
Web address: www.sjchs.org
Control: Church operated, Nongovernment, not–for–profit **Service:** General medical and surgical

Staffed Beds: 234

SMYRNA—Cobb County

⊞ **RIDGEVIEW INSTITUTE – SMYRNA (114012)**, 3995 South Cobb Drive SE, Zip 30080–6397; tel. 770/434–4567, (Nonreporting) **A**1 3 10
Primary Contact: Amy Alexander, Chief Executive Officer
CFO: Ruth Jenkins, Chief Financial Officer
CMO: Thomas Bradford Johns, M.D., Medical Director
CIO: Lynn Leger, Director Information Systems
CHR: Betty Sonderman, Manager Human Resources
Web address: www.ridgeviewinstitute.com
Control: Other not–for–profit (including NFP Corporation) **Service:** Psychiatric

Staffed Beds: 110

SNELLVILLE—Gwinnett County

⇧ **PIEDMONT EASTSIDE MEDICAL CENTER (110192)**, 1700 Medical Way, Zip 30078–2195; tel. 770/979–0200, (Nonreporting) **A**10 21 **S** Piedmont Healthcare, Roswell, GA
Primary Contact: Larry W. Ebert Jr, Chief Executive Officer
CMO: Michael O'Neill, M.D., Chief Medical Officer
CIO: Pattie Page, Director Marketing and Public Relations
CNO: Tracey Smithson, MSN, R.N., Chief Nursing Officer
Web address: www.eastsidemedical.com
Control: Corporation, Investor–owned (for–profit) **Service:** General medical and surgical

Staffed Beds: 310

SPRINGFIELD—Effingham County

⊞ **EFFINGHAM HEALTH SYSTEM (111306)**, 459 Georgia Highway 119 South, Zip 31329–3021, Mailing Address: P.O. Box 386, Zip 31329–0386; tel. 912/754–6451, (Total facility includes 105 beds in nursing home–type unit) **A**1 10 18 **F**3 6 11 15 18 24 29 34 35 40 43 45 50 57 59 77 81 85 97 107 110 111 114 115 119 126 127 128 130 133 135 144 147 149 154 **P**6
Primary Contact: Francine Witt, R.N., President and Chief Executive Officer
CFO: Matthew Moore, Director of Financial Reporting
CMO: Claude Sanks, Chief Medical Staff
CIO: Mary Pizzino, Chief Information Officer
CHR: Marie Murphy, Director Human Resources
CNO: Betsy Smith, Chief Nursing Officer
Web address: www.effinghamhospital.org
Control: Hospital district or authority, Government, Nonfederal **Service:** General medical and surgical

Staffed Beds: 130 **Admissions:** 509 **Census:** 89 **Outpatient Visits:** 74391 **Births:** 0 **Total Expense ($000):** 75309 **Payroll Expense ($000):** 25645 **Personnel:** 446

STATESBORO—Bulloch County

⊞ **EAST GEORGIA REGIONAL MEDICAL CENTER (110075)**, 1499 Fair Road, Zip 30458–1683, Mailing Address: P.O. Box 1048, Zip 30459–1048; tel. 912/486–1000, (Nonreporting) **A**1 10 **S** Community Health Systems, Inc., Franklin, TN
Primary Contact: Stephen G. Pennington, Chief Executive Officer
COO: Erin Smith, Chief Operating Officer
CFO: Christopher Hilton, Chief Financial Officer
CMO: Alan Scott, M.D., Chief of Staff
CIO: Brian Girardeau, Director Information System
CHR: Michael Black, Director Human Resources
CNO: Marie Burdette, Chief Nursing Officer
Web address: www.eastgeorgiaregional.com
Control: Corporation, Investor–owned (for–profit) **Service:** General medical and surgical

Staffed Beds: 149

Hospital, Medicare Provider Number, Address, Telephone, Approval, Facility, and Physician Codes, Health Care System

★ American Hospital Association (AHA) membership
☐ The Joint Commission accreditation
○ Healthcare Facilities Accreditation Program
◇ DNV Healthcare Inc. accreditation
⇧ Center for Improvement in Healthcare Quality Accreditation
△ Commission on Accreditation of Rehabilitation Facilities (CARF) accreditation

Hospitals, U.S. / GEORGIA

WILLINGWAY HOSPITAL, 311 Jones Mill Road, Zip 30458-4765; tel. 912/764-6236, (Nonreporting)
Primary Contact: Cherie Tolley, Chief Executive Officer
CMO: Robert W Mooney, M.D., Medical Director
Web address: www.willingway.com
Control: Corporation, Investor-owned (for-profit) **Service:** Substance Use Disorder

Staffed Beds: 40

STOCKBRIDGE—Henry County

⇧ **PIEDMONT HENRY HOSPITAL (110191)**, 1133 Eagle's Landing Parkway, Zip 30281-5099; tel. 678/604-5279, (Nonreporting) **A**2 10 21 **S** Piedmont Healthcare, Roswell, GA
Primary Contact: David Kent, Chief Executive Officer
COO: James Atkins, PharmD, Chief Operating Officer
CFO: Wesley James, Chief Financial Officer
CHR: Jana Warren, Human Resources Business Partner
CNO: Paula Yvonne Butts, Chief Nursing Officer
Web address: www.piedmont.org
Control: Other not-for-profit (including NFP Corporation) **Service:** General medical and surgical

Staffed Beds: 254

SWAINSBORO—Emanuel County

⇧ **EMANUEL MEDICAL CENTER (110109)**, 117 Kite Road, Zip 30401-3231, Mailing Address: P.O. Box 879, Zip 30401-0879; tel. 478/289-1100, (Nonreporting) **A**10 20 21
Primary Contact: Damien Scott, Chief Executive Officer
CFO: Jessica Johnson, Chief Financial Officer
CMO: Daryl McCartney, M.D., President Medical Staff
CIO: Tony Waters, Chief Information Officer
CHR: Jinny Newman, Director Human Resources
CNO: Ginger Hall, Chief Nursing Officer
Web address: www.emanuelmedical.org
Control: Hospital district or authority, Government, Nonfederal **Service:** General medical and surgical

Staffed Beds: 91

SYLVANIA—Screven County

OPTIM MEDICAL CENTER - SCREVEN (111312), 215 Mims Road, Zip 30467-2097; tel. 912/564-7426, (Nonreporting) **A**10 18 **S** National Surgical Healthcare, Chicago, IL
Primary Contact: Lagina Sheffield. Evans, R.N., Chief Executive Officer
CFO: Neil Orrill, Director of Finance
CMO: Heywood Kyle Gay, M.D., Physician
CIO: Christian Rekowski, Information Technology Manager
CHR: Natalie Tambon, Director of Human Resources
Web address: www.optimhealth.com
Control: Corporation, Investor-owned (for-profit) **Service:** General medical and surgical

Staffed Beds: 25

SYLVESTER—Worth County

★ ⇧ **PHOEBE WORTH MEDICAL CENTER (111328)**, 807 South Isabella Street, Zip 31791-7554, Mailing Address: P.O. Box 545, Zip 31791-0545; tel. 229/776-6961, (Nonreporting) **A**10 18 21 **S** Phoebe Putney Health System, Albany, GA
Primary Contact: Kim Gilman, Chief Executive Officer
CFO: Candace Guarnieri, Chief Financial Officer
CMO: Natu M Patel, M.D., Chief of Staff
CHR: Mandy Gordon, Human Resource Coordinator
CNO: Kim Gilman, Chief Nursing Officer
Web address: www.phoebeputney.com
Control: Other not-for-profit (including NFP Corporation) **Service:** General medical and surgical

Staffed Beds: 18

THOMASTON—Upson County

★ ⇧ **UPSON REGIONAL MEDICAL CENTER (110002)**, 801 West Gordon Street, Zip 30286-3426, Mailing Address: P.O. Box 1059, Zip 30286-0027; tel. 706/647-8111, **A**10 21 **F**3 11 13 15 18 19 20 22 28 29 30 31 34 35 36 40 45 46 49 50 54 57 59 60 61 64 65 66 68 70 76 77 78 79 80 81 82 85 86 87 89 97 98 103 107 108 109 111 114 115 118 119 124 126 127 129 130 131 132 135 148 154 156 167 169 **S** HealthTech Management Services, Plano, TX
Primary Contact: Jeffrey S. Tarrant, FACHE, Chief Executive Officer
CFO: John Williams, Chief Financial Officer
CIO: Johnathan Buice, Chief Information Officer
CHR: Laura Stokes, Human Resources Director
CNO: Lane Harrington, Chief Nursing Officer
Web address: www.urmc.org
Control: Other not-for-profit (including NFP Corporation) **Service:** General medical and surgical

Staffed Beds: 99 **Admissions:** 3882 **Census:** 57 **Outpatient Visits:** 74979 **Births:** 380 **Total Expense ($000):** 96241 **Payroll Expense ($000):** 38910 **Personnel:** 614

THOMASVILLE—Thomas County

ARCHBOLD MEDICAL CENTER See John D. Archbold Memorial Hospital

⊞ **JOHN D. ARCHBOLD MEMORIAL HOSPITAL (110038)**, 915 Gordon Avenue, Zip 31792-6614, Mailing Address: P.O. Box 1018, Zip 31799-1018; tel. 229/228-2000, (Total facility includes 64 beds in nursing home-type unit) **A**1 3 10 19 **F**3 8 11 12 13 15 18 20 22 26 28 29 30 31 32 34 35 38 40 43 45 46 47 48 49 50 51 54 56 57 58 59 60 61 63 64 65 66 67 70 73 74 75 76 77 78 79 80 81 82 84 85 86 87 90 91 92 93 96 97 98 100 101 102 103 104 107 108 110 111 114 115 116 117 119 120 121 123 124 126 128 129 130 131 132 135 143 144 145 146 147 148 149 154 164 **S** Archbold Medical Center, Thomasville, GA
Primary Contact: Darcy Craven, President and Chief Executive Officer
CFO: Skip Hightower, Senior Vice President and Chief Financial Officer
CIO: Tracy Gray, Senior Vice President Information Services
CHR: Zachariah P Wheeler, Senior Vice President Human Resources
CNO: Amy Griffin, Vice President Patient Care Services
Web address: www.archbold.org
Control: Other not-for-profit (including NFP Corporation) **Service:** General medical and surgical

Staffed Beds: 267 **Admissions:** 8757 **Census:** 193 **Outpatient Visits:** 244831 **Births:** 590 **Total Expense ($000):** 298109 **Payroll Expense ($000):** 108813 **Personnel:** 1477

THOMSON—McDuffie County

⇧ **PIEDMONT MCDUFFIE (110111)**, 2460 Washington Road, NE, Zip 30824; tel. 706/595-1411, (Nonreporting) **A**10 21 **S** Piedmont Healthcare, Roswell, GA
Primary Contact: Nicholas Wood, Administrator
CFO: Dave Belkoski, Chief Financial Officer
CNO: Danita Kiser, Chief Nursing Officer
Web address: www.universityhealth.org/mcduffie
Control: Other not-for-profit (including NFP Corporation) **Service:** General medical and surgical

Staffed Beds: 22

⇧ **UNIVERSITY HOSPITAL MCDUFFIE** See Piedmont Mcduffie

TIFTON—Tift County

⊞ **TIFT REGIONAL MEDICAL CENTER (110095)**, 901 East 18th Street, Zip 31794-3648, Mailing Address: Drawer 747, Zip 31793-0747; tel. 229/382-7120, **A**1 2 5 10 19 **F**3 8 9 11 12 13 15 18 20 22 26 28 29 30 31 33 34 35 40 45 47 49 50 51 54 57 59 60 63 64 68 70 71 74 75 76 77 78 79 81 82 84 85 86 87 89 92 93 97 100 104 107 108 110 111 114 115 118 119 120 121 123 126 129 130 131 132 135 143 144 146 147 148 149 154 156 167 169 **P**6 **S** Tift Regional Health System, Tifton, GA
Primary Contact: Christopher Dorman, President and Chief Executive Officer
CFO: Dennis L Crum, Senior Vice President and Chief Financial Officer
CMO: William Guest, M.D., Senior Vice President and Chief Medical Officer
CIO: Guy McAllister, Vice President and Chief Information Officer
CHR: Lori S Folsom, Assistant Vice President Human Resources
CNO: Carol Smith, Vice President Patient Care and Chief Nursing Officer
Web address: www.tiftregional.com
Control: Other not-for-profit (including NFP Corporation) **Service:** General medical and surgical

Staffed Beds: 181 **Admissions:** 10374 **Census:** 138 **Outpatient Visits:** 160211 **Births:** 1410 **Total Expense ($000):** 426090 **Payroll Expense ($000):** 166135 **Personnel:** 1987

Hospitals, U.S. / GEORGIA

TOCCOA—Stephens County

☐ **STEPHENS COUNTY HOSPITAL (110032)**, 163 Hospital Drive, Zip 30577-6820; tel. 706/282-4200, (Nonreporting) **A**1 3 10
Primary Contact: Van Loskoski, Chief Executive Officer
CFO: Richard W. Stokes, CPA, Chief Financial Officer
CNO: Deb Block, MSN, Director of Nursing
Web address: www.stephenscountyhospital.com
Control: Hospital district or authority, Government, Nonfederal **Service**: General medical and surgical

Staffed Beds: 188

VALDOSTA—Lowndes County

☐ **GREENLEAF BEHAVIORAL HEALTH HOSPITAL (114036)**, 2209 Pineview Drive, Zip 31602-7316; tel. 229/247-4357, (Nonreporting) **A**1 10 **S** Acadia Healthcare Company, Inc., Franklin, TN
Primary Contact: Michelle Neville, Chief Executive Officer
Web address: www.greenleafcounseling.net
Control: Corporation, Investor-owned (for-profit) **Service**: Psychiatric

Staffed Beds: 103

SMITH HOSPITAL See Smith Northview Hospital

⇧ **SOUTH GEORGIA MEDICAL CENTER (110122)**, 2501 North Patterson Street, Zip 31602-1735, Mailing Address: P.O. Box 1727, Zip 31603-1727; tel. 229/333-1000, (Includes SMITH NORTHVIEW HOSPITAL, 4280 North Valdosta Road, Valdosta, Georgia, Zip 31602, P O Box 10010, Zip 31604, tel. 229/671-2000; Leonard Carter, Campus Administrator) (Nonreporting) **A**2 3 5 10 19 21 **S** South Georgia Medical Center, Valdosta, GA
Primary Contact: Ronald Dean, President and Chief Executive Officer
COO: Randy Smith, Senior Vice President, Chief Operating Officer
CFO: Grant Byers, Senior Vice President and Chief Financial Officer
CIO: Bob Foster, Chief Information Officer
Web address: www.sgmc.org
Control: Hospital district or authority, Government, Nonfederal **Service**: General medical and surgical

Staffed Beds: 330

VIDALIA—Toombs County

⊞ **MEMORIAL HEALTH MEADOWS HOSPITAL (110128)**, 1 Meadows Parkway, Zip 30474-8759, Mailing Address: P.O. Box 1048, Zip 30475-1048; tel. 912/535-5555, (Nonreporting) **A**1 10 20 **S** HCA Healthcare, Nashville, TN
Primary Contact: Jared Kirby, Interim Chief Executive Officer
COO: James Nixon, Chief Operating Officer
CFO: Jared Kirby, Chief Financial Officer
CMO: Karen McColl, M.D., Chief Medical Officer
CIO: Charles Bondurant, Chief Information Officer
CNO: Jeffrey M Harden, Chief Nursing Officer
Web address: www.meadowsregional.org
Control: Other not-for-profit (including NFP Corporation) **Service**: General medical and surgical

Staffed Beds: 57

VILLA RICA—Carroll County

⊞ **TANNER MEDICAL CENTER–VILLA RICA (110015)**, 601 Dallas Highway, Zip 30180-1202; tel. 770/456-3000, (Includes WILLOWBROOKE AT TANNER, 20 Herrell Road, Villa Rica, Georgia, Zip 30180-5527, tel. 770/812-3266; Paula Gresham, Vice President, Hospital Administrator) (Nonreporting) **A**1 10 **S** Tanner Health System, Carrollton, GA
Primary Contact: Jerry Morris, Vice President and Administrator
CFO: Carol Crews, Senior Vice President and Chief Financial Officer
CMO: William Waters, M.D., IV, Executive Vice President
CIO: Terri Lee, Chief Information Officer
CHR: Shari W Gainey, Chief Human Resource Officer
CNO: Deborah Matthews, Senior Vice President
Web address: www.tanner.org
Control: Other not-for-profit (including NFP Corporation) **Service**: General medical and surgical

Staffed Beds: 132

WARM SPRINGS—Meriwether County

☐ **ROOSEVELT WARM SPRINGS LONG TERM ACUTE CARE HOSPITAL (112000)**, 6135 Roosevelt Highway, Zip 31830-2757, Mailing Address: P.O. Box 280, Zip 31830-2757; tel. 706/655-5291, (Nonreporting) **A**1 10
Primary Contact: Wanda Sims, Interim Chief Executive Officer
CFO: Susan Wilder, Director Financial Services
CMO: Carlos Parrado, M.D., Sr, Chief Medical Officer
CHR: Laura Stokes, Director Human Resources
CNO: Cathy Harbin, Chief Nursing Officer
Web address: www.augustahealth.org/roosevelt-warm-springs/rwsh
Control: Other not-for-profit (including NFP Corporation) **Service**: Acute long-term care hospital

Staffed Beds: 28

⊞ **ROOSEVELT WARM SPRINGS REHABILITATION AND SPECIALTY HOSPITALS (113028)**, 6135 Roosevelt Highway, Zip 31830-2757, Mailing Address: P.O. Box 280, Zip 31830-0280; tel. 706/655-5515, (Nonreporting) **A**1 10
Primary Contact: Wanda Sims, Interim Chief Executive Officer
CFO: Susan Wilder, Director Financial Services
CMO: Ara Chitchyan, M.D., Medical Director
CIO: Christen Carter, Director Public Relations
CHR: Laura Stokes, Director Human Resources
CNO: Cathy Harbin, Chief Nursing Officer
Web address: www.augustahealth.org/roosevelt-warm-springs/rwsh
Control: Other not-for-profit (including NFP Corporation) **Service**: Rehabilitation

Staffed Beds: 28

ROOSEVELT WARM SPRINGS REHABILITATION HOSPITAL See Roosevelt Warm Springs Rehabilitation and Specialty Hospitals

⊞ **WARM SPRINGS MEDICAL CENTER (111316)**, 5995 Spring Street, Zip 31830-2149, Mailing Address: P.O. Box 8, Zip 31830-0008; tel. 706/655-3331, (Total facility includes 79 beds in nursing home–type unit) **A**1 10 18 **F**3 15 29 30 34 35 40 41 57 59 64 65 68 87 107 110 114 119 127 128 130 133 135 146 149 154
Primary Contact: Karen Daniel, Chief Executive Officer
CFO: Patrick Flynn, Chief Financial Officer
CMO: Alan Thompson, M.D., President Medical Staff
CIO: Milo Varnadoe, Director Information Systems
CHR: Theresa Passarelli, Human Resources Generalist
CNO: Lynda Ligon, Chief Nursing Officer
Web address: www.warmspringsmc.org
Control: Partnership, Investor-owned (for-profit) **Service**: General medical and surgical

Staffed Beds: 104 **Admissions**: 337 **Census**: 88 **Outpatient Visits**: 7905 **Births**: 0 **Total Expense ($000)**: 17571 **Payroll Expense ($000)**: 6210 **Personnel**: 113

WARNER ROBINS—Houston County

★ ⇧ **HOUSTON MEDICAL CENTER (110069)**, 1601 Watson Boulevard, Zip 31093-3431, Mailing Address: P.O. Box 2886, Zip 31099-2886; tel. 478/922-4281, (Includes HOUSTON HEALTHCARE – PERRY, 1120 Morningside Drive, Perry, Georgia, Zip 31069-2906, tel. 478/987-3600; Todd Edenfield, R.N., Administrator) **A**5 10 13 21 **F**3 11 13 15 18 20 22 26 28 29 30 31 34 35 37 38 40 44 45 46 49 50 51 57 59 60 61 64 68 70 73 74 75 76 78 79 81 82 84 85 86 87 89 93 98 100 102 103 107 108 110 111 115 117 118 119 126 129 130 131 144 145 146 147 149 154 156 160 161 162 164 167 169
Primary Contact: Charles G. Briscoe, FACHE, President and Chief Executive Officer
COO: Charles G Briscoe, FACHE, Chief Operating Officer
CFO: Sean Whilden, Chief Financial Officer
CIO: George Curtis, Chief Information Officer
CHR: Michael O'Hara, Senior Executive Director Human Resources
Web address: www.hhc.org
Control: Other not-for-profit (including NFP Corporation) **Service**: General medical and surgical

Staffed Beds: 276 **Admissions**: 13189 **Census**: 169 **Outpatient Visits**: 307131 **Births**: 1971 **Total Expense ($000)**: 298820 **Payroll Expense ($000)**: 123499 **Personnel**: 1917

Hospital, Medicare Provider Number, Address, Telephone, Approval, Facility, and Physician Codes, Health Care System

★ American Hospital Association (AHA) membership
☐ The Joint Commission accreditation
○ Healthcare Facilities Accreditation Program
◇ DNV Healthcare Inc. accreditation
⇧ Center for Improvement in Healthcare Quality Accreditation
△ Commission on Accreditation of Rehabilitation Facilities (CARF) accreditation

© 2025 AHA Guide

Hospitals, U.S. / GEORGIA

WASHINGTON—Wilkes County

☐ **WILLS MEMORIAL HOSPITAL (111325)**, 120 Gordon Street, Zip 30673–1602, Mailing Address: P.O. Box 370, Zip 30673–0370; tel. 706/678-2151, (Nonreporting) **A**1 10 18
Primary Contact: Tracie Haughey, Chief Executive Officer and Chief Financial Officer
CFO: Tracie Haughey, Chief Executive Officer and Chief Financial Officer
CIO: David Harper, Chief Information Officer
CHR: Susan Pope, Director Human Resources
CNO: Angie Radford, R.N., Director of Nursing
Web address: www.willsmemorialhospital.com
Control: Hospital district or authority, Government, Nonfederal **Service**: General medical and surgical

Staffed Beds: 25

WAYCROSS—Ware County

✠ **MEMORIAL SATILLA HEALTH (110003)**, 1900 Tebeau Street, Zip 31501–6357, Mailing Address: P.O. Box 139, Zip 31502–0139; tel. 912/283-3030, (Nonreporting) **A**1 3 5 10 **S** HCA Healthcare, Nashville, TN
Primary Contact: K. Dale. Neely, FACHE, Chief Executive Officer
COO: Mark Roberts, Chief Operating Officer
CFO: Patrick Sloan, Chief Financial Officer
CIO: Barry Rudd, Chief Information Officer
CHR: Brigitte Churchill, Director of Human Resources
CNO: Holli Sweat, Associate Administrator and Chief Nursing Officer
Web address: www.memorialsatillahealth.com/
Control: Other not–for–profit (including NFP Corporation) **Service**: General medical and surgical

Staffed Beds: 122

WAYNESBORO—Burke County

☐ **BURKE MEDICAL CENTER (110113)**, 351 Liberty Street, Zip 30830–9686; tel. 706/554-4435, (Nonreporting) **A**1 10
Primary Contact: Michael Hester, Chief Executive Officer and Chief Financial Officer
CFO: Karen ONeal, Chief Financial Officer
CHR: Kim Anthony, Director Human Resources
CNO: Debra Burch, Chief Nursing Officer
Web address: https://www.burkehealth.com/
Control: Hospital district or authority, Government, Nonfederal **Service**: General medical and surgical

Staffed Beds: 40

WINDER—Barrow County

★ ⇧ **NORTHEAST GEORGIA MEDICAL CENTER BARROW (110045)**, 316 North Broad Street, Zip 30680–2150, Mailing Address: P.O. Box 688, Zip 30680–0688; tel. 770/867-3400, **A**10 21 **F**3 11 15 29 30 34 35 38 40 44 45 50 57 59 60 68 70 74 75 77 79 81 82 85 107 108 110 111 114 115 119 124 130 131 132 135 143 149 154 156 166 **S** Northeast Georgia Health System, Gainesville, GA
Primary Contact: John Neidenbach, Administrator
CMO: Jon Horn, M.D., Chief of Staff
CIO: Cory Crayton, Director Information Systems
CHR: Carlotta Hannah Newman, Human Resources Manager
CNO: Heather Standard, Chief Nursing Officer
Web address: www.barrowregional.com
Control: Other not–for–profit (including NFP Corporation) **Service**: General medical and surgical

Staffed Beds: 34 **Admissions**: 1289 **Census**: 11 **Outpatient Visits**: 41894 **Births**: 0 **Personnel**: 169

HAWAII

AIEA—Honolulu County

🏥 **PALI MOMI MEDICAL CENTER (120026)**, 98-1079 Moanalua Road, Zip 96701–4713; tel. 808/486–6000, **A**1 2 3 5 10 19 **F**3 12 15 18 20 22 26 29 31 34 35 36 40 43 44 45 46 49 50 58 59 60 61 63 64 65 68 70 74 75 77 78 79 80 81 84 85 86 87 92 93 107 108 110 111 115 118 119 126 130 131 132 135 146 147 148 149 154 156 167 **S** Hawaii Pacific Health, Honolulu, HI
Primary Contact: David T. Underriner, Executive Vice President of Oahu Operations, Chief Executive Officer
COO: Gloria Brooks, Chief Operating Officer
CFO: David Okabe, Executive Vice President, Chief Financial Officer and Treasurer
CMO: James Kakuda, M.D., Chief of Staff
CIO: Steve Robertson, Senior Vice President
CHR: Gail Lerch, R.N., Vice President Human Resources
CNO: Brigitte McKale, MSN, FACHE, Vice President and Chief Nurse Executive
Web address: www.palimomi.org
Control: Other not–for–profit (including NFP Corporation) **Service**: General medical and surgical

Staffed Beds: 118 **Admissions**: 5546 **Census**: 97 **Outpatient Visits**: 250152 **Births**: 0 **Total Expense ($000)**: 298085 **Payroll Expense ($000)**: 90887 **Personnel**: 1022

EWA BEACH—Honolulu County

HAWAII MEDICAL CENTER–WEST See Queen's Medical Center – West Oahu

🏥 **SUTTER HEALTH KAHI MOHALA (124001)**, 91–2301 Old Fort Weaver Road, Zip 96706–3602; tel. 808/671–8511, **A**1 10 **F**4 29 50 65 68 75 82 86 87 98 99 100 101 104 106 130 135 143 149 151 164
Primary Contact: Mark Linscott, Interim Administrator
CFO: Quin Ogawa, Chief Financial Officer
CMO: Steven Chaplin, M.D., Medical Director
CHR: Christina Enoka, Director Human Resources and Risk Management
CNO: Charles St. Louis, Director of Patient Care Services
Web address: www.kahimohala.org
Control: Other not–for–profit (including NFP Corporation) **Service**: Psychiatric

Staffed Beds: 88 **Admissions**: 363 **Census**: 66 **Outpatient Visits**: 0 **Births**: 0 **Total Expense ($000)**: 25829 **Payroll Expense ($000)**: 12826 **Personnel**: 190

HILO—Hawaii County

🏥 **HILO MEDICAL CENTER (120005)**, 1190 Waianuenue Avenue, Zip 96720–2089; tel. 808/932–3000, (Nonreporting) **A**1 2 3 5 10 20 **S** Hawaii Health Systems Corporation, Honolulu, HI
Primary Contact: Dan Brinkman, R.N., Chief Executive Officer
COO: Dan Brinkman, R.N., Chief Operating Officer
CMO: Ted Peskin, M.D., Acute Care Medical Director
CIO: Money Atwal, Chief Information Officer
CHR: Holly Ka'akimaka, Director Human Resources
CNO: Arthur Sampaga, Chief Nursing Officer
Web address: https://www.hilomedicalcenter.org/
Control: State, Government, Nonfederal **Service**: General medical and surgical

Staffed Beds: 199

HONOKAA—Hawaii County

★ **HALE HO'OLA HAMAKUA (121307)**, 45–547 Plumeria Street, Zip 96727–6902; tel. 808/932–4100, (Nonreporting) **A**10 18 **S** Hawaii Health Systems Corporation, Honolulu, HI
Primary Contact: Denise Mackey, Administrator
CMO: Bruce Graves, M.D., Chief of Staff
CNO: Gayle Green, Director of Nursing
Web address: www.halehoolahamakua.org
Control: State, Government, Nonfederal **Service**: General medical and surgical

Staffed Beds: 77

HONOLULU—Honolulu County

🏥 **KAISER PERMANENTE MEDICAL CENTER (120011)**, 3288 Moanalua Road, Zip 96819–1469; tel. 808/432–8000, **A**1 2 3 5 10 19 **F**3 12 13 15 17 18 19 20 21 22 24 26 29 30 31 32 34 35 36 37 38 40 41 44 45 46 47 48 49 50 51 54 55 56 57 58 59 60 61 64 65 68 70 72 73 74 75 76 77 78 79 80 81 82 84 85 86 87 88 89 92 93 94 100 102 107 108 110 111 114 115 119 126 130 131 141 143 146 148 149 154 162 164 167 169 **P**6 **S** Kaiser Foundation Hospitals, Oakland, CA
Primary Contact: Ed Chan, FACHE, Market President, Hawaii
CFO: Thomas Risse, Chief Financial Officer and Vice President Business Services
CMO: Keith Ogasawara, M.D., Associate Medical Director and Professional Chief of Staff
CIO: Donna Scannell, Vice President Information Technology
CHR: Jean Melnikoff, Vice President Human Resources
Web address: www.kaiserpermanente.org
Control: Other not–for–profit (including NFP Corporation) **Service**: General medical and surgical

Staffed Beds: 215 **Admissions**: 10132 **Census**: 145 **Outpatient Visits**: 78407 **Births**: 1441 **Personnel**: 1551

☐ **KAPIOLANI MEDICAL CENTER FOR WOMEN & CHILDREN (123300)**, 1319 Punahou Street, Zip 96826–1001; tel. 808/983–6000, **A**1 2 3 5 10 **F**3 13 15 19 21 23 25 27 29 31 32 34 35 36 39 40 41 43 44 48 50 53 54 55 57 58 59 63 64 65 70 72 73 74 75 76 77 78 79 81 83 84 85 87 88 89 91 92 93 94 96 97 107 108 110 111 115 119 126 129 130 131 132 134 135 136 146 147 148 149 154 156 167 169 **S** Hawaii Pacific Health, Honolulu, HI
Primary Contact: David T. Underriner, Executive Vice President of Oahu Operations, Chief Executive Officer
CFO: David Okabe, Senior Vice President, Chief Financial Officer and Treasurer
CIO: Steve Robertson, Vice President
CHR: Gail Lerch, R.N., Vice President
CNO: Mavis Hiroko Nikaido, Vice President of Patient Services and Chief Nurse Executive
Web address: www.kapiolani.org
Control: Other not–for–profit (including NFP Corporation) **Service**: General medical and surgical

Staffed Beds: 253 **Admissions**: 9735 **Census**: 156 **Outpatient Visits**: 228315 **Births**: 5513 **Total Expense ($000)**: 381200 **Payroll Expense ($000)**: 127571 **Personnel**: 1307

🏥 **KUAKINI MEDICAL CENTER (120007)**, 347 North Kuakini Street, Zip 96817–2381; tel. 808/536–2236, **A**1 2 3 5 10 **F**3 15 17 18 20 22 24 26 28 29 31 34 35 40 45 46 49 57 58 59 60 64 68 70 74 75 77 78 79 80 81 82 84 85 86 87 107 108 110 111 115 117 118 119 120 121 123 126 129 130 131 132 135 145 146 147 148 149 154 167 **P**1
Primary Contact: Gregg Oishi, President and Chief Executive Officer
CFO: Quin Ogawa, Vice President Finance and Chief Financial Officer
CMO: Nobuyuki Miki, M.D., Vice President Medical Services and Chief Medical Officer
CHR: Ann N. Choy, Manager Human Resources and Payroll
CNO: Virginia Walker, Vice President Nursing Services and Chief Nursing Officer
Web address: www.kuakini.org
Control: Other not–for–profit (including NFP Corporation) **Service**: General medical and surgical

Staffed Beds: 100 **Admissions**: 3079 **Census**: 68 **Outpatient Visits**: 41373 **Births**: 0 **Total Expense ($000)**: 147975 **Payroll Expense ($000)**: 57866 **Personnel**: 570

LEAHI HOSPITAL (122001), 3675 Kilauea Avenue, Zip 96816–2398; tel. 808/733–8000, (Nonreporting) **A**10 **S** Hawaii Health Systems Corporation, Honolulu, HI
Primary Contact: Derek Akiyoshi, Chief Executive Officer
CMO: Albert Yazawa, M.D., Regional Medical Director
CHR: Russel Higa, JD, Regional Director Human Resources
CNO: Amy Vasunaga, Chief Nurse Executive
Web address: www.hhsc.org
Control: State, Government, Nonfederal **Service**: Acute long–term care hospital

Staffed Beds: 126

Hospital, Medicare Provider Number, Address, Telephone, Approval, Facility, and Physician Codes, Health Care System

★ American Hospital Association (AHA) membership
☐ The Joint Commission accreditation
○ Healthcare Facilities Accreditation Program
◇ DNV Healthcare Inc. accreditation
⇑ Center for Improvement in Healthcare Quality Accreditation
△ Commission on Accreditation of Rehabilitation Facilities (CARF) accreditation

Hospitals, U.S. / HAWAII

REHABILITATION HOSPITAL OF THE PACIFIC (123025), 226 North Kuakini Street, Zip 96817–2488; tel. 808/531–3511, **A**1 10 **F**3 29 30 34 44 52 54 56 57 58 64 68 74 75 77 78 79 82 90 92 93 96 130 132 143 146 147 148 149
Primary Contact: Stephanie Nadolny, President and Chief Executive Officer
CFO: Wendy Manuel, Vice President and Chief Financial Officer
CMO: Shari Ann Oshiro, Chief Medical Director
CHR: Lori Yoshioka, Director of Human Resources
CNO: Brenda Hiromoto, Director of Nursing
Web address: www.rehabhospital.org
Control: Other not–for–profit (including NFP Corporation) **Service**: Rehabilitation

Staffed Beds: 82 **Admissions**: 1342 **Census**: 57 **Outpatient Visits**: 30962 **Births**: 0 **Total Expense ($000)**: 49974 **Payroll Expense ($000)**: 25368 **Personnel**: 345

SHRINERS HOSPITALS FOR CHILDREN–HONOLULU (123301), 1310 Punahou Street, Zip 96826–1099; tel. 808/941–4466, **A**1 3 5 10 **F**3 29 32 34 35 36 39 50 57 58 66 68 69 74 75 79 81 85 86 87 89 93 94 96 130 131 132 146 148 149 154 **P**6 **S** Shriners Hospitals for Children, Tampa, FL
Primary Contact: Andrew Graul, Administrator
CFO: Patricia Miyasawa, CPA, Director Fiscal Service
CMO: Craig Ono, M.D., Chief of Staff
CIO: Gregory A Wolf, Director Information Systems
CHR: Derek Ito, Director Human Resources
CNO: Anita Becker, R.N., Nurse Executive, Director of Patient Care Services
Web address: www.shrinershospitalsforchildren.org/honolulu
Control: Other not–for–profit (including NFP Corporation) **Service**: Children's orthopedic

Staffed Beds: 12 **Admissions**: 151 **Census**: 2 **Outpatient Visits**: 16299 **Births**: 0 **Total Expense ($000)**: 28924 **Payroll Expense ($000)**: 14136 **Personnel**: 146

STRAUB MEDICAL CENTER (120022), 888 South King Street, Zip 96813–3097; tel. 808/522–4000, **A**1 2 3 5 10 19 **F**3 5 15 16 18 20 21 22 23 24 26 27 28 29 31 34 35 40 44 45 46 47 48 49 50 54 56 58 59 60 61 63 64 65 68 70 74 75 77 78 79 80 81 84 85 86 87 92 93 97 100 102 104 107 108 110 111 115 119 126 130 131 132 135 144 145 146 147 148 149 154 156 167 **S** Hawaii Pacific Health, Honolulu, HI
Primary Contact: David T. Underriner, Executive Vice President of Oahu Operations, Chief Executive Officer
COO: Maureen Flannery, Vice President Clinic Operations
CFO: David Okabe, Executive Vice President, Chief Financial Officer and Treasurer
CMO: Randy Yates, M.D., Chief Medical Officer
CIO: Steve Robertson, Executive Vice President and Chief Information Officer
CHR: Gail Lerch, R.N., Executive Vice President Human Resources
CNO: Patricia Boeckmann, R.N., Chief Operating Officer and Chief Nursing Officer
Web address: www.straubhealth.org
Control: Other not–for–profit (including NFP Corporation) **Service**: General medical and surgical

Staffed Beds: 118 **Admissions**: 6703 **Census**: 135 **Outpatient Visits**: 775690 **Births**: 0 **Total Expense ($000)**: 437771 **Payroll Expense ($000)**: 102050 **Personnel**: 1588

THE QUEEN'S MEDICAL CENTER (120001), 1301 Punchbowl Street, Zip 96813–2499; tel. 808/691–1000, (Includes QUEEN'S MEDICAL CENTER – WEST OAHU, 91–2141 Fort Weaver Road, Ewa Beach, Hawaii, Zip 96706–1993, tel. 808/691–3000; Susan Murray, FACHE, Chief Operating Officer) **A**1 2 3 5 10 19 **F**3 4 5 11 12 13 15 17 18 19 20 21 22 24 26 28 29 30 34 35 37 38 39 40 43 44 46 47 49 50 51 54 55 56 57 58 59 60 61 62 63 64 66 68 70 71 73 74 75 76 77 78 79 81 82 84 85 86 87 89 93 96 97 98 99 100 102 104 105 107 108 110 111 115 117 118 119 120 121 124 126 129 130 131 132 135 138 139 144 146 147 148 149 150 152 153 154 156 157 160 167 **S** Queen's Health System, Honolulu, HI
Primary Contact: Jason Chang, President & Chief Executive Officer
CFO: Michel Riccioni, Chief Financial Officer
CMO: Whitney Limm, M.D., Executive Vice President and Chief Physician Executive
CIO: Brian Yoshii, Vice President Information Technology and Chief Information Officer
CHR: Nona Tamanaha, Vice President Human Resources
CNO: Kelly M Johnson, Chief Nursing Officer
Web address: https://www.queens.org/locations/hospitals/qmc/
Control: Other not–for–profit (including NFP Corporation) **Service**: General medical and surgical

Staffed Beds: 649 **Admissions**: 31373 **Census**: 523 **Outpatient Visits**: 712487 **Births**: 1345 **Total Expense ($000)**: 1411119 **Payroll Expense ($000)**: 548970 **Personnel**: 4908

TRIPLER ARMY MEDICAL CENTER, 1 Jarrett White Road, Zip 96859–5001; tel. 808/433–6661, (Nonreporting) **A**1 2 3 5 **S** Department of the Army, Office of the Surgeon General, Falls Church, VA
Primary Contact: Colonel Michael Ronn, Hospital Commander
COO: Major Elias B. Lozano, Executive Officer
CFO: Lieutenant Colonel Christopher A. Wodarz, Chief, Resource Management Division
CMO: Captain Andrew L. Findlay, Deputy Commander Clinical Services
CIO: Lieutenant Colonel Donna E Beed, Chief Information Management Division
CHR: Colonel James N. Davidson, Troop Commander
CNO: Colonel Jennifer L. Bedick, Deputy Commander Nursing
Web address: https://tripler.tricare.mil/
Control: Army, Government, federal **Service**: General medical and surgical

Staffed Beds: 143

KAHUKU—Honolulu County

KAHUKU MEDICAL CENTER (121304), 56–117 Pualalea Street, Zip 96731–2052; tel. 808/293–9221, (Nonreporting) **A**1 10 18
Primary Contact: Steve Nawahine, Chief Executive Officer
COO: Jerome Flores, Chief Financial Officer and Chief Operating Officer
CFO: Jerome Flores, Chief Financial Officer and Chief Operating Officer
CMO: P Douglas Nielson, M.D., Chief of Staff
Web address: www.kahuku.hhsc.org/
Control: Other not–for–profit (including NFP Corporation) **Service**: General medical and surgical

Staffed Beds: 21

KAHULUI—Maui County

HALE MAKUA See Hale Makua Health Services

KAILUA—Honolulu County

ADVENTIST HEALTH CASTLE (120006), 640 Ulukahiki Street, Zip 96734–4454; tel. 808/263–5500, **A**1 10 19 **F**3 8 12 13 15 18 20 22 24 26 29 30 31 34 35 37 39 40 43 48 49 50 51 54 55 59 64 68 70 73 74 75 76 78 79 81 84 85 87 93 97 98 102 104 107 108 110 111 115 118 119 126 127 130 131 132 135 144 146 147 148 149 154 156 157 167 **P**6 7 8 **S** Adventist Health, Roseville, CA
Primary Contact: Ryan Ashlock, Interim President
COO: Travis Clegg, Vice President, Operations
CFO: Heidar Thordarson, Chief Financial Officer
CMO: Alan Cheung, M.D., Vice President Medical Affairs
CHR: Todd Reese, Director Human Performance
CNO: Laura R. Westphal, R.N., Vice President Patient Care Services
Web address: www.castlemed.org
Control: Church operated, Nongovernment, not–for–profit **Service**: General medical and surgical

Staffed Beds: 152 **Admissions**: 6353 **Census**: 67 **Outpatient Visits**: 103526 **Births**: 878 **Total Expense ($000)**: 249276 **Payroll Expense ($000)**: 88029 **Personnel**: 1073

KAMUELA—Hawaii County

QUEEN'S NORTH HAWAII COMMUNITY HOSPITAL (120028), 67–1125 Mamalahoa Highway, Zip 96743–8496; tel. 808/885–4444, **A**1 3 5 10 20 **F**3 8 11 13 14 15 29 30 31 34 35 36 40 41 43 44 48 49 50 53 54 57 59 62 64 65 68 70 75 76 77 78 79 81 82 85 86 87 93 97 102 107 108 110 111 115 119 127 130 131 132 146 147 148 154 156 157 164 167 169 **S** Queen's Health System, Honolulu, HI
Primary Contact: Stephany Vaioleti, President
CFO: Michel Riccioni, Chief Financial Officer
CMO: Gary Goldberg, M.D., Chief Medical Officer
CNO: Miquel Noelani Simms, R.N., Chief Nursing Officer
Web address: www.nhch.com
Control: Other not–for–profit (including NFP Corporation) **Service**: General medical and surgical

Staffed Beds: 35 **Admissions**: 1903 **Census**: 21 **Outpatient Visits**: 101175 **Births**: 385 **Personnel**: 293

Hospitals, U.S. / HAWAII

KANEOHE—Honolulu County

☐ **HAWAII STATE HOSPITAL**, 45–710 Keaahala Road, Zip 96744–3597; tel. 808/247–2191, (Nonreporting) **A**1
Primary Contact: Marian Tsuji, Acting Administrator
COO: Anthony Fraiola, Associate Administrator Administrative and Support Services
CFO: Stephen Teeter, Business Manager
CMO: James Westphal, M.D., AMHD Medical Director
CIO: John Jansen, Management Information Specialist
CHR: Karen Hara, Personnel Management Specialist
CNO: Lani Tsuneishi, Nursing Services Manager
Web address: www.hawaii.gov/health/
Control: State, Government, Nonfederal **Service**: Psychiatric

Staffed Beds: 178

KAPAA—Kauai County

★ **SAMUEL MAHELONA MEMORIAL HOSPITAL (121306)**, 4800 Kawaihau Road, Zip 96746–1971; tel. 808/822–4961, (Nonreporting) **A**10 18 **S** Hawaii Health Systems Corporation, Honolulu, HI
Primary Contact: Lance Segawa, Chief Executive Officer
CFO: Michael Perel, Regional Chief Financial Officer
CMO: Gerald Tomory, M.D., Regional Medical Director
CIO: Sandra McMaster, Regional Chief Information Officer
CHR: Lani Aranio, Regional Director Human Resources
Web address: www.smmh.hhsc.org
Control: State, Government, Nonfederal **Service**: General medical and surgical

Staffed Beds: 71

KAUNAKAKAI—Maui County

✠ **MOLOKAI GENERAL HOSPITAL (121303)**, 280 Home Olu Place, Zip 96748–0408, Mailing Address: P.O. Box 408, Zip 96748–0408; tel. 808/553–5331, (Nonreporting) **A**1 10 18 **S** Queen's Health System, Honolulu, HI
Primary Contact: Janice Kalanihuia, President
CFO: Zessica L Apiki, Accountant
CMO: William Thomas, M.D., Jr, Medical Director Clinical and Internal Affairs
CIO: Sampson Wescoatt, Manager Information Technology
CHR: Alicia Teves, Coordinator Human Resources
Web address: www.queens.org
Control: Other not–for–profit (including NFP Corporation) **Service**: General medical and surgical

Staffed Beds: 15

KEALAKEKUA—Hawaii County

✠ **KONA COMMUNITY HOSPITAL (120019)**, 79–1019 Haukapila Street, Zip 96750–7920; tel. 808/322–9311, (Nonreporting) **A**1 10 20 **S** Hawaii Health Systems Corporation, Honolulu, HI
Primary Contact: Clayton McGhan, Interim West Hawaii Regional Chief Executive Officer
CFO: Dean Herzog, Chief Financial Officer
CMO: Richard McDowell, M.D., Medical Director
CHR: Kathryn Salomon, Director Human Resources
CNO: Patricia Kalua, Chief Nurse Executive
Web address: www.kch.hhsc.org
Control: State, Government, Nonfederal **Service**: General medical and surgical

Staffed Beds: 94

KOHALA—Hawaii County

★ **KOHALA HOSPITAL (121302)**, 54–383 Hospital Road, Zip 96755, Mailing Address: P.O. Box 10, Kapaau, Zip 96755–0010; tel. 808/889–6211, (Nonreporting) **A**10 18 **S** Hawaii Health Systems Corporation, Honolulu, HI
Primary Contact: Gino Amar, Administrator
CMO: Silvia Sonnenschein, M.D., Chief of Staff
Web address: www.koh.hhsc.org
Control: State, Government, Nonfederal **Service**: General medical and surgical

Staffed Beds: 28

KULA—Maui County

★ **KULA HOSPITAL (121308)**, 100 Keokea Place, Zip 96790–7450; tel. 808/878–1221, (Nonreporting) **A**10 18 **S** Kaiser Foundation Hospitals, Oakland, CA
Primary Contact: David Culbreth, Administrator
CFO: Nerissa Garrity, Chief Financial Officer
CMO: Nicole Apoliona, M.D., Medical Director
Web address: https://www.mauihealthsystem.org/kula-hospital/
Control: Other not–for–profit (including NFP Corporation) **Service**: General medical and surgical

Staffed Beds: 9

LANAI CITY—Maui County

★ **LANAI COMMUNITY HOSPITAL (121305)**, 628 Seventh Street, Zip 96763–0650; tel. 808/565–8450, (Nonreporting) **A**10 18 **S** Kaiser Foundation Hospitals, Oakland, CA
Primary Contact: David Culbreth, Administrator
Web address: https://www.mauihealthsystem.org/lanai-hospital/
Control: Other not–for–profit (including NFP Corporation) **Service**: General medical and surgical

Staffed Beds: 24

LIHUE—Kauai County

☐ **WILCOX MEDICAL CENTER (120014)**, 3–3420 Kuhio Highway, Zip 96766–1099; tel. 808/245–1100, **A**1 2 10 20 **F**3 13 15 28 29 31 32 34 35 37 40 41 43 44 45 49 50 53 56 57 58 59 61 63 64 70 74 75 76 77 78 79 81 82 84 85 86 87 93 107 108 110 111 114 115 119 126 130 131 132 133 135 145 146 147 148 149 154 156 167 169 **S** Hawaii Pacific Health, Honolulu, HI
Primary Contact: Jen Chahanovich, President and Chief Executive Officer
CFO: David Okabe, Executive Vice President, Chief Financial Officer and Treasurer
CMO: Craig Netzer, M.D., President Medical Staff
CIO: Steve Robertson, Executive Vice President Revenue Cycle Management and Chief Information Officer
CNO: Mary Ann England, Chief Nurse Executive
Web address: www.wilcoxhealth.org
Control: Other not–for–profit (including NFP Corporation) **Service**: General medical and surgical

Staffed Beds: 72 **Admissions**: 3365 **Census**: 45 **Outpatient Visits**: 133767 **Births**: 443 **Total Expense ($000)**: 147990 **Payroll Expense ($000)**: 42047 **Personnel**: 461

PAHALA—Hawaii County

★ **KA'U HOSPITAL (121301)**, 1 Kamani Street, Zip 96777, Mailing Address: P.O. Box 40, Zip 96777–0040; tel. 808/932–4200, (Nonreporting) **A**10 18 **S** Hawaii Health Systems Corporation, Honolulu, HI
Primary Contact: Denise Mackey, Administrator
CMO: Clifford Field, M.D., Medical Director
Web address: https://www.kauhospital.org/
Control: State, Government, Nonfederal **Service**: General medical and surgical

Staffed Beds: 21

WAILUKU—Maui County

✠ **MAUI MEMORIAL MEDICAL CENTER (120002)**, 221 Mahalani Street, Zip 96793–2581; tel. 808/298–2626, **A**1 10 20 **F**3 8 11 12 15 18 20 22 24 26 28 29 30 31 34 35 36 39 40 43 49 50 51 57 59 60 64 65 68 70 74 75 76 77 78 79 81 85 87 89 93 94 98 105 107 108 110 111 114 119 130 132 135 141 146 148 149 154 162 164 167 **S** Kaiser Foundation Hospitals, Oakland, CA
Primary Contact: Lynn Fulton, Chief Executive Officer
COO: Debbie Walsh, MSN, Chief Operating Officer
CIO: Dana Mendoza, Chief Information Officer
Web address: https://www.mauihealthsystem.org/maui-memorial/
Control: Other not–for–profit (including NFP Corporation) **Service**: General medical and surgical

Staffed Beds: 219 **Admissions**: 8421 **Census**: 204 **Outpatient Visits**: 70065 **Births**: 1271 **Total Expense ($000)**: 355085 **Payroll Expense ($000)**: 129317 **Personnel**: 1334

Hospitals, U.S. / HAWAII

WAIMEA—Kauai County

KAUAI VETERANS MEMORIAL HOSPITAL (121300), 4643 Waimea Canyon Road, Zip 96796, Mailing Address: P.O. Box 337, Zip 96796–0337; tel. 808/338–9431, (Nonreporting) **A** 1 10 18 **S** Hawaii Health Systems Corporation, Honolulu, HI
Primary Contact: Lance Segawa, Chief Executive Officer
CFO: Michael Perel, Regional Chief Financial Officer
CMO: Gerald Tomory, M.D., Regional Medical Director
CIO: Sandra McMaster, Regional Chief Information Officer
CHR: Solette Perry, Regional Director Human Resources
Web address: www.kvmh.hhsc.org
Control: State, Government, Nonfederal **Service**: General medical and surgical

Staffed Beds: 45

IDAHO

AMERICAN FALLS—Power County

★ ⇧ **POWER COUNTY HOSPITAL DISTRICT (131304)**, 510 Roosevelt Street, Zip 83211–1362, Mailing Address: P.O. Box 420, Zip 83211–0420; tel. 208/226–3200, (Total facility includes 21 beds in nursing home–type unit) **A**10 18 21 **F**29 34 40 50 59 64 65 68 75 77 93 97 102 107 115 127 128 130 133 135 143 146 154
Primary Contact: Dallas Clinger, Administrator
COO: Rock Roy, Professional Services Director
CFO: Jeremy Claunch, Chief Financial Officer
CMO: Spencer Garrett Seibold, M.D., Chief of Medical Staff
CIO: Jason Povey, Chief Information Officer
CHR: Kendra Sweat, Director Human Resources
CNO: June Mortenson, R.N., Director of Nursing
Web address: www.pchd.net
Control: Hospital district or authority, Government, Nonfederal **Service:** General medical and surgical

Staffed Beds: 31 **Admissions:** 75 **Census:** 5 **Births:** 0

ARCO—Butte County

⇧ **LOST RIVERS MEDICAL CENTER (131324)**, 551 Highland Drive, Zip 83213–9771, Mailing Address: P.O. Box 145, Zip 83213–0145; tel. 208/527–8206, (Nonreporting) **A**10 18 21
Primary Contact: Brad Huerta, Chief Executive Officer and Administrator
CFO: Jon Smith, Chief Financial Officer
CMO: Jeffrey Haskell, M.D., Chief Medical Staff
CHR: Tina Akins, Director Human Resources
CNO: Geri Cammack, R.N., Director of Nursing
Web address: www.lostriversmedical.com
Control: Hospital district or authority, Government, Nonfederal **Service:** General medical and surgical

Staffed Beds: 43

BLACKFOOT—Bingham County

⊞ **BINGHAM MEMORIAL HOSPITAL (131325)**, 98 Poplar Street, Zip 83221–1799; tel. 208/785–4100, (Nonreporting) **A**1 5 10 18
Primary Contact: Jake Erickson, Chief Executive Officer
CFO: Randy Nightengale, Chief Financial Officer
CIO: Robert Weis, Director Information Systems
CHR: Tara Preston, Director Human Resources
CNO: Carolyn Hansen, Chief Nursing Officer
Web address: www.binghammemorial.org
Control: Other not–for–profit (including NFP Corporation) **Service:** General medical and surgical

Staffed Beds: 85

⊞ **GROVE CREEK MEDICAL CENTER (130073)**, 350 North Meridian Street, Zip 83221–1625; tel. 208/782–0300, (Nonreporting) **A**1 10
Primary Contact: Jake Erickson, Chief Executive Officer
CIO: Robert Weis, Director Information Technology
CHR: Tara Preston, Director Human Resources
CNO: Nathan Buck, R.N., Nursing Manager
Web address: https://grovecreekmc.org/
Control: Corporation, Investor–owned (for–profit) **Service:** Obstetrics and gynecology

Staffed Beds: 8

☐ **STATE HOSPITAL SOUTH (134010)**, 700 East Alice Street, Zip 83221–4925, Mailing Address: P.O. Box 400, Zip 83221–0400; tel. 208/785–1200, (Nonreporting) **A**1 3 10
Primary Contact: Randy Rodriguez, Hospital Administrator
COO: Greg Horton, Director Support Services
CFO: Angela Loosli, Assistant Administrator, Operations
CMO: Kelly Palmer, D.O., Medical Director
CIO: Julie Sutton, Director Performance Improvement
CHR: Sheryl Donnelly, Human Resources Specialist
CNO: Randy Walker, Director Nursing Services
Web address: www.healthandwelfare.idaho.gov
Control: State, Government, Nonfederal **Service:** Psychiatric

Staffed Beds: 135

BOISE—Ada County

⊞ **BOISE VA MEDICAL CENTER**, 500 West Fort Street, Zip 83702–4598; tel. 208/422–1000, (Nonreporting) **A**1 3 5 **S** Department of Veterans Affairs, Washington, DC
Primary Contact: David P. Wood, FACHE, Medical Center Director
CFO: Ron Blanton, Chief Fiscal Services
CMO: Paul Lambert, M.D., Chief of Staff
CHR: Randy Turner, Chief Human Resource Management Services
Web address: www.boise.va.gov/
Control: Veterans Affairs, Government, federal **Service:** General medical and surgical

Staffed Beds: 92

☐ **INTERMOUNTAIN HOSPITAL (134002)**, 303 North Allumbaugh Street, Zip 83704–9208; tel. 208/377–8400, (Nonreporting) **A**1 10 **S** Universal Health Services, Inc., King of Prussia, PA
Primary Contact: Todd Hurt, Chief Executive Officer
CFO: JeDonne Hines, Chief Financial Officer
CHR: Nancy Nelson, Director Human Resources
Web address: www.intermountainhospital.com
Control: Corporation, Investor–owned (for–profit) **Service:** Psychiatric

Staffed Beds: 151

LIFEWAYS BEHAVIORAL HOSPITAL (134009), 8050 Northview Street, Zip 83704–7126; tel. 208/327–0504, (Nonreporting) **A**10
Primary Contact: David Fenton, Administrator
COO: Liz Johnsen, Chief Operations Officer
CFO: Steve Jensen, Chief Financial Officer
CMO: David Kent, M.D., Chief Medical Officer
CIO: Debra Alexander, Chief Information Officer
CHR: Christine Gray, Chief Human Resource Officer
Web address: https://www.lifeways.org/boise-idaho
Control: Corporation, Investor–owned (for–profit) **Service:** Psychiatric

Staffed Beds: 22

⊞ **SAINT ALPHONSUS REGIONAL MEDICAL CENTER (130007)**, 1055 N Curtis Rd, Zip 83706–1309, Mailing Address: 1055 North Curtis Road, Zip 83706–1309; tel. 208/367–2121, **A**1 2 3 5 10 19 **F**3 10 11 12 13 15 17 18 20 22 24 26 28 29 30 31 32 33 34 35 36 37 38 39 40 42 43 44 45 46 47 48 49 50 54 55 56 57 58 59 64 65 66 68 70 71 72 74 75 76 77 78 79 81 82 84 85 86 87 93 97 98 99 100 102 103 104 107 108 110 111 114 115 117 119 121 124 126 129 130 131 132 135 144 146 147 148 149 150 154 156 167 **S** Trinity Health, Livonia, MI
Primary Contact: David M. McFadyen, FACHE, President
CFO: Kenneth Fry, Chief Financial Officer
CMO: Steve Brown, M.D., Chief Quality Officer
CIO: Dwight Pond, TIS Boise
CHR: Teresa Sargent, Vice President Human Resources
CNO: Sherry Parks, R.N., MS, Chief Nursing Officer
Web address: www.saintalphonsus.org
Control: Other not–for–profit (including NFP Corporation) **Service:** General medical and surgical

Staffed Beds: 415 **Admissions:** 15774 **Census:** 237 **Outpatient Visits:** 1073638 **Births:** 1123 **Total Expense ($000):** 794488 **Payroll Expense ($000):** 346350 **Personnel:** 4365

⊞ **SAINT ALPHONSUS REGIONAL REHABILITATION HOSPITAL, AN AFFILIATE OF ENCOMPASS HEALTH (133028)**, 711 North Curtis Road, Zip 83706–1445; tel. 208/605–3000, (Nonreporting) **A**1 10 **S** Encompass Health Corporation, Birmingham, AL
Primary Contact: Joe Griffin, Chief Executive Officer
Web address: https://www.encompasshealth.com/locations/boiserehab
Control: Corporation, Investor–owned (for–profit) **Service:** Rehabilitation

Staffed Beds: 40

ST. LUKE'S BOISE MEDICAL CENTER See St. Luke's Regional Medical Center

---

Hospital, Medicare Provider Number, Address, Telephone, Approval, Facility, and Physician Codes, Health Care System

★ American Hospital Association (AHA) membership ○ Healthcare Facilities Accreditation Program ⇧ Center for Improvement in Healthcare Quality Accreditation
☐ The Joint Commission accreditation ◇ DNV Healthcare Inc. accreditation △ Commission on Accreditation of Rehabilitation Facilities (CARF) accreditation

Hospitals, U.S. / IDAHO

ST. LUKE'S REGIONAL MEDICAL CENTER (130006), 190 East Bannock Street, Zip 83712–6241; tel. 208/381–2222; (Includes ST. LUKE'S CHILDREN'S HOSPITAL, 190 East Bannock Street, Boise, Idaho, Zip 83712–6241, tel. 208/381-2222; ST. LUKE'S MERIDIAN MEDICAL CENTER, 520 South Eagle Road, Meridian, Idaho, Zip 83642, 520 S Eagle Road, Zip 83642–6351, tel. 208/706–5000; Dennis Mesaros, Administrator) (Total facility includes 19 beds in nursing home–type unit) **A**1 2 3 5 7 10 19 **F**3 7 8 11 12 13 15 17 18 19 20 21 22 23 24 25 26 27 28 29 30 31 32 34 35 36 37 40 41 43 46 47 48 49 50 51 53 54 55 56 57 58 59 60 62 63 64 65 68 70 71 72 74 75 76 77 78 79 81 82 84 87 88 89 90 91 93 97 100 105 107 108 110 111 114 115 116 117 118 119 120 121 124 126 127 128 129 130 131 132 134 135 136 144 146 147 148 149 154 167 **P**5 **S** St. Luke's Health System, Boise, ID
Primary Contact: Dennis Mesaros, Vice President, Population Health/Regional Acute Care Operations
CFO: Jeff Taylor, Vice President Finance
CMO: Jim Souza, Chief Medical Officer
CIO: Reid Stephan, Chief Information Officer
CHR: Phillip Johnson, Vice President, Chief Human Resources Officer
CNO: Barbara Hocking, Chief Nursing Officer
Web address: https://www.stlukesonline.org/communities-and-locations/facilities/hospitals-and-medical-centers/st-lukes-boise-medical-center
Control: Other not–for–profit (including NFP Corporation) **Service**: General medical and surgical

Staffed Beds: 604 **Admissions**: 27050 **Census**: 374 **Outpatient Visits**: 1620720 **Births**: 5182 **Total Expense ($000)**: 2289372 **Payroll Expense ($000)**: 841882 **Personnel**: 7504

★ **ST. LUKE'S REHABILITATION HOSPITAL (133025)**, 600 North Robbins Road, Zip 83702–4565, Mailing Address: P.O. Box 1100, Zip 83701–1100; tel. 208/489–4444, (Nonreporting) **A**5 10 **S** St. Luke's Health System, Boise, ID
Primary Contact: Nolan Hoffer, Administrator Rehabilitation Services
COO: Melissa Honsinger, Chief Operating Officer
CFO: Doug Lewis, Chief Financial Officer
CMO: Lee Kornfield, M.D., Medical Director
CIO: Scott Pyrah, Director Information Systems
CHR: Jim Atkins, Director Employee Services
Web address: www.idahoelksrehab.org
Control: Other not–for–profit (including NFP Corporation) **Service**: Rehabilitation

Staffed Beds: 30

☐ **TREASURE VALLEY HOSPITAL (130063)**, 8800 West Emerald Street, Zip 83704–8205; tel. 208/373–5000, (Nonreporting) **A**1 3 10
Primary Contact: Nick Genna, Administrator
CMO: Jeffrey Hessing, M.D., Medical Director
CHR: Kathleen Phelps, Director Human Resources
Web address: www.treasurevalleyhospital.com
Control: Corporation, Investor–owned (for–profit) **Service**: General medical and surgical

Staffed Beds: 9

VIBRA HOSPITAL OF BOISE (132002), 6651 West Franklin Road, Zip 83709–0914; tel. 877/801–2244, (Nonreporting) **A**1 10 **S** Vibra Healthcare, Mechanicsburg, PA
Primary Contact: Tammy Pettingill, Interim Chief Executive Officer
Web address: www.vhboise.com
Control: Corporation, Investor–owned (for–profit) **Service**: Acute long–term care hospital

Staffed Beds: 60

BONNERS FERRY—Boundary County

★ ⇧ **BOUNDARY COMMUNITY HOSPITAL (131301)**, 6640 Kaniksu Street, Zip 83805–7532; tel. 208/267–3141, (Nonreporting) **A**10 18 21
Primary Contact: April Bennett, Chief Executive Officer
CFO: Julie Leonard, Chief Financial Officer
CMO: Chuck Newhouse, M.D., Chief of Staff
CHR: Ann Coughlin, Director Human Resources
CNO: Tari Yourzek, Chief Nursing Officer
Web address: www.boundarycommunityhospital.org
Control: County, Government, Nonfederal **Service**: General medical and surgical

Staffed Beds: 48

BURLEY—Cassia County

CASSIA REGIONAL HOSPITAL (131326), 1501 Hiland Avenue, Zip 83318–2688; tel. 208/678–4444, **A**1 10 18 **F**3 7 9 12 13 15 18 28 29 31 34 35 37 38 40 41 43 44 45 47 50 54 59 63 64 65 68 70 75 76 77 78 79 81 85 86 87 89 90 92 93 97 100 101 102 104 107 108 110 111 115 118 119 126 128 129 130 131 132 133 135 141 146 147 148 149 150 154 157 164 169 **S** Intermountain Health, Salt Lake City, UT
Primary Contact: Michael Blauer, Administrator
CFO: Justin Wiser, Chief Financial Officer
CMO: Bernard Boehmer, M.D., Medical Director
CIO: Jared Gallup, Chief Information Officer
CHR: Eric Gochnour, Chief Human Resource Officer
CNO: Michele Pond–Bell, R.N., Nurse Administrator
Web address: www.cassiaregional.org
Control: Other not–for–profit (including NFP Corporation) **Service**: General medical and surgical

Staffed Beds: 25 **Admissions**: 1333 **Census**: 10 **Outpatient Visits**: 105962 **Births**: 550 **Total Expense ($000)**: 63628 **Payroll Expense ($000)**: 26959 **Personnel**: 294

CALDWELL—Canyon County

WEST VALLEY MEDICAL CENTER (130014), 1717 Arlington, Zip 83605–4802; tel. 208/459–4641, (Nonreporting) **A**1 3 5 10 **S** HCA Healthcare, Nashville, TN
Primary Contact: Travis Leach, FACHE, Chief Executive Officer
COO: Jennifer Opsut, Interim Chief Operating Officer
CFO: Kate Fowler, Chief Financial Officer
CMO: Richard Augustus, M.D., Chief Medical Officer
CIO: Jason Martinez, Director Information Technology
CHR: Senta Cornelius, Director Human Resources
CNO: Edith E Irving, R.N., MS, FACHE, Chief Nursing Officer
Web address: www.westvalleymedctr.com
Control: Corporation, Investor–owned (for–profit) **Service**: General medical and surgical

Staffed Beds: 105

CASCADE—Valley County

CASCADE MEDICAL CENTER (131308), 402 Lake Cascade Pkwy, Zip 83611–7702, Mailing Address: P.O. Box 1330, Zip 83611–1330; tel. 208/382–4242, **A**10 18 **F**5 28 35 40 57 59 64 65 66 68 75 77 89 93 97 104 107 115 119 127 130 133 135 144 147 154 160 165
Primary Contact: Tom Reinhardt, Chief Executive Officer
CFO: Penny Lancaster, Controller
CMO: Mikael Bedell, M.D., Medical Director
CNO: Teri Coombs, R.N., Director Nursing Services
Web address: www.cascademedicalcenter.net
Control: Hospital district or authority, Government, Nonfederal **Service**: General medical and surgical

Staffed Beds: 4 **Admissions**: 29 **Census**: 1 **Births**: 0

COEUR D ALENE—Kootenai County

NORTH IDAHO BEHAVIORAL HEALTH, DIVISION OF KOOTENAI MEDICAL CENTER See Kootenai Behavioral Health

COEUR D'ALENE—Kootenai County

★ ⇧ **KOOTENAI HEALTH (130049)**, 2003 Kootenai Health Way, Zip 83814–2677; tel. 208/625–4000, (Includes KOOTENAI BEHAVIORAL HEALTH, 2301 N Ironwood PL, Coeur D Alene, Idaho, Zip 83814–2696, 2301 North Ironwood Place, Coeur D'Alene, Zip 83814–2650, tel. 208/625–4800) **A**2 3 5 10 19 21 **F**3 4 5 7 9 11 13 14 15 17 18 20 22 24 26 28 29 30 31 32 34 35 37 40 41 43 44 45 46 47 48 49 50 51 53 54 56 57 58 59 60 63 64 65 68 70 71 72 74 75 76 77 78 79 81 82 83 84 85 86 87 89 91 93 95 96 97 98 99 100 101 102 104 107 108 110 111 114 115 116 117 119 121 124 126 127 129 130 131 132 133 135 143 144 145 146 148 149 154 156 169 **P**6
Primary Contact: Jameson C. Smith, FACHE, Chief Executive Officer
COO: Jeremy Evans, Vice President Operations
CFO: Kimberly Webb, Chief Financial Officer
CMO: Walter Fairfax, M.D., Chief Medical Officer
CHR: Daniel Klocko, Vice President Human Resources
Web address: www.kh.org
Control: Hospital district or authority, Government, Nonfederal **Service**: General medical and surgical

Staffed Beds: 375 **Admissions**: 17840 **Census**: 225 **Births**: 2226 **Total Expense ($000)**: 911464 **Payroll Expense ($000)**: 398233 **Personnel**: 3749

Hospitals, U.S. / IDAHO

COTTONWOOD—Idaho County

★ ⇧ **ST. MARY'S HEALTH (131321)**, 701 Lewiston Street, Zip 83522–9750, Mailing Address: P.O. Box 137, Zip 83522–0137; tel. 208/962–3251, **A**5 10 18 21 **F**7 13 34 59 64 128 133 146 148 154
Primary Contact: Lenne Bonner, President
CFO: Jyl Ruland, Chief Financial Officer
CHR: Debbie Schumacher, Chief Human Resource Officer
Web address: www.smh-cvhc.org/
Control: Other not-for-profit (including NFP Corporation) **Service**: General medical and surgical

Staffed Beds: 25 **Admissions**: 343 **Census**: 3 **Births**: 48

⇧ **ST. MARY'S HOSPITAL** See St. Mary's Health

DRIGGS—Teton County

★ ⇧ **TETON VALLEY HEALTH CARE (131313)**, 120 E Howard Avenue, Zip 83422–5112; tel. 208/354–2383, (Nonreporting) **A**10 18 21
Primary Contact: Troy Christensen, Chief Executive Officer
CFO: Wesley D White, Chief Financial Officer
CMO: Nathan Levanger, M.D., Chief of Staff
CHR: Dory Harris, Director Human Resource
CNO: Angela Booker, Director of Nursing Services
Web address: www.tvhcare.org
Control: Other not-for-profit (including NFP Corporation) **Service**: General medical and surgical

Staffed Beds: 13

EMMETT—Gem County

⇧ **VALOR HEALTH (131318)**, 1202 East Locust Street, Zip 83617–2715; tel. 208/365–3561, (Nonreporting) **A**10 18 21
Primary Contact: Brad Turpen, FACHE, Chief Executive Officer
CHR: Susan Vahlberg, Director Employee and Community Relations
Web address: www.wkmh.org
Control: County, Government, Nonfederal **Service**: General medical and surgical

Staffed Beds: 12

GOODING—Gooding County

★ ⇧ **NORTH CANYON MEDICAL CENTER (131302)**, 267 North Canyon Drive, Zip 83330–5500; tel. 208/934–4433, **A**10 18 21 **F**3 5 11 15 29 32 33 34 35 36 37 40 41 44 45 50 54 56 57 59 64 65 66 68 75 77 79 81 82 84 85 86 87 93 94 96 97 100 107 110 111 114 119 126 127 129 130 131 133 135 143 144 148 149 154 156 160 **P**6
Primary Contact: J'Dee Adams, Chief Executive Officer
CMO: Jennifer Olsen, M.D., Chief of Staff
CIO: Margie McLeod, Director Information Technology
CHR: Sara Otto, Chief Compliance Officer
CNO: Lisa Mangum, Chief Nursing Officer
Web address: https://northcanyon.org/locations/gooding/medical-center/
Control: Other not-for-profit (including NFP Corporation) **Service**: General medical and surgical

Staffed Beds: 18 **Admissions**: 348 **Census**: 3 **Outpatient Visits**: 58586 **Births**: 0 **Total Expense ($000)**: 58834 **Payroll Expense ($000)**: 24920 **Personnel**: 305

GRANGEVILLE—Idaho County

★ **SYRINGA HOSPITAL AND CLINICS (131315)**, 607 West Main Street, Zip 83530–1396; tel. 208/983–1700, **A**10 18 **F**3 7 12 13 29 34 35 40 43 45 50 57 59 63 64 65 76 81 87 89 93 97 102 107 115 119 127 130 133 146 148 156 160
Primary Contact: Abner King, Chief Executive Officer
CFO: Betty A Watson, Chief Financial Officer
CMO: Daniel Griffis, M.D., Chief Medical Officer
CIO: Darla Whitley, Manager Health Information Technology
CHR: Katy Eimers, Human Resources Officer
CNO: Cindy Daly, R.N., Director of Nursing
Web address: www.syringahospital.org
Control: Hospital district or authority, Government, Nonfederal **Service**: General medical and surgical

Staffed Beds: 14 **Admissions**: 255 **Census**: 2 **Outpatient Visits**: 17615 **Births**: 41 **Total Expense ($000)**: 24204 **Payroll Expense ($000)**: 11636 **Personnel**: 176

IDAHO FALLS—Bonneville County

✠ **EASTERN IDAHO REGIONAL MEDICAL CENTER (130018)**, 3100 Channing Way, Zip 83404–7533, Mailing Address: P.O. Box 2077, Zip 83403–2077; tel. 208/529–6111, (Nonreporting) **A**1 3 5 10 19 **S** HCA Healthcare, Nashville, TN
Primary Contact: Elizabeth Hunsicker, Chief Executive Officer
COO: Nicholas Manning, Chief Operating Officer
CFO: Aaron Martin, Chief Financial Officer
CMO: Patty Howell, M.D., Chief Medical Officer
CHR: Wendy Andersen, Director Human Resources
CNO: Brandi Allred, Chief Nursing Officer
Web address: www.eirmc.com
Control: Corporation, Investor-owned (for-profit) **Service**: General medical and surgical

Staffed Beds: 280

IDAHO FALLS COMMUNITY HOSPITAL (130074), 2327 Coronado Street, Zip 83404–7407, Mailing Address: 3270 East 17th Street # 217, Ammon, Zip 83406–6758; tel. 208/528–1000, (Nonreporting)
Primary Contact: James Adamson, Chief Executive Officer
COO: Casey Jackman, Chief Operating Officer
CFO: Russell Taylor, Comptroller
CMO: Joseph Anderson, Chief Medical Officer
Web address: www.idahofallscommunityhospital.com
Control: Partnership, Investor-owned (for-profit) **Service**: General medical and surgical

Staffed Beds: 88

MOUNTAIN VIEW HOSPITAL (130065), 2325 Coronado Street, Zip 83404–7407; tel. 208/557–2700, (Nonreporting) **A**5 10
Primary Contact: James Adamson, Chief Executive Officer
COO: Peter Fabrick, Vice President Clinical Operations
CHR: Eilene Horne, Manager Human Resources
Web address: www.mountainviewhospital.org
Control: Corporation, Investor-owned (for-profit) **Service**: General medical and surgical

Staffed Beds: 22

JEROME—Jerome County

★ **ST. LUKE'S JEROME (131310)**, 709 North Lincoln Street, Zip 83338–1851, Mailing Address: 709 North Lincoln Avenue, Zip 83338–1851; tel. 208/814–9500, **A**3 10 18 **F**3 7 15 29 40 50 57 59 64 65 68 75 77 86 87 89 97 107 110 111 114 119 127 130 133 135 143 148 154 **P**5 **S** St. Luke's Health System, Boise, ID
Primary Contact: Kevin Watson, Chief Operating Officer and Chief Nursing Officer
COO: Kevin Watson, Chief Operating Officer and Chief Nursing Officer
CMO: Elizabeth Sugden, M.D., Chief Medical Officer
CHR: Mark Stevens, Director Human Resources
CNO: Kevin Watson, Chief Operating Officer and Chief Nursing Officer
Web address: www.stlukesonline.org/jerome/
Control: Other not-for-profit (including NFP Corporation) **Service**: General medical and surgical

Staffed Beds: 25 **Admissions**: 305 **Census**: 6 **Outpatient Visits**: 34221 **Births**: 0 **Total Expense ($000)**: 20848 **Payroll Expense ($000)**: 12203 **Personnel**: 118

KELLOGG—Shoshone County

⇧ **SHOSHONE MEDICAL CENTER (131314)**, 25 Jacobs Gulch, Zip 83837–2023; tel. 208/784–1221, (Nonreporting) **A**10 18 21
Primary Contact: Paul Lewis, Chief Executive Officer
CFO: Donja Erdman, Chief Financial Officer
CMO: David Lawhorn, M.D., Chief Medical Officer
CIO: John Wohlman, Manager Information Systems
CHR: Dana Hemphill, Manager Human Resources
CNO: Karen Mann, R.N., Chief Nursing Officer
Web address: www.shoshonehealth.com
Control: Hospital district or authority, Government, Nonfederal **Service**: General medical and surgical

Staffed Beds: 25

Hospital, Medicare Provider Number, Address, Telephone, Approval, Facility, and Physician Codes, Health Care System

★ American Hospital Association (AHA) membership
☐ The Joint Commission accreditation
○ Healthcare Facilities Accreditation Program
◇ DNV Healthcare Inc. accreditation
⇧ Center for Improvement in Healthcare Quality Accreditation
△ Commission on Accreditation of Rehabilitation Facilities (CARF) accreditation

Hospitals, U.S. / IDAHO

KETCHUM—Blaine County

✠ **ST. LUKE'S WOOD RIVER MEDICAL CENTER (131323)**, 100 Hospital Drive, Zip 83340, Mailing Address: P.O. Box 100, Zip 83340–0100; tel. 208/727–8800, **A**1 3 5 10 18 **F**3 13 15 29 30 31 34 35 36 37 40 43 45 49 50 54 56 57 64 65 68 74 75 76 77 79 81 85 86 87 89 90 91 93 97 100 101 104 107 108 110 111 114 115 119 126 130 131 133 134 135 143 146 147 148 154 156 **P**5 **S** St. Luke's Health System, Boise, ID
Primary Contact: Almita Nunnelee, R.N., Chief Operating Officer and Chief Nursing Officer
COO: Almita Nunnelee, R.N., Chief Operating Officer and Chief Nursing Officer
CNO: Almita Nunnelee, R.N., Chief Operating Officer and Chief Nursing Officer
Web address: https://www.stlukesonline.org/communities-and-locations/facilities/hospitals-and-medical-centers/st-lukes-wood-river-medical-center
Control: Other not–for–profit (including NFP Corporation) **Service**: General medical and surgical

Staffed Beds: 25 **Admissions**: 837 **Census**: 7 **Outpatient Visits**: 123709 **Births**: 173 **Total Expense ($000)**: 88237 **Payroll Expense ($000)**: 42926 **Personnel**: 97

LEWISTON—Nez Perce County

✠ **ST. JOSEPH REGIONAL MEDICAL CENTER (130003)**, 415 Sixth Street, Zip 83501–2431; tel. 208/743–2511, **A**1 2 10 **F**15 18 20 22 26 29 30 31 34 37 38 40 43 45 46 49 57 59 64 65 68 69 70 74 75 76 77 78 79 81 85 87 89 90 91 92 93 94 96 97 98 100 107 108 109 110 111 112 114 115 117 118 119 120 121 123 126 129 132 146 148 149 154 167 **S** ScionHealth, Louisville, KY
Primary Contact: Edward E. Freysinger, Chief Executive Officer
COO: Taylor Rudd, Chief Operating Officer
CFO: Aaron Poole, Chief Financial Officer
CHR: Jordan Elben, Director of Human Resources
CNO: Holly Urban, R.N., MSN, RN, Interim Chief Nursing Officer
Web address: www.sjrmc.org
Control: Corporation, Investor–owned (for–profit) **Service**: General medical and surgical

Staffed Beds: 90 **Admissions**: 3691 **Census**: 37 **Outpatient Visits**: 90824 **Births**: 633 **Total Expense ($000)**: 170092 **Payroll Expense ($000)**: 51945 **Personnel**: 491

MALAD CITY—Oneida County

NELL J. REDFIELD MEMORIAL HOSPITAL (131303), 150 North 200 West, Zip 83252–1239, Mailing Address: Box 126, Zip 83252–0126; tel. 208/766–2231, (Nonreporting) **A**10 18
Primary Contact: John Williams, Administrator and Chief Executive Officer
CFO: Cindy Howard, Director Financial Services
CHR: Kathy Hubbard, Manager Human Resources
Web address: www.oneidahospital.com
Control: County, Government, Nonfederal **Service**: General medical and surgical

Staffed Beds: 11

MCCALL—Valley County

★ **ST. LUKE'S MCCALL (131312)**, 1000 State Street, Zip 83638–3704; tel. 208/634–2221, **A**5 10 18 **F**3 7 9 11 13 15 30 31 32 34 35 36 40 43 45 46 50 57 64 75 76 77 79 81 85 86 87 93 97 107 111 115 119 127 130 132 133 134 135 146 147 148 149 154 156 164 165 **P**5 **S** St. Luke's Health System, Boise, ID
Primary Contact: Amber Green, R.N., Chief Operating Officer and Chief Nursing Officer
COO: Amber Green, R.N., Chief Operating Officer and Chief Nursing Officer
CFO: Matt Groenig, Vice President Finance
CNO: Amber Green, R.N., Chief Operating Officer and Chief Nursing Officer
Web address: https://www.stlukesonline.org/communities-and-locations/facilities/hospitals-and-medical-centers/st-lukes-mccall-medical-center
Control: Other not–for–profit (including NFP Corporation) **Service**: General medical and surgical

Staffed Beds: 15 **Admissions**: 460 **Census**: 4 **Outpatient Visits**: 71359 **Births**: 102 **Total Expense ($000)**: 51071 **Payroll Expense ($000)**: 24962 **Personnel**: 227

MERIDIAN—Ada County

☐ **COTTONWOOD CREEK BEHAVIORAL HOSPITAL (134017)**, 2131 South Bonito Way, Zip 83642–1659; tel. 208/202–4700, (Nonreporting) **A**1 10 **S** Haven Behavioral Healthcare, Nashville, TN
Primary Contact: Kevan Finley, MS, Chief Executive Officer
CMO: Charles Novak, M.D., Medical Director
CHR: Alisha Ortega, Director, Human Resource
CNO: Ernesto Esparza, MSN, Director of Nursing
Web address: https://www.cottonwoodcreekboise.com/
Control: Corporation, Investor–owned (for–profit) **Service**: Psychiatric

Staffed Beds: 92

ST. LUKE'S MERIDIAN MEDICAL CENTER See St. Luke's Regional Medical Center, Boise

MONTPELIER—Bear Lake County

★ ⇑ **BEAR LAKE MEMORIAL HOSPITAL (131316)**, 164 South Fifth Street, Zip 83254–1597; tel. 208/847–1630, (Nonreporting) **A**10 18 21
Primary Contact: Arel Hunt, Chief Executive Officer
Web address: www.blmhospital.com
Control: County, Government, Nonfederal **Service**: General medical and surgical

Staffed Beds: 57

MOSCOW—Latah County

✠ **GRITMAN MEDICAL CENTER (131327)**, 700 South Main Street, Zip 83843–3056; tel. 208/882–4511, (Nonreporting) **A**1 10 18 **S** Ovation Healthcare, Brentwood, TN
Primary Contact: Kara Besst, President and Chief Executive Officer
CMO: John Brown, M.D., Chief Medical Officer
Web address: www.gritman.org
Control: Other not–for–profit (including NFP Corporation) **Service**: General medical and surgical

Staffed Beds: 25

MOUNTAIN HOME—Elmore County

✠ **ST. LUKE'S ELMORE (131311)**, 895 North Sixth East Street, Zip 83647–2207, Mailing Address: P.O. Box 1270, Zip 83647–1270; tel. 208/587–8401, (Total facility includes 27 beds in nursing home–type unit) **A**1 10 18 **F**3 7 13 15 29 30 34 35 40 45 50 57 64 68 75 76 77 81 85 87 97 107 111 119 127 128 129 130 133 135 146 147 149 154 **P**5 **S** St. Luke's Health System, Boise, ID
Primary Contact: Lisa Melchiorre, R.N., MS, Chief Operating Officer and Chief Nursing Officer
COO: Lisa Melchiorre, R.N., MS, Chief Operating Officer and Chief Nursing Officer
CFO: Tricia Senger, Chief Financial Officer
CNO: Lisa Melchiorre, R.N., MS, Chief Operating Officer and Chief Nursing Officer
Web address: www.stlukesonline.org/elmore/
Control: Other not–for–profit (including NFP Corporation) **Service**: General medical and surgical

Staffed Beds: 44 **Admissions**: 616 **Census**: 18 **Outpatient Visits**: 80687 **Births**: 175 **Total Expense ($000)**: 48675 **Payroll Expense ($000)**: 22287 **Personnel**: 218

NAMPA—Canyon County

✠ **SAINT ALPHONSUS MEDICAL CENTER – NAMPA (130013)**, 4300 East Flamingo Avenue, Zip 83686–6008; tel. 208/205–1000, **A**1 3 10 19 **F**3 11 12 13 14 15 18 20 22 28 29 30 31 32 34 35 37 39 40 41 42 43 44 45 46 47 48 49 50 51 53 57 59 64 65 66 68 69 70 71 72 74 75 76 77 78 79 81 82 84 85 86 87 92 100 107 108 110 111 115 118 119 120 121 123 126 127 129 130 131 132 134 135 141 143 144 145 146 147 148 149 154 164 167 **S** Trinity Health, Livonia, MI
Primary Contact: Clint Child, R.N., President
CFO: Lannie Checketts, Chief Financial Officer
CMO: Dustan Hughes, M.D., Vice President Medical Affairs
CIO: Daniel Wright, Director Information Technology
CHR: Stefanie Thiel, Senior Human Resources Business Partner
Web address: https://www.saintalphonsus.org/nampa
Control: Church operated, Nongovernment, not–for–profit **Service**: General medical and surgical

Staffed Beds: 106 **Admissions**: 6442 **Census**: 75

☐ **ST. LUKE'S NAMPA (130071)**, 9850 West St.Luke's Drive, Zip 83687; tel. 208/505–2000, **A**1 3 10 **F**3 7 11 13 15 18 20 28 29 30 31 35 40 43 45 50 51 64 68 70 72 75 76 77 81 84 85 87 107 108 110 111 114 115 118 119 126 130 135 146 157 167 **P**5 **S** St. Luke's Health System, Boise, ID
Primary Contact: Misty Robertson, R.N., FACHE, Chief Operating Officer and Chief Nursing Officer
COO: Misty Robertson, R.N., FACHE, Chief Operating Officer and Chief Nursing Officer
CNO: Misty Robertson, R.N., FACHE, Chief Operating Officer and Chief Nursing Officer
Web address: https://www.stlukesonline.org/communities-and-locations/facilities/hospitals-and-medical-centers/st-lukes-nampa-medical-center
Control: Other not–for–profit (including NFP Corporation) **Service**: General medical and surgical

Staffed Beds: 87 **Admissions**: 4715 **Census**: 53 **Outpatient Visits**: 227907 **Births**: 1378 **Total Expense ($000)**: 236474 **Payroll Expense ($000)**: 93035 **Personnel**: 858

Hospitals, U.S. / IDAHO

OROFINO—Clearwater County

★ ⇑ **CLEARWATER VALLEY HEALTH (131320)**, 301 Cedar, Zip 83544–9029; tel. 208/476–4555, (Nonreporting) **A**10 18 21
Primary Contact: Lenne Bonner, Chief Executive Officer
CFO: Jyl Ruland, Chief Financial Officer
CMO: Kelly McGrath, Chief Medical Officer
CHR: Debbie Schumacher, Chief Human Resource Officer
Web address: www.smh-cvhc.org
Control: Other not–for–profit (including NFP Corporation) **Service**: General medical and surgical

Staffed Beds: 23

STATE HOSPITAL NORTH, 300 Hospital Drive, Zip 83544–9034; tel. 208/476–8819, **F**98 106 154 163 165
Primary Contact: Teresa Shackelford, Administrator
CMO: Karla Eisele, M.D., Clinical Director
CIO: James Sarbacher, Chief Information Officer
CHR: Heather Vandenbark, Human Resources Specialist
Web address: https://healthandwelfare.idaho.gov/dhw/state-hospital-north
Control: State, Government, Nonfederal **Service**: Psychiatric

Staffed Beds: 60 **Admissions**: 211 **Census**: 45 **Outpatient Visits**: 0 **Births**: 0 **Total Expense ($000)**: 13988 **Payroll Expense ($000)**: 7814

POCATELLO—Bannock County

★ ⇑ **PORTNEUF MEDICAL CENTER (130028)**, 777 Hospital Way, Zip 83201–5175; tel. 208/239–1000, (Nonreporting) **A**3 5 10 21 **S** Ardent Health Services, Nashville, TN
Primary Contact: Nate Carter, Interim Chief Executive Officer and Chief Operating Officer
COO: Nate Carter, Interim Chief Executive Officer and Chief Operating Officer
CFO: John Abreu, Vice President and Chief Financial Officer
CMO: Dan Snell, Chief Medical Officer
CHR: Don Wadle, Interim Director Human Resources
CNO: Angela Treasure, Chief Nursing Officer
Web address: www.portmed.org
Control: Corporation, Investor–owned (for–profit) **Service**: General medical and surgical

Staffed Beds: 178

POST FALLS—Kootenai County

☐ **NORTHERN IDAHO ADVANCED CARE HOSPITAL (132001)**, 600 North Cecil Road, Zip 83854–6200; tel. 208/262–2800, (Nonreporting) **A**1 10 **S** Ernest Health, Inc., Albuquerque, NM
Primary Contact: Una Alderman, Chief Executive Officer
Web address: www.niach.ernesthealth.com
Control: Corporation, Investor–owned (for–profit) **Service**: Acute long–term care hospital

Staffed Beds: 40

☐ **NORTHWEST SPECIALTY HOSPITAL (130066)**, 1593 East Polston Avenue, Zip 83854–5326; tel. 208/262–2300, (Nonreporting) **A**1 10 **S** National Surgical Healthcare, Chicago, IL
Primary Contact: Rick Rasmussen, Chief Executive Officer
CIO: Craig McIntosh, Chief Information Officer
CHR: Gina Schneider, Director Human Resources
CNO: Christi Nance, R.N., MSN, Chief Nursing Officer
Web address: www.northwestspecialtyhospital.com
Control: Corporation, Investor–owned (for–profit) **Service**: Surgical

Staffed Beds: 32

☐ △ **REHABILITATION HOSPITAL OF THE NORTHWEST (133027)**, 3372 East Jenalan Avenue, Zip 83854–7787; tel. 208/262–8700, (Nonreporting) **A**1 7 10 **S** Ernest Health, Inc., Albuquerque, NM
Primary Contact: David Cox, Chief Executive Officer
Web address: https://rhn.ernesthealth.com/
Control: Corporation, Investor–owned (for–profit) **Service**: Rehabilitation

Staffed Beds: 25

PRESTON—Franklin County

★ ⇑ **FRANKLIN COUNTY MEDICAL CENTER (131322)**, 44 North First East Street, Zip 83263–1399; tel. 208/852–0137, (Nonreporting) **A**10 18
Primary Contact: Darin Dransfield, Chief Executive Officer
CFO: Paul Smart, CPA, Chief Financial Officer
CHR: Courtney Dursteler, Chief Human Resources Officer
CNO: Patrica Bowles, R.N., Chief Nursing Officer
Web address: www.fcmc.org
Control: County, Government, Nonfederal **Service**: General medical and surgical

Staffed Beds: 20

REXBURG—Madison County

⇑ **MADISON MEMORIAL HOSPITAL** See Madisonhealth

★ ⇑ **MADISONHEALTH (130025)**, 450 East Main Street, Zip 83440–2048, Mailing Address: P.O. Box 310, Zip 83440–0310; tel. 208/359–6900, **A**3 5 10 21 **F**3 11 28 29 31 34 39 40 41 43 45 50 54 57 68 70 72 75 76 77 78 79 81 82 85 87 91 93 97 98 100 107 108 111 115 118 119 126 129 130 131 132 146 147 148 149
Primary Contact: Rachel Ann. Gonzales, Chief Executive Officer
CMO: Clay Prince, M.D., Chief Medical Officer
CNO: Kevin K McEwan, R.N., Chief Nursing Officer
Web address: https://madisonhealth.org/
Control: County, Government, Nonfederal **Service**: General medical and surgical

Staffed Beds: 64 **Admissions**: 2487 **Census**: 23

RUPERT—Minidoka County

★ ⇑ **MINIDOKA MEMORIAL HOSPITAL (131319)**, 1224 Eighth Street, Zip 83350–1599; tel. 208/436–0481, **A**3 10 18 21 **F**1 3 7 10 15 29 34 40 45 46 62 64 65 68 75 77 79 81 82 83 84 87 107 110 111 119 126 127 129 130 131 133 146 147 148 149 150 154
Primary Contact: Tom Murphy, Chief Executive Officer
CFO: Jason Gibbons, Chief Financial Officer
CMO: Kevin Owens, M.D., Chief Medical Officer
CIO: Brody Beck, Director Information Technology
CHR: Desiree Carr, Director Human Resources
CNO: Erinn Neilson, Chief Nursing Officer
Web address: www.minidokamemorial.com
Control: County, Government, Nonfederal **Service**: General medical and surgical

Staffed Beds: 60 **Admissions**: 388 **Census**: 3 **Outpatient Visits**: 18842 **Births**: 0 **Total Expense ($000)**: 52010 **Payroll Expense ($000)**: 26709

SAINT MARIES—Benewah County

BENEWAH COMMUNITY HOSPITAL (131317), 229 South Seventh Street, Zip 83861–1803; tel. 208/245–5551, (Nonreporting) **A**10 18
Primary Contact: Chuck Lloyd, Chief Executive Officer
CFO: Lori Minier, Chief Financial Officer
CMO: William Wheeler, M.D., Chief of Staff
CIO: Joseph Getchius, Director Information Technology
CHR: Marlana Martin, Director Human Resources
CNO: Rhonda Smith, Chief Nursing Officer
Web address: www.bchmed.org
Control: County, Government, Nonfederal **Service**: General medical and surgical

Staffed Beds: 19

SALMON—Lemhi County

★ ⇑ **STEELE MEMORIAL MEDICAL CENTER (131305)**, 203 South Daisy Street, Zip 83467–4709; tel. 208/756–5600, **A**10 18 21 **F**3 11 13 15 28 29 31 32 34 35 40 41 43 44 45 46 47 50 54 57 59 64 65 68 75 76 77 78 79 81 82 87 89 90 93 97 107 108 110 111 115 119 127 128 131 133 135 146 148 149 154 157 167
Primary Contact: Preston Becker, Chief Executive Officer
CFO: Ryan Larson, CPA, Chief Financial Officer
CMO: Adam Deutchman, M.D., FACS, Chief Medical Officer
CHR: Ben Sessions, Human Resources Director
CNO: Kelly McNitt, R.N., Chief Nursing Officer
Web address: www.steelemh.org
Control: County, Government, Nonfederal **Service**: General medical and surgical

Staffed Beds: 18 **Admissions**: 367 **Census**: 4

Hospitals, U.S. / IDAHO

SANDPOINT—Bonner County

★ ⋔ **BONNER GENERAL HEALTH (131328)**, 520 North Third Avenue,
Zip 83864-1507; tel. 208/263-1441, (Nonreporting) **A**10 18 21
Primary Contact: John Hennessy, Chief Executive Officer
CMO: Samuel Uzabel, M.D., Chief Medical Officer
CIO: Jeremy Welser, Director Information Systems
CHR: Shannon Barnes, Chief Human Resource Officer
CNO: Tracy Lynn Autler, R.N., Chief Nursing and Quality Officer
Web address: www.bonnergeneral.org
Control: Other not-for-profit (including NFP Corporation) **Service**: General medical and surgical

Staffed Beds: 25

SODA SPRINGS—Caribou County

★ ⋔ **CARIBOU MEDICAL CENTER (131309)**, 300 South Third West,
Zip 83276-1598; tel. 208/547-3341, **A**10 18 21 **F**3 8 13 29 31 32 34 35 37 38 40 43 45 46 50 54 56 57 59 64 65 66 68 70 76 77 78 79 81 82 83 86 87 90 93 96 97 101 102 107 115 119 120 122 126 127 130 131 132 133 135 143 146 147 148 149 154 157 160 161 162 164 169
Primary Contact: Dillon Liechty, Interim Chief Executive Officer
CMO: John K Franson, M.D., Chief Medical Staff
CIO: Johnathan Inskeep, Chief Information Officer
CHR: Michael D Peck, Assistant Administrator
CNO: Brenda Bergholm, MSN, R.N., Chief Nursing Officer
Web address: https://cariboumc.org/
Control: Other not-for-profit (including NFP Corporation) **Service**: General medical and surgical

Staffed Beds: 11 **Admissions:** 246 **Census:** 3 **Births:** 40

⋔ **CARIBOU MEMORIAL HOSPITAL AND LIVING CENTER** See Caribou Medical Center

TWIN FALLS—Twin Falls County

✠ △ **ST. LUKE'S MAGIC VALLEY MEDICAL CENTER (130002)**, 801 Pole Line Road West, Zip 83301-5810, Mailing Address: P.O. Box 409, Zip 83303-0409; tel. 208/814-1000, **A**1 3 5 7 10 **F**3 7 8 11 13 15 18 20 22 28 29 30 32 34 35 37 38 40 43 45 46 48 49 50 51 54 56 57 59 62 63 64 65 68 70 71 72 74 75 76 77 79 81 82 84 85 87 89 90 91 92 93 96 97 98 100 101 104 107 108 110 111 115 116 117 118 119 126 129 130 131 132 135 143 144 146 147 148 154 156 161 164 167 169 **P**5 **S** St. Luke's Health System, Boise, ID
Primary Contact: Arlen Blaylock, Chief Operating Officer and Chief Nursing Officer
COO: Arlen Blaylock, Chief Operating Officer and Chief Nursing Officer
CIO: Melissa Capps, Site Leader Information Technology
CHR: Mark Stevens, Senior Director Human Resources
CNO: Arlen Blaylock, Chief Operating Officer and Chief Nursing Officer
Web address: www.stlukesonline.org
Control: Other not-for-profit (including NFP Corporation) **Service**: General medical and surgical

Staffed Beds: 224 **Admissions:** 9446 **Census:** 109 **Outpatient Visits:** 654794 **Births:** 1869 **Total Expense ($000):** 545436 **Payroll Expense ($000):** 191489 **Personnel:** 2026

WEISER—Washington County

★ ⋔ **WEISER MEMORIAL HOSPITAL (131307)**, 645 East Fifth Street,
Zip 83672-2202; tel. 208/549-0370, **A**10 18 21 **F**11 13 29 34 35 40 43 45 46 56 57 59 65 68 75 76 79 81 82 85 89 91 97 107 115 119 127 129 130 131 133 135 147 148 149 154 169 **S** St. Luke's Health System, Boise, ID
Primary Contact: Steven D. Hale, FACHE, Chief Executive Officer
CFO: Pam Stampfli, CPA, Chief Financial Officer
CMO: Jordan Blanchard, M.D., Chief of Medical Staff
CHR: Brenna Malone, Manager Human Resources
CNO: Jayme Skehan, R.N., MSN, Chief Nursing Officer
Web address: www.weisermemorialhospital.org
Control: Hospital district or authority, Government, Nonfederal **Service**: General medical and surgical

Staffed Beds: 13 **Admissions:** 244 **Census:** 1 **Outpatient Visits:** 14732 **Births:** 42 **Total Expense ($000):** 24225 **Payroll Expense ($000):** 10878

ILLINOIS

ALEDO—Mercer County

★ **GENESIS MEDICAL CENTER–ALEDO (141304)**, 409 NW Ninth Avenue, Zip 61231–1296; tel. 309/582–9100, **A**1 10 18 **F**3 11 15 28 29 34 35 40 45 46 55 56 59 64 65 81 82 87 89 93 97 104 107 108 110 115 119 127 128 130 131 133 144 146 149 154 **P**6 **S** Trinity Health, Livonia, MI
Primary Contact: Ted Rogalski, Administrator
CFO: Mark G Rogers, Vice President, Finance and Chief Financial Officer
CMO: Julio Santiago, M.D., Chief of Staff
CIO: Robert Frieden, Vice President, Information Services and Chief Information Officer
CHR: Tammy Hagedorn, Chief Human Resource Officer
CNO: Heidi Hess, Chief Nursing Officer
Web address: https://www.genesishealth.com/facilities/location-public-profile/medical-center-aledo/
Control: Other not–for–profit (including NFP Corporation) **Service**: General medical and surgical

Staffed Beds: 22 **Admissions**: 160 **Census**: 3 **Outpatient Visits**: 22510 **Births**: 0 **Total Expense ($000)**: 19280 **Payroll Expense ($000)**: 7275 **Personnel**: 91

ALTON—Madison County

★ **ALTON MEMORIAL HOSPITAL (140002)**, 1 Memorial Drive, Zip 62002–6722; tel. 618/463–7311, (Total facility includes 64 beds in nursing home–type unit) **A**1 3 5 10 **F**3 7 11 13 15 18 20 22 29 30 31 34 35 36 38 39 40 45 46 49 50 51 56 57 59 60 64 70 74 75 76 77 78 79 81 82 84 85 86 87 89 92 93 96 101 108 110 111 114 115 116 117 118 119 120 121 126 129 130 131 132 135 146 148 149 154 156 160 161 167 169 **S** BJC Health System, Saint Louis, MO
Primary Contact: David A. Braasch, FACHE, President
COO: Brad Goacher, Vice President Administration
CFO: Susan Koesterer, Vice President, Finance
CMO: Sebastian Rueckert, M.D., Vice President and Chief Medical Officer
CIO: Jerome Fox, Chief Information Officer
CHR: Bryan Hartwick, Vice President Human Resources
CNO: Debra Turpin, R.N., MSN, Vice President Patient Care Services and Chief Nursing Officer
Web address: www.altonmemorialhospital.org
Control: Other not–for–profit (including NFP Corporation) **Service**: General medical and surgical

Staffed Beds: 222 **Admissions**: 7215 **Census**: 116 **Outpatient Visits**: 258701 **Births**: 805 **Total Expense ($000)**: 185549 **Payroll Expense ($000)**: 71137 **Personnel**: 788

☐ **ALTON MENTAL HEALTH CENTER (144016)**, 4500 College Avenue, Zip 62002–5099; tel. 618/474–3800, (Nonreporting) **A**1 10 **S** Division of Mental Health, Department of Human Services, Springfield, IL
Primary Contact: Tonya Piephoff, Hospital Administrator
CFO: Susan Shobe, Director Administration and Support Services
CMO: Claudia Kachigion, M.D., Medical Director
Control: State, Government, Nonfederal **Service**: Psychiatric

Staffed Beds: 115

★ **OSF HEALTHCARE SAINT ANTHONY'S HEALTH CENTER (140052)**, 1 Saint Anthony's Way, Zip 62002–4579, Mailing Address: PO Box 340, Zip 62002–0340; tel. 618/474–6003, (Includes OSF HEALTHCARE SAINT CLARE'S HOSPITAL, 915 East Fifth Street, Alton, Illinois, Zip 62002–6434, tel. 618/463–5151) **A**1 2 10 **F**3 15 18 20 22 29 30 31 34 35 37 38 40 41 44 45 48 49 50 51 56 57 58 59 64 65 68 70 74 75 77 78 79 81 82 84 85 86 87 91 92 93 96 97 100 107 108 110 111 114 115 119 120 121 123 127 129 130 131 132 134 135 144 146 147 148 149 154 156 164 167 **S** OSF Healthcare, Peoria, IL
Primary Contact: Jerald W. Rumph, FACHE, President
COO: Sister M. Anselma Belongea, Chief Operating Officer
CFO: Mathew Hanley, Chief Financial Officer
CMO: Dennis Sands, Chief Medical Officer
CIO: Georgia Henke, Operational Account Manager
CHR: Robyn Grissom, Director of Human Resources
CNO: Colleen Becker, Chief Nursing Officer
Web address: www.osfsaintanthonys.org
Control: Church operated, Nongovernment, not–for–profit **Service**: General medical and surgical

Staffed Beds: 49 **Admissions**: 2366 **Census**: 23 **Outpatient Visits**: 124765 **Births**: 0 **Total Expense ($000)**: 99056 **Payroll Expense ($000)**: 30710 **Personnel**: 378

OSF SAINT CLARE'S HOSPITAL See OSF Healthcare Saint Clare's Hospital

ANNA—Union County

☐ **CHOATE MENTAL HEALTH CENTER (144038)**, 1000 North Main Street, Zip 62906–1699; tel. 618/833–5161, **A**1 10 **F**98 103 **S** Division of Mental Health, Department of Human Services, Springfield, IL
Primary Contact: Lori Gray, Chief Executive Officer
CMO: John Larcas, M.D., Acting Medical Director
CIO: Cindy Flamm, Manager Quality
CHR: Tammy Tellor, Acting Director Human Resources
Control: State, Government, Nonfederal **Service**: Psychiatric

Staffed Beds: 79 **Admissions**: 80 **Census**: 47 **Outpatient Visits**: 0 **Personnel**: 100

★ **DEACONESS ILLINOIS UNION COUNTY (141342)**, 517 North Main Street, Zip 62906–1696; tel. 618/833–4511, (Nonreporting) **A**1 10 18
Primary Contact: Harry Brockus, Chief Executive Officer
CFO: Terry Paligo, Chief Financial Officer
CMO: Christine Lucas, Chief of Staff
CIO: John Hegger, Director Information Systems
CHR: Tammy Davis, Director Human Resources
CNO: Tammy H. Wheaton, Interim Chief Nursing Officer
Web address: https://deaconessillinoisunioncounty.com/
Control: Corporation, Investor–owned (for–profit) **Service**: General medical and surgical

Staffed Beds: 25

ARLINGTON HEIGHTS—Cook County

★ △ **ENDEAVOR HEALTH NORTHWEST COMMUNITY HOSPITAL (140252)**, 800 West Central Road, Zip 60005–2392; tel. 847/618–1000, **A**1 2 7 10 **F**3 5 8 11 12 13 15 17 18 20 22 24 26 28 29 30 31 34 35 37 38 39 40 41 43 44 45 46 47 48 49 50 53 54 56 57 59 61 64 65 68 70 71 72 74 75 76 77 78 79 81 82 85 86 87 89 90 91 92 93 94 95 96 97 98 99 100 101 102 103 104 105 107 108 109 110 111 114 115 116 117 118 119 120 121 123 124 126 129 130 131 132 135 141 143 144 145 146 147 148 149 153 154 156 162 164 165 167 **S** Endeavor Health, Evanston, IL
Primary Contact: Michael Hartke, President
CFO: John Skeans, Chief Financial Officer
CMO: Alan Loren, M.D., Chief Medical Officer
CIO: Glen Malan, Vice President Information Technology and Chief Information Officer
CHR: Terry S Solem, Vice President of Human Resources
Web address: www.nch.org
Control: Other not–for–profit (including NFP Corporation) **Service**: General medical and surgical

Staffed Beds: 425 **Admissions**: 22316 **Census**: 286 **Outpatient Visits**: 628482 **Births**: 2375 **Total Expense ($000)**: 575867 **Payroll Expense ($000)**: 237555 **Personnel**: 3489

NORTHWEST COMMUNITY HEALTHCARE See Endeavor Health Northwest Community Hospital

AURORA—Du Page and Kane Counties County

AMITA HEALTH MERCY MEDICAL CENTER See Ascension Mercy

★ **ASCENSION MERCY (140174)**, 1325 North Highland Avenue, Zip 60506–1449; tel. 630/859–2222, (Nonreporting) **A**1 10 **S** Ascension Healthcare, Saint Louis, MO
Primary Contact: Fernando Gruta, President
COO: Roxann E. Barber, Regional Ambulatory Care and Ancillary Services Officer
CFO: Kevin Larkin, Regional Chief Financial Officer
CMO: Anil Gopinath, FACHE, M.D., Regional Chief Medical Officer
CHR: Michael O'Rourke, Regional Human Resource Officer
CNO: Grace McBride, Regional Chief Nursing Officer
Web address: https://healthcare.ascension.org/locations/illinois/ilchi/aurora-ascension-mercy
Control: Other not–for–profit (including NFP Corporation) **Service**: General medical and surgical

Staffed Beds: 292

Hospital, Medicare Provider Number, Address, Telephone, Approval, Facility, and Physician Codes, Health Care System

★ American Hospital Association (AHA) membership ○ Healthcare Facilities Accreditation Program ⇧ Center for Improvement in Healthcare Quality Accreditation
☐ The Joint Commission accreditation ◇ DNV Healthcare Inc. accreditation △ Commission on Accreditation of Rehabilitation Facilities (CARF) accreditation

Hospitals, U.S. / ILLINOIS

RUSH–COPLEY MEDICAL CENTER (140029), 2000 Ogden Avenue, Zip 60504–7222; tel. 630/978–6200, **A**1 2 3 5 7 10 **F**3 7 8 12 13 15 17 18 19 20 22 24 26 28 29 30 31 32 34 35 36 37 38 40 42 43 44 45 46 47 48 49 50 51 53 54 55 58 59 60 61 64 65 66 68 70 71 72 73 74 75 76 78 79 81 82 85 86 87 89 90 92 93 94 96 97 107 108 110 111 114 115 116 117 118 119 120 121 123 124 126 130 131 132 135 143 144 145 146 147 148 149 154 156 157 166 167 169 **P**6 **S** Rush University System for Health, Chicago, IL
Primary Contact: John A. Diederich, FACHE, President and Chief Executive Officer
COO: Mary Shilkaitis, Senior Vice President, Operations and Chief Operating Officer
CFO: Brenda VanWyhe, Senior Vice President Finance and Chief Financial Officer
CMO: Steve B Lowenthal, M.D., M.P.H., FACS, Senior Vice President Medical Affairs and Chief Medical Officer
CIO: Dennis DeMasie, Vice President Information Systems and Chief Information Officer
CNO: Abigail Lynn Hornbogen, MS, R.N., Vice President, Patient Care and Chief Nursing Officer
Web address: www.rushcopley.com
Control: Other not–for–profit (including NFP Corporation) **Service**: General medical and surgical

Staffed Beds: 210 **Admissions**: 12353 **Census**: 164 **Outpatient Visits**: 281620 **Births**: 2766 **Total Expense ($000)**: 373837 **Payroll Expense ($000)**: 152995 **Personnel**: 2171

BARRINGTON—Lake County

★ **ADVOCATE GOOD SHEPHERD HOSPITAL (140291)**, 450 West Highway 22, Zip 60010–1919; tel. 847/381–0123, **A**2 3 10 21 **F**3 11 12 13 15 17 18 20 22 24 26 28 29 30 31 34 35 36 43 45 46 47 48 49 50 54 57 59 63 64 65 68 70 74 75 76 77 78 79 81 82 84 85 87 89 92 93 94 96 107 108 110 111 114 115 116 117 118 119 120 121 123 124 126 129 130 131 132 135 144 146 148 154 156 164 165 167 169 **P**1 6 **S** Advocate Aurora Health, Downers Grove, IL
Primary Contact: Karen A. Lambert, FACHE, President
CFO: George Teufel, Vice President Finance
CMO: Barry Rosen, M.D., Vice President Medical Management
CIO: Chuck Malik, Director Information Systems
CHR: Jason Spigner, Vice President Human Resources
CNO: Marianne D Araujo, R.N., Ph.D., FACHE, Vice President Nursing and Chief Nurse Executive
Web address: www.advocatehealth.com/gshp/
Control: Church operated, Nongovernment, not–for–profit **Service**: General medical and surgical

Staffed Beds: 176 **Admissions**: 9491 **Census**: 104 **Outpatient Visits**: 221813 **Births**: 1025 **Total Expense ($000)**: 297977 **Payroll Expense ($000)**: 89767 **Personnel**: 1195

BELLEVILLE—St. Clair County

MEMORIAL HOSPITAL See Memorial Hospital Belleville

★ **MEMORIAL HOSPITAL BELLEVILLE (140185)**, 4500 Memorial Drive, Zip 62226–5399; tel. 618/233–7750, (Includes MEMORIAL HOSPITAL SHILOH, 1404 Cross Street, Shiloh, Illinois, Zip 62269–2988, tel. 618/607–1000; Deborah Graves, R.N., President) (Total facility includes 72 beds in nursing home–type unit) **A**10 11 19 **F**3 11 12 13 15 17 18 22 24 26 28 29 30 37 41 42 43 45 46 47 48 49 50 54 64 67 68 70 73 74 75 76 77 78 79 81 82 83 85 86 87 89 91 92 93 94 96 97 107 108 110 111 114 115 116 117 119 126 128 129 130 131 146 147 148 149 154 156 160 161 167 169 **P**6 **S** BJC Health System, Saint Louis, MO
Primary Contact: Deborah Graves, R.N., President
CFO: Jane Gusmano, Vice President Finance
CMO: Randolph Freeman, M.D., Vice President Medical Affairs
CIO: Jerome Fox, Senior Vice President and Chief Information Officer
CHR: John C Ziegler, FACHE, Vice President of Operations – Support
CNO: Teresa Halloran, Ph.D., R.N., Vice President Nursing Services
Web address: www.memhosp.com
Control: Other not–for–profit (including NFP Corporation) **Service**: General medical and surgical

Staffed Beds: 270 **Admissions**: 16312 **Census**: 254 **Outpatient Visits**: 300621 **Births**: 1289 **Total Expense ($000)**: 437573 **Payroll Expense ($000)**: 191865 **Personnel**: 1655

BENTON—Franklin County

FRANKLIN HOSPITAL DISTRICT (141321), 201 Bailey Lane, Zip 62812–1969; tel. 618/439–3161, **A**10 18 **F**3 11 29 34 35 40 45 56 57 59 63 68 75 77 81 97 107 115 119 127 130 133
Primary Contact: James Johnson, Chief Executive Officer
COO: Derek Johnson Sr, Chief Operating Officer
CFO: Rikki S Bonthron, Chief Financial Officer
CMO: Richard Rethorst, Chief of Medical Staff
CIO: David Williams, Director Information Technology
CNO: Terri Hermann, R.N., Chief Nursing Officer
Web address: www.franklinhospital.net
Control: Hospital district or authority, Government, Nonfederal **Service**: General medical and surgical

Staffed Beds: 16 **Admissions**: 617 **Census**: 3 **Outpatient Visits**: 47082 **Births**: 0 **Total Expense ($000)**: 28557 **Payroll Expense ($000)**: 10668 **Personnel**: 174

BERWYN—Cook County

MACNEAL HOSPITAL (140054), 3249 South Oak Park Avenue, Zip 60402–0715; tel. 708/783–9100, **A**1 3 5 7 8 10 19 **F**3 5 11 12 13 15 18 20 22 28 29 30 31 34 40 41 43 44 45 47 49 54 56 57 59 64 65 66 70 74 75 76 77 78 79 81 83 85 86 87 89 90 93 96 97 98 100 101 102 103 104 105 107 108 110 111 114 115 118 119 126 130 131 132 134 144 146 147 148 149 152 153 154 160 161 162 164 167 169 **P**6 **S** Trinity Health, Livonia, MI
Primary Contact: Pierre Monice, President
CMO: Charles Bareis, M.D., Medical Director
CIO: Tom Haslett, Interim Chief Information Officer
Web address: www.macneal.com
Control: Other not–for–profit (including NFP Corporation) **Service**: General medical and surgical

Staffed Beds: 300 **Admissions**: 9510 **Census**: 149 **Outpatient Visits**: 298594 **Births**: 707 **Personnel**: 1543

BLOOMINGTON—Mclean County

OSF ST. JOSEPH MEDICAL CENTER (140162), 2200 East Washington Street, Zip 61701–4323; tel. 309/308–6363, **A**1 2 3 10 **F**3 11 12 13 15 18 20 22 24 26 28 30 31 34 35 37 40 43 45 49 50 51 53 54 57 59 60 61 64 65 68 69 70 74 75 76 77 78 79 81 82 84 85 86 87 89 92 93 96 97 107 108 110 111 114 115 116 117 118 119 126 127 130 131 132 135 144 146 147 148 149 150 154 156 157 167 169 **S** OSF Healthcare, Peoria, IL
Primary Contact: Jennifer Ulrich, Interim President
CFO: John R Zell, Chief Financial Officer
CMO: Paul E Pedersen, M.D., Vice President and Chief Medical Officer
CHR: Kelley Wagner, Director Employee Relations
Web address: www.osfstjoseph.org
Control: Church operated, Nongovernment, not–for–profit **Service**: General medical and surgical

Staffed Beds: 149 **Admissions**: 6706 **Census**: 86 **Outpatient Visits**: 176368 **Births**: 756 **Total Expense ($000)**: 204727 **Payroll Expense ($000)**: 60460 **Personnel**: 984

BOLINGBROOK—Will County

ADVENTHEALTH BOLINGBROOK See Uchicago Medicine Adventhealth Bolingbrook

UCHICAGO MEDICINE ADVENTHEALTH BOLINGBROOK (140304), 500 Remington Boulevard, Zip 60440–4906; tel. 630/312–5000, **A**1 10 **F**3 12 13 15 18 19 20 22 26 28 29 30 31 34 35 40 43 45 49 50 56 57 59 64 68 70 73 74 76 78 79 81 82 85 87 97 98 100 101 102 103 107 108 110 111 114 116 117 119 126 146 149 167 **S** AdventHealth, Altamonte Springs, FL
Primary Contact: Kenneth Rose, President and Chief Executive Officer
CFO: Tristan Shaw, Chief Financial Officer
CMO: Richard Carroll, M.D., Chief Medical officer
CIO: John McLendon, Senior Vice President and Chief Information Officer
CHR: Katie Baio, Human Resource Director
CNO: Obed Cruz, Vice President and Chief Nursing Officer
Web address: https://www.adventhealth.com/hospital/adventhealth-bolingbrook
Control: Church operated, Nongovernment, not–for–profit **Service**: General medical and surgical

Staffed Beds: 134 **Admissions**: 6131 **Census**: 75 **Outpatient Visits**: 151439 **Births**: 733 **Total Expense ($000)**: 235376 **Payroll Expense ($000)**: 63539 **Personnel**: 850

BREESE—Clinton County

HSHS ST. JOSEPH'S HOSPITAL See HSHS St. Joseph's Hospital Breese

Hospitals, U.S. / ILLINOIS

☒ **HSHS ST. JOSEPH'S HOSPITAL BREESE (140145)**, 9515 Holy Cross Lane, Zip 62230–3618, Mailing Address: PO Box 99, Zip 62230–0099; tel. 618/526–4511, **A**1 10 **F**3 11 13 15 18 28 29 30 34 35 40 44 45 46 47 48 49 51 53 54 57 59 68 75 76 77 79 81 89 91 93 102 107 108 111 114 115 119 127 130 131 132 133 143 146 147 149 154 157 **S** HSHS Hospital Sisters Health System, Springfield, IL
Primary Contact: Chris Klay, FACHE, President and Chief Executive Officer, Southern Illinois Market
CFO: John Jeffries, Director Finance
CHR: Jed Driemeyer, Director of Human Resources
CNO: Zachary Yoder, Chief Nursing Officer
Web address: https://www.hshs.org/st-josephs-breese/
Control: Church operated, Nongovernment, not–for–profit **Service:** General medical and surgical

Staffed Beds: 52 **Admissions:** 1536 **Census:** 13 **Outpatient Visits:** 79473 **Births:** 491 **Total Expense ($000):** 57097 **Payroll Expense ($000):** 14460 **Personnel:** 199

CANTON—Fulton County

☒ **GRAHAM HOSPITAL (140001)**, 210 West Walnut Street, Zip 61520–2497; tel. 309/647–5240, (Nonreporting) **A**1 3 10 20
Primary Contact: Robert G. Senneff, FACHE, President and Chief Executive Officer
CFO: Eric Franz, Vice President, Finance and Chief Financial Officer
CIO: Alison Sours, Vice President Quality & Chief Information Officer
CHR: Canise A McComb, Director Human Resources
CNO: Teresa L McConkey, MSN, R.N., Vice President of Nursing and Chief Nursing Officer
Web address: www.grahamhealthsystem.org
Control: Other not–for–profit (including NFP Corporation) **Service:** General medical and surgical

Staffed Beds: 86

GRAHAM HOSPITAL ASSOCIATION See Graham Hospital

CARBONDALE—Jackson County

☒ **MEMORIAL HOSPITAL OF CARBONDALE (140164)**, 405 West Jackson Street, Zip 62901–1467, Mailing Address: P.O. Box 10000, Zip 62902–9000; tel. 618/549–0721, **A**1 2 3 5 10 13 19 **F**3 11 13 17 18 20 22 24 26 28 29 30 31 34 35 36 38 40 43 45 46 47 48 49 54 56 57 59 60 64 68 70 72 74 75 76 77 78 79 81 82 83 84 85 86 87 89 100 101 102 104 107 108 109 110 111 112 114 115 116 117 118 119 120 121 126 130 131 132 135 143 145 146 147 148 149 154 156 160 167 169 **S** Southern Illinois Healthcare, Carbondale, IL
Primary Contact: Craig A. Jesiolowski, FACHE, President and Chief Executive Officer
CFO: Michael Kasser, Vice President Chief Financial Officer and Treasurer
CMO: Marci Moore–Connelly, M.D., Vice President Chief Medical Officer
CIO: David Holland, Vice President Chief Innovation Officer
CHR: Pamela S Henderson, Vice President Human Resources
Web address: https://www.sih.net/locations/sih-memorial-hospital-of-carbondale
Control: Other not–for–profit (including NFP Corporation) **Service:** General medical and surgical

Staffed Beds: 175 **Admissions:** 8892 **Census:** 100 **Outpatient Visits:** 145118 **Births:** 2137 **Total Expense ($000):** 305111 **Payroll Expense ($000):** 79205 **Personnel:** 1261

CARLINVILLE—Macoupin County

★ ○ **CARLINVILLE AREA HOSPITAL (141347)**, 20733 North Broad Street, Zip 62626–1499; tel. 217/854–3141, **A**10 11 18 **F**3 11 15 28 29 34 35 40 45 50 57 59 64 77 79 81 91 93 107 110 111 115 127 129 133 148 149 150 154 167 **P**6 **S** HealthTech Management Services, Plano, TX
Primary Contact: Brian Burnside, FACHE, President and Chief Executive Officer
CFO: Mike Brown, Chief Financial Officer
CMO: Therese Polo, Medical Staff President
CIO: Jerod Cottingham, Director Information Systems
CHR: Tracy Koster, Director Human Resources
Web address: www.cahcare.com
Control: Other not–for–profit (including NFP Corporation) **Service:** General medical and surgical

Staffed Beds: 25 **Admissions:** 395 **Census:** 8 **Outpatient Visits:** 33719 **Births:** 0 **Total Expense ($000):** 44563 **Payroll Expense ($000):** 18834 **Personnel:** 221

CARROLLTON—Greene County

THOMAS H. BOYD MEMORIAL HOSPITAL (141300), 800 School Street, Zip 62016–1498; tel. 217/942–6946, (Nonreporting) **A**10 18
Primary Contact: Stace Holland, Chief Executive Officer
CHR: Lisa Eldridge, Human Resources Officer
Control: Other not–for–profit (including NFP Corporation) **Service:** General medical and surgical

Staffed Beds: 15

CARTHAGE—Hancock County

☐ **MEMORIAL HOSPITAL ASSOCIATION (141305)**, 1454 North County Road 2050, Zip 62321–3551, Mailing Address: P.O. Box 160, Zip 62321–0160; tel. 217/357–8500, (Nonreporting) **A**1 10 18
Primary Contact: Ada Bair, Chief Executive Officer
COO: Florine Dixon, Chief Operating Officer
CFO: Teresa Smith, Chief Financial Officer
CIO: Syndi Horn, Director Information Systems
CHR: Dan Smith, Director Human Resources
Web address: www.mhtlc.org
Control: Other not–for–profit (including NFP Corporation) **Service:** General medical and surgical

Staffed Beds: 18

CENTRALIA—Marion County

☒ **SSM HEALTH ST. MARY'S HOSPITAL CENTRALIA (140034)**, 400 North Pleasant Avenue, Zip 62801–3056; tel. 618/436–8000, **A**1 2 10 19 **F**3 4 5 11 12 15 18 28 29 30 31 32 34 35 38 40 44 45 46 50 51 54 55 56 57 59 61 64 68 70 74 75 77 78 79 80 81 82 84 85 86 87 89 90 91 92 93 94 98 99 100 101 102 103 104 105 107 108 110 111 114 115 118 119 120 121 123 124 127 129 130 131 132 135 144 146 147 148 149 152 153 154 156 157 160 161 162 164 165 167 **P**6 8 **S** SSM Health, Saint Louis, MO
Primary Contact: Damon R. Harbison, President
CFO: Matthew Kinsella, Chief Financial Officer
CMO: Rajendra Shroff, M.D., Administrative Medical Director
CIO: Steve Murphy, Director Information Systems
CHR: Brenda Alexander, System Vice President, Human Resources
Web address: https://www.ssmhealth.com/locations/st-marys-hospital-centralia
Control: Church operated, Nongovernment, not–for–profit **Service:** General medical and surgical

Staffed Beds: 115 **Admissions:** 3392 **Census:** 42 **Outpatient Visits:** 192718 **Births:** 0 **Total Expense ($000):** 101622 **Payroll Expense ($000):** 33187 **Personnel:** 407

CENTREVILLE—St. Clair County

☐ **TOUCHETTE REGIONAL HOSPITAL (140077)**, 5900 Bond Avenue, Zip 62207–2326; tel. 618/332–3060, (Nonreporting) **A**1 5 10
Primary Contact: Larry W. McCulley, Chief Executive Officer
COO: Tom Mikkelson, M.D., Interim Chief Operating Officer
CFO: John Majchrzak, Chief Financial Officer
CMO: Tom Mikkelson, M.D., Vice President Medical Affairs
Web address: www.touchette.org
Control: Other not–for–profit (including NFP Corporation) **Service:** General medical and surgical

Staffed Beds: 119

CHAMPAIGN—Champaign County

☐ **THE PAVILION (144029)**, 809 West Church Street, Zip 61820–3399; tel. 217/373–1700, (Nonreporting) **A**1 10 **S** Universal Health Services, Inc., King of Prussia, PA
Primary Contact: Shaun Doherty, Chief Executive Officer
CFO: Edith Frasca, Controller and Chief Financial Officer
Web address: www.pavilionhospital.com
Control: Corporation, Investor–owned (for–profit) **Service:** Psychiatric

Staffed Beds: 110

Hospital, Medicare Provider Number, Address, Telephone, Approval, Facility, and Physician Codes, Health Care System

★ American Hospital Association (AHA) membership
☐ The Joint Commission accreditation
○ Healthcare Facilities Accreditation Program
◇ DNV Healthcare Inc. accreditation
⇧ Center for Improvement in Healthcare Quality Accreditation
△ Commission on Accreditation of Rehabilitation Facilities (CARF) accreditation

© 2025 AHA Guide

Hospitals, U.S. / ILLINOIS

CHESTER—Randolph County

☐ **CHESTER MENTAL HEALTH CENTER**, Chester Road, Zip 62233-0031, Mailing Address: Box 31, Zip 62233-0031; tel. 618/826-4571, (Nonreporting) **A**1 **S**
Division of Mental Health, Department of Human Services, Springfield, IL
Primary Contact: Travis Nottmeier, Administrator
CFO: Sarah Imhoff, Business Administrator
CMO: Maitra Rupa, M.D., Acting Medical Director
CIO: Anthony Young, Information Services Specialist
CHR: Kim Holsapple, Human Resource Specialist
CNO: Jennifer Klingeman, Director of Nursing
Control: State, Government, Nonfederal **Service**: Psychiatric

Staffed Beds: 284

☐ **MEMORIAL HOSPITAL (141338)**, 1900 State Street, Zip 62233-1116, Mailing Address: P.O. Box 609, Zip 62233-0609; tel. 618/826-4581, (Nonreporting) **A**1 10 18
Primary Contact: Brett Bollmann, Chief Executive Officer
CFO: Gail Miesner, Chief Financial Officer
CMO: Alan Liefer, M.D., President Medical Staff
CIO: Becky Bunselmeyer, Director Information Services
CHR: May Rose, Director Human Resources
Web address: www.mhchester.com
Control: Hospital district or authority, Government, Nonfederal **Service**: General medical and surgical

Staffed Beds: 25

CHICAGO—Cook County

ADVOCATE BETHANY HOSPITAL See RML Specialty Hospital

★ ⇑ **ADVOCATE ILLINOIS MASONIC MEDICAL CENTER (140182)**, 836 West Wellington Avenue, Zip 60657-5147; tel. 773/975-1600, **A**2 3 5 8 10 21 **F**3 5 12 13 15 17 18 19 20 22 24 26 28 29 30 31 34 35 37 38 39 40 41 43 44 45 46 47 48 49 50 53 54 55 56 58 59 60 61 64 66 68 70 71 72 73 74 75 76 77 78 79 81 82 84 85 86 87 89 90 92 93 96 97 98 100 101 102 103 104 107 108 110 111 114 115 116 117 118 119 120 121 123 124 126 129 130 131 132 135 141 143 146 147 148 149 153 154 156 157 162 164 165 167 169 **P**1 6 **S** Advocate Aurora Health, Downers Grove, IL
Primary Contact: Susan Nordstrom. Lopez, President
CFO: Jack Gilbert, Vice President Finance and Facilities
CMO: Clifton Clarke, Vice President Medical Management
CIO: Chuck Malik, Director Information Systems
CHR: Katie Bata, Vice President Human Resources
Web address: www.advocatehealth.com/masonic
Control: Other not–for–profit (including NFP Corporation) **Service**: General medical and surgical

Staffed Beds: 315 **Admissions**: 11596 **Census**: 157 **Outpatient Visits**: 241698 **Births**: 1390 **Total Expense ($000)**: 615283 **Payroll Expense ($000)**: 162312 **Personnel**: 2143

★ ⇑ **ADVOCATE TRINITY HOSPITAL (140048)**, 2320 East 93rd Street, Zip 60617-3909; tel. 773/967-2000, **A**2 10 21 **F**3 13 15 18 20 22 24 26 28 29 30 31 34 35 40 45 46 49 50 53 55 56 57 59 60 63 64 65 68 70 74 75 76 77 78 79 81 82 84 87 89 92 93 100 107 110 111 114 115 119 130 132 135 146 148 154 156 164 165 167 169 **P**1 6 **S** Advocate Aurora Health, Downers Grove, IL
Primary Contact: Michelle Y. Blakely, Ph.D., FACHE, President
CFO: Maureen Morrison, Vice President, Finance
CMO: James Keller, M.D., Vice President, Medical Management
CIO: Bonita Brown-Roberts, Director Information Systems
CHR: Kristin Landini, Vice President, Human Resources
CNO: Gwendolyn Marie Oglesby-Odom, Chief Nursing Officer
Web address: https://www.advocatehealth.com/trin/
Control: Church operated, Nongovernment, not–for–profit **Service**: General medical and surgical

Staffed Beds: 138 **Admissions**: 5686 **Census**: 71 **Outpatient Visits**: 86431 **Births**: 652 **Total Expense ($000)**: 173748 **Payroll Expense ($000)**: 52601 **Personnel**: 786

AMITA HEALTH RESURRECTION MEDICAL CENTER See Ascension Resurrection

AMITA HEALTH SAINTS MARY & ELIZABETH MEDICAL CENTER See Ascension Saint Mary – Chicago

⊞ **ANN & ROBERT H. LURIE CHILDREN'S HOSPITAL OF CHICAGO (143300)**, 225 East Chicago Avenue, Zip 60611-2991; tel. 312/227-4000, **A**1 3 5 10 **F**3 5 8 9 11 12 17 18 19 20 21 22 23 24 25 26 27 28 29 30 31 32 33 34 35 36 37 38 39 40 41 43 44 45 46 48 49 50 51 52 54 55 57 58 59 60 61 63 64 65 68 71 72 74 75 78 79 81 82 84 85 86 87 88 89 91 92 93 94 95 96 97 98 99 100 101 102 104 105 107 108 111 114 115 116 117 118 119 124 126 129 130 131 132 134 136 137 138 139 141 142 144 146 148 149 150 151 153 154 164 165 167 169
Primary Contact: Thomas Shanley, M.D., President and Chief Executive Officer
COO: Michelle Stephenson, R.N., Executive Vice President & Chief Operations Officer
CFO: Ron Blaustein, Chief Financial Officer
CMO: Michael Kelleher, Chief Medical Officer
CIO: Lisa Dykstra, Senior Vice President and Chief Information Officer
CHR: Joani Duncan, Chief Human Resource Officer
CNO: Brian M Stahulak, R.N., Chief Nursing Officer
Web address: www.luriechildrens.org
Control: Other not–for–profit (including NFP Corporation) **Service**: Children's general medical and surgical

Staffed Beds: 354 **Admissions**: 10154 **Census**: 267 **Outpatient Visits**: 849779 **Births**: 0 **Total Expense ($000)**: 1273408 **Payroll Expense ($000)**: 612827 **Personnel**: 7700

⊞ **ASCENSION RESURRECTION (140117)**, 7435 West Talcott Avenue, Zip 60631-3746; tel. 773/774-8000, (Nonreporting) **A**1 3 5 10 13 19 **S** Ascension Healthcare, Saint Louis, MO
Primary Contact: Len Wilk, President
CFO: Colleen Koppenhaver, Interim Chief Financial Officer
CMO: David Bordo, M.D., Interim Co–Chief Executive Officer and Chief Medical Officer
CHR: Paula Zawojski, Regional Director, Human Resources
Web address: https://healthcare.ascension.org/locations/illinois/ilchi/chicago-ascension-resurrection
Control: Church operated, Nongovernment, not–for–profit **Service**: General medical and surgical

Staffed Beds: 337

⊞ **ASCENSION SAINT JOSEPH – CHICAGO (140224)**, 2900 North Lake Shore Drive, Zip 60657-6274; tel. 773/665-3000, (Nonreporting) **A**1 2 3 5 10 **S** Ascension Healthcare, Saint Louis, MO
Primary Contact: JOHN BAIRD, Chief Executive Officer
CFO: Stanley Kazmierczak, Controller
CMO: M Todd Grendon, M.D., President Medical Staff
CIO: George Chessum, Senior Vice President Information Systems and Chief Information Officer
CHR: Denise Brown, Vice President Human Resources
Web address: https://healthcare.ascension.org/locations/illinois/ilchi/chicago-ascension-saint-joseph-chicago-at-2900-n-lake-shore-dr
Control: Church operated, Nongovernment, not–for–profit **Service**: General medical and surgical

Staffed Beds: 338

ASCENSION SAINT JOSEPH – CHICAGO See Ascension Saint Joseph – Chicago

⊞ **ASCENSION SAINT MARY – CHICAGO (140180)**, 2233 West Division Street, Zip 60622-3086; tel. 312/770-2000, (Includes PRESENCE SAINTS MARY & ELIZABETH MEDICAL CENTER, CLAREMONT AVENUE, 1431 North Claremont Avenue, Chicago, Illinois, Zip 60622-1791, tel. 773/278-2000; Martin H. Judd, Regional President and Chief Executive Officer) (Nonreporting) **A**1 2 3 5 10 19 **S** Ascension Healthcare, Saint Louis, MO
Primary Contact: Ellis Hawkins, FACHE, President
CFO: Bob Cech, Regional Finance Officer
CMO: Laura Concannon, M.D., Regional Chief Medical Officer
CIO: Cheryl Rodenfels, System Vice President, IT Operations
CHR: Melanie Saenz, Regional Human Resources Officer
CNO: Suzanne Lambert, R.N., Regional Chief Nursing Officer and Support Services
Web address: https://healthcare.ascension.org/locations/illinois/ilchi/chicago-ascension-saint-mary
Control: Church operated, Nongovernment, not–for–profit **Service**: General medical and surgical

Staffed Beds: 441

BERNARD MITCHELL HOSPITAL See University of Chicago Medical Center, Chicago

CHICAGO LYING–IN (CLI) See University of Chicago Medical Center, Chicago

CHICAGO LYING–IN HOSPITAL See Chicago Lying–In (CLI)

Hospitals, U.S. / ILLINOIS

☐ **CHICAGO–READ MENTAL HEALTH CENTER (144010)**, 4200 North Oak Park Avenue, Zip 60634–1457; tel. 773/794–4000, **A**1 10 **F**98 **S** Division of Mental Health, Department of Human Services, Springfield, IL
Primary Contact: Ricardo Fernandez, Administrator
Control: State, Government, Nonfederal **Service:** Psychiatric

Staffed Beds: 160 **Admissions:** 246 **Census:** 16 **Outpatient Visits:** 312
Births: 0

COMER CHILDREN'S HOSPITAL See University of Chicago Medical Center, Chicago

☐ **COMMUNITY FIRST MEDICAL CENTER (140251)**, 5645 West Addison Street, Zip 60634–4403; tel. 773/282–7000, (Nonreporting) **A**1 3 10
Primary Contact: Barbara Martin, Chief Executive Officer
COO: Dennis FitzMaurice, Vice President, Professional Services
CFO: Richard Franco, Chief Financial Officer
CMO: David Bordo, M.D., Vice President and Chief Medical Officer
CIO: George Chessum, Senior Vice President and Chief Information Officer
CHR: Ivy McKinley, Regional Human Resources Officer
Web address: www.cfmedicalcenter.com
Control: Church operated, Nongovernment, not–for–profit **Service:** General medical and surgical

Staffed Beds: 279

★ ○ **ENDEAVOR HEALTH SWEDISH HOSPITAL (140114)**, 5145 North California Avenue, Zip 60625–3661; tel. 773/878–8200, **A**2 3 5 10 11 13 **F**3 9 12 13 15 18 20 22 26 28 29 30 31 32 34 35 36 38 39 40 44 45 46 47 49 50 53 55 56 57 58 59 60 64 65 68 70 73 74 75 76 78 79 81 82 84 85 86 87 90 92 93 94 96 97 98 100 102 103 104 107 110 111 114 115 116 117 118 119 120 121 123 126 129 130 131 132 134 135 136 143 144 146 147 148 154 156 164 167 169 **P**5 6 **S** Endeavor Health, Evanston, IL
Primary Contact: Jonathan Lind, President
CFO: Thomas J Garvey, Senior Vice President Operations and Chief Financial Officer
CMO: Bruce McNulty, Chief Medical Officer
CIO: Karen Sheehan, Vice President and Chief Information Officer
CNO: Kathryn Donofrio, Chief Nursing Officer
Web address: https://www.swedishcovenant.org
Control: Other not–for–profit (including NFP Corporation) **Service:** General medical and surgical

Staffed Beds: 255 **Admissions:** 9739 **Census:** 137 **Outpatient Visits:** 231728 **Births:** 1855 **Total Expense ($000):** 336829 **Payroll Expense ($000):** 133998 **Personnel:** 2060

☐ **GARFIELD PARK BEHAVIORAL HOSPITAL (144039)**, 520 North Ridgeway Avenue, Zip 60624–1232; tel. 773/265–3700, (Nonreporting) **A**1 3 10 **S** Universal Health Services, Inc., King of Prussia, PA
Primary Contact: Steven Airhart, Group Chief Executive Officer
CMO: Tina Mahera, M.D., Chief Medical Officer
CHR: Janice Clark, Manager Human Resources
Web address: www.garfieldparkhospital.com
Control: Corporation, Investor–owned (for–profit) **Service:** Children's hospital psychiatric

Staffed Beds: 88

GARFIELD PARK HOSPITAL See Garfield Park Behavioral Hospital

☐ **HARTGROVE BEHAVIORAL HEALTH SYSTEM (144026)**, 5730 West Roosevelt Road, Zip 60644–1580, Mailing Address: P.O. Box 61558, King of Prussia, PA, Zip 19406–0958; tel. 773/413–1700, (Nonreporting) **A**1 3 10 **S** Universal Health Services, Inc., King of Prussia, PA
Primary Contact: Steven Airhart, Chief Executive Officer
COO: Patrick Sanders, Chief Operating Officer
CFO: Joseph Remer, Chief Financial Officer
CMO: Teresa Poprawski, Chief Medical Officer
CHR: Alanna Barker, Director of Human Resources
CNO: Jody Bhambra, Chief Nursing Officer
Web address: www.hartgrovehospital.com
Control: Corporation, Investor–owned (for–profit) **Service:** Psychiatric

Staffed Beds: 160

HARTGROVE HOSPITAL See Hartgrove Behavioral Health System

★ ○ **HOLY CROSS HOSPITAL (140133)**, 2701 West 68th Street, Zip 60629–1882; tel. 773/884–9000, (Nonreporting) **A**3 10 11 **S** Sinai Chicago, Chicago, IL
Primary Contact: Jeen–Soo Chang, M.D., MS, President and Chief Medical Officer
CFO: Charles Weis, Executive Vice President and Chief Financial Officer
CMO: Jeen–Soo Chang, M.D., MS, President and Chief Medical Officer
CHR: Ann Hatches, Director, Human Resources
CNO: Deborah Davisson, MSN, Chief Nursing Officer and Vice President, Patient Care Services
Web address: https://www.sinaichicago.org/en/find-a-location/results/holy-cross-hospital/
Control: Other not–for–profit (including NFP Corporation) **Service:** General medical and surgical

Staffed Beds: 120

✠ **HUMBOLDT PARK HEALTH (140206)**, 1044 North Francisco Avenue, Zip 60622–2743; tel. 773/292–8200, (Nonreporting) **A**1 3 10
Primary Contact: Jose R. Sanchez, President and Chief Executive Officer
COO: Michelle Blakely, FACHE, Ph.D., Chief Operating Officer
CFO: Gary M Krugel, Chief Financial Officer
CIO: Stephen DePooter, Chief Information Officer
CHR: Neil Teatsorth, Vice President Human Resources
CNO: William Duffy, Interim Chief Nursing Officer
Web address: www.nahospital.org
Control: Other not–for–profit (including NFP Corporation) **Service:** General medical and surgical

Staffed Beds: 195

★ ○ **INSIGHT HOSPITAL AND MEDICAL CENTER (140158)**, 2525 South Michigan Avenue, Zip 60616–2333; tel. 312/567–2000, (Nonreporting) **A**3 10 11
Primary Contact: Atif Bawahab, Chief Executive Officer
CFO: Eric Krueger, Chief Financial Officer
CMO: Michael McDonnell, M.D., Chief Medical Officer
CIO: John Romeo, Chief Information Officer
Web address: https://insightchicago.com/
Control: Other not–for–profit (including NFP Corporation) **Service:** General medical and surgical

Staffed Beds: 402

INSTITUTE OF PSYCHIATRY See Stone Institute of Psychiatry

☐ **JACKSON PARK HOSPITAL AND MEDICAL CENTER (140177)**, 7531 Stony Island Avenue, Zip 60649–3993; tel. 773/947–7500, (Nonreporting) **A**1 3 10
Primary Contact: William Dorsey, M.D., Board Chairman and Chief Executive Officer
COO: Randall Smith, Executive Vice President
CFO: Kenneth Mcghee, Vice President of Finance
CMO: Bangalore Murthy, M.D., Director Medical Staff
CIO: Barry Mandell, Vice President, Special Projects
CHR: Tracey Jones, Director Human Resources
Web address: www.jacksonparkhospital.org
Control: Other not–for–profit (including NFP Corporation) **Service:** General medical and surgical

Staffed Beds: 118

✠ △ **JESSE BROWN VA MEDICAL CENTER**, 820 South Damen, Zip 60612–3776; tel. 312/569–8387, (Nonreporting) **A**1 3 5 7 **S** Department of Veterans Affairs, Washington, DC
Primary Contact: Clifford A. Smith, Ph.D., Acting Medical Center Director
COO: Michelle Blakely, FACHE, Ph.D., Associate Director
CFO: Kalpana Mehta, Chief Fiscal Services
CMO: Wendy W Brown, M.D., M.P.H., Chief of Staff
CIO: Howard Loewenstein, Chief Information Resource Management Services
CHR: Wayne Davis, Manager Human Resources
Web address: www.chicago.va.gov
Control: Veterans Affairs, Government, federal **Service:** General medical and surgical

Staffed Beds: 181

JESSE BROWN VETERANS AFFAIRS MEDICAL CENTER See Jesse Brown VA Medical Center

---

Hospital, Medicare Provider Number, Address, Telephone, Approval, Facility, and Physician Codes, Health Care System

★ American Hospital Association (AHA) membership   ○ Healthcare Facilities Accreditation Program   ⇑ Center for Improvement in Healthcare Quality Accreditation
☐ The Joint Commission accreditation   ◇ DNV Healthcare Inc. accreditation   △ Commission on Accreditation of Rehabilitation Facilities (CARF) accreditation

© 2025 AHA Guide   Hospitals **A189**

Hospitals, U.S. / ILLINOIS

JOHN H. STROGER JR. HOSPITAL OF COOK COUNTY (140124), 1969 West Ogden Avenue, Zip 60612–3714; tel. 312/864–6000, **A**1 2 3 5 8 10 11 **F**3 5 11 13 15 16 17 18 19 20 22 24 29 30 31 34 35 36 38 39 40 41 43 44 45 46 47 48 49 50 51 52 54 55 56 57 58 59 60 61 64 65 68 70 72 73 74 75 76 77 78 79 80 81 82 84 85 86 87 88 89 91 92 93 94 97 99 100 101 102 103 104 107 108 110 111 114 115 116 117 118 119 120 121 122 123 129 130 132 134 135 143 146 147 148 149 154 156 160 162 163 164 165 167 **S** Cook County Health and Hospitals System, Chicago, IL
Primary Contact: Donnica Austin, Chief Executive Officer
CMO: Claudia Fegan, M.D., Chief Medical Officer
CIO: Bala Hota, Interim Chief Information Officer
CHR: Paris I Partee, Associate Administrator and Director Human Resources
CNO: Antoinette Williams, Chief Nursing Officer
Web address: https://cookcountyhealth.org/locations/john-h-stroger-jr-hospital-of-cook-county/
Control: County, Government, Nonfederal **Service:** General medical and surgical

Staffed Beds: 414 **Admissions:** 14758 **Census:** 253 **Outpatient Visits:** 900112 **Births:** 952 **Total Expense ($000):** 1170241 **Payroll Expense ($000):** 485312 **Personnel:** 5477

JOHNSTON R. BOWMAN HEALTH CENTER See Rush University Medical Center, Chicago

KINDRED CHICAGO LAKESHORE (142009), 6130 North Sheridan Road, Zip 60660; tel. 773/381–1222, (Nonreporting) **A**1 **S** ScionHealth, Louisville, KY
Primary Contact: Kathy Kelly, Market Chief Executive Officer
Web address: www.kindredhealthcare.com
Control: Corporation, Investor–owned (for-profit) **Service:** Acute long–term care hospital

Staffed Beds: 103

KINDRED HOSPITAL–CHICAGO NORTH See Kindred Hospital Chicago North

LA RABIDA CHILDREN'S HOSPITAL (143301), 6501 South Promontory Drive, Zip 60649–1003; tel. 773/363–6700, **A**1 3 5 10 **F**3 29 32 34 35 38 41 50 55 57 59 64 65 74 75 77 79 86 87 91 93 96 97 99 100 101 104 119 130 132 134 143 146 148 149 154 156 164
Primary Contact: Rolla Sweis, PharmD, President and Chief Executive Officer
CFO: Mark Renfree, Chief Financial Officer
CMO: David Soglin, Chief Medical Officer
CIO: Sheelah Cabrera, Chief Information Officer
CHR: Frances Lefkow, Director Human Resources
Web address: www.larabida.org
Control: Other not–for–profit (including NFP Corporation) **Service:** Children's chronic disease

Staffed Beds: 30 **Admissions:** 122 **Census:** 27 **Outpatient Visits:** 31074 **Births:** 0 **Total Expense ($000):** 70049 **Payroll Expense ($000):** 36106 **Personnel:** 458

★ ○ **LORETTO HOSPITAL (140083)**, 645 South Central Avenue, Zip 60644–5059; tel. 773/626–4300, **A**3 10 11 **F**3 4 5 15 18 20 29 30 34 35 39 40 41 43 45 46 50 57 58 61 64 65 68 70 74 75 79 81 82 85 86 87 91 92 93 97 98 100 102 104 107 108 110 111 115 119 130 132 135 146 147 148 149 151 153 154 156 157 160 161 165 167
Primary Contact: Tesa Anewishki, President and Chief Executive Officer
CFO: John R. Morales, Interim Chief Financial Officer
CIO: Syed Haque, Vice President and Chief Information Officer
CHR: Chrystal Brown, Director Human Resources
CNO: Kimberly Wright, Executive Director, Nursing and Staff Development
Web address: www.lorettohospital.org
Control: Other not–for–profit (including NFP Corporation) **Service:** General medical and surgical

Staffed Beds: 177 **Admissions:** 3260 **Census:** 52 **Outpatient Visits:** 11736 **Births:** 0

LOUIS A. WEISS MEMORIAL HOSPITAL See Weiss Memorial Hospital

MERCY HOSPITAL AND MEDICAL CENTER See Insight Hospital and Medical Center

METHODIST HOSPITAL OF CHICAGO See Thorek Memorial Hospital Andersonville

□ **MONTROSE BEHAVIORAL HEALTH HOSPITAL (144043)**, 4720 North Clarendon Avenue, Zip 60640–5122; tel. 773/878–9700, (Nonreporting) **A**1
Primary Contact: Robert Hittmeier, Chief Executive Officer, Adolescent Hospital
COO: Patricia McClure–Chessier, Chief Administrative Officer
CFO: Kisha Scruggs–Morris, Chief Financial Officer
CMO: Joao Busnello, M.D., Chief Medical Officer
CHR: Linda Vestrand, Director, Human Resources
CNO: Ryan Diehl, Chief Nursing Officer
Web address: www.montrosebehavioral.com
Control: Corporation, Investor–owned (for–profit) **Service:** Psychiatric

Staffed Beds: 60

MOUNT SINAI HOSPITAL (140018), 1500 South Fairfield Avenue, Zip 60608–1729; tel. 773/542–2000, (Includes SINAI CHILDREN'S HOSPITAL, California Avenue at 15th Street, Chicago, Illinois, Zip 60608, tel. 773/542–2000) (Nonreporting) **A**1 2 3 5 10 **S** Sinai Chicago, Chicago, IL
Primary Contact: Sameer Shah, PharmD, President
CFO: Charles Weis, Chief Financial Officer
CMO: Mark Multach, M.D., Chief Medical Officer
CHR: Ann Hatches, Interim Director Human Resources
CNO: Michele A Mazurek, Chief Nursing Officer
Web address: www.sinai.org
Control: Other not–for–profit (including NFP Corporation) **Service:** General medical and surgical

Staffed Beds: 261

NORTHWESTERN MEMORIAL HOSPITAL (140281), 251 East Huron Street, Zip 60611–2908; tel. 312/926–2000, (Includes PRENTICE WOMEN'S HOSPITAL, 250 East Superior Street, Chicago, Illinois, Zip 60611, tel. 312/926–2000; STONE INSTITUTE OF PSYCHIATRY, 251 East Huron Street, Chicago, Illinois, Zip 60611, tel. 312/926–2000) **A**1 2 3 5 8 10 19 **F**3 4 6 9 11 12 13 14 15 17 18 20 22 24 26 28 29 30 31 33 34 35 36 37 38 39 40 41 43 44 45 46 47 48 49 50 51 52 54 55 56 57 58 59 60 61 64 65 66 68 70 72 73 74 75 76 77 78 79 80 81 82 84 85 86 87 92 93 94 96 97 98 100 101 102 103 104 107 108 110 111 112 114 115 116 117 118 119 120 121 123 126 129 130 131 132 134 135 136 137 138 139 140 141 142 144 145 146 147 148 149 150 154 156 157 162 163 165 167 168 169 **S** Northwestern Memorial HealthCare, Chicago, IL
Primary Contact: Thomas J. McAfee, President
CFO: Francis D Fraher, Vice President, Finance, Northwestern Memorial Hospital
CMO: Gary Noskin, Senior Vice President and Chief Medical Officer, Northwestern Memorial Hospital
CIO: Carl Christensen, Senior Vice President and Chief Information Officer, Northwestern Memorial HealthCare
CNO: Kristin Ramsey, R.N., Senior Vice President and Chief Nursing Executive, Northwestern Memorial Hospital
Web address: www.nm.org
Control: Other not–for–profit (including NFP Corporation) **Service:** General medical and surgical

Staffed Beds: 943 **Admissions:** 46966 **Census:** 800 **Outpatient Visits:** 2188776 **Births:** 11592 **Total Expense ($000):** 4188546 **Payroll Expense ($000):** 1276369 **Personnel:** 11913

PRENTICE WOMEN'S HOSPITAL See Northwestern Memorial Hospital, Chicago

PROVIDENT HOSPITAL OF COOK COUNTY (140300), 500 East 51st Street, Zip 60615–2494; tel. 312/572–2000, **A**1 3 10 **F**3 8 15 18 29 34 35 40 45 50 53 57 59 61 64 66 68 70 81 85 87 104 107 119 130 131 132 135 143 146 147 149 154 156 160 164 165 167 **S** Cook County Health and Hospitals System, Chicago, IL
Primary Contact: Arnold F. Turner, M.D., Chief Hospital Executive
CFO: Barbara Patterson, Chief Financial Officer
CMO: Aaron Hamb, M.D., Chief Medical Officer
CIO: Donna Hart, Chief Information Officer
Web address: https://cookcountyhealth.org/locations/provident-hospital-of-cook-county/
Control: County, Government, Nonfederal **Service:** General medical and surgical

Staffed Beds: 28 **Admissions:** 905 **Census:** 10 **Outpatient Visits:** 119782 **Births:** 0 **Total Expense ($000):** 78992 **Payroll Expense ($000):** 31585 **Personnel:** 290

○ **ROSELAND COMMUNITY HOSPITAL (140068)**, 45 West 111th Street, Zip 60628–4294; tel. 773/995–3000, (Nonreporting) **A**10 11
Primary Contact: Timothy Egan, President and Chief Executive Officer
CFO: Marlo Kemp, Vice President and Chief Financial Officer
CMO: Alan Jackson, M.D., Medical Director
CIO: Mariusz Mazek, Vice President Information Technology and Chief Information Officer
CHR: Paulette Clark, Chief Human Resource Officer
CNO: Jeraldene Shaffer, MSN, Chief Nursing Officer
Web address: www.roselandhospital.org
Control: Other not–for–profit (including NFP Corporation) **Service:** General medical and surgical

Staffed Beds: 134

□ **RUSH SPECIALTY HOSPITAL (140310)**, 516 South Loomis Street, Zip 60607; tel. 872/298–9199, (Nonreporting) **A**1 **S** Rush University System for Health, Chicago, IL
Primary Contact: Michael DeLaRosa, Chief Executive Officer
CNO: Rebecca Pedersen, Chief Nursing Officer
Web address: https://www.rush.edu/locations/rush-specialty-hospital
Control: Partnership, Investor–owned (for–profit) **Service:** Rehabilitation

Staffed Beds: 100

Hospitals, U.S. / ILLINOIS

☒ △ **RUSH UNIVERSITY MEDICAL CENTER (140119)**, 1653 West Congress Parkway, Zip 60612–3833; tel. 312/942–5000, (Includes JOHNSTON R. BOWMAN HEALTH CENTER, 700 South Paulina, Chicago, Illinois, Zip 60612, tel. 312/942–7000; RUSH CHILDREN'S HOSPITAL, 1653 W Congress Pkwy, Chicago, Illinois, Zip 60612–3833, 1653 Wes Congress Parkway, Zip 60612–3833, tel. 888/352–7874) **A**1 2 3 5 7 8 10 19 **F**2 3 5 6 8 9 11 12 13 14 15 17 18 19 20 21 22 23 24 25 26 27 29 30 31 32 33 34 35 36 37 38 39 40 41 43 44 45 46 47 48 49 50 51 52 53 54 55 56 57 58 59 60 61 62 63 64 65 66 68 70 71 72 73 74 75 76 77 78 79 81 82 83 84 85 86 87 88 89 90 91 92 94 95 96 97 98 99 100 101 102 103 104 105 106 107 108 110 111 114 115 116 117 118 119 120 121 123 124 125 126 129 130 131 132 135 136 138 139 141 142 145 146 147 148 149 150 152 153 154 156 157 160 161 162 163 164 166 167 169 **P**8 **S** Rush University System for Health, Chicago, IL
Primary Contact: Omar Lateef, D.O., President and Chief Executive Officer
CFO: Patricia Steeves O'Neil, Interim Senior Vice President, Acting Chief Financial Officer and Treasurer
CIO: Lac Tran, Senior Vice President Information Services
CHR: Mary Ellen Schopp, Senior Vice President Human Resources
CNO: Angelique Richard, R.N., Ph.D., Vice President Clinical Nursing, Chief Nursing Officer and Associate Dean for Practice, College of Nursing
Web address: www.rush.edu
Control: Other not–for–profit (including NFP Corporation) **Service**: General medical and surgical

Staffed Beds: 674 **Admissions**: 28842 **Census**: 486 **Outpatient Visits**: 680271 **Births**: 2593 **Total Expense ($000)**: 1985111 **Payroll Expense ($000)**: 786320 **Personnel**: 12027

☒ **SAINT ANTHONY HOSPITAL (140095)**, 2875 West 19th Street, Zip 60623–3596; tel. 773/484–1000, **A**1 3 10 **F**3 13 15 18 19 29 30 31 32 34 35 40 41 44 49 50 51 54 59 60 64 65 68 70 74 75 76 77 79 81 82 84 85 86 87 89 93 97 98 100 101 102 107 108 110 111 114 115 118 119 130 131 132 143 144 146 147 148 149 150 154 157 160 164 165 167 169
Primary Contact: Guy A. Medaglia, President and Chief Executive Officer
CFO: Justin Bynum, Chief Financial Officer
CIO: Mark Jennings, Chief Information Officer
CHR: Malinda Yvonne Carter, Vice President Human Resources
Web address: www.sahchicago.org
Control: Church operated, Nongovernment, not–for–profit **Service**: General medical and surgical

Staffed Beds: 151 **Admissions**: 5517 **Census**: 75 **Outpatient Visits**: 110671 **Births**: 1001 **Total Expense ($000)**: 130351 **Payroll Expense ($000)**: 71603 **Personnel**: 812

SAINT ELIZABETH HOSPITAL See Presence Saints Mary & Elizabeth Medical Center, Claremont Avenue

☒ △ **SCHWAB REHABILITATION HOSPITAL (143025)**, 1401 South California Avenue, Zip 60608–1858; tel. 773/522–2010, (Nonreporting) **A**1 3 5 7 10 **S** Sinai Chicago, Chicago, IL
Primary Contact: Julia Libcke, R.N., President
CFO: Charles Weis, Chief Financial Officer
CMO: Michelle Gittler, M.D., Medical Director
Web address: www.schwabrehab.org
Control: Other not–for–profit (including NFP Corporation) **Service**: Rehabilitation

Staffed Beds: 62

☒ **SHIRLEY RYAN ABILITYLAB (143026)**, 345 East Erie Street, Zip 60611–2654, Mailing Address: 355 East Erie Street, Zip 60611–2654; tel. 312/238–1000, (Nonreporting) **A**1 3 5 8 10
Primary Contact: Pablo Celnik, Chief Executive Officer
CFO: Ed Case, Executive Vice President and Chief Financial Officer
CMO: James Sliwa, M.D., Chief Medical Officer
CIO: Tim McKula, Vice President Information Systems and Chief Information Officer
CHR: Lois Huggins, Chief Human Resources Officer and Senior Vice President Human Resources
CNO: Karen M Colby, MS, Chief Nursing Officer
Web address: https://www.sralab.org/
Control: Other not–for–profit (including NFP Corporation) **Service**: Rehabilitation

Staffed Beds: 262

☐ **SHRINERS HOSPITALS FOR CHILDREN–CHICAGO (143302)**, 2211 North Oak Park Avenue, Zip 60707–3392; tel. 773/622–5400, (Nonreporting) **A**1 3 5 10 **S** Shriners Hospitals for Children, Tampa, FL
Primary Contact: Craig McGhee, FACHE, Midwest Market Administrator
CFO: Philip Magid, Director Fiscal Services
CMO: Jeffrey D. Ackman, M.D., Chief of Staff
CHR: James E Pawlowicz, Director Human Resources
CNO: Terry Wheat, R.N., M.P.H., Director of Patient Care Services
Web address: www.shrinershospitalsforchildren.org/Hospitals/Locations/Chicago.aspx
Control: Other not–for–profit (including NFP Corporation) **Service**: Children's orthopedic

Staffed Beds: 36

○ **SOUTH SHORE HOSPITAL (140181)**, 8012 South Crandon Avenue, Zip 60617–1124; tel. 773/356–5000, (Nonreporting) **A**10 11
Primary Contact: Leslie M. Rogers, President and Chief Executive Officer
CFO: Scott Spencer, Chief Financial Officer
CMO: James Bob Achebe, M.D., President Medical Staff
CIO: Jim Ritchie, Director Management Information Systems
CHR: Roger Rak, Director Human Resources
CNO: Laura Gonzalez, Interim Chief Nurse Executive
Web address: www.southshorehospital.com
Control: Other not–for–profit (including NFP Corporation) **Service**: General medical and surgical

Staffed Beds: 136

☐ **ST. BERNARD HOSPITAL AND HEALTH CARE CENTER (140103)**, 326 West 64th Street, Zip 60621–3146; tel. 773/962–3900, (Nonreporting) **A**1 3 10
Primary Contact: Charles Holland, President and Chief Executive Officer
COO: Roland Abellera, Vice President and Chief Operating Officer
CFO: James P Porter, Chief Financial Officer
CNO: Evelyn Jones, R.N., Vice President Nursing Services
Web address: www.stbernardhospital.com
Control: Church operated, Nongovernment, not–for–profit **Service**: General medical and surgical

Staffed Beds: 100

SWEDISH HOSPITAL See Endeavor Health Swedish Hospital

○ **THOREK MEMORIAL HOSPITAL (140115)**, 850 West Irving Park Road, Zip 60613–3077; tel. 773/525–6780, (Nonreporting) **A**3 10 11
Primary Contact: Ned Budd, President and Chief Executive Officer
COO: Peter N Kamberos, Chief Operating Officer
CMO: Ilona Carlos, M.D., President Medical Staff
CIO: Tony Vavarutsos, Director Information Systems
CHR: Brett Wakefield, Director Human Resources
CNO: Mary McCahill, Chief Nursing Officer
Web address: www.thorek.org
Control: Other not–for–profit (including NFP Corporation) **Service**: General medical and surgical

Staffed Beds: 134

○ **THOREK MEMORIAL HOSPITAL ANDERSONVILLE (140197)**, 5025 North Paulina Street, Zip 60640–2772; tel. 773/271–9040, (Nonreporting) **A**10 11
Primary Contact: Ned Budd, President and Chief Executive Officer
CFO: Jim Gregory, Controller
Web address: https://thorekandersonville.org/
Control: Other not–for–profit (including NFP Corporation) **Service**: General medical and surgical

Staffed Beds: 189

UNIVERSITY OF CHICAGO COMER CHILDREN'S HOSPITAL See Comer Children's Hospital

Hospitals, U.S. / ILLINOIS

UNIVERSITY OF CHICAGO MEDICAL CENTER (140088), 5841 South Maryland Avenue, Zip 60637-1443; tel. 773/702-1000, (Includes BERNARD MITCHELL HOSPITAL, 5815 South Maryland Avenue, Chicago, Illinois, Zip 60637, 5841 S. Maryland Ave., Zip 60637, tel. 773/702-1000; Sharon L O'Keefe, President, University of Chicago Medical Center; CHICAGO LYING-IN (CLI), 5815 South Maryland Avenue, Chicago, Illinois, Zip 60637, 5841 South Maryland Avenue, Zip 60637, tel. 773/702-1000, Sharon L O'Keefe, President, University of Chicago Medical Center; COMER CHILDREN'S HOSPITAL, 5721 South Maryland Avenue, Chicago, Illinois, Zip 60637, 5841 South Maryland Avenue, Zip 60637, tel. 773/702-1000; Sharon L O'Keefe, President, University of Chicago Medical Center) **A**1 2 3 5 8 10 19 **F**3 5 6 9 11 12 13 14 15 16 17 18 19 20 21 22 23 24 25 26 27 28 29 30 31 32 34 35 36 37 38 39 40 41 43 44 45 46 47 48 49 50 51 52 54 55 56 57 58 59 60 61 64 65 66 68 70 71 72 73 74 75 76 77 78 79 81 82 83 84 85 86 87 88 89 92 93 97 100 101 102 104 107 108 109 110 111 112 113 114 115 116 117 118 119 120 121 123 124 126 129 130 131 132 134 135 136 137 138 139 140 141 142 143 144 145 146 147 148 149 150 154 156 157 160 162 163 164 166 167 168 169 **S** University of Chicago Medicine, Chicago, IL
Primary Contact: Thomas E. Jackiewicz, President
COO: Jason Keeler, Executive Vice President and Chief Operating Officer
CFO: Ivan Samstein, Executive Vice President and Chief Financial Officer
CMO: Stephen Weber, M.D., Senior Vice President Clinical Effectiveness and Chief Medical Officer
CHR: Bob Hanley, Senior Vice President and Chief Human Resources Officer
Web address: www.uchospitals.org
Control: Other not-for-profit (including NFP Corporation) **Service:** General medical and surgical

Staffed Beds: 758 **Admissions:** 34067 **Census:** 655 **Outpatient Visits:** 949373 **Births:** 2716 **Total Expense ($000):** 2609291 **Payroll Expense ($000):** 929272 **Personnel:** 14047

UNIVERSITY OF ILLINOIS HOSPITAL (140150), 1740 West Taylor Street, Zip 60612-7232; tel. 312/996-7000, **A**1 2 3 5 8 10 19 **F**3 5 9 12 13 15 18 19 20 21 22 23 24 25 26 29 30 31 32 34 35 37 38 39 40 41 45 46 47 48 49 50 51 52 54 55 56 57 58 59 60 61 64 65 66 68 70 72 74 75 76 77 78 79 81 82 84 85 86 87 88 89 91 92 93 96 97 98 99 100 101 102 104 107 108 110 111 112 114 115 116 117 118 119 120 121 123 124 126 129 130 131 132 134 135 136 138 139 141 142 145 146 147 148 149 150 153 154 156 157 160 161 164 165 167 169
Primary Contact: Mark Rosenblatt, M.D., Ph.D., Chief Executive Officer
COO: David Loffing, Chief Operating Officer
CMO: Bernard Pygon, M.D., Chief Medical Officer
CIO: Audrius Polikaitis, Chief Information Officer
Web address: www.hospital.uillinois.edu/
Control: State, Government, Nonfederal **Service:** General medical and surgical

Staffed Beds: 432 **Admissions:** 16285 **Census:** 313 **Outpatient Visits:** 710311 **Births:** 1971 **Total Expense ($000):** 1282834 **Payroll Expense ($000):** 469086 **Personnel:** 6034

☐ **WEISS MEMORIAL HOSPITAL (140082)**, 4646 North Marine Drive, Zip 60640-5759; tel. 773/878-8700, (Nonreporting) **A**1 3 5 10 19
Primary Contact: Manoj Prasad, M.D., Group Chief Executive Officer
CFO: Jeffrey L Meigs, Chief Financial Officer
CIO: Thomas Crawford, Chicago Market Chief Information Officer
CHR: Keoni Nader, Director Human Resources
Web address: www.weisshospital.com
Control: Corporation, Investor-owned (for-profit) **Service:** General medical and surgical

Staffed Beds: 152

CLINTON—De Witt County

WARNER HOSPITAL AND HEALTH SERVICES (141303), 422 West White Street, Zip 61727-2272; tel. 217/935-9571, (Nonreporting) **A**10 18
Primary Contact: Paul Skowron, Chief Executive Officer
CFO: Donna Wisner, Chief Financial Officer
CMO: Brit Williams, M.D., President Medical Staff
CIO: Larry Schleicher, Manager Information Services
CHR: Sarah Gerke, Manager Human Resources
CNO: Heidi Cook, Chief Nursing Officer
Web address: www.djwhospital.org
Control: City, Government, Nonfederal **Service:** General medical and surgical

Staffed Beds: 25

CRYSTAL LAKE—Mchenry County

MERCY CRYSTAL LAKE HOSPITAL AND MEDICAL CENTER See Mercyhealth Hospital and Physician Clinic-Crystal Lake

MERCYHEALTH HOSPITAL AND PHYSICIAN CLINIC–CRYSTAL LAKE (140308), 875 South Route 31, Zip 60014, Mailing Address: 901 Grant Street, Harvard, Zip 60033-1821; tel. 608/756-6559, (Nonreporting) **A**10 **S** Mercy Health System, Janesville, WI
Primary Contact: Javon R. Bea, President and Chief Executive Officer
COO: Jennifer Hallatt, Vice President
CFO: Todd Anderson, Chief Financial Officer
CIO: Ali Olia, Vice President
CHR: Alen Brcic, Vice President
CNO: Kara Sankey, Chief Nursing Officer
Web address: https://www.mercyhealthsystem.org/locations/mercyhealth-hospital-and-physician-clinic-crystal-lake/
Control: Other not-for-profit (including NFP Corporation) **Service:** General medical and surgical

Staffed Beds: 13

DANVILLE—Vermilion County

OSF SACRED HEART MEDICAL CENTER (140093), 812 North Logan Avenue, Zip 61832-3788; tel. 217/443-5000, **A**1 5 10 19 **F**3 13 15 18 20 26 28 29 30 31 35 40 45 46 47 48 49 59 60 64 70 74 75 76 78 79 81 82 87 89 92 93 94 96 97 102 107 108 110 111 114 115 118 119 120 121 122 123 124 129 130 132 134 146 147 148 154 **S** OSF Healthcare, Peoria, IL
Primary Contact: J. T. Barnhart, President
CFO: Lucas Morton, Regional Chief Financial Officer
CMO: Vincent Kucich, FACHE, FACS, M.D., Chief Medical Officer
CIO: Paula Keele, Manager Information Systems
CHR: Michael Zimmerman, Human Resource Officer
CNO: Deborah McCarter, R.N., MSN, Vice President and Chief Nursing Officer
Web address: https://www.osfhealthcare.org/sacred-heart/
Control: Church operated, Nongovernment, not-for-profit **Service:** General medical and surgical

Staffed Beds: 115 **Admissions:** 2788 **Census:** 31 **Outpatient Visits:** 65346 **Births:** 17 **Total Expense ($000):** 104705 **Payroll Expense ($000):** 29338 **Personnel:** 388

VETERANS AFFAIRS ILLIANA HEALTH CARE SYSTEM, 1900 East Main Street, Zip 61832-5198; tel. 217/554-3000, (Nonreporting) **A**1 3 5 **S** Department of Veterans Affairs, Washington, DC
Primary Contact: Staci Williams, PharmD, Medical Center Director
COO: Diana Carranza, Associate Director
CFO: Becky Tissier, Chief Fiscal Service
CMO: Khiem Tran, M.D., Acting Chief of Staff
CIO: Frank D. Jackson III, Facility Chief Information Officer
CHR: Connie Ohl, Acting Chief Human Resources
Web address: www.danville.va.gov/
Control: Veterans Affairs, Government, federal **Service:** General medical and surgical

Staffed Beds: 172

DECATUR—Macon County

△ **DECATUR MEMORIAL HOSPITAL (140135)**, 2300 North Edward Street, Zip 62526-4192; tel. 217/876-8121, **A**1 2 3 5 7 10 19 **F**3 8 11 13 15 17 18 20 22 26 28 29 30 31 32 33 34 35 37 40 43 44 45 46 47 48 49 50 51 54 56 57 58 59 60 61 62 63 64 65 68 69 70 71 74 75 76 77 78 79 81 82 84 85 86 87 89 91 92 93 94 96 97 102 104 107 108 110 111 114 115 116 117 118 119 120 121 123 124 126 129 130 131 132 135 144 145 146 147 148 149 154 156 167 169 **P**5 **S** Memorial Health, Springfield, IL
Primary Contact: Drew Early, President and Chief Executive Officer
COO: John Ridley, Executive Vice President & Chief Operating Officer
CFO: Deborah L. Bragg, Senior Vice President, Finance
CMO: Larry T Hegland, M.D., Chief Medical Officer
CHR: Kevin Horath, Vice President Human Resources
Web address: www.dmhcares.com
Control: Other not-for-profit (including NFP Corporation) **Service:** General medical and surgical

Staffed Beds: 171 **Admissions:** 6540 **Census:** 83 **Outpatient Visits:** 212134 **Births:** 925 **Total Expense ($000):** 365396 **Payroll Expense ($000):** 158240 **Personnel:** 1553

Hospitals, U.S. / ILLINOIS

HSHS ST. MARY'S HOSPITAL (140166), 1800 East Lake Shore Drive, Zip 62521–3883; tel. 217/464–2966, **A**1 5 7 10 **F**3 11 15 18 20 22 28 29 30 31 34 35 40 44 45 50 54 56 57 59 64 66 70 74 75 77 78 79 81 82 85 86 87 91 92 93 96 100 101 102 104 105 107 108 110 111 114 115 117 119 120 121 123 124 126 129 130 131 132 141 146 148 149 150 154 165 167 **S** HSHS Hospital Sisters Health System, Springfield, IL
Primary Contact: Matthew Fry, FACHE, President and Chief Executive Officer, Central Illinois Market
CMO: Phil Barnell, Chief Medical Officer
CHR: Melissa Tipton, Human Resource Director
CNO: Robyn Reising, R.N., Chief Nursing Officer
Web address: https://www.hshs.org/st-marys-decatur/
Control: Church operated, Nongovernment, not-for-profit **Service**: General medical and surgical

Staffed Beds: 102 **Admissions**: 4757 **Census**: 73 **Outpatient Visits**: 135931 **Births**: 367 **Total Expense ($000)**: 195955 **Payroll Expense ($000)**: 41754 **Personnel**: 413

DEKALB—DeKalb County

NORTHWESTERN MEDICINE KISHWAUKEE HOSPITAL (140286), 1 Kish Hospital Drive, Zip 60115–9602, Mailing Address: P.O. Box 707, Zip 60115–0707; tel. 815/756–1521, **A**1 2 10 **F**3 8 11 15 17 18 20 22 26 28 29 30 31 32 33 34 35 36 38 40 41 43 44 45 46 48 49 50 51 53 54 55 57 58 59 60 64 65 68 70 71 73 74 75 76 77 78 79 80 81 82 84 85 86 87 89 93 94 96 97 98 100 101 102 104 107 108 110 111 114 115 117 118 119 120 121 123 124 126 129 130 131 132 135 144 145 146 147 148 149 150 154 157 158 162 167 169 **S** Northwestern Memorial HealthCare, Chicago, IL
Primary Contact: Maura O'Toole, President
COO: Brad Copple, Vice President, Operations
CFO: John Orsini, Senior Vice President, Chief Financial Officer
CMO: Michael Kulisz, D.O., Chief Medical Officer
CIO: Carl Christensen, Senior Vice President, Chief Information Officer
CNO: Pamela Duffy, MSN, R.N., Vice President Operations and Chief Nursing Officer
Web address: www.nm.org
Control: Other not-for-profit (including NFP Corporation) **Service**: General medical and surgical

Staffed Beds: 98 **Admissions**: 6285 **Census**: 68 **Outpatient Visits**: 467519 **Births**: 753 **Total Expense ($000)**: 371860 **Payroll Expense ($000)**: 131140 **Personnel**: 1534

DES PLAINES—Cook County

AMITA HEALTH HOLY FAMILY MEDICAL CENTER See Ascension Holy Family

ASCENSION HOLY FAMILY (142011), 100 North River Road, Zip 60016–1255; tel. 847/297–1800, (Nonreporting) **A**1 10 **S** Ascension Healthcare, Saint Louis, MO
Primary Contact: Yolande Wilson–Stubbs, President
CFO: Gene Yakovenko, Director of Finance
CMO: David Bordo, M.D., Chief Medical Officer
CIO: David Lundal, Senior Vice President Information Systems and Chief Information Officer
CHR: Ivy McKinley, Director Human Resources
Web address: https://healthcare.ascension.org/locations/illinois/ilchi/des-plaines-ascension-holy-family
Control: Church operated, Nongovernment, not-for-profit **Service**: Acute long-term care hospital

Staffed Beds: 178

CHICAGO BEHAVIORAL HOSPITAL (144040), 555 Wilson Lane, Zip 60016–4729; tel. 847/768–5430, (Nonreporting) **A**1 3 10
Primary Contact: Gerald M. Cholewa, MSN, R.N., Chief Executive Officer
CMO: Shiraz Butt, M.D., Medical Director
CHR: Betty Barnes, Director Human Resources
CNO: Barbara Preib, Director of Nursing
Web address: www.maryvilleacademy.org
Control: Church operated, Nongovernment, not-for-profit **Service**: Children's hospital psychiatric

Staffed Beds: 138

DIXON—Lee County

★ **KATHERINE SHAW BETHEA HOSPITAL (140012)**, 403 East First Street, Zip 61021–3187; tel. 815/288–5531, **A**3 5 10 **F**3 11 13 15 18 20 22 28 29 30 34 35 38 39 40 44 45 46 47 50 54 56 57 59 61 62 64 65 69 70 74 75 76 79 81 82 84 85 86 87 89 91 92 93 94 96 97 98 101 102 104 107 108 110 111 115 119 129 130 131 132 135 145 146 147 149 150 154 156 157 162 164 169 **P**6
Primary Contact: David Schreiner, Ph.D., President and Chief Executive Officer
CFO: Michael Kittoe, Chief Financial Officer
CMO: Pratip Nag, Vice President, Chief Medical Officer
CIO: Ray Sharp, Chief Information Officer
CHR: Christy Pierce, Director of Human Resources
CNO: Linda Clemen, Vice President and Chief Nursing Officer
Web address: www.ksbhospital.com
Control: Other not-for-profit (including NFP Corporation) **Service**: General medical and surgical

Staffed Beds: 64 **Admissions**: 2714 **Census**: 31 **Outpatient Visits**: 242921 **Births**: 325 **Total Expense ($000)**: 152129 **Payroll Expense ($000)**: 68100 **Personnel**: 750

DOWNERS GROVE—Dupage County

★ **ADVOCATE GOOD SAMARITAN HOSPITAL (140288)**, 3815 Highland Avenue, Zip 60515–1590; tel. 630/275–5900, **A**2 5 10 21 **F**3 5 11 12 13 15 17 18 20 22 24 26 28 29 30 31 32 34 35 36 37 38 40 41 43 44 45 46 47 49 50 53 54 55 56 57 59 60 63 64 65 68 70 72 74 75 76 77 78 79 80 81 82 84 85 86 87 89 93 97 98 100 101 102 103 104 105 107 108 109 110 111 114 115 118 119 120 121 123 124 126 129 130 131 132 135 143 144 145 146 147 148 149 152 153 154 156 157 160 161 162 164 165 167 169 **P**1 6 **S** Advocate Aurora Health, Downers Grove, IL
Primary Contact: Eric Rhodes, President
COO: Sandi Churchill, Vice President Business Development and Operations, Professional Services
CFO: Mary Treacy–Shiff, Vice President Finance
CMO: Charles Derus, M.D., Vice President Medical Management
CHR: Elizabeth Calby, Vice President Human Resources
Web address: www.advocatehealth.com/gsam
Control: Church operated, Nongovernment, not-for-profit **Service**: General medical and surgical

Staffed Beds: 349 **Admissions**: 15225 **Census**: 194 **Outpatient Visits**: 185573 **Births**: 1928 **Total Expense ($000)**: 382979 **Payroll Expense ($000)**: 119241 **Personnel**: 1660

DU QUOIN—Perry County

MARSHALL BROWNING HOSPITAL (141331), 900 North Washington Street, Zip 62832–1233, Mailing Address: P.O. Box 192, Zip 62832–0192; tel. 618/542–2146, (Nonreporting) **A**1 10 18
Primary Contact: Dan Eaves, Chief Executive Officer
CFO: Brice Harsy, Chief Financial Officer
CIO: Brian Schandl, Chief Information Officer
CHR: Sarah J. Dickey, Human Resource Director
CNO: Laurie Kellerman, MSN, Chief Clinical Officer
Web address: www.marshallbrowninghospital.com
Control: Other not-for-profit (including NFP Corporation) **Service**: General medical and surgical

Staffed Beds: 25

EDWARDSVILLE—Madison County

ANDERSON REHABILITATION INSTITUTE (143029), 3402 Anderson Healthcare Drive, Zip 62025; tel. 618/685–6000, (Nonreporting) **A**1
Primary Contact: Melissa Newbold Welge, Chief Executive Officer
Web address: https://www.andersonrehabinstitute.com/
Control: Partnership, Investor–owned (for–profit) **Service**: Rehabilitation

Staffed Beds: 34

Hospital, Medicare Provider Number, Address, Telephone, Approval, Facility, and Physician Codes, Health Care System

★ American Hospital Association (AHA) membership
☐ The Joint Commission accreditation
○ Healthcare Facilities Accreditation Program
◇ DNV Healthcare Inc. accreditation
⇧ Center for Improvement in Healthcare Quality Accreditation
△ Commission on Accreditation of Rehabilitation Facilities (CARF) accreditation

Hospitals, U.S. / ILLINOIS

EFFINGHAM—Effingham County

HSHS ST. ANTHONY'S MEMORIAL HOSPITAL (140032), 503 North Maple Street, Zip 62401-2099; tel. 217/342-2121, **A**1 2 5 10 **F**3 11 13 15 18 20 28 29 31 32 34 35 37 40 44 50 54 57 59 62 63 64 68 70 75 76 79 81 82 84 85 87 89 93 94 96 107 108 110 111 115 119 126 129 130 131 132 144 146 147 154 167 **S** HSHS Hospital Sisters Health System, Springfield, IL
Primary Contact: Matthew Fry, FACHE, President and Chief Executive Officer, Central Illinois Market
CFO: Dave Storm, Director Business Support
CNO: Kelly Sage, Chief Nursing Officer
Web address: https://www.hshs.org/st-anthonys/
Control: Church operated, Nongovernment, not-for-profit **Service:** General medical and surgical

Staffed Beds: 133 **Admissions:** 3488 **Census:** 30 **Outpatient Visits:** 135276 **Births:** 668 **Total Expense ($000):** 156511 **Payroll Expense ($000):** 46023 **Personnel:** 601

ELDORADO—Saline County

★ ○ **FERRELL HOSPITAL (141324)**, 1201 Pine Street, Zip 62930-1634; tel. 618/273-3361, (Nonreporting) **A**10 11 18
Primary Contact: Tony Keene, Chief Executive Officer
CFO: Kevin Fowler, Chief Financial Officer
CMO: Nate Oldham, M.D., Chief Medical Officer
CHR: Caleigh Bruce, Director of Human Resources/Chief Compliance Officer
CNO: Rachael Prather, Chief Nursing Officer
Web address: www.ferrellhosp.org
Control: Other not-for-profit (including NFP Corporation) **Service:** General medical and surgical

Staffed Beds: 25

ELGIN—Kane County

★ ⇧ **ADVOCATE SHERMAN HOSPITAL (140030)**, 1425 North Randall Road, Zip 60123-2300; tel. 847/742-9800, **A**2 3 10 21 **F**3 11 12 13 15 18 20 22 24 26 28 29 30 31 34 35 38 40 41 43 45 46 47 48 49 50 54 55 57 59 64 65 68 70 71 73 74 75 76 77 78 79 81 82 84 85 87 89 92 93 100 102 107 108 110 111 114 115 116 117 118 119 120 121 124 126 129 130 132 135 144 146 147 148 149 154 156 164 165 167 169 **P**1 6 **S** Advocate Aurora Health, Downers Grove, IL
Primary Contact: Sheri De Shazo, R.N., FACHE, President
CMO: Bruce Hyman, M.D., Vice President Clinical Performance
CHR: Melissa O'Neill, Vice President Human Resources
Web address: www.advocatehealth.com/sherman
Control: Other not-for-profit (including NFP Corporation) **Service:** General medical and surgical

Staffed Beds: 271 **Admissions:** 11949 **Census:** 135 **Outpatient Visits:** 320684 **Births:** 1765 **Total Expense ($000):** 335981 **Payroll Expense ($000):** 99145 **Personnel:** 1413

AMITA HEALTH SAINT JOSEPH HOSPITAL See Ascension Saint Joseph – Elgin

ASCENSION SAINT JOSEPH – ELGIN (140217), 77 North Airlite Street, Zip 60123-4912; tel. 847/695-3200, (Nonreporting) **A**1 10 **S** Ascension Healthcare, Saint Louis, MO
Primary Contact: Eva Balderrama, President
COO: Laurie Schachtner, Director Operations
CFO: Kevin Larkin, Chief Financial Officer
CMO: Anandita Gephart, M.D., Chief Medical Officer
CHR: Michael O'Rourke, Regional Human Resources Director
CNO: Erica Bentley, Vice President Nursing
Web address: https://healthcare.ascension.org/locations/illinois/ilchi/elgin-ascension-saint-joseph
Control: Other not-for-profit (including NFP Corporation) **Service:** General medical and surgical

Staffed Beds: 184

☐ **ELGIN MENTAL HEALTH CENTER (144037)**, 750 South State Street, Zip 60123-7692; tel. 847/742-1040, **A**1 3 5 10 **F**29 30 38 39 50 51 56 57 65 68 87 98 101 130 132 143 162 163 164 **S** Division of Mental Health, Department of Human Services, Springfield, IL
Primary Contact: Michelle Evans, Administrator
CFO: Tajudeen Ibrahim, Interim Business Administrator
CMO: Malini Patel, M.D., Medical Director
CIO: Kelly Callahan, Public Information Officer
CHR: Darek Williams, Director Human Resources
Web address: www.dhs.state.il.us
Control: State, Government, Nonfederal **Service:** Psychiatric

Staffed Beds: 427 **Admissions:** 542 **Census:** 411 **Outpatient Visits:** 0 **Births:** 0 **Total Expense ($000):** 71000 **Personnel:** 559

ELK GROVE VILLAGE—Cook County

ALEXIAN REHABILITATION HOSPITAL See Amita Health Rehabilitation Hospital

AMITA HEALTH ALEXIAN BROTHERS MEDICAL CENTER ELK GROVE VILLAGE See Ascension Alexian Brothers

ASCENSION ALEXIAN BROTHERS (140258), 800 Biesterfield Road, Zip 60007-3397; tel. 847/437-5500, (Includes AMITA HEALTH REHABILITATION HOSPITAL, 935 Beisner Road, Elk Grove Village, Illinois, Zip 60007, tel. 847/640-5600; John Dunkin, Executive Director) (Nonreporting) **A**1 2 3 5 10 19 **S** Ascension Healthcare, Saint Louis, MO
Primary Contact: Dan Doherty, Chief Executive Officer
COO: Laurence Dry, Chief Operating Officer, Acute Care Hospitals Northern Region
CFO: Henry Zeisel, Chief Financial Officer, Northern Region
CIO: Sherrie Russell, Senior Vice President & Chief Information Officer
CHR: Donald Russell, Senior Vice President and Chief Human Resources Officer
CNO: Chris Budzinsky, Vice President, Nursing and Chief Nursing Officer
Web address: https://healthcare.ascension.org/locations/illinois/ilchi/elk-grove-village-ascension-alexian-brothers
Control: Church operated, Nongovernment, not-for-profit **Service:** General medical and surgical

Staffed Beds: 376

ELMHURST—Dupage County

ELMHURST HOSPITAL See Endeavor Health Elmhurst Hospital

ENDEAVOR HEALTH ELMHURST HOSPITAL (140200), 155 East Brush Hill Road, Zip 60126-5658; tel. 331/221-1000, **A**1 2 3 5 10 **F**3 12 13 15 18 19 20 22 24 26 28 29 30 31 34 35 36 37 38 39 40 41 43 44 45 46 47 48 49 50 54 55 57 58 59 61 63 64 65 70 73 74 75 76 77 78 79 81 82 84 85 86 87 91 92 93 96 97 99 100 101 102 103 107 108 110 111 115 117 119 120 121 123 124 126 129 130 131 132 135 141 144 146 147 148 149 154 156 167 169 **P**3 6 8 **S** Endeavor Health, Evanston, IL
Primary Contact: Kimberley Darey, Chief Executive Officer
CMO: Ankur Singal, M.D., Chief Medical Officer
CHR: Robert Blazek, System Director, Human Resources Business Partners
CNO: Jean Lydon, MS, R.N., System Vice President Operations, Chief Nursing Officer
Web address: www.eehealth.org
Control: Other not-for-profit (including NFP Corporation) **Service:** General medical and surgical

Staffed Beds: 268 **Admissions:** 20010 **Census:** 222 **Outpatient Visits:** 626182 **Births:** 2907 **Total Expense ($000):** 475192 **Payroll Expense ($000):** 186179 **Personnel:** 2583

EUREKA—Woodford County

★ ⇧ **CARLE EUREKA HOSPITAL (141309)**, 101 South Major Street, Zip 61530-1246; tel. 309/467-2371, **A**10 18 21 **F**3 15 18 28 29 30 34 35 40 44 45 50 56 57 59 64 65 67 75 77 78 79 81 82 85 86 87 90 93 97 107 108 110 111 114 119 127 128 130 132 133 143 144 146 149 156 157 **S** Carle Health, Urbana, IL
Primary Contact: Anna Laible, Administrator
CFO: Aron Klein, Vice President of Finance
CMO: Steven K Jones, M.D., Medical Director
CIO: David Harper, Director, Site Information Systems
CHR: Antonio Coletta, Vice President Human Resources
CNO: Nancy Allen, R.N., MS, Director, Patient Services and Chief Nursing Executive
Web address: https://carle.org/locations/carle-eureka-hospital
Control: Other not-for-profit (including NFP Corporation) **Service:** General medical and surgical

Staffed Beds: 18 **Admissions:** 278 **Census:** 4 **Outpatient Visits:** 57689 **Births:** 0 **Total Expense ($000):** 27370 **Payroll Expense ($000):** 13892 **Personnel:** 117

EVANSTON—Cook County

AMITA HEALTH SAINT FRANCIS HOSPITAL EVANSTON See Ascension Saint Francis

ASCENSION SAINT FRANCIS (140080), 355 Ridge Avenue, Zip 60202-3399; tel. 847/316-4000, (Nonreporting) **A**1 2 3 5 10 19 **S** Ascension Healthcare, Saint Louis, MO
Primary Contact: Kendall Johnson, Interim Chief Executive Officer
CMO: David DiLoreto, M.D., Executive Vice President and Chief Medical Officer
CIO: George Chessum, Vice President Information Systems
CHR: Paul Skiem, Senior Vice President Human Resources
Web address: https://healthcare.ascension.org/locations/illinois/ilchi/evanston-ascension-saint-francis
Control: Church operated, Nongovernment, not-for-profit **Service:** General medical and surgical

Staffed Beds: 197

Hospitals, U.S. / ILLINOIS

☒ **ENDEAVOR HEALTH EVANSTON HOSPITAL (140010)**, 2650 Ridge Avenue, Zip 60201-1613; tel. 847/570-2000; (Includes ENDEAVOR HEALTH SKOKIE HOSPITAL, 9600 Gross Point Road, Skokie, Illinois, Zip 60076-1257, tel. 847/677-9600; Gustav E. Granchalek, President; NORTHSHORE EVANSTON HOSPITAL, 2650 Ridge Avenue, Evanston, Illinois, Zip 60201-1797, tel. 847/570-2000; Gabrielle Cummings, President; NORTHSHORE GLENBROOK HOSPITAL, 2100 Pfingsten Road, Glenview, Illinois, Zip 60025, tel. 847/657-5800; Maria Knecht, R.N., MSN, President; NORTHSHORE HIGHLAND PARK HOSPITAL, 718 Glenview Avenue, Highland Park, Illinois, Zip 60035-2497, tel. 847/432-8000; Nicole Fernandez, R.N., MS, President) **A**1 2 3 5 10 19 **F**3 5 6 9 11 12 13 14 15 17 18 20 22 24 26 28 29 30 31 32 34 35 36 37 38 39 40 43 44 45 46 47 48 49 50 51 54 55 56 57 58 59 60 61 64 65 66 68 70 72 74 75 76 77 78 79 81 82 84 85 86 87 89 91 92 93 96 97 98 99 100 101 102 103 104 105 107 108 110 111 114 115 116 117 118 119 120 121 123 124 126 129 130 131 132 134 135 136 141 144 145 146 147 148 149 152 153 154 156 157 160 162 164 165 167 169 **P**4 5 **S** Endeavor Health, Evanston, IL
Primary Contact: Gabrielle Cummings, President
CFO: Doug Welday, Chief Financial Officer
CIO: Steven Smith, Chief Information Officer
CHR: Bill Luehrs, Chief Human Resources Officer
CNO: Nancy Semerdjian, R.N., Chief Nursing Officer
Web address: www.northshore.org
Control: Other not-for-profit (including NFP Corporation) Service: General medical and surgical

Staffed Beds: 705 **Admissions:** 38835 **Census:** 442 **Outpatient Visits:** 1744181 **Births:** 4710 **Total Expense ($000):** 1864426 **Payroll Expense ($000):** 741652 **Personnel:** 9341

EVANSTON HOSPITAL See Endeavor Health Evanston Hospital

EVANSTON HOSPITAL See Northshore Evanston Hospital

EVERGREEN PARK—Cook County

☒ **OSF HEALTHCARE LITTLE COMPANY OF MARY MEDICAL CENTER (140179)**, 2800 West 95th Street, Zip 60805-2795; tel. 708/229-5270, **A**1 2 3 5 10 19 **F**3 5 11 12 13 15 18 22 26 29 30 31 34 35 38 40 45 46 47 49 50 54 56 57 59 60 62 63 64 65 70 72 74 75 76 77 78 79 81 82 83 84 85 86 87 92 93 94 100 101 102 104 105 107 108 110 111 114 115 119 120 121 124 126 129 130 131 132 133 135 146 147 148 149 150 152 153 154 156 157 160 162 167 169 **P**1 **S** OSF Healthcare, Peoria, IL
Primary Contact: Kathleen Kinsella, President
COO: Mary Freyer, Chief Operating Officer
CFO: Robert Tarola, Chief Financial Officer
CMO: Kent A W Armbruster, M.D., Vice President Medical Affairs
CIO: Darryl Mazzuca, Director Management Information Systems
CHR: Colleen M. Rohan, Director Human Resources
Web address: https://www.osfhealthcare.org/little-company-of-mary/
Control: Other not-for-profit (including NFP Corporation) Service: General medical and surgical

Staffed Beds: 217 **Admissions:** 10059 **Census:** 130 **Outpatient Visits:** 169555 **Births:** 961 **Total Expense ($000):** 288217 **Payroll Expense ($000):** 94743 **Personnel:** 1022

FAIRFIELD—Wayne County

☒ **FAIRFIELD MEMORIAL HOSPITAL (141311)**, 303 NW 11th Street, Zip 62837-1203; tel. 618/842-2611, (Total facility includes 30 beds in nursing home-type unit) **A**1 10 18 **F**3 11 15 28 29 30 34 35 38 40 43 50 57 59 64 69 70 71 75 77 79 81 82 85 87 92 93 97 104 107 119 127 128 133 146 153 156 164
Primary Contact: Mike Cooper, Chief Executive Officer
COO: Dana Shantel Taylor, Chief Operating Officer
CFO: Amy Marsh, Chief Financial Officer
CMO: Wesley Thompson, M.D., President Medical Staff
CIO: Brad August, Director Information Systems
CHR: Jill VanHyning, Director of Human Resources
CNO: Christina Baker, Chief Nursing Officer
Web address: www.fairfieldmemorial.org
Control: Other not-for-profit (including NFP Corporation) Service: General medical and surgical

Staffed Beds: 59 **Admissions:** 663 **Census:** 24 **Outpatient Visits:** 299056 **Births:** 0 **Total Expense ($000):** 55246 **Payroll Expense ($000):** 23568 **Personnel:** 336

FLORA—Clay County

☒ **CLAY COUNTY HOSPITAL (141351)**, 911 Stacy Burk Drive, Zip 62839-3241, Mailing Address: P.O. Box 280, Zip 62839-0280; tel. 618/662-2131, (Nonreporting) **A**1 10 18 **S** SSM Health, Saint Louis, MO
Primary Contact: Robert R. Sellers, President
COO: Jamie Veach, Chief Operating Officer
CFO: Mike Hobbs, Chief Financial Officer
CMO: Colleen Murphy, M.D., Chief of Staff
CIO: Phil Bute, Manager Information Technology
CHR: Chelsea Musgrave, Director of Human Resources
Web address: www.claycountyhospital.org
Control: County, Government, Nonfederal Service: General medical and surgical

Staffed Beds: 20

FOREST PARK—Cook County

☐ **RIVEREDGE HOSPITAL (144009)**, 8311 West Roosevelt Road, Zip 60130-2500; tel. 708/771-7000, (Nonreporting) **A**1 3 10 **S** Universal Health Services, Inc., King of Prussia, PA
Primary Contact: Allison Davenport, Chief Executive Officer
COO: Joseph Baw, Chief Operating Officer
CFO: Anne Kim, Chief Financial Officer
CMO: Aamir Safdar, M.D., Chief Medical Officer
CIO: Jocelyn Zavala, Senior Information Technology Coordinator
CHR: Joseph Rinke, Director of Human Resources
Web address: www.riveredgehospital.com
Control: Corporation, Investor-owned (for-profit) Service: Psychiatric

Staffed Beds: 210

FREEPORT—Stephenson County

★ **FHN MEMORIAL HOSPITAL (140160)**, 1045 West Stephenson Street, Zip 61032-4899; tel. 815/599-6000, **A**10 19 **F**3 14 15 18 20 22 28 29 30 31 34 35 40 44 45 49 50 55 57 58 59 63 64 66 70 73 74 75 76 77 78 79 81 84 85 86 87 89 93 94 97 107 108 109 110 111 114 118 119 120 121 123 126 129 130 146 147 149 150 154 156 167 169 **P**6
Primary Contact: Mark Gridley, FACHE, President and Chief Executive Officer
COO: Kathryn J Martinez, Chief Operating Officer and Chief Nursing Officer
CFO: Michael Clark, Executive Vice President and Chief Financial Officer
CMO: Keith Martin, M.D., Chief Medical Officer
CIO: Mike Williams, Chief Information Officer
CHR: Leonard M Carter, Chief Human Resources Officer
CNO: Kathryn J Martinez, Chief Operating Officer and Chief Nursing Officer
Web address: www.fhn.org
Control: Other not-for-profit (including NFP Corporation) Service: General medical and surgical

Staffed Beds: 100 **Admissions:** 3189 **Census:** 37 **Outpatient Visits:** 99120 **Births:** 251 **Total Expense ($000):** 140140 **Payroll Expense ($000):** 44271 **Personnel:** 525

GALENA—Jo Daviess County

★ **MIDWEST MEDICAL CENTER (141302)**, 1 Medical Center Drive, Zip 61036-8118; tel. 815/777-1340, (Nonreporting) **A**10 18
Primary Contact: Tracy Bauer, Chief Executive Officer
COO: Steve Busch, Chief Operating Officer
CMO: Grant Westenfelder, M.D., Chief Medical Officer
CHR: Melissa Conley, Director Human Resources
Web address: www.midwestmedicalcenter.org
Control: Other not-for-profit (including NFP Corporation) Service: General medical and surgical

Staffed Beds: 25

Hospital, Medicare Provider Number, Address, Telephone, Approval, Facility, and Physician Codes, Health Care System

★ American Hospital Association (AHA) membership
☐ The Joint Commission accreditation
○ Healthcare Facilities Accreditation Program
◇ DNV Healthcare Inc. accreditation
⑪ Center for Improvement in Healthcare Quality Accreditation
△ Commission on Accreditation of Rehabilitation Facilities (CARF) accreditation

Hospitals, U.S. / ILLINOIS

GALESBURG—Knox County

✠ **OSF ST. MARY MEDICAL CENTER (140064)**, 3333 North Seminary Street, Zip 61401–1299; tel. 309/344–3161, **A**1 10 **F**3 11 13 15 18 26 28 29 30 32 34 35 40 44 45 46 49 50 51 53 56 57 59 60 64 65 70 75 76 79 81 82 84 85 87 91 92 93 96 102 107 108 110 111 118 119 127 129 130 131 132 146 149 154 169 **S** OSF Healthcare, Peoria, IL
Primary Contact: Lisa DeKezel, R.N., President
COO: Don Shadensack, Vice President Clinical Services
CFO: Curt Lipe, Vice President, Chief Financial Officer
CMO: Clifford G Martin, M.D., Regional Vice President and Chief Medical Officer
CIO: Becky Lynch, Manager Business Entity Management and Information Systems
CHR: Jenny Jacobs, Director Human Resources
Web address: www.osfstmary.org
Control: Church operated, Nongovernment, not–for–profit **Service**: General medical and surgical

Staffed Beds: 83 **Admissions**: 3910 **Census**: 41 **Outpatient Visits**: 135996 **Births**: 607 **Total Expense ($000)**: 127164 **Payroll Expense ($000)**: 45413 **Personnel**: 606

GENESEO—Henry County

★ ⇑ **HAMMOND–HENRY HOSPITAL (141319)**, 600 North College Avenue, Zip 61254–1099; tel. 309/944–6431, (Nonreporting) **A**10 18 21 **S** Ovation Healthcare, Brentwood, TN
Primary Contact: David Smith, Chief Executive Officer
CFO: Jodie Criswell, Vice President of Fiscal Services
CIO: Heather Henry, Information Technology Manager
CHR: Hazel Butter, Manager Human Resources
Web address: www.hammondhenry.com
Control: Hospital district or authority, Government, Nonfederal **Service**: General medical and surgical

Staffed Beds: 61

GENEVA—Kane County

✠ **NORTHWESTERN MEDICINE DELNOR HOSPITAL (140211)**, 300 Randall Road, Zip 60134–4200; tel. 630/208–3000, **A**1 2 3 5 10 **F**3 11 12 13 15 17 18 20 22 26 28 29 30 31 33 34 35 36 37 38 39 40 41 43 44 45 46 47 48 49 50 51 53 55 57 59 62 64 65 68 70 73 74 75 76 77 78 79 81 82 84 85 86 87 89 92 93 94 96 97 100 101 102 104 105 107 108 110 111 114 115 116 117 118 119 120 121 123 126 130 131 132 135 146 147 148 149 153 154 156 157 167 169 **S** Northwestern Memorial HealthCare, Chicago, IL
Primary Contact: Emily Cochran. Jakacki, President
COO: Michael B Johnson, Vice President, Operations
CFO: Matt Flynn, Vice President/Chief Finanicial Officer
CMO: Mark Daniels, M.D., Vice President/Chief Medical Officer
CIO: Doug King, Senior Vice President and Chief Information Officer
CNO: Gina Reid Tinio, M.P.H., MS, Ph.D., Vice President, Chief Nurse Executive
Web address: www.nm.org
Control: Other not–for–profit (including NFP Corporation) **Service**: General medical and surgical

Staffed Beds: 159 **Admissions**: 10138 **Census**: 110 **Outpatient Visits**: 660424 **Births**: 1320 **Total Expense ($000)**: 565874 **Payroll Expense ($000)**: 193385 **Personnel**: 1837

GIBSON CITY—Ford County

★ ⇑ **GIBSON AREA HOSPITAL AND HEALTH SERVICES (141317)**, 1120 North Melvin Street, Zip 60936–1477, Mailing Address: P.O. Box 429, Zip 60936–0429; tel. 217/784–4251, (Total facility includes 37 beds in nursing home–type unit) **A**3 10 18 21 **F**3 5 7 9 11 13 15 18 28 29 31 37 39 40 44 45 46 50 53 56 59 64 65 69 70 71 74 75 76 77 78 79 81 82 85 87 89 92 93 96 97 100 102 104 107 108 110 111 115 119 124 126 127 128 129 130 131 132 133 135 143 144 146 147 148 149 154 156 160 162 167 169 **P**8 **S** Alliant Management Services, Louisville, KY
Primary Contact: Robert C. Schmitt II, CPA, FACHE, Chief Executive Officer
COO: Robin Rose, R.N., Chief Operating and Clinical Officer
CFO: Matthew Ertel, Chief Financial Officer
CMO: Mark Spangler, M.D., Chief Medical Officer
CHR: Ty Royal, Executive Director of Human Resources and Support Services
CNO: Barb Meyer, Executive Director of Nursing
Web address: www.gibsonhospital.org
Control: Other not–for–profit (including NFP Corporation) **Service**: General medical and surgical

Staffed Beds: 65 **Admissions**: 847 **Census**: 35 **Outpatient Visits**: 177916 **Births**: 241 **Total Expense ($000)**: 154756 **Payroll Expense ($000)**: 70995 **Personnel**: 937

GLENDALE HEIGHTS—DuPage County

ADVENTHEALTH GLENOAKS See Uchicago Medicine Adventhealth Glenoaks

✠ **UCHICAGO MEDICINE ADVENTHEALTH GLENOAKS (140292)**, 701 Winthrop Avenue, Zip 60139–1403; tel. 630/545–8000, **A**1 10 **F**3 5 15 18 20 22 24 26 29 31 34 35 40 41 43 44 45 47 48 49 50 51 56 57 59 64 68 70 73 74 75 77 78 79 81 82 86 87 91 93 97 98 100 101 102 103 105 107 108 110 111 114 119 126 130 132 135 146 148 149 150 152 154 157 160 161 164 167 **S** AdventHealth, Altamonte Springs, FL
Primary Contact: Vladimir Radivojevic, President and Chief Executive Officer
CMO: Richard Carroll, M.D., Vice President and Chief Medical Officer
CIO: Sherrie Russell, AMITA Health Senior Vice President and Chief Information Officer
CHR: Donald Russell, AMITA Health Senior Vice President and Chief Human Resources Officer
CNO: Suzette Mahneke, Associate Vice President of Nursing
Web address: https://www.uchicagomedicineadventhealth.org/uchicago-medicine-adventhealth-glenoaks
Control: Church operated, Nongovernment, not–for–profit **Service**: General medical and surgical

Staffed Beds: 143 **Admissions**: 4686 **Census**: 74 **Outpatient Visits**: 42280 **Births**: 142 **Total Expense ($000)**: 126106 **Payroll Expense ($000)**: 45938 **Personnel**: 643

GLENVIEW—Cook County

NORTHSHORE GLENBROOK HOSPITAL See Endeavor Health Evanston Hospital, Evanston

NORTHSHORE UNIVERSITY HEALTHSYSTEM–GLENBROOK HOSPITAL See Northshore Glenbrook Hospital

GRANITE CITY—Madison County

☐ **GATEWAY REGIONAL MEDICAL CENTER (140125)**, 2100 Madison Avenue, Zip 62040–4799; tel. 618/798–3000, (Nonreporting) **A**1 10 **S** American Healthcare Systems, Glendale, CA
Primary Contact: Aundrea Styles, R.N., Chief Executive Officer
COO: Michelle Waller, MSN, R.N., Chief Clinical and Operations Officer
CFO: Edward Maszak, Chief Financial Officer
CMO: George Mehjian, M.D., Chief Medical Officer
CIO: Dennis Kampwerth, Director Management Information Systems
CHR: Robert Boyd, Chief Human Resource Officer
CNO: Sam R White, Chief Nursing Officer
Web address: www.gatewayregional.net
Control: Corporation, Investor–owned (for–profit) **Service**: General medical and surgical

Staffed Beds: 127

GREENVILLE—Bond County

★ ○ **HSHS HOLY FAMILY HOSPITAL IN GREENVILLE (140137)**, 200 Healthcare Drive, Zip 62246–1154; tel. 618/664–1230, **A**10 11 **F**8 11 15 18 28 29 30 34 35 40 45 49 50 56 57 59 64 79 81 85 87 89 90 93 94 97 107 110 111 114 119 125 127 131 133 144 146 147 149 154 156 158 167 **S** HSHS Hospital Sisters Health System, Springfield, IL
Primary Contact: Chris Klay, FACHE, President and Chief Executive Officer, Southern Illinois Market
CFO: Mark S Ennen, Director of Finance
CHR: Vicki Kloeckner, Director Human Resources
CNO: Lorna Keaster, Interim Chief Nursing Officer
Web address: https://www.hshs.org/holy-family
Control: Church operated, Nongovernment, not–for–profit **Service**: General medical and surgical

Staffed Beds: 28 **Admissions**: 490 **Census**: 6 **Outpatient Visits**: 38919 **Births**: 0 **Total Expense ($000)**: 28979 **Payroll Expense ($000)**: 6298 **Personnel**: 87

HARRISBURG—Saline County

HARRISBURG MEDICAL CENTER (140210), 100 Dr Warren Tuttle Drive, Zip 62946-2718, Mailing Address: P.O. Box 428, Zip 62946-0428; tel. 618/253-7671, **A**1 10 20 **F**3 11 15 18 28 29 30 34 35 40 45 49 56 57 59 60 64 68 74 75 77 78 79 81 82 84 85 87 91 93 94 97 98 100 101 102 104 105 106 107 108 110 111 114 115 118 119 127 130 131 133 146 149 154 156 **S** Southern Illinois Healthcare, Carbondale, IL
Primary Contact: Rodney Smith, Vice President and Administrator
CFO: Warren Ladner, Senior Vice President, Chief Financial Officer
CMO: Marci Moore-Connelly, M.D., Senior Vice President, Chief Medical Officer
CIO: Denao Ruttino, Vice President, Chief Information Officer
CHR: Dorene L Ewell, Director of Human Resources and Development
CNO: Tera Lannom, Chief Nurse Executive
Web address: www.harrisburgmc.com
Control: Other not-for-profit (including NFP Corporation) **Service**: General medical and surgical

Staffed Beds: 77 **Admissions**: 1343 **Census**: 19 **Outpatient Visits**: 24737 **Births**: 0 **Total Expense ($000)**: 56031 **Payroll Expense ($000)**: 23043 **Personnel**: 374

HARVARD—Mchenry County

MERCYHEALTH HOSPITAL AND MEDICAL CENTER – HARVARD (141335), 901 Grant Street, Zip 60033-1898, Mailing Address: P.O. Box 850, Zip 60033-0850; tel. 815/943-5431, (Nonreporting) **A**1 10 18 **S** Mercy Health System, Janesville, WI
Primary Contact: Javon R. Bea, President and Chief Executive Officer
COO: Jennifer Hallatt, Chief Operating Officer
CFO: Shannon Dunphy-Alexander, Director
CMO: Tawfik Barakat, M.D., President, Medical Staff
CHR: Heather Niles, Director Human Resources Operations
CNO: Caryn Lynn Oleston, FACHE, MSN, R.N., Chief Nursing Officer
Web address: https://www.mercyhealthsystem.org/locations/mercyhealth-hospital-and-medical-center-harvard/
Control: Other not-for-profit (including NFP Corporation) **Service**: General medical and surgical

Staffed Beds: 58

HARVEY—Cook County

INGALLS MEMORIAL HOSPITAL See Uchicago Medicine Ingalls Memorial

UCHICAGO MEDICINE INGALLS MEMORIAL (140191), 1 Ingalls Drive, Zip 60426-3591; tel. 708/333-2300, (Nonreporting) **A**2 3 5 10 21 **S** University of Chicago Medicine, Chicago, IL
Primary Contact: Michael A. Antoniades, President
COO: Michael L Hicks, Senior Vice President and Chief Operating Officer
CFO: Michael Lawrence, Chief Financial Officer
Web address: https://www.uchicagomedicine.org/find-a-location/uchicago-medicine-at-ingalls-harvey
Control: Other not-for-profit (including NFP Corporation) **Service**: General medical and surgical

Staffed Beds: 288

HAVANA—Mason County

MASON DISTRICT HOSPITAL (141313), 615 North Promenade Street, Zip 62644-1243, Mailing Address: P.O. Box 530, Zip 62644-0530; tel. 309/543-4431, (Nonreporting) **A**1 10 18
Primary Contact: Dana Adcock, Chief Executive Officer
CMO: Tad A. Yetter, M.D., President Medical Staff
CIO: Aaron Coots, Information Technology Director
CHR: Anne Davis, Director Human Resources
CNO: Rhonda Hine, R.N., Interim Chief Nursing Executive
Web address: www.masondistricthospital.org
Control: Hospital district or authority, Government, Nonfederal **Service**: General medical and surgical

Staffed Beds: 20

HAZEL CREST—Cook County

★ **ADVOCATE SOUTH SUBURBAN HOSPITAL (140250)**, 17800 South Kedzie Avenue, Zip 60429-0989; tel. 708/799-8000, **A**2 10 **F**3 4 11 15 18 20 22 24 26 28 29 30 31 34 35 36 40 44 45 46 47 49 51 53 55 57 59 60 63 64 68 70 72 75 77 78 79 81 82 84 85 87 89 92 93 98 100 101 102 103 105 107 108 110 111 114 115 118 119 126 130 132 145 146 147 148 149 153 154 156 157 164 165 167 **P**1 6 **S** Advocate Aurora Health, Downers Grove, IL
Primary Contact: Michelle Y. Blakely, Ph.D., FACHE, President
COO: Karen Clark, MS, R.N., Vice President Operations
CFO: Brian Kelly, Vice President Finance
CMO: Richard Multack, D.O., Vice President Medical Management
CIO: Beth Turek, Site Manager Information Systems
CHR: Kristin Landini, Vice President Human Resources
CNO: Sharon A. Otten, Vice President Nursing
Web address: www.advocatehealth.com/ssub/
Control: Church operated, Nongovernment, not-for-profit **Service**: General medical and surgical

Staffed Beds: 217 **Admissions**: 8189 **Census**: 109 **Outpatient Visits**: 159820 **Births**: 0 **Total Expense ($000)**: 279576 **Payroll Expense ($000)**: 74294 **Personnel**: 1144

HERRIN—Williamson County

HERRIN HOSPITAL (140011), 201 South 14th Street, Zip 62948-3631; tel. 618/942-2171, **A**1 5 10 **F**3 11 12 18 28 29 30 34 35 38 40 45 47 49 51 54 56 57 59 60 64 68 70 74 75 77 78 79 81 82 84 85 86 87 90 92 93 100 107 108 111 114 115 119 126 130 131 132 135 143 146 148 149 154 156 160 167 **S** Southern Illinois Healthcare, Carbondale, IL
Primary Contact: Rodney Smith, Vice President and Administrator
CFO: Michael Kasser, Chief Financial Officer
CMO: Michelle Jenkins, M.D., President Medical Staff
CIO: David Holland, Chief Information Officer
CHR: Teresa A Lovellette, Manager Human Resources
Web address: www.sih.net
Control: Other not-for-profit (including NFP Corporation) **Service**: General medical and surgical

Staffed Beds: 114 **Admissions**: 5384 **Census**: 85 **Outpatient Visits**: 177602 **Births**: 0 **Total Expense ($000)**: 158389 **Payroll Expense ($000)**: 57000 **Personnel**: 994

HIGHLAND—Madison County

HSHS ST. JOSEPH'S HOSPITAL See HSHS St. Joseph's Hospital Highland

HSHS ST. JOSEPH'S HOSPITAL HIGHLAND (141336), 12866 Troxler Avenue, Zip 62249-1698; tel. 618/651-2600, **A**1 10 18 **F**3 11 15 28 29 30 34 35 37 40 41 44 45 47 49 51 57 59 64 67 75 79 81 84 86 87 93 97 107 108 110 111 114 119 124 126 129 130 131 133 143 146 147 154 156 157 167 **S** HSHS Hospital Sisters Health System, Springfield, IL
Primary Contact: Chris Klay, FACHE, President and Chief Executive Officer, Southern Illinois Market
COO: Teresa Cornelius, R.N., Chief Operating Officer and Chief Nursing Officer
CFO: David Nosacka, Southern Illinois Division Chief Financial Officer
CHR: Christie Silvey, Director People Services
CNO: Teresa Cornelius, R.N., Chief Operating Officer and Chief Nursing Officer
Web address: https://www.hshs.org/st-josephs-highland
Control: Church operated, Nongovernment, not-for-profit **Service**: General medical and surgical

Staffed Beds: 25 **Admissions**: 1349 **Census**: 17 **Outpatient Visits**: 60119 **Births**: 0 **Total Expense ($000)**: 45210 **Payroll Expense ($000)**: 12134 **Personnel**: 165

HIGHLAND PARK—Lake County

NORTHSHORE HIGHLAND PARK HOSPITAL See Endeavor Health Evanston Hospital, Evanston

NORTHSHORE UNIVERSITY HEALTHSYSTEM–HIGHLAND PARK HOSPITAL See Northshore Highland Park Hospital

Hospitals, U.S. / ILLINOIS

HILLSBORO—Montgomery County

★ ⇧ **HILLSBORO AREA HOSPITAL (141332)**, 1200 East Tremont Street, Zip 62049–1900; tel. 217/532–6111, (Nonreporting) **A**10 18 21 **S** HealthTech Management Services, Plano, TX
Primary Contact: Michael Alexander, FACHE, Chief Executive Officer
CFO: Terri L Carroll, Vice President Financial Services
CHR: Sharon Clark, Director Human Resources
Web address: www.hillsborohealth.org
Control: Other not–for–profit (including NFP Corporation) **Service:** General medical and surgical

Staffed Beds: 25

HINES—Cook County

△ **EDWARD HINES, JR. VETERANS AFFAIRS HOSPITAL**, 5000 South Fifth Avenue, Zip 60141–3030, Mailing Address: P.O. Box 5000, Zip 60141–5000; tel. 708/202–8387, (Nonreporting) **A**1 2 3 5 7 **S** Department of Veterans Affairs, Washington, DC
Primary Contact: James Doelling, Hospital Director
CFO: Yolanda Martinez, Chief Fiscal Services
CMO: Jack Bulmash, M.D., Chief of Staff
CIO: Robert Tanjuakio, Chief Information Resources Management
CNO: Marianne Locke, R.N., MSN, Associate Director Patient Care Services
Web address: www.hines.va.gov/
Control: Veterans Affairs, Government, federal **Service:** General medical and surgical

Staffed Beds: 157

JOHN J. MADDEN MENTAL HEALTH CENTER (144028), 1200 South First Avenue, Zip 60141–0800; tel. 708/338–7202, (Nonreporting) **A**1 3 5 10 **S** Division of Mental Health, Department of Human Services, Springfield, IL
Primary Contact: Patricia Hudson, Administrator
CFO: Janice Evans, Chief Financial Officer
Control: State, Government, Nonfederal **Service:** Psychiatric

Staffed Beds: 125

HINSDALE—DuPage County

ADVENTHEALTH HINSDALE See Uchicago Medicine Adventhealth Hinsdale

RML SPECIALTY HOSPITAL (142010), 5601 South County Line Road, Zip 60521–4875; tel. 630/286–4000, (Includes RML SPECIALTY HOSPITAL, 3435 West Van Buren Street, Chicago, Illinois, Zip 60624–3312, tel. 773/826–6300; James R. Prister, President and Chief Executive Officer) **A**1 3 5 10 **F**1 3 18 29 30 45 53 58 65 74 85 87 100 107 114 115 119 130 148 149 **P**6
Primary Contact: James R. Prister, President and Chief Executive Officer
COO: Ken Pawola, Chief Operating Officer
CFO: Tom Pater, Chief Financial Officer
CMO: John Brofman, M.D., Chief Medical Officer
CIO: Todd Prellberg, Chief Information Officer
CHR: Karen B. Murtaugh, Executive Director, Human Resources
CNO: Marti Edwards, MSN, R.N., Chief Nursing Officer
Web address: www.rmlspecialtyhospital.org
Control: Other not–for–profit (including NFP Corporation) **Service:** Acute long–term care hospital

Staffed Beds: 201 **Admissions:** 927 **Census:** 127 **Outpatient Visits:** 0 **Births:** 0 **Total Expense ($000):** 114872 **Payroll Expense ($000):** 50385 **Personnel:** 610

UCHICAGO MEDICINE ADVENTHEALTH HINSDALE (140122), 120 North Oak Street, Zip 60521–3890; tel. 630/856–6001, **A**1 2 3 5 10 13 **F**3 4 11 13 15 18 20 22 24 26 28 29 30 31 34 37 40 41 43 44 45 46 47 48 54 57 58 59 61 64 68 70 72 76 77 78 79 81 82 84 85 86 87 89 91 97 98 99 100 101 107 108 110 111 114 115 119 126 129 130 131 135 146 151 154 167 169 **S** AdventHealth, Altamonte Springs, FL
Primary Contact: Adam Maycock, President and Chief Executive Officer
CFO: Rebecca Mathis, Vice President and Chief Financial Officer
CMO: Bonny Chen, M.D., Vice President and Chief Medical Officer
CHR: Mary P Leurck, Human Resources Director
CNO: Mary S Murphy, MSN, Vice President and Chief Nursing Officer
Web address: https://www.uchicagomedicineadventhealth.org/uchicago-medicine-adventhealth-hinsdale
Control: Church operated, Nongovernment, not–for–profit **Service:** General medical and surgical

Staffed Beds: 246 **Admissions:** 9943 **Census:** 125 **Outpatient Visits:** 228484 **Births:** 2126 **Total Expense ($000):** 329556 **Payroll Expense ($000):** 103231 **Personnel:** 1259

HOFFMAN ESTATES—Cook County

ALEXIAN BROTHERS WOMEN & CHILDREN'S HOSPITAL See Amita Health Women & Children's Hospital

AMITA HEALTH ALEXIAN BROTHERS BEHAVIORAL HEALTH HOSPITAL See Ascension Alexian Brothers Behavioral Health Hospital

AMITA HEALTH ST. ALEXIUS MEDICAL CENTER HOFFMAN ESTATES See Ascension St. Alexius

ASCENSION ALEXIAN BROTHERS BEHAVIORAL HEALTH HOSPITAL (144031), 1650 Moon Lake Boulevard, Zip 60169–1010; tel. 847/882–1600, (Nonreporting) **A**1 10 **S** Ascension Healthcare, Saint Louis, MO
Primary Contact: Clayton Ciha, President and Chief Executive Officer
COO: Christopher Novak, Chief Operating Officer
CFO: David Jones, Chief Financial Officer
CMO: Christopher D'Agostino, Chief Medical Officer
CIO: Sherrie Russell, Vice President and Chief Information Officer
CNO: Beth Jelesky, MSN, Chief Nursing Officer
Web address: https://healthcare.ascension.org/locations/illinois/ilchi/hoffman-estates-ascension-alexian-brothers-behavioral-health-hospital
Control: Church operated, Nongovernment, not–for–profit **Service:** Psychiatric

Staffed Beds: 141

ASCENSION ST. ALEXIUS (140290), 1555 Barrington Road, Zip 60169–1019; tel. 847/843–2000, (Includes AMITA HEALTH WOMEN & CHILDREN'S HOSPITAL, 1555 Barrington Road, Hoffman Estates, Illinois, Zip 60169–1019, tel. 847/843–2000; Kevin Rath, Vice President and Executive Director) (Nonreporting) **A**1 2 3 5 10 19 **S** Ascension Healthcare, Saint Louis, MO
Primary Contact: Roxann E. Barber, President and Chief Executive Officer
COO: Laurence Dry, Chief Operating Officer, Acute Care Hospitals Northern Region
CFO: Henry Zeisel, Chief Financial Officer, Northern Region
CIO: Sherrie Russell, Senior Vice President and Chief Information Officer
CHR: Donald Russell, Senior Vice President and Chief Human Resources Officer
CNO: Chris Budzinsky, Vice President Nursing and Chief Nursing Officer Alexian Brothers Acute Care Ministries
Web address: https://healthcare.ascension.org/locations/illinois/ilchi/hoffman-estates-ascension-saint-alexius
Control: Church operated, Nongovernment, not–for–profit **Service:** General medical and surgical

Staffed Beds: 298

HOOPESTON—Vermilion County

★ ⇧ **CARLE HOOPESTON REGIONAL HEALTH CENTER (141316)**, 701 East Orange Street, Zip 60942–1801; tel. 217/283–5531, **A**3 5 10 18 21 **F**3 15 29 35 40 45 57 59 64 65 81 85 89 90 93 100 107 108 110 111 115 119 128 133 **S** Carle Health, Urbana, IL
Primary Contact: Heather Tucker, Administrator
CHR: Melodee Bowers, Director Human Resources
Web address: https://carle.org/locations/carle-hoopeston-regional-health-center
Control: Other not–for–profit (including NFP Corporation) **Service:** General medical and surgical

Staffed Beds: 13 **Admissions:** 406 **Census:** 5 **Outpatient Visits:** 234976 **Births:** 0 **Total Expense ($000):** 73095 **Payroll Expense ($000):** 31419 **Personnel:** 297

HOPEDALE—Tazewell County

HOPEDALE MEDICAL COMPLEX (141330), 107 Tremont Street, Zip 61747–7525, Mailing Address: PO Box 267, Zip 61747–7525; tel. 309/449–3321, (Total facility includes 45 beds in nursing home–type unit) **A**10 18 **F**10 15 18 28 29 30 32 34 35 40 45 48 49 50 51 53 56 57 59 64 65 67 70 74 78 79 81 82 93 97 107 110 115 119 129 130 131 133 145 146 147 148 149 157 158
Primary Contact: Matthew Rossi, M.D., Chief Executive Officer
COO: Mark F Rossi, Chief Operating Officer and General Counsel
CFO: Nicholas A. Penn, Chief Financial Officer
CHR: Andrea Halley, Vice President of Non–Clinical Operations/Director Human Resources
CNO: Timothy Sondag, Senior Nursing Officer
Web address: www.hopedalemc.com
Control: Other not–for–profit (including NFP Corporation) **Service:** General medical and surgical

Staffed Beds: 84 **Admissions:** 293 **Census:** 47 **Outpatient Visits:** 18433 **Births:** 0 **Total Expense ($000):** 36903 **Payroll Expense ($000):** 15321 **Personnel:** 263

HUNTLEY—Mchenry County

CENTEGRA HOSPITAL – HUNTLEY See Northwestern Medicine Huntley

Hospitals, U.S. / ILLINOIS

JACKSONVILLE—Morgan County

JACKSONVILLE MEMORIAL HOSPITAL (141352), 1600 West Walnut Street, Zip 62650–1136; tel. 217/245–9541, **A**1 3 10 18 **F**3 13 14 15 28 29 30 31 34 35 40 41 44 45 51 58 60 64 69 70 75 76 77 78 79 81 82 85 86 87 89 93 107 108 110 111 115 118 119 120 121 129 130 141 146 148 154 169 **P**5 **S** Memorial Health, Springfield, IL
Primary Contact: Michael Trevor. Huffman, Chief Executive Officer
CFO: Paul Eddington, CPA, Affiliate Vice President and Chief Financial Officer
CMO: Anthony Griffin, M.D., Chief Medical Officer
CIO: James Krug, Affiliate Vice President, Information Systems and Support Services
CHR: Dillon Woods, Director Human Resources
CNO: Leanna Wynn, Affiliate Vice President and Chief Nursing Officer
Web address: https://memorial.health/jacksonville-memorial-hospital/
Control: Other not–for–profit (including NFP Corporation) **Service**: General medical and surgical

Staffed Beds: 25 **Admissions**: 2442 **Census**: 32 **Outpatient Visits**: 90248 **Births**: 356 **Total Expense ($000)**: 117639 **Payroll Expense ($000)**: 47953 **Personnel**: 769

PASSAVANT AREA HOSPITAL See Jacksonville Memorial Hospital

JERSEYVILLE—Jersey County

JERSEY COMMUNITY HOSPITAL (140059), 400 Maple Summit Road, Zip 62052–2028, Mailing Address: P.O. Box 426, Zip 62052–0426; tel. 618/498–6402, **A**1 10 **F**3 5 7 11 15 18 26 28 29 34 35 36 38 40 41 45 46 47 48 50 51 53 54 56 57 59 64 65 68 70 71 75 79 81 82 83 84 85 87 97 100 101 104 107 110 111 115 119 126 127 129 130 131 133 146 147 148 149 154 156 160 161 169 **P**6
Primary Contact: Beth King, Chief Executive Officer
CMO: Michael McNear, M.D., Chief Medical Officer
CIO: Shane Winters, Chief Information Officer
CHR: Sharon K Sanford, Director Human Resources
CNO: Julie Smith, R.N., MSN, Director of Nursing
Web address: www.jch.org
Control: Hospital district or authority, Government, Nonfederal **Service**: General medical and surgical

Staffed Beds: 46 **Admissions**: 668 **Census**: 7 **Outpatient Visits**: 174365 **Births**: 0 **Total Expense ($000)**: 51705 **Payroll Expense ($000)**: 25685

JOLIET—Will County

AMITA HEALTH SAINT JOSEPH MEDICAL CENTER See Ascension Saint Joseph – Joliet

ASCENSION SAINT JOSEPH – JOLIET (140007), 333 North Madison Street, Zip 60435–8200; tel. 815/725–7133, (Nonreporting) **A**1 3 7 10 **S** Ascension Healthcare, Saint Louis, MO
Primary Contact: Barbara Martin, President
CFO: Deb Schimerowski, Regional Finance Officer
CMO: Gary Lipinski, M.D., Chief Medical Officer
CHR: Monica Simzyk, Regional Human Resource Officer
CNO: Lynn Watson, Interim Chief Nursing Officer
Web address: https://healthcare.ascension.org/locations/illinois/ilchi/joliet-ascension-saint-joseph
Control: Church operated, Nongovernment, not–for–profit **Service**: General medical and surgical

Staffed Beds: 485

KANKAKEE—Kankakee County

AMITA HEALTH ST. MARY'S HOSPITAL See Ascension St. Mary – Kankakee

ASCENSION ST. MARY – KANKAKEE (140155), 500 West Court Street, Zip 60901–3661; tel. 815/937–2400, (Nonreporting) **A**1 3 10 **S** Ascension Healthcare, Saint Louis, MO
Primary Contact: Otis L. Story Sr, President
CFO: Deb Schimerowski, Regional Chief Financial Officer
CMO: Kalisha Hill, M.D., Chief Medical Officer
CIO: Russell Soliman, Director Information Services
CHR: Monica Simzyk, Regional Chief Human Resources Officer
CNO: Karen M Gallagher, MSN, Chief Nursing Office, Vice President Operations
Web address: https://healthcare.ascension.org/locations/illinois/ilchi/kankakee-ascension-saint-mary
Control: Church operated, Nongovernment, not–for–profit **Service**: General medical and surgical

Staffed Beds: 182

RIVERSIDE MEDICAL CENTER (140186), 350 North Wall Street, Zip 60901–2901; tel. 815/933–1671, **A**2 3 5 7 10 21 **F**3 4 5 6 7 8 9 13 15 17 18 20 22 24 26 28 29 30 31 32 34 35 36 37 38 39 40 41 43 44 45 46 47 49 50 51 54 55 56 57 58 59 60 61 62 64 65 66 68 70 71 74 75 76 77 78 79 81 82 84 85 86 87 89 90 92 93 96 97 98 99 100 101 102 103 104 105 107 108 110 111 112 114 115 118 119 120 121 122 123 124 126 127 129 130 131 132 134 135 141 143 144 145 146 147 148 149 150 152 153 154 156 157 160 162 164 165 167 169
Primary Contact: Phillip M. Kambic, President and Chief Executive Officer
CFO: Patricia K. Vilt, CPA, Senior Vice President and Chief Financial Officer
CMO: Keith A Moss, Vice President & Chief Medical Informatics Officers
CIO: Kyle Hansen, Corporate Director Information Systems
CHR: Becky Kay Hinrichs, Vice President Human Resources
Web address: www.riversidehealthcare.org
Control: Other not–for–profit (including NFP Corporation) **Service**: General medical and surgical

Staffed Beds: 300 **Admissions**: 9380 **Census**: 130 **Outpatient Visits**: 668419 **Births**: 704 **Total Expense ($000)**: 425496 **Payroll Expense ($000)**: 180379 **Personnel**: 1972

KEWANEE—Henry County

OSF SAINT LUKE MEDICAL CENTER (141325), 1051 West South Street, Zip 61443–8354, Mailing Address: P.O. Box 747, Zip 61443–0747; tel. 309/852–7500, **A**10 18 **F**3 15 30 32 34 35 36 38 40 45 59 64 65 66 70 75 77 78 79 81 82 85 86 87 92 93 96 97 107 108 110 111 115 119 127 129 130 131 132 133 135 143 146 147 148 149 154 156 **S** OSF Healthcare, Peoria, IL
Primary Contact: Jackie Kernan, R.N., MSN, President
CFO: John Bowser, Vice President, Chief Financial Officer
CMO: Clifford G Martin, M.D., Regional Vice President and Chief Medical Officer
CHR: Renee A Salisbury, Director Human Resources
CNO: Shelley Wiborg, MS, R.N., Chief Nursing Officer
Web address: www.osfsaintluke.org
Control: Other not–for–profit (including NFP Corporation) **Service**: General medical and surgical

Staffed Beds: 25 **Admissions**: 373 **Census**: 4 **Outpatient Visits**: 85387 **Births**: 0 **Total Expense ($000)**: 39085 **Payroll Expense ($000)**: 15195 **Personnel**: 210

LA GRANGE—Cook County

ADVENTHEALTH LA GRANGE See Uchicago Medicine Adventhealth La Grange

UCHICAGO MEDICINE ADVENTHEALTH LA GRANGE (140065), 5101 South Willow Spring Road, Zip 60525–2600; tel. 708/245–9000, **A**1 2 3 5 10 19 **F**3 11 12 15 18 20 22 24 26 28 29 30 34 37 40 41 43 44 45 46 47 48 49 51 54 57 58 59 61 64 68 70 77 78 79 81 82 84 85 86 87 90 91 97 100 101 107 108 110 111 114 115 119 126 130 131 146 148 154 167 **S** AdventHealth, Altamonte Springs, FL
Primary Contact: Adam Maycock, President and Chief Executive Officer
CFO: Rebecca Mathis, Chief Financial Officer
CIO: Thomas Schoenig, Chief Information Officer
CHR: Garry Giertuga, Site Manager Human Resources
CNO: Mary S Murphy, MSN, Regional Chief Nursing Officer
Web address: https://www.uchicagomedicineadventhealth.org/uchicago-medicine-adventhealth-la-grange
Control: Church operated, Nongovernment, not–for–profit **Service**: General medical and surgical

Staffed Beds: 177 **Admissions**: 7343 **Census**: 106 **Outpatient Visits**: 83948 **Total Expense ($000)**: 220198 **Payroll Expense ($000)**: 63950 **Personnel**: 877

Hospital, Medicare Provider Number, Address, Telephone, Approval, Facility, and Physician Codes, Health Care System

★ American Hospital Association (AHA) membership
☐ The Joint Commission accreditation
○ Healthcare Facilities Accreditation Program
◇ DNV Healthcare Inc. accreditation
⇑ Center for Improvement in Healthcare Quality Accreditation
△ Commission on Accreditation of Rehabilitation Facilities (CARF) accreditation

© 2025 AHA Guide

Hospitals, U.S. / ILLINOIS

LAKE FOREST—Lake County

NORTHWESTERN MEDICINE LAKE FOREST HOSPITAL (140130), 1000 North Westmoreland Road, Zip 60045–1696, Mailing Address: 1000 N Westmoreland Road, Zip 60045–1658; tel. 847/234–5600, **A**1 2 3 5 10 **F**3 8 9 11 12 13 15 17 18 20 22 26 28 29 30 31 32 34 35 36 38 40 41 42 43 44 45 46 47 48 49 50 51 53 54 55 56 57 58 59 61 64 65 66 68 70 73 74 75 76 77 78 79 81 82 84 85 86 87 89 92 93 96 97 100 101 102 104 107 108 110 111 114 115 116 117 118 119 120 121 123 126 129 130 131 132 135 143 144 146 147 148 149 150 154 156 157 160 164 165 167 169 **S** Northwestern Memorial HealthCare, Chicago, IL
Primary Contact: Seamus Collins, President
CFO: Richard A. Franco, Vice President and Chief Financial Officer
CMO: Jeffrey D. Kopin, Senior Vice President and Chief Medical Officer
CNO: Denise Majeski, MSN, R.N., Vice President Operations and Chief Nurse Executive
Web address: https://www.nm.org/locations/lake-forest-hospital
Control: Other not–for–profit (including NFP Corporation) **Service:** General medical and surgical

Staffed Beds: 152 **Admissions:** 11742 **Census:** 127 **Outpatient Visits:** 754054 **Births:** 1752 **Total Expense ($000):** 888420 **Payroll Expense ($000):** 307968 **Personnel:** 2466

LAWRENCEVILLE—Lawrence County

LAWRENCE COUNTY MEMORIAL HOSPITAL (141344), 2200 West State Street, Zip 62439–1852; tel. 618/943–1000, (Nonreporting) **A**10 18
Primary Contact: Keith Miller, Chief Executive Officer
CFO: Larry Spore, Chief Financial Officer
CIO: Gary Theriac, Director Information Technology
CHR: Kim Alldredge, Director Human Resources
CNO: Rita Garvey, Chief Nursing Officer
Web address: www.lcmhosp.org
Control: Other not–for–profit (including NFP Corporation) **Service:** General medical and surgical

Staffed Beds: 25

LIBERTYVILLE—Lake County

★ **ADVOCATE CONDELL MEDICAL CENTER (140202)**, 801 South Milwaukee Avenue, Zip 60048–3199; tel. 847/362–2900, **A**2 10 21 **F**3 11 13 15 18 19 20 22 24 26 28 29 30 31 32 34 35 36 37 38 39 40 41 43 44 45 46 47 48 49 50 51 53 55 56 57 59 60 64 65 68 70 73 74 75 76 77 78 79 81 82 84 85 86 87 89 92 93 94 96 100 102 107 108 110 111 115 117 118 119 120 121 124 126 130 131 132 135 143 144 145 146 147 148 149 150 154 156 164 165 167 169 **P**1 6 **S** Advocate Aurora Health, Downers Grove, IL
Primary Contact: Matthew Lee. Primack, President
COO: Christian Wallis, Vice President Operations
CFO: Darrick Minzey, Vice President Finance
CMO: Debra Susie–Lattner, M.D., Vice President Medical Management
CIO: Rick Cornwall, HIT Site Coordinator
CHR: Sarah Stehly, Vice President Human Resources
CNO: Rachel Loberg, R.N., Chief Nursing Officer
Web address: www.advocatehealth.com/condell/
Control: Other not–for–profit (including NFP Corporation) **Service:** General medical and surgical

Staffed Beds: 275 **Admissions:** 13799 **Census:** 185 **Outpatient Visits:** 248882 **Births:** 962 **Total Expense ($000):** 369139 **Payroll Expense ($000):** 120081 **Personnel:** 1706

ENCOMPASS HEALTH REHABILITATION INSTITUTE OF LIBERTYVILLE (143031), 1201 American Way, Zip 60048; tel. 847/371–6500, (Nonreporting) **A**1 **S** Encompass Health Corporation, Birmingham, AL
Primary Contact: Gemma Fletcher, Interim Chief Executive Officer
CFO: Michael Brogan, Controller
CMO: Stephen Talty, M.D., Medical Director
CHR: Betty Shuman, Director Human Resources
CNO: Svetlana Janssen, Chief Nursing Officer
Web address: https://encompasshealth.com/libertyvillerehab
Control: Corporation, Investor–owned (for–profit) **Service:** Rehabilitation

Staffed Beds: 60

LINCOLN—Logan County

ABRAHAM LINCOLN MEMORIAL HOSPITAL See Lincoln Memorial Hospital

LINCOLN MEMORIAL HOSPITAL (141322), 200 Stahlhut Drive, Zip 62656–5066; tel. 217/732–2161, **A**1 5 10 18 **F**3 8 11 15 18 28 29 30 34 40 45 57 59 64 68 77 79 81 82 85 93 107 108 110 111 114 115 118 119 129 130 131 133 135 146 149 153 156 **P**5 **S** Memorial Health, Springfield, IL
Primary Contact: Dolan Dalpoas, FACHE, President and Chief Executive Officer
CMO: Amir J. Wahab, M.D., Medical Staff President
CIO: Keenan Leesman, Director Information Systems
CHR: Michelle Long, Regional Human Resource Manager
CNO: Roxanne Harling, Chief Nursing Officer
Web address: https://memorial.health/lincoln-memorial-hospital/overview
Control: Other not–for–profit (including NFP Corporation) **Service:** General medical and surgical

Staffed Beds: 25 **Admissions:** 819 **Census:** 15 **Outpatient Visits:** 45443 **Births:** 36 **Total Expense ($000):** 53204 **Payroll Expense ($000):** 21516 **Personnel:** 249

LITCHFIELD—Montgomery County

HSHS ST. FRANCIS HOSPITAL (141350), 1215 Franciscan Drive, Zip 62056–1799, Mailing Address: P.O. Box 1215, Zip 62056–0999; tel. 217/324–2191, **A**1 10 18 **F**3 8 11 13 15 18 28 29 30 31 34 35 40 44 45 46 50 56 57 59 64 68 70 74 75 76 77 78 79 81 82 85 86 87 92 93 107 111 114 117 118 119 129 132 133 134 135 146 147 148 149 154 167 169 **P**6 **S** HSHS Hospital Sisters Health System, Springfield, IL
Primary Contact: Matthew Fry, FACHE, President and Chief Executive Officer, Central Illinois Market
CFO: Marisa Murray, CPA, Director Finance
Web address: https://www.hshs.org/st-francis/
Control: Church operated, Nongovernment, not–for–profit **Service:** General medical and surgical

Staffed Beds: 25 **Admissions:** 1090 **Census:** 10 **Outpatient Visits:** 64385 **Total Expense ($000):** 50920 **Payroll Expense ($000):** 14316 **Personnel:** 191

MACOMB—McDonough County

MCDONOUGH DISTRICT HOSPITAL (140089), 525 East Grant Street, Zip 61455–3318; tel. 309/833–4101, (Nonreporting) **A**1 10 20
Primary Contact: William R. Murdock, President and Chief Executive Officer
CFO: Sherri Hitchcock, Chief Financial Officer
CIO: Travis Rath, Director Information Systems
CHR: William Corbin, Vice President and Chief Human Resources Officer
CNO: Amber Depoy, Interim Chief Nursing Officer
Web address: www.mdh.org
Control: Hospital district or authority, Government, Nonfederal **Service:** General medical and surgical

Staffed Beds: 48

MARION—Williamson County

☐ **DEACONESS ILLINOIS MEDICAL CENTER (140184)**, 3333 West DeYoung, Zip 62959–5884; tel. 618/998–7000, (Nonreporting) **A**1 10
Primary Contact: William Davis, Chief Administrative Officer
CFO: Jeff Thomas, Chief Financial Officer
CHR: Sam Hood, Director Human Resources
Web address: www.heartlandregional.com
Control: Corporation, Investor–owned (for–profit) **Service:** General medical and surgical

Staffed Beds: 92

MARION VETERANS AFFAIRS MEDICAL CENTER, 2401 West Main Street, Zip 62959–1188; tel. 618/997–5311, (Nonreporting) **A**1 **S** Department of Veterans Affairs, Washington, DC
Primary Contact: Zachary Sage, Director
COO: Frank Kehus, Associate Director for Operations
CFO: Connie McDonald, Chief Financial Officer
CMO: Michael Ladwig, M.D., Chief of Staff
CIO: Adam Powell, Program Manager
CHR: Tim Hartwell, Chief Human Resources
CNO: Rose Burke, Associate Director Patient Care Services
Web address: www.marion.va.gov
Control: Veterans Affairs, Government, federal **Service:** General medical and surgical

Staffed Beds: 63

Hospitals, U.S. / ILLINOIS

MARYVILLE—Madison County

ANDERSON HOSPITAL (140289), 6800 State Route 162, Zip 62062-8500; tel. 618/288-5711, **A**1 10 **F**3 8 11 13 15 18 20 22 28 29 30 31 34 35 40 49 57 59 62 64 70 74 75 76 78 79 81 82 85 93 107 110 111 115 117 119 120 121 123 126 129 130 132 144 146 147 148 149 154 156 167 169
Primary Contact: Lisa Spencer, R.N., MSN, President
COO: Michael Marshall, Chief Operating Officer
CFO: Michael Marshall, Vice President Finance and Chief Financial Officer
CMO: Charles A. Lane, Chief Medical Officer
CIO: Michael Ward, Director Information Services
CHR: Robin Steinmann, Chief Human Resources Officer
CNO: Lisa Spencer, R.N., MSN, Chief Nursing and Operating Officer
Web address: www.andersonhospital.org
Control: Other not–for–profit (including NFP Corporation) **Service**: General medical and surgical

Staffed Beds: 129 **Admissions**: 6147 **Census**: 61 **Outpatient Visits**: 192179 **Births**: 1340 **Total Expense ($000)**: 174498 **Payroll Expense ($000)**: 68342 **Personnel**: 1341

MATTOON—Coles County

SARAH BUSH LINCOLN HEALTH CENTER (140189), 1000 Health Center Drive, Zip 61938-9253; tel. 217/258-2525, (Nonreporting) **A**1 10 20
Primary Contact: Kimberly Uphoff, President and Chief Executive Officer
COO: Kimberly Uphoff, Vice President Operations
CFO: Dennis Pluard, Vice President Finance and Support Services
CMO: James Hildebrandt, D.O., Vice President Medical Affairs
CIO: Brian Murphy, Vice President Information Systems
CHR: Debbie Saddoris, Vice President Human Resources
CNO: Sandra Miller, MSN, R.N., Interim Vice President, Patient Care Continuum and Chief Nursing Officer
Web address: www.sarahbush.org
Control: Other not–for–profit (including NFP Corporation) **Service**: General medical and surgical

Staffed Beds: 141

MAYWOOD—Cook County

△ **LOYOLA UNIVERSITY MEDICAL CENTER (140276)**, 2160 South First Avenue, Zip 60153-3328; tel. 708/216-9000, (Includes RONALD MCDONALD CHILDREN'S HOSPITAL, 2160 South 1St Avenue, Maywood, Illinois, Zip 60153-3328, tel. 888/584-7888) **A**1 2 3 5 7 8 10 19 **F**3 5 6 7 8 9 11 12 13 14 15 16 17 18 19 20 21 22 23 24 25 26 27 28 29 30 31 32 33 34 35 36 37 38 39 40 41 43 44 45 46 47 48 49 50 51 54 55 56 57 58 59 60 61 64 65 66 68 70 71 72 74 75 76 77 78 79 80 81 82 84 85 86 87 88 89 92 93 96 97 100 101 102 104 107 108 110 111 115 116 117 118 119 120 121 123 124 126 129 130 131 132 134 135 136 137 138 139 140 141 142 143 144 145 146 147 148 149 150 154 156 160 162 164 167 169 **P**6 **S** Trinity Health, Livonia, MI
Primary Contact: Tad Gomez, MS, President
COO: Richard Freeman, FACS, M.D., Chief Clinical Officer
CFO: Melissa Lukasick, Chief Financial Officer
CMO: Kevin Smith, M.D., Interim Chief Medical Officer
CIO: Cynthia Davis, Chief Information Officer
CHR: Vicky Piper, Regional Vice President Human Resources
CNO: Peggy Norton–Rosko, R.N., MSN, Regional Chief Nursing Officer
Web address: www.loyolamedicine.org/Medical_Services/index.cfm
Control: Other not–for–profit (including NFP Corporation) **Service**: General medical and surgical

Staffed Beds: 500 **Admissions**: 18043 **Census**: 348 **Outpatient Visits**: 1236896 **Births**: 1124 **Personnel**: 6403

MCHENRY—Mchenry County

NORTHWESTERN MEDICINE MCHENRY (140116), 4201 Medical Center Drive, Zip 60050-8409; tel. 815/344-5000, (Includes NORTHWESTERN MEDICINE HUNTLEY, 10400 Haligus RD, Huntley, Illinois, Zip 60142-9553, 10400 Haligus Road, Zip 60142, tel. 224/654-0000; Thomas J. McAfee, Region President; NORTHWESTERN MEDICINE WOODSTOCK, 3701 Doty Road, Woodstock, Illinois, Zip 60098-7509, P O Box 1990, Zip 60098-1990, tel. 815/338-2500; Nick Rave, President) **A**1 2 3 5 10 **F**3 4 5 8 11 12 13 15 17 18 19 20 22 24 26 28 29 30 31 34 35 36 37 38 39 40 41 43 44 45 46 47 49 50 51 53 54 55 56 57 58 59 60 64 65 66 68 69 70 71 73 74 75 76 77 78 79 81 82 85 86 87 89 90 92 93 96 97 98 100 102 104 105 107 108 110 111 114 115 116 117 118 119 120 121 123 124 126 129 130 131 132 135 143 144 146 147 148 149 152 153 154 156 157 162 164 165 167 169 **S** Northwestern Memorial HealthCare, Chicago, IL
Primary Contact: Catie Schmit, President
CFO: David Tomlinson, Executive Vice President Chief Financial Officer and Chief Information Officer
CMO: Irfan Hafiz, Vice President Medical Affairs
CIO: David Tomlinson, Executive Vice President Chief Financial Officer and Chief Information Officer
CHR: Bernadette S Szczepanski, Senior Vice President, Human Resources
Web address: www.centegra.org
Control: Other not–for–profit (including NFP Corporation) **Service**: General medical and surgical

Staffed Beds: 327 **Admissions**: 20216 **Census**: 255 **Outpatient Visits**: 721463 **Births**: 1781 **Total Expense ($000)**: 854467 **Payroll Expense ($000)**: 327274 **Personnel**: 2871

MCLEANSBORO—Hamilton County

HAMILTON MEMORIAL HOSPITAL DISTRICT (141326), 611 South Marshall Avenue, Zip 62859-1213, Mailing Address: P.O. Box 429, Mc Leansboro, Zip 62859-0429; tel. 618/643-2361, (Nonreporting) **A**10 18
Primary Contact: Victoria Woodrow, Chief Executive Officer
CFO: Kent Mitchell, Chief Financial Officer
CIO: Mark Todd, Senior Systems Administrator
CHR: Sheila Thompson, Director Human Resources
CNO: Patty Blazier, Chief Nursing Officer
Web address: www.hmhospital.org
Control: Hospital district or authority, Government, Nonfederal **Service**: General medical and surgical

Staffed Beds: 25

MELROSE PARK—Cook County

△ **GOTTLIEB MEMORIAL HOSPITAL (140008)**, 701 West North Avenue, Zip 60160-1612; tel. 708/681-3200, **A**1 3 5 7 10 19 **F**3 12 15 18 20 22 28 29 30 31 34 40 43 44 45 47 53 54 56 57 59 60 64 65 66 68 70 74 75 77 78 79 81 85 86 87 90 92 93 96 97 102 107 110 111 115 119 126 128 129 130 131 132 143 146 148 149 150 164 167 **P**6 **S** Trinity Health, Livonia, MI
Primary Contact: Elizabeth Early, FACHE, President
CFO: Ellyn Chin, Vice President Finance
CMO: Gerald Luger, M.D., President Medical Staff
CIO: Maurita Adler, Director Information Services
CHR: Brett Wakefield, Vice President Human Resources
Web address: https://www.loyolamedicine.org/location/gmh
Control: Other not–for–profit (including NFP Corporation) **Service**: General medical and surgical

Staffed Beds: 154 **Admissions**: 5498 **Census**: 104 **Outpatient Visits**: 50652 **Births**: 0 **Personnel**: 807

MENDOTA—Lasalle County

★ **OSF SAINT PAUL MEDICAL CENTER (141310)**, 1401 East 12th Street, Zip 61342-9216; tel. 815/539-7461, **A**10 18 **F**3 11 15 28 29 30 31 34 40 49 57 59 64 69 70 77 79 81 82 85 93 107 110 111 115 127 129 130 133 146 148 149 154 **S** OSF Healthcare, Peoria, IL
Primary Contact: Dawn Trompeter, President
CMO: Leonardo Lopez, President Medical Staff
CHR: Kimberly Kennedy, Manager Human Resources
CNO: Heather Bomstad, MSN, R.N., Vice President Patient Care Services and Chief Nursing Officer
Web address: https://www.osfhealthcare.org/saint-paul
Control: Other not–for–profit (including NFP Corporation) **Service**: General medical and surgical

Staffed Beds: 25 **Admissions**: 565 **Census**: 7 **Outpatient Visits**: 77039 **Births**: 0 **Total Expense ($000)**: 37256 **Payroll Expense ($000)**: 17042 **Personnel**: 280

Hospital, Medicare Provider Number, Address, Telephone, Approval, Facility, and Physician Codes, Health Care System

★ American Hospital Association (AHA) membership   ○ Healthcare Facilities Accreditation Program   ⇑ Center for Improvement in Healthcare Quality Accreditation
□ The Joint Commission accreditation   ◇ DNV Healthcare Inc. accreditation   △ Commission on Accreditation of Rehabilitation Facilities (CARF) accreditation

© 2025 AHA Guide

Hospitals, U.S. / ILLINOIS

METROPOLIS—Massac County

★ **MASSAC MEMORIAL HOSPITAL (141323)**, 28 Chick Street, Zip 62960–2467, Mailing Address: P.O. Box 850, Zip 62960–0850; tel. 618/524–2176, **A**10 18 **F**3 7 11 15 18 28 29 34 40 44 45 50 54 56 59 64 71 75 81 82 93 96 97 104 107 110 111 115 119 127 129 132 133 143 148 149 153 154 162 164 165
Primary Contact: Donald Robbins, Chief Executive Officer
COO: Janet Vannatter, Chief Operating Officer
CFO: Lynn Goines, Chief Financial Officer
CMO: Jonathan Walters, M.D., Chief Medical Officer
CHR: Johnna Douglas, Manager, Human Resources
Web address: www.massachealth.org
Control: Hospital district or authority, Government, Nonfederal **Service**: General medical and surgical

Staffed Beds: 25 **Admissions**: 409 **Census**: 5 **Outpatient Visits**: 32399 **Births**: 0 **Total Expense ($000)**: 34077 **Payroll Expense ($000)**: 14342 **Personnel**: 217	

MOLINE—Rock Island County

▥ **QUAD CITIES REHABILITATION INSTITUTE, THE (143032)**, 653 52nd Avenue, Zip 61265–7058; tel. 309/581–3600, **A**1 **F**3 29 34 60 79 82 84 85 90 96 130 132 148 149 154 156 164 **S** Encompass Health Corporation, Birmingham, AL
Primary Contact: Angela Zaremba, Chief Executive Officer
COO: Alyssa Vanmelkebeke, Chief Nursing Officer
CFO: Lavern Balk, Chief Financial Officer
CMO: Albert Park, M.D., Chief Medical Officer
CIO: Hannah Wilson, HIMS Supervisor
CHR: Aaron Van Lauwe, Director, Human Resources
CNO: Alyssa Vanmelkebeke, Chief Nursing Officer
Web address: https://encompasshealth.com/locations/quadcitiesrehab
Control: Partnership, Investor–owned (for–profit) **Service**: Rehabilitation

Staffed Beds: 40 **Admissions**: 686 **Census**: 22 **Outpatient Visits**: 0 **Births**: 0 **Total Expense ($000)**: 11546 **Payroll Expense ($000)**: 6880 **Personnel**: 90

TRINITY MOLINE See Unitypoint Health – Trinity Moline

UNITYPOINT HEALTH – TRINITY MOLINE See Unitypoint Health – Trinity Rock Island, Rock Island

MONMOUTH—Warren County

★ **OSF HOLY FAMILY MEDICAL CENTER (141318)**, 1000 West Harlem Avenue, Zip 61462–1007; tel. 309/734–3141, **A**10 18 **F**11 15 28 29 30 34 40 45 46 57 59 64 65 68 75 81 85 87 93 97 107 110 115 118 119 127 129 130 132 133 145 146 148 154 156 **S** OSF Healthcare, Peoria, IL
Primary Contact: Lisa DeKezel, R.N., President
CFO: Theresa Springer, Chief Financial Officer
CMO: Clifford G Martin, M.D., Regional Vice President and Chief Medical Officer
CIO: Lew McCann, Director Management Information Systems
CHR: Jenny Jacobs, Director Human Resources
CNO: Shelley Wiborg, MS, R.N., Director of Nursing
Web address: www.osfholyfamily.org
Control: Church operated, Nongovernment, not–for–profit **Service**: General medical and surgical

Staffed Beds: 23 **Admissions**: 327 **Census**: 5 **Outpatient Visits**: 77062 **Births**: 0 **Total Expense ($000)**: 33723 **Payroll Expense ($000)**: 12738 **Personnel**: 192

MONTICELLO—Piatt County

▥ **KIRBY MEDICAL CENTER (141301)**, 1000 Medical Center Drive, Zip 61856–2116; tel. 217/762–2115, (Nonreporting) **A**1 3 10 18
Primary Contact: Steven Tenhouse, FACHE, Chief Executive Officer
COO: Mark Fred, R.N., Chief Operating Officer
CFO: Kimberly Alvis, CPA, Chief Financial Officer
CMO: Narain Mandhan, M.D., Chief Medical Officer
CIO: Mark Fred, R.N., Chief Operating Offier, Chief Information Officer
CHR: Andrew Buffenbarger, FACHE, Chief Compliance Officer, Director of Human Resources & Risk Management
CNO: Jennifer Moss, MS, R.N., Chief Clinical Officer
Web address: www.kirbyhealth.org
Control: Other not–for–profit (including NFP Corporation) **Service**: General medical and surgical

Staffed Beds: 16

MORRIS—Grundy County

★ ○ **MORRIS HOSPITAL & HEALTHCARE CENTERS (140101)**, 150 West High Street, Zip 60450–1497; tel. 815/942–2932, **A**10 11 **F**3 11 13 15 18 20 22 26 28 29 34 35 40 41 43 45 47 49 50 54 57 59 64 65 66 69 70 74 75 76 77 78 79 81 82 85 86 87 89 93 97 102 107 108 110 111 114 115 118 119 120 121 123 129 130 132 135 143 144 146 147 149 154 156 167 168 **P**6
Primary Contact: Thomas J. Dohm, President and Chief Executive Officer
CFO: Mary Lou Tate, Chief Financial Officer
CHR: Erin Murphy–Frobish, Vice President Human Resources
CNO: Kimberly Ann Landers, MS, RN, FACHE, Vice President Patient Care Services
Web address: www.morrishospital.org
Control: Other not–for–profit (including NFP Corporation) **Service**: General medical and surgical

Staffed Beds: 89 **Admissions**: 3529 **Census**: 37 **Outpatient Visits**: 309988 **Births**: 600 **Total Expense ($000)**: 229249 **Payroll Expense ($000)**: 107914 **Personnel**: 1085

MORRISON—Whiteside County

▥ **MORRISON COMMUNITY HOSPITAL (141329)**, 303 North Jackson Street, Zip 61270–3042; tel. 815/772–4003, (Nonreporting) **A**10 18
Primary Contact: Pam Pfister, Chief Executive Officer
COO: Pam Pfister, Chief Executive Officer
CFO: Cami Megli, Controller
CMO: Duncan Dinkha, M.D., Chief of Staff
CIO: Pam Pfister, Chief Executive Officer
CHR: Amber L Temple, Director Human Resources
Web address: www.morrisonhospital.com
Control: Hospital district or authority, Government, Nonfederal **Service**: General medical and surgical

Staffed Beds: 25

MOUNT CARMEL—Wabash County

▥ **WABASH GENERAL HOSPITAL (141327)**, 1418 College Drive, Zip 62863–2638; tel. 618/262–8621, (Nonreporting) **A**1 10 18 **S** Alliant Management Services, Louisville, KY
Primary Contact: Karissa Turner, President and Chief Executive Officer
COO: Karissa Turner, Vice President Operations
CFO: Lynn Leek, Executive Vice President of Finance and Chief Financial Officer
CMO: Levi McDaniel, M.D., Chief of Staff
CIO: Bobby Gage, Director Information Technology
CHR: Bridget Shepard, Vice President Human Resources
CNO: Tamara Gould, R.N., Vice President Clinical Services and Chief Nursing Officer
Web address: www.wabashgeneral.com
Control: County, Government, Nonfederal **Service**: General medical and surgical

Staffed Beds: 25

MOUNT VERNON—Jefferson County

▥ **DEACONESS ILLINOIS CROSSROADS (140294)**, 8 Doctors Park Road, Zip 62864–6224; tel. 618/244–5500, (Nonreporting) **A**1 10
Primary Contact: William Davis, Chief Administrative Officer
CIO: Bryan Delaney, Director Information Technology
CHR: Jessica Connaway, Director Human Resources
CNO: Stephanie Maines, Chief Nursing Officer
Web address: www.crossroadshospital.com
Control: Corporation, Investor–owned (for–profit) **Service**: General medical and surgical

Staffed Beds: 28

▥ **SSM HEALTH GOOD SAMARITAN HOSPITAL (140046)**, 1 Good Samaritan Way, Zip 62864–2402; tel. 618/242–4600, **A**1 2 5 10 19 **F**3 8 11 12 13 15 18 20 22 26 28 29 30 31 34 35 38 40 44 45 46 49 50 51 54 55 56 57 59 60 61 64 68 70 73 74 75 76 77 78 79 80 81 82 84 85 86 87 89 90 92 93 94 96 102 104 107 108 110 111 114 115 119 123 124 126 130 131 132 135 144 146 147 148 149 154 156 157 167 **P**6 8 **S** SSM Health, Saint Louis, MO
Primary Contact: Damon R. Harbison, President
COO: Mark A Clark, Vice President Operations
CFO: Deland Evischi, Regional Chief Financial Officer, Southern Illinois
CMO: Daniel Hoffman, M.D., Administrative Medical Director
CIO: Steve Murphy, FM–East Region IS
CHR: Thomas W Blythe, System Vice President Human Resources
CNO: Chris Adams, Vice President Patient Care Services
Web address: https://www.ssmhealth.com/locations/southern-illinois/good-samaritan-hospital-mt-vernon
Control: Church operated, Nongovernment, not–for–profit **Service**: General medical and surgical

Staffed Beds: 134 **Admissions**: 7844 **Census**: 89 **Outpatient Visits**: 230418 **Births**: 1309 **Total Expense ($000)**: 213685 **Payroll Expense ($000)**: 63242 **Personnel**: 810

Hospitals, U.S. / ILLINOIS

MURPHYSBORO—Jackson County

★ **ST. JOSEPH MEMORIAL HOSPITAL (141334)**, 2 South Hospital Drive, Zip 62966–3333; tel. 618/684–3156, **A**10 18 **F**3 11 18 28 29 30 31 34 35 40 45 49 56 57 59 60 64 68 75 77 78 79 81 82 84 85 86 87 93 104 107 111 119 129 130 132 133 135 146 148 149 154 156 160 **S** Southern Illinois Healthcare, Carbondale, IL
Primary Contact: Craig A. Jesiolowski, FACHE, Vice President and Administrator
CMO: Emily Hanson, M.D., President, Medical Staff
CIO: David Holland, Vice President Information Services
CHR: Kelly Stevens, Manager Human Resources
Web address: www.sih.net
Control: Other not–for–profit (including NFP Corporation) **Service**: General medical and surgical

Staffed Beds: 25 **Admissions**: 462 **Census**: 11 **Outpatient Visits**: 72664 **Births**: 0 **Total Expense ($000)**: 56896 **Payroll Expense ($000)**: 16324 **Personnel**: 286

NAPERVILLE—Dupage County

☒ **ENDEAVOR HEALTH EDWARD HOSPITAL (140231)**, 801 South Washington Street, Zip 60540–7499; tel. 630/527–3000, **A**1 2 10 **F**3 7 9 12 13 15 17 18 19 20 22 24 26 28 29 30 31 34 35 36 37 38 39 40 41 42 43 44 45 46 47 48 49 50 53 54 55 57 58 59 61 63 64 65 70 72 73 74 75 76 77 78 79 81 82 84 85 86 87 88 89 91 92 93 96 97 99 100 101 102 103 107 108 110 111 114 115 117 118 119 120 121 123 124 126 129 130 131 132 135 141 144 146 147 148 149 154 156 167 169 **P**8 **S** Endeavor Health, Evanston, IL
Primary Contact: Yvette Saba, R.N., President, Edward Hospital & South Institutes
CFO: Denise Chamberlain, Executive Vice President, Chief Financial Officer
CMO: Robert Payton, Chief Medical Officer
CHR: Chris Devereux, Human Resources Director, Business Partner
CNO: Patricia J Fairbanks, R.N., Vice President, Chief Nursing Officer
Web address: www.eehealth.org
Control: Other not–for–profit (including NFP Corporation) **Service**: General medical and surgical

Staffed Beds: 371 **Admissions**: 24925 **Census**: 267 **Outpatient Visits**: 697235 **Births**: 3457 **Total Expense ($000)**: 628960 **Payroll Expense ($000)**: 248528 **Personnel**: 2573

☒ **ENDEAVOR HEALTH LINDEN OAKS HOSPITAL (144035)**, 852 South West Street, Zip 60540–6400; tel. 630/305–5500, **A**1 10 **F**4 5 29 34 35 38 44 56 57 59 64 75 86 87 98 99 100 101 103 104 105 130 132 134 149 150 151 152 153 154 160 162 164 165 **P**6 8 **S** Endeavor Health, Evanston, IL
Primary Contact: Gina Sharp, FACHE, President
CFO: Kristen Refness, Director, Financial Operations
CMO: Barry Rabin, M.D., Regional Medical Director
CIO: David Pickering, System Director, Applications
CHR: Lisa Dixon, Business Partner and Human Resource Director
CNO: Patricia J Fairbanks, R.N., Vice President, Chief Nursing Officer
Web address: https://www.eehealth.org/services/behavioral-health
Control: Other not–for–profit (including NFP Corporation) **Service**: Psychiatric

Staffed Beds: 108 **Admissions**: 3485 **Census**: 75 **Outpatient Visits**: 68798 **Births**: 0 **Total Expense ($000)**: 57051 **Payroll Expense ($000)**: 34714 **Personnel**: 467

LINDEN OAKS HOSPITAL See Endeavor Health Linden Oaks Hospital

NASHVILLE—Washington County

☐ **WASHINGTON COUNTY HOSPITAL (141308)**, 705 South Grand Avenue, Zip 62263–1534; tel. 618/327–8236, (Nonreporting) **A**1 10 18 **S** SSM Health, Saint Louis, MO
Primary Contact: Brian Monsma, President
CFO: Jennifer Venable, Chief Financial Officer
CMO: Alfonso Urdaneta, M.D., President Medical Staff
CIO: Kim Larkin, Chief Information Officer
CHR: Barbara Gowler, Human Resources Manager
CNO: Stacie Hodge, Director of Nursing
Web address: www.washingtoncountyhospital.org
Control: Hospital district or authority, Government, Nonfederal **Service**: General medical and surgical

Staffed Beds: 32

NEW LENOX—Will County

☒ △ **SILVER CROSS HOSPITAL (140213)**, 1900 Silver Cross Boulevard, Zip 60451–9509, Mailing Address: 1900 Silver Cross Blvd, Zip 60451–9509; tel. 815/300–1100, **A**1 2 3 7 10 **F**3 11 13 15 17 18 20 22 24 26 28 29 30 34 35 37 40 42 43 44 45 46 47 48 49 50 51 54 56 57 58 59 60 62 63 64 65 70 71 72 73 74 75 76 77 78 79 81 84 85 86 87 89 90 97 107 108 109 110 111 112 113 114 115 116 117 119 120 121 123 124 126 129 130 131 132 135 144 145 146 147 148 149 150 154 156 157 167 169
Primary Contact: Michael Mutterer, R.N., President and Chief Executive Officer
CFO: Vincent Pryor, Senior Vice President and Chief Financial Officer
CMO: Christopher Udovich, M.D., Chief of Staff
CIO: Kevin Lane, Vice President Information Systems
CNO: Peggy Gricus, R.N., Vice President, Patient Care Services and Chief Nursing Officer
Web address: www.silvercross.org
Control: Other not–for–profit (including NFP Corporation) **Service**: General medical and surgical

Staffed Beds: 348 **Admissions**: 21067 **Census**: 255 **Outpatient Visits**: 281325 **Births**: 3113 **Total Expense ($000)**: 503700 **Payroll Expense ($000)**: 178638 **Personnel**: 2431

☐ **SILVER OAKS BEHAVIORAL HOSPITAL (144041)**, 1004 Pawlak Parkway, Zip 60451–9401; tel. 844/580–5000, (Nonreporting) **A**1 10
Primary Contact: Lindsay Pelletier, Chief Executive Officer
Web address: https://silveroaksbehavioralhospital.com
Control: Partnership, Investor–owned (for–profit) **Service**: Psychiatric

Staffed Beds: 110

NORMAL—Mclean County

BROMENN REGIONAL MEDICAL CENTER See Advocate Bromenn Regional Medical Center

★ ⇧ **CARLE BROMENN MEDICAL CENTER (140127)**, 1304 Franklin Avenue, Zip 61761–3558, Mailing Address: P.O. Box 2850, Bloomington, Zip 61702–2850; tel. 309/454–1400, (Includes ADVOCATE BROMENN REGIONAL MEDICAL CENTER, 1304 Franklin Avenue, Normal, Illinois, Zip 61761–3558, PO Box 2850, Bloomington, Zip 61702–2850, tel. 309/454–1400; Colleen Kannaday, FACHE, President) **A**2 3 5 10 13 19 21 **F**3 4 5 11 12 13 15 18 19 20 22 24 26 28 29 30 31 34 35 37 38 40 43 44 45 49 50 51 54 59 64 65 70 73 74 75 76 77 78 79 81 84 85 86 87 89 90 93 96 97 98 100 102 107 108 110 111 114 115 117 118 119 121 124 126 129 130 132 135 146 147 148 149 151 152 154 156 160 162 164 165 167 169 **S** Carle Health, Urbana, IL
Primary Contact: Colleen Kannaday, FACHE, President
CFO: Aron Klein, Vice President Finance
CMO: James Nevin, M.D., Vice President and Chief Medical Officer
CHR: Antonio Coletta, Vice President Human Resources
CNO: Laurie Round, MS, R.N., Vice President and Chief Nursing Officer
Web address: www.advocatehealth.com/bromenn
Control: Other not–for–profit (including NFP Corporation) **Service**: General medical and surgical

Staffed Beds: 179 **Admissions**: 8647 **Census**: 107 **Outpatient Visits**: 227783 **Births**: 1323 **Total Expense ($000)**: 254248 **Payroll Expense ($000)**: 90449 **Personnel**: 1095

NORTH CHICAGO—Lake County

☒ **CAPTAIN JAMES A. LOVELL FEDERAL HEALTH CARE CENTER**, 3001 Green Bay Road, Zip 60064–3049; tel. 847/688–1900, (Nonreporting) **A**1 3 5 **S** Department of Veterans Affairs, Washington, DC
Primary Contact: Robert G. Buckley, M.D., Medical Center Director
CFO: Barbara Meadows, Chief Financial Manager
CMO: Tariq Hassan, M.D., Associate Director of Patient Care
CIO: Jonathan Friedman, Public Affairs Officer
CHR: Amy Sanders, Chief Human Resources
CNO: Sarah Fouse, Associate Director of Patient Services
Web address: www.lovell.fhcc.va.gov
Control: Veterans Affairs, Government, federal **Service**: Other specialty treatment

Staffed Beds: 97

Hospital, Medicare Provider Number, Address, Telephone, Approval, Facility, and Physician Codes, Health Care System

★ American Hospital Association (AHA) membership ◯ Healthcare Facilities Accreditation Program ⇧ Center for Improvement in Healthcare Quality Accreditation
☐ The Joint Commission accreditation ◇ DNV Healthcare Inc. accreditation △ Commission on Accreditation of Rehabilitation Facilities (CARF) accreditation

© 2025 AHA Guide

Hospitals, U.S. / ILLINOIS

NORTHLAKE—Cook County

☒ **KINDRED HOSPITAL CHICAGO–NORTHLAKE (142008)**, 365 East North Avenue, Zip 60164–2628; tel. 708/345–8100, (Includes KINDRED HOSPITAL CHICAGO NORTH, 2544 West Montrose Avenue, Chicago, Illinois, Zip 60618–1589, tel. 773/267–2622; Richard Cerceo, Chief Executive Officer) (Nonreporting) **A**1 10 **S** ScionHealth, Louisville, KY
Primary Contact: Kathy Kelly, Market Chief Executive Officer
CFO: Chona Aban, Controller
CMO: Maher Najjar, M.D., Medical Director
CNO: Maria Suvacarov, Chief Clinical Officer
Web address: https://www.kindredhospitals.com/locations/ltac/kindred-hospital-chicago-northlake-campus
Control: Corporation, Investor–owned (for–profit) **Service:** Acute long–term care hospital

Staffed Beds: 94

O FALLON—St. Clair County

☒ **HSHS ST. ELIZABETH'S HOSPITAL (140187)**, 1 Saint Elizabeth Boulevard, Zip 62269–1099; tel. 618/234–2120, **A**1 2 3 5 10 **F**3 11 12 13 15 18 20 22 24 26 28 29 30 31 34 35 40 44 45 46 47 48 49 51 54 57 59 60 64 68 70 74 75 76 77 78 79 81 82 102 107 108 111 112 114 115 119 126 129 130 132 146 147 148 149 154 156 157 167 **S** HSHS Hospital Sisters Health System, Springfield, IL
Primary Contact: Chris Klay, FACHE, President and Chief Executive Officer, Southern Illinois Market and President and Chief Executive Of
CFO: David Nosacka, Chief Financial Officer
CMO: Shelly Harkins, M.D., Chief Medical Officer
CIO: Leslee Martin, Manager Information Technology
CHR: Jason T Snow, Director People Services
Web address: www.steliz.org
Control: Church operated, Nongovernment, not–for–profit **Service:** General medical and surgical

Staffed Beds: 144 **Admissions:** 10129 **Census:** 125 **Outpatient Visits:** 201405 **Births:** 841 **Total Expense ($000):** 305756 **Payroll Expense ($000):** 81450 **Personnel:** 971

OAK LAWN—Cook County

★ ⇧ **ADVOCATE CHRIST MEDICAL CENTER (140208)**, 4440 West 95th Street, Zip 60453–2699; tel. 708/684–8000, (Includes ADVOCATE HOPE CHILDREN'S HOSPITAL, 4440 West 95th Street, Oak Lawn, Illinois, Zip 60453–2600, tel. 708/684–8000) **A**2 3 5 8 10 21 **F**3 5 8 9 11 13 15 17 18 19 20 21 22 23 24 25 26 27 28 29 30 31 32 34 35 37 38 39 40 41 43 44 45 46 47 48 49 50 52 54 55 56 57 58 59 60 61 62 63 64 65 66 68 70 71 72 74 75 76 77 78 79 81 82 84 85 86 87 88 89 90 92 93 96 97 100 101 102 104 107 108 109 110 111 114 115 116 117 118 119 120 121 123 124 126 130 131 132 134 135 137 138 141 143 145 146 147 148 154 156 160 161 164 165 167 169 **P**1 6 **S** Advocate Aurora Health, Downers Grove, IL
Primary Contact: Mike Farrell, Interim President
CFO: Robert Pekofske, Vice President Finance
CMO: Robert Stein, M.D., Vice President Medical Management
CIO: Brian Banbury, Director Site Information Systems
Web address: https://www.advocatehealth.com/cmc/
Control: Other not–for–profit (including NFP Corporation) **Service:** General medical and surgical

Staffed Beds: 762 **Admissions:** 40031 **Census:** 670 **Outpatient Visits:** 362893 **Births:** 4015 **Total Expense ($000):** 1320774 **Payroll Expense ($000):** 417848 **Personnel:** 5606

OAK PARK—Cook County

☒ **RUSH OAK PARK HOSPITAL (140063)**, 520 South Maple Avenue, Zip 60304–1097; tel. 708/383–9300, **A**1 3 5 10 **F**3 11 12 15 18 20 22 26 28 29 31 33 34 35 37 40 45 50 56 57 58 59 64 65 70 74 75 77 78 79 81 82 85 87 91 92 93 96 97 107 108 110 111 114 115 119 120 121 126 129 130 131 141 145 146 147 148 149 154 164 167 **P**8 **S** Rush University System for Health, Chicago, IL
Primary Contact: Dino Rumoro, D.O., M.P.H., Chief Executive Officer
CFO: Elvy Yap, Director of Finance
CHR: Arlene Cruz, Director
Web address: www.roph.org
Control: Other not–for–profit (including NFP Corporation) **Service:** General medical and surgical

Staffed Beds: 87 **Admissions:** 4320 **Census:** 54 **Outpatient Visits:** 172521 **Births:** 0 **Total Expense ($000):** 188515 **Payroll Expense ($000):** 95130 **Personnel:** 883

☐ **WEST SUBURBAN MEDICAL CENTER (140049)**, 3 Erie Court, Zip 60302–2599; tel. 708/383–6200, (Nonreporting) **A**1 2 3 5 10 13
Primary Contact: Manoj Prasad, M.D., Group Chief Executive Officer
CFO: Jennifer Lamont, Chief Financial Officer
CMO: Robert Chase, M.D., Physician Advisor
CHR: Nancy Gunnell, Chief Human Resource Officer
CNO: Roslyn J Lennon, R.N., MS, Chief Nursing Officer
Web address: https://www.westsuburbanmc.com/
Control: Corporation, Investor–owned (for–profit) **Service:** General medical and surgical

Staffed Beds: 172

OLNEY—Richland County

★ ⇧ **CARLE RICHLAND MEMORIAL HOSPITAL (140147)**, 800 East Locust Street, Zip 62450–2553; tel. 618/395–2131, (Total facility includes 20 beds in nursing home–type unit) **A**10 20 21 **F**3 11 13 15 18 28 29 31 34 35 40 45 57 59 64 68 69 70 75 76 78 79 81 82 85 87 89 93 97 104 107 108 110 111 115 119 127 130 132 133 146 147 148 154 160 169 **S** Carle Health, Urbana, IL
Primary Contact: Gina R. Thomas, President
CMO: Brian Atwood, M.D., Associate Medical Director
CIO: Tim Gillespie, Manager Information Systems
CHR: Marsha Heath, Human Resources Manager
CNO: Gina R. Thomas, Chief Nursing Officer and Director of Patient Care Services
Web address: www.carlermh.com
Control: Other not–for–profit (including NFP Corporation) **Service:** General medical and surgical

Staffed Beds: 68 **Admissions:** 2055 **Census:** 28 **Outpatient Visits:** 127109 **Births:** 214 **Total Expense ($000):** 74780 **Payroll Expense ($000):** 36893 **Personnel:** 397

OLYMPIA FIELDS—Cook County

★ ○ **FRANCISCAN HEALTH OLYMPIA FIELDS (140172)**, 20201 South Crawford Avenue, Zip 60461–1010; tel. 708/747–4000, (Includes FRANCISCAN HEALTH OLYMPIA FIELDS, 20201 Crawford Avenue, Olympia Fields, Illinois, Zip 60461–1010, tel. 708/747–4000) (Nonreporting) **A**3 5 10 11 12 13 19 **S** Franciscan Health, Mishawaka, IN
Primary Contact: Raymond Grady, FACHE, Chief Executive Officer
CFO: Frank McHugh, Vice President Finance Chief Financial Officer
CIO: Stephen Maes, Director Information Systems
Web address: https://www.franciscanhealth.org/find-a-location/franciscan-health-olympia-fields-218593
Control: Church operated, Nongovernment, not–for–profit **Service:** General medical and surgical

Staffed Beds: 206

ST. JAMES HOSPITALS AND HEALTH CENTERS – OLYMPIA FIELDS CAMPUS
See Franciscan Health Olympia Fields

OTTAWA—Lasalle County

☒ **OSF SAINT ELIZABETH MEDICAL CENTER (140110)**, 1100 East Norris Drive, Zip 61350–1687; tel. 815/433–3100, **A**1 10 19 **F**3 11 13 15 18 28 29 30 34 35 40 42 45 48 49 53 56 57 59 68 70 75 76 77 79 81 82 84 85 86 87 93 94 98 99 100 101 102 104 105 107 108 110 111 115 116 117 118 119 120 121 129 130 131 132 135 143 144 146 148 149 153 154 155 156 157 160 162 164 165 167 **S** OSF Healthcare, Peoria, IL
Primary Contact: Dawn Trompeter, President
CFO: Brad Chamberlin, Director of Finance
CMO: Brian S Rosborough, M.D., Chief Medical Officer
CHR: Karen M Russell, Director of Employee Relations
CNO: Heather Bomstad, MSN, R.N., Vice President, Chief Nursing Officer
Web address: www.osfsaintelizabeth.org
Control: Church operated, Nongovernment, not–for–profit **Service:** General medical and surgical

Staffed Beds: 89 **Admissions:** 3842 **Census:** 41 **Outpatient Visits:** 176389 **Births:** 484 **Total Expense ($000):** 115285 **Payroll Expense ($000):** 53698 **Personnel:** 781

Hospitals, U.S. / ILLINOIS

PALOS HEIGHTS—Cook County

☒ **NORTHWESTERN MEDICINE PALOS HOSPITAL (140062)**, 12251 South 80th Avenue, Zip 60463-0930; tel. 708/923-4000, **A**1 2 5 10 **F**3 4 5 11 13 15 17 18 20 22 24 26 28 29 30 31 34 35 38 40 41 45 46 47 49 50 51 54 55 57 58 59 61 62 63 64 69 70 73 74 75 76 77 78 79 81 84 85 87 89 90 92 93 97 98 100 101 102 104 105 107 108 110 111 114 115 116 117 119 126 130 131 132 135 144 146 147 148 149 152 153 154 156 160 162 164 167 169 **S** Northwestern Memorial HealthCare, Chicago, IL
Primary Contact: Jeff Good, President
CFO: Hugh Rose, Vice President Fiscal Management
CIO: Peggy Carroll, Chief Information Officer
CHR: Mary Denisienko, Vice President Human Resources
Web address: https://www.nm.org/locations/palos-hospital
Control: Other not-for-profit (including NFP Corporation) **Service:** General medical and surgical

Staffed Beds: 406 **Admissions:** 17937 **Census:** 252 **Outpatient Visits:** 440695 **Births:** 691 **Total Expense ($000):** 612285 **Payroll Expense ($000):** 254416 **Personnel:** 2403

PANA—Christian County

★ ⇑ **PANA COMMUNITY HOSPITAL (141341)**, 101 East Ninth Street, Zip 62557-1785; tel. 217/562-2131, **A**10 18 21 **F**3 15 28 29 30 31 34 35 40 45 46 49 50 53 59 61 62 63 69 75 77 78 79 81 87 97 107 110 111 115 127 129 130 131 132 133 143 144 146 148 149 154 156 167
Primary Contact: Trina Casner, FACHE, President and Chief Executive Officer
CFO: James Moon, Chief Financial Officer
CMO: Alan Frigy, M.D., President Medical Staff
CIO: Dianne Bailey, Chief Information Officer
CHR: Luann A Funk, Administrative Assistant and Manager Human Resources
CNO: Vickie Coen, Chief Clinical Officer and Nurse Executive
Web address: www.panahospital.com
Control: Other not-for-profit (including NFP Corporation) **Service:** General medical and surgical

Staffed Beds: 22 **Admissions:** 292 **Census:** 4 **Outpatient Visits:** 44928 **Births:** 0 **Total Expense ($000):** 36508 **Payroll Expense ($000):** 15645 **Personnel:** 369

PARIS—Edgar County

☒ **PARIS COMMUNITY HOSPITAL (141320)**, 721 East Court Street, Zip 61944-2460; tel. 217/465-4141, **A**1 10 18 **F**3 7 12 15 18 26 28 29 30 31 32 34 35 40 45 50 54 56 57 59 60 62 64 65 69 71 74 75 77 78 79 81 82 85 86 87 93 94 97 99 100 101 103 104 107 108 110 111 115 118 119 127 130 131 132 133 135 143 144 146 147 148 149 150 154 156 157 160 164 165 169 **P**6 **S** Alliant Management Services, Louisville, KY
Primary Contact: Oliver Smith, President and Chief Executive Officer
CFO: Martin D. Adams, CPA, Vice President Finance and Chief Financial Officer
CIO: Ed Weeks, Manager Information Services
CHR: Nan Dunning, Human Resources Manager
CNO: Tiffany Turner, MSN, R.N., Vice President of Nursing and Chief Nursing Officer
Web address: https://www.myhorizonhealth.org/locations/paris-community-hospital/
Control: Other not-for-profit (including NFP Corporation) **Service:** General medical and surgical

Staffed Beds: 25 **Admissions:** 611 **Census:** 6 **Outpatient Visits:** 198627 **Births:** 0 **Total Expense ($000):** 124965 **Payroll Expense ($000):** 56517 **Personnel:** 718

PARK RIDGE—Cook County

★ △ ⇑ **ADVOCATE LUTHERAN GENERAL HOSPITAL (140223)**, 1775 Dempster Street, Zip 60068-1174; tel. 847/723-2210, **A**2 3 5 7 8 10 13 19 21 **F**2 3 4 5 6 8 9 11 13 15 17 18 19 20 22 24 26 28 29 30 31 32 34 35 37 38 39 40 41 43 44 45 46 47 48 49 50 52 53 55 56 57 58 59 60 61 63 64 65 66 68 69 70 71 72 74 75 76 77 78 79 80 81 82 84 85 86 87 88 89 90 92 93 94 96 97 98 99 100 101 102 103 104 105 107 108 110 111 115 116 117 118 119 120 121 123 124 126 129 130 131 132 134 135 136 143 144 146 147 148 149 150 152 153 154 156 157 160 161 162 164 165 167 169 **P**1 6 **S** Advocate Aurora Health, Downers Grove, IL
Primary Contact: Allison Wyler, President
CFO: Beth Hickey, Vice President, Finance
CMO: Leo Kelly, Vice President Medical Management
CIO: Mark Beitzel, Director Information Systems
CHR: Katie Bata, Vice President Human Resources
CNO: Jane Denten, MSN, R.N., Chief Nurse Executive
Web address: www.advocatehealth.com/luth/
Control: Other not-for-profit (including NFP Corporation) **Service:** General medical and surgical

Staffed Beds: 704 **Admissions:** 31147 **Census:** 508 **Outpatient Visits:** 369426 **Births:** 3597 **Total Expense ($000):** 944228 **Payroll Expense ($000):** 310433 **Personnel:** 4395

PEKIN—Tazewell County

☒ **CARLE HEALTH PEKIN HOSPITAL (140120)**, 600 South 13th Street, Zip 61554-4936; tel. 309/347-1151, (Data for 275 days) **A**1 10 **F**3 11 15 18 20 29 34 35 40 45 46 47 48 49 50 57 59 60 64 68 70 74 75 77 79 81 82 85 86 87 93 95 104 107 108 110 111 114 115 119 130 143 144 145 146 147 148 149 154 164 167 **S** Carle Health, Urbana, IL
Primary Contact: Keith Knepp, M.D., Regional President
COO: Jeanine R. Spain, R.N., MS, Vice President, Chief Operating Officer and Chief Nursing Officer
CFO: Steve Hall, Chief Financial Officer
CMO: Kathryn Kramer, M.D., President Medical Staff
CHR: Anne Dierker, Vice President Hospital Services
CNO: Jeanine R. Spain, R.N., MS, Vice President, Chief Operating Officer and Chief Nursing Officer
Web address: https://carle.org/locations/carle-health-pekin-hospital
Control: Other not-for-profit (including NFP Corporation) **Service:** General medical and surgical

Staffed Beds: 39 **Admissions:** 1356 **Census:** 20 **Outpatient Visits:** 47022 **Births:** 0 **Total Expense ($000):** 42343 **Payroll Expense ($000):** 14532 **Personnel:** 268

PEORIA—Peoria County

☒ **CARLE HEALTH METHODIST HOSPITAL (140209)**, 221 NE Glen Oak Avenue, Zip 61636-4310; tel. 309/672-5522, (Data for 275 days) **A**1 2 3 5 10 19 **F**3 9 11 12 13 15 17 18 20 22 24 26 29 30 31 32 34 35 36 38 40 43 44 45 46 47 49 50 53 54 56 57 58 59 60 62 63 64 68 70 73 74 75 76 77 78 79 81 82 84 85 86 87 89 90 92 93 96 98 99 100 101 102 104 105 107 108 110 111 115 116 117 118 119 120 121 126 127 129 130 131 132 134 135 136 145 146 147 148 149 150 153 154 156 162 164 167 169 **S** Carle Health, Urbana, IL
Primary Contact: Keith Knepp, M.D., Regional President
COO: Jeanine R. Spain, R.N., MS, Vice President, Chief Operating Officer and Chief Nursing Officer
CFO: Robert Quin, Regional Vice President Finance, and Chief Financial Officer
CMO: Gary Knepp, D.O., Regional Chief Medical Officer and Chief Quality Officer
CHR: Joy Ledbetter, Regional Chief Human Resources Officer
CNO: Jeanine R. Spain, R.N., MS, Vice President, Chief Operating Officer and Chief Nursing Officer
Web address: https://carle.org/locations/carle-health-methodist-hospital
Control: Other not-for-profit (including NFP Corporation) **Service:** General medical and surgical

Staffed Beds: 286 **Admissions:** 8676 **Census:** 199 **Outpatient Visits:** 370997 **Births:** 1261 **Total Expense ($000):** 406891 **Payroll Expense ($000):** 198794 **Personnel:** 2490

Hospital, Medicare Provider Number, Address, Telephone, Approval, Facility, and Physician Codes, Health Care System

★ American Hospital Association (AHA) membership ○ Healthcare Facilities Accreditation Program ⇑ Center for Improvement in Healthcare Quality Accreditation
□ The Joint Commission accreditation ◇ DNV Healthcare Inc. accreditation △ Commission on Accreditation of Rehabilitation Facilities (CARF) accreditation

Hospitals, U.S. / ILLINOIS

☐ **CARLE HEALTH PROCTOR HOSPITAL (140013)**, 5409 North Knoxville Avenue, Zip 61614–5069; tel. 309/691–1000, (Data for 275 days) **A**1 3 5 10 **F**3 4 5 11 15 18 20 22 28 29 30 34 40 45 51 53 57 59 60 64 68 70 74 75 79 81 85 86 87 93 98 103 104 107 108 110 111 114 115 118 119 130 132 135 143 145 146 148 149 150 151 152 154 160 167 **S** Carle Health, Urbana, IL
Primary Contact: Keith Knepp, M.D., Regional President
COO: Jeanine R. Spain, R.N., MS, Vice President, Chief Operating Officer and Chief Nursing Officer
CFO: Roger Armstrong, Vice President Finance and Chief Financial Officer
CHR: Linda K Buck, Vice President Human Resources
CNO: Jeanine R. Spain, R.N., MS, Vice President, Chief Operating Officer and Chief Nursing Officer
Web address: https://carle.org/locations/carle-health-proctor-hospital
Control: Other not–for–profit (including NFP Corporation) **Service**: General medical and surgical

Staffed Beds: 88 **Admissions**: 2321 **Census**: 40 **Outpatient Visits**: 43799 **Births**: 0 **Total Expense ($000)**: 98565 **Payroll Expense ($000)**: 28080 **Personnel**: 471

KINDRED HOSPITAL PEORIA See OSF Transitional Care Hospital

✠ **OSF SAINT FRANCIS MEDICAL CENTER (140067)**, 530 NE Glen Oak Avenue, Zip 61637–0001; tel. 309/655–2000, (Includes CHILDREN'S HOSPITAL OF ILLINOIS, 530 NE Glen Oak Avenue, Peoria, Illinois, Zip 61637–0001, tel. 309/655–7171; Kelly Nierstedt, President) **A**1 2 3 5 8 10 19 **F**3 9 11 12 13 15 17 18 19 20 21 22 23 24 25 26 27 28 29 30 31 32 34 35 37 38 39 40 41 43 44 45 46 47 48 49 50 51 52 54 56 57 58 59 60 64 65 66 70 71 72 73 74 75 76 77 78 79 80 81 82 83 84 85 86 87 88 89 90 92 93 95 96 100 102 104 105 107 108 109 110 111 112 114 115 116 117 118 119 120 121 124 126 129 130 132 137 138 142 145 146 147 148 149 153 154 167 168 169 **S** OSF Healthcare, Peoria, IL
Primary Contact: Michael Wells, President
CFO: Ken Harbaugh, Vice President and Chief Financial Officer
CMO: Robert T. Sparrow, M.D., Vice President, Chief Medical Officer
CHR: Jacki L. Fugitt, Director Employee Relations
CNO: Jennifer Croland, Chief Nursing Officer, Vice President Patient Care
Web address: www.osfsaintfrancis.org
Control: Church operated, Nongovernment, not–for–profit **Service**: General medical and surgical

Staffed Beds: 642 **Admissions**: 28139 **Census**: 463 **Outpatient Visits**: 644424 **Births**: 2426 **Total Expense ($000)**: 1225805 **Payroll Expense ($000)**: 355007 **Personnel**: 4503

✠ **OSF TRANSITIONAL CARE HOSPITAL (142013)**, 500 West Romeo B Garrett Avenue, Zip 61605–2301; tel. 309/680–1500, (Nonreporting) **A**1 10 **S** OSF Healthcare, Peoria, IL
Primary Contact: Christopher Curry, President
CMO: Michael Peil, M.D., Chief Medical Director
Web address: https://www.osftch.com/
Control: Corporation, Investor–owned (for–profit) **Service**: Acute long–term care hospital

Staffed Beds: 50

UNITYPOINT HEALTH – PEORIA See Carle Health Methodist Hospital

PEORIA HEIGHTS—Peoria County

SAINT CLAIRE HOME See Saint Clare Home

PINCKNEYVILLE—Perry County

PINCKNEYVILLE COMMUNITY HOSPITAL (141307), 5383 State Route 154, Zip 62274–1099, Mailing Address: PO Box 437, Zip 62274–1099; tel. 618/357–2187, (Nonreporting) **A**10 18
Primary Contact: Randall W. Dauby, Chief Executive Officer
COO: Bradley Futrell, Chief Operating Officer
CFO: Kara Jo Carson, Chief Financial Officer
CIO: Jeff Roberts, Director Information Technology
CHR: Christie Gajewski, Director Human Resources
CNO: Eva Hopp, Chief Nurse Executive
Web address: www.pvillehosp.org/
Control: Hospital district or authority, Government, Nonfederal **Service**: General medical and surgical

Staffed Beds: 17

PITTSFIELD—Pike County

★ ✠ **ILLINI COMMUNITY HOSPITAL (141315)**, 640 West Washington Street, Zip 62363–1350; tel. 217/285–2113, **A**10 18 21 **F**3 15 28 29 30 31 34 40 59 64 65 70 77 81 85 87 89 97 104 107 110 115 119 127 133 144 146 149 154 **P**6
Primary Contact: Holly A. Jones, Administrator
CFO: Tim Moore, Vice President Finance
CMO: Bashar Alzein, M.D., President Medical Staff
CHR: Becky Myers, Human Resources Specialist
CNO: Holly A Jones, Administrative Director Nursing Services
Web address: www.illinihospital.org
Control: Other not–for–profit (including NFP Corporation) **Service**: General medical and surgical

Staffed Beds: 25 **Admissions**: 458 **Census**: 5 **Outpatient Visits**: 95520 **Births**: 0 **Total Expense ($000)**: 34534 **Payroll Expense ($000)**: 15716 **Personnel**: 190

PONTIAC—Livingston County

✠ **OSF SAINT JAMES – JOHN W. ALBRECHT MEDICAL CENTER (140161)**, 2500 West Reynolds, Zip 61764–9774; tel. 815/842–2828, **A**1 10 20 **F**3 8 11 15 18 28 29 30 32 34 35 40 45 50 51 56 57 59 64 68 70 75 79 81 82 84 85 86 89 91 93 97 107 110 111 115 117 118 119 127 128 129 130 131 132 133 135 146 147 148 149 154 156 **S** OSF Healthcare, Peoria, IL
Primary Contact: Derrick A. Frazier, FACHE, President
CFO: Paula Corrigan, Vice President and Chief Financial Officer
CMO: John M. Rinker, Chief Medical Officer
CNO: Elizabeth Davidson, R.N., Vice President, Patient Care Services
Web address: www.osfsaintjames.org
Control: Church operated, Nongovernment, not–for–profit **Service**: General medical and surgical

Staffed Beds: 38 **Admissions**: 1289 **Census**: 12 **Outpatient Visits**: 81125 **Births**: 108 **Total Expense ($000)**: 61232 **Payroll Expense ($000)**: 30803 **Personnel**: 417

PRINCETON—Bureau County

★ **OSF SAINT CLARE MEDICAL CENTER (141337)**, 530 Park Avenue East, Zip 61356–2598; tel. 815/875–2811, **A**10 18 **F**11 15 18 28 30 31 32 34 35 40 45 48 49 51 56 57 59 64 65 66 70 75 77 78 79 81 82 86 87 93 97 100 104 107 108 110 111 115 118 119 127 129 130 131 132 133 144 145 146 148 149 153 154 156 **S** OSF Healthcare, Peoria, IL
Primary Contact: Jackie Kernan, R.N., MSN, President
COO: Chris J. Williams, FACHE, Vice President Operations
CFO: Mike DeFoe, Chief Financial Officer
CMO: T Doran, M.D., Chief of Staff
CIO: Karen Behrens, Director Technology Services
CHR: James Lewandowski, Vice President Human Resources
Web address: https://perrymemorial.org
Control: Other not–for–profit (including NFP Corporation) **Service**: General medical and surgical

Staffed Beds: 25 **Admissions**: 455 **Census**: 3 **Outpatient Visits**: 82651 **Births**: 0 **Total Expense ($000)**: 41818 **Payroll Expense ($000)**: 15302 **Personnel**: 223

PERRY MEMORIAL HOSPITAL See OSF Saint Clare Medical Center

QUINCY—Adams County

★ △ ✠ **BLESSING HOSPITAL (140015)**, 11th and Broadway, Zip 62305–7005, Mailing Address: P.O. Box 7005, Zip 62305–7005; tel. 217/223–1200, (Includes BLESSING HOSPITAL, 1005 Broadway Street, Quincy, Illinois, Zip 62301–2834, P O Box 7005, Zip 62305–7005, tel. 217/223–1200) (Total facility includes 20 beds in nursing home–type unit) **A**2 3 5 7 10 13 21 **F**3 5 8 11 12 13 15 17 18 20 22 24 26 28 29 30 31 32 33 34 35 37 40 43 44 45 48 49 50 53 54 56 57 58 59 61 62 63 64 66 68 70 73 74 75 76 77 78 79 81 82 84 85 86 87 89 90 96 97 98 99 100 101 102 104 105 107 108 110 111 112 114 115 118 119 120 121 123 124 126 127 128 129 130 131 132 135 144 146 147 148 149 152 153 154 156 160 162 164 165 167 168 169
Primary Contact: Brian Canfield, President and Chief Executive Officer
CFO: Patrick M Gerveler, Vice President Finance and Chief Financial Officer
CMO: George Liesmann, M.D., Chief Medical Officer
CHR: Michelle Zech, Chief Human Resources Officer
CNO: Jill K Mason, MS, R.N., Chief Nursing Officer
Web address: https://www.blessinghealth.org/
Control: Other not–for–profit (including NFP Corporation) **Service**: General medical and surgical

Staffed Beds: 352 **Admissions**: 14497 **Census**: 193 **Outpatient Visits**: 454868 **Births**: 1163 **Total Expense ($000)**: 604869 **Payroll Expense ($000)**: 266525 **Personnel**: 3130

ST MARY HOSPITAL See Blessing Hospital

Hospitals, U.S. / ILLINOIS

RED BUD—Randolph County

☐ **RED BUD REGIONAL HOSPITAL (141348)**, 325 Spring Street, Zip 62278-1105; tel. 618/282-3831, (Nonreporting) **A**1 10 18
Primary Contact: Jennifer Gregson, Chief Administrative Officer
CFO: Veronica Marin, Chief Financial Officer
CMO: Julie Kelley, M.D., Chief of Staff
CIO: Nick Behnken, IT Director
CHR: Lori Brooks, Director Human Resources
Web address: www.redbudregional.com
Control: Corporation, Investor-owned (for-profit) **Service:** General medical and surgical

Staffed Beds: 140

ROBINSON—Crawford County

★ ○ **CRAWFORD MEMORIAL HOSPITAL (141343)**, 1000 North Allen Street, Zip 62454-1167; tel. 618/544-3131, (Nonreporting) **A**10 11 18 **S** Ovation Healthcare, Brentwood, TN
Primary Contact: Douglas Florkowski, Chief Executive Officer
CFO: Richard Carlson, Chief Financial Officer
CMO: Gary Tennison, M.D., Chief of Staff
CIO: Tim Richard, IT Coordinator
CHR: Kristi Zane, Chief Human Resources Officer
CNO: Tammy Fralicker, MS, R.N., Chief Nursing Officer
Web address: www.crawfordmh.net
Control: Hospital district or authority, Government, Nonfederal **Service:** General medical and surgical

Staffed Beds: 25

ROCHELLE—Ogle County

✠ **ROCHELLE COMMUNITY HOSPITAL (141312)**, 900 North Second Street, Zip 61068-1764; tel. 815/562-2181, **A**1 10 18 **F**3 11 15 28 29 30 31 34 35 40 41 45 53 59 64 68 70 74 75 77 78 79 81 82 85 86 87 90 93 97 107 110 111 115 119 130 131 132 133 135 144 146 149 154 156 167 **P**6
Primary Contact: Karen Tracy, R.N., Chief Executive Officer
CFO: Lori Gutierrez, Chief Financial Officer
CMO: Michael Monfils, M.D., Chief of Medical Staff
CIO: Scott Stewart, Manager Information Services
CHR: Denise Bauer, Director of Human Resources
CNO: Rhonda Marks, Chief Nursing Officer
Web address: https://www.rochellehospital.com/
Control: Other not-for-profit (including NFP Corporation) **Service:** General medical and surgical

Staffed Beds: 17 **Admissions:** 363 **Census:** 3 **Outpatient Visits:** 39204 **Births:** 0 **Total Expense ($000):** 48287 **Payroll Expense ($000):** 20747 **Personnel:** 273

ROCK ISLAND—Rock Island County

ST ANTHONY CONTINUING CARE CTR See St. Anthony's Continuing Care Center

★ ⇧ **UNITYPOINT HEALTH – TRINITY ROCK ISLAND (140280)**, 2701 17th Street, Zip 61201-5393; tel. 309/779-5000, (Includes UNITYPOINT HEALTH – TRINITY MOLINE, 500 John Deere Road, Moline, Illinois, Zip 61265, tel. 309/779-5000) **A**10 19 21 **F**3 4 5 11 12 13 15 18 20 22 24 26 28 29 30 31 34 35 38 40 43 44 45 46 49 50 55 57 58 59 64 68 70 73 74 75 76 78 79 81 82 85 86 87 93 96 98 100 102 104 105 107 108 110 114 115 118 119 120 121 123 126 129 130 132 146 147 148 149 150 152 153 154 157 158 160 162 164 165 167 169 **S** UnityPoint Health, West Des Moines, IA
Primary Contact: Shawn Morrow, FACHE, Market President
COO: Barbara Weber, Chief Operating Officer
CFO: Katie A Marchik, Chief Financial Officer
CMO: Paul McLoone, M.D., Chief Medical Officer
CHR: Cara Fuller, Vice President Human Resources
CNO: Ginger L Renkiewicz, Chief Clinical Officer, Chief Nursing Executive, and Chief Quality Officer
Web address: https://www.unitypoint.org
Control: Other not-for-profit (including NFP Corporation) **Service:** General medical and surgical

Staffed Beds: 256 **Admissions:** 10625 **Census:** 131 **Outpatient Visits:** 498478 **Births:** 779 **Total Expense ($000):** 377546 **Payroll Expense ($000):** 134093 **Personnel:** 1481

ROCKFORD—Boone County

✠ **MERCYHEALTH JAVON BEA HOSPITAL – RIVERSIDE CAMPUS (140239)**, 8201 East Riverside Boulevard, Zip 61114-2300; tel. 815/971-7000, (Includes JAVON BEA HOSPITAL–ROCKTON, 2400 North Rockton Avenue, Rockford, Illinois, Zip 61103-3655, tel. 815/971-2292; Javon R. Bea, President and Chief Executive Officer) (Nonreporting) **A**1 2 3 5 **S** Mercy Health System, Janesville, WI
Primary Contact: Javon R. Bea, President and Chief Executive Officer
Web address: https://www.mercyhealthsystem.org/locations/javon-bea-hospital-riverside/
Control: Other not-for-profit (including NFP Corporation) **Service:** General medical and surgical

Staffed Beds: 188

ROCKFORD—Winnebago County

MERCYHEALTH HOSPITAL – ROCKTON AVENUE See Javon Bea Hospital–Rockton

✠ **OSF SAINT ANTHONY MEDICAL CENTER (140233)**, 5666 East State Street, Zip 61108-2425; tel. 815/226-2000, **A**1 2 3 10 19 **F**3 11 12 13 15 16 18 19 20 22 24 26 28 29 30 31 32 34 35 36 37 38 40 41 43 44 45 46 49 50 51 54 55 56 57 58 59 63 64 66 70 74 75 76 77 78 79 80 81 82 84 85 86 87 92 93 100 107 108 110 111 114 115 116 117 118 119 120 121 123 124 126 127 129 130 131 132 135 145 146 147 148 149 150 154 167 168 169 **P**6 **S** OSF Healthcare, Peoria, IL
Primary Contact: Paula A. Carynski, MS, R.N., President
COO: James Girardy, M.D., Vice President, Chief Surgical Officer
CFO: David Stenerson, Vice President and Chief Financial Officer
CMO: Harneet Bath, M.D., Vice President, Chief Medicine Officer
CIO: Kathy Peterson, Director Information Services
CHR: Karen C Brown, Vice President Chief Operating Officer
Web address: www.osfhealth.com
Control: Church operated, Nongovernment, not-for-profit **Service:** General medical and surgical

Staffed Beds: 241 **Admissions:** 10461 **Census:** 158 **Outpatient Visits:** 221742 **Births:** 372 **Total Expense ($000):** 412351 **Payroll Expense ($000):** 122666 **Personnel:** 1454

SWEDISHAMERICAN – A DIVISION OF UW HEALTH See UW Health Swedishamerican Hospital

✠ **UW HEALTH SWEDISHAMERICAN HOSPITAL (140228)**, 1401 East State Street, Zip 61104-2315; tel. 815/968-4400, **A**1 2 3 5 10 19 **F**3 5 13 15 17 18 20 22 24 26 28 29 30 31 34 35 36 38 39 40 43 44 45 46 48 49 50 51 54 55 56 57 58 59 61 64 65 68 70 71 72 74 76 77 78 79 81 84 85 86 87 89 92 93 98 99 100 102 105 107 108 110 111 115 118 119 124 126 129 130 132 135 146 147 148 149 151 154 156 162 164 167 169 **P**6 **S** UW Health, Madison, WI
Primary Contact: Travis Andersen, President and Chief Executive Officer
COO: Don Daniels, Executive Vice President and Chief Operating Officer
CFO: Patti DeWane, Chief Financial Officer and Treasurer
CMO: Mike Polizzotto, Chief Medical Officer
CIO: Sheryl Johnson, Chief Information Officer
CHR: Gerard Guinane, Vice President Human Resources
Web address: https://www.uwhealth.org/locations/swedishamerican
Control: Other not-for-profit (including NFP Corporation) **Service:** General medical and surgical

Staffed Beds: 339 **Admissions:** 16083 **Census:** 223 **Outpatient Visits:** 262168 **Births:** 2831 **Total Expense ($000):** 541980 **Payroll Expense ($000):** 226054 **Personnel:** 2364

✠ **VAN MATRE ENCOMPASS HEALTH REHABILITATION HOSPITAL (143028)**, 950 South Mulford Road, Zip 61108-4274; tel. 815/381-8500, (Nonreporting) **A**1 10 **S** Encompass Health Corporation, Birmingham, AL
Primary Contact: Scott J. Peterson, Interim Chief Executive Officer
CNO: Chrisi Karcz, Chief Nursing Officer
Web address: www.healthsouth.com
Control: Corporation, Investor-owned (for-profit) **Service:** Rehabilitation

Staffed Beds: 61

Hospital, Medicare Provider Number, Address, Telephone, Approval, Facility, and Physician Codes, Health Care System

★ American Hospital Association (AHA) membership ○ Healthcare Facilities Accreditation Program ⇧ Center for Improvement in Healthcare Quality Accreditation
☐ The Joint Commission accreditation ◇ DNV Healthcare Inc. accreditation △ Commission on Accreditation of Rehabilitation Facilities (CARF) accreditation

© 2025 AHA Guide

Hospitals, U.S. / ILLINOIS

ROSICLARE—Hardin County

★ **HARDIN COUNTY GENERAL HOSPITAL (141328)**, 6 Ferrell Road, Zip 62982, Mailing Address: P.O. Box 2467, Zip 62982-2467; tel. 618/285-6634, **A**10 18 **F**7 18 28 34 40 45 46 50 57 59 65 68 77 93 97 107 119 127 129 130 133 148 154
Primary Contact: Roby D. Williams, Chief Executive Officer
CFO: Janie Parker, Chief Financial Officer
CMO: Marcos N Sunga, M.D., Chief of Staff
CIO: Brian Casteel, Information Technology Technician
CNO: Courtney Spivey, Chief Nursing Officer
Web address: www.ilhcgh.org
Control: Other not-for-profit (including NFP Corporation) **Service**: General medical and surgical

Staffed Beds: 25 **Admissions**: 460 **Census**: 5 **Outpatient Visits**: 17616 **Births**: 0 **Total Expense ($000)**: 13569 **Payroll Expense ($000)**: 8155 **Personnel**: 114

RUSHVILLE—Schuyler County

★ **SARAH D. CULBERTSON MEMORIAL HOSPITAL (141333)**, 238 South Congress Street, Zip 62681-1472; tel. 217/322-4321, (Nonreporting) **A**10 18
Primary Contact: Gregg Snyder, Chief Executive Officer
CFO: Alan Palo, Chief Financial Officer
CMO: Marguerite Taillefer, M.D., Acting President Medical Staff
CIO: Dan Wise, Manager Information Technology
CNO: Lisa M Downs, R.N., Chief Nursing Officer
Web address: www.cmhospital.com
Control: Hospital district or authority, Government, Nonfederal **Service**: General medical and surgical

Staffed Beds: 22

SALEM—Marion County

★ ○ **SALEM TOWNSHIP HOSPITAL (141345)**, 1201 Ricker Drive, Zip 62881-4263; tel. 618/548-3194, (Nonreporting) **A**10 11 18
Primary Contact: James Timpe, Chief Executive Officer
CMO: Gautam Jha, M.D., Chief of Staff
CIO: Steve Turner, Director Information Technology
CHR: Diane Boswell, Director Human Resources and Marketing
CNO: Lisa Ambuehl, Chief Nursing Officer
Web address: www.sthcares.org
Control: City-county, Government, Nonfederal **Service**: General medical and surgical

Staffed Beds: 22

SANDWICH—Dekalb County

NORTHWESTERN MEDICINE VALLEY WEST HOSPITAL (141340), 1302 North Main Street, Zip 60548-2587; tel. 815/786-8484, **A**1 10 18 **F**3 11 13 15 18 28 29 30 31 34 35 36 38 40 41 44 45 46 49 50 51 57 58 59 60 64 68 70 71 73 74 75 77 78 79 81 82 84 85 87 89 93 102 104 107 108 110 111 115 119 129 130 131 133 135 146 147 148 149 150 154 169 **S** Northwestern Memorial HealthCare, Chicago, IL
Primary Contact: Maura O'Toole, President
COO: Brad Copple, Vice President Operations
CFO: Matthew J Flynn, Chief Financial Officer West Region
CMO: Michael Kulisz, D.O., Vice President, Chief Medical Officer
CIO: Heath Bell, Vice President, Information Services
CNO: Pamela Duffy, MSN, R.N., Vice President Operations and Chief Nursing Executive
Web address: www.nm.org
Control: Other not-for-profit (including NFP Corporation) **Service**: General medical and surgical

Staffed Beds: 19 **Admissions**: 474 **Census**: 6 **Outpatient Visits**: 32959 **Births**: 0 **Total Expense ($000)**: 45364 **Payroll Expense ($000)**: 14665 **Personnel**: 277

SHELBYVILLE—Shelby County

★ **HSHS GOOD SHEPHERD HOSPITAL (141354)**, 200 South Cedar Street, Zip 62565-1838; tel. 217/774-3961, **A**10 18 21 **F**3 15 28 29 30 34 35 40 45 50 57 59 64 77 79 81 97 107 108 110 115 118 119 127 129 131 132 133 146 154 **S** HSHS Hospital Sisters Health System, Springfield, IL
Primary Contact: Matthew Fry, FACHE, President and Chief Executive Officer, Central Illinois Market
CFO: Marilyn Sears, Chief Financial Officer
CMO: David Oligschlaeger, Medical Staff President
CIO: Ian Kuhlman, Manager Information Technology
CHR: Amy Koehler, Director Human Resources
CNO: Michelle Oliver, Chief Nursing Executive
Web address: https://www.hshs.org/good-shepherd
Control: Church operated, Nongovernment, not-for-profit **Service**: General medical and surgical

Staffed Beds: 30 **Admissions**: 318 **Census**: 5 **Outpatient Visits**: 24352 **Births**: 0 **Total Expense ($000)**: 19008 **Payroll Expense ($000)**: 5562 **Personnel**: 68

SHILOH—St. Clair County

REHABILITATION INSTITUTE OF SOUTHERN ILLINOIS, LLC, THE (143030), 2351 Frank Scott Pkwy East, Zip 62269-7457; tel. 618/206-7600, (Nonreporting) **A**1 10 **S** Encompass Health Corporation, Birmingham, AL
Primary Contact: Cassidy Hoelscher, Chief Executive Officer
CFO: Cindy Voss, Controlelr
CMO: Marc Sabatino, Medical Diretor
CNO: Deidra Dace-Murkey, Chief Nursing Officer
Web address: https://encompasshealth.com/locations/shilohrehab
Control: Partnership, Investor-owned (for-profit) **Service**: Rehabilitation

Staffed Beds: 40

SILVIS—Rock Island County

GENESIS MEDICAL CENTER, SILVIS (140275), 801 Illini Drive, Zip 61282-1893; tel. 309/281-4000, **A**1 10 **F**3 7 13 15 18 20 22 26 28 29 30 31 34 35 40 43 45 50 51 53 59 64 65 68 70 75 76 77 78 79 81 85 87 107 108 110 111 114 116 119 126 129 130 135 146 147 149 154 157 169 **S** Trinity Health, Livonia, MI
Primary Contact: Theresa Main, R.N., President
CFO: Mark G Rogers, Interim Vice President Finance and Chief Financial Officer
CMO: Peter Metcalf, M.D., President Medical Staff
CIO: Robert Frieden, Vice President Information Systems
CHR: Heidi Kahly-McMahon, Vice President Human Resources
Web address: www.genesishealth.com
Control: Other not-for-profit (including NFP Corporation) **Service**: General medical and surgical

Staffed Beds: 68 **Admissions**: 1859 **Census**: 21 **Outpatient Visits**: 172640 **Births**: 153 **Total Expense ($000)**: 108418 **Payroll Expense ($000)**: 31151 **Personnel**: 336

SKOKIE—Cook County

NORTHSHORE SKOKIE HOSPITAL See Endeavor Health Skokie Hospital

SPARTA—Randolph County

○ **SPARTA COMMUNITY HOSPITAL (141349)**, 818 East Broadway Street, Zip 62286-1820, Mailing Address: P.O. Box 297, Zip 62286-0297; tel. 618/443-2177, (Nonreporting) **A**10 11 18
Primary Contact: Joann Emge, Chief Executive Officer
CMO: Mark Pruess, M.D., Chief Medical Staff
CIO: Susan Gutjahr, Reimbursement Specialist
CHR: Darla Shawgo, Director Human Resources
CNO: Lori Clinton, Chief Nursing Officer
Web address: www.spartahospital.com
Control: Hospital district or authority, Government, Nonfederal **Service**: General medical and surgical

Staffed Beds: 25

SPRINGFIELD—Sangamon County

ANDREW MCFARLAND MENTAL HEALTH CENTER See Elizabeth Parsons Ware Packard Mental Health Center

Hospitals, U.S. / ILLINOIS

☐ **ELIZABETH PARSONS WARE PACKARD MENTAL HEALTH CENTER (144021)**, 901 East Southwind Road, Zip 62703–5125; tel. 217/786–6994, (Nonreporting) **A**1 10 **S** Division of Mental Health, Department of Human Services, Springfield, IL
Primary Contact: Lana Miller, Administrator
CFO: Jeff Frey, Business Administrator
CMO: Kasturi Kripakaran, M.D., Medical Director
CIO: Josh Kates, Information Technology Analyst
CNO: Frances Collins, Director of Nursing
Control: State, Government, Nonfederal **Service:** Psychiatric

Staffed Beds: 142

✠ **HSHS ST. JOHN'S HOSPITAL (140053)**, 800 East Carpenter Street, Zip 62769–0002; tel. 217/544–6464, (Includes ST. JOHN'S CHILDREN'S HOSPITAL, 800 East Carpenter Street, Springfield, Illinois, Zip 62769, tel. 217/544–6464) **A**1 2 3 5 10 19 **F**3 8 11 13 15 17 18 20 22 24 26 28 29 30 31 34 35 36 37 39 40 41 43 44 45 46 47 48 49 50 51 53 54 56 57 58 59 60 61 62 63 64 68 70 72 74 75 76 77 78 79 81 82 83 84 85 86 87 88 89 92 93 104 107 110 111 115 117 119 120 121 122 123 124 126 129 130 131 132 135 146 147 148 149 150 154 157 167 169 **S** HSHS Hospital Sisters Health System, Springfield, IL
Primary Contact: Matthew Fry, FACHE, President and Chief Executive Officer, Central Illinois Market and President and Chief Executive Off
CFO: Patty Allen, St. John's Vice President Finance
CIO: Ryan Leach, Chief Information Officer
CHR: Becky Puclik, Division Chief People Officer
CNO: Allison Kay Paul, R.N., Chief Nursing Officer
Web address: https://www.hshs.org/st-johns/
Control: Other not–for–profit (including NFP Corporation) **Service:** General medical and surgical

Staffed Beds: 442 **Admissions:** 21180 **Census:** 317 **Outpatient Visits:** 217208 **Births:** 2219 **Total Expense ($000):** 651910 **Payroll Expense ($000):** 161693 **Personnel:** 2063

✠ **LINCOLN PRAIRIE BEHAVIORAL HEALTH CENTER**, 5230 South Sixth Street, Zip 62703–5128; tel. 217/585–1180, (Nonreporting) **A**1 **S** Universal Health Services, Inc., King of Prussia, PA
Primary Contact: Tom DeMarco, Interim Chief Executive Officer
CFO: Chris Statz, Chief Financial Officer
CMO: Pamela Campbell, M.D., Medical Director
CNO: Renae Hale, Chief Nursing Officer
Web address: www.lincolnprairiebhc.com/
Control: Corporation, Investor–owned (for–profit) **Service:** Children's hospital psychiatric

Staffed Beds: 97

MEMORIAL MEDICAL CENTER See Springfield Memorial Hospital

✠ △ **SPRINGFIELD MEMORIAL HOSPITAL (140148)**, 701 North First Street, Zip 62781–0001; tel. 217/788–3000, **A**1 2 3 5 7 8 10 19 **F**3 8 11 12 13 14 15 16 17 18 20 22 24 26 28 29 30 31 32 34 35 36 37 40 43 44 45 46 47 48 49 50 51 54 55 57 58 59 60 61 63 64 65 68 69 70 74 75 76 77 78 79 81 82 84 85 86 87 89 90 91 92 93 96 97 98 100 101 102 104 105 107 110 111 114 115 116 117 118 119 120 121 123 124 126 129 130 131 132 134 135 138 141 145 146 147 148 149 153 154 156 167 **P**5 **S** Memorial Health, Springfield, IL
Primary Contact: Jay M. Roszhart, President and Chief Executive Officer
CFO: Robert W Kay, Senior Vice President and Chief Financial Officer
CMO: Rajesh G. Govindaiah, M.D., Chief Medical Officer
CIO: Jerry Miller, Vice President, Information Services
CHR: Robert F Scott, Vice President and Chief Human Resources Officer
CNO: Marsha A Prater, Ph.D., R.N., Chief Nursing Officer Emeritus
Web address: https://memorial.health/springfield-memorial-hospital/
Control: Other not–for–profit (including NFP Corporation) **Service:** General medical and surgical

Staffed Beds: 464 **Admissions:** 20938 **Census:** 345 **Outpatient Visits:** 512901 **Births:** 1089 **Total Expense ($000):** 799454 **Payroll Expense ($000):** 313814 **Personnel:** 3255

STAUNTON—Macoupin County

COMMUNITY HOSPITAL OF STAUNTON (141306), 400 Caldwell Street, Zip 62088–1499; tel. 618/635–2200, (Nonreporting) **A**10 18
Primary Contact: Larry Spour, Chief Executive Officer
CFO: Brian Engelke, Chief Financial Officer
CMO: Joshua Poos, M.D., President Medical Staff
CIO: Cheryl Horner, Supervisor Data Processing
CHR: Marilyn Herbeck, Coordinator Human Resources
CNO: Roberta Brown, Chief Nursing Officer
Web address: www.stauntonhospital.org
Control: Other not–for–profit (including NFP Corporation) **Service:** General medical and surgical

Staffed Beds: 25

STERLING—Whiteside County

✠ **CGH MEDICAL CENTER (140043)**, 100 East LeFevre Road, Zip 61081–1279; tel. 815/625–0400, **A**1 10 19 **F**3 7 8 11 13 15 18 20 22 28 29 30 31 33 34 35 40 45 47 50 51 57 59 60 62 64 68 70 74 76 77 78 79 81 82 84 85 86 87 89 93 97 98 102 107 108 110 111 112 115 116 117 118 119 124 129 130 132 135 144 145 146 147 148 149 156 157 164 167 169 **P**6
Primary Contact: Paul Steinke, D.O., President and Chief Executive Officer
CFO: Ben Schaab, Vice President, Chief Financial Officer
CIO: Randy Davis, Vice President and Chief Information Officer
CHR: Paul Steinke, D.O., President and Chief Executive Officer
CNO: Amy Berentes, R.N., MSN, Chief Nursing Officer
Web address: www.cghmc.com
Control: City, Government, Nonfederal **Service:** General medical and surgical

Staffed Beds: 96 **Admissions:** 3597 **Census:** 39 **Outpatient Visits:** 564704 **Births:** 452 **Total Expense ($000):** 266001 **Payroll Expense ($000):** 119180 **Personnel:** 1256

STREAMWOOD—Cook County

STREAMWOOD BEHAVIORAL HEALTH CENTER See Streamwood Behavioral Healthcare System

☐ **STREAMWOOD BEHAVIORAL HEALTHCARE SYSTEM (144034)**, 1400 East Irving Park Road, Zip 60107–3203; tel. 630/837–9000, **A**1 10 **F**3 64 68 87 98 99 100 101 104 105 130 135 149 153 154 160 162 163 164 **P**6 **S** Universal Health Services, Inc., King of Prussia, PA
Primary Contact: Ron Weglarz, PsyD, Chief Executive Officer
CMO: Joseph McNally, M.D., Medical Director
CHR: Joseph Rinke, Director Human Resources
CNO: Olieth Lightbourne, Chief Nursing Officer
Web address: www.streamwoodhospital.com
Control: Corporation, Investor–owned (for–profit) **Service:** Psychiatric

Staffed Beds: 178 **Admissions:** 3603 **Census:** 125 **Outpatient Visits:** 18332 **Births:** 0 **Total Expense ($000):** 41430 **Payroll Expense ($000):** 20707 **Personnel:** 221

SYCAMORE—Dekalb County

✠ **KINDRED HOSPITAL–SYCAMORE (142006)**, 225 Edward Street, Zip 60178–2137; tel. 815/895–2144, (Nonreporting) **A**1 10 **S** ScionHealth, Louisville, KY
Primary Contact: Kathy Kelly, Chief Executive Officer
CFO: Jay Schweikart, Chief Financial Officer
CMO: Manav Salwan, Medical Director
CNO: Beth Ann Navarro, Chief Clinical Officer
Web address: www.kindredhospitalsyc.com/
Control: Corporation, Investor–owned (for–profit) **Service:** Acute long–term care hospital

Staffed Beds: 69

Hospital, Medicare Provider Number, Address, Telephone, Approval, Facility, and Physician Codes, Health Care System

★ American Hospital Association (AHA) membership ○ Healthcare Facilities Accreditation Program ⇑ Center for Improvement in Healthcare Quality Accreditation
☐ The Joint Commission accreditation ◇ DNV Healthcare Inc. accreditation △ Commission on Accreditation of Rehabilitation Facilities (CARF) accreditation

© 2025 AHA Guide

Hospitals, U.S. / ILLINOIS

TAYLORVILLE—Christian County

TAYLORVILLE MEMORIAL HOSPITAL (141339), 201 East Pleasant Street, Zip 62568–1597; tel. 217/824–3331, **A** 1 3 5 10 18 **F** 3 8 11 15 18 28 29 30 34 40 45 59 64 68 79 81 82 93 107 108 110 111 115 118 119 129 133 135 146 149 153 156 **P** 5 **S** Memorial Health, Springfield, IL
Primary Contact: Kimberly L. Bourne, President and Chief Executive Officer
CFO: Christine Goldesberry–Curry, Director of Strategic Finance–CAH
CHR: Michelle Long, Regional Human Resource Manager
Web address: www.taylorvillememorial.org
Control: Other not–for–profit (including NFP Corporation) **Service**: General medical and surgical

Staffed Beds: 25 **Admissions**: 809 **Census**: 15 **Outpatient Visits**: 37362 **Births**: 0 **Total Expense ($000)**: 53460 **Payroll Expense ($000)**: 20033 **Personnel**: 248

TINLEY PARK—Cook County

MIRACARE BEHAVIORAL HEALTH CARE, 6775 Prosperi Drive, Zip 60477–4789; tel. 708/726–6472, (Nonreporting)
Primary Contact: Matthew Berry, Chief Executive Officer
COO: Matthew Berry, Chief Executive Officer
CFO: Matthew Berry, Chief Executive Officer
CMO: Martins Adeoye, M.D., Chief Medical Officer
CHR: Caitlin Varjavand, Chief Human Resources Officer
CNO: Christine Shannon, Chief Nursing Officer
Web address: www.miracaregroup.com
Control: Corporation, Investor–owned (for–profit) **Service**: Psychiatric

Staffed Beds: 30

URBANA—Champaign County

★ △ ⇧ **CARLE FOUNDATION HOSPITAL (140091)**, 611 West Park Street, Zip 61801–2529; tel. 217/383–3311, **A** 2 3 5 7 8 10 13 19 21 **F** 3 8 12 13 15 17 18 19 20 22 24 26 27 28 29 30 31 34 35 40 41 43 44 45 46 47 48 49 50 51 53 56 57 58 59 61 62 63 64 68 70 72 73 74 75 76 77 78 79 80 81 82 84 85 86 87 89 90 91 92 93 96 97 100 102 104 107 108 110 111 114 115 117 118 119 120 121 123 124 126 129 130 131 132 146 148 149 150 152 154 164 167 169 **S** Carle Health, Urbana, IL
Primary Contact: Elizabeth Angelo, President and Chief Nursing Officer
CFO: Dennis Hesch, Executive Vice President Finance, System Chief Financial Officer
CMO: Matthew Gibb, M.D., Executive Vice President and System Chief Medical Officer
CIO: Rick Rinehart, Vice President, Chief Information Officer
CHR: Laurence Fallon, JD, JD, Executive Vice President, Chief Legal and Human Resources Officer
CNO: Pamela Bigler, R.N., Senior Vice President of Clinical Partnerships and Programs
Web address: www.carle.org
Control: Other not–for–profit (including NFP Corporation) **Service**: General medical and surgical

Staffed Beds: 458 **Admissions**: 28947 **Census**: 395 **Outpatient Visits**: 1989895 **Births**: 2979 **Total Expense ($000)**: 1182507 **Payroll Expense ($000)**: 365604 **Personnel**: 4249

OSF HEART OF MARY MEDICAL CENTER (140113), 1400 West Park Street, Zip 61801–2396, Mailing Address: P.O. Box 6259, Peoria, Zip 61601; tel. 217/337–2000, **A** 1 3 5 10 19 **F** 3 8 12 15 18 20 22 24 26 28 29 30 35 40 45 46 48 49 57 59 60 64 68 70 73 74 75 76 79 81 82 84 87 89 90 92 94 96 97 98 100 102 107 108 110 111 112 113 114 115 119 126 130 132 146 147 148 154 **S** OSF Healthcare, Peoria, IL
Primary Contact: J. T. Barnhart, President
CFO: Lucas Morton, Regional Chief Financial Officer
CMO: Vincent Kucich, FACHE, FACS, M.D., Chief Medical Officer
CIO: Paula Keele, Manager Information Systems
CHR: Michael Zimmerman, Human Resource Officer
CNO: Deborah McCarter, R.N., MSN, Vice President and Chief Nursing Officer
Web address: www.presencehealth.org/covenant
Control: Church operated, Nongovernment, not–for–profit **Service**: General medical and surgical

Staffed Beds: 181 **Admissions**: 3770 **Census**: 53 **Outpatient Visits**: 39467 **Births**: 226 **Total Expense ($000)**: 124251 **Payroll Expense ($000)**: 35000 **Personnel**: 414

VANDALIA—Fayette County

FAYETTE COUNTY HOSPITAL See SBL Fayette County Hospital and Long Term Care

SBL FAYETTE COUNTY HOSPITAL AND LONG TERM CARE (141346), 650 West Taylor Street, Zip 62471–1296; tel. 618/283–1231, (Nonreporting) **A** 1 10 18 **S** Alliant Management Services, Louisville, KY
Primary Contact: Karen Dyer, Chief Executive Officer
CFO: David H Wiesman, Interim Chief Financial Officer
CMO: Joseph Blaser, Chief Medical Officer
CIO: Gary Hood, Chief Information Officer
CHR: Susan Crawford, Manager Human Resources
CNO: Marci Barth, Chief Nursing Officer
Web address: https://www.sblfch.org/
Control: Other not–for–profit (including NFP Corporation) **Service**: General medical and surgical

Staffed Beds: 110

WATSEKA—Iroquois County

IROQUOIS MEMORIAL HOSPITAL AND RESIDENT HOME (141353), 200 Fairman Avenue, Zip 60970–1644; tel. 815/432–5841, (Nonreporting) **A** 1 3 10 18
Primary Contact: Michael Tilstra, President and Chief Executive Officer
CFO: Dana Gilleland, Chief Financial Officer
CMO: John Tricou, M.D., Chief of Staff
CHR: Tera Bivins, Chief Human Resources Officer
CNO: Michelle Fairley, R.N., Chief Nursing Officer
Web address: www.imhrh.org
Control: Other not–for–profit (including NFP Corporation) **Service**: General medical and surgical

Staffed Beds: 60

WAUKEGAN—Lake County

LAKE BEHAVIORAL HOSPITAL (144042), 2615 Washington Street, Zip 60085–4988; tel. 847/249–3900, (Nonreporting) **A** 1 10
Primary Contact: Cindy DeMarco, Chief Executive Officer
CHR: Jackie Brewer, Director, Human Resources
CNO: Chad Carson, Director of Nursing
Web address: https://lakebehavioralhospital.com
Control: Corporation, Investor–owned (for–profit) **Service**: Psychiatric

Staffed Beds: 42

VISTA HEALTH See Vista Medical Center East

VISTA MEDICAL CENTER EAST (140084), 1324 North Sheridan Road, Zip 60085–2161; tel. 847/360–3000, (Nonreporting) **A** 1 3 5 10 **S** American Healthcare Systems, Glendale, CA
Primary Contact: Bianca Defilippi, Chief Executive Officer
COO: Kim Needham, Assistant Chief Executive Officer
CFO: Kerry Hill, Chief Financial Officer
CMO: Daniel Liesen, M.D., Chief Medical Officer
CHR: Michael R Isaacs, Vice President Human Resources
Web address: https://vistahealth.com/vista-medical-center-east/
Control: Corporation, Investor–owned (for–profit) **Service**: General medical and surgical

Staffed Beds: 190

WHEATON—DuPage County

△ **NORTHWESTERN MEDICINE MARIANJOY REHABILITATION HOSPITAL (143027)**, 26 West 171 Roosevelt Road, Zip 60187–0795, Mailing Address: P.O. Box 795, Zip 60187–0795; tel. 630/909–8000, **A** 1 3 5 7 10 **F** 3 29 30 34 35 36 44 50 53 54 57 58 60 64 68 74 75 77 79 82 86 87 90 91 92 93 94 95 96 100 119 130 131 132 143 146 148 149 154 **S** Northwestern Memorial HealthCare, Chicago, IL
Primary Contact: Anne Hubling, R.N., President and Chief Nurse Executive
COO: John Brady, Vice President Physician Services and Organizational Planning
CMO: Jeffrey Oken, Vice President of Medical Affairs
CIO: Robert Sinickas, Director Information Services
CHR: Teresa Chapman, Vice President Human Resources
Web address: https://www.nm.org/locations/marianjoy-rehabilitation-hospital
Control: Other not–for–profit (including NFP Corporation) **Service**: Rehabilitation

Staffed Beds: 125 **Admissions**: 2817 **Census**: 108 **Outpatient Visits**: 43271 **Births**: 0 **Total Expense ($000)**: 107748 **Payroll Expense ($000)**: 50937 **Personnel**: 689

WINFIELD—DuPage County

ALCOHOLISM TREATMENT CENTER See Behavioral Health Center

Hospitals, U.S. / ILLINOIS

☒ **NORTHWESTERN MEDICINE CENTRAL DUPAGE HOSPITAL (140242)**, 25 North Winfield Road, Zip 60190; tel. 630/933-1600, (Includes BEHAVIORAL HEALTH CENTER, 27 West 350 High Lake RD, Winfield, Illinois, Zip 60190-1262, 27 West 350 High Lake Road, Zip 60190, tel. 630/653-4000) **A**1 2 3 5 10 **F**3 4 5 6 7 8 12 13 15 17 18 19 20 22 24 26 28 29 30 31 32 34 35 36 37 38 39 40 41 43 44 45 46 47 48 49 50 51 54 55 56 57 58 59 64 65 68 70 71 72 73 74 75 76 77 78 79 81 82 84 85 86 87 88 89 91 92 93 96 97 98 99 100 101 102 103 104 105 106 107 108 110 111 112 114 115 116 117 118 119 120 121 122 123 124 126 129 130 131 132 135 144 145 146 147 148 149 152 153 154 156 157 160 161 162 164 165 167 169 **S** Northwestern Memorial HealthCare, Chicago, IL
Primary Contact: Kenneth Hedley, President
CFO: John Orsini, Executive Vice President and Chief Financial Officer
CIO: Daniel F Kinsella, Vice President and Chief Information Officer
Web address: www.nm.org
Control: Other not-for-profit (including NFP Corporation) **Service**: General medical and surgical

Staffed Beds: 429 **Admissions**: 22509 **Census**: 297 **Outpatient Visits**: 1080973 **Births**: 2676 **Total Expense ($000)**: 1453069 **Payroll Expense ($000)**: 499239 **Personnel**: 4873

WOODSTOCK—Mchenry County

NORTHWESTERN WOODSTOCK See Northwestern Medicine Woodstock

ZION—Lake County

☐ **CITY OF HOPE CHICAGO (140100)**, 2520 Elisha Avenue, Zip 60099-2587; tel. 847/872-4561, (Nonreporting) **A**1 2 3 10 **S** City of Hope, Schaumburg, IL
Primary Contact: Pete Govorchin, President and Chief Executive Officer
COO: Pete Govorchin, Senior Vice President Operations
CFO: Cecilia Taylor, Chief Financial Officer
CMO: Bradford Tan, M.D., Chief Medical Officer
CHR: Amy VanStrien, Director Talent Operations
Web address: www.cancercenter.com
Control: Corporation, Investor-owned (for-profit) **Service**: Cancer

Staffed Beds: 72

Hospital, Medicare Provider Number, Address, Telephone, Approval, Facility, and Physician Codes, Health Care System

★ American Hospital Association (AHA) membership   ○ Healthcare Facilities Accreditation Program   ⇧ Center for Improvement in Healthcare Quality Accreditation
☐ The Joint Commission accreditation   ◇ DNV Healthcare Inc. accreditation   △ Commission on Accreditation of Rehabilitation Facilities (CARF) accreditation

Hospitals, U.S. / INDIANA

INDIANA

ANDERSON—Madison County

☒ **ASCENSION ST. VINCENT ANDERSON (150088)**, 2015 Jackson Street, Zip 46016–4339; tel. 765/649–2511, (Nonreporting) **A**1 10 **S** Ascension Healthcare, Saint Louis, MO
Primary Contact: Marion Teixeira, Chief Executive Officer
CFO: Laura L Rose, Chief Financial Officer
CIO: Robert A. Pope, Director I
CHR: Ross Brodhead, Senior Director, Human Resource
Web address: https://healthcare.ascension.org/locations/indiana/ineva/anderson-ascension-st-vincent-anderson
Control: Church operated, Nongovernment, not–for–profit **Service**: General medical and surgical

Staffed Beds: 152

☒ **COMMUNITY HOSPITAL ANDERSON (150113)**, 1515 North Madison Avenue, Zip 46011–3453; tel. 765/298–4242, (Nonreporting) **A**1 2 3 10 **S** Community Health Network, Indianapolis, IN
Primary Contact: Marsha S. Meckel, R.N., Hospital Administrator
COO: Sherry Sidwell, Chief Operating Officer, Vice President Integrated Support Services
CFO: John B. Harris, Vice President Finance and Chief Financial Officer
CNO: Marsha S Meckel, R.N., Vice President Clinical Services and Chief Nursing Executive
Web address: https://www.ecommunity.com/locations/community-hospital-anderson
Control: Other not–for–profit (including NFP Corporation) **Service**: General medical and surgical

Staffed Beds: 118

ANGOLA—Steuben County

★ ⇑ **CAMERON MEMORIAL COMMUNITY HOSPITAL (151315)**, 416 East Maumee Street, Zip 46703–2015; tel. 260/665–2141, **A**10 18 21 **F**3 11 13 15 19 28 29 30 34 35 40 44 45 50 54 57 59 65 68 75 76 77 79 81 85 86 87 93 96 97 104 107 108 110 111 115 117 118 119 125 127 129 130 131 132 133 144 146 147 148 149 154 156 157 162 164 167 169 **P**6
Primary Contact: Angela Logan, Chief Executive Officer
CFO: Wendy Stamper, Controller
CMO: Jon Alley, D.O., President Medical Staff
CIO: Kris Keen, Chief Information Officer
CHR: Nancy Covell, Director Human Resources
Web address: www.cameronmch.com
Control: Other not–for–profit (including NFP Corporation) **Service**: General medical and surgical

Staffed Beds: 25 **Admissions**: 1206 **Census**: 12 **Outpatient Visits**: 206218 **Births**: 249 **Total Expense ($000)**: 104094 **Payroll Expense ($000)**: 40265 **Personnel**: 545

AUBURN—Dekalb County

NORTHEASTERN CENTER (154050), 1850 Wesley Road, Zip 46706–3653; tel. 260/927–0726, (Nonreporting) **A**10
Primary Contact: Jerry Hollister, Chief Executive Officer
Web address: www.necmh.org
Control: Other not–for–profit (including NFP Corporation) **Service**: Psychiatric

Staffed Beds: 16

★ **PARKVIEW DEKALB HOSPITAL (150045)**, 1316 East Seventh Street, Zip 46706–2515, Mailing Address: P.O. Box 542, Zip 46706–0542; tel. 260/925–4600, **A**10 **F**3 7 13 15 18 28 34 35 40 45 59 63 64 68 70 74 75 76 79 81 82 85 87 89 93 97 100 107 108 109 110 111 115 119 126 129 146 147 149 154 169 **S** Parkview Health, Fort Wayne, IN
Primary Contact: Natasha Eicher, President and Chief Executive Officer
CMO: Emilio Vazquez, M.D., Chief Medical Officer
CIO: Ed Hobbs, Director Information Services
CNO: Donna S Wisemore, R.N., Vice President and Chief Nursing Officer
Web address: www.dekalbhealth.com
Control: Other not–for–profit (including NFP Corporation) **Service**: General medical and surgical

Staffed Beds: 57 **Admissions**: 1576 **Census**: 11 **Outpatient Visits**: 58853 **Births**: 236 **Total Expense ($000)**: 79891 **Payroll Expense ($000)**: 20806 **Personnel**: 267

AVON—Hendricks County

☒ **INDIANA UNIVERSITY HEALTH WEST HOSPITAL (150158)**, 1111 North Ronald Reagan Parkway, Zip 46123–7085; tel. 317/217–3000, **A**1 2 3 5 10 **F**1 3 5 13 15 18 20 22 26 28 29 30 31 34 35 39 40 47 48 49 50 51 57 59 60 68 70 73 74 75 76 77 78 79 81 82 84 85 86 87 89 93 100 107 110 111 113 114 116 117 119 120 121 126 129 130 131 132 135 146 147 148 154 156 157 167 169 **S** Indiana University Health, Indianapolis, IN
Primary Contact: Doug Puckett, President
CMO: Andrew Nigh, M.D., Chief of Staff
CHR: Tamarah Brownlee, Vice President, Human Resources
CNO: Lisa Sparks, R.N., Chief Nursing Officer and Vice President Patient Care Services
Web address: www.iuhealth.org
Control: Other not–for–profit (including NFP Corporation) **Service**: General medical and surgical

Staffed Beds: 167 **Admissions**: 8873 **Census**: 116 **Outpatient Visits**: 184352 **Births**: 1105 **Total Expense ($000)**: 277672 **Payroll Expense ($000)**: 87613 **Personnel**: 998

BATESVILLE—Ripley County

☒ **MARGARET MARY HEALTH (151329)**, 321 Mitchell Avenue, Zip 47006–8909, Mailing Address: P.O. Box 226, Zip 47006–0226; tel. 812/934–6624, **A**1 2 10 18 **F**3 5 8 13 15 18 26 28 29 31 34 35 36 38 40 45 50 51 54 59 63 64 65 70 75 76 77 78 79 81 85 93 94 96 104 107 108 110 111 114 115 119 120 121 123 127 129 130 131 132 133 135 143 144 146 147 148 149 152 154 156 160 169
Primary Contact: Elizabeth Leising, Interim Chief Executive Officer and President
CFO: Brian Daeger, Chief Financial Officer and Vice President Financial Services
CMO: Charles McGovern, Chief of Staff
CIO: Trisha Prickel, Information Systems Director
CNO: Elizabeth Leising, Chief Nursing Officer and Vice President Patient Services
Web address: www.mmhealth.org
Control: Other not–for–profit (including NFP Corporation) **Service**: General medical and surgical

Staffed Beds: 25 **Admissions**: 1623 **Census**: 13 **Total Expense ($000)**: 128980 **Payroll Expense ($000)**: 51965 **Personnel**: 629

BEDFORD—Lawrence County

☒ **INDIANA UNIVERSITY HEALTH BEDFORD HOSPITAL (151328)**, 2900 West 16th Street, Zip 47421–3583; tel. 812/275–1200, **A**1 2 10 18 **F**15 18 28 29 30 31 34 35 38 40 41 45 46 47 48 49 50 57 59 64 68 70 74 75 77 78 79 81 85 86 87 93 102 107 108 110 111 115 118 119 129 130 132 133 135 146 149 154 156 157 **S** Indiana University Health, Indianapolis, IN
Primary Contact: Denzil Ross, FACHE, President
COO: Larry Bailey, FACHE, Chief Operating Officer
CFO: Mike Craig, Vice President, Chief Financial Officer
CMO: John Sparzo, M.D., Chief Medical Officer
CHR: Bruce Wade, Vice President Human Resources
CNO: Amy A Little, Vice President Patient Services
Web address: www.iuhealth.org
Control: Other not–for–profit (including NFP Corporation) **Service**: General medical and surgical

Staffed Beds: 25 **Admissions**: 1751 **Census**: 19 **Outpatient Visits**: 110515 **Births**: 0 **Total Expense ($000)**: 83210 **Payroll Expense ($000)**: 25544 **Personnel**: 295

BLOOMINGTON—Monroe County

☐ **BLOOMINGTON MEADOWS HOSPITAL (154041)**, 3600 North Prow Road, Zip 47404–1616; tel. 812/331–8000, (Nonreporting) **A**1 10 **S** Universal Health Services, Inc., King of Prussia, PA
Primary Contact: Kristen Primeau, Chief Executive Officer
CFO: Becky T. Nyberg, Chief Financial Officer
CMO: David Gilliam, M.D., Medical Director
CHR: Amanda Shettlesworth, Director Human Resources
CNO: Penny Caswell, Director of Nursing
Web address: www.bloomingtonmeadows.com
Control: Corporation, Investor–owned (for–profit) **Service**: Psychiatric

Staffed Beds: 71

Hospitals, U.S. / INDIANA

BLOOMINGTON REGIONAL REHABILITATION HOSPITAL (153049), 3050 North Lintel Drive, Zip 47404–8945; tel. 812/336–2815, (Nonreporting) **S** Ernest Health, Inc., Albuquerque, NM
Primary Contact: Jeff Stultz, Chief Executive Officer
Web address: https://brrh.ernesthealth.com/
Control: Corporation, Investor–owned (for–profit) **Service**: Rehabilitation

Staffed Beds: 50

✠ **INDIANA UNIVERSITY HEALTH BLOOMINGTON HOSPITAL (150051)**, 2651 East Discovery Parkway, Zip 47408–9059; tel. 812/336–6821, **A**1 2 5 10 19 **F**3 5 8 11 13 17 18 20 22 24 26 28 29 30 31 37 38 40 43 45 46 47 48 49 50 51 54 55 60 64 65 69 70 72 74 75 76 77 78 81 84 85 86 87 89 92 93 94 98 100 102 107 108 111 114 115 118 119 120 121 123 124 126 127 130 143 146 147 148 149 154 156 160 161 164 167 168 169 **P**6 **S** Indiana University Health, Indianapolis, IN
Primary Contact: Denzil Ross, FACHE, President
CFO: Mike Craig, Chief Financial Officer
CHR: Steven D Deckard, Vice President Human Resources
Web address: www.iuhealth.org
Control: Other not–for–profit (including NFP Corporation) **Service**: General medical and surgical

Staffed Beds: 201 Admissions: 11336 Census: 159 Outpatient Visits: 373694 Births: 1830 Total Expense ($000): 491804 Payroll Expense ($000): 162611 Personnel: 1719

☐ **MONROE HOSPITAL (150183)**, 4011 South Monroe Medical Park Boulevard, Zip 47403–8000; tel. 812/825–1111, **A**1 10 **F**3 15 18 29 30 34 35 40 41 44 45 46 47 48 50 56 57 59 64 65 68 70 75 78 79 80 81 82 85 86 87 91 97 107 108 109 110 111 114 115 119 135 148 149 154 156 164 167 **S** Prime Healthcare, Ontario, CA
Primary Contact: Nancy Bakewell, Administrator
CFO: Hilary Dolbee, Chief Financial Officer
CMO: Amandeep Singh, Chief Medical Officer
CIO: LaDonna Cagle, HIM Appeals Coordinator III
CHR: Karyn Batdorf, Director of Human Resources
CNO: Nancy Bakewell, Chief Nursing Officer
Web address: www.monroehospital.com
Control: Corporation, Investor–owned (for–profit) **Service**: General medical and surgical

Staffed Beds: 32 Admissions: 1425 Census: 13 Outpatient Visits: 17187 Births: 0 Total Expense ($000): 36264 Payroll Expense ($000): 16544 Personnel: 231

BLUFFTON—Wells County

✠ **BLUFFTON REGIONAL MEDICAL CENTER (150075)**, 303 South Main Street, Zip 46714–2503; tel. 260/824–3210, (Nonreporting) **A**1 10 19 **S** Community Health Systems, Inc., Franklin, TN
Primary Contact: Julie Thompson, Chief Adminstrative Officer and Chief Nursing Officer
COO: Julie Thompson, Chief Operating Officer and Chief Nursing Officer
CFO: Larry W DeBolt, Chief Financial Officer
CMO: Harish Ardeshna, Pulmonologist & Chief Medical Officer
CHR: Patricia Sprinkle, Vice President, Human Resources
CNO: Julie Thompson, Chief Operating Officer and Chief Nursing Officer
Web address: www.blufftonregional.com
Control: Corporation, Investor–owned (for–profit) **Service**: General medical and surgical

Staffed Beds: 52

BOONVILLE—Warrick County

✠ **ASCENSION ST. VINCENT WARRICK (151325)**, 1116 Millis Avenue, Zip 47601–2204; tel. 812/897–4800, (Nonreporting) **A**1 10 18 **S** Ascension Healthcare, Saint Louis, MO
Primary Contact: Marty Mattingly, Administrator
CFO: Crystal Heaton, Director of Finance
CNO: Karen Waters, Chief Nursing Officer
Web address: https://healthcare.ascension.org
Control: Other not–for–profit (including NFP Corporation) **Service**: General medical and surgical

Staffed Beds: 35

BRAZIL—Clay County

✠ **ASCENSION ST. VINCENT CLAY HOSPITAL (151309)**, 1206 East National Avenue, Zip 47834–2797, Mailing Address: 1206 East National Ave, Zip 47834–0489; tel. 812/442–2500, (Nonreporting) **A**1 10 18 **S** Ascension Healthcare, Saint Louis, MO
Primary Contact: Jerry Laue, Administrator
CFO: Wayne Knight, Director Finance
CMO: Stephen Tharp, Regional Chief Medical Officer
CHR: Lainie Collins, Human Resources Partner
CNO: Paulette Sue Gaskill, Executive Director of Nursing
Web address: www.stvincent.org
Control: Church operated, Nongovernment, not–for–profit **Service**: General medical and surgical

Staffed Beds: 25

BREMEN—Marshall County

★ **COMMUNITY HOSPITAL OF BREMEN (151300)**, 1020 High Road, Zip 46506–1093, Mailing Address: P.O. Box 8, Zip 46506–0008; tel. 574/546–2211, **A**10 18 **F**3 11 13 15 29 34 35 40 45 50 59 64 69 75 76 77 79 81 82 85 93 107 110 111 115 119 129 130 132 133 135 146 149 **S** Beacon Health System, South Bend, IN
Primary Contact: David Bailey, FACHE, President
CFO: Amy Lashbrook, Chief Financial Officer
CMO: Lindy Sergeant, Medical Staff President
CHR: Patricia Board, Vice President Human Resources
CNO: Sue Bettcher, R.N., Vice President of Nursing Services
Web address: www.bremenhospital.com
Control: Other not–for–profit (including NFP Corporation) **Service**: General medical and surgical

Staffed Beds: 21 Admissions: 432 Census: 7 Outpatient Visits: 39179 Births: 107 Total Expense ($000): 26700 Payroll Expense ($000): 10291 Personnel: 140

☐ **DOCTORS NEUROPSYCHIATRIC HOSPITAL (154058)**, 417 South Whitlock Street, Zip 46506–1626; tel. 574/546–0330, (Nonreporting) **A**1 10 **S** NeuroPsychiatric Hospitals, Mishawaka, IN
Primary Contact: Victor Chatuluka, Chief Executive Officer
COO: Christy Gilbert, President and Chief Operating Officer
CHR: Becky Holloway, Vice President, Human Resources
Web address: www.neuropsychiatrichospitals.net
Control: Individual, Investor–owned (for–profit) **Service**: Psychiatric

Staffed Beds: 37

CARMEL—Hamilton County

✠ **ASCENSION ST. VINCENT CARMEL HOSPITAL (150157)**, 13500 North Meridian Street, Zip 46032–1456; tel. 317/582–7000, (Nonreporting) **A**1 3 5 10 **S** Ascension Healthcare, Saint Louis, MO
Primary Contact: Chad Dilley, President
COO: Daniel LaReau, Executive Director, Operations and Information
CFO: Robert A. Bates, Chief Financial Officer
CMO: Steven Priddy, M.D., VP of Physician Affairs/Chief Medical Officer
CIO: Daniel LaReau, Executive Director, Operations and Information
CHR: Ross Brodhead, Senior Director, Human Resources
CNO: Ted Eads, Interim Chief Nursing Officer
Web address: https://www.stvincent.org
Control: Church operated, Nongovernment, not–for–profit **Service**: General medical and surgical

Staffed Beds: 121

FRANCISCAN HEALTH CARMEL (150182), 12188B North Meridian Street, Zip 46032–4840; tel. 317/705–4500, (Nonreporting) **A**10 **S** Franciscan Health, Mishawaka, IN
Primary Contact: Lori Price, R.N., President and Chief Executive Officer, Central Indiana Region
CFO: Keith A. Lauter, Chief Financial Officer
CMO: Christopher Doehring, M.D., Vice President of Medical Affairs
CIO: Rebecca Merkel, Privacy Officer
CHR: Corey Baute, Vice President of Human Resource
Web address: www.franciscanalliance.org/hospitals/carmel/Pages/default.aspx
Control: Other not–for–profit (including NFP Corporation) **Service**: General medical and surgical

Staffed Beds: 6

Hospital, Medicare Provider Number, Address, Telephone, Approval, Facility, and Physician Codes, Health Care System

★ American Hospital Association (AHA) membership
☐ The Joint Commission accreditation
○ Healthcare Facilities Accreditation Program
◇ DNV Healthcare Inc. accreditation
⇑ Center for Improvement in Healthcare Quality Accreditation
△ Commission on Accreditation of Rehabilitation Facilities (CARF) accreditation

© 2025 AHA Guide   Hospitals **A213**

Hospitals, U.S. / INDIANA

○ **INDIANA SPINE HOSPITAL**, 13219 North Meridian Street, Zip 46032-5480; tel. 317/795-2000, (Nonreporting) **A**5 11 12
Primary Contact: Hardy Sikand, Chief Executive Officer
CNO: Barbara Bridges, R.N., Chief Nursing Officer
Web address: https://indianaspinehospital.com
Control: Corporation, Investor-owned (for-profit) **Service**: General medical and surgical

Staffed Beds: 20

✠ **INDIANA UNIVERSITY HEALTH NORTH HOSPITAL (150161)**, 11700 North Meridian Street, Zip 46032-4656; tel. 317/688-2000, **A**1 3 5 10 **F**3 12 13 15 18 19 20 22 26 29 30 31 34 35 37 39 40 41 45 47 48 50 55 56 57 59 60 64 68 70 72 74 75 76 77 78 79 81 82 84 85 86 87 88 89 91 92 93 100 107 108 110 111 115 117 118 119 120 121 123 126 129 130 131 132 135 146 147 148 149 154 156 157 167 169 **S** Indiana University Health, Indianapolis, IN
Primary Contact: Soula Banich, President
COO: Randall C. Yust, Chief Operating Officer and Chief Financial Officer
CFO: Randall C. Yust, Chief Operating Officer and Chief Financial Officer
CMO: Paul Calkins, M.D., Chief Medical Officer
CIO: Steve Bodenham, Senior Manager Clinical Engineering
CHR: Steven E Kile, Vice President Human Resources
Web address: www.iuhealth.org/north
Control: Other not-for-profit (including NFP Corporation) **Service**: General medical and surgical

Staffed Beds: 165 **Admissions**: 9371 **Census**: 101 **Outpatient Visits**: 208653 **Births**: 2210 **Total Expense ($000)**: 322451 **Payroll Expense ($000)**: 96991 **Personnel**: 1011

○ **INDIANAPOLIS REHABILITATION HOSPITAL (153048)**, 1260 City Center Drive, Zip 46032-3810; tel. 463/333-9110, (Nonreporting) **A**10 **S** Nobis Rehabilitation Partners, Allen, TX
Primary Contact: Brandon Tudor, Chief Executive Officer
Web address: https://www.indianapolis-rehabhospital.com/
Control: Corporation, Investor-owned (for-profit) **Service**: Rehabilitation

Staffed Beds: 40

CLARKSVILLE—Clark County

★ **PAM HEALTH REHABILITATION HOSPITAL OF GREATER INDIANA (153046)**, 2101 Broadway Street, Zip 47129-7800; tel. 812/913-6880, (Nonreporting) **S** PAM Health, Enola, PA
Primary Contact: Waylon Maynard, Chief Executive Officer
CMO: Robert Thompson, M.D., Chief Medical Officer
CHR: Michelle Hendrickson, Human Resources Director
CNO: Gary Stallings, Chief Nursing Officer
Web address: https://pamhealth.com/
Control: Partnership, Investor-owned (for-profit) **Service**: Rehabilitation

Staffed Beds: 42

CLINTON—Vermillion County

○ **UNION HOSPITAL CLINTON (151326)**, 801 South Main Street, Zip 47842-2261; tel. 765/832-1234, **A**10 11 18 **F**3 11 15 18 29 30 34 35 40 45 50 57 59 64 65 68 70 75 81 85 86 87 91 93 97 107 108 110 115 119 130 133 146 156 157
Primary Contact: Steve M. Holman, FACHE, Chief Executive Officer
CFO: Wayne Hutson, Chief Financial Officer
CMO: John Albrecht, Chief of Staff
CIO: Jack Hill, Vice President and Chief Operating Officer
Web address: www.myunionhospital.org/unionhospital/union-hospital-clinton
Control: Other not-for-profit (including NFP Corporation) **Service**: General medical and surgical

Staffed Beds: 21 **Admissions**: 713 **Census**: 5 **Outpatient Visits**: 48834 **Births**: 0 **Total Expense ($000)**: 26364 **Payroll Expense ($000)**: 9011 **Personnel**: 113

COLUMBIA CITY—Whitley County

✠ **PARKVIEW WHITLEY HOSPITAL (150101)**, 1260 East State Road 205, Zip 46725-9492; tel. 260/248-9000, **A**1 10 **F**3 7 13 15 28 29 30 34 35 40 42 45 50 54 64 75 76 79 81 82 85 87 89 93 96 107 108 110 111 115 119 126 129 132 143 146 147 154 156 164 169 **S** Parkview Health, Fort Wayne, IN
Primary Contact: Scott F. Gabriel, President
COO: Scott F Gabriel, President
CFO: Lisa Peppler, Financial Manager
CMO: Jeffrey Brookes, M.D., Medical Director
Web address: www.parkview.com
Control: Other not-for-profit (including NFP Corporation) **Service**: General medical and surgical

Staffed Beds: 30 **Admissions**: 2020 **Census**: 14 **Outpatient Visits**: 83269 **Births**: 326 **Total Expense ($000)**: 92180 **Payroll Expense ($000)**: 25492 **Personnel**: 325

COLUMBUS—Bartholomew County

★ ○ **COLUMBUS REGIONAL HOSPITAL (150112)**, 2400 East 17th Street, Zip 47201-5360; tel. 812/379-4441, **A**2 10 11 19 **F**3 7 11 12 13 15 18 20 22 24 26 28 29 30 31 34 35 37 38 39 40 45 46 47 49 51 53 58 59 65 70 73 74 75 76 77 78 79 81 85 86 87 89 90 93 97 98 100 101 102 107 108 110 111 114 115 117 118 119 120 121 123 124 126 129 130 131 132 135 146 147 148 149 154 167 169 **P**6
Primary Contact: Jim Bickel, Chief Executive Officer
COO: Steve Baker, President and Chief Operating Officer
CFO: Marlene Weatherwax, Vice President and Chief Financial Officer
CMO: Thomas Sonderman, M.D., Vice President and Chief Medical Officer
CHR: Julie McGregor, Vice President, Human Resources and Organization Development
Web address: www.crh.org
Control: County, Government, Nonfederal **Service**: General medical and surgical

Staffed Beds: 250 **Admissions**: 9355 **Census**: 107 **Outpatient Visits**: 307184 **Births**: 1129 **Total Expense ($000)**: 379591 **Payroll Expense ($000)**: 120517 **Personnel**: 1772

CORYDON—Harrison County

★ ○ **HARRISON COUNTY HOSPITAL (151331)**, 1141 Hospital Drive N W, Zip 47112-1774; tel. 812/738-4251, **A**10 11 18 **F**3 7 13 15 18 28 29 34 35 40 45 46 49 56 57 59 64 70 76 77 79 81 82 85 87 90 93 97 107 108 110 111 115 119 127 129 131 133 144 146 154 156 169
Primary Contact: Lisa Clunie, Chief Executive Officer
CFO: Jeff Davis, Chief Financial Officer
CIO: Chuck Wiley, Manager Information Systems
CHR: Loren Haverstock, Manager Human Resources
CNO: Ruth Donahue, R.N., Chief Nursing Officer
Web address: www.hchin.org
Control: County, Government, Nonfederal **Service**: General medical and surgical

Staffed Beds: 25 **Admissions**: 899 **Census**: 7 **Outpatient Visits**: 48917 **Births**: 354 **Total Expense ($000)**: 65790 **Payroll Expense ($000)**: 29867 **Personnel**: 507

CRAWFORDSVILLE—Montgomery County

○ **FRANCISCAN HEALTH CRAWFORDSVILLE (150022)**, 1710 Lafayette Road, Zip 47933-1099; tel. 765/362-2800, (Nonreporting) **A**3 10 11 **S** Franciscan Health, Mishawaka, IN
Primary Contact: Carlos Vasquez, Chief Executive Officer
COO: Terrence Klein, Ph.D., Vice President and Chief Operating Officer
CFO: Keith A. Lauter, Vice President Finance
Web address: www.stclaremedical.com
Control: Other not-for-profit (including NFP Corporation) **Service**: General medical and surgical

Staffed Beds: 40

CROWN POINT—Lake County

✠ **AMG SPECIALTY HOSPITAL NORTHWEST INDIANA (152028)**, 9509 Georgia Street, Zip 46307-6518; tel. 219/472-2200, (Nonreporting) **A**1 10 **S** AMG Integrated Healthcare Management, Lafayette, LA
Primary Contact: Joe Bryant, Chief Executive Officer
CFO: Douglas Morris, Chief Financial Officer
CMO: Raja Devanathan, M.D., Chief Medical Officer
CNO: Robert Beard, Chief Clinical Officer
Web address: https://amgihm.com/locations/indiana-crown-point/
Control: Corporation, Investor-owned (for-profit) **Service**: Acute long-term care hospital

Staffed Beds: 40

○ **FRANCISCAN HEALTH CROWN POINT (150126)**, 1201 South Main Street, Zip 46307-8483; tel. 219/738-2100, (Nonreporting) **A**2 3 10 11 **S** Franciscan Health, Mishawaka, IN
Primary Contact: Daniel McCormick, M.D., President and Chief Executive Officer
CFO: Marc Golan, Chief Financial Officer
CIO: Tim Loosemore, Director
CNO: Carol E Schuster, R.N., Chief Nursing Officer and Vice President Patient Care Services
Web address: www.franciscanalliance.org
Control: Church operated, Nongovernment, not-for-profit **Service**: General medical and surgical

Staffed Beds: 254

Hospitals, U.S. / INDIANA

☐ **NEUROBEHAVIORAL HOSPITAL OF NW INDIANA/GREATER CHICAGO (154065),** 9330 Broadway, Zip 46307-9830; tel. 219/648-2400, (Nonreporting) **A**1 10 **S** NeuroPsychiatric Hospitals, Mishawaka, IN
Primary Contact: Jerome Phillips, Chief Executive Officer
COO: Christy Gilbert, President and Chief Operating Officer
CFO: Carlos Missagia, Chief Financial Officer
CHR: Becky Holloway, Vice President, Human Resources
Web address: https://www.neuropsychiatrichospitals.net
Control: Corporation, Investor-owned (for-profit) **Service:** Psychiatric

Staffed Beds: 70

○ **PINNACLE HOSPITAL (150166),** 9301 Connecticut Drive, Zip 46307-7486; tel. 219/756-2100, (Nonreporting) **A**10 11
Primary Contact: Haroon Naz, Chief Executive Officer
Web address: www.pinnaclehealthcare.net
Control: Partnership, Investor-owned (for-profit) **Service:** General medical and surgical

Staffed Beds: 18

DANVILLE—Hendricks County

★ ○ **HENDRICKS REGIONAL HEALTH (150005),** 1000 East Main Street, Zip 46122-1948, Mailing Address: P.O. Box 409, Zip 46122-0409; (Includes HENDRICKS REGIONAL HEALTH BROWNSBURG HOSPITAL, 5492 N Ronald Reagan Pkwy, Brownsburg, Indiana, Zip 46122-5618, tel. 317/456-9051) (Total facility includes 26 beds in nursing home-type unit) **A**2 5 10 11 **F**3 8 9 11 13 15 17 18 20 22 26 28 29 30 31 32 34 35 38 40 41 42 43 44 45 46 47 48 53 54 55 56 57 58 59 60 61 64 65 68 70 71 73 74 76 77 78 79 81 82 83 84 85 86 87 89 90 92 93 94 96 97 107 108 110 111 115 117 118 119 120 121 123 126 128 129 130 131 132 135 143 144 145 146 147 148 149 150 154 156 167 169 **P**6
Primary Contact: Michelle Fenoughty, M.D., President and Chief Executive Officer
COO: Yvonne Culpepper, MSN, R.N., Senior Vice President of Nursing and Professional Services, Chief Operating Officer and Chief Nursing Officer
CFO: Dennis Ressler, Vice President, Finance and Chief Financial Officer
CMO: Ryan Van Donselaar, Chief Medical Officer
CIO: Todd Davis, Executive Director of Information Systems
CHR: Nancy Foster, Vice President, Human Resources
CNO: Yvonne Culpepper, MSN, R.N., Senior Vice President of Nursing and Professional Services, Chief Operating Officer and Chief Nursing Officer
Web address: https://www.hendricks.org
Control: County, Government, Nonfederal **Service:** General medical and surgical

Staffed Beds: 161 Admissions: 5956 Census: 61 Outpatient Visits: 401811 Births: 1327 Total Expense ($000): 470693 Payroll Expense ($000): 213695 Personnel: 2113

DECATUR—Adams County

★ ○ **ADAMS MEMORIAL HOSPITAL (151330),** 1100 Mercer Avenue, Zip 46733-2303, Mailing Address: P.O. Box 151, Zip 46733-0151; tel. 260/724-2145, (Total facility includes 195 beds in nursing home-type unit) **A**10 11 18 **F**3 5 7 10 13 15 28 29 30 34 35 38 40 47 50 53 54 56 57 59 64 65 66 67 70 74 75 76 77 79 81 82 85 86 87 93 97 101 102 104 107 108 110 111 114 119 125 126 127 128 129 130 131 133 135 143 144 146 147 148 149 153 154 156 162 165 169
Primary Contact: Scott Smith, M.D., Chief Executive Officer and Chief Medical Officer
CFO: Dane Wheeler, Chief Financial Officer
CMO: Scott Smith, M.D., Chief Medical Officer
CIO: Nick Nelson, Director Support Services
CHR: Alison Kukelhan, Manager Human Resources
CNO: Theresa Bradtmiller DNP, RN, MSN, R.N., Nursing Talent and Development Leader
Web address: www.adamshospital.com
Control: County, Government, Nonfederal **Service:** General medical and surgical

Staffed Beds: 224 Admissions: 1283 Census: 157 Outpatient Visits: 197573 Births: 202 Total Expense ($000): 100723 Payroll Expense ($000): 49932 Personnel: 775

DYER—Lake County

○ **FRANCISCAN HEALTH DYER (150090),** 24 Joliet Street, Zip 46311-1799; tel. 219/865-2141, (Nonreporting) **A**3 10 11 19 **S** Franciscan Health, Mishawaka, IN
Primary Contact: Patrick J. Maloney, Chief Executive Officer
Control: Church operated, Nongovernment, not-for-profit **Service:** General medical and surgical

Staffed Beds: 341

EAST CHICAGO—Lake County

✠ **REGENCY HOSPITAL OF NORTHWEST INDIANA (152024),** 4321 Fir Street, 4th Floor, Zip 46312-3049; tel. 219/392-7799, (Includes REGENCY HOSPITAL OF PORTER COUNTY, 3630 Willow Creek Road, Portage, Indiana, Zip 46368, tel. 219/364-3800; Jessica Wilson, Chief Executive Officer) (Nonreporting) **A**1 10 **S** Select Medical Corporation, Mechanicsburg, PA
Primary Contact: Kristine Shields, MSN, R.N., Chief Executive Officer
Web address: www.regencyhospital.com/company/locations/indiana-northwest-indiana.aspx
Control: Corporation, Investor-owned (for-profit) **Service:** Acute long-term care hospital

Staffed Beds: 61

☐ △ **ST. CATHERINE HOSPITAL (150008),** 4321 Fir Street, Zip 46312-3097; tel. 219/392-1700, **A**1 2 7 10 **F**3 11 13 15 18 20 22 24 26 28 29 30 31 34 35 40 46 49 50 51 55 57 59 61 64 66 70 74 75 76 78 79 81 82 85 86 87 90 92 93 96 98 100 101 102 103 104 107 108 110 111 112 115 119 121 124 126 129 130 131 132 146 148 149 153 154 156 169 **S** Powers Health, Hammond, IN
Primary Contact: Leo Correa, Chief Executive Officer and Administrator
COO: Craig Bolda, Chief Operating Officer
CMO: John Griep, M.D., Chief Medical Director
CIO: Gary Weiner, Chief Information Officer
CNO: Paula C. Swenson, R.N., Vice President and Chief Nursing Officer
Web address: www.stcatherinehospital.org
Control: Other not-for-profit (including NFP Corporation) **Service:** General medical and surgical

Staffed Beds: 138 Admissions: 6220 Census: 85 Outpatient Visits: 186450 Births: 467 Total Expense ($000): 153799 Payroll Expense ($000): 60972 Personnel: 677

ELKHART—Elkhart County

✠ **ELKHART GENERAL HOSPITAL (150018),** 600 East Boulevard, Zip 46514-2499, Mailing Address: P.O. Box 1329, Zip 46515-1329; tel. 574/294-2621, **A**1 2 10 19 **F**3 11 12 13 15 17 18 20 22 24 26 28 29 30 31 34 35 37 40 43 46 48 49 50 59 60 64 65 67 68 70 72 74 75 76 77 78 79 81 82 84 85 86 87 89 90 91 92 93 98 100 102 104 107 108 110 111 114 115 116 117 118 119 120 121 123 126 129 130 131 132 134 135 145 146 147 148 155 156 167 169 **S** Beacon Health System, South Bend, IN
Primary Contact: Carl W. Risk II, President
CFO: Jeff Costello, Chief Financial Officer
CMO: Gene Grove, M.D., Chief of Staff
CIO: Mark Warlick, Chief Information Officer
CHR: Steven M Eller, Vice President Human Resources
Web address: www.egh.org
Control: Other not-for-profit (including NFP Corporation) **Service:** General medical and surgical

Staffed Beds: 214 Admissions: 9974 Census: 115 Outpatient Visits: 140725 Births: 1244 Total Expense ($000): 305773 Payroll Expense ($000): 101423 Personnel: 1362

ELWOOD—Madison County

✠ **ASCENSION ST. VINCENT MERCY (151308),** 1331 South 'A' Street, Zip 46036-1942; tel. 765/552-4600, (Nonreporting) **A**1 2 10 18 **S** Ascension Healthcare, Saint Louis, MO
Primary Contact: Ann C. Yates, R.N., MSN, Administrator and Chief Nursing Officer
CFO: John Arthur, Chief Financial Officer
CMO: Gary Brazel, M.D., Chief Medical Officer
CHR: Ross Brodhead, Manager Human Resources
CNO: Ann C Yates, R.N., MSN, Chief Nursing Officer
Web address: www.stvincent.org
Control: Church operated, Nongovernment, not-for-profit **Service:** General medical and surgical

Staffed Beds: 18

Hospital, Medicare Provider Number, Address, Telephone, Approval, Facility, and Physician Codes, Health Care System

★ American Hospital Association (AHA) membership   ○ Healthcare Facilities Accreditation Program   ⇧ Center for Improvement in Healthcare Quality Accreditation
☐ The Joint Commission accreditation   ◇ DNV Healthcare Inc. accreditation   △ Commission on Accreditation of Rehabilitation Facilities (CARF) accreditation

Hospitals, U.S. / INDIANA

EVANSVILLE—Vanderburgh County

△ **ASCENSION ST. VINCENT EVANSVILLE (150100)**, 3700 Washington Avenue, Zip 47714-0541; tel. 812/485-4000, (Nonreporting) **A**1 2 3 5 7 10 **S** Ascension Healthcare, Saint Louis, MO
Primary Contact: Alex Chang, President and Chief Executive Officer
COO: Gwynn Perlich, Chief Operating Officer
CFO: Craig Polkow, Vice President, Finance
CMO: Heidi Dunniway, M.D., Chief Medical Officer
CIO: Jose Diaz, Director Information Systems
CNO: Darcy Ellison, R.N., MSN, Senior Vice President, Chief Nursing Officer and Inpatient Flow
Web address: https://healthcare.ascension.org/locations/indiana/ineva/evansville-ascension-st-vincent-evansville
Control: Church operated, Nongovernment, not-for-profit **Service:** General medical and surgical

Staffed Beds: 384

○ **DEACONESS MIDTOWN HOSPITAL (150082)**, 600 Mary Street, Zip 47710-1658; tel. 812/450-5000, (Includes DEACONESS CROSS POINTE CENTER, 7200 East Indiana Street, Evansville, Indiana, Zip 47715, tel. 812/476-7200; Cheryl Rietman, Chief Administrative Officer; DEACONESS GATEWAY HOSPITAL, 4007 Gateway Blvd, Newburgh, Indiana, Zip 47630-8947, 4007 Gateway Boulevard, Zip 47630-8947, tel. 812/842-2000; Rebecca Malotte, Executive Director and Chief Nursing Officer) **A**1 2 3 5 10 11 19 **F**3 4 5 8 9 11 12 15 17 18 19 20 22 24 26 28 29 30 31 32 34 35 36 37 38 39 40 41 43 44 45 46 47 48 49 50 51 53 54 56 57 59 60 61 63 64 65 66 68 70 71 72 74 75 77 78 79 80 81 82 85 86 87 88 89 92 93 94 96 97 98 99 100 101 102 104 105 107 108 110 111 115 117 118 119 120 121 123 124 126 129 130 132 134 135 143 145 146 148 149 150 152 153 154 156 160 164 165 167 **P**1 8 **S** Deaconess Health System, Evansville, IN
Primary Contact: Shawn W. McCoy, Chief Executive Officer
CFO: Cheryl A Wathen, Interim Chief Financial Officer
CHR: Larry Pile, Director Human Resources
Web address: www.deaconess.com
Control: Other not-for-profit (including NFP Corporation) **Service:** General medical and surgical

Staffed Beds: 654 **Admissions:** 33978 **Census:** 597 **Outpatient Visits:** 640118 **Births:** 0 **Total Expense ($000):** 1169558 **Payroll Expense ($000):** 391949 **Personnel:** 3580

EVANSVILLE PSYCHIATRIC CHILDREN CENTER (15J200), 3300 East Morgan Avenue, Zip 47715-2232; tel. 812/477-6436, (Nonreporting) **A**10
Primary Contact: Carlene Oliver, Superintendent
COO: Melinda Kendle, Manager Business Office
CMO: Shannon Jones, M.D., Medical Director and Attending Psychiatrist
CIO: David Wirtz, Supervisor Information Technology
CHR: Jennifer Sontz, Director Human Resources
CNO: Elizabeth Angermeier, Director of Nursing
Web address: www.in.gov
Control: State, Government, Nonfederal **Service:** Children's hospital psychiatric

Staffed Beds: 20

□ **EVANSVILLE STATE HOSPITAL (154056)**, 3400 Lincoln Avenue, Zip 47714-0146; tel. 812/469-6800, (Nonreporting) **A**1 3 5 10
Primary Contact: Gene Schadler, Superintendent
CFO: Melinda Kendle, Director Fiscal Management
CMO: Melba Briones, M.D., Medical Director
CIO: David Wirtz, Senior LAN Administrator
CHR: Jennifer Sontz, Director Human Resources
Control: State, Government, Nonfederal **Service:** Psychiatric

Staffed Beds: 168

SELECT SPECIALTY HOSPITAL–EVANSVILLE (152014), 400 SE 4th Street, Zip 47713-1206; tel. 812/421-2500, (Nonreporting) **A**1 10 **S** Select Medical Corporation, Mechanicsburg, PA
Primary Contact: Robyn Baehl, Interim Chief Executive Officer
CNO: Robyn Baehl, Chief Nursing Officer
Web address: www.selectspecialtyhospitals.com/company/locations/evansville.aspx
Control: Corporation, Investor-owned (for-profit) **Service:** Acute long-term care hospital

Staffed Beds: 51

FISHERS—Hamilton County

ASCENSION ST. VINCENT FISHERS (150181), 13861 Olio Road, Zip 46037-3487; tel. 317/415-9000, (Nonreporting) **A**1 10 **S** Ascension Healthcare, Saint Louis, MO
Primary Contact: Jeralene Hudson, Director
CMO: Craig Wilson, Chief Medical Officer
Web address: www.stvincent.org
Control: Other not-for-profit (including NFP Corporation) **Service:** General medical and surgical

Staffed Beds: 46

IU HEALTH SAXONY HOSPITAL See Indiana University Health Saxony Hospital

FORT WAYNE—Allen County

DUPONT HOSPITAL (150150), 2520 East Dupont Road, Zip 46825-1675; tel. 260/416-3000, (Nonreporting) **A**1 10 **S** Community Health Systems, Inc., Franklin, TN
Primary Contact: Brent Parsons, Chief Executive Officer
COO: Darrick Hoopingarner, Chief Operating Officer
CFO: Brian Schneider, Chief Financial Officer
CIO: Janis Gray, Chief Information Officer
CNO: Kimberly Fulkerson, Chief Nursing Officer
Web address: https://www.theduponthospital.com/hospitals
Control: Partnership, Investor-owned (for-profit) **Service:** General medical and surgical

Staffed Beds: 131

LUTHERAN DOWNTOWN HOSPITAL (150047), 700 Broadway, Zip 46802-1493; tel. 260/425-3000, (Nonreporting) **A**1 3 10 **S** Community Health Systems, Inc., Franklin, TN
Primary Contact: Perry Gay, Chief Executive Officer
COO: Vince Green, Chief Operating Officer
CHR: Steve Heggen, Administrative Director Human Resources
Web address: https://www.lutherandowntownhospital.com/
Control: Corporation, Investor-owned (for-profit) **Service:** General medical and surgical

Staffed Beds: 191

LUTHERAN HOSPITAL OF INDIANA (150017), 7950 West Jefferson Boulevard, Zip 46804-4140; tel. 260/435-7001, **A**1 2 3 5 10 **F**3 7 11 12 13 15 17 18 20 23 24 26 28 29 30 31 32 34 35 40 41 43 44 45 46 47 48 49 50 51 54 57 58 59 60 64 65 68 70 72 74 75 76 77 78 79 80 81 84 85 86 87 88 89 91 92 93 94 96 107 108 109 110 111 112 113 114 115 116 117 118 119 120 121 122 123 124 126 129 130 132 137 138 141 144 145 146 147 154 **S** Community Health Systems, Inc., Franklin, TN
Primary Contact: Lorie Ailor, Chief Executive Officer
CFO: Cully Chapman, Chief Financial Officer
CIO: Keith A. Neuman, Chief Information Officer
CHR: Maria Kurtz, Director Human Resources
CNO: Angela Logan, Chief Nursing Officer
Web address: www.lutheranhospital.com
Control: Corporation, Investor-owned (for-profit) **Service:** General medical and surgical

Staffed Beds: 407 **Admissions:** 17164 **Census:** 251

ORTHOPAEDIC HOSPITAL OF LUTHERAN HEALTH NETWORK (150168), 7952 West Jefferson Boulevard, Zip 46804-4140; tel. 260/435-2999, (Nonreporting) **A**1 10 **S** Community Health Systems, Inc., Franklin, TN
Primary Contact: Lorie Ailor, Chief Executive Officer, Chief Administrative Officer, Network Vice President Orthopedics and Sports
CFO: Amy Hochstetler, Chief Financial Officer
CMO: Kevin Rahn, President Medical Staff
CIO: Keith A. Neuman, Chief Information Officer
CHR: Maria Kurtz, Director Human Resources
CNO: Marci Hamilton, Chief Nursing Officer
Web address: www.theorthohospital.com
Control: Corporation, Investor-owned (for-profit) **Service:** Orthopedic

Staffed Beds: 43

PARKVIEW HOSPITAL See Parkview Hospital Randallia

PARKVIEW NORTH HOSPITAL See Parkview Regional Medical Center

Hospitals, U.S. / INDIANA

⊞ **PARKVIEW ORTHO HOSPITAL (150167)**, 11130 Parkview Circle Drive, Zip 46845–1735; tel. 260/672–5000, **A**1 10 **F**3 8 29 30 34 37 50 58 65 68 75 79 81 82 84 85 86 87 90 91 93 94 96 107 111 119 126 135 141 149 **S** Parkview Health, Fort Wayne, IN
Primary Contact: Marceline Rogers, Senior Vice President, Chief Operating Officer, Service Line Leader
Web address: www.parkview.com
Control: Corporation, Investor–owned (for–profit) **Service**: Orthopedic

Staffed Beds: 37 **Admissions**: 617 **Census**: 3 **Births**: 0 **Total Expense ($000)**: 118161 **Payroll Expense ($000)**: 22246 **Personnel**: 317

⊞ △ **PARKVIEW REGIONAL MEDICAL CENTER (150021)**, 11109 Parkview Plaza Drive, Zip 46845–1701; tel. 260/266–1000, (Includes PARKVIEW HOSPITAL RANDALLIA, 2200 Randallia Drive, Fort Wayne, Indiana, Zip 46805–4699, tel. 260/373–4000; PARKVIEW REGIONAL MEDICAL CENTER, 11109 Parkview Plaza Drive, Fort Wayne, Indiana, Zip 46845, tel. 260/266–1000) **A**1 2 3 7 10 19 **F**3 5 7 8 11 12 13 15 17 18 19 20 22 24 26 28 29 30 31 32 34 35 37 39 40 41 43 44 45 46 47 48 49 50 51 54 55 56 57 58 59 60 61 62 63 64 65 68 70 72 73 74 75 76 78 79 80 81 82 83 84 85 86 87 88 89 90 91 92 93 95 96 98 99 100 101 102 104 105 107 108 110 111 114 115 119 120 121 123 124 126 129 130 131 132 135 141 144 146 147 148 149 153 154 155 156 164 167 168 169 **S** Parkview Health, Fort Wayne, IN
Primary Contact: John Bowen, President
Web address: www.parkview.com
Control: Other not–for–profit (including NFP Corporation) **Service**: General medical and surgical

Staffed Beds: 823 **Admissions**: 47996 **Census**: 653 **Outpatient Visits**: 784146 **Births**: 2096 **Total Expense ($000)**: 1831991 **Payroll Expense ($000)**: 457027 **Personnel**: 4857

⊞ **REHABILITATION HOSPITAL OF FORT WAYNE (153030)**, 7970 West Jefferson Boulevard, Zip 46804–4140; tel. 260/435–6100, **A**1 10 **F**28 29 34 44 50 51 68 74 75 77 79 82 84 85 86 87 90 91 92 94 95 96 100 119 130 135 148 149 157 160 161 164 **S** Select Medical Corporation, Mechanicsburg, PA
Primary Contact: Fabian Polo, Ph.D., Chief Executive Officer
COO: Shelley Boxell, R.N., Interim Chief Operating Officer
CFO: Edward Romero, Chief Financial Officer
CMO: Preeti Dembla, Chief Medical Officer and Medical Director
CIO: Janis Gray, Chief Information Officer
CHR: Deborah Giardina, Director Human Resources and Medical Staff Services
CNO: Shelley Boxell, R.N., Chief Nursing Officer
Web address: https://www.selectrehabilitationhospital.com/locations-and-tours/select-medical-rehabilitation-hospital-at-lutheran-hospital
Control: Partnership, Investor–owned (for–profit) **Service**: Rehabilitation

Staffed Beds: 36 **Admissions**: 675 **Census**: 22 **Personnel**: 173

⊞ **VETERANS AFFAIRS NORTHERN INDIANA HEALTH CARE SYSTEM**, 2121 Lake Avenue, Zip 46805–5100; tel. 260/426–5431, (Includes VETERANS AFFAIRS NORTHERN INDIANA HEALTH CARE SYSTEM–MARION CAMPUS, 1700 East 38th Street, Marion, Indiana, Zip 46953–4589, tel. 765/674–3321) (Nonreporting) **A**1 **S** Department of Veterans Affairs, Washington, DC
Primary Contact: Anthony Colon, Director
COO: Helen Rhodes, R.N., Associate Director Operations
CFO: Jay H Vandermark, Chief Financial Officer
CMO: Ajay Dhawan, M.D., Chief of Staff
CIO: David Troyer, Chief Information Officer
CHR: Brian Flynn, Chief Human Resources Officer
Web address: www.northernindiana.va.gov/
Control: Veterans Affairs, Government, federal **Service**: General medical and surgical

Staffed Beds: 175

FRANKFORT—Clinton County

⊞ **INDIANA UNIVERSITY HEALTH FRANKFORT (151316)**, 1300 South Jackson Street, Zip 46041–3313; tel. 765/656–3000, **A**1 3 10 18 **F**3 11 15 18 28 29 30 34 35 40 45 50 57 59 61 64 68 75 79 81 85 86 93 107 110 111 114 119 129 133 146 148 154 157 167 **S** Indiana University Health, Indianapolis, IN
Primary Contact: Mary Minier, Chief Operating Officer
CFO: Wayne Knight, Chief Financial Officer
CMO: Stephen Tharp, Medical Director
CHR: Krista Wright, Director Human Resources
Web address: https://iuhealth.org/find-locations/iu-health-frankfort-hospital
Control: Other not–for–profit (including NFP Corporation) **Service**: General medical and surgical

Staffed Beds: 12 **Admissions**: 302 **Census**: 3 **Outpatient Visits**: 29815 **Births**: 0 **Total Expense ($000)**: 28586 **Payroll Expense ($000)**: 7921 **Personnel**: 104

INDIANA UNIVERSITY HEALTH METHODIST HOSPITAL See Indiana University Health University Hospital, Indianapolis

METHODIST HOSPITAL See Indiana University Health Methodist Hospital

FRANKLIN—Johnson County

★ ○ **JOHNSON MEMORIAL HOSPITAL (150001)**, 1125 West Jefferson Street, Zip 46131–2140, Mailing Address: P.O. Box 549, Zip 46131–0549; tel. 317/736–3300, **A**5 10 11 **F**3 12 13 15 18 20 28 29 30 31 34 35 36 40 44 45 49 50 53 54 55 57 59 64 65 68 70 74 75 76 77 78 79 81 85 87 90 92 93 95 96 97 102 104 105 107 108 110 111 113 114 115 118 119 129 130 131 132 134 135 144 146 147 148 154 156 169
Primary Contact: David Dunkle, President and Chief Executive Officer and Vice President Medical Affairs
COO: Steve Wohlford, Chief Operating Officer
CFO: Tim Balasia, Chief Financial Officer
CMO: David Dunkle, President and Chief Executive Officer and Vice President Medical Affairs
CIO: Scott Krodel, Vice President Information Systems
CHR: Judy Ware, Director Human Resources
CNO: Anita M. Keller, R.N., MSN, Chief Nursing Officer
Web address: www.johnsonmemorial.org
Control: County, Government, Nonfederal **Service**: General medical and surgical

Staffed Beds: 58 **Admissions**: 1860 **Census**: 17 **Outpatient Visits**: 169256 **Births**: 314 **Total Expense ($000)**: 129041 **Payroll Expense ($000)**: 54097 **Personnel**: 728

GARY—Lake County

□ △ **METHODIST HOSPITALS (150002)**, 600 Grant Street, Zip 46402–6099; tel. 219/886–4000, (Includes SOUTHLAKE CAMPUS, 8701 Broadway, Merrillville, Indiana, Zip 46410, tel. 219/738–5500) **A**1 2 3 5 7 10 **F**3 8 11 12 13 15 18 20 22 24 26 28 29 30 31 34 35 37 40 45 46 47 48 49 50 51 54 55 57 58 59 61 62 64 67 70 72 73 74 75 76 77 78 79 81 82 85 86 87 89 90 91 92 93 96 98 100 101 102 103 107 108 110 111 114 115 118 119 120 121 123 124 126 130 132 134 135 147 148 149 154 156 167 169 **P**6
Primary Contact: Matthew Doyle, CPA, President and Chief Executive Officer
CFO: Lauren Trumbo, System Chief Financial Officer/Vice President of Finance
CIO: Timothy Diamond, Chief Information Officer
CHR: Alex Horvath, Vice President Human Resources
CNO: James M Renneker, FACHE, MSN, R.N., Vice President and Chief Nursing Officer
Web address: www.methodisthospitals.org
Control: Other not–for–profit (including NFP Corporation) **Service**: General medical and surgical

Staffed Beds: 524 **Admissions**: 11289 **Census**: 223 **Outpatient Visits**: 344739 **Births**: 1056 **Total Expense ($000)**: 430542 **Payroll Expense ($000)**: 164056 **Personnel**: 2012

GOSHEN—Elkhart County

⊞ **GOSHEN HEALTH (150026)**, 200 High Park Avenue, Zip 46526–4899, Mailing Address: P.O. Box 139, Zip 46527–0139; tel. 574/533–2141, **A**1 2 3 10 **F**3 8 11 12 13 15 18 20 22 26 28 29 30 31 34 35 36 37 38 40 45 46 47 48 49 51 56 57 58 59 61 62 63 64 65 68 70 71 74 75 76 77 78 79 81 82 83 85 86 87 89 91 92 93 94 97 102 107 108 109 110 111 114 115 116 117 118 119 120 121 123 124 126 129 130 131 132 135 144 146 147 148 149 154 156 167 169
Primary Contact: Randal Christophel, President and Chief Executive Officer
COO: Robert T Myers, Chief Operating Officer
CFO: Lisa Wine, Chief Financial Officer
CMO: Randall Cammenga, M.D., Vice President Medical Affairs
CHR: Alan Weldy, Vice President Human Resources, Compliance and Legal Services
Web address: https://goshenhealth.com/Home
Control: Other not–for–profit (including NFP Corporation) **Service**: General medical and surgical

Staffed Beds: 105 **Admissions**: 4711 **Census**: 45 **Outpatient Visits**: 159641 **Births**: 1008 **Total Expense ($000)**: 290054 **Payroll Expense ($000)**: 86614 **Personnel**: 1763

Hospital, Medicare Provider Number, Address, Telephone, Approval, Facility, and Physician Codes, Health Care System

★ American Hospital Association (AHA) membership   ○ Healthcare Facilities Accreditation Program   ⇑ Center for Improvement in Healthcare Quality Accreditation
□ The Joint Commission accreditation   ◇ DNV Healthcare Inc. accreditation   △ Commission on Accreditation of Rehabilitation Facilities (CARF) accreditation

© 2025 AHA Guide

Hospitals, U.S. / INDIANA

OAKLAWN PSYCHIATRIC CENTER (154031), 330 Lakeview Drive, Zip 46528–9365, Mailing Address: P.O. Box 809, Zip 46527–0809; tel. 574/533–1234, (Nonreporting) **A**10
Primary Contact: Laurie N. Nafziger, President and Chief Executive Officer
CFO: Joseph Barkman, Vice President Financial Services
CMO: Daniel Kinsey, M.D., Medical Director
CIO: Jennifer Glick, Manager Clinical Informatics
CHR: Jill Seifer, Vice President Human Resources
CNO: Elaine G Miller, Director of Nursing
Web address: www.oaklawn.org
Control: Other not–for–profit (including NFP Corporation) **Service:** Psychiatric

Staffed Beds: 16

GREENCASTLE—Putnam County

○ **PUTNAM COUNTY HOSPITAL (151333)**, 1542 South Bloomington Street, Zip 46135–2297; tel. 765/653–5121, (Nonreporting) **A**2 10 11 18
Primary Contact: Dennis Weatherford, Chief Executive Officer
CFO: Kevin Fowler, Director Finance
Web address: www.pchosp.org/
Control: County, Government, Nonfederal **Service:** General medical and surgical

Staffed Beds: 25

GREENFIELD—Hancock County

★ ○ **HANCOCK REGIONAL HOSPITAL (150037)**, 801 North State Street, Zip 46140–1270, Mailing Address: P.O. Box 827, Zip 46140–0827; tel. 317/462–5544, **A**2 10 11 **F**3 5 8 11 13 15 18 20 22 28 29 30 31 32 34 35 36 37 38 39 40 41 44 45 46 48 50 51 53 54 55 59 62 63 65 66 70 73 74 75 76 78 79 81 82 83 84 85 86 87 89 93 97 100 101 102 104 107 108 110 111 114 115 116 119 120 121 123 124 127 129 130 131 132 134 135 144 145 146 147 148 149 150 153 154 156 164 165 167 169 **P**6 8
Primary Contact: Steven V. Long, FACHE, President and Chief Executive Officer
CFO: Rick Edwards, Vice President and Chief Financial Officer
CMO: Michael Fletcher, M.D., Vice President and Chief Medical Officer
CIO: Jon Miller, Director Accounting and Information Services
CHR: Laura L Nichols, Director Human Resources
Web address: www.hancockregional.org
Control: County, Government, Nonfederal **Service:** General medical and surgical

Staffed Beds: 68 **Admissions:** 2815 **Census:** 32 **Outpatient Visits:** 187051 **Births:** 430 **Total Expense ($000):** 205074 **Payroll Expense ($000):** 71042 **Personnel:** 1129

GREENSBURG—Decatur County

★ ⇑ **DECATUR COUNTY MEMORIAL HOSPITAL (151332)**, 720 North Lincoln Street, Zip 47240–1398; tel. 812/663–1171, (Total facility includes 219 beds in nursing home–type unit) **A**2 10 18 21 **F**3 7 13 15 28 29 30 31 34 35 36 38 40 44 45 51 54 57 59 64 65 67 71 74 75 76 77 78 79 80 81 85 87 89 93 96 97 101 104 107 108 110 111 115 118 119 127 128 129 130 131 132 133 135 143 144 147 149 154 156 167 169 **P**8
Primary Contact: Rex McKinney, President and Chief Executive Officer
CFO: Catherine Keck, Chief Financial Officer
CMO: Jennifer Fletcher, Chief of Staff
CHR: Amy Lynn Wickens, Executive Director Human Resources
CNO: Kathy Stephens, Vice President of Patient Care
Web address: www.dcmh.net
Control: County, Government, Nonfederal **Service:** General medical and surgical

Staffed Beds: 322 **Admissions:** 1487 **Census:** 198 **Outpatient Visits:** 91571 **Births:** 184 **Total Expense ($000):** 98603 **Payroll Expense ($000):** 36014 **Personnel:** 578

GREENWOOD—Johnson County

□ △ **COMMUNITY REHABILITATION HOSPITAL SOUTH (153044)**, 607 Greenwood Springs Drive, Zip 46143–6377; tel. 317/215–3800, (Nonreporting) **A**1 7 **S** Community Health Network, Indianapolis, IN
Primary Contact: Michelle Russell, Chief Executive Officer
CFO: Amber Riggs, Controller
CMO: Shiva Gangadhar, M.D., Medical Director
CIO: Michelle Russell, Chief Executive Officer
CHR: Diana Pope, Director, Human Resources
Web address: www.communityrehabhospitalsouth.com
Control: Partnership, Investor–owned (for–profit) **Service:** Rehabilitation

Staffed Beds: 37

□ **VALLE VISTA HEALTH SYSTEM (154024)**, 898 East Main Street, Zip 46143–1400; tel. 317/887–1348, (Nonreporting) **A**1 10 **S** Universal Health Services, Inc., King of Prussia, PA
Primary Contact: Kristen Primeau, Chief Executive Officer
CFO: Tim Sides, Chief Financial Officer
CMO: Jennifer Comer, M.D., Medical Director
CIO: Karen Hayden, Director Health Information Services, Performance Improvement and Risk Management
CHR: Ismael Santos, Director Human Resources
Web address: www.vallevistahospital.com
Control: Corporation, Investor–owned (for–profit) **Service:** Psychiatric

Staffed Beds: 122

HAMMOND—Lake County

FRANCISCAN HEALTH HAMMOND (150004), 5454 Hohman Avenue, Zip 46320–1999; tel. 219/932–2300, (Includes SAINT MARGARET MERCY HEALTHCARE CENTERS–NORTH CAMPUS, 5454 Hohman Avenue, Hammond, Indiana, Zip 46320, tel. 219/932–2300) (Nonreporting) **A**10 **S** Franciscan Health, Mishawaka, IN
Primary Contact: Patrick J. Maloney, Chief Executive Officer
CFO: Marc Golan, Chief Financial Officer
Web address: https://www.franciscanhealth.org/healthcare-facilities/franciscan-health-hammond-18
Control: Church operated, Nongovernment, not–for–profit **Service:** General medical and surgical

Staffed Beds: 406

SAINT MARGARET HOSP & HLTH CTR See Saint Margaret Mercy Healthcare Centers–North Campus

HOBART—Lake County

□ **ST. MARY MEDICAL CENTER (150034)**, 1500 South Lake Park Avenue, Zip 46342–6699; tel. 219/942–0551, **A**1 2 10 **F**3 8 11 12 13 15 18 20 22 24 26 28 29 30 31 34 35 36 37 38 39 40 44 46 47 49 50 51 54 55 57 58 59 64 65 68 70 74 75 76 77 78 79 81 82 84 85 86 87 89 90 91 92 93 94 107 108 111 114 115 116 117 118 119 120 121 122 123 126 129 130 131 132 135 144 146 148 149 156 157 167 **S** Powers Health, Hammond, IN
Primary Contact: Janice L. Ryba, JD, Chief Executive Officer
CFO: Mary Sudicky, Chief Financial Officer
CIO: Gary Weiner, Vice President Information Technology and Chief Information Officer
CHR: Tony Ferracane, Vice President Human Resources
Web address: www.comhs.org
Control: Other not–for–profit (including NFP Corporation) **Service:** General medical and surgical

Staffed Beds: 200 **Admissions:** 8573 **Census:** 115 **Outpatient Visits:** 615569 **Births:** 571 **Total Expense ($000):** 288804 **Payroll Expense ($000):** 85026 **Personnel:** 1004

HUNTINGTON—Huntington County

✚ **PARKVIEW HUNTINGTON HOSPITAL (150091)**, 2001 Stults Road, Zip 46750–1291; tel. 260/355–3000, **A**1 10 **F**3 7 13 15 28 29 30 32 34 37 40 45 50 57 64 68 69 70 75 76 77 78 79 81 85 86 87 93 96 97 107 108 111 119 129 130 131 132 134 135 146 148 154 **S** Parkview Health, Fort Wayne, IN
Primary Contact: Doug R. Selig, MSN, R.N., President
CMO: Jeffrey Brooks, M.D., Chief Medical Officer
CIO: Ron Double, Chief Information Officer
CHR: Dena M Jacquay, Chief Human Resource Officer
CNO: Doug R Selig, MSN, R.N., Vice President of Patient Services
Web address: www.parkview.com
Control: Other not–for–profit (including NFP Corporation) **Service:** General medical and surgical

Staffed Beds: 36 **Admissions:** 1953 **Census:** 14 **Outpatient Visits:** 62367 **Births:** 410 **Total Expense ($000):** 70249 **Payroll Expense ($000):** 19882 **Personnel:** 239

INDIANAPOLIS—Hamilton County

✚ **ASCENSION ST. VINCENT HEART CENTER (150153)**, 10580 North Meridian Street, Zip 46290–1028; tel. 317/583–5000, (Nonreporting) **A**1 3 10 **S** Ascension Healthcare, Saint Louis, MO
Primary Contact: Lori Shannon, President
CFO: Becky Jacobson, Vice President Finance
CIO: Jeremy Long, Chief Information Officer
Web address: www.bestheartcare.com/
Control: Partnership, Investor–owned (for–profit) **Service:** Heart

Staffed Beds: 80

Hospitals, U.S. / INDIANA

INDIANAPOLIS—Marion County

☒ **ASCENSION ST. VINCENT INDIANAPOLIS HOSPITAL (150084)**, 2001 West 86th Street, Zip 46260-1991, Mailing Address: P.O. Box 40970, Zip 46240-0970; tel. 317/338-2345, (Includes PEYTON MANNING CHILDREN'S HOSPITAL AT ST. VINCENT, 2001 West 86th Street, Indianapolis, Indiana, Zip 46260-1902, P O Box 40970, Zip 46240-0970, tel. 317/415-8111; PEYTON MANNING CHILDREN'S HOSPITAL, 1707 West 86th Street, Indianapolis, Indiana, Zip 46240, P O Box 40407, Zip 46240, tel. 317/415-5500; ST. VINCENT STRESS CENTER, 8401 Harcourt RD, Indianapolis, Indiana, Zip 46260-2036, P O Box 80160, Zip 46280, tel. 317/338-4600; Sheila Mishler, Chief Executive Officer; ST. VINCENT WOMEN'S HOSPITAL, 8111 Township Line Road, Indianapolis, Indiana, Zip 46260-8043, tel. 317/415-8111; Anne Coleman, Administrator) (Nonreporting) **A**1 3 5 8 10 19 **S** Ascension Healthcare, Saint Louis, MO
Primary Contact: Daniel A. Parod, President Central Region
COO: Erica Wehrmeister, Chief Operating Officer
CIO: Randy Cox, Chief Information Officer
CHR: Audra Pratt, Chief Human Resource Officer
CNO: Cynthia D Adams, Ph.D., R.N., Chief Nursing Officer
Web address: www.stvincent.org
Control: Church operated, Nongovernment, not-for-profit **Service**: General medical and surgical

Staffed Beds: 787

☒ **ASCENSION ST. VINCENT SETON SPECIALTY HOSPITAL (152020)**, 8050 Township Line Road, Zip 46260-2478; tel. 317/415-8500, (Nonreporting) **A**1 3 10 **S** Ascension Healthcare, Saint Louis, MO
Primary Contact: Daniel A. Parod, President Central Region
CMO: Alain Broccard, M.D., Chief Medical Officer
Web address: www.stvincent.org/
Control: Church operated, Nongovernment, not-for-profit **Service**: Acute long-term care hospital

Staffed Beds: 72

☐ **COMMUNITY FAIRBANKS RECOVERY CENTER (150179)**, 8102 Clearvista Parkway, Zip 46256-4698; tel. 317/849-8222, (Nonreporting) **A**1 3 10
Primary Contact: Cathy Boggs, Executive Director and Administrator
CFO: Barb Elliott, Chief Financial Officer
CMO: Dennis Rhyne, M.D., Acting Medical Director
CIO: Randy Walls, Manager Information Services
CHR: Sharon Baker, Director Support Services
CNO: Jennifer M Horstman, R.N., Chief Nursing Officer and Chief Information Officer
Web address: www.fairbankscd.org
Control: Other not-for-profit (including NFP Corporation) **Service**: Substance Use Disorder

Staffed Beds: 86

☒ **COMMUNITY HOSPITAL EAST (150074)**, 1500 North Ritter Avenue, Zip 46219-3095; tel. 317/355-1411, (Includes COMMUNITY HEART AND VASCULAR HOSPITAL, 8075 North Shadeland Avenue, Indianapolis, Indiana, Zip 46250-2693, tel. 317/621-8000; Kathleen R Krusie, FACHE, President) (Nonreporting) **A**1 2 3 10 13 19 **S** Community Health Network, Indianapolis, IN
Primary Contact: Paige Dooley, R.N., MSN, Hospital Administrator, Vice President and Chief Nurse Executive
CNO: Paige Dooley, R.N., MSN, Hospital Administrator, Vice President and Chief Nurse Executive
Web address: www.ecommunity.com/east/
Control: Other not-for-profit (including NFP Corporation) **Service**: General medical and surgical

Staffed Beds: 163

☒ △ **COMMUNITY HOSPITAL NORTH (150169)**, 7150 Clearvista Drive, Zip 46256-1695, Mailing Address: 7250 Clearvista Drive, Suite 200, Zip 46256-1695; tel. 317/355-2469, **A**1 3 5 7 10 **F**3 11 13 29 30 31 34 35 40 41 43 44 45 46 47 48 49 50 55 56 57 59 61 64 65 70 72 74 75 76 78 79 80 81 82 84 85 87 96 98 101 103 107 108 111 114 119 120 130 132 145 146 147 148 156 167 **S** Community Health Network, Indianapolis, IN
Primary Contact: Jennifer Hindman, Vice President, Hospital Administrator
CFO: Amy Campbell, Chief Financial Officer
CMO: Wesley Wong, M.D., Acting Vice President Medical and Academic Affairs
CIO: Ron Thieme, Ph.D., Chief Knowledge and Information Officer
CHR: Steve Pearcy, Director Human Resources
Web address: www.ecommunity.com/north
Control: Other not-for-profit (including NFP Corporation) **Service**: General medical and surgical

Staffed Beds: 352 **Admissions**: 23420 **Census**: 349

☒ **COMMUNITY HOSPITAL SOUTH (150128)**, 1402 East County Line Road South, Zip 46227-0963; tel. 317/887-7000, (Nonreporting) **A**1 3 5 10 19 **S** Community Health Network, Indianapolis, IN
Primary Contact: Anita Capps, R.N., Hospital Administrator and Chief Nurse Executive
COO: Nichole Goddard, Chief Operating Officer, South Region
CFO: Leslie Yoder, Executive Director, Finance
CMO: Randy Lee, M.D., Senior Vice President Medical Affairs
CHR: Edie Garriott, Director Human Resources
CNO: Anita Capps, R.N., Chief Nursing Executive
Web address: www.ecommunity.com
Control: Other not-for-profit (including NFP Corporation) **Service**: General medical and surgical

Staffed Beds: 161

☐ **COMMUNITY REHABILITATION HOSPITAL NORTH (153043)**, 7343 Clearvista Drive, Zip 46256-4602; tel. 317/585-5400, **A**1 10 **F**29 90 91 95 96 **S** Community Health Network, Indianapolis, IN
Primary Contact: Roxanne Stacy, Chief Executive Officer
Web address: https://www.communityrehabhospitalnorth.com/
Control: Partnership, Investor-owned (for-profit) **Service**: Rehabilitation

Staffed Beds: 60 **Admissions**: 1741 **Census**: 55 **Outpatient Visits**: 0 **Births**: 0 **Total Expense ($000)**: 25313 **Payroll Expense ($000)**: 11470

☒ **ESKENAZI HEALTH (150024)**, 720 Eskenazi Avenue, Zip 46202-5166; tel. 317/880-0000, **A**1 3 5 8 10 19 **F**5 9 13 15 16 18 20 22 26 28 29 30 31 32 34 35 36 37 38 39 40 43 45 46 47 48 49 50 53 56 57 58 59 60 61 64 65 66 68 69 70 71 72 74 75 76 77 78 79 81 82 84 86 87 94 97 98 99 100 101 102 103 104 105 107 108 110 111 115 116 117 119 126 132 134 135 143 146 147 148 149 150 151 153 154 156 157 158 160 162 163 164 165 167 169
Primary Contact: Lisa E. Harris, M.D., Chief Executive Officer
COO: Neil Johnson, Chief Operating Officer
CMO: David W Crabb, M.D., Chief Medical Officer
CIO: Scott Morris, Vice President Information Systems
CHR: Christia Hicks, Vice President Human Resources
CNO: Lee Ann Blue, MSN, R.N., Chief Nursing Officer and Executive Vice President Patient Care Services
Web address: www.eskenazihealth.edu
Control: Hospital district or authority, Government, Nonfederal **Service**: General medical and surgical

Staffed Beds: 359 **Admissions**: 16132 **Census**: 228 **Outpatient Visits**: 1109800 **Births**: 3246 **Total Expense ($000)**: 953554 **Payroll Expense ($000)**: 369716 **Personnel**: 4455

FAIRBANKS See Community Fairbanks Recovery Center

☐ **FRANCISCAN HEALTH INDIANAPOLIS (150162)**, 8111 South Emerson Avenue, Zip 46237-8601; tel. 317/528-5000, (Nonreporting) **A**2 3 5 10 11 19 **S** Franciscan Health, Mishawaka, IN
Primary Contact: Lori Price, R.N., President and Chief Executive Officer, Central Indiana Region
CFO: Keith A. Lauter, Regional Chief Financial Officer
CMO: Christopher Doehring, M.D., Vice President Medical Affairs
CIO: Barbara Coulter, Director Information Systems
CHR: Corey Baute, Vice President Human Resources
Web address: https://www.franciscanhealth.org/find-a-location/franciscan-health-indianapolis-218334
Control: Church operated, Nongovernment, not-for-profit **Service**: General medical and surgical

Staffed Beds: 485

INDIANA HEART HOSPITAL See Community Heart and Vascular Hospital

---

Hospital, Medicare Provider Number, Address, Telephone, Approval, Facility, and Physician Codes, Health Care System

★ American Hospital Association (AHA) membership
☐ The Joint Commission accreditation
○ Healthcare Facilities Accreditation Program
◇ DNV Healthcare Inc. accreditation
⇑ Center for Improvement in Healthcare Quality Accreditation
△ Commission on Accreditation of Rehabilitation Facilities (CARF) accreditation

Hospitals, U.S. / INDIANA

☒ △ **INDIANA UNIVERSITY HEALTH UNIVERSITY HOSPITAL (150056)**, 550 University Boulevard, Zip 46202–5149, Mailing Address: P.O. Box 1367, Zip 46206–1367; tel. 317/944–5000, (Includes INDIANA UNIVERSITY HEALTH METHODIST HOSPITAL, 1300 S Jackson ST, Frankfort, Indiana, Zip 46041–3313, 1701 Senate Boulevard, Indianapolis, Zip 46202–1239, tel. 317/962–2000; Ryan Nagy, M.D., President; INDIANA UNIVERSITY HEALTH SAXONY HOSPITAL, 13000 East 136th Street, Fishers, Indiana, Zip 46037–9478, tel. 317/678–2000; Doug Puckett, President; INDIANA UNIVERSITY HOSPITAL, 550 North University Boulevard, Indianapolis, Indiana, Zip 46202–5262, tel. 317/274–5000; RILEY HOSPITAL FOR CHILDREN AT INDIANA UNIVERSITY HEALTH, 702 Barnhill Drive, Indianapolis, Indiana, Zip 46202–5128, 705 Riley Hospital Drive, Zip 46202–5109, tel. 317/274–5000; Gil Peri, President) **A**1 2 3 5 7 8 10 19 **F**3 5 6 13 15 16 17 18 19 20 21 22 23 24 25 26 27 28 29 30 31 32 33 34 35 36 37 38 39 40 41 42 43 44 45 46 47 48 49 50 51 52 53 54 55 56 57 58 59 60 61 62 63 64 65 68 69 70 71 72 73 74 75 76 77 78 79 80 81 82 83 84 85 86 87 88 89 90 91 92 93 94 95 96 97 98 99 100 101 102 103 105 107 108 109 110 111 112 113 114 115 116 117 118 119 120 121 123 124 126 129 130 131 132 134 135 136 137 138 139 140 141 142 144 145 146 147 148 149 150 151 153 154 157 160 161 162 164 166 167 169 **S** Indiana University Health, Indianapolis, IN
Primary Contact: Ryan Nagy, M.D., President
COO: Elizabeth Linden, MSN, R.N., Chief Operating Officer and Vice President
Web address: www.iuhealth.org
Control: Other not-for-profit (including NFP Corporation) **Service**: General medical and surgical

Staffed Beds: 1329 **Admissions**: 47356 **Census**: 958 **Outpatient Visits**: 1188170 **Births**: 3474 **Total Expense ($000)**: 5241024 **Payroll Expense ($000)**: 1506669 **Personnel**: 16479

INDIANA UNIVERSITY HOSPITAL See Indiana University Health University Hospital, Indianapolis

INDIANA UNIVERSITY MED CENTER See Indiana University Hospital

☒ **KINDRED HOSPITAL INDIANAPOLIS NORTH (152013)**, 8060 Knue Road, Zip 46250–1976; tel. 317/813–8900, (Nonreporting) **A**1 10 **S** ScionHealth, Louisville, KY
Primary Contact: Nakia Tremble, Chief Executive Officer
CFO: Chad Watson, Market Controller
CHR: Jeffrey Herdelin, Vice President Human Resources
CNO: Teresa Richardson, Chief Clinical Officer
Web address: www.kindredindynorth.com/
Control: Corporation, Investor-owned (for-profit) **Service**: Acute long-term care hospital

Staffed Beds: 45

☒ **KINDRED HOSPITAL–INDIANAPOLIS (152007)**, 1700 West 10th Street, Zip 46222–3802; tel. 317/636–4400, (Nonreporting) **A**1 10 **S** ScionHealth, Louisville, KY
Primary Contact: Judy K. Weaver, MS, Interim Chief Executive Officer
COO: Angela Lynne Rotert, Chief Clinical Officer
CFO: William Brenner, Chief Financial Officer
CHR: Joe Housh, District Director Human Resources
Web address: www.kindredhospitalindy.com/
Control: Corporation, Investor-owned (for-profit) **Service**: Acute long-term care hospital

Staffed Beds: 26

☐ **NEURODIAGNOSTIC INSTITUTE AND ADVANCED TREATMENT CENTER (154008)**, 5435 East 16th Street, Zip 46218–4869; tel. 317/941–4000, (Nonreporting) **A**1 3 10
Primary Contact: Matthew Foster, Chief Executive Officer and Superintendent
CNO: Cynthia Wilson, Director, NDI Advanced Treatment Center, Nursing and BHRA Unit Services
Web address: https://www.in.gov/fssa/dmha/index.htm
Control: State, Government, Nonfederal **Service**: Psychiatric

Staffed Beds: 318

☐ **NEUROPSYCHIATRIC HOSPITAL OF INDIANAPOLIS (154063)**, 6720 Parkdale Place, Zip 46254–4668; tel. 317/744–9200, (Nonreporting) **A**1 10 **S** NeuroPsychiatric Hospitals, Mishawaka, IN
Primary Contact: Kathryn Stanley, Interim Chief Executive Officer
COO: Christy Gilbert, President and Chief Operating Officer
CFO: Carlos Missagia, Chief Financial Officer
CHR: Becky Holloway, Vice President, Human Resources
Web address: https://www.neuropsychiatrichospitals.net
Control: Individual, Investor-owned (for-profit) **Service**: Psychiatric

Staffed Beds: 50

☐ **OPTIONS BEHAVIORAL HEALTH SYSTEM (154057)**, 5602 Caito Drive, Zip 46226–1346; tel. 317/544–4340, (Nonreporting) **A**1 10 **S** Acadia Healthcare Company, Inc., Franklin, TN
Primary Contact: Ryan Cassedy, Chief Executive Officer
Web address: www.optionsbehavioralhealthsystem.com/
Control: Corporation, Investor-owned (for-profit) **Service**: Psychiatric

Staffed Beds: 84

○ **ORTHOINDY HOSPITAL (150160)**, 8400 Northwest Boulevard, Zip 46278–1381; tel. 317/956–1000, (Nonreporting) **A**3 10 11
Primary Contact: John Ryan, JD, Chief Executive Officer
COO: Stacie Vance, Chief Nursing Officer and
CFO: Anthony Gioia, Chief Financial Officer
CMO: Joseph Randolph, M.D., Chairman Medical Executive Committee
CIO: Paul Frey, Director Information Technology Applications
CHR: Kristy Hensley, Director Human Resources
CNO: Stacie Vance, Chief Nursing Officer and Vice President Operations
Web address: www.orthoindy.com
Control: Corporation, Investor-owned (for-profit) **Service**: Orthopedic

Staffed Beds: 38

☐ △ **REHABILITATION HOSPITAL OF INDIANA (153028)**, 4141 Shore Drive, Zip 46254–2607; tel. 317/329–2000, (Nonreporting) **A**1 3 5 7 10 **S** Indiana University Health, Indianapolis, IN
Primary Contact: Monte Spence, Interim Chief Executive Officer
COO: Monte Spence, Chief Operating Officer
CFO: Marjorie Basey, Chief Financial Officer
CMO: Flora Hammond, M.D., Chief Medical Affairs
CIO: Gary Skinner, Director Information Technology
CHR: Joni Brown, Director Human Resources
CNO: Debra Cordes, Chief Nursing Officer
Web address: www.rhin.com
Control: Other not-for-profit (including NFP Corporation) **Service**: Rehabilitation

Staffed Beds: 83

☒ △ **RICHARD L. ROUDEBUSH VETERANS AFFAIRS MEDICAL CENTER**, 1481 West Tenth Street, Zip 46202–2884; tel. 317/554–0000, (Nonreporting) **A**1 2 3 5 7 **S** Department of Veterans Affairs, Washington, DC
Primary Contact: Michael E. Hershman, Director
COO: Ginny L. Creasman, Associate Director
CFO: Colin Lennon, Chief Financial Officer
CMO: Imtiaz A Munshi, M.D., Chief of Staff
CIO: Steve Stoner, Chief Information Officer
CHR: Chari Weddle, Chief Human Resource Management Service
CNO: Patricia Mathis, Associate Director Patient Care Service
Web address: www.indianapolis.va.gov
Control: Veterans Affairs, Government, federal **Service**: General medical and surgical

Staffed Beds: 159

RILEY HOSPITAL FOR CHILDREN See Riley Hospital For Children At Indiana University Health

RILEY HOSPITAL FOR CHILDREN AT INDIANA UNIVERSITY HEALTH See Indiana University Health University Hospital, Indianapolis

ST VINCENT CHILDREN'S HOSPITAL See Peyton Manning Children's Hospital At St. Vincent

ST. VINCENT PEDIATRIC REHABILITATION CENTER See Peyton Manning Children's Hospital

WOMEN'S HOSPITAL–INDIANAPOLIS See St. Vincent Women's Hospital

JASPER—Dubois County

☒ **MEMORIAL HOSPITAL AND HEALTH CARE CENTER (150115)**, 800 West Ninth Street, Zip 47546–2516; tel. 812/996–2345, (Nonreporting) **A**1 2 3 5 10 19 **S** American Province of Little Company of Mary Sisters, Evergreen Park, IL
Primary Contact: E Kyle. Bennett, President and Chief Executive Officer
CFO: Ted Miller, Vice President and Chief Financial Officer
CMO: Stan Tretter, M.D., Chief Medical Officer
CIO: Mathew P. Gaug, Vice President Information Systems and Chief Information Officer
CHR: Richard Pea, Director Human Resources
Web address: www.mhhcc.org
Control: Church operated, Nongovernment, not-for-profit **Service**: General medical and surgical

Staffed Beds: 137

JEFFERSONVILLE—Clark County

⊞ **NORTON CLARK HOSPITAL (150009)**, 1220 Missouri Avenue, Zip 47130-3743; Mailing Address: P.O. Box 69, Zip 47131-0600; tel. 812/282-6631, (Nonreporting) **A**1 2 3 5 10 **S** Norton Healthcare, Louisville, KY
Primary Contact: Kathleen Exline, R.N., Chief Administrative Officer
COO: Joey Waddell, Chief Operating Officer
CMO: William Templeton, M.D., III, Medical Director
CIO: Larry Reverman, Director Information Systems
CHR: Scott Hicks, Vice President
CNO: Kathy Neuner, R.N., Chief Nursing Officer
Web address: www.clarkmemorial.org
Control: County, Government, Nonfederal **Service**: General medical and surgical

Staffed Beds: 185

☐ **WELLSTONE REGIONAL HOSPITAL (154051)**, 2700 Vissing Park Road, Zip 47130-5989; tel. 812/284-8000, (Nonreporting) **A**1 10 **S** Universal Health Services, Inc., King of Prussia, PA
Primary Contact: Jessica Campbell, Chief Executive Officer
CFO: Patricia Ellison, Chief Financial Officer
CMO: Asad Ismail, M.D., Medical Director
CIO: Timothy Wise, Director, Information Technology
CHR: Tiffany Pierce, Director Human Resources
CNO: Carrie Dodson, Director of Nursing
Web address: www.wellstonehospital.com
Control: Corporation, Investor-owned (for-profit) **Service**: Psychiatric

Staffed Beds: 100

KENDALLVILLE—Noble County

⊞ **PARKVIEW NOBLE HOSPITAL (150146)**, 401 Sawyer Road, Zip 46755-2568; tel. 260/347-8700, **A**1 10 **F**3 7 13 15 28 29 34 35 40 45 46 47 50 54 57 59 64 70 74 75 76 79 81 82 85 87 93 97 107 108 110 111 114 118 119 129 130 132 135 143 145 146 148 154 156 169 **S** Parkview Health, Fort Wayne, IN
Primary Contact: Jordi K. Disler, Market President
COO: Gary W Adkins, Chief Executive Officer
CFO: Kem Prince, Manager of Finance
CMO: Gerald Warrener, M.D., Chief Medical Officer
CIO: Ron Double, Chief Information Officer
CHR: Bruce Buttermore, Manager Human Resources
CNO: Catherine Byrd, Vice President Patient Services
Web address: www.parkview.com
Control: Other not-for-profit (including NFP Corporation) **Service**: General medical and surgical

Staffed Beds: 31 **Admissions**: 1943 **Census**: 13 **Outpatient Visits**: 63454 **Births**: 277 **Total Expense ($000)**: 66939 **Payroll Expense ($000)**: 19480 **Personnel**: 218

KNOX—Starke County

⊞ **NORTHWEST HEALTH – STARKE (150102)**, 102 East Culver Road, Zip 46534-2216, Mailing Address: P.O. Box 339, Zip 46534-0339; tel. 574/772-6231, (Nonreporting) **A**1 10 **S** Community Health Systems, Inc., Franklin, TN
Primary Contact: Simon Ratliff, Chief Executive Officer
COO: Jeff Vice, Chief Operating Officer
CFO: Drew Keesbury, Chief Financial Officer
CMO: A N Damodaran, M.D., President Medical Staff
CIO: Ashley Norem, Chief Information Systems
CHR: Doug Jesch, Director Human Resources
Web address: https://www.nwhealthstarke.com/
Control: Corporation, Investor-owned (for-profit) **Service**: General medical and surgical

Staffed Beds: 15

KOKOMO—Howard County

⊞ **ASCENSION ST. VINCENT KOKOMO (150010)**, 1907 West Sycamore Street, Zip 46901-4197; tel. 765/452-5611, (Nonreporting) **A**1 10 **S** Ascension Healthcare, Saint Louis, MO
Primary Contact: Don Damron, Chief Executive Officer
CMO: David L Williams, M.D., Chief Medical Officer
CIO: Jeffrey Scott, Chief Information Officer
CHR: Cindy Babb, Executive Director Human Resources and Organizational Effectiveness
CNO: Kathleen K Peoples, R.N., MS, Vice President of Nursing
Web address: www.stvincent.org/stjoseph
Control: Church operated, Nongovernment, not-for-profit **Service**: General medical and surgical

Staffed Beds: 117

⊞ **COMMUNITY HOWARD REGIONAL HEALTH (150007)**, 3500 South Lafountain Street, Zip 46902-3803, Mailing Address: P.O. Box 9011, Zip 46904-9011; tel. 765/453-0702, (Nonreporting) **A**1 2 10 **S** Community Health Network, Indianapolis, IN
Primary Contact: Derek McMichael, Administrator
COO: Theodore Brown, Chief Operating Officer
CFO: Theodore Brown, Vice President Financial Services
CIO: Kevin Purvis, Chief Information Officer
CHR: Michael L Williams, FACHE, Vice President Human Resources
CNO: Melodi Greene, R.N., MS, Chief Nursing Officer
Web address: https://www.ecommunity.com/locations/community-howard-regional-health
Control: Other not-for-profit (including NFP Corporation) **Service**: General medical and surgical

Staffed Beds: 201

LA PORTE—Laporte County

⊞ **NORTHWEST HEALTH – LA PORTE (150006)**, 1007 Lincolnway, Zip 46350-3201, Mailing Address: P.O. Box 250, Zip 46352-0250; tel. 219/326-1234, (Nonreporting) **A**1 2 3 10 19 **S** Community Health Systems, Inc., Franklin, TN
Primary Contact: Simon Ratliff, Chief Executive Officer
CFO: Drew Keesbury, Chief Financial Officer
Web address: https://www.nwhealthlaporte.com
Control: Corporation, Investor-owned (for-profit) **Service**: General medical and surgical

Staffed Beds: 84

LAFAYETTE—Tippecanoe County

FRANCISCAN HEALTH – LAFAYETTE CENTRAL See Franciscan Health Lafayette Central

○ **FRANCISCAN HEALTH LAFAYETTE EAST (150109)**, 1701 South Creasy Lane, Zip 47905-4972; tel. 765/502-4000, (Includes FRANCISCAN HEALTH LAFAYETTE CENTRAL, 1501 Hartford Street, Lafayette, Indiana, Zip 47904-2134, tel. 765/423-6011; Terrance E. Wilson, President and Chief Executive Officer) (Nonreporting) **A**2 3 10 11 19 **S** Franciscan Health, Mishawaka, IN
Primary Contact: Terrance E. Wilson, President and Chief Executive Officer
Web address: www.ste.org
Control: Other not-for-profit (including NFP Corporation) **Service**: General medical and surgical

Staffed Beds: 203

Hospitals, U.S. / INDIANA

☒ **INDIANA UNIVERSITY HEALTH ARNETT HOSPITAL (150173)**, 5165 McCarty Lane, Zip 47905–8764, Mailing Address: P.O. Box 5545, Zip 47903–5545; tel. 765/448–8000, **A**1 2 3 5 10 19 **F**3 11 12 13 15 17 18 20 22 24 26 28 29 30 31 34 35 40 43 45 46 49 50 51 54 56 57 59 61 64 65 68 69 70 72 74 75 76 77 78 79 81 82 84 85 87 89 92 93 97 100 104 107 108 110 111 114 115 116 117 118 119 120 121 126 129 130 131 132 135 144 145 146 147 148 154 156 167 169 **P**6 **S** Indiana University Health, Indianapolis, IN
Primary Contact: Arthur Vasquez, President
CFO: Cara Breidster, Chief Financial Officer
CMO: Jeffrey P Brown, M.D., Chief Medical Officer
CIO: Rusty McGill, System Director Information Technology
CHR: Koreen H Kyhnell, Vice President Human Resources
Web address: www.iuhealth.org
Control: Other not–for–profit (including NFP Corporation) **Service**: General medical and surgical

Staffed Beds: 199 **Admissions:** 11601 **Census:** 128 **Outpatient Visits:** 217922 **Births:** 1546 **Total Expense ($000):** 604868 **Payroll Expense ($000):** 254304 **Personnel:** 2004

☒ **LAFAYETTE REGIONAL REHABILITATION HOSPITAL (153042)**, 950 Park East Boulevard, Zip 47905–0792; tel. 765/447–4040, (Nonreporting) **A**1 10 **S** Ernest Health, Inc., Albuquerque, NM
Primary Contact: Logan Savage, Chief Executive Officer
Web address: www.lrrh.ernesthealth.com
Control: Corporation, Investor–owned (for–profit) **Service**: Rehabilitation

Staffed Beds: 40

ST ELIZABETH MED CENTER See St. Elizabeth Medical Center

☐ **SYCAMORE SPRINGS (154059)**, 833 Park East Boulevard, Zip 47905–0785; tel. 765/743–4400, (Nonreporting) **A**1 10 **S** Springstone, Louisville, KY
Primary Contact: Denise Sullivan, Chief Executive Officer
CFO: Michael Huth, Chief Financial Officer
CMO: Nizar El Khalili, M.D., Medical Director
CHR: Pam Sichts, Director Human Resources
CNO: Brooke Lavignette, Director of Nursing
Web address: www.sycamorespringshealth.com
Control: Corporation, Investor–owned (for–profit) **Service**: Psychiatric

Staffed Beds: 48

LAGRANGE—Lagrange County

☒ **PARKVIEW LAGRANGE HOSPITAL (151323)**, 207 North Townline Road, Zip 46761–1325; tel. 260/463–9000, **A**1 10 18 **F**3 15 17 26 29 30 34 35 40 45 50 51 57 59 63 64 70 75 76 79 81 82 83 84 85 86 87 89 90 93 96 107 108 109 110 111 114 118 119 128 130 132 133 143 146 148 156 **S** Parkview Health, Fort Wayne, IN
Primary Contact: Jordi K. Disler, President
CFO: Vickie Stanski, Financial Manager
CMO: Jeffrey Brookes, M.D., Chief Medical Officer
CIO: Ron Double, Chief Information Technology Officer
CHR: Bruce Buttermore, Director Human Resources
CNO: Jared Beasley, R.N., Vice President Patient Care
Web address: www.parkview.com
Control: Other not–for–profit (including NFP Corporation) **Service**: General medical and surgical

Staffed Beds: 25 **Admissions:** 991 **Census:** 8 **Outpatient Visits:** 30806 **Births:** 139 **Total Expense ($000):** 39771 **Payroll Expense ($000):** 10884 **Personnel:** 119

LAWRENCEBURG—Dearborn County

COMMUNITY MENTAL HEALTH CENTER See Incompass Healthcare

★ **INCOMPASS HEALTHCARE (154011)**, 285 Bielby Road, Zip 47025–1055; tel. 812/537–1302, (Nonreporting) **A**10
Primary Contact: Greg Duncan, President and Chief Executive Officer
COO: Diane Young, Chief Operating Manager
CFO: Georgii Zhirkin, Chief Financial Officer
CMO: Hasan Bakhtier, M.D., Medical Director
CIO: John McKinley, Director, Information Technology
CHR: Emily Walston, Chief Human Resources Officer
Web address: https://incompasshc.org/
Control: Other not–for–profit (including NFP Corporation) **Service**: Psychiatric

Staffed Beds: 16

○ **ST. ELIZABETH DEARBORN (150086)**, 600 Wilson Creek Road, Zip 47025–2751; tel. 812/537–1010, **A**10 11 **F**3 11 13 15 18 20 28 29 30 34 35 40 44 45 46 47 49 50 53 59 64 70 75 76 78 79 81 85 86 87 92 93 101 102 107 108 110 111 115 116 117 118 119 129 130 131 132 135 146 148 149 164 167 169 **S** St. Elizabeth Healthcare, Edgewood, KY
Primary Contact: Garren Colvin, Chief Executive Officer
CMO: Nancy A. Kennedy, M.D., Chief Medical Officer
CIO: Kathy Dickman, Director of Information Systems
CNO: Angela K. Scudder, MSN, R.N., Vice President Patient Care Services
Web address: https://www.stelizabeth.com/location/details/st-elizabeth-dearborn
Control: Church operated, Nongovernment, not–for–profit **Service**: General medical and surgical

Staffed Beds: 61 **Admissions:** 3564 **Census:** 35 **Outpatient Visits:** 143451 **Births:** 274 **Total Expense ($000):** 100502 **Payroll Expense ($000):** 40415 **Personnel:** 432

LEBANON—Boone County

☒ **WITHAM HEALTH SERVICES (150104)**, 2605 North Lebanon Street, Zip 46052–1476, Mailing Address: P.O. Box 1200, Zip 46052–3005; tel. 765/485–8000, **A**1 3 10 **F**3 7 8 13 15 18 20 22 24 28 29 30 34 40 42 44 45 53 54 56 57 59 64 65 69 70 75 76 77 79 81 82 83 85 86 87 89 90 91 93 94 97 98 103 107 111 116 119 121 128 129 130 131 132 135 143 144 146 147 148 154 156 169 **P**1
Primary Contact: Kelly Braverman, FACHE, President and Chief Executive Officer
CFO: George Pogas, CPA, Senior Vice President and Chief Financial Officer
CMO: Anthony Steele, M.D., Chief Medical Officer
CIO: George Pogas, CPA, Senior Vice President and Chief Financial Officer
CHR: Gary A Deater, Vice President Administration, Human Resources and Risk Management
CNO: Julie Hawkins, MSN, R.N., Chief Nursing Officer
Web address: www.witham.org
Control: County, Government, Nonfederal **Service**: General medical and surgical

Staffed Beds: 78 **Admissions:** 2663 **Census:** 41 **Outpatient Visits:** 152439 **Births:** 341 **Total Expense ($000):** 175142 **Payroll Expense ($000):** 73027 **Personnel:** 868

LINTON—Greene County

☒ **GREENE COUNTY GENERAL HOSPITAL (151317)**, 1185 North 1000 West, Zip 47441–5282; tel. 812/847–2281, **A**1 10 18 **F**3 13 15 26 27 28 29 30 31 34 35 40 41 44 45 56 57 58 59 64 65 66 67 68 70 75 76 77 78 79 81 85 86 87 89 90 93 96 97 107 108 110 111 114 119 127 128 130 131 133 135 144 147 148 149 154 156 160 164 167 169 **P**6
Primary Contact: Brenda Reetz, FACHE, Chief Executive Officer
COO: Kyle Cross, Director of Support Services
CFO: Rebecca Wittmer, CPA, Chief Financial Officer
CMO: Mike Gamble, M.D., Chief Medical Officer
CIO: Dylan Morris, Director of Information Technology
CHR: Robin M. Rose, Director of Human Resources
CNO: Jill Raines, R.N., Chief of Clinical Quality
Web address: www.greenecountyhospital.com
Control: County, Government, Nonfederal **Service**: General medical and surgical

Staffed Beds: 25 **Admissions:** 564 **Census:** 6 **Outpatient Visits:** 957466 **Births:** 79 **Total Expense ($000):** 64282 **Payroll Expense ($000):** 27542 **Personnel:** 409

LOGANSPORT—Cass County

4C HEALTH (154035), 1015 Michigan Avenue, Zip 46947–1526; tel. 574/722–5151, (Nonreporting) **A**10
Primary Contact: Carrie Cadwell, PsyD, Chief Executive Officer
CFO: Jason Cadwell, Chief Financial Officer
CMO: John Yarling, M.D., Medical Director
CIO: Becky Mulis, Director of Health Information Management Systems
CHR: Steve Curry, Regional Director Human Resources
CNO: Donna Henry, Vice President of Nursing Services
Web address: https://www.4chealthin.org/
Control: Other not–for–profit (including NFP Corporation) **Service**: Psychiatric

Staffed Beds: 15

FOUR COUNTY COUNSELING CENTER See 4C Health

Hospitals, U.S. / INDIANA

○ **LOGANSPORT MEMORIAL HOSPITAL (150072)**, 1101 Michigan Avenue, Zip 46947–1528, Mailing Address: P.O. Box 7013, Zip 46947–7013; tel. 574/753–7541, (Nonreporting) **A**10 11 20
Primary Contact: Tara McVay, Chief Executive Officer
CFO: Sherri Gehlhausen, Chief Financial Officer
CMO: Kamlesh Kaul, M.D., Chief of Staff
CIO: Dan Hildebrand, Chief Information Officer
CHR: Lynda J Shrock, Vice President Human Resources
CNO: Tara McVay, Chief Nursing Officer
Web address: www.logansportmemorial.org
Control: County, Government, Nonfederal **Service**: General medical and surgical

Staffed Beds: 33

☐ **LOGANSPORT STATE HOSPITAL**, 1098 South State Road 25, Zip 46947–6723; tel. 574/722–4141, (Nonreporting) **A**1
Primary Contact: Gregory Grostefon, Superintendent
CFO: Misty Moss, Director Business Administration
CMO: Danny Meadows, M.D., Medical Director
CIO: Joe McIntosh, Director Management Information Systems
CHR: Dianne Renner, Director Human Resources
Web address: https://www.in.gov/fssa/dmha/state-psychiatric-hospitals/
Control: State, Government, Nonfederal **Service**: Psychiatric

Staffed Beds: 170

MADISON—Jefferson County

KING'S DAUGHTERS' HEALTH See Norton King's Daughters' Health

☐ **MADISON STATE HOSPITAL (154019)**, 711 Green Road, Zip 47250–2199; tel. 812/265–2611, (Nonreporting) **A**1 10
Primary Contact: Alicia Isaacs, Superintendent and Medical Director
CFO: Carolyn Copeland, Business Administrator
CIO: Ric Martin, Information Specialist
Web address: www.in.gov/fssa/msh
Control: State, Government, Nonfederal **Service**: Psychiatric

Staffed Beds: 120

★ ○ **NORTON KING'S DAUGHTERS' HEALTH (150069)**, 1373 East State Road 62, Zip 47250–3357, Mailing Address: P.O. Box 447, Zip 47250–0447; tel. 812/801–0800, **A**2 10 11 **F**3 7 8 12 13 15 18 28 29 30 31 32 34 35 40 42 45 48 50 55 56 57 59 62 63 64 65 68 70 75 76 77 78 79 81 82 84 85 86 87 91 93 94 97 107 108 110 111 115 119 120 121 123 129 130 131 132 134 135 143 144 145 146 147 148 149 150 156 167 169
Primary Contact: Carol Dozier, President and Chief Executive Officer
CFO: John Price, Chief Financial Officer
CIO: Linda Darnell, Director Management Information Systems
CHR: Susan Kay Poling, Director Human Resources
CNO: Jennifer Lynn Liter, Vice President of Inpatient Services
Web address: www.kdhhs.org
Control: Other not–for–profit (including NFP Corporation) **Service**: General medical and surgical

Staffed Beds: 60 **Admissions**: 2315 **Census**: 27 **Outpatient Visits**: 238991 **Births**: 363 **Total Expense ($000)**: 163410 **Payroll Expense ($000)**: 56886 **Personnel**: 721

MARION—Grant County

GRANT–BLACKFORD MENTAL HEALTH CENTER See Radiant Health

MARION GENERAL HOSPITAL See Marion Health

★ ○ △ **MARION HEALTH (150011)**, 441 North Wabash Avenue, Zip 46952–2690; tel. 765/660–6000, (Includes MARION HEALTH EAST, 911 Marion Health Drive, Gas City, Indiana, Zip 46933–1302, 441 North Wabash Avenue, Marion, Zip 46952–2612, tel. 765/660–7300; Stephanie Hilton–Siebert, FACHE, MSN, Chief Executive Officer) **A**2 3 7 10 11 **F**7 8 11 13 15 20 22 28 29 30 31 34 35 40 44 45 50 54 57 59 64 68 69 70 76 78 79 81 86 87 89 90 93 96 129 130 135 143 144 146 148 149 154 156 157 164
Primary Contact: Stephanie Hilton–Siebert, FACHE, MSN, President and Chief Executive Officer
CFO: Tony Roberts, CPA, Chief Financial Officer
CMO: Shankaran Srikanth, M.D., Chief Medical Officer
CIO: Emmanuel Ndow, Chief Information Officer
CHR: Karen Jones, Administrative Director of Human Resources
CNO: Cynthia Futrell, MSN, R.N., Chief Nursing Officer
Web address: https://www.marionhealth.com/
Control: Other not–for–profit (including NFP Corporation) **Service**: General medical and surgical

Staffed Beds: 146 **Admissions**: 3875 **Census**: 43 **Outpatient Visits**: 240159 **Births**: 411 **Total Expense ($000)**: 210246 **Payroll Expense ($000)**: 79792 **Personnel**: 1018

⊞ **RADIANT HEALTH (154021)**, 505 North Wabash Avenue, Zip 46952–2608; tel. 765/662–3971, (Nonreporting) **A**1 10
Primary Contact: Lisa Dominisse, President and Chief Executive Officer
Web address: https://getradiant.org
Control: Other not–for–profit (including NFP Corporation) **Service**: Psychiatric

Staffed Beds: 16

VETERANS AFFAIRS MED CENTER See Veterans Affairs Northern Indiana Health Care System–Marion Campus

VETERANS AFFAIRS NORTHERN INDIANA HEALTH CARE SYSTEM–MARION CAMPUS See Veterans Affairs Northern Indiana Health Care System, Fort Wayne

MERRILLVILLE—Lake County

REGIONAL MENTAL HEALTH CENTER (154020), 8555 Taft Street, Zip 46410–6123; tel. 219/769–4005, (Nonreporting) **A**3 5 10
Primary Contact: William Trowbridge, President and Chief Executive Officer
Web address: www.regionalmentalhealth.org/
Control: Corporation, Investor–owned (for–profit) **Service**: Psychiatric

Staffed Beds: 16

SOUTHLAKE CAMPUS See Methodist Hospitals, Gary

SOUTHLAKE CAMPUS See Southlake Campus

MICHIGAN CITY—Laporte County

○ **FRANCISCAN HEALTH MICHIGAN CITY (150015)**, 301 West Homer Street, Zip 46360–4358; tel. 219/879–8511, (Nonreporting) **A**2 10 11 19 **S** Franciscan Health, Mishawaka, IN
Primary Contact: Dean Mazzoni, President and Chief Executive Officer
CFO: Marc Golan, Regional Chief Financial Officer
CIO: Tim Loosemore, Regional Director Information Systems
CHR: John Barrett, Regional Director Human Resources
Web address: www.franciscanalliance.org
Control: Church operated, Nongovernment, not–for–profit **Service**: General medical and surgical

Staffed Beds: 171

MISHAWAKA—St. Joseph County

☐ **MEDICAL BEHAVIORAL HOSPITAL OF MISHAWAKA (154061)**, 1625 East Jefferson Boulevard, Zip 46545–7103; tel. 574/255–1400, (Nonreporting) **A**1 10 **S** NeuroPsychiatric Hospitals, Mishawaka, IN
Primary Contact: Ted Paarlberg, Chief Executive Officer
COO: Christy Gilbert, President and Chief Operating Officer
CFO: Carlos Missagia, Chief Financial Officer
CHR: Becky Holloway, Vice President, Human Resources
Web address: https://www.neuropsychiatrichospitals.net/
Control: Individual, Investor–owned (for–profit) **Service**: Psychiatric

Staffed Beds: 30

Hospital, Medicare Provider Number, Address, Telephone, Approval, Facility, and Physician Codes, Health Care System

★ American Hospital Association (AHA) membership
☐ The Joint Commission accreditation
○ Healthcare Facilities Accreditation Program
◇ DNV Healthcare Inc. accreditation
⇑ Center for Improvement in Healthcare Quality Accreditation
△ Commission on Accreditation of Rehabilitation Facilities (CARF) accreditation

Hospitals, U.S. / INDIANA

REHABILITATION HOSPITAL OF NORTHERN INDIANA (153047), 4807 Edison Lakes Parkway, Zip 46545-1112; tel. 574/243-7727, (Nonreporting) **S** Ernest Health, Inc., Albuquerque, NM
Primary Contact: Cindie McPhie, Chief Executive Officer
Web address: https://rhni.ernesthealth.com/
Control: Corporation, Investor-owned (for-profit) **Service**: Rehabilitation

Staffed Beds: 50

✠ **SAINT JOSEPH HEALTH SYSTEM (150012)**, 5215 Holy Cross Parkway, Zip 46545-1469; tel. 574/335-5000, (Nonreporting) **A**1 3 5 10 19 **S** Trinity Health, Livonia, MI
Primary Contact: Shawn Vincent, Chief Executive Officer
COO: Christopher J Karam, Chief Operating Officer
CFO: Kevin J Higdon, Chief Financial Officer
CMO: Genevieve Lankowicz, M.D., Chief Medical Officer
CIO: Gary L Miller, Senior Director Information Systems
CHR: Kurt A Meyer, Chief Human Resource Officer
CNO: Kenneth C Hall, R.N., Chief Nursing Officer
Web address: www.sjmed.com
Control: Other not-for-profit (including NFP Corporation) **Service**: General medical and surgical

Staffed Beds: 270

UNITY MEDICAL & SURGICAL HOSPITAL See Unity Physicians Hospital

○ **UNITY PHYSICIANS HOSPITAL (150177)**, 4455 Edison Lakes Parkway, Zip 46545-1442; tel. 574/231-6800, (Nonreporting) **A**10 11
Primary Contact: John M. Day, Chief Executive Officer
COO: Donald Allen, Chief Operating Officer
CFO: Matthew M Sherwood, Chief Financial Officer
CMO: Viraj Patel, M.D., Chief Medical Officer
CIO: Richard Leighton, Financial Application Analyst
CHR: Emyle Kruyer-Collins, Chief Human Resources Officer
CNO: Sylvia K Coffing, R.N., MSN, Chief Nursing and Compliance Officer
Web address: https://www.unityphysicianshospital.com/
Control: Partnership, Investor-owned (for-profit) **Service**: Surgical

Staffed Beds: 15

MONTICELLO—White County

✠ **INDIANA UNIVERSITY HEALTH WHITE MEMORIAL HOSPITAL (151312)**, 720 South Sixth Street, Zip 47960-8182; tel. 574/583-7111, **A**1 3 10 18 **F**3 11 15 28 29 30 31 34 35 40 45 50 59 64 70 75 77 78 79 81 84 85 93 107 108 110 111 114 119 129 133 135 146 147 148 149 150 167 **S** Indiana University Health, Indianapolis, IN
Primary Contact: Mary Minier, Chief Operating Officer
CMO: Adel Khdour, M.D., Chief Medical Officer
CIO: Michelle Baker, Director Information Systems
CHR: JoEllyn Brockmeyer, Director Human Resources
CNO: Robin C Smith, Chief Nursing Officer
Web address: www.iuhealth.org/white-memorial
Control: Other not-for-profit (including NFP Corporation) **Service**: General medical and surgical

Staffed Beds: 24 **Admissions:** 622 **Census:** 7 **Outpatient Visits:** 48083 **Births:** 0 **Total Expense ($000):** 43326 **Payroll Expense ($000):** 10376 **Personnel:** 150

MOORESVILLE—Morgan County

○ **FRANCISCAN HEALTH MOORESVILLE (150057)**, 1201 Hadley Road, Zip 46158-1789; tel. 317/831-1160, (Nonreporting) **A**3 5 10 11 **S** Franciscan Health, Mishawaka, IN
Primary Contact: Lori Price, R.N., President and Chief Executive Officer, Central Indiana Region
COO: Trish Weber, R.N., FACHE, Vice President and Chief Operating Officer
CIO: Barbara Coulter, Director Information Systems
CHR: John Ross, Vice President
Web address: www.franciscanalliance.org/hospitals/mooresville/Pages/default.aspx
Control: Church operated, Nongovernment, not-for-profit **Service**: General medical and surgical

Staffed Beds: 115

MUNCIE—Delaware County

CENTRAL INDIANA AMG SPECIALTY HOSPITAL (152025), 2401 West University Avenue, 8th Floor, Zip 47303-3428; tel. 765/751-5253, (Includes AMG SPECIALTY HOSPITAL – CENTRAL INDIANA HANCOCK CAMPUS, 801 N. State Street, 3rd Floor West, Greenfield, Indiana, Zip 46140-1270, tel. 317/477-6789; William Hedge, Chief Executive Officer) (Nonreporting) **A**10 22
Primary Contact: William Hedge, Chief Executive Officer
CNO: Lisa G. Hayes, Chief Clinical Officer
Web address: www.amgmuncie.com/
Control: Corporation, Investor-owned (for-profit) **Service**: Acute long-term care hospital

Staffed Beds: 32

✠ **INDIANA UNIVERSITY HEALTH BALL MEMORIAL HOSPITAL (150089)**, 2401 West University Avenue, Zip 47303-3499; tel. 765/747-3111, **A**1 2 3 5 10 19 **F**3 4 5 8 11 12 13 15 17 18 20 22 24 26 28 29 30 31 32 33 34 35 36 38 40 43 44 45 46 47 48 49 50 51 53 54 55 56 57 58 59 60 61 64 65 66 70 72 73 74 75 76 77 78 79 81 82 83 84 85 86 87 89 90 92 93 94 96 97 98 100 101 102 104 107 108 110 111 114 115 117 118 119 120 121 123 124 126 129 130 131 132 140 141 146 147 148 149 154 156 157 160 161 162 165 167 169 **S** Indiana University Health, Indianapolis, IN
Primary Contact: Jeffrey C. Bird, M.D., President
COO: Lori Luther, CPA, Chief Operating Officer
CMO: Peter Voss, M.D., Chief Medical Officer
CHR: Ann M. McGuire, Regional Vice President Human Resources
CNO: Carla C. Cox, Chief Nursing Officer
Web address: www.iuhealth.org
Control: Other not-for-profit (including NFP Corporation) **Service**: General medical and surgical

Staffed Beds: 325 **Admissions:** 15298 **Census:** 217 **Outpatient Visits:** 250505 **Births:** 1287 **Total Expense ($000):** 518926 **Payroll Expense ($000):** 156670 **Personnel:** 1840

MERIDIAN HEALTH SERVICES (154053), 240 North Tillotson Avenue, Zip 47304; tel. 765/747-3281, (Nonreporting) **A**10
Primary Contact: Seth Warren, President and Chief Executive Officer
CMO: Sarfraz Khan, Medical Director
Web address: www.meridianhs.org
Control: Other not-for-profit (including NFP Corporation) **Service**: Psychiatric

Staffed Beds: 20

MUNSTER—Lake County

□ △ **COMMUNITY HOSPITAL (150125)**, 901 Macarthur Boulevard, Zip 46321-2959; tel. 219/836-1600, **A**1 2 7 10 **F**8 11 12 13 15 17 18 20 22 24 26 28 29 30 31 34 35 37 39 40 46 47 48 49 50 51 53 54 55 57 58 59 60 64 68 70 72 74 75 76 78 79 81 82 84 85 86 87 89 92 93 94 97 107 108 109 110 111 114 115 116 117 118 119 120 121 122 126 129 130 131 132 144 146 148 149 150 156 167 **S** Powers Health, Hammond, IN
Primary Contact: Randy Neiswonger, Chief Operating Officer
CFO: Daniel R. O'Brien, Vice President and Chief Financial Officer
CMO: David Robinson, President Medical and Dental Staff
CIO: Gary Weiner, Vice President Information Technology, Chief Information Officer
CHR: Debbie Brandt, Director Human Resources
CNO: Ronda McKay, R.N., Vice President Patient Care Services, Chief Nursing Officer
Web address: www.comhs.org
Control: Other not-for-profit (including NFP Corporation) **Service**: General medical and surgical

Staffed Beds: 509 **Admissions:** 17877 **Census:** 232 **Outpatient Visits:** 1012457 **Births:** 1660 **Total Expense ($000):** 578376 **Payroll Expense ($000):** 208279 **Personnel:** 2225

○ **FRANCISCAN HEALTHCARE MUNSTER (150165)**, 701 Superior Avenue, Zip 46321-4037; tel. 219/924-1300, (Nonreporting) **A**3 10 11 **S** Franciscan Health, Mishawaka, IN
Primary Contact: Patrick J. Maloney, Chief Executive Officer
CFO: Harold E Collins, JD, Chief Financial Officer
CMO: Vijay D Gupta, M.D., President and Chief Executive Officer
CIO: Steven Krause, Manager Information Technology
Web address: www.franciscanphysicianshospital.org
Control: Partnership, Investor-owned (for-profit) **Service**: General medical and surgical

Staffed Beds: 32

Hospitals, U.S. / INDIANA

NEW ALBANY—Floyd County

○ **BAPTIST HEALTH FLOYD (150044)**, 1850 State Street, Zip 47150–4997; tel. 812/949–5500, **A**2 3 5 10 11 **F**3 7 12 13 15 17 18 20 22 24 26 28 29 30 31 32 33 34 35 36 37 40 44 45 46 47 49 50 51 53 54 55 57 58 59 60 62 64 65 70 72 74 75 76 77 78 79 81 82 84 85 86 87 89 92 93 100 104 107 108 109 110 111 114 115 116 117 118 119 120 121 123 124 126 129 130 131 132 135 143 144 145 146 147 148 149 154 156 157 167 169 **P**6 **S** Baptist Health, Louisville, KY
Primary Contact: Mike K. Schroyer, FACHE, MSN, R.N., President
COO: Mark Truman, Vice President of Operations
CMO: Richard Phillips, Chief Medical Officer
CIO: Brian Cox, Director Information Systems
CNO: Kelly McMinoway, R.N., Vice President, Nursing
Web address: www.baptisthealth.com/floyd
Control: Other not-for-profit (including NFP Corporation) Service: General medical and surgical

Staffed Beds: 237 **Admissions:** 11968 **Census:** 151 **Outpatient Visits:** 244760 **Births:** 1018 **Total Expense ($000):** 384461 **Payroll Expense ($000):** 125901 **Personnel:** 1549

☐ **PHYSICIANS' MEDICAL CENTER (150172)**, 4023 Reas Lane, Zip 47150–2228; tel. 812/206–7660, **A**1 3 5 10 **F**3 12 29 45 49 51 79 81 82 85 89 126 149
Primary Contact: Dennis Medley, Chief Executive Officer and Administrator
COO: Rob Jones, Director of Nursing and Operations
CFO: Dennis Medley, Chief Executive Officer
CMO: Perry Cassady, M.D., Medical Director
CIO: Rob Jones, Director of Nursing and Operations
CHR: Mary Arntz, Manager Business Office and Executive Assistant
CNO: Rob Jones, Director of Nursing and Operations
Web address: www.pmcindiana.com
Control: Partnership, Investor-owned (for-profit) Service: Surgical

Staffed Beds: 19 **Admissions:** 1581 **Census:** 4 **Births:** 0 **Total Expense ($000):** 47711 **Payroll Expense ($000):** 13901 **Personnel:** 222

☐ △ **SOUTHERN INDIANA REHABILITATION HOSPITAL (153037)**, 3104 Blackiston Boulevard, Zip 47150–9579; tel. 812/941–8300, (Nonreporting) **A**1 7 10
Primary Contact: Jill Bosa, Chief Executive Officer
CFO: Robert Steltenpohl, Vice President
CMO: John C Shaw, M.D., Medical Director
CHR: Lisa Burris, Director Human Resources
CNO: Suzann Byers, Director of Nursing
Web address: https://vrhsouthernindiana.com/
Control: Other not-for-profit (including NFP Corporation) Service: Rehabilitation

Staffed Beds: 60

NEW CASTLE—Henry County

★ ○ **HENRY COMMUNITY HEALTH (150030)**, 1000 North 16th Street, Zip 47362–4319, Mailing Address: P.O. Box 490, Zip 47362–0490; tel. 765/521–0890, (Nonreporting) **A**10 11
Primary Contact: Brian K. Ring, Chief Executive Officer
CFO: Darin Brown, Chief Financial Officer
CMO: Arun Tewari, M.D., Chief Medical Officer
CIO: Mike Spencer, Chief Information Officer
CHR: Deanna Malott, Director Human Resources
CNO: Shelley Wilson, R.N., Chief Nursing Officer
Web address: https://www.hchcares.org/
Control: County, Government, Nonfederal Service: General medical and surgical

Staffed Beds: 49

NEWBURGH—Warrick County

☐ **BRENTWOOD SPRINGS (154055)**, 4488 Roslin Road, Zip 47630; tel. 812/858–7200, (Nonreporting) **A**1 10 **S** Springstone, Louisville, KY
Primary Contact: Kim Retzner, Chief Executive Officer
Web address: https://brentwoodsprings.com
Control: Partnership, Investor-owned (for-profit) Service: Psychiatric

Staffed Beds: 48

✠ **ENCOMPASS HEALTH DEACONESS REHABILITATION HOSPITAL (153025)**, 9355 Warrick Trail, Zip 47630–0015; tel. 812/476–9983, **A**1 3 10 **F**3 28 29 60 75 87 90 91 94 95 96 130 132 143 148 149 156 **S** Encompass Health Corporation, Birmingham, AL
Primary Contact: Blake Bunner, Chief Executive Officer
CFO: Rhonda Ramsey, Controller
CMO: Mohammed Adeel, Medical Director
CHR: Wendy Gumbel, Director of Human Resources
CNO: Trish Draeger, Chief Nursing Officer
Web address: www.healthsouthdeaconess.com
Control: Corporation, Investor-owned (for-profit) Service: Rehabilitation

Staffed Beds: 98 **Admissions:** 2521 **Census:** 88 **Outpatient Visits:** 0 **Births:** 0

THE HEART HOSPITAL AT DEACONESS GATEWAY See Deaconess Gateway Hospital

★ ○ **THE WOMEN'S HOSPITAL (150149)**, 4199 Gateway Boulevard, Zip 47630–8940; tel. 812/842–4200, **A**3 10 11 **F**3 13 15 29 34 35 36 40 50 55 57 59 64 72 75 76 77 78 81 84 85 86 87 93 110 119 126 130 132 134 135 147 149 154 160 162 169 **P**6 **S** Deaconess Health System, Evansville, IN
Primary Contact: Christina M. Ryan, R.N., Chief Executive Officer
CFO: Tina Cady, Controller
CIO: Jenny Skelton, System Integration Manager
CHR: Jerri Sue Traylor, Director Human Resources
CNO: Christina M Ryan, R.N., Chief Executive Officer and Chief Nursing Officer
Web address: www.deaconess.com
Control: Partnership, Investor-owned (for-profit) Service: Obstetrics and gynecology

Staffed Beds: 74 **Admissions:** 3771 **Census:** 53 **Outpatient Visits:** 57011 **Births:** 3104 **Total Expense ($000):** 124249 **Payroll Expense ($000):** 54159 **Personnel:** 510

NOBLESVILLE—Hamilton County

○ △ **RIVERVIEW HEALTH (150059)**, 395 Westfield Road, Zip 46060–1425, Mailing Address: P.O. Box 220, Zip 46061–0220; tel. 317/773–0760, (Includes RIVERVIEW HEALTH WESTFIELD HOSPITAL, 17600 Shamrock Boulevard, Westfield, Indiana, Zip 46074–7002, tel. 317/214–5555; David W Hyatt, FACHE, Chief Executive Officer) **A**5 7 10 11 **F**3 11 13 15 18 20 22 26 28 29 30 31 34 35 37 40 42 45 49 50 51 53 54 56 57 59 60 64 65 70 73 74 75 76 77 78 79 81 82 85 86 87 89 90 92 93 94 96 97 104 107 108 110 111 114 115 118 119 120 121 123 124 126 129 130 131 132 144 146 147 148 149 154 167 169
Primary Contact: David W. Hyatt, FACHE, Chief Executive Officer
COO: Lawrence Christman, Chief Financial Officer and Chief Operating Officer
CMO: Eric Marcotte, M.D., Chief Medical Officer
CIO: Brant Bucciarelli, Chief Information Officer
CHR: Ann Kuzee, Executive Director Human Resources
CNO: Joyce Wood, Vice President Organizational Improvement and Chief Nursing Officer
Web address: www.riverview.org
Control: County, Government, Nonfederal Service: General medical and surgical

Staffed Beds: 150 **Admissions:** 3759 **Census:** 48 **Outpatient Visits:** 506032 **Births:** 549 **Total Expense ($000):** 295282 **Payroll Expense ($000):** 99378 **Personnel:** 1300

NORTH VERNON—Jennings County

✠ **ASCENSION ST. VINCENT JENNINGS (151303)**, 301 Henry Street, Zip 47265–1097; tel. 812/352–4200, (Nonreporting) **A**1 10 18 **S** Ascension Healthcare, Saint Louis, MO
Primary Contact: Christina Crank, Administrator, Chief Nursing Officer
CFO: Joseph Kubala, Chief Financial Officer
CMO: Jennifer Stanley, M.D., Chief Medical Officer
CHR: Kathryn Johnson, Manager Human Resources, Marketing and Public Relations
Web address: www.stvincent.org
Control: Other not-for-profit (including NFP Corporation) Service: General medical and surgical

Staffed Beds: 17

Hospital, Medicare Provider Number, Address, Telephone, Approval, Facility, and Physician Codes, Health Care System
★ American Hospital Association (AHA) membership ○ Healthcare Facilities Accreditation Program ⇑ Center for Improvement in Healthcare Quality Accreditation ☐ The Joint Commission accreditation ◇ DNV Healthcare Inc. accreditation △ Commission on Accreditation of Rehabilitation Facilities (CARF) accreditation

© 2025 AHA Guide

Hospitals, U.S. / INDIANA

PAOLI—Orange County

INDIANA UNIVERSITY HEALTH PAOLI HOSPITAL (151306), 642 West Hospital Road, Zip 47454–9672; tel. 812/723–2811, **A**1 10 18 **F**3 13 15 18 29 30 35 40 45 50 53 57 59 64 65 68 76 77 81 85 87 89 93 97 100 107 110 111 114 119 127 129 130 133 135 144 146 148 149 150 154 **S** Indiana University Health, Indianapolis, IN
Primary Contact: Denzil Ross, FACHE, Chief Operating Officer
COO: Michele A Ridge, R.N., Chief Operating Officer and Chief Nursing Officer
CMO: Jose Lopez, M.D., Medical Staff President
CNO: Michele A Ridge, R.N., Chief Operating Officer and Chief Nursing Officer
Web address: www.iuhealth.org/paoli
Control: Other not–for–profit (including NFP Corporation) **Service**: General medical and surgical

Staffed Beds: 24 **Admissions**: 540 **Census**: 5 **Outpatient Visits**: 50631 **Births**: 119 **Total Expense ($000)**: 33757 **Payroll Expense ($000)**: 12221 **Personnel**: 143

PERU—Miami County

DUKES MEMORIAL HOSPITAL (151318), 275 West 12th Street, Zip 46970–1638; tel. 765/472–8000, (Nonreporting) **A**1 10 18 **S** Community Health Systems, Inc., Franklin, TN
Primary Contact: Debra Close, Chief Executive Officer
CFO: Adam Cumbo, Chief Financial Officer
CMO: Neil Stalker, M.D., Chief of Staff
Web address: www.dukesmemorialhosp.com
Control: Corporation, Investor–owned (for–profit) **Service**: General medical and surgical

Staffed Beds: 28

PLYMOUTH—Marshall County

MICHIANA BEHAVIORAL HEALTH CENTER (154047), 1800 North Oak Drive, Zip 46563–3492; tel. 574/936–3784, (Nonreporting) **A**1 10 **S** Universal Health Services, Inc., King of Prussia, PA
Primary Contact: Brian Gray, Chief Executive Officer
CFO: Jeff Calvin, Chief Financial Officer
CMO: Robert Raster, M.D., Medical Director
CIO: Leslie McLaughlin, Director of Business Development
CHR: Becky Nowicki, Director Human Resources
CNO: Brandi Richard, Chief Nursing Officer
Web address: https://michianabehavioralhealth.com
Control: Corporation, Investor–owned (for–profit) **Service**: Psychiatric

Staffed Beds: 75

PLYMOUTH MEDICAL CENTER (150076), 1915 Lake Avenue, Zip 46563–9366, Mailing Address: P.O. Box 670, Zip 46563–0670; tel. 574/948–4000, (Nonreporting) **A**1 10 **S** Trinity Health, Livonia, MI
Primary Contact: Christopher J. Karam, President
CFO: Janice Dunn, Chief Financial Officer
CMO: Stephen Anderson, M.D., Chief Medical Officer
CIO: Gary L Miller, Regional Director Information Systems
CHR: Kurt A Meyer, Chief Human Resources Officer
Web address: www.sjmed.com
Control: Other not–for–profit (including NFP Corporation) **Service**: General medical and surgical

Staffed Beds: 48

PORTLAND—Jay County

INDIANA UNIVERSITY HEALTH JAY HOSPITAL (151320), 500 West Votaw Street, Zip 47371–1322; tel. 260/726–7131, **A**1 10 18 **F**3 11 15 28 29 30 31 32 34 35 40 44 45 50 53 57 59 75 77 81 85 86 87 93 97 104 107 110 111 114 115 119 129 130 132 133 135 146 147 153 154 157 160 161 162 164 165 169 **S** Indiana University Health, Indianapolis, IN
Primary Contact: Christina Marie. Schemenaur, Vice President, Chief Operating Officer and Chief Nursing Officer
CHR: Linda Guise, Senior Human Resource Consultant
Web address: www.iuhealth.org
Control: Other not–for–profit (including NFP Corporation) **Service**: General medical and surgical

Staffed Beds: 21 **Admissions**: 355 **Census**: 4 **Outpatient Visits**: 63095 **Births**: 0 **Total Expense ($000)**: 41974 **Payroll Expense ($000)**: 11936 **Personnel**: 179

PRINCETON—Gibson County

DEACONESS GIBSON HOSPITAL (151319), 1808 Sherman Drive, Zip 47670–9931; tel. 812/385–3401, **A**1 10 18 **F**3 11 15 28 29 31 34 35 40 44 45 49 50 53 57 59 62 65 68 70 75 77 78 81 82 85 89 93 100 102 107 110 111 115 119 127 129 130 132 133 135 146 148 149 156 167 **S** Deaconess Health System, Evansville, IN
Primary Contact: Lois Morgan, R.N., MSN, Chief Administrative Officer, Chief Nursing Officer
CMO: M. S. Krishna, M.D., Chief of Medical Staff
CIO: Jarad Lear, Interim Director of Information Services
CNO: Lois Morgan, R.N., MSN, Chief Administrative Officer, Chief Nursing Officer
Web address: https://www.deaconess.com/Deaconess-Gibson-Hospital
Control: Other not–for–profit (including NFP Corporation) **Service**: General medical and surgical

Staffed Beds: 25 **Admissions**: 333 **Census**: 6 **Outpatient Visits**: 49337 **Births**: 0 **Total Expense ($000)**: 42715 **Payroll Expense ($000)**: 14050 **Personnel**: 154

RENSSELAER—Jasper County

FRANCISCAN HEALTH RENSSELEAR (151324), 1104 East Grace Street, Zip 47978–3296; tel. 219/866–5141, (Nonreporting) **A**10 18 **S** Franciscan Health, Mishawaka, IN
Primary Contact: Carlos Vasquez, Vice President and Chief Operating Officer
CFO: Jeffrey D Webb, CPA, Chief Financial Officer
CIO: Kirby Reed, Director Information Systems
CHR: Deana Brown, Director Administrative Services
CNO: Stacie Klingler, R.N., Vice President of Patient Services
Web address: www.franciscanhealth.org
Control: Church operated, Nongovernment, not–for–profit **Service**: General medical and surgical

Staffed Beds: 46

RICHMOND—Wayne County

REID HEALTH (150048), 1100 Reid Parkway, Zip 47374–1157; tel. 765/983–3000, (Includes REID HEALTH CARE PAVILION, 450 Erie Avenue, Connersville, Indiana, Zip 47331–3176, tel. 765/827–7890; Craig C. Kinyon, President and Chief Executive Officer) **A**2 3 5 10 21 **F**3 4 5 7 8 11 13 15 18 20 22 24 26 28 29 30 31 34 35 37 38 40 42 43 44 45 49 50 51 53 54 55 56 57 58 59 61 63 64 65 66 68 69 70 71 74 75 76 77 78 79 81 82 83 84 85 86 87 89 90 91 92 93 94 95 96 98 99 100 101 102 104 106 107 108 110 111 114 115 116 117 118 119 120 121 123 124 126 127 129 130 131 132 135 143 144 146 147 148 149 151 154 156 160 162 164 167 169 **P**6
Primary Contact: Craig C. Kinyon, President and Chief Executive Officer
CFO: Christopher D. Knight, Vice President Finance and Chief Financial Officer
CMO: Thomas Huth, M.D., Vice President Medical Affairs
CIO: Tim Love, Director Information Services
CHR: Scott C Rauch, Vice President Human Resources
CNO: Misti Foust–Cofield, R.N., Vice President and Chief Nursing Officer
Web address: www.reidhealth.org
Control: Other not–for–profit (including NFP Corporation) **Service**: General medical and surgical

Staffed Beds: 203 **Admissions**: 11224 **Census**: 129 **Outpatient Visits**: 379364 **Births**: 611 **Total Expense ($000)**: 678222 **Payroll Expense ($000)**: 302998 **Personnel**: 3505

RICHMOND STATE HOSPITAL (154018), 498 NW 18th Street, Zip 47374–2851; tel. 765/966–0511, (Nonreporting) **A**1 10
Primary Contact: Paul Stanley, Superintendent
CFO: Dave Shelford, Assistant Superintendent
CMO: Donald Graber, M.D., Medical Director
CIO: Robert Boatman, Director Information Technology
CHR: Sarah Witt, Director Human Resources
Web address: www.richmondstatehospital.org
Control: State, Government, Nonfederal **Service**: Psychiatric

Staffed Beds: 179

ROCHESTER—Fulton County

WOODLAWN HOSPITAL (151313), 1400 East Ninth Street, Zip 46975–8937; tel. 574/223–3141, (Nonreporting) **A**10 11 18
Primary Contact: Alan Fisher, Chief Executive Officer
CFO: John Kraft, Chief Financial Officer
Web address: www.woodlawnhospital.com
Control: County, Government, Nonfederal **Service**: General medical and surgical

Staffed Beds: 25

Hospitals, U.S. / INDIANA

RUSHVILLE—Rush County

★ **RUSH MEMORIAL HOSPITAL (151304)**, 1300 North Main Street, Zip 46173–1198; tel. 765/932–4111, (Nonreporting) **A**3 10 18
Primary Contact: Bradley Smith, President and Chief Executive Officer
COO: Gretchen Smith, Vice President of Operations, Risk and Compliance, and Chief Operating Officer
CFO: Karen Meyer, Vice President Finance and Chief Financial Officer
CMO: Donald Snyder, M.D., Chief Medical Officer
CIO: Jim Boyer, Vice President Information Technology and Chief Information Officer
CHR: Brian R Bane, Vice President Human Resources
CNO: Carrie Tressler, Vice President of Nursing and Chief Nursing Officer
Web address: www.rushmemorial.com
Control: County, Government, Nonfederal **Service**: General medical and surgical

Staffed Beds: 25

SALEM—Washington County

ASCENSION ST. VINCENT SALEM (151314), 911 North Shelby Street, Zip 47167–1694; tel. 812/883–5881, (Nonreporting) **A**1 10 18 **S** Ascension Healthcare, Saint Louis, MO
Primary Contact: Donna Cassidy, Hospital Administrator
CFO: Joseph Kubala, Director Financial and Support Services
CMO: S E Kemker, M.D., President Medical Staff
CIO: Jeremy Long, Manager Information Systems
CHR: Val Potter, Director Human Resources
Web address: www.stvincent.org/St-Vincent-Salem/Default.aspx
Control: Other not–for–profit (including NFP Corporation) **Service**: General medical and surgical

Staffed Beds: 25

SCOTTSBURG—Scott County

NORTON SCOTT HOSPITAL (151334), 1451 North Gardner Street, Zip 47170, Mailing Address: Box 430, Zip 47170–0430; tel. 812/752–3456, (Nonreporting) **A**1 10 18 **S** Norton Healthcare, Louisville, KY
Primary Contact: Bruce J. Tassin, Interim Chief Executive Officer
COO: Scott Edwards, Chief Operating Officer
CFO: Angela Doan, Chief Financial Officer
CNO: Dawn Mays, Chief Nursing Officer
Web address: www.scottmemorial.com
Control: County, Government, Nonfederal **Service**: General medical and surgical

Staffed Beds: 35

SEYMOUR—Jackson County

SCHNECK MEDICAL CENTER (150065), 411 West Tipton Street, Zip 47274–2363, Mailing Address: P.O. Box 2349, Zip 47274–5000; tel. 812/522–2349, **A**1 2 10 **F**3 5 12 13 15 18 28 29 30 31 34 35 36 37 40 47 49 56 57 59 62 63 64 65 68 69 70 74 75 76 77 78 79 81 82 84 85 87 89 93 97 100 101 104 107 110 111 114 115 119 120 121 123 124 126 127 129 130 131 132 133 135 144 146 147 148 154 160 169
Primary Contact: Eric Fish, M.D., President and Chief Executive Officer
CFO: Deborah Mann, CPA, Vice President Finance and Chief Financial Officer
CMO: D. Ryan Stone, D.O., Chief Medical Officer
CIO: Craig Rice, Chief Information Officer
CHR: Kathy Covert, MSN, Vice President Workforce Development and Organizational Development
CNO: Amy Pettit, R.N., Vice President of Patient Care Services and Chief Nursing Officer
Web address: www.schneckmed.org
Control: County, Government, Nonfederal **Service**: General medical and surgical

Staffed Beds: 84 **Admissions**: 2096 **Census**: 21 **Outpatient Visits**: 432480 **Births**: 835 **Total Expense ($000)**: 197290 **Payroll Expense ($000)**: 92697 **Personnel**: 1144

SHELBYVILLE—Shelby County

★ ○ **MAJOR HOSPITAL (150097)**, 150 West Washington Street, Zip 46176–1236, Mailing Address: 2451 Intelliplex Drive, Zip 46176; tel. 317/392–3211, (Nonreporting) **A**2 10 11
Primary Contact: John M. Horner, President and Chief Executive Officer
CFO: Ralph Mercuri, Vice President and Chief Financial Officer
CMO: Douglas S Carter, M.D., Vice President and Chief Medical Officer
CIO: Carol Huesman, Chief Information Officer
CHR: Nicki Sparling, Manager Human Resources
CNO: Valerie L Miller, MSN, R.N., Director of Nursing
Web address: www.majorhospital.org
Control: City–county, Government, Nonfederal **Service**: General medical and surgical

Staffed Beds: 71

SOUTH BEND—St. Joseph County

DOR–A–LIN OF SOUTH BEND See Saint Joseph's Care Center Notre Dame

MEMORIAL CHILDREN'S HOSPITAL See Beacon Children's Hospital

MEMORIAL HOSPITAL OF SOUTH BEND (150058), 615 North Michigan Street, Zip 46601–1033; tel. 574/647–1000, (Includes BEACON CHILDREN'S HOSPITAL, 615 North Michigan Street, South Bend, Indiana, Zip 46601, tel. 574/647–1000) **A**1 2 3 5 10 **F**3 7 8 13 15 17 18 19 20 22 24 26 28 29 30 31 34 35 36 37 38 40 42 43 45 46 47 48 49 50 55 56 58 59 60 61 63 64 65 67 68 70 72 73 74 75 76 77 78 79 81 82 84 85 86 87 88 89 90 91 92 93 96 98 99 100 102 103 107 108 110 111 114 115 116 118 119 120 121 123 124 126 129 130 131 132 135 145 146 147 148 149 150 154 155 156 167 **S** Beacon Health System, South Bend, IN
Primary Contact: Larry A. Tracy Jr, FACHE, President
CFO: Jeff Costello, Chief Financial Officer, Beacon Health System
CMO: Cheryl Wibbens, M.D., Vice President Medical Staff Affairs
CIO: Mark Warlick, Chief Information Officer
CHR: Steven M Eller, Chief Human Resources Officer
Web address: www.beaconhealthsystem.org
Control: Other not–for–profit (including NFP Corporation) **Service**: General medical and surgical

Staffed Beds: 426 **Admissions**: 18004 **Census**: 253 **Outpatient Visits**: 229000 **Births**: 2509 **Total Expense ($000)**: 569388 **Payroll Expense ($000)**: 197344 **Personnel**: 2626

SULLIVAN—Sullivan County

★ ○ **SULLIVAN COUNTY COMMUNITY HOSPITAL (151327)**, 2200 North Section Street, Zip 47882–7523, Mailing Address: P.O. Box 10, Zip 47882–0010; tel. 812/268–4311, **A**10 11 18 **F**3 5 8 11 13 15 28 29 32 34 35 40 44 45 47 48 50 53 56 57 59 61 65 69 70 75 76 77 78 79 81 82 86 87 93 94 96 97 107 108 110 111 114 119 127 129 130 131 133 146 147 148 154 156 160 161 169 **S** Ovation Healthcare, Brentwood, TN
Primary Contact: Michelle Franklin, Chief Executive Officer
CFO: Jim Bishop, Chief Financial Officer
CMO: Divyesh Purohit, M.D., Chief of Staff
CIO: Hap Beckes, Director Information Systems
CHR: Denise Hart, Director Human Resources
CNO: Lori Resler, R.N., Chief Nurse
Web address: www.schosp.com
Control: County, Government, Nonfederal **Service**: General medical and surgical

Staffed Beds: 25 **Admissions**: 409 **Census**: 4 **Outpatient Visits**: 72058 **Births**: 122 **Total Expense ($000)**: 56568 **Payroll Expense ($000)**: 27722 **Personnel**: 370

TELL CITY—Perry County

★ ○ **PERRY COUNTY MEMORIAL HOSPITAL (151322)**, 8885 State Road 237, Zip 47586–2750; tel. 812/547–7011, (Nonreporting) **A**10 11 18 **S** Alliant Management Services, Louisville, KY
Primary Contact: Jared M. Stimpson, Chief Executive Officer
CMO: James Rogan, M.D., Chief Medical Officer
CIO: Debbie Kleeman, Director Information Systems
CHR: Marchelle Heslep, Human Resources Director
Web address: www.pchospital.org
Control: County, Government, Nonfederal **Service**: General medical and surgical

Staffed Beds: 25

Hospital, Medicare Provider Number, Address, Telephone, Approval, Facility, and Physician Codes, Health Care System

★ American Hospital Association (AHA) membership
☐ The Joint Commission accreditation
○ Healthcare Facilities Accreditation Program
◇ DNV Healthcare Inc. accreditation
⇧ Center for Improvement in Healthcare Quality Accreditation
△ Commission on Accreditation of Rehabilitation Facilities (CARF) accreditation

Hospitals, U.S. / INDIANA

TERRE HAUTE—Vigo County

★ **HAMILTON CENTER (154009)**, 620 Eighth Avenue, Zip 47804–2744; tel. 812/231–8323, (Nonreporting) **A**10
Primary Contact: Melvin Burks, Chief Executive Officer
COO: Robb Johnson, Director Operations
CFO: Renee Utley, Chief Financial Officer
CMO: Ahsan Mahmood, M.D., Chief Medical Officer
CIO: Hans Eilbracht, Chief Information Officer
CHR: Margie Anshutz, Chief Development Officer
CNO: Rose Christy, Executive Director of Medical Services
Web address: www.hamiltoncenter.org
Control: Other not–for–profit (including NFP Corporation) **Service:** Psychiatric

Staffed Beds: 16

□ **HARSHA BEHAVIORAL CENTER (154054)**, 1980 East Woodsmall Drive, Zip 47802–4937; tel. 866/644–8880, (Nonreporting) **A**1 10
Primary Contact: Roopam Harshawat, President and Chief Executive Officer
COO: Holly Near, Chief Administrative Officer
CFO: Holly Near, Chief Administrative Officer
CMO: Paras Harshawat, M.D., Medical Director
CHR: Karen Hunt, Executive Director
CNO: Cindy Dowers, Chief Nursing Officer
Web address: www.harshacenter.com
Control: Corporation, Investor–owned (for–profit) **Service:** Psychiatric

Staffed Beds: 44

⊞ **TERRE HAUTE REGIONAL HOSPITAL (150046)**, 3901 South Seventh Street, Zip 47802–5709; tel. 812/232–0021, (Nonreporting) **A**1 2 10 **S** HCA Healthcare, Nashville, TN
Primary Contact: Mark Casanova, Chief Executive Officer
COO: Andrea Gwyn, Chief Operating Officer
CIO: Mike Kuckewich, Director Information Systems
CNO: Angela Ellis, R.N., Chief Nursing Officer
Web address: www.regionalhospital.com
Control: Corporation, Investor–owned (for–profit) **Service:** General medical and surgical

Staffed Beds: 278

★ ○ **UNION HOSPITAL (150023)**, 1606 North Seventh Street, Zip 47804–2780; tel. 812/238–7000, **A**2 3 5 10 11 19 **F**3 8 13 15 17 18 20 22 24 26 28 29 30 31 34 35 36 40 43 45 46 47 48 49 50 51 53 54 57 59 64 68 70 71 72 73 74 75 76 77 78 79 81 85 86 87 89 90 91 92 93 94 95 96 97 107 108 110 111 112 114 115 116 117 118 119 120 121 123 124 126 127 130 131 132 135 144 146 147 149 154 157 167 169
Primary Contact: Steve M. Holman, FACHE, President and Chief Executive Officer
CFO: Wayne Hutson, Executive Vice President and Chief Financial Officer
CMO: John Bolinger, M.D., Vice President Medical Affairs
CIO: Kym Pfrank, Senior Vice President and Chief Operating Officer
CHR: Sally Zuel, Vice President Human Resources
Web address: https://www.myunionhealth.org/
Control: Other not–for–profit (including NFP Corporation) **Service:** General medical and surgical

Staffed Beds: 280 **Admissions:** 14661 **Census:** 203 **Outpatient Visits:** 349708 **Births:** 1790 **Total Expense ($000):** 593297 **Payroll Expense ($000):** 148350 **Personnel:** 1856

TIPTON—Tipton County

⊞ **INDIANA UNIVERSITY HEALTH TIPTON HOSPITAL (151311)**, 1000 South Main Street, Zip 46072–9799; tel. 765/675–8500, **A**1 10 18 **F**3 11 15 18 28 29 30 31 34 35 39 40 50 57 59 68 70 75 77 78 79 81 82 83 84 85 86 87 93 97 102 107 108 110 111 115 119 129 130 131 132 133 135 146 147 148 154 156 **S** Indiana University Health, Indianapolis, IN
Primary Contact: Doug Puckett, President
CFO: Randall C. Yust, Chief Financial Officer NCR
CMO: Larry Hopkins, Chief Medical Officer
CHR: Shelley E Huff, Regional Program Manager
CNO: Jo Ellen Scott, R.N., MS, Senior Vice President of Patient Care Services and Chief Nursing Officer
Web address: www.iuhealth.org
Control: Other not–for–profit (including NFP Corporation) **Service:** General medical and surgical

Staffed Beds: 25 **Admissions:** 493 **Census:** 5 **Outpatient Visits:** 35815 **Births:** 0 **Total Expense ($000):** 42369 **Payroll Expense ($000):** 11492 **Personnel:** 155

VALPARAISO—Porter County

⊞ **NORTHWEST HEALTH – PORTER (150035)**, 85 East U. S. Highway 6, Zip 46383–8947; tel. 219/983–8300, (Nonreporting) **A**1 5 10 19 **S** Community Health Systems, Inc., Franklin, TN
Primary Contact: James Leonard, M.D., Chief Executive Officer
COO: Sarah Hunter, Interim Chief Operating Officer
CFO: Jeffrey Daneff, Chief Financial Officer
CMO: Ramireddy K Tummuru, M.D., Chief Medical Officer
CIO: Robert Richardson, Information Technology Administrator
CHR: Angie Hampton, Director Human Resources
CNO: Judy Davidson, R.N., I, Chief Nursing Officer
Web address: www.porterhealth.com
Control: Corporation, Investor–owned (for–profit) **Service:** General medical and surgical

Staffed Beds: 446

PORTER–STARKE SERVICES (154052), 601 Wall Street, Zip 46383–2512; tel. 219/531–3500, **A**10 **F**5 29 32 34 35 38 39 50 56 57 59 65 98 101 102 104 130 135 153 154 156 157 158 160 162 164 165
Primary Contact: Matthew J. Burden, President and Chief Executive Officer
CFO: Mary Idstein, Chief Financial Officer
CMO: Anand Popli, Medical Director
Web address: www.porterstarke.org
Control: Other not–for–profit (including NFP Corporation) **Service:** Psychiatric

Staffed Beds: 16 **Admissions:** 470 **Census:** 6 **Outpatient Visits:** 110625 **Births:** 0 **Total Expense ($000):** 34414 **Payroll Expense ($000):** 20658 **Personnel:** 19

VINCENNES—Knox County

⊞ **GOOD SAMARITAN HOSPITAL (150042)**, 520 South Seventh Street, Zip 47591–1038; tel. 812/882–5220, **A**1 2 3 5 10 19 **F**3 5 7 8 11 13 14 15 18 20 22 28 29 30 31 34 35 38 44 46 47 49 50 51 53 57 58 59 60 62 63 64 65 68 70 71 74 76 77 78 79 80 81 82 83 84 85 87 89 90 93 94 97 98 100 101 102 104 107 108 110 111 115 118 119 120 121 123 126 127 129 130 131 132 135 143 144 146 147 148 149 153 154 157 160 161 162 163 165 167 168 169 **P**4 6
Primary Contact: Robert D. McLin, President and Chief Executive Officer
COO: Adam Thacker, Chief Operating Officer
CFO: Thomas M Cook, Chief Financial Officer
CMO: Charles C Hedde, M.D., Chief Medical Officer
CIO: Daniel Scott, Director of Information Systems
CHR: Dean Wagoner, Director Human Resources
CNO: Karen S. Haak, R.N., MSN, Chief Nursing Officer
Web address: www.gshvin.org/goodsamaritan
Control: County, Government, Nonfederal **Service:** General medical and surgical

Staffed Beds: 156 **Admissions:** 5361 **Census:** 69 **Outpatient Visits:** 37718 **Births:** 398 **Total Expense ($000):** 277053 **Payroll Expense ($000):** 112557 **Personnel:** 1509

WABASH—Wabash County

⊞ **PARKVIEW WABASH HOSPITAL (151310)**, 10 John Kissinger Drive, Zip 46992–1648; tel. 260/563–3131, **A**1 10 18 **F**3 5 7 15 29 30 31 34 35 38 40 44 45 46 50 53 57 59 64 68 69 75 77 78 79 81 85 86 87 89 91 93 97 100 101 102 107 108 109 110 111 115 119 127 128 129 132 133 134 144 146 149 153 154 156 160 161 162 167 169 **S** Parkview Health, Fort Wayne, IN
Primary Contact: Debra Potempa, MSN, R.N., President
CMO: Tod Sider, M.D., Chief of Staff
CNO: Cathy Allyson Wolfe, Vice President Patient Care and Chief Nursing Officer
Web address: https://www.parkview.com/locations/parkview-wabash-hospital/parkview-wabash-hospital
Control: Other not–for–profit (including NFP Corporation) **Service:** General medical and surgical

Staffed Beds: 18 **Admissions:** 1272 **Census:** 10 **Outpatient Visits:** 46607 **Births:** 1 **Total Expense ($000):** 64404 **Payroll Expense ($000):** 14546 **Personnel:** 164

WARSAW—Kosciusko County

KOSCIUSKO COMMUNITY HOSPITAL See Lutheran Kosciusko Hospital

✠ **LUTHERAN KOSCIUSKO HOSPITAL (150133)**, 2101 East Dubois Drive, Zip 46580-3288; tel. 574/267-3200, (Nonreporting) **A**1 10 19 **S** Community Health Systems, Inc., Franklin, TN
Primary Contact: Lynn M. Mergen, Chief Executive Officer
CFO: Douglas J BeMent, Chief Financial Officer
CMO: Patrick Silveus, M.D., Medical Director
CIO: Tammy Lukens, Director Information
CHR: Joe Jarboe, Director Human Resources
CNO: Kim Finch, Chief Nursing Officer
Web address: https://www.lutherankosciuskohospital.com/
Control: Corporation, Investor-owned (for-profit) Service: General medical and surgical

Staffed Beds: 72

★ **OTIS R. BOWEN CENTER FOR HUMAN SERVICES (154014)**, 2621 East Jefferson Street, Zip 46580-3880; tel. 574/267-7169, **A**10 **F**5 29 34 35 38 50 54 56 57 59 65 66 68 69 75 86 98 101 102 104 106 130 132 135 147 152 153 154 160 164 165 **P**1
Primary Contact: Robert Ryan, President and Chief Executive Officer
Web address: www.bowencenter.org
Control: Other not-for-profit (including NFP Corporation) Service: Psychiatric

Staffed Beds: 20 **Admissions:** 650 **Census:** 11 **Outpatient Visits:** 860293 **Births:** 0 **Total Expense ($000):** 98294 **Payroll Expense ($000):** 64512 **Personnel:** 68

WASHINGTON—Daviess County

✠ △ **DAVIESS COMMUNITY HOSPITAL (150061)**, 1314 East Walnut Street, Zip 47501-2860, Mailing Address: P.O. Box 760, Zip 47501-0760; tel. 812/254-2760, (Nonreporting) **A**1 7 10 **S** Ascension Healthcare, Saint Louis, MO
Primary Contact: Tracy Conroy, Chief Executive Officer
COO: Keith Miller, Chief Operating Officer
CFO: Amanda Rodewald, Interim Chief Financial Officer
CNO: Nancy Devine, Chief Nursing Officer
Web address: www.dchosp.org
Control: County, Government, Nonfederal Service: General medical and surgical

Staffed Beds: 72

WEST LAFAYETTE—Tippecanoe County

✠ **RIVER BEND HOSPITAL (154005)**, 2900 North River Road, Zip 47906-3744; tel. 765/464-0400, (Nonreporting) **A**1 10
Primary Contact: Stephanie Long, President and Chief Executive Officer
COO: Tom Gillian, Chief Operating Officer
CFO: Jeff Nagy, Chief Financial Officer
CMO: Richard Rahdert, M.D., Medical Director
CIO: Craig Anderson, Director Management Information Systems
CHR: Jan Shaw, Director Personnel
CNO: Megan Gibson, Nurse Manager
Web address: www.nchsi.com/riverbendhospital.cfm
Control: Other not-for-profit (including NFP Corporation) Service: Psychiatric

Staffed Beds: 16

WILLIAMSPORT—Warren County

✠ **ASCENSION ST. VINCENT WILLIAMSPORT (151307)**, 412 North Monroe Street, Zip 47993-1049; tel. 765/762-4000, (Nonreporting) **A**1 10 18 **S** Ascension Healthcare, Saint Louis, MO
Primary Contact: Melanie Jane. Craigin, Chief Executive Officer and Administrator
CFO: Janet Merritt, Chief Financial Officer
Web address: www.stvincent.org
Control: Other not-for-profit (including NFP Corporation) Service: General medical and surgical

Staffed Beds: 16

WINAMAC—Pulaski County

★ ○ **PULASKI MEMORIAL HOSPITAL (151305)**, 616 East 13th Street, Zip 46996-1117, Mailing Address: P.O. Box 279, Zip 46996-0279; tel. 574/946-2100, **A**10 11 18 **F**3 11 15 28 29 30 31 34 35 40 45 50 56 57 59 64 65 75 77 78 79 80 81 85 87 93 96 97 100 104 107 110 111 115 119 127 128 130 131 132 133 135 146 147 148 153 154 160 169 **P**6
Primary Contact: Steve Jarosinski, Chief Executive Officer
CFO: Gregg Malott, Chief Financial Officer
CIO: Jeff Boer, Director Information Technology
CHR: Mark Fenn, Director Human Resources
CNO: Linda Webb, R.N., Chief Nursing Executive
Web address: www.pmhnet.com
Control: County, Government, Nonfederal Service: General medical and surgical

Staffed Beds: 19 **Admissions:** 286 **Census:** 4 **Outpatient Visits:** 31473 **Births:** 0 **Total Expense ($000):** 41743 **Payroll Expense ($000):** 19856 **Personnel:** 284

WINCHESTER—Randolph County

✠ **ASCENSION ST. VINCENT RANDOLPH (151301)**, 473 Greenville Avenue, Zip 47394-9436; tel. 765/584-0004, (Nonreporting) **A**1 10 18 **S** Ascension Healthcare, Saint Louis, MO
Primary Contact: Rodney Stevens, Administrator
CFO: John Arthur, Chief Financial Officer
CNO: Carla Fouse, Chief Nursing Officer
Web address: www.stvincent.org
Control: Other not-for-profit (including NFP Corporation) Service: General medical and surgical

Staffed Beds: 25

IOWA

ALBIA—Monroe County

★ **MONROE COUNTY HOSPITAL AND CLINICS (161342)**, 6580 165th Street, Zip 52531–8793; tel. 641/932–2134, **A**10 18 **F**7 11 15 28 29 31 34 40 43 47 50 59 77 81 93 107 110 114 119 127 130 132 133 154 **P**6 **S** MercyOne, Clive, IA
Primary Contact: Veronica Fuhs, Chief Executive Officer
Web address: www.mchalbia.com
Control: County, Government, Nonfederal **Service**: General medical and surgical

Staffed Beds: 25 **Admissions**: 179 **Census**: 3 **Outpatient Visits**: 57778 **Births**: 0 **Total Expense ($000)**: 32244 **Payroll Expense ($000)**: 14180 **Personnel**: 158	

ALGONA—Kossuth County

★ **KOSSUTH REGIONAL HEALTH CENTER (161353)**, 1515 South Phillips Street, Zip 50511–3649; tel. 515/295–2451, **A**10 18 **F**3 11 13 15 17 28 29 30 32 34 35 36 40 41 43 45 50 56 57 59 62 63 64 65 70 75 76 77 81 82 84 86 87 92 93 97 100 107 110 114 119 127 130 131 132 133 146 147 148 149 156 169 **P**6 **S** Trinity Health, Livonia, MI
Primary Contact: Darlene M. Elbert, R.N., MS, Chief Executive Officer
CFO: Collete McConnell, Chief Financial Officer
CMO: Michael Lampe, M.D., Chief of Staff
CIO: Nancy Erickson, Administrator Information Systems
CHR: Paula Seely, Manager Human Resources
Web address: www.krhc.com
Control: County, Government, Nonfederal **Service**: General medical and surgical

Staffed Beds: 23 **Admissions**: 981 **Census**: 12 **Outpatient Visits**: 122933
Births: 137 **Total Expense ($000)**: 40517 **Payroll Expense ($000)**: 15793
Personnel: 220

AMES—Story County

★ ⇧ **MARY GREELEY MEDICAL CENTER (160030)**, 1111 Duff Avenue, Zip 50010–5745; tel. 515/239–2011, **A**2 5 10 19 21 **F**3 7 11 12 13 15 17 18 20 22 26 28 29 30 31 34 35 36 37 38 40 43 45 46 47 48 49 50 53 55 57 58 59 61 62 63 64 65 69 70 72 74 75 76 77 78 79 81 82 84 85 86 87 89 90 92 93 96 98 100 101 102 104 107 108 110 111 114 115 116 119 120 121 123 124 126 129 130 131 132 135 146 147 148 149 156 164 167
Primary Contact: Brian Dieter, President and Chief Executive Officer
CFO: Gary Botine, Vice President, Chief Financial Officer
CIO: Scott Carlson, Director
CHR: Betsy V Schoeller, Director Human Resources and Education
Web address: www.mgmc.org
Control: City, Government, Nonfederal **Service**: General medical and surgical

Staffed Beds: 196 **Admissions**: 8502 **Census**: 109 **Outpatient Visits**: 171218
Births: 1431 **Total Expense ($000)**: 228220 **Payroll Expense ($000)**: 90913
Personnel: 1326

ANAMOSA—Jones County

★ ⇧ **UNITYPOINT HEALTH – JONES REGIONAL MEDICAL CENTER (161306)**, 1795 Highway 64 East, Zip 52205–2112; tel. 319/462–6131, **A**10 18 21 **F**3 7 8 11 15 28 29 30 31 34 35 40 43 45 46 50 51 53 57 59 65 68 71 75 77 78 79 81 82 83 84 87 90 91 92 93 96 97 102 104 107 110 111 114 116 118 119 126 127 128 129 130 131 132 133 135 144 146 147 148 149 154 156 157 **S** UnityPoint Health, West Des Moines, IA
Primary Contact: Eric Briesemeister, Chief Executive Officer
CFO: Rachel Von Behren, Director Financial Services
CMO: Victor Salas, M.D., President Medical Staff
CHR: Donna Condry, Director Human Resources
Web address: www.jonesregional.org
Control: Other not–for–profit (including NFP Corporation) **Service**: General medical and surgical

Staffed Beds: 22 **Admissions**: 354 **Census**: 5 **Outpatient Visits**: 168509
Births: 0 **Total Expense ($000)**: 44462 **Payroll Expense ($000)**: 21197
Personnel: 168

ATLANTIC—Cass County

CASS COUNTY HEALTH SYSTEM See Cass Health

★ **CASS HEALTH (161376)**, 1501 East Tenth Street, Zip 50022–1997; tel. 712/243–3250, **A**10 18 **F**3 13 15 28 29 31 34 35 40 45 50 57 59 64-65 70 75 76 77 78 79 81 82 85 92 93 97 102 107 108 110 111 115 118 119 124 127 130 131 132 133 135 146 147 148 154 169 **P**6
Primary Contact: Brett Altman, FACHE, Chief Executive Officer
COO: Alison Bruckner, Chief Operating Officer
CFO: Abbey Stangl, Chief Financial Officer
CMO: Todd Bean, Chief Medical Officer
CIO: Jeff Osegard, Chief Information Officer
CHR: Denise Coder, Chief Human Resource Officer
Web address: www.casshealth.org
Control: County, Government, Nonfederal **Service**: General medical and surgical

Staffed Beds: 25 **Admissions**: 1009 **Census**: 10 **Outpatient Visits**: 140837
Births: 131 **Total Expense ($000)**: 63416 **Payroll Expense ($000)**: 29057
Personnel: 315

AUDUBON—Audubon County

AUDUBON COUNTY MEMORIAL HOSPITAL AND CLINICS (161330), 515 Pacific Avenue, Zip 50025–1056; tel. 712/563–2611, **A**10 18 **F**3 15 28 29 31 34 40 43 45 46 47 49 50 53 55 56 57 59 64 65 78 79 81 82 85 86 87 89 91 93 97 107 110 114 127 128 130 133 149 156 169 **P**6
Primary Contact: Suzanne Cooner, MSN, R.N., Chief Executive Officer
CFO: Melinda Alt, Chief Financial Officer
CMO: Jeffrey Maire, M.D., Chief of Staff
CIO: Nathan Moser, Information Technology Engineer
CNO: Lisa Paulsen, R.N., Chief Nursing Officer
Web address: www.acmhhosp.org
Control: County, Government, Nonfederal **Service**: General medical and surgical

Staffed Beds: 17 **Admissions**: 127 **Census**: 2 **Outpatient Visits**: 20990
Births: 0 **Total Expense ($000)**: 17298 **Payroll Expense ($000)**: 6942
Personnel: 92

BELMOND—Wright County

★ ⇧ **IOWA SPECIALTY HOSPITAL-BELMOND (161301)**, 403 1st Street SE, Zip 50421–1201; tel. 641/444–3223, **A**10 18 21 **F**5 7 11 12 15 28 29 32 34 35 40 43 50 56 57 59 62 63 64 65 67 68 70 75 77 79 81 82 85 87 89 92 93 96 97 103 104 107 110 111 115 119 127 128 129 130 131 133 134 135 146 148 149 150 154 160 162 **P**6 **S** Iowa Specialty Hospitals & Clinics, Clarion, IA
Primary Contact: Amy McDaniel, Chief Executive Officer
CFO: Greg Polzin, Chief Financial Officer
CMO: Charles B Brindle, M.D., Chief Medical Staff
CHR: Holly Martin, Director Human Resource
CNO: Lisa Weatherwax, R.N., Chief Nursing Officer
Web address: www.iowaspecialtyhospital.com
Control: City, Government, Nonfederal **Service**: General medical and surgical

Staffed Beds: 22 **Admissions**: 546 **Census**: 3 **Outpatient Visits**: 76270
Births: 0 **Total Expense ($000)**: 48426 **Payroll Expense ($000)**: 17647
Personnel: 245

BETTENDORF—Scott County

☐ **EAGLE VIEW BEHAVIORAL HEALTH (164006)**, 770 Tanglefoot Lane, Zip 52722–1608; tel. 536/396–2100, (Nonreporting) **A**1 10
Primary Contact: Burton Carriker, Chief Executive Officer
COO: Dwight Lacy, Chief Operating Officer
CFO: David Westmoreland, Divisional Chief Financial Officer
CMO: Joan James, M.D., Medical Director
CIO: Russ Haskett, Vice President Information Technology
CHR: Kellie Kerns, Director, Human Resources
CNO: Benjamin Lalli, Director of Nursing
Web address: https://eagleviewbh.com/
Control: Corporation, Investor–owned (for–profit) **Service**: Psychiatric

Staffed Beds: 56

Hospitals, U.S. / IOWA

★ ⇧ **UNITYPOINT HEALTH – TRINITY BETTENDORF (160104)**, 4500 Utica Ridge Road, Zip 52722–1626; tel. 563/742–5000, **A**10 21 **F**3 11 13 15 18 20 22 26 29 30 34 35 37 40 44 45 48 50 57 59 64 68 70 73 74 76 79 81 82 85 86 87 89 93 96 107 108 110 114 119 126 130 132 146 147 148 149 150 154 157 167 169 **S** UnityPoint Health, West Des Moines, IA
Primary Contact: Shawn Morrow, FACHE, Market President–UnityPoint Health Quad Cities
COO: Barbara Weber, Chief Operating Officer
CFO: Greg Pagliuzza, Chief Financial Officer
CMO: Paul McLoone, M.D., Chief Medical Officer
CHR: Cara Fuller, Vice President Human Resources
CNO: Jean B Doerge, MS, R.N., Chief Nursing Executive
Web address: https://www.unitypoint.org/locations/unitypoint–health–trinity–bettendorf
Control: Other not–for–profit (including NFP Corporation) **Service**: General medical and surgical

Staffed Beds: 90 **Admissions**: 3911 **Census**: 36 **Outpatient Visits**: 76821 **Births**: 1005 **Total Expense ($000)**: 93444 **Payroll Expense ($000)**: 31504 **Personnel**: 308

BLOOMFIELD—Davis County

★ **DAVIS COUNTY HOSPITAL AND CLINICS (161327)**, 509 North Madison Street, Zip 52537–1271; tel. 641/664–2145, **A**3 10 18 **F**3 7 15 28 29 34 35 40 44 45 50 57 59 63 64 65 69 75 81 84 85 86 87 97 107 110 111 115 119 127 132 133 135 146 154 **P**6 **S** MercyOne, Clive, IA
Primary Contact: Veronica Fuhs, Chief Executive Officer
CFO: Kendra Warning, Chief Financial Officer
CMO: Robert Floyd, D.O., Chief Medical Staff
CIO: Kendra Warning, Chief Financial Officer
CHR: Pam Young, Director Human Resources
CNO: Susan Kay Pankey, Chief Nursing Officer
Web address: www.daviscountyhospital.org
Control: County, Government, Nonfederal **Service**: General medical and surgical

Staffed Beds: 13 **Admissions**: 168 **Census**: 2 **Outpatient Visits**: 47193 **Births**: 0 **Total Expense ($000)**: 32946 **Payroll Expense ($000)**: 13411 **Personnel**: 144

BOONE—Boone County

★ **BOONE COUNTY HOSPITAL (161372)**, 1015 Union Street, Zip 50036–4821; tel. 515/432–3140, **A**10 18 **F**1 2 3 4 7 11 13 15 16 17 28 29 30 31 34 35 37 40 43 45 50 56 57 59 62 64 65 67 69 70 72 73 75 76 77 78 79 80 81 82 85 86 87 88 89 90 91 93 97 98 107 110 111 114 119 127 128 131 132 133 134 145 146 147 148 156 166 167 **P**6
Primary Contact: Mikaela Kienitz, Chief Executive Officer
CFO: Chris Torres, Chief Financial Officer
CIO: Paul Sliva, Chief Information Officer
CHR: Kim Schwartz, Assistant Administrator Human Resources and Operations
Web address: www.boonehospital.com
Control: County, Government, Nonfederal **Service**: General medical and surgical

Staffed Beds: 25 **Admissions**: 399 **Census**: 5 **Outpatient Visits**: 151377 **Births**: 84 **Total Expense ($000)**: 53301 **Payroll Expense ($000)**: 24655 **Personnel**: 332

BRITT—Hancock County

★ **HANCOCK COUNTY HEALTH SYSTEM (161307)**, 532 First Street NW, Zip 50423–1227; tel. 641/843–5000, **A**10 18 **F**3 15 29 34 35 36 40 41 43 44 45 46 50 53 56 57 59 62 64 65 75 77 81 82 85 93 97 100 104 107 108 110 111 114 119 130 131 132 133 135 146 148 149 154 156 164 165 169 **P**1 **S** Trinity Health, Livonia, MI
Primary Contact: Laura Zwiefel, Chief Executive officer/Chief Nursing Officer
CFO: Julia C Bowman, Chief Financial Officer
CMO: Catherine Butler, M.D., Chief Medical Staff
CHR: Denise Jakoubeck, Director Human Resources
Web address: www.trusthchs.com/hancock-county-health-system
Control: County, Government, Nonfederal **Service**: General medical and surgical

Staffed Beds: 25 **Admissions**: 346 **Census**: 8 **Outpatient Visits**: 22442 **Births**: 0 **Total Expense ($000)**: 29101 **Payroll Expense ($000)**: 10672 **Personnel**: 180

CARROLL—Carroll County

★ **ST. ANTHONY REGIONAL HOSPITAL (160005)**, 311 South Clark Street, Zip 51401–3038, Mailing Address: P.O. Box 628, Zip 51401–0628; tel. 712/792–3581, (Total facility includes 79 beds in nursing home–type unit) **A**10 20 **F**6 10 11 13 15 28 29 30 31 34 35 37 38 39 40 43 44 45 46 50 51 56 57 59 60 61 62 63 64 65 67 68 69 70 74 75 76 77 78 79 81 82 84 85 86 87 89 93 97 98 100 101 102 103 104 107 108 110 111 115 118 119 120 121 122 123 125 126 127 130 131 132 133 134 135 145 146 147 148 154 156 169 **P**6
Primary Contact: Allen K. Anderson, President and Chief Executive Officer
CFO: Eric Salmonson, Vice President and Chief Financial Officer
CMO: Kyle Ulveling, M.D., Chief of Staff
CIO: Chad Lawson, Chief Information Officer
CHR: Anna Fitzpatrick, Director Human Resources
Web address: www.stanthonyhospital.org
Control: Church operated, Nongovernment, not–for–profit **Service**: General medical and surgical

Staffed Beds: 155 **Admissions**: 1889 **Census**: 93 **Outpatient Visits**: 116032 **Births**: 351 **Total Expense ($000)**: 101794 **Payroll Expense ($000)**: 40154 **Personnel**: 594

CEDAR FALLS—Black Hawk County

▣ **MERCYONE CEDAR FALLS MEDICAL CENTER (160040)**, 515 College Street, Zip 50613–2500; tel. 319/268–3000, **A**1 10 **F**3 7 8 11 12 15 29 30 35 40 43 44 46 53 57 59 64 68 70 75 77 79 81 91 93 97 107 110 111 119 130 131 132 146 167 **S** Trinity Health, Livonia, MI
Primary Contact: Ryan Meyer, Chief Operating Officer
COO: Ryan Meyer, Chief Operating Officer
CFO: Timothy Huber, Vice President Finance
CMO: Matthew Sojka, M.D., Vice President Medical Affairs
CIO: Marge Ray, Director Information Systems
CHR: Suzanne M. Burt, Chief Human Resources Officer
CNO: Kelly Richards, Vice President and Chief Nursing Officer
Web address: www.MercyOne.org
Control: Church operated, Nongovernment, not–for–profit **Service**: General medical and surgical

Staffed Beds: 35 **Admissions**: 524 **Census**: 6 **Outpatient Visits**: 42816 **Births**: 0 **Total Expense ($000)**: 33248 **Payroll Expense ($000)**: 10269 **Personnel**: 149

CEDAR RAPIDS—Linn County

★ △ ⇧ **MERCY MEDICAL CENTER – CEDAR RAPIDS (160079)**, 701 Tenth Street SE, Zip 52403–1292; tel. 319/398–6011, (Total facility includes 55 beds in nursing home–type unit) **A**2 3 5 7 10 21 **F**3 4 5 6 11 12 13 15 18 19 20 22 24 26 28 29 30 31 34 35 37 38 40 42 43 44 45 46 48 49 50 51 54 55 56 57 58 59 60 62 63 64 65 67 68 70 72 74 75 76 78 79 81 82 84 85 86 87 88 89 90 91 92 93 96 98 100 101 102 103 104 107 108 110 114 115 116 117 118 119 120 121 123 124 126 130 131 132 134 135 145 146 147 148 149 150 153 154 162 164 165 167 169 **P**8
Primary Contact: Tim Quinn, M.D., President and Chief Executive Officer
CFO: Nathan Van Genderen, Executive Vice President and Chief Financial Officer
CIO: Jeff Cash, Senior Vice President and Chief Information Officer
CHR: Nancy L Hill–Davis, Senior Vice President and Chief Talent Officer
CNO: Mary Brobst, R.N., MSN, Senior Vice President Patient Care Services and Chief Nursing Officer
Web address: www.mercycare.org
Control: Church operated, Nongovernment, not–for–profit **Service**: General medical and surgical

Staffed Beds: 305 **Admissions**: 10156 **Census**: 165 **Outpatient Visits**: 581691 **Births**: 700 **Total Expense ($000)**: 452417 **Payroll Expense ($000)**: 192119 **Personnel**: 1969

Hospital, Medicare Provider Number, Address, Telephone, Approval, Facility, and Physician Codes, Health Care System

★ American Hospital Association (AHA) membership
□ The Joint Commission accreditation
○ Healthcare Facilities Accreditation Program
◇ DNV Healthcare Inc. accreditation
⇧ Center for Improvement in Healthcare Quality Accreditation
△ Commission on Accreditation of Rehabilitation Facilities (CARF) accreditation

Hospitals, U.S. / IOWA

★ △ ⇧ **UNITYPOINT HEALTH – ST. LUKE'S HOSPITAL (160045)**, 1026 'A' Avenue NE, Zip 52402–3026, Mailing Address: P.O. Box 3026, Zip 52406–3026; tel. 319/369–7211, **A**2 3 5 7 10 21 **F**3 5 11 12 13 15 18 19 20 22 24 26 28 29 30 31 32 34 35 37 39 40 43 44 45 46 48 49 50 51 55 57 58 59 60 61 63 64 65 68 70 72 74 76 77 78 79 81 82 84 85 86 87 89 90 91 92 93 95 96 98 99 100 101 103 104 105 107 108 110 115 117 118 119 120 121 123 124 126 130 132 134 135 145 146 148 149 152 153 154 157 165 167 169 **P**6 **S** UnityPoint Health, West Des Moines, IA
Primary Contact: Casey Greene, Market President–UnityPoint Health Cedar Rapids
CFO: Michael G. Heinrich, Senior Vice President and Chief Financial Officer
CMO: Dustin Arnold, D.O., Chief Medical Officer
CHR: Susan L Slattery, Director Human Resources
CNO: Carmen Kleinsmith, MSN, R.N., Chief Nurse Executive
Web address: www.unitypoint.org
Control: Other not–for–profit (including NFP Corporation) **Service**: General medical and surgical

Staffed Beds: 318 **Admissions**: 13724 **Census**: 186 **Outpatient Visits**: 597665 **Births**: 2268 **Total Expense ($000)**: 427741 **Payroll Expense ($000)**: 182095 **Personnel**: 1892

CENTERVILLE—Appanoose County

★ **MERCYONE CENTERVILLE MEDICAL CENTER (161377)**, 1 St Joseph's Drive, Zip 52544–8055; tel. 641/437–4111, (Total facility includes 19 beds in nursing home–type unit) **A**10 18 **F**3 7 11 12 15 28 29 30 31 34 39 40 43 45 46 50 51 57 59 63 64 67 70 75 77 78 79 81 82 85 93 107 110 115 119 127 129 130 131 132 133 144 148 149 154 156 157 **P**6 **S** Trinity Health, Livonia, MI
Primary Contact: Nicole Clapp, R.N., MSN, FACHE, President
CHR: Tonya Clawson, Manager Human Resources
CNO: Sherri L Doggett, Vice President Patient Services
Web address: www.mercycenterville.org
Control: Church operated, Nongovernment, not–for–profit **Service**: General medical and surgical

Staffed Beds: 44 **Admissions**: 590 **Census**: 22 **Outpatient Visits**: 133207 **Births**: 0 **Total Expense ($000)**: 46841 **Payroll Expense ($000)**: 19980 **Personnel**: 225

CHARITON—Lucas County

★ **LUCAS COUNTY HEALTH CENTER (161341)**, 1200 North Seventh Street, Zip 50049–1258; tel. 641/774–3000, **A**10 18 **F**3 11 15 28 29 30 31 34 40 43 44 45 46 47 50 55 64 66 70 75 81 85 87 93 97 107 110 115 119 127 130 131 132 133 143 145 146 148 156 **S** UnityPoint Health, West Des Moines, IA
Primary Contact: Brian Sims, FACHE, Chief Executive Officer
COO: Lori Johnson, Chief Operating Officer
CFO: Jay Christensen, FACHE, Chief Financial Officer
CMO: David Marcowitz, M.D., Chief of Staff
CIO: Terri Black, Network Manager
CHR: Lana Kuball, Director Administrative Services
CNO: JoBeth Lawless, Chief Nursing Officer, Nursing Services and Director Emergency Management Services
Web address: www.lchcia.com
Control: County, Government, Nonfederal **Service**: General medical and surgical

Staffed Beds: 23 **Admissions**: 188 **Census**: 2 **Outpatient Visits**: 30854 **Births**: 0 **Total Expense ($000)**: 28755 **Payroll Expense ($000)**: 12732 **Personnel**: 187

CHARLES CITY—Floyd County

★ **FLOYD COUNTY MEDICAL CENTER (161347)**, 800 Eleventh Street, Zip 50616–3499; tel. 641/228–6830, **A**10 18 **F**11 13 15 28 29 34 35 40 45 50 57 59 64 75 76 79 81 84 86 87 91 93 96 97 107 111 115 119 127 130 132 133 146 148 149 154 156 169
Primary Contact: Dawnett Willis, Chief Executive Officer
CFO: Craig Carstens, Chief Financial Officer
CHR: Don Nosbisch, Director Human Resources
CNO: Viva Boerschel, Director of Nursing
Web address: www.fcmc.us.com/
Control: County, Government, Nonfederal **Service**: General medical and surgical

Staffed Beds: 25 **Admissions**: 663 **Census**: 8 **Outpatient Visits**: 38036 **Births**: 91 **Total Expense ($000)**: 40015 **Payroll Expense ($000)**: 16418 **Personnel**: 219

CHEROKEE—Cherokee County

☐ **CHEROKEE MENTAL HEALTH INSTITUTE (164002)**, 1251 West Cedar Loop, Zip 51012–1599; tel. 712/225–2594, **A**1 10 **F**29 30 68 75 98 99 100 101 130 135 149 154 163
Primary Contact: Chris Tosteberg, Superintendent
CFO: Tony Morris, Business Manager
CHR: Mary Ann Hanson, Director Personnel
Web address: www.dhs.state.ia.us
Control: State, Government, Nonfederal **Service**: Psychiatric

Staffed Beds: 36 **Admissions**: 215 **Census**: 25 **Outpatient Visits**: 65 **Births**: 0 **Total Expense ($000)**: 19602 **Payroll Expense ($000)**: 9390 **Personnel**: 163

★ ⇧ **CHEROKEE REGIONAL MEDICAL CENTER (161362)**, 300 Sioux Valley Drive, Zip 51012–1205; tel. 712/225–5101, (Total facility includes 30 beds in nursing home–type unit) **A**10 18 21 **F**7 10 11 13 15 28 29 31 34 35 40 43 45 53 56 57 59 62 63 64 65 67 68 69 75 76 77 78 81 86 87 89 90 93 96 97 107 111 114 119 125 127 128 129 130 131 132 133 135 146 147 148 154 156 169 **P**6 **S** UnityPoint Health, West Des Moines, IA
Primary Contact: Gary W. Jordan, FACHE, Chief Executive Officer
CFO: Joan Bierman, Vice President Finance
CIO: Kevin Naslund, Manager Information Technology
CHR: Theresa Conley, Manager Human Resources
CNO: Christy Syndergaard, Vice President Nursing
Web address: www.cherokeermc.org
Control: Other not–for–profit (including NFP Corporation) **Service**: General medical and surgical

Staffed Beds: 55 **Admissions**: 498 **Census**: 30 **Outpatient Visits**: 63193 **Births**: 62 **Total Expense ($000)**: 53108 **Payroll Expense ($000)**: 24353 **Personnel**: 295

CLARINDA—Page County

★ ⇧ **CLARINDA REGIONAL HEALTH CENTER (161352)**, 220 Essie Davison Drive, Zip 51632–2915, Mailing Address: P.O. Box 217, Zip 51632–0217; tel. 712/542–2176, **A**10 18 21 **F**3 7 8 11 15 18 28 29 31 32 34 35 36 40 41 43 44 45 50 57 59 64 65 68 69 74 75 77 78 79 81 82 84 85 86 87 92 93 97 100 101 104 107 110 111 114 115 118 119 127 128 129 130 131 132 133 135 143 146 147 148 149 150 154 155 156 160
Primary Contact: Charles Nordyke, Chief Executive Officer
COO: Elaine Otte, Chief Operating Officer
CFO: Milton Trabal, Chief Financial Officer
CMO: Autumn Morales, Chief Medical Staff Officer
CIO: Richard Morgan-Fine, IT Director
CHR: Melissa Walter, Director Human Resources
CNO: Sherrie L Laubenthal, R.N., Chief Nursing Officer
Web address: www.clarindahealth.com
Control: City, Government, Nonfederal **Service**: General medical and surgical

Staffed Beds: 25 **Admissions**: 525 **Census**: 7 **Outpatient Visits**: 85143 **Births**: 0 **Total Expense ($000)**: 50010 **Payroll Expense ($000)**: 24418 **Personnel**: 373

CLARION—Wright County

★ ⇧ **IOWA SPECIALTY HOSPITAL–CLARION (161302)**, 1316 South Main Street, Zip 50525–2019; tel. 515/532–2811, **A**10 18 21 **F**3 5 11 13 15 28 29 32 34 35 37 38 40 43 50 54 56 57 59 64 65 68 69 71 75 76 77 79 81 82 85 86 87 92 93 96 97 103 104 107 110 111 115 117 119 125 127 130 131 133 134 135 146 147 148 149 154 156 157 160 162 169 **P**4 6 **S** Iowa Specialty Hospitals & Clinics, Clarion, IA
Primary Contact: Steven J. Simonin, President and Chief Executive Officer
COO: Kirk Rier, Chief Operating Officer
CFO: Greg Polzin, Chief Financial Officer
CMO: Dennis Colby, M.D., Chief of Staff
CHR: Holly Martin, Human Resources Leader
CNO: Abby Young, Chief Nursing Officer
Web address: www.iowaspecialtyhospital.com
Control: City, Government, Nonfederal **Service**: General medical and surgical

Staffed Beds: 25 **Admissions**: 1286 **Census**: 8 **Outpatient Visits**: 87592 **Births**: 626 **Total Expense ($000)**: 77093 **Payroll Expense ($000)**: 27808 **Personnel**: 378

Hospitals, U.S. / IOWA

CLINTON—Clinton County

☒ **MERCYONE CLINTON MEDICAL CENTER (160080)**, 1410 North Fourth Street, Zip 52732–2940; tel. 563/244–5555, (Includes MERCY SERVICES FOR AGING, 600 14th Avenue North, Clinton, Iowa, Zip 52732, tel. 563/244–3888) **A**1 10 **F**3 11 13 15 18 20 22 28 29 30 31 34 35 36 38 40 44 45 47 49 50 53 56 57 59 60 61 62 63 64 68 70 74 75 76 77 78 79 80 81 82 84 85 87 89 93 98 100 101 102 107 108 110 111 115 118 119 121 123 129 130 132 143 144 146 147 148 149 154 160 169 **P**6 **S** Trinity Health, Livonia, MI
Primary Contact: Mellissa Wood, Chief Operating Officer, Chief Nursing Officer
CFO: Tonya Johnson, Director of Finance
CMO: Ashton Nickles, DPM, Chief Medical Officer
CHR: Shane Buer, Vice President, Human Resources
Web address: www.mercyclinton.com
Control: Church operated, Nongovernment, not–for–profit **Service**: General medical and surgical

Staffed Beds: 73 **Admissions**: 3063 **Census**: 31 **Outpatient Visits**: 173053
Births: 271 **Total Expense ($000)**: 136264 **Payroll Expense ($000)**: 56807
Personnel: 737

SAMARITAN SERVICES FOR AGING See Mercy Services For Aging

CLIVE—Polk County

☐ **CLIVE BEHAVIORAL HEALTH (164007)**, 1450 NW 114th Street, Zip 50325–7039; tel. 515/553–6200, **A**1 3 10 **F**5 29 35 38 50 59 64 75 87 98 99 100 101 102 104 105 130 135 149 153 154 162 164 **P**6 **S** Universal Health Services, Inc., King of Prussia, PA
Primary Contact: Kevin Pettit, Chief Executive Officer
CFO: Mark A VanderLinden, Chief Financial Officer
CMO: Sasha Khosravi, D.O., Chief Medical Officer
Web address: www.clivebehavioral.com
Control: Corporation, Investor–owned (for–profit) **Service**: Psychiatric

Staffed Beds: 54 **Admissions**: 2409 **Census**: 48 **Outpatient Visits**: 5831
Births: 0 **Total Expense ($000)**: 24619 **Payroll Expense ($000)**: 10627
Personnel: 147

☐ △ **MERCYONE CLIVE REHABILITATION HOSPITAL (163025)**, 1401 Campus Drive, Zip 50325–6500; tel. 515/381–6519, **A**1 7 10 **F**3 29 30 56 90 95 96 132 143 148
Primary Contact: Nicole Nigg, Chief Executive Officer
Web address: www.mercydesmoines.org
Control: Partnership, Investor–owned (for–profit) **Service**: Rehabilitation

Staffed Beds: 50 **Admissions**: 1149 **Census**: 35 **Outpatient Visits**: 0
Births: 0 **Total Expense ($000)**: 19243 **Payroll Expense ($000)**: 8779
Personnel: 138

CORALVILLE—Johnson County

☐ **EASTERN IOWA REHABILITATION HOSPITAL (163026)**, 2801 Heartland Drive, Zip 52241–2733; tel. 319/645–4001, **A**1 **F**3 29 90 91 95 96 149
Primary Contact: Robin Honomichl, Chief Executive Officer
Web address: https://www.easterniowarehabhospital.com/
Control: Partnership, Investor–owned (for–profit) **Service**: Rehabilitation

Staffed Beds: 40 **Admissions**: 388 **Census**: 11 **Outpatient Visits**: 0
Births: 0 **Total Expense ($000)**: 7596 **Payroll Expense ($000)**: 3833
Personnel: 24

IOWA MEDICAL AND CLASSIFICATION CENTER, 2700 Coral Ridge Avenue, Zip 52241–4708, Mailing Address: 2700 Coral Rigde Avenue, Zip 52241; tel. 319/626–2391, (Nonreporting) **A**3
Primary Contact: James McKinney, Warden
Web address: www.oakdaleprison.com/
Control: State, Government, Nonfederal **Service**: Psychiatric

Staffed Beds: 20

MERCY IOWA CITY REHABILITATION HOSPITAL See Eastern Iowa Rehabilitation Hospital

☒ **UNIVERSITY OF IOWA HEALTH NETWORK REHABILITATION HOSPITAL (163027)**, 2450 Coral Court, Zip 52241–2975; tel. 319/645–3300, **A**1 10 **F**3 29 30 44 68 77 79 86 90 91 92 95 96 100 132 146 148 149 164 **S** Encompass Health Corporation, Birmingham, AL
Primary Contact: Angela Zaremba, Chief Executive Officer
CFO: Gary Ward, Controller
CMO: Philip Chen, M.D., Medical Director
CIO: Nicole Gerdts, Director, Quality and Risk
CHR: Beth Nissen, Human Resources Director
CNO: Brenda Bell, Chief Nursing Officer
Web address: www.uihnrehab.com
Control: Corporation, Investor–owned (for–profit) **Service**: Rehabilitation

Staffed Beds: 40 **Admissions**: 947 **Census**: 30 **Outpatient Visits**: 0
Births: 0 **Total Expense ($000)**: 16989 **Payroll Expense ($000)**: 9709
Personnel: 107

UNIVERSITY OF IOWA REHABILITATION HOSPITAL, A VENTURE WITH ENCOMPASS HEALTH See University of Iowa Health Network Rehabilitation Hospital

CORNING—Adams County

★ **CHI HEALTH MERCY CORNING (161304)**, 603 Rosary Drive, Zip 50841–1683; tel. 641/322–3121, **A**10 18 **F**3 11 15 28 29 30 31 34 35 40 43 45 46 48 49 50 53 56 57 59 64 65 69 75 77 78 79 81 82 85 89 96 97 107 110 115 119 127 129 130 132 133 135 146 147 149 153 154 157 **P**6 **S** CommonSpirit Health, Chicago, IL
Primary Contact: Alicia Reed, President
CMO: Maen Haddadin, M.D., President Medical Staff
CIO: Kenneth Lawonn, Senior Vice President and Chief Information Officer
CHR: Sandra Lammers, Coordinator Human Resources and Finance
Web address: www.chihealth.com/en/location-search/mercy-corning.html
Control: Church operated, Nongovernment, not–for–profit **Service**: General medical and surgical

Staffed Beds: 12 **Admissions**: 178 **Census**: 5 **Outpatient Visits**: 20376
Births: 0 **Total Expense ($000)**: 16680 **Payroll Expense ($000)**: 5593
Personnel: 103

CORYDON—Wayne County

★ **WAYNE COUNTY HOSPITAL AND CLINIC SYSTEM (161358)**, 417 South East Street, Zip 50060–1860, Mailing Address: P.O. Box 305, Zip 50060–0305; tel. 641/872–2260, **A**10 18 **F**7 13 15 28 29 31 34 35 40 43 51 56 57 59 60 64 70 75 76 77 78 79 81 85 87 89 91 92 93 97 107 110 115 119 126 127 130 131 133 144 147 148 149 154 169 **P**6 **S** MercyOne, Clive, IA
Primary Contact: Daren Relph, Chief Executive Officer
COO: Michael Thomas, Associate Administrator
CFO: Diane Hook, Chief Financial Officer
CMO: Joel Baker, D.O., Chief Medical Officer
CIO: Laurie Ehrich, Chief Communications Officer
CHR: Dave Carlyle, Director Human Resources
CNO: Sheila Mattly, Chief Nursing Officer
Web address: www.waynecountyhospital.org
Control: County, Government, Nonfederal **Service**: General medical and surgical

Staffed Beds: 25 **Admissions**: 560 **Census**: 5 **Outpatient Visits**: 30031
Births: 174 **Total Expense ($000)**: 41630 **Payroll Expense ($000)**: 18194
Personnel: 274

COUNCIL BLUFFS—Pottawattamie County

☒ **CHI HEALTH MERCY COUNCIL BLUFFS (160028)**, 800 Mercy Drive, Zip 51503–3128; tel. 712/328–5000, **A**1 2 3 10 **F**3 5 11 13 15 18 20 22 26 28 29 30 31 34 35 37 40 41 43 45 47 48 49 50 57 59 68 70 72 74 76 77 78 79 81 82 84 85 87 89 91 93 98 99 100 101 102 104 105 107 108 110 111 114 115 119 126 129 130 132 146 147 154 167 169 **S** CommonSpirit Health, Chicago, IL
Primary Contact: Derek Havens, Interim President
CFO: Jeanette Wojtalewicz, Chief Financial Officer
CMO: Joseph Hoagbin, M.D., Chief Quality Officer
CIO: Thomas Haley, Information Technology Services Site Director
CHR: Nancy Wallace, Senior Vice President Human Resources
Web address: https://www.chihealth.com/locations/mercy-council-bluffs
Control: Church operated, Nongovernment, not–for–profit **Service**: General medical and surgical

Staffed Beds: 146 **Admissions**: 4923 **Census**: 60 **Outpatient Visits**: 77763
Births: 415 **Total Expense ($000)**: 113154 **Payroll Expense ($000)**: 41190
Personnel: 447

Hospital, Medicare Provider Number, Address, Telephone, Approval, Facility, and Physician Codes, Health Care System

★ American Hospital Association (AHA) membership ○ Healthcare Facilities Accreditation Program ⇑ Center for Improvement in Healthcare Quality Accreditation
☐ The Joint Commission accreditation ◇ DNV Healthcare Inc. accreditation △ Commission on Accreditation of Rehabilitation Facilities (CARF) accreditation

Hospitals, U.S. / IOWA

☒ **METHODIST JENNIE EDMUNDSON HOSPITAL (160047)**, 933 East Pierce Street, Zip 51503–4652, Mailing Address: P.O. Box 2C, Zip 51502–3002; tel. 712/396–6000, **A**1 2 3 5 10 **F**3 11 13 15 18 20 22 26 28 29 30 31 34 35 40 41 43 44 45 46 47 49 50 51 55 57 58 59 61 64 68 70 73 74 75 76 78 79 81 82 85 86 87 89 92 93 98 100 101 102 107 108 110 111 113 115 118 119 120 121 123 126 129 130 131 145 146 147 148 149 156 162 164 167 169 **S** Nebraska Methodist Health System, Inc., Omaha, NE
Primary Contact: David Burd, President and Chief Executive Officer
CFO: Jeff Francis, Vice President Finance and Chief Financial Officer
CMO: Scott Bomgaars, M.D., Vice President Medical Affairs
CIO: Steven Zuber, Vice President
CHR: Holly Huerter, Vice President Human Resources
CNO: Jenene Vandenburg, Vice President Patient Services and Chief Nursing Officer
Web address: www.bestcare.org
Control: Other not–for–profit (including NFP Corporation) **Service:** General medical and surgical

Staffed Beds: 133 **Admissions:** 6257 **Census:** 75 **Outpatient Visits:** 72697 **Births:** 691 **Total Expense ($000):** 137620 **Payroll Expense ($000):** 58383 **Personnel:** 744

CRESCO—Howard County

★ **REGIONAL HEALTH SERVICES OF HOWARD COUNTY (161328)**, 235 Eighth Avenue West, Zip 52136–1098; tel. 563/547–2101, **A**10 18 **F**3 7 11 13 15 28 29 34 35 36 38 40 43 44 45 47 48 50 53 56 57 59 62 63 64 65 68 75 76 77 81 82 85 87 89 96 104 107 110 115 119 127 128 130 131 132 133 146 147 149 150 154 156 169 **P**7 **S** Trinity Health, Livonia, MI
Primary Contact: Robin M. Schluter, Chief Executive Officer
CFO: Greg Burkel, Chief Financial Officer
CMO: Paul Jensen, M.D., Chief of Staff
CIO: Greg Burkel, Chief Financial Officer
CHR: Jennalee Pedretti, Vice President Operations
CNO: Carol Kerian–Masters, R.N., Chief Nursing Officer
Web address: www.rhshc.org
Control: County, Government, Nonfederal **Service:** General medical and surgical

Staffed Beds: 19 **Admissions:** 309 **Census:** 3 **Outpatient Visits:** 31221 **Births:** 70 **Total Expense ($000):** 45087 **Payroll Expense ($000):** 15048 **Personnel:** 209

CRESTON—Union County

★ ⇧ **GREATER REGIONAL HEALTH (161365)**, 1700 West Townline Street Suite 3, Zip 50801–1099; tel. 641/782–7091, **A**10 18 21 **F**3 7 8 11 12 13 15 28 29 31 34 35 37 40 43 44 45 47 48 50 51 56 57 59 64 65 66 68 70 74 75 76 77 78 79 81 82 85 86 93 96 97 102 104 107 108 110 111 115 119 120 121 122 123 124 125 126 127 129 131 133 143 144 146 147 148 149 154 156 167 169 **P**6 **S** UnityPoint Health, West Des Moines, IA
Primary Contact: Monte Neitzel, Chief Executive Officer
CFO: Matt McCutchan, Chief Financial Officer
CMO: Steve Reeves, M.D., Chief Medical Staff
CIO: Karla Alford, Chief Information Officer
CHR: Amy Rieck, Human Resources Officer
CNO: Amanda Mohr, Chief Nursing Officer
Web address: www.greaterregional.org
Control: County, Government, Nonfederal **Service:** General medical and surgical

Staffed Beds: 25 **Admissions:** 945 **Census:** 9 **Outpatient Visits:** 147171 **Births:** 191 **Total Expense ($000):** 93004 **Payroll Expense ($000):** 44504 **Personnel:** 495

DAVENPORT—Scott County

☒ △ **GENESIS MEDICAL CENTER – DAVENPORT (160033)**, 1227 East Rusholme Street, Zip 52803–2498; tel. 563/421–1000, (Includes GENESIS MEDICAL CENTER–EAST CAMPUS, 1227 East Rusholme Street, Davenport, Iowa, Zip 52803, tel. 563/421–1000; GENESIS MEDICAL CENTER–WEST CAMPUS, 1401 West Central Park, Davenport, Iowa, Zip 52804–1769, tel. 563/421–1000) **A**1 2 3 5 7 10 19 **F**3 11 12 13 15 17 18 20 22 24 26 28 29 30 31 40 42 43 46 47 48 49 64 68 72 74 75 76 77 78 79 81 82 84 89 90 92 93 95 98 99 104 107 111 114 115 118 119 120 121 123 124 126 129 130 131 132 135 146 147 148 154 167 **S** Trinity Health, Livonia, MI
Primary Contact: Jordan Voigt, President MercyOne Eastern Division
CFO: Joe Malas, CPA, Eastern Division Vice President, Chief Financial Officer
CMO: Christopher Crome, M.D., Chief Medical Officer, Genesis Health System
CIO: Robert Frieden, Vice President Information Systems
CHR: Heidi Kahly–McMahon, Vice President Human Resources Genesis Health System
Web address: www.genesishealth.com
Control: Other not–for–profit (including NFP Corporation) **Service:** General medical and surgical

Staffed Beds: 344 **Admissions:** 15425 **Census:** 185 **Outpatient Visits:** 228719 **Births:** 2085 **Total Expense ($000):** 421490 **Payroll Expense ($000):** 119246 **Personnel:** 1447

MERCY HOSPITAL See Genesis Medical Center–West Campus

☒ **SELECT SPECIALTY HOSPITAL–QUAD CITIES (162001)**, 1227 East Rusholme Street, Zip 52803–2459; tel. 563/468–2000, **A**1 10 **F**1 3 29 45 75 85 119 130 148 **S** Select Medical Corporation, Mechanicsburg, PA
Primary Contact: Codie Dillie, Chief Executive Officer
Web address: www.selectmedicalcorp.com
Control: Corporation, Investor–owned (for–profit) **Service:** Acute long–term care hospital

Staffed Beds: 35 **Admissions:** 279 **Census:** 20 **Outpatient Visits:** 0 **Births:** 0 **Total Expense ($000):** 15692 **Payroll Expense ($000):** 7617 **Personnel:** 82

ST LUKE'S HOSPITAL See Genesis Medical Center–East Campus

DE WITT—Clinton County

☒ **GENESIS MEDICAL CENTER, DEWITT (161313)**, 1118 11th Street, Zip 52742–1296; tel. 563/659–4200, **A**1 10 18 **F**3 11 28 29 30 34 35 38 40 41 43 44 45 50 57 59 64 68 69 79 81 83 92 93 107 110 115 119 127 128 129 130 132 133 148 149 154 164 **P**6 **S** Trinity Health, Livonia, MI
Primary Contact: Ted Rogalski, Administrator
CMO: Steven Fowler, M.D., President Medical Staff
CHR: Kristin Nicholson, Coordinator Human Resources
CNO: Wanda Haack, MSN, R.N., Chief Nursing Officer
Web address: www.genesishealth.com
Control: Other not–for–profit (including NFP Corporation) **Service:** General medical and surgical

Staffed Beds: 13 **Admissions:** 185 **Census:** 3 **Outpatient Visits:** 29737 **Births:** 0 **Total Expense ($000):** 20519 **Payroll Expense ($000):** 6941 **Personnel:** 105

DECORAH—Winneshiek County

WINNESHIEK MEDICAL CENTER See Winnmed

☒ **WINNMED (161371)**, 901 Montgomery Street, Zip 52101–2325; tel. 563/382–2911, **A**1 10 18 **F**3 7 11 13 15 28 29 31 34 35 36 38 40 43 44 45 50 56 57 59 61 62 63 64 65 68 69 75 76 77 78 79 81 82 86 87 93 94 97 101 104 107 110 111 115 119 128 129 130 131 132 133 135 144 146 147 148 149 150 153 154 156 164 169 **S** Mayo Clinic, Rochester, MN
Primary Contact: Steve Robert. Slessor, Chief Administrative Officer
COO: David Rooney, Administrator Operations
CMO: Thomas Marquardt, M.D., Interim Chief Medical Officer
CHR: Laurie Bulman, Director Human Resources
CNO: Kathy Moritz, Chief Nursing Officer
Web address: https://winnmed.org/
Control: County, Government, Nonfederal **Service:** General medical and surgical

Staffed Beds: 30 **Admissions:** 894 **Census:** 9 **Outpatient Visits:** 150491 **Births:** 248 **Total Expense ($000):** 77073 **Payroll Expense ($000):** 29364 **Personnel:** 437

DENISON—Crawford County

★ ⇧ **CRAWFORD COUNTY MEMORIAL HOSPITAL (161369)**, 100 Medical Parkway, Zip 51442–2299; tel. 712/265–2500, **A**10 18 21 **F**3 7 8 13 15 17 28 29 31 34 35 40 45 50 56 57 59 64 65 67 68 70 75 76 77 81 82 85 87 89 93 97 101 107 110 111 115 119 127 128 133 135 143 148 156 169 **P**6
Primary Contact: Erin Muck, Chief Executive Officer
CFO: Rachel Melby, Vice President, Chief Financial Officer
CIO: Angie Anderson, Director Information Technology
CHR: Brad L. Bonner, Executive Director, Human Resources and General Counsel
Web address: www.ccmhia.com
Control: County, Government, Nonfederal **Service:** General medical and surgical

Staffed Beds: 25 **Admissions:** 474 **Census:** 4 **Outpatient Visits:** 81652 **Births:** 87 **Total Expense ($000):** 39802 **Payroll Expense ($000):** 19838 **Personnel:** 274

DES MOINES—Polk County

BLANK CHILDREN'S HOSPITAL See Unitypoint Health – Blank Children's Hospital

☒ **BROADLAWNS MEDICAL CENTER (160101)**, 1801 Hickman Road, Zip 50314–1597; tel. 515/282–2200, **A**1 3 5 10 **F**3 5 11 13 15 18 29 30 31 32 34 35 38 39 40 43 44 48 50 53 54 56 57 58 59 64 65 66 68 70 74 75 76 77 78 79 81 82 85 86 87 92 93 94 97 98 100 101 102 104 105 106 107 110 111 114 119 126 127 129 130 131 132 135 144 146 147 148 153 154 156 162 164 165 169 **P**6
Primary Contact: Proctor Lureman, President and Chief Executive Officer
CFO: Karl Vilums, Chief Financial Officer, Executive Vice President
CMO: Tammara Chance, D.O., Chief Medical Officer
CHR: Julie Kilgore, Vice President, Human Resources
CNO: Lance Schmitt, R.N., Chief Nursing Officer and Vice President, Nursing
Web address: www.broadlawns.org
Control: County, Government, Nonfederal **Service:** General medical and surgical

Staffed Beds: 140 **Admissions:** 2844 **Census:** 69 **Outpatient Visits:** 307443 **Births:** 822 **Total Expense ($000):** 235285 **Payroll Expense ($000):** 111562 **Personnel:** 1127

Hospitals, U.S. / IOWA

DEPT OF VETERANS AFF MED CTR See Des Moines Division

DES MOINES DIVISION See VA Central Iowa Health Care System–Des Moines, Des Moines

JOHN STODDARD CANCER CENTER See Unity Point Health – John Stoddard Cancer Center

MERCYONE DES MOINES MEDICAL CENTER (160083), 1111 6th Avenue, Zip 50314–2611; tel. 515/247–3121, (Includes MERCYONE WEST DES MOINES MEDICAL CENTER, 1755 59th Place, West Des Moines, Iowa, Zip 50266–7737, tel. 515/358–8000) **A**1 2 3 5 10 13 **F**3 5 6 7 8 9 11 12 13 15 17 18 19 20 21 22 23 24 25 26 27 28 29 30 31 32 34 35 36 38 39 40 41 43 44 46 48 49 50 53 54 55 56 57 58 59 60 61 62 63 64 65 66 68 70 71 72 73 74 75 76 77 78 79 81 82 84 85 86 87 88 89 91 92 93 94 96 97 98 99 100 101 102 103 104 105 107 108 110 111 114 115 116 117 118 119 120 121 123 124 126 129 130 131 132 134 135 143 144 145 146 147 148 149 150 153 154 156 157 158 160 164 165 167 169 **P**6 **S** Trinity Health, Livonia, MI
Primary Contact: Kurt Andersen, M.D., President – Central Iowa Division
COO: Vanessa Freitag, Chief Operating Officer
CFO: Terri Donovan, Vice President of Finance
CIO: James Strother, Site Director Information Technology Systems
CHR: Donna R Hoffman, Chief Human Resource Officer
CNO: Jennifer Misajet, Interim Chief Nursing Officer
Web address: www.mercydesmoines.org
Control: Church operated, Nongovernment, not–for–profit **Service:** General medical and surgical

Staffed Beds: 620 **Admissions:** 23242 **Census:** 405 **Outpatient Visits:** 210629 **Births:** 3684 **Total Expense ($000):** 869859 **Payroll Expense ($000):** 317749 **Personnel:** 3359

SELECT SPECIALTY HOSPITAL–DES MOINES (162003), 1111 6th Avenue, 4th Floor Main, Zip 50314–2610; tel. 515/247–4400, **A**1 10 **F**1 29 75 148 **S** Select Medical Corporation, Mechanicsburg, PA
Primary Contact: Sam Ayres, Chief Executive Officer
Web address: www.selectspecialtyhospitals.com
Control: Corporation, Investor–owned (for–profit) **Service:** Acute long–term care hospital

Staffed Beds: 30 **Admissions:** 263 **Census:** 17 **Outpatient Visits:** 0 **Births:** 0 **Total Expense ($000):** 10707 **Payroll Expense ($000):** 6088 **Personnel:** 84

UNITYPOINT HEALTH – DES MOINES See Unitypoint Health–Iowa Lutheran Hospital

★ △ ⇑ **UNITYPOINT HEALTH–DES MOINES (160082)**, 1200 Pleasant Street, Zip 50309–1406; tel. 515/241–6212, (Includes POWELL CONVALESCENT CENTER, 1200 Pleasant, Des Moines, Iowa, Zip 50309, tel. 515/263–5612; UNITY POINT HEALTH – JOHN STODDARD CANCER CENTER, 1221 Pleasant Street, Des Moines, Iowa, Zip 50309–1423, tel. 515/241–6212; UNITYPOINT HEALTH – BLANK CHILDREN'S HOSPITAL, 1200 Pleasant Street, Des Moines, Iowa, Zip 50309–1406, tel. 515/241–5437; Steve R. Stephenson, M.D., President and Chief Operating Officer; UNITYPOINT HEALTH – METHODIST WEST HOSPITAL, 1660 60th Street, West Des Moines, Iowa, Zip 50266–7700, tel. 515/343–1000; David A. Stark, FACHE, President and Chief Executive Officer; UNITYPOINT HEALTH–IOWA LUTHERAN HOSPITAL, 700 East University Avenue, Des Moines, Iowa, Zip 50316–2392, tel. 515/263–5612; David A. Stark, FACHE, President and Chief Executive Officer; YOUNKER MEMORIAL REHABILITATION CENTER, 1200 Pleasant Road, Des Moines, Iowa, Zip 50308, tel. 515/263–5612) **A**2 3 5 7 10 19 21 **F**3 4 5 7 8 11 12 13 15 17 18 20 22 24 26 28 29 30 31 32 34 35 37 38 39 40 41 43 44 45 46 47 48 49 50 54 55 56 57 58 59 60 61 64 65 66 68 70 72 74 75 76 77 78 79 81 82 84 85 86 87 88 89 90 91 92 93 95 96 97 98 99 100 101 102 103 104 105 106 107 108 111 115 116 117 118 119 120 121 123 124 126 130 131 132 134 135 138 143 146 148 149 152 153 154 156 157 162 163 164 165 166 167 169 **P**6 **S** UnityPoint Health, West Des Moines, IA
Primary Contact: Jon Rozenfeld, Market President, UnityPoint Health – Des Moines
COO: Eric L Lothe, FACHE, Executive Vice President and Chief Operating Officer
CFO: Thomas Mathews, Chief Financial Officer
CMO: Mark Purtle, M.D., Vice President Medical Affairs
CHR: Joyce McDaniel, Vice President Human Resources and Education
Web address: www.unitypoint.org
Control: Other not–for–profit (including NFP Corporation) **Service:** General medical and surgical

Staffed Beds: 672 **Admissions:** 33869 **Census:** 524 **Outpatient Visits:** 455983 **Births:** 3550 **Total Expense ($000):** 1036626 **Payroll Expense ($000):** 459400 **Personnel:** 5218

△ **VA CENTRAL IOWA HEALTH CARE SYSTEM–DES MOINES**, 3600 30th Street, Zip 50310–5753; tel. 515/699–5999, (Includes DES MOINES DIVISION, 3600 30th Street, Des Moines, Iowa, Zip 50310–5774, tel. 515/699–5999; KNOXVILLE DIVISION, 1515 West Pleasant, Knoxville, Iowa, Zip 50138–3399, tel. 515/842–3101) (Total facility includes 60 beds in nursing home–type unit) **A**1 3 5 7 **F**2 3 4 5 6 8 11 12 15 18 20 24 28 29 30 31 33 34 35 36 37 38 39 40 44 45 46 50 53 54 55 56 57 59 60 61 62 63 64 65 66 70 71 74 75 77 78 79 81 82 83 84 85 86 87 93 94 96 97 98 100 101 102 104 106 107 108 110 111 114 115 117 118 119 127 128 129 130 132 135 137 138 139 140 141 142 143 144 146 147 148 149 150 154 156 157 160 161 164 169 **S** Department of Veterans Affairs, Washington, DC
Primary Contact: Lisa Curnes, R.N., Medical Center Director/Chief Executive Officer
CMO: Fredrick Bahls, M.D., Chief of Staff
CIO: James Danuser, Chief Information Officer
CHR: Sabrina Owen, Human Resources Officer
Web address: www.centraliowa.va.gov/
Control: Veterans Affairs, Government, federal **Service:** General medical and surgical

Staffed Beds: 141 **Admissions:** 3064 **Census:** 108 **Outpatient Visits:** 419454 **Births:** 0 **Total Expense ($000):** 394552 **Payroll Expense ($000):** 159064 **Personnel:** 1728

DUBUQUE—Dubuque County

△ **MERCYONE DUBUQUE MEDICAL CENTER (160069)**, 250 Mercy Drive, Zip 52001–7360; tel. 563/589–8000, (Total facility includes 36 beds in nursing home–type unit) **A**1 5 7 10 19 **F**3 4 5 8 11 13 15 18 20 22 24 26 28 29 30 31 32 34 35 36 38 39 40 43 44 49 50 51 53 56 57 58 59 61 62 64 65 67 70 71 72 74 75 76 77 78 79 80 81 82 84 85 86 87 89 90 91 93 97 98 99 100 101 102 103 104 107 108 110 111 114 115 117 118 119 126 128 129 130 131 132 134 135 144 146 147 148 149 150 154 156 160 164 167 169 **P**8 **S** Trinity Health, Livonia, MI
Primary Contact: Kay Takes, R.N., President
CFO: Tonya Johnson, Director of Finance
CIO: Joe Billmeyer, Director, Information Services
CHR: Kathryn Roberts, Director Human Resources
CNO: Robert Wethal, R.N., Vice President Patient Care Services and Chief Nursing Officer
Web address: www.mercydubuque.com
Control: Church operated, Nongovernment, not–for–profit **Service:** General medical and surgical

Staffed Beds: 197 **Admissions:** 7558 **Census:** 118 **Outpatient Visits:** 45219 **Births:** 683 **Total Expense ($000):** 191699 **Payroll Expense ($000):** 65168 **Personnel:** 1096

★ △ ⇑ **UNITYPOINT HEALTH – FINLEY HOSPITAL (160117)**, 350 North Grandview Avenue, Zip 52001–6393; tel. 563/582–1881, **A**7 10 21 **F**3 13 15 18 20 22 28 29 30 31 32 34 35 37 40 43 44 50 51 55 56 57 58 59 62 64 65 68 70 72 74 75 76 77 78 79 81 82 85 86 87 90 91 93 96 98 100 102 103 104 107 108 110 111 114 115 116 117 118 119 120 121 123 124 126 129 130 132 135 146 148 149 153 154 156 167 169 **S** UnityPoint Health, West Des Moines, IA
Primary Contact: Jennifer Havens, R.N., FACHE, Market President, UnityPoint Health – Dubuque
CMO: Bryan Pechous, M.D., Vice President Medical Affairs
CIO: Tim Loeffelholz, Account Executive Information Technology
CHR: Karla Waldbillig, Director Human Resources
CNO: Mary Peters, Chief Nursing Executive
Web address: www.unitypoint.org
Control: Other not–for–profit (including NFP Corporation) **Service:** General medical and surgical

Staffed Beds: 82 **Admissions:** 4216 **Census:** 48 **Outpatient Visits:** 95403 **Births:** 595 **Total Expense ($000):** 141846 **Payroll Expense ($000):** 62688 **Personnel:** 574

Hospital, Medicare Provider Number, Address, Telephone, Approval, Facility, and Physician Codes, Health Care System

★ American Hospital Association (AHA) membership
☐ The Joint Commission accreditation
○ Healthcare Facilities Accreditation Program
◇ DNV Healthcare Inc. accreditation
⇑ Center for Improvement in Healthcare Quality Accreditation
△ Commission on Accreditation of Rehabilitation Facilities (CARF) accreditation

Hospitals, U.S. / IOWA

DYERSVILLE—Dubuque County

★ **MERCYONE DYERSVILLE MEDICAL CENTER (161378)**, 1111 Third Street SW, Zip 52040-1725; tel. 563/875-7101, **A**10 18 **F**11 15 28 29 30 34 35 36 40 50 53 56 57 59 64 65 75 77 79 81 85 89 93 107 114 119 130 131 133 135 146 147 149 167 **P**8 **S** Trinity Health, Livonia, MI
Primary Contact: Kay Takes, R.N., President
CFO: Robert Shafer, Vice President Finance
Web address: www.mercydubuque.com/mercy-dyersville
Control: Church operated, Nongovernment, not-for-profit **Service**: General medical and surgical

Staffed Beds: 8 **Admissions**: 55 **Census**: 1 **Outpatient Visits**: 3736 **Births**: 0 **Total Expense ($000)**: 7628 **Payroll Expense ($000)**: 3310 **Personnel**: 55

ELKADER—Clayton County

★ **MERCYONE ELKADER MEDICAL CENTER (161319)**, 901 Davidson Street NW, Zip 52043-9015; tel. 563/245-7000, **A**10 18 **F**7 11 15 28 29 34 35 40 43 45 50 57 59 64 67 68 75 81 85 87 91 93 102 107 110 111 114 119 128 129 131 133 146 **S** Trinity Health, Livonia, MI
Primary Contact: Christopher Brady, Interim Chief Executive Officer
CFO: Patricia Borel, Chief Financial Officer
CIO: Jonathan Holliday, Manager Information Technology
CHR: Angie Gerndt, Human Resources Manager
CNO: Natalie Shea, Chief Nursing Officer
Web address: www.centralcommunityhospital.com
Control: Other not-for-profit (including NFP Corporation) **Service**: General medical and surgical

Staffed Beds: 15 **Admissions**: 168 **Census**: 3 **Outpatient Visits**: 15378 **Births**: 0 **Total Expense ($000)**: 12216 **Payroll Expense ($000)**: 5499 **Personnel**: 92

EMMETSBURG—Palo Alto County

★ **PALO ALTO COUNTY HEALTH SYSTEM (161357)**, 3201 First Street, Zip 50536-2516; tel. 712/852-5500, (Total facility includes 22 beds in nursing home-type unit) **A**10 18 **F**3 5 7 11 13 15 28 29 30 34 35 40 43 45 46 50 57 59 62 63 64 65 67 69 75 76 77 81 82 84 85 87 93 97 104 107 110 114 119 127 130 131 132 133 143 146 153 154 156 158 160 169 **S** Trinity Health, Livonia, MI
Primary Contact: Jonathan Moe, Chief Executive Officer
CFO: Collette Johnson, Chief Financial Officer
CMO: Madhan Prabhakaran, M.D., Chief Medical Officer
CHR: Tara Helle, Human Resources Lead
CNO: Sara Travis, Chief Nursing Officer and Assistant Administrator
Web address: https://www.mercyonenorthiowaaffiliates.org/pachs/
Control: County, Government, Nonfederal **Service**: General medical and surgical

Staffed Beds: 40 **Admissions**: 481 **Census**: 26 **Outpatient Visits**: 46792 **Births**: 73 **Total Expense ($000)**: 32028 **Payroll Expense ($000)**: 13874 **Personnel**: 245

ESTHERVILLE—Emmet County

★ **AVERA HOLY FAMILY HOSPITAL (161351)**, 826 North Eighth Street, Zip 51334-1598; tel. 712/362-2631, **A**10 18 **F**3 11 15 28 29 30 31 34 35 37 40 45 55 57 59 64 65 69 75 77 78 79 81 85 87 93 97 107 110 111 114 119 130 131 132 133 146 154 156 **P**6 **S** Avera Health, Sioux Falls, SD
Primary Contact: Deborah L. Herzberg, R.N., MS, FACHE, Chief Executive Officer
CFO: Shannon Adams, Chief Financial Officer
CMO: Anthony Cook, M.D., Chief of Staff
CHR: Janette Jensen, Manager Human Resources
CNO: Cathi Rae Scharnberg, R.N., M.P.H., Vice President Patient Services
Web address: www.avera-holyfamily.org
Control: Church operated, Nongovernment, not-for-profit **Service**: General medical and surgical

Staffed Beds: 22 **Admissions**: 423 **Census**: 5 **Outpatient Visits**: 26992 **Births**: 0 **Total Expense ($000)**: 26613 **Payroll Expense ($000)**: 10743 **Personnel**: 136

FAIRFIELD—Jefferson County

★ **JEFFERSON COUNTY HEALTH CENTER (161364)**, 2000 S Main, Zip 52556-9572, Mailing Address: P.O. Box 588, Zip 52556-0010; tel. 641/472-4111, **A**10 18 **F**1 4 11 15 16 17 28 29 30 31 40 43 45 50 57 67 68 70 72 73 75 76 77 78 79 80 81 82 85 88 89 90 93 98 102 107 111 115 119 127 128 129 132 133 143 144 148 154 166 167
Primary Contact: Bryan Hunger, Chief Executive Officer
CFO: Brent Feickert, Chief Financial Officer
CIO: Tim Belec, Chief Information Officer
CHR: Nanette Everly, Manager Human Resources and Administrative Assistant
Web address: www.jeffersoncountyhealthcenter.org
Control: County, Government, Nonfederal **Service**: General medical and surgical

Staffed Beds: 25 **Admissions**: 709 **Census**: 11 **Outpatient Visits**: 134074 **Births**: 0 **Total Expense ($000)**: 58311 **Payroll Expense ($000)**: 23565 **Personnel**: 322

FORT DODGE—Webster County

★ ⇧ **UNITYPOINT HEALTH – TRINITY REGIONAL MEDICAL CENTER (160016)**, 802 Kenyon Road, Zip 50501-5795; tel. 515/573-3101, **A**2 10 21 **F**3 11 13 15 18 20 22 26 28 29 30 31 32 34 35 38 40 43 44 45 47 49 50 53 57 59 64 68 70 75 76 77 81 82 84 85 86 87 89 93 96 101 102 104 107 108 110 111 115 118 119 120 121 123 127 129 130 135 146 147 149 150 153 156 164 165 167 169 **P**6 **S** UnityPoint Health, West Des Moines, IA
Primary Contact: Leah Glasgo, R.N., Market President, UnityPoint Health – Fort Dodge
COO: Troy Martens, Chief Operating Officer
CHR: Ted W Vaughn, Director Human Resources
CNO: Debra Shriver, R.N., MSN, Chief Nurse Executive
Web address: www.trmc.org
Control: Other not-for-profit (including NFP Corporation) **Service**: General medical and surgical

Staffed Beds: 49 **Admissions**: 3442 **Census**: 39 **Outpatient Visits**: 453152 **Births**: 462 **Total Expense ($000)**: 167870 **Payroll Expense ($000)**: 81788 **Personnel**: 511

FORT MADISON—Lee County

FORT MADISON COMMUNITY HOSPITAL See Southeast Iowa Regional Medical Center, Fort Madison Campus

GREENFIELD—Adair County

★ **ADAIR COUNTY HEALTH SYSTEM (161310)**, 609 SE Kent Street, Zip 50849-9454; tel. 641/743-2123, **A**10 18 **F**3 7 8 11 15 28 29 32 34 35 40 43 45 50 59 64 65 69 81 97 107 108 110 115 119 127 133 143 144 148 154 156 **S** MercyOne, Clive, IA
Primary Contact: Catherine Hillestad, Chief Executive Officer
CFO: Heather Shaull, Chief Financial Officer
CMO: Jessica Kennedy, D.O., Chief Medical Officer
CIO: Gary Bateman, Chief Information Technology
CHR: Angie Frankl, Director Human Resources
CNO: Cindy K Peeler, R.N., Chief Nursing Officer
Web address: www.adaircountyhealthsystem.org
Control: County, Government, Nonfederal **Service**: General medical and surgical

Staffed Beds: 4 **Admissions**: 106 **Census**: 1 **Outpatient Visits**: 36386 **Births**: 0 **Total Expense ($000)**: 18223 **Payroll Expense ($000)**: 6077 **Personnel**: 107

GRINNELL—Poweshiek County

★ ⇧ **UNITYPOINT HEALTH – GRINNELL REGIONAL MEDICAL CENTER (160147)**, 210 Fourth Avenue, Zip 50112-1898; tel. 641/236-7511, **A**10 21 **F**3 12 13 15 28 29 32 34 35 36 40 43 44 45 46 47 50 53 54 56 57 59 61 62 64 65 66 67 70 75 76 77 78 80 81 85 86 87 89 93 97 107 110 111 115 119 126 127 129 130 131 132 133 134 135 147 148 149 150 154 156 167 169 **S** UnityPoint Health, West Des Moines, IA
Primary Contact: David-Paul Cavazos, Chief Executive Officer
CIO: David L Ness, Vice President Operations
CHR: Debra S. Nowachek, Director Human Resources
CNO: Doris Rindels, Vice President Operations
Web address: www.grmc.us
Control: Other not-for-profit (including NFP Corporation) **Service**: General medical and surgical

Staffed Beds: 49 **Admissions**: 1310 **Census**: 13 **Outpatient Visits**: 91759 **Births**: 246 **Total Expense ($000)**: 64326 **Payroll Expense ($000)**: 34132 **Personnel**: 317

GRUNDY CENTER—Grundy County

★ ⇧ **GRUNDY COUNTY MEMORIAL HOSPITAL (161303)**, 201 East 'J' Avenue, Zip 50638-2096; tel. 319/824-5421, **A**10 18 21 **F**3 15 28 29 34 35 40 43 50 57 59 63 64 68 69 75 78 79 81 82 86 87 93 107 110 111 115 117 119 126 128 129 130 131 132 133 135 146 148 154 156 **S** UnityPoint Health, West Des Moines, IA
Primary Contact: Adam Scherling, President
COO: Ryan Bingman, Director Operations
CFO: Lisa Zinkula, Chief Financial Officer
CMO: Douglas Cooper, M.D., Chief Medical Officer
CIO: Steve Bantz, Manager Information Technology
CHR: Keagan Brunscheon, Manager, Human Resources
CNO: Jody Schipper, Director of Nursing
Web address: https://www.unitypoint.org
Control: County, Government, Nonfederal **Service**: General medical and surgical

Staffed Beds: 25 **Admissions**: 264 **Census**: 4 **Outpatient Visits**: 59226 **Births**: 0 **Total Expense ($000)**: 25182 **Payroll Expense ($000)**: 11206 **Personnel**: 144

Hospitals, U.S. / IOWA

GUTHRIE CENTER—Guthrie County

★ **GUTHRIE COUNTY HOSPITAL (161314)**, 710 North 12th Street, Zip 50115-1544; tel. 641/332-2201, **A**10 18 **F**11 15 18 28 29 34 35 40 43 45 53 56 57 59 64 69 75 79 81 85 93 107 110 114 119 128 130 132 133 143 148 154 156 **P**6 **S** UnityPoint Health, West Des Moines, IA
Primary Contact: Chris Stipe, Chief Executive Officer
COO: Lisa Wolfe, Chief Operating Officer
CFO: Troy Eller, Chief Financial Officer
CMO: Donald Fillman, M.D., Chief Medical Officer
CIO: Jeff Cobb, Information Technologist
CHR: Kimberly Myers, Director Human Resources
Web address: www.guthriecountyhospital.org
Control: County, Government, Nonfederal **Service**: General medical and surgical

Staffed Beds: 17 **Admissions**: 320 **Census**: 3 **Outpatient Visits**: 57294
Births: 0 **Total Expense ($000)**: 23003 **Payroll Expense ($000)**: 9679
Personnel: 176

GUTTENBERG—Clayton County

★ **GUTTENBERG MUNICIPAL HOSPITAL AND CLINICS (161312)**, 200 Main Street, Zip 52052-9108, Mailing Address: P.O. Box 550, Zip 52052-0550; tel. 563/252-1121, **A**10 18 **F**3 7 11 15 28 29 34 35 40 43 45 50 56 57 59 64 68 77 79 81 85 89 93 97 100 104 107 110 111 115 119 126 127 128 130 131 132 133 134 154 **P**6 **S** MercyOne, Clive, IA
Primary Contact: Tim Ahlers, Chief Executive Officer
COO: Lisa Manson, Director Ambulatory Services
CFO: Jill DeMoss, Finance Manager
CMO: Chris Hugo, M.D., Chief of Staff
CIO: Scott R Pauls, Director Information Technology- HealthNet Connect
CHR: Chelsea Greene, Manager Human Resources
Web address: www.guttenberghospital.org
Control: City, Government, Nonfederal **Service**: General medical and surgical

Staffed Beds: 18 **Admissions**: 253 **Census**: 4 **Outpatient Visits**: 54206
Births: 0 **Total Expense ($000)**: 24095 **Payroll Expense ($000)**: 11514
Personnel: 153

HAMBURG—Fremont County

GEORGE C. GRAPE COMMUNITY HOSPITAL (161324), 2959 US Highway 275, Zip 51640-5067; tel. 712/382-1515, (Total facility includes 6 beds in nursing home–type unit) **A**10 18 **F**7 14 15 18 28 31 34 35 40 43 45 50 53 57 59 62 64 65 68 74 75 77 78 79 81 82 85 91 93 107 110 115 119 128 129 130 133 135 148 154
Primary Contact: Cristin Hendrickson, Chief Executive Officer
CFO: Hilary Christiansen, Chief Financial Officer
CMO: Kelli Woltemath, D.O., Chief Medical Staff
CIO: Craig Wells, Chief Information Officer
CHR: Jackie Wertz, Director Human Resources
CNO: Gloria Mattice, R.N., Director Patient Care
Web address: www.grapehospital.com
Control: Other not–for–profit (including NFP Corporation) **Service**: General medical and surgical

Staffed Beds: 25 **Admissions**: 127 **Census**: 2 **Outpatient Visits**: 13308
Births: 0 **Total Expense ($000)**: 14609 **Payroll Expense ($000)**: 5434
Personnel: 134

HAMPTON—Franklin County

★ **FRANKLIN GENERAL HOSPITAL (161308)**, 1720 Central Avenue East, Suite A, Zip 50441-1867; tel. 641/456-5000, (Total facility includes 52 beds in nursing home–type unit) **A**10 18 **F**3 7 10 11 15 28 30 34 40 43 57 59 63 64 65 67 68 75 77 81 82 85 86 89 90 93 103 107 111 115 119 127 128 129 130 131 132 133 135 146 147 148 154 156 **S** Trinity Health, Livonia, MI
Primary Contact: Kim Price, Chief Executive Officer
CFO: Lee Elbert, Chief Financial Officer
CHR: Victoria Kruse, Manager Human Resources
CNO: Ronda Reimer, Chief Nursing Officer and Assistant Administrator
Web address: www.franklingeneral.com
Control: County, Government, Nonfederal **Service**: General medical and surgical

Staffed Beds: 77 **Admissions**: 355 **Census**: 43 **Outpatient Visits**: 33063
Births: 0 **Total Expense ($000)**: 25582 **Payroll Expense ($000)**: 8097
Personnel: 165

HARLAN—Shelby County

★ **MYRTUE MEDICAL CENTER (161374)**, 1213 Garfield Avenue, Zip 51537-2057; tel. 712/755-5161, **A**10 18 **F**3 4 5 11 13 15 28 29 31 32 34 35 38 40 43 45 46 50 53 56 57 59 62 63 64 65 68 75 76 77 78 79 81 85 87 92 93 97 99 101 102 103 104 107 110 115 119 127 128 129 130 131 132 133 135 146 148 154 156 157 162 164 165 **P**6
Primary Contact: Barry Jacobsen, CPA, Chief Executive Officer
CFO: Kristy Hansen, CPA, Chief Financial Officer
CMO: Sarah M. Devine, M.D., Chief of Staff
CIO: Jeffrey Sundholm, Chief Information Officer
CHR: Jill Mages, Chief Human Resource Officer
CNO: Karen Buman, MSN, Chief Nursing Officer
Web address: www.myrtuemedical.org
Control: County, Government, Nonfederal **Service**: General medical and surgical

Staffed Beds: 25 **Admissions**: 759 **Census**: 7 **Outpatient Visits**: 134580
Births: 91 **Total Expense ($000)**: 52831 **Payroll Expense ($000)**: 21057
Personnel: 378

HAWARDEN—Sioux County

★ **HAWARDEN REGIONAL HEALTHCARE (161311)**, 1111 11th Street, Zip 51023-1999; tel. 712/551-3100, **A**10 18 **F**3 11 15 28 29 35 40 43 45 57 59 64 65 68 75 77 79 81 82 85 87 93 97 102 107 110 115 127 128 129 130 131 132 133 148 154 156 **S** Trinity Health, Livonia, MI
Primary Contact: Jayson Pullman, Chief Executive Officer
CFO: Jessica Hughes, Director Finance
CMO: Dale Nystrom, M.D., Chief Medical Officer, Physician
CHR: Maggie Hofer, Human Resources Representative
Web address: www.hawardenregionalhealthcare.com/
Control: City, Government, Nonfederal **Service**: General medical and surgical

Staffed Beds: 14 **Admissions**: 258 **Census**: 4 **Outpatient Visits**: 29304
Births: 0 **Total Expense ($000)**: 17531 **Payroll Expense ($000)**: 5727
Personnel: 103

HUMBOLDT—Humboldt County

★ **HUMBOLDT COUNTY MEMORIAL HOSPITAL (161334)**, 1000 North 15th Street, Zip 50548-1008; tel. 515/332-4200, (Total facility includes 28 beds in nursing home–type unit) **A**10 18 **F**7 8 10 11 12 14 15 28 29 34 35 40 41 43 45 47 50 59 62 63 64 65 68 75 77 81 82 85 93 96 102 107 110 115 119 128 129 130 133 135 156 167 **S** UnityPoint Health, West Des Moines, IA
Primary Contact: Michelle Sleiter, Chief Executive Officer
CFO: AJ Mason, Chief Financial Officer
CHR: Mary Moritz, Administrator Human Resources
Web address: www.humboldthospital.org
Control: County, Government, Nonfederal **Service**: General medical and surgical

Staffed Beds: 49 **Admissions**: 457 **Census**: 31 **Outpatient Visits**: 124152
Births: 0 **Total Expense ($000)**: 28303 **Payroll Expense ($000)**: 12028
Personnel: 249

IDA GROVE—Ida County

★ **HORN MEMORIAL HOSPITAL (161354)**, 701 East Second Street, Zip 51445-1699; tel. 712/364-3311, **A**10 18 **F**11 15 28 29 34 35 40 43 44 45 50 57 59 62 63 64 65 66 68 75 77 79 81 82 85 86 87 89 93 97 100 107 108 110 111 115 117 119 127 128 129 130 131 132 133 146 147 148 149 154 **P**6
Primary Contact: Glen Winekauf, Chief Executive Officer
CFO: Marcia Fehring, Chief Financial Officer
CIO: Robbie Todd, Director Information Technology
CHR: Lorraine Davis, Vice President Human Resources
CNO: Jo Hayes, Chief Nursing Officer
Web address: www.hornmemorialhospital.org
Control: Other not–for–profit (including NFP Corporation) **Service**: General medical and surgical

Staffed Beds: 20 **Admissions**: 224 **Census**: 4 **Outpatient Visits**: 50331
Births: 0 **Total Expense ($000)**: 28495 **Payroll Expense ($000)**: 11287
Personnel: 180

Hospitals, U.S. / IOWA

INDEPENDENCE—Buchanan County

★ **BUCHANAN COUNTY HEALTH CENTER (161335)**, 1600 First Street East, Zip 50644-3155; tel. 319/332-0999, (Total facility includes 39 beds in nursing home–type unit) **A**10 18 **F**3 11 15 28 29 32 34 35 40 43 45 50 53 56 57 59 64 65 67 75 77 79 81 82 84 85 86 87 91 93 97 101 104 107 110 111 114 119 125 127 128 129 130 131 132 133 135 144 146 148 154 156 160 165 167 **P**6
Primary Contact: Wade Weis, Chief Executive Officer
CFO: Tony Fortmann, Chief Financial Officer
CNO: Rachel Goldenstein, R.N., Chief Nursing Officer
Web address: https://bchealth.org/
Control: County, Government, Nonfederal **Service**: General medical and surgical

| **Staffed Beds**: 58 **Admissions**: 236 **Census**: 36 **Outpatient Visits**: 96260 **Births**: 0 **Total Expense ($000)**: 51016 **Payroll Expense ($000)**: 19772 **Personnel**: 295 |

☐ **INDEPENDENCE MENTAL HEALTH INSTITUTE (164003)**, 2277 Iowa Avenue, Zip 50644-9106; tel. 319/334-2583, (Nonreporting) **A**1 10
Primary Contact: Bhasker J. Dave, M.D., Superintendent
CFO: Kevin Jimmerson, Business Manager
CMO: Bhasker J Dave, M.D., Superintendent
Web address: https://dhs.iowa.gov/mhds/mental-health/in-patient/mental-health-institutes/independence
Control: State, Government, Nonfederal **Service**: Psychiatric

| **Staffed Beds**: 56 |

IOWA CITY—Johnson County

⊞ **IOWA CITY VA HEALTH SYSTEM**, 601 Highway 6 West, Zip 52246-2208; tel. 319/338-0581, (Nonreporting) **A**1 3 5 **S** Department of Veterans Affairs, Washington, DC
Primary Contact: Judith Johnson-Mekota, FACHE, Director
COO: Kevin Kosek, Associate Director Operations
CFO: Jennifer Ruppert, Chief Financial Officer
CMO: Richard A Charlat, Chief of Staff
CIO: Dwight Schuessler, Chief Information Officer
CHR: Dan Helle, Human Resources Officer
CNO: Dawn Oxley, R.N., Associate Director Patient Care Services and Nurse Executive
Web address: www.iowacity.va.gov/
Control: Veterans Affairs, Government, federal **Service**: General medical and surgical

| **Staffed Beds**: 66 |

MERCYONE IOWA CITY See University of Iowa Health Care Medical Center Downtown

UNIVERSITY HOSPITAL SCHOOL See Center For Disabilities and Development

UNIVERSITY OF IOWA CHILDREN'S HOSPITAL See University of Iowa Stead Family Children's Hospital

⊞ **UNIVERSITY OF IOWA HEALTH CARE MEDICAL CENTER DOWNTOWN (160029)**, 500 East Market Street, Zip 52245-2689; tel. 319/688-7525, (Nonreporting) **A**1 10 **S** University of Iowa Health Care, Iowa City, IA
Primary Contact: Jennifer Miller, Chief Administrative Officer
CFO: Douglas Davenport, Interim Chief Financial Officer
CMO: Martin Izakovic, M.D., Vice President Medical Staff Affairs and Chief Medical Officer
CHR: Dena M Brockhouse, Director Human Resources
CNO: Cindy L Penney, R.N., Vice President Nursing
Web address: www.mercyiowacity.org
Control: Church operated, Nongovernment, not-for-profit **Service**: General medical and surgical

| **Staffed Beds**: 194 |

⊞ **UNIVERSITY OF IOWA HOSPITALS & CLINICS (160058)**, 200 Hawkins Drive, Zip 52242-1009; tel. 319/356-1616, (Includes CENTER FOR DISABILITIES AND DEVELOPMENT, 200 Hawkins Drive, Iowa City, Iowa, Zip 52242, tel. 319/356-1347; CHEMICAL DEPENDENCY CENTER, 200 Hawkins Drive, Iowa City, Iowa, Zip 52242-1007, tel. 319/384-8765; STATE PSYCHIATRIC HOSPITAL, 200 Hawkins Drive, Iowa City, Iowa, Zip 52242, tel. 319/356-4658; UNIVERSITY OF IOWA STEAD FAMILY CHILDREN'S HOSPITAL, 200 Hawkins Drive, Iowa City, Iowa, Zip 52242-1009, tel. 888/573-5437; Jim Leste, Chief Administrative Officer) **A**1 2 3 5 8 10 19 **F**3 4 5 6 7 8 9 11 12 13 14 15 16 17 18 19 20 21 22 23 24 25 26 27 28 29 30 31 32 33 34 35 36 37 38 39 40 41 43 44 45 46 47 48 49 50 51 52 53 54 55 56 57 58 59 60 61 62 63 64 65 66 68 70 72 73 74 75 76 77 78 79 80 81 82 83 84 85 86 87 88 89 90 91 92 93 94 96 97 98 99 100 101 102 103 104 105 106 107 108 109 110 111 114 115 116 117 118 119 120 121 123 124 126 127 129 130 131 132 135 136 137 138 139 140 141 142 143 144 145 146 147 148 151 152 153 154 155 156 160 161 162 163 164 165 167 169 **P**1 **S** University of Iowa Health Care, Iowa City, IA
Primary Contact: Bradley Haws, Chief Executive Officer
COO: Jody Reyes, R.N., Chief Operating Officer, Clinical Enterprise
CFO: Mark Henrichs, Chief Financial Officer
CMO: Theresa Brennan, M.D., Chief Medical Officer
CIO: Lee Carmen, Associate Vice President Health Care Information Systems
CHR: Jana Wessels, Associate Vice President Human Resources
CNO: Kimberly D. Hunter, MSN, R.N., Chief Nurse Executive
Web address: www.uihealthcare.org
Control: State, Government, Nonfederal **Service**: General medical and surgical

| **Staffed Beds**: 810 **Admissions**: 30705 **Census**: 664 **Outpatient Visits**: 1659225 **Births**: 3072 **Total Expense ($000)**: 2433943 **Payroll Expense ($000)**: 676132 **Personnel**: 9975 |

UNIVERSITY OF IOWA HOSPITALS AND CLINICS See University of Iowa Hospitals & Clinics

IOWA FALLS—Hardin County

★ **HANSEN FAMILY HOSPITAL (161380)**, 920 South Oak, Zip 50126-9506; tel. 641/648-4631, **A**10 18 **F**3 7 11 15 18 28 29 30 33 34 40 41 43 45 50 53 57 59 64 65 75 77 81 82 85 86 87 89 93 97 100 102 104 107 110 115 119 127 128 129 131 133 135 146 149 156 **S** Trinity Health, Livonia, MI
Primary Contact: George Von Mock, Chief Executive Officer/Administrator
CFO: Mike White, Chief Financial Officer
CMO: George Pfaltzgraff, Chief Medical Officer
CHR: Cheri Geitz, Director Human Resources
CNO: Katie Rieks, Chief Nursing Officer
Web address: www.hansenfamilyhospital.com
Control: City, Government, Nonfederal **Service**: General medical and surgical

| **Staffed Beds**: 21 **Admissions**: 222 **Census**: 3 **Outpatient Visits**: 53938 **Births**: 0 **Total Expense ($000)**: 31756 **Payroll Expense ($000)**: 9550 **Personnel**: 161 |

JEFFERSON—Greene County

★ **GREENE COUNTY MEDICAL CENTER (161325)**, 1000 West Lincolnway, Zip 50129-1645; tel. 515/386-2114, (Total facility includes 60 beds in nursing home–type unit) **A**10 18 **F**3 11 15 18 28 29 31 32 34 35 36 40 46 50 55 56 57 59 63 64 65 67 68 75 77 79 81 82 85 89 93 97 101 104 107 110 114 119 125 127 128 130 131 132 133 146 147 149 150 154 156 **S** UnityPoint Health, West Des Moines, IA
Primary Contact: Chad Butterfield, Chief Executive Officer
COO: Christa Simons, Chief Operating Officer
CFO: Heather Paris, Chief Administrator Officer and Chief Financial Officer
CMO: Michael Line, Chief Medical Officer
CIO: Roger Overby, Executive Director Information Systems
CHR: Cathy Krieger, Human Resources Director
Web address: www.gcmchealth.com
Control: County, Government, Nonfederal **Service**: General medical and surgical

| **Staffed Beds**: 77 **Admissions**: 176 **Census**: 7 **Outpatient Visits**: 31661 **Births**: 0 **Total Expense ($000)**: 30362 **Payroll Expense ($000)**: 11356 **Personnel**: 180 |

KEOSAUQUA—Van Buren County

★ **VAN BUREN COUNTY HOSPITAL (161337)**, 304 Franklin Street, Zip 52565-1164; tel. 319/293-3171, **A**10 18 **F**3 7 11 15 18 28 29 32 34 35 40 43 45 50 56 57 59 64 65 74 75 77 81 82 87 89 93 97 102 107 110 115 119 127 128 130 132 133 135 143 147 148 154 156 157 169 **P**6 **S** MercyOne, Clive, IA
Primary Contact: Garen Carpenter, Chief Executive Officer
CFO: Kara McEntee, Chief Financial Officer
CIO: Chris McEntee, Network Specialist
CNO: Rhonda Fellows, R.N., Chief Nursing Officer
Web address: www.vbch.org
Control: County, Government, Nonfederal **Service**: General medical and surgical

| **Staffed Beds**: 10 **Admissions**: 332 **Census**: 4 **Outpatient Visits**: 24651 **Births**: 0 **Total Expense ($000)**: 22473 **Payroll Expense ($000)**: 10531 **Personnel**: 167 |

Hospitals, U.S. / IOWA

KNOXVILLE—Marion County

DEPT OF VETERANS AFF MED CTR See Knoxville Division

KNOXVILLE DIVISION See VA Central Iowa Health Care System–Des Moines, Des Moines

★ **KNOXVILLE HOSPITAL & CLINICS (161355)**, 1002 South Lincoln Street, Zip 50138-3155; tel. 641/842-2151, **A**10 18 **F**3 8 11 15 28 29 31 40 43 45 47 48 49 50 54 57 59 64 65 75 78 79 81 82 85 87 92 97 107 108 110 111 114 119 129 132 133 144 146 148 154 169 **P**6
Primary Contact: Kevin Kincaid, Chief Executive Officer
CFO: Maggie Hamilton–Beyer, Chief Financial Officer
CMO: Brent Hoehns, M.D., Chief of Medical Staff
CIO: Thom Richards, Director Information Technology
CNO: Jan M Myers, Chief Nursing Officer
Web address: www.knoxvillehospital.org
Control: Other not–for–profit (including NFP Corporation) **Service**: General medical and surgical

> **Staffed Beds**: 25 **Admissions**: 531 **Census**: 5 **Outpatient Visits**: 109659
> **Births**: 0 **Total Expense ($000)**: 44692 **Payroll Expense ($000)**: 16498
> **Personnel**: 259

LAKE CITY—Calhoun County

★ **STEWART MEMORIAL COMMUNITY HOSPITAL (161350)**, 1301 West Main, Zip 51449-1585; tel. 712/464-3171, **A**10 18 **F**3 7 11 12 13 15 28 29 30 31 34 40 43 45 50 59 64 65 69 70 75 78 79 81 82 86 89 93 94 107 110 115 119 127 130 133 135 147 154 156 169 **P**6 **S** UnityPoint Health, West Des Moines, IA
Primary Contact: Linn Block, Chief Executive Officer
CFO: Jim Henkenius, Chief Financial Officer
CHR: Bill Albright, Director Human Resources
Web address: www.stewartmemorial.org
Control: Other not–for–profit (including NFP Corporation) **Service**: General medical and surgical

> **Staffed Beds**: 25 **Admissions**: 346 **Census**: 3 **Outpatient Visits**: 45991
> **Births**: 86 **Total Expense ($000)**: 37288 **Payroll Expense ($000)**: 17521
> **Personnel**: 221

LE MARS—Plymouth County

★ **FLOYD VALLEY HEALTHCARE (161368)**, 714 Lincoln Street NE, Zip 51031-3314; tel. 712/546-7871, **A**10 18 **F**3 10 11 13 15 28 29 31 32 34 35 40 43 45 50 57 59 62 64 65 68 76 78 81 85 86 87 90 93 107 110 111 115 119 128 129 130 132 133 135 146 148 154 156 157 160 167 169 **S** Avera Health, Sioux Falls, SD
Primary Contact: Dustin Wright, Chief Executive Officer
CFO: Daryl Friedenbach, Director Fiscal Services
CMO: Andrew Geha, D.O., President Medical Staff
CIO: Jacob Jorgensen, Chief Information Officer
CHR: Mary Helen Gibson, Director Human Resources
CNO: Lorrie Mortensen, MSN, R.N., Director, Patient Care
Web address: www.floydvalley.org
Control: City, Government, Nonfederal **Service**: General medical and surgical

> **Staffed Beds**: 25 **Admissions**: 553 **Census**: 5 **Outpatient Visits**: 91961
> **Births**: 101 **Total Expense ($000)**: 47727 **Payroll Expense ($000)**: 19346
> **Personnel**: 336

LEON—Decatur County

DECATUR COUNTY HOSPITAL (161340), 1405 NW Church Street, Zip 50144-1299; tel. 641/446-4871, **A**10 18 **F**3 7 11 28 29 31 34 35 40 41 45 50 56 57 59 64 68 69 71 74 75 78 79 81 82 85 93 102 104 107 111 114 117 119 130 132 133 143 146 148 149 154 157 **P**6 **S** MercyOne, Clive, IA
Primary Contact: Mike Johnston, Chief Executive Officer
CFO: Tara Spidle, Chief Financial Officer
CMO: Ed Wehling, Chief Medical Staff
CHR: Jo Beth Smith, Vice President Human Resources
Web address: www.decaturcountyhospital.org
Control: County, Government, Nonfederal **Service**: General medical and surgical

> **Staffed Beds**: 11 **Admissions**: 249 **Census**: 3 **Outpatient Visits**: 32620
> **Births**: 0 **Total Expense ($000)**: 22609 **Payroll Expense ($000)**: 7079
> **Personnel**: 107

MANCHESTER—Delaware County

★ **REGIONAL MEDICAL CENTER (161343)**, 709 West Main Street, Zip 52057-1526, Mailing Address: P.O. Box 359, Zip 52057-0359; tel. 563/927-3232, **A**5 10 18 **F**3 7 11 13 15 17 28 29 34 35 36 40 43 44 50 53 57 59 61 62 64 65 66 68 70 75 76 77 79 81 82 85 86 89 93 94 97 100 104 107 110 111 114 119 126 127 128 129 130 131 132 133 144 146 148 153 154 162 169 **P**6
Primary Contact: Danette Kramer, Chief Executive Officer
COO: Amy Mensen, Chief Operating Officer
CFO: Danette Kramer, Chief Financial Officer
CNO: Heather Ries, Chief Nursing Officer
Web address: www.regmedctr.org
Control: County, Government, Nonfederal **Service**: General medical and surgical

> **Staffed Beds**: 25 **Admissions**: 740 **Census**: 6 **Outpatient Visits**: 192424
> **Births**: 248 **Total Expense ($000)**: 67285 **Payroll Expense ($000)**: 31490
> **Personnel**: 412

MANNING—Carroll County

★ **MANNING REGIONAL HEALTHCARE CENTER (161332)**, 1550 6th Street, Zip 51455-1093; tel. 712/655-2072, **A**10 18 **F**3 4 5 11 15 18 29 31 32 34 35 40 45 50 56 57 59 64 65 75 78 81 82 85 93 97 100 104 107 114 119 128 129 130 132 133 135 147 148 149 152 153 154 156 157 160 169 **P**6 **S** MercyOne, Clive, IA
Primary Contact: Shannon Black, Chief Executive Officer
CFO: Amy McLaughlin, CPA, Chief Financial Officer
CMO: Douglas McLaws, D.O., Chief Medical Officer
CIO: Kim C Jahn, Chief Plant Operations and Chief Information Officer
CHR: Shelli Lorenzen, Chief Human Resources Officer
CNO: Michelle Andersen, R.N., Chief Nursing Officer
Web address: www.mrhcia.com
Control: Other not–for–profit (including NFP Corporation) **Service**: General medical and surgical

> **Staffed Beds**: 25 **Admissions**: 145 **Census**: 2 **Outpatient Visits**: 26003
> **Births**: 0 **Total Expense ($000)**: 17870 **Payroll Expense ($000)**: 6937
> **Personnel**: 120

MAQUOKETA—Jackson County

✠ **JACKSON COUNTY REGIONAL HEALTH CENTER (161329)**, 601 Hospital Dr, Zip 52060; tel. 563/652-2474, **A**1 10 18 **F**3 7 11 15 28 34 40 43 45 50 53 64 75 81 82 85 87 93 107 110 114 119 128 129 133 146 148 156 **S** Trinity Health, Livonia, MI
Primary Contact: Patrick Peters, Administrator/Chief Executive Officer
CFO: Donna Roeder, Chief Financial Officer
CHR: Shannon Langenberg, Director Human Resources
Web address: www.jcrhc.org
Control: County, Government, Nonfederal **Service**: General medical and surgical

> **Staffed Beds**: 12 **Admissions**: 189 **Census**: 3 **Outpatient Visits**: 18424
> **Births**: 0 **Total Expense ($000)**: 21487 **Payroll Expense ($000)**: 7308
> **Personnel**: 129

MARENGO—Iowa County

★ **COMPASS MEMORIAL HEALTHCARE (161317)**, 300 West May Street, Zip 52301-1261; tel. 319/642-5543, **A**10 18 **F**3 8 15 28 29 31 34 35 38 40 43 45 50 59 64 65 67 75 77 78 79 81 85 87 89 93 96 97 107 110 111 115 127 128 130 131 132 133 146 148 154 169 **P**6 **S** UnityPoint Health, West Des Moines, IA
Primary Contact: Barry Goettsch, FACHE, Chief Executive Officer
COO: Mikaela Gehring, Chief Operating Officer
CFO: Matthew Murphy, Chief Financial Officer
CHR: Lesa Waddell, Director Human Resources
CNO: Teresa Sauerbrei, Chief Nursing Officer
Web address: www.compassmemorial.org
Control: Other not–for–profit (including NFP Corporation) **Service**: General medical and surgical

> **Staffed Beds**: 25 **Admissions**: 332 **Census**: 3 **Outpatient Visits**: 40335
> **Births**: 0 **Total Expense ($000)**: 37510 **Payroll Expense ($000)**: 15525
> **Personnel**: 225

Hospital, Medicare Provider Number, Address, Telephone, Approval, Facility, and Physician Codes, Health Care System

★ American Hospital Association (AHA) membership ○ Healthcare Facilities Accreditation Program ⇑ Center for Improvement in Healthcare Quality Accreditation
☐ The Joint Commission accreditation ◇ DNV Healthcare Inc. accreditation △ Commission on Accreditation of Rehabilitation Facilities (CARF) accreditation

Hospitals, U.S. / IOWA

MARSHALLTOWN—Marshall County

★ ⇧ **UNITYPOINT HEALTH – MARSHALLTOWN (160001)**, 55 UnityPoint Way, Zip 50158-4749; tel. 641/754-5151, **A**10 21 **F**3 7 11 12 15 28 29 30 40 43 50 64 68 69 75 79 81 82 85 86 87 102 107 108 110 111 114 115 119 127 129 130 135 146 148 149 154 156 167 **P**6 **S** UnityPoint Health, West Des Moines, IA
Primary Contact: Jenni Friedly, Market President, UnityPoint Health – Waterloo
CMO: Russell Adams, M.D., Chief Medical Officer
CHR: Jill Petermeier, Senior Executive Human Resources
Web address: https://marshalltown.unitypoint.org
Control: Other not–for–profit (including NFP Corporation) **Service:** General medical and surgical

Staffed Beds: 16 **Admissions:** 840 **Census:** 9 **Outpatient Visits:** 222183 **Births:** 0 **Total Expense ($000):** 73481 **Payroll Expense ($000):** 33206 **Personnel:** 341

MASON CITY—Cerro Gordo County

✣ **MERCYONE NORTH IOWA MEDICAL CENTER (160064)**, 1000 Fourth Street SW, Zip 50401-2800; tel. 641/428-7000, (Total facility includes 26 beds in nursing home-type unit) **A**1 3 5 10 13 **F**3 4 5 11 12 13 15 18 20 22 24 26 28 29 30 31 32 34 35 37 40 43 45 50 51 53 54 55 56 57 58 59 61 62 63 64 68 69 70 71 72 74 75 76 77 78 79 81 82 84 85 86 87 89 90 91 92 93 97 98 99 100 101 102 103 104 107 108 110 111 115 116 117 118 119 120 121 123 124 126 127 128 129 130 131 135 143 146 147 148 149 151 153 154 156 157 162 164 167 169 **P**1 6 **S** Trinity Health, Livonia, MI
Primary Contact: Chad Boore, Chief Operations Officer
COO: Diane Fischels, Senior Vice President and Chief Operating Officer
CMO: Paul Manternach, M.D., Senior Vice President Physician Integration and Chief Medical Officer
CIO: Terry Chartier, Director, Information Systems
CHR: Julie Kline, Chief Human Resource Officer
CNO: Kim Chamberlin, Vice President Patient Services and Chief Nursing Officer
Web address: www.mercynorthiowa.com
Control: Church operated, Nongovernment, not–for–profit **Service:** General medical and surgical

Staffed Beds: 238 **Admissions:** 9181 **Census:** 130 **Outpatient Visits:** 436964 **Births:** 709 **Total Expense ($000):** 501303 **Payroll Expense ($000):** 189657 **Personnel:** 1859

MISSOURI VALLEY—Harrison County

★ **CHI HEALTH MISSOURI VALLEY (161309)**, 631 North Eighth Street, Zip 51555-1102; tel. 712/642-2784, **A**10 18 **F**3 34 40 43 55 64 65 81 97 100 104 107 108 109 110 111 112 113 114 115 116 117 118 119 120 121 122 123 124 126 127 129 130 133 135 145 146 154 167 **S** CommonSpirit Health, Chicago, IL
Primary Contact: David J. Jones, Market President, Critical Access Hospitals (NE, IA, MN)
CMO: Daniel Richter, M.D., Chief of Staff
CIO: Ravae Smallwood, IS Coordinator
CHR: Heidi Winters, Business Partner Human Resources
CNO: Darcy Behrendt, R.N., Vice President, Patient Care Services
Web address: www.chihealth.com/chi-health-missouri-valley
Control: Other not–for–profit (including NFP Corporation) **Service:** General medical and surgical

Staffed Beds: 12 **Admissions:** 352 **Census:** 7 **Outpatient Visits:** 32480 **Births:** 0 **Total Expense ($000):** 22923 **Payroll Expense ($000):** 8813 **Personnel:** 78

MOUNT AYR—Ringgold County

RINGGOLD COUNTY HOSPITAL (161373), 504 North Cleveland Street, Zip 50854-2201; tel. 641/464-3226, **A**10 18 **F**3 7 15 28 29 31 34 36 40 43 45 50 59 65 81 82 85 87 93 97 100 107 110 119 127 133 135 148 154 156 157 169 **P**6 **S** MercyOne, Clive, IA
Primary Contact: Nicholle Gilbertson, Chief Executive Officer
CFO: Teresa Roberts, Chief Financial Officer
CIO: Beth Kosman, Director Health Information Management
CHR: Mitzi Hymbaugh, Chief Personnel
Web address: www.rchmtayr.org
Control: County, Government, Nonfederal **Service:** General medical and surgical

Staffed Beds: 16 **Admissions:** 218 **Census:** 3 **Outpatient Visits:** 42110 **Births:** 0 **Total Expense ($000):** 26476 **Payroll Expense ($000):** 10866 **Personnel:** 133

MOUNT PLEASANT—Henry County

★ **HENRY COUNTY HEALTH CENTER (161356)**, 407 South White Street, Zip 52641-2263; tel. 319/385-3141, (Total facility includes 49 beds in nursing home-type unit) **A**10 18 **F**3 15 28 29 31 34 35 40 41 43 45 50 53 59 64 70 75 78 79 81 86 87 89 93 97 104 107 108 110 115 118 119 127 128 130 131 132 133 146 147 154 156 169
Primary Contact: Teresa Colgan, Chief Executive Officer
CFO: David Muhs, Chief Financial Officer
CMO: Joel Ryon, M.D., Chief of Staff
CHR: Lynn Humphreys, Director Human Resources
Web address: www.hchc.org
Control: Other not–for–profit (including NFP Corporation) **Service:** General medical and surgical

Staffed Beds: 74 **Admissions:** 298 **Census:** 32 **Outpatient Visits:** 48172 **Births:** 0 **Total Expense ($000):** 41025 **Payroll Expense ($000):** 16001 **Personnel:** 212

MUSCATINE—Muscatine County

★ ⇧ **UNITYPOINT HEALTH – TRINITY MUSCATINE (160013)**, 1518 Mulberry Avenue, Zip 52761-3499; tel. 563/264-9100, **A**5 10 20 21 **F**5 11 15 18 28 29 34 38 40 43 45 50 56 59 61 64 65 66 68 69 75 81 85 87 97 102 107 108 110 111 114 119 127 129 130 131 134 147 148 149 154 156 **S** UnityPoint Health, West Des Moines, IA
Primary Contact: Shawn Morrow, FACHE, Market President, UnityPoint Health – Quad Cities
COO: Barbara Weber, Chief Operating Officer
CFO: Katie A Marchik, Vice President, Consolidated Services, UnityPoint Health and Chief Financial Officer, Trinity Regional Health System
CMO: Manasi Nadkarni, M.D., Vice President Medical Affairs
CIO: Sean Liddell, Manager Regional Service Information Technology
CHR: Karla Blaser, Director Human Resources
CNO: Pam Askew, R.N., Vice President Patient Care Services
Web address: www.unitypoint.org/quadcities/trinity-muscatine.aspx
Control: Other not–for–profit (including NFP Corporation) **Service:** General medical and surgical

Staffed Beds: 24 **Admissions:** 901 **Census:** 7 **Outpatient Visits:** 74416 **Births:** 0 **Total Expense ($000):** 56085 **Payroll Expense ($000):** 16466 **Personnel:** 271

NEVADA—Story County

★ ⇧ **STORY COUNTY MEDICAL CENTER (161333)**, 640 South 19th Street, Zip 50201-2902; tel. 515/382-2111, **A**10 18 21 **F**3 7 11 28 29 32 34 35 36 40 43 50 53 57 59 64 65 71 75 77 81 85 87 97 100 107 114 116 119 127 130 133 146 147 154 **S** UnityPoint Health, West Des Moines, IA
Primary Contact: Nathan Thompson, Chief Executive Officer
CFO: Jane Ramthun, Chief Financial Officer
CMO: Arthur Check, M.D., Chief Medical Officer
CHR: Jessica Lingo, Human Resource Generalist
CNO: Beth Rehbein, Chief Nursing and Quality Officer
Web address: www.storymedical.org
Control: County, Government, Nonfederal **Service:** General medical and surgical

Staffed Beds: 17 **Admissions:** 219 **Census:** 6 **Outpatient Visits:** 63116 **Births:** 0 **Total Expense ($000):** 29695 **Payroll Expense ($000):** 12675 **Personnel:** 160

NEW HAMPTON—Chickasaw County

★ **MERCYONE NEW HAMPTON MEDICAL CENTER (161331)**, 308 North Maple Avenue, Zip 50659-1142; tel. 641/394-4121, **A**10 18 **F**3 15 28 34 35 40 43 45 48 50 56 59 64 65 68 77 79 81 85 91 92 93 97 107 110 115 119 131 133 146 149 154 **S** Trinity Health, Livonia, MI
Primary Contact: Aaron Flugum, Chief Executive Officer
CFO: Jennifer Rapenske, Manager Financial Services
CMO: Daniel Paul McQuillen, M.D., Chief of Medical Staff
CIO: Terry Chartier, Director, Information Systems
CNO: Cheryl Kay Haggerty, Chief Nursing Officer, Assistant Chief Executive Officer
Web address: www.mercynewhampton.com
Control: Church operated, Nongovernment, not–for–profit **Service:** General medical and surgical

Staffed Beds: 11 **Admissions:** 273 **Census:** 4 **Outpatient Visits:** 22398 **Births:** 0 **Total Expense ($000):** 19428 **Payroll Expense ($000):** 9406 **Personnel:** 99

NEWTON—Jasper County

★ **MERCYONE NEWTON MEDICAL CENTER (160032)**, 204 North Fourth Avenue East, Zip 50208–3100; tel. 641/792–1273, **A**10 **F**3 11 13 15 17 28 29 30 31 34 35 40 43 44 45 50 57 59 63 64 70 75 76 77 78 79 81 82 85 89 90 93 94 96 107 108 110 111 115 119 128 129 130 131 132 133 145 146 147 148 149 154 169 **S** Trinity Health, Livonia, MI
Primary Contact: Chad Kelley, Chief Operating Officer
CMO: Holly Melahoures, D.O., Chief Medical Officer
CIO: Heather Wolf, Manager Human Resources, Employee Health, InformationTechnology, Support Servicess
CHR: Heather Wolf, Manager Human Resources, Employee Health, Information Technology, Support Services
CNO: Melissa Doehrmann, Director Patient Care Services
Web address: www.skiffmed.com
Control: Other not–for–profit (including NFP Corporation) **Service**: General medical and surgical

Staffed Beds: 34 **Admissions**: 680 **Census**: 6 **Outpatient Visits**: 94617
Births: 112 **Total Expense ($000)**: 40525 **Payroll Expense ($000)**: 11302
Personnel: 183

OELWEIN—Fayette County

★ **MERCYONE OELWEIN MEDICAL CENTER (161338)**, 201 Eighth Avenue SE, Zip 50662–2447; tel. 319/283–6000, **A**10 18 **F**1 3 4 7 11 15 16 17 28 29 30 34 35 40 57 59 67 69 70 73 75 76 79 80 88 89 90 93 97 98 107 110 111 119 127 128 130 132 133 146 147 166 **S** Trinity Health, Livonia, MI
Primary Contact: Ryan Meyer, Chief Operating Officer
CFO: Timothy Huber, Vice President Finance
CMO: Matthew Sojka, M.D., Vice President Medical Affairs
CHR: Suzanne M. Burt, Chief Human Resources Officer
CNO: Kelly Richards, Vice President and Chief Nursing Officer
Web address: www.wheatoniowa.org
Control: Church operated, Nongovernment, not–for–profit **Service**: General medical and surgical

Staffed Beds: 56 **Admissions**: 207 **Census**: 3 **Outpatient Visits**: 20089
Births: 0 **Total Expense ($000)**: 14618 **Payroll Expense ($000)**: 5813
Personnel: 100

ONAWA—Monona County

★ **BURGESS HEALTH CENTER (161359)**, 1600 Diamond Street, Zip 51040–1548; tel. 712/423–2311, **A**10 18 **F**3 7 11 15 28 29 31 32 34 35 40 45 50 53 56 57 59 62 63 64 65 68 75 77 78 79 80 81 82 85 93 97 100 104 107 110 111 115 119 127 130 132 133 135 146 147 148 149 154 156 167 **P**6
Primary Contact: Lynn Wold, Chief Executive Officer
CFO: Johnathan Wilker, Vice President of Finance and Chief Financial Officer
CMO: John Garred, M.D., Sr, Chief Medical Officer
CIO: Grady Warner, Director of Information Technology
CHR: Erin Brekke, Director Human Resources
CNO: Patty Sandmann, Senior Director of Nursing
Web address: www.burgesshc.org
Control: Other not–for–profit (including NFP Corporation) **Service**: General medical and surgical

Staffed Beds: 15 **Admissions**: 473 **Census**: 5 **Outpatient Visits**: 44268
Births: 0 **Total Expense ($000)**: 35541 **Payroll Expense ($000)**: 16908
Personnel: 303

ORANGE CITY—Sioux County

★ **ORANGE CITY AREA HEALTH SYSTEM (161360)**, 1000 Lincoln Circle SE, Zip 51041–1862; tel. 712/737–4984, (Total facility includes 89 beds in nursing home–type unit) **A**10 18 **F**3 7 10 11 13 15 18 28 29 31 34 35 40 45 50 53 56 57 59 62 63 64 67 68 70 75 76 77 78 79 81 82 85 86 87 89 93 97 100 101 102 104 107 110 111 114 119 120 125 127 130 131 132 133 146 147 148 154 156 169 **P**6 **S** Sanford Health, Sioux Falls, SD
Primary Contact: Martin W. Guthmiller, Chief Executive Officer
COO: Daniel P McCarty, Chief Operating Officer
CFO: Dina Baas, Director Financial Services
CMO: Alan Laird, M.D., Chief Medical Officer
CHR: Jason Jauron, Director Human Resources
CNO: Laurie Gebauer, Director Patient Care
Web address: www.ochealthsystem.org
Control: City, Government, Nonfederal **Service**: General medical and surgical

Staffed Beds: 114 **Admissions**: 788 **Census**: 94 **Outpatient Visits**: 82303
Births: 202 **Total Expense ($000)**: 62813 **Payroll Expense ($000)**: 29086
Personnel: 464

OSAGE—Mitchell County

★ **MITCHELL COUNTY REGIONAL HEALTH CENTER (161323)**, 616 North Eighth Street, Zip 50461–1498; tel. 641/732–6000, **A**10 18 **F**3 7 8 11 15 28 29 34 35 40 43 45 50 56 57 59 63 64 65 68 75 77 79 81 82 89 90 93 107 110 115 119 127 129 130 132 133 146 148 154 156 **P**1 **S** Trinity Health, Livonia, MI
Primary Contact: Shelly Russell, Chief Executive Officer
CFO: Gregory Burkel, Chief Financial Officer
CMO: Jeff Nasstrom, D.O., Chief of Staff
CHR: Angie Konig, Senior Director Human Resources
CNO: Judy Brown, Chief Nursing Officer
Web address: www.mcrhc.com
Control: County, Government, Nonfederal **Service**: General medical and surgical

Staffed Beds: 23 **Admissions**: 340 **Census**: 5 **Outpatient Visits**: 78998
Births: 0 **Total Expense ($000)**: 32780 **Payroll Expense ($000)**: 13139
Personnel: 220

OSCEOLA—Clarke County

★ ⇑ **CLARKE COUNTY HOSPITAL (161348)**, 800 South Fillmore Street, Zip 50213–1619; tel. 641/342–2184, **A**10 18 21 **F**3 7 11 15 18 28 29 31 34 35 40 44 45 51 57 59 64 65 67 68 75 77 78 79 81 82 89 90 93 94 96 97 101 104 105 107 110 111 115 116 117 118 119 128 130 131 132 133 135 143 146 148 154 156 162 164 165 169 **P**6 **S** UnityPoint Health, West Des Moines, IA
Primary Contact: Brian G. Evans, FACHE, Chief Executive Officer
CFO: Michael Thilges, Chief Financial Officer
CMO: George Fotiadis, M.D., Chief of Staff
CIO: Dennis Blazek, Chief Information Officer
CHR: Kate Emanuel, Director Human Resources
Web address: www.clarkehosp.org
Control: County, Government, Nonfederal **Service**: General medical and surgical

Staffed Beds: 25 **Admissions**: 324 **Census**: 9 **Outpatient Visits**: 64419
Births: 0 **Total Expense ($000)**: 34053 **Payroll Expense ($000)**: 13645
Personnel: 201

OSKALOOSA—Mahaska County

⊞ **MAHASKA HEALTH (161379)**, 1229 'C' Avenue East, Zip 52577–4298; tel. 641/672–3100, **A**1 10 18 **F**3 7 11 13 15 18 19 28 29 34 35 40 43 45 46 48 50 54 56 57 59 63 64 65 68 70 74 75 76 77 79 81 82 84 85 86 87 93 97 102 107 110 111 115 119 126 129 130 131 133 135 146 147 148 149 154 156 167 169
Primary Contact: Kevin DeRonde, Chief Executive Officer
COO: Erin Baldwin, M.P.H., Chief Operating Officer
CMO: Matt Whitis, Chief Medical Officer
CHR: Sarah S. Dickey, Executive Director, Human Resource People and Culture
Web address: www.mahaskahealth.com
Control: County, Government, Nonfederal **Service**: General medical and surgical

Staffed Beds: 22 **Admissions**: 1156 **Census**: 14 **Outpatient Visits**: 143380
Births: 181 **Total Expense ($000)**: 76508 **Payroll Expense ($000)**: 42242
Personnel: 409

OTTUMWA—Wapello County

⊞ △ **OTTUMWA REGIONAL HEALTH CENTER (160089)**, 1001 Pennsylvania Avenue, Zip 52501–2186; tel. 641/684–2300, **A**1 7 10 **F**3 7 11 13 15 18 20 22 26 28 29 30 34 35 40 41 43 44 45 46 50 51 56 57 59 60 64 75 76 77 79 81 82 85 87 89 90 93 96 98 102 107 108 110 111 114 115 118 119 120 121 123 126 129 130 135 146 147 148 154 164 169 **S** Lifepoint Health, Brentwood, TN
Primary Contact: William Kiefer, Chief Executive Officer
COO: Dennis Hunger, Chief Operating Officer
CMO: Sandro Younadam, M.D., Chief Medical Officer
CIO: Scott Garrett, Director of IS
CHR: Lidia Bryant, Director Human Resources
CNO: Bryan Harkness, R.N., Chief Nursing Officer
Web address: www.ottumwaregionalhealth.com
Control: Corporation, Investor–owned (for–profit) **Service**: General medical and surgical

Staffed Beds: 68 **Admissions**: 1917 **Census**: 27 **Outpatient Visits**: 103846
Births: 297 **Total Expense ($000)**: 72288 **Payroll Expense ($000)**: 18661
Personnel: 279

Hospital, Medicare Provider Number, Address, Telephone, Approval, Facility, and Physician Codes, Health Care System

★ American Hospital Association (AHA) membership
□ The Joint Commission accreditation
○ Healthcare Facilities Accreditation Program
◇ DNV Healthcare Inc. accreditation
⇑ Center for Improvement in Healthcare Quality Accreditation
△ Commission on Accreditation of Rehabilitation Facilities (CARF) accreditation

Hospitals, U.S. / IOWA

PELLA—Marion County

☒ **PELLA REGIONAL HEALTH CENTER (161367)**, 404 Jefferson Street, Zip 50219-1257; tel. 641/628-3150, **A**1 10 18 **F**3 11 13 15 18 28 29 30 32 34 35 40 43 45 50 51 53 59 62 63 64 65 67 70 75 76 77 78 79 81 82 84 85 87 93 94 97 102 107 108 110 111 115 119 126 127 129 130 131 133 144 146 147 148 149 154 156 157 167 169
Primary Contact: Robert D. Kroese, FACHE, Chief Executive Officer
COO: Robert D Kroese, FACHE, Chief Executive Officer
CFO: Bruce Heifner, Chief Financial Officer
CIO: Cristina Thomas, Chief Information Systems
CHR: Ashley Arkema, Director of Human Resources
Web address: www.pellahealth.org
Control: Other not-for-profit (including NFP Corporation) **Service:** General medical and surgical

Staffed Beds: 25 **Admissions:** 1279 **Census:** 13 **Outpatient Visits:** 168197 **Births:** 607 **Total Expense ($000):** 77967 **Payroll Expense ($000):** 27405 **Personnel:** 659

PERRY—Dallas County

★ **DALLAS COUNTY HOSPITAL (161322)**, 610 10th Street, Zip 50220-2221; tel. 515/465-3547, **A**10 18 **F**15 18 28 31 34 35 40 41 43 45 47 50 56 57 59 65 68 75 78 79 81 82 85 87 89 93 107 110 114 119 127 128 130 132 133 135 146 148 154 156 **S** MercyOne, Clive, IA
Primary Contact: Angela Mortoza, Chief Executive Officer
CFO: Randy Loomis, Chief Financial Officer
CMO: Steven Sohn, M.D., President Medical Staff
CIO: Jake Wendler, Chief Information Officer
CHR: Sherry Smith, Manager Human Resources
CNO: Tonya Summerson, Chief Clinical Officer
Web address: www.dallascohospital.org
Control: County, Government, Nonfederal **Service:** General medical and surgical

Staffed Beds: 17 **Admissions:** 120 **Census:** 2 **Outpatient Visits:** 55623 **Births:** 0 **Total Expense ($000):** 24440 **Payroll Expense ($000):** 6987 **Personnel:** 126

POCAHONTAS—Pocahontas County

★ **POCAHONTAS COMMUNITY HOSPITAL (161305)**, 606 NW Seventh Street, Zip 50574-1099; tel. 712/335-3501, **A**10 18 **F**7 15 28 29 30 31 34 35 40 43 45 50 59 64 67 75 77 79 81 82 85 90 93 107 110 115 119 128 129 130 132 133 135 146 148 **S** UnityPoint Health, West Des Moines, IA
Primary Contact: James D. Roetman, President and Chief Executive Officer
CFO: Lynn Raveling, Chief Financial Officer
CIO: Justin Romo, Director of Information Technology
CNO: Susie Aden, Director, Inpatient Services
Web address: www.pocahontashospital.org
Control: City, Government, Nonfederal **Service:** General medical and surgical

Staffed Beds: 20 **Admissions:** 182 **Census:** 3 **Outpatient Visits:** 23548 **Births:** 0 **Total Expense ($000):** 14362 **Payroll Expense ($000):** 4928 **Personnel:** 73

PRIMGHAR—O'brien County

★ **MERCYONE PRIMGHAR MEDICAL CENTER (161300)**, 255 North Welch Avenue, Zip 51245-7765, Mailing Address: P.O. Box 528, Zip 51245-0528; tel. 712/957-2300, **A**10 18 **F**11 18 34 35 40 43 45 50 53 57 59 64 67 81 85 86 89 97 100 107 119 127 128 129 130 133 150 154 169 **P**6 **S** Trinity Health, Livonia, MI
Primary Contact: Thomas A. Clark, President, MercyOne Western Division
CFO: Sue E McCauley, Director Finance
CMO: Shailesh Desai, M.D., Chief of Staff
Web address: https://www.mercyone.org/primghar/
Control: Hospital district or authority, Government, Nonfederal **Service:** General medical and surgical

Staffed Beds: 14 **Admissions:** 48 **Census:** 1 **Outpatient Visits:** 16247 **Births:** 0 **Total Expense ($000):** 8928 **Payroll Expense ($000):** 4312 **Personnel:** 38

RED OAK—Montgomery County

★ **MONTGOMERY COUNTY MEMORIAL HOSPITAL (161363)**, 2301 Eastern Avenue, Zip 51566-1300, Mailing Address: P.O. Box 498, Zip 51566-0498; tel. 712/623-7000, **A**10 18 **F**3 8 11 12 15 28 29 30 31 34 35 40 43 45 50 53 55 56 57 59 64 65 68 69 70 71 74 75 77 78 79 81 82 84 85 86 87 93 97 100 102 105 107 110 111 114 115 118 119 127 129 130 132 133 135 146 147 148 149 154 156 167 169
Primary Contact: Ron Kloewer, Chief Executive Officer
CFO: Rick J Leinen, Chief Financial Officer
CMO: Warren Hayes, Chief of Staff
CHR: Shayla Jennings, Human Resources Director
CNO: Diane McGrew, Chief Nurse Executive
Web address: www.mcmh.org
Control: County, Government, Nonfederal **Service:** General medical and surgical

Staffed Beds: 25 **Admissions:** 417 **Census:** 4 **Outpatient Visits:** 48117 **Births:** 0 **Total Expense ($000):** 49243 **Payroll Expense ($000):** 22816 **Personnel:** 336

ROCK RAPIDS—Lyon County

★ **AVERA MERRILL PIONEER HOSPITAL (161321)**, 1100 South 10th Avenue, Zip 51246-2020; tel. 712/472-5400, **A**10 18 **F**3 11 15 28 31 32 34 35 38 40 41 44 45 50 57 59 63 64 65 68 75 81 85 86 93 97 100 102 107 110 115 119 127 131 132 133 144 146 148 154 156 **P**6 **S** Avera Health, Sioux Falls, SD
Primary Contact: Craig Hohn, Chief Executive Officer
Web address: https://www.avera.org
Control: Other not-for-profit (including NFP Corporation) **Service:** General medical and surgical

Staffed Beds: 11 **Admissions:** 112 **Census:** 2 **Outpatient Visits:** 7695 **Births:** 0 **Total Expense ($000):** 9953 **Payroll Expense ($000):** 4243 **Personnel:** 65

ROCK VALLEY—Sioux County

★ **HEGG HEALTH CENTER AVERA (161336)**, 1202 21st Avenue, Zip 51247-1497; tel. 712/476-8000, (Total facility includes 55 beds in nursing home–type unit) **A**10 18 22 **F**3 15 28 29 31 34 35 36 40 41 43 44 45 50 53 57 59 62 64 65 67 68 75 77 78 79 81 82 85 89 91 93 96 97 107 110 115 119 128 130 131 132 133 144 147 148 154 156 164 169 **S** Avera Health, Sioux Falls, SD
Primary Contact: Glenn Zevenbergen, Chief Executive Officer
CFO: Bill Slater, Chief Financial Officer
CMO: Jon Engbers, M.D., President
CHR: Tammy Faber, Director Human Resources
Web address: www.hegghc.org
Control: Other not-for-profit (including NFP Corporation) **Service:** General medical and surgical

Staffed Beds: 72 **Admissions:** 248 **Census:** 54 **Outpatient Visits:** 26099 **Births:** 0 **Total Expense ($000):** 26233 **Payroll Expense ($000):** 12912 **Personnel:** 170

SAC CITY—Sac County

★ **LORING HOSPITAL (161370)**, 211 Highland Avenue, Zip 50583-2424; tel. 712/662-7105, **A**10 18 **F**3 11 15 28 29 34 35 40 43 45 50 57 59 64 75 77 81 86 87 93 102 107 110 115 125 130 133 146 149 156 **S** UnityPoint Health, West Des Moines, IA
Primary Contact: Matt Johnson, Chief Executive Officer
CMO: Les Marczewski, M.D., Chief Medical Officer
CIO: Leah Snyder, Director Health Information Services
CHR: Becky Pontious, Human Resources/Accounting
CNO: Nicole Wiggins, R.N., Chief Clinical Officer
Web address: www.loringhospital.org
Control: Other not-for-profit (including NFP Corporation) **Service:** General medical and surgical

Staffed Beds: 25 **Admissions:** 131 **Census:** 1 **Outpatient Visits:** 27200 **Births:** 0 **Total Expense ($000):** 16734 **Payroll Expense ($000):** 6147 **Personnel:** 107

Hospitals, U.S. / IOWA

SHELDON—O'brien County

★ **SANFORD SHELDON MEDICAL CENTER (161381)**, 118 North Seventh Avenue, Zip 51201-1235, Mailing Address: P.O. Box 250, Zip 51201-0250; tel. 712/324-5041, (Total facility includes 68 beds in nursing home-type unit) **A**10 18 **F**3 11 13 15 28 29 30 31 32 34 35 40 43 45 56 57 59 61 62 63 64 65 66 67 75 76 77 78 81 84 85 86 89 93 94 96 97 100 101 104 107 110 111 114 119 127 130 131 133 135 148 149 154 156 167 169 **P**6 **S** Sanford Health, Sioux Falls, SD
Primary Contact: Richard E. Nordahl, Senior Director
CFO: Stanley Knobloch, Director of Finance
CMO: Scott Lichty, M.D., Physician
CIO: Jason Brown, Director Information Systems
CHR: Dianne Wolthuizen, Director Human Resources
CNO: Joni DeKok, Chief Nursing Officer
Web address: www.sanfordsheldon.org
Control: Other not-for-profit (including NFP Corporation) **Service**: General medical and surgical

Staffed Beds: 93 **Admissions**: 647 **Census**: 58 **Outpatient Visits**: 48615
Births: 124 **Total Expense ($000)**: 35133 **Payroll Expense ($000)**: 16744
Personnel: 219

SHENANDOAH—Page County

★ **SHENANDOAH MEDICAL CENTER (161366)**, 300 Pershing Avenue, Zip 51601-2355; tel. 712/246-1230, **A**10 18 **F**3 5 13 15 18 28 29 31 34 36 38 40 41 43 45 46 48 49 50 53 55 56 57 59 64 65 68 69 70 74 75 76 77 78 79 81 85 87 89 91 92 93 97 101 102 104 107 108 110 115 118 119 120 121 123 127 129 130 131 132 133 135 144 146 147 148 149 154 160 161 164 169 **P**6
Primary Contact: Matt Sells, Chief Executive Officer
CFO: Kaley Neal, Chief Financial Officer
CMO: Heather Babe, M.D., Chief of Staff
CIO: Chuck Dougherty, Chief Information Officer
CHR: Keli Royal, Chief Human Resources Officer
CNO: Laura Stofferson, Chief Nursing Officer
Web address: www.smchospital.com/
Control: Other not-for-profit (including NFP Corporation) **Service**: General medical and surgical

Staffed Beds: 25 **Admissions**: 425 **Census**: 4 **Outpatient Visits**: 224048
Births: 114 **Total Expense ($000)**: 53579 **Payroll Expense ($000)**: 23449
Personnel: 307

SIBLEY—Osceola County

★ **OSCEOLA REGIONAL HEALTH CENTER (161345)**, 600 9th Avenue North, Zip 51249-1012, Mailing Address: P.O. Box 258, Zip 51249-0258; tel. 712/754-2574, **A**10 18 **F**3 8 9 10 11 12 15 18 26 28 29 31 34 35 40 43 45 46 50 53 56 57 59 61 62 64 65 67 68 75 77 78 79 81 82 84 85 86 87 89 107 108 110 114 119 125 128 130 131 132 133 135 143 144 145 146 147 148 149 154 156 **S** Avera Health, Sioux Falls, SD
Primary Contact: Joe Heitritter, Chief Executive Officer
CMO: Gregory J Kosters, D.O., Chief Medical Officer
CHR: Emily VanKekerix, Director Human Resources
CNO: Wendy Marco, R.N., Chief Nursing Officer
Web address: www.osceolacommunityhospital.org
Control: Other not-for-profit (including NFP Corporation) **Service**: General medical and surgical

Staffed Beds: 25 **Admissions**: 127 **Census**: 2 **Outpatient Visits**: 15276
Births: 0 **Total Expense ($000)**: 14263 **Payroll Expense ($000)**: 5069
Personnel: 90

SIGOURNEY—Keokuk County

KEOKUK COUNTY HOSPITAL & CLINICS (161315), 23019 Highway 149, Zip 52591-8341; tel. 641/622-2720, **A**10 18 **F**2 3 7 11 12 15 28 29 30 34 35 38 40 43 44 50 56 57 59 64 65 66 75 77 82 83 84 85 86 87 91 93 97 102 104 107 110 114 129 130 131 132 133 135 143 144 146 147 148 149 154 156 157 160 165 **P**5
Primary Contact: Matthew Ives, Chief Executive Officer and Chief Financial Officer
CFO: Matthew Ives, Interim Chief Executive Officer and Chief Financial Officer
Web address: www.kchc.net
Control: County, Government, Nonfederal **Service**: General medical and surgical

Staffed Beds: 14 **Admissions**: 41 **Census**: 3 **Outpatient Visits**: 23697
Births: 0 **Total Expense ($000)**: 15806 **Payroll Expense ($000)**: 8291
Personnel: 101

SIOUX CENTER—Sioux County

★ **SIOUX CENTER HEALTH (161346)**, 1101 9th Street SE, Zip 51250; tel. 712/722-8107, (Total facility includes 99 beds in nursing home-type unit) **A**10 18 **F**3 5 8 10 12 13 15 18 26 28 29 30 31 34 35 37 40 41 43 45 50 56 57 59 62 63 64 65 67 68 74 75 76 77 78 79 80 81 82 83 85 86 87 89 93 96 97 100 101 104 107 108 110 111 114 119 125 126 128 130 131 132 133 144 146 147 148 149 154 156 157 160 164 169 **P**6 **S** Avera Health, Sioux Falls, SD
Primary Contact: Cory D. Nelson, Administrator
CFO: Kari Timmer, Chief Financial Officer
CHR: Theresa Tucker, Human Resources Officer
Web address: www.siouxcenterhealth.org
Control: Other not-for-profit (including NFP Corporation) **Service**: General medical and surgical

Staffed Beds: 118 **Admissions**: 699 **Census**: 80 **Outpatient Visits**: 75560
Births: 261 **Total Expense ($000)**: 62675 **Payroll Expense ($000)**: 25805
Personnel: 431

SIOUX CITY—Woodbury County

✠ **MERCYONE SIOUXLAND MEDICAL CENTER (160153)**, 801 Fifth Street, Zip 51101-1326, Mailing Address: P.O. Box 3168, Zip 51102-3168; tel. 712/279-2010, **A**1 3 5 10 19 **F**3 5 8 11 12 15 17 18 20 22 24 26 28 29 30 31 32 34 35 37 40 43 44 45 49 50 56 57 59 64 65 67 68 70 71 74 75 77 78 79 81 82 84 85 87 89 90 91 92 93 96 97 98 100 102 107 108 110 111 115 119 126 127 128 129 130 144 145 146 148 149 150 154 156 157 166 167 **S** Trinity Health, Livonia, MI
Primary Contact: Thomas A. Clark, President, MercyOne Western Division
CFO: Jesica Hanson, Vice President Finance and Chief Financial Officer
CMO: Keith Vollstedt, M.D., Chief Medical Officer
CIO: Steve Larson, M.D., Director Information Systems
CHR: Julie Anfinson, Chief Human Resources Officer
CNO: Tracy Larson, MS, Vice President Patient Care Services and Chief Nursing Officer
Web address: www.mercysiouxcity.com
Control: Church operated, Nongovernment, not-for-profit **Service**: General medical and surgical

Staffed Beds: 152 **Admissions**: 6167 **Census**: 103 **Outpatient Visits**: 178966 **Births**: 0 **Total Expense ($000)**: 282631 **Payroll Expense ($000)**: 86527 **Personnel**: 1197

★ ⇑ **UNITYPOINT HEALTH – ST. LUKES'S SIOUX CITY (160146)**, 2720 Stone Park Boulevard, Zip 51104-3734; tel. 712/279-3500, **A**3 5 10 19 21 **F**3 11 13 15 17 18 20 22 26 28 29 30 31 34 35 39 40 43 45 49 50 51 54 56 57 58 59 60 64 68 70 72 73 74 75 76 77 78 79 81 82 84 85 86 88 89 90 91 92 93 96 97 98 102 104 105 107 108 110 111 114 115 118 119 126 129 130 132 135 142 143 144 145 146 147 149 154 156 157 164 167 **P**6 **S** UnityPoint Health, West Des Moines, IA
Primary Contact: Jane Arnold, Market President, UnityPoint Health – Sioux City
COO: Brenda Larsen, R.N., Vice President Operations
CFO: James Gobell, Chief Financial Officer
CMO: John Jones, M.D., Chief Medical Officer
CIO: James Gobell, Chief Financial Officer
CHR: Tammy Hartnett, Employee Relations Manager
CNO: Priscilla Stokes, MS, R.N., Vice President Patient Care and Hospital Operations
Web address: https://www.unitypoint.org/locations/unitypoint-health-stlukes
Control: Other not-for-profit (including NFP Corporation) **Service**: General medical and surgical

Staffed Beds: 188 **Admissions**: 9191 **Census**: 125 **Outpatient Visits**: 94240 **Births**: 2225 **Total Expense ($000)**: 220328 **Payroll Expense ($000)**: 102049 **Personnel**: 1038

Hospital, Medicare Provider Number, Address, Telephone, Approval, Facility, and Physician Codes, Health Care System

★ American Hospital Association (AHA) membership ○ Healthcare Facilities Accreditation Program ⇑ Center for Improvement in Healthcare Quality Accreditation
☐ The Joint Commission accreditation ◇ DNV Healthcare Inc. accreditation △ Commission on Accreditation of Rehabilitation Facilities (CARF) accreditation

© 2025 AHA Guide

Hospitals, U.S. / IOWA

SPENCER—Clay County

★ **SPENCER HOSPITAL (160112)**, 1200 First Avenue East, Suite 1, Zip 51301–4342; tel. 712/264–6111, **A**10 22 **F**3 7 8 11 13 15 28 29 30 31 34 35 40 43 45 50 53 57 59 60 62 63 64 65 70 75 76 77 78 79 81 82 85 86 87 93 96 98 107 108 109 110 111 115 118 119 120 121 123 126 127 129 130 131 132 133 135 144 146 147 148 149 156 167
Primary Contact: Brenda Marie. Tiefenthaler, R.N., MSN, President and Chief Executive Officer
CFO: Stacy E Mol, CPA, Director Finance
CMO: Sonia Sather, M.D., President Medical Staff
CHR: Stephen Deutsch, Vice President Operations and Support
Web address: www.spencerhospital.org
Control: City, Government, Nonfederal **Service**: General medical and surgical

Staffed Beds: 64 **Admissions**: 1893 **Census**: 21 **Outpatient Visits**: 111640
Births: 265 **Total Expense ($000)**: 120365 **Payroll Expense ($000)**: 31425
Personnel: 480

SPIRIT LAKE—Dickinson County

★ **LAKES REGIONAL HEALTHCARE (160124)**, 2301 Highway 71 South, Zip 51360–0159; tel. 712/336–1230, **A**10 **F**3 7 11 13 15 28 29 30 31 34 35 37 40 41 43 45 50 54 57 59 62 63 64 65 70 75 76 77 78 79 81 85 89 91 93 97 107 110 111 115 119 126 128 129 130 132 133 135 143 146 148 149 152 154 156 169 **P**5 **S** Avera Health, Sioux Falls, SD
Primary Contact: Jason Harrington, FACHE, President and Chief Executive Officer
CFO: Steve Alger, Senior Vice President and Chief Financial Officer
CMO: Zachary A. Borus, M.D., Medical Chief of Staff
CIO: Derek Larson, Information Technology Network
CHR: Sonja Hamm, Vice President Human and Foundation Resources
CNO: Christopher Ingraham, Chief Nursing Officer
Web address: www.lakeshealth.org
Control: County, Government, Nonfederal **Service**: General medical and surgical

Staffed Beds: 30 **Admissions**: 1137 **Census**: 11 **Outpatient Visits**: 141959
Births: 231 **Total Expense ($000)**: 59806 **Payroll Expense ($000)**: 17624
Personnel: 254

STORM LAKE—Buena Vista County

⊞ **BUENA VISTA REGIONAL MEDICAL CENTER (161375)**, 1525 West Fifth Street, Zip 50588–3027, Mailing Address: P.O. Box 309, Zip 50588–0309; tel. 712/732–4030, **A**1 10 18 **F**3 7 8 11 13 15 18 28 29 30 31 34 37 40 43 45 53 55 56 57 59 63 64 68 70 74 75 76 77 78 79 81 82 84 85 86 87 93 96 98 103 104 107 108 110 111 115 117 118 119 124 126 128 129 130 131 132 133 135 146 147 148 149 169 **S** UnityPoint Health, West Des Moines, IA
Primary Contact: Steven Colerick, Chief Executive Officer
CFO: Krista Ketcham, Chief Financial Officer
CMO: Seth Harrer, M.D., Chief of Staff
CIO: Steve Spurlock, Director Information Systems
CHR: Carrie Turnquist, Director Human Resources
Web address: www.bvrmc.org
Control: County, Government, Nonfederal **Service**: General medical and surgical

Staffed Beds: 35 **Admissions**: 948 **Census**: 11 **Outpatient Visits**: 76343
Births: 356 **Total Expense ($000)**: 66043 **Payroll Expense ($000)**: 23962
Personnel: 329

SUMNER—Bremer County

★ **COMMUNITY MEMORIAL HOSPITAL (161320)**, 909 West First Street, Zip 50674–1203, Mailing Address: P.O. Box 148, Zip 50674–0148; tel. 563/578–3275, **A**10 18 **F**3 11 15 28 29 34 40 45 57 59 64 65 77 81 82 85 86 97 107 110 115 119 128 129 131 133 135 146 148 149 154 156 **P**6 **S** UnityPoint Health, West Des Moines, IA
Primary Contact: Dawn Everding, Chief Hospital Administrator/Chief Financial Officer
CFO: Dawn Everding, Chief Hospital Administrator and Chief Financial Officer
CMO: Jeff Roske, D.O., Chief Medical Staff
CHR: Robin Elliott, Personnel Officer
CNO: Lynne Niemann, Director Nurses and Patient Care
Web address: www.cmhsumner.org
Control: Other not–for–profit (including NFP Corporation) **Service**: General medical and surgical

Staffed Beds: 16 **Admissions**: 133 **Census**: 2 **Outpatient Visits**: 45943
Births: 0 **Total Expense ($000)**: 17428 **Payroll Expense ($000)**: 6106
Personnel: 91

VINTON—Benton County

★ **VIRGINIA GAY HOSPITAL (161349)**, 502 North 9th Avenue, Zip 52349–2299; tel. 319/472–6200, (Total facility includes 40 beds in nursing home–type unit) **A**10 18 **F**3 29 34 40 43 45 53 57 59 62 64 65 66 75 81 85 86 87 91 92 97 104 107 110 111 114 119 125 127 129 130 131 132 133 143 146 148 149 154 156 **P**6 **S** UnityPoint Health, West Des Moines, IA
Primary Contact: Barry Dietsch, Interim executive leader (Currently CFO)
CFO: Barry Dietsch, Chief Financial Officer
CMO: Brian Meeker, D.O., President Medical Staff
CIO: Sherri Isbell, Chief Information Officer
CHR: Kim Frank, Chief Human Resources Officer
CNO: Tina M Eden, Director of Nursing
Web address: www.myvgh.org
Control: Other not–for–profit (including NFP Corporation) **Service**: General medical and surgical

Staffed Beds: 65 **Admissions**: 333 **Census**: 35 **Outpatient Visits**: 86281
Births: 0 **Total Expense ($000)**: 36250 **Payroll Expense ($000)**: 16655
Personnel: 273

WASHINGTON—Washington County

★ **WASHINGTON COUNTY HOSPITAL AND CLINICS (161344)**, 400 East Polk Street, Zip 52353–1237, Mailing Address: P.O. Box 909, Zip 52353–0909; tel. 319/653–5481, **A**10 18 **F**3 15 18 28 29 37 40 43 45 50 59 64 74 75 81 85 86 92 93 96 97 107 110 111 115 119 127 132 133 146 147 148 154 156 **P**6
Primary Contact: Todd Patterson, Chief Executive Officer
CFO: Steve Sanders, Chief Financial Officer
CMO: Matt Prihoda, M.D., Chief of Staff
CIO: Makyla Maize, Director Information Services
CHR: Tracy Ousey, Director Human Resources
CNO: Andrea Leyden RN, Chief Nursing Officer
Web address: www.wchc.org
Control: County, Government, Nonfederal **Service**: General medical and surgical

Staffed Beds: 22 **Admissions**: 1089 **Census**: 4 **Outpatient Visits**: 64531
Births: 0 **Total Expense ($000)**: 49748 **Payroll Expense ($000)**: 22101
Personnel: 309

WATERLOO—Black Hawk County

⊞ △ **MERCYONE WATERLOO MEDICAL CENTER (160067)**, 3421 West Ninth Street, Zip 50702–5401; tel. 319/272–8000, **A**1 2 3 5 7 10 **F**3 4 5 7 11 13 15 18 19 20 22 26 28 29 30 31 33 34 35 40 43 44 45 46 48 49 50 51 53 56 57 58 59 60 61 62 64 68 70 71 72 74 75 76 77 78 79 81 82 86 87 89 90 93 97 98 99 100 101 102 103 104 107 108 110 111 114 115 116 118 119 120 126 127 129 130 131 132 135 143 144 146 147 148 152 154 156 162 167 169 **S** Trinity Health, Livonia, MI
Primary Contact: Ryan Meyer, Chief Operating Officer
COO: Ryan Meyer, Vice President Operations
CFO: Timothy Huber, Vice President Finance
CMO: Matthew Sojka, M.D., Vice President, Medical Affairs
CIO: Marge Ray, Director Information Systems
CHR: Suzanne M. Burt, Chief Human Resources Officer
CNO: Kelly Richards, Vice President and Chief Nursing Officer
Web address: https://www.mercyone.org/location/mercyone-waterloo-medical-center-1
Control: Church operated, Nongovernment, not–for–profit **Service**: General medical and surgical

Staffed Beds: 242 **Admissions**: 6499 **Census**: 92 **Outpatient Visits**: 679104 **Births**: 953 **Total Expense ($000)**: 326585 **Payroll Expense ($000)**: 160308 **Personnel**: 1794

★ △ ⇑ **UNITYPOINT HEALTH – ALLEN HOSPITAL (160110)**, 1825 Logan Avenue, Zip 50703–1916; tel. 319/235–3941, **A**3 5 7 10 19 21 **F**3 5 11 13 15 18 20 22 24 26 28 29 30 31 34 35 36 40 43 45 46 47 49 50 51 54 57 59 60 64 66 68 70 72 74 75 76 77 78 79 81 82 84 85 86 87 88 89 90 91 92 93 96 98 100 101 102 103 104 107 108 110 111 114 115 118 119 126 129 130 132 135 146 147 148 149 153 160 161 165 167 169 **P**6 **S** UnityPoint Health, West Des Moines, IA
Primary Contact: Jenni Friedly, Market President, UnityPoint Health – Waterloo
CFO: Craig Flanagan, Chief Financial Officer
CMO: Timothy Horrigan, M.D., Chief Quality Officer
CIO: Daniel Norman, Regional Service Manager
CHR: Steven Sesterhenn, Vice President
CNO: Mary Hagen, R.N., MSN, VP and Chief Nursing Officer
Web address: www.unitypoint.org/waterloo
Control: Other not–for–profit (including NFP Corporation) **Service**: General medical and surgical

Staffed Beds: 201 **Admissions**: 10858 **Census**: 128 **Outpatient Visits**: 616279
Births: 1283 **Total Expense ($000)**: 338657 **Payroll Expense ($000)**: 134947
Personnel: 1413

Hospitals, U.S. / IOWA

WAUKON—Allamakee County

★ **VETERANS MEMORIAL HOSPITAL (161318)**, 40 First Street SE, Zip 52172–2099; tel. 563/568–3411, **A**10 18 **F**3 7 11 13 15 28 34 36 40 43 45 57 59 62 64 65 68 75 76 77 79 81 86 93 97 100 102 104 107 110 111 115 119 128 130 131 132 133 144 146 147 148 149 154 156 169 **P**6
Primary Contact: Michael F. Coyle, Chief Executive Officer
CFO: Scott Knode, Chief Financial Officer
CHR: Erin Berns, Director Human Resources
Web address: https://www.veteransmemorialhospital.com
Control: County, Government, Nonfederal **Service:** General medical and surgical

Staffed Beds: 20 **Admissions:** 519 **Census:** 6 **Outpatient Visits:** 53006 **Births:** 68 **Total Expense ($000):** 22824 **Payroll Expense ($000):** 12411 **Personnel:** 212

WAVERLY—Bremer County

⊞ **WAVERLY HEALTH CENTER (161339)**, 312 Ninth Street SW, Zip 50677–2999; tel. 319/352–4120, **A**1 10 18 **F**3 7 9 11 12 13 15 28 29 34 35 37 40 43 45 48 50 57 59 64 75 76 81 82 85 86 97 100 102 104 107 110 111 114 119 127 130 132 133 135 144 146 147 154 156 164 169 **P**6
Primary Contact: Jodi Geerts, Chief Executive Officer
COO: Heidi Solheim, Chief Operating Officer
CFO: Lisa Bennett, Chief Financial Officer
CMO: Clay Dahlquist, M.D., Chief Medical Officer
CIO: Jerry Tiedt, Director Information Systems
CHR: Angie Tye, Director Human Resources
CNO: Kelly Hilsenbeck, MSN, R.N., Chief Nursing Officer
Web address: www.waverlyhealthcenter.org
Control: City, Government, Nonfederal **Service:** General medical and surgical

Staffed Beds: 25 **Admissions:** 746 **Census:** 6 **Outpatient Visits:** 115562 **Births:** 196 **Total Expense ($000):** 72699 **Payroll Expense ($000):** 32013 **Personnel:** 347

WEBSTER CITY—Hamilton County

★ **VAN DIEST MEDICAL CENTER (161361)**, 2350 Hospital Drive, Zip 50595–6600, Mailing Address: P.O. Box 430, Zip 50595–0430; tel. 515/832–9400, **A**10 18 **F**3 7 8 10 11 15 28 29 31 40 43 45 50 64 65 68 75 77 78 81 82 85 89 90 93 96 97 107 110 111 115 119 127 128 129 130 133 146 147 154 156 157 169 **P**6 **S** MercyOne, Clive, IA
Primary Contact: Lisa Carolyn. Ridge, Chief Executive Officer
CFO: Ashley Allers, Chief Financial Officer
CMO: Nicole Ehn, M.D., Chief of Staff
CIO: Vickie A Wickham, R.N., MSN, Senior Director of Information Services
CHR: Jodie Harker, Director Human Resources
CNO: Amy K McDonough, Chief Nursing Officer
Web address: www.vandiestmc.org
Control: County, Government, Nonfederal **Service:** General medical and surgical

Staffed Beds: 25 **Admissions:** 581 **Census:** 10 **Outpatient Visits:** 73653 **Births:** 0 **Total Expense ($000):** 36711 **Payroll Expense ($000):** 16921 **Personnel:** 224

WEST BURLINGTON—Des Moines County

GREAT RIVER MEDICAL CENTER See Southeast Iowa Regional Medical Center, West Burlington Campus

★ △ **SOUTHEAST IOWA REGIONAL MEDICAL CENTER, WEST BURLINGTON CAMPUS (160057)**, 1221 South Gear Avenue, Zip 52655–1681; tel. 319/768–1000, (Includes SOUTHEAST IOWA REGIONAL MEDICAL CENTER, FORT MADISON CAMPUS, 5445 Avenue O, Fort Madison, Iowa, Zip 52627–9611, P O Box 174, Zip 52627–0174, tel. 319/372–6530; Shelby Burchett, Chief Executive Officer) (Total facility includes 160 beds in nursing home–type unit) **A**5 7 10 22 **F**3 5 7 11 13 15 17 18 20 22 28 29 30 31 32 34 35 36 38 40 43 45 48 50 53 54 57 59 60 62 63 64 65 67 68 69 70 72 73 74 75 76 77 78 79 81 82 84 85 86 87 89 90 91 92 93 94 96 97 98 100 101 102 104 107 108 110 111 114 115 116 117 118 119 120 121 123 128 129 130 131 132 133 143 144 146 147 148 149 154 156 157 164 167 169 **P**6
Primary Contact: Michael Jerry. McCoy, M.D., President and Chief Executive Officer
CFO: Jeremy Alexander, Chief Financial Officer
CMO: Michael Jerry McCoy, M.D., Chief Medical Officer
CIO: Levi Nathan Gause, M.D., Chief Information Officer and Vice President Health System Informatics
CHR: James M. Kammerer, Vice President Support Services
CNO: Teresa Colgan, Vice President Nursing
Web address: https://www.greatriverhealth.org/
Control: Other not–for–profit (including NFP Corporation) **Service:** General medical and surgical

Staffed Beds: 352 **Admissions:** 5803 **Census:** 146 **Outpatient Visits:** 1250219 **Births:** 818 **Total Expense ($000):** 363630 **Payroll Expense ($000):** 137306 **Personnel:** 1798

WEST DES MOINES—Polk County

MERCY MEDICAL CENTER – WEST LAKES See Mercyone West Des Moines Medical Center

METHODIST WEST HOSPITAL See Unitypoint Health – Methodist West Hospital

WEST UNION—Fayette County

★ **GUNDERSEN PALMER LUTHERAN HOSPITAL AND CLINICS (161316)**, 112 Jefferson Street, Zip 52175–1022; tel. 563/422–3811, **A**10 18 **F**3 11 13 15 28 29 30 31 32 34 35 36 38 40 43 44 45 50 56 57 59 62 63 64 65 68 75 76 77 78 79 81 82 85 86 87 89 91 93 96 100 101 104 107 110 111 115 119 127 128 129 130 131 132 133 135 146 148 154 156 169 **P**6
Primary Contact: Patrice Kuennen, Chief Executive Officer
CFO: Joni Gisleson, Director Finance
CMO: Chaudri Rasool, D.O., Chief of Staff
CIO: Kurt Chicken, Director Support Services
CNO: Kathy Begalske, Chief Nursing Officer
Web address: www.palmerlutheran.org
Control: Other not–for–profit (including NFP Corporation) **Service:** General medical and surgical

Staffed Beds: 25 **Admissions:** 309 **Census:** 5 **Outpatient Visits:** 89324 **Births:** 69 **Total Expense ($000):** 39961 **Payroll Expense ($000):** 19968 **Personnel:** 205

WINTERSET—Madison County

★ **MADISON COUNTY HEALTH CARE SYSTEM (161326)**, 300 West Hutchings Street, Zip 50273–2109; tel. 515/462–2373, **A**10 18 **F**3 15 18 28 31 35 37 40 43 45 59 64 78 79 81 89 93 97 107 110 114 119 127 128 130 131 133 135 146 149 154 156 **P**6
Primary Contact: Marcia Hendricks, FACHE, R.N., Chief Executive Officer
CFO: Audra Ford, Chief Financial Officer
CMO: Joe Kimball, D.O., Chief of Staff
CIO: Dan VandenBosch, Chief Information Officer
CHR: Jennifer Jackson, Director Human Resources
CNO: Kim Hulbert, R.N., R.N., Chief Clinical Officer
Web address: www.madisonhealth.com
Control: County, Government, Nonfederal **Service:** General medical and surgical

Staffed Beds: 12 **Admissions:** 254 **Census:** 3 **Outpatient Visits:** 69416 **Births:** 0 **Total Expense ($000):** 27976 **Payroll Expense ($000):** 12305 **Personnel:** 145

Hospital, Medicare Provider Number, Address, Telephone, Approval, Facility, and Physician Codes, Health Care System

★ American Hospital Association (AHA) membership
□ The Joint Commission accreditation
○ Healthcare Facilities Accreditation Program
◇ DNV Healthcare Inc. accreditation
⇑ Center for Improvement in Healthcare Quality Accreditation
△ Commission on Accreditation of Rehabilitation Facilities (CARF) accreditation

KANSAS

ABILENE—Dickinson County

★ **MEMORIAL HEALTH SYSTEM (171381)**, 511 NE Tenth Street, Zip 67410–2153; tel. 785/263–2100, (Total facility includes 75 beds in nursing home–type unit) **A**10 18 **F**3 11 15 18 28 29 34 35 40 45 53 57 59 62 63 64 68 69 75 77 81 85 87 89 93 97 98 103 104 107 108 110 111 115 119 127 128 129 130 131 132 133 146 148 149 154 158 169 **S** Salina Regional Health Center, Salina, KS
Primary Contact: Harold Courtois, Chief Executive Officer
CFO: Elgin Glanzer, Chief Financial Officer
CMO: W L Short, M.D., Chief Medical Officer
CIO: Blaine Cappel, Director Information Systems
CNO: Brenda L. Moffitt, Chief Nursing Officer
Web address: www.mhsks.org
Control: Hospital district or authority, Government, Nonfederal **Service:** General medical and surgical

Staffed Beds: 110 **Admissions:** 536 **Census:** 83 **Outpatient Visits:** 66629 **Births:** 0 **Total Expense ($000):** 51691 **Payroll Expense ($000):** 21924 **Personnel:** 364

ANDOVER—Butler County

KANSAS MEDICAL CENTER (170197), 1124 West 21st Street, Zip 67002–5500; tel. 316/300–4000, (Nonreporting) **A**10
Primary Contact: Badr Idbeis, M.D., Chief Executive Officer
COO: Daryl W Thornton, Chief Operating Officer
CFO: Steven N Hadley, Chief Financial Officer
CMO: G. Whitney Reader, M.D., Chief Medical Officer
CIO: Mike Buffington, Manager Information Technology
CHR: Norm Nevins, Manager Human Resources
CNO: Janet Kaiser, R.N., Chief Nursing Officer
Web address: www.ksmedcenter.com/
Control: Corporation, Investor–owned (for–profit) **Service:** General medical and surgical

Staffed Beds: 58

ANTHONY—Harper County

HOSPITAL DISTRICT 6 – PATTERSON HEALTH CENTER See Patterson Health Center

★ **PATTERSON HEALTH CENTER (171346)**, 485 N KS Hwy 2, Zip 67003–2526; tel. 620/914–1200, **A**10 18 **F**3 5 10 15 28 29 34 35 38 40 45 50 53 57 59 64 67 71 75 77 81 93 97 107 108 110 127 128 130 132 133 135 146 148 154 157 164 **P**6
Primary Contact: Sarah Teaff, Chief Executive Officer
COO: Lori Allen, Chief Operating Officer
CNO: Teresa Tomlin, R.N., Chief Nursing Officer
Web address: www.pattersonhc.org
Control: Hospital district or authority, Government, Nonfederal **Service:** General medical and surgical

Staffed Beds: 16 **Admissions:** 243 **Census:** 4 **Outpatient Visits:** 90559 **Births:** 0 **Total Expense ($000):** 26041 **Payroll Expense ($000):** 9327 **Personnel:** 149

ARKANSAS CITY—Cowley County

★ **SOUTH CENTRAL KANSAS MEDICAL CENTER (170779)**, 6401 Patterson Parkway, Zip 67005–5701; tel. 620/442–2500, (Nonreporting) **A**10
Primary Contact: Shannon Gray, Interim Administrator
CFO: Shannon Gray, Chief Financial Officer
CMO: Kamran Shahzada, M.D., Chief Medical Staff
CHR: Clayton Pappan, Director Human Resources and Marketing
CNO: Patricia Davis, Chief Nursing Officer
Web address: www.sckrmc.org
Control: City, Government, Nonfederal

Staffed Beds: 44

ASHLAND—Clark County

★ **ASHLAND HEALTH CENTER (171304)**, 709 Oak Street, Zip 67831–0188, Mailing Address: P.O. Box 188, Zip 67831–0188; tel. 620/635–2241, **A**10 18 **F**2 30 34 40 53 59 62 64 68 85 87 93 107 127 128 133 143 154 156 166 **P**6 **S** Great Plains Health Alliance, Inc., Wichita, KS
Primary Contact: Sandrea Wright, Chief Executive Officer
CFO: Debbie Filson, Chief Financial Officer
CMO: Daniel Shuman, D.O., Chief Medical Officer
CIO: Alan Romans, Director Information Technology
CHR: Debbie Filson, Chief Financial Officer
CNO: Patty Young, R.N., Chief Nursing Officer
Web address: www.ashlandhc.org
Control: Hospital district or authority, Government, Nonfederal **Service:** General medical and surgical

Staffed Beds: 25 **Admissions:** 84 **Census:** 14 **Outpatient Visits:** 8175 **Births:** 0 **Total Expense ($000):** 12223 **Payroll Expense ($000):** 4136 **Personnel:** 61

ATCHISON—Atchison County

★ ○ **AMBERWELL HEALTH (171382)**, 800 Raven Hill Drive, Zip 66002–9204; tel. 913/367–2131, (Nonreporting) **A**10 11 18
Primary Contact: Jared Abel, Chief Executive Officer
COO: Sandra Leggett, Chief Operating Officer
CFO: Gary R Foll, Chief Financial Officer
CMO: McGarrett Groth, Chief of Staff
CIO: Terry Davis, Manager Information Systems
CHR: Jill Wenger, Chief Human Resources Officer
Web address: https://amberwellhealth.org
Control: Other not–for–profit (including NFP Corporation) **Service:** General medical and surgical

Staffed Beds: 25

ATWOOD—Rawlins County

★ **RAWLINS COUNTY HEALTH CENTER (171307)**, 707 Grant Street, Zip 67730–1526, Mailing Address: P.O. Box 47, Zip 67730–0047; tel. 785/626–3211, **A**10 18 **F**3 28 29 34 40 41 43 45 50 53 59 64 65 66 67 77 81 83 84 85 87 93 97 107 115 127 128 130 133 148 156 **P**6
Primary Contact: Craig Loveless, Chief Executive Officer
COO: Ryan Marvin, Support Services Director
CFO: Heather Prideaux, Chief Financial Officer
CIO: Destiny Schroeder, Information Systems Director
CHR: Tara Bowles, Employee Relations Director
Web address: www.rchc.us
Control: County, Government, Nonfederal **Service:** General medical and surgical

Staffed Beds: 15 **Admissions:** 158 **Census:** 1 **Outpatient Visits:** 33590 **Births:** 0 **Total Expense ($000):** 8957 **Payroll Expense ($000):** 3581 **Personnel:** 57

BELLEVILLE—Republic County

★ **REPUBLIC COUNTY HOSPITAL (171361)**, 2420 'G' Street, Zip 66935–2400; tel. 785/527–2254, **A**10 18 **F**3 13 15 28 29 30 31 34 35 40 43 45 56 57 59 64 68 75 76 77 79 81 82 85 86 87 89 91 93 94 104 107 108 110 115 119 128 129 130 131 133 148 153 156 **S** Great Plains Health Alliance, Inc., Wichita, KS
Primary Contact: Daniel J. Kelly, Chief Executive Officer
CFO: Barry Bottger, Chief Financial Officer
Web address: www.rphospital.org
Control: Other not–for–profit (including NFP Corporation) **Service:** General medical and surgical

Staffed Beds: 25 **Admissions:** 547 **Census:** 15 **Outpatient Visits:** 18383 **Births:** 37 **Total Expense ($000):** 20235 **Payroll Expense ($000):** 8588 **Personnel:** 142

Hospitals, U.S. / KANSAS

BELOIT—Mitchell County

MITCHELL COUNTY HOSPITAL HEALTH SYSTEMS (171375), 400 West 8th Street, Zip 67420–1605, Mailing Address: P.O. Box 399, Zip 67420–0399; tel. 785/738–2266, (Total facility includes 36 beds in nursing home–type unit) **A**10 18 **F**2 3 11 13 15 28 29 31 34 35 40 43 45 48 50 56 59 63 64 68 70 76 77 79 81 82 85 87 91 93 107 108 109 110 111 115 119 128 129 130 132 133 135 148 149 153 156 169
Primary Contact: Janelle Kircher, MSN, R.N., Chief Executive Officer
CFO: Eldon Koepke, Chief Financial Officer
CIO: Nate Richards, Director Information Technology
CHR: Phyllis Oetting, Director Human Resources
CNO: Jan Kemmerer, Director of Nursing
Web address: www.mchks.com
Control: County, Government, Nonfederal **Service**: General medical and surgical

Staffed Beds: 61 **Admissions**: 888 **Census**: 42 **Outpatient Visits**: 11810 **Births**: 53 **Total Expense ($000)**: 29767 **Payroll Expense ($000)**: 13850 **Personnel**: 237

BURLINGTON—Coffey County

★ **COFFEY COUNTY HOSPITAL (171385)**, 801 North 4th Street, Zip 66839–2602; tel. 620/364–2121, (Nonreporting) **A**10 18
Primary Contact: Stacy Augustyn, MSN, R.N., Chief Executive Officer
CFO: Jim Van Hoet, Chief Financial Officer
CMO: John Shell, M.D., Chief Medical Officer
CIO: Adam Haag, Manager Information Technology
CHR: Theresa Thoele, Director Human Resources
Web address: www.coffeyhealth.org
Control: County, Government, Nonfederal **Service**: General medical and surgical

Staffed Beds: 49

CALDWELL—Sumner County

★ **CALDWELL REGIONAL MEDICAL CENTER (171329)**, 761 West 175th Street South, Zip 67022–1654; tel. 620/845–6492, **A**10 18 **F**3 7 11 12 29 34 40 50 56 57 59 64 65 66 67 68 81 87 92 93 97 102 107 115 119 127 128 130 133 134 135 146 147 148 149 154 157
Primary Contact: Christopher Graham, Chief Executive Officer
CMO: Jim Blunk, D.O., Chief Medical Officer
CIO: Trey Watson, Network Administrator
Web address: https://www.crmcks.com/
Control: Hospital district or authority, Government, Nonfederal **Service**: General medical and surgical

Staffed Beds: 16 **Admissions**: 199 **Census**: 2 **Outpatient Visits**: 7676 **Births**: 0 **Total Expense ($000)**: 9978 **Payroll Expense ($000)**: 3477 **Personnel**: 66

SUMNER COUNTY HOSPITAL DISTRICT 1 See Caldwell Regional Medical Center

CHANUTE—Neosho County

★ ⇑ **NEOSHO MEMORIAL REGIONAL MEDICAL CENTER (171380)**, 629 South Plummer, Zip 66720–1928, Mailing Address: P.O. Box 426, Zip 66720–0426; tel. 620/431–4000, **A**10 18 21 **F**3 7 11 13 15 28 29 30 40 43 45 46 47 48 50 55 59 62 63 64 70 71 76 79 81 85 97 107 108 110 111 114 119 126 127 129 130 133 143 146 147 149 154 162 167 **P**3 8 **S** Ovation Healthcare, Brentwood, TN
Primary Contact: Dennis Franks, FACHE, Chief Executive Officer
COO: Wendy Brazil, Chief Operating Officer
CFO: Katie Tinsley, Chief Financial Officer
CMO: Charles Van Houden, M.D., Chief Medical Officer
CIO: Gretchen Keller, Director Health Information
CHR: R C Rowan, Director Human Resources
CNO: Jennifer Newton, R.N., Chief Nursing Officer
Web address: www.nmrmc.com
Control: County, Government, Nonfederal **Service**: General medical and surgical

Staffed Beds: 25 **Admissions**: 1275 **Census**: 11 **Outpatient Visits**: 61221 **Births**: 342 **Total Expense ($000)**: 62549 **Payroll Expense ($000)**: 28418 **Personnel**: 353

CLAY CENTER—Clay County

★ **CLAY COUNTY MEDICAL CENTER (171371)**, 617 Liberty Street, Zip 67432–1564, Mailing Address: P.O. Box 512, Zip 67432–0512; tel. 785/632–2144, **A**10 18 **F**3 13 15 18 28 29 30 34 40 45 50 53 55 57 59 63 64 68 74 75 76 77 78 79 81 82 84 86 87 93 96 97 104 107 108 111 115 116 119 127 130 132 133 135 146 147 148 149 154
Primary Contact: Austin M. Gillard, FACHE, Chief Executive Officer
CFO: James Garbarino, Chief Financial Officer
CIO: Chris Wolf, Director Information Technology
CHR: Cindy Rush, Director Human Resources
CNO: Sara Beikman, Director of Nursing
Web address: www.ccmcks.org
Control: County, Government, Nonfederal **Service**: General medical and surgical

Staffed Beds: 25 **Admissions**: 518 **Census**: 6 **Outpatient Visits**: 94305 **Births**: 66 **Total Expense ($000)**: 37248 **Payroll Expense ($000)**: 16671 **Personnel**: 244

COFFEYVILLE—Montgomery County

★ ⇑ **COFFEYVILLE REGIONAL MEDICAL CENTER (170145)**, 1400 West Fourth, Zip 67337–3306; tel. 620/251–1200, **A**10 20 21 **F**3 7 11 13 15 18 28 29 30 31 34 35 40 45 50 57 59 64 65 70 74 76 77 78 79 81 82 85 87 93 97 107 108 110 111 114 115 118 119 120 121 123 127 131 133 146 147 149 154 164 167 169 **P**6
Primary Contact: Brian Lawrence, Chief Executive Officer
CIO: Kris Penco, Director Information Systems
CHR: Becky A McCune, Director Human Resources, Community Relations and Education
CNO: Sarah M Hoy, Chief Nursing Officer
Web address: https://www.crmcinc.org
Control: Other not-for-profit (including NFP Corporation) **Service**: General medical and surgical

Staffed Beds: 25 **Admissions**: 900 **Census**: 7 **Outpatient Visits**: 72319 **Births**: 183 **Total Expense ($000)**: 52153 **Payroll Expense ($000)**: 21533 **Personnel**: 330

COLBY—Thomas County

★ **CITIZENS MEDICAL CENTER (171362)**, 100 East College Drive, Zip 67701–3799; tel. 785/462–7511, (Total facility includes 60 beds in nursing home–type unit) **A**10 18 **F**3 11 12 13 15 28 29 30 31 34 35 38 40 43 45 50 53 55 56 57 59 64 65 67 68 75 76 77 78 81 82 85 86 87 90 93 97 107 108 110 111 115 119 127 128 130 131 132 133 135 144 146 147 148 149 154 156 157 169 **P**6
Primary Contact: David McCorkle, Chief Executive Officer
CMO: Kelly Gabel, Chief of Staff
CIO: Jacee Dobbs, Chief Information Officer
CHR: Margaret Kummer, Chief Human Resource Officer
CNO: Jenny Niblock, Chief Clinical Officer
Web address: www.cmciks.com
Control: Other not-for-profit (including NFP Corporation) **Service**: General medical and surgical

Staffed Beds: 85 **Admissions**: 613 **Census**: 54 **Outpatient Visits**: 239058 **Births**: 187 **Personnel**: 375

COLDWATER—Comanche County

★ **COMANCHE COUNTY HOSPITAL (171312)**, 202 South Frisco Street, Zip 67029–9101, Mailing Address: HC 65, Box 8A, Zip 67029–9500; tel. 620/582–2144, **A**10 18 **F**3 11 30 31 40 53 59 61 68 75 78 93 102 107 128 133 156 166 **P**6 **S** Great Plains Health Alliance, Inc., Wichita, KS
Primary Contact: Lisa Brooks, Administrator
CMO: Daniel Schowengerdt, M.D., Chief of Staff
CIO: LaNell Wagnon, Director Medical Records
CNO: Sandra Dobrinski, Director of Nursing
Web address: www.gpha.com
Control: County, Government, Nonfederal **Service**: General medical and surgical

Staffed Beds: 12 **Admissions**: 103 **Census**: 1 **Outpatient Visits**: 8849 **Births**: 0 **Total Expense ($000)**: 7063 **Payroll Expense ($000)**: 3236 **Personnel**: 45

Hospital, Medicare Provider Number, Address, Telephone, Approval, Facility, and Physician Codes, Health Care System

★ American Hospital Association (AHA) membership ◯ Healthcare Facilities Accreditation Program ⇑ Center for Improvement in Healthcare Quality Accreditation
☐ The Joint Commission accreditation ◇ DNV Healthcare Inc. accreditation △ Commission on Accreditation of Rehabilitation Facilities (CARF) accreditation

© 2025 AHA Guide

Hospitals, U.S. / KANSAS

COLUMBUS—Cherokee County

★ **MERCY HOSPITAL COLUMBUS (171308)**, 220 North Pennsylvania Avenue, Zip 66725-1110; tel. 620/429-2545, **A**10 18 **F**3 11 29 40 41 64 67 77 89 91 93 107 119 128 133 **S** Mercy, Chesterfield, MO
Primary Contact: Angie Saporito, Administrator
Web address: https://www.mercy.net/practice/mercy-hospital-columbus/
Control: Church operated, Nongovernment, not-for-profit **Service**: General medical and surgical

> **Staffed Beds**: 6 **Admissions**: 89 **Census**: 1 **Outpatient Visits**: 6207
> **Births**: 0 **Total Expense ($000)**: 5466 **Payroll Expense ($000)**: 3260
> **Personnel**: 31

CONCORDIA—Cloud County

CLOUD COUNTY HEALTH CENTER See North Central Kansas Medical Center

★ **NORTH CENTRAL KANSAS MEDICAL CENTER (171349)**, 155 West College Drive, Zip 66901; tel. 785/243-1234, **A**10 18 **F**3 11 15 28 31 34 35 40 41 45 56 57 59 64 65 74 75 77 79 81 82 85 86 87 93 96 97 102 107 108 111 114 118 119 127 130 133 135 146 148 154 **P**6 **S** Salina Regional Health Center, Salina, KS
Primary Contact: David Garnas, Administrator
CFO: Pamela Blochlinger, Acting Vice President Finance
CMO: Justin Poore, D.O., Chief Medical Staff
CIO: Jenny Bergstrom, Project Manager Information Technology
CHR: Dawn Thoman, Vice President Human Resources
CNO: Michelle Metro, Vice President Nursing
Web address: https://www.nckmed.com/
Control: Other not-for-profit (including NFP Corporation) **Service**: General medical and surgical

> **Staffed Beds**: 25 **Admissions**: 232 **Census**: 4 **Outpatient Visits**: 42094
> **Births**: 0 **Total Expense ($000)**: 27910 **Payroll Expense ($000)**: 11384
> **Personnel**: 145

COUNCIL GROVE—Morris County

★ **MORRIS COUNTY HOSPITAL (171379)**, 600 North Washington Street, Zip 66846-1422; tel. 620/767-6811, **A**10 18 **F**3 7 11 13 15 18 28 34 35 36 40 45 50 57 59 64 65 68 70 76 77 79 81 82 87 93 94 96 107 110 111 119 127 129 130 131 132 133 144 146 148 154 156 169 **P**6
Primary Contact: Kevin Alan. Leeper, Chief Executive Officer
CFO: Ron Christenson, Chief Financial Officer
CMO: Lora Siegle, M.D., Chief Medical Officer
CIO: Bill Lauer, Chief Information Officer
CHR: Don Zimmerman, Director Human Resources
CNO: Stephanne Wolf, Chief Nursing Officer
Web address: www.mrcohosp.com
Control: County, Government, Nonfederal **Service**: General medical and surgical

> **Staffed Beds**: 21 **Admissions**: 251 **Census**: 3 **Outpatient Visits**: 19916
> **Births**: 16 **Total Expense ($000)**: 17444 **Payroll Expense ($000)**: 7428
> **Personnel**: 142

DERBY—Sedgwick County

☐ **ROCK REGIONAL HOSPITAL (170204)**, 3251 North Rock Road, Zip 67037-3850; tel. 316/425-2400, (Nonreporting) **A**1 10
Primary Contact: Ben Quinton, Chief Executive Officer
Web address: https://rockregionalhospitalderby.com
Control: Corporation, Investor-owned (for-profit) **Service**: General medical and surgical

> **Staffed Beds**: 15

DIGHTON—Lane County

★ **LANE COUNTY HOSPITAL (171303)**, 235 West Vine, Zip 67839-0969, Mailing Address: P.O. Box 969, Zip 67839-0969; tel. 620/397-5321, **A**10 18 **F**40 59 77 93 97 107 127 128 133 156 166 **P**6 **S** Great Plains Health Alliance, Inc., Wichita, KS
Primary Contact: Marcia Gabel, Chief Financial Officer and Co-Chief Executive Officer
CFO: Marcia Gabel, Chief Financial Officer
CMO: Paul Chinburg, M.D., Medical Director
CHR: Dina Casey, Human Resources Officer
CNO: Jennifer Whipple, Director Nursing
Web address: www.lanecountyhospital.com/
Control: County, Government, Nonfederal **Service**: General medical and surgical

> **Staffed Beds**: 25 **Admissions**: 74 **Census**: 19 **Outpatient Visits**: 9092
> **Births**: 0 **Total Expense ($000)**: 7657 **Payroll Expense ($000)**: 3481
> **Personnel**: 64

DODGE CITY—Ford County

✠ **ST. CATHERINE HOSPITAL – DODGE CITY (170175)**, 3001 Avenue 'A', Zip 67801-6508, Mailing Address: P.O. Box 1478, Zip 67801-1478; tel. 620/225-8400, **A**1 5 10 20 **F**3 13 15 18 20 22 28 29 30 40 45 46 50 60 65 70 74 75 76 77 79 81 87 89 93 96 97 107 108 109 110 111 112 114 115 119 130 147 148 149 154 167 169 **P**6 **S** CommonSpirit Health, Chicago, IL
Primary Contact: Twilla Lee, Chief Executive Officer
COO: John Fitzthum, Chief Operating Officer and Admiistrator
CFO: Mark Massey, Chief Financial Officer
CMO: Merrill Conant, M.D., Chief of Staff
CIO: Shawna Culver, Director Information Systems
CHR: Corry Israel, Director Human Resources
CNO: Marsha Jamison, Chief Nursing Officer
Web address: https://www.centura.org/location/st-catherine-hospital-dodge-city
Control: Church operated, Nongovernment, not-for-profit **Service**: General medical and surgical

> **Staffed Beds**: 99 **Admissions**: 1459 **Census**: 10 **Outpatient Visits**: 42626
> **Births**: 548 **Total Expense ($000)**: 40864 **Payroll Expense ($000)**: 14653
> **Personnel**: 123

EL DORADO—Butler County

✠ **SUSAN B. ALLEN MEMORIAL HOSPITAL (170017)**, 720 West Central Avenue, Zip 67042-2112; tel. 316/321-3300, **A**1 10 **F**3 11 13 15 28 34 35 40 45 55 57 59 62 64 68 69 70 75 76 79 81 85 89 92 93 96 107 108 110 111 115 119 120 121 123 133 144 146 148 149 154 167 169
Primary Contact: Melissa K. Hall, Chief Executive Officer
CFO: Gene Kaberline, Chief Financial Officer
CMO: Paige Dodson, M.D., M.P.H., Chief Medical Officer
CHR: D. Gay Kimble, Chief Human Resource Officer
CNO: Cecilia B Goebel, R.N., Chief Nursing Officer
Web address: www.sbamh.com
Control: Other not-for-profit (including NFP Corporation) **Service**: General medical and surgical

> **Staffed Beds**: 20 **Admissions**: 570 **Census**: 5 **Outpatient Visits**: 264905
> **Births**: 159 **Total Expense ($000)**: 38250 **Payroll Expense ($000)**: 14581
> **Personnel**: 154

ELKHART—Morton County

★ **MORTON COUNTY HEALTH SYSTEM (170166)**, 445 Hilltop Street, Zip 67950-0937, Mailing Address: P.O. Box 937, Zip 67950-0937; tel. 620/697-2141, **A**10 20 22 **F**3 5 28 29 34 38 40 57 59 63 64 86 87 93 94 104 107 108 115 127 130 131 133 147 148 154 160 167
Primary Contact: Lisa Swenson, Chief Executive Officer
CHR: Sonja May, Director Human Resources
Web address: www.mchswecare.com
Control: County, Government, Nonfederal **Service**: General medical and surgical

> **Staffed Beds**: 25 **Admissions**: 125 **Census**: 1 **Outpatient Visits**: 11278
> **Births**: 0 **Total Expense ($000)**: 9621 **Payroll Expense ($000)**: 5711
> **Personnel**: 75

ELLINWOOD—Barton County

★ **ELLINWOOD DISTRICT HOSPITAL (171301)**, 605 North Main Street, Zip 67526-1440; tel. 620/564-2548, **A**10 18 **F**11 40 64 65 93 107 127 128 133 154 156 **P**6 **S** Great Plains Health Alliance, Inc., Wichita, KS
Primary Contact: Kile Magner, Administrator
CFO: Summer Zink, Chief Financial Officer
CMO: Charlie Joslin, M.D., Chief of Staff
CIO: Becky L Burns, Manager Health Information Management
CHR: Chris Robl, Human Resources
CNO: Jill Ritchie, Director of Nursing
Web address: www.ellinwooddistricthospital.org
Control: Other not-for-profit (including NFP Corporation) **Service**: General medical and surgical

> **Staffed Beds**: 25 **Admissions**: 202 **Census**: 6 **Outpatient Visits**: 15256
> **Births**: 0 **Total Expense ($000)**: 10384 **Payroll Expense ($000)**: 4622
> **Personnel**: 91

Hospitals, U.S. / KANSAS

ELLSWORTH—Ellsworth County

★ **ELLSWORTH COUNTY MEDICAL CENTER (171327)**, 1604 Aylward Street, Zip 67439-0087, Mailing Address: P.O. Box 87, Zip 67439-0087; tel. 785/472-3111, (Nonreporting) **A**10 18
Primary Contact: James B. Kirkbride, Chief Executive Officer
CFO: Preston Sauers, Chief Financial Officer
CIO: Lynette Dick, Director of Support Services
CHR: Christa N Bohnen, Director Human Resources
CNO: Amanda Thrasher, Director Nursing
Web address: www.ewmed.com
Control: County, Government, Nonfederal **Service**: General medical and surgical

Staffed Beds: 19

EMPORIA—Lyon County

○ **NEWMAN REGIONAL HEALTH (171384)**, 1201 West 12th Avenue, Zip 66801-2597; tel. 620/343-6800, **A**10 11 18 **F**3 11 13 15 17 18 20 22 26 28 29 31 39 40 41 43 45 51 53 59 61 63 64 65 68 70 72 73 76 77 78 79 81 82 84 85 86 87 89 90 96 102 107 108 111 114 118 119 127 129 130 131 132 133 135 144 145 146 147 148 149 156 169 **P**6
Primary Contact: Cathy Pimple, MS, Chief Executive Officer
CFO: Holly French, Chief Financial Officer
CHR: Tabatha Tafoya, Director Human Resources
CNO: Julia Pyle, R.N., Chief Nursing Officer
Web address: www.newmanrh.org
Control: County, Government, Nonfederal **Service**: General medical and surgical

Staffed Beds: 35 **Admissions**: 1456 **Census**: 21 **Outpatient Visits**: 134068
Births: 345 **Total Expense ($000)**: 87707 **Payroll Expense ($000)**: 39547
Personnel: 479

EUREKA—Greenwood County

GREENWOOD COUNTY HOSPITAL (171339), 100 West 16th Street, Zip 67045-1064; tel. 620/583-7451, (Nonreporting) **A**10 18
Primary Contact: Sandra Dickerson, Chief Executive Officer
CFO: Melody Curnutt, CPA, Chief Financial Officer
CMO: Mark Basham, M.D., Chief Medical Officer
CIO: Jason Clark, Director Information Systems
CHR: Janel M Palmer, Director Human Resources
CNO: Rebecca Randall, Chief Nursing Officer
Web address: www.gwch.org
Control: County, Government, Nonfederal **Service**: General medical and surgical

Staffed Beds: 25

FREDONIA—Wilson County

★ **FREDONIA REGIONAL HOSPITAL (171374)**, 1527 Madison Street, Zip 66736-1751, Mailing Address: P.O. Box 579, Zip 66736-0579; tel. 620/378-2121, **A**10 18 **F**3 7 11 15 30 40 57 59 81 82 85 93 104 107 110 111 115 119 128 133 156 166 **S** Great Plains Health Alliance, Inc., Wichita, KS
Primary Contact: Johnathan Durrett, Chief Executive Officer
CFO: Tracy Row, Manager Business Office
CMO: Jennifer McKenney, M.D., Chief Medical Officer
CIO: Tyler Row, Director Information Technology
CHR: Debbie Marr, Administrative Assistant and Director Human Resources
CNO: Ryan Duft, R.N., Chief Nursing Officer
Web address: www.fredoniaregionalhospital.org
Control: City, Government, Nonfederal **Service**: General medical and surgical

Staffed Beds: 25 **Admissions**: 180 **Census**: 2 **Outpatient Visits**: 32874
Births: 0 **Total Expense ($000)**: 14724 **Payroll Expense ($000)**: 5289
Personnel: 129

GALENA—Cherokee County

★ ⇧ **MERCY SPECIALTY HOSPITAL SOUTHEAST KANSAS (170203)**, 1619 West 7th Street, Zip 66739; tel. 620/783-1732, (Nonreporting) **A**10 21 **S** Mercy, Chesterfield, MO
Primary Contact: Joseph Caputo, Vice President, Operations
Web address: www.premiersurgicalinstitute.com/
Control: City, Government, Nonfederal **Service**: General medical and surgical

Staffed Beds: 25

GARDEN CITY—Finney County

⊞ **ST. CATHERINE HOSPITAL (170023)**, 401 East Spruce Street, Zip 67846-5679; tel. 620/272-2222, **A**1 10 20 **F**3 13 15 18 20 22 29 30 31 34 35 39 40 45 51 59 63 64 65 68 69 70 72 74 75 76 77 78 79 81 82 83 84 85 86 87 89 90 91 92 93 94 96 97 98 100 102 107 108 109 110 111 112 113 114 115 118 119 130 131 146 147 148 149 154 156 167 169 **P**6 **S** CommonSpirit Health, Chicago, IL
Primary Contact: Twilla Lee, Chief Executive Officer
CFO: Amanda Vaughan, Chief Financial Officer
CMO: Anita Toussi, M.D., Ph.D., Chief Medical Officer
CIO: Lance Kellenbarger, Site Director Information Systems
CHR: Kathy E. Morrison, Executive Director Human Resources
CNO: Margaret Elizabeth Prewitt, Vice President Patient Services and Chief Nursing Officer
Web address: www.StCatherineHosp.org
Control: Church operated, Nongovernment, not-for-profit **Service**: General medical and surgical

Staffed Beds: 100 **Admissions**: 3009 **Census**: 36 **Outpatient Visits**: 67767
Births: 696 **Total Expense ($000)**: 83773 **Payroll Expense ($000)**: 27124
Personnel: 239

GARDNER—Johnson County

△ **MEADOWBROOK REHABILITATION HOSPITAL (173033)**, 427 West Main Street, Zip 66030-1183; tel. 913/856-8747, (Nonreporting) **A**7 10
Primary Contact: Matt Tait, JD, Chief Executive Officer
CFO: Kelly Taul, Business Manager
CMO: David Edalati, M.D., Medical Director
CHR: Carrie Moore, Director Human Resources
CNO: Lisa Perez, R.N., Director Nursing
Web address: https://meadowbrookrh.com/
Control: Partnership, Investor-owned (for-profit) **Service**: Rehabilitation

Staffed Beds: 96

GARNETT—Anderson County

★ **ANDERSON COUNTY HOSPITAL (171316)**, 421 South Maple, Zip 66032-1334, Mailing Address: P.O. Box 309, Zip 66032-0309; tel. 785/448-3131, (Total facility includes 30 beds in nursing home-type unit) **A**10 18 **F**3 4 7 11 15 18 29 30 34 35 40 43 44 45 50 56 59 64 65 67 68 75 77 79 81 82 85 86 87 93 96 97 102 104 107 108 110 111 115 118 119 127 130 131 133 135 146 147 148 149 154 164 167 **P**6 **S** BJC Health System, Saint Louis, MO
Primary Contact: William Patton, Administrator
CFO: Vicki L Mills, Chief Financial Officer
CMO: Mackenzie Peterson, M.D., Chief of Staff
CHR: Karen Gillespie, Director Human Resources
CNO: Margo L Williams, R.N., Chief Nursing Officer
Web address: https://www.saintlukeskc.org/locations/anderson-county-hospital
Control: Other not-for-profit (including NFP Corporation) **Service**: General medical and surgical

Staffed Beds: 40 **Admissions**: 262 **Census**: 28 **Outpatient Visits**: 30964
Births: 0 **Total Expense ($000)**: 32807 **Payroll Expense ($000)**: 13201
Personnel: 209

GIRARD—Crawford County

★ **GIRARD MEDICAL CENTER (171376)**, 302 North Hospital Drive, Zip 66743-2000; tel. 620/724-8291, **A**10 18 **F**3 6 8 11 12 15 17 28 29 34 35 40 43 44 45 47 50 53 56 57 59 62 64 65 68 70 75 81 86 87 89 93 98 100 101 103 104 107 114 119 127 128 130 133 144 146 148 149 154 164 165 **P**6
Primary Contact: Ruth Duling, Chief Executive Officer
CFO: Holly Koch, Chief Financial Officer
CIO: Jeff Barnes, Director Information Technology
CHR: Gregory Sullivan, Manager Human Resources
CNO: Joyce Geier, Director Nursing
Web address: www.girardmedicalcenter.com
Control: Hospital district or authority, Government, Nonfederal **Service**: General medical and surgical

Staffed Beds: 35 **Admissions**: 476 **Census**: 8 **Outpatient Visits**: 24821
Births: 0 **Total Expense ($000)**: 24203 **Payroll Expense ($000)**: 11476
Personnel: 189

Hospital, Medicare Provider Number, Address, Telephone, Approval, Facility, and Physician Codes, Health Care System

★ American Hospital Association (AHA) membership
□ The Joint Commission accreditation
○ Healthcare Facilities Accreditation Program
◇ DNV Healthcare Inc. accreditation
⇧ Center for Improvement in Healthcare Quality Accreditation
△ Commission on Accreditation of Rehabilitation Facilities (CARF) accreditation

© 2025 AHA Guide

Hospitals, U.S. / KANSAS

GOODLAND—Sherman County

★ **GOODLAND REGIONAL MEDICAL CENTER (171370)**, 220 West Second Street, Zip 67735-1602; tel. 785/890-3625, **A**10 18 **F**3 11 15 19 28 29 31 40 44 45 50 57 59 68 69 77 78 85 87 93 97 107 110 115 119 127 128 130 131 133 148 169 **P**6
Primary Contact: Craig Loveless, Chief Executive Officer
CMO: Travis Daise, M.D., Chief Medical Officer
CHR: Kim Horineck, Chief Human Resource Officer
Web address: www.goodlandregional.com
Control: County, Government, Nonfederal **Service**: General medical and surgical

Staffed Beds: 25 **Admissions**: 387 **Census**: 4 **Outpatient Visits**: 57366 **Births**: 0 **Total Expense ($000)**: 33534 **Payroll Expense ($000)**: 7969 **Personnel**: 125	

GREAT BEND—Barton County

UNIVERSITY OF KANSAS HEALTH SYSTEM GREAT BEND CAMPUS (170191), 514 Cleveland Street, Zip 67530-3562; tel. 620/792-8833, **A**10 20 **F**3 13 15 29 30 40 43 46 55 59 62 63 76 79 81 82 89 93 97 107 108 111 115 119 124 127 130 131 144 147 167 169 **S** The University of Kansas Health System, Kansas City, KS
Primary Contact: John Worden, Interim Administrator
CFO: Timothy Latimer, Chief Financial Officer
CMO: Randall Hildebrand, M.D., Chief Medical Officer
CHR: Laura Maneth, Human Resources Businss Partner
CNO: Melissa A Jensen, Director, Nursing and Clinical Operations
Web address: www.gbregional.com
Control: Other not-for-profit (including NFP Corporation) **Service**: General medical and surgical

Staffed Beds: 33 **Admissions**: 1045 **Census**: 9 **Outpatient Visits**: 88600 **Births**: 234 **Total Expense ($000)**: 66061 **Payroll Expense ($000)**: 29354 **Personnel**: 379

GREENSBURG—Kiowa County

★ ⇑ **KIOWA COUNTY MEMORIAL HOSPITAL (171332)**, 721 West Kansas Avenue, Zip 67054-1633; tel. 620/723-3341, **A**10 18 21 **F**3 7 34 40 50 53 59 64 68 107 114 127 133 149 154 156 167 **P**6
Primary Contact: Morgan Allison, Chief Executive Officer
CFO: Ron Tucker, Business Office Manager
CMO: Nizar Kibar, M.D., Chief Medical Staff
CIO: Jeremy Steven Hoover, Chief Information Officer
CHR: Cathy McFall, Human Resources Manager
CNO: Vanessa Kirk, Director of Nursing
Web address: www.kcmh.net
Control: County, Government, Nonfederal **Service**: General medical and surgical

Staffed Beds: 15 **Admissions**: 161 **Census**: 7 **Outpatient Visits**: 11677 **Births**: 1 **Total Expense ($000)**: 12405 **Payroll Expense ($000)**: 5274

HANOVER—Washington County

★ **HANOVER HOSPITAL (171365)**, 205 South Hanover, Zip 66945-8924, Mailing Address: P.O. Box 38, Zip 66945-0038; tel. 785/337-2214, **A**10 18 **F**2 3 28 34 40 45 50 59 64 67 69 81 97 107 115 127 128 130 133 143 148 154 169 **P**6
Primary Contact: Brittni Oehmke, Administrator
CFO: Sheryl Adam, Chief Financial Officer
Control: Hospital district or authority, Government, Nonfederal **Service**: General medical and surgical

Staffed Beds: 25 **Admissions**: 69 **Census**: 2 **Outpatient Visits**: 8000 **Births**: 0 **Total Expense ($000)**: 7721 **Payroll Expense ($000)**: 3207 **Personnel**: 45

HAYS—Ellis County

★ ⇑ **HAYS MEDICAL CENTER (170013)**, 2220 Canterbury Drive, Zip 67601-2370; tel. 785/623-5000, **A**10 21 **F**3 11 12 13 15 18 20 22 24 26 28 29 30 31 32 34 35 36 37 38 40 41 43 45 51 53 55 56 57 59 60 63 64 65 66 68 69 70 71 72 73 75 76 77 78 79 80 81 82 84 85 86 87 89 90 93 96 97 107 108 110 111 115 118 119 120 121 123 124 126 127 129 130 131 135 144 146 147 148 149 154 156 167 169 **P**4
Primary Contact: Edward Herrman, R.N., FACHE, President and Chief Executive Officer
COO: Bryce A Young, Chief Operating Officer
CFO: Michelle Beckner, Chief Financial Officer
CIO: Scott Rohleder, Chief Information Officer
CHR: Bryce A Young, Chief Operating Officer
Web address: www.haysmed.com
Control: Other not-for-profit (including NFP Corporation) **Service**: General medical and surgical

Staffed Beds: 105 **Admissions**: 4050 **Census**: 52 **Outpatient Visits**: 190784 **Births**: 560 **Total Expense ($000)**: 241595 **Payroll Expense ($000)**: 98127 **Personnel**: 1114

HIAWATHA—Brown County

★ **AMBERWELL HIAWATHA (171341)**, 300 Utah Street, Zip 66434-2314; tel. 785/742-2131, (Nonreporting) **A**10 18
Primary Contact: Jared Abel, Chief Executive Officer
CFO: Jenny Knudson, Controller
CMO: Steffen Shamburg, M.D., Chief of Staff
CIO: Sharese Moser, Director, Finance
CHR: Alison Keri, Director Human Resources
CNO: Lisa Thompson, MSN, R.N., Director of Nursing
Web address: www.hch-ks.org
Control: Other not-for-profit (including NFP Corporation) **Service**: General medical and surgical

Staffed Beds: 25

HIAWATHA COMMUNITY HOSPITAL See Amberwell Hiawatha

HILL CITY—Graham County

★ **GRAHAM COUNTY HOSPITAL (171325)**, 304 West Prout Street, Zip 67642-1435; tel. 785/421-2121, **A**10 18 **F**3 11 34 40 50 53 59 64 67 68 81 84 93 107 115 127 128 133 148 149 154
Primary Contact: Melissa Atkins, CPA, Chief Executive Officer
CHR: Donella Belleau, Director Human Resources
Web address: www.grahamcountyhospital.org
Control: County, Government, Nonfederal **Service**: General medical and surgical

Staffed Beds: 15 **Admissions**: 215 **Census**: 3 **Outpatient Visits**: 7791 **Births**: 0 **Total Expense ($000)**: 10324 **Payroll Expense ($000)**: 4762 **Personnel**: 75

HILLSBORO—Marion County

HILLSBORO COMMUNITY HOSPITAL (171357), 701 South Main Street, Zip 67063-1553; tel. 620/947-3114, **A**10 18 **F**1 3 12 15 29 34 35 40 45 50 57 59 64 65 67 68 75 90 93 97 107 114 119 127 128 130 131 133 148 149 154 **P**6
Primary Contact: Mark Rooker, Chief Executive Officer
COO: Johna Magnuson, Director Nursing
CIO: Marsha Setzkorn-Meyer, Director Public Relations and Marketing
CHR: Wendy McCarty, Director Human Resources
Web address: https://www.hillsborohospital.com/
Control: Corporation, Investor-owned (for-profit) **Service**: General medical and surgical

Staffed Beds: 8 **Admissions**: 253 **Census**: 4 **Outpatient Visits**: 13314 **Births**: 0 **Total Expense ($000)**: 8469 **Payroll Expense ($000)**: 3579 **Personnel**: 68

HOISINGTON—Barton County

CLARA BARTON HOSPITAL See Clara Barton Medical Center

★ **CLARA BARTON MEDICAL CENTER (171333)**, 250 West Ninth Street, Zip 67544-1706; tel. 620/653-2114, (Nonreporting) **A**10 18
Primary Contact: Jay Tusten, President and Chief Executive Officer
CMO: Nathan Knackstedt, D.O., Chief of Staff
CHR: John Moshier, Director Human Resources
CNO: Jane Schepmann, Vice President and Chief Nursing Officer
Web address: www.clarabartonhospital.org
Control: Other not-for-profit (including NFP Corporation) **Service**: General medical and surgical

Staffed Beds: 23

HOLTON—Jackson County

★ **HOLTON COMMUNITY HOSPITAL (171319)**, 1110 Columbine Drive, Zip 66436-8824; tel. 785/364-2116, **A**10 18 **F**3 11 12 15 18 28 29 34 40 43 45 50 59 62 63 64 65 75 77 78 79 81 82 87 93 97 107 110 114 119 127 130 131 132 133 135 146 147 154 156 157 **P**3
Primary Contact: Carrie L. Lutz, Chief Executive Officer
CFO: Bart Kenton, Chief Financial Officer
CMO: Joel Hutchsin, M.D., Chief Medical Staff
CIO: Holli Peters, Director Health Information Management
CHR: Gretchen Snavely, Director Human Resources
CNO: Mandy Bontrager, Director Nursing
Web address: www.holtonhospital.com
Control: Other not-for-profit (including NFP Corporation) **Service**: General medical and surgical

Staffed Beds: 14 **Admissions**: 220 **Census**: 3 **Outpatient Visits**: 47132 **Births**: 0 **Total Expense ($000)**: 26650 **Payroll Expense ($000)**: 11534 **Personnel**: 165

HOXIE—Sheridan County

SHERIDAN COUNTY HEALTH COMPLEX (171347), 826 18th Street, Zip 67740–0167, Mailing Address: P.O. Box 167, Zip 67740–0167; tel. 785/675–3281, (Total facility includes 32 beds in nursing home–type unit) **A**10 18 **F**3 7 10 11 29 34 35 40 45 50 53 56 57 59 64 65 66 67 69 75 81 82 85 87 92 93 97 100 101 107 115 119 125 130 133 143 147 148 149 154
Primary Contact: Chad Koster, Chief Executive Officer
CFO: Michael O'Dell, Chief Financial Officer
CMO: Victor Nemechek, M.D., Chief of Staff and Chief Medical Officer
CHR: Shelby Moss, Human Resource Officer
CNO: Hannah Schoendaler, Chief Nursing Officer
Web address: www.sheridancountyhospital.com
Control: County, Government, Nonfederal **Service**: General medical and surgical

Staffed Beds: 50 **Admissions**: 139 **Census**: 32 **Outpatient Visits**: 6315
Births: 0 **Total Expense ($000)**: 16611 **Payroll Expense ($000)**: 8647
Personnel: 136

HUGOTON—Stevens County

STEVENS COUNTY HOSPITAL (171335), 1006 South Jackson Street, Zip 67951–2858, Mailing Address: P.O. Box 10, Zip 67951–0010; tel. 620/544–8511, (Nonreporting) **A**10 18
Primary Contact: Jennifer Featherston, Chief Executive Officer
CMO: Samer Al–hashmi, M.D., Chief Medical Staff
Web address: www.stevenscountyhospital.com/
Control: County, Government, Nonfederal **Service**: General medical and surgical

Staffed Beds: 94

HUTCHINSON—Reno County

▣ △ **HUTCHINSON REGIONAL MEDICAL CENTER (170020)**, 1701 East 23rd Avenue, Zip 67502–1191; tel. 620/665–2000, (Nonreporting) **A**1 7 10
Primary Contact: Benjamin Anderson, President and Chief Executive Officer
COO: Nicholas Baldetti, Chief Operating Officer and Chief Quality Officer
CFO: Cameron Meyer, CPA, Chief Financial Officer
CMO: Thomas Smith, M.D., Vice President Medical Affairs
CIO: Calvin Wright, Chief Information Officer
CHR: Jed M. Liuzza, Chief Human Resources Officer
CNO: Jonna Jenkins, Vice President of Patient Care Services, Chief Nursing Officer
Web address: www.hutchregional.com
Control: Other not–for–profit (including NFP Corporation) **Service**: General medical and surgical

Staffed Beds: 146

SUMMIT SURGICAL (170198), 1818 East 23rd Avenue, Zip 67502–1106; tel. 620/663–4800, (Nonreporting) **A**10
Primary Contact: Randy Roatch, Chief Executive Officer
COO: Nancy Corwin, Chief Operating Officer
CNO: Nancy Corwin, Chief Nursing Officer
Web address: www.summitks.com
Control: Partnership, Investor–owned (for–profit) **Service**: Surgical

Staffed Beds: 10

IOLA—Allen County

▣ **ALLEN COUNTY REGIONAL HOSPITAL (171373)**, 3066 N. Kentucky St, Zip 66749, Mailing Address: P.O. Box 540, Zip 66749–0540; tel. 620/365–1000, **A**1 10 18 **F**3 4 11 15 18 29 30 31 34 35 40 43 44 45 50 56 59 64 65 68 75 77 78 79 81 82 85 86 87 93 96 97 102 104 107 108 110 111 115 118 119 127 130 131 133 135 146 148 149 154 164 167 **P**6 **S** BJC Health System, Saint Louis, MO
Primary Contact: William Patton, Administrator
CFO: Larry Peterson, Chief Financial Officer
CMO: Brian Wolfe, Chief of Staff
CHR: Paula Sell, Director Human Resources
Web address: https://www.saintlukeskc.com/locations/allen-county-regional-hospital
Control: Other not–for–profit (including NFP Corporation) **Service**: General medical and surgical

Staffed Beds: 10 **Admissions**: 363 **Census**: 6 **Outpatient Visits**: 29946
Births: 0 **Total Expense ($000)**: 30874 **Payroll Expense ($000)**: 10423
Personnel: 150

JETMORE—Hodgeman County

★ **HODGEMAN COUNTY HEALTH CENTER (171369)**, 809 Bramley Street, Zip 67854–9320, Mailing Address: P.O. Box 310, Zip 67854–0310; tel. 620/357–8361, (Total facility includes 17 beds in nursing home–type unit) **A**10 18 **F**3 29 32 33 40 50 53 55 57 59 64 67 68 81 82 93 97 107 115 125 127 130 133 143 147 148 149 **P**6
Primary Contact: Allen E. Van Driel, Interim Chief Executive Officer
CFO: Stacey Briggs, Chief Financial Officer
CHR: Vanessa A Bamberger, Human Resources Manager
Web address: www.hchconline.org
Control: County, Government, Nonfederal **Service**: General medical and surgical

Staffed Beds: 25 **Admissions**: 180 **Census**: 18 **Outpatient Visits**: 4905
Births: 0 **Total Expense ($000)**: 10237 **Payroll Expense ($000)**: 5250
Personnel: 73

JOHNSON—Stanton County

STANTON COUNTY HOSPITAL (171343), 404 North Chestnut Street, Zip 67855–5001, Mailing Address: P.O. Box 779, Zip 67855–0779; tel. 620/492–6250, (Total facility includes 25 beds in nursing home–type unit) **A**10 18 **F**11 13 34 35 40 41 45 50 54 56 57 59 64 68 75 76 82 86 87 93 97 107 114 127 130 131 133 143 154 **P**6
Primary Contact: Camille Davidson, Administrator and Chief Executive Officer
CMO: Bill Troup, M.D., Chief of Staff
CIO: Marco Medina, Chief Information Officer
CNO: Marianne Mills, R.N., Chairperson
Web address: www.stantoncountyhospital.com
Control: County, Government, Nonfederal **Service**: General medical and surgical

Staffed Beds: 40 **Admissions**: 180 **Census**: 26 **Outpatient Visits**: 12403
Births: 8 **Total Expense ($000)**: 19869 **Payroll Expense ($000)**: 5268
Personnel: 113

JUNCTION CITY—Geary County

▣ **IRWIN ARMY COMMUNITY HOSPITAL**, 600 Caisson Hill Road, Zip 66442–7037; tel. 785/239–7000, (Nonreporting) **A**1 5 **S** Department of the Army, Office of the Surgeon General, Falls Church, VA
Primary Contact: Colonel Edgar Arroyo, Hospital Commander
CMO: Lieutenant Colonel Mark S Ochoa, M.D., Deputy Commander, Clinical Services
CIO: David Dougherty, Chief Information Management Officer
CHR: Hope Brunton, Chief Manpower Branch
Web address: https://irwin.tricare.mil
Control: Army, Government, federal **Service**: General medical and surgical

Staffed Beds: 44

▣ **STORMONT VAIL HEALTH – FLINT HILLS CAMPUS (170074)**, 1102 St Mary's Road, Zip 66441–4196, Mailing Address: P.O. Box 490, Zip 66441–0490; tel. 785/238–4131, (Data for 273 days) **A**1 10 **F**3 11 13 15 29 32 34 35 40 45 50 59 64 65 75 76 77 79 81 82 85 86 87 97 107 108 109 110 111 113 115 117 118 119 127 128 130 132 133 135 144 146 148 149 154 156 169
Primary Contact: Tracy Duran, Administrator
CFO: Preston Trecek, Controller
CMO: Jimmy Jenkins, M.D., Chief Medical Officer
CIO: Kyle Ibarra, Director Information Systems
CHR: Loren Streit, Director Human Resources
Web address: https://www.stormontvail.com/flinthillscampus/
Control: Other not–for–profit (including NFP Corporation) **Service**: General medical and surgical

Staffed Beds: 23 **Admissions**: 530 **Census**: 5 **Outpatient Visits**: 38030
Births: 163 **Total Expense ($000)**: 30525 **Payroll Expense ($000)**: 15277
Personnel: 267

KANSAS CITY—Wyandotte County

☐ **KVC PRAIRIE RIDGE PSYCHIATRIC HOSPITAL**, 4300 Brenner Drive, Zip 66104–1163; tel. 913/334–0294, (Nonreporting) **A**1
Primary Contact: Jason R. Hooper, President and Chief Executive Officer
CMO: Vishal Adma, M.D., Medical Director
Web address: www.kvc.org
Control: Other not–for–profit (including NFP Corporation) **Service**: Children's hospital psychiatric

Staffed Beds: 122

Hospital, Medicare Provider Number, Address, Telephone, Approval, Facility, and Physician Codes, Health Care System

★ American Hospital Association (AHA) membership ○ Healthcare Facilities Accreditation Program ⇑ Center for Improvement in Healthcare Quality Accreditation
☐ The Joint Commission accreditation ◇ DNV Healthcare Inc. accreditation △ Commission on Accreditation of Rehabilitation Facilities (CARF) accreditation

Hospitals, U.S. / KANSAS

☐ **PROVIDENCE MEDICAL CENTER (170146)**, 8929 Parallel Parkway, Zip 66112–1689; tel. 913/596–4000, **A**1 3 10 **F**3 13 15 17 18 20 22 24 28 29 30 31 34 35 40 41 43 44 45 49 53 56 57 59 64 70 72 74 75 76 77 78 79 81 82 84 85 87 93 97 102 107 108 110 111 114 119 120 121 123 124 126 129 130 131 132 135 143 146 147 148 149 156 167 **P**6 **S** Prime Healthcare, Ontario, CA
Primary Contact: Karen Orr, Administrator and Chief Nursing Officer
CFO: David Dulny, Chief Financial Officer
CMO: Sabato Sisillo, M.D., Chief Medical Officer
CIO: Charles Soeken, Director Information Technology
CHR: Brenda Farwell, Director Human Resources
CNO: Karen Orr, Chief Nursing Officer
Web address: www.providencekc.com
Control: Individual, Investor–owned (for–profit) **Service:** General medical and surgical

Staffed Beds: 161 **Admissions:** 5358 **Census:** 69 **Outpatient Visits:** 154154 **Births:** 205 **Total Expense ($000):** 139180 **Payroll Expense ($000):** 53952 **Personnel:** 495

※ **SELECT SPECIALTY HOSPITAL–KANSAS CITY (172005)**, 1731 North 90th Street, Zip 66112–1515; tel. 913/732–5900, **A**1 10 **F**1 3 29 34 45 46 57 74 75 78 79 94 148 **S** Select Medical Corporation, Mechanicsburg, PA
Primary Contact: Brent Hanson, Chief Executive Officer
Web address: www.selectspecialtyhospitals.com
Control: Corporation, Investor–owned (for–profit) **Service:** Acute long–term care hospital

Staffed Beds: 40 **Admissions:** 348 **Census:** 29 **Outpatient Visits:** 0 **Births:** 0 **Total Expense ($000):** 22270 **Payroll Expense ($000):** 11250 **Personnel:** 159

※ **THE UNIVERSITY OF KANSAS HOSPITAL (170040)**, 4000 Cambridge Street, MS 3011, Zip 66160–8501; tel. 913/588–5000, (Includes THE UNIVERSITY OF KANSAS HOSPITAL – INDIAN CREEK CAMPUS, 10720 Nall Avenue, Overland Park, Kansas, Zip 66211–1206, tel. 913/754–5000) **A**1 2 3 5 8 10 19 **F**3 5 8 9 12 13 15 16 17 18 20 22 24 26 28 29 30 31 32 34 35 36 37 38 39 40 41 43 44 45 46 47 48 49 50 51 52 54 55 57 58 59 60 61 64 65 68 70 72 74 75 76 77 78 79 80 81 82 83 84 85 86 87 88 89 90 92 93 96 97 98 99 100 101 102 104 107 108 110 111 112 114 115 116 117 118 119 120 121 122 123 124 126 129 130 131 132 134 135 136 137 138 139 141 142 144 145 146 147 148 149 154 156 157 160 161 162 164 165 167 169 **P**6 **S** The University of Kansas Health System, Kansas City, KS
Primary Contact: Bob Page, Chief Executive Officer
COO: Tammy Peterman, R.N., MS, Executive Vice President, Chief Operating Officer and Chief Nursing Officer
CFO: David Vranicar, Vice Chancellor for Finance and Chief Financial Officer
CMO: Lou Wetzel, M.D., Chief of Staff
CIO: Chris Hansen, Senior Vice President and Chief Information Officer
CHR: Alisa Ford, Vice President Human Resources
CNO: Tammy Peterman, R.N., MS, Executive Vice President, Chief Operating Officer and Chief Nursing Officer
Web address: www.kumed.com
Control: Hospital district or authority, Government, Nonfederal **Service:** General medical and surgical

Staffed Beds: 1005 **Admissions:** 45753 **Census:** 775 **Outpatient Visits:** 2189688 **Births:** 2689 **Total Expense ($000):** 3579778 **Payroll Expense ($000):** 1589010 **Personnel:** 12977

KINGMAN—Kingman County

★ **KINGMAN COMMUNITY HOSPITAL (171378)**, 750 Avenue D West, Zip 67068–0376; tel. 620/532–3147, **A**10 18 **F**3 11 15 18 28 29 31 32 34 35 38 40 44 45 50 53 56 57 59 64 65 71 75 77 78 81 86 87 93 97 104 107 109 114 119 127 128 129 130 131 133 143 146 147 148 154 156 164 165 167 169 **P**6
Primary Contact: Preston Sauers, Chief Executive Officer
CFO: Kent Hudson, Chief Financial Officer
CIO: Jay Gehring, Director Information Systems
CHR: Nancy Stucky, Director Human Resources and Public Relations
CNO: Nita McFarland, Director of Nursing
Web address: www.kchks.com
Control: Other not–for–profit (including NFP Corporation) **Service:** General medical and surgical

Staffed Beds: 23 **Admissions:** 301 **Census:** 4 **Outpatient Visits:** 25349 **Births:** 0 **Total Expense ($000):** 18268 **Payroll Expense ($000):** 8135 **Personnel:** 119

KINSLEY—Edwards County

⇧ **EDWARDS COUNTY MEDICAL CENTER (171317)**, 620 West Eighth Street, Zip 67547–2329, Mailing Address: P.O. Box 99, Zip 67547–0099; tel. 620/659–3621, (Nonreporting) **A**10 18 21
Primary Contact: Jimmie W. Hansel, Ph.D., Chief Executive Officer
CHR: Tammy K Lampe, Director Human Resources
Web address: www.edwardscohospital.com
Control: County, Government, Nonfederal **Service:** General medical and surgical

Staffed Beds: 12

KIOWA—Barber County

★ **KIOWA DISTRICT HEALTHCARE (171331)**, 1002 South Fourth Street, Zip 67070–1825, Mailing Address: P.O. Box 184, Zip 67070–0184; tel. 620/825–4131, (Total facility includes 28 beds in nursing home–type unit) **A**10 18 **F**2 3 12 34 40 41 45 55 56 57 59 64 65 67 69 81 84 85 87 91 92 93 97 107 114 119 127 128 133 148 150 154 **P**6
Primary Contact: Janell Goodno, Chief Executive Officer
CFO: Robin Lewis, Chief Financial Officer
CMO: Paul Wilhelm, M.D., Chief of Staff
CHR: Tara Girty, Director Human Resources
Web address: www.k-d-h.com
Control: Hospital district or authority, Government, Nonfederal **Service:** General medical and surgical

Staffed Beds: 39 **Admissions:** 233 **Census:** 25 **Outpatient Visits:** 9684 **Births:** 0 **Total Expense ($000):** 12037 **Payroll Expense ($000):** 6668 **Personnel:** 90

LA CROSSE—Rush County

★ **RUSH COUNTY MEMORIAL HOSPITAL (171342)**, 801 Locust Street, Zip 67548–9673, Mailing Address: P.O. Box 520, Zip 67548–0520; tel. 785/222–2545, (Total facility includes 18 beds in nursing home–type unit) **A**10 **F**3 40 53 64 67 77 92 93 107 127 128 133 154
Primary Contact: Robert Ladd, M.D., Interim Chief Executive Officer
CMO: Robert Ladd, M.D., Medical Director
CHR: Brenda Legleiter, Director Quality and Human Resources
Web address: www.rushcountymemorialhospital.com
Control: County, Government, Nonfederal **Service:** General medical and surgical

Staffed Beds: 25 **Admissions:** 105 **Census:** 18 **Births:** 0 **Personnel:** 53

LAKIN—Kearny County

★ **KEARNY COUNTY HOSPITAL (171313)**, 500 Thorpe Street, Zip 67860–9625; tel. 620/355–7111, (Total facility includes 75 beds in nursing home–type unit) **A**10 18 **F**2 3 6 10 13 28 29 34 35 40 45 50 56 57 58 59 64 67 68 69 75 76 79 81 82 85 86 87 89 93 97 107 110 111 114 119 125 127 128 130 131 132 133 143 149 154 156 169 **P**6
Primary Contact: Marley Lyn. Koons, Chief Executive Officer
COO: Shari Campbell, Chief Operating Officer
CFO: Kelly Ann Speckman, Chief Financial Officer
CIO: Tony Salcido, Director of Information Technology
CHR: Laci Williams, Director Human Resources
CNO: Robin Allaman, Chief Nursing Officer
Web address: www.kearnycountyhospital.com
Control: County, Government, Nonfederal **Service:** General medical and surgical

Staffed Beds: 100 **Admissions:** 517 **Census:** 56 **Outpatient Visits:** 45673 **Births:** 343 **Total Expense ($000):** 26479 **Payroll Expense ($000):** 12851 **Personnel:** 177

LARNED—Pawnee County

☐ **LARNED STATE HOSPITAL (174006)**, 1301 Kansas Highway 264, Zip 67550; tel. 620/285–2131, **A**1 10 **F**3 29 30 38 50 53 82 86 87 97 98 100 101 102 103 130 132 135 148 149 156 163 164 165 **P**6
Primary Contact: Thomas Kinlen, Superintendent
COO: Steve Spain, Chief Operating Officer
CMO: Sayed Jehan, M.D., Interim Medical Director
CIO: Sid Smith, Director Information Resources
CHR: Kerri Barnard, Director Human Resources
CNO: Holly Hertel, Director Nursing
Web address: www.larnedstatehospital.org
Control: State, Government, Nonfederal **Service:** Psychiatric

Staffed Beds: 518 **Admissions:** 813 **Census:** 405 **Outpatient Visits:** 0 **Births:** 0 **Total Expense ($000):** 103825 **Payroll Expense ($000):** 35062 **Personnel:** 514

★ **PAWNEE VALLEY COMMUNITY HOSPITAL (171345)**, 923 Carroll Avenue, Zip 67550–2429; tel. 620/285–3161, **A**10 18 **F**3 11 15 28 29 30 32 34 40 43 45 46 56 57 59 65 68 77 81 82 84 85 86 87 93 97 102 107 110 111 115 119 127 129 130 131 133 135 146 147 148 149 154 156 **P**6
Primary Contact: Melanie D. Urban, Administrator
COO: Bryce A Young, Chief Operating Officer
CFO: George Harms, Chief Financial Officer
CMO: David Sanger, M.D., Chief Medical Officer
CHR: Bruce Whittington, Vice President Human Resources
Web address: www.pawneevalleyhospital.com
Control: County, Government, Nonfederal **Service**: General medical and surgical

Staffed Beds: 22 **Admissions**: 208 **Census**: 6 **Outpatient Visits**: 53368 **Births**: 0 **Total Expense ($000)**: 18318 **Payroll Expense ($000)**: 8757 **Personnel**: 109

LAWRENCE—Douglas County

✠ **LMH HEALTH (170137)**, 325 Maine Street, Zip 66044–1360; tel. 785/505–5000, (Total facility includes 17 beds in nursing home–type unit) **A**1 2 3 5 10 20 **F**3 11 13 15 18 19 20 22 26 28 29 30 31 34 35 38 39 40 43 44 45 49 50 51 54 55 56 57 59 61 64 65 67 69 70 73 74 75 76 77 78 79 81 82 84 85 86 87 89 90 93 94 96 97 100 102 107 108 110 111 114 115 118 119 120 124 126 128 129 130 131 132 135 145 146 147 148 154 156 169
Primary Contact: Russell W. Johnson, President and Chief Executive Officer
CFO: Debra L Cartwright, Senior Vice President, Chief Financial Officer
CMO: Kirk Sloan, M.D., Senior Vice President and Chief Medical Officer
CIO: Michael Williams, Vice President and Chief Information Officer
CHR: Colleen Browne, Vice President and Chief People Officer
CNO: Traci Hoopingarner, R.N., Chief Nursing Officer
Web address: www.lmh.org
Control: Other not–for–profit (including NFP Corporation) **Service**: General medical and surgical

Staffed Beds: 142 **Admissions**: 6455 **Census**: 77 **Outpatient Visits**: 188985 **Births**: 853 **Total Expense ($000)**: 356293 **Payroll Expense ($000)**: 149539 **Personnel**: 1121

LEAVENWORTH—Douglas County

DWIGHT D. EISENHOWER VETERANS AFFAIRS MEDICAL CENTER See Veterans Affairs Eastern Kansas Health Care System–Dwight D. Eisenhower Veterans Affairs Medical Center

LEAVENWORTH—Leavenworth County

☐ **SAINT JOHN HOSPITAL (170009)**, 3500 South Fourth Street, Zip 66048–5043; tel. 913/680–6000, **A**1 10 **F**3 15 18 29 30 34 35 40 44 45 46 50 54 56 57 59 64 68 70 74 75 77 79 82 85 87 93 97 98 100 102 103 107 108 110 114 115 119 130 133 144 146 148 149 154 157 168 **P**6 **S** Prime Healthcare, Ontario, CA
Primary Contact: Billie Leonard, Chief Executive Officer
CFO: David Dulny, Chief Financial Officer
CMO: Sabato Sisillo, M.D., Chief Medical Officer
CIO: Charles Soeken, Director Information Technology
CHR: Brenda Farwell, Director Human Resources
CNO: Jodi Fincher, R.N., Vice President Patient Care Services
Web address: https://www.stjohnleavenworth.com/
Control: Individual, Investor–owned (for–profit) **Service**: General medical and surgical

Staffed Beds: 51 **Admissions**: 1233 **Census**: 22 **Outpatient Visits**: 50556 **Births**: 0 **Total Expense ($000)**: 35907 **Payroll Expense ($000)**: 16479 **Personnel**: 153

VETERANS AFFAIRS EASTERN KANSAS HEALTH CARE SYSTEM–DWIGHT D. EISENHOWER VETERANS AFFAIRS MEDICAL CENTER See Eastern Kansas HCS, Topeka

LEAWOOD—Johnson County

☐ **DOCTOR'S HOSPITAL (170194)**, 4901 College Boulevard, Zip 66211–1602; tel. 913/529–1801, (Nonreporting) **A**1 10
Primary Contact: Phil Harness, Chief Executive Officer
Web address: www.dshospital.net
Control: Partnership, Investor–owned (for–profit) **Service**: General medical and surgical

Staffed Beds: 9

○ **KANSAS CITY ORTHOPAEDIC INSTITUTE (170188)**, 3651 College Boulevard, Zip 66211–1910; tel. 913/338–4100, **A**3 5 10 11 **F**77 79 81 82 93 111 119 131 144 154 **P**5
Primary Contact: Gene Austin, Chief Executive Officer
CIO: Jim Leveling, Director Information Technology
CHR: Laura Sinclair, Director Human Resources
Web address: www.kcoi.com
Control: Partnership, Investor–owned (for–profit) **Service**: Orthopedic

Staffed Beds: 17 **Admissions**: 922 **Census**: 5 **Outpatient Visits**: 197997 **Births**: 0

LENEXA—Johnson County

☐ **MINIMALLY INVASIVE SURGERY HOSPITAL (170199)**, 11217 Lakeview Avenue, Zip 66219–1399; tel. 913/322–7401, (Nonreporting) **A**1 10
Primary Contact: Parajeet Sabharrwal, Chief Executive Officer
Web address: www.mishhospital.com
Control: Corporation, Investor–owned (for–profit) **Service**: Surgical

Staffed Beds: 9

LEOTI—Wichita County

★ **WICHITA COUNTY HEALTH CENTER (171306)**, 211 East Earl Street, Zip 67861–9620; tel. 620/375–2233, (Total facility includes 17 beds in nursing home–type unit) **A**10 18 **F**1 2 3 11 29 34 35 40 41 45 50 56 57 59 64 69 75 77 86 87 93 97 102 107 119 127 128 130 133 135 146 148 154 156 166 **P**6 **S** Great Plains Health Alliance, Inc., Wichita, KS
Primary Contact: Teresa Clark, Chief Executive Officer and Administrator
CFO: Janice Campas, Chief Financial Officer
CMO: Jeffrey Alpert, M.D., Medical Director
CHR: Patti Whalen, Manager Human Resources
Web address: www.wichitacountyhealthcenter.com
Control: County, Government, Nonfederal **Service**: General medical and surgical

Staffed Beds: 42 **Admissions**: 130 **Census**: 24 **Outpatient Visits**: 6550 **Births**: 0 **Total Expense ($000)**: 11697 **Payroll Expense ($000)**: 5024 **Personnel**: 84

LIBERAL—Seward County

☐ **SOUTHWEST MEDICAL CENTER (170068)**, 315 West 15th Street, Zip 67901–2455, Mailing Address: Box 1340, Zip 67905–1340; tel. 620/624–1651, (Nonreporting) **A**1 10
Primary Contact: Amber Williams, Chief Executive Officer
CFO: Amber Williams, Chief Financial Officer, Vice President of Finance
CHR: Lisa L Mathes, Human Resources Director
CNO: Jo L Harrison, Vice President of Patient Care Services
Web address: www.swmedcenter.com
Control: County, Government, Nonfederal **Service**: General medical and surgical

Staffed Beds: 101

LINCOLN—Lincoln County

LINCOLN COUNTY HOSPITAL (171360), 624 North Second Street, Zip 67455–1738, Mailing Address: P.O. Box 406, Zip 67455–0406; tel. 785/524–4403, (Nonreporting) **A**10 18
Primary Contact: Tawnya Seitz, Chief Executive Officer and Chief Financial Officer
CFO: Tawnya Seitz, Chief Executive Officer and Chief Financial Officer
CNO: Christa Haesemeyer, Chief Nursing Officer
Web address: www.lincolncountyhospital.net
Control: County, Government, Nonfederal **Service**: General medical and surgical

Staffed Beds: 14

LINDSBORG—Mcpherson County

★ **LINDSBORG COMMUNITY HOSPITAL (171358)**, 605 West Lincoln Street, Zip 67456–2328; tel. 785/227–3308, **A**10 18 **F**3 11 12 28 29 36 40 53 59 64 65 67 81 87 93 97 107 114 119 128 130 133 144 148 154 160 **P**6 **S** Salina Regional Health Center, Salina, KS
Primary Contact: Larry Van Der Wege, Administrator
CFO: Laraine Gengler, Chief Financial Officer
CIO: Jeremy Snapp, Director Information Systems
CHR: Brad Malm, Director Human Resources and Education
CNO: Beth Hedberg, R.N., Director Nursing
Web address: www.lindsborghospital.org
Control: Other not–for–profit (including NFP Corporation) **Service**: General medical and surgical

Staffed Beds: 12 **Admissions**: 194 **Census**: 5 **Outpatient Visits**: 38757 **Births**: 0 **Total Expense ($000)**: 16604 **Payroll Expense ($000)**: 7247 **Personnel**: 114

Hospitals, U.S. / KANSAS

LYONS—Rice County

★ **HOSPITAL DISTRICT NO 1 OF RICE COUNTY (171330)**, 619 South Clark Street, Zip 67554–3003, Mailing Address: P.O. Box 828, Zip 67554–0828; tel. 620/257–5173, (Nonreporting) **A**10 18
Primary Contact: George M. Stover, Chief Executive Officer
CFO: Terry Pound, Chief Financial Officer
CMO: Kristina Darnauer, M.D., Chief of Staff
CNO: Judy Hogdson, R.N., Chief Nursing Officer
Web address: www.ricecountyhospital.com
Control: Hospital district or authority, Government, Nonfederal **Service**: General medical and surgical

Staffed Beds: 25

MANHATTAN—Riley County

⊞ **ASCENSION VIA CHRISTI HOSPITAL, MANHATTAN (170142)**, 1823 College Avenue, Zip 66502–3346; tel. 785/776–3322, **A**1 10 19 **F**3 11 12 13 15 18 22 28 29 30 31 34 35 37 40 41 44 45 49 50 51 55 56 64 67 70 76 89 90 156 **S** Ascension Healthcare, Saint Louis, MO
Primary Contact: Robert C. Copple, FACHE, President
CFO: James Fraser, Administrator Finance
CIO: Andy Gagnon, Manager Information Technology
CHR: Renee Reed, Director Human Resources
CNO: Jennifer Goehring, R.N., Assistant Chief Nursing Officer
Web address: https://www.viachristi.org/manhattan
Control: Other not–for–profit (including NFP Corporation) **Service**: General medical and surgical

Staffed Beds: 94 **Admissions**: 4170 **Census**: 39 **Outpatient Visits**: 103511
Births: 1028 **Total Expense ($000)**: 96728 **Payroll Expense ($000)**: 33314

MANHATTAN SURGICAL (170190), 1829 College Avenue, Zip 66502–3381; tel. 785/776–5100, **A**10 **F**24 29 37 45 51 64 68 78 79 81 82 85 97 107 115 119 120 121 123 126
Primary Contact: Melissa Westcott, CPA, Interim Chief Executive Officer and Chief Financial Officer
CFO: Melissa Westcott, CPA, Chief Financial Oficer
CNO: Jane Alderson, R.N., Chief Nursing Officer
Web address: www.manhattansurgical.com
Control: Partnership, Investor–owned (for–profit) **Service**: Surgical

Staffed Beds: 13 **Admissions**: 458 **Census**: 2 **Outpatient Visits**: 10980
Births: 0 **Total Expense ($000)**: 42751 **Payroll Expense ($000)**: 9910
Personnel: 114

MANKATO—Jewell County

JEWELL COUNTY HOSPITAL (171309), 100 Crestvue Avenue, Zip 66956–2407, Mailing Address: P.O. Box 327, Zip 66956–0327; tel. 785/378–3137, **A**10 18 **F**2 3 29 40 50 64 75 77 87 93 107 127 128 130 133 148 156 **P**6
Primary Contact: Doyle L. McKimmy, FACHE, Chief Executive Officer
COO: Eric Borden, Chief Operating Officer and Chief Financial Officer
CFO: Eric Borden, Chief Operating Officer and Chief Financial Officer
Web address: https://www.jewellcohospital.org/
Control: County, Government, Nonfederal **Service**: General medical and surgical

Staffed Beds: 25 **Admissions**: 107 **Census**: 17 **Outpatient Visits**: 7977
Births: 0 **Total Expense ($000)**: 8956 **Payroll Expense ($000)**: 4170
Personnel: 58

MARION—Marion County

ST. LUKE HOSPITAL AND LIVING CENTER (171356), 535 South Freeborn, Zip 66861–1256; tel. 620/382–2177, (Nonreporting) **A**10 18
Primary Contact: Alex Haines, Chief Executive Officer
CFO: Bev Reid, Chief Financial Officer
CMO: Don Hodson, M.D., Chief Medical Officer
CIO: Jeff Methvin, Manager Information Technology
CHR: Sharon Zogelman, Director Human Resources
Web address: www.slhmarion.org
Control: Hospital district or authority, Government, Nonfederal **Service**: General medical and surgical

Staffed Beds: 39

MARYSVILLE—Marshall County

★ **COMMUNITY MEMORIAL HEALTHCARE (171363)**, 708 North 18th Street, Zip 66508–1338; tel. 785/562–2311, **A**10 18 **F**3 13 15 28 29 34 35 40 45 47 50 57 59 62 64 69 75 76 79 81 87 97 107 108 110 111 115 119 127 128 129 130 131 132 133 135 146 169 **P**6
Primary Contact: Curtis R. Hawkinson, Chief Executive Officer
CFO: Daniel Fehr, Chief Financial Officer
CMO: Shane Thoreson, M.D., Chief Medical Officer
CIO: Scott Keller, Director Information Technology
CHR: Jessie Schneider, Director Human Resources
CNO: Diane Luebcke, R.N., Director Nursing
Web address: www.cmhcare.org
Control: Other not–for–profit (including NFP Corporation) **Service**: General medical and surgical

Staffed Beds: 25 **Admissions**: 543 **Census**: 7 **Outpatient Visits**: 30989
Births: 40 **Total Expense ($000)**: 29321 **Payroll Expense ($000)**: 12288
Personnel: 182

MCPHERSON—McPherson County

★ **MCPHERSON HOSPITAL, INC. (170105)**, 1000 Hospital Drive, Zip 67460–2326; tel. 620/241–2250, **A**10 **F**3 7 11 13 15 28 29 34 35 40 43 45 50 53 59 64 65 70 75 76 77 81 82 85 86 87 89 97 107 110 111 115 119 127 129 130 144 146 147 154 156 164 167 169 **P**6
Primary Contact: Tanner Wealand, CPA, President and Chief Executive Officer
COO: Charity Clark, Chief Operating Officer
CFO: Tanner Wealand, CPA, Chief Financial Officer and Interim Chief Executive Officer
CMO: Esther Rettig, M.D., Chief Medical Officer
CHR: Cathy Dunham, Chief Human Resources Officer
Web address: www.mcphersoncenterforhealth.org
Control: Other not–for–profit (including NFP Corporation) **Service**: General medical and surgical

Staffed Beds: 32 **Admissions**: 939 **Census**: 7 **Outpatient Visits**: 114251
Births: 134 **Total Expense ($000)**: 44747 **Payroll Expense ($000)**: 20403
Personnel: 332

MEADE—Meade County

★ **MEADE DISTRICT HOSPITAL (171321)**, 510 East Carthage Street, Zip 67864–6401, Mailing Address: P.O. Box 820, Zip 67864–0820; tel. 620/873–2141, (Nonreporting) **A**10 18
Primary Contact: Dawn Unruh, R.N., Chief Executive Officer
CIO: Matt Bobo, Chief Information Officer
Web address: www.meadehospital.com
Control: Hospital district or authority, Government, Nonfederal **Service**: General medical and surgical

Staffed Beds: 65

MEDICINE LODGE—Barber County

MEDICINE LODGE MEMORIAL HOSPITAL (171334), 710 North Walnut Street, Zip 67104–1019; tel. 620/886–3771, **A**10 18 **F**3 7 11 40 44 45 56 64 81 93 107 119 127 128 133 148 154 156 166 **P**6 **S** Great Plains Health Alliance, Inc., Wichita, KS
Primary Contact: Ashley Taylor, Administrator
CFO: Thomas G Lee, Chief Financial Officer
CHR: Johnnie Davis, Director Human Resources
CNO: Kathryn I. Burns, R.N., Director of Nursing
Web address: www.mlmh.net/
Control: Hospital district or authority, Government, Nonfederal **Service**: General medical and surgical

Staffed Beds: 25 **Admissions**: 166 **Census**: 15 **Outpatient Visits**: 17285
Births: 0 **Total Expense ($000)**: 12540 **Payroll Expense ($000)**: 5940
Personnel: 88

Hospitals, U.S. / KANSAS

MERRIAM—Johnson County

✠ **ADVENTHEALTH SHAWNEE MISSION (170104)**, 9100 West 74th Street, Zip 66204–4004, Mailing Address: Box 2923, Shawnee Mission, Zip 66201–1323; tel. 913/676–2000, **A**1 2 3 5 10 **F**3 4 5 8 11 12 13 15 17 18 20 22 24 26 28 29 30 31 32 33 34 35 36 38 40 42 45 46 47 48 49 53 54 55 56 57 58 59 62 64 65 70 72 74 75 76 77 78 79 80 81 82 84 85 86 87 89 93 96 97 98 100 101 102 103 104 105 107 108 110 111 115 117 118 119 120 121 123 124 126 129 130 131 132 133 135 141 142 144 145 146 147 148 149 152 153 154 156 157 160 162 164 165 167 169 **P**6 **S** AdventHealth, Altamonte Springs, FL
Primary Contact: Alan Verrill, M.D., President and Chief Executive Officer
CFO: Karsten Randolph, Executive Vice President and Chief Financial Officer
CMO: Sherri Martin, M.D., President Medical Staff
CIO: Mike Allen, Director Information Services
CHR: Brad Hoffman, Administrative Director Human Resources
CNO: Sheri Hawkins, Chief Nursing Officer
Web address: www.shawneemission.org
Control: Church operated, Nongovernment, not–for–profit **Service:** General medical and surgical

Staffed Beds: 430 **Admissions:** 17439 **Census:** 206 **Outpatient Visits:** 611446 **Births:** 4394 **Total Expense ($000):** 598713 **Payroll Expense ($000):** 239695 **Personnel:** 3001

MINNEAPOLIS—Ottawa County

★ **OTTAWA COUNTY HEALTH CENTER (171328)**, 215 East Eighth, Zip 67467–1902, Mailing Address: P.O. Box 290, Zip 67467–0290; tel. 785/392–2122, **A**10 18 **F**28 29 34 35 40 53 56 64 81 85 86 93 107 114 128 130 133 143 154 156 **S** Great Plains Health Alliance, Inc., Wichita, KS
Primary Contact: Jody Parks, Administrator
CFO: Cheryl Lanoue, Chief Financial Officer
CIO: Linda Wright, Director Information
CNO: Marlene Gawith, Director of Nursing
Web address: www.ottawacountyhealthcenter.com
Control: Other not–for–profit (including NFP Corporation) **Service:** General medical and surgical

Staffed Beds: 25 **Admissions:** 177 **Census:** 16 **Outpatient Visits:** 9215 **Births:** 0 **Total Expense ($000):** 8726 **Payroll Expense ($000):** 3660 **Personnel:** 73

MINNEOLA—Ford County

★ **MINNEOLA DISTRICT HOSPITAL (171368)**, 212 Main Street, Zip 67865–8511, Mailing Address: P.O. Box 127, Zip 67865–0127; tel. 620/885–4264, (Nonreporting) **A**10 18
Primary Contact: Deborah Bruner, Chief Executive Officer and Administrator
CFO: Marion Zirger, Chief Financial Officer
CMO: Tony Luna, M.D., Chief of Staff
CHR: Vena Harris, Director Human Resources
CNO: Amanda Stout, Chief Nursing Officer
Web address: www.minneolahealthcare.com
Control: Hospital district or authority, Government, Nonfederal **Service:** General medical and surgical

Staffed Beds: 50

MOUNDRIDGE—Mcpherson County

★ **MERCY HOSPITAL INC. (170780)**, 218 East Pack Street, Zip 67107–8815, Mailing Address: P.O. Box 180, Zip 67107–0180; tel. 620/345–6391, **A**10 **F**3 29 30 34 35 40 45 50 59 64 67 77 81 86 87 91 92 93 107 108 114 128 130 133 146 149
Primary Contact: Aaron Herbel, Administrator
CFO: Trevor Wiebe, Business Office Manager, Information Technology
CNO: Lorie Friesen, Director of Nursing
Web address: https://www.mercyh.org
Control: Church operated, Nongovernment, not–for–profit **Service:** General medical and surgical

Staffed Beds: 12 **Admissions:** 239 **Census:** 4 **Outpatient Visits:** 10325 **Births:** 0 **Total Expense ($000):** 5648 **Payroll Expense ($000):** 2980 **Personnel:** 51

MULVANE—Sedgwick County

✠ **ASCENSION VIA CHRISTI ST. FRANCIS (170122)**, 211 N College Ave, Zip 67110, Mailing Address: 929 North St Francis Street, Wichita, Zip 67214–3882; tel. 316/268–5000, (Includes GOOD SHEPHERD CAMPUS, 8901 East Orme, Wichita, Kansas, Zip 67207, tel. 316/858–0333; ST. FRANCIS CAMPUS, 929 North St Francis Street, Wichita, Kansas, Zip 67214–3882, tel. 316/268–5000; Robyn Chadwick, President; ST. JOSEPH CAMPUS, 3600 East Harry Street, Wichita, Kansas, Zip 67218–3713, tel. 316/685–1111; Claudio J Ferraro, President) **A**1 3 5 10 13 19 **F**3 7 11 12 13 15 16 17 18 20 21 22 23 24 26 27 28 29 30 31 32 34 35 37 38 40 42 43 44 45 46 48 49 50 51 54 56 57 58 59 60 61 62 64 68 70 72 74 75 76 77 78 79 80 81 82 84 85 86 87 88 89 92 93 97 98 99 100 101 102 103 104 105 107 108 110 111 115 118 119 120 121 123 124 126 130 131 132 135 136 141 142 143 146 148 153 154 162 164 167 169 **S** Ascension Healthcare, Saint Louis, MO
Primary Contact: Joy Scott, Market Administrator
CFO: Jeff Seirer, Interim Chief Financial Officer
CMO: Darrell Youngman, D.O., Chief Medical Officer
CHR: Judy Espinoza, Chief Human Resources Officer
CNO: Amy Katherine Renn, Vice President, Nursing
Web address: www.via–christi.org
Control: Church operated, Nongovernment, not–for–profit **Service:** General medical and surgical

Staffed Beds: 669 **Admissions:** 27650 **Census:** 447 **Outpatient Visits:** 259917 **Births:** 2536 **Total Expense ($000):** 710934 **Payroll Expense ($000):** 220645 **Personnel:** 3615

NEODESHA—Wilson County

★ **WILSON MEDICAL CENTER (171344)**, 2600 Ottawa Road, Zip 66757–1897, Mailing Address: P.O. Box 360, Zip 66757–0360; tel. 620/325–2611, **A**10 18 **F**3 8 15 29 30 32 40 41 45 50 53 57 59 81 82 89 90 93 96 97 107 108 110 115 119 127 128 130 131 133 141 148 154 157 **S** Ovation Healthcare, Brentwood, TN
Primary Contact: Tom Hood, Chief Executive Officer
CFO: John Gutschenritter, Chief Financial Officer
CIO: Kevin Myers, Director Information Technology
CHR: Laura L Dean, Director Human Resources
CNO: Temple Monroe, Director Nursing Operations
Web address: www.wilsonmedical.org
Control: County, Government, Nonfederal **Service:** General medical and surgical

Staffed Beds: 15 **Admissions:** 204 **Census:** 4 **Outpatient Visits:** 34979 **Births:** 0 **Total Expense ($000):** 21407 **Payroll Expense ($000):** 9457 **Personnel:** 143

NESS CITY—Ness County

★ **NESS COUNTY HOSPITAL DISTRICT NO 2 (171336)**, 312 Custer Street, Zip 67560–1654; tel. 785/798–2291, (Total facility includes 30 beds in nursing home–type unit) **A**10 18 **F**7 15 40 45 55 59 62 64 68 77 81 93 100 102 111 115 119 125 127 133 148 154 **P**6
Primary Contact: Aaron Kuehn, Administrator
CFO: Debra Frank, Chief Financial Officer
CMO: Mikhail Imseis, M.D., Chief of Staff
CIO: Vicki Howe, Health Information Management
CHR: Shelly McDonald, Chief Human Resources Officer
CNO: Cindy Maier, R.N., Director of Nursing
Web address: www.nchospital.org
Control: Hospital district or authority, Government, Nonfederal **Service:** General medical and surgical

Staffed Beds: 52 **Admissions:** 193 **Census:** 38 **Outpatient Visits:** 11299 **Births:** 0 **Total Expense ($000):** 16484 **Payroll Expense ($000):** 5588 **Personnel:** 101

NEWTON—Harvey County

★ ○ △ **NMC HEALTH (170103)**, 600 Medical Center Drive, Zip 67114–8780, Mailing Address: P.O. Box 308, Zip 67114–0308; tel. 316/283–2700, (Nonreporting) **A**3 5 7 10 11
Primary Contact: Vallerie L. Gleason, President and Chief Executive Officer
COO: Todd Tangeman, Chief Operating Officer
CFO: Todd Kasitz, Vice President Finance
CIO: Mike Cottle, Information Technology Director
CHR: Todd Tangeman, Chief Operating Officer and Chief Human Resource Officer
CNO: Heather Porter, Chief Clinical Officer
Web address: www.newtonmedicalcenter.com
Control: Other not–for–profit (including NFP Corporation) **Service:** General medical and surgical

Staffed Beds: 99

Hospital, Medicare Provider Number, Address, Telephone, Approval, Facility, and Physician Codes, Health Care System

★ American Hospital Association (AHA) membership ○ Healthcare Facilities Accreditation Program ⇈ Center for Improvement in Healthcare Quality Accreditation
☐ The Joint Commission accreditation ◇ DNV Healthcare Inc. accreditation △ Commission on Accreditation of Rehabilitation Facilities (CARF) accreditation

Hospitals, U.S. / KANSAS

☐ **PRAIRIE VIEW (174016)**, 1901 East First Street, Zip 67114–5010, Mailing Address: P.O. Box 467, Zip 67114–0467; tel. 316/284–6400, (Nonreporting) **A**1 10
Primary Contact: Jessie Kaye, Chief Executive Officer
CFO: Lisa Ramsey, Chief Financial Officer
CMO: Gary Fast, M.D., Medical Director
CIO: Chad Roth, Director Information Services
CHR: Joy Robb, Vice President Human Resources
CNO: Patrick Flaming, R.N., Director Inpatient Operations
Web address: www.prairieview.org
Control: Other not–for–profit (including NFP Corporation) **Service**: Psychiatric

Staffed Beds: 38

NORTON—Norton County

★ **NORTON COUNTY HOSPITAL (171348)**, 102 East Holme, Zip 67654–1406, Mailing Address: P.O. Box 250, Zip 67654–0250; tel. 785/877–3351, **A**10 18 **F**13 15 28 29 34 35 40 43 45 56 59 64 67 69 71 81 82 87 107 110 115 119 127 128 129 133 148 154 167
Primary Contact: Kevin Faughnder, Chief Executive Officer
CHR: Shannan Hempler, Director Human Resources
Web address: www.ntcohosp.com
Control: County, Government, Nonfederal **Service**: General medical and surgical

Staffed Beds: 25 **Admissions**: 225 **Census**: 3 **Outpatient Visits**: 30790 **Births**: 23 **Total Expense ($000)**: 19239 **Payroll Expense ($000)**: 8683 **Personnel**: 111

OAKLEY—Logan County

LOGAN COUNTY HOSPITAL (171326), 211 Cherry Street, Zip 67748–1201; tel. 785/672–3211, **A**10 18 **F**3 28 29 34 35 36 40 41 44 45 48 50 53 56 57 59 64 66 67 68 75 81 82 89 92 93 96 97 107 119 125 127 128 130 133 135 143 144 148 154 160 **P**6
Primary Contact: Aimee Zimmerman, R.N., Chief Executive Officer
CFO: Bonnie Hagel, Chief Financial Officer
CMO: Celeste Rains, D.O., Chief of Staff
CIO: Russ Kahle, Chief Information Officer
CHR: Steve Allison, Director Human Resources
CNO: Marcia Kruse, R.N., Director Nursing
Web address: www.logancountyhospital.org
Control: County, Government, Nonfederal **Service**: General medical and surgical

Staffed Beds: 25 **Admissions**: 252 **Census**: 5 **Outpatient Visits**: 14130 **Births**: 0 **Total Expense ($000)**: 15718 **Payroll Expense ($000)**: 7621

OBERLIN—Decatur County

DECATUR HEALTH SYSTEMS (171352), 810 West Columbia Street, Zip 67749–2450, Mailing Address: P.O. Box 268, Zip 67749–0268; tel. 785/475–2208, **A**10 18 **F**3 15 29 34 40 41 45 50 53 54 56 57 59 64 68 69 77 81 82 83 84 86 89 93 97 102 107 110 114 125 127 130 133 135 148 149 154 158
Primary Contact: Julie Smith, Chief Executive Officer
COO: Kristopher Matthews, Chief Operating Officer
CFO: Amanda Fortin, Manager Finance
CMO: Elizabeth Sliter, M.D., Chairman Medical Staff
Web address: www.decaturhealthsystems.org
Control: Other not–for–profit (including NFP Corporation) **Service**: General medical and surgical

Staffed Beds: 12 **Admissions**: 238 **Census**: 2 **Outpatient Visits**: 6562 **Births**: 0 **Total Expense ($000)**: 12221 **Payroll Expense ($000)**: 5012 **Personnel**: 83

OLATHE—Johnson County

☐ **COTTONWOOD SPRINGS HOSPITAL (174020)**, 13351 South Arapaho Drive, Zip 66062–1520; tel. 913/353–3000, (Nonreporting) **A**1 10 **S** Springstone, Louisville, KY
Primary Contact: Jason Toalson, Chief Executive Officer
Web address: www.cottonwoodsprings.com
Control: Corporation, Investor–owned (for–profit) **Service**: Psychiatric

Staffed Beds: 72

☐ **OLATHE MEDICAL CENTER (170049)**, 20333 West 151st Street, Zip 66061–5350; tel. 913/791–4200, **A**1 2 3 10 **F**3 11 12 13 15 18 20 22 24 26 28 29 30 31 34 35 39 40 45 46 47 48 49 51 56 57 58 59 60 61 62 63 64 65 68 70 73 74 75 76 77 78 79 80 81 82 84 85 86 87 89 91 92 93 107 108 110 111 115 116 117 118 119 120 121 123 124 126 129 130 131 132 135 145 146 147 148 149 154 156 167 169 **S** The University of Kansas Health System, Kansas City, KS
Primary Contact: Jason Hannagan, Chief Executive Officer, Southwest Kansas City Market, and Senior Vice President, Kansas City Divisi
COO: Jeffrey Dossett, Southwest Kansas City Market Chief Operating Officer
CFO: Nora Loesche, Southwest Kansas City Market Finance Director
CMO: Eric Bradstreet, M.D., Chief of Medical Staff
CIO: Nicholas Sindorf, Southwest Kansas City Market Vice President and Chief Information Officer
CHR: Janelle Lee, Vice President Human Resources
CNO: Gail Schuetz, Associate Chief Nursing Officer
Web address: www.olathehealth.org
Control: Other not–for–profit (including NFP Corporation) **Service**: General medical and surgical

Staffed Beds: 268 **Admissions**: 10725 **Census**: 107 **Outpatient Visits**: 356454 **Births**: 1323 **Personnel**: 1360

ONAGA—Pottawatomie County

★ **COMMUNITY HEALTHCARE SYSTEM (171354)**, 120 West Eighth Street, Zip 66521–9574; tel. 785/889–4272, (Total facility includes 67 beds in nursing home–type unit) **A**10 18 **F**2 3 5 10 11 12 13 15 28 29 31 32 34 35 36 40 43 45 50 53 56 57 59 62 64 65 67 68 74 75 77 81 82 84 85 86 87 93 97 99 100 101 102 103 104 105 106 107 110 111 114 119 125 127 128 130 131 132 133 134 135 143 144 145 146 147 148 149 151 152 153 154 156 169 **P**6
Primary Contact: Lorraine R. Meyer, Interim Chief Executive Officer
COO: Lorraine R Meyer, Chief Operating Officer
CFO: Monica Holthaus, Chief Financial Officer
CMO: Nicholas Cahoj, M.D., Chief of Staff
CIO: Dominic Freeman, Chief Information Officer
CHR: Terry D. Bernatis, Director Human Resources
CNO: Andrea Lutz, Director of Ancillary Services
Web address: www.chcsks.org
Control: Other not–for–profit (including NFP Corporation) **Service**: General medical and surgical

Staffed Beds: 103 **Admissions**: 425 **Census**: 48 **Outpatient Visits**: 93501 **Births**: 70 **Total Expense ($000)**: 37254 **Payroll Expense ($000)**: 20702 **Personnel**: 335

OSAWATOMIE—Miami County

OSAWATOMIE STATE HOSPITAL AT ADAIR ACUTE CARE (174022), 500 State Hospital Drive, Zip 66064–1813, Mailing Address: P.O. Box 500, Zip 66064–0500; tel. 913/755–7000, (Nonreporting) **A**10
Primary Contact: Ashley Byram, Superintendent
CHR: Dezerae Curran, Director Human Resources
Web address: www.srskansas.org/osh/osh-rmhf_info.html
Control: State, Government, Nonfederal **Service**: Psychiatric

Staffed Beds: 176

OSBORNE—Osborne County

OSBORNE COUNTY MEMORIAL HOSPITAL (171364), 424 West New Hampshire Street, Zip 67473–2314, Mailing Address: P.O. Box 70, Zip 67473–0070; tel. 785/346–2121, (Nonreporting) **A**10 18 **S** Great Plains Health Alliance, Inc., Wichita, KS
Primary Contact: Doris Brown, Chief Executive Officer
CFO: Linda Murphy, Chief Financial Officer
CMO: Erin Baxa, M.D., Chief Medical Officer
CNO: Monica Mullender, Director of Nursing
Web address: www.ocmh.org
Control: County, Government, Nonfederal **Service**: General medical and surgical

Staffed Beds: 25

OTTAWA—Franklin County

✠ **ADVENTHEALTH OTTAWA (170014)**, 1301 South Main Street, Zip 66067–3598; tel. 785/229–8200, **A**1 10 20 **F**3 11 15 18 28 29 30 31 34 35 40 41 43 44 45 50 54 56 57 59 64 65 68 70 74 75 77 78 79 81 82 85 86 87 89 92 93 94 96 97 107 108 110 111 115 118 119 127 129 130 131 146 147 148 149 154 **P**6 **S** AdventHealth, Altamonte Springs, FL
Primary Contact: Shawn Perry, Chief Financial Officer
CFO: Shawn Perry, Chief Financial Officer
Web address: https://www.adventhealth.com/hospital/adventhealth-ottawa
Control: Church operated, Nongovernment, not–for–profit **Service**: General medical and surgical

Staffed Beds: 30 **Admissions**: 1154 **Census**: 9 **Outpatient Visits**: 82926 **Births**: 128 **Total Expense ($000)**: 56749 **Payroll Expense ($000)**: 22595 **Personnel**: 264

Hospitals, U.S. / KANSAS

OVERLAND PARK—Johnson County

✠ **ADVENTHEALTH SOUTH OVERLAND PARK**, 7820 West 165th Street, Zip 66223–2925; tel. 913/373–1100, **A**1 5 **F**3 8 11 12 13 15 18 20 22 29 30 34 35 36 37 40 41 44 45 47 59 60 64 70 72 73 75 76 77 79 81 85 86 87 89 90 93 100 102 103 107 108 110 111 115 119 126 130 131 145 146 147 149 154 157 167 169 **S** AdventHealth, Altamonte Springs, FL
Primary Contact: Dallas Purkeypile, Chief Executive Officer
COO: Jimmy Bolanos, Chief Operating Officer
CFO: Jeff Prusia, Chief Financial Officer
CMO: Michale Jean–Francois, Chief Medical Officer
Web address: https://www.adventhealth.com/hospital/adventhealth-south-overland-park
Control: Church operated, Nongovernment, not–for–profit **Service**: General medical and surgical

Staffed Beds: 41 **Admissions**: 1962 **Census**: 16 **Outpatient Visits**: 21577 **Births**: 461 **Total Expense ($000)**: 72079 **Payroll Expense ($000)**: 23883 **Personnel**: 223

✠ **CHILDREN'S MERCY HOSPITAL KANSAS (173300)**, 5808 West 110th Street, Zip 66211–2504; tel. 913/696–8000, **A**1 3 10 **F**3 7 9 19 27 29 32 34 35 38 40 41 44 48 50 55 57 59 64 65 68 75 77 79 81 82 85 87 89 93 97 99 100 104 107 111 115 117 118 119 129 130 131 132 134 144 146 148 150 154 156 157 164 167
Primary Contact: Paul D. Kempinski, MS, FACHE, Chief Executive Officer
COO: Jodi Coombs, R.N., Executive Vice President, Chief Operating Officer
CFO: David Cauble, Executive Vice President and Chief Financial Officer
CIO: Chad Mills, Senior Vice President, Chief Information Officer
CHR: Robin Faulk, Senior Vice President, Chief Human Resources Officer
Web address: https://www.childrensmercy.org/locations/childrens-mercy-hospital-kansas/
Control: Other not–for–profit (including NFP Corporation) **Service**: Children's general medical and surgical

Staffed Beds: 42 **Admissions**: 373 **Census**: 5 **Outpatient Visits**: 140789 **Births**: 0 **Total Expense ($000)**: 133894 **Payroll Expense ($000)**: 66481 **Personnel**: 740

HEARTLAND SURGICAL SPECIALTY HOSPITAL See The University of Kansas Hospital – Indian Creek Campus

JOHNSON COUNTY REHABILITATION HOSPITAL (173034), 11325 College Boulevard, Zip 66210; tel. 913/372–7800, (Nonreporting) **A**10 **S** Nobis Rehabilitation Partners, Allen, TX
Primary Contact: Krista Jackson, Chief Executive Officer
Web address: https://www.johnsoncounty-rehab.com/
Control: Corporation, Investor–owned (for–profit) **Service**: Rehabilitation

Staffed Beds: 40

☐ **KPC PROMISE HOSPITAL OF OVERLAND PARK (172004)**, 6509 West 103rd Street, Zip 66212–1728; tel. 913/649–3701, (Nonreporting) **A**1 10 **S** KPC Healthcare, Inc., Santa Ana, CA
Primary Contact: Patricia Ann. Wors, Chief Executive Officer
CFO: William Scott, Chief Financial Officer
CHR: Darren Enochs, Director Human Resources
Web address: www.overlandpark.kpcph.com
Control: Corporation, Investor–owned (for–profit) **Service**: Acute long–term care hospital

Staffed Beds: 104

✠ **MENORAH MEDICAL CENTER (170182)**, 5721 West 119th Street, Zip 66209–3722; tel. 913/498–6000, **A**1 2 3 5 10 **F**3 12 13 15 18 20 22 24 26 28 29 30 31 35 37 38 40 45 46 47 48 49 51 55 58 59 60 64 68 70 72 74 75 76 77 78 79 81 82 84 85 87 90 93 102 107 108 110 111 114 115 116 117 119 120 121 124 126 129 130 132 135 145 146 148 149 154 167 **S** HCA Healthcare, Nashville, TN
Primary Contact: Kirk McCarty, R.N., MSN, Chief Executive Officer
CFO: Deborah Gafford, Chief Financial Officer
CMO: James Cheray, M.D., Chief Medical Officer
CIO: Christina McGinnis, Director Information Technology
CHR: Amy Hunt, Director Human Resources
CNO: Kelly Reno, R.N., Chief Nursing Officer
Web address: www.menorahmedicalcenter.com
Control: Corporation, Investor–owned (for–profit) **Service**: General medical and surgical

Staffed Beds: 190 **Admissions**: 8760 **Census**: 112 **Outpatient Visits**: 68842 **Births**: 682 **Personnel**: 932

✠ **OVERLAND PARK REGIONAL MEDICAL CENTER (170176)**, 10500 Quivira Road, Zip 66215–2306, Mailing Address: P.O. Box 15959, Zip 66215–5959; tel. 913/541–5000, **A**1 2 3 5 10 **F**3 8 13 15 17 18 19 20 22 24 26 28 29 30 31 34 35 37 40 41 42 43 45 49 50 52 55 56 57 59 60 61 64 65 67 70 72 73 74 75 76 77 78 79 81 82 83 84 85 86 87 88 89 91 92 93 107 108 110 111 114 115 119 126 129 130 131 135 144 145 146 147 149 154 156 167 169 **P**6 **S** HCA Healthcare, Nashville, TN
Primary Contact: Matt Sogard, Chief Executive Officer
COO: Patrick Rafferty, Chief Operating Officer
CFO: Steven R Cleary, Chief Financial Officer
CMO: George D. Stamos, M.D., Chief Medical Officer
CHR: Connie Miller, Vice President Human Resources
Web address: www.oprmc.com
Control: Corporation, Investor–owned (for–profit) **Service**: General medical and surgical

Staffed Beds: 281 **Admissions**: 13989 **Census**: 184 **Outpatient Visits**: 111732 **Births**: 2867 **Personnel**: 987

✠ **REHABILITATION HOSPITAL OF OVERLAND PARK (173032)**, 5100 Indian Creek Parkway, Zip 66207–4115; tel. 913/544–1957, **A**1 3 10 **F**3 29 34 35 56 58 64 75 77 79 82 86 87 90 91 93 94 95 96 130 131 132 135 143 148 149 154 164 **P**8 **S** PAM Health, Enola, PA
Primary Contact: Megan Hall, Chief Executive Officer
Web address: https://postacutemedical.com/facilities/find-facility/rehabilitation-hospitals/pam-rehabilitation-hospital-overland
Control: Corporation, Investor–owned (for–profit) **Service**: Rehabilitation

Staffed Beds: 45 **Admissions**: 1205 **Census**: 40 **Outpatient Visits**: 15135 **Births**: 0 **Total Expense ($000)**: 25872 **Payroll Expense ($000)**: 12397 **Personnel**: 287

✠ **SAINT LUKE'S SOUTH HOSPITAL (170185)**, 12300 Metcalf Avenue, Zip 66213–1324; tel. 913/317–7000, (Includes SAINT LUKE'S COMMUNITY HOSPITAL AT LEAWOOD, 13200 State Line Road, Leawood, Kansas, Zip 66209, tel. 913/222–8380; Bobby Olm–Shipman, Chief Executive Officer) **A**1 2 10 **F**3 12 15 18 20 22 26 28 29 30 31 34 35 38 39 40 42 44 45 48 49 50 54 56 58 59 60 61 64 65 68 70 74 75 77 78 79 80 81 84 85 86 87 89 90 92 93 94 95 96 100 102 107 108 110 111 114 115 116 117 118 119 126 130 131 132 135 141 146 147 148 149 154 164 167 168 **S** BJC Health System, Saint Louis, MO
Primary Contact: Bobby Olm–Shipman, Chief Executive Officer
COO: Anna Sahli, Vice President of Operations
CFO: Matt Marino, Chief Financial Officer
CMO: Michael Davenport, D.O., President, Medical Staff
CIO: Deborah Gash, Chief Information Officer
CHR: Carol Ferrara, Director Human Resources
CNO: Julia Woods, MSN, Vice President and Chief Nursing Officer
Web address: www.saintlukeshealthsystem.org/south
Control: Other not–for–profit (including NFP Corporation) **Service**: General medical and surgical

Staffed Beds: 142 **Admissions**: 6330 **Census**: 107 **Outpatient Visits**: 142060 **Births**: 0 **Total Expense ($000)**: 259167 **Payroll Expense ($000)**: 69891 **Personnel**: 857

PAOLA—Miami County

☐ **MIAMI COUNTY MEDICAL CENTER (170109)**, 2100 Baptiste Drive, Zip 66071–1314, Mailing Address: P.O. Box 365, Zip 66071–0365; tel. 913/294–2327, **A**1 10 **F**3 11 15 18 28 29 34 40 43 57 59 64 68 75 77 79 81 85 87 93 100 107 108 110 111 115 119 127 130 131 135 145 146 147 148 149 154 156 169 **S** The University of Kansas Health System, Kansas City, KS
Primary Contact: Paul W. Luce, R.N., MSN, Administrator
CFO: Monica Lubeck, Senior Vice President and Chief Financial Officer
CMO: Kelly Rhodes–Stark, Chief Medical Officer
CHR: Janelle Lee, Vice President Human Resources
CNO: Aubree Slayman, Director Patient Services
Web address: https://www.olathehealth.org/locations/miami-county-medical-center/
Control: Other not–for–profit (including NFP Corporation) **Service**: General medical and surgical

Staffed Beds: 18 **Admissions**: 418 **Census**: 2 **Outpatient Visits**: 60516 **Births**: 0 **Personnel**: 139

Hospital, Medicare Provider Number, Address, Telephone, Approval, Facility, and Physician Codes, Health Care System

★ American Hospital Association (AHA) membership   ○ Healthcare Facilities Accreditation Program   ⇧ Center for Improvement in Healthcare Quality Accreditation
☐ The Joint Commission accreditation   ◇ DNV Healthcare Inc. accreditation   △ Commission on Accreditation of Rehabilitation Facilities (CARF) accreditation

Hospitals, U.S. / KANSAS

PARSONS—Labette County

★ ○ **LABETTE HEALTH (170120)**, 1902 South US Highway 59, Zip 67357-7404; tel. 620/421-4880, **A**10 11 **F**3 11 13 15 29 30 34 40 42 43 50 53 59 62 70 74 75 76 77 79 81 86 90 93 97 107 108 110 111 114 119 126 127 129 130 133 143 144 146 147 148 149 154 156 169 **P**6
Primary Contact: Brian A. Williams, Chief Executive Officer
CHR: Christina Sykes, Director Human Resources
Web address: www.labettehealth.com
Control: County, Government, Nonfederal **Service:** General medical and surgical

> **Staffed Beds:** 56 **Admissions:** 1427 **Census:** 14 **Outpatient Visits:** 121370
> **Births:** 248 **Total Expense ($000):** 98523 **Payroll Expense ($000):** 44220
> **Personnel:** 684

PARSONS STATE HOSPITAL AND TRAINING CENTER, 2601 Gabriel Avenue, Zip 67357-2341, Mailing Address: P.O. Box 738, Zip 67357-0738; tel. 620/421-6550, **F**35 67 75 130 146 **P**6
Primary Contact: Jerry A. Rea, Ph.D., Superintendent
CFO: John Spare, Accountant
CMO: Rema Menon, M.D., Clinical Director
CIO: Ron Malmstrom, Information Research Specialist
CHR: Tim B Posch, Business Manager and Director Personnel
Web address: www.pshtc.org
Control: State, Government, Nonfederal **Service:** Intellectual disabilities

> **Staffed Beds:** 172 **Admissions:** 10 **Census:** 148 **Outpatient Visits:** 0
> **Births:** 0 **Total Expense ($000):** 33758 **Payroll Expense ($000):** 22228
> **Personnel:** 501

PHILLIPSBURG—Phillips County

★ **PHILLIPS COUNTY HEALTH SYSTEMS (171353)**, 1150 State Street, Zip 67661-1743; tel. 785/543-5226, (Nonreporting) **A**10 18
Primary Contact: Tara Overmiller, Chief Executive Officer
COO: Tara Overmiller, Chief Operating Officer
CFO: Krystal Schwenn, Chief Financial Officer
CMO: Doak Doolittle, M.D., Chief of Staff
CIO: Steven Seems, Director of Information Technology
CHR: Peggy Fabin, Director Human Resources
CNO: Vickie Gibbs, Director Nursing
Web address: www.phillipshospital.org
Control: Other not-for-profit (including NFP Corporation) **Service:** General medical and surgical

> **Staffed Beds:** 25

PITTSBURG—Crawford County

⬚ **MERCY HOSPITAL PITTSBURG (170006)**, 1 Mt. Carmel Way, Zip 66762-7587; tel. 620/231-6100, **A**1 3 5 10 **F**3 11 12 13 15 18 20 22 26 28 29 30 31 34 35 40 42 43 45 46 47 48 50 51 53 54 56 57 59 62 64 68 69 70 75 76 78 79 81 82 84 85 86 89 90 93 107 108 109 110 111 112 114 115 116 117 118 119 120 121 123 124 126 129 130 131 132 133 135 145 146 147 148 154 156 157 167 169 **S** Mercy, Chesterfield, MO
Primary Contact: Drew Talbott, President
CFO: Mike Joy, Administrator, Finance
CIO: Missy McDown, Director Information Systems
CHR: Laurie Johnson, Director – Human Resources
Web address: https://www.mercy.net/practice/mercy-hospital-pittsburg/
Control: Church operated, Nongovernment, not-for-profit **Service:** General medical and surgical

> **Staffed Beds:** 89 **Admissions:** 2627 **Census:** 30 **Outpatient Visits:** 83126
> **Births:** 570 **Total Expense ($000):** 104576 **Payroll Expense ($000):** 38593
> **Personnel:** 320

PLAINVILLE—Rooks County

★ **ROOKS COUNTY HEALTH CENTER (171311)**, 1210 North Washington Street, Zip 67663-1632, Mailing Address: P.O. Box 389, Zip 67663-0389; tel. 785/434-4553, (Nonreporting) **A**10 18
Primary Contact: Jeff VanDyke, Interim Chief Executive Officer
COO: William D Stahl, Chief Operating Officer
CFO: Frank A Rajewski, Chief Financial Officer
CMO: Lynn Fisher, M.D., Chief of Staff
CHR: Cindi Knipp, Director Human Resources
Web address: www.rookscountyhealthcenter.com
Control: Hospital district or authority, Government, Nonfederal **Service:** General medical and surgical

> **Staffed Beds:** 22

PRATT—Pratt County

★ ⇈ **PRATT REGIONAL MEDICAL CENTER (170027)**, 200 Commodore Street, Zip 67124-2903; tel. 620/672-7451, **A**10 20 21 **F**3 7 11 13 15 28 29 30 31 34 40 45 49 50 54 56 57 59 62 64 68 70 75 76 77 79 81 82 85 86 87 93 107 108 114 118 119 124 126 127 130 131 133 144 146 147 148 149 154 155 156 167
Primary Contact: Tammy Smith, R.N., President and Chief Executive Officer
CFO: Vincent Scot Wilczek, Controller
CIO: Vikki Mader, Director Health Information Services
CHR: Kenneth A Brown, Vice President and Chief Human Resource Officer
CNO: Tracy Johnson, Vice President Patient Care Services/Chief Nursing Officer
Web address: www.prmc.org
Control: Other not-for-profit (including NFP Corporation) **Service:** General medical and surgical

> **Staffed Beds:** 39 **Admissions:** 1267 **Census:** 10 **Outpatient Visits:** 47650
> **Births:** 221 **Total Expense ($000):** 58518 **Payroll Expense ($000):** 25820
> **Personnel:** 318

QUINTER—Gove County

GOVE COUNTY MEDICAL CENTER (171367), 520 West Fifth Street, Zip 67752-0129, Mailing Address: P.O. Box 129, Zip 67752-0129; tel. 785/754-3341, **A**10 18 **F**3 11 13 28 29 40 45 75 76 81 82 86 93 107 115 119 129 132 133 143 148 156 169
Primary Contact: Conner Mikhail. Fiscarelli, Chief Executive Officer
CFO: Alan Waites, Chief Financial Officer
CIO: Brad Mullins, Director Information Technology
CHR: Valerie Schneider, Director Human Resources
CNO: Renee Wagoner, R.N., Director of Nursing
Web address: www.govecountymedicalcenter.org
Control: County, Government, Nonfederal **Service:** General medical and surgical

> **Staffed Beds:** 21 **Admissions:** 325 **Census:** 5 **Outpatient Visits:** 10892
> **Births:** 54 **Total Expense ($000):** 20131 **Payroll Expense ($000):** 7414
> **Personnel:** 124

RANSOM—Ness County

★ **GRISELL MEMORIAL HOSPITAL DISTRICT ONE (171300)**, 210 South Vermont Avenue, Zip 67572-9525; tel. 785/731-2231, **A**10 18 **F**3 40 67 69 85 93 97 127 128 133 156 **P**6 **S** Great Plains Health Alliance, Inc., Wichita, KS
Primary Contact: Frank Safrit, Ph.D., MSN, Chief Executive Officer
CMO: Allen McLain, M.D., Chief of Staff
CNO: Joni Pfaff, Chief Nursing Officer
Web address: www.grisellmemorialhospital.org
Control: Hospital district or authority, Government, Nonfederal **Service:** General medical and surgical

> **Staffed Beds:** 25 **Admissions:** 62 **Census:** 16 **Outpatient Visits:** 5110
> **Births:** 0 **Total Expense ($000):** 8142 **Payroll Expense ($000):** 3117
> **Personnel:** 58

RUSSELL—Russell County

★ **RUSSELL REGIONAL HOSPITAL (171350)**, 200 South Main Street, Zip 67665-2920; tel. 785/483-3131, (Total facility includes 20 beds in nursing home-type unit) **A**10 18 **F**9 11 15 29 33 34 35 40 45 46 50 53 57 59 64 65 67 69 75 77 81 82 85 87 93 97 107 108 109 110 111 115 119 127 129 130 131 133 135 145 146 147 148 149 154 **P**6
Primary Contact: David Caudill, Chief Executive Officer
CFO: Kevin Kreutzer, Chief Financial Officer
CMO: Tyrel Somers, M.D., Chief Medical Officer
CIO: David Schraeder, Director Information Systems
CNO: Deb Strobel, R.N., Chief Nursing Officer
Web address: www.russellhospital.org
Control: Other not-for-profit (including NFP Corporation) **Service:** General medical and surgical

> **Staffed Beds:** 35 **Admissions:** 414 **Census:** 25 **Outpatient Visits:** 19312
> **Births:** 0 **Total Expense ($000):** 23305 **Payroll Expense ($000):** 10884
> **Personnel:** 169

SABETHA—Nemaha County

★ **SABETHA COMMUNITY HOSPITAL (171338)**, 14th and Oregon Streets, Zip 66534-0229, Mailing Address: P.O. Box 229, Zip 66534-0229; tel. 785/284-2121, **A**10 18 **F**3 11 13 15 28 34 35 40 43 45 50 56 57 59 62 63 64 68 75 76 77 78 79 81 82 84 85 86 93 107 110 114 119 128 130 132 133 146 148 156 **P**6 **S** Great Plains Health Alliance, Inc., Wichita, KS
Primary Contact: James Longabaugh, M.D., Chief Executive Officer
CFO: Lori Lackey, Chief Financial Officer
CIO: Garrett Colglazier, Director Health Information Management
CHR: Julie K Holthaus, Director Human Resources
CNO: Rhonda Spellmeier, R.N., Director of Nursing
Web address: www.sabethahospital.com
Control: Other not-for-profit (including NFP Corporation) **Service:** General medical and surgical

Staffed Beds: 25 **Admissions:** 293 **Census:** 4 **Outpatient Visits:** 35335 **Births:** 13 **Total Expense ($000):** 19250 **Payroll Expense ($000):** 8302 **Personnel:** 114

SAINT FRANCIS—Cheyenne County

★ **CHEYENNE COUNTY HOSPITAL (171310)**, 210 West First Street, Zip 67756-3540, Mailing Address: P.O. Box 547, Zip 67756-0547; tel. 785/332-2104, **A**10 18 **F**3 8 11 13 28 29 34 40 57 59 64 65 66 68 76 77 81 82 89 97 107 119 127 128 133 148 156 166 **P**6 **S** Great Plains Health Alliance, Inc., Wichita, KS
Primary Contact: Jeremy Clingenpeel, Chief Executive Officer
CFO: Heidi Tice, Chief Financial Officer
CMO: Mary Beth Miller, M.D., Chief of Staff
CIO: Carol Sloper, Manager Information Technology
CHR: Sara Wilson, Director Human Resources
CNO: Judith Ann Hodgson, Chief Nursing Officer
Web address: www.cheyennecountyhospital.com
Control: Other not-for-profit (including NFP Corporation) **Service:** General medical and surgical

Staffed Beds: 16 **Admissions:** 263 **Census:** 3 **Outpatient Visits:** 28430 **Births:** 39 **Total Expense ($000):** 17376 **Payroll Expense ($000):** 5129 **Personnel:** 84

SALINA—Saline County

ASBURY-SALINA REG MEDICAL CTR See Salina Regional Health Center–Santa Fe Campus

★ ○ **SALINA REGIONAL HEALTH CENTER (170012)**, 400 South Santa Fe Avenue, Zip 67401-4198, Mailing Address: P.O. Box 5080, Zip 67402-5080; tel. 785/452-7000, (Includes SALINA REGIONAL HEALTH CENTER– PENN CAMPUS, 139 North Penn Street, Salina, Kansas, Zip 67401, P O Box 5080, Zip 67402-5080, tel. 913/452-7000; SALINA REGIONAL HEALTH CENTER– SANTA FE CAMPUS, 400 South Santa Fe Avenue, Salina, Kansas, Zip 67401, Box 5080, Zip 67402-5080, tel. 913/452-7000) **A**3 5 10 11 20 **F**3 11 13 15 18 19 20 22 24 28 29 30 31 34 35 40 43 45 46 47 48 49 51 53 54 55 57 58 59 60 64 65 68 70 72 73 74 76 77 78 79 81 85 86 87 89 90 93 98 100 101 102 104 105 107 110 111 115 117 118 119 120 121 123 124 126 129 130 131 135 143 144 146 147 148 149 153 154 167 **P**6 **S** Salina Regional Health Center, Salina, KS
Primary Contact: Joel Phelps, President and Chief Executive Officer
CFO: Joe Tallon, Vice President Finance
CIO: Larry Barnes, Vice President Information Technology
CHR: David Moody, Vice President Human Resources
Web address: www.srhc.com
Control: Other not-for-profit (including NFP Corporation) **Service:** General medical and surgical

Staffed Beds: 214 **Admissions:** 6799 **Census:** 83 **Outpatient Visits:** 628033 **Births:** 1093 **Total Expense ($000):** 333757 **Payroll Expense ($000):** 132635 **Personnel:** 1626

SALINA SURGICAL HOSPITAL (170187), 401 South Santa Fe Avenue, Zip 67401-4143, Mailing Address: 401 South Sante Fe Avenue, Zip 67401-4143; tel. 785/827-0610, **A**5 10 **F**3 29 45 48 49 51 59 79 81 85 131 166
Primary Contact: LuAnn Puvogel, R.N., Chief Executive Officer
CFO: Elizabeth Bishop, Business Office Manager
CMO: Michael Johnson, M.D., Medical Director
CIO: Earl Akers, Supervisor Information Technology
CHR: Elizabeth Bishop, Business Office Manager
CNO: Jolene Glavin, R.N., MSN, Director Nursing
Web address: www.salinasurgical.com/
Control: Partnership, Investor-owned (for-profit) **Service:** Surgical

Staffed Beds: 16 **Admissions:** 639 **Census:** 4 **Outpatient Visits:** 9365 **Births:** 0 **Total Expense ($000):** 24969 **Payroll Expense ($000):** 7659 **Personnel:** 110

ST JOHN'S REGIONAL HEALTH CTR See Salina Regional Health Center– Penn Campus

SATANTA—Haskell County

★ **SATANTA DISTRICT HOSPITAL AND LONG TERM CARE (171324)**, 401 South Cheyenne Street, Zip 67870-0159, Mailing Address: P.O. Box 159, Zip 67870-0159; tel. 620/649-2761, (Total facility includes 34 beds in nursing home-type unit) **A**10 18 **F**3 11 40 43 45 57 64 67 68 75 81 87 93 104 107 119 127 128 130 133 156 **P**4 **S** Great Plains Health Alliance, Inc., Wichita, KS
Primary Contact: Tina Pendergraft, Chief Executive Officer
CFO: Libby Anderson, Chief Financial Officer
CMO: Virgilio Taduran, M.D., Chief Medical Officer
CIO: Ben Leppke, Chief Information Officer
CHR: Samantha Hett, Manager Human Resources
Web address: www.satantahospital.org
Control: Hospital district or authority, Government, Nonfederal **Service:** General medical and surgical

Staffed Beds: 59 **Admissions:** 107 **Census:** 32 **Outpatient Visits:** 19060 **Births:** 0 **Total Expense ($000):** 16624 **Payroll Expense ($000):** 7334 **Personnel:** 117

SCOTT CITY—Scott County

★ **SCOTT COUNTY HOSPITAL (171372)**, 201 East Albert Avenue, Zip 67871-1203; tel. 620/872-5811, **A**10 18 **F**7 13 15 28 29 34 40 41 45 50 56 57 59 64 65 68 69 74 75 76 77 81 82 85 87 93 94 97 100 107 108 109 110 111 112 115 119 127 128 129 130 131 132 133 135 146 147 148 149 156 157 169 **P**6
Primary Contact: David Mark. Burnett, President and Chief Executive Officer
CMO: Matthew Lightner, M.D., Chief Medical Staff
CHR: Whisper Carson, Manager Human Resource
CNO: Jeri Grove, Chief Nursing Officer
Web address: www.scotthospital.net
Control: County, Government, Nonfederal **Service:** General medical and surgical

Staffed Beds: 23 **Admissions:** 587 **Census:** 8 **Outpatient Visits:** 31275 **Births:** 61 **Total Expense ($000):** 28491 **Payroll Expense ($000):** 13930 **Personnel:** 214

SEDAN—Chautauqua County

SEDAN CITY HOSPITAL (171318), 300 North Street, Zip 67361-1051, Mailing Address: P.O. Box 'C', Zip 67361-0427; tel. 620/725-3115, **A**10 18 **F**3 29 34 40 57 64 93 107 119 128 130 133 148
Primary Contact: Michelle Williams, Administrator
CFO: Jennifer Seever, Regional Chief Financial Officer
CMO: James McDermott, M.D., Chief of Staff
Web address: https://sedancityhospital.org/
Control: City, Government, Nonfederal **Service:** General medical and surgical

Staffed Beds: 20 **Admissions:** 108 **Census:** 2 **Outpatient Visits:** 9241 **Births:** 0 **Total Expense ($000):** 5510 **Payroll Expense ($000):** 2092 **Personnel:** 31

Hospitals, U.S. / KANSAS

SENECA—Nemaha County

★ **NEMAHA VALLEY COMMUNITY HOSPITAL (171315)**, 1600 Community Drive, Zip 66538–9739; tel. 785/336–6181, **A**10 18 **F**3 11 12 13 15 28 34 35 40 50 57 59 64 65 76 81 85 93 97 107 111 114 119 127 129 130 131 133 135 146 147 156 164 169 **P**6
Primary Contact: Kiley Floyd, Chief Executive Officer
CFO: Abbie Thomas, Chief Financial Officer
CMO: Tony Bartkoski, M.D., Chief of Medical Staff
CHR: Ronnette Worthley, Manager Human Resource
CNO: Lynda Cross, R.N., Director of Nurses
Web address: www.nemvch.org
Control: Other not–for–profit (including NFP Corporation) **Service:** General medical and surgical

Staffed Beds: 18 **Admissions:** 366 **Census:** 4 **Outpatient Visits:** 41915 **Births:** 42 **Total Expense ($000):** 21906 **Payroll Expense ($000):** 10592 **Personnel:** 139

SHAWNEE MISSION—Johnson County

MID–AMERICA REHABILITATION HOSPITAL (173026), 5701 West 110th Street, Zip 66211–2503, Mailing Address: Overland Park, tel. 913/491–2400, (Nonreporting) **A**1 10 **S** Encompass Health Corporation, Birmingham, AL
Primary Contact: Tiffany Kiehl, Chief Executive Officer
CFO: Richard Lane, Chief Financial Officer
CMO: Cielo Dehning, M.D., Medical Director
CNO: Amy McKay, Chief Nursing Officer
Web address: www.midamericarehabhospital.com
Control: Corporation, Investor–owned (for–profit) **Service:** Rehabilitation

Staffed Beds: 98

SMITH CENTER—Smith County

★ **SMITH COUNTY MEMORIAL HOSPITAL (171377)**, 921 East Highway 36, Zip 66967–9582; tel. 785/282–6845, **A**10 18 **F**3 13 15 28 29 30 31 34 40 43 45 53 64 65 68 69 75 76 81 85 89 91 93 107 110 114 119 127 128 130 133 135 154 156 **P**6 **S** Great Plains Health Alliance, Inc., Wichita, KS
Primary Contact: Sarah Jane. Ragsdale, R.N., Chief Executive Officer
CFO: Avery Aiken, Chief Financial Officer
CIO: Tammy Gaston, Chief Information Officer
CHR: Julie Haresnape, Coordinator Human Resources
Web address: www.scmhks.org
Control: Other not–for–profit (including NFP Corporation) **Service:** General medical and surgical

Staffed Beds: 16 **Admissions:** 608 **Census:** 5 **Outpatient Visits:** 32587 **Births:** 48 **Total Expense ($000):** 25451 **Payroll Expense ($000):** 8697 **Personnel:** 145

STAFFORD—Stafford County

★ **STAFFORD COUNTY HOSPITAL (171323)**, 502 South Buckeye Street, Zip 67578–2035, Mailing Address: P.O. Box 190, Zip 67578–0190; tel. 620/234–5221, (Nonreporting) **A**10 18
Primary Contact: Todd Taylor, Chief Executive Officer
Web address: www.staffordcounty.org
Control: County, Government, Nonfederal **Service:** General medical and surgical

Staffed Beds: 25

SYRACUSE—Hamilton County

HAMILTON COUNTY HOSPITAL (171322), 700 North Huser Street, Zip 67878–0948, Mailing Address: P.O. Box 948, Zip 67878–0948; tel. 620/384–7461, (Nonreporting) **A**10 18
Primary Contact: Kelly Holder, Administrator
CMO: Richard Carter, M.D., Chief Medical Director
CNO: Malachi Lones, Chief Nursing Officer
Web address: www.myhch.org
Control: County, Government, Nonfederal **Service:** General medical and surgical

Staffed Beds: 25

TOPEKA—Shawnee County

COLMERY–O'NEIL VETERANS AFFAIRS MEDICAL CENTER See Veterans Affairs Eastern Kansas Health Care System–Colmery–O'Neil Veterans Affairs Medical Center

EASTERN KANSAS HCS, 2200 South West Gage Boulevard, Zip 66622–0002, Mailing Address: LVN–4101 4th Street Trafficway, Leavenworth, Zip 66048; tel. 785/350–3111, (Includes VETERANS AFFAIRS EASTERN KANSAS HEALTH CARE SYSTEM–COLMERY–O'NEIL VETERANS AFFAIRS MEDICAL CENTER, 2200 South West Gage Boulevard, Topeka, Kansas, Zip 66622–0002, tel. 785/350–3111; VETERANS AFFAIRS EASTERN KANSAS HEALTH CARE SYSTEM–DWIGHT D. EISENHOWER VETERANS AFFAIRS MEDICAL CENTER, 4101 South 4th Street Trafficway, Leavenworth, Kansas, Zip 66048–5055, tel. 913/682–2000) (Total facility includes 29 beds in nursing home–type unit) **A**1 3 5 **F**3 4 5 7 8 10 12 18 26 28 29 30 31 33 35 36 38 39 40 45 46 50 53 54 56 57 58 59 61 62 63 64 65 66 67 68 70 74 75 77 78 79 81 82 83 84 86 87 93 94 97 100 101 102 104 105 107 108 111 114 115 116 117 118 119 127 128 129 130 132 133 135 143 145 146 147 148 149 150 152 153 154 155 158 160 164 165 167 168 169 **S** Department of Veterans Affairs, Washington, DC
Primary Contact: Anthony Rudy. Klopfer, FACHE, Director
COO: John Moon, Associate Director
CMO: Rajeev Trehan, M.D., M.P.H., Chief of Staff
CIO: Joni Davin, Director Information and Business Management Service Line
Web address: www.topeka.va.gov/
Control: Veterans Affairs, Government, federal **Service:** General medical and surgical

Staffed Beds: 125 **Admissions:** 3101 **Census:** 120 **Outpatient Visits:** 301972 **Births:** 0 **Total Expense ($000):** 320996 **Payroll Expense ($000):** 167398 **Personnel:** 1953

KANSAS NEUROLOGICAL INSTITUTE, 3107 West 21st Street, Zip 66604–3298; tel. 785/296–5301, (Nonreporting)
Primary Contact: Brent Widick, Superintendent
CFO: Sara Hoyer, Director Administrative Services
CMO: Mary Gingrich, Director Health Care Services
CIO: Cheryl Fuller, Director Information Resources
CHR: Shawna Mercer, Director Human Resources
Web address: www.kdads.ks.gov/state-hospitals-and-institutions/kansas-neurological-institute
Control: State, Government, Nonfederal **Service:** Intellectual disabilities

Staffed Beds: 142

KANSAS REHABILITATION HOSPITAL (173025), 1504 SW Eighth Avenue, Zip 66606–1632; tel. 785/235–6600, **A**1 10 **F**29 60 75 86 90 91 95 96 130 132 148 149 **S** Encompass Health Corporation, Birmingham, AL
Primary Contact: Barry Muninger, Chief Executive Officer
CMO: Joseph Sankoorikal, M.D., Chief Medical Staff
CHR: Dina Cox, Director Human Resources
CNO: Carol Swanger, Chief Nursing Officer
Web address: www.kansasrehabhospital.com
Control: Corporation, Investor–owned (for–profit) **Service:** Rehabilitation

Staffed Beds: 47 **Admissions:** 1069 **Census:** 36 **Outpatient Visits:** 0 **Births:** 0 **Total Expense ($000):** 19913 **Payroll Expense ($000):** 10135 **Personnel:** 128

STORMONT VAIL HEALTH (170086), 1500 SW Tenth Avenue, Zip 66604–1353; tel. 785/354–6000, **A**1 2 10 19 **F**3 8 11 12 13 15 17 18 19 20 22 24 26 28 29 30 31 34 35 37 40 43 44 45 46 47 49 50 51 54 55 56 57 58 59 60 61 64 65 68 70 71 72 74 75 76 77 78 79 81 82 84 85 86 87 88 89 91 92 93 97 98 99 100 101 102 103 104 105 107 108 110 111 112 114 115 116 117 118 119 120 121 123 126 129 130 131 132 135 143 144 145 146 147 148 149 150 153 154 156 167 169
Primary Contact: Rob Kenagy, M.D., President and Chief Executive Officer
CFO: Robert Langland, Senior Vice President and Chief Financial Officer
CMO: Kevin Dishman, M.D., Chief Medical Officer
CIO: Judy Corzine, Vice President of IT & Chief Information Officer
CHR: Darlene Stone, Senior Vice President and Chief Experience Officer
CNO: Carol Perry, R.N., Vice President and Chief Nursing Officer
Web address: www.stormontvail.org
Control: Other not–for–profit (including NFP Corporation) **Service:** General medical and surgical

Staffed Beds: 398 **Admissions:** 18537 **Census:** 238 **Outpatient Visits:** 162985 **Births:** 1517 **Total Expense ($000):** 884821 **Payroll Expense ($000):** 467098 **Personnel:** 4965

Hospitals, U.S. / KANSAS

✠ **UNIVERSITY OF KANSAS HEALTH SYSTEM ST. FRANCIS CAMPUS (170016)**, 1700 SW 7th Street, Zip 66606-1690; tel. 785/295-8000, **A**1 2 3 5 10 19 **F**3 8 12 13 15 18 20 22 24 26 28 29 31 34 35 37 38 40 44 45 46 47 48 49 50 51 54 55 56 57 58 59 61 65 70 71 73 74 75 76 77 78 79 81 82 85 86 87 89 90 92 93 95 96 97 107 108 110 111 115 116 117 118 119 120 121 123 126 127 129 130 131 132 146 147 148 149 154 156 167 169 **P**6 **S** Ardent Health Services, Nashville, TN
Primary Contact: Scott Campbell, Chief Executive Officer
CFO: Samuel Moore, Chief Financial Officer
CMO: Jaquelyn Hyland, M.D., Chief Medical Officer
CIO: Jamie Hilliard, Director of Information Technology
CHR: Steve Saffa, Director Human Resources
CNO: Adam Meier, MSN, R.N., Chief Nursing Officer
Web address: https://kutopeka.com/
Control: Partnership, Investor-owned (for-profit) **Service**: General medical and surgical

Staffed Beds: 131 **Admissions**: 7278 **Census**: 80 **Outpatient Visits**: 176501 **Births**: 889 **Total Expense ($000)**: 311616 **Payroll Expense ($000)**: 75503 **Personnel**: 1052

VETERANS AFFAIRS EASTERN KANSAS HEALTH CARE SYSTEM–COLMERY–O'NEIL VETERANS AFFAIRS MEDICAL CENTER See Eastern Kansas HCS, Topeka

TRIBUNE—Greeley County

★ **GREELEY COUNTY HEALTH SERVICES (171359)**, 506 Third Street, Zip 67879-9684, Mailing Address: P.O. Box 338, Zip 67879-0338; tel. 620/376-4221, (Nonreporting) **A**10 18
Primary Contact: Trice Watts, Chief Financial Officer and Chief Executive Officer
CFO: Trice Watts, Chief Financial Officer
CMO: Wendel Ellis, D.O., Chief Medical Staff
CIO: Shanon Schneider, Chief Information Officer
CHR: Katelyn Reynolds, Manager Human Resources
CNO: Janie Schmidt, Director of Nursing
Web address: www.mygchs.com
Control: Other not-for-profit (including NFP Corporation) **Service**: General medical and surgical

Staffed Beds: 50

ULYSSES—Grant County

★ **BOB WILSON MEMORIAL GRANT COUNTY HOSPITAL (170110)**, 415 North Main Street, Zip 67880-2133; tel. 620/356-1266, **A**10 20 **F**3 13 29 30 40 76 81 93 97 107 111 119 127 128 130 133 154 **P**6 **S** CommonSpirit Health, Chicago, IL
Primary Contact: Twilla Lee, Chief Executive Officer
CFO: Amanda Vaughan, Chief Financial Officer
CIO: Chris Moffet, Director Information Services
CHR: Tammy Oxford, Director Human Resources
Web address: www.bwmgch.com
Control: Church operated, Nongovernment, not-for-profit **Service**: General medical and surgical

Staffed Beds: 26 **Admissions**: 202 **Census**: 3 **Outpatient Visits**: 10570 **Births**: 0 **Total Expense ($000)**: 8664 **Payroll Expense ($000)**: 3501 **Personnel**: 29

WAKEENEY—Trego County

★ **TREGO COUNTY-LEMKE MEMORIAL HOSPITAL (171355)**, 320 North 13th Street, Zip 67672-2099; tel. 785/743-2182, (Total facility includes 37 beds in nursing home-type unit) **A**10 18 **F**3 8 10 11 15 28 29 34 40 45 53 57 59 62 64 67 69 71 81 86 89 93 107 110 114 127 128 130 133 143 146 148 154 156 166 **P**6 **S** Great Plains Health Alliance, Inc., Wichita, KS
Primary Contact: Jeremy Rabe, Chief Executive Officer
CFO: ReChelle Horinek, Chief Financial Officer
CMO: Gordon Lang, M.D., Chief of Staff
CHR: Jeff Bieker, Director Human Resource
CNO: Sandy Purinton, Chief Nursing Officer
Web address: www.tclmh.org
Control: County, Government, Nonfederal **Service**: General medical and surgical

Staffed Beds: 62 **Admissions**: 215 **Census**: 34 **Outpatient Visits**: 30042 **Births**: 0 **Total Expense ($000)**: 18279 **Payroll Expense ($000)**: 8666 **Personnel**: 141

WAMEGO—Pottawatomie County

★ **WAMEGO HEALTH CENTER (171337)**, 711 Genn Drive, Zip 66547-1179; tel. 785/456-2295, **A**10 18 **F**3 11 15 28 29 30 34 40 56 59 64 65 75 77 81 93 97 107 114 119 127 130 131 132 133 143 146 147 148 149 167 **P**6 **S** Ascension Healthcare, Saint Louis, MO
Primary Contact: Brian Howells, Administrator
COO: Brian Smith, Director of Operations
CFO: Keith Zachariasen, Chief Financial Officer
CMO: Roland Darey, M.D., Medical Director
CIO: Wes Janzen, Chief Information Officer
CHR: Renee Reed, Director Human Resources
CNO: Tresha Flanary, R.N., Chief Clinical Services Officer
Web address: https://wamegohealthcenter.org/
Control: Other not-for-profit (including NFP Corporation) **Service**: General medical and surgical

Staffed Beds: 8 **Admissions**: 150 **Census**: 4 **Outpatient Visits**: 46685 **Births**: 0 **Total Expense ($000)**: 14202 **Payroll Expense ($000)**: 7127 **Personnel**: 80

WASHINGTON—Washington County

WASHINGTON COUNTY HOSPITAL (171351), 304 East Third Street, Zip 66968-2033; tel. 785/325-2211, (Nonreporting) **A**10 18
Primary Contact: Roxanne Schottel, Chief Executive Officer
CFO: Roxanne Schottel, Chief Executive Officer
CNO: Kelly Otott, R.N., Chief Nursing Officer
Web address: www.washingtoncountyhospital.net
Control: County, Government, Nonfederal **Service**: General medical and surgical

Staffed Beds: 18

WICHITA—Sedgwick County

✠ **ASCENSION VIA CHRISTI HOSPITAL ON ST. TERESA (170200)**, 14800 West St. Teresa, Zip 67235-9602; tel. 316/796-7000, **A**1 10 **F**3 8 18 20 22 29 30 34 35 37 40 45 50 64 68 70 75 78 79 81 85 87 92 93 100 107 108 111 114 118 119 126 130 146 148 167 **S** Ascension Healthcare, Saint Louis, MO
Primary Contact: Laurie Labarca, President
Web address: www.via-christi.org/st-teresa
Control: Church operated, Nongovernment, not-for-profit **Service**: General medical and surgical

Staffed Beds: 35 **Admissions**: 2261 **Census**: 23 **Outpatient Visits**: 44404 **Births**: 0 **Total Expense ($000)**: 45422 **Payroll Expense ($000)**: 13873 **Personnel**: 216

ASCENSION VIA CHRISTI HOSPITAL ST. FRANCIS See St. Francis Campus

✠ **ASCENSION VIA CHRISTI REHABILITATION HOSPITAL (173028)**, 1151 North Rock Road, Zip 67206-1262; tel. 316/634-3400, **A**1 10 **F**11 29 30 34 35 44 50 54 57 59 64 77 86 87 90 92 93 95 96 100 119 129 130 131 132 143 146 148 **S** Ascension Healthcare, Saint Louis, MO
Primary Contact: Laurie Labarca, President
CMO: Kevin Rieg, M.D., President Medical Staff
CNO: Cindy Hagerty, Assistant Chief Nurse Officer and Administrator of Operations
Web address: www.via-christi.org
Control: Church operated, Nongovernment, not-for-profit **Service**: Rehabilitation

Staffed Beds: 30 **Admissions**: 854 **Census**: 27 **Outpatient Visits**: 93177 **Births**: 0 **Total Expense ($000)**: 26404 **Payroll Expense ($000)**: 8993 **Personnel**: 173

CHILDREN'S CENTER AT WESLEY See Wesley Children's Hospital

GALICHIA HEART HOSPITAL See Wesley Woodlawn Hospital & Er

KANSAS HEART HOSPITAL (170186), 3601 North Webb Road, Zip 67226-8129; tel. 316/630-5000, **A**10 **F**3 17 18 20 22 24 26 29 67 70 81 107 115 119
Primary Contact: Thomas L. Ashcom, M.D., Ph.D., Chief Executive Officer
COO: Joyce Heismeyer, Chief Operating Officer
CFO: Steve Smith, Chief Financial Officer
CHR: Teresa E Wolfe, Manager Human Resources
CNO: Susan Bradford, Director Nursing
Web address: www.kansasheart.com
Control: Partnership, Investor-owned (for-profit) **Service**: Heart

Staffed Beds: 54 **Admissions**: 1564 **Census**: 16 **Outpatient Visits**: 0 **Births**: 0 **Personnel**: 211

Hospitals, U.S. / KANSAS

KANSAS SPINE & SPECIALTY HOSPITAL (170196), 3333 North Webb Road, Zip 67226–8123; tel. 316/462–5000, **A**10 **F**3 29 79 81 82 85 87 107 111 114 126 149 154 **P**2
Primary Contact: Scott Chapman, Chief Executive Officer
CFO: Jennifer Gerken, R.N., Chief Financial Officer
CIO: Michael Knocke, Chief Information Officer
CHR: Angela L. Anderson, Manager Human Resource
CNO: Theresa Edwards, R.N., Chief Nursing Officer
Web address: www.ksspine.com
Control: Corporation, Investor–owned (for–profit) **Service**: General medical and surgical

Staffed Beds: 35 **Admissions**: 1536 **Census**: 10 **Outpatient Visits**: 11408
Births: 0 **Personnel**: 211

○ **KANSAS SURGERY AND RECOVERY CENTER (170183)**, 2770 North Webb Road, Zip 67226–8112; tel. 316/634–0090, **A**3 10 11 **F**37 51 64 68 78 79 81 85 87 93 107 111 114 119 126 130
Primary Contact: Ely Bartal, M.D., Chief Executive Officer
CFO: Ashley Simon, Chief Financial Officer
CMO: Ely Bartal, M.D., Chief Executive Officer and Medical Director
CIO: Jonathan Wells, Supervisor Information Technology
CNO: Becky Bailey, R.N., Director Nursing
Web address: www.ksrc.org
Control: Partnership, Investor–owned (for–profit) **Service**: Surgical

Staffed Beds: 28 **Admissions**: 440 **Census**: 2 **Outpatient Visits**: 16415
Births: 0 **Total Expense ($000)**: 50214 **Payroll Expense ($000)**: 14313
Personnel: 205

✠ **ROBERT J. DOLE DEPARTMENT OF VETERANS AFFAIRS MEDICAL AND REGIONAL OFFICE CENTER**, 5500 East Kellogg, Zip 67218–1607; tel. 316/685–2221, (Nonreporting) **A**1 3 5 **S** Department of Veterans Affairs, Washington, DC
Primary Contact: Michael D. Payne, Medical Center Director
CFO: Ronald Dreher, Finance Officer
CMO: Kent Murray, M.D., Chief of Staff
CIO: Sharon Williamson, Chief Information Technology
CHR: Nancy Gerstner, Manager Human Resources
Web address: www.wichita.va.gov
Control: Veterans Affairs, Government, federal **Service**: General medical and surgical

Staffed Beds: 61

✠ **SELECT SPECIALTY HOSPITAL–WICHITA (172007)**, 929 North St Francis Street, Zip 67214–3821; tel. 316/261–8303, **A**1 2 10 **F**1 3 29 34 45 46 57 74 75 78 79 94 148 **S** Select Medical Corporation, Mechanicsburg, PA
Primary Contact: Eric Christensen, Chief Executive Officer
CHR: Renee Schaffer, Coordinator Human Resources
CNO: Lindsey Cahoj, Chief Nursing Officer
Web address: www.selectspecialtyhospitals.com/company/locations/wichita.aspx
Control: Corporation, Investor–owned (for–profit) **Service**: Acute long–term care hospital

Staffed Beds: 48 **Admissions**: 464 **Census**: 37 **Outpatient Visits**: 0
Births: 0 **Total Expense ($000)**: 27499 **Payroll Expense ($000)**: 12307
Personnel: 212

VIA CHRISTI BEHAVIORAL HEALTH CENTER See Good Shepherd Campus

VIA CHRISTI ST. JOSEPH See St. Joseph Campus

✠ **WESLEY MEDICAL CENTER (170123)**, 550 North Hillside, Zip 67214–4976; tel. 316/962–2000, (Includes WESLEY CHILDREN'S HOSPITAL, 550 North Hillside Street, Wichita, Kansas, Zip 67214–4910, tel. 316/962–2000; WESLEY WOODLAWN HOSPITAL & ER, 2610 North Woodlawn, Wichita, Kansas, Zip 67220, tel. 316/858–2610; Cathan Riding, Interim Chief Operating Officer) (Nonreporting) **A**1 2 3 5 10 19 **S** HCA Healthcare, Nashville, TN
Primary Contact: Bill Voloch, President and Chief Executive Officer
CFO: Bradley Schultz, Chief Financial Officer
CMO: Francie H Ekengren, M.D., Chief Medical Officer
CIO: Jeffrey Schauf, Director Information Systems
CHR: Jennifer Krier, Vice President Human Resources
CNO: Jane Taylor Ritter, R.N., Chief Nursing Officer
Web address: www.wesleymc.com
Control: Corporation, Investor–owned (for–profit) **Service**: General medical and surgical

Staffed Beds: 573

WICHITA VAMC See Robert J. Dole Department of Veterans Affairs Medical and Regional Office Center

WINCHESTER—Jefferson County

★ **F. W. HUSTON MEDICAL CENTER (171314)**, 408 Delaware Street, Zip 66097–4003; tel. 913/774–4340, (Nonreporting) **A**10 18
Primary Contact: Heidi Pickerell, Chief Executive Officer
CFO: Jason Johnson, Controller
CMO: William Greiner, M.D., Chief of Staff
CIO: Jason Johnson, Controller
CHR: Melody Keirns, Manager Human Resources
CNO: Heather R Aranda, R.N., MSN, Chief Nursing Officer
Web address: https://fwhuston.com/
Control: Other not–for–profit (including NFP Corporation) **Service**: General medical and surgical

Staffed Beds: 69

WINFIELD—Cowley County

★ **WILLIAM NEWTON HOSPITAL (171383)**, 1300 East Fifth Street, Zip 67156–2407; tel. 620/221–2300, (Nonreporting) **A**5 10 18
Primary Contact: Brian Barta, Chief Executive Officer
COO: Shona Salzman, Chief Operating Officer
CMO: Bryan Dennett, M.D., Chief of Staff
CIO: Randy Mayo, Director Information Technology
CHR: Cathy McClurg, Director Human Resources
CNO: Deborah Marrs, Chief Nursing Officer
Web address: https://www.wnhcares.org/
Control: Other not–for–profit (including NFP Corporation) **Service**: General medical and surgical

Staffed Beds: 25

KENTUCKY

ALBANY—Clinton County

THE MEDICAL CENTER AT ALBANY (181333), 723 Burkesville Road, Zip 42602-1654; tel. 606/387-8000, (Nonreporting) **A**10 18 **S** Med Center Health, Bowling Green, KY
Primary Contact: Laura Belcher, FACHE, Administrator
CFO: Ronald G. Sowell, FACHE, Executive Vice President, Chief Financial Officer
CIO: Mark Brookman, Chief Information Officer
CHR: Lynn Williams, Vice President, Human Resources
Web address: www.chc.net/services/hospitals/the_medical_center_at_albany.aspx
Control: Other not-for-profit (including NFP Corporation) **Service**: General medical and surgical

Staffed Beds: 42

ASHLAND—Boyd County

KING'S DAUGHTERS MEDICAL CENTER See UK King's Daughters Medical Center

UK KING'S DAUGHTERS MEDICAL CENTER (180009), 2201 Lexington Avenue, Zip 41101-2874, Mailing Address: P.O. Box 151, Zip 41105-0151; tel. 606/408-4000, (Total facility includes 137 beds in nursing home-type unit) **A**1 2 3 5 10 **F**3 4 5 7 11 12 13 15 17 18 20 22 24 26 28 29 30 31 33 34 35 36 37 39 40 41 45 46 47 48 49 51 53 54 55 57 58 59 61 62 65 69 70 71 72 73 74 75 76 77 78 79 81 82 84 85 87 89 90 92 93 97 98 100 101 102 104 107 108 109 110 111 112 113 114 115 116 117 118 119 126 127 128 129 130 131 132 134 135 143 144 145 146 148 149 154 156 157 160 161 162 164 167 169 **S** UK Healthcare, Lexington, KY
Primary Contact: Sara Marks, President and Chief Executive Officer
COO: Sara Marks, Senior Vice President and Chief Operating Officer
CFO: Paul L McDowell, Vice President Finance and Chief Financial Officer
CMO: Phil Fioret, M.D., Vice President Medical Affairs
CIO: David Oliver, Director Information Systems
Web address: https://www.kingsdaughtershealth.com/locations/kings-daughters-medical-center/
Control: State, Government, Nonfederal **Service**: General medical and surgical

Staffed Beds: 630 **Admissions**: 18484 **Census**: 338 **Outpatient Visits**: 1671524 **Births**: 1176 **Total Expense ($000)**: 884102 **Payroll Expense ($000)**: 393430 **Personnel**: 4841

BARBOURVILLE—Knox County

BARBOURVILLE ARH HOSPITAL (181328), 80 Hospital Drive, Zip 40906-7363, Mailing Address: P.O. Box 10, Zip 40906-0010; tel. 606/546-4175, (Nonreporting) **A**10 18 21
Primary Contact: Beau Masterson, Chief Executive Officer
CFO: Amanda Ellis, Chief Financial Officer
CMO: Kamran Hasni, M.D., Chief of Medical Staff
CIO: Evan Davis, Director Technology and Environmental Services
CHR: Janet Wilder, Director Human Resources
CNO: Brenda Graham, Chief Nursing Officer
Web address: https://www.arh.org/locations/barbourville.aspx
Control: Other not-for-profit (including NFP Corporation) **Service**: General medical and surgical

Staffed Beds: 25

BARDSTOWN—Nelson County

CHI FLAGET MEMORIAL HOSPITAL See Chi Saint Joseph Health – Flaget Memorial Hospital

CHI SAINT JOSEPH HEALTH – FLAGET MEMORIAL HOSPITAL (180025), 4305 New Shepherdsville Road, Zip 40004-9019; tel. 502/350-5000, (Nonreporting) **A**1 2 3 5 10 **S** CommonSpirit Health, Chicago, IL
Primary Contact: Jennifer Nolan, President and Chief Executive Officer
CFO: Jim Wentz, Chief Financial Officer
CMO: Mickey Anderson, M.D., Vice President Medical Affairs
CHR: Tanja Oquendo, Chief Human Resources Officer
CNO: Norma Goss, R.N., Chief Nursing Officer
Web address: https://www.chisaintjosephhealth.org/
Control: Other not-for-profit (including NFP Corporation) **Service**: General medical and surgical

Staffed Beds: 42

BENTON—Marshall County

MARSHALL COUNTY HOSPITAL (181327), 615 Old Symsonia Road, Zip 42025-5042; tel. 270/527-4800, (Nonreporting) **A**1 10 18
Primary Contact: David G. Fuqua, Chief Executive Officer
CFO: Janice Kelley, Chief Financial Officer
CMO: Edwin Perez, M.D., Chief of Medical Staff
CIO: Dave Cope, Director Information Systems
CHR: Janice Bone, Human Resources
Web address: www.marshallcountyhospital.org
Control: Hospital district or authority, Government, Nonfederal **Service**: General medical and surgical

Staffed Beds: 25

BEREA—Madison County

CHI SAINT JOSEPH BEREA See Chi Saint Joseph Health – Saint Joseph Berea

CHI SAINT JOSEPH HEALTH – SAINT JOSEPH BEREA (181329), 305 Estill Street, Zip 40403-1909; tel. 859/986-3151, (Nonreporting) **A**1 10 18 **S** CommonSpirit Health, Chicago, IL
Primary Contact: John C. Yanes, President
CFO: Christy Spitser, Vice President Finance
CMO: Joshua Huffman, M.D., Chief Medical Staff
CHR: Sandra Turqueza, Human Resources Business Partner
CNO: Leslie Adams, Chief Nursing Executive
Web address: www.kentuckyonehealth.org/berea
Control: Other not-for-profit (including NFP Corporation) **Service**: General medical and surgical

Staffed Beds: 25

BOWLING GREEN—Warren County

COMMONWEALTH REGIONAL SPECIALTY HOSPITAL (182005), 250 Park Street, 6th Floor, Zip 42101-1760, Mailing Address: P.O. Box 90010, Zip 42102-9010; tel. 270/796-6200, (Nonreporting) **A**10 **S** Med Center Health, Bowling Green, KY
Primary Contact: Christa Atkins, Administrator
CFO: Ronald G. Sowell, FACHE, Executive Vice President
CMO: Doug Thomson, M.D., Chief Medical Officer
CIO: Jean Cherry, Executive Vice President
CHR: Lynn Williams, Vice President Human Resources
Web address: www.commonwealthregionalspecialtyhospital.org
Control: Other not-for-profit (including NFP Corporation) **Service**: Acute long-term care hospital

Staffed Beds: 28

RIVENDELL BEHAVIORAL HEALTH HOSPITAL (184017), 1035 Porter Pike, Zip 42103-9581; tel. 270/843-1199, (Nonreporting) **A**1 3 10 **S** Universal Health Services, Inc., King of Prussia, PA
Primary Contact: Jeremy Wagoner, Chief Executive Officer
CFO: Tim Gore, Chief Financial Officer
Web address: www.rivendellbehavioral.com
Control: Corporation, Investor-owned (for-profit) **Service**: Psychiatric

Staffed Beds: 125

SOUTHERN KENTUCKY REHABILITATION HOSPITAL (183029), 1300 Campbell Lane, Zip 42104-4162; tel. 270/594-5980, (Nonreporting) **A**1 7 10 **S** Vibra Healthcare, Mechanicsburg, PA
Primary Contact: Stuart Locke, Chief Executive Officer
COO: Dana Lewis, Director Clinical Services
CMO: Jim Farrage, M.D., Medical Director
CHR: Suzanne Cornett, Director Human Resources
Web address: www.skyrehab.com
Control: Corporation, Investor-owned (for-profit) **Service**: Rehabilitation

Staffed Beds: 60

Hospitals, U.S. / KENTUCKY

☐ **THE MEDICAL CENTER AT BOWLING GREEN (180013)**, 250 Park Street, Zip 42101–1795, Mailing Address: P.O. Box 90010, Zip 42102–9010; tel. 270/745–1000, (Nonreporting) **A**1 2 3 5 8 10 19 **S** Med Center Health, Bowling Green, KY
Primary Contact: Connie Smith, FACHE, MSN, R.N., Chief Executive Officer
CFO: Ronald G. Sowell, FACHE, Executive Vice President
CIO: Mark Brookman, Chief Information Officer
CHR: Lynn Williams, Vice President Human Resources
Web address: www.themedicalcenter.org
Control: Other not–for–profit (including NFP Corporation) **Service**: General medical and surgical

Staffed Beds: 337

✠ **TRISTAR GREENVIEW REGIONAL HOSPITAL (180124)**, 1801 Ashley Circle, Zip 42104–3362; tel. 270/793–1000, (Nonreporting) **A**1 2 10 19 **S** HCA Healthcare, Nashville, TN
Primary Contact: Michael Sherrod, Chief Executive Officer
COO: Sam Younger, Chief Operating Officer
CMO: Wayne Bush, M.D., Chief of Staff
CIO: Cyndi Talley, Director Information Systems
CHR: Judy Fulkerson, Director Human Resources
Web address: www.greenviewhospital.com
Control: Corporation, Investor–owned (for–profit) **Service**: General medical and surgical

Staffed Beds: 211

BURKESVILLE—Cumberland County

CUMBERLAND COUNTY HOSPITAL (181317), 299 Glasgow Road, Zip 42717–9696, Mailing Address: P.O. Box 280, Zip 42717–0280; tel. 270/864–2511, (Nonreporting) **A**10 18
Primary Contact: Richard Neikirk, Chief Executive Officer
COO: Steve Burns, Chief Operating Officer
CFO: Rick Capps, Chief Financial Officer
CMO: Christian Konsavage, M.D., Chief of Staff
CHR: Martha Young, Director Human Resources
CNO: Susan S Flowers, MSN, R.N., Chief Nursing Officer
Web address: www.cchospital.org
Control: Other not–for–profit (including NFP Corporation) **Service**: General medical and surgical

Staffed Beds: 25

CADIZ—Trigg County

TRIGG COUNTY HOSPITAL (181304), 254 Main Street, Zip 42211–9153, Mailing Address: P.O. Box 312, Zip 42211–0312; tel. 270/522–3215, (Nonreporting) **A**10 18
Primary Contact: John Sumner, Chief Executive Officer
CMO: Stuart Harris, M.D., Chief of Staff
CHR: Janet James, Director Human Resources
Web address: www.trigghospital.org
Control: County, Government, Nonfederal **Service**: General medical and surgical

Staffed Beds: 18

CAMPBELLSVILLE—Taylor County

✠ **TAYLOR REGIONAL HOSPITAL (180087)**, 1700 Old Lebanon Road, Zip 42718–9600; tel. 270/465–3561, (Nonreporting) **A**1 2 10
Primary Contact: Michael Everett, Chief Executive Officer
COO: Amy Christine Smith, R.N., Chief Operating Officer
CFO: Paul Phillips, Chief Financial Officer
CIO: Christopher Michael Gibbs, Director Information Management Systems
CHR: Andrea Settle, Director Human Resources
CNO: Dana M. Garrett, R.N., Nursing Services Administrator
Web address: www.trhosp.org
Control: Hospital district or authority, Government, Nonfederal **Service**: General medical and surgical

Staffed Beds: 90

CARROLLTON—Carroll County

★ **CARROLL COUNTY MEMORIAL HOSPITAL (181310)**, 309 11th Street, Zip 41008–1400; tel. 502/732–4321, (Nonreporting) **A**10 18 **S** Alliant Management Services, Louisville, KY
Primary Contact: Kim Haverly, Chief Executive Officer
CMO: Winston Yap, M.D., Chief Medical Officer
CHR: Kimberly Adams, Manager Human Resources
CNO: Lisa Penick, R.N., Chief Nursing Officer
Web address: www.ccmhosp.com
Control: County, Government, Nonfederal **Service**: General medical and surgical

Staffed Beds: 25

COLUMBIA—Adair County

☐ **T.J. HEALTH COLUMBIA (180149)**, 901 Westlake Drive, Zip 42728–1123, Mailing Address: P.O. Box 1269, Zip 42728–6269; tel. 270/384–4753, (Nonreporting) **A**1 10
Primary Contact: Neil Thornbury, Chief Executive Officer
CFO: David R Hayes, Chief Financial Officer
CMO: Charles Giles, M.D., President Medical Staff
CHR: Tonya Grant, Director Human Resources
CNO: Gidgett Warren, Director of Nursing
Web address: www.healthiercolumbia.org/
Control: Hospital district or authority, Government, Nonfederal **Service**: General medical and surgical

Staffed Beds: 32

CORBIN—Whitley County

⚕ **BAPTIST HEALTH CORBIN (180080)**, 1 Trillium Way, Zip 40701–8420; tel. 606/528–1212, (Nonreporting) **A**10 19 21 **S** Baptist Health, Louisville, KY
Primary Contact: Anthony Powers, Interim President and Vice President of Patient Services
CFO: Pamela K. Jones, Executive Director of Finance
CMO: David Worthy, M.D., Vice President and Chief Medical Officer
CIO: Rodney Richardson, Director of Information Technology
CHR: Tim Perry, Executive Director of Human Resources
CNO: Sherrie Mays, MSN, R.N., Vice President and Chief Nursing Officer
Web address: www.baptisthealth.com/corbin
Control: Other not–for–profit (including NFP Corporation) **Service**: General medical and surgical

Staffed Beds: 273

★ **CONTINUECARE HOSPITAL AT BAPTIST HEALTH CORBIN (182006)**, 1 Trillium Way, Lower Level, Zip 40701–8727; tel. 606/523–5150, **A**10 22 **F**1 3 29 30 148 **S** Community Hospital Corporation, Plano, TX
Primary Contact: Pam Harrison, MSN, Chief Executive Officer
COO: Wilson Weber, Chief Operating Officer
CFO: Lisa Young, CPA, Chief Financial Officer
CMO: Steve Morton, M.D., Chief Medical Officer
CIO: Brian Doerr, Chief Information Officer
CHR: Amie Marcum, Human Resources Coordinator
CNO: Pam Harrison, MSN, Chief Nursing Officer
Web address: www.continuecare.com
Control: Other not–for–profit (including NFP Corporation) **Service**: Acute long–term care hospital

Staffed Beds: 32 **Admissions**: 236 **Census**: 22 **Outpatient Visits**: 0 **Births**: 0 **Total Expense ($000)**: 11413 **Payroll Expense ($000)**: 5762 **Personnel**: 66

COVINGTON—Kenton County

ST. ELIZABETH MEDICAL CENTER–NORTH See St. Elizabeth Covington

CYNTHIANA—Harrison County

✠ **HARRISON MEMORIAL HOSPITAL (180079)**, 1210 KY Highway 36E, Zip 41031–7498; tel. 859/234–2300, (Nonreporting) **A**1 2 10
Primary Contact: Kathy Tussey, R.N., Chief Executive Officer
CFO: David Mellett, Chief Financial Officer
CMO: Stephen Toadvine, M.D., Chief Medical Officer
CIO: Martha Sullivan, Chief Information Officer
CNO: Wendy Reeder, R.N., Chief Nursing Officer
Web address: www.harrisonmemhosp.com
Control: Other not–for–profit (including NFP Corporation) **Service**: General medical and surgical

Staffed Beds: 34

DANVILLE—Boyle County

☐ **EPHRAIM MCDOWELL REGIONAL MEDICAL CENTER (180048)**, 217 South Third Street, Zip 40422–1823; tel. 859/239–1000, (Nonreporting) **A**1 2 3 10 19 **S** Ephraim McDowell Health, Danville, KY
Primary Contact: Daniel E. McKay, Chief Executive Officer
CFO: William R Snapp III, Executive Vice President Finance and Chief Financial Officer
CMO: Kryder Van Buskirk III, Medical Staff President at EMRMC
CIO: Gary Neat, Chief Information Officer
CHR: Libby Mayes, Human Resource Director
Web address: www.emrmc.org
Control: Other not–for–profit (including NFP Corporation) **Service**: General medical and surgical

Staffed Beds: 159

Hospitals, U.S. / KENTUCKY

☒ **SELECT SPECIALTY HOSPITAL–CENTRAL KENTUCKY (182003)**, 217 South 3rd Street, Fourth Floor, Zip 40422-1823; tel. 859/712-7072, (Nonreporting) **A1 10 S** Select Medical Corporation, Mechanicsburg, PA
Primary Contact: Josh Greeman, Chief Executive Officer
CMO: Fadi Bacha, M.D., Chief Medical Officer
CHR: Tina Kirkland–Rose, Coordinator Human Resources
CNO: Katie Meredith, Chief Nursing Officer
Web address: www.lexington.selectspecialtyhospitals.com/
Control: Corporation, Investor–owned (for–profit) **Service**: Acute long–term care hospital

Staffed Beds: 41

EDGEWOOD—Kenton County

☒ **ENCOMPASS HEALTH REHABILITATION HOSPITAL OF NORTHERN KENTUCKY (183027)**, 201 Medical Village Drive, Zip 41017-3407; tel. 859/341-2044, (Nonreporting) **A1 10 S** Encompass Health Corporation, Birmingham, AL
Primary Contact: Dean Blevins, Chief Executive Officer
CFO: Lisa McGue, Controller
CMO: Neal Moser, M.D., Medical Director
CHR: Bridgette Keith, Director Human Resources
CNO: Terri Ballard, Chief Nursing Officer
Web address: www.healthsouthkentucky.com
Control: Partnership, Investor–owned (for–profit) **Service**: Rehabilitation

Staffed Beds: 40

☐ **ST. ELIZABETH EDGEWOOD (180035)**, 1 Medical Village Drive, Zip 41017-3403; tel. 859/301-2000, (Includes ST. ELIZABETH COVINGTON, 1500 James Simpson Jr. Way, Covington, Kentucky, Zip 41014-1585, tel. 859/655-8800) **A1** 2 3 5 10 19 **F3** 8 9 13 15 17 18 20 22 24 26 28 29 30 31 34 35 36 37 38 40 42 44 45 46 47 48 49 50 51 52 54 55 57 58 59 60 61 63 64 65 70 71 72 73 74 75 76 77 78 79 80 81 82 83 84 85 86 87 92 93 96 97 101 102 107 108 110 111 114 115 117 118 119 120 121 123 124 126 129 130 131 132 135 141 145 146 147 148 149 150 154 162 164 167 169 **S** St. Elizabeth Healthcare, Edgewood, KY
Primary Contact: Garren Colvin, Chief Executive Officer
CMO: Karl Schmitt, M.D., Chief of Staff
CIO: Alex Rodriguez, Vice President and Chief Information Officer
CHR: Martin Oscadal, Vice President Human Resources
Web address: www.stelizabeth.com
Control: Church operated, Nongovernment, not–for–profit **Service**: General medical and surgical

Staffed Beds: 546 Admissions: 26046 Census: 362 Outpatient Visits: 1727719 Births: 4149 Total Expense ($000): 1299554 Payroll Expense ($000): 433575 Personnel: 3569

ELIZABETHTOWN—Hardin County

☐ **BAPTIST HEALTH HARDIN (180012)**, 913 North Dixie Avenue, Zip 42701-2503; tel. 270/737-1212, **A1** 2 5 10 19 **F3** 7 8 11 12 13 15 17 18 20 22 24 28 29 30 31 32 34 35 36 37 39 40 44 45 48 49 50 51 52 54 57 58 59 60 64 65 68 70 71 72 74 75 76 77 78 79 80 81 82 84 85 86 87 89 93 94 96 98 104 107 110 111 114 115 117 118 119 120 121 124 126 127 128 129 130 131 132 134 135 144 146 147 148 149 154 156 167 169 **S** Baptist Health, Louisville, KY
Primary Contact: Robert L. Ramey, President
COO: Tom Carrico, Vice President of Operations
CMO: John Godfrey, M.D., Vice President and Chief Executive Officer
CIO: Trey Hyberger, Director Information Technology
CHR: Myra Covault, Associate Vice President of Human Resources
CNO: Sharon Wright, R.N., Vice President and Chief Nursing Officer
Web address: www.hmh.net
Control: Other not–for–profit (including NFP Corporation) **Service**: General medical and surgical

Staffed Beds: 268 Admissions: 15255 Census: 155 Outpatient Visits: 508569 Births: 1121 Total Expense ($000): 407423 Payroll Expense ($000): 123377 Personnel: 1570

☒ **ENCOMPASS HEALTH REHABILITATION HOSPITAL OF LAKEVIEW (183028)**, 134 Heartland Drive, Zip 42701-2778; tel. 270/769-3100, (Nonreporting) **A1 10 S** Encompass Health Corporation, Birmingham, AL
Primary Contact: David Fredericks, Chief Executive Officer
CFO: Scott Hart, Controller
CMO: Toni Abang, M.D., Medical Director
CHR: Janet Morris, Director Human Resources
CNO: Amy Logsdon, Chief Nursing Officer
Web address: www.healthsouthlakeview.com
Control: Corporation, Investor–owned (for–profit) **Service**: Rehabilitation

Staffed Beds: 40

ERLANGER—Kenton County

☒ **SUN BEHAVIORAL KENTUCKY (184006)**, 820 Dolwick Drive, Zip 41018, Mailing Address: 3900 Olympic Blvd., Ste 400, Zip 41018; tel. 859/429-5188, (Nonreporting) **A1 10**
Primary Contact: Jason Staats, Chief Executive Officer
COO: Carol Parke, Chief Operating Officer, SUN Kentucky
Web address: https://www.sunkentucky.com/
Control: Corporation, Investor–owned (for–profit) **Service**: Psychiatric

Staffed Beds: 197

FLEMINGSBURG—Fleming County

☒ **FLEMING COUNTY HOSPITAL (181332)**, 55 Foundation Drive, Zip 41041-9815, Mailing Address: P.O. Box 388, Zip 41041-0388; tel. 606/849-5000, (Nonreporting) **A1 10 18 S** Lifepoint Health, Brentwood, TN
Primary Contact: Joseph G. Koch, Chief Executive Officer
CFO: Theresa Fite, R.N., Chief Financial Officer
CMO: Samuel Gehring, M.D., Chief of Staff
CIO: Don Daugherty, Director Information Systems
CHR: Marsha Mitchell, Director Human Resources
Web address: www.flemingcountyhospital.org
Control: Other not–for–profit (including NFP Corporation) **Service**: General medical and surgical

Staffed Beds: 51

FLORENCE—Boone County

☐ △ **GATEWAY REHABILITATION HOSPITAL (183030)**, 5940 Merchant Street, Zip 41042-1158; tel. 859/426-2400, (Nonreporting) **A1 7 10 S** Vibra Healthcare, Mechanicsburg, PA
Primary Contact: Jennifer Jones, Chief Executive Officer
CFO: Margaret Cesarez, Chief Financial Officer
CNO: Jenna Wellbrock, Chief Nursing Officer
Web address: www.gatewayflorence.com/
Control: Corporation, Investor–owned (for–profit) **Service**: Rehabilitation

Staffed Beds: 40

☐ **ST. ELIZABETH FLORENCE (180045)**, 4900 Houston Road, Zip 41042-4824; tel. 859/212-5200, (Total facility includes 10 beds in nursing home–type unit) **A1 10 F3** 11 12 15 20 28 29 30 34 35 38 40 44 45 46 47 48 49 50 55 57 59 60 61 63 64 65 70 74 75 77 78 79 80 81 82 84 85 86 87 92 93 100 101 102 107 108 110 111 115 118 119 126 128 129 130 132 141 145 146 147 148 149 150 154 164 167 **S** St. Elizabeth Healthcare, Edgewood, KY
Primary Contact: Garren Colvin, Chief Executive Officer
COO: Chris Carle, Senior Vice President and Chief Operating Officer
CMO: George Hall, M.D., Vice President Medical Affairs
CIO: Alex Rodriguez, Vice President and Chief Information Officer
CHR: Martin Oscadal, Senior Vice President Human Resources
Web address: www.stelizabeth.com
Control: Church operated, Nongovernment, not–for–profit **Service**: General medical and surgical

Staffed Beds: 154 Admissions: 8767 Census: 116 Outpatient Visits: 215916 Births: 0 Total Expense ($000): 224898 Payroll Expense ($000): 90978 Personnel: 937

FORT CAMPBELL—Christian County

☒ **COLONEL FLORENCE A. BLANCHFIELD ARMY COMMUNITY HOSPITAL**, 650 Joel Drive, Zip 42223-5318; tel. 270/798-8400, (Nonreporting) **A1 3 S** Department of the Army, Office of the Surgeon General, Falls Church, VA
Primary Contact: Colonel Samuel L. Preston, Commander
CHR: Major Travis Burchett, Troop Commander Human Resources
Web address: https://blanchfield.tricare.mil/
Control: Army, Government, federal **Service**: General medical and surgical

Staffed Beds: 66

FORT THOMAS—Campbell County

☒ **SELECT SPECIALTY HOSPITAL–NORTHERN KENTUCKY (182004)**, 85 North Grand Avenue, Zip 41075-1793; tel. 859/572-3880, (Nonreporting) **A1 10 S** Select Medical Corporation, Mechanicsburg, PA
Primary Contact: Candace Moehringer, Chief Executive Officer
Web address: www.selectspecialtyhospitals.com
Control: Corporation, Investor–owned (for–profit) **Service**: Acute long–term care hospital

Staffed Beds: 33

Hospital, Medicare Provider Number, Address, Telephone, Approval, Facility, and Physician Codes, Health Care System

★ American Hospital Association (AHA) membership ○ Healthcare Facilities Accreditation Program ⇑ Center for Improvement in Healthcare Quality Accreditation
☐ The Joint Commission accreditation ◇ DNV Healthcare Inc. accreditation △ Commission on Accreditation of Rehabilitation Facilities (CARF) accreditation

© 2025 AHA Guide

Hospitals, U.S. / KENTUCKY

☐ **ST. ELIZABETH FORT THOMAS (180001)**, 85 North Grand Avenue, Zip 41075–1796; tel. 859/572-3100, (Includes ST. ELIZABETH FALMOUTH, 512 South Maple Avenue, Falmouth, Kentucky, Zip 41040–1422, tel. 859/572-3500; Garren Colvin, Chief Executive Officer) (Total facility includes 26 beds in nursing home–type unit) **A**1 10 **F**3 5 11 15 18 20 28 29 30 31 34 35 39 40 44 45 46 47 48 49 50 51 55 56 57 58 59 60 61 63 64 65 70 71 74 75 77 78 79 80 81 82 83 84 85 86 87 91 92 93 101 102 107 108 110 111 115 118 119 120 121 123 126 128 129 130 132 135 141 146 147 148 149 150 152 154 164 167 **S** St. Elizabeth Healthcare, Edgewood, KY
Primary Contact: Garren Colvin, Chief Executive Officer
COO: Thomas Saalfeld, Senior Vice President and Chief Operating Officer
CMO: George Hall, M.D., Vice President Medical Affairs
CIO: Alex Rodriguez, Vice President and Chief Information Officer
CHR: Martin Oscadal, Senior Vice President Human Resources
Web address: www.stelizabeth.com
Control: Church operated, Nongovernment, not–for–profit **Service**: General medical and surgical

Staffed Beds: 132 **Admissions**: 6491 **Census**: 89 **Outpatient Visits**: 150916 **Births**: 0 **Total Expense ($000)**: 155573 **Payroll Expense ($000)**: 68351 **Personnel**: 627

FRANKFORT—Franklin County

✠ **FRANKFORT REGIONAL MEDICAL CENTER (180127)**, 299 King's Daughters Drive, Zip 40601–4186; tel. 502/875-5240, (Nonreporting) **A**1 10 19 **S** HCA Healthcare, Nashville, TN
Primary Contact: John Ballard, Chief Executive Officer
COO: Ashley Hickel, Chief Operating Officer
CMO: Willis P McKee, M.D., Jr, Chief Medical Officer
CIO: Craig Willard, Director Information Technology and Systems
CHR: Bev Young, Director Human Resources
Web address: www.frankfortregional.com
Control: Corporation, Investor–owned (for–profit) **Service**: General medical and surgical

Staffed Beds: 130

FRANKLIN—Simpson County

☐ **MEDICAL CENTER AT FRANKLIN (181318)**, 1100 Brookhaven Road, Zip 42134–2746; tel. 270/598-4800, (Nonreporting) **A**1 10 18 **S** Med Center Health, Bowling Green, KY
Primary Contact: Annette Runyon, Vice President and Administrator
CFO: Ronald G. Sowell, FACHE, Executive Vice President
CIO: Mark Brookman, Vice President and Chief Information Officer
Web address: www.themedicalcenterfranklin.org
Control: Other not–for–profit (including NFP Corporation) **Service**: General medical and surgical

Staffed Beds: 25

GEORGETOWN—Scott County

✠ **GEORGETOWN COMMUNITY HOSPITAL (180101)**, 1140 Lexington Road, Zip 40324–9362; tel. 502/868-1100, (Nonreporting) **A**1 2 10 **S** Lifepoint Health, Brentwood, TN
Primary Contact: Clifford Wilson, Chief Executive Officer, Market President Central Kentucky
CFO: Patrick C Bolander, Chief Financial Officer
CMO: Brian Allen, M.D., President Medical Staff
CHR: Marrianne Slonina, Director Human Resources
Web address: www.georgetowncommunityhospital.com
Control: Corporation, Investor–owned (for–profit) **Service**: General medical and surgical

Staffed Beds: 58

GLASGOW—Barren County

☐ **T. J. SAMSON COMMUNITY HOSPITAL (180017)**, 1301 North Race Street, Zip 42141–3483; tel. 270/651-4444, (Nonreporting) **A**1 2 3 5 10
Primary Contact: Neil Thornbury, Chief Executive Officer
COO: Margie Gentry, Controller
CFO: Mei Deng, Chief Financial Officer
CIO: Chad Friend, Director
CHR: LaDonna Rogers, Executive Vice President Human Resources
CNO: Megan Calkins, R.N., Chief Nursing Officer
Web address: www.tjsamson.org
Control: Other not–for–profit (including NFP Corporation) **Service**: General medical and surgical

Staffed Beds: 114

GREENSBURG—Green County

☐ **JANE TODD CRAWFORD HOSPITAL (181325)**, 202–206 Milby Street, Zip 42743–1100, Mailing Address: P.O. Box 220, Zip 42743–0220; tel. 270/932-4211, (Nonreporting) **A**10 18
Primary Contact: Rex A. Tungate, Chief Executive Officer
CFO: Richard Hendershot, Chief Financial Officer
CMO: Shane DeSimone, M.D., Chief of Staff
CHR: Mary Ann Quinn, Administrative Assistant
CNO: Roxie Montgomery, Director of Nursing
Web address: www.janetoddhospital.com
Control: County, Government, Nonfederal **Service**: General medical and surgical

Staffed Beds: 45

GREENVILLE—Muhlenberg County

✠ **OWENSBORO HEALTH MUHLENBERG COMMUNITY HOSPITAL (180004)**, 440 Hopkinsville Street, Zip 42345–1124, Mailing Address: P.O. Box 387, Zip 42345–0378; tel. 270/338-8000, (Total facility includes 45 beds in nursing home–type unit) **A**1 10 **F**3 7 11 18 26 28 29 34 35 40 45 46 49 57 59 62 64 65 70 74 75 77 79 81 82 83 84 85 86 87 92 93 97 107 108 111 114 115 116 117 118 119 120 127 128 129 130 131 133 135 144 145 154 156 **S** Owensboro Health, Owensboro, KY
Primary Contact: Ed Heath, FACHE, Chief Executive Officer
CMO: Vincent P Genovese, M.D., President Medical Staff
CIO: Alan Trail, Director Information Systems
CHR: Lisa R Hope, Director Human Resources
CNO: Kathy Mitchell, Chief Nursing Officer
Web address: www.ww.owensborohealth.org/
Control: Other not–for–profit (including NFP Corporation) **Service**: General medical and surgical

Staffed Beds: 135 **Admissions**: 1090 **Census**: 60 **Outpatient Visits**: 72510 **Births**: 0 **Total Expense ($000)**: 53663 **Payroll Expense ($000)**: 25265 **Personnel**: 400

HARDINSBURG—Breckinridge County

☐ **BRECKINRIDGE MEMORIAL HOSPITAL (181319)**, 1011 Old Highway 60, Zip 40143–2597; tel. 270/756-7000, (Nonreporting) **A**1 10 18 **S** Alliant Management Services, Louisville, KY
Primary Contact: Angela Portman, Chief Executive Officer
CFO: Amy Andell, Chief Financial Officer
CMO: Brian O'Donoghue, M.D., Chief Medical Officer
CIO: Bruce Elder, Information Technology
CHR: James Turpin, Chief Human Resource Officer
Web address: www.breckinridgehealth.org/
Control: Other not–for–profit (including NFP Corporation) **Service**: General medical and surgical

Staffed Beds: 43

HARLAN—Harlan County

⇑ **HARLAN ARH HOSPITAL (180050)**, 81 Ball Park Road, Zip 40831–1792; tel. 606/573-8100, (Nonreporting) **A**2 3 5 10 21 **S** Appalachian Regional Healthcare, Inc., Lexington, KY
Primary Contact: Joseph Horton, Community Chief Executive Officer
CFO: Brad Burkhart, Assistant Administrator
CHR: Sabra Howard, Manager Human Resources
Web address: www.arh.org
Control: Other not–for–profit (including NFP Corporation) **Service**: General medical and surgical

Staffed Beds: 103

HARRODSBURG—Mercer County

☐ **EPHRAIM MCDOWELL JAMES B. HAGGIN MEMORIAL HOSPITAL (181302)**, 464 Linden Avenue, Zip 40330–1862; tel. 859/734-5441, (Nonreporting) **A**1 10 18 **S** Ephraim McDowell Health, Danville, KY
Primary Contact: Lynne Warner Lynn, R.N., Administrator
CFO: Tony Patterson, Chief Financial Officer
Web address: www.hagginhosp.org
Control: Other not–for–profit (including NFP Corporation) **Service**: General medical and surgical

Staffed Beds: 25

HARTFORD—Ohio County

OHIO COUNTY HOSPITAL (181323), 1211 Main Street, Zip 42347-1619; tel. 270/298-7411, (Nonreporting) A1 10 18 S Ovation Healthcare, Brentwood, TN
Primary Contact: Shellie Dube. Shouse, Chief Executive Officer
CFO: John Tichenor, Chief Financial Officer
CMO: Joshua Skibba, Chief Medical Officer
CHR: Sue Wydick, Director Human Resources
CNO: Athena Minor, Chief Nursing Officer
Web address: www.ohiocountyhospital.com
Control: Other not-for-profit (including NFP Corporation) **Service**: General medical and surgical

Staffed Beds: 25

HAZARD—Perry County

⇑ **HAZARD ARH REGIONAL MEDICAL CENTER (180029)**, 100 Medical Center Drive, Zip 41701-9421; tel. 606/439-6600, (Nonreporting) A2 3 5 10 19 21 S Appalachian Regional Healthcare, Inc., Lexington, KY
Primary Contact: Brian Springate, Chief Executive Officer
CMO: J D Miller, M.D., Chief Medical Officer
CIO: Jeff Brady, Director Information Systems
CHR: Sheila Cornett, Manager Human Resources
Web address: www.arh.org
Control: Other not-for-profit (including NFP Corporation) **Service**: General medical and surgical

Staffed Beds: 358

HENDERSON—Henderson County

DEACONESS HENDERSON HOSPITAL (180056), 1305 North Elm Street, Zip 42420-2775, Mailing Address: P.O. Box 48, Zip 42419-0048; tel. 270/827-7700, A1 2 10 13 F3 7 11 13 15 18 24 28 29 30 31 34 35 40 45 46 47 48 49 51 54 57 59 60 64 68 70 72 74 75 76 77 78 79 81 82 85 86 93 98 107 108 110 111 115 118 119 126 127 129 130 135 146 147 148 149 154 156 164 167 169 S Deaconess Health System, Evansville, IN
Primary Contact: Linda E. White, Chief Administrative Officer
CFO: David Massengale, Vice President and Chief Financial Officer
CMO: John Logan, M.D., Chief Medical Officer
CIO: Randy McCleese, Chief Information Officer
CHR: Ty Kahle, Vice President Human Resources
Web address: https://www.deaconess.com/Deaconess-Henderson-Hospital
Control: Other not-for-profit (including NFP Corporation) **Service**: General medical and surgical

Staffed Beds: 123 **Admissions**: 3371 **Census**: 37 **Outpatient Visits**: 37577 **Births**: 416 **Total Expense ($000)**: 122209 **Payroll Expense ($000)**: 35233 **Personnel**: 485

HOPKINSVILLE—Christian County

☐ **CUMBERLAND HALL HOSPITAL (184014)**, 270 Walton Way, Zip 42240-6808; tel. 270/886-1919, (Nonreporting) A1 10 S Universal Health Services, Inc., King of Prussia, PA
Primary Contact: Jessica Estes, Chief Executive Officer
CFO: Mark Wallace, Chief Financial Officer
CMO: Deepak Patel, M.D., Medical Director
CIO: Patricia Gray, Director Health Information Management
CHR: Kelly Hagy, Director Human Resources
CNO: Denise Lyons, Chief Nursing Officer
Web address: www.cumberlandhallhospital.com
Control: Corporation, Investor-owned (for-profit) **Service**: Psychiatric

Staffed Beds: 97

☐ **JENNIE STUART MEDICAL CENTER (180051)**, 320 West 18th Street, Zip 42240-1965, Mailing Address: P.O. Box 2400, Zip 42241-2400; tel. 270/887-0100, (Nonreporting) A1 10 20
Primary Contact: Eric A. Lee, President and Chief Executive Officer
CMO: Casey Covington, M.D., President Elect, Medical Staff
CIO: Jerry Houston, Director Information Systems
CHR: Austin Moss, Vice President Human Resources
Web address: www.jsmc.org
Control: Other not-for-profit (including NFP Corporation) **Service**: General medical and surgical

Staffed Beds: 139

☐ **WESTERN STATE HOSPITAL (184002)**, Russellville Road, Zip 42240-3017, Mailing Address: P.O. Box 2200, Zip 42241-2200; tel. 270/889-6025, (Nonreporting) A1 10
Primary Contact: Jessica Cates, Interim Facility Director
CFO: Jessica Cates, Fiscal Manager
CMO: Nayyar Iqbal, M.D., Director Medical Staff
CIO: Valerie Majors, Director Information Services
CHR: James L Hayes, Director Human Resources
CNO: Jill Thomas, Director of Nursing
Web address: www.westernstatehospital.ky.gov
Control: State, Government, Nonfederal **Service**: Psychiatric

Staffed Beds: 160

HORSE CAVE—Hart County

★ **THE MEDICAL CENTER AT CAVERNA (181314)**, 1501 South Dixie Street, Zip 42749-1477; tel. 270/786-2191, (Nonreporting) A10 18 S Med Center Health, Bowling Green, KY
Primary Contact: Alan B. Alexander, FACHE, Vice President and Administrator
CFO: Ronald G. Sowell, FACHE, Executive Vice President and Chief Financial Officer
CIO: Mark Brookman, Vice President, Chief Information Officer
CHR: Lynn Williams, Vice President, Human Resources
CNO: Penny Nole, Director of Patient Care Services
Web address: www.TheMedicalCenterCaverna.org
Control: Other not-for-profit (including NFP Corporation) **Service**: General medical and surgical

Staffed Beds: 25

HYDEN—Leslie County

⇑ **MARY BRECKINRIDGE ARH HOSPITAL (181316)**, 130 Kate Ireland Drive, Zip 41749-9071, Mailing Address: P.O. Box 447-A, Zip 41749-0717; tel. 606/672-2901, (Nonreporting) A10 18 21 S Appalachian Regional Healthcare, Inc., Lexington, KY
Primary Contact: Mallie S. Noble, Chief Executive Officer
COO: Nathan W Lee, Chief Executive Officer
CFO: Robert Besten, Chief Financial Officer
CMO: Roy Varghese, M.D., Chief of Staff
CIO: Frank Baker, Chief Information Officer
CHR: Beulah Couch, Director Human Resources
Web address: www.frontiernursing.org
Control: Other not-for-profit (including NFP Corporation) **Service**: General medical and surgical

Staffed Beds: 25

IRVINE—Estill County

MERCY HEALTH – MARCUM AND WALLACE (181301), 60 Mercy Court, Zip 40336-1331; tel. 606/723-2115, (Nonreporting) A10 18 S Bon Secours Mercy Health, Cincinnati, OH
Primary Contact: Trena Stocker, President
CFO: Lori Witt, Site Finance Director
CMO: Maher Kassis, M.D., Chief Medical Staff
CHR: Dana Stepp, Human Resources Officer
Web address: www.marcumandwallace.org
Control: Church operated, Nongovernment, not-for-profit **Service**: General medical and surgical

Staffed Beds: 25

JACKSON—Breathitt County

☐ **KENTUCKY RIVER MEDICAL CENTER (180139)**, 540 Jett Drive, Zip 41339-9622; tel. 606/666-6000, (Nonreporting) A1 10 20 S Quorum Health, Brentwood, TN
Primary Contact: Susie Robinette, MSN, Chief Executive Officer
CFO: Michael Ackley, Chief Financial Officer
CMO: Eunice Johnson, M.D., Chief Medical Staff
CIO: Diana Tyra, Director Health Information
CHR: Naomi Mitchell, Director Human Resources
CNO: Susie Robinette, MSN, Chief Nursing Officer
Web address: www.kentuckyrivermc.com
Control: Corporation, Investor-owned (for-profit) **Service**: General medical and surgical

Staffed Beds: 54

Hospitals, U.S. / KENTUCKY

LA GRANGE—Oldham County

☐ **BAPTIST HEALTH LA GRANGE (180138)**, 1025 New Moody Lane, Zip 40031–9154; tel. 502/222–5388, (Nonreporting) **A**1 2 5 10 **S** Baptist Health, Louisville, KY
Primary Contact: Clint Kaho, President
CFO: Jim Morris, Vice President Finance
CMO: Matt McDanald, M.D., Chief Medical Officer
CHR: Kayla Batts, Manager Human Resources
CNO: Nathan Wilson, R.N., Vice President and Chief Nursing Officer
Web address: www.baptisthealthlagrange.com
Control: Other not–for–profit (including NFP Corporation) **Service:** General medical and surgical

Staffed Beds: 65

LEBANON—Marion County

✠ **SPRING VIEW HOSPITAL (180024)**, 320 Loretto Road, Zip 40033–1300; tel. 270/692–3161, (Nonreporting) **A**1 10 **S** Lifepoint Health, Brentwood, TN
Primary Contact: Reba Celsor, Chief Executive Officer
CFO: Denise Thomas, Chief Financial Officer
CHR: Joe Voboril, Director, Human Resources
CNO: Tonia McCarthy, Chief Nursing Officer
Web address: www.springviewhospital.com
Control: Corporation, Investor–owned (for–profit) **Service:** General medical and surgical

Staffed Beds: 47

LEITCHFIELD—Grayson County

✠ **OWENSBORO HEALTH TWIN LAKES REGIONAL MEDICAL CENTER (180070)**, 910 Wallace Avenue, Zip 42754–2414; tel. 270/259–9400, **A**1 10 **F**5 13 15 18 19 26 28 29 30 34 35 40 45 50 53 56 59 64 65 68 70 74 75 76 77 79 81 87 92 93 97 98 107 108 110 111 115 118 119 127 129 133 146 147 148 154 161 167 169 **S** Alliant Management Services, Louisville, KY
Primary Contact: Ashley Herrington, Chief Executive Officer
CFO: Scott Arndell, Chief Financial Officer
CIO: Robbie Lindsey, Chief Information Officer
CNO: Cathy Joy Stewart, Vice President Patient Care Services and Chief Nursing Officer
Web address: https://www.owensborohealth.org/locations/profile/owensboro-health-twin-lakes-medical-center
Control: Other not–for–profit (including NFP Corporation) **Service:** General medical and surgical

Staffed Beds: 57 **Admissions:** 1599 **Census:** 14 **Outpatient Visits:** 96195 **Births:** 350 **Total Expense ($000):** 47079 **Payroll Expense ($000):** 20199 **Personnel:** 278

TWIN LAKES REGIONAL MEDICAL CENTER See Owensboro Health Twin Lakes Regional Medical Center

LEXINGTON—Fayette County

☐ **BAPTIST HEALTH LEXINGTON (180103)**, 1740 Nicholasville Road, Zip 40503–1499; tel. 859/260–6100, **A**1 2 3 5 10 **F**3 7 8 11 12 13 15 17 18 20 22 24 26 28 29 30 31 34 35 36 40 42 44 45 46 47 48 49 51 54 55 56 57 58 59 60 64 65 68 70 72 74 75 76 77 79 81 82 84 85 86 87 92 93 97 107 108 110 111 114 115 117 118 119 120 121 124 126 129 130 131 132 135 143 144 146 147 148 149 154 156 157 160 167 169 **S** Baptist Health, Louisville, KY
Primary Contact: Christopher Roty, President
CFO: Stephanie Doom, Chief Financial Officer
CMO: James Borders, M.D., Chief Medical Officer
CIO: Lisa Fluty, Director Information Services
CHR: Lynette Walker, R.N., Ph.D., Regional Vice President, Human Resources
CNO: Dee Beckman, MSN, R.N., Chief Nursing Officer
Web address: www.baptisthealthlexington.com
Control: Other not–for–profit (including NFP Corporation) **Service:** General medical and surgical

Staffed Beds: 434 **Admissions:** 19500 **Census:** 277 **Outpatient Visits:** 410864 **Births:** 4075 **Total Expense ($000):** 737006 **Payroll Expense ($000):** 213299 **Personnel:** 2226

CHI SAINT JOSEPH EAST See Chi Saint Joseph Health – Saint Joseph East

✠ **CHI SAINT JOSEPH HEALTH (180010)**, 1 St Joseph Drive, Zip 40504–3754; tel. 859/313–1000, (Nonreporting) **A**1 2 5 10 **S** CommonSpirit Health, Chicago, IL
Primary Contact: Christy Spitser, Interim President
COO: Jason Adams, Chief Operating Officer
CFO: Melinda S Evans, Vice President Finance
CIO: Janie Fergus, Director and Chief Information Officer
Web address: https://www.chisaintjosephhealth.org/saint-joseph-hospital
Control: Church operated, Nongovernment, not–for–profit **Service:** General medical and surgical

Staffed Beds: 307

✠ **CHI SAINT JOSEPH HEALTH – SAINT JOSEPH EAST (180143)**, 150 North Eagle Creek Drive, Zip 40509–1805; tel. 859/967–5000, (Includes WOMEN'S HOSPITAL SAINT JOSEPH EAST, 170 North Eagle Creek Drive, Lexington, Kentucky, Zip 40509–9087, tel. 859/572–3500) (Nonreporting) **A**1 2 10 **S** CommonSpirit Health, Chicago, IL
Primary Contact: Jennifer Nolan, President
COO: Jason Adams, Chief Operating Officer
CFO: Melinda S Evans, Vice President Finance
CIO: Janie Fergus, Director and Chief Information Officer
Web address: www.sjhlex.org
Control: Church operated, Nongovernment, not–for–profit **Service:** General medical and surgical

Staffed Beds: 150

✠ **CONTINUING CARE HOSPITAL (182002)**, 1 Saint Joseph Drive, Zip 40504–3742; tel. 859/967–5744, (Nonreporting) **A**1 2 10 **S** CommonSpirit Health, Chicago, IL
Primary Contact: Robert C. Desotelle, President and Chief Executive Officer
CMO: Michael Miedler, M.D., Chief Medical Officer
CNO: Regina Masters, R.N., MSN, Director of Nursing
Web address: www.kentuckyonehealth.org
Control: Church operated, Nongovernment, not–for–profit **Service:** Acute long–term care hospital

Staffed Beds: 23

☐ **EASTERN STATE HOSPITAL (184004)**, 1350 Bull Lea Road, Zip 40511; tel. 859/246–8000, **A**1 3 5 10 **F**30 35 38 98 101 103 130 132 135 146 149 164 P6 **S** UK Healthcare, Lexington, KY
Primary Contact: Lindsey Jasinski, Chief Administrative Officer
CFO: Susan M Griffith, Finance Business Partner Specialist
CMO: Andrew Cooley, M.D., Chief Medical Officer
CIO: Steve Kincaid, Information Technology Manager
CHR: Stephanie DeRossette, Human Resources Business Partner
CNO: Marc Anthony Woods, Chief Nursing Officer for Behavioral Health
Web address: https://ukhealthcare.uky.edu/
Control: State, Government, Nonfederal **Service:** Psychiatric

Staffed Beds: 179 **Admissions:** 3224 **Census:** 135 **Outpatient Visits:** 0 **Births:** 0 **Total Expense ($000):** 63851 **Payroll Expense ($000):** 37290 **Personnel:** 428

✠ **ENCOMPASS HEALTH CARDINAL HILL REHABILITATION HOSPITAL (183026)**, 2050 Versailles Road, Zip 40504–1405; tel. 859/254–5701, (Total facility includes 36 beds in nursing home–type unit) **A**1 3 5 10 **F**3 28 29 56 58 60 75 87 90 91 95 96 128 130 132 146 148 149 **S** Encompass Health Corporation, Birmingham, AL
Primary Contact: Susan Hart, Chief Executive Officer
CFO: Marty Lautner, Vice President Finance and Chief Financial Officer
CMO: William Lester, M.D., Vice President Medical Affairs
CIO: LouAnn Hyder, Director Information Integrity Management
CHR: Barry K Lindeman, Director Human Resources
CNO: Maureen Couture, Chief Nursing Officer and Vice President Nursing
Web address: https://encompasshealth.com/locations/cardinalhillrehab
Control: Corporation, Investor–owned (for–profit) **Service:** Rehabilitation

Staffed Beds: 232 **Admissions:** 4578 **Census:** 165 **Outpatient Visits:** 0 **Births:** 0 **Total Expense ($000):** 82743 **Payroll Expense ($000):** 37234 **Personnel:** 395

FEDERAL MEDICAL CENTER, 3301 Leestown Road, Zip 40511–8799; tel. 859/255–6812, (Nonreporting)
Primary Contact: Francisco Quintana, Warden
CFO: Mike Kinsel, Controller
CMO: Michael Growse, M.D., Clinical Director
Control: Department of Justice, Government, federal **Service:** Hospital unit of an institution (prison hospital, college infirmary, etc.)

Staffed Beds: 22

✠ **LEXINGTON VAMC**, 1101 Veterans Drive, Zip 40502–2235; tel. 859/281–4901, (Nonreporting) **A**1 3 5 **S** Department of Veterans Affairs, Washington, DC
Primary Contact: Russell Armstead, Executive Director
CFO: Patricia Swisshelm, Acting Chief Fiscal Service
CMO: Patricia Breeden, M.D., Chief of Staff
CIO: Jeffrey Sutton, Chief Information Officer
CHR: Laura Faulkner, Chief Human Resource Management Service
CNO: Mary Kelly McCullough, Associate Director Patient Care Services
Web address: www.lexington.va.gov/
Control: Veterans Affairs, Government, federal **Service:** General medical and surgical

Staffed Beds: 159

Hospitals, U.S. / KENTUCKY

☐ **RIDGE BEHAVIORAL HEALTH SYSTEM (184009)**, 3050 Rio Dosa Drive, Zip 40509–1540; tel. 859/269–2325, (Nonreporting) **A**1 3 5 10 **S** Universal Health Services, Inc., King of Prussia, PA
Primary Contact: Keith Rankin, Chief Executive Officer and Managing Director
CFO: Richard McDowell, Chief Financial Officer
CMO: Michael Rieser, M.D., Medical Director
CNO: Georgia Swank, Chief Nursing Officer
Web address: www.ridgebhs.com
Control: Corporation, Investor–owned (for–profit) **Service**: Psychiatric

Staffed Beds: 110

UK HEALTHCARE GOOD SAMARITAN See UK Healthcare Good Samaritan Hospital

✠ **UNIVERSITY OF KENTUCKY ALBERT B. CHANDLER HOSPITAL (180067)**, 800 Rose Street, Zip 40536–0293; tel. 859/323–5000, (Includes KENTUCKY CHILDREN'S HOSPITAL, 800 Rose Street, Lexington, Kentucky, Zip 40536–0293, N–100 - 800 Rose Street, Zip 40536–0293, tel. 859/257–1000; UK HEALTHCARE GOOD SAMARITAN HOSPITAL, 310 South Limestone Street, Lexington, Kentucky, Zip 40508–3008, tel. 859/226–7000; Eric Monday, Co–Chief Executive Officer, Executive Vice President for Health Affairs) **A**1 2 3 5 8 10 **F**3 5 6 7 9 11 12 13 15 16 17 18 19 20 21 22 23 24 25 26 27 28 29 30 31 32 34 35 36 37 38 39 40 41 43 44 45 46 47 48 49 50 51 54 55 57 58 59 60 61 64 65 66 68 70 72 73 74 75 76 77 78 79 81 82 84 85 86 87 88 89 91 92 93 94 95 96 97 98 99 100 101 102 103 104 107 108 110 111 114 115 116 117 118 119 120 121 123 124 126 127 129 130 131 132 134 135 136 137 138 139 140 141 142 143 144 145 146 147 148 149 150 154 155 157 160 162 163 164 165 167 169 **P**6 **S** UK Healthcare, Lexington, KY
Primary Contact: Robert DiPaola, Executive Vice President for Health Affairs
COO: Peter N. Gilbert, Senior Vice President and Chief Operations Officer
CHR: Kimberly P Wilson, Director Human Resources
Web address: www.ukhealthcare.uky.edu
Control: State, Government, Nonfederal **Service**: General medical and surgical

Staffed Beds: 1168 **Admissions**: 41474 **Census**: 888 **Outpatient Visits**: 1424581 **Births**: 2486 **Total Expense ($000)**: 2557836 **Payroll Expense ($000)**: 784010 **Personnel**: 12866

LIBERTY—Casey County

☐ **CASEY COUNTY HOSPITAL (181309)**, 187 Wolford Avenue, Zip 42539–3278; tel. 606/787–6275, (Nonreporting) **A**1 10 18
Primary Contact: Rex A. Tungate, Chief Executive Officer
CFO: Richard Hendershot, Chief Financial Officer
CMO: Housam Haddad, M.D., Chief of Staff
CHR: Mary Ann Quinn, Administrative Assistant
CNO: Sue Antle, Director of Nursing
Web address: www.caseycountyhospital.com
Control: County, Government, Nonfederal **Service**: General medical and surgical

Staffed Beds: 24

LONDON—Laurel County

✠ **CHI SAINT JOSEPH HEALTH – SAINT JOSEPH LONDON (180011)**, 1001 Saint Joseph Lane, Zip 40741–8345; tel. 606/330–6000, (Nonreporting) **A**1 10 19 **S** CommonSpirit Health, Chicago, IL
Primary Contact: John C. Yanes, President
CFO: Christy Spitser, Vice President Finance and Business Development
CMO: Shelley Stanko, M.D., Chief Medical Officer
CHR: Sandra Turqueza, Senior Human Resources Business Partner
CNO: Lewis Stephen O'Neal, R.N., MSN, Chief Nursing Officer
Web address: www.saintjosephhealthsystem.org
Control: Church operated, Nongovernment, not–for–profit **Service**: General medical and surgical

Staffed Beds: 116

CHI SAINT JOSEPH LONDON See Chi Saint Joseph Health – Saint Joseph London

LOUISA—Lawrence County

☐ **THREE RIVERS MEDICAL CENTER (180128)**, 2485 Highway 644, Zip 41230–9242, Mailing Address: P.O. Box 769, Zip 41230–0769; tel. 606/638–9451, (Nonreporting) **A**1 10 20 **S** Quorum Health, Brentwood, TN
Primary Contact: Greg Kiser, Chief Executive Officer
CFO: Michael Ackley, Chief Financial Officer
CHR: Pat Hart, Director Human Resources
CNO: Catherine Heston, Chief Nursing Officer
Web address: www.threeriversmedicalcenter.com
Control: Corporation, Investor–owned (for–profit) **Service**: General medical and surgical

Staffed Beds: 90

LOUISVILLE—Jefferson County

AUDUBON HOSPITAL See Norton Audubon Hospital

☐ △ **BAPTIST HEALTH LOUISVILLE (180130)**, 4000 Kresge Way, Zip 40207–4676; tel. 502/897–8100, **A**1 2 3 5 7 10 **F**3 5 7 8 11 12 13 15 17 18 20 22 24 26 28 29 30 31 34 35 36 37 40 44 45 46 47 48 49 50 51 54 56 57 58 59 61 64 65 70 72 74 75 76 78 79 81 82 83 84 85 86 87 90 91 92 93 96 100 101 102 104 105 107 108 110 111 114 115 116 117 118 119 120 121 123 124 126 129 130 132 135 141 143 146 147 148 149 153 154 156 157 167 169 **P**6 **S** Baptist Health, Louisville, KY
Primary Contact: Jonathan Velez, President
COO: Clint Kaho, Vice President
CFO: Jim Morris, Vice President Finance
CMO: Kenneth Anderson, M.D., Vice President and Chief Medical Officer
CIO: Shari Price, Director Information Services
CHR: Kim Scaglione, Vice President Human Resources
CNO: Karen Newman, Ed.D., MSN, R.N., Vice President and Chief Nursing Officer
Web address: www.baptisthealthlouisville.com
Control: Other not–for–profit (including NFP Corporation) **Service**: General medical and surgical

Staffed Beds: 473 **Admissions**: 22223 **Census**: 324 **Outpatient Visits**: 368542 **Births**: 3038 **Total Expense ($000)**: 724532 **Payroll Expense ($000)**: 259316 **Personnel**: 2843

☐ **CENTRAL STATE HOSPITAL (184015)**, 10510 LaGrange Road, Zip 40223–1228; tel. 502/253–7060, (Nonreporting) **A**1 3 5 10
Primary Contact: Matt Mooring, Hospital Director
CFO: Robert Underhill, Director of Business Services
CMO: Vital Shah, M.D., Associate Director and Chief Medical Officer
CIO: Randy Spicer, Information Technology Supervisor
CHR: Sonya Wheatley, Human Resources Manager
CNO: Jennifer Fowler
Control: State, Government, Nonfederal **Service**: Psychiatric

Staffed Beds: 112

FRAZIER INSTITUTE See UOFL Health – Frazier Rehabilitation Institute

KINDRED HOSPITAL LOUISVILLE AT JEWISH HOSPITAL See Kindred Hospital–Louisville, Louisville

✠ **KINDRED HOSPITAL–LOUISVILLE (182001)**, 1313 Saint Anthony Place, Zip 40204–1740; tel. 502/587–7001, (Includes KINDRED HOSPITAL LOUISVILLE AT JEWISH HOSPITAL, 200 Abraham Flexner Way, 2nd Floor, Louisville, Kentucky, Zip 40202–2877, tel. 502/587–3999; Tim Phoenix, Chief Executive Officer) (Nonreporting) **A**1 3 5 10 **S** ScionHealth, Louisville, KY
Primary Contact: Tim Phoenix, Chief Executive Officer
Web address: www.kindredlouisville.com
Control: Corporation, Investor–owned (for–profit) **Service**: Acute long–term care hospital

Staffed Beds: 117

LOUISVILLE VAMC See Robley Rex Department of Veterans Affairs Medical Center

★ ⇧ **NORTON CHILDREN'S HOSPITAL (189801)**, 231 East Chestnut Street, Zip 40202–1821; tel. 502/629–6000, **A**2 3 5 8 10 21 **F**3 4 7 8 9 11 16 17 18 19 20 21 22 23 24 25 26 27 28 29 30 31 32 34 35 36 37 38 39 40 41 42 43 44 45 47 48 49 50 51 54 55 57 58 59 60 61 64 65 66 68 70 72 73 74 75 78 79 80 81 82 84 85 86 87 88 89 90 91 92 93 96 97 98 99 100 101 102 105 107 108 111 115 116 117 119 126 127 129 130 131 132 134 136 137 138 144 145 146 148 149 150 154 155 156 164 167 **S** Norton Healthcare, Louisville, KY
Primary Contact: Diane M. Scardino, Chief Administrative Officer
CNO: Erik Martin, R.N., Vice President Patient Care Services and Chief Nursing Officer
Web address: https://nortonchildrens.com/location/hospitals/norton-childrens-hospital/
Control: Other not–for–profit (including NFP Corporation) **Service**: Children's general medical and surgical

Staffed Beds: 287 **Admissions**: 9290 **Census**: 195 **Outpatient Visits**: 146128 **Births**: 0 **Total Expense ($000)**: 473662 **Payroll Expense ($000)**: 154426 **Personnel**: 1778

NORTON HEALTHCARE PAVILION See Norton Hospital, Louisville

Hospital, Medicare Provider Number, Address, Telephone, Approval, Facility, and Physician Codes, Health Care System

★ American Hospital Association (AHA) membership
☐ The Joint Commission accreditation
○ Healthcare Facilities Accreditation Program
◇ DNV Healthcare Inc. accreditation
⇧ Center for Improvement in Healthcare Quality Accreditation
△ Commission on Accreditation of Rehabilitation Facilities (CARF) accreditation

Hospitals, U.S. / KENTUCKY

★ ⇑ **NORTON HOSPITAL (180088)**, 200 East Chestnut Street, Zip 40202–1800, Mailing Address: P.O. Box 35070, Zip 40232–5070; tel. 502/629–8000, (Includes NORTON AUDUBON HOSPITAL, 1 Audubon Plaza Drive, Louisville, Kentucky, Zip 40217–1318, P O Box 17550, Zip 40217–0550, tel. 502/636–7111; Randy Hamilton, Chief Administrative Officer; NORTON BROWNSBORO HOSPITAL, 4960 Norton Healthcare Boulevard, Louisville, Kentucky, Zip 40241–2831, tel. 502/446–8000; Jeremy Sprecher, Chief Administrative Officer; NORTON HEALTHCARE PAVILION, 315 East Broadway, Louisville, Kentucky, Zip 40202–1703, tel. 502/629–2000; NORTON WOMEN'S AND CHILDREN'S HOSPITAL, 4001 Dutchmans Lane, Louisville, Kentucky, Zip 40207–4799, tel. 502/893–1000; Tammy L. McClanahan, Chief Administrative Officer) **A** 2 3 5 8 10 21 **F** 3 4 5 6 7 9 11 12 13 14 15 17 18 20 22 23 24 26 28 29 30 31 34 35 36 37 38 39 40 41 42 44 45 46 47 48 49 50 51 52 53 54 55 56 57 58 59 60 61 62 64 65 66 68 69 70 71 72 73 74 75 76 77 78 79 81 82 83 84 85 86 87 89 90 91 92 93 95 96 97 98 100 101 102 103 104 105 107 108 110 111 114 115 116 117 119 120 121 123 124 126 127 129 130 131 132 133 134 135 136 143 144 146 147 148 149 150 154 156 157 160 161 162 164 165 167 168 169 **S** Norton Healthcare, Louisville, KY
Primary Contact: Matthew Ayers, Chief Administrative Officer
CFO: Carl Amorose, Vice President Finance
Web address: www.nortonhealthcare.com/nortonhospital
Control: Other not–for–profit (including NFP Corporation) **Service**: General medical and surgical

Staffed Beds: 1272 **Admissions**: 58253 **Census**: 843 **Outpatient Visits**: 625992 **Births**: 8477 **Total Expense ($000)**: 1665425 **Payroll Expense ($000)**: 574982 **Personnel**: 6237

NORTON MEDICAL PAVILION See Norton Healthcare Pavilion

NORTON SOUTHWEST HOSPITAL See Norton Brownsboro Hospital

NORTON WOMEN'S AND KOSAIR CHILDREN'S HOSPITAL See Norton Women's and Children's Hospital

▣ **ROBLEY REX DEPARTMENT OF VETERANS AFFAIRS MEDICAL CENTER**, 800 Zorn Avenue, Zip 40206–1499; tel. 502/287–4000, (Nonreporting) **A** 1 3 5 **S** Department of Veterans Affairs, Washington, DC
Primary Contact: Jo–Ann M. Ginsberg, R.N., MSN, Medical Center Executive Director
CFO: Barbara Roberts, Chief Financial Officer
CMO: Marylee Rothschild, M.D., Chief of Staff
CIO: Augustine Bittner, Chief Information Officer
CHR: Angela Dutton, Chief Human Resources Management Service
CNO: Kathy Berger, R.N., Chief Nursing Officer
Web address: www.louisville.va.gov
Control: Veterans Affairs, Government, federal **Service**: General medical and surgical

Staffed Beds: 119

☐ **THE BROOK AT DUPONT (184007)**, 1405 Browns Lane, Zip 40207–4608; tel. 502/896–0495, (Nonreporting) **A** 1 10 **S** Universal Health Services, Inc., King of Prussia, PA
Primary Contact: Shane Koch, Chief Executive Officer
Web address: www.thebrookhospitals.com/
Control: Corporation, Investor–owned (for–profit) **Service**: Psychiatric

Staffed Beds: 88

☐ **THE BROOK HOSPITAL – KMI (184008)**, 8521 Old LaGrange Road, Zip 40242–3800; tel. 502/426–6380, (Nonreporting) **A** 1 10 **S** Universal Health Services, Inc., King of Prussia, PA
Primary Contact: Sherri Flood, Chief Executive Officer
COO: Kim Peabody, Chief Operating Officer
CFO: Glenn Brewer, Chief Financial Officer
CMO: Timothy Burke, M.D., Medical Director
CIO: John Ford, Information Technology Director
CHR: Christina Taylor, Director Human Resources
CNO: John Bisig, Chief Nursing Officer
Web address: www.thebrookhospitals.com
Control: Corporation, Investor–owned (for–profit) **Service**: Psychiatric

Staffed Beds: 110

▣ △ **UOFL HEALTH – JEWISH HOSPITAL (180040)**, 200 Abraham Flexner Way, Zip 40202–1886; tel. 502/587–4011, (Includes UOFL HEALTH – FRAZIER REHABILITATION INSTITUTE, 220 Abraham Flexner Way, Louisville, Kentucky, Zip 40202–1887, tel. 502/582–7400; Cathy Spalding, Administrator; UOFL HEALTH – SOUTH HOSPITAL, 1903 West Hebron Lane, Shepherdsville, Kentucky, Zip 40165–7425, tel. 502/955–3000; Dorie Shelburne, Chief Executive Officer) **A** 1 3 5 7 10 22 **F** 3 8 12 15 17 18 20 22 24 26 28 29 30 34 37 40 42 44 45 46 47 48 49 50 51 54 56 59 60 64 65 67 68 70 74 75 77 79 81 82 84 85 86 87 90 91 92 93 94 96 107 108 109 110 111 112 113 114 115 118 119 126 130 131 137 138 139 140 141 142 146 149 154 156 157 167 **S** UofL Health, Louisville, KY
Primary Contact: John Walsh, FACHE, Chief Administrative Officer
CFO: Ronald Farr, Chief Financial Officer
CMO: James P Ketterhagen, M.D., Senior Vice President and Chief Medical Officer
CIO: Thomas Wittman, Chief Information Officer
CHR: Julie McGregor, Vice President and Chief People Officer
CNO: Cheryl Fugatte, MSN, Vice President and Chief Nursing Officer
Web address: https://www.kindredhealthcare.com/locations/transitional-care-hospitals/kindred-hospital-louisville-at-jewish-hospital
Control: Other not–for–profit (including NFP Corporation) **Service**: General medical and surgical

Staffed Beds: 458 **Admissions**: 15286 **Census**: 351 **Outpatient Visits**: 174436 **Births**: 0 **Total Expense ($000)**: 639677 **Payroll Expense ($000)**: 164879 **Personnel**: 2335

▣ **UOFL HEALTH – MARY AND ELIZABETH HOSPITAL (180037)**, 1850 Bluegrass Avenue, Zip 40215–1199; tel. 502/361–6000, **A** 1 3 5 10 **F** 3 4 11 12 15 18 20 22 28 29 30 34 35 36 39 40 44 45 46 47 49 50 51 53 57 59 60 64 68 70 74 75 78 79 81 82 85 87 93 107 108 110 111 114 115 118 119 130 132 135 146 147 148 149 154 164 167 **S** UofL Health, Louisville, KY
Primary Contact: Melisa Adkins, Chief Executive Officer
COO: Shane Fitzgerald, Chief Operating Officer
CFO: Elaine Hayes, Controller
CMO: Val Slayton, M.D., Vice President Medical Affairs
CHR: Julie McGregor, Director Human Resources
Web address: https://uoflhealth.org/locations/mary-elizabeth-hospital/
Control: Other not–for–profit (including NFP Corporation) **Service**: General medical and surgical

Staffed Beds: 199 **Admissions**: 6264 **Census**: 84 **Outpatient Visits**: 82428 **Births**: 0 **Total Expense ($000)**: 188100 **Payroll Expense ($000)**: 53140 **Personnel**: 1051

▣ **UOFL HEALTH – PEACE HOSPITAL (184000)**, 2020 Newburg Road, Zip 40205–1879; tel. 502/479–4500, **A** 1 3 5 10 **F** 5 29 30 35 50 56 68 69 98 99 103 104 105 130 132 143 149 152 153 154 157 164 **S** UofL Health, Louisville, KY
Primary Contact: Aundrea Lewis, Interim Chief Executive Officer
COO: Abbey Roach, Chief Operating Officer, Vice President
CFO: Beckie Kistler, Director of Finance
CHR: Jan Ostbloom, Human Resources Consultant
Web address: www.kentuckyonehealth.org/our-lady-of-peace
Control: Other not–for–profit (including NFP Corporation) **Service**: Psychiatric

Staffed Beds: 261 **Admissions**: 6406 **Census**: 202 **Outpatient Visits**: 23233 **Births**: 0 **Total Expense ($000)**: 104201 **Payroll Expense ($000)**: 47133 **Personnel**: 916

▣ **UOFL HEALTH – UOFL HOSPITAL (180141)**, 530 South Jackson Street, Zip 40202–3611; tel. 502/562–3000, **A** 1 2 3 5 8 10 **F** 3 5 8 13 15 16 17 18 20 22 26 27 29 30 31 34 35 36 38 40 43 44 45 46 47 48 49 50 51 56 57 58 59 60 61 64 66 68 70 71 72 73 74 75 76 77 78 79 80 81 82 84 85 86 87 91 92 93 96 98 100 101 102 107 108 110 111 114 115 117 118 119 120 121 123 124 126 130 135 136 145 146 147 148 149 150 151 154 156 160 162 164 **S** UofL Health, Louisville, KY
Primary Contact: Kenneth P. Marshall, Chief Executive Officer
CFO: Kirk Strack, Assistant Chief Financial Officer
CMO: Mark P Pfeifer, M.D., Senior Vice President and Chief Medical Officer
CIO: Troy May, Chief Information Officer
CNO: Mary Jane Adams, R.N., MSN, Senior Vice President and Chief Nursing Officer
Web address: www.ulh.org
Control: Other not–for–profit (including NFP Corporation) **Service**: General medical and surgical

Staffed Beds: 340 **Admissions**: 15361 **Census**: 306 **Outpatient Visits**: 200945 **Births**: 1726 **Total Expense ($000)**: 861388 **Payroll Expense ($000)**: 191013 **Personnel**: 2488

Hospitals, U.S. / KENTUCKY

MADISONVILLE—Hopkins County

☐ **BAPTIST HEALTH DEACONESS MADISONVILLE, INC. (180093)**, 900 Hospital Drive, Zip 42431-1694; tel. 270/825-5100, (Nonreporting) **A**1 2 3 5 10 **S** Baptist Health, Louisville, KY
Primary Contact: Alisa Coleman, President
COO: Kevin Moser, Vice President of Operations
CFO: Kim Ashby, Vice President of Finance
CMO: Wayne Lipson, M.D., Chief Physician Executive
CIO: Karla Durham, Director of Information Systems
CHR: Lorie A. Oglesby, Director of Human Resources
CNO: Denise Dunn, R.N., Chief Nursing Officer
Web address: www.baptisthealthmadisonville.com
Control: Other not-for-profit (including NFP Corporation) **Service**: General medical and surgical

Staffed Beds: 165

BAPTIST HEALTH MADISONVILLE See Baptist Health Deaconess Madisonville, Inc.

★ **CONTINUECARE HOSPITAL AT MADISONVILLE (182009)**, 900 Hospital Drive, 4th Floor, Zip 42431-1644; tel. 270/825-5450, **A**10 22 **F**1 3 29 85 **S** Community Hospital Corporation, Plano, TX
Primary Contact: Michelle Mullen, Chief Executive Officer
CNO: Michelle Mullen, Chief Nursing Officer
Web address: www.continuecare.org/madisonville/
Control: Other not-for-profit (including NFP Corporation) **Service**: Acute long-term care hospital

Staffed Beds: 35 **Admissions**: 200 **Census**: 12 **Outpatient Visits**: 0 **Births**: 0 **Total Expense ($000)**: 7075 **Payroll Expense ($000)**: 3183 **Personnel**: 48

MANCHESTER—Clay County

⊞ **ADVENTHEALTH MANCHESTER (180043)**, 210 Marie Langdon Drive, Zip 40962-6388; tel. 606/598-5104, (Nonreporting) **A**1 10 **S** AdventHealth, Altamonte Springs, FL
Primary Contact: Jamie Couch, Interim Chief Executive Officer
CMO: Jeff Newswanger, M.D., Chief Medical Officer
CHR: Joe Skula, Director Human Resources
Web address: www.manchestermemorial.org
Control: Church operated, Nongovernment, not-for-profit **Service**: General medical and surgical

Staffed Beds: 27

MARION—Crittenden County

CRITTENDEN COMMUNITY HOSPITAL (180779), 520 West Gum Street, Zip 42064-1516, Mailing Address: P.O. Box 386, Zip 42064-0386; tel. 270/965-5281, (Nonreporting) **A**10
Primary Contact: Shawn Bright, Chief Executive Officer
COO: Robin Curnel, MSN, Chief Operating Officer and Chief Nursing Officer
CFO: Karen Paris, Controller
CMO: Steven Burkhart, M.D., Chief Medical Officer
CIO: Reese Baker, Director Information Systems
CHR: Jan Gregory, Chief of Human Resources
CNO: Robin Curnel, MSN, Chief Operating Officer and Chief Nursing Officer
Web address: www.crittenden-health.org
Control: Other not-for-profit (including NFP Corporation)

Staffed Beds: 48

CRITTENDEN COUNTY HOSPITAL See Crittenden Community Hospital

MARTIN—Floyd County

★ ⇈ **ARH OUR LADY OF THE WAY (181305)**, 11203 Main Street, Zip 41649; tel. 606/285-6400, (Nonreporting) **A**10 18 21 **S** Appalachian Regional Healthcare, Inc., Lexington, KY
Primary Contact: Rocco K. Massey, Interim Chief Executive Officer
CFO: Robert Brock, Vice President Finance
CMO: John Triplett, D.O., President Medical Staff
CIO: Chris Dye, Director Information Systems
Web address: https://www.arh.org/portfolio_page/arh-our-lady-of-the-way-hospital/
Control: Church operated, Nongovernment, not-for-profit **Service**: General medical and surgical

Staffed Beds: 25

MAYFIELD—Graves County

⊞ **JACKSON PURCHASE MEDICAL CENTER (180116)**, 1099 Medical Center Circle, Zip 42066-1159; tel. 270/251-4100, (Nonreporting) **A**1 10 19 **S** Lifepoint Health, Brentwood, TN
Primary Contact: David Anderson, Chief Executive Officer
CMO: Rudy Triana, M.D., Chief of Staff
CIO: Randy McDaniel, Information Systems Director
CHR: Tressa B Hargrove, Director Human Resources
CNO: Perry W. Ballard MSN, RN, Chief Nursing Officer
Web address: www.jacksonpurchase.com
Control: Corporation, Investor-owned (for-profit) **Service**: General medical and surgical

Staffed Beds: 227

MAYSVILLE—Mason County

⊞ **MEADOWVIEW REGIONAL MEDICAL CENTER (180019)**, 989 Medical Park Drive, Zip 41056-8750; tel. 606/759-5311, (Nonreporting) **A**1 2 3 10 20 **S** Lifepoint Health, Brentwood, TN
Primary Contact: Joseph G. Koch, Chief Executive Officer
CFO: Clayton Kolodziejczyk, Chief Financial Officer
CMO: Eric Lohman, M.D., Chief of Staff
CHR: Diana Kennedy, Director Human Resources
Web address: www.meadowviewregional.com
Control: Corporation, Investor-owned (for-profit) **Service**: General medical and surgical

Staffed Beds: 100

MCDOWELL—Floyd County

⇈ **MCDOWELL ARH HOSPITAL (181331)**, Route 122, Zip 41647, Mailing Address: P.O. Box 247, Zip 41647-0247; tel. 606/377-3400, (Nonreporting) **A**10 18 21 **S** Appalachian Regional Healthcare, Inc., Lexington, KY
Primary Contact: Danita Hampton, Chief Executive Officer
CMO: Mary A Hall, Chief Medical Staff
CIO: Jeff Brady, Director Information Systems
CHR: Stephanie Owens, Manager Human Resources
Web address: www.arh.org
Control: Other not-for-profit (including NFP Corporation) **Service**: General medical and surgical

Staffed Beds: 25

MIDDLESBORO—Bell County

⇈ **MIDDLESBORO ARH HOSPITAL (180020)**, 3600 West Cumberland Avenue, Zip 40965-2614, Mailing Address: P.O. Box 340, Zip 40965-0340; tel. 606/242-1100, (Nonreporting) **A**2 10 21 **S** Appalachian Regional Healthcare, Inc., Lexington, KY
Primary Contact: Michael Slusher, FACHE, Community Chief Executive Officer
CFO: Joseph Horton, Assistant Administrator
CMO: Robert Thomas, M.D., Chief of Staff
CHR: Christopher Thompson, Human Resources Manager
CNO: Vicki Thompson, MSN, Community Chief Nursing Officer
Web address: www.arh.org/middlesboro
Control: Other not-for-profit (including NFP Corporation) **Service**: General medical and surgical

Staffed Beds: 46

MONTICELLO—Wayne County

○ **WAYNE COUNTY HOSPITAL (181321)**, 166 Hospital Street, Zip 42633-2416; tel. 606/348-9343, **A**10 11 18 **F**3 8 15 29 30 40 47 75 81 107 108 114 119 127 133 135 146 **P**6
Primary Contact: Joseph Murrell, Chief Executive Officer
CFO: Anne Sawyer, Chief Financial Officer
CMO: David Mayer, Chief of Staff
CIO: Angela Burton, Privacy Officer
CHR: Mollie Dick, Coordinator Human Resources
CNO: Lora Elam, R.N., Chief Nursing Officer
Web address: www.waynehospital.org
Control: Other not-for-profit (including NFP Corporation) **Service**: General medical and surgical

Staffed Beds: 25 **Admissions**: 190 **Census**: 2 **Outpatient Visits**: 11557 **Births**: 0 **Total Expense ($000)**: 21255 **Payroll Expense ($000)**: 9007 **Personnel**: 197

Hospital, Medicare Provider Number, Address, Telephone, Approval, Facility, and Physician Codes, Health Care System

★ American Hospital Association (AHA) membership
☐ The Joint Commission accreditation
○ Healthcare Facilities Accreditation Program
◇ DNV Healthcare Inc. accreditation
⇈ Center for Improvement in Healthcare Quality Accreditation
△ Commission on Accreditation of Rehabilitation Facilities (CARF) accreditation

© 2025 AHA Guide

Hospitals, U.S. / KENTUCKY

MOREHEAD—Rowan County

ST. CLAIRE REGIONAL MEDICAL CENTER (180018), 222 Medical Circle, Zip 40351-1179; tel. 606/783-6500, **A**1 2 3 5 10 13 **F**3 12 13 15 18 20 22 28 29 30 31 34 35 36 38 39 40 45 46 47 48 49 50 51 54 57 58 59 60 62 63 64 65 68 70 74 75 76 77 78 79 81 82 83 84 85 87 90 92 93 94 97 98 100 102 103 104 107 110 111 114 115 118 119 120 124 127 129 130 131 132 135 144 145 146 147 148 149 154 157 160 161 164 165 167 169 **P**6 **S** UK Healthcare, Lexington, KY
Primary Contact: Donald H. Lloyd II, President and Chief Executive Officer
CFO: Chris McClurg, Vice President Finance and Chief Financial Officer
CMO: William L Melahn, M.D., Vice President Medical Affairs and Chief Medical Officer
CIO: Andy Price, Chief Information Officer
CNO: Kathleen Lerae Wilson DNP, RN, Vice President Patient Services and Chief Nursing Officer
Web address: www.st-claire.org
Control: State, Government, Nonfederal Service: General medical and surgical

Staffed Beds: 149 Admissions: 4924 Census: 53 Outpatient Visits: 90841 Births: 334 Total Expense ($000): 222620 Payroll Expense ($000): 102172 Personnel: 1252

MORGANFIELD—Union County

DEACONESS UNION COUNTY HOSPITAL (181306), 4604 Highway 60 West, Zip 42437-9570; tel. 270/389-5000, **A**1 10 18 **F**3 11 15 29 34 35 40 44 45 53 57 59 64 65 68 75 81 86 93 107 110 114 119 127 133 146 148 149 154 164 **S** Deaconess Health System, Evansville, IN
Primary Contact: Amber Powell, Chief Administrative Officer
CFO: David Massengale, Chief Financial Officer
CMO: William Clapp, M.D., Chief of Medical Staff
CIO: Randy McCleese, Chief Information Officer
CHR: Ty Kahle, Assistant Vice President Human Resources
CNO: Peggy F Creighton, R.N., Director of Nursing
Web address: https://www.deaconess.com/Deaconess-Union-County-Hospital
Control: Other not-for-profit (including NFP Corporation) Service: General medical and surgical

Staffed Beds: 25 Admissions: 373 Census: 8 Outpatient Visits: 26826 Births: 0 Total Expense ($000): 22895 Payroll Expense ($000): 7515 Personnel: 99

METHODIST HOSPITAL UNION COUNTY See Deaconess Union County Hospital

MOUNT STERLING—Montgomery County

CHI SAINT JOSEPH HEALTH – SAINT JOSEPH MOUNT STERLING (180064), 225 Falcon Drive, Zip 40353-1158, Mailing Address: P.O. Box 7, Zip 40353-0007; tel. 859/497-5000, (Nonreporting) **A**1 10 **S** CommonSpirit Health, Chicago, IL
Primary Contact: John C. Yanes, President
CFO: Amanda Kinman, Director of Finance
CMO: Jeff McGinnis, M.D., President Medical Staff
CIO: Jeff Ryder, Director Information Systems
CHR: Annette Saadat, Human Resources Business Partner
CNO: Cinda Fluke, R.N., Chief Nursing Officer
Web address: https://www.chisaintjosephhealth.org/
Control: Other not-for-profit (including NFP Corporation) Service: General medical and surgical

Staffed Beds: 42

SAINT JOSEPH MOUNT STERLING See Chi Saint Joseph Health – Saint Joseph Mount Sterling

MOUNT VERNON—Rockcastle County

ROCKCASTLE REGIONAL HOSPITAL AND RESPIRATORY CARE CENTER (180115), 145 Newcomb Avenue, Zip 40456-2728, Mailing Address: P.O. Box 1310, Zip 40456-1310; tel. 606/256-2195, (Nonreporting) **A**1 2 3 10
Primary Contact: Stephen A. Estes, Chief Executive Officer
CFO: Charles Black Jr, Chief Financial Officer
CMO: Jon A Arvin, M.D., Chief Medical Officer
CIO: Maleigha Amyx, Chief Information Officer
CHR: Carmen Poynter, Director Human Resources
CNO: Tammy Brock, MSN, R.N., Chief Nursing Officer
Web address: www.rockcastleregional.org
Control: Other not-for-profit (including NFP Corporation) Service: General medical and surgical

Staffed Beds: 105

MURRAY—Calloway County

MURRAY–CALLOWAY COUNTY HOSPITAL (180027), 803 Poplar Street, Zip 42071-2432; tel. 270/762-1100, **A**1 2 10 19 **F**3 7 12 13 15 17 18 20 22 26 28 29 30 31 32 34 35 40 44 45 47 48 49 50 51 53 57 59 63 64 65 67 68 70 71 74 75 76 77 78 79 81 82 85 87 89 90 92 93 96 97 98 100 103 104 107 108 110 111 115 118 119 121 123 129 130 131 132 135 143 146 147 148 149 154 167
Primary Contact: Colonel Jerome Penner, FACHE, Chief Executive Officer
COO: John R Wilson, Chief Operating Officer
CFO: John Bradford, Chief Financial Officer
CIO: Brian Benedict, Director of Information Technology
CHR: John R Wilson, Vice President, Human Resources
CNO: Jeffrey L Eye, R.N., MSN, Vice President Patient Care Services
Web address: www.murrayhospital.org
Control: City–county, Government, Nonfederal Service: General medical and surgical

Staffed Beds: 121 Admissions: 3169 Census: 36 Births: 483 Total Expense ($000): 166031 Payroll Expense ($000): 64635

OWENSBORO—Daviess County

MERCY HOSPITAL See Healthpark

OWENSBORO HEALTH REGIONAL HOSPITAL (180038), 1201 Pleasant Valley Road, Zip 42303; tel. 270/417-2000, (Includes HEALTHPARK, 1006 Ford Avenue, Owensboro, Kentucky, Zip 42301, P O Box 2839, Zip 42302, tel. 270/688-5433) (Total facility includes 30 beds in nursing home–type unit) **A**1 2 3 5 7 10 **F**3 5 11 13 15 17 18 20 22 24 26 28 29 30 31 32 34 35 40 43 44 45 46 49 53 54 56 57 58 59 61 62 64 65 66 70 72 74 75 76 77 78 79 81 82 83 84 85 86 87 89 90 91 92 93 97 98 100 101 102 103 104 105 107 108 110 111 114 115 116 117 118 119 120 121 123 124 126 127 128 129 130 131 132 135 144 145 146 147 148 149 153 154 156 162 164 165 167 169 **S** Owensboro Health, Owensboro, KY
Primary Contact: Mark A. Marsh, President and Chief Executive Officer
COO: Beth Steele, MSN, R.N., Chief Operating Officer
CFO: John Hackbarth, CPA, Senior Vice President Finance and Chief Financial Officer
CMO: Francis DuFrayne, M.D., Chief Medical Officer
CHR: Mia Suter, Chief Administration Officer
CNO: Joni Sims, Chief Nursing Officer
Web address: www.owensborohealth.org
Control: Other not-for-profit (including NFP Corporation) Service: General medical and surgical

Staffed Beds: 362 Admissions: 16341 Census: 217 Outpatient Visits: 1204872 Births: 2122 Total Expense ($000): 603214 Payroll Expense ($000): 195813 Personnel: 2057

★ **RIVERVALLEY BEHAVIORAL HEALTH HOSPITAL (184013)**, 1000 Industrial Drive, Zip 42301-8715; tel. 270/689-6500, (Nonreporting) **A**10
Primary Contact: Wanda Figueroa Peralta, President and Chief Executive Officer
COO: Michelle Parks, Administrator
CFO: J Michael Mountain, Chief Financial Officer
CMO: David Harmon, D.O., Vice President Medical Services
CIO: Travis Taggart, Director Information Technology
CHR: Cathryn H Gaddis, Director Human Resources
Web address: www.rvbh.com
Control: Other not-for-profit (including NFP Corporation) Service: Children's hospital psychiatric

Staffed Beds: 80

PADUCAH—Mccracken County

BAPTIST HEALTH PADUCAH (180104), 2501 Kentucky Avenue, Zip 42003-3200; tel. 270/575-2100, **A**1 2 10 19 **F**3 11 12 13 15 17 18 20 22 24 26 28 29 30 31 32 34 35 40 45 46 48 50 51 57 58 59 64 65 68 70 72 73 74 75 76 77 78 79 81 82 84 85 86 87 89 91 92 93 96 107 108 109 110 111 112 113 114 115 116 117 118 119 120 121 124 126 130 131 132 134 135 145 146 147 148 149 154 156 157 167 169 **S** Baptist Health, Louisville, KY
Primary Contact: Kenneth Boyd, President
COO: Bonnie W Schrock, FACHE, Chief Operating Officer
CMO: Bradley W. Housman, M.D., Chief Medical Officer
CIO: Jay Orazine, Director Information Services
CNO: Sharon Freyer, R.N., Chief Nursing Officer
Web address: https://www.baptisthealth.com/paducah/
Control: Other not-for-profit (including NFP Corporation) Service: General medical and surgical

Staffed Beds: 182 Admissions: 8340 Census: 103 Outpatient Visits: 202350 Births: 904 Total Expense ($000): 358200 Payroll Expense ($000): 99888 Personnel: 1197

★ **CONTINUECARE HOSPITAL AT BAPTIST HEALTH PADUCAH (182008)**, 2501 Kentucky Avenue, 5th Floor, Zip 42003–3813; tel. 270/575–2598, **A**10 22 **F**1 3 29 34 35 148 **S** Community Hospital Corporation, Plano, TX
Primary Contact: Lee Gentry, FACHE, Chief Executive Officer
CNO: Mary Lou Young, Chief Nursing Officer
Web address: www.continuecare.org/paducah//
Control: Other not–for–profit (including NFP Corporation) **Service**: Acute long–term care hospital

Staffed Beds: 37 **Admissions**: 207 **Census**: 15 **Outpatient Visits**: 0 **Births**: 0 **Total Expense ($000)**: 8764 **Payroll Expense ($000)**: 3895 **Personnel**: 39

LOURDES HOSPITAL See Mercy Health – Lourdes Hospital

△ **MERCY HEALTH – LOURDES HOSPITAL (180102)**, 1530 Lone Oak Road, Zip 42003–7900, Mailing Address: P.O. Box 7100, Zip 42002–7100; tel. 270/444–2444, (Nonreporting) **A**1 2 7 10 19 **S** Bon Secours Mercy Health, Cincinnati, OH
Primary Contact: Michael Yungmann, President and Chief Executive Officer
CHR: Kim Lindsey, Chief Human Resources Officer
Web address: www.lourdes-pad.org
Control: Church operated, Nongovernment, not–for–profit **Service**: General medical and surgical

Staffed Beds: 281

PAINTSVILLE—Johnson County

⇑ **PAINTSVILLE ARH HOSPITAL (180078)**, 625 James S. Trimble Boulevard, Zip 41240–0000; tel. 606/789–3511, (Nonreporting) **A**10 21 **S** Appalachian Regional Healthcare, Inc., Lexington, KY
Primary Contact: Kathy Stumbo, Chief Executive Officer
CFO: Pattie Major, Chief Financial Officer
CMO: F K Belhasen, M.D., Medical Director
CHR: Carla J. Stapleton, Director Human Resources
Web address: www.pbhrmc.com
Control: Other not–for–profit (including NFP Corporation) **Service**: General medical and surgical

Staffed Beds: 72

⇑ **PAUL B. HALL REGIONAL MEDICAL CENTER** See Paintsville Arh Hospital

PARIS—Bourbon County

✠ **BOURBON COMMUNITY HOSPITAL (180046)**, 9 Linville Drive, Zip 40361–2196; tel. 859/987–3600, (Nonreporting) **A**1 10 **S** Lifepoint Health, Brentwood, TN
Primary Contact: Tommy Haggard, Chief Executive Officer
CFO: Michael Snedegar, Chief Financial Officer
CMO: C. Ray Young, M.D., Chief Medical Officer
CIO: Phil Osborne, Director Information Technology
CHR: Roger K Davis, Director Human Resources
Web address: www.bourbonhospital.com
Control: Corporation, Investor–owned (for–profit) **Service**: General medical and surgical

Staffed Beds: 58

PIKEVILLE—Pike County

☐ **PIKEVILLE MEDICAL CENTER (180044)**, 911 Bypass Road, Zip 41501–1689; tel. 606/218–3500, (Nonreporting) **A**1 2 3 5 10
Primary Contact: Donovan Blackburn, Chief Executive Officer and Vice President of Board of Directors
COO: Kansas Justice, Senior Vice President and Chief Operating Officer
CFO: Michelle Hagy, Senior Vice President and Chief Financial Officer
CMO: Aaron Crum, M.D., Chief Medical Officer, Assistant Chief Executive Officer and Senior Vice President
CIO: Tony Damron, Senior Vice President and Chief Information Officer
CNO: Michelle L. Rainey, Senior Vice President and Chief Nursing Officer
Web address: www.pikevillehospital.org
Control: Other not–for–profit (including NFP Corporation) **Service**: General medical and surgical

Staffed Beds: 328

PINEVILLE—Bell County

PINEVILLE COMMUNITY HEALTH CENTER (180154), 850 Riverview Avenue, Zip 40977–1452; tel. 606/337–3051, (Nonreporting) **A**10 22
Primary Contact: Michael Frey, Chief Executive Officer
CFO: Colan Kelly, Chief Financial Officer
CMO: Michael Peterson, M.D., Chief of Staff
CIO: David Hall, Chief Information Officer
CHR: Josh Collett, Director Human Resources
CNO: Dinah Jarvis, Director of Nursing
Web address: https://www.pinevillehospital.org/
Control: Other not–for–profit (including NFP Corporation) **Service**: General medical and surgical

Staffed Beds: 150

PRESTONSBURG—Floyd County

⇑ **HIGHLANDS ARH REGIONAL MEDICAL CENTER (180005)**, 5000 Kentucky Route 321, Zip 41653–1273, Mailing Address: P.O. Box 668, Zip 41653–0668; tel. 606/886–8511, (Nonreporting) **A**2 3 10 19 21 **S** Appalachian Regional Healthcare, Inc., Lexington, KY
Primary Contact: Jonathan Koonce, Chief Executive Officer
COO: Justin Turner, Chief Operating Officer
CIO: Mike Roberts, Chief Technology Officer
Web address: https://providers.arh.org/location/highlands-arh-regional-medical-center/loc0000132808
Control: Other not–for–profit (including NFP Corporation) **Service**: General medical and surgical

Staffed Beds: 139

PRINCETON—Caldwell County

★ **CALDWELL MEDICAL CENTER (181322)**, 100 Medical Center Drive, Zip 42445–2430, Mailing Address: P.O. Box 410, Zip 42445–0410; tel. 270/365–0300, (Nonreporting) **A**10 18 **S** Ovation Healthcare, Brentwood, TN
Primary Contact: Daniel Odegaard, FACHE, Chief Executive Officer
CHR: Rhonda Burns, Director Human Resources
CNO: Douglas James, Chief Nursing Officer
Web address: www.caldwellhosp.org
Control: Other not–for–profit (including NFP Corporation) **Service**: General medical and surgical

Staffed Beds: 25

RADCLIFF—Hardin County

☐ **LINCOLN TRAIL BEHAVIORAL HEALTH SYSTEM (184012)**, 3909 South Wilson Road, Zip 40160–8944, Mailing Address: P.O. Box 369, Zip 40159–0369; tel. 270/351–9444, (Nonreporting) **A**1 10 **S** Universal Health Services, Inc., King of Prussia, PA
Primary Contact: Leslie Flechler, Chief Executive Officer
CFO: Debbie Ditto, CPA, Controller
CMO: Muhammad W. Sajid, M.D., Medical Director
CHR: Charlotte C Davis, Director Human Resources
Web address: www.lincolnbehavioral.com
Control: Corporation, Investor–owned (for–profit) **Service**: Psychiatric

Staffed Beds: 140

RICHMOND—Madison County

○ **BAPTIST HEALTH RICHMOND (180049)**, 801 Eastern Bypass, Zip 40475–2405, Mailing Address: P.O. Box 1600, Zip 40476–2603; tel. 859/623–3131, (Nonreporting) **A**10 11 19 **S** Baptist Health, Louisville, KY
Primary Contact: Greg Donavan. Gerard, President
CMO: Richard Shelton, M.D., Chief Medical Officer
CIO: Kelly Bonzo, Director
CHR: Joy M Benedict, Director Human Resources
CNO: Melinda Lee Blair, Vice President and Chief Nursing Officer
Web address: www.baptisthealthrichmond.com
Control: Other not–for–profit (including NFP Corporation) **Service**: General medical and surgical

Staffed Beds: 58

Hospital, Medicare Provider Number, Address, Telephone, Approval, Facility, and Physician Codes, Health Care System

★ American Hospital Association (AHA) membership   ○ Healthcare Facilities Accreditation Program   ⇑ Center for Improvement in Healthcare Quality Accreditation
☐ The Joint Commission accreditation   ◇ DNV Healthcare Inc. accreditation   △ Commission on Accreditation of Rehabilitation Facilities (CARF) accreditation

Hospitals, U.S. / KENTUCKY

RUSSELL SPRINGS—Russell County

★ **RUSSELL COUNTY HOSPITAL (181330)**, 153 Dowell Road, Zip 42642–4579, Mailing Address: P.O. Box 1610, Zip 42642–1610; tel. 270/866–4141, (Nonreporting) **A**3 10 18
Primary Contact: Scott Thompson, Chief Executive Officer
CFO: Janie Landis, Chief Financial Officer
CMO: Jerry D. Westerfield, M.D., Chief of Medical Staff
CIO: Monte Monsanto, Chief Information Systems
CHR: Jennifer Goode, Director Human Resources
CNO: Judy Chenoweth, Chief Nursing Officer
Web address: www.russellcohospital.org
Control: County, Government, Nonfederal **Service**: General medical and surgical

Staffed Beds: 25

RUSSELLVILLE—Logan County

LOGAN MEMORIAL HOSPITAL See The Medical Center At Russellville

THE MEDICAL CENTER AT RUSSELLVILLE (180066), 1625 South Nashville Road, Zip 42276–8834, Mailing Address: P.O. Box 10, Zip 42276–0010; tel. 270/726–4011, (Nonreporting) **A**1 10 **S** Med Center Health, Bowling Green, KY
Primary Contact: Andrew Bedi, Chief Executive Officer
CIO: Randy Compton, Information Technology and System Director
CHR: Susan Renodin Deaton, Human Resources Director
CNO: Deborah Brown, Chief Nursing Officer
Web address: https://medcenterhealth.org/hospitals/russellville/
Control: Corporation, Investor–owned (for–profit) **Service**: General medical and surgical

Staffed Beds: 46

SALEM—Livingston County

LIVINGSTON HOSPITAL AND HEALTHCARE SERVICES (181320), 131 Hospital Drive, Zip 42078–8043; tel. 270/988–2299, (Nonreporting) **A**10 18
Primary Contact: Shane Whittington, Chief Executive Officer
CMO: William Guyette, M.D., President Medical Staff
CIO: Shannan Landreth, Information Systems
CHR: Carla Wiggins, Director Human Resources
CNO: Joanna Stone, Chief Nursing Officer
Web address: www.lhhs.org
Control: Other not–for–profit (including NFP Corporation) **Service**: General medical and surgical

Staffed Beds: 25

SCOTTSVILLE—Allen County

☐ **MEDICAL CENTER AT SCOTTSVILLE (181324)**, 456 Burnley Road, Zip 42164–6355; tel. 270/622–2800, (Nonreporting) **A**1 10 18 **S** Med Center Health, Bowling Green, KY
Primary Contact: Eric Hagan, R.N., Executive Vice President and Administrator
CFO: Ronald G. Sowell, FACHE, Chief Financial Officer
CIO: Mark Brookman, Chief Information Officer
CHR: Lynn Williams, Vice President Human Resources
Web address: www.themedicalcenterscottsville.org/
Control: Other not–for–profit (including NFP Corporation) **Service**: General medical and surgical

Staffed Beds: 135

SHELBYVILLE—Shelby County

UOFL HEALTH – SHELBYVILLE HOSPITAL (180016), 727 Hospital Drive, Zip 40065–1699; tel. 502/647–4000, **A**1 10 **F**3 11 15 18 26 27 28 29 34 35 40 41 44 45 50 57 59 68 70 75 77 79 81 85 87 91 93 94 107 108 110 111 115 119 129 131 132 146 148 149 154 167 **S** UofL Health, Louisville, KY
Primary Contact: Aaron Garofola, Chief Executive Officer
CFO: Erika McGimsey, Controller
CMO: Tony Perez, M.D., President Medical Staff
CHR: Cindy Stewart Rattray, Director Human Resources
Web address: www.kentuckyonehealth.org/jewish-hospital-shelbyville
Control: Other not–for–profit (including NFP Corporation) **Service**: General medical and surgical

Staffed Beds: 32 **Admissions**: 741 **Census**: 8 **Outpatient Visits**: 38269
Births: 0 **Total Expense ($000)**: 37980 **Payroll Expense ($000)**: 14340
Personnel: 253

SOMERSET—Pulaski County

LAKE CUMBERLAND REGIONAL HOSPITAL (180132), 305 Langdon Street, Zip 42503–2750, Mailing Address: P.O. Box 620, Zip 42502–0620; tel. 606/679–7441, (Nonreporting) **A**1 2 3 5 10 13 **S** Lifepoint Health, Brentwood, TN
Primary Contact: Carolyn Sparks, Chief Executive Officer
COO: Elizabeth Jones, Chief Operating Officer
CFO: Steve Sloan, Chief Financial Officer
CMO: Michael Citak, M.D., Chief Medical Officer
CIO: Thomas Gilbert, Director Information Technology Services
CHR: James Hughes, Director Human Resources
CNO: Sheryl Glasscock, Chief Nursing Officer
Web address: www.lakecumberlandhospital.com
Control: Corporation, Investor–owned (for–profit) **Service**: General medical and surgical

Staffed Beds: 283

SOUTH WILLIAMSON—Pike County

TUG VALLEY ARH REGIONAL MEDICAL CENTER (180069), 260 Hospital Drive, Zip 41503–4072; tel. 606/237–1710, (Nonreporting) **A**2 10 19 21 **S** Appalachian Regional Healthcare, Inc., Lexington, KY
Primary Contact: Paula Vaughan, Chief Executive Officer
CMO: J D Miller, M.D., Vice President Medical Affairs
CIO: Jeff Brady, Chief Information Officer
Web address: www.arh.org/locations/tug_valley/about_us.aspx
Control: Other not–for–profit (including NFP Corporation) **Service**: General medical and surgical

Staffed Beds: 123

STANFORD—Lincoln County

☐ **EPHRAIM MCDOWELL FORT LOGAN HOSPITAL (181315)**, 110 Metker Trail, Zip 40484–1020; tel. 606/365–4600, (Nonreporting) **A**1 10 18 **S** Ephraim McDowell Health, Danville, KY
Primary Contact: Jason Dean, Administrator
CFO: William R Snapp III, Vice President and Chief Financial Officer
CMO: James Turpin, Chief of Staff
CIO: Gary Neat, Director Information Systems
CHR: Carl Metz, Vice President
Web address: www.fortloganhospital.org
Control: Other not–for–profit (including NFP Corporation) **Service**: General medical and surgical

Staffed Beds: 25

TOMPKINSVILLE—Monroe County

☐ **MONROE COUNTY MEDICAL CENTER (180105)**, 529 Capp Harlan Road, Zip 42167–1840; tel. 270/487–9231, (Nonreporting) **A**1 10 20
Primary Contact: Andrea McLerran, Chief Executive Officer
CFO: Rickie F Brown, Chief Financial Officer
CIO: Paul McKiddy, Director Information Technology
CHR: Sue Page, Director Human Resources
Web address: www.mcmccares.com
Control: Other not–for–profit (including NFP Corporation) **Service**: General medical and surgical

Staffed Beds: 49

VERSAILLES—Woodford County

★ **BLUEGRASS COMMUNITY HOSPITAL (181308)**, 360 Amsden Avenue, Zip 40383–1286; tel. 859/873–3111, (Nonreporting) **A**10 18 **S** Lifepoint Health, Brentwood, TN
Primary Contact: David P. Steitz, Chief Executive Officer
CFO: Shellie Shouse, Chief Financial Officer
CMO: Michele Welling, M.D., Chief of Staff
CHR: Marcia Carter, Director Human Resources
CNO: Kathy Russell, R.N., Chief Nursing Officer
Web address: www.bluegrasscommunityhospital.com
Control: Other not–for–profit (including NFP Corporation) **Service**: General medical and surgical

Staffed Beds: 16

Hospitals, U.S. / KENTUCKY

WEST LIBERTY—Morgan County

⇧ **MORGAN COUNTY ARH HOSPITAL (181307)**, 476 Liberty Road, Zip 41472–2049, Mailing Address: P.O. Box 579, Zip 41472–0579; tel. 606/743–3186, (Nonreporting) **A**10 18 21 **S** Appalachian Regional Healthcare, Inc., Lexington, KY
Primary Contact: Allie Archer, Chief Executive Officer and Chief Nursing Officer
COO: Paul V Miles, Chief Operating Officer
CMO: J D Miller, M.D., Vice President Medical Affairs
CIO: Jeff Brady, Director Information Systems
CHR: Lisa Redding, Manager Human Resources
CNO: Allie Archer, Chief Executive Officer and Chief Nursing Officer
Web address: www.arh.org
Control: Other not–for–profit (including NFP Corporation) **Service**: General medical and surgical

Staffed Beds: 25

WHITESBURG—Letcher County

⇧ **WHITESBURG ARH HOSPITAL (180002)**, 240 Hospital Road, Zip 41858–7627; tel. 606/633–3500, (Nonreporting) **A**3 5 10 20 21 **S** Appalachian Regional Healthcare, Inc., Lexington, KY
Primary Contact: Ellen Wright, Chief Executive Officer
COO: Paul V Miles, Vice President Administration
CMO: Ricky M Collins, M.D., Chief of Staff
CIO: Brent Styer, Director Information Technology
CHR: Daniel Fitzpatrick, Director Human Resources
Web address: https://www.arh.org/portfolio_page/whitesburg-arh-hospital/
Control: Other not–for–profit (including NFP Corporation) **Service**: General medical and surgical

Staffed Beds: 90

WILLIAMSTOWN—Grant County

☐ **ST. ELIZABETH GRANT (181311)**, 238 Barnes Road, Zip 41097–9482; tel. 859/824–8240, **A**1 10 18 **F**15 18 26 28 29 30 31 34 35 38 40 44 45 50 57 59 63 64 65 74 75 78 79 84 93 101 102 107 108 110 111 115 119 128 129 130 131 132 133 135 141 146 148 149 154 164 **S** St. Elizabeth Healthcare, Edgewood, KY
Primary Contact: Garren Colvin, Chief Executive Officer
Web address: www.stelizabeth.com
Control: Church operated, Nongovernment, not–for–profit **Service**: General medical and surgical

Staffed Beds: 17 **Admissions**: 165 **Census**: 2 **Outpatient Visits**: 70387
Births: 0 **Total Expense ($000)**: 38255 **Payroll Expense ($000)**: 13337
Personnel: 104

WINCHESTER—Clark County

⊞ **CLARK REGIONAL MEDICAL CENTER (180092)**, 175 Hospital Drive, Zip 40391–9591; tel. 859/745–3500, (Nonreporting) **A**1 2 3 10 **S** Lifepoint Health, Brentwood, TN
Primary Contact: Matt Smith, Chief Executive Officer
CFO: Samantha Patrick, Chief Financial Officer
CMO: Enio Kuvliev, M.D., Chief of Staff
CHR: Elizabeth Spencer, Director, Human Resources
CNO: Barbara Kinder, R.N., Chief Clinical Officer
Web address: www.clarkregional.org
Control: Corporation, Investor–owned (for–profit) **Service**: General medical and surgical

Staffed Beds: 79

Hospital, Medicare Provider Number, Address, Telephone, Approval, Facility, and Physician Codes, Health Care System

★ American Hospital Association (AHA) membership
☐ The Joint Commission accreditation
○ Healthcare Facilities Accreditation Program
◇ DNV Healthcare Inc. accreditation
⇧ Center for Improvement in Healthcare Quality Accreditation
△ Commission on Accreditation of Rehabilitation Facilities (CARF) accreditation

LOUISIANA

ABBEVILLE—Vermilion Parish

ABBEVILLE GENERAL HOSPITAL (190034), 118 North Hospital Drive, Zip 70510-4077, Mailing Address: P.O. Box 580, Zip 70511-0580; tel. 337/893-5466, **A**1 10 **F**3 13 15 29 30 31 34 37 39 40 45 49 50 51 54 59 60 64 65 66 70 75 76 78 79 81 82 85 86 87 89 97 98 100 102 103 104 107 108 110 111 114 115 119 126 127 128 130 133 144 149 154 156 160 164 167 169 **P**6
Primary Contact: Michael Bertrand, Chief Executive Officer
COO: Tom Pigott, Chief Operating Officer
CFO: William T. Hair, Chief Financial Officer
CMO: Weston Miller, M.D., Chief Medical Officer
CIO: Charles W Guidry, Chief Information Officer
CNO: Heidi Broussard, Chief Nursing Officer
Web address: www.abbgen.net
Control: Hospital district or authority, Government, Nonfederal **Service**: General medical and surgical

Staffed Beds: 60 Admissions: 2063 Census: 26 Outpatient Visits: 122459
Births: 294 Total Expense ($000): 71554 Payroll Expense ($000): 33451
Personnel: 430

ALEXANDRIA—Rapides Parish

CENTRAL LOUISIANA SURGICAL HOSPITAL (190298), 651 North Bolton Avenue, Zip 71301-7449, Mailing Address: P.O. Box 8646, Zip 71306-1646; tel. 318/443-3511, (Nonreporting) **A**10 21 **S** CHRISTUS Health, Irving, TX
Primary Contact: Erin Roes, R.N., MSN, Chief Executive Officer
COO: Erin Roes, R.N., MSN, Chief Operating Officer
CFO: Steven Schaeffer, Director of Finance
CMO: Renick Webb, M.D., Chief Medical Director
CHR: Debbie Norman, Director Human Resources
CNO: Carol Wells, R.N., MSN, Chief Nursing Officer
Web address: www.clshospital.com
Control: Corporation, Investor-owned (for-profit) **Service**: Surgical

Staffed Beds: 24

CHRISTUS DUBUIS HOSPITAL OF ALEXANDRIA (192012), 3330 Masonic Drive, 4th Floor, Zip 71301-3841; tel. 318/448-4938, (Nonreporting) **A**1 10 **S** LHC Group, Lafayette, LA
Primary Contact: George Patrick. DeRouen, Administrator
CNO: Kimberly Bennett, R.N., Director of Nursing
Web address: https://lhcgroup.com/locations/christus-dubuis-hospital-of-alexandria/
Control: Church operated, Nongovernment, not-for-profit **Service**: Acute long-term care hospital

Staffed Beds: 25

CHRISTUS ST. FRANCES CABRINI HOSPITAL (190019), 3330 Masonic Drive, Zip 71301-3899; tel. 318/487-1122, **A**1 2 10 **F**3 11 12 13 15 18 20 22 24 26 28 29 30 31 34 35 40 45 46 49 57 58 59 64 66 70 72 74 75 76 78 79 81 82 84 85 86 87 89 90 91 93 98 102 104 105 107 108 110 111 114 115 116 117 118 119 120 121 124 126 129 130 131 132 135 144 146 147 148 149 156 167 **S** CHRISTUS Health, Irving, TX
Primary Contact: Monte A. Wilson, President and Chief Executive Officer
COO: Lisa R. Lauve, R.N., Regional Chief Nursing Executive and Chief Operating Officer
CFO: Jason R. Miller, Chief Financial Officer
CHR: Wendy Chandler, Regional Vice President Human Resources
CNO: Shannon C. Forrest, R.N., Chief Nursing Officer
Web address: www.cabrini.org/
Control: Church operated, Nongovernment, not-for-profit **Service**: General medical and surgical

Staffed Beds: 293 Admissions: 12487 Census: 191 Outpatient Visits: 269398 Births: 1112 Total Expense ($000): 354655 Payroll Expense ($000): 111761 Personnel: 1312

COMPASS BEHAVIORAL CENTER OF ALEXANDRIA (194106), 6410 Masonic Drve, Zip 71301-2319; tel. 318/442-3163, **A**10 **F**29 54 98 100 102 153 154 **S** Compass Health, Crowley, LA
Primary Contact: Jeremy Autin, Chief Executive Officer
CNO: Cheryl Lachney, Director of Nursing
Web address: https://www.compasshealthcare.com
Control: Corporation, Investor-owned (for-profit) **Service**: Psychiatric

Staffed Beds: 18 Admissions: 531 Census: 13 Outpatient Visits: 0
Births: 0

ENCOMPASS HEALTH REHABILITATION HOSPITAL OF ALEXANDRIA (193031), 104 North Third Street, Zip 71301-8581; tel. 318/449-1370, (Nonreporting) **A**1 10 **S** Encompass Health Corporation, Birmingham, AL
Primary Contact: Joanna Williams, Chief Executive Officer
CFO: Brenda Forbes, Interim Controller
CMO: Vasudeva Dhulipala, M.D., Medical Director
CHR: Suzie Wagner, Director Human Resources
Web address: https://encompasshealth.com/alexandriarehab
Control: Partnership, Investor-owned (for-profit) **Service**: Rehabilitation

Staffed Beds: 47

LONGLEAF HOSPITAL (194022), 44 Versailles Boulevard, Zip 71303-3960; tel. 318/445-5111, **A**1 10 **F**4 5 29 34 35 38 50 57 64 98 99 100 101 102 103 132 143 151 153 154 157 160 164 **P**5 **S** Acadia Healthcare Company, Inc., Franklin, TN
Primary Contact: Jared Ferguson, Chief Executive Officer
CFO: Ashley Knippers, Chief Financial Officer
CNO: Felicia Wigley, R.N., Director of Nursing
Web address: www.longleafhospital.com
Control: Corporation, Investor-owned (for-profit) **Service**: Psychiatric

Staffed Beds: 139 Admissions: 5135 Census: 114 Outpatient Visits: 0
Births: 0

OCEANS BEHAVIORAL HOSPITAL OF ALEXANDRIA (194096), 2621 North Bolton Avenue, Zip 71303-4506; tel. 318/448-8473, (Nonreporting) **A**1 10 **S** Oceans Healthcare, Plano, TX
Primary Contact: Justin McDaniel, R.N., Administrator
Web address: https://oceanshealthcare.com/ohc-location/alexandria/
Control: Corporation, Investor-owned (for-profit) **Service**: Psychiatric

Staffed Beds: 24

RAPIDES REGIONAL MEDICAL CENTER (190026), 211 Fourth Street, Zip 71301-8421; tel. 318/769-3000, (Nonreporting) **A**1 3 5 10 **S** HCA Healthcare, Nashville, TN
Primary Contact: Vernon Jones II, Chief Executive Officer
CFO: William Davis, Chief Financial Officer
CMO: Sara Kelly, D.O., Chief Medical Officer
CHR: Stephen W Scull, Vice President Ethics and Compliance officer
CNO: Katlin Bolton, R.N., Chief Nursing Officer
Web address: www.rapidesregional.com
Control: Partnership, Investor-owned (for-profit) **Service**: General medical and surgical

Staffed Beds: 365

RIVERSIDE HOSPITAL (192043), 13 Heyman Lane, Zip 71303-3574; tel. 318/767-2900, (Nonreporting) **A**1 10
Primary Contact: Amy Perry Grimes, Chief Executive Officer
COO: Amy Perry Grimes, Chief Operating Officer
CNO: Michael Parham, R.N., Chief Nursing Officer
Web address: www.riversidehospital.net
Control: Corporation, Investor-owned (for-profit) **Service**: Acute long-term care hospital

Staffed Beds: 27

AMITE—Tangipahoa Parish

HOOD MEMORIAL HOSPITAL (191309), 301 Walnut Street, Zip 70422-2098; tel. 985/748-9485, (Nonreporting) **A**10 18
Primary Contact: Michael Whittington, R.N., Chief Executive Officer
CFO: Mike Estay, Chief Financial Officer
CMO: Richard Bridges, M.D., Chief of Staff
CIO: Schley Harvin, Information Technology Technician
CHR: Alicia Chatelain, Director Human Resource
CNO: Todd Acosta, R.N., Chief Nursing Officer
Web address: www.hoodmemorial.com
Control: Hospital district or authority, Government, Nonfederal **Service**: General medical and surgical

Staffed Beds: 25

Hospitals, U.S. / LOUISIANA

ARCADIA—Bienville Parish

BIENVILLE MEDICAL CENTER (191320), 1175 Pine Street, Suite 200, Zip 71001-3122; tel. 318/263-4700, (Nonreporting) **A**5 10 18 **S** Allegiance Health Management, Shreveport, LA
Primary Contact: Kirk Lemoine, Chief Executive Officer
Web address: www.bienvillemedicalcenter.net/
Control: Other not-for-profit (including NFP Corporation) **Service**: General medical and surgical

Staffed Beds: 21

BASTROP—Morehouse Parish

☐ **CYPRESS GROVE BEHAVIORAL HEALTH (194083)**, 4673 Eugene Ware Boulevard, Zip 71220-1425; tel. 318/281-2448, (Nonreporting) **A**1 10
Primary Contact: Tony Lambert, Administrator
COO: Christine Murphy, MS, Chief Operating Officer
CFO: Paul Coburn, Chief Financial Officer
CMO: Tommy Dansby, Chief Medical Officer
CHR: Lindsay Cobb, Director Human Resources
CNO: Shelly Hoard RN, Director of Nursing
Web address: https://ldh.la.gov/index.cfm/directory/detail/18238/catid/169
Control: Corporation, Investor-owned (for-profit) **Service**: Psychiatric

Staffed Beds: 60

★ **MOREHOUSE GENERAL HOSPITAL (190116)**, 323 West Walnut Avenue, Zip 71220-4521, Mailing Address: P.O. Box 1060, Zip 71221-1060; tel. 318/283-3600, (Nonreporting) **A**10
Primary Contact: Elmore Patterson, Chief Executive Officer
COO: John Bowie, Chief Operating Officer
CFO: Jason Bonner, Interim Chief Financial, Accounting Analyst
CMO: John Coats, M.D., Chief Medical Staff
CIO: B J Vail, Director Information Systems
CHR: Debbie Spann, Director Human Resources
CNO: Janet Ashlock, Chief Nursing Officer
Web address: www.mghospital.com
Control: Hospital district or authority, Government, Nonfederal **Service**: General medical and surgical

Staffed Beds: 59

STERLINGTON REHABILITATION HOSPITAL (193069), 370 W Hickory Ave, Zip 71220-4442, Mailing Address: P.O. Box 627, Sterlington, Zip 71280-0627; tel. 318/665-9950, **A**10 **F**28 34 35 56 59 64 65 66 75 86 90 91 93 96 97 104 127 130 143 147 148 153 154 **P**5
Primary Contact: Catherine M. Waldrop, Administrator
Web address: https://sterlingtonrehab.com/
Control: Corporation, Investor-owned (for-profit) **Service**: Rehabilitation

Staffed Beds: 10 **Admissions:** 210 **Census:** 7 **Outpatient Visits:** 631
Births: 0 **Total Expense ($000):** 8605 **Payroll Expense ($000):** 5438
Personnel: 57

BASTROP—Ouachita Parish

RIVERBEND REHABILITATION HOSPITAL (193058), 323 W Walnut Ave, Zip 71220-4521, Mailing Address: 4310 South Grand Street, Monroe, Zip 71202-6322; tel. 318/654-8300, (Nonreporting) **A**10
Primary Contact: Stephen J. Florentine, Administrator
CMO: Jeffery Combetta, M.D., Medical Director
CHR: Rhonda Church, Director Human Resources
Web address: www.dss.state.la.us/directory/office/9151
Control: Corporation, Investor-owned (for-profit) **Service**: Rehabilitation

Staffed Beds: 12

BATON ROUGE—East Baton Rouge Parish

☐ **APOLLO BEHAVIORAL HEALTH HOSPITAL (194105)**, 9938 Airline Highway, Zip 70816-8193; tel. 225/663-2881, (Nonreporting) **A**1 10
Primary Contact: Gopinath Gopalam, Administrator and Chief Executive Officer
CNO: Clay Aguillard, R.N., Director of Nursing
Web address: www.apollo-bhh.com/about-us
Control: Other not-for-profit (including NFP Corporation) **Service**: Psychiatric

Staffed Beds: 24

☐ **BATON ROUGE BEHAVIORAL HOSPITAL (194107)**, 4040 North Boulevard, Zip 70806-3829; tel. 225/300-8470, (Nonreporting) **A**1 10 **S** Oglethorpe Recovery and Behavioral Hospitals, Tampa, FL
Primary Contact: Larry Godfrey, Chief Executive Officer
COO: James O'Shea, Chief Operating Officer
CFO: Warren Knight, Chief Financial Officer
CMO: Richard Capiola, M.D., Chief Medical Officer
CNO: Francine Mineau, Chief Nursing Officer
Web address: www.batonrougebehavioral.com
Control: Corporation, Investor-owned (for-profit) **Service**: Psychiatric

Staffed Beds: 15

BATON ROUGE GEN HEALTH CENTER See Baton Rouge General Medical Center–Bluebonnet

☐ **BATON ROUGE GENERAL MEDICAL CENTER (190065)**, 8585 Picardy Avenue, Zip 70809-3679; tel. 225/763-4000, (Includes BATON ROUGE GENERAL MEDICAL CENTER–BLUEBONNET, 8585 Picardy Avenue, Baton Rouge, Louisiana, Zip 70809-3679, P O Box 84330, Zip 70884-4330, tel. 225/763-4000; Edgardo J. Tenreiro, FACHE, President, Chief Executive Officer and Chief Operating Officer; BATON ROUGE GENERAL–ASCENSION, 14105 Highway 73, Suites 100 & 201, Prairieville, Louisiana, Zip 70769-3626, tel. 225/402-2600; Edgardo J. Tenreiro, FACHE, President and Chief Executive Officer) (Nonreporting) **A**1 2 3 5 10 19 **S** General Health System, Baton Rouge, LA
Primary Contact: Edgardo J. Tenreiro, FACHE, President and Chief Executive Officer
COO: Stephen Mumford, Chief Operating Officer
CFO: Kendall Johnson, Chief Financial Officer
CIO: Bennett Cheramie, Vice President Information Technology
CHR: Paul Douglas, Vice President Human Resources
CNO: Monica Nijoka, Chief Nursing Officer
Web address: www.brgeneral.org
Control: Other not-for-profit (including NFP Corporation) **Service**: General medical and surgical

Staffed Beds: 360

☐ **BATON ROUGE REHABILITATION HOSPITAL (193028)**, 8595 United Plaza Boulevard, Zip 70809-2251; tel. 225/927-0567, (Nonreporting) **A**1 10
Primary Contact: Trisha Guidry, Administrator
CFO: Nicholas Hluchy, Business Analyst, Support Services Manager
CMO: Catalina R. Negulescu, M.D., Medical Officer
CIO: Laura Simon, R.N., MSN, Director Quality Operations and Nursing
CHR: Michelle Smith, Coordinator Human Resources
CNO: Laura Simon, R.N., MSN, Director, Quality Operations and Nursing
Web address: www.brrehab.com
Control: Corporation, Investor-owned (for-profit) **Service**: Rehabilitation

Staffed Beds: 80

BETHESDA REHABILITATION HOSPITAL (193092), 7414 Sumrall Drive, Zip 70812-1240; tel. 225/767-2034, (Nonreporting) **A**10
Primary Contact: Lionel Murphy, Chief Executive Officer
CNO: Yolanda Scales, R.N., Director of Nursing
Control: Corporation, Investor-owned (for-profit) **Service**: Rehabilitation

Staffed Beds: 18

☐ **KPC PROMISE HOSPITAL OF BATON ROUGE (192004)**, 5130 Mancuso Lane, Zip 70809-3583; tel. 225/490-9600, (Nonreporting) **A**1 10 **S** KPC Healthcare, Inc., Santa Ana, CA
Primary Contact: LaTeka Tanette. Johnson, Chief Executive Officer
COO: Michael R Sanders, MS, Chief Operating Officer
CFO: Trina Arceneaux, Assistant Chief Financial Officer
CMO: Subhaker Gummadi, M.D., Chief Medical Staff
CIO: Charmaine T Mosby, Area Director Health Information Management
CHR: Marilyn Hamilton, Director Human Resources
CNO: Larrie Arceneaux, Chief Clinical Officer
Web address: www.batonrouge.kpcph.com/
Control: Corporation, Investor-owned (for-profit) **Service**: Acute long-term care hospital

Staffed Beds: 54

☐ **OCEANS BEHAVIORAL HOSPITAL OF BATON ROUGE – SOUTH (194086)**, 11135 Florida Boulevard, Zip 70815-2013; tel. 225/356-7030, (Nonreporting) **A**1 10 **S** Oceans Healthcare, Plano, TX
Primary Contact: Valerie Dalton, R.N., Administrator
Web address: www.obhbr.info/
Control: Corporation, Investor-owned (for-profit) **Service**: Psychiatric

Staffed Beds: 20

Hospital, Medicare Provider Number, Address, Telephone, Approval, Facility, and Physician Codes, Health Care System

★ American Hospital Association (AHA) membership ◯ Healthcare Facilities Accreditation Program ⇑ Center for Improvement in Healthcare Quality Accreditation
☐ The Joint Commission accreditation ◇ DNV Healthcare Inc. accreditation △ Commission on Accreditation of Rehabilitation Facilities (CARF) accreditation

Hospitals, U.S. / LOUISIANA

☩ **OCHSNER MEDICAL CENTER – BATON ROUGE (190202)**, 17000 Medical Center Drive, Zip 70816–3224; tel. 225/752–2470, **A**1 10 **F**3 11 12 13 15 18 20 22 24 26 28 29 30 31 34 35 36 40 41 42 44 45 46 47 48 49 51 54 57 58 59 60 61 64 65 68 70 72 74 75 76 77 78 79 81 82 84 85 86 87 93 97 102 104 107 108 110 111 114 116 117 119 126 129 130 131 132 135 144 146 147 148 154 165 167 169 **P**6 **S** Ochsner Health, New Orleans, LA
Primary Contact: Charles D. Daigle, Chief Executive Officer
CFO: Stephen Pepitone, Interim Chief Financial Officer
CMO: F Ralph Dauterive, M.D., Vice President Medical Affairs
CHR: Amanda Seals, Assistant Vice President, Human Resource Business Partner
Web address: https://www.ochsner.org/locations/ochsner-medical-center-baton-rouge
Control: Other not–for–profit (including NFP Corporation) **Service**: General medical and surgical

Staffed Beds: 169 **Admissions**: 7662 **Census**: 88 **Outpatient Visits**: 102970 **Births**: 1572 **Total Expense ($000)**: 390269 **Payroll Expense ($000)**: 131192 **Personnel**: 1526

☩ **OUR LADY OF THE LAKE REGIONAL MEDICAL CENTER (190064)**, 5000 Hennessy Boulevard, Zip 70808–4375; tel. 225/765–6565, (Includes OUR LADY OF THE LAKE ASCENSION, 1125 West Highway 30, Gonzales, Louisiana, Zip 70737–5004, tel. 225/647–5000; Charles L. Spicer Jr, FACHE, President; OUR LADY OF THE LAKE CHILDREN'S HOSPITAL, 8300 Constantin Boulevard, Baton Rouge, Louisiana, Zip 70809–3489, tel. 225/374–1300; Jonathan Brouk, President) **A**1 2 3 5 8 10 **F**3 8 12 14 15 17 18 20 22 24 26 28 29 30 31 32 34 35 38 39 40 41 42 43 44 45 46 47 48 49 50 51 53 54 55 57 58 59 60 61 64 65 66 67 68 70 72 74 75 77 78 79 80 81 82 84 85 87 88 89 90 95 96 97 98 99 100 101 102 103 104 107 108 110 111 115 116 117 118 119 126 127 128 129 130 131 135 144 146 147 148 149 150 154 156 158 162 164 165 167 **P**6 **S** Franciscan Missionaries of Our Lady Health System, Inc., Baton Rouge, LA
Primary Contact: Charles L. Spicer Jr, FACHE, President, Baton Rouge Market and Northshore Market
COO: Logan Austin, Chief Operating Officer
CFO: Jennifer Clowers, Regional Chief Financial Officer
CMO: Catherine O'Neal, M.D., Chief Medical Officer
CIO: Avery Cloud, Chief Information Officer
CNO: Nicole Telhiard, Senior Vice President, Patient Care Services
Web address: https://www.fmolhs.org/locations/greater-baton-rouge/our-lady-of-the-lake-regional-medical-center
Control: Church operated, Nongovernment, not–for–profit **Service**: General medical and surgical

Staffed Beds: 875 **Admissions**: 34972 **Census**: 519 **Outpatient Visits**: 514857 **Births**: 0 **Total Expense ($000)**: 1342880 **Payroll Expense ($000)**: 338993 **Personnel**: 5855

☐ **REGIONS BEHAVIORAL HOSPITAL (194115)**, 8416 Cumberland Place, Zip 70806–6543; tel. 225/408–6060, (Nonreporting) **A**1 10
Primary Contact: Robert Stephen. Richardson Jr, Administrator
COO: Marc Crawford, Chief Operating Officer
CHR: Julia Perry, Director Human Resources
Web address: https://www.regionsbh.com/
Control: Corporation, Investor–owned (for–profit) **Service**: Psychiatric

Staffed Beds: 24

SAGE REHABILITATION HOSPITAL (193078), 8000 Summa Avenue, Zip 70809–3423, Mailing Address: P.O. Box 82681, Zip 70884–2681; tel. 225/819–0703, (Nonreporting) **A**10 **S** The Carpenter Health Network, Baton Rouge, LA
Primary Contact: Leonard Greg. Crider, Administrator
CMO: Christopher Belleau, M.D., Medical Director
CHR: Kathy Ringe, Director Human Resources
CNO: Beth Sibley, Director of Nursing
Web address: www.sage-rehab.org
Control: Individual, Investor–owned (for–profit) **Service**: Rehabilitation

Staffed Beds: 45

☐ **SEASIDE HEALTH SYSTEM – BATON ROUGE (194103)**, 4363 Convention Street, Zip 70806–3906, Mailing Address: 4363 Convention Stret, Zip 70806–3906; tel. 225/238–3043, **A**1 10 **F**4 5 29 38 68 98 100 101 102 104 105 106 132 135 143 149 151 152 154 160 164 165
Primary Contact: Clay Aguillard, R.N., Chief Executive Officer
Web address: https://www.seasidehc.com/
Control: Corporation, Investor–owned (for–profit) **Service**: Psychiatric

Staffed Beds: 50 **Admissions**: 1912 **Census**: 38 **Outpatient Visits**: 0 **Births**: 0 **Personnel**: 63

☐ **SURGICAL SPECIALTY CENTER OF BATON ROUGE (190251)**, 8080 Bluebonnet Boulevard, Zip 70810–7827; tel. 225/408–8080, (Nonreporting) **A**1 10
Primary Contact: Ann Heine, Chief Executive Officer
CFO: Kathryn Ponder, Chief Financial Officer
CNO: Kari Ulrich, R.N., Chief Nursing Officer, Director Operating Room
Web address: www.sscbr.com
Control: Corporation, Investor–owned (for–profit) **Service**: Surgical

Staffed Beds: 14

THE GENERAL (190316), 3600 Florida Street, Suite 2020, Zip 70806–3842; tel. 225/381–6393, (Nonreporting) **A**10 **S** General Health System, Baton Rouge, LA
Primary Contact: Edgardo J. Tenreiro, FACHE, President and Chief Executive Officer
CMO: Aaron DeWitt, Chief Medical Officer
CNO: Angela Clouatre, MSN, R.N., Chief Nursing Officer
Control: Other not–for–profit (including NFP Corporation) **Service**: General medical and surgical

Staffed Beds: 137

THE NEUROMEDICAL CENTER REHABILITATION HOSPITAL (193090), 10101 Park Rowe Avenue, Suite 500, Zip 70810–1685; tel. 225/906–2999, (Nonreporting) **A**10 **S** AMG Integrated Healthcare Management, Lafayette, LA
Primary Contact: Bradley Pevey, Chief Executive Officer
Web address: www.theneuromedicalcenter.com
Control: Corporation, Investor–owned (for–profit) **Service**: Rehabilitation

Staffed Beds: 23

THE SPINE HOSPITAL OF LOUISIANA AT THE NEUROMEDICAL CENTER (190266), 10105 Park Rowe Circle, Suite 250, Zip 70810–1684; tel. 225/763–9900, (Nonreporting) **A**10
Primary Contact: Terri Hicks, Chief Executive Officer
CFO: Allison Doherty, Chief Financial Officer
CMO: Greg Fautheree, M.D., Medical Director
CIO: Jeremy Deprato, Director Information Technology
CHR: Kimberly Jones, Director Human Resources
CNO: Kim Pettijohn, R.N., MSN, Chief Nursing Officer
Web address: www.theneuromedicalcenter.com
Control: Corporation, Investor–owned (for–profit) **Service**: Surgical

Staffed Beds: 23

☩ **WOMAN'S HOSPITAL (190128)**, 100 Woman's Way, Zip 70817–5100, Mailing Address: P.O. Box 95009, Zip 70895–9009; tel. 225/927–1300, **A**1 2 3 5 10 **F**3 11 12 13 15 29 31 32 34 35 36 38 40 44 45 50 53 55 58 59 60 61 66 68 70 72 74 76 77 78 81 85 86 87 97 100 104 107 108 109 110 111 115 116 117 118 119 120 121 123 124 126 130 132 146 147 149 154 156 157 160 162 167 169 **P**6
Primary Contact: Rene J. Ragas, FACHE, President and Chief Executive Officer
COO: Stephanie Anderson, Executive Vice President and Chief Operating Officer
CFO: Nina Dusang, Chief Financial Officer
CMO: Dore Binder, M.D., Chief Medical Officer
CIO: Paul Kirk, Vice President
CHR: Donna L Bodin, Vice President
CNO: Cheri Barker Johnson, MSN, Executive Vice President/Chief Nursing Officer
Web address: www.womans.org
Control: Other not–for–profit (including NFP Corporation) **Service**: Obstetrics and gynecology

Staffed Beds: 228 **Admissions**: 10890 **Census**: 142 **Outpatient Visits**: 152381 **Births**: 7941 **Total Expense ($000)**: 432968 **Payroll Expense ($000)**: 164375 **Personnel**: 2279

BERNICE—Union Parish

REEVES MEMORIAL MEDICAL CENTER (191326), 409 First Street, Zip 71222–4001, Mailing Address: P.O. Box 697, Zip 71222–0697; tel. 318/285–9066, (Nonreporting) **A**5 10 18
Primary Contact: David Caston, Chief Executive Officer
COO: Beth Jones, Chief Operating Officer
CFO: Robert Welch, Chief Financial Officer
CMO: R Brian Harris, M.D., Chief of Staff
CIO: Scott Dickson, Director Information Technology
CHR: Robin Adams, Director Human Resources
CNO: Beth Jones, Director of Nursing
Web address: www.reevesmemorial.com/
Control: Hospital district or authority, Government, Nonfederal **Service**: General medical and surgical

Staffed Beds: 11

Hospitals, U.S. / LOUISIANA

BOGALUSA—Washington Parish

OUR LADY OF THE ANGELS HOSPITAL (190312), 433 Plaza Street, Zip 70427–3793; tel. 985/730–6700, (Includes BOGALUSA COMMUNITY MEDICAL CENTER, 433 Plaza Street, Bogalusa, Louisiana, Zip 70427–3793, tel. 985/730–6700) **A**1 3 5 10 **F**3 13 15 28 29 30 34 35 40 45 47 49 50 57 59 61 64 65 66 70 74 75 76 77 79 81 85 87 91 93 98 100 104 107 110 111 115 119 130 135 148 149 154 160 167 169 **S** Franciscan Missionaries of Our Lady Health System, Inc., Baton Rouge, LA
Primary Contact: Charles L. Spicer Jr, FACHE, President, Baton Rouge Market and Northshore Market
CFO: Brooke Cummings, Chief Financial Officer
CMO: Brian J. Galofaro, M.D., Chief Medical Officer
CIO: Mike Gilly, Chief Information Officer
CHR: Christi Brown, Director Human Resources
CNO: Mark Kellar, R.N., Interim Chief Nursing Officer
Web address: www.oloah.org
Control: Other not–for–profit (including NFP Corporation) **Service**: General medical and surgical

Staffed Beds: 46 **Admissions**: 1965 **Census**: 23 **Outpatient Visits**: 119056
Births: 250 **Total Expense ($000)**: 79894 **Payroll Expense ($000)**: 30692
Personnel: 461

BOSSIER CITY—Bossier Parish

CORNERSTONE SPECIALTY HOSPITALS BOSSIER CITY (192006), 4900 Medical Drive, Zip 71112–4521; tel. 318/747–9500, (Nonreporting) **A**1 10 **S** ScionHealth, Louisville, KY
Primary Contact: Sheri Burnette, R.N., Chief Executive Officer
CMO: James Jackson, M.D., Chief of Staff
CNO: Tamara Grimm, R.N., Chief Clinical Officer and Chief Nursing Officer
Web address: www.chghospitals.com/
Control: Corporation, Investor–owned (for–profit) **Service**: Acute long–term care hospital

Staffed Beds: 54

PATHWAY REHABILITATION HOSPITAL OF BOSSIER (193094), 4900 Medical Drive, Zip 71112–4521; tel. 318/841–5555, (Nonreporting) **A**10 21
Primary Contact: James Manning, Administrator
Web address: www.pathrehab.com
Control: Corporation, Investor–owned (for–profit) **Service**: Rehabilitation

Staffed Beds: 24

PROMISE HOSPITAL OF BOSSIER CITY See Promise Hospital of Louisiana – Bossier City Campus

RED RIVER BEHAVIORAL CENTER (194079), 2800 Melrose Avenue, Zip 71111–5870; tel. 318/549–2033, (Nonreporting) **A**10
Primary Contact: Rod Baronet, Chief Executive Officer
CNO: John Crumpler, R.N., Director of Nursing
Web address: www.redriverbc.com
Control: Partnership, Investor–owned (for–profit) **Service**: Psychiatric

Staffed Beds: 20

WILLIS–KNIGHT BOSSIER See Willis Knight Bossier

BREAUX BRIDGE—St. Martin Parish

GENESIS BEHAVIORAL HOSPITAL (194089), 606 Latiolais Drive, Zip 70517–4231, Mailing Address: PO BOX 159, Zip 70517–0159; tel. 337/442–6254, (Nonreporting) **A**10
Primary Contact: William Arledge, Administrator and Chief Financial Officer
COO: Gretchen Kaltenbach, R.N., Chief Operating Officer
CFO: William Arledge, Administrator and Chief Financial Officer
Web address: www.genesisbh.com/
Control: Corporation, Investor–owned (for–profit) **Service**: Psychiatric

Staffed Beds: 18

OCHSNER ST. MARTIN HOSPITAL (191302), 210 Champagne Boulevard, Zip 70517–3700, Mailing Address: P.O. Box 357, Zip 70517–0357; tel. 337/332–2178, **A**10 18 **F**3 8 15 18 20 22 28 29 30 34 35 40 45 50 57 59 64 68 75 77 81 87 91 93 96 107 108 110 111 114 115 119 127 130 133 148 149 154 156 **S** Ochsner Health, New Orleans, LA
Primary Contact: Jennifer Vicknair, R.N., Assistant Vice President, Nursing and Hospital Administration
CFO: Shadelle Huval, Director Finance
CHR: Rena B Mouisset, Director Human Resources and Contract Compliance
Web address: www.stmartinhospital.org
Control: Other not–for–profit (including NFP Corporation) **Service**: General medical and surgical

Staffed Beds: 25 **Admissions**: 551 **Census**: 17 **Outpatient Visits**: 33291
Births: 0 **Total Expense ($000)**: 32389 **Payroll Expense ($000)**: 13976
Personnel: 178

BROUSSARD—Lafayette Parish

OCEANS BEHAVIORAL HOSPITAL OF BROUSSARD (194073), 418 Albertson Parkway, Zip 70518–4971; tel. 337/237–6444, (Nonreporting) **A**1 10 **S** Oceans Healthcare, Plano, TX
Primary Contact: Amy Dysart–Credeur, Administrator
Web address: www.obhb.info/
Control: Corporation, Investor–owned (for–profit) **Service**: Psychiatric

Staffed Beds: 38

BUNKIE—Avoyelles Parish

BEACON BEHAVIORAL HOSPITAL (194112), 323 Evergreen Street, Zip 71322–1307; tel. 318/346–3143, (Nonreporting) **A**10
Primary Contact: Sean Wendell, CPA, Chief Executive Officer
CNO: Charlene Kessler, R.N., Director of Nursing
Web address: www.beaconbh.com
Control: Other not–for–profit (including NFP Corporation) **Service**: Psychiatric

Staffed Beds: 17

BUNKIE GENERAL HOSPITAL (191311), 427 Evergreen Street, Zip 71322; tel. 318/346–6681, (Nonreporting) **A**10 18
Primary Contact: Linda F. Deville, Chief Executive Officer
CFO: Layla Chase, Interim Chief Financial Officer
CMO: Mohit Srivastava, M.D., Chief of Staff
CIO: Kiland Jackson, Chief Information Officer
CHR: Tina Louise Juneau, Director Human Resources
CNO: Corey Jeansonne, Chief Nursing Officer
Web address: https://www.mercybh.com/
Control: Hospital district or authority, Government, Nonfederal **Service**: General medical and surgical

Staffed Beds: 18

CHALMETTE—Saint Bernard Parish

ST. BERNARD PARISH HOSPITAL (190308), 8000 West Judge Perez Drive, Zip 70043–1668; tel. 504/826–9500, **A**1 10 **F**3 20 22 29 34 35 40 41 43 44 45 50 53 57 59 64 65 70 77 79 81 82 86 87 93 107 108 111 115 119 130 135 146 148 154 156 167 **S** Ochsner Health, New Orleans, LA
Primary Contact: Alanna Fast, Chief Executive Officer
CFO: Anthony Bonnecarrere, Controller
CMO: Paul Verrette, M.D., Chief Medical Officer
CIO: Zane Looney, Chief Information Officer
CHR: Melody M O'Connell, Director Human Resources
CNO: Janice Kishner, R.N., FACHE, Chief Clinical Officer
Web address: www.sbph.net
Control: Hospital district or authority, Government, Nonfederal **Service**: General medical and surgical

Staffed Beds: 24 **Admissions**: 1246 **Census**: 12 **Outpatient Visits**: 43506
Births: 0 **Total Expense ($000)**: 87986 **Payroll Expense ($000)**: 24338
Personnel: 292

Hospital, Medicare Provider Number, Address, Telephone, Approval, Facility, and Physician Codes, Health Care System

★ American Hospital Association (AHA) membership
☐ The Joint Commission accreditation
○ Healthcare Facilities Accreditation Program
◇ DNV Healthcare Inc. accreditation
⇑ Center for Improvement in Healthcare Quality Accreditation
△ Commission on Accreditation of Rehabilitation Facilities (CARF) accreditation

Hospitals, U.S. / LOUISIANA

CHURCH POINT—Acadia Parish

ACADIA–ST. LANDRY HOSPITAL (191319), 810 South Broadway Street, Zip 70525-4497; tel. 337/684-5435, (Nonreporting) **A**10 18
Primary Contact: Michael LeJeune, Chief Executive Officer
CFO: Tiffany Young, Chief Financial Officer
CMO: Ty Hargroder, M.D., Chief of Staff
CNO: Phyllis Faul, R.N., Chief Nursing Officer
Web address: www.aslh.org
Control: Other not-for-profit (including NFP Corporation) **Service**: General medical and surgical

Staffed Beds: 25

COLUMBIA—Caldwell Parish

CALDWELL MEMORIAL HOSPITAL (190190), 411 Main Street, Zip 71418-6704, Mailing Address: P.O. Box 899, Zip 71418-0899; tel. 318/649-6111, (Nonreporting) **A**5 10
Primary Contact: Danielle H. Williams, Administrator
COO: Lisa Patrick, Chief Operating Officer
CFO: William H Clark, Chief Financial Officer
CNO: Debbie Bailes, R.N., Director of Nursing
Web address: https://www.mycaldwellmemorial.com/
Control: Other not-for-profit (including NFP Corporation) **Service**: General medical and surgical

Staffed Beds: 47

CITIZENS MEDICAL CENTER (190184), 7939 US Highway 165, Zip 71418-1079, Mailing Address: P.O. Box 1079, Zip 71418-1079; tel. 318/649-6106, (Nonreporting) **A**5 10
Primary Contact: Steve Barbo, R.N., Chief Executive Officer
Web address: www.citizensmedcenter.com/
Control: Hospital district or authority, Government, Nonfederal **Service**: General medical and surgical

Staffed Beds: 40

COUSHATTA—Red River Parish

CHRISTUS COUSHATTA HEALTH CARE CENTER (191312), 1635 Marvel Street, Zip 71019-9022, Mailing Address: P.O. Box 589, Zip 71019-0589; tel. 318/932-2000, **A**1 10 18 **F**3 8 15 28 29 30 34 39 40 45 59 68 81 107 110 119 127 130 133 148 154 **S** CHRISTUS Health, Irving, TX
Primary Contact: Brandon Hillman, R.N., Administrator
CFO: Bryan Pannagl, Chief Financial Officer
CMO: Jonathan Weisul, M.D., Vice President Medical Affairs and Chief Medical Officer
CIO: Bruce Honea, Director Information Services
CHR: Donnette Craig, Director Human Resources
CNO: Celia Carr, MSN, R.N., Director of Nursing
Web address: www.christuscoushatta.org
Control: Church operated, Nongovernment, not-for-profit **Service**: General medical and surgical

Staffed Beds: 25 **Admissions**: 441 **Census**: 7 **Outpatient Visits**: 24022 **Births**: 0 **Total Expense ($000)**: 24091 **Payroll Expense ($000)**: 9458 **Personnel**: 149

SPECIALTY REHABILITATION HOSPITAL OF COUSHATTA (193080), 1110 Ringgold Avenue Suite B, Zip 71019-9073; tel. 318/932-1770, (Nonreporting) **A**10
Primary Contact: Craig Ball, Chief Executive Officer
COO: Charlie Ball, Chief Operating Officer
CFO: Connie Ball, Chief Financial Officer
CMO: Jalal Joudeh, M.D., Chief Medical Officer
CHR: Denise Logan, Director Human Resources
Web address: www.specialtyhealthcare.com
Control: Individual, Investor-owned (for-profit) **Service**: Rehabilitation

Staffed Beds: 12

COVINGTON—St. Tammany Parish

AMG PHYSICAL REHABILITATION HOSPITAL (193097), 5025 Keystone Boulevard, Suite 200, Zip 70433; tel. 985/888-0301, (Nonreporting) **A**10 22 **S** AMG Integrated Healthcare Management, Lafayette, LA
Primary Contact: Stephanie Dawsey, R.N., Chief Executive Officer
Web address: www.amgcovingtonprh.com/
Control: Partnership, Investor-owned (for-profit) **Service**: Rehabilitation

Staffed Beds: 24

⇑ **AVALA (190267)**, 67252 Industry Lane, Zip 70433-8704; tel. 985/809-9888, (Nonreporting) **A**10 21
Primary Contact: J. William. Hankins, Chief Executive Officer
COO: Jay Buras, Chief Operating Officer
CFO: Stacey Zimmer, Chief Financial Officer
CMO: Samer Shamieh, M.D., Chief Medical Officer
CHR: Pam Collins, Director Human Resources
CNO: Joy Melgar, MSN, R.N., Chief Nursing Officer
Web address: www.fairwaymedical.com
Control: Corporation, Investor-owned (for-profit) **Service**: General medical and surgical

Staffed Beds: 21

☐ **COVINGTON BEHAVIORAL HEALTH (194069)**, 201 Greenbrier Boulevard, Zip 70433-7236; tel. 985/893-2970, (Nonreporting) **A**1 10 **S** Acadia Healthcare Company, Inc., Franklin, TN
Primary Contact: Dustin Thiels, Group Chief Executive Officer
CFO: Jan Adams, Chief Financial Officer
CMO: Jason Coe, M.D., Medical Director
Web address: https://www.covingtonbh.com/
Control: Corporation, Investor-owned (for-profit) **Service**: Psychiatric

Staffed Beds: 84

LAKEVIEW REGIONAL MEDICAL CENTER See Lakeview Hospital

⊞ **PAM SPECIALTY HOSPITAL OF COVINGTON (192048)**, 20050 Crestwood Boulevard, Zip 70433-5207; tel. 985/875-7525, **A**1 10 **F**1 29 64 75 130 143 154 **S** PAM Health, Enola, PA
Primary Contact: Tim Burke, Chief Executive Officer
COO: John Bauer, Chief Operating Officer
CFO: Karick Stober, Chief Financial Officer
CMO: Adam Burick, M.D., Chief Medical Officer
CIO: Bryan Munchel, Senior Vice President and Chief Information Officer
Web address: www.postacutemedical.com
Control: Partnership, Investor-owned (for-profit) **Service**: Acute long-term care hospital

Staffed Beds: 26 **Admissions**: 603 **Census**: 26 **Outpatient Visits**: 0 **Births**: 0 **Total Expense ($000)**: 17942 **Payroll Expense ($000)**: 8198 **Personnel**: 113

⊞ **ST. TAMMANY HEALTH SYSTEM (190045)**, 1202 South Tyler Street, Zip 70433-2330; tel. 985/898-4000, **A**1 2 3 10 **F**3 8 11 12 13 15 18 20 22 24 26 28 29 30 31 34 35 37 38 40 41 42 43 44 45 46 48 49 50 54 55 56 57 59 62 63 64 65 70 71 72 74 75 76 77 78 79 81 82 84 85 86 87 88 89 92 93 96 97 107 108 109 110 111 114 115 119 123 124 126 129 130 132 135 146 147 148 149 154 156 167 **P**6
Primary Contact: Joan M. Coffman, FACHE, President and Chief Executive Officer
COO: Sharon A Toups, Senior Vice President and Chief Operating Officer
CFO: Sandra P Dipietro, Chief Financial Officer
CMO: Robert Capitelli, M.D., Senior Vice President and Chief Medical Officer
CIO: Craig Doyle, Director and Chief Information Officer
CHR: Carolyn Adema, Senior Vice President
CNO: Kerry K. Milton, R.N., Chief Nursing Officer
Web address: www.stph.org
Control: Hospital district or authority, Government, Nonfederal **Service**: General medical and surgical

Staffed Beds: 255 **Admissions**: 12574 **Census**: 160 **Outpatient Visits**: 542573 **Births**: 2068 **Total Expense ($000)**: 454398 **Payroll Expense ($000)**: 199507 **Personnel**: 2385

CROWLEY—Acadia Parish

★ **OCHSNER ACADIA GENERAL HOSPITAL (190044)**, 1305 Crowley Rayne Highway, Zip 70526-8202; tel. 337/783-3222, **A**10 **F**3 15 29 31 40 45 56 60 70 78 79 81 82 85 89 107 108 110 111 115 119 124 126 148 149 167 **S** Ochsner Health, New Orleans, LA
Primary Contact: Caroline Marceaux, MSN, R.N., Assistant Vice President, Nursing and Hospital Administration
CMO: Robert J. Aertker, M.D., III, Chief of Staff
CNO: Caroline Marceaux, MSN, R.N., Assistant Vice President, Nursing and Hospital Administration
Web address: www.acadiageneral.com
Control: Other not-for-profit (including NFP Corporation) **Service**: General medical and surgical

Staffed Beds: 30 **Admissions**: 1509 **Census**: 22 **Outpatient Visits**: 26435 **Births**: 0 **Total Expense ($000)**: 59155 **Payroll Expense ($000)**: 17052 **Personnel**: 250

Hospitals, U.S. / LOUISIANA

CUT OFF—Lafourche Parish

★ ⇧ **LADY OF THE SEA GENERAL HOSPITAL (191325)**, 200 West 134th Place, Zip 70345-4143; tel. 985/632-6401, (Nonreporting) **A**10 18 21
Primary Contact: Lloyd Guidry, Chief Executive Officer
CFO: Jacquelyn Richoux, Chief Financial Officer
CMO: William Crenshaw, M.D., Chief of Staff
CIO: Bennie Smith, Chief Information Officer
CHR: Bennie Smith, Director Human Resources and Risk Management
CNO: Holly Griffin, R.N., Chief Nursing Officer
Web address: www.losgh.org
Control: Hospital district or authority, Government, Nonfederal **Service**: General medical and surgical

Staffed Beds: 25

DE RIDDER—Beauregard Parish

⊞ **BEAUREGARD HEALTH SYSTEM (190050)**, 600 South Pine Street, Zip 70634-4942, Mailing Address: P.O. Box 730, Zip 70634-0730; tel. 337/462-7100, **A**1 10 **F**3 11 13 15 18 20 22 28 29 30 31 34 35 39 40 45 46 50 53 57 64 70 75 76 78 81 85 89 91 93 96 107 108 110 111 114 119 127 129 130 133 144 148 154 156 169 **P**6
Primary Contact: Traci Thibodeaux, Chief Executive Officer
CFO: Jarred Veillon, Chief Financial Officer
CMO: David Jones, M.D., Chief Medical Officer
CIO: Meg Jackson, Director Information Technology
CHR: Kelli C Broocks, Director Human Resources, Public Relations and Physician Recruitment
CNO: Kie McNabb, Chief Nursing Officer
Web address: www.beauregard.org
Control: Hospital district or authority, Government, Nonfederal **Service**: General medical and surgical

Staffed Beds: 49 **Admissions**: 1069 **Census**: 11 **Outpatient Visits**: 48361 **Births**: 300 **Total Expense ($000)**: 61235 **Payroll Expense ($000)**: 23405 **Personnel**: 393

DELHI—Richland Parish

DELHI HOSPITAL (191323), 407 Cincinnati Street, Zip 71232-3007; tel. 318/878-5171, (Nonreporting) **A**10 18
Primary Contact: Jinger Greer, CPA, Interim Administrator
CFO: Jinger Greer, CPA, Chief Financial Officer
CIO: Barbra Hutchison, Director Medical Records
CHR: Patsy Stout, Director Personnel
Web address: www.delhihospital.com
Control: Hospital district or authority, Government, Nonfederal **Service**: General medical and surgical

Staffed Beds: 25

RICHLAND PARISH HOSPITAL–DELHI See Delhi Hospital

DENHAM SPRINGS—Livingston Parish

SAGE SPECIALTY HOSPITAL (LTAC) (192008), 8375 Florida Boulevard, Zip 70726-7806; tel. 225/665-2664, (Includes SAGE SPECIALTY HOSPITAL, 8225 Summa Avenue, Building B, Baton Rouge, Louisiana, Zip 70809-3422, tel. 225/208-0300; Sybil J. Miles, R.N., Administrator) (Nonreporting) **A**10 **S** The Carpenter Health Network, Baton Rouge, LA
Primary Contact: Sharon Faulkner, R.N., Administrator
CFO: Jessica McGee, Chief Financial Officer
CMO: Durwin Walker, M.D., Chief Medical Officer
CHR: Kim Hernandez, Chief Human Resources Officer
CNO: Sharon Faulkner, R.N., Chief Nursing Officer
Web address: https://www.thecarpenterhealthnetwork.com/locations/sage-specialty-hospital/
Control: Individual, Investor–owned (for–profit) **Service**: Acute long–term care hospital

Staffed Beds: 36

DEQUINCY—Calcasieu Parish

DEQUINCY MEMORIAL HOSPITAL (191307), 110 West Fourth Street, Zip 70633-3508, Mailing Address: P.O. Box 1166, Zip 70633-1166; tel. 337/786-1200, (Nonreporting) **A**10 18
Primary Contact: F. Peter. Savoy III, Chief Executive Officer
CMO: Jalal Joudeh, M.D., Chief of Staff
CNO: Darrell Ross, Chief Nursing Officer
Web address: www.dequincymemorial.com/
Control: Corporation, Investor–owned (for–profit) **Service**: General medical and surgical

Staffed Beds: 29

DERIDDER—Beauregard Parish

⊞ **OCEANS BEHAVIORAL HOSPITAL OF DERIDDER (194081)**, 1420 Blankenship Drive, Zip 70634-4604; tel. 337/460-9472, (Nonreporting) **A**1 10 **S** Oceans Healthcare, Plano, TX
Primary Contact: Nicholas D. Guillory, MSN, Interim Administrator, Executive Vice President, Regional Operations
CNO: Amy Daniels, R.N., Director of Nursing
Web address: https://oceanshealthcare.com/ohc-location/deridder/
Control: Corporation, Investor–owned (for–profit) **Service**: Psychiatric

Staffed Beds: 20

DONALDSONVILLE—Ascension Parish

⊞ **PREVOST MEMORIAL HOSPITAL (191308)**, 301 Memorial Drive, Zip 70346-4376; tel. 225/473-7931, (Nonreporting) **A**1 10 18
Primary Contact: Shelton Anthony, Hospital Administrator
CFO: John Montanio, Chief Financial Officer
CMO: Glenn Schexnayder, M.D., Chief of Staff
CHR: Linda Cataldo, Human Resources Secretary
Web address: https://www.prevosthospital.com/
Control: Hospital district or authority, Government, Nonfederal **Service**: General medical and surgical

Staffed Beds: 25

EUNICE—Saint Landry Parish

ACADIAN MEDICAL CENTER (190318), 3501 Highway 190, Zip 70535-5129; tel. 337/580-7500, (Nonreporting) **A**10
Primary Contact: David Ingram, Chief Executive Officer
CFO: John Fougere, Chief Financial Officer
CMO: Randy Miller, M.D., Chief, Medical Staff
CIO: Kristie Bertrand, Director Health Information Management
CHR: Cody Ardoan, Director Human Resources
CNO: Julie Paul, R.N., Chief Nursing Officer
Web address: www.acadianmedicalcenter.com
Control: Corporation, Investor–owned (for–profit) **Service**: General medical and surgical

Staffed Beds: 30

FARMERVILLE—Union Parish

★ **UNION GENERAL HOSPITAL (191301)**, 901 James Avenue, Zip 71241-2234, Mailing Address: P.O. Box 398, Zip 71241-0398; tel. 318/368-9751, (Nonreporting) **A**5 10 18
Primary Contact: Dianne Davidson, Chief Executive Officer
COO: Amanda Whiddon, Chief Operating Officer
CFO: Brad Adcock, Chief Financial Officer
CHR: Sheri Taylor, Director Human Resources
CNO: Darra Jung, Director of Nursing
Web address: https://www.uniongen.org/
Control: Other not–for–profit (including NFP Corporation) **Service**: General medical and surgical

Staffed Beds: 15

Hospital, Medicare Provider Number, Address, Telephone, Approval, Facility, and Physician Codes, Health Care System

★ American Hospital Association (AHA) membership ○ Healthcare Facilities Accreditation Program ⇧ Center for Improvement in Healthcare Quality Accreditation
□ The Joint Commission accreditation ◇ DNV Healthcare Inc. accreditation △ Commission on Accreditation of Rehabilitation Facilities (CARF) accreditation

© 2025 AHA Guide

Hospitals, U.S. / LOUISIANA

FERRIDAY—Concordia Parish

TRINITY MEDICAL (191318), 6569 Highway 84, Zip 71334; tel. 318/757–6551, **A**10 18 **F**3 15 29 34 35 40 45 50 57 64 65 68 70 75 77 81 87 93 96 102 107 110 111 115 119 127 133 149 **P**6
Primary Contact: Nekeisha Smith, Chief Executive Officer
COO: Neely Greene, Chief Operating Officer
CFO: Spencer Holder, Chief Financial Officer
CMO: Carrie Bonomo, M.D., Chief of Staff
CHR: Debra Stephens, Director Personnel
CNO: John Woodruff, R.N., Director of Nursing
Web address: https://www.trinitymed.com/
Control: Hospital district or authority, Government, Nonfederal **Service**: General medical and surgical

Staffed Beds: 23 **Admissions**: 721 **Census**: 11 **Outpatient Visits**: 26643 **Births**: 0 **Total Expense ($000)**: 31290 **Payroll Expense ($000)**: 9958 **Personnel**: 179

FORT POLK—Vernon Parish

BAYNE–JONES ARMY COMMUNITY HOSPITAL, 1585 3rd Street, Building 283, Zip 71459–5102; tel. 337/531–3928, (Nonreporting) **A**1 **S** Department of the Army, Office of the Surgeon General, Falls Church, VA
Primary Contact: Colonel Aristotle A. Vaseliades, FACHE, Commanding Officer
COO: Larry R. Patterson, Deputy Commander Administration
CFO: Captain Dustin Mullins, Chief Resource Management
CIO: Major William Callahan, Chief Information Management Division
CHR: Captain Dustin Mullins, Chief Human Resources
CNO: Colonel Michael Szymaniak, Deputy Commander for Nursing
Web address: https://bayne-jones.tricare.mil/
Control: Army, Government, federal **Service**: General medical and surgical

Staffed Beds: 13

FRANKLIN—St. Mary Parish

BAYOU BEND HEALTH SYSTEM (191310), 1097 Northwest Boulevard, Zip 70538–3407, Mailing Address: P.O. Box 577, Zip 70538–0577; tel. 337/828–0760, (Nonreporting) **A**1 10 18
Primary Contact: Stephanie A. Guidry, Chief Executive Officer
CFO: Mary Bevier, Chief Financial Officer
CMO: Jesus Chua, M.D., Chief of Staff
CIO: John Spradlin, Information Systems Director
CHR: Elmo Vinas, Director Human Resources
CNO: Robert Raheem, R.N., Chief Nursing Officer
Web address: www.bayoubendhealth.org
Control: Hospital district or authority, Government, Nonfederal **Service**: General medical and surgical

Staffed Beds: 22

FRANKLIN FOUNDATION HOSPITAL See Bayou Bend Health System

FRANKLINTON—Washington Parish

RIVERSIDE MEDICAL CENTER (191313), 1900 Main Street, Zip 70438–3688; tel. 985/839–4431, **A**1 10 18 **F**3 11 15 18 20 22 26 28 29 31 34 35 39 40 45 46 56 57 59 63 64 65 70 75 77 81 85 86 87 93 97 107 110 111 114 119 127 128 129 130 133 135 146 148 149 154 **P**6
Primary Contact: Darrell Lee. Lavender, Chief Executive Officer
CFO: Patty Mizell, Chief Financial Officer
CMO: Chris Foret, M.D., Chief of Staff
Web address: www.rmchospital.com
Control: Hospital district or authority, Government, Nonfederal **Service**: General medical and surgical

Staffed Beds: 25 **Admissions**: 113 **Census**: 1 **Outpatient Visits**: 36611 **Births**: 0 **Total Expense ($000)**: 33611 **Payroll Expense ($000)**: 14294 **Personnel**: 247

GONZALES—Ascension Parish

ASCENSION GONZALES REHABILITATION HOSPITAL See United Medical Rehabilitation Hospital – Gonzales

ST. ELIZABETH HOSPITAL See Our Lady of The Lake Ascension

ST. JAMES BEHAVIORAL HEALTH HOSPITAL (194088), 3136 South Saint Landry Avenue, Zip 70737–5801; tel. 225/647–7524, (Nonreporting) **A**1 10
Primary Contact: Andrew Hines, Administrator
COO: Wendell Smith, Chief Operating Officer
CFO: Rama Kongara, Chief Financial Officer
CMO: Lance Bullock, M.D., Medical Director
CHR: Dessa Frederick, Manager Human Resources
Web address: www.sjbhh.net
Control: Corporation, Investor–owned (for-profit) **Service**: Psychiatric

Staffed Beds: 10

GREENSBURG—St. Helena Parish

ST. HELENA PARISH HOSPITAL (191300), 16874 Highway 43, Zip 70441–4834; tel. 225/222–6111, (Nonreporting) **A**5 10 18
Primary Contact: Naveed Awan, FACHE, Chief Executive Officer
CFO: Theresa Brinkhaus, Chief Financial Officer
CMO: Anjanette Varnado, M.D., Chief Medical Officer
CHR: Lorraine L Ballard, Director Human Resources
CNO: Julie Morgan, Director of Nursing
Web address: www.sthelenaparishhospital.com
Control: Hospital district or authority, Government, Nonfederal **Service**: General medical and surgical

Staffed Beds: 16

GRETNA—Jefferson Parish

MEADOWCREST HOSPITAL See Ochsner Medical Center – West Bank

UNITED MEDICAL HEALTHWEST NEW ORLEANS, LLC (193074), 3201 Wall Boulevard, Suite B, Zip 70056–7755; tel. 504/433–5551, (Nonreporting) **A**10 **S** United Medical Rehabilitation Hospitals, Gretna, LA
Primary Contact: Gayla Bryant, R.N., Administrator
CMO: Kenneth Williams, M.D., Medical Director
Web address: https://umrhospital.com/locations/new-orleans/
Control: Individual, Investor–owned (for-profit) **Service**: Rehabilitation

Staffed Beds: 26

HAMMOND—Tangipahoa Parish

CYPRESS POINTE SURGICAL HOSPITAL (190303), 42570 South Airport Road, Zip 70403–0946; tel. 985/510–6200, (Nonreporting) **A**10 21
Primary Contact: Albert Geldenhuys, Chief Executive Officer
COO: Scott Boudreaux, Chief Operating Officer
CFO: Albert Geldenhuys, Chief Financial Officer
CNO: Denise Fortenberry, Chief Nursing Officer and Chief Compliance Officer
Web address: www.cpsh.org
Control: Corporation, Investor–owned (for-profit) **Service**: Surgical

Staffed Beds: 30

NORTH OAKS MEDICAL CENTER (190015), 15790 Paul Vega, MD, Drive, Zip 70403–1436, Mailing Address: P.O. Box 2668, Zip 70404–2668; tel. 985/345–2700, **A**1 3 10 19 **F**3 12 13 15 18 20 22 24 26 28 29 30 31 32 34 37 40 43 45 46 49 50 54 56 57 58 59 63 64 68 70 72 73 74 75 76 77 78 79 81 82 84 85 86 87 89 93 94 96 102 107 108 110 111 114 115 118 119 126 129 130 131 132 135 146 147 148 149 154 156 167 169 **S** North Oaks Health System, Hammond, LA
Primary Contact: Michele Kidd. Sutton, FACHE, President and Chief Executive Officer
COO: Michael Watkins, Chief Operating Officer
CFO: Mark Anderson, Chief Financial Officer
CMO: Robert Peltier, M.D., Chief Medical Officer
CIO: Doug Bankston, Director Technical Services
CHR: Jeff Jarreau, Chief Human Resources Officer
CNO: Kirsten S Riney, MSN, R.N., Chief Nursing Officer
Web address: www.northoaks.org
Control: Hospital district or authority, Government, Nonfederal **Service**: General medical and surgical

Staffed Beds: 248 **Admissions**: 10109 **Census**: 143 **Outpatient Visits**: 327596 **Births**: 1059 **Total Expense ($000)**: 395267 **Payroll Expense ($000)**: 200473 **Personnel**: 2019

NORTH OAKS REHABILITATION HOSPITAL (193044), 1900 South Morrison Boulevard, Zip 70403–5742; tel. 985/542–7777, **A**1 7 10 **F**29 56 75 86 87 90 130 132 143 154 **S** North Oaks Health System, Hammond, LA
Primary Contact: Mac Barrient Jr, Administrator
CFO: Mark Anderson, Chief Financial Officer
CMO: Robert Peltier, M.D., Senior Vice President, Chief Medical Officer, North Oaks Health System
CIO: Herbert Robinson, M.D., Vice President, Chief Medical Information Officer, North Oaks Health System
CHR: Jeff Jarreau, Senior Vice President, Human Resources, North Oaks Health System
Web address: www.northoaks.org
Control: Hospital district or authority, Government, Nonfederal **Service**: Rehabilitation

Staffed Beds: 27 **Admissions**: 497 **Census**: 15 **Outpatient Visits**: 0 **Births**: 0 **Total Expense ($000)**: 8083 **Payroll Expense ($000)**: 2867 **Personnel**: 38

Hospitals, U.S. / LOUISIANA

☒ **PAM SPECIALTY HOSPITAL OF HAMMOND (192036)**, 42074 Veterans Avenue, Zip 70403-1408; tel. 985/902-8148, **A**1 10 **F**1 29 60 75 77 148 149 **S** PAM Health, Enola, PA
Primary Contact: Nicholas Paul. Mendez, Chief Executive Officer and Director of Nursing
Web address: www.postacutemedical.com/facilities/find-facility/specialty-hospitals/PAM-Specialty-Hospital-Hammond
Control: Partnership, Investor-owned (for-profit) **Service**: Acute long-term care hospital

Staffed Beds: 40 **Admissions**: 372 **Census**: 22 **Outpatient Visits**: 0 **Births**: 0 **Total Expense ($000)**: 14028 **Payroll Expense ($000)**: 6015 **Personnel**: 141

UNITED MEDICAL REHABILITATION HOSPITAL-HAMMOND (193079), 15717 Belle Drive, Zip 70403-1439; tel. 985/340-5998, (Includes UNITED MEDICAL REHABILITATION HOSPITAL – GONZALES, 333 East Worthy Road, Gonzales, Louisiana, Zip 70737-4234, tel. 225/450-2231; Warren Swenson, Interim Executive Officer and Chief Financial Officer) (Nonreporting) **A**10 **S** United Medical Rehabilitation Hospitals, Gretna, LA
Primary Contact: Karen Crayton, Chief Executive Officer
CFO: Krystal Howard, System Chief Financial Officer
CMO: Luis Franco, M.D., Medical Director
CHR: Mark Gros, Director Human Resources
CNO: Lindsay Dietsch, R.N., Director of Nursing
Web address: https://umrhospital.com/locations/hammond/
Control: Corporation, Investor-owned (for-profit) **Service**: Rehabilitation

Staffed Beds: 20

HOMER—Claiborne Parish

CLAIBORNE MEMORIAL MEDICAL CENTER (190114), 620 East College Street, Zip 71040-3202; tel. 318/927-2024, (Nonreporting) **A**5 10
Primary Contact: Tina Haynes, Chief Executive Officer
CFO: Michael Fontenot, Chief Financial Officer
CMO: Mark Haynes, M.D., Chief of Staff
CIO: Angie Costakis, Chief Information Officer
CHR: William Colvin, Human Resources Officer
CNO: Lee Jones, R.N., Chief Nursing Officer
Web address: www.clairbornemedical.com/
Control: City, Government, Nonfederal **Service**: General medical and surgical

Staffed Beds: 57

HOUMA—Terrebonne Parish

AMG SPECIALTY HOSPITAL-HOUMA (192037), 629 Dunn Street, Zip 70360-4707; tel. 985/274-0001, (Nonreporting) **A**10 22 **S** AMG Integrated Healthcare Management, Lafayette, LA
Primary Contact: Rachelle Economides, R.N., Chief Executive Officer
Web address: www.amghouma.com/
Control: Corporation, Investor-owned (for-profit) **Service**: Acute long-term care hospital

Staffed Beds: 40

COMPASS BEHAVIORAL CENTER OF HOUMA (194109), 4701 West Park Avenue, Zip 70364-4426; tel. 985/876-1715, (Nonreporting) **A**10 **S** Compass Health, Crowley, LA
Primary Contact: Alaina Richards, Chief Executive Officer
Web address: https://www.compasshealthcare.com/locations/compass-behavioral-center-of-houma-2/
Control: Corporation, Investor-owned (for-profit) **Service**: Psychiatric

Staffed Beds: 20

☒ **LEONARD J. CHABERT MEDICAL CENTER (190183)**, 1978 Industrial Boulevard, Zip 70363-7094; tel. 985/873-2200, **A**1 3 5 10 **F**3 15 18 20 24 26 29 31 34 35 38 40 44 45 46 48 49 50 51 57 58 59 61 64 65 66 70 74 77 78 79 81 84 85 86 87 89 91 93 96 97 98 100 101 102 107 108 110 111 115 119 130 146 147 149 154 156 164 167 **S** Ochsner Health, New Orleans, LA
Primary Contact: Fernis LeBlanc, Chief Executive Officer
COO: Kendrick Duet, Chief Operating Officer
CNO: Jana Semere, Chief Nursing Officer
Web address: www.ochsner.org/locations/leonard-j-chabert-medical-center
Control: Hospital district or authority, Government, Nonfederal **Service**: General medical and surgical

Staffed Beds: 45 **Admissions**: 1763 **Census**: 29 **Outpatient Visits**: 48007 **Births**: 0 **Total Expense ($000)**: 299733 **Payroll Expense ($000)**: 38664 **Personnel**: 547

☐ **PHYSICIANS MEDICAL CENTER (190241)**, 218 Corporate Drive, Zip 70360-2768; tel. 985/853-1390, (Nonreporting) **A**1 10
Primary Contact: Phyllis Peoples, Chief Executive Officer
CNO: Megan Picou Duval, Chief Nursing Officer
Web address: www.physicianshouma.com/
Control: Partnership, Investor-owned (for-profit) **Service**: Surgical

Staffed Beds: 15

☒ △ **TERREBONNE GENERAL HEALTH SYSTEM (190008)**, 8166 Main Street, Zip 70360-3498; tel. 985/873-4141, **A**1 2 3 5 7 10 19 **F**3 11 13 14 15 17 18 20 22 24 26 29 30 31 34 40 44 46 49 50 53 57 58 59 64 65 68 70 72 74 75 76 77 78 79 81 84 85 86 87 89 90 91 92 93 96 97 102 107 108 109 110 111 112 115 116 117 118 119 121 123 124 129 130 131 132 134 135 143 146 147 148 149 154 156 157 169 **P**6
Primary Contact: Phyllis L. Peoples, President and Chief Executive Officer
COO: Diane Yeates, FACHE, Chief Operating Officer
CFO: Meggan Murray, Assistant Vice President Finance
CIO: Jeff Sardella, Director Information Technology
CHR: Mickie Rousseau, Director Human Resources
CNO: Teresita McNabb, FACHE, R.N., Vice President Nursing Services
Web address: www.tgmc.com
Control: Hospital district or authority, Government, Nonfederal **Service**: General medical and surgical

Staffed Beds: 152 **Admissions**: 5490 **Census**: 79 **Outpatient Visits**: 143331 **Births**: 1314 **Total Expense ($000)**: 249681 **Payroll Expense ($000)**: 98241 **Personnel**: 1006

INDEPENDENCE—Tangipahoa Parish

☐ **LALLIE KEMP MEDICAL CENTER (191321)**, 52579 Highway 51 South, Zip 70443-2231; tel. 985/878-9421, (Nonreporting) **A**1 3 5 10 18
Primary Contact: Lisa G. Bruhl, Hospital Administrator
CFO: Chad Thompson, Chief Financial Officer
CMO: Kathy Willis, M.D., Medical Director
CIO: Charles Tate, Director Information Technology
CHR: Diane Farnham, Acting Director Human Resources
CNO: Vicki Hirsch, R.N., Director of Nursing
Web address: www.lsuhospitals.org/Hospitals/LK/LK.aspx
Control: State, Government, Nonfederal **Service**: General medical and surgical

Staffed Beds: 24

JACKSON—East Feliciana Parish

☐ **EASTERN LOUISIANA MENTAL HEALTH SYSTEM (194008)**, 4502 Highway 10, Zip 70748-3507, Mailing Address: P.O. Box 498, Zip 70748-0498; tel. 225/634-0100, (Nonreporting) **A**1 3 10 **S** Louisiana State Hospitals, Baton Rouge, LA
Primary Contact: Laura Lott, Chief Executive Officer
CMO: John W Thompson, M.D., Chief of Staff
CIO: Deborah Brandon, Director Total Quality Management
CHR: Vikki Riggle, Director Human Resources
CNO: Mary Fontenelle, Executive Nurse Director
Web address: www.new.dhh.louisiana.gov/index.cfm/directory/detail/219
Control: State, Government, Nonfederal **Service**: Psychiatric

Staffed Beds: 693

VILLA FELICIANA MEDICAL COMPLEX (190199), 5002 Highway 10, Zip 70748-3627, Mailing Address: P.O. Box 438, Zip 70748-0438; tel. 225/634-4017, (Nonreporting) **A**10
Primary Contact: Patrick Eckler, Administrator
CFO: Kim Jelks, Fiscal Officer
CMO: John F Piker, M.D., Medical Director
CIO: Michael James, Information Technology Technical Support Specialist 1
CHR: Sandra Delatte, Director Human Resources
CNO: Linda Williams, Director of Nursing
Web address: www.ldh.la.gov/index.cfm/directory/detail/535
Control: State, Government, Nonfederal **Service**: Other specialty treatment

Staffed Beds: 299

Hospital, Medicare Provider Number, Address, Telephone, Approval, Facility, and Physician Codes, Health Care System

★ American Hospital Association (AHA) membership ◯ Healthcare Facilities Accreditation Program ⇧ Center for Improvement in Healthcare Quality Accreditation
☐ The Joint Commission accreditation ◇ DNV Healthcare Inc. accreditation △ Commission on Accreditation of Rehabilitation Facilities (CARF) accreditation

© 2025 AHA Guide

Hospitals, U.S. / LOUISIANA

LA

JEFFERSON—Jefferson Parish

✠ △ **OCHSNER REHABILITATON HOSPITAL WEST CAMPUS (193099)**, 2614 Jefferson Highway, Floors 4 & 5, Zip 70121-3828; tel. 504/291-5100, **A**1 7 10 **F**3 29 34 44 68 87 90 91 95 96 130 132 148 **S** Select Medical Corporation, Mechanicsburg, PA
Primary Contact: Laurel DuPont, Chief Executive Officer
CNO: Ronnie B. King, Chief Nursing Officer
Web address: https://www.ochsner.org/services/rehabilitation
Control: Corporation, Investor-owned (for-profit) **Service**: Rehabilitation

> **Staffed Beds**: 56 **Admissions**: 1067 **Census**: 43 **Outpatient Visits**: 0
> **Births**: 0 **Personnel**: 172

JENA—La Salle Parish

★ **LASALLE GENERAL HOSPITAL (190145)**, 187 Ninth Street, Zip 71342-3901, Mailing Address: P.O. Box 2780, Zip 71342-2780; tel. 318/992-9200, **A**3 5 10 **F**3 7 11 18 29 33 34 35 40 53 57 59 62 64 93 97 98 100 103 104 107 108 110 111 115 119 127 130 133 149 154 **P**6
Primary Contact: Lana B. Francis, Chief Executive Officer
CHR: Allyson Fannin, Human Resources Officer
CNO: Carolyn Francis, R.N., MSN, Director of Nursing
Web address: www.lasallegeneralhospital.com
Control: Hospital district or authority, Government, Nonfederal **Service**: General medical and surgical

> **Staffed Beds**: 46 **Admissions**: 735 **Census**: 16 **Outpatient Visits**: 60012
> **Births**: 0 **Total Expense ($000)**: 27554 **Payroll Expense ($000)**: 11053
> **Personnel**: 235

JENNINGS—Jefferson Davis Parish

JENNINGS SENIOR CARE HOSPITAL (194082), 1 Hospital Drive, Suite 201, Zip 70546-3641; tel. 337/824-1558, **A**10 **F**56 64 69 98 99 100 103 153 **S** Compass Health, Crowley, LA
Primary Contact: Chad Hoffpauir, Chief Executive Officer
CFO: Kirk Perron, Controller
Web address: https://www.compasshealthcare.com/locations/jennings-senior-care-hospital/
Control: Corporation, Investor-owned (for-profit) **Service**: Psychiatric

> **Staffed Beds**: 36 **Admissions**: 557 **Census**: 20 **Outpatient Visits**: 0
> **Births**: 0 **Personnel**: 54

✠ **OCHSNER AMERICAN LEGION HOSPITAL (190053)**, 1634 Elton Road, Zip 70546-3614; tel. 337/616-7000, (Nonreporting) **A**1 10 **S** Ochsner Health, New Orleans, LA
Primary Contact: Dana D. Williams, Chief Executive Officer
CHR: Ruth Carnes, Director Human Resources
CNO: Brooke Broussard Hornsby, Chief Nursing Officer
Web address: www.jalh.com
Control: Other not-for-profit (including NFP Corporation) **Service**: General medical and surgical

> **Staffed Beds**: 41

✠ **REHABILITATION HOSPITAL OF JENNINGS (193067)**, 1 Hospital Drive, Suite 101, Zip 70546-3641; tel. 337/821-5353, (Nonreporting) **A**10
Primary Contact: Michael Holland, M.D., Chief Executive Officer
Web address: www.jenningsrehab.com
Control: Partnership, Investor-owned (for-profit) **Service**: Rehabilitation

> **Staffed Beds**: 16

JONESBORO—Jackson Parish

★ **JACKSON PARISH HOSPITAL (191317)**, 165 Beech Springs Road, Zip 71251-2059; tel. 318/259-4435, (Nonreporting) **A**10 18
Primary Contact: John Morgan, R.N., Chief Executive Officer
CFO: Bill Stansbury, Chief Financial Officer
CMO: W. James (Jamie) Slusher, M.D., Chief of Staff
CIO: Monie Phillips III, Director Clinical Informatics
CHR: Phillip Thomas Jr, Director Human Resources
CNO: Christy Wyatt, R.N., Interim Chief Nursing Officer
Web address: www.jacksonparishhospital.com
Control: Hospital district or authority, Government, Nonfederal **Service**: General medical and surgical

> **Staffed Beds**: 25

KAPLAN—Vermilion Parish

★ **OCHSNER ABROM KAPLAN MEMORIAL HOSPITAL (191322)**, 1310 West Seventh Street, Zip 70548-2910; tel. 337/643-8300, **A**10 18 **F**3 15 29 34 40 57 59 60 64 65 68 77 81 87 91 93 98 100 103 105 107 108 110 111 115 119 127 130 133 135 149 154 **P**6 8 **S** Ochsner Health, New Orleans, LA
Primary Contact: Jennifer Gerard, R.N., Assistant Vice President, Nursing and Hospital Administration
CFO: Michael G. Johnson, CPA, Chief Financial Officer
CMO: Scott Bergeaux, M.D., Chief Medical Staff
CIO: Michael Cardiff, Systems Supervisor
CHR: Linda Guidry, Human Resources Generalist
CNO: Jennifer Gerard, R.N., Chief Nursing Officer
Web address: https://www.ochsner.org/locations/ochsner-abrom-kaplan-memorial-hospital
Control: Other not-for-profit (including NFP Corporation) **Service**: General medical and surgical

> **Staffed Beds**: 20 **Admissions**: 601 **Census**: 12 **Outpatient Visits**: 20817
> **Births**: 0 **Total Expense ($000)**: 27684 **Payroll Expense ($000)**: 11073
> **Personnel**: 122

KENNER—Jefferson Parish

☐ **OCEANS BEHAVIORAL HOSPITAL OF GREATER NEW ORLEANS (194098)**, 716 Village Road, Zip 70065-2751; tel. 504/464-8895, (Includes OCEANS BEHAVIORAL HOSPITAL GREATER NEW ORLEANS – MARRERO, 4500 Wichers Drive, Marrero, Louisiana, Zip 70072-3184, tel. 504/349-1661; Deborah Spiers, Administrator) (Nonreporting) **A**1 10 **S** Oceans Healthcare, Plano, TX
Primary Contact: Deborah Spiers, Administrator
Web address: www.obhgno.info/
Control: Corporation, Investor-owned (for-profit) **Service**: Psychiatric

> **Staffed Beds**: 30

✠ **OCHSNER MEDICAL CENTER – KENNER (190274)**, 180 West Esplanade Avenue, Zip 70065-6001; tel. 504/468-8600, **A**1 3 5 10 **F**3 15 18 20 22 26 29 30 31 34 35 37 38 40 41 42 45 44 46 49 50 51 54 56 57 58 59 60 61 64 65 68 70 72 74 75 76 77 78 79 81 82 84 85 86 87 93 97 102 107 108 110 111 114 116 117 119 120 126 129 130 131 135 143 146 147 148 154 157 167 169 **S** Ochsner Health, New Orleans, LA
Primary Contact: Stephen Robinson Jr, FACHE, Chief Executive Officer
COO: Thomas Rhodes, Chief Operating Officer (River Region)
CFO: Tara Alleman, Chief Financial Officer
CMO: James Tebbe, M.D., Vice President Medical Affairs
CIO: Dere Krummel, Director Information Systems
Web address: https://www.ochsner.org/locations/ochsner-medical-center-kenner/
Control: Other not-for-profit (including NFP Corporation) **Service**: General medical and surgical

> **Staffed Beds**: 111 **Admissions**: 6180 **Census**: 66 **Outpatient Visits**: 74314
> **Births**: 1049 **Total Expense ($000)**: 192637 **Payroll Expense ($000)**: 81110 **Personnel**: 913

☐ **PERIMETER BEHAVIORAL HOSPITAL OF NEW ORLEANS (194113)**, 3639 Loyola Drive, Zip 70065; tel. 504/305-2700, **A**1 10 **F**98 100 101 103 105 153 162 **S** Perimeter Healthcare, Alpharetta, GA
Primary Contact: Gary Burns, Chief Executive Officer
COO: Debbie Tullier, Regional Vice President, Operations
CNO: Gerard Oncale, Director of Nursing
Web address: https://www.perimeterhealthcare.com/new-orleans
Control: Partnership, Investor-owned (for-profit) **Service**: Psychiatric

> **Staffed Beds**: 36 **Admissions**: 1253 **Census**: 28 **Outpatient Visits**: 0
> **Births**: 0 **Total Expense ($000)**: 8694 **Payroll Expense ($000)**: 4310
> **Personnel**: 76

KENTWOOD—Tangipahoa Parish

SOUTHEAST REGIONAL MEDICAL CENTER (192058), 719 Avenue G, Zip 70444-2601; tel. 337/603-6364, (Nonreporting) **A**10
Primary Contact: Mark Murphy, Administrator
Control: Corporation, Investor-owned (for-profit) **Service**: Acute long-term care hospital

> **Staffed Beds**: 14

KINDER—Allen Parish Parish

ALLEN PARISH COMMUNITY HEALTHCARE (190133), 108 Sixth Avenue, Zip 70648-3187, Mailing Address: P.O. Box 1670, Zip 70648-1670; tel. 337/738-2527, (Nonreporting) **A**10
Primary Contact: Jackie Costley. Reviel, R.N., Chief Executive Officer
COO: Terry Willet, Chief Financial Officer
CFO: Stephen Thames, Chief Financial Officer
CMO: Ejiro Ughouwa, M.D., Chief of Staff
CIO: Bill Marcantel, Chief Information Systems
CHR: Amand Lambert, Director Human Resources
CNO: Terra Bailey, Chief Nursing Officer
Web address: www.allenparishhospital.com
Control: Hospital district or authority, Government, Nonfederal **Service**: General medical and surgical

Staffed Beds: 49

LA PLACE—St. John the Baptist Parish

RIVER PLACE BEHAVIORAL HEALTH (194114), 500 Rue De Sante, Zip 70068-5418; tel. 985/303-2327, (Nonreporting) **A**1 10 **S** Acadia Healthcare Company, Inc., Franklin, TN
Primary Contact: Dustin Thiels, Group Chief Executive Officer
CFO: Muriel Osburn, Chief Financial Officer
CNO: Shannon Gabriel, Chief Nursing Officer
Web address: www.riverplacebh.com
Control: Corporation, Investor-owned (for-profit) **Service**: Psychiatric

Staffed Beds: 48

LACOMBE—St. Tammany Parish

BEACON BEHAVIORAL HOSPITAL – NORTHSHORE (194080), 64026 Highway 434, Suite 300, Zip 70445-5417; tel. 985/882-0226, (Nonreporting) **A**10
Primary Contact: Sean Wendell, CPA, Chief Executive Officer
Web address: www.magnoliabh.com/
Control: Corporation, Investor-owned (for-profit) **Service**: Psychiatric

Staffed Beds: 22

△ **NORTHSHORE REHABILITATION HOSPITAL (713025)**, 64030 State Highway 434, Zip 70445; tel. 985/218-4660, **A**1 7 10 **F**3 29 30 34 35 44 58 59 65 68 74 77 86 87 90 91 95 96 130 132 143 148 149 154 157 **S** Select Medical Corporation, Mechanicsburg, PA
Primary Contact: Laurel DuPont, Chief Executive Officer
CNO: Lena Riordan, R.N., Chief Nursing Officer
Web address: www.northshore-rehab.com
Control: Partnership, Investor-owned (for-profit) **Service**: Rehabilitation

Staffed Beds: 30 Admissions: 571 Census: 21 Outpatient Visits: 0 Births: 0 Personnel: 97

LAFAYETTE—Lafayette Parish

☐ **ACADIANA REHABILITATION (193096)**, 314 Youngsville Highway, Zip 70508-4524; tel. 337/330-2051, (Nonreporting) **A**1 10
Primary Contact: Angelique Richardson, Chief Executive Officer
Web address: https://acadianarehabilitation.com/
Control: Partnership, Investor-owned (for-profit) **Service**: Rehabilitation

Staffed Beds: 24

AMG SPECIALTY HOSPITAL–LAFAYETTE (192029), 4811 Ambassador Caffery Parkway, 4th Floor, Zip 70508-7265; tel. 337/839-9880, (Nonreporting) **A**10 22 **S** AMG Integrated Healthcare Management, Lafayette, LA
Primary Contact: April Ebeling, Chief Executive Officer
CFO: Jessica McGee, Chief Financial Officer
CMO: Maximo LaMarche, M.D., Chief Medical Officer
CNO: Mary Bollich, Director of Nurses
Web address: www.amglafayette.com
Control: Corporation, Investor-owned (for-profit) **Service**: Acute long-term care hospital

Staffed Beds: 18

COMPASS BEHAVIORAL CENTER OF LAFAYETTE (194085), 312 Youngsville Highway, Zip 70508; tel. 337/534-4655, (Nonreporting) **A**10 **S** Compass Health, Crowley, LA
Primary Contact: Andre' Robichaux, Chief Executive Officer
Web address: www.compasshealthcare.com
Control: Corporation, Investor-owned (for-profit) **Service**: Psychiatric

Staffed Beds: 24

HEART HOSPITAL OF LAFAYETTE See Our Lady of Lourdes Heart Hospital

IBERIA REHABILITATION HOSPITAL See Acadiana Rehabilitation

LAFAYETTE GENERAL SOUTHWEST See Lafayette General Orthopedic Hospital

LAFAYETTE GENERAL SURGICAL HOSPITAL See Ochsner Lafayette General Surgical Hospital

LAFAYETTE PHYSICAL REHABILITATION HOSPITAL (193093), 307 Polly Lane, Zip 70508-4960; tel. 337/314-1111, (Nonreporting) **A**10 22 **S** AMG Integrated Healthcare Management, Lafayette, LA
Primary Contact: Kevin M. Romero, Chief Executive Officer
Web address: www.lafayettephysicalrehab.com/
Control: Corporation, Investor-owned (for-profit) **Service**: Rehabilitation

Staffed Beds: 24

LHC GROUP – HOME HEALTHCARE, 901 Hugh Wallis Road South, Zip 70508-2511; tel. 337/233-1307, (Nonreporting) **S** LHC Group, Lafayette, LA
Primary Contact: Keith G. Myers, Chairman and Chief Executive Officer
Control: Corporation, Investor-owned (for-profit) **Service**: Other specialty treatment

Staffed Beds: 25

LOUISIANA EXTENDED CARE HOSPITAL OF LAFAYETTE (192032), 2810 Ambassador Caffery Parkway, 6th Floor, Zip 70506-5906; tel. 337/289-8180, (Includes EUNICE EXTENDED CARE HOSPITAL, 3879 Highway 190, Eunice, Louisiana, Zip 70535-7900, tel. 337/546-0024; Chris Fox, Division President) (Nonreporting) **A**10 **S** LHC Group, Lafayette, LA
Primary Contact: Chris Fox, Division President
CMO: David Ashton Reed, M.D., Chief Medical Officer
CNO: Belinda Trahan, Chief Nursing Officer
Web address: https://lhcgroup.com/locations/louisiana-extended-care-hospital-of-lafayette-2/
Control: Other not-for-profit (including NFP Corporation) **Service**: Acute long-term care hospital

Staffed Beds: 42

OCHSNER LAFAYETTE GENERAL MEDICAL CENTER (190002), 1214 Coolidge Boulevard, Zip 70503-2696, Mailing Address: P.O. Box 52009 OCS, Zip 70505-2009; tel. 337/289-7991, (Includes LAFAYETTE BEHAVIORAL HEALTH, 302 Dulles Drive, Lafayette, Louisiana, Zip 70506-3008, tel. 337/289-8595; Sandra Armand, Director; LAFAYETTE GENERAL ORTHOPEDIC HOSPITAL, 2810 Ambassador Caffery Parkway, Lafayette, Louisiana, Zip 70506-5906, tel. 337/981-2949; Jude Fontenot, Administrator; LAFAYETTE SURGICAL SPECIALTY HOSPITAL, 1101 Kaliste Saloom Road, Lafayette, Louisiana, Zip 70508-5705, tel. 337/769-4100; Buffy H. Domingue, Chief Executive Officer; OCHSNER LAFAYETTE GENERAL SURGICAL HOSPITAL, 1000 West Pinhook Road, Suite 100, Lafayette, Louisiana, Zip 70503-2460, tel. 337/289-8095; Kenneth M. LeBaron, R.N., Administrator) **A**1 2 3 5 10 19 **F**3 8 11 12 13 15 18 20 22 24 26 28 29 30 31 34 35 37 40 41 43 45 46 47 48 49 50 53 54 55 56 57 58 59 64 65 70 72 74 75 76 77 78 79 81 82 84 85 87 89 90 92 93 96 98 107 108 110 111 115 117 118 119 120 121 123 124 126 129 130 131 132 135 145 147 148 149 154 167 169 **S** Ochsner Health, New Orleans, LA
Primary Contact: Al J. Patin, R.N., Chief Executive Officer
COO: Jude Fontenot, Chief Operating Officer
CFO: Kim Hebert, Chief Financial Officer
CMO: Stephen G. Rees, M.D., Vice President Medical Affairs
CIO: Michael Dozier, Vice President, Chief Information Officer
CHR: Sheena Bouquet Ronsonet, Vice President
CNO: Renee D. Delahoussaye, R.N., Vice President, Chief Nursing Officer
Web address: www.lafayettegeneral.com
Control: Other not-for-profit (including NFP Corporation) **Service**: General medical and surgical

Staffed Beds: 527 Admissions: 20651 Census: 328 Outpatient Visits: 166101 Births: 3378 Total Expense ($000): 647043 Payroll Expense ($000): 216780 Personnel: 2396

Hospital, Medicare Provider Number, Address, Telephone, Approval, Facility, and Physician Codes, Health Care System

★ American Hospital Association (AHA) membership
☐ The Joint Commission accreditation
◇ Healthcare Facilities Accreditation Program
◇ DNV Healthcare Inc. accreditation
⇑ Center for Improvement in Healthcare Quality Accreditation
△ Commission on Accreditation of Rehabilitation Facilities (CARF) accreditation

Hospitals, U.S. / LOUISIANA

☒ **OCHSNER UNIVERSITY HOSPITAL & CLINICS (190006)**, 2390 West Congress Street, Zip 70506–4298; tel. 337/261–6000, **A**1 2 3 10 **F**3 8 9 11 12 15 18 19 20 22 29 30 31 34 35 40 45 49 50 55 56 59 61 64 65 66 68 70 75 78 79 81 85 87 97 100 104 107 108 110 111 115 119 124 129 131 132 135 142 144 147 148 149 154 156 167 **S** Ochsner Health, New Orleans, LA
Primary Contact: Glenn Dailey, Chief Executive Officer
CMO: James B Falterman, M.D., Jr, Medical Director
CIO: Michael Dozier, Senior Vice President, Chief Information Officer
CHR: Sheena Bouquet Ronsonet, Vice President Human Resources
CNO: Laurence Marie Vincent, Chief Nursing Officer
Web address: https://www.ochsner.org/locations/ochsner-university-hospital-and-clinics
Control: Other not–for–profit (including NFP Corporation) **Service:** General medical and surgical

Staffed Beds: 52 **Admissions:** 2425 **Census:** 31 **Outpatient Visits:** 231123 **Births:** 0 **Total Expense ($000):** 180303 **Payroll Expense ($000):** 81233 **Personnel:** 775

☒ **OUR LADY OF LOURDES REGIONAL MEDICAL CENTER (190102)**, 4801 Ambassador Caffery Parkway, Zip 70508–6917; tel. 337/470–2000, (Includes OUR LADY OF LOURDES HEART HOSPITAL, 1105 Kaliste Saloom Road, Lafayette, Louisiana, Zip 70508–5705, tel. 337/521–1000; Michelle B. Crain, R.N., MSN, Vice President; OUR LADY OF LOURDES WOMEN'S AND CHILDREN'S HOSPITAL, 4600 Ambassador Caffery Parkway, Lafayette, Louisiana, Zip 70508–6923, P O Box 88030, Zip 70598–8030, tel. 337/521–9100; Donna F. Landry, Interim President, Acadiana Market) **A**1 2 3 5 10 **F**3 8 9 11 12 13 15 16 17 18 19 20 22 24 26 28 29 30 31 32 34 35 38 39 40 41 42 43 46 48 49 50 51 53 54 55 56 57 58 59 60 61 64 65 66 67 70 72 74 75 76 77 78 79 81 82 84 85 86 87 88 89 90 93 94 96 107 108 110 111 114 115 117 118 119 126 127 129 130 132 134 135 143 144 146 147 148 149 150 154 167 169 **P**6 **S** Franciscan Missionaries of Our Lady Health System, Inc., Baton Rouge, LA
Primary Contact: Stephanie Manson, FACHE, President, Acadiana Market
COO: Donna F. Landry, Chief Operating Officer
CFO: Jeremy Rogers, FACHE, Chief Financial Officer
CIO: Ryan J Latiolais, Director Information Systems
CHR: Jennifer Lynch Trahan, Assistant Vice President Human Resources
CNO: Gilbert Glenn Humbert, R.N., Jr, Market Chief Nursing Officer
Web address: www.lourdesrmc.com
Control: Church operated, Nongovernment, not–for–profit **Service:** General medical and surgical

Staffed Beds: 393 **Admissions:** 17787 **Census:** 269 **Outpatient Visits:** 203115 **Births:** 2481 **Total Expense ($000):** 527969 **Payroll Expense ($000):** 186527 **Personnel:** 2281

⇑ **PARK PLACE SURGICAL HOSPITAL (190255)**, 4811 Ambassador Caffery Parkway, Zip 70508–6917; tel. 337/237–8119, (Nonreporting) **A**10 21
Primary Contact: J. Brandon. Moore, FACHE, Chief Executive Officer
Web address: www.parkplacesurgery.com/
Control: Partnership, Investor–owned (for–profit) **Service:** Surgical

Staffed Beds: 10

UNIVERSITY MEDICAL CENTER–PSYCHIATRIC UNIT See Lafayette Behavioral Health

☐ **VERMILION BEHAVIORAL HEALTH SYSTEMS - NORTH CAMPUS (194044)**, 2520 North University Avenue, Zip 70507–5306; tel. 337/234–5614, (Includes VERMILION BEHAVIORAL HEALTH SYSTEMS - SOUTH CAMPUS, 1131 Rue De Belier, Lafayette, Louisiana, Zip 70506–6532, tel. 337/991–0571) **A**1 10 **F**98 99 151 **S** Acadia Healthcare Company, Inc., Franklin, TN
Primary Contact: Amy Apperson, R.N., Chief Executive Officer
CFO: Natalie Lemelle, Chief Financial Officer
CMO: Bob Winston, M.D., Medical Director
CHR: Claire Rowland, Director Human Resources
CNO: Pam Whittington, R.N., Director of Nursing
Web address: www.acadiavermilion.com
Control: Corporation, Investor–owned (for–profit) **Service:** Psychiatric

Staffed Beds: 78 **Admissions:** 3058 **Census:** 63 **Births:** 0

VERMILION BEHAVIORAL HEALTH SYSTEMS SOUTH See Vermilion Behavioral Health Systems – South Campus

WOMEN'S AND CHILDREN'S HOSPITAL See Our Lady of Lourdes Women's and Children's Hospital

LAKE CHARLES—Calcasieu Parish

☒ **CHRISTUS OCHSNER LAKE AREA HOSPITAL (190201)**, 4200 Nelson Road, Zip 70605–4118; tel. 337/474–6370, **A**1 10 **F**3 8 11 12 13 15 29 30 31 32 34 35 40 41 50 55 56 57 58 59 60 61 64 65 68 72 76 78 79 80 81 86 87 93 97 107 108 110 111 114 115 118 119 126 130 132 135 146 147 157 167 **S** CHRISTUS Health, Irving, TX
Primary Contact: Paul Trevino, Chief Executive Officer, CHRISTUS Ochsner Health Southwestern LA
CFO: Nikki Martin, Chief Financial Officer
CIO: Aaron Cook, Director Information Services
CHR: Lisa Friday, Director Human Resources
CNO: Jane Rawls, R.N., Interim Chief Nursing Officer
Web address: www.Lakeareamc.com
Control: Church operated, Nongovernment, not–for–profit **Service:** Obstetrics and gynecology

Staffed Beds: 88 **Admissions:** 2044 **Census:** 19 **Outpatient Visits:** 72543 **Births:** 1353 **Total Expense ($000):** 79775 **Payroll Expense ($000):** 22599 **Personnel:** 306

☒ △ **CHRISTUS OCHSNER ST. PATRICK (190027)**, 524 Dr Michael Debakey Drive, Zip 70601–5799, Mailing Address: P.O. Box 3401, Zip 70602–3401; tel. 337/436–2511, **A**1 2 7 10 19 **F**3 11 17 18 20 22 24 26 28 29 30 31 32 34 35 37 38 40 44 45 46 47 48 49 50 56 57 59 61 64 65 70 74 75 78 79 81 84 85 86 87 89 90 93 96 97 98 100 101 102 103 104 105 107 108 110 115 118 119 120 121 122 123 124 126 130 131 135 146 147 148 154 161 163 164 167 **S** CHRISTUS Health, Irving, TX
Primary Contact: Paul Trevino, Chief Executive Officer, CHRISTUS Ochsner Health Southwestern LA
CFO: Nikki Martin, Chief Financial Officer
CMO: Timothy Haman, M.D., Vice President Medical Affairs
CHR: Shelly Aguillard, Vice President Human Resources
CNO: Jane Rawls, R.N., Interim Chie Nursing Officer
Web address: www.christusochsner.org
Control: Church operated, Nongovernment, not–for–profit **Service:** General medical and surgical

Staffed Beds: 162 **Admissions:** 6551 **Census:** 98 **Outpatient Visits:** 98573 **Births:** 0 **Total Expense ($000):** 195826 **Payroll Expense ($000):** 56283 **Personnel:** 766

☒ **CORNERSTONE SPECIALTY HOSPITALS SOUTHWEST LOUISIANA (192013)**, 524 Doctor Michael Debakey Drive, Zip 70601–5725; tel. 337/310–6000, (Nonreporting) **A**1 10 **S** ScionHealth, Louisville, KY
Primary Contact: Darren Williams, Chief Executive Officer
CFO: Amy Bryant, Chief Financial Officer
CNO: Jeffrey Clark, Chief Nursing Officer
Web address: www.chghospitals.com/sulphur/
Control: Partnership, Investor–owned (for–profit) **Service:** Acute long–term care hospital

Staffed Beds: 28

★ ⇑ **LAKE CHARLES MEMORIAL HOSPITAL (190060)**, 1701 Oak Park Boulevard, Zip 70601–8911; tel. 337/494–3000, (Includes LAKE CHARLES MEMORIAL HOSPITAL FOR WOMEN, 1900 West Gauthier Road, Lake Charles, Louisiana, Zip 70605–7170, tel. 337/480–7000; Bernita Loyd Brown, Vice President and Administrator) (Nonreporting) **A**2 3 5 10 19 21
Primary Contact: Devon Hyde, President and Chief Executive Officer
CFO: Dawn Johnson–Hatcher, Interim Chief Financial Officer, Vice President Finance
CMO: William A. Brown, Chief Medical Officer
CIO: Steve M Stanic, Chief Information Officer
CHR: Ginger Consigney, Vice President Human Resources
Web address: www.lcmh.com
Control: Other not–for–profit (including NFP Corporation) **Service:** General medical and surgical

Staffed Beds: 335

OCEANS BEHAVIORAL HOSPITAL OF LAKE CHARLES (194090), 4250 5th Avenue, Zip 70607–3900; tel. 337/474–7581, (Nonreporting) **A**10 **S** Oceans Healthcare, Plano, TX
Primary Contact: Misty Kelly, Chief Executive Officer and Administrator
COO: Nicholas D Guillory, MSN, Chief Operating Officer
Web address: www.obhlc.info/
Control: Corporation, Investor–owned (for–profit) **Service:** Psychiatric

Staffed Beds: 40

Hospitals, U.S. / LOUISIANA

LAKE PROVIDENCE—East Carroll Parish

EAST CARROLL PARISH HOSPITAL (190208), 336 North Hood Street, Zip 71254-2140; tel. 318/559-4023, (Nonreporting) **A**10
Primary Contact: LaDonna Englerth, Administrator and Chief Executive Officer
CNO: Katie Pippin, R.N., Director of Nursing
Control: Hospital district or authority, Government, Nonfederal **Service**: General medical and surgical

Staffed Beds: 11

LECOMPTE—Rapides Parish

☐ **MERCY BEHAVIORAL HOSPITAL LLC (194118)**, 2810 US 71 South, Zip 71347; tel. 318/290-3900, **A**1 10 **F**29 38 50 56 98 100 101 102 122 130 135 149 154 161 164
Primary Contact: Felicia Powers, Chief Executive Officer
COO: Russell Kahn, Administrator
CMO: Joan Brunson, M.D., Medical Director
CNO: Tanya Fontenot, Director of Nursing
Web address: https://www.mercybh.com/
Control: State, Government, Nonfederal **Service**: Psychiatric

Staffed Beds: 25 **Admissions**: 240 **Census**: 7 **Outpatient Visits**: 0 **Births**: 0
Personnel: 21

LEESVILLE—Vernon Parish

BYRD REGIONAL HOSPITAL (190164), 1020 West Fertitta Boulevard, Zip 71446-4645; tel. 337/239-9041, (Nonreporting) **A**5 10 **S** Allegiance Health Management, Shreveport, LA
Primary Contact: Kevin J. Quinn, Chief Executive Officer
CFO: Kimberly Bridges, Chief Financial Officer
CMO: Thomas Tom Dobbins, M.D., Chief of Staff
CHR: Karolyne Christian, Director Human Resources
CNO: Amy Keene, R.N., Chief Nursing Officer
Web address: www.byrdregional.com
Control: Corporation, Investor-owned (for-profit) **Service**: General medical and surgical

Staffed Beds: 60

☐ **CLEARSKY REHABILITATION HOSPITAL OF LEESVILLE (193086)**, 900 South 6th Street, Zip 71446-4723; tel. 337/392-8118, (Nonreporting) **A**1 10 **S** ClearSky Health, West Lake Hills, TX
Primary Contact: Lacey Sandel, Chief Executive Officer
CMO: Gregory D Lord, M.D., Chief Medical Officer
CHR: Melanie Packer, Administrative Assistant, Director of Human Resources
Web address: https://www.clearskyhealth.com/Leesville
Control: Corporation, Investor-owned (for-profit) **Service**: Rehabilitation

Staffed Beds: 16

☐ **CLEARSKY REHABILITATION HOSPITAL OF ROSEPINE (193050)**, 8088 Hawks Road, Zip 71446-6649; tel. 337/462-8880, (Nonreporting) **A**1 10 **S** ClearSky Health, West Lake Hills, TX
Primary Contact: Robert LaFleur, Chief Executive Officer
Web address: https://www.clearskyhealth.com/Rosepine/
Control: Corporation, Investor-owned (for-profit) **Service**: Rehabilitation

Staffed Beds: 20

LULING—St. Charles Parish

SPECIALTY REHABILITATION HOSPITAL See Premier Rehabilitation

✠ **ST. CHARLES PARISH HOSPITAL (190079)**, 1057 Paul Maillard Road, Zip 70070-4349, Mailing Address: P.O. Box 87, Zip 70070-0087; tel. 985/785-6242, **A**1 3 10 **F**3 7 11 15 18 20 22 24 28 29 30 31 34 35 40 45 50 51 54 57 59 60 64 68 70 75 78 79 81 82 85 86 87 93 96 97 98 100 102 104 107 108 110 111 115 119 130 131 135 143 146 148 154 157 **S** Ochsner Health, New Orleans, LA
Primary Contact: Keith Dacus, MSC, Chief Executive Officer
CFO: Peter Torsch, Chief Financial Officer
CMO: Vadakkipalayam N. Devarajan, Chief Medical Staff
CIO: Angela Boudreaux, Director Information Technology
CHR: Karen Ann Judlin, Director Human Resources
CNO: Jarrett Fuselier, Assistant Vice President Nursing
Web address: https://www.ochsner.org/locations/st-charles-parish-hospital/
Control: Hospital district or authority, Government, Nonfederal **Service**: General medical and surgical

Staffed Beds: 39 **Admissions**: 1837 **Census**: 29 **Outpatient Visits**: 59119
Births: 0 **Total Expense ($000)**: 113091 **Payroll Expense ($000)**: 34076
Personnel: 408

LUTCHER—St. James Parish

BEACON BEHAVIORAL HOSPITAL (194102), 2471 Louisiana Avenue, Zip 70071-5413; tel. 225/258-6103, (Nonreporting) **A**10
Primary Contact: Sean Wendell, CPA, Chief Executive Officer
CNO: Kamara Holmes, Director of Nursing
Web address: www.beaconbh.com
Control: Individual, Investor-owned (for-profit) **Service**: Psychiatric

Staffed Beds: 24

✠ **ST. JAMES PARISH HOSPITAL (191305)**, 1645 Lutcher Avenue, Zip 70071-5150; tel. 225/869-5512, **A**1 10 18 **F**29 34 35 40 45 46 50 51 57 59 64 75 77 80 81 85 93 96 97 107 108 110 111 114 119 129 130 132 133 144 146 149 154
Primary Contact: MaryEllen Pratt, FACHE, Chief Executive Officer
COO: Jeremy Martin, Chief Operating Officer
CFO: Tracy L George, Chief Financial Officer
CHR: Lisa Faucheux, Director Human Resources
CNO: Rhonda Zeringue, R.N., Chief Nursing Officer
Web address: www.sjph.org
Control: Hospital district or authority, Government, Nonfederal **Service**: General medical and surgical

Staffed Beds: 25 **Admissions**: 262 **Census**: 5 **Outpatient Visits**: 55113
Births: 1 **Total Expense ($000)**: 32871 **Payroll Expense ($000)**: 14255
Personnel: 267

MAMOU—Evangeline Parish

✠ **SAVOY MEDICAL CENTER (190025)**, 801 Poinciana Avenue, Zip 70554-2298; tel. 337/468-5261, (Nonreporting) **A**1 10 **S** CHRISTUS Health, Irving, TX
COO: Gerald Fuselier, Chief Operating Officer
CFO: Shelly Soileau, Chief Financial Officer
CMO: Greg Savoy, M.D., Chief Medical Officer
CIO: Daniel LaHaye, Director of Operations
CHR: Annette Thibodeaux, Director Human Resources
Web address: www.savoymedical.com/
Control: City, Government, Nonfederal **Service**: General medical and surgical

Staffed Beds: 60

MANDEVILLE—St. Tammany Parish

COVINGTON TRACE ER & HOSPITAL, 4107 Highway 59, Zip 70471-1962; tel. 985/951-3650, (Nonreporting) **A**22
Primary Contact: Matthew Bernard, M.D., Chief Executive Officer
COO: Sarah Gallaher, Chief Operating Officer
CMO: Matthew Bernard, M.D., Chief Medical Officer
CNO: Dan Flynn, Chief Nursing Officer
Web address: https://covingtonhospital.com/
Control: Corporation, Investor-owned (for-profit) **Service**: General medical and surgical

Staffed Beds: 10

NORTHLAKE BEHAVIORAL HEALTH SYSTEM (194007), 23515 Highway 190, Zip 70448-7334; tel. 985/626-6300, **A**10 **F**5 10 34 35 38 64 71 75 86 87 98 99 100 101 104 105 106 130 132 135 143 153 154 158 160 161 162 163 164 165
Primary Contact: James Buckley, Chief Executive Officer
CFO: Wayne D. Thompson, Chief Financial Officer
CMO: Hyon Su Kim, M.D., Medical Director
CIO: Archie Carriere, Information Technology Technician
CHR: Nicole Messa-Gill, Manager Human Resources
CNO: Jo Nell King, Director of Nursing
Web address: https://northlakebh.org/
Control: Other not-for-profit (including NFP Corporation) **Service**: Psychiatric

Staffed Beds: 105 **Admissions**: 1069 **Census**: 89 **Outpatient Visits**: 2561
Births: 0 **Total Expense ($000)**: 25317 **Payroll Expense ($000)**: 11797
Personnel: 227

Hospital, Medicare Provider Number, Address, Telephone, Approval, Facility, and Physician Codes, Health Care System

★ American Hospital Association (AHA) membership
☐ The Joint Commission accreditation
○ Healthcare Facilities Accreditation Program
◇ DNV Healthcare Inc. accreditation
⇧ Center for Improvement in Healthcare Quality Accreditation
△ Commission on Accreditation of Rehabilitation Facilities (CARF) accreditation

Hospitals, U.S. / LOUISIANA

MANSFIELD—De Soto Parish

★ **DE SOTO REGIONAL HEALTH SYSTEM (190118)**, 207 Jefferson Street, Zip 71052-2603, Mailing Address: P.O. Box 1636, Zip 71052-1636; tel. 318/872-4610, (Nonreporting) **A**10 20 **S** Willis Knighton Health, Shreveport, LA
Primary Contact: Todd Eppler, FACHE, Chief Executive Officer
COO: Christopher Davis, Chief Operating Officer
CFO: Tanika Nash, Chief Financial Officer
CMO: Benjamin Leggio, M.D., Chief Medical Officer
CNO: Heidi Richardson, Chief Nursing Officer
Web address: www.desoregional.com
Control: Other not-for-profit (including NFP Corporation) **Service**: General medical and surgical

Staffed Beds: 10

MANY—Sabine Parish

SABINE MEDICAL CENTER (190218), 240 Highland Drive, Zip 71449-3718; tel. 318/256-5691, (Nonreporting) **A**10 20 **S** Allegiance Health Management, Shreveport, LA
Primary Contact: Dale Anderson, Chief Executive Officer
COO: Doug Plummer, Chief Operating Officer
CFO: Frances F Hopkins, Chief Financial Officer
CNO: Karen Ford, Chief Nursing Officer
Web address: www.sabinemedicalcenter.net
Control: Individual, Investor-owned (for-profit) **Service**: General medical and surgical

Staffed Beds: 24

MARKSVILLE—Avoyelles Parish

AVOYELLES HOSPITAL (190099), 4231 Highway 1192, Zip 71351-4711, Mailing Address: P.O. Box 249, Zip 71351-0249; tel. 318/253-8611, (Includes FREEDOM BEHAVIORAL MARKSVILLE, 426 North Washington Street, Marksville, Louisiana, Zip 71351-2426, P.O. Box 249, Zip 71351-0249, tel. 318/409-0635; Timothey Curry, Chief Executive Officer) **A**5 10 **F**3 15 18 24 29 30 34 35 40 45 54 56 57 64 68 70 79 81 82 85 87 89 91 97 100 107 108 110 114 119 127 130 133 147 148 149 154 164 165
Primary Contact: Timothey Curry, Chief Executive Officer
CFO: Christina White, Financial Manager
CMO: James L. Bordelon, M.D., Jr, Chief of Staff
CIO: Blaine Brouillette, Director Information Technology
CHR: Allison Ferguson, Director Human Resources
CNO: Cindy K. Juneau, Chief Nursing Officer
Web address: https://avoyelleshospital.ahmgt.com/
Control: Corporation, Investor-owned (for-profit) **Service**: General medical and surgical

Staffed Beds: 18 **Admissions**: 1402 **Census**: 6 **Outpatient Visits**: 46952 **Births**: 0 **Total Expense ($000)**: 27434 **Payroll Expense ($000)**: 14519 **Personnel**: 219

COMPASS BEHAVIORAL CENTER OF MARKSVILLE, 137 Dr. Childress Drive, Zip 71351; tel. 318/256-3332, **F**56 98 103 153 **S** Compass Health, Crowley, LA
Primary Contact: Jeremy Autin, Chief Executive Officer
Web address: https://www.compasshealthcare.com/locations/
Control: State, Government, Nonfederal **Service**: Psychiatric

Staffed Beds: 18 **Admissions**: 201 **Census**: 11 **Outpatient Visits**: 0 **Births**: 0 **Personnel**: 21

MARRERO—Jefferson Parish

BRIDGEPOINT CONTINUING CARE HOSPITAL (192007), 1101 Medical Center Boulevard, 7th Floor, Zip 70072-3147; tel. 504/349-6836, (Nonreporting) **A**10 **S** BridgePoint Healthcare, Washington, DC
Primary Contact: Anthony DiGerolamo, R.N., MSN, Chief Executive Officer
Web address: https://www.bridgepointhealthcare.com/
Control: Corporation, Investor-owned (for-profit) **Service**: Acute long-term care hospital

Staffed Beds: 56

△ **WEST JEFFERSON MEDICAL CENTER (190039)**, 1101 Medical Center Boulevard, Zip 70072-3191; tel. 504/347-5511, (Nonreporting) **A**1 3 5 7 10 **S** LCMC Health, New Orleans, LA
Primary Contact: Rob Calhoun, President and Chief Executive Officer
COO: Eli Smith, Chief Operating Officer
CFO: Chad Miller, Chief Financial Officer
CMO: Robert Chugden, M.D., Chief Medical Officer
CHR: Floyd Riedlinger, Director Human Resources
CNO: Monica Bologna, R.N., Chief Nursing Officer
Web address: www.wjmc.org
Control: Other not-for-profit (including NFP Corporation) **Service**: General medical and surgical

Staffed Beds: 252

METAIRIE—Jefferson Parish

DOCTORS HOSP OF JEFFERSON See Doctors Hospital of Jefferson

△ **EAST JEFFERSON GENERAL HOSPITAL (190176)**, 4200 Houma Boulevard, Zip 70006-2996; tel. 504/503-4000, (Includes DOCTORS HOSPITAL OF JEFFERSON, 4320 Houma Boulevard, Metairie, Louisiana, Zip 70006-2973, tel. 504/849-4000; LAKESIDE HOSPITAL, 4700 South I 10 Service Road West, Metairie, Louisiana, Zip 70001-1269, tel. 504/780-4200; Thomas Patrias, FACHE, Chief Executive Officer; LAKEVIEW HOSPITAL, 95 Judge Tanner Boulevard, Covington, Louisiana, Zip 70433-7507, tel. 985/867-3800; Benjamin Richaud, Chief Executive Officer) **A**1 3 5 7 10 **F**3 7 8 11 12 13 14 15 17 18 20 22 24 26 28 29 30 31 34 35 36 37 39 40 44 45 46 47 48 49 50 51 53 54 55 56 57 58 59 64 65 70 72 73 74 75 76 77 78 79 81 82 84 85 86 87 88 90 91 92 93 96 97 98 102 103 107 108 110 111 114 115 116 117 118 119 120 121 123 124 126 128 129 130 131 132 135 136 138 139 141 142 145 146 147 148 149 154 156 160 164 167 169 **P**6 7 **S** LCMC Health, New Orleans, LA
Primary Contact: Gregory Nielsen, Chief Executive Officer
COO: Michael McKendall, Vice President, Operations
CFO: James Wentz, Chief Financial Officer
CMO: Jennifer Meyer, M.D., Chief Medical Officer
CHR: Frank Martinez, Senior Vice President Human Resources
CNO: Ruby Brewer RN, Senior Vice President, Chief Nursing and Quality Officer
Web address: https://www.lcmchealth.org/east-jefferson-general-hospital/
Control: Other not-for-profit (including NFP Corporation) **Service**: General medical and surgical

Staffed Beds: 540 **Admissions**: 28783 **Census**: 327 **Outpatient Visits**: 529893 **Births**: 2488 **Total Expense ($000)**: 1103370 **Payroll Expense ($000)**: 366235

TULANE-LAKESIDE HOSPITAL See Lakeside Hospital

MINDEN—Webster Parish

☐ **MINDEN MEDICAL CENTER (190144)**, 1 Medical Plaza Place, Zip 71055-3330, Mailing Address: P.O. Box 5003, Zip 71058-5003; tel. 318/377-2321, (Nonreporting) **A**1 5 10 19 **S** Allegiance Health Management, Shreveport, LA
Primary Contact: Keith Cox, Chief Executive Officer
CFO: Jade E. Andrews, Regional Chief Financial Officer
CMO: G Max Stell, M.D., Medical Director
CIO: Mace Morgan, Director Information Systems
CHR: Mary Winget, Director Human Resources
CNO: Patricia Bailey, Chief Nursing Officer
Web address: www.mindenmedicalcenter.com
Control: Corporation, Investor-owned (for-profit) **Service**: General medical and surgical

Staffed Beds: 77

MONROE—Ouachita Parish

ALLEGIANCE BEHAVIORAL HEALTH CENTERS See Freedom Behavioral Hospital of Monroe

⇧ **MONROE SURGICAL HOSPITAL (190245)**, 2408 Broadmoor Boulevard, Zip 71201-2963; tel. 318/410-0002, (Nonreporting) **A**10 21
Primary Contact: Robyn Hemphill, Chief Executive Officer and Chief Nursing Officer
CNO: Sharon R. Tackett, R.N., Chief Nursing Officer
Web address: www.monroesurgical.com
Control: Corporation, Investor-owned (for-profit) **Service**: Surgical

Staffed Beds: 10

☐ **OCHSNER LSU HEALTH SHREVEPORT - MONROE MEDICAL CENTER (190011)**, 4864 Jackson Street, Zip 71202-6497, Mailing Address: P.O. Box 1881, Zip 71210-8005; tel. 318/330-7000, **A**1 3 5 10 **F**3 13 15 18 20 22 26 29 30 31 32 34 35 38 39 40 43 44 45 49 50 51 57 59 60 61 64 65 68 70 72 74 75 76 77 78 79 81 84 85 86 87 89 93 97 98 100 102 104 107 108 110 111 114 115 119 126 130 131 132 134 135 144 146 147 149 150 154 157 160 161 162 164 165 167 169 **S** Ochsner Health, New Orleans, LA
Primary Contact: Mark A. Randolph, Chief Executive Officer
COO: Jonathan Phillips, Chief Operating Officer
CFO: Dorothy Whittington, Chief Financial Officer
CMO: Michael O'Neal, M.D., Chief Medical Officer
CIO: Jessie Frank, Assistant Vice President, Information Services
CHR: Rob Hartmann, Assistant Director Human Resources Management
CNO: Traci S. Jordan, MS, R.N., Chief Nursing Officer
Web address: www.uhsystem.com
Control: Other not-for-profit (including NFP Corporation) **Service**: General medical and surgical

Staffed Beds: 127 **Admissions**: 5120 **Census**: 71 **Outpatient Visits**: 136980 **Births**: 1104 **Total Expense ($000)**: 160787 **Payroll Expense ($000)**: 55516 **Personnel**: 684

SPECIALTY HOSPITAL (192016), 309 Jackson Street, 7th Floor, Zip 71201-7407, Mailing Address: P.O. Box 1532, Zip 71210-1532; tel. 318/966-7045, (Nonreporting) **A**10 **S** LHC Group, Lafayette, LA
Primary Contact: Cleta Munholland, Administrator
COO: Pamela Chappell, R.N., Assistant Administrator
CNO: Jerry Rogers, R.N., Director Nurses and Infection Control
Web address: www.lhcgroup.com
Control: Church operated, Nongovernment, not–for–profit **Service:** Acute long–term care hospital

Staffed Beds: 32

ST. FRANCIS MEDICAL CENTER (190125), 309 Jackson Street, Zip 71201-7407, Mailing Address: P.O. Box 1901, Zip 71210-1901; tel. 318/966-4000, **A**1 3 5 8 10 **F**1 3 4 12 13 15 16 17 18 19 20 21 22 23 24 25 26 27 28 29 30 31 32 34 35 37 39 40 43 44 45 46 49 50 54 55 56 57 59 64 65 67 68 69 70 71 72 73 74 75 76 77 78 79 80 81 84 85 87 88 89 90 92 93 96 97 98 107 108 110 111 114 115 118 119 124 126 128 129 130 131 132 135 146 147 148 154 155 156 157 166 167 169 **P**8 **S** Franciscan Missionaries of Our Lady Health System, Inc., Baton Rouge, LA
Primary Contact: Thomas Gullatt, M.D., President
COO: Jeremy Rogers, FACHE, Vice President and Chief Operating Officer
CFO: Jeremy Rogers, FACHE, Chief Operating Officer and Chief Financial Officer
CMO: John Bruchhaus, M.D., Chief Medical Officer
CNO: Kayla Johnson, R.N., Vice President Patient Care Services and Chief Nursing Officer
Web address: www.stfran.com
Control: Church operated, Nongovernment, not–for–profit **Service:** General medical and surgical

Staffed Beds: 321 **Admissions:** 12712 **Census:** 193 **Outpatient Visits:** 194138 **Births:** 2168 **Total Expense ($000):** 347296 **Payroll Expense ($000):** 132419 **Personnel:** 1543

MORGAN CITY—St. Mary Parish

OCHSNER ST. MARY (190014), 1125 Marguerite Street, Zip 70380-1855, Mailing Address: P.O. Box 2308, Zip 70381-2308; tel. 985/384-2200, **A**1 10 20 **F**3 11 15 18 29 34 35 38 40 44 45 57 59 70 74 75 77 79 81 85 87 89 90 91 93 96 97 98 100 101 102 107 108 110 111 115 119 130 132 134 135 146 147 149 154 164 167 **S** Ochsner Health, New Orleans, LA
Primary Contact: Jennifer Wise, Hospital Administrator, Chief Nursing Officer
COO: Don Knight, Assistant Administrator and Risk Manager
CFO: Debbie Kyzar, Interim Chief Financial Officer
CMO: Eric Melancon, Chief of Staff
CIO: Rene Bilello, Manager Information System
CHR: Timothy Hebert, Director Human Resources
CNO: Jennifer Wise, Chief Nursing Officer
Web address: https://www.ochsner.org
Control: Other not–for–profit (including NFP Corporation) **Service:** General medical and surgical

Staffed Beds: 47 **Admissions:** 1450 **Census:** 24 **Outpatient Visits:** 31404 **Births:** 33 **Total Expense ($000):** 44471 **Payroll Expense ($000):** 21548 **Personnel:** 280

NAPOLEONVILLE—Assumption Parish

ASSUMPTION COMMUNITY HOSPITAL See Our Lady of The Lake Assumption Community Hospital

★ **OUR LADY OF THE LAKE ASSUMPTION COMMUNITY HOSPITAL (190779)**, 135 Highway 402, Zip 70390-2217; tel. 985/369-3600, (Nonreporting) **A**10 **S** Franciscan Missionaries of Our Lady Health System, Inc., Baton Rouge, LA
Primary Contact: Brian Frank. Tripode, Senior Director Assumption Administrator
CHR: Tonia Pierre, Coordinator Human Resources
CNO: Donna Mullings, Director of Nursing
Web address: https://ololrmc.com/about-us/assumption-community-hospital/
Control: Other not–for–profit (including NFP Corporation)

Staffed Beds: 6

NATCHITOCHES—Natchitoches Parish

☐ **LOUISIANA EXTENDED CARE HOSPITAL OF NATCHITOCHES (192035)**, 501 Keyser Avenue, Zip 71457-6018; tel. 318/354-2044, (Nonreporting) **A**1 10 **S** LHC Group, Lafayette, LA
Primary Contact: TameKia Colbert, Administrator
CNO: Meghan Castille, R.N., Director of Nursing
Web address: https://lhcgroup.com/locations/louisiana-extended-care-hospital-of-natchitoches/
Control: Corporation, Investor–owned (for–profit) **Service:** Acute long–term care hospital

Staffed Beds: 21

NATCHITOCHES REGIONAL MEDICAL CENTER (190007), 501 Keyser Avenue, Zip 71457-6036, Mailing Address: P.O. Box 2009, Zip 71457-2009; tel. 318/214-4200, (Nonreporting) **A**1 3 10 20 **S** CHRISTUS Health, Irving, TX
Primary Contact: D. Kirk. Soileau, FACHE, Chief Executive Officer
CFO: Brad McCormick, Chief Financial Officer
CMO: Phyllis Mason, M.D., Chief Medical Officer
CIO: Christopher Golden, Director Information Systems
CHR: Ernie Scott, Director Human Resources
CNO: Dawna DeBlieux, Vice President Patient Care Services and Chief Nurse Executive
Web address: www.nrmchospital.org
Control: Hospital district or authority, Government, Nonfederal **Service:** General medical and surgical

Staffed Beds: 91

NEW IBERIA—Iberia Parish

☐ **IBERIA MEDICAL CENTER (190054)**, 2315 East Main Street, Zip 70560-4031, Mailing Address: P.O. Box 13338, Zip 70562-3338; tel. 337/364-0441, **A**1 10 **F**3 11 13 15 18 20 22 28 29 30 31 34 39 40 45 46 47 48 49 50 53 57 64 70 72 74 75 76 78 79 81 85 89 90 93 97 98 103 107 108 110 111 115 119 127 130 135 146 147 149 153 154 167 169 **P**6 **S** HealthTech Management Services, Plano, TX
Primary Contact: Dionne Viator, CPA, FACHE, President and Chief Executive Officer
COO: Shane P Myers, Chief Operating Officer
CFO: Amy Langlinias, Chief Financial Officer
CMO: Shawn Baquet, Chief of Staff
CIO: Vance Robinson, Chief Information Officer
CHR: Lori Spann, Director Human Resources
CNO: Sandy Morein, Chief Nursing Officer
Web address: www.iberiamedicalcenter.com
Control: Hospital district or authority, Government, Nonfederal **Service:** General medical and surgical

Staffed Beds: 166 **Admissions:** 4454 **Census:** 64 **Outpatient Visits:** 127313 **Births:** 368 **Total Expense ($000):** 131342 **Payroll Expense ($000):** 45064 **Personnel:** 525

NEW ORLEANS—Jefferson Parish

OCHSNER EXTENDED CARE HOSPITAL (192015), 2614 Jefferson Highway, 2nd Floor, Zip 70121-3828; tel. 504/314-4242, (Nonreporting) **A**10 **S** LHC Group, Lafayette, LA
Primary Contact: Len McDade, Chief Executive Officer
CMO: Jeremiah Newsom, M.D., Medical Director
CNO: Erika Plaisance, Chief Nursing Officer
Web address: www.lhcgroup.com/
Control: Corporation, Investor–owned (for–profit) **Service:** Acute long–term care hospital

Staffed Beds: 32

OCHSNER MEDICAL CENTER (190036), 1514 Jefferson Highway, Zip 70121-2429; tel. 504/842-3000, (Includes OCHSNER BAPTIST, A CAMPUS OF OCHSNER MEDICAL CENTER, 2700 Napoleon Avenue, New Orleans, Louisiana, Zip 70115-6914, tel. 504/899-9311; Beth Walker, Chief Executive Officer; OCHSNER HOSPITAL FOR ORTHOPEDICS & SPORTS MEDICINE, 1221 South Clearview Parkway, New Orleans, Louisiana, Zip 70121-1011, tel. 504/842-6684; OCHSNER MEDICAL CENTER – WEST BANK, 2500 Belle Chasse Highway, Gretna, Louisiana, Zip 70056-7127, tel. 504/392-3131; Mary Deynoodt, Interim Chief Executive Officer and Chief Operating Officer; OCHSNER MEDICAL CENTER FOR CHILDREN, 1514 Jefferson Highway, New Orleans, Louisiana, Zip 70121-2429, tel. 504/842-3000) (Total facility includes 30 beds in nursing home–type unit) **A**1 2 3 8 10 19 **F**3 4 5 6 7 8 9 11 12 13 14 15 17 18 19 20 21 22 23 24 25 26 27 28 29 30 31 32 33 34 35 36 37 38 40 41 42 44 45 46 47 48 49 50 51 53 54 55 56 57 58 59 60 61 63 64 65 68 70 71 72 73 74 75 76 77 78 79 80 81 82 84 85 86 87 88 89 91 92 93 94 96 97 98 99 100 101 102 104 107 108 110 111 112 114 115 116 117 118 119 120 121 123 124 126 128 129 130 131 132 134 135 136 137 138 139 140 141 142 145 146 147 148 153 154 155 156 157 160 162 165 167 169 **P**6 **S** Ochsner Health, New Orleans, LA
CMO: Patrick J Quinlan, M.D., Chief Executive Officer, Ochsner Clinic Foundation & International Services, Exec. Director Ochsner Center for Community
CIO: Lynn Witherspoon, Vice President and Chief Information Officer
CHR: Joan Mollohan, Vice President Human Resources
Web address: www.ochsner.org
Control: Other not–for–profit (including NFP Corporation) **Service:** General medical and surgical

Staffed Beds: 852 **Admissions:** 39603 **Census:** 642 **Outpatient Visits:** 383875 **Births:** 4280 **Total Expense ($000):** 2454156 **Payroll Expense ($000):** 897936 **Personnel:** 10113

Hospital, Medicare Provider Number, Address, Telephone, Approval, Facility, and Physician Codes, Health Care System

★ American Hospital Association (AHA) membership
☐ The Joint Commission accreditation
○ Healthcare Facilities Accreditation Program
◇ DNV Healthcare Inc. accreditation
⇧ Center for Improvement in Healthcare Quality Accreditation
△ Commission on Accreditation of Rehabilitation Facilities (CARF) accreditation

Hospitals, U.S. / LOUISIANA

☐ **RIVER OAKS HOSPITAL (194031)**, 1525 River Oaks Road West, Zip 70123–2162; tel. 504/734–1740; (Includes RIVER OAKS CHILD AND ADOLESCENT HOSPITAL, 1525 River Oaks Road West, New Orleans, Louisiana, Zip 70123–2162, tel. 504/734–1740) (Nonreporting) **A**1 10 **S** Universal Health Services, Inc., King of Prussia, PA
Primary Contact: Josh Sumrall, Chief Executive Officer
CFO: Linda Weymouth, Chief Financial Officer
CMO: Lincoln Paine, M.D., Medical Director
CIO: Vincent Chatelain, Director Business Development
CHR: Wanda Hoffmann, Director Human Resources
CNO: Brady Rivet, MSN, R.N., Chief Nursing Officer
Web address: www.riveroakshospital.com
Control: Corporation, Investor–owned (for–profit) **Service**: Psychiatric

Staffed Beds: 126

NEW ORLEANS—Orleans Parish

BEACON BEHAVIORAL HOSPITAL – NEW ORLEANS (194084), 14500 Hayne Boulevard, Suite 200, Zip 70128–1751; tel. 504/210–0460, (Includes BEACON BEHAVIORAL HOSPITAL – WESTBANK, 4201 Woodland Drive, New Orleans, Louisiana, Zip 70131–7339, tel. 504/342–4511; Sean Wendell, CPA, Chief Executive Officer) (Nonreporting) **A**10
Primary Contact: Sean Wendell, CPA, Chief Executive Officer
Web address: https://www.beaconbh.com/
Control: Corporation, Investor–owned (for–profit) **Service**: Psychiatric

Staffed Beds: 24

BLIANT SPECIALTY HOSPITAL (192030), 14500 Hayne Boulevard, Suite 100, Zip 70128–1751; tel. 504/210–3000, (Nonreporting) **A**10
Primary Contact: Juanita Bates. Bonds, M.D., President and Chief Executive Officer
CMO: Ricardo Febry, M.D., Medical Director
CHR: Nicole Wilson, Manager Human Resources
CNO: Tamara White, R.N., Director of Nursing
Web address: www.bliantspecialtyhospital.com
Control: Corporation, Investor–owned (for–profit) **Service**: Acute long–term care hospital

Staffed Beds: 73

☐ △ **CHILDREN'S HOSPITAL NEW ORLEANS (193300)**, 200 Henry Clay Avenue, Zip 70118–5720; tel. 504/899–9511, (Includes CHILDREN'S HOSPITAL BEHAVIORAL HEALTH CENTER, 210 State Street, Building 10, New Orleans, Louisiana, Zip 70118–5735, tel. 504/869–7200; John R. Nickens IV, Chief Executive Officer) (Nonreporting) **A**1 3 5 7 10 **S** LCMC Health, New Orleans, LA
Primary Contact: Lucio Fragoso, President and Chief Executive Officer
CFO: Mathew Timmons, Senior Vice President and Chief Operating Officer
CIO: David Singer, Chief Information Officer
CHR: Wendy L Willis, Vice President Human Resources
CNO: Lindsey Casey, MSN, R.N., Senior Vice President, Chief Nursing Officer
Web address: www.chnola.org
Control: Other not–for–profit (including NFP Corporation) **Service**: Children's general medical and surgical

Staffed Beds: 226

COBALT REHABILITATION HOSPITAL OF NEW ORLEANS (193098), 3801 Bienville Street, Zip 70119; tel. 504/930–3500, (Nonreporting) **A**10
Primary Contact: James Munson, R.N., Chief Executive Officer
Web address: www.curahealth.com/inpatient-rehabilitation-facilities/cobalt-rehabilitation-new-orleans/
Control: Partnership, Investor–owned (for–profit) **Service**: Rehabilitation

Staffed Beds: 60

☐ **COMMUNITY CARE HOSPITAL (194056)**, 1421 General Taylor Street, Zip 70115–3717; tel. 504/899–2500, (Nonreporting) **A**1 10
Primary Contact: Paul B. Kavanaugh, President and Chief Executive Officer
CNO: Christine Richmond, Director of Nursing
Web address: www.communitycarehospital.com
Control: State, Government, Nonfederal **Service**: Psychiatric

Staffed Beds: 36

MEMORIAL MEDICAL CENTER See Ochsner Baptist, A Campus of Ochsner Medical Center

⊞ **NEW ORLEANS EAST HOSPITAL (190313)**, 5620 Read Boulevard, Zip 70127–3106, Mailing Address: 5620 Read Blvd, Zip 70127–3106; tel. 504/592–6600, (Nonreporting) **A**1 10 **S** LCMC Health, New Orleans, LA
Primary Contact: Takeisha C. Davis, M.D., M.P.H., President and Chief Executive Officer
COO: Courtney J. Marbley, Chief Operating Officer
CFO: Danielle S. Willis, CPA, Interim Chief Financial Officer, Manager Finance
CMO: Candace Robinson, Chief Medical Officer
CHR: Brion Stanford, Director Human Resources
CNO: Martha Smith, R.N., Chief Nursing Officer
Web address: www.noehospital.org
Control: Hospital district or authority, Government, Nonfederal **Service**: General medical and surgical

Staffed Beds: 34

ST. CHARLES SURGICAL HOSPITAL (190300), 1717 Saint Charles Avenue, Zip 70130–5223; tel. 504/529–6600, (Nonreporting) **A**10 22
Primary Contact: Penny Banks, R.N., Administrator
Web address: www.scsh.com
Control: Corporation, Investor–owned (for–profit) **Service**: Surgical

Staffed Beds: 39

⊞ △ **TOURO INFIRMARY (190046)**, 1401 Foucher Street, Zip 70115–3593; tel. 504/897–7011, (Includes TOURO REHABILITATION CENTER, 1401 Foucher Street, New Orleans, Louisiana, Zip 70115–3515, tel. 504/897–8560; Susan E. Andrews, Chief Executive Officer) (Nonreporting) **A**1 2 3 5 7 10 **S** LCMC Health, New Orleans, LA
Primary Contact: Christopher Lege, Chief Executive Officer
COO: Stephen Baldwin, Chief Operating Officer
CFO: Jay M Pennisson, Chief Financial Officer
CIO: Leann Hughes-Mickel, Chief Information Officer
CHR: Cindy Mousa, Director Human Resources
CNO: Patricia A Rosenberg, R.N., MSN, Chief Nursing Officer
Web address: https://www.lcmchealth.org/touro/
Control: Other not–for–profit (including NFP Corporation) **Service**: General medical and surgical

Staffed Beds: 280

☐ **UNIVERSITY MEDICAL CENTER (190005)**, 2000 Canal Street, Zip 70112–3018; tel. 504/702–3000, **A**1 2 3 5 8 10 **F**3 4 5 8 11 12 15 16 18 20 22 24 26 29 30 31 34 35 39 40 43 45 46 47 49 50 51 55 56 57 58 59 60 61 63 64 65 66 70 74 75 77 78 79 81 83 84 85 86 87 91 92 93 94 97 98 100 102 104 107 108 110 111 112 114 115 116 117 118 119 123 126 129 130 135 141 142 145 146 147 148 149 150 153 154 156 160 162 163 164 165 167 **S** LCMC Health, New Orleans, LA
Primary Contact: John R. Nickens IV, President and Chief Executive Officer
COO: Thomas Patrias, FACHE, Chief Operating Officer
CFO: Christine Williams, Chief Financial Officer
CNO: Allison Guste, Chief Nursing Officer
Web address: www.umcno.org
Control: Other not–for–profit (including NFP Corporation) **Service**: General medical and surgical

Staffed Beds: 386 Admissions: 12896 Census: 265 Outpatient Visits: 411448 Total Expense ($000): 850037 Payroll Expense ($000): 192748 Personnel: 2294

NEW ROADS—Pointe Coupee Parish

⊞ **POINTE COUPEE GENERAL HOSPITAL (191316)**, 2202 False River Drive, Zip 70760–2614; tel. 225/638–6331, (Nonreporting) **A**1 10 18
Primary Contact: Chad E. Olinde, CPA, Chief Executive Officer
CFO: John Cazayoux, Chief Financial Officer
CMO: Paul Rachal, M.D., Chief Medical Officer
CIO: Anthony Sauro, Chief Information Officer
CHR: Lisa Patterson, Director Human Resources
CNO: Valerie Sparks Jarreau, R.N., Chief Nursing Officer
Web address: www.pcgh.org
Control: Hospital district or authority, Government, Nonfederal **Service**: General medical and surgical

Staffed Beds: 23

OAK GROVE—West Carroll Parish

WEST CARROLL MEMORIAL HOSPITAL (190081), 706 Ross Street, Zip 71263–9798; tel. 318/428–3237, (Nonreporting) **A**5 10
Primary Contact: R. Randall. Morris, Administrator
Control: Other not–for–profit (including NFP Corporation) **Service**: General medical and surgical

Staffed Beds: 21

OAKDALE—Allen Parish

OAKDALE COMMUNITY HOSPITAL (190106), 130 North Hospital Drive, Zip 71463–3035, Mailing Address: P.O. Box 629, Zip 71463–0629; tel. 318/335–3700, (Nonreporting) **A**5 10
Primary Contact: Kevin Ardoin, Chief Executive Officer
CFO: John Lawless, Chief Financial Officer
CMO: Tommy Davis, M.D., Chief of Staff
CIO: Monica King, Chief Information Officer
CHR: Becky Johnson, Director Human Resources
CNO: Patricia Erwin, R.N., Chief Nursing Officer
Web address: www.oakdalecommunityhospital.ahmgt.com/
Control: Partnership, Investor–owned (for–profit) **Service**: General medical and surgical

Staffed Beds: 49

Hospitals, U.S. / LOUISIANA

OLLA—Caldwell Parish

HARDTNER MEDICAL CENTER (191315), 1102 North Pine Road, Zip 71465–4804; tel. 318/495–3131, (Nonreporting) **A**5 10 18
Primary Contact: Paul G. Mathews, CPA, Chief Executive Officer
CIO: Sarah Thompson, Director Health Information Management
CNO: Cherry B Salter, Director of Nursing
Web address: www.hardtnermedical.com
Control: Hospital district or authority, Government, Nonfederal **Service**: General medical and surgical

Staffed Beds: 35

OPELOUSAS—St. Landry Parish

☐ **OCEANS BEHAVIORAL HOSPITAL OF OPELOUSAS (194095)**, 1310 Heather Drive, Zip 70570–7714; tel. 337/948–8820, (Nonreporting) **A**1 10 **S** Oceans Healthcare, Plano, TX
Primary Contact: Cayle P. Guillory, Administrator
CNO: Daphne Frame, R.N., Director of Nursing
Web address: https://oceanshealthcare.com/ohc-location/opelousas/
Control: Corporation, Investor–owned (for–profit) **Service**: Psychiatric

Staffed Beds: 20

OPELOUSAS GENERAL HEALTH STSTEM–SOUTH CAMPUS See Opelousas General Health System–South Campus

✠ **OPELOUSAS GENERAL HEALTH SYSTEM (190017)**, 539 East Prudhomme Street, Zip 70570–6499, Mailing Address: P.O. Box 1389, Zip 70571–1389; tel. 337/948–3011, (Includes OPELOUSAS GENERAL HEALTH SYSTEM–SOUTH CAMPUS, 3983 I-49 South Service Road, Opelousas, Louisiana, Zip 70570–8975, tel. 337/948–2100; James B Juneau, Interim Chief Executive Officer) **A**1 2 10 19 **F**3 13 15 28 29 31 34 37 40 44 45 48 49 50 57 60 64 68 70 76 77 78 79 80 81 85 87 89 90 91 93 96 97 98 100 103 104 105 107 108 110 111 112 114 115 116 117 119 121 126 129 130 131 132 146 147 148 149 153 167 **P**6
Primary Contact: Lance Armentor, Chief Executive Officer
COO: Bob Hardy, Chief Operating Officer
CFO: Shelly Soileau, Chief Financial Officer
CMO: Hunt Deblanc, M.D., Chief of Staff
CIO: Jared Lormand, Vice President Information Technology
CHR: Suzanne F Kidder, Human Resources Officer
CNO: Kimberly Probus, Chief Nursing Officer
Web address: www.opelousasgeneral.com
Control: Other not–for–profit (including NFP Corporation) **Service**: General medical and surgical

Staffed Beds: 197 **Admissions:** 4609 **Census:** 60 **Outpatient Visits:** 144898 **Births:** 802 **Total Expense ($000):** 190452 **Payroll Expense ($000):** 76947 **Personnel:** 969

PINEVILLE—Rapides Parish

✠ **ALEXANDRIA VA MEDICAL CENTER**, 2495 Shreveport Highway, 71 N, Zip 71360–4044, Mailing Address: P.O. Box 69004, Alexandria, Zip 71306–9004; tel. 318/473–0010, (Nonreporting) **A**1 3 5 **S** Department of Veterans Affairs, Washington, DC
Primary Contact: Peter C. Dancy Jr, FACHE, Medical Center Director
CFO: Bianca A. Obey, Chief Financial Officer
CMO: Robert Bernard, M.D., Chief of Staff
CIO: Robin McBryde, Chief Information Officer
CHR: Alex Love, Acting Manager Human Resources
CNO: Amy Lesniewski, Associate Director Patient Care Services
Web address: www.alexandria.va.gov/
Control: Veterans Affairs, Government, federal **Service**: General medical and surgical

Staffed Beds: 119

☐ **CENTRAL LOUISIANA STATE HOSPITAL (194025)**, 242 West Shamrock Avenue, Zip 71360–6439, Mailing Address: P.O. Box 5031, Zip 71361–5031; tel. 318/484–6200, (Nonreporting) **A**1 10 **S** Louisiana State Hospitals, Baton Rouge, LA
Primary Contact: Celeste Gauthier, Mental Hospital Administrator 2
COO: Paul Benoit, Associate Administrator
CFO: Tina Darbonne, Chief Financial Officer
CMO: Joel Breving, M.D., Medical Director
CIO: William Haynes, Director Information Technology
CHR: Tom Crout, MS, Director Human Resources
Web address: www.dhh.louisiana.gov/index.cfm/directory/detail/217
Control: State, Government, Nonfederal **Service**: Psychiatric

Staffed Beds: 120

PLAQUEMINE—Iberville Parish

ACCORD REHABILITATION HOSPITAL (193070), 59213 Riverwest Drive, Zip 70764–6552; tel. 225/687–8100, (Nonreporting) **A**10
Primary Contact: Julene McAlister, Administrator
Web address: https://ldh.la.gov/index.cfm/directory/detail/18233/catid/169
Control: Other not–for–profit (including NFP Corporation) **Service**: Rehabilitation

Staffed Beds: 8

RACELAND—Lafourche Parish

✠ **OCHSNER ST. ANNE GENERAL HOSPITAL (191324)**, 4608 Highway 1, Zip 70394–2623; tel. 985/537–6841, **A**1 10 18 **F**3 29 34 35 38 40 44 45 50 56 57 59 64 65 68 70 74 75 76 77 79 81 82 85 86 87 97 98 100 102 104 107 110 111 114 119 127 130 133 135 146 147 149 154 156 160 161 162 164 169 **S** Ochsner Health, New Orleans, LA
Primary Contact: Fernis LeBlanc, Chief Executive Officer, Bayou Region
CNO: Renata Schexnaydre, Chief Nursing Officer
Web address: www.ochsner.org/locations/ochsner-st-anne
Control: Other not–for–profit (including NFP Corporation) **Service**: General medical and surgical

Staffed Beds: 28 **Admissions:** 1534 **Census:** 17 **Outpatient Visits:** 27236 **Births:** 420 **Total Expense ($000):** 55060 **Payroll Expense ($000):** 22460 **Personnel:** 265

RAYVILLE—Richland Parish

RICHARDSON MEDICAL CENTER (190151), 254 Highway 3048, Zip 71269–0388, Mailing Address: P.O. Box 388, Zip 71269–0388; tel. 318/728–4181, (Nonreporting) **A**5 10
Primary Contact: James W. Barrett Jr, Chief Executive Officer
COO: Butch Tolbert, Chief Operating Officer
CFO: Donna Eldridge, Chief Financial Officer
CMO: David Thompson, M.D., Chief of Staff
CHR: Rita Brown, Director Human Resources
CNO: Mark Siratt, Director of Nursing
Web address: www.richardsonmed.org
Control: Hospital district or authority, Government, Nonfederal **Service**: General medical and surgical

Staffed Beds: 38

RUSTON—Lincoln Parish

★ **NORTHERN LOUISIANA MEDICAL CENTER (190086)**, 401 East Vaughn Avenue, Zip 71270–5950; tel. 318/254–2100, (Includes GREEN CLINIC SURGICAL HOSPITAL, 1118 Farmerville Street, Ruston, Louisiana, Zip 71270–5914, tel. 318/232–7700; Chad Conner, Administrator) (Nonreporting) **A**5 10 19 **S** Allegiance Health Management, Shreveport, LA
Primary Contact: Kathy Hall, R.N., Chief Executive Officer
CFO: Michael Lockridge, Chief Financial Officer
CMO: Gregg Arena, M.D., Chief of Staff
CIO: Heather Nolan, Director Information Services
CHR: Tonya Duggan, Director Human Resources
CNO: Jennifer Carpenter, Chief Nursing Officer
Web address: www.northernlouisianamedicalcenter.com
Control: Other not–for–profit (including NFP Corporation) **Service**: General medical and surgical

Staffed Beds: 91

☐ **RUSTON REGIONAL SPECIALTY HOSPITAL (192022)**, 1401 Ezell Street, Zip 71270–7218; tel. 318/251–3126, (Nonreporting) **A**1 10
Primary Contact: Mark J. Rice, Administrator
Web address: www.rustonregional.com/
Control: Corporation, Investor–owned (for–profit) **Service**: Acute long–term care hospital

Staffed Beds: 55

SERENITY SPRINGS SPECIALTY HOSPITAL (194074), 1495 Frazier Road, Zip 71270–1632; tel. 318/202–3860, (Nonreporting) **A**10
Primary Contact: Adrian Williams, Chief Executive Officer
Web address: www.serenityhospital.com
Control: Corporation, Investor–owned (for–profit) **Service**: Psychiatric

Staffed Beds: 18

Hospital, Medicare Provider Number, Address, Telephone, Approval, Facility, and Physician Codes, Health Care System

★ American Hospital Association (AHA) membership
☐ The Joint Commission accreditation
◇ Healthcare Facilities Accreditation Program
◇ DNV Healthcare Inc. accreditation
⇧ Center for Improvement in Healthcare Quality Accreditation
△ Commission on Accreditation of Rehabilitation Facilities (CARF) accreditation

© 2025 AHA Guide

Hospitals, U.S. / LOUISIANA

SAINT FRANCISVILLE—West Feliciana Parish

WEST FELICIANA HOSPITAL (191306), 5266 Commerce Street, Zip 70775, Mailing Address: P.O. Box 368, Zip 70775-0368; tel. 225/635-3811, (Nonreporting) **A**1 10 18
Primary Contact: Lee J. Chastant III, Chief Executive Officer
CFO: Linda Harvey, Chief Financial Officer
CHR: Neta F Leake, Administrative Assistant Human Resources
CNO: Angel Noble, Chief Nursing Officer
Web address: www.wfph.org
Control: Hospital district or authority, Government, Nonfederal **Service**: General medical and surgical

Staffed Beds: 12

SHREVEPORT—Caddo Parish

BRENTWOOD HOSPITAL (194020), 1006 Highland Avenue, Zip 71101-4103; tel. 318/678-7500, (Nonreporting) **A**1 3 5 10 **S** Universal Health Services, Inc., King of Prussia, PA
Primary Contact: William C. Weaver, Group Chief Executive Officer
CFO: Kae Bell, Chief Financial Officer
CMO: Colonel Daniel Feeney, M.D., Medical Director
CHR: Talicia Johnson, Director Human Resources
CNO: Ravon Dominique, Chief Nursing Officer
Web address: www.brentwoodbehavioral.com
Control: Corporation, Investor-owned (for-profit) **Service**: Psychiatric

Staffed Beds: 238

CHRISTUS HEALTH SHREVEPORT-BOSSIER (190041), 1453 East Bert Kouns Industrial Loop, Zip 71105-6800; tel. 318/681-5000, (Includes CHRISTUS BOSSIER EMERGENCY HOSPITAL, 2531 Viking Drive, Bossier City, Louisiana, Zip 71111, tel. 318/681-7000; Jennifer Varnadore, Administrator; CHRISTUS HIGHLAND MEDICAL CENTER, 1453 East Bert Kouns Industrial Loop, Shreveport, Louisiana, Zip 71105-6050, tel. 318/681-5000; Casey Robertson, President and Chief Executive Officer; CHRISTUS IN-PATIENT REHABILITATION CENTER SHREVEPORT-BOSSIER, 1035 Margaret Place, Shreveport, Louisiana, Zip 71101-4315, tel. 318/681-4434; Casey Robertson, President and Chief Executive Officer) **A**1 2 3 10 19 **F**3 11 12 13 15 17 24 27 28 29 30 31 32 34 35 37 40 42 45 46 47 48 49 50 51 54 55 56 57 58 59 60 61 64 70 72 73 75 76 77 78 79 80 81 82 84 85 86 87 90 93 96 97 102 107 108 110 111 114 115 116 117 119 120 121 123 124 126 130 131 132 134 135 146 147 148 149 154 156 157 167 **S** CHRISTUS Health, Irving, TX
Primary Contact: Casey Robertson, President and Chief Executive Officer
COO: Joshua Lamb, Vice President Operations
CFO: Glen Boles, Chief Financial Officer
CMO: Richard Michael, M.D., Vice President Medical Affairs
CIO: Mary Merryman, Regional Director Information Management
CHR: Wendy Chandler, Vice President Human Resources
CNO: Ginger Disante, Chief Nursing Executive
Web address: www.christushealthsb.org
Control: Church operated, Nongovernment, not-for-profit **Service**: General medical and surgical

Staffed Beds: 214 **Admissions:** 9774 **Census:** 125 **Outpatient Visits:** 253137 **Births:** 863 **Total Expense ($000):** 297679 **Payroll Expense ($000):** 89299 **Personnel:** 1032

CHRISTUS SCHUMPERT HIGHLAND See Christus Highland Medical Center

ENCOMPASS HEALTH REHABILITATION HOSPITAL (713028), 8650 Millicent Way, Zip 71115-2228; tel. 318/642-8100, (Nonreporting) **A**1 3 10 **S** Encompass Health Corporation, Birmingham, AL
Primary Contact: Christopher Phillips, Chief Executive Officer
CFO: Michelle Watson, Chief Financial Officer
CMO: Christina Reynolds, M.D., Medical Director
CHR: Veleaka Broadwater, Director Human Resource
CNO: Raven White Foate, Chief Nursing Officer
Web address: www.encompasshealth.com
Control: Corporation, Investor-owned (for-profit) **Service**: Rehabilitation

Staffed Beds: 40

INTENSIVE SPECIALTY HOSPITAL - SHREVEPORT CAMPUS (192010), 1800 Irving Place, Zip 71101-4608; tel. 318/425-4096, (Includes PROMISE HOSPITAL OF LOUISIANA - BOSSIER CITY CAMPUS, 2525 Viking Drive, Bossier City, Louisiana, Zip 71111-2103, tel. 318/841-2525) (Nonreporting) **A**1 10
COO: Anthony Jones, Chief Operating Officer
Web address: https://intensivespecialty.com/portfolio-items/welcome-to-promise/
Control: Corporation, Investor-owned (for-profit) **Service**: Acute long-term care hospital

Staffed Beds: 146

LOUISIANA BEHAVIORAL HEALTH (194116), 9320 Linwood Avenue, Zip 71106-7003, Mailing Address: 3905 Hedgcoxe Road, Unit 250249, Plano, TX, Zip 75025-0840; tel. 318/644-8830, (Nonreporting) **A**10 **S** Oceans Healthcare, Plano, TX
Primary Contact: Lee Edge, Administrator
CFO: Eric Elliott, Chief Financial Officer
Web address: www.oceanshealthcare.com
Control: Corporation, Investor-owned (for-profit) **Service**: Psychiatric

Staffed Beds: 89

OCHSNER LSU HEALTH SHREVEPORT - ACADEMIC MEDICAL CENTER (190098), 1501 Kings Highway, Zip 71103-4228, Mailing Address: P.O. Box 33932, Zip 71130-3932; tel. 318/675-5000, (Includes CHILDREN'S HOSPITAL OF SHREVEPORT, 1501 Kings Highway, Shreveport, Louisiana, Zip 71103-4228, PO Box 33932, Zip 71130-3932, tel. 318/675-5000) **A**1 2 3 5 10 19 **F**3 5 9 15 16 17 18 19 20 21 22 23 24 25 26 27 29 30 31 32 34 35 38 39 40 41 43 44 45 46 47 48 49 50 51 54 55 57 58 59 60 61 64 65 68 70 74 75 77 78 79 81 82 84 85 86 87 88 93 97 100 102 104 107 108 109 110 111 114 115 118 119 120 121 123 124 126 129 130 131 132 134 135 136 146 147 148 149 150 154 157 160 162 163 164 165 167 **S** Ochsner Health, New Orleans, LA
Primary Contact: Chris Mangin, Chief Executive Officer
COO: Stephen Randall, Chief Operating Officer
CFO: Harold White, Vice Chancellor
CIO: Marcus Hobgood, Director Information Services
CHR: David Fuqua, Director Human Resources Management
Web address: www.lsuhscshreveport.edu
Control: Other not-for-profit (including NFP Corporation) **Service**: General medical and surgical

Staffed Beds: 251 **Admissions:** 10750 **Census:** 193 **Outpatient Visits:** 430451 **Births:** 9 **Total Expense ($000):** 735193 **Payroll Expense ($000):** 185107 **Personnel:** 1921

OCHSNER LSU HEALTH SHREVEPORT - ST. MARY MEDICAL CENTER, LLC (190317), 1 Saint Mary Place, Zip 71101-4307; tel. 318/626-0050, **A**1 3 5 **F**3 8 13 15 18 19 29 30 31 32 34 35 38 39 44 48 50 54 55 57 59 64 65 68 70 71 72 74 75 76 78 79 81 82 84 85 86 87 88 89 93 97 100 104 107 110 111 114 115 119 126 129 130 131 132 134 135 146 147 148 149 150 154 156 157 160 162 164 165 169 **S** Ochsner Health, New Orleans, LA
Primary Contact: Riley Waddell, Chief Executive Officer
CFO: Lauri Walton, Interim Chief Financial Officer, Controller
CMO: LaTashia Upton, M.D., Chief Medical Officer
CIO: Jodie Crouch, Assistant Vice President, Information Services
CHR: Rob Lindsey, Vice President Strategic, Business Partner
CNO: Chasity Teer, Chief Nursing Officer
Web address: www.ochsnerlsuhs.org
Control: Other not-for-profit (including NFP Corporation) **Service**: Obstetrics and gynecology

Staffed Beds: 133 **Admissions:** 5832 **Census:** 70 **Outpatient Visits:** 201418 **Births:** 2406 **Total Expense ($000):** 147264 **Payroll Expense ($000):** 52809 **Personnel:** 780

OVERTON BROOKS VETERANS' ADMINISTRATION MEDICAL CENTER, 510 East Stoner Avenue, Zip 71101-4295; tel. 318/221-8411, (Nonreporting) **A**1 3 5 **S** Department of Veterans Affairs, Washington, DC
Primary Contact: Richard Crockett, Director
CFO: Kim Lane, Chief Fiscal Service
CIO: Janey Taylor, Chief Information and Technology
CHR: Michael L Palmier, Chief Human Resources Management
Web address: www.shreveport.va.gov/
Control: Veterans Affairs, Government, federal **Service**: General medical and surgical

Staffed Beds: 119

PAM SPECIALTY HOSPITAL OF SHREVEPORT (192011), 1541 Kings Highway, 10th Floor, Zip 71103-4228; tel. 318/212-2200, **A**1 3 10 **F**1 3 29 60 148 149 **S** PAM Health, Enola, PA
Primary Contact: Marc B. Pearce, Chief Executive Officer
Web address: www.postacutemedical.com
Control: Partnership, Investor-owned (for-profit) **Service**: Acute long-term care hospital

Staffed Beds: 24 **Admissions:** 318 **Census:** 20 **Outpatient Visits:** 0 **Births:** 0 **Total Expense ($000):** 13268 **Payroll Expense ($000):** 5255 **Personnel:** 73

PHYSICIANS BEHAVIORAL HOSPITAL (194094), 2025 Desoto Street, Zip 71103-4717; tel. 318/550-0520, (Nonreporting) **A**10
Primary Contact: Brad Mabry, Administrator
Web address: https://pbhospital.com/
Control: Corporation, Investor-owned (for-profit) **Service**: Psychiatric

Staffed Beds: 24

Hospitals, U.S. / LOUISIANA

PROMISE HOSPITAL OF LOUISIANA – SHREVEPORT CAMPUS See Intensive Specialty Hospital – Shreveport Campus

SHREVEPORT –OVERTON BROOKS VA MEDICAL CENTER See Overton Brooks Veterans' Administration Medical Center

SHREVEPORT REHABILITATION HOSPITAL (713029), 1451 Fern Circle, Zip 71105–4177; tel. 318/232–8880, (Nonreporting) **A**10 **S** Nobis Rehabilitation Partners, Allen, TX
Primary Contact: Brent Martin, Chief Executive Officer
Web address: https://www.shreveport-rehabhospital.com/
Control: Corporation, Investor–owned (for–profit) **Service:** Rehabilitation

Staffed Beds: 40

SPECIALISTS HOSPITAL SHREVEPORT (190278), 1500 Line Avenue, Zip 71101–4639; tel. 318/213–3800, (Nonreporting) **A**10
Primary Contact: Devin Jenkins, MSN, Chief Executive Officer and Chief Operating Officer
COO: Devin Jenkins, MSN, Chief Operating Officer
CFO: Eric Cripps, Chief Financial Officer
CMO: Val Irion, M.D., Medical Director
CHR: Crystal Lawson, Director Human Resource
CNO: Michelle Reeves, R.N., Director of Nursing
Web address: www.specialistshospitalshreveport.com/
Control: Corporation, Investor–owned (for–profit) **Service:** Orthopedic

Staffed Beds: 15

△ **WILLIS KNIGHTON NORTH (190111)**, 2600 Greenwood Road, Zip 71103–3908, Mailing Address: P.O. Box 32600, Zip 71130–2600; tel. 318/212–4000, (Includes WILLIS KNIGHT BOSSIER, 2400 Hospital Drive, Bossier City, Louisiana, Zip 71111–2385, tel. 318/212–7000; Vincent Sedminik, Vice President and Administrator; WILLIS KNIGHTON PIERREMONT, 8001 Youree Drive, Shreveport, Louisiana, Zip 71115, tel. 318/212–3000; WILLIS KNIGHTON SOUTH, 2510 Bert Kouns Industrial Loop, Shreveport, Louisiana, Zip 71118, tel. 318/212–5000; Keri Elrod, Administrator) (Total facility includes 123 beds in nursing home–type unit) **A**1 2 3 5 7 10 19 **F**3 4 5 7 8 12 13 15 17 18 20 22 24 26 28 29 30 31 32 34 35 37 38 39 40 45 46 47 48 49 50 51 52 53 54 55 56 57 58 59 60 62 63 64 65 66 70 72 74 75 76 77 78 79 81 82 84 85 86 87 88 89 90 91 92 93 94 96 97 98 100 101 102 104 107 108 109 110 111 112 114 115 116 117 118 119 120 121 122 123 124 125 126 127 128 129 130 131 132 135 138 139 142 143 144 147 148 149 152 153 154 156 167 169 **S** Willis Knighton Health, Shreveport, LA
Primary Contact: Jaf Fielder, President and Chief Executive Officer
CMO: Dan Moller, M.D., Chief Medical Officer
CNO: Denise Jones, R.N., Chief Nursing Officer
Web address: www.wkhs.com
Control: Other not–for–profit (including NFP Corporation) **Service:** General medical and surgical

Staffed Beds: 813 **Admissions:** 47964 **Census:** 565 **Outpatient Visits:** 979610 **Births:** 2392 **Personnel:** 6252

WILLIS–KNIGHTON NORTH See Willis Knighton North

WILLIS–KNIGHTON PIERREMONT See Willis Knighton Pierremont

WILLIS–KNIGHTON SOUTH See Willis Knighton South

SLIDELL—St. Tammany Parish

OCHSNER MEDICAL CENTER – NORTH SHORE See Slidell Memorial Hospital East

SLIDELL MEMORIAL HOSPITAL (190040), 1001 Gause Boulevard, Zip 70458–2987; tel. 985/280–2200, **A**1 2 3 5 10 **F**3 8 11 12 13 15 17 18 20 22 24 26 28 29 30 31 32 34 35 38 40 45 46 47 49 54 56 57 59 64 65 70 72 75 76 77 78 79 81 82 85 86 87 91 93 96 97 102 107 108 110 111 114 115 116 117 118 119 120 121 124 129 130 132 135 146 148 154 167 169 **S** Ochsner Health, New Orleans, LA
Primary Contact: Sandy Badinger, Chief Executive Officer
COO: Claire Chitwood, Chief Operating Officer
CFO: Patrick Bolander, Chief Financial Officer
CMO: James Newcomb, M.D., Vice President Medical Affairs
CIO: Holly Sanchez, Chief Information Officer
CNO: Ray Holmes, Chief Nursing Officer
Web address: www.slidellmemorial.org
Control: Hospital district or authority, Government, Nonfederal **Service:** General medical and surgical

Staffed Beds: 202 **Admissions:** 10304 **Census:** 113 **Outpatient Visits:** 202226 **Births:** 1068 **Total Expense ($000):** 341786 **Payroll Expense ($000):** 93168 **Personnel:** 646

SLIDELL MEMORIAL HOSPITAL EAST (190204), 100 Medical Center Drive, Zip 70461–5520; tel. 985/649–7070, (Nonreporting) **A**1 3 10 **S** Ochsner Health, New Orleans, LA
Primary Contact: Sandy Badinger, Chief Executive Officer
CFO: Alisha Neal, Chief Financial Officer
CMO: James Newcomb, M.D., Vice President Medical
CHR: Terri Joseph-Taylor, Chief Human Resource Manager
CNO: Cheryl Woods, Chief Nursing Officer
Web address: https://www.ochsner.org/locations/slidell-memorial-hospital-east
Control: Other not–for–profit (including NFP Corporation) **Service:** General medical and surgical

Staffed Beds: 77

SOUTHERN SURGICAL HOSPITAL (190270), 1700 Lindberg Drive, Zip 70458–8062; tel. 985/641–0600, (Nonreporting) **A**1 10
Primary Contact: Michael J. Pisciotta, Chief Executive Officer
CFO: Michael J Maurin, Chief Financial Officer
CMO: J Gosey, M.D., Medical Director
CIO: Buddy Graves, Chief Information Officer
CHR: Lorrie Alfred, Director Human Resources
Web address: www.sshla.com/
Control: Corporation, Investor–owned (for–profit) **Service:** Surgical

Staffed Beds: 37

STERLING SURGICAL HOSPITAL (190256), 989 Robert Boulevard, Zip 70458–2009; tel. 985/690–8200, (Nonreporting) **A**10
Primary Contact: Erin Dianne. Diamond, R.N., Chief Executive Officer
Web address: www.sterlingsurgical.net/
Control: Corporation, Investor–owned (for–profit) **Service:** Surgical

Staffed Beds: 10

SPRINGHILL—Webster Parish

SPRINGHILL MEDICAL CENTER (190088), 2001 Doctors Drive, Zip 71075–4526, Mailing Address: P.O. Box 920, Zip 71075–0920; tel. 318/539–1000, (Nonreporting) **A**1 10 20 **S** Willis Knighton Health, Shreveport, LA
Primary Contact: Peter B. Johnson, Chief Executive Officer
COO: Dana R. Jones, R.N., MSN, Chief Operating Officer
CFO: Brian Griffin, Chief Financial Officer
CMO: Jerry W. Sessions, M.D., Chief Medical Staff
CHR: Ashley Ortego, Director Human Resources and Marketing
CNO: Kristin B Cole, R.N., Chief Nursing Officer
Web address: www.smccare.com
Control: Other not–for–profit (including NFP Corporation) **Service:** General medical and surgical

Staffed Beds: 32

SULPHUR—Calcasieu Parish

WEST CALCASIEU CAMERON HOSPITAL (190013), 701 Cypress Street, Zip 70663–5000, Mailing Address: P.O. Box 2509, Zip 70664–2509; tel. 337/527–7034, (Nonreporting) **A**1 10
Primary Contact: Janie D. Fruge, FACHE, Chief Executive Officer
CFO: Jobie James, Chief Financial Officer
CIO: Michael Klenke, Chief Information Security Officer
CHR: Christi Kingsley, Vice President Human Resources
CNO: Robbin Odom, R.N., MSN, Chief Nursing Officer
Web address: https://wcch.com/
Control: Hospital district or authority, Government, Nonfederal **Service:** General medical and surgical

Staffed Beds: 79

TALLULAH—Madison Parish

MADISON PARISH HOSPITAL (191314), 900 Johnson Street, Zip 71282–4537; tel. 318/574–2374, (Nonreporting) **A**10 18
Primary Contact: William Ermann, Chief Executive Officer
CFO: W Robert Laurents, CPA, Chief Financial Officer
CMO: Lawrence Chenier, Chief Medical Officer
CIO: Charles Whitaker, Director Information Technology
CHR: Chasity Whitaker, Administrative Assistant
CNO: Susan Gaines, Chief Nursing Officer
Web address: www.madisonparishhospital.com
Control: Other not–for–profit (including NFP Corporation) **Service:** General medical and surgical

Staffed Beds: 25

Hospital, Medicare Provider Number, Address, Telephone, Approval, Facility, and Physician Codes, Health Care System

★ American Hospital Association (AHA) membership
☐ The Joint Commission accreditation
○ Healthcare Facilities Accreditation Program
◇ DNV Healthcare Inc. accreditation
⇑ Center for Improvement in Healthcare Quality Accreditation
△ Commission on Accreditation of Rehabilitation Facilities (CARF) accreditation

Hospitals, U.S. / LOUISIANA

THIBODAUX—Lafourche Parish

☒ △ **THIBODAUX REGIONAL HEALTH SYSTEM (190004)**, 602 North Acadia Road, Zip 70301-4847, Mailing Address: P.O. Box 1118, Zip 70302-1118; tel. 985/447-5500, **A**1 2 7 10 **F**3 8 11 12 13 15 18 19 20 22 24 28 29 31 32 34 37 39 40 46 49 50 53 57 59 62 64 70 73 74 75 76 78 79 81 82 85 86 87 89 90 92 93 96 97 104 107 108 110 111 115 116 117 119 120 121 123 124 126 127 129 130 131 132 134 141 144 146 147 148 149 154 156 167 169 **S** Ovation Healthcare, Brentwood, TN
Primary Contact: Greg K. Stock, FACHE, Chief Executive Officer
COO: Eric Degravelle, Vice President Professional Services
CFO: Stephen H East, Chief Financial Officer
CIO: Bernie Clement, Chief Information Officer
CHR: Casey Peltier, Director Human Resources
CNO: Danna Caillouet, R.N., Chief Nursing Officer
Web address: www.thibodaux.com
Control: Other not-for-profit (including NFP Corporation) **Service**: General medical and surgical

Staffed Beds: 138 **Admissions**: 6020 **Census**: 73 **Outpatient Visits**: 432096 **Births**: 939 **Total Expense ($000)**: 278154 **Payroll Expense ($000)**: 111227 **Personnel**: 1158

VIDALIA—Concordia Parish

☐ **RIVERBRIDGE SPECIALTY HOSPITAL (192028)**, 209 Front Street, Zip 71373-2837; tel. 318/336-6500, (Nonreporting) **A**1 10
Primary Contact: Michael Harrell, R.N., Chief Executive Officer
COO: Howard B Koslow, President and Chief Executive Officer
CFO: James Hopwood, Chief Financial Officer
CMO: Randy Tillman, M.D., Chief Medical Staff
CIO: Robert Greene, Director Information Technology
CHR: Roxan Houghton, Director Human Resources
CNO: Regetta Woods, Chief Nursing Officer and Chief Clinical Officer
Web address: www.riverbridgela.com
Control: Corporation, Investor-owned (for-profit) **Service**: Acute long-term care hospital

Staffed Beds: 40

VILLE PLATTE—Evangeline Parish

☐ **MERCY REGIONAL MEDICAL CENTER (190167)**, 800 East Main Street, Zip 70586-4618; tel. 337/363-5684, (Nonreporting) **A**1 10 **S** Allegiance Health Management, Shreveport, LA
Primary Contact: Ashley Fontenot, Chief Executive Officer
CFO: Jessica Broussard, Chief Financial Officer
CMO: Zebediah Stearns, M.D., Chief of Staff
CIO: Courtney Bieber, Director Information Systems
CHR: Cody Ardoin, Director Human Resources
CNO: Natalie Brignac, Chief Nursing Officer
Web address: www.mercyregionalmedicalcenter.com/
Control: Corporation, Investor-owned (for-profit) **Service**: General medical and surgical

Staffed Beds: 30

VIVIAN—Caddo Parish

★ **NORTH CADDO MEDICAL CENTER (191304)**, 815 South Pine Street, Zip 71082-3353, Mailing Address: P.O. Box 792, Zip 71082-0792; tel. 318/375-3235, (Nonreporting) **A**3 5 10 18
Primary Contact: David C. Jones, Administrator
CFO: Dakota Robinson, Interim Chief Financial Officer and Controller
CMO: John H Haynes, M.D., Jr, Chief of Medical Staff
Web address: www.ncmcla.com/
Control: Hospital district or authority, Government, Nonfederal **Service**: General medical and surgical

Staffed Beds: 27

WEST MONROE—Ouachita Parish

★ **CORNERSTONE SPECIALTY HOSPITALS WEST MONROE (192031)**, 6198 Cypress Street, Zip 71291-9010; tel. 318/396-5600, (Nonreporting) **A**10 22 **S** ScionHealth, Louisville, KY
Primary Contact: Chris Simpson, Chief Executive Officer
CFO: Kurt Schultz, Chief Financial Officer
CMO: Khaled Shafici, M.D., President Medical Staff
CHR: Dan Perkins, Corporate Director Human Resources
Web address: www.chghospitals.com/chwm.html
Control: Corporation, Investor-owned (for-profit) **Service**: Acute long-term care hospital

Staffed Beds: 40

⇈ **GLENWOOD REGIONAL MEDICAL CENTER (190160)**, 503 McMillan Road, Zip 71291-5327; tel. 318/329-4200, (Includes GLENWOOD SURGERY CENTER, 1275 Glenwood DR, West Monroe, Louisiana, Zip 71291-5539, 503 McMillan Road, Zip 71291-5327, tel. 318/322-1339) (Nonreporting) **A**10 19 21 **S** Steward Health Care System, LLC, Dallas, TX
Primary Contact: Jonathan Turton, FACHE, President
COO: Lori Mathieu, MSN, Chief Nursing Officer and Chief Operating Officer
CFO: John DeSantis, Interim Chief Financial Officer
CMO: Steve McMahan, M.D., Chief Medical Officer
CIO: Ronnie Maxwell, Director Information Systems
CHR: Jan Walker, Director Human Resources
CNO: Lori Mathieu, MSN, Chief Nursing Officer and Chief Operating Officer
Web address: https://www.glenwoodregional.org/
Control: Corporation, Investor-owned (for-profit) **Service**: General medical and surgical

Staffed Beds: 278

OUACHITA COMMUNITY HOSPITAL See Glenwood Surgery Center

WINNFIELD—Winn Parish

WINN PARISH MEDICAL CENTER (190090), 301 West Boundary Avenue, Zip 71483-3427, Mailing Address: P.O. Box 152, Zip 71483-0152; tel. 318/648-3000, (Nonreporting) **A**5 10
Primary Contact: Monica Lewis, Chief Executive Officer
CFO: Sheri McNeely, Chief Financial Officer
CMO: Eric Dupree, M.D., Chief of Staff
CHR: Ashley S. Files, Director Human Resources, Public Relations and Marketing
CNO: Sabrina Khulmann, R.N., Chief Nursing Officer
Web address: https://winnparishmedical.ahmgt.com/
Control: Partnership, Investor-owned (for-profit) **Service**: General medical and surgical

Staffed Beds: 60

WINNSBORO—Franklin Parish

FRANKLIN MEDICAL CENTER (190140), 2106 Loop Road, Zip 71295-3344, Mailing Address: P.O. Box 1300, Zip 71295-1300; tel. 318/435-9411, (Nonreporting) **A**3 10
Primary Contact: Blake Kramer, Administrator
CFO: William E Page, CPA, Chief Financial Officer
CMO: Jay Busby, M.D., President Medical Staff
CIO: Judy Ogden, Director Information Technology
Web address: www.fmc-cares.com
Control: Hospital district or authority, Government, Nonfederal **Service**: General medical and surgical

Staffed Beds: 42

ZACHARY—East Baton Rouge Parish

AMG SPECIALTY HOSPITAL-ZACHARY (192041), 4601 McHugh Road, Building B, Zip 70791-5348; tel. 225/683-1600, (Nonreporting) **A**10 22 **S** AMG Integrated Healthcare Management, Lafayette, LA
Primary Contact: John Derrick. Landreneau, R.N., Chief Executive Officer
Web address: www.amgzachary.com/
Control: Corporation, Investor-owned (for-profit) **Service**: Acute long-term care hospital

Staffed Beds: 16

☒ **LANE REGIONAL MEDICAL CENTER (190020)**, 6300 Main Street, Zip 70791-4037; tel. 225/658-4000, **A**1 10 **F**3 8 11 12 13 15 20 22 26 29 34 35 36 40 45 46 50 54 57 59 62 64 68 70 73 75 76 77 79 80 81 85 87 90 93 100 107 108 110 111 114 115 119 130 132 144 145 146 148 149 154 167 169 **P**5
Primary Contact: Larry R. Meese Jr, FACHE, Chief Executive Officer
COO: David S. Beck, Chief Operating Officer
CFO: Michael Devall, Chief Financial Officer
CIO: Todd Walters, Director, Information Technology
CNO: Staci Sullivan, R.N., Chief Nursing Officer
Web address: www.lanermc.org
Control: Hospital district or authority, Government, Nonfederal **Service**: General medical and surgical

Staffed Beds: 92 **Admissions**: 3189 **Census**: 39 **Outpatient Visits**: 90698 **Births**: 321 **Total Expense ($000)**: 138597 **Payroll Expense ($000)**: 43540 **Personnel**: 512

MAINE

AUGUSTA—Kennebec County

MAINE VETERANS AFFAIRS MEDICAL CENTER, 1 VA Center, Zip 04330–6719; tel. 207/623–8411, (Nonreporting) **A**1 3 5 **S** Department of Veterans Affairs, Washington, DC
Primary Contact: Tracye B. Davis, FACHE, Medical Center Director
CFO: Daniel Howard, Chief Financial Officer
CMO: Timothy J Richardson, M.D., Chief of Staff
CIO: Richard McNaughton, Chief Information Management Service
CHR: Christine Miller, Chief Human Resources Management Services
Web address: www.maine.va.gov/
Control: Veterans Affairs, Government, federal **Service**: General medical and surgical

Staffed Beds: 109

MAINEGENERAL MEDICAL CENTER (200039), 35 Medical Center Parkway, Zip 04330; tel. 207/626–1000, (Includes MAINEGENERAL MEDICAL CENTER–AUGUSTA CAMPUS, 35 Medical Center Parkway, Augusta, Maine, Zip 04330–9988, tel. 207/626–1000; Chuck Hays, President and Chief Executive Officer) **A**1 2 3 10 **F**3 4 5 8 11 12 13 15 17 18 20 26 28 29 30 31 34 35 36 40 42 44 45 46 47 48 49 50 51 54 55 56 57 58 59 61 64 65 70 73 74 75 76 77 78 79 81 82 84 85 86 87 89 90 92 93 96 97 98 99 100 101 102 104 107 108 110 114 115 116 117 118 119 120 121 123 124 126 129 130 131 132 134 135 144 145 146 147 148 149 153 154 156 160 165 167 169 **P**6 8
Primary Contact: Nathan Howell, President and Chief Executive Officer
COO: Paul Stein, Chief Operating Officer
CFO: Terry Brann, Chief Financial Officer
CMO: Steve Diaz, M.D., Chief Medical Officer
CIO: Daniel Burgess, Chief Information Officer
CHR: Rebecca Lamey, Vice President Human Resources
CNO: Jennifer Riggs, R.N., Chief Nurse Officer
Web address: www.mainegeneral.org
Control: Other not–for–profit (including NFP Corporation) **Service**: General medical and surgical

Staffed Beds: 198 **Admissions:** 8531 **Census:** 161 **Outpatient Visits:** 847439 **Births:** 1012 **Total Expense ($000):** 659376 **Payroll Expense ($000):** 271108 **Personnel:** 3640

MAINEGENERAL MEDICAL CENTER–AUGUSTA CAMPUS See Mainegeneral Medical Center, Augusta

MID–MAINE GENERAL MEDICAL CTR See Mainegeneral Medical Center–Augusta Campus

RIVERVIEW PSYCHIATRIC CENTER (204008), 250 Arsenal Street, Zip 04330–5742; tel. 207/624–3900, (Nonreporting) **A**1 10
Primary Contact: Stephanie George-Ray, Superintendent
COO: David Lovejoy, Chief Operations Officer
CFO: Samantha Kavanaugh, Chief Financial Officer
CMO: Brendan Kirby, M.D., Medical Director
CHR: Aimee Rice, Human Resources Manager
CNO: Roland Pushard, Director of Nursing
Web address: www.state.me.us/dhhs/riverview
Control: State, Government, Nonfederal **Service**: Psychiatric

Staffed Beds: 92

BANGOR—Penobscot County

DOROTHEA DIX PSYCHIATRIC CENTER (204004), 656 State Street, Zip 04401–5609, Mailing Address: P.O. Box 926, Zip 04402–0926; tel. 207/941–4000, (Nonreporting) **A**1 10
Primary Contact: Carolyn Dimek, Superintendent
CMO: Michelle Gardner, M.D., Clinical Director
CHR: Tamra Hanson, Human Resource Manager
CNO: Christine Bellatty, Acting Director of Nursing
Web address: www.maine.gov/dhhs/ddpc/index.shtml
Control: State, Government, Nonfederal **Service**: Psychiatric

Staffed Beds: 100

NORTHERN LIGHT EASTERN MAINE MEDICAL CENTER (200033), 489 State Street, Zip 04401–6674, Mailing Address: P.O. Box 404, Zip 04402–0404; tel. 207/973–7000, **A**1 2 3 5 10 13 **F**3 11 12 13 15 17 18 19 20 22 24 26 28 29 30 31 32 34 35 36 37 39 40 43 44 45 46 47 48 49 50 51 53 54 55 56 57 58 59 60 61 64 65 68 70 72 74 75 76 77 78 79 80 81 82 84 85 86 87 88 89 92 93 96 97 100 102 104 107 108 110 111 115 117 118 119 120 121 123 124 126 129 130 131 132 144 145 146 147 148 149 154 156 167 169 **P**6 **S** Northern Light Health, Brewer, ME
Primary Contact: Gregory LaFrancois, President
CMO: James Raczek, M.D., Sr. Vice President of Operations and Chief Medical Officer
CIO: Catherine Bruno, FACHE, Chief Information Officer
CHR: Greg Howat, Vice President Human Resources
Web address: https://northernlighthealth.org/Eastern-Maine-Medical-Center
Control: Other not-for-profit (including NFP Corporation) **Service**: General medical and surgical

Staffed Beds: 361 **Admissions:** 15684 **Census:** 277 **Outpatient Visits:** 782439 **Births:** 1398 **Total Expense ($000):** 1051036 **Payroll Expense ($000):** 359525 **Personnel:** 3498

★ ⇧ **ST. JOSEPH HOSPITAL (200001)**, 360 Broadway, Zip 04401–3979, Mailing Address: P.O. Box 403, Zip 04402–0403; tel. 207/262–1000, (Nonreporting) **A**10 21 **S** Covenant Health, Tewksbury, MA
Primary Contact: Mary Prybylo, R.N., MSN, FACHE, President
CFO: Michael Hendrix, Chief Financial Officer
CMO: William Wood, M.D., Vice President Medical Affairs
CHR: Paige A Hagerstrom, System Director of Talent Management
CNO: Dianne Swandal, R.N., MSN, Vice President Patient Care
Web address: www.sjhhealth.com
Control: Church operated, Nongovernment, not–for–profit **Service**: General medical and surgical

Staffed Beds: 78

THE ACADIA HOSPITAL (204006), 268 Stillwater Avenue, Zip 04401–3945, Mailing Address: P.O. Box 422, Zip 04402–0422; tel. 207/973–6100, **A**1 3 10 **F**5 29 30 34 43 50 56 58 59 64 74 75 77 87 98 99 100 101 104 130 132 143 149 153 154 160 164 165 **P**6 **S** Northern Light Health, Brewer, ME
Primary Contact: Mark Lukens, President
CFO: Marie Suitter, Chief Financial Officer
CMO: Anthony Ng, M.D., Vice President and Chief Medical Officer
CIO: Jeanne Paradis, Director Information Services
CHR: Paul Bolin, Vice President and Chief Human Resources Officer
CNO: Wayne Steller, Vice President Chief Nursing Officer
Web address: https://northernlighthealth.org/Our-System/Acadia-Hospital/Locations/Hospital
Control: Other not-for-profit (including NFP Corporation) **Service**: Psychiatric

Staffed Beds: 78 **Admissions:** 1589 **Census:** 60 **Outpatient Visits:** 133906 **Births:** 0 **Total Expense ($000):** 67526 **Payroll Expense ($000):** 35644 **Personnel:** 522

BAR HARBOR—Hancock County

★ **MOUNT DESERT ISLAND HOSPITAL (201304)**, 10 Wayman Lane, Zip 04609–1625, Mailing Address: P.O. Box 8, Zip 04609–0008; tel. 207/288–5081, **A**10 18 **F**3 5 6 8 10 11 13 15 28 29 31 34 35 36 39 40 50 54 56 57 59 63 64 65 70 72 73 74 75 76 77 78 79 81 82 84 85 87 91 92 93 97 100 104 107 110 111 115 118 119 125 127 130 131 132 133 135 145 146 147 148 154 156 160 167 169
Primary Contact: Christina Maguire, President and Chief Executive Officer
COO: Christina Maguire, Senior Vice President, Chief Operating Officer and Chief Financial Officer
CFO: Christina Maguire, Senior Vice President, Chief Operating Officer and Chief Financial Officer
CMO: Stuart Davidson, M.D., Chief Medical Officer
CIO: Tom Mockus, Director Information Services
CHR: Sara O'Connell, Director Human Resources
CNO: Karen Mueller, R.N., Chief Nursing Officer
Web address: www.mdihospital.org
Control: Other not-for-profit (including NFP Corporation) **Service**: General medical and surgical

Staffed Beds: 25 **Admissions:** 743 **Census:** 9 **Outpatient Visits:** 210630 **Births:** 60 **Total Expense ($000):** 82848 **Payroll Expense ($000):** 37256 **Personnel:** 400

Hospital, Medicare Provider Number, Address, Telephone, Approval, Facility, and Physician Codes, Health Care System

★ American Hospital Association (AHA) membership ○ Healthcare Facilities Accreditation Program ⇧ Center for Improvement in Healthcare Quality Accreditation
☐ The Joint Commission accreditation ◇ DNV Healthcare Inc. accreditation △ Commission on Accreditation of Rehabilitation Facilities (CARF) accreditation

Hospitals, U.S. / MAINE

BELFAST—Waldo County

WALDO COUNTY GENERAL HOSPITAL (201312), 118 Northport Avenue, Zip 04915-6072, Mailing Address: P.O. Box 287, Zip 04915-0287; tel. 207/338-2500, **A**5 10 18 **F**3 5 11 12 13 15 18 26 29 31 34 35 36 39 40 45 46 50 52 55 56 57 59 63 64 65 70 74 75 76 77 78 79 81 82 84 85 87 90 93 97 107 110 111 115 117 119 125 127 129 130 131 132 133 135 145 146 147 148 149 154 156 160 169 **S** MaineHealth, Portland, ME
Primary Contact: Denise Needham, PharmD, President
CFO: Linda Drinkwater, Chief Financial Officer
CMO: Kent Clark, M.D., Chief Medical Affairs and Quality
CIO: David Felton, Manager Information Systems
CHR: Karen Littlefield, Director Human Resources
CNO: Paula Delahanty, Regional Chief Nursing Officer
Web address: www.wcgh.org
Control: Other not-for-profit (including NFP Corporation) **Service**: General medical and surgical

Staffed Beds: 31 **Admissions**: 1145 **Census**: 21 **Outpatient Visits**: 113406 **Births**: 110 **Total Expense ($000)**: 126523 **Payroll Expense ($000)**: 52430 **Personnel**: 643

BIDDEFORD—York County

SOUTHERN MAINE HEALTH CARE – BIDDEFORD MEDICAL CENTER (200019), 1 Medical Center Drive, Zip 04005-9496, Mailing Address: P.O. Box 626, Zip 04005-0626; tel. 207/283-7000, (Nonreporting) **A**1 2 3 10 **S** MaineHealth, Portland, ME
Primary Contact: Britt Crewse, CPA, Southern Region President
COO: Patricia Aprile, Chief Operating Officer
CFO: Norman Belair, Senior Vice President and Chief Financial Officer
CMO: Michael Albaum, M.D., Senior Vice President and Chief Medical Officer
CIO: Ralph Johnson, Chief Information Officer
CHR: Yvonne McAllister, Senior Director Human Resources
CNO: Joanna Salamone, Senior Vice President Clinical Services and Chief Nursing Officer
Web address: www.smhc.org
Control: Other not-for-profit (including NFP Corporation) **Service**: General medical and surgical

Staffed Beds: 155

BLUE HILL—Hancock County

★ **NORTHERN LIGHT BLUE HILL HOSPITAL (201300)**, 57 Water Street, Zip 04614-5231; tel. 207/374-3400, **A**10 18 **F**3 15 18 28 29 32 33 34 35 36 38 40 44 50 59 64 65 75 77 79 82 84 85 86 87 93 96 97 100 102 104 107 108 110 111 115 119 130 133 135 146 147 148 149 154 156 157 160 169 **P**6 **S** Northern Light Health, Brewer, ME
Primary Contact: John Ronan, President
CFO: Wendy Jones, Interim Chief Financial Officer
CHR: David Wheaton, Director Human Resources
CNO: Kathy Lirakis, R.N., Chief Nursing Officer
Web address: www.bhmh.org
Control: Other not-for-profit (including NFP Corporation) **Service**: General medical and surgical

Staffed Beds: 10 **Admissions**: 487 **Census**: 10 **Outpatient Visits**: 86033 **Births**: 0 **Total Expense ($000)**: 42078 **Payroll Expense ($000)**: 15098 **Personnel**: 195

BRIDGTON—Cumberland County

BRIDGTON HOSPITAL (201310), 10 Hospital Drive, Zip 04009-1148; tel. 207/647-6000, (Nonreporting) **A**10 18 **S** Central Maine HealthCare, Lewiston, ME
Primary Contact: Stephany Jacques, R.N., President
COO: Robert Slattery, Vice President of Operations
CHR: Kirk Miklavic, Director Human Resources
Web address: https://www.cmhc.org/bridgton-hospital/
Control: Other not-for-profit (including NFP Corporation) **Service**: General medical and surgical

Staffed Beds: 22

BRUNSWICK—Cumberland County

MID COAST HOSPITAL (200021), 123 Medical Center Drive, Zip 04011-2652; tel. 207/373-6000, **A**1 2 3 10 **F**3 5 11 12 13 15 18 20 28 29 30 31 32 34 35 36 40 41 44 46 47 48 49 51 53 54 56 57 58 59 61 64 65 66 68 70 74 75 76 77 78 79 81 82 84 85 86 87 89 92 93 97 98 101 102 103 105 107 108 110 111 115 119 129 130 131 132 134 135 144 146 147 148 149 150 152 153 154 156 160 167 169 **S** MaineHealth, Portland, ME
Primary Contact: Christopher Bowe, M.D., President
COO: Philip A Ortolani, Vice President Operations
CFO: Robert N McCue, Vice President Finance
CMO: Scott Mills, M.D., Vice President Medical Staff Administration and Chief Medical Officer
CIO: Gale Stoy, Manager Information Systems
CHR: Coleen M Farrell, Vice President Human Resources
CNO: Deborah MacLeod, MS, R.N., Vice President Nursing and Patient Care Services
Web address: www.midcoasthealth.com
Control: Other not-for-profit (including NFP Corporation) **Service**: General medical and surgical

Staffed Beds: 93 **Admissions**: 4479 **Census**: 69 **Outpatient Visits**: 227461 **Births**: 535 **Total Expense ($000)**: 255673 **Payroll Expense ($000)**: 110355 **Personnel**: 1287

CALAIS—Washington County

★ **CALAIS COMMUNITY HOSPITAL (201305)**, 24 Hospital Lane, Zip 04619-1398; tel. 207/454-9201, (Nonreporting) **A**10 18
Primary Contact: Steve Lail, Chief Executive Officer
COO: Lynnette Parr, Chief Operating Officer
CFO: Lynnette Parr, Vice President Financial Services, Chief Financial Officer
CIO: Dee Dee Travis, Vice President Community Relations
CNO: John Marshall, Chief Nursing Officer
Web address: www.calaishospital.org
Control: Other not-for-profit (including NFP Corporation) **Service**: General medical and surgical

Staffed Beds: 10

CARIBOU—Aroostook County

CARY MEDICAL CENTER (200031), 163 Van Buren Road, Suite 1, Zip 04736-3567; tel. 207/498-3111, (Total facility includes 9 beds in nursing home-type unit) **A**1 10 **F**3 8 11 13 15 28 29 31 32 34 35 36 38 40 43 44 51 53 54 56 57 59 61 64 67 68 70 75 76 77 78 79 81 82 84 85 86 87 89 90 93 97 107 108 111 115 118 121 130 131 132 135 144 146 147 148 156 169 **S** Ovation Healthcare, Brentwood, TN
Primary Contact: Kris A. Doody, Chief Executive Officer
COO: Chelsea Lee Desrosiers, CPA, Chief Operating Officer
CFO: Chelsea Lee Desrosiers, CPA, Chief Financial Officer
CMO: Regen Gallagher, D.O., Chief Medical Officer
CIO: Tim Conroy, Chief Information Officer
CHR: Paula A. Parent, Chief Nursing Officer and Director of Human Resources
Web address: www.carymedicalcenter.org
Control: City, Government, Nonfederal **Service**: General medical and surgical

Staffed Beds: 47 **Admissions**: 1267 **Census**: 32 **Outpatient Visits**: 62749 **Births**: 203 **Total Expense ($000)**: 69378 **Payroll Expense ($000)**: 28074 **Personnel**: 421

DAMARISCOTTA—Lincoln County

★ **LINCOLNHEALTH (201302)**, 35 Miles Street, Zip 04543-4047; tel. 207/563-1234, (Includes LINCOLNHEALTH MILES CAMPUS, 35 Miles Street, Damariscotta, Maine, Zip 04543-4047, tel. 207/563-1234; LINCOLNHEALTH ST. ANDREWS CAMPUS, 6 Saint Andrews Lane, Boothbay Harbor, Maine, Zip 04538-1731, P O Box 417, Zip 04538-0417, tel. 207/633-2121) (Total facility includes 66 beds in nursing home-type unit) **A**10 18 **F**3 5 10 11 13 15 29 30 31 32 34 35 40 44 45 50 57 59 64 65 67 70 75 76 78 79 81 84 85 86 87 93 96 97 107 108 110 111 114 115 119 125 127 128 130 131 132 133 135 144 146 147 148 149 154 156 160 169 **P**6 **S** MaineHealth, Portland, ME
Primary Contact: Cynthia Wade RN, BSN, President
CFO: Wayne Printy, Chief Financial Officer
CIO: David Felton, Regional Chief Information Officer
CHR: Thomas R Girard, Vice President Human Resources
CNO: Christine Anderson, Chief Nursing Officer and Vice President of Patient Care Services
Web address: www.lchcare.org
Control: Other not-for-profit (including NFP Corporation) **Service**: General medical and surgical

Staffed Beds: 91 **Admissions**: 1314 **Census**: 69 **Outpatient Visits**: 132884 **Births**: 120 **Total Expense ($000)**: 126628 **Payroll Expense ($000)**: 51294 **Personnel**: 479

Hospitals, U.S. / MAINE

DOVER–FOXCROFT—Piscataquis County

★ **NORTHERN LIGHT MAYO HOSPITAL (201309)**, 897 West Main Street, Zip 04426–1099; tel. 207/564–8401, **A**10 18 **F**3 5 7 11 13 15 18 28 29 30 31 34 35 40 45 50 57 59 64 65 71 75 76 77 78 79 80 81 82 85 86 87 93 96 97 100 102 104 107 110 111 114 119 127 129 130 133 134 135 146 147 148 149 154 156 160 162 164 165 169 **P**6 **S** Northern Light Health, Brewer, ME
Primary Contact: Marie E. Vienneau, President
CFO: Nancy Glidden, Chief Financial Officer and Vice President Finance
CMO: Challa Reddy, M.D., President Medical Staff
CHR: James R Godley, Vice President of Human Resources
CNO: Denise Scuderi, Vice President Patient Care Services
Web address: www.mayohospital.com
Control: Other not–for–profit (including NFP Corporation) **Service**: General medical and surgical

Staffed Beds: 25 **Admissions**: 793 **Census**: 9 **Outpatient Visits**: 116353
Births: 103 **Total Expense ($000)**: 61019 **Payroll Expense ($000)**: 27197
Personnel: 332

ELLSWORTH—Hancock County

✠ **NORTHERN LIGHT MAINE COAST HOSPITAL (200050)**, 50 Union Street, Zip 04605–1599; tel. 207/664–5311, **A**1 10 20 **F**3 13 15 18 28 29 31 32 34 35 36 38 40 44 45 50 51 59 64 65 70 75 76 77 78 79 81 82 84 85 86 87 93 96 97 100 102 104 107 108 110 111 115 119 129 130 131 133 135 146 147 148 149 154 156 157 160 169 **P**6 **S** Northern Light Health, Brewer, ME
Primary Contact: John Ronan, President
CFO: Chris Frauenhofer, Chief Financial Officer
CMO: Sheena Whittaker, M.D., Chief Medical Officer
CIO: Scott Burtchell, Director Information Systems
CHR: Noah Lundy, Director of Human Resources
CNO: Kristin Cyr, R.N., MSN, Senior Nursing Executive and Vice President of Patient Care Services
Web address: www.mainehospital.org
Control: Other not–for–profit (including NFP Corporation) **Service**: General medical and surgical

Staffed Beds: 45 **Admissions**: 1501 **Census**: 25 **Outpatient Visits**: 201929
Births: 184 **Total Expense ($000)**: 111430 **Payroll Expense ($000)**: 36580
Personnel: 446

FARMINGTON—Franklin County

✠ **FRANKLIN MEMORIAL HOSPITAL (200037)**, 111 Franklin Health Commons, Zip 04938–6144; tel. 207/778–6031, **A**1 10 20 **F**3 5 7 13 15 18 28 29 30 31 34 35 38 40 45 50 51 58 59 61 64 68 70 76 77 78 79 81 82 85 87 89 93 97 100 104 107 108 110 114 119 127 131 133 135 143 149 154 156 157 160 165 169 **S** MaineHealth, Portland, ME
Primary Contact: Barbara Sergio, President
CFO: Daniel Bazemore, Chief Financial Officer
CMO: Michael Rowland, M.D., Vice President Medical Affairs
CIO: Ralph Johnson, Chief Information Officer
CHR: Joline Hart, Vice President Human Resources
Web address: www.mainehealth.org/franklin-community-health-network/locations/franklin-memorial-hospital
Control: Other not–for–profit (including NFP Corporation) **Service**: General medical and surgical

Staffed Beds: 25 **Admissions**: 1776 **Census**: 19 **Outpatient Visits**: 243023
Births: 228 **Total Expense ($000)**: 129461 **Payroll Expense ($000)**: 53213
Personnel: 730

FORT FAIRFIELD—Aroostook County

COMMUNITY GENERAL HEALTH CENTER See The Aroostook Medical Center, Presque Isle

COMMUNITY GENERAL HOSPITAL See Community General Health Center

FORT KENT—Aroostook County

✠ **NORTHERN MAINE MEDICAL CENTER (200052)**, 194 East Main Street, Zip 04743–1497; tel. 207/834–3155, (Total facility includes 45 beds in nursing home–type unit) **A**1 3 10 20 **F**3 15 18 29 31 34 40 45 50 54 57 59 64 67 68 70 75 77 78 79 81 82 85 86 87 89 98 99 100 101 102 103 104 107 108 110 111 115 119 127 128 130 131 132 133 135 146 147 148 156
Primary Contact: Jeff S. Zewe, R.N., President and Chief Executive Officer
CFO: Cindy Daigle, Chief Financial Officer
CMO: Michael Sullivan, M.D., Chief Medical Officer
CIO: Adam Landry, Director of Information Systems
CHR: Robin Damboise, Director Human Resources
CNO: Alain Bois, R.N., Director of Nursing
Web address: www.nmmc.org
Control: Other not–for–profit (including NFP Corporation) **Service**: General medical and surgical

Staffed Beds: 81 **Admissions**: 1345 **Census**: 69 **Outpatient Visits**: 47838
Births: 22 **Total Expense ($000)**: 74503 **Payroll Expense ($000)**: 33817
Personnel: 390

GREENVILLE—Piscataquis County

★ **NORTHERN LIGHT CA DEAN HOSPITAL (201301)**, 364 Pritham Avenue, Zip 04441–1395, Mailing Address: P.O. Box 1129, Zip 04441–1129; tel. 207/695–5200, **A**10 18 **F**3 7 11 15 18 28 29 30 34 35 40 45 50 53 54 56 59 64 71 77 85 87 93 97 102 104 107 114 119 127 130 133 143 148 154 169 **P**6 **S** Northern Light Health, Brewer, ME
Primary Contact: Marie E. Vienneau, President
CFO: Edward Olivier, Chief Financial Officer
CMO: Darin Peck, M.D., Chief of Staff
Web address: www.cadean.org
Control: Other not–for–profit (including NFP Corporation) **Service**: General medical and surgical

Staffed Beds: 14 **Admissions**: 196 **Census**: 11 **Outpatient Visits**: 43192
Births: 0 **Total Expense ($000)**: 22477 **Payroll Expense ($000)**: 10980
Personnel: 132

HOULTON—Aroostook County

✠ **HOULTON REGIONAL HOSPITAL (201308)**, 20 Hartford Street, Zip 04730–1891; tel. 207/532–2900, **A**1 10 18 **F**3 11 13 15 28 29 30 34 40 43 46 59 65 75 76 77 80 81 85 93 96 97 107 108 110 114 119 127 129 130 132 133 135 146 148 149 154 169 **P**6
Primary Contact: Shauna Cameron, FACHE, Chief Executive Officer
CFO: Cynthia Thompson, Chief Financial Officer
CMO: Brian Griffin, Director of Medical Affairs
Web address: www.houlton.net/hrh
Control: Other not–for–profit (including NFP Corporation) **Service**: General medical and surgical

Staffed Beds: 25 **Admissions**: 838 **Census**: 15 **Outpatient Visits**: 85073
Births: 94 **Total Expense ($000)**: 53308 **Payroll Expense ($000)**: 22248
Personnel: 319

LEWISTON—Androscoggin County

☐ △ **CENTRAL MAINE MEDICAL CENTER (200024)**, 300 Main Street, Zip 04240–7027; tel. 207/795–0111, (Nonreporting) **A**1 2 3 5 7 10 13 19 **S** Central Maine HealthCare, Lewiston, ME
Primary Contact: Steven G. Littleson, FACHE, President and Chief Executive Officer
CMO: David Lauver, M.D., Chief Division Hospital Based Care
CIO: Denis Tanguay, Chief Information Officer
CHR: Kirk Miklavic, Director, Human Resources
Web address: www.cmmc.org
Control: Other not–for–profit (including NFP Corporation) **Service**: General medical and surgical

Staffed Beds: 190

Hospitals, U.S. / MAINE

★ △ ⇑ **ST. MARY'S REGIONAL MEDICAL CENTER (200034)**, 93 Campus Avenue, Zip 04240–6030, Mailing Address: P.O. Box 291, Zip 04243–0291; tel. 207/777–8100, (Nonreporting) **A**2 3 5 7 10 21 **S** Covenant Health, Tewksbury, MA
Primary Contact: Cindy Segar-Miller, FACHE, R.N., President
CFO: Michael Hendrix, Chief Financial Officer
CMO: Christopher Bowe, M.D., Chief Medical Officer, Medical Affairs
CIO: Karen Bowling, Chief Information Officer
CHR: Nicole Morin–Scribner, Director Human Resources
CNO: Karen Clark, Vice President Patient Care Services
Web address: www.stmarysmaine.com
Control: Other not–for–profit (including NFP Corporation) **Service**: General medical and surgical

Staffed Beds: 350

LINCOLN—Penobscot County

★ **PENOBSCOT VALLEY HOSPITAL (201303)**, 7 Transalpine Road, Zip 04457–4222, Mailing Address: P.O. Box 368, Zip 04457–0368; tel. 207/794–3321, (Nonreporting) **A**10 18
Primary Contact: Melissa Pelkey, Chief Executive Officer
CFO: Ann Marie Rush, Chief Financial Officer
CHR: Sarah Loman, Director Human Resources
Web address: www.pvhme.org
Control: Other not–for–profit (including NFP Corporation) **Service**: General medical and surgical

Staffed Beds: 25

MACHIAS—Washington County

★ **DOWN EAST COMMUNITY HOSPITAL (201311)**, 11 Hospital Drive, Zip 04654–3325; tel. 207/255–3356, **A**10 18 **F**3 13 15 29 34 35 40 45 57 64 65 74 76 77 79 81 82 83 85 89 93 94 96 97 107 110 111 115 119 127 130 133 146 147 148 154 160 169
Primary Contact: Steve Lail, Chief Executive Officer
CMO: Aziz Massaad, M.D., Medical Staff President
CHR: Ernestine O Reisman, Vice President Human Resources
CNO: Stephanie Lakeman Baillargeon, R.N., Chief Nursing Officer
Web address: www.dech.org
Control: Other not–for–profit (including NFP Corporation) **Service**: General medical and surgical

Staffed Beds: 25 **Admissions**: 530 **Census**: 7 **Outpatient Visits**: 43776 **Births**: 112 **Total Expense ($000)**: 63607 **Payroll Expense ($000)**: 24082 **Personnel**: 251

MARS HILL—Aroostook County

AROOSTOOK HEALTH CENTER See The Aroostook Medical Center, Presque Isle

MILLINOCKET—Penobscot County

★ **MILLINOCKET REGIONAL HOSPITAL (201307)**, 200 Somerset Street, Zip 04462–1298; tel. 207/723–5161, **A**10 18 **F**3 5 15 26 29 31 34 35 40 41 45 50 53 56 59 65 68 75 77 78 79 80 81 82 85 87 93 96 97 107 108 110 114 118 119 127 128 130 131 132 133 135 154 156 160
Primary Contact: Robert Peterson, FACHE, Chief Executive Officer
CFO: Catherine LeMay, Vice President Finance
CMO: Daniel Herbert, M.D., Medical Administrative Officer
CHR: Lisa Arsenault, Vice President Human Resources and Compliance
CNO: Mary Tatro Esq, Chief Nursing Officer
Web address: www.mrhme.org
Control: Other not–for–profit (including NFP Corporation) **Service**: General medical and surgical

Staffed Beds: 25 **Admissions**: 401 **Census**: 4 **Outpatient Visits**: 25105 **Births**: 2 **Total Expense ($000)**: 31101 **Payroll Expense ($000)**: 13986 **Personnel**: 157

NORWAY—Oxford County

★ **MAINEHEALTH STEPHENS HOSPITAL (201315)**, 181 Main Street, Zip 04268–5664; tel. 207/743–5933, **A**3 10 18 **F**3 5 7 13 15 28 29 31 34 35 36 40 45 54 59 64 65 68 75 76 77 78 80 81 84 85 87 89 93 96 97 100 107 108 110 111 115 118 119 127 130 132 135 143 147 148 149 154 160 167 169 **S** MaineHealth, Portland, ME
Primary Contact: Jeff Noblin, FACHE, President
CMO: James Eshleman, D.O., President Medical Staff
CHR: Roberta Metivier, Vice President Human Resources and Administrator, Western Main Nursing Home
Web address: https://mainehealth.org
Control: Other not–for–profit (including NFP Corporation) **Service**: General medical and surgical

Staffed Beds: 25 **Admissions**: 1410 **Census**: 16 **Outpatient Visits**: 103873 **Births**: 207 **Total Expense ($000)**: 103894 **Payroll Expense ($000)**: 41819 **Personnel**: 430

PITTSFIELD—Somerset County

⊞ **NORTHERN LIGHT SEBASTICOOK VALLEY HOSPITAL (201313)**, 447 North Main Street, Zip 04967–3707; tel. 207/487–4000, **A**1 10 18 **F**3 7 11 15 18 28 29 30 32 34 35 40 45 46 50 51 57 59 64 65 70 75 77 79 81 87 93 97 100 104 107 108 111 115 119 127 129 130 132 133 135 143 146 147 148 149 154 156 **P**6 **S** Northern Light Health, Brewer, ME
Primary Contact: Randy Clark, President
COO: Michael D. Peterson, FACHE, Chief Operating Officer
CMO: Robert Schlager, M.D., Chief Medical Officer
CIO: Michael D. Peterson, FACHE, Chief Operating Officer
CHR: Tammy Hatch, Manager
Web address: www.sebasticookvalleyhealth.org
Control: Other not–for–profit (including NFP Corporation) **Service**: General medical and surgical

Staffed Beds: 25 **Admissions**: 864 **Census**: 12 **Outpatient Visits**: 125436 **Births**: 0 **Total Expense ($000)**: 54812 **Payroll Expense ($000)**: 21097 **Personnel**: 255

PORTLAND—Cumberland County

BRIGHTON CAMPUS–MAINE MED CTR See Maine Medical Center, Brighton Campus

⊞ **MAINEHEALTH MAINE MEDICAL CENTER (200009)**, 22 Bramhall Street, Zip 04102–3175; tel. 207/662–0111, (Includes BARBARA BUSH CHILDREN'S HOSPITAL, 22 Bramhall Street, Portland, Maine, Zip 04102–3134, tel. 207/662–0111; Richard W Petersen, President and Chief Executive Officer; MAINE MEDICAL CENTER, BRIGHTON CAMPUS, 335 Brighton Avenue, Portland, Maine, Zip 04102–9735, P O Box 9735, Zip 04102–9735, tel. 207/879–8000; Richard W Petersen, President and Chief Executive Officer) (Nonreporting) **A**1 2 3 5 8 10 **S** MaineHealth, Portland, ME
Primary Contact: Britt Crewse, CPA, Southern Region President
COO: Kathryn Cope, Chief Operating Officer
CFO: Lou Inzana, Chief Financial Officer and MaineHealth Associate Chief Financial Officer
CMO: Joel Botler, M.D., Chief Medical Officer
CIO: Don MacMillan, MS, Senior Director of Information Services, Regional Chief Information Officer
CHR: Margo Peffer, Vice President, Human Resources
Web address: www.mmc.org
Control: Other not–for–profit (including NFP Corporation) **Service**: General medical and surgical

Staffed Beds: 758

⊞ **NEW ENGLAND REHABILITATION HOSPITAL OF PORTLAND (203025)**, 335 Brighton Avenue, Zip 04102–2363; tel. 207/775–4000, (Nonreporting) **A**1 3 10 **S** Encompass Health Corporation, Birmingham, AL
Primary Contact: Nabarun Kundu, Chief Executive Officer
CFO: James Paladino, Controller
CMO: Thomas Morrione, Medical Director
CHR: Mary Cote, Director Human Resources
CNO: Sharon Kuhrt, Chief Nursing Officer
Web address: www.nerhp.org
Control: Partnership, Investor–owned (for–profit) **Service**: Rehabilitation

Staffed Beds: 90

⊞ **NORTHERN LIGHT MERCY HOSPITAL (200008)**, 175 Fore River Parkway, Zip 04102–2779; tel. 207/879–3000, **A**1 2 10 **F**3 5 11 13 15 18 20 29 30 31 34 35 36 40 44 45 48 49 50 51 54 55 56 57 59 61 64 65 70 74 75 76 77 78 79 81 82 84 85 86 87 93 96 97 100 102 104 107 108 110 111 115 117 119 126 130 132 135 143 144 146 147 148 149 154 156 160 164 167 169 **P**6 **S** Northern Light Health, Brewer, ME
Primary Contact: Charles D. Therrien, President
CFO: Michael Hachey, Senior Vice President and Chief Financial Officer
CIO: Craig Dreher, Chief Information Officer
CHR: Elizabeth B Christensen, Director Human Resources
CNO: Bette Neville, R.N., MSN, Vice President and Chief Nursing Officer
Web address: https://northernlighthealth.org/Mercy-Hospital
Control: Other not–for–profit (including NFP Corporation) **Service**: General medical and surgical

Staffed Beds: 77 **Admissions**: 3627 **Census**: 45 **Outpatient Visits**: 426139 **Births**: 660 **Total Expense ($000)**: 279011 **Payroll Expense ($000)**: 118977 **Personnel**: 1259

THE BARBARA BUSH CHILDREN'S HOSPITAL See Barbara Bush Children's Hospital

Hospitals, U.S. / MAINE

PRESQUE ISLE—Aroostook County

☒ **THE AROOSTOOK MEDICAL CENTER (200018)**, 140 Academy Street, Zip 04769–3171, Mailing Address: P.O. Box 151, Zip 04769–0151; tel. 207/768–4000, (Includes AROOSTOOK HEALTH CENTER, 15 Highland Ave, Mars Hill, Maine, Zip 04758–3133, 15 Highland Avenue, Zip 04758, tel. 207/768–4900; ARTHUR R. GOULD MEMORIAL HOSPITAL, 140 Academy ST, Presque Isle, Maine, Zip 04769–3102, P O Box 151, Zip 04769, tel. 207/768–4000; COMMUNITY GENERAL HEALTH CENTER, 3 Green Street, Fort Fairfield, Maine, Zip 04742, tel. 207/768–4700) (Total facility includes 30 beds in nursing home–type unit) **A**1 10 **F**3 7 12 13 15 18 20 28 29 30 31 32 34 35 36 38 40 45 50 51 53 54 56 57 59 60 61 64 65 67 68 70 74 75 76 78 79 81 82 84 85 86 87 90 91 93 96 97 100 102 104 107 108 110 111 115 116 117 118 119 120 121 123 124 128 129 130 131 132 133 134 135 143 144 146 147 148 149 150 154 156 167 169 **P**6 **S** Northern Light Health, Brewer, ME
Primary Contact: Jay Reynolds, M.D., President
COO: Jay Reynolds, M.D., Chief Medical Officer and Chief Clinical Officer
CFO: C Bruce Sandstrom, Vice President and Chief Financial Officer
CMO: Jay Reynolds, M.D., Chief Medical Officer and Chief Clinical Officer
CIO: Kyle Johnson, Chief Information Officer
CHR: Joseph Siddiqui, Vice President Human Resources
Web address: https://northernlighthealth.org/A-R-Gould-Hospital
Control: Other not–for–profit (including NFP Corporation) **Service**: General medical and surgical

Staffed Beds: 125 **Admissions:** 1805 **Census:** 65 **Outpatient Visits:** 316015 **Births:** 175 **Total Expense ($000):** 170722 **Payroll Expense ($000):** 72660 **Personnel:** 873

ROCKPORT—Knox County

☐ **MAINEHEALTH PEN BAY MEDICAL CENTER (200063)**, 6 Glen Cove Drive, Zip 04856–4240; tel. 207/921–8000, **A**1 3 10 20 **F**3 4 5 13 15 18 28 29 30 31 32 34 35 36 38 40 44 45 46 47 48 49 50 55 56 58 59 64 65 68 70 74 75 76 77 78 79 81 82 83 84 85 86 87 89 91 92 93 94 96 97 98 100 104 107 108 110 111 115 116 117 118 119 130 131 132 135 144 146 147 148 149 154 156 157 160 165 167 169 **S** MaineHealth, Portland, ME
Primary Contact: Denise Needham, PharmD, President
COO: Eric Waters, Vice President Operations
CFO: Maura Kelly, Vice President Fiscal Services
CMO: Dana L Goldsmith, M.D., Vice President Medical Affairs
CIO: Brooks Betts, Director Information Systems and Chief Information Officer
CHR: Thomas R Girard, Vice President Human Resources
CNO: Paula Delahanty, Regional Chief Nursing Officer
Web address: www.penbayhealthcare.org
Control: Other not–for–profit (including NFP Corporation) **Service**: General medical and surgical

Staffed Beds: 163 **Admissions:** 2751 **Census:** 100 **Outpatient Visits:** 138432 **Births:** 209 **Total Expense ($000):** 215908 **Payroll Expense ($000):** 83616 **Personnel:** 727

RUMFORD—Oxford County

RUMFORD HOSPITAL (201306), 420 Franklin Street, Zip 04276–2145; tel. 207/369–1000, (Nonreporting) **A**3 10 18 **S** Central Maine HealthCare, Lewiston, ME
Primary Contact: Stephany Jacques, R.N., President
CNO: Becky Hall, R.N., Director Nursing
Web address: https://www.cmhc.org/rumford-hospital/
Control: Other not–for–profit (including NFP Corporation) **Service**: General medical and surgical

Staffed Beds: 25

SKOWHEGAN—Somerset County

★ **REDINGTON–FAIRVIEW GENERAL HOSPITAL (201314)**, 46 Fairview Avenue, Zip 04976, Mailing Address: PO Box 468, Zip 04976–0468; tel. 207/474–5121, **A**10 18 **F**3 7 11 13 15 28 29 30 31 34 35 40 45 47 50 53 57 59 65 70 74 75 76 77 79 81 82 84 85 91 92 93 97 107 108 110 114 115 118 119 130 131 132 133 134 135 146 147 148 154 156 160 169 **P**6
Primary Contact: Richard D. Willett, Chief Executive Officer
CFO: Elmer H Doucette, Chief Financial Officer
CMO: Gust Stringos, M.D., Medical Staff Director
CHR: Lisa G. Landry, Human Resources Director
Web address: www.rfgh.net
Control: Other not–for–profit (including NFP Corporation) **Service**: General medical and surgical

Staffed Beds: 25 **Admissions:** 1057 **Census:** 12 **Outpatient Visits:** 91847 **Births:** 115 **Total Expense ($000):** 140332 **Payroll Expense ($000):** 59306 **Personnel:** 766

WATERVILLE—Kennebec County

★ ○ **NORTHERN LIGHT INLAND HOSPITAL (200041)**, 200 Kennedy Memorial Drive, Zip 04901–4595; tel. 207/861–3000, **A**10 11 **F**3 13 15 18 28 29 30 34 35 36 40 43 44 45 50 51 56 59 64 65 70 74 75 76 77 79 81 82 84 85 86 87 92 93 96 97 100 102 104 107 108 110 111 115 119 127 130 132 135 144 146 147 148 149 154 156 162 164 169 **P**6 **S** Northern Light Health, Brewer, ME
Primary Contact: Tricia Costigan, FACHE, President
COO: Daniel Booth, Vice President Operations and Chief Human Resources Officer
CFO: Chris Frauenhofer, Vice President of Finance
CMO: Nishan Chobanian, M.D., Vice President of the Practices and Senior Physician Executive
CIO: Kevin Dieterich, Director Information Services
CHR: Daniel Booth, Vice President Operations
CNO: Courtney L. Cook, Vice President of Nursing and Patient Care Services
Web address: https://northernlighthealth.org/inland-hospital
Control: Other not–for–profit (including NFP Corporation) **Service**: General medical and surgical

Staffed Beds: 35 **Admissions:** 1043 **Census:** 20 **Outpatient Visits:** 181449 **Births:** 283 **Total Expense ($000):** 84770 **Payroll Expense ($000):** 30658 **Personnel:** 379

WESTBROOK—Cumberland County

☒ **MAINEHEALTH BEHAVIORAL HEALTH AT SPRING HARBOR (204005)**, 123 Andover Road, Zip 04092–3850; tel. 207/761–2200, **A**1 3 10 **F**75 80 87 98 99 100 103 105 130 135 154 160 164 **S** MaineHealth, Portland, ME
Primary Contact: Kelly Barton, President
CMO: Girard Robinson, M.D., Senior Vice President Medical and Clinical Affairs
CIO: Susan Moulton, Director Health Information Management
CHR: Timothy McNulty, Director Human Resources
Web address: www.springharbor.org
Control: Other not–for–profit (including NFP Corporation) **Service**: Psychiatric

Staffed Beds: 95 **Admissions:** 1288 **Census:** 64 **Outpatient Visits:** 863 **Births:** 0 **Total Expense ($000):** 45718 **Payroll Expense ($000):** 20481 **Personnel:** 253

YORK—York County

★ **YORK HOSPITAL (200020)**, 15 Hospital Drive, Zip 03909–1099; tel. 207/363–4321, (Nonreporting) **A**10
Primary Contact: Patrick Taylor, M.D., President and Chief Executive Officer
CFO: Robin LaBonte, Leader Financial Care
CMO: Jennifer Cutts, M.D., Chief Medical Officer
CIO: Robin LaBonte, Leader Financial Care
CHR: Olivia Chayer, Director, Human Resources
Web address: www.yorkhospital.com
Control: Other not–for–profit (including NFP Corporation) **Service**: General medical and surgical

Staffed Beds: 58

Hospital, Medicare Provider Number, Address, Telephone, Approval, Facility, and Physician Codes, Health Care System

★ American Hospital Association (AHA) membership
☐ The Joint Commission accreditation
○ Healthcare Facilities Accreditation Program
◇ DNV Healthcare Inc. accreditation
⇑ Center for Improvement in Healthcare Quality Accreditation
△ Commission on Accreditation of Rehabilitation Facilities (CARF) accreditation

MARYLAND

ANNAPOLIS—Anne Arundel County

ANNE ARUNDEL MEDICAL CENTER See Luminis Health Anne Arundel Medical Center

LUMINIS HEALTH ANNE ARUNDEL MEDICAL CENTER (210023), 2001 Medical Parkway, Zip 21401–3019; tel. 443/481–1000, (Total facility includes 40 beds in nursing home–type unit) **A**1 2 3 5 8 10 **F**3 4 9 11 12 13 14 15 18 20 22 24 26 28 29 30 31 32 34 35 37 38 39 40 41 44 45 46 47 48 49 50 54 55 56 57 58 59 60 61 63 64 65 66 68 70 72 74 75 76 77 78 79 81 82 84 85 86 87 89 91 92 93 94 96 98 100 101 102 104 105 107 108 110 111 115 119 123 124 126 129 130 131 132 135 146 147 148 149 150 153 154 156 157 164 165 166 167 169 **S** Luminis Health, Annapolis, MD
Primary Contact: Sherry B. Perkins, Ph.D., R.N., President
COO: Jennifer Harrington, Chief Operating Officer
CFO: Robert Reilly, Vice President and Chief Financial Officer
CMO: Stephen Selinger, M.D., Chief Medical Officer
CIO: Barbara Baldwin, Chief Information Officer
CHR: Julie McGovern, Vice President Human Resources
CNO: Christine Frost, Chief Nursing Officer
Web address: www.aahs.org
Control: Other not–for–profit (including NFP Corporation) **Service**: General medical and surgical

Staffed Beds: 480 Admissions: 22506 Census: 312 Outpatient Visits: 168709 Births: 5369 Total Expense ($000): 655836 Payroll Expense ($000): 232433 Personnel: 2506

BALTIMORE—Baltimore City County

ASCENSION SAINT AGNES (210011), 900 South Caton Avenue, Zip 21229–5201; tel. 667/234–6000, (Nonreporting) **A**1 2 3 5 10 **S** Ascension Healthcare, Saint Louis, MO
Primary Contact: Beau Higginbotham, Interim Chief Executive Officer, Chief Strategy Officer and Chief Operating Officer
COO: Beau Higginbotham, Chief Operating Officer
CFO: Scott Furniss, Vice President and Chief Financial Officer
CMO: Nancy Hammond, M.D., Vice President, Chief Medical Officer
CHR: James Bobbitt, Vice President Human Resources, Group Ministry Market
CNO: Yolanda Copeland, R.N., Senior Vice President Patient Care Services and Chief Nursing Officer
Web address: https://healthcare.ascension.org/locations/maryland/mdbal/baltimore-ascension-saint-agnes-hospital
Control: Church operated, Nongovernment, not–for–profit **Service**: General medical and surgical

Staffed Beds: 367

JOHNS HOPKINS BAYVIEW MEDICAL CENTER (210029), 4940 Eastern Avenue, Zip 21224–2780; tel. 410/550–0100, **A**1 3 5 7 8 10 **F**1 2 3 4 5 6 8 9 11 12 13 15 16 17 18 22 26 28 29 30 31 32 34 35 36 38 40 41 43 44 45 46 47 48 49 50 51 54 55 56 57 58 59 60 61 64 65 66 67 68 70 72 74 75 76 77 78 79 80 81 82 84 85 86 87 89 90 92 93 96 97 98 99 100 101 102 103 104 107 108 110 111 115 116 117 118 119 120 121 123 126 128 130 131 132 134 135 141 143 146 147 148 149 153 154 157 160 164 165 166 167 169 **S** Johns Hopkins Health System, Baltimore, MD
Primary Contact: Jennifer Nickoles, President
CIO: Sandy Reckert, Director Communications and Public Affairs
CHR: Craig R Brodian, Vice President Human Resources
Web address: www.hopkinsbayview.org
Control: Other not–for–profit (including NFP Corporation) **Service**: General medical and surgical

Staffed Beds: 461 Admissions: 17101 Census: 298 Outpatient Visits: 358201 Births: 1351 Total Expense ($000): 668916 Payroll Expense ($000): 227010 Personnel: 2620

JOHNS HOPKINS HOSPITAL (210009), 1800 Orleans Street, Zip 21287; tel. 410/955–5000, (Includes JOHNS HOPKINS CHILDREN'S CENTER, 1800 Orleans ST, Baltimore, Maryland, Zip 21287–0010, 1800 Orleans Street, Zip 21287, tel. 410/955–5000) **A**1 2 3 5 7 8 10 **F**3 4 5 6 7 8 9 11 13 14 15 16 17 18 19 20 21 22 23 24 25 26 27 28 29 30 31 32 34 35 36 38 39 40 41 43 44 45 46 47 48 49 50 51 52 54 55 56 57 58 59 60 61 63 64 65 66 68 70 72 74 75 76 77 78 79 80 81 82 83 84 85 86 87 88 89 90 91 92 93 94 95 96 97 98 99 100 101 102 103 104 105 106 107 108 109 110 111 112 113 114 115 116 117 118 119 120 121 123 124 126 129 130 131 132 133 134 135 136 137 138 139 140 141 142 143 145 146 147 148 149 150 151 152 153 154 155 156 157 160 162 164 165 166 167 169 **S** Johns Hopkins Health System, Baltimore, MD
Primary Contact: Redonda G. Miller, M.D., President
COO: Charles B. Reuland, Sc.D., Executive Vice President and Chief Operatng Officer
CFO: Ronald J Werthman, Senior Vice President Finance, Chief Financial Officer and Treasurer
CIO: Stephanie L Reel, Senior Vice President Information Services
CHR: Bonnie Windsor, Senior Vice President Human Resources
CNO: Deborah Baker, Vice President, Nursing
Web address: www.hopkinsmedicine.org
Control: Other not–for–profit (including NFP Corporation) **Service**: General medical and surgical

Staffed Beds: 1042 Admissions: 38962 Census: 866 Outpatient Visits: 557538 Births: 2525 Total Expense ($000): 3083500 Payroll Expense ($000): 778335 Personnel: 10525

KENNEDY KRIEGER INSTITUTE (213301), 707 North Broadway, Zip 21205–1890; tel. 443/923–9200, (Nonreporting) **A**1 3 5 7 10
Primary Contact: Bradley Schlaggar, M.D., President and Chief Executive Officer
COO: James M Anders Jr, Administrator and Chief Operating Officer
CFO: Michael J Neuman, Vice President Finance
CMO: Michael V Johnston, M.D., Chief Medical Officer and Senior Vice President Medical Programs
CIO: Kenneth Davis, Assistant Vice President Information Systems
CHR: Michael Loughran, Vice President Human Resources
Web address: www.kennedykrieger.org
Control: Other not–for–profit (including NFP Corporation) **Service**: Children's other specialty

Staffed Beds: 45

KESWICK–HOME FOR INCURABLES See Keswick Multi-Care Center

LEVINDALE HEBREW GERIATRIC CENTER AND HOSPITAL (210064), 2434 West Belvedere Avenue, Zip 21215–5267; tel. 410/601–2400, (Nonreporting) **A**1 7 10 **S** LifeBridge Health, Baltimore, MD
Primary Contact: Sharon Hendricks, Chief Administrative Officer
CMO: Susan M Levy, M.D., Vice President Medical Affairs
CIO: Tressa Springmann, Vice President and Chief Information Officer
CHR: Cheryl T. Boyer, Vice President Human Resources
CNO: Candy Hamner, Vice President and Chief Nursing Officer
Web address: www.sinai-balt.com
Control: Other not–for–profit (including NFP Corporation) **Service**: Acute long–term care hospital

Staffed Beds: 490

LEVINDALE HEBREW HOSPITAL AND NURSING See Levindale Hebrew Geriatric Center and Hospital

MEDSTAR GOOD SAMARITAN HOSPITAL (210056), 5601 Loch Raven Boulevard, Zip 21239–2995; tel. 443/444–8000, **A**1 2 3 5 7 10 **F**3 5 6 9 11 15 17 18 28 29 30 31 34 35 38 40 44 45 50 51 53 56 57 58 59 61 64 65 66 68 70 71 74 75 77 78 80 81 82 84 85 86 87 90 91 92 93 94 95 96 97 100 101 102 104 107 108 110 111 115 117 118 119 120 121 123 129 130 132 135 145 146 147 148 149 150 154 156 157 160 164 165 167 **P**6 **S** MedStar Health, Columbia, MD
Primary Contact: Thomas J. Senker, FACHE, President
CFO: Deana Stout, Vice President Financial Services
Web address: www.goodsam-md.org
Control: Other not–for–profit (including NFP Corporation) **Service**: General medical and surgical

Staffed Beds: 187 Admissions: 7770 Census: 139 Outpatient Visits: 203398 Births: 0 Total Expense ($000): 286696 Payroll Expense ($000): 128323 Personnel: 1503

Hospitals, U.S. / MARYLAND

MEDSTAR HARBOR HOSPITAL (210034), 3001 South Hanover Street, Zip 21225–1290; tel. 410/350–3200, **A**1 2 3 5 10 **F**3 5 9 13 15 18 29 30 34 35 36 38 40 44 45 49 50 51 54 55 56 57 58 59 61 64 65 66 68 70 71 73 74 75 76 77 78 79 81 82 84 85 86 87 89 92 93 94 97 98 100 102 104 105 107 108 110 111 115 118 119 130 131 132 135 143 146 147 148 149 150 152 153 154 156 157 160 162 164 165 167 169 **P**6 **S** MedStar Health, Columbia, MD
Primary Contact: Jill Donaldson, President
CFO: David R Pitman, Vice President Finance
CMO: Allan Birenberg, Vice President Medical Affairs
CIO: Cynthia Tanebaum, Director Information Services
CHR: Karen Evelius, Director Human Resources
CNO: Lenora Addison, Vice President Patient Care and Nursing
Web address: www.harborhospital.org
Control: Other not–for–profit (including NFP Corporation) **Service**: General medical and surgical

Staffed Beds: 123 **Admissions:** 6306 **Census:** 88 **Outpatient Visits:** 67795 **Births:** 1004 **Total Expense ($000):** 202129 **Payroll Expense ($000):** 86882 **Personnel:** 1110

MEDSTAR UNION MEMORIAL HOSPITAL (210024), 201 East University Parkway, Zip 21218–2895; tel. 410/554–2000, **A**1 2 3 5 10 **F**3 5 9 11 15 17 18 20 22 24 26 28 29 30 34 35 37 38 39 40 44 45 50 51 53 54 55 56 57 58 59 61 64 65 66 69 70 71 74 75 77 78 79 80 81 82 84 85 86 87 91 92 93 94 96 97 100 101 102 104 105 107 108 110 111 115 118 119 126 130 131 132 135 141 143 145 146 148 149 150 153 154 156 157 160 164 165 167 **P**6 **S** MedStar Health, Columbia, MD
Primary Contact: Thomas J. Senker, FACHE, President
COO: Neil MacDonald, Vice President, Operations
CFO: Deana Stout, Vice President, Finance
CMO: Stuart Bell, M.D., Vice President, Medical Affairs
CIO: Janet Decker, Assistant Vice President, Information Systems
CHR: Ashley Handwerk, Director, Human Resources
CNO: Karen Owings, MSN, Vice President, Patient Care Services
Web address: www.medstarunionmemorial.org
Control: Other not–for–profit (including NFP Corporation) **Service**: General medical and surgical

Staffed Beds: 192 **Admissions:** 8792 **Census:** 134 **Outpatient Visits:** 114905 **Births:** 0 **Total Expense ($000):** 444771 **Payroll Expense ($000):** 160925 **Personnel:** 1994

MERCY MEDICAL CENTER (210008), 301 St Paul Place, Zip 21202–2165; tel. 410/332–9000, **A**1 2 3 5 10 **F**3 4 5 11 12 13 14 15 16 29 30 31 34 35 36 37 39 40 41 44 45 46 47 48 49 50 51 55 57 58 59 64 65 66 68 70 72 74 75 76 77 78 79 81 82 84 85 86 87 89 92 93 94 97 100 102 107 108 110 111 114 115 116 117 118 119 120 121 123 124 126 128 130 131 132 135 141 142 143 144 145 146 147 148 149 150 154 156 157 158 160 167 169 **P**6
Primary Contact: David N. Maine, M.D., President and Chief Executive Officer
COO: Susan D Finlayson, MSN, R.N., Senior Vice President of MMC Operations
CFO: Justin Deibel, Senior Vice President and Chief Financial Officer
CMO: Wilma Rowe, M.D., Senior Vice President Medical Affairs
CIO: Kathleen Perry, Senior Vice President and Chief Information Officer
CHR: Tammy Janus, Senior Vice President Human Resources
CNO: Kim Bushnell, R.N., Vice President, Patient Care Services
Web address: www.mdmercy.com
Control: Church operated, Nongovernment, not–for–profit **Service**: General medical and surgical

Staffed Beds: 205 **Admissions:** 9426 **Census:** 132 **Outpatient Visits:** 272605 **Births:** 2286 **Total Expense ($000):** 579752 **Payroll Expense ($000):** 223411 **Personnel:** 4121

MT. WASHINGTON PEDIATRIC HOSPITAL (213300), 1708 West Rogers Avenue, Zip 21209–4545; tel. 410/578–8600, (Nonreporting) **A**1 3 5 7 10 **S** University of Maryland Medical System, Baltimore, MD
Primary Contact: Scott M. Klein, M.D., Chief Executive Officer
CFO: Mary Miller, Vice President Finance and Business Development
CMO: Richard Katz, M.D., Vice President Medical Affairs
CIO: Tim Brady, Director Information Systems
CHR: Thomas J Ellis, Vice President Human Resources
Web address: www.mwph.org
Control: Other not–for–profit (including NFP Corporation) **Service**: Children's other specialty

Staffed Beds: 61

SINAI HOSPITAL OF BALTIMORE (210012), 2401 West Belvedere Avenue, Zip 21215–5271; tel. 410/601–9000, **A**1 2 3 5 7 10 **F**2 3 5 6 8 9 12 13 15 17 18 19 20 22 24 26 29 30 31 32 34 35 37 38 39 40 41 43 44 46 47 49 50 51 52 54 55 56 57 58 59 60 61 63 64 65 66 67 68 70 72 74 75 76 77 78 79 80 81 82 83 84 85 86 87 88 89 90 91 92 93 94 95 96 97 98 100 101 102 104 107 108 110 111 114 115 116 117 118 119 120 121 123 124 126 130 131 132 134 135 141 142 146 147 148 149 150 154 156 157 160 161 162 165 167 169 **S** LifeBridge Health, Baltimore, MD
Primary Contact: Amy Shlossman, President and Chief Operating Officer, Senior Vice President, Lifebridge Health
CFO: David Krajewski, Senior Vice President and Chief Financial Officer
CMO: Daniel C Silverman, M.D., Vice President and Chief Medical Officer
CIO: Karen Barker, Vice President and Chief Information Officer
CHR: Cheryl T. Boyer, Vice President Human Resources
CNO: Linda Kosnik, R.N., MSN, Chief Nursing Officer and Vice President, Patient Care Services
Web address: https://www.lifebridgehealth.org/main/sinai-hospital
Control: Other not–for–profit (including NFP Corporation) **Service**: General medical and surgical

Staffed Beds: 477 **Admissions:** 15264 **Census:** 335 **Outpatient Visits:** 143000 **Births:** 1733 **Total Expense ($000):** 965396 **Payroll Expense ($000):** 330890 **Personnel:** 4694

UNIVERSITY OF MARYLAND MEDICAL CENTER (210002), 22 South Greene Street, Zip 21201–1595; tel. 410/328–9199, (Includes UNIVERSITY OF MARYLAND HOSPITAL FOR CHILDREN, 22 South Greene Street, Baltimore, Maryland, Zip 21201–1544, tel. 800/492–5538) **A**1 2 3 8 10 **F**3 5 6 7 8 11 12 13 14 15 17 18 19 20 21 22 23 24 25 26 27 28 29 30 31 32 34 35 36 37 38 39 40 41 43 44 45 46 47 48 49 50 51 52 54 55 56 57 58 59 60 61 63 64 65 66 68 70 71 72 74 75 76 77 78 79 81 82 84 85 86 87 88 89 91 92 93 94 96 97 98 99 100 101 102 103 104 105 107 108 110 111 114 115 116 117 118 119 120 121 123 124 126 129 130 131 132 134 135 136 137 138 139 140 141 142 143 144 145 146 147 148 149 150 151 153 154 155 156 157 160 162 164 165 167 169 **S** University of Maryland Medical System, Baltimore, MD
Primary Contact: Bert W. O'Malley Jr, President and Chief Executive Officer
COO: Ron V. Cummins, Senior Vice President and Chief Operating Officer
CMO: Jonathan Gottlieb, M.D., Senior Vice President and Chief Medical Officer
CHR: R Keith Allen, Senior Vice President Human Resources
Web address: www.umm.edu
Control: Other not–for–profit (including NFP Corporation) **Service**: General medical and surgical

Staffed Beds: 658 **Admissions:** 23666 **Census:** 551 **Outpatient Visits:** 286017 **Births:** 1942 **Total Expense ($000):** 2022919 **Payroll Expense ($000):** 664172 **Personnel:** 7780

UNIVERSITY OF MARYLAND MEDICAL CENTER MIDTOWN CAMPUS (210038), 827 Linden Avenue, Zip 21201–4606; tel. 410/225–8000, **A**1 3 5 10 **F**1 2 3 4 5 11 18 20 29 30 32 34 35 38 39 40 44 45 46 47 49 50 54 55 56 57 58 59 60 61 64 65 66 68 70 71 74 75 77 78 79 81 82 84 85 86 87 91 93 94 96 97 98 100 101 102 104 105 107 108 111 114 115 116 117 118 126 129 130 131 132 133 135 143 144 146 147 148 149 150 153 154 156 157 160 161 162 164 165 167 **P**7 **S** University of Maryland Medical System, Baltimore, MD
Primary Contact: Rebecca A. Altman, R.N., Senior Vice President and Chief Administrative Officer
COO: Donald Ray, Vice President Operations
CFO: Craig Fleischmann, Vice President Finance
CMO: W Eugene Egerton, M.D., Chief Medical Officer
CHR: Paula Henderson, Vice President Human Resources
Web address: www.ummidtown.org/
Control: Other not–for–profit (including NFP Corporation) **Service**: General medical and surgical

Staffed Beds: 125 **Admissions:** 3969 **Census:** 102 **Outpatient Visits:** 92619 **Births:** 0 **Total Expense ($000):** 266647 **Payroll Expense ($000):** 100546 **Personnel:** 1223

Hospital, Medicare Provider Number, Address, Telephone, Approval, Facility, and Physician Codes, Health Care System

★ American Hospital Association (AHA) membership
☐ The Joint Commission accreditation
○ Healthcare Facilities Accreditation Program
◇ DNV Healthcare Inc. accreditation
⇧ Center for Improvement in Healthcare Quality Accreditation
△ Commission on Accreditation of Rehabilitation Facilities (CARF) accreditation

Hospitals, U.S. / MARYLAND

UNIVERSITY OF MARYLAND REHABILITATION & ORTHOPAEDIC INSTITUTE (210058), 2200 Kernan Drive, Zip 21207–6697; tel. 410/448–2500, (Nonreporting) **A**1 3 5 7 10 **S** University of Maryland Medical System, Baltimore, MD
Primary Contact: Julie Nemens, Chief Administrative Officer
CFO: W Walter Augustin, CPA, III, Vice President Financial Services and Chief Financial Officer
CMO: John P. Straumanis, M.D., Vice President Medical Affairs and Chief Medical Officer
CIO: Linda Hines, Vice President Information Technology and Information Systems
CHR: Paula Henderson, Vice President Human Resources
CNO: Cheryl D Lee, R.N., MSN, Vice President of Patient Care Services and Chief Nursing Officer
Web address: www.umrehabortho.org
Control: Other not–for–profit (including NFP Corporation) **Service**: Rehabilitation

Staffed Beds: 117

VETERANS AFFAIRS MARYLAND HEALTH CARE SYSTEM–BALTIMORE DIVISION, 10 North Greene Street, Zip 21201–1524; tel. 410/605–7001, (Includes VETERANS AFFAIRS MARYLAND HEALTH CARE SYSTEM–PERRY POINT DIVISION, Circle Drive, Perry Point, Maryland, Zip 21902, tel. 410/642–2411; Adam M. Robinson, M.D., Director) (Nonreporting) **A**1 2 3 5 **S** Department of Veterans Affairs, Washington, DC
Primary Contact: Jonathan R. Eckman, Medical Center Director
CFO: Major Tom Scheffler, Chief Fiscal Officer
CMO: Dorothy Snow, M.D., Chief of Staff
CIO: Sharon Zielinski, Chief Information Resource Officer
CHR: Jeff Craig, Chief Human Resource Management
Web address: www.maryland.va.gov/
Control: Veterans Affairs, Government, federal **Service**: General medical and surgical

Staffed Beds: 394

BALTIMORE—Baltimore County

GBMC HEALTHCARE (210044), 6701 North Charles Street, Zip 21204–6892; tel. 443/849–2000, (Total facility includes 27 beds in nursing home–type unit) **A**1 2 3 5 10 **F**3 8 11 12 13 20 26 29 30 31 34 35 38 40 41 44 45 46 47 48 49 50 51 53 54 55 57 58 59 60 61 64 65 68 70 72 74 75 76 77 78 79 80 81 82 83 84 85 86 87 89 92 93 96 97 102 104 108 114 115 119 120 121 123 124 126 128 129 130 132 135 142 145 146 147 148 149 150 154 156 157 167 169 **P**6
Primary Contact: John B. Chessare, M.D., M.P.H., FACHE, President and Chief Executive Officer
COO: Keith R Poisson, Executive Vice President and Chief Operating Officer
CFO: Eric L Melchior, Executive Vice President and Chief Financial Officer
CMO: John R Saunders, M.D., Senior Vice President Medical Affairs and Chief Medical Officer
CHR: Deloris Simpson–Tuggle, Vice President Human Resources and Organizational Development and Chief Human Resources Officer
CNO: Jody Porter, R.N., Senior Vice President Patient Care Services and Chief Nursing Officer
Web address: www.gbmc.org
Control: Other not–for–profit (including NFP Corporation) **Service**: General medical and surgical

Staffed Beds: 376 **Admissions**: 13501 **Census**: 166 **Outpatient Visits**: 547429 **Births**: 3759 **Total Expense ($000)**: 624194 **Payroll Expense ($000)**: 227206 **Personnel**: 3177

GREATER BALTIMORE MEDICAL CENTER See GBMC Healthcare

MEDSTAR FRANKLIN SQUARE MEDICAL CENTER (210015), 9000 Franklin Square Drive, Zip 21237–3901; tel. 443/777–7000, **A**1 2 3 5 8 10 **F**3 5 9 11 12 13 15 18 20 22 26 28 29 30 31 32 34 35 36 37 38 40 44 45 46 47 48 49 50 51 54 55 56 57 58 59 60 64 65 66 68 70 71 72 74 75 76 77 78 79 80 81 82 84 85 86 87 92 93 94 97 98 99 100 101 102 103 104 107 108 110 111 114 115 118 119 120 121 123 124 126 129 130 131 132 134 135 145 146 147 148 149 154 156 160 162 164 165 167 169 **P**6 **S** MedStar Health, Columbia, MD
Primary Contact: Stuart M. Levine, M.D., President
CFO: Robert P Lally Jr, Vice President Finance
CMO: Tony Sclama, M.D., Vice President Medical Affairs
CIO: Stephen Mannion, Assistant Vice President Information Systems Customer Service
CNO: Lawrence F Strassner III, Ph.D., FACHE, R.N., MS, Senior Vice President Operations and Chief Nursing Officer
Web address: www.medstarfranklin.org
Control: Other not–for–profit (including NFP Corporation) **Service**: General medical and surgical

Staffed Beds: 392 **Admissions**: 16575 **Census**: 268 **Outpatient Visits**: 200869 **Births**: 2148 **Total Expense ($000)**: 568135 **Payroll Expense ($000)**: 215943 **Personnel**: 2680

SHEPPARD PRATT (214000), 6501 North Charles Street, Zip 21204–6819, Mailing Address: P.O. Box 6815, Zip 21285–6815; tel. 410/938–3000, **A**1 3 5 10 **F**4 6 29 30 34 35 36 38 44 50 55 56 57 58 59 64 68 75 77 82 86 87 98 99 100 101 103 104 105 106 130 131 132 135 143 144 146 149 150 153 154 162 164 165
Primary Contact: Harsh Trivedi, M.D., President and Chief Executive Officer
COO: Stephen Merz, Chief Operating Officer
CFO: Kelly Savoca, Chief Financial Officer
CIO: Matthew Knudsen, Director, Information Systems
CHR: Cathy Doughty, Vice President Human Resources
CNO: Ernestine Y. Cosby, Vice President Clinical Services and Chief Nursing Officer
Web address: www.sheppardpratt.org
Control: Other not–for–profit (including NFP Corporation) **Service**: Psychiatric

Staffed Beds: 341 **Admissions**: 8341 **Census**: 304 **Outpatient Visits**: 77681 **Births**: 0 **Total Expense ($000)**: 198314 **Payroll Expense ($000)**: 118436 **Personnel**: 1290

SPRING GROVE HOSPITAL CENTER (214018), 55 Wade Avenue, Zip 21228–4663; tel. 410/402–6000, (Nonreporting) **A**1 3 5 10
Primary Contact: Marie Rose. Alam, M.D., Chief Executive Officer
CFO: Edward Swartz, Chief Financial Officer
CMO: Kelly Phillips, M.D., M.P.H., Clinical Director and Chief Staff
Web address: https://health.maryland.gov/springgrove/Pages/home.aspx
Control: State, Government, Nonfederal **Service**: Psychiatric

Staffed Beds: 377

BEL AIR—Harford County

UNIVERSITY OF MARYLAND UPPER CHESAPEAKE MEDICAL CENTER (210049), 500 Upper Chesapeake Drive, Zip 21014–4324; tel. 443/643–1000, **A**1 2 3 5 10 **F**3 13 15 18 20 22 28 29 30 40 41 50 51 60 63 68 70 75 76 77 78 79 81 82 84 85 89 92 93 94 100 101 102 107 111 114 115 116 117 119 120 121 126 130 146 147 148 154 156 157 164 167 **S** University of Maryland Medical System, Baltimore, MD
Primary Contact: Elizabeth Wise, FACHE, MSN, President and Chief Executive Officer
CMO: Peggy Vaughan, M.D., Senior Vice President Medical Affairs
CIO: Rick Casteel, Vice President Management Information Systems and Chief Information Officer
CHR: Toni M Shivery, Vice President Human Resources
Web address: www.uchs.org
Control: Other not–for–profit (including NFP Corporation) **Service**: General medical and surgical

Staffed Beds: 211 **Admissions**: 11748 **Census**: 150 **Outpatient Visits**: 141914 **Births**: 1278 **Total Expense ($000)**: 303952 **Payroll Expense ($000)**: 125758 **Personnel**: 1393

BERLIN—Worcester County

ATLANTIC GENERAL HOSPITAL (210061), 9733 Healthway Drive, Zip 21811–1155; tel. 410/641–1100, (Nonreporting) **A**1 2 10
Primary Contact: Donald R. Owrey, President and Chief Executive Officer
COO: Kim Justice, Vice President Planning and Operations
CFO: Cheryl Nottingham, Chief Financial Officer
CMO: Sally Dowling, M.D., Vice President Medical Affairs
CIO: Jonathan Bauer, Vice President Information Systems and Chief Information Officer
CHR: Jim Brannon, Vice President Human Resources
Web address: www.atlanticgeneral.org
Control: Other not–for–profit (including NFP Corporation) **Service**: General medical and surgical

Staffed Beds: 59

BETHESDA—Montgomery County

NATIONAL INSTITUTES OF HEALTH CLINICAL CENTER See Nih Clinical Center

NIH CLINICAL CENTER, 9000 Rockville Pike, Building 10, Room 6–2551, Zip 20892–1504; tel. 301/496–4000, (Includes CHILDREN'S INN AT NIH, 7 West Drive, Bethesda, Maryland, Zip 20814–1509, tel. 301/496–5672) (Nonreporting) **A**1 3 5 8
Primary Contact: Major General James K. Gilman, M.D., Chief Executive Officer
COO: Captain Pius Aiyelawo, Chief Operating Officer
CFO: Maria Joyce, Chief Financial Officer
CMO: David K Henderson, M.D., Deputy Director Clinical Care
CIO: Jon W McKeeby, Chief Information Officer
CHR: Bonnie Tuma, Human Resources Team Lead
CNO: Clare Hastings, R.N., Ph.D., Chief Nurse Officer
Web address: https://clinicalcenter.nih.gov/
Control: Department of Defense, Government, federal **Service**: Other specialty treatment

Staffed Beds: 121

Hospitals, U.S. / MARYLAND

☒ **SUBURBAN HOSPITAL (210022)**, 8600 Old Georgetown Road, Zip 20814–1497; tel. 301/896–3100, **A**1 2 3 5 10 **F**3 5 15 17 18 20 22 24 26 28 29 30 31 34 35 36 37 38 39 40 41 43 44 45 49 50 56 58 59 60 65 68 70 71 74 75 77 78 79 80 81 82 84 87 89 92 93 98 100 101 102 104 105 107 110 111 115 118 119 124 126 130 132 135 146 148 149 152 153 154 155 156 157 160 164 165 167 **S** Johns Hopkins Health System, Baltimore, MD
Primary Contact: LeighAnn Sidone, R.N., President and Chief Executive Officer
COO: Joseph Linstrom, Vice President Operations
CFO: Marty Basso, Senior Vice President Finance
CMO: Eric D Dobkin, M.D., Vice President Medical Affairs
CIO: Jason Cole, Senior Director, Management Information Systems
CHR: Queenie C. Plater, Vice President, Human Resources National Capital Region Johns Hopkins Medicine
CNO: LeighAnn Sidone, R.N., Chief Nursing Officer
Web address: www.suburbanhospital.org
Control: Other not–for–profit (including NFP Corporation) **Service**: General medical and surgical

Staffed Beds: 232 **Admissions**: 12039 **Census**: 181 **Births**: 0
Total Expense ($000): 384510 **Payroll Expense ($000)**: 147086
Personnel: 1659

THE CHILDREN'S INN AT NIH See Children's Inn At Nih

☒ **WALTER REED NATIONAL MILITARY MEDICAL CENTER**, 8901 Rockville Pike, Zip 20889; tel. 301/295–4611, (Nonreporting) **A**1 2 3 5 **S** Bureau of Medicine and Surgery, Department of the Navy, Falls Church, VA
Primary Contact: Captain Melissa Austin, Hospital Director
CFO: Commander Joseph Pickel, Director Resource Management
CIO: Commander Cayetano Thornton, Chief Information Officer
CHR: Captain Jaime Carroll, Department Head
Web address: https://walterreed.tricare.mil/
Control: Navy, Government, federal **Service**: General medical and surgical

Staffed Beds: 251

BOWIE—Prince George's County

REHABILITATION HOSPITAL OF BOWIE (213030), 17351 Melford Boulevard, Zip 20715; tel. 240/548–1300, (Data for 201 days) **F**3 29 60 77 90 91 92 94 95 96 148 149 **P**5 **S** Encompass Health Corporation, Birmingham, AL
Primary Contact: Joseph Williams, Chief Executive Officer
Web address: https://encompasshealth.com/locations/bowierehab
Control: Corporation, Investor–owned (for–profit) **Service**: Rehabilitation

Staffed Beds: 40 **Admissions**: 469 **Census**: 25 **Outpatient Visits**: 0 **Births**: 0
Total Expense ($000): 12597 **Payroll Expense ($000)**: 6852 **Personnel**: 76

CAMBRIDGE—Dorchester County

☐ **EASTERN SHORE HOSPITAL CENTER (214002)**, 5262 Woods Road, Zip 21613–3796; tel. 410/221–2300, (Nonreporting) **A**1 10
Primary Contact: Forrest Daniels, Chief Executive Officer
COO: William Webb, Assistant Superintendent
CFO: William Webb, Assistant Superintendent
CMO: Evangeline Garcia, M.D., Clinical Director
CHR: Cassandra Stanley, Director Personnel
CNO: Lisa Hines, Director of Performance Improvement
Web address: www.dhmh.state.md.us/eshc
Control: State, Government, Nonfederal **Service**: Psychiatric

Staffed Beds: 80

CHESTERTOWN—Kent County

☒ **UNIVERSITY OF MARYLAND SHORE MEDICAL CENTER AT CHESTERTOWN (210030)**, 100 Brown Street, Zip 21620–1499; tel. 410/778–3300, (Nonreporting) **A**1 10 **S** University of Maryland Medical System, Baltimore, MD
Primary Contact: Aaron Royston, Vice President, Rural Health Transformation and Executive Director
COO: Robert A Frank, Senior Vice President of Operations
CFO: Joanne A Hahey, Vice President Finance and Chief Financial Officer
CMO: William Huffner, M.D., Chief Medical Officer
CIO: Elizabeth Fish, Senior Director Site Executive and Information Technology
CHR: Susan Coe, Vice President Human Resources
CNO: Ruth Ann Jones, Ed.D., MSN, R.N., Senior Vice President, Chief Nursing Officer
Web address: https://www.umms.org/shore/locations/medical-center-chestertown
Control: Other not–for–profit (including NFP Corporation) **Service**: General medical and surgical

Staffed Beds: 30

CLINTON—Prince George's County

☒ **MEDSTAR SOUTHERN MARYLAND HOSPITAL CENTER (210062)**, 7503 Surratts Road, Zip 20735–3358; tel. 301/868–8000, **A**1 2 3 5 10 **F**3 13 15 18 20 22 26 28 29 30 34 35 37 38 39 40 44 45 46 47 48 49 50 51 57 58 59 61 64 65 66 68 70 71 74 75 76 77 78 79 81 82 84 85 86 87 93 98 100 101 102 104 105 107 108 110 111 114 115 118 119 120 121 124 126 129 130 132 135 141 143 146 147 148 149 154 156 162 164 167 169 **P**6 **S** MedStar Health, Columbia, MD
Primary Contact: Stephen T. Michaels, M.D., FACHE, President
CFO: Daniel Feeley, Interim Chief Financial Officer
CMO: Yvette Johnson–Threat, Vice President Medical Affairs
CIO: Lou Mavromatis, Vice President Information Technology
CHR: Paul Zeller, Vice President Human Resources
Web address: www.medstarsouthernmaryland.org
Control: Other not–for–profit (including NFP Corporation) **Service**: General medical and surgical

Staffed Beds: 168 **Admissions**: 10223 **Census**: 142 **Outpatient Visits**: 75688 **Births**: 953 **Total Expense ($000)**: 307135 **Payroll Expense ($000)**: 143471 **Personnel**: 1209

COLUMBIA—Howard County

HOWARD COUNTY GENERAL HOSPITAL See Johns Hopkins Howard County Medical Center

☒ **JOHNS HOPKINS HOWARD COUNTY MEDICAL CENTER (210048)**, 5755 Cedar Lane, Zip 21044–2999; tel. 410/740–7890, **A**1 3 5 10 **F**3 8 11 13 15 18 20 22 26 28 29 30 31 32 34 35 36 39 40 41 44 45 46 47 49 50 51 55 56 57 58 59 60 61 64 65 68 70 72 74 75 76 77 78 79 81 82 84 85 86 87 89 91 92 93 96 98 99 100 101 102 103 104 107 108 110 111 115 118 119 126 130 131 132 134 135 146 147 148 149 154 156 162 164 165 167 169 **S** Johns Hopkins Health System, Baltimore, MD
Primary Contact: Mohammed Shafeeq. Ahmed, M.D., President
COO: Ryan Brown, Vice President, Operations
CFO: Claro M Pio Roda, Dr.PH, Vice President, Finance and Chief Financial Officer
CMO: Jeanette Nazarian, M.D., Vice President, Medical Affairs and Chief Medical Officer
CHR: Theresa Forget, Executive Director, Human Resources
CNO: Ronald Langlotz, Vice President, Nursing and Chief Nursing Officer
Web address: www.hcgh.org
Control: Other not–for–profit (including NFP Corporation) **Service**: General medical and surgical

Staffed Beds: 243 **Admissions**: 14241 **Census**: 171 **Outpatient Visits**: 116838 **Births**: 2557 **Total Expense ($000)**: 331214 **Payroll Expense ($000)**: 119691 **Personnel**: 1658

CRISFIELD—Somerset County

MCCREADY FOUNDATION See Tidalhealth Mccready

CUMBERLAND—Allegany County

☐ **THOMAS B. FINAN CENTER (214012)**, 10102 Country Club Road SE, Zip 21502–8339; Mailing Address: P.O. Box 1722, Zip 21501–1722; tel. 301/777–2405, (Nonreporting) **A**1 10
Primary Contact: Lesa Diehl, Chief Executive Officer
COO: Craig Alexander, Chief Operating Officer
CFO: Gina Spears, Chief Financial Officer
CMO: David Millis, M.D., Clinical Director
CIO: Jim Taylor, Computer Network Specialist II
CHR: Chris Loney, Director Personnel
CNO: Gayle Walter, Director of Nursing
Web address: https://health.maryland.gov/finan/Pages/home.aspx
Control: State, Government, Nonfederal **Service**: Psychiatric

Staffed Beds: 88

Hospital, Medicare Provider Number, Address, Telephone, Approval, Facility, and Physician Codes, Health Care System

★ American Hospital Association (AHA) membership
☐ The Joint Commission accreditation
◯ Healthcare Facilities Accreditation Program
◇ DNV Healthcare Inc. accreditation
⇑ Center for Improvement in Healthcare Quality Accreditation
△ Commission on Accreditation of Rehabilitation Facilities (CARF) accreditation

Hospitals, U.S. / MARYLAND

△ **UPMC WESTERN MARYLAND (210027)**, 12500 Willowbrook Road SE, Zip 21502–6393, Mailing Address: P.O. Box 539, Zip 21501–0539; tel. 240/964–7000, **A**1 3 7 10 20 **F**3 5 11 13 14 15 17 18 19 20 22 24 26 28 29 30 31 32 34 35 38 39 40 41 43 44 45 49 50 51 53 54 56 57 58 59 60 62 63 64 65 66 68 70 73 74 75 76 77 78 79 80 81 84 85 86 87 89 90 93 94 96 97 98 100 101 102 103 104 106 107 108 110 114 115 119 120 121 124 126 129 130 132 134 135 143 144 146 147 148 149 150 153 154 156 160 162 164 165 167 169 **P**6 **S** UPMC, Pittsburgh, PA
Primary Contact: Michele R. Martz, CPA, President
COO: Nancy D. Adams, R.N., Senior Vice President and Chief Operating Officer
CFO: Kimberly S. Repac, Senior Vice President and Chief Financial Officer
CMO: Gerald Goldstein, M.D., Senior Vice President and Chief Medical Officer
CIO: William J. Byers, Chief Information Officer
CHR: Jennifer J. Williams, Director, Human Resources
CNO: James M. Karstetter, R.N., II, Vice President and Chief Nursing Officer
Web address: www.wmhs.com
Control: Other not–for–profit (including NFP Corporation) **Service**: General medical and surgical

Staffed Beds: 233 **Admissions**: 9025 **Census**: 134 **Outpatient Visits**: 558993 **Births**: 867 **Total Expense ($000)**: 353680 **Payroll Expense ($000)**: 150085 **Personnel**: 1734

EASTON—Talbot County

△ **UNIVERSITY OF MARYLAND SHORE MEDICAL CENTER AT EASTON (210037)**, 219 South Washington Street, Zip 21601–2996; tel. 410/822–1000, (Includes UNIVERSITY OF MARYLAND SHORE MEDICAL CENTER AT CAMBRIDGE, 715 Cambridge Marketplace Boulevard, Cambridge, Maryland, Zip 21613–2567, tel. 443/225–7500) (Nonreporting) **A**1 2 3 7 10 **S** University of Maryland Medical System, Baltimore, MD
Primary Contact: Kenneth D. Kozel, FACHE, President and Chief Executive Officer
COO: Robert A Frank, Senior Vice President of Operations
CFO: Joanne A Hahey, Senior Vice President and Chief Financial Officer
CMO: William Huffner, M.D., Chief Medical Officer
CIO: Elizabeth Fish, Chief Information Officer
CHR: Susan Coe, Regional Vice President Human Resources
CNO: Ruth Ann Jones, Ed.D., MSN, R.N., Senior Vice President, Chief Nursing Officer
Web address: www.shorehealth.org
Control: Other not–for–profit (including NFP Corporation) **Service**: General medical and surgical

Staffed Beds: 132

ELKTON—Cecil County

CHRISTIANACARE, UNION HOSPITAL (210032), 106 Bow Street, Zip 21921–5596; tel. 410/398–4000, **A**1 2 10 **F**3 11 12 13 15 18 24 26 29 30 31 34 35 38 40 44 45 46 47 50 51 53 54 57 59 61 64 69 70 74 75 76 77 78 79 81 82 84 85 86 87 89 92 93 97 98 100 102 104 107 108 110 111 114 115 117 118 119 130 131 132 135 146 147 148 149 154 156 164 167 169 **P**6 **S** ChristianaCare, Wilmington, DE
Primary Contact: Janice E. Nevin, M.D., M.P.H., President and Chief Executive Officer
CFO: Laurie Beyer, Senior Vice President and Chief Financial Officer
CMO: Cydney Teal, M.D., Vice President Medical Affairs
CIO: Anne Lara, Chief Information Officer
CHR: Terrence Lovell, Vice President Human Resources
Web address: www.uhcc.com
Control: Other not–for–profit (including NFP Corporation) **Service**: General medical and surgical

Staffed Beds: 84 **Admissions**: 6034 **Census**: 75 **Outpatient Visits**: 94002 **Births**: 384 **Total Expense ($000)**: 192302 **Payroll Expense ($000)**: 96940 **Personnel**: 1044

FORT WASHINGTON—Prince George's County

ADVENTIST HEALTHCARE FORT WASHINGTON MEDICAL CENTER (210060), 11711 Livingston Road, Zip 20744; tel. 301/292–7000, **A**1 3 10 **F**34 40 44 45 47 49 50 51 57 59 61 64 68 70 74 75 77 79 81 85 86 87 100 107 108 114 118 119 126 130 135 148 149 156 157 164 167 **S** Adventist HealthCare, Gaithersburg, MD
Primary Contact: Eunmee Shim, R.N., MSN, President, Fort Washington and Adventist Ambulatory Networks
COO: Anna Leah Cazes, Senior Vice President, Chief Operating Officer and Chief Nursing Officer
CFO: Vanessa Murray, Director of Finance
CMO: Kenneth Fisher, M.D., President, Medical Staff
CIO: Stephen Tim–Young, Director Information Technology
CHR: Tammy J. Woodfork, Corporate Director Human Resources
Web address: https://www.adventisthealthcare.com/locations/profile/fort-washington-medical-center/
Control: Church operated, Nongovernment, not–for–profit **Service**: General medical and surgical

Staffed Beds: 27 **Admissions**: 1910 **Census**: 25 **Outpatient Visits**: 25897 **Births**: 1 **Total Expense ($000)**: 57984 **Payroll Expense ($000)**: 25124 **Personnel**: 280

FREDERICK—Frederick County

FREDERICK HEALTH (210005), 400 West Seventh Street, Zip 21701–4593; tel. 240/566–3300, **A**1 2 10 **F**3 8 11 12 13 15 18 20 22 26 28 29 30 31 34 35 37 38 40 41 44 45 46 48 49 50 53 54 56 57 58 59 61 62 63 64 65 68 70 71 72 74 75 76 77 78 79 81 82 84 85 86 87 89 93 98 100 102 105 107 108 111 114 115 119 120 121 123 124 126 129 130 131 132 135 146 147 148 149 150 152 153 154 157 160 167 169
Primary Contact: Thomas A. Kleinhanzl, President and Chief Executive Officer
COO: Cheryl Cioffi, R.N., Senior Vice President, Chief Operating Officer and Chief Nursing Officer
CFO: Hannah Jacobs, Senior Vice President and Chief Financial Officer
CMO: Manuel Casiano, M.D., Senior Vice President Medical Affairs
CIO: David Quirke, Vice President Information Services
CNO: Cheryl Cioffi, R.N., Senior Vice President, Chief Operating Officer and Chief Nursing Officer
Web address: www.fmh.org
Control: Other not–for–profit (including NFP Corporation) **Service**: General medical and surgical

Staffed Beds: 279 **Admissions**: 14292 **Census**: 193 **Outpatient Visits**: 338013 **Births**: 2426 **Total Expense ($000)**: 411877 **Payroll Expense ($000)**: 189397 **Personnel**: 2199

GERMANTOWN—Montgomery County

HOLY CROSS GERMANTOWN HOSPITAL (210065), 19801 Observation Drive, Zip 20876–4070; tel. 301/557–6000, **A**1 3 10 **F**3 12 13 18 29 30 37 40 45 48 49 50 51 60 61 68 70 74 75 76 77 79 81 85 87 98 100 102 107 108 109 111 115 118 119 126 130 131 132 146 147 149 154 157 167 169 **S** Trinity Health, Livonia, MI
Primary Contact: Louis Damiano, M.D., Chief Executive Officer
CMO: Blair Eig, M.D., Vice President and Chief Medical Officer, Medical Affairs
CNO: Kimberly Elliott, Chief Nursing Officer
Web address: https://www.holycrosshealth.org/location/holy-cross-germantown-hospital
Control: Church operated, Nongovernment, not–for–profit **Service**: General medical and surgical

Staffed Beds: 95 **Admissions**: 6059 **Census**: 74 **Outpatient Visits**: 37583 **Births**: 1860 **Total Expense ($000)**: 139881 **Payroll Expense ($000)**: 55384 **Personnel**: 622

GLEN BURNIE—Anne Arundel County

UNIVERSITY OF MARYLAND BALTIMORE WASHINGTON MEDICAL CENTER (210043), 301 Hospital Drive, Zip 21061–5899; tel. 410/787–4000, **A**1 2 3 5 10 **F**3 11 13 15 18 20 22 26 28 29 30 31 34 35 37 38 40 41 44 45 46 47 48 49 50 51 54 55 56 57 58 59 60 61 63 64 65 68 70 74 75 76 77 78 79 81 82 83 84 85 86 87 89 93 98 100 101 102 105 107 108 111 114 115 116 117 118 119 120 121 123 124 126 130 131 132 135 146 147 148 149 150 154 156 160 161 164 167 169 **P**6 **S** University of Maryland Medical System, Baltimore, MD
Primary Contact: Kathleen McCollum, President and Chief Executive Officer
COO: John H. Greely, Senior Vice President and Chief Operating Officer
CFO: Al Pietsch, CPA, Senior Vice President and Chief Financial Officer
CMO: Jason Heavner, M.D., Senior Vice President and Chief Medical Officer
CHR: Kathy Poehler, Vice President, Human Resources
CNO: Catherine Whitaker, MSN, R.N., Vice President and Chief Nursing Officer
Web address: www.mybwmc.org
Control: Other not–for–profit (including NFP Corporation) **Service**: General medical and surgical

Staffed Beds: 266 **Admissions**: 15613 **Census**: 210 **Outpatient Visits**: 200113 **Births**: 1914 **Total Expense ($000)**: 554772 **Payroll Expense ($000)**: 256772 **Personnel**: 2841

HAGERSTOWN—Washington County

☐ **BROOK LANE (214003)**, 13121 Brook Lane Drive, Zip 21742–1435, Mailing Address: P.O. Box 1945, Zip 21742–1945; tel. 301/733–0330, (Nonreporting) **A**1 10
Primary Contact: Jeffery D. O'Neal, FACHE, Chief Executive Officer
COO: Jason Allen, Chief Operating Officer
CFO: David Schey, Chief Financial Officer
CMO: David Gonzalez, M.D., Medical Director
CIO: Robert Fritz, Chief Information Officer
CHR: Nicole Twigg, Director Human Resources
CNO: Jason Allen, Director Patient Care Services
Web address: www.brooklane.org
Control: Other not–for–profit (including NFP Corporation) **Service**: Psychiatric

Staffed Beds: 57

BROOK LANE HEALTH SERVICES See Brook Lane

Hospitals, U.S. / MARYLAND

☒ △ **MERITUS HEALTH (210001)**, 11116 Medical Campus Road, Zip 21742–6710; tel. 301/790–8000, **A**1 2 3 5 7 10 13 **F**3 5 11 12 13 15 17 18 20 22 26 28 29 30 31 34 35 38 40 43 44 49 51 52 54 55 56 57 58 59 60 61 62 64 65 70 71 74 75 76 77 78 79 81 82 83 84 85 86 87 89 90 93 94 96 97 98 99 100 101 102 103 104 107 108 110 111 114 115 118 119 120 121 123 129 130 131 132 135 143 144 145 146 147 148 153 154 155 156 157 160 162 164 165 167 169
Primary Contact: Maulik Joshi, President and Chief Executive Officer
COO: Carrie Adams, Chief Operating Officer
CFO: Thomas T. Chan, Chief Financial Officer
CHR: Laura Minteer, Chief Human Resource Officer
Web address: www.meritushealth.com
Control: Other not–for–profit (including NFP Corporation) **Service**: General medical and surgical

Staffed Beds: 327 **Admissions**: 14059 **Census**: 170 **Outpatient Visits**: 196709 **Births**: 1929 **Total Expense ($000)**: 390071 **Payroll Expense ($000)**: 180064 **Personnel**: 2110

MERITUS MEDICAL CENTER See Meritus Health

☐ △ **WESTERN MARYLAND HOSPITAL CENTER (212002)**, 1500 Pennsylvania Avenue, Zip 21742–3194; tel. 301/745–4200, (Nonreporting) **A**1 7 10
Primary Contact: Michele Fleming, Chief Executive Officer
COO: David Davis, Chief Operating Officer
CFO: Kelly Edmonds, Chief Financial Officer
CMO: Monica Stallworth, M.D., Chief of Staff
CIO: Ron Keplinger, Chief Information Officer
CHR: David Davis, Chief Operating Officer
Web address: www.wmhc.us
Control: State, Government, Nonfederal **Service**: Acute long–term care hospital

Staffed Beds: 55

JESSUP—Howard County

☐ **CLIFTON T. PERKINS HOSPITAL CENTER**, 8450 Dorsey Run Road, Zip 20794–9486; tel. 410/724–3000, (Nonreporting) **A**1 3 5
Primary Contact: Paula A. Langmead, Acting Chief, Hospital Administration
COO: Thomas D Lewis, Chief Operating Officer
CFO: George Parnel, Chief Financial Officer
CMO: Muhammed Ajanah, M.D., Clinical Director
CIO: Chanda Hamilton, Chief Information Officer
CHR: Beverly Stacie, Director Human Resources
Web address: https://health.maryland.gov/perkins/Pages/home.aspx
Control: State, Government, Nonfederal **Service**: Psychiatric

Staffed Beds: 250

LA PLATA—Charles County

☒ **UNIVERSITY OF MARYLAND CHARLES REGIONAL MEDICAL CENTER (210035)**, 5 Garrett Avenue, Zip 20646–5960, Mailing Address: P.O. Box 1070, Zip 20646–1070; tel. 301/609–4000, (Nonreporting) **A**1 10 **S** University of Maryland Medical System, Baltimore, MD
Primary Contact: Noel A. Cervino, President and Chief Executive Officer
CFO: Albert Zanger, Vice President, Chief Financial Officer
CMO: Joseph Moser, M.D., Chief Medical Officer
CIO: Elizabeth Fish, Information Technology Site Executive
CHR: Stacey M Cook, MS, Vice President, Human Resources
CNO: Dana Levy, Chief Nursing Officer
Web address: https://www.umms.org/charles
Control: Other not–for–profit (including NFP Corporation) **Service**: General medical and surgical

Staffed Beds: 108

LANHAM—Prince George's County

☒ **LUMINIS HEALTH DOCTORS COMMUNITY MEDICAL CENTER (210051)**, 8118 Good Luck Road, Zip 20706–3574; tel. 301/552–8118, **A**1 3 10 **F**3 9 11 12 15 18 20 26 28 29 30 31 34 35 36 37 38 39 40 41 44 45 46 47 49 50 51 53 54 57 58 59 60 61 63 64 65 66 68 70 74 75 77 78 79 81 82 84 85 86 87 91 92 93 94 96 97 98 101 102 104 107 108 110 111 115 119 124 126 129 130 131 132 135 146 147 148 149 150 153 156 157 164 165 167 169 **S** Luminis Health, Annapolis, MD
Primary Contact: Deneen Richmond, R.N., President
CFO: Camille Bash, Chief Financial Officer
CMO: Sunil I. Madan, M.D., Chief Medical Officer and Chief Population Health Officer
CIO: Joyce Hanscome, Chief Information Officer
CHR: Paul Hagens, Vice President Human Resources
CNO: Crystal Beckford, Chief Nursing Officer
Web address: www.dchweb.org
Control: Other not–for–profit (including NFP Corporation) **Service**: General medical and surgical

Staffed Beds: 210 **Admissions**: 9080 **Census**: 151 **Outpatient Visits**: 55583 **Births**: 0 **Total Expense ($000)**: 246712 **Payroll Expense ($000)**: 92263 **Personnel**: 982

LARGO—Prince George's County

UNIVERSITY OF MARYLAND CAPITAL REGION HEALTH PRINCE GEORGE'S HOSPITAL CENTER See University of Maryland Capital Region Medical Center

☐ **UNIVERSITY OF MARYLAND CAPITAL REGION MEDICAL CENTER (210003)**, 901 Harry S Truman Drive North, Zip 20774–5477; tel. 301/618–2000, (Includes GLADYS SPELLMAN SPECIALTY HOSPITAL AND NURSING CENTER, 3001 Hospital Drive, Sixth Floor, Cheverly, Maryland, Zip 20785–1189, tel. 301/618–6666; Trudy Hall, M.D., Vice President, Medical Affairs; UNIVERSITY OF MARYLAND CAPITAL REGION HEALTH AT LAUREL MEDICAL CENTER, 7300 Van Dusen Road, Laurel, Maryland, Zip 20707–9463, tel. 301/725–4300; Trudy Hall, M.D., Vice President Medical Affairs and Interim Chief Executive Officer) (Nonreporting) **A**1 3 5 10 **S** University of Maryland Medical System, Baltimore, MD
Primary Contact: Nathaniel Richardson Jr, President and Chief Executive Officer
CFO: William Brosius, Chief Financial Officer
CIO: Henry Archibong, Vice President, Information Services and Technology
CHR: Veronica Ford, Vice President Human Resources
CNO: Katie Boston–Leary, Vice President and Chief Nursing Officer, UMPGHC
Web address: https://www.umms.org/capital/locations/um-capital-region-medical-center
Control: Other not–for–profit (including NFP Corporation) **Service**: General medical and surgical

Staffed Beds: 245

LAUREL—Prince George's County

UNIVERSITY OF MARYLAND CAPITAL REGION HEALTH AT LAUREL REGIONAL MEDICAL CENTER See University of Maryland Capital Region Health At Laurel Medical Center

LEONARDTOWN—St. Mary's County

☒ **MEDSTAR ST. MARY'S HOSPITAL (210028)**, 25500 Point Lookout Road, Zip 20650–2015, Mailing Address: PO Box 527, Zip 20650–0527; tel. 301/475–6001, **A**1 2 3 10 **F**3 12 13 15 18 28 29 30 31 32 34 35 36 37 38 39 40 44 45 48 50 51 53 54 56 57 59 63 64 65 68 70 71 74 75 76 77 78 79 81 82 84 85 86 87 89 93 98 100 101 102 104 105 107 108 110 111 114 115 116 117 118 119 126 129 130 132 134 135 143 146 147 148 149 150 154 156 160 161 162 164 167 169 **P**6 **S** MedStar Health, Columbia, MD
Primary Contact: Mimi Novello, President and Chief Medical Officer
CMO: Mimi Novello, President and Chief Medical Officer
CIO: Donald Sirk, Director Information Systems
CNO: Dawn Yeitrakis, Vice President, Nursing
Web address: www.medstarstmarys.org
Control: Other not–for–profit (including NFP Corporation) **Service**: General medical and surgical

Staffed Beds: 92 **Admissions**: 6102 **Census**: 70 **Outpatient Visits**: 124547 **Births**: 1113 **Total Expense ($000)**: 201540 **Payroll Expense ($000)**: 93375 **Personnel**: 1003

Hospital, Medicare Provider Number, Address, Telephone, Approval, Facility, and Physician Codes, Health Care System

★ American Hospital Association (AHA) membership ◯ Healthcare Facilities Accreditation Program ⇧ Center for Improvement in Healthcare Quality Accreditation
☐ The Joint Commission accreditation ◇ DNV Healthcare Inc. accreditation △ Commission on Accreditation of Rehabilitation Facilities (CARF) accreditation

© 2025 AHA Guide

Hospitals, U.S. / MARYLAND

OAKLAND—Garrett County

GARRETT REGIONAL MEDICAL CENTER (210017), 251 North Fourth Street, Zip 21550–1375; tel. 301/533–4000, (Total facility includes 10 beds in nursing home–type unit) **A**1 10 **F**3 5 11 13 28 29 30 31 32 34 35 38 40 45 50 51 56 57 59 64 65 68 70 75 76 77 78 79 81 82 83 84 85 87 89 90 98 100 102 104 107 108 114 119 128 130 132 135 141 146 147 148 149 154 156 160 **P**6 **S** West Virginia University Health System, Morgantown, WV
Primary Contact: Mark G. Boucot, FACHE, President and Chief Executive Officer
CFO: Tracy Lipscomb, CPA, Vice President Financial Services and Chief Financial Officer
CMO: Marjorie Fridkin, M.D., Chief Medical Officer
CIO: Steven Peterson, Chief Information Officer, Vice President of Operations
CHR: Laura M Waters, Vice President Human Resources
CNO: Kendra Thayer, MSN, R.N., Chief Nursing Officer, Vice President Clinical Services
Web address: https://www.gcmh.com
Control: Other not–for–profit (including NFP Corporation) **Service**: General medical and surgical

Staffed Beds: 53 **Admissions**: 1397 **Census**: 12 **Outpatient Visits**: 55703 **Births**: 232 **Total Expense ($000)**: 73508 **Payroll Expense ($000)**: 35489 **Personnel**: 394

OLNEY—Montgomery County

MEDSTAR MONTGOMERY MEDICAL CENTER (210018), 18101 Prince Philip Drive, Zip 20832–1512; tel. 301/774–8882, **A**1 2 3 5 10 **F**3 4 5 11 12 13 15 18 20 26 28 29 30 31 34 35 37 38 40 41 44 45 46 48 49 50 51 53 55 56 57 58 59 61 65 67 68 70 73 74 75 76 77 78 79 81 82 84 85 86 87 89 92 93 97 98 99 100 101 102 104 105 107 108 110 111 114 115 118 119 120 121 123 124 126 129 130 131 132 134 135 146 147 148 149 152 153 154 156 160 162 164 165 167 169 **P**6 **S** MedStar Health, Columbia, MD
Primary Contact: Emily M. Briton, President
CFO: David A Havrilla, Chief Financial Officer
CMO: Frederick Finelli, M.D., Vice President Medical Affairs
CIO: Chistiane Brown, Assistant Vice President
CHR: Kevin Mell, Vice President Operations
Web address: www.medstarmontgomery.org
Control: Other not–for–profit (including NFP Corporation) **Service**: General medical and surgical

Staffed Beds: 102 **Admissions**: 5202 **Census**: 80 **Outpatient Visits**: 64634 **Births**: 575 **Total Expense ($000)**: 198205 **Payroll Expense ($000)**: 83436 **Personnel**: 890

PERRY POINT—Cecil County

VETERANS AFFAIRS MARYLAND HEALTH CARE SYSTEM–PERRY POINT DIVISION See Veterans Affairs Maryland Health Care System–Baltimore Division, Baltimore

VETERANS AFFAIRS MED CENTER See Veterans Affairs Maryland Health Care System–Perry Point Division

PRINCE FREDERICK—Calvert County

CALVERTHEALTH MEDICAL CENTER (210039), 100 Hospital Road, Zip 20678–4017; tel. 410/535–4000, **A**1 2 10 **F**3 12 13 18 20 26 28 29 30 31 34 35 38 40 43 45 46 47 48 49 50 51 54 56 57 59 64 65 66 70 71 74 75 76 77 78 79 81 85 86 87 89 93 98 99 100 101 102 104 105 107 108 111 112 114 115 119 124 126 127 130 132 134 135 146 147 148 149 154 156 157 160 164 167 169
Primary Contact: Jeremy Bradford, President and Chief Executive Officer
COO: Anthony M. Bladen, Executive Vice President, Chief Operating Officer
CFO: Carolyn Heithaus, Chief Financial Officer
CMO: J Michael Brooks, M.D., Chief Medical Officer
CHR: Diane Couchman, Interim Vice President, Human Resources
CNO: Melissa Hall, MSN, R.N., Vice President of Clinical Affairs and Chief Nursing Officer
Web address: www.calverthealthmedicine.org/
Control: Other not–for–profit (including NFP Corporation) **Service**: General medical and surgical

Staffed Beds: 80 **Admissions**: 5264 **Census**: 58 **Outpatient Visits**: 88009 **Births**: 559 **Total Expense ($000)**: 160773 **Payroll Expense ($000)**: 69588 **Personnel**: 1032

RANDALLSTOWN—Baltimore County

NORTHWEST HOSPITAL (210040), 5401 Old Court Road, Zip 21133–5185; tel. 410/521–2200, **A**1 2 3 10 **F**3 9 11 12 15 18 28 29 30 31 34 35 38 39 40 44 45 49 51 55 56 58 60 61 63 64 67 68 70 74 75 77 78 79 81 82 83 84 85 87 93 94 96 97 98 100 101 102 107 108 110 111 114 115 118 119 126 128 130 131 132 134 143 146 147 148 149 150 154 156 157 167 **S** LifeBridge Health, Baltimore, MD
Primary Contact: Craig Carmichael, President and Chief Operating Officer, Senior Vice President, LifeBridge Health
COO: Craig Carmichael, President and Chief Operating Officer, Senior Vice President, LifeBridge Health
CFO: David McCormick, Chief Financial Officer, Northwest Hospital, Assistant Vice President, Finance, LifeBridge Health
CIO: Tressa Springmann, Vice President and Chief Information Officer
CHR: Tracie Oden, Vice President, Human Resources
CNO: Kim Bushnell, R.N., Vice President, Patient Care Services and Chief Nursing Officer, Northwest
Web address: https://www.lifebridgehealth.org/main/northwest-hospital
Control: Other not–for–profit (including NFP Corporation) **Service**: General medical and surgical

Staffed Beds: 210 **Admissions**: 8197 **Census**: 160 **Outpatient Visits**: 58775 **Births**: 0 **Total Expense ($000)**: 313097 **Payroll Expense ($000)**: 97571 **Personnel**: 1236

ROCKVILLE—Montgomery County

ADVENTIST BEHAVIORAL HEALTH ROCKVILLE See Adventist Behavioral Health and Wellness Services

ADVENTIST HEALTHCARE REHABILITATION (213029), 9909 Medical Center Drive, Zip 20850–6361; tel. 240/864–6000, **A**1 7 10 **F**3 28 29 30 34 35 50 53 56 57 58 59 60 64 68 74 75 77 87 90 93 94 96 130 131 146 149 154 **S** Adventist HealthCare, Gaithersburg, MD
Primary Contact: Brent Reitz, President, Post Acute Care Services
COO: Jason Makaroff, Chief Operating Officer and Associate Vice President
CMO: Terrence P Sheehan, M.D., Medical Director
CHR: Carrie Hibbard, Human Resource Business Partner
CNO: Valerie Summerlin, R.N., MS, Chief Nursing Officer
Web address: https://www.adventisthealthcare.com/locations/profile/rehabilitation-rockville/
Control: Church operated, Nongovernment, not–for–profit **Service**: Rehabilitation

Staffed Beds: 97 **Admissions**: 2161 **Census**: 87 **Outpatient Visits**: 68693 **Births**: 0 **Total Expense ($000)**: 64044 **Payroll Expense ($000)**: 35988 **Personnel**: 478

ADVENTIST HEALTHCARE SHADY GROVE MEDICAL CENTER (210057), 9901 Medical Center Drive, Zip 20850–3395; tel. 240/826–6000, (Includes ADVENTIST BEHAVIORAL HEALTH AND WELLNESS SERVICES, 14901 Broschart Road, Rockville, Maryland, Zip 20850–3318, tel. 301/251–4500; John Sackett, President SGMC and Executive Vice President and Chief Operating Officer) **A**1 3 5 10 **F**3 5 10 12 13 15 18 19 20 22 26 28 29 30 31 34 35 39 40 41 42 44 45 46 47 48 49 50 51 54 57 58 64 66 68 70 72 74 75 76 77 78 79 81 82 84 85 86 87 89 98 99 100 101 102 103 104 105 107 111 114 115 116 117 118 119 120 121 124 126 130 132 143 146 147 148 149 153 154 156 164 167 169 **P**8 **S** Adventist HealthCare, Gaithersburg, MD
Primary Contact: Daniel Cochran, President
COO: Eunmee Shim, R.N., MSN, Vice President Operations
CFO: Daniel Cochran, Vice President and Chief Financial Officer
CMO: Kevin Smothers, M.D., Vice President Chief Medical Officer
CIO: christopher Ghion, Vice President and Chief Information Officer
CNO: Joan M Vincent, MSN, MS, R.N., Vice President Patient Care Services and Chief Nurse Executive
Web address: www.adventisthealthcare.com
Control: Church operated, Nongovernment, not–for–profit **Service**: General medical and surgical

Staffed Beds: 339 **Admissions**: 16809 **Census**: 254 **Outpatient Visits**: 105380 **Births**: 3801 **Total Expense ($000)**: 473985 **Payroll Expense ($000)**: 187615 **Personnel**: 2190

Hospitals, U.S. / MARYLAND

SALISBURY—Wicomico County

DEER'S HEAD HOSPITAL CENTER (212003), 351 Deer's Head Hospital Road, Zip 21801–3201, Mailing Address: PO Box 2018, Zip 21802–2018; tel. 410/543–4000, (Total facility includes 38 beds in nursing home–type unit) **A1** 10 **F3** 6 11 28 29 30 44 50 56 57 59 60 61 65 68 75 77 82 84 85 86 87 91 93 94 96 128 130 132 135 146 148 149 154 164
Primary Contact: Mary Beth Waide, R.N., JD, MS, Chief Executive Officer
COO: Luanne Dashield, Chief Operating Officer
CFO: Kenneth Waller, Fiscal Administrator
CMO: Robert Coker, M.D., Medical Director
CIO: Mac Beattie, Computer Network Specialist
CHR: Andre Harmon, Chief Human Resource Officer
CNO: Cheri Porcelli, MSN, R.N., Chief Nursing Officer
Web address: https://health.maryland.gov/deershead/Pages/Home.aspx
Control: State, Government, Nonfederal **Service**: Chronic disease

Staffed Beds: 44 **Admissions**: 26 **Census**: 33 **Outpatient Visits**: 4875 **Births**: 0 **Total Expense ($000)**: 24366 **Payroll Expense ($000)**: 11411 **Personnel**: 169

ENCOMPASS HEALTH REHABILITATION HOSPITAL OF SALISBURY (213028), 220 Tilghman Road, Zip 21804–1921; tel. 410/546–4600, (Nonreporting) **A1** 7 10 **S** Encompass Health Corporation, Birmingham, AL
Primary Contact: W. Mark. Rader, Chief Executive Officer
CFO: Karen Rounsley, Controller
CHR: Belinda Thompson, Coordinator Human Resources
CNO: Belle Goslee, Chief Nursing Officer
Web address: www.healthsouthchesapeake.com
Control: Corporation, Investor–owned (for–profit) **Service**: Rehabilitation

Staffed Beds: 54

TIDALHEALTH PENINSULA See Tidalhealth Peninsula Regional

TIDALHEALTH PENINSULA REGIONAL (210019), 100 East Carroll Street, Zip 21801–5422; tel. 410/546–6400, (Includes TIDALHEALTH MCCREADY, 201 Hall Highway, Crisfield, Maryland, Zip 21817–1299, tel. 410/968–1200; Kathleen Harrison, Chief Executive Officer) **A1** 2 3 5 10 **F3** 8 10 11 12 13 15 17 18 20 22 24 26 28 29 30 31 32 34 35 37 40 43 44 45 46 47 48 49 50 51 53 54 57 58 59 60 61 64 65 66 68 70 71 73 74 75 76 77 78 79 81 82 84 85 86 87 89 92 93 97 98 100 102 104 105 107 108 110 111 114 115 118 119 120 121 123 124 126 129 130 132 134 135 143 144 145 146 147 148 149 153 154 156 167 169 **S** TidalHealth, Salisbury, MD
Primary Contact: Steven E. Leonard, President and Chief Executive Officer
COO: Cindy Lunsford, Executive Vice President and Chief Operating Officer
CFO: Bruce Ritchie, Vice President of Finance and Chief Financial Officer
CMO: Charles B Silvia, M.D., Chief Medical Officer and Vice President Medical Affairs
CIO: Raymond Adkins, Chief Information Officer
CHR: Scott Peterson, Vice President of People and Organizational Development
CNO: Karen C Poisker, MSN, Vice President Patient Care Services and Chief Nursing Officer
Web address: https://www.tidalhealth.org/our-locations/tidalhealth-peninsula-regional
Control: Other not–for–profit (including NFP Corporation) **Service**: General medical and surgical

Staffed Beds: 281 **Admissions**: 15790 **Census**: 199 **Outpatient Visits**: 408409 **Births**: 2145 **Total Expense ($000)**: 489455 **Payroll Expense ($000)**: 190935 **Personnel**: 3309

SILVER SPRING—Montgomery County

ADVENTIST HEALTHCARE WHITE OAK MEDICAL CENTER (210016), 11890 Healing Way, Zip 20904; tel. 240/637–4000, (Includes ADVENTIST HEALTHCARE WASHINGTON ADVENTIST HOSPITAL, 7600 Carroll Avenue, Takoma Park, Maryland, Zip 20912–6392, tel. 301/891–7600; Erik Wangsness, President and Chief Executive Officer) **A1** 3 5 7 10 **F3** 12 13 18 20 22 24 26 29 30 31 34 35 40 44 45 46 49 50 51 53 57 58 59 61 64 65 68 70 73 74 75 76 77 78 79 81 82 84 85 87 100 107 108 111 115 118 119 126 130 135 141 144 146 147 148 149 157 164 167 169 **S** Adventist HealthCare, Gaithersburg, MD
Primary Contact: Anthony Stahl, FACHE, Ph.D., President
Web address: https://www.adventisthealthcare.com
Control: Other not–for–profit (including NFP Corporation) **Service**: General medical and surgical

Staffed Beds: 194 **Admissions**: 9998 **Census**: 154 **Outpatient Visits**: 45174 **Births**: 1864 **Total Expense ($000)**: 303679 **Payroll Expense ($000)**: 104622 **Personnel**: 1156

HOLY CROSS HOSPITAL (210004), 1500 Forest Glen Road, Zip 20910–1487; tel. 301/754–7000, **A1** 2 3 5 10 **F3** 11 12 13 15 18 20 22 26 29 30 31 37 40 41 45 46 47 48 49 50 51 58 60 64 67 68 69 70 71 72 73 74 75 76 77 78 79 81 82 84 85 87 89 92 93 102 107 110 111 118 119 120 121 124 126 130 146 147 148 149 167 **S** Trinity Health, Livonia, MI
Primary Contact: Louis Damiano, M.D., Chief Executive Officer
CFO: Anne Gillis, Chief Financial Officer
CMO: Blair Eig, M.D., Senior Vice President Medical Affairs
CIO: Matthew Trimmer, Director Information Services
CHR: J Manuel Ocasio, Vice President Human Resources
CNO: Celia Guarino, R.N., MSN, Vice President and Chief Nursing Officer
Web address: www.holycrosshealth.org
Control: Church operated, Nongovernment, not–for–profit **Service**: General medical and surgical

Staffed Beds: 453 **Admissions**: 20928 **Census**: 431 **Outpatient Visits**: 97559 **Births**: 10745 **Total Expense ($000)**: 529814 **Payroll Expense ($000)**: 244043 **Personnel**: 2236

SILVER SPRING—Prince George's County

SAINT LUKE INSTITUTE, 8901 New Hampshire Avenue, Zip 20903–3611; tel. 301/445–7970, (Nonreporting)
Primary Contact: Father David Songy, O.F.M.Cap., President and Chief Executive Officer
COO: Sister Danile Lynch, Chief Operating Officer
Web address: www.sli.org
Control: Other not–for–profit (including NFP Corporation) **Service**: Psychiatric

Staffed Beds: 52

SYKESVILLE—Carroll County

SPRINGFIELD HOSPITAL CENTER (214004), 6655 Sykesville Road, Zip 21784–7966; tel. 410/970–7000, (Nonreporting) **A1** 3 10
Primary Contact: Paula A. Langmead, Chief Executive Officer
COO: Daniel Triplett, Acting Chief Operating Officer
CFO: Keith Hardesty, Chief Financial Officer
CMO: Kim Bright, M.D., Clinical Director
CIO: Denise Maskell, Chief Information Officer
CNO: Gloria Merek, Director of Nursing
Web address: www.dhmh.state.md.us/springfield
Control: State, Government, Nonfederal **Service**: Psychiatric

Staffed Beds: 220

TAKOMA PARK—Montgomery County

WASHINGTON ADVENTIST HOSPITAL See Adventist Healthcare Washington Adventist Hospital

TOWSON—Baltimore County

UNIVERSITY OF MARYLAND ST. JOSEPH MEDICAL CENTER (210063), 7601 Osler Drive, Zip 21204–7582; tel. 410/337–1000, **A1** 2 3 5 10 **F3** 8 11 13 15 17 18 20 22 24 26 28 29 31 34 35 36 37 40 41 44 45 46 47 48 49 50 54 55 56 57 58 59 60 61 64 65 68 70 72 74 75 76 77 78 79 81 82 84 85 86 87 89 91 92 93 94 96 97 98 100 101 102 103 104 105 107 108 110 111 114 115 118 119 120 121 123 124 126 129 130 131 132 135 143 144 146 147 148 149 153 154 156 157 165 167 169 **P8 S** University of Maryland Medical System, Baltimore, MD
Primary Contact: Thomas Smyth, President and Chief Executive Officer
CMO: Gail Cunningham, Chief Medical Officer
CIO: Thomas Gronert, Chief Information Officer
CNO: Nicole Beeson, Senior Vice President, Patient Care Services and Chief Nursing Officer
Web address: www.stjosephtowson.com/home.aspx
Control: Other not–for–profit (including NFP Corporation) **Service**: General medical and surgical

Staffed Beds: 286 **Admissions**: 12847 **Census**: 159 **Outpatient Visits**: 85629 **Births**: 2230 **Total Expense ($000)**: 386960 **Payroll Expense ($000)**: 143653 **Personnel**: 1607

Hospital, Medicare Provider Number, Address, Telephone, Approval, Facility, and Physician Codes, Health Care System

★ American Hospital Association (AHA) membership
□ The Joint Commission accreditation
○ Healthcare Facilities Accreditation Program
◇ DNV Healthcare Inc. accreditation
⇧ Center for Improvement in Healthcare Quality Accreditation
△ Commission on Accreditation of Rehabilitation Facilities (CARF) accreditation

Hospitals, U.S. / MARYLAND

WESTMINSTER—Carroll County

CARROLL HOSPITAL (210033), 200 Memorial Avenue, Zip 21157-5799; tel. 410/848-3000, **A**1 2 3 10 **F**3 7 11 13 15 18 19 20 22 26 28 29 30 31 32 34 35 36 37 38 39 40 44 45 49 50 51 54 55 56 57 58 59 61 62 63 64 66 67 68 70 72 74 75 76 77 78 79 81 82 83 84 85 86 87 89 96 97 98 99 100 101 102 104 105 106 107 108 109 110 111 114 115 116 117 119 120 121 126 127 130 131 132 134 135 143 146 147 148 149 150 153 154 155 156 157 160 162 164 167 169 **S** LifeBridge Health, Baltimore, MD
Primary Contact: Garrett W. Hoover, FACHE, President and Chief Operating Officer, Senior Vice President LifeBridge Health
COO: Garrett W Hoover, FACHE, President and Chief Operating Officer, Senior Vice President LifeBridge Health
CFO: Kevin Kelbly, Senior Vice President Finance and Corporate Fiscal Affairs
CMO: Mark Olszyk, M.D., Vice President Medical Affairs and Chief Medical Officer
CHR: Holly Phipps Adams, Vice President of Human Resources
CNO: Stephanie Reid, R.N., Vice President of Patient Care Services and Chief Nursing Officer
Web address: www.carrollhospitalcenter.org
Control: Other not-for-profit (including NFP Corporation) **Service**: General medical and surgical

Staffed Beds: 163 **Admissions**: 9177 **Census**: 124 **Outpatient Visits**: 80457 **Births**: 1027 **Total Expense ($000)**: 275947 **Payroll Expense ($000)**: 104335 **Personnel**: 1366

CARROLL HOSPITAL CENTER See Carroll Hospital

MASSACHUSETTS

ATHOL—Worcester County

ATHOL HOSPITAL (221303), 2033 Main Street, Zip 01331–3598;
tel. 978/249–3511, **A**1 10 18 **F**40 42 107 114 115 **S** Heywood Healthcare, Gardner, MA
Primary Contact: Rozanna Penney, Co–Chief Executive Officer
COO: Michael Grimmer, Chief Operating Officer
CFO: Robert Crosby, Chief Financial Officer
CMO: Mohsen Noreldin, M.D., President Medical Staff
CIO: Carol Roosa, Vice President Information Services and Chief Information Officer
CNO: Lucille Songer, Chief Nursing Officer
Web address: www.atholhospital.org
Control: Other not–for–profit (including NFP Corporation)

Staffed Beds: 25 **Admissions**: 550 **Census**: 11 **Outpatient Visits**: 33253
Total Expense ($000): 40713 **Payroll Expense ($000)**: 11095

ATTLEBORO—Bristol County

ARBOUR–FULLER HOSPITAL (224021), 200 May Street, Zip 02703–5520;
tel. 508/761–8500, (Nonreporting) **A**1 5 10 **S** Universal Health Services, Inc., King of Prussia, PA
Primary Contact: Rachel Legend, Chief Executive Officer
CFO: James Rollins, Chief Financial Officer
CMO: Aminadav Zakai, M.D., Medical Director
CHR: Brian Jenkins, Director Human Resources
Web address: www.arbourhealth.com
Control: Corporation, Investor–owned (for–profit) **Service**: Psychiatric

Staffed Beds: 46

★ ⇧ **STURDY MEMORIAL HOSPITAL (220008)**, 211 Park Street,
Zip 02703–3137, Mailing Address: PO Box 2963, Zip 02703–0963;
tel. 508/222–5200, **A**2 3 10 21 **F**3 13 15 18 28 29 31 34 35 37 40 41 45 46 49 50 51 56 57 59 61 64 65 68 70 74 75 76 77 78 79 81 82 85 86 87 93 97 107 108 110 111 114 115 116 119 126 129 130 131 132 135 144 146 147 148 149 150 154 156 157 164 167 169
Primary Contact: Aimee Brewer, MPH, President and Chief Executive Officer
CFO: Amy Pfeffer, Chief Financial Officer
CMO: Brian Kelly, M.D., Vice President Medical Affairs and Medical Director
CHR: Cheryl Barrows, Vice President Human Resources
CNO: David Spoor, R.N., Senior Vice President, Patient Care Services and Chief Nursing Officer
Web address: www.sturdymemorial.org
Control: Other not–for–profit (including NFP Corporation) **Service**: General medical and surgical

Staffed Beds: 126 **Admissions**: 7244 **Census**: 92 **Outpatient Visits**: 171486 **Births**: 570 **Total Expense ($000)**: 256606 **Payroll Expense ($000)**: 110735 **Personnel**: 1254

BEDFORD—Middlesex County

BEDFORD VAMC See Bedford Veterans Affairs Medical Center, Edith Nourse Rogers Memorial Veterans Hospital

BEDFORD VETERANS AFFAIRS MEDICAL CENTER, EDITH NOURSE ROGERS MEMORIAL VETERANS HOSPITAL, 200 Springs Road, Zip 01730–1198, Mailing Address: 200 Springs Road Bldg 3, Zip 01730–1198; tel. 781/687–2000, (Nonreporting) **A**1 3 5 **S** Department of Veterans Affairs, Washington, DC
Primary Contact: Joan Clifford, R.N., FACHE, Medical Center Director and Chief Executive Officer
COO: Kendra Lee, JD, Chief Operating Officer
CFO: Edward Koetting, Chief Financial Officer
CMO: Dan Berlowitz, M.D., M.P.H., Acting Chief of Staff
CNO: Mary Ann Petrillo, R.N., MSN, Acting Associate Director Nursing and Patient Clinical Services
Web address: www.bedford.va.gov
Control: Veterans Affairs, Government, federal **Service**: Psychiatric

Staffed Beds: 23

BELMONT—Middlesex County

MCLEAN HOSPITAL (224007), 115 Mill Street, Zip 02478–1064;
tel. 617/855–2000, **A**1 3 5 10 **F**4 5 29 30 53 68 77 86 98 100 101 103 104 105 106 111 119 130 132 152 153 154 160 164 **P**6 **S** Mass General Brigham, Boston, MA
Primary Contact: Scott L. Rauch, M.D., President and Psychiatrist in Chief
COO: Michele L Gougeon, Executive Vice President and Chief Operating Officer
CFO: David A Lagasse, Senior Vice President Fiscal Affairs
CMO: Joseph Gold, M.D., Chief Medical Officer
CHR: Lisa D. Pratt, Vice President, Human Resources
CNO: Linda Flaherty, R.N., Senior Vice President, Patient Care Services
Web address: www.mcleanhospital.org
Control: Other not–for–profit (including NFP Corporation) **Service**: Psychiatric

Staffed Beds: 309 **Admissions**: 6321 **Census**: 264 **Outpatient Visits**: 60771 **Births**: 0 **Total Expense ($000)**: 356467 **Payroll Expense ($000)**: 165203 **Personnel**: 2098

BEVERLY—Essex County

BEVERLY HOSPITAL (220033), 85 Herrick Street, Zip 01915–1777;
tel. 978/922–3000, (Includes ADDISON GILBERT HOSPITAL, 298 Washington Street, Gloucester, Massachusetts, Zip 01930–4887, tel. 978/283–4000) (Nonreporting) **A**1 2 3 5 10 19 **S** Beth Israel Lahey Health, Cambridge, MA
Primary Contact: Tom Sands, FACHE, President
COO: Pauline Pike, Chief Operating Officer
CFO: Connie Woodworth, Vice President Finance
CMO: Peter H Short, M.D., Senior Vice President Medical Affairs
CIO: Robert Laramie, Chief Information Officer
CHR: Althea C Lyons, Vice President Human Resources and Development
Web address: www.beverlyhospital.org
Control: Other not–for–profit (including NFP Corporation) **Service**: General medical and surgical

Staffed Beds: 320

BOSTON—Suffolk County

ARBOUR HOSPITAL (224013), 49 Robinwood Avenue, Zip 02130–2156;
tel. 617/522–4400, (Nonreporting) **A**1 10 **S** Universal Health Services, Inc., King of Prussia, PA
Primary Contact: Stephen P. Fahey, Chief Executive Officer
Web address: https://arbourhospital.com/
Control: Other not–for–profit (including NFP Corporation) **Service**: Psychiatric

Staffed Beds: 118

BETH ISRAEL DEACONESS MEDICAL CENTER (220086), 330 Brookline Avenue, Zip 02215–5491; tel. 617/667–7000, **A**1 2 3 5 8 10 19 **F**3 5 6 7 9 12 13 15 17 18 20 22 24 26 29 30 31 34 35 36 37 38 40 43 44 45 46 47 48 49 50 51 52 54 55 56 57 58 59 60 61 63 64 65 66 68 70 71 72 73 74 75 76 77 78 79 81 82 84 85 87 92 93 97 98 100 102 103 104 107 108 109 110 111 112 113 114 115 116 117 118 119 120 121 123 124 126 129 130 131 132 136 137 138 139 141 142 143 144 145 146 147 148 149 150 154 156 157 160 162 163 167 169 **P**8 **S** Beth Israel Lahey Health, Cambridge, MA
Primary Contact: Peter J. Healy, Divisional President, Metro Boston and President of Beth Israel Deaconess Medical Center
CFO: Steven P Fischer, Chief Financial Officer
CMO: Anthony Weiss, M.D., Chief Medical Officer
CHR: Judi Bieber, Senior Vice President Human Resources
CNO: Marsha L. Maurer, R.N., MS, Chief Nursing Officer Patient Care Services
Web address: www.bidmc.harvard.edu
Control: Other not–for–profit (including NFP Corporation) **Service**: General medical and surgical

Staffed Beds: 756 **Admissions**: 31386 **Census**: 635 **Outpatient Visits**: 1213618 **Births**: 4697 **Total Expense ($000)**: 2632415 **Payroll Expense ($000)**: 890533 **Personnel**: 10949

Hospitals, U.S. / MASSACHUSETTS

☐ **BOSTON CHILDREN'S HOSPITAL (223302)**, 300 Longwood Avenue, Zip 02115–5737; tel. 617/355–6000, **A**1 3 5 8 10 **F**3 5 7 12 14 17 19 21 23 25 27 28 29 30 31 32 34 35 37 38 39 40 41 43 44 45 46 48 49 50 51 55 58 59 60 61 64 65 68 70 72 74 75 77 78 79 81 82 84 85 86 87 88 89 91 92 93 97 98 99 100 104 106 107 108 110 111 112 113 114 115 116 117 118 119 126 129 130 131 132 133 135 136 137 138 139 140 141 142 146 148 149 154 155 157 160 161 164 167 **P**3
Primary Contact: Kevin B. Churchwell, M.D., Chief Executive Officer
COO: Kevin B Churchwell, M.D., President and Chief Operating Officer
CFO: Douglas M Vanderslice, Senior Vice President and Chief Financial Officer
CIO: Heather Nelson, Senior Vice President and Chief Information Officer
Web address: www.childrenshospital.org/
Control: Other not–for–profit (including NFP Corporation) Service: Children's general medical and surgical

Staffed Beds: 513 **Admissions:** 28306 **Census:** 383 **Outpatient Visits:** 592030 **Births:** 0 **Total Expense ($000):** 2705934 **Payroll Expense ($000):** 988890 **Personnel:** 13277

✠ **BOSTON MEDICAL CENTER (220031)**, 1 Boston Medical Center Place, Zip 02118–2908; tel. 617/638–8000, **A**1 2 3 5 8 10 19 **F**2 3 4 5 8 9 12 13 15 17 18 19 20 22 24 26 28 29 30 31 32 33 34 35 36 37 38 40 41 42 43 44 45 46 47 48 49 50 51 54 55 56 57 58 59 61 62 64 65 66 68 70 71 74 75 76 77 78 79 80 81 82 84 85 86 87 88 89 92 93 94 96 97 98 99 100 101 102 103 104 107 108 110 111 114 115 117 118 119 120 121 123 124 126 129 130 131 132 134 135 136 138 142 144 145 146 147 148 149 150 151 154 156 157 158 160 162 163 164 166 167 169 **P**7
Primary Contact: Anthony Hollenberg, M.D., President
COO: Joe Camillus, Chief Operating Officer
CFO: Ronald E Bartlett, Chief Financial Officer
CHR: Stephanie Lovell, Vice President and General Counsel
Web address: www.bmc.org
Control: Other not–for–profit (including NFP Corporation) Service: General medical and surgical

Staffed Beds: 594 **Admissions:** 24340 **Census:** 481 **Outpatient Visits:** 1291158 **Births:** 2960 **Total Expense ($000):** 2417596 **Payroll Expense ($000):** 699273 **Personnel:** 8574

✠ **BRIGHAM AND WOMEN'S FAULKNER HOSPITAL (220119)**, 1153 Centre Street, Zip 02130–3446; tel. 617/983–7000, **A**1 3 5 10 19 **F**3 4 5 12 15 18 28 29 30 34 35 37 38 40 45 46 47 48 49 50 56 57 58 59 61 63 68 70 74 75 77 79 81 82 84 87 93 96 98 100 101 102 103 104 105 107 108 110 111 119 126 129 130 132 146 149 150 152 153 154 156 157 164 167 168 **S** Mass General Brigham, Boston, MA
Primary Contact: Kevin T. Giordano, President
CFO: Gerard Hadley, Vice President Finance for Brigham & Women's Faulkner Hospital and Vice President Finance and Controller
CIO: Catherine Schroeder, Deputy Chief Information Officer
CHR: Laura Barnett, Executive Director, Human Resources
CNO: Cori Loescher, R.N., Chief Nursing Officer and Vice President of Patient Care Services
Web address: www.brighamandwomensfaulkner.org/index.asp
Control: Other not–for–profit (including NFP Corporation) Service: General medical and surgical

Staffed Beds: 163 **Admissions:** 8443 **Census:** 135 **Outpatient Visits:** 238783 **Births:** 0 **Total Expense ($000):** 375214 **Payroll Expense ($000):** 166481 **Personnel:** 1560

✠ **BRIGHAM AND WOMEN'S HOSPITAL (220110)**, 75 Francis Street, Zip 02115–6110; tel. 617/732–5500, **A**1 2 3 5 8 10 19 **F**3 5 6 8 9 11 12 13 14 15 16 17 18 20 22 24 26 28 29 30 31 33 34 35 36 37 38 39 40 43 44 45 46 47 48 49 50 51 52 54 55 56 57 58 59 60 61 64 65 66 68 70 71 72 73 74 75 76 77 78 79 81 82 83 84 85 86 87 92 93 97 100 101 102 104 105 107 108 110 111 112 114 115 116 117 118 119 120 121 122 123 124 126 129 130 131 132 133 134 135 136 137 138 139 140 141 142 143 144 145 146 147 148 149 150 152 153 154 156 157 165 167 168 169 **P**6 **S** Mass General Brigham, Boston, MA
Primary Contact: Giles W. Boland, M.D., President
COO: Kevin T. Giordano, Chief Operating Officer
CIO: Adam Landman, M.D., Chief Information Officer
CHR: Sabrina Williams, Interim Vice President Human Resources
CNO: Madelyn Pearson, R.N., Senior Vice President Patient Care Services and Chief Nursing Officer
Web address: www.brighamandwomens.org
Control: Other not–for–profit (including NFP Corporation) Service: General medical and surgical

Staffed Beds: 885 **Admissions:** 39380 **Census:** 802 **Outpatient Visits:** 1569551 **Births:** 6966 **Total Expense ($000):** 3284914 **Payroll Expense ($000):** 1167962 **Personnel:** 16850

✠ **DANA–FARBER CANCER INSTITUTE (220162)**, 450 Brookline Avenue, Zip 02215–5418; tel. 617/632–3000, **A**1 2 3 5 8 10 **F**3 5 11 15 29 30 31 32 34 35 36 44 50 54 55 56 57 58 59 64 65 66 68 71 75 77 78 82 83 84 85 86 87 100 101 104 107 108 110 111 114 115 117 118 119 120 121 123 124 130 132 134 135 136 144 146 147 148 149 150 154 160 164 **P**6
Primary Contact: Laurie H. Glimcher, President and Chief Executive Officer
CFO: Michael L. Reney, Senior Vice President for Finance and Chief Financial Officer
CMO: Craig A. Bunnell, Chief Medical Officer
CIO: Naomi Lenane, Chief Information Officer
CHR: Deborah Hicks, Senior Vice President, Chief People and Culture Officer
CNO: Anne H Gross, Senior Vice President, Patient Care Services and Chief Nursing Officer
Web address: www.dana-farber.org
Control: Other not–for–profit (including NFP Corporation) Service: Cancer

Staffed Beds: 30 **Admissions:** 1338 **Census:** 28 **Outpatient Visits:** 601373 **Births:** 0 **Total Expense ($000):** 2989082 **Payroll Expense ($000):** 764037 **Personnel:** 7165

☐ **DR. SOLOMON CARTER FULLER MENTAL HEALTH CENTER (224040)**, 85 East Newton Street, Zip 02118–2340; tel. 617/626–8700, (Nonreporting) **A**1 3 5 10
Primary Contact: Theresa M. Harrison, Site Director
Web address: https://www.mass.gov/service-details/metro-boston-area
Control: State, Government, Nonfederal Service: Psychiatric

Staffed Beds: 32

✠ **MASSACHUSETTS EYE AND EAR (220075)**, 243 Charles Street, Zip 02114–3002; tel. 617/523–7900, **A**1 3 5 10 **F**3 8 11 29 30 31 34 35 36 40 41 44 50 54 55 56 57 58 59 64 65 66 68 74 75 77 78 81 82 85 86 87 89 107 111 114 119 126 129 130 132 141 146 **P**6 **S** Mass General Brigham, Boston, MA
Primary Contact: CarolAnn Williams, President
CIO: Leo Hill, Chief Information Officer
CHR: Martha Pyle Farrell, Vice President Human Resources and General Counsel
CNO: Kathleen Charbonnier, MSN, R.N., Interim Chief Nursing Officer
Web address: www.masseyeandear.org
Control: Other not–for–profit (including NFP Corporation) Service: Eye, ear, nose and throat

Staffed Beds: 41 **Admissions:** 1127 **Census:** 12 **Outpatient Visits:** 543114 **Births:** 0 **Total Expense ($000):** 363611 **Payroll Expense ($000):** 91204 **Personnel:** 2089

✠ **MASSACHUSETTS GENERAL HOSPITAL (220071)**, 55 Fruit Street, Zip 02114–2696, Mailing Address: 55 Fruit Street, Bulfinch 310, Zip 02114–2696; tel. 617/726–2000, (Includes MASSGENERAL HOSPITAL FOR CHILDREN, 55 Fruit Street, Boston, Massachusetts, Zip 02114–2621, tel. 888/644–3248) **A**1 3 5 8 10 19 **F**3 4 5 6 8 9 11 12 13 14 15 16 17 18 19 20 21 22 23 24 25 26 27 28 29 31 32 33 34 35 36 37 38 39 40 41 43 44 45 46 47 48 49 50 51 52 53 54 55 56 57 58 59 60 61 62 64 65 66 68 70 71 72 73 74 75 76 77 78 79 80 81 82 84 85 86 87 88 89 90 91 92 93 94 96 97 98 99 100 101 102 103 104 107 108 110 111 112 113 114 115 116 117 118 119 120 121 122 123 124 126 129 130 131 132 134 136 137 138 139 140 141 142 143 144 145 146 147 148 149 150 151 153 154 156 157 160 161 162 163 164 165 166 167 169 **P**6 7 **S** Mass General Brigham, Boston, MA
Primary Contact: Marcela G. del Carmen, President
CFO: Sally Mason Boemer, Senior Vice President Finance
CMO: Britain Nicholson, M.D., Chief Medical Officer
CIO: Keith Jennings, Chief Information Officer
CHR: Jovita Thomas–Williams, Senior Vice President of Human Resources
CNO: Jeanette R Ives Erickson, MS, R.N., Senior Vice President Patient Care and Chief Nurse
Web address: www.massgeneral.org
Control: Other not–for–profit (including NFP Corporation) Service: General medical and surgical

Staffed Beds: 1040 **Admissions:** 44902 **Census:** 954 **Outpatient Visits:** 943693 **Births:** 3760 **Total Expense ($000):** 5513952 **Payroll Expense ($000):** 1526275 **Personnel:** 27633

Hospitals, U.S. / MASSACHUSETTS

✣ **NEW ENGLAND BAPTIST HOSPITAL (220088)**, 125 Parker Hill Avenue, Zip 02120–2847; tel. 617/754–5800, **A**1 3 5 10 19 **F**3 8 9 18 29 34 35 37 44 50 53 54 57 58 59 64 65 70 74 75 79 81 82 86 87 92 93 97 100 107 108 111 115 119 126 130 131 141 146 148 149 154 157 **P**8 **S** Beth Israel Lahey Health, Cambridge, MA
Primary Contact: David Passafaro, President
CFO: Thomas Gheringhelli, Senior Vice President, Chief Financial Officer
CHR: Linda Thompson, Senior Vice President, Human Resources and Service Excellence
CNO: Mary Sullivan Smith, R.N., MS, Senior Vice President, Chief Operating Officer and Chief Nursing Officer
Web address: www.nebh.org
Control: Other not–for–profit (including NFP Corporation) **Service**: Orthopedic

> **Staffed Beds**: 113 **Admissions**: 3007 **Census**: 24 **Outpatient Visits**: 105154 **Births**: 0 **Total Expense ($000)**: 242794 **Payroll Expense ($000)**: 75530 **Personnel**: 984

☐ **SHRINERS HOSPITALS FOR CHILDREN–BOSTON (223304)**, 51 Blossom Street, Zip 02114–2601; tel. 617/722–3000, (Nonreporting) **A**1 3 5 10 **S** Shriners Hospitals for Children, Tampa, FL
Primary Contact: Frances Marthone, Ph.D., MSN, R.N., Administrator
CFO: Maria Chung, CPA, Director Fiscal Services
CMO: Matthias B Donelan, M.D., Chief of Staff
CIO: Mary Dolan, Regional Director Information Services and HIPAA Security Official
CHR: John Donlin, Regional Director Human Resources – Boston, Erie, and Springfield
Web address: www.shrinershospitalsforchildren.org/Hospitals/Locations/Boston
Control: Other not–for–profit (including NFP Corporation) **Service**: Children's other specialty

> **Staffed Beds**: 9

✣ **TUFTS MEDICAL CENTER (220116)**, 800 Washington Street, Zip 02111–1552; tel. 617/636–5000, **A**1 2 3 5 8 10 19 **F**3 4 5 9 12 13 14 15 17 18 19 20 21 22 23 24 26 27 28 29 30 31 32 33 34 35 36 37 40 43 44 45 46 47 49 50 51 52 55 56 57 58 59 61 64 65 68 70 71 72 74 75 76 77 78 79 81 82 83 84 85 86 87 92 93 97 98 100 101 102 104 105 107 108 110 111 114 115 116 117 118 119 120 121 123 124 126 129 130 131 132 134 135 136 137 138 139 141 142 143 146 147 148 149 154 156 157 160 162 163 164 165 167 169 **P**5 **S** Tufts Medicine, Burlington, MA
Primary Contact: Michael J. Dandorph, Chief Executive Officer
CFO: Kristine Hanscom, Chief Financial Officer
CMO: David Fairchild, M.D., Chief Medical Officer
CIO: William Shickolovich, Chief Information Officer
CNO: Therese M. Hudson–Jinks, R.N., MSN, Chief Nursing Officer
Web address: www.tuftsmedicalcenter.org
Control: Other not–for–profit (including NFP Corporation) **Service**: General medical and surgical

> **Staffed Beds**: 302 **Admissions**: 15414 **Census**: 276 **Outpatient Visits**: 398103 **Births**: 1424 **Total Expense ($000)**: 1236815 **Payroll Expense ($000)**: 444995 **Personnel**: 5097

BRADFORD—Essex County

✣ **WHITTIER REHABILITATION HOSPITAL (222047)**, 145 Ward Hill Avenue, Zip 01835–6928; tel. 978/372–8000, (Nonreporting) **A**1 10 **S** Whittier Health Network, Haverhill, MA
Primary Contact: Robert Iannaco, Administrator
Web address: www.whittierhealth.com
Control: Partnership, Investor–owned (for–profit) **Service**: Acute long–term care hospital

> **Staffed Beds**: 60

BRAINTREE—Norfolk County

✣ **ENCOMPASS HEALTH REHABILITATION HOSPITAL OF BRAINTREE (223027)**, 250 Pond Street, Zip 02184–5351; tel. 781/348–2500, (Nonreporting) **A**1 5 10 **S** Encompass Health Corporation, Birmingham, AL
Primary Contact: Cynthia Page, FACHE, Chief Executive Officer
CFO: Barry Leonard I, Vice President of Finance
CMO: Arthur Williams, M.D., Medical Director
CHR: Cathryn Wigman, Director Human Resources
CNO: Jinia Drinkwater, R.N., Director Patient Care Services
Web address: www.braintreerehabhospital.com
Control: Corporation, Investor–owned (for–profit) **Service**: Rehabilitation

> **Staffed Beds**: 187

BRIDGEWATER—Plymouth County

BRIDGEWATER STATE HOSPITAL, 20 Administration Road, Zip 02324–3201; tel. 508/279–4521, (Nonreporting) **A**3 5
Primary Contact: Stephen Kennedy, Superintendent
CFO: Diane Wholley, Director Fiscal Services
Control: State, Government, Nonfederal **Service**: Psychiatric

> **Staffed Beds**: 350

BRIGHTON—Suffolk County

✣ **FRANCISCAN CHILDREN'S (223300)**, 30 Warren Street, Zip 02135–3680; tel. 617/254–3800, (Nonreporting) **A**1 3 10
Primary Contact: Joseph Mitchell, M.D., President and Chief Executive Officer
COO: Donna Polselli, Chief Operating Officer
CFO: Alex Denucci, Chief Financial Officer
CMO: Jane E O'Brien, M.D., Medical Director
CIO: Sean McKeon, Director, Information Technology
CHR: Nancy Murphy, Vice President, Human Resources
CNO: Mary Lou Kelleher, R.N., MSN, Vice President, Nursing
Web address: www.franciscanhospital.org
Control: Other not–for–profit (including NFP Corporation) **Service**: Children's rehabilitation

> **Staffed Beds**: 81

☐ **ST. ELIZABETH'S MEDICAL CENTER (220036)**, 736 Cambridge Street, Zip 02135–2997; tel. 617/789–3000, (Nonreporting) **A**1 2 3 5 10 19 **S** Steward Health Care System, LLC, Dallas, TX
Primary Contact: Marisela Marrero, M.D., President
CMO: Dicken S.C. Ko, M.D., Vice President of Medical Affairs and Chief Medical Officer
CIO: Joseph Schmitt, Chief Information Officer
CHR: Claudia Henderson, Chief Human Resources
Web address: www.semc.org/
Control: Corporation, Investor–owned (for–profit) **Service**: General medical and surgical

> **Staffed Beds**: 338

BROCKTON—Plymouth County

CARDINAL CUSHING GEN HOSPITAL See Good Samaritan Medical Center – Cushing Campus

☐ **GOOD SAMARITAN MEDICAL CENTER (220111)**, 235 North Pearl Street, Zip 02301–1794; tel. 508/427–3000, {Includes GOOD SAMARITAN MEDICAL CENTER – CUSHING CAMPUS, 235 North Pearl Street, Brockton, Massachusetts, Zip 02401–1794, tel. 508/427–3000) (Nonreporting) **A**1 2 3 5 10 19 **S** Steward Health Care System, LLC, Dallas, TX
Primary Contact: Matthew Hesketh, President
COO: Donna Rubinate, R.N., Chief Operating Officer
CFO: Thomas Whalen, Vice President Finance
CMO: Scott Stewart, M.D., Vice President Medical Management
CIO: Lori Caswell, Director Information Technology
CHR: David J Cronin, Regional Vice President Human Resources
Web address: www.goodsamaritanmedical.org
Control: Corporation, Investor–owned (for–profit) **Service**: General medical and surgical

> **Staffed Beds**: 190

✣ **SIGNATURE HEALTHCARE BROCKTON HOSPITAL (220052)**, 680 Centre Street, Zip 02302–3395; tel. 508/941–7000, (Data for 130 days) **A**1 2 3 10 **F**3 5 12 13 15 17 18 20 22 28 29 30 31 34 35 38 40 44 45 46 47 48 49 50 51 52 54 57 58 59 61 64 65 68 70 71 73 74 75 76 78 79 81 82 85 86 87 89 92 93 97 98 100 102 107 108 110 111 114 115 116 117 118 119 120 121 122 123 124 130 131 132 135 144 146 147 148 149 154 161 167 **P**6 8
Primary Contact: Robert Haffey, R.N., Chief Executive Officer and President
CFO: Kevin G Murphy, Chief Financial Officer
CIO: Gerald Greeley, Chief Information Officer
CHR: David Fisher, Vice President Human Resources
CNO: Kim Walsh, Chief Nursing Officer
Web address: www.signature-healthcare.org
Control: Other not–for–profit (including NFP Corporation) **Service**: General medical and surgical

> **Staffed Beds**: 216 **Admissions**: 3619 **Census**: 149 **Outpatient Visits**: 480031 **Births**: 496 **Total Expense ($000)**: 317198 **Payroll Expense ($000)**: 114847 **Personnel**: 1619

Hospital, Medicare Provider Number, Address, Telephone, Approval, Facility, and Physician Codes, Health Care System

★ American Hospital Association (AHA) membership ◯ Healthcare Facilities Accreditation Program ⇑ Center for Improvement in Healthcare Quality Accreditation
☐ The Joint Commission accreditation ◇ DNV Healthcare Inc. accreditation △ Commission on Accreditation of Rehabilitation Facilities (CARF) accreditation

Hospitals, U.S. / MASSACHUSETTS

☒ **VETERANS AFFAIRS BOSTON HEALTHCARE SYSTEM BROCKTON DIVISION**, 940 Belmont Street, Zip 02301–5596; tel. 508/583-4500, (Includes VETERANS AFFAIRS MEDICAL CENTER WEST ROXBURY DIVISION, 1400 Vfw Pkwy, West Roxbury, Massachusetts, Zip 02132–4927, 1400 VVF Parkway, West Roxbury, Boston, Zip 02132, tel. 617/323-7700; William H Kelleher, Director) (Nonreporting) **A**1 3 5 **S** Department of Veterans Affairs, Washington, DC
Primary Contact: Vincent Ng, Director
CFO: Joe Costa, Acting Chief Fiscal Officer
Web address: www.boston.va.gov/
Control: Veterans Affairs, Government, federal **Service**: General medical and surgical

Staffed Beds: 375

BROOKLINE—Norfolk County

☐ **ARBOUR H. R. I. HOSPITAL (224018)**, 227 Babcock Street, Zip 02446–6799; tel. 617/731-3200, (Nonreporting) **A**1 10 **S** Universal Health Services, Inc., King of Prussia, PA
Primary Contact: Kurt Gunther, Chief Executive Officer
CFO: Diane Airosus, Chief Financial Officer
CMO: Krishnaswamy Gajaraj, M.D., Medical Director
CHR: Katherine McCarthy, Director Human Resources
Web address: www.HRIHospital.com
Control: Corporation, Investor-owned (for-profit) **Service**: Psychiatric

Staffed Beds: 76

☐ **BOURNEWOOD HEALTH SYSTEMS (224022)**, 300 South Street, Zip 02467–3658; tel. 617/469-0300, (Nonreporting) **A**1 3 5 10
Primary Contact: Marcia Fowler, Chief Executive Officer
CFO: Michael Gale, Chief Financial Officer
CMO: Carmel Heinsohn, M.D., Medical Director
CHR: Paula Berardi, Manager Human Resources
Web address: www.bournewood.com
Control: Corporation, Investor-owned (for-profit) **Service**: Psychiatric

Staffed Beds: 90

BURLINGTON—Middlesex County

☒ **LAHEY HOSPITAL & MEDICAL CENTER (220171)**, 41 Mall Road, Zip 01805–0001, Mailing Address: 31 Mall Road, Zip 01805–0001; tel. 781/744-5100, (Includes LAHEY MEDICAL CENTER, PEABODY, 1 Essex Center Drive, Peabody, Massachusetts, Zip 01960–2901, tel. 978/538-4000) **A**1 2 3 5 8 10 19 **F**3 5 6 7 8 9 11 12 15 17 18 20 22 24 26 28 29 30 31 34 35 36 37 38 40 43 44 45 46 47 48 49 50 51 52 54 55 56 57 58 59 60 61 64 65 68 70 74 75 77 78 79 81 82 84 85 86 87 91 92 93 96 97 100 101 102 104 107 108 109 110 111 114 115 116 117 118 119 120 121 122 123 124 126 129 130 131 132 135 136 138 139 141 142 143 144 145 146 147 148 149 150 153 154 156 157 162 164 167 168 **P**6 **S** Beth Israel Lahey Health, Cambridge, MA
Primary Contact: Susan Moffatt-Bruce, President
COO: Richard R Bias, Chief Operating Officer
CFO: Timothy P. O'Connor, Executive Vice President and Chief Financial Officer
CMO: Timothy Liesching, M.D., Chief Medical Officer
CIO: Bruce Metz, Ph.D., Senior Vice President and Chief Information Officer
CHR: Elizabeth P. Conrad, Senior Vice President and Chief Human Resource Officer
Web address: www.lahey.org
Control: Other not-for-profit (including NFP Corporation) **Service**: General medical and surgical

Staffed Beds: 358 **Admissions**: 21618 **Census**: 328 **Outpatient Visits**: 1222732 **Births**: 0 **Total Expense ($000)**: 1082657 **Payroll Expense ($000)**: 408472 **Personnel**: 4162

CAMBRIDGE—Middlesex County

☒ **CAMBRIDGE HEALTH ALLIANCE (220011)**, 1493 Cambridge Street, Zip 02139–1099; tel. 617/665-1000, (Includes CAMBRIDGE HOSPITAL, 1493 Cambridge Street, Cambridge, Massachusetts, Zip 02139–1099, tel. 617/498-1000; SOMERVILLE HOSPITAL, 230 Highland Ave, Somerville, Massachusetts, Zip 02143–1408, 230 Highland Avenue, Zip 02143, tel. 617/666-4400; WHIDDEN MEMORIAL HOSPITAL, 103 Garland Street, Everett, Massachusetts, Zip 02149–5095, tel. 617/389-6270) **A**1 2 3 5 8 10 **F**5 8 11 12 13 15 29 30 31 32 34 35 36 38 39 40 44 45 46 47 48 49 50 51 56 57 58 59 61 64 65 66 68 70 75 76 77 78 79 81 82 86 87 89 93 97 98 100 101 102 104 107 108 110 111 114 115 119 126 129 130 131 132 134 135 141 143 145 146 147 148 149 150 153 154 156 160 164 167 169 **P**6
Primary Contact: Assaad Sayah, M.D., Chief Executive Officer
CFO: Jill I Batty, Chief Financial Officer
CMO: Assaad Sayah, M.D., Chief Medical Officer
CIO: Brian Herrick, M.D., Chief Information Officer
CHR: Joy U Curtis, Senior Vice President Human Resources
CNO: Elizabeth Cadigan, R.N., MSN, Senior Vice President Patient Care Services and Chief Nursing Officer
Web address: www.challiance.org
Control: County, Government, Nonfederal **Service**: General medical and surgical

Staffed Beds: 299 **Admissions**: 8218 **Census**: 169 **Outpatient Visits**: 752252 **Births**: 1271 **Total Expense ($000)**: 946425 **Payroll Expense ($000)**: 444355

☒ **MOUNT AUBURN HOSPITAL (220002)**, 330 Mount Auburn Street, Zip 02138–5597; tel. 617/492-3500, (Nonreporting) **A**1 2 3 5 8 10 19 **S** Beth Israel Lahey Health, Cambridge, MA
Primary Contact: Edwin Huang, M.D., Interim President
COO: Nicholas T Dileso, R.N., Chief Operating Officer
CFO: William Sullivan
CIO: Kendall White, Chief Information Officer
CHR: Tom Fabiano, Director Human Resources
CNO: Deborah Baker, Vice President, Patient Care Services
Web address: www.mountauburnhospital.org
Control: Other not-for-profit (including NFP Corporation) **Service**: General medical and surgical

Staffed Beds: 198

☒ **SPAULDING HOSPITAL FOR CONTINUING MEDICAL CARE CAMBRIDGE (222000)**, 1575 Cambridge Street, Zip 02138–4308; tel. 617/876-4344, **A**1 10 **F**1 3 7 28 29 30 31 50 54 60 64 68 74 75 77 78 85 86 87 91 92 93 94 100 119 129 130 131 132 146 148 149 154 157 **S** Mass General Brigham, Boston, MA
Primary Contact: Ross Zafonte, D.O., President
CFO: Claudia Reed, Interim Chief Financial Officer
CMO: Jonathon Schwartz, M.D., Chief Medical Officer
CIO: John Campbell, Chief Information Officer
CHR: Jack Carroll, Director Human Resources
Web address: www.spauldingnetwork.org
Control: Other not-for-profit (including NFP Corporation) **Service**: Acute long-term care hospital

Staffed Beds: 116 **Admissions**: 883 **Census**: 107 **Outpatient Visits**: 4010 **Births**: 0 **Total Expense ($000)**: 104276 **Payroll Expense ($000)**: 54623 **Personnel**: 514

CANTON—Norfolk County

☐ **PAPPAS REHABILITATION HOSPITAL FOR CHILDREN (222025)**, 3 Randolph Street, Zip 02021–2351; tel. 781/828-2440, (Nonreporting) **A**1 10 **S** Massachusetts Department of Public Health, Boston, MA
Primary Contact: Brian V. Devin, Chief Executive Officer
CFO: Sharon Porter, Chief Financial Officer
CMO: Aruna Sachdev, M.D., Medical Director
CIO: Robert Lima, Director Information Systems
CHR: Trish Scully, Manager Employment Services
Web address: www.prhc.us/
Control: State, Government, Nonfederal **Service**: Children's acute long-term Care

Staffed Beds: 80

CHARLESTOWN—Suffolk County

☒ △ **SPAULDING REHABILITATION HOSPITAL (223034)**, 300 First Avenue, Zip 02129–3109; tel. 617/952-5000, **A**1 3 5 7 10 **F**3 7 28 29 30 34 35 36 50 54 57 58 60 64 68 71 74 75 77 82 86 87 90 91 92 93 94 95 96 100 119 130 131 132 146 148 149 154 157 158 **S** Mass General Brigham, Boston, MA
Primary Contact: Ross Zafonte, D.O., President
COO: Maureen Banks, Chief Operating Officer
CFO: Amy Guay, Chief Financial Officer
CMO: Cheri Blauwet, Chief Medical Officer
CIO: John Campbell, Chief Information Officer
CHR: Russell Averna, Vice President Human Resources
CNO: Maureen Banks, Chief Nursing Officer
Web address: www.spauldingrehab.org
Control: Other not-for-profit (including NFP Corporation) **Service**: Rehabilitation

Staffed Beds: 132 **Admissions**: 2566 **Census**: 123 **Outpatient Visits**: 417598 **Births**: 0 **Total Expense ($000)**: 208058 **Payroll Expense ($000)**: 92743 **Personnel**: 1212

CLINTON—Worcester County

CLINTON HOSPITAL See Umass Memorial Healthalliance–Clinton Hospital

Hospitals, U.S. / MASSACHUSETTS

CONCORD—Middlesex County

✠ **EMERSON HOSPITAL (220084)**, 133 Old Road to Nine Acre Corner, Zip 01742–9120; tel. 978/369–1400, **A**1 10 19 **F**3 5 7 8 11 12 13 14 15 18 28 29 30 31 32 34 35 36 37 38 40 45 48 49 50 51 54 57 58 59 60 62 64 65 68 70 73 74 75 76 77 78 79 81 82 85 86 87 89 93 97 98 100 102 105 107 108 110 111 114 115 118 119 126 129 130 131 132 135 144 145 146 148 152 153 154 156 157 160 161 167 169
Primary Contact: Christine C. Schuster, R.N., President and Chief Executive Officer
CFO: Michael Hachey, Senior Vice President and Chief Financial Officer
CMO: Barrett Kitch, M.D., Senior Vice President, Clinical Affairs and Chief Medical Officer
CIO: Renee Fosberg, Chief Information Officer
CNO: Joyce Welsh, R.N., MS, Vice President of Clinical Services and Chief Nursing Officer
Web address: www.emersonhospital.org
Control: Other not–for–profit (including NFP Corporation) **Service**: General medical and surgical

Staffed Beds: 155 **Admissions**: 7717 **Census**: 95 **Outpatient Visits**: 341393 **Births**: 1435 **Total Expense ($000)**: 367287 **Payroll Expense ($000)**: 177955 **Personnel**: 1367

DARTMOUTH—Bristol County

☐ **SOUTHCOAST BEHAVIORAL HEALTH (224041)**, 581 Faunce Corner Road, Zip 02747–1242; tel. 508/207–9800, (Nonreporting) **A**1 10 **S** Acadia Healthcare Company, Inc., Franklin, TN
Primary Contact: Darcy Lichnerowicz, Chief Executive Officer
Web address: www.southcoastbehavioral.com
Control: Corporation, Investor–owned (for–profit) **Service**: Psychiatric

Staffed Beds: 120

EAST SANDWICH—Barnstable County

✠ △ **SPAULDING REHABILITATION HOSPITAL CAPE COD (223032)**, 311 Service Road, Zip 02537–1370; tel. 508/833–4000, **A**1 7 10 **F**3 28 29 30 32 34 35 36 50 60 64 74 75 77 79 82 90 91 92 93 94 96 130 131 132 135 146 147 148 149 **S** Mass General Brigham, Boston, MA
Primary Contact: Ross Zafonte, D.O., President
COO: Stephanie Nadolny, Vice President of Hospital Operations
CFO: Claudia Reed, Interim Chief Financial Officer
CMO: David Lowell, M.D., Chief Medical Officer
CIO: John Campbell, Chief Information Officer
CHR: Russell Averna, Vice President of Human Resources
Web address: www.spauldingrehab.org
Control: Other not–for–profit (including NFP Corporation) **Service**: Rehabilitation

Staffed Beds: 48 **Admissions**: 1160 **Census**: 43 **Outpatient Visits**: 135749 **Births**: 0 **Total Expense ($000)**: 55873 **Payroll Expense ($000)**: 29052 **Personnel**: 360

EVERETT—Middlesex County

WHIDDEN MEMORIAL HOSPITAL See Cambridge Health Alliance, Cambridge

FALL RIVER—Bristol County

CHARLTON MEMORIAL HOSPITAL See Southcoast Hospitals Group, Fall River

☐ **DR. J. CORRIGAN MENTAL HEALTH CENTER (224028)**, 49 Hillside Street, Zip 02720–5266; tel. 508/235–7200, (Nonreporting) **A**1 3 10 **S** Massachusetts Department of Mental Health, Boston, MA
Primary Contact: Frank O'Reilly, Director
Control: State, Government, Nonfederal **Service**: Psychiatric

Staffed Beds: 16

☐ **SAINT ANNE'S HOSPITAL (220020)**, 795 Middle Street, Zip 02721–1798; tel. 508/674–5741, (Nonreporting) **A**1 2 3 10 19 **S** Steward Health Care System, LLC, Dallas, TX
Primary Contact: Michael Bushell, President
CMO: John Conlon, M.D., Chief Medical Officer
CIO: Julie Berry, Chief Information Officer
CHR: Sandra Dellicker, Director of Human Resources
CNO: Carole Billington, R.N., MSN, Vice President Operations, Chief Nursing Officer
Web address: www.saintanneshospital.org
Control: Corporation, Investor–owned (for–profit) **Service**: General medical and surgical

Staffed Beds: 160

✠ **SOUTHCOAST HOSPITALS GROUP (220074)**, 363 Highland Avenue, Zip 02720–3703; tel. 508/679–3131, (Includes CHARLTON MEMORIAL HOSPITAL, 363 Highland Avenue, Fall River, Massachusetts, Zip 02720–3703, tel. 508/679–3131; David McCready, President and Chief Executive Officer; ST. LUKE'S HOSPITAL, 101 Page ST, New Bedford, Massachusetts, Zip 02740–3464, 101 Page Street, Zip 02740, tel. 508/997–1515; David McCready, President and Chief Executive Officer; TOBEY HOSPITAL, 43 High ST, Wareham, Massachusetts, Zip 02571–2097, 43 High Street, Zip 02571, tel. 508/295–0880; David McCready, President and Chief Executive Officer) **A**1 2 3 5 10 **F**3 11 12 13 14 15 17 18 20 22 24 26 28 29 30 31 34 35 37 40 41 43 44 45 46 47 48 49 50 51 54 56 57 58 59 60 61 64 65 68 70 71 73 74 75 76 77 78 79 81 82 84 85 86 87 89 90 91 92 93 96 97 100 102 104 107 108 110 111 114 115 116 117 118 119 120 121 123 124 126 130 131 132 134 135 146 147 148 149 154 156 157 160 167 169
Primary Contact: David McCready, President and Chief Executive Officer
COO: Renee Clark, M.D., Executive Vice President and Chief Operating Officer
CFO: Wade Broughman, Chief Financial Officer
CIO: Jim Feen, Senior Vice President and Chief Information Officer
CHR: Lauren De Simon Johnson, Senior Vice President, Chief Human Resources Officer
CNO: Jacqueline G Somerville, R.N., Ph.D., Senior Vice President and Chief Nursing Officer
Web address: www.southcoast.org
Control: Other not–for–profit (including NFP Corporation) **Service**: General medical and surgical

Staffed Beds: 505 **Admissions**: 29394 **Census**: 415 **Outpatient Visits**: 972867 **Births**: 3149 **Total Expense ($000)**: 1034083 **Payroll Expense ($000)**: 412466 **Personnel**: 3409

FALMOUTH—Barnstable County

✠ **FALMOUTH HOSPITAL (220135)**, 100 Ter Heun Drive, Zip 02540–2599; tel. 508/548–5300, **A**1 2 10 **F**3 8 11 15 18 28 29 30 34 35 38 40 45 50 51 54 58 61 64 65 68 70 74 75 77 79 81 82 85 86 87 93 96 99 100 101 102 103 104 107 108 110 111 115 119 120 121 123 124 129 130 131 132 144 146 147 148 149 150 154 160 161 162 164 167 169 **S** Cape Cod Healthcare, Inc., Hyannis, MA
Primary Contact: Carter Hunt, Chief Executive Officer
CFO: Michael Connors, Senior Vice President and Chief Financial Officer
CMO: Alex Heard, M.D., Chief Medical Officer
CIO: Paul Solverson, Senior Vice President and Chief Information Officer
CHR: Emily Schorer, Vice President, Human Resources
CNO: Mary Johnson, Chief Nursing Officer
Web address: www.capecodhealth.org
Control: Other not–for–profit (including NFP Corporation) **Service**: General medical and surgical

Staffed Beds: 81 **Admissions**: 4890 **Census**: 61 **Outpatient Visits**: 163628 **Births**: 0 **Total Expense ($000)**: 180988 **Payroll Expense ($000)**: 81205 **Personnel**: 549

FRAMINGHAM—Middlesex County

FRAMINGTON UNION HOSPITAL See Framingham Union Hospital

✠ **METROWEST MEDICAL CENTER (220175)**, 115 Lincoln Street, Zip 01702–6342; tel. 508/383–1000, (Includes FRAMINGHAM UNION HOSPITAL, 115 Lincoln ST, Framingham, Massachusetts, Zip 01702–6358, 115 Lincoln Street, Zip 01702, tel. 508/383–1000) (Nonreporting) **A**1 3 5 10 19 **S** TENET Healthcare Corporation, Dallas, TX
Primary Contact: John Whitlock Jr, CPA, Chief Executive Officer
COO: Melinda Darrigo, Interim Chief Operating Officer
CFO: Stephanie Jackman–Havey, Chief Financial Officer
CMO: Michele Sinopoli, M.D., Chief Medical Officer
CNO: Erin Truman, Associate Chief Nursing Officer
Web address: www.mwmc.com
Control: Corporation, Investor–owned (for–profit) **Service**: General medical and surgical

Staffed Beds: 351

Hospital, Medicare Provider Number, Address, Telephone, Approval, Facility, and Physician Codes, Health Care System

★ American Hospital Association (AHA) membership   ○ Healthcare Facilities Accreditation Program   ⇑ Center for Improvement in Healthcare Quality Accreditation
☐ The Joint Commission accreditation   ◇ DNV Healthcare Inc. accreditation   △ Commission on Accreditation of Rehabilitation Facilities (CARF) accreditation

© 2025 AHA Guide

Hospitals, U.S. / MASSACHUSETTS

GARDNER—Worcester County

HEYWOOD HOSPITAL (220095), 242 Green Street, Zip 01440–1373; tel. 978/632–3420, **A**1 5 10 **F**3 8 12 14 15 18 19 26 29 30 31 34 35 38 40 45 57 59 60 61 62 68 70 76 78 79 81 82 89 93 98 100 102 103 104 105 133 148 153 154 156 160 169 **P**5 8 **S** Heywood Healthcare, Gardner, MA
Primary Contact: Rozanna Penney, Co–Chief Executive Officer
CHR: Thomas Cady, Vice President Human Resources
Web address: www.heywood.org
Control: Other not–for–profit (including NFP Corporation) **Service**: General medical and surgical

Staffed Beds: 173 **Admissions**: 3456 **Census**: 57 **Outpatient Visits**: 84034 **Births**: 316 **Total Expense ($000)**: 188276 **Payroll Expense ($000)**: 68233 **Personnel**: 772

GEORGETOWN—Essex County

BALDPATE HOSPITAL (224033), 83 Baldpate Road, Zip 01833–2303; tel. 978/352–2131, (Nonreporting) **A**10
Primary Contact: Lucille M. Batal, Administrator
Web address: www.detoxma.com/
Control: Corporation, Investor–owned (for–profit) **Service**: Psychiatric

Staffed Beds: 59

GLOUCESTER—Essex County

ADDISON GILBERT HOSPITAL See Beverly Hospital, Beverly

GREAT BARRINGTON—Berkshire County

FAIRVIEW HOSPITAL (221302), 29 Lewis Avenue, Zip 01230–1713; tel. 413/528–0790, (Nonreporting) **A**1 5 10 18 **S** Berkshire Health Systems, Inc., Pittsfield, MA
Primary Contact: Eugene A. Dellea, President
COO: Doreen M Sylvia–Hutchinson, Vice President Operations and Chief Nurse Executive
CFO: Anthony Rinaldi, Executive Vice President
CMO: Brian Burke, M.D., President Medical Staff
CHR: Laura Farkas, Director Human Resources
Web address: www.bhs1.org/body_fh.cfm?id=39
Control: Other not–for–profit (including NFP Corporation) **Service**: General medical and surgical

Staffed Beds: 24

GREENFIELD—Franklin County

BAYSTATE FRANKLIN MEDICAL CENTER (220016), 164 High Street, Zip 01301–2613; tel. 413/773–0211, **A**1 3 5 10 **F**3 8 11 12 13 15 18 28 29 30 31 34 35 37 38 40 50 51 52 57 59 64 70 74 75 76 77 78 79 81 82 83 84 85 87 89 93 97 98 100 104 105 107 108 110 111 114 119 124 126 129 130 131 146 147 148 149 154 160 161 164 167 169 **S** Baystate Health, Inc., Springfield, MA
Primary Contact: Ronald Bryant, President
CFO: Andrea Nathanson, Director Finance
CMO: Thomas Higgins, M.D., Chief Medical Officer
CHR: Kerry Damon, Director Human Resources
CNO: Jodi Stack, R.N., MSN, Chief Nursing Officer and Chief Administrative Officer
Web address: www.baystatehealth.org
Control: Other not–for–profit (including NFP Corporation) **Service**: General medical and surgical

Staffed Beds: 80 **Admissions**: 4399 **Census**: 54 **Outpatient Visits**: 52286 **Births**: 433 **Total Expense ($000)**: 128488 **Payroll Expense ($000)**: 42054 **Personnel**: 721

HAVERHILL—Essex County

HOLY FAMILY HOSPITAL AT MERRIMACK VALLEY See Holy Family Hospital At Merrimack Valley

WHITTIER PAVILION (224039), 76 Summer Street, Zip 01830–5814; tel. 978/373–8222, (Nonreporting) **A**10 **S** Whittier Health Network, Haverhill, MA
Primary Contact: Alfred J. Arcidi, M.D., Chief Executive Officer
Web address: www.whittierhealth.com
Control: Partnership, Investor–owned (for–profit) **Service**: Psychiatric

Staffed Beds: 65

HOLYOKE—Hampden County

HOLYOKE MEDICAL CENTER (220024), 575 Beech Street, Zip 01040–2223; tel. 413/534–2500, (Nonreporting) **A**2 5 10 21
Primary Contact: Spiros Hatiras, FACHE, President and Chief Executive Officer
CFO: Michael J Koziol, Chief Financial Officer
CMO: Karen Ferroni, M.D., Medical Director
CIO: Carl Cameron, Director Information Systems
CHR: Mary Kelleher, Vice President Human Resources
CNO: Colleen Desai, Chief Nursing Officer
Web address: www.holyokehealth.com
Control: Other not–for–profit (including NFP Corporation) **Service**: General medical and surgical

Staffed Beds: 107

MIRAVISTA BEHAVIORAL HEALTH CENTER (224046), 1233 Main Street, Zip 01040–5381; tel. 413/536–5111, (Nonreporting)
Primary Contact: Michael P. Krupa, Ed.D., Chief Executive Officer
Control: Other not–for–profit (including NFP Corporation) **Service**: Psychiatric

Staffed Beds: 202

VALLEY SPRINGS BEHAVIORAL HEALTH HOSPITAL (224047), 45 Lower Westfield Road, Zip 01040–2747; tel. 413/315–4100, (Nonreporting) **A**1
Primary Contact: Roy Sasenaraine, Chief Executive Officer
Web address: www.valleyspringsbh.com
Control: Corporation, Investor–owned (for–profit) **Service**: Psychiatric

Staffed Beds: 150

HYANNIS—Barnstable County

CAPE COD HOSPITAL (220012), 27 Park Street, Zip 02601–5230; tel. 508/771–1800, **A**1 2 3 5 10 20 **F**3 11 13 14 15 17 18 20 22 24 26 28 29 30 31 34 35 37 38 40 45 49 50 51 54 57 58 61 64 65 68 70 74 75 76 77 78 79 81 82 85 86 87 89 93 97 98 99 100 101 102 103 104 105 107 108 110 111 115 119 120 121 123 124 126 130 131 132 144 146 147 148 149 150 153 154 160 161 162 164 167 169 **S** Cape Cod Healthcare, Inc., Hyannis, MA
Primary Contact: Michael K. Lauf, President and Chief Executive Officer
CFO: Michael Connors, Senior Vice President and Chief Financial Officer
CMO: Donald Guadagnoli, M.D., Chief Medical Officer
CIO: Paul Solverson, Senior Vice President and Chief Information Officer
CHR: Emily Schorer, Senior Vice President Human Resources
CNO: Judith Quinn, Vice President Patient Care Services
Web address: www.capecodhealth.org
Control: Other not–for–profit (including NFP Corporation) **Service**: General medical and surgical

Staffed Beds: 259 **Admissions**: 16256 **Census**: 214 **Outpatient Visits**: 417957 **Births**: 934 **Total Expense ($000)**: 654915 **Payroll Expense ($000)**: 265503 **Personnel**: 1693

JAMAICA PLAIN—Suffolk County

LEMUEL SHATTUCK HOSPITAL (222006), 170 Morton Street, Zip 02130–3735; tel. 617/522–8110, (Nonreporting) **A**1 3 5 10 **S** Massachusetts Department of Public Health, Boston, MA
Primary Contact: Justin Douglas, R.N., MSN, Chief Executive Officer
CFO: Mike Donovan, Chief Financial Officer
CMO: Kenneth Freedman, M.D., Chief Medical Officer
CIO: Kathryn Noonan, Director Information Management
CHR: Jill Sampson, Director Human Resources
Web address: www.mass.gov/shattuckhospital
Control: State, Government, Nonfederal **Service**: Acute long–term care hospital

Staffed Beds: 260

LAWRENCE—Essex County

LAWRENCE GENERAL HOSPITAL (220010), 1 General Street, Zip 01841–2961, Mailing Address: P.O. Box 189, Zip 01842–0389; tel. 978/683–4000, (Nonreporting) **A**1 3 5 10 19
Primary Contact: Abha Agrawal, M.D., FACHE, President and Chief Executive Officer
COO: Robin Hynds, MSN, R.N., Executive Vice President and Chief Operating Officer
CFO: Felix V. Mercado, Chief Financial Officer
CMO: Pracha Eamranond, M.D., Senior Vice President Population Health and Medical Affairs
CHR: Cynthia Phelan, Vice President Human Resources
CNO: Karen O. Moore, FACHE, Senior Vice President Operations and Chief Nursing Officer
Web address: www.lawrencegeneral.org
Control: Other not–for–profit (including NFP Corporation) **Service**: General medical and surgical

Staffed Beds: 186

Hospitals, U.S. / MASSACHUSETTS

LEEDS—Hampshire County

VETERANS AFFAIRS CENTRAL WESTERN MASSACHUSETTS HEALTHCARE SYSTEM, 421 North Main Street, Zip 01053–9764; tel. 413/582–3000, (Nonreporting) **A**1 3 5 **S** Department of Veterans Affairs, Washington, DC
Primary Contact: Jonathan Kerr, Acting Director
COO: Joyce Fredrick, Associate Director
CFO: Andrew McMahon, Chief Fiscal Officer
CMO: Neil Nusbaum, M.D., Chief of Staff
CIO: Michael Marley, Chief Information Officer
CHR: Pablo Feliciano, Manager Human Resources
Web address: www.centralwesternmass.va.gov/
Control: Veterans Affairs, Government, federal **Service**: Psychiatric

Staffed Beds: 52

LEOMINSTER—Worcester County

UMASS MEMORIAL HEALTHALLIANCE–CLINTON HOSPITAL (220001), 60 Hospital Road, Zip 01453–2205; tel. 978/466–2000, (Includes UMASS MEMORIAL HEALTHALLIANCE–CLINTON HOSPITAL, 201 Highland Street, Clinton, Massachusetts, Zip 01510–1096, tel. 978/368–3000; Charles E Cavagnaro III, M.D., Interim President) (Nonreporting) **A**1 2 3 5 10 **S** UMass Memorial Health Care, Inc., Worcester, MA
Primary Contact: Charles E. Cavagnaro III, M.D., Interim President
COO: Paul MacKinnon, MS, R.N., Chief Operating Officer
CFO: John Edward Bronhard, CPA, II, Corporate Vice President, Chief Financial Officer and Treasurer
CMO: Daniel H O'Leary, M.D., Chief Medical Officer
CHR: Julie DeBono, Director, Human Resources
CNO: Judith Thorpe, R.N., MSN, Vice President and Chief Nursing Officer
Web address: www.healthalliance.com
Control: Other not–for–profit (including NFP Corporation) **Service**: General medical and surgical

Staffed Beds: 152

LONGMEADOW—Hampden County

JEWISH HOME FOR THE AGED See Jewish Nursing Home of Western Massachusetts

LOWELL—Middlesex County

LOWELL GENERAL HOSPITAL (220063), 295 Varnum Avenue, Zip 01854–2134; tel. 978/937–6000, (Includes LOWELL GENERAL HOSPITAL, SAINTS CAMPUS, 1 Hospital DR, Lowell, Massachusetts, Zip 01852–1311, 295 Varnum Ave, Zip 01854–2134, tel. 978/458–1411; Normand E. Deschene, FACHE, Chief Executive Officer) **A**1 2 3 5 10 19 **F**3 7 11 12 13 15 18 20 22 26 28 29 30 31 32 33 34 35 36 37 40 41 43 44 45 46 47 48 49 50 51 54 56 57 58 59 60 61 64 65 68 70 71 73 74 75 76 77 78 79 81 82 84 85 86 87 89 93 97 100 107 108 110 114 115 118 119 120 121 123 124 126 129 130 131 132 134 143 144 146 147 148 149 154 156 157 167 169 **P**6 8 **S** Tufts Medicine, Burlington, MA
Primary Contact: Amy J. Hoey, R.N., MS, President
CFO: Susan Green, Senior Vice President Finance, Chief Financial Officer
CMO: Arthur Lauretano, M.D., Chief Medical Officer
CIO: Brian Sandager, Chief Information Officer
CNO: Cecelia Lynch, R.N., MS, Vice President Patient Care Services and Chief Nursing Officer
Web address: www.lowellgeneral.org
Control: Other not–for–profit (including NFP Corporation) **Service**: General medical and surgical

Staffed Beds: 297 **Admissions**: 16304 **Census**: 258 **Outpatient Visits**: 600000 **Births**: 1757 **Total Expense ($000)**: 570354 **Payroll Expense ($000)**: 240318 **Personnel**: 2550

SAINTS MEDICAL CENTER See Lowell General Hospital, Saints Campus

LUDLOW—Hampden County

ENCOMPASS HEALTH REHABILITATION HOSPITAL OF WESTERN MASSACHUSETTS (223030), 222 State Street, Zip 01056–3437; tel. 413/308–3300, (Nonreporting) **A**1 10 **S** Encompass Health Corporation, Birmingham, AL
Primary Contact: John R. Hunt, Chief Executive Officer
CFO: John Flaherty, Chief Financial Officer
CMO: Adnan Dahdul, M.D., Medical Director
CHR: Mary Mazza, Director Human Resources
CNO: Deborah Santos, R.N., Chief Nursing Officer
Web address: www.healthsouthrehab.org
Control: Corporation, Investor–owned (for–profit) **Service**: Rehabilitation

Staffed Beds: 53

LYNN—Essex County

UNION CAMPUS See Salem Hospital, Salem

UNION HOSPITAL See Union Campus

MARLBOROUGH—Middlesex County

UMASS MEMORIAL–MARLBOROUGH HOSPITAL (220049), 157 Union Street, Zip 01752–1297; tel. 508/481–5000, (Nonreporting) **A**1 3 5 10 **S** UMass Memorial Health Care, Inc., Worcester, MA
Primary Contact: Charles E. Cavagnaro III, M.D., Interim President
COO: John Kelly, R.N., Chief Nursing Officer and Chief Operating Officer
CFO: Steven McCue, Chief Financial Officer
CMO: Habib Sioufi, M.D., Chief Medical Officer
CHR: Francis Meringolo, Vice President Human Resources
CNO: John Kelly, R.N., Chief Nursing Officer and Chief Operating Officer
Web address: www.marlboroughhospital.org
Control: Other not–for–profit (including NFP Corporation) **Service**: General medical and surgical

Staffed Beds: 63

MEDFORD—Middlesex County

LAWRENCE MEMORIAL HOSPITAL OF MEDFORD See Melrosewakefield Healthcare, Melrose

MELROSE—Middlesex County

MELROSEWAKEFIELD HEALTHCARE (220070), 585 Lebanon Street, Zip 02176–3225; tel. 781/979–3000, (Includes LAWRENCE MEMORIAL HOSPITAL OF MEDFORD, 170 Governors Avenue, Medford, Massachusetts, Zip 02155–1643, tel. 781/306–6000; MELROSE–WAKEFIELD HOSPITAL, 585 Lebanon ST, Melrose, Massachusetts, Zip 02176–3225, 585 Lebanon Street, Zip 02176, tel. 781/979–3000; Michael V Sack, FACHE, Chief Executive Officer) **A**1 3 10 19 **F**3 12 13 15 18 20 22 26 28 29 30 34 35 36 37 38 40 43 45 46 47 48 49 50 51 54 55 56 57 58 59 61 62 63 64 65 70 72 74 75 76 77 78 79 81 82 84 85 86 87 93 97 98 100 101 102 103 104 107 108 110 111 114 115 118 119 120 121 123 124 126 129 130 131 132 135 144 146 147 148 149 153 154 156 157 160 161 164 165 167 169 **S** Tufts Medicine, Burlington, MA
Primary Contact: Kelly Corbi, President and Chief Executive Officer
CFO: Michael P. Connelly, CPA, FACHE, Executive Vice President and Chief Financial Officer
CMO: Steven P. Sbardella, M.D., FABC, President Clinical Operations and Chief Medical Officer
CHR: David P. Ryan, Vice President Human Resources
CNO: Deborah L Cronin–Waelde, MSN, R.N., Senior Vice President Clinical Operations and Chief Nursing Officer
Web address: www.melrosewakefield.org
Control: Other not–for–profit (including NFP Corporation) **Service**: General medical and surgical

Staffed Beds: 216 **Admissions**: 8108 **Census**: 141 **Outpatient Visits**: 296619 **Births**: 727 **Total Expense ($000)**: 286457 **Payroll Expense ($000)**: 127922 **Personnel**: 1190

Hospitals, U.S. / MASSACHUSETTS

METHUEN—Essex County

☐ **HOLY FAMILY HOSPITAL (220080)**, 70 East Street, Zip 01844-4597;
tel. 978/687-0151, (Includes HOLY FAMILY HOSPITAL AT MERRIMACK
VALLEY, 140 Lincoln Avenue, Haverhill, Massachusetts, Zip 01830-6798,
tel. 978/374-2000) (Nonreporting) **A**1 2 3 10 19 **S** Steward Health Care System,
LLC, Dallas, TX
COO: Martha M McDrury, R.N., Chief Operating Officer and Chief Nursing Officer
CFO: Jeffrey P. Dion, Vice President and Chief Financial Officer
CHR: Patricia Gauron, Director Human Resources
CNO: Martha M McDrury, R.N., Chief Operating Officer and Chief Nursing Officer
Web address: www.stewardhealth.org/Holy-Family-Hospital
Control: Corporation, Investor-owned (for-profit) **Service:** General medical and surgical

Staffed Beds: 329

MILFORD—Worcester County

✠ **MILFORD REGIONAL MEDICAL CENTER (220090)**, 14 Prospect Street,
Zip 01757-3003; tel. 508/473-1190, (Includes WHITINSVILLE MEDICAL CENTER,
18 Granite ST, Whitinsville, Massachusetts, Zip 01588-1908, 18 Granite Street,
Zip 01588, tel. 508/234-6311) **A**1 2 3 5 10 **F**3 11 12 13 15 18 20 26 29 30 31
32 34 35 40 41 45 46 50 51 57 59 64 68 70 74 75 76 77 79 80 81 84 85 86
87 93 96 107 108 110 115 118 119 126 130 131 132 134 135 145 146 147
148 149 154 167 169
Primary Contact: Edward Kelly, Chief Executive Officer and President
COO: Peggy Novick, Vice President, Clinical Support and Outpatient Services
CFO: Jeanne Lynskey, Vice President and Chief Financial Officer
CMO: Mary Czymbor, Chief Medical Officer
CIO: Nicole Heim, Chief Information Officer
CHR: Linda Greason, Vice President Human Resources
CNO: Nancy Tomaso, Vice President, Patient Care Services
Web address: www.milfordregional.org
Control: Other not-for-profit (including NFP Corporation) **Service:** General medical and surgical

Staffed Beds: 148 **Admissions:** 9204 **Census:** 98 **Outpatient Visits:** 455068 **Births:** 1056 **Total Expense ($000):** 294602 **Payroll Expense ($000):** 119863 **Personnel:** 961

MILTON—Norfolk County

✠ **BETH ISRAEL DEACONESS HOSPITAL–MILTON (220108)**, 199 Reedsdale
Road, Zip 02186-3926; tel. 617/696-4600, (Nonreporting) **A**1 3 10 **S** Beth Israel
Lahey Health, Cambridge, MA
Primary Contact: Richard W. Fernandez, President and Chief Executive Officer
CIO: Jean Fernandez, Chief Information Officer
CHR: Kathleen Harrington, Vice President Human Resources
Web address: www.miltonhospital.org
Control: Other not-for-profit (including NFP Corporation) **Service:** General medical and surgical

Staffed Beds: 100

NANTUCKET—Nantucket County

✠ **NANTUCKET COTTAGE HOSPITAL (220177)**, 57 Prospect Street,
Zip 02554-2799; tel. 508/825-8100, (Nonreporting) **A**1 10 20 **S** Mass General
Brigham, Boston, MA
Primary Contact: Amy Lee, President
COO: Amy Lee, Chief Operating Officer
CFO: Aaron Fishman, Vice President, Finance
CMO: Barbara Malone, M.D., Chief Medical Officer
CIO: Terry Hughes, Director Information Systems
CHR: Cristina Hickey-Toedtmann, Senior Director, Human Resources
CNO: Aimee Carew Lyons, Ph.D., R.N., Chief Nursing Officer
Web address: www.nantuckethospital.org
Control: Other not-for-profit (including NFP Corporation) **Service:** General medical and surgical

Staffed Beds: 14

NEEDHAM—Norfolk County

✠ **BETH ISRAEL DEACONESS HOSPITAL–NEEDHAM (220083)**, 148 Chestnut
Street, Zip 02492; tel. 781/453-3000, **A**1 2 3 5 10 **F**3 8 15 29 30 34 35 40
45 46 47 48 50 51 60 64 65 68 69 70 74 75 77 79 81 85 87 93 100 102 107
108 110 111 114 115 118 119 129 130 131 145 146 148 149 154 157 167
P1 **S** Beth Israel Lahey Health, Cambridge, MA
Primary Contact: John M. Fogarty, President and Chief Executive Officer
CFO: Brian Smith, Chief Financial Officer
CMO: Peter Ostrow, M.D., President Medical Staff
Web address: www.bidneedham.org/
Control: Other not-for-profit (including NFP Corporation) **Service:** General medical and surgical

Staffed Beds: 80 **Admissions:** 4385 **Census:** 53 **Outpatient Visits:** 232782 **Births:** 0 **Total Expense ($000):** 140040 **Payroll Expense ($000):** 60384 **Personnel:** 719

NEW BEDFORD—Bristol County

ST LUKE'S HOSP OF NEW BEDFORD See St. Luke's Hospital

ST. LUKE'S HOSPITAL See Southcoast Hospitals Group, Fall River

✠ **VIBRA HOSPITAL OF SOUTHEASTERN MASSACHUSETTS (222043)**, 4499
Acushnet Avenue, Zip 02745-4707; tel. 508/995-6900, (Nonreporting) **A**1 10 **S**
Vibra Healthcare, Mechanicsburg, PA
Primary Contact: Edward B. Leary, Chief Executive Officer
CFO: Cheryl Perry, Chief Financial Officer
CMO: Albert Loerinc, M.D., Medical Director
CHR: Ilene Mirabella, Director Human Resources
CNO: Emmanuel Berthil, Chief Clinical Officer
Web address: www.newbedfordrehab.com
Control: Corporation, Investor-owned (for-profit) **Service:** Acute long-term care hospital

Staffed Beds: 90

NEWBURYPORT—Essex County

✠ **ANNA JAQUES HOSPITAL (220029)**, 25 Highland Avenue, Zip 01950-3894;
tel. 978/463-1000, (Nonreporting) **A**1 2 10 **S** Beth Israel Lahey Health,
Cambridge, MA
Primary Contact: Glenn Focht, M.D., President
COO: Christine Kipp, R.N., MSN, Interim Chief Nursing Officer and Chief Operating Officer
CFO: Nicole Mulkern, Assistant Chief Financial Officer
CMO: Michael Patmas, M.D., Interim Chief Medical Officer
CIO: Robert Buchanan, Chief Information Officer
CHR: Mariana Bugallo-Muros, Vice President, Human Resources
CNO: Christine Kipp, R.N., MSN, Interim Chief Nursing Officer and Chief Operating Officer
Web address: www.ajh.org
Control: Other not-for-profit (including NFP Corporation) **Service:** General medical and surgical

Staffed Beds: 123

NEWTON LOWER FALLS—Middlesex County

✠ **NEWTON–WELLESLEY HOSPITAL (220101)**, 2014 Washington Street,
Zip 02462-1699; tel. 617/243-6000, (Includes MASSGENERAL FOR CHILDREN
AT NEWTON–WELLESLEY HOSPITAL, 2000 Washington Street, Newton,
Massachusetts, Zip 02462-1650, tel. 617/243-6585) **A**1 2 3 5 10 19 **F**3 8 9
12 15 18 19 26 28 29 30 31 34 35 37 38 40 41 44 45 46 47 48 49 50 51 52
53 54 55 56 57 58 59 60 63 64 65 68 70 72 74 75 76 77 78 79 81 82 84 85
87 89 92 93 97 98 100 101 102 107 108 110 111 114 115 116 117 118 119
126 129 130 131 132 135 146 147 148 149 150 154 156 164 167 168 169
P1 6 **S** Mass General Brigham, Boston, MA
Primary Contact: Ellen Moloney, President and Chief Operating Officer
COO: Ellen Moloney, President and Chief Operating Officer
CMO: Timothy Foster, Acting Chief Medical Officer
CIO: Beth Downie, Chief Information Officer
CHR: Beth Taylor, Vice President, Human Resources
Web address: www.nwh.org
Control: State, Government, Nonfederal **Service:** General medical and surgical

Staffed Beds: 314 **Admissions:** 18416 **Census:** 220 **Outpatient Visits:** 609072 **Births:** 3864 **Total Expense ($000):** 819104 **Payroll Expense ($000):** 377804 **Personnel:** 3081

NORTHAMPTON—Hampshire County

✠ **COOLEY DICKINSON HOSPITAL (220015)**, 30 Locust Street, Zip 01060-2093,
Mailing Address: P.O. Box 5001, Zip 01061-5001; tel. 413/582-2000, **A**1 10 19
F3 11 12 13 15 18 20 22 26 28 29 30 31 34 35 36 38 40 46 49 50 51 54 55
57 59 60 61 64 68 70 74 75 76 77 78 79 81 84 85 86 87 89 93 94 96 98 100
107 108 110 111 115 119 120 121 130 131 132 144 146 147 148 149 154
157 160 167 169 **P**6 8 **S** Mass General Brigham, Boston, MA
CFO: Laurie Lamoureux, Director of Finance
CMO: Estevan Garcia, M.D., Chief Medical Officer
CIO: Lee Martinez, Chief Information Officer
CHR: Lori A Kerwood, Director Human Resources
Web address: www.cooleydickinson.org
Control: Other not-for-profit (including NFP Corporation) **Service:** General medical and surgical

Staffed Beds: 140 **Admissions:** 5670 **Census:** 82 **Outpatient Visits:** 283495 **Births:** 592 **Total Expense ($000):** 245293 **Payroll Expense ($000):** 97729 **Personnel:** 1597

Hospitals, U.S. / MASSACHUSETTS

OAK BLUFFS—Dukes County

✠ **MARTHA'S VINEYARD HOSPITAL (221300)**, 1 Hospital Road, Zip 02557, Mailing Address: P.O. Box 1477, Zip 02557–1477; tel. 508/693–0410, (Total facility includes 34 beds in nursing home–type unit) **A** 1 10 18 **F** 3 5 13 15 18 28 29 30 31 37 40 44 45 48 50 51 59 60 64 68 69 70 74 75 76 77 78 79 81 82 85 86 87 89 91 93 97 107 110 111 115 119 127 128 130 133 135 146 147 149 154 160 169 **P** 6 **S** Mass General Brigham, Boston, MA
Primary Contact: Denise Schepici, M.P.H., Chief Executive Officer and President
CFO: Edward Olivier, Chief Financial Officer
CMO: Pieter Pil, M.D., Chief Medical Staff
CHR: Christine Gould, Director Human Resources
CNO: Carol A Bardwell, R.N., MSN, Chief Nurse Executive
Web address: www.mvhospital.com/
Control: Other not–for–profit (including NFP Corporation) **Service:** General medical and surgical

Staffed Beds: 86 **Admissions:** 1135 **Census:** 37 **Outpatient Visits:** 463127 **Births:** 117 **Total Expense ($000):** 114760 **Payroll Expense ($000):** 68612 **Personnel:** 519

PALMER—Hampden County

✠ **BAYSTATE WING HOSPITAL (220030)**, 40 Wright Street, Zip 01069–1138; tel. 413/283–7651, **A** 1 3 5 10 **F** 3 11 15 18 29 34 35 36 38 40 44 45 46 49 50 54 56 57 59 61 64 65 67 68 74 75 79 81 82 85 86 87 93 97 98 100 101 103 104 107 108 110 115 119 130 132 135 144 146 147 148 149 154 160 164 165 169 **S** Baystate Health, Inc., Springfield, MA
Primary Contact: Ronald Bryant, President
CFO: Keary T Allicon, Vice President Finance and Chief Financial Officer
CMO: David L Maguire, M.D., Vice President Medical Affairs
CIO: Kenneth Riley, Director Information Systems
CHR: Thomas Guilfoil, Director Human Resources
Web address: www.baystatewinghospital.org/
Control: Other not–for–profit (including NFP Corporation) **Service:** General medical and surgical

Staffed Beds: 74 **Admissions:** 3763 **Census:** 59 **Outpatient Visits:** 134823 **Births:** 0 **Total Expense ($000):** 108477 **Payroll Expense ($000):** 36504 **Personnel:** 616

PEMBROKE—Plymouth County

☐ **PEMBROKE HOSPITAL (224027)**, 199 Oak Street, Zip 02359–1953; tel. 781/829–7000, (Nonreporting) **A** 1 10 **S** Universal Health Services, Inc., King of Prussia, PA
Primary Contact: Steven Baroletti, Chief Executive Officer
CFO: Diane Airosus, Chief Financial Officer
CMO: Gary Jacobson, M.D., Chief Medical Officer
Web address: https://pembrokehospital.com/
Control: Partnership, Investor–owned (for–profit) **Service:** Psychiatric

Staffed Beds: 115

PITTSFIELD—Berkshire County

✠ **BERKSHIRE MEDICAL CENTER (220046)**, 725 North Street, Zip 01201–4124; tel. 413/447–2000, (Includes HILLCREST HOSPITAL, 165 Tor Court, Pittsfield, Massachusetts, Zip 01201–3099, Box 1155, Zip 01202–1155, tel. 413/443–4761) **A** 1 2 3 5 10 12 13 **F** 3 4 5 8 12 13 14 15 17 18 20 22 26 28 29 30 31 32 34 35 37 38 40 42 43 44 45 46 48 49 50 51 53 54 55 56 57 58 59 60 61 62 63 64 65 68 70 71 74 75 76 77 78 79 81 82 83 85 86 87 89 90 92 93 95 96 97 98 100 101 102 104 105 107 108 110 111 114 115 116 117 118 119 120 121 122 123 124 126 127 129 130 131 132 134 135 144 145 146 147 148 149 150 152 153 154 156 157 160 162 164 167 169 **P** 8 **S** Berkshire Health Systems, Inc., Pittsfield, MA
Primary Contact: Darlene Rodowicz, President and Chief Executive Officer
CFO: Scott St. George, Chief Financial Officer
CIO: William Young, Chief Information Officer
CHR: Arthur D Milano, Vice President Human Resources
CNO: Brenda E Cadorette, Chief Nursing Officer
Web address: www.berkshirehealthsystems.org
Control: Other not–for–profit (including NFP Corporation) **Service:** General medical and surgical

Staffed Beds: 272 **Admissions:** 11293 **Census:** 163 **Outpatient Visits:** 415769 **Births:** 570 **Total Expense ($000):** 625457 **Payroll Expense ($000):** 229172 **Personnel:** 2631

PLYMOUTH—Plymouth County

✠ **BETH ISRAEL DEACONESS HOSPITAL–PLYMOUTH (220060)**, 275 Sandwich Street, Zip 02360, Mailing Address: 36 Cordage Park Circle, Suite 322, Zip 02360; tel. 508/746–2000, (Nonreporting) **A** 1 2 5 10 19 **S** Beth Israel Lahey Health, Cambridge, MA
Primary Contact: Kevin B. Coughlin, President and Chief Executive Officer
CFO: Jason Radzevich, Vice President Finance
CMO: Tenny Thomas, M.D., Chief Medical Officer
CNO: Donna Doherty, R.N., Vice President of Nursing and Chief Nursing Officer
Web address: www.bidplymouth.org
Control: Other not–for–profit (including NFP Corporation) **Service:** General medical and surgical

Staffed Beds: 170

POCASSET—Barnstable County

☐ **POCASSET MENTAL HEALTH CENTER (224031)**, 830 County Road, Zip 02559–2110; tel. 508/564–9600, (Nonreporting) **A** 1 10
Primary Contact: Naomi Tavares–Silva, Center Director
Web address: https://www.mass.gov/locations/pocasset-mental-health-center
Control: State, Government, Nonfederal **Service:** Psychiatric

Staffed Beds: 24

ROCHDALE—Worcester County

KINDRED HOSPITAL PARK VIEW–CENTRAL MASSACHUSETTS See Vibra Hospital of Western Massachusetts–Central Campus

★ **VIBRA HOSPITAL OF WESTERN MASSACHUSETTS–CENTRAL CAMPUS (222046)**, 111 Huntoon Memorial Hwy, Zip 01542–1305, Mailing Address: 111 Huntoon Memorial Highway, Zip 01542; tel. 508/892–6000, (Nonreporting) **A** 10 **S** Vibra Healthcare, Mechanicsburg, PA
Primary Contact: Edward B. Leary, Chief Executive Officer
Web address: https://vhwmasscentral.com/
Control: Corporation, Investor–owned (for–profit) **Service:** Acute long–term care hospital

Staffed Beds: 10

ROSLINDALE—Suffolk County

★ △ **HEBREW REHABILITATION CENTER (222007)**, 1200 Centre Street, Zip 02131–1097; tel. 617/363–8000, (Total facility includes 675 beds in nursing home–type unit) **A** 7 10 **F** 1 2 6 10 29 30 35 50 58 59 60 64 65 68 69 75 77 82 83 84 93 97 100 104 119 125 128 130 132 143 146 148 149 154 158 **P** 6
Primary Contact: Ernest I. Mandel, M.D., Executive Vice President Health Care and Hebrew Senior Living Chief Medical Officer and Chief Qualit
COO: Brian Murphy, Senior Director Admissions and Referral Services
CFO: Lise Paul, Vice President Reimbursement and Network Planning
CMO: Ernest I. Mandel, M.D., Executive Vice President Health Care and Hebrew Senior Living Chief Medical Officer and Chief Quality Officer
CIO: Eric Rogers, Chief Information Officer
CHR: Deborah Lemmerman, Chief People Officer
CNO: Tammy B. Retalic, R.N., MS, Chief Nursing Officer
Web address: www.hebrewseniorlife.org
Control: Other not–for–profit (including NFP Corporation) **Service:** Acute long–term care hospital

Staffed Beds: 725 **Admissions:** 849 **Census:** 641 **Outpatient Visits:** 60821 **Births:** 0 **Total Expense ($000):** 153038 **Payroll Expense ($000):** 85639 **Personnel:** 1154

SALEM—Essex County

NORTH SHORE CHILDREN'S HOSPITAL See Massgeneral For Children At North Shore Medical Center

NORTH SHORE MEDICAL CENTER See Salem Hospital

Hospitals, U.S. / MASSACHUSETTS

☒ **SALEM HOSPITAL (220035)**, 81 Highland Avenue, Zip 01970–2714; tel. 978/741–1200, (Includes MASSGENERAL FOR CHILDREN AT NORTH SHORE MEDICAL CENTER, 57 Highland Avenue, Salem, Massachusetts, Zip 01970–6508, tel. 978/745–2100; SALEM CAMPUS, 81 Highland Ave, Salem, Massachusetts, Zip 01970–2714, 81 Highland Avenue, Zip 01970, tel. 978/741–1200; Robert G Norton, President; UNION CAMPUS, 500 Lynnfield Street, Lynn, Massachusetts, Zip 01904–1487, tel. 781/581–9200; Robert G Norton, President) **A**1 3 5 10 **F**5 12 13 15 16 18 20 22 26 28 29 30 32 34 35 36 38 40 41 43 44 45 46 47 48 49 50 51 55 56 57 59 60 64 68 70 73 74 75 76 77 79 81 82 84 85 86 87 88 92 98 99 100 101 102 103 104 105 107 108 110 111 114 115 119 126 129 130 132 135 143 145 146 147 148 149 150 152 153 154 156 157 160 162 164 167 168 169 **P**6 8 **S** Mass General Brigham, Boston, MA
Primary Contact: Roxanne C. Ruppel, President and Chief Operating Officer
CFO: Sally Mason Boemer, Chief Financial Officer
CMO: Mitchell S Rein, M.D., Chief Medical Officer
CIO: Fran X. Hinckley, Chief Information Officer
CHR: Arthur Bowes, Senior Vice President Human Resources
CNO: Cheryl Bhima Merrill, MSN, R.N., Senior Vice President Patient Care Services and Chief Nursing Officer
Web address: https://salem.massgeneralbrigham.org/
Control: Other not–for–profit (including NFP Corporation) **Service:** General medical and surgical

Staffed Beds: 367 **Admissions:** 17940 **Census:** 308 **Outpatient Visits:** 589467 **Births:** 1370 **Total Expense ($000):** 611786 **Payroll Expense ($000):** 284168 **Personnel:** 2553

SALEM HOSPITAL See Salem Campus

SOMERVILLE—Middlesex County

SOMERVILLE HOSPITAL See Cambridge Health Alliance, Cambridge

SOUTH WEYMOUTH—Norfolk County

☒ **SOUTH SHORE HOSPITAL (220100)**, 55 Fogg Road, Zip 02190–2432; tel. 781/624–8000, **A**1 3 5 10 19 **F**3 7 8 11 12 13 15 17 18 20 22 24 26 28 29 30 31 32 34 35 36 37 40 41 43 44 45 46 49 50 51 53 54 55 57 58 59 60 62 64 65 68 70 71 72 73 74 75 76 78 79 81 82 84 85 86 87 89 91 92 93 96 107 108 110 111 113 114 115 118 119 124 126 129 130 132 134 135 143 146 147 148 149 150 154 156 162 164 167 169
Primary Contact: Allen L. Smith, M.D., President and Chief Executive Officer
COO: Joseph Cahill, Executive Vice President and Chief Operating Officer
CFO: Stephen Jenney, Vice President of Finance
CMO: John Stevenson, M.D., Senior Vice President and Chief Medical Officer
CIO: Del Dixon, Chief Information Officer
CHR: Robert Wheeler, Vice President Human Resources
Web address: www.southshorehospital.org
Control: Other not–for–profit (including NFP Corporation) **Service:** General medical and surgical

Staffed Beds: 394 **Admissions:** 29658 **Census:** 350 **Outpatient Visits:** 539364 **Births:** 3585 **Total Expense ($000):** 820299 **Payroll Expense ($000):** 392223 **Personnel:** 4112

SOUTHBRIDGE—Worcester County

HARRINGTON HOSPITAL See Umass Memorial Health – Harrington

☒ **UMASS MEMORIAL HEALTH – HARRINGTON (220019)**, 100 South Street, Zip 01550–4051; tel. 508/765–9771, (Nonreporting) **A**1 2 5 10 **S** UMass Memorial Health Care, Inc., Worcester, MA
Primary Contact: Edward H. Moore, President
COO: Kristin Morales, Chief Operating Officer
CMO: Arthur Russo, M.D., Director Medical Affairs
CIO: Harry Lemieux, Chief Information Officer
CHR: Christopher Canniff, Executive Director, Human Resources
CNO: Thomas W. Hijeck, R.N., MS, Vice President Nursing Services and Chief Nursing Officer
Web address: www.harringtonhospital.org
Control: Other not–for–profit (including NFP Corporation) **Service:** General medical and surgical

Staffed Beds: 119

SPRINGFIELD—Hampden County

☒ **BAYSTATE MEDICAL CENTER (220077)**, 759 Chestnut Street, Zip 01199–0001; tel. 413/794–0000, (Includes BAYSTATE CHILDREN'S HOSPITAL, 759 Chestnut Street, Springfield, Massachusetts, Zip 01199–1001, tel. 413/794–0000) **A**1 3 5 8 10 19 **F**3 8 12 13 14 15 17 18 19 20 22 24 26 28 29 30 31 32 34 35 37 38 40 41 43 44 45 46 47 48 49 50 51 52 54 55 56 57 58 59 60 61 64 65 66 68 70 72 73 74 75 76 77 78 79 81 82 83 84 85 86 87 88 89 92 93 96 97 98 99 100 101 102 103 104 105 107 108 109 110 111 114 115 118 119 120 121 123 124 126 129 130 131 132 135 138 143 145 146 147 148 149 154 156 157 162 164 167 169 **S** Baystate Health, Inc., Springfield, MA
Primary Contact: Sam Skura, President
COO: Tejas Gandhi, Ph.D., Chief Operating Officer
CFO: Dennis Chalke, Senior Vice President, Chief Financial Officer and Treasurer
CMO: Andrew Artenstein, M.D., Chief Physician Executive, Chief Academic Officer and President, Baystate Medical Practices
CIO: Joel L. Vengco, MS, Vice President, Chief Information Officer
CHR: Paula C Squires, Senior Vice President, Chief Human Resources Officer and Chief Human Resources Officer
CNO: Joanne Miller, R.N., MSN, Chief Nursing Officer
Web address: www.baystatehealth.org/bmc
Control: Other not–for–profit (including NFP Corporation) **Service:** General medical and surgical

Staffed Beds: 746 **Admissions:** 39313 **Census:** 662 **Outpatient Visits:** 646708 **Births:** 4275 **Total Expense ($000):** 1734363 **Payroll Expense ($000):** 577974 **Personnel:** 8721

☒ △ **MERCY MEDICAL CENTER (220066)**, 271 Carew Street, Zip 01104–2398, Mailing Address: P.O. Box 9012, Zip 01102–9012; tel. 413/748–9000, (Nonreporting) **A**1 2 7 10 **S** Trinity Health, Livonia, MI
Primary Contact: Deborah Bitsoli, CPA, President
CFO: Thomas W. Robert, Senior Vice President of Finance and Chief Financial Officer
CMO: Robert Roose, M.D., Chief Medical Officer
CHR: Leonard F Pansa, Senior Vice President Human Resources and Administrative Services
CNO: Susan Pettorini–D'Amico, R.N., Chief Nursing Officer
Web address: www.mercycares.com
Control: Other not–for–profit (including NFP Corporation) **Service:** General medical and surgical

Staffed Beds: 334

SHRINERS HOSPITALS FOR CHILDREN–SPRINGFIELD (223303), 516 Carew Street, Zip 01104–2396; tel. 413/787–2000, (Nonreporting) **A**5 10 **S** Shriners Hospitals for Children, Tampa, FL
Primary Contact: Frances Marthone, Ph.D., MSN, R.N., Administrator
CFO: Richard Fulkerson, Director Fiscal Services
CMO: David M Drvaric, M.D., Chief of Staff
CIO: Eric Kamens, Regional Director Information Systems
CHR: John Donlin, Director Human Resources
CNO: Diane Brunelle, MSN, R.N., Director Patient Care Services and Chief Nursing Officer
Web address: www.shrinershospitalsforchildren.org/Hospitals/Locations/Springfield.aspx
Control: Other not–for–profit (including NFP Corporation) **Service:** Children's orthopedic

Staffed Beds: 10

STOCKBRIDGE—Berkshire County

☒ **AUSTEN RIGGS CENTER**, 25 Main Street, Zip 01262, Mailing Address: P.O. Box 962, Zip 01262–0962; tel. 413/298–5511, (Nonreporting) **A**1
Primary Contact: Eric M. Plakun, M.D., Medical Center Director and Chief Executive Officer
COO: Chauncey Collins, Chief Operating Officer and Chief Financial Officer
CFO: Chauncey Collins, Chief Operating Officer and Chief Financial Officer
CIO: Ave Schwartz, Chief Information Officer
CHR: Bertha Mary Connelley, Director Human Resources
CNO: Barbara Turner, Director of Nursing
Web address: www.austenriggs.net
Control: Other not–for–profit (including NFP Corporation) **Service:** Psychiatric

Staffed Beds: 67

Hospitals, U.S. / MASSACHUSETTS

STOUGHTON—Norfolk County

★ **PAM HEALTH SPECIALTY HOSPITAL OF STOUGHTON (222002)**, 909 Sumner Street, 1st Floor, Zip 02072-3396; tel. 781/297-8200, **A**10 22 **F**1 3 29 98 100 148 **S** PAM Health, Enola, PA
Primary Contact: Shawn Todd, Interim Chief Executive Officer
Web address: https://pamhealth.com/index.php/facilities/find-facility/specialty-hospitals/pam-health-specialty-hospital-stoughton
Control: Individual, Investor-owned (for-profit) **Service**: Acute long-term care hospital

Staffed Beds: 152 **Admissions**: 330 **Census**: 51 **Outpatient Visits**: 0
Births: 0 **Total Expense ($000)**: 27583 **Payroll Expense ($000)**: 12189
Personnel: 151

TAUNTON—Bristol County

☐ **MORTON HOSPITAL AND MEDICAL CENTER (220073)**, 88 Washington Street, Zip 02780-2465; tel. 508/828-7000, (Nonreporting) **A**1 10 **S** Steward Health Care System, LLC, Dallas, TX
Primary Contact: Heidi Taylor, President
COO: Donna Maher, R.N., Chief Operating Officer
CMO: Charles Thayer, M.D., Chief Medical Officer
CNO: Lisa Coggins, Chief Nursing Officer
Web address: www.mortonhospital.org
Control: Other not-for-profit (including NFP Corporation) **Service**: General medical and surgical

Staffed Beds: 153

☐ **TAUNTON STATE HOSPITAL (224001)**, 60 Hodges Avenue Extension, Zip 02780-3034, Mailing Address: PO Box 4007, Zip 02780-0997; tel. 508/977-3000, (Nonreporting) **A**1 10 **S** Massachusetts Department of Mental Health, Boston, MA
Primary Contact: Joyce O'Connor, Chief Operating Officer
CHR: Trish Scully, Director Human Resources
Web address: https://www.mass.gov/locations/taunton-state-hospital
Control: State, Government, Nonfederal **Service**: Psychiatric

Staffed Beds: 45

TEWKSBURY—Middlesex County

☐ **TEWKSBURY HOSPITAL (222003)**, 365 East Street, Zip 01876-1998; tel. 978/851-7321, (Nonreporting) **A**1 3 10 **S** Massachusetts Department of Public Health, Boston, MA
Primary Contact: Betsy L. Schwechheimer, Chief Executive Officer
CFO: Maureen DiPalma, Chief Financial Officer
CMO: James DeVita, M.D., Chief Medical Officer
CNO: Janice E Bishop, R.N., Chief Nursing Officer
Web address: www.mass.gov
Control: State, Government, Nonfederal **Service**: Acute long-term care hospital

Staffed Beds: 357

TURNERS FALLS—Franklin County

FARREN MEMORIAL HOSPITAL See Farren Care Center

WALTHAM—Middlesex County

☐ **WALDEN BEHAVIORAL CARE (224038)**, 9 Hope Avenue, Zip 02453-2741; tel. 781/647-6700, (Nonreporting) **A**1 3 10
Primary Contact: Stuart Koman, Ph.D., President and Chief Executive Officer
COO: Paula Vass, Vice President Clinical Operations
CFO: Lawrence Behan, Vice President Administration and Finance, Chief Financial Officer
CMO: James Greenblatt, M.D., Chief Medical Officer, Vice President Medical Clinical Services
CIO: Lawrence Behan, Vice President Administration and Finance, Chief Financial Officer
CHR: Carol Pender, Assistant Vice President Human Resources
Web address: https://www.waldeneatingdisorders.com/eating-disorder-treatment-programs/inpatient/
Control: Corporation, Investor-owned (for-profit) **Service**: Psychiatric

Staffed Beds: 51

WAREHAM—Plymouth County

TOBEY HOSPITAL See Southcoast Hospitals Group, Fall River

WEST ROXBURY—Suffolk County

⊞ △ **VETERANS AFFAIRS BOSTON HEALTHCARE SYSTEM**, 1400 VFW Parkway, Zip 02132-4927; tel. 617/323-7700, (Nonreporting) **A**1 2 3 5 7 8 **S** Department of Veterans Affairs, Washington, DC
Primary Contact: Vincent Ng, Medical Center Director
CFO: Joe Costa, Chief Financial Officer
CMO: Brian Hoffman, M.D., Chief Medical Services
CIO: David M Goodman, Ph.D., Chief Information Officer
CHR: William Warfield, Chief Human Resources Management
CNO: Cecilia McVey, Chief, Nursing Service
Web address: www.boston.va.gov/
Control: Veterans Affairs, Government, federal **Service**: General medical and surgical

Staffed Beds: 491

VETERANS AFFAIRS MEDICAL CENTER See Veterans Affairs Medical Center West Roxbury Division

VETERANS AFFAIRS MEDICAL CENTER WEST ROXBURY DIVISION See Veterans Affairs Boston Healthcare System Brockton Division, Brockton

WESTBOROUGH—Worcester County

☐ **WESTBOROUGH BEHAVIORAL HEALTHCARE HOSPITAL (224044)**, 300 Friberg Parkway, Zip 01581-3900; tel. 508/329-6112, (Nonreporting) **A**1 10 **S** Signature Healthcare Services, Corona, CA
Primary Contact: Michelle Lynn, Chief Executive Officer
Web address: https://www.westboroughbehavioral.com/
Control: Corporation, Investor-owned (for-profit) **Service**: Psychiatric

Staffed Beds: 120

☐ **WHITTIER REHABILITATION HOSPITAL (222048)**, 150 Flanders Road, Zip 01581-1017; tel. 508/871-2000, (Nonreporting) **A**1 10 **S** Whittier Health Network, Haverhill, MA
Primary Contact: Rebecca Roman, Administrator
Web address: www.whittierhealth.com
Control: Partnership, Investor-owned (for-profit) **Service**: Acute long-term care hospital

Staffed Beds: 60

WESTFIELD—Hampden County

⊞ **BAYSTATE NOBLE HOSPITAL (220065)**, 115 West Silver Street, Zip 01085-3628; tel. 413/568-2811, **A**1 3 5 10 **F**3 15 18 28 29 34 37 38 40 45 47 50 51 57 59 65 67 68 74 75 77 80 81 85 87 90 93 97 98 100 101 102 105 107 108 109 110 111 114 115 119 130 146 147 154 157 162 165 **S** Baystate Health, Inc., Springfield, MA
Primary Contact: Ronald Bryant, President
CFO: John Shaver, Chief Financial Officer
CMO: Stanley Strzempko, M.D., Vice President Medical Affairs and Chief Medical Officer
CIO: Steven Cummings, Chief Operating Officer and Chief Information Officer
CHR: Joanne Ollson, Vice President Human Resources
Web address: www.baystatehealth.org/locations/noble-hospital
Control: Other not-for-profit (including NFP Corporation) **Service**: General medical and surgical

Staffed Beds: 85 **Admissions**: 3691 **Census**: 48 **Outpatient Visits**: 40727
Births: 0 **Total Expense ($000)**: 81064 **Payroll Expense ($000)**: 33050
Personnel: 460

☐ **WESTERN MASSACHUSETTS HOSPITAL (222023)**, 91 East Mountain Road, Zip 01085-1801; tel. 413/562-4131, (Nonreporting) **A**1 10 **S** Massachusetts Department of Public Health, Boston, MA
Primary Contact: Valenda M. Liptak, Chief Executive Officer
CMO: Chabilal Neergheen, M.D., Medical Director
CHR: James E Duggan, Director Human Resources
Web address: www.mass.gov/eohhs/gov/departments/dph/programs/western-massachusetts-hospital.html
Control: State, Government, Nonfederal **Service**: Acute long-term care hospital

Staffed Beds: 80

WHITINSVILLE—Worcester County

WHITINSVILLE HOSPITAL See Whitinsville Medical Center

WHITINSVILLE MEDICAL CENTER See Milford Regional Medical Center, Milford

---

Hospital, Medicare Provider Number, Address, Telephone, Approval, Facility, and Physician Codes, Health Care System

★ American Hospital Association (AHA) membership
☐ The Joint Commission accreditation
○ Healthcare Facilities Accreditation Program
◇ DNV Healthcare Inc. accreditation
⇑ Center for Improvement in Healthcare Quality Accreditation
△ Commission on Accreditation of Rehabilitation Facilities (CARF) accreditation

© 2025 AHA Guide

Hospitals, U.S. / MASSACHUSETTS

WINCHESTER—Middlesex County

✠ **WINCHESTER HOSPITAL (220105)**, 41 Highland Avenue, Zip 01890–1496; tel. 781/729–9000, (Nonreporting) **A**1 2 3 5 10 **S** Beth Israel Lahey Health, Cambridge, MA
Primary Contact: Al Campbell, FACHE, R.N., President
CFO: Matthew Woods, Vice President Finance
CHR: Stephanie M Bettinelli, Vice President of Human Resources
Web address: www.winchesterhospital.org
Control: Other not–for–profit (including NFP Corporation) **Service**: General medical and surgical

Staffed Beds: 194

WOBURN—Middlesex County

✠ **ENCOMPASS HEALTH REHABILITATION HOSPITAL OF NEW ENGLAND (223026)**, 2 Rehabilitation Way, Zip 01801–6098; tel. 781/935–5050, (Nonreporting) **A**1 3 10 **S** Encompass Health Corporation, Birmingham, AL
Primary Contact: David Coggins, MS, Chief Executive Officer
CFO: Barbara Polizzotti, Controller
CHR: Lauren Healey, Human Resources Director
CNO: Deborah Rich, R.N., Chief Nursing Officer
Web address: www.newenglandrehab.com
Control: Corporation, Investor–owned (for–profit) **Service**: Rehabilitation

Staffed Beds: 210

WORCESTER—Worcester County

ADCARE HOSPITAL OF WORCESTER (220062), 107 Lincoln Street, Zip 01605–2499; tel. 508/799–9000, (Nonreporting) **A**3 5 10
Primary Contact: Andrea Dayotas, Interim Chief Executive Officer
CFO: Christine Judycki–Crepeault, Chief Financial Officer
CMO: Ronald F Pike, M.D., Medical Director
CHR: Joan L. Bertrand, Vice President Human Resources
CNO: Judith Richards, Director of Nursing
Web address: https://adcare.com/locations/adcare-hospital/
Control: Other not–for–profit (including NFP Corporation) **Service**: Substance Use Disorder

Staffed Beds: 114

✠ **FAIRLAWN REHABILITATION HOSPITAL (223029)**, 189 May Street, Zip 01602–4339; tel. 508/791–6351, (Nonreporting) **A**1 3 5 10 **S** Encompass Health Corporation, Birmingham, AL
Primary Contact: Peter Lancette, Chief Executive Officer
CFO: John Flaherty, Controller
CMO: Debra Twehous, Medical Director
CIO: Jennifer Jozefiak, Information Officer
CHR: Rosalie Lawless, Director Human Resources
CNO: Lisa Perales, Chief Nursing Officer
Web address: www.fairlawnrehab.org
Control: Corporation, Investor–owned (for–profit) **Service**: Rehabilitation

Staffed Beds: 110

☐ **HOSPITAL FOR BEHAVIORAL MEDICINE (224045)**, 100 Century Drive, Zip 01606–1244; tel. 774/420–3939, (Nonreporting) **A**1 10
Primary Contact: Michelle Lynn, Chief Executive Officer
Web address: https://www.hospitalforbehavioralmedicine.com/
Control: Corporation, Investor–owned (for–profit) **Service**: Psychiatric

Staffed Beds: 120

✠ **SAINT VINCENT HOSPITAL (220176)**, 123 Summer Street, Zip 01608–1216; tel. 508/363–5000, (Nonreporting) **A**1 2 3 5 10 19 **S** TENET Healthcare Corporation, Dallas, TX
Primary Contact: Carolyn Jackson, Chief Executive Officer
COO: Darrin Cook, Chief Operating Officer
CFO: Tina Kovacs, Interim Chief Financial Officer
CMO: Michele Sinopoli, M.D., Chief Medical Officer
CHR: Christian Bartholomew, Chief Human Resources Officer
CNO: Denise Kvapil, Chief Nursing Officer
Web address: www.stvincenthospital.com
Control: Corporation, Investor–owned (for–profit) **Service**: General medical and surgical

Staffed Beds: 288

✠ **UMASS MEMORIAL MEDICAL CENTER (220163)**, 119 Belmont Street, Zip 01605–2982; tel. 508/334–1000, (Includes HAHNEMANN CAMPUS, 281 Lincoln ST, Worcester, Massachusetts, Zip 01605–2138, 281 Lincoln Street, Zip 01605, tel. 508/334–1000; MEMORIAL CAMPUS, 119 Belmont ST, Worcester, Massachusetts, Zip 01605–2903, 119 Belmont Street, Zip 01605, tel. 508/334–1000; UMASS MEMORIAL CHILDREN'S MEDICAL CENTER, 55 Lake Avenue North, Worcester, Massachusetts, Zip 01655–0002, tel. 508/334–1000; UNIVERSITY CAMPUS, 55 Lake Avenue North, Worcester, Massachusetts, Zip 01655–0002, tel. 508/334–1000) **A**1 2 3 5 8 10 19 **F**3 4 6 7 8 9 12 13 14 15 17 18 19 20 22 24 26 29 30 31 32 38 40 41 43 45 46 47 48 49 50 51 52 55 56 59 60 61 63 64 65 67 68 70 71 72 73 74 75 76 77 78 79 80 81 82 84 85 86 87 88 89 90 92 97 98 99 100 101 102 104 107 108 110 114 115 118 119 120 121 123 124 126 127 130 131 132 135 136 138 139 141 145 146 147 148 149 150 154 156 160 167 168 169 **S** UMass Memorial Health Care, Inc., Worcester, MA
Primary Contact: Justin Precourt, Interim President and Chief Nursing Officer
COO: Andrew Sussman, M.D., Chief Operating Officer
CFO: Therese Day, Chief Financial Officer
CMO: Charles E Cavagnaro, M.D., III, Interim Chief Medical officer
CIO: George Brenkle, Chief Information Officer
CNO: Justin Precourt, Chief Nursing Officer
Web address: www.umassmemorial.org
Control: Other not–for–profit (including NFP Corporation) **Service**: General medical and surgical

Staffed Beds: 720 **Admissions**: 37000 **Census**: 822 **Outpatient Visits**: 1100000 **Births**: 4800 **Total Expense ($000)**: 2409795 **Payroll Expense ($000)**: 686984 **Personnel**: 6150

WORCESTER HAHNEMANN HOSPITAL See Hahnemann Campus

WORCESTER MEMORIAL HOSPITAL See Memorial Campus

☐ **WORCESTER RECOVERY CENTER AND HOSPITAL (224032)**, 309 Belmont Street, Zip 01604–1695; tel. 508/368–3300, (Nonreporting) **A**1 3 5 10 **S** Massachusetts Department of Mental Health, Boston, MA
Primary Contact: Jacqueline Ducharme, Chief Operating Officer and Interim Chief Executive Officer
COO: Jacqueline Ducharme
CIO: Ron Medciros, Director Applied Information Technology
Web address: https://www.mass.gov/locations/worcester-recovery-center-and-hospital-wrch
Control: State, Government, Nonfederal **Service**: Psychiatric

Staffed Beds: 126

Hospitals, U.S. / MICHIGAN

MICHIGAN

ADRIAN—Lenawee County

★ ○ **PROMEDICA CHARLES AND VIRGINIA HICKMAN HOSPITAL (230005)**, 5640 North Adrian Hwy, Zip 49221–8318; tel. 517/577–0000, **A**10 11 **F**3 8 11 13 15 18 19 26 28 29 30 31 34 35 38 39 40 45 48 50 51 53 56 57 59 60 62 63 64 65 70 74 76 77 78 79 81 82 85 87 92 93 95 97 100 101 102 104 107 108 109 110 111 114 115 119 126 127 129 130 135 141 146 147 148 149 154 156 157 167 **S** ProMedica Health System, Toledo, OH
Primary Contact: Julie Yaroch, D.O., President, ProMedica Charles and Virginia Hickman Hospital
Web address: https://www.promedica.org
Control: Other not–for–profit (including NFP Corporation) Service: General medical and surgical

> Staffed Beds: 50 Admissions: 2807 Census: 27 Outpatient Visits: 119924 Births: 445 Total Expense ($000): 123696 Payroll Expense ($000): 31624 Personnel: 542

ALLEGAN—Allegan County

ASCENSION ALLEGAN HOSPITAL See Ascension Borgess Allegan Hospital

⊞ **ASCENSION BORGESS ALLEGAN HOSPITAL (231328)**, 555 Linn Street, Zip 49010–1524; tel. 269/673–8424, **A**1 3 10 18 **F**3 15 28 29 30 31 34 35 40 43 45 47 48 50 59 75 77 78 79 81 82 85 86 87 93 96 97 100 101 102 104 107 108 110 115 118 119 127 129 130 131 132 133 135 144 146 149 153 154 156 **S** Ascension Healthcare, Saint Louis, MO
Primary Contact: Dean Kindler, M.D., Regional President and Chief Executive Officer
CMO: Nabil Nouna, M.D., Chief of Staff
CNO: Kathy Chapman, R.N., Chief Clinical Officer and Vice President of Patient Services
Web address: https://healthcare.ascension.org/locations/michigan/mikal/allegan-ascension-borgess-allegan-hospital
Control: Church operated, Nongovernment, not–for–profit Service: General medical and surgical

> Staffed Beds: 25 Admissions: 414 Census: 7 Outpatient Visits: 84754 Births: 0 Total Expense ($000): 40088 Payroll Expense ($000): 13175 Personnel: 120

ALMA—Gratiot County

⊞ △ **MYMICHIGAN MEDICAL CENTER ALMA (230030)**, 300 East Warwick Drive, Zip 48801–1014; tel. 989/463–1101, **A**1 2 3 5 7 10 19 **F**3 12 13 15 18 20 24 26 28 29 31 34 35 36 38 40 42 43 44 45 46 48 50 56 57 58 59 62 64 65 68 70 74 75 76 77 78 79 81 82 85 86 87 89 90 91 92 93 96 97 98 101 103 104 105 107 108 110 111 115 118 119 120 121 127 129 130 131 132 135 144 146 147 148 149 153 154 156 157 162 168 169 **S** MyMichigan Health, Midland, MI
Primary Contact: Marita Hattem-Schiffman, FACHE, Regional President
CFO: Jeff Provenzano, Vice President and Chief Financial Officer
CNO: LeeAnn Chadwick, Chief Nursing Officer
Web address: www.midmichigan.org/gratiot
Control: Other not–for–profit (including NFP Corporation) Service: General medical and surgical

> Staffed Beds: 97 Admissions: 4075 Census: 66 Outpatient Visits: 150871 Births: 457 Total Expense ($000): 122644 Payroll Expense ($000): 38229 Personnel: 566

MYMICHIGAN MEDICAL CENTER–GRATIOT See Mymichigan Medical Center Alma

ALPENA—Alpena County

MIDMICHIGAN MEDICAL CENTER - ALPENA See Mymichigan Medical Center Alpena

⊞ **MYMICHIGAN MEDICAL CENTER ALPENA (230036)**, 1501 West Chisholm Street, Zip 49707–1401; tel. 989/356–7000, **A**1 2 3 10 **F**3 11 13 15 20 28 29 30 31 34 35 40 42 43 44 45 46 47 48 49 50 59 60 62 64 65 70 71 75 76 77 78 79 81 82 85 86 87 90 92 93 96 97 98 100 101 102 104 107 110 111 114 115 118 119 129 130 131 132 135 144 146 147 148 149 154 156 160 162 164 165 167 169 **S** MyMichigan Health, Midland, MI
Primary Contact: Hunter Nostrant, FACHE, President
CMO: Thomas Thornton, M.D., Vice President of Medical Affairs
CNO: Debra Pokorzynski, Vice President of Nursing
Web address: www.midmichigan.org
Control: Other not–for–profit (including NFP Corporation) Service: General medical and surgical

> Staffed Beds: 86 Admissions: 4131 Census: 49 Outpatient Visits: 179361 Births: 380 Total Expense ($000): 226630 Payroll Expense ($000): 55422 Personnel: 806

ANN ARBOR—Washtenaw County

C.S. MOTT CHILDREN'S HOSPITAL See C. S. Mott Children's Hospital

⊞ **UNIVERSITY OF MICHIGAN MEDICAL CENTER (230046)**, 1500 East Medical Center Drive, Zip 48109; tel. 734/936–4000, (Includes C. S. MOTT CHILDREN'S HOSPITAL, 1540 East Hospital Drive, Ann Arbor, Michigan, Zip 48109–5475, tel. 734/936–4000; Luanne M. Thomas Ewald, Chief Operating Officer) **A**1 2 3 8 10 19 **F**3 5 6 8 9 11 12 13 15 16 17 18 19 20 21 22 23 24 25 26 27 28 29 30 31 32 34 35 36 37 38 39 40 41 43 44 45 46 47 48 49 50 51 52 53 54 55 56 57 58 59 60 61 62 64 65 66 68 69 70 71 72 74 75 76 77 78 79 80 81 82 83 84 85 86 87 88 89 90 91 92 93 94 95 96 97 98 99 100 101 102 103 104 107 108 110 111 112 114 115 116 117 118 119 120 121 123 124 126 127 129 130 131 132 134 135 136 137 138 139 140 141 142 145 146 147 148 149 150 151 153 154 156 160 162 163 164 165 167 169 **S** University of Michigan Health, Ann Arbor, MI
Primary Contact: David C. Miller, M.D., M.P.H., Executive Vice Dean for Clinical Affairs and President, UM Health System
COO: T. Anthony Denton, JD, Senior Vice President and Chief Environmental Social and Governance Officer
CFO: Paul Castillo, Chief Financial Officer
CMO: Jeffrey Desmond, M.D., Chief Medical Officer
CIO: Andrew Rosenberg, M.D., Chief Information Officer
CHR: Deloris Hunt, Chief Human Resources Officer
CNO: Marge Calarco, Chief Nursing Executive
Web address: www.med.umich.edu
Control: Other not–for–profit (including NFP Corporation) Service: General medical and surgical

> Staffed Beds: 1102 Admissions: 48127 Census: 899 Outpatient Visits: 3674453 Births: 5321 Total Expense ($000): 5422344 Payroll Expense ($000): 1678371 Personnel: 18130

⊞ **VETERANS AFFAIRS ANN ARBOR HEALTHCARE SYSTEM**, 2215 Fuller Road, Zip 48105–2399; tel. 734/769–7100, (Nonreporting) **A**1 3 5 **S** Department of Veterans Affairs, Washington, DC
Primary Contact: Ginny L. Creasman, Director
COO: Himanshu Singh, M.D., Associate Director
CFO: Joel Wallinga, Chief Financial Officer
CMO: Eric Young, M.D., Chief of Staff
CIO: Rob Whitehurst, Chief, Office of Information and Technology
CHR: Stephanie Hunter, Chief Human Resources Officer
CNO: Stacey Breedveld, R.N., MSN, Associate Director for Patient Care
Web address: www.annarbor.va.gov
Control: Veterans Affairs, Government, federal Service: General medical and surgical

> Staffed Beds: 156

AUBURN HILLS—Oakland County

HAVENWYCK HOSPITAL See Havenwyck Hospital, Inc.

Hospital, Medicare Provider Number, Address, Telephone, Approval, Facility, and Physician Codes, Health Care System

★ American Hospital Association (AHA) membership ○ Healthcare Facilities Accreditation Program ⇧ Center for Improvement in Healthcare Quality Accreditation
☐ The Joint Commission accreditation ◇ DNV Healthcare Inc. accreditation △ Commission on Accreditation of Rehabilitation Facilities (CARF) accreditation

© 2025 AHA Guide

Hospitals, U.S. / MICHIGAN

☐ **HAVENWYCK HOSPITAL, INC. (234023)**, 1525 University Drive, Zip 48326–2673; tel. 248/373–9200, **A**1 10 **F**29 34 35 38 50 64 98 99 101 103 104 105 106 130 149 153 154 164 **P**5 **S** Universal Health Services, Inc., King of Prussia, PA
Primary Contact: Jaime White, Chief Executive Officer
CFO: Steve Sacharski, Chief Financial Officer
CMO: Hani Mekhael, M.D., Chief Staff
CHR: Amy Giannosa, Director Human Resources
CNO: Mitzi Sawicki, Director of Nursing
Web address: www.havenwyckhospital.com
Control: Corporation, Investor–owned (for–profit) **Service**: Psychiatric

Staffed Beds: 243 **Admissions**: 5514 **Census**: 211 **Outpatient Visits**: 5978 **Births**: 0 **Total Expense ($000)**: 48968 **Payroll Expense ($000)**: 28115 **Personnel**: 429

BAD AXE—Huron County

★ **MCLAREN THUMB REGION (231340)**, 1100 South Van Dyke Road, Zip 48413–9615; tel. 989/269–9521, **A**10 18 **F**5 8 11 13 15 18 20 28 29 31 32 34 40 43 45 54 59 64 68 74 75 76 77 78 79 81 87 93 97 100 107 108 110 111 115 119 121 127 129 130 133 146 147 148 149 154 160 **S** McLaren Health Care Corporation, Grand Blanc, MI
Primary Contact: Connie L. Koutouzos, R.N., MSN, President and Chief Executive Officer
CFO: Kevin J Cawley, Interim Chief Financial Officer
CMO: Craig McManaman, M.D., Chief of Staff
CHR: Nancy Bouck, Senior Director, Human Resources
CNO: Jane Christner, Chief Nursing Officer
Web address: https://www.mclaren.org/thumb-region/mclaren-thumb-region-home
Control: Other not–for–profit (including NFP Corporation) **Service**: General medical and surgical

Staffed Beds: 16 **Admissions**: 815 **Census**: 5 **Outpatient Visits**: 41984 **Births**: 276 **Total Expense ($000)**: 40417 **Payroll Expense ($000)**: 17325 **Personnel**: 222

BATTLE CREEK—Calhoun County

BATTLE CREEK ADVENTIST HOSP See Fieldstone Center

⊞ **BATTLE CREEK VETERANS AFFAIRS MEDICAL CENTER**, 5500 Armstrong Road, Zip 49037–7314; tel. 269/966–5600, (Nonreporting) **A**1 3 5 **S** Department of Veterans Affairs, Washington, DC
Primary Contact: Michelle Martin, Executive Medical Center Director
COO: Edward G. Dornoff, Associate Director
CFO: James M. Rupert, Chief Fiscal Services
CMO: Wilfredo Rodriguez, M.D., Chief of Staff
CIO: Scott Hershberger, Acting Chief Information Management Services
CHR: Palma Simkins, Chief Human Resources Management Services
CNO: Kay Bower, Associate Director for Patient Care Services
Web address: www.battlecreek.va.gov/
Control: Veterans Affairs, Government, federal **Service**: Psychiatric

Staffed Beds: 208

⊞ **BRONSON BATTLE CREEK HOSPITAL (230075)**, 300 North Avenue, Zip 49017–3307; tel. 269/245–8000, (Includes FIELDSTONE CENTER, 165 North Washington Avenue, Battle Creek, Michigan, Zip 49037, tel. 269/245–8570; MAIN CAMPUS, 300 North Avenue, Battle Creek, Michigan, Zip 49017, tel. 616/966–8000) **A**1 2 3 5 10 19 **F**3 5 9 11 15 18 28 29 30 31 32 34 35 36 37 38 40 41 43 44 45 50 51 54 55 56 57 59 60 61 64 65 66 68 70 74 75 76 77 78 79 81 82 83 85 86 87 93 97 98 102 104 107 108 110 111 114 115 117 118 119 120 121 123 124 126 129 130 131 132 134 135 143 144 146 147 148 149 150 154 162 167 169 **P**6 **S** Bronson Healthcare Group, Kalamazoo, MI
Primary Contact: Bill Manns, President and Chief Executive Officer
COO: Joseph du Lac, Senior Vice President, Chief Operating Officer
CMO: Daniel Stewart, M.D., Vice President Medical Affairs
CHR: John Hayden, Senior Vice President and Human Resources Officer
CNO: Susan Watson, MSN, R.N., Vice President
Web address: www.bronsonhealth.com
Control: Other not–for–profit (including NFP Corporation) **Service**: General medical and surgical

Staffed Beds: 164 **Admissions**: 7513 **Census**: 90 **Outpatient Visits**: 455438 **Births**: 740 **Total Expense ($000)**: 325999 **Payroll Expense ($000)**: 161529 **Personnel**: 1178

⊞ **SELECT SPECIALTY HOSPITAL – BATTLE CREEK (232035)**, 300 North Avenue, 6th Floor, Zip 49017–3307; tel. 269/245–4675, (Nonreporting) **A**1 10 **S** Select Medical Corporation, Mechanicsburg, PA
Primary Contact: Kenneth C. LePage, FACHE, Chief Executive Officer
Web address: www.battlecreek.selectspecialtyhospitals.com/
Control: Corporation, Investor–owned (for–profit) **Service**: Acute long–term care hospital

Staffed Beds: 25

SELECT SPECIALTY HOSPITAL–BATTLE CREEK See Select Specialty Hospital – Battle Creek

BAY CITY—Bay County

BAY REGIONAL MEDICAL CENTER–WEST CAMPUS See Mclaren Bay Region–West Campus

⊞ **MCLAREN BAY REGION (230041)**, 1900 Columbus Avenue, Zip 48708–6831; tel. 989/894–3000, (Includes MCLAREN BAY REGION–WEST CAMPUS, 3250 East Midland Road, Bay City, Michigan, Zip 48706, tel. 989/667–6750; Monica Baranski, MS, R.N., President) **A**1 3 5 10 13 19 **F**3 4 11 13 15 17 18 20 22 24 26 28 29 30 31 32 34 35 36 38 43 44 45 46 47 48 49 50 54 57 58 59 64 65 68 70 73 74 75 76 78 79 81 82 85 86 87 89 90 92 93 96 97 98 100 102 103 105 107 108 110 111 114 115 119 120 121 123 124 126 129 130 131 132 135 141 143 144 146 147 148 149 154 157 167 **S** McLaren Health Care Corporation, Grand Blanc, MI
Primary Contact: James Carter, Interim Chief Executive Officer
COO: Mitch Southwick, Chief Operating Officer
CFO: Damon Sorensen, Chief Financial Officer
CMO: Jason White, M.D., Chief Medical Officer
CIO: Ronald Strachan, Chief Information Officer
CHR: Carolyn Potter, Chief Human Resources Officer
Web address: www.mclaren.org/bayregion
Control: Other not–for–profit (including NFP Corporation) **Service**: General medical and surgical

Staffed Beds: 352 **Admissions**: 11280 **Census**: 193 **Outpatient Visits**: 271699 **Births**: 483 **Total Expense ($000)**: 310400 **Payroll Expense ($000)**: 123593 **Personnel**: 3160

☐ **MCLAREN BAY SPECIAL CARE (232020)**, 3250 East Midland Road, Suite 1, Zip 48706–2835; tel. 989/667–6851, **A**1 10 **F**1 3 29 30 79 85 87 96 130 148 **S** McLaren Health Care Corporation, Grand Blanc, MI
Primary Contact: Jeffrey Robinson, President and Chief Executive Officer
CMO: Janet Sutton, D.O., Medical Director
CIO: Greg Jacobs, Manager
CHR: Carolyn Potter, Vice President Human Resources
Web address: www.mclaren/bayspecialcare
Control: Other not–for–profit (including NFP Corporation) **Service**: Acute long–term care hospital

Staffed Beds: 26 **Admissions**: 174 **Census**: 11 **Outpatient Visits**: 0 **Births**: 0 **Total Expense ($000)**: 6071 **Payroll Expense ($000)**: 3774 **Personnel**: 62

BIG RAPIDS—Mecosta County

⊞ **COREWELL HEALTH BIG RAPIDS HOSPITAL (230093)**, 605 Oak Street, Zip 49307–2099; tel. 231/796–8691, **A**1 3 10 20 **F**1 3 13 15 16 17 28 29 34 35 40 43 44 45 50 54 57 64 65 67 68 70 75 76 77 79 80 81 87 88 89 90 92 93 96 97 102 107 108 110 115 118 119 126 127 130 131 132 143 144 146 147 148 149 154 156 157 160 164 166 169 **P**6 **S** Corewell Health, Grand Rapids, MI
Primary Contact: Drew H. Dostal, FACHE, Regional Market Leader
CFO: Thomas Khoerl, Vice President Finance
CMO: Christopher Skinner, Chief of Staff
CIO: Patrick Whiteside, Manager Information Services
CHR: Melonie Jackson, Human Resource Business Partner
CNO: Caroline A Ring, Chief Nursing Officer
Web address: https://www.spectrumhealth.org/locations/big-rapids-hospital
Control: Other not–for–profit (including NFP Corporation) **Service**: General medical and surgical

Staffed Beds: 49 **Admissions**: 2170 **Census**: 18 **Outpatient Visits**: 198433 **Births**: 415 **Total Expense ($000)**: 87493 **Payroll Expense ($000)**: 33113 **Personnel**: 422

SPECTRUM HEALTH BIG RAPIDS HOSPITAL See Corewell Health Big Rapids Hospital

Hospitals, U.S. / MICHIGAN

BRIGHTON—Livingston County

★ **ASCENSION BRIGHTON CENTER FOR RECOVERY (230279)**, 12851 Grand River Road, Zip 48116–8506; tel. 810/227–1211, **A**10 **F**4 5 29 30 35 36 38 44 68 75 82 86 87 100 104 130 132 135 146 149 153 154 160 161 164 **S** Ascension Healthcare, Saint Louis, MO
Primary Contact: Barbara Shoup, R.N., Hospital Administrator
CFO: Marie Allard, Finance Manager
CMO: Ismael David Yanga, M.D., Chief Medical Officer
CIO: Frank Sanzone, Manager Information Technology
CHR: Marney Daugherty, Worklife Services Consultant
CNO: Barbara Shoup, R.N., Chief Nursing Officer
Web address: https://healthcare.ascension.org/locations/michigan/midet/brighton-ascension-brighton-center-for-recovery
Control: Church operated, Nongovernment, not–for–profit **Service:** Substance Use Disorder

Staffed Beds: 63 **Admissions:** 1490 **Census:** 47 **Outpatient Visits:** 16991 **Births:** 0 **Total Expense ($000):** 15528 **Payroll Expense ($000):** 7073 **Personnel:** 107

CADILLAC—Wexford County

MUNSON HEALTHCARE CADILLAC HOSPITAL (230081), 400 Hobart Street, Zip 49601–2389; tel. 231/876–7200, **A**1 10 20 **F**3 11 13 15 18 28 29 30 31 34 35 36 38 39 40 43 44 45 48 49 50 51 57 59 60 62 64 65 68 70 74 75 76 77 78 79 81 85 86 87 92 93 97 100 101 102 104 107 108 110 111 115 118 119 127 129 130 131 132 135 144 146 147 148 149 154 156 157 164 165 169 **P**6 8 **S** Munson Healthcare, Traverse City, MI
Primary Contact: Peter Marinoff Jr, Munson Healthcare Cadillac Hospital Community President and Munson Healthcare South Region President
COO: Michael Zdrodowski, Vice President of Operations and Ambulatory Services
CFO: Kristin Ellis, Controller
CMO: Joe Santangelo, M.D., Vice President of Medical Affairs
CIO: Randi Terry, Site Director Management Information Systems
CHR: Kelley Whittington-Geppert, Director Human Resources
CNO: Kathryn Bandfield-Keough, Vice President Patient Care Services
Web address: www.mercyhealthcadillac.com/welcome-cadillac
Control: Other not–for–profit (including NFP Corporation) **Service:** General medical and surgical

Staffed Beds: 49 **Admissions:** 2248 **Census:** 25 **Outpatient Visits:** 172648 **Births:** 308 **Total Expense ($000):** 121468 **Payroll Expense ($000):** 41072 **Personnel:** 464

CARO—Tuscola County

☐ **CARO CENTER (234025)**, 2000 Chambers Road, Zip 48723–9296; tel. 989/673–3191, **A**1 10 **F**29 38 39 75 77 86 87 98 100 103 135 164
Primary Contact: Rose Laskowski, R.N., Director
COO: Rose Laskowski, R.N., Director
CFO: Mary Jo Drzewiecki–Burger, Administrative Manager
CMO: William Clark, M.D., Chief Clinical Affairs
CIO: Michele Wills, Registered Health Information Administrator
CHR: Barbara Frank, Human Resource Specialist
Control: State, Government, Nonfederal **Service:** Psychiatric

Staffed Beds: 100 **Admissions:** 74 **Census:** 96 **Outpatient Visits:** 0 **Births:** 0

★ **MCLAREN CARO REGION (231329)**, 401 North Hooper Street, Zip 48723–1476, Mailing Address: P.O. Box 435, Zip 48723–0435; tel. 989/673–3141, **A**10 18 **F**5 11 15 29 31 32 34 35 40 43 45 59 74 75 77 79 81 87 93 97 100 107 108 110 115 119 121 127 129 133 146 147 148 149 154 160 **S** McLaren Health Care Corporation, Grand Blanc, MI
Primary Contact: Connie L. Koutouzos, R.N., MSN, President and Chief Executive Officer
CFO: Ron Srebinski, Chief Financial Officer
CMO: T Gard Adams, M.D., Chief of Staff
CHR: Allyson Joyce, Vice President Human Resources
CNO: Kelly Whittaker, Vice President Nursing
Web address: https://www.mclaren.org/caro-region/mclaren-caro-region-home
Control: Other not–for–profit (including NFP Corporation) **Service:** General medical and surgical

Staffed Beds: 10 **Admissions:** 231 **Census:** 3 **Outpatient Visits:** 22978 **Births:** 0 **Total Expense ($000):** 19003 **Payroll Expense ($000):** 8710 **Personnel:** 94

CARSON CITY—Montcalm County

UNIVERSITY OF MICHIGAN HEALTH–SPARROW CARSON (230208), 406 East Elm Street, PO Box 879, Zip 48811–9693; tel. 989/584–3131, **A**1 3 10 19 **F**3 15 18 20 30 31 34 35 40 45 46 50 57 59 64 65 70 75 78 79 81 82 85 86 87 93 97 107 108 110 111 115 118 119 126 127 129 130 146 147 148 149 156 **P**6 8 **S** University of Michigan Health, Ann Arbor, MI
Primary Contact: Mark Brisboe, President
CFO: Richard Reid, Vice President Chief Finance Officer
CMO: Robert Seals, D.O., Medical Director
CIO: Richard Terry, Vice President & Chief Information Officer
CHR: Georgette Russell, Vice President of Talent & Organizational Effectiveness
Web address: www.carsoncityhospital.com
Control: Other not–for–profit (including NFP Corporation) **Service:** General medical and surgical

Staffed Beds: 48 **Admissions:** 423 **Census:** 3 **Outpatient Visits:** 128039 **Births:** 0 **Total Expense ($000):** 50222 **Payroll Expense ($000):** 23091 **Personnel:** 253

CASS CITY—Tuscola County

★ ⇧ **HILLS & DALES HEALTHCARE (231316)**, 4675 Hill Street, Zip 48726–1099; tel. 989/872–2121, (Nonreporting) **A**10 18 21 **S** Aspire Rural Health System, Cass City, MI
Primary Contact: Andy Daniels Esq, FACHE, Co–CEO, Aspire Rural Health System
CFO: Kenneth Baranski, Chief Financial Officer
CMO: Donald Robbins, M.D., Jr, Chief Staff
CNO: Jennifer TerBush, Vice President, Patient Services
Web address: https://hdhlth.org/
Control: Other not–for–profit (including NFP Corporation) **Service:** General medical and surgical

Staffed Beds: 25

CHARLEVOIX—Charlevoix County

MUNSON HEALTHCARE CHARLEVOIX HOSPITAL (231322), 14700 Lake Shore Drive, Zip 49720–1999; tel. 231/547–4024, **A**1 10 18 **F**3 11 13 14 15 18 26 28 29 30 31 34 35 40 43 50 55 59 64 65 75 76 77 78 79 81 85 87 93 97 100 104 107 108 110 111 115 116 117 118 119 127 129 130 131 132 133 135 144 146 147 149 154 156 164 169 **P**6 8 **S** Munson Healthcare, Traverse City, MI
Primary Contact: Joanne Schroeder, FACHE, Munson Healthcare Charlevoix Hospital President and Chief Executive Officer
COO: John Singer IV, Chief Operating Officer
CFO: Robert Wilcox, Chief Financial Officer
CMO: James Jeakle, Chief Medical Officer
CIO: David Priest, Director Information Systems
CHR: Patty Fitzgerald, Staff Services
CNO: Bernadette Cole, R.N., Chief Nursing Officer
Web address: www.cah.org
Control: Other not–for–profit (including NFP Corporation) **Service:** General medical and surgical

Staffed Beds: 25 **Admissions:** 608 **Census:** 5 **Outpatient Visits:** 69795 **Births:** 170 **Total Expense ($000):** 72153 **Payroll Expense ($000):** 24224 **Personnel:** 238

CHARLOTTE—Eaton County

UNIVERSITY OF MICHIGAN HEALTH–SPARROW EATON (231327), 321 East Harris Street, Zip 48813–1629; tel. 517/543–1050, **A**1 3 10 18 **F**3 7 15 18 26 28 29 34 35 36 40 45 46 50 53 59 64 65 75 77 79 81 82 85 87 92 93 97 102 107 108 110 115 118 119 124 126 127 129 130 131 143 144 146 147 149 154 156 **P**6 **S** University of Michigan Health, Ann Arbor, MI
Primary Contact: Linda Reetz, R.N., President
CFO: Kim Capps, Chief Financial Officer
CMO: Hugh Lindsey, M.D., Chief Medical Officer
CIO: Kevin Neugent, Chief Information Officer
CHR: Mandy Rood, Vice President Human Resources
CNO: Maureen Hillary, Chief Nursing Officer
Web address: www.hgbhealth.com
Control: Other not–for–profit (including NFP Corporation) **Service:** General medical and surgical

Staffed Beds: 25 **Admissions:** 881 **Census:** 8 **Outpatient Visits:** 194131 **Births:** 0 **Total Expense ($000):** 64221 **Payroll Expense ($000):** 31518 **Personnel:** 386

Hospital, Medicare Provider Number, Address, Telephone, Approval, Facility, and Physician Codes, Health Care System

★ American Hospital Association (AHA) membership
☐ The Joint Commission accreditation
○ Healthcare Facilities Accreditation Program
◇ DNV Healthcare Inc. accreditation
⇧ Center for Improvement in Healthcare Quality Accreditation
△ Commission on Accreditation of Rehabilitation Facilities (CARF) accreditation

Hospitals, U.S. / MICHIGAN

CHELSEA—Washtenaw County

✠ **CHELSEA HOSPITAL (230259)**, 775 South Main Street, Zip 48118–1383; tel. 734/593–6000, **A**1 2 3 5 10 **F**3 5 8 11 12 15 18 29 30 31 34 35 40 45 50 51 56 57 59 64 65 70 74 75 77 78 79 81 82 84 85 86 87 90 91 92 93 97 98 100 101 102 103 104 107 110 111 114 115 119 120 121 126 130 131 132 134 135 144 146 148 149 154 156 167 **P**6 **S** Trinity Health, Livonia, MI
Primary Contact: Ben Miles, President
CFO: Barb Fielder, Vice President Finance
CMO: Randall T Forsch, M.D., M.P.H., Chief Medical Officer
CHR: Jeremy Stephens, Vice President and Chief Human Resources Officer
Web address: https://www.stjoeshealth.org/location/chelsea-hospital
Control: Church operated, Nongovernment, not–for–profit **Service**: General medical and surgical

Staffed Beds: 120 Admissions: 4549 Census: 67 Outpatient Visits: 162758 Births: 0 Total Expense ($000): 189749 Payroll Expense ($000): 78492 Personnel: 895

ST. JOSEPH MERCY CHELSEA See Chelsea Hospital

CLARE—Clare County

✠ **MYMICHIGAN MEDICAL CENTER CLARE (230180)**, 703 North McEwan Street, Zip 48617–1440; tel. 989/802–5000, **A**1 10 **F**3 11 15 18 20 28 29 30 34 35 40 43 45 50 53 57 58 59 61 64 75 77 79 80 81 85 86 87 93 97 107 108 110 111 115 118 119 127 129 130 135 144 146 148 154 156 157 160 **S** MyMichigan Health, Midland, MI
Primary Contact: Marita Hattem–Schiffman, FACHE, Regional President
CFO: Jeff Provenzano, Vice President and Chief Financial Officer
CMO: David Bremer, D.O., Chief of Staff
CIO: Michael Larson, Vice President Chief Information Officer
CNO: Glenn King, R.N., MSN, Vice President, Chief Nursing Officer
Web address: www.midmichigan.org
Control: Other not–for–profit (including NFP Corporation) **Service**: General medical and surgical

Staffed Beds: 49 Admissions: 737 Census: 6 Outpatient Visits: 134343 Births: 0 Total Expense ($000): 56576 Payroll Expense ($000): 18344 Personnel: 291

MYMICHIGAN MEDICAL CENTER–CLARE See Mymichigan Medical Center Clare

CLINTON TOWNSHIP—Macomb County

✠ **HENRY FORD MACOMB HOSPITAL (230047)**, 15855 19 Mile Road, Zip 48038–6324; tel. 586/263–2300, (Includes HENRY FORD MACOMB HOSPITAL – MOUNT CLEMENS CAMPUS, 215 North Avenue, Mount Clemens, Michigan, Zip 48043, tel. 586/466–9300; ST. JOSEPH'S MERCY HOSPITAL–WEST, 15855 19 Mile Road, Clinton Township, Michigan, Zip 48038, tel. 586/263–2707; ST. JOSEPH'S MERCY–NORTH, 80650 North Van Dyke, Romeo, Michigan, Zip 48065, tel. 810/798–3551) **A**1 2 3 5 10 13 **F**3 5 7 8 11 12 13 15 17 18 20 22 24 26 28 29 30 31 32 34 35 36 38 40 41 43 44 45 46 47 49 50 51 54 56 57 58 59 60 61 62 63 64 65 66 68 69 70 71 73 74 75 76 77 78 79 81 82 83 84 85 86 87 89 90 92 93 94 95 96 97 98 100 101 102 103 107 108 110 111 114 115 116 117 118 119 120 121 123 124 126 130 131 132 134 135 144 146 147 148 149 150 152 154 156 157 167 169 **P**6 **S** Henry Ford Health, Detroit, MI
Primary Contact: Shanna Johnson, FACHE, Interim President
COO: Gary Beaulac, Chief Operating Officer
CFO: Terry Goodbalian, Vice President Finance and Chief Financial Officer
CMO: Charles Kelly, D.O., Vice President Medical Affairs and Chief Medical Officer
CHR: Joel Gibson, Vice President Human Resources
Web address: www.henryfordmacomb.com
Control: Other not–for–profit (including NFP Corporation) **Service**: General medical and surgical

Staffed Beds: 345 Admissions: 18629 Census: 259 Outpatient Visits: 607554 Births: 1408 Total Expense ($000): 619873 Payroll Expense ($000): 222544 Personnel: 2895

ST JOSEPH'S MERCY HOSPITAL See St. Joseph's Mercy Hospital–West

COLDWATER—Branch County

✠ **PROMEDICA COLDWATER REGIONAL HOSPITAL (230022)**, 274 East Chicago Street, Zip 49036–2041; tel. 517/279–5400, **A**1 10 13 19 **F**3 11 15 18 28 29 31 35 40 43 45 46 48 50 64 70 76 77 78 79 81 82 87 92 93 94 97 98 100 104 107 108 110 111 115 118 119 127 129 130 131 132 134 135 146 147 148 149 154 162 164 167 **P**6 8 **S** ProMedica Health System, Toledo, OH
Primary Contact: Dan Schwanke, FACHE, Interim President
COO: Mary R Rose, R.N., Chief Clinical Officer
CFO: Amy Crouch, Chief Financial Officer
CMO: Joudat Daoud, M.D., Chief of Staff
CIO: Joel Lederman, Director Information Systems
CHR: Amy Jensen, Director Human Resources
CNO: Mary Rose, Chief Nursing Officer
Web address: https://www.promedica.org/location/promedica-coldwater-regional-hospital?utm_campaign=reputation-management&utm_segment=gmb_listing-link&utm_source=google&utm_medium=organic-search
Control: Other not–for–profit (including NFP Corporation) **Service**: General medical and surgical

Staffed Beds: 62 Admissions: 2614 Census: 31 Outpatient Visits: 119614 Births: 228 Total Expense ($000): 96242 Payroll Expense ($000): 31489 Personnel: 351

COMMERCE TOWNSHIP—Oakland County

✠ **DMC HURON VALLEY–SINAI HOSPITAL (230277)**, 1 William Carls Drive, Zip 48382–2201; tel. 248/937–3300, (Nonreporting) **A**1 3 5 10 19 **S** TENET Healthcare Corporation, Dallas, TX
Primary Contact: Lance Beus, Chief Executive Officer
CFO: William Lantzy, Chief Financial Officer
CHR: Nicole Williams, Director of Human Resources Operations
CNO: Lori Stallings–Sicard, R.N., Chief Nursing Officer
Web address: www.hvsh.org
Control: Corporation, Investor–owned (for–profit) **Service**: General medical and surgical

Staffed Beds: 156

DEARBORN—Wayne County

✠ **COREWELL HEALTH DEARBORN HOSPITAL (230020)**, 18101 Oakwood Boulevard, Zip 48124–4089; tel. 313/593–7000, **A**1 2 3 5 10 19 **F**3 11 12 13 15 17 18 20 22 24 26 28 29 30 31 32 34 35 37 38 39 40 41 43 44 45 46 47 49 50 54 55 56 57 58 59 60 61 64 65 68 70 72 74 75 76 77 78 79 80 81 82 84 85 86 87 89 92 93 96 97 100 102 107 108 110 111 114 115 117 118 119 120 121 123 124 126 129 130 131 132 146 147 149 154 167 **P**6 **S** Corewell Health, Grand Rapids, MI
Primary Contact: Debra Guido–Allen, R.N., FACHE, President
COO: Carolyn Wilson, Chief Operating Officer
CFO: Timothy Jodway, Chief Financial Administrator
CMO: Paolo G Marciano, M.D., Chief Medical Officer
CIO: Subra Sripada, Executive Vice President, Chief Transformation Officer and Chief Information Officer
CHR: Sherry Huffman, Administrator Human Resources
CNO: Mary Ellen Kochis, MSN, R.N., Administrator Nursing Operations
Web address: https://www.beaumont.org/locations/beaumont-hospital-dearborn
Control: Other not–for–profit (including NFP Corporation) **Service**: General medical and surgical

Staffed Beds: 486 Admissions: 22673 Census: 355 Outpatient Visits: 192084 Births: 4412 Total Expense ($000): 655376 Payroll Expense ($000): 237041 Personnel: 3095

COREWELL HEALTH'S BEAUMONT HOSPITAL, DEARBORN See Corewell Health Dearborn Hospital

DECKERVILLE—Sanilac County

⇧ **DECKERVILLE COMMUNITY HOSPITAL (231311)**, 3559 Pine Street, Zip 48427–7703, Mailing Address: P.O. Box 126, Zip 48427–0126; tel. 810/376–2835, (Nonreporting) **A**10 18 21 **S** Aspire Rural Health System, Cass City, MI
Primary Contact: Angela McConnachie, MSN, R.N., Co–Chief Executive Officer, Aspire Rural Health System
CFO: Kim Gentner, Chief Financial Officer
CMO: Josh White, Chief Medical Officer
Web address: www.deckervillehosp.org
Control: Other not–for–profit (including NFP Corporation) **Service**: General medical and surgical

Staffed Beds: 15

Hospitals, U.S. / MICHIGAN

DETROIT—Wayne County

✚ **ASCENSION ST. JOHN HOSPITAL (230165)**, 22101 Moross Road, Zip 48236–2148; tel. 313/343–4000, **A**1 2 3 5 10 19 **F**3 8 9 11 12 13 15 17 18 19 20 22 24 26 28 29 30 31 32 34 35 36 37 38 39 40 41 42 43 44 45 46 47 48 49 50 51 54 55 56 57 58 59 60 61 63 64 65 66 67 68 70 72 73 74 75 76 77 78 79 81 82 84 85 86 87 88 89 90 91 92 93 94 95 96 97 98 100 101 102 107 108 110 111 114 115 118 119 120 121 123 124 126 130 131 132 134 135 138 141 144 146 147 148 149 150 154 156 157 160 162 164 167 169 **S** Ascension Healthcare, Saint Louis, MO
Primary Contact: Kevin Grady, M.D., East Region President
CIO: Ralph Tenney, Chief Information Officer
CHR: Joanne E Tuscany, Director Human Resources
Web address: https://healthcare.ascension.org/Locations/Michigan/MIDET/Detroit-Ascension-St-John-Hospital
Control: Church operated, Nongovernment, not–for–profit **Service:** General medical and surgical

Staffed Beds: 562 **Admissions:** 27967 **Census:** 410 **Outpatient Visits:** 956946 **Births:** 2869 **Total Expense ($000):** 1057745 **Payroll Expense ($000):** 340277 **Personnel:** 2930

☐ **BCA STONECREST CENTER (234038)**, 15000 Gratiot Avenue, Zip 48205–1973; tel. 313/245–0600, **A**1 10 **F**98 99 100 101 103 130 149 164 **S** Acadia Healthcare Company, Inc., Franklin, TN
Primary Contact: Steve Savage, Chief Executive Officer
Web address: www.stonecrestcenter.com
Control: Corporation, Investor–owned (for–profit) **Service:** Psychiatric

Staffed Beds: 182 **Admissions:** 3677 **Census:** 171 **Outpatient Visits:** 0 **Births:** 0 **Total Expense ($000):** 45628 **Payroll Expense ($000):** 22023 **Personnel:** 372

✚ △ **DMC CHILDREN'S HOSPITAL OF MICHIGAN (233300)**, 3901 Beaubien Street, Zip 48201–2119; tel. 313/745–5852, **A**1 3 5 7 10 **F**3 7 8 11 16 17 18 19 20 21 22 23 24 25 26 27 29 30 31 32 34 35 37 38 39 40 41 42 43 44 45 46 48 49 50 54 55 57 58 59 60 61 64 65 66 72 74 75 76 78 79 80 81 82 84 85 86 87 88 89 90 91 93 96 97 100 107 108 111 114 115 119 120 121 123 124 126 129 130 131 132 136 137 138 139 141 146 148 149 154 156 167 **S** TENET Healthcare Corporation, Dallas, TX
Primary Contact: Archie Drake, Chief Executive Officer
COO: Heath M Roberts, Chief Operating Officer
CFO: Lisa Hutchings, Chief Financial Officer
CMO: Rudolph Valentini, M.D., Chief Medical Officer
CHR: Jonita Edwards, Director Human Resources
CNO: Brenda VanWallaghen, Interim Chief Nursing Officer
Web address: www.chmkids.org
Control: Corporation, Investor–owned (for–profit) **Service:** Children's general medical and surgical

Staffed Beds: 227 **Admissions:** 8608 **Census:** 128 **Outpatient Visits:** 266191 **Births:** 0 **Total Expense ($000):** 383542 **Payroll Expense ($000):** 122214 **Personnel:** 1838

✚ **DMC DETROIT RECEIVING HOSPITAL & UNIVERSITY HEALTH CENTER (230273)**, 4201 Saint Antoine Street, Zip 48201–2153; tel. 313/745–3000, **A**1 3 5 10 19 **F**3 16 18 29 30 34 35 38 39 40 41 43 44 49 50 56 57 58 59 60 61 64 65 66 70 74 75 77 79 81 82 84 86 87 93 97 98 100 102 104 107 114 115 119 129 130 131 135 144 146 148 149 150 154 166 169 **S** TENET Healthcare Corporation, Dallas, TX
Primary Contact: Joshua Hester, Chief Executive Officer
COO: Tina Wood, Chief Operations Officer
CMO: Karen Carbone, M.D., Chief Medical Officer
CIO: Michael LeRoy, Senior Vice President and Chief Information Officer
Web address: www.dmc.org
Control: Corporation, Investor–owned (for–profit) **Service:** General medical and surgical

Staffed Beds: 584 **Admissions:** 10307 **Census:** 201 **Outpatient Visits:** 107701 **Births:** 0 **Total Expense ($000):** 281127 **Payroll Expense ($000):** 93552

✚ **DMC HARPER UNIVERSITY HOSPITAL (230104)**, 3990 John 'R' Street, Zip 48201–2018; tel. 313/745–8040, (Includes DMC HUTZEL WOMEN'S HOSPITAL, 3980 John R Street, Detroit, Michigan, Zip 48201, tel. 313/745–7555; Brittany Lavis, Chief Executive Officer) **A**1 3 5 10 19 **F**12 13 17 22 24 26 29 30 34 40 44 45 46 49 51 57 58 59 60 68 70 72 74 75 76 77 79 81 82 84 85 87 93 107 111 115 116 117 119 126 129 130 146 149 169 **S** TENET Healthcare Corporation, Dallas, TX
Primary Contact: Joshua Hester, Chief Executive Officer
COO: Tina Wood, Chief Operating Officer
CMO: Karen Carbone, M.D., Chief Medical Officer
CIO: Michael LeRoy, Senior Vice President and Chief Information Officer
CNO: Christine Bowen, R.N., Chief Nursing Officer
Web address: www.harperhospital.org
Control: Corporation, Investor–owned (for–profit) **Service:** General medical and surgical

Staffed Beds: 224 **Admissions:** 11163 **Census:** 162 **Outpatient Visits:** 115026 **Births:** 2921 **Total Expense ($000):** 382042 **Payroll Expense ($000):** 114421

✚ △ **DMC REHABILITATION INSTITUTE OF MICHIGAN (233027)**, 261 Mack Avenue, Zip 48201–2495; tel. 313/745–1203, (Nonreporting) **A**1 3 5 7 10 **S** TENET Healthcare Corporation, Dallas, TX
Primary Contact: Christina Michajyszyn, FACHE, Chief Executive Officer
CFO: Dan Babb, Chief Financial Officer
CMO: Ali Bitar, M.D., Vice President Medical Affairs
CHR: Paul Sturgis, Director Human Resources
Web address: www.rimrehab.org
Control: Corporation, Investor–owned (for–profit) **Service:** Rehabilitation

Staffed Beds: 69

✚ **DMC SINAI–GRACE HOSPITAL (230024)**, 6071 West Outer Drive, Zip 48235–2679; tel. 313/966–3300, (Nonreporting) **A**1 3 5 10 12 13 19 **S** TENET Healthcare Corporation, Dallas, TX
Primary Contact: Gary Purushotham, Chief Executive Officer
CFO: Jeffery Wright, Chief Financial Officer
CHR: Joi Little, Chief Human Resources Officer
CNO: Dixie Lee Aune, Chief Nursing Officer
Web address: www.sinaigrace.org
Control: Corporation, Investor–owned (for–profit) **Service:** General medical and surgical

Staffed Beds: 424

✚ **HENRY FORD HOSPITAL (230053)**, 2799 West Grand Boulevard, Zip 48202–2608; tel. 313/916–2600, **A**1 2 3 5 8 10 19 **F**3 4 5 8 9 11 12 13 15 17 18 19 20 22 24 26 28 29 30 31 32 33 34 35 36 37 38 39 40 41 42 43 44 45 46 47 48 49 50 51 52 54 55 56 58 59 60 61 62 63 64 65 66 68 69 70 71 72 73 74 75 76 77 78 79 80 81 82 84 85 86 87 93 97 98 99 100 101 102 103 104 105 106 107 108 110 111 112 113 114 115 116 117 118 119 120 121 122 124 126 129 130 131 132 134 135 136 137 138 139 140 141 142 143 144 146 147 148 149 150 152 153 154 156 160 167 **P**6 **S** Henry Ford Health, Detroit, MI
Primary Contact: Steven Kalkanis, M.D., Chief Executive Officer
CFO: Joseph Schmitt III, Senior Vice President Finance and Chief Financial Officer
CIO: Mary Alice Annecharico, System Vice President and Chief Information Officer
CHR: Antonina Ramsey, Senior Vice President and Chief Human Resource Officer
CNO: Gwen Gnam, R.N., MSN, Chief Nursing Officer
Web address: www.henryfordhealth.org
Control: Other not–for–profit (including NFP Corporation) **Service:** General medical and surgical

Staffed Beds: 769 **Admissions:** 31791 **Census:** 533 **Outpatient Visits:** 3419144 **Births:** 2326 **Total Expense ($000):** 2925515 **Payroll Expense ($000):** 1382770 **Personnel:** 10301

HUTZEL WOMEN'S HOSPITAL See Dmc Hutzel Women's Hospital

✚ △ **JOHN D. DINGELL DEPARTMENT OF VETERANS AFFAIRS MEDICAL CENTER**, 4646 John 'R' Street, Zip 48201–1932; tel. 313/576–1000, (Nonreporting) **A**1 2 3 5 7 **S** Department of Veterans Affairs, Washington, DC
Primary Contact: Chris Cauley, FACHE, Interim Medical Center Director
COO: Annette Walker, Associate Director
CMO: Scott Gruber, M.D., Chief of Staff
CIO: Jonathan Small, Chief Operations Information and Technology
CHR: Kathleen Osinski, Chief Human Resources Service
Web address: www.detroit.va.gov/
Control: Veterans Affairs, Government, federal **Service:** General medical and surgical

Staffed Beds: 157

Hospital, Medicare Provider Number, Address, Telephone, Approval, Facility, and Physician Codes, Health Care System

★ American Hospital Association (AHA) membership ○ Healthcare Facilities Accreditation Program ⇑ Center for Improvement in Healthcare Quality Accreditation
☐ The Joint Commission accreditation ◇ DNV Healthcare Inc. accreditation △ Commission on Accreditation of Rehabilitation Facilities (CARF) accreditation

Hospitals, U.S. / MICHIGAN

☐ **KARMANOS CANCER CENTER (230297)**, 4100 John 'R' Street, Zip 48201-2013; tel. 313/576-8670, **A**1 3 5 10 **F**3 14 15 29 30 31 34 35 36 39 44 45 46 47 48 49 50 54 55 57 58 59 63 64 65 68 74 75 77 78 79 80 81 82 83 84 85 86 87 107 108 109 110 111 114 115 116 117 118 119 120 121 123 124 126 130 132 135 136 146 147 148 149 154 157 167 **P**4 5
Primary Contact: Brian Gamble, President
CMO: George Yoo, M.D., Chief Medical Officer
CIO: Scott McCarter, Chief Information Officer
CHR: David Jansen, Vice President Human Resources
Web address: www.karmanos.org
Control: Other not-for-profit (including NFP Corporation) **Service:** Cancer

Staffed Beds: 87 **Admissions:** 2242 **Census:** 57 **Outpatient Visits:** 271227 **Births:** 0 **Total Expense ($000):** 426633 **Payroll Expense ($000):** 92012 **Personnel:** 1030

STONECREST CENTER See Bca Stonecrest Center

DOWAGIAC—Cass County

⊞ **ASCENSION BORGESS-LEE HOSPITAL (231315)**, 420 West High Street, Zip 49047-1943; tel. 269/782-8681, **A**1 10 18 **F**3 11 15 18 28 29 30 34 35 40 41 50 54 59 64 65 68 70 75 77 78 79 81 85 86 87 93 97 100 104 107 108 110 114 119 127 128 130 132 133 135 146 148 149 154 **S** Ascension Healthcare, Saint Louis, MO
Primary Contact: Dean Kindler, M.D., Regional President and Chief Executive Officer
CIO: James Keller, Chief Information Officer
Web address: https://healthcare.ascension.org/locations/michigan/mikal/dowagiac-ascension-borgess-lee-hospital
Control: Church operated, Nongovernment, not-for-profit **Service:** General medical and surgical

Staffed Beds: 25 **Admissions:** 451 **Census:** 6 **Outpatient Visits:** 32124 **Births:** 0 **Total Expense ($000):** 21798 **Payroll Expense ($000):** 8430 **Personnel:** 55

EAST CHINA—St. Clair County

⊞ **ASCENSION RIVER DISTRICT HOSPITAL (230241)**, 4100 River Road, Zip 48054-2909; tel. 810/329-7111, **A**1 3 10 **F**3 7 11 13 15 18 29 30 35 36 40 43 44 45 49 50 60 64 65 68 70 75 77 79 81 82 85 87 92 93 107 108 110 115 119 130 141 146 147 149 154 156 164 167 **S** Ascension Healthcare, Saint Louis, MO
Primary Contact: Kevin Grady, M.D., East Region President
CMO: H Lee Bacheldor, D.O., Chief Medical Officer
CHR: Dawn Beindit, Labor Relations Partner
Web address: https://healthcare.ascension.org/Locations/Michigan/MIDET/East-China-Township-Ascension-River-District-Hospital
Control: Church operated, Nongovernment, not-for-profit **Service:** General medical and surgical

Staffed Beds: 12 **Admissions:** 624 **Census:** 4 **Outpatient Visits:** 64051 **Total Expense ($000):** 38187 **Payroll Expense ($000):** 17367 **Personnel:** 134

EATON RAPIDS—Eaton County

★ ⇧ **EATON RAPIDS MEDICAL CENTER (231324)**, 1500 South Main Street, Zip 48827-1952, Mailing Address: P.O. Box 130, Zip 48827-0130; tel. 517/663-2671, **A**10 18 21 **F**3 11 14 15 18 28 29 34 35 40 41 43 45 50 57 59 64 65 66 68 75 77 81 85 86 87 91 93 96 97 107 110 115 119 126 127 129 131 133 146 148 149 154 157 167 **P**5 6
Primary Contact: Timothy Johnson, President and Chief Executive Officer
CFO: Shari Glynn, Vice President Finance and Chief Financial Officer
CMO: Ashok K Gupta, M.D., Chief of Staff
CIO: Mark Rodge, Director Information Systems
CHR: Laurie Field, Director Human Resources
Web address: www.eatonrapidsmedicalcenter.org
Control: Other not-for-profit (including NFP Corporation) **Service:** General medical and surgical

Staffed Beds: 20 **Admissions:** 687 **Census:** 4 **Outpatient Visits:** 58700 **Births:** 0 **Total Expense ($000):** 37232 **Payroll Expense ($000):** 15252 **Personnel:** 211

ESCANABA—Delta County

⊞ **OSF ST. FRANCIS HOSPITAL AND MEDICAL GROUP (231337)**, 3401 Ludington Street, Zip 49829-1377; tel. 906/399-1741, **A**1 10 18 **F**3 11 13 15 18 28 29 30 31 34 35 40 43 44 45 53 57 59 62 63 64 65 66 70 75 76 77 78 79 81 82 84 85 86 87 92 93 96 97 101 102 104 107 108 110 111 115 117 119 127 129 130 131 132 133 144 146 147 148 149 154 160 167 169 **S** OSF Healthcare, Peoria, IL
Primary Contact: Kelly Jefferson, MSN, President
COO: Kelly Jefferson, MSN, Vice President, Operations
CFO: Fred Wagner, Chief Financial Officer
CMO: Mark Povich, D.O., Medical Director
CIO: Mark Irving, Manager Management Information Systems
CHR: Elizabeth Zorza, Assistant Administrator
CNO: Joy Hopkins, Vice President Patient Care Services
Web address: www.osfstfrancis.org
Control: Church operated, Nongovernment, not-for-profit **Service:** General medical and surgical

Staffed Beds: 25 **Admissions:** 1531 **Census:** 15 **Outpatient Visits:** 175633 **Births:** 289 **Total Expense ($000):** 104395 **Payroll Expense ($000):** 33190 **Personnel:** 410

FARMINGTON HILLS—Oakland County

⊞ **COREWELL HEALTH FARMINGTON HILLS HOSPITAL (230151)**, 28050 Grand River Avenue, Zip 48336-5933; tel. 248/471-8000, **A**1 2 3 5 10 12 13 19 **F**3 9 11 13 15 18 20 22 28 29 30 31 34 35 36 38 39 40 41 42 43 44 45 46 47 48 49 50 51 54 56 57 58 59 60 61 64 65 68 70 74 75 76 77 78 79 80 81 82 84 85 86 87 90 92 93 96 97 98 100 102 103 107 110 111 114 115 118 119 120 121 123 126 130 131 132 145 146 147 148 149 154 160 167 **P**6 **S** Corewell Health, Grand Rapids, MI
Primary Contact: Derk F. Pronger, President
COO: Carolyn Wilson, R.N., Chief Operating Officer
CFO: Barbara Hrit, Controller
CMO: Michael Rebock, Chief Medical Officer
CIO: Subra Sripada, Executive Vice President, Chief Transportation Officer and Chief Information Officer
CHR: Dalph Watson, Director of Human Resources
CNO: Kim Guesman, R.N., Chief Nursing Officer
Web address: https://www.beaumont.org/locations/beaumont-hospital-farmington-hills
Control: Other not-for-profit (including NFP Corporation) **Service:** General medical and surgical

Staffed Beds: 305 **Admissions:** 11418 **Census:** 166 **Outpatient Visits:** 195424 **Births:** 594 **Total Expense ($000):** 429813 **Payroll Expense ($000):** 128386 **Personnel:** 1821

COREWELL HEALTH'S BEAUMONT HOSPITAL, FARMINGTON HILLS See Corewell Health Farmington Hills Hospital

FERNDALE—Oakland County

⊞ **HENRY FORD KINGSWOOD HOSPITAL (234011)**, 10300 West Eight Mile Road, Zip 48220-2100; tel. 248/398-3200, **A**1 10 **F**34 44 50 58 59 68 75 86 87 97 98 99 101 135 149 164 **P**6 **S** Henry Ford Health, Detroit, MI
Primary Contact: Cathrine Frank, M.D., Chairperson
CMO: Robert Lagrou, D.O., Medical Director
CNO: Cheryl Taylor, R.N., Director of Nursing
Web address: www.henryford.com
Control: Other not-for-profit (including NFP Corporation) **Service:** Psychiatric

Staffed Beds: 98 **Admissions:** 2539 **Census:** 72 **Outpatient Visits:** 0 **Births:** 0 **Total Expense ($000):** 28080 **Payroll Expense ($000):** 18658 **Personnel:** 246

FLINT—Genesee County

⊞ **HURLEY MEDICAL CENTER (230132)**, 1 Hurley Plaza, Zip 48503-5993; tel. 810/262-9000, (Includes HURLEY CHILDREN'S HOSPITAL, 1 Hurley Plaza, Flint, Michigan, Zip 48503-5902, tel. 313/745-7555) **A**1 3 5 8 10 **F**3 5 11 12 13 15 16 17 18 19 20 22 26 28 29 30 31 32 35 39 40 41 43 45 46 49 50 52 54 55 56 57 58 59 61 64 66 70 72 74 75 76 77 78 79 80 81 82 84 85 86 87 88 89 90 93 96 97 98 100 101 102 104 107 108 110 111 114 115 118 119 120 121 123 124 126 129 130 131 132 135 141 143 144 146 147 148 154 156 160 167 169 **P**6
Primary Contact: Melany Gavulic, R.N., President & Chief Executive Officer
COO: Melany Gavulic, R.N., Senior Vice President Operations & COO
CFO: Keith David Poniers, Vice President and Chief Financial Officer
CMO: Michael Jaggi, D.O., Vice President and Chief Medical Officer
CIO: Gary Townsend, Chief Information Officer
CHR: Beth Brophy, Interim VP for Human Resources
CNO: Teresa Bourque, Sr. Administrator for Nursing/Chief Nurse
Web address: www.hurleymc.org
Control: City, Government, Nonfederal **Service:** General medical and surgical

Staffed Beds: 418 **Admissions:** 15559 **Census:** 292 **Outpatient Visits:** 450568 **Births:** 2213 **Total Expense ($000):** 497036 **Payroll Expense ($000):** 179561 **Personnel:** 2188

Hospitals, U.S. / MICHIGAN

☐ **MCLAREN FLINT (230141)**, 401 South Ballenger Highway, Zip 48532–3685; tel. 810/342–2000, **A**1 3 5 8 10 19 **F**3 8 11 12 13 15 17 18 20 22 24 26 28 29 30 31 34 35 36 37 38 39 40 42 43 44 45 46 47 48 49 50 54 55 56 57 58 59 60 61 64 66 68 70 74 75 76 77 78 79 81 82 85 86 87 90 91 93 95 96 97 98 100 101 102 105 107 108 110 111 114 115 118 119 120 121 122 123 124 126 130 131 132 135 141 144 145 146 147 148 149 154 164 167 **S** McLaren Health Care Corporation, Grand Blanc, MI
Primary Contact: Chris Candela, President and Chief Executive Officer
COO: Brent Wheeler, Vice President of Operations
CFO: Fred Korte, Chief Financial Officer
CMO: Binesh Patel, M.D., Chief Medical Officer
CIO: Ronald Strachan, Chief Information Officer
CHR: Rachelle Hulett, Vice President Human Resources
CNO: James Williams, Vice President and Chief Nursing Officer
Web address: www.mclaren.org/flint
Control: Other not–for–profit (including NFP Corporation) **Service**: General medical and surgical

Staffed Beds: 349 **Admissions**: 15045 **Census**: 231 **Outpatient Visits**: 260279 **Births**: 269 **Total Expense ($000)**: 470999 **Payroll Expense ($000)**: 203691 **Personnel**: 2090

⊞ **SELECT SPECIALTY HOSPITAL – FLINT (232012)**, 401 South Ballenger Highway, 5th Floor Central, Zip 48532–3638; tel. 810/342–4545, (Nonreporting) **A**1 10 **S** Select Medical Corporation, Mechanicsburg, PA
Primary Contact: Christina DeBlouw, R.N., Chief Executive Officer
CMO: Jitendra P. Katneni, M.D., Medical Director
CHR: Gayle Barthel, Coordinator Human Resources
CNO: Kathleen Gallardo, Chief Nursing Officer
Web address: www.selectspecialtyhospitals.com/company/locations/flint.aspx
Control: Corporation, Investor–owned (for–profit) **Service**: Acute long–term care hospital

Staffed Beds: 26

SELECT SPECIALTY HOSPITAL–FLINT See Select Specialty Hospital – Flint

FRANKFORT—Benzie County

★ **MUNSON HEALTHCARE PAUL OLIVER MEMORIAL HOSPITAL (231300)**, 224 Park Avenue, Zip 49635–9658; tel. 231/352–2200, (Total facility includes 35 beds in nursing home–type unit) **A**10 18 **F**2 6 11 15 29 30 34 35 38 40 43 44 45 50 53 56 57 59 60 62 65 68 75 77 79 81 86 87 93 100 101 102 104 107 110 111 115 119 127 130 131 132 133 135 143 146 149 154 156 157 164 165 **P**6 8 **S** Munson Healthcare, Traverse City, MI
Primary Contact: Kelly Tomaszewski, R.N., MSN, President and Chief Executive Officer Manistee and Paul Oliver
CMO: George Ryckman, D.O., Chief of Staff
CHR: Julie Banktson, Manager Human Resources
Web address: https://www.munsonhealthcare.org/paul-oliver-memorial-hospital/paul-oliver-home
Control: Other not–for–profit (including NFP Corporation) **Service**: General medical and surgical

Staffed Beds: 43 **Admissions**: 70 **Census**: 23 **Outpatient Visits**: 47109 **Births**: 0 **Total Expense ($000)**: 24612 **Payroll Expense ($000)**: 11003 **Personnel**: 187

PAUL OLIVER MEMORIAL HOSPITAL See Munson Healthcare Paul Oliver Memorial Hospital

FREMONT—Newaygo County

⊞ **COREWELL HEALTH GERBER HOSPITAL (231338)**, 212 South Sullivan Avenue, Zip 49412–1548; tel. 231/924–3300, **A**1 2 3 5 10 18 **F**3 11 13 15 28 29 30 31 32 34 35 36 40 43 45 50 53 59 64 70 75 76 77 78 79 81 86 87 93 96 107 108 110 111 115 119 126 127 129 130 131 132 135 146 147 156 **S** Corewell Health, Grand Rapids, MI
COO: Shelly Johnson, Chief Operating Officer
CFO: John Sella, Controller
CMO: Jordan Sall, Chief of Staff
CIO: Jeremy Vronko, Manager Information Services
CHR: Jill Vasquez, Senior Business Partner
Web address: www.spectrumhealth.org
Control: Other not–for–profit (including NFP Corporation) **Service**: General medical and surgical

Staffed Beds: 25 **Admissions**: 1736 **Census**: 13 **Outpatient Visits**: 213874 **Births**: 439 **Total Expense ($000)**: 106564 **Payroll Expense ($000)**: 36911 **Personnel**: 447

SPECTRUM HEALTH GERBER MEMORIAL See Corewell Health Gerber Hospital

GARDEN CITY—Wayne County

★ ○ **GARDEN CITY HOSPITAL (230244)**, 6245 Inkster Road, Zip 48135–4001; tel. 734/421–3300, (Nonreporting) **A**3 5 10 11 12 13 **S** Prime Healthcare, Ontario, CA
Primary Contact: Saju George, Regional Chief Executive Officer – Prime Healthcare Michigan Market
CFO: Gina Butcher, Chief Financial Officer
CMO: H. Rex Reuttinger, D.O., Chief Medical Officer, Administration
CIO: Randall Sanborn, Director Information Systems
CHR: Josie Ciccone, Director, Human Resources
Web address: www.gch.org
Control: Corporation, Investor–owned (for–profit) **Service**: General medical and surgical

Staffed Beds: 190

GAYLORD—Otsego County

⊞ **MUNSON HEALTHCARE OTSEGO MEMORIAL HOSPITAL (230133)**, 825 North Center Avenue, Zip 49735–1592; tel. 989/731–2100, (Total facility includes 34 beds in nursing home–type unit) **A**1 10 20 **F**3 11 13 15 28 29 31 32 34 35 36 38 39 40 43 44 45 46 50 51 54 56 57 59 62 64 65 68 70 75 76 77 78 79 81 82 85 86 87 93 96 97 101 102 107 108 110 111 115 118 119 124 126 127 128 130 131 132 134 135 144 146 147 148 149 154 156 157 169 **P**6 8 **S** Munson Healthcare, Traverse City, MI
Primary Contact: Robert Richardson, Interim President and Chief Executive Officer
COO: James Flickema, Vice President Market Development
CFO: Robert Courtois, Vice President Finance
CMO: Kevin Smith, D.O., Chief of Staff
CIO: Timothy Hella, Chief Information Officer
CHR: Terra Deming, Director Human Resources
CNO: Diane Fisher, R.N., VP, Patient Care Services
Web address: www.myomh.org
Control: Other not–for–profit (including NFP Corporation) **Service**: General medical and surgical

Staffed Beds: 80 **Admissions**: 1538 **Census**: 40 **Outpatient Visits**: 116976 **Births**: 327 **Total Expense ($000)**: 112898 **Payroll Expense ($000)**: 43537 **Personnel**: 393

GLADWIN—Gladwin County

MIDMICHIGAN MEDICAL CENTER–GLADWIN See Mymichigan Medical Center Gladwin

⊞ **MYMICHIGAN MEDICAL CENTER GLADWIN (231325)**, 515 Quarter Street, Zip 48624–1959; tel. 989/426–9286, **A**1 10 18 **F**3 7 15 18 26 28 29 31 34 35 40 45 46 48 49 50 57 59 62 64 77 78 79 81 91 92 93 107 108 110 111 114 115 119 127 129 130 132 135 144 154 156 157 168 169 **S** MyMichigan Health, Midland, MI
Primary Contact: Raymond Stover, Regional President
CFO: Jeff Provenzano, Vice President and Chief Financial Officer
CMO: Cheryl Loubert, M.D., Chief Medical Staff
CIO: Dan Waltz, Vice President and Chief Information Officer
CNO: Glenn King, R.N., MSN, Vice President and Chief Nursing Officer
Web address: www.midmichigan.org
Control: Other not–for–profit (including NFP Corporation) **Service**: General medical and surgical

Staffed Beds: 25 **Admissions**: 306 **Census**: 3 **Outpatient Visits**: 63038 **Births**: 0 **Total Expense ($000)**: 32477 **Payroll Expense ($000)**: 9073 **Personnel**: 192

GRAND BLANC—Genesee County

⊞ **ASCENSION GENESYS HOSPITAL (230197)**, 1 Genesys Parkway, Zip 48439–8066; tel. 810/606–5000, **A**1 2 3 5 10 12 13 **F**3 11 12 13 18 20 22 24 26 28 29 30 31 34 35 40 43 44 45 46 47 48 49 50 58 59 61 63 64 68 70 73 74 75 76 77 78 79 81 82 84 85 86 87 90 91 92 93 96 97 100 102 107 108 110 111 115 118 119 126 129 130 132 135 145 146 147 148 149 154 164 167 169 **P**5 6 8 **S** Ascension Healthcare, Saint Louis, MO
Primary Contact: Douglas Apple, M.D., Chief Clinical Officer Ascension Michigan & Interim President and CEO Ascension Genesys
CFO: Nancy Haywood, Chief Financial Officer
CMO: Charles Husson, Regional Chief Medical Officer
CNO: Julie A Gorczyca, R.N., Chief Nursing Officer
Web address: www.genesys.org
Control: Church operated, Nongovernment, not–for–profit **Service**: General medical and surgical

Staffed Beds: 379 **Admissions**: 16778 **Census**: 243 **Outpatient Visits**: 188367 **Births**: 1385 **Total Expense ($000)**: 411951 **Payroll Expense ($000)**: 152228 **Personnel**: 1817

Hospital, Medicare Provider Number, Address, Telephone, Approval, Facility, and Physician Codes, Health Care System

★ American Hospital Association (AHA) membership ○ Healthcare Facilities Accreditation Program ⇑ Center for Improvement in Healthcare Quality Accreditation
☐ The Joint Commission accreditation ◇ DNV Healthcare Inc. accreditation △ Commission on Accreditation of Rehabilitation Facilities (CARF) accreditation

© 2025 AHA Guide

Hospitals, U.S. / MICHIGAN

GRAND HAVEN—Ottawa County

⇑ **NORTH OTTAWA COMMUNITY HOSPITAL** See Trinity Health Grand Haven Hospital

★ ⇑ **TRINITY HEALTH GRAND HAVEN HOSPITAL (230174)**, 1309 Sheldon Road, Zip 49417-2488; tel. 616/842-3600, **A**10 21 **F**3 7 11 12 15 29 30 34 35 37 40 43 45 46 47 50 51 57 59 63 64 65 68 70 71 74 75 77 79 81 83 84 85 86 87 92 107 108 110 115 116 118 119 124 126 129 130 132 135 143 144 145 146 148 149 154 157 167 168
Primary Contact: Gary Allore, President
CFO: Mark Gross, Vice President Finance and Chief Financial Officer
CMO: Haney Assaad, Vice President Medical Affairs
CHR: Tim F Gengle, Director Human Resources
CNO: Cindy Van Kampen, Chief Nursing Officer
Web address: www.noch.org
Control: Other not-for-profit (including NFP Corporation) **Service**: General medical and surgical

Staffed Beds: 36 **Admissions**: 669 **Census**: 6 **Outpatient Visits**: 80375 **Births**: 0 **Total Expense ($000)**: 51624 **Payroll Expense ($000)**: 19051 **Personnel**: 382

GRAND RAPIDS—Kent County

COREWELL HEALTH BUTTERWORTH HOSPITAL (230038), 100 Michigan Street NE, Zip 49503-2560; tel. 616/391-1774, (Includes COREWELL HEALTH BLODGETT HOSPITAL, 1840 Wealthy Street SE, Grand Rapids, Michigan, Zip 49506-2921, tel. 616/774-7444; Andrea M. Leslie, MSN, R.N., Senior Vice President, Hospital Operations; COREWELL HEALTH HELEN DEVOS CHILDREN'S HOSPITAL, 100 Michigan Street NE, Grand Rapids, Michigan, Zip 49503-2560, tel. 616/391-9000; Robert Connors, M.D., President, Helen DeVos Children's Hospital; SPECTRUM HEALTH, 100 Michigan Street NE, Grand Rapids, Michigan, Zip 49503-2551, tel. 616/391-1774) **A**1 2 3 5 8 10 19 **F**1 3 5 8 9 11 12 13 14 15 16 17 18 19 20 21 22 23 24 25 26 27 28 29 30 31 32 34 35 36 37 38 40 41 43 44 45 46 47 48 49 50 51 54 55 56 58 59 60 61 62 63 64 65 68 70 71 72 73 74 75 76 77 78 79 80 81 82 83 84 85 86 87 88 89 90 92 93 96 97 98 99 100 101 102 104 107 108 110 111 112 113 114 115 117 118 119 120 121 123 124 126 128 129 130 131 132 134 135 136 137 138 140 141 143 145 146 147 148 149 150 152 154 155 156 157 160 161 164 166 167 169 **S** Corewell Health, Grand Rapids, MI
Primary Contact: Alejandro Quiroga, M.D., President of Corewell Health West
COO: Brian Brasser, Chief Operating Officer
CFO: Leslie Flake, Senior Vice President, Finance
CMO: Josh Kooistra, M.D., Senior Vice President, Chief Medical Officer
CIO: Jason Joseph, Vice President, Information Services
CHR: Nicole McConnell, Senior Vice President, Human Resources, SHDS
CNO: Shawn Ulreich, MSN, R.N., Vice President Clinical Operations and Chief Nursing Executive
Web address: https://www.spectrumhealth.org/locations/butterworth-hospital
Control: Other not-for-profit (including NFP Corporation) **Service**: General medical and surgical

Staffed Beds: 1599 **Admissions**: 56895 **Census**: 1152 **Outpatient Visits**: 1615827 **Births**: 7712 **Total Expense ($000)**: 2712163 **Payroll Expense ($000)**: 764337 **Personnel**: 10605

FOREST VIEW PSYCHIATRIC HOSPITAL (234030), 1055 Medical Park Drive SE, Zip 49546-3607; tel. 616/942-9610, **A**1 3 10 **F**75 87 98 99 100 101 104 105 130 135 149 154 **S** Universal Health Services, Inc., King of Prussia, PA
Primary Contact: Michael Nanzer, FACHE, Chief Executive Officer
COO: Scott Miles, Chief Operating Officer
CFO: Carl Caley, Chief Financial Officer
CMO: James VanHaren, M.D., Medical Director
CHR: Mike Henderson, Human Resources Director
CNO: Jo ell Harris, R.N., Chief Nursing Officer
Web address: www.forestviewhospital.com
Control: Corporation, Investor-owned (for-profit) **Service**: Psychiatric

Staffed Beds: 108 **Admissions**: 3342 **Census**: 88 **Outpatient Visits**: 15400 **Births**: 0 **Total Expense ($000)**: 29769 **Payroll Expense ($000)**: 14788 **Personnel**: 227

GRAND VALLEY NURSING CENTRE See Grand Valley Health Center

HELEN DEVOS CHILDREN'S HOSPITAL See Corewell Health Helen Devos Children's Hospital

△ **MARY FREE BED REHABILITATION HOSPITAL (233026)**, 235 Wealthy Street SE, Zip 49503-5247; tel. 616/840-8000, **A**1 3 5 7 10 **F**12 28 29 30 31 33 34 35 36 38 44 50 53 54 56 57 58 59 60 62 63 64 65 66 68 71 74 75 77 78 79 81 82 86 87 90 91 92 93 94 95 96 119 130 131 132 135 142 143 146 147 148 149 154 156 157 168 **P**6
Primary Contact: Kent Riddle, Chief Executive Officer
CFO: Randall DeNeff, Vice President Finance
CMO: Michael Jakubowski, M.D., Chief Medical Officer
CIO: Jeff Burns, Manager of Information Technology
CHR: Karen S. Powell, Vice President, Human Resources
CNO: Ingrid Cheslek, R.N., Chief Nursing Officer
Web address: www.maryfreebed.com
Control: Other not-for-profit (including NFP Corporation) **Service**: Rehabilitation

Staffed Beds: 156 **Admissions**: 2452 **Census**: 109 **Outpatient Visits**: 232785 **Births**: 0 **Total Expense ($000)**: 191345 **Payroll Expense ($000)**: 129378 **Personnel**: 1822

PINE REST CHRISTIAN MENTAL HEALTH SERVICES (234006), 300 68th Street SE, Zip 49548-6927, Mailing Address: P.O. Box 165, Zip 49501-0165; tel. 616/455-5000, **A**1 3 5 10 **F**4 5 6 29 30 32 34 35 38 56 58 59 66 68 75 77 82 86 87 98 99 100 101 102 103 104 105 106 130 132 134 135 144 146 149 150 152 153 154 158 160 162 163 164 165 169 **P**6
Primary Contact: Mark C. Eastburg, Ph.D., President and Chief Executive Officer
COO: Robert Nykamp, Vice President and Chief Operating Officer
CFO: Paul H Karsten, Vice President Finance and Chief Financial Officer
CMO: Alan Armstrong, M.D., Chief Medical Officer
Web address: www.pinerest.org
Control: Other not-for-profit (including NFP Corporation) **Service**: Psychiatric

Staffed Beds: 345 **Admissions**: 9368 **Census**: 162 **Outpatient Visits**: 396187 **Births**: 0 **Total Expense ($000)**: 201919 **Personnel**: 1890

△ **SELECT SPECIALTY HOSPITAL – COREWELL HEALTH GRAND RAPIDS (232029)**, 1840 Wealthy Street, Southeast, Zip 49506-2921; tel. 616/774-3800, (Nonreporting) **A**1 3 7 10 **S** Select Medical Corporation, Mechanicsburg, PA
Primary Contact: Matthew J. Campbell Esq, Regional Chief Executive Officer
Web address: https://grandrapids.selectspecialtyhospitals.com
Control: Corporation, Investor-owned (for-profit) **Service**: Acute long-term care hospital

Staffed Beds: 36

SPECTRUM HEALTH – BUTTERWORTH See Spectrum Health

SPECTRUM HEALTH – BLODGETT CAMPUS See Corewell Health Blodgett Hospital

TRINITY HEALTH GRAND RAPIDS HOSPITAL (230059), 200 Jefferson Avenue Southeast, Zip 49503-4598, Mailing Address: 200 Jefferson Avenue SE, Zip 49503-4598; tel. 616/685-5000, (Includes MERCY HEALTH ROCKFORD, 6050 Northland Drive NE, Rockford, Michigan, Zip 49341-9244, tel. 616/685-7950) **A**1 2 3 5 10 19 **F**3 6 12 13 15 18 20 22 26 28 29 30 31 34 35 36 37 38 40 42 43 44 45 46 48 49 50 54 55 56 57 58 59 60 61 64 66 68 70 72 74 75 76 77 78 79 81 82 84 85 86 87 92 93 96 97 98 100 101 102 104 107 108 110 111 114 115 116 117 118 119 120 121 123 124 126 129 130 132 135 138 144 146 147 148 149 153 154 156 160 161 164 165 167 169 **P**1 **S** Trinity Health, Livonia, MI
Primary Contact: Matt Biersack, M.D., President
COO: Randall J Wagner, Chief Operating Officer
CFO: Steve Eavenson, Vice President Finance
CIO: Jim Keller, Site Director Information Services
CHR: Thomas L Karel, Vice President Organization and Talent Effectiveness
CNO: Elizabeth A Murphy, R.N., FACHE, Chief Nursing Officer
Web address: https://www.mercyhealth.com/location/mercy-health-saint-marys
Control: Church operated, Nongovernment, not-for-profit **Service**: General medical and surgical

Staffed Beds: 303 **Admissions**: 15390 **Census**: 208 **Outpatient Visits**: 779439 **Births**: 1890 **Total Expense ($000)**: 649547 **Payroll Expense ($000)**: 219977 **Personnel**: 3541

TRINITY HEALTH SAINT MARY'S – GRAND RAPIDS See Trinity Health Grand Rapids Hospital

Hospitals, U.S. / MICHIGAN

GRAYLING—Crawford County

☒ **MUNSON HEALTHCARE GRAYLING HOSPITAL (230058)**, 1100 East Michigan Avenue, Zip 49738–1312; tel. 989/348–5461, (Total facility includes 39 beds in nursing home–type unit) **A**1 10 20 **F**2 3 6 11 13 15 18 28 29 30 31 32 34 35 36 38 40 43 44 45 48 49 50 51 56 57 59 62 65 68 70 74 75 76 77 78 79 81 85 86 87 92 93 97 100 101 102 104 107 108 110 111 115 118 119 127 129 130 131 132 135 146 147 148 149 154 156 157 164 169 **P**6 8 **S** Munson Healthcare, Traverse City, MI
Primary Contact: Kirsten Korth–White, Munson Healthcare Grayling Hospital President and Chief Executive Officer and MHC East Region Presid
CFO: Lori Shively, Vice President of Finance
CMO: Vince Schultz, M.D., Chief Medical Officer
CNO: Carla Gardner, Director of Nursing
Web address: https://www.munsonhealthcare.org/grayling-hospital/grayling-home
Control: Other not–for–profit (including NFP Corporation) **Service**: General medical and surgical

Staffed Beds: 110 **Admissions**: 1762 **Census**: 46 **Outpatient Visits**: 123316 **Births**: 300 **Total Expense ($000)**: 96179 **Payroll Expense ($000)**: 36936 **Personnel**: 384

GREENVILLE—Montcalm County

☒ **COREWELL HEALTH GREENVILLE HOSPITAL (230035)**, 615 South Bower Street, Zip 48838–2614; tel. 616/754–4691, (Total facility includes 70 beds in nursing home–type unit) **A**1 2 3 10 **F**3 5 12 13 15 18 22 26 27 28 29 30 31 34 35 40 43 44 45 47 48 49 50 51 54 56 57 59 64 65 68 70 75 76 77 78 79 81 85 87 93 97 102 104 107 108 110 111 115 119 126 127 128 129 130 131 132 133 134 135 146 147 148 149 154 156 157 160 164 167 169 **S** Corewell Health, Grand Rapids, MI
Primary Contact: Drew H. Dostal, FACHE, Regional Market Leader
COO: Priscilla Mahar, Chief Operating Officer
CFO: Ryan K Johnson, Controller
CMO: Kevin O'Connor, D.O., President, Medical Staff
CIO: David Dutmers, Manager, Information Services
CHR: Jennifer Nelson, Senior Human Resource Business Partner
Web address: www.spectrumhealth.org
Control: Other not–for–profit (including NFP Corporation) **Service**: General medical and surgical

Staffed Beds: 119 **Admissions**: 2712 **Census**: 67 **Outpatient Visits**: 287970 **Births**: 484 **Total Expense ($000)**: 141148 **Payroll Expense ($000)**: 50772 **Personnel**: 598

SPECTRUM HEALTH UNITED HOSPITAL See Corewell Health Greenville Hospital

GROSSE POINTE—Wayne County

☒ **COREWELL HEALTH BEAUMONT GROSSE POINTE HOSPITAL (230089)**, 468 Cadieux Road, Zip 48230–1507; tel. 313/473–1000, **A**1 2 3 5 10 **F**3 11 12 13 15 18 20 22 26 28 29 30 31 33 34 35 36 39 40 41 42 43 45 46 47 48 49 50 54 55 57 58 59 60 61 64 65 68 70 74 75 76 77 78 79 80 81 82 84 85 86 87 91 92 93 100 102 104 107 108 110 111 115 117 118 119 120 121 123 126 129 130 131 132 135 145 146 147 148 149 150 154 156 157 167 169 **S** Corewell Health, Grand Rapids, MI
Primary Contact: Derk F. Pronger, President
COO: Carolyn Wilson, R.N., Chief Operating Officer
CFO: Maria Miller, Controller
CMO: Nicholas Gilpin, D.O., Chief Medical Director, Infection Control and Section Head of Infectious Disease
CIO: Subra Sripada, Executive Vice President, Chief Transportation Officer and Chief Information Officer
CHR: Pandora Walker, Director, Human Resources
Web address: https://www.beaumont.org/locations/beaumont-hospital-grosse-pointe
Control: Other not–for–profit (including NFP Corporation) **Service**: General medical and surgical

Staffed Beds: 280 **Admissions**: 9223 **Census**: 108 **Outpatient Visits**: 269378 **Births**: 524 **Total Expense ($000)**: 266663 **Payroll Expense ($000)**: 91233 **Personnel**: 1360

HANCOCK—Houghton County

☒ **UP HEALTH SYSTEM – PORTAGE (230108)**, 500 Campus Drive, Zip 49930–1569; tel. 906/483–1000, (Total facility includes 60 beds in nursing home–type unit) **A**1 10 20 **F**3 13 15 18 28 29 31 34 35 40 43 46 50 53 54 56 57 59 60 64 65 67 68 70 75 76 77 78 79 81 85 86 87 89 93 97 100 107 108 110 111 115 116 119 128 129 130 131 132 133 144 145 146 148 149 154 156 157 164 167 **P**6 **S** Lifepoint Health, Brentwood, TN
Primary Contact: Ryan Heinonen, MSN, R.N., Chief Executive Officer
CFO: Steve Bishop, Chief Financial Officer
CMO: Mary Beth Hines, D.O., Chief Medical Officer
CHR: Robbyn Lucier, Director Human Resources
Web address: www.portagehealth.org
Control: Corporation, Investor–owned (for–profit) **Service**: General medical and surgical

Staffed Beds: 96 **Admissions**: 1125 **Census**: 72 **Outpatient Visits**: 96491 **Births**: 208 **Total Expense ($000)**: 83885 **Payroll Expense ($000)**: 35715 **Personnel**: 362

HARBOR BEACH—Huron County

HARBOR BEACH COMMUNITY HOSPITAL See Harbor Beach Community Hospital Inc.

HARBOR BEACH COMMUNITY HOSPITAL INC. (231313), 210 South First Street, Zip 48441–1236; tel. 989/479–3201, (Nonreporting) **A**10 18
Primary Contact: Jill Wehner, President and Chief Executive Officer
CMO: Richard Lloyd, D.O., Chief of Staff
CIO: Tami Nickrand, Director Information Technology
CHR: Tina Osantoski, Director Human Resources
CNO: Deb Geiger, Executive Director of Acute Care
Web address: www.hbch.org
Control: Other not–for–profit (including NFP Corporation) **Service**: General medical and surgical

Staffed Beds: 45

HASTINGS—Barry County

☒ **COREWELL HEALTH PENNOCK HOSPITAL (231339)**, 1009 West Green Street, Zip 49058–1710; tel. 269/945–3451, **A**1 3 10 18 **F**3 12 13 15 29 30 31 32 34 35 36 39 40 43 44 45 47 48 49 50 53 54 57 59 64 65 68 70 74 75 76 77 79 81 82 85 86 87 89 92 93 96 97 100 107 108 110 111 115 119 125 126 127 130 131 132 135 144 146 147 148 149 154 **S** Corewell Health, Grand Rapids, MI
Primary Contact: Bill Hoefer, FACHE, Regional Market Leader
COO: Carla Wilson–Neil, FACHE, Chief Operating Officer
CFO: Micheal King, Controller
CMO: Douglas Smendik, M.D., Hospital Medical Director
CIO: Teri VanTongeren, Director Information Services
CHR: Sherri Thrasher, Executive Human Resources Partner
CNO: Steve Marzolf, R.N., Chief Nursing Officer
Web address: https://www.spectrumhealth.org/locations/pennock
Control: Other not–for–profit (including NFP Corporation) **Service**: General medical and surgical

Staffed Beds: 25 **Admissions**: 1507 **Census**: 12 **Outpatient Visits**: 229656 **Births**: 285 **Total Expense ($000)**: 99105 **Payroll Expense ($000)**: 34881 **Personnel**: 402

SPECTRUM HEALTH PENNOCK See Corewell Health Pennock Hospital

HILLSDALE—Hillsdale County

★ ○ **HILLSDALE HOSPITAL (230037)**, 168 South Howell Street, Zip 49242–2081; tel. 517/437–4451, (Total facility includes 38 beds in nursing home–type unit) **A**10 11 19 **F**3 11 12 13 15 28 29 30 34 35 38 40 45 46 48 49 50 57 59 62 64 70 74 75 76 77 79 81 82 87 93 97 98 102 105 106 107 110 111 115 119 127 128 130 131 132 135 146 147 148 154 156 167 169 **P**8
Primary Contact: Jeremiah J. Hodshire, President and Chief Executive Officer
CFO: Mark Gross, Chief Finance Officer
CMO: Nichole Ellis, Chief Medical Officer
CIO: Sheila Puffenberger, Manager Information Technology
CHR: Stacy Feltz, Manager Human Resource
CNO: Loren Corbin, Chief Nursing Officer
Web address: www.hillsdalehospital.com
Control: Other not–for–profit (including NFP Corporation) **Service**: General medical and surgical

Staffed Beds: 92 **Admissions**: 2157 **Census**: 50 **Outpatient Visits**: 115359 **Births**: 391 **Total Expense ($000)**: 80414 **Payroll Expense ($000)**: 30241 **Personnel**: 614

Hospital, Medicare Provider Number, Address, Telephone, Approval, Facility, and Physician Codes, Health Care System

★ American Hospital Association (AHA) membership ○ Healthcare Facilities Accreditation Program ⇑ Center for Improvement in Healthcare Quality Accreditation
☐ The Joint Commission accreditation ◇ DNV Healthcare Inc. accreditation △ Commission on Accreditation of Rehabilitation Facilities (CARF) accreditation

© 2025 AHA Guide

Hospitals, U.S. / MICHIGAN

HOLLAND—Ottawa County

★ ⓗ **HOLLAND HOSPITAL (230072)**, 602 Michigan Avenue, Zip 49423-4999; tel. 616/392-5141, (Nonreporting) **A**3 10 21
Primary Contact: Patti J. VanDort, MSN, R.N., Chief Executive Officer
CFO: Alex Roehling, Chief Financial Officer
CMO: William Vandervliet, M.D., Vice President Medical Affairs
CIO: Randy J Paruch, Director, Information Systems
CHR: Sandra Trammell, Vice President, Human Resources and Support Services
CNO: Joseph Bonello, R.N., Chief Nursing Officer
Web address: www.hollandhospital.org
Control: Other not-for-profit (including NFP Corporation) **Service**: General medical and surgical

Staffed Beds: 130

HOWELL—Livingston County

ST. JOSEPH MERCY LIVINGSTON HOSPITAL See Trinity Health Livingston Hospital

⊞ **TRINITY HEALTH LIVINGSTON HOSPITAL (230069)**, 620 Byron Road, Zip 48843-1093; tel. 517/545-6000, **A**1 2 3 5 10 **F**3 8 11 12 15 18 28 29 30 31 34 35 40 41 42 43 45 50 51 54 56 57 59 61 63 64 65 66 68 70 74 75 77 78 79 81 82 84 85 86 87 93 97 100 107 108 110 111 115 117 118 119 120 121 123 126 129 130 131 132 134 135 145 146 147 148 149 154 156 157 160 164 167 169 **S** Trinity Health, Livonia, MI
Primary Contact: John F. O'Malley, FACHE, President
CFO: Kathy O'Connor, Vice President Finance and Controller
CMO: Rosalie Tocco-Bradley, Ph.D., M.D., Chief Medical Officer
CHR: Tonia Schemer, Interim Chief Human Resources
Web address: www.stjoeslivingston.org/livingston
Control: Church operated, Nongovernment, not-for-profit **Service**: General medical and surgical

Staffed Beds: 42 **Admissions**: 3418 **Census**: 32 **Outpatient Visits**: 328556
Births: 0 **Total Expense ($000)**: 169825 **Payroll Expense ($000)**: 58166
Personnel: 560

IONIA—Ionia County

⊞ **UNIVERSITY OF MICHIGAN HEALTH-SPARROW IONIA (231331)**, 3565 South State Road, Zip 48846-1870; tel. 616/523-1400, **A**1 3 10 18 **F**3 15 18 29 31 34 35 40 43 45 50 54 57 59 64 65 68 70 75 77 78 79 81 85 93 97 107 108 110 111 115 116 119 127 129 130 131 146 148 149 154 156 **P**6 **S** University of Michigan Health, Ann Arbor, MI
Primary Contact: Linda Reetz, R.N., President
COO: Kevin A Price, Vice President and Chief Operating Officer
CMO: Amy Jentz, M.D., Chief of Staff
CIO: Bob Neal, Information Technology
CHR: Debbie Olsen, Human Resource Partner
Web address: www.sparrow.org/sparrowionia
Control: Other not-for-profit (including NFP Corporation) **Service**: General medical and surgical

Staffed Beds: 22 **Admissions**: 672 **Census**: 6 **Outpatient Visits**: 153543
Births: 0 **Total Expense ($000)**: 57571 **Payroll Expense ($000)**: 25975
Personnel: 290

IRON MOUNTAIN—Dickinson County

IRON MOUNTAIN VAMC See Oscar G. Johnson Department of Veterans Affairs Medical Facility

⊞ **MARSHFIELD MEDICAL CENTER - DICKINSON (230055)**, 1721 South Stephenson Avenue, Zip 49801-3637; tel. 906/774-1313, **A**1 10 20 **F**3 11 13 15 18 28 29 31 32 34 35 40 43 45 46 50 56 57 59 62 63 64 65 67 70 75 76 77 78 79 81 85 86 87 89 92 97 107 108 110 111 114 115 118 119 120 121 123 126 127 129 130 131 133 135 145 146 147 148 149 154 156 157 160 167 169 **P**6 **S** Marshfield Clinic Health System, Marshfield, WI
Primary Contact: Amanda Shelast, FACHE, President
COO: Peggy Freeman, Chief Physicians Services Officer
CMO: Don Kube, M.D., Chief Medical Officer
CIO: Dean Decremer, Information Systems Manager
CHR: Paula Swartout, Human Resources Manager
CNO: Susan Hadley, MS, Chief Nursing Officer
Web address: www.dchs.org
Control: Other not-for-profit (including NFP Corporation) **Service**: General medical and surgical

Staffed Beds: 49 **Admissions**: 1751 **Census**: 21 **Outpatient Visits**: 149514
Births: 321 **Total Expense ($000)**: 137802 **Payroll Expense ($000)**: 48964
Personnel: 416

⊞ **OSCAR G. JOHNSON DEPARTMENT OF VETERANS AFFAIRS MEDICAL FACILITY**, 325 East 'H' Street, Zip 49801-4792; tel. 906/774-3300, (Nonreporting) **A**1 **S** Department of Veterans Affairs, Washington, DC
Primary Contact: John P. Shealey, Medical Center Director
Web address: www.ironmountain.va.gov/
Control: Veterans Affairs, Government, federal **Service**: General medical and surgical

Staffed Beds: 27

IRON RIVER—Iron County

⊞ **ASPIRUS IRON RIVER HOSPITAL (231318)**, 1400 West Ice Lake Road, Zip 49935-9526; tel. 906/265-6121, **A**1 10 18 **F**11 15 28 29 31 32 34 35 40 45 48 56 57 59 64 65 66 68 70 75 77 78 79 81 85 87 93 97 100 107 108 110 111 115 119 127 128 132 133 135 146 147 148 149 154 156 **S** Aspirus, Inc., Wausau, WI
Primary Contact: Rae Kaare, Chief Administrative Officer
CFO: Glenn E Dobson, Vice President, Finance and Chief Financial Officer
CMO: Nasseem Rizkalla, M.D., Chief Medical Officer
CHR: Carol Bastianello, Director Human Resources
CNO: Nancy Lynn Ponozzo, MSN, R.N., Chief Nursing Officer
Web address: www.aspirus.org
Control: Other not-for-profit (including NFP Corporation) **Service**: General medical and surgical

Staffed Beds: 7 **Admissions**: 428 **Census**: 4 **Outpatient Visits**: 39441
Births: 0 **Total Expense ($000)**: 40128 **Payroll Expense ($000)**: 13048
Personnel: 142

ASPIRUS IRON RIVER HOSPITALS & CLINICS, INC. See Aspirus Iron River Hospital

IRONWOOD—Gogebic County

ASPIRUS IRONWOOD HOSPITAL See Aspirus Ironwood Hospital & Clinics, Inc.

⊞ **ASPIRUS IRONWOOD HOSPITAL & CLINICS, INC. (231333)**, N10561 Grandview Lane, Zip 49938-9622; tel. 906/932-2525, **A**1 10 18 **F**3 11 13 15 28 29 31 34 38 40 41 43 45 50 56 57 59 62 63 64 70 76 77 78 79 81 85 87 89 93 97 104 107 108 110 115 119 120 121 122 123 127 129 130 132 133 135 144 146 147 148 149 153 154 156 164 167 169 **S** Aspirus, Inc., Wausau, WI
Primary Contact: Paula L. Chermside, Chief Administrative Officer
COO: Paula L. Chermside, Chief Administrative Officer
CFO: Mick Hagwell, Chief Financial Officer
CMO: Chris Pogliano, M.D., Chief Medical Staff
CHR: Keri Van Epern, Manager Human Resources
CNO: Grace Tousignant, R.N., MSN, Chief Nursing Officer
Web address: www.aspirus.org
Control: Other not-for-profit (including NFP Corporation) **Service**: General medical and surgical

Staffed Beds: 25 **Admissions**: 831 **Census**: 8 **Outpatient Visits**: 68420
Births: 116 **Total Expense ($000)**: 68136 **Payroll Expense ($000)**: 24847
Personnel: 155

ISHPEMING—Marquette County

⊞ **UP HEALTH SYSTEM - BELL (231321)**, 901 Lakeshore Drive, Zip 49849-1367; tel. 906/486-4431, **A**1 10 18 **F**3 11 13 15 17 29 30 34 40 50 53 57 59 64 65 68 70 72 75 76 77 79 81 82 85 87 88 89 92 93 96 97 107 108 110 114 119 129 133 135 144 145 146 147 149 156 167 169 **P**6 **S** Lifepoint Health, Brentwood, TN
Primary Contact: Mitchell D. Leckelt, FACHE, Chief Executive Officer
CFO: Teresa J Perry, Chief Financial Officer
CMO: Douglas LaBelle, M.D., Chief Medical Officer
CIO: Mike Brady, Director Information Technology
CHR: Tami Ketchem, Human Resource Director
CNO: June Hanson, Chief Nursing Officer
Web address: www.bellhospital.org
Control: Corporation, Investor-owned (for-profit) **Service**: General medical and surgical

Staffed Beds: 25 **Admissions**: 865 **Census**: 9 **Outpatient Visits**: 59821
Births: 259 **Total Expense ($000)**: 56281 **Payroll Expense ($000)**: 16559
Personnel: 246

UP HEALTH SYSTEM-BELL See Up Health System - Bell

JACKSON—Jackson County

DUANE L. WATERS HOSPITAL, 3857 Cooper Street, Zip 49201-7521; tel. 517/780-5600, (Nonreporting)
Primary Contact: Carol Griffes, Administrator
Control: State, Government, Nonfederal **Service**: Hospital unit of an institution (prison hospital, college infirmary, etc.)

Staffed Beds: 150

Hospitals, U.S. / MICHIGAN

✠ **HENRY FORD JACKSON HOSPITAL (230092)**, 205 North East Avenue, Zip 49201–1753; tel. 517/205–4800, **A**1 2 3 5 10 12 13 **F**3 4 5 8 9 11 12 13 15 17 18 20 22 24 26 28 29 30 31 34 35 37 38 40 43 45 46 47 48 49 50 51 53 56 57 58 59 62 63 64 65 68 70 71 73 74 75 76 77 78 79 80 81 82 84 85 87 89 93 98 99 100 102 103 104 105 106 107 108 110 111 115 118 119 120 121 123 124 129 130 131 132 133 143 146 147 148 149 152 153 154 156 157 160 164 167 169 **P**6 **S** Henry Ford Health, Detroit, MI
Primary Contact: Emily Moorhead, FACHE, President, Henry Ford Hospital and Central Market Operations
COO: Ondrea Bates, Senior Vice President, Operations and Continuum of Care
CFO: Kevin Leonard, Vice President, Finance
CMO: Ray King, M.D., Senior Vice President, Medical Affairs and Chief Medical Officer
CIO: Aaron Wootton, Vice President, Health Information Systems and Chief Information Officer
CHR: Patricia Seagram, Vice President Human Resources
CNO: Wendy Kim, Vice President, Nursing and Chief Nursing Officer
Web address: www.allegiancehealth.org
Control: Other not–for–profit (including NFP Corporation) **Service:** General medical and surgical

Staffed Beds: 362 **Admissions:** 16055 **Census:** 209 **Outpatient Visits:** 1051930 **Births:** 1087 **Total Expense ($000):** 764330 **Payroll Expense ($000):** 326778 **Personnel:** 3420

KALAMAZOO—Kalamazoo County

✠ **ASCENSION BORGESS HOSPITAL (230117)**, 1521 Gull Road, Zip 49048–1640; tel. 269/226–7000, (Includes ASCENSION BORGESS–PIPP HOSPITAL, 411 Naomi Street, Plainwell, Michigan, Zip 49080–1222, tel. 269/685–6811; Donna Cassidy, Administrator) **A**1 3 5 10 19 **F**3 7 8 9 11 12 13 15 17 18 20 22 24 26 29 30 31 32 34 35 36 37 38 40 43 44 45 46 47 49 50 51 53 54 56 57 58 59 60 61 64 65 68 70 73 74 75 76 77 78 79 81 82 83 84 85 86 87 90 91 92 93 96 97 98 100 101 102 103 104 107 110 111 114 115 118 119 126 127 129 130 131 132 135 143 144 145 146 147 148 149 150 154 156 157 162 164 167 169 **P**6 8 **S** Ascension Healthcare, Saint Louis, MO
Primary Contact: Dean Kindler, M.D., Regional President and Chief Executive Officer
COO: Mark Anthony, Executive Vice President and Chief Operating Officer
CHR: Laura Lentenbrink, Vice President, Human Resources
Web address: https://healthcare.ascension.org/locations/michigan/mikal/kalamazoo-ascension-borgess-hospital
Control: Church operated, Nongovernment, not–for–profit **Service:** General medical and surgical

Staffed Beds: 393 **Admissions:** 12338 **Census:** 176 **Outpatient Visits:** 283006 **Births:** 548 **Total Expense ($000):** 545548 **Payroll Expense ($000):** 159703 **Personnel:** 1413

✠ **BRONSON METHODIST HOSPITAL (230017)**, 601 John Street, Zip 49007–5346; tel. 269/341–6000, (Includes CHILDREN'S HOSPITAL AT BRONSON, 601 John Street, Kalamazoo, Michigan, Zip 49007–5341, tel. 269/341–7654) **A**1 2 3 5 10 19 **F**3 5 8 9 11 15 16 17 18 19 20 22 24 26 28 29 30 31 32 34 35 36 37 38 40 41 43 44 45 46 47 48 49 50 51 54 55 56 57 59 60 61 64 65 66 68 70 73 74 75 76 77 78 79 80 81 82 83 85 86 87 88 89 93 97 102 104 107 108 110 111 115 117 118 119 126 129 130 131 132 134 135 141 143 146 147 148 149 150 154 157 162 167 169 **P**6 **S** Bronson Healthcare Group, Kalamazoo, MI
Primary Contact: Bill Manns, President and Chief Executive Officer
COO: Kimberly Kay Hatchel, Senior Vice President, Chief Operating Officer
CHR: John Hayden, Vice President and Chief Human Resources Officer
CNO: Denise Neely, Vice President and Chief Nursing Officer
Web address: www.bronsonhealth.com
Control: Other not–for–profit (including NFP Corporation) **Service:** General medical and surgical

Staffed Beds: 415 **Admissions:** 24431 **Census:** 321 **Outpatient Visits:** 1538216 **Births:** 3597 **Total Expense ($000):** 1187516 **Payroll Expense ($000):** 558705 **Personnel:** 4142

☐ **KALAMAZOO PSYCHIATRIC HOSPITAL (234026)**, 1312 Oakland Drive, Zip 49008–1205; tel. 269/337–3000, (Nonreporting) **A**1 10
Primary Contact: Lance Bettison, Hospital Director
CMO: V.R. Kanaparti, M.D., Director Medical Services
CIO: Brian Bayer, Information Technology Site Leader
CHR: Holly Hiday, Director Human Resources
CNO: Kathleen Millard, Acting Director Nursing
Control: State, Government, Nonfederal **Service:** Psychiatric

Staffed Beds: 203

THE CHILDREN'S HOSPITAL AT BRONSON See Children's Hospital At Bronson

KALKASKA—Kalkaska County

★ **KALKASKA MEMORIAL HEALTH CENTER (231301)**, 419 South Coral Street, Zip 49646–2503; tel. 231/258–7500, (Total facility includes 104 beds in nursing home–type unit) **A**10 18 **F**2 3 10 11 15 29 30 31 32 34 35 36 38 40 44 45 48 50 53 56 57 59 60 62 65 68 75 78 79 81 86 87 93 97 100 101 102 104 107 110 115 119 125 127 128 130 131 132 133 134 135 143 144 146 147 148 149 154 156 157 164 **P**6 8 **S** Munson Healthcare, Traverse City, MI
Primary Contact: Kevin L. Rogols, FACHE, Administrator/CEO
CHR: Kimberly Babcock, Administrative Director of Operations
CNO: Christine Bissonette, R.N., Service Line Director for Acute Services
Web address: www.munsonhealthcare.org
Control: Hospital district or authority, Government, Nonfederal **Service:** General medical and surgical

Staffed Beds: 112 **Admissions:** 461 **Census:** 78 **Outpatient Visits:** 87799 **Births:** 0 **Total Expense ($000):** 73426 **Payroll Expense ($000):** 36769 **Personnel:** 576

L'ANSE—Baraga County

☐ **BARAGA COUNTY MEMORIAL HOSPITAL (231307)**, 18341 U.S. Highway 41, Zip 49946–8024; tel. 906/524–3300, (Nonreporting) **A**1 10 18
Primary Contact: Rob Stowe, Chief Executive Officer
CFO: Gail Jestila–Peltola, Chief Financial Officer
CMO: Sharon Gilliland, Chief of Staff
CIO: Taylor Makela, Director Information Technology
CHR: Janelle E Beeler, Human Resource Manager
CNO: Bonny Cotter, Chief Nursing Officer
Web address: www.bcmh.org
Control: County, Government, Nonfederal **Service:** General medical and surgical

Staffed Beds: 15

LANSING—Ingham County

INGHAM REGIONAL MEDICAL CENTER, GREENLAWN CAMPUS See Mclaren Greater Lansing

INGHAM REGIONAL ORTHOPEDIC HOSPITAL, PENNSYLVANIA CAMPUS See Mclaren Orthopedic Hospital

☐ **MCLAREN GREATER LANSING (230167)**, 2900 Collins Road, Zip 48910–8394; tel. 517/975–6000, (Includes MCLAREN GREATER LANSING, 401 West Greenlawn Avenue, Lansing, Michigan, Zip 48910–2819, tel. 517/795–6000; MCLAREN ORTHOPEDIC HOSPITAL, 2727 South Pennsylvania Avenue, Lansing, Michigan, Zip 48910–3490, tel. 517/975–6000; Casey Kandow, Interim President and Chief Executive Officer) (Nonreporting) **A**1 3 5 10 13 19 **S** McLaren Health Care Corporation, Grand Blanc, MI
Primary Contact: Kirk M. Ray, President and Chief Executive Officer
COO: Casey Kandow, Chief Operating Officer
CFO: Dale Thompson, Chief Financial Officer
CMO: Linda Peterson, M.D., Vice President Medical Affairs
CHR: Amy Dorr, Vice President Human Resources
Web address: www.mclaren.org
Control: Other not–for–profit (including NFP Corporation) **Service:** General medical and surgical

Staffed Beds: 321

SPARROW REGIONAL CHILDREN'S CENTER See Sparrow Children's Center

✠ △ **SPARROW SPECIALTY HOSPITAL (232037)**, 1215 East Michigan Avenue, 8 West Tower, Zip 48912; tel. 517/364–4840, **A**1 7 10 **F**1 3 29 30 60 68 85 100 101 119 130 148 149 **P**6 **S** University of Michigan Health, Ann Arbor, MI
Primary Contact: Tina Gross, MSN, R.N., President and Chief Nursing Officer
CFO: David Przybylski, Controller
CMO: Paul Entler, D.O., Medical Director
CHR: Paul Sturgis, Chief Human Resource Officer
CNO: Tina Gross, MSN, R.N., President and Chief Nursing Officer
Web address: www.sparrowspecialty.org
Control: Other not–for–profit (including NFP Corporation) **Service:** Acute long–term care hospital

Staffed Beds: 30 **Admissions:** 416 **Census:** 27 **Outpatient Visits:** 0 **Births:** 0 **Total Expense ($000):** 17109 **Payroll Expense ($000):** 7803 **Personnel:** 69

Hospital, Medicare Provider Number, Address, Telephone, Approval, Facility, and Physician Codes, Health Care System

★ American Hospital Association (AHA) membership
☐ The Joint Commission accreditation
◯ Healthcare Facilities Accreditation Program
◇ DNV Healthcare Inc. accreditation
⇑ Center for Improvement in Healthcare Quality Accreditation
△ Commission on Accreditation of Rehabilitation Facilities (CARF) accreditation

Hospitals, U.S. / MICHIGAN

✠ **UNIVERSITY OF MICHIGAN HEALTH–SPARROW LANSING (230230)**, 1215 East Michigan Avenue, Zip 48912–1811; tel. 517/364–1000, (Includes SPARROW CHILDREN'S CENTER, 1215 East Michigan Avenue, Lansing, Michigan, Zip 48912–1811, tel. 517/364–1000) **A**1 2 3 5 10 13 **F**3 11 12 13 15 18 20 22 24 26 28 29 30 31 34 35 36 37 38 40 41 42 43 44 45 46 49 50 51 54 55 56 57 58 59 60 63 64 65 67 70 72 74 75 76 77 78 79 81 82 83 84 85 86 87 88 89 90 91 92 93 94 96 97 98 100 101 102 103 104 105 107 108 109 110 111 114 115 116 117 118 119 120 121 123 124 126 129 130 131 132 135 144 146 147 148 149 154 156 167 169 **P**1 6 **S** University of Michigan Health, Ann Arbor, MI
Primary Contact: Denny Martin, D.O., President, University of Michigan Health–Sparrow Lansing
COO: Joseph Ruth, Executive Vice President and Chief Operating Officer
CFO: Paula Reichle, Senior Vice President and Chief Operating Officer
CMO: Brian D. Schroeder, M.D., Senior Vice President and Chief Medical Officer
CIO: Thomas Bres, Senior Vice President and Chief Administrative Officer
CHR: Paul Sturgis, Vice President and Chief Human Resources Officer
CNO: Mary Lou Wesley, R.N., Senior Vice President and Chief Nursing Officer
Web address: https://www.sparrow.org/our-hospitals-services/sparrow-hospitals/sparrow-hospital
Control: Other not–for–profit (including NFP Corporation) **Service**: General medical and surgical

Staffed Beds: 535 **Admissions**: 25589 **Census**: 400 **Outpatient Visits**: 1073600 **Births**: 3231 **Total Expense ($000)**: 1127197 **Payroll Expense ($000)**: 540209 **Personnel**: 5175

LAPEER—Lapeer County

☐ **MCLAREN LAPEER REGION (230193)**, 1375 North Main Street, Zip 48446–1350; tel. 810/667–5500, (Total facility includes 19 beds in nursing home–type unit) **A**1 10 **F**3 12 13 15 18 20 26 28 29 30 31 34 35 40 43 44 45 49 54 56 57 59 61 64 68 70 74 76 77 79 81 82 84 85 86 87 92 93 94 97 98 100 101 102 107 108 110 111 114 115 118 119 126 128 129 130 131 135 143 144 146 148 149 154 157 167 169 **S** McLaren Health Care Corporation, Grand Blanc, MI
Primary Contact: Tim Vargas, President and Chief Executive Officer
CFO: Benjamin Brow, Vice President of Finance
CMO: Gary Salem, M.D., Vice President Medical Affairs
CIO: Gayle Consiglio, Chief Information Officer
CHR: Amy Dorr, Vice President Human Resources
Web address: https://www.mclaren.org/lapeer-region/mclaren-lapeer-region-home
Control: Other not–for–profit (including NFP Corporation) **Service**: General medical and surgical

Staffed Beds: 131 **Admissions**: 7138 **Census**: 72 **Outpatient Visits**: 145829 **Births**: 137 **Total Expense ($000)**: 131821 **Payroll Expense ($000)**: 60187 **Personnel**: 657

LAURIUM—Houghton County

✠ **ASPIRUS KEWEENAW HOSPITAL (231319)**, 205 Osceola Street, Zip 49913–2134; tel. 906/337–6500, **A**1 10 18 **F**3 5 8 11 13 15 18 28 29 30 31 34 35 36 40 43 45 52 53 56 57 59 61 64 65 66 68 70 75 76 77 78 79 81 82 85 87 89 93 97 107 108 110 115 118 119 127 130 131 132 133 135 146 147 148 149 154 156 160 167 169 **S** Aspirus, Inc., Wausau, WI
Primary Contact: Matt Krause, Chief Administrative Officer
CFO: Andrew Costic, Vice President of Regional Finance
CMO: Michael Luoma, M.D., Chief of Staff
CHR: Chad Rowe, Human Resource Director
CNO: Grace Tousignant, R.N., MSN, Chief Nursing Officer
Web address: www.aspirus.org
Control: Other not–for–profit (including NFP Corporation) **Service**: General medical and surgical

Staffed Beds: 18 **Admissions**: 834 **Census**: 10 **Outpatient Visits**: 51103 **Births**: 174 **Total Expense ($000)**: 66720 **Payroll Expense ($000)**: 23497 **Personnel**: 170

LINCOLN PARK—Wayne County

VIBRA HOSPITAL – TAYLOR CAMPUS See Vibra Hospitals of Southeastern Michigan – Taylor Campus

✠ **VIBRA HOSPITALS OF SOUTHEASTERN MICHIGAN – TAYLOR CAMPUS (232019)**, 26400 West Outer Drive, Zip 48146–2088, Mailing Address: 1000 Telegraph Rd 2nd Fl, Taylor, Zip 48180; tel. 313/386–2000, (Nonreporting) **A**1 10 **S** Vibra Healthcare, Mechanicsburg, PA
Primary Contact: Brooke Saunders, Vice President of Southeastern Market
COO: Cindy Brassinger, Chief Operating Officer
CFO: Douglas Morris, Chief Financial Officer
CHR: Karen D Gray, Director Human Resources
Web address: www.vhsemichigan.com/
Control: Corporation, Investor–owned (for–profit) **Service**: Acute long–term care hospital

Staffed Beds: 220

LIVONIA—Wayne County

ST. MARY MERCY LIVONIA HOSPITAL See Trinity Health Livonia Hospital

✠ **TRINITY HEALTH LIVONIA HOSPITAL (230002)**, 36475 Five Mile Road, Zip 48154–1988; tel. 734/655–4800, **A**1 2 3 5 10 **F**3 4 5 8 11 12 13 15 18 20 22 26 28 29 30 31 34 35 38 40 43 44 45 46 47 49 50 51 54 55 56 57 58 59 63 64 68 70 74 75 76 77 78 79 81 84 85 86 87 90 92 93 97 98 100 101 102 104 107 108 110 111 114 115 116 117 118 119 120 121 126 129 130 131 132 135 143 144 145 146 147 148 149 153 154 156 160 164 165 167 169 **P**6 **S** Trinity Health, Livonia, MI
Primary Contact: Shannon Striebich, FACHE, President & Chief Executive Officer, Trinity Health Michigan Market
CFO: Mike Samyn, Vice President, Finance and Chief Financial Officer
CMO: Matthew Griffin, M.D., Chief Medical Officer
CIO: Janet Yim, Director Information Services
CHR: Kenneth Antczak, Vice President Human Resources
Web address: https://www.stjoeshealth.org/location/trinity-health-livonia-hospital
Control: Church operated, Nongovernment, not–for–profit **Service**: General medical and surgical

Staffed Beds: 304 **Admissions**: 18272 **Census**: 237 **Outpatient Visits**: 279446 **Births**: 750 **Total Expense ($000)**: 408314 **Payroll Expense ($000)**: 168648 **Personnel**: 1829

LUDINGTON—Mason County

✠ **COREWELL HEALTH LUDINGTON HOSPITAL (230110)**, 1 Atkinson Drive, Zip 49431–1906, Mailing Address: 1 Atkinson Dr, Zip 49431; tel. 231/843–2591, **A**1 10 20 **F**3 8 11 13 15 28 29 31 32 35 37 38 40 70 75 76 77 78 79 81 82 83 84 86 87 90 91 126 127 129 131 135 146 156 164 **P**6 **S** Corewell Health, Grand Rapids, MI
Primary Contact: Drew H. Dostal, FACHE, Regional Market Leader, North Region
CFO: Kerri Nelson, Chief Financial Officer
CMO: Steve Strbich, D.O., Chief of Staff
CIO: Jeremy Vronko, Manager, Information Services
CHR: Jill Vasquez, Manager Human Resources
CNO: Meleah Mariani, Chief Nursing Officer
Web address: https://www.spectrumhealth.org/locations/ludington-hospital
Control: Other not–for–profit (including NFP Corporation) **Service**: General medical and surgical

Staffed Beds: 30 **Admissions**: 1852 **Census**: 19 **Outpatient Visits**: 214962 **Births**: 256 **Total Expense ($000)**: 111578 **Payroll Expense ($000)**: 38454 **Personnel**: 468

SPECTRUM HEALTH LUDINGTON HOSPITAL See Corewell Health Ludington Hospital

MADISON HEIGHTS—Oakland County

ST. JOHN PROVIDENCE MACOMB–OAKLAND HOSPITAL, OAKLAND CENTER See St. John Macomb–Oakland Hospital, Madison Heights Campus

MANISTEE—Manistee County

✠ **MUNSON HEALTHCARE MANISTEE HOSPITAL (230303)**, 1465 East Parkdale Avenue, Zip 49660–9709; tel. 231/398–1000, **A**1 10 20 **F**3 11 15 28 29 31 34 35 36 38 39 40 44 45 48 50 53 54 57 59 62 64 65 68 74 75 77 78 79 81 85 86 87 92 93 97 101 107 108 110 111 115 118 119 127 129 130 131 132 135 146 147 148 149 154 156 157 164 169 **P**6 8 **S** Munson Healthcare, Traverse City, MI
Primary Contact: Kelly Tomaszewski, R.N., MSN, President and Chief Executive Officer Manistee and Paul Oliver
COO: Donn J Lemmer, Chief Financial Officer and Chief Operating Officer
CFO: Donn J Lemmer, Chief Financial Officer and Chief Operating Officer
CMO: Marion Fuller, Chief of Staff
CHR: Kim Weckesser, Director Human Resources
CNO: Thomas Kane, R.N., Vice President Patient Services and Chief Nursing Officer
Web address: https://www.munsonhealthcare.org/manistee-hospital/manistee-home
Control: Other not–for–profit (including NFP Corporation) **Service**: General medical and surgical

Staffed Beds: 45 **Admissions**: 707 **Census**: 7 **Outpatient Visits**: 63121 **Births**: 0 **Total Expense ($000)**: 58873 **Payroll Expense ($000)**: 21754 **Personnel**: 197

Hospitals, U.S. / MICHIGAN

MANISTIQUE—Schoolcraft County

★ **SCHOOLCRAFT MEMORIAL HOSPITAL (231303)**, 7870W US Highway 2, Zip 49854–8992; tel. 906/341–3200, **A**10 18 **F**3 11 12 15 18 19 28 29 30 31 32 34 35 40 41 45 50 56 57 59 62 63 64 65 68 70 75 77 78 79 81 82 85 90 93 97 100 107 108 110 114 115 118 119 127 129 130 131 132 133 146 148 154 156 **P**6
Primary Contact: Andrew Bertapelle, MSN, R.N., Chief Executive Officer
CMO: John P Galey, M.D., Chief Medical Officer
CIO: Kent La Croix, Chief Information Officer
CHR: Fawn Freeborn, Human Resources Generalist
CNO: Cindy Olli, R.N., Chief Nursing Officer
Web address: www.scmh.org
Control: Other not–for–profit (including NFP Corporation) **Service**: General medical and surgical

Staffed Beds: 12 **Admissions**: 308 **Census**: 4 **Outpatient Visits**: 55863 **Births**: 0 **Total Expense ($000)**: 55698 **Payroll Expense ($000)**: 24968 **Personnel**: 333

MARLETTE—Sanilac County

○ ⇧ **MARLETTE REGIONAL HOSPITAL (231330)**, 2770 Main Street, Zip 48453–1141, Mailing Address: P.O. Box 307, Zip 48453–0307; tel. 989/635–4000, (Nonreporting) **A**10 11 18 21 **S** Aspire Rural Health System, Cass City, MI
Primary Contact: Angela McConnachie, MSN, R.N., Co–CEO, Aspire Rural Health System
CFO: James L Singles, Chief Financial Officer
CMO: Daniel Kulick, M.D., Chief of Staff
CIO: Paul Gugel, Manager Information Technology
CHR: Connie Kennedy, Director Human Resources
CNO: Hilda Hebberd, R.N., MSN, Senior Director Clinical Services
Web address: www.marletteregionalhospital.org
Control: Other not–for–profit (including NFP Corporation) **Service**: General medical and surgical

Staffed Beds: 74

MARQUETTE—Marquette County

⊞ **UP HEALTH SYSTEM – MARQUETTE (230054)**, 850 West Baraga Avenue, Zip 49855–4550; tel. 906/228–9440, **A**1 2 3 5 10 **F**3 5 7 12 13 14 15 18 19 20 22 24 26 28 29 30 31 32 34 35 38 40 43 45 46 43 45 50 55 56 57 58 59 60 64 65 68 70 72 74 75 76 77 78 79 81 82 84 85 86 87 89 90 93 94 98 99 100 101 104 107 108 110 111 115 117 118 119 120 121 123 124 126 129 130 131 132 135 146 147 148 149 154 155 156 157 165 167 **P**6 **S** Lifepoint Health, Brentwood, TN
Primary Contact: Tonya Darner, Chief Executive Officer
COO: Christine Anne Stryker, Chief Nursing Officer and Chief Operating Officer
CFO: Henrietta Skeens, CPA, Chief Financial Officer
CMO: Lisa Long, M.D., Physician, Vice Chief of Staff
CIO: Tracey Elmblad, Director of IT
CHR: Lucy Grove, Human Resources Director
CNO: Christine Anne Stryker, Chief Nursing Officer and Chief Operating Officer
Web address: www.mgh.org
Control: Corporation, Investor–owned (for–profit) **Service**: General medical and surgical

Staffed Beds: 211 **Admissions**: 7914 **Census**: 136 **Outpatient Visits**: 281802 **Births**: 466 **Total Expense ($000)**: 389220 **Payroll Expense ($000)**: 113713 **Personnel**: 1255

MARSHALL—Calhoun County

★ ⇧ **OAKLAWN HOSPITAL (230217)**, 200 North Madison Street, Zip 49068–1199; tel. 269/781–4271, **A**10 21 **F**3 11 13 15 29 30 31 35 37 38 40 43 45 53 54 60 63 64 70 75 76 79 81 82 85 86 87 93 96 97 98 100 102 104 107 108 110 111 115 119 126 129 130 131 132 148 149 154 162 164 167 169
Primary Contact: Gregg M. Beeg, FACHE, President and Chief Executive Officer
COO: Sharon Thomas–Boyd, Chief Operating Officer
CFO: Andrew J. Poole III, Interim Chief Financial Officer
CNO: Theresa Dawson, MSN, R.N., Chief Nursing Officer
Web address: www.oaklawnhospital.org
Control: Other not–for–profit (including NFP Corporation) **Service**: General medical and surgical

Staffed Beds: 94 **Admissions**: 2567 **Census**: 26 **Outpatient Visits**: 156268 **Births**: 595 **Total Expense ($000)**: 176019 **Payroll Expense ($000)**: 77079 **Personnel**: 897

MIDLAND—Midland County

MIDMICHIGAN MEDICAL CENTER–MIDLAND See Mymichigan Medical Center Midland

⊞ **MYMICHIGAN MEDICAL CENTER MIDLAND (230222)**, 4000 Wellness Drive, Zip 48670–2000; tel. 989/839–3000, **A**1 2 3 5 10 **F**3 7 8 11 12 13 15 17 18 20 22 24 26 28 29 31 32 34 35 36 37 38 40 42 43 45 46 47 48 49 50 53 54 56 57 58 59 60 61 62 63 64 65 68 69 70 71 73 74 75 76 77 78 79 80 81 82 84 85 86 87 89 91 92 93 94 97 98 100 101 102 104 105 107 108 109 110 111 114 115 116 117 118 119 120 121 122 123 124 126 127 129 130 131 132 135 143 144 146 147 148 149 154 156 157 160 164 167 168 169 **S** MyMichigan Health, Midland, MI
Primary Contact: Chuck H. Sherwin, FACHE, President
CFO: Scott D Currie, Vice President and Chief Financial Officer
CMO: Margueritte Kuhn, M.D., Vice President Medical Affairs
CIO: C Harlan Goodrich, Vice President and Chief Information Officer
CNO: Jan Penney, R.N., Vice President and Chief Nursing Officer
Web address: https://www.mymichigan.org/locations/profile/medicalcenter-midland/
Control: Other not–for–profit (including NFP Corporation) **Service**: General medical and surgical

Staffed Beds: 270 **Admissions**: 12740 **Census**: 155 **Outpatient Visits**: 341363 **Births**: 1335 **Total Expense ($000)**: 589511 **Payroll Expense ($000)**: 185284 **Personnel**: 2548

MONROE—Monroe County

⊞ **PROMEDICA MONROE REGIONAL HOSPITAL (230099)**, 718 North Macomb Street, Zip 48162–7815; tel. 734/240–8400, **A**1 2 3 5 10 12 13 **F**3 11 12 13 15 18 20 21 22 28 29 30 34 35 36 37 38 40 41 43 44 45 46 49 50 51 53 56 57 59 65 69 70 71 73 74 75 76 77 78 79 81 82 85 86 87 89 92 93 97 98 100 101 102 104 107 108 109 110 111 113 114 115 116 117 119 121 124 126 128 129 130 135 141 146 147 148 149 154 156 164 167 **S** ProMedica Health System, Toledo, OH
Primary Contact: Darrin Arquette, President, Regional Acute Care, Michigan and President, ProMedica Monroe Regional Hospital
CNO: Maurine Weis, Vice President Patient Care Services and Chief Nursing Officer
Web address: www.promedica.org
Control: Other not–for–profit (including NFP Corporation) **Service**: General medical and surgical

Staffed Beds: 120 **Admissions**: 5346 **Census**: 67 **Outpatient Visits**: 206766 **Births**: 446 **Total Expense ($000)**: 166311 **Payroll Expense ($000)**: 53518 **Personnel**: 845

MOUNT CLEMENS—Macomb County

□ **MCLAREN MACOMB (230227)**, 1000 Harrington Boulevard, Zip 48043–2992; tel. 586/493–8000, **A**1 3 5 10 12 13 19 **F**3 8 11 12 13 15 18 19 20 22 24 26 28 29 30 31 34 35 36 37 40 41 43 45 46 47 48 49 50 51 54 55 56 57 62 63 64 65 66 68 70 71 74 75 76 77 78 79 81 82 84 85 87 89 92 93 94 96 98 100 102 103 107 110 111 114 115 118 119 120 121 123 124 126 129 130 131 132 135 145 146 147 148 149 154 156 167 **P**8 **S** McLaren Health Care Corporation, Grand Blanc, MI
Primary Contact: Tracey Franovich, R.N., President and Chief Executive Officer
COO: Sue Durst, R.N., MS, Vice President Plant Operations
CMO: Dennis J. Cunningham, M.D., Chief Medical Officer
Web address: https://www.mclaren.org/macomb/mclaren-macomb-home
Control: Other not–for–profit (including NFP Corporation) **Service**: General medical and surgical

Staffed Beds: 304 **Admissions**: 12801 **Census**: 183 **Outpatient Visits**: 221918 **Births**: 992 **Total Expense ($000)**: 350115 **Payroll Expense ($000)**: 136546

Hospital, Medicare Provider Number, Address, Telephone, Approval, Facility, and Physician Codes, Health Care System

★ American Hospital Association (AHA) membership   ○ Healthcare Facilities Accreditation Program   ⇧ Center for Improvement in Healthcare Quality Accreditation
□ The Joint Commission accreditation   ◇ DNV Healthcare Inc. accreditation   △ Commission on Accreditation of Rehabilitation Facilities (CARF) accreditation

Hospitals, U.S. / MICHIGAN

✚ **SELECT SPECIALTY HOSPITAL – MACOMB COUNTY (232023)**, 215 North Avenue, Zip 48043-1700; tel. 586/307-9000, (Includes SELECT SPECIALTY HOSPITAL–GROSSE POINTE, 468 Cadieux Road, 3 North East, Grosse Pointe, Michigan, Zip 48230-1507, 22101 Moross Road, 6th Floor, Detroit, Zip 48236, tel. 313/473-6131; Zaahra Butt, Chief Executive Officer; SELECT SPECIALTY HOSPITAL–PONTIAC, 44405 Woodward Avenue, 8th Floor, Pontiac, Michigan, Zip 48341-5023, tel. 248/452-5202; Brandon Young, Chief Executive Officer) (Nonreporting) **A**1 10 **S** Select Medical Corporation, Mechanicsburg, PA
Primary Contact: Jon P. O'Malley, Chief Executive Officer
CFO: Sharon Ryan, Regional Controller
CMO: Arsenio V Deleon, M.D., Chief Medical Officer
CHR: Katelyn Andre, Human Resource Coordinator
CNO: Lydia Alaszewski, Chief Nursing Officer
Web address: www.macomb.selectspecialtyhospitals.com/
Control: Corporation, Investor–owned (for–profit) **Service:** Acute long–term care hospital

Staffed Beds: 96

SELECT SPECIALTY HOSPITAL–MACOMB COUNTY See Select Specialty Hospital – Macomb County

ST JOSEPH'S MERCY HOSP–EAST See Henry Ford Macomb Hospital – Mount Clemens Campus

MOUNT PLEASANT—Isabella County

☐ **MCLAREN CENTRAL MICHIGAN (230080)**, 1221 South Drive, Zip 48858-3257; tel. 989/772-6700, **A**1 10 19 **F**3 10 11 13 15 18 20 26 28 29 31 32 34 35 40 41 43 44 45 48 50 51 54 56 57 59 61 62 64 65 68 70 74 75 76 77 78 79 81 82 85 86 87 89 96 97 100 107 108 110 111 115 116 117 118 119 120 121 123 124 125 127 130 132 135 143 144 145 146 147 149 154 156 157 158 167 169 **S** McLaren Health Care Corporation, Grand Blanc, MI
Primary Contact: Robert G. David, President and Chief Executive Officer
CMO: Ashok Vashishta, M.D., Vice President Medical Affairs
CIO: Nicolette Zalud, Customer Site Manager
CHR: Carolyn Potter, Vice President Human Resources
CNO: Sheri Myers, Vice President Patient Care Services
Web address: https://www.mclaren.org/central-michigan/mclaren-central-michigan-home
Control: Other not–for–profit (including NFP Corporation) **Service:** General medical and surgical

Staffed Beds: 49 **Admissions:** 1869 **Census:** 17 **Outpatient Visits:** 109150 **Births:** 424 **Total Expense ($000):** 164740 **Payroll Expense ($000):** 78800 **Personnel:** 796

MUNISING—Alger County

MUNISING MEMORIAL HOSPITAL (231308), 1500 Sand Point Road, Zip 49862-1406; tel. 906/387-4110, (Nonreporting) **A**10 18
Primary Contact: Jim Parker, FACHE, Chief Executive Officer
CFO: Wendy Rautio, Chief Financial Officer
CMO: Christine Krueger, M.D., Chief of Staff
CNO: Andrea Wills, R.N., Chief Nursing Executive
Web address: www.munisingmemorial.org
Control: Other not–for–profit (including NFP Corporation) **Service:** General medical and surgical

Staffed Beds: 11

MUSKEGON—Muskegon County

✚ **TRINITY HEALTH MUSKEGON HOSPITAL (230066)**, 1500 East Sherman Boulevard, Zip 49444-1849; tel. 231/672-2000, **A**1 2 3 5 10 12 13 20 **F**3 5 7 11 12 13 15 18 20 22 24 26 28 29 30 31 34 35 37 40 43 44 45 46 49 50 51 54 55 56 57 58 59 61 64 68 70 71 74 75 76 77 78 79 81 82 84 86 87 89 90 92 93 96 97 98 100 107 108 110 111 114 115 116 117 118 119 120 121 123 124 126 127 129 130 131 132 143 144 146 147 148 149 154 156 160 161 167 169 **P**6 7 **S** Trinity Health, Livonia, MI
Primary Contact: Gary Allore, President
Web address: https://www.trinityhealthmichigan.org/location/trinity-health-muskegon-hospital
Control: Church operated, Nongovernment, not–for–profit **Service:** General medical and surgical

Staffed Beds: 348 **Admissions:** 17431 **Census:** 256 **Outpatient Visits:** 1539414 **Births:** 863 **Total Expense ($000):** 731538 **Payroll Expense ($000):** 324878 **Personnel:** 3357

NEW BALTIMORE—Macomb County

HARBOR OAKS HOSPITAL (234021), 35031 23 Mile Road, Zip 48047-3649; tel. 586/725-5777, (Nonreporting) **A**10 **S** Acadia Healthcare Company, Inc., Franklin, TN
Primary Contact: Anne Long, Chief Executive Officer
CFO: Michael Ferguson, Chief Financial Officer
CMO: James D. Adamo, M.D., Medical Director
CHR: Zena Ridley, Director Human Resources
CNO: Leeann Duncan, Director Patient Care Services
Web address: www.harboroaks.com
Control: Corporation, Investor–owned (for–profit) **Service:** Psychiatric

Staffed Beds: 99

NEWBERRY—Luce County

★ ⚕ **HELEN NEWBERRY JOY HOSPITAL & HEALTHCARE CENTER (231304)**, 502 West Harrie Street, Zip 49868-1209; tel. 906/293-9200, (Total facility includes 39 beds in nursing home–type unit) **A**10 18 21 **F**3 15 28 29 31 34 35 40 43 45 53 57 59 64 65 75 78 79 81 87 93 97 107 108 110 115 118 119 127 128 129 130 131 132 133 143 148 149 154 160 **P**6
Primary Contact: Helen Johnson, Chief Executive Officer
CFO: Kenneth G Landau, CPA, Chief Financial Officer
CMO: Michael Gregory Beaulieu, M.D., Chief Medical Officer
CIO: Howard Bliss, Director of Information Systems
CNO: Joe Johnson, Chief Nursing Officer
Web address: www.hnjh.org
Control: County, Government, Nonfederal **Service:** General medical and surgical

Staffed Beds: 64 **Admissions:** 303 **Census:** 25 **Outpatient Visits:** 33422 **Births:** 0 **Total Expense ($000):** 37925 **Payroll Expense ($000):** 12876 **Personnel:** 171

NILES—Berrien County

LAKELAND HOSPITAL, NILES See Corewell Health Niles Hospital

NORTHVILLE—Wayne County

HAWTHORN CENTER, 18471 Haggerty Road, Zip 48168-9575; tel. 248/735-6771, (Nonreporting) **A**3
Primary Contact: George Mellows, Facility Director
CIO: Robert W Bailey, Chief Information Officer
Web address: https://www.michigan.gov
Control: State, Government, Nonfederal **Service:** Children's hospital psychiatric

Staffed Beds: 69

NOVI—Oakland County

PROVIDENCE – PROVIDENCE PARK HOSPITAL, NOVI CAMPUS See Ascension Providence Hospital, Southfield Campus, Southfield

PROVIDENCE PARK HOSPITAL See Providence – Providence Park Hospital, Novi Campus

OWOSSO—Shiawassee County

✚ **MEMORIAL HEALTHCARE (230121)**, 826 West King Street, Zip 48867-2120; tel. 989/723-5211, (Total facility includes 21 beds in nursing home–type unit) **A**1 10 **F**3 10 11 13 15 28 29 30 31 32 34 35 36 38 40 43 45 50 51 53 54 56 57 58 59 62 63 64 65 69 70 74 75 76 77 78 79 81 82 84 85 87 89 93 97 98 100 101 102 107 108 110 111 115 119 126 127 128 129 130 131 132 143 144 146 147 148 149 154 156 **P**6
Primary Contact: Brian Long, FACHE, President and Chief Executive Officer
COO: Tim Susterich, Chief Financial Officer and Chief Operating Officer
CFO: Tim Susterich, Chief Financial Officer and Chief Operating Officer
CMO: Wael Salman, M.D., Vice President Medical Affairs
CIO: Tom Kurtz, Vice President Information Services and Chief Information Officer
Web address: www.memorialhealthcare.org
Control: Other not–for–profit (including NFP Corporation) **Service:** General medical and surgical

Staffed Beds: 126 **Admissions:** 3796 **Census:** 60 **Outpatient Visits:** 252511 **Births:** 431 **Total Expense ($000):** 284947 **Payroll Expense ($000):** 111371 **Personnel:** 1405

PAW PAW—Van Buren County

☒ **BRONSON LAKEVIEW HOSPITAL (231332)**, 408 Hazen Street, Zip 49079-1019, Mailing Address: P.O. Box 209, Zip 49079-0209; tel. 269/657-3141, **A**1 10 18 **F**3 5 6 9 11 15 18 29 30 32 34 35 37 38 40 41 44 45 50 54 56 57 59 60 61 64 65 66 68 74 75 77 79 81 82 85 86 87 93 97 98 102 103 107 108 110 111 115 118 119 127 129 130 131 132 133 134 135 143 146 147 148 149 150 154 169 **P**6 **S** Bronson Healthcare Group, Kalamazoo, MI
Primary Contact: Bill Manns, President and Chief Executive Officer, Bronson Healthcare Group
COO: Matthew N. Dommer, M.D., Vice President Medical Affairs and Chief Operating Officer
CFO: Becky East, CPA, Senior Vice President, Chief Financial Officer
CMO: Matthew N. Dommer, M.D., Vice President Medical Affairs and Chief Operating Officer
CIO: Ash Goel, Senior Vice President Information Technology and Chief Information/Medical Informatics Officer
CHR: John Hayden, Senior Vice President and Chief Human Resources Officer
CNO: Kirk Richardson, R.N., Senior Vice President, Chief Operating Officer, and Chief Nursing Officer
Web address: www.bronsonhealth.com/lakeview
Control: Other not-for-profit (including NFP Corporation) **Service:** General medical and surgical

Staffed Beds: 26 Admissions: 867 Census: 10 Outpatient Visits: 193325 Births: 0 Total Expense ($000): 63179 Payroll Expense ($000): 34583 Personnel: 288

PETOSKEY—Emmet County

☐ **MCLAREN NORTHERN MICHIGAN (230105)**, 416 Connable Avenue, Zip 49770-2297; tel. 231/487-4000, **A**1 10 **F**3 12 13 15 17 18 20 22 24 26 28 29 30 31 32 34 35 36 38 40 42 43 44 45 48 49 50 51 53 57 58 59 60 64 68 70 74 75 76 77 78 79 81 82 85 86 87 89 90 91 93 94 96 98 107 108 110 111 114 115 119 120 121 123 124 126 129 130 132 135 148 149 154 157 167 **S** McLaren Health Care Corporation, Grand Blanc, MI
Primary Contact: Garfield Atchison, President and Chief Executive Officer
CFO: David Bellamy, Chief Financial Officer
CMO: Kirk Lufkin, M.D., VPMA
CIO: David Bellamy, Chief Financial Officer
CHR: Gene Kaminski, Vice President Human Resources and Hospitality Services
Web address: www.northernhealth.org
Control: Other not-for-profit (including NFP Corporation) **Service:** General medical and surgical

Staffed Beds: 200 Admissions: 7472 Census: 85 Outpatient Visits: 206499 Births: 354 Total Expense ($000): 240047 Payroll Expense ($000): 83548 Personnel: 855

PIGEON—Huron County

☒ **SCHEURER HEALTH (231310)**, 170 North Caseville Road, Zip 48755-9781; tel. 989/453-3223, (Total facility includes 19 beds in nursing home–type unit) **A**1 10 18 **F**3 7 8 10 11 15 28 29 30 31 32 34 35 37 40 43 44 45 50 51 54 56 57 59 64 65 68 69 75 77 78 79 81 85 86 87 91 93 97 107 108 110 115 118 119 125 127 130 131 132 133 134 144 146 149 154 156 164 167 **P**6 8
Primary Contact: Ross Ramsey, M.D., President and Chief Executive Officer
CFO: Terry Lutz, Chief Financial Officer
CMO: Ross Ramsey, M.D., Chief of Staff
CHR: Gregory S. Foy, Risk Manager
CNO: Kendra Kretzschmer, Patient Care System Leader
Web address: www.scheurer.org
Control: Other not-for-profit (including NFP Corporation) **Service:** General medical and surgical

Staffed Beds: 44 Admissions: 324 Census: 17 Outpatient Visits: 50662 Births: 0 Total Expense ($000): 58422 Payroll Expense ($000): 26126 Personnel: 340

PLAINWELL—Allegan County

BORGESS–PIPP HOSPITAL See Ascension Borgess–Pipp Hospital

PONTIAC—Oakland County

☐ **MCLAREN OAKLAND (230207)**, 50 North Perry Street, Zip 48342-2253; tel. 248/338-5000, (Nonreporting) **A**1 3 5 10 12 **S** McLaren Health Care Corporation, Grand Blanc, MI
Primary Contact: Lorenzo Suter, President and Chief Executive Officer
COO: Nicholle Mehr, Vice President Operations
CFO: Lynn Marcotte, Chief Financial Officer
CMO: Steven Calkin, D.O., Vice President Medical Affairs
CIO: Kelly Finley, Customer Site Executive
CHR: Dwan Cosby, Manager Human Resources
CNO: Calandra Anderson, Vice President Patient Care and Chief Nursing Officer
Web address: www.mclaren.org/oakland
Control: Other not-for-profit (including NFP Corporation) **Service:** General medical and surgical

Staffed Beds: 277

☐ **PIONEER SPECIALTY HOSPITAL (232039)**, 50 North Perry Street, 6th Floor, Zip 48342-2217; tel. 248/338-5430, **A**1 10 **F**1 18 29
Primary Contact: Denise Wayne, Chief Executive Officer
Web address: www.pioneerspecialtyhospital.com
Control: Individual, Investor-owned (for-profit) **Service:** Acute long-term care hospital

Staffed Beds: 42 Admissions: 139 Census: 15 Outpatient Visits: 0 Births: 0 Total Expense ($000): 9281 Payroll Expense ($000): 5015 Personnel: 113

PONTIAC GENERAL HOSPITAL (230013), 461 West Huron Street, Zip 48341-1601; tel. 248/857-7200, (Nonreporting) **A**3 10
Primary Contact: Robert Barrow, Chief Executive Officer
COO: Dennis Franks, Vice President Operations
CFO: Dennis Franks, Interim Chief Financial Officer
CMO: Ray Breitenbach, M.D., Chief of Staff
CIO: Albert Sinisi, Director Information Systems
Web address: www.pontiacgeneral.com
Control: Other not-for-profit (including NFP Corporation) **Service:** General medical and surgical

Staffed Beds: 85

ST. JOSEPH MERCY OAKLAND See Trinity Health Oakland Hospital

☒ **TRINITY HEALTH OAKLAND HOSPITAL (230029)**, 44405 Woodward Avenue, Zip 48341-5023; tel. 248/858-3000, **A**1 2 3 5 10 19 **F**3 10 11 12 13 17 18 19 20 22 24 26 28 29 30 31 34 35 36 38 39 40 43 44 45 46 48 49 50 53 54 55 56 57 58 59 61 62 63 64 65 70 72 74 75 76 77 78 79 81 82 84 85 86 87 89 90 92 93 96 97 98 100 102 104 105 107 108 109 110 111 114 115 118 119 126 129 130 131 132 135 146 147 148 149 153 154 156 162 164 167 169 **P**6 7 **S** Trinity Health, Livonia, MI
Primary Contact: Shannon Striebich, FACHE, President and Chief Executive Officer of Trinity Health Michigan Market
CFO: Michael Gusho, Chief Financial Officer
CMO: Fabian Fregoli, M.D., Chief Medical Officer
CIO: Robert Jones, Director Management Information Systems
CHR: Ane McNeil, Vice President Human Resources
CNO: Douglas R Dascenzo, R.N., Chief Nursing Officer
Web address: https://www.stjoeshealth.org/location/trinity-health-oakland-hospital
Control: Church operated, Nongovernment, not-for-profit **Service:** General medical and surgical

Staffed Beds: 389 Admissions: 18751 Census: 273 Outpatient Visits: 301642 Births: 1963 Total Expense ($000): 515687 Payroll Expense ($000): 205293 Personnel: 2201

Hospital, Medicare Provider Number, Address, Telephone, Approval, Facility, and Physician Codes, Health Care System

★ American Hospital Association (AHA) membership
☐ The Joint Commission accreditation
○ Healthcare Facilities Accreditation Program
◇ DNV Healthcare Inc. accreditation
⇑ Center for Improvement in Healthcare Quality Accreditation
△ Commission on Accreditation of Rehabilitation Facilities (CARF) accreditation

Hospitals, U.S. / MICHIGAN

PORT HURON—St. Clair County

LAKE HURON MEDICAL CENTER (230031), 2601 Electric Avenue, Zip 48060–6518; tel. 810/985–1500, **A**1 10 **F**3 12 15 18 20 28 29 30 31 34 35 40 43 45 46 47 48 49 50 51 54 56 57 58 59 60 64 66 70 74 75 77 78 79 81 85 86 87 90 91 93 96 97 107 108 110 111 114 115 119 120 121 123 126 130 131 132 135 146 147 148 149 154 156 167 **S** Prime Healthcare, Ontario, CA
Primary Contact: Jose Kottoor, Chief Executive Officer
COO: Ken Sanger, R.N., Chief Nursing Officer and Chief Operations Officer
CFO: Chris Fulks, Vice President Finance
CMO: Sridhar Reddy, M.D., Chief Medical Officer
CIO: Jefferey Wagner, Director, Information Technology
CHR: Debra A Seifert, Director Human Resources
CNO: Ken Sanger, R.N., Chief Nursing Officer and Chief Operations Officer
Web address: https://www.mylakehuron.com
Control: Corporation, Investor–owned (for–profit) **Service**: General medical and surgical

Staffed Beds: 68 Admissions: 3307 Census: 42 Outpatient Visits: 102124
Births: 0 Total Expense ($000): 69311 Payroll Expense ($000): 25532

MARWOOD MANOR See Marwood Manor Nursing Home

MCLAREN PORT HURON (230216), 1221 Pine Grove Avenue, Zip 48060–3511; tel. 810/987–5000, (Nonreporting) **A**1 3 10 19 **S** McLaren Health Care Corporation, Grand Blanc, MI
Primary Contact: Eric Cecava, President and Chief Executive Officer
COO: John Liston, Chief Operating Officer
CFO: Bridget Sholtis, Chief Financial Officer
CMO: Michael W Tawney, D.O., Vice President Medical Affairs
CIO: John McGrath, Chief Information Officer
CHR: Doris A Seidl, Vice President Human Resources
CNO: Christine R Sansom, Chief Nursing Officer
Web address: www.porthuronhospital.org
Control: Other not–for–profit (including NFP Corporation) **Service**: General medical and surgical

Staffed Beds: 186

REED CITY—Osceola County

COREWELL HEALTH REED CITY HOSPITAL (231323), 300 North Patterson Road, Zip 49677–8041; tel. 231/832–3271, **A**1 2 10 18 **F**1 3 8 15 16 17 29 31 34 35 38 40 43 44 45 50 59 64 65 67 68 70 72 73 75 77 78 80 87 88 89 92 96 97 102 107 110 114 115 119 127 128 129 130 143 146 148 149 154 156 157 164 166 **P**6 **S** Corewell Health, Grand Rapids, MI
Primary Contact: Drew H. Dostal, FACHE, Regional Market Leader, North Region
COO: Cathy Rybicki, Chief Operating Officer
CFO: Thomas Knoerl, Vice President Finance
CMO: Thomas Campana, M.D., Chief of Staff
CIO: Brandi Johnson, Site Manager Technology Information Systems
CHR: Kris Miller, Senior Human Resources Business Partner
Web address: www.spectrumhealth.org/reedcity
Control: Other not–for–profit (including NFP Corporation) **Service**: General medical and surgical

Staffed Beds: 64 Admissions: 285 Census: 36 Outpatient Visits: 86961
Births: 0 Total Expense ($000): 67778 Payroll Expense ($000): 16592
Personnel: 236

SPECTRUM HEALTH REED CITY HOSPITAL See Corewell Health Reed City Hospital

ROCHESTER—Oakland County

ASCENSION PROVIDENCE ROCHESTER HOSPITAL (230254), 1101 West University Drive, Zip 48307–1831; tel. 248/652–5000, **A**1 3 5 10 19 **F**3 11 13 15 17 18 20 22 24 26 28 29 30 32 34 35 36 37 38 40 43 44 45 46 49 50 51 53 54 56 57 58 59 60 61 63 64 65 66 68 70 74 75 76 77 78 79 80 81 82 85 86 87 90 93 97 98 100 107 108 110 111 114 115 119 126 129 130 131 132 135 141 143 146 147 148 149 154 156 157 162 164 167 169 **P**4 6 8 **S** Ascension Healthcare, Saint Louis, MO
Primary Contact: Michael Wiemann, M.D., Regional President & Chief Executive Officer, Ascension Metro West Region
COO: Tomasine Marx, Chief Financial Officer and Chief Operating Officer
CFO: Tomasine Marx, Chief Financial Officer and Chief Operating Officer
CMO: Sheryl Wissman, M.D., Chief Medical Officer
CIO: Ralph Tenney, Chief Information Officer
CHR: Ann Vano, Vice President, Human Resources
Web address: https://healthcare.ascension.org/Locations/Michigan/MIROC/Rochester-Ascension-Providence-Rochester-Hospital
Control: Church operated, Nongovernment, not–for–profit **Service**: General medical and surgical

Staffed Beds: 226 Admissions: 11420 Census: 143 Outpatient Visits: 177009 Births: 696 Total Expense ($000): 269685 Payroll Expense ($000): 99558 Personnel: 870

ROMEO—Macomb County

ST JOSEPH'S–TRI COUNTY HOSP See St. Joseph's Mercy–North

ST. JOSEPH'S MERCY–NORTH See Henry Ford Macomb Hospital, Clinton Township

ROYAL OAK—Oakland County

COREWELL HEALTH WILLIAM BEAUMONT UNIVERSITY HOSPITAL (230130), 3601 West Thirteen Mile Road, Zip 48073–6712; tel. 248/898–5000, (Includes BEAUMONT CHILDREN'S HOSPITAL, 3601 West 13 Mile Road, Royal Oak, Michigan, Zip 48073–6712, tel. 248/898–5000) **A**1 2 3 5 10 19 **F**3 6 11 12 13 15 17 18 19 20 22 24 26 28 29 30 31 32 34 35 36 37 38 39 40 41 43 44 45 46 47 48 49 50 54 55 56 57 58 59 60 61 64 65 66 68 70 71 72 74 75 76 77 78 79 80 81 82 83 84 85 86 87 88 89 90 91 92 93 94 95 96 97 100 101 102 107 108 110 111 113 114 115 116 117 118 119 120 121 122 123 124 126 129 130 131 132 134 135 138 139 141 142 145 146 147 148 149 150 154 156 157 160 161 167 169 **P**6 **S** Corewell Health, Grand Rapids, MI
Primary Contact: Daniel Carey, M.D., President
CMO: Leslie Rocher, Senior Vice President and Chief Medical Officer
CIO: Subra Sripada, Executive Vice President, Chief Transportation Officer and Chief Information Officer
CHR: Michael L Dixon, Vice President, Human Resources
CNO: Anne Stewart, Vice President and Chief Nursing Officer
Web address: https://www.beaumont.org/locations/beaumont-hospital-royal-oak
Control: Other not–for–profit (including NFP Corporation) **Service**: General medical and surgical

Staffed Beds: 1049 Admissions: 48621 Census: 764 Outpatient Visits: 1081364 Births: 5638 Total Expense ($000): 1445454 Payroll Expense ($000): 455071 Personnel: 7458

SAGINAW—Saginaw County

★ △ **ALEDA E. LUTZ DEPARTMENT OF VETERANS AFFAIRS MEDICAL CENTER**, 1500 Weiss Street, Zip 48602–5298; tel. 989/497–2500, **A**3 5 7 **F**5 8 30 33 35 36 38 39 45 46 50 53 54 59 61 62 63 64 65 74 75 77 81 82 83 84 86 87 90 91 93 94 96 97 100 101 104 107 119 127 128 130 132 135 143 144 145 147 148 149 153 154 156 157 158 160 161 164 **S** Department of Veterans Affairs, Washington, DC
Primary Contact: Roy Samsel, Medical Center Director
COO: Stephanie Young, Associate Director
CFO: Jeff Drew, Fiscal Officer
CMO: Gregory Movsesian, M.D., Acting Chief of Staff
CIO: Angie Schmus, Chief Information Technology
CHR: Thomas Stredney, Chief Human Resources Management Service
CNO: Penny Holland, Associate Director for Patient Care Services
Web address: www.saginaw.va.gov/
Control: Veterans Affairs, Government, federal **Service**: General medical and surgical

Staffed Beds: 41 Admissions: 1379 Census: 23 Births: 0 Personnel: 710

★ ○ △ **COVENANT HEALTHCARE (230070)**, 1447 North Harrison Street, Zip 48602–4727; tel. 989/583–0000, (Includes COVENANT MEDICAL CENTER–COOPER, 700 Cooper Avenue, Saginaw, Michigan, Zip 48602–5399, tel. 989/583–0000; Beth Charlton, R.N., President and Chief Executive Officer, Covenant Healthcare; COVENANT MEDICAL CENTER–HARRISON, 1447 North Harrison Street, Saginaw, Michigan, Zip 48602–4785, tel. 989/583–0000; Beth Charlton, R.N., President and Chief Executive Officer, Covenant Healthcare; COVENANT MEDICAL CENTER, 515 N. Michigan Avenue, Saginaw, Michigan, Zip 48602–4316, tel. 989/583–6000; Beth Charlton, R.N., President and Chief Executive Officer, Covenant Healthcare) **A**2 3 5 7 10 11 19 **F**3 8 11 12 13 15 17 18 19 20 22 24 25 26 27 28 29 30 31 35 36 40 41 42 43 45 46 47 48 49 50 54 57 58 59 60 61 62 63 64 65 70 72 74 75 76 77 78 79 81 82 83 84 86 87 88 89 90 91 92 93 94 97 107 108 110 111 113 114 115 118 119 120 121 123 124 126 128 129 130 131 132 135 143 144 146 147 148 155 167 169
Primary Contact: Beth Charlton, R.N., President and Chief Executive Officer
COO: Daniel M George, Executive Vice President, Operations
CFO: Kevin Albosta, Vice President, Chief Financial Officer
CMO: John Kosanovich, M.D., Executive Vice President Physician Enterprise and Chief Executive Officer, Covenant Medical Group
CHR: Kevin Birchmeier, Director Human Resources
Web address: www.covenanthealthcare.com
Control: Other not–for–profit (including NFP Corporation) **Service**: General medical and surgical

Staffed Beds: 524 Admissions: 23105 Census: 375 Outpatient Visits: 458768 Births: 2707 Total Expense ($000): 752473 Payroll Expense ($000): 388028 Personnel: 3806

Hospitals, U.S. / MICHIGAN

☐ **HEALTHSOURCE SAGINAW INC. (230275)**, 3340 Hospital Road, Zip 48603-9622; tel. 989/790-7700, (Total facility includes 192 beds in nursing home-type unit) **A**1 3 5 10 **F**4 30 90 91 93 96 98 99 100 101 103 128 130 143 146 149 154 161 164
Primary Contact: Michelle Trevillian, President and Chief Executive Officer
CFO: Glen Chipman, Chief Financial Officer
CMO: Daniel Duffy, D.O., Chief Medical Director
CIO: Greg Sieg, Support Services Executive
CHR: Krystal Hadaway, Director Human Resources
CNO: Susan Graham, R.N., Nurse Executive
Web address: www.healthsourcesaginaw.org
Control: Other not-for-profit (including NFP Corporation) **Service:** Psychiatric

Staffed Beds: 242 **Admissions:** 2807 **Census:** 215 **Outpatient Visits:** 4801 **Births:** 0 **Total Expense ($000):** 54906 **Payroll Expense ($000):** 26853 **Personnel:** 672

HEALTHSOURCE SAGINAW, INC. See Healthsource Saginaw Inc.

✠ **MYMICHIGAN MEDICAL CENTER SAGINAW (230077)**, 800 South Washington Avenue, Zip 48601-2594; tel. 989/907-8000, (Nonreporting) **A**1 2 3 5 10 19 **S** MyMichigan Health, Midland, MI
Primary Contact: Michael Erickson, Northern Region President
CFO: Nancy Haywood, Chief Financial Officer
CMO: Raghu Sarvepalli, M.D., Vice President of Medical Affairs
CHR: Paula Coffee, Director Human Resources
CNO: Bernie Jore, Chief Nursing Officer
Web address: https://healthcare.ascension.org/locations/michigan/misag/saginaw-ascension-st-marys-hospital?intent_source=location_title&result_position=1
Control: Church operated, Nongovernment, not-for-profit **Service:** General medical and surgical

Staffed Beds: 210

SAGINAW GENERAL HOSPITAL See Covenant Medical Center-Harrison

✠ **SELECT SPECIALTY HOSPITAL – SAGINAW (232033)**, 1447 North Harrison Street, 8th Floor, Zip 48602-4785; tel. 989/583-4235, (Nonreporting) **A**1 10 **S** Select Medical Corporation, Mechanicsburg, PA
Primary Contact: Kelly Ann. DeBolt, R.N., Chief Executive Officer
CNO: Shannon Sequin, MSN, Chief Nursing Officer
Web address: www.selectspecialtyhospitals.com/company/locations/saginaw.aspx
Control: Corporation, Investor-owned (for-profit) **Service:** Acute long-term care hospital

Staffed Beds: 25

SELECT SPECIALTY HOSPITAL-SAGINAW See Select Specialty Hospital – Saginaw

ST LUKE'S HOSPITAL See Covenant Medical Center-Cooper

ST. MARY'S OF MICHIGAN See Mymichigan Medical Center Saginaw

SAINT IGNACE—Mackinac County

★ ⇑ **MACKINAC STRAITS HEALTH SYSTEM, INC. (231306)**, 1140 North State Street, Zip 49781-1048; tel. 906/643-8585, (Total facility includes 48 beds in nursing home-type unit) **A**10 18 21 **F**3 8 15 28 29 31 40 42 45 51 54 56 59 64 65 74 75 77 78 79 81 91 93 97 107 110 111 115 119 126 127 128 130 133 135 146 147 148 154 156 167
Primary Contact: Karen Cheeseman, President and Chief Executive Officer
CFO: Ryan Speas, Chief Financial Officer
CMO: Loretta Leja, M.D., Chief of Staff
CHR: Kevin McElroy, Chief Human Resources Officer
Web address: www.mackinacstraitshealth.org
Control: Other not-for-profit (including NFP Corporation) **Service:** General medical and surgical

Staffed Beds: 63 **Admissions:** 277 **Census:** 50 **Outpatient Visits:** 45604 **Births:** 0 **Total Expense ($000):** 63874 **Payroll Expense ($000):** 19739 **Personnel:** 158

SAINT JOHNS—Clinton County

☐ **CEDAR CREEK HOSPITAL OF MICHIGAN (234043)**, 101 W Townsend Road, Zip 48879-9200; tel. 989/403-6022, **A**1 10 **F**98 154 **S** Universal Health Services, Inc., King of Prussia, PA
Primary Contact: Steven Vernon, Chief Executive Officer
Web address: www.cedarcreekhospital.com
Control: Corporation, Investor-owned (for-profit) **Service:** Psychiatric

Staffed Beds: 58 **Admissions:** 2145 **Census:** 47 **Outpatient Visits:** 0 **Total Expense ($000):** 17484 **Payroll Expense ($000):** 7820

✠ **SPARROW CLINTON HOSPITAL (231326)**, 805 South Oakland Street, Zip 48879-2253; tel. 989/227-3400, **A**1 10 18 **F**3 15 18 26 28 29 31 34 35 40 43 45 50 53 59 64 68 70 75 77 78 79 81 85 93 97 107 108 110 111 115 119 129 130 131 133 146 148 149 154 156 **P**6 **S** University of Michigan Health, Ann Arbor, MI
Primary Contact: Mark Brisboe, President
COO: Kevin A Price, Vice President and Chief Operating Officer
CMO: Christopher Beal, M.D., Chief of Staff
Web address: https://www.sparrow.org/our-hospitals-services/sparrow-hospitals/sparrow-clinton-hospital
Control: Other not-for-profit (including NFP Corporation) **Service:** General medical and surgical

Staffed Beds: 25 **Admissions:** 742 **Census:** 7 **Outpatient Visits:** 110505 **Births:** 0 **Total Expense ($000):** 54059 **Payroll Expense ($000):** 23189 **Personnel:** 243

SAINT JOSEPH—Berrien County

COREWELL HEALTH LAKELAND HOSPITAL See Corewell Health Lakeland Hospitals

✠ **COREWELL HEALTH LAKELAND HOSPITALS (230021)**, 1234 Napier Avenue, Zip 49085-2158; tel. 269/983-8300, (Includes COREWELL HEALTH NILES HOSPITAL, 31 North Saint Joseph Avenue, Niles, Michigan, Zip 49120, tel. 269/683-5510; Debra Johnson, R.N., Chief Administrator) (Total facility includes 111 beds in nursing home-type unit) **A**1 2 3 5 10 13 19 **F**1 3 4 12 13 15 18 19 20 22 24 26 28 29 30 31 34 35 37 38 40 43 45 46 48 49 50 51 54 55 56 58 59 60 61 62 63 64 65 68 70 74 75 76 77 78 79 81 84 85 86 87 89 93 96 97 98 100 102 107 111 114 115 117 119 120 121 123 124 126 127 128 129 130 131 135 146 147 148 149 154 156 164 167 169 **P**1 **S** Corewell Health, Grand Rapids, MI
Primary Contact: Natalie Baggio, R.N., President and Chief Operating Officer
CFO: Timothy Calhoun, Vice President Finance and Chief Financial Officer
CMO: Stephen Hempel, M.D., President Medical Staff
CIO: Emily Gallay, Vice President and Chief Information Officer
Web address: www.lakelandhealth.org
Control: Other not-for-profit (including NFP Corporation) **Service:** General medical and surgical

Staffed Beds: 407 **Admissions:** 12008 **Census:** 249 **Outpatient Visits:** 414030 **Births:** 1306 **Total Expense ($000):** 534017 **Payroll Expense ($000):** 188557 **Personnel:** 2122

SALINE—Washtenaw County

☐ **CENTER FOR FORENSIC PSYCHIATRY (234041)**, 8303 Platt Rd, Zip 48176-9773, Mailing Address: P.O. Box 2060, Ann Arbor, Zip 48106-2060; tel. 734/429-2531, (Nonreporting) **A**1 3 10
Primary Contact: Diane Heisel, Acting Director
Web address: www.michigan.gov
Control: County, Government, Nonfederal **Service:** Psychiatric

Staffed Beds: 210

SANDUSKY—Sanilac County

MCKENZIE HEALTH SYSTEM (231314), 120 North Delaware Street, Zip 48471-1087; tel. 810/648-3770, (Nonreporting) **A**10 18
Primary Contact: Steve Barnett, FACHE, President and Chief Executive Officer
COO: Billi Jo Hennika, Vice President Operations
CFO: Amy Ruedisueli, Vice President of Finance
CMO: James C. Sams, Chief of Staff
CHR: Carrie Krampits, Director Human Resources
CNO: Patricia Schafsnitz, Director of Nursing Services
Web address: www.mckenziehealth.org
Control: Other not-for-profit (including NFP Corporation) **Service:** General medical and surgical

Staffed Beds: 25

Hospital, Medicare Provider Number, Address, Telephone, Approval, Facility, and Physician Codes, Health Care System

★ American Hospital Association (AHA) membership   ○ Healthcare Facilities Accreditation Program   ⇑ Center for Improvement in Healthcare Quality Accreditation
☐ The Joint Commission accreditation   ◇ DNV Healthcare Inc. accreditation   △ Commission on Accreditation of Rehabilitation Facilities (CARF) accreditation

© 2025 AHA Guide

Hospitals, U.S. / MICHIGAN

SAULT SAINTE MARIE—Chippewa County

★ ⇧ **MYMICHIGAN MEDICAL CENTER SAULT (230239)**, 500 Osborn Boulevard, Zip 49783-1884; tel. 906/635-4460, (Total facility includes 43 beds in nursing home–type unit) **A**10 20 21 **F**3 11 12 13 15 18 28 29 30 31 34 35 36 38 40 43 44 50 51 53 54 55 56 57 59 60 61 64 65 66 68 70 74 75 76 77 78 79 81 82 85 86 87 92 93 96 97 98 100 101 104 106 107 108 110 111 115 119 126 127 128 129 130 131 132 133 135 143 144 146 147 148 149 154 156 160 162 164 166 169 **P**6 **S** MyMichigan Health, Midland, MI
Primary Contact: Kevin Kalchik, CPA, President
COO: Marla Bunker, Vice President Nursing and Chief Operating Officer
CMO: Paula Rechner, M.D., Chief Medical Officer
CIO: Sandy DePlonty, Chief Information Officer and Senior Director, Ancillary Services
CNO: Marla Bunker, Vice President Nursing and Chief Operating Officer
Web address: www.warmemorialhospital.org
Control: Other not–for–profit (including NFP Corporation) **Service**: General medical and surgical

Staffed Beds: 97 Admissions: 2489 Census: 70 Outpatient Visits: 260912 Births: 301 Total Expense ($000): 134994 Payroll Expense ($000): 58561 Personnel: 689

⇧ **WAR MEMORIAL HOSPITAL** See Mymichigan Medical Center Sault

SHELBY—Oceana County

MERCY HEALTH, LAKESHORE CAMPUS See Trinity Health Shelby Hospital

⊞ **TRINITY HEALTH SHELBY HOSPITAL (231320)**, 72 South State Street, Zip 49455-1299; tel. 231/861-2156, **A**1 10 18 **F**3 11 15 29 30 34 35 40 43 45 49 50 57 59 64 68 81 84 87 97 100 107 110 111 114 119 127 129 132 146 154 **S** Trinity Health, Livonia, MI
Primary Contact: Gary Allore, President
Web address: www.mercyhealthmuskegon.com
Control: Church operated, Nongovernment, not–for–profit **Service**: General medical and surgical

Staffed Beds: 24 Admissions: 405 Census: 3 Outpatient Visits: 101920 Births: 0 Total Expense ($000): 36726 Payroll Expense ($000): 16655 Personnel: 210

SHERIDAN—Montcalm County

○ **SHERIDAN COMMUNITY HOSPITAL (231312)**, 301 North Main Street, Zip 48884-9235, Mailing Address: P.O. Box 279, Zip 48884-0279; tel. 989/291-3261, **A**10 11 18 **F**3 4 8 11 15 30 34 35 40 44 45 50 57 59 64 75 77 81 84 86 87 90 93 97 107 110 111 114 115 119 126 127 130 133 141 144 146 148 149 152 154 **P**6
Primary Contact: Lili Petricevic, Chief Executive Officer
COO: Steve Scott, Chief Operating Officer
CMO: Maria Charlotte Alvarez, M.D., Chief of Staff
CIO: David Bussler, Chief Information Officer
CHR: Sharon Bowers, R.N., Manager of Community, Public and Employee Relations
CNO: Kim Christensen, Interim Chief Nursing Executive
Web address: www.sheridanhospital.com
Control: Other not–for–profit (including NFP Corporation) **Service**: General medical and surgical

Staffed Beds: 19 Admissions: 119 Census: 2 Outpatient Visits: 14608 Births: 0 Total Expense ($000): 17222 Payroll Expense ($000): 8349 Personnel: 133

SOUTH HAVEN—Van Buren County

⊞ **BRONSON SOUTH HAVEN HOSPITAL (230085)**, 955 South Bailey Avenue, Zip 49090-6743; tel. 269/637-5271, **A**1 10 **F**3 5 9 11 15 18 28 29 30 32 34 35 38 40 41 44 50 53 54 56 57 59 60 61 64 65 66 68 74 75 77 79 82 86 87 93 97 102 107 108 110 111 115 118 119 127 130 131 132 133 134 135 143 146 147 148 149 150 154 169 **P**6 **S** Bronson Healthcare Group, Kalamazoo, MI
Primary Contact: Bill Manns, President and Chief Executive Officer
CFO: Mark Gross, Executive Vice President and Chief Financial Officer
CMO: Allan Caudill, M.D., Chief of Staff
CIO: Dennis Sorenson, Supervisor Information Technology
CHR: Kim Wise, Director Human Resources
CNO: Donna Cassidy, Chief Nursing Executive
Web address: https://www.bronsonhealth.com/locations/bronson-south-haven-hospital/
Control: Other not–for–profit (including NFP Corporation) **Service**: General medical and surgical

Staffed Beds: 8 Admissions: 465 Census: 4 Outpatient Visits: 116694 Total Expense ($000): 38770 Payroll Expense ($000): 21239 Personnel: 220

SOUTHFIELD—Oakland County

⊞ **ASCENSION PROVIDENCE HOSPITAL, SOUTHFIELD CAMPUS (230019)**, 16001 West Nine Mile Road, Zip 48075; tel. 248/849-3000, (Includes PROVIDENCE – PROVIDENCE PARK HOSPITAL, NOVI CAMPUS, 47601 Grand River Avenue, Novi, Michigan, Zip 48374-1233, tel. 248/465-4100; Brant Russell, R.N., President and Chief Executive Officer) **A**1 2 3 5 10 19 **F**3 11 12 13 15 17 18 20 22 24 26 28 29 30 31 34 35 36 37 38 39 40 43 44 45 46 47 48 49 50 51 54 55 56 57 58 59 60 61 63 64 65 68 70 72 74 75 76 77 78 79 80 81 82 84 85 86 87 90 91 92 93 96 97 98 100 101 102 107 108 110 111 114 115 118 119 120 121 123 124 126 129 130 131 132 135 139 141 146 147 148 149 150 154 156 157 164 167 169 **S** Ascension Healthcare, Saint Louis, MO
Primary Contact: Michael Wiemann, M.D., Regional President & CEO, Ascension Metro West Region
CFO: Douglas Winner, Chief Financial Officer, Acute Care Operations
CHR: Ann Vano, Vice President Human Resources
Web address: https://healthcare.ascension.org/locations/michigan/midet/southfield-ascension-providence-hospital-southfield-campus
Control: Church operated, Nongovernment, not–for–profit **Service**: General medical and surgical

Staffed Beds: 628 Admissions: 33624 Census: 440 Outpatient Visits: 877974 Births: 3011 Total Expense ($000): 928094 Payroll Expense ($000): 322328 Personnel: 3225

⊞ **STRAITH HOSPITAL FOR SPECIAL SURGERY (230071)**, 23901 Lahser Road, Zip 48033-6035; tel. 248/357-3360, **A**1 10 **F**64 79 81 82 89 107 119 126 **P**6
Primary Contact: Bradley Bescoe, President and Chief Executive Officer
COO: Lamia Alfatlawi, Chief Operating Officer
CNO: Michelle Holder, Nurse Executive
Web address: www.straith.org/
Control: Other not–for–profit (including NFP Corporation) **Service**: Surgical

Staffed Beds: 34 Admissions: 298 Census: 5 Outpatient Visits: 7122 Births: 0 Total Expense ($000): 18772 Payroll Expense ($000): 7760 Personnel: 87

★ ○ **SURGEONS CHOICE MEDICAL CENTER (230301)**, 22401 Foster Winter Drive, Zip 48075-3724; tel. 248/423-5100, (Nonreporting) **A**3 10 11
Primary Contact: Steven Craig, Ph.D., Chief Executive Officer
CMO: John Jack Ryan, M.D., Chief Medical Officer
CIO: William Moncrief, ORH IT Client Executive
CHR: Gordon Meyer, Director Human Resources
CNO: Lola Evans, Director of Nursing
Web address: https://surgeonschoice.com/
Control: Corporation, Investor–owned (for–profit) **Service**: Surgical

Staffed Beds: 71

STANDISH—Arenac County

⊞ **MYMICHIGAN MEDICAL CENTER STANDISH (231305)**, 805 West Cedar Street, Zip 48658-9526; tel. 989/846-4521, (Nonreporting) **A**1 10 18 **S** MyMichigan Health, Midland, MI
Primary Contact: Michael Erickson, Northern Region President
CFO: Tony Doud, Controller
CMO: Jaya Sankaran, M.D., Chief of Staff
CIO: Tammy Copes, Director Information Systems
CHR: Renee Reetz, Director Human Resources
Web address: www.stmarysofmichigan.org/standish
Control: Other not–for–profit (including NFP Corporation) **Service**: General medical and surgical

Staffed Beds: 54

STURGIS—St. Joseph County

★ **STURGIS HOSPITAL (230779)**, 916 Myrtle Street, Zip 49091-2326; tel. 269/651-7824, (Nonreporting) **A**10
Primary Contact: Jeremy Gump, Interim Chief Executive Officer
COO: Robert J. Morin, Chief Financial Officer and Chief Operating Officer
CFO: Robert J. Morin, Chief Financial Officer and Chief Operating Officer
CMO: James Grannell, Chief Medical Officer
CIO: Rita Denison, Director of Information Systems
CHR: Mary Kay Schultz, Director Human Resources
CNO: Charlotte J Pavilanis, R.N., Vice President of Clinical Services and Chief Nursing Officer
Web address: www.sturgishospital.com
Control: Other not–for–profit (including NFP Corporation)

Staffed Beds: 49

Hospitals, U.S. / MICHIGAN

TAWAS CITY—Iosco County

☒ **MYMICHIGAN MEDICAL CENTER TAWAS (230100)**, 200 Hemlock Street, Zip 48763–9237, Mailing Address: P.O. Box 659, Zip 48764–0659; tel. 989/362–3411, (Nonreporting) **A**1 10 20 **S** MyMichigan Health, Midland, MI
Primary Contact: Michael Erickson, Northern Region President
CFO: Tony Doud, Controller
CHR: Nancy Bodenner, Director Human Resources
Web address: https://healthcare.ascension.org/locations/michigan/mitaw/tawas-city-ascension-st-joseph-hospital
Control: Other not–for–profit (including NFP Corporation) **Service:** General medical and surgical

Staffed Beds: 47

TAYLOR—Wayne County

☒ **COREWELL HEALTH TAYLOR HOSPITAL (230270)**, 10000 Telegraph Road, Zip 48180–3330; tel. 313/295–5000, **A**1 3 5 10 **F**3 11 15 29 30 34 35 37 38 40 44 46 49 50 56 57 59 60 61 64 65 68 70 74 75 79 81 82 84 85 86 87 90 92 93 96 97 100 101 102 107 108 111 114 117 118 119 126 130 131 132 135 146 147 148 149 150 154 164 168 **P**6 **S** Corewell Health, Grand Rapids, MI
Primary Contact: Kristine Donahue, R.N., President
COO: Carolyn Wilson, R.N., Chief Operating Officer
CFO: Mark Deming, Administrator, Finance and Support
CMO: Kassem Charara, Chief Medical Officer
CIO: Subra Sripada, Exec. Vice President, Chief Transformation Officer and Chief Information Officer
CHR: Karen Krolicki, Director, Human Resources
Web address: https://www.beaumont.org/locations/beaumont-hospital-taylor
Control: Other not–for–profit (including NFP Corporation) **Service:** General medical and surgical

Staffed Beds: 148 **Admissions:** 6586 **Census:** 116 **Outpatient Visits:** 71270 **Births:** 0 **Total Expense ($000):** 181012 **Payroll Expense ($000):** 70976 **Personnel:** 996

COREWELL HEALTH'S BEAUMONT HOSPITAL, TAYLOR See Corewell Health Taylor Hospital

THREE RIVERS—St. Joseph County

BEACON HEALTH SYSTEM – THREE RIVERS HEALTH SYSTEM, INC. See Three Rivers Health System, Inc.

★ ○ **THREE RIVERS HEALTH SYSTEM, INC. (230015)**, 701 South Health Parkway, Zip 49093–8352; tel. 269/278–1145, **A**3 10 11 **F**3 4 11 13 15 28 29 31 32 34 40 45 50 60 62 63 65 70 75 76 77 79 81 90 93 96 97 107 108 110 111 115 116 119 127 129 130 131 132 133 144 147 148 154 156 160 169 **S** Beacon Health System, South Bend, IN
Primary Contact: Maria Behr, President
COO: Maria Behr, Vice President Operations
CIO: Dave Parks, Chief Information Officer
CHR: Pauletta Wagner, Manager, Human Resources
CNO: Hope Bailey, Vice President Nursing
Web address: www.threerivershealth.org
Control: Other not–for–profit (including NFP Corporation) **Service:** General medical and surgical

Staffed Beds: 60 **Admissions:** 1301 **Census:** 14 **Outpatient Visits:** 18447 **Births:** 252 **Total Expense ($000):** 68450 **Payroll Expense ($000):** 27121 **Personnel:** 366

TRAVERSE CITY—Grand Traverse County

☒ **MUNSON MEDICAL CENTER (230097)**, 1105 Sixth Street, Zip 49684–2386; tel. 231/935–5000, **A**1 2 3 5 10 13 **F**3 4 5 10 12 13 15 17 18 20 22 24 26 28 29 30 31 34 35 36 39 40 43 44 45 46 47 48 49 50 53 54 55 56 57 58 59 60 61 62 63 64 65 68 70 72 74 75 76 77 78 79 81 85 86 87 89 90 92 93 97 98 100 101 102 104 107 108 110 111 115 116 117 118 119 120 121 123 124 126 129 130 131 132 134 135 141 142 143 144 146 147 148 149 154 156 157 160 164 165 167 169 **P**6 8 **S** Munson Healthcare, Traverse City, MI
Primary Contact: Joseph Hurshe, MMc President & Chief Executive Officer
CFO: Mark A Helper, Corporate Vice President and Chief Financial Officer
CMO: Kevin Omilusik, M.D., Chief Medical Officer
CIO: Christopher J Podges, Vice President and Chief Information Officer
Web address: www.munsonhealthcare.org
Control: Other not–for–profit (including NFP Corporation) **Service:** General medical and surgical

Staffed Beds: 442 **Admissions:** 18509 **Census:** 321 **Outpatient Visits:** 631528 **Births:** 1724 **Total Expense ($000):** 813536 **Payroll Expense ($000):** 299010 **Personnel:** 2766

TRENTON—Wayne County

☒ **COREWELL HEALTH TRENTON HOSPITAL (230176)**, 5450 Fort Street, Zip 48183–4625; tel. 734/671–3800, **A**1 3 5 10 12 13 **F**3 8 11 12 13 15 18 20 22 26 28 29 30 34 35 38 40 43 44 45 46 47 49 50 56 57 59 60 61 64 65 68 70 74 75 76 78 79 80 81 82 84 85 87 91 92 93 100 102 107 108 110 111 114 115 117 118 119 126 130 131 132 135 146 147 148 149 150 154 157 167 169 **P**6 **S** Corewell Health, Grand Rapids, MI
Primary Contact: Kristine Donahue, R.N., President
COO: Carolyn Wilson, R.N., Executive Vice President, Chief Operating Officer
CFO: Shawn Beggs, Administrator, Finance
CMO: Jonathan Kaper, Chief Medical Officer
CHR: Michelle Corra, Administrator, Human Resources
CNO: Susan G Schulz, Chief Nursing Officer
Web address: https://www.beaumont.org/locations/beaumont-hospital-trenton
Control: Other not–for–profit (including NFP Corporation) **Service:** General medical and surgical

Staffed Beds: 172 **Admissions:** 9379 **Census:** 112 **Outpatient Visits:** 67442 **Births:** 653 **Total Expense ($000):** 203745 **Payroll Expense ($000):** 77198 **Personnel:** 1077

COREWELL HEALTH'S BEAUMONT HOSPITAL, TRENTON See Corewell Health Trenton Hospital

TROY—Oakland County

☒ **COREWELL HEALTH BEAUMONT TROY HOSPITAL (230269)**, 44201 Dequindre Road, Zip 48085–1117; tel. 248/964–5000, **A**1 2 3 5 10 13 19 **F**3 5 8 11 12 13 15 17 18 19 20 22 24 26 28 29 30 31 32 34 35 36 37 38 39 40 41 43 44 45 46 47 48 49 50 53 54 55 56 57 58 59 60 63 66 68 70 72 74 75 76 77 78 79 80 81 82 84 85 86 87 89 90 91 92 93 96 97 100 102 104 107 108 110 111 114 115 117 118 119 120 121 123 124 126 129 130 131 132 135 141 142 145 146 147 148 149 150 154 157 160 161 162 165 167 **P**6 **S** Corewell Health, Grand Rapids, MI
Primary Contact: Nancy Susick, MSN, President
COO: Carolyn Wilson, R.N., Chief Operating Officer
CFO: Mark Leonard, Vice President Finance
CMO: James Lynch, M.D., Senior Vice President and Chief Medical Officer
CIO: Subra Sripada, Executive Vice President, Chief Transportation Officer and Chief Information Officer
CHR: Lisa Ouelette, Director Human Resources
Web address: https://www.beaumont.org/locations/beaumont-hospital-troy
Control: Other not–for–profit (including NFP Corporation) **Service:** General medical and surgical

Staffed Beds: 521 **Admissions:** 33490 **Census:** 428 **Outpatient Visits:** 513784 **Births:** 3791 **Total Expense ($000):** 745105 **Payroll Expense ($000):** 273852 **Personnel:** 4131

COREWELL HEALTH'S BEAUMONT HOSPITAL, TROY See Corewell Health Beaumont Troy Hospital

WARREN—Macomb County

ASCENSION MACOMB–OAKLAND HOSPITAL See Ascension Macomb–Oakland Hospital, Warren Campus

---

Hospital, Medicare Provider Number, Address, Telephone, Approval, Facility, and Physician Codes, Health Care System

★ American Hospital Association (AHA) membership   ○ Healthcare Facilities Accreditation Program   ⇑ Center for Improvement in Healthcare Quality Accreditation
☐ The Joint Commission accreditation   ◇ DNV Healthcare Inc. accreditation   △ Commission on Accreditation of Rehabilitation Facilities (CARF) accreditation

© 2025 AHA Guide

Hospitals, U.S. / MICHIGAN

ASCENSION MACOMB–OAKLAND HOSPITAL, WARREN CAMPUS (230195), 11800 East 12 Mile Road, Zip 48093–3472; tel. 586/573–5000, (Includes ST. JOHN MACOMB–OAKLAND HOSPITAL, MADISON HEIGHTS CAMPUS, 27351 Dequindre, Madison Heights, Michigan, Zip 48071–3487, tel. 248/967–7000; Terry Hamilton, President; ST. JOHN MACOMB–OAKLAND HOSPITAL, WARREN CAMPUS, 11800 E 12 Mile RD, Warren, Michigan, Zip 48093–3472, 11800 East Twelve Mile Road, Zip 48093–3472, tel. 586/573–5000; Terry Hamilton, President) **A**1 2 3 5 10 12 19 **F**3 11 12 15 18 20 22 26 28 29 30 31 33 34 35 36 38 39 40 43 44 45 46 47 48 49 50 51 54 56 57 58 59 60 61 63 64 65 68 70 74 75 77 78 79 80 81 82 84 85 86 87 90 91 92 93 96 97 98 100 101 102 107 108 110 111 115 118 119 121 123 126 129 130 131 132 135 141 146 147 148 149 150 154 157 164 167 **S** Ascension Healthcare, Saint Louis, MO
Primary Contact: Kevin Grady, M.D., East Region President
COO: William Mott, Chief Operating Officer
CFO: Patrick McGuire, Chief Financial Officer, Michigan Market
CMO: Gary L Berg, D.O., Chief Medical Officer
CIO: Ralph Tenney, Chief Information Officer
CHR: Joanne E Tuscany, Senior Director Human Resources
CNO: Kim Ronnisch, Vice President Nursing and Chief Nursing Officer
Web address: https://healthcare.ascension.org/locations/michigan/midet/warren-ascension-macomboakland-hospital-warren-campus
Control: Church operated, Nongovernment, not–for–profit **Service**: General medical and surgical

Staffed Beds: 479 **Admissions**: 23889 **Census**: 349 **Outpatient Visits**: 242246 **Births**: 404 **Total Expense ($000)**: 503739 **Payroll Expense ($000)**: 202921 **Personnel**: 1706

BEHAVIORAL CENTER OF MICHIGAN (234042), 4050 East 12 Mile Road, Zip 48092–2534; tel. 586/261–2266, (Nonreporting) **A**1 10
Primary Contact: Ryan Gunabalan, Chief Executive Officer
COO: Efren Lusterio, Director of Nursing
CFO: Mark Corey, Chief Financial Officer
CMO: Eleanor Medina, M.D., Chief Medical Officer
CIO: Kashmira Khade, Coordinator Non–Clinical Services
CHR: Erin R Youngblood, Chief Human Resources Officer
Web address: www.behavioralcenter.com
Control: Corporation, Investor–owned (for–profit) **Service**: Psychiatric

Staffed Beds: 42

INSIGHT SURGICAL HOSPITAL (230264), 21230 Dequindre, Zip 48091–2287; tel. 586/427–1000, (Nonreporting) **A**1 10
Primary Contact: Atif Bawahab, Chief Executive Officer
CMO: Benjamin Paolucci, D.O., Chief of Staff
CHR: Dawn Meiers, Coordinator Medical Staff and Personnel Services
Web address: https://www.insightsurgicalhospital.com/
Control: Corporation, Investor–owned (for–profit) **Service**: Surgical

Staffed Beds: 13

ST. JOHN MACOMB–OAKLAND HOSPITAL See St. John Macomb–Oakland Hospital, Warren Campus

WATERVLIET—Berrien County

COREWELL HEALTH WATERVLIET HOSPITAL (230078), 400 Medical Park Drive, Zip 49098–9225; tel. 269/463–3111, **A**1 7 10 **F**3 11 15 18 29 30 34 35 40 43 45 50 54 57 59 64 65 68 75 77 79 81 87 90 93 94 96 97 107 110 114 115 119 127 130 131 135 144 146 148 149 154 156 **P**1 **S** Corewell Health, Grand Rapids, MI
Primary Contact: Christine Fox, MSN, R.N., Interim Chief Nursing Officer
CFO: Timothy Calhoun, Vice President Finance, Chief Financial Officer
CIO: Norma Tirado, Vice President, Human Resources and Health Information Technology
CHR: Norma Tirado, Vice President, Human Resources and Health Information Technology
CNO: Connie Harmon, Director of Nursing
Web address: https://www.spectrumhealthlakeland.org/locations/Detail/corewell-health-watervliet-hospital/f3a140ad-c230-6723-add8-ff0000ca780f
Control: Other not–for–profit (including NFP Corporation) **Service**: General medical and surgical

Staffed Beds: 44 **Admissions**: 409 **Census**: 14 **Outpatient Visits**: 121514 **Births**: 0 **Total Expense ($000)**: 47427 **Payroll Expense ($000)**: 22133 **Personnel**: 260

SPECTRUM HEALTH LAKELAND WATERVLIET HOSPITAL See Corewell Health Watervliet Hospital

WAYNE—Wayne County

COREWELL HEALTH WAYNE HOSPITAL (230142), 33155 Annapolis Street, Zip 48184–2405; tel. 734/467–4000, **A**1 3 5 10 **F**3 11 12 13 15 18 20 22 26 28 29 30 31 34 38 40 42 43 44 45 46 47 49 50 54 57 59 60 61 64 65 68 70 74 75 76 77 78 79 81 82 84 85 86 87 91 92 93 96 100 102 107 108 110 111 115 117 118 119 126 130 131 132 134 135 143 146 147 148 149 154 167 **P**6 8 **S** Corewell Health, Grand Rapids, MI
Primary Contact: Kristine Donahue, R.N., President
COO: Carolyn Wilson, R.N., Chief Operating Officer
CFO: Jacqueline Nash, Controller
CMO: Ashok Jain, M.D., Senior Vice President and Chief Medical Officer
CIO: Subra Sripada, Executive Vice President, Chief Transformation Officer and Chief Information Officer
CHR: Robert L James, Director Human Resources
CNO: Diane L Hartley, Director of Patient Care Services
Web address: https://www.beaumont.org/locations/beaumont-hospital-wayne
Control: Other not–for–profit (including NFP Corporation) **Service**: General medical and surgical

Staffed Beds: 99 **Admissions**: 6135 **Census**: 82 **Outpatient Visits**: 163016 **Births**: 497 **Total Expense ($000)**: 170966 **Payroll Expense ($000)**: 68569 **Personnel**: 813

COREWELL HEALTH'S BEAUMONT HOSPITAL, WAYNE See Corewell Health Wayne Hospital

WEST BLOOMFIELD—Oakland County

HENRY FORD WEST BLOOMFIELD HOSPITAL (230302), 6777 West Maple Road, Zip 48322–3013; tel. 248/325–1000, **A**1 2 3 10 **F**3 11 12 13 15 18 20 22 26 28 29 30 31 32 34 35 36 37 38 40 41 43 44 45 46 49 50 51 54 55 56 57 58 59 60 61 62 63 64 65 68 70 73 74 75 76 77 78 79 80 81 82 84 85 86 87 89 92 93 96 97 99 100 101 103 107 108 110 111 114 115 116 117 118 119 120 121 123 124 125 126 130 131 132 134 141 145 146 147 148 149 150 154 156 157 167 169 **P**6 **S** Henry Ford Health, Detroit, MI
Primary Contact: Shanna Johnson, FACHE, President
COO: Karen Harris, R.N., Chief Nursing and Operations Officer
CFO: Terry Goodbalian, Regional Chief Financial Officer
CMO: Betty Chu, M.D., Chief Medical Officer and Vice President of Medical Affairs
CIO: Mary Alice Annecharico, System Vice President and Chief Information Officer
CNO: Karen Harris, R.N., Chief Nursing and Operations Officer
Web address: https://www.henryford.com/locations/west-bloomfield
Control: Other not–for–profit (including NFP Corporation) **Service**: General medical and surgical

Staffed Beds: 191 **Admissions**: 13336 **Census**: 154 **Outpatient Visits**: 202351 **Births**: 2005 **Total Expense ($000)**: 386850 **Payroll Expense ($000)**: 154147 **Personnel**: 1971

WEST BRANCH—Ogemaw County

MIDMICHIGAN MEDICAL CENTER – WEST BRANCH See Mymichigan Medical Center West Branch

MYMICHIGAN MEDICAL CENTER WEST BRANCH (230095), 2463 South M–30, Zip 48661–1199; tel. 989/345–3660, **A**1 10 20 **F**3 7 11 13 15 18 20 26 28 29 30 31 34 35 38 40 45 46 50 59 64 70 75 76 77 79 81 93 96 107 108 110 111 114 115 116 118 119 135 144 146 148 149 154 156 164 167 **P**2 **S** MyMichigan Health, Midland, MI
Primary Contact: Raymond Stover, Regional President
CFO: Kathy Kohr, Chief Financial Officer
CMO: Mark Weber, M.D., President Medical Staff
CHR: Kent Allen, Director Human Resources
CNO: Nicole Gillette, R.N., Chief Nursing Officer
Web address: https://www.mymichigan.org/locations/profile/medicalcenter-westbranch/
Control: Other not–for–profit (including NFP Corporation) **Service**: General medical and surgical

Staffed Beds: 86 **Admissions**: 1662 **Census**: 15 **Outpatient Visits**: 60194 **Births**: 56 **Total Expense ($000)**: 104239 **Payroll Expense ($000)**: 22756 **Personnel**: 274

WESTLAND—Wayne County

WALTER P. REUTHER PSYCHIATRIC HOSPITAL (234035), 30901 Palmer Road, Zip 48186–5389; tel. 734/367–8400, (Nonreporting) **A**1 3 10
Primary Contact: Richard T. Young, FACHE, Director
CMO: H. Bandla, M.D., Chief Clinical Affairs
CHR: Deborah Moore, Director Human Resources
Web address: www.mhweb.org/wayne/reuther.htm
Control: State, Government, Nonfederal **Service**: Psychiatric

Staffed Beds: 239

Hospitals, U.S. / MICHIGAN

WYANDOTTE—Wayne County

HENRY FORD WYANDOTTE HOSPITAL (230146), 2333 Biddle Avenue, Zip 48192-4668; tel. 734/246-6000, **A**1 2 3 5 7 10 19 **F**3 8 11 12 13 15 18 19 20 22 26 28 29 30 31 32 34 35 36 40 41 42 43 44 45 46 47 49 50 51 53 54 56 57 58 59 60 61 62 63 64 65 66 70 73 74 75 76 77 78 79 80 81 82 84 85 86 87 90 92 93 96 97 98 100 102 107 108 111 112 114 115 116 117 118 119 126 128 129 130 131 132 135 144 146 147 148 149 154 156 157 167 169 **P**6 **S** Henry Ford Health, Detroit, MI
Primary Contact: Rand O'Leary, FACHE, President
CFO: Terry Goodbalian, Vice President, Finance and Chief Financial Officer
CMO: Brooke Mattern Buckley, M.D., FACS, Chief Medical Officer
CIO: Mary Alice Annecharico, System Vice President and Chief Information Officer
CNO: Josephine Sclafani Wahl, R.N., MS, FACHE, VP, Patient Care Services & CNO
Web address: https://www.henryford.com/locations/wyandotte
Control: Other not-for-profit (including NFP Corporation) **Service**: General medical and surgical

Staffed Beds: 310 **Admissions**: 13381 **Census**: 187 **Outpatient Visits**: 418077 **Births**: 1412 **Total Expense ($000)**: 386173 **Payroll Expense ($000)**: 165585 **Personnel**: 1915

SELECT SPECIALTY HOSPITAL – DOWNRIVER (232031), 2333 Biddle Avenue, 8th Floor, Zip 48192-4668; tel. 734/246-5500, (Includes SELECT SPECIALTY HOSPITAL–NORTHWEST DETROIT, 6071 West Outer Drive, Detroit, Michigan, Zip 48235-2624, tel. 313/966-4747; Marilouise Riska, Chief Executive Officer) (Nonreporting) **A**1 10 **S** Select Medical Corporation, Mechanicsburg, PA
Primary Contact: John Ponczocha, Chief Executive Officer
CMO: Roderick Boyer, M.D., Medical Director
CHR: Barb Wierzbicki, Manager Human Resources
CNO: Angela Kudla, MSN, R.N., Chief Nursing Officer
Web address: www.downriver.selectspecialtyhospitals.com/
Control: Corporation, Investor-owned (for-profit) **Service**: Acute long-term care hospital

Staffed Beds: 35

SELECT SPECIALTY HOSPITAL–DOWNRIVER See Select Specialty Hospital – Downriver

WYOMING—Kent County

METRO HEALTH – UNIVERSITY OF MICHIGAN HEALTH See University of Michigan Health – West

UNIVERSITY OF MICHIGAN HEALTH – WEST (230236), 5900 Byron Center Avenue SW, Zip 49519-9606, Mailing Address: P.O. Box 916, Zip 49509-0916; tel. 616/252-7200, **A**3 5 10 11 13 19 **F**3 12 13 15 18 19 20 22 24 26 28 29 30 31 34 35 37 40 43 44 45 46 48 49 50 54 57 58 59 64 65 66 70 74 75 76 77 78 79 80 81 85 86 87 92 97 101 104 107 108 110 111 115 119 126 129 130 131 132 135 144 146 147 148 149 150 154 156 160 162 164 165 167 169 **S** University of Michigan Health, Ann Arbor, MI
Primary Contact: Ronald Grifka, M.D., FACC, President
CFO: Kris Kurtz, Chief Financial Officer
CIO: Joshua Wilda, Chief Information Officer
CNO: Steve Polega, Chief Nursing Officer
Web address: https://uofmhealthwest.org/
Control: Other not-for-profit (including NFP Corporation) **Service**: General medical and surgical

Staffed Beds: 208 **Admissions**: 8843 **Census**: 93 **Outpatient Visits**: 648287 **Births**: 1742 **Total Expense ($000)**: 569840 **Payroll Expense ($000)**: 237176 **Personnel**: 2518

YPSILANTI—Washtenaw County

FOREST HEALTH MEDICAL CENTER (230144), 135 South Prospect Street, Zip 48198-7914; tel. 734/547-4700, **A**1 10 **F**12 30 64 74 75 81 82 85 111 119 130 132 149
Primary Contact: Trevor J. Dyksterhouse, President
COO: Andrea Walrath, Chief Operating Officer
CFO: David Althoen, Director Financial Planning and Analysis
CMO: Jason Adams, M.D., Medical Staff President
CIO: Andrea Walrath, Chief Operating Officer
CHR: Amy Mohr, Coordinator Human Resources
Web address: www.fhmc-mi.com
Control: Corporation, Investor-owned (for-profit) **Service**: General medical and surgical

Staffed Beds: 24 **Admissions**: 349 **Census**: 2 **Outpatient Visits**: 16049 **Births**: 0 **Personnel**: 40

SELECT SPECIALTY HOSPITAL – ANN ARBOR (232024), 5301 East Huron River Drive, 7th Floor, Zip 48197-1051; tel. 734/712-6751, (Nonreporting) **A**1 10 **S** Select Medical Corporation, Mechanicsburg, PA
Primary Contact: Michael Grace, Chief Executive Officer
CMO: Hamid Halimi, M.D., Medical Director
CHR: Cindy Hardick, Human Resources Coordinator
CNO: Tim Varney, R.N., Chief Nursing Officer
Web address: www.annarbor.selectspecialtyhospitals.com/
Control: Corporation, Investor-owned (for-profit) **Service**: Acute long-term care hospital

Staffed Beds: 36

ST. JOSEPH MERCY ANN ARBOR See Trinity Health Ann Arbor Hospital

TRINITY HEALTH ANN ARBOR HOSPITAL (230156), 5301 Mcauley Drive, Zip 48197-1051; Mailing Address: P.O. Box 995, Ann Arbor, Zip 48106-0995; tel. 734/712-3456, **A**1 2 3 5 10 19 **F**3 4 5 8 11 12 13 15 17 18 20 22 24 26 28 29 30 31 32 34 35 36 37 38 40 41 43 44 45 46 47 48 49 50 51 53 54 55 56 57 58 59 61 64 65 66 68 70 71 72 73 74 75 76 77 78 79 80 81 82 83 84 85 86 87 89 90 91 92 93 94 95 96 97 98 100 101 102 103 104 105 107 108 109 110 111 114 115 117 118 119 120 121 123 124 126 129 130 131 132 134 135 143 144 145 146 147 148 149 153 154 156 157 160 162 163 164 165 166 167 169 **S** Trinity Health, Livonia, MI
Primary Contact: Alonzo Lewis, President
CFO: Kathy O'Connor, Vice President Finance
CMO: Rosalie Tocco-Bradley, Ph.D., M.D., Chief Medical Officer
Web address: https://www.trinityhealthmichigan.org/location/trinity-health-ann-arbor-hospital
Control: Church operated, Nongovernment, not-for-profit **Service**: General medical and surgical

Staffed Beds: 537 **Admissions**: 35561 **Census**: 433 **Outpatient Visits**: 1098881 **Births**: 3958 **Total Expense ($000)**: 1015504 **Payroll Expense ($000)**: 364592 **Personnel**: 4623

ZEELAND—Ottawa County

COREWELL HEALTH ZEELAND HOSPITAL (230003), 8333 Felch Street, Zip 49464-2608; tel. 616/772-4644, **A**1 2 10 **F**3 12 13 15 18 29 32 34 35 39 40 43 44 45 50 57 59 64 65 68 70 74 75 76 79 81 85 86 87 93 100 107 108 110 111 115 116 119 126 129 130 131 132 134 135 144 145 146 149 154 164 169 **S** Corewell Health, Grand Rapids, MI
Primary Contact: Bill Hoefer, FACHE, President and Regional Market Leader
CFO: Ryan J. Powers, Vice President Finance
CMO: Ruel R. Lirio, M.D., Clinical Physician Advisor
CIO: Imran Syed, Manager Technology Information Services
CHR: Jennifer F Becksvoort, Senior Human Resource Business Partner
CNO: Linda Schaltz, MSN, R.N., Chief Nursing Officer
Web address: www.spectrumhealth.org/zeeland
Control: Other not-for-profit (including NFP Corporation) **Service**: General medical and surgical

Staffed Beds: 55 **Admissions**: 2607 **Census**: 18 **Outpatient Visits**: 122513 **Births**: 722 **Total Expense ($000)**: 90583 **Payroll Expense ($000)**: 23140 **Personnel**: 323

SPECTRUM HEALTH ZEELAND COMMUNITY HOSPITAL See Corewell Health Zeeland Hospital

---

Hospital, Medicare Provider Number, Address, Telephone, Approval, Facility, and Physician Codes, Health Care System

★ American Hospital Association (AHA) membership
☐ The Joint Commission accreditation
○ Healthcare Facilities Accreditation Program
◇ DNV Healthcare Inc. accreditation
⇑ Center for Improvement in Healthcare Quality Accreditation
△ Commission on Accreditation of Rehabilitation Facilities (CARF) accreditation

Hospitals, U.S. / MINNESOTA

MINNESOTA

ADA—Norman County

★ **ESSENTIA HEALTH–ADA (241313)**, 201 9th Street West, Zip 56510–1279; tel. 218/784–5000, **A**10 18 **F**7 15 28 29 34 35 40 41 45 56 57 59 64 65 77 79 81 82 87 89 93 97 104 107 127 130 131 133 135 154 156 169 **P**6 **S** Essentia Health, Duluth, MN
Primary Contact: Erin Stoltman, Administrator
CMO: Jeff Peterson, M.D., Chief of Staff
CHR: Shayla Hennenberg, Director Human Resources
Web address: www.essentiahealth.org
Control: Other not–for–profit (including NFP Corporation) **Service:** General medical and surgical

Staffed Beds: 14 **Admissions:** 67 **Census:** 1 **Outpatient Visits:** 12113
Births: 0 **Total Expense ($000):** 9205 **Payroll Expense ($000):** 4107
Personnel: 38

AITKIN—Aitkin County

✠ **RIVERWOOD HEALTHCARE CENTER (241305)**, 200 Bunker Hill Drive, Zip 56431–1865; tel. 218/927–2121, (Nonreporting) **A**1 10 18
Primary Contact: Ken Westman, Chief Executive Officer
COO: Cindi Baker, Chief Operating Officer
CFO: Casey R Johnson, Chief Financial Officer
CMO: Mark Heggem, M.D., Chief Medical Officer
CIO: Daryl Kallevig, Chief Information Officer
CHR: Cindi Hills, Director Human Resources
CNO: Carla Zupko, R.N., Chief Nursing Officer
Web address: www.riverwoodhealthcare.org
Control: Other not–for–profit (including NFP Corporation) **Service:** General medical and surgical

Staffed Beds: 25

ALBERT LEA—Freeborn County

☐ **MAYO CLINIC HEALTH SYSTEM – ALBERT LEA AND AUSTIN (240043)**, 404 West Fountain Street, Zip 56007–2473; tel. 507/373–2384, (Includes MAYO CLINIC HEALTH SYSTEM – ALBERT LEA AND AUSTIN, 1000 First Drive NW, Austin, Minnesota, Zip 55912–2904, tel. 507/433–7351) **A**1 3 5 10 20 **F**3 4 5 9 11 12 13 15 18 28 29 30 31 32 34 35 36 38 40 43 44 45 46 47 50 56 57 58 59 64 65 68 70 71 74 75 76 77 78 79 81 82 85 86 87 89 93 94 96 97 98 99 100 101 102 103 104 106 107 108 110 111 115 119 120 126 129 130 131 132 135 146 147 148 149 150 153 154 156 160 161 162 164 165 169 **S** Mayo Clinic, Rochester, MN
Primary Contact: Mark Ciota, M.D., Chief Executive Officer
CMO: John Grzybowski, M.D., Medical Director
CHR: Monica Fleegel, Director Human Resources
CNO: Lori Routh, R.N., Nurse Administrator
Web address: www.almedcenter.org
Control: Other not–for–profit (including NFP Corporation) **Service:** General medical and surgical

Staffed Beds: 80 **Admissions:** 3253 **Census:** 37 **Outpatient Visits:** 260015
Births: 616

ALEXANDRIA—Douglas County

★ ○ **ALOMERE HEALTH (240030)**, 111 17th Avenue East, Zip 56308–3798; tel. 320/762–1511, **A**2 10 11 **F**3 8 11 13 15 28 29 30 31 32 34 35 36 40 43 50 57 61 64 65 68 70 76 77 78 79 81 82 85 86 87 89 91 93 97 107 108 111 115 117 118 119 126 129 130 131 132 135 144 146 148 149 154 156 157 169 **P**6
Primary Contact: Carl P. Vaagenes, Chief Executive Officer
CFO: Nate Meyer, Chief Financial Officer
CMO: Dan Kryder, M.D., Chief Medical Officer
CHR: Shelly Gompf, Director Human Resources
CNO: Margaret L Kalina, R.N., KalinaDirector of Patient Services and Chief Nursing Officer
Web address: https://alomerehealth.com/
Control: County, Government, Nonfederal **Service:** General medical and surgical

Staffed Beds: 98 **Admissions:** 2563 **Census:** 22 **Outpatient Visits:** 279706
Births: 594 **Total Expense ($000):** 194940 **Payroll Expense ($000):** 55763
Personnel: 707

ALEXANDRIA—Sherburne County

☐ **COMMUNITY BEHAVIORAL HEALTH HOSPITAL – ALEXANDRIA (244012)**, 1610 8th Avenue East, Zip 56308–2472; tel. 320/335–6201, (Nonreporting) **A**1 10 **S** Minnesota Department of Human Services, Saint Paul, MN
Primary Contact: Kimberly Jutz, Administrator
CFO: Shirley Jacobson, Chief Financial Officer
Web address: www.health.state.mn.us
Control: State, Government, Nonfederal **Service:** Psychiatric

Staffed Beds: 16

ANNANDALE—Wright County

☐ **COMMUNITY BEHAVIORAL HEALTH HOSPITAL – ANNANDALE (244011)**, 400 Annandale Boulevard, Zip 55302–3141; tel. 651/259–3850, (Nonreporting) **A**1 10 **S** Minnesota Department of Human Services, Saint Paul, MN
Primary Contact: Bill Stoner, Site Administrator
CMO: Shabeer A Ahmed, M.D., Clinical Director
CNO: Lennetta M Reynolds, Administrative Supervisor
Web address: www.health.state.mn.us
Control: State, Government, Nonfederal **Service:** Psychiatric

Staffed Beds: 16

ANOKA—Anoka County

ANOKA METRO REGIONAL TREATMENT CENTER (244002), 3301 Seventh Avenue, Zip 55303–4516, Mailing Address: 3301 Seventh Avenue North, Zip 55303–4516; tel. 651/431–5000, (Nonreporting) **A**10 **S** Minnesota Department of Human Services, Saint Paul, MN
Primary Contact: Kathryn Kallas, Interim Administrator
Web address: www.health.state.mn.us
Control: State, Government, Nonfederal **Service:** Psychiatric

Staffed Beds: 200

APPLETON—Swift County

APPLETON AREA HEALTH (241341), 30 South Behl Street, Zip 56208–1699; tel. 320/289–2422, (Nonreporting) **A**10 18
Primary Contact: Greg Miner, Chief Executive Officer
CFO: Anne Kells, Interim Chief Financial Officer
Web address: www.appletonareahealth.com
Control: City, Government, Nonfederal **Service:** General medical and surgical

Staffed Beds: 15

ARLINGTON—Sibley County

★ ⇑ **RIDGEVIEW SIBLEY MEDICAL CENTER (241311)**, 601 West Chandler Street, Zip 55307–2127; tel. 507/964–2271, **A**10 18 21 **F**3 7 15 28 29 31 34 35 40 43 45 46 56 57 59 62 63 64 65 66 77 78 81 86 87 93 96 97 107 110 115 119 127 128 130 131 133 135 144 154 169 **P**6 **S** Ridgeview Medical Center, Waconia, MN
Primary Contact: Stacey Lee, CPA, JD, Vice President/Administrator
COO: Ben Nielsen, Vice President, Chief Operating Officer
CFO: Aaron Bloomquist, Vice President, Chief Financial Officer
CMO: Matthew Herold, Vice President, Chief Medical Officer
CIO: Andy Kester, Vice President, Chief Information Officer
CHR: Sara Christiansen, Interim Director Human Resources
CNO: Elaine Arion, Vice President, Chief Nursing Officer
Web address: www.sibleymedical.org
Control: Other not–for–profit (including NFP Corporation) **Service:** General medical and surgical

Staffed Beds: 6 **Admissions:** 154 **Census:** 2 **Outpatient Visits:** 32505
Births: 0 **Total Expense ($000):** 16577 **Payroll Expense ($000):** 6575
Personnel: 83

Hospitals, U.S. / MINNESOTA

AURORA—St. Louis County

★ **ESSENTIA HEALTH NORTHERN PINES (241340)**, 5211 Highway 110, Zip 55705–1599; tel. 218/229–2211, (Total facility includes 33 beds in nursing home–type unit) **A**10 18 **F**3 28 29 34 40 43 50 56 57 59 64 65 75 81 82 85 87 93 96 97 100 102 107 127 128 130 133 135 148 149 154 157 **S** Essentia Health, Duluth, MN
Primary Contact: Diana Kallberg, Administrator
CFO: Kevin Boren, Chief Financial Officer
CMO: Michelle Oman, D.O., Chief Medical Officer
CHR: Kim Carlson, Director Human Resources
CNO: Cindy Loe, R.N., Director of Nursing
Web address: www.essentiahealth.org/NorthernPines/FindaClinic/Essentia-HealthNorthern-Pines-36.aspx
Control: Other not–for–profit (including NFP Corporation) **Service:** General medical and surgical

Staffed Beds: 49 **Admissions:** 289 **Census:** 35 **Outpatient Visits:** 31661 **Births:** 0 **Total Expense ($000):** 20446 **Payroll Expense ($000):** 9662 **Personnel:** 84

AUSTIN—Mower County

MAYO CLINIC HEALTH SYSTEM–ALBERT LEA AND AUSTIN See Mayo Clinic Health System – Albert Lea and Austin

BAGLEY—Clearwater County

★ **SANFORD BAGLEY MEDICAL CENTER (241328)**, 203 Fourth Street NW, Zip 56621–8307; tel. 218/694–6501, (Nonreporting) **A**10 18 **S** Sanford Health, Sioux Falls, SD
Primary Contact: Carrie Krump, Senior Director
CMO: Andre Spence, Chief Medical Staff
CNO: Stephanie McKnight, Hospital Nursing Manager
Web address: www.sanfordhealth.org
Control: Other not–for–profit (including NFP Corporation) **Service:** General medical and surgical

Staffed Beds: 8

BAUDETTE—Lake of The Woods County

★ **CHI LAKEWOOD HEALTH (241301)**, 600 Main Avenue South, Zip 56623–2855; tel. 218/634–2120, (Nonreporting) **A**10 18 **S** CommonSpirit Health, Chicago, IL
Primary Contact: Jeffry Stampohar, President
CFO: Jay Ross, Vice President of Finance
CMO: Justin Quo, Chief of Staff
CIO: Dan Leadbetter, Information Technology Systems Site Lead
CNO: Danielle Abel, Vice President of Patient Care Services
Web address: www.lakewoodhealthcenter.org
Control: Church operated, Nongovernment, not–for–profit **Service:** General medical and surgical

Staffed Beds: 55

BAXTER—Crow Wing County

☐ **COMMUNITY BEHAVIORAL HEALTH HOSPITAL – BAXTER (244015)**, 14241 Grand Oaks Drive, Zip 56425–8749; tel. 218/316–3101, (Nonreporting) **A**1 10 **S** Minnesota Department of Human Services, Saint Paul, MN
Primary Contact: Ryan D. Cerney, Administrator
Web address: www.business.explorebrainerdlakes.com/list/member/community-behavioral-health-hospital-baxter-8647
Control: State, Government, Nonfederal **Service:** Psychiatric

Staffed Beds: 16

BEMIDJI—Beltrami County

☐ **COMMUNITY BEHAVIORAL HEALTH HOSPITAL – BEMIDJI (244014)**, 800 Bemidji Avenue North, Zip 56601–3054; tel. 218/308–2400, (Nonreporting) **A**1 10 **S** Minnesota Department of Human Services, Saint Paul, MN
Primary Contact: Larry A. Laudon, Administrator
Control: State, Government, Nonfederal **Service:** Psychiatric

Staffed Beds: 16

◈ **SANFORD BEMIDJI MEDICAL CENTER (240100)**, 1300 Anne Street NW, Zip 56601–5103; tel. 218/751–5430, (Total facility includes 78 beds in nursing home–type unit) **A**1 2 10 **F**3 8 11 13 15 17 18 20 22 26 28 29 30 31 32 33 34 35 38 40 41 43 45 46 49 50 51 53 54 56 57 58 59 60 61 62 63 64 65 68 70 73 74 75 76 77 78 79 81 82 83 84 85 86 87 88 89 90 91 93 94 96 97 101 102 104 107 108 110 111 114 115 118 119 120 121 123 124 126 127 128 129 130 131 132 134 135 144 146 147 148 149 153 154 155 156 157 169 **P**6 **S** Sanford Health, Sioux Falls, SD
Primary Contact: Karla Eischens, Chief Executive Officer
CMO: Daniel DeKrey, M.D., Chief of Staff
CIO: Dan Moffatt, Chief Information Officer
Web address: www.sanfordhealth.org/bemidji
Control: Other not–for–profit (including NFP Corporation) **Service:** General medical and surgical

Staffed Beds: 196 **Admissions:** 5337 **Census:** 116 **Outpatient Visits:** 297301 **Births:** 761 **Total Expense ($000):** 392393 **Payroll Expense ($000):** 161599 **Personnel:** 1508

BENSON—Swift County

★ **CENTRACARE – BENSON (241365)**, 1815 Wisconsin Avenue, Zip 56215–1653; tel. 320/843–4232, (Data for 181 days) **A**10 18 **F**3 15 28 29 31 34 35 40 45 50 56 59 65 68 81 82 93 97 107 110 111 114 119 127 129 130 131 133 135 146 148 154 169 **S** CentraCare Health, Saint Cloud, MN
Primary Contact: Melissa McGinty–Thompson, Administrator, Chief Nursing Officer and Clinical Officer
CMO: Richard Horecka, Chief Medical Officer
CNO: Melissa McGinty–Thompson, Chief Nursing Officer
Web address: https://www.centracare.com/locations/centracare-benson-hospital/
Control: Other not–for–profit (including NFP Corporation) **Service:** General medical and surgical

Staffed Beds: 11 **Admissions:** 57 **Census:** 1 **Outpatient Visits:** 10797 **Births:** 0 **Total Expense ($000):** 8850 **Payroll Expense ($000):** 2929 **Personnel:** 91

BIGFORK—Itasca County

★ **BIGFORK VALLEY HOSPITAL (241316)**, 258 Pine Tree Drive, Zip 56628, Mailing Address: P.O. Box 258, Zip 56628–0258; tel. 218/743–3177, (Nonreporting) **A**10 18
Primary Contact: Nathan Hough, Chief Executive Officer
CFO: Christine Lokken, Chief Financial Officer
CMO: Edwin Anderson, M.D., Chief of Staff and Chief Medical Officer
CIO: Amanda Niemala, Director of Information Services
CHR: Angela Kleffman, Director of Ancillary Services
CNO: Nancy Probst, R.N., Chief Nursing Officer
Web address: www.bigforkvalley.org
Control: Hospital district or authority, Government, Nonfederal **Service:** General medical and surgical

Staffed Beds: 67

BLUE EARTH—Faribault County

⇧ **UNITED HOSPITAL DISTRICT (241369)**, 515 South Moore Street, Zip 56013–2158, Mailing Address: P.O. Box 160, Zip 56013–0160; tel. 507/526–3273, (Nonreporting) **A**10 18 21
Primary Contact: Richard M. Ash, Chief Executive Officer
CFO: Patrick Justin, Chief Financial Officer
CMO: Bob Karp, M.D., Chief Medical Officer
CIO: Mary Hynes, Manager Information Services
CHR: Shanna Gudahl, Manager Human Resources
CNO: Candace Arends, R.N., Chief Nursing Officer
Web address: www.uhd.org
Control: Hospital district or authority, Government, Nonfederal **Service:** General medical and surgical

Staffed Beds: 25

Hospital, Medicare Provider Number, Address, Telephone, Approval, Facility, and Physician Codes, Health Care System

★ American Hospital Association (AHA) membership ○ Healthcare Facilities Accreditation Program ⇧ Center for Improvement in Healthcare Quality Accreditation
☐ The Joint Commission accreditation ◇ DNV Healthcare Inc. accreditation △ Commission on Accreditation of Rehabilitation Facilities (CARF) accreditation

Hospitals, U.S. / MINNESOTA

BRAINERD—Crow Wing County

✠ **ESSENTIA HEALTH–ST. JOSEPH'S MEDICAL CENTER (240075)**, 523 North Third Street, Zip 56401-3098; tel. 218/829-2861, **A**1 2 10 **F**3 4 5 11 13 15 18 20 22 26 28 29 30 31 32 34 35 40 43 45 49 50 51 54 57 59 64 65 70 74 75 76 77 78 79 81 82 84 85 86 87 89 91 93 96 97 98 100 102 105 107 111 115 118 119 126 129 130 131 132 135 144 145 146 147 148 152 154 160 167 **S** Essentia Health, Duluth, MN
Primary Contact: Todd DeFreece, Senior Vice President of Operations
COO: Mike Larson, Chief Operating Officer
CFO: Dave Pilot, Chief Financial Officer
CMO: Peter Henry, M.D., Chief Medical Officer
CIO: Pam Marlatt, Business Systems Director
CHR: Sarah Carlson, Director Human Resources
CNO: Patricia DeLong, Chief Nursing Officer
Web address: https://www.essentiahealth.org/find-facility/profile/essentia-health-st-josephs-medical-center-brainerd/
Control: Church operated, Nongovernment, not-for-profit **Service**: General medical and surgical

Staffed Beds: 127 **Admissions**: 4332 **Census**: 53 **Outpatient Visits**: 105894 **Births**: 371 **Total Expense ($000)**: 257091 **Payroll Expense ($000)**: 105393 **Personnel**: 846

BRECKENRIDGE—Wilkin County

★ **CHI ST. FRANCIS HEALTH (241377)**, 2400 St Francis Drive, Zip 56520-1025; tel. 218/643-3000, (Nonreporting) **A**10 18 **S** CommonSpirit Health, Chicago, IL
Primary Contact: David A. Nelson, President and Chief Executive Officer
CFO: Joshua Senger, Chief Financial Officer
CHR: Gail Grant, Director Human Resources
CNO: Alice Pesonen-Johnson, Chief Nursing Officer
Web address: www.sfcare.org
Control: Church operated, Nongovernment, not-for-profit **Service**: General medical and surgical

Staffed Beds: 105

BROOKLYN PARK—Hennepin County

☐ **PRAIRIECARE BROOKLYN PARK (244016)**, 9400 Zane Avenue North, Zip 55443, Mailing Address: 12915 63rd Avenue North, Maple Grove, Zip 55369-6001; tel. 763/383-5800, (Nonreporting) **A**1 3 10
Primary Contact: Todd Archbold, Chief Executive Officer
Web address: www.prairie-care.com
Control: Corporation, Investor-owned (for-profit) **Service**: Psychiatric

Staffed Beds: 50

BUFFALO—Wright County

✠ **BUFFALO HOSPITAL (240076)**, 303 Catlin Street, Zip 55313-1947; tel. 763/682-1212, **A**1 2 10 **F**3 13 15 28 29 30 34 35 36 37 40 41 43 44 45 51 57 59 60 75 76 77 79 80 81 85 86 87 93 100 102 107 110 111 114 115 119 126 129 130 131 132 135 146 148 149 150 154 **S** Allina Health, Minneapolis, MN
Primary Contact: Joshua Shepherd, President
COO: Heather Johnson, Director of Finance, Operations and Business Development
CFO: Heather Johnson, Director of Finance, Operations and Business Development
CMO: Corey Martin, M.D., Director Medical Affairs
CIO: Jonathan Cloutier, Manager, Information Services
CNO: Gretchen A Frederick, R.N., Director Patient Care Services
Web address: www.buffalohospital.org
Control: Other not-for-profit (including NFP Corporation) **Service**: General medical and surgical

Staffed Beds: 39 **Admissions**: 2142 **Census**: 17 **Outpatient Visits**: 68840 **Births**: 541 **Total Expense ($000)**: 87485 **Payroll Expense ($000)**: 34849 **Personnel**: 303

BURNSVILLE—Dakota County

✠ **M HEALTH FAIRVIEW RIDGES HOSPITAL (240207)**, 201 East Nicollet Boulevard, Zip 55337-5799; tel. 952/892-2000, **A**1 2 3 5 10 **F**3 13 15 18 20 22 28 29 30 31 34 40 43 44 45 46 49 50 53 55 57 59 64 65 68 70 72 73 74 75 76 77 78 79 81 82 84 85 86 87 89 93 96 107 108 110 111 114 115 116 117 118 119 126 130 132 146 148 149 154 167 169 **S** Fairview Health Services, Minneapolis, MN
Primary Contact: Jeoff Will, Executive Vice President, Chief Operating Officer
COO: Brian A Knapp, Vice President Operations
CFO: Alan Lem, Vice President Finance
CMO: Paul Kettler, M.D., Vice President Medical Affairs
CHR: Michelle LeDell, Director Human Resource
CNO: Julie Silkey, R.N., Vice President Patient Care
Web address: https://mhealthfairview.org/locations/m-health-fairview-ridges-hospital
Control: Other not-for-profit (including NFP Corporation) **Service**: General medical and surgical

Staffed Beds: 173 **Admissions**: 10750 **Census**: 138 **Outpatient Visits**: 137946 **Births**: 1889 **Total Expense ($000)**: 310168 **Payroll Expense ($000)**: 141484 **Personnel**: 1453

CAMBRIDGE—Isanti County

✠ **CAMBRIDGE MEDICAL CENTER (240020)**, 701 South Dellwood Street, Zip 55008-1920; tel. 763/689-7700, **A**1 2 10 **F**3 5 15 18 28 29 30 31 34 35 37 40 41 43 45 56 57 59 60 64 75 77 78 79 80 81 85 86 87 93 98 100 102 104 105 107 110 111 115 119 126 129 130 131 132 135 146 148 149 153 154 156 **S** Allina Health, Minneapolis, MN
Primary Contact: Joshua Shepherd, President
CFO: Nancy Treacy, Director Finance
CHR: Diane Rasmussen, Director Human Resources
CNO: Sherri Abrahamson-Baty, Director Patient Care Services
Web address: www.allina.com/ahs/cambridge.nsf
Control: Other not-for-profit (including NFP Corporation) **Service**: General medical and surgical

Staffed Beds: 35 **Admissions**: 1883 **Census**: 21 **Outpatient Visits**: 63350 **Births**: 0 **Total Expense ($000)**: 88323 **Payroll Expense ($000)**: 35136 **Personnel**: 285

CANBY—Yellow Medicine County

★ **SANFORD CANBY MEDICAL CENTER (241347)**, 112 St Olaf Avenue South, Zip 56220-1433; tel. 507/223-7277, (Nonreporting) **A**10 18 **S** Sanford Health, Sioux Falls, SD
Primary Contact: Lori Sisk, R.N., Chief Executive Officer
CFO: Allison Nelson, Chief Financial Officer
CMO: Maritza Lopez, M.D., Chief of Staff
CIO: Cheryl L Ferguson, Associate Administrator
Web address: www.sanfordcanby.org
Control: Other not-for-profit (including NFP Corporation) **Service**: General medical and surgical

Staffed Beds: 68

CANNON FALLS—Goodhue County

☐ **MAYO CLINIC HEALTH SYSTEM IN CANNON FALLS (241346)**, 32021 County Road 24 Boulevard, Zip 55009-1898; tel. 507/263-4221, (Nonreporting) **A**1 10 18 **S** Mayo Clinic, Rochester, MN
Primary Contact: Kenneth F. Ackerman, FACHE, Hospital Administrator
Web address: www.mayoclinichealthsystem.org/locations/cannon-falls
Control: Other not-for-profit (including NFP Corporation) **Service**: General medical and surgical

Staffed Beds: 15

CASS LAKE—Cass County

★ **U. S. PUBLIC HEALTH SERVICE INDIAN HOSPITAL (241358)**, 425 7th Street North West, Zip 56633; tel. 218/335-3200, (Nonreporting) **A**10 18 **S** U. S. Indian Health Service, Rockville, MD
Primary Contact: Andrew Joseph. Lankowicz, Chief Executive Officer, Cass Lake Service Unit
CMO: Antonio Guimaraes, M.D., Clinical Director
CHR: Terrance Lascano, Administrative Officer
CNO: Roberta A Williams, Director of Nursing
Web address: www.ihs.gov
Control: PHS, Indian Service, Government, federal **Service**: General medical and surgical

Staffed Beds: 9

Hospitals, U.S. / MINNESOTA

CLOQUET—Carlton County

★ **COMMUNITY MEMORIAL HOSPITAL (241364)**, 512 Skyline Boulevard, Zip 55720–1199; tel. 218/879–4641, (Nonreporting) **A**10 18
Primary Contact: Rick Breuer, Chief Executive Officer and Administrator
CFO: Brad Anderson, Chief Financial Officer
CIO: Sam Jacobson, Director Management Information Systems
Web address: www.cloquethospital.com
Control: Other not–for–profit (including NFP Corporation) **Service:** General medical and surgical

Staffed Beds: 69

COOK—St. Louis County

★ **COOK HOSPITAL & CARE CENTER (241312)**, 10 Fifth Street SE, Zip 55723–9745; tel. 218/666–5945, (Total facility includes 28 beds in nursing home–type unit) **A**10 18 **F**1 3 4 11 15 16 17 28 29 34 35 40 43 50 53 56 57 63 64 67 68 70 72 73 77 80 81 88 89 90 93 96 98 110 115 128 130 133 146 148 149 154 166
Primary Contact: Teresa Debevec, Chief Executive Officer and Administrator
COO: Julie Lesemann, Chief Operating Officer and Assistant Administrator
CFO: Kaylee S. Hoard, Chief Financial Officer
Web address: www.cookhospital.org
Control: Hospital district or authority, Government, Nonfederal **Service:** General medical and surgical

Staffed Beds: 42 **Admissions:** 129 **Census:** 27 **Outpatient Visits:** 11002 **Births:** 0 **Total Expense ($000):** 17639 **Payroll Expense ($000):** 6831 **Personnel:** 103

COON RAPIDS—Anoka County

▣ **MERCY HOSPITAL (240115)**, 4050 Coon Rapids Boulevard, Zip 55433–2586; tel. 763/236–6000, (Includes MERCY HOSPITAL–UNITY CAMPUS, 550 Osborne Road NE, Fridley, Minnesota, Zip 55432–2799, tel. 763/236–5000; Michael Eric Johnston, FACHE, President) **A**1 2 3 5 10 **F**2 3 4 5 11 13 15 16 17 18 20 22 24 26 28 29 30 31 34 35 36 37 38 40 41 43 45 46 49 53 55 56 57 59 64 65 70 74 75 76 77 78 79 81 82 84 85 86 87 89 93 96 97 98 100 102 103 104 105 107 108 110 111 114 115 116 118 119 126 130 131 132 135 143 146 148 149 152 153 154 160 161 167 **S** Allina Health, Minneapolis, MN
Primary Contact: Michael Eric. Johnston, FACHE, President Southern Market, Mercy Hospital
COO: Daniel Steffen, Vice President, Operations
CFO: Phillip Krolik, Vice President, Finance
CMO: Jay MacGregor, Vice President Medical Affairs
CHR: Jim McGlade, Vice President, Human Resources
Web address: www.allinamercy.org
Control: Other not–for–profit (including NFP Corporation) **Service:** General medical and surgical

Staffed Beds: 479 **Admissions:** 27914 **Census:** 351 **Outpatient Visits:** 248947 **Births:** 2797 **Total Expense ($000):** 879091 **Payroll Expense ($000):** 320034 **Personnel:** 2567

CROOKSTON—Polk County

GLENMORE FOUNDATION See Glenmore Recovery Center

▣ **RIVERVIEW HEALTH (241320)**, 323 South Minnesota Street, Zip 56716–1601; tel. 218/281–9200, (Nonreporting) **A**1 10 18
Primary Contact: Carrie Michalski, President and Chief Executive Officer
COO: Chris Bruggeman, Chief Operating Officer
CFO: Betty Arvidson, Chief Financial Officer
CMO: Colin Fennell, M.D., Chief Medical Officer
CIO: Nichole Beauchane, Director Information Technology
CHR: Jean Tate, Vice President Human Resources
CNO: April Grunhovd, Vice President of Patient Care Services and Chief Nursing Officer
Web address: www.riverviewhealth.org
Control: Other not–for–profit (including NFP Corporation) **Service:** General medical and surgical

Staffed Beds: 49

CROSBY—Crow Wing County

☐ **CUYUNA REGIONAL MEDICAL CENTER (241353)**, 320 East Main Street, Zip 56441–1690; tel. 218/546–7000, (Nonreporting) **A**1 2 3 10 18
Primary Contact: Amy Hart, Chief Executive Officer
CFO: Katie Berg, Chief Financial Officer
CMO: Robert Westin, M.D., Chief Medical Officer
CHR: Caity Eggen, Chief Human Resource Officer
CNO: Renee Steffin, Chief Nursing Officer
Web address: www.cuyunamed.org
Control: Hospital district or authority, Government, Nonfederal **Service:** General medical and surgical

Staffed Beds: 142

DAWSON—Lac Qui Parle County

JOHNSON MEMORIAL HEALTH SERVICES (241314), 1282 Walnut Street, Zip 56232–2333; tel. 320/769–4323, (Nonreporting) **A**10 18
Primary Contact: Kathy Johnson, Interim Chief Executive Officer
CFO: Crystal Bothun, Chief Financial Officer
CMO: Erik Shelstad, M.D., Chief of Staff
CIO: Steve Coubal, Manager Information Technology and Systems
CHR: Megan Lynch, Manager Human Resources
Web address: www.jmhsmn.org
Control: Hospital district or authority, Government, Nonfederal **Service:** General medical and surgical

Staffed Beds: 65

DEER RIVER—Itasca County

★ **ESSENTIA HEALTH–DEER RIVER (241360)**, 115 10th Avenue NE, Zip 56636–8795; tel. 218/246–2900, (Total facility includes 32 beds in nursing home–type unit) **A**10 18 **F**3 11 15 28 29 31 32 34 35 40 43 45 50 54 56 57 59 62 64 65 75 77 78 79 81 82 83 85 91 92 93 96 97 107 108 110 115 118 119 125 128 129 130 131 133 135 146 147 148 149 154 156 160 169 **P**6 **S** Essentia Health, Duluth, MN
Primary Contact: Amanda Reed, Administrator
CMO: David Goodall, M.D., Chief Medical Staff
CHR: Brittany Mohler, Director Human Resources
Web address: www.essentiahealth.org
Control: Other not–for–profit (including NFP Corporation) **Service:** General medical and surgical

Staffed Beds: 48 **Admissions:** 391 **Census:** 23 **Outpatient Visits:** 45531 **Births:** 0 **Total Expense ($000):** 40764 **Payroll Expense ($000):** 15347 **Personnel:** 137

DETROIT LAKES—Becker County

▣ **ESSENTIA HEALTH ST. MARY'S – DETROIT LAKES (240101)**, 1027 Washington Avenue, Zip 56501–3409; tel. 218/847–5611, (Total facility includes 94 beds in nursing home–type unit) **A**1 10 20 **F**1 3 4 10 12 13 15 16 17 18 28 29 30 31 32 33 34 35 40 41 43 45 54 56 57 59 62 63 64 65 67 70 72 73 75 76 77 78 79 80 81 82 87 88 89 90 91 93 96 97 98 100 104 107 110 111 114 115 118 119 125 126 127 128 129 130 131 135 144 147 148 149 154 156 160 162 164 166 167 169 **S** Essentia Health, Duluth, MN
Primary Contact: Tanner Goodrich, Senior Vice President, Operations – West Market
CFO: Ryan Hill, Senior Financial Advisor
CMO: Richard Vetter, M.D., Associate Chief
CIO: Ken Gilles, Associate Chief Information Officer
CHR: Diane Sundrud, Human Resource Service Partner
CNO: Kay Larson, R.N., Chief Nursing Officer
Web address: www.essentiahealth.org
Control: Other not–for–profit (including NFP Corporation) **Service:** General medical and surgical

Staffed Beds: 130 **Admissions:** 2006 **Census:** 86 **Outpatient Visits:** 158201 **Births:** 470 **Total Expense ($000):** 156312 **Payroll Expense ($000):** 72020 **Personnel:** 585

Hospital, Medicare Provider Number, Address, Telephone, Approval, Facility, and Physician Codes, Health Care System

★ American Hospital Association (AHA) membership ◯ Healthcare Facilities Accreditation Program ⇑ Center for Improvement in Healthcare Quality Accreditation
☐ The Joint Commission accreditation ◇ DNV Healthcare Inc. accreditation △ Commission on Accreditation of Rehabilitation Facilities (CARF) accreditation

Hospitals, U.S. / MINNESOTA

DULUTH—St. Louis County

★ ⇧ **ASPIRUS ST. LUKE's HOSPITAL (240047)**, 915 East First Street, Zip 55805-2193; tel. 218/249-5555, (Nonreporting) **A**2 3 5 10 19 21 **S** Aspirus, Inc., Wausau, WI
Primary Contact: Nicholas Van Deelen, M.D., President
CIO: Clark Averill, Director Information Technology
CHR: Marla Halvorson, Vice President, Chief Human Resources Officer
CNO: Theresa Hannu, Vice President, Chief Nursing Officer
Web address: www.slhduluth.com
Control: Other not-for-profit (including NFP Corporation) **Service**: General medical and surgical

Staffed Beds: 267

△ **ESSENTIA HEALTH DULUTH (240019)**, 502 East Second Street, Zip 55805-1982; tel. 218/727-8762, **A**1 3 7 10 **F**3 5 11 12 15 29 30 31 32 34 35 36 37 49 50 51 52 54 55 56 57 59 61 64 65 74 75 77 78 79 81 82 84 85 86 87 90 91 92 93 94 96 97 98 99 100 101 103 104 105 107 108 110 111 114 115 116 117 118 119 120 121 123 124 126 130 131 132 134 135 141 144 146 147 148 149 151 153 154 157 160 164 165 167 169 **P**6 **S** Essentia Health, Duluth, MN
Primary Contact: David C. Herman, M.D., Chief Executive Officer
COO: Bradley Beard, Chief Operating Officer
CFO: Kevin Boren, Chief Financial Officer
CMO: Hugh Renier, M.D., Vice President Medical Affairs
CIO: Dennis Dassenko, Chief Information Officer
CHR: Diane Davidson, Senior Vice President Human Resources
CNO: Sandee Carlson, Director of Nursing
Web address: www.smdcmedicalcenter.org
Control: Other not-for-profit (including NFP Corporation) **Service**: General medical and surgical

Staffed Beds: 154 **Admissions**: 3524 **Census**: 88 **Outpatient Visits**: 563845 **Births**: 0 **Total Expense ($000)**: 555998 **Payroll Expense ($000)**: 272976 **Personnel**: 1679

ESSENTIA HEALTH ST. MARY'S MEDICAL CENTER (240002), 407 East Third Street, Zip 55805-1984; tel. 218/786-4000, (Includes ST. MARY'S CHILDREN'S HOSPITAL, 407 East Third Street, Duluth, Minnesota, Zip 55805-1950, tel. 218/786-5437) **A**1 2 3 5 10 19 **F**3 11 12 13 17 18 20 22 24 26 28 29 30 34 35 37 38 40 41 43 45 46 47 48 49 50 57 59 63 65 67 70 72 74 76 78 79 81 83 84 85 86 87 88 89 91 102 107 108 111 115 119 126 129 130 132 135 141 146 149 154 157 **S** Essentia Health, Duluth, MN
Primary Contact: Krista Skorupa, President, East Market
CMO: Hugh Renier, M.D., Vice President Medical Affairs
CIO: Tess Jettergren, Director Clinical Informatics
CHR: Glen Porter, Vice President Human Resources
Web address: https://www.essentiahealth.org/find-facility/profile/essentia-health-st-marys-medical-center-duluth/
Control: Other not-for-profit (including NFP Corporation) **Service**: General medical and surgical

Staffed Beds: 329 **Admissions**: 17247 **Census**: 226 **Outpatient Visits**: 134868 **Births**: 1308 **Total Expense ($000)**: 496336 **Payroll Expense ($000)**: 194421 **Personnel**: 1870

⇧ **ST. LUKE'S HOSPITAL** See Aspirus St. Luke's Hospital

EDINA—Hennepin County

M HEALTH FAIRVIEW SOUTHDALE HOSPITAL (240078), 6401 France Avenue South, Zip 55435-2199; tel. 952/924-5000, **A**1 2 3 5 10 **F**3 15 17 18 20 22 24 26 28 29 30 31 37 40 43 44 45 46 49 50 51 63 68 70 72 74 75 76 78 79 81 84 85 87 92 100 102 107 108 110 111 115 116 117 118 119 120 121 123 124 126 130 146 148 149 154 167 169 **S** Fairview Health Services, Minneapolis, MN
Primary Contact: Jeoff Will, Executive Vice President, Chief Operating Officer
COO: Jeoff Will, Chief Operating Officer, Acute Care Hospitals
CFO: Alan Lem, Vice President Finance
CHR: Michelle LeDell, Director Human Resources
Web address: https://mhealthfairview.org/locations/m-health-fairview-southdale-hospital
Control: Other not-for-profit (including NFP Corporation) **Service**: General medical and surgical

Staffed Beds: 349 **Admissions**: 17686 **Census**: 238 **Outpatient Visits**: 149302 **Births**: 2998 **Total Expense ($000)**: 586107 **Payroll Expense ($000)**: 253044 **Personnel**: 2522

ELBOW LAKE—Grant County

★ **ELBOW LAKE MEDICAL CENTER (241379)**, 1411 Highway 79 East, Zip 56531-4645; tel. 218/685-7300, (Nonreporting) **A**10 18
Primary Contact: Kent D. Mattson, Chief Executive Officer
CFO: Brett Longtin, Chief Financial Officer
CMO: Phillip Walter Holmes, M.D., Chief of Staff
CHR: Kim Blank, Director Human Resources
CNO: Alycia Athey, Director of Nursing
Web address: https://www.lrhc.org/clinics/elbow-lake-medical-center/
Control: Other not-for-profit (including NFP Corporation) **Service**: General medical and surgical

Staffed Beds: 9

PRAIRE RIDGE HEALTHCARE See Elbow Lake Medical Center

ELY—St. Louis County

★ **ELY-BLOOMENSON COMMUNITY HOSPITAL (241318)**, 328 West Conan Street, Zip 55731-1198; tel. 218/365-3271, **A**10 18 **F**3 15 28 31 40 45 53 62 64 81 107 110 115 119 126 130 133 148 149 154
Primary Contact: Patricia Banks, Chief Executive Officer
CHR: Rochelle Sjoberg, Chief Human Resources Officer
CNO: Rebecca Holmstrom, Chief Nursing Officer
Web address: www.ebch.org
Control: Other not-for-profit (including NFP Corporation) **Service**: General medical and surgical

Staffed Beds: 21 **Admissions**: 451 **Census**: 1 **Outpatient Visits**: 5630 **Births**: 0 **Total Expense ($000)**: 30426 **Payroll Expense ($000)**: 9385 **Personnel**: 116

FAIRMONT—Martin County

☐ **MAYO CLINIC HEALTH SYSTEM IN FAIRMONT (240166)**, 800 Medical Center Drive, Zip 56031-4575; tel. 507/238-8100, **A**1 10 20 **F**3 5 9 12 13 15 18 28 29 30 31 32 34 35 38 40 43 44 45 50 57 59 63 64 65 71 74 75 76 77 78 79 81 85 86 87 91 93 94 96 97 101 102 104 107 108 110 111 115 116 117 118 119 129 130 131 132 134 135 146 147 149 154 160 161 162 164 165 169 **S** Mayo Clinic, Rochester, MN
Primary Contact: Amy Long, Administrator
COO: Gayle B Hansen, R.N., Chief Operating Officer
CFO: Brian Suter, Chief Financial Officer
CMO: Rufus Rodriguez, M.D., Medical Director
Web address: https://www.mayoclinichealthsystem.org/locations/fairmont
Control: Other not-for-profit (including NFP Corporation) **Service**: General medical and surgical

Staffed Beds: 25 **Admissions**: 987 **Census**: 10 **Outpatient Visits**: 66688 **Births**: 137

FARIBAULT—Rice County

ALLINA HEALTH FARIBAULT MEDICAL CENTER (240071), 200 State Avenue, Zip 55021-6345; tel. 507/334-6451, **A**1 2 10 **F**3 12 13 15 28 31 40 41 43 45 64 75 76 77 78 79 80 81 85 87 91 93 100 102 105 107 110 111 119 126 130 131 132 143 146 147 149 153 154 **S** Allina Health, Minneapolis, MN
Primary Contact: Whitney Johnson, President
COO: Rick Miller, Director, Operations and Finance
CFO: Rick Miller, Chief Financial Officer
CMO: Amy Elliott, M.D., Director Medical Affairs
Web address: https://www.allinahealth.org/allina-health-faribault-medical-center
Control: Other not-for-profit (including NFP Corporation) **Service**: General medical and surgical

Staffed Beds: 32 **Admissions**: 1286 **Census**: 10 **Outpatient Visits**: 38882 **Births**: 255 **Total Expense ($000)**: 59666 **Payroll Expense ($000)**: 22016 **Personnel**: 182

DISTRICT ONE HOSPITAL See Allina Health Faribault Medical Center

FERGUS FALLS—Otter Tail County

☐ **COMMUNITY BEHAVIORAL HEALTH HOSPITAL – FERGUS FALLS (244013)**, 1801 West Alcott Avenue, Zip 56537-2661, Mailing Address: P.O. Box 478, Zip 56538-0478; tel. 218/332-5001, (Nonreporting) **A**1 10 **S** Minnesota Department of Human Services, Saint Paul, MN
Primary Contact: Leah Voigt. Potter, Hospital Administrator
Control: State, Government, Nonfederal **Service**: Psychiatric

Staffed Beds: 16

✠ **LAKE REGION HEALTHCARE CORPORATION (240052)**, 712 South Cascade Street, Zip 56537–2900, Mailing Address: P.O. Box 728, Zip 56538–0728; tel. 218/736–8000, (Nonreporting) **A**1 10 20
Primary Contact: Kent D. Mattson, Chief Executive Officer
CFO: Brett Longtin, Chief Financial Officer
CMO: Greg Smith, Chief Medical Officer
CIO: Wade A Jyrkas, Director Computer Information Systems
CHR: Kim Blank, Director Human Resources
Web address: www.lrhc.org
Control: Other not–for–profit (including NFP Corporation) **Service**: General medical and surgical

Staffed Beds: 166

FOSSTON—Polk County

★ **ESSENTIA HEALTH–FOSSTON (241357)**, 900 Hilligoss Boulevard SE, Zip 56542–1599; tel. 218/435–1133, (Total facility includes 50 beds in nursing home–type unit) **A**10 18 **F**3 7 10 13 14 15 18 28 29 30 31 34 35 40 50 56 59 62 63 65 68 70 75 76 77 78 79 80 81 82 84 87 93 97 104 107 110 114 127 128 130 131 132 133 135 148 149 154 156 169 **P**6 **S** Essentia Health, Duluth, MN
CFO: Kim Bodensteiner, Chief Financial Officer
CHR: Diane Sundrud, Director Human Resources
Web address: www.essentiahealth.org
Control: Other not–for–profit (including NFP Corporation) **Service**: General medical and surgical

Staffed Beds: 68 **Admissions**: 221 **Census**: 33 **Outpatient Visits**: 27921
Births: 0 **Total Expense ($000)**: 29867 **Payroll Expense ($000)**: 13190
Personnel: 136

FRIDLEY—Anoka County

UNITY HOSPITAL See Mercy Hospital–Unity Campus

GLENCOE—Mcleod County

★ **GLENCOE REGIONAL HEALTH (241355)**, 1805 Hennepin Avenue North, Zip 55336–1416; tel. 320/864–3121, (Nonreporting) **A**10 18 **S** HealthPartners, Bloomington, MN
Primary Contact: Ben Davis, President and Chief Executive Officer
CFO: John C Doidge, Vice President Finance
CMO: Kristine Knudten, M.D., Vice President Medical Affairs
CIO: Ryan Lake, Director Information Technology
CHR: Jill Hatlestad, Vice President Human Resources and Marketing
Web address: www.grhsonline.org
Control: Other not–for–profit (including NFP Corporation) **Service**: General medical and surgical

Staffed Beds: 133

GLENWOOD—Pope County

★ **GLACIAL RIDGE HEALTH SYSTEM (241376)**, 10 Fourth Avenue SE, Zip 56334–1898; tel. 320/634–4521, **A**10 18 **F**11 13 15 17 28 31 34 35 40 41 43 45 53 59 62 63 64 75 76 77 79 81 93 107 110 111 115 119 127 130 133 146 148 149 154 155 **P**6
Primary Contact: Kirk A. Stensrud, Chief Executive Officer
CFO: Kyle Chase, Chief Financial Officer
CMO: Gustave Mellgren, M.D., Chief of Staff
CIO: Jeff Ofstedal, Manager Information Technology
CHR: Gordon Paulson, Manager Human Resources
CNO: Lynn Flesner, Director of Nursing
Web address: www.glacialridge.org
Control: Hospital district or authority, Government, Nonfederal **Service**: General medical and surgical

Staffed Beds: 22 **Admissions**: 557 **Census**: 5 **Outpatient Visits**: 22373
Births: 115 **Total Expense ($000)**: 50674 **Payroll Expense ($000)**: 24931
Personnel: 366

GOLDEN VALLEY—Hennepin County

✠ **REGENCY HOSPITAL OF MINNEAPOLIS (242005)**, 1300 Hidden Lakes Parkway, Zip 55422–4286; tel. 763/588–2750, (Nonreporting) **A**1 10 **S** Select Medical Corporation, Mechanicsburg, PA
Primary Contact: Sean Stricker, President and Chief Executive Officer
CMO: Alaka Nagaraj, M.D., Medical Director
CNO: Caren Gaytko, Chief Nursing Officer
Web address: www.regencyhospital.com
Control: Corporation, Investor–owned (for–profit) **Service**: Acute long–term care hospital

Staffed Beds: 92

GRACEVILLE—Big Stone County

★ **ESSENTIA HEALTH–GRACEVILLE (241321)**, 115 West Second Street, Zip 56240–4845, Mailing Address: P.O. Box 157, Zip 56240–0157; tel. 320/748–7223, (Total facility includes 40 beds in nursing home–type unit) **A**10 18 **F**3 15 28 30 33 34 40 43 56 57 59 62 64 65 68 75 77 81 82 85 87 93 97 107 110 127 128 133 135 146 147 148 149 154 156 169 **S** Essentia Health, Duluth, MN
Primary Contact: Debra Stueve, Administrator
CMO: Arthur Van Vranken, M.D., Chief Medical Officer
CIO: Brad Tostenson, Chief Information Officer
CHR: Jenny Lee, Human Resources Generalist
CNO: Jill Johnsrud, Director of Nursing
Web address: www.essentiahealth.org/HolyTrinityHospital/FindaClinic/Essentia-HealthHoly-Trinity-Hospital-96.aspx
Control: Other not–for–profit (including NFP Corporation) **Service**: General medical and surgical

Staffed Beds: 55 **Admissions**: 82 **Census**: 19 **Outpatient Visits**: 6938
Births: 0 **Total Expense ($000)**: 11319 **Payroll Expense ($000)**: 5202
Personnel: 73

GRAND MARAIS—Cook County

★ **NORTH SHORE HEALTH (241317)**, 515 5th Avenue West, Zip 55604–3017; tel. 218/387–3040, (Total facility includes 37 beds in nursing home–type unit) **A**10 18 **F**3 7 15 28 30 31 40 45 56 59 62 64 75 78 89 93 107 110 111 115 119 128 130 133 148 154
Primary Contact: Kimber L. Wraalstad, FACHE, Chief Executive Officer and Administrator
CFO: Vera Schumann, Director of Finance and Controller
CMO: Milan Schmidt, Medical Director
CIO: Greg Johnson, IT Coordinator
CHR: Michele Starkey, Director Human Resources
CNO: Fred Andrews, Director of Nursing
Web address: https://www.northshorehealthgm.org/
Control: Hospital district or authority, Government, Nonfederal **Service**: General medical and surgical

Staffed Beds: 53 **Admissions**: 121 **Census**: 29 **Outpatient Visits**: 11767
Births: 0 **Total Expense ($000)**: 24015 **Payroll Expense ($000)**: 6971
Personnel: 94

GRAND RAPIDS—Itasca County

✠ **GRAND ITASCA CLINIC AND HOSPITAL (240064)**, 1601 Golf Course Road, Zip 55744–8648; tel. 218/326–5000, **A**1 3 10 20 **F**3 11 13 15 18 28 29 31 32 33 34 35 36 40 43 44 48 50 51 53 57 59 62 64 65 68 70 75 76 77 78 81 82 85 86 87 89 93 96 97 100 107 108 110 111 115 118 119 129 130 131 132 135 146 147 148 149 154 156 167 169 **P**6 **S** Fairview Health Services, Minneapolis, MN
Primary Contact: Jean MacDonell, President and Chief Executive Officer
CFO: Todd Christensen, Vice President, Finance
CMO: Dan Soular, M.D., Vice President, Medical Affairs
CHR: Katherine Burns–Chistenson, Human Resource Director
CNO: Sandy Lenarz, Chief Nursing Officer
Web address: www.granditasca.org
Control: Other not–for–profit (including NFP Corporation) **Service**: General medical and surgical

Staffed Beds: 39 **Admissions**: 1728 **Census**: 15 **Outpatient Visits**: 254474
Births: 379 **Total Expense ($000)**: 120349 **Payroll Expense ($000)**: 61177
Personnel: 591

Hospitals, U.S. / MINNESOTA

GRANITE FALLS—Yellow Medicine County

★ **AVERA GRANITE FALLS (241343)**, 345 Tenth Avenue, Zip 56241–1499; tel. 320/564–3111, (Total facility includes 48 beds in nursing home–type unit) **A**10 18 **F**3 7 13 15 28 29 31 40 56 59 65 75 76 77 81 89 107 110 115 118 119 125 128 130 133 143 154 169 **P**6 **S** Avera Health, Sioux Falls, SD
Primary Contact: Thomas Kooiman, Chief Executive Officer
CFO: Val Hoffman, Chief Financial Officer
CIO: Kris Wilke, Manager Health Information
CHR: Sue Tollefson, Coordinator Payroll Personnel
CNO: Patty Massman, Director of Nursing
Web address: https://www.avera.org/locations/avera-granite-falls-health-center/
Control: Church operated, Nongovernment, not–for–profit **Service**: General medical and surgical

Staffed Beds: 73 **Admissions**: 248 **Census**: 49 **Outpatient Visits**: 18748
Births: 6 **Total Expense ($000)**: 28368 **Payroll Expense ($000)**: 13522
Personnel: 148

HALLOCK—Kittson County

★ **KITTSON HEALTHCARE (241336)**, 1010 South Birch Street, Zip 56728–4215, Mailing Address: P.O. Box 700, Zip 56728–0700; tel. 218/843–3612, (Nonreporting) **A**10 18
Primary Contact: Andrea Swenson, Chief Executive Officer
CMO: Thomas Lohstreter, M.D., Chief of Staff
CIO: Holly Knutson, Manager Information Technology
CHR: Carlene Cole, Manager Human Resources
CNO: Tawnya Sorenson, Director of Nursing
Web address: https://kittsonhc.org
Control: Other not–for–profit (including NFP Corporation) **Service**: General medical and surgical

Staffed Beds: 75

KITTSON MEMORIAL HEALTHCARE CENTER See Kittson Healthcare

HENDRICKS—Lincoln County

★ **HENDRICKS COMMUNITY HOSPITAL ASSOCIATION (241339)**, 503 East Lincoln Street, Zip 56136–9598, Mailing Address: P.O. Box 106, Zip 56136–0106; tel. 507/275–3134, (Nonreporting) **A**10 18
Primary Contact: Jeffrey Gollaher, Chief Executive Officer
CMO: Tabb McCluskey, M.D., Chief Medical Officer
CHR: Lynn R Olson, Director Human Resources
Web address: www.hendrickshosp.org
Control: Other not–for–profit (including NFP Corporation) **Service**: General medical and surgical

Staffed Beds: 59

HIBBING—St. Louis County

⊞ **FAIRVIEW RANGE (240040)**, 750 East 34th Street, Zip 55746–4600; tel. 218/262–4881, **A**1 2 10 **F**3 11 13 15 18 28 29 30 31 32 33 34 35 36 40 43 44 45 50 56 57 58 59 62 63 64 65 68 70 75 76 77 78 79 81 82 83 84 85 86 87 89 93 97 98 100 102 104 105 107 108 110 111 115 116 118 119 120 121 123 125 129 130 131 132 135 143 144 145 146 147 148 149 150 154 156 160 167 168 169 **P**5 **S** Fairview Health Services, Minneapolis, MN
Primary Contact: Jean MacDonell, President and Chief Executive Officer
CFO: Tom Fink, Vice President Regional Finance Officer
CMO: Susan Rudberg, M.D., Chief Medical Officer
CIO: Jessica Valento, Director Information Systems
CHR: Mitchell S Vincent, Vice President Organizational Support
CNO: Sherry Burg, Chief Nursing Officer
Web address: www.range.fairview.org
Control: Other not–for–profit (including NFP Corporation) **Service**: General medical and surgical

Staffed Beds: 72 **Admissions**: 2093 **Census**: 35 **Outpatient Visits**: 51628
Total Expense ($000): 135083 **Payroll Expense ($000)**: 68439
Personnel: 663

HUTCHINSON—Mcleod County

⊞ **HUTCHINSON HEALTH (240187)**, 1095 Highway 15 South, Zip 55350–3182; tel. 320/234–5000, (Nonreporting) **A**1 10 20 **S** HealthPartners, Bloomington, MN
Primary Contact: Jim Lyons, President
CFO: Pamela Larson, Division Director Financial Services
CMO: Brian Pollman, Chief Medical Officer
CIO: Tara Nelson, Chief Clinic Officer
CHR: Rebecca Streich, Manager Human Resources and Education Manager
CNO: Susan Karnitz, Chief Nursing Director
Web address: www.hutchhealth.com
Control: Other not–for–profit (including NFP Corporation) **Service**: General medical and surgical

Staffed Beds: 36

INTERNATIONAL FALLS—Koochiching County

RAINY LAKE MEDICAL CENTER (241322), 1400 Highway 71, Zip 56649–2189; tel. 218/283–4481, (Nonreporting) **A**10 18
Primary Contact: Robert Pastor II, R.N., Chief Executive Officer
CFO: Melissa Marcotte, Chief Financial Officer
CIO: Michael Blesi, Director Information Technology
CNO: Donita Ettestad, R.N., MS, Chief Nursing Officer
Web address: www.rainylakemedical.com
Control: Other not–for–profit (including NFP Corporation) **Service**: General medical and surgical

Staffed Beds: 16

JACKSON—Jackson County

★ **SANFORD JACKSON MEDICAL CENTER (241315)**, 1430 North Highway, Zip 56143–1093; tel. 507/847–2420, (Nonreporting) **A**10 18 **S** Sanford Health, Sioux Falls, SD
Primary Contact: Dawn Schnell, Administrator and Chief Executive Officer
CFO: Gail Eike, Chief Financial Officer
CMO: Sister Marie Paul Lockerd, M.D., Chief Medical Officer
CNO: Dawn Schnell, Chief Nursing Officer
Web address: www.sanfordjackson.org
Control: Other not–for–profit (including NFP Corporation) **Service**: General medical and surgical

Staffed Beds: 16

LAKE CITY—Goodhue County

☐ **MAYO CLINIC HEALTH SYSTEM IN LAKE CITY (241338)**, 500 West Grant Street, Zip 55041–1143; tel. 651/345–3321, (Nonreporting) **A**1 10 18 **S** Mayo Clinic, Rochester, MN
Primary Contact: Brian Whited, M.D., Physician Executive
Web address: https://www.mayoclinichealthsystem.org/locations/lake-city
Control: Other not–for–profit (including NFP Corporation) **Service**: General medical and surgical

Staffed Beds: 101

LE SUEUR—Le Sueur County

★ **RIDGEVIEW LE SUEUR MEDICAL CENTER (241375)**, 621 South Fourth Street, Zip 56058–2298; tel. 507/665–3375, **A**10 18 **F**3 7 15 34 40 43 45 56 59 62 63 79 81 87 91 93 97 107 115 127 130 133 144 154 167 169 **S** Ridgeview Medical Center, Waconia, MN
Primary Contact: Stacey Lee, CPA, JD, Vice President and Administrator
CFO: Cole Schlauderaff, Director, Finance
CMO: Matthew Herold, Vice President, Chief Medical Officer
CHR: Bonnie Barnhardt, Executive Director Human Resources
CNO: Kelly Wendt, Director, Patient Care
Web address: www.mvhc.org
Control: Other not–for–profit (including NFP Corporation) **Service**: General medical and surgical

Staffed Beds: 19 **Admissions**: 119 **Census**: 12 **Outpatient Visits**: 12327
Total Expense ($000): 13566 **Payroll Expense ($000)**: 4697
Personnel: 66

LITCHFIELD—Meeker County

★ **MEEKER MEMORIAL HOSPITAL AND CLINICS (241366)**, 612 South Sibley Avenue, Zip 55355–3398; tel. 320/693–4500, (Nonreporting) **A**10 18 **S** CentraCare Health, Saint Cloud, MN
Primary Contact: Mary Ellen Wells, FACHE, Chief Executive Officer
CFO: Stephen Plaisance, Chief Financial Officer
CMO: Tim Peterson, M.D., Chief of Staff
CIO: Troy Bruning, Director Information Technology
CHR: Cindi Twardy, Manager Human Resources
CNO: Joan Bitz, Chief Nursing Officer
Web address: www.meekermemorial.org
Control: County, Government, Nonfederal **Service**: General medical and surgical

Staffed Beds: 38

Hospitals, U.S. / MINNESOTA

LITTLE FALLS—Morrison County

☒ **CHI ST. GABRIEL'S HEALTH (241370)**, 815 Second Street SE, Zip 56345-3596; tel. 320/632-5441, (Nonreporting) **A**1 10 18 **S** CommonSpirit Health, Chicago, IL
Primary Contact: Steve Smith, President and Chief Executive Officer
CFO: Steve Smith, President and Chief Financial Officer
CMO: Susan Okoniewski, M.D., Chief of Staff
Web address: www.stgabriels.com
Control: Church operated, Nongovernment, not-for-profit **Service:** General medical and surgical

Staffed Beds: 25

LONG PRAIRIE—Todd County

★ **CENTRACARE - LONG PRAIRIE (241326)**, 50 CentraCare Drive, Zip 56347-2100; tel. 320/732-2141, (Total facility includes 60 beds in nursing home-type unit) **A**5 10 18 **F**13 15 28 29 31 34 35 40 43 45 50 53 57 59 64 65 68 75 76 77 78 79 81 85 87 91 93 96 97 100 101 102 107 108 110 111 115 119 127 128 130 131 133 135 146 148 149 154 156 164 169 **S** CentraCare Health, Saint Cloud, MN
Primary Contact: Jose Alba, President
CFO: Larry Knutson, Director Finance
CMO: Rene Eldidy, M.D., Chief of Staff
Web address: www.centracare.com
Control: Other not-for-profit (including NFP Corporation) **Service:** General medical and surgical

Staffed Beds: 74 **Admissions:** 539 **Census:** 23 **Outpatient Visits:** 34291 **Births:** 85 **Total Expense ($000):** 40675 **Payroll Expense ($000):** 17631 **Personnel:** 134

LUVERNE—Rock County

★ **SANFORD LUVERNE MEDICAL CENTER (241371)**, 1600 North Kniss Avenue, Zip 56156-1067; tel. 507/283-2321, (Nonreporting) **A**10 18 **S** Sanford Health, Sioux Falls, SD
Primary Contact: Tammy Loosbrock, Chief Executive Officer and Administrator
COO: Nancy E Drenth, R.N., Director Ancillary Services
CMO: Judy S Chesley, M.D., Chief of Staff
CNO: Nyla H Sandbulte, R.N., Director of Nursing
Web address: https://www.sanfordhealth.org/locations/sanford-luverne-medical-center
Control: Other not-for-profit (including NFP Corporation) **Service:** General medical and surgical

Staffed Beds: 18

MADELIA—Watonwan County

MADELIA COMMUNITY HOSPITAL See Madelia Health

☐ **MADELIA HEALTH (241323)**, 121 Drew Avenue SE, Zip 56062-1899; tel. 507/642-3255, (Nonreporting) **A**1 10 18
Primary Contact: David Frank. Walz, Chief Executive Officer
CFO: Donna M Klinkner, Chief Financial Officer
CMO: Todd Gavin, Chief Medical Officer
CIO: Valerie Juhl, Director of Health
CHR: Donna M Klinkner, Chief Financial Officer
CNO: Deidre Hruby, Director of Patient Care
Web address: https://www.madeliahealth.org/
Control: Other not-for-profit (including NFP Corporation) **Service:** General medical and surgical

Staffed Beds: 21

MADISON—Lac Qui Parle County

MADISON HEALTHCARE SERVICES (241372), 900 Second Avenue, Zip 56256-1006; tel. 320/598-7556, (Nonreporting) **A**10 18
Primary Contact: Erik Bjerke, Chief Executive Officer
CFO: Carol Borgerson, Chief Financial Officer
CIO: Jerry Harberts, Information Technologist
CHR: Kelly Johnson, Director Human Resources
Web address: www.mlhmn.org/
Control: Other not-for-profit (including NFP Corporation) **Service:** General medical and surgical

Staffed Beds: 12

MAHNOMEN—Mahnomen County

MAHNOMEN HEALTH (240779), 414 West Jefferson Avenue, Zip 56557-4912, Mailing Address: PO Box 396, Zip 56557-0396; tel. 218/935-2511, (Nonreporting) **A**10 **S** Sanford Health, Sioux Falls, SD
Primary Contact: Dale K. Kruger, Chief Executive Officer
CFO: Mary Pazdernik, Chief Financial Officer
CMO: Anju Gurung, M.D., Chief Medical Officer
CHR: Kristi Stall, Chief Human Resources Officer
Web address: www.mahnomenhealthcenter.com
Control: City-county, Government, Nonfederal

Staffed Beds: 50

MAHNOMEN HEALTH CENTER See Mahnomen Health

MANKATO—Blue Earth County

☒ **MAYO CLINIC HEALTH SYSTEM IN MANKATO (240093)**, 1025 Marsh Street, Zip 56001-4752; tel. 507/625-4031, **A**1 2 3 5 10 **F**3 4 5 9 12 13 15 17 18 19 20 22 24 26 28 29 30 31 32 34 35 36 37 38 40 43 44 45 46 48 49 50 53 55 57 58 59 60 61 63 64 65 70 71 73 74 75 76 77 78 79 80 81 82 84 85 86 87 89 91 92 93 94 96 97 98 100 101 102 104 107 108 110 111 115 116 117 118 119 120 121 123 124 126 129 130 131 132 134 135 144 146 147 148 149 154 156 160 161 162 164 165 167 169 **S** Mayo Clinic, Rochester, MN
Primary Contact: James Hebl, M.D., Regional Vice President
CMO: Gokhan Anil, Chief Medical Officer
CIO: Sarah Daniels, Vice President, Information Technology
CHR: Beth Dittbenner, Regional Director, Human Resources
CNO: Lisa McConnell, Chief Nursing Officer
Web address: https://www.mayoclinichealthsystem.org/locations/mankato
Control: Other not-for-profit (including NFP Corporation) **Service:** General medical and surgical

Staffed Beds: 156 **Admissions:** 7704 **Census:** 104 **Outpatient Visits:** 280077 **Births:** 1257

MAPLE GROVE—Hennepin County

⇧ **MAPLE GROVE HOSPITAL (240214)**, 9875 Hospital Drive, Zip 55369-4648; tel. 763/581-1000, (Nonreporting) **A**3 5 10 21 **S** North Memorial Health Care, Robbinsdale, MN
Primary Contact: Trevor Sawallish, Chief Executive Officer
CMO: Pamela Doorenbos, M.D., Vice President, Medical Affairs
CNO: Wendy Ulferts, Vice President and Chief Nursing Officer
Web address: www.maplegrovehospital.org
Control: Other not-for-profit (including NFP Corporation) **Service:** General medical and surgical

Staffed Beds: 108

MAPLEWOOD—Ramsey County

☒ **M HEALTH FAIRVIEW ST. JOHN'S HOSPITAL (240210)**, 1575 Beam Avenue, Zip 55109-1126; tel. 651/232-7000, **A**1 2 3 5 10 **F**3 5 12 13 15 18 20 22 24 26 28 29 30 31 34 35 36 37 38 40 42 43 44 45 46 49 50 51 54 55 58 61 63 64 68 70 72 74 75 76 77 78 79 81 82 83 84 85 86 87 93 100 107 108 110 111 114 115 116 117 119 120 121 123 126 130 131 132 135 146 147 148 149 167 169 **S** Fairview Health Services, Minneapolis, MN
Primary Contact: Jeoff Will, Executive Vice President, Chief Operating Officer
COO: M. Osman Akhtar, Chief Operating Officer
CMO: Mark Welton, M.D., Chief Medical Officer
CIO: Alistair Jacques, Chief Information Officer, Senior Vice President
CHR: Carolyn Jacobson, Chief Human Resources Officer
Web address: https://www.fairview.org/locations/healtheast-st-johns-hospital
Control: Other not-for-profit (including NFP Corporation) **Service:** General medical and surgical

Staffed Beds: 199 **Admissions:** 12275 **Census:** 165 **Outpatient Visits:** 152854 **Births:** 2296 **Total Expense ($000):** 438826 **Payroll Expense ($000):** 188590 **Personnel:** 1935

Hospital, Medicare Provider Number, Address, Telephone, Approval, Facility, and Physician Codes, Health Care System

★ American Hospital Association (AHA) membership ○ Healthcare Facilities Accreditation Program ⇧ Center for Improvement in Healthcare Quality Accreditation
☐ The Joint Commission accreditation ◇ DNV Healthcare Inc. accreditation △ Commission on Accreditation of Rehabilitation Facilities (CARF) accreditation

Hospitals, U.S. / MINNESOTA

MARSHALL—Lyon County

★ ○ **AVERA MARSHALL REGIONAL MEDICAL CENTER (241359)**, 300 South Bruce Street, Zip 56258-3900; tel. 507/532-9661, (Total facility includes 76 beds in nursing home–type unit) **A**2 10 11 18 **F**3 11 12 13 15 18 28 29 30 31 34 35 40 41 43 45 50 54 56 57 59 60 62 63 64 65 70 75 76 77 78 79 81 82 84 85 87 89 97 98 101 102 104 107 110 111 115 119 120 121 123 126 128 129 130 131 132 133 144 146 147 148 149 156 157 162 164 169 **P**6 **S** Avera Health, Sioux Falls, SD
Primary Contact: Debbie Streier, Regional President and Chief Executive Officer
CMO: Timothy Mok, Chief Medical Officer
CHR: Sonya J Kayser, Human Resources Officer
CNO: Dodie Derynck, Chief Nursing Officer
Web address: www.avera.org
Control: Church operated, Nongovernment, not-for-profit **Service**: General medical and surgical

Staffed Beds: 111 **Admissions**: 1480 **Census**: 84 **Outpatient Visits**: 76859 **Births**: 399 **Total Expense ($000)**: 134839 **Payroll Expense ($000)**: 63413 **Personnel**: 546

MELROSE—Stearns County

★ **CENTRACARE – MELROSE (241330)**, 525 Main Street West, Zip 56352-1043; tel. 320/256-4231, (Total facility includes 141 beds in nursing home–type unit) **A**5 10 18 **F**3 10 13 15 28 29 31 34 35 40 43 44 45 50 57 59 60 64 65 68 75 76 77 78 79 81 85 87 91 93 96 97 100 101 102 107 108 110 111 115 119 121 123 127 128 130 131 132 133 135 146 148 149 154 156 164 167 169 **P**6 **S** CentraCare Health, Saint Cloud, MN
Primary Contact: Jennifer Tschida, President
COO: Gerry Gilbertson, FACHE, Chief Operating Officer
CMO: Dante Beretta, M.D., Chief of Staff
CIO: Janet Kruzel, Business Office Manager
CHR: Joyce Chan, Chief Human Resources Officer
CNO: Keri Wimmer, R.N., Patient Care Director
Web address: www.centracare.com
Control: Other not-for-profit (including NFP Corporation) **Service**: General medical and surgical

Staffed Beds: 155 **Admissions**: 494 **Census**: 68 **Outpatient Visits**: 41324 **Births**: 102 **Total Expense ($000)**: 51550 **Payroll Expense ($000)**: 24701 **Personnel**: 157

MINNEAPOLIS—Hennepin County

△ **ABBOTT NORTHWESTERN HOSPITAL (240057)**, 800 East 28th Street, Zip 55407-3799; tel. 612/863-4000, (Includes PHILLIPS EYE INSTITUTE, 2215 Park Avenue, Minneapolis, Minnesota, Zip 55404-3756, tel. 612/775-8800; Daniel S Conrad, M.D., President; SISTER KENNY REHABILITATION INSTITUTE, 810 East 27th Street, Minneapolis, Minnesota, Zip 55407, tel. 612/874-4000) (Total facility includes 56 beds in nursing home–type unit) **A**1 2 3 5 7 8 10 **F**3 12 13 15 17 18 19 20 22 24 26 28 29 30 31 34 35 36 37 38 40 41 42 43 45 46 47 48 49 51 52 53 54 55 56 57 58 59 60 61 64 65 68 70 74 75 76 77 78 79 80 81 82 84 85 86 87 90 91 92 93 95 96 97 98 99 100 102 104 105 107 108 109 110 111 112 113 114 115 116 117 118 119 120 121 123 124 126 128 130 131 132 135 137 138 144 145 146 147 148 149 153 154 157 160 161 162 167 **S** Allina Health, Minneapolis, MN
Primary Contact: David Joos, President
COO: Kelly Spratt, Vice President, Operations
CFO: Brian Weinreis, Vice President Operations and Finance
CHR: Margaret Butler, Vice President Human Resources
Web address: www.abbottnorthwestern.com
Control: Other not-for-profit (including NFP Corporation) **Service**: General medical and surgical

Staffed Beds: 704 **Admissions**: 30916 **Census**: 533 **Outpatient Visits**: 427310 **Births**: 3928 **Total Expense ($000)**: 1704516 **Payroll Expense ($000)**: 690125 **Personnel**: 5163

CHILDREN'S HEALTH CARE See Children's Hospitals and Clinics of Minnesota

CHILDREN'S HOSPITALS AND CLINICS OF MINNESOTA See Children's Minnesota

□ **CHILDREN'S MINNESOTA (243302)**, 2525 Chicago Avenue South, Zip 55404-4518; tel. 612/813-6100, (Includes CHILDREN'S HOSPITALS AND CLINICS OF MINNESOTA, 345 North Smith Avenue, Saint Paul, Minnesota, Zip 55102-2346, tel. 651/220-6000; Robert Bonar Jr, Chief Executive Officer) (Nonreporting) **A**1 3 5 10
Primary Contact: Marc Gorelick, M.D., President and Chief Executive Officer
COO: Trevor Sawallish, Senior Vice President Clinical Operations and Chief Operating Officer
CFO: Brenda McCormick, Chief Financial Officer, Senior Vice President
CMO: Emily Chapman, Chief Medical Officer
CIO: Sam Githinji, Chief Information Security Officer
CHR: Laurin Cathey, Senior Vice President, Chief Human Resource Officer
CNO: Caronline Njau, Chief Nursing Officer & Senior Vice President, Patient Care
Web address: www.childrensmn.org
Control: Other not-for-profit (including NFP Corporation) **Service**: Children's general medical and surgical

Staffed Beds: 429

FAIRVIEW RIVERSIDE HOSPITAL See M Health Fairview University of Minnesota Medical Center, Minneapolis

□ △ **HENNEPIN HEALTHCARE (240004)**, 701 Park Avenue South, Zip 55415-1829; tel. 612/873-3000, (Includes HCMC DEPARTMENT OF PEDIATRICS, 701 Park Avenue, Minneapolis, Minnesota, Zip 55415-1623, tel. 612/873-2064) **A**1 2 3 5 7 8 10 **F**3 5 7 8 12 13 15 16 18 20 22 24 26 28 29 30 31 32 33 34 35 36 38 39 40 41 43 44 45 46 47 48 49 50 51 53 54 55 56 57 58 59 61 62 65 66 68 70 72 74 75 76 77 78 79 82 84 85 86 87 88 89 90 92 93 94 96 97 98 100 101 102 104 105 106 107 108 110 111 112 114 115 116 117 118 119 120 121 126 129 130 131 132 134 135 138 139 140 141 144 145 146 147 148 149 150 152 153 154 156 157 160 162 164 165 167 169 **P**6
Primary Contact: Jennifer DeCubellis, Chief Executive Officer
CFO: Derrick O. Hollings, Chief Financial Officer
CMO: Dan Hoody, M.D., MSC, Interim Chief Medical Officer
CIO: Joanne Sunquist, Chief Information Officer
CHR: Walter Chesley, Senior Vice President Human Resources
CNO: Lori J. Brown, R.N., FACHE, Chief Nursing Officer
Web address: www.hcmc.org
Control: County, Government, Nonfederal **Service**: General medical and surgical

Staffed Beds: 446 **Admissions**: 16592 **Census**: 348 **Outpatient Visits**: 98818 **Births**: 1758 **Total Expense ($000)**: 1398722 **Payroll Expense ($000)**: 737981 **Personnel**: 6134

△ **M HEALTH FAIRVIEW UNIVERSITY OF MINNESOTA MEDICAL CENTER (240080)**, 2450 Riverside Avenue, Zip 55454-1400; tel. 612/624-8618, (Includes FAIRVIEW RIVERSIDE HOSPITAL, 2312 South Sixth Street, Minneapolis, Minnesota, Zip 55454, tel. 612/371-6300; ST. MARY'S HOSPITAL AND REHABILITATION CENTER, 2414 South Seventh Street, Minneapolis, Minnesota, Zip 55454, tel. 612/338-2229; UNIVERSITY OF MINNESOTA HOSPITAL AND CLINIC, 420 Delaware St SE, Minneapolis, Minnesota, Zip 55455-0341, 420 SE Delaware Street, Zip 55455-0392, tel. 612/626-3000; UNIVERSITY OF MINNESOTA MASONIC CHILDREN'S HOSPITAL, 420 Delaware Street, SE, Minneapolis, Minnesota, Zip 55455-0341, tel. 888/543-7866) (Total facility includes 24 beds in nursing home–type unit) **A**1 2 3 5 7 8 10 19 **F**3 4 5 11 12 13 15 17 18 19 20 21 22 23 24 25 26 27 28 29 30 31 32 33 34 35 36 37 38 39 40 41 43 44 45 46 47 48 49 50 51 52 55 56 57 58 59 60 61 63 64 65 68 70 72 74 75 76 77 78 79 80 81 82 84 85 86 87 88 89 90 91 92 93 94 96 97 98 99 100 101 102 103 104 105 106 107 108 109 110 111 112 113 114 115 116 117 118 119 120 121 123 124 126 128 129 130 131 132 134 135 136 137 138 139 140 141 142 145 146 147 148 149 151 152 153 154 156 157 160 162 164 165 166 167 169 **S** Fairview Health Services, Minneapolis, MN
Primary Contact: Jeoff Will, Executive Vice President, Chief Operating Officer
CMO: Barbara Gold, M.D., Chief Medical Officer
CHR: Don Moschkau, Senior Director Human Resources
Web address: www.fairview.org
Control: Other not-for-profit (including NFP Corporation) **Service**: General medical and surgical

Staffed Beds: 903 **Admissions**: 27404 **Census**: 654 **Outpatient Visits**: 448887 **Births**: 2099 **Total Expense ($000)**: 2117739 **Payroll Expense ($000)**: 788967 **Personnel**: 6424

Hospitals, U.S. / MINNESOTA

✦ △ **MINNEAPOLIS VA HEALTH CARE SYSTEM**, 1 Veterans Drive, Zip 55417-2399, Mailing Address: One Veterans Drive, Zip 55417-2399; tel. 612/725-2000, (Nonreporting) **A**1 2 3 5 7 8 **S** Department of Veterans Affairs, Washington, DC
Primary Contact: Patrick J. Kelly, FACHE, Director
COO: Kurt Thielen, Associate Director
CFO: LeAnn Stomberg, Chief Financial Officer
CMO: Kent Crossley, M.D., Chief of Staff
CIO: Brian Bornick, Chief Information Officer
CHR: Tom Johnson, Chief Human Resource Officer
CNO: Helen Pearlman, Nurse Executive
Web address: www.minneapolis.va.gov
Control: Veterans Affairs, Government, federal **Service**: General medical and surgical

Staffed Beds: 264

MINNEAPOLIS VAMC See Minneapolis VA Health Care System

SISTER KENNY INSTITUTE See Sister Kenny Rehabilitation Institute

SISTER KENNY REHABILITATION INSTITUTE See Abbott Northwestern Hospital, Minneapolis

ST. MARY'S HOSPITAL AND REHABILITATION CENTER See M Health Fairview University of Minnesota Medical Center, Minneapolis

THE HCMC DEPARTMENT OF PEDIATRICS See Hcmc Department of Pediatrics

UNIVERSITY OF MINNESOTA CHILDREN'S HOSPITAL, FAIRVIEW See University of Minnesota Masonic Children's Hospital

UNIVERSITY OF MINNESOTA HOSPITAL AND CLINIC See M Health Fairview University of Minnesota Medical Center, Minneapolis

UNIVERSITY OF MN HOSPITAL See University of Minnesota Hospital and Clinic

MONTEVIDEO—Chippewa County

CCM HEALTH (241325), 824 North 11th Street, Zip 56265-1683; tel. 320/269-8877, (Nonreporting) **A**10 18
Primary Contact: Brian A. Lovdahl, Chief Executive Officer
CFO: Darlene Boike, Chief Financial Officer
CIO: Jeff Plemel, Director Health Information
CHR: Vonnie Erickson, Human Resource Manager
CNO: Terry Anderson, R.N., Director of Nursing Services
Web address: www.montevideomedical.com
Control: City-county, Government, Nonfederal **Service**: General medical and surgical

Staffed Beds: 25

MONTICELLO—Wright County

★ ⇧ **CENTRACARE – MONTICELLO (241362)**, 1013 Hart Boulevard, Zip 55362-8230; tel. 763/295-2945, (Total facility includes 50 beds in nursing home–type unit) **A**10 18 21 **F**3 13 15 18 28 30 31 34 40 43 44 45 51 59 64 69 70 74 76 77 78 79 81 85 87 98 100 103 107 108 110 111 114 115 117 118 119 120 121 126 128 129 130 133 135 146 148 149 154 156 **S** CentraCare Health, Saint Cloud, MN
Primary Contact: John Hering, M.D., President and Chief Medical Officer
CFO: Jason Weaver, Director Finance
CMO: John Hering, M.D., Chief Medical Officer
CNO: Lynn Christian, MSN, R.N., Senior Director Acute Care Nursing
Web address: https://www.centracare.com/locations/centracare-monticello/
Control: Other not-for-profit (including NFP Corporation) **Service**: General medical and surgical

Staffed Beds: 73 **Admissions**: 1139 **Census**: 56 **Outpatient Visits**: 45114
Births: 245 **Total Expense ($000)**: 86841 **Payroll Expense ($000)**: 41473
Personnel: 434

MOOSE LAKE—Carlton County

★ **ESSENTIA HEALTH MOOSE LAKE (241350)**, 4572 County Road 61, Zip 55767-9405; tel. 218/485-4481, **A**10 18 **F**3 7 8 11 13 15 28 29 31 34 35 40 41 43 45 46 53 57 59 62 64 68 75 76 77 78 79 81 82 85 86 87 93 107 111 114 118 119 130 131 132 133 135 144 146 148 149 154 156 167 169 **P**6 **S** Essentia Health, Duluth, MN
Primary Contact: Sam Barney, Administrator
CMO: Andrea Kramer, Chief Medical Officer
CHR: Sonya Towle, Director Human Resources
CNO: Donita Korpela, R.N., Director of Patient Care Services
Web address: https://www.essentiahealth.org/find-facility/profile/essentia-health-moose-lake/
Control: Other not-for-profit (including NFP Corporation) **Service**: General medical and surgical

Staffed Beds: 25 **Admissions**: 594 **Census**: 5 **Outpatient Visits**: 29143
Births: 91 **Total Expense ($000)**: 39717 **Payroll Expense ($000)**: 16116
Personnel: 144

MORA—Kanabec County

✦ **WELIA HEALTH (241367)**, 301 South Highway 65 South, Zip 55051-1899; tel. 320/679-1212, **A**1 10 18 **F**3 7 11 13 15 28 31 34 35 40 43 51 53 55 64 68 70 75 76 77 78 79 81 84 85 87 93 94 97 107 108 110 111 115 119 126 127 130 131 132 133 135 143 144 146 147 148 149 154 160
Primary Contact: Randy Ulseth, Chief Executive Officer
COO: Sandy Zutz-Wiczek, Chief Operating Officer
CFO: Josh Asp, Chief Financial Officer
CMO: Brian Niskanen, Chief Medical Officer
CNO: Diane Bankers, Chief Nursing Officer
Web address: https://www.weliahealth.org
Control: Other not-for-profit (including NFP Corporation) **Service**: General medical and surgical

Staffed Beds: 25 **Admissions**: 1055 **Census**: 9 **Outpatient Visits**: 177816
Births: 242 **Total Expense ($000)**: 115359 **Payroll Expense ($000)**: 45454
Personnel: 487

MORRIS—Stevens County

★ **STEVENS COMMUNITY MEDICAL CENTER (241363)**, 400 East First Street, Zip 56267-1408; tel. 320/589-1313, **A**10 18 **F**3 10 11 13 15 28 29 31 34 35 40 43 44 45 50 54 57 59 64 68 70 75 76 77 79 81 85 86 87 89 97 100 104 107 110 111 115 119 126 127 128 130 131 133 135 144 146 148 149 154 162 164 166 169 **P**6
Primary Contact: Kerrie McEvilly, President and Chief Executive Officer
CHR: Karla Larson, Director Human Resources
Web address: www.scmcinc.org
Control: Other not-for-profit (including NFP Corporation) **Service**: General medical and surgical

Staffed Beds: 25 **Admissions**: 439 **Census**: 3 **Outpatient Visits**: 78396
Births: 64 **Total Expense ($000)**: 47156 **Payroll Expense ($000)**: 20795
Personnel: 242

NEW PRAGUE—Scott County

☐ **MAYO CLINIC HEALTH SYSTEM IN NEW PRAGUE (241361)**, 301 Second Street NE, Zip 56071-1799; tel. 952/758-4431, (Nonreporting) **A**1 3 10 18 **S** Mayo Clinic, Rochester, MN
Primary Contact: James Hebl, M.D., Regional Vice President
Web address: www.mayoclinichealthsystem.org/locations/new-prague
Control: Other not-for-profit (including NFP Corporation) **Service**: General medical and surgical

Staffed Beds: 17

Hospitals, U.S. / MINNESOTA

NEW ULM—Brown County

✠ **NEW ULM MEDICAL CENTER (241378)**, 1324 Fifth Street North, Zip 56073–1553; tel. 507/217–5000, **A**1 2 3 5 10 18 **F**3 13 28 29 31 32 34 35 36 40 41 43 45 54 55 59 64 65 74 75 76 77 78 79 80 81 82 85 87 93 97 98 100 102 104 106 107 110 111 115 118 119 124 126 129 130 131 132 146 148 149 154 **S** Allina Health, Minneapolis, MN
Primary Contact: Toby Freier, President
COO: Carisa Buegler, Director of Operations
CFO: Michael Grand, Director of Finance
CMO: Andrew Reeves, M.D., Director Medical Affairs
CHR: Katie Slette, Director Human Resources
CNO: Jennifer Brehmer, Director Patient Care
Web address: www.newulmmedicalcenter.com
Control: Other not–for–profit (including NFP Corporation) **Service**: General medical and surgical

Staffed Beds: 34 **Admissions**: 1775 **Census**: 17 **Outpatient Visits**: 111479 **Births**: 292 **Total Expense ($000)**: 125591 **Payroll Expense ($000)**: 41126 **Personnel**: 396

NORTHFIELD—Dakota County

★ **NORTHFIELD HOSPITAL AND CLINICS (240014)**, 2000 North Avenue, Zip 55057–1498; tel. 507/646–1000, (Nonreporting) **A**2 10
Primary Contact: Steve Underdahl, President and Chief Executive Officer
COO: Jerry Ehn, Chief Operating Officer
CFO: Scott D Edin, Vice President, Finance and Chief Financial Officer
CMO: Jeff Meland, M.D., Vice President, Chief Medical Officer
CHR: Jeffrey S. Mutz, Human Resources Director
CNO: Tammy A. Hayes, R.N., MS, Chief Nurse Executive, Hospital and Long Term Care Center Administrator
Web address: www.northfieldhospital.org
Control: City, Government, Nonfederal **Service**: General medical and surgical

Staffed Beds: 77

OLIVIA—Renville County

HEALTHPARTNERS OLIVIA HOSPITAL & CLINIC (241306), 100 Healthy Way, Zip 56277–1117; tel. 320/523–1261, (Nonreporting) **A**10 18 **S** HealthPartners, Bloomington, MN
Primary Contact: Nathan Pulscher, President
CIO: Cherry Weigel, Director Health Information Management
Web address: https://oliviahospital.com/
Control: County, Government, Nonfederal **Service**: General medical and surgical

Staffed Beds: 16

ONAMIA—Mille Lacs County

★ **MILLE LACS HEALTH SYSTEM (241356)**, 200 North Elm Street, Zip 56359–7901; tel. 320/532–3154, (Total facility includes 57 beds in nursing home–type unit) **A**10 18 **F**3 5 7 11 15 18 28 31 33 40 43 45 50 56 59 62 63 65 81 82 93 97 98 102 103 104 107 114 127 128 129 130 133 135 144 148 149 151 154 156 157 160
Primary Contact: Bill Nelson, Chief Executive Officer
COO: Kim Kucera, Chief Operating Officer
CFO: Andy Knutson, Chief Financial Officer
CMO: Thomas H Bracken, M.D., Vice President Medical Affairs
Web address: www.mlhealth.org
Control: Other not–for–profit (including NFP Corporation) **Service**: General medical and surgical

Staffed Beds: 85 **Admissions**: 488 **Census**: 46 **Outpatient Visits**: 24348 **Births**: 0 **Total Expense ($000)**: 57216 **Payroll Expense ($000)**: 26409 **Personnel**: 334

ORTONVILLE—Big Stone County

★ **ORTONVILLE AREA HEALTH SERVICES (241342)**, 450 Eastvold Avenue, Zip 56278–1133; tel. 320/839–2502, (Nonreporting) **A**10 18 **S** Sanford Health, Sioux Falls, SD
Primary Contact: Allan Ross, Chief Excecutive Officer
CMO: Stacy Longnecker, Chief of Staff
CIO: Barbara Voecks, Chief Information Officer
CHR: Kim McCrea, Chief Human Resources Officer
CNO: Jennifer Wiik, Chief Nursing Officer
Web address: www.oahs.us
Control: City, Government, Nonfederal **Service**: General medical and surgical

Staffed Beds: 90

OWATONNA—Steele County

✠ **OWATONNA HOSPITAL (240069)**, 2250 NW 26th Street, Zip 55060–5503; tel. 507/451–3850, **A**1 3 5 10 **F**3 11 28 29 40 41 43 45 75 76 77 79 80 81 85 87 93 98 102 107 119 126 129 130 131 143 146 149 154 **S** Allina Health, Minneapolis, MN
Primary Contact: Whitney Johnson, President
COO: Mark T Gillen, Director of Operations
CFO: Mark T Gillen, Director Finance and Operations
CNO: Anne Draeger, Chief Nursing Officer
Web address: https://www.allinahealth.org/owatonna-hospital
Control: Other not–for–profit (including NFP Corporation) **Service**: General medical and surgical

Staffed Beds: 40 **Admissions**: 1911 **Census**: 22 **Outpatient Visits**: 30923 **Births**: 363 **Total Expense ($000)**: 62105 **Payroll Expense ($000)**: 21431 **Personnel**: 191

PARK RAPIDS—Hubbard County

✠ **CHI ST. JOSEPH'S HEALTH (241380)**, 600 Pleasant Avenue, Zip 56470–1431; tel. 218/732–3311, (Nonreporting) **A**1 10 18 **S** CommonSpirit Health, Chicago, IL
Primary Contact: Benjamin Koppelman, President
CFO: Jay Ross, Chief Financial Officer
CMO: Kia Parsi, M.D., Chief Medical Officer
CHR: John Tormanen, Director Mission and Human Resources
CNO: Deb Haagenson, R.N., Vice President of Patient Care
Web address: www.sjahs.org
Control: Church operated, Nongovernment, not–for–profit **Service**: General medical and surgical

Staffed Beds: 25

PAYNESVILLE—Stearns County

★ **CENTRACARE – PAYNESVILLE (241349)**, 200 West 1st Street, Zip 56362–1496; tel. 320/243–3767, **A**5 10 18 **F**3 10 13 15 29 31 34 40 43 45 54 56 57 59 64 65 68 75 76 81 85 89 93 107 110 111 115 119 125 127 130 133 135 145 146 148 149 154 156 158 164 169 **S** CentraCare Health, Saint Cloud, MN
Primary Contact: Craig Henneman, President
CFO: Jennifer Holtz, Director Finance
CMO: Timothy Malling, M.D., Chief of Staff
CHR: Paulette Hagen, Human Resources and Administrative Services Director
CNO: Rachel A Walz, Director Patient Care
Web address: https://www.centracare.com/locations/centracare-paynesville/
Control: Other not–for–profit (including NFP Corporation) **Service**: General medical and surgical

Staffed Beds: 14 **Admissions**: 372 **Census**: 6 **Outpatient Visits**: 45929 **Births**: 49 **Total Expense ($000)**: 38590 **Payroll Expense ($000)**: 18814 **Personnel**: 131

PERHAM—Otter Tail County

✠ **PERHAM HEALTH (241373)**, 1000 Coney Street West, Zip 56573–1108; tel. 218/347–4500, (Nonreporting) **A**1 10 18 **S** Sanford Health, Sioux Falls, SD
Primary Contact: Chuck Hofius, FACHE, Chief Executive Officer
CFO: Justine Anderson, Chief Financial Officer
CMO: Tim Studer, President Medical Staff
CIO: Jim Rieber, Director Information Systems
CHR: Sadie Christiansen, Director Human Resources
CNO: Sonda Tolle, R.N., Vice President Patient Services
Web address: www.perhamhealth.org
Control: Hospital district or authority, Government, Nonfederal **Service**: General medical and surgical

Staffed Beds: 119

PIPESTONE—Pipestone County

★ **PIPESTONE COUNTY MEDICAL CENTER (241374)**, 916 4th Avenue SW, Zip 56164–1890; tel. 507/825–5811, (Nonreporting) **A**10 18 **S** Avera Health, Sioux Falls, SD
Primary Contact: Bradley D. Burris, Chief Executive Officer
CFO: Sandy Schlechter, Chief Financial Officer
CHR: Judy Raschke, Director Human Resources
CNO: Jessica Smidt, R.N., Director of Nursing
Web address: www.pcmchealth.org
Control: County, Government, Nonfederal **Service**: General medical and surgical

Staffed Beds: 18

Hospitals, U.S. / MINNESOTA

PRINCETON—Sherburne County

✠ **M HEALTH FAIRVIEW NORTHLAND MEDICAL CENTER (240141)**, 911 Northland Drive, Zip 55371–2173; tel. 763/389–1313, **A**1 5 10 **F**3 13 15 18 28 29 30 31 34 35 40 41 43 45 50 51 57 59 64 69 70 75 76 77 78 79 81 82 85 86 87 93 96 101 107 110 111 115 119 126 130 131 146 148 149 154 156 164 167 169 **S** Fairview Health Services, Minneapolis, MN
Primary Contact: Jeoff Will, Executive Vice President, Chief Operating Officer
CFO: Tim Lynch, Director of Finance
CMO: Greg Schoen, M.D., Regional Medical Director
Web address: https://mhealthfairview.org/locations/m-health-fairview-northland-medical-center
Control: Other not–for–profit (including NFP Corporation) **Service**: General medical and surgical

Staffed Beds: 23 **Admissions**: 1488 **Census**: 14 **Outpatient Visits**: 62926 **Births**: 356 **Total Expense ($000)**: 87917 **Payroll Expense ($000)**: 33547 **Personnel**: 371

RED LAKE—Beltrami County

✠ **RED LAKE INDIAN HEALTH SERVICE HOSPITAL (240206)**, 24760 Hospital Drive, Zip 56671, Mailing Address: P.O. Box 497, Zip 56671–0497; tel. 218/679–3912, (Nonreporting) **A**1 10 **S** U. S. Indian Health Service, Rockville, MD
Primary Contact: Mary Ann. Cook, Chief Executive Officer, Red Lake Service Unit
CMO: Paul Ditmanson, M.D., Clinical Director
CNO: Mary Ann Cook, Director of Nursing
Web address: www.rlnnredlakehospital.com/
Control: PHS, Indian Service, Government, federal **Service**: General medical and surgical

Staffed Beds: 19

RED WING—Goodhue County

□ **MAYO CLINIC HEALTH SYSTEM IN RED WING (240018)**, 701 Hewitt Boulevard, Zip 55066–2848, Mailing Address: P.O. Box 95, Zip 55066–0095; tel. 651/267–5000, **A**1 3 5 10 **F**3 9 11 13 15 18 28 29 30 31 32 34 35 36 38 40 43 44 45 47 50 56 57 59 63 64 65 71 74 75 76 77 78 79 80 81 82 85 86 87 93 94 96 97 100 101 102 104 107 108 110 111 115 119 130 131 132 134 135 146 147 148 149 154 156 160 161 162 164 169 **S** Mayo Clinic, Rochester, MN
Primary Contact: Brian Whited, M.D., Physician Executive
Web address: www.mayoclinichealthsystem.org/locations/red-wing
Control: Other not–for–profit (including NFP Corporation) **Service**: General medical and surgical

Staffed Beds: 22 **Admissions**: 1324 **Census**: 11 **Outpatient Visits**: 129476 **Births**: 310

REDWOOD FALLS—Redwood County

CARRIS HEALTH – REDWOOD See Centracare – Redwood

★ **CENTRACARE – REDWOOD (241351)**, 101 Caring Way, Zip 56283; tel. 507/637–4500, **A**10 18 **F**3 5 13 15 28 29 31 34 35 40 43 45 50 56 59 65 68 76 81 82 85 93 97 107 110 111 114 119 127 129 130 131 133 135 146 148 154 156 160 165 169 **S** CentraCare Health, Saint Cloud, MN
Primary Contact: Carnie Allex, President
CFO: Thomas Richard, Director Budget and Revenue Cycle
CIO: Tom Balko, Manager Information Systems
CHR: Jody Rindfleisch, Manager Human Resources
CNO: Dawn Allen, R.N., Chief Clinical Officer
Web address: https://www.centracare.com/locations/centracare-redwood-hospital/
Control: Other not–for–profit (including NFP Corporation) **Service**: General medical and surgical

Staffed Beds: 14 **Admissions**: 524 **Census**: 4 **Outpatient Visits**: 51943 **Births**: 121 **Total Expense ($000)**: 49685 **Payroll Expense ($000)**: 20559 **Personnel**: 147

ROBBINSDALE—Hennepin County

△ ⇑ **NORTH MEMORIAL HEALTH HOSPITAL (240001)**, 3300 Oakdale Avenue North, Zip 55422–2926; tel. 763/520–5200, (Nonreporting) **A**3 5 7 10 21 **S** North Memorial Health Care, Robbinsdale, MN
Primary Contact: Trevor Sawallish, Chief Executive Officer
COO: Steve Horstmann, Vice President Operations
CFO: Daniel Fromm, Chief Financial Officer
CMO: Andrew Houlton, M.D., Chief Medical Officer
CIO: Bradford Newton, Chief Information Officer
CHR: Melissa Smith, Interim Vice President Human Resources
Web address: www.northmemorial.com
Control: Other not–for–profit (including NFP Corporation) **Service**: General medical and surgical

Staffed Beds: 358

ROCHESTER—Olmsted County

□ **COMMUNITY BEHAVIORAL HEALTH HOSPITAL – ROCHESTER (244017)**, 251 Wood Lake Drive SE, Zip 55904–5530; tel. 507/206–2561, (Nonreporting) **A**1 **S** Minnesota Department of Human Services, Saint Paul, MN
Primary Contact: James Pierce, Chief Executive Officer
CFO: Shirley Jacobson, Chief Financial Officer
CMO: Peter S Millen, Chief Medical Officer MHSATS
CIO: Thomas Baden Jr, Chief Information Officer
CHR: Connie Jones, Director Human Resources
CNO: Pamela R Bajari, R.N., Nurse Executive MHSATS
Web address: www.health.state.mn.us
Control: State, Government, Nonfederal **Service**: Psychiatric

Staffed Beds: 8

MAYO CLINIC – SAINT MARYS HOSPITAL See Mayo Clinic Hospital – Saint Marys Campus

✠ △ **MAYO CLINIC HOSPITAL – ROCHESTER (240010)**, 1216 Second Street SW, Zip 55902–1906; tel. 507/255–5123, (Includes MAYO CLINIC HOSPITAL – METHODIST CAMPUS, 201 West Center Street, Rochester, Minnesota, Zip 55902–3084, tel. 507/266–7890; MAYO CLINIC HOSPITAL – SAINT MARYS CAMPUS, 1216 Second Street SW, Rochester, Minnesota, Zip 55902–1970, tel. 507/255–5123; Kenneth F. Ackerman, FACHE, Chair, Hospital Operation; MAYO EUGENIO LITTA CHILDREN'S HOSPITAL, 200 First Street, SW, Rochester, Minnesota, Zip 55905–0001, tel. 507/255–5123) **A**1 2 3 5 7 8 10 **F**1 3 4 5 6 7 8 9 11 12 13 14 15 17 18 19 20 21 22 23 24 25 26 27 28 29 30 31 32 33 34 35 36 37 38 39 40 41 43 44 45 46 47 48 49 50 51 52 53 54 55 56 57 58 59 60 61 62 63 64 65 68 70 71 72 74 75 76 77 78 79 80 81 82 83 84 85 86 87 88 89 90 91 92 93 94 95 96 97 98 99 100 101 102 103 104 105 107 108 110 111 112 114 115 116 117 118 119 120 121 122 123 124 126 129 130 131 132 134 135 136 137 138 139 140 141 142 143 145 146 147 148 149 150 152 153 154 155 157 160 161 162 164 165 166 167 169 **S** Mayo Clinic, Rochester, MN
Primary Contact: Lindsey Lehman, Associate Administrator, Hospital Operations
COO: Natalie Caine, Chief Administrative Officer
CFO: Adam Horst, Chief Financial Officer
CMO: Daniel Brown, M.D., Ph.D., Medical Director, Hospital Operations
CIO: Christopher J. Ross, Chief Information Technology Officer
CHR: Paula Menkosky, Chief Human Resources Officer
CNO: Sherry Wolf, R.N., Chief Nursing Office, RST
Web address: www.mayoclinic.org
Control: Other not–for–profit (including NFP Corporation) **Service**: General medical and surgical

Staffed Beds: 1304 **Admissions**: 51064 **Census**: 923 **Outpatient Visits**: 474700 **Births**: 2368

Hospital, Medicare Provider Number, Address, Telephone, Approval, Facility, and Physician Codes, Health Care System

★ American Hospital Association (AHA) membership ○ Healthcare Facilities Accreditation Program ⇑ Center for Improvement in Healthcare Quality Accreditation
□ The Joint Commission accreditation ◇ DNV Healthcare Inc. accreditation △ Commission on Accreditation of Rehabilitation Facilities (CARF) accreditation

Hospitals, U.S. / MINNESOTA

★ ⓗ **OLMSTED MEDICAL CENTER (240006)**, 1650 Fourth Street SE, Zip 55904–4717, Mailing Address: 210 Ninth Street SE, Zip 55904–6756; tel. 507/288–3443, **A**5 10 21 **F**3 5 11 12 13 15 18 28 29 30 34 35 37 40 44 45 46 48 50 51 53 54 56 57 58 59 64 65 68 70 74 75 76 77 79 81 82 84 85 86 87 92 93 96 97 100 102 104 107 108 110 111 115 119 126 129 130 131 132 135 146 147 148 149 154 156 160 161 162 164 165 167 169 **P**6
Primary Contact: Tim W. Weir, FACHE, Chief Executive Officer
COO: Robert Cunningham, Chief Operations Officer
CFO: Kevin A Higgins, Chief Financial Officer
CMO: Randy Hemann, M.D., Chief Medical Officer
CIO: Tom Ogg, Chief Information Officer
CHR: Tom Hunsberger, Director Human Resources
CNO: Sharon L Schneller, Chief Nursing Officer
Web address: www.olmmed.org
Control: Other not–for–profit (including NFP Corporation) Service: General medical and surgical

Staffed Beds: 47 **Admissions:** 1770 **Census:** 13 **Outpatient Visits:** 354344 **Births:** 887 **Total Expense ($000):** 266538 **Payroll Expense ($000):** 130663 **Personnel:** 956

ROCHESTER METHODIST HOSPITAL See Mayo Clinic Hospital – Methodist Campus

ROSEAU—Roseau County

☒ **LIFECARE MEDICAL CENTER (241344)**, 715 Delmore Drive, Zip 56751–1599; tel. 218/463–2500, (Total facility includes 80 beds in nursing home–type unit) **A**1 10 18 **F**3 7 10 11 13 15 28 29 30 31 32 34 35 36 40 43 45 53 56 57 59 62 63 64 65 68 75 76 77 81 82 84 85 86 93 104 107 110 111 115 118 119 128 129 130 132 133 135 144 146 147 148 149 156 169 **P**6
Primary Contact: Keith Okeson, President and Chief Executive Officer
COO: Shannon Carlson, Chief Operating Officer
CFO: Cathy Huss, Chief Financial Officer
CIO: Kevin Schumacher, Director of Information Systems
CHR: Lois Slick, Director of Human Resources
CNO: Nathan Brovold, Chief Nursing Officer
Web address: www.lifecaremedicalcenter.org
Control: Other not–for–profit (including NFP Corporation) Service: General medical and surgical

Staffed Beds: 105 **Admissions:** 475 **Census:** 67 **Outpatient Visits:** 48241 **Births:** 148 **Total Expense ($000):** 55893 **Payroll Expense ($000):** 25730 **Personnel:** 316

SAINT CLOUD—Stearns County

☒ **CENTRACARE – ST. CLOUD HOSPITAL (240036)**, 1406 Sixth Avenue North, Zip 56303–1901; tel. 320/251–2700, **A**1 2 3 5 8 10 **F**3 5 11 12 13 14 15 17 18 19 20 22 24 26 28 29 30 31 32 34 35 36 37 38 39 40 43 44 45 46 47 48 49 50 51 54 56 57 58 59 60 61 62 63 64 66 68 69 70 72 74 75 76 77 78 79 80 81 82 84 85 86 87 88 89 90 92 93 96 97 98 99 100 101 102 103 104 105 107 108 110 111 115 117 118 119 120 121 122 123 124 126 129 130 131 132 134 135 141 144 145 146 147 148 149 150 151 156 157 160 161 162 164 167 169 **S** CentraCare Health, Saint Cloud, MN
Primary Contact: Joy Plamann, R.N., Senior Vice President Central Operations, President CentraCare – St. Cloud Hospital
CMO: Mark Matthias, M.D., Vice President, Medical Affairs, and Physician Vice President, Acute Care Division
CIO: Amy Porwoll, Vice President of Information Systems
CHR: Joe Kalkman, Chief Administrative Officer, Chief Human Resources Officer, Executive Vice President
Web address: www.centracare.com
Control: Other not–for–profit (including NFP Corporation) Service: General medical and surgical

Staffed Beds: 477 **Admissions:** 23280 **Census:** 307 **Outpatient Visits:** 424297 **Births:** 2611 **Total Expense ($000):** 944826 **Payroll Expense ($000):** 420396 **Personnel:** 3569

☒ **ST. CLOUD VA HEALTH CARE SYSTEM**, 4801 Veterans Drive, Zip 56303–2099; tel. 320/252–1670, (Nonreporting) **A**1 3 **S** Department of Veterans Affairs, Washington, DC
Primary Contact: Cheryl Thieschafer, Interim Health Care System Director
CFO: Joseph Schmitz, Chief Financial Officer
CMO: Scott C. Bartley, M.D., Chief of Staff
CIO: Denise Hanson, Information Technology Specialist
CHR: Lisa Rosendahl, Director Human Resources
CNO: Meri Hauge, R.N., MSN, Associate Director of Patient Care Services and Nurse Executive
Web address: https://www.va.gov/st-cloud-health-care/about-us/
Control: Veterans Affairs, Government, federal Service: Psychiatric

Staffed Beds: 240

ST. CLOUD VAMC See St. Cloud VA Health Care System

SAINT JAMES—Watonwan County

☐ **MAYO CLINIC HEALTH SYSTEM IN SAINT JAMES (241333)**, 1101 Moulton and Parsons Drive, Zip 56081–5550; tel. 507/375–3261, (Nonreporting) **A**1 10 18 **S** Mayo Clinic, Rochester, MN
Primary Contact: James Hebl, M.D., Regional Vice President
COO: Richard Grace, Chief Administrative Officer
CFO: James Tarasovich, Chief Financial Officer
CMO: Jennifer Langbehn, Medical Director
CHR: Gayle B Hansen, R.N., Chief Integration Officer
Web address: www.mayoclinichealthsystem.org/locations/st-james
Control: Other not–for–profit (including NFP Corporation) Service: General medical and surgical

Staffed Beds: 13

SAINT LOUIS PARK—Hennepin County

☐ **PARK NICOLLET METHODIST HOSPITAL (240053)**, 6500 Excelsior Boulevard, Zip 55426–4702; tel. 952/993–5000, (Nonreporting) **A**1 2 3 5 10 **S** HealthPartners, Bloomington, MN
Primary Contact: Jennifer Myster, President
COO: Michael Kaupa, Executive Vice President and Chief Operating Officer
CFO: Sheila McMillan, Chief Financial Officer
CMO: Steven Connelly, M.D., President and Chief Medical Officer
CIO: Julie Flaschenriem, Chief Information Officer
CHR: Paul Dominski, Vice President Human Resources
CNO: Melissa Fritz, R.N., Chief Nursing Officer
Web address: www.parknicollet.com
Control: Other not–for–profit (including NFP Corporation) Service: General medical and surgical

Staffed Beds: 370

SAINT PAUL—Ramsey County

CHILDREN'S HOSPITAL & CLINICS See Children's Hospitals and Clinics of Minnesota

☒ △ **GILLETTE CHILDREN'S SPECIALTY HEALTHCARE (243300)**, 200 University Avenue East, Zip 55101–2507; tel. 651/291–2848, **A**1 3 5 7 10 **F**3 19 29 30 35 36 39 43 48 50 54 55 58 64 65 68 69 74 77 79 81 82 84 85 86 87 88 89 90 91 92 93 94 95 96 107 111 115 119 127 129 130 131 136 141 142 146 148 149 154 164 **P**6
Primary Contact: Barbara Walczyk-Joers, President and Chief Executive Officer
COO: Thomas Harris, Chief Operating POfficer
CFO: Patrick Nolan, Vice President Finance and Chief Financial Officer
CMO: Micah Niermann, Chief Medical Officer
CIO: Timothy Getsay, Chief of Performance and Integration
CHR: Kit Brady, Vice President of People Strategy
CNO: Karen Brill, R.N., Chief Nursing Officer, Vice President Care
Web address: www.gillettechildrens.org
Control: Other not–for–profit (including NFP Corporation) Service: Children's other specialty

Staffed Beds: 60 **Admissions:** 2122 **Census:** 26 **Outpatient Visits:** 144621 **Births:** 0 **Total Expense ($000):** 310530 **Payroll Expense ($000):** 141279 **Personnel:** 1170

★ **M HEALTH FAIRVIEW BETHESDA HOSPITAL (242024)**, 45 West 10th Street, Zip 55102–1053; tel. 651/232–3000, **A**5 **F**1 30 35 50 63 68 75 77 84 87 107 108 119 130 146 148 149 **S** Fairview Health Services, Minneapolis, MN
Primary Contact: James Hereford, Executive Vice President, Chief Operating Officer
Web address: www.fairview.org
Control: Other not–for–profit (including NFP Corporation) Service: Acute long–term care hospital

Staffed Beds: 24 **Admissions:** 197 **Census:** 24 **Outpatient Visits:** 149 **Births:** 0 **Total Expense ($000):** 36738 **Payroll Expense ($000):** 20785 **Personnel:** 184

☐ △ **REGIONS HOSPITAL (240106)**, 640 Jackson Street, Zip 55101–2595; tel. 651/254–3456, (Nonreporting) **A**1 3 5 7 8 10 **S** HealthPartners, Bloomington, MN
Primary Contact: Emily Blomberg, President
CFO: Heidi Conrad, Vice President and Chief Financial Officer
CMO: Charles Fazio, Chief Health Officer and Medical Director Health Plan
CIO: Kari Toft, Vice President, Chief Information Officer
CHR: Alicia Gilbert, Vice President
CNO: Chris Boese, Vice President and Chief Nursing Officer
Web address: www.regionshospital.com
Control: Other not–for–profit (including NFP Corporation) Service: General medical and surgical

Staffed Beds: 457

Hospitals, U.S. / MINNESOTA

△ **UNITED HOSPITAL (240038)**, 333 North Smith Avenue, Zip 55102–2389; tel. 651/241–8000, (Includes UNITED HOSPITAL – HASTINGS REGINA CAMPUS, 1175 Nininger Road, Hastings, Minnesota, Zip 55033–1098, tel. 651/480–4100); Jill Ostrem, President) **A**1 2 3 5 7 10 **F**3 12 13 15 18 20 22 24 26 28 29 30 31 34 35 36 37 40 41 43 44 45 46 47 48 49 51 53 54 56 58 59 60 61 64 65 70 74 75 76 77 78 79 80 81 82 84 85 86 87 90 91 92 93 94 96 97 98 100 102 103 104 105 107 108 109 110 111 112 113 114 115 118 119 120 121 123 124 126 129 130 131 132 135 143 146 147 148 149 153 154 156 162 167 **S** Allina Health, Minneapolis, MN
Primary Contact: Jill Ostrem, President
CFO: John Bien, Vice President Finance
CMO: Jose Bernard, Vice President Medical Affairs
CHR: Jim McGlade, Director Human Resources
CNO: Tracy L Kirby, MS, R.N., Vice President Patient Care Services and Chief Nursing Officer
Web address: www.allina.com
Control: Other not–for–profit (including NFP Corporation) **Service**: General medical and surgical

Staffed Beds: 467 **Admissions**: 23042 **Census**: 316 **Outpatient Visits**: 264087 **Births**: 3081 **Total Expense ($000)**: 928053 **Payroll Expense ($000)**: 386425 **Personnel**: 2559

SAINT PETER—Nicollet County

★ ⇪ **RIVER'S EDGE HOSPITAL AND CLINIC (241334)**, 1900 North Sunrise Drive, Zip 56082–5376; tel. 507/931–2200, **A**10 18 21 **F**3 7 28 29 34 35 37 40 43 45 51 53 57 68 89 133 144 149 154 156 **S** Ovation Healthcare, Brentwood, TN
Primary Contact: Paula Meskan, R.N., Chief Executive Officer
CFO: Jake Halstenson, Chief Financial Officer
CIO: Kevin Schaefer, Manager Information Services
CHR: Jackie Kimmet, Chief Human Resource Officer
CNO: Paula Meskan, R.N., Chief Nursing Officer
Web address: www.rehc.org
Control: City, Government, Nonfederal **Service**: Surgical

Staffed Beds: 25 **Admissions**: 1162 **Census**: 8 **Births**: 0

SANDSTONE—Pine County

★ **ESSENTIA HEALTH SANDSTONE (241309)**, 705 Lundorff Drive, Zip 55072–5009; tel. 320/245–2212, **A**10 18 **F**3 7 15 28 29 30 31 34 35 40 43 45 59 64 65 75 77 80 81 82 85 87 91 92 93 107 110 115 119 129 132 133 135 144 146 148 149 154 156 **S** Essentia Health, Duluth, MN
Primary Contact: Sam Barney, Administrator
CMO: Erika Miles, Chief Medical Officer
Web address: https://www.essentiahealth.org/find-facility/profile/essentia-health-sandstone/?utm_campaign=website-link&utm_medium=organic&utm_source=local-listing
Control: Hospital district or authority, Government, Nonfederal **Service**: General medical and surgical

Staffed Beds: 9 **Admissions**: 182 **Census**: 3 **Outpatient Visits**: 20058 **Births**: 0 **Total Expense ($000)**: 21507 **Payroll Expense ($000)**: 8246 **Personnel**: 69

SAUK CENTRE—Stearns County

★ **CENTRACARE – SAUK CENTRE (241368)**, 425 North Elm Street, Zip 56378–1010; tel. 320/352–2221, (Total facility includes 60 beds in nursing home–type unit) **A**5 10 18 **F**3 13 15 28 29 31 34 35 40 43 45 50 57 59 64 65 68 75 76 77 78 79 81 85 91 93 96 97 101 102 107 108 110 115 119 125 127 128 129 130 131 133 135 146 148 149 154 156 169 **S** CentraCare Health, Saint Cloud, MN
Primary Contact: Adam Paulson, President
Web address: https://www.centracare.com/locations/centracare-sauk-centre/
Control: Other not–for–profit (including NFP Corporation) **Service**: General medical and surgical

Staffed Beds: 74 **Admissions**: 531 **Census**: 39 **Outpatient Visits**: 33319 **Births**: 58 **Total Expense ($000)**: 39412 **Payroll Expense ($000)**: 17669 **Personnel**: 148

SHAKOPEE—Scott County

⊞ **ST. FRANCIS REGIONAL MEDICAL CENTER (240104)**, 1455 St Francis Avenue, Zip 55379–3380; tel. 952/428–3000, **A**1 2 5 10 **F**3 13 15 28 29 30 31 34 35 36 38 40 41 43 45 46 50 57 58 59 64 75 76 77 78 79 80 81 82 84 85 86 87 93 100 102 107 108 110 111 114 115 116 117 118 119 120 121 124 126 129 130 131 143 144 146 147 148 149 154 169 **S** Allina Health, Minneapolis, MN
Primary Contact: Amy L. Jerdee, R.N., President
CFO: Cynthia Vincent, Vice President Finance and Operations
CMO: Monte Johnson, Vice President, Medical Affairs
CIO: Joe Delveaux, Manager Information Services
CHR: Sally Haack, Vice President and Director of Human Resources
CNO: Debora Ryan, R.N., Vice President Patient Care
Web address: www.stfrancis-shakopee.com
Control: Other not–for–profit (including NFP Corporation) **Service**: General medical and surgical

Staffed Beds: 89 **Admissions**: 5468 **Census**: 52 **Outpatient Visits**: 100951 **Births**: 880 **Total Expense ($000)**: 204488 **Payroll Expense ($000)**: 75940 **Personnel**: 636

SLAYTON—Murray County

★ **MURRAY COUNTY MEDICAL CENTER (241319)**, 2042 Juniper Avenue, Zip 56172–1017; tel. 507/836–6111, (Nonreporting) **A**10 18 **S** Sanford Health, Sioux Falls, SD
Primary Contact: Luke Schryvers, Chief Executive Officer
CFO: Renee Logan, Chief Financial Officer
CMO: Joyce Tarbet, M.D., Chief Medical Officer
CIO: Justin Keller, Chief Information Officer
CHR: Nancy Andert, Director Human Resources
Web address: www.murraycountymed.org
Control: County, Government, Nonfederal **Service**: General medical and surgical

Staffed Beds: 20

SLEEPY EYE—Brown County

SLEEPY EYE MEDICAL CENTER (241327), 400 Fourth Avenue NW, Zip 56085–1109, Mailing Address: P.O. Box 323, Zip 56085–0323; tel. 507/794–3571, (Nonreporting) **A**10 18
Primary Contact: Todd Consbruck, Administrator
CNO: Karee Schmiesing, Director of Nursing
Web address: www.semedicalcenter.org
Control: City, Government, Nonfederal **Service**: General medical and surgical

Staffed Beds: 16

SPRING GROVE—Houston County

TWEETEN LUTHERAN HLTH CARE CTR See Tweeten Health Services

STAPLES—Todd County

LAKEWOOD HEALTH SYSTEM (241329), 49725 County 83, Zip 56479–5280; tel. 218/894–1515, (Nonreporting) **A**10 18
Primary Contact: Lisa Bjerga, President and Chief Executive Officer
CMO: John Halfen, M.D., Medical Director
CHR: Janet Jacobson, Director Human Resources
CNO: Teresa Fisher, Chief Nursing Officer
Web address: www.lakewoodhealthsystem.com
Control: Other not–for–profit (including NFP Corporation) **Service**: General medical and surgical

Staffed Beds: 124

STILLWATER—Washington County

☐ **LAKEVIEW HOSPITAL (240066)**, 927 Churchill Street West, Zip 55082–6605; tel. 651/439–5330, (Nonreporting) **A**1 3 5 10 **S** HealthPartners, Bloomington, MN
Primary Contact: Brandi Lunneborg, Chief Executive Officer
CFO: Douglas E Johnson, Chief Financial Officer
CMO: Thomas Anderson, Vice President Medical Affairs
CIO: Emad Awwad, Director Care Delivery Sites Information Systems and Technology
CHR: Angy Duchesneau, Senior Director Human Resources
CNO: Robbi Hagelberg, Vice President Nursing Services and Chief Nursing Officer
Web address: www.lakeview.org
Control: Other not–for–profit (including NFP Corporation) **Service**: General medical and surgical

Staffed Beds: 67

Hospital, Medicare Provider Number, Address, Telephone, Approval, Facility, and Physician Codes, Health Care System

★ American Hospital Association (AHA) membership
☐ The Joint Commission accreditation
◯ Healthcare Facilities Accreditation Program
◇ DNV Healthcare Inc. accreditation
⇪ Center for Improvement in Healthcare Quality Accreditation
△ Commission on Accreditation of Rehabilitation Facilities (CARF) accreditation

Hospitals, U.S. / MINNESOTA

THIEF RIVER FALLS—Pennington County

★ **SANFORD BEHAVIORAL HEALTH CENTER (244018)**, 120 LaBree Avenue South, Zip 56701–2819, Mailing Address: 3001 Sanford Parkway, Zip 56701–2819; tel. 218/683–4349, (Nonreporting) **A**10 **S** Sanford Health, Sioux Falls, SD
Primary Contact: Heather Bregier, Administrator, Chief Executive Officer
COO: Rob Lovejoy, Chief Operating Officer
Web address: www.sanfordhealth.org/Locations/1766896362
Control: Other not–for–profit (including NFP Corporation) **Service:** Psychiatric

Staffed Beds: 16

★ **SANFORD THIEF RIVER FALLS MEDICAL CENTER (241381)**, 3001 Sanford Parkway, Zip 56701–2700; tel. 218/681–4747, (Nonreporting) **A**10 18 **S** Sanford Health, Sioux Falls, SD
Primary Contact: Tyler Ust, Adminstrator, Chief Executive Officer
COO: Rob Lovejoy, Director, Operations
CMO: Brook Redd, M.D., Chief of Staff
CNO: Janell Hudson, Director, Nursing and Clinical Services
Web address: www.sanfordhealth.org
Control: Other not–for–profit (including NFP Corporation) **Service:** General medical and surgical

Staffed Beds: 25

TRACY—Lyon County

★ **SANFORD TRACY MEDICAL CENTER (241303)**, 251 Fifth Street East, Zip 56175–1536; tel. 507/629–8400, (Nonreporting) **A**10 18 **S** Sanford Health, Sioux Falls, SD
Primary Contact: Stacy Barstad, Chief Executive Officer
CMO: Muhammad Ali, M.D., Chief Medical Officer
CIO: Janet Theisen, Chief Information Officer
CHR: Becky Foster, Employee Relations Specialist
CNO: Jeri Schons, R.N., Chief Nursing Officer
Web address: www.sanfordtracy.org
Control: Other not–for–profit (including NFP Corporation) **Service:** General medical and surgical

Staffed Beds: 10

TWO HARBORS—Lake County

★ **ASPIRUS LAKE VIEW HOSPITAL (241308)**, 325 11th Avenue, Zip 55616–1360; tel. 218/834–7300, (Nonreporting) **A**10 18 **S** Aspirus, Inc., Wausau, WI
Primary Contact: Greg Ruberg, FACHE, President and Chief Executive Officer
Web address: www.lvmhospital.com
Control: Other not–for–profit (including NFP Corporation) **Service:** General medical and surgical

Staffed Beds: 25

LAKE VIEW HOSPITAL See Aspirus Lake View Hospital

TYLER—Lincoln County

AVERA TYLER (241348), 240 Willow Street, Zip 56178–1166; tel. 507/247–5521, (Total facility includes 30 beds in nursing home–type unit) **A**10 18 **F**7 34 35 40 57 59 64 65 75 81 97 107 108 119 127 128 133 **P**6 **S** Avera Health, Sioux Falls, SD
Primary Contact: Thomas Kooiman, Administrator
CNO: Kris Vollmer, Director Patient Care Services
Web address: www.avera.org
Control: Church operated, Nongovernment, not–for–profit **Service:** General medical and surgical

Staffed Beds: 50 **Admissions:** 159 **Census:** 31 **Outpatient Visits:** 9100 **Births:** 0 **Total Expense ($000):** 12730 **Payroll Expense ($000):** 6798 **Personnel:** 62

VIRGINIA—St. Louis County

☧ **ESSENTIA HEALTH–VIRGINIA (240084)**, 901 Ninth Street North, Zip 55792–2398; tel. 218/741–3340, (Total facility includes 77 beds in nursing home–type unit) **A**1 10 **F**3 11 13 15 18 28 29 30 31 34 35 40 41 43 45 47 48 56 59 63 64 65 70 75 76 77 81 84 85 87 89 90 93 96 97 104 107 108 110 111 115 119 127 128 129 130 132 135 144 146 147 148 149 154 157 169 **S** Essentia Health, Duluth, MN
Primary Contact: Sam Stone, Campus Administrator
CFO: Steven Feltman, CPA, Chief Financial Officer
CMO: Michelle Oman, D.O., Chief Medical Officer
Web address: www.essentiahealth.org
Control: Other not–for–profit (including NFP Corporation) **Service:** General medical and surgical

Staffed Beds: 124 **Admissions:** 1345 **Census:** 49 **Outpatient Visits:** 162084 **Births:** 204 **Total Expense ($000):** 138639 **Payroll Expense ($000):** 54929 **Personnel:** 411

WABASHA—Wabasha County

★ **GUNDERSEN SAINT ELIZABETH'S HOSPITAL & CLINICS (241335)**, 1200 Grant Boulevard West, Zip 55981–1042; tel. 651/565–4531, (Total facility includes 100 beds in nursing home–type unit) (Data for 304 days) **A**10 18 **F**3 6 8 10 11 12 15 18 28 30 34 35 40 43 45 46 49 50 53 56 59 62 64 65 68 75 77 79 81 85 93 94 96 97 100 102 104 107 110 115 119 127 128 130 131 132 133 135 146 147 148 149 150 154 156 169 **P**6
Primary Contact: Jim Root, Administrator
CFO: John Wolfe, Chief Financial Officer
CMO: Brian E. Kelly, M.D., President Medical Staff
CNO: Kathy Lueders, R.N., Director of Nursing–Acute Care
Web address: https://www.gundersenhealth.org/st-elizabeths/
Control: Other not–for–profit (including NFP Corporation) **Service:** General medical and surgical

Staffed Beds: 112 **Admissions:** 329 **Census:** 101 **Outpatient Visits:** 33768 **Births:** 0 **Total Expense ($000):** 38727 **Payroll Expense ($000):** 21550 **Personnel:** 275

WACONIA—Carver County

★ ⇧ **RIDGEVIEW MEDICAL CENTER (240056)**, 500 South Maple Street, Zip 55387–1791; tel. 952/442–2191, **A**2 10 21 **F**3 7 12 13 15 18 20 22 28 29 30 31 32 34 35 36 40 41 42 43 45 46 48 49 54 56 57 58 59 62 63 64 65 70 71 72 74 75 76 77 78 79 81 82 84 85 86 87 89 93 96 97 107 108 110 111 114 115 118 119 126 127 129 130 131 132 135 144 146 147 148 149 154 156 167 169 **S** Ridgeview Medical Center, Waconia, MN
Primary Contact: Michael Phelps, President and Chief Executive Officer
COO: Ben Nielsen, Vice President, Chief Operating Officer
CFO: Aaron Bloomquist, Vice President, Chief Financial Officer
CMO: Matthew Herold, Vice President, Chief Medical Officer
CIO: Andy Kester, Vice President, Chief Information Officer
CHR: Sarah M Hastings, Executive Director
CNO: Elaine Arion, Vice President, Chief Nursing Officer
Web address: www.ridgeviewmedical.org
Control: Other not–for–profit (including NFP Corporation) **Service:** General medical and surgical

Staffed Beds: 104 **Admissions:** 6581 **Census:** 61 **Outpatient Visits:** 463786 **Births:** 1486 **Total Expense ($000):** 337849 **Payroll Expense ($000):** 170256 **Personnel:** 1694

WADENA—Wadena County

☧ **ASTERA HEALTH (241354)**, 421 11th Street NW, Zip 56482–1044, Mailing Address: 415 Jefferson Street North, Zip 56482–1297; tel. 218/631–3510, **A**1 10 18 **F**3 7 11 13 15 17 18 28 29 31 33 34 35 36 40 43 45 48 50 54 57 59 64 65 68 70 75 76 77 79 81 85 86 87 89 93 97 104 107 108 110 111 114 115 118 119 126 127 129 130 131 133 135 146 147 148 149 154 156 160 167 169 **P**6
Primary Contact: Joel Beiswenger, Chief Executive Officer
CFO: Kim Aagard, Chief Financial Officer
CMO: John Pate, M.D., Chief Medical Officer
CIO: Bill Blaha, Manager Information Technology
CHR: Bryan Pederson, Human Resources Manager
CNO: Kathy Kleen, Chief Nursing Officer
Web address: https://asterahealth.org/
Control: Other not–for–profit (including NFP Corporation) **Service:** General medical and surgical

Staffed Beds: 18 **Admissions:** 633 **Census:** 5 **Outpatient Visits:** 108971 **Births:** 147 **Total Expense ($000):** 90592 **Payroll Expense ($000):** 33970 **Personnel:** 381

TRI–COUNTY HOSPITAL See Astera Health

Hospitals, U.S. / MINNESOTA

WARREN—Marshall County

★ **NORTH VALLEY HEALTH CENTER (241337)**, 300 West Good Samaritan Drive, Zip 56762–1412; tel. 218/745–4211, (Nonreporting) **A**10 18
Primary Contact: Jon E. Linnell, Chief Executive Officer
CFO: Mitchell Kotrba, Chief Financial Officer
CNO: Sara Marie Kazmierczak, R.N., Director of Nursing
Web address: www.northvalleyhealth.org
Control: Other not–for–profit (including NFP Corporation) **Service**: General medical and surgical

Staffed Beds: 20

WASECA—Waseca County

☐ **MAYO CLINIC HEALTH SYSTEM IN WASECA (241345)**, 501 North State Street, Zip 56093–2811; tel. 507/835–1210, (Nonreporting) **A**1 5 10 18 **S** Mayo Clinic, Rochester, MN
Primary Contact: Paul Travis, Regional Chair – Administration
CMO: Christopher Schimming, M.D., Medical Director
Web address: https://www.mayoclinichealthsystem.org/locations/waseca
Control: Other not–for–profit (including NFP Corporation) **Service**: General medical and surgical

Staffed Beds: 12

WESTBROOK—Cottonwood County

★ **SANFORD WESTBROOK MEDICAL CENTER (241302)**, 920 Bell Avenue, Zip 56183–9669, Mailing Address: P.O. Box 188, Zip 56183–0188; tel. 507/274–6121, (Nonreporting) **A**10 18 **S** Sanford Health, Sioux Falls, SD
Primary Contact: Stacy Barstad, Chief Executive Officer
COO: Gordon Kopperud, Director Operations
CIO: Janet Theisen, Chief Information Officer
CHR: Becky Foster, Employee Relations Specialist
Web address: www.sanfordwestbrook.org
Control: Other not–for–profit (including NFP Corporation) **Service**: General medical and surgical

Staffed Beds: 5

WHEATON—Traverse County

★ **SANFORD WHEATON MEDICAL CENTER (241304)**, 401 12th Street North, Zip 56296–1099; tel. 320/563–8226, (Nonreporting) **A**10 18 **S** Sanford Health, Sioux Falls, SD
Primary Contact: Chelsie Falk, Chief Executive Officer
CFO: Shane Ayres, Chief Financial Officer
CHR: Brenda Petersen, Human Resources
Web address: www.sanfordhealth.org
Control: Other not–for–profit (including NFP Corporation) **Service**: General medical and surgical

Staffed Beds: 12

WILLMAR—Kandiyohi County

⊞ **CENTRACARE – RICE MEMORIAL HOSPITAL (240088)**, 301 Becker Avenue SW, Zip 56201–3395; tel. 320/235–4543, (Total facility includes 78 beds in nursing home–type unit) **A**1 2 10 **F**3 8 11 13 28 29 30 31 34 35 39 40 43 45 47 48 50 57 59 60 64 65 70 73 75 76 77 78 79 81 82 85 86 87 89 90 93 97 98 100 101 104 107 108 115 116 117 118 119 121 126 128 130 132 143 146 148 149 150 154 162 164 165 167 169 **S** CentraCare Health, Saint Cloud, MN
Primary Contact: Michael Schramm, Chief Executive Officer
CFO: Bill Fenske, Chief Financial Officer
CMO: Kenneth Flowe, M.D., Chief Medical Officer
CIO: Teri Beyer, Chief Information Officer, Quality
Web address: https://www.centracare.com/locations/centracare-rice-memorial-hospital/
Control: Other not–for–profit (including NFP Corporation) **Service**: General medical and surgical

Staffed Beds: 164 **Admissions**: 2659 **Census**: 82 **Outpatient Visits**: 104546 **Births**: 599 **Total Expense ($000)**: 142831 **Payroll Expense ($000)**: 64955 **Personnel**: 640

☐ **CHILD AND ADOLESCENT BEHAVIORAL HEALTH SERVICES (244005)**, 1701 Technology Drive Northeast, Zip 56201–2275; tel. 320/231–5421, (Nonreporting) **A**1 10
Primary Contact: Michael Gallagher, Administrator
Web address: www.dhs.state.mn.us
Control: County, Government, Nonfederal **Service**: Psychiatric

Staffed Beds: 8

WINDOM—Cottonwood County

★ **WINDOM AREA HEALTH (241332)**, 2150 Hospital Drive, Zip 56101–0339, Mailing Address: P.O. Box 339, Zip 56101–0339; tel. 507/831–2400, (Nonreporting) **A**10 18 **S** Sanford Health, Sioux Falls, SD
Primary Contact: Shelby Medina, Chief Executive Officer
CIO: Lori Ling, Information Technician
CHR: Emily Masters, Chief Human Relations Officer
CNO: Kari Witte, Director Patient Care
Web address: www.windomareahospital.com
Control: City, Government, Nonfederal **Service**: General medical and surgical

Staffed Beds: 18

WINONA—Winona County

★ **WINONA HEALTH (240044)**, 855 Mankato Avenue, Zip 55987–4868, Mailing Address: P.O. Box 5600, Zip 55987–0600; tel. 507/454–3650, **A**2 10 20 **F**3 6 10 11 13 15 28 29 30 31 34 35 36 38 40 43 45 50 56 57 58 59 60 61 62 63 64 65 70 75 76 77 78 79 81 82 83 84 85 86 87 93 94 96 97 100 101 102 104 107 108 110 111 115 116 119 126 127 129 130 131 132 133 135 144 146 147 148 149 153 154 156 169
Primary Contact: Rachelle H. Schultz, Ed.D., President and Chief Executive Officer
COO: Robin Hoeg, Chief Operating Officer
CFO: Jan Brosnahan, Chief Financial Officer
CMO: Mike Donnenwerth, DPM, Chief Medical Officer
CIO: Luke Keninger, Information Technology Client Leader
CHR: Chad Decker, Director Human Resources
CNO: Sara S Gabrick, R.N., Chief Nursing Officer
Web address: www.winonahealth.org
Control: Other not–for–profit (including NFP Corporation) **Service**: General medical and surgical

Staffed Beds: 38 **Admissions**: 1171 **Census**: 11 **Outpatient Visits**: 125958 **Births**: 179 **Total Expense ($000)**: 122193 **Payroll Expense ($000)**: 53562 **Personnel**: 676

WINSTED—McLeod County

ST MARY'S HOSPITAL AND HOME See Health One St Mary's

WOODBURY—Washington County

⊞ **M HEALTH FAIRVIEW WOODWINDS HOSPITAL (240213)**, 1925 Woodwinds Drive, Zip 55125–4445; tel. 651/232–0228, **A**1 3 10 **F**3 13 15 28 29 30 31 35 36 37 38 40 43 49 50 59 64 68 70 74 75 76 77 78 79 81 85 86 87 93 94 96 97 100 102 107 108 110 111 115 118 119 120 121 124 126 130 132 146 149 154 167 169 **P**6 **S** Fairview Health Services, Minneapolis, MN
Primary Contact: Jeoff Will, Executive Vice President, Chief Operating Officer
CMO: Kevin C. Garrett, M.D., Medical Executive, East Region
CHR: Carolyn Jacobson, Chief Human Resource Officer
CNO: Debra J. Hurd, MS, R.N., Vice President and Chief Nursing Officer
Web address: https://www.mhealthfairview.org/locations/M-Health-Fairview-Woodwinds-Hospital--Woodbury
Control: Other not–for–profit (including NFP Corporation) **Service**: General medical and surgical

Staffed Beds: 86 **Admissions**: 7199 **Census**: 75 **Outpatient Visits**: 91045 **Births**: 2023 **Total Expense ($000)**: 237658 **Payroll Expense ($000)**: 92975 **Personnel**: 782

WOODWINDS HEALTH CAMPUS See M Health Fairview Woodwinds Hospital

Hospitals, U.S. / MINNESOTA

WORTHINGTON—Nobles County

★ **SANFORD WORTHINGTON MEDICAL CENTER (240022)**, 1018 Sixth Avenue, Zip 56187–2202, Mailing Address: P.O. Box 997, Zip 56187–0997; tel. 507/372–2941, (Nonreporting) **A**10 20 **S** Sanford Health, Sioux Falls, SD
Primary Contact: Jennifer Weg, MS, R.N., Executive Director
CFO: Linda Wagner, Chief Financial Officer
CMO: Charles Dike, M.D., Chief of Staff
CIO: Brad Klassen, Information Technology Coordinator
CNO: Gwen Post, R.N., Chief Nursing Officer
Web address: www.sanfordhealth.org
Control: Other not–for–profit (including NFP Corporation) **Service**: General medical and surgical

Staffed Beds: 48

WYOMING—Chisago County

⊞ **M HEALTH FAIRVIEW LAKES MEDICAL CENTER (240050)**, 5200 Fairview Boulevard, Zip 55092–8013; tel. 651/982–7000, **A**1 10 **F**3 11 13 15 18 28 29 30 31 34 35 40 41 43 45 50 51 57 59 64 67 70 75 76 77 81 82 84 85 86 87 89 93 96 101 107 110 111 115 119 126 130 131 144 146 148 149 154 156 164 167 169 **S** Fairview Health Services, Minneapolis, MN
Primary Contact: Jeoff Will, Executive Vice President, Chief Operating Officer
CFO: Tim Lynch, Director of Finance
CMO: Greg Schoen, M.D., Vice President Medical Affairs
Web address: www.fairview.org/
Control: Other not–for–profit (including NFP Corporation) **Service**: General medical and surgical

Staffed Beds: 38 **Admissions**: 2758 **Census**: 27 **Outpatient Visits**: 93086 **Births**: 476 **Total Expense ($000)**: 113558 **Payroll Expense ($000)**: 50959 **Personnel**: 564

MISSISSIPPI

ABERDEEN—Monroe County

MONROE REGIONAL HOSPITAL (251302), 400 South Chestnut Street, Zip 39730–3335, Mailing Address: P.O. Box 548, Zip 39730–0548; tel. 662/369–2455, (Nonreporting) **A**3 10 18 22
Primary Contact: Christopher Chandler, Chief Executive Officer
CFO: Julie Gieger, Chief Financial Officer
CMO: Kevin Hayes, M.D., Chief of Staff
CHR: Lee Rob, Director Human Resources
Control: Other not–for–profit (including NFP Corporation) **Service:** General medical and surgical

Staffed Beds: 35

ACKERMAN—Choctaw County

⇑ **CHOCTAW REGIONAL MEDICAL CENTER (251334)**, 8613 Highway 12, Zip 39735–8708; tel. 662/285–6235, (Total facility includes 60 beds in nursing home–type unit) **A**10 18 21 **F**3 29 34 40 43 57 59 64 65 87 89 93 104 107 114 119 127 128 130 133 153 154
Primary Contact: Steve Marinelli, Chief Executive Officer
Web address: www.choctawregional.com
Control: County, Government, Nonfederal **Service:** General medical and surgical

Staffed Beds: 75 **Admissions:** 143 **Census:** 51 **Outpatient Visits:** 37389
Births: 0 **Total Expense ($000):** 20009 **Payroll Expense ($000):** 9975
Personnel: 180

AMORY—Monroe County

★ ⇑ **NORTH MISSISSIPPI MEDICAL CENTER GILMORE–AMORY (250025)**, 1105 Earl Frye Boulevard, Zip 38821–5500, Mailing Address: P.O. Box 459, Zip 38821–0459; tel. 662/256–7111, (Nonreporting) **A**10 21 **S** North Mississippi Health Services, Inc., Tupelo, MS
Primary Contact: Jamie Rodgers, Administrator
CFO: Bert Pickard, Chief Financial Officer
CMO: William Rogers, Chief Medical Officer
CIO: Jeff Wideman, Director Information Systems
CHR: Angie L Weaver, Director Human Resources
CNO: Ronda Sweet, Chief Nursing Officer
Web address: https://www.nmhs.net/locations/profile/north-mississippi-medical-center-gilmore-amory/
Control: Other not–for–profit (including NFP Corporation) **Service:** General medical and surgical

Staffed Beds: 95

BATESVILLE—Panola County

PANOLA MEDICAL CENTER (250781), 303 Medical Center Drive, Zip 38606–8608; tel. 662/563–5611, (Nonreporting) **A**10
Primary Contact: Quentin Whitwell, Interim Chief Executive Officer
CMO: Michael R. Hovens, M.D., Chief Medical Officer
CIO: Will Morris, Director Information Technology
CHR: Arthur A Wasek, Director Human Resources
Web address: https://www.panolamed.com/
Control: Corporation, Investor–owned (for–profit)

Staffed Beds: 106

BAY SAINT LOUIS—Hancock County

☒ **OCHSNER MEDICAL CENTER – HANCOCK (250162)**, 149 Drinkwater Boulevard, Zip 39520–1658, Mailing Address: Bay St Louis, tel. 228/467–8600, (Nonreporting) **A**1 10 **S** Ochsner Health, New Orleans, LA
Primary Contact: Jeffery Edge, Chief Executive Officer
CFO: Thomas Ramsey, Chief Financial Officer
CIO: Craig Hodges, Director Information Services
CHR: Cathy Benvenutti, Human Resource Director
Web address: https://www.ochsner.org/locations/ochsner-medical-center-hancock
Control: Other not–for–profit (including NFP Corporation) **Service:** General medical and surgical

Staffed Beds: 102

BAY SPRINGS—Jasper County

★ **JASPER GENERAL HOSPITAL (250018)**, 15 'A' South Sixth Street, Zip 39422–9738, Mailing Address: P.O. Box 527, Zip 39422–0527; tel. 601/764–2101, (Total facility includes 110 beds in nursing–type unit) **A**10 **F**10 55 59 62 64 119 128 133
Primary Contact: Eric Jordan, Chief Executive Officer
CFO: Steve Green, Comptroller
CMO: A K Lay, M.D., Jr, Chief Medical Officer
CHR: Beth Gable, Administrative Assistant
CNO: Becky Ulmer, R.N., Director of Nursing
Web address: www.jaspergeneralhospital.com
Control: County, Government, Nonfederal **Service:** General medical and surgical

Staffed Beds: 122 **Admissions:** 117 **Census:** 86 **Outpatient Visits:** 18588
Births: 0 **Total Expense ($000):** 14654 **Payroll Expense ($000):** 7297
Personnel: 168

BILOXI—Harrison County

☒ **BILOXI VA MEDICAL CENTER**, 400 Veterans Avenue, Zip 39531–2410; tel. 228/523–5000, (Nonreporting) **A**1 3 5 **S** Department of Veterans Affairs, Washington, DC
Primary Contact: Stephanie Repasky, PsyD, Interim Medical Center Director
COO: Alexander Murray, Interim Associate Director
CFO: John D Williams Jr, Chief Financial Officer
CMO: Kenneth B Simon, M.D., Chief of Staff
CIO: David D Wagner, Chief Information Management Service
CHR: Andrew Roberts, Interim Chief Human Resources Officer
CNO: Deatosha D. Haynes, Interim Associates Director for Patient
Web address: www.biloxi.va.gov/
Control: Veterans Affairs, Government, federal **Service:** General medical and surgical

Staffed Beds: 83

GULF COAST HCS See Biloxi VA Medical Center

☒ **MERIT HEALTH BILOXI (250007)**, 150 Reynoir Street, Zip 39530–4199, Mailing Address: P.O. Box 128, Zip 39533–0128; tel. 228/432–1571, (Nonreporting) **A**1 10 **S** Community Health Systems, Inc., Franklin, TN
Primary Contact: Travis Sisson, Chief Executive Officer
CFO: Chad Miller, Chief Financial Officer
CMO: John Nelson, Chief of Staff
CIO: George Bickel, Director, Information Systems
CHR: Angela Thompson, Director of Human Resources
CNO: Rachael Williams, Chief Nursing Officer
Web address: www.merithealthbiloxi.com
Control: Corporation, Investor–owned (for–profit) **Service:** General medical and surgical

Staffed Beds: 124

☐ **OCEANS BEHAVIORAL HOSPITAL BILOXI (254012)**, 180 Debuys Road, Zip 39531–4402; tel. 228/388–0600, (Nonreporting) **A**1 10 **S** Oceans Healthcare, Plano, TX
Primary Contact: Cliff Hermes, Administrator
Web address: https://oceanshealthcare.com/biloxi
Control: Corporation, Investor–owned (for–profit) **Service:** Psychiatric

Staffed Beds: 55

Hospital, Medicare Provider Number, Address, Telephone, Approval, Facility, and Physician Codes, Health Care System

★ American Hospital Association (AHA) membership ○ Healthcare Facilities Accreditation Program ⇑ Center for Improvement in Healthcare Quality Accreditation
☐ The Joint Commission accreditation ◇ DNV Healthcare Inc. accreditation △ Commission on Accreditation of Rehabilitation Facilities (CARF) accreditation

Hospitals, U.S. / MISSISSIPPI

BOONEVILLE—Prentiss County

✠ **BAPTIST MEMORIAL HOSPITAL–BOONEVILLE (250044)**, 100 Hospital Street, Zip 38829–3359; tel. 662/720–5000, **A**1 10 **F**3 15 17 28 29 30 34 35 40 43 51 56 57 58 63 65 68 70 74 75 77 81 85 86 87 89 90 93 98 103 104 107 108 111 115 118 119 130 132 133 145 146 148 153 154 **S** Baptist Memorial Health Care Corporation, Memphis, TN
Primary Contact: Ann Bishop, Chief Executive Officer and Administrator
CFO: Donavan Leonard, Chief Financial Officer
CMO: Nathan Baldwin, M.D., President Medical Staff
CIO: Linda Chaffin, Director Medical Review
CHR: Shannon Bolen, Director Human Resources
Web address: www.bmhcc.org/booneville
Control: Other not–for–profit (including NFP Corporation) **Service**: General medical and surgical

Staffed Beds: 68 Admissions: 1238 Census: 34 Outpatient Visits: 24488 Births: 0 Total Expense ($000): 23705 Payroll Expense ($000): 9459 Personnel: 188

BRANDON—Rankin County

✠ **MERIT HEALTH RANKIN (250096)**, 350 Crossgates Boulevard, Zip 39042–2698; tel. 601/825–2811, **A**1 5 10 **F**15 29 35 39 40 43 60 70 79 81 87 90 93 97 98 103 104 107 108 111 119 129 130 146 153 154 **P**1 5 **S** Community Health Systems, Inc., Franklin, TN
Primary Contact: Heather Sistrunk, R.N., Chief Executive Officer
CFO: Christy Wilson, Chief Financial Officer
CMO: Edward Rigdon, M.D., Chief Medical Officer
CIO: Heather Holmes, Director Health Information Systems
CHR: Joy M Hutson, Director Human Resources
CNO: Cynthia Ellis, Chief Nursing Officer
Web address: www.merithealthrankin.com/
Control: Corporation, Investor–owned (for–profit) **Service**: General medical and surgical

Staffed Beds: 55 Admissions: 1629 Census: 27 Outpatient Visits: 32067 Births: 0 Total Expense ($000): 32239 Payroll Expense ($000): 12693 Personnel: 188

BROOKHAVEN—Lincoln County

★ ⇑ **KING'S DAUGHTERS MEDICAL CENTER (250057)**, 427 Highway 51 North, Zip 39601–2350, Mailing Address: P.O. Box 948, Zip 39602–0948; tel. 601/833–6011, **A**3 10 20 21 **F**7 11 13 15 17 29 30 34 35 40 41 45 53 57 59 64 65 68 70 73 74 75 76 77 79 80 81 82 85 86 89 93 96 97 107 108 110 111 114 115 119 126 129 130 131 132 135 143 145 146 147 148 149 154 156 164 165 167 **S** Ovation Healthcare, Brentwood, TN
Primary Contact: Scott Christensen, FACHE, Chief Executive Officer
COO: Thomas Hood, Chief Operating Officer
CMO: Jeffrey Ross, M.D., Chief Medical Officer
CIO: Carl Smith, Chief Information Officer
CHR: Celine H Craig, Chief Human Resource and Regulatory Officer
CNO: Cheri Brooks, R.N., Chief Nursing Officer
Web address: www.kdmc.org
Control: Other not–for–profit (including NFP Corporation) **Service**: General medical and surgical

Staffed Beds: 37 Admissions: 2213 Census: 17 Births: 752 Total Expense ($000): 94808 Payroll Expense ($000): 40824 Personnel: 573

CALHOUN CITY—Calhoun County

★ **BAPTIST MEMORIAL HOSPITAL – CALHOUN (251331)**, 140 Burke–Calhoun City Road, Zip 38916–9690; tel. 662/628–6611, (Total facility includes 120 beds in nursing home–type unit) **A**10 18 **F**3 30 40 43 56 68 71 103 107 114 119 127 130 133 153 154 **S** Baptist Memorial Health Care Corporation, Memphis, TN
Primary Contact: Christopher Threadgill, M.D., Chief Executive Officer and Administrator
CFO: Kenneth Conley, Chief Financial Officer
CMO: Bruce Longest, M.D., President Medical Staff
Web address: www.baptistonline.org/calhoun/
Control: Other not–for–profit (including NFP Corporation) **Service**: General medical and surgical

Staffed Beds: 145 Admissions: 214 Census: 96 Outpatient Visits: 12109 Births: 0 Total Expense ($000): 15370 Payroll Expense ($000): 6504 Personnel: 104

CANTON—Madison County

✠ **MERIT HEALTH MADISON (250038)**, 161 River Oaks Drive, Zip 39046–5375, Mailing Address: PO Box 1607, Zip 39046–5375; tel. 601/855–4000, **A**1 3 5 10 **F**15 29 39 43 70 81 82 87 89 93 108 111 119 133 146 **S** Community Health Systems, Inc., Franklin, TN
Primary Contact: David Henry, FACHE, Chief Executive Officer
CFO: Shea Sutherland, Chief Financial Officer
CMO: Vibha Vig, Chief of Staff
CIO: Rick Hartzog, Chief Information Officer
CHR: Jackie Williams, Director Human Resources
CNO: Tim Lolley, MSN, Chief Nursing Officer
Web address: www.merithealthmadison.com
Control: Corporation, Investor–owned (for–profit) **Service**: General medical and surgical

Staffed Beds: 33 Admissions: 1204 Census: 14 Outpatient Visits: 37717 Births: 0 Total Expense ($000): 32626 Payroll Expense ($000): 12847 Personnel: 191

CARTHAGE—Leake County

★ **BAPTIST MEDICAL CENTER – LEAKE (251315)**, 1100 Highway 16 E, Zip 39051–3809, Mailing Address: 1100 Hwy 16 East, Zip 39051–0909; tel. 601/267–1100, **A**10 18 **F**3 11 15 29 34 35 40 43 45 56 57 59 64 68 81 87 107 110 111 114 127 130 133 146 148 149 153 154 167 **P**6 **S** Baptist Memorial Health Care Corporation, Memphis, TN
Primary Contact: Daryl W. Weaver, Chief Executive Officer and Administrator
COO: C Gerald Cotton, Interim Chief Operating Officer
CFO: David Jackson, Chief Financial Officer
CMO: Doug Perry, M.D., Chief of Staff
Web address: www.mbhs.com/locations/baptist-medical-center-leake/
Control: Other not–for–profit (including NFP Corporation) **Service**: General medical and surgical

Staffed Beds: 25 Admissions: 596 Census: 14 Outpatient Visits: 25883 Births: 0 Total Expense ($000): 15120 Payroll Expense ($000): 9728

CENTREVILLE—Wilkinson County

✠ **FIELD MEMORIAL COMMUNITY HOSPITAL (251309)**, 178 Highway 24, Zip 39631–4171; tel. 601/890–0500, (Nonreporting) **A**1 10 18
Primary Contact: Richard Williams, Administrator and Chief Executive Officer
CIO: Locke Wheeles, Information Technology Manager
CHR: Dana McNabb, Human Resources Manager
CNO: Robin Walker, Chief Nursing Officer
Web address: www.fhsms.org
Control: County, Government, Nonfederal **Service**: General medical and surgical

Staffed Beds: 16

CHARLESTON—Tallahatchie County

⇑ **TALLAHATCHIE GENERAL HOSPITAL (251304)**, 201 South Market, Zip 38921–2236, Mailing Address: P.O. Box 230, Zip 38921–0240; tel. 662/647–5535, (Total facility includes 98 beds in nursing home-type unit) **A**10 18 21 **F**29 40 43 53 86 87 93 130 133 143 **P**6
Primary Contact: Jim Blackwood, Chief Executive Officer
CFO: Sammie Bell Jr, Chief Financial Officer
Control: County, Government, Nonfederal **Service**: General medical and surgical

Staffed Beds: 116 Admissions: 360 Census: 96 Outpatient Visits: 2676 Births: 0 Total Expense ($000): 39182 Payroll Expense ($000): 17154 Personnel: 134

CLARKSDALE—Coahoma County

⇑ **DELTA HEALTH – NORTHWEST REGIONAL (250042)**, 1970 Hospital Drive, Zip 38614–7202, Mailing Address: P.O. Box 1218, Zip 38614–1218; tel. 662/627–3211, **A**10 21 **F**3 13 15 17 29 35 40 43 53 57 59 60 65 70 73 76 78 79 80 81 89 90 93 97 107 108 109 110 111 115 119 130 131 148 154 167 **S** Delta Health System, Greenville, MS
Primary Contact: Janet Benzing, Chief Administrative Officer
CFO: Charles H. Hester, CPA, Jr, Chief Financial Officer
CMO: Richard Brownstein, M.D., Chief of Staff
CIO: Adrienne Taylor, Director of Health Information Management
CHR: Devasha Patterson, Director of Human Resources
Web address: www.northwestmsmedicalcenter.org
Control: Other not–for–profit (including NFP Corporation) **Service**: General medical and surgical

Staffed Beds: 181 Admissions: 907 Census: 8 Births: 505 Total Expense ($000): 35379 Payroll Expense ($000): 19158 Personnel: 137

Hospitals, U.S. / MISSISSIPPI

CLEVELAND—Bolivar County

⊠ **BOLIVAR MEDICAL CENTER (250093)**, 901 East Sunflower Road, Zip 38732-2833, Mailing Address: P.O. Box 1380, Zip 38732-1380; tel. 662/846-0061, (Total facility includes 30 beds in nursing home–type unit) **A**1 10 20 **F**3 8 11 13 15 18 29 30 34 35 39 40 41 43 45 46 51 57 59 70 73 76 79 81 87 88 89 93 94 96 103 107 108 109 110 111 115 116 118 119 120 128 130 133 146 148 **S** ScionHealth, Louisville, KY
Primary Contact: James Young, Chief Executive Officer
CMO: Mark Blackwood, M.D., Chief of Staff
CIO: Cagri Sapmaz, Information Technology Director
CHR: Ben Bufkin, Human Resource Director
CNO: Joann McCollum, Chief Nursing Officer
Web address: www.bolivarmedical.com
Control: Corporation, Investor-owned (for-profit) **Service**: General medical and surgical

Staffed Beds: 124 **Admissions**: 2459 **Census**: 54 **Outpatient Visits**: 44713 **Births**: 338 **Total Expense ($000)**: 45964 **Payroll Expense ($000)**: 19847 **Personnel**: 419

COLLINS—Covington County

★ ⇧ **COVINGTON COUNTY HOSPITAL (251325)**, 701 South Holly Avenue, Zip 39428-3894, Mailing Address: P.O. Box 1149, Zip 39428-1149; tel. 601/765-6711, (Total facility includes 60 beds in nursing home–type unit) **A**10 18 21 **F**2 3 7 29 34 35 39 40 43 45 50 54 57 59 64 65 66 68 81 89 93 94 103 104 105 107 114 119 127 130 133 143
Primary Contact: Gregg Gibbes, Chief Executive Officer
CFO: Delilah Hudson, Controller
CMO: Word Johnston, Medical Director
CHR: Beverly K Ponder, Executive Assistant and Human Resources Coordinator
CNO: Martha Lynn Scott, Chief Patient Care Officer
Web address: www.covingtoncountyhospital.com
Control: County, Government, Nonfederal **Service**: General medical and surgical

Staffed Beds: 95 **Admissions**: 282 **Census**: 58 **Outpatient Visits**: 27566 **Births**: 0 **Total Expense ($000)**: 45113 **Payroll Expense ($000)**: 21668 **Personnel**: 287

COLUMBIA—Marion County

MARION GENERAL HOSPITAL (250085), 1560 Sumrall Road, Zip 39429-2654, Mailing Address: P.O. Box 630, Zip 39429-0630; tel. 601/736-6303, **A**10 **F**11 29 34 35 39 40 43 57 59 65 66 68 70 81 85 87 92 97 107 114 119 127 130 133 146 148 149 154
Primary Contact: Alaina Cedillo, Administrator
CMO: Mark Stevens, M.D., Chief Medical Staff
CIO: Donny Bracey, Director Information Services
CNO: Patricia Reid, Director of Nursing
Web address: https://www.forresthealth.org/our-locations/marion-general-hospital/
Control: County, Government, Nonfederal **Service**: General medical and surgical

Staffed Beds: 49 **Admissions**: 472 **Census**: 11 **Outpatient Visits**: 13311 **Births**: 0 **Total Expense ($000)**: 14677 **Payroll Expense ($000)**: 7154 **Personnel**: 102

COLUMBUS—Lowndes County

⊠ **BAPTIST MEMORIAL HOSPITAL–GOLDEN TRIANGLE (250100)**, 2520 Fifth Street North, Zip 39705-2095, Mailing Address: P.O. Box 1307, Zip 39703-1307; tel. 662/244-1000, **A**1 2 3 5 10 19 **F**3 4 5 7 11 12 13 15 17 18 20 22 24 26 28 29 30 31 34 38 39 40 43 45 49 51 57 59 60 64 70 73 75 76 77 78 79 80 81 84 85 87 88 89 91 93 94 96 98 100 102 104 105 106 107 108 109 110 111 114 115 116 117 118 119 120 121 123 124 126 128 129 130 132 134 146 147 148 149 153 154 156 157 160 167 **S** Baptist Memorial Health Care Corporation, Memphis, TN
Primary Contact: Robert Coleman, Chief Executive Officer and Administrator
CFO: David Webb, Chief Financial Officer
CMO: John E Reed, M.D., Medical Director
CIO: Sheila Bardwell, Director Information Systems
CHR: Bob McCallister, Director Human Resources
CNO: Mary Ellen Sumrall, R.N., Chief Nursing Officer
Web address: www.baptistonline.org/golden-triangle/
Control: Other not-for-profit (including NFP Corporation) **Service**: General medical and surgical

Staffed Beds: 244 **Admissions**: 9303 **Census**: 112 **Outpatient Visits**: 143623 **Births**: 832 **Total Expense ($000)**: 211289 **Payroll Expense ($000)**: 71047 **Personnel**: 1078

CORINTH—Alcorn County

⊠ ⇧ **MAGNOLIA REGIONAL HEALTH CENTER (250009)**, 611 Alcorn Drive, Zip 38834-9321; tel. 662/293-1000, **A**1 3 5 10 19 21 **F**13 15 17 22 24 29 30 35 39 40 43 51 53 60 62 63 70 75 76 77 78 81 82 86 87 89 93 98 100 101 102 103 107 108 111 116 118 119 127 129 130 131 132 143 146 147 148 **P**7 8
Primary Contact: James M. Hobson, Chief Executive Officer
CIO: David Parker, VP Information Technology
CHR: Regenia Brown, Vice President Human Resources
CNO: Pam B Wallis, MSN, Vice President Nursing Services
Web address: www.mrhc.org
Control: City-county, Government, Nonfederal **Service**: General medical and surgical

Staffed Beds: 124 **Admissions**: 5929 **Census**: 72 **Outpatient Visits**: 221532 **Births**: 443 **Total Expense ($000)**: 151759 **Payroll Expense ($000)**: 91811 **Personnel**: 1024

DE KALB—Kemper County

JOHN C. STENNIS MEMORIAL HOSPITAL See Ochsner Stennis Hospital

★ **OCHSNER STENNIS HOSPITAL (251335)**, 14365 Highway 16 West, Zip 39328-7974; tel. 769/486-1000, (Nonreporting) **A**3 10 18 **S** Ochsner Health, New Orleans, LA
Primary Contact: Kristin Molony, Chief Executive Officer
Web address: https://www.ochsnerrush.org/hospitals/ochsner-stennis-hospital/
Control: Other not-for-profit (including NFP Corporation) **Service**: General medical and surgical

Staffed Beds: 25

EUPORA—Webster County

★ ⇧ **NORTH MISSISSIPPI MEDICAL CENTER–EUPORA (250020)**, 70 Medical Plaza, Zip 39744-4018; tel. 662/258-6221, (Nonreporting) **A**10 20 21 **S** North Mississippi Health Services, Inc., Tupelo, MS
Primary Contact: Robin Mixon, Administrator
CFO: Adonna Mitchell, Director Fiscal Services
CMO: Charles A. Ozborn, M.D., Chief of Staff
CIO: Helen Reed, Director Health Information
CHR: Lesley Gore, Human Resources Director
Web address: www.nmhs.net/eupora
Control: Other not-for-profit (including NFP Corporation) **Service**: General medical and surgical

Staffed Beds: 74

FAYETTE—Jefferson County

★ **JEFFERSON COUNTY HOSPITAL (250780)**, 870 South Main Street, Zip 39069-5695, Mailing Address: P.O. Box 577, Zip 39069-0577; tel. 601/786-3401, **A**10 **F**40 98 103 105 107 130 133
Primary Contact: Linda St. Julien, Chief Executive Officer
CMO: Khar Omolara, M.D., Chief Medical Staff
CHR: Patricia Selmon, Director Public Relations and Chief Human Resources
Web address: https://www.jeffhospital.com/
Control: County, Government, Nonfederal **Service**: General medical and surgical

Staffed Beds: 12 **Admissions**: 272 **Census**: 9 **Outpatient Visits**: 3420 **Births**: 0 **Total Expense ($000)**: 12587 **Payroll Expense ($000)**: 3957 **Personnel**: 72

FLOWOOD—Rankin County

☐ **BRENTWOOD BEHAVIORAL HEALTHCARE OF MISSISSIPPI (254007)**, 3531 Lakeland Drive, Zip 39232-8839; tel. 601/936-2024, (Nonreporting) **A**1 5 10 **S** Universal Health Services, Inc., King of Prussia, PA
Primary Contact: Alison G. Land, Chief Executive Officer
Web address: www.brentwoodjackson.com
Control: Corporation, Investor-owned (for-profit) **Service**: Psychiatric

Staffed Beds: 105

Hospital, Medicare Provider Number, Address, Telephone, Approval, Facility, and Physician Codes, Health Care System

★ American Hospital Association (AHA) membership
☐ The Joint Commission accreditation
◯ Healthcare Facilities Accreditation Program
◇ DNV Healthcare Inc. accreditation
⇧ Center for Improvement in Healthcare Quality Accreditation
△ Commission on Accreditation of Rehabilitation Facilities (CARF) accreditation

© 2025 AHA Guide

Hospitals, U.S. / MISSISSIPPI

☒ **MERIT HEALTH RIVER OAKS (250138)**, 1030 River Oaks Drive, Zip 39232–9553, Mailing Address: P.O. Box 5100, Jackson, Zip 39296–5100; tel. 601/932–1030, (Nonreporting) **A**1 3 5 10 **S** Community Health Systems, Inc., Franklin, TN
Primary Contact: Sam Dean, Chief Executive Officer
CIO: Pat Jones, Director Information Systems
CHR: Warren Weed, Director Human Resources
CNO: Shelly L. Cordum, MSN, R.N., Chief Nursing Officer
Web address: https://www.merithealthriveroaks.com/
Control: Corporation, Investor-owned (for-profit) **Service**: General medical and surgical

Staffed Beds: 118

☒ **MERIT HEALTH WOMAN'S HOSPITAL (250136)**, 1026 North Flowood Drive, Zip 39232–9532, Mailing Address: 1026 North Flowood Drive, Zip 39232; tel. 601/932–1000, (Nonreporting) **A**1 5 10 **S** Community Health Systems, Inc., Franklin, TN
Primary Contact: Heather Sistrunk, R.N., Chief Executive Officer
CFO: Nick Renda, Chief Financial Officer
CMO: Ed Barham, M.D., Chief of Staff
CHR: Warren Weed, Director Associate Relations
CNO: Linda Atwood, Chief Nursing Officer
Web address: www.merithealthwomanshospital.com
Control: Corporation, Investor-owned (for-profit) **Service**: Obstetrics and gynecology

Staffed Beds: 60

FOREST—Scott County

★ ⇑ **LACKEY MEMORIAL HOSPITAL (251300)**, 330 Broad Street, Zip 39074–3508, Mailing Address: P.O. Box 428, Zip 39074–0428; tel. 601/469–4151, (Nonreporting) **A**10 18 21
Primary Contact: Sydney Sawyer, R.N., Chief Executive Officer
CFO: Julie Gieger, Chief Financial Officer
CMO: John Paul Lee, M.D., Chief of Staff
CIO: Eddie Pope, Chief Information Officer
CHR: Donn Paul, Chief Human Resources
Web address: www.lackeymemorialhospital.com
Control: Other not-for-profit (including NFP Corporation) **Service**: General medical and surgical

Staffed Beds: 55

GREENVILLE—Washington County

★ **ALLEGIANCE SPECIALTY HOSPITAL OF GREENVILLE (252013)**, 300 South Washington Avenue, 3rd Floor, Zip 38701–4719; tel. 662/332–7344, **A**10 **F**1 3 29 85 98 103 104 130 149 153 154 165 **S** Allegiance Health Management, Shreveport, LA
Primary Contact: Vearnail Herzog, Chief Executive Officer
CMO: Parvez Karim, M.D., Chief Medical Officer
CIO: Sharon Scott, Health Information Director
CHR: Sharon Taylor, Human Resources Director
CNO: John Read, Chief Nursing Officer
Web address: www.ahmgt.com
Control: Corporation, Investor-owned (for-profit) **Service**: Acute long-term care hospital

Staffed Beds: 53 **Admissions**: 399 **Census**: 23 **Outpatient Visits**: 0 **Births**: 0 **Total Expense ($000)**: 10287 **Payroll Expense ($000)**: 4644 **Personnel**: 107

★ **DELTA HEALTH–THE MEDICAL CENTER (250082)**, 1400 East Union Street, Zip 38704–5247; tel. 662/378–3783, (Includes THE KING'S DAUGHTERS HOSPITAL, 300 Washington Avenue, Greenville, Mississippi, Zip 38701–3614, P O Box 1857, Zip 38702–1857, tel. 662/378–2020; Scott Christensen, FACHE, Chief Executive Officer) (Nonreporting) **A**3 10 **S** Delta Health System, Greenville, MS
Primary Contact: Iris Stacker, Chief Executive Officer
CFO: Scott Goodin, Interim Chief Financial Officer
CHR: Chrissy Nicholson, Vice President of Human Resources
CNO: Amy Walker, MSN, Chief Nursing Officer
Web address: https://www.deltahealthsystem.org/
Control: County, Government, Nonfederal **Service**: General medical and surgical

Staffed Beds: 171

GREENWOOD—Leflore County

☒ △ **GREENWOOD LEFLORE HOSPITAL (250099)**, 1401 River Road, Zip 38930–4030, Mailing Address: Drawer 1410, Zip 38935–1410; tel. 662/459–7000, (Nonreporting) **A**1 7 10 19
Primary Contact: Gary Marchand, Interim Chief Executive Officer
CFO: Dawne Holmes, Chief Financial Officer
CMO: Abhash Thakur, M.D., Chief of Staff
CHR: Key Britt, Associate Director
Web address: www.glh.org
Control: City-county, Government, Nonfederal **Service**: General medical and surgical

Staffed Beds: 149

GRENADA—Grenada County

⇑ **UNIVERSITY OF MISSISSIPPI MEDICAL CENTER GRENADA (250168)**, 960 Avent Drive, Zip 38901–5230; tel. 662/227–7000, **A**10 21 **F**13 15 17 29 30 32 34 35 39 40 43 44 46 50 51 54 57 59 60 64 65 66 70 73 76 77 78 79 80 81 82 84 85 87 89 90 93 97 107 108 110 111 115 116 118 119 124 127 130 133 139 143 146 147 148 149 154 156 167 **P**6 **S** University Hospitals and Health System, Jackson, MS
Primary Contact: Dodie McElmurray, FACHE, Chief Executive Officer
COO: Molly B. Brown, Chief Operating Officer
CFO: Scott Whittemore, Chief Financial Officer
CIO: John Farrish, Health Information Director
CHR: Claudette Hathcock, Administrative Director Human Resources
Web address: www.glmc.net/
Control: State, Government, Nonfederal **Service**: General medical and surgical

Staffed Beds: 126 **Admissions**: 1819 **Census**: 23 **Outpatient Visits**: 64788 **Births**: 381 **Total Expense ($000)**: 59171 **Payroll Expense ($000)**: 20831 **Personnel**: 290

GULFPORT—Harrison County

☒ △ **ENCOMPASS HEALTH REHABILITATION HOSPITAL, A PARTNER OF MEMORIAL HOSPITAL AT GULFPORT (253027)**, 4500 13th Street, Suite 900, Zip 39501–2515; tel. 228/822–6965, **A**1 7 10 **F**28 29 74 79 82 90 **S** Encompass Health Corporation, Birmingham, AL
Primary Contact: Mark Studdard, Interim Chief Executive Officer
Web address: www.healthsouthgulfport.com
Control: Corporation, Investor-owned (for-profit) **Service**: Rehabilitation

Staffed Beds: 43 **Admissions**: 1347 **Census**: 43 **Outpatient Visits**: 0 **Births**: 0 **Total Expense ($000)**: 21416 **Payroll Expense ($000)**: 10073 **Personnel**: 140

☐ **GULFPORT BEHAVIORAL HEALTH SYSTEM (254011)**, 11150 Highway 49 North, Zip 39503–4110; tel. 228/831–1700, (Nonreporting) **A**1 10 **S** Universal Health Services, Inc., King of Prussia, PA
Primary Contact: Dean Doty, Chief Executive Officer
Web address: www.gulfportmemorial.com
Control: Corporation, Investor-owned (for-profit) **Service**: Psychiatric

Staffed Beds: 90

☐ **MEMORIAL HOSPITAL AT GULFPORT (250019)**, 4500 13th Street, Zip 39501–2569, Mailing Address: P.O. Box 1810, Zip 39502–1810; tel. 228/867–4000, **A**1 2 3 5 10 19 **F**2 11 12 13 15 17 18 20 22 24 28 29 30 31 34 35 40 43 44 45 46 47 48 49 50 53 54 57 59 64 65 68 70 71 72 73 74 76 77 78 79 80 81 82 84 85 87 89 107 108 110 111 114 115 116 117 118 119 120 121 123 124 126 130 132 145 146 148 149
Primary Contact: Kent Nicaud, President and Chief Executive Officer
CFO: Craig Faerber, Interim Chief Financial Officer
CIO: Chris Belmont, Chief Information Officer
CHR: Myron McCoo, Vice President, Human Resources
CNO: Jennifer Dumal, R.N., Senior Vice President, Patient Care Services and Chief Nursing Officer
Web address: www.gulfportmemorial.com
Control: City-county, Government, Nonfederal **Service**: General medical and surgical

Staffed Beds: 276 **Admissions**: 13981 **Census**: 192 **Outpatient Visits**: 1060073 **Births**: 1699 **Total Expense ($000)**: 585308 **Payroll Expense ($000)**: 289820 **Personnel**: 3430

Hospitals, U.S. / MISSISSIPPI

✣ **SELECT SPECIALTY HOSPITAL–GULFPORT (252005)**, 4500 13th Street, 3rd Floor, Zip 39501–2515; tel. 228/575–7500, **A**1 10 **F**1 29 75 82 87 90 **S** Select Medical Corporation, Mechanicsburg, PA
Primary Contact: John O'Keefe, Chief Executive Officer
Web address: www.selectspecialtyhospitals.com/company/locations/gulfcoast.aspx
Control: Corporation, Investor–owned (for–profit) **Service**: Acute long–term care hospital

Staffed Beds: 36 **Admissions**: 387 **Census**: 32 **Outpatient Visits**: 0
Births: 0 **Personnel**: 133

⇑ **SINGING RIVER GULFPORT (250123)**, 15200 Community Road, Zip 39503–3085, Mailing Address: P.O. Box 1240, Zip 39502–1240; tel. 228/575–7000, (Nonreporting) **A**10 21
Primary Contact: Heather Rowley, R.N., Administrator
CMO: T. Paul Mace, Chief Medical Officer
CIO: Chris Oubre, Information Technology Director
CHR: Michael Pocchiari, Director Human Resources
CNO: Cheryl Thompson, Chief Nursing Officer
Web address: https://singingriverhealthsystem.com/locations/gulfporthospital/
Control: Other not–for–profit (including NFP Corporation) **Service**: General medical and surgical

Staffed Beds: 130

HATTIESBURG—Forrest County

★ △ ⇑ **FORREST GENERAL HOSPITAL (250078)**, 6051 US Highway 49, Zip 39401–7200, Mailing Address: P.O. Box 16389, Zip 39404–6389; tel. 601/288–7000, (Includes PINE GROVE BEHAVIORAL HEALTH AND ADDICTION SERVICES, 2255 Broadway Drive, Hattiesburg, Mississippi, Zip 39402–3254, tel. 888/574–4673; Debbie F Sanford, R.N., MS, Administrator) (Nonreporting) **A**2 3 5 7 10 19 21
Primary Contact: Andy Woodard, President and Chief Executive Officer
COO: Douglas A Jones, Chief Operating Officer
CMO: Steven E Farrell, M.D., Chief Medical Officer
CHR: Troy P Daniels, Chief Human Resources Officer
CNO: Micah Rehm, Chief Nursing Officer
Web address: www.forrestgeneral.com
Control: County, Government, Nonfederal **Service**: General medical and surgical

Staffed Beds: 547

HATTIESBURG—Lamar County

✣ **MERIT HEALTH WESLEY (250094)**, 5001 Hardy Street, Zip 39402–1308, Mailing Address: P.O. Box 16509, Zip 39404–6509; tel. 601/268–8000, (Nonreporting) **A**1 3 5 10 12 13 19 **S** Community Health Systems, Inc., Franklin, TN
Primary Contact: Travis Sisson, Chief Executive Officer
COO: Rick Kolaczek, Chief Operating Officer
CFO: Randy Humphrey, Chief Financial Officer
CMO: William Reno, M.D., III, President Medical Staff
CIO: Jesse Folds, Director of Information Technologies
CHR: Terry Trigg, Director Human Resources
Web address: https://www.merithealthwesley.com/
Control: Corporation, Investor–owned (for–profit) **Service**: General medical and surgical

Staffed Beds: 211

HAZLEHURST—Copiah County

★ **COPIAH COUNTY MEDICAL CENTER (251327)**, 27190 Highway 28, Zip 39083–2228; tel. 601/574–7000, (Nonreporting) **A**10 18
Primary Contact: Benjamin Lott, Chief Executive Officer
CFO: Kortney Gaddy, CPA, Chief Financial Officer
CNO: Alison Mathis, Chief Nursing Officer
Web address: www.myccmc.org/
Control: County, Government, Nonfederal **Service**: General medical and surgical

Staffed Beds: 25

HOLLY SPRINGS—Marshall County

ALLIANCE HEALTHCARE SYSTEM (250779), 1430 Highway 4 East, Zip 38635–2140, Mailing Address: P.O. Box 6000, Zip 38634–6000; tel. 662/252–1212, (Nonreporting) **A**10
Primary Contact: Perry E. Williams Sr, Administrator and Chief Executive Officer
COO: Cecelia Bost, Chief Operating Officer
CFO: William F Magee, Chief Financial Officer
CMO: Subbu Rayudu, M.D., Chief of Staff
CIO: Saul Mbenga, Manager Information Technology
CHR: Judy Eggers, Manager Human Resources
Web address: https://www.alliancehcs.org/
Control: Corporation, Investor–owned (for–profit) **Service**: General medical and surgical

Staffed Beds: 40

HOUSTON—Chickasaw County

TRACE REGIONAL HOSPITAL (250017), Highway 8 East, Zip 38851–9396, Mailing Address: P.O. Box 626, Zip 38851–0626; tel. 662/456–3700, **A**10 **F**15 26 28 34 35 54 57 59 64 65 68 90 98 103 105 106 107 111 115 119 127 130 133 135 149 154 156 **P**6
Primary Contact: Sheila Brockman, Chief Executive Officer
CFO: Pamela W Cook, Chief Financial Officer
CMO: Bill Brohawn, Chief of Staff
CHR: Sherry Craig, Director Human Resources
CNO: Marianne Johnson, Chief Nursing Officer
Web address: www.traceregional.com
Control: Corporation, Investor–owned (for–profit) **Service**: General medical and surgical

Staffed Beds: 35 **Admissions**: 277 **Census**: 10 **Outpatient Visits**: 242
Births: 0 **Total Expense ($000)**: 16403 **Payroll Expense ($000)**: 7618
Personnel: 108

INDIANOLA—Sunflower County

★ **SOUTH SUNFLOWER COUNTY HOSPITAL (250095)**, 121 East Baker Street, Zip 38751–2498; tel. 662/635–7201, **A**3 10 20 **F**8 13 15 34 40 43 50 61 64 65 76 80 81 85 89 107 119 127 133 **P**8
Primary Contact: Courtney Phillips, Chief Executive Officer
COO: Holly H. Sparks, Chief Clinical Officer
CFO: Katie Yates, Chief Financial Officer
CMO: Eric Lessmann, Chief of Staff
CIO: Benjamin Rosenthal, Information Systems Director
CHR: Meredith Taylor, Controller
Web address: www.southsunflower.com
Control: County, Government, Nonfederal **Service**: General medical and surgical

Staffed Beds: 46 **Admissions**: 696 **Census**: 11 **Outpatient Visits**: 59800
Births: 190 **Total Expense ($000)**: 19760 **Payroll Expense ($000)**: 5888
Personnel: 131

IUKA—Tishomingo County

★ ⇑ **NORTH MISSISSIPPI MEDICAL CENTER–IUKA (250002)**, 1777 Curtis Drive, Zip 38852–1001, Mailing Address: P.O. Box 860, Zip 38852–0860; tel. 662/423–6051, (Nonreporting) **A**10 21 **S** North Mississippi Health Services, Inc., Tupelo, MS
Primary Contact: Barry L. Keel, Administrator
CFO: Betty Moore, Business Manager
CMO: Margaret Glynn, M.D., Chief Medical Officer
CHR: Jane Chamblee, Manager Human Resources
Web address: www.nmhs.net
Control: Other not–for–profit (including NFP Corporation) **Service**: General medical and surgical

Staffed Beds: 48

Hospital, Medicare Provider Number, Address, Telephone, Approval, Facility, and Physician Codes, Health Care System

★ American Hospital Association (AHA) membership ○ Healthcare Facilities Accreditation Program ⇑ Center for Improvement in Healthcare Quality Accreditation
☐ The Joint Commission accreditation ◇ DNV Healthcare Inc. accreditation △ Commission on Accreditation of Rehabilitation Facilities (CARF) accreditation

© 2025 AHA Guide

Hospitals, U.S. / MISSISSIPPI

JACKSON—Hinds County

G.V. (SONNY) MONTGOMERY DEPARTMENT OF VETERANS AFFAIRS MEDICAL CENTER, 1500 East Woodrow Wilson Drive, Zip 39216-5199; tel. 601/362-4471, (Nonreporting) **A**1 3 5 **S** Department of Veterans Affairs, Washington, DC
Primary Contact: Kai Mentzer, Interim Director
COO: Jed Fillingim, Acting Chief Operating Officer and Associate Director
CFO: Joy Willis, Acting Chief Fiscal Service
CMO: Kent Kirchner, M.D., Chief of Staff
CIO: Robert Wolak, Chief Information Resource Management Service
CHR: Sam Evans, Chief Human Resources Management
Web address: www.jackson.va.gov/
Control: Veterans Affairs, Government, federal **Service**: General medical and surgical

Staffed Beds: 61

MERIT HEALTH CENTRAL (250072), 1850 Chadwick Drive, Zip 39204-3479, Mailing Address: P.O. Box 59001, Zip 39284-9001; tel. 601/376-1000, (Nonreporting) **A**1 3 10 **S** Community Health Systems, Inc., Franklin, TN
Primary Contact: Vincent Brummett, Chief Administrative Officer
COO: Tom Wills, R.N., Chief Operating Officer
CFO: Justin Stroud, Chief Financial Officer
CMO: Greg Oden, Chief Medical Officer
CIO: Tracy Holifield, Director Information Systems
CHR: Sean Jones, Director Human Resources
CNO: Laura Knight, Chief Nursing Officer
Web address: www.merithealthcentral.com/
Control: Corporation, Investor-owned (for-profit) **Service**: General medical and surgical

Staffed Beds: 319

△ **METHODIST REHABILITATION CENTER (250152)**, 1350 Woodrow Wilson Drive, Zip 39216-5198; tel. 601/981-2611, (Nonreporting) **A**1 5 7 10
Primary Contact: David McMillin, President and Chief Executive Officer
COO: Joseph M Morette, Executive Vice President
CFO: Gary Armstrong, President and Chief Financial Officer
CIO: Gary Armstrong, President and Chief Financial Officer
CHR: Steve Hope, Vice President Corporate Services
Web address: www.methodistrehab.org
Control: Other not-for-profit (including NFP Corporation) **Service**: Rehabilitation

Staffed Beds: 184

MISSISSIPPI BAPTIST MEDICAL CENTER (250102), 1225 North State Street, Zip 39202-2064; tel. 601/968-1000, (Nonreporting) **A**1 2 3 5 10 19 **S** Baptist Memorial Health Care Corporation, Memphis, TN
Primary Contact: Bobbie K. Ware, R.N., FACHE, Chief Executive Officer and Administrator
COO: Bobbie K. Ware, R.N., FACHE, Vice President Patient Care and Chief Nursing Officer
CFO: William Thompson, Chief Financial Officer
CMO: Michael Maples, M.D., Vice President and Chief Medical Officer
CHR: Lee Ann Foreman, Vice President Human Resources
CNO: Bobbie K. Ware, R.N., FACHE, Vice President Patient Care and Chief Nursing Officer
Web address: www.mbhs.org
Control: Other not-for-profit (including NFP Corporation) **Service**: General medical and surgical

Staffed Beds: 425

SELECT SPECIALTY HOSPITAL - BELHAVEN (252003), 1225 North State Street, 5th Floor, Zip 39202-2097; tel. 601/968-1000, **A**1 10 **F**1 77 130 **S** Select Medical Corporation, Mechanicsburg, PA
Primary Contact: Cris Bourn, Chief Executive Officer
CFO: Russell W York, Vice President and Chief Financial Officer
CHR: Lee Ann Foreman, Vice President Human Resources
Web address: https://www.selectspecialtyhospitals.com/locations-and-tours/ms/jackson/belhaven/
Control: Corporation, Investor-owned (for-profit) **Service**: Acute long-term care hospital

Staffed Beds: 36 **Admissions**: 327 **Census**: 31 **Outpatient Visits**: 0 **Births**: 0 **Total Expense ($000)**: 19049 **Payroll Expense ($000)**: 9006 **Personnel**: 120

SELECT SPECIALTY HOSPITAL–JACKSON (252007), 5903 Ridgewood Road, Suite 100, Zip 39211-3700; tel. 601/899-3800, **A**1 3 10 **F**1 107 119 **P**7 **S** Select Medical Corporation, Mechanicsburg, PA
Primary Contact: Robert Shannon. Canard, Chief Executive Officer
CFO: Melissa Smith, Controller
CIO: Jacqueline Barnes, Manager Health Information
CHR: Vicki Watson, Manager Human Resources
Web address: www.selectspecialtyhospitals.com/company/locations/jackson.aspx
Control: Corporation, Investor-owned (for-profit) **Service**: Acute long-term care hospital

Staffed Beds: 53 **Admissions**: 607 **Census**: 50 **Outpatient Visits**: 0 **Births**: 0 **Total Expense ($000)**: 28983 **Payroll Expense ($000)**: 16068 **Personnel**: 187

ST. DOMINIC–JACKSON MEMORIAL HOSPITAL (250048), 969 Lakeland Drive, Zip 39216-4606; tel. 601/200-2000, **A**1 2 3 5 10 **F**3 4 10 11 12 13 15 17 29 30 31 34 37 40 43 45 46 49 50 51 53 54 57 58 59 60 61 64 66 70 71 72 73 74 75 76 77 78 79 80 81 82 83 84 85 86 87 89 90 93 94 96 97 98 100 107 108 110 111 114 115 116 117 118 119 120 121 123 124 125 126 130 131 141 146 147 148 149 154 164 167 **P**1 4 **S** Franciscan Missionaries of Our Lady Health System, Inc., Baton Rouge, LA
Primary Contact: Jeremy M. Tinnerello, R.N., MSN, Jackson Market President
CFO: Sam Scott, Vice President Financial Services
CMO: Eric A McVey, M.D., III, Executive Vice President Medical Affairs and Quality
CIO: Keith Van Camp, Vice President Information Services
CHR: Frank Lenior, Vice President Human Resources
Web address: www.stdom.com
Control: Church operated, Nongovernment, not-for-profit **Service**: General medical and surgical

Staffed Beds: 660 **Admissions**: 21371 **Census**: 355 **Outpatient Visits**: 144046 **Births**: 1620 **Total Expense ($000)**: 594905 **Payroll Expense ($000)**: 227066 **Personnel**: 2039

UNIVERSITY OF MISSISSIPPI MEDICAL CENTER (250001), 2500 North State Street, Zip 39216-4505; tel. 601/984-1000, (Includes BLAIR E. BATSON HOSPITAL FOR CHILDREN, 2500 North State Street Room W019, Jackson, Mississippi, Zip 39216-4500, tel. 601/984-1000; CHILDREN'S HEALTHCARE OF MISSISSIPPI, 2500 North State Street, Jackson, Mississippi, Zip 39216-4500, tel. 601/984-1000; Guy Giesecke, Chief Executive Officer) **A**1 2 3 5 8 10 13 19 **F**6 7 8 9 11 12 14 15 17 18 19 20 21 22 23 24 25 26 27 28 29 30 31 32 34 35 38 39 40 41 43 45 46 47 48 49 50 52 53 54 55 56 57 58 59 60 61 62 64 65 66 68 70 71 72 73 74 75 76 77 78 79 80 81 82 84 85 86 87 88 89 90 92 93 94 97 98 99 100 101 102 103 104 107 108 110 111 112 114 115 116 117 118 119 120 121 123 124 126 130 131 132 134 135 136 137 138 139 141 142 143 144 146 147 148 149 152 154 155 156 **P**6 **S** University Hospitals and Health System, Jackson, MS
Primary Contact: Britt Crewse, CPA, Chief Executive Officer
CFO: Dan Janicak, Chief Financial Officer
CMO: William H Cleland, M.D., Chief Medical Officer
CHR: Paula Henderson, Chief Human Resources Officer
CNO: Ellen Dempsey Hansen, Chief Nursing Officer
Web address: www.umc.edu
Control: State, Government, Nonfederal **Service**: General medical and surgical

Staffed Beds: 733 **Admissions**: 28380 **Census**: 604 **Outpatient Visits**: 536216 **Births**: 2357 **Total Expense ($000)**: 989008 **Payroll Expense ($000)**: 305519 **Personnel**: 5954

KEESLER AFB—Harrison County

U. S. AIR FORCE MEDICAL CENTER KEESLER, 301 Fisher Street, Room 1A132, Zip 39534-2519; tel. 228/376-2550, (Nonreporting) **A**1 3 5 **S** Department of the Air Force, Washington, DC
Primary Contact: Christopher J. Estridge, Commander
COO: Brigadier General James Dougherty, Commander
CFO: Major Brenda Yi, Director Medical Resource Management and Chief Financial Officer
CMO: Colonel James Gasque, M.D., Chief Hospital Services
CIO: Major Samuel Silverthorne, Chief Information Officer
CHR: Major Brenda Yi, Director Medical Resource Management and Chief Financial Officer
Web address: https://keesler.tricare.mil/
Control: Air Force, Government, federal **Service**: General medical and surgical

Staffed Beds: 56

Hospitals, U.S. / MISSISSIPPI

KOSCIUSKO—Attala County

★ ⇑ **BAPTIST MEDICAL CENTER – ATTALA (251336)**, 220 Highway 12 West, Zip 39090–3208, Mailing Address: 220 Hwy 12 West, Zip 39090–0887; tel. 662/289–4311, **A**10 18 21 **F**2 3 15 30 34 40 45 81 93 107 108 110 114 118 119 127 133 135 148 **S** Baptist Memorial Health Care Corporation, Memphis, TN
Primary Contact: Mac Flynt, Chief Executive Officer and Administrator
CHR: Stephanie Washington, Human Resources Director
CNO: Allison Schuler, R.N., Chief Nursing Officer
Web address: www.mbhs.org/locations/baptist-medical-center-attala/
Control: Other not–for–profit (including NFP Corporation) **Service**: General medical and surgical

Staffed Beds: 25 **Admissions**: 386 **Census**: 4 **Outpatient Visits**: 21918
Births: 0 **Total Expense ($000)**: 12015 **Payroll Expense ($000)**: 7717
Personnel: 142

LAUREL—Jones County

★ ⇑ **SOUTH CENTRAL REGIONAL MEDICAL CENTER (250058)**, 1220 Jefferson Street, Zip 39440–4374, Mailing Address: 1220 Jefferson St, Zip 39440–4355; tel. 601/426–4000, (Nonreporting) **A**10 21
Primary Contact: Gregg Gibbes, President and Chief Executive Officer
CFO: Tom Canizaro, Vice President and Chief Financial Officer
CMO: Willus Mark Horne, M.D., Chief Medical Officer
CIO: Dell Blakeney, Vice President and Chief Information Officer
CHR: Janet Staples, Vice President Human Resources
CNO: Beth W Endom, R.N., MSN, Vice President and Chief Nursing Officer
Web address: www.scrmc.com
Control: County, Government, Nonfederal **Service**: General medical and surgical

Staffed Beds: 436

LEAKESVILLE—Greene County

GREENE COUNTY HOSPITAL (250782), 1017 Jackson Avenue, Zip 39451–9105; tel. 601/394–4139, (Nonreporting) **A**10
Primary Contact: Richard P. Daughdrill, R.N., Administrator
CFO: Debbie Brannan, Chief Financial Officer
CMO: Jay Pinkerton, M.D., Chief of Staff
CHR: Carla Shows, Payroll Clerk
CNO: Tabatha Pinter, Director of Nursing
Web address: www.georgeregional.com
Control: County, Government, Nonfederal

Staffed Beds: 7

LEXINGTON—Holmes County

⇑ **UNIVERSITY OF MISSISSIPPI MEDICAL CENTER HOLMES COUNTY (251319)**, 239 Bowling Green Road, Zip 39095–5167; tel. 601/496–5200, (Nonreporting) **A**10 18 21 **S** University Hospitals and Health System, Jackson, MS
Primary Contact: Dodie McElmurray, FACHE, Chief Executive Officer
COO: Paige Lawrence, Assistant Administrator
CFO: Scott Whittemore, Chief Financial Officer
CMO: Mark Smothers, M.D., Chief Medical Officer
CIO: Sammuel Townsend, LAN Administrator
CHR: Claudette Hathcock, Human Resources Director
Web address: www.ummchealth.com/holmes/
Control: State, Government, Nonfederal **Service**: General medical and surgical

Staffed Beds: 25

LOUISVILLE—Winston County

WINSTON MEDICAL CENTER (250027), 562 East Main Street, Zip 39339–2742, Mailing Address: P.O. Box 967, Zip 39339–0967; tel. 662/773–6211, (Nonreporting) **A**3 10 20
Primary Contact: Michael Nester, Chief Executive Officer
Web address: www.winstonmedical.org
Control: Other not–for–profit (including NFP Corporation) **Service**: General medical and surgical

Staffed Beds: 120

LUCEDALE—George County

GEORGE REGIONAL HOSPITAL (250036), 859 Winter Street, Zip 39452–6603, Mailing Address: P.O. Box 607, Zip 39452–0607; tel. 601/947–3161, (Nonreporting) **A**10
Primary Contact: Greg Havard, Chief Executive Officer
CFO: Debbie Brannan, Chief Financial Officer
CMO: Jay Pinkerton, M.D., Chief Medical Officer
CIO: Anthoney Fryfogle, Chief Information Officer
CHR: Carla Shows, Human Resource and Payroll Clerk
CNO: Tabatha Pinter, Director of Nursing
Web address: www.georgeregional.com
Control: County, Government, Nonfederal **Service**: General medical and surgical

Staffed Beds: 48

MACON—Noxubee County

NOXUBEE GENERAL HOSPITAL (251307), 606 North Jefferson Street, Zip 39341–2242, Mailing Address: P.O. Box 480, Zip 39341–0480; tel. 662/726–4231, (Total facility includes 60 beds in nursing home–type unit) **A**10 18 **F**89 111 119 128 130 133
Primary Contact: Meg Ebert, Administrator
Web address: https://www.ngcah.com/
Control: County, Government, Nonfederal **Service**: General medical and surgical

Staffed Beds: 110 **Admissions**: 231 **Census**: 56 **Outpatient Visits**: 21981
Births: 0 **Total Expense ($000)**: 16273 **Payroll Expense ($000)**: 8346
Personnel: 86

MAGEE—Simpson County

★ **MAGEE GENERAL HOSPITAL (250124)**, 300 Third Avenue SE, Zip 39111–3698; tel. 601/849–5070, **A**10 **F**15 29 35 40 43 81 89 107 108 111 119 130 133 146
Primary Contact: Gregg Gibbes, Chief Executive Officer
CMO: Kelli Smith, M.D., Chief of Staff
CIO: Kirby Craft, Chief Information Officer
CHR: Steve Beckham, Director Human Resources
CNO: Cindy McIntyre, R.N., Administrative Director Clinical Services
Web address: www.mghosp.org
Control: Other not–for–profit (including NFP Corporation) **Service**: General medical and surgical

Staffed Beds: 32 **Admissions**: 591 **Census**: 9 **Outpatient Visits**: 12154
Births: 0 **Total Expense ($000)**: 15731 **Payroll Expense ($000)**: 8243
Personnel: 155

MAGNOLIA—Pike County

BEACHAM MEMORIAL HOSPITAL (250049), 205 North Cherry Street, Zip 39652–2819, Mailing Address: P.O. Box 351, Zip 39652–0351; tel. 601/783–2351, **A**10 **F**3 34 35 36 57 59 65 68 98 100 101 103 107 127 130 133 148
Primary Contact: Sarah Chisolm, Chief Executive Officer
CMO: Lucius Lampton, M.D., Medical Director
CHR: Jackie McKenzie, Director Administrative Services
Web address: www.beachammemorial.org
Control: Corporation, Investor–owned (for–profit) **Service**: General medical and surgical

Staffed Beds: 31 **Admissions**: 778 **Census**: 14 **Outpatient Visits**: 0
Births: 0 **Total Expense ($000)**: 5906 **Payroll Expense ($000)**: 2786
Personnel: 66

Hospitals, U.S. / MISSISSIPPI

MCCOMB—Pike County

★ ⇧ **SOUTHWEST MISSISSIPPI REGIONAL MEDICAL CENTER (250097)**, 215 Marion Avenue, Zip 39648–2705, Mailing Address: P.O. Box 1307, Zip 39649–1307; tel. 601/249–5500, **A**3 10 19 21 **F**8 13 15 17 18 20 22 28 29 30 31 34 35 37 39 40 43 45 46 49 50 53 57 59 64 65 70 72 73 75 76 77 78 79 81 84 85 86 87 93 94 107 108 109 110 111 112 114 115 117 118 119 120 121 123 126 127 129 130 131 132 154 156 157 167 **P**6 **S** Southwest Health Systems, Mccomb, MS
Primary Contact: Charla Rowley, Chief Executive Officer
CFO: Mallory Ginn, Chief Financial Officer
CMO: Kevin Richardson, M.D., Chief of Staff
CIO: David Hamilton, Chief Information Officer
CHR: Don Haskins, Administrative Director Human Resources
CNO: Michelle Gough MSN, RN–B, Chief Nursing Officer
Web address: www.smrmc.com
Control: Hospital district or authority, Government, Nonfederal **Service**: General medical and surgical

Staffed Beds: 93 **Admissions**: 3681 **Census**: 42 **Outpatient Visits**: 83701
Births: 466 **Total Expense ($000)**: 156455 **Payroll Expense ($000)**: 67701
Personnel: 876

MEADVILLE—Franklin County

FRANKLIN COUNTY MEMORIAL HOSPITAL (251330), 40 Union Church Road, Zip 39653–8336, Mailing Address: P.O. Box 636, Zip 39653–0636; tel. 601/384–5801, (Nonreporting) **A**10 18
Primary Contact: Mike Boleware, Administrator
Web address: www.fcmh.net
Control: County, Government, Nonfederal **Service**: General medical and surgical

Staffed Beds: 25

MENDENHALL—Simpson County

SIMPSON GENERAL HOSPITAL (251317), 1842 Simpson Highway 149, Zip 39114–3438; tel. 601/847–2221, (Nonreporting) **A**10 18
Primary Contact: Gregg Gibbes, Chief Executive Officer
COO: Al Gary, COO
CFO: Al Gary, COO
CMO: Chip Holbrook, M.D., Chief of Staff
CHR: Randall Neely, CEO
CNO: Sharon Burnham, Director of Nursing
Web address: https://www.simpsongeneral.com/
Control: Other not–for–profit (including NFP Corporation) **Service**: General medical and surgical

Staffed Beds: 35

MERIDIAN—Lauderdale County

☐ **ALLIANCE HEALTH CENTER (250151)**, 5000 Highway 39 North, Zip 39301–1021; tel. 601/483–6211, (Nonreporting) **A**1 3 10 **S** Universal Health Services, Inc., King of Prussia, PA
Primary Contact: Jay Shehi, Chief Executive Officer
CFO: Robert Jackson, Chief Financial Officer
CMO: Terry Jordan, M.D., Chief of Staff
CIO: Brenda Smith, Director Financial Services
CHR: Shrea Johnson, Director Human Resources
Web address: www.alliancehealthcenter.com
Control: Corporation, Investor–owned (for–profit) **Service**: Psychiatric

Staffed Beds: 154

ANDERSON REGIONAL HEALTH SYSTEM See Baptist Anderson Regional Medical Center

ANDERSON REGIONAL HEALTH SYSTEM SOUTH See Baptist Anderson Regional Medical Center – South

✠ **BAPTIST ANDERSON REGIONAL MEDICAL CENTER (250104)**, 2124 14th Street, Zip 39301–4040; tel. 601/553–6000, **A**1 2 3 10 19 **F**3 9 11 12 13 15 17 18 20 22 24 28 29 30 31 34 35 38 40 43 44 45 46 47 48 49 50 53 57 58 59 64 65 69 70 72 74 75 76 77 78 79 81 85 86 87 89 92 93 107 108 110 111 115 118 119 120 121 123 124 126 129 130 131 132 135 145 146 148 149 154 156 167 **S** Baptist Memorial Health Care Corporation, Memphis, TN
Primary Contact: John G. Anderson, FACHE, Chief Executive Officer and Administrator
CFO: Steven Brown, Vice President Finance
CMO: Scot Bell, Chief Medical Officer
CHR: Joel Windham, Vice President Human Resources
CNO: Matt Edwards, Vice President Nursing Services and Chief Nursing Officer
Web address: www.andersonregional.org
Control: Other not–for–profit (including NFP Corporation) **Service**: General medical and surgical

Staffed Beds: 170 **Admissions**: 6778 **Census**: 92 **Outpatient Visits**: 165823 **Births**: 898 **Total Expense ($000)**: 150872 **Payroll Expense ($000)**: 71219 **Personnel**: 1113

✠ △ **BAPTIST ANDERSON REGIONAL MEDICAL CENTER – SOUTH (250081)**, 1102 Constitution Avenue, Zip 39301–4001; tel. 601/553–6000, **A**1 7 10 **F**11 29 30 34 35 44 50 57 59 60 64 65 68 90 98 **S** Baptist Memorial Health Care Corporation, Memphis, TN
Primary Contact: John G. Anderson, FACHE, Chief Executive Officer and Administrator
CFO: Steven Brown, Vice President Finance
CIO: Steve Taylor, Chief Information Officer
CHR: Joel Windham, Vice President Human Resources
Web address: www.andersonregional.org
Control: Other not–for–profit (including NFP Corporation) **Service**: General medical and surgical

Staffed Beds: 58 **Admissions**: 1123 **Census**: 42 **Outpatient Visits**: 38232
Births: 0 **Total Expense ($000)**: 20989 **Payroll Expense ($000)**: 7771
Personnel: 79

☐ **EAST MISSISSIPPI STATE HOSPITAL**, 1818 College Drive, Zip 39307, Mailing Address: Box 4128, West Station, Zip 39304–4128; tel. 601/482–6186, (Total facility includes 130 beds in nursing home–type unit) **A**1 3 5 **F**4 29 30 39 60 65 82 86 87 98 103 106 128 130 135 143 146 149 160 164 **S** Mississippi State Department of Mental Health, Jackson, MS
Primary Contact: Charles Carlisle, Director
CFO: Geri Doggett, Director Business
CMO: Gloria Gomez, M.D., Medical Director
CIO: Scotty Taylor, Information Technology Director
CHR: Shearmaine Calaway, Director Human Resources
CNO: Diane Nobles, Nurse Executive
Web address: www.emsh.state.ms.us
Control: State, Government, Nonfederal **Service**: Psychiatric

Staffed Beds: 250 **Admissions**: 475 **Census**: 222 **Births**: 0 **Total Expense ($000)**: 57470 **Payroll Expense ($000)**: 18621 **Personnel**: 288

★ ⇧ **OCHSNER RUSH MEDICAL CENTER (250069)**, 1314 19th Avenue, Zip 39301–4195; tel. 601/483–0011, (Nonreporting) **A**3 5 10 19 21 **S** Ochsner Health, New Orleans, LA
Primary Contact: Larkin Kennedy, Chief Executive Officer
COO: Jason Payne, Executive Vice President and Chief Operating Officer
CMO: W Scot Bell, M.D., Chief Medical Officer
CIO: Mike Peavy, Chief Information Officer
CHR: Donnie Smith, Director Human Resources
CNO: Casey Bland, Director of Nursing
Web address: www.rushhealthsystems.org/rfh/
Control: Other not–for–profit (including NFP Corporation) **Service**: General medical and surgical

Staffed Beds: 182

★ **OCHSNER SPECIALTY HOSPITAL (252004)**, 1314 19th Avenue, Zip 39301–4116; tel. 601/703–4211, (Nonreporting) **A**3 10 **S** Ochsner Health, New Orleans, LA
Primary Contact: Kawanda Johnson, Ph.D., MSN, Administrator and Executive Vice President
CFO: David Butler, Chief Financial Officer
CMO: John Johnston, Chief Medical Officer
CIO: Mike Peavy, Chief Information Officer
CHR: Scott Vincent, Chief Human Resource Officer
CNO: Ashley Roy, Vice President of Nursing Services
Web address: www.specialtyhospitalofmeridian.com/shm/
Control: Other not–for–profit (including NFP Corporation) **Service**: Acute long–term care hospital

Staffed Beds: 30

✠ **REGENCY HOSPITAL OF MERIDIAN (252006)**, 1102 Constitution Avenue, 2nd Floor, Zip 39301–4001; tel. 601/484–7900, (Nonreporting) **A**1 10 **S** Select Medical Corporation, Mechanicsburg, PA
Primary Contact: Eliza Gavin, Chief Executive Officer
Web address: www.regencyhospital.com
Control: Corporation, Investor–owned (for–profit) **Service**: Acute long–term care hospital

Staffed Beds: 40

MONTICELLO—Lawrence County

★ **LAWRENCE COUNTY HOSPITAL (251305)**, Highway 84 East, Zip 39654–0788, Mailing Address: P.O. Box 788, Zip 39654–0788; tel. 601/587–4051, **A**10 18 **F**18 34 40 43 50 57 59 64 87 107 115 119 127 133 149 153 **P**5 **S** Southwest Health Systems, Mccomb, MS
Primary Contact: Phillip W. Langston, Administrator
CFO: Jennifer Moak, Business Office Manager
Web address: www.smrmc.com
Control: County, Government, Nonfederal **Service**: General medical and surgical

Staffed Beds: 25 **Admissions**: 378 **Census**: 9 **Outpatient Visits**: 12463
Births: 0 **Total Expense ($000)**: 12145 **Payroll Expense ($000)**: 6992
Personnel: 114

Hospitals, U.S. / MISSISSIPPI

MORTON—Scott County

★ **OCHSNER SCOTT REGIONAL (251323)**, 317 Highway 13 South, Zip 39117-3353, Mailing Address: P.O. Box 259, Zip 39117-0259; tel. 601/732-6301, (Nonreporting) **A**10 18 **S** Ochsner Health, New Orleans, LA
Primary Contact: Heather Davis, Administrator
CHR: Amy Sugg, Director Human Resources
Web address: www.scottregional.org/srh/
Control: Other not-for-profit (including NFP Corporation) **Service**: General medical and surgical

Staffed Beds: 25

SCOTT REGIONAL HOSPITAL See Ochsner Scott Regional

NATCHEZ—Adams County

⊞ △ **MERIT HEALTH NATCHEZ (250084)**, 54 Seargent 'S' Prentiss Drive, Zip 39120-4726; tel. 601/443-2100, **A**1 7 10 20 **F**13 15 17 18 26 28 29 35 40 43 45 46 47 60 70 73 74 75 76 77 78 79 81 82 85 86 87 89 90 92 93 94 107 108 109 110 111 112 114 115 116 118 119 126 129 130 131 132 133 134 146 147 156 **P**5 **S** Community Health Systems, Inc., Franklin, TN
Primary Contact: Kevin Samrow, Chief Executive Officer
CFO: Charles Mack, Vice President Finance and Chief Financial Officer
CMO: Leslie England, Chief of Staff
CIO: Leslie Makoro, Director Information management Systems
CHR: Jean E Juchnowicz, Director Human Resources
CNO: Lee Hinson, Chief Nursing Officer
Web address: https://www.merithealthnatchez.com/
Control: Corporation, Investor-owned (for-profit) **Service**: General medical and surgical

Staffed Beds: 81 **Admissions**: 2624 **Census**: 35 **Outpatient Visits**: 52267 **Births**: 583 **Total Expense ($000)**: 51532 **Payroll Expense ($000)**: 22300 **Personnel**: 340

NEW ALBANY—Union County

⊞ **BAPTIST MEMORIAL HOSPITAL–UNION COUNTY (250006)**, 200 Highway 30 West, Zip 38652-3112; tel. 662/538-7631, **A**1 2 3 10 **F**3 11 13 15 28 29 30 31 34 35 39 40 45 51 57 59 64 68 70 75 76 77 78 79 81 84 85 86 87 91 93 96 107 108 110 111 115 116 117 118 119 124 130 132 133 135 146 147 148 149 154 156 **S** Baptist Memorial Health Care Corporation, Memphis, TN
Primary Contact: Ann Bishop, Chief Executive Officer and Administrator
CFO: Kim High, Chief Financial Officer
CMO: H F Mason, M.D., Chief Medical Officer
CIO: Missy Coltharp, Director
CHR: Lori Goode, Director Human Resources
Web address: www.baptistonline.org/union-county/
Control: Other not-for-profit (including NFP Corporation) **Service**: General medical and surgical

Staffed Beds: 101 **Admissions**: 2990 **Census**: 29 **Outpatient Visits**: 94754 **Births**: 782 **Total Expense ($000)**: 118959 **Payroll Expense ($000)**: 24329 **Personnel**: 422

OCEAN SPRINGS—Jackson County

OCEAN SPRINGS HOSPITAL See Singing River Ocean Springs

SINGING RIVER OCEAN SPRINGS See Singing River Health System, Pascagoula

OLIVE BRANCH—Desoto County

★ ⇑ **METHODIST HEALTHCARE OLIVE BRANCH HOSPITAL (250167)**, 4250 Bethel Road, Zip 38654-8737; tel. 662/932-9000, (Nonreporting) **A**10 21 **S** Methodist Le Bonheur Healthcare, Memphis, TN
Primary Contact: David G. Baytos, President
CFO: Kris Sanders, Chief Financial Officer
CHR: Robin Mathis, Director Human Resources
CNO: Annelise Jensen, Vice President and Chief Nursing Officer
Web address: www.methodisthealth.org/olivebranch
Control: Church operated, Nongovernment, not-for-profit **Service**: General medical and surgical

Staffed Beds: 57

PARKWOOD BEHAVIORAL HEALTH SYSTEM (254005), 8135 Goodman Road, Zip 38654-2103; tel. 662/895-4900, (Nonreporting) **A**1 10 **S** Universal Health Services, Inc., King of Prussia, PA
Primary Contact: Alicia Plunkett, Chief Executive Officer
CFO: David Denegri, Chief Financial Officer
CMO: Paul King, M.D., Medical Director
CHR: Julie Dorman, Human Resources Director
CNO: Alicia Plunkett, Chief Nurse Executive
Web address: www.parkwoodbhs.com
Control: Corporation, Investor-owned (for-profit) **Service**: Psychiatric

Staffed Beds: 148

OXFORD—Lafayette County

⊞ △ **BAPTIST MEMORIAL HOSPITAL–NORTH MISSISSIPPI (250034)**, 2301 South Lamar Boulevard, Zip 38655-5373, Mailing Address: P.O. Box 946, Zip 38655-6002; tel. 662/232-8100, (Nonreporting) **A**1 2 3 5 7 10 19 **S** Baptist Memorial Health Care Corporation, Memphis, TN
Primary Contact: Brian Welton, Chief Executive Officer and Administrator
CFO: Dana Williams, Chief Financial Officer
CMO: Dennis P Morgan, Chief of Staff
CIO: Linda Britt, Director Information Systems
CHR: Josh Lowery, Director of Human Resources
CNO: Mark Ottens, Chief Nursing Officer
Web address: www.baptistonline.org/north-mississippi/
Control: Other not-for-profit (including NFP Corporation) **Service**: General medical and surgical

Staffed Beds: 184

PASCAGOULA—Jackson County

△ ⇑ **SINGING RIVER HEALTH SYSTEM (250040)**, 2809 Denny Avenue, Zip 39581-5301; tel. 228/809-5000, (Includes SINGING RIVER OCEAN SPRINGS, 3109 Bienville Boulevard, Ocean Springs, Mississippi, Zip 39564-4361, tel. 228/818-1111; Heath Thompson, R.N., Administrator; SINGING RIVER PASCAGOULA, 2809 Denny Avenue, Pascagoula, Mississippi, Zip 39581-5301, tel. 228/809-5000; Laurin St. Pe, Administrator – Singing River Hospital) (Nonreporting) **A**2 3 7 10 19 21
Primary Contact: Laurin St. Pe, Interim Chief Executive Officer
COO: Laurin St. Pe, Chief Operating Officer
CFO: Sandra Albrecht, Interim Chief Financial Officer
CMO: Randy Roth, Chief Medical Officer
CHR: Craig Summerlin, Chief Human Resources Officer
CNO: Susan Russell, Chief Nursing Officer
Web address: www.singingriverhealthsystem.com
Control: County, Government, Nonfederal **Service**: General medical and surgical

Staffed Beds: 361

SINGING RIVER HOSPITAL See Singing River Pasagoula

PHILADELPHIA—Neshoba County

⇑ **CHOCTAW HEALTH CENTER (250127)**, 210 Hospital Circle, Zip 39350-6781; tel. 601/656-2211, (Nonreporting) **A**10 21
Primary Contact: Mary Harrison, Interim Health Director
CFO: Myrna Hancock, Director Financial Services
CMO: Juantina Johnson, Chief of Staff
CIO: Raymond Willis, IT Manager
CHR: Anna Denson, Human Resources Specialist
CNO: Regina Isaac, Director of Nursing
Web address: https://www.choctawhealthcenter.org/
Control: Public Health Service other than 47, Government, federal **Service**: General medical and surgical

Staffed Beds: 26

★ ⇑ **NESHOBA GENERAL (250043)**, 1001 Holland Avenue, Zip 39350-2161, Mailing Address: P.O. Box 648, Zip 39350-0648; tel. 601/663-1200, (Nonreporting) **A**10 20 21
Primary Contact: Lee McCall, Chief Executive Officer
CFO: Scott McNair, Chief Financial Officer
CMO: Heather Cannon, M.D., Medical Director
CHR: Hedda Stewart, Director Human Resources
CNO: Scott Breazeale, Chief Nursing Officer
Web address: www.neshobageneral.com
Control: County, Government, Nonfederal **Service**: General medical and surgical

Staffed Beds: 193

Hospital, Medicare Provider Number, Address, Telephone, Approval, Facility, and Physician Codes, Health Care System

★ American Hospital Association (AHA) membership
☐ The Joint Commission accreditation
◯ Healthcare Facilities Accreditation Program
◇ DNV Healthcare Inc. accreditation
⇑ Center for Improvement in Healthcare Quality Accreditation
△ Commission on Accreditation of Rehabilitation Facilities (CARF) accreditation

Hospitals, U.S. / MISSISSIPPI

PICAYUNE—Pearl River County

HIGHLAND COMMUNITY HOSPITAL (250117), 130 Highland Parkway, Zip 39466-5574, Mailing Address: P.O. Box 909, Zip 39466-0909; tel. 601/358-9400, (Nonreporting) **A**10
Primary Contact: Bryan K. Maxie, Administrator
CMO: Robert Lopez, Chief Medical Officer
CHR: Cynthia Render-Leach, Director Human Resources
CNO: Kim Varnado, R.N., Chief Nursing Officer
Web address: www.highlandch.com
Control: County, Government, Nonfederal **Service**: General medical and surgical

Staffed Beds: 49

PONTOTOC—Pontotoc County

★ ⇑ **NORTH MISSISSIPPI MEDICAL CENTER–PONTOTOC (251308)**, 176 South Main Street, Zip 38863-3311, Mailing Address: P.O. Box 790, Zip 38863-0790; tel. 662/488-7640, (Nonreporting) **A**10 18 21 **S** North Mississippi Health Services, Inc., Tupelo, MS
Primary Contact: Jamie Rodgers, Administrator
CFO: M Denise Heard, Director Business Services
CHR: P. Marie Barnes, Director, Human Resources
CNO: Cathy Waldrop, Director, Hospital Nursing Services
Web address: https://www.nmhs.net/locations/profile/north-mississippi-medical-center-pontotoc/
Control: Other not-for-profit (including NFP Corporation) **Service**: General medical and surgical

Staffed Beds: 69

POPLARVILLE—Pearl River County

★ **PEARL RIVER COUNTY HOSPITAL (251333)**, 305 West Moody Street, Zip 39470-7338, Mailing Address: P.O. Box 392, Zip 39470-0392; tel. 601/795-4543, (Nonreporting) **A**10 18
Primary Contact: Shawn Carpenter, Chief Executive Officer
CNO: Lisa Brown, Director of Nursing
Web address: www.prc-med.com
Control: County, Government, Nonfederal **Service**: General medical and surgical

Staffed Beds: 124

PORT GIBSON—Claiborne County

★ **CLAIBORNE COUNTY MEDICAL CENTER (251320)**, 123 McComb Avenue, Zip 39150-2915, Mailing Address: P.O. Box 1004, Zip 39150-1004; tel. 601/437-5141, (Nonreporting) **A**10 18
Primary Contact: Ada Ratliff, Chief Executive Officer
CFO: Linda Caho-Mooney, Chief Financial Officer
CIO: Ada Ratliff, Chief Information Officer
Control: County, Government, Nonfederal **Service**: General medical and surgical

Staffed Beds: 32

PRENTISS—Jefferson Davis County

★ **JEFFERSON DAVIS COMMUNITY HOSPITAL (251326)**, 1102 Rose Street, Zip 39474-5200, Mailing Address: P.O. Box 1288, Zip 39474-1288; tel. 601/792-4276, (Total facility includes 55 beds in nursing home-type unit) **A**10 18 **F**29 34 35 39 40 43 53 55 57 59 64 65 66 68 87 89 92 97 104 107 114 119 127 130 133 148 149 153 154 164
Primary Contact: Alaina Cedillo, Administrator
CHR: Diane Daughdrill, Director Human Resources
Web address: https://www.forresthealth.org/our-locations/jefferson-davis-community-hospital/
Control: County, Government, Nonfederal **Service**: General medical and surgical

Staffed Beds: 80 **Admissions**: 101 **Census**: 47 **Outpatient Visits**: 10295 **Births**: 0 **Total Expense ($000)**: 11324 **Payroll Expense ($000)**: 5412 **Personnel**: 109

PURVIS—Lamar County

☐ **SOUTH MISSISSIPPI STATE HOSPITAL (254008)**, 823 Highway 589, Zip 39475-4194; tel. 601/794-0100, (Nonreporting) **A**1 10 **S** Mississippi State Department of Mental Health, Jackson, MS
Primary Contact: Sabrina Young, Director
CFO: Andy Tucker, Chief Financial Officer
CMO: Allen Harris, M.D., Clinical Director
CIO: Sabrina Young, Administrative Support Director
CHR: Kelly Reid, Human Resources Director
CNO: Pam Brinson, Nurse Executive
Web address: www.smsh.ms.gov
Control: State, Government, Nonfederal **Service**: Psychiatric

Staffed Beds: 50

QUITMAN—Clarke County

H. C. WATKINS MEMORIAL HOSPITAL See Ochsner Watkins Hospital

★ **OCHSNER WATKINS HOSPITAL (251316)**, 605 South Archusa Avenue, Zip 39355-2331; tel. 601/776-6925, (Nonreporting) **A**10 18 **S** Ochsner Health, New Orleans, LA
Primary Contact: Kawanda Johnson, Ph.D., MSN, Administrator
CMO: O Wayne Byrd, M.D., Chief of Staff
CIO: Melinda Smith, Chief Information Systems
CHR: Leigh Moore, Administrative Assistant Human Resources
Web address: https://www.ochsnerrush.org/hospitals/ochsner-watkins-hospital/
Control: Other not-for-profit (including NFP Corporation) **Service**: General medical and surgical

Staffed Beds: 25

RALEIGH—Smith County

PATIENTS CHOICE MEDICAL CENTER OF SMITH COUNTY (250163), 347 Magnolia Drive, Zip 39153-6011; tel. 601/782-9997, (Nonreporting) **A**10
Primary Contact: Paulette Butler, Chief Executive Officer
Web address: https://www.patientschoicesc.com/
Control: Corporation, Investor-owned (for-profit) **Service**: General medical and surgical

Staffed Beds: 29

RICHTON—Perry County

PERRY COUNTY GENERAL HOSPITAL (250783), 206 Bay Avenue, Zip 39476-2941; tel. 601/788-6316, (Nonreporting) **A**10
Primary Contact: David Paris, Chief Executive Officer
Web address: www.pcghospital.com
Control: Other not-for-profit (including NFP Corporation)

Staffed Beds: 22

RIPLEY—Tippah County

★ **TIPPAH COUNTY HOSPITAL (251337)**, 1005 City Avenue North, Zip 38663-1414, Mailing Address: P.O. Box 499, Zip 38663-0499; tel. 662/837-9221, (Total facility includes 40 beds in nursing home-type unit) **A**10 18 **F**40 43 53 81 104 107 119 127 128 130 133 **P**1
Primary Contact: Patrick Chapman, Ed.D., Chief Executive Officer
CFO: Stephanie McAlister, Controller
CMO: Troy Cappleman, M.D., Chief of Staff
CHR: Heather Taylor, Human Resources Manager
CNO: Carol Anne Hurt, Chief Nursing Officer
Web address: www.tippahcountyhospital.com/
Control: County, Government, Nonfederal **Service**: General medical and surgical

Staffed Beds: 55 **Admissions**: 383 **Census**: 38 **Outpatient Visits**: 10055 **Births**: 0 **Total Expense ($000)**: 18881 **Payroll Expense ($000)**: 6911 **Personnel**: 169

ROLLING FORK—Sharkey County

SHARKEY-ISSAQUENA COMMUNITY HOSPITAL (250784), 108 South Fourth Street, Zip 39159-5146, Mailing Address: P.O. Box 339, Zip 39159-0339; tel. 662/873-4395, **A**10 **F**40 53 98 103 104 105 107 133
Primary Contact: Jerry Keever, Administrator
Control: County, Government, Nonfederal **Service**: General medical and surgical

Staffed Beds: 29 **Admissions**: 129 **Census**: 2 **Outpatient Visits**: 0 **Births**: 0 **Total Expense ($000)**: 19372 **Payroll Expense ($000)**: 5527 **Personnel**: 69

RULEVILLE—Sunflower County

★ **NORTH SUNFLOWER MEDICAL CENTER (251318)**, 840 North Oak Avenue, Zip 38771-3227, Mailing Address: P.O. Box 369, Zip 38771-0369; tel. 662/756-2711, (Nonreporting) **A**10 18
Primary Contact: Billy Marlow, Executive Director and Administrator
COO: Rodney Clark, Chief Operating Officer
CFO: Daniel Ceja, Interim Chief Financial Officer
CMO: Ronald Brent Roberts, M.D., Chief of Medical Staff
CIO: Roger Goss, Chief Information Officer
CHR: Robbie Taylor, Director Human Resources
CNO: Hannah Barrett, Director of Nursing
Web address: www.northsunflower.com
Control: County, Government, Nonfederal **Service**: General medical and surgical

Staffed Beds: 95

Hospitals, U.S. / MISSISSIPPI

SENATOBIA—Tate County

HIGHLAND HILLS MEDICAL CENTER (250172), 401 Getwell Drive, Zip 38668–2213; tel. 662/612–0311, **A**10 **F**15 29 40 107
Primary Contact: Joshua Hammons, Chief Executive Officer
Web address: https://highlandhillsmc.com/
Control: County, Government, Nonfederal **Service**: General medical and surgical

> **Staffed Beds**: 15 **Admissions**: 290 **Census**: 2 **Outpatient Visits**: 13476
> **Births**: 0 **Total Expense ($000)**: 43282 **Payroll Expense ($000)**: 18983
> **Personnel**: 172

SOUTHAVEN—Desoto County

☒ △ **BAPTIST MEMORIAL HOSPITAL–DESOTO (250141)**, 7601 Southcrest Parkway, Zip 38671–4742; tel. 662/772–4000, (Nonreporting) **A**1 2 3 7 10 19 **S** Baptist Memorial Health Care Corporation, Memphis, TN
Primary Contact: Brian Hogan, Chief Executive Officer and Administrator
CFO: Joe McWherter, Chief Financial Officer
CMO: Joann Wood, M.D., Chief Medical Officer
CHR: Walter Banks, Director Human Resources
CNO: Randy White, Chief Nursing Officer
Web address: www.baptistonline.com/desoto/
Control: Other not–for–profit (including NFP Corporation) **Service**: General medical and surgical

> **Staffed Beds**: 247

STARKVILLE—Oktibbeha County

★ ⇑ **OCH REGIONAL MEDICAL CENTER (250050)**, 400 Hospital Road, Zip 39759–2163, Mailing Address: P.O. Box 1506, Zip 39760–1506; tel. 662/323–4320, (Nonreporting) **A**10 21
Primary Contact: James H. Jackson Jr, Chief Executive Officer
COO: Mike Andrews, Associate Administrator and Chief Operating Officer
CFO: Susan Russell, Chief Financial Officer
CMO: W. Todd Smith, M.D., Chief Medical Officer
CIO: Charles Greene, Chief Information Technology Officer
CHR: Mike Andrews, Associate Administrator and Chief Operating Officer
CNO: Michelle Welander, FACHE, R.N., Chief Nursing Officer
Web address: www.och.org
Control: County, Government, Nonfederal **Service**: General medical and surgical

> **Staffed Beds**: 55

TUPELO—Lee County

★ △ ⇑ **NORTH MISSISSIPPI MEDICAL CENTER – TUPELO (250004)**, 830 South Gloster Street, Zip 38801–4934; tel. 662/377–3136, (Nonreporting) **A**2 3 5 7 8 10 21 **S** North Mississippi Health Services, Inc., Tupelo, MS
Primary Contact: David C. Wilson, President and Chief Operation Officer
CFO: Sharon Nobles, Chief Financial Officer
CMO: Jeremy Blanchard, M.D., Chief Medical Officer
CIO: James Weldon, Chief Information Officer
Web address: www.nmhs.net
Control: Other not–for–profit (including NFP Corporation) **Service**: General medical and surgical

> **Staffed Beds**: 741

☐ **NORTH MISSISSIPPI STATE HOSPITAL (254009)**, 1937 Briar Ridge Road, Zip 38804–5963; tel. 662/690–4200, (Nonreporting) **A**1 10 **S** Mississippi State Department of Mental Health, Jackson, MS
Primary Contact: Paul A. Callens, Ph.D., Director
CFO: Joe Rials, Director Fiscal Services
CMO: Ken Lippincott, M.D., Chief of Staff
CIO: James Wilhite, Director Systems Information
Web address: www.nmsh.state.ms.us
Control: State, Government, Nonfederal **Service**: Psychiatric

> **Staffed Beds**: 50

OCEANS BEHAVIORAL HOSPITAL OF TUPELO (254013), 4579 South Eason Boulevard, Suite B, Zip 38801–6539, Mailing Address: 3905 Hedgcoxe Road, Unit 250249, Plano, TX, Zip 75025–0840; tel. 662/268–4418, (Nonreporting) **A**10 **S** Oceans Healthcare, Plano, TX
Primary Contact: Stuart Archer, Chief Executive Officer
CFO: Eric Elliott, Chief Financial Officer
Web address: www.oceanshealthcare.com
Control: Corporation, Investor–owned (for–profit) **Service**: Psychiatric

> **Staffed Beds**: 34

TYLERTOWN—Walthall County

WALTHALL COUNTY GENERAL HOSPITAL See Walthall General Hospital

★ **WALTHALL GENERAL HOSPITAL (251324)**, 100 Hospital Drive, Zip 39667–2099; tel. 601/876–2122, (Nonreporting) **A**10 18
Primary Contact: Nacole Dillon, Administrator
Web address: www.co.walthall.ms.us/walthall-general-hospital.html
Control: County, Government, Nonfederal **Service**: General medical and surgical

> **Staffed Beds**: 25

UNION—Newton County

LAIRD HOSPITAL See Ochsner Laird Hospital

★ **OCHSNER LAIRD HOSPITAL (251322)**, 25117 Highway 15, Zip 39365–9099; tel. 601/774–8214, (Nonreporting) **A**5 10 18 **S** Ochsner Health, New Orleans, LA
Primary Contact: Thomas G. Bartlett III, Administrator
COO: Morris A Reece, EVP/COO
CFO: Jennifer Flint, Chief Financial Officer
CMO: John Mutziger, M.D., Chief Medical Officer
CIO: Angela Sherrill, Chief Information Officer
CHR: Donnie Smith, Chief Human Resources Officer
CNO: Pam Rigdon, Director Nursing
Web address: www.lairdhospital.com/lh/
Control: Other not–for–profit (including NFP Corporation) **Service**: General medical and surgical

> **Staffed Beds**: 25

VICKSBURG—Warren County

☒ **MERIT HEALTH RIVER REGION (250031)**, 2100 Highway 61 North, Zip 39183–8211, Mailing Address: P.O. Box 590, Zip 39181–0590; tel. 601/883–5000, (Includes RIVER REGION WEST CAMPUS, 1111 North Frontage Road, Vicksburg, Mississippi, Zip 39180–5102, tel. 601/883–5000) (Nonreporting) **A**1 10 **S** Community Health Systems, Inc., Franklin, TN
Primary Contact: David R. Fox, FACHE, Chief Executive Officer
CFO: John Milazzo, Chief Financial Officer
CMO: W Briggs Hopson, M.D., Clinical Medical Director
CIO: J B White, Director Information Systems
CHR: Hal Harrington, Vice President Human Resources
CNO: Laurie Morrow Neely, Chief Nursing Officer
Web address: www.riverregion.com
Control: Corporation, Investor–owned (for–profit) **Service**: General medical and surgical

> **Staffed Beds**: 361

VICKSBURG MEDICAL CENTER See River Region West Campus

WATER VALLEY—Yalobusha County

YALOBUSHA GENERAL HOSPITAL (250061), 630 South Main, Zip 38965–3468, Mailing Address: P.O. Box 728, Zip 38965–0728; tel. 662/473–1411, (Total facility includes 122 beds in nursing home–type unit) **A**3 10 **F**128
Primary Contact: Terry Varner, Administrator
COO: Ashlee Langdon, Controller
CHR: Katie Rotenberry–Baggett, Administrative Assistant and Human Resources
Web address: www.yalobushageneral.com/
Control: County, Government, Nonfederal **Service**: General medical and surgical

> **Staffed Beds**: 148 **Admissions**: 286 **Census**: 99 **Outpatient Visits**: 25891
> **Births**: 0 **Total Expense ($000)**: 27403 **Payroll Expense ($000)**: 15235
> **Personnel**: 111

WAYNESBORO—Wayne County

⇑ **WAYNE GENERAL HOSPITAL (250077)**, 950 Matthew Drive, Zip 39367–2590, Mailing Address: P.O. Box 1249, Zip 39367–1249; tel. 601/735–5151, **A**3 10 20 21 **F**3 7 70 76 89
Primary Contact: Kathy Waddell, Administrator
Web address: www.waynegeneralhospital.org
Control: County, Government, Nonfederal **Service**: General medical and surgical

> **Staffed Beds**: 49 **Admissions**: 1257 **Census**: 19 **Outpatient Visits**: 50956
> **Births**: 174 **Total Expense ($000)**: 35677 **Payroll Expense ($000)**: 20649
> **Personnel**: 395

Hospital, Medicare Provider Number, Address, Telephone, Approval, Facility, and Physician Codes, Health Care System

★ American Hospital Association (AHA) membership
☐ The Joint Commission accreditation
○ Healthcare Facilities Accreditation Program
◇ DNV Healthcare Inc. accreditation
⇑ Center for Improvement in Healthcare Quality Accreditation
△ Commission on Accreditation of Rehabilitation Facilities (CARF) accreditation

© 2025 AHA Guide

Hospitals, U.S. / MISSISSIPPI

WEST POINT—Clay County

★ ⇧ **NORTH MISSISSIPPI MEDICAL CENTER–WEST POINT (250067)**, 150 Medical Center Drive, Zip 39773–0428; tel. 662/495–2300, **A**10 21 **F**11 13 15 28 29 30 31 32 34 35 40 43 45 48 53 57 59 65 70 72 75 76 78 79 81 85 86 87 89 97 107 108 109 110 114 119 120 127 129 132 133 135 145 146 147 148 **S** North Mississippi Health Services, Inc., Tupelo, MS
Primary Contact: Barry L. Keel, Administrator
CFO: Kay Lawler, Business Office Manager
CMO: B Keith Watson, M.D., Chief Medical Staff
CIO: Stacie Griggs, MIS Analyst
CHR: Lauren Hollis, Chief Human Resources Officer
CNO: Pamela White, Chief Nursing Officer
Web address: www.nmhs.net/westpoint
Control: Other not–for–profit (including NFP Corporation) **Service**: General medical and surgical

Staffed Beds: 49 **Admissions**: 1128 **Census**: 15 **Outpatient Visits**: 100605 **Births**: 248 **Total Expense ($000)**: 46677 **Payroll Expense ($000)**: 20592 **Personnel**: 235

WHITFIELD—Rankin County

✠ **MISSISSIPPI STATE HOSPITAL (254010)**, 3550 Highway 468 West, Zip 39193–5529, Mailing Address: P.O. Box 157–A, Zip 39193–0157; tel. 601/351–8000, (Includes WHITFIELD MEDICAL SURGICAL HOSPITAL, 3550 Highway 468 West, Building 60, Whitfield, Mississippi, Zip 39193–5529, P O Box 157A, Zip 39193–0157, tel. 601/351–8023) (Nonreporting) **A**1 3 5 10 **S** Mississippi State Department of Mental Health, Jackson, MS
Primary Contact: James G. Chastain, FACHE, Director
COO: Kelly R Breland, CPA, Director Support Services
CFO: Alicia Harris, Director Fiscal Services
CMO: Duncan Stone, D.D.S., Chief Medical Staff
CIO: Bart Uharriet, Director Information Services
CHR: Katie Storr, Director of Human Resources
CNO: Jackie Yates, R.N., Nurse Executive
Web address: www.msh.state.ms.us
Control: State, Government, Nonfederal **Service**: Psychiatric

Staffed Beds: 259

WIGGINS—Stone County

MEMORIAL HOSPITAL AT STONE COUNTY (251303), 1434 East Central Avenue, Zip 39577–9602; tel. 601/928–6600, **A**10 **F**5 7 29 34 35 40 43 46 57 59 64 89 97 107 112 114 115 119 130
Primary Contact: Kevin Holland, Administrator
Web address: https://www.gulfportmemorial.com/schospital
Control: City–county, Government, Nonfederal **Service**: General medical and surgical

Staffed Beds: 25 **Admissions**: 399 **Census**: 3 **Births**: 0 **Total Expense ($000)**: 8104 **Payroll Expense ($000)**: 4770 **Personnel**: 79

WINONA—Montgomery County

TYLER HOLMES MEMORIAL HOSPITAL (251312), 409 Tyler Holmes Drive, Zip 38967–1599; tel. 662/283–4114, **A**10 18 **F**11 15 29 34 35 40 43 50 57 59 64 68 87 104 107 111 115 119 127 130 133 148 149 153 **P**8
Primary Contact: Cori Bailey, Chief Executive Officer
CFO: Cori Bailey, Accountant
CMO: Eddie Rutherford, Director of Pharmacy
CHR: Becky Corley, Director Human Resources
Web address: www.thmh.org/
Control: County, Government, Nonfederal **Service**: General medical and surgical

Staffed Beds: 25 **Admissions**: 399 **Census**: 8 **Outpatient Visits**: 11998 **Births**: 0 **Total Expense ($000)**: 19578 **Payroll Expense ($000)**: 10471 **Personnel**: 142

YAZOO CITY—Yazoo County

★ **BAPTIST MEDICAL CENTER – YAZOO (251313)**, 823 Grand Avenue, Zip 39194–3233; tel. 662/746–2261, **A**10 18 **F**3 8 11 15 29 34 40 45 46 56 57 59 65 68 81 97 107 111 114 119 127 133 145 148 153 154 167 **S** Baptist Memorial Health Care Corporation, Memphis, TN
Primary Contact: Mac Flynt, Chief Executive Officer and Administrator
COO: Marsha Jones, R.N., Director Nursing
CFO: James L Miller, Chief Financial Officer
CMO: Marion Sigrest, M.D., Chief of Staff
CIO: Benton D Estes, Materials Management
CHR: Stephanie Washington, Director Community Relations and Human Resources
CNO: Marsha Jones, R.N., Director of Nursing
Web address: www.mbhs.org/locations/baptist-medical-center-yazoo/
Control: Other not–for–profit (including NFP Corporation) **Service**: General medical and surgical

Staffed Beds: 25 **Admissions**: 519 **Census**: 10 **Outpatient Visits**: 27661 **Births**: 1 **Personnel**: 143

MISSOURI

ALBANY—Gentry County

★ **MOSAIC MEDICAL CENTER – ALBANY (261328)**, 705 North College Street, Zip 64402–1433; tel. 660/726–3941, **A**10 18 **F**3 11 15 18 28 29 30 32 34 35 39 40 41 44 45 50 53 56 57 59 64 65 66 68 74 75 77 79 81 82 84 85 86 87 89 90 93 97 103 104 107 108 110 111 115 119 127 128 130 131 132 133 135 143 146 148 149 154 156 169 **P**6 **S** Mosaic Life Care, Saint Joseph, MO
Primary Contact: Katie Dias, D.O., President
CMO: Angelia Martin, M.D., Chief of Staff
CIO: James Crouch, Vice President Technical Services
CHR: Vickie Cline, Director Human Resources
CNO: Miranda Floyd, R.N., Chief Nursing Officer
Web address: https://www.mymlc.com/Main/Location/albany-mo/mosaic-medical-center-albany/
Control: Other not–for–profit (including NFP Corporation) **Service:** General medical and surgical

Staffed Beds: 19 **Admissions:** 251 **Census:** 4 **Outpatient Visits:** 30224
Births: 0 **Total Expense ($000):** 25705 **Payroll Expense ($000):** 10850
Personnel: 129

APPLETON CITY—St. Clair County

★ **ELLETT MEMORIAL HOSPITAL (261301)**, 610 North Ohio Avenue, Zip 64724–1609, Mailing Address: P.O. Box 6, Zip 64724–0006; tel. 660/476–2111, **A**10 18 **F**3 7 11 40 90 107 111 114 119 127 128 130 133 143 146 147 154
Primary Contact: Laura Smith, R.N., Chief Executive Officer
CMO: Richard R Dailey, D.O., President Medical Staff
CIO: Gina Raybourn, Director Health Information
CHR: Cathy Grishow, Director Human Resources
Web address: www.ellettmemorial.com
Control: Hospital district or authority, Government, Nonfederal **Service:** General medical and surgical

Staffed Beds: 12 **Admissions:** 121 **Census:** 2 **Outpatient Visits:** 2032
Births: 0 **Total Expense ($000):** 10160 **Payroll Expense ($000):** 4821
Personnel: 71

AURORA—Lawrence County

✠ **MERCY HOSPITAL AURORA (261316)**, 500 Porter Street, Zip 65605–2365; tel. 417/678–2122, **A**1 10 18 **F**3 11 13 15 28 29 30 34 35 40 41 45 50 57 59 64 65 75 76 77 81 85 86 87 89 93 94 96 107 110 111 114 119 129 130 132 133 148 149 154 169 **S** Mercy, Chesterfield, MO
Primary Contact: Valerie Davis, Administrator
CMO: Christie Hurt, M.D., Chief of Staff and Medical Director
CHR: George Roden, Vice President Human Resources
Web address: www.stjohns.com/aboutus/aurora.aspx
Control: Church operated, Nongovernment, not–for–profit **Service:** General medical and surgical

Staffed Beds: 25 **Admissions:** 734 **Census:** 9 **Outpatient Visits:** 40632
Births: 104 **Total Expense ($000):** 24020 **Payroll Expense ($000):** 12148
Personnel: 147

BELTON—Cass County

✠ **BELTON REGIONAL MEDICAL CENTER (260214)**, 17065 South 71 Highway, Zip 64012–4631; tel. 816/348–1200, **A**1 2 3 10 **F**3 15 29 30 31 34 35 37 40 43 45 57 59 65 68 70 74 75 77 78 79 81 82 85 90 93 107 108 110 111 118 119 126 129 130 131 132 146 149 154 **S** HCA Healthcare, Nashville, TN
Primary Contact: Todd Krass, Chief Executive Officer
CFO: Ronnie Thompson, Chief Financial Officer
CIO: Sarah Richardson, Director Information Systems
CHR: Jessica Sulzen, Director Human Resources
CNO: Robyn Miller, Chief Nursing Officer
Web address: www.beltonregionalmedicalcenter.com
Control: Corporation, Investor–owned (for–profit) **Service:** General medical and surgical

Staffed Beds: 62 **Admissions:** 3406 **Census:** 32 **Outpatient Visits:** 34241
Births: 0 **Total Expense ($000):** 77185 **Payroll Expense ($000):** 27821
Personnel: 333

BETHANY—Harrison County

★ **HARRISON COUNTY COMMUNITY HOSPITAL (261312)**, 2600 Miller Street, Zip 64424–2701; tel. 660/425–2211, **A**10 18 **F**3 11 12 15 18 28 29 34 35 40 41 44 45 49 50 53 56 57 59 62 64 65 67 68 75 77 82 85 87 89 90 92 93 96 97 102 103 104 107 108 110 111 115 119 127 128 129 130 131 133 135 143 147 148 149 150 153 154 156 157 165 169
Primary Contact: Christina L. Gillespie, Chief Executive Officer
CFO: Lee Ann Miles, Chief Financial Officer
CMO: Terry E. Hall, Chief of Staff
CIO: Will Holt, Director Information Technology
CHR: Cathie Chalfant, Director Human Resources
CNO: Crystal Hicks, R.N., Chief Nursing Officer
Web address: www.hcchospital.org
Control: Hospital district or authority, Government, Nonfederal **Service:** General medical and surgical

Staffed Beds: 19 **Admissions:** 377 **Census:** 6 **Outpatient Visits:** 29432
Births: 0 **Total Expense ($000):** 30292 **Payroll Expense ($000):** 13065
Personnel: 197

BLUE SPRINGS—Jackson County

□ **ST. MARY'S MEDICAL CENTER (260193)**, 201 Northwest R D Mize Road, Zip 64014–2518; tel. 816/228–5900, **A**1 3 5 10 **F**3 15 18 20 22 26 28 29 30 34 35 37 40 44 45 49 50 53 56 57 59 64 68 70 74 75 77 79 80 81 82 85 86 87 90 93 96 107 108 110 111 115 119 129 130 135 146 148 149 154 167 **S** Prime Healthcare, Ontario, CA
Primary Contact: Kelly Pearce, R.N., FACHE, Chief Executive Officer
Web address: www.stmaryskc.com/
Control: Corporation, Investor–owned (for–profit) **Service:** General medical and surgical

Staffed Beds: 83 **Admissions:** 3371 **Census:** 35 **Outpatient Visits:** 36768
Births: 0 **Total Expense ($000):** 79705 **Payroll Expense ($000):** 27268
Personnel: 364

BOLIVAR—Polk County

✠ **CITIZENS MEMORIAL HOSPITAL (260195)**, 1500 North Oakland Avenue, Zip 65613–3011; tel. 417/326–6000, **A**1 10 20 **F**3 4 5 7 11 13 15 18 20 22 26 28 29 31 34 35 40 43 44 51 56 57 58 59 64 66 70 71 74 75 76 77 78 79 80 81 82 85 86 87 89 90 93 94 96 97 98 99 100 102 103 104 107 108 110 111 115 117 118 119 126 127 128 129 130 131 132 133 135 143 146 147 148 149 151 154 155 156 160 161 169 **P**6
Primary Contact: Michael Calhoun, Chief Executive Officer
COO: Jeff Miller, Safety Officer
CMO: Ronald A. Evans, M.D., Chief Medical Officer
CIO: Denni McColm, Chief Information Officer
CHR: Jeremy MacLaughlin, Director Human Resources
CNO: Lesa Stock, R.N., Chief Clinical Officer
Web address: www.citizensmemorial.com
Control: Hospital district or authority, Government, Nonfederal **Service:** General medical and surgical

Staffed Beds: 72 **Admissions:** 2717 **Census:** 31 **Outpatient Visits:** 458200
Births: 525 **Total Expense ($000):** 212137 **Payroll Expense ($000):** 99206
Personnel: 1334

BONNE TERRE—St. Francois County

★ **PARKLAND HEALTH CENTER–BONNE TERRE (260779)**, 7245 Raider Road, Zip 63628; tel. 573/358–1400, **A**10 **F**3 11 29 30 34 35 40 50 57 59 68 75 77 86 90 102 107 119 129 130 143 146 149 154 157 160 161 164 167 **S** BJC Health System, Saint Louis, MO
Primary Contact: Annette D. Schnabel, FACHE, President
CFO: Cheri L. Goldsmith, Director Financial Services
Web address: www.parklandhealthcenter.org
Control: Other not–for–profit (including NFP Corporation) **Service:** General medical and surgical

Staffed Beds: 3 **Admissions:** 9 **Census:** 1 **Outpatient Visits:** 10456
Births: 0 **Personnel:** 31

Hospital, Medicare Provider Number, Address, Telephone, Approval, Facility, and Physician Codes, Health Care System

★ American Hospital Association (AHA) membership
□ The Joint Commission accreditation
○ Healthcare Facilities Accreditation Program
◇ DNV Healthcare Inc. accreditation
⇑ Center for Improvement in Healthcare Quality Accreditation
△ Commission on Accreditation of Rehabilitation Facilities (CARF) accreditation

Hospitals, U.S. / MISSOURI

BRANSON—Taney County

△ ⇑ **COX MEDICAL CENTER BRANSON (260094)**, 525 Branson Landing Boulevard, Zip 65616-2052, Mailing Address: P.O. Box 650, Zip 65615-0650; tel. 417/335-7000, **A**7 10 21 **F**3 11 13 15 17 18 20 22 26 28 29 30 31 32 34 35 40 45 48 50 53 56 57 59 62 64 65 66 68 70 74 75 76 77 78 79 80 81 84 85 86 87 89 90 93 98 105 107 108 110 111 114 117 118 119 120 121 123 127 129 130 131 132 135 144 146 147 148 149 150 154 156 160 161 **P**6 **S** CoxHealth, Springfield, MO
Primary Contact: William K. Mahoney, FACHE, President and Senior Vice President, Community Hospital Group
CFO: David Strong, Chief Financial Officer/Vice President Finance
CMO: James Duff, M.D., Chief Medical Officer
CHR: Carol Murrow, Vice President Business Development
CNO: Lynne Yaggy, MSN, R.N., Vice President, Chief Nursing Officer
Web address: www.coxhealth.com
Control: Other not-for-profit (including NFP Corporation) **Service**: General medical and surgical

Staffed Beds: 106 **Admissions**: 6004 **Census**: 80 **Outpatient Visits**: 177864 **Births**: 528 **Total Expense ($000)**: 211630 **Payroll Expense ($000)**: 73486 **Personnel**: 1129

BRIDGETON—St. Louis County

✠ △ **SSM HEALTH DEPAUL HOSPITAL – ST. LOUIS (260104)**, 12303 De Paul Drive, Zip 63044-2512; tel. 314/344-6000, (Total facility includes 52 beds in nursing home-type unit) **A**1 2 5 7 10 19 **F**3 4 5 8 11 12 13 15 17 18 20 22 24 26 28 29 30 31 34 35 38 40 44 45 49 50 51 53 55 56 57 58 59 60 61 64 65 70 73 74 75 76 78 79 82 84 85 86 87 89 98 99 100 101 102 104 105 107 108 110 111 114 115 117 118 119 120 121 122 126 128 129 130 132 135 144 146 147 148 149 153 154 164 165 169 **S** SSM Health, Saint Louis, MO
Primary Contact: Deborah Berini, President
CFO: Eileen Lamm, Regional Chief Financial Officer
CIO: James Hamner, Regional Information Technology Director
CHR: Rodney Lacy, Leader Human Resources
Web address: https://www.ssmhealth.com/locations/st-louis/depaul-hospital-st-louis
Control: Church operated, Nongovernment, not-for-profit **Service**: General medical and surgical

Staffed Beds: 523 **Admissions**: 18288 **Census**: 383 **Outpatient Visits**: 227568 **Births**: 743 **Total Expense ($000)**: 591262 **Payroll Expense ($000)**: 228145 **Personnel**: 1251

SSM REHABILITATION HOSPITAL See SSM Select Rehabilitation Hospital

BROOKFIELD—Linn County

PERSHING MEMORIAL HOSPITAL (261307), 130 East Lockling Avenue, Zip 64628-2337, Mailing Address: P.O. Box 408, Zip 64628-0408; tel. 660/258-2222, **A**10 **F**3 11 15 22 29 30 34 40 45 57 59 64 75 77 81 85 89 93 97 107 115 119 127 129 130 133 146 149 154 **P**6
Primary Contact: Karla Clubine, Chief Executive Officer
CFO: Gary R Tandy, Chief Financial Officer
CMO: B K Knowles, D.O., Chief of Staff
CIO: Elaine Sutton, Chief Information Officer
CHR: Amy Sayre, Director Human Resources
Web address: www.phsmo.org
Control: Other not-for-profit (including NFP Corporation) **Service**: General medical and surgical

Staffed Beds: 25 **Admissions**: 280 **Census**: 4 **Outpatient Visits**: 19752 **Births**: 0 **Total Expense ($000)**: 21373 **Payroll Expense ($000)**: 8082 **Personnel**: 118

BUTLER—Bates County

★ **BATES COUNTY MEMORIAL HOSPITAL (260034)**, 615 West Nursery Street, Zip 64730-1840, Mailing Address: P.O. Box 370, Zip 64730-0370; tel. 660/200-7000, **A**10 20 **F**3 7 11 15 18 28 29 30 31 34 40 45 50 59 64 68 70 77 78 79 81 87 90 93 107 108 109 110 111 115 116 118 119 127 129 130 132 133 148 154 155 **P**6
Primary Contact: Greg Weaver, Chief Executive Officer
CFO: Terri Floyd, Chief Financial Officer
CMO: James Patterson, M.D., Chief of Medical Staff
CIO: Marcia Cook, Director Information Technology
CHR: Melinda R Jackson, Director Human Resources
CNO: Rebecca Tarver, Chief Nursing Officer
Web address: www.bcmhospital.com
Control: County, Government, Nonfederal **Service**: General medical and surgical

Staffed Beds: 49 **Admissions**: 323 **Census**: 4 **Outpatient Visits**: 48944 **Births**: 0 **Total Expense ($000)**: 46635 **Payroll Expense ($000)**: 17627 **Personnel**: 276

CAMERON—Clinton County

CAMERON REGIONAL MEDICAL CENTER (260057), 1600 East Evergreen, Zip 64429-2400, Mailing Address: P.O. Box 557, Zip 64429-0557; tel. 816/632-2101, **A**3 5 10 **F**3 11 12 13 15 28 29 30 31 34 35 39 45 46 47 49 56 57 59 61 62 63 64 68 69 70 74 75 76 77 78 79 81 82 83 86 87 89 90 93 94 98 100 107 110 111 115 119 127 128 129 130 131 133 143 146 147 148 154 156
Primary Contact: Joseph F. Abrutz Jr, Administrator
CFO: Rosa Patti, Chief Financial Officer
CIO: Bill Walser, Coordinator Technology
CHR: Pat Bestgen, Manager Human Resources
Web address: www.cameronregional.org
Control: Other not-for-profit (including NFP Corporation) **Service**: General medical and surgical

Staffed Beds: 60 **Admissions**: 1329 **Census**: 24 **Outpatient Visits**: 328920 **Births**: 94 **Total Expense ($000)**: 72591 **Payroll Expense ($000)**: 33868 **Personnel**: 538

CAPE GIRARDEAU—Cape Girardeau County

LANDMARK HOSPITAL OF CAPE GIRARDEAU (262015), 3255 Independence Street, Zip 63701-4914; tel. 573/335-1091, (Nonreporting) **A**10 22 **S** Landmark Hospitals, Cape Girardeau, MO
Primary Contact: Deborah Sabella, R.N., Chief Executive Officer
COO: Michael L Norman, Executive Vice President and Chief Operating Officer
CFO: Richard H Hogan, CPA, Chief Financial Officer
CMO: William Fritsch, M.D., Medical Director
CIO: Renee Hesselrode, Director Health Information Management
CHR: Angela Kisner, Director Human Resources and Coordinator Medical Staff
Web address: www.landmarkhospitals.com
Control: Partnership, Investor-owned (for-profit) **Service**: Acute long-term care hospital

Staffed Beds: 30

✠ **MERCY HOSPITAL SOUTHEAST (260110)**, 1701 Lacey Street, Zip 63701-5230; tel. 573/334-4822, **A**1 5 10 19 **F**3 13 15 17 18 20 22 24 26 28 29 30 31 32 34 35 37 40 47 48 49 50 51 53 54 57 58 59 60 63 65 70 72 73 74 75 76 77 78 79 80 81 84 85 86 87 89 90 92 93 96 107 108 109 110 111 115 117 119 120 121 123 124 126 127 128 130 131 135 146 147 148 149 154 169 **S** Mercy, Chesterfield, MO
Primary Contact: Ryan Geib, President, Mercy Southeast Communities
CFO: Bruce Fairbanks, Vice President and Chief Financial Officer
CMO: Matt Shoemaker, D.O., Vice President and Chief Medical Officer
CHR: Lincoln Scott, Vice President Human Resources
Web address: www.sehealth.org/
Control: Other not-for-profit (including NFP Corporation) **Service**: General medical and surgical

Staffed Beds: 130 **Admissions**: 6815 **Census**: 97 **Outpatient Visits**: 518184 **Births**: 774 **Total Expense ($000)**: 468876 **Payroll Expense ($000)**: 151250 **Personnel**: 1735

✠ **SAINT FRANCIS MEDICAL CENTER (260183)**, 211 St Francis Drive, Zip 63703-5049; tel. 573/331-3000, **A**1 2 3 10 19 **F**3 11 13 15 17 18 20 22 24 26 28 29 30 31 34 35 40 43 44 45 46 49 50 51 53 55 57 59 60 61 63 65 70 72 73 74 75 76 77 78 79 80 81 82 84 85 86 87 89 90 92 93 107 108 110 111 114 115 116 117 118 119 120 121 123 124 126 129 130 131 132 142 144 145 146 147 148 149 157 167 169 **P**6
Primary Contact: Justin Davison, President and Chief Executive Officer
CMO: James Schell, M.D., Vice President Medical Affairs
CHR: Teri Kreitzer, Director Human Resources
CNO: Jeannie Fadler, R.N., Vice President Patient Care Services
Web address: www.sfmc.net
Control: Other not-for-profit (including NFP Corporation) **Service**: General medical and surgical

Staffed Beds: 306 **Admissions**: 8537 **Census**: 117 **Outpatient Visits**: 243368 **Births**: 1123 **Total Expense ($000)**: 569893 **Payroll Expense ($000)**: 304088 **Personnel**: 2689

CARROLLTON—Carroll County

★ **CARROLL COUNTY MEMORIAL HOSPITAL (261332)**, 1502 North Jefferson Street, Zip 64633-1948; tel. 660/542-1695, **A**10 18 **F**3 11 15 18 28 29 31 34 35 38 40 45 50 53 59 62 64 65 68 69 74 75 77 78 79 81 82 90 93 96 97 103 104 107 108 110 111 115 119 125 127 128 129 130 131 133 143 146 148 149 154 165 167 **P**6
Primary Contact: Scott D. Thoreson, FACHE, Chief Executive Officer
COO: Tim Braun, Chief Operation Officer
CFO: Amy Ireland, Chief Financial Officer
CMO: Richard Smith, Chief of Staff
CIO: Bill Bollinger, Chief Information Officer
CHR: Michael Schubach, Chief People Officer
CNO: Jeanne Rector, Chief Nursing Officer
Web address: www.carrollcountyhospital.org
Control: Other not-for-profit (including NFP Corporation) **Service**: General medical and surgical

Staffed Beds: 25 **Admissions**: 326 **Census**: 4 **Outpatient Visits**: 34864 **Births**: 0 **Total Expense ($000)**: 40782 **Payroll Expense ($000)**: 15581 **Personnel**: 245

CARTHAGE—Jasper County

★ **MERCY HOSPITAL CARTHAGE (261338)**, 3125 Dr Russell Smith Way, Zip 64836-7402; tel. 417/358-8121, **A**10 18 **F**3 6 7 8 11 12 15 28 29 30 31 34 35 40 45 50 53 59 64 67 68 69 74 75 79 81 85 86 89 107 108 110 111 115 119 127 128 129 130 132 133 135 146 147 149 154 156 **P**6 **S** Mercy, Chesterfield, MO
Primary Contact: Jeremy Drinkwitz, President, Mercy Joplin Communities
CFO: Douglas Culver, Chief Financial Officer
CIO: Cheryl Lease-Homeyer, Lead Information Technology Business Partner
CHR: Colette St. Peter, Senior Manager Human Resources
Web address: https://www.mercy.net/practice/mercy-hospital-carthage/
Control: Church operated, Nongovernment, not-for-profit **Service**: General medical and surgical

Staffed Beds: 25 **Admissions**: 834 **Census**: 15 **Outpatient Visits**: 86032 **Births**: 0 **Total Expense ($000)**: 53813 **Payroll Expense ($000)**: 20549 **Personnel**: 239

CASSVILLE—Barry County

MERCY HOSPITAL CASSVILLE (261317), 94 Main Street, Zip 65625-1610; tel. 417/847-6000, **A**1 10 18 **F**3 11 15 28 29 30 34 35 40 41 45 50 53 57 59 64 68 75 77 81 89 93 103 107 108 110 111 114 119 132 133 135 148 149 153 154 **S** Mercy, Chesterfield, MO
Primary Contact: Valerie Davis, Administrator
CFO: Sherry Clouse Day, CPA, Chief Financial Officer
CMO: Jamie Zengotita, M.D., Chief Medical Staff
CHR: George Roden, Vice President Human Resources
Web address: www.mercy.net/northwestarar/practice/mercy-hospital-cassville
Control: Church operated, Nongovernment, not-for-profit **Service**: General medical and surgical

Staffed Beds: 18 **Admissions**: 417 **Census**: 5 **Outpatient Visits**: 38760 **Births**: 0 **Total Expense ($000)**: 19234 **Payroll Expense ($000)**: 9224 **Personnel**: 111

CHESTERFIELD—St. Louis County

△ **MERCY REHABILITATION HOSPITAL ST. LOUIS (263029)**, 14561 North Outer Forty Road, Zip 63017; tel. 314/881-4000, **A**1 7 10 **F**16 29 30 90 148 **S** Kindred Healthcare, Chesterfield, MO
Primary Contact: Joseph Koehler, Market Chief Executive Officer
CMO: Siresha Samudrala, M.D., Medical Director
Web address: https://www.mercy.net/practice/mercy-rehabilitation-hospital-st-louis/
Control: Partnership, Investor-owned (for-profit) **Service**: Rehabilitation

Staffed Beds: 90 **Admissions**: 1871 **Census**: 62 **Outpatient Visits**: 0 **Births**: 0 **Total Expense ($000)**: 29607 **Payroll Expense ($000)**: 15119 **Personnel**: 157

ST. LUKE'S HOSPITAL (260179), 232 South Woods Mill Road, Zip 63017-3417; tel. 314/434-1500, **A**1 2 3 5 10 **F**3 11 13 15 17 18 20 22 24 26 28 29 30 31 34 35 36 38 39 40 44 45 46 49 50 51 52 53 54 56 57 58 59 60 61 62 63 64 65 66 68 70 71 73 74 75 76 77 78 79 81 82 84 85 86 87 89 90 93 97 107 110 111 114 115 117 118 119 120 121 123 124 126 128 129 130 131 132 135 142 144 145 146 147 148 149 154 156 160 167 169 **S** St. Luke's Hospital, Chesterfield, MO
Primary Contact: Andrew Bagnall, FACHE, President and Chief Executive Officer
COO: Diane Ray, R.N., FACHE, Senior Vice President and Chief Operating Officer; Network Chief Nursing Officer
CFO: Scott H. Johnson, Executive Vice President and Chief Financial Officer
CIO: William Meyers, Chief Information Officer
CHR: Janette L. Taaffe, Vice President, Human Resource
CNO: Diane Ray, R.N., FACHE, Senior Vice President and Chief Operating Officer; Network Chief Nursing Officer
Web address: www.stlukes-stl.com
Control: Other not-for-profit (including NFP Corporation) **Service**: General medical and surgical

Staffed Beds: 488 **Admissions**: 14089 **Census**: 196 **Outpatient Visits**: 43224 **Births**: 1356 **Total Expense ($000)**: 582022 **Payroll Expense ($000)**: 239604 **Personnel**: 3226

△ **ST. LUKE'S REHABILITATION HOSPITAL (263030)**, 14709 Olive Boulevard, Zip 63017-2221; tel. 314/317-5700, **A**1 7 10 **F**3 29 34 68 74 75 79 86 87 90 91 94 96 100 119 130 132 135 148 154 **S** PAM Health, Enola, PA
Primary Contact: Bruce Eady, R.N., MSN, Chief Executive Officer
Web address: https://postacutemedical.com/facilities/find-facility/rehabilitation-hospitals/St-Lukes-Rehabilitation-Hospital
Control: Partnership, Investor-owned (for-profit) **Service**: Rehabilitation

Staffed Beds: 35 **Admissions**: 913 **Census**: 28 **Outpatient Visits**: 0 **Births**: 0 **Total Expense ($000)**: 16982 **Payroll Expense ($000)**: 4933 **Personnel**: 128

CHILLICOTHE—Livingston County

HEDRICK MEDICAL CENTER (261321), 2799 North Washington Street, Zip 64601-2902; tel. 660/646-1480, **A**1 10 18 **F**3 4 11 13 15 18 28 29 30 31 34 35 40 44 45 50 59 64 67 68 69 70 74 75 76 77 78 79 81 82 85 86 87 89 90 92 93 96 97 102 104 107 108 110 111 115 118 119 127 128 130 131 133 141 146 147 148 149 154 169 **S** BJC Health System, Saint Louis, MO
Primary Contact: Catherine Hamilton, MSN, R.N., Administrator
CFO: Janet Buckman, Chief Financial Officer
CHR: Lisa A Hecker, Director Human Resources
CNO: Catherine Hamilton, MSN, R.N., Chief Nursing Officer
Web address: www.saintlukeskc.org
Control: Other not-for-profit (including NFP Corporation) **Service**: General medical and surgical

Staffed Beds: 21 **Admissions**: 789 **Census**: 12 **Outpatient Visits**: 72856 **Births**: 117 **Total Expense ($000)**: 61527 **Payroll Expense ($000)**: 24346 **Personnel**: 327

CLINTON—Henry County

GOLDEN VALLEY MEMORIAL HEALTHCARE (260175), 1600 North Second Street, Zip 64735-1192; tel. 660/885-5511, **A**1 10 **F**3 7 11 12 13 15 17 18 28 29 30 31 34 35 37 38 40 45 47 48 49 53 57 59 62 63 64 65 68 70 74 75 76 77 78 79 81 85 86 87 89 90 93 96 107 108 111 115 117 118 120 121 123 124 127 129 130 131 132 133 143 146 147 148 149 154 156 164
Primary Contact: Craig Thompson, FACHE, Chief Executive Officer
CFO: Tammy R Nadler, Chief Financial Officer
CIO: Mike Gaul, Director Information Technology
CHR: Greg Shannon, Chief Human Resources Officer
CNO: Lynnette Hayes, Chief Nursing Officer
Web address: www.gvmh.org
Control: Hospital district or authority, Government, Nonfederal **Service**: General medical and surgical

Staffed Beds: 49 **Admissions**: 1978 **Census**: 18 **Outpatient Visits**: 209664 **Births**: 301 **Total Expense ($000)**: 144721 **Payroll Expense ($000)**: 58327 **Personnel**: 958

Hospital, Medicare Provider Number, Address, Telephone, Approval, Facility, and Physician Codes, Health Care System

★ American Hospital Association (AHA) membership
☐ The Joint Commission accreditation
○ Healthcare Facilities Accreditation Program
◇ DNV Healthcare Inc. accreditation
⇧ Center for Improvement in Healthcare Quality Accreditation
△ Commission on Accreditation of Rehabilitation Facilities (CARF) accreditation

© 2025 AHA Guide

Hospitals, U.S. / MISSOURI

COLUMBIA—Boone County

BOONE HOSPITAL CENTER (260068), 1600 East Broadway, Zip 65201–5844; tel. 573/815–8000, **A**1 3 5 10 **F**3 4 7 11 12 13 15 17 18 19 20 22 24 26 27 28 29 30 31 32 34 35 36 37 38 39 40 41 45 46 47 48 49 50 51 52 53 54 55 56 57 58 59 60 61 63 64 65 68 70 71 72 73 74 75 76 77 78 79 80 81 82 83 84 85 86 87 89 90 91 93 94 96 97 100 101 102 103 107 108 110 111 115 117 118 119 126 129 130 131 132 134 135 141 143 146 147 148 149 150 154 155 156 157 160 161 164 167 169 **P**6
Primary Contact: Brady Dubois, Chief Executive Officer
COO: Christian Jones, Chief Operating Officer
CFO: Randy Morrow, Vice President and Chief Operating Officer
CMO: Robin Blount, Chief Medical Officer
CHR: Michelle Zvanut, Vice President Human Resources
Web address: https://boone.health/
Control: Other not–for–profit (including NFP Corporation) **Service**: General medical and surgical

Staffed Beds: 281 **Admissions**: 12841 **Census**: 158 **Outpatient Visits**: 256480 **Births**: 1360 **Total Expense ($000)**: 357152 **Payroll Expense ($000)**: 114058 **Personnel**: 1665

CENTERPOINTE HOSPITAL OF COLUMBIA (264032), 1201 International Drive, Zip 65202; tel. 573/615–2001, (Nonreporting) **A**1 10
Primary Contact: Robert Marsh, Chief Executive Officer
Web address: www.centerpointehospitalcolumbia.com
Control: Corporation, Investor–owned (for–profit) **Service**: Psychiatric

Staffed Beds: 56

COLUMBIA REGIONAL HOSPITAL See Women's and Children's Hospital

COLUMBIA VAMC See Harry S. Truman Memorial Veterans' Hospital

ELLIS FISCHEL CANCER CENTER See University Hospital, Columbia

ELLIS FISCHEL CANCER CTR See Ellis Fischel Cancer Center

HARRY S. TRUMAN MEMORIAL VETERANS' HOSPITAL, 800 Hospital Drive, Zip 65201–5275; tel. 573/814–6000, (Nonreporting) **A**1 3 5 **S** Department of Veterans Affairs, Washington, DC
Primary Contact: Christopher Myhaver, FACHE, Medical Center Director
COO: Robert G Ritter, FACHE, Associate Director
CFO: Deborah Henderson, Acting Chief Financial Officer
CMO: Lana Zerrer, M.D., Chief of Staff
CIO: Donna Krause, Chief Information Officer
CHR: Jimmy Powell, Manager Human Resources
Web address: www.columbiamo.va.gov
Control: Veterans Affairs, Government, federal **Service**: General medical and surgical

Staffed Beds: 130

LANDMARK HOSPITAL OF COLUMBIA (262020), 604 Old 63 North, Zip 65201–6308; tel. 573/499–6600, (Nonreporting) **A**10 22 **S** Landmark Hospitals, Cape Girardeau, MO
Primary Contact: Kerry Ashment, Chief Executive Officer
Web address: https://www.landmarkhospitals.com/critical-care-hospital-system/columbia-mo/
Control: Partnership, Investor–owned (for–profit) **Service**: Rehabilitation

Staffed Beds: 23

RUSK REHABILITATION HOSPITAL (263027), 315 Business Loop 70 West, Zip 65203–3248; tel. 573/817–2703, (Nonreporting) **A**1 3 5 10 **S** Encompass Health Corporation, Birmingham, AL
Primary Contact: Monica Gooch, Chief Executive Officer
CFO: Jeff Reese, Chief Financial Officer
CMO: Gregory Worsowicz, M.D., Medical Director
CHR: Robin Prater, Director Human Resources
CNO: Lori Mann, R.N., MSN, Chief Nursing Officer
Web address: https://www.encompasshealth.com/locations/ruskrehab
Control: Partnership, Investor–owned (for–profit) **Service**: Rehabilitation

Staffed Beds: 60

UNIVERSITY HOSPITAL (260141), 1 Hospital Drive, Zip 65212–0001; tel. 573/882–4141, (Includes ELLIS FISCHEL CANCER CENTER, 115 Business Loop 70 West, Columbia, Missouri, Zip 65203, tel. 573/882–5460; WOMEN'S AND CHILDREN'S HOSPITAL, 404 Keene Street, Columbia, Missouri, Zip 65201–6626, tel. 573/875–9000; Kimberly Reeks, Director) **A**2 3 5 8 10 19 21 **F**3 5 7 9 11 12 13 15 17 18 19 20 22 24 26 28 29 30 31 32 33 34 35 36 37 38 39 40 41 43 44 45 46 47 48 49 50 51 52 54 55 56 57 58 59 60 61 64 65 66 68 70 71 72 74 75 76 77 78 79 80 81 82 83 84 85 86 87 88 89 91 92 93 96 97 98 99 100 101 102 104 107 108 110 111 114 115 116 117 118 119 120 121 123 124 126 129 130 131 132 134 135 138 141 142 143 144 145 146 147 148 149 151 154 157 160 161 162 164 166 167 169 **S** University of Missouri Health Care, Columbia, MO
Primary Contact: Ric A. Ransom, Chief Executive Officer
COO: Katrina Lambrecht, JD, Chief Operating Officer
CFO: Kevin Necas, Chief Financial Officer
CMO: Stevan Whitt, M.D., Chief Medical Officer
Web address: www.muhealth.org
Control: State, Government, Nonfederal **Service**: General medical and surgical

Staffed Beds: 600 **Admissions**: 27282 **Census**: 446 **Outpatient Visits**: 1238736 **Births**: 2514 **Total Expense ($000)**: 1408435 **Payroll Expense ($000)**: 463924 **Personnel**: 6002

UNIVERSITY OF MISSOURI HEALTH CARE See University Hospital

DEXTER—Stoddard County

MERCY HOSPITAL STODDARD (260160), 1200 North One Mile Road, Zip 63841–1000; tel. 573/624–5566, **A**10 **F**11 15 28 29 31 34 39 40 45 59 65 70 75 77 78 81 85 89 90 93 97 98 107 110 111 115 118 119 127 130 133 135 146 154 **S** Mercy, Chesterfield, MO
Primary Contact: Sue Ann Williams, Chief Executive Officer
Web address: www.sehealth.org
Control: Other not–for–profit (including NFP Corporation) **Service**: General medical and surgical

Staffed Beds: 36 **Admissions**: 1350 **Census**: 13 **Outpatient Visits**: 92120 **Births**: 0 **Total Expense ($000)**: 53945 **Payroll Expense ($000)**: 17803 **Personnel**: 228

EL DORADO SPRINGS—Cedar County

CEDAR COUNTY MEMORIAL HOSPITAL (261323), 1401 South Park Street, Zip 64744–2037; tel. 417/876–2511, **A**10 18 **F**3 11 18 28 29 34 35 40 45 46 50 56 57 59 65 74 77 81 83 90 93 97 102 107 110 111 114 119 127 129 130 133 148 154 165 **P**6
Primary Contact: Terry Nichols, Chief Executive Officer
CFO: Carla Gilbert, Director Finance
CMO: R. John Torontow, M.D., Chief Medical Staff
CIO: Lois Willmore, Supervisor Health Information Management
CHR: Diana Pyle, Director Human Resources and Executive Assistant to Chief Executive Officer
CNO: Drew Alexander, Chief Nursing Officer
Web address: https://www.ccmh.co/
Control: County, Government, Nonfederal **Service**: General medical and surgical

Staffed Beds: 25 **Admissions**: 283 **Census**: 4 **Outpatient Visits**: 12248 **Births**: 0 **Total Expense ($000)**: 17698 **Payroll Expense ($000)**: 5045 **Personnel**: 132

EXCELSIOR SPRINGS—Clay County

EXCELSIOR SPRINGS HOSPITAL (261322), 1700 Rainbow Boulevard, Zip 64024–1190; tel. 816/630–6081, (Nonreporting) **A**10 18
Primary Contact: Kristen DeHart, Chief Executive Officer
CMO: Paul Torres, M.D., Medical Staff President
CHR: Kim Schweizer, Director Human Resources
Web address: www.ESHospital.org
Control: City, Government, Nonfederal **Service**: General medical and surgical

Staffed Beds: 20

Hospitals, U.S. / MISSOURI

FAIRFAX—Atchison County

★ ⇧ **COMMUNITY HOSPITAL–FAIRFAX (261303)**, 26136 US Highway 59, Zip 64446–9105, Mailing Address: P.O. Box 107, Zip 64446–0107; tel. 660/686–2211, **A**10 18 21 **F**11 15 18 28 29 30 34 40 45 50 57 59 64 75 76 79 81 85 87 89 93 96 97 101 103 104 107 110 111 114 119 127 130 132 133 148 149
Primary Contact: Julie L. Jones, R.N., Chief Executive Officer
COO: Ann Schlueter, Chief Operating Officer
CFO: Jon Davis, Chief Financial Officer
CMO: Richard Aron Burke, M.D., Chief Medical Officer
CIO: Chris Hedlund, Director Information Systems
Web address: www.fairfaxmed.com
Control: Other not–for–profit (including NFP Corporation) **Service**: General medical and surgical

Staffed Beds: 18 **Admissions**: 304 **Census**: 5 **Outpatient Visits**: 3042 **Births**: 50 **Total Expense ($000)**: 23327 **Payroll Expense ($000)**: 9244 **Personnel**: 55

FARMINGTON—St. Francois County

✠ **PARKLAND HEALTH CENTER – FARMINGTON COMMUNITY (260163)**, 1101 West Liberty Street, Zip 63640–1921; tel. 573/756–6451, **A**1 10 **F**3 11 13 15 18 20 22 26 28 29 30 31 34 35 40 45 46 49 50 53 57 58 59 60 64 65 68 69 70 75 76 77 78 79 81 85 86 87 90 93 97 102 107 108 110 111 115 116 118 119 127 130 141 143 146 147 148 149 154 156 157 160 161 164 167 169 **S** BJC Health System, Saint Louis, MO
Primary Contact: Annette D. Schnabel, FACHE, President, Parkland Health Center Corporation
COO: Steven R Marler, Assistant Administrator
CFO: Cheri L. Goldsmith, Director Financial Services
CMO: Scott Kirkley, M.D., BJC Chief Medical Officer Group Liaison
Web address: www.parklandhealthcenter.org
Control: Other not–for–profit (including NFP Corporation) **Service**: General medical and surgical

Staffed Beds: 104 **Admissions**: 4251 **Census**: 41 **Outpatient Visits**: 27180 **Births**: 487 **Total Expense ($000)**: 136589 **Payroll Expense ($000)**: 52798 **Personnel**: 552

☐ **SOUTHEAST MISSOURI MENTAL HEALTH CENTER (264005)**, 1010 West Columbia Street, Zip 63640–2997; tel. 573/218–6792, **A**1 10 **F**4 11 30 38 53 65 75 86 87 97 98 101 106 130 132 135 143 146 157 163
Primary Contact: Donna Anderson, Chief Executive Officer
CMO: Jay Englehart, M.D., Medical Director
CHR: Mark Remspecher, Director Human Resources
Web address: https://dmh.mo.gov/smmhc
Control: City, Government, Nonfederal **Service**: Psychiatric

Staffed Beds: 348 **Admissions**: 29 **Census**: 316 **Outpatient Visits**: 0 **Births**: 0 **Total Expense ($000)**: 97039 **Payroll Expense ($000)**: 50026 **Personnel**: 915

FENTON—St. Louis County

✠ **SSM HEALTH ST. CLARE HOSPITAL – FENTON (260081)**, 1015 Bowles Avenue, Zip 63026–2394; tel. 636/496–2000, **A**1 3 5 10 19 **F**3 11 12 13 15 17 18 20 22 24 28 29 30 31 34 43 48 49 53 54 56 57 58 59 61 64 70 73 74 75 76 78 79 81 82 84 85 86 87 89 100 102 105 107 108 110 111 120 121 126 129 130 132 135 144 146 147 148 149 153 164 167 **S** SSM Health, Saint Louis, MO
Primary Contact: Kyle Crate, President
COO: Lee Bernstein, Regional Executive Vice President and Chief Operating Officer
CFO: Hal Holder, Regional Chief Financial Officer–Hospital Operations
CMO: Timothy J Pratt, M.D., Vice President Medical Affairs and Chief Medical Officer
CIO: Michael Paasch, Vice President, Regional Chief Information Officer
CHR: Renee Roach, System Vice President, Human Resources
CNO: Wayne Laramie, Vice President Nursing
Web address: www.ssmstclare.com
Control: Other not–for–profit (including NFP Corporation) **Service**: General medical and surgical

Staffed Beds: 184 **Admissions**: 10119 **Census**: 117 **Outpatient Visits**: 138936 **Births**: 992 **Total Expense ($000)**: 250390 **Payroll Expense ($000)**: 101721 **Personnel**: 740

FESTUS—Jefferson County

✠ **MERCY HOSPITAL JEFFERSON (260023)**, 1400 US Highway 61 South, Zip 63028–4100, Mailing Address: P.O. Box 350, Crystal City, Zip 63019–0350; tel. 636/933–1000, **A**1 10 **F**3 4 8 11 12 13 15 18 20 22 28 29 30 31 34 35 38 40 44 45 49 50 51 53 54 57 59 60 62 63 64 68 70 74 75 76 77 78 79 81 82 84 85 86 87 89 90 93 96 98 100 101 102 103 104 105 107 108 110 111 115 116 118 119 120 121 123 129 130 131 132 135 146 148 149 152 153 154 157 160 161 162 164 167 169 **S** Mercy, Chesterfield, MO
Primary Contact: Dan Eckenfels, President, Mercy Jefferson Communities
COO: Michele C. Meyer, R.N., Vice President of Operations
CFO: Scott Martinez, Executive Director Finance
CMO: Mark Briete, M.D., Vice President Medical Affairs
CIO: Jan Poneta, Director Information Services
CHR: Saundra G Turner, Director Human Resources
Web address: www.mercy.net/crystalcitymo
Control: Other not–for–profit (including NFP Corporation) **Service**: General medical and surgical

Staffed Beds: 209 **Admissions**: 11184 **Census**: 132 **Outpatient Visits**: 149560 **Births**: 521 **Total Expense ($000)**: 183217 **Payroll Expense ($000)**: 94611 **Personnel**: 1172

FORT LEONARD WOOD—Pulaski County

✠ **GENERAL LEONARD WOOD ARMY COMMUNITY HOSPITAL**, 4430 Missouri Avenue, Zip 65473–8952, Mailing Address: PO Box 4430, Zip 65473–8952; tel. 573/596–0414, (Nonreporting) **A**1 **S** Department of the Army, Office of the Surgeon General, Falls Church, VA
Primary Contact: Colonel Stacey S. Amos, Hospital Commander/Ozark Market Director
CFO: Major Michael Hogan, Chief Resource Management
CMO: Lieutenant Colonel John Lowery, M.D., Deputy Commander Clinical Services
CHR: Major Sandra Roper, Chief Human Resources
Web address: www.glwach.amedd.army.mil/
Control: Army, Government, federal **Service**: General medical and surgical

Staffed Beds: 46

FREDERICKTOWN—Madison County

MADISON MEDICAL CENTER (261302), 611 West Main Street, Zip 63645–1111; tel. 573/783–3341, (Total facility includes 80 beds in nursing home–type unit) **A**10 18 **F**6 11 15 18 28 35 45 59 64 67 70 77 78 79 81 85 87 92 93 97 103 107 111 119 127 128 130 133 144 146
Primary Contact: Lisa Twidwell, Chief Executive Officer
CMO: P A George, M.D., Chief of Staff
CHR: Jennifer Penuel, Director Human Resources
Web address: www.madisonmedicalcenter.net
Control: County, Government, Nonfederal **Service**: General medical and surgical

Staffed Beds: 97 **Admissions**: 336 **Census**: 70 **Outpatient Visits**: 52632 **Births**: 0 **Total Expense ($000)**: 22773 **Payroll Expense ($000)**: 11351 **Personnel**: 242

FULTON—Callaway County

☐ **FULTON STATE HOSPITAL (264004)**, 600 East Fifth Street, Zip 65251–1753; tel. 573/592–4100, **A**1 3 5 10 **F**3 4 11 29 30 39 44 53 56 57 59 75 77 98 103 130 132 135 143 146 149 163 164
Primary Contact: Russell DeTrempe, Chief Executive Officer
COO: Andrew Atkinson, Chief Operating Officer
CFO: Susie Kemp, Chief Financial Officer
CMO: Sanjiv Sethi, M.D., Medical Director
CIO: Keith Jones, Chief Information Officer
CHR: Lori French, Manager Human Resources
CNO: Susan Knoepflein, Chief Nurse Executive
Web address: www.dmh.missouri.gov/fulton
Control: State, Government, Nonfederal **Service**: Psychiatric

Staffed Beds: 450 **Admissions**: 89 **Census**: 397 **Outpatient Visits**: 48 **Births**: 0 **Total Expense ($000)**: 133110 **Payroll Expense ($000)**: 54327 **Personnel**: 930

Hospital, Medicare Provider Number, Address, Telephone, Approval, Facility, and Physician Codes, Health Care System

★ American Hospital Association (AHA) membership ○ Healthcare Facilities Accreditation Program ⇧ Center for Improvement in Healthcare Quality Accreditation
☐ The Joint Commission accreditation ◇ DNV Healthcare Inc. accreditation △ Commission on Accreditation of Rehabilitation Facilities (CARF) accreditation

Hospitals, U.S. / MISSOURI

HANNIBAL—Marion County

HANNIBAL REGIONAL HOSPITAL (260025), 6000 Hospital Drive, Zip 63401–6887, Mailing Address: P.O. Box 551, Zip 63401–0551; tel. 573/248–1300, **A**1 2 10 **F**3 13 15 18 20 22 26 28 29 31 34 35 40 48 49 57 59 62 64 70 71 73 74 76 78 79 81 84 85 86 87 89 90 92 107 108 110 111 115 117 118 119 120 121 123 124 126 129 130 132 135 148 154 164 167 169 **P**1
Primary Contact: C Todd. Ahrens, FACHE, President and Chief Executive Officer
COO: Aaron Zook, Vice President–Operations
CFO: Rob Gasaway, Vice President Finance
CMO: Pranav Parikh, M.D., Vice President & Chief Medical Officer
CIO: Jeff W. Evans, Vice President Information and Technology
CHR: Susan R. Wathen, Vice President Human Resources
CNO: Patricia Brawner, Vice President–Nursing
Web address: https://hospital.hannibalregional.org/
Control: Other not–for–profit (including NFP Corporation) **Service**: General medical and surgical

Staffed Beds: 99 **Admissions**: 5301 **Census**: 61 **Outpatient Visits**: 76488 **Births**: 531 **Total Expense ($000)**: 260982 **Payroll Expense ($000)**: 122797 **Personnel**: 1000

HARRISONVILLE—Cass County

CASS REGIONAL MEDICAL CENTER (261324), 2800 East Rock Haven Road, Zip 64701–4411; tel. 816/380–3474, **A**1 10 18 **F**3 11 12 15 17 18 26 28 29 30 31 34 35 39 40 43 44 45 46 48 50 54 56 57 59 65 66 70 74 75 77 78 79 81 82 85 86 87 93 96 97 98 103 107 110 111 115 119 127 129 130 131 132 133 135 145 146 147 148 149 154 156 161 **P**6
Primary Contact: John Christopher. Lang, FACHE, Chief Executive Officer
CFO: Brent Probasco, Chief Financial Officer
CIO: Lester Vohs, Manager Information Systems
CHR: Carla Wallen, Manager Human Resources
CNO: Twila Buckner, R.N., Chief Nursing Officer
Web address: www.cassregional.org
Control: County, Government, Nonfederal **Service**: General medical and surgical

Staffed Beds: 35 **Admissions**: 893 **Census**: 13 **Outpatient Visits**: 14751 **Births**: 0 **Total Expense ($000)**: 87606 **Payroll Expense ($000)**: 31329 **Personnel**: 410

HAYTI—Pemiscot County

PEMISCOT MEMORIAL HEALTH SYSTEM (260070), 946 East Reed Street, Zip 63851–1245, Mailing Address: P.O. Box 489, Zip 63851–0489; tel. 573/359–1372, (Total facility includes 66 beds in nursing home–type unit) **A**10 **F**3 29 30 34 40 50 57 59 64 67 68 70 75 81 82 87 90 93 97 98 103 107 111 119 127 128 130 133 147 148 149 150 154 156 167 **P**6
Primary Contact: David Ketchum, PharmD, Chief Executive Officer
CFO: Leigha Ward, Chief Financial Officer
CHR: Jackie Powell, Director Human Resources
Web address: www.pemiscot.org/
Control: County, Government, Nonfederal **Service**: General medical and surgical

Staffed Beds: 115 **Admissions**: 473 **Census**: 21 **Outpatient Visits**: 25480 **Births**: 0 **Total Expense ($000)**: 36234 **Payroll Expense ($000)**: 10299 **Personnel**: 156

HERMANN—Gasconade County

HERMANN AREA DISTRICT HOSPITAL (261314), 509 West 18th Street, Zip 65041–1547, Mailing Address: P.O. Box 470, Zip 65041–0470; tel. 573/486–2191, **A**10 18 **F**3 11 12 15 18 28 29 34 35 40 41 44 45 56 57 59 64 67 75 77 79 81 85 86 87 89 90 93 96 97 104 107 110 111 114 119 127 128 129 130 133 143 146 148 154
Primary Contact: William Hellebusch, Administrator
COO: Matt Siebert, Assistant Administrator Ancillary Services
CFO: Christine Lewis, Assistant Administrator, Finance
CMO: Michael Rothermich, M.D., Chief of Staff
CIO: Dee Vaughan, Director Information Technology
CNO: Sue Daller, R.N., Assistant Administrator Nursing
Web address: www.hadh.org
Control: Hospital district or authority, Government, Nonfederal **Service**: General medical and surgical

Staffed Beds: 24 **Admissions**: 314 **Census**: 8 **Outpatient Visits**: 3616 **Births**: 0 **Total Expense ($000)**: 19995 **Payroll Expense ($000)**: 8791 **Personnel**: 170

HOUSTON—Texas County

TEXAS COUNTY MEMORIAL HOSPITAL (260024), 1333 South Sam Houston Boulevard, Zip 65483–2046; tel. 417/967–3311, **A**10 20 **F**3 7 13 15 28 29 34 40 45 50 56 57 59 62 63 64 70 76 81 85 89 90 93 97 107 110 111 115 119 127 128 129 130 133 143 148 149 169
Primary Contact: Bill Bridges, Chief Executive Officer
CFO: Linda Pamperien, Chief Financial Officer
CMO: Charles Mueller, M.D., Chief of Staff
CHR: Anita Kuhn, Controller
CNO: Courtney Owens, R.N., Chief Nursing Officer
Web address: www.tcmh.org
Control: County, Government, Nonfederal **Service**: General medical and surgical

Staffed Beds: 47 **Admissions**: 943 **Census**: 9 **Outpatient Visits**: 11787 **Births**: 0 **Total Expense ($000)**: 41706 **Payroll Expense ($000)**: 21482 **Personnel**: 343

INDEPENDENCE—Jackson County

CENTERPOINT MEDICAL CENTER (260095), 19600 East 39th Street, Zip 64057–2301; tel. 816/698–7000, **A**1 2 3 5 10 **F**3 8 12 13 15 18 20 22 24 26 28 29 30 31 34 35 38 40 43 46 47 48 49 50 52 54 55 56 57 59 60 64 68 70 72 74 75 76 77 78 79 80 81 82 85 86 87 90 92 93 107 108 110 111 114 115 116 117 118 119 120 121 123 124 126 129 130 131 132 144 145 146 147 148 149 154 167 169 **P**6 **S** HCA Healthcare, Nashville, TN
Primary Contact: John McDonald, FACHE, Chief Executive Officer
CFO: James H Brown, Chief Financial Officer
CMO: Christopher Sullivan, M.D., Chief Medical Officer
CIO: Carl Sifers, Director Information Technology and System Services
CHR: Kyla Stoltz, Vice President Human Resources
Web address: www.centerpointmedical.com
Control: Corporation, Investor–owned (for–profit) **Service**: General medical and surgical

Staffed Beds: 285 **Admissions**: 16680 **Census**: 211 **Outpatient Visits**: 161360 **Births**: 1065 **Total Expense ($000)**: 333297 **Payroll Expense ($000)**: 107779 **Personnel**: 1015

JEFFERSON CITY—Cole County

★ **CAPITAL REGION MEDICAL CENTER (260047)**, 1125 Madison Street, Zip 65101–5200, Mailing Address: P.O. Box 1128, Zip 65102–1128; tel. 573/632–5000, **A**3 5 10 12 13 19 **F**3 11 13 15 17 18 20 22 24 26 28 29 30 31 34 35 36 38 45 46 47 48 49 51 53 57 58 59 60 61 62 64 65 68 70 73 74 75 76 77 78 79 80 81 82 85 87 89 90 92 93 96 97 100 104 107 108 110 111 115 118 119 120 121 123 126 129 130 131 135 144 146 147 148 149 150 154 167 **S** University of Missouri Health Care, Columbia, MO
Primary Contact: John Dennis. Hamilton, Interim Chief Operating Officer
CFO: Mike Rundle, Interim Site Leader for Finance
CMO: Mitchell Godbee, Chief of Staff
CIO: Jason Cecil, Vice President, Information
CHR: Sarah Morrow, Vice President Human Resources
CNO: Debra Jean Deeken, R.N., Interim Chief Nursing Officer
Web address: www.crmc.org
Control: Other not–for–profit (including NFP Corporation) **Service**: General medical and surgical

Staffed Beds: 114 **Admissions**: 4566 **Census**: 52 **Outpatient Visits**: 38769 **Births**: 606 **Total Expense ($000)**: 264915 **Payroll Expense ($000)**: 102563 **Personnel**: 1257

SSM HEALTH ST. MARY'S HOSPITAL – JEFFERSON CITY (260011), 2505 Mission Drive, Zip 65109; tel. 573/681–3000, **A**1 10 19 **F**3 7 11 13 15 17 18 20 22 26 28 29 30 31 34 35 40 41 45 46 47 48 49 50 51 53 57 59 68 70 73 74 75 76 77 78 79 81 82 84 85 86 87 89 90 91 93 97 98 99 101 102 104 107 111 115 116 117 118 119 120 121 123 124 127 129 130 131 132 135 144 146 148 149 150 153 154 155 156 157 162 164 167 169 **S** SSM Health, Saint Louis, MO
Primary Contact: Kenneth C. DeBoer, Regional President for Mid–Missouri
COO: Justin Morley, Vice President of Operations
CFO: James Stratton, Vice President Finance
CMO: Stephen Stewart, M.D., Vice President Medical Affairs
CHR: Susan Mankoski, Vice President Human Resources
CNO: Alice M Chatley, R.N., MSN, Vice President Acute Care Services
Web address: https://www.ssmhealth.com/locations/mid-missouri/st-marys-hospital-jefferson-city
Control: Church operated, Nongovernment, not–for–profit **Service**: General medical and surgical

Staffed Beds: 86 **Admissions**: 5354 **Census**: 68 **Outpatient Visits**: 92736 **Births**: 750 **Total Expense ($000)**: 172037 **Payroll Expense ($000)**: 57662 **Personnel**: 658

JOPLIN—Newton County

★ ○ **FREEMAN HEALTH SYSTEM (260137)**, 1102 West 32nd Street, Zip 64804–3503; tel. 417/347–1111, (Includes FREEMAN HOSPITAL EAST, 932 East 34th Street, Joplin, Missouri, Zip 64804–3999, 1102 West 32nd Street, Zip 64804–3999, tel. 417/347–1111; Paula F Baker, President and Chief Executive Officer) **A**3 5 10 11 13 19 **F**3 11 12 13 15 17 18 20 22 24 26 28 30 31 34 35 40 43 44 45 46 47 48 49 50 51 54 56 57 58 59 60 61 62 64 65 66 68 70 72 73 74 75 76 77 78 79 81 82 84 85 86 87 89 90 92 93 94 96 97 98 100 102 103 107 108 110 111 115 117 119 120 121 124 126 129 130 131 132 144 145 146 147 148 154 156 162 167 169 **S** Freeman Health System, Joplin, MO
Primary Contact: Paula F. Baker, President and Chief Executive Officer
CFO: Steve W Graddy, Chief Financial Officer
CIO: Skip Rollins, Chief Information Officer
CHR: Mary Frerer, Chief Human Resources Officer
Web address: www.freemanhealth.com
Control: Other not–for–profit (including NFP Corporation) **Service:** General medical and surgical

Staffed Beds: 376 **Admissions:** 14981 **Census:** 215 **Outpatient Visits:** 644280 **Births:** 1708 **Total Expense ($000):** 656928 **Payroll Expense ($000):** 298799 **Personnel:** 3297

LANDMARK HOSPITAL OF JOPLIN (262016), 2040 West 32nd Street, Zip 64804–3512; tel. 417/627–1300, (Nonreporting) **A**10 22 **S** Landmark Hospitals, Cape Girardeau, MO
Primary Contact: Robert Samples, Chief Executive Officer
CMO: Jack Rhoads, M.D., Medical Director
CHR: Janice Nordstrom, Director Human Resources
CNO: Stephanie Slater–Nesuold, Director of Nursing
Web address: www.landmarkhospitals.com
Control: Partnership, Investor–owned (for–profit) **Service:** Acute long–term care hospital

Staffed Beds: 28

⊞ **MERCY HOSPITAL JOPLIN (260001)**, 100 Mercy Way, Zip 64804–1626; tel. 417/781–2727, (Includes ST. JOHN'S REHABILITATION CENTER, 2727 McClelland Boulevard, Joplin, Missouri, Zip 64804, tel. 417/659–6716) **A**1 2 10 19 **F**3 5 7 11 12 13 14 15 17 18 19 20 22 24 26 28 29 30 31 34 35 38 39 40 43 44 45 46 47 48 49 51 54 57 58 59 60 61 64 65 66 67 70 72 73 74 75 76 77 78 79 81 84 85 86 87 89 93 94 97 98 100 101 102 104 107 108 110 111 114 115 119 120 121 123 124 126 127 129 130 131 132 135 144 146 147 148 154 156 169 **P**6 **S** Mercy, Chesterfield, MO
Primary Contact: Jeremy Drinkwitz, President, Mercy Joplin Communities
CMO: Jesse Hatfield, M.D., Chief Medical Officer
CHR: Timothy Murphy, Vice President Human Resources
CNO: Kelli Bigando, Chief Nursing Officer
Web address: www.mercy.net/joplinmo
Control: Church operated, Nongovernment, not–for–profit **Service:** General medical and surgical

Staffed Beds: 221 **Admissions:** 12925 **Census:** 148 **Outpatient Visits:** 188136 **Births:** 1370 **Total Expense ($000):** 254956 **Payroll Expense ($000):** 98794 **Personnel:** 981

OAK HILL HOSPITAL See Freeman Hospital East

KANSAS CITY—Clay County

☐ **SIGNATURE PSYCHIATRIC HOSPITAL (264030)**, 2900 Clay Edwards Drive, Zip 64116–3235; tel. 816/691–5101, (Nonreporting) **A**1 10
Primary Contact: Casey Webb, Chief Executive Officer
CFO: Robert Jackson, Chief Financial Officer
CMO: Azfar Malik, M.D., Chief Medical Officer
CIO: Tariq Nazir, Interim Director Information Technology
CHR: Maria Griffith, Director Human Resources
Web address: www.sphkc.net
Control: Corporation, Investor–owned (for–profit) **Service:** Psychiatric

Staffed Beds: 76

KANSAS CITY—Jackson County

☐ **CENTER FOR BEHAVIORAL MEDICINE (264008)**, 1000 East 24th Street, Zip 64108–2776; tel. 816/512–7000, (Total facility includes 25 beds in nursing home–type unit) **A**1 3 5 10 **F**4 29 53 65 75 87 98 106 128 135 143 149 163 164
Primary Contact: Megan Roedel, Chief Operating Officer
COO: Megan Roedel, Chief Operating Officer
CFO: Tyler Rinehart, Chief Financial Officer
CMO: Maheshkumar Patel, M.D., Medical Director
CIO: Robert Curren, Director Information Technology
CHR: Silva Ward, Director Human Resources
CNO: John Tucker, Chief Nursing Executive
Web address: www.dmhonline.dmh.state.mo.us
Control: State, Government, Nonfederal **Service:** Psychiatric

Staffed Beds: 90 **Admissions:** 110 **Census:** 76 **Outpatient Visits:** 0 **Births:** 0 **Total Expense ($000):** 32635 **Payroll Expense ($000):** 19487 **Personnel:** 263

⊞ △ **CHILDREN'S MERCY KANSAS CITY (263302)**, 2401 Gillham Road, Zip 64108–4619; tel. 816/234–3000, **A**1 3 5 7 8 10 **F**3 7 8 9 11 12 13 14 16 19 20 21 22 23 24 25 26 27 28 29 30 31 32 34 35 36 38 39 40 41 43 44 49 50 53 54 55 57 58 59 60 61 62 64 65 68 72 73 74 75 76 77 78 79 81 82 84 85 86 87 88 89 90 91 92 93 94 96 97 99 100 104 107 111 115 117 118 119 129 130 131 132 133 134 136 137 138 139 141 142 144 146 148 149 150 154 155 156 157 164 167 169
Primary Contact: Paul D. Kempinski, MS, FACHE, President and Chief Executive Officer
COO: Jo W. Stueve, Executive Vice President and Co–Chief Operating Officer
CFO: Jim Simaras, Executive Vice President and Chief Financial Officer
CMO: Charles Roberts, M.D., Executive Vice President and Executive Medical Director
CIO: David Chou, Vice President, Chief Information and Digital Officer
Web address: www.childrensmercy.org
Control: Other not–for–profit (including NFP Corporation) **Service:** Children's general medical and surgical

Staffed Beds: 338 **Admissions:** 13747 **Census:** 257 **Outpatient Visits:** 458512 **Births:** 200 **Total Expense ($000):** 1609785 **Payroll Expense ($000):** 802207 **Personnel:** 7270

CRITTENTON CHILDREN'S CENTER See Saint Luke's Hospital of Kansas City Crittenton Children's Center

⊞ **KANSAS CITY VA MEDICAL CENTER**, 4801 East Linwood Boulevard, Zip 64128–2226; tel. 816/861–4700, (Nonreporting) **A**1 3 5 **S** Department of Veterans Affairs, Washington, DC
Primary Contact: Paul Hopkins, Director
CFO: Bryan Bieri, Manager Finance
CMO: Ahmad Batrash, Chief of Staff
CIO: Eddie Johnson, Chief Information Technology Officer
CHR: Kathi Nippert, Acting Chief Human Resources Officer
Web address: www.kansascity.va.gov/
Control: Veterans Affairs, Government, federal **Service:** General medical and surgical

Staffed Beds: 97

KANSAS CITY VAMC See Kansas City VA Medical Center

⊞ **KINDRED HOSPITAL NORTHLAND (262018)**, 500 Northwest 68th Street, Zip 64118–2455; tel. 816/420–6300, (Nonreporting) **A**1 10 **S** ScionHealth, Louisville, KY
Primary Contact: Laura Inge, MSN, R.N., Chief Executive Officer
CFO: Brett Stevenson, Controller
CMO: Sean R Muldoon, M.D., Senior Vice President and Chief Medical Officer–Kindred Healthcare, Hospital Division
Web address: www.khnorthland.com
Control: Corporation, Investor–owned (for–profit) **Service:** Acute long–term care hospital

Staffed Beds: 42

Hospital, Medicare Provider Number, Address, Telephone, Approval, Facility, and Physician Codes, Health Care System

★ American Hospital Association (AHA) membership ○ Healthcare Facilities Accreditation Program ⇧ Center for Improvement in Healthcare Quality Accreditation
☐ The Joint Commission accreditation ◇ DNV Healthcare Inc. accreditation △ Commission on Accreditation of Rehabilitation Facilities (CARF) accreditation

Hospitals, U.S. / MISSOURI

☒ **RESEARCH MEDICAL CENTER (260027)**, 2316 East Meyer Boulevard, Zip 64132–1136; tel. 816/276–4000, (Includes RESEARCH PSYCHIATRIC CENTER, 2323 East 63rd Street, Kansas City, Missouri, Zip 64130–3462, tel. 816/444–8161; Shannon Griggs, Interim Chief Executive Officer) **A**1 2 3 5 10 **F**3 8 11 13 15 16 17 18 20 22 24 26 28 29 30 31 34 35 36 38 39 40 43 45 46 47 48 49 50 52 54 55 56 57 58 59 61 65 68 70 72 73 74 75 76 77 78 79 80 81 84 85 86 87 90 92 93 96 97 98 99 100 101 102 103 104 105 107 108 110 111 114 115 116 117 118 119 120 121 123 124 126 130 131 132 138 139 141 142 143 147 148 149 150 153 154 156 164 165 167 169 **P**6 **S** HCA Healthcare, Nashville, TN
Primary Contact: Kirk McCarty, R.N., MSN, Chief Executive Officer
COO: Jessica Marin, Chief Operating Officer
CFO: John Krajicek, Chief Financial Officer
CIO: Shawn Kegley, Director Information Services
CHR: Charlotte O'Neal, Vice President Human Resources
Web address: https://hcamidwest.com/locations/research-medical-center/
Control: Corporation, Investor–owned (for–profit) **Service**: General medical and surgical

Staffed Beds: 442 **Admissions**: 17986 **Census**: 292 **Outpatient Visits**: 143088 **Births**: 696 **Total Expense ($000)**: 611735 **Payroll Expense ($000)**: 160989 **Personnel**: 2506

☒ **SAINT LUKE'S HOSPITAL OF KANSAS CITY (260138)**, 4401 Wornall Road, Zip 64111–3220; tel. 816/932–3800, (Includes SAINT LUKE'S HOSPITAL OF KANSAS CITY CRITTENTON CHILDREN'S CENTER, 10918 Elm Avenue, Kansas City, Missouri, Zip 64134–4108, tel. 816/765–6600; Carmen Parker–Bradshaw, Vice President and Administrator) **A**1 2 3 5 8 10 **F**3 4 5 6 8 9 11 12 13 15 17 18 20 22 24 26 28 29 30 31 32 34 35 36 37 38 39 40 43 44 45 46 47 49 50 55 56 57 58 59 60 61 64 65 66 68 70 72 73 74 75 76 77 78 79 80 81 82 84 85 86 87 89 90 91 92 93 94 95 96 97 98 99 100 101 102 103 104 106 107 108 110 111 112 114 115 116 117 118 119 120 121 123 124 126 129 130 131 132 134 135 137 138 139 141 145 146 147 148 149 150 151 153 154 155 158 162 164 167 168 169 **S** BJC Health System, Saint Louis, MO
Primary Contact: Jani L. Johnson, R.N., MSN, Chief Executive Officer
COO: Brad Simmons, Chief Operating Officer
CFO: Amy Nachtigal, Chief Financial Officer
CMO: Peter Holt, M.D., Director Medical Affairs
CIO: Deborah Gash, Chief Information Officer
CHR: Doris Rogers, Vice President Human Resources
Web address: www.saint-lukes.org
Control: Other not–for–profit (including NFP Corporation) **Service**: General medical and surgical

Staffed Beds: 500 **Admissions**: 19884 **Census**: 345 **Outpatient Visits**: 294536 **Births**: 2005 **Total Expense ($000)**: 1100776 **Payroll Expense ($000)**: 269352 **Personnel**: 3724

☐ **ST. JOSEPH MEDICAL CENTER (260085)**, 1000 Carondelet Drive, Zip 64114–4673; tel. 816/942–4400, **A**1 10 **F**3 11 12 15 17 18 20 22 24 26 28 29 30 31 35 36 40 56 60 63 64 68 70 74 75 76 77 78 79 80 81 82 85 87 90 93 98 102 103 107 108 109 110 111 114 115 119 129 130 132 135 146 148 149 156 **S** Prime Healthcare, Ontario, CA
Primary Contact: Jodi Fincher, R.N., Chief Executive Officer
CFO: Debra Cartwright, Chief Financial Officer
CMO: Tommy Ko, M.D., Chief Medical Officer
CIO: Cheryl Johnson, Regional Chief Information Officer
CHR: Donna Sumner, Director, Human Resources and Organizational Development
CNO: Greg Simpson, Chief Nursing Officer
Web address: www.stjosephkc.com/
Control: Individual, Investor–owned (for–profit) **Service**: General medical and surgical

Staffed Beds: 129 **Admissions**: 5560 **Census**: 73 **Outpatient Visits**: 73944 **Births**: 0 **Total Expense ($000)**: 155904 **Payroll Expense ($000)**: 49225 **Personnel**: 895

☒ **UNIVERSITY HEALTH–LAKEWOOD MEDICAL CENTER (260102)**, 7900 Lee's Summit Road, Zip 64139–1236, Mailing Address: 2301 Holmes Street, Zip 64108–2640; tel. 816/404–7000, (Total facility includes 188 beds in nursing home–type unit) **A**1 3 5 10 **F**1 3 4 6 13 15 18 29 30 32 34 35 36 38 39 40 44 45 50 53 56 57 58 59 64 65 66 67 68 70 73 74 75 76 77 78 79 81 82 85 86 87 89 90 93 96 97 98 99 100 101 102 103 104 107 111 115 119 126 128 129 130 131 143 146 147 148 149 150 153 154 156 164 165 169 **S** University Health, Kansas City, MO
Primary Contact: Charlie Shields, Chief Executive Officer
COO: Lynette Wheeler, MSN, Chief Operating Officer
CFO: Allen Johnson, Chief Financial Officer
CMO: Mark Steele, M.D., Chief Medical Officer
CIO: Mitzi Cardenas, Executive Chief Administrative Officer
CHR: Ruth Pullins, Chief Human Resources Officer
Web address: www.trumed.org
Control: Other not–for–profit (including NFP Corporation) **Service**: General medical and surgical

Staffed Beds: 305 **Admissions**: 3715 **Census**: 212 **Outpatient Visits**: 203352 **Births**: 1395 **Total Expense ($000)**: 213745 **Payroll Expense ($000)**: 85046 **Personnel**: 892

☒ **UNIVERSITY HEALTH–TRUMAN MEDICAL CENTER (260048)**, 2301 Holmes Street, Zip 64108–2640; tel. 816/404–1000, **A**1 2 3 5 8 10 **F**3 4 5 8 12 13 14 15 17 18 20 22 26 28 29 30 31 34 35 36 38 40 43 44 45 46 48 49 50 52 53 54 55 57 58 59 60 61 64 65 66 68 70 72 74 75 76 77 78 79 81 82 84 85 86 87 89 90 92 93 97 98 99 100 101 102 103 104 106 107 108 110 111 115 119 126 129 130 131 132 134 135 142 143 146 147 148 149 150 151 152 154 156 157 158 160 161 162 164 165 167 169 **S** University Health, Kansas City, MO
Primary Contact: Charlie Shields, President and Chief Executive Officer
CFO: Allen Johnson, Chief Financial Officer
CMO: Mark Steele, M.D., Chief Medical Officer
CIO: Mitzi Cardenas, Executive Chief Administrative Officer
CHR: Ruth Pullins, Chief Human Resources Officer
Web address: www.trumed.org
Control: Other not–for–profit (including NFP Corporation) **Service**: General medical and surgical

Staffed Beds: 258 **Admissions**: 10525 **Census**: 191 **Outpatient Visits**: 443928 **Births**: 1771 **Total Expense ($000)**: 613788 **Payroll Expense ($000)**: 225796 **Personnel**: 2883

KANSAS CITY—Platte County

☒ **SAINT LUKE'S NORTH HOSPITAL – BARRY ROAD (260062)**, 5830 NW Barry Road, Zip 64154–2778; tel. 816/891–6000, (Includes SAINT LUKE'S NORTH HOSPITAL–SMITHVILLE CAMPUS, 601 South 169 Highway, Smithville, Missouri, Zip 64089–9317, tel. 816/532–3700; Darren Bass, FACHE, Chief Executive Officer, North Region) **A**1 2 3 10 **F**3 4 11 12 13 15 18 20 22 26 28 29 30 31 34 35 38 40 44 45 46 49 50 56 58 59 60 61 64 68 69 70 73 74 75 76 77 78 79 80 81 82 84 85 86 87 89 90 91 92 93 96 98 100 101 102 103 107 108 110 111 114 115 116 117 118 119 126 129 130 131 132 135 141 146 147 148 149 154 162 164 167 168 169 **S** BJC Health System, Saint Louis, MO
Primary Contact: Darren Bass, FACHE, Chief Executive Officer, North Region
CFO: Julie Murphy, Chief Financial Officer
CMO: Leonardo J Lozada, M.D., Chief Physician Executive
CIO: Matt Stadler, Information Services Site Manager
CHR: Donna Kunz, System Director Human Resources
CNO: Amy Brummer, MSN, Chief Nursing Officer
Web address: www.saint-lukes.org
Control: Other not–for–profit (including NFP Corporation) **Service**: General medical and surgical

Staffed Beds: 125 **Admissions**: 7290 **Census**: 87 **Outpatient Visits**: 114800 **Births**: 643 **Total Expense ($000)**: 208319 **Payroll Expense ($000)**: 64302 **Personnel**: 795

KIRKSVILLE—Adair County

★ ○ **NORTHEAST REGIONAL MEDICAL CENTER (260022)**, 315 South Osteopathy Street, Zip 63501–6401, Mailing Address: P.O. Box C8502, Zip 63501–8599; tel. 660/785–1000, (Nonreporting) **A**3 5 10 11 12 13 **S** Community Health Systems, Inc., Franklin, TN
Primary Contact: Patrick Avila, Chief Executive Officer
CFO: Carol Cross, CPA, Chief Financial Officer
CMO: Benjamin Schrant, M.D., Chief of Staff
CIO: Chad Tatro, Supervisor Information Systems
CHR: Jim Bergman, Director Human Resources
CNO: Peggy Parks, R.N., Chief Nursing Officer
Web address: www.nermc.com
Control: Corporation, Investor–owned (for–profit) **Service**: General medical and surgical

Staffed Beds: 55

Hospitals, U.S. / MISSOURI

LAKE SAINT LOUIS—St. Charles County

☒ △ **SSM HEALTH ST. JOSEPH HOSPITAL – LAKE SAINT LOUIS (260200)**, 100 Medical Plaza, Zip 63367–1366; tel. 636/625–5200, **A**1 2 7 10 **F**3 11 13 15 17 18 20 22 28 29 30 31 34 35 36 38 40 41 43 44 45 46 49 50 51 53 54 55 56 57 59 60 63 64 68 70 73 74 75 76 78 79 81 82 84 85 87 89 102 107 108 110 111 115 116 118 119 129 130 132 134 135 146 147 148 149 156 157 164 167 169 **S** SSM Health, Saint Louis, MO
Primary Contact: Jerald W. Rumph, FACHE, President
COO: Lee Bernstein, Regional Executive Vice President of Hospital and Chief Operating Officer
CFO: Hal Holder, Regional Chief Financial Officer
CMO: Michael Handler, M.D., Vice President Medical Affairs and Chief Medical Officer
CIO: Sharon Gardner, Manager Information Systems
CHR: Renee Roach, System Vice President
Web address: https://www.ssmhealth.com/locations/st-louis/st-joseph-hospital-lake-saint-louis
Control: Church operated, Nongovernment, not–for–profit **Service**: General medical and surgical

Staffed Beds: 213 **Admissions**: 10389 **Census**: 116 **Outpatient Visits**: 142472 **Births**: 1086 **Total Expense ($000)**: 236760 **Payroll Expense ($000)**: 100604 **Personnel**: 670

LAMAR—Barton County

⇑ **COX BARTON COUNTY MEMORIAL HOSPITAL (261325)**, 29 NW First Lane, Zip 64759–8105; tel. 417/681–5100, **A**10 18 21 **F**3 11 15 18 28 29 30 34 40 44 45 50 57 59 64 68 70 74 75 77 81 84 85 86 89 90 92 93 97 100 107 108 110 111 114 119 127 128 129 130 132 133 146 148 149 154 156 **P**6 **S** CoxHealth, Springfield, MO
Primary Contact: Andrea McKay, President
CIO: Brad Butler, Network Administrator
CNO: Rosie Hubbard, R.N., Administrative Director of Nursing
Web address: www.bcmh.net
Control: Other not–for–profit (including NFP Corporation) **Service**: General medical and surgical

Staffed Beds: 25 **Admissions**: 575 **Census**: 8 **Outpatient Visits**: 43824 **Births**: 0 **Total Expense ($000)**: 27852 **Payroll Expense ($000)**: 13330 **Personnel**: 174

LEBANON—Laclede County

☒ **MERCY HOSPITAL LEBANON (260059)**, 100 Hospital Drive, Zip 65536–9210; tel. 417/533–6100, **A**1 10 20 **F**3 11 15 28 29 30 31 35 40 45 47 48 50 65 68 70 76 77 78 79 81 84 85 87 89 90 93 94 100 102 107 108 110 111 115 119 129 130 131 146 147 148 149 154 **S** Mercy, Chesterfield, MO
Primary Contact: Jason Wilson, Administrator, Mercy Hospital Lebanon
CNO: Judy O'Connor-Snyder, R.N., Chief Nursing Officer
Web address: www.mercy.net/practice/mercy-hospital-lebanon
Control: Church operated, Nongovernment, not–for–profit **Service**: General medical and surgical

Staffed Beds: 58 **Admissions**: 1570 **Census**: 12 **Outpatient Visits**: 28087 **Births**: 184 **Total Expense ($000)**: 79517 **Payroll Expense ($000)**: 35212 **Personnel**: 384

LEE'S SUMMIT—Jackson County

☒ **LEE'S SUMMIT MEDICAL CENTER (260190)**, 2100 SE Blue Parkway, Zip 64063–1007; tel. 816/282–5000, **A**1 2 3 5 10 **F**3 12 15 18 20 22 28 29 30 31 34 37 40 48 49 50 57 59 64 70 74 75 77 78 79 80 81 82 85 87 90 107 110 111 115 119 126 129 130 145 146 148 149 154 167 **S** HCA Healthcare, Nashville, TN
Primary Contact: Gabriel Clements, Chief Executive Officer
CFO: John Heurtin, Chief Financial Officer
CIO: Andrew Beechy, Manager Information Technology Systems
CHR: Linda Duncan, Director Human Resources
CNO: Paige Baker, MSN, R.N., Chief Nursing Officer
Web address: www.leessummitmedicalcenter.com
Control: Corporation, Investor–owned (for–profit) **Service**: General medical and surgical

Staffed Beds: 88 **Admissions**: 5932 **Census**: 68 **Outpatient Visits**: 36352 **Births**: 0 **Total Expense ($000)**: 141833 **Payroll Expense ($000)**: 43596 **Personnel**: 566

SAINT LUKE'S EAST HOSPITAL (260216), 100 NE Saint Luke's Boulevard, Zip 64086–6000; tel. 816/347–5000, **A**1 2 10 **F**3 4 12 13 15 18 20 22 24 26 28 29 30 31 34 35 38 40 44 45 46 47 49 50 51 56 58 59 60 61 64 65 70 72 73 74 75 76 77 78 79 80 81 82 84 85 86 87 89 90 93 94 96 97 100 102 103 107 108 110 111 114 115 117 118 119 120 121 123 126 129 130 131 132 135 141 145 146 147 148 149 154 164 167 168 169 **S** BJC Health System, Saint Louis, MO
Primary Contact: Bobby Olm–Shipman, President and Chief Executive Officer
CFO: Joseph P Stasi, Chief Financial Officer
CHR: John Clabaugh, Director Human Resources
CNO: Gloria Solis, R.N., MSN, Chief Nursing Officer
Web address: www.saintlukeskc.org
Control: Other not–for–profit (including NFP Corporation) **Service**: General medical and surgical

Staffed Beds: 238 **Admissions**: 13854 **Census**: 168 **Outpatient Visits**: 154312 **Births**: 1966 **Total Expense ($000)**: 349275 **Payroll Expense ($000)**: 102604 **Personnel**: 1243

LEXINGTON—Lafayette County

☒ **LAFAYETTE REGIONAL HEALTH CENTER (261320)**, 1500 State Street, Zip 64067–1107; tel. 660/259–2203, **A**1 2 10 18 **F**3 11 15 18 29 30 31 40 70 75 77 78 81 85 93 107 108 110 111 114 119 127 133 147 149 **P**6 **S** HCA Healthcare, Nashville, TN
Primary Contact: Darrel Box, Chief Executive Officer
COO: Daniel Astleford, Vice President Operations
CFO: Teri James, Chief Financial Officer
CIO: Keith Richcreek, Manager Technical Services
CHR: Stephen Davidson, Director Human Resources
CNO: Kim Leakey, R.N., Chief Nursing Officer
Web address: www.lafayetteregionalhealthcenter.com
Control: Corporation, Investor–owned (for–profit) **Service**: General medical and surgical

Staffed Beds: 25 **Admissions**: 783 **Census**: 7 **Outpatient Visits**: 21384 **Births**: 0 **Total Expense ($000)**: 34450 **Payroll Expense ($000)**: 10664 **Personnel**: 198

LIBERTY—Clay County

☒ **LIBERTY HOSPITAL (260177)**, 2525 Glenn Hendren Dive, Zip 64068–9600, Mailing Address: P.O. Box 1002, Zip 64069–1002; tel. 816/781–7200, **A**1 2 3 10 **F**3 8 11 13 15 17 18 20 22 24 26 28 29 30 31 33 34 35 37 40 43 45 47 48 49 51 55 59 61 62 63 64 65 69 70 73 74 75 76 77 78 79 80 81 82 83 84 85 86 87 90 92 93 96 107 108 110 111 114 115 117 119 126 129 130 131 132 144 146 147 148 149 156 167
Primary Contact: Raghu Adiga, M.D., President and Chief Executive Officer
CFO: Dan Williams, Vice President Finance and Support
CMO: Raghu Adiga, M.D., Chief Medical Officer
CIO: Paul Klehn, Chief Information Technology Officer
CHR: Nancy E Cattell, Vice President Human Resources
Web address: www.Libertyhospital.org
Control: Hospital district or authority, Government, Nonfederal **Service**: General medical and surgical

Staffed Beds: 177 **Admissions**: 7906 **Census**: 90 **Outpatient Visits**: 458880 **Births**: 1540 **Total Expense ($000)**: 324589 **Payroll Expense ($000)**: 167711 **Personnel**: 1704

LOUISIANA—Pike County

☒ **PIKE COUNTY MEMORIAL HOSPITAL (261333)**, 2305 Georgia Street, Zip 63353–2559; tel. 573/754–5531, **A**1 10 18 **F**3 5 7 11 15 18 28 29 30 34 35 40 45 50 53 54 56 57 59 64 65 68 74 75 77 79 81 85 86 87 89 90 93 97 107 110 115 127 130 131 132 133 143 144 147 148 149 154 156
Primary Contact: Tylie Mills, R.N., Chief Executive Officer
CFO: Ann Tran, Chief Financial Officer
CIO: Jeremy Gruen, Director Information Systems
CHR: Layne Ebers, Director Human Resources and Marketing
CNO: Dolly Giles, Chief Nursing Officer
Web address: www.pcmh-mo.org
Control: County, Government, Nonfederal **Service**: General medical and surgical

Staffed Beds: 25 **Admissions**: 179 **Census**: 5 **Outpatient Visits**: 6129 **Births**: 0 **Total Expense ($000)**: 24377 **Payroll Expense ($000)**: 12194 **Personnel**: 152

Hospital, Medicare Provider Number, Address, Telephone, Approval, Facility, and Physician Codes, Health Care System

★ American Hospital Association (AHA) membership
☐ The Joint Commission accreditation
◯ Healthcare Facilities Accreditation Program
◇ DNV Healthcare Inc. accreditation
⇑ Center for Improvement in Healthcare Quality Accreditation
△ Commission on Accreditation of Rehabilitation Facilities (CARF) accreditation

Hospitals, U.S. / MISSOURI

MACON—Macon County

SAMARITAN HOSPITAL (261313), 1205 North Missouri Street, Zip 63552–2095; tel. 660/385–8700, **A**10 18 **F**3 7 8 11 28 29 34 35 40 45 46 53 56 57 59 63 64 65 68 75 77 79 81 82 87 89 90 93 97 107 111 115 119 127 128 129 130 133 146 148 154 169
Primary Contact: Jill Williams, Chief Executive Officer
CHR: Suzanne Britt, Director Human Resources
Web address: www.samaritanhospital.net
Control: County, Government, Nonfederal **Service**: General medical and surgical

Staffed Beds: 25 **Admissions**: 326 **Census**: 7 **Outpatient Visits**: 41680
Births: 0 **Total Expense ($000)**: 28817 **Payroll Expense ($000)**: 10913
Personnel: 189

MARSHALL—Saline County

★ **FITZGIBBON HOSPITAL (260142)**, 2305 South 65 Highway, Zip 65340–0250, Mailing Address: P.O. Box 250, Zip 65340–0250; tel. 660/886–7431, **A**10 20 **F**3 11 13 15 30 31 33 34 35 40 45 56 57 59 62 63 64 65 68 70 75 76 77 78 79 81 85 87 89 90 93 98 104 107 108 110 111 115 119 120 121 127 128 130 131 132 133 146 147 148 154 167 169
Primary Contact: Angela P. Littrell, CPA, President and Chief Executive Officer
CMO: Darin L. Haug, D.O., Chief Medical Officer
CIO: Tom Jones, Chief Information Officer
CHR: Jessica Henderson, Manager Human Resources
CNO: Angela Igo, MSN, R.N., Chief Nursing Officer
Web address: www.fitzgibbon.org
Control: Other not–for–profit (including NFP Corporation) **Service**: General medical and surgical

Staffed Beds: 52 **Admissions**: 1671 **Census**: 17 **Outpatient Visits**: 126472
Births: 275 **Total Expense ($000)**: 67556 **Payroll Expense ($000)**: 24389
Personnel: 413

MARYLAND HEIGHTS—St. Louis County

⇑ **CENTER FOR BEHAVIORAL HEALTH MARYLAND HEIGHTS (264035)**, 11100 Ayrshire Drive, Zip 63043–1973; tel. 314/528–2700, (Nonreporting) **A**10 21
Primary Contact: Laura Outlaw, Chief Executive Officer
Web address: https://marylandheightsbehavioralhealth.com/
Control: Corporation, Investor–owned (for–profit) **Service**: Psychiatric

Staffed Beds: 16

★ **RANKEN JORDAN PEDIATRIC BRIDGE HOSPITAL (263303)**, 11365 Dorsett Road, Zip 63043–3411; tel. 314/872–6400, **A**3 5 10 **F**1 3 12 16 29 30 32 34 35 44 50 53 64 75 77 80 86 87 89 90 91 92 93 96 98 99 104 146 148 149 154 **P**6
Primary Contact: Shawn Dryden, FACHE, President and Chief Executive Officer
CFO: Kenneth Marx, Chief Financial Officer
CMO: Nicholas Holekamp, M.D., Chief Medical Officer
CHR: Erin Bachelier, Human Resource Administrator
Web address: www.rankenjordan.org
Control: Other not–for–profit (including NFP Corporation) **Service**: Children's rehabilitation

Staffed Beds: 60 **Admissions**: 254 **Census**: 48 **Outpatient Visits**: 9656
Births: 0 **Total Expense ($000)**: 52341 **Payroll Expense ($000)**: 27776
Personnel: 326

MARYVILLE—Nodaway County

✠ **MOSAIC MEDICAL CENTER – MARYVILLE (260050)**, 2016 South Main Street, Zip 64468–2655; tel. 660/562–2600, **A**1 10 20 **F**3 11 15 18 28 29 30 31 34 35 38 40 45 57 59 64 65 68 70 75 76 77 78 79 81 82 84 85 86 89 90 93 96 97 98 102 103 104 107 110 111 115 116 117 118 119 127 128 130 131 132 133 135 146 148 149 154 156 161 164 167 169 **S** Mosaic Life Care, Saint Joseph, MO
Primary Contact: Nate Blackford, President
COO: Frank Grispino, Vice President Operations
CFO: Jocelyn Skidmore, Director Finance
CMO: Shirley Harris, M.D., President Medical Staff
CIO: Dave Lewis, Director Information Services
CHR: Krista Barcus, Human Resources Leader
CNO: Debbie Hoffman, Vice President Patient Services
Web address: www.mymosaiclifecare.org
Control: Other not–for–profit (including NFP Corporation) **Service**: General medical and surgical

Staffed Beds: 50 **Admissions**: 1346 **Census**: 15 **Outpatient Visits**: 142912
Births: 184 **Total Expense ($000)**: 91540 **Payroll Expense ($000)**: 37577
Personnel: 411

MEMPHIS—Scotland County

★ **SCOTLAND COUNTY HOSPITAL (261310)**, 450 Sigler Avenue, Zip 63555–1726, Mailing Address: 450 E Sigler Avenue, Zip 63555–1726; tel. 660/465–8511, (Nonreporting) **A**10 18
Primary Contact: Meagan Weber, Chief Executive Officer
COO: Brent Peirick, Chief Operating Officer
CFO: Sheryl Templeton, Chief Financial Officer
CIO: Ken McMinn, Director Information Technology
CHR: Missy Smith, Coordinator Human Resources
CNO: Carla Cook, Director of Nursing
Web address: www.scotlandcountyhospital.com
Control: Hospital district or authority, Government, Nonfederal **Service**: General medical and surgical

Staffed Beds: 25

MILAN—Sullivan County

★ **SULLIVAN COUNTY MEMORIAL HOSPITAL (261306)**, 630 West Third Street, Zip 63556–1076; tel. 660/265–4212, **A**10 18 **F**28 29 33 34 35 40 57 59 65 67 68 77 81 93 97 107 111 114 119 127 128 133 148 154 **P**5
Primary Contact: Martha Gragg, R.N., MSN, Chief Executive Officer
COO: Amy J Michael, Chief Operating Officer
CMO: Dale Essmyer, M.D., Chief of Staff
CIO: Vern Johnson, Director Information Technology
CHR: Rae A. Ashby, Director Human Resources
CNO: Tina Sears, Director Patient Care Services
Web address: www.scmhospital.org
Control: County, Government, Nonfederal **Service**: General medical and surgical

Staffed Beds: 25 **Admissions**: 162 **Census**: 9 **Outpatient Visits**: 7384
Births: 0 **Total Expense ($000)**: 12188 **Payroll Expense ($000)**: 5109
Personnel: 88

MOBERLY—Randolph County

✠ **MOBERLY REGIONAL MEDICAL CENTER (260074)**, 1515 Union Avenue, Zip 65270–9449; tel. 660/263–8400, (Nonreporting) **A**1 3 5 10 20 **S** Community Health Systems, Inc., Franklin, TN
Primary Contact: Michael D. Hall, Chief Executive Officer
COO: Tracey Matheis, Chief Operating Officer
CFO: Tracey Matheis, Chief Financial Officer
CMO: Heather Gessling, M.D., Chief Medical Officer
CHR: Michael Turner, Director Human Resources
CNO: Patsy Lewellen, Interim Chief Nursing Officer
Web address: https://www.moberlyregionalmedicalcenter.com
Control: Corporation, Investor–owned (for–profit) **Service**: General medical and surgical

Staffed Beds: 99

MONETT—Lawrence County

⇑ **COX MONETT HOSPITAL, INC (261329)**, 1000 East US Highway 60, Zip 65708–8258; tel. 417/235–3144, **A**10 18 21 **F**3 11 15 18 28 29 30 31 32 34 35 40 45 50 56 57 59 64 68 70 75 77 79 81 85 89 90 93 107 110 111 115 119 127 128 129 130 131 133 135 144 146 148 149 154 156 **P**6 **S** CoxHealth, Springfield, MO
Primary Contact: Andrea McKay, President
CFO: Josh Powell, Facility Controller
CMO: Frank Romero, M.D., Vice President Medical Affairs and Chief Medical Officer
CHR: Debra Isenmann, Human Resources Generalist
CNO: Heidi Clark, Administrative Director of Nursing
Web address: www.coxhealth.com
Control: Other not–for–profit (including NFP Corporation) **Service**: General medical and surgical

Staffed Beds: 25 **Admissions**: 997 **Census**: 10 **Outpatient Visits**: 133064
Births: 191 **Total Expense ($000)**: 62770 **Payroll Expense ($000)**: 27246
Personnel: 338

Hospitals, U.S. / MISSOURI

MOUNTAIN VIEW—Howell County

MERCY ST. FRANCIS HOSPITAL (261335), 100 West Highway 60, Zip 65548-7125; tel. 417/934-7000, **A**1 10 18 **F**3 11 15 28 29 30 34 40 41 45 50 59 64 65 75 81 85 93 107 110 111 114 119 129 131 133 146 148 149 150 154 **S** Mercy, Chesterfield, MO
Primary Contact: Valerie Davis, Administrator, Mercy Hospital Aurora
CFO: Sherry Clouse Day, CPA, Chief Financial Officer
CMO: Barry Spoon, M.D., Chief of Staff
CHR: Tracy Smith, Director Human Resources
Web address: https://www.mercy.net/practice/mercy-st-francis-hospital/
Control: Church operated, Nongovernment, not-for-profit **Service**: General medical and surgical

Staffed Beds: 20 **Admissions**: 191 **Census**: 3 **Outpatient Visits**: 24432 **Births**: 0 **Total Expense ($000)**: 16914 **Payroll Expense ($000)**: 8967 **Personnel**: 96

NEOSHO—Newton County

★ **FREEMAN NEOSHO HOSPITAL (261331)**, 113 West Hickory Street, Zip 64850-1705; tel. 417/455-4352, **A**3 10 18 **F**3 11 15 28 30 34 35 40 44 45 50 56 57 59 64 68 70 75 77 81 85 86 87 90 93 97 107 110 111 114 119 127 130 131 132 133 154 156 **S** Freeman Health System, Joplin, MO
Primary Contact: Renee Denton, Chief Operating Officer
CFO: Steve W Graddy, Chief Financial Officer
CMO: Rodney McFarland, M.D., Medical Director
CIO: Sue Annesser, Director Information Systems
CHR: Mary Frerer, Chief Human Resources Officer
Web address: www.freemanhealth.com
Control: Other not-for-profit (including NFP Corporation) **Service**: General medical and surgical

Staffed Beds: 25 **Admissions**: 665 **Census**: 8 **Outpatient Visits**: 79312 **Births**: 2 **Total Expense ($000)**: 35478 **Payroll Expense ($000)**: 15240 **Personnel**: 182

NEVADA—Vernon County

☐ **HEARTLAND BEHAVIORAL HEALTH SERVICES (264013)**, 1500 West Ashland Street, Zip 64772-1710; tel. 417/667-2666, (Nonreporting) **A**1 10 **S** Universal Health Services, Inc., King of Prussia, PA
Primary Contact: Alyson Wysong-Harder, Chief Executive Officer
CFO: Wendy Duvall, Chief Financial Officer
CMO: Ahmad Tarar, M.D., Medical Director
CHR: Carri Compton, Administrative Officer
CNO: Amanda Sloniker, Director of Nursing
Web address: www.heartlandbehavioral.com
Control: Corporation, Investor-owned (for-profit) **Service**: Psychiatric

Staffed Beds: 69

NEVADA REGIONAL MEDICAL CENTER (260061), 800 South Ash Street, Zip 64772-3223; tel. 417/667-3355, **A**3 10 20 22 **F**3 11 13 14 15 18 26 27 28 29 30 32 34 35 40 45 50 54 59 64 65 66 68 70 73 74 75 76 77 81 82 83 85 86 87 89 90 91 93 94 96 97 98 99 101 102 103 104 107 108 110 111 115 119 127 128 129 130 131 133 143 144 146 147 148 154 169 **P**6
Primary Contact: Jason Anglin, Chief Executive Officer
CMO: Warren Lovinger, M.D., Chief Medical Officer
CIO: Marci Hardin, Manager Information Technology
CHR: Heather Brockmeyer, Human Resource Administrative Officer
CNO: Cory Vokoun, Chief Nursing Officer
Web address: www.nrmchealth.com
Control: City, Government, Nonfederal **Service**: General medical and surgical

Staffed Beds: 71 **Admissions**: 1745 **Census**: 22 **Outpatient Visits**: 11140 **Births**: 292 **Total Expense ($000)**: 47940 **Payroll Expense ($000)**: 25653 **Personnel**: 288

NORTH KANSAS CITY—Clay County

NORTH KANSAS CITY HOSPITAL (260096), 2800 Clay Edwards Drive, Zip 64116-3220; tel. 816/691-2000, **A**1 2 3 5 10 **F**3 11 12 13 15 17 18 20 22 24 26 28 29 30 31 34 35 37 40 43 45 46 47 48 49 50 51 53 57 58 59 60 64 70 72 74 75 76 77 78 79 80 81 82 84 85 86 87 89 90 93 96 107 108 110 111 115 117 118 119 120 121 123 124 126 129 130 131 132 135 136 146 147 148 149 154 156 166 167 168
Primary Contact: Stephen Reintjes Sr, M.D., President and Chief Executive Officer
COO: Kerri Jenkins, Senior Vice President and Chief Operating Officer
CFO: Henry Seybold, Senior Vice President and Chief Financial Officer
CMO: Steven Starr, Interim Chief Medical Officer
CIO: Kristen Guillaume, Vice President and Chief Information Officer
CHR: Dawn Bryant, Vice President Human Resources
CNO: Sarah G Oakley, R.N., MSN, Vice President Nursing
Web address: www.nkch.org
Control: City, Government, Nonfederal **Service**: General medical and surgical

Staffed Beds: 287 **Admissions**: 19116 **Census**: 248 **Outpatient Visits**: 342328 **Births**: 1817 **Total Expense ($000)**: 607472 **Payroll Expense ($000)**: 245709 **Personnel**: 2593

O FALLON—St. Charles County

PROGRESS WEST HOSPITAL (260219), 2 Progress Point Parkway, Zip 63368-2205; tel. 636/344-1000, **A**1 5 10 **F**3 13 15 18 20 22 26 28 29 30 34 35 40 41 45 46 49 51 57 59 60 70 73 74 75 76 77 79 81 85 86 87 89 107 108 110 111 115 118 119 130 132 135 146 147 148 149 154 156 169 **S** BJC Health System, Saint Louis, MO
Primary Contact: Gregory Patterson, President
COO: Gregory Patterson, Vice President and Chief Operating Officer
CFO: Glen Schwaegel, Chief Financial Officer
CMO: Dane Glueck, M.D., Chief of Staff
CHR: Michael J Miller, Director Human Resources
Web address: www.progresswest.org
Control: Other not-for-profit (including NFP Corporation) **Service**: General medical and surgical

Staffed Beds: 77 **Admissions**: 4660 **Census**: 46 **Outpatient Visits**: 91096 **Births**: 886 **Total Expense ($000)**: 120316 **Payroll Expense ($000)**: 50282 **Personnel**: 448

OSAGE BEACH—Camden County

LAKE REGIONAL HEALTH SYSTEM (260186), 54 Hospital Drive, Zip 65065-3050; tel. 573/348-8000, (Total facility includes 16 beds in nursing home-type unit) **A**1 3 10 **F**3 11 12 13 15 17 18 20 22 24 28 29 30 31 32 34 35 38 39 40 43 44 45 46 48 49 50 51 53 57 59 60 62 63 64 65 68 70 73 74 75 76 77 78 79 81 82 84 85 86 87 89 93 96 107 108 111 115 120 121 123 126 127 128 129 130 131 132 145 146 148 149 150 154 **P**6
Primary Contact: Kevin G. McRoberts, FACHE, Chief Executive Officer
CFO: Paula Littleton, Chief Financial Officer
CMO: Harbaksh Sangha, M.D., Chief Medical Officer
CIO: Patrick Neece, Chief Information Officer
CHR: Tom Williams, Vice President Human Resources
CNO: Melissa Hunter, Chief Nursing Officer
Web address: www.lakeregional.com
Control: Other not-for-profit (including NFP Corporation) **Service**: General medical and surgical

Staffed Beds: 121 **Admissions**: 5367 **Census**: 58 **Outpatient Visits**: 372928 **Births**: 652 **Total Expense ($000)**: 279240 **Payroll Expense ($000)**: 113664 **Personnel**: 163

★ ⇧ **OSAGE BEACH CENTER FOR BEHAVIORAL HEALTH, LLC (264031)**, 840 Passover Road, Zip 65065; tel. 573/302-0319, **A**10 21 **F**50 68 75 77 86 98 101 103 130 135 154 162 164
Primary Contact: Lydia Porter, Administrator
CNO: Lorri Steffen, Director of Nursing
Web address: www.osagebeachccd.com
Control: Corporation, Investor-owned (for-profit) **Service**: Psychiatric

Staffed Beds: 16 **Admissions**: 621 **Census**: 13 **Outpatient Visits**: 0 **Births**: 0 **Total Expense ($000)**: 4391 **Payroll Expense ($000)**: 2617 **Personnel**: 36

Hospital, Medicare Provider Number, Address, Telephone, Approval, Facility, and Physician Codes, Health Care System

★ American Hospital Association (AHA) membership ○ Healthcare Facilities Accreditation Program ⇧ Center for Improvement in Healthcare Quality Accreditation
☐ The Joint Commission accreditation ◇ DNV Healthcare Inc. accreditation △ Commission on Accreditation of Rehabilitation Facilities (CARF) accreditation

Hospitals, U.S. / MISSOURI

PERRYVILLE—Perry County

MERCY HOSPITAL PERRY (261311), 434 North West Street, Zip 63775–1398; tel. 573/547–2536, (Nonreporting) A1 10 18 S Mercy, Chesterfield, MO
Primary Contact: Christopher M. Wibbenmeyer, FACHE, President and Chief Executive Officer
CFO: Randall Wolf, Vice President Finance
CMO: Michael Steele, M.D., Chief of Staff
CIO: Michael Jobin, Chief Information Officer
Web address: https://www.mercy.net/practice/mercy-hospital-perry/
Control: Other not–for–profit (including NFP Corporation) **Service**: General medical and surgical

Staffed Beds: 25

PERRY COUNTY MEMORIAL HOSPITAL See Mercy Hospital Perry

PILOT KNOB—Iron County

IRON COUNTY MEDICAL CENTER (261336), 301 North Highway 21, Zip 63663–0548, Mailing Address: P.O. Box 548, Zip 63663–0548; tel. 573/546–1260, A10 18 F3 11 18 28 29 34 35 38 40 41 45 50 51 57 59 68 77 81 90 93 97 100 107 111 115 119 127 130 133 135 149 154
Primary Contact: Bruce Harrison, Chief Executive Officer
COO: Erika Griggs, Chief Operating Officer
CNO: Travis W. Moore, R.N., Director of Nursing and Compliance Officer
Web address: www.icmedcenter.org/
Control: Hospital district or authority, Government, Nonfederal **Service**: General medical and surgical

Staffed Beds: 15 **Admissions**: 292 **Census**: 6 **Outpatient Visits**: 33800
Births: 0 **Total Expense ($000)**: 19629 **Payroll Expense ($000)**: 7270
Personnel: 100

POPLAR BLUFF—Butler County

JOHN J. PERSHING VETERANS' ADMINISTRATION MEDICAL CENTER, 1500 North Westwood Boulevard, Zip 63901–3318; tel. 573/686–4151, (Nonreporting) A1 S Department of Veterans Affairs, Washington, DC
Primary Contact: James Warren, Interim Medical Center Director
COO: Seth Barlage, Associate Medical Center Director
CFO: Kristy Williams, Manager Finance
CMO: Vijayachandran Nair, M.D., Chief of Staff
CIO: Michael Gustin, Information Technology
CHR: Genise Denton, Manager Human Resources
CNO: Chandra Miller, Director of Nursing
Web address: www.poplarbluff.va.gov
Control: Veterans Affairs, Government, federal **Service**: General medical and surgical

Staffed Beds: 58

POPLAR BLUFF REGIONAL MEDICAL CENTER (260119), 3100 Oak Grove Road, Zip 63901, Mailing Address: P.O. Box 88, Zip 63902–0088; tel. 573/776–2000, (Nonreporting) A1 3 5 10 S Community Health Systems, Inc., Franklin, TN
Primary Contact: Clyde Wood, Chief Executive Officer
COO: Tony Torres, Chief Operating Officer
CFO: Jeff Kurcab, Chief Financial Officer
CHR: Denise Rushin, Director Human Resources
CNO: Timothy O'Neal, Chief Nursing Officer
Web address: www.poplarbluffregional.com
Control: Individual, Investor–owned (for–profit) **Service**: General medical and surgical

Staffed Beds: 274

POPLAR BLUFF VAMC See John J. Pershing Veterans' Administration Medical Center

POTOSI—Washington County

WASHINGTON COUNTY MEMORIAL HOSPITAL (261308), 300 Health Way, Zip 63664–1420; tel. 573/438–5451, A10 18 F3 5 15 28 29 31 33 34 35 36 40 43 45 47 50 57 59 64 65 74 79 81 85 87 90 91 92 93 97 98 101 104 107 108 111 115 119 127 129 130 131 133 135 143 144 145 146 148 151 152 154 160 161 166
Primary Contact: Michele C. Meyer, R.N., Chief Executive Officer
CFO: Debra Pratt, Chief Financial Officer
CMO: Jonathan Borchers, M.D., Chief Medical Officer
CIO: Jim Smith, Director Information Systems
CHR: Christy Aubuchon, Director Personnel
CNO: Beverly Williams, R.N., Chief Nursing Officer
Web address: www.wcmhosp.org
Control: County, Government, Nonfederal **Service**: General medical and surgical

Staffed Beds: 25 **Admissions**: 679 **Census**: 10 **Outpatient Visits**: 33880
Births: 0 **Total Expense ($000)**: 27222 **Payroll Expense ($000)**: 11417
Personnel: 216

RICHMOND—Ray County

★ **RAY COUNTY HOSPITAL AND HEALTHCARE (261327)**, 904 Wollard Boulevard, Zip 64085–2229; tel. 816/470–5432, A10 18 F3 11 15 28 29 31 44 45 56 64 68 75 77 78 79 81 85 87 90 93 104 107 108 110 111 115 117 119 128 130 133 154 P6
Primary Contact: Jeff Bloemker, Chief Executive Officer
CFO: David Usher, Chief Financial Officer
CHR: Donna Strain, Director Human Resources
Web address: www.raycountyhospital.com
Control: County, Government, Nonfederal **Service**: General medical and surgical

Staffed Beds: 25 **Admissions**: 258 **Census**: 4 **Outpatient Visits**: 10128
Births: 0 **Total Expense ($000)**: 25583 **Payroll Expense ($000)**: 11363
Personnel: 208

RICHMOND HEIGHTS—St. Louis County

△ **SSM SELECT REHABILITATION HOSPITAL (263031)**, 1027 Bellevue Avenue, 3rd Floor, Zip 63117–1851, Mailing Address: 1027 Bellevue Avenue, Zip 63117–1851; tel. 314/768–5300, (Includes SSM HEALTH REHABILITATION HOSPITAL – LAKE SAINT LOUIS, 100 Medical Plaza, Fifth Floor, Lake Saint Louis, Missouri, Zip 63367–1366, tel. 636/755–6500; Sarah Larkin, Chief Executive Officer; SSM SELECT REHABILITATION HOSPITAL, 12380 De Paul Drive, Bridgeton, Missouri, Zip 63044–2511, tel. 314/447–9700; John Grubbs, Chief Executive Officer) A1 7 10 F3 28 29 64 90 91 93 95 96 130 131 132 143 148 149 154 S Select Medical Corporation, Mechanicsburg, PA
Primary Contact: Cole Silverman, Chief Executive Officer
Web address: www.ssm-select.com
Control: Partnership, Investor–owned (for–profit) **Service**: Rehabilitation

Staffed Beds: 125 **Admissions**: 3243 **Census**: 115 **Outpatient Visits**: 0
Births: 0 **Total Expense ($000)**: 165407 **Payroll Expense ($000)**: 96781
Personnel: 1399

ROLLA—Phelps County

△ **PHELPS HEALTH (260017)**, 1000 West Tenth Street, Zip 65401–2905; tel. 573/458–8899, (Total facility includes 12 beds in nursing home–type unit) A1 2 7 10 F3 7 8 11 13 15 18 20 22 26 28 29 30 31 34 35 39 40 45 46 47 51 56 57 60 62 63 64 65 68 70 73 74 75 76 77 78 79 81 85 89 90 93 94 98 102 107 111 115 119 120 121 123 126 128 129 130 132 135 142 143 146 147 148 149 154 155 167 169
Primary Contact: Jason Shenefield, FACHE, President, Chief Executive Officer
COO: Keri S. Brookshire–Heavin, Senior Vice President, Chief Operating Officer and Chief Nursing Officer
CFO: Jana Cook, Vice President and Chief Financial Officer
CMO: Donald James, D.O., Senior Vice President and Chief Medical Officer
CIO: Jeff McKune, Chief Health Informatics Officer
CHR: Frank A. Lazzaro III, Chief Human Resources Officer
CNO: Keri S. Brookshire–Heavin, Senior Vice President, Chief Operating Officer and Chief Nursing Officer
Web address: https://phelpshealth.org/
Control: County, Government, Nonfederal **Service**: General medical and surgical

Staffed Beds: 153 **Admissions**: 6697 **Census**: 81 **Outpatient Visits**: 275120 **Births**: 690 **Total Expense ($000)**: 326429 **Payroll Expense ($000)**: 144687 **Personnel**: 1836

SAINT CHARLES—St. Charles County

CENTERPOINTE HOSPITAL (264012), 4801 Weldon Spring Parkway, Zip 63304–9101; tel. 636/441–7300, (Nonreporting) A1 10
Primary Contact: Karen Kasten, Chief Executive Officer
CFO: Tom Croffut, Chief Financial Officer
CMO: Azfar Malik, M.D., Chief Medical Officer
CIO: Jennifer Bourn, Director, Health Information Services and Medical Staff Services
CHR: Kelli White, Director, Human Resources
Web address: www.centerpointehospital.com
Control: Corporation, Investor–owned (for–profit) **Service**: Children's hospital psychiatric

Staffed Beds: 87

SSM HEALTH ST. JOSEPH – ST. CHARLES (260005), 300 First Capitol Drive, Zip 63301–2844; tel. 636/947–5000, (Includes SSM HEALTH ST. JOSEPH – WENTZVILLE, 500 Medical Drive, Wentzville, Missouri, Zip 63385–3421, tel. 636/327–1000; Douglas Barton, M.D., Interim President) A1 2 3 10 19 F3 4 5 8 11 15 18 20 22 26 28 29 30 31 34 35 38 40 41 44 45 49 50 53 54 55 57 58 59 60 62 63 64 65 67 68 70 74 75 77 78 79 81 82 84 85 86 87 90 92 97 98 99 100 101 102 104 105 107 108 111 114 115 118 119 126 128 129 130 132 135 144 145 146 147 148 149 150 153 154 161 164 165 167 S SSM Health, Saint Louis, MO
Primary Contact: Jacob Brooks, President
COO: Michael E. Bowers, Regional Executive Vice President and Chief Operating Officer
CFO: Karen Rewerts, System Vice President Finance
CMO: Douglas Barton, M.D., Chief Medical Officer
CIO: Margaret Feilner, Director Information Services
CHR: Debbie G Walkenhorst, System Vice President Talent Management
Web address: https://www.ssmhealth.com/locations/st-joseph-hospital-st-charles
Control: Church operated, Nongovernment, not–for–profit **Service**: General medical and surgical

Staffed Beds: 212 **Admissions**: 9697 **Census**: 153 **Outpatient Visits**: 184000 **Births**: 0 **Total Expense ($000)**: 340841 **Payroll Expense ($000)**: 148434 **Personnel**: 853

SELECT SPECIALTY HOSPITAL–ST. LOUIS (262013), 300 First Capitol Drive, Unit 1, Zip 63301–2844; tel. 636/947–5010, (Includes SELECT SPECIALTY HOSPITAL – TOWN AND COUNTRY, 3015 North Ballas Road, Fifth Floor, Saint Louis, Missouri, Zip 63131–2329, tel. 314/996–6500; Jeff Halbert, Chief Executive Officer) A1 10 F1 29 74 75 148 S Select Medical Corporation, Mechanicsburg, PA
Primary Contact: James W. McClung, Chief Executive Officer
Web address: https://www.selectspecialtyhospitals.com/locations-and-tours/mo/st-charles/st-louis/
Control: Corporation, Investor–owned (for–profit) **Service**: Acute long–term care hospital

Staffed Beds: 33 **Admissions**: 279 **Census**: 29 **Outpatient Visits**: 0 **Births**: 0 **Total Expense ($000)**: 21870 **Payroll Expense ($000)**: 10771 **Personnel**: 120

SAINT JOSEPH—Buchanan County

★ **LONG–TERM ACUTE CARE HOSPITAL, MOSAIC LIFE CARE AT ST. JOSEPH (262019)**, 5325 Faraon Street, Zip 64506–3488; tel. 816/271–6000, A10 F1 3 29 85 130 148 149 150 S Mosaic Life Care, Saint Joseph, MO
Primary Contact: Dana Anderson, R.N., Administrator
CNO: Douglas Schmitz, Director of Nursing
Web address: https://www.mymosaiclifecare.org/General/Long-Term-Acute-Care-Hospital/
Control: Other not–for–profit (including NFP Corporation) **Service**: Acute long–term care hospital

Staffed Beds: 39 **Admissions**: 173 **Census**: 20 **Outpatient Visits**: 0 **Births**: 0 **Total Expense ($000)**: 13833 **Payroll Expense ($000)**: 4985 **Personnel**: 62

MOSAIC LIFE CARE AT ST. JOSEPH – MEDICAL CENTER (260006), 5325 Faraon Street, Zip 64506–3488; tel. 816/271–6000, A1 2 10 20 F3 9 11 12 13 15 17 18 20 22 24 26 28 29 30 31 32 33 34 35 36 37 39 40 43 45 46 47 48 49 50 51 53 54 56 57 58 59 61 62 63 64 65 70 73 74 75 76 78 79 80 81 82 84 85 86 87 89 90 92 93 94 96 97 98 100 101 102 103 104 107 108 110 111 115 116 117 118 119 120 121 123 124 126 129 130 131 132 134 135 141 143 144 145 146 147 148 149 150 153 154 167 169 P6 S Mosaic Life Care, Saint Joseph, MO
Primary Contact: Tony A. Claycomb, R.N., President
COO: Curt Kretzinger, Chief Operating Officer
CFO: Dwain Stilson, Chief Financial Officer
CHR: Michael Pulido, Chief Administrative Officer
Web address: https://www.mymlc.com
Control: Other not–for–profit (including NFP Corporation) **Service**: General medical and surgical

Staffed Beds: 348 **Admissions**: 13377 **Census**: 183 **Outpatient Visits**: 1066216 **Births**: 1333 **Total Expense ($000)**: 724497 **Payroll Expense ($000)**: 309186 **Personnel**: 3478

☐ **NORTHWEST MISSOURI PSYCHIATRIC REHABILITATION CENTER (264007)**, 3505 Frederick Avenue, Zip 64506–2914; tel. 816/387–2300, A1 3 5 10 F4 11 29 30 53 65 75 77 86 87 97 98 101 103 130 132 135 143 146 149 163 164 P6
Primary Contact: Tara C. Tubbesing, Chief Operating Officer
COO: Mary Attebury, Chief Operating Officer
CFO: Randy Riley, Fiscal and Administrative Manager
CMO: James B Reynolds, M.D., Medical Director
CIO: Robert Curren, Western Region Chief Information Technology Officer
CHR: Mary Blakey Gorman, Director Human Resources
CNO: Pam Nold, Chief Nurse Executive
Web address: https://dmh.mo.gov
Control: State, Government, Nonfederal **Service**: Psychiatric

Staffed Beds: 108 **Admissions**: 27 **Census**: 105 **Outpatient Visits**: 0 **Births**: 0 **Total Expense ($000)**: 23463 **Payroll Expense ($000)**: 14974 **Personnel**: 309

SAINT LOUIS—St. Louis City County

BARNES–JEWISH HOSPITAL (260032), 1 Barnes–Jewish Hospital Plaza, Zip 63110–1003; tel. 314/747–3000, (Includes BARNES–JEWISH HOSPITAL PSYCHIATRIC SUPPORT CENTER, 5355 Delmar Boulevard, Saint Louis, Missouri, Zip 63112–3146, tel. 314/286–1700) (Total facility includes 120 beds in nursing home–type unit) A1 2 3 5 8 10 19 F3 4 5 8 9 11 12 13 15 16 17 18 20 22 24 26 28 29 30 31 34 35 36 37 38 39 40 41 43 44 45 46 47 48 49 50 51 52 53 54 55 56 57 58 59 60 61 63 64 65 66 68 70 71 73 74 75 76 77 78 79 80 81 82 83 84 85 86 87 89 90 91 92 93 94 96 97 98 100 101 103 104 107 108 109 110 111 112 114 115 116 117 118 119 120 121 122 123 124 126 128 129 130 131 132 134 135 136 137 138 139 140 141 142 143 145 146 147 148 149 150 154 156 157 158 160 161 162 163 164 165 167 169 P6 S BJC Health System, Saint Louis, MO
Primary Contact: John Lynch, M.D., President
COO: Angelleen Peters–Lewis, Ph.D., R.N., Vice President and Chief Operating Officer
CFO: Mark Krieger, Vice President and Chief Financial Officer
CHR: Betsy Rodriguez, Vice President Human Resources
Web address: www.barnesjewish.org
Control: Other not–for–profit (including NFP Corporation) **Service**: General medical and surgical

Staffed Beds: 1401 **Admissions**: 52965 **Census**: 1102 **Outpatient Visits**: 101731 **Births**: 3548 **Total Expense ($000)**: 2850319 **Payroll Expense ($000)**: 1071346 **Personnel**: 9766

KINDRED HOSPITAL–ST. LOUIS (262010), 4930 Lindell Boulevard, Zip 63108–1510; tel. 314/361–8700, (Includes KINDRED HOSPITAL ST. LOUIS SOUTH, 10018 Kennerly Road, 3rd Floor, Saint Louis, Missouri, Zip 63128, tel. 314/525–8100; Larry Rodgers, Market Chief Executive Officer) (Nonreporting) A1 10 S ScionHealth, Louisville, KY
Primary Contact: Larry Rodgers, Market Chief Executive Officer
COO: Dakota Redd, R.N., Chief Clinical Officer
CFO: Maureen Roach, Senior Chief Financial Officer
CMO: Michael Holtzman, M.D., Medical Director
CIO: Thomas C Christman, Director Plant Operations
CHR: Cindy Sander, Coordinator Human Resources
Web address: www.kindredstlouis.com/
Control: Corporation, Investor–owned (for–profit) **Service**: Acute long–term care hospital

Staffed Beds: 98

Hospitals, U.S. / MISSOURI

SSM CARDINAL GLENNON CHILDREN'S HOSPITAL See SSM Health Cardinal Glennon Children's Hospital

SSM HEALTH CARDINAL GLENNON CHILDREN'S HOSPITAL (263300), 1465 South Grand Boulevard, Zip 63104-1095; tel. 314/577-5600, **A**1 3 5 10 **F**3 11 12 16 18 19 21 23 25 27 29 30 31 32 34 35 38 39 40 41 43 44 45 46 47 48 49 50 51 54 55 57 59 60 61 64 66 68 72 73 74 75 77 78 79 80 81 82 84 85 86 87 88 89 90 93 94 97 99 100 101 104 115 118 119 124 126 129 130 131 136 137 138 139 141 142 144 146 148 150 154 156 167 **S** SSM Health, Saint Louis, MO
Primary Contact: Hossain Marandi, M.D., FACHE, President
CFO: Karen Rewerts, System Vice President of Finance
CMO: John Peter, M.D., Vice President Medical Affairs
CIO: Michael Paasch, Regional Vice President and Chief Information Officer
CHR: Debbie G Walkenhorst, Network Vice President
Web address: www.cardinalglennon.com
Control: Church operated, Nongovernment, not-for-profit **Service:** Children's general medical and surgical

Staffed Beds: 176 **Admissions:** 5607 **Census:** 118 **Outpatient Visits:** 249120 **Births:** 0 **Total Expense ($000):** 389924 **Payroll Expense ($000):** 126835 **Personnel:** 1449

SSM HEALTH SAINT LOUIS UNIVERSITY HOSPITAL (260105), 1201 South Grand Boulevard, Zip 63104-1016, Mailing Address: P.O. Box 15250, Zip 63110-0250; tel. 314/577-8000, (Includes SSM HEALTH SAINT LOUIS UNIVERSITY HOSPITAL-SOUTH, 1755 South Grand Boulevard, Saint Louis, Missouri, Zip 63104-1540, tel. 314/577-6027; Raymond Alvey, Chief Financial Officer) **A**1 2 3 5 8 10 19 **F**3 4 6 8 9 11 14 15 17 18 20 22 24 26 28 29 30 31 34 35 36 37 38 40 43 44 45 46 47 48 49 50 51 55 56 57 58 59 60 61 63 64 65 68 70 74 75 77 78 79 81 82 84 85 86 87 90 91 92 93 94 96 97 98 100 101 102 104 107 108 110 111 112 113 114 115 116 117 118 119 121 123 124 126 129 130 131 132 135 136 138 139 141 142 146 147 148 149 150 156 157 160 161 167 **S** SSM Health, Saint Louis, MO
Primary Contact: Steven M. Scott, M.P.H., FACHE, President
COO: Gretchen Leiterman, Chief Operating Officer
CFO: Raymond Alvey, Chief Financial Officer
CMO: Matthew Broom, Vice President of Medical Affairs and Chief Medical Officer
CIO: Patrick Brennan, Director Information System Technology
CNO: Rita Fowler, Vice President of Nursing and Chief Nursing Officer
Web address: https://www.ssmhealth.com
Control: Church operated, Nongovernment, not-for-profit **Service:** General medical and surgical

Staffed Beds: 406 **Admissions:** 16576 **Census:** 344 **Outpatient Visits:** 203992 **Births:** 0 **Total Expense ($000):** 885412 **Payroll Expense ($000):** 264953 **Personnel:** 1729

SSM HEALTH SAINT LOUIS UNIVERSITY HOSPITAL – SOUTH CAMPUS See SSM Health Saint Louis University Hospital-South

ST. LOUIS CHILDREN'S HOSPITAL (263301), 1 Children's Place, Zip 63110-1002; tel. 314/454-6000, **A**1 3 5 7 8 10 **F**3 7 8 11 12 16 17 19 20 21 22 23 24 25 26 27 29 30 31 32 33 34 35 36 37 38 39 40 41 43 44 45 46 47 48 49 50 51 52 54 57 58 59 60 61 62 63 64 65 66 70 71 72 73 74 75 77 78 79 81 82 83 84 85 86 87 88 89 90 91 92 93 94 95 96 98 99 100 101 102 104 107 108 109 111 114 115 117 118 119 126 129 130 131 132 134 136 137 138 139 140 141 142 143 145 146 148 149 150 154 155 156 164 165 167 **S** BJC Health System, Saint Louis, MO
Primary Contact: Trisha Lollo, President
CFO: Michele McKee, Vice President and Chief Financial Officer
CMO: F Sessions Cole, M.D., Chief Medical Officer
CNO: Peggy Gordin, Vice President, Patient Care Services and Chief Nursing Officer
Web address: www.stlouischildrens.org
Control: Other not-for-profit (including NFP Corporation) **Service:** Children's general medical and surgical

Staffed Beds: 355 **Admissions:** 12362 **Census:** 298 **Outpatient Visits:** 312152 **Births:** 0 **Total Expense ($000):** 996623 **Payroll Expense ($000):** 365060 **Personnel:** 3833

ST. LOUIS FORENSIC TREATMENT CENTER (264010), 5300 Arsenal Street, Zip 63139-1463; tel. 314/877-6501, **A**1 10 **F**11 30 39 65 68 75 86 87 98 100 101 130 143 146 157 163 164
Primary Contact: Felix T. Vincenz, Ph.D., Chief Executive Officer
CFO: James D Martin, Chief Financial Officer
CMO: Roy Wilson, M.D., Medical Director
CHR: Michael McFarlane, Chief Human Resource Officer
CNO: Deborah Mokry, Chief Nurse Executive
Web address: www.dmh.missouri.gov
Control: State, Government, Nonfederal **Service:** Psychiatric

Staffed Beds: 255 **Admissions:** 130 **Census:** 239 **Outpatient Visits:** 0 **Births:** 0 **Total Expense ($000):** 81302 **Payroll Expense ($000):** 30395 **Personnel:** 621

ST. LOUIS FORENSIC TREATMENT CENTER (264025), 5351 Delmar, Zip 63112-3198; tel. 314/877-0501, (Nonreporting) **A**10
Primary Contact: Laurent D. Javois, Regional Executive Officer
COO: Michael Bruce Anderson, Ph.D., Chief Operating Officer
CFO: James D Martin, Chief Financial Officer
CMO: Davinder Hayreh, M.D., Medical Director
CHR: Michael McFarlane, Director Human Resources
CNO: Sarah Jones, Chief Nurse Executive
Web address: www.dmh.missouri.gov/mpc
Control: State, Government, Nonfederal **Service:** Psychiatric

Staffed Beds: 50

ST. LOUIS PSYCHIATRIC REHABILITATION CENTER See St. Louis Forensic Treatment Center

ST. LOUIS REGIONAL PSYCHIATRIC STABILIZATION CENTER See Barnes-Jewish Hospital Psychiatric Support Center

THE REHABILITATION INSTITUTE OF ST. LOUIS (263028), 4455 Duncan Avenue, Zip 63110-1111; tel. 314/658-3800, **A**1 3 5 7 10 **F**29 34 35 44 56 60 64 68 74 75 79 87 90 91 94 100 103 130 132 143 148 149 150 **S** Encompass Health Corporation, Birmingham, AL
Primary Contact: Jeffrey Reese, Chief Executive Officer
CMO: David Carr, M.D., Physician Medical Director
CHR: Heather Savage, Director Human Resources
CNO: Angelina Sherman, R.N., MSN, Chief Nursing Officer
Web address: www.rehabinstitutestl.com
Control: Partnership, Investor-owned (for-profit) **Service:** Rehabilitation

Staffed Beds: 136 **Admissions:** 2587 **Census:** 96 **Outpatient Visits:** 0 **Births:** 0 **Total Expense ($000):** 56351 **Payroll Expense ($000):** 31049 **Personnel:** 314

VA ST. LOUIS HEALTH CARE SYSTEM, 915 North Grand Boulevard, Zip 63106-1621, Mailing Address: 1 Jefferson Barracks Dr BLDG 57, Zip 63125; tel. 314/652-4100, (Nonreporting) **A**1 3 5 7 **S** Department of Veterans Affairs, Washington, DC
Primary Contact: Candace Ifabiyi, FACHE, Medical Center Director
CFO: Karen Westerheide, Chief Financial Officer
CIO: Steve Warmbold, Director Information Management Service Line
CHR: Marie Lewis, Human Resources Liaison
CNO: Richard Holt, R.N., Associate Director Patient Care Services
Web address: www.stlouis.va.gov/
Control: Veterans Affairs, Government, federal **Service:** General medical and surgical

Staffed Beds: 240

VETERANS AFFAIRS ST. LOUIS HEALTH CARE SYSTEM See VA St. Louis Health Care System

SAINT LOUIS—St. Louis County

BARNES-JEWISH WEST COUNTY HOSPITAL (260162), 12634 Olive Boulevard, Zip 63141-6337; tel. 314/996-8000, **A**1 3 5 10 **F**3 8 12 15 29 34 35 37 40 45 46 47 49 50 51 54 59 60 64 65 68 70 75 77 78 79 81 82 85 93 96 107 110 111 115 117 119 120 121 123 126 129 130 131 141 146 148 149 154 156 167 **S** BJC Health System, Saint Louis, MO
Primary Contact: Angelleen Peters-Lewis, Ph.D., R.N., President
CFO: Diane M Glen, Assistant Administrator
CMO: Sam B Bhayani, M.D., Chief Medical Officer
CNO: Yoany Finetti, R.N., Vice President Patient Care Services Chief Nurse Officer
Web address: www.barnesjewishwestcounty.org
Control: Other not-for-profit (including NFP Corporation) **Service:** General medical and surgical

Staffed Beds: 100 **Admissions:** 3869 **Census:** 35 **Outpatient Visits:** 27046 **Births:** 0 **Total Expense ($000):** 257499 **Payroll Expense ($000):** 85509 **Personnel:** 737

Hospitals, U.S. / MISSOURI

✦ **CHRISTIAN HOSPITAL (260180)**, 11133 Dunn Road, Zip 63136–6119; tel. 314/653–5000, **A**1 3 10 19 **F**3 4 5 7 11 15 17 18 20 22 24 26 28 29 30 31 34 35 36 38 40 44 45 46 47 49 50 51 53 56 57 58 59 60 63 64 65 68 69 70 71 74 75 77 78 79 80 81 82 83 84 85 86 87 90 92 93 94 96 102 103 104 105 107 108 109 110 111 114 115 117 118 119 120 121 123 124 126 129 130 131 132 135 143 146 147 148 149 152 153 154 160 161 167 **P**6 **S** BJC Health System, Saint Louis, MO
Primary Contact: Rick Stevens, FACHE, President
COO: Douglas Black, Vice President of Operations
CMO: Sebastian Rueckert, M.D., Chief Medical Officer
CIO: Michael Kelly, Vice President
CHR: Bryan Hartwick, Vice President Human Resources
CNO: Jennifer Cordia, Vice President and Chief Nursing Executive
Web address: www.christianhospital.org
Control: Other not–for–profit (including NFP Corporation) **Service**: General medical and surgical

Staffed Beds: 232 **Admissions**: 12397 **Census**: 203 **Outpatient Visits**: 270400 **Births**: 0 **Total Expense ($000)**: 420052 **Payroll Expense ($000)**: 184269 **Personnel**: 1427

☐ **HAWTHORN CHILDREN PSYCHIATRIC HOSPITAL (264028)**, 1901 Pennsylvania, Zip 63133–1325, Mailing Address: 1901 Pennsylvania Avenue, Zip 63133–1325; tel. 314/512–7800, **A**1 3 5 10 **F**98 99 106 143 **P**6
Primary Contact: Michael McFarlane, Chief Executive Officer
COO: Michael McFarlane, Chief Operating Officer
CFO: James D Martin, Chief Financial Officer
CMO: Joshua Calhoun, M.D., Medical Director
CNO: Melody Chilese, Chief Nurse Executive
Web address: www.dmh.missouri.gov/hcph/
Control: State, Government, Nonfederal **Service**: Children's hospital psychiatric

Staffed Beds: 28 **Admissions**: 36 **Census**: 17 **Outpatient Visits**: 0 **Births**: 0 **Total Expense ($000)**: 18606 **Payroll Expense ($000)**: 5237 **Personnel**: 190

KINDRED HOSPITAL ST. LOUIS–ST. ANTHONY'S See Kindred Hospital St. Louis South

✦ △ **MERCY HOSPITAL SOUTH (260077)**, 10010 Kennerly Road, Zip 63128–2106; tel. 314/525–1000, **A**1 2 3 5 7 10 **F**3 4 5 8 11 12 13 15 17 18 20 22 24 26 28 29 30 31 33 34 35 36 38 40 41 43 44 45 46 47 49 50 53 54 60 62 63 64 65 68 69 70 73 74 75 76 77 78 79 80 81 82 84 85 86 87 89 90 91 92 93 96 97 98 99 100 101 102 103 104 105 106 107 108 109 110 111 114 115 116 117 118 119 120 121 123 124 126 129 130 132 135 143 146 147 148 149 153 154 156 157 167 169 **S** Mercy, Chesterfield, MO
Primary Contact: Sean Hogan, FACHE, President, Mercy South St. Louis Communities
Web address: www.stanthonysmedcenter.com
Control: Other not–for–profit (including NFP Corporation) **Service**: General medical and surgical

Staffed Beds: 536 **Admissions**: 26974 **Census**: 392 **Outpatient Visits**: 309328 **Births**: 1189 **Total Expense ($000)**: 552115 **Payroll Expense ($000)**: 247210 **Personnel**: 2314

✦ **MERCY HOSPITAL ST. LOUIS (260020)**, 615 South New Ballas Road, Zip 63141–8277; tel. 314/251–6000, (Includes MERCY CHILDREN'S HOSPITAL ST. LOUIS, 615 South New Ballas Road, Saint Louis, Missouri, Zip 63141–8221, tel. 314/251–6000; MERCY HEART AND VASCULAR HOSPITAL, 625 South New Ballas Road, Saint Louis, Missouri, Zip 63141–8240, tel. 314/251–1100; David Meiners, President) **A**1 2 3 5 8 10 **F**3 4 5 8 12 13 14 15 16 17 18 19 20 22 24 25 26 27 28 29 30 31 32 33 34 35 36 38 39 40 41 43 45 46 47 48 49 50 51 52 53 54 55 56 57 58 59 60 61 64 66 68 69 70 71 72 73 74 75 76 77 78 79 80 81 82 84 85 86 87 88 89 90 92 93 94 96 97 98 99 100 101 102 103 104 105 106 107 108 110 111 114 115 116 117 118 119 120 121 122 123 124 126 129 130 131 132 134 135 143 146 147 148 149 153 154 156 157 160 161 162 164 167 169 **S** Mercy, Chesterfield, MO
Primary Contact: David Meiners, President
CFO: Cheryl Matejka, Chief Financial Officer
CMO: Paul Hintze, M.D., Vice President Medical Affairs
CIO: Eugene Roth, Vice President Information Services
CHR: Rocky Ruello, Vice President Human Resources
Web address: www.mercy.net/stlouismo
Control: Other not–for–profit (including NFP Corporation) **Service**: General medical and surgical

Staffed Beds: 831 **Admissions**: 42451 **Census**: 614 **Outpatient Visits**: 869336 **Births**: 8367 **Total Expense ($000)**: 1201532 **Payroll Expense ($000)**: 420662 **Personnel**: 5117

✦ **MERCY REHABILITATION HOSPITAL SOUTH (263034)**, 10114 Kennerly Road, Zip 63128–2183; tel. 314/948–2000, **A**10 **F**29 30 60 90 148 **S** Lifepoint Health, Brentwood, TN
Primary Contact: Daniel Vogel Jr, Chief Executive Officer
CFO: Ryan Friley, CPA, Area Controller
CMO: Jennifer Page, M.D., Medical Director
CHR: Brooke Doherty, Director, People Services
CNO: Rhonda Morse, Chief Nursing Officer
Web address: https://www.mercy.net/practice/mercy-rehabilitation-hospital-south/
Control: Partnership, Investor–owned (for–profit) **Service**: Rehabilitation

Staffed Beds: 50 **Admissions**: 912 **Census**: 27 **Outpatient Visits**: 0 **Births**: 0 **Total Expense ($000)**: 13144 **Payroll Expense ($000)**: 8898 **Personnel**: 244

✦ **MISSOURI BAPTIST MEDICAL CENTER (260108)**, 3015 North Ballas Road, Zip 63131–2329; tel. 314/996–5000, **A**1 2 3 5 10 19 **F**3 11 13 14 15 17 18 19 20 22 24 26 28 29 30 31 34 35 36 40 41 45 46 47 48 49 50 51 54 56 57 58 59 60 63 64 65 67 68 69 70 72 73 74 75 76 77 78 79 81 82 83 85 87 89 90 92 93 94 97 99 100 101 102 107 108 110 111 114 115 116 117 118 119 120 121 123 124 126 130 131 132 145 146 147 148 149 154 156 157 162 164 167 169 **P**6 **S** BJC Health System, Saint Louis, MO
Primary Contact: Ann Abad, President
COO: Michael Kelly, Vice President Operations
CFO: Amy Desart, Vice President, Chief Financial Officer
CMO: Mitchell Botney, M.D., Vice President Medical Affairs and Chief Medical Officer
CIO: Tracie Jones, Director Information Services
CHR: Cyndy Donato, Vice President, Human Resources
CNO: Pamela Brouder, Associate Chief Nursing Officer
Web address: www.missouribaptist.org
Control: Other not–for–profit (including NFP Corporation) **Service**: General medical and surgical

Staffed Beds: 351 **Admissions**: 21464 **Census**: 287 **Outpatient Visits**: 412640 **Births**: 3475 **Total Expense ($000)**: 787944 **Payroll Expense ($000)**: 251046 **Personnel**: 2355

☐ **SHRINERS HOSPITALS FOR CHILDREN–ST. LOUIS (263304)**, 4400 Clayton Avenue, Zip 63110–1624; tel. 314/432–3600, **A**1 3 5 10 **F**3 29 58 64 74 75 79 81 85 86 89 93 94 130 131 143 146 154 **S** Shriners Hospitals for Children, Tampa, FL
Primary Contact: Mark Venable, Administrator
CFO: Sandra K. Lawson, Interim Director Fiscal Services
CMO: Perry L Schoenecker, M.D., Chief of Staff
CIO: Jeanne Hall, Director Information Systems
CHR: Mark Venable, Director Human Resources
Web address: https://www.shrinershospitalsforchildren.org
Control: Other not–for–profit (including NFP Corporation) **Service**: Children's orthopedic

Staffed Beds: 12 **Admissions**: 213 **Census**: 2 **Outpatient Visits**: 9376 **Births**: 0 **Total Expense ($000)**: 28629 **Payroll Expense ($000)**: 8007 **Personnel**: 123

✦ **SSM HEALTH ST. MARY'S HOSPITAL – ST. LOUIS (260091)**, 6420 Clayton Road, Zip 63117–1811; tel. 314/768–8000, **A**1 2 3 5 10 19 **F**3 13 15 18 20 22 26 28 29 30 31 34 35 37 38 40 44 45 46 48 49 50 51 52 55 56 57 58 59 60 61 64 66 70 72 73 74 75 76 78 79 82 85 86 87 97 98 100 101 102 103 104 107 108 110 111 115 119 120 121 126 129 130 132 135 143 144 146 147 148 149 153 154 156 167 **S** SSM Health, Saint Louis, MO
Primary Contact: Steven M. Scott, M.P.H., FACHE, President
CFO: Karen Rewerts, System Vice President of Finance
CMO: Stephen Kelly, M.D., Chief Medical Officer
CIO: Michael Paasch, Regional Chief Information Officer
Web address: https://www.ssmhealth.com/locations/st-marys-hospital-st-louis
Control: Church operated, Nongovernment, not–for–profit **Service**: General medical and surgical

Staffed Beds: 394 **Admissions**: 14265 **Census**: 206 **Outpatient Visits**: 217240 **Births**: 2225 **Total Expense ($000)**: 478413 **Payroll Expense ($000)**: 168443 **Personnel**: 1210

ST. JOHN'S MERCY CHILDREN'S HOSPITAL See Mercy Children's Hospital St. Louis

Hospitals, U.S. / MISSOURI

✠ **ST. LUKE'S DES PERES HOSPITAL (260176)**, 2345 Dougherty Ferry Road, Zip 63122-3313; tel. 314/966-9100, **A**1 3 5 10 12 13 **F**2 3 12 18 20 22 29 30 34 35 36 40 44 49 51 60 64 68 70 75 77 79 81 85 86 87 93 107 111 115 119 130 132 142 149 154 167 **S** St. Luke's Hospital, Chesterfield, MO
Primary Contact: Andrew Bagnall, FACHE, President and Chief Executive Officer
CFO: Steven Downs, Chief Financial Officer
CIO: Mary Estes, Director Information Systems
CHR: Kathaleen Clutts, Chief Human Resources Officer
CNO: Mary Ann Hampton, MSN, R.N., Chief Nursing Officer
Web address: https://www.stlukes-stl.com/desperes/
Control: Other not–for–profit (including NFP Corporation) **Service**: General medical and surgical

Staffed Beds: 55 **Admissions**: 1931 **Census**: 18 **Outpatient Visits**: 14776 **Births**: 0 **Total Expense ($000)**: 95205 **Payroll Expense ($000)**: 28662 **Personnel**: 331

SAINT PETERS—St. Charles County

✠ △ **BARNES–JEWISH ST. PETERS HOSPITAL (260191)**, 10 Hospital Drive, Zip 63376-1659; tel. 636/916-9000, **A**1 3 5 7 10 **F**2 3 15 18 20 22 26 28 29 30 31 34 35 40 45 46 49 51 57 59 60 64 70 74 75 77 78 79 81 85 86 87 93 107 108 110 111 115 118 119 120 121 123 124 126 129 130 132 135 146 147 148 149 154 156 167 **S** BJC Health System, Saint Louis, MO
Primary Contact: Gregory Patterson, President
CFO: Glen Schwaegel, Vice President and Chief Financial Officer
CMO: Feliipe Orellana, Chief Medical Officer
CIO: Cindy Gross, Director of Finance
CHR: Michael J Miller, Director Human Resources
CNO: Lauren Beckmann, Vice President Patient Services and Chief Nursing Officer
Web address: www.bjsph.org/
Control: Other not–for–profit (including NFP Corporation) **Service**: General medical and surgical

Staffed Beds: 102 **Admissions**: 6517 **Census**: 81 **Outpatient Visits**: 115520 **Births**: 0 **Total Expense ($000)**: 202567 **Payroll Expense ($000)**: 75455 **Personnel**: 672

SALEM—Dent County

★ **SALEM MEMORIAL DISTRICT HOSPITAL (261318)**, 35629 Highway 72, Zip 65560-7217, Mailing Address: P.O. Box 774, Zip 65560-0774; tel. 573/729-6626, (Total facility includes 18 beds in nursing home–type unit) **A**10 18 **F**3 7 11 15 29 30 34 35 40 41 45 56 57 59 64 67 68 75 77 81 87 89 93 100 107 110 111 115 119 127 128 130 133 149
Primary Contact: Brooke Bollman, Chief Executive Officer
CFO: Kayla Chamberlain, Chief Financial Officer
CMO: John Demorlis, M.D., Chief Medical Staff
CHR: Jodie Gorman, Director Human Resources
CNO: Ashley Sullins, Chief Nursing Officer
Web address: www.smdh.net
Control: Hospital district or authority, Government, Nonfederal **Service**: General medical and surgical

Staffed Beds: 43 **Admissions**: 577 **Census**: 26 **Outpatient Visits**: 25224 **Births**: 0 **Total Expense ($000)**: 30610 **Payroll Expense ($000)**: 12881 **Personnel**: 192

SEDALIA—Pettis County

✠ **BOTHWELL REGIONAL HEALTH CENTER (260009)**, 601 East 14th Street, Zip 65301-5972, Mailing Address: P.O. Box 1706, Zip 65302-1706; tel. 660/826-8833, **A**1 3 5 10 **F**3 9 11 13 15 18 20 26 28 29 30 31 34 35 38 40 45 46 50 51 54 56 57 59 64 65 68 70 73 74 75 76 77 78 79 80 81 82 86 87 89 90 92 93 97 107 108 110 111 115 118 119 120 121 123 124 127 129 130 131 132 133 146 147 148 149 154 156 164 167 169
Primary Contact: Lori Wightman, R.N., FACHE, Chief Executive Officer
COO: Thomas Bailey, Chief Operating Officer
CMO: Philip Fracica, M.D., Chief Medical Officer
CIO: Tom Fairfax, Director Information Systems
CHR: Deb Clemmer, Vice President Human Resources
CNO: Michele Laas, R.N., Chief Nursing Officer
Web address: www.brhc.org
Control: City, Government, Nonfederal **Service**: General medical and surgical

Staffed Beds: 74 **Admissions**: 3011 **Census**: 33 **Outpatient Visits**: 110376 **Births**: 456 **Total Expense ($000)**: 156231 **Payroll Expense ($000)**: 62025 **Personnel**: 738

SIKESTON—Scott County

☐ **MISSOURI DELTA MEDICAL CENTER (260113)**, 1008 North Main Street, Zip 63801-5044; tel. 573/471-1600, **A**1 5 10 **F**3 11 13 15 28 29 30 31 33 34 35 37 40 45 50 51 54 56 59 60 62 63 64 68 70 74 75 76 77 78 79 81 82 84 85 87 89 90 93 94 97 98 99 102 103 104 107 110 111 115 116 118 119 126 127 129 130 131 132 144 146 147 148 149 153 154 164 169
Primary Contact: Jason Schrumpf, FACHE, Chief Executive Officer
CFO: Greg Carda, Vice President Finance
Web address: www.missouridelta.com
Control: Other not–for–profit (including NFP Corporation) **Service**: General medical and surgical

Staffed Beds: 108 **Admissions**: 3521 **Census**: 49 **Outpatient Visits**: 23121 **Births**: 455 **Total Expense ($000)**: 144849 **Payroll Expense ($000)**: 59814 **Personnel**: 876

SMITHVILLE—Clay County

SAINT LUKE'S NORTHLAND HOSPITAL-SMITHVILLE CAMPUS See Saint Luke's North Hospital–Smithville Campus

SPRINGFIELD—Greene County

⇑ **COX MEDICAL CENTERS** See Cox North Hospital

★ △ ⇑ **COX NORTH HOSPITAL (260040)**, 1423 North Jefferson Street, Zip 65802-1988; tel. 417/269-3000, (Includes COX MEDICAL CENTER NORTH, 1423 North Jefferson Avenue, Springfield, Missouri, Zip 65802, tel. 417/269-3000; COX MEDICAL CENTER SOUTH, 3801 South National Avenue, Springfield, Missouri, Zip 65807, tel. 417/269-6000) **A**3 5 7 10 19 21 **F**3 4 5 7 11 12 13 15 17 18 19 20 22 24 26 28 29 30 31 32 34 35 38 39 40 41 42 43 44 45 46 47 48 49 50 51 52 53 54 55 56 57 58 59 60 61 62 64 65 68 69 70 71 72 73 74 75 76 77 78 79 80 81 82 84 85 86 87 88 89 90 91 92 93 94 96 98 99 100 101 102 103 104 107 108 110 111 114 115 116 117 118 119 120 121 124 126 128 129 130 131 134 135 143 144 146 147 148 149 150 152 154 155 156 160 161 162 167 168 **P**6 **S** CoxHealth, Springfield, MO
Primary Contact: Ashley Kimberling–Casad, President of Springfield Hospitals
CFO: Jacob McWay, Senior Vice President and Chief Financial Officer
CMO: Frank Romero, M.D., Chief Medical Officer
CHR: John Hursh, Vice President Human Resources
Web address: www.coxhealth.com
Control: Other not–for–profit (including NFP Corporation) **Service**: General medical and surgical

Staffed Beds: 734 **Admissions**: 33547 **Census**: 522 **Outpatient Visits**: 2424408 **Births**: 3486 **Total Expense ($000)**: 1686546 **Payroll Expense ($000)**: 551767 **Personnel**: 10087

☐ **LAKELAND BEHAVIORAL HEALTH SYSTEM (264024)**, 440 South Market Street, Zip 65806-2026; tel. 417/865-5581, **A**1 10 **F**98 99 103 130 135 149 164 **S** Acadia Healthcare Company, Inc., Franklin, TN
Primary Contact: Nathan Duncan, Chief Executive Officer
COO: Randy Fox, Director Performance Improvement and Risk Management
CFO: Rick Crump, Chief Financial Officer
CMO: Richard Aiken, M.D., Medical Director
CIO: Brad Strothkamp, Chief Information Systems
CHR: Dave England, Director Human Resources
Web address: https://www.lakelandbehavioralhealth.com/
Control: Corporation, Investor-owned (for-profit) **Service**: Psychiatric

Staffed Beds: 206 **Admissions**: 1910 **Census**: 171 **Outpatient Visits**: 3200 **Births**: 0 **Total Expense ($000)**: 33299 **Payroll Expense ($000)**: 20549 **Personnel**: 420

LESTER E. COX MEDICAL CENTER NORTH See Cox Medical Center North

LESTER E. COX MEDICAL CENTER SOUTH See Cox Medical Center South

Hospitals, U.S. / MISSOURI

✠ **MERCY HOSPITAL SPRINGFIELD (260065)**, 1235 East Cherokee Street, Zip 65804–2263; tel. 417/820–2000, (Includes MERCY CHILDREN'S HOSPITAL SPRINGFIELD, 1235 East Cherokee Street, Springfield, Missouri, Zip 65804–2203, tel. 417/820–2000; MERCY ORTHOPEDIC HOSPITAL SPRINGFIELD, 3050 E River Bluff Blvd, Ozark, Missouri, Zip 65721–8807, 3050 East Riverbluff Boulevard, Zip 65721, tel. 417/820–5611; Robert Steele, M.D., President) **A**1 2 3 5 10 **F**3 4 7 8 9 11 12 13 15 16 17 18 19 20 22 24 26 27 28 29 30 31 32 34 35 37 38 39 40 41 43 45 46 47 48 49 50 51 52 53 54 55 56 57 58 59 60 61 62 63 64 65 66 67 68 70 71 72 73 74 75 76 77 78 79 80 81 82 83 84 85 86 87 88 89 90 91 92 93 94 96 97 98 100 102 104 107 111 114 115 116 117 118 119 120 121 123 124 126 129 130 131 132 133 135 143 146 147 148 149 155 156 157 162 164 167 168 169 **S** Mercy, Chesterfield, MO
Primary Contact: John Myers, President, Mercy Springfield Communities
COO: Taylor Warwick, Chief Operating Officer
CFO: Scott Reynolds, Vice President Finance
CMO: Sadaf Sohrab, M.D., Chief Medical Officer
CIO: Lori Sturgill, Vice President Business Partnership
CHR: Tanya Maricn, Interim Vice President Human Resources
CNO: Marie Moore, Chief Nursing Officer
Web address: www.mercy.net/springfieldmo
Control: Church operated, Nongovernment, not–for–profit **Service**: General medical and surgical

Staffed Beds: 504 **Admissions:** 31702 **Census:** 457 **Outpatient Visits:** 579808 **Births:** 3020 **Total Expense ($000):** 990921 **Payroll Expense ($000):** 414748 **Personnel:** 4397

☐ △ **MERCY REHABILITATION HOSPITAL SPRINGFIELD (263032)**, 5904 South Southwood Road, Zip 65804–5234; tel. 417/227–9000, **A**1 7 10 **F**29 30 90 95 96
Primary Contact: Brent Yates, Chief Executive Officer
CFO: Melissa Campbell, Chief Financial Officer and Controller
CMO: Hollis Bell, M.D., Esq, Medical Director
CHR: Melissa Mooney, Director Human Resources
CNO: Paul Moore, R.N., Chief Clinical Officer
Web address: www.mercy.net
Control: Partnership, Investor–owned (for–profit) **Service**: Rehabilitation

Staffed Beds: 60 **Admissions:** 1433 **Census:** 43 **Outpatient Visits:** 0 **Births:** 0 **Total Expense ($000):** 19053 **Payroll Expense ($000):** 9182 **Personnel:** 93

☐ **PERIMETER BEHAVIORAL HOSPITAL OF SPRINGFIELD (264033)**, 2828 North National Avenue, Zip 65803–4306; tel. 417/799–7474, (Nonreporting) **A**1 10 **S** Perimeter Healthcare, Alpharetta, GA
Primary Contact: Alyssa Ingle, Chief Executive Officer
Web address: https://www.perimeterhealthcare.com/springfield
Control: Corporation, Investor–owned (for–profit) **Service**: Psychiatric

Staffed Beds: 32

✠ **SELECT SPECIALTY HOSPITAL–SPRINGFIELD (262017)**, 1630 East Primrose Street, Zip 65804–7929; tel. 417/885–4700, **A**1 10 **F**1 3 29 45 85 107 114 119 148 **S** Select Medical Corporation, Mechanicsburg, PA
Primary Contact: Elizabeth Hallam, R.N., Chief Executive Officer
CHR: Tonya Eddington, Coordinator Human Resources
Web address: www.selectspecialtyhospitals.com/company/locations/springfield.aspx
Control: Corporation, Investor–owned (for–profit) **Service**: Acute long–term care hospital

Staffed Beds: 44 **Admissions:** 483 **Census:** 31 **Outpatient Visits:** 0 **Births:** 0 **Total Expense ($000):** 22252 **Payroll Expense ($000):** 10188 **Personnel:** 182

ST. JOHN'S CHILDREN'S HOSPITAL See Mercy Children's Hospital Springfield

STE GENEVIEVE—Ste. Genevieve County

★ **STE. GENEVIEVE COUNTY MEMORIAL HOSPITAL (261330)**, 800 Ste Genevieve Drive, Zip 63670–1434, Mailing Address: 800 Saiinte Genevieve Drive, Sainte Genevieve, Zip 63670–1434; tel. 573/883–2751, **A**10 18 **F**3 4 11 13 14 15 18 28 29 31 34 35 40 50 53 55 56 57 59 62 64 65 75 76 77 78 79 81 82 86 89 92 107 110 111 115 119 124 127 129 130 131 132 133 135 146 147 148 154 160 167 169 **P**5 6
Primary Contact: John Steve Pautler, FACHE, Chief Executive Officer
CFO: Susan Eckenfels, Chief Financial Officer
CMO: Joseph Sharlow, M.D., Chief of Staff
CHR: Sarah Hi Kelley, Executive Director of Human Resources and Support Services
CNO: Rita Brumfield, R.N., MSN, Chief Nursing Officer
Web address: www.stegenevievehospital.org
Control: County, Government, Nonfederal **Service**: General medical and surgical

Staffed Beds: 25 **Admissions:** 752 **Census:** 10 **Outpatient Visits:** 7944 **Births:** 154 **Total Expense ($000):** 69618 **Payroll Expense ($000):** 28575 **Personnel:** 413

SULLIVAN—Crawford County

★ **MISSOURI BAPTIST SULLIVAN HOSPITAL (261337)**, 751 Sappington Bridge Road, Zip 63080–2354; tel. 573/468–4186, **A**10 18 **F**3 7 11 12 13 15 28 29 30 31 34 35 40 45 50 56 57 59 63 64 65 70 75 76 77 78 79 81 82 83 85 86 87 89 90 93 97 98 102 103 104 107 111 115 119 127 129 130 131 133 146 148 149 154 167 169 **S** BJC Health System, Saint Louis, MO
Primary Contact: Lisa Lochner, President
CFO: Angela Wilks, Finance Director
CMO: Alison Baker, M.D., Chief of Staff
CHR: Kathleen Reed, Manager Human Resources
CNO: Carmen J. Bartolotta, R.N., Vice President, Patient Care Services and Chief Nursing Officer
Web address: www.missouribaptistsullivan.org
Control: Other not–for–profit (including NFP Corporation) **Service**: General medical and surgical

Staffed Beds: 35 **Admissions:** 2257 **Census:** 24 **Outpatient Visits:** 110840 **Births:** 197 **Total Expense ($000):** 71868 **Payroll Expense ($000):** 29361 **Personnel:** 415

TRENTON—Grundy County

✠ **WRIGHT MEMORIAL HOSPITAL (261309)**, 191 Iowa Boulevard, Zip 64683–8343; tel. 660/358–5700, **A**1 10 18 **F**3 4 11 15 18 28 29 30 31 34 35 40 44 45 50 56 59 64 65 68 74 75 77 78 79 81 82 85 86 87 89 90 93 96 97 102 104 107 108 110 111 115 119 127 128 130 131 133 141 146 148 149 154 **S** BJC Health System, Saint Louis, MO
Primary Contact: Catherine Hamilton, MSN, R.N., Administrator
CFO: Leslie Reed, Chief Financial Officer
CMO: Gerald C Zabielski, M.D., Chief Medical Staff
CHR: Jenny Donovan, Director Human Resources
Web address: www.saintlukeshealthsystem.org
Control: Other not–for–profit (including NFP Corporation) **Service**: General medical and surgical

Staffed Beds: 10 **Admissions:** 342 **Census:** 6 **Outpatient Visits:** 41488 **Births:** 0 **Total Expense ($000):** 37907 **Payroll Expense ($000):** 13699 **Personnel:** 171

TROY—Lincoln County

✠ **MERCY HOSPITAL LINCOLN (261319)**, 1000 East Cherry Street, Zip 63379–1513; tel. 636/528–8551, **A**1 10 18 **F**3 11 15 18 28 29 30 34 35 40 44 45 50 51 59 63 64 65 68 70 75 77 79 81 85 86 87 90 93 104 107 110 111 113 114 119 127 128 129 130 131 133 135 144 146 147 148 149 154 156 157 164 167 **S** Mercy, Chesterfield, MO
Primary Contact: Alan Smith, Administrator
CFO: Mark Thorn, FACHE, Executive Director, Finance
CIO: Travis Boyd, Manager, Information Technology
CHR: Mary Kay Kunza, Manager Human Resources
Web address: www.mercy.net
Control: Other not–for–profit (including NFP Corporation) **Service**: General medical and surgical

Staffed Beds: 18 **Admissions:** 776 **Census:** 8 **Outpatient Visits:** 68576 **Births:** 0 **Total Expense ($000):** 40133 **Payroll Expense ($000):** 24649 **Personnel:** 238

Hospital, Medicare Provider Number, Address, Telephone, Approval, Facility, and Physician Codes, Health Care System

★ American Hospital Association (AHA) membership   ○ Healthcare Facilities Accreditation Program   ⇑ Center for Improvement in Healthcare Quality Accreditation
☐ The Joint Commission accreditation   ◇ DNV Healthcare Inc. accreditation   △ Commission on Accreditation of Rehabilitation Facilities (CARF) accreditation

Hospitals, U.S. / MISSOURI

UNIONVILLE—Putnam County

★ **PUTNAM COUNTY MEMORIAL HOSPITAL (261305)**, 1926 Oak Street, Zip 63565–1180, Mailing Address: P.O. Box 389, Zip 63565–0389; tel. 660/947–2411, **A**10 18 **F**3 4 5 15 18 29 32 34 35 39 40 50 57 59 64 75 77 82 85 90 93 97 98 102 107 110 111 115 119 127 128 130 131 133 135 143 147 148 149 152 154 156 160 161 167 **P**3 5 6
Primary Contact: Arlene G. Pickens, Chief Executive Officer
COO: Jerry Cummings, Chief Operating Officer
CMO: Dawn Ann Fairley, M.D., Chief of Staff
CHR: Debbie Douglas, Director Human Resources
CNO: Nathan Baughman, Chief Nursing Officer
Web address: www.pcmhosp.com
Control: County, Government, Nonfederal **Service**: General medical and surgical

Staffed Beds: 15 **Admissions**: 209 **Census**: 3 **Outpatient Visits**: 5072
Births: 0 **Total Expense ($000)**: 12078 **Payroll Expense ($000)**: 5351
Personnel: 91

WARRENSBURG—Johnson County

☐ **WESTERN MISSOURI MEDICAL CENTER (260097)**, 403 Burkarth Road, Zip 64093–3101; tel. 660/747–2500, **A**1 10 20 **F**3 8 11 13 15 18 28 29 30 31 32 34 35 40 43 45 47 53 57 59 60 61 64 65 68 70 74 75 76 77 78 79 81 82 85 87 89 90 93 97 102 107 108 110 111 115 117 118 119 126 127 129 130 131 132 133 135 144 146 147 148 149 154 156 167 169
Primary Contact: Darinda Dick, MSN, R.N., President and Chief Executive Officer
CFO: Dean Ohmart, Vice President Financial Services and Chief Financial Officer
CIO: Bill Ladd, Director Information Services
CHR: Dennis Long, Director Human Resources
Web address: www.wmmc.com
Control: County, Government, Nonfederal **Service**: General medical and surgical

Staffed Beds: 45 **Admissions**: 2152 **Census**: 19 **Outpatient Visits**: 24096
Births: 599 **Total Expense ($000)**: 128526 **Payroll Expense ($000)**: 54896
Personnel: 660

WASHINGTON—Franklin County

✠ **MERCY HOSPITAL WASHINGTON (260052)**, 901 East Fifth Street, Zip 63090–3127; tel. 636/239–8000, **A**1 10 **F**3 8 11 12 13 14 15 17 18 20 22 26 28 29 30 31 32 34 35 39 40 43 44 46 48 49 50 51 52 53 54 56 57 59 61 64 66 68 69 70 73 74 75 76 77 78 79 80 81 82 85 86 87 89 92 93 94 96 97 100 101 102 103 104 107 108 110 111 114 115 116 117 118 119 120 121 123 127 129 130 131 132 134 135 143 146 147 148 149 153 154 156 157 164 167 **S** Mercy, Chesterfield, MO
Primary Contact: Eric Eoloff, President, Mercy Washington
CFO: Cheryl Matejka, Chief Financial Officer
CMO: Thomas Riechers, M.D., Chief Medical Staff
CIO: Michael McCreary, Chief of Services
CHR: Barbara Grayson, Vice President Human Resources
CNO: Anna Landon, Chief Nursing Officer
Web address: www.mercy.net
Control: Other not–for–profit (including NFP Corporation) **Service**: General medical and surgical

Staffed Beds: 97 **Admissions**: 6933 **Census**: 61 **Outpatient Visits**: 249624
Births: 723 **Total Expense ($000)**: 169610 **Payroll Expense ($000)**: 76645
Personnel: 843

WENTZVILLE—St. Charles County

SSM HEALTH ST. JOSEPH – WENTZVILLE See SSM Health St. Joseph – St. Charles, Saint Charles

SSM ST. JOSEPH – WENTZVILLE See SSM Health St. Joseph – Wentzville

WEST PLAINS—Howell County

✠ **OZARKS HEALTHCARE (260078)**, 1100 Kentucky Avenue, Zip 65775–2029, Mailing Address: P.O. Box 1100, Zip 65775–1100; tel. 417/256–9111, **A**1 5 10 **F**2 3 11 13 15 17 18 20 22 28 29 30 31 38 40 44 45 63 70 76 82 83 89 90 98 120 121 123 124 **P**8
Primary Contact: Thomas W. Keller, President and Chief Executive Officer
CFO: Nichole Cook, Chief Financial Officer
CIO: EZ Niles, Executive Director of Information Technology
CHR: Connie Schott, Vice President, Human Resources
CNO: Lacey Carter, MSN, Chief Nursing Officer
Web address: https://www.ozarkshealthcare.com/
Control: Other not–for–profit (including NFP Corporation) **Service**: General medical and surgical

Staffed Beds: 103 **Admissions**: 5001 **Census**: 50 **Outpatient Visits**: 68856
Births: 520 **Total Expense ($000)**: 237182 **Payroll Expense ($000)**: 93546
Personnel: 930

WINDSOR—Henry County

⚙ **ROYAL OAKS HOSPITAL (264020)**, 307 North Main, Zip 65360–1449; tel. 660/647–2182, (Nonreporting) **A**3 5 10 21
Primary Contact: Alan W. Greiman, Chief Executive Officer and President
CFO: Jake Matthew Krafve, Chief Financial Officer
CMO: Syed Arshad Husain, M.D., Executive Vice President and Chief Medical Officer
CIO: Richard Colvert, Chief Information Officer
CHR: Diane Coletta, Vice President Human Resources
CNO: Saundra Overton, R.N., Chief Nursing Officer
Web address: www.compasshealthnetwork.org
Control: Other not–for–profit (including NFP Corporation) **Service**: Psychiatric

Staffed Beds: 48

MONTANA

ANACONDA—Deer Lodge County

★ **COMMUNITY HOSPITAL OF ANACONDA (271335)**, 401 West Pennsylvania Street, Zip 59711; tel. 406/563-8500, (Total facility includes 32 beds in nursing home-type unit) **A**3 10 18 **F**3 13 15 29 31 34 35 40 41 43 45 46 47 50 51 54 56 57 59 62 63 64 65 66 68 70 75 76 77 78 79 81 82 85 87 89 93 97 99 100 101 102 104 107 111 115 119 126 128 130 131 132 133 143 144 146 148 154 156 160 162 164 165 167 169 **P**6
Primary Contact: Jo Ellen Villa, R.N., Chief Executive Officer
CFO: Meg Hickey-Boynton, Chief Financial Officer
CMO: Freddy Bartoletti, M.D., Chief of Staff
CHR: Meg Hickey-Boynton, Director Human Resources and Marketing
CNO: Jamie Johnson, R.N., Vice President Nursing
Web address: www.communityhospitalofanaconda.org
Control: Other not-for-profit (including NFP Corporation) **Service:** General medical and surgical

Staffed Beds: 57 **Admissions:** 878 **Census:** 30 **Outpatient Visits:** 89517
Births: 129 **Total Expense ($000):** 92940 **Payroll Expense ($000):** 41348
Personnel: 342

BAKER—Fallon County

FALLON MEDICAL COMPLEX (271301), 202 South 4th Street West, Zip 59313-9156, Mailing Address: P.O. Box 820, Zip 59313-0820; tel. 406/778-3331, **A**10 18 **F**3 11 15 32 34 40 56 57 59 62 64 65 66 68 69 75 93 97 107 110 114 119 127 128 130 133 146 148 149 **P**6
Primary Contact: David Espeland, Chief Executive Officer
CFO: Selena Nelson, Chief Financial Officer
CMO: Darryl Espeland, D.O., Chief Medical Staff
CIO: Susan Stevens, Information Technology Specialist
CHR: Theresa Myers, Personnel Director
CNO: Susan Lunde, R.N., Director of Nursing
Web address: www.fallonmedical.org
Control: Other not-for-profit (including NFP Corporation) **Service:** General medical and surgical

Staffed Beds: 25 **Admissions:** 81 **Census:** 16 **Outpatient Visits:** 13025
Births: 0 **Total Expense ($000):** 12372 **Payroll Expense ($000):** 3927
Personnel: 78

BIG SANDY—Chouteau County

★ **BIG SANDY MEDICAL CENTER (271311)**, 166 Montana Avenue East, Zip 59520-8474, Mailing Address: P.O. Box 530, Zip 59520-0530; tel. 406/378-2188, **A**10 18 **F**3 11 29 33 34 35 40 53 56 59 77 93 104 127 133 143 144 148 156
Primary Contact: Ron Wiens, Chief Executive Officer
CFO: Nora Grubb, Chief Financial Officer
Web address: www.bsmc.org
Control: Other not-for-profit (including NFP Corporation) **Service:** General medical and surgical

Staffed Beds: 25 **Admissions:** 66 **Census:** 18 **Outpatient Visits:** 3102
Births: 0 **Total Expense ($000):** 6144 **Payroll Expense ($000):** 2487
Personnel: 50

BIG SKY—Gallatin County

⇧ **BOZEMAN HEALTH BIG SKY MEDICAL CENTER (271389)**, 334 Town Center Avenue, Suite 161529, Zip 59716, Mailing Address: P.O. Box 161529, Zip 59716-1529; tel. 406/995-6995, **A**10 18 21 **F**3 29 34 35 38 40 43 57 59 65 85 87 93 102 104 107 111 115 119 133 144 154 162 164
Primary Contact: Chris Darnell, Administrator
Web address: https://www.bigskymedicalcenter.org/
Control: Other not-for-profit (including NFP Corporation) **Service:** General medical and surgical

Staffed Beds: 8 **Admissions:** 51 **Census:** 1 **Outpatient Visits:** 23526
Births: 0 **Total Expense ($000):** 18576 **Payroll Expense ($000):** 5863
Personnel: 74

BIG TIMBER—Sweet Grass County

★ **PIONEER MEDICAL CENTER (271313)**, 301 West Seventh Avenue, Zip 59011-7893, Mailing Address: P.O. Box 1228, Zip 59011-1228; tel. 406/932-4603, **A**10 18 **F**2 7 10 28 29 34 40 56 57 59 63 64 65 67 68 82 93 97 107 119 127 128 133 135 146 154
Primary Contact: Ian Peterson, Chief Executive Officer
CFO: Kyle Gee, Chief Financial Officer
CMO: Benjamin P Bullington, M.D., Chief of Staff
CHR: Miki Gregorich, Director Human Resources
CNO: Randi Pike, Director of Nursing
Web address: www.pmcmt.org/
Control: Other not-for-profit (including NFP Corporation) **Service:** General medical and surgical

Staffed Beds: 25 **Admissions:** 88 **Census:** 1 **Outpatient Visits:** 10943
Births: 0 **Total Expense ($000):** 10636 **Payroll Expense ($000):** 3227
Personnel: 82

BILLINGS—Yellowstone County

☐ **ADVANCED CARE HOSPITAL OF MONTANA (272001)**, 3528 Gabel Road, Zip 59102-7307; tel. 406/373-8000, (Nonreporting) **A**1 10 **S** Ernest Health, Inc., Albuquerque, NM
Primary Contact: Aubrey Peterschick, Chief Executive Officer
Web address: www.achm.ernesthealth.com
Control: Corporation, Investor-owned (for-profit) **Service:** Acute long-term care hospital

Staffed Beds: 40

★ ⇧ **BILLINGS CLINIC (270004)**, 2800 10th Avenue North, Zip 59107, Mailing Address: P.O. Box 37000, Zip 59107-7000; tel. 406/657-4000, **A**2 3 5 8 10 19 21 **F**3 7 8 9 11 12 13 15 17 18 19 20 22 24 26 27 28 29 30 31 32 34 35 36 38 40 41 43 44 45 46 47 48 49 50 51 52 54 55 56 57 58 59 60 61 62 64 65 66 68 70 72 74 75 76 77 78 79 80 81 82 84 85 86 87 89 91 92 93 97 98 99 100 101 102 103 104 105 107 108 110 111 114 115 116 117 118 119 120 121 124 126 129 130 131 132 134 135 136 144 146 147 148 149 153 154 155 156 162 164 167 169 **P**6
Primary Contact: Clint Seger, M.D., Chief Executive Officer
COO: Greg Titensor, MSN, R.N., Vice President, Operations
CFO: Priscilla Needham, CPA, Chief Financial Officer
CMO: Michelle Pierson, M.D., Chief Medical Officer
CIO: Brian Jones, Chief Information Officer
CHR: Gerele Dawn Pelton, Interim Chief Human Resources Officer
CNO: Shannon S. Holland, R.N., MSN, Chief Nursing Officer
Web address: www.billingsclinic.com
Control: Other not-for-profit (including NFP Corporation) **Service:** General medical and surgical

Staffed Beds: 312 **Admissions:** 14933 **Census:** 226 **Outpatient Visits:** 925623 **Births:** 747 **Total Expense ($000):** 1028089 **Payroll Expense ($000):** 526785 **Personnel:** 3664

SCL HEALTH – ST. VINCENT HEALTHCARE See SCL Health Mt – St. Vincent Healthcare

Hospitals, U.S. / MONTANA

✠ **SCL HEALTH MT – ST. VINCENT HEALTHCARE (270049)**, 1233 North 30th Street, Zip 59101–0165, Mailing Address: P.O. Box 35200, Zip 59107–5200; tel. 406/237–7000, **A**1 2 3 5 10 **F**3 7 9 11 12 13 15 18 19 20 22 24 26 28 29 30 31 34 35 40 41 43 45 46 47 48 49 50 55 56 59 60 61 64 68 70 71 72 74 75 76 78 79 81 82 84 85 86 87 88 89 93 94 100 107 108 110 111 115 116 117 119 120 121 123 124 126 129 130 135 145 146 147 148 149 154 155 167 169 **S** Intermountain Health, Salt Lake City, UT
Primary Contact: Lee Boyles, President, MT|WY Market and President, St. Vincent Regional Hospital
COO: Krikor Jansezian, Ph.D., Chief Operating Officer
CFO: Pam Palagi, Regional Vice President, Finance
CIO: Al Rooney, Director Information Systems
CHR: James Ritchey, Montana Region, Vice President Human Resources
CNO: BJ Gilmore, Chief Nursing Officer
Web address: https://www.sclhealth.org/locations/st-vincent-healthcare/
Control: Other not–for–profit (including NFP Corporation) **Service:** General medical and surgical

Staffed Beds: 277 **Admissions:** 12224 **Census:** 172 **Outpatient Visits:** 194107 **Births:** 1828 **Total Expense ($000):** 565722 **Payroll Expense ($000):** 140017 **Personnel:** 1502

☐ **THE REHABILITATION HOSPITAL OF MONTANA (273025)**, 3572 Hesper Road, Zip 59102–6891; tel. 406/413–6200, (Nonreporting) **A**1 10 **S** Kindred Healthcare, Salt Lake City, UT
Primary Contact: Belle Widgeon, Chief Executive Officer
Web address: https://www.rehabhospitalofmontana.com/
Control: Partnership, Investor–owned (for–profit) **Service:** Rehabilitation

Staffed Beds: 34

BOZEMAN—Gallatin County

⇧ **BOZEMAN HEALTH** See Bozeman Health Deaconess Regional Medical Center

★ ⇧ **BOZEMAN HEALTH DEACONESS REGIONAL MEDICAL CENTER (270057)**, 915 Highland Boulevard, Zip 59715–6902; tel. 406/585–5000, **A**2 10 20 21 **F**3 13 18 20 22 28 29 30 31 34 35 37 38 40 43 45 46 47 48 49 51 56 57 59 61 64 65 70 72 74 75 76 77 78 79 81 82 84 85 86 87 93 97 100 102 104 107 108 111 115 118 119 120 121 123 124 126 129 130 131 132 135 146 147 148 149 154 156 162 164 167 169
Primary Contact: Kathryn Bertany, M.D., President and Chief Executive Officer
COO: Kallie Kujawa, Chief Operating Officer
CFO: Brad Ludford, Chief Financial Officer
CIO: Tamara Havenhill–Jacobs, Chief Information Officer
CNO: Kiera Pattison, R.N., Interim Chief Nursing Officer
Web address: www.bozemandeaconess.org
Control: Other not–for–profit (including NFP Corporation) **Service:** General medical and surgical

Staffed Beds: 139 **Admissions:** 6299 **Census:** 72 **Outpatient Visits:** 538318 **Births:** 1290 **Total Expense ($000):** 450699 **Payroll Expense ($000):** 103017 **Personnel:** 1668

BUTTE—Silver Bow County

✠ **SCL HEALTH MT – ST. JAMES HEALTHCARE (270017)**, 400 South Clark Street, Zip 59701–2328; tel. 406/723–2500, **A**1 2 10 **F**3 11 13 15 18 19 20 22 28 29 30 31 34 35 40 41 43 45 47 48 49 50 51 53 56 57 59 64 65 68 70 71 72 74 75 76 77 78 79 81 82 86 87 89 93 94 97 107 108 110 111 114 115 117 118 119 120 121 123 124 126 130 131 132 133 135 146 147 148 149 156 157 167 169 **S** Intermountain Health, Salt Lake City, UT
Primary Contact: Karen Costello, Chief Executive Officer
CFO: David Brain, Interim Vice President Finance
CMO: Dennis Salisbury, M.D., Vice President for Medical Affairs
CNO: Mary Winters, Interim Chief Nursing Officer
Web address: https://www.sclhealth.org/locations/st-james-healthcare/
Control: Other not–for–profit (including NFP Corporation) **Service:** General medical and surgical

Staffed Beds: 73 **Admissions:** 2687 **Census:** 33 **Outpatient Visits:** 82820 **Births:** 255 **Total Expense ($000):** 149984 **Payroll Expense ($000):** 42378 **Personnel:** 688

CHESTER—Liberty County

★ **LOGAN HEALTH CHESTER (271334)**, 315 West Madison Avenue, Zip 59522, Mailing Address: P.O. Box 705, Zip 59522–0705; tel. 406/759–5181, **A**10 18 **F**3 10 29 34 35 40 43 57 59 64 81 91 93 97 107 119 127 130 133 148 154
Primary Contact: Cherie Taylor, President
CMO: Gladys Young, M.D., Chief of Staff
CHR: Bev Halter, Director Human Resources and Payroll
CNO: Shirley Morkrid, Chief Nursing Officer
Web address: https://www.logan.org/health/locations/logan-health-chester
Control: Other not–for–profit (including NFP Corporation) **Service:** General medical and surgical

Staffed Beds: 25 **Admissions:** 46 **Census:** 1 **Outpatient Visits:** 13766 **Births:** 0 **Total Expense ($000):** 8548 **Payroll Expense ($000):** 3518 **Personnel:** 67

CHOTEAU—Teton County

BENEFIS TETON MEDICAL CENTER (271307), 915 4th Street North West, Zip 59422–9123; tel. 406/466–5763, **A**10 18 **F**2 34 40 41 43 53 56 57 59 64 93 97 107 115 127 128 133 154 **S** Benefis Health System, Great Falls, MT
Primary Contact: Louie King, Chief Executive Officer
Web address: www.tetonmedicalcenter.net
Control: Other not–for–profit (including NFP Corporation) **Service:** General medical and surgical

Staffed Beds: 25 **Admissions:** 70 **Census:** 20 **Outpatient Visits:** 9701 **Births:** 0 **Total Expense ($000):** 10139 **Payroll Expense ($000):** 3744 **Personnel:** 54

CIRCLE—McCone County

★ **MCCONE COUNTY HEALTH CENTER (271305)**, 605 Sullivan Avenue, Zip 59215, Mailing Address: P.O. Box 48, Zip 59215–0048; tel. 406/485–3381, **A**10 18 **F**2 3 11 34 40 41 57 58 65 69 86 87 93 133 135 143 146 149 154 164
Primary Contact: Jacque Gardner, Chief Executive Officer
Web address: www.mcconehealth.org/
Control: County, Government, Nonfederal **Service:** General medical and surgical

Staffed Beds: 25 **Admissions:** 39 **Census:** 18 **Outpatient Visits:** 962 **Births:** 0 **Total Expense ($000):** 5135 **Payroll Expense ($000):** 1769 **Personnel:** 27

COLUMBUS—Stillwater County

★ **STILLWATER BILLINGS CLINIC (271330)**, 44 West Fourth Avenue North, Zip 59019–0959, Mailing Address: P.O. Box 959, Zip 59019–0959; tel. 406/322–5316, **A**10 18 **F**3 15 28 29 34 40 43 45 46 57 59 64 65 75 79 93 97 107 110 127 133 144 147 154 156
Primary Contact: Luke Kobold, Chief Executive Officer
Web address: www.billingsclinic.com
Control: Other not–for–profit (including NFP Corporation) **Service:** General medical and surgical

Staffed Beds: 10 **Admissions:** 338 **Census:** 4 **Outpatient Visits:** 11269 **Births:** 0 **Total Expense ($000):** 14072 **Payroll Expense ($000):** 6632 **Personnel:** 84

CONRAD—Pondera County

LOGAN HEALTH – CONRAD (271324), 805 Sunset Boulevard, Zip 59425–1717, Mailing Address: P.O. Box 668, Zip 59425–0668; tel. 406/271–3211, (Total facility includes 59 beds in nursing home–type unit) **A**10 18 **F**3 6 28 29 34 40 41 45 53 55 56 57 59 62 63 64 65 66 68 93 97 100 107 110 111 114 115 119 125 127 129 130 131 133 143 144 148 149 154 158 169
Primary Contact: Vicki Newmiller, President
CFO: Brigid Burke, Chief Financial Officer
CMO: Jay Taylor, M.D., Chief of Medical Staff
CIO: Sean Kavanagh, Director Information Technology
CHR: Patrick Johnson, Director Human Resources
CNO: Laura Erickson, R.N., Chief Nursing Officer
Web address: www.ponderamedical.org
Control: Other not–for–profit (including NFP Corporation) **Service:** General medical and surgical

Staffed Beds: 79 **Admissions:** 39 **Census:** 40 **Outpatient Visits:** 8010 **Births:** 1 **Total Expense ($000):** 20596 **Payroll Expense ($000):** 8077 **Personnel:** 91

PONDERA MEDICAL CENTER See Logan Health – Conrad

Hospitals, U.S. / MONTANA

CROW AGENCY—Big Horn County

✠ **CROW/NORTHERN CHEYENNE HOSPITAL (271339)**, 10110 South 7650 East, Zip 59022–0009, Mailing Address: P.O. Box 9, Zip 59022–0009; tel. 406/638–2626, (Nonreporting) **A**1 10 18 **S** U. S. Indian Health Service, Rockville, MD
Primary Contact: Darren Crowe, Chief Executive Officer
CMO: Jim Upchurch, M.D., Chief Medical Officer
CIO: Melanie Falls Down, Site Manager
Web address: https://www.ihs.gov/billings/healthcarefacilities/crow/
Control: PHS, Indian Service, Government, federal **Service:** General medical and surgical

Staffed Beds: 24

CULBERTSON—Roosevelt County

★ **ROOSEVELT MEDICAL CENTER (271308)**, 818 Second Avenue East, Zip 59218, Mailing Address: P.O. Box 419, Zip 59218–0419; tel. 406/787–6401, (Total facility includes 25 beds in nursing home–type unit) **A**10 18 **F**2 3 7 29 32 34 35 40 56 57 59 65 69 77 82 93 97 107 127 128 133 143 146 147 154 156
Primary Contact: Audrey Stromberg, Administrator
CFO: Jennifer Kessner, Financial Director
CMO: Don Helland, M.D., Chief Medical Officer
CIO: Brian Fordyce, Director Information Technology
CHR: Elizabeth Raaum, Manger Business Office
CNO: Jessica Schmitz, Director of Nursing
Web address: www.roosmem.org
Control: Other not–for–profit (including NFP Corporation) **Service:** General medical and surgical

Staffed Beds: 29 **Admissions:** 71 **Census:** 22 **Outpatient Visits:** 12003 **Births:** 0 **Total Expense ($000):** 8239 **Payroll Expense ($000):** 3490
Personnel: 59

CUT BANK—Glacier County

★ **LOGAN HEALTH – CUT BANK (271337)**, 802 Second Street SE, Zip 59427–3329; tel. 406/873–2251, **A**10 18 **F**3 11 32 34 35 40 45 57 59 65 68 77 81 85 89 93 107 115 127 128 133 147 148 149 154 156 169 **S** Ovation Healthcare, Brentwood, TN
Primary Contact: Cherie Taylor, President
CFO: Treasure Berkram, Chief Financial Officer
CMO: Robert Clary, M.D., Medical Director
CHR: Ashley Kimmet, Human Resources
CNO: Crystal Losing, Chief Nursing Officer
Web address: https://www.logan.org/health/locations/logan-health-cut-bank
Control: Other not–for–profit (including NFP Corporation) **Service:** General medical and surgical

Staffed Beds: 8 **Admissions:** 48 **Census:** 1 **Outpatient Visits:** 9460 **Births:** 0 **Total Expense ($000):** 11548 **Payroll Expense ($000):** 6515
Personnel: 77

DEER LODGE—Powell County

DEER LODGE MEDICAL CENTER (271314), 1100 Hollenbeck Lane, Zip 59722–2317; tel. 406/846–2212, **A**3 10 18 **F**7 14 15 18 28 29 31 32 33 34 35 36 38 40 43 44 45 50 57 59 64 65 66 68 75 77 79 81 82 91 93 97 100 102 107 111 115 119 127 131 133 148 149 154 156 **P**6
Primary Contact: Tony Pfaff, Chief Executive Officer
CFO: Jaena Richards, Chief Financial Officer
CMO: Michelle Corbin, M.D., Chief of Staff
CIO: Chris Foster, Director Health Information Management
Web address: www.dlmed.org/
Control: Other not–for–profit (including NFP Corporation) **Service:** General medical and surgical

Staffed Beds: 16 **Admissions:** 203 **Census:** 4 **Outpatient Visits:** 23042 **Births:** 0 **Total Expense ($000):** 23101 **Payroll Expense ($000):** 9050
Personnel: 125

DILLON—Beaverhead County

★ **BARRETT HOSPITAL & HEALTHCARE (271318)**, 600 Mt Highway 91 South, Zip 59725–7379; tel. 406/683–3000, **A**3 5 10 18 **F**3 13 15 28 29 31 34 40 45 50 55 57 59 62 63 64 65 75 76 77 79 80 81 82 83 84 85 87 89 93 96 97 107 110 111 115 119 129 130 131 132 133 135 146 148 154 156 169 **S** HealthTech Management Services, Plano, TX
Primary Contact: Taylor Rose, Chief Executive Officer
CFO: Dick Achter, Chief Financial Officer
CMO: Carol Kennedy, Chief Clinical Officer
CIO: Dick Achter, Chief Financial Officer
CHR: Geoff Roach, Director Human Resources
Web address: www.barretthospital.org
Control: Other not–for–profit (including NFP Corporation) **Service:** General medical and surgical

Staffed Beds: 18 **Admissions:** 473 **Census:** 6 **Outpatient Visits:** 25006 **Births:** 71 **Total Expense ($000):** 40518 **Payroll Expense ($000):** 16602
Personnel: 201

EKALAKA—Carter County

DAHL MEMORIAL HEALTHCARE ASSOCIATION (271302), 215 Sandy Street, Zip 59324, Mailing Address: P.O. Box 46, Zip 59324–0046; tel. 406/775–8730, (Nonreporting) **A**10 18
Primary Contact: Ryan Tooke, Chief Executive Officer
CMO: Darryl Espeland, D.O., Medical Director
CIO: Davie Ann Barrere, Coordinator Information Technology
CHR: Melissa Matthews, Director Human Resources
CNO: Patricia Rogers, Director of Nursing
Web address: www.dahlmemorial.com
Control: Other not–for–profit (including NFP Corporation) **Service:** General medical and surgical

Staffed Beds: 25

ENNIS—Madison County

MADISON VALLEY MEDICAL CENTER (271329), 305 North Main Street, Zip 59729–8001; tel. 406/682–4222, **A**10 18 **F**3 7 11 15 18 19 28 29 32 34 35 38 40 43 44 46 57 59 65 68 71 77 82 91 93 94 97 102 107 110 114 115 117 119 127 128 131 133 143 148 149 154 156 168 **P**3 6
Primary Contact: Allen Rohrback, Chief Executive Officer
CMO: Cindy Sharp, M.D., Chief Medical Officer
CIO: Bo Nix, Chief Information Officer
Web address: www.mvmedcenter.org
Control: Hospital district or authority, Government, Nonfederal **Service:** General medical and surgical

Staffed Beds: 10 **Admissions:** 87 **Census:** 1 **Births:** 0

FORSYTH—Rosebud County

★ **ROSEBUD HEALTH CARE CENTER (271327)**, 383 North 17th Avenue, Zip 59327–0268, Mailing Address: P.O. Box 268, Zip 59327–0268; tel. 406/346–2161, (Nonreporting) **A**10 18
Primary Contact: Mindy Price, R.N., Chief Executive Officer
CMO: William Anderson, Medical Director
CHR: Dee Raymond, Director Human Resources
CNO: Jeanne Maciag, Director of Nursing
Web address: www.rosebudhealthcare.com/
Control: Other not–for–profit (including NFP Corporation) **Service:** General medical and surgical

Staffed Beds: 55

Hospital, Medicare Provider Number, Address, Telephone, Approval, Facility, and Physician Codes, Health Care System

★ American Hospital Association (AHA) membership
☐ The Joint Commission accreditation
○ Healthcare Facilities Accreditation Program
◇ DNV Healthcare Inc. accreditation
⇑ Center for Improvement in Healthcare Quality Accreditation
△ Commission on Accreditation of Rehabilitation Facilities (CARF) accreditation

Hospitals, U.S. / MONTANA

FORT BENTON—Chouteau County

MISSOURI RIVER MEDICAL CENTER (271304), 1501 St Charles Street, Zip 59442-0249, Mailing Address: P.O. Box 249, Zip 59442-0249; tel. 406/622-3331, (Data for 183 days) **A**10 18 **F**30 34 40 50 57 63 68 77 80 128 **S** Benefis Health System, Great Falls, MT
Primary Contact: Louie King, President, Harry Bold Nursing Home Administrator
CMO: Jace Bird, M.D., Chief Medical Officer
CIO: Bryan Cartwright, Chief Information Technology Officer
CHR: Carolyn Johnsrud, Manager Human Resources
CNO: Janice Woodhouse, Director of Nursing
Web address: www.mrmcfb.org
Control: Other not-for-profit (including NFP Corporation) **Service**: General medical and surgical

Staffed Beds: 25 **Admissions**: 20 **Census**: 21 **Outpatient Visits**: 2747 **Births**: 0 **Total Expense ($000)**: 5079 **Payroll Expense ($000)**: 1977 **Personnel**: 68

FORT HARRISON—Lewis and Clark County

FORT HARRISON VA MEDICAL CENTER, 3687 Veterans Drive, Zip 59636-9703, Mailing Address: P.O. Box 1500, Zip 59636-1500; tel. 406/442-6410, (Nonreporting) **A**1 **S** Department of Veterans Affairs, Washington, DC
Primary Contact: Duane B. Gill, Acting Director
CFO: Brian Gustafson, Chief Financial Officer
CMO: Kurt Werner, M.D., Chief of Staff
CIO: Paul Gauthier, Chief Information Resources Management
CHR: Aggie Hamilton, Chief Human Resources
Web address: www.montana.va.gov/
Control: Veterans Affairs, Government, federal **Service**: General medical and surgical

Staffed Beds: 69

MONTANA HCS See Fort Harrison VA Medical Center

GLASGOW—Valley County

FRANCES MAHON DEACONESS HOSPITAL (271316), 621 Third Street South, Zip 59230-2699; tel. 406/228-3500, **A**1 10 18 **F**3 7 10 13 15 28 29 31 34 35 40 43 53 56 57 59 61 64 70 75 76 78 79 81 82 86 87 89 93 100 102 107 108 110 111 115 118 119 127 130 131 133 145 149 154 169 **P**6
Primary Contact: Nick Dirkes, Chief Executive Officer
COO: Ellen Guttenberg, Chief Operating Officer
CFO: Cami Kalinski, Chief Financial Officer
CMO: Kevin Ross, M.D., Chief of Medical Staff
CIO: David L Nixdorf, Director Support Services
CHR: Ben Thoeny, Director Human Resources
CNO: Brenda Koessl, R.N., Director of Nursing Services
Web address: www.fmdh.org
Control: Other not-for-profit (including NFP Corporation) **Service**: General medical and surgical

Staffed Beds: 25 **Admissions**: 440 **Census**: 4 **Outpatient Visits**: 38309 **Births**: 82 **Total Expense ($000)**: 36296 **Payroll Expense ($000)**: 15112 **Personnel**: 195

GLENDIVE—Dawson County

★ **GLENDIVE MEDICAL CENTER (271332)**, 202 Prospect Drive, Zip 59330-1999; tel. 406/345-3306, (Total facility includes 36 beds in nursing home-type unit) **A**10 18 **F**3 10 11 13 15 28 30 31 34 35 37 40 43 45 50 57 59 61 63 65 67 68 70 75 76 78 81 89 91 93 97 98 100 102 104 105 107 111 115 117 119 126 127 128 130 131 132 133 135 144 146 148 154 156 162 169 **P**6
Primary Contact: Parker Powell, Chief Executive Officer
CFO: Barbara Markham, Chief Financial Officer
CMO: Joseph M Leal, M.D., Jr, Chief of Staff
CIO: Barbara Markham, Chief Financial Officer
CHR: Joetta J Pearcy, Director, Human Resources
Web address: www.gmc.org
Control: Other not-for-profit (including NFP Corporation) **Service**: General medical and surgical

Staffed Beds: 61 **Admissions**: 895 **Census**: 43 **Outpatient Visits**: 27084 **Births**: 73 **Total Expense ($000)**: 62625 **Payroll Expense ($000)**: 25901 **Personnel**: 514

GREAT FALLS—Cascade County

BENEFIS HEALTH CARE–EAST CAMP See Benefis Health Care–East Campus

BENEFIS HEALTH CARE–WEST CAMP See Benefis Health Care–West Campus

△ **BENEFIS HEALTH SYSTEM (270012)**, 1101 26th Street South, Zip 59405-5104; tel. 406/455-5000, (Includes BENEFIS HEALTH CARE–EAST CAMPUS, 1101 26th Street, Great Falls, Montana, Zip 59405, tel. 406/455-5000; BENEFIS HEALTH CARE–WEST CAMPUS, 500 15th Avenue South, Great Falls, Montana, Zip 59405, tel. 406/455-5000) (Total facility includes 210 beds in nursing home–type unit) **A**2 7 10 **F**3 4 5 6 8 9 10 11 12 13 15 18 20 22 24 26 28 29 30 31 32 34 35 36 37 38 40 43 45 46 47 48 49 50 52 53 54 55 56 57 58 59 61 62 63 64 65 70 71 72 73 74 75 76 77 78 79 81 82 83 84 85 86 87 88 89 90 91 92 93 95 96 97 98 100 101 102 104 105 107 110 111 115 117 119 120 121 123 124 126 127 128 129 130 131 132 133 135 143 144 146 147 148 149 152 153 154 155 158 160 161 162 163 164 167 169 **P**8 **S** Benefis Health System, Great Falls, MT
Primary Contact: John H. Goodnow, Chief Executive Officer
CFO: Forrest Ehlinger, System Chief Financial Officer
CMO: Gregory Tierney, M.D., President, BMG and BHS Chief Medical Officer
CIO: Mark Simon, System Chief Information Officer
CNO: Rayn Ginnaty, Vice President Nursing
Web address: www.benefis.org
Control: Other not-for-profit (including NFP Corporation) **Service**: General medical and surgical

Staffed Beds: 508 **Admissions**: 10185 **Census**: 363 **Outpatient Visits**: 630713 **Births**: 1276 **Total Expense ($000)**: 594996 **Payroll Expense ($000)**: 269828 **Personnel**: 2897

⇑ **GREAT FALLS CLINIC HOSPITAL (270086)**, 3010 15th Avenue South, Zip 59405-5240, Mailing Address: 3010 15th Street South, Zip 59405-5240; tel. 406/216-8000, **A**10 21 **F**3 8 15 18 20 22 24 29 30 31 35 40 42 45 46 58 59 60 65 68 70 78 79 81 82 107 108 111 112 114 115 119 120 121 126 129 130 131 147 154
Primary Contact: Wayne Gillis, Chief Executive Officer
CFO: Paul Hanson, Chief Financial Officer
CMO: David Kluge, M.D., Chief of Staff
CHR: Sally Callery, Director Human Resources
CNO: Rachel Pahut, Chief Nursing Officer
Web address: www.gfclinic.com/location/great-falls-clinic-hospital/
Control: Corporation, Investor-owned (for-profit) **Service**: General medical and surgical

Staffed Beds: 46 **Admissions**: 1395 **Census**: 15 **Outpatient Visits**: 103672 **Births**: 0 **Total Expense ($000)**: 123145 **Payroll Expense ($000)**: 33073 **Personnel**: 632

HAMILTON—Ravalli County

★ **BITTERROOT HEALTH – DALY HOSPITAL (271340)**, 1200 Westwood Drive, Zip 59840-2345; tel. 406/363-2211, **A**10 18 **F**3 7 11 13 15 28 29 31 37 40 41 43 48 49 54 63 64 70 74 76 77 78 79 81 82 85 86 87 91 93 94 97 107 110 111 115 119 124 126 127 129 130 131 133 143 144 146 147 148 149 154 167 169
Primary Contact: John Bishop, Chief Executive Officer
COO: Troy Hanson, Chief Operating Officer
CFO: Trevor Lewis, Chief Financial Officer
CMO: April Weinberger, M.D., Chief Medical Officer
CIO: Robert Weissenbach, Chief Information Officer
CHR: Rebecca Conroy Bargfrede, Chief Transformational Officer
CNO: Kathy Padilla, Chief Nursing Officer
Web address: https://www.bitterroothealth.org/about-us/who-we-are/
Control: Other not-for-profit (including NFP Corporation) **Service**: General medical and surgical

Staffed Beds: 25 **Admissions**: 1646 **Census**: 14 **Outpatient Visits**: 171378 **Births**: 114 **Total Expense ($000)**: 109052 **Payroll Expense ($000)**: 57454 **Personnel**: 698

MARCUS DALY MEMORIAL HOSPITAL See Bitterroot Health – Daly Hospital

HARDIN—Big Horn County

★ **BIG HORN HOSPITAL (271338)**, 17 North Miles Avenue, Zip 59034-2323; tel. 406/665-2310, **A**10 18 **F**3 15 29 34 40 41 43 59 64 67 89 90 93 107 110 111 114 119 130 133 143 146 149 154
Primary Contact: Kristi Gatrell, Chief Executive Officer
CFO: Roxie Cain, Chief Financial Officer
CNO: Kirsten Willoughby, Director of Nursing
Control: Other not-for-profit (including NFP Corporation) **Service**: General medical and surgical

Staffed Beds: 18 **Admissions**: 118 **Census**: 11 **Outpatient Visits**: 7639 **Births**: 5 **Total Expense ($000)**: 19607 **Payroll Expense ($000)**: 8791 **Personnel**: 102

Hospitals, U.S. / MONTANA

HARLEM—Blaine County

☒ **FORT BELKNAP SERVICE UNIT (271315)**, 669 Agency Main Street, Zip 59526-9455; tel. 406/353-3100, (Nonreporting) **A**1 10 18 **S** U. S. Indian Health Service, Rockville, MD
Primary Contact: Lieutenant Commander Matthew Frye, Acting Chies Executive Officer
CMO: Ethel L Moore, M.D., Director of Medical Affairs
CIO: Mikki Grant, Chief Information Officer
CHR: Charlotte Lamebull, Administrative Officer
CNO: Diana Hunter, Director of Nursing
Web address: www.ihs.gov
Control: PHS, Indian Service, Government, federal **Service**: General medical and surgical

Staffed Beds: 6

HARLOWTON—Wheatland County

★ **WHEATLAND MEMORIAL HEALTHCARE (271321)**, 530 Third Street North West, Zip 59036, Mailing Address: P.O. Box 287, Zip 59036-0287; tel. 406/632-4351, **A**10 18 **F**29 64 65 67 82 87 90 91 93 97 107 114 119 127 128 133 143 147 148 149 154 **P**3
Primary Contact: Donna Neste, Chief Executive Officer
CFO: Doug Lewis, Chief Financial Officer
CMO: Kathy Jutila, M.D., Chief of Staff
CIO: Ray Hetherington, Network Administrator
CHR: Peggy Hiner, Director Human Resources
CNO: Lauri Ann Cooney, Director Nursing
Web address: www.wheatlandmemorial.org
Control: Other not-for-profit (including NFP Corporation) **Service**: General medical and surgical

Staffed Beds: 18 **Admissions**: 42 **Census**: 1 **Outpatient Visits**: 30436 **Births**: 0 **Total Expense ($000)**: 10176 **Payroll Expense ($000)**: 3497 **Personnel**: 52

HAVRE—Hill County

★ **NORTHERN MONTANA HOSPITAL (271348)**, 30 13th Street, Zip 59501-5222, Mailing Address: PO Box 1231, Zip 59501-1231; tel. 406/265-2211, (Total facility includes 115 beds in nursing home-type unit) **A**10 18 **F**2 5 10 11 13 15 28 29 34 35 36 38 40 43 45 53 56 57 59 60 63 64 68 70 75 76 77 78 79 81 82 84 85 89 93 97 99 101 102 103 104 107 108 110 111 115 118 119 126 127 128 129 130 132 133 135 146 148 153 154 156 164 166 169 **P**6
Primary Contact: David Henry, President and Chief Executive Officer
CFO: Kim Lucke, Vice President Finance
CNO: Eric Koch, Chief Nursing Officer
Web address: www.nmhcare.org
Control: Other not-for-profit (including NFP Corporation) **Service**: General medical and surgical

Staffed Beds: 154 **Admissions**: 1176 **Census**: 82 **Outpatient Visits**: 90820 **Births**: 217 **Total Expense ($000)**: 79854 **Payroll Expense ($000)**: 40682 **Personnel**: 460

HELENA—Lewis and Clark County

☒ **SHODAIR CHILDREN'S HOSPITAL (274004)**, 2755 Colonial Drive, Zip 59601-4926, Mailing Address: P.O. Box 5539, Zip 59604-5539; tel. 406/444-7500, **A**1 10 **F**55 98 99 100 104 106 130 149 154 **P**6
Primary Contact: Craig E. Aasved, Chief Executive Officer
CMO: Heather Zaluski, M.D., President Medical Staff
CIO: Judy Jackson, Director Health Information Management and Privacy Officer
CNO: Christine Bates, Chief Nursing Officer
Web address: www.shodair.org
Control: Other not-for-profit (including NFP Corporation) **Service**: Children's hospital psychiatric

Staffed Beds: 82 **Admissions**: 661 **Census**: 33 **Outpatient Visits**: 18256 **Births**: 0 **Total Expense ($000)**: 36579 **Payroll Expense ($000)**: 20054 **Personnel**: 276

★ ⇧ **ST. PETER'S HEALTH (270003)**, 2475 Broadway, Zip 59601-4928, Mailing Address: 2475 Broadway st, Zip 59601-4928; tel. 406/442-2480, **A**10 20 21 **F**3 5 7 13 15 18 20 22 28 29 30 31 34 35 38 40 41 43 46 49 50 54 56 57 59 60 62 63 64 68 70 71 72 73 74 75 76 77 78 79 81 82 83 84 85 86 88 89 92 93 97 98 100 101 102 103 104 107 108 109 110 111 112 115 116 117 119 121 123 124 126 127 129 130 132 133 135 144 146 147 148 149 150 154 157 160 162 164 167 169
Primary Contact: Wade C. Johnson, MS, FACHE, Chief Executive Officer
CFO: John Green, Vice President Finance
CMO: Shelly Harkins, M.D., Chief Medical Officer
CHR: Karla Smith, Director Human Resources
CNO: Cheryl Hunt Esq, Chief Nursing Officer
Web address: www.stpetes.org
Control: Other not-for-profit (including NFP Corporation) **Service**: General medical and surgical

Staffed Beds: 123 **Admissions**: 5789 **Census**: 72 **Outpatient Visits**: 262287 **Births**: 659 **Total Expense ($000)**: 321231 **Payroll Expense ($000)**: 145638 **Personnel**: 1597

JORDAN—Garfield County

GARFIELD COUNTY HEALTH CENTER (271310), 332 Leavitt Avenue, Zip 59337, Mailing Address: P.O. Box 389, Zip 59337-0389; tel. 406/557-2500, (Nonreporting) **A**10 18
Primary Contact: Paul Claybrook, CEO/Administrator
COO: Earline Lawrence, Chief Operating Officer
CFO: Charlotte Herbold, Manager Business Officer
CMO: David M. Kidder, D.O., Chief Medical Officer
CIO: Charlotte Herbold, Manager Business Officer
CNO: Sarah Nordlund, Director of Nursing
Web address: www.garfieldco.us/garfield-county-health-center.html
Control: County, Government, Nonfederal **Service**: General medical and surgical

Staffed Beds: 32

KALISPELL—Flathead County

GLACIER VIEW HOSPITAL See Pathways Treatment Center

★ △ **LOGAN HEALTH (270051)**, 310 Sunnyview Lane, Zip 59901-3129; tel. 406/752-5111, (Includes PATHWAYS TREATMENT CENTER, 200 Heritage Way, Kalispell, Montana, Zip 59901, tel. 406/756-3950) **A**2 3 5 7 10 **F**3 4 5 7 8 13 15 18 19 20 22 24 26 28 29 30 31 33 34 35 36 40 43 44 46 47 48 49 50 51 54 55 56 57 58 59 60 62 63 64 70 71 72 74 75 76 77 78 79 80 81 82 83 84 85 86 87 88 89 90 91 92 93 94 96 97 98 99 100 101 102 103 104 105 107 110 111 114 115 116 117 118 119 120 121 122 123 124 126 129 130 131 132 143 144 146 147 148 149 151 152 153 154 155 156 157 164 167 169 **P**6
Primary Contact: Kevin Abel, Chief Executive Officer
COO: Ted W Hirsch, Senior Executive Director
CFO: Tracey Talley, Chief Financial and Information Officer
CHR: Deb Wilson, Director Human Resources
CNO: Ryan Pitts, Chief Nursing Officer
Web address: https://www.krh.org/
Control: Other not-for-profit (including NFP Corporation) **Service**: General medical and surgical

Staffed Beds: 212 **Admissions**: 8363 **Census**: 108 **Outpatient Visits**: 778188 **Births**: 627 **Total Expense ($000)**: 533425 **Payroll Expense ($000)**: 240528 **Personnel**: 2328

LEWISTOWN—Fergus County

★ **CENTRAL MONTANA MEDICAL CENTER (271345)**, 408 Wendell Avenue, Zip 59457-2261; tel. 406/535-7711, **A**3 10 18 **F**3 7 11 13 15 28 29 31 34 35 40 43 45 53 59 62 63 64 65 75 76 77 81 84 85 89 93 97 100 107 108 110 111 115 119 129 130 131 132 133 148 154 156 167 **P**6
Primary Contact: Cody Langbehn, Chief Executive Officer
CFO: Alan Aldrich, Chief Financial Officer
CHR: Torie A Lynch, Manager Human Resources
CNO: Karen White, Chief Nursing Officer
Web address: https://www.cmmc.health/
Control: Other not-for-profit (including NFP Corporation) **Service**: General medical and surgical

Staffed Beds: 25 **Admissions**: 429 **Census**: 7 **Outpatient Visits**: 28642 **Births**: 84 **Total Expense ($000)**: 48175 **Payroll Expense ($000)**: 20646 **Personnel**: 266

Hospital, Medicare Provider Number, Address, Telephone, Approval, Facility, and Physician Codes, Health Care System

★ American Hospital Association (AHA) membership
☐ The Joint Commission accreditation
○ Healthcare Facilities Accreditation Program
◇ DNV Healthcare Inc. accreditation
⇧ Center for Improvement in Healthcare Quality Accreditation
△ Commission on Accreditation of Rehabilitation Facilities (CARF) accreditation

Hospitals, U.S. / MONTANA

LIBBY—Lincoln County

★ **CABINET PEAKS MEDICAL CENTER (271320)**, 209 Health Park Drive, Zip 59923–2130; tel. 406/283–7000, **A**3 5 10 18 **F**3 11 13 15 17 28 29 30 31 34 35 40 43 45 50 54 56 57 59 64 70 75 76 77 79 81 82 84 85 86 87 89 93 97 102 107 110 111 115 119 127 128 129 130 131 132 133 135 146 147 148 154 156 169 **P**6 **S** Ovation Healthcare, Brentwood, TN
Primary Contact: Tadd S. Greenfield, Chief Executive Officer
CMO: Jay Maloney, M.D., Chief of Staff
Web address: https://www.cabinetpeaks.org/
Control: Other not–for–profit (including NFP Corporation) **Service**: General medical and surgical

Staffed Beds: 25 **Admissions**: 606 **Census**: 6 **Outpatient Visits**: 154650 **Births**: 109 **Total Expense ($000)**: 42463 **Payroll Expense ($000)**: 16806 **Personnel**: 249

LIVINGSTON—Park County

★ **LIVINGSTON HEALTHCARE (271317)**, 320 Alpenglow Lane, Zip 59047–8506; tel. 406/222–3541, **A**5 10 18 **F**3 12 13 15 28 29 30 31 34 35 38 40 41 43 45 46 50 55 56 57 59 62 63 64 65 66 67 70 75 76 78 81 84 85 86 87 89 93 97 100 101 104 107 108 110 111 115 119 124 127 128 129 130 132 133 144 146 147 148 149 154 156 160 162 165 167 169 **P**6
Primary Contact: Bruce Whitfield, CPA, Chief Executive Officer
CFO: Kris Kester, Chief Financial Officer
CMO: D. Scott Coleman, M.D., Medical Director
CIO: Jody Duran, Manager Information Systems
CHR: Vicki Axtell, Director Human Resources
CNO: Dave Noble, Director of Nursing
Web address: www.livingstonhealthcare.org
Control: Other not–for–profit (including NFP Corporation) **Service**: General medical and surgical

Staffed Beds: 25 **Admissions**: 902 **Census**: 10 **Outpatient Visits**: 63643 **Births**: 134 **Total Expense ($000)**: 77804 **Payroll Expense ($000)**: 29356 **Personnel**: 435

MALTA—Phillips County

★ **PHILLIPS COUNTY HOSPITAL (271312)**, 311 South 8th Avenue East, Zip 59538–0640, Mailing Address: P.O. Box 640, Zip 59538–0640; tel. 406/654–1100, **A**10 18 **F**40 59 62 64 93 97 107 119 127 128 133 148 154
Primary Contact: Jo Tharp, Interim Chief Executive Officer
CFO: Stephanie Denham, Chief Financial Officer and Human Resources Officer
CMO: Ed Medina, M.D., Medical Director
CHR: Stephanie Denham, Chief Financial Officer and Human Resources Officer
CNO: Lonna Crowder, Director of Nursing
Web address: www.pchospital.us/
Control: Other not–for–profit (including NFP Corporation) **Service**: General medical and surgical

Staffed Beds: 6 **Admissions**: 87 **Census**: 1 **Outpatient Visits**: 13860 **Births**: 0 **Personnel**: 35

MILES CITY—Custer County

⊞ **HOLY ROSARY HEALTHCARE (271347)**, 2600 Wilson Street, Zip 59301–5094; tel. 406/233–2600, (Total facility includes 64 beds in nursing home–type unit) **A**1 10 18 **F**1 3 13 15 28 29 30 31 32 34 35 40 41 43 50 55 56 59 63 64 65 67 68 70 75 76 77 78 79 81 82 84 85 87 89 93 94 97 100 102 107 108 110 111 115 119 127 128 130 131 132 133 135 146 147 148 149 154 156 157 167 **S** Intermountain Health, Salt Lake City, UT
Primary Contact: Karen Costello, President
CFO: Travis Scheving, Chief Financial Officer
CHR: Cathy Rodenbaugh, Director Human Resources
CNO: Lisa Sanford, VP Patient Care/CNO
Web address: https://www.sclhealth.org/locations/holy-rosary-healthcare/
Control: Other not–for–profit (including NFP Corporation) **Service**: General medical and surgical

Staffed Beds: 89 **Admissions**: 962 **Census**: 62 **Outpatient Visits**: 36981 **Births**: 200 **Total Expense ($000)**: 64587 **Payroll Expense ($000)**: 23621 **Personnel**: 216

MISSOULA—Missoula County

⊞ **COMMUNITY MEDICAL CENTER (270023)**, 2827 Fort Missoula Road, Zip 59804–7408; tel. 406/728–4100, **A**1 2 3 5 10 19 **F**3 13 15 17 18 20 21 22 26 28 29 30 31 34 35 36 40 43 45 46 47 48 49 51 54 55 57 59 60 63 64 65 68 70 72 75 76 78 79 81 82 83 84 85 87 88 89 90 91 92 93 94 96 97 106 107 108 114 115 117 118 119 120 121 122 123 124 126 130 132 134 135 141 143 144 145 146 147 148 149 154 156 167 169 **P**1 **S** Lifepoint Health, Brentwood, TN
Primary Contact: Robert Gomes, FACHE, Chief Executive Officer
COO: Sandy Leggett, R.N., MSN, Chief Operations Officer
CFO: Sandee Mahoney, Chief Financial Officer
CMO: Bonnie Stephans, M.D., Chief Medical Officer
CNO: Hollie Nagel, MSN, Chief Nursing Officer
Web address: www.communitymed.org
Control: Corporation, Investor–owned (for–profit) **Service**: General medical and surgical

Staffed Beds: 135 **Admissions**: 4563 **Census**: 65 **Outpatient Visits**: 104170 **Births**: 1185 **Total Expense ($000)**: 218861 **Payroll Expense ($000)**: 66287 **Personnel**: 669

⊞ **PROVIDENCE ST. PATRICK HOSPITAL (270014)**, 500 West Broadway, Zip 59802–4096, Mailing Address: P.O. Box 4587, Zip 59806–4587; tel. 406/543–7271, **A**1 3 5 10 19 **F**3 11 12 13 15 17 18 20 22 24 26 28 29 30 31 34 35 38 40 43 50 51 53 54 57 58 59 64 65 68 70 72 74 75 76 77 78 79 81 82 84 85 86 87 89 92 93 97 98 99 100 101 102 104 105 107 108 110 111 114 115 117 118 119 120 121 124 126 127 129 130 132 134 135 141 144 145 146 148 149 154 156 157 162 164 165 166 167 168 169 **P**6 **S** Providence, Renton, WA
Primary Contact: William Calhoun, FACHE, Chief Executive
CFO: Kirk Bodlovic, WMSA Chief Financial Officer
CHR: Karyn Trainor, Director Human Resources
CNO: Carol Bensen, MSN, R.N., Chief Nursing Officer
Web address: https://www.providence.org/locations/MT/st-patrick-hospital
Control: Church operated, Nongovernment, not–for–profit **Service**: General medical and surgical

Staffed Beds: 211 **Admissions**: 9909 **Census**: 139 **Outpatient Visits**: 278538 **Births**: 365 **Total Expense ($000)**: 314427 **Payroll Expense ($000)**: 108168 **Personnel**: 1589

PHILIPSBURG—Missoula County

★ **GRANITE COUNTY MEDICAL CENTER (271303)**, 310 South Sansome Street, Zip 59858, Mailing Address: P.O. Box 729, Zip 59858–0729; tel. 406/859–3271, (Nonreporting) **A**10 18
Primary Contact: Brian Huso, Chief Executive Officer
CFO: Susan Ossello, Chief Financial Officer
CMO: John Moore, M.D., Medical Director
Web address: www.gcmedcenter.org/
Control: County, Government, Nonfederal **Service**: General medical and surgical

Staffed Beds: 25

PLAINS—Sanders County

★ **CLARK FORK VALLEY HOSPITAL (271323)**, 10 Kruger Road, Zip 59859, Mailing Address: P.O. Box 768, Zip 59859–0768; tel. 406/826–4800, (Total facility includes 28 beds in nursing home–type unit) **A**3 10 18 **F**3 11 13 15 29 30 32 34 35 36 40 43 44 45 50 57 58 59 62 63 64 65 70 75 76 77 79 81 82 83 84 85 86 87 89 91 93 97 100 101 102 104 107 110 114 115 118 119 127 128 129 130 132 133 135 143 144 146 147 148 149 154 156 165 166 169 **P**6
Primary Contact: Gregory S. Hanson, M.D., President and Chief Executive Officer
CFO: Carla A. Neiman, Chief Financial Officer
CMO: Ronald Black, M.D., Chief Medical Officer
CIO: Carla A. Neiman, Chief Financial Officer
CHR: Barry Fowler, Director Human and System Resources
CNO: Lisa Eberhardt, Chief Nursing Officer
Web address: www.cfvh.org
Control: Other not–for–profit (including NFP Corporation) **Service**: General medical and surgical

Staffed Beds: 44 **Admissions**: 413 **Census**: 13 **Outpatient Visits**: 27480 **Births**: 25 **Total Expense ($000)**: 30410 **Payroll Expense ($000)**: 13757 **Personnel**: 199

PLENTYWOOD—Sheridan County

SHERIDAN MEMORIAL HOSPITAL (271322), 440 West Laurel Avenue, Zip 59254–1596; tel. 406/765–3700, (Nonreporting) **A**10 18
Primary Contact: Kody Nelson, Chief Executive Officer
CHR: Roxy Kleppen, Director Human Resource
Web address: www.sheridanmemorial.net/
Control: Other not–for–profit (including NFP Corporation) **Service**: General medical and surgical

Staffed Beds: 19

Hospitals, U.S. / MONTANA

POLSON—Lake County

✠ **PROVIDENCE ST. JOSEPH MEDICAL CENTER (271343)**, 6 Thirteenth Avenue East, Zip 59860–5315, Mailing Address: P.O. Box 1010, Zip 59860–1010; tel. 406/883–5377, **A**1 3 10 18 **F**3 5 10 11 13 15 28 29 30 31 34 35 40 43 45 50 53 54 59 64 65 75 76 77 79 81 82 85 86 87 89 93 97 104 107 110 115 119 127 128 130 131 133 144 146 147 148 149 154 160 161 162 164 169 **P**6 **S** Providence, Renton, WA
Primary Contact: Devin Huntley, Chief Operating Officer
COO: Devin Huntley, Chief Operating Officer
CFO: Kirk Bodlovic, Vice President and Chief Financial Officer
CMO: Kelly Bagnell, M.D., Chief of Staff
Web address: www.saintjoes.org
Control: Church operated, Nongovernment, not–for–profit **Service**: General medical and surgical

Staffed Beds: 22 **Admissions**: 509 **Census**: 6 **Outpatient Visits**: 51539
Births: 116 **Total Expense ($000)**: 37965 **Payroll Expense ($000)**: 22144
Personnel: 287

POPLAR—Richland County

★ **POPLAR COMMUNITY HOSPITAL (271300)**, 211 H Street, Zip 59255–9519, Mailing Address: P.O. Box 38, Zip 59255–0038; tel. 406/768–6100, (Nonreporting) **A**10 18
Primary Contact: Michael Post, Chief Executive Officer
CHR: Annie Block, Director Human Resources
Web address: www.nemhs.net
Control: Other not–for–profit (including NFP Corporation) **Service**: General medical and surgical

Staffed Beds: 20

RED LODGE—Carbon County

★ **BEARTOOTH BILLINGS CLINIC (271326)**, 2525 North Broadway Avenue, Zip 59068–9222, Mailing Address: P.O. Box 590, Zip 59068–0590; tel. 406/446–2345, **A**10 18 **F**3 15 18 29 34 35 40 43 45 56 59 62 63 64 65 68 75 77 81 84 85 86 87 91 93 94 96 97 107 110 114 119 130 131 133 146 147 148 149 154 156 169
Primary Contact: Abby Lotz, MSN, R.N., Chief Executive Officer
CFO: Kyle Gee, Chief Financial Officer
CMO: William George, M.D., Chief of Staff
CHR: Katie Nordstrom, Director Human Resources
CNO: Bridgett Chartier, Director of Nursing
Web address: www.beartoothbillingsclinic.org
Control: Other not–for–profit (including NFP Corporation) **Service**: General medical and surgical

Staffed Beds: 10 **Admissions**: 147 **Census**: 4 **Outpatient Visits**: 124922
Births: 0 **Total Expense ($000)**: 18805 **Payroll Expense ($000)**: 7144
Personnel: 142

RONAN—Lake County

★ **ST. LUKE COMMUNITY HEALTHCARE (271325)**, 107 Sixth Avenue SW, Zip 59864–2634; tel. 406/676–4441, (Total facility includes 75 beds in nursing home–type unit) **A**3 10 18 **F**1 2 13 15 28 29 30 31 34 40 43 45 53 54 56 57 59 61 64 65 67 68 75 76 78 79 81 82 85 93 97 107 108 110 111 115 119 127 128 129 130 131 132 133 135 144 145 147 148 154 156 160 161 169 **P**6
Primary Contact: Steve J. Todd, Chief Executive Officer
CFO: Paul Soukup, Chief Financial Officer
CMO: Edred T. Vizcarra, M.D., Chief of Staff
CHR: Theresa L. Jones, Manager Human Resources
CNO: Leah Emerson, Director of Nursing
Web address: www.stlukehealthcare.org
Control: Other not–for–profit (including NFP Corporation) **Service**: General medical and surgical

Staffed Beds: 100 **Admissions**: 709 **Census**: 47 **Outpatient Visits**: 72425
Births: 75 **Total Expense ($000)**: 48214 **Payroll Expense ($000)**: 29200
Personnel: 348

ROUNDUP—Musselshell County

★ **ROUNDUP MEMORIAL HEALTHCARE (271346)**, 1202 Third Street West, Zip 59072–1816, Mailing Address: P.O. Box 40, Zip 59072–0040; tel. 406/323–2301, **A**10 18 **F**3 34 40 43 57 59 62 64 65 93 97 107 114 119 127 130 133 154
Primary Contact: Rick Schroeder, Interim Chief Executive Officer
CFO: Kyle Gee, Regional Vice President Financial Operations
CMO: Mark Ward, M.D., Chief of Staff
CNO: Emily Shoup, Director Nursing Services
Web address: www.rmhmt.org/
Control: Hospital district or authority, Government, Nonfederal **Service**: General medical and surgical

Staffed Beds: 25 **Admissions**: 48 **Census**: 1 **Outpatient Visits**: 7934
Births: 0 **Total Expense ($000)**: 14371 **Payroll Expense ($000)**: 4533
Personnel: 84

SAINT MARY—Glacier County

✠ **BLACKFEET COMMUNITY HOSPITAL (270074)**, 760 New Hospital Circle, Zip 59417–0760, Mailing Address: P.O. Box 760, Browning, Zip 59417–0760; tel. 406/338–6100, (Nonreporting) **A**1 3 10 **S** U. S. Indian Health Service, Rockville, MD
Primary Contact: Lisa Racine–Wells, Interim Chief Executive Officer
CFO: Cleo Main, Finance Officer
CMO: Neil Sun Rhodes, M.D., Chief Medical Officer
CNO: Susan Head, Director Nursing Services
Web address: www.ihs.gov
Control: PHS, Indian Service, Government, federal **Service**: General medical and surgical

Staffed Beds: 25

SCOBEY—Daniels County

★ **DANIELS MEMORIAL HEALTHCARE CENTER (271342)**, 105 Fifth Avenue East, Zip 59263, Mailing Address: P.O. Box 400, Zip 59263–0400; tel. 406/487–2296, **A**10 18 **F**2 11 29 34 40 43 44 50 56 57 59 64 65 67 69 71 85 87 91 93 97 100 104 107 115 119 127 130 133 143 146 147 148 154 **P**6
Primary Contact: Kody Brinton, Chief Executive Officer
CMO: Don Sawdey, M.D., Medical Director
CHR: Edith Huda, Director Human Resources
CNO: Kathy Ware, Director of Nursing
Web address: www.danielsmemorialhealthcare.org
Control: Other not–for–profit (including NFP Corporation) **Service**: General medical and surgical

Staffed Beds: 25 **Admissions**: 78 **Census**: 2 **Outpatient Visits**: 573
Births: 1 **Total Expense ($000)**: 10717 **Payroll Expense ($000)**: 3693
Personnel: 68

SHELBY—Toole County

★ **LOGAN HEALTH SHELBY (271328)**, 640 Park Avenue, Zip 59474–1663, Mailing Address: P.O. Box 915, Zip 59474–0915; tel. 406/434–3200, (Data for 275 days) **A**10 18 **F**3 13 17 28 29 34 40 41 45 50 59 70 77 81 87 89 93 102 107 111 114 119 129 130 133 148 154 167
Primary Contact: Vicki Newmiller, President
CMO: Justin Hooker, M.D., Chief of Staff
CIO: Jayce Yarn, Director Information Technology
CHR: Cindy Lamb, Director Human Resources
CNO: Crystal Rattler, Director of Nursing
Web address: https://www.logan.org/health/locations/logan-health-shelby
Control: Other not–for–profit (including NFP Corporation) **Service**: General medical and surgical

Staffed Beds: 21 **Admissions**: 63 **Census**: 1 **Outpatient Visits**: 4816
Births: 0 **Total Expense ($000)**: 8426 **Payroll Expense ($000)**: 3508
Personnel: 110

Hospital, Medicare Provider Number, Address, Telephone, Approval, Facility, and Physician Codes, Health Care System

★ American Hospital Association (AHA) membership
☐ The Joint Commission accreditation
◯ Healthcare Facilities Accreditation Program
◇ DNV Healthcare Inc. accreditation
⇑ Center for Improvement in Healthcare Quality Accreditation
△ Commission on Accreditation of Rehabilitation Facilities (CARF) accreditation

Hospitals, U.S. / MONTANA

SHERIDAN—Madison County

RUBY VALLEY MEDICAL CENTER (271319), 220 East Crofoot Street, Zip 59749–7714, Mailing Address: P.O. Box 336, Zip 59749–0336; tel. 406/842–5453, (Nonreporting) **A**10 18
Primary Contact: Landon Dybdal, Chief Executive Officer
CFO: Dennis Holschbach, Chief Financial Officer
CMO: Roman Hendrickson, M.D., Medical Director
CHR: Jenny Rohrback, Director Human Resource
CNO: Brenda Green, Director of Nursing
Web address: www.rubyvalleyhospital.com/
Control: Hospital district or authority, Government, Nonfederal **Service**: General medical and surgical

Staffed Beds: 5

SIDNEY—Richland County

★ **SIDNEY HEALTH CENTER (271344)**, 216 14th Avenue SW, Zip 59270–3586; tel. 406/488–2100, (Total facility includes 51 beds in nursing home–type unit) **A**10 18 **F**2 3 7 11 13 15 17 28 29 30 31 34 35 36 40 41 45 50 55 56 57 59 62 64 67 70 75 76 77 78 79 81 82 84 85 86 87 89 90 93 96 97 107 108 110 111 115 119 120 121 122 123 124 127 128 129 130 131 132 133 135 145 146 147 148 149 154 156 164 167 169 **P**6
Primary Contact: Jennifer Doty, Chief Executive Officer
CFO: Tina Montgomery, Chief Financial Officer
CMO: Rajohn Karanjai, M.D., Chief Medical Officer
CIO: Brian Fay, Director Information Systems
CHR: Lisa Aisenbrey, Administrator Human Resources and Support Services
Web address: www.sidneyhealth.org
Control: Other not–for–profit (including NFP Corporation) **Service**: General medical and surgical

Staffed Beds: 76 **Admissions**: 1353 **Census**: 62 **Outpatient Visits**: 59978
Births: 238 **Total Expense ($000)**: 101142 **Payroll Expense ($000)**: 34142
Personnel: 489

SUPERIOR—Mineral County

MINERAL COMMUNITY HOSPITAL (271331), 1208 6th Avenue East, Zip 59872–9618; tel. 406/822–4841, **A**10 18 **F**3 15 29 32 34 35 40 43 45 55 56 57 59 64 65 68 69 92 93 97 100 102 107 115 128 131 133 144 147 148 149 154 156 164 169
Primary Contact: Laurel Chambers Haskins, Chief Executive Officer
CFO: Cliff Case, Chief Financial Officer
CMO: Roger Pafford, M.D., Medical Director
CHR: Stacy Conrow–Ververis, Director Human Resources
CNO: Jenifer Mitchell, R.N., Director of Nursing Services
Web address: www.mineralcommunityhospital.com/
Control: Hospital district or authority, Government, Nonfederal **Service**: General medical and surgical

Staffed Beds: 25 **Admissions**: 124 **Census**: 4 **Outpatient Visits**: 6009
Births: 0 **Total Expense ($000)**: 11369 **Payroll Expense ($000)**: 5372
Personnel: 78

TERRY—Prairie County

★ **PRAIRIE COUNTY HOSPITAL DISTRICT (271309)**, 312 South Adams Avenue, Zip 59349–0156, Mailing Address: P.O. Box 156, Zip 59349–0156; tel. 406/635–5511, (Nonreporting) **A**10 18
Primary Contact: Burt Keltner, Administrator
CFO: Mia Amore Talon, Chief Financial Officer
CNO: Susan Morgan, Director of Nursing Services
Web address: www.prairiecommunityhospital.org/
Control: Hospital district or authority, Government, Nonfederal **Service**: General medical and surgical

Staffed Beds: 22

TOWNSEND—Broadwater County

BILLINGS CLINIC BROADWATER (271333), 110 North Oak Street, Zip 59644–2306; tel. 406/266–3186, **A**10 18 **F**7 34 35 40 57 59 64 65 67 75 77 82 86 87 93 97 100 107 115 119 128 133 154 **P**6
Primary Contact: Jennifer Clowes, Chief Executive Officer
CMO: Carol Bridges, M.D., Medical Director
CHR: April Campbell, Director Human Resources
CNO: Fran Wright, Director of Nursing
Web address: https://www.billingsclinic.com/billings-clinic-broadwater/
Control: Other not–for–profit (including NFP Corporation) **Service**: General medical and surgical

Staffed Beds: 18 **Admissions**: 134 **Census**: 18 **Outpatient Visits**: 6608
Births: 0 **Total Expense ($000)**: 10540 **Payroll Expense ($000)**: 5390
Personnel: 68

BROADWATER HEALTH CENTER See Billings Clinic Broadwater

WARM SPRINGS—Deer Lodge County

MONTANA STATE HOSPITAL (274086), 100 Garnet Way, Zip 59756–9705, Mailing Address: P.O. Box 300, tel. 406/693–7000, (Nonreporting) **A**10
Primary Contact: Carter Anderson, Administrator
CFO: Tracey Thun, Director Business and Support Services
CMO: Thomas Gray, M.D., Medical Director
CIO: Melinda Bridgewater, Director, Information Services
CHR: Todd Thun, Director Human Resources
CNO: Dave Olson, Director of Nursing
Web address: www.msh.mt.gov
Control: State, Government, Nonfederal **Service**: Psychiatric

Staffed Beds: 270

WHITE SULPHUR SPRINGS—Meagher County

MOUNTAINVIEW MEDICAL CENTER (271306), 16 West Main Street, Zip 59645–9036, Mailing Address: P.O. Box 'Q', Zip 59645–0817; tel. 406/547–3321, **A**10 18 **F**3 33 35 40 43 56 59 64 65 82 84 87 91 93 97 107 114 119 130 133 135 144 148 154
Primary Contact: Rob Brandt, Chief Executive Officer
Web address: www.mvmc.org
Control: Other not–for–profit (including NFP Corporation) **Service**: General medical and surgical

Staffed Beds: 25 **Admissions**: 93 **Census**: 11 **Outpatient Visits**: 7435
Births: 0 **Total Expense ($000)**: 7552 **Payroll Expense ($000)**: 3868
Personnel: 45

WHITEFISH—Flathead County

★ **LOGAN HEALTH – WHITEFISH (271336)**, 1600 Hospital Way, Zip 59937–7849; tel. 406/863–3500, **A**10 18 **F**3 13 15 28 29 30 31 34 35 37 40 43 45 50 51 54 56 59 64 65 68 70 76 79 81 85 87 97 104 107 111 115 119 126 127 129 130 133 144 146 154 156 169 **P**6
Primary Contact: Kevin Abel, Chief Executive Officer
COO: Christina Bogers, Chief Clinical Officer
CFO: David Richhart, Chief Financial Officer
CMO: Jason Cohen, M.D., Chief Medical Officer
CIO: Michael Barnes, Chief Information Officer
CHR: Joseph Schmier, Interim Director Human Resources
Web address: www.nvhosp.org
Control: Other not–for–profit (including NFP Corporation) **Service**: General medical and surgical

Staffed Beds: 25 **Admissions**: 1464 **Census**: 12 **Outpatient Visits**: 86652
Births: 569 **Total Expense ($000)**: 93177 **Payroll Expense ($000)**: 36262
Personnel: 381

NORTH VALLEY HOSPITAL See Logan Health – Whitefish

WOLF POINT—Roosevelt County

★ **TRINITY HOSPITAL (271341)**, 315 Knapp Street, Zip 59201–1826; tel. 406/653–6500, (Nonreporting) **A**10 18
Primary Contact: Michael Post, Chief Executive Officer
Web address: www.nemhs.net
Control: Other not–for–profit (including NFP Corporation) **Service**: General medical and surgical

Staffed Beds: 82

NEBRASKA

AINSWORTH—Brown County

BROWN COUNTY HOSPITAL (281325), 945 East Zero Street,
Zip 69210–1547; tel. 402/387–2800, (Nonreporting) **A**10 18
Primary Contact: Mirya Hallock, Chief Executive Officer
CFO: Tad Stearns, Chief Financial Officer
CMO: Melvin Campbell, M.D., Medical Staff Chairman
CIO: Mike Depko, Director Information Technology
CHR: Lisa Fischer, Director Human Resources
CNO: Brandy Bussinger, Director of Nursing
Web address: www.browncountyhospital.org
Control: County, Government, Nonfederal **Service:** General medical and surgical

Staffed Beds: 18

ALBION—Boone County

★ **BOONE COUNTY HEALTH CENTER (281334)**, 723 West Fairview Street, Zip 68620–1725, Mailing Address: P.O. Box 151, Zip 68620–0151; tel. 402/395–2191, (Nonreporting) **A**10 18
Primary Contact: Caleb Poore, President and Chief Executive Officer
CFO: Rita Liss, Vice President Fiscal Services and Chief Financial Officer
CIO: Kenyon Woodward, Chief Information Officer
CHR: Jennifer Beierman, Director Human Resources
CNO: Cindy Lesiak, Vice President Patient Care Services and Director of Nursing
Web address: www.boonecohealth.org
Control: County, Government, Nonfederal **Service:** General medical and surgical

Staffed Beds: 25

ALLIANCE—Box Butte County

✢ **BOX BUTTE GENERAL HOSPITAL (281360)**, 2101 Box Butte Avenue, Zip 69301–4445, Mailing Address: P.O. Box 810, Zip 69301–0810; tel. 308/762–6660, **A**1 10 18 **F**3 5 11 13 15 28 29 31 32 34 35 36 38 40 43 47 48 50 51 53 57 59 60 64 68 69 75 77 78 79 81 82 85 86 87 92 93 96 97 100 101 104 107 108 110 111 114 118 119 122 127 130 131 132 133 134 135 146 148 149 154 156 169
Primary Contact: Lori Mazanec, Chief Executive Officer
COO: Jim Bargen, Chief Operating Officer
CFO: Michael O'Dell, Chief Financial Officer
CHR: Lisa L Hillyer, Human Resources Manager
CNO: Jordan Colwell, R.N., Chief Nursing Officer
Web address: www.bbgh.org
Control: County, Government, Nonfederal **Service:** General medical and surgical

Staffed Beds: 25 **Admissions:** 578 **Census:** 10 **Outpatient Visits:** 79501
Births: 134 **Total Expense ($000):** 54487 **Payroll Expense ($000):** 19471
Personnel: 263

ALMA—Harlan County

★ **HARLAN COUNTY HEALTH SYSTEM (281300)**, 717 North Brown Street, Zip 68920–2132, Mailing Address: P.O. Box 836, Zip 68920–0836; tel. 308/928–2151, (Nonreporting) **A**10 18 **S** Great Plains Health Alliance, Inc., Wichita, KS
Primary Contact: Stacy Neubauer, R.N., Chief Executive Officer
CFO: Heidi Cushing, Chief Financial Officer
CMO: Cameron Knackstedt, D.O., Chief Medical Staff
CIO: Michael Andrews, Coordinator Information Systems
CHR: Ana Schluntz, Director of Human Resources
Web address: www.harlancountyhealth.com
Control: County, Government, Nonfederal **Service:** General medical and surgical

Staffed Beds: 19

ATKINSON—Holt County

WEST HOLT MEDICAL SERVICES (281343), 406 West Neely Street, Zip 68713–4801; tel. 402/925–2811, (Nonreporting) **A**10 18 **S** Faith Regional Health Services, Norfolk, NE
Primary Contact: Jeremy Bauer, Chief Executive Officer
CFO: Taylor McCormick, Chief Financial Officer
CMO: John Tubbs, M.D., Chief of Staff
CIO: Mark Johnson, Chief Information Officer
CHR: Margaret Linse, Administrative Secretary and Director Human Resources
CNO: Jennifer Rystrom, R.N., Chief Nursing Officer
Web address: www.westholtmed.org
Control: Other not-for-profit (including NFP Corporation) **Service:** General medical and surgical

Staffed Beds: 15

AUBURN—Nemaha County

★ ⇑ **NEMAHA COUNTY HOSPITAL (281324)**, 2022 13th Street, Zip 68305–1799; tel. 402/274–4366, **A**3 10 18 21 **F**3 12 15 28 29 30 31 34 35 40 43 64 68 74 75 77 78 79 81 85 86 87 93 94 107 110 111 114 117 119 128 129 130 131 133 135 141 148 149 156
Primary Contact: Marty Fattig, Chief Executive Officer
COO: Kermit Moore, R.N., Chief Operating Officer and Chief Nursing Officer
CFO: Stacy Taylor, Chief Financial Officer
CIO: Kathy McNaughton, Chief Information Officer
CHR: Susan Shupp, Chief Human Resources Officer
Web address: www.nchnet.org
Control: County, Government, Nonfederal **Service:** General medical and surgical

Staffed Beds: 16 **Admissions:** 147 **Census:** 2 **Outpatient Visits:** 26120
Births: 0 **Total Expense ($000):** 17124 **Payroll Expense ($000):** 6398
Personnel: 80

AURORA—Hamilton County

★ **MEMORIAL COMMUNITY HEALTH (281320)**, 1423 Seventh Street, Zip 68818–1197; tel. 402/694–3171, (Nonreporting) **A**10 18
Primary Contact: Justin Wolf, Chief Executive Officer
CFO: Phil Fendt, Chief Financial Officer
CMO: Jeff Muilenburg, Chief of Staff
CIO: Brad Tiede, Director Information Systems
CHR: Laura Teichmeier, Director Human Resources
CNO: Lindy Mosel, Director of Nursing
Web address: www.memorialcommunityhealth.org
Control: Other not-for-profit (including NFP Corporation) **Service:** General medical and surgical

Staffed Beds: 63

BASSETT—Rock County

ROCK COUNTY HOSPITAL (281333), 102 East South Street, Zip 68714–5508; tel. 402/684–3366, (Total facility includes 30 beds in nursing home–type unit) **A**10 18 **F**7 11 15 28 40 53 62 81 84 107 110 119 127 128 133 154
Primary Contact: Stacey A. Knox, Administrator
CMO: John Tubbs, M.D., Chief of Staff
CIO: Cal Alder, Director Information Technology
CHR: Jackie Carpenter, Office Manager
CNO: Katie Ogier, Director of Nursing
Web address: www.rockcountyhospital.com
Control: County, Government, Nonfederal **Service:** General medical and surgical

Staffed Beds: 54 **Admissions:** 172 **Census:** 29 **Outpatient Visits:** 7023
Births: 0 **Total Expense ($000):** 13503 **Payroll Expense ($000):** 6284
Personnel: 99

Hospital, Medicare Provider Number, Address, Telephone, Approval, Facility, and Physician Codes, Health Care System

★ American Hospital Association (AHA) membership   ○ Healthcare Facilities Accreditation Program   ⇑ Center for Improvement in Healthcare Quality Accreditation
☐ The Joint Commission accreditation   ◇ DNV Healthcare Inc. accreditation   △ Commission on Accreditation of Rehabilitation Facilities (CARF) accreditation

Hospitals, U.S. / NEBRASKA

BEATRICE—Gage County

★ **BEATRICE COMMUNITY HOSPITAL AND HEALTH CENTER (281364)**, 4800 Hospital Parkway, Zip 68310–6906, Mailing Address: P.O. Box 278, Zip 68310–0278; tel. 402/228–3344, **A**10 18 **F**3 28 29 30 31 34 35 40 45 50 57 64 65 68 69 70 75 76 78 79 81 82 84 85 87 93 104 107 108 110 111 114 119 126 127 129 130 131 132 133 135 144 146 147 148 149 156 169
Primary Contact: Richard Haraldson, CPA, FACHE, Chief Executive Officer
CFO: Chad Jurgens, Senior Executive, Financial Services
CMO: Steven Paulmeyer, M.D., Senior Executive, Medical Services
CHR: Kathryn G. Humble, Senior Executive, Human Resource Services
CNO: Tasha N. Hesman, R.N., Senior Executive, Patient Care Services
Web address: www.beatricecommunityhospital.com
Control: Other not–for–profit (including NFP Corporation) **Service:** General medical and surgical

Staffed Beds: 25 **Admissions:** 921 **Census:** 9 **Outpatient Visits:** 202996 **Births:** 215 **Total Expense ($000):** 88305 **Payroll Expense ($000):** 40954 **Personnel:** 472

BELLEVUE—Sarpy County

☐ **NEBRASKA MEDICINE – BELLEVUE (280132)**, 2500 Bellevue Medical Center Drive, Zip 68123–1591; tel. 402/763–3000, **A**1 3 5 10 **F**3 15 18 20 22 26 28 29 30 31 34 35 37 38 40 41 44 45 47 48 49 50 51 53 55 56 57 58 59 63 64 65 68 70 74 75 77 78 79 81 82 84 85 86 87 91 92 93 96 97 107 108 110 111 114 115 119 130 131 132 135 141 143 145 146 147 148 149 150 154 164 167 169 **P**5 6 8
Primary Contact: Julie L. Lazure, R.N., MSN, Vice President, Nurse Executive
CFO: Stephanie Daubert, Chief Financial Officer
CMO: Jeffrey D. Akerson, M.D., Chief Medical Officer
CIO: Brian Lancaster, Executive Director Information Management
CNO: Ray D. Dial, Director of Nursing
Web address: www.nebraskamed.com
Control: Other not–for–profit (including NFP Corporation) **Service:** General medical and surgical

Staffed Beds: 80 **Admissions:** 4425 **Census:** 53 **Outpatient Visits:** 118262 **Births:** 0 **Total Expense ($000):** 105996 **Payroll Expense ($000):** 46050 **Personnel:** 399

BENKELMAN—Dundy County

★ **DUNDY COUNTY HOSPITAL (281340)**, 1313 North Cheyenne Street, Zip 69021–3074, Mailing Address: P.O. Box 626, Zip 69021–0626; tel. 308/423–2204, (Nonreporting) **A**10 18
Primary Contact: Kristopher Mathews, Chief Executive Officer
COO: Wendy Elkins, Director Operations
CFO: Renee Fink, CPA, Chief Financial Officer
CMO: Jose Garcia, M.D., Chief Medical Staff
CIO: David Craw, Coordinator Information Technology
CHR: Sandy Noffsinger, Executive Assistant, Risk Manager and Director Marketing
CNO: Laken Vrbas, R.N., Director of Nursing
Web address: www.dchbenkelman.com
Control: County, Government, Nonfederal **Service:** General medical and surgical

Staffed Beds: 12

BLAIR—Washington County

★ **MEMORIAL COMMUNITY HOSPITAL AND HEALTH SYSTEM (281359)**, 810 North 22nd Street, Zip 68008–1199, Mailing Address: P.O. Box 250, Zip 68008–0250; tel. 402/426–2182, **A**10 18 **F**3 13 15 28 29 31 32 34 35 40 41 43 44 45 55 57 59 64 65 67 68 75 76 77 78 79 81 82 85 93 97 107 110 111 115 119 127 128 129 130 131 132 133 135 144 146 147 148 149 153 154 169 **P**5 6 7
Primary Contact: Manuela Banner, FACHE, R.N., President and Chief Executive Officer
CFO: Jennifer Newby, Vice President of Operational Finance and Chief Financial Officer
CMO: John F. Simonson, M.D., Medical Director
CIO: Matt Baker, Director of Information Technology
CHR: Kristine Nielsen, Manager Human Resources
CNO: Amy Zimmer, Vice President of Patient Care Services and Chief Nursing Executive
Web address: www.mchhs.org
Control: Other not–for–profit (including NFP Corporation) **Service:** General medical and surgical

Staffed Beds: 17 **Admissions:** 460 **Census:** 8 **Outpatient Visits:** 61825 **Births:** 54 **Total Expense ($000):** 47049 **Payroll Expense ($000):** 23024 **Personnel:** 239

BRIDGEPORT—Morrill County

MORRILL COUNTY COMMUNITY HOSPITAL (281318), 1313 'S' Street, Zip 69336–0579; tel. 308/262–1616, (Nonreporting) **A**10 18
Primary Contact: Robin Stuart, Chief Executive Officer
CFO: Connie Christensen, Chief Financial Officer
CMO: John Post, M.D., Medical Director
CIO: Lori Shengle, Director Information Technology
CHR: Rhea Basa, Director Human Resources
CNO: Sylvia Marie Lichius, R.N., Chief Nursing Officer
Web address: www.morrillcountyhospital.com
Control: County, Government, Nonfederal **Service:** General medical and surgical

Staffed Beds: 8

BROKEN BOW—Custer County

JENNIE M. MELHAM MEMORIAL MEDICAL CENTER (281365), 145 Memorial Drive, Zip 68822–1378, Mailing Address: P.O. Box 250, Zip 68822–0250; tel. 308/872–4100, (Nonreporting) **A**10 18
Primary Contact: Kyle Kellum, President and Chief Executive Officer
CFO: Tim Schuckman, Chief Financial Officer
CIO: Tim Schuckman, Chief Financial Officer
CHR: Teri Sell, Payroll and Personnel Coordinator
CNO: Shelly Amsberry, Director of Nursing
Web address: https://www.melham.org
Control: Other not–for–profit (including NFP Corporation) **Service:** General medical and surgical

Staffed Beds: 12

CALLAWAY—Custer County

★ **CALLAWAY DISTRICT HOSPITAL (281335)**, 211 East Kimball, Zip 68825–2589, Mailing Address: P.O. Box 100, Zip 68825–0100; tel. 308/836–2228, (Nonreporting) **A**10 18
Primary Contact: Brett Eggleston, Chief Executive Officer
COO: Cassie Penn, Chief Operating Officer
CFO: Caleb Kelly Poore, Chief Financial Officer
CHR: Toni French, Manager Human Resources
Web address: www.callawayhospital.org
Control: Hospital district or authority, Government, Nonfederal **Service:** General medical and surgical

Staffed Beds: 12

CAMBRIDGE—Furnas County

★ **TRI VALLEY HEALTH SYSTEM (281348)**, 1305 West Highway 6 and 34, Zip 69022–0488, Mailing Address: P.O. Box 488, Zip 69022–0488; tel. 308/697–3329, (Nonreporting) **A**10 18
Primary Contact: Clay Jordan, R.N., Chief Executive Officer
CFO: Diana Swindler, Chief Financial Officer
CMO: Shiuvaun Jaeger, M.D., Chief of Staff
CIO: Ciprian Galarneau, Director Information Systems
CHR: Tammy Claussen, Chief Human Resource Officer
Web address: www.trivalleyhealth.com
Control: Other not–for–profit (including NFP Corporation) **Service:** General medical and surgical

Staffed Beds: 52

CENTRAL CITY—Merrick County

★ **MERRICK MEDICAL CENTER (281328)**, 1715 26th Street, Zip 68826–9620; tel. 308/946–3015, (Nonreporting) **A**10 18 **S** Bryan Health, Lincoln, NE
Primary Contact: Jodi Mohr, Chief Executive Officer
CHR: Shauna Graham, Director of Professional Services Human Resources, Marketing Foundation
Web address: https://www.bryanhealth.com
Control: County, Government, Nonfederal **Service:** General medical and surgical

Staffed Beds: 20

CHADRON—Dawes County

★ **CHADRON COMMUNITY HOSPITAL AND HEALTH SERVICES (281341)**, 825 Centennial Drive, Zip 69337–9400; tel. 308/432–5586, (Nonreporting) **A**10 18
Primary Contact: Sean Wolfe, Interim Chief Executive Officer
CFO: Jennifer L Brown, Chief Financial Officer
CMO: Ed Pelton, Chief of Staff
CHR: Ellen Krueger, Director Human Resources
CNO: Jeff Boman, Chief Nursing Officer
Web address: www.chadronhospital.com
Control: Other not–for–profit (including NFP Corporation) **Service:** General medical and surgical

Staffed Beds: 25

Hospitals, U.S. / NEBRASKA

COLUMBUS—Platte County

✣ **COLUMBUS COMMUNITY HOSPITAL (280111)**, 4600 38th Street, Zip 68601-1664, Mailing Address: P.O. Box 1800, Zip 68602-1800; tel. 402/564-7118, **A**1 3 10 20 **F**3 13 15 18 20 22 26 28 29 30 31 34 35 36 37 38 40 41 43 44 45 46 48 50 53 56 57 58 59 60 62 63 64 65 68 69 70 71 75 76 77 78 79 81 82 85 86 87 91 93 94 96 100 101 104 107 108 109 110 111 115 118 119 120 121 123 124 126 127 129 130 131 132 133 135 146 148 149 154 156 167 **P**8
Primary Contact: Michael T. Hansen, FACHE, President and Chief Executive Officer
COO: James P Goulet, Vice President Operations
CFO: Chad Van Cleave, Chief Financial Officer
CMO: Mark Howerter, M.D., Chief Medical Officer
CIO: Cheryl Tira, Director Information Systems
CHR: Scott E Messersmith, Director Human Resources
CNO: Tawny Sandifer, R.N., MSN, Chief Nursing Officer, Vice President of Patient Care Services
Web address: www.columbushosp.org
Control: Other not-for-profit (including NFP Corporation) **Service**: General medical and surgical

Staffed Beds: 50 **Admissions**: 1674 **Census**: 18 **Outpatient Visits**: 65777 **Births**: 512 **Total Expense ($000)**: 138485 **Payroll Expense ($000)**: 59905 **Personnel**: 912

COZAD—Dawson County

★ **COZAD COMMUNITY HEALTH SYSTEM (281327)**, 300 East 12th Street, Zip 69130-1505, Mailing Address: P.O. Box 108, Zip 69130-0108; tel. 308/784-2261, (Nonreporting) **A**10 18
Primary Contact: Robert Dyer, Chief Executive Officer
Web address: www.cozadhealthcare.com
Control: Hospital district or authority, Government, Nonfederal **Service**: General medical and surgical

Staffed Beds: 20

CREIGHTON—Knox County

★ **AVERA CREIGHTON HOSPITAL (281331)**, 1503 Main Street, Zip 68729-3007, Mailing Address: P.O. Box 186, Zip 68729-0186; tel. 402/358-5700, (Total facility includes 47 beds in nursing home–type unit) **A**10 18 **F**15 18 28 29 34 35 40 41 43 45 47 50 53 56 59 65 67 68 77 79 81 82 89 93 97 100 102 104 107 108 110 115 127 128 129 131 133 143 146 149 154 **P**6 **S** Avera Health, Sioux Falls, SD
Primary Contact: Theresa L. Guenther, Chief Executive Officer
CHR: Jane E. Miller, Director Human Resources
CNO: Jean M. Henes, MSN, R.N., Director of Nursing
Web address: www.avera.org/creighton/
Control: Other not-for-profit (including NFP Corporation) **Service**: General medical and surgical

Staffed Beds: 70 **Admissions**: 165 **Census**: 37 **Outpatient Visits**: 7814 **Births**: 0 **Total Expense ($000)**: 19426 **Payroll Expense ($000)**: 10631 **Personnel**: 129

CRETE—Saline County

★ **CRETE AREA MEDICAL CENTER (281354)**, 2910 Betten Drive, Zip 68333-3084, Mailing Address: P.O. Box 220, Zip 68333-0220; tel. 402/826-2102, (Nonreporting) **A**10 18 **S** Bryan Health, Lincoln, NE
Primary Contact: Stephanie Boldt, President and Chief Executive Officer
CFO: Julie Lacy, Chief Financial Officer
CMO: Russell Ebke, M.D., Chief of Staff
CIO: Drew Kotil, Director Information Technology
CHR: Bobbie Wilson, Director Human Resources
CNO: April R. Gaines, Chief Nursing Officer
Web address: www.creteareamedicalcenter.com
Control: Other not-for-profit (including NFP Corporation) **Service**: General medical and surgical

Staffed Beds: 24

DAVID CITY—Butler County

★ **BUTLER COUNTY HEALTH CARE CENTER (281332)**, 372 South Ninth Street, Zip 68632-2116; tel. 402/367-1200, (Nonreporting) **A**10 18
Primary Contact: Donald T. Naiberk, Administrator and Chief Executive Officer
CFO: Jodi Prochaska, Chief Financial Officer
CMO: Victor Thoendel, M.D., Chief Medical Officer
CIO: Cindy Neesen, Director of Information Technology
CHR: Andra Vandenberg, Director Human Resources
CNO: Sue M Birkel, R.N., Director of Nursing
Web address: www.bchccnet.org
Control: County, Government, Nonfederal **Service**: General medical and surgical

Staffed Beds: 20

ELKHORN—Douglas County

METHODIST WOMEN'S HOSPITAL See Nebraska Methodist Hospital, Omaha

FAIRBURY—Jefferson County

★ **JEFFERSON COMMUNITY HEALTH AND LIFE (281319)**, 2200 'H' Street, Zip 68352-1119, Mailing Address: P.O. Box 277, Zip 68352-0277; tel. 402/729-3351, (Nonreporting) **A**10 18
Primary Contact: William L. Welch, FACHE, Interim Chief Executive Officer
CFO: Chance Klasek, CPA, Chief Financial Officer
CIO: Dennis Ahl, Director Information Technology
CHR: Sandra A. Bauer, Director Human Resources
CNO: Erin L. Starr, Chief Nursing Officer
Web address: www.jchealthandlife.org
Control: Other not-for-profit (including NFP Corporation) **Service**: General medical and surgical

Staffed Beds: 57

FALLS CITY—Richardson County

★ ⇑ **COMMUNITY MEDICAL CENTER, INC. (281352)**, 3307 Barada Street, Zip 68355-2470, Mailing Address: P.O. Box 399, Zip 68355-0399; tel. 402/245-2428, **A**10 18 21 **F**3 5 15 28 31 34 35 40 43 45 59 75 78 79 81 82 85 93 97 107 111 114 119 127 130 133 135 154 160 169 **P**6
Primary Contact: Ryan C. Larsen, FACHE, Chief Executive Officer
CFO: Randy Willy, Chief Financial Officer
CMO: Daniel Samani, M.D.
CIO: Joe Buckminster, Manager Information Technology
CHR: Shannon Weinmann, Director Human Resources
CNO: Ivy Campbell, Director of Nursing
Web address: www.cmcfc.org
Control: Other not-for-profit (including NFP Corporation) **Service**: General medical and surgical

Staffed Beds: 24 **Admissions**: 581 **Census**: 6 **Outpatient Visits**: 60771 **Births**: 0 **Total Expense ($000)**: 33221 **Payroll Expense ($000)**: 11641 **Personnel**: 188

FRANKLIN—Franklin County

★ **FRANKLIN COUNTY MEMORIAL HOSPITAL (281311)**, 1406 'Q' Street, Zip 68939-0315, Mailing Address: 1406 Q Street, Zip 68939-0315; tel. 308/425-6221, (Nonreporting) **A**10 18
Primary Contact: Theresa Rizzo, Administrator
CFO: Amy Kahrs, Director of Finance
CMO: Linda Mazour, M.D., President
CIO: Cathy Webber, Director of Health Information Management
CNO: Kari Yelken, R.N., Director of Nursing
Web address: www.fcmh.com
Control: County, Government, Nonfederal **Service**: General medical and surgical

Staffed Beds: 14

Hospital, Medicare Provider Number, Address, Telephone, Approval, Facility, and Physician Codes, Health Care System

★ American Hospital Association (AHA) membership ◯ Healthcare Facilities Accreditation Program ⇑ Center for Improvement in Healthcare Quality Accreditation
☐ The Joint Commission accreditation ◇ DNV Healthcare Inc. accreditation △ Commission on Accreditation of Rehabilitation Facilities (CARF) accreditation

© 2025 AHA Guide

Hospitals, U.S. / NEBRASKA

FREMONT—Dodge County

METHODIST FREMONT HEALTH (280077), 450 East 23rd Street, Zip 68025-2387; tel. 402/721-1610, (Nonreporting) **A**1 2 3 5 10 20 **S** Nebraska Methodist Health System, Inc., Omaha, NE
Primary Contact: William Vobejda, President and Chief Executive Officer
CFO: Jeff Francis, Vice President, Chief Financial Officer
CIO: Kent Sona, Vice President, Chief Information Officer
CHR: Bethany Childers, Director Human Resources
CNO: Melinda Johanna Kentfield, R.N., Chief Nursing Officer
Web address: www.fremonthealth.com
Control: Other not-for-profit (including NFP Corporation) **Service**: General medical and surgical

Staffed Beds: 181

FRIEND—Saline County

FRIEND COMMUNITY HEALTHCARE SYSTEM (280779), 905 Second Street, Zip 68359-1133; tel. 402/947-2541, (Nonreporting) **A**10
Primary Contact: Jared Chaffin, Chief Executive Officer and Chief Financial Officer
CFO: Jared Chaffin, Chief Executive Officer and Chief Financial Officer
CMO: Roger Meyer, M.D., Chief of Staff
CIO: Ron TeBrink, Chief Information Officer
CHR: Shyanne Scholl, Interim Human Resources Director
CNO: Dayna Pulver, Director of Nursing
Web address: www.friendmed.org/
Control: City, Government, Nonfederal

Staffed Beds: 17

GENEVA—Fillmore County

★ **FILLMORE COUNTY HOSPITAL (281301)**, 1900 'F' Street, Zip 68361-1325, Mailing Address: P.O. Box 193, Zip 68361-0193; tel. 402/759-3167, **A**10 18 **F**3 7 11 13 15 28 29 31 34 39 40 41 45 46 47 48 49 50 56 57 59 64 67 75 76 77 79 81 82 85 87 92 93 94 101 102 104 107 110 115 119 126 128 130 131 132 133 143 148 149 153 154 162 164 **P**6
Primary Contact: Christopher Nichols, Chief Executive Officer
COO: Debbie Domann, Director of Operations
CFO: Dayle Harlow, Chief Financial Officer
CMO: Jason Bespalec, M.D., Chief of Staff
CIO: Tyler Gewecke, Information Technology Technician
CHR: Abby Alfs, Chief Human Resources Officer
Web address: www.fhsofgeneva.org
Control: County, Government, Nonfederal **Service**: General medical and surgical

Staffed Beds: 20 **Admissions**: 298 **Census**: 3 **Outpatient Visits**: 30418 **Births**: 18 **Total Expense ($000)**: 27050 **Payroll Expense ($000)**: 11278 **Personnel**: 172

GENOA—Nance County

GENOA MEDICAL FACILITIES (281312), 706 Ewing Avenue, Zip 68640-3035, Mailing Address: P.O. Box 310, Zip 68640-0310; tel. 402/993-2283, (Nonreporting) **A**10 18 **S** Faith Regional Health Services, Norfolk, NE
Primary Contact: Amanda Roebuck, Chief Executive Officer
CFO: Angie Sutton, Chief Financial Officer
CMO: Brian Buhlke, M.D., Medical Director
CHR: Brianna Molt, Human Resources Director
Web address: www.genoamedical.org/
Control: City-county, Government, Nonfederal **Service**: General medical and surgical

Staffed Beds: 58

GORDON—Sheridan County

GORDON MEMORIAL HEALTH SERVICES (281358), 300 East Eighth Street, Zip 69343-1123; tel. 308/282-0401, (Nonreporting) **A**10 18
Primary Contact: Megan Heath, Chief Executive Officer and Chief Nursing Officer
CMO: Christopher P. Costa, M.D., Chief of Staff
CIO: Ray Waldron, Director Information Technology
CNO: Megan Heath, Chief Nursing Officer
Web address: www.gordonmemorial.org
Control: Hospital district or authority, Government, Nonfederal **Service**: General medical and surgical

Staffed Beds: 25

GOTHENBURG—Dawson County

★ **GOTHENBURG HEALTH (281313)**, 910 20th Street, Zip 69138-1237, Mailing Address: P.O. Box 469, Zip 69138-0469; tel. 308/537-3661, **A**10 18 **F**3 13 15 28 29 32 34 35 40 43 50 53 56 57 59 64 65 76 77 81 85 89 93 97 100 101 102 104 107 111 114 115 119 122 127 130 131 133 135 148 154 156 157 164 169
Primary Contact: Mick Brant, FACHE, Chief Executive Officer
CFO: Michael Pracheil, Chief Financial Officer
CMO: Carol Shackleton, M.D., Medical Director
CIO: Tinna Marie Therrien, R.N., Chief Information Officer and Senior Director Ancillary Services
CHR: Jim Imler, Director Human Resources
CNO: Susan Moore, MS, R.N., Chief Nursing Officer
Web address: www.gothenburghealth.org
Control: Hospital district or authority, Government, Nonfederal **Service**: General medical and surgical

Staffed Beds: 14 **Admissions**: 607 **Census**: 2 **Outpatient Visits**: 2344 **Births**: 61 **Personnel**: 183

GRAND ISLAND—Hall County

CHI HEALTH SAINT FRANCIS (280023), 2620 West Faidley Avenue, Zip 68803-4297, Mailing Address: P.O. Box 9804, Zip 68802-9804; tel. 308/384-4600, (Includes ST. FRANCIS MEDICAL PLAZA, 2116 West Faidley Avenue, Grand Island, Nebraska, Zip 68803, P O Box 9804, Zip 68802, tel. 308/384-4600) (Nonreporting) **A**1 2 3 5 10 19 **S** CommonSpirit Health, Chicago, IL
Primary Contact: Steven M. Schieber, FACHE, President
CFO: Lisa Webb, Vice President Operational Finance
CMO: Shu-Ming Wang, MD, Vice President Medical Affairs
CHR: Nancy Wallace, Vice President Human Resources, CHI Health
CNO: Beth Bartlett, MSN, R.N., Vice President Nursing
Web address: https://www.chihealth.com/locations/st-francis
Control: Church operated, Nongovernment, not-for-profit **Service**: General medical and surgical

Staffed Beds: 165

★ **GRAND ISLAND REGIONAL MEDICAL CENTER (280139)**, 3533 Prairieview Street, Zip 68803-4409; tel. 308/675-5000, (Nonreporting) **A**3 10 22 **S** Bryan Health, Lincoln, NE
Primary Contact: Drew Waterman, Chief Executive Officer
CFO: Derick Lorentz, Chief Financial Officer
CMO: Ryan Crouch, M.D., Chief Medical Officer
CIO: Mark Blinde, Director, Information Technology
CHR: Kari Fluckey, Director of Human Resources
CNO: Tiffani Arndt, Chief Nursing Officer
Web address: www.giregional.org
Control: Other not-for-profit (including NFP Corporation) **Service**: General medical and surgical

Staffed Beds: 67

SAINT FRANCIS MEMORIAL HEALTH CENTER See St. Francis Medical Plaza

GRANT—Perkins County

★ **PERKINS COUNTY HEALTH SERVICES (281356)**, 900 Lincoln Avenue, Zip 69140-3095; tel. 308/352-7200, (Nonreporting) **A**10 18
Primary Contact: Neil A. Hilton, FACHE, Chief Executive Officer
CMO: Ruth Demmel, M.D., Chief Medical Officer
CIO: Jennifer Baumgartner, Chief Information Officer
CHR: Julie Bevard, Vice President Human Resources
CNO: Dana McArtor, R.N., Director of Nursing
Web address: www.pchsgrant.com
Control: Hospital district or authority, Government, Nonfederal **Service**: General medical and surgical

Staffed Beds: 20

HASTINGS—Adams County

MARY LANNING HEALTHCARE (280032), 715 North St Joseph Avenue, Zip 68901-4497; tel. 402/463-4521, (Nonreporting) **A**1 2 3 5 10
Primary Contact: Eric A. Barber, President and Chief Executive Officer
COO: Mark Callahan, Chief Operating Officer
CFO: Shawn A Nordby, Chief Financial Officer
CMO: Abel Luksan, M.D., Chief Medical Officer
CIO: Lisa Nonneman, Director Information Technology Services
CHR: Michelle Hopkins, Vice President of Human Resources
CNO: Ronda S Ehly, R.N., Chief Nursing Officer
Web address: www.marylanning.org
Control: Other not-for-profit (including NFP Corporation) **Service**: General medical and surgical

Staffed Beds: 148

Hospitals, U.S. / NEBRASKA

HEBRON—Thayer County

★ **THAYER COUNTY HEALTH SERVICES (281304)**, 120 Park Avenue, Zip 68370–2019, Mailing Address: P.O. Box 49, Zip 68370–0049; tel. 402/768–6041, (Nonreporting) **A**10 18
Primary Contact: Brian Rokusek, President and Chief Executive Officer
COO: Amanda R Vandervoort, Chief Operating Officer
CFO: Michael Defoe, Chief Financial Officer
CMO: Leann Heinrichs, M.D., Chief of Staff
CIO: Rich Neyenhouse, Director Information Technology
CHR: Tamara Brose, Director Human Resources
CNO: Jamie Koch, R.N., Chief Nursing Officer
Web address: www.thayercountyhealth.com
Control: County, Government, Nonfederal **Service**: General medical and surgical

Staffed Beds: 19

HENDERSON—York County

HENDERSON HEALTH CARE SERVICES (281308), 1621 Front Street, Zip 68371–8902; tel. 402/723–4512, (Nonreporting) **A**10 18
Primary Contact: Cheryl Brown, Chief Executive Officer
CMO: James M Ohrt, M.D., Director Medical Staff
CHR: Lynette Friesen, Manager Human Resources
CNO: Carrie Peterson, Director of Nursing
Web address: www.hendersonhealthcare.org/getpage.php?name=message
Control: Other not-for-profit (including NFP Corporation) **Service**: General medical and surgical

Staffed Beds: 56

HOLDREGE—Phelps County

★ ⇧ **PHELPS MEMORIAL HEALTH CENTER (281362)**, 1215 Tibbals Street, Zip 68949–1255; tel. 308/995–2211, (Nonreporting) **A**10 18 21 **S** Ovation Healthcare, Brentwood, TN
Primary Contact: Mark Harrel, Chief Executive Officer
CFO: Loren D Schroder, Chief Financial Officer
CMO: Stuart Embury, M.D., Chief Medical Officer
CIO: Leora Smith, Information System and Health Information Management Team Leader
CHR: Cindy Jackson, Director Human Resources
Web address: www.phelpsmemorial.com
Control: Other not-for-profit (including NFP Corporation) **Service**: General medical and surgical

Staffed Beds: 25

IMPERIAL—Chase County

CHASE COUNTY COMMUNITY HOSPITAL (281351), 600 West 12th Street, Zip 69033–3130, Mailing Address: P.O. Box 819, Zip 69033–0819; tel. 308/882–7111, (Nonreporting) **A**10 18
Primary Contact: Abigail Cyboron, Chief Executive Officer
CMO: Jonathan Richman, M.D., Chief of Staff
CIO: Jen Harris, Director Health Information Management
CHR: Julie Sharp, Supervisor Human Resources
CNO: Kathy Geier, Director of Nursing
Web address: www.chasecountyhospital.com
Control: County, Government, Nonfederal **Service**: General medical and surgical

Staffed Beds: 20

KEARNEY—Buffalo County

▣ **CHI HEALTH GOOD SAMARITAN (280009)**, 10 East 31st Street, Zip 68847–2926, Mailing Address: P.O. Box 1990, Zip 68848–1990; tel. 308/865–7100, (Includes RICHARD H. YOUNG BEHAVIORAL HEALTH CENTER, 1755 Prairie View Place, Kearney, Nebraska, Zip 68848, P O Box 1750, Zip 68848–1705, tel. 308/865–2000; Lacey Witt, Director) (Nonreporting) **A**1 2 3 5 10 19 **S** CommonSpirit Health, Chicago, IL
Primary Contact: Curt Coleman, FACHE, President
CFO: Lisa Webb, Vice President for Operational Finance
CMO: Dennis Edwards, M.D., Vice President Medical Affairs
CIO: Katie Gartner, Director Health Information Management
CHR: Aaron Austin, Division Vice President, Human Resources
CNO: Kimber Bonner, R.N., Vice President Patient Care Services
Web address: www.chihealthgoodsamaritan.org
Control: Church operated, Nongovernment, not-for-profit **Service**: General medical and surgical

Staffed Beds: 252

★ ○ **KEARNEY REGIONAL MEDICAL CENTER (280134)**, 804 22nd Avenue, Zip 68845–2206; tel. 855/404–5762, (Nonreporting) **A**10 11 **S** Bryan Health, Lincoln, NE
Primary Contact: Douglas Edward. Koch, Chief Executive Officer
COO: Danny Van Ranken, Chief Operating Officer
CFO: Steve Regier, Chief Financial Officer
CHR: Steve Beck, MS, Chief Human Resource Officer
CNO: Adrienne Carney, R.N., Director Nursing and Surgical Services
Web address: www.kearneyregional.com
Control: Other not-for-profit (including NFP Corporation) **Service**: General medical and surgical

Staffed Beds: 92

RICHARD H. YOUNG HOSPITAL See Richard H. Young Behavioral Health Center

KIMBALL—Kimball County

★ **KIMBALL HEALTH SERVICES (281305)**, 255 West 4th Street, Zip 69145; tel. 308/235–1952, (Nonreporting) **A**10 18
Primary Contact: Cassie Gasseling, Chief Executive Officer
CFO: Cassie Gasseling, Chief Financial Officer
CMO: James Plate, M.D., Chief of Staff
CIO: Charles Walker, Director Information Technology
CHR: Jim Imler, Director Human Resources
CNO: Trevor Mohren, Chief Nursing Officer
Web address: www.kimballhealth.org
Control: County, Government, Nonfederal **Service**: General medical and surgical

Staffed Beds: 10

LEXINGTON—Dawson County

★ ⇧ **LEXINGTON REGIONAL HEALTH CENTER (281361)**, 1201 North Erie Street, Zip 68850–1560, Mailing Address: PO Box 980, Zip 68850–0980; tel. 308/324–5651, (Nonreporting) **A**3 5 10 18 21
Primary Contact: Wade Eschenbrenner, Interim Chief Executive Officer
COO: Jim Hain, Chief Operating Officer
CFO: Wade Eschenbrenner, Chief Financial Officer
CMO: Francisca Acosta–Carlson, M.D., Chief of Staff
CIO: Robb Hanna, Executive Director Information Technology
CHR: Jill Denker, Executive Director Human Resources
CNO: Nicole Thorell, R.N., MSN, Chief Nursing Officer
Web address: www.lexingtonregional.org
Control: Hospital district or authority, Government, Nonfederal **Service**: General medical and surgical

Staffed Beds: 25

LINCOLN—Lancaster County

▣ △ **BRYAN MEDICAL CENTER (280003)**, 1600 South 48th Street, Zip 68506–1299; tel. 402/481–1111, (Includes BRYAN MEDICAL CENTER–EAST, 1600 South 48th Street, Lincoln, Nebraska, Zip 68506–1299, tel. 402/481–1111; Eric Mooss, Chief Executive Officer; BRYAN MEDICAL CENTER–WEST, 2300 South 16th Street, Lincoln, Nebraska, Zip 68502–3781, tel. 402/475–1011; Eric Mooss, Chief Executive Officer) (Nonreporting) **A**1 2 3 5 7 10 19 **S** Bryan Health, Lincoln, NE
Primary Contact: Eric Mooss, President and Chief Executive Officer
COO: Travis Gregg, FACHE, Chief Operating Officer
CMO: John Trapp, Vice President Medical Affairs
CNO: Adrienne Olson, R.N., FACHE, Chief Nursing Officer and Vice President, Patient Care Services
Web address: www.bryanhealth.com
Control: Other not-for-profit (including NFP Corporation) **Service**: General medical and surgical

Staffed Beds: 557

BRYANLGH MEDICAL CENTER–EAST See Bryan Medical Center–East

BRYANLGH MEDICAL CENTER–WEST See Bryan Medical Center–West

▣ **CHI HEALTH NEBRASKA HEART (280128)**, 7500 South 91st Street, Zip 68526–9437; tel. 402/327–2700, (Nonreporting) **A**1 10 **S** CommonSpirit Health, Chicago, IL
Primary Contact: Rick Thompson, M.D., FACS, FACC, President
Web address: www.CHIhealthNebraskaHeart.com
Control: Church operated, Nongovernment, not-for-profit **Service**: Heart

Staffed Beds: 54

Hospital, Medicare Provider Number, Address, Telephone, Approval, Facility, and Physician Codes, Health Care System

★ American Hospital Association (AHA) membership
□ The Joint Commission accreditation
○ Healthcare Facilities Accreditation Program
◇ DNV Healthcare Inc. accreditation
⇧ Center for Improvement in Healthcare Quality Accreditation
△ Commission on Accreditation of Rehabilitation Facilities (CARF) accreditation

Hospitals, U.S. / NEBRASKA

CHI HEALTH ST ELIZABETH (280020), 555 South 70th Street, Zip 68510–2494; tel. 402/219–8000, (Nonreporting) **A**1 2 3 5 10 **S** CommonSpirit Health, Chicago, IL
Primary Contact: Tyler DeJong, President
CFO: Tyler DeJong, Vice President, Operational Finance
CMO: Jason Kruger, Chief Medical Officer and Vice President
CIO: Richard Bohaty, Director Information Technology
CHR: Nancy Wallace, Senior Vice President, Chief Human Resources Officer
CNO: Elizabeth A Raetz, R.N., MSN, Vice President Nursing and Chief Nursing Officer
Web address: https://www.chihealth.com/locations/st-elizabeth
Control: Church operated, Nongovernment, not–for–profit **Service:** General medical and surgical

Staffed Beds: 235

LINCOLN DIVISION See Veterans Affairs Nebraska–Western Iowa Health Care System – Lincoln, Lincoln

LINCOLN REGIONAL CENTER (284003), 801 West Prospector Place, Zip 68522–2299, Mailing Address: P.O. Box 94949, Zip 68509–4949; tel. 402/471–4444, (Nonreporting) **A**1 3 10
Primary Contact: Jess Russell–Berring, Hospital Administrator
COO: Stacey Werth–Sweeney, Facility Operating Officer
CFO: Randy Willey, Business Manager
CMO: Vijay Dewan, M.D., Clinical Director
CHR: Scott Rasmussen, Director Human Resources
Web address: www.hhs.state.ne.us/beh/rc
Control: State, Government, Nonfederal **Service:** Psychiatric

Staffed Beds: 190

LINCOLN SURGICAL HOSPITAL (280127), 1710 South 70th Street, Suite 200, Zip 68506–1677; tel. 402/484–9090, (Nonreporting) **A**10
Primary Contact: Robb Linafelter, Chief Executive Officer
Web address: www.lincolnsurgery.com
Control: Corporation, Investor–owned (for–profit) **Service:** Surgical

Staffed Beds: 7

MADONNA REHABILITATION HOSPITAL (283025), 5401 South Street, Zip 68506–2134; tel. 402/489–7102, (Total facility includes 79 beds in nursing home–type unit) **A**3 5 10 **F**1 3 29 30 32 34 50 57 58 59 65 71 74 75 86 87 90 91 92 93 95 96 100 107 115 119 128 130 131 132 143 146 148 149 154 157 164 **P**6
Primary Contact: Paul Dongilli Jr, Ph.D., FACHE, President and Chief Executive Officer
CFO: Victor J Witkowicz, Senior Vice President and Chief Financial Officer
CMO: Julie Lyon, M.D., Chief Medical Officer
CIO: David Rolfe, Chief Information Officer
CHR: Lou Ann Manske, Vice President Human Resources
Web address: www.madonna.org
Control: Other not–for–profit (including NFP Corporation) **Service:** Rehabilitation

Staffed Beds: 146 **Admissions:** 724 **Census:** 136 **Outpatient Visits:** 60698 **Births:** 0 **Total Expense ($000):** 50032 **Payroll Expense ($000):** 29413 **Personnel:** 884

MADONNA REHABILITATION HOSPITAL See Madonna Rehabilitation Specialty Hospital Lincoln

MADONNA REHABILITATION SPECIALTY HOSPITAL LINCOLN (282000), 5401 South Street, Zip 68506–2150; tel. 402/413–3000, (Nonreporting) **A**10
Primary Contact: Paul Dongilli Jr, Ph.D., FACHE, President and Chief Executive Officer
CFO: Ken Hopkins, Vice President and Chief Executive Officer
CMO: Julie Lyon, M.D., Chief Medical Officer
Web address: www.madonna.org/
Control: Other not–for–profit (including NFP Corporation) **Service:** Acute long–term care hospital

Staffed Beds: 300

NEBRASKA PENAL AND CORRECTIONAL HOSPITAL, 14th and Pioneer Streets, Zip 68501, Mailing Address: P.O. Box 94661, Zip 94661; tel. 402/471–3161, (Nonreporting)
Primary Contact: Randy T. Kohl, M.D., Deputy Director, Health Services
Web address: www.corrections.nebraska.gov
Control: State, Government, Nonfederal **Service:** Hospital unit of an institution (prison hospital, college infirmary, etc.)

Staffed Beds: 12

VETERANS AFFAIRS MED CENTER See Lincoln Division

VETERANS AFFAIRS NEBRASKA–WESTERN IOWA HEALTH CARE SYSTEM – LINCOLN, 600 South 70th Street, Zip 68510–2493; tel. 402/489–3802, (Includes LINCOLN DIVISION, 600 South 70th Street, Lincoln, Nebraska, Zip 68510–2493, tel. 402/489–3802) (Nonreporting) **S** Department of Veterans Affairs, Washington, DC
Primary Contact: Eileen M. Kingston, R.N., Acting Director, Chief Executive Officer
CIO: David Daiker, Chief Information Resource Management
CHR: Dave Peters, Chief Human Resources Officer
Web address: www.nebraska.va.gov/
Control: Veterans Affairs, Government, federal **Service:** General medical and surgical

Staffed Beds: 132

LYNCH—Boyd County

NIOBRARA VALLEY HOSPITAL (281303), 401 South Fifth Street, Zip 68746–0118, Mailing Address: P.O. Box 118, Zip 68746–0118; tel. 402/569–2451, (Nonreporting) **A**10 18 **S** Faith Regional Health Services, Norfolk, NE
Primary Contact: Kelly Kalkowski, Chief Executive Officer
CFO: Martha Nelson, Chief Financial Officer
CMO: James Keil, M.D., Chief Medical Officer
CHR: Trudy Nelson, Chief Human Resource Officer
CNO: Debra Dawn Hanzlik, R.N., Director of Nursing
Web address: www.nvhcares.org
Control: Other not–for–profit (including NFP Corporation) **Service:** General medical and surgical

Staffed Beds: 20

MCCOOK—Red Willow County

COMMUNITY HOSPITAL (281363), 1301 East 'H' Street, Zip 69001–1328, Mailing Address: P.O. Box 1328, Zip 69001–1328; tel. 308/344–2650, (Nonreporting) **A**3 5 10 18 21
Primary Contact: Troy Bruntz, CPA, President and Chief Executive Officer
CFO: Sean Wolfe, Vice President Finance and Chief Financial Officer
CMO: Jason Blomstedt, Chief of Staff
CIO: Lori Beeby, Vice President Support Services
CHR: Leanne R Miller, Director Human Resources
Web address: www.chmccook.org
Control: Other not–for–profit (including NFP Corporation) **Service:** General medical and surgical

Staffed Beds: 25

MINDEN—Kearney County

KEARNEY COUNTY HEALTH SERVICES (281306), 727 East First Street, Zip 68959–1705; tel. 308/832–3400, (Nonreporting) **A**3 10 18
Primary Contact: Luke David. Poore, Chief Executive Officer
CFO: Gavin Blum, Chief Financial Officer
CMO: Douglas Althouse, Chief Medical Officer
CHR: Rebecca L Cooke, Director Human Resources
CNO: Kendra Brown, MSN, R.N., Chief Nursing Officer
Web address: www.kchs.org
Control: County, Government, Nonfederal **Service:** General medical and surgical

Staffed Beds: 10

NEBRASKA CITY—Otoe County

CHI HEALTH ST. MARY'S (281342), 1301 Grundman Boulevard, Zip 68410; tel. 402/873–3321, **A**10 18 **F**3 13 15 18 28 29 31 34 35 40 43 44 45 57 59 64 66 68 69 74 75 76 77 78 79 81 82 85 86 87 92 96 97 107 108 110 111 115 118 119 127 128 129 132 133 135 146 147 148 149 150 154 156 160 169 **S** CommonSpirit Health, Chicago, IL
Primary Contact: Daniel DeFreece, M.D., President
CFO: Tim H. Schnack, Vice President Operations Finance
CMO: Jonathan Stelling, M.D., Vice President Medical Affairs
CNO: Brenda Jean Sebek, R.N., Administrator
Web address: www.chihealthstmarys.com
Control: Church operated, Nongovernment, not–for–profit **Service:** General medical and surgical

Staffed Beds: 18 **Admissions:** 375 **Census:** 6 **Outpatient Visits:** 45444 **Births:** 86 **Total Expense ($000):** 32534 **Payroll Expense ($000):** 10289 **Personnel:** 215

NELIGH—Antelope County

★ **ANTELOPE MEMORIAL HOSPITAL (281326)**, 102 West 9th Street, Zip 68756-1114, Mailing Address: P.O. Box 229, Zip 68756-0229; tel. 402/887-4151, (Nonreporting) **A**10 18
Primary Contact: Diane Brugger, FACHE, Chief Executive Officer
CFO: Martha Nelson, Chief Financial Officer
CMO: Roger Rudloff, M.D., President Medical Staff
CIO: Kevin Trease, Chief Information Officer
CHR: Megan Becklun, Director Human Resources
CNO: Merry Sprout, R.N., Chief Nursing Officer
Web address: www.amhne.org/
Control: Other not-for-profit (including NFP Corporation) **Service**: General medical and surgical

Staffed Beds: 23

NORFOLK—Madison County

▣ **FAITH REGIONAL HEALTH SERVICES (280125)**, 2700 West Norfolk Avenue, Zip 68701-4438, Mailing Address: P.O. Box 869, Zip 68702-0869; tel. 402/371-4880, (Includes EAST CAMPUS, 1500 Koenigstein Avenue, Norfolk, Nebraska, Zip 68701, tel. 402/371-3402; WEST CAMPUS, 2700 Norfolk Avenue, Norfolk, Nebraska, Zip 68701, P O Box 869, Zip 68702-0869; tel. 402/371-4880) (Nonreporting) **A**1 2 5 10 20 **S** Faith Regional Health Services, Norfolk, NE
Primary Contact: Kelly Driscoll, R.N., FACHE, President and Chief Executive Officer
CMO: Dean O French, M.D., Chief of Staff
CIO: Brian Sterud, Chief Information Officer
CHR: Janet M Pinkelman, Director Human Resources
Web address: www.frhs.org
Control: Other not-for-profit (including NFP Corporation) **Service**: General medical and surgical

Staffed Beds: 199

NORTH PLATTE—Lincoln County

★ **GREAT PLAINS HEALTH (280065)**, 601 West Leota Street, Zip 69101-6598, Mailing Address: P.O. Box 1167, Zip 69103-1167; tel. 308/568-8000, (Nonreporting) **A**2 3 5 10 22
Primary Contact: Ivan Mitchell, Chief Executive Officer
COO: Danelle Franzen, Chief Operating Officer
CFO: Summer Owen, Chief Financial Officer
CIO: Brandon Kelliher, Chief Information Officer
CHR: Jayne Johnson, Director Human Resources
CNO: Tamara Martin-Linnard, R.N., Chief Clinical Officer
Web address: www.gphealth.org
Control: Other not-for-profit (including NFP Corporation) **Service**: General medical and surgical

Staffed Beds: 72

O'NEILL—Holt County

★ **AVERA ST. ANTHONY'S HOSPITAL (281329)**, 300 North Second Street, Zip 68763-1514, Mailing Address: P.O. Box 270, Oneill, Zip 68763-0270; tel. 402/336-2611, **A**10 18 **F**3 8 13 15 28 29 30 31 32 34 35 38 40 43 45 50 59 60 64 65 74 75 76 77 78 79 81 82 84 85 86 91 93 107 110 111 119 120 127 129 130 131 132 133 135 143 147 148 154 156 169 **S** Avera Health, Sioux Falls, SD
Primary Contact: John Kozyra, Chief Executive Officer
CFO: Michael Garman, Chief Financial Officer
CIO: Michael Garman, Chief Financial Officer
CHR: Kathryn Benson, Human Resources Partner
Web address: www.avera.org/st-anthonys
Control: Church operated, Nongovernment, not-for-profit **Service**: General medical and surgical

Staffed Beds: 25 **Admissions**: 694 **Census**: 8 **Outpatient Visits**: 31824
Births: 149 **Total Expense ($000)**: 40400 **Payroll Expense ($000)**: 18143
Personnel: 191

OGALLALA—Keith County

▣ **OGALLALA COMMUNITY HOSPITAL (281355)**, 2601 North Spruce Street, Zip 69153-2465; tel. 308/284-4011, **A**1 10 18 **F**3 13 15 29 31 34 40 43 45 59 65 68 75 77 79 81 85 87 93 97 107 110 111 115 119 127 130 132 133 148 149 154 169 **S** Banner Health, Phoenix, AZ
Primary Contact: Timothy Gullingsrud, Chief Executive Officer
CFO: Dena Klockman, Chief Financial Officer
CMO: Jeff Bacon, D.O., Chief Medical Officer
CHR: Gracie Ramos, Chief Human Resources Officer
CNO: Linda Baldwin, Chief Nursing Officer
Web address: https://www.bannerhealth.com/locations/ogallala/ogallala-community-hospital
Control: Other not-for-profit (including NFP Corporation) **Service**: General medical and surgical

Staffed Beds: 18 **Admissions**: 299 **Census**: 3 **Outpatient Visits**: 17580
Births: 62 **Total Expense ($000)**: 26184 **Payroll Expense ($000)**: 11173
Personnel: 101

OMAHA—Douglas County

☐ **BOYS TOWN NATIONAL RESEARCH HOSPITAL (283300)**, 555 North 30th Street, Zip 68131-2198; tel. 531/355-6510, (Nonreporting) **A**1 3 5 10
Primary Contact: Jason Bruce, Executive Vice President of Healthcare and Director of Boys Town National Research Hospital and Clin
CFO: Anna McCaslin, Director Finance
CMO: Edward M. Kolb, M.D., Medical Director
CNO: Lori S. Umberger, Chief Nursing Officer
Web address: www.boystownhospital.org
Control: Other not-for-profit (including NFP Corporation) **Service**: Children's general medical and surgical

Staffed Beds: 141

▣ **CHI HEALTH CREIGHTON UNIVERSITY MEDICAL CENTER – BERGAN MERCY (280060)**, 7500 Mercy Road, Zip 68124-2319; tel. 402/398-6060, (Includes LASTING HOPE RECOVERY CENTER, 415 South 25th Avenue, Omaha, Nebraska, Zip 68131, tel. 402/717-5300; Robin Conyers, Administrator) (Nonreporting) **A**1 2 3 5 8 10 **S** CommonSpirit Health, Chicago, IL
Primary Contact: Dennis Bierle, President
CFO: Tim H. Schnack, Vice President Financial Services
CMO: Devin Fox, M.D., Vice President Medical Operations
CIO: Anna M. Turman, Division Vice President, Chief Information Officer
CHR: Aaron Austin, Division Vice President Human Resources Administration
Web address: www.chihealth.com/chi-health-bergan-mercy
Control: Church operated, Nongovernment, not-for-profit **Service**: General medical and surgical

Staffed Beds: 385

▣ △ **CHI HEALTH IMMANUEL (280081)**, 6901 North 72nd Street, Zip 68122-1799; tel. 402/572-2121, (Nonreporting) **A**1 2 3 5 7 10 **S** CommonSpirit Health, Chicago, IL
Primary Contact: Anthony Ashby, President
COO: Anthony Ashby, Vice President and Chief Operating Officer
CFO: Tim H. Schnack, Chief Financial Officer
CMO: Joseph Hoagbin, M.D., Chief Medical Officer
CHR: Nancy Wallace, Vice President Human Resources
Web address: www.alegent.com/immanuel
Control: Church operated, Nongovernment, not-for-profit **Service**: General medical and surgical

Staffed Beds: 276

▣ **CHI HEALTH LAKESIDE (280130)**, 6901 N 72nd St, Zip 68122, Mailing Address: 16901 Lakeside Hills Court, Zip 68130-2318; tel. 402/717-8000, (Nonreporting) **A**1 2 3 5 10 **S** CommonSpirit Health, Chicago, IL
Primary Contact: Mark E. Longacre, President
CFO: Nick O'Tool, Vice President Operational Finance
CMO: Patricia Murdock-Langan, M.D., Chief Medical Officer
CIO: Thomas Haley, Information Technology Systems Site Director
CHR: Nancy Wallace, Division Senior Vice President, Chief Human Resource Officer
Web address: https://www.chihealth.com/en/location-search/lakeside.html
Control: Church operated, Nongovernment, not-for-profit **Service**: General medical and surgical

Staffed Beds: 137

Hospital, Medicare Provider Number, Address, Telephone, Approval, Facility, and Physician Codes, Health Care System

★ American Hospital Association (AHA) membership
☐ The Joint Commission accreditation
○ Healthcare Facilities Accreditation Program
◇ DNV Healthcare Inc. accreditation
⇑ Center for Improvement in Healthcare Quality Accreditation
△ Commission on Accreditation of Rehabilitation Facilities (CARF) accreditation

Hospitals, U.S. / NEBRASKA

CHILDREN'S NEBRASKA (283301), 8200 Dodge Street, Zip 68114–4113; tel. 402/955–5400, **A**1 3 5 10 **F**3 7 8 11 12 13 17 19 21 23 25 27 29 30 31 32 33 34 35 37 39 40 41 43 45 46 47 48 49 50 53 54 55 57 58 59 60 62 63 65 69 71 72 74 75 77 78 79 81 82 84 85 87 88 89 92 93 97 100 104 107 108 111 112 114 115 118 119 124 126 129 130 131 137 143 144 145 146 148 149 154 155 156 157 164 167 **P**6
Primary Contact: Chanda Chacon, M.P.H., FACHE, President and Chief Executive Officer
COO: Kathy L English, R.N., MSN, Executive Vice President and Chief Operating Officer
CFO: Amy Hatcher, Executive Vice President and Chief Financial Officer
CMO: Christopher Maloney, M.D., Senior Vice President, Medical Affairs and Chief Medical Officer
CIO: Jerry Vuchak, Senior Vice President, Chief Information Officer
CHR: Janel Allen, Senior Vice President and Chief Human Resources Officer
CNO: Pam Johnson Carlson, R.N., Chief Nursing Officer
Web address: www.childrensomaha.org
Control: Other not–for–profit (including NFP Corporation) **Service:** Children's general medical and surgical

Staffed Beds: 205 **Admissions:** 4260 **Census:** 113 **Outpatient Visits:** 495159 **Births:** 0 **Total Expense ($000):** 663339 **Payroll Expense ($000):** 288543 **Personnel:** 3026

★ ○ **DOUGLAS COUNTY COMMUNITY MENTAL HEALTH CENTER (284009)**, 4102 Woolworth Avenue, Zip 68105–1899; tel. 402/444–7449, (Nonreporting) **A**5 10 11
Primary Contact: Sherry L. Glasnapp, Director
CFO: DeDe Will, Director Finance
CMO: Sidney A. Kauzlarich, M.D., Medical Director
CIO: Dianne Wallace, County Information Manager
CHR: Karen Buche, Chief Human Resource Officer
CNO: Marti Christensen, Director of Psychiatric Nursing
Web address: www.co.douglas.ne.us
Control: County, Government, Nonfederal **Service:** Psychiatric

Staffed Beds: 16

△ **MADONNA REHABILITATION SPECIALTY HOSPITAL OMAHA (282003)**, 17500 Burke Street, Zip 68118–2244; tel. 844/403–3131, (Includes MADONNA REHABILITATION HOSPITAL, 17500 Burke Street, Omaha, Nebraska, Zip 68118–2244, tel. 844/403–3131; Paul Dongilli Jr, Ph.D., FACHE, President and Chief Executive Officer) **A**5 7 10 **F**1 3 29 30 32 34 35 36 50 56 57 58 59 60 64 65 71 75 86 87 90 91 92 93 95 96 100 107 115 118 119 130 131 132 143 146 148 149 154 157 **P**6
Primary Contact: Paul Dongilli Jr, Ph.D., FACHE, President and Chief Executive Officer
CMO: Julie Lyon, M.D., Chief Medical Officer
Web address: https://www.madonna.org
Control: Other not–for–profit (including NFP Corporation) **Service:** Rehabilitation

Staffed Beds: 109 **Admissions:** 1280 **Census:** 82 **Outpatient Visits:** 27563 **Births:** 0 **Total Expense ($000):** 83572 **Payroll Expense ($000):** 49131 **Personnel:** 423

MERCY CARE CENTER See Alegent Health Mercy Care Center

MIDWEST SURGICAL HOSPITAL (280131), 7915 Farnam Drive, Zip 68114–4504; tel. 402/399–1900, (Nonreporting) **A**10 22
Primary Contact: Charles Livingston, Chief Executive Officer
Web address: www.mwsurgicalhospital.com
Control: Corporation, Investor–owned (for–profit) **Service:** Surgical

Staffed Beds: 19

NEBRASKA MEDICINE – NEBRASKA MEDICAL CENTER (280013), 987400 Nebraska Medical Center, Zip 68198–7400; tel. 402/552–2000, **A**1 2 3 5 8 10 **F**3 5 6 8 9 11 12 13 15 17 18 20 22 24 26 28 29 30 31 32 34 35 36 37 38 39 40 41 43 44 45 46 47 48 49 50 51 53 54 55 56 57 58 59 60 61 62 63 64 65 66 68 70 71 72 74 75 76 77 78 79 80 81 82 84 85 86 87 88 89 91 92 93 94 96 97 98 100 102 103 104 107 108 110 111 113 114 115 116 117 118 119 120 121 123 124 126 127 129 130 131 132 134 135 136 137 138 139 140 141 142 143 144 145 146 147 148 149 150 153 154 156 160 161 162 164 166 167 169 **P**5 6 8
Primary Contact: James Linder, M.D., Chief Executive Officer
COO: Michael A Ash, President, Chief Operating Officer
CFO: Stephanie Daubert, Chief Financial Officer
CMO: Harris Frankel, M.D., Chief Medical Officer, Chief Compliance Officer
CHR: Frank Venuto, Chief Human Capital Officer
CNO: Kelly Vaughn, Chief Nursing Officer
Web address: www.nebraskamed.com
Control: Other not–for–profit (including NFP Corporation) **Service:** General medical and surgical

Staffed Beds: 624 **Admissions:** 26268 **Census:** 520 **Outpatient Visits:** 1242634 **Births:** 1914 **Total Expense ($000):** 2191931 **Payroll Expense ($000):** 951557 **Personnel:** 8154

△ **NEBRASKA METHODIST HOSPITAL (280040)**, 8303 Dodge Street, Zip 68114–4199; tel. 402/354–4000, (Includes METHODIST WOMEN'S HOSPITAL, 707 North 190th Plaza, Elkhorn, Nebraska, Zip 68022–3974, tel. 402/815–4000; Josie Abboud, R.N., FACHE, President and Chief Executive Officer) **A**1 2 3 5 7 10 **F**3 11 12 13 15 17 18 20 22 24 26 28 29 30 31 34 35 40 45 46 47 48 49 50 51 52 54 55 57 58 59 64 65 66 68 70 71 72 73 74 75 76 77 78 79 80 81 82 83 84 85 86 87 90 91 92 93 95 96 100 101 102 104 107 108 110 111 114 115 116 117 118 119 120 121 123 124 126 127 129 130 132 135 142 143 146 147 148 149 150 154 156 157 167 169 **S** Nebraska Methodist Health System, Inc., Omaha, NE
Primary Contact: Josie Abboud, R.N., FACHE, President and Chief Executive Officer
CFO: Linda K Burt, Corporate Vice President Finance
CMO: William Shiffermiller, M.D., Vice President Medical Affairs
CHR: Holly Huerter, Vice President Human Resources
CNO: Teri Tipton Bruening, MSN, Chief Nursing Officer and Vice President Patient Care Services
Web address: www.bestcare.org
Control: Other not–for–profit (including NFP Corporation) **Service:** General medical and surgical

Staffed Beds: 448 **Admissions:** 20186 **Census:** 312 **Outpatient Visits:** 233667 **Births:** 4935 **Total Expense ($000):** 647564 **Payroll Expense ($000):** 262911 **Personnel:** 3045

NEBRASKA SPINE HOSPITAL (280133), 6901 North 72nd Street, Suite 20300, Zip 68122–1755, Mailing Address: 6901 North 72nd Street, Zip 68122–1709; tel. 402/572–3000, (Nonreporting) **A**1 10
Primary Contact: Christopher M. Palumbo, Chief Executive Officer
Web address: www.nebraskaspinehospital.com
Control: Partnership, Investor–owned (for–profit) **Service:** Orthopedic

Staffed Beds: 34

NEBRASKA–WESTERN IOWA HCS See Omaha VA Medical Center

OMAHA VA MEDICAL CENTER, 4101 Woolworth Avenue, Zip 68105–1873; tel. 402/346–8800, (Nonreporting) **A**1 2 3 5 **S** Department of Veterans Affairs, Washington, DC
Primary Contact: Eileen M. Kingston, R.N., Acting Director, Chief Executive Officer
COO: Denise Harrison, Associate Director
CFO: Kirk Kay, Chief Financial Officer
CMO: Grace Stringfellow, M.D., Chief of Staff
CIO: Jennifer Rosenbalm, Manager Business Office
CNO: Eileen M Kingston, R.N., Nurse Executive, Associate Director Patient Care
Web address: www.nebraska.va.gov/
Control: Veterans Affairs, Government, federal **Service:** General medical and surgical

Staffed Beds: 104

□ **ORTHONEBRASKA HOSPITAL (280129)**, 2808 South 143rd Plaza, Zip 68144–5611; tel. 402/609–1600, (Nonreporting) **A**1 10
Primary Contact: Levi Scheppers, Chief Executive Officer
CMO: Ian Crabb, M.D., Chief Medical Officer
CIO: Tim Pugsley, Chief Information Officer
CHR: Lori L Thompson, Manager Human Resources
Web address: www.neorthohospital.com
Control: Partnership, Investor–owned (for–profit) **Service:** Orthopedic

Staffed Beds: 24

SELECT SPECIALTY HOSPITAL–OMAHA (282001), 1870 South 75th Street, Zip 68124–1700; tel. 402/361–5700, (Nonreporting) **A**1 10 **S** Select Medical Corporation, Mechanicsburg, PA
Primary Contact: Kathryn Triplett, MSN, Chief Executive Officer
COO: Joel White, Chief Operating Officer
CMO: Guillermo Huerta, M.D., Chief Medical Officer
CHR: Laurna Hoss, Human Resource Coordinator
CNO: Amanda Wellman, MSN, R.N., Chief Nursing Officer
Web address: https://omaha.selectspecialtyhospitals.com
Control: Corporation, Investor–owned (for–profit) **Service:** Acute long–term care hospital

Staffed Beds: 56

ORD—Valley County

VALLEY COUNTY HEALTH SYSTEM (281353), 2707 L Street, Zip 68862–1275; tel. 308/728–4200, (Nonreporting) **A**10 18
Primary Contact: Nancy Glaubke, Chief Executive Officer
CFO: Chelsea Ortmeier, Chief Financial Officer
CMO: Jennifer Bengston, M.D., Chief Medical Officer
CIO: Jeff Geaghan, Chief Information Officer
CHR: Danielle Proskocil, Director Human Resources
CNO: Vicki Bredthauer, R.N., Director of Nursing
Web address: www.valleycountyhealthsystem.org
Control: County, Government, Nonfederal **Service:** General medical and surgical

Staffed Beds: 16

Hospitals, U.S. / NEBRASKA

OSCEOLA—Polk County

ANNIE JEFFREY MEMORIAL COUNTY HEALTH CENTER (281314), 531 Beebe Street, Zip 68651-5537, Mailing Address: P.O. Box 428, Zip 68651-0428; tel. 402/747-2031, (Nonreporting) **A**10 18
Primary Contact: Marcus Augustin, Chief Executive Officer
CFO: Joseph W Lohrman, Chief Executive Officer
CMO: David Jameson, M.D., Chief of Staff
CIO: Frank Vrba, Chief Information Officer
CHR: Sue Leif, R.N., Director Human Resources
Web address: www.ajhc.org
Control: County, Government, Nonfederal **Service:** General medical and surgical

Staffed Beds: 16

OSHKOSH—Garden County

★ **REGIONAL WEST GARDEN COUNTY (281310)**, 1100 West Second Street, Zip 69154-6152; tel. 308/772-3283, (Nonreporting) **A**10 18
Primary Contact: Bradley C. Howell, Chief Executive Officer
CFO: Jennifer Moffat, Staff Accountant
CMO: Steve Boyer, M.D., Chief Medical Officer
CHR: Ricca Sanford, Director Human Resources
CNO: Trish Davison, R.N., Chief Nursing Officer
Web address: www.gchealth.org
Control: County, Government, Nonfederal **Service:** General medical and surgical

Staffed Beds: 10

OSMOND—Pierce County

★ **OSMOND GENERAL HOSPITAL (281347)**, 402 North Maple Street, Zip 68765-5726, Mailing Address: P.O. Box 429, Zip 68765-0429; tel. 402/748-3393, (Nonreporting) **A**10 18
Primary Contact: Lon Knievel, Chief Executive Officer
CFO: Jodi Aschoff, Chief Financial Officer
CMO: David Mwebe, M.D., Chief of Staff
CNO: Kristen Colsden, Director of Nursing
Web address: www.osmondhospital.com
Control: Other not-for-profit (including NFP Corporation) **Service:** General medical and surgical

Staffed Beds: 20

PAPILLION—Sarpy County

✠ **CHI HEALTH MIDLANDS (280105)**, 11111 South 84th Street, Zip 68046-4122; tel. 402/593-3000, (Nonreporting) **A**1 2 3 10 **S** CommonSpirit Health, Chicago, IL
Primary Contact: Mark E. Longacre, FACHE, President
CFO: Tyler DeJong, Vice President, Operational Finance
CMO: Patricia Murdock-Langan, M.D., Chief Medical Officer
CIO: Thomas Haley, Information Technology Systems Site Director
CHR: Nancy Wallace, Division Senior Vice President, Chief Human Resource Officer
CNO: Brenda Bergman-Evans, Chief Nursing Officer
Web address: www.CHIhealth.com
Control: Church operated, Nongovernment, not-for-profit **Service:** General medical and surgical

Staffed Beds: 58

PAWNEE CITY—Pawnee County

★ **PAWNEE COUNTY MEMORIAL HOSPITAL AND RURAL HEALTH CLINIC (281302)**, 600 'I' Street, Zip 68420-3001, Mailing Address: P.O. Box 433, Zip 68420-0433; tel. 402/852-2231, (Nonreporting) **A**10 18
Primary Contact: John Werner, Chief Executive Officer
CFO: Michaela Parks, Director of Finance
CHR: Jennifer Bartels, Director Human Resources
CNO: Kelly Findlay, Director of Nurses
Web address: www.pawneehospital.com
Control: County, Government, Nonfederal **Service:** General medical and surgical

Staffed Beds: 11

PENDER—Thurston County

★ **PENDER COMMUNITY HOSPITAL (281349)**, 100 Hospital Drive, Zip 68047-0100, Mailing Address: P.O. Box 100, Zip 68047-0100; tel. 402/385-3083, (Nonreporting) **A**10 18 **S** Trinity Health, Livonia, MI
Primary Contact: Laura Gamble, Chief Executive Officer
COO: Shane Schuster, Chief Operating Officer
CFO: Kim Hixson, Chief Financial Officer
CMO: Matt Timm, M.D., Chief Medical Officer
CIO: Teresa Heise, Coordinator Management Information Systems
CHR: Nancy Suhr, Manager Human Resources
CNO: Katie Peterson, R.N., Chief Nursing Officer
Web address: www.pendercommunityhospital.com
Control: Hospital district or authority, Government, Nonfederal **Service:** General medical and surgical

Staffed Beds: 61

PLAINVIEW—Pierce County

★ **CHI HEALTH PLAINVIEW (281346)**, 704 North Third Street, Zip 68769-2047, Mailing Address: P.O. Box 489, Zip 68769-0489; tel. 402/582-4245, (Nonreporting) **A**10 18 **S** CommonSpirit Health, Chicago, IL
Primary Contact: Connie Peters, R.N., President
CFO: Tim H. Schnack, Chief Financial Officer
CMO: Steve Peterson, M.D., Chief of Staff
CHR: Diane Blair, Human Resources and Admissions
CNO: Debra K Rutledge, R.N., Vice President Nursing Services
Web address: www.alegentcreighton.com/plainview-hospital
Control: Church operated, Nongovernment, not-for-profit **Service:** General medical and surgical

Staffed Beds: 15

RED CLOUD—Webster County

WEBSTER COUNTY COMMUNITY HOSPITAL (281316), 621 North Franklin Street, Zip 68970-2260, Mailing Address: P.O. Box 465, Zip 68970-0465; tel. 402/746-5600, (Nonreporting) **A**10 18
Primary Contact: LaMont Cook, Chief Executive Officer
CFO: Marcia Olson, Business Office Manager
CMO: Amy Springer, Medical Director
CHR: Marcia Olson, Business Office Manager
CNO: Candace Peters, R.N., Director of Nursing
Web address: www.websterhospital.org
Control: County, Government, Nonfederal **Service:** General medical and surgical

Staffed Beds: 13

SAINT PAUL—Howard County

★ **HOWARD COUNTY MEDICAL CENTER (281338)**, 1113 Sherman Street, Zip 68873-1546, Mailing Address: P.O. Box 406, Zip 68873-0406; tel. 308/754-4421, (Nonreporting) **A**10 18
Primary Contact: Arlan D. Johnson, Chief Executive Officer
COO: Jillyn Klein, Chief Operating Officer
CFO: Morgan Meyer, Chief Financial Officer
CMO: Angela Brennan, M.D., Chief of Staff
CIO: Cheryl Watson, Chief Information Officer
CHR: Leslie Belzer, Director Human Resources
CNO: Janelle Morgan, Interim Director of Nursing
Web address: www.hcmc.us.com
Control: County, Government, Nonfederal **Service:** General medical and surgical

Staffed Beds: 10

SCHUYLER—Colfax County

★ **CHI HEALTH SCHUYLER (281323)**, 104 West 17th Street, Zip 68661-1304; tel. 402/352-2441, (Nonreporting) **A**10 18 **S** CommonSpirit Health, Chicago, IL
Primary Contact: Connie Peters, R.N., President
CFO: Tim H. Schnack, Chief Financial Officer
CIO: Kenneth Lawonn, Senior Vice President and Chief Information Officer
CHR: Nancy Wallace, Vice President Human Resources
Web address: www.alegent.org
Control: Church operated, Nongovernment, not-for-profit **Service:** General medical and surgical

Staffed Beds: 25

Hospital, Medicare Provider Number, Address, Telephone, Approval, Facility, and Physician Codes, Health Care System

★ American Hospital Association (AHA) membership
☐ The Joint Commission accreditation
○ Healthcare Facilities Accreditation Program
◇ DNV Healthcare Inc. accreditation
⇧ Center for Improvement in Healthcare Quality Accreditation
△ Commission on Accreditation of Rehabilitation Facilities (CARF) accreditation

Hospitals, U.S. / NEBRASKA

SCOTTSBLUFF—Scotts Bluff County

△ **REGIONAL WEST MEDICAL CENTER (280061)**, 4021 Avenue 'B', Zip 69361–4695; tel. 308/635–3711, (Nonreporting) **A**2 3 5 7 10 22
Primary Contact: Melvin McNea, President and Chief Executive Officer
COO: Amanda Vick, R.N., Chief Operating Officer
CFO: Jeanne McKerrigan, Chief Financial Officer
CMO: Lisa Scheppers, Chief Medical Officer
CIO: Montie Hodge, Vice President Information Technology and Chief Information Officer
CHR: Brenda J Forge, Vice President, Human Resources
CNO: Erika Carmody, Interim Chief Nursing Officer
Web address: www.rwhs.org
Control: Other not–for–profit (including NFP Corporation) **Service**: General medical and surgical

Staffed Beds: 135

SEWARD—Seward County

★ **MEMORIAL HEALTH CARE SYSTEMS (281339)**, 300 North Columbia Avenue, Zip 68434–2228; tel. 402/643–2971, (Nonreporting) **A**10 18
Primary Contact: Roger J. Reamer, Chief Executive Officer
CFO: Greg Jerger, Chief Financial Officer
CMO: James Plasek, M.D., Chief of Staff
CIO: Mark Criner, Director Information Technology
CHR: Corey Mann, Director Human Resources
Web address: www.mhcs.us
Control: Other not–for–profit (including NFP Corporation) **Service**: General medical and surgical

Staffed Beds: 24

SIDNEY—Cheyenne County

★ **SIDNEY REGIONAL MEDICAL CENTER (281357)**, 1000 Pole Creek Crossing, Zip 69162–1799; tel. 308/254–5825, (Nonreporting) **A**10 18
Primary Contact: Jason Petik, Chief Executive Officer
CMO: Mandy Shaw, M.D., Chief of Staff
CIO: Jennifer Brockhaus, Chief Information Officer
CHR: Catherine T Arterburn, R.N., Vice President Human Resources
CNO: Julie A Slagle, R.N., MSN, Vice President Patient Care Services
Web address: www.sidneyrmc.com
Control: Other not–for–profit (including NFP Corporation) **Service**: General medical and surgical

Staffed Beds: 88

SUPERIOR—Nuckolls County

★ **BRODSTONE MEMORIAL HOSPITAL (281315)**, 520 East Tenth Street, Zip 68978–1225, Mailing Address: P.O. Box 187, Zip 68978–0187; tel. 402/879–3281, **A**10 18 **F**3 5 11 13 15 28 29 30 31 32 34 35 40 44 45 48 50 53 57 59 64 65 68 70 74 75 76 77 78 79 81 82 85 87 89 92 93 94 96 97 100 101 104 107 110 111 115 117 119 127 128 129 130 131 132 133 135 146 148 149 153 154 156 157 160 164 167 169 **P**6
Primary Contact: Treg Vyzourek, Chief Executive Officer
COO: Dena C Alvarez, R.N., Chief Operating Officer and Chief Compliance Officer
CFO: Crystal Wyatt, Chief Financial Officer
CMO: Timothy Blecha, M.D., Medical Director
CIO: Tim Hiatt, Chief Information Officer
CHR: Beth A Schlichtman, Chief Human Resources Officer
CNO: Candice M. Thompson, R.N., MSN, Chief Nursing Officer
Web address: https://www.brodstonehealthcare.org/
Control: Other not–for–profit (including NFP Corporation) **Service**: General medical and surgical

Staffed Beds: 25 **Admissions**: 519 **Census**: 5 **Outpatient Visits**: 40343 **Births**: 29 **Total Expense ($000)**: 36561 **Payroll Expense ($000)**: 14956 **Personnel**: 246

SYRACUSE—Otoe County

★ **SYRACUSE AREA HEALTH (281309)**, 2731 Healthcare Drive, Zip 68446, Mailing Address: P.O. Box N, Zip 68446–0518; tel. 402/269–2011, **A**10 18 **F**3 8 11 15 28 29 34 35 37 40 41 43 45 50 53 57 59 64 65 75 77 79 81 82 85 87 89 91 92 93 94 96 97 107 110 111 115 119 126 127 128 130 131 133 146 148 154 156 157 169
Primary Contact: Michael Harvey, FACHE, President and Chief Executive Officer
CFO: Karrie Beach, Vice President Finance
CMO: James Steckelberg, M.D., Chief Medical Staff
CIO: Matthew Steinblock, Director Information Systems
CHR: Nancy R. Brack, Vice President Human Resources
CNO: Derek Greenwald, Chief Nursing Officer
Web address: www.syracuseareahealth.com
Control: Hospital district or authority, Government, Nonfederal **Service**: General medical and surgical

Staffed Beds: 10 **Admissions**: 219 **Census**: 2 **Outpatient Visits**: 31676 **Births**: 0 **Total Expense ($000)**: 28799 **Payroll Expense ($000)**: 12656 **Personnel**: 176

TECUMSEH—Johnson County

★ **JOHNSON COUNTY HOSPITAL (281350)**, 202 High Street, Zip 68450–2443, Mailing Address: P.O. Box 599, Zip 68450–0599; tel. 402/335–3361, (Nonreporting) **A**10 18
Primary Contact: Mary Kent, Administrator
CMO: Benjamin Biehl, M.D., Chief Medical Officer
CIO: Joseph Randall Stollar, Chief Information Officer
CHR: Susan Hessheimer, Director Human Resources
CNO: Matthew Snyder, R.N., Director of Nursing
Web address: www.jchosp.com
Control: County, Government, Nonfederal **Service**: General medical and surgical

Staffed Beds: 18

VALENTINE—Cherry County

CHERRY COUNTY HOSPITAL (281344), 510 North Green Street, Zip 69201–1932; tel. 402/376–2525, (Nonreporting) **A**10 18
Primary Contact: Nancy J. Hicks–Arsenault, R.N., Interim Chief Executive Officer
CFO: Peggy Snell, Chief Finance Officer
CNO: Laura Willert, Interim Chief Nursing Officer
Web address: www.cherrycountyhospital.org
Control: County, Government, Nonfederal **Service**: General medical and surgical

Staffed Beds: 25

WAHOO—Saunders County

★ **SAUNDERS MEDICAL CENTER (281307)**, 1760 County Road J, Zip 68066–4152; tel. 402/443–4191, (Nonreporting) **A**10 18 **S** Bryan Health, Lincoln, NE
Primary Contact: Julie A. Rezac, R.N., Chief Executive Officer
CFO: Chase Manstedt, Chief Financial Officer
CMO: Andrew Opp, M.D., Medical Chief of Staff
CIO: Carrie Stephens, Director Information Technology
CNO: Destiny Bader, Director of Nursing
Web address: www.saundersmedicalcenter.com
Control: County, Government, Nonfederal **Service**: General medical and surgical

Staffed Beds: 16

WAYNE—Wayne County

★ **PROVIDENCE MEDICAL CENTER (281345)**, 1200 Providence Road, Zip 68787–1299; tel. 402/375–3800, **A**10 18 **F**3 7 13 15 28 29 30 31 34 35 36 40 44 50 53 57 59 62 63 64 65 68 75 76 77 81 84 85 93 96 107 110 111 115 119 128 130 131 132 133 135 146 148 154 167 169
Primary Contact: Nicole Haglund, Interim Chief Executive Officer and Chief Nursing Officer
COO: Kristine A Giese, Chief Operating Officer
CFO: Bruce Craven, Chief Financial Officer
CNO: Nicole Haglund, Vice President of Nursing Services
Web address: www.providencemedical.com
Control: Other not–for–profit (including NFP Corporation) **Service**: General medical and surgical

Staffed Beds: 21 **Admissions**: 303 **Census**: 4 **Outpatient Visits**: 17515 **Births**: 62 **Total Expense ($000)**: 30059 **Payroll Expense ($000)**: 10861 **Personnel**: 165

Hospitals, U.S. / NEBRASKA

WEST POINT—Cuming County

★ **FRANCISCAN HEALTHCARE (281322)**, 430 North Monitor Street,
Zip 68788–1555; tel. 402/372–2404, (Nonreporting) **A**10 18 **S** Franciscan
Sisters of Christian Charity Sponsored Ministries, Inc., Manitowoc, WI
Primary Contact: Tyler Toline, FACHE, Chief Executive Officer
CFO: Alisa A. Brunsing, Chief Financial Officer
CMO: Thomas W. Cohee, M.D., Chief of Staff
CIO: Jeff Geaghan, Chief Information Officer
CHR: Terri Ridder, Director Human Resources
CNO: Dara Schlecht, Chief Nursing Officer
Web address: www.fcswp.org
Control: Church operated, Nongovernment, not–for–profit **Service**: General medical and surgical

Staffed Beds: 25

ST. FRANCIS MEMORIAL HOSPITAL See Franciscan Healthcare

WINNEBAGO—Thurston County

TWELVE CLANS UNITY HOSPITAL (280059), Highway 7577, Zip 68071;
tel. 402/745–3950, (Nonreporting) **A**10
Primary Contact: David Edwards, Chief Executive Officer
CFO: Beth Wewel, Chief Financial Officer
Control: PHS, Indian Service, Government, federal **Service**: General medical and surgical

Staffed Beds: 30

YORK—York County

★ **YORK GENERAL (281336)**, 2222 North Lincoln Avenue, Zip 68467–1095;
tel. 402/362–6671, (Nonreporting) **A**10 18
Primary Contact: James P. Ulrich Jr, FACHE, Chief Executive Officer
COO: Jenny Obermier, Senior Vice President, Chief Operating Officer and Chief Nursing Officer
CFO: Bob McQuistan, Vice President Finance
CMO: Patrick Hotovy, M.D., Chief of Staff
CIO: Chris Kraft, Director Information Systems
CHR: Cathy Norquest, Director Human Resources
CNO: Jenny Obermier, Senior Vice President, Chief Operating Officer and Chief Nursing Officer
Web address: www.yorkgeneral.org
Control: Other not–for–profit (including NFP Corporation) **Service**: General medical and surgical

Staffed Beds: 154

Hospital, Medicare Provider Number, Address, Telephone, Approval, Facility, and Physician Codes, Health Care System

★ American Hospital Association (AHA) membership   ○ Healthcare Facilities Accreditation Program   ⇧ Center for Improvement in Healthcare Quality Accreditation
□ The Joint Commission accreditation   ◇ DNV Healthcare Inc. accreditation   △ Commission on Accreditation of Rehabilitation Facilities (CARF) accreditation

© 2025 AHA Guide

Hospitals, U.S. / NEVADA

NEVADA

BATTLE MOUNTAIN—Lander County

BATTLE MOUNTAIN GENERAL HOSPITAL (291303), 535 South Humboldt Street, Zip 89820-1988; tel. 775/635-2550, (Nonreporting) **A**10 18
Primary Contact: Jason Bleak, Chief Executive Officer
CFO: Cindy Fagg, Fiscal Officer
CMO: Mark S. Meyers, M.D., Chief of Staff
CIO: Terry Dunn, Director Information Technology
CHR: Lori Sherbondy, Director Human Resources
CNO: Kelley Price, R.N., Chief Nursing Officer
Web address: www.bmgh.org
Control: Hospital district or authority, Government, Nonfederal **Service**: General medical and surgical

Staffed Beds: 7

BOULDER CITY—Clark County

★ **BOULDER CITY HOSPITAL (291309)**, 901 Adams Boulevard, Zip 89005-2213; tel. 702/293-4111, (Nonreporting) **A**10 18
Primary Contact: Thomas Maher, Chief Executive Officer and Administrator
COO: Rae Cummings, Chief Operating Officer
CFO: Douglas Lewis, Chief Financial Officer
CMO: Craig Jorgenson, M.D., Chief of Staff
CHR: Belinda McGraw, Director Human Resources
CNO: Andre Pastian, R.N., MSN, Chief Nursing Officer
Web address: www.bchcares.org
Control: Other not-for-profit (including NFP Corporation) **Service**: General medical and surgical

Staffed Beds: 82

CALIENTE—Lincoln County

GROVER C. DILS MEDICAL CENTER (291312), 700 North Spring Street, Zip 89008, Mailing Address: P.O. Box 1010, Zip 89008-1010; tel. 775/726-3171, (Nonreporting) **A**10 18
Primary Contact: Melissa S. Rowe, Chief Executive Officer
CFO: Sherlyn Fackrell, Finance Controller
CMO: R William Katschke, M.D., Jr, Medical Director
CHR: Rozanne Mangum, Administrative Assistant and Director Human Resources
Web address: www.gcdmc.org
Control: Other not-for-profit (including NFP Corporation) **Service**: Other specialty treatment

Staffed Beds: 20

CARSON CITY—Carson City County

★ **CARSON TAHOE HEALTH (290019)**, 1600 Medical Parkway, Zip 89703-4625, Mailing Address: P.O. Box 2168, Zip 89702-2168; tel. 775/445-8672, (Includes SIERRA SURGERY HOSPITAL, 1400 Medical Parkway, Carson City, Nevada, Zip 89703-4624, tel. 775/883-1700; Ken Doran, Interim Chief Executive Officer) **A**3 10 22 **F**3 5 8 11 12 13 15 17 18 20 22 24 26 28 29 30 31 34 35 38 40 42 45 46 47 49 50 51 54 56 57 59 64 65 68 70 74 75 76 77 78 79 81 82 84 85 86 87 89 93 96 98 100 101 102 103 104 105 107 108 110 111 115 116 117 118 119 126 130 132 135 143 144 146 147 148 149 152 153 154 156 160 162 164 165 169
Primary Contact: Michelle L. Joy, FACHE, President and Chief Executive Officer
CFO: Katie Kucera, Chief Financial Officer
CMO: Jeffrey Sanders, M.D., Chief of Staff
CHR: Jim Lewandowski, Interim Director of Human Resources
CNO: Anna Anders, R.N., MSN, Vice President and Chief Nursing Officer
Web address: www.carsontahoe.com
Control: Other not-for-profit (including NFP Corporation) **Service**: General medical and surgical

Staffed Beds: 211 **Admissions:** 11563 **Census:** 155 **Outpatient Visits:** 250759 **Births:** 909 **Total Expense ($000):** 336323 **Payroll Expense ($000):** 104547 **Personnel:** 1300

ELKO—Elko County

⊞ **NORTHEASTERN NEVADA REGIONAL HOSPITAL (290008)**, 2001 Errecart Boulevard, Zip 89801-8333; tel. 775/738-5151, (Nonreporting) **A**1 10 20 **S** Lifepoint Health, Brentwood, TN
Primary Contact: Steve Simpson, Chief Executive Officer
CFO: Greg Hexem, Chief Financial Officer
CIO: Jeff Morgan, Director Information Systems
CHR: Laura Elliott, Director Human Resources
CNO: Alice A Allen, R.N., MS, Chief Nursing Officer
Web address: www.nnrhospital.com
Control: Corporation, Investor-owned (for-profit) **Service**: General medical and surgical

Staffed Beds: 75

ELY—White Pine County

⊞ **WILLIAM BEE RIRIE HOSPITAL (291302)**, 1500 Avenue 'H', Zip 89301-2699; tel. 775/289-3001, **A**1 10 18 **F**12 13 15 18 20 22 26 31 32 34 35 36 40 45 46 48 50 57 59 65 70 76 81 82 89 97 107 111 115 119 127 130 131 133 135 146 147 149 160 161 169
Primary Contact: Matthew Walker, Chief Executive Officer and Administrator
CMO: G N Christensen, M.D., Chief Medical Officer
CIO: Destin Brandis, Chief Information Officer
CHR: Vicki Pereace, Manager Human Resources
Web address: www.wbrhely.org/getpage.php?name=index
Control: Hospital district or authority, Government, Nonfederal **Service**: General medical and surgical

Staffed Beds: 25 **Admissions:** 250 **Census:** 2 **Outpatient Visits:** 5873 **Births:** 52 **Total Expense ($000):** 35600 **Payroll Expense ($000):** 15800 **Personnel:** 267

FALLON—Churchill County

⊞ **BANNER CHURCHILL COMMUNITY HOSPITAL (291313)**, 801 East Williams Avenue, Zip 89406-3052; tel. 775/423-3151, **A**1 10 18 **F**3 7 11 13 15 29 31 34 40 41 44 45 47 59 64 65 68 70 75 76 81 85 86 87 89 93 97 107 110 111 115 119 127 130 146 149 154 164 167 169 **S** Banner Health, Phoenix, AZ
Primary Contact: Robert H. Carnahan II, R.N., Chief Executive Officer
CFO: Steve Fraker, Chief Financial Officer
CMO: Brent Aikin, D.O., Chief Medical Officer
CHR: Darlene Hanefeld, Chief Human Resources Officer
CNO: LeGay Marie Naseath, Chief Nursing Officer
Web address: www.bannerhealth.com/churchill
Control: Other not-for-profit (including NFP Corporation) **Service**: General medical and surgical

Staffed Beds: 25 **Admissions:** 1433 **Census:** 14 **Outpatient Visits:** 56784 **Births:** 255 **Total Expense ($000):** 64222 **Payroll Expense ($000):** 28721 **Personnel:** 296

GARDNERVILLE—Douglas County

★ **CARSON VALLEY MEDICAL CENTER (291306)**, 1107 Hwy 395, Zip 89410, Mailing Address: 1107 Highway 395, Zip 89410; tel. 775/782-1500, **A**3 10 18 **F**3 15 24 26 29 30 31 34 35 38 39 40 45 50 54 56 57 59 61 64 65 66 70 74 75 77 78 79 81 82 85 87 93 97 100 104 107 108 110 111 114 119 127 128 129 130 131 132 133 144 146 147 148 149 153 154 156 157 165 **P**6 **S** Renown Health, Reno, NV
Primary Contact: Jeffrey Prater, Chief Executive Officer
COO: Shannon Albert, Director of Operations
CFO: Colleen Reid, Chief Financial Officer
CMO: Evan Easley, M.D., Chief Medical Officer
CIO: Jason Roberts, Director Information System
CHR: Lisa Tremaine, Manager Human Resources
CNO: Andrea Highfill, Chief Nursing Officer
Web address: www.cvmchospital.org
Control: Other not-for-profit (including NFP Corporation) **Service**: General medical and surgical

Staffed Beds: 23 **Admissions:** 1037 **Census:** 9 **Births:** 0 **Personnel:** 416

Hospitals, U.S. / NEVADA

HAWTHORNE—Mineral County

MOUNT GRANT GENERAL HOSPITAL (291300), 200 South A Street, Zip 89415, Mailing Address: P.O. Box 1510, Zip 89415-1510; tel. 775/945-2461, (Total facility includes 24 beds in nursing home-type unit) **A**10 18 **F**3 5 29 34 40 56 57 59 64 65 68 87 93 97 107 111 114 115 119 127 130 133 143 146 147 149 154 156 160 161 **P**6
Primary Contact: Denise L. Ferguson, Administrator
Web address: www.mgghnv.org/
Control: Hospital district or authority, Government, Nonfederal **Service:** General medical and surgical

Staffed Beds: 35 **Admissions:** 174 **Census:** 25 **Births:** 0 **Total Expense ($000):** 18557 **Payroll Expense ($000):** 7506 **Personnel:** 133

HENDERSON—Clark County

DIGNITY HEALTH REHABILITATION HOSPITAL (293035), 2930 Siena Heights Drive, Zip 89052-3871; tel. 725/726-2000, **A**1 10 **F**29 30 34 44 50 58 68 74 77 82 86 87 90 91 92 93 94 95 96 100 130 132 148 157 **S** Select Medical Corporation, Mechanicsburg, PA
Primary Contact: Linda Tautz, Chief Executive Officer
Web address: https://www.dignityhealthrehab.com
Control: Partnership, Investor-owned (for-profit) **Service:** Rehabilitation

Staffed Beds: 60 **Admissions:** 1531 **Census:** 54 **Outpatient Visits:** 0 **Births:** 0 **Personnel:** 248

ENCOMPASS HEALTH REHABILITATION HOSPITAL OF HENDERSON (293032), 10301 Jeffreys Street, Zip 89052-3922; tel. 702/939-9400, (Nonreporting) **A**1 10 **S** Encompass Health Corporation, Birmingham, AL
Primary Contact: Varsha Chauhan, Chief Executive Officer
CFO: Robert Bollard, Chief Financial Officer
Web address: www.hendersonrehabhospital.com
Control: Corporation, Investor-owned (for-profit) **Service:** Rehabilitation

Staffed Beds: 90

HENDERSON HOSPITAL (290057), 1050 West Galleria Drive, Zip 89011; tel. 702/963-7000, (Nonreporting) **A**1 3 10 **S** Universal Health Services, Inc., King of Prussia, PA
Primary Contact: Samuel Kaufman, Chief Executive Officer
COO: Ryan Tingey, Chief Operating Officer
CNO: Tina Coker, MSN, Chief Nursing Officer
Web address: www.hendersonhospital.com/
Control: Corporation, Investor-owned (for-profit) **Service:** General medical and surgical

Staffed Beds: 145

★ **KINDRED HOSPITAL LAS VEGAS-SAHARA (292002)**, 102 East Mead Parkway, 3rd Floor, Zip 89015; tel. 702/871-1418, (Includes KINDRED HOSPITAL-FLAMINGO, 2250 East Flamingo Road, Las Vegas, Nevada, Zip 89119, tel. 702/784-4300) (Nonreporting) **A**10 **S** ScionHealth, Louisville, KY
Primary Contact: Robin Hager, Chief Executive Officer
CFO: William Lysaght, Chief Financial Officer
CMO: Paul Stewart, M.D., Medical Director
CHR: Jim Sturgeon, Area Director Human Resources
Web address: www.kindredhospitallvs.com/
Control: Corporation, Investor-owned (for-profit) **Service:** Acute long-term care hospital

Staffed Beds: 238

SEVEN HILLS HOSPITAL (294012), 3021 West Horizon Ridge Parkway, Zip 89052-3990; tel. 702/646-5000, **A**3 5 10 **F**4 5 29 98 99 101 103 105 130 135 149 152 153 154 160 161 **S** Acadia Healthcare Company, Inc., Franklin, TN
Primary Contact: Amanda Butler, Chief Executive Officer
CFO: Chantel Hughes, Chief Financial Officer
CMO: Jonathan Wirjo, M.D., Medical Director
CIO: Jessica Raub, Director Health Information Management
CHR: Teresa Sulit, Director of Human Resources
CNO: Rustin Park, Director of Nursing
Web address: www.sevenhillsbi.com
Control: Corporation, Investor-owned (for-profit) **Service:** Psychiatric

Staffed Beds: 134 **Admissions:** 4416 **Census:** 75 **Outpatient Visits:** 7281 **Births:** 0 **Personnel:** 201

ST. ROSE DOMINICAN HOSPITALS – ROSE DE LIMA CAMPUS (290012), 102 East Lake Mead Parkway, Zip 89015-5524; tel. 702/616-5000, **A**1 10 **F**3 7 29 40 107 149 154 155 **S** CommonSpirit Health, Chicago, IL
Primary Contact: Tom Burns, Chief Operating Officer and Chief Nurse Executive
COO: Teressa Conley, Vice President and Chief Operating Officer
CFO: Kevin Walters, Chief Financial Officer
CMO: Stephen K Jones, M.D., Vice President Medical Staff Affairs
Web address: www.strosehospitals.org
Control: Corporation, Investor-owned (for-profit) **Service:** General medical and surgical

Staffed Beds: 20 **Admissions:** 536 **Census:** 3 **Outpatient Visits:** 69059 **Births:** 0 **Total Expense ($000):** 54636 **Payroll Expense ($000):** 15955 **Personnel:** 198

ST. ROSE DOMINICAN HOSPITALS – SIENA CAMPUS (290045), 3001 St Rose Parkway, Zip 89052; tel. 702/616-5000, (Nonreporting) **A**1 3 5 10 19 **S** CommonSpirit Health, Chicago, IL
Primary Contact: Katherine Vergos, FACHE, President and Chief Executive Officer
COO: Ryan Christensen, Chief Operatng Officer
CFO: Brian Kleven, Chief Financial Officer
CMO: G. Rodney Buzzas, M.D., Chief Medical Officer
CIO: Russ Patterson, Director Information Technology
CHR: Linda Gerstenberger, Vice President Human Resources
CNO: Beth Carlson, R.N., Chief Nurse Executive
Web address: www.strosehospitals.com
Control: Church operated, Nongovernment, not-for-profit **Service:** General medical and surgical

Staffed Beds: 326

INCLINE VILLAGE—Washoe County

★ ○ **INCLINE VILLAGE COMMUNITY HOSPITAL (291301)**, 880 Alder Avenue, Zip 89451-8335; tel. 775/833-4100, **A**10 11 18 **F**29 34 35 40 50 57 59 64 68 79 81 93 97 107 114 119 127 164 **S** Tahoe Forest Health System, Truckee, CA
Primary Contact: Louis James. Ward, Chief Operating Officer and Administrator
CFO: Crystal Betts, Chief Financial Officer
CIO: Mark Griffiths, Director Management Information Systems
CHR: Jayne O'Flanagan, Director Human Resources
Web address: https://www.tfhd.com/ivch/ivch
Control: Hospital district or authority, Government, Nonfederal **Service:** General medical and surgical

Staffed Beds: 4 **Admissions:** 1 **Census:** 1

LAS VEGAS—Clark County

AMG SPECIALTY HOSPITAL – LAS VEGAS (292007), 4015 Mcleod Drive, Zip 89121-4305; tel. 702/433-2200, (Nonreporting) **A**10 22 **S** AMG Integrated Healthcare Management, Lafayette, LA
Primary Contact: Vicki Davis, Chief Executive Officer
CMO: Anthony Pollard, D.O., Chief Medical Officer
Web address: www.amgihm.com/locations/#map_top
Control: Partnership, Investor-owned (for-profit) **Service:** Acute long-term care hospital

Staffed Beds: 24

□ **CENTENNIAL HILLS HOSPITAL MEDICAL CENTER (290054)**, 6900 North Durango Drive, Zip 89149-4409; tel. 702/835-9700, (Nonreporting) **A**1 3 5 10 **S** Universal Health Services, Inc., King of Prussia, PA
Primary Contact: Craig McCoy, Chief Executive Officer and Managing Director
Web address: www.centennialhillshospital.com
Control: Corporation, Investor-owned (for-profit) **Service:** General medical and surgical

Staffed Beds: 165

□ **DESERT PARKWAY BEHAVIORAL HEALTHCARE HOSPITAL (294013)**, 3247 South Maryland Parkway, Zip 89109-2412; tel. 702/776-3500, (Nonreporting) **A**1 10 **S** Signature Healthcare Services, Corona, CA
Primary Contact: Jordan Peterson, Chief Executive Officer
Web address: https://www.desertparkway.com/
Control: Individual, Investor-owned (for-profit) **Service:** Psychiatric

Staffed Beds: 152

Hospital, Medicare Provider Number, Address, Telephone, Approval, Facility, and Physician Codes, Health Care System

★ American Hospital Association (AHA) membership ○ Healthcare Facilities Accreditation Program ⇧ Center for Improvement in Healthcare Quality Accreditation
□ The Joint Commission accreditation ◇ DNV Healthcare Inc. accreditation △ Commission on Accreditation of Rehabilitation Facilities (CARF) accreditation

Hospitals, U.S. / NEVADA

DESERT WILLOW TREATMENT CENTER, 6171 West Charleston Boulevard, Zip 89146–1126; tel. 702/486–8900, (Nonreporting) **A**3 5
Primary Contact: Susie Miller, Deputy Administrator
Web address: www.dcfs.nv.gov/
Control: State, Government, Nonfederal **Service**: Psychiatric

Staffed Beds: 20

☐ **DESERT WINDS HOSPITAL (294016)**, 5900 West Rochelle Avenue, Zip 89103–3304; tel. 702/522–7922, (Nonreporting) **A**1
Primary Contact: Shelly Mirato, Chief Executive Officer
CFO: Andrew Brick–Turin, Chief Financial Officer
Web address: https://desertwindshospital.com/
Control: Individual, Investor–owned (for–profit) **Service**: Psychiatric

Staffed Beds: 154

⊞ **ENCOMPASS HEALTH REHABILITATION HOSPITAL OF DESERT CANYON (293033)**, 9175 West Oquendo Road, Zip 89148–1234; tel. 702/252–7342, **A**1 5 10 **F**3 29 56 60 68 74 75 79 82 84 86 87 90 91 96 119 130 132 146 148 149 154 156 **S** Encompass Health Corporation, Birmingham, AL
Primary Contact: Michele Butts, Chief Executive Officer
CMO: Bevins Chue, M.D., Medical Director
CNO: Timothy Murphy, R.N., Chief Nursing Officer
Web address: www.healthsouthdesertcanyon.com
Control: Corporation, Investor–owned (for–profit) **Service**: Rehabilitation

Staffed Beds: 50 **Admissions**: 1037 **Census**: 41 **Outpatient Visits**: 0
Births: 0 **Personnel**: 156

⊞ **ENCOMPASS HEALTH REHABILITATION HOSPITAL OF LAS VEGAS (293026)**, 1250 South Valley View Boulevard, Zip 89102–1861; tel. 702/877–8898, (Nonreporting) **A**1 10 **S** Encompass Health Corporation, Birmingham, AL
Primary Contact: Tij Von Nieda, Chief Executive Officer
CFO: Raymond Hardy, Controller
CMO: John D. Reneau, Medical Director
CHR: Cheryl Ballew, Human Resources Director
CNO: Susan Ramirez, Chief Nursing Officer
Web address: www.healthsouthlasvegas.com
Control: Corporation, Investor–owned (for–profit) **Service**: Rehabilitation

Staffed Beds: 79

HARMON MEDICAL AND REHABILITATION HOSPITAL (290042), 2170 East Harmon Avenue, Zip 89119–7840; tel. 702/794–0100, (Nonreporting) **A**3 10 **S** Fundamental Long Term Care Holdings, LLC, Sparks Glencoe, MD
Primary Contact: Robert McClay, Chief Executive Officer
Control: Corporation, Investor–owned (for–profit) **Service**: Rehabilitation

Staffed Beds: 118

☐ **HORIZON SPECIALTY HOSPITAL (292003)**, 640 Desert Lane, Zip 89106–4207; tel. 702/382–3155, **A**1 10 **F**1 3 18 19 29 70 75 82 146 148 149 154 157 **S** Fundamental Long Term Care Holdings, LLC, Sparks Glencoe, MD
Primary Contact: Darrin Cook, Chief Executive Officer and Administrator
CFO: Darnell Bennett, Director Finance
CMO: Syed Rahman, M.D., Chief of Staff
CIO: Azena Ansi, Manager Health Information Management
CHR: Melvin Layugan, Director Human Resources
Web address: www.horizonspecialtyhosp.com/
Control: Corporation, Investor–owned (for–profit) **Service**: Acute long–term care hospital

Staffed Beds: 79 **Admissions**: 744 **Census**: 56 **Outpatient Visits**: 0
Births: 0

⊞ **MOUNTAINVIEW HOSPITAL (290039)**, 3100 North Tenaya Way, Zip 89128–0436; tel. 702/255–5000, (Nonreporting) **A**1 3 5 10 **S** HCA Healthcare, Nashville, TN
Primary Contact: Hiral Patel, M.D., Chief Executive Officer
CFO: Carl H. James, Chief Financial Officer
CMO: Jack Collier, M.D., Chief of Staff
CHR: Robert Nettles, Director Human Resources
Web address: www.mountainview-hospital.com
Control: Corporation, Investor–owned (for–profit) **Service**: General medical and surgical

Staffed Beds: 407

ORTHOPEDIC SPECIALTY HOSPITAL OF NEVADA (290056), 8656 West Patrick Lane, Zip 89148–5043; tel. 702/777–7100, (Nonreporting) **A**10
Primary Contact: Melissa War, Chief Executive Officer
Web address: www.mountainsedgehospital.com/
Control: Other not–for–profit (including NFP Corporation) **Service**: General medical and surgical

Staffed Beds: 130

⊞ **PAM REHABILITATION HOSPITAL OF CENTENNIAL HILLS (293034)**, 6166 North Durango Drive, Zip 89149–3912; tel. 725/223–4100, **A**1 10 **F**3 28 29 60 64 67 68 74 75 82 90 93 94 95 96 130 132 135 143 148 149 154 156 **S** PAM Health, Enola, PA
Primary Contact: Dan Kunde, Chief Executive Officer
Web address: www.postacutemedical.com/facilities/find-facility/rehabilitation-hospitals/pam-rehabilitation-hospital-centennial-hills
Control: Partnership, Investor–owned (for–profit) **Service**: Rehabilitation

Staffed Beds: 44 **Admissions**: 1243 **Census**: 41 **Outpatient Visits**: 10923
Births: 0 **Total Expense ($000)**: 25216 **Payroll Expense ($000)**: 12295
Personnel: 188

⊞ **PAM SPECIALTY HOSPITAL OF LAS VEGAS (292006)**, 2500 North Tenaya, Zip 89128–0482; tel. 702/562–2021, **A**1 10 **F**1 3 18 28 29 45 60 65 68 78 79 82 96 107 114 119 148 149 167 **S** PAM Health, Enola, PA
Primary Contact: Adrian Campos, Chief Executive Officer
CFO: Anna Rich, Chief Financial Officer
CMO: C Dean Milne, D.O., Medical Director
CNO: Robin Wolf, Chief Nursing Officer
Web address: https://pamhealth.com/facilities/find-facility/specialty-hospitals/PAM-Specialty-Hospital-of-Las-Vegas
Control: Partnership, Investor–owned (for–profit) **Service**: Acute long–term care hospital

Staffed Beds: 73 **Admissions**: 712 **Census**: 48 **Outpatient Visits**: 0
Births: 0 **Total Expense ($000)**: 31864 **Payroll Expense ($000)**: 14737
Personnel: 216

⊞ **SOUTHERN HILLS HOSPITAL AND MEDICAL CENTER (290047)**, 9300 West Sunset Road, Zip 89148–4844; tel. 702/880–2100, (Nonreporting) **A**1 3 10 19 **S** HCA Healthcare, Nashville, TN
Primary Contact: Alexis Mussi, Chief Executive Officer
CFO: Jennifer Le, Chief Financial Officer
CMO: Joseph C. Corcoran, D.O., Division Chief Medical Officer
CIO: Gary Sharp, Director Information Technology
CHR: Jennifer McDonnell, Director, Human Resources
Web address: www.southernhillshospital.com
Control: Corporation, Investor–owned (for–profit) **Service**: General medical and surgical

Staffed Beds: 252

☐ **SOUTHERN NEVADA ADULT MENTAL HEALTH SERVICES (294002)**, 6161 West Charleston Boulevard, Zip 89146–1126; tel. 702/486–6000, (Nonreporting) **A**1 3 5 10
Primary Contact: Jo Malay, M.P.H., R.N., Hospital Administrator
Web address: www.mhds.state.nv.us
Control: State, Government, Nonfederal **Service**: Psychiatric

Staffed Beds: 274

☐ **SPRING MOUNTAIN SAHARA (294010)**, 5460 West Sahara, Zip 89146–3307; tel. 702/216–8900, (Nonreporting) **A**1 10 **S** Universal Health Services, Inc., King of Prussia, PA
Primary Contact: Purcell Dye, Ph.D., Chief Executive Officer
Web address: www.springmountainsahara.com
Control: Corporation, Investor–owned (for–profit) **Service**: Psychiatric

Staffed Beds: 30

⊞ **SPRING MOUNTAIN TREATMENT CENTER (294011)**, 7000 West Spring Mountain Road, Zip 89117–3816; tel. 702/873–2400, (Nonreporting) **A**1 3 10 **S** Universal Health Services, Inc., King of Prussia, PA
Primary Contact: Purcell Dye, Ph.D., Chief Executive Officer
CFO: Sherilene DeLeon, Chief Financial Officer
CMO: Jerome Nwokike, M.D., Medical Director
CNO: Norma Ferris, R.N., MS, Chief Nursing Officer
Web address: www.springmountaintreatmentcenter.com/
Control: Corporation, Investor–owned (for–profit) **Service**: Psychiatric

Staffed Beds: 110

Hospitals, U.S. / NEVADA

☐ **SPRING VALLEY HOSPITAL MEDICAL CENTER (290046)**, 5400 South Rainbow Boulevard, Zip 89118-1859; tel. 702/853-3000, **A**1 3 10 **F**3 12 13 18 20 22 24 26 29 36 37 40 42 45 47 48 49 50 60 64 70 72 74 75 76 77 79 81 85 86 87 90 100 102 105 107 108 111 115 118 119 126 130 144 146 147 148 149 167 169 **P**6 **S** Universal Health Services, Inc., King of Prussia, PA
Primary Contact: Claude Wise, Chief Executive Officer and Managing Director
COO: Matthew Wheelus, Chief Operating Officer
CFO: Carl Caley, Chief Financial Officer
CMO: S. Daniel, M.D., Chief Medical Officer
CHR: Angelique Ford, Administrator Human Resources
CNO: Margaret Covelli, R.N., Chief Nursing Officer
Web address: www.springvalleyhospital.com
Control: Corporation, Investor-owned (for-profit) **Service:** General medical and surgical

Staffed Beds: 430 **Admissions:** 17472 **Census:** 249 **Outpatient Visits:** 55163 **Births:** 1497 **Personnel:** 1167

✠ **ST. ROSE DOMINICAN HOSPITALS – SAN MARTIN CAMPUS (290053)**, 8280 West Warm Springs Road, Zip 89113-3612; tel. 702/492-8000, (Nonreporting) **A**1 3 10 19 **S** CommonSpirit Health, Chicago, IL
Primary Contact: Tom Burns, President and Chief Executive Officer
CFO: Dev Ramsamy, Chief Financial Officer
CMO: Robert Pretzlaff, M.D., Chief Medical Officer
CIO: Russ Patterson, Site Manager Information Technology
CHR: Linda Gerstenberger, Vice President Human Resources
CNO: Jalyn McKelleb, MSN, R.N., Chief Nursing Executive Officer
Web address: www.strosehospitals.org
Control: Church operated, Nongovernment, not-for-profit **Service:** General medical and surgical

Staffed Beds: 147

☐ **SUMMERLIN HOSPITAL MEDICAL CENTER (290041)**, 657 Town Center Drive, Zip 89144-6367; tel. 702/233-7000, (Nonreporting) **A**1 3 10 **S** Universal Health Services, Inc., King of Prussia, PA
Primary Contact: Robert S. Freymuller, Chief Executive Officer
Web address: www.summerlinhospital.com
Control: Corporation, Investor-owned (for-profit) **Service:** General medical and surgical

Staffed Beds: 148

✠ △ **SUNRISE HOSPITAL AND MEDICAL CENTER (290003)**, 3186 South Maryland Parkway, Zip 89109-2306, Mailing Address: P.O. Box 98530, Zip 89193; tel. 702/731-8000, (Nonreporting) **A**1 2 3 5 7 10 19 **S** HCA Healthcare, Nashville, TN
Primary Contact: Todd Sklamberg, President
CMO: Katherine Keeley, M.D., Chief of Staff
CIO: Alan Burt, Director Information Services
CNO: Cynthia J Johnson, R.N., Chief Nurse Officer
Web address: www.sunrisehospital.com
Control: Corporation, Investor-owned (for-profit) **Service:** General medical and surgical

Staffed Beds: 762

✠ **UNIVERSITY MEDICAL CENTER (290007)**, 1800 West Charleston Boulevard, Zip 89102-2386; tel. 702/383-2000, (Includes CHILDREN'S HOSPITAL OF NEVADA AT UMC, 800 Hope PL, Las Vegas, Nevada, Zip 89102-2321, 800 Hope Place, Zip 89106, tel. 702/383-2000) (Nonreporting) **A**1 3 5 8 10
Primary Contact: Mason Van Houweling, Chief Executive Officer
COO: Anthony Marinello, Chief Operating Officer
CFO: Jennifer Wakem, Chief Financial Officer
CMO: Frederick Lippmann, Chief of Staff
CIO: Lonnie Richardson, Chief Information Officer
CHR: Kurt Houser, Chief Human Resources Officer
CNO: Debra Fox, Chief Nursing Officer
Web address: www.umcsn.com
Control: County, Government, Nonfederal **Service:** General medical and surgical

Staffed Beds: 508

☐ **VALLEY HOSPITAL MEDICAL CENTER (290021)**, 620 Shadow Lane, Zip 89106-4119; tel. 702/388-4000, (Nonreporting) **A**1 3 5 10 12 13 **S** Universal Health Services, Inc., King of Prussia, PA
Primary Contact: Collin McLaughlin, Chief Executive Officer
CFO: Betsy A Sponsler, Chief Financial Officer
CMO: Dost Wattoo, M.D., Chief of Staff
CIO: Tom Schoenig, Regional Director Information Services
CHR: Dana Thorne, Administrator Human Resources
Web address: www.valleyhospital.net
Control: Corporation, Investor-owned (for-profit) **Service:** General medical and surgical

Staffed Beds: 306

VEGAS VALLEY REHABILITATION HOSPITAL See Southern Nevada Medical and Rehabilitation Center

LOVELOCK—Pershing County

★ **PERSHING GENERAL HOSPITAL (291304)**, 855 Sixth Street, Zip 89419, Mailing Address: P.O. Box 661, Zip 89419-0661; tel. 775/273-2621, (Nonreporting) **A**10 18
Primary Contact: Brandon Chadock, Interim Chief Executive Officer
CFO: Marjorie Skinner, Director Finance
CMO: Yousri Gadallah, M.D., Chief Medical Officer
CIO: Jim Weeldreyer, Manager Information Technology
CHR: Jeff Meyers, HR Generalist
Web address: www.pershinghospital.org
Control: Hospital district or authority, Government, Nonfederal **Service:** General medical and surgical

Staffed Beds: 38

MESQUITE—Clark County

☐ **MESA VIEW REGIONAL HOSPITAL (291307)**, 1299 Bertha Howe Avenue, Zip 89027-7500; tel. 702/346-8040, **A**1 10 18 **F**3 15 40 45 59 70 75 81 85 87 97 107 108 110 111 115 119 132 133 135 144 146 147 149 154 157 167 **P**6 **S** Quorum Health, Brentwood, TN
Primary Contact: Kelly Adams, Chief Executive Officer
CFO: Mitchell Fransen, Chief Financial Officer
CHR: Steve Siegrist, Director of Human Resources
CNO: Leslie Woodson, Chief Nursing Officer
Web address: www.mesaviewhospital.com
Control: Corporation, Investor-owned (for-profit) **Service:** General medical and surgical

Staffed Beds: 25 **Admissions:** 1009 **Census:** 9 **Outpatient Visits:** 50437 **Births:** 0 **Total Expense ($000):** 37001 **Payroll Expense ($000):** 13143 **Personnel:** 239

NELLIS AFB—Clark County

✠ **MIKE O'CALLAGHAN FEDERAL HOSPITAL**, 4700 Las Vegas Boulevard North, Suite 2419, Zip 89191-6600; tel. 702/653-2000, (Nonreporting) **A**1 3 5 **S** Department of the Air Force, Washington, DC
Primary Contact: Colonel Brent Johnson, Commander
COO: Colonel Linnes L Chester, USAF, MSC, Administrator
CFO: Major Kari Turkal-Barrett, Flight Commander Resource Management Officer
CMO: Lieutenant Colonel Markham Brown, M.D., Chief Medical Staff
CIO: Major Kevin Seeley, Chief Information Officer
Web address: https://tricare.mil/
Control: Air Force, Government, federal **Service:** General medical and surgical

Staffed Beds: 46

NORTH LAS VEGAS—Clark County

★ ⇧ **DIGNITY ST. ROSE – CRAIG RANCH (290058)**, 1550 West Craig Road, Suite 100, Zip 89032-0327, Mailing Address: 8686 New Trails Drive, Suite 100, The Woodlands, TX, Zip 77381-1188; tel. 702/777-3615, (Nonreporting) **A**10 21 **S** CommonSpirit Health, Chicago, IL
Primary Contact: Linda Tautz, Market Chief Executive Officer
COO: Vanessa Smith, Chief Operating Officer
CFO: Mark Kopser, Interim Chief Financial Officer
Web address: https://www.strosenh.org/locations/north-las-vegas/
Control: Corporation, Investor-owned (for-profit) **Service:** General medical and surgical

Staffed Beds: 8

Hospital, Medicare Provider Number, Address, Telephone, Approval, Facility, and Physician Codes, Health Care System

★ American Hospital Association (AHA) membership ○ Healthcare Facilities Accreditation Program ⇧ Center for Improvement in Healthcare Quality Accreditation
☐ The Joint Commission accreditation ◇ DNV Healthcare Inc. accreditation △ Commission on Accreditation of Rehabilitation Facilities (CARF) accreditation

© 2025 AHA Guide

Hospitals, U.S. / NEVADA

NORTH LAS VEGAS VA MEDICAL CENTER, 6900 North Pecos Road, Zip 89086–4400; tel. 702/791–9000, (Nonreporting) **A**1 3 5 **S** Department of Veterans Affairs, Washington, DC
Primary Contact: William J. Caron, Medical Center Director
CFO: Richard O Hays, Chief Fiscal Service
CMO: Ramanujam Komanduri, M.D., Chief of Staff
Web address: www.lasvegas.va.gov/
Control: Veterans Affairs, Government, federal **Service**: General medical and surgical

Staffed Beds: 222

NORTH VISTA HOSPITAL (290005), 1409 East Lake Mead Boulevard, Zip 89030–7197; tel. 702/649–7711, (Nonreporting) **A**10 21 **S** Prime Healthcare, Ontario, CA
Primary Contact: Vincenzo Variale, Chief Executive Officer
CFO: Peter S Miller, Chief Financial Officer
CHR: Abayomi Fibiyi, Chief Human Resources Officer
Web address: www.northvistahospital.com
Control: Corporation, Investor–owned (for–profit) **Service**: General medical and surgical

Staffed Beds: 177

SOUTHERN NEVADA HCS See North Las Vegas VA Medical Center

PAHRUMP—Nye County

DESERT VIEW HOSPITAL (291311), 360 South Lola Lane, Zip 89048–0884; tel. 775/751–7500, **A**3 10 18 **F**3 29 45 46 49 64 65 75 81 93 107 110 111 114 115 118 119 148 149 157 **S** Universal Health Services, Inc., King of Prussia, PA
Primary Contact: Susan Davila, Chief Executive Officer
CFO: Ryan Eggleston, Chief Financial Officer
CMO: Fredric Siegel, M.D., Chief of Staff
CIO: Chad Andres, Chief Information Officer
CHR: Lisa Doty, Manager Human Resources
CNO: Markeeta Araujo, Chief Nursing Officer
Web address: www.desertviewhospital.com
Control: Corporation, Investor–owned (for–profit) **Service**: General medical and surgical

Staffed Beds: 25 **Admissions**: 1279 **Census**: 12 **Outpatient Visits**: 62961 **Births**: 0 **Personnel**: 144

RENO—Washoe County

IOANNIS A. LOUGARIS VETERANS' ADMINISTRATION MEDICAL CENTER, 975 Kirman Avenue, Zip 89502–0993; tel. 775/786–7200, (Nonreporting) **A**1 3 5 **S** Department of Veterans Affairs, Washington, DC
Primary Contact: Thomas Talamante, Medical Center Director
CFO: Kelly Manson, Chief Financial Officer
CMO: Steven Brilliant, M.D., Chief of Staff
CIO: Jack Smith, Acting Chief Information Resources Management Service
CHR: Debbie Jenkins, Chief Human Resources Management Service
Web address: www.reno.va.gov/
Control: Veterans Affairs, Government, federal **Service**: General medical and surgical

Staffed Beds: 130

RENO BEHAVIORAL HEALTHCARE HOSPITAL (294015), 6940 Sierra Center Parkway, Zip 89511–2209; tel. 877/787–8518, (Nonreporting) **A**1 10 **S** Signature Healthcare Services, Corona, CA
Primary Contact: Don Butterfield, Interim Chief Executive Officer
Web address: www.renobehavioral.com
Control: Corporation, Investor–owned (for–profit) **Service**: Psychiatric

Staffed Beds: 70

RENOWN REGIONAL MEDICAL CENTER (290001), 1155 Mill Street, Zip 89502–1576; tel. 775/982–4100, (Includes RENOWN CHILDREN'S HOSPITAL, 1155 Mill Street, Reno, Nevada, Zip 89502–1576, 1155 Mill Street – N11, Zip 89502–1576, tel. 775/982–4100; Larry Duncan, Vice President and Administrator Children's Hospital) **A**1 2 3 5 8 10 **F**3 11 12 13 15 17 18 19 20 21 22 23 24 25 26 27 28 29 30 31 32 34 35 37 38 39 40 41 43 44 45 47 48 49 50 51 54 55 56 57 58 59 61 62 63 64 65 66 68 70 71 72 73 74 75 76 77 78 79 80 81 82 84 85 86 87 88 89 92 100 102 104 107 108 109 110 111 114 115 116 117 118 119 120 121 123 124 126 130 132 135 141 143 145 146 148 149 150 152 153 154 157 160 162 164 167 169 **S** Renown Health, Reno, NV
Primary Contact: Chris Nicholas, Chief Executive Officer
COO: Amy S. McCombs, MSN, R.N., Chief Operating Officer
CFO: Katie Kucera, interim Chief Financial Officer Acute Services
CMO: Adnan Akbar, Chief Medical Officer, Acute Care
CNO: Jennifer Richards, Ph.D., R.N., Chief Nursing Officer Acute Services
Web address: www.renown.org
Control: Other not–for–profit (including NFP Corporation) **Service**: General medical and surgical

Staffed Beds: 616 **Admissions**: 33428 **Census**: 457 **Outpatient Visits**: 611436 **Births**: 4070 **Total Expense ($000)**: 1059140 **Payroll Expense ($000)**: 384368 **Personnel**: 5170

RENOWN REHABILITATION HOSPITAL, 1495 Mill Street, Zip 89502–1479; tel. 775/982–3500, **A**1 7 **F**29 34 35 36 54 58 77 82 90 91 92 93 94 95 96 107 130 132 148 149 154 164 **S** Renown Health, Reno, NV
Primary Contact: Seth M. Langevin, Vice President and Administrator
CFO: Ann Beck, Chief Financial Officer
CNO: Jennifer Richards, Ph.D., R.N., Chief Nursing Officer
Web address: www.renown.org
Control: Other not–for–profit (including NFP Corporation) **Service**: Rehabilitation

Staffed Beds: 62 **Admissions**: 1052 **Census**: 37 **Outpatient Visits**: 24262 **Births**: 0 **Total Expense ($000)**: 31778 **Payroll Expense ($000)**: 17503 **Personnel**: 407

RENOWN SOUTH MEADOWS MEDICAL CENTER (290049), 10101 Double 'R' Boulevard, Zip 89521–5931; tel. 775/982–7000, **A**1 10 **F**3 12 18 28 29 30 35 38 40 44 45 46 47 49 57 68 70 74 75 79 80 81 82 85 87 92 93 107 108 111 119 126 130 131 135 145 146 149 150 157 167 **S** Renown Health, Reno, NV
Primary Contact: Samuel Weller, Chief Executive Officer
CFO: Ann Beck, Chief Financial Officer
CMO: Adnan Akbar, Chief Medical Officer, Acute Care
CNO: Jennifer Richards, Ph.D., R.N., Chief Nursing Officer
Web address: www.renown.org
Control: Other not–for–profit (including NFP Corporation) **Service**: General medical and surgical

Staffed Beds: 60 **Admissions**: 3892 **Census**: 40 **Outpatient Visits**: 94616 **Births**: 0 **Total Expense ($000)**: 128089 **Payroll Expense ($000)**: 41681 **Personnel**: 1054

RIVERSIDE HOSP – SKILLED CARE See Riverside Hospital Skilled Care

SAINT MARY'S REGIONAL MEDICAL CENTER (290009), 235 West Sixth Street, Zip 89503–4548; tel. 775/770–3000, (Nonreporting) **A**1 5 10 **S** Prime Healthcare, Ontario, CA
Primary Contact: Derrick Glum, Chief Executive Officer
CFO: John R Deakyne, Chief Financial Officer
CIO: Cindy Mullins, Director Information Technology
CHR: David Milovich, Vice President Human Resources
Web address: https://www.saintmarysreno.com/
Control: Corporation, Investor–owned (for–profit) **Service**: General medical and surgical

Staffed Beds: 305

VETERANS AFFAIRS SIERRA NEVADA HEALTH CARE SYSTEM See Ioannis A. Lougaris Veterans' Administration Medical Center

WILLOW SPRINGS CENTER, 690 Edison Way, Zip 89502–4135; tel. 775/858–3303, (Nonreporting) **A**3 5
Primary Contact: Pamela Alba, Chief Executive Officer
CFO: Charette Godoy, Chief Financial Officer
CMO: Dana Arlien, M.D., Chief Medical Officer
CIO: Wallace Marsh, Director of Information Technology
CHR: Kristine Anglin, Human Resources Manager
CNO: Riva Rios, Chief Nursing Officer
Web address: www.willowspringscenter.com
Control: Corporation, Investor–owned (for–profit) **Service**: Children's hospital psychiatric

Staffed Beds: 116

Hospitals, U.S. / NEVADA

SPARKS—Washoe County

☐ **NORTHERN NEVADA ADULT MENTAL HEALTH SERVICES (294000)**, 480 Galletti Way, Zip 89431–5564; tel. 775/688–2001, **A**1 3 5 10 **F**98 130 149 154
Primary Contact: Cody Phinney, Administrator
CFO: Elizabeth O'Brien, Chief Financial Officer
CIO: Lois Repass, Quality Assurance Specialist and Coordinator Performance Improvement
Web address: www.mhds.state.nv.us/
Control: State, Government, Nonfederal **Service**: Psychiatric

Staffed Beds: 30 **Admissions**: 232 **Census**: 14 **Births**: 0

☐ **NORTHERN NEVADA MEDICAL CENTER (290032)**, 2375 East Prater Way, Zip 89434–9641; tel. 775/331–7000, **A**1 10 19 **F**1 3 15 18 20 22 24 26 28 29 30 34 35 37 38 40 42 45 46 47 48 49 50 51 56 57 58 59 60 61 65 68 70 75 79 81 82 84 85 86 87 90 92 93 96 97 98 101 102 103 104 107 108 109 110 111 115 118 119 126 129 130 131 132 133 135 146 148 149 150 154 164 167 **S** Universal Health Services, Inc., King of Prussia, PA
Primary Contact: Helen Lidholm, Chief Executive Officer
COO: Philip Reber, Chief Operations Officer
CFO: Shawn Curtis, Chief Financial Officer
CHR: Patricia Downs, Director Human Resources
CNO: Carla Adams, Chief Nursing Officer
Web address: www.nnmc.com
Control: Corporation, Investor–owned (for–profit) **Service**: General medical and surgical

Staffed Beds: 124 **Admissions**: 5668 **Census**: 82

⊠ **PAM SPECIALTY HOSPITAL OF RENO (292004)**, 2375 East Prater Way, Zip 89434–9641; tel. 775/355–5600, **A**1 10 **F**1 3 12 29 74 79 120 148 154 **P**5 **S** PAM Health, Enola, PA
Primary Contact: sarah castle, Chief Executive Officer
COO: Gary Brooks, Chief Operating Officer
Web address: https://postacutemedical.com/
Control: Partnership, Investor–owned (for–profit) **Service**: Acute long–term care hospital

Staffed Beds: 24 **Admissions**: 302 **Census**: 20 **Outpatient Visits**: 0
Births: 0 **Total Expense ($000)**: 13621 **Payroll Expense ($000)**: 5988
Personnel: 61

WINNEMUCCA—Humboldt County

★ **HUMBOLDT GENERAL HOSPITAL (291308)**, 118 East Haskell Street, Zip 89445–3299; tel. 775/623–5222, (Total facility includes 42 beds in nursing home–type unit) **A**3 5 10 18 **F**3 6 7 11 12 14 15 28 29 32 34 35 37 38 40 41 44 45 50 56 57 59 61 64 65 68 70 75 76 77 79 81 82 87 89 97 100 101 102 104 105 107 108 109 110 111 115 119 126 127 128 130 132 133 135 144 147 148 149 154 156 162 164 169 **P**6
Primary Contact: Robyn Dunckhorst, R.N., Chief Executive Officer
CFO: Sandi Lehman, Chief Financial Officer
CMO: Brad Granath, M.D., Chief of Staff
CHR: Rose Marie Green, Director Human Resources
CNO: Darlene Bryan, R.N., Chief Nursing Officer
Web address: www.hghospital.org
Control: County, Government, Nonfederal **Service**: General medical and surgical

Staffed Beds: 73 **Admissions**: 789 **Census**: 44 **Outpatient Visits**: 168214
Births: 184 **Total Expense ($000)**: 80632 **Payroll Expense ($000)**: 31638
Personnel: 397

YERINGTON—Lyon County

SOUTH LYON MEDICAL CENTER (291314), 213 South Whitacre, Zip 89447–2561, Mailing Address: P.O. Box 940, Zip 89447–0940; tel. 775/463–2301, (Nonreporting) **A**10 18
Primary Contact: Toni A. Inserra, Administrator
CFO: David Bezard, Chief Financial Officer
Web address: www.southlyonmedicalcenter.org
Control: Other not–for–profit (including NFP Corporation) **Service**: General medical and surgical

Staffed Beds: 31

Hospital, Medicare Provider Number, Address, Telephone, Approval, Facility, and Physician Codes, Health Care System

★ American Hospital Association (AHA) membership ○ Healthcare Facilities Accreditation Program ⇑ Center for Improvement in Healthcare Quality Accreditation
☐ The Joint Commission accreditation ◇ DNV Healthcare Inc. accreditation △ Commission on Accreditation of Rehabilitation Facilities (CARF) accreditation

© 2025 AHA Guide

Hospitals, U.S. / NEW HAMPSHIRE

NEW HAMPSHIRE

BERLIN—Coos County

★ **ANDROSCOGGIN VALLEY HOSPITAL (301310)**, 59 Page Hill Road, Zip 03570-3531; tel. 603/752-2200, **A**10 18 **F**3 8 11 12 13 15 17 28 29 30 34 40 41 45 47 57 59 61 64 67 68 70 74 75 76 77 79 81 82 85 89 92 93 102 107 108 110 115 119 128 129 130 131 132 133 146 147 149 154 156 167 169 **P**6 **S** Ovation Healthcare, Brentwood, TN
Primary Contact: Michael D. Peterson, FACHE, President and Chief Executive Officer
CMO: Keith M Shute, M.D., Senior Vice President Medical Affairs and Clinical Services
CIO: Linda M Laperle, Vice President Administrative Services
CHR: James A Wheeler, Vice President Human Relations and Community Development
Web address: www.avhnh.org
Control: Other not-for-profit (including NFP Corporation) **Service**: General medical and surgical

Staffed Beds: 25 **Admissions**: 781 **Census**: 10 **Outpatient Visits**: 91406 **Births**: 81 **Total Expense ($000)**: 83743 **Payroll Expense ($000)**: 27555 **Personnel**: 331

CLAREMONT—Sullivan County

★ **VALLEY REGIONAL HOSPITAL (301308)**, 243 Elm Street, Zip 03743-4921; tel. 603/542-7771, **A**10 18 **F**3 11 14 15 28 29 31 34 35 38 40 43 45 49 50 54 57 59 64 68 75 77 79 81 83 84 85 87 93 97 107 110 114 118 119 130 131 132 133 135 144 146 147 149 154 156 157 **P**6
Primary Contact: Jocelyn Caple, M.D., Interim President and Chief Executive Officer
CFO: Jean Shaw, Chief Financial Officer
CMO: Oliver Herfort, M.D., Chief Medical Officer
CIO: Patricia Witthaus, Director Information Services
CHR: Cheryl Cavanaugh, Senior Director Human Resources
Web address: www.vrh.org
Control: Other not-for-profit (including NFP Corporation) **Service**: General medical and surgical

Staffed Beds: 25 **Admissions**: 776 **Census**: 12 **Outpatient Visits**: 73118 **Births**: 0 **Total Expense ($000)**: 61893 **Payroll Expense ($000)**: 22629 **Personnel**: 267

COLEBROOK—Coos County

★ **UPPER CONNECTICUT VALLEY HOSPITAL (301300)**, 181 Corliss Lane, Zip 03576-3207; tel. 603/237-4971, **A**10 18 **F**3 14 15 28 29 34 35 40 45 50 55 56 57 59 64 67 68 75 78 79 81 82 84 85 86 93 102 107 110 111 115 119 128 130 146 147 148 149 156 167 **S** Ovation Healthcare, Brentwood, TN
Primary Contact: Greg Cook, President and Chief Executive Officer
CFO: Celeste Pitts, Chief Financial Officer
CMO: Tom Cochran, Chief Medical Officer
CIO: Heather Pollard-Leighton, Director of Administrative Services
CHR: Heidi L Saari, Director, Human Resources
CNO: Lindsay Lea, Chief Nursing Officer
Web address: www.ucvh.org
Control: Other not-for-profit (including NFP Corporation) **Service**: General medical and surgical

Staffed Beds: 16 **Admissions**: 234 **Census**: 3 **Outpatient Visits**: 28366 **Births**: 0 **Total Expense ($000)**: 30494 **Payroll Expense ($000)**: 9275 **Personnel**: 126

CONCORD—Merrimack County

★ ⚕ **CONCORD HOSPITAL (300001)**, 250 Pleasant Street, Zip 03301-2598; tel. 603/225-2711, **A**2 3 5 10 21 **F**3 5 8 13 14 15 17 18 20 22 24 26 28 29 30 31 32 34 35 37 38 39 40 43 44 45 46 47 48 49 50 51 54 55 56 57 58 59 61 64 65 66 68 70 71 73 74 75 76 77 78 79 80 81 82 83 84 85 86 87 89 91 92 93 96 97 98 101 102 104 105 107 108 110 111 114 115 118 119 120 121 123 124 126 129 130 132 134 135 144 145 146 147 148 149 150 152 153 154 156 157 160 164 165 167 169 **P**6
Primary Contact: Robert P. Steigmeyer, President and Chief Executive Officer
COO: Timothy P. Jones, Chief Operating Officer
CFO: Bruce R. Burns, Chief Financial Officer
CMO: David F. Green, M.D., Chief Medical Officer
CIO: Deane Morrison, Chief Information Officer
CHR: Robin A. Moore, Chief Human Resources Officer
Web address: www.concordhospital.org
Control: Other not-for-profit (including NFP Corporation) **Service**: General medical and surgical

Staffed Beds: 244 **Admissions**: 11199 **Census**: 162 **Outpatient Visits**: 585135 **Births**: 1334 **Total Expense ($000)**: 752693 **Payroll Expense ($000)**: 374303 **Personnel**: 3024

ENCOMPASS HEALTH REHABILITATION HOSPITAL OF CONCORD (303027), 254 Pleasant Street, Zip 03301-2508; tel. 603/226-9800, **A**1 10 **F**3 28 29 34 35 50 56 74 78 79 82 86 87 90 91 93 95 96 130 135 148 149 **S** Encompass Health Corporation, Birmingham, AL
Primary Contact: Sharon Hartl, Chief Executive Officer
CMO: Muhammad Salmanullah, Chief Medical Director
CHR: Myra Nixon, Director Human Resources
CNO: Joseph Adamski, Chief Nursing Officer
Web address: www.healthsouthrehabconcordnh.com
Control: Corporation, Investor-owned (for-profit) **Service**: Rehabilitation

Staffed Beds: 50 **Admissions**: 1249 **Census**: 41 **Outpatient Visits**: 3918 **Births**: 0 **Total Expense ($000)**: 19355 **Payroll Expense ($000)**: 12333 **Personnel**: 133

NEW HAMPSHIRE HOSPITAL (304000), 36 Clinton Street, Zip 03301-2359; tel. 603/271-5300, **A**1 3 5 10 **F**3 29 30 35 38 44 50 53 56 57 58 59 65 74 75 86 87 98 101 103 106 130 132 135 146 149 156 163 164 **P**6
Primary Contact: Ellen M. Lapointe, Chief Executive Officer
COO: Timothy Whitman, Chief Operating Officer
CFO: Bret Mason, Chief Financial Officer
CIO: David Wieters, Director of Information Systems
CHR: Mark Bussiere, Administrator Human Resources
CNO: Rosemary Costanzo, Chief Nursing Officer
Web address: www.dhhs.nh.gov/dcbcs/nhh/
Control: State, Government, Nonfederal **Service**: Psychiatric

Staffed Beds: 154 **Admissions**: 823 **Census**: 146 **Outpatient Visits**: 0 **Births**: 0 **Total Expense ($000)**: 118576 **Payroll Expense ($000)**: 38550 **Personnel**: 567

DERRY—Rockingham County

PARKLAND MEDICAL CENTER (300017), 1 Parkland Drive, Zip 03038-2750; tel. 603/432-1500, (Nonreporting) **A**1 2 10 **S** HCA Healthcare, Nashville, TN
Primary Contact: Jeff Scionti, Interim Chief Executive Officer
CFO: Jacob Wisemann, Chief Financial Officer
CMO: Edward Yourtee, M.D., Chief Medical Officer
CIO: Brad George, Director Information Systems
CHR: Mary G Lahti, Director Human Resources
CNO: Eileen Keefe, Chief Nursing Officer
Web address: www.parklandmedicalcenter.com
Control: Corporation, Investor-owned (for-profit) **Service**: General medical and surgical

Staffed Beds: 86

DOVER—Strafford County

WENTWORTH-DOUGLASS HOSPITAL (300018), 789 Central Avenue, Zip 03820-2526; tel. 603/742-5252, **A**1 2 10 19 **F**3 5 8 12 13 15 17 18 19 20 22 26 28 29 30 31 32 34 35 36 38 39 40 41 43 44 45 46 47 48 49 50 51 52 53 54 55 57 58 59 61 63 64 65 68 70 73 74 75 76 77 78 79 81 82 84 85 86 87 89 91 92 93 94 96 97 100 101 102 104 107 108 110 111 114 115 118 119 120 121 122 123 124 126 129 130 131 132 134 135 143 144 145 146 147 148 149 154 156 160 169 **P**6 8 **S** Mass General Brigham, Boston, MA
Primary Contact: Darin Roark, President and Chief Executive Officer
CFO: Joel Degenaars, Chief Financial Officer
CMO: Paul Cass, D.O., Chief Medical & Clinical Integration Officer
CIO: Jeffrey Pollock, Chief Information Officer
CHR: Erin J Flanigan, Vice President Human Resources
CNO: Sheila Woolley, R.N., M.P.H., Vice President, Patient Care Services
Web address: www.wdhospital.com
Control: Other not-for-profit (including NFP Corporation) **Service**: General medical and surgical

Staffed Beds: 173 **Admissions**: 10095 **Census**: 118 **Outpatient Visits**: 478063 **Births**: 1522 **Total Expense ($000)**: 470788 **Payroll Expense ($000)**: 172929 **Personnel**: 3003

Hospitals, U.S. / NEW HAMPSHIRE

EXETER—Rockingham County

★ ⇑ **EXETER HOSPITAL (300023)**, 5 Alumni Drive, Zip 03833-2128; tel. 603/778-7311, **A**2 5 10 19 21 **F**3 13 14 15 18 20 22 26 28 29 30 31 34 35 37 38 40 43 44 45 46 47 48 49 50 51 52 54 55 57 58 59 64 65 70 74 75 76 77 78 79 80 81 84 85 86 87 89 93 100 107 108 110 111 114 115 117 118 119 120 121 123 124 126 129 130 131 132 135 143 145 146 147 148 149 156 160 165 169 **S** Beth Israel Lahey Health, Cambridge, MA
Primary Contact: Debra Cresta, President
COO: Sean K O'Neil, Chief Operations Officer
CFO: Kevin J O'Leary, Senior Vice President and Chief Financial Officer
CMO: Richard Hollister, President of Medical Staff
CIO: David Briden, Chief Information Officer
CHR: Christopher M Callahan, Vice President Human Resources
CNO: Susan Burns-Tisdale, Senior Vice President Clinical Operations, Interim CNO
Web address: https://www.exeterhospital.com/
Control: Other not-for-profit (including NFP Corporation) **Service**: General medical and surgical
Staffed Beds: 99 **Admissions**: 4894 **Census**: 66 **Outpatient Visits**: 271910 **Births**: 557 **Total Expense ($000)**: 295221 **Payroll Expense ($000)**: 109466 **Personnel**: 959

FRANKLIN—Merrimack County

★ ⇑ **CONCORD HOSPITAL – FRANKLIN (301306)**, 15 Aiken Avenue, Zip 03235-1299; tel. 603/934-2060, (Total facility includes 10 beds in nursing home-type unit) **A**10 18 21 **F**3 5 11 15 29 30 32 34 35 40 44 45 46 47 48 49 50 59 61 64 65 68 74 75 77 83 84 85 87 93 96 97 98 100 101 102 107 110 114 119 127 128 132 133 146 154 156 157 160 164 165 **P**6
Primary Contact: Kevin L. McCarthy, Chief Administrative Officer
CFO: Henry D Lipman, Senior Vice President, Financial Strategy and External Relations
CMO: Peter Doane, M.D., Chief Medical Officer
CIO: Kevin Irish, Chief Information Officer
CHR: Cass Walker, Vice President Administrative & Support Services
CNO: Patti Strohla, R.N., Chief Nursing Officer
Web address: www.lrgh.org
Control: Other not-for-profit (including NFP Corporation) **Service**: General medical and surgical
Staffed Beds: 30 **Admissions**: 545 **Census**: 10 **Outpatient Visits**: 42853 **Births**: 0 **Personnel**: 113

HAMPSTEAD—Rockingham County

☐ **HAMPSTEAD HOSPITAL & RESIDENTIAL TREATMENT FACILITY (304001)**, 218 East Road, Zip 03841-2305; tel. 603/329-5311, (Nonreporting) **A**1 3 10
Primary Contact: Justin Looser, Chief Executive Officer
COO: Cynthia A Gove, Chief Operating Officer
CFO: Cherie Clough-Berry, Vice President, Finance
CMO: Michael Knight, M.D., Medical Director
CIO: Sandra J Lucia, Director Health Information and Corporate Compliance Officer
CHR: Lisa M Ryan, Coordinator Human Resources
CNO: Julie D'Apollo, R.N., Director of Nursing
Web address: www.hampsteadhospital.com
Control: Other not-for-profit (including NFP Corporation) **Service**: Psychiatric
Staffed Beds: 60

KEENE—Cheshire County

▣ **CHESHIRE MEDICAL CENTER (300019)**, 580 Court Street, Zip 03431-1718; tel. 603/354-5400, **A**1 3 5 10 19 **F**3 4 5 12 13 15 18 28 29 30 31 34 35 36 38 40 41 44 45 46 49 50 54 55 56 57 58 59 64 65 68 70 74 75 76 77 78 79 80 81 82 84 85 86 87 89 90 91 92 93 96 97 100 104 107 108 110 111 115 118 119 120 121 123 130 131 132 133 135 144 146 147 148 149 151 154 156 160 161 167 169 **S** Dartmouth Health, Lebanon, NH
Primary Contact: Joseph L. Perras, M.D., President and Chief Executive Officer
COO: Kathy Willbarger, Chief Operating Officer
CMO: Gina O'Brien, M.D., Interim Chief Medical Officer
CIO: Peter Malloy, Chief Information Officer
CHR: Julie Green, Vice President Human Resources
CNO: Anne Tyrol, R.N., Chief Nursing Officer
Web address: https://www.cheshiremed.org/
Control: Other not-for-profit (including NFP Corporation) **Service**: General medical and surgical
Staffed Beds: 94 **Admissions**: 5168 **Census**: 54 **Outpatient Visits**: 446430 **Births**: 401 **Total Expense ($000)**: 288390 **Payroll Expense ($000)**: 144785 **Personnel**: 1369

LACONIA—Belknap County

★ ⇑ **CONCORD HOSPITAL – LACONIA (300005)**, 80 Highland Street, Zip 03246-3298; tel. 603/524-3211, **A**10 21 **F**3 5 11 12 15 18 28 29 30 32 34 35 37 39 40 44 45 46 47 48 49 50 54 56 59 61 62 64 65 68 70 75 77 78 81 82 83 84 85 86 87 92 93 96 97 107 108 110 111 114 118 119 123 130 132 146 147 148 154 156 157 160 **P**6
Primary Contact: Kevin L. McCarthy, Chief Administrative Officer and Vice President, Support Services
CMO: Peter Doane, M.D., Chief Medical Officer
CIO: Kevin Irish, Chief Information Officer
CHR: Cass Walker, Vice President Administrative & Support Services
Web address: www.lrgh.org
Control: Other not-for-profit (including NFP Corporation) **Service**: General medical and surgical
Staffed Beds: 51 **Admissions**: 2774 **Census**: 39 **Outpatient Visits**: 187056 **Births**: 0 **Personnel**: 751

LANCASTER—Coos County

★ **WEEKS MEDICAL CENTER (301303)**, 173 Middle Street, Zip 03584-3508; tel. 603/788-4911, **A**5 10 18 **F**3 5 11 15 18 28 29 31 32 34 35 36 40 45 50 51 56 57 59 62 63 64 65 66 67 68 75 77 78 79 81 82 84 85 86 87 91 92 93 94 97 100 102 104 107 108 110 111 115 116 117 118 119 127 128 130 131 132 133 134 135 146 147 148 154 156 160 168 169 **P**6 **S** Ovation Healthcare, Brentwood, TN
Primary Contact: Matthew Streeter, Interim President & Chief Executive Officer
CMO: Lars Nielson, M.D., Chief Medical Officer
CIO: Darrell Bodnar, Director Information
CHR: Linda Rexford, Director Human Resources
CNO: Donna Walker, Chief Nurse Executive
Web address: www.weeksmedical.org
Control: Other not-for-profit (including NFP Corporation) **Service**: General medical and surgical
Staffed Beds: 25 **Admissions**: 527 **Census**: 8 **Outpatient Visits**: 124238 **Births**: 0 **Total Expense ($000)**: 84338 **Payroll Expense ($000)**: 28125 **Personnel**: 411

LEBANON—Grafton County

★ **ALICE PECK DAY MEMORIAL HOSPITAL (301305)**, 10 Alice Peck Day Drive, Zip 03766-2650; tel. 603/448-3121, **A**3 5 10 18 **F**3 5 10 11 14 15 29 30 34 35 36 37 40 41 44 45 50 56 59 64 65 74 75 77 79 81 82 85 87 92 93 96 97 102 107 110 111 112 115 119 125 128 129 130 131 133 146 147 148 149 154 156 160 **P**6 **S** Dartmouth Health, Lebanon, NH
Primary Contact: Susan E. Mooney, M.D., MS, President and Chief Executive Officer
CFO: Todd P Roberts, Vice President Finance
CMO: Michael T. Lynch, M.D., Chief Medical Officer
CIO: Kristin Kneisel, Interim Director, Information Services
CNO: Barbra Brown, MS, R.N., Interim Chief Nursing Officer and Vice President of Nursing
Web address: www.alicepeckday.org
Control: Other not-for-profit (including NFP Corporation) **Service**: General medical and surgical
Staffed Beds: 23 **Admissions**: 952 **Census**: 14 **Outpatient Visits**: 72051 **Births**: 0 **Total Expense ($000)**: 95636 **Payroll Expense ($000)**: 49062 **Personnel**: 405

CHILDREN'S HOSPITAL AT DARTMOUTH See Children's Hospital At Dartmouth-Hitchcock

---

Hospital, Medicare Provider Number, Address, Telephone, Approval, Facility, and Physician Codes, Health Care System

★ American Hospital Association (AHA) membership
☐ The Joint Commission accreditation
○ Healthcare Facilities Accreditation Program
◇ DNV Healthcare Inc. accreditation
⇑ Center for Improvement in Healthcare Quality Accreditation
△ Commission on Accreditation of Rehabilitation Facilities (CARF) accreditation

© 2025 AHA Guide

Hospitals, U.S. / NEW HAMPSHIRE

✱ **DARTMOUTH–HITCHCOCK MEDICAL CENTER (300003)**, 1 Medical Center Drive, Zip 03756–1000; tel. 603/650–5000, (Includes CHILDREN'S HOSPITAL AT DARTMOUTH–HITCHCOCK, 1 Medical Center DR, Lebanon, New Hampshire, Zip 03756–1000, One Medical Center Drive, Zip 03756, tel. 603/650–5000) **A**1 2 3 5 8 10 **F**3 5 7 8 9 11 12 13 14 15 16 17 18 19 20 22 24 25 26 28 29 30 31 32 33 34 35 36 37 38 40 41 43 44 45 46 47 48 49 50 51 53 54 55 56 57 58 59 60 61 63 64 65 68 70 72 73 74 75 76 77 78 79 80 81 82 83 84 85 86 87 88 89 91 92 93 96 97 98 99 100 101 102 103 104 107 108 110 111 112 113 114 115 116 117 118 119 120 121 123 124 126 129 130 131 132 134 135 136 138 139 141 142 143 144 145 146 147 148 149 150 152 153 154 155 156 157 160 161 162 164 167 169 **P**6 **S** Dartmouth Health, Lebanon, NH
Primary Contact: Joanne M. Conroy, M.D., Chief Executive Officer and President
COO: Patrick Jordan III, Chief Operating Officer
CFO: Daniel Jantzen, Chief Financial Officer
CMO: Jonathan Huntington, M.D., Ph.D., M.P.H., Chief Medical Officer
CHR: Aimee M. Claiborne, Chief Human Resources Officer
CNO: Susan A. Reeves, Ed.D., R.N., Chief Nursing Executive
Web address: www.hitchcock.org
Control: Other not–for–profit (including NFP Corporation) **Service:** General medical and surgical

Staffed Beds: 438 **Admissions:** 19210 **Census:** 363 **Outpatient Visits:** 1274395 **Births:** 1372 **Total Expense ($000):** 2273901 **Payroll Expense ($000):** 939837 **Personnel:** 7033

LITTLETON—Grafton County

★ **LITTLETON REGIONAL HEALTHCARE (301302)**, 600 Saint Johnsbury Road, Zip 03561–3442; tel. 603/444–9000, (Nonreporting) **A**10 18 **S** Ovation Healthcare, Brentwood, TN
Primary Contact: Robert F. Nutter, President and Chief Executive Officer
CFO: Jeffrey C. Hebert, Vice President Finance, Chief Financial Officer
CIO: Scott Vachon, Director Information Technology
CHR: Georgene Novak, Director Human Resources
Web address: www.littletonhospital.org
Control: Other not–for–profit (including NFP Corporation) **Service:** General medical and surgical

Staffed Beds: 25

MANCHESTER—Hillsborough County

★ ⇧ **CATHOLIC MEDICAL CENTER (300034)**, 100 McGregor Street, Zip 03102–3770; tel. 603/668–3545, **A**2 3 5 10 21 **F**3 9 12 13 15 17 18 20 22 24 26 28 29 30 31 34 35 36 37 38 39 40 41 43 44 45 46 47 48 49 50 51 52 53 54 57 58 59 60 64 65 66 67 68 70 71 73 74 75 76 77 78 79 80 81 82 83 84 85 86 87 93 94 97 100 104 107 110 111 114 115 118 119 124 126 129 130 131 132 135 143 144 145 146 147 148 149 154 156 160 162 164 167 169
Primary Contact: Alexander J. Walker, President and Chief Executive Officer
CFO: Edward L Dudley III, Executive Vice President and Chief Financial Officer
CMO: William H. Goodman, Vice President Medical Affairs, Chief Medical Officer
CIO: Thomas Della Flora, Vice President and Chief Information Officer
CHR: Merryll Rosenfeld, Vice President, Human Resources
CNO: Robert A Duhaime, R.N., Senior Vice President Clinical Operations and Chief Nursing Officer
Web address: www.catholicmedicalcenter.org
Control: Other not–for–profit (including NFP Corporation) **Service:** General medical and surgical

Staffed Beds: 262 **Admissions:** 11229 **Census:** 167 **Outpatient Visits:** 186652 **Births:** 1005 **Total Expense ($000):** 516933 **Payroll Expense ($000):** 214498 **Personnel:** 2227

★ ⇧ **ELLIOT HOSPITAL (300012)**, 1 Elliot Way, Zip 03103–3502; tel. 603/669–5300, **A**2 3 5 10 21 **F**3 5 8 9 11 12 13 15 17 18 20 22 26 28 29 30 31 32 34 35 36 37 38 39 40 41 43 44 45 46 47 48 49 50 51 53 54 55 56 57 58 59 62 63 64 65 68 70 72 74 75 76 77 78 79 81 82 83 84 85 86 87 89 93 94 96 97 98 100 101 102 103 104 105 107 108 110 111 114 115 118 119 120 121 123 124 126 129 130 131 132 135 144 146 147 148 149 152 153 154 156 157 160 162 164 165 167 169 **P**6 **S** SolutionHealth, Manchester, NH
Primary Contact: W. Gregory. Baxter, M.D., President and Chief Executive Officer
COO: Joseph Tate Curti, Chief Operating Officer
CFO: Richard Elwell, Senior Vice President and Chief Financial Officer
CMO: W. Gregory Baxter, M.D., Senior Vice President Medical Affairs and Chief Medical Officer
CIO: Denise Purington, Vice President and Chief Information Officer
CHR: Catherine Bardier, Vice President, Human Resources
CNO: Martha Leighton, Senior Vice President and Chief Nursing Officer
Web address: www.elliothospital.org
Control: Other not–for–profit (including NFP Corporation) **Service:** General medical and surgical

Staffed Beds: 292 **Admissions:** 12913 **Census:** 218 **Outpatient Visits:** 566119 **Births:** 2230 **Total Expense ($000):** 564996 **Payroll Expense ($000):** 182302 **Personnel:** 2897

★ **MANCHESTER VETERANS AFFAIRS MEDICAL CENTER**, 718 Smyth Road, Zip 03104–4098; tel. 603/624–4366, (Nonreporting) **A**3 5 **S** Department of Veterans Affairs, Washington, DC
Primary Contact: Major Kevin Forrest, FACHE, Medical Center Director
COO: Richard T Rose, Associate Director
CFO: Frank Ryan, Chief Financial Officer
CMO: Andrew Breuder, M.D., Chief of Staff
CIO: John Foote, Chief Information Officer
CHR: Mary Ellen Kenney, Chief Human Services
Web address: www.manchester.va.gov/
Control: Veterans Affairs, Government, federal **Service:** Rehabilitation

Staffed Beds: 44

NASHUA—Hillsborough County

★ ⇧ **SOUTHERN NEW HAMPSHIRE MEDICAL CENTER (300020)**, 8 Prospect Street, Zip 03060–3925, Mailing Address: P.O. Box 2014, Zip 03061–2014; tel. 603/577–2000, **A**2 3 5 10 21 **F**1 3 4 11 13 15 16 17 18 20 22 26 28 29 30 31 34 35 40 43 45 49 50 51 52 57 59 61 65 67 68 70 72 73 74 75 76 77 78 79 80 81 84 85 86 87 88 89 90 93 96 98 100 102 104 105 107 110 111 115 118 119 126 128 129 130 131 132 135 143 146 147 148 149 150 153 154 156 160 161 166 167 169 **S** SolutionHealth, Manchester, NH
Primary Contact: Colin T. McHugh, President and Chief Executive Officer
COO: Tate Curti, Senior Vice President and Chief Operating Officer
CFO: Paul Trainor, Senior Vice President Finance and Chief Financial Officer
CMO: Timothy Scherer, M.D., Chief Medical Officer
CIO: Andrew Watt, M.D., Vice President, Information Technology & Services, Chief Information Officer, Chief Medical Information Officer
CNO: Cheryl Gagne I, Vice President Patient Care Services and Chief Nursing Officer
Web address: www.snhhs.org
Control: Other not–for–profit (including NFP Corporation) **Service:** General medical and surgical

Staffed Beds: 172 **Admissions:** 7041 **Census:** 101 **Outpatient Visits:** 240606 **Births:** 1154 **Total Expense ($000):** 295416 **Payroll Expense ($000):** 108754 **Personnel:** 1317

★ ⇧ **ST. JOSEPH HOSPITAL (300011)**, 172 Kinsley Street, Zip 03060–3648; tel. 603/882–3000, (Nonreporting) **A**2 5 10 21 **S** Covenant Health, Tewksbury, MA
Primary Contact: John Albert. Jurczyk, FACHE, President
CFO: Richard Plamondon, Vice President Finance and Chief Financial Officer
CIO: Keith A Choinka, Vice President Information Systems and Chief Information Officer
Web address: www.stjosephhospital.com
Control: Church operated, Nongovernment, not–for–profit **Service:** General medical and surgical

Staffed Beds: 159

NEW LONDON—Merrimack County

★ **NEW LONDON HOSPITAL (301304)**, 273 County Road, Zip 03257–5736; tel. 603/526–2911, **A**3 5 10 18 **F**3 5 7 11 15 18 29 30 31 32 34 35 36 38 40 44 45 50 53 54 56 57 59 64 75 77 80 81 86 87 93 96 97 102 104 107 110 114 115 119 126 127 128 130 131 132 133 146 147 149 150 154 160 167 169 **P**6 **S** Dartmouth Health, Lebanon, NH
Primary Contact: Lauren Geddes Wirth, Interim President and Chief Executive Officer
CFO: Lisa Cohen, Chief Financial Officer
CMO: Lauren Geddes Wirth, Chief Medical Officer
CIO: David Foss, Chief Information Officer
CHR: Shari Bostwick, Director Human Resources
CNO: Karen Lewis Beinhaur, Chief Nursing Officer
Web address: www.newlondonhospital.org
Control: Other not–for–profit (including NFP Corporation) **Service:** General medical and surgical

Staffed Beds: 25 **Admissions:** 1708 **Census:** 19 **Outpatient Visits:** 277765 **Births:** 0 **Total Expense ($000):** 87409 **Payroll Expense ($000):** 46198 **Personnel:** 498

Hospitals, U.S. / NEW HAMPSHIRE

NORTH CONWAY—Carroll County

★ **MEMORIAL HOSPITAL (301307)**, 3073 White Mountain Highway, Zip 03860-7101; tel. 603/356-5461, (Nonreporting) **A**10 18 **S** MaineHealth, Portland, ME
Primary Contact: Bradley J. Chapman, President
CFO: Diana J. McLaughlin, Chief Financial Officer
CMO: Ray Rabideau, M.D., Senior Vice President and Chief Medical Officer
CIO: Curtis Kerbs, Regional Chief Information Officer
CHR: Melanie Sleime, Director Human Resources
CNO: Kristine Dascoulias, Chief Nursing Officer
Web address: www.memorialhospitalnh.org
Control: Other not-for-profit (including NFP Corporation) **Service**: General medical and surgical

Staffed Beds: 70

PETERBOROUGH—Hillsborough County

★ **MONADNOCK COMMUNITY HOSPITAL (301309)**, 452 Old Street Road, Zip 03458-1295; tel. 603/924-7191, **A**5 10 18 **F**3 11 13 15 28 29 31 34 35 36 38 40 41 44 50 59 62 64 65 70 71 75 76 77 78 79 81 82 85 86 87 89 91 92 93 96 97 99 100 101 102 104 107 110 114 119 127 130 131 132 133 135 146 147 148 149 154 156 162 165 167 169 **P**6
Primary Contact: Cynthia K. McGuire, FACHE, President and Chief Executive Officer
CFO: Richard Scheinblum, Chief Financial Officer
CMO: Michael Lindberg, M.D., Chief Medical Officer
CIO: Peter A Johnson, Interim Chief Information Officer
CHR: John Sansone, Vice President, Human Resources
CNO: Vicki Campanile, R.N., MS, Chief Nursing Officer
Web address: www.monadnockhospital.org
Control: Other not-for-profit (including NFP Corporation) **Service**: General medical and surgical

Staffed Beds: 25 **Admissions**: 1122 **Census**: 10 **Outpatient Visits**: 76016 **Births**: 262 **Total Expense ($000)**: 95395 **Payroll Expense ($000)**: 41734 **Personnel**: 418

PLYMOUTH—Grafton County

★ **SPEARE MEMORIAL HOSPITAL (301311)**, 16 Hospital Road, Zip 03264-1199; tel. 603/536-1120, **A**5 10 18 **F**3 12 13 15 28 29 30 31 32 34 35 40 45 47 48 50 53 54 57 59 64 70 75 76 77 78 79 81 85 87 93 97 107 110 111 114 115 119 127 129 130 131 133 144 146 147 148 154 169
Primary Contact: Michelle McEwen, President and Chief Executive Officer
CFO: Travis Boucher, Chief Financial Officer
CMO: Joseph Ebner, M.D., Chief Medical Officer
CHR: Laurie J Bolognani, Human Resources Officer
CNO: Kristine Hering, R.N., Chief Nursing Officer
Web address: www.spearehospital.com
Control: Other not-for-profit (including NFP Corporation) **Service**: General medical and surgical

Staffed Beds: 25 **Admissions**: 1076 **Census**: 12 **Outpatient Visits**: 71927 **Births**: 173 **Total Expense ($000)**: 78630 **Payroll Expense ($000)**: 24748 **Personnel**: 379

PORTSMOUTH—Rockingham County

✠ **PORTSMOUTH REGIONAL HOSPITAL (300029)**, 333 Borthwick Avenue, Zip 03801-7128; tel. 603/436-5110, (Nonreporting) **A**1 2 3 5 10 **S** HCA Healthcare, Nashville, TN
Primary Contact: John Skevington, Interim President & Chief Executive Officer
COO: Matthew Larkin, Chief Operating Officer
CFO: Richard Senger, Chief Financial Officer
CMO: Brian Sanders, M.D., Chief Medical Officer
CIO: Ed Sovetskhy, Director Information Services
CHR: Jackie Brayton, Vice President Human Resources
Web address: www.portsmouthhospital.com
Control: Corporation, Investor-owned (for-profit) **Service**: General medical and surgical

Staffed Beds: 220

ROCHESTER—Strafford County

✠ **FRISBIE MEMORIAL HOSPITAL (300014)**, 11 Whitehall Road, Zip 03867-3297; tel. 603/332-5211, (Nonreporting) **A**1 10 **S** HCA Healthcare, Nashville, TN
Primary Contact: Megan Gray, Interim Chief Executive Officer and Chief Nursing Officer
CFO: Robert K. Cochrane, Vice President Finance and Chief Financial Officer
CMO: Trevor Eide, M.D., Chief Medical Officer
CNO: John L Levitow Jr, Vice President Patient Care Services and Chief Nursing Officer
Web address: www.frisbiehospital.com
Control: Corporation, Investor-owned (for-profit) **Service**: General medical and surgical

Staffed Beds: 80

SALEM—Rockingham County

☐ **NORTHEAST REHABILITATION HOSPITAL (303026)**, 70 Butler Street, Zip 03079-3925; tel. 603/893-2900, **A**1 10 **F**28 29 64 68 74 75 77 82 87 90 93 96 131 133 147 148 149 154 157
Primary Contact: Charles D. Champagne, Chief Executive Officer
CMO: A Deniz Ozel, M.D., Chief Medical Officer
CHR: Shirley G Lussier, Vice President Human Resources
CNO: Helene Thibodeau, R.N., MSN, Vice President Patient Care Services
Web address: www.northeastrehab.com
Control: Corporation, Investor-owned (for-profit) **Service**: Rehabilitation

Staffed Beds: 135 **Admissions**: 3040 **Census**: 113 **Outpatient Visits**: 182797 **Births**: 0 **Total Expense ($000)**: 101856 **Payroll Expense ($000)**: 58003 **Personnel**: 734

WOLFEBORO—Carroll County

★ **HUGGINS HOSPITAL (301312)**, 240 South Main Street, Zip 03894-4455, Mailing Address: P.O. Box 912, Zip 03894-0912; tel. 603/569-7500, **A**10 18 **F**3 8 15 28 29 34 35 36 37 40 45 50 53 57 59 64 65 68 70 75 79 81 85 86 87 93 96 97 107 108 110 115 119 130 131 132 133 135 147 148 149 154 156 160 164 **P**6
Primary Contact: Jeremy Roberge, CPA, President and Chief Executive Officer
CMO: John Boornazian, M.D., Chief Medical Officer
CIO: Pam McGovern, Director Technology
CHR: Laura Stauss, Director of Human Resources
Web address: www.hugginshospital.org
Control: Other not-for-profit (including NFP Corporation) **Service**: General medical and surgical

Staffed Beds: 25 **Admissions**: 836 **Census**: 9 **Outpatient Visits**: 147239 **Births**: 0 **Total Expense ($000)**: 97760 **Payroll Expense ($000)**: 41328 **Personnel**: 427

WOODSVILLE—Grafton County

★ **COTTAGE HOSPITAL (301301)**, 90 Swiftwater Road, Zip 03785-1421, Mailing Address: P.O. Box 2001, Zip 03785-2001; tel. 603/747-9000, **A**10 18 **F**3 8 11 15 28 29 34 36 40 41 43 44 45 50 54 56 57 59 64 70 75 77 79 81 86 87 93 97 105 104 107 110 115 119 127 130 131 132 133 147 148 154 156 166 **P**6
Primary Contact: Holly McCormack, R.N., Chief Executive Officer
COO: Lori Hughes, R.N., MSN, Chief Nursing Officer, Vice President Operations and Patient Care Services
CFO: Steven L Plant, Chief Financial Officer
CIO: Rick Fredrick, Director Information Technology
CNO: Lori Hughes, R.N., MSN, Chief Nursing Officer, Vice President Operations and Patient Care Services
Web address: www.cottagehospital.org
Control: Other not-for-profit (including NFP Corporation) **Service**: General medical and surgical

Staffed Beds: 35 **Admissions**: 685 **Census**: 19 **Outpatient Visits**: 29982 **Births**: 0 **Total Expense ($000)**: 42194 **Payroll Expense ($000)**: 19372 **Personnel**: 201

Hospital, Medicare Provider Number, Address, Telephone, Approval, Facility, and Physician Codes, Health Care System

★ American Hospital Association (AHA) membership   ○ Healthcare Facilities Accreditation Program   ⇑ Center for Improvement in Healthcare Quality Accreditation
☐ The Joint Commission accreditation   ◇ DNV Healthcare Inc. accreditation   △ Commission on Accreditation of Rehabilitation Facilities (CARF) accreditation

Hospitals, U.S. / NEW JERSEY

NEW JERSEY

ATLANTIC CITY—Atlantic County

⇧ **ACUITY SPECIALTY HOSPITAL OF NEW JERSEY** See Select Specialty Hospital – Atlantic City

ATLANTICARE REGIONAL MEDICAL CENTER See Atlanticare Regional Medical Center, Atlantic City Campus

ATLANTICARE REGIONAL MEDICAL CENTER, ATLANTIC CITY CAMPUS (310064), 1925 Pacific Avenue, Zip 08401–6713; tel. 609/441–8994, (Includes ATLANTICARE REGIONAL MEDICAL CENTER, MAINLAND CAMPUS, 65 W Jimmie Leeds Road, Pomona, New Jersey, Zip 08240–9102, 65 West Jimmie Leeds Road, Zip 08240, tel. 609/652–1000; Michael Charlton, President and Chief Executive Officer) (Nonreporting) **A**1 2 3 5 10 **S** AtlantiCare, Egg Harbor Township, NJ
Primary Contact: Kevin McDonnell, Chief Hospital Executive
CFO: Walter Greiner, Chief Financial Officer
CMO: Marilouise Vendetti, M.D., Chief Medical Officer
CIO: Christopher A Scanzera, Vice President and Chief Information Officer
CHR: Richard Lovering, Corporate Vice President Human Resources and Organizational Development
Web address: https://www.atlanticare.org/location/atlanticare-regional-medical-center-atlantic-city-campus
Control: Other not–for–profit (including NFP Corporation) **Service:** General medical and surgical

Staffed Beds: 593

★ ⇧ **SELECT SPECIALTY HOSPITAL – ATLANTIC CITY (312023)**, 1925 Pacific Avenue, 7th Floor, Zip 08401–6713; tel. 609/441–2122, (Nonreporting) **A**10 21 **S** Select Medical Corporation, Mechanicsburg, PA
Primary Contact: Joanne McGovern, MSN, R.N., Chief Executive Officer
CFO: Cheryl Lambert, Chief Financial Officer
CHR: Maria Ciro, Director Human Resources
Web address: www.acuityhealthcare.net
Control: Corporation, Investor–owned (for–profit) **Service:** Acute long–term care hospital

Staffed Beds: 30

BAYONNE—Hudson County

☐ **CAREPOINT HEALTH BAYONNE MEDICAL CENTER (310025)**, 29th Street & Avenue E, Zip 07002–4699, Mailing Address: 29 East 29 Street, Zip 07002–4699; tel. 201/858–5000, (Nonreporting) **A**1 2 3 5 10 12 13 **S** CarePoint Health, Jersey City, NJ
Primary Contact: Mohammad Zubair, M.D., Chief Hospital Executive
CFO: Gary Bryant, Chief Financial Officer
CIO: Joel Taylor, Chief Information Officer
CHR: Jennifer Dobin, Executive Vice President Human Resources
Web address: www.carepointhealth.org
Control: Corporation, Investor–owned (for–profit) **Service:** General medical and surgical

Staffed Beds: 178

BELLE MEAD—Somerset County

HACKENSACK MERIDIAN HEALTH CARRIER CLINIC (314012), 252 County Route 601, Zip 08502–0147, Mailing Address: P.O. Box 147, Zip 08502–0147; tel. 908/281–1000, **A**1 5 10 **F**4 5 29 30 38 75 98 99 100 101 102 103 104 106 130 132 149 151 153 154 160 161 162 165 **S** Hackensack Meridian Health, Edison, NJ
Primary Contact: Patricia Toole, President and Chief Executive Officer
CFO: Randolph Jacobson, Chief Financial Officer
CMO: Umesh Mehta, M.D., Chief Medical Officer
CIO: Peter Schwartz, Director Information Systems
CNO: Shaun Sweeney, R.N., Vice President Patient Care Services
Web address: www.carrierclinic.org
Control: Other not–for–profit (including NFP Corporation) **Service:** Psychiatric

Staffed Beds: 363 **Admissions:** 4039 **Census:** 220 **Outpatient Visits:** 3080 **Births:** 0 **Total Expense ($000):** 100617 **Payroll Expense ($000):** 69195 **Personnel:** 796

BELLEVILLE—Essex County

CLARA MAASS MEDICAL CENTER (310009), 1 Clara Maass Drive, Zip 07109–3557; tel. 973/450–2000, **A**1 3 10 **F**3 8 11 12 13 15 18 19 20 22 28 29 30 31 34 35 36 38 39 40 41 46 49 50 51 53 55 56 57 58 59 60 61 63 64 65 66 68 69 70 71 73 74 75 76 77 78 79 81 82 83 84 85 86 87 89 91 92 93 94 96 98 100 101 102 103 107 108 111 114 115 118 119 120 121 123 124 126 129 130 131 132 133 134 135 143 146 148 149 150 154 156 157 160 161 162 164 165 167 169 **S** RWJBarnabas Health, West Orange, NJ
Primary Contact: Mary Ellen Clyne, Ph.D., President and Chief Executive Officer
COO: Jeffrey J. Holt, Chief Operating Officer
CMO: Frank Dos Santos, D.O., Chief Medical Officer
CIO: Michael McTigue, Chief Information Officer
CHR: Jim Rolek, Chief Human Resources Officer, Vice President
CNO: Bonnie Geissler, R.N., Chief Nursing Officer, Vice President Patient Care Services
Web address: www.barnabashealth.org/hospitals/clara_maass/index.html
Control: Other not–for–profit (including NFP Corporation) **Service:** General medical and surgical

Staffed Beds: 380 **Admissions:** 13087 **Census:** 215 **Outpatient Visits:** 141918 **Births:** 1735 **Total Expense ($000):** 374596 **Payroll Expense ($000):** 146572 **Personnel:** 1514

BERKELEY HEIGHTS—Union County

CORNERSTONE BEHAVIORAL HEALTH HOSPITAL OF UNION COUNTY (314027), 40 Watchung Way, Zip 07922–2600; tel. 908/790–5300, **A**10 **F**30 65 68 69 87 98 100 101 105 130 132 135 143 149 154 164 165 **P**4 5 7 8
Primary Contact: Paul Herskovitz, Administrator
Web address: https://ucnj.org/cornerstone-behavioral-health-hospital-of-union-county/
Control: County, Government, Nonfederal **Service:** Psychiatric

Staffed Beds: 44 **Admissions:** 206 **Census:** 33 **Outpatient Visits:** 0 **Births:** 0 **Personnel:** 113

RUNNELLS SPECIALIZED HOSPITAL OF UNION COUNTY See Runnells Center For Rehabilitation and Healthcare

BLACKWOOD—Camden County

☐ **NORTHBROOK BEHAVIORAL HEALTH HOSPITAL (314018)**, 425 Woodbury Turnersville Road, Zip 08012–2960; tel. 856/374–6500, (Nonreporting) **A**1 10
Primary Contact: Avi Feigenbaum, Chief Executive Officer
Web address: www.northbrookbhh.com
Control: Corporation, Investor–owned (for–profit) **Service:** Psychiatric

Staffed Beds: 153

BOONTON TOWNSHIP—Morris County

SAINT CLARE'S HOSPITAL/BOONTON TOWNSHIP See Saint Clare's Denville Hospital, Denville

ST CLARE'S HOSPITAL/BOONTON See Saint Clare's Hospital/Boonton Township

BRICK—Ocean County

HACKENSACK MERIDIAN HEALTH SHORE REHABILITATION INSTITUTE See Johnson Rehabilitation Institute At Hackensack Meridian Health Ocean Medical Center

△ **JOHNSON REHABILITATION INSTITUTE AT HACKENSACK MERIDIAN HEALTH OCEAN MEDICAL CENTER (313033)**, 425 Jack Martin Boulevard, Zip 08724–7732; tel. 732/836–4500, **A**1 5 7 10 **F**29 36 50 58 68 74 75 77 90 91 93 94 95 96 130 132 148 149 **S** Hackensack Meridian Health, Edison, NJ
Primary Contact: Kerri Fitzgerald, Executive Director
CFO: Richard C. Smith, Senior Vice President Finance
CMO: Lisa Luciano, D.O., Medical Director
CNO: Maria Clohsey, Director of Nursing
Web address: www.shorerehabilitationinstitute.com
Control: Other not–for–profit (including NFP Corporation) **Service:** Rehabilitation

Staffed Beds: 40 **Admissions:** 894 **Census:** 33 **Outpatient Visits:** 18471 **Births:** 0 **Total Expense ($000):** 21792 **Payroll Expense ($000):** 12896 **Personnel:** 127

Hospitals, U.S. / NEW JERSEY

BRICK TOWNSHIP—Ocean County

✠ **HACKENSACK MERIDIAN HEALTH OCEAN UNIVERSITY MEDICAL CENTER (310052)**, 425 Jack Martin Boulevard, Zip 08724–7732; tel. 732/840–2200, **A**1 2 3 5 10 **F**3 11 12 13 15 18 20 22 26 28 29 30 31 34 35 36 37 38 40 41 42 44 45 46 47 48 49 50 51 54 55 56 57 58 59 60 63 64 65 68 70 73 74 75 76 77 78 79 81 82 84 85 86 87 91 92 93 94 95 96 100 102 104 107 108 109 110 111 114 115 116 117 118 119 120 121 122 123 124 126 129 130 131 132 141 144 146 147 148 149 154 155 162 165 167 **S** Hackensack Meridian Health, Edison, NJ
Primary Contact: Frank Citara, Chief Hospital Executive
COO: Regina Foley, R.N., FACHE, Vice President Nursing and Operations
CFO: Robert Palermo, Vice President Finance
CMO: Patricia Fisher, M.D., Chief Medical Officer
CIO: Rebecca Weber, Senior Vice President and Chief Information Officer
CHR: Sherrie String, Senior Vice President Human Resources
Web address: www.meridianhealth.com
Control: Other not–for–profit (including NFP Corporation) Service: General medical and surgical

Staffed Beds: 313 **Admissions:** 15664 **Census:** 227 **Outpatient Visits:** 193670 **Births:** 1114 **Total Expense ($000):** 510101 **Payroll Expense ($000):** 231192 **Personnel:** 2030

BRIDGETON—Cumberland County

BRIDGETON HEALTH CENTER See Inspira Medical Center–Vineland, Vineland

BRIDGETON HOSPITAL See Bridgeton Health Center

BROWNS MILLS—Burlington County

⇑ **DEBORAH HEART AND LUNG CENTER (310031)**, 200 Trenton Road, Zip 08015–1705; tel. 609/893–6611, **A**3 5 10 13 21 **F**3 8 11 17 18 19 20 22 24 26 28 29 30 32 34 35 36 39 45 46 50 54 55 56 57 58 59 60 64 65 66 68 70 75 77 78 81 82 84 85 87 93 94 100 101 107 108 111 115 116 117 118 119 124 126 129 130 132 135 143 146 147 148 149 154 156 157 167 **P**1 7
Primary Contact: Jim Andrews, President and Chief Executive Officer
COO: Joseph Manni, Executive Vice President and Chief Operating Officer
CFO: Thomas Percello, Executive Vice President, Finance and Chief Financial Officer
CMO: Lynn McGrath, M.D., Vice President Medical Affairs
CIO: Richard Temple, Chief Information Officer
CHR: Marion Stamopoulos, Vice President Human Resources
CNO: Rita Zenna, R.N., Vice President Patient Care Services
Web address: www.deborah.org
Control: Other not–for–profit (including NFP Corporation) Service: Heart

Staffed Beds: 89 **Admissions:** 3406 **Census:** 51 **Outpatient Visits:** 98642 **Births:** 0 **Total Expense ($000):** 244620 **Payroll Expense ($000):** 104562 **Personnel:** 1025

CAMDEN—Camden County

✠ **COOPER UNIVERSITY HEALTH CARE (310014)**, 1 Cooper Plaza, Zip 08103–1489; tel. 856/342–2000, (Includes CHILDEN'S REGIONAL HOSPITAL AT COOPER, 3 Cooper Plz, Camden, New Jersey, Zip 08103–1438, Three Cooper Plaza, Zip 08103, tel. 800/826–6737) **A**1 2 3 5 8 10 13 **F**3 5 7 8 9 11 12 13 15 17 18 20 22 24 26 29 30 31 32 34 35 36 37 38 39 40 41 43 44 45 46 47 48 49 50 51 54 55 56 57 58 59 60 61 64 65 66 68 70 72 73 74 76 77 78 79 80 81 82 84 85 86 87 88 89 93 96 97 98 100 101 102 104 107 108 110 111 114 115 116 117 118 119 120 121 123 124 126 130 131 132 135 144 145 146 147 148 149 150 154 155 157 160 162 167 169 **P**6
Primary Contact: Anthony J. Mazzarelli, JD, M.D., Co–President and Chief Executive Officer
CFO: Douglas E. Shirley, Senior Executive Vice President and Chief Financial Officer
CHR: Elizabeth Green, Chief Human Resources Officer
CNO: Kathleen Devine, R.N., Senior Vice President and Chief Nursing Executive
Web address: www.cooperhealth.org
Control: Other not–for–profit (including NFP Corporation) Service: General medical and surgical

Staffed Beds: 596 **Admissions:** 30040 **Census:** 539 **Outpatient Visits:** 434320 **Births:** 1849 **Total Expense ($000):** 1543554 **Payroll Expense ($000):** 521218 **Personnel:** 8701

THE CHILDEN'S REGIONAL HOSPITAL AT COOPER See Childen's Regional Hospital At Cooper

✠ **VIRTUA OUR LADY OF LOURDES HOSPITAL (310029)**, 1600 Haddon Avenue, Zip 08103–3117; tel. 856/757–3500, **A**1 3 5 10 **F**3 13 15 17 18 20 22 24 26 28 29 30 31 34 40 45 46 47 49 50 55 56 57 58 59 60 61 64 65 70 73 74 75 76 77 78 80 81 85 87 90 93 96 100 107 108 110 111 114 115 117 118 119 126 130 132 134 138 139 141 142 146 147 148 149 154 167 169 **S** Virtua Health, Marlton, NJ
Primary Contact: Mark Nessel, Executive Vice President and Chief Operating Officer
COO: Mark Nessel, Executive Vice President and Chief Operating Officer
CFO: Michael Hammond, Chief Financial Officer
CMO: Alan R Pope, M.D., Chief Medical Officer
CIO: Maureen Hetu, Chief Information Officer
CHR: Jennifer L Moughan, Chief Human Resources Officer
CNO: Audrey Jadczak, R.N., FACHE, Vice President Chief Nursing Officer
Web address: https://www.lourdesnet.org/locations/hospitals/our-lady-of-lourdes-medical-center/
Control: Other not–for–profit (including NFP Corporation) Service: General medical and surgical

Staffed Beds: 325 **Admissions:** 12487 **Census:** 191 **Outpatient Visits:** 112944 **Births:** 644 **Total Expense ($000):** 476450 **Payroll Expense ($000):** 130378 **Personnel:** 1464

CAPE MAY COURT HOUSE—Cape May County

✠ **COOPER UNIVERSITY HOSPITAL CAPE REGIONAL (310011)**, 2 Stone Harbor Boulevard, Zip 08210–9990; tel. 609/463–2000, (Nonreporting) **A**1 10
Primary Contact: Joanne Carrocino, FACHE, President and Chief Executive Officer
CFO: Mark Gill, Vice President Finance and Chief Financial Officer
CMO: Andrea C.S. McCoy, M.D., Chief Medical Officer
CIO: Richard Wheatley, Chief Information Officer
CHR: Byron Hunter, Vice President Human Resources
CNO: Rosemary Dunn, R.N., Chief Nursing Officer
Web address: www.caperegional.com
Control: Other not–for–profit (including NFP Corporation) Service: General medical and surgical

Staffed Beds: 178

CEDAR GROVE—Essex County

☐ **ESSEX COUNTY HOSPITAL CENTER (314020)**, 204 Grove Avenue, Zip 07009–1436; tel. 973/571–2800, (Nonreporting) **A**1 10
Primary Contact: Frank J. Del Gaudio, Department and Hospital Center Director
CFO: Jacqueline Campoverde, Business Manager
CMO: Bolivar Pascual, M.D., Medical Director
CIO: Vijay Prakash, Information Technology Officer
CHR: Marlon Brown, Human Resources
CNO: Fern Papalia, Director of Nursing
Web address: www.essexcountynj.org
Control: County, Government, Nonfederal Service: Psychiatric

Staffed Beds: 180

CHESTER—Morris County

KESSLER INSTITUTE FOR REHABILITATION See Kessler Institute For Rehabilitation, West Orange

WELKIND FACILITY See Kessler Institute For Rehabilitation

CRANFORD—Union County

CRANFORD HEALTH AND EC CENTER See Cranford Health and Extended Care Center

---

Hospital, Medicare Provider Number, Address, Telephone, Approval, Facility, and Physician Codes, Health Care System

★ American Hospital Association (AHA) membership
☐ The Joint Commission accreditation
○ Healthcare Facilities Accreditation Program
◇ DNV Healthcare Inc. accreditation
⇑ Center for Improvement in Healthcare Quality Accreditation
△ Commission on Accreditation of Rehabilitation Facilities (CARF) accreditation

© 2025 AHA Guide

Hospitals, U.S. / NEW JERSEY

DENVILLE—Morris County

☐ **SAINT CLARE'S DENVILLE HOSPITAL (310050)**, 25 Pocono Road, Zip 07834-2954; tel. 973/625-6000, (Includes SAINT CLARE'S HOSPITAL/BOONTON TOWNSHIP, 130 Powerville RD, Boonton Township, New Jersey, Zip 07005-8705, 130 Powerville Road, Zip 07005, tel. 973/316-1800; Brian Finestein, Chief Executive Officer; SAINT CLARE'S HOSPITAL/DENVILLE, 25 Pocono RD, Denville, New Jersey, Zip 07834-2954, 25 Pocono Road, Zip 07834, tel. 973/625-6000; SAINT CLARE'S HOSPITAL/DOVER, 400 West Blackwell Street, Dover, New Jersey, Zip 07801-3311, tel. 973/989-3000; Brian Finestein, Chief Executive Officer) (Nonreporting) **A**1 3 10 **S** Prime Healthcare, Ontario, CA
Primary Contact: Brian Ulery, Chief Executive Officer
CFO: Thomas G. Scott, CPA, Chief Financial Officer
CMO: Neil Udani, M.D., Chief Medical Officer
CIO: Tero Caamano, Director Information Technology
CHR: Karen Sosnowski, Director, Human Resources
CNO: Jan Bednar, R.N., MS, Chief Nursing Officer
Web address: https://saintclares.com/locations/saint-clares-denville-hospital/
Control: Church operated, Nongovernment, not-for-profit **Service**: General medical and surgical

Staffed Beds: 412

SAINT CLARE'S HOSPITAL/DENVILLE See Saint Clare's Denville Hospital, Denville

ST CLARE'S HOSPITAL/DENVILLE See Saint Clare's Hospital/Denville

DOVER—Morris County

✣ **KINDRED HOSPITAL–NEW JERSEY MORRIS COUNTY (312020)**, 400 West Blackwell Street, Zip 07801-2525; tel. 973/537-3818, (Includes KINDRED HOSPITAL EAST NEW JERSEY, 350 Boulevard, Passaic, New Jersey, Zip 07055-2840, tel. 973/636-7200; Alice M. O'Connor, Chief Executive Officer; KINDRED HOSPITAL NEW JERSEY – RAHWAY, 865 Stone ST, Rahway, New Jersey, Zip 07065-2742, 865 Stone Street, Zip 07065, tel. 732/669-8200; Patrick J O'Connor, Chief Executive Officer) (Nonreporting) **A**1 10 **S** ScionHealth, Louisville, KY
Primary Contact: Andrew P. Donet, Chief Executive Officer
CFO: Stephen D. Farber, Chief Financial Officer
CMO: Sean R Muldoon, M.D., Chief Medical Officer
Web address: www.khmorriscounty.com/
Control: Corporation, Investor-owned (for-profit) **Service**: Acute long-term care hospital

Staffed Beds: 45

ST. CLARE'S HOSPITAL/DOVER See Saint Clare's Hospital/Dover

EAST ORANGE—Essex County

☐ **CAREWELL HEALTH MEDICAL CENTER (310083)**, 300 Central Avenue, Zip 07018-2897; tel. 973/672-8400, **A**1 10 **F**4 12 15 18 29 30 34 35 38 40 45 46 49 50 55 59 60 70 74 77 79 81 82 86 87 93 97 98 100 101 102 104 107 108 111 114 119 147 151 154 156 158 160 164 167 **P**6 **S** Prospect Medical Holdings, Los Angeles, CA
Primary Contact: Paige Dworak, FACHE, President and Chief Executive Officer
COO: Rodemil Fuentes, Chief Operating Officer
CFO: Don Alcuino, Chief Financial Officer
CMO: Anuj Mehta, M.D., Chief Medical Officer
CIO: Jeff Kridel, Senior Director, Information Technology Operations
CHR: Jennifer Dobin, Chief Human Resources Officer
CNO: Chris Coruna, Chief Nursing Officer
Web address: https://carewellhealth.com/
Control: Partnership, Investor-owned (for-profit) **Service**: General medical and surgical

Staffed Beds: 150 **Admissions**: 4635 **Census**: 66 **Outpatient Visits**: 50819 **Births**: 0 **Total Expense ($000)**: 106470 **Payroll Expense ($000)**: 48823 **Personnel**: 615

EAST ORANGE GENERAL HOSPITAL See Carewell Health Medical Center

VETERANS ADM MEDICAL CENTER See East Orange Division

✣ △ **VETERANS AFFAIRS NEW JERSEY HEALTH CARE SYSTEM**, 385 Tremont Avenue, Zip 07018-1095; tel. 973/676-1000, (Includes EAST ORANGE DIVISION, 385 Tremont Avenue, East Orange, New Jersey, Zip 07018-1095, tel. 973/676-1000; LYONS DIVISION, 151 Knollcroft Road, Lyons, New Jersey, Zip 07939-9998, tel. 908/647-0180) (Nonreporting) **A**1 2 3 5 7 **S** Department of Veterans Affairs, Washington, DC
Primary Contact: Patricia O'Kane, Associate Director
CFO: Tyrone Taylor, Chief Financial Officer
CMO: Steven L Lieberman, M.D., Chief of Staff
CIO: Kamesha Scarlett, Chief Information Resource Management
CHR: Nancy Hamilton, Chief Human and Learning Resources
CNO: Patrick J Troy, R.N., MSN, Associate Director Patient Care Services
Web address: www.newjersey.va.gov/
Control: Veterans Affairs, Government, federal **Service**: General medical and surgical

Staffed Beds: 343

EDISON—Middlesex County

✣ **HACKENSACK MERIDIAN HEALTH JFK MEDICAL CENTER (310108)**, 65 James Street, Zip 08818; tel. 732/321-7000, **A**1 2 3 5 10 **F**3 5 6 7 8 11 12 13 14 15 18 20 22 26 28 29 30 31 34 35 36 37 38 39 40 41 42 44 45 46 47 48 49 50 51 53 54 56 57 58 59 60 61 63 64 65 66 68 69 70 71 73 74 75 76 77 78 79 81 82 84 85 86 87 89 91 92 93 94 95 96 97 100 101 102 104 107 108 109 110 111 113 114 115 116 117 118 119 121 123 124 126 129 130 131 132 135 141 143 144 145 146 147 148 149 153 154 156 162 164 165 167 168 169 **S** Hackensack Meridian Health, Edison, NJ
Primary Contact: Amie D. Thornton, Chief Hospital Executive
COO: Scott Gebhard, Executive VP and Chief Operating Officer
CFO: Richard C. Smith, Senior Vice President and Chief Financial Officer
CMO: William F. Oser, M.D., Senior Vice President and Chief Medical Officer
CIO: Indranil Ganguly, Vice President and Chief Information Officer
CHR: Shirley Higgins Bowers, Senior Vice President Human Resources
CNO: James Lindquist, Chief Nursing Officer
Web address: www.jfkmc.org
Control: Other not-for-profit (including NFP Corporation) **Service**: General medical and surgical

Staffed Beds: 372 **Admissions**: 19546 **Census**: 294 **Outpatient Visits**: 318981 **Births**: 1483 **Total Expense ($000)**: 798481 **Payroll Expense ($000)**: 319131 **Personnel**: 2954

★ △ **JFK JOHNSON REHABILITATION INSTITUTE AT HACKENSACK MERIDIAN HEALTH (310105)**, 65 James Street, Zip 08818; tel. 732/321-7050, **A**3 7 10 **F**3 9 28 29 30 35 36 44 50 53 54 58 64 68 74 77 82 87 90 91 92 93 94 95 96 130 131 132 143 146 149 150 154 157 **S** Hackensack Meridian Health, Edison, NJ
Primary Contact: Anthony Cuzzola, Vice President, Administrator
COO: Scott Gebhard, Chief Operating Officer
CFO: Richard C. Smith, Chief Financial Officer
CMO: William F. Oser, M.D., Chief Medical Officer
CIO: Neal Ganguly, Chief Information Officer
CNO: James Lindquist, Chief Nursing Officer
Web address: www.njrehab.org
Control: Other not-for-profit (including NFP Corporation) **Service**: Rehabilitation

Staffed Beds: 90 **Admissions**: 1655 **Census**: 73 **Outpatient Visits**: 104330 **Births**: 0 **Total Expense ($000)**: 87709 **Payroll Expense ($000)**: 54817 **Personnel**: 554

ROOSEVELT HOSPITAL See Roosevelt Care Center

ELIZABETH—Union County

CAREONE AT TRINITAS REGIONAL MEDICAL CENTER (312018), 225 Williamson Street, Zip 07202-3625; tel. 908/994-5288, (Nonreporting) **A**10
Primary Contact: Grant Welson, Chief Executive Officer, CareOne Hospital Division
Web address: www.care-one.com/locations/ltach-careone-at-trinitas-regional-medical-center/
Control: Other not-for-profit (including NFP Corporation) **Service**: Acute long-term care hospital

Staffed Beds: 25

TRINITAS HOSPITAL – JERSEY STREET CAMPUS See Trinitas Hospital

TRINITAS HOSPITAL – NEW POINT CAMPUS See Trinitas Regional Medical Center – New Point Campus

Hospitals, U.S. / NEW JERSEY

☒ **TRINITAS REGIONAL MEDICAL CENTER (310027)**, 225 Williamson Street, Zip 07202-3625; tel. 908/994-5000, (Includes TRINITAS HOSPITAL, 225 Williamson ST, Elizabeth, New Jersey, Zip 07202-3625, 225 Williamson Street, Zip 07207, tel. 908/994-5000; Gary S Horan, FACHE, President and Chief Executive Officer; TRINITAS REGIONAL MEDICAL CENTER – NEW POINT CAMPUS, 655 E Jersey ST, Elizabeth, New Jersey, Zip 07206-1259, 655 East Jersey Street, Zip 07206, tel. 908/994-5000; Gary S Horan, FACHE, President and Chief Executive Officer) (Total facility includes 124 beds in nursing home–type unit) **A**1 2 3 5 10 **F**3 5 7 8 11 13 15 17 18 20 22 28 29 30 31 32 34 35 36 38 40 44 45 46 48 49 55 56 57 58 59 60 61 64 65 66 68 70 73 74 75 76 77 78 79 81 82 84 85 86 87 91 93 97 98 99 100 101 102 103 104 105 106 107 108 110 111 115 117 118 119 120 121 123 124 126 128 129 130 132 134 135 141 143 146 147 148 149 153 154 157 160 164 167 169 **S** RWJBarnabas Health, West Orange, NJ
Primary Contact: Nancy DiLiegro, Ph.D., FACHE, President and Chief Executive Officer
CFO: Karen Lumpp, Senior Vice President and Chief Financial Officer
CMO: John D'Angelo, D.O., Vice President, Chief Medical Officer
CHR: Glenn Nacion, Vice President Human Resources
CNO: Mary McTigue, DNP, RNC, CENP, Vice President Patient Care Services and Chief Nursing Officer
Web address: www.trinitasrmc.com
Control: Other not–for–profit (including NFP Corporation) **Service**: General medical and surgical

Staffed Beds: 449 **Admissions**: 9343 **Census**: 271 **Outpatient Visits**: 283443 **Births**: 1133 **Total Expense ($000)**: 355261 **Payroll Expense ($000)**: 161069 **Personnel**: 1973

ENGLEWOOD—Bergen County

☒ **ENGLEWOOD HEALTH (310045)**, 350 Engle Street, Zip 07631-1898; tel. 201/894-3000, **A**1 2 3 5 10 **F**3 4 5 6 7 8 9 11 12 13 15 17 18 19 20 22 24 26 28 29 30 31 32 34 35 36 37 38 39 40 41 44 45 46 47 48 49 50 51 54 55 56 57 58 59 60 61 62 63 64 65 68 70 71 72 73 74 75 76 77 78 79 80 81 82 83 84 85 86 87 89 91 92 93 94 96 97 98 100 101 102 103 104 107 108 110 111 114 115 116 117 118 119 120 121 123 124 126 129 130 131 132 133 134 135 141 143 144 145 146 147 148 149 150 154 156 157 160 161 162 164 165 167 169
Primary Contact: Warren Geller, President and Chief Executive Officer
COO: Helene Wolk, Senior Vice President Operations and Chief Operating Officer
CFO: Anthony T Orlando, Senior Vice President Finance
CIO: Ravikanth Koganti, Vice President Information Technology
CHR: Patricia Wilson, Senior Vice President Human Resources
CNO: Kathleen A. Kaminsky, MS, R.N., Senior Vice President Patient Care Services
Web address: www.englewoodhealth.org
Control: Other not–for–profit (including NFP Corporation) **Service**: General medical and surgical

Staffed Beds: 301 **Admissions**: 15603 **Census**: 187 **Outpatient Visits**: 3057805 **Births**: 2924 **Total Expense ($000)**: 1079151 **Payroll Expense ($000)**: 227112 **Personnel**: 3719

FLEMINGTON—Hunterdon County

☐ **HUNTERDON HEALTHCARE (310005)**, 2100 Wescott Drive, Zip 08822-4604; tel. 908/788-6100, **A**1 2 3 5 10 13 **F**3 5 8 11 12 13 14 15 17 18 20 22 26 28 29 30 31 32 33 34 35 36 37 38 40 44 45 46 47 48 49 50 51 54 55 56 57 58 59 60 61 62 63 64 65 66 68 70 73 74 75 76 77 78 79 81 82 84 85 86 87 89 93 96 97 98 100 101 102 104 105 107 108 109 110 111 114 115 116 117 118 119 120 121 123 126 129 130 131 132 134 135 143 144 146 147 148 149 150 153 154 156 157 160 161 162 164 165 167 169 **P**6
Primary Contact: Patrick J. Gavin, M.P.H., President and Chief Executive Officer
COO: Lawrence N Grand, MS, R.N., Chief Operating Officer
CMO: Robert Coates, M.D., Vice President, Medical Affairs
CIO: Edmund Siy, Chief Information Officer
CHR: Violet Kocsis, Chief Human Resources Officer
CNO: Patricia Steingall, MS, R.N., Vice President, Patient Care Services
Web address: www.hunterdonhealthcare.org
Control: Other not–for–profit (including NFP Corporation) **Service**: General medical and surgical

Staffed Beds: 184 **Admissions**: 7597 **Census**: 95 **Outpatient Visits**: 895865 **Births**: 933 **Total Expense ($000)**: 424812 **Payroll Expense ($000)**: 214944 **Personnel**: 2173

FREEHOLD—Monmouth County

☒ **CENTRASTATE HEALTHCARE SYSTEM (310111)**, 901 West Main Street, Zip 07728-2549; tel. 732/431-2000, **A**1 2 3 5 10 **F**3 11 12 13 15 18 20 22 28 29 30 31 32 34 35 36 37 38 39 40 41 45 46 47 49 56 57 58 59 64 65 70 73 74 75 76 77 78 79 81 82 84 86 87 89 92 93 98 100 101 102 107 108 110 114 115 118 119 120 121 123 126 129 130 131 132 134 135 146 147 148 149 154 156 160 161 167 169 **P**1
Primary Contact: Thomas W. Scott, FACHE, FABC, President and Chief Executive Officer
CFO: John Dellocono, Senior Vice President and Chief Financial Officer
CMO: Jack H Dworkin, M.D., Vice President Medical Affairs and Chief Medical Officer
CIO: John Ulett, Vice President and Chief Information Officer
CHR: Fran Keane, Vice President Human Resources
CNO: Linda W Geisler, R.N., FACHE, Vice President Patient Services
Web address: www.centrastate.com
Control: Other not–for–profit (including NFP Corporation) **Service**: General medical and surgical

Staffed Beds: 240 **Admissions**: 11115 **Census**: 169 **Outpatient Visits**: 232049 **Births**: 752 **Total Expense ($000)**: 387148 **Payroll Expense ($000)**: 141194 **Personnel**: 1879

HACKENSACK—Bergen County

☒ △ **HACKENSACK MERIDIAN HEALTH HACKENSACK UNIVERSITY MEDICAL CENTER (310001)**, loading dock A(off Essex street), Zip 07601-1914, Mailing Address: 30 Prospect Avenue, Zip 07601-1914; tel. 201/996-2000, (Includes THE JOSEPH M. SANZARI CHILDREN'S HOSPITAL, 30 Prospect Avenue, Hackensack, New Jersey, Zip 07601-1914, tel. 201/996-2000) **A**1 2 3 5 7 8 10 **F**3 5 6 7 8 9 11 12 13 15 17 18 19 20 22 24 26 28 29 30 31 32 33 34 35 36 37 38 39 40 41 43 44 45 46 47 48 49 50 51 52 53 54 55 56 57 58 59 60 61 63 64 65 66 68 69 70 71 72 73 74 75 76 77 78 79 81 82 84 85 86 87 88 89 91 92 93 94 96 97 98 100 101 102 103 104 107 108 109 110 111 112 113 114 115 116 117 118 119 120 121 123 124 126 129 130 131 132 134 135 138 141 142 143 145 146 147 148 149 150 153 154 155 156 157 158 160 161 162 163 164 165 167 168 169 **S** Hackensack Meridian Health, Edison, NJ
Primary Contact: Mark Sparta, FACHE, President and Chief Hospital Executive
COO: Jason Kreitner, FACHE, Senior Vice President and Chief Operarting Officer
CFO: Robert Glenning, Executive Vice President Finance and Chief Financial Officer
CMO: Peter A Gross, M.D., Senior Vice President and Chief Medical Officer
CHR: Nancy R Corcoran, Senior Vice President Human Resources and Quality Service
CNO: Ramonita Jimenez, R.N., Chief Nursing Officer
Web address: www.hackensackumc.org
Control: Other not–for–profit (including NFP Corporation) **Service**: General medical and surgical

Staffed Beds: 793 **Admissions**: 38288 **Census**: 653 **Outpatient Visits**: 542563 **Births**: 4885 **Total Expense ($000)**: 2491644 **Payroll Expense ($000)**: 895300 **Personnel**: 7732

HACKETTSTOWN—Warren County

☒ **HACKETTSTOWN MEDICAL CENTER (310115)**, 651 Willow Grove Street, Zip 07840-1799; tel. 908/852-5100, **A**1 2 3 10 **F**3 5 11 12 15 18 28 29 30 31 34 35 36 38 40 41 44 45 47 49 50 53 54 56 57 60 63 64 65 68 70 74 75 77 78 79 81 82 84 85 86 87 93 94 100 101 102 104 107 108 110 115 116 117 118 119 120 130 132 135 141 144 146 148 149 154 156 164 165 167 **S** Atlantic Health System, Morristown, NJ
Primary Contact: Robert H. Adams, President, Western Region
COO: Donna Watridge, R.N., Director of Operations
CFO: Robert Peterson, CPA, Chief Financial Officer
CMO: Geralda Xavier, M.D., Chief Medical Officer
CIO: Dorothy Cox, Manager Information Systems
CHR: Kimberly McGovern, Manager Human Resources
CNO: Donna Watridge, R.N., Chief Nursing Officer
Web address: www.atlantichealth.org
Control: Other not–for–profit (including NFP Corporation) **Service**: General medical and surgical

Staffed Beds: 104 **Admissions**: 3763 **Census**: 52 **Outpatient Visits**: 75306 **Births**: 0 **Total Expense ($000)**: 135167 **Payroll Expense ($000)**: 60688 **Personnel**: 647

Hospital, Medicare Provider Number, Address, Telephone, Approval, Facility, and Physician Codes, Health Care System

★ American Hospital Association (AHA) membership ○ Healthcare Facilities Accreditation Program ⇑ Center for Improvement in Healthcare Quality Accreditation
☐ The Joint Commission accreditation ◇ DNV Healthcare Inc. accreditation △ Commission on Accreditation of Rehabilitation Facilities (CARF) accreditation

Hospitals, U.S. / NEW JERSEY

HAMILTON—Mercer County

☒ **ROBERT WOOD JOHNSON UNIVERSITY HOSPITAL AT HAMILTON (310110)**, 1 Hamilton Health Place, Zip 08690-3599; tel. 609/586-7900, **A**1 2 10 **F**3 11 12 15 18 20 22 26 28 29 30 31 32 34 35 36 37 40 45 46 47 49 50 51 54 55 56 57 58 59 64 65 66 68 69 70 74 75 78 79 81 82 84 85 86 87 90 92 93 94 95 96 97 100 107 108 110 111 114 115 116 117 119 120 121 124 126 129 130 131 132 135 143 144 145 146 147 148 149 150 154 156 160 161 167 **S** RWJBarnabas Health, West Orange, NJ
Primary Contact: Lisa Breza, R.N., Chief Administrative Officer
COO: Barbara H Smith, Senior Vice President & Chief Operating Officer
CMO: Ronald Ryder, D.O., President of the Medical Staff
CIO: L. Gill Gottle, Senior Vice President and Chief Financial Officer
CNO: Lisa Breza, R.N., Vice President and Chief Nursing Officer
Web address: www.rwjhamilton.org
Control: Other not-for-profit (including NFP Corporation) **Service**: General medical and surgical

Staffed Beds: 164 **Admissions**: 6902 **Census**: 89 **Outpatient Visits**: 144774 **Births**: 0 **Total Expense ($000)**: 220691 **Payroll Expense ($000)**: 77317 **Personnel**: 860

HAMMONTON—Camden County

☐ **ANCORA PSYCHIATRIC HOSPITAL (314005)**, 301 Spring Garden Road, Zip 08037-9699; tel. 609/561-1700, (Nonreporting) **A**1 3 10 **S** Division of Mental Health and Addiction Services, Department of Human Services, State of New Jersey, Trenton, NJ
Primary Contact: Christopher Morrison, Chief Executive Officer
CFO: John Holmes, Business Manager
CIO: Charlene Ruberti, Director Information Technology Development
CHR: Alfred Filipini, Manager Human Resources
Web address: https://www.state.nj.us/humanservices/dmhas/resources/services/treatment/aph.html
Control: State, Government, Nonfederal **Service**: Psychiatric

Staffed Beds: 515

HOBOKEN—Hudson County

☐ **CAREPOINT HEALTH HOBOKEN UNIVERSITY MEDICAL CENTER (310040)**, 308 Willow Avenue, Zip 07030-3889; tel. 201/418-1000, (Nonreporting) **A**1 3 5 10 **S** CarePoint Health, Jersey City, NJ
Primary Contact: Robert P. Beauvais, Chief Hospital Executive
COO: Ann P. Logan, R.N., Ph.D., Chief Hospital Executive
CMO: Meika Roberson, M.D., Chief Medical Officer
CIO: Joel Taylor, Chief Information Officer
CHR: Roberto Gonzalez, Executive Director Human Resources
Web address: www.hobokenumc.com
Control: Corporation, Investor-owned (for-profit) **Service**: General medical and surgical

Staffed Beds: 228

HOLMDEL—Monmouth County

☒ **HACKENSACK MERIDIAN HEALTH BAYSHORE COMMUNITY HOSPITAL (310112)**, 727 North Beers Street, Zip 07733-1598; tel. 732/739-5900, **A**1 2 5 10 **F**3 12 15 18 20 22 28 29 30 32 34 35 38 39 40 41 44 45 46 49 50 51 54 56 57 58 59 60 61 62 63 64 65 68 70 74 75 77 79 81 82 84 85 86 87 92 93 94 97 100 101 102 107 108 110 111 114 115 116 117 118 126 129 130 131 132 134 135 141 146 147 148 149 150 154 156 167 **S** Hackensack Meridian Health, Edison, NJ
Primary Contact: Caitlin Miller, MS, Chief Hospital Executive
CMO: Ian Leber, M.D., Chief Medical Officer
CIO: Rebecca Weber, Senior Vice President and Chief Information Officer
CHR: Sherrie String, Senior Vice President Human Resources
CNO: Linda Walsh, R.N., MSN, Vice President Chief Nursing Executive
Web address: https://www.bayshoremedicalcenter.org/
Control: Other not-for-profit (including NFP Corporation) **Service**: General medical and surgical

Staffed Beds: 175 **Admissions**: 7001 **Census**: 96 **Outpatient Visits**: 82467 **Births**: 0 **Total Expense ($000)**: 190134 **Payroll Expense ($000)**: 87674 **Personnel**: 878

JERSEY CITY—Hudson County

☐ **CAREPOINT HEALTH CHRIST HOSPITAL (310016)**, 176 Palisade Avenue, Zip 07306-1196; Mailing Address: 176 Palisades Avenue, Zip 07306-1196; tel. 201/795-8200, (Nonreporting) **A**1 2 3 5 10 12 13 **S** CarePoint Health, Jersey City, NJ
Primary Contact: Marie Theresa Duffy, Chief Hospital Executive, Executive Vice President System Clinical Integration and Standards
COO: Marie Theresa Duffy, Chief Hospital Executive, Executive Vice President System Clinical Integration and Standards
CFO: Gary Bryant, Executive Vice President and Chief Financial Officer
CHR: Josiane Deroncerey, Director Human Resources
CNO: Denise Cimmino, MSN, R.N., Assistant Vice President, Nursing and Patient Care Services
Web address: www.carepointhealth.org
Control: Other not-for-profit (including NFP Corporation) **Service**: General medical and surgical

Staffed Beds: 376

★ ⇧ **JERSEY CITY MEDICAL CENTER (310074)**, 355 Grand Street, Zip 07302-4321; tel. 201/915-2000, **A**2 3 5 10 13 21 **F**3 5 6 7 8 11 13 15 17 18 20 22 24 26 29 30 31 34 35 38 39 40 41 42 43 45 46 47 48 49 50 54 55 56 57 59 60 61 64 65 66 68 70 71 72 73 74 75 76 77 78 79 81 82 84 85 87 89 91 92 93 96 97 98 100 101 102 104 105 106 107 108 110 111 112 114 115 118 119 126 129 130 132 143 146 147 148 149 150 152 153 154 156 157 158 162 163 164 165 167 169 **S** RWJBarnabas Health, West Orange, NJ
Primary Contact: Michael Prilutsky, President and Chief Executive Officer
CFO: Paul R Goldberg, Chief Financial Officer
CMO: Kenneth Garay, M.D., Chief Medical Officer
CIO: Stephen Li, Vice President Management Information Systems
CHR: Mary Cataudella, Corporate Director Human Resources
CNO: Joanne Reich, R.N., Chief Nursing Officer
Web address: www.barnabashealth.org/Jersey-City-Medical-Center.aspx
Control: Other not-for-profit (including NFP Corporation) **Service**: General medical and surgical

Staffed Beds: 352 **Admissions**: 15846 **Census**: 217 **Outpatient Visits**: 246062 **Births**: 2118 **Total Expense ($000)**: 550452 **Payroll Expense ($000)**: 196001 **Personnel**: 2245

LAKEWOOD—Ocean County

☒ **MONMOUTH MEDICAL CENTER, SOUTHERN CAMPUS (310084)**, 600 River Avenue, Zip 08701-5237; tel. 732/363-1900, **A**1 2 10 **F**3 11 12 15 18 28 29 30 31 34 35 36 38 40 41 44 49 50 51 55 56 57 58 59 60 63 64 65 66 68 70 71 74 75 77 78 79 81 82 84 85 87 92 93 97 98 100 101 102 103 104 107 108 110 112 115 116 117 119 130 131 132 135 143 145 146 148 149 154 156 157 162 164 165 167 **S** RWJBarnabas Health, West Orange, NJ
Primary Contact: Eric Carney, President and Chief Executive Officer
COO: Jonathan Tango, Vice President, Operations
CFO: Nikolas Alexiades, Chief Financial Officer
CMO: Rajesh Mohan, M.D., Chief Medical Officer
CIO: Ray Duarte, Director, Information Technology and Services
CHR: Richard Kiernan, Regional Chief Human Resources Officer
CNO: Judy Colorado, R.N., Chief Nursing Officer
Web address: www.rwjbarnabashealth.org/monmouth-medical-center-southern-campus.aspx
Control: Other not-for-profit (including NFP Corporation) **Service**: General medical and surgical

Staffed Beds: 132 **Admissions**: 5661 **Census**: 97 **Outpatient Visits**: 70437 **Births**: 0 **Total Expense ($000)**: 153470 **Payroll Expense ($000)**: 61400 **Personnel**: 575

☐ **SPECIALTY HOSPITAL OF CENTRAL JERSEY (312017)**, 600 River Avenue, 4 and 5 West, Zip 08701-5237; tel. 732/942-3588, (Nonreporting) **A**1 10
Primary Contact: Maureen Rogers, Executive Director
CFO: Kristin Prentiss, Chief Financial Officer
CMO: Howard Lebowitz, M.D., Chief Medical Officer
CHR: Mary Pat Napolitano, Director Human Resources
CNO: Judy Boccellato, R.N., MSN, Chief Nursing Officer
Web address: www.acutecarehs.com
Control: Corporation, Investor-owned (for-profit) **Service**: Acute long-term care hospital

Staffed Beds: 50

Hospitals, U.S. / NEW JERSEY

LAWRENCEVILLE—Mercer County

☐ **ST. LAWRENCE REHABILITATION HOSPITAL (313027)**, 2381 Lawrenceville Road, Zip 08648–2025; tel. 609/896–9500, (Nonreporting) **A**1 10
Primary Contact: Thomas W. Boyle, President and Chief Executive Officer
COO: Shirley Pukala, R.N., Assistant Administrator Operations
CMO: Kevin McGuigan, M.D., Medical Director
CIO: Joseph Castronuevo, Director Information Management
CHR: John Levi, Director Human Resources
CNO: Hsiu–chin Brix, R.N., Director of Nursing
Web address: https://lawrencerehabhospital.com
Control: Church operated, Nongovernment, not–for–profit **Service:** Rehabilitation

Staffed Beds: 116

LIVINGSTON—Essex County

⊞ **COOPERMAN BARNABAS MEDICAL CENTER (310076)**, 94 Old Short Hills Rd, Zip 07039–5672; tel. 973/322–5000, **A**1 2 3 5 8 10 13 **F**3 6 8 11 12 13 14 16 17 18 19 20 22 24 26 28 29 30 31 32 34 35 36 37 38 39 40 41 44 46 47 48 49 50 52 53 54 55 56 57 58 59 60 61 63 64 65 66 68 69 70 71 72 73 74 75 76 77 78 79 80 81 82 84 85 86 87 88 89 91 92 93 94 96 97 100 101 102 107 108 111 114 115 118 119 120 121 123 124 126 129 130 131 132 134 135 138 141 142 143 144 145 146 147 148 149 150 154 156 160 162 167 169 **P**6 **S** RWJBarnabas Health, West Orange, NJ
Primary Contact: Richard Davis, President and Chief Executive Officer
COO: Jennifer A O'Neill, R.N., Chief Operating Officer
CMO: Gregory Rokosz, D.O., Senior Vice President Medical and Academic Affairs
CIO: Michael McTigue, Chief Information Officer
CHR: Arnold D Manzo, Vice President Human Resources
CNO: Maggie Lundberg, R.N., Chief Nursing Officer
Web address: www.barnabashealth.org/hospitals/saint_barnabas/index.html
Control: Other not–for–profit (including NFP Corporation) **Service:** General medical and surgical

Staffed Beds: 565 **Admissions:** 30431 **Census:** 491 **Outpatient Visits:** 325063 **Births:** 6383 **Total Expense ($000):** 1168446 **Payroll Expense ($000):** 365218 **Personnel:** 3754

SAINT BARNABAS MEDICAL CENTER See Cooperman Barnabas Medical Center

LONG BRANCH—Monmouth County

⊞ **MONMOUTH MEDICAL CENTER, LONG BRANCH CAMPUS (310075)**, 300 Second Avenue, Zip 07740–6303; tel. 732/222–5200, (Includes CHILDREN'S HOSPITAL AT MONMOUTH MEDICAL CENTER, 300 Second Avenue, Long Branch, New Jersey, Zip 07740–6303, tel. 732/222-5200) **A**1 2 3 5 8 10 **F**3 9 11 12 13 15 18 20 22 28 29 30 31 34 35 37 38 39 40 41 44 45 46 47 48 49 50 51 54 55 56 57 58 59 60 61 63 64 66 68 70 72 73 74 75 76 77 78 79 81 82 84 85 86 87 88 89 96 97 98 99 100 101 102 104 105 107 108 109 110 111 114 115 117 118 119 120 121 123 124 126 129 130 132 135 141 143 145 146 147 148 149 153 154 156 157 162 164 165 167 169 **S** RWJBarnabas Health, West Orange, NJ
Primary Contact: Eric Carney, President and Chief Executive Officer
CMO: Eric Burkett, M.D., Vice President Medical Affairs
CIO: Chris Butler, Chief Information Officer
CHR: Richard Kiernan, Vice President Human Resources
CNO: Diann Johnston, R.N., MSN, Vice President of Patient Care Services
Web address: www.barnabashealth.org/hospitals/monmouth_medical/index.html
Control: Other not–for–profit (including NFP Corporation) **Service:** General medical and surgical

Staffed Beds: 303 **Admissions:** 18215 **Census:** 207 **Outpatient Visits:** 191313 **Births:** 6722 **Total Expense ($000):** 500446 **Payroll Expense ($000):** 194075 **Personnel:** 2017

THE CHILDREN'S HOSPITAL AT MONMOUTH MEDICAL CENTER See Children's Hospital At Monmouth Medical Center

LYONS—Somerset County

LYONS DIVISION See Veterans Affairs New Jersey Health Care System, East Orange

VETERANS AFFAIRS NEW JERSEY HEALTH CARE SYSTEM See Lyons Division

MADISON—Morris County

ATLANTIC REHABILITATION INSTITUTE (313038), 4 Giralda Farms, Zip 07940; tel. 973/549–7440, **A**10 **F**3 29 35 68 87 90 91 95 96 130 132 148 149 154 164 **P**5 **S** Atlantic Health System, Morristown, NJ
Primary Contact: Saif Salim, Chief Executive Officer
CFO: Donna Kutasinski–Martin, Controller
CMO: Joseph Rempson, Medical Director
CHR: Victor Vena, Director of Human Resources
CNO: Alissa Getts, Chief Nursing Officer
Web address: www.AtlanticRehabInstitute.com
Control: Partnership, Investor–owned (for–profit) **Service:** Rehabilitation

Staffed Beds: 38 **Admissions:** 999 **Census:** 33 **Outpatient Visits:** 0 **Births:** 0 **Total Expense ($000):** 18470 **Payroll Expense ($000):** 8910 **Personnel:** 115

MANAHAWKIN—Ocean County

⊞ **HACKENSACK MERIDIAN HEALTH SOUTHERN OCEAN MEDICAL CENTER (310113)**, 1140 Route 72 West, Zip 08050–2499; tel. 609/597–6011, **A**1 2 5 10 **F**3 11 12 13 18 20 22 26 28 29 30 31 32 34 35 36 38 39 40 44 45 46 47 48 49 50 51 54 55 56 57 58 59 60 61 63 64 65 66 68 70 71 74 75 76 77 78 79 81 82 84 85 86 87 92 93 94 96 97 100 101 102 107 108 110 111 114 115 116 119 120 121 123 126 128 130 131 132 134 135 145 146 147 148 149 154 156 164 167 169 **S** Hackensack Meridian Health, Edison, NJ
Primary Contact: Michele Morrison, R.N., M.P.H., President and Chief Hospital Executive
CFO: Joseph M Lemaire, Executive Vice President
CMO: Theodore Zaleski, M.D., Vice President Clinical Effectiveness
CIO: Rebecca Weber, Senior Vice President and Chief Information Officer
CHR: Susan Tillman–Taylor, Manager Human Resources
CNO: Donna Ciufo, R.N., Vice President and Chief Nurse Executive
Web address: www.soch.com
Control: Other not–for–profit (including NFP Corporation) **Service:** General medical and surgical

Staffed Beds: 156 **Admissions:** 8528 **Census:** 98 **Outpatient Visits:** 112710 **Births:** 385 **Total Expense ($000):** 226953 **Payroll Expense ($000):** 93221 **Personnel:** 857

MARLTON—Burlington County

⊞ △ **KESSLER MARLTON REHABILITATION (313032)**, 92 Brick Road, Zip 08053–2177; tel. 856/988–8778, **A**1 7 10 **F**3 28 29 34 35 36 44 53 57 58 64 68 74 75 77 78 79 82 84 85 86 87 90 91 92 93 94 95 96 100 119 130 131 132 148 149 154 164 **S** Select Medical Corporation, Mechanicsburg, PA
Primary Contact: Kenneth Turley, Chief Executive Officer
CFO: Stuart Moss, Chief Financial Officer
CMO: Kenneth Wu, M.D., Medical Director
CHR: Joanne Cernava, Director Human Resources
CNO: Chris Kreeley, Director Nursing
Web address: www.marltonrehab.com
Control: Corporation, Investor–owned (for–profit) **Service:** Rehabilitation

Staffed Beds: 61 **Admissions:** 1573 **Census:** 59 **Outpatient Visits:** 12437 **Births:** 0 **Personnel:** 288

⊞ **VIRTUA MARLTON**, 90 Brick Road, Zip 08053–2177; tel. 856/355–6000, **A**1 3 5 **F**3 4 12 18 20 22 26 29 30 31 34 40 45 46 47 49 50 55 59 60 61 64 70 74 75 77 78 79 80 81 85 87 92 93 96 100 107 108 111 115 118 119 126 130 146 148 149 154 167 168 **S** Virtua Health, Marlton, NJ
Primary Contact: Dennis W. Pullin, FACHE, President and Chief Executive Officer
CFO: Robert Segin, Executive Vice President & Chief Financial Officer
CMO: John Matsinger, D.O., Chief Medical Officer
CIO: Thomas Gordon, Chief Information Officer
CHR: Rhonda R Jordan, Chief Human Resources Officer
Web address: www.virtua.org
Control: Other not–for–profit (including NFP Corporation) **Service:** General medical and surgical

Staffed Beds: 187 **Admissions:** 8002 **Census:** 111 **Outpatient Visits:** 41429 **Births:** 0 **Total Expense ($000):** 168399 **Payroll Expense ($000):** 59894 **Personnel:** 651

Hospital, Medicare Provider Number, Address, Telephone, Approval, Facility, and Physician Codes, Health Care System

★ American Hospital Association (AHA) membership ○ Healthcare Facilities Accreditation Program ⇧ Center for Improvement in Healthcare Quality Accreditation
☐ The Joint Commission accreditation ◇ DNV Healthcare Inc. accreditation △ Commission on Accreditation of Rehabilitation Facilities (CARF) accreditation

Hospitals, U.S. / NEW JERSEY

☐ **WEISMAN CHILDREN'S REHABILITATION HOSPITAL (313302)**, 92 Brick Road 3rd Floor, Zip 08053–2177; tel. 856/489–4520, (Nonreporting) **A**1 3 10
Primary Contact: Patricia Oliver, Administrator
CMO: Connie Domingo, M.D., Medical Director
CIO: Darren Pedersen, Coordinator Information Technology
CHR: Jill Koerner, Manager Employee Relations
CNO: Daniel William Pfeffer, Chief Nurse Executive
Web address: www.weismanchildrens.com
Control: Corporation, Investor–owned (for–profit) **Service:** Children's rehabilitation

Staffed Beds: 24

MONTCLAIR—Essex County

✠ **HACKENSACK MERIDIAN MOUNTAINSIDE MEDICAL CENTER (310054)**, 1 Bay Avenue, Zip 07042–4898; tel. 973/429–6000, **A**1 2 3 5 10 **F**3 12 13 15 17 18 20 22 24 28 29 30 31 32 34 35 38 39 40 44 45 46 47 48 49 50 51 52 54 55 56 57 58 59 60 64 65 68 70 73 74 75 76 77 78 79 80 81 82 84 85 86 87 93 94 96 97 98 100 101 102 103 104 105 107 108 110 111 114 115 116 117 118 119 121 124 126 129 130 131 132 135 141 144 146 147 148 149 153 154 157 164 167 169 **P**5 **S** Ardent Health Services, Nashville, TN
Primary Contact: Tim O'Brien, Chief Executive Officer
COO: Valarie McPherson, MSN, R.N., Chief Operating Officer and Chief Nursing Officer
CFO: Linda Chen, Chief Financial Officer
CMO: Valerie Alluson, M.D., Chief Medical Officer
CIO: Max Siu, Chief Information Officer
CNO: Valarie McPherson, MSN, R.N., Chief Operating Officer and Chief Nursing Officer
Web address: www.mountainsidenow.com
Control: Partnership, Investor–owned (for–profit) **Service:** General medical and surgical

Staffed Beds: 184 **Admissions:** 9820 **Census:** 122 **Outpatient Visits:** 140670 **Births:** 900 **Total Expense ($000):** 256089 **Payroll Expense ($000):** 100068 **Personnel:** 1149

MORRIS PLAINS—Morris County

☐ **GREYSTONE PARK PSYCHIATRIC HOSPITAL (314016)**, 59 Koch Avenue, Zip 07950–4400; tel. 973/538–1800, **A**1 3 5 10 **F**30 39 68 77 87 98 103 130 132 135 143 146 149 154 163 164 **S** Division of Mental Health and Addiction Services, Department of Human Services, State of New Jersey, Trenton, NJ
Primary Contact: Joshua Belsky, Chief Executive Officer
COO: Stacey Provenzano, Chief Operating Officer
CFO: Jack Frey, Acting Business Manager
CMO: Cherry Monroy-Miller, M.D., Acting Medical Director
CIO: David Saleem, Director Information Technology
CHR: James Frey Jr, Acting Manager Human Resources
Web address: https://www.state.nj.us/humanservices/involved/nurses/mentalhph/greystone.html
Control: State, Government, Nonfederal **Service:** Psychiatric

Staffed Beds: 468 **Admissions:** 167 **Census:** 396 **Outpatient Visits:** 0 **Births:** 0 **Total Expense ($000):** 111837 **Payroll Expense ($000):** 87855 **Personnel:** 1220

MORRISTOWN—Morris County

✠ **MORRISTOWN MEDICAL CENTER (310015)**, 100 Madison Avenue, Zip 07960–6136; tel. 973/971–5000, (Includes GORYEB CHILDREN'S HOSPITAL, 100 Madison Avenue, Morristown, New Jersey, Zip 07960–6136, tel. 973/971–5000) **A**1 2 3 5 10 **F**3 5 6 8 9 11 12 13 15 17 18 19 20 22 24 26 28 29 30 31 32 33 34 35 36 37 38 39 40 41 43 44 45 46 47 48 49 50 51 52 53 54 55 56 57 58 59 60 61 64 65 66 68 70 72 73 74 75 76 77 78 79 81 82 83 84 85 86 87 88 89 91 92 93 94 95 96 97 98 100 101 102 103 104 107 108 110 111 115 117 118 119 120 121 123 124 126 129 130 131 132 134 135 141 143 145 146 147 148 149 150 153 154 156 157 160 162 164 165 167 169 **S** Atlantic Health System, Morristown, NJ
Primary Contact: Trish O'Keefe, Ph.D., R.N., President
CFO: Joseph D'Auria, Director Finance
CNO: Carol S. Jones, MSN, R.N., Interim Chief Nursing Officer
Web address: www.atlantichealth.org/Morristown/
Control: Other not–for–profit (including NFP Corporation) **Service:** General medical and surgical

Staffed Beds: 746 **Admissions:** 38926 **Census:** 621 **Outpatient Visits:** 759331 **Births:** 5347 **Total Expense ($000):** 2101526 **Payroll Expense ($000):** 968821 **Personnel:** 9503

MOUNT HOLLY—Burlington County

VIRTUA MEMORIAL See Virtua Mount Holly Hospital

✠ **VIRTUA MOUNT HOLLY HOSPITAL (310057)**, 175 Madison Avenue, Zip 08060–2099; tel. 609/267–0700, **A**1 3 5 10 **F**3 4 11 12 13 15 18 19 20 21 22 26 28 29 30 31 34 40 41 45 46 48 50 54 55 58 59 60 61 64 70 73 74 75 76 77 78 79 80 81 82 85 87 89 91 92 93 96 98 100 101 102 107 108 110 111 118 119 120 121 123 126 129 130 135 145 146 147 148 149 154 164 167 168 169 **S** Virtua Health, Marlton, NJ
Primary Contact: Dennis W. Pullin, FACHE, President and Chief Executive Officer
CFO: Robert Segin, Chief Financial Officer
CMO: James P Dwyer, D.O., Executive Vice President and Chief Medical Officer
CHR: E D Dunn, Vice President Human Resources
Web address: www.virtua.org
Control: Other not–for–profit (including NFP Corporation) **Service:** General medical and surgical

Staffed Beds: 334 **Admissions:** 15403 **Census:** 192 **Outpatient Visits:** 154827 **Births:** 1937 **Total Expense ($000):** 384242 **Payroll Expense ($000):** 128542 **Personnel:** 1365

MULLICA HILL—Gloucester County

★ ⇑ **INSPIRA MEDICAL CENTER MULLICA HILL (310069)**, 700 Mullica Hill Road, Zip 08062–4413; tel. 856/508–1000, (Includes INSPIRA MEDICAL CENTER MANNINGTON, 310 Woodstown Road, Salem, New Jersey, Zip 08079–2080, tel. 856/935–1000; Amy B. Mansue, President and Chief Executive Officer; INSPIRA MEDICAL CENTER–ELMER, 501 West Front Street, Elmer, New Jersey, Zip 08318–2101, tel. 856/363–1000; Amy B. Mansue, President and Chief Executive Officer) **A**3 21 **F**1 3 4 13 15 16 17 18 20 22 28 29 30 31 32 34 35 40 42 45 46 47 49 50 51 57 58 59 64 66 67 70 72 73 74 75 76 78 80 81 82 84 87 88 89 90 98 101 102 107 108 110 111 114 115 116 117 118 119 120 121 123 124 126 128 130 132 135 145 146 147 148 149 154 156 161 164 166 167 168 169 **S** Inspira Health Network, Mullica Hill, NJ
Primary Contact: Amy B. Mansue, President and Chief Executive Officer
Web address: https://www.inspirahealthnetwork.org/MullicaHill
Control: Other not–for–profit (including NFP Corporation) **Service:** General medical and surgical

Staffed Beds: 309 **Admissions:** 14459 **Census:** 190 **Outpatient Visits:** 200442 **Births:** 1527 **Total Expense ($000):** 468812 **Payroll Expense ($000):** 190357 **Personnel:** 2484

NEPTUNE—Monmouth County

✠ **HACKENSACK MERIDIAN HEALTH JERSEY SHORE UNIVERSITY MEDICAL CENTER (310073)**, 1945 Route 33, Zip 07754–0397; tel. 732/775–5500, (Includes K. HOVNANIAN CHILDREN'S HOSPITAL, 1945 State Route 33, Neptune, New Jersey, Zip 07753–4859, tel. 800/560–9990) **A**1 2 3 5 8 10 **F**3 5 6 9 11 12 13 14 15 16 17 18 19 20 22 24 26 28 29 30 31 32 34 35 36 37 38 39 40 41 43 44 45 46 47 49 50 51 52 54 55 56 57 58 59 60 61 63 64 65 66 68 69 70 71 72 73 74 75 76 77 78 79 80 81 82 84 85 86 87 88 89 91 92 93 94 96 97 98 99 100 101 102 103 104 105 107 108 109 111 112 114 115 116 117 118 119 120 121 123 124 126 129 130 131 132 134 135 136 141 142 143 144 145 146 147 148 149 150 151 152 153 154 156 157 160 161 162 163 164 165 167 168 169 **S** Hackensack Meridian Health, Edison, NJ
Primary Contact: Vito Buccellato, Chief Hospital Executive
COO: Robert H Adams, Vice President Operations
CMO: David Kountz, M.D., Senior Vice President Medical Affairs
CIO: Rebecca Weber, Senior Vice President and Chief Information Officer
Web address: www.meridianhealth.com
Control: Other not–for–profit (including NFP Corporation) **Service:** General medical and surgical

Staffed Beds: 622 **Admissions:** 29279 **Census:** 492 **Outpatient Visits:** 273161 **Births:** 3512 **Total Expense ($000):** 1298286 **Payroll Expense ($000):** 523923 **Personnel:** 4131

NEW BRUNSWICK—Middlesex County

☐ **CHILDREN'S SPECIALIZED HOSPITAL (313300)**, 200 Somerset Street, Zip 08901–1942; tel. 732/258–7000, (Includes CHILDREN'S SPECIALIZED HOSPITAL, 200 Somerset Street, New Brunswick, New Jersey, Zip 08901–1942, tel. 732/258–7134; Matthew B. McDonald III, President and Chief Executive Officer) (Total facility includes 89 beds in nursing home–type unit) **A**1 3 5 10 **F**29 32 35 54 64 65 74 78 82 90 91 93 94 97 104 130 132 146 154 **S** RWJBarnabas Health, West Orange, NJ
Primary Contact: Matthew B. McDonald III, President and Chief Executive Officer
COO: Charles Chianese, Vice President, Chief Operating Officer
CFO: Joseph J Dobosh Jr, Vice President and Chief Financial Officer
CMO: Colin O'Reilly, D.O., Vice President and Chief Medical Officer
CHR: Lisa Knothe, Vice President, Chief Human Resources Officer
CNO: Kelly Keefe Marcoux, MSN, Vice President, Patient Care Services and Chief Nursing Officer
Web address: www.childrens-specialized.org
Control: Other not–for–profit (including NFP Corporation) **Service:** Children's rehabilitation

Staffed Beds: 158 **Admissions:** 569 **Census:** 119 **Outpatient Visits:** 252812 **Births:** 0 **Total Expense ($000):** 189550 **Payroll Expense ($000):** 110096 **Personnel:** 1406

Hospitals, U.S. / NEW JERSEY

✠ **ROBERT WOOD JOHNSON UNIVERSITY HOSPITAL (310038)**, 1 Robert Wood Johnson Place, Zip 08903–2601; tel. 732/828–3000, (Includes BRISTOL–MYERS SQUIBB CHILDREN'S HOSPITAL, One Robert Wood Johnson PL, New Brunswick, New Jersey, Zip 08901–1928, P.O. Box 2601, Zip 08903–2601, tel. 732/828–3000) **A**1 2 3 5 8 10 **F**3 5 6 7 9 11 12 13 14 17 18 19 20 22 24 26 28 29 30 31 32 34 35 37 38 39 40 41 43 44 45 46 47 48 49 50 51 52 53 54 55 56 57 58 59 60 61 62 63 64 65 66 68 70 72 73 74 75 76 77 79 81 82 84 85 86 87 88 89 91 92 93 94 96 97 100 101 102 104 107 108 109 110 111 112 114 115 116 117 118 119 120 121 122 123 124 126 130 131 132 134 135 136 137 138 141 142 143 144 145 146 147 148 149 150 154 155 156 157 158 164 167 168 169 **S** RWJBarnabas Health, West Orange, NJ
Primary Contact: Bill Arnold, Executive Vice President, RWJBarnabas Health, President Southern Region, Chief Executive Officer, Ro
CFO: Brian M Reilly, Chief Financial Officer
CMO: Stanley Trooskin, M.D., Chief Medical Officer
CIO: Robert G Irwin, Vice President Information Systems
CHR: Martin S Everhart, Senior Vice President Human Resources
CNO: Courtney Vose, R.N., Senior Vice President, Chief Nursing Officer
Web address: www.rwjuh.edu
Control: Other not–for–profit (including NFP Corporation) **Service**: General medical and surgical

Staffed Beds: 660 **Admissions:** 33035 **Census:** 557 **Outpatient Visits:** 311517 **Births:** 2497 **Total Expense ($000):** 1786819 **Payroll Expense ($000):** 673494 **Personnel:** 5371

✠ **SAINT PETER'S HEALTHCARE SYSTEM (310070)**, 254 Easton Avenue, Zip 08901–1780; tel. 732/745–8600, (Includes THE CHILDREN'S HOSPITAL AT SAINT PETER'S UNIVERSITY, 254 Easton Avenue, New Brunswick, New Jersey, Zip 08901–1766, tel. 732/565–5437) **A**1 2 3 5 8 10 **F**3 12 13 15 17 19 20 22 26 27 29 30 31 32 34 35 37 38 39 40 41 44 45 46 47 49 50 51 54 55 56 57 58 59 60 61 63 64 65 66 67 68 70 71 72 73 74 75 76 77 78 79 81 82 83 84 85 86 87 88 89 91 92 93 94 96 97 100 101 102 104 105 107 108 110 111 114 115 118 119 120 121 123 124 126 129 130 131 132 134 135 143 145 146 147 148 149 150 153 154 156 157 167 169 **P**6
Primary Contact: Leslie D. Hirsch, FACHE, President and Chief Executive Officer
CFO: Garrick J Stoldt, Vice President and Chief Financial Officer
CIO: Jordan Tannenbaum, Chief Information Officer and Chief Medical Information Officer
CHR: Harry Dieuveuil, Vice President and Chief Human Resources Officer
CNO: Linda Carroll, Chief Nursing Officer and Vice President, Patient Care Services
Web address: https://www.saintpetershcs.com/
Control: Church operated, Nongovernment, not–for–profit **Service**: General medical and surgical

Staffed Beds: 352 **Admissions:** 18149 **Census:** 234 **Outpatient Visits:** 286235 **Births:** 5637 **Total Expense ($000):** 565069 **Payroll Expense ($000):** 280624 **Personnel:** 2898

SAINT PETER'S UNIVERSITY HOSPITAL See Saint Peter's Healthcare System

THE BRISTOL–MYERS SQUIBB CHILDREN'S HOSPITAL See Bristol–Myers Squibb Children's Hospital

NEW LISBON—Burlington County

BUTTONWOOD HOSPITAL OF BURLINGTON See Aspen Hills Healthcare Center

NEWARK—Essex County

⇑ **COLUMBUS HOSPITAL LTACH** See Silver Lake Hospital Ltach

✠ **NEWARK BETH ISRAEL MEDICAL CENTER (310002)**, 201 Lyons Avenue at Osborne Terrace, Zip 07112–2027; tel. 973/926–7000, (Includes CHILDREN'S HOSPITAL OF NEW JERSEY, 201 Lyons Avenue, Newark, New Jersey, Zip 07112–2027, tel. 973/926–7000; Darrell K. Terry Sr, M.P.H., FACHE, President and Chief Executive Officer) **A**1 2 3 5 8 10 12 13 **F**3 12 13 14 15 17 18 19 20 21 22 23 24 25 26 27 28 29 30 31 32 34 35 37 38 39 40 41 44 45 46 47 48 49 50 53 55 56 57 58 59 60 61 64 65 66 68 70 71 72 73 74 75 76 77 78 79 80 81 82 84 85 86 87 88 89 91 92 93 94 97 98 99 100 101 102 104 107 108 109 110 111 114 115 117 118 119 120 121 123 126 129 130 131 132 135 137 140 141 143 145 146 147 148 149 153 154 156 157 162 164 165 167 169 **S** RWJBarnabas Health, West Orange, NJ
Primary Contact: Darrell K. Terry Sr, M.P.H., FACHE, President and Chief Executive Officer
CFO: Deborah Dente, Site Finance Officer
CMO: Jeremias Murillo, M.D., Chief Medical Officer
CHR: Zach Lipner, Vice President Human Resources
CNO: Mary Fuhro, Chief Nursing Officer
Web address: www.barnabashealth.org/hospitals/newark_beth_israel/index.html
Control: Other not–for–profit (including NFP Corporation) **Service**: General medical and surgical

Staffed Beds: 356 **Admissions:** 18886 **Census:** 363 **Outpatient Visits:** 286413 **Births:** 2772 **Total Expense ($000):** 810968 **Payroll Expense ($000):** 352203 **Personnel:** 3116

☐ **SAINT MICHAEL'S MEDICAL CENTER (310096)**, 111 Central Avenue, Zip 07102–1909; tel. 973/877–5000, (Nonreporting) **A**1 3 5 10 13 **S** Prime Healthcare, Ontario, CA
Primary Contact: Alan Sickles, M.D., Chief Executive Officer
COO: Dennis Pettigrew, Chief Operating Officer
CFO: Carolyn Allen, Chief Financial Officer
CMO: Claudia Komer, M.D., Chief Medical Officer
CIO: Tom Addington, Chief Information Officer
CHR: Dennis W. Sparks, Vice President Human Resources
CNO: Nancy Bisco–Flora, Chief Nursing Officer
Web address: https://www.smmcnj.com/
Control: Church operated, Nongovernment, not–for–profit **Service**: General medical and surgical

Staffed Beds: 147

⇑ **SILVER LAKE HOSPITAL LTACH (312024)**, 495 North Thirteenth Street, Zip 07107–1317; tel. 973/587–7777, (Nonreporting) **A**10 21
Primary Contact: Karli Kohut, President and Chief Executive Officer
CFO: Alexey Gololobov, Chief Financial Officer
CHR: Patrice Ricciardi, Director Human Resources
CNO: Arthur Kharonov, Vice President Nursing
Web address: www.silverlakehospital.org
Control: Corporation, Investor–owned (for–profit) **Service**: Acute long–term care hospital

Staffed Beds: 63

✠ **UNIVERSITY HOSPITAL (310119)**, 150 Bergen Street, Zip 07103–2496; tel. 973/972–4300, **A**1 2 3 5 8 10 **F**3 5 7 8 11 12 13 15 17 18 20 22 24 26 28 29 30 31 32 34 35 37 39 40 41 43 44 45 46 47 49 50 51 55 56 57 58 59 60 61 64 65 66 68 70 71 72 74 75 76 77 78 79 81 82 83 84 85 87 88 89 92 93 94 97 98 100 101 102 105 107 108 110 111 114 115 116 117 118 119 120 121 123 124 126 130 131 135 139 143 146 147 148 149 150 154 156 157 160 161 163 167 169
Primary Contact: Edward Jimenez, President and Chief Executive Officer
COO: Nancy Hamstra, Chief Operating Officer
CFO: Thomas M Daly, CPA, Chief Financial Officer
CMO: William Holubek, M.D., Chief Medical Officer
CIO: Richard Tunnell, Chief Information Officer
CHR: Gerard Garcia, Chief Human Resource Officer
CNO: Carl Kirton, Ph.D., Chief Nursing Officer
Web address: www.uhnj.org
Control: State, Government, Nonfederal **Service**: General medical and surgical

Staffed Beds: 411 **Admissions:** 17579 **Census:** 306 **Outpatient Visits:** 350387 **Births:** 1477 **Total Expense ($000):** 830320 **Payroll Expense ($000):** 403883 **Personnel:** 3528

Hospitals, U.S. / NEW JERSEY

NEWTON—Sussex County

NEWTON MEDICAL CENTER (310028), 175 High Street, Zip 07860-1004; tel. 973/383-2121, **A**1 2 10 **F**3 5 8 11 12 13 15 18 19 20 22 28 29 30 31 32 34 35 36 38 40 41 44 45 47 49 50 52 53 54 56 57 59 60 63 64 65 68 69 70 73 74 75 76 77 78 79 80 81 82 84 85 86 87 91 92 93 94 96 98 100 101 102 104 107 108 110 115 116 117 118 119 120 130 132 134 135 141 146 148 154 156 164 165 167 169 **S** Atlantic Health System, Morristown, NJ
Primary Contact: Robert H. Adams, President, Western Region
CFO: Kevin Lenahan, Director Corporate Accounting, Budgets, Grants and Reimbursements
CMO: Geralda Xavier, M.D., Chief Medical Officer
CIO: Linda Reed, Vice President Information Systems and Chief Information Officer
CHR: Andrew L Kovach, Vice President Human Resources and Chief Administrative Officer
Web address: www.atlantichealth.org/newton/
Control: Other not-for-profit (including NFP Corporation) **Service**: General medical and surgical

Staffed Beds: 154 **Admissions**: 7414 **Census**: 111 **Outpatient Visits**: 100031 **Births**: 498 **Total Expense ($000)**: 240112 **Payroll Expense ($000)**: 122526 **Personnel**: 1210

NORTH BERGEN—Hudson County

HACKENSACK MERIDIAN HEALTH PALISADES MEDICAL CENTER (310003), 7600 River Road, Zip 07047-6217; tel. 201/854-5000, **A**1 3 5 10 12 13 **F**3 7 11 12 13 15 18 26 29 30 34 35 38 39 40 44 45 46 49 50 54 56 57 59 60 63 64 65 68 70 73 74 75 76 77 78 79 81 82 85 87 92 93 94 97 100 101 102 104 107 108 110 111 115 119 129 130 131 132 141 143 146 147 148 149 154 156 157 162 164 167 169 **S** Hackensack Meridian Health, Edison, NJ
Primary Contact: Lisa Iachetti, President and Chief Hospital Executive
COO: David J Berkowitz, Vice President and Chief Operating Officer
CFO: John Calandriello, Vice President and Chief Financial Officer
CMO: Suresh Raina, M.D., Vice President Medical Staff and Chief Medical Officer
CIO: Albert Porco, Director Management Information Systems
CNO: Ruben D Fernandez, R.N., Vice President and Chief Nursing Officer
Web address: www.palisadesmedical.org
Control: Other not-for-profit (including NFP Corporation) **Service**: General medical and surgical

Staffed Beds: 168 **Admissions**: 5870 **Census**: 73 **Outpatient Visits**: 102710 **Births**: 829 **Total Expense ($000)**: 207791 **Payroll Expense ($000)**: 104598 **Personnel**: 980

OLD BRIDGE—Middlesex County

OLD BRIDGE DIVISION See Old Bridge Medical Center

PARAMUS—Bergen County

BERGEN NEW BRIDGE MEDICAL CENTER (310058), 230 East Ridgewood Avenue, Zip 07652-4142; tel. 201/967-4000, (Total facility includes 574 beds in nursing home-type unit) **A**1 3 5 10 **F**1 3 4 5 6 7 8 10 12 15 17 18 20 22 28 29 30 32 34 35 38 40 44 45 46 50 56 57 59 61 64 65 66 68 70 71 74 75 77 81 82 85 86 87 90 92 93 97 98 99 100 101 102 103 104 105 106 107 108 109 110 111 114 115 118 119 128 130 132 133 134 135 146 147 148 149 150 152 153 154 156 160 163 164 165 167 **P**5
Primary Contact: Deborah D. Visconi, MS, President and Chief Executive Officer
COO: Susan Mendelowitz, R.N., FACHE, Executive Vice President and Chief Operating Officer
CFO: Connie Magdangal, Executive Vice President and Chief Financial Officer
CMO: Robert M Harris, M.D., President Medical and Dental Staff
CIO: Ronald Li, Vice President Management Information Systems
CHR: Guy Mennonna, Senior Vice President Human Resources
Web address: www.bergenregional.com
Control: Hospital district or authority, Government, Nonfederal **Service**: Acute long-term care hospital

Staffed Beds: 1020 **Admissions**: 10018 **Census**: 701 **Outpatient Visits**: 246865 **Births**: 0 **Total Expense ($000)**: 259237 **Payroll Expense ($000)**: 141813 **Personnel**: 1483

VALLEY HOSPITAL (310012), 4 Valley Health Plaza, Zip 07652; tel. 201/447-8000, **A**1 2 3 10 **F**3 7 8 11 12 13 15 17 18 19 20 22 24 26 28 29 30 31 32 34 35 36 37 38 40 41 44 45 46 47 48 49 50 51 52 53 54 55 56 57 58 59 60 61 64 65 66 68 70 71 72 73 74 75 76 77 78 79 80 81 82 83 84 85 86 87 88 89 91 92 93 94 96 97 100 102 107 108 110 111 115 117 118 119 120 121 123 124 126 129 130 131 132 134 135 141 143 145 146 147 148 149 154 156 164 167 169
Primary Contact: Robert William. Brenner, M.D., FACHE, President and Chief Executive Officer, President, Valley Health
COO: Peter Diestel, Senior Vice President and Chief Operating Officer
CFO: Richard Keenan, Senior Vice President Finance and Chief Financial Officer
CMO: Joseph Yallowitz, M.D., Vice President and Chief Medical Officer
CIO: Eric R Carey, Vice President Information Systems and Chief Information Officer
CHR: Jose Balderrama, Vice President Human Resources
CNO: Charles Vannoy, R.N., Vice President Patient Care Services and Chief Nursing Officer
Web address: www.valleyhealth.com
Control: Other not-for-profit (including NFP Corporation) **Service**: General medical and surgical

Staffed Beds: 446 **Admissions**: 28735 **Census**: 327 **Outpatient Visits**: 376807 **Births**: 3602 **Total Expense ($000)**: 877781 **Payroll Expense ($000)**: 326071 **Personnel**: 4061

PASSAIC—Passaic County

KINDRED HOSPITAL EAST NEW JERSEY See Kindred Hospital-New Jersey Morris County, Dover

KINDRED HOSPITAL NEW JERSEY – WAYNE See Kindred Hospital East New Jersey

ST. MARY'S GENERAL HOSPITAL (310006), 350 Boulevard, Zip 07055-2840; tel. 973/365-4300, (Nonreporting) **A**1 3 5 10 **S** Prime Healthcare, Ontario, CA
Primary Contact: Edward Condit, President and Chief Executive Officer
CFO: Nicholas Lanza, Controller
CMO: Ronald Poblete, M.D., President Medical and Dental Staff
CHR: Cathy Lynch-Kilic, Vice President Human Resources
Web address: www.smh-passaic.org
Control: Other not-for-profit (including NFP Corporation) **Service**: General medical and surgical

Staffed Beds: 287

PATERSON—Passaic County

★ ⇑ **ST. JOSEPH'S UNIVERSITY MEDICAL CENTER (310019)**, 703 Main Street, Zip 07503-2691; tel. 973/754-2000, (Includes ST. JOSEPH'S CHILDREN'S HOSPITAL, 703 Main Street, Paterson, New Jersey, Zip 07503-2621, tel. 973/754-2500; Dustin Riccio, M.D., President and Chief Executive Officer; ST. JOSEPH'S WAYNE HOSPITAL, 224 Hamburg Turnpike, Wayne, New Jersey, Zip 07470-2100, tel. 973/942-6900; Daniel B Kline, Vice President, Site Administrator) (Nonreporting) **A**2 3 5 10 13 21
Primary Contact: Dustin Riccio, M.D., President and Chief Executive Officer
CFO: David Alexander, Senior Vice President and Chief Financial Officer
CMO: James Labagnara, M.D., Vice President Medical Affairs
CIO: Linda Reed, Vice President and Chief Information Officer
CHR: John P Bruno, Senior Vice President Human Resources
CNO: Judy Padula, MSN, R.N., Vice President Patient Care Services and Chief Nursing Officer
Web address: www.stjosephshealth.org
Control: Church operated, Nongovernment, not-for-profit **Service**: General medical and surgical

Staffed Beds: 995

PEAPACK—Somerset County

MATHENY MEDICAL AND EDUCATIONAL CENTER (312014), 65 Highland Avenue, Zip 07977, Mailing Address: P.O. Box 339, Zip 07977-0339; tel. 908/234-0011, **A**1 10 **F**2 29 30 33 39 64 79 84 89 91 93 94 97 100 130 143 146 147 149
Primary Contact: William Kent, President and Chief Executive Officer
COO: Christopher King, Director Operations and Administrative Services
CFO: Wayne Guberman, Director Finance
CMO: Gary E Eddey, M.D., Medical Director
CIO: Ron Daniel, Manager Information Systems
CHR: Nancy Petrillo, Director Human Resources
Web address: www.matheny.org
Control: Other not-for-profit (including NFP Corporation) **Service**: Rehabilitation

Staffed Beds: 101 **Admissions**: 8 **Census**: 99 **Outpatient Visits**: 0 **Personnel**: 601

Hospitals, U.S. / NEW JERSEY

PENNINGTON—Mercer County

★ ⇑ **CAPITAL HEALTH MEDICAL CENTER–HOPEWELL (310044)**, 1 Capital Way, Zip 08534–2520; tel. 609/303–4000, **A** 2 3 5 10 21 **F** 3 12 13 15 18 20 22 28 29 30 31 34 35 37 40 41 42 44 45 46 47 48 49 50 51 53 54 55 56 57 58 59 60 61 64 65 68 70 72 73 74 75 76 77 78 79 81 82 84 85 86 87 91 92 93 96 97 100 101 102 104 107 108 110 111 112 115 117 118 119 120 121 123 124 126 129 130 132 135 143 145 146 147 148 149 150 154 156 157 162 169 **P**6 **S** Capital Health, Trenton, NJ
Primary Contact: Al Maghazehe, Ph.D., FACHE, President and Chief Executive Officer
CFO: Shane Fleming, Chief Financial Officer
CMO: Eugene McMahon, Senior Vice President and Chief Medical Officer
CIO: Eugene Grochala, Vice President Information Systems
CHR: Scott Clemmensen, Vice President Human Resources and Leadership Enhancement
CNO: Deborah Mican, R.N., Chief Nursing Officer
Web address: www.capitalhealth.org
Control: Other not–for–profit (including NFP Corporation) **Service**: General medical and surgical

Staffed Beds: 220 **Admissions**: 15125 **Census**: 183 **Outpatient Visits**: 222070 **Births**: 3728 **Personnel**: 3124

PERTH AMBOY—Middlesex County

✠ **HACKENSACK MERIDIAN HEALTH RARITAN BAY MEDICAL CENTER (312025)**, 530 New Brunswick Avenue, Zip 08861–3654; tel. 732/442–3700, (Includes OLD BRIDGE MEDICAL CENTER, 1 Hospital Plaza, Old Bridge, New Jersey, Zip 08857–3012, tel. 732/360–1000; Patricia Carroll, President and Chief Hospital Executive; RARITAN BAY MEDICAL CENTER, 530 New Brunswick Avenue, Perth Amboy, New Jersey, Zip 08861–3685, tel. 732/442–3700; Patricia Carroll, President and Chief Hospital Executive) **A** 1 3 5 10 **F** 3 12 13 15 18 20 22 29 30 31 34 35 36 38 40 44 45 46 50 51 53 58 59 60 61 63 64 65 68 70 73 74 75 76 77 78 79 81 84 85 86 87 91 92 93 96 97 98 101 102 103 104 107 108 110 111 114 115 119 126 130 131 132 135 141 146 147 148 149 154 156 162 164 165 167 169 **S** Hackensack Meridian Health, Edison, NJ
Primary Contact: Patricia Carroll, President and Chief Hospital Executive
COO: Thomas Shanahan, CPA, Chief Operating Officer
CFO: Thomas Shanahan, CPA, Chief Financial Officer and Senior Vice President
CMO: Louis Brusco, M.D., Chief Medical Officer
CHR: Vincent Costantino, Vice President Operations and Human Resources
Web address: www.rbmc.org
Control: Other not–for–profit (including NFP Corporation) **Service**: General medical and surgical

Staffed Beds: 308 **Admissions**: 11996 **Census**: 155 **Outpatient Visits**: 130380 **Births**: 944 **Total Expense ($000)**: 310012 **Payroll Expense ($000)**: 146153 **Personnel**: 1542

PERTH AMBOY DIVISION See Raritan Bay Medical Center

PHILLIPSBURG—Warren County

☐ **ST. LUKE'S HOSPITAL – WARREN CAMPUS (310060)**, 185 Roseberry Street, Zip 08865–1690; tel. 908/847–6700, (Nonreporting) **A** 1 3 5 10 13 **S** St. Luke's University Health Network, Bethlehem, PA
Primary Contact: Trevor Micklos, President
COO: Alice Wilson, FACHE, Vice President Administration
CMO: Edward Gilkey, M.D., Vice President Medical Affairs
CHR: Morgan G Mahl, Director Human Resources
CNO: Gail Newton, R.N., MSN, Vice President Patient Care Services
Web address: www.slhn.org
Control: Other not–for–profit (including NFP Corporation) **Service**: General medical and surgical

Staffed Beds: 92

PISCATAWAY—Middlesex County

RUTGERS UNIVERSITY BEHAVIORAL HEALTHCARE (314011), 671 Hoes Lane West, Zip 08854–8021; tel. 732/235–5900, (Nonreporting) **A** 3 5 10
Primary Contact: Frank A. Ghinassi, Ph.D., President and Chief Executive Officer
COO: Rosemarie Rosati, Chief Operating Officer
CFO: Alan Weinkrantz, Chief Financial Officer, Finance
CMO: Theresa Miskimen, M.D., Vice President Medical Services
CIO: Adam Levinson, Associate Director, Information Services
CNO: Michele A Miller, R.N., MSN, Vice President, Acute and Nursing Services
Web address: www.ubhc.rutgers.edu
Control: State, Government, Nonfederal **Service**: Psychiatric

Staffed Beds: 48

PLAINSBORO—Middlesex County

✠ △ **PENN MEDICINE PRINCETON MEDICAL CENTER (310010)**, 1 Plainsboro Road, Zip 08536–1913; tel. 609/853–7100, **A** 1 2 3 5 7 10 **F** 3 4 5 8 10 12 13 14 15 18 20 22 26 28 29 30 31 32 34 35 36 37 38 39 40 44 45 46 47 49 50 51 53 54 55 56 57 58 59 60 61 62 63 64 65 68 70 72 73 74 75 76 77 78 79 81 82 84 85 86 87 89 90 91 92 93 94 96 97 98 100 101 102 104 105 107 108 110 111 115 116 117 118 119 120 121 123 124 126 129 130 131 132 134 135 141 142 145 146 147 148 149 150 152 153 154 156 157 160 162 164 165 167 **P**6 **S** University of Pennsylvania Health System, Philadelphia, PA
Primary Contact: James Demetriades, Chief Executive Officer
COO: James Demetriades, Vice President, Operations
CMO: Donald Denny, M.D., Senior Vice President, Medical Affairs
CIO: Anne Searle, Chief Information Officer
CHR: Marcia M Telthorster, M.Ed, Vice President Human Resources
CNO: Barbara Christiano, Vice President, Patient Care Services and Chief Nursing Officer
Web address: www.princetonhcs.org
Control: Other not–for–profit (including NFP Corporation) **Service**: General medical and surgical

Staffed Beds: 435 **Admissions**: 17081 **Census**: 279 **Outpatient Visits**: 286538 **Births**: 2121 **Total Expense ($000)**: 551328 **Payroll Expense ($000)**: 215882 **Personnel**: 2836

POMONA—Atlantic County

ATLANTICARE REGIONAL MEDICAL CENTER, MAINLAND CAMPUS See Atlanticare Regional Medical Center, Atlantic City Campus, Atlantic City

ATLANTICARE REGIONAL MEDICAL CENTER–MAINLAND DIVISION See Atlanticare Regional Medical Center, Mainland Campus

POMPTON PLAINS—Morris County

✠ **CHILTON MEDICAL CENTER (310017)**, 97 West Parkway, Zip 07444–1696; tel. 973/831–5000, **A** 1 2 10 **F** 3 11 12 13 15 18 20 22 26 28 29 30 31 32 34 35 37 38 39 40 41 44 45 46 47 49 50 53 54 55 56 57 58 59 60 61 64 65 66 68 70 73 74 75 76 77 78 79 81 82 84 85 86 87 89 93 96 97 100 102 104 107 108 110 111 114 115 116 118 119 120 121 123 124 126 129 130 131 135 141 146 147 148 149 150 154 156 164 165 167 169 **S** Atlantic Health System, Morristown, NJ
Primary Contact: Maureen Schneider, Ph.D., R.N., FACHE, President
CFO: Michael Richetti, Chief Financial Officer
CMO: Charles Ross, M.D., Vice President Medical Affairs
CIO: Karen S Smith, Director Information Services
CHR: Julia McGovern, Vice President Human Resources
Web address: https://www.atlantichealth.org/locations/hospitals/chilton-medical-center.html
Control: Other not–for–profit (including NFP Corporation) **Service**: General medical and surgical

Staffed Beds: 177 **Admissions**: 7908 **Census**: 106 **Outpatient Visits**: 128313 **Births**: 665 **Total Expense ($000)**: 318028 **Payroll Expense ($000)**: 160222 **Personnel**: 1350

RAHWAY—Union County

KINDRED HOSPITAL NEW JERSEY – RAHWAY See Kindred Hospital–New Jersey Morris County, Dover

✠ **ROBERT WOOD JOHNSON UNIVERSITY HOSPITAL RAHWAY (310024)**, 865 Stone Street, Zip 07065–2797; tel. 732/381–4200, **A** 1 10 **F** 3 11 12 15 17 20 28 29 30 31 34 35 38 40 45 46 47 48 49 50 51 53 56 57 59 60 64 68 70 74 75 77 79 81 86 87 92 93 97 100 101 102 107 108 110 111 114 116 117 118 119 126 129 130 132 143 146 147 148 149 154 156 167 **S** RWJBarnabas Health, West Orange, NJ
Primary Contact: Kirk C. Tice, President and Chief Executive Officer
CFO: Peter Bihuniak, Vice President Finance
CMO: Juan Baez, M.D., President Medical Staff
CIO: Denine Izzi, Senior Director Information Technology
CHR: Barbara M Mullery, Vice President Administration
CNO: Ann Marie Shears, Vice President Patient Care Services
Web address: www.rwjuhr.com
Control: Other not–for–profit (including NFP Corporation) **Service**: General medical and surgical

Staffed Beds: 92 **Admissions**: 5005 **Census**: 72 **Outpatient Visits**: 83133 **Total Expense ($000)**: 137775 **Payroll Expense ($000)**: 58816 **Personnel**: 592

Hospital, Medicare Provider Number, Address, Telephone, Approval, Facility, and Physician Codes, Health Care System

★ American Hospital Association (AHA) membership ○ Healthcare Facilities Accreditation Program ⇑ Center for Improvement in Healthcare Quality Accreditation
☐ The Joint Commission accreditation ◇ DNV Healthcare Inc. accreditation △ Commission on Accreditation of Rehabilitation Facilities (CARF) accreditation

Hospitals, U.S. / NEW JERSEY

RED BANK—Monmouth County

HACKENSACK MERIDIAN HEALTH RIVERVIEW MEDICAL CENTER (310034), 1 Riverview Plaza, Zip 07701–1864; tel. 732/741-2700, **A**1 2 5 7 10 **F**3 5 9 11 13 15 18 20 22 26 28 29 30 31 32 34 35 36 37 38 39 40 41 44 45 46 47 49 50 51 54 55 56 57 58 59 60 61 63 64 65 66 68 70 71 73 74 75 76 77 78 79 81 82 84 85 86 87 90 91 92 93 94 96 97 98 99 100 101 102 103 104 105 107 108 110 111 114 115 116 117 118 119 120 121 123 124 126 130 131 132 135 141 144 145 146 147 148 149 150 152 153 154 157 162 164 165 167 169 **S** Hackensack Meridian Health, Edison, NJ
Primary Contact: Timothy J. Hogan, FACHE, President, Chief Hospital Executive
CFO: Joseph M Lemaire, Executive Vice President Finance
CMO: Joseph Reichman, M.D., Vice President Medical Affairs and Clinical Effectiveness
CIO: Rebecca Weber, Senior Vice President Information Technology
CHR: Sherrie String, Senior Vice President Human Resources
CNO: Rebecca Graboso, Vice President and Chief Nurse Executive
Web address: www.riverviewmedicalcenter.com
Control: Other not–for–profit (including NFP Corporation) **Service**: General medical and surgical

Staffed Beds: 274 **Admissions**: 10936 **Census**: 155 **Outpatient Visits**: 121074 **Births**: 1368 **Total Expense ($000)**: 374744 **Payroll Expense ($000)**: 162987 **Personnel**: 1361

ROCHELLE PARK—Bergen County

SELECT SPECIALTY HOSPITAL-NORTHEAST NEW JERSEY (312019), 96 Parkway, Zip 07662–4200; tel. 201/221-2352, (Nonreporting) **A**1 10 **S** Select Medical Corporation, Mechanicsburg, PA
Primary Contact: Oleg Rivkin, Chief Executive Officer
Web address: www.northeastnewjersey.selectspecialtyhospitals.com/about/
Control: Corporation, Investor–owned (for–profit) **Service**: Acute long–term care hospital

Staffed Beds: 62

SADDLE BROOK—Bergen County

KESSLER INSTITUTE FOR REHABILITATION See Kessler Institute For Rehabilitation, West Orange

SECAUCUS—Hudson County

HUDSON COUNTY MEADOWVIEW PSYCHIATRIC HOSPITAL (314024), 595 County Avenue, Zip 07094–2605; tel. 201/369-5252, **A**1 10 **F**29 34 50 57 65 75 87 98 101 130 132 135 143 149 160 161 164 **P**6
Primary Contact: Lucy Rubino, Hospital Administrator and Chief Executive Officer
Web address: www.hudsoncountynj.org
Control: County, Government, Nonfederal **Service**: Psychiatric

Staffed Beds: 84 **Admissions**: 196 **Census**: 74 **Outpatient Visits**: 0 **Births**: 0 **Total Expense ($000)**: 32536 **Payroll Expense ($000)**: 15296 **Personnel**: 168

HUDSON REGIONAL HOSPITAL (310118), 55 Meadowlands Parkway, Zip 07094–2977; tel. 201/392-3100, (Nonreporting) **A**10 21
Primary Contact: Nizar Kifaieh, M.D., President and Chief Executive Officer
COO: Lynn McVey, Chief Operating Officer
CMO: Michael Sciarra, M.D., Chief Medical Officer
CHR: Elizabeth Garrity, Director Human Resources
CNO: Felicia Karsos, R.N., Chief Nursing Officer
Web address: www.hudsonregionalhospital.com/
Control: Partnership, Investor–owned (for–profit) **Service**: General medical and surgical

Staffed Beds: 104

SOMERS POINT—Atlantic County

SHORE MEDICAL CENTER (310047), 100 Medical Center Way, Zip 08244; tel. 609/653-3500, (Nonreporting) **A**1 2 10
Primary Contact: Ronald W. Johnson, FACHE, President and Chief Executive Officer
COO: Linda S Kenwood, R.N., MSN, Chief Nursing Officer and Chief Operating Officer
CFO: James T Foley, CPA, Vice President and Chief Financial Officer
CMO: Jeanne M Rowe, M.D., Chief Medical Officer
CIO: Fred Banner, Chief Information Officer
CHR: Alan L Beatty, Vice President Human Resources
CNO: Linda S Kenwood, R.N., MSN, Chief Nursing Officer and Chief Operating Officer
Web address: www.shoremedicalcenter.org
Control: Other not–for–profit (including NFP Corporation) **Service**: General medical and surgical

Staffed Beds: 198

SOMERVILLE—Somerset County

ROBERT WOOD JOHNSON UNIVERSITY HOSPITAL SOMERSET (310048), 110 Rehill Avenue, Zip 08876–2598; tel. 908/685-2200, **A**1 2 3 5 10 **F**3 7 11 13 14 15 18 20 22 26 28 29 30 31 34 35 36 38 40 44 45 46 47 48 49 50 51 55 56 57 58 59 61 62 63 65 66 68 70 73 74 75 76 77 78 79 81 82 84 85 86 87 92 93 97 98 100 101 102 104 105 107 108 109 110 111 114 115 116 117 118 119 120 121 123 124 126 129 130 131 132 134 143 145 146 149 150 153 154 156 162 164 165 167 169 **S** RWJBarnabas Health, West Orange, NJ
Primary Contact: Deidre A. Blaus, Interim Chief Administrative Officer
CMO: Salvatore Moffa, M.D., Vice President, Medical Affairs and Chief Medical Officer
CIO: Jordan Ruch, Vice President and Chief Information Officer
CHR: Anastasia Jacobs, Chief Human Resources Officer
CNO: Lynn Kearney, Vice President Nursing
Web address: www.rwjbh.org
Control: Other not–for–profit (including NFP Corporation) **Service**: General medical and surgical

Staffed Beds: 331 **Admissions**: 13045 **Census**: 195 **Outpatient Visits**: 194952 **Births**: 812 **Total Expense ($000)**: 401875 **Payroll Expense ($000)**: 149794 **Personnel**: 1624

STRATFORD—Camden County

JEFFERSON STRATFORD HOSPITAL (310086), 18 East Laurel Road, Zip 08084–1327; tel. 856/346-6000, (Includes JEFFERSON STRATFORD HOSPITAL, 18 E Laurel RD, Stratford, New Jersey, Zip 08084–1327, 18 East Laurel Road, Zip 08084, tel. 609/346-6000; Richard Galup, Chief Operating Officer; JEFFERSON WASHINGTON TOWNSHIP HOSPITAL, 435 Hurffville Cross Keys RD, Turnersville, New Jersey, Zip 08012–2453, 435 Hurffville–Cross Keys Road, Zip 08012, tel. 856/582-2500; John W Graham, FACHE, Chief Administrative Officer) **A**1 2 3 5 10 12 **F**3 4 8 11 12 13 15 18 20 22 29 30 31 32 34 35 38 39 40 41 44 45 46 49 50 51 54 55 56 57 58 59 60 61 62 63 64 65 66 70 72 73 74 75 76 77 78 79 81 82 84 85 86 87 89 92 93 97 98 99 100 101 102 103 104 105 107 108 110 111 114 115 116 117 119 120 121 123 124 126 129 130 131 132 134 141 146 147 148 149 154 155 156 157 164 165 167 169 **P**6 **S** Jefferson Health, Philadelphia, PA
Primary Contact: Richard Galup, Chief Operating Officer
CFO: Glenn Zirbser, Senior Vice President Finance and Chief Financial Officer
CMO: David Condoluci, M.D., Senior Vice President and Chief Medical Officer
CIO: Thomas Balcavage, Vice President Chief Patient Safety and Quality Officer
CNO: Helene M Burns, R.N., Senior Vice President and Chief Nursing Officer
Web address: https://www.jeffersonhealth.org/locations/stratford-hospital
Control: Other not–for–profit (including NFP Corporation) **Service**: General medical and surgical

Staffed Beds: 565 **Admissions**: 25558 **Census**: 333 **Outpatient Visits**: 246608 **Births**: 900 **Total Expense ($000)**: 721935 **Payroll Expense ($000)**: 247247 **Personnel**: 4215

JEFFERSON STRATFORD HOSPITAL See Jefferson Stratford Hospital, Stratford

KENNEDY UNIVERSITY HOSPITAL – STRATFORD See Jefferson Stratford Hospital

SUMMIT—Union County

OVERLOOK MEDICAL CENTER (310051), 99 Beauvoir Avenue, Zip 07901–3533; tel. 908/522-2000, **A**1 2 3 5 10 **F**3 5 6 8 9 11 12 13 15 17 18 19 20 22 28 29 30 31 32 34 35 36 37 38 39 40 41 42 44 45 46 47 48 49 50 51 53 54 55 56 57 58 59 60 61 63 64 65 66 68 69 70 71 72 73 74 75 76 77 78 79 81 82 84 85 86 87 88 89 91 92 93 94 95 96 97 98 100 101 102 103 104 105 107 108 110 111 113 115 116 117 118 119 120 121 123 124 126 130 131 132 134 135 141 143 145 146 147 148 149 150 151 152 153 154 156 157 160 161 162 164 165 167 169 **S** Atlantic Health System, Morristown, NJ
Primary Contact: Stephanie L. Schwartz, FACHE, President
CFO: Kevin Lenahan, Vice President Finance and Chief Financial Officer
CMO: John R Audett, M.D., Medical Director Clinical Affairs
CIO: Elizabeth Lindsay–Wood, Interim Chief Information Officer
Web address: www.atlantichealth.org/Overlook
Control: Other not–for–profit (including NFP Corporation) **Service**: General medical and surgical

Staffed Beds: 513 **Admissions**: 19867 **Census**: 288 **Outpatient Visits**: 314691 **Births**: 2275 **Total Expense ($000)**: 1056118 **Payroll Expense ($000)**: 518057 **Personnel**: 4876

SUMMIT OAKS HOSPITAL (314001), 19 Prospect Street, Zip 07901–2530; tel. 908/522-7000, (Nonreporting) **A**1 10 **S** Universal Health Services, Inc., King of Prussia, PA
Primary Contact: Y. Brooke. Tillman, Chief Executive Officer
Web address: www.summitoakshospital.com/
Control: Corporation, Investor–owned (for–profit) **Service**: Psychiatric

Staffed Beds: 124

Hospitals, U.S. / NEW JERSEY

TEANECK—Bergen County

✠ **HOLY NAME MEDICAL CENTER (310008)**, 718 Teaneck Road, Zip 07666–4281; tel. 201/833–3000, **A**1 2 3 10 **F**2 3 5 7 11 12 13 15 18 19 20 22 28 29 30 31 32 34 35 36 37 38 39 40 44 45 46 47 48 49 50 51 53 54 55 56 57 58 59 60 62 63 64 65 66 68 70 71 73 74 75 76 77 78 79 80 81 82 83 84 85 86 87 89 91 92 93 94 96 97 98 100 101 102 103 107 108 109 110 111 114 115 116 117 118 119 120 121 123 124 126 129 130 131 132 133 135 143 145 146 147 148 149 154 156 157 160 162 164 165 167 168 169 **P**4 7
Primary Contact: Michael Maron, President and Chief Executive Officer
CFO: Ryan Kennedy, Chief Financial Officer
CMO: Adam D Jarrett, M.D., Executive Vice President and Chief Medical Officer
CIO: Michael Skvarenina, Assistant Vice President Information Systems
CHR: April Rodgers, Vice President, Human Resources
CNO: Sheryl A Slonim, Executive Vice President and Chief Nursing Officer
Web address: www.holyname.org
Control: Other not–for–profit (including NFP Corporation) Service: General medical and surgical

Staffed Beds: 317 **Admissions:** 16027 **Census:** 177 **Outpatient Visits:** 338536 **Births:** 1414 **Total Expense ($000):** 468073 **Payroll Expense ($000):** 204159 **Personnel:** 2159

TINTON FALLS—Monmouth County

✠ **ENCOMPASS HEALTH REHABILITATION HOSPITAL OF TINTON FALLS, A JOINT VENTURE WITH MONMOUTH MEDICAL CENTER (313035)**, 2 Centre Plaza, Zip 07724–9744; tel. 732/460–5320, (Nonreporting) **A**1 10 **S** Encompass Health Corporation, Birmingham, AL
Primary Contact: Beth Sarfaty, Chief Executive Officer
CFO: Lynne Traister, Controller
CMO: Todd Cooperman, M.D., Medical Director
CHR: Anita Saum, Director Human Resources
Web address: www.rehabnjtintonfalls.com/
Control: Corporation, Investor–owned (for–profit) Service: Rehabilitation

Staffed Beds: 60

TOMS RIVER—Ocean County

✠ △ **COMMUNITY MEDICAL CENTER (310041)**, 99 Route 37 West, Zip 08755–6423; tel. 732/557–8000, **A**1 2 3 5 7 10 **F**3 11 12 13 15 18 20 22 26 28 29 30 31 32 34 35 36 37 38 39 40 41 43 44 48 49 50 54 55 56 57 58 59 60 61 63 64 65 69 70 73 74 75 76 77 78 79 81 82 83 84 85 86 87 89 93 96 97 100 102 107 108 109 110 111 114 115 118 119 120 121 123 124 126 129 130 131 132 133 134 135 143 146 147 148 149 154 156 157 167 169 **S** RWJBarnabas Health, West Orange, NJ
Primary Contact: Patrick Ahearn, Chief Executive Officer
CFO: Christopher Reidy, Site Financial Officer
CMO: Meika Neblett, M.D., Chief Medical Officer
CIO: Shaun Fitzsimmons, Director Information Technology Services
CHR: Vanessa Smith, Chief Human Resources Officer
CNO: Donna Bonacorso, R.N., Chief Nursing Officer
Web address: https://www.rwjbh.org/community-medical-center/
Control: Other not–for–profit (including NFP Corporation) Service: General medical and surgical

Staffed Beds: 353 **Admissions:** 21974 **Census:** 332 **Outpatient Visits:** 197893 **Births:** 1785 **Total Expense ($000):** 524006 **Payroll Expense ($000):** 194778 **Personnel:** 2182

✠ **ENCOMPASS HEALTH REHABILITATION HOSPITAL OF TOMS RIVER (313029)**, 14 Hospital Drive, Zip 08755–6470; tel. 732/244–3100, (Nonreporting) **A**1 10 **S** Encompass Health Corporation, Birmingham, AL
Primary Contact: Josette Meyers, Area Chief Executive Officer
COO: Patricia Ostaszewski, MS, Chief Executive Officer
CFO: Janet Turso, Controller
CMO: Carol Sonatore, D.O., Medical Director
CIO: Coleen Rossi, Director Quality Services
CHR: Lori Munyan, Director, Human Resources
CNO: Susan Castor, Chief Nursing Officer
Web address: www.rehabnjtomsriver.com/
Control: Corporation, Investor–owned (for–profit) Service: Rehabilitation

Staffed Beds: 92

✠ **RWJBARNABAS HEALTH BEHAVIORAL HEALTH CENTER (314022)**, 1691 Highway 9, Zip 08754; tel. 732/914–1688, **A**1 10 **F**35 68 98 100 101 103 104 153 154 **S** RWJBarnabas Health, West Orange, NJ
Primary Contact: Deanna Sperling, R.N., President and Chief Executive Officer
Web address: https://www.rwjbh.org/our-locations/behavioral-health-center/barnabas-health-behavioral-health-center/
Control: Other not–for–profit (including NFP Corporation) Service: Psychiatric

Staffed Beds: 40 **Admissions:** 1067 **Census:** 30 **Outpatient Visits:** 3874 **Births:** 0 **Total Expense ($000):** 12517 **Payroll Expense ($000):** 6301 **Personnel:** 395

TRENTON—Mercer County

★ ⇑ **CAPITAL HEALTH REGIONAL MEDICAL CENTER (310092)**, 750 Brunswick Avenue, Zip 08638–4143; tel. 609/394–6000, **A**3 5 10 21 **F**3 4 7 15 18 29 30 32 34 35 38 40 42 43 44 45 46 48 50 54 56 57 58 59 60 61 64 65 66 68 70 72 73 74 75 76 77 79 81 84 85 86 87 91 92 93 96 97 98 100 101 102 104 105 107 108 111 112 114 115 118 119 130 132 135 143 145 146 147 148 149 150 154 156 157 164 166 **P**6 **S** Capital Health, Trenton, NJ
Primary Contact: Al Maghazehe, Ph.D., FACHE, President and Chief Executive Officer
CFO: Shane Fleming, Chief Financial Officer
CMO: Eugene McMahon, Senior Vice President and Chief Medical Officer
CIO: Eugene Grochala, Vice President Information Systems
CHR: Scott Clemmensen, Vice President Human Resources and Leadership Enhancement
CNO: Gina Mumolie, Senior Vice President Hospital Administration
Web address: www.capitalhealth.org
Control: Other not–for–profit (including NFP Corporation) Service: General medical and surgical

Staffed Beds: 216 **Admissions:** 8250 **Census:** 165 **Outpatient Visits:** 160774 **Births:** 0

☐ **TRENTON PSYCHIATRIC HOSPITAL (314013)**, Route 29 and Sullivan Way, Zip 08628–3425, Mailing Address: P.O. Box 7500, West Trenton, Zip 08628–0500; tel. 609/633–1500, (Nonreporting) **A**1 3 10 **S** Division of Mental Health and Addiction Services, Department of Human Services, State of New Jersey, Trenton, NJ
Primary Contact: Maria Christensen, Chief Executive Officer
CFO: Joseph Canale, Business Manager
CMO: Lawrence Rossi, M.D., Clinical Director
CIO: Scott Eustace, Director Health Information Technology
CHR: Marybeth Longo, Manager Human Resources
CNO: Colleen Birkhofer, Chief Nursing Officer
Web address: https://nj.gov/
Control: State, Government, Nonfederal Service: Psychiatric

Staffed Beds: 431

TURNERSVILLE—Gloucester County

JEFFERSON WASHINGTON TOWNSHIP HOSPITAL See Jefferson Stratford Hospital, Stratford

KENNEDY UNIVERSITY HOSPITAL – WASHINGTON TOWNSHIP See Jefferson Washington Township Hospital

VINELAND—Cumberland County

✠ **ENCOMPASS HEALTH REHABILITATION HOSPITAL OF VINELAND (313036)**, 1237 West Sherman Avenue, Zip 08360–6920; tel. 856/696–7100, (Nonreporting) **A**1 3 10 **S** Encompass Health Corporation, Birmingham, AL
Primary Contact: Monica B. Titus, R.N., Chief Executive Officer
CHR: Dawn Pearson, Director Human Resources
Web address: www.healthsouthvineland.com
Control: Corporation, Investor–owned (for–profit) Service: Rehabilitation

Staffed Beds: 41

Hospital, Medicare Provider Number, Address, Telephone, Approval, Facility, and Physician Codes, Health Care System

★ American Hospital Association (AHA) membership   ○ Healthcare Facilities Accreditation Program   ⇑ Center for Improvement in Healthcare Quality Accreditation
☐ The Joint Commission accreditation   ◇ DNV Healthcare Inc. accreditation   △ Commission on Accreditation of Rehabilitation Facilities (CARF) accreditation

© 2025 AHA Guide

Hospitals, U.S. / NEW JERSEY

★ ⇑ **INSPIRA MEDICAL CENTER–VINELAND (310032)**, 1505 West Sherman Avenue, Zip 08360–6912; tel. 856/641–8000; (Includes BRIDGETON HEALTH CENTER, 333 Irving Avenue, Bridgeton, New Jersey, Zip 08302–2100, tel. 856/575–4500) **A**2 3 5 10 12 13 21 **F**1 3 4 7 8 12 13 15 16 17 18 20 22 28 29 30 31 32 34 35 39 40 42 45 46 47 49 50 51 57 58 59 64 66 67 70 72 73 74 75 76 78 80 81 82 84 85 86 87 88 89 90 93 94 98 99 101 102 103 107 108 110 111 114 115 116 117 119 120 121 123 124 126 128 130 132 135 145 146 147 148 149 154 155 156 161 162 164 166 167 168 169 **S** Inspira Health Network, Mullica Hill, NJ
Primary Contact: Amy B. Mansue, President and Chief Executive Officer
CFO: Thomas Baldosaro, Chief Financial Officer
CMO: Steven C Linn, M.D., Chief Medical Officer
CIO: Thomas Pacek, Vice President Information Systems and Chief Information Officer
CHR: Anneliese McMenamin, Chief Human Resource Officer
Web address: www.inspirahealthnetwork.org/?id=5280&sid=1
Control: Other not–for–profit (including NFP Corporation) **Service**: General medical and surgical

Staffed Beds: 343 **Admissions**: 15693 **Census**: 255 **Outpatient Visits**: 376814 **Births**: 1643 **Total Expense ($000)**: 614169 **Payroll Expense ($000)**: 270803 **Personnel**: 3118

VOORHEES—Camden County

⊞ **VIRTUA VOORHEES (310022)**, 100 Bowman Drive, Zip 08043–9612; tel. 856/325–3000, (Includes VOORHEES PEDIATRIC FACILITY, 1304 Laurel Oak Road, Voorhees, New Jersey, Zip 08043–4310, tel. 888/873–5437) **A**1 3 5 10 **F**3 4 13 15 18 19 29 30 31 34 37 39 40 41 45 46 49 50 54 55 59 61 64 70 72 73 74 75 76 77 78 79 80 81 85 87 88 89 92 93 96 100 107 108 110 111 115 116 117 118 119 126 129 130 132 146 147 148 149 154 167 168 169 **S** Virtua Health, Marlton, NJ
Primary Contact: Dennis W. Pullin, FACHE, President and Chief Executive Officer
COO: Paul E Minnick, R.N., MSN, Senior Vice President and Chief Operating Officer
CFO: Robert Rosvold, Director Finance
CMO: James P Dwyer, D.O., Executive Vice President and Chief Medical Officer
CIO: Alfred Campanella, Chief Information Officer
Web address: www.virtua.org
Control: Other not–for–profit (including NFP Corporation) **Service**: General medical and surgical

Staffed Beds: 402 **Admissions**: 23933 **Census**: 286 **Outpatient Visits**: 318851 **Births**: 6482 **Total Expense ($000)**: 760168 **Payroll Expense ($000)**: 248233 **Personnel**: 2271

WAYNE—Passaic County

WAYNE GENERAL HOSPITAL See St. Joseph's Wayne Hospital

WEST ORANGE—Essex County

GROTTA CENTER FOR SENIOR CARE See Summit Ridge Nursing and Rehabilitation Center

KESSLER INSTITUTE FOR REHABILITATION See Kessler Institute For Rehabilitation, West Orange

⊞ △ **KESSLER INSTITUTE FOR REHABILITATION (313025)**, 1199 Pleasant Valley Way, Zip 07052–1424; tel. 973/731–3600, (Includes KESSLER INSTITUTE FOR REHABILITATION, 1199 Pleasant Valley Way, West Orange, New Jersey, Zip 07052–1424, tel. 973/731–3600; Sam Bayoumy, Interim Chief Executive Officer; KESSLER INSTITUTE FOR REHABILITATION, 201 Pleasant Hill Road, Chester, New Jersey, Zip 07930–2141, tel. 973/252–6300; Neel Patel, Chief Executive Officer; KESSLER INSTITUTE FOR REHABILITATION, 300 Market Street, Saddle Brook, New Jersey, Zip 07663–5309, tel. 201/368–6000; Philip J. Driscoll, Chief Executive Officer) **A**1 3 5 7 10 **F**3 28 29 34 35 36 44 53 57 58 60 64 68 74 75 77 78 79 82 86 87 90 91 92 93 94 95 96 100 119 130 131 132 146 148 149 154 157 164 **P**6 **S** Select Medical Corporation, Mechanicsburg, PA
Primary Contact: Michelle O'Keefe, Chief Executive Officer
CMO: Bruce M Gans, M.D., Executive Vice President and Chief Medical Officer
CHR: Ken Caldera, Director Human Resources
Web address: www.kessler-rehab.com
Control: Corporation, Investor–owned (for–profit) **Service**: Rehabilitation

Staffed Beds: 336 **Admissions**: 6192 **Census**: 261 **Outpatient Visits**: 91560 **Births**: 0 **Personnel**: 1563

WESTAMPTON—Burlington County

☐ **HAMPTON BEHAVIORAL HEALTH CENTER (314021)**, 650 Rancocas Road, Zip 08060–5613; tel. 609/267–7000, **A**1 10 **F**3 30 35 50 98 99 103 105 130 132 143 149 153 154 **P**6 **S** Universal Health Services, Inc., King of Prussia, PA
Primary Contact: Craig Hilton, Chief Executive Officer and Managing Director
COO: Joanne Wijaya, MSN, R.N., Chief Operating Officer and Risk Manager
CFO: Melissa Zinni, Chief Financial Officer
CMO: Anusuya Balasundaram, M.D., Medical Director
CHR: Lori DeCelis, Director Human Resources
CNO: Kathleena Cohen, MSN, R.N., Director of Nursing
Web address: www.hamptonhospital.com
Control: Corporation, Investor–owned (for–profit) **Service**: Psychiatric

Staffed Beds: 120 **Admissions**: 2470 **Census**: 102 **Outpatient Visits**: 10985 **Births**: 0 **Total Expense ($000)**: 32659 **Payroll Expense ($000)**: 22268 **Personnel**: 246

WESTWOOD—Bergen County

CAREONE AT HACKENSACK UNIVERSITY MEDICAL CENTER AT PASCACK VALLEY, 250 Old Hook Road, Zip 07675–3123, Mailing Address: 250 Old Hook Road, 4 Central, Zip 07675–3123; tel. 201/781–1555, (Nonreporting)
Primary Contact: Grant Welson, Chief Executive Officer, CareOne Hospital Division
Web address: www.care-one.com/locations/ltach-careone-at-hackensack-university-medical-center-pascack-valley/
Control: Other not–for–profit (including NFP Corporation) **Service**: Acute long–term care hospital

Staffed Beds: 25

⊞ **HACKENSACK MERIDIAN HEALTH PASCACK VALLEY MEDICAL CENTER (310130)**, 250 Old Hook Road, Zip 07675–3123; tel. 201/383–1035, **A**1 10 **F**3 12 13 15 18 20 28 29 30 34 35 37 40 44 45 46 47 49 50 51 57 59 60 64 68 70 73 74 75 76 77 78 79 81 82 85 87 93 107 108 110 111 115 119 126 129 130 135 141 146 147 148 149 154 156 157 167 169 **S** Ardent Health Services, Nashville, TN
Primary Contact: Michael Bell, Chief Executive Officer
COO: Colleen Smorra, Assistant Administrator
CFO: Jason Pritchard, Chief Financial Officer
CMO: George Lin, M.D., Physician Advisor
CIO: Anthony Teri, Director Information Technology
CNO: Susan Giordano, Chief Nursing Officer
Web address: www.hackensackumcpv.com/
Control: Partnership, Investor–owned (for–profit) **Service**: General medical and surgical

Staffed Beds: 128 **Admissions**: 3970 **Census**: 38 **Outpatient Visits**: 59941 **Births**: 961 **Total Expense ($000)**: 107666 **Payroll Expense ($000)**: 41782 **Personnel**: 475

WILLINGBORO—Burlington County

ACUITY SPECIALTY HOSPITAL OF SOUTHERN NEW JERSEY See Select Specialty Hospital – Willingboro

⊞ **SELECT SPECIALTY HOSPITAL – WILLINGBORO (312022)**, 218 A Sunset Road, Zip 08046–1110, Mailing Address: 220 Sunset Road, Zip 08046–1110; tel. 609/835–3650, (Nonreporting) **A**1 10 **S** Select Medical Corporation, Mechanicsburg, PA
Primary Contact: Shawn Dilmore, Market Chief Executive Officer
CMO: Edward G. Hamaty, D.O., Chief Medical Officer
CHR: Lisa M Sinnott, Director Human Resources
CNO: Eddie Perez, R.N., Chief Clinical Officer and Chief Nurse Executive
Web address: https://www.selectspecialtyhospitals.com/locations-and-tours/nj/willingboro/willingboro/?ty=xt&tab=our-team-heading
Control: Corporation, Investor–owned (for–profit) **Service**: Acute long–term care hospital

Staffed Beds: 53

Hospitals, U.S. / NEW JERSEY

☒ **VIRTUA WILLINGBORO HOSPITAL (310061)**, 218–A Sunset Road, Zip 08046–1162; tel. 609/835–2900, **A**1 3 10 **F**3 4 11 15 18 29 30 31 34 40 45 46 48 50 54 55 58 59 60 61 64 70 74 75 77 78 81 85 87 91 92 93 98 100 101 102 107 108 110 111 114 118 119 126 130 135 145 146 148 149 154 164 167 168 **S** Virtua Health, Marlton, NJ
Primary Contact: John Kirby, Senior Vice President, Virtua Health and President of Virtua Mount Holly and Virtua Willingboro hosp
CFO: Michael Hammond, Chief Financial Officer
CMO: Alan R Pope, M.D., Vice President, Medical Affairs
CIO: Mike Elfert, Director Information Services
CNO: Audrey Jadczak, R.N., FACHE, Vice President/Chief Nursing Officer
Web address: https://www.lourdesnet.org/locations/hospitals/lourdes-medical-center-of-burlington-county/
Control: Other not–for–profit (including NFP Corporation) **Service**: General medical and surgical

Staffed Beds: 169 **Admissions**: 5406 **Census**: 78 **Outpatient Visits**: 57165 **Births**: 0 **Total Expense ($000)**: 125154 **Payroll Expense ($000)**: 46072 **Personnel**: 494

WYCKOFF—Bergen County

☒ **CHRISTIAN HEALTH (314019)**, 301 Sicomac Avenue, Zip 07481–2194; tel. 201/848–5200, (Total facility includes 304 beds in nursing home–type unit) **A**1 10 **F**6 30 34 35 56 57 58 69 84 87 98 99 101 103 104 105 128 132 143 146 153 154
Primary Contact: Douglas A. Struyk, CPA, President and Chief Executive Officer
COO: Steve Dumke, FACHE, Executive Vice President and Chief Operating Officer
CFO: Kevin Stagg, Executive Vice President Finance and Chief Financial Officer
CMO: Allen M. Khademi, M.D., Vice President Medical Affairs
CIO: Ed Rizgallah, Vice President Information Services and Chief Information Officer
CHR: Bob Zierold, Senior Vice President, Chief Human Resources Officer
CNO: Rebecca Dauerman, R.N., Vice President, Administrator Mental Health Services and Chief Nursing Officer
Web address: https://www.christianhealthnj.org/
Control: Other not–for–profit (including NFP Corporation) **Service**: Psychiatric

Staffed Beds: 457 **Admissions**: 2105 **Census**: 386 **Outpatient Visits**: 79907 **Births**: 0 **Total Expense ($000)**: 87786 **Payroll Expense ($000)**: 49985 **Personnel**: 736

NEW MEXICO

ACOMA—Bergen County

ACOMA–CANONCITO–LAGUNA HOSPITAL (320070), 80B Veterans Boulevard, Zip 87034, Mailing Address: P.O. Box 130, San Fidel, Zip 87049–0130; tel. 505/552–5300, (Nonreporting) **A**10 **S** U. S. Indian Health Service, Rockville, MD
Primary Contact: Delaine Alley, Chief Executive Officer
Web address: www.ihs.gov/albuquerque/index.cfm?module=dsp_abq_acoma_canoncito_laguna
Control: PHS, Indian Service, Government, federal **Service**: General medical and surgical

Staffed Beds: 6

ALAMOGORDO—Otero County

★ △ ⇑ **GERALD CHAMPION REGIONAL MEDICAL CENTER (320004)**, 2669 North Scenic Drive, Zip 88310–8799; tel. 575/439–6100, **A**3 5 7 10 13 20 21 **F**3 8 11 12 13 18 20 22 26 28 29 30 31 34 35 37 38 40 43 44 45 50 51 57 59 62 63 64 68 70 74 75 76 77 78 79 81 82 83 85 86 87 91 96 97 98 100 101 102 103 104 105 107 108 111 114 115 117 119 120 121 123 129 130 131 132 144 145 146 147 148 149 153 154 156 160 162 164 167 169 **S** CHRISTUS Health, Irving, TX
Primary Contact: Robert J. Heckert Jr, Chief Executive Officer
CFO: Bashar Naser, Chief Financial Officer
CMO: Lee Saltzgaber, Chief Medical Officer
CIO: Ana Castro, Director Information Technology
CHR: Karen O'Brien, Director Human Resources
CNO: Robert Eldon Middleton, MSN, R.N., III, Vice President Ancillary Services, Chief Administrative Officer, Chief Construction Executive
Web address: www.gcrmc.org
Control: Other not–for–profit (including NFP Corporation) **Service**: General medical and surgical

Staffed Beds: 98 **Admissions**: 3987 **Census**: 50 **Outpatient Visits**: 112508 **Births**: 482 **Total Expense ($000)**: 269736 **Payroll Expense ($000)**: 83934 **Personnel**: 1030

ALBUQUERQUE—Bernalillo County

AMG SPECIALTY HOSPITAL–ALBUQUERQUE (322003), 5400 Gibson Boulevard SE, 3rd Floor, Zip 87108–4729, Mailing Address: 5400 Gibson Boulevad SE, 3rd Floor, Zip 87108–4729; tel. 505/842–5550, (Nonreporting) **A**10 22 **S** AMG Integrated Healthcare Management, Lafayette, LA
Primary Contact: Kendra Camp, R.N., Chief Executive Officer
CMO: Jeffrey Ross, M.D., Medical Director
CHR: Robin Stendel–Freels, Coordinator Human Resources
Web address: www.amgalbuquerque.com/
Control: Partnership, Investor–owned (for–profit) **Service**: Acute long–term care hospital

Staffed Beds: 24

☐ **CENTRAL DESERT BEHAVIORAL HEALTH HOSPITAL (324014)**, 1525 North Renaissance Boulevard North East, Zip 87107–6827; tel. 505/243–3387, (Nonreporting) **A**1
Primary Contact: Kelley Whitaker, Chief Executive Officer
CFO: Irene Torres, Chief Financial Officer
CHR: Kimberly Lokke, Chief Human Resources Officer
CNO: Emma Argueta, Chief Nursing Officer
Web address: www.centraldesertbh.com
Control: Other not–for–profit (including NFP Corporation) **Service**: Psychiatric

Staffed Beds: 64

⊞ **ENCOMPASS HEALTH REHABILITATION HOSPITAL OF ALBUQUERQUE (323027)**, 7000 Jefferson Street NE, Zip 87109–4313; tel. 505/344–9478, **A**1 10 **F**29 90 96 143 148 149 **S** Encompass Health Corporation, Birmingham, AL
Primary Contact: LaDessa Forrest, Chief Executive Officer
CFO: Michelle Martinez, Controller
CMO: Joseph Michael Long, M.D., Medical Director
CHR: Kristen Hernandez, Director Human Resources
CNO: Susan Blanchard, R.N., Chief Nursing Officer
Web address: www.encompasshealth.com/albuquerquerehab
Control: Corporation, Investor–owned (for–profit) **Service**: Rehabilitation

Staffed Beds: 60 **Admissions**: 1497 **Census**: 53 **Births**: 0

☐ **HAVEN BEHAVIORAL SENIOR CARE OF ALBUQUERQUE (324013)**, 5400 Gibson Boulevard SE, 4th Floor, Box #8, Zip 87108–4729; tel. 505/254–4502, **A**1 10 **F**5 98 103 105 152 153 154 **S** Haven Behavioral Healthcare, Nashville, TN
Primary Contact: Kathleen Dostalik, Chief Executive Officer
Web address: https://albuquerque.havenbehavioral.com/
Control: Corporation, Investor–owned (for–profit) **Service**: Psychiatric

Staffed Beds: 48 **Admissions**: 1366 **Census**: 26 **Outpatient Visits**: 4724 **Births**: 0 **Total Expense ($000)**: 11689 **Payroll Expense ($000)**: 6269 **Personnel**: 228

KASEMAN PRESBYTERIAN HOSPITAL See Presbyterian Kaseman Hospital

⊞ **KINDRED HOSPITAL–ALBUQUERQUE (322002)**, 700 High Street NE, Zip 87102–2565; tel. 505/242–4444, **A**1 10 **F**1 3 50 60 70 85 87 107 130 135 148 149 160 **P**5 **S** ScionHealth, Louisville, KY
Primary Contact: Lisa Cochran, Chief Executive Officer
CFO: Sheila Bova, Chief Financial Officer
CMO: Jon Marinaro, M.D., Chief Medical Officer
CHR: Donald Whitney, Director Human Resources
CNO: Diane Nelson, R.N., Chief Nursing Officer
Web address: www.kindredalbuquerque.com/
Control: Corporation, Investor–owned (for–profit) **Service**: Acute long–term care hospital

Staffed Beds: 57 **Admissions**: 326 **Census**: 43 **Outpatient Visits**: 0 **Births**: 0

★ ⇑ **LOVELACE MEDICAL CENTER (320009)**, 601 Martin Luther King Avenue NE, Zip 87102–3619; tel. 505/727–8000, (Includes HEART HOSPITAL OF NEW MEXICO, 504 Elm Street, Albuquerque, New Mexico, Zip 87102, tel. 505/724–2000; Brian Miller, Chief Executive Officer) **A**3 10 19 21 **F**3 17 18 20 22 24 26 28 29 30 31 35 37 38 40 45 46 49 50 51 56 57 58 59 60 64 65 67 68 70 74 75 77 78 79 81 82 84 85 87 98 100 105 107 108 109 111 114 115 117 118 119 120 121 124 126 130 132 146 148 149 154 157 167 **S** Ardent Health Services, Nashville, TN
Primary Contact: Brian Miller, Chief Executive Officer
COO: Denzil Ross, FACHE, Chief Operating Officer
CHR: Helen V Nielsen, Director Human Resources
Web address: https://lovelace.com/location/lovelace-medical-center
Control: Corporation, Investor–owned (for–profit) **Service**: General medical and surgical

Staffed Beds: 247 **Admissions**: 10515 **Census**: 146

★ △ ⇑ **LOVELACE UNM REHABILITATION HOSPITAL (323028)**, 505 Elm Street NE, Zip 87102–2500; tel. 505/727–4700, (Nonreporting) **A**3 5 7 10 21 **S** Ardent Health Services, Nashville, TN
Primary Contact: Troy Greer, Interim Chief Executive Officer
CFO: Andrea Solin, Chief Financial Officer
CHR: Helen V Nielsen, Director Human Resources
CNO: Cynthia Rankin, Chief Nursing Officer
Web address: https://lovelace.com/location/lovelace-rehabilitation-hospital
Control: Corporation, Investor–owned (for–profit) **Service**: Rehabilitation

Staffed Beds: 62

★ ⇑ **LOVELACE WESTSIDE HOSPITAL (320074)**, 10501 Golf Course Road NW, Zip 87114–5000; tel. 505/727–8000, **A**10 21 **F**3 12 13 15 29 30 34 39 40 41 49 51 57 59 68 70 75 76 79 81 85 93 107 110 111 115 119 130 133 135 146 148 **S** Ardent Health Services, Nashville, TN
Primary Contact: Amy Blasing, R.N., MSN, Chief Executive Officer
CFO: Andrea Solin, Chief Financial Officer
CNO: Brenda Holley, R.N., Chief Nursing Officer
Web address: https://lovelace.com/location/lovelace-westside-hospital
Control: Corporation, Investor–owned (for–profit) **Service**: General medical and surgical

Staffed Beds: 80 **Admissions**: 1746 **Census**: 18

Hospitals, U.S. / NEW MEXICO

★ ⭧ **LOVELACE WOMEN'S HOSPITAL (320017)**, 4701 Montgomery Boulevard NE, Zip 87109–1251; tel. 505/727-7800, (Nonreporting) **A**3 10 21 **S** Ardent Health Services, Nashville, TN
Primary Contact: Amy Blasing, R.N., MSN, Chief Executive Officer
COO: Janelle Raborn, Chief Operating Officer
CFO: Joseph Sereno, Chief Financial Officer
CHR: Carol Shelton, Director Human Resources
CNO: Brenda Holley, R.N., Chief Nursing Officer
Web address: www.lovelace.com/albuquerque-hospital/lovelace-womens-hospital#.UDZ17KDhf48
Control: Corporation, Investor-owned (for-profit) **Service**: General medical and surgical

Staffed Beds: 78

NEW MEXICO HCS See Raymond G. Murphy Department of Veterans Affairs Medical Center

⊞ **PRESBYTERIAN HOSPITAL (320021)**, 1100 Central Avenue SE, Zip 87106–4934, Mailing Address: P.O. Box 26666, Zip 87125–6666; tel. 505/841-1234, (Includes PRESBYTERIAN KASEMAN HOSPITAL, 8300 Constitution Avenue NE, Albuquerque, New Mexico, Zip 87110-7624, P O Box 26666, Zip 87125-6666, tel. 505/291-2000; Doyle Boykin, R.N., MSN, Administrator; PRESBYTERIAN RUST MEDICAL CENTER, 2400 Unser Boulevard SE, Rio Rancho, New Mexico, Zip 87124-4740, tel. 505/253-7878; Jeff McBee, Administrator) **A**1 2 3 5 10 19 **F**3 5 12 13 15 17 18 19 20 21 22 23 24 25 26 27 28 29 30 31 32 34 35 38 40 43 44 45 46 47 48 49 50 51 53 54 55 56 57 58 59 60 62 63 64 65 67 68 70 72 74 75 76 77 78 79 80 81 82 83 84 85 86 87 88 89 92 93 97 98 99 100 101 102 104 107 108 111 114 115 116 117 118 119 120 124 125 129 130 132 135 138 139 142 143 144 146 147 148 149 150 153 154 156 157 160 162 164 165 167 169 **S** Presbyterian Healthcare Services, Albuquerque, NM
Primary Contact: Jon Wade, Hospital Chief Executive Officer
CFO: Dale Maxwell, Executive Vice President and Chief Financial Officer
CMO: Jayne McCormick, M.D., Chief Medical Officer CDS
CIO: Lee Marley, Vice President, Information Services Chief Application Officer
CHR: Lee Patchell, Lead Human Resources Business Partner
CNO: Ann L Wright, R.N., MSN, Assistant Central Delivery System CNO
Web address: www.phs.org
Control: Other not-for-profit (including NFP Corporation) **Service**: General medical and surgical

Staffed Beds: 744 **Admissions:** 40387 **Census:** 607 **Outpatient Visits:** 349737 **Births:** 3590 **Total Expense ($000):** 1388241 **Payroll Expense ($000):** 407564 **Personnel:** 4287

⊞ △ **RAYMOND G. MURPHY DEPARTMENT OF VETERANS AFFAIRS MEDICAL CENTER**, 1501 San Pedro SE, Zip 87108–5153; tel. 505/265-1711, (Nonreporting) **A**1 2 3 5 7 8 **S** Department of Veterans Affairs, Washington, DC
Primary Contact: Robert W. McKenrick, Medical Center Director
CFO: Michael McNeill, Chief Financial Management
CMO: Meghan Gerety, M.D., Chief of Staff
CIO: Ronald Ferrell, Chief Information Officer
CHR: Melvin Hooker, Chief Human Resources
Web address: www.albuquerque.va.gov/
Control: Veterans Affairs, Government, federal **Service**: General medical and surgical

Staffed Beds: 175

TURQUOISE LODGE HOSPITAL, 5901 Zuni Road SE, Zip 87108–3073; tel. 505/841-8978, (Nonreporting)
Primary Contact: Shauna Hartley, Administrator
CFO: Juliette Aragon, Finance Director
CIO: Eric Gurule, Chief Information Officer
CHR: Mario Lechuga, Director Human Resources
CNO: Debra Jane Green, R.N., Director of Nursing
Web address: www.health.state.nm.us
Control: State, Government, Nonfederal **Service**: Substance Use Disorder

Staffed Beds: 20

UNIV OF NEW MEXICO HOSPITAL See Mental Health Center

⊞ **UNIVERSITY OF NEW MEXICO HOSPITALS (320001)**, 2211 Lomas Boulevard NE, Zip 87106–2745; tel. 505/272-2121, (Includes CARRIE TINGLEY HOSPITAL, 1127 University Boulevard NE, Albuquerque, New Mexico, Zip 87102-1715, tel. 505/272-5200; Doris Tinagero, Executive Director; MENTAL HEALTH CENTER, 2600 Marble NE, Albuquerque, New Mexico, Zip 87131-2600, tel. 505/272-2800; UNIVERSITY OF NEW MEXICO CHILDREN'S PSYCHIATRIC HOSPITAL, 1001 Yale Boulevard NE, Albuquerque, New Mexico, Zip 87131-3830, tel. 505/272-2890; UNM CHILDREN'S HOSPITAL, 2211 Lomas Boulevard, NE, 3rd Floor of UNM Hospital, Albuquerque, New Mexico, Zip 87106-2745, tel. 505/272-2111; UNM SANDOVAL REGIONAL MEDICAL CENTER, A CAMPUS OF UNM HOSPITAL, 3001 Broadmoor Boulevard NE, Rio Rancho, New Mexico, Zip 87131, tel. 505/994-7000; Jamie A. Silva-Steele, FACHE, R.N., President and Chief Executive Officer) **A**1 2 3 5 8 10 19 **F**3 5 8 9 11 13 15 16 17 18 19 20 21 22 23 24 25 26 27 28 29 30 31 32 34 35 38 40 41 43 44 45 46 47 48 49 50 51 54 56 57 59 60 61 62 63 64 65 68 70 72 73 74 75 76 77 78 79 81 82 84 85 86 87 88 89 92 93 94 95 96 97 107 108 110 111 113 114 115 116 117 118 119 126 129 130 131 132 135 136 138 144 146 147 148 151 155 156 160 161 162 163 165 167 169
Primary Contact: Kathleen R. Becker, M.P.H., JD, Chief Executive Officer
COO: Michael Chicarelli, R.N., Chief Operating Officer
CFO: Bonnie White, Chief Financial Officer
CMO: Steve McLaughlin, M.D., Chief Medical Officer
CIO: Dawn Harrington, Chief Information Officer
CHR: Sara Frasch, Chief Human Resource Officer
CNO: Mary E. Perez, MSN, Chief Nursing Officer
Web address: www.unm.edu
Control: State, Government, Nonfederal **Service**: General medical and surgical

Staffed Beds: 512 **Admissions:** 33911 **Census:** 472 **Outpatient Visits:** 661506 **Births:** 2891 **Total Expense ($000):** 1442631 **Payroll Expense ($000):** 583050 **Personnel:** 6721

UNM CHILDREN'S PSYCH HOSPITAL See University of New Mexico Children's Psychiatric Hospital

ARTESIA—Eddy County

★ ⭧ **ARTESIA GENERAL HOSPITAL (320030)**, 702 North 13th Street, Zip 88210–1199; tel. 575/748-3333, (Nonreporting) **A**3 10 20 21
Primary Contact: Joe Salgado, M.D., Interim Chief Executive Officer
COO: Jose Luis Gurrola, Chief Operating Officer
CFO: Carl Hollingsworth, Chief Financial Officer
CMO: Joe Salgado, M.D., Chief of Staff
CIO: Eric Jimenez, Chief Information Officer
CHR: Bruce Hinshaw, Director Human Resources
CNO: Wendi Hulett, Chief Nursing Officer
Web address: www.artesiageneral.com
Control: Other not-for-profit (including NFP Corporation) **Service**: General medical and surgical

Staffed Beds: 30

CARLSBAD—Eddy County

⊞ **CARLSBAD MEDICAL CENTER (320063)**, 2430 West Pierce Street, Zip 88220–3597; tel. 575/887-4100, (Nonreporting) **A**1 10 **S** Community Health Systems, Inc., Franklin, TN
Primary Contact: Nicholas Arledge, Chief Executive Officer
CFO: Craig Morse, Chief Financial Officer
CIO: Thomas Motejzik, Director Information Systems
CNO: Connie Shofner, Chief Nursing Officer
Web address: www.carlsbadmedicalcenter.com
Control: Corporation, Investor-owned (for-profit) **Service**: General medical and surgical

Staffed Beds: 99

Hospitals, U.S. / NEW MEXICO

CLAYTON—Union County

★ **UNION COUNTY GENERAL HOSPITAL (321304)**, 300 Wilson Street, Zip 88415-3304, Mailing Address: P.O. Box 489, Zip 88415-0489; tel. 575/374-2585, (Nonreporting) **A**10 18 **S** Community Hospital Corporation, Plano, TX
Primary Contact: Tammie Chavez Stump, R.N., Chief Executive Officer
CFO: Alexander B Altman III, Chief Financial Officer
CMO: Daniel Radunsky, M.D., Medical Staff President
CIO: Kelsey Lawrence, Manager Information Technology
CHR: Jill Swagerty, Director Human Resources
CNO: Stacye Bradley, R.N., Chief Nursing Officer
Web address: www.ucgh.net
Control: Other not-for-profit (including NFP Corporation) **Service**: General medical and surgical

Staffed Beds: 25

CLOVIS—Curry County

✠ **PLAINS REGIONAL MEDICAL CENTER (320022)**, 2100 North Doctor Martin Luther King Boulevard, Zip 88101-9412, Mailing Address: P.O. Box 1688, Zip 88102-1688; tel. 575/769-2141, **A**1 10 **F**3 11 13 15 18 29 30 31 35 40 45 50 51 56 62 63 64 65 68 69 70 76 77 78 79 81 84 85 87 89 93 97 107 108 110 111 114 115 116 119 120 121 123 129 130 135 146 147 148 149 154 167 **S** Presbyterian Healthcare Services, Albuquerque, NM
Primary Contact: Bill Priest, Chief Executive Officer
CMO: Brian Willmon, M.D., Medical Director
CHR: Cindy Duncan, Manager Human Resources
CNO: Terri A Marney, R.N., Director of Nursing
Web address: www.phs.org
Control: Other not-for-profit (including NFP Corporation) **Service**: General medical and surgical

Staffed Beds: 54 **Admissions**: 2475 **Census**: 22

CROWNPOINT—McKinley County

★ **U. S. PUBLIC HEALTH SERVICE INDIAN HOSPITAL (320062)**, Route 9 and State Road 371, Zip 87313, Mailing Address: P.O. Box 358, Zip 87313-0358; tel. 505/786-5291, (Nonreporting) **A**10 **S** U. S. Indian Health Service, Rockville, MD
Primary Contact: Anslem Roanhorse, Chief Executive Officer
CFO: Darlene Kirk, Manager Finance
CMO: John Johnson, M.D., Clinical Director
CIO: Jimmy Burbank, Chief Information Officer
CHR: Christina Bitsilly, Human Resource Specialist
CNO: Alex Daniels, Chief Nurse Executive
Web address: www.ihs.gov
Control: PHS, Indian Service, Government, federal **Service**: General medical and surgical

Staffed Beds: 12

DEMING—Luna County

☐ **MIMBRES MEMORIAL HOSPITAL (321309)**, 900 West Ash Street, Zip 88030-4098, Mailing Address: P.O. Box 710, Zip 88031-0710; tel. 575/546-5800, (Nonreporting) **A**1 10 18 **S** Quorum Health, Brentwood, TN
Primary Contact: Duke Young, Chief Executive Officer
CFO: Trisha Smith, Chief Financial Officer
CHR: Johanna Gramer, Director Human Resources
CNO: Joy Harrell, R.N., Chief Nursing Officer
Web address: www.mimbresmemorial.com
Control: Corporation, Investor-owned (for-profit) **Service**: General medical and surgical

Staffed Beds: 25

ESPANOLA—Rio Arriba County

✠ **PRESBYTERIAN ESPANOLA HOSPITAL (320011)**, 1010 Spruce Street, Zip 87532-2746; tel. 505/753-7111, **A**1 3 10 20 **F**3 5 7 13 15 29 30 34 40 45 50 57 59 68 70 73 76 79 81 85 89 93 107 110 111 114 115 119 129 146 147 149 154 156 157 160 169 **S** Presbyterian Healthcare Services, Albuquerque, NM
Primary Contact: Brenda Romero, Hospital Chief
CFO: Lupe Lucero, Manager Business Office
CMO: Fernando Bayardo, M.D., Chief Medical Officer
CHR: Joshua Griffith, Manager Human Resources
CNO: Nancy Santiesteban, Director Patient Care Services
Web address: www.phs.org
Control: Other not-for-profit (including NFP Corporation) **Service**: General medical and surgical

Staffed Beds: 48 **Admissions**: 1798 **Census**: 16 **Outpatient Visits**: 45607
Births: 258 **Total Expense ($000)**: 91903 **Payroll Expense ($000)**: 36101
Personnel: 347

FARMINGTON—San Juan County

LIFECOURSE REHABILITATION HOSP See San Juan Regional Medical Center Rehabilitation Hospital

★ ⇑ **SAN JUAN REGIONAL MEDICAL CENTER (320005)**, 801 West Maple Street, Zip 87401-5630; tel. 505/609-2000, (Includes SAN JUAN REGIONAL MEDICAL CENTER REHABILITATION HOSPITAL, 525 South Schwartz Avenue, Farmington, New Mexico, Zip 87401-5955, tel. 505/609-2625) **A**10 21 **F**3 7 11 13 15 18 20 22 26 28 29 30 31 34 40 43 45 46 48 49 50 51 53 54 57 59 60 61 64 68 70 74 75 76 78 79 80 81 82 85 86 87 89 90 93 96 98 100 104 107 108 110 111 114 115 116 117 118 119 120 121 126 130 143 144 146 147 148 154 155 156 167
Primary Contact: Jason Rounds, FACHE, President and Chief Executive Officer
CFO: John W. Mayer, Chief Financial Officer
CMO: Melania Yeats, M.D., Chief Medical Officer
CIO: Sheri Rawlings, Chief Information Officer
CHR: Elizabeth Volkerding, Director Workforce Excellence
CNO: Suzanne E Smith, R.N., MSN, Chief Nursing Officer
Web address: www.sanjuanregional.com
Control: Other not-for-profit (including NFP Corporation) **Service**: General medical and surgical

Staffed Beds: 130 **Admissions**: 7634 **Census**: 88

GALLUP—McKinley County

✠ **GALLUP INDIAN MEDICAL CENTER (320061)**, 516 East Nizhoni Boulevard, Zip 87301-5748, Mailing Address: P.O. Box 1337, Zip 87301; tel. 505/722-1000, (Nonreporting) **A**1 3 5 10 **S** U. S. Indian Health Service, Rockville, MD
Primary Contact: Captain Katrina Leslie-Puhuyaoma, D.D.S., Chief Executive Officer
CFO: Agnes Kee, Financial Manager
CMO: Douglas G Peter, M.D., Chief Medical Officer
CIO: Adrian C Haven, Site Manager
CHR: Karen Lee, Director Human Resources
CNO: Selva Thompson, R.N., Chief Nurse Executive
Web address: https://www.ihs.gov/navajo/healthcarefacilities/gallup/
Control: PHS, Indian Service, Government, federal **Service**: General medical and surgical

Staffed Beds: 57

★ **REHOBOTH MCKINLEY CHRISTIAN HEALTH CARE SERVICES (320038)**, 1901 Red Rock Drive, Zip 87301-5683; tel. 505/863-7000, **A**5 10 22 **F**3 5 11 15 18 29 35 40 45 50 53 54 60 68 70 79 81 87 89 93 97 107 111 115 119 122 127 133 141 146 149 157
Primary Contact: William D. Patten Jr, Interim Chief Executive Officer
CFO: Blaise Bondi, Interim Chief Financial Officer
CIO: Randy Myers, Chief Information Officer
CHR: Ronnye Etcitty, Director Human Resources
CNO: Bill Norton, Chief Nursing Officer
Web address: www.rmch.org
Control: Other not-for-profit (including NFP Corporation) **Service**: General medical and surgical

Staffed Beds: 22 **Admissions**: 816 **Census**: 14 **Outpatient Visits**: 51499
Births: 0 **Total Expense ($000)**: 69945 **Payroll Expense ($000)**: 24376
Personnel: 371

GRANTS—Cibola County

✠ **CIBOLA GENERAL HOSPITAL (321308)**, 1016 East Roosevelt Avenue, Zip 87020-2118; tel. 505/287-4446, **A**1 10 18 **F**3 13 15 29 30 34 40 45 46 50 56 57 59 64 65 66 68 70 75 76 77 81 85 93 97 107 110 115 119 129 130 133 135 147 148 **S** Ovation Healthcare, Brentwood, TN
Primary Contact: Maria A. Atencio, R.N., Acting Chief Executive Officer and Chief Nursing Officer
CFO: Ed Brown, Chief Financial Officer
CMO: Janice Shipley, M.D., Chief Medical Officer
CIO: Rick Smith, Director Information Services
CHR: Sheila Cox, Director Human Resources
CNO: Maria A Atencio, R.N., Acting Chief Executive Officer and Chief Nursing Officer
Web address: www.cibolahospital.com
Control: Other not-for-profit (including NFP Corporation) **Service**: General medical and surgical

Staffed Beds: 25 **Admissions**: 1571 **Census**: 9

Hospitals, U.S. / NEW MEXICO

HOBBS—Lea County

COVENANT HEALTH HOBBS HOSPITAL (320065), 5419 North Lovington Highway, Zip 88240-9125, Mailing Address: P.O. Box 3000, Zip 88241-9501; tel. 575/492-5000, **A**1 10 **F**3 13 15 29 30 34 40 45 50 57 59 68 70 76 77 81 87 93 107 110 111 130 131 135 147 148 154 169 **S** Providence, Renton, WA
Primary Contact: Rachel Slade, Chief Executive Officer
CFO: Jorge Latibeaudiere, Chief Financial Officer
CMO: Chris Driskill, M.D., Chief of Staff
CHR: Laurie Russell, Director Human Resources
CNO: Eric Simmermon, Chief Nursing Officer
Web address: https://www.providence.org/locations/covenant-health/hobbs-hospital
Control: Other not-for-profit (including NFP Corporation) **Service**: General medical and surgical

Staffed Beds: 34 **Admissions**: 1027 **Census**: 8 **Outpatient Visits**: 68549 **Births**: 208 **Total Expense ($000)**: 59814 **Payroll Expense ($000)**: 10663 **Personnel**: 128

HOBBS HOSPITAL See Covenant Health Hobbs Hospital

LAS CRUCES—Dona Ana County

ADVANCED CARE HOSPITAL OF SOUTHERN NEW MEXICO (322004), 4451 East Lohman Avenue, Zip 88011-8267; tel. 575/521-6600, (Nonreporting) **A**1 10 **S** Ernest Health, Inc., Albuquerque, NM
Primary Contact: Sabrina Martin, Chief Executive Officer
COO: Christina Salazar, Chief Operating Officer
Web address: https://achsnm.ernesthealth.com/
Control: Corporation, Investor-owned (for-profit) **Service**: Acute long-term care hospital

Staffed Beds: 40

MEMORIAL MEDICAL CENTER (320018), 2450 South Telshor Boulevard, Zip 88011-5076; tel. 575/522-8641, (Nonreporting) **A**1 2 3 5 10 **S** Lifepoint Health, Brentwood, TN
Primary Contact: John Harris, Chief Executive Officer
COO: Mary Armijo, Chief Operating Officer
CFO: Steve Winegeart, Chief Financial Officer
CMO: Dolores Gomez, M.D., Chief Medical Officer
CHR: Laura Pierce, Director Human Resources
CNO: Caryn Iverson, MSN, Chief Nursing Officer
Web address: www.mmclc.org
Control: Corporation, Investor-owned (for-profit) **Service**: General medical and surgical

Staffed Beds: 173

MESILLA VALLEY HOSPITAL (324010), 3751 Del Rey Boulevard, Zip 88012-8526; tel. 575/382-3500, (Nonreporting) **A**1 10 **S** Universal Health Services, Inc., King of Prussia, PA
Primary Contact: Anna Laliotis, Chief Executive Officer
CFO: Dana McRimmon, Chief Financial Officer
CMO: Arthur L. Ramirez, M.D., Medical Director
CIO: Rebecca Mumpower, Director Marketing
CHR: Linda Moya, Director Human Resources
CNO: Veronica Hughes, Chief Nursing Officer
Web address: www.mesillavalleyhospital.com
Control: Corporation, Investor-owned (for-profit) **Service**: Psychiatric

Staffed Beds: 115

MOUNTAINVIEW REGIONAL MEDICAL CENTER (320085), 4311 East Lohman Avenue, Zip 88011-8255; tel. 575/556-7600, (Nonreporting) **A**1 3 5 10 12 13 **S** Community Health Systems, Inc., Franklin, TN
Primary Contact: Matthew Conrad, Interim Chief Executive Officer and Chief Operating Officer
COO: Matthew Conrad, Chief Operating Officer
CFO: Andrew McDonald, Chief Finance Officer
CIO: Donald Harlow, Director of Information Services
CHR: Delilah Doss, Director, Human Resources
CNO: Gayle Nash, R.N., M.P.H., Chief Nursing Officer
Web address: www.mountainviewregional.com
Control: Corporation, Investor-owned (for-profit) **Service**: General medical and surgical

Staffed Beds: 168

REHABILITATION HOSPITAL OF SOUTHERN NEW MEXICO (323032), 4441 East Lohman Avenue, Zip 88011-8267; tel. 575/521-6400, (Nonreporting) **A**1 10 **S** Ernest Health, Inc., Albuquerque, NM
Primary Contact: Sabrina Martin, Chief Executive Officer
CFO: Elizabeth Striplin, Chief Financial Officer
CMO: Kimberly Encapera, M.D., Medical Director
CHR: Yolanda Mendoza, Director Human Resources
CNO: Carole Carson, Director of Nursing Operations
Web address: www.rhsnm.ernesthealth.com
Control: Corporation, Investor-owned (for-profit) **Service**: Rehabilitation

Staffed Beds: 40

★ **THREE CROSSES REGIONAL HOSPITAL (320091)**, 2560 Samaritan Drive, Zip 88001-1170, Mailing Address: 2560 Samaritan DR, Zip 88001-1170; tel. 800/421-8274, (Nonreporting) **A**10
Primary Contact: John Lanning, Chief Executive Officer
Control: Partnership, Investor-owned (for-profit) **Service**: General medical and surgical

Staffed Beds: 20

LAS VEGAS—San Miguel County

ALTA VISTA REGIONAL HOSPITAL (320003), 104 Legion Drive, Zip 87701-4804; tel. 505/426-3500, (Nonreporting) **A**1 10 **S** Quorum Health, Brentwood, TN
Primary Contact: Robert Nelson, Chief Executive Officer
CMO: Nancy Wright, M.D., Chief Medical Staff
CIO: Laird Thornton, Director Information Systems
CHR: Michael Freeman, Director Human Resources
CNO: Rhonda Clark, Interim Chief Nursing Officer
Web address: www.altavistaregionalhospital.com
Control: Corporation, Investor-owned (for-profit) **Service**: General medical and surgical

Staffed Beds: 54

NEW MEXICO BEHAVIORAL HEALTH INSTITUTE AT LAS VEGAS, 3695 Hot Springs Boulevard, Zip 87701-9549; tel. 505/454-2100, (Nonreporting) **A**1
Primary Contact: Frances Tweed, R.N., Executive Director and Administrator
COO: Charles Jaramillo, Chief Operating Officer
CFO: Darlene Martinez, Director Finance
CMO: Daniel Collins, M.D., Clinical Director
CNO: Mabel Arguello-Vasquez, R.N., Executive Nurse Administrator
Web address: www.nmbhi.org
Control: State, Government, Nonfederal **Service**: Psychiatric

Staffed Beds: 257

LOS ALAMOS—Los Alamos County

LOS ALAMOS MEDICAL CENTER (320033), 3917 West Road, Zip 87544-2293, Mailing Address: PO Box 1663, Zip 87545; tel. 505/661-9500, **A**1 10 20 **F**3 8 11 13 15 28 29 31 34 40 45 46 57 59 70 76 78 81 85 87 90 93 97 107 108 110 111 115 119 130 133 147 149 154 **S** Lifepoint Health, Brentwood, TN
Primary Contact: Tracie Stratton, Chief Executive Officer
CFO: James McGonnell, Chief Financial Officer
CMO: Justin Green, M.D., Ph.D., FACS, Chief Medical Officer
CIO: Rob Mulikin, Director Information Systems
CHR: Jacqueline Carroll, Director Human Resources
CNO: Donald Ayers Hislop, R.N., Jr, Chief Nursing Officer
Web address: www.losalamosmedicalcenter.com
Control: Corporation, Investor-owned (for-profit) **Service**: General medical and surgical

Staffed Beds: 24 **Admissions**: 376 **Census**: 4

LOVINGTON—Lea County

★ ⇑ **NOR-LEA HOSPITAL DISTRICT (321305)**, 1600 North Main Avenue, Zip 88260-2871; tel. 575/396-6611, (Nonreporting) **A**10 18 21
Primary Contact: David B. Shaw, Chief Executive Officer and Administrator
COO: Dan Hamilton, Chief Operating Officer
CFO: Allyson Roberts, CPA, Chief Financial Officer
CMO: Ronald Hopkins, D.O., Chief of Staff
CIO: Brent Kelley, Director Information Technology
CHR: Angela Carrejo, Director Human Resources
Web address: www.norlea.org/
Control: Hospital district or authority, Government, Nonfederal **Service**: General medical and surgical

Staffed Beds: 25

Hospital, Medicare Provider Number, Address, Telephone, Approval, Facility, and Physician Codes, Health Care System

★ American Hospital Association (AHA) membership
☐ The Joint Commission accreditation
○ Healthcare Facilities Accreditation Program
◇ DNV Healthcare Inc. accreditation
⇑ Center for Improvement in Healthcare Quality Accreditation
△ Commission on Accreditation of Rehabilitation Facilities (CARF) accreditation

Hospitals, U.S. / NEW MEXICO

MESCALERO—Otero County

MESCALERO PUBLIC HEALTH SERVICE INDIAN HOSPITAL (320058), 318 Abalone Loop, Zip 88340, Mailing Address: Box 210, Zip 88340–0210; tel. 505/464–3801, (Nonreporting) **A**10 **S** U. S. Indian Health Service, Rockville, MD
Primary Contact: Dorlynn Simmons, Chief Executive Officer
CFO: Rainey Enjady, Administrative Officer
CIO: Kathy Murphy, Site Manager
Web address: www.ihs.gov
Control: PHS, Indian Service, Government, federal **Service**: General medical and surgical

Staffed Beds: 13

PORTALES—Roosevelt County

★ ⇑ **ROOSEVELT GENERAL HOSPITAL (320084)**, 42121 US Highway 70, Zip 88130, Mailing Address: P.O. Box 868, Zip 88130–0868; tel. 575/359–1800, (Nonreporting) **A**10 21
Primary Contact: Kaye Green, FACHE, Chief Executive Officer
CFO: Eva Steven, Chief Financial Officer
CMO: Les Donaldson, M.D., Chief of Staff
CHR: Cindy Duncan, Director Human Resources
Web address: www.myrgh.org
Control: Hospital district or authority, Government, Nonfederal **Service**: General medical and surgical

Staffed Beds: 24

ROOSEVELT GENERAL HOSPITAL See Plains Regional Medical Center–Portales

RATON—Colfax County

★ **MINERS' COLFAX MEDICAL CENTER (321307)**, 200 Hospital Drive, Zip 87740–2099; tel. 575/445–7700, (Includes MINERS' COLFAX MEDICAL CENTER, 203 Hospital DR, Raton, New Mexico, Zip 87740–2012, Box 1067, Zip 87740, tel. 575/445–3661; Bo Beames, Chief Executive Officer) (Nonreporting) **A**10 18
Primary Contact: Bo Beames, Chief Executive Officer
CFO: Albino Martinez, Director Budget and Finance
CIO: Richard Laner Jr, Manager Information Systems
CHR: Jamie Johnson, Director Human Resources
Web address: www.minershosp.com
Control: County, Government, Nonfederal **Service**: General medical and surgical

Staffed Beds: 25

MINERS' HOSPITAL OF NEW MEXICO See Miners' Colfax Medical Center

RIO RANCHO—Sandoval County

☐ **CLEARSKY REHABILITATION HOSPITAL OF RIO RANCHO (323033)**, 2401 Westside Boulevard Southeast, Zip 87124–4983; tel. 505/295–6358, (Nonreporting) **A**1 **S** ClearSky Health, West Lake Hills, TX
Primary Contact: Shawn Wilbur, Chief Executive Officer
Web address: www.clearskyhealth.com/riorancho
Control: Corporation, Investor–owned (for–profit) **Service**: Rehabilitation

Staffed Beds: 25

UNM SANDOVAL REGIONAL MEDICAL CENTER, INC. See Unm Sandoval Regional Medical Center, A Campus of Unm Hospital

ROSWELL—Chaves County

⊞ **EASTERN NEW MEXICO MEDICAL CENTER (320006)**, 405 West Country Club Road, Zip 88201–5209; tel. 575/622–8170, (Nonreporting) **A**1 10 19 **S** Community Health Systems, Inc., Franklin, TN
Primary Contact: Warren Yehl, Chief Executive Officer
CFO: Adelane Kelly, Chief Financial Officer
CMO: Richard Pinon, Chief Medical Officer
CIO: Deepak Surl, Chief Information Officer
CHR: Sheila Nunez, Director Human Resources
CNO: Kathy Williams, Chief Nursing Officer
Web address: www.enmmc.com
Control: Corporation, Investor–owned (for–profit) **Service**: General medical and surgical

Staffed Beds: 162

★ ⇑ **LOVELACE REGIONAL HOSPITAL – ROSWELL (320086)**, 117 East 19th Street, Zip 88201–5151; tel. 575/627–7000, **A**10 21 **F**3 13 17 18 22 29 34 40 45 57 59 70 76 79 81 82 85 89 90 91 93 107 111 119 127 130 146 147 154 **S** Ardent Health Services, Nashville, TN
Primary Contact: Nicholas Shirilla, Chief Executive Officer
CFO: Andrea Solin, Interim Chief Financial Officer
CNO: Christy Escandon, R.N., Chief Nursing Officer
Web address: www.lovelace.com
Control: Corporation, Investor–owned (for–profit) **Service**: General medical and surgical

Staffed Beds: 27 **Admissions**: 1668 **Census**: 10

☐ **NEW MEXICO REHABILITATION CENTER (323026)**, 72 Gail Harris Street, Zip 88203–8116; tel. 575/347–3400, (Includes PECOS VALLEY LODGE, 31 Gail Harris Avenue, Roswell, New Mexico, Zip 88201, tel. 505/347–5491) (Nonreporting) **A**1 10
Primary Contact: Matthew Rael, Administrator
CFO: Curtis Gant, Chief Financial Officer
CMO: Thomas Massaro, M.D., Chief Medical Officer
CIO: Dennis Hoefs, Manager Information Technology
CHR: Cynthia Trujillo, Director Human Resources
Control: State, Government, Nonfederal **Service**: Rehabilitation

Staffed Beds: 41

RUIDOSO—Lincoln County

⊞ **LINCOLN COUNTY MEDICAL CENTER (321306)**, 211 Sudderth Drive, Zip 88345–6043, Mailing Address: P.O. Box 8000, Zip 88355–8000; tel. 575/257–8200, **A**1 10 18 **F**3 7 11 13 15 18 28 29 31 34 35 39 40 45 46 48 50 53 56 57 59 64 65 68 70 76 77 78 79 81 85 87 91 93 97 107 110 111 115 119 127 130 131 132 133 135 146 148 154 160 169 **S** Presbyterian Healthcare Services, Albuquerque, NM
Primary Contact: Todd Oberheu, Hospital Chief Executive
CFO: Dudley McCauley, Controller
CMO: Gary Jackson, D.O., Medical Director
CHR: Susanne Johnston, Manager Human Resources
Web address: www.phs.org
Control: Other not–for–profit (including NFP Corporation) **Service**: General medical and surgical

Staffed Beds: 25 **Admissions**: 1291 **Census**: 12 **Outpatient Visits**: 32273 **Births**: 145 **Total Expense ($000)**: 68300 **Payroll Expense ($000)**: 28690 **Personnel**: 313

SANTA FE—Santa Fe County

⊞ △ **CHRISTUS ST. VINCENT REGIONAL MEDICAL CENTER (320002)**, 455 Saint Michaels Drive, Zip 87505–7601, Mailing Address: P.O. Box 2107, Zip 87505; tel. 505/983–3361, (Includes CHRISTUS ST. VINCENT PHYSICIANS MEDICAL CENTER, 2990 Rodeo Park Drive East, Santa Fe, New Mexico, Zip 87505, tel. 505/428–5400; J. Alex Valdez, JD, President and Chief Executive Officer) **A**1 3 5 7 10 **F**3 8 11 13 15 18 20 21 22 24 26 28 29 30 31 32 34 35 36 37 38 40 41 43 45 46 47 48 49 50 51 54 55 56 57 58 59 60 61 63 64 65 66 68 70 73 74 75 76 77 78 79 81 82 83 84 85 86 87 89 90 91 92 93 96 97 98 100 101 102 104 107 108 109 110 111 112 113 114 115 119 120 121 124 126 129 130 131 132 135 144 146 147 148 149 150 154 156 167 169 **S** CHRISTUS Health, Irving, TX
Primary Contact: Lillian Montoya, President and Chief Executive Officer
COO: Hope Wade, Chief Operating Officer
CMO: David Gonzales, Chief Medical Officer
CIO: Ron Dekeyzer, Regional Director Information Systems
CHR: Pearl Mohnkern, Vice President and Director Human Resources
Web address: www.stvin.org
Control: Other not–for–profit (including NFP Corporation) **Service**: General medical and surgical

Staffed Beds: 175 **Admissions**: 11424 **Census**: 149 **Outpatient Visits**: 245885 **Births**: 846 **Total Expense ($000)**: 560189 **Payroll Expense ($000)**: 206667 **Personnel**: 2017

PHS SANTA FE INDIAN HOSPITAL (320057), 1700 Cerrillos Road, Zip 87505–3554; tel. 505/988–9821, (Nonreporting) **A**5 10 **S** U. S. Indian Health Service, Rockville, MD
Primary Contact: Leslie Dye, Chief Executive Officer
CMO: Bret Smoker, M.D., Clinical Director
CIO: Vernita Jones, Site Manager
Control: PHS, Indian Service, Government, federal **Service**: General medical and surgical

Staffed Beds: 4

PHYSICIANS MEDICAL CENTER OF SANTA FE HOSPITAL See Christus St. Vincent Physicians Medical Center

Hospitals, U.S. / NEW MEXICO

☐ **PRESBYTERIAN SANTA FE MEDICAL CENTER (320090)**, 4801 Beckner Road, Zip 87507–3641; tel. 505/772–1234, **A**1 10 **F**3 11 13 18 19 29 30 34 35 39 40 44 45 50 51 54 57 59 64 65 68 70 74 75 76 77 79 81 82 84 85 93 97 100 104 107 108 111 115 119 126 130 131 144 146 147 149 154 156 160 169 **S** Presbyterian Healthcare Services, Albuquerque, NM
Primary Contact: John Adams, Hospital Chief Executive officer
Web address: https://santa-fe-medical-center.phs.org/Pages/default.aspx
Control: Other not–for–profit (including NFP Corporation) **Service:** General medical and surgical

Staffed Beds: 36 **Admissions:** 1809 **Census:** 17 **Outpatient Visits:** 43654 **Births:** 345 **Total Expense ($000):** 123095 **Payroll Expense ($000):** 41451 **Personnel:** 463

SANTA ROSA—Guadalupe County

★ **GUADALUPE COUNTY HOSPITAL (320779)**, 117 Camino de Vida, Zip 88435–2267; tel. 575/472–3417, **A**10 **F**3 34 35 40 59 65 66 68 107 119 122
CFO: Bret Goebel, Chief Financial Officer
CMO: Randal Brown, M.D., Chief of Medical Staff
CIO: Emilio Campos, Department Head Information Technology
CHR: Colleen Gallegos, Director Human Resources
CNO: Mandelyn Cordova, R.N., Director of Nurses
Web address: www.gchnm.org
Control: Other not–for–profit (including NFP Corporation)

Staffed Beds: 10 **Admissions:** 21 **Census:** 1 **Outpatient Visits:** 6774 **Births:** 2 **Total Expense ($000):** 9693 **Payroll Expense ($000):** 2530 **Personnel:** 43

SANTA TERESA—Dona Ana County

✠ **PEAK BEHAVIORAL HEALTH SERVICES (324012)**, 5065 McNutt Road, Zip 88008–9442; tel. 575/589–3000, (Nonreporting) **A**1 10 **S** Strategic Behavioral Health, LLC, Memphis, TN
Primary Contact: Sandra Emanuel, Chief Executive Officer
COO: Doug Ginn, Executive Vice President Operations
CFO: Espie Herrara, Chief Financial Officer
CHR: Norma Oaxaca, Director Human Resources
Web address: www.peakbehavioral.com/
Control: Corporation, Investor–owned (for–profit) **Service:** Psychiatric

Staffed Beds: 120

SHIPROCK—San Juan County

✠ **NORTHERN NAVAJO MEDICAL CENTER (320059)**, Highway 491 North, Zip 87420–0160, Mailing Address: P.O. Box 160, Zip 87420–0160; tel. 505/368–6001, (Nonreporting) **A**1 3 10 **S** U. S. Indian Health Service, Rockville, MD
Primary Contact: Captain Katrina Leslie–Puhuyaoma, D.D.S., Chief Executive Officer
CFO: Shawn Morgan, Finance Officer
CMO: Ira Salom, M.D., Clinical Director
CIO: Roland Chapman, Chief Information Officer
CHR: Gloria Redhorse–Charley, Director Human Resources
CNO: Lavenia Diswood, R.N., Chief Nurse Executive
Web address: www.ihs.gov/
Control: PHS, Indian Service, Government, federal **Service:** General medical and surgical

Staffed Beds: 68

SILVER CITY—Grant County

✠ **GILA REGIONAL MEDICAL CENTER (321311)**, 1313 East 32nd Street, Zip 88061–7251; tel. 575/538–4000, (Nonreporting) **A**1 10 18 **S** HealthTech Management Services, Plano, TX
Primary Contact: Robert Whitaker, Chief Executive Officer
CFO: Paul Rogers, Interim Chief Financial Officer
CIO: David Furnas, Chief Information Officer
CHR: Barbara Barela, Director Human Resources
CNO: Patricia Sheyka, Chief Nursing Officer
Web address: www.grmc.org
Control: County, Government, Nonfederal **Service:** General medical and surgical

Staffed Beds: 25

SOCORRO—Socorro County

✠ **SOCORRO GENERAL HOSPITAL (321301)**, 1202 Highway 60 West, Zip 87801–3914, Mailing Address: P.O. Box 1009, Zip 87801–1009; tel. 575/835–1140, (Nonreporting) **A**1 10 18 **S** Presbyterian Healthcare Services, Albuquerque, NM
Primary Contact: Veronica Pound, R.N., Hospital Chief Executive Officer, Chief Nursing Officer and Director, Home Health Care and Hospice
CFO: Scott Shannon, Director Finance
CMO: Darla Bejnar, M.D., Chief Medical Officer
CHR: Pam Miller–Balfour, Director Human Resources
CNO: Veronica Pound, R.N., Hospital Chief Executive Officer, Chief Nursing Officer and Director, Home Health Care and Hospice
Web address: www.phs.org
Control: Other not–for–profit (including NFP Corporation) **Service:** General medical and surgical

Staffed Beds: 24

TAOS—Taos County

★ ⑪ **HOLY CROSS HOSPITAL (321310)**, 1397 Weimer Road, Zip 87571–6253; tel. 575/758–8883, (Nonreporting) **A**3 10 18 21 **S** Ovation Healthcare, Brentwood, TN
Primary Contact: James Kiser, Chief Executive Officer
COO: Margaret Lynch, Chief of Support Operations
CFO: Steve Rozenboom, Chief Financial Officer
CHR: Judy Marshall, Director Human Resources
CNO: Denise Clark, Chief Nursing Officer
Web address: www.taoshospital.org
Control: Other not–for–profit (including NFP Corporation) **Service:** General medical and surgical

Staffed Beds: 25

TRUTH OR CONSEQUENCES—Sierra County

★ **SIERRA VISTA HOSPITAL (321300)**, 800 East Ninth Avenue, Zip 87901–1961; tel. 575/894–2111, **A**10 18 **F**3 5 7 11 15 18 29 40 43 45 46 50 64 65 75 77 81 97 100 104 107 110 111 115 127 128 129 130 133 135 143 154 157 **S** Ovation Healthcare, Brentwood, TN
Primary Contact: Frank Corcoran, R.N., Chief Executive Officer
CFO: Bret Gobel, Chief Financial Officer
CMO: James F Malcolmson, M.D., Chief of Staff
CIO: Dan Morrell, Manager Information Systems
CHR: Mindee Holguin, Manager Human Resources
CNO: Palmer Greene, R.N., Chief Nursing Officer
Web address: www.svhnm.org
Control: City–county, Government, Nonfederal **Service:** General medical and surgical

Staffed Beds: 11 **Admissions:** 331 **Census:** 4 **Outpatient Visits:** 11998 **Births:** 0 **Total Expense ($000):** 36713 **Payroll Expense ($000):** 11692 **Personnel:** 168

TUCUMCARI—Quay County

★ **DR. DAN C. TRIGG MEMORIAL HOSPITAL (321302)**, 301 East Miel De Luna Avenue, Zip 88401–3810, Mailing Address: P.O. Box 608, Zip 88401–0608; tel. 575/461–7000, (Nonreporting) **A**10 18 **S** Presbyterian Healthcare Services, Albuquerque, NM
Primary Contact: Vickie Gutierrez, Hospital Administrator and Chief Nursing Officer
CMO: Darrell Willis, M.D., Chief of Staff
CNO: Vickie Gutierrez, Hospital Administrator and Chief Nursing Officer
Web address: www.phs.org
Control: Other not–for–profit (including NFP Corporation) **Service:** General medical and surgical

Staffed Beds: 5

ZUNI—McKinley County

✠ **U. S. PUBLIC HEALTH SERVICE INDIAN HOSPITAL (320060)**, Route 301 North B Street, Zip 87327, Mailing Address: P.O. Box 467, Zip 87327–0467; tel. 505/782–4431, (Nonreporting) **A**1 10 **S** U. S. Indian Health Service, Rockville, MD
Primary Contact: Jean Othole, Chief Executive Officer
CFO: Clyde Yatsattie, Administrative Officer
CMO: David Kessler, M.D., Clinical Director
CHR: Cynthia Tsalate, Human Resource Specialist
Web address: www.ihs.gov
Control: PHS, Indian Service, Government, federal **Service:** General medical and surgical

Staffed Beds: 32

Hospital, Medicare Provider Number, Address, Telephone, Approval, Facility, and Physician Codes, Health Care System

★ American Hospital Association (AHA) membership   ○ Healthcare Facilities Accreditation Program   ⑪ Center for Improvement in Healthcare Quality Accreditation
☐ The Joint Commission accreditation   ◇ DNV Healthcare Inc. accreditation   △ Commission on Accreditation of Rehabilitation Facilities (CARF) accreditation

© 2025 AHA Guide

Hospitals, U.S. / NEW YORK

NEW YORK

ALBANY—Albany County

☐ **ALBANY MEDICAL CENTER (330013)**, 43 New Scotland Avenue, Zip 12208–3478; tel. 518/262–3125, (Includes ALBANY MEDICAL CENTER SOUTH–CLINICAL CAMPUS, 25 Hackett Boulevard, Albany, New York, Zip 12208–3499, tel. 518/242–1200; Timothy W Duffy, General Director) (Nonreporting) **A**1 2 3 5 8 10 19
Primary Contact: Dennis McKenna, M.D., President and Chief Executive Officer
COO: Bernadette R Pedlow, Senior Vice President Business and Chief Operating Officer
CFO: Frances Spreer–Albert, Chief Financial Officer and Executive Vice President
CMO: Dennis McKenna, M.D., Interim Vice President Medical Affairs
CIO: Kristopher Kusche, Vice President and Chief Information Officer
Web address: www.amc.edu
Control: Other not-for-profit (including NFP Corporation) **Service:** General medical and surgical

Staffed Beds: 789

✠ **ALBANY STRATTON VETERANS AFFAIRS MEDICAL CENTER**, 113 Holland Avenue, Zip 12208–3473; tel. 518/626–5000, (Nonreporting) **A**1 2 3 5 8 **S** Department of Veterans Affairs, Washington, DC
Primary Contact: Darlene DeLancey, Director
CFO: Gerard Scorzelli, Chief Financial Officer
CMO: Lourdes Irizarry, M.D., Chief of Staff
CIO: Ron Diaz, Manager Operations
CHR: Kenneth Kio, Manager Human Resources
CNO: Deborah Spath, R.N., MSN, Associate Director Patient and Nurses Services
Web address: www.albany.va.gov/
Control: Veterans Affairs, Government, federal **Service:** General medical and surgical

Staffed Beds: 110

☐ **CAPITAL DISTRICT PSYCHIATRIC CENTER (334046)**, 75 New Scotland Avenue, Zip 12208–3474; tel. 518/549–6000, (Nonreporting) **A**1 3 5 10 **S** New York State Office of Mental Health, Albany, NY
Primary Contact: Deborah Murray, Executive Director
COO: Catherine McGregor, Deputy Director Facility and Administrative Services
CMO: Kren K Shriver, M.D., Clinical Director
CNO: Charlene Puorto, Chief Nursing Officer
Web address: https://omh.ny.gov/omhweb/facilities/cdpc/index.htm
Control: State, Government, Nonfederal **Service:** Psychiatric

Staffed Beds: 100

CHILD'S HOSPITAL See Albany Medical Center South–Clinical Campus

MEMORIAL HOSPITAL See Samaritan Hospital – Albany Memorial Campus

✠ **ST. PETER'S HOSPITAL (330057)**, 315 South Manning Boulevard, Zip 12208–1789; tel. 518/525–1550, **A**1 2 3 5 10 **F**3 4 5 8 11 12 13 15 17 18 19 20 22 24 26 27 28 29 30 31 34 35 36 37 38 39 40 44 45 46 47 48 49 50 51 53 54 55 56 57 59 60 61 63 64 65 66 68 70 71 72 73 74 75 76 77 78 79 80 81 84 85 86 87 92 93 97 100 107 108 109 110 111 114 115 116 117 118 119 120 121 123 124 126 129 130 132 133 135 143 145 146 147 148 149 152 156 160 162 167 **S** Trinity Health, Livonia, MI
Primary Contact: Steven Hanks, M.D., President and Chief Executive Officer
CFO: Lori Santos, Chief Financial Officer
CMO: Robert Cella, M.D., Chief Medical Officer
CHR: Judy Gray, Vice President Human Resources
CNO: Jane O'Rourke, R.N., Chief Nursing Officer, Vice President Operations
Web address: https://www.sphp.com/location/st-peters-hospital
Control: Other not-for-profit (including NFP Corporation) **Service:** General medical and surgical

Staffed Beds: 482 **Admissions:** 27686 **Census:** 335 **Outpatient Visits:** 310389 **Births:** 2991 **Total Expense ($000):** 702260 **Payroll Expense ($000):** 245959

ALEXANDRIA BAY—Jefferson County

RIVER HOSPITAL (331309), 4 Fuller Street, Zip 13607–1316; tel. 315/482–2511, (Nonreporting) **A**10 18
Primary Contact: Kelley Tiernan, Interim Chief Executive Officer
COO: William Connor, Assistant Administrator and Director Human Resources
CFO: Traci Mintonye, Chief Financial Officer
CMO: Prasad Yitta, M.D., Medical Director
CIO: John Smithers, Network Specialist
CHR: William Connor, Assistant Administrator and Director Human Resources
CNO: Ann Narrow, Director of Nursing
Web address: www.riverhospital.org
Control: Other not-for-profit (including NFP Corporation) **Service:** General medical and surgical

Staffed Beds: 11

AMITYVILLE—Suffolk County

☐ **BRUNSWICK PSYCH CENTER (334026)**, 81 Louden Avenue, Zip 11701–2736; tel. 631/789–7421, (Nonreporting) **A**1 10
Primary Contact: Mini Singh, Chief Executive Officer
Control: Corporation, Investor-owned (for-profit) **Service:** Psychiatric

Staffed Beds: 124

✠ **SOUTH OAKS HOSPITAL (334027)**, 400 Sunrise Highway, Zip 11701–2508; tel. 631/264–4000, **A**1 10 **F**4 5 30 53 68 98 99 101 102 104 105 135 153 154 160 161 164 **S** Northwell Health, Lake Success, NY
Primary Contact: Michael Scarpelli, Executive Director
CMO: Tina Walch, M.D., Medical Director
CHR: Irene Calvin, Vice President Human Resources
Web address: www.longislandhome.org
Control: Other not-for-profit (including NFP Corporation) **Service:** Psychiatric

Staffed Beds: 202 **Admissions:** 3135 **Census:** 149 **Outpatient Visits:** 82615 **Total Expense ($000):** 113160 **Payroll Expense ($000):** 66098 **Personnel:** 748

AMSTERDAM—Montgomery County

✠ **ST. MARY'S HEALTHCARE (330047)**, 427 Guy Park Avenue, Zip 12010–1054; tel. 518/842–1900, (Includes ST. MARY'S HEALTHCARE, 427 Guy Park Avenue, Amsterdam, New York, Zip 12010–1054, tel. 518/842–1900) (Nonreporting) **A**1 10
Primary Contact: Jeffrey M. Methven, President and Chief Executive Officer
CFO: Rick Henze, Chief Financial Officer
CMO: William Mayer, M.D., Vice President Medical Staff Services
CHR: Albert Turo, Vice President Human Resources
CNO: Michele M Walsh, Chief Nursing Officer
Web address: www.smha.org
Control: Church operated, Nongovernment, not-for-profit **Service:** General medical and surgical

Staffed Beds: 290

ST. MARY'S HEALTHCARE See St. Mary's Healthcare, Amsterdam

ST. MARY'S HOSPITAL AMSTERDAM See St. Mary's Healthcare

AUBURN—Cayuga County

✠ **AUBURN COMMUNITY HOSPITAL (330235)**, 17 Lansing Street, Zip 13021–1943; tel. 315/255–7011, (Nonreporting) **A**1 10 20
Primary Contact: Scott A. Berlucchi, FACHE, President
CFO: Jason Lesch, Chief Financial Officer
CMO: Michael Wilson, M.D., Chief Medical Officer
CIO: Christopher Ryan, Chief Information Officer
CHR: Linda Daly, Vice President Human Resources
CNO: Tammy Sunderlin, Director of Nursing
Web address: www.auburnhospital.org
Control: Other not-for-profit (including NFP Corporation) **Service:** General medical and surgical

Staffed Beds: 179

BATAVIA—Genesee County

GENESEE MEMORIAL HOSPITAL See United Memorial Medical Center–North Street

Hospitals, U.S. / NEW YORK

ST JEROME HOSPITAL See United Memorial Medical Center–Bank Street

★ ⇑ **UNITED MEMORIAL MEDICAL CENTER (330073)**, 127 North Street, Zip 14020–1631; tel. 585/343–6030, (Includes UNITED MEMORIAL MEDICAL CENTER–BANK STREET, 16 Bank Street, Batavia, New York, Zip 14020–2260, tel. 585/343–6030; UNITED MEMORIAL MEDICAL CENTER–NORTH STREET, 127 North Street, Batavia, New York, Zip 14020–1697, tel. 585/343–6030) **A**3 5 10 13 21 **F**3 4 8 13 15 17 18 28 29 30 31 34 35 40 49 50 51 54 57 59 64 65 68 70 74 75 76 77 78 79 81 82 84 85 86 87 93 97 107 111 114 115 119 120 121 122 126 127 129 130 131 132 135 144 146 147 148 149 154 156 157 **S** Rochester Regional Health, Rochester, NY
Primary Contact: Daniel P. Ireland, FACHE, President and Chief Operating Officer, Finger Lakes Rural Hospitals
CFO: Robert Chiavetta, Vice President Finance
CMO: Tara L Gellasch, Chief Medical Officer
CIO: Chad Caccamise, Director Information Services
CHR: Eileen Herkimer, Director Human Resources
CNO: Marilyn Almeter, Chief Nursing Officer
Web address: www.ummc.org
Control: Other not–for–profit (including NFP Corporation) **Service:** General medical and surgical

Staffed Beds: 113 **Admissions:** 4601 **Census:** 68 **Outpatient Visits:** 328338 **Births:** 397 **Total Expense ($000):** 150733 **Payroll Expense ($000):** 76581 **Personnel:** 664

✠ **VETERANS AFFAIRS WESTERN NEW YORK HEALTHCARE SYSTEM–BATAVIA DIVISION**, 222 Richmond Avenue, Zip 14020–1288; tel. 585/297–1000, (Nonreporting) **A**1 **S** Department of Veterans Affairs, Washington, DC
Primary Contact: Michael J. Swartz, FACHE, Interim Director
Web address: www.buffalo.va.gov/batavia.asp
Control: Veterans Affairs, Government, federal **Service:** General medical and surgical

Staffed Beds: 128

BATH—Steuben County

✠ **BATH VETERANS AFFAIRS MEDICAL CENTER**, 76 Veterans Avenue, Zip 14810–0842; tel. 607/664–4000, (Nonreporting) **A**1 **S** Department of Veterans Affairs, Washington, DC
Primary Contact: Bruce Tucker, Medical Center Director
CFO: Jill Haynes, Financial Coach
CMO: Robert Babcock, M.D., Interim Chief of Staff
CHR: Susan DeSalvo, Manager Human Resources
Web address: www.bath.va.gov
Control: Veterans Affairs, Government, federal **Service:** General medical and surgical

Staffed Beds: 127

✠ **IRA DAVENPORT MEMORIAL HOSPITAL (330144)**, 7571 State Route 54, Zip 14810–9590; tel. 607/776–8500, (Nonreporting) **A**1 10 **S** Arnot Health, Elmira, NY
Primary Contact: Elizabeth Weir, MSN, R.N., Site Administrator and Vice President of Nursing
CFO: Ronald J Kintz, Chief Financial Officer
CMO: Dennis O'Connor, M.D., Medical Director
CIO: Gregg Martin, Chief Information Officer
CHR: Dave Stanbro, Director Human Resources
CNO: Linda Donley, Vice President Operations
Web address: www.arnothealth.org
Control: Other not–for–profit (including NFP Corporation) **Service:** General medical and surgical

Staffed Beds: 135

BAY SHORE—Suffolk County

✠ **SOUTH SHORE UNIVERSITY HOSPITAL (330043)**, 301 East Main Street, Zip 11706–8458; tel. 631/968–3000, **A**1 2 3 5 10 19 **F**3 8 11 12 13 15 17 18 20 22 24 26 28 29 30 31 32 34 35 36 37 38 40 41 43 44 45 46 47 48 49 50 51 53 54 56 57 58 59 60 61 62 63 64 65 66 68 70 71 73 74 75 76 77 78 79 81 82 84 85 86 87 89 92 93 96 97 100 102 107 108 111 114 115 119 126 129 130 131 132 134 135 145 146 147 148 149 154 156 157 160 164 167 169 **S** Northwell Health, Lake Success, NY
Primary Contact: Irene Macyk, R.N., MS, Ph.D., Executive Director
CFO: Michele Cusack, Senior Vice President and Chief Financial Officer
CMO: Jay Enden, M.D., Medical Director
CHR: Anne J Barrett, Associate Executive Director Human Resources
Web address: https://www.northwell.edu/find-care/locations/southside-hospital
Control: Other not–for–profit (including NFP Corporation) **Service:** General medical and surgical

Staffed Beds: 322 **Admissions:** 23051 **Census:** 300 **Outpatient Visits:** 183203 **Births:** 2626 **Total Expense ($000):** 1040846 **Payroll Expense ($000):** 522508 **Personnel:** 3782

SOUTHSIDE HOSPITAL See South Shore University Hospital

BELLEROSE—Queens County, See New York City

BETHPAGE—Nassau County

✠ **ST. JOSEPH HOSPITAL (330332)**, 4295 Hempstead Turnpike, Zip 11714–5769; tel. 516/579–6000, **A**1 3 5 10 **F**3 12 18 20 22 29 30 31 34 35 37 40 44 45 49 50 51 57 59 64 65 70 74 75 78 79 81 82 84 85 86 87 93 107 108 111 114 115 119 126 130 132 141 146 149 156 167 168 **S** Catholic Health Services of Long Island, Rockville Centre, NY
Primary Contact: Christopher Nelson, President
CFO: John Morahan, Vice President Finance
CMO: Howard Sussman, M.D., Chief Medical Officer
CNO: Barbara Gibbons, Vice President Patient Care Services
Web address: www.stjosephhospital.chsli.org/
Control: Church operated, Nongovernment, not–for–profit **Service:** General medical and surgical

Staffed Beds: 121 **Admissions:** 6345 **Census:** 86 **Outpatient Visits:** 55021 **Births:** 0 **Total Expense ($000):** 182202 **Payroll Expense ($000):** 72280 **Personnel:** 827

BINGHAMTON—Broome County

BINGHAMTON GENERAL HOSPITAL See United Health Services Hospitals–Binghamton, Binghamton

☐ **GREATER BINGHAMTON HEALTH CENTER (334012)**, 425 Robinson Street, Zip 13904–1735; tel. 607/724–1391, (Nonreporting) **A**1 3 10 **S** New York State Office of Mental Health, Albany, NY
Primary Contact: David Peppel, Executive Director
CFO: Cherry Randall, Business Officer
CHR: Renee O'Brien, Director Human Resources
Web address: www.omh.ny.gov/omhweb/facilities/bipc/facility.htm
Control: State, Government, Nonfederal **Service:** Psychiatric

Staffed Beds: 86

✠ **GUTHRIE LOURDES HOSPITAL (330011)**, 169 Riverside Drive, Zip 13905–4246; tel. 607/798–5111, (Nonreporting) **A**1 2 3 5 10 13 19 **S** Guthrie Clinic, Sayre, PA
Primary Contact: Kathryn Connerton, President and Chief Executive Officer
CFO: Sean Mills, Chief Financial Officer
CMO: Richard Blansky, M.D., Chief Medical Officer
CIO: Thomas Ellerson, Chief Information Officer
CHR: Mary Hughs, Chief Human Resources Officer
Web address: www.lourdes.com
Control: Church operated, Nongovernment, not–for–profit **Service:** General medical and surgical

Staffed Beds: 197

☐ **UNITED HEALTH SERVICES HOSPITALS–BINGHAMTON (330394)**, 10–42 Mitchell Avenue, Zip 13903–1678; tel. 607/763–6000, (Includes BINGHAMTON GENERAL HOSPITAL, 10–42 Mitchell Avenue, Binghamton, New York, Zip 13903, tel. 607/762–2200; John M. Carrigg, President and Chief Executive Officer; WILSON MEMORIAL REGIONAL MEDICAL CENTER, 33–57 Harrison Street, Johnson City, New York, Zip 13790, tel. 607/763–6000; John M. Carrigg, President and Chief Executive Officer) (Nonreporting) **A**1 2 3 5 8 19 **S** United Health Services, Binghamton, NY
Primary Contact: John M. Carrigg, President and Chief Executive Officer
COO: John M. Carrigg, Executive Vice President and Chief Operating Officer
CFO: David MacDougall, Chief Financial Officer
CMO: Rajesh J Dave', M.D., Executive Vice President and Chief Medical Officer
CIO: Susan Carman, Chief Information Officer
CNO: E. Kay Boland, R.N., MS, Vice President and Chief Nursing Officer
Web address: www.uhs.net
Control: Other not–for–profit (including NFP Corporation) **Service:** General medical and surgical

Staffed Beds: 464

BRENTWOOD—Suffolk County

☐ **PILGRIM PSYCHIATRIC CENTER (334013)**, 998 Crooked Hill Road, Zip 11717–1019; tel. 631/761–3500, (Nonreporting) **A**1 10 **S** New York State Office of Mental Health, Albany, NY
Primary Contact: Kathy O'Keefe, Executive Director
Web address: www.omh.ny.gov/omhweb/facilities/pgpc/facility.htm
Control: State, Government, Nonfederal **Service:** Psychiatric

Staffed Beds: 569

Hospital, Medicare Provider Number, Address, Telephone, Approval, Facility, and Physician Codes, Health Care System

★ American Hospital Association (AHA) membership
☐ The Joint Commission accreditation
○ Healthcare Facilities Accreditation Program
◇ DNV Healthcare Inc. accreditation
⇑ Center for Improvement in Healthcare Quality Accreditation
△ Commission on Accreditation of Rehabilitation Facilities (CARF) accreditation

© 2025 AHA Guide

Hospitals, U.S. / NEW YORK

BRONX—Bronx County, See New York City

BRONXVILLE—Westchester County

LAWRENCE HOSPITAL CENTER See New York–Presbyterian/Lawrence Hospital

BROOKLYN—Kings County, See New York City

BUFFALO—Erie County

BRYLIN HOSPITALS (334022), 1263 Delaware Avenue, Zip 14209–2402; tel. 716/886–8200, (Nonreporting) **A**10
Primary Contact: Eric D. Pleskow, President and Chief Executive Officer
CFO: E Paul Hettich, Chief Financial Officer
CMO: Maria Cartagena, M.D., Chief Medical Officer
CIO: Pawel Wieczorek, Director Information Technology
Web address: www.brylin.com
Control: Corporation, Investor–owned (for–profit) **Service**: Psychiatric

Staffed Beds: 88

☐ **BUFFALO PSYCHIATRIC CENTER (334052)**, 400 Forest Avenue, Zip 14213–1298; tel. 716/885–2261, (Nonreporting) **A**1 3 5 10 **S** New York State Office of Mental Health, Albany, NY
Primary Contact: Beatrix Souza, Chief Executive Officer
COO: Celia Spacone, M.D., Director Operations
CFO: Pamela Esposito, Director Administration
CMO: Jeffery Grace, M.D., Clinical Director
CIO: Anne Buchheit, Coordinator Mental Health Local Information Systems
CHR: Charles Siewert, Director Human Resources
CNO: Susan Fallis, Chief Nursing Officer
Web address: www.omh.ny.gov
Control: State, Government, Nonfederal **Service**: Psychiatric

Staffed Beds: 240

CHILDREN'S HOSPITAL See Women and Children's Hospital

△ **ERIE COUNTY MEDICAL CENTER (330219)**, 462 Grider Street, Zip 14215–3098; tel. 716/898–3000, (Nonreporting) **A**1 2 3 5 7 10 19
Primary Contact: Thomas J. Quatroche Jr, President and Chief Executive Officer
COO: Andrew L Davis Jr, Chief Operating Officer
CFO: Michael Sammarco, M.D., Chief Financial Officer
CMO: Brian Murray, M.D., Medical Director
CIO: Leslie Feidt, Chief Information Officer
CHR: Kathleen O'Hara, Vice President Human Resources
CNO: Karen Ziemianski, R.N., MS, Senior Vice President Nursing
Web address: www.ecmc.edu
Control: Hospital district or authority, Government, Nonfederal **Service**: General medical and surgical

Staffed Beds: 889

⇑ **KALEIDA HEALTH (330005)**, 100 High Street, Zip 14203–1154; tel. 716/859–5600, (Includes DE GRAFF MEDICAL PARK, 445 Tremont Street, North Tonawanda, New York, Zip 14120–0750, P O Box 0750, Zip 14120–0750, tel. 716/694–4500; Donald Boyd, Chief Executive Officer; MILLARD FILLMORE SUBURBAN HOSPITAL, 1540 Maple Road, Williamsville, New York, Zip 14221, tel. 716/688–3100; Donald Boyd, Chief Executive Officer; WOMEN AND CHILDREN'S HOSPITAL, 219 Bryant Street, Buffalo, New York, Zip 14222–2099, tel. 716/878–7000; Cheryl Klass, President) (Nonreporting) **A**2 3 5 10 19 21
Primary Contact: Donald Boyd, President and Chief Executive Officer
CMO: Michael Mineo, M.D., Interim Chief Medical Officer
CIO: Robert Diamond, Senior Vice President and Chief Operating Officer
Web address: www.kaleidahealth.org
Control: Other not–for–profit (including NFP Corporation) **Service**: General medical and surgical

Staffed Beds: 1368

MERCY HOSPITAL (330279), 565 Abbott Road, Zip 14220–2095; tel. 716/826–7000, (Nonreporting) **A**1 3 5 10 **S** Catholic Health System, Buffalo, NY
Primary Contact: Martin W. Boryszak, President
CFO: James H Dunlop, CPA, Jr, Senior Vice President Finance and Chief Financial Officer
CMO: Timothy Gabryel, M.D., Vice President Medical Affairs and Medical Director
CIO: Michael Galang, M.D., Chief Information Officer
CHR: Joseph A Scrivo Jr, Director Human Resources
Web address: www.chsbuffalo.org
Control: Church operated, Nongovernment, not–for–profit **Service**: General medical and surgical

Staffed Beds: 369

NAZARETH NURSING HOME See Nazareth Home

☐ **ROSWELL PARK COMPREHENSIVE CANCER CENTER (330354)**, 665 Elm Street, Zip 14203–1104; tel. 716/845–2300, **A**1 2 3 5 10 **F**3 14 15 29 30 31 32 34 35 36 38 39 44 45 46 47 48 49 50 54 55 57 58 59 63 64 67 70 74 75 77 78 79 80 81 82 84 85 86 87 90 91 92 93 94 96 98 107 108 110 111 112 114 115 116 117 118 119 120 121 123 124 126 130 132 134 135 136 141 145 146 147 148 149 154 157 160 164 167 **P**6
Primary Contact: Candace Johnson, Ph.D., President and Chief Executive Officer
COO: Shirley Johnson, Chief Clinical Operations Officer
CFO: Gregory McDonald, Vice President Finance and Chief Financial Officer
CMO: Boris Kuvshinoff, M.D., II, Chief Medical Officer
CIO: Thomas Furlani, M.D., Chief Information Officer
CHR: Errol A. Douglas, MS, Vice President, Human Resources
CNO: Andrew Storer, Ph.D., R.N., Chief Nursing Officer and Senior Vice President for Patient Care Services
Web address: www.roswellpark.org
Control: Hospital district or authority, Government, Nonfederal **Service**: Cancer

Staffed Beds: 142 **Admissions**: 5258 **Census**: 120 **Outpatient Visits**: 294413 **Births**: 0 **Total Expense ($000)**: 928750 **Payroll Expense ($000)**: 323274 **Personnel**: 3840

SISTERS OF CHARITY HOSPITAL OF BUFFALO (330078), 2157 Main Street, Zip 14214–2692; tel. 716/862–1000, (Includes ELIZABETH SETON CHILDREN'S CENTER, 300 Corporate Boulevard South, Yonkers, New York, Zip 10701–6862, tel. 914/294–6300; ST. JOSEPH HOSPITAL, 2605 Harlem Road, Cheektowaga, New York, Zip 14225–4097, tel. 716/891–2400) (Nonreporting) **A**1 3 5 10 13 19 **S** Catholic Health System, Buffalo, NY
Primary Contact: Meghan Aldrich, President
CFO: James H Dunlop, CPA, Jr, Chief Financial Officer
CMO: Nady Shehata, M.D., Vice President Medical Affairs
CIO: Michael Galang, M.D., Chief Information Officer
CHR: David DeLorenzo, Senior Director Human Resources
CNO: Jessica Visser, R.N., Chief Nursing Officer
Web address: www.chsbuffalo.org
Control: Church operated, Nongovernment, not–for–profit **Service**: General medical and surgical

Staffed Beds: 321

ST FRANCIS HOSPITAL OF BUFFALO See St. Francis of Buffalo

VETERANS AFFAIRS WESTERN NEW YORK HEALTHCARE SYSTEM–BUFFALO DIVISION, 3495 Bailey Avenue, Zip 14215–1129; tel. 716/834–9200, (Nonreporting) **A**1 3 5 **S** Department of Veterans Affairs, Washington, DC
Primary Contact: Michael J. Swartz, FACHE, Executive Director, Veterans Affairs Western New York Healthcare System
CFO: Susan Gage, Financial Manager
CMO: Ali El–Solh, M.D., Interim Chief of Staff
CIO: Margaret Senker, Chief Information Officer
Web address: www.buffalo.va.gov/index.asp
Control: Veterans Affairs, Government, federal **Service**: General medical and surgical

Staffed Beds: 127

WOMEN AND CHILDREN'S HOSPITAL See Kaleida Health, Buffalo

CALLICOON—Sullivan County

⇑ **GARNET HEALTH MEDICAL CENTER – CATSKILLS, CALLICOON CAMPUS (331303)**, 8881 Route 97, Zip 12723; tel. 845/887–5530, (Nonreporting) **A**10 18 21 **S** Garnet Health, Middletown, NY
Primary Contact: Jerry Dunlavey, Chief Executive Officer
CNO: Suzanne Lange–Ahmed, Chief Nursing Officer
Web address: https://www.garnethealth.org/locations/garnet-health-medical-center-catskills-callicoon-campus
Control: Other not–for–profit (including NFP Corporation) **Service**: General medical and surgical

Staffed Beds: 10

CANANDAIGUA—Ontario County

F. F. THOMPSON HOSPITAL (330074), 350 Parrish Street, Zip 14424–1731; tel. 585/396–6000, **A**1 3 5 10 **F**3 13 15 18 28 29 30 34 37 40 45 51 53 55 56 57 64 65 70 75 76 77 81 82 85 107 108 110 111 114 115 119 126 130 131 135 137 138 140 144 145 146 147 148 149 154 167 **S** University of Rochester Medical Center, Rochester, NY
Primary Contact: Michael Stapleton, R.N., MS, FACHE, President and Chief Executive Officer
COO: Kurt Koczent, Executive Vice President and Chief Operating Officer
CFO: Mark Prunoske, Chief Financial Officer and Senior Vice President Finance
CMO: David Baum, M.D., Senior Vice President Medical Services
CHR: Jennifer DeVault, Vice President Associate Services
CNO: Hazel Robertshaw, R.N., Ph.D., Chief Nursing Officer, Vice President Patient Services
Web address: www.thompsonhealth.com
Control: Other not–for–profit (including NFP Corporation) **Service**: General medical and surgical

Staffed Beds: 87 **Admissions**: 5005 **Census**: 65 **Outpatient Visits**: 476690 **Births**: 738 **Total Expense ($000)**: 212806 **Payroll Expense ($000)**: 98885 **Personnel**: 1538

CARMEL—Putnam County

ARMS ACRES, 75 Seminary Hill Road, Zip 10512–1921; tel. 845/225–3400, (Nonreporting) **A**3
Primary Contact: Patrice Wallace–Moore, Chief Executive Officer and Executive Director
CFO: Jason Burczeuski, Controller
CMO: Fred Hesse, M.D., Medical Director
CIO: Dolores Watson, Director Health Information Management
CHR: Kim Halpin, Director Human Resources
CNO: Barbara Klein, R.N., Director of Nursing
Web address: www.armsacres.com
Control: Corporation, Investor–owned (for–profit) **Service**: Substance Use Disorder

Staffed Beds: 160

PUTNAM HOSPITAL (330273), 670 Stoneleigh Avenue, Zip 10512–3997; tel. 845/279–5711, **A**1 3 10 **F**3 8 12 13 15 18 28 29 30 31 34 35 37 38 40 41 44 45 46 50 51 54 55 56 57 59 64 65 68 70 74 75 76 77 78 79 81 82 84 85 87 92 93 96 98 100 102 104 105 107 108 110 111 114 115 118 119 120 121 126 129 130 131 132 135 141 143 146 147 149 154 156 157 160 161 162 164 165 167 169 **S** Nuvance Health, Danbury, CT
Primary Contact: Mark Hirko, M.D., FACS, President
CFO: Joseph Hart, Director Finance and Support Services
CNO: Luanne Convery, Vice President Patient Care Services
Web address: https://www.nuvancehealth.org/locations/putnam-hospital
Control: Other not–for–profit (including NFP Corporation) **Service**: General medical and surgical

Staffed Beds: 62 **Admissions**: 3072 **Census**: 47 **Outpatient Visits**: 78220 **Births**: 17 **Total Expense ($000)**: 148922 **Payroll Expense ($000)**: 56261 **Personnel**: 560

PUTNAM HOSPITAL CENTER See Putnam Hospital

CARTHAGE—Jefferson County

CARTHAGE AREA HOSPITAL (331318), 1001 West Street, Zip 13619–9703; tel. 315/493–1000, (Nonreporting) **A**1 10 18
Primary Contact: Richard Duvall, Chief Executive Officer
COO: Natalie Burnham, Chief Operating Officer
CFO: Rob Bloom, Chief Financial Officer
CMO: Michael Gordon, M.D., Chief Medical Officer
CIO: John Cranker, Chief Information Officer
CHR: Diana Chamberlain, Director Human Resources
CNO: Steven Olson, Administrator Patient Care Services
Web address: www.carthagehospital.com
Control: Other not–for–profit (including NFP Corporation) **Service**: General medical and surgical

Staffed Beds: 25

CATSKILL—Greene County

COLUMBIA–GREENE LONG TERM CARE See Kaaterskill Care

CLIFTON SPRINGS—Ontario County

★ ⇧ **CLIFTON SPRINGS HOSPITAL AND CLINIC (330265)**, 2 Coulter Road, Zip 14432–1189; tel. 315/462–9561, (Total facility includes 108 beds in nursing home–type unit) **A**3 10 21 **F**3 4 5 15 18 28 29 30 31 34 36 37 38 39 40 44 45 46 47 48 50 54 56 57 59 60 64 68 70 71 75 77 78 79 81 82 85 86 87 90 93 97 98 100 101 102 104 107 108 110 115 118 119 120 121 123 126 128 130 131 132 141 145 146 148 149 154 156 160 161 165 167 **S** Rochester Regional Health, Rochester, NY
Primary Contact: Daniel P. Ireland, FACHE, President and Chief Operating Officer, Finger Lakes Rural Hospitals
CFO: Sharon Kelley, Chief Financial Officer
CIO: Joel Majauskas, Chief Information Officer
CHR: Kathy Babb, Manager Human Resources
CNO: Donna P Smith, R.N., Vice President Chief Operating Officer and Chief Nursing Officer
Web address: www.cliftonspringshospital.org
Control: Other not–for–profit (including NFP Corporation) **Service**: General medical and surgical

Staffed Beds: 194 **Admissions**: 3059 **Census**: 169 **Outpatient Visits**: 170327 **Births**: 0 **Total Expense ($000)**: 123918 **Payroll Expense ($000)**: 62231 **Personnel**: 491

COBLESKILL—Schoharie County

COBLESKILL REGIONAL HOSPITAL (331320), 178 Grandview Drive, Zip 12043–5144; tel. 518/254–3456, (Nonreporting) **A**1 10 18 **S** Bassett Healthcare Network, Cooperstown, NY
Primary Contact: Susan Oakes Ferrucci, MS, Chief Hospital Executive
CFO: James Vielkind, Chief Financial Officer
CMO: Roy Korn, M.D., Medical Director
CIO: Bridgette West, Director Patient Access Services
Web address: www.bassett.org
Control: Other not–for–profit (including NFP Corporation) **Service**: General medical and surgical

Staffed Beds: 25

COOPERSTOWN—Otsego County

BASSETT MEDICAL CENTER (330136), 1 Atwell Road, Zip 13326–1394; tel. 607/547–3456, (Nonreporting) **A**1 2 3 5 8 10 **S** Bassett Healthcare Network, Cooperstown, NY
Primary Contact: Henry Weil, M.D., President
COO: Ronette Wiley, R.N., Executive Vice President and Chief Operating Officer
CFO: Paul G. Swinko Jr, Corporate Vice President and Chief Financial Officer
CMO: Nicholas Hellenthal, M.D., Chief Medical Officer
CIO: Amelia Marley, Chief Information Officer
CHR: Sara Z Albright, Vice President Human Resources
Web address: www.bassett.org
Control: Other not–for–profit (including NFP Corporation) **Service**: General medical and surgical

Staffed Beds: 152

CORNING—Steuben County

GUTHRIE CORNING HOSPITAL (330277), 1 Guthrie Drive, Zip 14830–3696; tel. 607/937–7200, (Nonreporting) **A**1 3 10 **S** Guthrie Clinic, Sayre, PA
Primary Contact: Paul VerValin, President
CFO: Francis M Macafee, Vice President Finance and Chief Financial Officer
CMO: Chris Wentzel, M.D., Interim Medical Director
CHR: Laura Manning, Administrative Director
CNO: Debra Raupers, MSN, R.N., Chief Nursing Officer
Web address: https://www.guthrie.org/locations/guthrie-corning-hospital
Control: Other not–for–profit (including NFP Corporation) **Service**: General medical and surgical

Staffed Beds: 65

CORNWALL—Orange County

CORNWALL HOSPITAL See St. Luke's Cornwall Hospital – Cornwall Campus

ST. LUKE'S CORNWALL HOSPITAL – CORNWALL CAMPUS See Montefiore St. Luke's Cornwall, Newburgh

CORTLAND—Cortland County

GUTHRIE CORTLAND REGIONAL MEDICAL CENTER (330175), 134 Homer Avenue, Zip 13045–1206; tel. 607/756–3500, (Nonreporting) **A**1 3 10 20
Primary Contact: Jennifer Yartym, President
COO: Tracy Gates, Vice President Operations and Chief Operating Officer
CFO: Denise Wrinn, Vice President Finance and Chief Financial Officer
CMO: Russell Firman, M.D., Chief Medical Officer
CIO: Robert J Duthe, Director Information Systems and Chief Information Officer
CNO: Mary Wright, Vice President Nursing Services and Chief Nursing Officer
Web address: www.cortlandregional.org
Control: Other not–for–profit (including NFP Corporation) **Service**: General medical and surgical

Staffed Beds: 149

Hospitals, U.S. / NEW YORK

CORTLANDT MANOR—Westchester County

NEW YORK–PRESBYTERIAN/HUDSON VALLEY HOSPITAL (330267), 1980 Crompond Road, Zip 10567–4182; tel. 914/737–9000, **A**1 2 10 **F**3 8 11 12 13 15 18 20 22 26 28 29 30 31 34 35 36 37 40 41 44 45 46 47 49 51 54 55 56 57 59 60 64 68 70 73 74 75 76 77 78 79 81 82 84 85 87 89 93 94 102 107 108 110 111 114 115 116 117 119 120 124 126 129 130 131 145 146 147 148 149 154 156 160 162 167 **S** New York–Presbyterian, New York, NY
Primary Contact: Paul Dunphey, President
COO: Deborah Neuendorf, Vice President Administration
CFO: Mark Webster, Vice President Finance
CMO: William Higgins, M.D., Vice President Medical Affairs
CIO: Bud Sorbello, Director Management Information Systems
CHR: Jeane L Costella, Vice President
CNO: Kathleen Webster, R.N., MSN, Vice President Patient Services
Web address: www.hvhc.org
Control: Other not–for–profit (including NFP Corporation) **Service**: General medical and surgical

Staffed Beds: 128 **Admissions**: 7659 **Census**: 96 **Outpatient Visits**: 159963 **Births**: 806 **Total Expense ($000)**: 368863 **Payroll Expense ($000)**: 125151 **Personnel**: 950

CUBA—Allegany County

CUBA MEMORIAL HOSPITAL (331301), 140 West Main Street, Zip 14727–1398; tel. 585/968–2000, (Nonreporting) **A**10 18
Primary Contact: Norma Kerling, Interim Chief Executive Officer and Chief Clinical Officer
CFO: Jack Ormond, Chief Financial Officer
Web address: www.cubamemorialhospital.com
Control: Other not–for–profit (including NFP Corporation) **Service**: General medical and surgical

Staffed Beds: 81

DANSVILLE—Livingston County

NICHOLAS H. NOYES MEMORIAL HOSPITAL (330238), 111 Clara Barton Street, Zip 14437–9503; tel. 585/335–6001, (Nonreporting) **A**1 10 **S** University of Rochester Medical Center, Rochester, NY
Primary Contact: John Teeters, M.D., President and Chief Executive Officer
CFO: Mark Prunoske, Chief Financial Officer
CMO: Douglas Mayhle, M.D., Medical Director
CIO: John Dorak, Director, Information Systems
CHR: Cassie Weitzel, Director, Human Resources
CNO: Tamara West, R.N., MSN, Vice President Patient Care
Web address: www.noyes-health.org
Control: Other not–for–profit (including NFP Corporation) **Service**: General medical and surgical

Staffed Beds: 67

DELHI—Delaware County

O'CONNOR HOSPITAL (331305), 460 Andes Road, State Route 28, Zip 13753–7407; tel. 607/746–0300, (Nonreporting) **A**1 10 18 **S** Bassett Healthcare Network, Cooperstown, NY
Primary Contact: Susan Oakes Ferrucci, MS, Chief Hospital Executive
CFO: Sue E. Andrews, Chief Financial Officer
CMO: Peter L Sosnow, Medical Director
CHR: Barbara Green, Director Human Resources
CNO: Debra Neale, R.N., Chief Nursing Officer
Web address: https://www.bassett.org/locations/oconnor-hospital
Control: Other not–for–profit (including NFP Corporation) **Service**: General medical and surgical

Staffed Beds: 23

DIX HILLS—Suffolk County

SAGAMORE CHILDREN'S PSYCHIATRIC CENTER (334064), 197 Half Hollow Road, Zip 11746–5861; tel. 631/370–1700, (Nonreporting) **A**1 10 **S** New York State Office of Mental Health, Albany, NY
Primary Contact: Kathy O'Keefe, Interim Executive Director
COO: Cathy Stein, Chief Inpatient Services
CFO: Jane Alexander, Director Facility Administrative Services
CIO: Bryan Doherty, Management Information Technology Services I
CHR: Nancy Angell, Associate Administrator Personnel
CNO: Sandra King, Chief Nursing Officer
Web address: www.omh.ny.gov
Control: State, Government, Nonfederal **Service**: Children's hospital psychiatric

Staffed Beds: 54

DOBBS FERRY—Westchester County

COMMUNITY HOSPITAL AT DOBBS FERRY See St. John's Riverside Hospital – Dobbs Ferry Pavilion

DUNKIRK—Chautauqua County

★ **BROOKS–TLC HOSPITAL SYSTEM, INC. (330229)**, 529 Central Avenue, Zip 14048–2599; tel. 716/366–1111, (Nonreporting) **A**10 20 21
Primary Contact: Kenneth R. Morris, President and Chief Executive Officer
CHR: Tracie Luther, Director Employee and Labor Relations
CNO: Julie Morton, Chief Nursing Officer and Chief Clinical Officer
Web address: www.brookshospital.org
Control: Other not–for–profit (including NFP Corporation) **Service**: General medical and surgical

Staffed Beds: 65

EAST MEADOW—Nassau County

NASSAU UNIVERSITY MEDICAL CENTER (330027), 2201 Hempstead Turnpike, Zip 11554–1859; tel. 516/572–0123, (Nonreporting) **A**1 3 5 10 12 13
Primary Contact: Megan C. Ryan, Interim Chief Executive Officer and Chief Legal Officer
CIO: Farooq Ajmal, Vice President and Chief Information Officer
CHR: Maureen Roarty, Executive Vice President Human Resources
CNO: Kathy Skarka, MSN, R.N., Executive Vice President Patient Care Services
Web address: www.nuhealth.net
Control: Hospital district or authority, Government, Nonfederal **Service**: General medical and surgical

Staffed Beds: 481

ELIZABETHTOWN—Essex County

THE UNIVERSITY OF VERMONT HEALTH NETWORK ELIZABETHTOWN COMMUNITY HOSPITAL (331302), 75 Park Street, Zip 12932, Mailing Address: P.O. Box 277, Zip 12932–0277; tel. 518/873–6377, (Includes UNIVERSITY OF VERMONT HEALTH NETWORK ELIZABETHTOWN COMMUNITY HOSPITAL – TICONDEROGA CAMPUS, 1019 Wicker Street, Ticonderoga, New York, Zip 12883–1097, tel. 518/585–2831; Robert Ortmyer, President) (Nonreporting) **A**1 10 18 **S** The University of Vermont Health Network, Burlington, VT
Primary Contact: Robert Ortmyer, President
COO: Matthew Nolan, Chief Operating Officer
CFO: Alan Chardavoyne, Chief Financial Officer
CMO: Jun Chon, M.D., Chief Medical Officer
CIO: Darrin Goodrow, Chief Information Officer
CHR: Michelle Meachem, Director Human Resources
CNO: Julie Tromblee, R.N., Chief Nursing Officer
Web address: www.ech.org
Control: Other not–for–profit (including NFP Corporation) **Service**: General medical and surgical

Staffed Beds: 25

ELLENVILLE—Ulster County

★ **ELLENVILLE REGIONAL HOSPITAL (331310)**, 10 Healthy Way, Zip 12428–5612; tel. 845/647–6400, (Nonreporting) **A**10 18
Primary Contact: Steven L. Kelley, President and Chief Executive Officer
CFO: Robert Rue, Chief Financial Officer
CMO: Walter Sperling, M.D., Medical Director
CHR: Deborah Briggs, Vice President Human Resources, Marketing, Volunteer Services and Community Relations
CNO: Ann Marie Guntlow, Chief Nursing Officer
Web address: www.ellenvilleregional.org
Control: Other not–for–profit (including NFP Corporation) **Service**: General medical and surgical

Staffed Beds: 25

ELMHURST—Queens County, See New York City

ELMIRA—Chemung County

ARNOT OGDEN MEDICAL CENTER (330090), 600 Roe Avenue, Zip 14905–1629; tel. 607/737–4100, (Includes ARNOT MEDICAL CENTER – ST. JOSEPH'S CAMPUS, 555 Saint Josephs Blvd, Elmira, New York, Zip 14901–3223, 555 St. Joseph's Boulevard, Zip 14901–3223, tel. 607/733–6541; Jonathan I Lawrence, President and Chief Executive Officer) (Nonreporting) **A**1 3 5 10 12 13 **S** Arnot Health, Elmira, NY
Primary Contact: Jonathan I. Lawrence, President and Chief Executive Officer
CFO: Ronald J Kintz, Vice President and Treasurer
CMO: Kenneth Herzl–Betz, M.D., Chief Medical Officer
CIO: Gregg Martin, Chief Information Officer
CHR: Dave Stanbro, Director Human Resources
CNO: Sandra Mac McCarthy, Chief Nursing Officer
Web address: www.arnothealth.org
Control: Other not–for–profit (including NFP Corporation) **Service**: General medical and surgical

Staffed Beds: 322

Hospitals, U.S. / NEW YORK

☐ **ELMIRA PSYCHIATRIC CENTER (334045)**, 100 Washington Street, Zip 14901–2898; tel. 607/737–4739, (Nonreporting) **A** 1 3 10 **S** New York State Office of Mental Health, Albany, NY
Primary Contact: David Peppel, Executive Director
COO: Karen Patterson, Deputy Director Operations
CFO: J. Paul Bedzyk, Deputy Director Administration
CMO: Kurt Hahn, M.D., Acting Clinical Director
CIO: Jeremy Newcomer, Director Information Services
CHR: Patricia Santulli, Director Human Resources
CNO: Pam Seeley, Chief Nursing Officer
Web address: www.omh.ny.gov/omhweb/facilities/elpc/facility.htm
Control: State, Government, Nonfederal **Service:** Psychiatric

Staffed Beds: 59

FAR ROCKAWAY—Queens County, See New York City

FLUSHING—Queens County, See New York City

FOREST HILLS—Queens County, See New York City

FRESH MEADOWS—Queens County

CORNERSTONE OF MEDICAL ARTS CENTER HOSPITAL, 159–05 Union Turnpike, Zip 11366–1950; tel. 212/755–0200, (Nonreporting)
Primary Contact: Thomas C. Puzo, President and Chief Executive Officer
CFO: Jeff OniFather, Chief Financial Officer
CMO: Sami Kaddouri, M.D., Medical Director
CHR: Gloria Burtch, Director Human Resources
Web address: www.cornerstoneny.com
Control: Corporation, Investor–owned (for–profit) **Service:** Substance Use Disorder

Staffed Beds: 162

GENEVA—Ontario County

✠ **GENEVA GENERAL HOSPITAL (330058)**, 196 North Street, Zip 14456–1694; tel. 315/787–4000, **A** 1 3 10 **F** 3 8 11 15 17 18 29 32 34 35 40 45 50 54 59 60 61 64 70 74 75 77 79 81 85 86 87 92 93 94 96 97 100 107 108 110 115 118 119 130 131 132 135 146 147 149 154 167 **P** 6 **S** Finger Lakes Health, Geneva, NY
Primary Contact: Jose Acevedo, M.D., President and Chief Executive Officer
CFO: Pamela Johnson, Treasurer and Chief Financial Officer
CMO: Jason Feinberg, M.D., Vice President Medical Affairs and Chief Medical Officer
CIO: Guy W Mosher III, Manager Information Systems
CHR: Patrick R Boyle, Vice President Human Resources
CNO: Ardelle Bigos, R.N., MSN, Vice President Nursing
Web address: www.flhealth.org
Control: Other not–for–profit (including NFP Corporation) **Service:** General medical and surgical

Staffed Beds: 50 **Admissions:** 2545 **Census:** 36 **Outpatient Visits:** 512090 **Births:** 0 **Total Expense ($000):** 121687 **Payroll Expense ($000):** 69625 **Personnel:** 634

GLEN COVE—Nassau County

✠ **GLEN COVE HOSPITAL (330181)**, 101 St Andrews Lane, Zip 11542–2254; tel. 516/674–7300, **A** 1 3 5 10 **F** 3 5 8 9 11 15 17 18 28 29 30 32 33 34 35 36 38 39 40 45 46 47 48 49 50 51 54 55 56 57 58 59 60 61 63 64 65 66 68 69 70 74 75 77 78 79 81 84 85 86 87 90 91 92 93 94 95 96 97 100 102 104 107 110 111 115 118 119 121 126 130 131 132 135 143 146 147 148 149 152 154 156 165 166 167 **S** Northwell Health, Lake Success, NY
Primary Contact: Kerri Scanlon, R.N., Executive Director
COO: Michele Frankel, Associate Executive Director Finance
CFO: Michele Frankel, Associate Executive Director Finance
CNO: Theresa Anne Dillman, MSN, R.N., Chief Nursing Officer, Associate Executive Director, Patient Services
Web address: www.northshorelij.com
Control: Other not–for–profit (including NFP Corporation) **Service:** General medical and surgical

Staffed Beds: 148 **Admissions:** 6081 **Census:** 135 **Outpatient Visits:** 84018 **Births:** 0 **Total Expense ($000):** 243267 **Payroll Expense ($000):** 134258 **Personnel:** 1167

GLEN OAKS—Queens County, See New York City

GLENS FALLS—Warren County

★ ⇑ **GLENS FALLS HOSPITAL (330191)**, 100 Park Street, Zip 12801–4413; tel. 518/926–1000, **A** 2 3 5 10 19 21 **F** 3 6 8 11 13 15 18 20 22 26 28 29 30 31 32 34 35 36 37 38 40 41 43 44 45 46 47 49 50 53 54 55 57 58 59 64 68 70 71 73 74 75 76 77 78 79 81 82 84 85 86 87 92 93 94 96 97 98 100 102 107 108 110 111 114 115 118 119 120 121 123 124 126 127 130 131 132 135 144 146 148 154 167 **P** 6
Primary Contact: Paul Scimeca, President and Chief Executive Officer
CFO: Mitchell Amado, Senior Vice President Finance and Chief Financial Officer
CMO: Howard P Fritz, M.D., Vice President, Medical Affairs and Chief Medical Officer
CNO: Donna Kirker, R.N., MS, Vice President Patient Services and Chief Nursing Officer
Web address: www.glensfallshospital.org
Control: Other not–for–profit (including NFP Corporation) **Service:** General medical and surgical

Staffed Beds: 243 **Admissions:** 12060 **Census:** 149 **Outpatient Visits:** 696213 **Births:** 1044 **Total Expense ($000):** 395442 **Payroll Expense ($000):** 172292 **Personnel:** 1887

GLENVILLE—Schenectady County

CONIFER PARK, 79 Glenridge Road, Zip 12302–4523; tel. 518/399–6446, (Nonreporting)
Primary Contact: Jeanne Gluchowski, Executive Director
COO: Jeanne Gluchowski, Executive Director
CFO: Jason Burczeuski, Controller
CMO: John Melbourne, M.D., Medical Director
CIO: Amy Kentera, Chief Information Officer
CHR: Maureen Fowler, Director Human Resources
Web address: www.coniferpark.com/
Control: Corporation, Investor–owned (for–profit) **Service:** Substance Use Disorder

Staffed Beds: 225

GLOVERSVILLE—Fulton County

★ ⇑ **NATHAN LITTAUER HOSPITAL AND NURSING HOME (330276)**, 99 East State Street, Zip 12078–1203; tel. 518/725–8621, (Total facility includes 84 beds in nursing home–type unit) **A** 10 21 **F** 3 8 11 13 15 18 28 29 30 31 32 34 35 36 37 40 45 50 53 54 57 59 61 64 65 70 74 75 76 77 78 79 81 82 84 85 86 87 89 93 96 97 107 108 110 115 118 119 128 129 130 131 132 135 144 145 146 147 149 154 156 167 **P** 6
Primary Contact: Sean Fadale, FACHE, President and Chief Executive Officer
CMO: Frederick Goldberg, M.D., Vice President Medical Affairs and Chief Medical Officer
CIO: Martin Brown, Vice President Information Services and Chief Information Officer
CNO: Stephanie Fishel, Vice President Patient Care Services and Chief Nursing Officer
Web address: www.nlh.org
Control: Other not–for–profit (including NFP Corporation) **Service:** General medical and surgical

Staffed Beds: 141 **Admissions:** 2276 **Census:** 81 **Outpatient Visits:** 244657 **Births:** 314 **Total Expense ($000):** 132050 **Payroll Expense ($000):** 64615 **Personnel:** 800

GOUVERNEUR—St. Lawrence County

★ ⇑ **GOUVERNEUR HOSPITAL (331315)**, 77 West Barney Street, Zip 13642–1040; tel. 315/287–1000, (Nonreporting) **A** 5 10 18 21 **S** Rochester Regional Health, Rochester, NY
Primary Contact: Katherine Schleider, Interim President, Gouverneur Hospital, Senior Vice President of Operations, St. Lawrence Health
CFO: Richard T Lang, Chief Financial Officer
CMO: George Dodds, M.D., Medical Director
CNO: Jennifer Shaver, Director of Nursing
Web address: www.gvnrhospital.org
Control: Other not–for–profit (including NFP Corporation) **Service:** General medical and surgical

Staffed Beds: 25

GREENPORT—Suffolk County

EASTERN LONG ISLAND HOSPITAL See Stony Brook Eastern Long Island Hospital

---

Hospital, Medicare Provider Number, Address, Telephone, Approval, Facility, and Physician Codes, Health Care System

★ American Hospital Association (AHA) membership   ○ Healthcare Facilities Accreditation Program   ⇑ Center for Improvement in Healthcare Quality Accreditation
☐ The Joint Commission accreditation   ◇ DNV Healthcare Inc. accreditation   △ Commission on Accreditation of Rehabilitation Facilities (CARF) accreditation

© 2025 AHA Guide   Hospitals **A443**

Hospitals, U.S. / NEW YORK

HAMILTON—Madison County

COMMUNITY MEMORIAL HOSPITAL (331316), 150 Broad Street, Zip 13346–9518; tel. 315/824–1100, (Nonreporting) **A**1 10 18
Primary Contact: Jeffrey Coakley, President and Chief Executive Officer
CFO: Christopher W Graham, Chief Financial Officer
CMO: Robert Delorme, Vice President Medical Affairs
CHR: Jennifer Montana, Manager Human Resources
CNO: Denise Hummer, R.N., Vice President Administrative Services
Web address: www.communitymemorial.org
Control: Other not–for–profit (including NFP Corporation) **Service**: General medical and surgical

Staffed Beds: 29

HARRIS—Sullivan County

GARNET HEALTH MEDICAL CENTER – CATSKILLS, HARRIS CAMPUS (330386), 68 Harris Bushville Road, Zip 12742–5030, Mailing Address: P.O. Box 800, Zip 12742–0800; tel. 845/794–3300, (Nonreporting) **A**2 3 10 21 **S** Garnet Health, Middletown, NY
Primary Contact: Jerry Dunlavey, Chief Executive Officer
CFO: Rick Caprico, Chief Financial Officer
CMO: Gerard Galarneau, M.D., Regional Chief Medical Officer
Web address: https://www.garnethealth.org/locations/garnet-health-medical-center-catskills-harris-campus
Control: Other not–for–profit (including NFP Corporation) **Service**: General medical and surgical

Staffed Beds: 67

HOLLISWOOD—Queens County, See New York City

HORNELL—Steuben County

ST. JAMES HOSPITAL (330151), 7329 Seneca Road North, Zip 14843; tel. 607/247–2200, (Nonreporting) **A**1 10 20 **S** University of Rochester Medical Center, Rochester, NY
Primary Contact: Wendy Disbrow, President and Chief Executive Officer
CFO: Jim Wright, Interim Chief Financial Officer
CMO: John Carroll, M.D., Chief Medical Officer
CIO: Jason Soles, Manager Information Systems
CHR: Jennifer Spike, Director Human Resources
CNO: Kathleen Brodbeck MSN, RN–B, Chief Nursing Officer
Web address: www.stjamesmercy.org
Control: Other not–for–profit (including NFP Corporation) **Service**: General medical and surgical

Staffed Beds: 15

HUDSON—Columbia County

★ **COLUMBIA MEMORIAL HOSPITAL (330094)**, 71 Prospect Avenue, Zip 12534–2907; tel. 518/828–7601, (Nonreporting) **A**3 10 19 21
Primary Contact: Dorothy M. Urschel, President and Chief Executive Officer
CFO: Bryan Mahoney, Chief Financial Officer
CMO: Lawrence Perl, M.D., Chief Medical Officer
CIO: Bonnie Ratliff, Chief Information Officer
CNO: Mary Ellen Plass, MS, R.N., Senior Vice President and Chief Nursing Officer
Web address: www.columbiamemorialhealth.org
Control: Other not–for–profit (including NFP Corporation) **Service**: General medical and surgical

Staffed Beds: 192

HUNTINGTON—Suffolk County

HUNTINGTON HOSPITAL (330045), 270 Park Avenue, Zip 11743–2799; tel. 631/351–2000, **A**1 2 3 10 **F**3 8 12 13 17 18 19 20 22 26 29 30 31 32 34 35 36 37 38 39 40 41 43 44 45 46 47 48 49 50 51 54 55 56 57 58 59 60 61 63 64 65 66 68 69 70 73 74 75 76 77 78 79 81 82 84 85 86 87 89 92 97 98 100 101 102 103 104 107 108 110 111 115 118 119 126 130 132 145 146 147 148 149 150 154 156 157 160 161 167 169 **S** Northwell Health, Lake Success, NY
Primary Contact: Nick Fitterman, M.D., Executive Director
CIO: David Lombardi, Site Chief Information Officer
CHR: Lisa Khavkin, Vice President Human Resources
CNO: Susan Knoepffler, R.N., Vice President Nursing
Web address: https://huntington.northwell.edu
Control: Other not–for–profit (including NFP Corporation) **Service**: General medical and surgical

Staffed Beds: 284 **Admissions**: 19125 **Census**: 240 **Outpatient Visits**: 84378 **Births**: 1962 **Total Expense ($000)**: 670739 **Payroll Expense ($000)**: 339719 **Personnel**: 2494

ITHACA—Tompkins County

☐ **CAYUGA MEDICAL CENTER AT ITHACA (330307)**, 101 Dates Drive, Zip 14850–1342; tel. 607/274–4011, (Nonreporting) **A**1 2 3 5 10 20 **S** Cayuga Health System, Ithaca, NY
Primary Contact: Martin Stallone, M.D., President and Chief Executive Officer
CFO: John Collett, Vice President and Chief Financial Officer
CMO: David M Evelyn, M.D., Vice President Medical Affairs
CIO: Brett Mello, Chief Information Officer
CHR: Brian Forrest, Vice President Human Resources
Web address: www.cayugamed.org
Control: Other not–for–profit (including NFP Corporation) **Service**: General medical and surgical

Staffed Beds: 159

JACKSON HEIGHTS—Queens County, See New York City

JAMAICA—Queens County, See New York City

JAMESTOWN—Chautauqua County

UPMC CHAUTAUQUA (330239), 207 Foote Avenue, Zip 14701–7077, Mailing Address: P.O. Box 840, Zip 14702–0840; tel. 716/487–0141, **A**1 10 **F**3 4 5 7 8 12 13 15 18 19 20 28 29 31 34 35 38 40 45 50 59 68 70 75 76 77 79 81 82 84 87 89 93 98 99 100 101 102 104 107 108 110 115 117 119 124 126 130 132 135 143 146 147 148 149 153 154 156 157 160 161 164 165 167 **S** UPMC, Pittsburgh, PA
Primary Contact: Brian Durniok, President
CFO: Bradley Dinger, Chief Financial Officer
CMO: Marlene Garone, M.D., Vice President Medical Affairs and Medical Director
CIO: Keith Robison, Chief Information Officer
CHR: Karen Bohall, Director Human Resources
Web address: www.wcahospital.org
Control: Other not–for–profit (including NFP Corporation) **Service**: General medical and surgical

Staffed Beds: 130 **Admissions**: 5324 **Census**: 90 **Outpatient Visits**: 190639 **Births**: 670 **Total Expense ($000)**: 96238 **Payroll Expense ($000)**: 41712 **Personnel**: 764

JOHNSON CITY—Broome County

WILSON MEMORIAL REG MED CTR See Wilson Memorial Regional Medical Center

WILSON MEMORIAL REGIONAL MEDICAL CENTER See United Health Services Hospitals–Binghamton, Binghamton

KATONAH—Westchester County

☐ **FOUR WINDS HOSPITAL (334002)**, 800 Cross River Road, Zip 10536–3549; tel. 914/763–8151, (Nonreporting) **A**1 3 10
Primary Contact: Moira Morrissey Esq, Chief Executive Officer
COO: Moira Morrissey Esq, Chief Operating Officer and General Counsel
CFO: Barry S Weinstein, Chief Financial Officer
CMO: Jonathan Bauman, M.D., Chief Medical Officer
CIO: Barry S Weinstein, Chief Financial Officer
CHR: Susan Cusano, Director Human Resources
Web address: www.fourwindshospital.com
Control: Partnership, Investor–owned (for–profit) **Service**: Psychiatric

Staffed Beds: 181

KENMORE—Erie County

CATHERINE MCAULEY MANOR See Mcauley Residence

KENMORE MERCY HOSPITAL (330102), 2950 Elmwood Avenue, Zip 14217–1390; tel. 716/447–6100, (Nonreporting) **A**1 3 10 **S** Catholic Health System, Buffalo, NY
Primary Contact: Walter Ludwig, President
CFO: James H Dunlop, CPA, Jr, Executive Vice President and Chief Financial Officer
CMO: James Fitzpatrick, M.D., Vice President Medical Affairs
CHR: Laura Cianflone, Director Human Resources
Web address: www.chsbuffalo.org
Control: Church operated, Nongovernment, not–for–profit **Service**: General medical and surgical

Staffed Beds: 258

KINGSTON—Ulster County

HEALTH ALLIANCE HOSPITAL – BROADWAY CAMPUS (330004), 396 Broadway, Zip 12401–4692; tel. 845/331–3131, (Nonreporting) **A**3 10 **S** WMCHealth, Valhalla, NY
Primary Contact: Michael Doyle, M.D., Executive Director and Chief Medical Officer
COO: Robert Seidman, Chief Operating Officer
CFO: Steven J Haas, Chief Financial Officer
CMO: Frank Ehrlich, M.D., Chief Medical Officer
CIO: John Finch, Vice President Information Services
CHR: Greg M Howard, Director Human Resource
Web address: www.hahv.org
Control: Other not–for–profit (including NFP Corporation) **Service**: General medical and surgical

Staffed Beds: 150

⇧ **HEALTH ALLIANCE HOSPITAL – MARY'S AVENUE CAMPUS (330224)**, 105 Marys Avenue, Zip 12401–5894; tel. 845/338–2500, (Nonreporting) **A**10 19 21 **S** WMCHealth, Valhalla, NY
Primary Contact: Michael Doyle, M.D., Executive Director and Chief Medical Officer
COO: Robert Seidman, Chief Operating Officer
CFO: Steven J Haas, Chief Financial Officer
CMO: Frank Ehrlich, M.D., Chief Medical Officer
CIO: John Finch, Chief Information and Community Officer
CHR: Greg M Howard, Vice President Human Resources
Web address: www.hahv.org
Control: Other not–for–profit (including NFP Corporation) **Service**: General medical and surgical

Staffed Beds: 105

LEWISTON—Niagara County

MOUNT ST. MARY'S HOSPITAL AND HEALTH CENTER (330188), 5300 Military Road, Zip 14092–1903; tel. 716/298–2017, (Nonreporting) **A**1 10 **S** Catholic Health System, Buffalo, NY
Primary Contact: Charles J. Urlaub, President
Web address: https://www.chsbuffalo.org/mount-st-marys-hospital/
Control: Other not–for–profit (including NFP Corporation) **Service**: General medical and surgical

Staffed Beds: 135

LITTLE FALLS—Herkimer County

LITTLE FALLS HOSPITAL (331311), 140 Burwell Street, Zip 13365–1725; tel. 315/823–1000, (Nonreporting) **A**1 10 18 **S** Bassett Healthcare Network, Cooperstown, NY
Primary Contact: Susan Oakes Ferrucci, MS, Chief Hospital Executive
CMO: Louis Oceguera, M.D., Medical Director
CIO: Duane Merry, Chief Information Officer
CHR: Christine Pirri, Vice President Human Resources
CNO: Heidi Camardello, Vice President Patient Care Services and Chief Nursing Officer
Web address: www.bassett.org
Control: Other not–for–profit (including NFP Corporation) **Service**: General medical and surgical

Staffed Beds: 25

LITTLE NECK—Queens County, See New York City

LOCKPORT—Niagara County

LOCKPORT MEMORIAL HOSPITAL See Eastern Niagara Hospital Lockport

LONG ISLAND CITY—Queens County, See New York City

LOWVILLE—Lewis County

LEWIS COUNTY GENERAL HOSPITAL (331317), 7785 North State Street, Zip 13367–1297; tel. 315/376–5200, (Total facility includes 160 beds in nursing home–type unit) **A**1 10 18 **F**3 11 13 29 30 34 35 36 40 45 50 56 57 59 62 63 70 75 76 77 79 81 82 93 96 97 107 110 111 115 119 127 128 129 130 132 133 141 143 145 146 147 154 160 167 **P**3
Primary Contact: Gerald R. Cayer, Chief Executive Officer
CFO: Jeffrey Hellinger, Chief Financial Officer
CMO: Sean Patrick Harney, Chief Medical Officer, Employed Provider Clinics
CIO: Rob Uttendorfsky, Director Information Management
CHR: Jessica Skiff, Director Human Resources
CNO: Neva Bossard, Chief Nursing Officer
Web address: www.lcgh.net
Control: County, Government, Nonfederal **Service**: General medical and surgical

Staffed Beds: 185 **Admissions:** 985 **Census:** 132 **Outpatient Visits:** 148649 **Births:** 0 **Total Expense ($000):** 87888 **Payroll Expense ($000):** 34065 **Personnel:** 522

MALONE—Franklin County

THE UNIVERSITY OF VERMONT HEALTH NETWORK – ALICE HYDE MEDICAL CENTER (331321), 133 Park Street, Zip 12953–1243, Mailing Address: P.O. Box 729, Zip 12953–0729; tel. 518/483–3000, (Total facility includes 165 beds in nursing home–type unit) **A**1 10 18 **F**3 10 11 15 18 28 29 31 34 35 39 40 45 57 59 64 67 75 77 78 79 81 82 84 85 86 87 90 92 93 96 97 107 108 110 111 115 119 121 127 128 129 130 131 133 141 146 147 149 154 156 157 160 164 169 **S** The University of Vermont Health Network, Burlington, VT
Primary Contact: Michelle LeBeau, President
COO: Matthew Jones, Chief Operating Officer and Senior Vice President
CFO: Christopher Hickey, Chief Financial Officer and Senior Vice President
CMO: Kent Hall, M.D., Chief Medical Officer
CIO: Justin Miller, Chief Information Officer and Associate Vice President
CHR: Emily Campbell, Assistant Vice President People and Patient Experience
CNO: Rebecca Shutts, R.N., Chief Nursing Officer
Web address: www.UVMHealth.org/AHMC
Control: Other not–for–profit (including NFP Corporation) **Service**: General medical and surgical

Staffed Beds: 196 **Admissions:** 932 **Census:** 134 **Outpatient Visits:** 208877 **Births:** 0 **Total Expense ($000):** 106342 **Payroll Expense ($000):** 60521 **Personnel:** 490

MANHASSET—Nassau County

MANHASSET AMBULATORY CARE CTR See Manhasset Ambulatory Care Pavilion

NORTH SHORE UNIVERSITY HOSPITAL (330106), 300 Community Drive, Zip 11030–3816; tel. 516/562–0100, (Includes SYOSSET HOSPITAL, 221 Jericho Turnpike, Syosset, New York, Zip 11791–4515, tel. 516/496–6500; Kerri Scanlon, R.N., Executive Director) **A**1 2 3 5 8 10 19 **F**3 5 6 7 8 9 11 12 13 15 17 18 20 22 24 26 28 29 30 31 34 35 36 37 38 39 40 41 43 44 45 46 47 48 49 50 51 52 53 54 55 56 57 58 59 60 61 62 63 64 65 66 68 69 70 71 72 73 74 75 76 77 78 79 80 81 82 83 84 85 86 87 91 92 93 94 96 97 100 101 102 104 107 108 110 111 112 114 115 116 117 118 119 126 129 130 131 132 134 135 136 137 138 139 140 141 142 143 144 145 146 147 148 149 150 152 154 156 157 167 169 **S** Northwell Health, Lake Success, NY
Primary Contact: Jon Sendach, Executive Director
CMO: Michael Gitman, M.D., Medical Director
CIO: Nympha Meindel, R.N., Chief Information Officer
CHR: Debra Bierman, Associate Executive Director Human Resources
CNO: Irene Macyk, R.N., MS, Ph.D., Chief Nursing Officer
Web address: https://www.northwell.edu/find-care/locations/north-shore-university-hospital
Control: Other not–for–profit (including NFP Corporation) **Service**: General medical and surgical

Staffed Beds: 815 **Admissions:** 48187 **Census:** 792 **Outpatient Visits:** 1186511 **Births:** 6084 **Total Expense ($000):** 3571740 **Payroll Expense ($000):** 1858187 **Personnel:** 12624

Hospitals, U.S. / NEW YORK

MANHATTAN—New York County, See New York City

MARCY—Oneida County

☐ **CENTRAL NEW YORK PSYCHIATRIC CENTER**, 9005 Old River Road, Zip 13403–3000, Mailing Address: P.O. Box 300, Zip 13403–0300; tel. 315/765–3600, (Nonreporting) **A**1 3 **S** New York State Office of Mental Health, Albany, NY
Primary Contact: Danielle Dill, Executive Director
Web address: www.omh.ny.gov
Control: State, Government, Nonfederal **Service**: Psychiatric

Staffed Beds: 226

MARGARETVILLE—Delaware County

⇑ **MARGARETVILLE HOSPITAL (331304)**, 42084 State Highway 28, Zip 12455–2820; tel. 845/586–2631, (Nonreporting) **A**10 18 21 **S** WMCHealth, Valhalla, NY
Primary Contact: Edward McNamara, Executive Director
CHR: Linda Mead, Director Human Resources
Web address: www.margaretvillehospital.org
Control: Other not-for-profit (including NFP Corporation) **Service**: General medical and surgical

Staffed Beds: 15

MASSENA—St. Lawrence County

★ ⇑ **MASSENA HOSPITAL, INC. (330223)**, 1 Hospital Drive, Zip 13662–1097; tel. 315/764–1711, (Nonreporting) **A**10 21 **S** Rochester Regional Health, Rochester, NY
Primary Contact: Brent Bishop, Associate Chief Operating Officer
CMO: Nimesh Desai, M.D., Medical Director
CHR: Jonnie Dorothy, Senior Director Human Resources
CNO: Ralene North, Chief Nurse Executive
Web address: www.massenahospital.org
Control: City, Government, Nonfederal **Service**: General medical and surgical

Staffed Beds: 25

MEDINA—Orleans County

ORLEANS COMMUNITY HEALTH (331319), 200 Ohio Street, Zip 14103–1095; tel. 585/798–2000, (Nonreporting) **A**10 18
Primary Contact: Marc Shurtz, Interim Chief Executive Officer and Chief Financial Officer
CMO: Dale Sponaugle, M.D., Medical Staff President
CHR: Mary Williams, Director Human Resources
CNO: Paula Dresser, Chief Nursing Officer
Web address: www.medinamemorial.org
Control: State, Government, Nonfederal **Service**: General medical and surgical

Staffed Beds: 55

MIDDLETOWN—Orange County

△ ⇑ **GARNET HEALTH MEDICAL CENTER (330126)**, 707 East Main Street, Zip 10940–2650; tel. 845/333–1000, (Nonreporting) **A**2 3 5 7 10 12 13 19 21 **S** Garnet Health, Middletown, NY
Primary Contact: Jonathan Schiller, President and Chief Executive Officer
COO: Timothy P Selz, Vice President
CFO: Mitch Amodo, Vice President and Chief Financial Officer
CMO: Leroy Floyd, M.D., Chief Medical Officer
CHR: Deborah Carr, Vice President Human Resources
Web address: https://www.garnethealth.org/locations/garnet-health-medical-center
Control: Other not-for-profit (including NFP Corporation) **Service**: General medical and surgical

Staffed Beds: 410

MINEOLA—Nassau County

CHILDREN'S MEDICAL CENTER AT WINTHROP UNIVERSITY HOSPITAL See Children's Medical Center

NYU WINTHROP HOSPITAL See NYU Langone Hospital – Long Island

MONTOUR FALLS—Schuyler County

☐ **SCHUYLER HOSPITAL (331313)**, 220 Steuben Street, Zip 14865–9709; tel. 607/535–7121, (Nonreporting) **A**1 10 18 **S** Cayuga Health System, Ithaca, NY
Primary Contact: Jasmine Canestaro, Assistant Vice President, Operations
CMO: Michael Eisman, M.D., Medical Director
Web address: www.schuylerhospital.org
Control: Other not-for-profit (including NFP Corporation) **Service**: General medical and surgical

Staffed Beds: 145

MONTROSE—Westchester County

✣ **VETERANS AFFAIRS HUDSON VALLEY HEALTH CARE SYSTEM**, 2094 Albany Post Road, Zip 10548–1454, Mailing Address: P.O. Box 100, Zip 10548–0100; tel. 914/737–4400, (Includes VETERAN AFFAIRS HUDSON VALLEY HEALTH CARE SYSTEM–CASTLE POINT CAMPUS, 41 Castle Point RD, Wappingers Falls, New York, Zip 12590–7004, 41 Castle Point Road, Wappingers, Zip 12590, tel. 914/831–2000; VETERANS AFFAIRS HUDSON VALLEY HEALTH CARE SYSTEM–MONTROSE CAMPUS, 2094 Albany Post RD, Montrose, New York, Zip 10548–1454, 2094 Albany Post Road, Zip 10548, tel. 914/737–4400) (Nonreporting) **A**1 3 5 **S** Department of Veterans Affairs, Washington, DC
Primary Contact: Dawn M. Schaal, Medical Center Director
COO: John M Grady, Associate Director
CFO: John Walsh, Chief Fiscal Services
CMO: Joanne J Malina, M.D., Chief of Staff
CIO: Thomas Rooney, Chief Information Resource Management
CHR: Dardanella Russell, Chief Human Resources Management Service
Web address: www.hudsonvalley.va.gov/
Control: Veterans Affairs, Government, federal **Service**: Psychiatric

Staffed Beds: 166

VETERANS AFFAIRS HUDSON VALLEY HEALTH CARE SYSTEM–MONTROSE DIVISION See Veterans Affairs Hudson Valley Health Care System–Montrose Campus

MOUNT KISCO—Westchester County

✣ **NORTHERN WESTCHESTER HOSPITAL (330162)**, 400 East Main Street, Zip 10549–3477, Mailing Address: 400 East Main Street, G-02, Zip 10549–3477; tel. 914/666–1200, **A**1 2 3 5 10 **F**3 12 13 15 17 18 20 22 26 28 29 30 31 34 35 36 37 40 46 47 48 49 50 51 53 54 55 57 58 59 60 61 64 65 68 70 72 73 74 75 76 77 78 79 81 82 84 85 86 87 89 91 92 93 97 98 100 101 102 107 108 109 110 111 114 115 119 120 121 124 126 129 130 131 132 135 146 147 148 149 154 167 169 **S** Northwell Health, Lake Success, NY
Primary Contact: Derek Anderson, Executive Director
CFO: John Partenza, Vice President and Treasurer
CMO: Sherri Sandel, D.O., Chief Medical Director
CIO: Sue Prince, Director Information Systems
CNO: Lauraine Szekely, R.N., Senior Vice President, Patient Care
Web address: www.nwhc.net
Control: Other not-for-profit (including NFP Corporation) **Service**: General medical and surgical

Staffed Beds: 199 **Admissions**: 9423 **Census**: 103 **Outpatient Visits**: 143617 **Births**: 2128 **Total Expense ($000)**: 455132 **Payroll Expense ($000)**: 220679 **Personnel**: 1753

MOUNT VERNON—Westchester County

☐ **MONTEFIORE MOUNT VERNON (330086)**, 12 North Seventh Avenue, Zip 10550–2098; tel. 914/664–8000, **A**1 10 **F**3 5 15 18 29 30 31 34 35 40 45 50 59 61 64 65 66 68 70 74 75 77 78 79 81 84 85 86 87 92 97 98 100 102 104 107 111 114 115 118 119 130 132 135 147 148 154 156 160 165 **P**5 **S** Montefiore Health System, Bronx, NY
Primary Contact: Regginald Jordan, Executive Director
CFO: Albert M Farina, Chief Financial Officer
CMO: Gary Ishkanian, M.D., Vice President Medical Affairs
CIO: Barbara Cooke, Director Health Information Systems
CHR: Dennis H Ashley, Vice President Human Resources
Web address: www.montefiorehealthsystem.org/landing.cfm?id=17
Control: Other not-for-profit (including NFP Corporation) **Service**: General medical and surgical

Staffed Beds: 33 **Admissions**: 2059 **Census**: 35 **Outpatient Visits**: 103150 **Births**: 0 **Total Expense ($000)**: 93517 **Payroll Expense ($000)**: 38878 **Personnel**: 402

NEW HAMPTON—Orange County

☐ **MID–HUDSON FORENSIC PSYCHIATRIC CENTER (334061)**, Route 17M, Zip 10958, Mailing Address: P.O. Box 158, Zip 10958–0158; tel. 845/374–8700, **A**1 3 10 **F**29 30 38 39 40 68 77 82 86 87 98 100 130 135 149 163 **S** New York State Office of Mental Health, Albany, NY
Primary Contact: Kristin Orlando, Chief Executive Officer
Web address: www.omh.ny.gov
Control: State, Government, Nonfederal **Service**: Psychiatric

Staffed Beds: 285 **Admissions**: 346 **Census**: 172 **Outpatient Visits**: 0 **Births**: 0 **Total Expense ($000)**: 128127 **Payroll Expense ($000)**: 53793 **Personnel**: 540

Hospitals, U.S. / NEW YORK

NEW HYDE PARK—Queens County, See New York City

NEW HYDE PARK—Queens County

✠ **LONG ISLAND JEWISH MEDICAL CENTER (330195)**, 270–05 76th Avenue, Zip 11040-1496; tel. 718/470-7000, (Includes LONG ISLAND JEWISH FOREST HILLS, 102–01 66th Road, Forest Hills, New York, Zip 11375-2029, tel. 718/830-4000; Lorraine Chambers Lewis, Executive Director; LONG ISLAND JEWISH VALLEY STREAM, 900 Franklin Avenue, Valley Stream, New York, Zip 11580-2190, tel. 516/256-6000; David Seligman, Executive Director; MANHASSET AMBULATORY CARE PAVILION, 1554 Northern Boulevard, Manhasset, New York, Zip 11030, tel. 516/365-2070; STEVEN AND ALEXANDRA COHEN CHILDREN'S MEDICAL CENTER OF NEW YORK, 270–05 76th Avenue, New Hyde Park, New York, Zip 11040, tel. 718/470-3000; ZUCKER HILLSIDE HOSPITAL, 75–59 263rd Street, Glen Oaks, New York, Zip 11004, tel. 718/470-8000) (Total facility includes 120 beds in nursing home–type unit) **A**1 2 3 5 8 10 19 **F**2 3 4 5 6 7 8 9 11 12 13 14 15 17 18 19 20 21 22 23 24 25 26 27 28 29 30 31 32 34 35 36 37 38 39 40 41 44 45 46 47 48 49 50 51 52 53 54 55 56 57 58 59 60 61 62 63 64 65 66 67 68 70 71 72 73 74 75 76 77 78 79 80 81 82 83 84 85 86 87 88 89 92 93 94 96 97 98 99 100 101 102 103 104 105 107 108 109 110 111 112 114 115 116 117 118 119 120 121 123 124 126 128 129 130 131 132 134 135 136 138 141 142 143 144 145 146 147 148 149 151 152 153 154 156 157 158 160 162 164 165 167 169 **S** Northwell Health, Lake Success, NY
Primary Contact: Michael Gitman, M.D., Executive Director
CIO: John Bosco, Senior Vice President and Chief Information Officer
CHR: Maxine Cenac Carrington, Senior Vice President and Chief Human Resources Officer
CNO: Marybeth McManus, Chief Nursing Officer
Web address: www.lij.edu
Control: Other not–for–profit (including NFP Corporation) **Service**: General medical and surgical

Staffed Beds: 1508 **Admissions**: 79388 **Census**: 1370 **Outpatient Visits**: 861928 **Births**: 9522 **Total Expense ($000)**: 4003639 **Payroll Expense ($000)**: 1997353 **Personnel**: 15049

NEW ROCHELLE—Westchester County

✠ **MONTEFIORE NEW ROCHELLE (330184)**, 16 Guion Place, Zip 10801-5502; tel. 914/365-5000, (Total facility includes 150 beds in nursing home–type unit) **A**1 3 5 10 19 **F**3 12 13 14 15 18 29 30 31 32 34 35 40 45 50 55 59 60 64 65 66 68 70 74 75 76 77 78 79 81 82 84 85 86 87 90 92 93 97 100 107 108 110 111 114 115 119 126 128 129 130 132 135 147 149 154 156 157 **P**5 **S** Montefiore Health System, Bronx, NY
Primary Contact: Anthony Alfano, Vice President Executive Director
CMO: Daniela Levi, Chief Medical Officer
CHR: Emy Velez, Director of Human Resources
CNO: Danielle Kennedy, Director of Nursing
Web address: www.montefiorehealthsystem.org
Control: Other not–for–profit (including NFP Corporation) **Service**: General medical and surgical

Staffed Beds: 234 **Admissions**: 5468 **Census**: 222 **Outpatient Visits**: 84743 **Births**: 576 **Total Expense ($000)**: 234446 **Payroll Expense ($000)**: 101210 **Personnel**: 1042

UNITED HOME See United Hebrew Geriatric Center

NEW YORK—Kings County

☐ **BROOKDALE HOSPITAL MEDICAL CENTER (330233)**, 125 Worth Street, 4th Fl Ste 418, Zip 10013, Mailing Address: One Brookdale Plaza, Brooklyn, Zip 11212-3139; tel. 718/240-5000, (Nonreporting) **A**1 3 10
Primary Contact: Chris Paras, Interim Executive Director
CFO: James Porter, Chief Financial Officer
CIO: David Reitzel, Chief Information Officer
Web address: https://onebrooklynhealth.org/
Control: Other not–for–profit (including NFP Corporation) **Service**: General medical and surgical

Staffed Beds: 808

NEW YORK (Includes all hospitals located within the five boroughs)
  BRONX – Bronx County (Mailing Address – Bronx)
  BROOKLYN – Kings County (Mailing Address – Brooklyn)
  MANHATTAN – New York County (Mailing Address – New York)
  QUEENS – Queens County (Mailing Addresses – Bellerose, Elmhurst, Far Rockaway, Flushing, Forest Hills, Glen Oaks, Holliswood, Jackson Heights, Jamaica, Little Neck, Long Island City, New Hyde Park, and Queens Village)
  RICHMOND VALLEY – Richmond County (Mailing Address – Staten Island)

BETH ABRAHAM HOSPITAL See Beth Abraham Health Services

BETH ISRAEL MEDICAL CENTER–KINGS HIGHWAY DIVISION See Mount Sinai Beth Israel Brooklyn

☐ **BRONX PSYCHIATRIC CENTER (334053)**, 1500 Waters Place, Zip 10461-2796; tel. 718/931-0600, (Nonreporting) **A**1 3 5 10 **S** New York State Office of Mental Health, Albany, NY
Primary Contact: Precious Stepney, Executive Director
CFO: Robert Erway, Director for Administration
Web address: www.omh.ny.gov
Control: State, Government, Nonfederal **Service**: Psychiatric

Staffed Beds: 156

✠ **BRONXCARE HEALTH SYSTEM (330009)**, 1276 Fulton Avenue, Zip 10456-3499; tel. 718/590-1800, (Includes BRONX–LEBANON SPECIAL CARE CENTER, 1265 Fulton Ave, Bronx, New York, Zip 10456-3401, 1265 Fulton Avenue, Zip 10465, tel. 718/579-7000; Octavio Marin, Vice President Long Term Care and Ambulatory Care Services; CONCOURSE DIVISION, 1650 Grand Concourse, Bronx, New York, Zip 10457-7606, 1276 Fulton Ave, Zip 10456-3402, tel. 718/590-1800; Miguel A Fuentes Jr, President and Chief Executive Officer; FULTON DIVISION, 1276 Fulton Avenue, Bronx, New York, Zip 10456, 1650 Grand Concourse, Zip 10457-7606, tel. 718/590-1800; Miguel A Fuentes Jr, President and Chief Executive Officer; HIGHBRIDGE WOODYCREST CENTER, 936 Woodycrest Ave, Bronx, New York, Zip 10452-5503, 936 Woodycrest Avenue, Zip 10452, tel. 718/579-8875; Leonardo Vicent III, Executive Director) (Total facility includes 240 beds in nursing home–type unit) **A**1 3 5 10 **F**3 4 5 7 8 11 12 13 14 15 17 18 19 20 21 22 23 26 28 29 30 31 32 34 35 36 37 38 39 40 41 43 44 45 46 47 48 49 50 51 52 54 55 56 57 58 59 60 61 62 64 65 66 68 70 71 72 73 74 75 76 77 78 79 81 82 83 84 85 86 87 88 89 91 92 93 97 98 99 100 101 102 103 104 105 106 107 108 109 110 111 114 115 118 119 120 121 126 128 129 130 131 132 133 134 135 144 145 146 147 148 149 150 151 152 153 154 156 157 160 161 162 163 164 165 167 169
Primary Contact: Miguel A. Fuentes Jr, President and Chief Executive Officer
CFO: Victor DeMarco, Chief Financial Officer
CMO: Milton A Gumbs, M.D., Vice President and Medical Director
CIO: Ivan Durbak, Chief Information Officer
CHR: Selena Griffin–Mahon, Assistant Vice President Human Resources
CNO: Patricia Cahill, Vice President, Patient Care Services and Chief Nursing Officer
Web address: www.bronxcare.org
Control: Other not–for–profit (including NFP Corporation) **Service**: General medical and surgical

Staffed Beds: 859 **Admissions**: 24636 **Census**: 717 **Outpatient Visits**: 900280 **Births**: 1415 **Total Expense ($000)**: 1034379 **Payroll Expense ($000)**: 455485 **Personnel**: 3991

☐ **BROOKLYN HOSPITAL CENTER (330056)**, 121 DeKalb Avenue, Zip 11201-5425; tel. 718/250-8000, **A**1 3 5 10 **F**3 4 5 7 8 12 14 15 17 18 19 20 22 26 29 30 31 32 34 35 38 39 40 41 44 46 47 48 49 50 51 54 55 56 57 58 59 60 61 64 65 66 68 70 72 74 75 76 77 79 80 81 85 87 88 89 90 92 93 94 97 102 104 107 108 109 110 111 114 115 116 117 119 123 126 129 130 131 135 143 144 146 147 148 149 150 152 154 156 157 160 161 162 165 167 169
Primary Contact: Gary G. Terrinoni, President and Chief Executive Officer
COO: John Gupta, Executive Vice President and Chief Operating Officer
CIO: Irene Farrelly, Vice President and Chief Information Officer
CHR: Ira Warm, Senior Vice President Human Resources
Web address: www.tbh.org
Control: Other not–for–profit (including NFP Corporation) **Service**: General medical and surgical

Staffed Beds: 292 **Admissions**: 11405 **Census**: 196 **Outpatient Visits**: 260910 **Births**: 1291 **Total Expense ($000)**: 533917 **Payroll Expense ($000)**: 253925 **Personnel**: 2406

✠ **CALVARY HOSPITAL (332006)**, 1740 Eastchester Road, Zip 10461-2392; tel. 718/518-2000, (Includes CALVARY HOSPITAL BROOKLYN CAMPUS, 150 55th Street, 3rd Floor, Brooklyn, New York, Zip 11220-2508, tel. 718/630-6666; Jeffrey Menkes, President and Chief Executive Officer) (Nonreporting) **A**1 3 5 10
Primary Contact: Jeffrey Menkes, President and Chief Executive Officer
CFO: Andrew Greco, Chief Financial Officer
CMO: Michael J Brescia, M.D., Executive Medical Director
CIO: Patrick Martin, Director Information Systems
CHR: Michael T Troncone, Chief Human Resources Officer
CNO: Margaret Pelkowski, R.N., Vice President Patient Care Services
Web address: www.calvaryhospital.org
Control: Church operated, Nongovernment, not–for–profit **Service**: Acute long–term care hospital

Staffed Beds: 225

Hospital, Medicare Provider Number, Address, Telephone, Approval, Facility, and Physician Codes, Health Care System

★ American Hospital Association (AHA) membership   ○ Healthcare Facilities Accreditation Program   ⇑ Center for Improvement in Healthcare Quality Accreditation
☐ The Joint Commission accreditation   ◇ DNV Healthcare Inc. accreditation   △ Commission on Accreditation of Rehabilitation Facilities (CARF) accreditation

Hospitals, U.S. / NEW YORK

☐ **CHILDREN'S HOSP OF NEW YORK** See Morgan Stanley Children's Hospital of New York–Presbyterian

COLER MEMORIAL HOSPITAL See Coler Rehabilitation and Nursing Care Center

COLUMBIA PRESBYTERIAN MED CTR See New York–Presbyterian/Columbia University Medical Center

CONCOURSE DIVISION See Bronxcare Health System, Bronx

CONCOURSE NURSING HOME See Concourse Regabilitation and Nursing Center

☐ **CREEDMOOR PSYCHIATRIC CENTER (334004)**, 79–25 Winchester Boulevard, Zip 11427–2128; tel. 718/264–3600, (Nonreporting) **A**1 3 5 10 **S** New York State Office of Mental Health, Albany, NY
Primary Contact: Martha Sullivan, M.D., Executive Director
CFO: Viodelda Ho–Shing, Deputy Director Administration
CIO: Ed Yunusov, Chief Information Officer
CHR: Adrienne Jones, Director Human Resources
CNO: Marie S Jean–Louis, R.N., Chief Nursing Officer
Web address: www.omh.ny.gov
Control: State, Government, Nonfederal **Service**: Psychiatric

Staffed Beds: 322

EINSTEIN–WEILER HOSPITAL See Jack D Weiler Hospital of Albert Einstein College of Medicine

☒ **FLUSHING HOSPITAL MEDICAL CENTER (330193)**, 4500 Parsons Boulevard, Zip 11355–2205; tel. 718/670–5000, **A**1 3 5 10 19 **F**3 4 5 7 12 13 15 17 18 19 29 30 31 32 34 35 36 39 40 41 45 49 50 55 56 57 59 60 61 63 64 65 68 70 71 72 73 74 75 76 77 78 79 81 82 84 85 87 89 91 92 93 97 98 100 101 104 107 110 111 114 115 119 126 130 132 135 140 147 148 149 150 154 156 160 162 164 167 169 **S** MediSys Health Network, Jamaica, NY
Primary Contact: Bruce J. Flanz, President and Chief Executive Officer
COO: Robert V Levine, Executive Vice President and Chief Operating Officer
CFO: Mounir F Doss, Executive Vice President and Chief Financial Officer
CIO: Tony Gatto, Director Management Information Systems
Web address: www.flushinghospital.org
Control: Other not–for–profit (including NFP Corporation) **Service**: General medical and surgical

Staffed Beds: 293 Admissions: 11364 Census: 147 Outpatient Visits: 168988 Births: 2479 Total Expense ($000): 1003741 Payroll Expense ($000): 167548 Personnel: 1754

FOREST HILLS HOSPITAL See Long Island Jewish Forest Hills

FULTON DIVISION See Bronxcare Health System, Bronx

GOLDWATER MEMORIAL HOSPITAL See Henry J. Carter Specialty Hospital & Nursing Facility

GOUVERNEUR HOSPITAL See NYC Health + Hospitals/Gouverneur

☐ **GRACIE SQUARE HOSPITAL (334048)**, 420 East 76th Street, Zip 10021–3396; tel. 212/988–4400, (Nonreporting) **A**1 10
Primary Contact: David Wyman, President and Chief Executive Officer
Web address: www.nygsh.org
Control: Other not–for–profit (including NFP Corporation) **Service**: Psychiatric

Staffed Beds: 157

HEBREW HOME FOR AGED–RIVERDALE See Hebrew Home For The Aged At Riverdale

HEBREW HOSP FOR CHRONIC SICK See Hebrew Hospital Home, Inc.

HENRY J. CARTER SPECIALTY HOSPITAL & NURSING FACILITY See NYC Health + Hospitals/Henry J Carter Specialty Hospital and Medical Center, New York

HOLY FAMILY HOME FOR THE AGED See Holy Family Home

☒ **HOSPITAL FOR SPECIAL SURGERY (330270)**, 535 East 70th Street, Zip 10021–4898, Mailing Address: 535 East 70th Street, Belaire 10–08, Zip 10021–4898; tel. 212/606–1000, **A**1 3 5 8 10 19 **F**3 8 9 12 29 30 32 33 34 35 36 37 38 44 50 53 54 56 57 58 59 64 66 68 70 74 75 77 79 80 81 82 84 85 86 87 89 91 92 93 94 97 100 107 111 114 115 119 126 130 131 132 134 141 142 143 146 147 148 149 154 164 **P**8
Primary Contact: Bryan T. Kelly, M.D., President and Chief Executive Officer
COO: Mary Cassai, Executive Vice President and Chief Operating Officer
CFO: Stacey Malakoff, Executive Vice President and Chief Financial Officer
CIO: Jamie Nelson, Vice President and Chief Information Officer
CHR: Bruce Slawitsky, Vice President Human Resources
CNO: Stephanie J Goldberg, MSN, R.N., Senior Vice President and Chief Nursing Officer
Web address: www.hss.edu
Control: Other not–for–profit (including NFP Corporation) **Service**: Orthopedic

Staffed Beds: 166 Admissions: 10807 Census: 83 Outpatient Visits: 708955 Births: 0 Total Expense ($000): 1510260 Payroll Expense ($000): 726319 Personnel: 5975

☐ **INTERFAITH MEDICAL CENTER (330397)**, 1545 Atlantic Avenue, Zip 11213–1122; tel. 718/613–4000, (Nonreporting) **A**1 3 5 10
Primary Contact: Sandra Scott, M.D., Interim Chief Executive Officer
CMO: Jochanan Weisenfreund, M.D., Senior Vice President Academic and Medical Affairs
CHR: Venra Mathurin, Vice President Human Resources
Web address: www.interfaithmedical.com
Control: Other not–for–profit (including NFP Corporation) **Service**: General medical and surgical

Staffed Beds: 243

JACK D WEILER HOSPITAL OF ALBERT EINSTEIN COLLEGE OF MEDICINE See Montefiore Medical Center, Bronx

☒ **JAMAICA HOSPITAL MEDICAL CENTER (330014)**, 8900 Van Wyck Expressway, Zip 11418–2832; tel. 718/206–6000, (Total facility includes 228 beds in nursing home–type unit) **A**1 3 5 10 13 19 **F**3 7 11 13 15 17 18 19 20 22 26 29 30 31 32 34 35 36 38 39 40 41 43 44 45 49 50 52 53 54 55 56 57 58 59 60 61 64 65 66 68 70 71 72 73 74 75 76 77 78 79 80 81 82 83 84 85 86 87 89 90 92 93 96 97 98 100 101 102 104 107 108 110 111 114 115 118 119 128 129 130 131 132 134 135 143 144 146 147 149 150 154 156 157 165 167 **S** MediSys Health Network, Jamaica, NY
Primary Contact: Bruce J. Flanz, President and Chief Executive Officer
COO: William Lynch, Executive Vice President and Chief Operating Officer
CFO: Mounir F Doss, Executive Vice President and Chief Financial Officer
CMO: Antonietta Morisco, M.D., Medical Director, Chairman Anesthesiology
CIO: Sami Boshut, Chief Information Officer
CHR: Trina Cornet, JD, Vice President Human Resources
CNO: Kathleen Scher, Ed.D., R.N., Chief Nursing Officer
Web address: www.Jamaicahospital.org
Control: Other not–for–profit (including NFP Corporation) **Service**: General medical and surgical

Staffed Beds: 612 Admissions: 15871 Census: 493 Outpatient Visits: 435118 Births: 1533 Total Expense ($000): 810802 Payroll Expense ($000): 366331 Personnel: 3706

☒ △ **JAMES J. PETERS VETERANS AFFAIRS MEDICAL CENTER**, 130 West Kingsbridge Road, Zip 10468–3904; tel. 718/584–9000, (Nonreporting) **A**1 2 3 5 7 **S** Department of Veterans Affairs, Washington, DC
Primary Contact: Balavenkatesh Kanna, M.D., M.P.H., FACHE, Medical Center Director
CFO: Gregory Angelo, Chief Fiscal Program
CIO: Linda Bund, Chief Information Officer and Director Education
CNO: Kathleen Capitulo, Ph.D., R.N., Chief Nurse Executive
Web address: www.bronx.va.gov/
Control: Veterans Affairs, Government, federal **Service**: General medical and surgical

Staffed Beds: 311

☐ **KINGSBORO PSYCHIATRIC CENTER (334063)**, 681 Clarkson Avenue, Zip 11203–2125; tel. 718/221–7395, (Nonreporting) **A**1 3 5 10 **S** New York State Office of Mental Health, Albany, NY
Primary Contact: Deborah Parchment, Executive Director
CFO: Yinusa Awolowo, Business Officer
CMO: Jeffery Lucey, M.D., Clinical Director
CIO: George Gavora, Director Program Evaluation
CHR: Vera Thompson, Director Human Resources
CNO: Deborah Denigris, Chief Nursing Officer
Web address: www.omh.ny.gov/omhweb/facilities/kbpc/facility/htm
Control: State, Government, Nonfederal **Service**: Psychiatric

Staffed Beds: 290

☐ **KIRBY FORENSIC PSYCHIATRIC CENTER (334060)**, 600 East 125th Street, Zip 10035–6000; tel. 646/672–5800, (Nonreporting) **A**1 3 5 10 **S** New York State Office of Mental Health, Albany, NY
Primary Contact: Brian Belfi, M.D., Executive Director
Web address: https://www.omh.ny.gov/omhweb/facilities/krpc/
Control: Other not–for–profit (including NFP Corporation) **Service**: Psychiatric

Staffed Beds: 193

Hospitals, U.S. / NEW YORK

★ **LENOX HILL HOSPITAL (330119)**, 100 East 77th Street, Zip 10075–1850; tel. 212/434–2000, (Includes MANHATTAN EYE, EAR AND THROAT HOSPITAL, 210 East 64th Street, New York, New York, Zip 10021–9885, tel. 212/838–9200; Philip P Rosenthal, Executive Director) **A**1 2 3 5 8 10 19 **F**3 5 7 8 9 11 12 13 14 15 17 18 20 22 24 25 29 30 31 32 33 34 35 36 37 39 40 42 44 45 46 47 48 49 50 51 52 54 55 56 57 58 59 60 61 62 64 65 66 68 70 71 72 73 74 75 76 77 78 79 81 82 83 84 85 86 87 89 91 92 93 94 97 98 100 101 102 103 104 107 108 110 111 114 115 116 117 118 119 120 121 123 124 126 129 130 131 132 134 135 141 143 144 145 147 148 149 150 154 155 162 164 165 167 168 169 **S** Northwell Health, Lake Success, NY
Primary Contact: Daniel Baker, Executive Director
CIO: Beth Dituro, Divisional Chief Information Officer
Web address: https://lenoxhill.northwell.edu/
Control: Other not–for–profit (including NFP Corporation) **Service**: General medical and surgical

Staffed Beds: 446 **Admissions:** 28465 **Census:** 326 **Outpatient Visits:** 286111 **Births:** 3787 **Total Expense ($000):** 1916809 **Payroll Expense ($000):** 921207 **Personnel:** 5786

LI JEWISH–HILLSIDE MED CENTER See Zucker Hillside Hospital

★ **MAIMONIDES MEDICAL CENTER (330194)**, 4802 Tenth Avenue, Zip 11219–2916; tel. 718/283–6000, (Includes MAIMONIDES INFANTS AND CHILDREN'S HOSPITAL OF BROOKLYN, 4802 Tenth Avenue, Brooklyn, New York, Zip 11219–2916, tel. 718/283–6000) **A**1 2 3 5 8 10 13 19 **F**3 7 8 9 11 12 13 14 15 17 19 20 22 24 26 28 29 30 31 32 34 35 37 38 39 40 41 42 43 45 46 47 48 49 50 51 52 54 55 56 57 58 59 60 61 64 65 66 68 70 72 74 75 76 77 78 79 81 82 84 85 86 87 88 89 91 92 93 94 96 97 98 99 100 101 102 103 104 107 108 110 111 114 115 116 117 118 119 120 121 123 124 126 129 130 131 132 135 145 146 147 148 149 150 154 156 159 160 162 163 164 165 167 169 **P**5 6
Primary Contact: Kenneth Gibbs, President and Chief Executive Officer
COO: Mark McDougle, Executive Vice President and Chief Operating Officer
CFO: Robert Naldi, Chief Financial Officer
CMO: Samuel Kopel, M.D., Medical Director
CIO: Walter Fahey, Chief Information Officer
Web address: www.maimonidesmed.org/
Control: Other not–for–profit (including NFP Corporation) **Service**: General medical and surgical

Staffed Beds: 646 **Admissions:** 29623 **Census:** 506 **Outpatient Visits:** 570262 **Births:** 5757 **Total Expense ($000):** 1774772 **Payroll Expense ($000):** 826582 **Personnel:** 6476

MANHATTAN EET HOSPITAL See Manhattan Eye, Ear and Throat Hospital

☐ **MANHATTAN PSYCHIATRIC CENTER–WARD'S ISLAND (334054)**, 600 East 125th Street, Zip 10035–6000; tel. 646/672–6767, (Nonreporting) **A**1 3 5 10 **S** New York State Office of Mental Health, Albany, NY
Primary Contact: Brian Belfi, M.D., Executive Director
Web address: www.omh.ny.gov
Control: State, Government, Nonfederal **Service**: Psychiatric

Staffed Beds: 745

MARGARET TIETZ CNTR FOR NRSG See Margaret Tietz Center For Nursing

★ **MEMORIAL SLOAN KETTERING CANCER CENTER (330154)**, 1275 York Avenue, Zip 10065–6007; tel. 212/639–2000, **A**1 2 3 5 8 10 **F**3 5 8 11 14 15 18 29 31 32 34 35 36 37 39 44 45 46 47 48 49 50 54 55 56 57 58 59 60 61 64 66 68 70 71 74 75 77 78 79 81 82 84 85 86 87 88 89 90 92 94 96 98 99 100 103 104 107 108 110 111 112 114 115 117 118 119 120 121 123 124 126 130 132 135 136 142 143 144 145 146 147 148 149 154 157 160 161 167 **P**6
Primary Contact: Selwyn Vickers, M.D., President
COO: Shelly Anderson, Hospital President
CFO: Michael Gutnick, Executive Vice President and Chief Financial Officer
CMO: Lisa DeAngelis, M.D., Acting Physician–in–Chief
CIO: Patricia Skarulis, Senior Vice President and Chief Information Systems Officer
CHR: Kerry Bessey, Senior Vice President and Chief Human Resources Officer
Web address: www.mskcc.org
Control: Other not–for–profit (including NFP Corporation) **Service**: Cancer

Staffed Beds: 512 **Admissions:** 25244 **Census:** 485 **Outpatient Visits:** 2055712 **Births:** 0 **Total Expense ($000):** 6045363 **Payroll Expense ($000):** 2008700 **Personnel:** 21635

★ **MONTEFIORE MEDICAL CENTER (330059)**, 111 East 210th Street, Zip 10467–2401; tel. 718/920–4321, (Includes CHILDREN'S HOSPITAL OF MONTEFIORE, 3415 Bainbridge Avenue, Bronx, New York, Zip 10467–2403, tel. 718/741–2426; JACK D WEILER HOSPITAL OF ALBERT EINSTEIN COLLEGE OF MEDICINE, 1825 Eastchester Road, Bronx, New York, Zip 10461–2373, tel. 718/904–2000; MONTEFIORE MEDICAL CENTER – NORTH DIVISION, 600 East 233rd Street, Bronx, New York, Zip 10466–2697, tel. 718/920–9000) **A**1 2 3 5 8 10 19 **F**3 5 6 7 8 9 12 13 14 15 17 18 19 20 21 22 23 24 25 26 27 28 29 30 31 32 34 35 36 37 38 39 40 41 42 43 44 45 46 47 48 49 50 51 52 53 54 55 56 57 58 59 60 61 62 63 64 65 66 68 70 71 72 73 74 75 76 77 78 79 80 81 82 83 84 85 86 87 88 89 90 91 92 93 94 96 97 98 99 100 101 102 103 104 107 108 110 111 114 115 116 117 118 119 120 121 123 124 126 129 130 131 132 134 135 136 137 138 139 140 141 142 143 144 145 146 147 148 149 150 153 154 156 157 160 161 162 163 164 165 166 167 169 **P**5 **S** Montefiore Health System, Bronx, NY
Primary Contact: Philip O. Ozuah, M.D., Ph.D., Chief Executive Officer
CFO: Colleen M Blye, Executive Vice President and Chief Financial Officer
CMO: Gary Kalkut, M.D., Senior Vice President and Chief Medical Officer
CIO: Jack Wolf, Vice President Information Systems
Web address: www.montefiore.org
Control: Other not–for–profit (including NFP Corporation) **Service**: General medical and surgical

Staffed Beds: 1294 **Admissions:** 80046 **Census:** 1325 **Outpatient Visits:** 4265319 **Births:** 4198 **Total Expense ($000):** 5006441 **Payroll Expense ($000):** 2280728 **Personnel:** 19866

MORGAN STANLEY CHILDREN'S HOSPITAL OF NEW YORK–PRESBYTERIAN See New York–Presbyterian Hospital, New York

★ **MOUNT SINAI BETH ISRAEL (330169)**, 281 First Avenue, Zip 10003–2925; tel. 212/420–2000, (Includes MOUNT SINAI BETH ISRAEL BROOKLYN, 3201 Kings Highway, Brooklyn, New York, Zip 11234, tel. 718/252–3000; Lin H Mo, M.P.H., President) **A**1 2 3 5 8 10 19 **F**3 4 5 7 8 9 11 12 15 17 18 20 22 26 29 30 31 32 34 35 36 38 39 40 41 44 45 46 47 48 49 50 51 53 54 55 56 57 58 59 60 61 63 64 65 66 68 70 71 74 75 77 78 79 81 82 83 84 85 86 87 92 93 97 98 100 101 102 103 104 105 107 108 110 111 114 115 116 117 118 119 120 121 123 124 126 129 130 131 132 134 135 141 143 144 145 146 147 148 149 150 153 154 156 157 160 162 164 165 167 169 **S** Mount Sinai Health System, New York, NY
Primary Contact: Elizabeth Sellman, President and Chief Operating Officer
COO: Elizabeth Sellman, President and Chief Operating Officer
CFO: Donald Scanlon, Chief Corporate Services, Mount Sinai Health System
CIO: Kumar Chatani, Senior Vice President and Chief Information Officer Mount Sinai Health System
CHR: Jane Maksoud, R.N., Senior Vice President Human Resources and Labor Relations, Mount Sinai Health System
CNO: Mary Walsh, R.N., MSN, Vice President Patient Care Services and Chief Nursing Officer
Web address: www.bethisraelny.org
Control: Other not–for–profit (including NFP Corporation) **Service**: General medical and surgical

Staffed Beds: 441 **Admissions:** 21523 **Census:** 384 **Outpatient Visits:** 543411 **Births:** 0 **Total Expense ($000):** 1188020 **Payroll Expense ($000):** 417523 **Personnel:** 4841

MOUNT SINAI HOSPITAL OF QUEENS See Mount Sinai Queens

★ **MOUNT SINAI MORNINGSIDE (330046)**, 1111 Amsterdam Avenue, Zip 10025–1716; tel. 212/523–4000, (Includes MOUNT SINAI WEST HOSPITAL, 1000 Tenth Avenue, New York, New York, Zip 10019, tel. 212/523–4000; Evan Flatow, M.D., President) **A**1 2 3 5 8 10 19 **F**3 4 5 7 8 9 11 12 13 15 17 18 20 22 24 26 29 30 31 32 35 36 37 38 39 40 41 43 44 45 46 47 48 49 50 51 52 54 55 56 57 58 59 60 61 62 63 64 65 66 68 70 71 72 73 74 75 76 77 78 79 81 82 83 84 85 86 87 90 92 96 97 98 99 100 101 102 103 104 107 108 110 111 112 114 115 116 117 118 119 120 121 123 124 126 129 130 131 132 134 135 141 143 144 145 146 147 148 149 150 153 154 156 157 160 161 162 164 165 167 168 169 **S** Mount Sinai Health System, New York, NY
Primary Contact: Evan Flatow, M.D., President
COO: Kevin Molloy, Senior Vice President and Chief Operating Officer
CFO: Donald Scanlon, Chief Corporate Services, Mount Sinai Health System
CIO: Kumar Chatani, Chief Information Officer, Mount Sinai Health System
CHR: Jane Maksoud, R.N., Senior Vice President Human Resources and Labor Relations, Mount Sinai Health System
CNO: Mary Walsh, R.N., MSN, Vice President Patient Care Services and Chief Nursing Officer
Web address: https://www.mountsinai.org/locations/morningside
Control: Other not–for–profit (including NFP Corporation) **Service**: General medical and surgical

Staffed Beds: 737 **Admissions:** 38269 **Census:** 647 **Outpatient Visits:** 423491 **Births:** 4520 **Total Expense ($000):** 1696613 **Payroll Expense ($000):** 647003 **Personnel:** 6294

Hospital, Medicare Provider Number, Address, Telephone, Approval, Facility, and Physician Codes, Health Care System

★ American Hospital Association (AHA) membership   ◯ Healthcare Facilities Accreditation Program   ⇑ Center for Improvement in Healthcare Quality Accreditation
☐ The Joint Commission accreditation   ◇ DNV Healthcare Inc. accreditation   △ Commission on Accreditation of Rehabilitation Facilities (CARF) accreditation

© 2025 AHA Guide

Hospitals, U.S. / NEW YORK

MOUNT SINAI ROOSEVELT HOSPITAL See Mount Sinai West Hospital

MOUNT SINAI WEST HOSPITAL See Mount Sinai Morningside, New York

☐ **NEW YORK CITY CHILDREN'S CENTER (334067)**, 74–03 Commonwealth Boulevard, Zip 11426–1890; tel. 718/264–4506, (Includes BRONX CHILDREN'S PSYCHIATRIC CENTER, 1000 Waters Place, Bronx, New York, Zip 10461–2799, tel. 718/239–3600; BROOKLYN CHILDREN'S PSYCHIATRIC CENTER, 1819 Bergen Street, Brooklyn, New York, Zip 11233–4513, tel. 718/221–4500) (Nonreporting) **A**1 3 **S** New York State Office of Mental Health, Albany, NY
Primary Contact: Kanika Jefferies, Executive Director
CMO: David M Rube, M.D., Clinical Director
CIO: Ed Yunusov, Coordinator Facility Information Center
Web address: www.omh.ny.gov/omhweb/facilities/nyccc/
Control: State, Government, Nonfederal **Service**: Children's hospital psychiatric

Staffed Beds: 92

☐ **NEW YORK COMMUNITY HOSPITAL (330019)**, 2525 Kings Highway, Zip 11229–1705; tel. 718/692–5300, **A**1 3 10 **F**3 8 12 18 20 22 29 30 31 34 35 40 44 45 46 47 48 49 50 51 57 59 60 68 70 74 75 77 78 79 81 82 84 85 87 100 107 111 114 119 130 135 143 146 148 149 154 156 164 167 **P**6
Primary Contact: Barry Stern, President and Chief Executive Officer
COO: Una E Morrissey, R.N., MSN, Senior Vice President Operations, Chief Operating Officer and Chief Nursing Officer
CFO: Leonardo Tamburello, Chief Financial Officer
CMO: Herbert Rader, M.D., Advisor for Medical Affairs
CIO: Edward B. Stolyar, D.O., Divisional Chief Informational Officer
CHR: Raquel Collado, Vice President Human Resources
CNO: Una E Morrissey, R.N., MSN, Senior Vice President Operations, Chief Operating Officer and Chief Nursing Officer
Web address: www.nych.com
Control: Other not–for–profit (including NFP Corporation) **Service**: General medical and surgical

Staffed Beds: 134 **Admissions**: 5875 **Census**: 88 **Outpatient Visits**: 37294 **Births**: 0 **Total Expense ($000)**: 149731 **Payroll Expense ($000)**: 68320 **Personnel**: 406

NEW YORK DOWNTOWN HOSPITAL See New York Presbyterian Lower Manhattan Hospital

✠ **NEW YORK EYE AND EAR INFIRMARY OF MOUNT SINAI (330100)**, 310 East 14th Street, Zip 10003–4201; tel. 212/979–4000, **A**1 3 5 8 10 **F**3 8 29 30 34 35 44 50 54 57 58 59 64 66 68 75 81 82 87 107 119 129 130 142 143 146 149 154 157 **P**5 **S** Mount Sinai Health System, New York, NY
Primary Contact: James C. Tsai, M.D., President
CFO: Donald Scanlon, Chief Corporate Services, Mount Sinai Health System
CIO: Kumar Chatani, Chief Information Officer, Mount Sinai Health System
CHR: Jane Maksoud, R.N., Senior Vice President Human Resources and Labor Relations, Mount Sinai Health System
Web address: www.nyee.edu
Control: Other not–for–profit (including NFP Corporation) **Service**: Eye, ear, nose and throat

Staffed Beds: 13 **Admissions**: 312 **Census**: 2 **Outpatient Visits**: 109727 **Total Expense ($000)**: 140653 **Payroll Expense ($000)**: 49699 **Personnel**: 457

NEW YORK FOUNDLING HOSPITAL See New York Foundling

✠ **NEW YORK–PRESBYTERIAN QUEENS (330055)**, 56–45 Main Street, Zip 11355–5045; tel. 718/670–1231, **A**1 2 3 5 10 19 **F**3 8 12 13 15 17 18 19 20 22 24 26 29 30 31 32 34 35 37 39 40 41 43 44 45 46 47 48 49 50 51 54 55 56 57 58 59 60 66 68 70 71 72 73 74 75 76 77 78 79 80 81 82 84 85 87 89 91 92 93 96 97 100 101 102 107 108 110 111 114 115 118 119 120 121 123 124 126 130 131 141 145 146 147 148 149 154 167 169 **S** New York–Presbyterian, New York, NY
Primary Contact: Stacey Petrower, President
COO: Robert Blenderman, Senior Vice President and Chief Operating Officer
CFO: Kevin J Ward, Vice President and Chief Financial Officer
CMO: Amir Jaffer, M.D., Senior Vice President Medical Affairs
CIO: Mark Greaker, Chief Information Officer
CHR: Lorraine S Orlando, Vice President Human Resources
CNO: Alan M. Levin, MSN, R.N., Chief Nursing Officer
Web address: https://www.nyp.org/queens
Control: Other not–for–profit (including NFP Corporation) **Service**: General medical and surgical

Staffed Beds: 512 **Admissions**: 26548 **Census**: 429 **Outpatient Visits**: 406764 **Births**: 2305 **Total Expense ($000)**: 987216 **Payroll Expense ($000)**: 398455 **Personnel**: 3324

☐ **NEW YORK STATE PSYCHIATRIC INSTITUTE (334009)**, 1051 Riverside Drive, Zip 10032–1007; tel. 646/774–5000, (Nonreporting) **A**1 3 5 10 **S** New York State Office of Mental Health, Albany, NY
COO: Janelle Dierkens, Chief Administration Officer
CFO: Jonathan Segal, Chief Financial Officer
CMO: David Lowenthal, M.D., Clinical Director
CIO: Joseph Grun, Chief Information Officer
CHR: Rebecca Dechabert, Acting Director Personnel
Web address: www.nyspi.org
Control: State, Government, Nonfederal **Service**: Psychiatric

Staffed Beds: 58

NEW YORK WEILL CORNELL MED CTR See New York–Presbyterian Hospital/Weill Cornell Medical Center

✠ △ **NEW YORK–PRESBYTERIAN HOSPITAL (330101)**, 525 East 68th Street, Zip 10065–4870; tel. 212/746–5454, (Includes MORGAN STANLEY CHILDREN'S HOSPITAL OF NEW YORK–PRESBYTERIAN, 3959 Broadway, New York, New York, Zip 10032–3784, tel. 212/305–2500; NEW YORK PRESBYTERIAN LOWER MANHATTAN HOSPITAL, 170 William Street, New York, New York, Zip 10038–2649, tel. 212/312–5000; Robert E Kelly, M.D., President; NEW YORK–PRESBYTERIAN HOSPITAL, WESTCHESTER DIVISION, 21 Bloomingdale Road, White Plains, New York, Zip 10605, tel. 914/682–9100; NEW YORK–PRESBYTERIAN HOSPITAL/WEILL CORNELL MEDICAL CENTER, 525 East 68th Street, New York, New York, Zip 10021–4885, tel. 212/746–5454; NEW YORK–PRESBYTERIAN/COLUMBIA UNIVERSITY MEDICAL CENTER, 161 Fort Washington Avenue, New York, New York, Zip 10032, tel. 212/305–2500; NEW YORK–PRESBYTERIAN/LAWRENCE HOSPITAL, 55 Palmer Avenue, Bronxville, New York, Zip 10708–3403, tel. 914/787–1000; Michael Fosina, M.P.H., FACHE, President; NEWYORK–PRESBYTERIAN BROOKLYN METHODIST HOSPITAL, 506 Sixth Street, Brooklyn, New York, Zip 11215–3609, tel. 718/780–3000; Robert Guimento, President; PAYNE WHITNEY PSYCHIATRIC CLINIC, 525 East 68th Street, New York, New York, Zip 10021, tel. 212/746–3800; PHYLLIS AND DAVID KOMANSKY CENTER FOR CHILDREN'S HEALTH, 525 East 68th Street, New York, New York, Zip 10065–4870, tel. 212/746–5454; THE ALLEN PAVILION, 5141 Broadway, New York, New York, Zip 10032, tel. 212/932–5000) **A**1 2 3 5 7 8 10 19 **F**3 4 5 6 7 8 9 11 12 13 14 15 16 17 18 19 20 21 22 23 24 25 26 27 28 29 30 31 32 34 35 36 37 38 39 40 41 43 44 45 46 47 48 49 50 51 52 54 55 56 57 58 59 60 61 62 63 64 65 66 68 70 71 72 73 74 75 76 77 78 79 80 81 82 83 84 85 86 87 88 89 90 92 93 94 96 97 98 99 100 101 102 103 104 105 107 108 110 111 112 114 115 116 117 118 119 120 121 123 124 126 129 130 131 132 134 135 136 137 138 139 140 141 142 143 144 145 146 147 148 149 150 152 153 154 156 157 160 161 162 164 165 167 169 **S** New York–Presbyterian, New York, NY
Primary Contact: Steven J. Corwin, M.D., President and Chief Executive Officer
COO: Colleen Koch, M.D., MS, Group Senior Vice President and Chief Operating Officer
CHR: G Thomas Ferguson, Senior Vice President and Chief Human Resources Officer
CNO: Rosemary Ventura, M.D., Chief Nursing Informatics Officer
Web address: www.nyp.org
Control: Other not–for–profit (including NFP Corporation) **Service**: General medical and surgical

Staffed Beds: 3018 **Admissions**: 142006 **Census**: 2639 **Outpatient Visits**: 2355283 **Births**: 21011 **Total Expense ($000)**: 9804553 **Payroll Expense ($000)**: 4554936 **Personnel**: 34423

NORTH CENTRAL BRONX HOSPITAL See NYC Health + Hospitals/North Central Bronx

✠ **NYC HEALTH + HOSPITALS/BELLEVUE (330204)**, 462 First Avenue, Zip 10016–9198; tel. 212/562–4141, **A**1 2 3 5 10 **F**3 5 10 11 12 13 15 17 18 19 20 22 24 26 28 29 30 31 32 33 34 35 36 37 38 39 40 41 43 45 46 47 48 49 50 51 52 53 55 56 57 58 59 61 62 64 65 66 68 70 71 74 75 76 77 78 79 81 82 83 84 85 86 87 88 89 90 92 93 94 96 97 98 99 100 101 102 103 104 105 107 108 110 111 114 115 118 119 126 130 131 132 135 144 146 147 148 149 153 154 156 160 161 162 163 164 166 167 169 **S** NYC Health + Hospitals, New York, NY
Primary Contact: William Hicks, Chief Executive Officer
COO: Michael Rawlings, Interim Chief Operating Officer
CFO: Rebecca J Fischer, Chief Financial Officer
CMO: Nathan Link, M.D., Medical Director
CIO: James Carr, Chief Information Officer
CNO: Kim K Mendez, Ed.D., R.N., Chief Nurse Officer
Web address: www.nyc.gov/bellevue
Control: City, Government, Nonfederal **Service**: General medical and surgical

Staffed Beds: 853 **Admissions**: 27717 **Census**: 680 **Outpatient Visits**: 757506 **Births**: 1405 **Total Expense ($000)**: 1538873 **Payroll Expense ($000)**: 476689 **Personnel**: 4862

NYC HEALTH + HOSPITALS/CONEY ISLAND See NYC Health + Hospitals/South Brooklyn Health

Hospitals, U.S. / NEW YORK

NYC HEALTH + HOSPITALS/ELMHURST (330128), 79–01 Broadway, Zip 11373–1329; tel. 718/334–4000, (Nonreporting) **A**1 2 3 5 10 **S** NYC Health + Hospitals, New York, NY
Primary Contact: Helen Arteaga. Landaverde, Chief Executive Officer
COO: Wayne Zimmermann, Chief Operating Officer
CFO: David Guzman, Chief Financial Officer
CMO: Jasmin Moshirpur, M.D., Dean and Medical Director
CIO: Jeannith Michelen, Chief Implementation Officer
CHR: Peter Maris, Director Human Resources
CNO: Joann Bernadette Gull, Chief Nursing Officer
Web address: https://www.nychealthandhospitals.org/locations/elmhurst/
Control: City, Government, Nonfederal **Service:** General medical and surgical

Staffed Beds: 512

NYC HEALTH + HOSPITALS/HARLEM (330240), 506 Lenox Avenue, Zip 10037–1802; tel. 212/939–1000, **A**1 3 5 10 **F**1 3 4 5 8 11 12 13 15 16 17 18 19 29 30 32 34 35 38 39 40 41 43 44 45 46 47 49 50 52 53 55 57 58 59 60 61 64 65 67 68 70 72 73 74 75 76 77 79 80 81 82 84 85 86 87 88 89 90 93 94 96 97 98 100 102 104 107 108 110 111 114 115 118 119 128 130 132 134 135 141 144 146 147 148 149 154 156 160 162 163 164 165 166 167 169 **S** NYC Health + Hospitals, New York, NY
Primary Contact: Georges Leconte, Chief Executive Officer
Web address: www.nyc.gov/html/hhc/harlem
Control: City, Government, Nonfederal **Service:** General medical and surgical

Staffed Beds: 241 **Admissions:** 11173 **Census:** 192 **Outpatient Visits:** 334346 **Births:** 702 **Total Expense ($000):** 638769 **Payroll Expense ($000):** 192926 **Personnel:** 1949

NYC HEALTH + HOSPITALS/HENRY J CARTER SPECIALTY HOSPITAL AND MEDICAL CENTER (332008), 1752 Park Avenue, Zip 10035; tel. 646/686–0000, (Includes COLER REHABILITATION AND NURSING CARE CENTER, 900 Main Street, Roosevelt Island, New York, New York, Zip 10044–0066, tel. 212/848–6300; Robert K. Hughes, Chief Executive Officer; HENRY J. CARTER SPECIALTY HOSPITAL & NURSING FACILITY, 1752 Park Ave, New York, New York, Zip 10035–2811, 1752 Park Avenue, Zip 10035, tel. 646/686–0000; Floyd R Long, Chief Executive Officer) (Total facility includes 164 beds in nursing home–type unit) **A**1 3 5 10 **F**1 3 11 28 29 30 39 56 58 60 68 74 75 77 79 84 85 87 100 107 114 119 128 130 132 135 146 148 149 **S** NYC Health + Hospitals, New York, NY
Primary Contact: Floyd R. Long, Executive Director
CFO: Manuela Brito, Chief Financial Officer Post Acute Care
CMO: Vasudeva Raju, M.D., Suffix, Chief, Long Term Acute Care Medicine
CIO: Steve ONeill, Chief Information Officer
CHR: Jamie Grecco, Director Human Resources Post Acute
CNO: Stanlee Richards, R.N., MS, Chief Nurse Executive
Web address: www.nychealthandhospitals.org/Carter
Control: City, Government, Nonfederal **Service:** Acute long–term care hospital

Staffed Beds: 365 **Admissions:** 927 **Census:** 255 **Outpatient Visits:** 350 **Births:** 0 **Total Expense ($000):** 163079 **Payroll Expense ($000):** 40731 **Personnel:** 405

NYC HEALTH + HOSPITALS/JACOBI (330127), 1400 Pelham Parkway South, Zip 10461–1197; tel. 718/918–5000, (Includes NYC HEALTH + HOSPITALS/NORTH CENTRAL BRONX, 3424 Kossuth Avenue, Bronx, New York, Zip 10467–2489, tel. 718/519–3500; Christopher Mastromano, Chief Executive Officer) **A**1 2 3 5 10 **F**1 3 4 5 11 12 13 15 16 17 18 20 22 26 29 30 31 32 34 35 38 39 40 41 43 44 45 46 47 49 50 51 52 53 55 56 57 58 59 60 61 63 64 65 66 68 70 72 73 74 75 76 77 78 79 80 81 82 84 85 86 87 88 89 90 92 93 94 96 97 98 100 101 102 103 104 105 107 108 110 111 114 115 116 117 118 119 128 130 131 132 134 135 141 144 145 146 147 148 149 150 153 154 156 157 160 162 164 165 166 167 169 **S** NYC Health + Hospitals, New York, NY
Primary Contact: Christopher Mastromano, Chief Executive Officer
COO: Jordana Ane Bailey, Chief Operating Officer
CFO: Ellen Barlis, Chief Financial Officer
CMO: Michael Zinaman, M.D., Acting Chief Medical Officer
CIO: Md Alam, Chief Information Officer
CHR: Jamie Grecco, Chief Human Resource Executive
CNO: Suzanne Pennacchio, MSN, R.N., Chief Nursing Officer
Web address: www.nyc.gov/html/hhc/jacobi/home.html
Control: City, Government, Nonfederal **Service:** General medical and surgical

Staffed Beds: 520 **Admissions:** 25466 **Census:** 483 **Outpatient Visits:** 688392 **Births:** 2777 **Total Expense ($000):** 1314381 **Payroll Expense ($000):** 434065 **Personnel:** 4514

NYC HEALTH + HOSPITALS/KINGS COUNTY (330202), 451 Clarkson Avenue, Zip 11203–2054; tel. 718/245–3131, **A**1 2 3 5 10 19 **F**3 5 9 11 12 13 15 17 18 29 30 31 32 34 35 38 39 40 41 43 45 46 47 48 49 50 51 53 56 57 58 59 60 61 64 65 68 70 71 72 73 74 75 76 77 78 79 81 82 84 85 86 87 88 89 90 91 92 93 94 96 97 98 99 100 101 102 104 105 106 107 108 110 111 115 116 117 118 119 120 121 123 126 129 130 131 132 133 134 135 142 143 144 145 146 147 148 149 150 153 154 156 157 160 164 167 169 **P**6 **S** NYC Health + Hospitals, New York, NY
Primary Contact: Sheldon Mcleod, Chief Executive Officer
CNO: Opal Sinclair–Chung, R.N., MS, Chief Nursing Officer, Deputy Executive Director
Web address: www.nyc.gov/html/hhc/kchc/html/home/home.shtml
Control: City, Government, Nonfederal **Service:** General medical and surgical

Staffed Beds: 505 **Admissions:** 16329 **Census:** 424 **Outpatient Visits:** 646716 **Births:** 1331 **Total Expense ($000):** 1180638 **Payroll Expense ($000):** 466727 **Personnel:** 5370

NYC HEALTH + HOSPITALS/LINCOLN (330080), 234 East 149th Street, Zip 10451–5504, Mailing Address: 234 East 149th Street, Room 2D3, Zip 10451–5504; tel. 718/579–5700, **A**1 5 10 **F**3 5 15 24 25 29 30 31 32 34 35 38 39 40 41 43 45 46 49 50 51 55 56 57 58 59 60 61 64 65 66 68 70 71 72 73 74 75 76 77 78 79 81 82 84 85 87 88 89 92 93 97 98 100 101 102 104 107 108 110 111 115 117 119 126 130 132 134 135 146 147 148 149 150 156 160 161 164 167 169 **S** NYC Health + Hospitals, New York, NY
Primary Contact: Christopher Roker, Chief Executive Officer
CFO: Caswell Samms, Network Chief Financial Officer
CMO: Anita Soni, M.D., Chief Medical Officer
CIO: James Carr, Chief Information Officer
CHR: Jeannith Michelen, Senior Associate Executive Director
Web address: https://www.nychealthhospitals.org/
Control: City, Government, Nonfederal **Service:** General medical and surgical

Staffed Beds: 319 **Admissions:** 14668 **Census:** 214 **Outpatient Visits:** 589403 **Births:** 1466 **Total Expense ($000):** 852547 **Payroll Expense ($000):** 301362 **Personnel:** 4344

NYC HEALTH + HOSPITALS/METROPOLITAN (330199), 1901 First Avenue, Zip 10029–7404; tel. 212/423–6262, (Nonreporting) **A**1 3 5 10 **S** NYC Health + Hospitals, New York, NY
Primary Contact: Cristina Contreras, Chief Executive Officer
COO: William Norberto Wang, M.D., Chief Operating Officer
CFO: Edie Coleman, Chief Financial Officer
CMO: John T Pellicone, M.D., Chief Medical Officer
CIO: Md Alam, Chief Information Officer
CHR: April Alexander, Director Human Resources
CNO: Noreen Bridget Brennan, Chief Nursing Officer
Web address: www.nyc.gov/html/hhc/mhc/html/home/home.shtml
Control: City, Government, Nonfederal **Service:** General medical and surgical

Staffed Beds: 281

NYC HEALTH + HOSPITALS/QUEENS (330231), 82–68 164th Street, Zip 11432–1104; tel. 718/883–3000, **A**1 2 3 5 10 **F**3 5 8 9 11 13 15 18 19 28 29 30 31 32 34 35 38 39 40 41 45 46 47 49 50 52 53 54 55 56 58 59 60 61 64 65 66 68 70 71 72 73 74 75 76 77 78 79 81 82 86 87 93 94 97 98 100 101 102 104 105 107 108 110 111 114 115 116 117 118 119 120 121 123 124 129 130 132 141 143 144 146 147 148 149 152 153 154 156 160 162 163 164 165 169 **S** NYC Health + Hospitals, New York, NY
Primary Contact: Neil J. Moore, Chief Executive Officer
COO: Dean Milhaltses, Chief Operating Officer
CFO: Brian Stacey, Chief Financial Officer
CMO: Jasmin Moshirpur, M.D., Chief Medical Officer
CIO: Vincent Smith, Chief Information Officer
CHR: Jeannith Michelen, Senior Associate Executive Director
CNO: Joan Gabriele, Deputy Executive Director
Web address: www.nyc.gov/html/hhc/qhc/html/home/home.shtml
Control: City, Government, Nonfederal **Service:** General medical and surgical

Staffed Beds: 253 **Admissions:** 10993 **Census:** 204 **Outpatient Visits:** 544576 **Births:** 1390 **Total Expense ($000):** 605829 **Payroll Expense ($000):** 198126 **Personnel:** 1902

Hospital, Medicare Provider Number, Address, Telephone, Approval, Facility, and Physician Codes, Health Care System

★ American Hospital Association (AHA) membership
☐ The Joint Commission accreditation
○ Healthcare Facilities Accreditation Program
◇ DNV Healthcare Inc. accreditation
⇑ Center for Improvement in Healthcare Quality Accreditation
△ Commission on Accreditation of Rehabilitation Facilities (CARF) accreditation

Hospitals, U.S. / NEW YORK

NYC HEALTH + HOSPITALS/SOUTH BROOKLYN HEALTH (330196), 2601 Ocean Parkway, Zip 11235–7795; tel. 718/616–3000, **A**1 3 5 10 12 13 **F**3 5 11 12 13 15 17 18 20 22 29 30 31 34 35 38 39 40 41 44 45 46 47 48 49 50 51 54 56 57 58 59 60 61 64 65 66 68 70 73 74 75 76 77 78 79 81 82 83 84 85 86 87 91 92 93 94 96 97 98 100 102 104 107 108 110 111 114 115 118 119 120 121 126 130 132 141 145 146 147 148 149 150 154 156 160 161 164 165 167 169 **P**6 **S** NYC Health + Hospitals, New York, NY
Primary Contact: Svetlana Lipyanskaya, Chief Executive Officer
COO: Mei Kong, Chief Operating Officer
CMO: Wehbeh Wehbeh, M.D., Chief Medical Officer
CIO: Robert Kee, Chief Information Officer
CHR: Andrew Campbell, Associate Executive Director
CNO: Patricia Ruiz, R.N., Chief Nursing Officer
Web address: https://www.nychealthandhospitals.org/Coneylsland/
Control: City, Government, Nonfederal **Service**: General medical and surgical

Staffed Beds: 307 **Admissions**: 13665 **Census**: 272 **Outpatient Visits**: 497020 **Births**: 1495 **Total Expense ($000)**: 685594 **Payroll Expense ($000)**: 221816 **Personnel**: 2807

NYC HEALTH + HOSPITALS/WOODHULL (330396), 760 Broadway, Zip 11206–5383; tel. 718/963–8000, **A**1 3 5 10 **F**3 5 11 12 13 15 19 29 30 31 32 34 35 36 37 38 39 40 41 44 45 46 49 50 52 55 56 57 58 59 60 61 64 65 66 68 70 71 72 73 74 75 76 77 78 79 80 81 82 84 85 86 87 89 93 94 97 98 100 101 102 104 107 108 110 111 115 118 119 126 130 132 134 135 141 146 147 149 150 154 156 160 161 164 165 167 169 **P**6 **S** NYC Health + Hospitals, New York, NY
Primary Contact: Gregory Calliste, Ph.D., FACHE, Chief Executive Officer
CFO: Erika Soiman, CPA, Chief Financial Officer
CMO: Edward Fishkin, M.D., Medical Director
CHR: Irma Suarez, Deputy Executive Director
CNO: Angela Imelda Edwards, R.N., Chief Nurse Executive
Web address: https://www.nychealthandhospitals.org/Woodhull/
Control: City–county, Government, Nonfederal **Service**: General medical and surgical

Staffed Beds: 243 **Admissions**: 7221 **Census**: 178 **Outpatient Visits**: 455508 **Births**: 1342 **Total Expense ($000)**: 575746 **Payroll Expense ($000)**: 195635 **Personnel**: 2047

NYU CHILDREN'S HOSPITAL See Hassenfeld Childrens Hospital of New York At Nyu Langone Medical Center

NYU LANGONE HOSPITALS (330214), 550 First Avenue, Zip 10016–6402; tel. 212/263–7300, (Includes HASSENFELD CHILDRENS HOSPITAL OF NEW YORK AT NYU LANGONE MEDICAL CENTER, 550 First Avenue, New York, New York, Zip 10016–6401, tel. 212/263–7300; NYU LANGONE HOSPITAL – LONG ISLAND, 259 First Street, Mineola, New York, Zip 11501–3957, tel. 516/663–0333; John F Collins, President and Chief Executive Officer; NYU LANGONE HOSPITAL–BROOKLYN, 150 55th Street, Brooklyn, New York, Zip 11220–2559, tel. 718/630–7000; Bret Rudy, M.D., Executive Director and Senior Vice President; NYU LANGONE ORTHOPEDIC HOSPITAL, 301 East 17th Street, New York, New York, Zip 10003–3890, tel. 212/598–6000; David A Dibner, FACHE, Senior Vice President Hospital Operations and Musculoskeletal Strategic Areas; RUSK INSTITUTE AT NYU–HJD, 301 E 17th ST, New York, New York, Zip 10003–3804, tel. 212/598–6000; David A Dibner, FACHE, Senior Vice President Hospital Operations and Musculoskeletal Strategic Areas) **A**1 2 3 5 7 8 10 13 19 **F**3 5 6 7 8 9 11 12 13 15 17 18 19 20 21 22 23 24 25 26 27 28 29 30 31 32 34 35 36 37 38 39 40 41 42 43 44 45 46 47 48 49 50 51 52 53 54 55 56 57 58 59 60 61 62 64 65 66 67 68 70 72 73 74 75 76 77 78 79 80 81 82 84 85 86 87 88 89 90 91 92 93 95 96 97 98 100 101 102 103 104 107 108 109 110 111 112 113 114 115 116 117 118 119 120 121 123 124 126 129 130 131 132 134 135 136 137 138 139 140 141 142 144 145 146 147 148 149 150 153 154 156 157 160 161 162 164 167 168 169 **P**5 6
Primary Contact: Robert I. Grossman, M.D., Chief Executive Officer
COO: Robert J. Cerfolio, M.D., Chief Operating Officer
CFO: Daniel J. Widawsky, Chief Financial Officer
CMO: Fritz Francois, M.D., Chief Medical Officer
CIO: Nader Mherabi, Senior Vice President and Vice Dean, Chief Information Officer
CHR: Nancy Sanchez, Senior Vice President and Vice Dean Human Resources
Web address: www.nyumedicalcenter.org
Control: Other not–for–profit (including NFP Corporation) **Service**: General medical and surgical

Staffed Beds: 1799 **Admissions**: 108618 **Census**: 1471 **Outpatient Visits**: 2530971 **Births**: 14339 **Total Expense ($000)**: 8099163 **Payroll Expense ($000)**: 2504009 **Personnel**: 25514

NYU LANGONE MEDICAL CENTER'S HOSPITAL FOR JOINT DISEASES See NYU Langone Orthopedic Hospital

NYU LUTHERAN (NYU HOSPITALS CENTER) See NYU Langone Hospital–Brooklyn

OUR LADY OF MERCY MED CENTER See Montefiore Medical Center – North Division

PAYNE WHITNEY PSYCHIATRIC CLINIC See New York–Presbyterian Hospital, New York

RICHMOND UNIVERSITY MEDICAL CENTER (330028), 355 Bard Avenue, Zip 10310–1664; tel. 718/818–1234, (Nonreporting) **A**1 2 3 5 10
Primary Contact: Daniel J. Messina, Ph.D., FACHE, President and Chief Executive Officer
CMO: Edward Arsura, M.D., Chief Medical Officer
CHR: Patricia Caldari, Vice President
Web address: www.rumcsi.org
Control: Other not–for–profit (including NFP Corporation) **Service**: General medical and surgical

Staffed Beds: 255

ROCKEFELLER UNIVERSITY HOSPITAL (330387), 1230 York Avenue, Zip 10065–6399; tel. 212/327–8000, (Nonreporting) **A**10
Primary Contact: James G. Krueger, M.D., Ph.D., Chief Executive Officer
CMO: Barbara O'Sullivan, M.D., M.P.H., Medical Director
Web address: www.rucares.org
Control: Other not–for–profit (including NFP Corporation) **Service**: Other specialty treatment

Staffed Beds: 14

RUSK INSTITUTE See Rusk Institute At Nyu–Hjd

SEA VIEW HOSPITAL REHABILITATION CENTER AND HOME See NYC Health + Hospitals/Sea View

SOUTH BEACH PSYCHIATRIC CENTER (334043), 777 Seaview Avenue, Zip 10305–3409; tel. 718/667–2300, **A**1 3 5 10 **F**29 30 34 35 50 59 65 75 86 87 97 98 99 100 101 130 132 135 146 149 156 157 164 **S** New York State Office of Mental Health, Albany, NY
Primary Contact: Doreen Piazza, MS, Executive Director
CHR: George Bouquio, Director Human Resources
Web address: www.omh.ny.gov/omhweb/facilities/sbpc/facility.htm
Control: State, Government, Nonfederal **Service**: Psychiatric

Staffed Beds: 235 **Admissions**: 208 **Census**: 224 **Outpatient Visits**: 0 **Births**: 0 **Total Expense ($000)**: 168893 **Payroll Expense ($000)**: 68506 **Personnel**: 658

ST. ALBANS PRIMARY AND EXTENDED CARE CENTER See Veterans Affairs New York Harbor Healthcare System – St. Albans Community Living Center

ST. BARNABAS HOSPITAL (330399), 4422 Third Avenue, Zip 10457–2545; tel. 718/960–9000, **A**1 3 5 10 12 13 19 **F**3 4 5 11 12 13 15 18 19 20 22 26 29 30 31 32 34 35 36 38 39 40 41 43 44 45 46 47 49 50 51 53 54 55 56 57 58 59 60 61 64 65 66 68 70 71 72 74 75 76 77 78 79 81 82 83 84 85 86 87 89 91 92 93 94 97 98 100 101 102 104 107 108 110 111 114 115 117 119 129 130 131 132 134 135 143 146 147 148 149 150 154 156 157 160 162 165 167 169
Primary Contact: David A. Perlstein, M.D., President and Chief Executive Officer
COO: Len Walsh, Executive Vice President and Chief Operating Officer
CFO: Todd Gorlewski, Senior Vice President and Chief Financial Officer
CIO: Jitendra Barmecha, M.D., M.P.H., Senior Vice President and Chief Information Officer
CHR: Marc Wolf, Assistant Vice President Human Resources
CNO: Denise Richardson, R.N., MSN, Senior Vice President and Chief Nursing Officer
Web address: www.sbhny.org
Control: Other not–for–profit (including NFP Corporation) **Service**: General medical and surgical

Staffed Beds: 422 **Admissions**: 13952 **Census**: 242 **Outpatient Visits**: 472154 **Births**: 615 **Total Expense ($000)**: 545069 **Payroll Expense ($000)**: 264402 **Personnel**: 2587

ST JOHN'S EPISCOPAL HOME See St John's Episcopal Homes For The Aged & Blind

Hospitals, U.S. / NEW YORK

☐ **ST. JOHN'S EPISCOPAL HOSPITAL (330395)**, 327 Beach 19th Street, Zip 11691–4423; tel. 718/869–7000, (Nonreporting) **A**1 3 5 10 12 13 19
Primary Contact: Gerard W. Walsh, Chief Executive Officer
COO: Christopher Parker, R.N., Executive Vice President and Chief Operating Officer
CFO: Kathleen Garcia, Controller
CMO: Raymond Pastore, M.D., Chief Medical Officer
CIO: Michael J Piro, Chief Information Officer
CHR: Roger Franco, Director Human Resources
CNO: Hermelina Zabala, MSN, R.N., MSN, RN, Senior Vice President, Patient Care Services and Chief Nursing Officer
Web address: www.ehs.org
Control: Church operated, Nongovernment, not–for–profit **Service**: General medical and surgical

Staffed Beds: 213

✠ △ **STATEN ISLAND UNIVERSITY HOSPITAL (330160)**, 475 Seaview Avenue, Zip 10305–3436; tel. 718/226–9000, **A**1 2 3 5 7 8 10 **F**3 5 7 8 11 12 13 14 15 16 17 18 19 20 22 24 26 28 29 30 31 32 34 35 38 39 40 41 43 44 45 46 47 48 49 50 51 52 53 54 55 56 57 58 59 60 61 63 64 65 66 68 70 71 72 73 74 75 76 77 78 79 81 82 84 85 86 87 88 89 90 92 93 94 96 97 98 100 101 102 104 105 107 108 110 111 114 116 117 118 119 120 121 123 124 126 129 130 131 132 134 135 145 146 147 148 153 154 160 161 162 164 165 167 169 **S** Northwell Health, Lake Success, NY
Primary Contact: Brahim Ardolic, M.D., Chief Executive Officer
CFO: Thomas Reca Sr, Deputy Executive Director and Chief Financial Officer
CMO: Theodore Maniatis, M.D., Medical Director
CIO: Kathy Kania, Associate Executive Director and Chief Information Officer
CHR: Margaret DiAlto, Regional Chief Human Resource Officer
CNO: Terry Pando, R.N., Associate Executive Director and Chief Nursing Officer
Web address: www.siuh.edu
Control: Other not–for–profit (including NFP Corporation) **Service**: General medical and surgical

Staffed Beds: 595 **Admissions**: 36457 **Census**: 557 **Outpatient Visits**: 706245 **Births**: 2984 **Total Expense ($000)**: 1435272 **Payroll Expense ($000)**: 672608 **Personnel**: 5686

STEVEN AND ALEXANDRA COHEN CHILDREN'S MEDICAL CENTER OF NEW YORK See Long Island Jewish Medical Center, New Hyde Park

☐ **SUNY DOWNSTATE HEALTH SCIENCES UNIVERSITY (330350)**, 445 Lenox Road, Zip 11203–2017, Mailing Address: 450 Clarkson Avenue, MSC#1, Zip 11203–2012; tel. 718/270–1000, (Nonreporting) **A**1 3 5 8 10
Primary Contact: Wayne J. Riley, M.D., M.P.H., President
COO: Patricia A Winston, FACHE, MS, R.N., Senor Vice President, Hospital Administration
CFO: Richard B. Miller, Ph.D., Vice President Hospital Affairs and Chief Financial Officer
CMO: Michael Lucchesi, M.D., Chief Medical Officer; Chair, Emergency Medicine
CIO: Dennis Sutterfield, Chief Information Officer
CHR: Maria Silas, Manager Human Resources
CNO: Margaret G. Jackson, R.N., Vice President Patient Care Services and Chief Nursing Officer
Web address: www.downstate.edu
Control: State, Government, Nonfederal **Service**: General medical and surgical

Staffed Beds: 286

TERENCE CARDINAL COOKE HEALTH CARE CENTER (330410), 1249 Fifth Avenue, Zip 10029–4413; tel. 212/360–1000, (Nonreporting) **A**5 10
Primary Contact: Mitch Marsh, Interim Executive Director
COO: Neil Pollack, Senior Administrator
CFO: Ann Marie Covone, Senior Vice President and Chief Financial Officer
CMO: Anthony Lechich, M.D., Chief Medical Officer
CIO: Mitze Amoroso, Chief Information Officer
CHR: Hugo A Pizarro, Vice President Human Resources
CNO: Monica McGibbon, Chief Nursing Officer
Web address: www.tcchcc.org/
Control: Church operated, Nongovernment, not–for–profit **Service**: Acute long–term care hospital

Staffed Beds: 28

THE ALLEN PAVILION See New York–Presbyterian Hospital, New York

THE CHILDREN'S HOSPITAL OF MONTEFIORE See Children's Hospital of Montefiore

✠ **THE MOUNT SINAI HOSPITAL (330024)**, 1 Gustave L Levy Place, Zip 10029–0310; tel. 212/241–6500, (Includes KRAVIS CHILDREN'S HOSPITAL, 1184 5th Ave, New York, New York, Zip 10029–6503, One Gustave L Levy Place, Zip 10029–0312, tel. 212/241–9500; MOUNT SINAI QUEENS, 25–10 30th Avenue, Long Island City, New York, Zip 11102–2448, tel. 718/932–1000; Caryn A Schwab, Executive Director) **A**1 2 3 5 8 10 **F**3 4 6 7 8 9 11 12 13 14 15 17 18 19 20 21 22 23 24 25 26 27 28 29 30 31 32 33 34 35 36 37 38 39 40 41 42 43 44 45 46 47 48 49 50 51 52 54 55 56 57 58 59 60 61 62 63 64 65 66 68 70 71 72 73 74 75 76 77 78 79 80 81 82 83 84 85 86 87 88 89 90 91 92 93 95 96 97 98 100 101 102 103 104 105 107 108 110 111 112 114 115 116 117 118 119 120 121 123 124 126 129 130 131 132 134 135 136 137 138 139 140 141 142 143 144 145 146 147 148 149 150 154 156 157 161 162 164 165 167 168 169 **S** Mount Sinai Health System, New York, NY
Primary Contact: David L. Reich, M.D., President and Chief Operating Officer
COO: Jonathan Kyriacou, Chief Operating Officer
CFO: Donald Scanlon, Chief Financial Officer
CMO: Vicki L. LoPachin, M.D., Chief Medical Officer
CIO: Kumar Chatani, Senior Vice President and Chief Information Officer Mount Sinai Health System
CHR: Jane Maksoud, R.N., Senior Vice President Human Resources and Labor Relations
Web address: www.mountsinai.org
Control: Other not–for–profit (including NFP Corporation) **Service**: General medical and surgical

Staffed Beds: 1194 **Admissions**: 57291 **Census**: 1065 **Outpatient Visits**: 1138068 **Births**: 6398 **Total Expense ($000)**: 3880963 **Payroll Expense ($000)**: 1510083 **Personnel**: 13117

VETERANS AFFAIRS NY HARBOR HEALTHCARE SYSTEM – MANHATTAN CAMPUS See Veterans Affairs New York Harbor Healthcare System – Manhattan Campus

✠ △ **VETERANS AFFAIRS NEW YORK HARBOR HEALTHCARE SYSTEM**, 800 Poly Place, Zip 11209–7104; tel. 718/630–3500, (Includes VETERANS AFFAIRS NEW YORK HARBOR HEALTHCARE SYSTEM – MANHATTAN CAMPUS, 423 East 23rd Street, New York, New York, Zip 10010–5050, tel. 212/686–7500; Martina A Parauda, Director) (Nonreporting) **A**1 2 3 5 7 8 **S** Department of Veterans Affairs, Washington, DC
Primary Contact: Timothy Graham, JD, Medical Center Director
CFO: Andre Chance, Chief Financial Officer
CMO: Patrick C. Malloy, M.D., Chief of Staff
CIO: Luis Barrios, Chief Information Officer
CHR: Kevin Grundig, Chief Human Resource Officer
CNO: Cynthia A. Caroselli, R.N., Ph.D., Chief Nursing Officer
Web address: www.nyharbor.va.gov
Control: Veterans Affairs, Government, federal **Service**: General medical and surgical

Staffed Beds: 316

☐ **WYCKOFF HEIGHTS MEDICAL CENTER (330221)**, 374 Stockholm Street, Zip 11237–4006; tel. 718/963–7272, **A**1 3 5 10 13 **F**3 7 8 12 13 15 18 19 20 22 26 29 30 31 32 34 35 39 40 41 45 46 49 50 51 54 57 59 61 63 64 65 68 70 72 74 75 76 78 79 81 82 84 85 87 89 90 92 93 97 100 104 107 110 111 114 115 119 120 121 126 130 131 141 146 147 148 154 162 167 169 **P**1 4 5 7 8
Primary Contact: Ramon J. Rodriguez, President and Chief Executive Officer
COO: David Rock, Executive Vice President and Chief Operating Officer
CFO: Frank A Vutrano, Chief Financial Officer
CMO: Gustavo Del Toro, M.D., Chief Medical Officer
CIO: Jebashini Jesurasa, Vice President, Chief Information Technology Officer
CHR: Margaret E Cornelius, Vice President Human Resources
CNO: Catherine A Gallogly–Simon, R.N., MS, Chief Nursing Officer
Web address: www.wyckoffhospital.org
Control: Other not–for–profit (including NFP Corporation) **Service**: General medical and surgical

Staffed Beds: 213 **Admissions**: 12165 **Census**: 153 **Outpatient Visits**: 238743 **Births**: 914 **Total Expense ($000)**: 483891 **Payroll Expense ($000)**: 220829 **Personnel**: 1992

ZUCKER HILLSIDE HOSPITAL See Long Island Jewish Medical Center, New Hyde Park

---

Hospital, Medicare Provider Number, Address, Telephone, Approval, Facility, and Physician Codes, Health Care System

★ American Hospital Association (AHA) membership
☐ The Joint Commission accreditation
○ Healthcare Facilities Accreditation Program
◇ DNV Healthcare Inc. accreditation
⇑ Center for Improvement in Healthcare Quality Accreditation
△ Commission on Accreditation of Rehabilitation Facilities (CARF) accreditation

Hospitals, U.S. / NEW YORK

NEWARK—Wayne County

★ ⇑ **NEWARK–WAYNE COMMUNITY HOSPITAL (330030)**, 1200 Driving Park Avenue, Zip 14513–1057, Mailing Address: P.O. Box 111, Zip 14513–0111; tel. 315/332–2022, (Total facility includes 180 beds in nursing home–type unit) **A**3 10 21 **F**3 11 13 15 18 29 30 34 35 37 38 40 44 45 46 47 48 50 54 56 57 59 63 64 68 70 74 75 76 79 81 85 86 87 89 90 93 97 100 102 107 108 110 111 115 118 119 126 128 130 131 141 145 146 148 149 154 169 **S** Rochester Regional Health, Rochester, NY
Primary Contact: Daniel P. Ireland, FACHE, President and Chief Operating Officer, Finger Lakes Rural Hospitals
CFO: Tom Crilly, Executive Vice President, Chief Financial Officer, Rochester Regional Health
CMO: Robert Mayo, M.D., Executive Vice President, Chief Medical Officer, Rochester Regional Health
CIO: John Glynn, Executive Vice President, Chief Information Officer, Rochester Regional Health
CHR: Janine Schue, Executive Vice President, Chief Human Resources Officer, Rochester Regional Health
CNO: Theresa Glessner, Chief Nursing Officer, Eastern Region
Web address: www.rochesterregional.org
Control: Other not–for–profit (including NFP Corporation) **Service**: General medical and surgical

Staffed Beds: 268 **Admissions**: 4973 **Census**: 231 **Outpatient Visits**: 145435 **Births**: 484 **Total Expense ($000)**: 120354 **Payroll Expense ($000)**: 71729 **Personnel**: 572

NEWBURGH—Orange County

⊞ **MONTEFIORE ST. LUKE'S CORNWALL (330264)**, 70 Dubois Street, Zip 12550–4851; tel. 845/561–4400, (Includes ST. LUKE'S CORNWALL HOSPITAL – CORNWALL CAMPUS, 19 Laurel Avenue, Cornwall, New York, Zip 12518–1499, tel. 845/534–7711; ST. LUKE'S CORNWALL HOSPITAL – NEWBURGH CAMPUS, 70 Dubois Street, Newburgh, New York, Zip 12550–4898, tel. 845/561–4400; Daniel J. Maughan MSN,RN, C, President and Chief Executive Officer) **A**1 2 3 5 10 19 **F**3 11 12 13 15 17 18 20 22 26 28 29 31 34 35 37 40 43 45 46 49 51 54 57 59 60 61 64 68 70 72 74 75 76 77 78 79 81 82 84 85 86 87 89 93 94 97 100 102 107 108 110 111 114 115 117 118 119 120 121 123 124 126 129 130 131 132 146 147 148 149 154 156 167 **P**5 **S** Montefiore Health System, Bronx, NY
Primary Contact: Daniel J. Maughan MSN,RN, C, President and Chief Executive Officer
CFO: Thomas Gibney, Senior Vice President and Chief Financial Officer
CMO: Christine Jelalian, M.D., Medical Director
CIO: Dwayne Simmons, Interim Chief Information Officer
CHR: Daniel Bengyak, Vice President, Administrative Services
CNO: Margaret Deyo–Allers, Vice President, Chief Nursing Officer
Web address: https://www.montefioreslc.org/
Control: Other not–for–profit (including NFP Corporation) **Service**: General medical and surgical

Staffed Beds: 201 **Admissions**: 10374 **Census**: 114 **Outpatient Visits**: 149739 **Births**: 1109 **Total Expense ($000)**: 279699 **Payroll Expense ($000)**: 99795 **Personnel**: 1018

ST. LUKE'S HOSPITAL See St. Luke's Cornwall Hospital – Newburgh Campus

NIAGARA FALLS—Niagara County

○ **NIAGARA FALLS MEMORIAL MEDICAL CENTER (330065)**, 621 Tenth Street, Zip 14301–1813, Mailing Address: P.O. Box 708, Zip 14302–0708; tel. 716/278–4000, (Nonreporting) **A**3 5 10 11 13
Primary Contact: Joseph A. Ruffolo, President and Chief Executive Officer
CFO: Richard G Braun, CPA, Jr, Executive Vice President and Chief Financial Officer
CMO: Fatma Patel, M.D., Vice President Medical Affairs
CIO: Diane Martin–Pratt, Director Information Systems
CNO: Pamela Levering, Chief Nursing Officer
Web address: www.nfmmc.org
Control: Other not–for–profit (including NFP Corporation) **Service**: General medical and surgical

Staffed Beds: 288

NORTH TONAWANDA—Niagara County

DE GRAFF MEDICAL PARK See Kaleida Health, Buffalo

NORTHPORT—Suffolk County

⊞ **NORTHPORT VETERANS AFFAIRS MEDICAL CENTER**, 79 Middleville Road, Zip 11768–2200; tel. 631/261–4400, (Nonreporting) **A**1 2 3 5 **S** Department of Veterans Affairs, Washington, DC
Primary Contact: Antonio Sanchez, M.D., Executive Director
COO: Michael McCully, Chief Operating Officer
CFO: Mary Pat Hessman, Chief Fiscal
CIO: Robert Ziskin, Chief Information Officer
CHR: Wilmino Sainbert, Chief Human Resources Management Service
Web address: www.northport.va.gov/index.asp
Control: Veterans Affairs, Government, federal **Service**: General medical and surgical

Staffed Beds: 213

NORWICH—Chenango County

★ ○ **UHS CHENANGO MEMORIAL HOSPITAL (330033)**, 179 North Broad Street, Zip 13815–1097; tel. 607/337–4111, **A**10 11 20 **F**3 8 11 13 15 17 18 28 29 32 34 35 38 40 45 47 50 54 56 57 59 61 64 65 67 68 70 74 75 76 77 79 81 82 85 86 87 89 90 93 97 107 108 110 111 115 119 126 127 128 130 132 133 144 146 147 148 154 156 169 **S** United Health Services, Binghamton, NY
Primary Contact: Drake M. Lamen, M.D., President and Chief Executive Officer
COO: Christina A Kisacky, Vice President, Operations
CFO: Peggy Swartwood, Assistant Vice President, Finance and Controller
CIO: Richard Stone, Manager, Technical Services
CNO: David Finney, R.N., Vice President Nursing
Web address: https://www.nyuhs.org/locations/uhs-chenango-memorial-hospital/
Control: Other not–for–profit (including NFP Corporation) **Service**: General medical and surgical

Staffed Beds: 37 **Admissions**: 1231 **Census**: 35 **Outpatient Visits**: 399689 **Births**: 202 **Total Expense ($000)**: 90889 **Payroll Expense ($000)**: 25445 **Personnel**: 370

NYACK—Rockland County

⊞ **MONTEFIORE NYACK HOSPITAL (330104)**, 160 North Midland Avenue, Zip 10960–1998; tel. 845/348–2000, **A**1 2 10 **F**3 4 5 8 9 11 12 15 19 20 22 26 28 29 30 31 34 35 37 38 39 40 41 43 44 45 46 49 50 51 55 57 58 59 60 61 62 63 64 65 66 68 70 72 74 75 76 77 78 79 81 82 83 84 85 86 87 89 91 92 94 97 98 100 101 102 104 107 108 110 111 115 117 118 119 120 121 123 124 126 129 130 132 135 145 146 147 148 149 154 156 157 160 161 164 165 166 167 **P**6 **S** Montefiore Health System, Bronx, NY
Primary Contact: Mark Geller, M.D., President and Chief Executive Officer
COO: Michael Novak, Vice President and Chief Operating Officer
CFO: John Burke, Chief Financial Officer
CMO: Anthony Matejicka, D.O., M.P.H., Vice President, Chief Medical Officer
CHR: Mary K Shinick, Vice President Human Resources
CNO: Kathleen Lunney, MS, R.N., Vice President Patient Care Services and Chief Nursing Officer
Web address: https://www.montefiorenyack.org/
Control: Other not–for–profit (including NFP Corporation) **Service**: General medical and surgical

Staffed Beds: 250 **Admissions**: 12000 **Census**: 205 **Outpatient Visits**: 160000 **Births**: 1500

OCEANSIDE—Nassau County

⊞ **MOUNT SINAI SOUTH NASSAU (330198)**, 1 Healthy Way, Zip 11572–1551; tel. 516/632–3000, (Total facility includes 20 beds in nursing home–type unit) **A**1 2 3 5 10 12 13 **F**3 5 7 8 11 12 13 15 17 18 19 20 22 26 28 29 30 31 32 34 35 36 37 38 40 42 43 44 45 46 47 49 50 54 55 56 57 58 59 60 61 62 64 65 66 68 70 73 74 75 76 77 78 79 81 82 83 84 85 86 87 89 91 92 93 97 98 100 101 102 103 104 105 107 108 110 111 114 115 117 118 119 120 121 123 124 126 128 129 130 131 132 135 145 146 147 148 149 153 154 156 157 160 162 164 165 167 168 169 **S** Mount Sinai Health System, New York, NY
Primary Contact: Adhi Sharma, M.D., President
COO: William E. Allison, Senior Vice President and Chief Operating Officer, Administration
CFO: John Pohlman, Senior Vice President and Chief Financial Officer
CMO: Adhi Sharma, M.D., Senior Vice President, Medical Affairs and Chief Medical Officer
CIO: Noah Caldwell, Vice President and Chief Information Officer
CHR: Paul D. Giordano, Senior Vice President, Human Resources
CNO: Stacey A Conklin, Chief Nursing Officer
Web address: www.southnassau.org
Control: Other not–for–profit (including NFP Corporation) **Service**: General medical and surgical

Staffed Beds: 363 **Admissions**: 18342 **Census**: 294 **Outpatient Visits**: 276354 **Births**: 2180 **Total Expense ($000)**: 748546 **Payroll Expense ($000)**: 367327 **Personnel**: 3294

Hospitals, U.S. / NEW YORK

OGDENSBURG—St. Lawrence County

⇧ **CLAXTON–HEPBURN MEDICAL CENTER (330211)**, 214 King Street, Zip 13669-1142; tel. 315/393-3600, (Nonreporting) **A**2 10 20 21
Primary Contact: Richard Duvall, President and Chief Executive Officer
COO: Brandon Bowline, Chief Operating Officer
CIO: James Flood, Director Information Systems
CHR: Lou-Ann McNally, Executive Director Human Resources and Staff Development
CNO: David Ferris, Chief Nursing Officer and Vice President Patient Care Services
Web address: www.claxtonhepburn.org
Control: Other not-for-profit (including NFP Corporation) **Service**: General medical and surgical

Staffed Beds: 97

☐ **ST. LAWRENCE PSYCHIATRIC CENTER (334003)**, 1 Chimney Point Drive, Zip 13669-2291; tel. 315/541-2001, (Nonreporting) **A**1 3 10 **S** New York State Office of Mental Health, Albany, NY
Primary Contact: Aimee Dean, Executive Director
CMO: Harishankar Sanghi, M.D., Clinical Director
CHR: Rosie Turnbull, Director Human Resources
Web address: www.omh.ny.gov/omhweb/facilities/slpc/facility.htm
Control: State, Government, Nonfederal **Service**: Psychiatric

Staffed Beds: 146

OLEAN—Cattaraugus County

★ ⇧ **OLEAN GENERAL HOSPITAL (330103)**, 515 Main Street, Zip 14760-1513; tel. 716/373-2600, (Includes BRADFORD REGIONAL MEDICAL CENTER, 116 Interstate Parkway, Bradford, Pennsylvania, Zip 16701-1036, tel. 814/368-4143; Jill Owens, M.D., President) (Nonreporting) **A**3 5 10 21
Primary Contact: Jill Owens, M.D., President
COO: David J DiBacco, Interim Chief Operating Officer
CMO: Henri Lamothe, Chief Medical Officer
CIO: Jason Yaworsky, Senior Vice President Information Systems and Chief Information Officer
CHR: Timothy M McNamara, Senior Vice President Human Resources
Web address: www.ogh.org
Control: Other not-for-profit (including NFP Corporation) **Service**: General medical and surgical

Staffed Beds: 289

ONEIDA—Madison County

☐ **ONEIDA HEALTHCARE (330115)**, 321 Genesee Street, Zip 13421-2611; tel. 315/363-6000, (Nonreporting) **A**1 10
Primary Contact: Felissa Koernig, President and Chief Executive Officer
COO: Mary Parry, Vice President Operations and Chief Operating Officer
CFO: Jeremiah Sweet, Chief Financial Officer
CMO: Thomas Chmelicek, M.D., Chief Medical Officer
CIO: Mohammed J. Mere, Chief Information Officer
CHR: Anne L English, Vice President Human Resources
CNO: Rhonda L Reader, R.N., Chief Nursing Officer
Web address: www.oneidahealth.org
Control: Other not-for-profit (including NFP Corporation) **Service**: General medical and surgical

Staffed Beds: 231

ONEONTA—Otsego County

★ ⇧ **AURELIA OSBORN FOX MEMORIAL HOSPITAL (330085)**, 1 Norton Avenue, Zip 13820-2629; tel. 607/432-2000, (Nonreporting) **A**10 21 **S** Bassett Healthcare Network, Cooperstown, NY
Primary Contact: Staci Thompson, President and Chief Executive Officer
COO: Gary Smith, Chief Operating Officer
CFO: Paul G. Swinko Jr, Chief Finanial Officer
CMO: Reginald Q. Knight, Chief Medical Officer
CHR: Jennie Gliha, Chief Human Resource Officer
CNO: Joan MacDonald, R.N., MSN, Chief Nursing Officer, Vice President Nursing Services
Web address: www.bassett.org/ao-fox-hospital/
Control: Other not-for-profit (including NFP Corporation) **Service**: General medical and surgical

Staffed Beds: 184

ORANGEBURG—Rockland County

☐ **ROCKLAND CHILDREN'S PSYCHIATRIC CENTER (334066)**, 599 Convent Road, Zip 10962-1162; tel. 845/359-7400, (Nonreporting) **A**1 3 5 10 **S** New York State Office of Mental Health, Albany, NY
Primary Contact: Rebecca Leland, Executive Director
COO: Kenneth Perrotte, Director Operations
CFO: Peter Gorey, Administrative Coordinator
CMO: Sadhana Sardana, M.D., Clinical Director
CIO: Mary Pivonka, Director Quality Management
Web address: www.omh.ny.gov/
Control: State, Government, Nonfederal **Service**: Children's hospital psychiatric

Staffed Beds: 54

☐ **ROCKLAND PSYCHIATRIC CENTER (334015)**, 140 Old Orangeburg Road, Zip 10962-1157; tel. 845/359-1000, (Nonreporting) **A**1 3 5 10 **S** New York State Office of Mental Health, Albany, NY
Primary Contact: Janet J. Monroe, R.N., Executive Director
Web address: www.omh.ny.gov/
Control: State, Government, Nonfederal **Service**: Psychiatric

Staffed Beds: 337

ORCHARD PARK—Erie County

ORCHARD PARK NURSING HOME See Father Baker Manor

OSSINING—Westchester County

OSSINING CORRECTIONAL FACILITIES HOSPITAL, 354 Hunter Street, Zip 10562-5498; tel. 914/941-0108, (Nonreporting) **A**3
Primary Contact: Riza Ferdous, Health Services Director
Control: State, Government, Nonfederal **Service**: Hospital unit of an institution (prison hospital, college infirmary, etc.)

Staffed Beds: 25

OSWEGO—Oswego County

✠ **OSWEGO HOSPITAL (330218)**, 110 West Sixth Street, Zip 13126-2507; tel. 315/349-5511, (Nonreporting) **A**1 10 20
Primary Contact: Michael Backus, President and Chief Executive Officer
CFO: Eric Campbell, Chief Financial Officer
CMO: Renato Mandanas, M.D., Chief Medical Officer
CIO: Barry W. Ryle, Chief Information Officer
CHR: James E Marco Jr, Interim Vice President, Human Resources
CNO: Valerie Favata, R.N., MS, Chief Nursing Officer
Web address: www.oswegohealth.org
Control: Other not-for-profit (including NFP Corporation) **Service**: General medical and surgical

Staffed Beds: 90

PATCHOGUE—Suffolk County

★ ⇧ **LONG ISLAND COMMUNITY HOSPITAL (330141)**, 101 Hospital Road, Zip 11772-4897; tel. 631/654-7100, **A**3 5 10 13 21 **F**3 5 12 15 17 18 20 22 26 28 29 30 34 35 40 43 45 46 47 49 50 51 54 57 59 60 63 64 66 68 70 74 75 77 78 79 81 82 84 85 87 98 100 101 102 107 110 111 114 115 118 119 124 129 130 135 146 147 148 149 154 160 161 165 167
Primary Contact: Marc Adler, M.D., Senior Vice President and Chief of Hospital Operations
COO: Matthew Brian Peddie, Vice President and Chief Operating Officer
CFO: Brenda Farrell, Vice President Finance
CMO: Nejat Zeyneloglu, Vice President and Chief Quality Medical Officer
CIO: Joseph Wood, Vice President and Chief Information Officer
CNO: Debra Grimm, MS, R.N., Vice President and Chief Nursing Officer
Web address: https://licommunityhospital.org/
Control: Other not-for-profit (including NFP Corporation) **Service**: General medical and surgical

Staffed Beds: 161 **Admissions**: 8344 **Census**: 119 **Outpatient Visits**: 98882 **Births**: 0 **Total Expense ($000)**: 320566 **Payroll Expense ($000)**: 115801 **Personnel**: 1518

Hospital, Medicare Provider Number, Address, Telephone, Approval, Facility, and Physician Codes, Health Care System

★ American Hospital Association (AHA) membership ○ Healthcare Facilities Accreditation Program ⇧ Center for Improvement in Healthcare Quality Accreditation
☐ The Joint Commission accreditation ◇ DNV Healthcare Inc. accreditation △ Commission on Accreditation of Rehabilitation Facilities (CARF) accreditation

Hospitals, U.S. / NEW YORK

PENN YAN—Yates County

SOLDIERS AND SAILORS MEMORIAL HOSPITAL (331314), 418 North Main Street, Zip 14527–1085; tel. 315/531–2000, **A**10 18 **F**3 11 15 18 28 29 32 34 35 38 40 54 56 59 64 69 75 87 93 94 96 97 100 101 102 104 107 110 115 119 128 130 132 133 135 146 154 **P**6 **S** Finger Lakes Health, Geneva, NY
Primary Contact: Jose Acevedo, M.D., President and Chief Executive Officer
COO: Lina Brennan, Site Administrator
CFO: Pamela Johnson, Treasurer and Chief Financial Officer
CMO: Jason Feinberg, M.D., Vice President Medical Affairs and Chief Medical Officer
CIO: Guy W Mosher III, Manager Information Systems
CHR: Patrick R Boyle, Vice President Human Resources
Web address: www.flhealth.org
Control: Other not–for–profit (including NFP Corporation) **Service**: General medical and surgical

> **Staffed Beds:** 139 **Admissions:** 1003 **Census:** 111 **Outpatient Visits:** 232228 **Births:** 0 **Total Expense ($000):** 48354 **Payroll Expense ($000):** 27034 **Personnel:** 267

PLAINVIEW—Nassau County

PLAINVIEW HOSPITAL (330331), 888 Old Country Road, Zip 11803–4978; tel. 516/719–3000, **A**1 3 5 10 12 13 **F**3 8 15 17 18 20 22 29 30 31 34 35 36 38 40 44 45 46 49 50 51 57 58 59 60 63 64 65 68 69 70 71 74 75 78 79 81 84 85 86 87 97 100 101 102 107 108 110 111 114 115 119 126 130 132 135 146 148 149 154 157 167 **S** Northwell Health, Lake Success, NY
Primary Contact: Kerri Scanlon, R.N., Executive Director
CMO: Alan Mensch, M.D., Senior Vice President Medical Affairs
Web address: https://www.planview.com/
Control: Other not–for–profit (including NFP Corporation) **Service**: General medical and surgical

> **Staffed Beds:** 156 **Admissions:** 8259 **Census:** 113 **Outpatient Visits:** 56654 **Births:** 0 **Total Expense ($000):** 295481 **Payroll Expense ($000):** 152731 **Personnel:** 1256

PLATTSBURGH—Clinton County

THE UNIVERSITY OF VERMONT HEALTH NETWORK–CHAMPLAIN VALLEY PHYSICIANS HOSPITAL (330250), 75 Beekman Street, Zip 12901–1438; tel. 518/561–2000, (Nonreporting) **A**1 2 3 5 10 **S** The University of Vermont Health Network, Burlington, VT
Primary Contact: Michelle LeBeau, President and Chief Operating Officer
COO: Michelle LeBeau, President and Chief Operating Officer
CFO: Joyce Rafferty, Vice President Finance
CMO: Kent Hall, M.D., Vice President and Chief Medical Officer
CIO: Wouter Rietsema, M.D., Chief Quality and Information Officer
CHR: Dean Civitello, Vice President, Human Resources, Public Relations and Development
Web address: https://profiles.health.ny.gov/hospital/view/103048
Control: Other not–for–profit (including NFP Corporation) **Service**: General medical and surgical

> **Staffed Beds:** 254

PORT JEFFERSON—Suffolk County

MATHER HOSPITAL (330185), 75 North Country Road, Zip 11777–2190; tel. 631/473–1320, **A**1 2 3 5 10 **F**5 8 11 12 14 15 18 20 22 26 29 30 31 34 35 36 37 38 40 44 45 46 49 51 55 56 57 59 60 64 65 69 70 74 75 77 78 79 81 82 84 85 86 87 93 98 100 101 102 103 104 105 107 108 110 111 114 115 118 119 124 126 129 130 132 146 147 148 152 160 164 167 **S** Northwell Health, Lake Success, NY
Primary Contact: Kevin M. McGeachy, Executive Director
COO: Kevin J Murray, Senior Vice President
CFO: Joseph Wisnoski, Chief Financial Officer
CMO: Joan Faro, M.D., Chief Medical Officer
CIO: Thomas Heiman, Vice President Information Services and Chief Information Officer
CHR: Diane Marotta, Vice President Human Resources
CNO: Marie Mulligan, R.N., MSN, Chief Nursing Officer, Vice President Nursing
Web address: www.matherhospital.com
Control: Other not–for–profit (including NFP Corporation) **Service**: General medical and surgical

> **Staffed Beds:** 248 **Admissions:** 10243 **Census:** 158 **Outpatient Visits:** 155153 **Births:** 0 **Total Expense ($000):** 460522 **Payroll Expense ($000):** 246726 **Personnel:** 2342

ST. CHARLES HOSPITAL (330246), 200 Belle Terre Road, Zip 11777–1928; tel. 631/474–6000, **A**1 2 3 5 7 10 **F**3 4 5 8 11 12 13 15 17 28 29 30 31 32 34 35 36 37 38 39 40 41 44 45 46 47 48 49 50 51 54 56 57 58 59 64 65 66 70 72 73 74 75 76 77 78 79 80 81 82 84 85 86 87 89 90 91 92 93 95 96 97 107 108 110 111 114 115 119 126 129 130 131 134 135 141 142 146 147 148 149 151 153 154 157 160 167 169 **S** Catholic Health Services of Long Island, Rockville Centre, NY
Primary Contact: James O'Connor, President
COO: Ronald Weingartner, Vice President Administration
CFO: Kathleen Vasil, Vice President Finance
CMO: Michael Sauter, M.D., Chief Medical Officer
CIO: Felix Pabon–Ramirez, Chief Information Officer
CNO: Nicolette Fiore–Lopez, Ph.D., R.N., Chief Nursing Officer
Web address: https://www.chsli.org/st-charles-hospital
Control: Church operated, Nongovernment, not–for–profit **Service**: General medical and surgical

> **Staffed Beds:** 243 **Admissions:** 9120 **Census:** 161 **Outpatient Visits:** 208504 **Births:** 1195 **Total Expense ($000):** 251907 **Payroll Expense ($000):** 105048 **Personnel:** 1005

PORT JERVIS—Orange County

BON SECOURS COMMUNITY HOSPITAL (330135), 160 East Main Street, Zip 12771–2245; tel. 184/499–0381, (Nonreporting) **A**1 3 10 **S** WMCHealth, Valhalla, NY
Primary Contact: Mary Leahy, M.D., Chief Executive Officer
CHR: Kim Hirkaler, Director Human Resources
Web address: www.bonsecourscommunityhosp.org
Control: Church operated, Nongovernment, not–for–profit **Service**: General medical and surgical

> **Staffed Beds:** 143

POTSDAM—St. Lawrence County

CANTON–POTSDAM HOSPITAL (330197), 50 Leroy Street, Zip 13676–1799; tel. 315/265–3300, (Nonreporting) **A**10 20 21 **S** Rochester Regional Health, Rochester, NY
Primary Contact: Donna McGregor, FACHE, President
COO: Katherine Schleider, St. Lawrence Health Senior Vice President, Operations
CMO: Robert T Rogers, M.D., II, Medical Director
CIO: Lyndon Allen, Director Information Systems
CHR: Michael Katz, Vice President Human Resources
CNO: Jan Carroll, MSN, M.P.H., R.N., Chief Nursing Officer
Web address: https://www.stlawrencehealthsystem.org/canton-potsdam-hospital
Control: Other not–for–profit (including NFP Corporation) **Service**: General medical and surgical

> **Staffed Beds:** 94

POUGHKEEPSIE—Dutchess County

SAINT FRANCIS HOSPITAL AND HEALTH CENTERS See Midhudson Regional Hospital of Westchester Medical Center

VASSAR BROTHERS MEDICAL CENTER (330023), 45 Reade Place, Zip 12601–3947; tel. 845/454–8500, **A**1 3 5 10 19 **F**3 8 13 15 17 18 20 22 24 26 28 29 30 31 34 35 36 37 40 41 43 44 45 46 47 48 49 50 51 54 55 57 58 59 60 64 65 68 70 72 73 74 75 76 77 78 79 81 82 84 85 86 87 89 92 93 96 101 102 107 108 109 110 111 114 115 116 117 118 119 120 121 124 126 130 131 132 135 141 143 145 146 147 148 149 150 154 157 160 161 162 164 167 169 **S** Nuvance Health, Danbury, CT
Primary Contact: Susan Browning, President
COO: Cindy Czaplinski, MSN, R.N., Vice President Operations
CFO: Antonio Perugino, Vice President Finance, Hospitals
CMO: William V. Begg, M.D., III, Vice President Medical Affairs
CNO: Lore Bogolin, MSN, R.N., Vice President Patient Care Services and Chief Nursing Officer
Web address: https://www.nuvancehealth.org/locations/vassar-brothers-medical-center
Control: Other not–for–profit (including NFP Corporation) **Service**: General medical and surgical

> **Staffed Beds:** 329 **Admissions:** 19022 **Census:** 273 **Outpatient Visits:** 286820 **Births:** 2460 **Total Expense ($000):** 799434 **Payroll Expense ($000):** 242059 **Personnel:** 2398

Hospitals, U.S. / NEW YORK

QUEENS—Queens County, See New York City

QUEENS VILLAGE—Queens County, See New York City

RHINEBECK—Dutchess County

🏥 △ **NORTHERN DUTCHESS HOSPITAL (330049)**, 6511 Springbrook Avenue, Zip 12572–3709, Mailing Address: P.O. Box 5002, Zip 12572–5002; tel. 845/876–3001, **A**1 3 7 10 **F**3 12 13 15 18 20 28 29 30 31 34 35 36 37 40 44 45 46 47 48 50 54 56 57 59 60 64 68 70 74 75 76 77 78 79 81 82 84 85 86 87 90 93 96 101 107 108 110 111 115 118 119 126 129 130 131 132 135 141 143 146 147 148 149 154 156 157 160 161 164 167 169 **S** Nuvance Health, Danbury, CT
Primary Contact: Denise George, R.N., President
CMO: John Sabia, M.D., Vice President Medical Affairs
Web address: https://www.nuvancehealth.org/locations/northern-dutchess-hospital
Control: Other not-for-profit (including NFP Corporation) **Service:** General medical and surgical

Staffed Beds: 75 **Admissions:** 5008 **Census:** 61 **Outpatient Visits:** 95904 **Births:** 970 **Total Expense ($000):** 179278 **Payroll Expense ($000):** 59618 **Personnel:** 618

RICHMOND VALLEY—Richmond County, See New York City

RIVERHEAD—Suffolk County

🏥 **PECONIC BAY MEDICAL CENTER (330107)**, 1300 Roanoke Avenue, Zip 11901–2031; tel. 631/548–6000, **A**1 3 5 10 12 13 **F**3 7 11 12 13 15 18 20 22 26 28 29 30 31 34 35 37 40 41 43 44 45 50 51 53 54 56 57 58 59 60 64 68 70 74 75 76 77 78 79 80 81 82 84 85 86 87 93 96 100 102 107 108 110 111 115 118 119 126 130 131 132 143 146 147 148 149 150 154 157 160 167 169 **S** Northwell Health, Lake Success, NY
Primary Contact: Amy E. Loeb, Ed.D., R.N., Executive Director
COO: Ronald McManus, Senior Vice President Clinical Services and Business Entities
CFO: Michael F. O'Donnell, CPA, Chief Financial Officer
CIO: Arthur Crowe, Director Information Systems
CHR: Monica Chestnut-Rauls, Vice President Human Resources
Web address: www.pbmchealth.org
Control: Other not-for-profit (including NFP Corporation) **Service:** General medical and surgical

Staffed Beds: 144 **Admissions:** 11023 **Census:** 123 **Outpatient Visits:** 209317 **Births:** 497 **Total Expense ($000):** 390267 **Payroll Expense ($000):** 194778 **Personnel:** 1453

ROCHESTER—Monroe County

🏥 **HIGHLAND HOSPITAL (330164)**, 1000 South Avenue, Zip 14620–2733; tel. 585/473–2200, **A**1 3 5 10 19 **F**3 12 13 15 18 26 29 30 34 35 36 37 40 44 45 46 47 49 50 54 55 56 57 58 59 60 63 64 65 66 68 70 74 75 76 77 78 79 81 83 84 85 86 87 91 92 93 97 100 107 108 110 111 114 115 118 119 120 121 122 123 126 130 132 135 141 145 146 147 148 149 154 156 167 169 **P**5 6 **S** University of Rochester Medical Center, Rochester, NY
Primary Contact: Steven I. Goldstein, President and Chief Executive Officer
COO: Cindy Becker, Vice President and Chief Operating Officer
CFO: Carrie Fuller Spencer, Chief Financial Officer
CMO: Raymond Mayewski, M.D., Chief Medical Officer
CIO: Tom Barnett, Chief Information Officer
CHR: Amy S. Galiana, Chief Human Resource Officer
Web address: https://www.urmc.rochester.edu/highland
Control: Other not-for-profit (including NFP Corporation) **Service:** General medical and surgical

Staffed Beds: 238 **Admissions:** 14488 **Census:** 238 **Outpatient Visits:** 515288 **Births:** 2630 **Total Expense ($000):** 509095 **Payroll Expense ($000):** 227097 **Personnel:** 2464

★ 🏥 **ROCHESTER GENERAL HOSPITAL (330125)**, 1425 Portland Avenue, Zip 14621–3099; tel. 585/922–4000, **A**3 5 8 10 19 21 **F**3 8 9 11 12 13 15 17 18 20 22 24 26 29 30 31 32 34 35 37 38 39 40 41 44 45 46 47 48 49 50 51 52 53 54 55 56 57 58 59 60 61 63 64 65 66 68 70 71 73 74 75 76 77 78 79 80 81 82 84 85 86 87 89 92 93 96 97 98 100 101 102 103 104 107 108 110 111 114 115 116 117 118 119 120 121 123 124 126 127 129 130 131 132 134 135 141 144 145 146 147 148 149 150 154 156 157 158 162 164 165 167 169 **S** Rochester Regional Health, Rochester, NY
Primary Contact: Tammy Snyder, President and Chief Executive Officer
COO: Tammy Snyder, President and Chief Operating Officer
CMO: Robert Mayo, M.D., Chief Medical Officer
CIO: John Glynn, Chief Information Officer
CHR: Janine Schue, Senior Vice President Human Resources
CNO: Shari McDonald, Chief Nursing Officer
Web address: https://www.rochesterregional.org/
Control: Other not-for-profit (including NFP Corporation) **Service:** General medical and surgical

Staffed Beds: 608 **Admissions:** 26542 **Census:** 501 **Outpatient Visits:** 3366163 **Births:** 1599 **Total Expense ($000):** 1740261 **Payroll Expense ($000):** 818172 **Personnel:** 5239

☐ **ROCHESTER PSYCHIATRIC CENTER (334020)**, 1111 Elmwood Avenue, Zip 14620–3005; tel. 585/241–1200, (Nonreporting) **A**1 3 5 10 **S** New York State Office of Mental Health, Albany, NY
Primary Contact: Philip Griffin, Director of Operations
COO: Joseph Coffey, Director Facility Administration
CFO: Rosanne Minnis, Business Officer
CMO: Laurence Guttmacher, M.D., Clinical Director
CIO: Lori Hintz, Coordinator Information Systems
CHR: Colomba Misseritti, Director Human Resources
CNO: Christopher Kirisits, Chief Nursing Officer
Web address: www.omh.ny.gov/omhweb/facilities/ropc/facility.htm
Control: State, Government, Nonfederal **Service:** Psychiatric

Staffed Beds: 180

🏥 △ **STRONG MEMORIAL HOSPITAL OF THE UNIVERSITY OF ROCHESTER (330285)**, 601 Elmwood Avenue, Zip 14642–0002, Mailing Address: 601 Elmwood Avenue, Box 612, Zip 14642–0002; tel. 585/275–2100, (Includes GOLISANO CHILDREN'S HOSPITAL, 601 Elmwood Avenue, Rochester, New York, Zip 14610, tel. 585/275–2182) **A**1 2 3 5 7 8 10 19 **F**3 5 6 8 9 11 12 13 14 15 16 17 18 19 20 21 22 23 24 25 26 27 28 29 30 31 32 33 34 35 36 38 39 40 41 42 43 44 45 46 47 48 49 50 51 52 53 54 55 56 57 58 59 60 61 63 64 65 66 68 70 71 72 73 74 75 76 77 78 79 80 81 82 83 84 85 86 87 88 89 90 91 92 93 94 95 96 97 98 99 100 101 102 103 104 105 107 108 110 111 112 114 115 116 117 118 119 120 121 123 124 126 127 129 130 131 132 134 135 136 137 138 139 141 142 143 144 145 146 147 148 149 150 152 153 154 156 157 160 162 163 164 165 166 167 169 **P**5 6 **S** University of Rochester Medical Center, Rochester, NY
Primary Contact: Steven I. Goldstein, President and Chief Executive Officer
COO: Kathleen M Parrinello, Ph.D., Chief Operating Officer
CFO: David L. Kirshner, Chief Financial Officer
CMO: Raymond Mayewski, M.D., Chief Medical Officer
CIO: D Jerome Powell, M.D., Chief Information Officer
CHR: Charles J Murphy, Associate Vice President Human Resources
Web address: www.urmc.rochester.edu
Control: Other not-for-profit (including NFP Corporation) **Service:** General medical and surgical

Staffed Beds: 916 **Admissions:** 38395 **Census:** 899 **Outpatient Visits:** 2271679 **Births:** 2646 **Total Expense ($000):** 3181880 **Payroll Expense ($000):** 1059585 **Personnel:** 13183

Hospital, Medicare Provider Number, Address, Telephone, Approval, Facility, and Physician Codes, Health Care System

★ American Hospital Association (AHA) membership ○ Healthcare Facilities Accreditation Program 🛡 Center for Improvement in Healthcare Quality Accreditation
☐ The Joint Commission accreditation ◇ DNV Healthcare Inc. accreditation △ Commission on Accreditation of Rehabilitation Facilities (CARF) accreditation

© 2025 AHA Guide

Hospitals, U.S. / NEW YORK

★ △ ⇑ **UNITY HOSPITAL (330226)**, 1555 Long Pond Road, Zip 14626–4182; tel. 585/723–7000, (Total facility includes 120 beds in nursing home–type unit) **A**3 5 7 10 19 21 **F**3 4 5 12 13 18 20 22 26 28 29 30 31 34 35 37 38 39 40 41 44 45 46 47 48 49 50 55 56 57 59 60 61 63 64 65 66 68 70 71 73 74 75 76 77 78 79 80 81 82 83 84 85 86 87 90 91 92 93 96 97 100 101 102 104 107 108 111 114 115 118 119 120 121 126 128 129 130 131 132 134 135 141 144 146 147 148 149 150 152 153 154 156 157 158 160 161 164 165 166 167 169 **S** Rochester Regional Health, Rochester, NY
Primary Contact: Jill Graziano, R.N., Senior Vice President, President and Chief Operating Officer
CFO: Tom Crilly, Executive Vice President and Chief Financial Officer
CMO: James Haley, M.D., Senior Vice President and Chief Medical Officer
CIO: John Glynn, Senior Vice President and Chief Information Officer
CHR: Maryalice Keller, Vice President Brand and Talent Management
CNO: Jane McCormack, R.N., MSN, Vice President, Chief Nursing Officer and Nursing and Patient Care Services
Web address: www.unityhealth.org
Control: Other not–for–profit (including NFP Corporation) **Service:** General medical and surgical

Staffed Beds: 523 **Admissions:** 18553 **Census:** 442 **Outpatient Visits:** 915020 **Births:** 1368 **Total Expense ($000):** 729233 **Payroll Expense ($000):** 375985 **Personnel:** 2613

ROCKVILLE CENTRE—Nassau County

✠ **MERCY MEDICAL CENTER (330259)**, 1000 North Village Avenue, Zip 11570–1000; tel. 516/705–2525, **A**1 2 3 5 10 13 **F**3 5 8 11 12 13 15 18 20 22 26 29 30 31 34 35 37 38 40 44 45 46 48 49 50 51 54 55 56 57 59 60 64 65 68 70 72 74 75 76 77 78 79 81 82 83 84 85 86 87 90 93 96 97 98 100 101 102 104 105 107 108 110 111 115 119 126 130 132 135 141 142 143 146 147 149 153 154 156 158 160 161 162 164 165 167 168 169 **S** Catholic Health Services of Long Island, Rockville Centre, NY
Primary Contact: Joseph Manopella, President
CFO: William C Armstrong, Senior Vice President and Chief Financial Officer
CMO: John Reilly, M.D., Vice President Medical Affairs and Chief Medical Officer
CHR: Allison Cianciotto Croyle, Vice President of Human Resources
CNO: Beth Vlahavas, R.N., MSN, Vice President Patient Care Services and Chief Nursing Officer
Web address: www.mercymedicalcenter.chsli.org
Control: Church operated, Nongovernment, not–for–profit **Service:** General medical and surgical

Staffed Beds: 207 **Admissions:** 10293 **Census:** 158 **Outpatient Visits:** 122772 **Births:** 937 **Total Expense ($000):** 346545 **Payroll Expense ($000):** 143506 **Personnel:** 1558

ROME—Oneida County

★ ○ **ROME HEALTH (330215)**, 1500 North James Street, Zip 13440–2844; tel. 315/338–7000, (Total facility includes 80 beds in nursing home–type unit) **A**3 5 10 11 **F**3 5 8 12 13 15 18 22 26 29 30 34 35 37 38 40 44 45 49 50 51 54 55 56 57 59 64 70 74 75 76 77 78 79 80 81 82 85 87 89 90 93 97 98 102 103 107 108 109 110 111 112 113 114 115 116 117 119 120 121 122 123 124 127 128 129 130 131 132 135 144 147 148 149 154 157 160 169
Primary Contact: AnneMarie Czyz, R.N., Ed.D., President and Chief Executive Officer
COO: Ryan Thompson, Vice President, Chief Operating Officer
CFO: Dewey R Rowlands, Vice President and Chief Financial Officer
CMO: Cristain Andrade, M.D., Vice President, Chief Medical Officer
CIO: Mark Rowan, Vice President, Chief Information Officer
CHR: Michelle Podesiwck, Director Human Resources
CNO: Ashley Edwards, Chief Nursing Officer
Web address: www.romehospital.org
Control: Other not–for–profit (including NFP Corporation) **Service:** General medical and surgical

Staffed Beds: 178 **Admissions:** 4269 **Census:** 83 **Outpatient Visits:** 176346 **Births:** 659 **Total Expense ($000):** 114555 **Payroll Expense ($000):** 48304 **Personnel:** 809

ROSLYN—Nassau County

✠ **ST. FRANCIS HOSPITAL AND HEART CENTER (330182)**, 100 Port Washington Boulevard, Zip 11576–1353; tel. 516/562–6000, **A**1 2 3 5 10 **F**3 7 8 11 12 14 15 17 18 19 20 21 22 23 24 26 27 28 29 30 31 34 35 38 39 40 41 44 45 46 47 49 50 53 54 55 56 57 58 59 60 61 62 63 64 65 66 68 70 71 74 75 77 78 79 80 81 82 83 84 85 86 87 97 100 107 108 109 110 111 115 116 117 118 119 120 121 123 124 126 130 131 132 135 141 143 146 147 148 149 154 156 164 167 **P**5 6 **S** Catholic Health Services of Long Island, Rockville Centre, NY
Primary Contact: Charles Lucore, M.D., President
CFO: William C Armstrong, Vice President and Chief Financial Officer
CMO: Jack Soterakis, M.D., Executive Vice President Medical Affairs
CHR: Barbara Fierro, Director, Human Resources
CNO: Ann S Cella, R.N., Senior Vice President, Patient Care Services
Web address: www.stfrancisheartcenter.com/index.html
Control: Church operated, Nongovernment, not–for–profit **Service:** General medical and surgical

Staffed Beds: 321 **Admissions:** 19769 **Census:** 271 **Outpatient Visits:** 262344 **Births:** 0 **Total Expense ($000):** 841126 **Payroll Expense ($000):** 343963 **Personnel:** 3167

SARANAC LAKE—Franklin County

★ ○ **ADIRONDACK HEALTH (330079)**, 2233 State Route 86, Zip 12983–5644, Mailing Address: P.O. Box 471, Zip 12983–0471; tel. 518/891–4141, **A**10 11 **F**3 12 13 15 18 28 29 31 34 35 37 38 39 40 41 43 45 46 49 50 53 54 55 56 57 59 60 64 65 70 71 75 76 77 78 79 81 82 84 85 86 87 89 92 93 94 96 97 98 101 102 103 104 107 108 110 111 114 119 126 127 128 129 130 131 135 147 148 153 154 156 162 164 165 167 169 **S** Ovation Healthcare, Brentwood, TN
Primary Contact: Aaron Kramer, Chief Executive Officer
COO: Patti Hammond, Chief Operating Officer
CFO: Tristan Glanville, Chief Financial Officer
CMO: Joahd Toure', M.D., Chief Medical Officer
CHR: Michael D Lee, Chief Human Resources Officer
CNO: Linda McClarigan, R.N., Chief Nursing Officer
Web address: www.adirondackhealth.org
Control: Other not–for–profit (including NFP Corporation) **Service:** General medical and surgical

Staffed Beds: 68 **Admissions:** 2034 **Census:** 29 **Outpatient Visits:** 161065 **Births:** 192 **Total Expense ($000):** 131964 **Payroll Expense ($000):** 59559 **Personnel:** 638

SARATOGA SPRINGS—Saratoga County

☐ **FOUR WINDS HOSPITAL (334049)**, 30 Crescent Avenue, Zip 12866–5142; tel. 518/584–3600, **A**1 10 **F**98 99 100 103 105 153 154
Primary Contact: Moira Morrissey Esq, Chief Executive Officer
CFO: Juanita Wheeler–Moore, Director Financial Services
CMO: Kevin P. Martin, M.D., Chief Medical Officer
CIO: Susan Snowdon, Director Information Technology
CHR: Susan M Kirchner, Director Human Resources
CNO: James Colamaria, Director of Nursing
Web address: www.fourwindshospital.com
Control: Individual, Investor–owned (for–profit) **Service:** Psychiatric

Staffed Beds: 88 **Admissions:** 2454 **Census:** 87 **Outpatient Visits:** 0 **Births:** 0 **Total Expense ($000):** 38254 **Payroll Expense ($000):** 24350 **Personnel:** 328

✠ **SARATOGA HOSPITAL (330222)**, 211 Church Street, Zip 12866–1003; tel. 518/587–3222, **A**1 2 3 10 19 **F**3 5 8 11 12 13 15 17 18 20 22 26 28 29 30 31 32 34 35 36 38 39 40 44 45 46 47 48 49 50 51 53 54 56 57 58 59 60 61 64 65 66 68 70 74 75 76 77 78 79 81 82 84 85 86 87 92 93 94 96 97 98 100 101 102 104 107 108 110 111 115 116 117 119 120 121 123 124 126 129 130 131 132 135 144 146 147 148 149 154 156 157 160 161 162 164 165 167 169 **P**6
Primary Contact: Jill Johnson VanKuren, President and Chief Executive Officer
CFO: Gary Foster, Vice President and Chief Financial Officer
CMO: Richard Falivena, D.O., M.P.H., Vice President and Chief Medical Officer
CIO: John Mangona, Vice President, Chief Information Officer and Compliance Officer
CNO: Toni Bishop–McWain, Vice President Chief Nursing Officer
Web address: www.saratogahospital.org
Control: Other not–for–profit (including NFP Corporation) **Service:** General medical and surgical

Staffed Beds: 171 **Admissions:** 9668 **Census:** 130 **Outpatient Visits:** 800580 **Births:** 755 **Total Expense ($000):** 520622 **Payroll Expense ($000):** 261951 **Personnel:** 2801

SCHENECTADY—Schenectady County

BELLEVUE WOMAN'S HOSPITAL See Bellevue Woman's Care Center

ELLIS HOSPITAL HEALTH CENTER See Ellis Medicine, Schenectady

ELLIS HOSPITAL MCCLELLAN CAMPUS See Ellis Hospital Health Center

✠ **ELLIS MEDICINE (330153)**, 1101 Nott Street, Zip 12308–2425; tel. 518/243–4000, (Includes BELLEVUE WOMAN'S CARE CENTER, 2210 Troy Road, Schenectady, New York, Zip 12309–4797, tel. 518/346–9400; ELLIS HOSPITAL HEALTH CENTER, 600 McClellan Street, Schenectady, New York, Zip 12304–1090, tel. 518/382–2000) (Nonreporting) **A**1 3 5 10 13
Primary Contact: Paul A. Milton, President and Chief Executive Officer
COO: Paul A Milton, Executive Vice President and Chief Operating Officer
CFO: Marc Mesick, Vice President and Chief Financial Officer
CMO: David Liebers, M.D., Chief Medical Officer and Vice President Medical Affairs
CIO: Ron McKinnon, Chief Information Officer
CHR: Joseph Giansante, Vice President Human Resources
Web address: www.ellismedicine.org
Control: Other not–for–profit (including NFP Corporation) **Service:** General medical and surgical

Staffed Beds: 541

Hospitals, U.S. / NEW YORK

✣ △ **SUNNYVIEW REHABILITATION HOSPITAL (330406)**, 1270 Belmont Avenue, Zip 12308–2104; tel. 518/382–4500, **A** 1 3 7 10 28 29 30 34 35 36 38 39 44 50 53 56 57 58 59 60 64 65 68 74 75 77 79 82 84 86 87 90 91 92 93 94 95 96 100 119 130 131 132 135 146 148 149 154 156 157 164 **P**6 **S** Trinity Health, Livonia, MI
Primary Contact: Kim Baker, Senior Vice President, Hospital Operations
CFO: Kristin Signor, Director Finance
CMO: Lynne T Nicolson, M.D., Medical Director
CIO: Patrick Clark, Manager Information Technology
CHR: Meghan Glowa, Director Human Resources
Web address: www.sunnyview.org
Control: Other not-for-profit (including NFP Corporation) **Service:** Rehabilitation

Staffed Beds: 115 **Admissions:** 2115 **Census:** 85 **Outpatient Visits:** 85456 **Births:** 0 **Total Expense ($000):** 62854 **Payroll Expense ($000):** 36093 **Personnel:** 523

SLEEPY HOLLOW—Westchester County

✣ **PHELPS MEMORIAL HOSPITAL CENTER (330261)**, 701 North Broadway, Zip 10591–1020; tel. 914/366–3000, **A**1 2 3 5 10 **F**3 4 5 8 9 11 12 13 15 18 28 29 30 31 34 35 36 37 39 40 41 45 46 47 48 49 50 51 55 56 57 58 59 60 61 64 65 68 70 74 75 76 77 78 79 81 82 84 85 86 87 89 90 93 94 96 97 98 100 101 102 104 105 107 108 110 111 114 115 118 119 120 121 124 125 129 130 131 132 135 146 147 148 149 152 153 154 156 158 160 167 169 **S** Northwell Health, Lake Success, NY
Primary Contact: Beata Mastalerz, Executive Director
CFO: Vincent DeSantis, Vice President Finance
CNO: Mary McDermott, MSN, MS, R.N., Senior Vice President Patient Care Services and Chief Nursing Officer
Web address: www.phelpshospital.org
Control: Other not-for-profit (including NFP Corporation) **Service:** General medical and surgical

Staffed Beds: 149 **Admissions:** 7262 **Census:** 125 **Outpatient Visits:** 192737 **Births:** 819 **Total Expense ($000):** 454434 **Payroll Expense ($000):** 250416 **Personnel:** 1922

SMITHTOWN—Suffolk County

✣ **ST. CATHERINE OF SIENA HOSPITAL (330401)**, 50 Route 25–A, Zip 11787–1348; tel. 631/862–3000, (Total facility includes 240 beds in nursing home-type unit) **A**1 3 5 10 **F**3 11 12 13 15 17 18 20 22 26 29 30 31 34 35 37 38 40 44 45 46 49 50 51 55 56 57 59 60 64 65 68 70 72 74 75 76 77 78 79 81 84 85 86 87 97 98 100 101 102 104 107 108 110 111 115 118 119 126 128 129 130 132 134 135 141 142 146 147 148 149 154 157 160 162 164 165 166 167 168 169 **S** Catholic Health Services of Long Island, Rockville Centre, NY
Primary Contact: Declan Doyle, President
COO: Dominick Pernice, Chief Operating Officer
CNO: Mary Jane Finnegan, Chief Nursing Officer
Web address: www.stcatherines.chsli.org/
Control: Church operated, Nongovernment, not-for-profit **Service:** General medical and surgical

Staffed Beds: 522 **Admissions:** 11200 **Census:** 343 **Outpatient Visits:** 67508 **Births:** 489 **Total Expense ($000):** 292376 **Payroll Expense ($000):** 128652 **Personnel:** 1318

ST. CATHERINE OF SIENA MEDICAL CENTER See St. Catherine of Siena Hospital

SPRINGVILLE—Erie County

BERTRAND CHAFFEE HOSPITAL (330111), 224 East Main Street, Zip 14141–1497; tel. 716/592–2871, (Nonreporting) **A**10
Primary Contact: Theresa Donahue, Chief Executive Officer
CMO: J Matthew Baker, M.D., President Medical Staff
CHR: Mary Beth Brown, Director Human Resources
Web address: www.chaffeehospitalandhome.com
Control: Other not-for-profit (including NFP Corporation) **Service:** General medical and surgical

Staffed Beds: 24

STAR LAKE—St. Lawrence County

★ **CLIFTON–FINE HOSPITAL (331307)**, 1014 Oswegatchie Trail, Zip 13690–3143; tel. 315/848–3351, (Nonreporting) **A**10 18
Primary Contact: Dierdra Sorrell, R.N., MSN, Chief Executive Officer
COO: Cathy Rice, Director Support Services
CFO: Heather Cockayne, Chief Financial Officer
CMO: David Welch, M.D., Medical Director
CIO: Joe Deeter, MS, Director Information Systems
CNO: John Schaffer, R.N., Director of Nursing
Web address: www.cliftonfinehospital.org
Control: Other not-for-profit (including NFP Corporation) **Service:** General medical and surgical

Staffed Beds: 20

STATEN ISLAND—Richmond County, See New York City

STONY BROOK—Suffolk County

STONY BROOK CHILDREN'S HOSPITAL See Stony Brook Children's Hospital

✣ **STONY BROOK UNIVERSITY HOSPITAL (330393)**, 101 Nicolls Road, Zip 11794–8410; tel. 631/444–1077, (Includes STONY BROOK CHILDREN'S HOSPITAL, 100 Nicolls Road, Stony Brook, New York, Zip 11794–0001; tel. 631/444–4000; STONY BROOK EASTERN LONG ISLAND HOSPITAL, 201 Manor Place, Greenport, New York, Zip 11944–1298, tel. 631/477–1000; Paul J. Connor III, Chief Administrative Officer; STONY BROOK SOUTHAMPTON HOSPITAL, 240 Meeting House Lane, Southampton, New York, Zip 11968–5090, tel. 631/726–8200; Frederic Weinbaum, M.D., Interim Chief Administrative Officer, Chief Medical Officer and Chief Operating Officer) **A**1 2 3 5 8 10 19 **F**3 4 5 6 7 8 9 11 12 13 14 15 16 17 18 19 20 22 24 26 28 29 30 31 32 34 35 36 37 38 39 40 41 43 44 45 46 47 48 49 50 51 52 53 54 55 56 57 58 59 60 61 62 64 65 66 68 70 71 72 73 74 75 76 77 78 79 81 82 84 85 86 87 88 89 91 92 93 96 97 98 99 100 101 102 103 104 107 108 110 111 114 115 116 117 118 119 120 121 122 123 124 126 129 130 131 132 134 135 136 138 141 143 144 145 146 147 148 149 150 151 154 156 157 158 160 161 164 166 167 169 **P**7
Primary Contact: Carol Gomes, MS, FACHE, Chief Executive Officer and Chief Operating Officer
COO: Carol Gomes, MS, FACHE, Chief Executive Officer and Chief Operating Officer
CFO: Gary E Bie, CPA, Chief Financial Officer
CMO: Jonathan Buscaglia, M.D., Chief Medical Officer
CIO: Jim Murry, Chief Information Officer
CHR: Luis de Onis, Interim Chief Human Resources Officer
CNO: Mary Ann T Donohue, Ph.D., R.N., Chief Patient Care Services Officer
Web address: https://www.stonybrookmedicine.edu/sbuh
Control: State, Government, Nonfederal **Service:** General medical and surgical

Staffed Beds: 874 **Admissions:** 38677 **Census:** 711 **Outpatient Visits:** 554123 **Births:** 4873 **Total Expense ($000):** 2055544 **Payroll Expense ($000):** 908388 **Personnel:** 8384

SUFFERN—Rockland County

✣ **GOOD SAMARITAN REGIONAL MEDICAL CENTER (330158)**, 255 Lafayette Avenue, Zip 10901–4869; tel. 845/368–5000, (Nonreporting) **A**1 2 5 10 **S** WMCHealth, Valhalla, NY
Primary Contact: Mary Leahy, M.D., Chief Executive Officer
CMO: Rodney W Williams, M.D., JD, MS, Vice President Medical Affairs
CIO: Deborah K Marshall, Vice President Public Relations
CHR: Pamela Tarulli, Senior Vice President Human Resources
Web address: www.goodsamhosp.org
Control: Church operated, Nongovernment, not-for-profit **Service:** General medical and surgical

Staffed Beds: 308

SYOSSET—Nassau County

NORTH SHORE UNIVERSITY HOSPITAL AT SYOSSET See Syosset Hospital

SYRACUSE—Onondaga County

COMMUNITY–GENERAL HOSPITAL OF GREATER SYRACUSE See Upstate University Hospital At Community General

---

Hospital, Medicare Provider Number, Address, Telephone, Approval, Facility, and Physician Codes, Health Care System

★ American Hospital Association (AHA) membership
☐ The Joint Commission accreditation
○ Healthcare Facilities Accreditation Program
◇ DNV Healthcare Inc. accreditation
⇧ Center for Improvement in Healthcare Quality Accreditation
△ Commission on Accreditation of Rehabilitation Facilities (CARF) accreditation

Hospitals, U.S. / NEW YORK

★ ⇧ **CROUSE HEALTH (330203)**, 736 Irving Avenue, Zip 13210–1690; tel. 315/470–7375, (Nonreporting) **A**3 5 10 21
Primary Contact: Seth Kronenberg, M.D., President and Chief Executive Officer
CFO: Kevin Randall, Chief Financial Officer
CIO: Kim Rose, Chief Information Technology
CHR: John Bergemann, Director Human Resources
CNO: Betty O'Connor, Chief Nursing Officer
Web address: www.crouse.org
Control: Other not–for–profit (including NFP Corporation) **Service**: General medical and surgical

Staffed Beds: 487

☐ **RICHARD H. HUTCHINGS PSYCHIATRIC CENTER (334001)**, 620 Madison Street, Zip 13210–2319; tel. 315/426–3632, (Nonreporting) **A**1 3 5 10 **S** New York State Office of Mental Health, Albany, NY
Primary Contact: Thomas Umina, M.D., Executive Director
CFO: Robert Stapleton, Director Administration
CMO: Mark Cattalani, M.D., Clinical Director
CIO: Neil Nemi, Administrator Facility Information Center
CHR: Katherine Herron, Director Human Resources
Web address: www.omh.ny.gov
Control: State, Government, Nonfederal **Service**: Psychiatric

Staffed Beds: 131

★ ⇧ **ST. JOSEPH'S HOSPITAL HEALTH CENTER (330140)**, 301 Prospect Avenue, Zip 13203–1807; tel. 315/448–5111, (Nonreporting) **A**3 5 10 19 21 **S** Trinity Health, Livonia, MI
Primary Contact: Meredith Price, Senior Vice President, Acute Operations
COO: Janet L. Ready, Chief Operating Officer
CFO: Meredith Price, Vice President Fiscal Services and Chief Financial Officer
CMO: Joseph W Spinale, D.O., Chief Medical Officer
CIO: Charles Fennell, Vice President Information Management
CHR: Erika Duncan, Vice President Human Resources
Web address: www.sjhsyr.org
Control: Other not–for–profit (including NFP Corporation) **Service**: General medical and surgical

Staffed Beds: 451

✠ △ **SYRACUSE VETERANS AFFAIRS MEDICAL CENTER**, 800 Irving Avenue, Zip 13210–2716; tel. 315/425–4400, (Nonreporting) **A**1 3 5 7 **S** Department of Veterans Affairs, Washington, DC
Primary Contact: Michael DelDuca, Associate Medical Center Director
CFO: Deborah Angell, Chief Financial Officer
CMO: Syed Asif Ali, M.D., Chief of Staff
CIO: James Stenson, Chief Information Officer
CHR: Mark Antinelli, Manager Human Resources
CNO: Cheryl Czajkowski, Associate Director Patient and Nursing Services
Web address: www.syracuse.va.gov/
Control: Veterans Affairs, Government, federal **Service**: General medical and surgical

Staffed Beds: 103

★ ⇧ **UPSTATE UNIVERSITY HOSPITAL (330241)**, 750 East Adams Street, Zip 13210–2342; tel. 315/464–5540, (Includes GOLISANO CHILDREN'S HOSPITAL, 750 East Adams Street, Syracuse, New York, Zip 13210–2342, tel. 315/464–4570; UPSTATE UNIVERSITY HOSPITAL AT COMMUNITY GENERAL, 4900 Broad Road, Syracuse, New York, Zip 13215–2293, tel. 315/492–5011; Robert J. Corona Jr., Chief Executive Officer) **A**2 3 5 8 10 19 21 **F**3 6 9 12 13 15 16 17 18 19 20 22 24 25 26 28 29 30 31 33 34 35 36 37 38 39 40 41 43 44 45 46 47 48 49 50 51 52 53 54 55 56 58 59 61 64 65 66 68 69 70 71 74 75 76 78 79 81 82 84 85 86 87 88 89 90 92 93 95 96 97 98 99 100 102 104 107 108 109 110 111 112 114 115 118 119 120 121 123 124 126 128 129 130 131 132 135 136 138 141 142 145 146 147 148 149 150 153 154 157 160 162 167 168 169
Primary Contact: Robert J. Corona Jr., Chief Executive Officer
CFO: Stuart M. Wright, CPA, Chief Financial Officer
CMO: Amy Tucker, M.D., Chief Medical Officer
CIO: Mark Zeman, Chief Information Officer
CHR: Eric Frost, Associate Vice President Human Resources
CNO: Scott Jessie, Chief Nursing Officer
Web address: www.upstate.edu/hospital
Control: State, Government, Nonfederal **Service**: General medical and surgical

Staffed Beds: 632 **Admissions**: 30728 **Census**: 536 **Outpatient Visits**: 1036834 **Births**: 922 **Total Expense ($000)**: 1935540 **Payroll Expense ($000)**: 556579 **Personnel**: 6193

TICONDEROGA—Essex County

MOSES LUDINGTON HOSPITAL See University of Vermont Health Network Elizabethtown Community Hospital – Ticonderoga Campuss

TROY—Rensselaer County

BURDETT BIRTH CENTER (330409), 2215 Burdett Avenue, Suite 200, Zip 12180–2466; tel. 518/271–3393, (Nonreporting) **A**10 **S** Trinity Health, Livonia, MI
Primary Contact: JoAnn Lionarons, Director
Web address: www.burdettbirthcenter.org/
Control: Church operated, Nongovernment, not–for–profit **Service**: Obstetrics and gynecology

Staffed Beds: 15

★ **SAMARITAN HOSPITAL – MAIN CAMPUS (330180)**, 2215 Burdett Avenue, Zip 12180–2475; tel. 518/271–3300, (Includes SAMARITAN HOSPITAL – ALBANY MEMORIAL CAMPUS, 600 Northern Boulevard, Albany, New York, Zip 12204–1083, tel. 518/471–3221; Kim Baker, Senior Vice President Hospital Operations; SAMARITAN HOSPITAL – ST. MARY'S CAMPUS, 1300 Massachusetts Avenue, Troy, New York, Zip 12180–1695, tel. 518/268–5000; Kim Baker, Senior Vice President Hospital Operations) **A**3 5 10 19 **F**3 8 11 12 15 17 18 20 22 26 28 29 30 31 32 34 36 38 40 42 44 45 46 47 48 49 50 51 55 56 57 59 60 63 64 65 66 68 70 73 74 75 76 77 78 79 80 81 84 85 87 93 94 97 98 100 101 102 103 104 107 108 109 111 114 119 120 121 123 126 130 132 135 145 146 147 148 149 150 153 154 164 167 **S** Trinity Health, Livonia, MI
Primary Contact: Steven Hanks, M.D., President and Chief Executive Officer, St. Joseph's Health and St. Peter's Health Partners
CFO: Daniel A Kochie, CPA, Chief Financial Officer
CMO: Daniel C Silverman, M.D., Chief Medical Officer, Acute Care Troy
CIO: Karen LeBlanc, Director, Applications
CNO: Jacqueline Priore, Chief Nursing Officer
Web address: www.sphp.com/sam
Control: Other not–for–profit (including NFP Corporation) **Service**: General medical and surgical

Staffed Beds: 321 **Admissions**: 11177 **Census**: 158 **Outpatient Visits**: 266583 **Births**: 824 **Total Expense ($000)**: 411108 **Payroll Expense ($000)**: 169384

SETON HEALTH ST. MARY'S HOSPITAL See Samaritan Hospital – St. Mary's Campus

SETON HLTH SYST–ST MARY'S See Seton Health System–St. Mary's Hospital

UTICA—Oneida County

FAXTON–ST LUKE'S HEALTHCARE See Faxton Campus

☐ **MOHAWK VALLEY PSYCHIATRIC CENTER (334021)**, 1400 Noyes Street, Zip 13502–3854; tel. 315/738–3800, **A**1 3 10 **F**3 29 50 59 77 82 98 99 100 101 104 106 130 149 153 154 164 165 **S** New York State Office of Mental Health, Albany, NY
Primary Contact: Anthony Gonzalez, Executive Director
Web address: https://omh.ny.gov/omhweb/facilities/mvpc/
Control: State, Government, Nonfederal **Service**: Children's hospital psychiatric

Staffed Beds: 27 **Admissions**: 247 **Census**: 18 **Births**: 0

ST LUKE'S MEM HOSPITAL CENTER See St. Luke's Campus

ST. LUKE'S CAMPUS See Wynn Hospital, Utica

★ △ **WYNN HOSPITAL (330044)**, 111 Hospital Drive, Zip 13502, Mailing Address: P.O. Box 479, Zip 13503–0479; tel. 315/917–9966, (Includes FAXTON CAMPUS, 1676 Sunset Avenue, Utica, New York, Zip 13502–5475, tel. 315/624–6000; ST. LUKE'S CAMPUS, 1656 Champlin Ave, Utica, New York, Zip 13502–4830, P O Box 479, Zip 13503–0479, tel. 315/624–6000) (Nonreporting) **A**2 3 7 10 21
Primary Contact: Darlene Stromstad, FACHE, President and Chief Executive Officer
COO: Robert Scholefield, MS, R.N., Executive Vice President and Chief Operating Officer
CFO: Louis Aiello, Senior Vice President and Chief Financial Officer
CMO: Fred Talarico, Chief Medical Officer
CIO: Tammy Canfield, Chief Information Officer
CHR: Allison Marie Wollen, Chief Human Resources Officer
CNO: Jerome Mendoza Dayao, MS, R.N., Chief Nursing Officer
Web address: https://www.mvhealthsystem.org/wynn-hospital/
Control: Other not–for–profit (including NFP Corporation) **Service**: General medical and surgical

Staffed Beds: 266

VALHALLA—Westchester County

✠ **BLYTHEDALE CHILDREN'S HOSPITAL (333301)**, 95 Bradhurst Avenue, Zip 10595–1697; tel. 914/592–7555, (Nonreporting) **A**1 3 5 10
Primary Contact: Larry L. Levine, President and Chief Executive Officer
COO: Maureen Desimone, Chief Operating Officer
CFO: John Canning, Chief Financial Officer
CMO: Joelle Mast, Ph.D., M.D., Chief Medical Officer
CHR: Ronald Gallo, Director Human Resources
Web address: www.blythedale.org
Control: Other not–for–profit (including NFP Corporation) **Service**: Children's rehabilitation

Staffed Beds: 92

Hospitals, U.S. / NEW YORK

⇧ **WESTCHESTER MEDICAL CENTER (330234)**, 100 Woods Road,
Zip 10595–1530; tel. 914/493–7000, (Includes MARIA FARERI CHILDREN'S
HOSPITAL, 100 Woods Road, Valhalla, New York, Zip 10595–1652,
tel. 866/962–7337; MIDHUDSON REGIONAL HOSPITAL OF WESTCHESTER
MEDICAL CENTER, 241 North Road, Poughkeepsie, New York, Zip 12601–1154,
tel. 845/483–5000; Paul S Hochenberg, Executive Director) (Nonreporting) **A**2 3 5
8 10 19 21 **S** WMCHealth, Valhalla, NY
Primary Contact: Michael D. Israel, President and Chief Executive Officer
COO: Gary F Brudnicki, Senior Executive Vice President, Chief Operating Officer
and Chief Financial Officer
CFO: Gary F Brudnicki, Senior Executive Vice President, Chief Operating Officer
and Chief Financial Officer
CMO: Renee Garrick, M.D., Executive Medical Director
CIO: John Moustakakis, Senior Vice President Information Systems and Chief
Information Officer
CHR: Jordy Rabinowitz, Senior Vice President Human Resources Operations
CNO: Phyllis M. Yezzo, R.N., MS, Senior Vice President, Chief Nurse Executive
Web address: www.wmchealth.org
Control: Hospital district or authority, Government, Nonfederal **Service:** General
medical and surgical

Staffed Beds: 915

VALLEY STREAM—Nassau County

FRANKLIN HOSPITAL See Long Island Jewish Valley Stream

WALTON—Delaware County

UHS DELAWARE VALLEY HOSPITAL (331312), 1 Titus Place,
Zip 13856–1498; tel. 607/865–2100, **A**10 18 **F**3 11 15 18 29 30 34 35 40 41
44 45 50 57 59 64 65 66 75 77 79 87 97 104 107 110 111 115 119 130 133
146 148 149 154 156 160 **S** United Health Services, Binghamton, NY
Primary Contact: Rolland Bojo, R.N., President and Chief Executive Officer
CFO: Lucinda Rider, CFO
CMO: John Giannone, M.D., Delaware Valley Hospital Medical Director
CHR: Cynthia Gardepe, Director, Human Resources
CNO: Victoria Conkling, Vice President, Patient Services and Chief Nursing Officer
Web address: www.uhs.net/locations/
Control: Other not-for-profit (including NFP Corporation) **Service:** General
medical and surgical

Staffed Beds: 21 **Admissions:** 421 **Census:** 10 **Outpatient Visits:** 192386
Births: 0 **Total Expense ($000):** 33422 **Payroll Expense ($000):** 10963
Personnel: 162

WAPPINGERS FALLS—Dutchess County

**VETERAN AFFAIRS HUDSON VALLEY HEALTH CARE SYSTEM–CASTLE
POINT CAMPUS** See Veterans Affairs Hudson Valley Health Care System,
Montrose

**VETERAN AFFAIRS HUDSON VALLEY HEALTH CARE SYSTEM–CASTLE
POINT DIVISION** See Veteran Affairs Hudson Valley Health Care System–Castle
Point Campus

WARSAW—Wyoming County

☐ **WYOMING COUNTY COMMUNITY HOSPITAL (330008)**, 400 North Main
Street, Zip 14569–1025; tel. 585/786–2233, (Total facility includes 138 beds in
nursing home–type unit) **A**1 10 20 **F**3 11 13 15 18 28 29 30 34 35 36 38 40 44
45 46 47 49 50 56 57 59 60 64 65 68 70 74 75 76 77 79 81 82 87 90 91 92
93 96 97 98 100 102 103 107 108 109 110 111 114 119 128 130 131 133
135 146 147 149 154 157
Primary Contact: David A. Kobis, Chief Executive Officer
COO: Michael Corcimiglia, Chief Operating Officer
CFO: Amy Chase, Chief Financial Officer
CMO: Mandip Panesar, M.D., Medical Director
CIO: Dan Flint, Director Healthcare Information Systems
CHR: Daniel Farberman, Director Human Resource
CNO: Connie Almeter, Chief Nursing Officer
Web address: www.wcchs.net
Control: County, Government, Nonfederal **Service:** General medical and surgical

Staffed Beds: 222 **Admissions:** 1975 **Census:** 157 **Outpatient
Visits:** 130845 **Births:** 80 **Total Expense ($000):** 83998 **Payroll Expense
($000):** 36621 **Personnel:** 540

WARWICK—Orange County

✣ **ST. ANTHONY COMMUNITY HOSPITAL (330205)**, 15 Maple Avenue,
Zip 10990–1028; tel. 845/986–2276, (Nonreporting) **A**1 10 **S** WMCHealth,
Valhalla, NY
Primary Contact: Mary Leahy, M.D., Chief Executive Officer
Web address: www.stanthonycommunityhosp.org
Control: Church operated, Nongovernment, not-for-profit **Service:** General
medical and surgical

Staffed Beds: 60

WATERTOWN—Jefferson County

✣ **SAMARITAN MEDICAL CENTER (330157)**, 830 Washington Street,
Zip 13601–4034; tel. 315/785–4000, (Nonreporting) **A**1 3 5 10 12 13 20
Primary Contact: Thomas H. Carman, President and Chief Executive Officer
CFO: Sean Mills, Chief Financial Officer
CMO: Mario Victoria, M.D., Vice President, Medical Affairs
CIO: M Andrew Short, Vice President Information Services
CHR: Thomas Shatraw, Director Human Resources
CNO: Kimberly Thibert, R.N., MSN, Vice President Patient Care Services and Chief
Nursing Officer
Web address: www.samaritanhealth.com
Control: Other not-for-profit (including NFP Corporation) **Service:** General
medical and surgical

Staffed Beds: 174

WELLSVILLE—Allegany County

✣ **JONES MEMORIAL HOSPITAL (330096)**, 191 North Main Street,
Zip 14895–1150, Mailing Address: P.O. Box 72, Zip 14895–0072;
tel. 585/593–1100, **A**1 10 20 **F**3 11 13 17 28 29 30 31 34 35 36 40 43 50
57 59 61 64 68 70 72 73 75 76 77 78 79 81 85 89 93 97 107 111 114 119
127 129 130 131 132 133 144 146 147 149 154 156 157 169 **S** University of
Rochester Medical Center, Rochester, NY
Primary Contact: James Helms, President and Chief Executive Officer
CMO: Kevin McCormick, M.D., Associate Medical Director
CHR: Carrie Walker, Executive Director Human Resources
CNO: Donna Bliven, Vice President Patient Care Services and Chief Nursing Officer
Web address: www.jmhny.org
Control: Other not-for-profit (including NFP Corporation) **Service:** General
medical and surgical

Staffed Beds: 33 **Admissions:** 1096 **Census:** 15 **Outpatient Visits:** 141754
Births: 392 **Total Expense ($000):** 71876 **Payroll Expense ($000):** 28627
Personnel: 392

WEST HAVERSTRAW—Rockland County

☐ **HELEN HAYES HOSPITAL (330405)**, 51–55 Route 9W, Zip 10993–1127;
tel. 845/786–4000, (Nonreporting) **A**1 3 10
Primary Contact: Edmund Coletti, Chief Executive Officer
COO: Kathleen Martucci, Chief Operating Officer
CFO: Lori A. Meszler, Chief Financial Officer
CIO: Virgil Ennis, Chief Information Officer
CHR: Patrick J. Ryan, Chief Human Resources Officer
Web address: www.helenhayeshospital.org
Control: State, Government, Nonfederal **Service:** Rehabilitation

Staffed Beds: 155

WEST ISLIP—Suffolk County

✣ **GOOD SAMARITAN HOSPITAL MEDICAL CENTER (330286)**, 1000 Montauk
Highway, Zip 11795–4927; tel. 631/376–3000, **A**1 2 3 5 10 13 **F**3 11 12 13 15
17 18 19 20 22 24 26 28 29 30 31 32 34 35 38 39 40 41 43 44 45 46 49 50
52 54 55 56 57 58 59 61 64 65 66 70 72 73 74 75 76 77 78 79 80 81 82 84
85 86 87 88 89 93 94 100 101 102 107 108 110 111 115 117 118 119 120
121 123 124 126 129 130 131 132 134 135 141 142 146 147 148 149 150
154 156 162 164 166 167 168 169 **S** Catholic Health Services of Long Island,
Rockville Centre, NY
Primary Contact: Justin Lundbye, President
CFO: Dan Macksood, Regional Senior Vice President and Chief Financial Officer
CMO: Jerome Weiner, M.D., Senior Vice President Medical Affairs
CHR: Lori Spina, Vice President Human Resources
Web address: www.good-samaritan-hospital.org
Control: Other not-for-profit (including NFP Corporation) **Service:** General
medical and surgical

Staffed Beds: 409 **Admissions:** 24477 **Census:** 334 **Outpatient
Visits:** 285077 **Births:** 2412 **Total Expense ($000):** 904250 **Payroll
Expense ($000):** 415153 **Personnel:** 3097

Hospital, Medicare Provider Number, Address, Telephone, Approval, Facility, and Physician Codes, Health Care System

★ American Hospital Association (AHA) membership
☐ The Joint Commission accreditation
○ Healthcare Facilities Accreditation Program
◇ DNV Healthcare Inc. accreditation
⇧ Center for Improvement in Healthcare Quality Accreditation
△ Commission on Accreditation of Rehabilitation Facilities (CARF) accreditation

Hospitals, U.S. / NEW YORK

WEST POINT—Orange County

☒ **KELLER ARMY COMMUNITY HOSPITAL,** 900 Washington Road, Zip 10996–1197, Mailing Address: U S Military Academy, Building 900, Zip 10996–1197; tel. 845/938–5169, (Nonreporting) **A**1 3 5 **S** Department of the Army, Office of the Surgeon General, Falls Church, VA
Primary Contact: Colonel Amy L. Jackson, Commander
CIO: Patrick McGuinness, Chief Information Management
CHR: Margaret Greco, Chief Human Resources
Web address: https://keller.tricare.mil/
Control: Army, Government, federal **Service:** General medical and surgical

Staffed Beds: 12

WEST SENECA—Erie County

☐ **WESTERN NEW YORK CHILDREN'S PSYCHIATRIC CENTER (334065),** 1010 East and West Road, Zip 14224–3602; tel. 716/677–7000, (Nonreporting) **A**1 3 5 10 **S** New York State Office of Mental Health, Albany, NY
Primary Contact: David Thomas. Privett, Executive Director
CMO: Patrick Stein, M.D., Clinical Director
CIO: Dan Hrubiak, Associate Computer Program Analyst
CHR: Charles Siewert, Director Human Resources
Web address: www.omh.ny.gov
Control: State, Government, Nonfederal **Service:** Children's hospital psychiatric

Staffed Beds: 46

WESTFIELD—Chautauqua County

★ **WESTFIELD MEMORIAL HOSPITAL (330166),** 189 East Main Street, Zip 14787–1195; tel. 716/326–4921, **A**10 **F**3 11 15 18 28 29 34 35 40 44 50 64 75 79 81 85 87 93 97 102 107 108 110 115 118 119 135 141 146 147 148 149 154 156 157 **S** Allegheny Health Network, Pittsburgh, PA
Primary Contact: Rodney Buchanan, MSN, R.N., Interim President
COO: Patricia Ballman, Director
CFO: Tina Gowen, System Controller
CMO: Russell Elwell, M.D., Medical Director
CIO: Cindy Harper, Manager Patient Data
Web address: https://www.ahn.org/locations/westfield-memorial-hospital
Control: Other not–for–profit (including NFP Corporation) **Service:** General medical and surgical

Staffed Beds: 4 **Admissions:** 146 **Census:** 1 **Outpatient Visits:** 24198 **Births:** 0 **Total Expense ($000):** 13644 **Payroll Expense ($000):** 5402 **Personnel:** 74

WHITE PLAINS—Westchester County

☒ △ **BURKE REHABILITATION HOSPITAL (333030),** 785 Mamaroneck Avenue, Zip 10605–2523; tel. 914/597–2500, **A**1 3 5 7 10 **F**3 9 11 28 29 30 34 35 36 44 50 53 54 56 57 58 59 64 68 74 75 77 79 82 86 87 90 91 92 93 94 95 96 100 119 130 131 132 135 146 148 149 154 156 157 **S** Montefiore Health System, Bronx, NY
Primary Contact: Scott Edelman, Executive Director and Chief Executive Officer
COO: Brian M Swift, Senior Administrator Plant Operations
CFO: John Stewart, Director Finance
CIO: Cathy Dwyer, Senior Administrator Information Systems
CHR: Annette Bucci, Vice President Human Resources
CNO: Marie Spencer, Chief Nursing Officer and Senior Administrator
Web address: www.burke.org
Control: Other not–for–profit (including NFP Corporation) **Service:** Rehabilitation

Staffed Beds: 150 **Admissions:** 2916 **Census:** 118 **Outpatient Visits:** 156760 **Births:** 0 **Total Expense ($000):** 128567 **Payroll Expense ($000):** 71792 **Personnel:** 803

NEW YORK–PRESBYTERIAN HOSPITAL, WESTCHESTER DIVISION See New York–Presbyterian Hospital, New York

☒ **WHITE PLAINS HOSPITAL CENTER (330304),** 41 East Post Road, Zip 10601–4699; tel. 914/681–0600, **A**1 2 3 5 10 19 **F**3 7 8 9 11 12 13 15 17 18 19 20 22 24 26 29 30 31 32 34 35 36 37 38 39 40 41 42 44 45 46 47 49 50 51 53 54 55 56 57 58 59 60 61 63 64 65 66 68 70 72 73 74 75 76 77 78 79 81 82 84 85 86 87 89 92 93 94 96 97 100 101 102 107 108 110 111 114 115 117 118 119 120 121 123 124 126 129 130 131 132 134 143 144 145 146 147 148 149 150 154 156 157 160 164 167 169 **P**6 **S** Montefiore Health System, Bronx, NY
Primary Contact: Susan Fox, President and Chief Executive Officer
COO: Edward F Leonard, Executive Vice President and Chief Operating Officer
CFO: Joseph Guarracino, Senior Vice President and Chief Financial Officer
CMO: Michael Palumbo, M.D., Executive Vice President and Medical Director
CIO: Rick McCarthy, Chief Information Officer
CHR: Diane Woolley, Senior Vice President, Chief Human Resources Officer
CNO: Leigh McMahon, MS, R.N., Executive Vice President Patient Care Services and Chief Nursing Officer
Web address: www.wphospital.org
Control: Other not–for–profit (including NFP Corporation) **Service:** General medical and surgical

Staffed Beds: 292 **Admissions:** 21712 **Census:** 273 **Outpatient Visits:** 507475 **Births:** 2296 **Total Expense ($000):** 1200508 **Payroll Expense ($000):** 580528 **Personnel:** 4263

WILLIAMSVILLE—Erie County

MILLARD FILLMORE SUBURBAN HOSPITAL See Kaleida Health, Buffalo

ST FRANCIS HOME See St. Francis of Williamsville

YONKERS—Westchester County

ANDRUS PAVILION See St. John's Riverside Hospital, Yonkers

ELIZABETH SETON PEDIATRIC CENTER See Elizabeth Seton Children's Center

☒ **SAINT JOSEPH'S MEDICAL CENTER (330006),** 127 South Broadway, Zip 10701–4006; tel. 914/378–7000, (Nonreporting) **A**1 3 5 10
Primary Contact: Michael J. Spicer, President and Chief Executive Officer
COO: Frances Casola, Senior Vice President Operations
CFO: Frank Hagan, Senior Vice President Finance
CMO: James Neuendorf, M.D., Medical Director
CIO: Deborah Di Bernardo, Chief Information Officer
CHR: Dean Civitello, Vice President Human Resources
CNO: Margaret M Cusumano, R.N., MSN, Vice President Patient Care Services and Chief Nursing Officer
Web address: www.saintjosephs.org
Control: Other not–for–profit (including NFP Corporation) **Service:** General medical and surgical

Staffed Beds: 276

☐ **ST. JOHN'S RIVERSIDE HOSPITAL (330208),** 967 North Broadway, Zip 10701–1399; tel. 914/964–4444, (Includes ANDRUS PAVILION, 967 North Broadway, Yonkers, New York, Zip 10701–1399, tel. 914/964–4444; ST. JOHN'S RIVERSIDE HOSPITAL – DOBBS FERRY PAVILION, 128 Ashford Avenue, Dobbs Ferry, New York, Zip 10522–1896, tel. 914/693–0700; ST. JOHN'S RIVERSIDE HOSPITAL – PARK CARE PAVILION, 2 Park Avenue, Yonkers, New York, Zip 10703–3497, tel. 914/964–7300) **A**1 3 5 10 19 **F**3 4 5 8 11 12 13 15 18 29 30 31 34 35 36 37 40 41 45 49 50 51 54 55 56 57 59 60 61 64 68 70 72 74 75 76 77 78 79 81 82 84 85 87 92 93 94 97 107 108 110 111 114 115 118 119 124 126 129 130 132 135 146 147 148 149 152 154 160 164 167
Primary Contact: Ronald J. Corti, President and Chief Executive Officer
COO: Lynn M. Nelson, R.N., R.N., Chief Nursing Officer and Chief Operating Officer
CFO: Dennis M. Keane, Vice President Finance and Chief Financial Officer
CMO: Paul Antonecchia, M.D., Vice President Medical Affairs and Chief Medical Officer
CIO: Peter Weidner, Director Information Technology
CHR: Marc Leff, Vice President Human Resources
CNO: Lynn M. Nelson, R.N., R.N., Chief Nursing Officer and Chief Operating Officer
Web address: www.riversidehealth.org
Control: Other not–for–profit (including NFP Corporation) **Service:** General medical and surgical

Staffed Beds: 378 **Admissions:** 15208 **Census:** 230 **Outpatient Visits:** 278037 **Births:** 1132 **Total Expense ($000):** 366310 **Payroll Expense ($000):** 163895 **Personnel:** 1757

YONKERS GENERAL HOSPITAL See St. John's Riverside Hospital – Park Care Pavilion

Hospitals, U.S. / NORTH CAROLINA

NORTH CAROLINA

AHOSKIE—Hertford County

ECU HEALTH ROANOKE–CHOWAN HOSPITAL (340099), 500 South Academy Street, Zip 27910–3261, Mailing Address: P.O. Box 1385, Zip 27910–1385; tel. 252/209–3000, **A**1 2 3 10 20 **F**3 10 11 13 15 29 30 31 34 35 40 43 44 45 56 57 59 64 68 70 75 76 77 78 79 81 82 83 84 85 86 87 89 92 93 98 100 101 102 103 107 108 110 111 114 118 119 121 123 129 130 132 146 148 149 154 156 164 **S** ECU Health, Greenville, NC
Primary Contact: Brian Harvill, President
CFO: Jon Graham, Chief Finance Officer
CMO: David Lingle, Directors Council Chairman and Chief of Staff
CHR: Debbie Sisler, Director, Human Resource
Web address: https://locations.ecuhealth.org/Details/180
Control: Other not–for–profit (including NFP Corporation) **Service**: General medical and surgical

Staffed Beds: 110 **Admissions:** 3933 **Census:** 54 **Outpatient Visits:** 63619 **Births:** 273 **Total Expense ($000):** 93022 **Payroll Expense ($000):** 31124 **Personnel:** 521

VIDANT ROANOKE–CHOWAN HOSPITAL See ECU Health Roanoke–Chowan Hospital

ALBEMARLE—Stanly County

ATRIUM HEALTH STANLY (340119), 301 Yadkin Street, Zip 28001–3441, Mailing Address: P.O. Box 1489, Zip 28002–1489; tel. 704/984–4000, **A**1 2 10 **F**3 13 15 28 29 30 31 32 34 35 40 44 45 46 49 50 59 64 66 68 70 75 76 78 79 81 82 84 85 86 87 93 98 100 101 102 107 110 111 114 115 119 120 121 123 129 130 131 132 146 148 149 156 169 **P**6 **S** Atrium Health, Inc., Charlotte, NC
Primary Contact: Brian Freeman, FACHE, Senior Vice President, President West Area
CFO: Nick Samilo, Vice President Fiscal Services and Chief Financial Officer
CMO: Paul D'Amico, M.D., Chief of Staff
CNO: Marietta Kaye Abernathy, Chief Nursing Officer
Web address: www.stanly.org
Control: Hospital district or authority, Government, Nonfederal **Service**: General medical and surgical

Staffed Beds: 109 **Admissions:** 4314 **Census:** 51 **Outpatient Visits:** 109722 **Births:** 349 **Total Expense ($000):** 100685 **Payroll Expense ($000):** 52241 **Personnel:** 576

ASHEBORO—Randolph County

RANDOLPH HEALTH (340123), 364 White Oak Street, Zip 27203–5400, Mailing Address: P.O. Box 1048, Zip 27204–1048; tel. 336/625–5151, **A**1 10 19 **F**3 13 15 28 29 30 34 35 40 44 45 49 50 57 59 62 64 68 70 75 76 77 79 80 81 85 86 87 91 92 93 94 96 97 107 110 111 115 118 119 120 121 130 131 135 143 146 148 149 167 **S** American Healthcare Systems, Glendale, CA
Primary Contact: Tim Ford, President and Chief Executive Officer
CMO: Charles West, M.D., Chief Medical Officer
CIO: Angela Burgess, Chief Information Officer
Web address: https://www.randolphhealth.org/
Control: Corporation, Investor–owned (for–profit) **Service**: General medical and surgical

Staffed Beds: 70 **Admissions:** 5084 **Census:** 52 **Outpatient Visits:** 72209 **Births:** 671 **Personnel:** 970

ASHEVILLE—Buncombe County

ASHEVILLE SPECIALTY HOSPITAL (342017), 428 Biltmore Avenue, 4th Floor, Zip 28801–4502; tel. 828/213–5400, (Nonreporting) **A**1 10 **S** HCA Healthcare, Nashville, TN
Primary Contact: Julie A. Dikos, President and Chief Executive Officer
CFO: Gregg Dixon, Chief Financial Officer
CMO: Ronnie Jacobs, M.D., Chief Medical Officer
CIO: Megan Serzan, Director of Quality, Compliance, Risk & Safety
CNO: Josephine Picker, MSN, R.N., Director of Nursing
Web address: www.missionhospitals.org/acute-care
Control: Partnership, Investor–owned (for–profit) **Service**: Acute long–term care hospital

Staffed Beds: 34

CAREPARTNERS REHABILITATION HOSPITAL (343025), 68 Sweeten Creek Road, Zip 28803–2318, Mailing Address: P.O. Box 15025, Zip 28813–0025; tel. 828/277–4800, (Nonreporting) **A**1 3 10 **S** HCA Healthcare, Nashville, TN
Primary Contact: Tracy Buchanan, Chief Executive Officer and President
CFO: Gregg Dixon, Chief Financial Officer
CMO: Michael Parmer, Chief Medical Officer
CIO: Jennifer Scott, Director of Informatics
CHR: Katy Pless, Director of Human Resources
CNO: Cathleen Adams, Chief Nursing Officer
Web address: www.carepartners.org
Control: Other not–for–profit (including NFP Corporation) **Service**: Rehabilitation

Staffed Beds: 80

CHARLES GEORGE VETERANS AFFAIRS MEDICAL CENTER, 1100 Tunnel Road, Zip 28805–2087; tel. 828/298–7911, (Total facility includes 73 beds in nursing home–type unit) **A**1 3 5 **F**3 4 5 6 7 8 9 18 20 22 26 28 29 30 31 33 35 36 38 39 40 44 45 47 48 49 50 51 54 55 56 57 58 59 60 61 62 63 64 65 70 74 75 77 78 79 81 82 83 84 85 86 87 91 92 93 94 96 97 98 100 101 102 104 105 106 107 108 111 114 115 119 120 124 126 127 128 129 130 131 132 135 143 144 145 146 147 148 149 152 153 154 156 157 158 160 161 164 165 167 168 **S** Department of Veterans Affairs, Washington, DC
Primary Contact: Stephanie Young, Medical Center Director
CFO: Margaret Wilkes, Chief Fiscal Officer
CIO: Carla McLendon, Director Information Resource Management Services
CHR: James Sitlinger, Chief Human Resources Management
CNO: David Przestrzelski, Associate Director, Patient Care Services and Chief Nursing Executive
Web address: www.asheville.va.gov/
Control: Veterans Affairs, Government, federal **Service**: General medical and surgical

Staffed Beds: 188 **Admissions:** 4465 **Census:** 125 **Outpatient Visits:** 580247 **Births:** 0 **Total Expense ($000):** 746966 **Payroll Expense ($000):** 259350 **Personnel:** 2483

MEMORIAL MISSION HOSPITAL See Mission Hospital

MISSION HOSPITAL (340002), 509 Biltmore Avenue, Zip 28801–4690; tel. 828/213–1111, (Includes MISSION CHILDREN'S HOSPITAL, 509 Biltmore Avenue, Asheville, North Carolina, Zip 28801–4601, tel. 828/213–1111; MISSION HOSPITAL – ST. JOSEPH'S CAMPUS, 428 Biltmore Avenue, Asheville, North Carolina, Zip 28801–9839, tel. 828/213–1111; MISSION HOSPITAL, 509 Biltmore Avenue, Asheville, North Carolina, Zip 28801–4690, tel. 828/213–1111; Chad Patrick, Chief Executive Officer) (Nonreporting) **A**1 2 3 5 10 19 **S** HCA Healthcare, Nashville, TN
Primary Contact: Chad Patrick, Chief Executive Officer
CFO: Paul L McDowell, Deputy Chief Financial Officer
CIO: Jon Brown, Chief Information Officer
CHR: Sheila M Meadows, Chief Human Resources Officer
Web address: www.mission-health.org
Control: Other not–for–profit (including NFP Corporation) **Service**: General medical and surgical

Staffed Beds: 763

ST. JOSEPH'S HOSPITAL See Mission Hospital – St. Joseph's Campus

BERMUDA RUN—Davie County

ATRIUM HEALTH WAKE FOREST BAPTIST DAVIE MEDICAL CENTER (340187), 329 NC Highway 801 North, Zip 27006; tel. 336/998–1300, **A**1 5 10 **F**3 15 18 28 29 30 34 35 37 40 45 50 56 57 59 64 65 68 74 75 77 79 81 85 87 93 102 107 110 111 115 119 130 131 146 154 **P**6 **S** Atrium Health, Inc., Charlotte, NC
Primary Contact: Cathleen Wheatley, President
CFO: Danny Squires, Chief Financial Officer
CMO: Bret Nicks, M.D., Chief Medical Officer and Chief of Staff
CIO: William Showalter, Senior Vice President and Chief Information Officer, Information Technology Services
CHR: Jennifer Bandy, Human Resource Business Partner
CNO: Susan T. Bachmeier, MSN, R.N., Chief Nursing Officer
Web address: www.wakehealth.edu/Davie-Medical-Center
Control: Other not–for–profit (including NFP Corporation) **Service**: General medical and surgical

Staffed Beds: 38 **Admissions:** 1891 **Census:** 12 **Outpatient Visits:** 109588 **Births:** 0 **Total Expense ($000):** 90310 **Payroll Expense ($000):** 35899 **Personnel:** 378

Hospital, Medicare Provider Number, Address, Telephone, Approval, Facility, and Physician Codes, Health Care System

★ American Hospital Association (AHA) membership
□ The Joint Commission accreditation
○ Healthcare Facilities Accreditation Program
◇ DNV Healthcare Inc. accreditation
⇑ Center for Improvement in Healthcare Quality Accreditation
△ Commission on Accreditation of Rehabilitation Facilities (CARF) accreditation

Hospitals, U.S. / NORTH CAROLINA

BLACK MOUNTAIN—Buncombe County

JULIAN F. KEITH ALCOHOL AND DRUG ABUSE TREATMENT CENTER (344023), 201 Tabernacle Road, Zip 28711-2599; tel. 828/669-3400, (Nonreporting) **A**3 10
Primary Contact: Erin Bowman, Director
CFO: Jackie Maurer, Fiscal Officer
CMO: Anthony Burnett, M.D., Medical Director
CHR: Faye Hamlin, Manager Human Resources
Web address: www.ncdhhs.gov/divisions/dsohf/julian-f-keith-alcohol-and-drug-abuse-treatment-center
Control: State, Government, Nonfederal **Service**: Substance Use Disorder

Staffed Beds: 80

BLOWING ROCK—Watauga County

BLOWING ROCK HOSPITAL See Blowing Rock Rehabilitation & Davant Extended Care Center

BOLIVIA—Brunswick County

NOVANT HEALTH BRUNSWICK MEDICAL CENTER (340158), 240 Hospital Drive NE, Zip 28422-8346; tel. 910/721-1000, (Nonreporting) **A**1 10 **S** Novant Health, Winston Salem, NC
Primary Contact: Heather King, President and Chief Operating Officer
CMO: Thomas Zweng, Executive Vice President and Chief Medical Officer
CIO: David B Garrett, Senior Vice President and Chief Information Officer
CNO: Lorna J Ward, MSN, R.N., Chief Nursing Officer
Web address: https://www.novanthealth.org
Control: Other not–for–profit (including NFP Corporation) **Service**: General medical and surgical

Staffed Beds: 54

BOONE—Watauga County

WATAUGA MEDICAL CENTER (340051), 336 Deerfield Road, Zip 28607-5008, Mailing Address: P.O. Box 2600, Zip 28607-2600; tel. 828/262-4100, (Nonreporting) **A**1 2 3 10 **S** UNC Health, Chapel Hill, NC
Primary Contact: Charles Mantooth, President and Chief Executive Officer
CFO: Kevin B May, Chief Financial Officer
CMO: Herman A Godwin, M.D., Jr, Senior Vice President and Medical Director
CIO: Mike Quinto, Chief Information Officer
CHR: Amy J. Crabbe, Senior Vice President Human Resources
Web address: https://apprhs.org/contact-us
Control: Other not–for–profit (including NFP Corporation) **Service**: General medical and surgical

Staffed Beds: 99

BREVARD—Transylvania County

TRANSYLVANIA REGIONAL HOSPITAL (341319), 260 Hospital Drive, Zip 28712-3378; tel. 828/884-9111, (Nonreporting) **A**1 3 10 18 **S** HCA Healthcare, Nashville, TN
Primary Contact: Michele Pilon, President and Chief Nursing Officer
CFO: Theresa M Parker, Regional Finance Director
CMO: Mark Lemel, Chief of Staff
CIO: Ed Coye, Director Information Technology
CHR: Susan Stevens, Human Resources Strategic Business Partner
CNO: Melina Arrowood, Chief Nursing Officer
Web address: www.trhospital.org
Control: Other not–for–profit (including NFP Corporation) **Service**: General medical and surgical

Staffed Beds: 30

BRYSON CITY—Swain County

SWAIN COMMUNITY HOSPITAL, A DUKE LIFEPOINT HOSPITAL (341305), 45 Plateau Street, Zip 28713-4200; tel. 828/488-2155, (Nonreporting) **A**1 10 18 **S** Lifepoint Health, Brentwood, TN
Primary Contact: Ashley Hindman, Chief Executive Officer
CMO: David Zimmerman, M.D., Chief of Staff
CNO: LaCrystal Gordon, Chief Nursing Officer
Web address: https://www.myswaincommunity.com
Control: Other not–for–profit (including NFP Corporation) **Service**: General medical and surgical

Staffed Beds: 25

BURGAW—Pender County

★ ⇑ **NOVANT HEALTH PENDER MEDICAL CENTER (341307)**, 507 East Freemont Street, Zip 28425-5131; tel. 910/259-5451, (Nonreporting) **A**10 18 21 **S** Novant Health, Winston Salem, NC
Primary Contact: Ruth Glaser, President and Chief Operating Officer
CFO: Morrison Hall, Chief Financial Officer
CMO: Heather Davis, M.D., Chief of Staff
CIO: Ashley Hernandez, Chief Information Technology Officer
CHR: Lori McKoy, Business Partner
CNO: Cynthia Faulkner, R.N., Chief Nursing Executive
Web address: www.pendermemorial.org
Control: County, Government, Nonfederal **Service**: General medical and surgical

Staffed Beds: 64

BURLINGTON—Alamance County

CONE HEALTH ALAMANCE REGIONAL MEDICAL CENTER (340070), 1240 Huffman Mill Road, Zip 27215-8700, Mailing Address: P.O. Box 202, Zip 27216-0202; tel. 336/538-7000, **A**1 10 19 **F**3 8 13 15 18 20 22 24 26 28 29 30 31 32 34 35 36 37 38 39 40 44 45 46 47 49 50 53 54 56 57 58 59 60 64 65 68 70 73 74 75 76 77 78 79 81 82 84 85 86 87 89 91 93 94 96 97 98 100 101 102 103 107 108 110 111 115 117 118 119 120 121 123 126 130 131 132 135 144 145 146 147 148 154 156 167 **S** Cone Health, Greensboro, NC
Primary Contact: Mark Gordon, President
CFO: Rex Street, Senior Vice President and Chief Financial Officer
CMO: Andrew Lamb, M.D., Chief of Staff
CIO: Terri Andrews, Director Information Technology
Web address: www.armc.com
Control: Other not–for–profit (including NFP Corporation) **Service**: General medical and surgical

Staffed Beds: 195 Admissions: 10856 Census: 129 Outpatient Visits: 180462 Births: 1067 Total Expense ($000): 315291 Payroll Expense ($000): 84987 Personnel: 1205

BURNSVILLE—Yancey County

YANCEY COMMUNITY MEDICAL CENTER See Blue Ridge Medical Center – Yancey Campus

BUTNER—Granville County

☐ **CENTRAL REGIONAL HOSPITAL (344004)**, 300 Veazey Road, Zip 27509-1668; tel. 919/764-2000, (Nonreporting) **A**1 3 5 10
Primary Contact: Walter Edwin. Beal, Chief Executive Officer
COO: Cliff Hood, Chief Operating Officer
CFO: Pamela Richardson, Business Manager
CMO: Alan Cook, Chief Medical Officer
CIO: Joe Thurber, Director Information Technology
CHR: Kathleen Tardif, Director of Human Resources
CNO: Diana Holmes, Chief Nursing Officer
Control: State, Government, Nonfederal **Service**: Psychiatric

Staffed Beds: 398

CAMP LEJEUNE—Onslow County

NAVAL HOSPITAL CAMP LEJEUNE, 100 Brewster Boulevard, Zip 28547-2538, Mailing Address: P.O. Box 10100, Zip 28547-0100; tel. 910/450-4300, (Nonreporting) **A**1 3 5 **S** Bureau of Medicine and Surgery, Department of the Navy, Falls Church, VA
Primary Contact: Captain Reginald S. Ewing III, Commanding Officer
Web address: https://camp-lejeune.tricare.mil/
Control: Navy, Government, federal **Service**: General medical and surgical

Staffed Beds: 117

CARY—Wake County

WAKEMED CARY HOSPITAL (340173), 1900 Kildaire Farm Road, Zip 27518-6616; tel. 919/350-8000, **A**1 10 **F**3 5 7 11 12 13 15 18 20 22 24 26 28 29 30 32 34 35 36 37 38 40 42 43 44 45 46 47 48 49 50 53 54 56 57 58 59 60 61 62 64 65 66 68 70 73 74 75 76 77 78 79 81 82 85 86 87 92 100 101 102 107 108 110 111 114 115 119 126 129 130 132 135 144 146 147 148 149 150 154 156 160 162 164 165 169 **S** WakeMed Health & Hospitals, Raleigh, NC
Primary Contact: Thomas J. Gough, Executive Vice President & Chief Operating Officer
CMO: West Paul, M.D., Ph.D., Senior Vice President, Chief Quality and Medical Staff Officer
CIO: Denton Arledge, Vice President and Chief Information Officer
CNO: Cindy Boily, MSN, R.N., Senior Vice President and Chief Nursing Officer
Web address: www.wakemed.org
Control: Other not–for–profit (including NFP Corporation) **Service**: General medical and surgical

Staffed Beds: 208 Admissions: 13915 Census: 175 Outpatient Visits: 125335 Births: 2993 Total Expense ($000): 346547 Payroll Expense ($000): 146374 Personnel: 1355

Hospitals, U.S. / NORTH CAROLINA

CHAPEL HILL—Orange County

⊞ △ **UNIVERSITY OF NORTH CAROLINA HOSPITALS (340061)**, 101 Manning Drive, Zip 27514-4220; tel. 984/974-1000, (Includes N.C. WOMEN'S HOSPITAL, 101 Manning Drive, Chapel Hill, North Carolina, Zip 27514-4220, tel. 984/974-1000; Janet Hadar, President; NORTH CAROLINA CHILDREN'S HOSPITAL, 101 Manning Drive, Chapel Hill, North Carolina, Zip 27514-4220, tel. 984/974-1000; UNC HEALTH CARE HILLSBOROUGH CAMPUS, 430 Waterstone Drive, Hillsborough, North Carolina, Zip 27278-9078, tel. 984/215-2000; Janet Hadar, President; UNC LINEBERGER COMPREHENSIVE CANCER CENTER, 450 West Drive, Chapel Hill, North Carolina, Zip 27599-5020, tel. 919/966-3036) **A**1 2 3 5 7 8 10 19 **F**3 5 6 7 8 9 11 12 13 14 15 16 17 18 19 20 21 22 23 24 25 26 27 28 29 30 31 32 34 35 36 37 38 39 40 41 43 44 45 46 47 48 49 50 51 53 54 55 56 57 58 59 60 61 62 63 64 65 66 68 70 72 73 74 75 76 77 78 79 80 81 82 83 84 85 86 87 88 89 90 91 92 93 94 95 96 97 98 99 100 101 102 103 104 106 107 108 110 111 114 115 116 117 118 119 120 121 123 124 126 129 130 131 132 134 135 136 137 138 139 140 141 142 143 145 146 147 148 149 150 154 155 156 157 160 161 162 163 164 165 166 167 168 169 **S** UNC Health, Chapel Hill, NC
Primary Contact: Janet Hadar, President
CMO: Tony Lindsey, M.D., Chief of Staff
CIO: Tracy Parham
CHR: Scott Doak, System Vice President, Human Resources
CNO: Catherine Madigan, Chief Nursing Executive
Web address: www.unchealthcare.org
Control: State, Government, Nonfederal **Service:** General medical and surgical

Staffed Beds: 1001 **Admissions:** 37303 **Census:** 817 **Outpatient Visits:** 1023784 **Births:** 4110 **Total Expense ($000):** 2513402 **Payroll Expense ($000):** 790916 **Personnel:** 9800

CHARLOTTE—Mecklenburg County

★ △ ⇧ **ATRIUM HEALTH PINEVILLE (340098)**, 10628 Park Road, Zip 28210-8407; tel. 704/667-1000, **A**2 3 7 10 21 **F**3 13 17 18 20 22 24 26 28 29 30 31 40 42 44 45 49 50 56 60 64 68 70 73 74 75 76 77 78 79 81 82 84 85 86 87 90 91 92 93 100 107 111 114 115 118 119 120 121 123 126 129 130 132 135 145 146 147 148 149 156 167 168 169 **P**6 **S** Atrium Health, Inc., Charlotte, NC
Primary Contact: Alicia Campbell, Vice President, Facility Executive
Web address: www.carolinashealthcare.org/pineville
Control: Hospital district or authority, Government, Nonfederal **Service:** General medical and surgical

Staffed Beds: 307 **Admissions:** 21182 **Census:** 300 **Outpatient Visits:** 198051 **Births:** 2502 **Total Expense ($000):** 465374 **Payroll Expense ($000):** 216812 **Personnel:** 2054

⊞ **ATRIUM HEALTH UNIVERSITY CITY (340166)**, 8800 North Tryon Street, Zip 28262-3300, Mailing Address: P.O. Box 560727, Zip 28256-0727; tel. 704/863-6000, **A**1 2 3 10 **F**3 8 13 18 26 29 30 31 34 40 42 43 44 45 49 50 54 57 59 60 64 68 70 72 74 75 76 78 79 81 82 84 85 86 87 93 107 111 115 119 120 126 129 130 131 132 146 148 149 164 167 168 169 **P**6 **S** Atrium Health, Inc., Charlotte, NC
Primary Contact: William H. Leonard, President
CFO: Greg A Gombar, Chief Financial Officer
CIO: John Knox, Senior Vice President and Chief Information Officer
Web address: www.carolinashealthcare.org/university
Control: Hospital district or authority, Government, Nonfederal **Service:** General medical and surgical

Staffed Beds: 104 **Admissions:** 8171 **Census:** 118 **Outpatient Visits:** 186922 **Births:** 1583 **Total Expense ($000):** 219873 **Payroll Expense ($000):** 109374 **Personnel:** 1068

⊞ △ **ATRIUM HEALTH'S CAROLINAS MEDICAL CENTER (340113)**, 1000 Blythe Boulevard, Zip 28203-5871, Mailing Address: P.O. Box 32861, Zip 28232-2861; tel. 704/355-2000, (Includes CAROLINAS MEDICAL CENTER–MERCY, 2001 Vail Avenue, Charlotte, North Carolina, Zip 28207-1289, tel. 704/304-5000; Scott Jones, Vice President and Facility Executive; LEVINE CHILDREN'S HOSPITAL, 1000 Blythe Boulevard, Charlotte, North Carolina, Zip 28203, tel. 704/381-2000; Callie F. Dobbins, R.N., MSN, Vice President and Facility Executive) **A**1 2 3 5 7 8 10 **F**3 4 5 7 8 12 13 17 18 19 20 21 22 23 24 25 26 27 28 29 30 31 32 33 34 35 36 37 38 39 40 41 42 43 44 45 46 47 48 49 50 52 54 55 56 57 59 60 61 64 65 66 68 70 71 72 73 74 75 76 77 78 79 80 81 82 84 85 86 87 88 89 90 93 97 98 99 100 101 102 104 105 107 111 112 114 115 116 117 118 119 120 121 123 124 126 130 131 132 134 135 136 137 138 139 141 142 145 146 147 148 149 154 155 156 160 161 162 163 164 165 167 168 169 **P**6 **S** Atrium Health, Inc., Charlotte, NC
Primary Contact: D. Channing. Roush, Facility Executive
CHR: Jim Dunn, Ph.D., FACHE, Chief Human Resource Officer
Web address: www.carolinashealthcare.org/cmc
Control: Hospital district or authority, Government, Nonfederal **Service:** General medical and surgical

Staffed Beds: 1279 **Admissions:** 59182 **Census:** 1192 **Outpatient Visits:** 1230399 **Births:** 7191 **Total Expense ($000):** 3060749 **Payroll Expense ($000):** 1175492 **Personnel:** 11882

★ **CAROLINAS CONTINUECARE HOSPITAL AT PINEVILLE (342015)**, 10648 Park Road, Zip 28210; tel. 704/667-8050, **A**10 22 **F**1 3 20 29 34 35 45 46 59 65 74 75 77 82 83 85 91 96 130 148 **S** Community Hospital Corporation, Plano, TX
Primary Contact: Derek Murzyn, Market Chief Executive Officer
CFO: Joanne Tyo, Chief Financial Officer
CMO: Joseph Lang, M.D., Chief of Staff
CHR: Doug Gallagher, Director Human Resources
CNO: Teshia Davis, Chief Clinical Officer
Web address: www.continuecare.com/pineville
Control: Other not-for-profit (including NFP Corporation) **Service:** Acute long-term care hospital

Staffed Beds: 40 **Admissions:** 392 **Census:** 34 **Outpatient Visits:** 0 **Births:** 0 **Total Expense ($000):** 19765 **Payroll Expense ($000):** 9760 **Personnel:** 85

CAROLINAS MED CENTER–PINEVILLE See Carolinas Medical Center–Mercy

⊞ △ **CAROLINAS REHABILITATION (343026)**, 1100 Blythe Boulevard, Zip 28203-5864; tel. 704/355-4300, **A**1 3 7 10 **F**3 11 29 30 31 34 35 36 50 53 54 55 57 58 59 60 64 65 68 74 75 78 79 82 84 86 87 90 91 92 93 94 95 96 119 129 130 131 132 143 144 146 147 148 149 150 154 157 **P**1 2 3 4 5 6 7 8 **S** Atrium Health, Inc., Charlotte, NC
Primary Contact: Robert G. Larrison, President
CFO: William Hopkins, Director Finance
CMO: William Bockenek, M.D., Chief Medical Officer
CHR: Deonca Leach, Director, Human Resources
CNO: Susan Chase, Vice President
Web address: www.carolinashealthcare.org/rehabilitation
Control: Other not-for-profit (including NFP Corporation) **Service:** Rehabilitation

Staffed Beds: 150 **Admissions:** 2906 **Census:** 121 **Outpatient Visits:** 93862 **Births:** 0 **Total Expense ($000):** 127120 **Payroll Expense ($000):** 55922 **Personnel:** 828

⊞ **NOVANT HEALTH BALLANTYNE MEDICAL CENTER (340195)**, 10905 Providence Road West, Zip 28277; tel. 980/488-4000, (Nonreporting) **A**1 10 **S** Novant Health, Winston Salem, NC
Primary Contact: Joy Greear, President and Chief Operating Officer
COO: Benjamin Brodersen, President and Chief Operating Officer
CFO: Geoffrey Gardner, Senior Vice President Operational Finance and Revenue Cycle
CMO: Pamela A. Oliver, M.D., Executive Vice President and Chief Medical Officer
CIO: Onyeka Nchege, Executive Vice President and Chief Digital and Information Officer
CHR: Mary Bell, Vice President People and Culture
CNO: Michael Vaccaro, Senior Vice President Nursing
Web address: https://www.novanthealth.org/locations/medical-centers/ballantyne-medical-center/
Control: Other not-for-profit (including NFP Corporation) **Service:** General medical and surgical

Staffed Beds: 36

Hospitals, U.S. / NORTH CAROLINA

★ **NOVANT HEALTH CHARLOTTE ORTHOPAEDIC HOSPITAL (340153)**, 1901 Randolph Road, Zip 28207-1195; tel. 704/316-2000, (Nonreporting) **A**10 **S** Novant Health, Winston Salem, NC
Primary Contact: Jamie Feinour, President and Chief Operating Officer
CMO: Thomas Zweng, Executive Vice President and Chief Medical Officer
CIO: David B Garrett, Senior Vice President and Chief Information Officer
Web address: www.novanthealth.org
Control: Other not-for-profit (including NFP Corporation) **Service**: Orthopedic

Staffed Beds: 15

NOVANT HEALTH MINT HILL MEDICAL CENTER (340190), 8201 Healthcare Loop, Zip 28215-7072; tel. 980/302-1000, (Nonreporting) **A**1 2 10 **S** Novant Health, Winston Salem, NC
Primary Contact: Joy Greear, President and Chief Operating Officer
Web address: https://www.novanthealth.org
Control: Other not-for-profit (including NFP Corporation) **Service**: General medical and surgical

Staffed Beds: 36

NOVANT HEALTH PRESBYTERIAN MEDICAL CENTER (340053), 200 Hawthorne Lane, Zip 28204-2528, Mailing Address: P.O. Box 33549, Zip 28233-3549; tel. 704/384-4000, (Includes PRESBYTERIAN HEMBY CHILDREN'S HOSPITAL, 200 Hawthorne Lane, Charlotte, North Carolina, Zip 28204-2515, tel. 704/384-5134) (Total facility includes 6 beds in nursing home-type unit) **A**1 2 3 10 **F**3 7 12 17 18 19 20 21 22 23 24 26 28 29 30 31 32 34 35 37 38 40 41 43 44 45 46 47 48 49 51 53 55 57 58 59 61 63 64 65 66 68 69 70 71 72 74 75 76 77 78 79 80 81 82 84 85 86 87 88 89 90 93 96 98 99 100 102 104 105 107 108 110 111 115 116 117 118 119 120 121 123 124 126 128 130 131 132 134 136 142 143 145 146 147 148 149 150 153 154 156 164 165 167 169 **S** Novant Health, Winston Salem, NC
Primary Contact: Saad Ehtisham, FACHE, Senior Vice President and President Novant Health Presbyterian Medical Center & Greater Charlotte Ma
CMO: Thomas Zweng, Executive Vice President and Chief Medical Officer
CIO: David B Garrett, Senior Vice President Information Technology
Web address: www.novanthealth.org
Control: Other not-for-profit (including NFP Corporation) **Service**: General medical and surgical

Staffed Beds: 588 **Admissions**: 24554 **Census**: 482 **Outpatient Visits**: 238202 **Births**: 5897 **Total Expense ($000)**: 1304425 **Payroll Expense ($000)**: 377050 **Personnel**: 3179

CHEROKEE—Swain County

CHEROKEE INDIAN HOSPITAL (340156), 1 Hospital Road, Zip 28719; tel. 828/497-9163, (Nonreporting) **A**1 3 10
Primary Contact: Casey Cooper, Chief Executive Officer
COO: Beth Greene, Chief Operating Officer
CFO: Chrissy Arch, Chief Financial Officer
CMO: Michael E Toedt, M.D., Director Clinical Services
CIO: Anthony Taylor, Manager Information Technology
Web address: www.cherokeehospital.org
Control: Other not-for-profit (including NFP Corporation) **Service**: General medical and surgical

Staffed Beds: 15

CLINTON—Sampson County

SAMPSON REGIONAL MEDICAL CENTER (340024), 607 Beaman Street, Zip 28328-2697, Mailing Address: P.O. Box 260, Zip 28329-0260; tel. 910/592-8511, **A**1 3 5 10 12 13 **F**3 7 13 14 15 29 34 35 40 45 50 51 59 64 70 75 76 77 79 81 82 85 86 87 89 93 107 110 111 114 115 119 130 132 133 144 146 154
Primary Contact: Shawn Howerton, M.D., Chief Executive Officer and President, Medical Staff
COO: Geraldine H Shipp, Director of Risk Management
CFO: Jerry Heinzman, Senior Vice President and Chief Financial Officer
CMO: Shawn Howerton, M.D., Chief Executive Officer and President, Medical Staff
CIO: Kelly Lucas, Chief Information Officer
CHR: Michael W. Gilpin, Vice President Human Resources
Web address: www.sampsonrmc.org
Control: County, Government, Nonfederal **Service**: General medical and surgical

Staffed Beds: 67 **Admissions**: 2419 **Census**: 23 **Outpatient Visits**: 138759 **Births**: 397 **Total Expense ($000)**: 70112 **Payroll Expense ($000)**: 30462 **Personnel**: 468

CLYDE—Haywood County

HAYWOOD REGIONAL MEDICAL CENTER (340184), 262 Leroy George Drive, Zip 28721-7430; tel. 828/456-7311, (Nonreporting) **A**1 2 3 10 **S** Lifepoint Health, Brentwood, TN
Primary Contact: Chris Brown, Chief Executive Officer
CFO: Rose Coyne, Interim CFO
CMO: Tyson Smith, M.D., Chief Medical Officer
CIO: Greg Copen, Chief Information Officer
CHR: Janet Millsaps, Vice President Human Resources
Web address: www.haymed.org
Control: Hospital district or authority, Government, Nonfederal **Service**: General medical and surgical

Staffed Beds: 146

COLUMBUS—Polk County

△ **ST. LUKE'S HOSPITAL (341322)**, 101 Hospital Drive, Zip 28722-6418; tel. 828/894-3311, (Nonreporting) **A**1 7 10 18 **S** Atrium Health, Inc., Charlotte, NC
Primary Contact: Alex Bell, Interim Chief Executive Officer
CFO: Elizabeth Presnell, Assistant Vice President of Finance
CMO: James Holleman, M.D., Chief of Staff
CIO: Nick Whichard, Chief Information Officer
CHR: Amy Norville, Vice President Support Services
CNO: Katherine Hefner, MSN, Chief Nursing Officer
Web address: www.saintlukeshospital.com
Control: Other not-for-profit (including NFP Corporation) **Service**: General medical and surgical

Staffed Beds: 35

CONCORD—Cabarrus County

△ **ATRIUM HEALTH CABARRUS (340001)**, 920 Church Street North, Zip 28025-2983; tel. 704/403-3000, **A**1 2 3 5 7 10 **F**3 5 6 8 9 11 12 13 15 17 18 20 22 24 26 28 29 30 31 32 34 35 36 38 40 42 43 44 45 46 47 48 49 50 54 55 56 57 58 59 60 61 64 65 68 70 71 72 73 74 75 76 77 78 79 80 81 82 84 85 86 87 89 92 93 94 96 97 98 100 101 102 103 104 105 107 110 111 114 115 116 117 118 119 120 121 123 124 126 130 131 132 135 146 147 148 149 150 154 156 164 165 167 168 169 **P**6 **S** Atrium Health, Inc., Charlotte, NC
Primary Contact: Asha Rodriguez, Vice President and Facility Executive
COO: Bill Hubbard, Vice President, Operations
CFO: Rodney Ball, Vice President Finance
CIO: Lisa Sykes, Manager, Information Services
CHR: Lesley Chambless, Assistant Vice President Workforce Relations
Web address: www.carolinashealthcare.org/northeast
Control: Hospital district or authority, Government, Nonfederal **Service**: General medical and surgical

Staffed Beds: 526 **Admissions**: 29462 **Census**: 405 **Outpatient Visits**: 431807 **Births**: 2801 **Total Expense ($000)**: 727335 **Payroll Expense ($000)**: 332121 **Personnel**: 3106

DANBURY—Stokes County

★ **LIFEBRITE COMMUNITY HOSPITAL OF STOKES (341317)**, 1570 NC 8 & 89 Highway North, Zip 27016, Mailing Address: P.O. Box 10, Zip 27016-0010; tel. 336/593-2831, (Nonreporting) **A**10 18 21 **S** LifeBrite Hospital Group, LLC, Lilburn, GA
Primary Contact: Pamela P. Tillman, Administrator
COO: Samantha Freeman-Brown, Assistant Administrator, Respiratory Director
CMO: Kirk S. Sanders, M.D., Chief of Staff
CIO: Ada Ashley, HIM Director
CHR: Shannon Manring, Director Human Resources
CNO: Pamela P. Tillman, Administrator
Web address: www.lifebritestokes.com
Control: Corporation, Investor-owned (for-profit) **Service**: General medical and surgical

Staffed Beds: 65

Hospitals, U.S. / NORTH CAROLINA

DUNN—Harnett County

☒ **HARNETT HEALTH SYSTEM (340071)**, 800 Tilghman Drive, Zip 28334–5599, Mailing Address: P.O. Box 1706, Zip 28335–1706; tel. 910/892–1000, (Includes CENTRAL HARNETT HOSPITAL, 215 Brightwater Drive, Lillington, North Carolina, Zip 27546, tel. 910/892–1000) (Nonreporting) **A**1 3 5 10 12 13 **S** Cape Fear Valley Health System, Fayetteville, NC
Primary Contact: Cory Hess, President and Chief Executive Officer
COO: Kenneth E Bryan, FACHE, President and Chief Executive Officer
CFO: Lynn Lambert, Chief Financial Officer
CIO: Tim Krieger, Director Information Systems
CHR: Sondra Davis, Vice President Human Resources & System Development
CNO: Vicki Allen, R.N., MS, Vice President Patient Care Services and Chief Nursing Officer
Web address: www.myharnetthealth.org/
Control: Other not–for–profit (including NFP Corporation) **Service**: General medical and surgical

Staffed Beds: 114

DURHAM—Durham County

☒ **DUKE REGIONAL HOSPITAL (340155)**, 3643 North Roxboro Street, Zip 27704–2763; tel. 919/470–4000, **A**1 3 5 10 19 **F**3 8 11 12 13 15 17 18 20 22 24 26 29 30 31 34 35 40 44 45 50 51 56 57 58 59 60 64 66 68 70 73 74 75 76 77 78 79 80 81 82 84 85 86 87 90 96 98 100 101 102 104 107 108 110 111 115 118 119 120 121 123 124 126 130 131 132 135 146 147 148 149 154 164 167 169 **P**6 **S** Duke University Health System, Durham, NC
Primary Contact: Devdutta Sangvai, M.D., President
COO: Jason A. Carter, Chief Operating Officer
CFO: Jonathan B Hoy, Chief Financial Officer
CMO: Adia Ross, M.D., M.P.H., Chief Medical Officer
CIO: Terry Mears, Director Information Systems
CHR: Dexter Nolley, Chief Human Resources Officer
CNO: Victoria K Orto, R.N., Chief Nursing and Patient Care Services Officer
Web address: www.dukehealth.org
Control: Other not–for–profit (including NFP Corporation) **Service**: General medical and surgical

Staffed Beds: 274 **Admissions**: 15866 **Census**: 274 **Outpatient Visits**: 236000 **Births**: 2710 **Total Expense ($000)**: 560647 **Payroll Expense ($000)**: 238545 **Personnel**: 2562

☒ **DUKE UNIVERSITY HOSPITAL (340030)**, 2301 Erwin Road, Zip 27705–4699, Mailing Address: P.O. Box 3814, Zip 27710–3708; tel. 919/684–8111, (Includes DUKE CHILDREN'S HOSPITAL & HEALTH CENTER, 2301 Erwin Road, Durham, North Carolina, Zip 27710–0001, PO Box 3708, Zip 27702, tel. 919/684–8111) **A**1 2 5 8 10 19 **F**3 6 7 9 11 12 13 15 17 18 19 20 21 22 23 24 25 26 27 28 29 30 31 32 34 35 36 37 39 40 41 43 44 45 46 47 48 49 50 54 55 56 57 58 59 60 61 64 65 66 68 70 72 73 74 75 76 77 78 79 80 81 82 84 85 86 87 88 89 91 92 93 94 96 97 99 100 101 102 103 104 107 108 110 111 112 114 115 116 117 118 119 120 121 123 124 126 129 130 131 132 135 136 137 138 139 140 141 142 143 145 146 147 148 149 154 155 156 157 164 167 169 **P**1 6 **S** Duke University Health System, Durham, NC
Primary Contact: Greg Pauly, President
COO: Mary Martin, FACHE, Chief Operating Officer
CFO: Sabrina Olsen, Chief Financial Officer
CMO: Lisa C Pickett, M.D., Chief Medical Officer
CIO: Jeffrey Ferranti, M.D., Chief Information Officer
CHR: Deborah Page, Chief Human Resources Officer
Web address: www.dukehealth.org
Control: Other not–for–profit (including NFP Corporation) **Service**: General medical and surgical

Staffed Beds: 1041 **Admissions**: 41549 **Census**: 906 **Outpatient Visits**: 1264297 **Births**: 3946 **Total Expense ($000)**: 3298986 **Payroll Expense ($000)**: 882812 **Personnel**: 12699

☒ **DURHAM VA HEALTH CARE SYSTEM**, 508 Fulton Street, Zip 27705–3897; tel. 919/286–0411, (Nonreporting) **A**1 3 5 **S** Department of Veterans Affairs, Washington, DC
Primary Contact: Alyshia Smith, R.N., Medical Center Director
COO: Sara Haigh, Associate Director
CFO: David Kuboushek, Chief, Fiscal Service
CMO: John D Shelburne, M.D., Chief of Staff
CIO: Toby Dickerson, Chief Information Resources Management Services
CHR: Jerry Freeman, Chief, Human Resources Management Services
Web address: www.durham.va.gov/
Control: Veterans Affairs, Government, federal **Service**: General medical and surgical

Staffed Beds: 286

☐ **NORTH CAROLINA SPECIALTY HOSPITAL (340049)**, 3916 Ben Franklin Boulevard, Zip 27704–2383, Mailing Address: PO Box 15819, Zip 27704–2383; tel. 919/956–9300, (Nonreporting) **A**1 10 **S** National Surgical Healthcare, Chicago, IL
Primary Contact: Randi L. Shults, Chief Executive Officer
CFO: Bill Wilson, Chief Financial Officer
CMO: David Musante, M.D., Medical Director
CHR: Sarah Bohlin, Human Resources Director
CNO: John Medlin, Chief Nursing Officer
Web address: www.ncspecialty.com
Control: Partnership, Investor–owned (for–profit) **Service**: Surgical

Staffed Beds: 18

☒ **SELECT SPECIALTY HOSPITAL–DURHAM (342018)**, 3643 North Roxboro Road, 6th Floor, Zip 27704–2702; tel. 984/569–4040, (Nonreporting) **A**1 10 **S** Select Medical Corporation, Mechanicsburg, PA
Primary Contact: Ian Hodge, Chief Executive Officer
CHR: Michael Stinson, Human Resources Coordinator
CNO: Cole Oren, R.N., Chief Nursing Officer
Web address: https://durham.selectspecialtyhospitals.com/
Control: Corporation, Investor–owned (for–profit) **Service**: Acute long–term care hospital

Staffed Beds: 30

VERITAS COLLABORATIVE, 4024 Stirrup Creek Drive, Zip 27703–9464; tel. 919/908–9730, (Nonreporting) **S** Veritas Collaborative, Durham, NC
Primary Contact: Cindy Skocik, Chief Operating Officer
Web address: https://veritascollaborative.com
Control: Partnership, Investor–owned (for–profit) **Service**: Psychiatric

Staffed Beds: 40

VERITAS COLLABORATIVE, 615 Douglas Street, Suite 500, Zip 27705–6616; tel. 919/908–9730, (Nonreporting) **S** Veritas Collaborative, Durham, NC
Primary Contact: Becca Eckstein, Executive Director
Web address: https://veritascollaborative.com
Control: Partnership, Investor–owned (for–profit) **Service**: Psychiatric

Staffed Beds: 25

EDEN—Rockingham County

★ ⇑ **UNC HEALTH ROCKINGHAM (340060)**, 117 East King's Highway, Zip 27288–5201; tel. 336/623–9711, (Total facility includes 79 beds in nursing home–type unit) **A**10 21 **F**3 6 11 13 15 18 29 30 34 35 36 38 40 44 45 46 48 49 50 54 56 57 59 64 65 67 68 70 74 75 76 77 78 79 81 84 85 86 87 89 91 93 101 102 107 108 110 111 115 116 117 119 128 130 131 143 144 146 147 148 149 154 157 164 167 169 **P**6 **S** UNC Health, Chapel Hill, NC
Primary Contact: Steven E. Eblin, Chief Executive Officer
CFO: LaTonya Brown, Interim Chief Operating Officer and Chief Financial Officer
CIO: Wade Williams, Chief Information Officer
CHR: Janine Eanes, Senior Human Resources Business Partner
CNO: JoAnn P. Smith, R.N., Chief Nursing Officer, and Vice President Patient Care Services
Web address: www.uncrockingham.org
Control: Other not–for–profit (including NFP Corporation) **Service**: General medical and surgical

Staffed Beds: 127 **Admissions**: 2087 **Census**: 91 **Outpatient Visits**: 60931 **Births**: 369 **Total Expense ($000)**: 65973 **Payroll Expense ($000)**: 27554 **Personnel**: 449

EDENTON—Chowan County

☒ **ECU HEALTH CHOWAN HOSPITAL (341318)**, 211 Virginia Road, Zip 27932–9668, Mailing Address: P.O. Box 629, Zip 27932–0629; tel. 252/482–8451, **A**1 3 10 18 **F**3 11 13 15 28 29 30 31 34 35 40 45 46 57 59 64 70 74 75 76 77 78 79 81 82 84 85 93 107 108 110 111 114 119 130 132 135 146 147 148 **S** ECU Health, Greenville, NC
Primary Contact: Brian Harvill, President
CMO: William Hope IV, Chief of Medical Staff
CIO: Brian White, Director Strategic Operations
CHR: Nicole Spell, Director Human Resources
CNO: Cindy Coker, Vice President, Patient Care Services
Web address: https://locations.ecuhealth.org/details/120
Control: Other not–for–profit (including NFP Corporation) **Service**: General medical and surgical

Staffed Beds: 19 **Admissions**: 1482 **Census**: 18 **Outpatient Visits**: 44465 **Births**: 328 **Total Expense ($000)**: 59012 **Payroll Expense ($000)**: 19019 **Personnel**: 289

Hospital, Medicare Provider Number, Address, Telephone, Approval, Facility, and Physician Codes, Health Care System

★ American Hospital Association (AHA) membership
☐ The Joint Commission accreditation
○ Healthcare Facilities Accreditation Program
◇ DNV Healthcare Inc. accreditation
⇑ Center for Improvement in Healthcare Quality Accreditation
△ Commission on Accreditation of Rehabilitation Facilities (CARF) accreditation

© 2025 AHA Guide

Hospitals, U.S. / NORTH CAROLINA

VIDANT CHOWAN HOSPITAL See ECU Health Chowan Hospital

ELIZABETH CITY—Pasquotank County

★ ⇑ **SENTARA ALBEMARLE MEDICAL CENTER (340109)**, 1144 North Road Street, Zip 27909–3473; tel. 252/335–0531, **A**2 10 21 **F**3 13 15 18 20 22 26 28 29 30 31 34 35 37 40 41 44 45 46 47 48 50 51 57 58 59 60 61 64 65 68 70 71 74 75 76 77 78 79 81 84 85 86 87 91 92 93 94 96 97 100 102 107 108 110 111 114 115 118 119 121 126 130 131 132 141 146 147 148 149 154 156 162 164 169 **S** Sentara Health, Virginia Beach, VA
Primary Contact: Teresa C. Watson, Division President
CFO: Craig Lewis, Chief Financial Officer
CMO: Charles Nicholson, Vice President, Medical Affairs
CHR: Deborah Ferguson, Director, Human Resources
CNO: JAIME CARROLL, R.N., Vice President Nursing
Web address: https://www.sentara.com/hospitalslocations/locations/new-sentara-albemarle-medical-center.aspx
Control: Other not–for–profit (including NFP Corporation) **Service**: General medical and surgical

Staffed Beds: 98 **Admissions**: 4670 **Census**: 60 **Outpatient Visits**: 140928
Births: 364 **Total Expense ($000)**: 165332 **Payroll Expense ($000)**: 50886
Personnel: 516

ELIZABETHTOWN—Bladen County

CAPE FEAR VALLEY BLADEN COUNTY HOSPITAL (341315), 501 South Poplar Street, Zip 28337–9375, Mailing Address: P.O. Box 398, Zip 28337–0398; tel. 910/862–5100, (Nonreporting) **A**1 10 18 **S** Cape Fear Valley Health System, Fayetteville, NC
Primary Contact: Spencer Cummings, President and Chief Executive Officer
CFO: Stephen Fife, President and Chief Financial Officer
CIO: Craig Kellum, Director Management Information Systems
CHR: Brenda E. Hubbard, Corporate Director, Human Resources
CNO: Traci R. Preston, Director of Nursing
Web address: https://www.capefearvalley.com/bladen/home.html
Control: County, Government, Nonfederal **Service**: General medical and surgical

Staffed Beds: 25

ELKIN—Surry County

HUGH CHATHAM HEALTH (340097), 180 Parkwood Drive, Zip 28621–2430, Mailing Address: P.O. Box 560, Zip 28621–0560; tel. 336/527–7000, **A**1 3 10 **F**3 11 13 15 26 28 29 30 34 35 36 40 44 49 50 53 57 59 62 64 68 70 74 75 76 77 79 81 83 85 87 93 94 100 101 102 104 107 108 110 111 114 115 119 125 130 132 143 144 146 147 148 149 154 156 167 169 **P**6
Primary Contact: Paul Hammes, Chief Executive Officer
COO: Mary Blackburn, Vice President Operations and Chief Practice Officer
CFO: Donald E Trippel, Chief Financial Officer
CMO: Dominick Carbone, M.D., Chief of Staff
CIO: Lee Powe, Director Management Information Systems
CHR: Kathy Poteate, Human Resources Manager
CNO: Paula Moore, R.N., Chief Clinical Officer
Web address: www.hughchatham.org
Control: Other not–for–profit (including NFP Corporation) **Service**: General medical and surgical

Staffed Beds: 81 **Admissions**: 2834 **Census**: 28 **Outpatient Visits**: 357655
Births: 388 **Total Expense ($000)**: 140225 **Payroll Expense ($000)**: 62156
Personnel: 880

HUGH CHATHAM MEMORIAL HOSPITAL See Hugh Chatham Health

FAYETTEVILLE—Cumberland County

△ **CAPE FEAR VALLEY MEDICAL CENTER (340028)**, 1638 Owen Drive, Zip 28304–3431, Mailing Address: P.O. Box 2000, Zip 28302–2000; tel. 910/615–4000, (Includes BEHAVIORAL HEALTH CARE OF CAPE FEAR VALLEY HEALTH SYSTEM, 711 Executive Pl, Fayetteville, North Carolina, Zip 28305–5193, 711 Executive Place, Zip 28301, tel. 910/615–3700; CAPE FEAR VALLEY REHABILITATION CENTER, 1638 Owen Drive, Fayetteville, North Carolina, Zip 28304, tel. 910/615–4000) (Nonreporting) **A**1 2 3 5 7 8 10 12 13 19 **S** Cape Fear Valley Health System, Fayetteville, NC
Primary Contact: Michael Nagowski, Chief Executive Officer
COO: Daniel R Weatherly, Chief Operating Officer
CFO: Sandra Williams, Chief Financial Officer
CMO: Samuel A Fleishman, M.D., Chief Medical Officer
CIO: Phillip E. Wood Jr, Chief Information Officer
CNO: Deborah Marshburn, Chief Nursing Executive
Web address: www.capefearvalley.com
Control: Other not–for–profit (including NFP Corporation) **Service**: General medical and surgical

Staffed Beds: 634

CUMBERLAND HOSPITAL See Behavioral Health Care of Cape Fear Valley Health System

FAYETTEVILLE VETERANS AFFAIRS MEDICAL CENTER, 2300 Ramsey Street, Zip 28301–3899; tel. 910/488–2120, (Nonreporting) **A**1 3 5 **S** Department of Veterans Affairs, Washington, DC
Primary Contact: Marri Fryar, Executive Director
COO: James Galkowski, Associate Director for Operations
CFO: Patrick Bullard, Chief Financial Officer
CMO: Greg Antoine, M.D., Chief of Staff
CIO: Kenneth Williams, Chief Information Officer
CHR: Joseph Whaley, Chief, Human Resources Management Service
CNO: Joyce Alexander-Hines, R.N., MSN, Associate Director, Patient Care Services
Web address: www.fayettevillenc.va.gov
Control: Veterans Affairs, Government, federal **Service**: General medical and surgical

Staffed Beds: 52

HIGHSMITH–RAINEY SPECIALTY HOSPITAL (342014), 150 Robeson Street, Zip 28301–5570; tel. 910/615–1000, (Nonreporting) **A**1 10 **S** Cape Fear Valley Health System, Fayetteville, NC
Primary Contact: Michael Tart, President
Web address: www.capefearvalley.com
Control: Other not–for–profit (including NFP Corporation) **Service**: Acute long–term care hospital

Staffed Beds: 66

SOUTHEASTERN REGIONAL REHABILITATION CENTER See Cape Fear Valley Rehabilitation Center

FORT BRAGG—Cumberland County

WOMACK ARMY MEDICAL CENTER, 2817 Reilly Road, Zip 28310–7302; tel. 910/907–6000, (Nonreporting) **A**1 3 5 **S** Department of the Army, Office of the Surgeon General, Falls Church, VA
Primary Contact: Colonel David R. Zinnante, Commander
CIO: Mary Peters, Chief Information Officer
Web address: https://womack.tricare.mil/
Control: Army, Government, federal **Service**: General medical and surgical

Staffed Beds: 156

FRANKLIN—Macon County

ANGEL MEDICAL CENTER (341326), 124 One Center Court, Zip 28734–0192, Mailing Address: P.O. Box 1209, Zip 28744–0569; tel. 828/524–8411, **A**1 3 10 18 **F**3 15 18 28 29 34 35 38 40 45 49 50 54 56 57 64 68 70 71 77 79 81 85 93 97 107 108 110 111 115 119 124 127 128 131 133 135 143 144 146 148 149 154 155 156 167 **P**7 **S** HCA Healthcare, Nashville, TN
Primary Contact: Clint Kendall, R.N., Chief Executive Officer and Chief Nursing Officer
COO: Martin Wadewitz, Chief Operations Officer/Vice President, Operations
CIO: Ed Coye, Director Information Technology Mission Health System Hospitals
CHR: Teresa Mallonee, Director Human Resources
Web address: www.angelmed.org
Control: Corporation, Investor–owned (for–profit) **Service**: General medical and surgical

Staffed Beds: 35 **Admissions**: 1731 **Census**: 18 **Outpatient Visits**: 66081
Births: 0 **Total Expense ($000)**: 53705 **Payroll Expense ($000)**: 19425

GARNER—Wake County

☐ **STRATEGIC BEHAVIORAL HEALTH, LLC (344035)**, 3200 Waterfield Drive, Zip 27529–7727; tel. 919/800–4400, (Nonreporting) **A**1 10 **S** Strategic Behavioral Health, LLC, Memphis, TN
Primary Contact: Andre Cromwell, Chief Executive Officer
CMO: Karen Miles, M.D., Medical Director
CHR: Christina Meeker, Director Human Resources
CNO: Shawanna Royal, R.N., Director Nursing
Web address: www.sbcraleigh.com/
Control: Corporation, Investor–owned (for–profit) **Service**: Children's hospital psychiatric

Staffed Beds: 50

Hospitals, U.S. / NORTH CAROLINA

GASTONIA—Gaston County

★ **CAROMONT REGIONAL MEDICAL CENTER (340032)**, 2525 Court Drive, Zip 28054–2140, Mailing Address: P.O. Box 1747, Zip 28053–1747; tel. 704/834–2000, **A**1 2 3 10 **F**3 13 15 17 18 20 22 24 26 28 29 30 31 34 35 40 41 42 43 44 45 46 47 48 49 50 54 57 58 59 60 64 67 68 70 71 72 73 74 75 76 78 79 81 82 83 87 89 92 93 94 96 98 99 100 102 107 108 110 111 114 115 117 118 119 120 121 123 124 126 129 130 131 132 135 146 148 149 154 167 169
Primary Contact: Chris Peek, Chief Executive Officer
COO: Kathleen Besson, Executive Vice President and Chief Operating Officer
CFO: David O'Connor, Executive Vice President and Chief Financial Officer
CMO: Todd Davis, M.D., Executive Vice President, Chief Medical Officer
CIO: Robin Lynn Lang, Vice President, Chief Information Officer
CHR: Joel Riddle, Senior Director Human Resources
CNO: Scott E. Wells, MSN, R.N., Vice President Patient Care Services
Web address: www.caromonthealth.org
Control: Other not-for-profit (including NFP Corporation) **Service**: General medical and surgical

Staffed Beds: 476 **Admissions**: 22662 **Census**: 339 **Outpatient Visits**: 294026 **Births**: 1830 **Total Expense ($000)**: 596307 **Payroll Expense ($000)**: 274783 **Personnel**: 2717

GOLDSBORO—Wayne County

□ **CHERRY HOSPITAL (344026)**, 1401 West Ash Street, Zip 27530–1057; tel. 919/947–7000, (Nonreporting) **A**1 3 10
Primary Contact: Tim Miller, Chief Executive Officer
CFO: Susie Sherrod Sanders, Chief Financial Officer
CMO: Jim Mayo, M.D., Clinical Director
CIO: Mike Letchworth, Manager Information Systems
CHR: Carol Thornton, Director Human Resources
CNO: Debbie Wall, Chief Nursing Officer
Web address: https://www.ncdhhs.gov/divisions/dsohf/cherry-hospital
Control: State, Government, Nonfederal **Service**: Psychiatric

Staffed Beds: 243

★ **UNC HEALTH WAYNE (340010)**, 2700 Wayne Memorial Drive, Zip 27534–9494, Mailing Address: P.O. Box 8001, Zip 27533–8001; tel. 919/736–1110, **A**1 5 10 **F**3 8 13 15 18 20 22 28 29 30 31 34 35 39 40 45 47 49 50 57 58 59 60 64 66 68 70 71 73 74 75 76 77 78 79 81 85 86 87 89 92 93 96 101 102 107 108 110 111 114 118 119 126 129 130 132 145 146 147 148 156 167 **S** UNC Health, Chapel Hill, NC
Primary Contact: Jessie Tucker III, Ph.D., FACHE, President and Chief Executive Officer
COO: Howard Whitfield, Chief Operating Officer
CFO: Rebecca W Craig, Vice President and Chief Financial Officer
CIO: Lori Cole, Director Information Technology
Web address: https://www.wayneunc.org/locations/profile/wayne-unc-health-care/
Control: Other not-for-profit (including NFP Corporation) **Service**: General medical and surgical

Staffed Beds: 230 **Admissions**: 9264 **Census**: 133 **Outpatient Visits**: 153629 **Births**: 1212 **Total Expense ($000)**: 281439 **Payroll Expense ($000)**: 124344 **Personnel**: 1476

GREENSBORO—Guilford County

CHARTER GREENSBORO HEALTH SYST See Behavioral Health Center

★ △ **CONE HEALTH MOSES CONE HOSPITAL (340091)**, 1200 North Elm Street, Zip 27401–1020; tel. 336/832–7000, (Includes ANNIE PENN HOSPITAL, 618 South Main Street, Reidsville, North Carolina, Zip 27320–5094, tel. 336/951–4000; Cynthia B Farrand, President; BEHAVIORAL HEALTH CENTER, 700 Walter Reed Drive, Greensboro, North Carolina, Zip 27403–1129, tel. 336/832–9600; CONE HEALTH, 1200 North Elm Street, Greensboro, North Carolina, Zip 27401, tel. 336/832–7000; Judith A Schanel, R.N., MSN, FACHE, Chief Operating Officer; WESLEY LONG COMMUNITY HOSPITAL, 501 North Elam Avenue, Greensboro, North Carolina, Zip 27403, tel. 336/832–1000; Paul A Jeffrey, President; WOMEN'S HOSPITAL OF GREENSBORO, 801 Green Valley Road, Greensboro, North Carolina, Zip 27408, tel. 336/832–6500) (Total facility includes 92 beds in nursing home–type unit) **A**1 3 5 7 10 19 **F**1 3 5 7 8 12 13 15 17 18 20 22 24 26 28 29 30 31 32 34 35 36 37 39 40 41 43 44 45 46 47 49 50 53 54 55 56 57 58 59 60 61 63 64 65 66 68 70 71 72 74 75 76 77 78 79 81 82 83 84 85 86 87 88 89 90 92 93 95 96 97 98 99 100 101 102 103 104 105 107 108 110 111 115 116 117 118 119 120 121 123 124 126 127 128 129 130 131 132 134 135 144 145 146 147 148 149 152 153 154 156 167 **S** Cone Health, Greensboro, NC
Primary Contact: Preston W. Hammock, President
CFO: Andy Barrow, Chief Financial Officer
CMO: William Bowman, M.D., Vice President Medical Affairs
CIO: Steve Horsley, Vice President and Chief Information Officer
CHR: Noel F Burt, Ph.D., Chief Human Resources Officer
Web address: www.conehealth.com/locations/moses-cone-hospital/
Control: Other not-for-profit (including NFP Corporation) **Service**: General medical and surgical

Staffed Beds: 875 **Admissions**: 41323 **Census**: 483 **Outpatient Visits**: 964384 **Births**: 5951 **Total Expense ($000)**: 2426231 **Payroll Expense ($000)**: 896279 **Personnel**: 9806

GREENSBORO HOSPITAL See Women's Hospital of Greensboro

★ **KINDRED HOSPITAL–GREENSBORO (342012)**, 2401 Southside Boulevard, Zip 27406–3311; tel. 336/271–2800, (Nonreporting) **A**1 10 **S** ScionHealth, Louisville, KY
Primary Contact: Preston Bryant, Chief Executive Officer
CFO: Anthony Grate, Controller
CMO: Saad Amin, Medical Director Hospital
CIO: Little Shuford, Health Information Manager
CNO: Anne Correll, Chief Clinical Officer
Web address: https://www.kindredhospitals.com/locations/ltac/kindred-hospital-greensboro
Control: Corporation, Investor-owned (for-profit) **Service**: Acute long–term care hospital

Staffed Beds: 101

MOSES H. CONE MEMORIAL HOSPITAL See Cone Health Moses Cone Hospital

MOSES H. CONE MEMORIAL HOSPITAL See Cone Health

★ **SELECT SPECIALTY HOSPITAL–GREENSBORO (342020)**, 1200 North Elm Street, 5th Floor, Zip 27401–1004; tel. 336/832–8571, (Nonreporting) **A**1 10 **S** Select Medical Corporation, Mechanicsburg, PA
Primary Contact: Bradley Jordan, Chief Executive Officer
CHR: Karen Tracey, Chief Human Resources
CNO: Robin Clark, Chief Nursing Officer
Web address: www.selectspecialtyhospitals.com/company/locations/greensboro.aspx
Control: Corporation, Investor-owned (for-profit) **Service**: Acute long–term care hospital

Staffed Beds: 30

Hospitals, U.S. / NORTH CAROLINA

GREENVILLE—Pitt County

✠ △ **ECU HEALTH MEDICAL CENTER (340040)**, 2100 Stantonsburg Road, Zip 27834–2818, Mailing Address: P.O. Box 6028, Zip 27835–6028; tel. 252/847–4100, (Includes ECU HEALTH BEAUFORT HOSPITAL, 628 East 12th Street, Washington, North Carolina, Zip 27889–3409, tel. 252/975–4100; Dennis Campbell II, R.N., President; JAMES AND CONNIE MAYNARD CHILDREN'S HOSPITAL, 2101 Stantonsburg Road, Greenville, North Carolina, Zip 27834–2817, tel. 252/847–5712; UNIVERSITY HEALTH SYSTEMS CHILDREN'S HOSPITAL, 2100 Stantonsburg Road, Greenville, North Carolina, Zip 27834–2818, PO Box 6028, Zip 27835–6028, tel. 252/847–4100) **A**1 2 3 5 7 8 10 **F**3 7 8 11 12 13 14 15 17 18 19 20 21 22 23 24 25 26 27 28 29 30 31 35 37 38 40 41 43 44 45 46 47 48 49 50 51 55 58 60 61 68 70 72 73 74 76 78 79 81 83 84 86 87 88 89 90 91 92 93 94 95 98 100 101 102 103 107 108 110 111 115 117 118 124 129 130 138 139 145 146 148 154 155 163 164 168 169 **S** ECU Health, Greenville, NC
Primary Contact: Jay Briley, FACHE, President
CMO: Paul Shackelford, M.D., Chief Medical Officer
CHR: Tyree Walker, Chief Human Resources Officer
Web address: https://locations.ecuhealth.org/Details/163
Control: Other not–for–profit (including NFP Corporation) **Service**: General medical and surgical

Staffed Beds: 913 **Admissions**: 35862 **Census**: 641 **Outpatient Visits**: 298353 **Births**: 3916 **Total Expense ($000)**: 1541981 **Payroll Expense ($000)**: 470563

VIDANT MEDICAL CENTER See ECU Health Medical Center

□ **WALTER B. JONES ALCOHOL AND DRUG ABUSE TREATMENT CENTER (344033)**, 2577 West Fifth Street, Zip 27834–7813; tel. 252/830–3426, (Nonreporting) **A**1 10
Primary Contact: Ben Gregory, Chief Executive Officer
CFO: Roy Carlton, Chief Financial Officer
CMO: Sonya Longest, M.D., Chief Medical Officer
CIO: Jed Hayn, Chief Information Officer
CHR: Amy Marion, Chief Human Resource Officer
CNO: Linda Roy, R.N., Chief Nursing Officer
Web address: www.ncdhhs.gov
Control: State, Government, Nonfederal **Service**: Substance Use Disorder

Staffed Beds: 80

HENDERSON—Vance County

✠ **MARIA PARHAM HEALTH, DUKE LIFEPOINT HEALTHCARE (340132)**, 566 Ruin Creek Road, Zip 27536–2927; tel. 252/438–4143, (Nonreporting) **A**1 2 3 5 10 **S** Lifepoint Health, Brentwood, TN
Primary Contact: Bert Beard, Chief Executive Officer
CFO: Jim Chatman, Chief Financial Officer
CMO: Shauna Guthrie, M.D., Chief Medical Officer
CIO: Randy Williams, Director Management Information Systems
Web address: www.mariaparham.com
Control: Other not–for–profit (including NFP Corporation) **Service**: General medical and surgical

Staffed Beds: 116

HENDERSONVILLE—Henderson County

✠ **ADVENTHEALTH HENDERSONVILLE (340023)**, 100 Hospital Drive, Zip 28792–5272; tel. 828/684–8501, (Nonreporting) **A**1 2 3 10 19 **S** AdventHealth, Altamonte Springs, FL
Primary Contact: Brandon M. Nudd, President and Chief Executive Officer
COO: Beverly Ann Knapp, Chief Operating Officer
CFO: Ella Stenstrom, Vice President and Chief Financial Officer
CMO: Teresa Herbert, M.D., Chief Medical Officer
CIO: Lee Strickland, Regional Director Information Technology
CHR: Sharon J Campbell, Director, Human Resources
CNO: Roland Eugene Joy Jr, Vice President and Chief Nursing Officer
Web address: www.adventhealth.com/hospital/adventhealth-hendersonville
Control: Other not–for–profit (including NFP Corporation) **Service**: General medical and surgical

Staffed Beds: 103

★ ⇑ **UNC HEALTH PARDEE (340017)**, 800 North Justice Street, Zip 28791–3410; tel. 828/696–1000, (Nonreporting) **A**2 3 10 19 21 **S** UNC Health, Chapel Hill, NC
Primary Contact: James M. Kirby II, President and Chief Executive Officer
CFO: Andrew R. Wampler, Chief Financial Officer
CMO: Robert Kiskaddon, M.D., Chief Medical Officer
Web address: https://www.pardeehospital.org/
Control: County, Government, Nonfederal **Service**: General medical and surgical

Staffed Beds: 158

HICKORY—Catawba County

✠ △ **CATAWBA VALLEY MEDICAL CENTER (340143)**, 810 Fairgrove Church Road SE, Zip 28602–9643; tel. 828/326–3000, (Nonreporting) **A**1 7 10
Primary Contact: Dennis B. Johnson, Chief Executive Officer
CFO: Pamela J Gallagher, Chief Financial Officer
CMO: Andrew Chesson, Chief Medical Officer
CIO: Tim Blanchat, Chief Information Officer
CHR: Phyllis M. Johnston, Vice President
Web address: www.catawbavalleymc.org
Control: County, Government, Nonfederal **Service**: General medical and surgical

Staffed Beds: 253

✠ **FRYE REGIONAL MEDICAL CENTER (340116)**, 420 North Center Street, Zip 28601–5049, Mailing Address: 1950 11th Street Crt. NW, Zip 28601; tel. 828/315–5000, (Includes FRYE REGIONAL MEDICAL CENTER–SOUTH CAMPUS, 1 3rd Street NW, Hickory, North Carolina, Zip 28601–6134, 420 North Center St., Zip 28603, tel. 828/315–5777) (Nonreporting) **A**1 10 19 **S** Lifepoint Health, Brentwood, TN
Primary Contact: Philip Greene, M.D., Chief Executive Officer
CFO: Jamey Stoner, Chief Financial Officer
CNO: Michelle Dickerson, Chief Nursing Officer
Web address: www.fryemedctr.com
Control: Corporation, Investor–owned (for–profit) **Service**: General medical and surgical

Staffed Beds: 271

TEN BROECK HOSPITAL See Frye Regional Medical Center–South Campus

HIGH POINT—Guilford County

✠ △ **ATRIUM HEALTH WAKE FOREST BAPTIST HIGH POINT MEDICAL CENTER (340004)**, 601 North Elm Street, Zip 27262–4398, Mailing Address: P.O. Box HP–5, Zip 27261–1899; tel. 336/878–6000, **A**1 2 3 7 10 19 **F**3 4 8 12 13 15 17 18 20 22 24 26 28 29 30 31 32 34 35 36 38 39 40 44 45 47 48 49 50 53 54 55 57 58 59 60 61 66 67 68 70 73 74 75 76 77 78 79 81 82 84 85 86 87 89 90 91 92 93 96 98 100 101 102 104 107 108 109 110 111 114 115 116 117 118 119 120 121 123 124 126 130 131 132 135 145 146 147 148 149 154 167 **P**6 **S** Atrium Health, Inc., Charlotte, NC
Primary Contact: James Hoekstra, M.D., President
COO: Gregory W Taylor, M.D., Vice President and Chief Operating Officer
CMO: L Dale Williams, M.D., Vice President and Chief Medical Director
CIO: Nancy Waters, Interim Chief Information Officer
CHR: Katherine Burns, Vice President Human Resources
CNO: Tammi Erving–Mengel, R.N., MSN, Vice President, Chief Nursing Officer
Web address: www.highpointregional.com
Control: Other not–for–profit (including NFP Corporation) **Service**: General medical and surgical

Staffed Beds: 277 **Admissions**: 14364 **Census**: 178 **Outpatient Visits**: 198642 **Births**: 1342 **Total Expense ($000)**: 391957 **Payroll Expense ($000)**: 171741 **Personnel**: 1459

HIGHLANDS—Macon County

✠ **HIGHLANDS–CASHIERS HOSPITAL (341316)**, 190 Hospital Drive, Zip 28741–7600, Mailing Address: P O Drawer 190, Zip 28741–0190; tel. 828/526–1200, (Nonreporting) **A**1 10 18 **S** HCA Healthcare, Nashville, TN
Primary Contact: Tom Neal, Chief Executive Officer and Chief Nursing Officer
CFO: Lena Cochran, Director of Finance
CHR: Ruby Rowland, Strategic Partner
CNO: Cindy Pierson, Interim Chief Nursing Officer
Web address: www.hchospital.org
Control: Other not–for–profit (including NFP Corporation) **Service**: General medical and surgical

Staffed Beds: 24

HUNTERSVILLE—Mecklenburg County

✠ **NOVANT HEALTH HUNTERSVILLE MEDICAL CENTER (340183)**, 10030 Gilead Road, Zip 28078–7545, Mailing Address: P.O. Box 3508, Zip 28070–3508; tel. 704/316–4000, (Nonreporting) **A**1 2 3 5 10 **S** Novant Health, Winston Salem, NC
Primary Contact: Mike Riley, President and Chief Operating Officer
CMO: Thomas Zweng, Executive Vice President and Chief Medical Officer
CIO: David B Garrett, Senior Vice President and Chief Information Officer
CNO: Katrina King, R.N., Senior Director, Nursing
Web address: www.novanthealth.org
Control: Other not–for–profit (including NFP Corporation) **Service**: General medical and surgical

Staffed Beds: 91

Hospitals, U.S. / NORTH CAROLINA

JACKSONVILLE—Onslow County

☐ **BRYNN MARR HOSPITAL (344016)**, 192 Village Drive, Zip 28546–7299; tel. 910/577–1400, (Nonreporting) **A**1 10 **S** Universal Health Services, Inc., King of Prussia, PA
Primary Contact: Cynthia Waun, Chief Executive Officer
CFO: David Warmerdam, Chief Financial Officer
CMO: Ashraf Mikhail, M.D., Medical Director
CHR: Jennifer Gier, Director Human Resources
CNO: Sheila Maraan, Director of Nursing
Web address: www.brynnmarr.org
Control: Corporation, Investor–owned (for–profit) **Service**: Psychiatric

Staffed Beds: 99

✠ **ONSLOW MEMORIAL HOSPITAL (340042)**, 317 Western Boulevard, Zip 28546–6379, Mailing Address: P.O. Box 1358, Zip 28541–1358; tel. 910/577–2345, (Nonreporting) **A**1 2 10 20 **S** UNC Health, Chapel Hill, NC
Primary Contact: Penney Burlingame Deal, FACHE, R.N., Chief Executive Officer
CMO: Steven Spencer, M.D., Chief Medical Officer
CIO: Rob Lowe, Director, Healthcare Information Management
CHR: Taylor Flowers, Senior Vice President Human Resources
CNO: Rose Morgan, MS, Interim Chief Nursing Officer
Web address: www.onslow.org
Control: Hospital district or authority, Government, Nonfederal **Service**: General medical and surgical

Staffed Beds: 149

JEFFERSON—Ashe County

✠ **ASHE MEMORIAL HOSPITAL (341325)**, 200 Hospital Avenue, Zip 28640–9244; tel. 336/846–7101, (Nonreporting) **A**1 10 18 **S** Novant Health, Winston Salem, NC
Primary Contact: Brian Yates, Chief Executive Officer
COO: Joe Thore, Chief Operating Officer
CFO: Charles Wright, Chief Financial Officer
CMO: Jayne Leonard, M.D., Family Medicine
CIO: BJ Maynard, Chief Information Officer
CHR: Lana Smith, Human Resources Director
CNO: Sara Houser, Chief Nursing Officer
Web address: www.ashememorial.org
Control: Other not–for–profit (including NFP Corporation) **Service**: General medical and surgical

Staffed Beds: 25

KENANSVILLE—Duplin County

✠ **ECU HEALTH DUPLIN HOSPITAL (340120)**, 401 North Main Street, Zip 28349–8801, Mailing Address: P.O. Box 278, Zip 28349–0278; tel. 910/296–0941, (Nonreporting) **A**1 10 **S** ECU Health, Greenville, NC
Primary Contact: Jeffery Dial, Chief Executive Officer
COO: Matthew Gitzinger, Director of Operations
CFO: Lucinda Crawford, Vice President Financial Services
CMO: Dyrek Miller, M.D., Chief Medical Staff
CIO: Lucinda Crawford, Vice President Financial Services
CHR: Pansy Chase, Director Human Resources
CNO: Sue O. Taylor, Vice President Nursing
Web address: www.vidanthealth.com
Control: Other not–for–profit (including NFP Corporation) **Service**: General medical and surgical

Staffed Beds: 81

VIDANT DUPLIN HOSPITAL See ECU Health Duplin Hospital

KINGS MOUNTAIN—Cleveland County

CAROLINAS HEALTHCARE SYSTEM KINGS MOUNTAIN See Atrium Health Kings Mountain

KINSTON—Lenoir County

✠ **UNC HEALTH LENOIR (340027)**, 100 Airport Road, Zip 28501–1634, Mailing Address: P.O. Box 1678, Zip 28503–1678; tel. 252/522–7000, **A**1 2 10 **F**3 8 11 12 13 18 20 28 29 30 31 34 35 40 44 45 47 48 50 53 57 59 60 64 65 68 70 71 74 75 76 77 78 79 81 82 85 86 87 90 93 96 101 102 104 107 108 111 114 115 119 120 121 123 129 130 132 135 146 147 148 149 154 156 167 169 **S** UNC Health, Chapel Hill, NC
Primary Contact: Crystal Hayden, FACHE, R.N., President and Chief Executive Officer
CFO: Jeffrey A. Wakefield, CPA, Vice President and Chief Financial Officer
CMO: Claire Paris, M.D., Vice President and Chief Medical Officer
CIO: Karl Vanderstouw, Vice President, Support Services
CHR: Jim Dobbins, Vice President and Chief Human Resources Officer
CNO: Shirley S. Harkey, M.D., R.N., FACHE, Interim Vice President and Chief Nursing Officer
Web address: https://www.unclenoir.org/
Control: Other not–for–profit (including NFP Corporation) **Service**: General medical and surgical

Staffed Beds: 169 **Admissions**: 4577 **Census**: 67 **Outpatient Visits**: 182348 **Births**: 280 **Total Expense ($000)**: 130981 **Payroll Expense ($000)**: 61538 **Personnel**: 785

LAURINBURG—Scotland County

✠ **SCOTLAND HEALTH CARE SYSTEM (340008)**, 500 Lauchwood Drive, Zip 28352–5599; tel. 910/291–7000, **A**1 2 3 5 10 **F**3 11 13 15 18 28 29 31 34 37 40 45 50 54 57 59 63 64 70 71 73 74 75 76 77 78 79 81 83 84 85 86 87 89 90 92 93 96 97 107 110 111 114 115 119 120 121 123 126 127 130 132 135 144 146 147 148 149 154 156 157 167 168 169 **S** Atrium Health, Inc., Charlotte, NC
Primary Contact: David L. Pope, President and Chief Executive Officer
CFO: Matthew Pracht, Vice President Finance
CMO: Cheryl Davis, M.D., Chief Medical Officer
CIO: Chip Reklis, Director Information Systems
CHR: Ann Locklear, Vice President, Human Resources
CNO: Bebe Holt, Chief Nursing Officer
Web address: www.scotlandhealth.org
Control: Other not–for–profit (including NFP Corporation) **Service**: General medical and surgical

Staffed Beds: 104 **Admissions**: 5818 **Census**: 66 **Outpatient Visits**: 116747 **Births**: 774 **Total Expense ($000)**: 238276 **Payroll Expense ($000)**: 90367 **Personnel**: 1182

LELAND—Brunswick County

☐ **CAROLINA DUNES BEHAVIORAL HEALTH (344030)**, 2050 Mercantile Drive, Zip 28451–4053; tel. 910/371–2500, **A**1 3 10 **F**29 38 87 98 99 100 101 103 106 130 149 154 164 **S** Strategic Behavioral Health, LLC, Memphis, TN
Primary Contact: Steve McCabe, Chief Executive Officer
CHR: Kelly Pace, Director Human Resource
CNO: Brooke Cook, Director of Nursing
Web address: https://www.carolinadunesbh.com/
Control: Corporation, Investor–owned (for–profit) **Service**: Psychiatric

Staffed Beds: 116 **Admissions**: 1090 **Census**: 13 **Outpatient Visits**: 0 **Total Expense ($000)**: 19983 **Payroll Expense ($000)**: 11884 **Personnel**: 156

LENOIR—Caldwell County

CALDWELL UNC HEALTH CARE See UNC Health Caldwell

✠ **UNC HEALTH CALDWELL (340041)**, 321 Mulberry Street SW, Zip 28645–5720, Mailing Address: P.O. Box 1890, Zip 28645–1890; tel. 828/757–5100, **A**1 10 **F**3 8 11 15 18 20 22 28 29 30 31 34 35 37 40 45 46 48 49 50 53 54 55 57 59 64 65 70 75 76 77 78 79 81 82 85 86 87 93 97 98 100 102 104 105 107 108 109 110 111 114 119 120 121 122 123 129 131 132 135 145 146 147 148 149 153 154 156 165 167 **P**6 **S** UNC Health, Chapel Hill, NC
Primary Contact: David Lowry, M.D., Chief Executive Officer
CFO: Karen Shadowens, Chief Financial Officer
CIO: Deborah Purcell, Director of Information Technology
CNO: Jerrell Suddreth, Chief Nursing Officer
Web address: www.caldwellmemorial.org
Control: Other not–for–profit (including NFP Corporation) **Service**: General medical and surgical

Staffed Beds: 109 **Admissions**: 3725 **Census**: 57 **Outpatient Visits**: 46755 **Births**: 6 **Total Expense ($000)**: 168740 **Payroll Expense ($000)**: 70797 **Personnel**: 954

Hospital, Medicare Provider Number, Address, Telephone, Approval, Facility, and Physician Codes, Health Care System

★ American Hospital Association (AHA) membership
☐ The Joint Commission accreditation
○ Healthcare Facilities Accreditation Program
◇ DNV Healthcare Inc. accreditation
⇑ Center for Improvement in Healthcare Quality Accreditation
△ Commission on Accreditation of Rehabilitation Facilities (CARF) accreditation

© 2025 AHA Guide

Hospitals, U.S. / NORTH CAROLINA

LEXINGTON—Davidson County

✠ **ATRIUM HEALTH WAKE FOREST BAPTIST LEXINGTON MEDICAL CENTER (340096)**, 250 Hospital Drive, Zip 27292–6728, Mailing Address: P.O. Box 1817, Zip 27293–1817; tel. 336/248–5161, **A**1 3 5 10 **F**3 15 18 28 29 30 31 34 35 39 40 45 46 50 57 58 59 61 64 65 68 70 74 75 78 79 81 82 85 87 91 92 93 97 102 107 108 110 111 114 115 116 117 119 120 121 123 126 129 130 131 146 147 148 154 156 **P**6 **S** Atrium Health, Inc., Charlotte, NC
Primary Contact: Chad J. Brown, Dr.PH, FACHE, M.P.H., President, South and West Areas
CFO: Danny Squires, Assistant Vice President and Chief Financial Officer Network Hospital
CMO: Raghava Nagaraj, M.D., Chief Medical Officer
CIO: Will Showalter, Senior Vice President and Chief information Officer
Web address: https://www.wakehealth.edu/locations/hospitals/lexington-medical-center
Control: Other not–for–profit (including NFP Corporation) **Service**: General medical and surgical

Staffed Beds: 75 **Admissions**: 3416 **Census**: 40 **Outpatient Visits**: 100075 **Births**: 0 **Total Expense ($000)**: 116329 **Payroll Expense ($000)**: 56079 **Personnel**: 511

LINCOLNTON—Lincoln County

✠ **ATRIUM HEALTH LINCOLN (340145)**, 433 McAlister Road, Zip 28092–4147, Mailing Address: PO Box 677, Zip 28093–0677; tel. 980/212–2000, **A**1 10 **F**3 8 13 15 18 29 30 31 34 35 39 40 44 45 50 51 57 59 64 70 73 74 75 76 77 78 79 81 82 84 85 87 93 96 107 110 111 114 115 119 129 130 131 146 148 149 150 154 156 167 168 169 **P**6 **S** Atrium Health, Inc., Charlotte, NC
Primary Contact: Tri Tang, Vice President
CFO: Jarrett L Morris, Controller
CMO: Vineet Goel, Chief Medical Officer
CIO: Jarrett L Morris, Controller and Chief Information Officer
CHR: Lesley Chambless, Assistant Vice President Human Resources
CNO: Elaine S Haynes, R.N., MSN, Vice President Patient Services and Chief Nursing Executive
Web address: https://atriumhealth.org/locations/detail/atrium-health-lincoln
Control: Hospital district or authority, Government, Nonfederal **Service**: General medical and surgical

Staffed Beds: 101 **Admissions**: 5294 **Census**: 56 **Outpatient Visits**: 111348 **Births**: 520 **Total Expense ($000)**: 116233 **Payroll Expense ($000)**: 54525 **Personnel**: 643

LINVILLE—Lincoln County

★ **APPALACHIAN REGIONAL BEHAVIORAL HEALTH (344034)**, 432 Hospital Drive, Zip 28646, Mailing Address: PO Box 767, Zip 28646; tel. 828/737–7071, (Nonreporting) **A**3 **S** UNC Health, Chapel Hill, NC
Primary Contact: Stephanie Greer, President, Avery Healthcare Market
Web address: https://apprhs.org/appalachian-regional-behavioral-health/
Control: Other not–for–profit (including NFP Corporation) **Service**: Psychiatric

Staffed Beds: 27

LUMBERTON—Robeson County

★ ⇧ **UNC HEALTH SOUTHEASTERN (340050)**, 300 West 27th Street, Zip 28358–3075, Mailing Address: P.O. Box 1408, Zip 28359–1408; tel. 910/671–5000, (Total facility includes 100 beds in nursing home–type unit) **A**2 3 5 10 12 13 21 **F**3 6 7 8 9 11 12 13 15 17 18 20 22 24 26 28 29 30 31 35 36 37 38 40 44 45 46 48 49 50 53 55 56 58 59 60 63 64 65 68 70 72 73 76 77 78 79 81 82 84 85 86 87 89 91 93 94 95 98 100 102 105 107 108 111 114 116 117 118 119 120 121 122 123 124 126 127 128 129 130 131 132 135 144 146 147 148 152 154 156 157 160 162 164 167 **P**6 **S** UNC Health, Chapel Hill, NC
Primary Contact: Christopher Ellington, President and Chief Executive Officer
CFO: C Thomas Johnson III, Vice President Finance and Chief Financial Officer
CMO: Barry Williamson, President Medical Staff
CHR: Susan Hayes, Director Human Resources
CNO: Renae Taylor, Chief Nursing Officer
Web address: www.srmc.org
Control: Other not–for–profit (including NFP Corporation) **Service**: General medical and surgical

Staffed Beds: 335 **Admissions**: 11735 **Census**: 196 **Outpatient Visits**: 242140 **Births**: 1257 **Total Expense ($000)**: 373929 **Payroll Expense ($000)**: 119798 **Personnel**: 1799

MARION—Mcdowell County

✠ **MISSION HOSPITAL MCDOWELL (340087)**, 430 Rankin Drive, Zip 28752–6568, Mailing Address: P.O. Box 730, Zip 28752–0730; tel. 828/659–5000, (Nonreporting) **A**1 3 10 **S** HCA Healthcare, Nashville, TN
Primary Contact: Lee Higginbotham, Chief Executive Officer
CFO: Clint Stewart, Regional Director of Finance East
CMO: Rex Henderson, M.D., Chief of Staff
CIO: Pam Blevins, R.N., Director Information Technology Member Hospitals Mission
CHR: Tonya Revels, Senior Strategic Business Partner
CNO: Kathy Hefner, Chief Nursing Officer
Web address: https://missionhealth.org/member-hospitals/mcdowell/
Control: Other not–for–profit (including NFP Corporation) **Service**: General medical and surgical

Staffed Beds: 30

MATTHEWS—Mecklenburg County

✠ **NOVANT HEALTH MATTHEWS MEDICAL CENTER (340171)**, 1500 Matthews Township Parkway, Zip 28105–4656; tel. 704/384–6500, (Nonreporting) **A**1 2 10 **S** Novant Health, Winston Salem, NC
Primary Contact: Jason Bernd, President and Chief Operating Officer
CMO: Thomas Zweng, Executive Vice President and Chief Medical Officer
CIO: David B Garrett, Senior Vice President and Chief Information Officer
CNO: Tracy B Forster, R.N., Senior Director of Nursing
Web address: https://www.novanthealth.org
Control: Other not–for–profit (including NFP Corporation) **Service**: General medical and surgical

Staffed Beds: 117

MONROE—Union County

✠ **ATRIUM HEALTH UNION (340130)**, 600 Hospital Drive, Zip 28112–6000, Mailing Address: P.O. Box 5003, Zip 28111–5003; tel. 980/993–3100, **A**1 2 3 10 **F**3 8 13 18 20 22 26 28 29 30 31 34 35 40 42 44 45 49 50 56 57 59 60 64 68 70 72 74 75 76 77 78 79 81 82 84 85 87 89 93 107 111 114 115 116 117 118 119 120 121 126 129 130 131 132 135 146 148 149 156 167 169 **P**6 **S** Atrium Health, Inc., Charlotte, NC
Primary Contact: Denise White, MSN, Vice President, Facility Executive
COO: Dave Anderson, FACHE, Vice President Administration
CFO: John G Moore, Vice President and Chief Financial Officer
CMO: Craig M Slater, M.D., Chief Medical Officer
CIO: Lisa Sykes, Director Information Services
CHR: Rhonda McFarland, Director Human Resources
CNO: Denise White, MSN, Chief Nurse Executive and Vice President Facility Executive
Web address: https://atriumhealth.org/locations/detail/atrium-health-union
Control: Hospital district or authority, Government, Nonfederal **Service**: General medical and surgical

Staffed Beds: 182 **Admissions**: 12525 **Census**: 174 **Outpatient Visits**: 232926 **Births**: 1177 **Total Expense ($000)**: 313677 **Payroll Expense ($000)**: 149219 **Personnel**: 1405

MOORESVILLE—Iredell County

✠ **LAKE NORMAN REGIONAL MEDICAL CENTER (340129)**, 171 Fairview Road, Zip 28117–9500, Mailing Address: P.O. Box 3250, Zip 28117–3250; tel. 704/660–4000, (Nonreporting) **A**1 10 19 **S** Community Health Systems, Inc., Franklin, TN
Primary Contact: Alec Grabowski, Chief Executive Officer
CFO: Claire Polk, Chief Financial Officer
CHR: Stephanie Williams, Market Director Human Resources
CNO: Tammy Marie Moore, Chief Nursing Officer
Web address: www.lnrmc.com
Control: Corporation, Investor–owned (for–profit) **Service**: General medical and surgical

Staffed Beds: 123

Hospitals, U.S. / NORTH CAROLINA

MOREHEAD CITY—Carteret County

☒ **CARTERET HEALTH CARE (340142)**, 3500 Arendell Street, Zip 28557-2901, Mailing Address: P.O. Box 1619, Zip 28557-1619; tel. 252/499-6000, **A**1 2 10 **F**3 7 11 12 13 15 18 20 22 28 29 30 31 34 35 37 40 45 46 54 57 59 62 63 64 65 68 70 74 75 76 77 78 79 81 82 84 85 86 87 89 91 93 97 107 108 110 111 114 115 118 119 120 121 123 129 130 132 135 143 145 146 148 149 154 156 167 **P**6
Primary Contact: Kyle Marek, President
CFO: Joanie King, Chief Financial Officer
CMO: Clyde Brooks, M.D., Chief Medical Officer
CIO: Kyle Marek, Vice President General Services and Chief Information Officer
CHR: Elizabeth Beswick, Vice President Human Resources and Public Relations
Web address: https://www.carterethealth.org/
Control: County, Government, Nonfederal **Service:** General medical and surgical

Staffed Beds: 104 **Admissions:** 6009 **Census:** 69 **Outpatient Visits:** 192760 **Births:** 849 **Total Expense ($000):** 190757 **Payroll Expense ($000):** 68971 **Personnel:** 1050

MORGANTON—Burke County

☐ **BROUGHTON HOSPITAL (344025)**, 1000 South Sterling Street, Zip 28655-3999; tel. 828/433-2111, (Nonreporting) **A**1 3 10
Primary Contact: Vivian Streater, Co-Acting Chief Executive Officer
CFO: Bea Tullis, Chief Financial Officer and Budget Officer
CMO: George Krebs, M.D., Chief Medical Officer
CIO: Darin Kiracofe, Director Information Resource Management
CHR: Jean Buchanan, Director Human Resources
CNO: Vivian Streater, Chief Nursing Officer and Co-Acting Chief Executive Officer
Web address: www.ncdhhs.gov/dsohf/broughton
Control: State, Government, Nonfederal **Service:** Psychiatric

Staffed Beds: 297

CAROLINAS HEALTHCARE SYSTEM – BLUE RIDGE – MORGANTON See UNC Health Blue Ridge – Morganton

☒ **UNC HEALTH BLUE RIDGE (340075)**, 2201 South Sterling Street, Zip 28655-4058; tel. 828/580-5000, (Includes UNC HEALTH BLUE RIDGE – MORGANTON, 2201 South Sterling Street, Morganton, North Carolina, Zip 28655-4058; tel. 828/580-5000; Gary Paxson, FACHE, President and Chief Executive Officer; UNC HEALTH BLUE RIDGE – VALDESE, 720 Malcolm Boulevard, Valdese, North Carolina, Zip 28690-2872, P O Box 700, Zip 28690-0700, tel. 828/580-5000; Gary Paxson, FACHE, President and Chief Executive Officer) **A**1 2 3 5 10 13 **F**3 8 13 15 18 20 22 28 29 30 31 34 35 40 45 47 49 50 53 54 56 57 59 64 68 69 70 71 72 74 76 77 78 81 82 85 86 87 93 96 97 98 100 107 110 111 114 115 118 119 120 121 122 123 124 126 129 130 131 132 135 142 144 146 147 148 149 150 154 167 169 **P**6 7 **S** UNC Health, Chapel Hill, NC
Primary Contact: Gary Paxson, FACHE, President and Chief Executive Officer
COO: Jonathan Mercer, FACHE, Senior Vice President, Chief Operating Officer
CFO: Robert G. Fritts, Chief Financial Officer and Senior Vice President
CMO: Anthony Frank, M.D., Senior Vice President and Chief Medical Officer
CHR: Lorinnsa Bridges-Kee, Vice President Human Resources
CNO: Barry Nelson, MSN, Vice President Nursing, Chief Nurse Executive
Web address: https://www.unchealthblueridge.org/
Control: Other not-for-profit (including NFP Corporation) **Service:** General medical and surgical

Staffed Beds: 156 **Admissions:** 7170 **Census:** 95 **Outpatient Visits:** 194932 **Births:** 971 **Total Expense ($000):** 280458 **Payroll Expense ($000):** 117872 **Personnel:** 1426

MOUNT AIRY—Surry County

☒ **NORTHERN REGIONAL HOSPITAL (340003)**, 830 Rockford Street, Zip 27030-5365, Mailing Address: P.O. Box 1101, Zip 27030-1101; tel. 336/719-7000, (Nonreporting) **A**1 10
Primary Contact: Chris A. Lumsden, President and Chief Executive Officer
CFO: Andrea Hickling, Vice President of Finance and Chief Financial Officer
CMO: Druery DeVore, Chief of Medical Staff
CIO: Rodney Bond, Director of Information Technology
CHR: Julia Nelson, Vice President of Human Resources
CNO: Robin Hodgin, R.N., Vice President of Patient Services and Chief Nursing Officer
Web address: www.northernhospital.com
Control: Hospital district or authority, Government, Nonfederal **Service:** General medical and surgical

Staffed Beds: 108

MURPHY—Cherokee County

⇧ **ERLANGER WESTERN CAROLINA HOSPITAL (341328)**, 3990 US Highway 64 East Alt, Zip 28906-7917; tel. 828/837-8161, **A**10 18 21 **F**3 8 15 18 28 29 40 45 47 50 53 59 64 70 77 79 81 93 97 100 104 107 108 110 111 114 115 118 119 127 131 133 141 142 144 146 148 149 154 155 157 167 **S** Erlanger Health System, Chattanooga, TN
Primary Contact: Stephanie Boynton, Vice President and Chief Executive Officer
COO: Toni Lovingood, Chief Operating Officer
CMO: Jeffrey H Martin, M.D., Chief of Staff
CIO: Connie Stalcup, Manager Information Systems
CHR: Russ Paine, Human Resources Officer
CNO: Teresa Bowleg, R.N., Chief Nursing Officer
Web address: https://www.erlanger.org
Control: Other not-for-profit (including NFP Corporation) **Service:** General medical and surgical

Staffed Beds: 25 **Admissions:** 946 **Census:** 14 **Outpatient Visits:** 221527 **Births:** 2 **Total Expense ($000):** 63749 **Payroll Expense ($000):** 26985 **Personnel:** 396

NAGS HEAD—Dare County

☒ **THE OUTER BANKS HOSPITAL (341324)**, 4800 South Croatan Highway, Zip 27959-9704; tel. 252/449-4500, **A**1 2 10 18 **F**3 13 15 28 29 30 31 34 35 36 38 40 45 46 48 50 55 57 59 64 68 71 73 75 76 77 78 79 81 82 84 85 86 87 93 96 107 108 109 110 111 115 119 124 130 132 133 135 144 146 147 154 156 167 **P**8 **S** ECU Health, Greenville, NC
Primary Contact: Ronald A. Sloan, FACHE, President
CFO: Todd Warlitner, Vice President Business Operations
CMO: Roger Lever, M.D., President Medical Staff
CHR: Mary Kelley, Director Human Resources
CNO: Marcia Bryant, R.N., MSN, RN, Vice President, Clinical Operations
Web address: https://locations.outerbankshealth.org/Details/132
Control: Other not-for-profit (including NFP Corporation) **Service:** General medical and surgical

Staffed Beds: 21 **Admissions:** 1159 **Census:** 8

NEW BERN—Craven County

☒ △ **CAROLINAEAST HEALTH SYSTEM (340131)**, 2000 Neuse Boulevard, Zip 28560-3499, Mailing Address: 2000 Neuse Blvd, Zip 28560; tel. 252/633-8281, **A**1 2 7 10 **F**3 7 11 13 15 17 18 20 22 24 26 28 29 30 31 34 35 36 39 40 45 46 47 48 49 53 54 57 58 59 62 64 67 70 74 75 76 77 78 79 81 84 85 86 87 89 90 91 92 93 94 96 98 100 101 102 104 107 108 110 111 114 115 117 118 119 120 121 123 126 130 132 135 141 142 143 146 147 148 149
Primary Contact: Michael C. Smith, President and Chief Executive Officer
CFO: Tammy M. Sherron, Vice President Finance
CMO: Ronald B May, M.D., Vice President Medical Affairs
CIO: Ronald B May, M.D., Vice President Medical Affairs
CHR: Bruce A Martin, Vice President Human Resources
CNO: Rosanne Leahy, Vice President Nursing Services
Web address: www.carolinaeasthealth.com
Control: Hospital district or authority, Government, Nonfederal **Service:** General medical and surgical

Staffed Beds: 226 **Admissions:** 12731 **Census:** 197 **Outpatient Visits:** 180118 **Births:** 1001 **Total Expense ($000):** 413557 **Payroll Expense ($000):** 130688 **Personnel:** 2570

NEWLAND—Avery County

☒ **CHARLES A. CANNON JR. MEMORIAL HOSPITAL (341323)**, 434 Hospital Drive, Zip 28646, Mailing Address: P.O. Box 767, Linville, Zip 28646-0767; tel. 828/737-7000, (Nonreporting) **A**1 3 10 18 **S** UNC Health, Chapel Hill, NC
Primary Contact: Stephanie Greer, President, Avery Healthcare Market
CFO: Kevin B May, System Director Finance
CMO: Thomas M Haizlip, M.D., Jr, Chief of Staff
CIO: Nathan White, Chief Information Officer
CHR: Amy J. Crabbe, Vice President People Services
Web address: https://apprhs.org/cannon/
Control: Other not-for-profit (including NFP Corporation) **Service:** General medical and surgical

Staffed Beds: 31

Hospital, Medicare Provider Number, Address, Telephone, Approval, Facility, and Physician Codes, Health Care System

★ American Hospital Association (AHA) membership
☐ The Joint Commission accreditation
○ Healthcare Facilities Accreditation Program
◇ DNV Healthcare Inc. accreditation
⇧ Center for Improvement in Healthcare Quality Accreditation
△ Commission on Accreditation of Rehabilitation Facilities (CARF) accreditation

Hospitals, U.S. / NORTH CAROLINA

NORTH WILKESBORO—Wilkes County

ATRIUM HEALTH WAKE FOREST BAPTIST WILKES MEDICAL CENTER (340064), 1370 West 'D' Street, Zip 28659–3506, Mailing Address: P.O. Box 609, Zip 28659–0609; tel. 336/651–8100, (Total facility includes 10 beds in nursing home–type unit) **A**1 10 **F**3 13 15 18 28 29 30 31 34 35 39 40 45 49 57 59 60 64 65 67 68 70 74 75 77 78 79 81 85 87 92 93 107 108 110 111 114 115 119 124 128 129 130 131 135 146 147 148 149 154 169 **P**6 **S** Atrium Health, Inc., Charlotte, NC
Primary Contact: Chad J. Brown, Dr.PH, FACHE, M.P.H., President
CFO: Barry Wald, Chief Financial Officer
CMO: Richard Barber, M.D., Chief Medical Officer
CIO: William Hofman, Manager Information Technology
CHR: Vanya Baker, Director
CNO: Sandy Sheppard, Vice President Patient Services
Web address: www.wilkesregional.com/
Control: Other not–for–profit (including NFP Corporation) **Service**: General medical and surgical

Staffed Beds: 80 **Admissions:** 4126 **Census:** 48 **Outpatient Visits:** 83356 **Births:** 262 **Total Expense ($000):** 122365 **Payroll Expense ($000):** 54793 **Personnel:** 569

OXFORD—Granville County

GRANVILLE HEALTH SYSTEM (340127), 1010 College Street, Zip 27565–2507, Mailing Address: P.O. Box 947, Zip 27565–0947; tel. 919/690–3000, (Nonreporting) **A**1 10
Primary Contact: Adam McConnell, Interim Chief Executive Officer
COO: Cristina Rigsbee Carroll, Chief Operating Officer
CFO: Adam McConnell, Chief Financial Officer
CMO: Richard Pacca, M.D., Chief of Staff
CIO: Geoff Tanthorey, Director, Information Systems
CHR: Scott Thomas, Administrative Director Human Resources and Communications
CNO: Bill Hughes, Chief Nursing Officer
Web address: www.ghshospital.org
Control: County, Government, Nonfederal **Service**: General medical and surgical

Staffed Beds: 142

PINEHURST—Moore County

★ △ ⊓ **FIRSTHEALTH MOORE REGIONAL HOSPITAL (340115)**, 155 Memorial Drive, Zip 28374–8710, Mailing Address: P.O. Box 3000, Zip 28374–3000; tel. 910/715–1000, (Includes FIRSTHEALTH MOORE REGIONAL HOSPITAL – HOKE, 6408 Fayetteville Road, Raeford, North Carolina, Zip 28376–7977, tel. 910/878–6000; Susan R Beaty, R.N., Administrator; FIRSTHEALTH MOORE REGIONAL HOSPITAL – RICHMOND, 925 Long Drive, Rockingham, North Carolina, Zip 28379–4835, tel. 910/417–3000; John J Jackson, President) (Nonreporting) **A**2 5 7 10 19 21 **S** FirstHealth of the Carolinas, Pinehurst, NC
Primary Contact: Mickey W. Foster, Chief Executive Officer
CMO: John F Krahnert, M.D., Chief Medical Officer
CIO: David B Dillehunt, Chief Information Officer
CHR: Daniel F Biediger, Vice President Human Resources
Web address: www.firsthealth.org
Control: Other not–for–profit (including NFP Corporation) **Service**: General medical and surgical

Staffed Beds: 362

PLYMOUTH—Washington County

WASHINGTON REGIONAL MEDICAL CENTER (341314), 958 US Highway 64 East, Zip 27962–9591, Mailing Address: PO Box 707, Zip 27962–9591; tel. 252/793–4135, (Nonreporting) **A**10 18
Primary Contact: Amanze Ugoji, M.D., Chief Executive Officer
CMO: Robert Venable, M.D., Chief Medical Staff
CIO: Christina Craft, Director Information Systems
CNO: Kimberly Manning, Chief Nursing Officer
Web address: https://www.washingtonregionalmedical.org/
Control: County, Government, Nonfederal **Service**: General medical and surgical

Staffed Beds: 25

RAEFORD—Hoke County

HOKE HOSPITAL (340188), 210 Medical Pavilion Drive, Zip 28376–9111; tel. 910/904–8000, (Nonreporting) **A**1 10 **S** Cape Fear Valley Health System, Fayetteville, NC
Primary Contact: Chris Tart, PharmD, President
CNO: Sheri Dahman, Chief Nursing Officer
Web address: https://www.capefearvalley.com/hospitals/hoke.html
Control: Other not–for–profit (including NFP Corporation) **Service**: General medical and surgical

Staffed Beds: 29

RALEIGH—Wake County

CENTRAL PRISON HOSPITAL, 1300 Western Boulevard, Zip 27606–2148; tel. 919/743–2440, (Nonreporting) **A**3 5
Primary Contact: Chad Lovett Lovett, Chief Executive Officer
CMO: Olushola Metiko, M.D., Medical Director
CHR: Bruce McKinney, Business Officer, Administrative Services
CNO: Cindy J McLean, R.N., MSN, Director of Nursing
Web address: https://www.ncdps.gov/index2.cfm?a=000003,002240,002381,002252
Control: State, Government, Nonfederal **Service**: Hospital unit of an institution (prison hospital, college infirmary, etc.)

Staffed Beds: 230

DUKE RALEIGH HOSPITAL (340073), 3400 Wake Forest Road, Zip 27609–7373; tel. 919/954–3000, **A**1 2 3 5 10 **F**3 11 15 18 20 22 24 26 28 29 30 31 34 35 37 39 40 44 45 46 47 49 50 51 54 55 56 57 58 59 60 64 68 70 74 75 77 78 79 80 81 82 84 85 86 87 92 93 94 96 100 102 103 107 108 110 111 114 115 117 118 119 120 121 123 124 126 129 130 131 132 135 141 142 146 147 148 149 154 164 167 **P**1 6 **S** Duke University Health System, Durham, NC
Primary Contact: Barbara Griffith, M.D., President
COO: Brian Sloan, Chief Operating Officer
CFO: Leigh Bleecker, Chief Financial Officer
CMO: Michael Spiritos, Chief Medical Officer
CHR: Alyson Gordon, Chief Human Resources Officer
Web address: www.dukeraleighhospital.org
Control: Other not–for–profit (including NFP Corporation) **Service**: General medical and surgical

Staffed Beds: 220 **Admissions:** 10204 **Census:** 151 **Outpatient Visits:** 397299 **Births:** 1 **Total Expense ($000):** 657740 **Payroll Expense ($000):** 177092 **Personnel:** 2351

HOLLY HILL HOSPITAL (344014), 3019 Falstaff Road, Zip 27610–1812; tel. 919/250–7000, (Nonreporting) **A**1 10 **S** Universal Health Services, Inc., King of Prussia, PA
Primary Contact: Kevin Poitinger, Chief Executive Officer and Managing Director
COO: Jessica Knudsen, Chief Operating Officer and Director Performance Improvement and Risk Management
CFO: Ron Howard, Chief Financial Officer
CMO: Thomas Cornwall, M.D., Medical Director
CHR: Ebuni McFall–Roberts, Director Human Resources
CNO: Michael Hartley, MS, Chief Nursing Officer
Web address: www.hollyhillhospital.com
Control: Corporation, Investor–owned (for–profit) **Service**: Psychiatric

Staffed Beds: 285

LARRY B. ZIEVERINK, SR. ALCOHOLISM TREATMENT CENTER, 3000 Falstaff Road, Zip 27610–1897; tel. 919/250–1500, (Nonreporting)
Primary Contact: Martin D. Woodward, Director Acute Care Services
COO: Martin D Woodward, Director Acute Care Services
CFO: Paul Gross, Human Services and Finance Officer
CMO: Enrique Lopez, M.D., Medical Director
CIO: Wil A Glenn, Director Communications
Web address: www.wakegov.com/humanservices/locations/lbz/Pages/default.aspx
Control: County, Government, Nonfederal **Service**: Substance Use Disorder

Staffed Beds: 34

TRIANGLE SPRINGS HOSPITAL (344032), 10901 World Trade Boulevard, Zip 27617–4203; tel. 919/372–4408, (Nonreporting) **A**1 10 **S** Springstone, Louisville, KY
Primary Contact: Amanda Johanson, Chief Executive Officer
Web address: https://www.trianglesprings.com
Control: Corporation, Investor–owned (for–profit) **Service**: Psychiatric

Staffed Beds: 77

Hospitals, U.S. / NORTH CAROLINA

☒ **UNC HEALTH REX (340114)**, 4420 Lake Boone Trail, Zip 27607-6599; tel. 919/784-3100, (Total facility includes 227 beds in nursing home-type unit) **A**1 2 3 5 10 **F**3 7 8 11 12 13 15 17 18 20 22 24 26 28 29 30 31 34 35 36 40 44 45 46 47 48 49 50 53 54 55 56 57 58 59 64 65 66 68 70 71 72 73 74 75 76 77 78 79 81 82 84 85 86 87 89 92 93 96 100 102 107 108 110 111 114 115 116 117 118 119 120 121 123 126 128 129 130 131 132 135 142 143 144 145 146 147 148 149 154 156 157 167 168 169 **P**6 **S** UNC Health, Chapel Hill, NC
Primary Contact: Kirsten Riggs, Interim President and Chief Operating Officer
COO: Kirsten Riggs, Chief Operating Officer
CFO: Andrew Zukowski, Chief Financial Officer
CMO: Linda H. Butler, M.D., Chief Medical Officer
CIO: Tracy Parham, Health Care System Chief Information Officer
CHR: Scott Doak, Vice President, Human Resources
Web address: www.rexhealth.com
Control: Other not-for-profit (including NFP Corporation) **Service**: General medical and surgical

Staffed Beds: 716 **Admissions**: 31151 **Census**: 582 **Outpatient Visits**: 1538336 **Births**: 7377 **Total Expense ($000)**: 1502960 **Payroll Expense ($000)**: 604506 **Personnel**: 6057

WAKEMED NORTH FAMILY HEALTH AND WOMEN'S HOSPITAL See Wakemed North Hospital

☒ △ **WAKEMED RALEIGH CAMPUS (340069)**, 3000 New Bern Avenue, Zip 27610-1295; tel. 919/350-8000, (Includes WAKEMED NORTH HOSPITAL, 10000 Falls of Neuse Road, Raleigh, North Carolina, Zip 27614-7838, tel. 919/350-8000; Valerie Barlow, Senior Vice President and Administrator) **A**1 3 5 7 8 10 **F**3 5 7 11 12 13 15 17 18 19 20 22 24 25 26 27 28 29 30 31 32 34 35 36 37 38 40 41 42 43 44 46 47 48 49 50 53 54 55 56 57 58 59 60 61 62 64 65 66 67 70 71 72 73 74 75 76 77 78 79 81 82 85 86 87 88 89 90 91 92 93 94 95 96 97 100 101 102 104 107 108 110 111 114 115 119 126 129 130 131 132 135 144 146 147 148 149 150 154 156 160 161 162 164 165 168 169 **S** WakeMed Health & Hospitals, Raleigh, NC
Primary Contact: Rebecca Andrews, Senior Vice President and Administrator
COO: Denise Wilder Warren, R.N., Executive Vice President and Chief Operating Officer
CMO: West Paul, M.D., Ph.D., Senior Vice President and Chief Quality and Medical Staff Officer
CIO: Peter Marks, Vice President & Chief Information Officer
CNO: Cindy Boily, MSN, R.N., Senior Vice President and Chief Nursing Officer
Web address: www.wakemed.org
Control: Other not-for-profit (including NFP Corporation) **Service**: General medical and surgical

Staffed Beds: 714 **Admissions**: 38182 **Census**: 613 **Outpatient Visits**: 566279 **Births**: 6059 **Total Expense ($000)**: 1733236 **Payroll Expense ($000)**: 955015 **Personnel**: 8758

REIDSVILLE—Rockingham County

ANNIE PENN HOSPITAL See Cone Health Moses Cone Hospital, Greensboro

ANNIE PENN MEMORIAL HOSPITAL See Annie Penn Hospital

ROANOKE RAPIDS—Halifax County

☒ **ECU HEALTH NORTH HOSPITAL (340151)**, 250 Smith Church Road, Zip 27870-4914, Mailing Address: P.O. Box 1089, Zip 27870-1089; tel. 252/535-8011, (Nonreporting) **A**1 3 10 20 **S** ECU Health, Greenville, NC
Primary Contact: Dennis Campbell II, R.N., Interim President
CFO: Sherry Jensen, Vice President, Financial Services
CIO: Robert Gordon, Manager, Information Services
CHR: Thomas Mastroianni, Director, Human Resources
Web address: https://www.ecuhealth.org/
Control: Other not-for-profit (including NFP Corporation) **Service**: General medical and surgical

Staffed Beds: 204

VIDANT NORTH HOSPITAL See ECU Health North Hospital

ROCKINGHAM—Richmond County

FIRSTHEALTH RICHMOND MEMORIAL HOSPITAL See Firsthealth Moore Regional Hospital – Richmond

ROCKY MOUNT—Nash County

☒ **PAM SPECIALTY HOSPITAL OF ROCKY MOUNT (342013)**, 1051 Noell Lane, Zip 27804-1761; tel. 252/451-2300, **A**1 10 **F**1 3 29 30 60 91 130 148 **S** PAM Health, Enola, PA
Primary Contact: Robyn Perkerson, R.N., Administrator
COO: Robyn Perkerson, R.N., Administrator
CMO: Daniel Crocker, M.D., Chief Medical Officer
CHR: Vicky Goode, Director Human Resources
Web address: www.lifecare-hospitals.com
Control: Corporation, Investor-owned (for-profit) **Service**: Acute long-term care hospital

Staffed Beds: 43 **Admissions**: 344 **Census**: 35 **Outpatient Visits**: 0 **Births**: 0 **Total Expense ($000)**: 22322 **Payroll Expense ($000)**: 9981 **Personnel**: 113

☒ △ **UNC HEALTH NASH (340147)**, 2460 Curtis Ellis Drive, Zip 27804-2237; tel. 252/962-8000, **A**1 2 7 10 **F**3 4 11 13 15 17 18 20 22 26 28 29 30 31 34 35 38 40 41 44 45 49 50 55 57 59 60 63 64 65 68 70 73 74 75 76 77 78 79 81 82 85 86 87 90 93 98 100 101 102 104 107 108 110 111 114 115 117 118 119 120 121 123 126 129 130 131 132 135 146 147 148 149 154 156 160 161 164 167 **S** UNC Health, Chapel Hill, NC
Primary Contact: L. Lee. Isley, FACHE, Ph.D., President and Chief Executive Officer
CFO: Shawn Hartley, Chief Financial Officer
CMO: Anne Shriner, M.D., Senior Vice President, Chief Medical Officer
CHR: Katie Davison, Vice President, Human Resources
Web address: www.nhcs.org
Control: Hospital district or authority, Government, Nonfederal **Service**: General medical and surgical

Staffed Beds: 224 **Admissions**: 12501 **Census**: 171 **Outpatient Visits**: 360984 **Births**: 1034 **Total Expense ($000)**: 310303 **Payroll Expense ($000)**: 129140 **Personnel**: 1902

ROXBORO—Person County

☒ **PERSON MEMORIAL HOSPITAL (340159)**, 615 Ridge Road, Zip 27573-4629; tel. 336/599-2121, (Nonreporting) **A**1 10 **S** Lifepoint Health, Brentwood, TN
Primary Contact: Bert Beard, Chief Executive Officer
CFO: Jessi Ayers, Chief Financial Officer
CIO: Rhonda M. Elliott, Director Information Technology and Meaningful Use
CHR: Mary Barksdale, Director Human Resources
CNO: Lynn Peoples, Interim Chief Nursing Officer
Web address: www.personhospital.com
Control: Partnership, Investor-owned (for-profit) **Service**: General medical and surgical

Staffed Beds: 77

RUTHERFORDTON—Rutherford County

☒ **RUTHERFORD REGIONAL HEALTH SYSTEM (340013)**, 288 South Ridgecrest Avenue, Zip 28139-2838; tel. 828/286-5000, (Nonreporting) **A**1 10 **S** Lifepoint Health, Brentwood, TN
Primary Contact: Susan C. Shugart, FACHE, Chief Executive Officer
COO: John Domansky, Vice President Operations
CFO: John Bostwick, Chief Financial Officer
CIO: Tommy Finley, Chief Information Officer
CHR: Robin B Callas, Vice President Human Resources
CNO: Anne Melton, Interim Chief Nursing Officer
Web address: www.rutherfordhosp.org
Control: Partnership, Investor-owned (for-profit) **Service**: General medical and surgical

Staffed Beds: 68

SALISBURY—Rowan County

☒ **NOVANT HEALTH ROWAN MEDICAL CENTER (340015)**, 612 Mocksville Avenue, Zip 28144-2799; tel. 704/210-5000, (Nonreporting) **A**1 2 5 10 19 **S** Novant Health, Winston Salem, NC
Primary Contact: Gary Blabon, President and Chief Operating Officer
CMO: Thomas Zweng, Executive Vice President and Chief Medical Officer
CIO: David B Garrett, Senior Vice President and Chief Information Officer
CNO: Cora Greene, Senior Director, Chief Nursing Officer
Web address: https://www.novanthealth.org/rowan-medical-center.aspx
Control: Other not-for-profit (including NFP Corporation) **Service**: General medical and surgical

Staffed Beds: 149

Hospitals, U.S. / NORTH CAROLINA

W. G. (BILL) HEFFNER VETERANS AFFAIRS MEDICAL CENTER, 1601 Brenner Avenue, Zip 28144–2559; tel. 704/638–9000, (Nonreporting) **A**1 3 5 **S** Department of Veterans Affairs, Washington, DC
Primary Contact: Kevin Amick, Executive Director
CFC: Steve Patil, Chief Financial Officer
CIO: Deborah Gunn, Chief Information Officer
CHR: Sandra Fischer, Director Human Resources
Web address: www.salisbury.va.gov
Control: Veterans Affairs, Government, federal **Service**: Psychiatric

Staffed Beds: 95

SANFORD—Lee County

CENTRAL CAROLINA HOSPITAL (340020), 1135 Carthage Street, Zip 27330–4162; tel. 919/774–2100, (Nonreporting) **A**1 5 10 **S** Lifepoint Health, Brentwood, TN
Primary Contact: Dave Santoemma, Chief Executive Officer
CFO: Jessi Ayers, Chief Financial Officer
CIC: Jimmy Whitaker, Director Information Systems
CHR: Deanna Lamb, Director Human Resources
CNO: Elizabeth Skarbinski, Chief Nursing Officer, Patient Safety Officer
Web address: www.centralcarolinahosp.com
Control: Corporation, Investor–owned (for–profit) **Service**: General medical and surgical

Staffed Beds: 55

SHELBY—Cleveland County

ATRIUM HEALTH CLEVELAND (340021), 201 East Grover Street, Zip 28150–3917; tel. 980/487–3000, (Includes ATRIUM HEALTH KINGS MOUNTAIN, 706 West King Street, Kings Mountain, North Carolina, Zip 28086–2708, tel. 980/487–5000; Veronica Poole–Adams, R.N., Interim West Market President) **A**1 2 3 10 19 **F**3 4 8 13 15 18 20 28 29 30 31 32 34 35 39 40 43 44 45 47 48 49 50 55 56 57 59 60 64 65 70 71 74 75 76 77 78 79 80 81 82 84 85 86 87 89 93 98 100 107 110 111 114 115 118 119 120 121 123 126 129 130 131 132 135 146 147 148 149 154 156 164 167 168 169 P6 **S** Atrium Health, Inc., Charlotte, NC
Primary Contact: Veronica Poole–Adams, R.N., Interim West Market President
CFO: Christine M Martin, Vice President and Chief Financial Officer
CMO: Charles M Tomlinson, M.D., Chief Medical Officer
CHR: Debra Kale, Vice President Human Resources
CNO: Veronica Poole–Adams, R.N., Vice President, Facility Executive and Chief Nursing Executive
Web address: www.clevelandregional.org
Control: Hospital district or authority, Government, Nonfederal **Service**: General medical and surgical

Staffed Beds: 244 Admissions: 12569 Census: 185 Outpatient Visits: 260120 Births: 1226 Total Expense ($000): 302624 Payroll Expense ($000): 149342 Personnel: 1556

SILER CITY—Chatham County

UNC HEALTH CHATHAM (341311), 475 Progress Boulevard, Zip 27344–6787, Mailing Address: P.O. Box 649, Zip 27344–0649; tel. 919/799–4000, **A**1 10 18 **F**3 13 15 18 28 29 34 35 40 45 46 59 68 70 75 76 77 79 81 84 85 86 92 93 107 110 111 115 119 130 133 135 147 150 156 169 **S** UNC Health, Chapel Hill, NC
Primary Contact: Jeffery C. Strickler, R.N., President
CFO: Jeff LeGay, Chief Financial Officer
CMO: Andrew Hannapel, Chief Medical Officer
CIO: Deborah Taylor, Chief Information Officer
CHR: Jodie Sartor Solow, Director of Human Resources
CNO: Tammy Needham, Chief Nursing Officer
Web address: https://www.chathamhospital.org/ch/
Control: Other not–for–profit (including NFP Corporation) **Service**: General medical and surgical

Staffed Beds: 21 Admissions: 1082 Census: 11 Outpatient Visits: 51733 Births: 141 Total Expense ($000): 47220 Payroll Expense ($000): 13057 Personnel: 170

SMITHFIELD—Johnston County

UNC HEALTH JOHNSTON (340090), 509 North Bright Leaf Blvd, Zip 27577–4407, Mailing Address: P.O. Box 1376, Zip 27577–1376; tel. 919/934–8171, **A**1 2 10 **F**3 11 13 15 17 18 20 22 26 28 29 30 31 32 34 35 38 40 45 49 50 53 57 59 61 62 63 64 66 68 70 73 74 75 76 79 81 82 85 86 87 89 92 93 98 100 107 108 110 111 114 115 119 120 121 126 130 132 145 146 147 148 149 154 156 167 **S** UNC Health, Chapel Hill, NC
Primary Contact: Tom Williams, Chief Executive Officer
COO: Ruth Marler, Chief Nursing Officer and Chief Operating Officer
CFO: Edward A Klein, Chief Financial Officer
CMO: Rodney McCaskill, M.D., Interim Chief Medical Officer
CIO: Teresa Chappell, Chief Information Officer
CHR: Timothy A Hays, Vice President Human Resources
CNO: Ruth Marler, Chief Nursing Officer and Chief Operating Officer
Web address: www.johnstonhealth.org
Control: Hospital district or authority, Government, Nonfederal **Service**: General medical and surgical

Staffed Beds: 153 Admissions: 10868 Census: 138 Outpatient Visits: 174430 Births: 1959 Total Expense ($000): 322344 Payroll Expense ($000): 133251 Personnel: 1709

SOUTHPORT—Brunswick County

★ **DOSHER MEMORIAL HOSPITAL (341327)**, 924 North Howe Street, Zip 28461–3099; tel. 910/457–3800, (Nonreporting) **A**10 18 21
Primary Contact: Lynda Stanley, President and Chief Executive Officer
CFO: Daniel J. Porter, Senior Vice President and Chief Financial Officer
CMO: Brad L Hilaman, M.D., Chief Medical Officer
CIO: Susan Shomaker, Director Information Management Systems
CHR: Deanna Parker, Director Human Resources
Web address: www.dosher.org
Control: Other not–for–profit (including NFP Corporation) **Service**: General medical and surgical

Staffed Beds: 12

SPARTA—Alleghany County

ALLEGHANY HEALTH (341320), 233 Doctors Street, Zip 28675–9247; tel. 336/372–5511, **A**1 10 18 **F**3 15 18 28 29 30 34 35 40 43 45 59 64 67 77 78 79 81 82 87 90 93 97 107 111 114 119 129 130 131 133 135 146 154
Primary Contact: Kathryn Doby, Chief Administrative Officer
CFO: Brett Liverman, Chief Financial Officer
CMO: Joe Arocha, Chief of Staff
CIO: Darlene Keith, Chief Information Systems
CHR: Courtney Bennett, Human Resource Manager
CNO: Wendy Orton, Chief Nursing Officer
Web address: www.amhsparta.org
Control: Other not–for–profit (including NFP Corporation) **Service**: General medical and surgical

Staffed Beds: 3 Admissions: 148 Census: 2 Outpatient Visits: 16116 Births: 0 Total Expense ($000): 15657 Payroll Expense ($000): 5980 Personnel: 138

ALLEGHANY MEMORIAL HOSPITAL See Alleghany Health

SPRUCE PINE—Mitchell County

BLUE RIDGE REGIONAL HOSPITAL (341329), 125 Hospital Drive, Zip 28777–3035; tel. 828/765–4201, (Includes BLUE RIDGE MEDICAL CENTER – YANCEY CAMPUS, 800 Medical Campus Drive, Burnsville, North Carolina, Zip 28714–9010, tel. 828/682–0200) (Nonreporting) **A**1 3 10 18 **S** HCA Healthcare, Nashville, TN
Primary Contact: Tonia Hale, R.N., Chief Executive Officer and Chief Nursing Officer
CFO: Clint Stewart, Chief Financial Officer
CMO: Jennifer Larson, M.D., Chief of Staff
CIO: Pam Blevins, R.N., Director, Clinical Informatics
CNO: Tonia Hale, R.N., Chief Executive Officer and Chief Nursing Officer
Web address: https://missionhealth.org/member-hospitals/blue-ridge/
Control: Other not–for–profit (including NFP Corporation) **Service**: General medical and surgical

Staffed Beds: 21

Hospitals, U.S. / NORTH CAROLINA

STATESVILLE—Iredell County

DAVIS REGIONAL MEDICAL CENTER (344036), 218 Old Mocksville Road, Zip 28625-1930, Mailing Address: P.O. Box 1823, Zip 28687-1823; tel. 704/873-0281, (Nonreporting) **A**1 10 **S** Community Health Systems, Inc., Franklin, TN
Primary Contact: Alec Grabowski, Chief Executive Officer
CFO: Hugh Tobin, Chief Financial Officer
CMO: Christopher Lariscy, M.D., Chief of Staff
CIO: Janie Stikeleather, Director Marketing and Community Relations
CNO: Tammy Marie Moore, Chief Nursing Officer
Web address: www.davisregional.com
Control: Corporation, Investor-owned (for-profit) **Service**: General medical and surgical

Staffed Beds: 144

★ ⇑ **IREDELL HEALTH SYSTEM (340039)**, 557 Brookdale Drive, Zip 28677-4107, Mailing Address: P.O. Box 1828, Zip 28687-1828; tel. 704/873-5661, (Total facility includes 48 beds in nursing home–type unit) **A**2 10 21 **F**3 8 11 13 15 17 18 20 22 28 29 30 31 32 34 35 37 40 41 44 45 47 49 50 54 56 57 58 59 60 62 64 68 70 74 75 76 77 78 79 81 82 85 86 87 89 91 93 97 104 107 108 110 111 115 116 117 118 119 120 121 123 126 127 128 130 132 135 144 146 147 148 154 156 167
Primary Contact: John Green, President and Chief Executive Officer
CFO: Skip Smith, Vice President Finance
CMO: Joseph Mazzola, D.O., Vice President of Medical Affairs
CIO: Kyle Smith, Director Information Systems
CHR: Cindy Smale, Director, Human Resources
CNO: Becky Wagner DNP, RN, Vice President Nursing and Patient Care Services
Web address: www.iredellhealth.org
Control: Other not-for-profit (including NFP Corporation) **Service**: General medical and surgical

Staffed Beds: 199 **Admissions**: 6716 **Census**: 87 **Outpatient Visits**: 120344 **Births**: 669 **Total Expense ($000)**: 235454 **Payroll Expense ($000)**: 110273 **Personnel**: 1435

SYLVA—Jackson County

HARRIS REGIONAL HOSPITAL (340016), 68 Hospital Road, Zip 28779-2722; tel. 828/586-7000, (Nonreporting) **A**1 10 **S** Lifepoint Health, Brentwood, TN
Primary Contact: Ashley Hindman, Chief Executive Officer
CHR: Janet Millsaps, Chief Human Resources Officer
CNO: LaCrystal Gordon, Chief Nursing Officer
Web address: https://www.myharrisregional.com/
Control: Other not-for-profit (including NFP Corporation) **Service**: General medical and surgical

Staffed Beds: 86

TARBORO—Edgecombe County

ECU HEALTH EDGECOMBE HOSPITAL (340107), 111 Hospital Drive, Zip 27886-2011; tel. 252/641-7700, (Nonreporting) **A**1 2 3 10 **S** ECU Health, Greenville, NC
Primary Contact: Patrick Heins, President
CFO: Charles Alford, Vice President Financial Services
CMO: Barry Bunn, M.D., Chief of Staff
CHR: David Prafka, Ed.D., Director of Human Resources
Web address: https://locations.ecuhealth.org/Details/118
Control: Other not-for-profit (including NFP Corporation) **Service**: General medical and surgical

Staffed Beds: 117

VIDANT EDGECOMBE HOSPITAL See ECU Health Edgecombe Hospital

THOMASVILLE—Davidson County

NOVANT HEALTH THOMASVILLE MEDICAL CENTER (340085), 207 Old Lexington Road, Zip 27360-3428, Mailing Address: P.O. Box 789, Zip 27361-0789; tel. 336/472-2000, (Nonreporting) **A**1 2 3 10 **S** Novant Health, Winston Salem, NC
Primary Contact: Jonathan D. Applebaum, President and Chief Operating Officer
CMO: Thomas Zweng, Executive Vice President and Chief Medical Officer
CIO: David B Garrett, Senior Vice President and Chief Information Officer
CNO: Nancy Pearson, MSN, R.N., Director, Nursing
Web address: www.thomasvillemedicalcenter.org
Control: Other not-for-profit (including NFP Corporation) **Service**: General medical and surgical

Staffed Beds: 87

TROY—Montgomery County

★ ⇑ **FIRSTHEALTH MONTGOMERY MEMORIAL HOSPITAL (341303)**, 520 Allen Street, Zip 27371-2802; tel. 910/571-5000, (Nonreporting) **A**10 18 21 **S** FirstHealth of the Carolinas, Pinehurst, NC
Primary Contact: Rebecca W. Carter, MSN, R.N., FACHE, President
CFO: Bryan Hawkins, Controller
CIO: David B Dillehunt, Chief Information Officer
CHR: Tina H Thompson, Coordinator Human Resources
CNO: Pam Gaddy, Director, Patient Care Services and Chief Nursing Officer
Web address: www.firsthealth.org
Control: Other not-for-profit (including NFP Corporation) **Service**: General medical and surgical

Staffed Beds: 5

VALDESE—Burke County

CAROLINAS HEALTHCARE SYSTEM – BLUE RIDGE – VALDESE CAMPUS See UNC Health Blue Ridge – Valdese

WADESBORO—Anson County

ATRIUM HEALTH ANSON (340084), 2301 US Highway 74 W, Zip 28170-7554, Mailing Address: 2301 U.S Highway 74 West, Zip 28170; tel. 704/994-4500, **A**1 10 **F**3 15 18 29 34 35 40 45 50 57 59 75 81 87 93 97 107 110 115 119 129 130 131 132 135 149 156 **P**6 **S** Atrium Health, Inc., Charlotte, NC
Primary Contact: Seth Chandler. Goldwire, Interim Chief Executive Officer
CFO: Jeff Griffin, Assistant Vice President Finance
CMO: Edward Blasko, Chief of Staff
CIO: Lisa Sykes, IS/Communications Director
CHR: Rhonda McFarland, Director Human Resources
CNO: Denise White, MSN, Chief Nurse Executive
Web address: www.carolinashealthcare.org/anson
Control: Hospital district or authority, Government, Nonfederal **Service**: General medical and surgical

Staffed Beds: 15 **Admissions**: 497 **Census**: 4 **Outpatient Visits**: 41474 **Births**: 0 **Total Expense ($000)**: 23051 **Payroll Expense ($000)**: 11805 **Personnel**: 136

WASHINGTON—Beaufort County

VIDANT BEAUFORT HOSPITAL See ECU Health Beaufort Hospital

WHITEVILLE—Columbus County

★ ⇑ **COLUMBUS REGIONAL HEALTHCARE SYSTEM (340068)**, 500 Jefferson Street, Zip 28472-3634; tel. 910/642-8011, (Nonreporting) **A**10 19 21 **S** Atrium Health, Inc., Charlotte, NC
Primary Contact: Jason Beck, President and Chief Executive Officer
CFO: Carl Biber, Chief Financial Officer
CMO: Samuel N Wheatley, Chief Medical Officer
CIO: Lisa Ward, Director Information Systems
CHR: Andrea West, MS, Vice President of Human Resources
CNO: Terri Veneziano, Interim Chief Nursing Officer
Web address: www.crhealthcare.org/
Control: Hospital district or authority, Government, Nonfederal **Service**: General medical and surgical

Staffed Beds: 85

WILMINGTON—New Hanover County

CAPE FEAR MEMORIAL HOSPITAL See Cape Fear Hospital

Hospitals, U.S. / NORTH CAROLINA

★ △ ⇑ **NOVANT HEALTH NEW HANOVER REGIONAL MEDICAL CENTER (340141)**, 2131 South 17th Street, Zip 28401-7483, Mailing Address: P.O. Box 9000, Zip 28402-9000; tel. 910/343-7000, (Includes CAPE FEAR HOSPITAL, 5301 Wrightsville Avenue, Wilmington, North Carolina, Zip 28403-6599, tel. 910/452-8100) **A**2 3 5 7 10 21 **F**3 7 8 11 12 13 15 17 18 20 22 24 26 28 29 30 31 34 35 36 37 39 40 42 43 44 45 46 47 48 49 50 53 54 56 57 58 59 60 61 64 65 66 68 70 72 73 74 75 76 77 78 79 81 82 84 85 86 87 88 89 90 92 93 94 96 97 98 100 101 102 107 108 110 111 114 115 116 117 118 119 120 121 123 124 126 130 131 132 135 144 146 147 148 149 154 155 167 168 169 **S** Novant Health, Winston Salem, NC
Primary Contact: Ernest L. Bovio Jr, Senior Vice President & President Novant Health New Hanover Regional Medical Center & Coastal Market
COO: Laurie Whalin, PharmD, Chief Operating Officer
CFO: Edwin J Ollie, Executive Vice President and Chief Financial Officer
CMO: Sam Spicer, M.D., Vice President Medical Affairs
CHR: Keith A Strawn, Vice President Human Resources
Web address: https://www.novanthealth.org/locations/medical-centers/new-hanover-regional-medical-center/
Control: Other not-for-profit (including NFP Corporation) **Service**: General medical and surgical

Staffed Beds: 697 **Admissions**: 37796 **Census**: 679 **Outpatient Visits**: 521772 **Births**: 4463 **Total Expense ($000)**: 1662995 **Payroll Expense ($000)**: 548556 **Personnel**: 6546

WILMINGTON TREATMENT CENTER (340168), 2520 Troy Drive, Zip 28401-7643; tel. 910/762-2727, (Nonreporting) **A**10 **S** Acadia Healthcare Company, Inc., Franklin, TN
Primary Contact: Robert Pitts, Executive Director
COO: Paige Bottom, Director Operations
CFO: Virginia Powell, Director Finance
CMO: Patrick Martin, M.D., Medical Director
Web address: www.wilmtreatment.com
Control: Corporation, Investor-owned (for-profit) **Service**: Substance Use Disorder

Staffed Beds: 44

WILSON—Wilson County

WILMED NURSING CARE CENTER See Wilmed Nursing Care Center

WILSON MEDICAL CENTER (340126), 1705 Tarboro Street, SW, Zip 27893-3428; tel. 252/399-8040, (Nonreporting) **A**1 2 10 19 **S** Lifepoint Health, Brentwood, TN
Primary Contact: Christopher Munton, Chief Executive Officer
CMO: Rick Guarino, M.D., Vice President Medical Affairs
CIO: Brian Dietrick, Director Information Systems
CHR: Denise O'Hara, Vice President Human Resources
Web address: www.wilmed.org
Control: Other not-for-profit (including NFP Corporation) **Service**: General medical and surgical

Staffed Beds: 130

WINDSOR—Bertie County

ECU HEALTH BERTIE HOSPITAL (341304), 1403 South King Street, Zip 27983-9666, Mailing Address: P.O. Box 40, Zip 27983-0040; tel. 252/794-6600, **A**1 10 18 **F**3 15 29 30 34 35 40 45 46 47 48 49 57 59 64 77 79 81 82 93 94 97 107 110 114 119 127 132 135 146 148 154 156 **S** ECU Health, Greenville, NC
Primary Contact: Brian Harvill, President
CMO: William Ballance, Chief of Medical Staff
CIO: Brian White, Director Strategic Planning
CHR: Nicole Spell, Director Human Resources
Web address: https://locations.ecuhealth.org/Details/126
Control: Other not-for-profit (including NFP Corporation) **Service**: General medical and surgical

Staffed Beds: 6 **Admissions**: 307 **Census**: 3 **Outpatient Visits**: 27129 **Births**: 0 **Total Expense ($000)**: 21274 **Payroll Expense ($000)**: 8755 **Personnel**: 101

VIDANT BERTIE HOSPITAL See ECU Health Bertie Hospital

WINSTON SALEM—Forsyth County

BRENNER CHILDREN'S HOSPITAL & HEALTH SERVICES See Atrium Health Wake Forest Baptist, Winston-Salem

NOVANT HEALTH REHABILITATION HOSPITAL, AN AFFILIATE OF ENCOMPASS HEALTH (343027), 2475 Hillcrest Center Circle, Zip 27103-3048; tel. 336/754-3500, (Nonreporting) **A**1 10 **S** Encompass Health Corporation, Birmingham, AL
Primary Contact: Christopher Fuller, Chief Executive Officer
Web address: https://www.encompasshealth.com/locations/novanthealthrehab
Control: Corporation, Investor-owned (for-profit) **Service**: Rehabilitation

Staffed Beds: 60

WINSTON-SALEM—Forsyth County

△ **ATRIUM HEALTH WAKE FOREST BAPTIST (340047)**, Medical Center Boulevard, Zip 27157-0001; tel. 336/716-2011, (Includes BRENNER CHILDREN'S HOSPITAL & HEALTH SERVICES, 300 Center Boulevard, Winston Salem, North Carolina, Zip 27157, One Medical Center Boulevard, Zip 27157, tel. 336/716-2255) **A**1 2 3 5 7 8 10 19 **F**3 6 7 9 11 12 13 15 16 17 18 19 20 21 22 23 24 25 26 27 28 29 30 31 32 34 35 36 37 38 40 41 43 44 45 46 47 48 49 50 52 53 54 55 56 57 58 59 60 61 62 64 65 66 68 70 72 74 75 76 77 78 79 81 82 84 85 86 87 88 89 90 91 92 93 96 97 98 99 100 101 102 103 104 107 108 110 111 113 114 115 116 117 118 119 120 121 123 124 126 127 129 130 131 132 133 134 135 136 137 138 141 142 143 145 146 147 148 149 150 151 153 154 155 156 157 160 162 164 165 167 168 169 **P**6 **S** Atrium Health, Inc., Charlotte, NC
Primary Contact: Julie Ann. Freischlag, M.D., FACS, Chief Executive Officer
CMO: Russell M Howerton, M.D., Chief Medical Officer
CHR: Cheryl Locke, Vice President and Chief Human Resource Officer
Web address: www.wakehealth.edu
Control: Other not-for-profit (including NFP Corporation) **Service**: General medical and surgical

Staffed Beds: 814 **Admissions**: 44532 **Census**: 719 **Outpatient Visits**: 1134243 **Births**: 3380 **Total Expense ($000)**: 2723004 **Payroll Expense ($000)**: 894044 **Personnel**: 10927

NOVANT HEALTH FORSYTH MEDICAL CENTER (340014), 3333 Silas Creek Parkway, Zip 27103-3090; tel. 336/718-5000, (Includes KERNERSVILLE MEDICAL CENTER, 1750 Kernersville Medical Parkway, Kernersville, North Carolina, Zip 27284-7146, tel. 336/564-4000; Chad Setliff, Senior Vice President, President Novant Health Forsyth Medical Center and Greater Winston-Salem Mark; NOVANT HEALTH CLEMMONS MEDICAL CENTER, 6915 Village Medical Circle, Clemmons, North Carolina, Zip 27012-8002, tel. 336/893-1000; Chad Setliff, Senior Vice President, President Novant Health Forsyth Medical Center and Greater Winston-Salem Mark) **A**1 2 3 5 10 19 **F**3 5 8 11 13 15 17 18 20 22 24 26 28 29 30 31 34 35 37 38 40 44 45 46 48 49 51 53 54 55 57 59 64 65 68 70 71 72 74 76 77 78 79 80 81 82 83 84 85 86 87 89 93 98 100 102 104 105 107 108 110 111 112 115 116 117 118 119 120 121 123 124 126 131 135 136 143 146 147 148 149 152 153 154 156 157 160 161 162 164 165 167 **S** Novant Health, Winston Salem, NC
Primary Contact: Chad Setliff, Senior Vice President, President Novant Health Forsyth Medical Center and Greater Winston-Salem Mark
CMO: Thomas Zweng, Executive Vice President and Chief Medical Officer
CIO: David B Garrett, Senior Vice President and Chief Information Officer
CNO: Loraine Frank-Lightfoot, Vice President and Market Chief Nursing Officer
Web address: https://www.novanthealth.org
Control: Other not-for-profit (including NFP Corporation) **Service**: General medical and surgical

Staffed Beds: 915 **Admissions**: 31858 **Census**: 651 **Outpatient Visits**: 635258 **Births**: 4293 **Total Expense ($000)**: 1295835 **Payroll Expense ($000)**: 434614 **Personnel**: 4784

NOVANT HEALTH MEDICAL PARK HOSPITAL (340148), 1950 South Hawthorne Road, Zip 27103-3993; tel. 336/718-0600, (Nonreporting) **A**1 2 10 **S** Novant Health, Winston Salem, NC
Primary Contact: Alisha C. Hutchens, President and Chief Operating Officer
CMO: Thomas Zweng, Executive Vice President and Chief Medical Officer
CIO: David B Garrett, Senior Vice President and Chief Information Officer
CNO: Carol A Smith, R.N., Director Operations and Nursing
Web address: https://www.novanthealth.org/medical-park-hospital.aspx
Control: Other not-for-profit (including NFP Corporation) **Service**: General medical and surgical

Staffed Beds: 21

OLD VINEYARD BEHAVIORAL HEALTH SERVICES (344007), 3637 Old Vineyard Road, Zip 27104-4842; tel. 336/794-3550, (Nonreporting) **A**1 10 **S** Universal Health Services, Inc., King of Prussia, PA
Primary Contact: Kelly S. Thacker, Chief Executive Officer
CFO: Ernest C Priddy III, Chief Financial Officer
CMO: Raj Thotakura, M.D., Medical Director
CHR: Jackie Pennino, Director Human Resources
CNO: Susan Evans, Chief Nursing Officer
Web address: www.oldvineyardbhs.com
Control: Corporation, Investor-owned (for-profit) **Service**: Psychiatric

Staffed Beds: 158

WAKE FOREST BAPTIST MEDICAL CENTER See Atrium Health Wake Forest Baptist

NORTH DAKOTA

ASHLEY—Mcintosh County

★ **ASHLEY MEDICAL CENTER (351322)**, 612 North Center Avenue, Zip 58413–7013, Mailing Address: P.O. Box 450, Zip 58413–0450; tel. 701/288–3433, (Nonreporting) **A**10 18
Primary Contact: Eric Heupel, Chief Executive Officer
CMO: Udom Tinsa, M.D., Medical Director
Web address: www.amctoday.org
Control: Other not–for–profit (including NFP Corporation) **Service**: General medical and surgical

Staffed Beds: 50

BELCOURT—Rolette County

QUENTIN N. BURDICK MEMORIAL HEALTHCARE FACILITY (350063), 1300 Hospital Loop, Zip 58316, Mailing Address: P.O. Box 160, Zip 58316–0160; tel. 701/477–6111, **A**1 10 **F**3 5 7 8 13 15 29 32 34 35 39 40 43 45 59 64 65 75 76 81 82 89 97 107 110 111 114 119 130 135 143 147 149 154 156 160 164 **S** U. S. Indian Health Service, Rockville, MD
Primary Contact: Shelly Harris, Chief Executive Officer
CFO: Deland Davis, Chief Financial Officer
CMO: Paula Bercier, M.D., Chief Medical Officer
CIO: Chance Wilkie, Information Technology Specialist
CHR: Donna Belgarde, Human Resources Specialist
CNO: Lynelle Hunt, Director of Nursing
Web address: www.ihs.gov
Control: PHS, Indian Service, Government, federal **Service**: General medical and surgical

Staffed Beds: 27 **Admissions**: 310 **Census**: 4 **Outpatient Visits**: 114577 **Births**: 103 **Total Expense ($000)**: 88358 **Payroll Expense ($000)**: 31093 **Personnel**: 387

BISMARCK—Burleigh County

CHI ST. ALEXIUS HEALTH See Chi St. Alexius Health Bismarck

CHI ST. ALEXIUS HEALTH BISMARCK (350002), 900 East Broadway, Zip 58501–4586, Mailing Address: P.O. Box 5510, Zip 58506–5510; tel. 701/530–7000, (Nonreporting) **A**1 2 3 5 10 **S** CommonSpirit Health, Chicago, IL
Primary Contact: Reed Reyman, President
CFO: Stephanie Kaul, Interim Chief Financial Officer
CMO: J'Patrick Fahn, D.O., Chief Medical Officer
CIO: Todd Bortke, Director Information Systems
CHR: Mellissa Nordsven, Director, Human Resources
CNO: Raumi Kudrna, Chief Nursing Officer
Web address: https://www.chistalexiushealth.org/locations/bismarck
Control: Church operated, Nongovernment, not–for–profit **Service**: General medical and surgical

Staffed Beds: 237

SANFORD MEDICAL CENTER BISMARCK (350015), 300 North Seventh Street, Zip 58501–4439, Mailing Address: P.O. Box 5525, Zip 58506–5525; tel. 701/323–6000, **A**1 2 3 5 10 19 **F**3 8 9 11 12 13 15 17 18 20 22 24 26 28 29 30 31 32 33 34 35 36 37 38 40 43 44 45 49 51 53 54 55 56 57 58 59 60 61 62 63 64 65 66 68 69 70 71 72 73 74 75 76 77 78 79 81 82 84 85 86 87 88 89 92 93 96 97 98 100 101 102 104 107 108 110 111 115 118 119 126 129 130 131 132 134 135 138 141 142 146 147 148 149 150 154 156 157 169 **P**6 **S** Sanford Health, Sioux Falls, SD
Primary Contact: Todd Schaffer, M.D., President and Chief Executive Officer
CFO: Kirk Cristy, Vice President Finance
CMO: Chris Meeker, M.D., Chief Medical Officer
CHR: Leah Kelsch, Executive Director
CNO: Patrick Schultz, Vice President Nursing
Web address: https://www.sanfordhealth.org/locations/sanford-medical-center-bismarck
Control: Other not–for–profit (including NFP Corporation) **Service**: General medical and surgical

Staffed Beds: 241 **Admissions**: 13213 **Census**: 144 **Outpatient Visits**: 258795 **Births**: 1595 **Total Expense ($000)**: 788884 **Payroll Expense ($000)**: 331157 **Personnel**: 2970

BOTTINEAU—Bottineau County

SMP HEALTH – ST. ANDREW'S (351307), 316 Ohmer Street, Zip 58318–1045; tel. 701/228–9300, (Nonreporting) **A**10 18 **S** Sisters of Mary of the Presentation Health System, Fargo, ND
Primary Contact: Christopher Albertson, President and Chief Executive Officer
CFO: Sean Rinkenberger, Chief Financial Officer
CMO: Jessica Skjolden, M.D., Chief of Staff
CHR: Brenda Arneson, Administrative Assistant
CNO: Karla Spence, Director of Nursing
Web address: https://smphealth.org/standrews/
Control: Church operated, Nongovernment, not–for–profit **Service**: General medical and surgical

Staffed Beds: 25

ST. ANDREW'S HEALTH CENTER See SMP Health – St. Andrew's

BOWMAN—Bowman County

SOUTHWEST HEALTHCARE SERVICES (351313), 802 2nd Street Northwest, Zip 58623–4483, Mailing Address: P O Drawer 'C', Zip 58623; tel. 701/523–5265, (Nonreporting) **A**10 18
Primary Contact: Dennis Goebel, Chief Executive Officer
Web address: www.swhealthcare.net
Control: Other not–for–profit (including NFP Corporation) **Service**: General medical and surgical

Staffed Beds: 55

CANDO—Towner County

★ **TOWNER COUNTY MEDICAL CENTER (351331)**, State Highway 281 North, Zip 58324, Mailing Address: P.O. Box 688, Zip 58324–0688; tel. 701/968–4411, (Nonreporting) **A**10 18
Primary Contact: Ben Bucher, Chief Executive Officer
CFO: Tammy Larson, Chief Financial Officer
CMO: Russ Petty, M.D., Chief of Staff
CIO: David Fite, Director Information Technology
CHR: Pat Klingenberg, Director Human Resources
Web address: www.tcmedcenter.org
Control: Other not–for–profit (including NFP Corporation) **Service**: General medical and surgical

Staffed Beds: 55

CARRINGTON—Foster County

★ **CHI ST ALEXIUS HEALTH CARRINGTON (351318)**, 800 North Fourth Street, Zip 58421–1217, Mailing Address: P.O. Box 461, Zip 58421–0461; tel. 701/652–3141, **A**10 18 **F**3 5 7 8 11 15 29 40 43 45 47 56 59 68 75 81 82 97 100 102 104 107 108 109 110 114 115 127 128 130 133 135 144 146 147 149 154 156 160 169 **S** CommonSpirit Health, Chicago, IL
Primary Contact: Jodi Lynn. Hovdenes, R.N., President
COO: Brenda Rask, Vice President Operations
CFO: Kurt Sargent, CPA, Vice President, Operational Finance
CIO: Keith Stauffer, Regional Chief Information Officer
CHR: Carol Risovi, Human Resources
Web address: https://www.chistalexiushealth.org/locations/carrington
Control: Church operated, Nongovernment, not–for–profit **Service**: General medical and surgical

Staffed Beds: 25 **Admissions**: 257 **Census**: 2 **Outpatient Visits**: 15529 **Births**: 3

Hospitals, U.S. / NORTH DAKOTA

CAVALIER—Pembina County

★ **PEMBINA COUNTY MEMORIAL HOSPITAL AND WEDGEWOOD MANOR (351319)**, 301 Mountain Street East, Zip 58220–4015, Mailing Address: P.O. Box 380, Zip 58220–0380; tel. 701/265–8461, (Nonreporting) **A**10 18
Primary Contact: Lisa LeTexier, Chief Executive Officer
CFO: Katie Werner, Chief Financial Officer
CMO: K S Sumra, M.D., Chief of Staff
CIO: Robert Heidt, Director Information Systems
CHR: Chelsey Terault, Manager Human Resources
CNO: ArvaDell Sharp, Director of Nursing
Web address: www.cavalierhospital.com
Control: Other not–for–profit (including NFP Corporation) **Service:** General medical and surgical

Staffed Beds: 70

COOPERSTOWN—Griggs County

COOPERSTOWN MEDICAL CENTER See Dakota Regional Medical Center

DAKOTA REGIONAL MEDICAL CENTER (351306), 107 12th Street S, Zip 58425–4501; tel. 701/786–1700, **A**10 18 **F**10 15 28 29 34 35 40 41 43 50 57 59 60 64 67 69 75 77 84 85 89 90 92 97 100 102 104 107 114 127 128 129 130 131 133 135 154 156 169
Primary Contact: Nikki Lindsey, Administrator and Chief Executive Officer
CMO: Jeffrey Peterson, M.D., Medical Director
CHR: Pamela VenHuizen, Chief Human Resources Officer
Web address: https://www.dakotaregional.com/
Control: Other not–for–profit (including NFP Corporation) **Service:** General medical and surgical

Staffed Beds: 9 **Admissions:** 54 **Census:** 3 **Outpatient Visits:** 1459 **Births:** 0 **Personnel:** 34

CROSBY—Divide County

★ **ST. LUKE'S MEDICAL CENTER (351325)**, 702 First Street Southwest, Zip 58730–3329, Mailing Address: P.O. Box 10, Zip 58730–0010; tel. 701/965–6384, (Nonreporting) **A**10 18
Primary Contact: Jody Nelson, Chief Executive Officer
Web address: www.dcstlukes.org/
Control: Other not–for–profit (including NFP Corporation) **Service:** General medical and surgical

Staffed Beds: 50

DEVILS LAKE—Ramsey County

✠ **CHI ST. ALEXIUS HEALTH DEVILS LAKE (351333)**, 1031 Seventh Street NE, Zip 58301–2798; tel. 701/662–2131, (Nonreporting) **A**1 10 18 **S** CommonSpirit Health, Chicago, IL
Primary Contact: Mariann Doeling, R.N., President
CFO: Kurt Sargent, CPA, Vice President Operational Finance
CMO: Richard Johnson, M.D., Chief of Medical Staff
CHR: Bonnie Mattern, Director Human Resources
CNO: Aaron Johnson, Vice President Patient Care Services and Chief Nursing Officer
Web address: https://www.chistalexiushealth.org/locations/devils-lake
Control: Other not–for–profit (including NFP Corporation) **Service:** General medical and surgical

Staffed Beds: 25

DICKINSON—Stark County

✠ **CHI ST. ALEXIUS HEALTH DICKINSON (351336)**, 2500 Fairway Street, Zip 58601–4399; tel. 701/456–4000, (Nonreporting) **A**1 10 18 **S** CommonSpirit Health, Chicago, IL
Primary Contact: Carol Enderle, R.N., MSN, President
CFO: Stephanie Franken, Vice President Operational Finance
CHR: Denise Lutz, Chief Human Resources Officer
CNO: DeeAnna Opstedahl, R.N., Vice President Patient Care Services
Web address: https://www.chistalexiushealth.org/locations/dickinson
Control: Church operated, Nongovernment, not–for–profit **Service:** General medical and surgical

Staffed Beds: 25

ELGIN—Grant County

JACOBSON MEMORIAL HOSPITAL CARE CENTER (351314), 601 East Street North, Zip 58533–7105, Mailing Address: P.O. Box 367, Zip 58533–0367; tel. 701/584–2792, (Nonreporting) **A**10 18
Primary Contact: Scott Brooks, Chief Executive Officer
CFO: Scott Ostenson, Chief Financial Officer
CMO: Deepak Goyal, M.D., Chief of Staff
CHR: Rynae Golke, Director Human Resources
CNO: Connie Gustafson, Director of Nursing
Web address: www.jacobsonhospital.org
Control: Other not–for–profit (including NFP Corporation) **Service:** General medical and surgical

Staffed Beds: 25

FARGO—Cass County

✠ **ESSENTIA HEALTH FARGO (350070)**, 3000 32nd Avenue South, Zip 58103–6132; tel. 701/364–8000, **A**1 2 3 5 10 19 **F**3 9 11 12 13 15 17 18 19 20 22 24 26 28 29 30 31 32 33 34 35 36 38 40 43 44 45 46 47 48 49 50 51 52 54 55 56 57 58 59 60 61 64 65 67 70 72 74 75 76 77 78 79 81 82 84 85 86 87 89 91 92 93 97 100 104 107 108 109 110 111 112 113 114 115 116 117 118 119 120 121 122 123 124 126 127 129 130 131 132 135 144 145 146 147 148 149 154 156 157 162 164 167 168 169 **P**6 **S** Essentia Health, Duluth, MN
Primary Contact: Mark Thompson, M.D., President
COO: Al Hurley, West Region Chief Operating Officer
CFO: Dennis Fuhrman, Vice President Finance
CMO: Michael Briggs, M.D., Chief Medical Officer
CIO: Ken Gilles, Chief Information Officer
CHR: Keith Wahlund, Vice President Human Resources
Web address: https://www.essentiahealth.org/find-facility/profile/essentia-health-fargo/
Control: Other not–for–profit (including NFP Corporation) **Service:** General medical and surgical

Staffed Beds: 156 **Admissions:** 8519 **Census:** 118 **Outpatient Visits:** 195596 **Births:** 1199 **Total Expense ($000):** 565793 **Payroll Expense ($000):** 244031 **Personnel:** 1905

FARGO NURSING HOME See Rosewood On Broadway

✠ **FARGO VA MEDICAL CENTER**, 2101 Elm Street North, Zip 58102; tel. 701/232–3241, (Nonreporting) **A**1 3 5 **S** Department of Veterans Affairs, Washington, DC
Primary Contact: Breton Weintraub, Medical Center Director
COO: Dale DeKrey, MS, Associate Director Operations and Resources
CFO: Roger Sayler, Finance Officer
CMO: J Brian Hancock, M.D., Chief of Staff
CIO: Raymond Nelson, Acting Chief Information Resource Management
CHR: Jason Wells, Chief Human Resources Management Service
CNO: Julie Bruhn, R.N., MS, Associate Director Patient Care and Nurse Executive
Web address: www.fargo.va.gov
Control: Veterans Affairs, Government, federal **Service:** General medical and surgical

Staffed Beds: 38

FARGO VAMC See Fargo VA Medical Center

MERITCARE SOUTH UNIVERSITY See Sanford South University

★ △ **PAM REHABILITATION HOSPITAL OF FARGO (353026)**, 4671 38th Avenue South, Zip 58104; tel. 701/404–5100, **A**7 22 **F**29 34 56 57 60 64 68 74 75 77 79 82 86 87 90 132 135 143 148 149 154 **S** PAM Health, Enola, PA
Primary Contact: Jessica Franke, Chief Executive Officer
Web address: https://pamhealth.com/facilities/find-facility/rehabilitation-hospitals/pam-rehabilitation-hospital-fargo
Control: Partnership, Investor–owned (for–profit) **Service:** Rehabilitation

Staffed Beds: 42 **Admissions:** 1245 **Census:** 40 **Outpatient Visits:** 4961 **Births:** 0 **Total Expense ($000):** 23860 **Payroll Expense ($000):** 12121 **Personnel:** 188

☐ **PRAIRIE ST. JOHN'S (354004)**, 510 4th Street South, Zip 58103–1914; tel. 701/476–7200, (Nonreporting) **A**1 3 5 10 **S** Universal Health Services, Inc., King of Prussia, PA
Primary Contact: Ty Hegland, Chief Executive Officer
COO: Jennifer Faul, Chief Operating Officer
CFO: Tom Eide, Chief Financial Officer
CMO: Eduardo Meza, M.D., Medical Director
CHR: Michelle A Parkinson, Director Human Resources
CNO: Jacki Toppen, Director of Nursing
Web address: www.prairie-stjohns.com
Control: Partnership, Investor–owned (for–profit) **Service:** Psychiatric

Staffed Beds: 94

Hospitals, U.S. / NORTH DAKOTA

✠ △ **SANFORD MEDICAL CENTER FARGO (350011)**, 801 Broadway North, Zip 58122-3641; tel. 701/234-2000, (Includes SANFORD SOUTH UNIVERSITY, 1720 South University Drive, Fargo, North Dakota, Zip 58103-4994, tel. 701/234-2000; Nate White, Executive Vice President) **A**1 2 3 5 7 10 19 **F**3 5 7 8 9 11 12 13 15 17 18 19 20 21 22 23 24 25 26 27 28 29 30 31 32 33 34 35 36 37 38 39 40 43 44 45 46 47 48 49 50 51 52 53 54 55 56 57 58 59 60 61 62 63 64 65 66 67 68 70 71 72 74 75 76 78 79 80 81 82 83 84 85 86 87 88 89 90 91 92 93 94 96 97 98 99 100 101 102 103 104 105 107 108 110 111 112 114 115 116 117 118 119 120 121 123 124 126 129 130 131 132 135 138 141 142 143 144 145 146 147 148 149 150 152 153 154 155 156 157 160 162 163 165 167 169 **P**6 **S** Sanford Health, Sioux Falls, SD
Primary Contact: Tiffany Lawrence, President and Chief Executive Officer
COO: Brittany Sachdeva, Vice President of Operations
CMO: Douglas Griffin, M.D., Vice President Medical Officer
CIO: Arlyn Broekhuis, Chief Information Officer
CNO: Theresa Larson, MSN, R.N., Vice President, Nursing and Clinical Services
Web address: www.sanfordhealth.org
Control: Other not-for-profit (including NFP Corporation) **Service**: General medical and surgical

Staffed Beds: 530 **Admissions**: 25997 **Census**: 334 **Outpatient Visits**: 379382 **Births**: 2743 **Total Expense ($000)**: 1650913 **Payroll Expense ($000)**: 638197 **Personnel**: 5328

✠ **VIBRA HOSPITAL OF FARGO (352004)**, 5225 23rd Avenue South, 7th Floor, Zip 58103-4940; tel. 701/241-9099, (Nonreporting) **A**1 10 **S** Vibra Healthcare, Mechanicsburg, PA
Primary Contact: Custer Huseby, Chief Executive Officer
Web address: www.vhfargo.com
Control: Corporation, Investor-owned (for-profit) **Service**: Acute long-term care hospital

Staffed Beds: 31

FORT YATES—Sioux County

✠ **STANDING ROCK SERVICE UNIT, FORT YATES HOSPITAL, INDIAN HEALTH SERVICE, DHHS (350064)**, 10 North River Road, Zip 58538, Mailing Address: P.O. Box 'J', Zip 58538; tel. 701/854-3831, (Nonreporting) **A**1 10 **S** U. S. Indian Health Service, Rockville, MD
Primary Contact: Jana Gipp, Chief Executive Officer
CFO: Byron Wilcox, Chief Financial Management Officer
CMO: Sara Jumping Eagle, Clinical Director
CNO: Joelle Keepseagle, Director of Nursing
Web address: www.ihs.gov
Control: PHS, Indian Service, Government, federal **Service**: General medical and surgical

Staffed Beds: 14

GARRISON—Mclean County

★ **CHI ST. ALEXIUS HEALTH GARRISON (351303)**, 407 Third Avenue SE, Zip 58540-7235; tel. 701/463-2275, (Nonreporting) **A**5 10 18 **S** CommonSpirit Health, Chicago, IL
Primary Contact: Adam Maus, Administrator
CMO: Vern Harchenko, M.D., Chief of Staff
CNO: Beth Hetletved, Director of Nurses
Web address: https://www.chistalexiushealth.org/locations/garrison
Control: Other not-for-profit (including NFP Corporation) **Service**: General medical and surgical

Staffed Beds: 50

CHI ST. ALEXIUS HEALTH-GARRISON MEMORIAL HOSPITAL See Chi St. Alexius Health Garrison

GRAFTON—Walsh County

★ **UNITY MEDICAL CENTER (351320)**, 164 West 13th Street, Zip 58237-1896; tel. 701/352-1620, (Nonreporting) **A**10 18
Primary Contact: Alan O'Neil, Chief Executive Officer
CFO: Rachel Ray, Chief Financial Officer
Web address: www.unitymedcenter.com
Control: Other not-for-profit (including NFP Corporation) **Service**: General medical and surgical

Staffed Beds: 14

GRAND FORKS—Grand Forks County

✠ △ **ALTRU HEALTH SYSTEM (350019)**, 1200 South Columbia Road, Zip 58201-4036, Mailing Address: P.O. Box 6002, Zip 58206-6002; tel. 701/780-5000, (Includes ALTRU HOSPITAL, 1200 South Columbia Road, Grand Forks, North Dakota, Zip 58201, PO Box 6002, Zip 58206-6002, tel. 701/780-5000; ALTRU REHABILITATION CENTER, 1300 South Columbia Road, Grand Forks, North Dakota, Zip 58201, tel. 701/780-2311) (Nonreporting) **A**1 2 3 5 7 10 20
Primary Contact: Todd Forkel, Chief Executive Officer
COO: Meghan Compton, Executive Vice President, Chief Clinic Operations Officer
CIO: Mark Waind, Executive Vice President, Chief Information Officer
CHR: Kellee J. Fisk, Chief People and Strategy Officer
CNO: Janice L. Hamscher, MSN, Executive Vice President, Chief Nursing Officer
Web address: www.altru.org
Control: Other not-for-profit (including NFP Corporation) **Service**: General medical and surgical

Staffed Beds: 299

ALTRU REHAB CENTER See Altru Rehabilitation Center

☐ **ALTRU REHABILITATION HOSPITAL (353027)**, 4500 S Washington Street, Suite B, Zip 58201-7217; tel. 701/732-7400, (Nonreporting) **A**1 **S** Encompass Health Corporation, Birmingham, AL
Primary Contact: Luke Lawrimore, Chief Executive Officer
Web address: https://encompasshealth.com/locations/grandforksrehab
Control: Corporation, Investor-owned (for-profit) **Service**: Rehabilitation

Staffed Beds: 40

UNITED HOSPITAL See Altru Hospital

HARVEY—Wells County

SMP HEALTH – ST. ALOISIUS (351327), 325 East Brewster Street, Zip 58341-1653; tel. 701/324-4651, (Nonreporting) **A**10 18 **S** Sisters of Mary of the Presentation Health System, Fargo, ND
Primary Contact: Ryan Mickelsen, President and Chief Executive Officer
COO: Colleen Cannon, Chief Financial Officer and Chief Operational Officer
CFO: Colleen Cannon, Chief Operating Officer and Chief Financial Officer
Web address: https://smphealth.org/staloisius/
Control: Church operated, Nongovernment, not-for-profit **Service**: General medical and surgical

Staffed Beds: 110

ST. ALOISIUS MEDICAL CENTER See SMP Health – St. Aloisius

HAZEN—Mercer County

★ **SAKAKAWEA MEDICAL CENTER (351310)**, 510 Eighth Avenue NE, Zip 58545-4637; tel. 701/748-2225, (Nonreporting) **A**10 18
Primary Contact: Kurt Waldbillig, Chief Executive Officer
CFO: Renae Snyder, Chief Financial Officer
CMO: Jacinta Klindworth, Chief Medical Officer
CHR: Laurie Miller, Executive Assistant
Web address: www.smcnd.org
Control: Other not-for-profit (including NFP Corporation) **Service**: General medical and surgical

Staffed Beds: 18

HETTINGER—Adams County

WEST RIVER REGIONAL MEDICAL CENTER (351330), 1000 Highway 12, Zip 58639-7530; tel. 701/567-4561, (Nonreporting) **A**3 5 10 18
Primary Contact: Alyson Kornele, Chief Executive Officer
CFO: Nathan Stadheim, Chief Financial Officer
CMO: Jennifer Shefield, M.D., Chief of Staff
CIO: Julia Gochenour, Manager Information Systems
CHR: Tera Fried, Manager Human Resources
CNO: Barbara Stadheim, Chief Nursing Officer
Web address: www.wrhs.com
Control: Other not-for-profit (including NFP Corporation) **Service**: General medical and surgical

Staffed Beds: 25

HILLSBORO—Traill County

HILLSBORO NURSING HOME See Hillsboro Community Nursing Home

Hospital, Medicare Provider Number, Address, Telephone, Approval, Facility, and Physician Codes, Health Care System

★ American Hospital Association (AHA) membership   ○ Healthcare Facilities Accreditation Program   ⇑ Center for Improvement in Healthcare Quality Accreditation
☐ The Joint Commission accreditation   ◇ DNV Healthcare Inc. accreditation   △ Commission on Accreditation of Rehabilitation Facilities (CARF) accreditation

Hospitals, U.S. / NORTH DAKOTA

★ **SANFORD HILLSBORO MEDICAL CENTER (351329)**, 12 Third Street SE, Zip 58045–4840, Mailing Address: P.O. Box 609, Zip 58045–0609; tel. 701/636–3200, (Nonreporting) **A**10 18 **S** Sanford Health, Sioux Falls, SD
Primary Contact: Jac McTaggart, Chief Executive Officer
CFO: Scott Awalt, Chief Financial Officer
CMO: Charles J Breen, M.D., Medical Director
CHR: Jenny Jacobson, Manager Human Resources
Web address: https://www.sanfordhealth.org/locations/sanford-hillsboro-medical-center
Control: Other not–for–profit (including NFP Corporation) **Service**: General medical and surgical

Staffed Beds: 46

JAMESTOWN—Stutsman County

⊞ **JAMESTOWN REGIONAL MEDICAL CENTER (351335)**, 2422 20th Street SW, Zip 58401–6201; tel. 701/952–1050, (Nonreporting) **A**1 10 18
Primary Contact: Michael Delfs, President and Chief Executive Officer
CFO: Beverly Fiferlick, Chief Financial Officer
CMO: Bradly Skari, Chief of Staff
CIO: Jeff Gunkel, Chief Information Officer
CHR: Lesley Erlandson, Human Resources Manager
CNO: Trisha Jungels, R.N., Chief Nursing Officer and Vice President Clinical Services
Web address: https://www.jrmcnd.com
Control: Other not–for–profit (including NFP Corporation) **Service**: General medical and surgical

Staffed Beds: 25

☐ **NORTH DAKOTA STATE HOSPITAL (354003)**, 2605 Circle Drive SE, Zip 58401–6905; tel. 701/253–3964, (Nonreporting) **A**1 3 5 10
Primary Contact: Aaron Olson, Chief Executive Officer
COO: Ken Schulz, Chief Operating Officer
CIO: Amy Shape, Information Technology
CNO: Leah Schulz, Director of Nursing
Web address: www.nd.gov/
Control: State, Government, Nonfederal **Service**: Psychiatric

Staffed Beds: 100

KENMARE—Ward County

TRINITY KENMARE COMMUNITY HOSPITAL (351305), 317 First Avenue NW, Zip 58746–7104, Mailing Address: P.O. Box 697, Zip 58746–0697; tel. 701/385–4296, (Nonreporting) **A**10 18 **S** Trinity Health, Minot, ND
Primary Contact: Danielle Alsadon, Clinic/Hospital Manager
COO: Bev Heninger, Director of Nursing
CFO: Dennis Empey, Chief Financial Officer
CMO: Buki Oni, M.D., Chief Medical Officer
CIO: David Wanner, Director Information Technology
CHR: Ranae Ehlke, Administrative Secretary and Coordinator Risk Management and Human Resources
CNO: Bev Heninger, Director of Nursing
Web address: www.kenmarend.net/hospital.htm
Control: Other not–for–profit (including NFP Corporation) **Service**: General medical and surgical

Staffed Beds: 25

LANGDON—Cavalier County

CAVALIER COUNTY MEMORIAL HOSPITAL AND CLINICS See Langdon Prairie Health

★ **LANGDON PRAIRIE HEALTH (351323)**, 909 Second Street, Zip 58249–2407; tel. 701/256–6100, (Nonreporting) **A**10 18
Primary Contact: Wayne Reid, Chief Executive Officer
COO: Darla Roder, Chief Operating Officer
CFO: Richard Fromme, Chief Financial Officer
CMO: Lynne Didrikson, M.D., Chief Medical Officer
CHR: Linda Benoit, Human Resource Officer
CNO: Jamie Nienhuis, Chief Nursing Officer
Web address: https://www.lph.hospital/
Control: Other not–for–profit (including NFP Corporation) **Service**: General medical and surgical

Staffed Beds: 20

LINTON—Emmons County

★ **LINTON REGIONAL MEDICAL CENTER (351328)**, 518 North Broadway, Zip 58552–7308, Mailing Address: P.O. Box 850, Zip 58552–0850; tel. 701/254–4511, (Nonreporting) **A**10 18
Primary Contact: Lukas Fischer, R.N., Chief Executive Officer
CMO: John Knecht, Chief Medical Staff
CHR: Sue Meidinger, Manager Business Office
Web address: www.lintonhospital.com
Control: Other not–for–profit (including NFP Corporation) **Service**: General medical and surgical

Staffed Beds: 14

LISBON—Ransom County

★ **CHI LISBON HEALTH (351311)**, 905 Main Street, Zip 58054–4334, Mailing Address: P.O. Box 353, Zip 58054–0353; tel. 701/683–6400, (Nonreporting) **A**10 18 **S** CommonSpirit Health, Chicago, IL
Primary Contact: Becki Thompson, Administrator
COO: Sheri Heinisch, Compliance Officer
CFO: Amber Stowman, Controller
CHR: Janet Froemke, Human Resources Officer
Web address: www.lisbonhospital.com
Control: Church operated, Nongovernment, not–for–profit **Service**: General medical and surgical

Staffed Beds: 25

MANDAN—Morton County

⊞ **VIBRA HOSPITAL OF CENTRAL DAKOTAS (352005)**, 1000 18th Street NW, Zip 58554–1612; tel. 701/667–2000, (Nonreporting) **A**1 10 **S** Vibra Healthcare, Mechanicsburg, PA
Primary Contact: Scott Schneider, Chief Executive Officer
Web address: www.vhcentraldakotas.com
Control: Corporation, Investor–owned (for–profit) **Service**: Acute long–term care hospital

Staffed Beds: 41

MAYVILLE—Traill County

★ **SANFORD MAYVILLE MEDICAL CENTER (351309)**, 42 Sixth Avenue SE, Zip 58257–1598; tel. 701/786–3800, (Nonreporting) **A**10 18 **S** Sanford Health, Sioux Falls, SD
Primary Contact: Jac McTaggart, Chief Executive Officer
CFO: Shauna Slabik, Chief Financial Officer
CMO: Jane Ostlig, Chief Medical Officer
Web address: www.unionhospital.com
Control: Other not–for–profit (including NFP Corporation) **Service**: General medical and surgical

Staffed Beds: 10

MCVILLE—Nelson County

NELSON COUNTY HEALTH SYSTEM (351308), 200 Main Street, Zip 58254, Mailing Address: P.O. Box 367, Zip 58254–0367; tel. 701/322–4328, (Nonreporting) **A**10 18
Primary Contact: Samantha Harding, Chief Executive Officer
CMO: Erling Martinson, M.D., Medical Director
Web address: www.nelsoncountyhealthsystem.org
Control: Other not–for–profit (including NFP Corporation) **Service**: General medical and surgical

Staffed Beds: 49

MINOT—Ward County

☐ △ **TRINITY HEALTH (350006)**, 1 Burdick Expressway West, Zip 58701–4406, Mailing Address: P.O. Box 5020, Zip 58702–5020; tel. 701/857–5766, (Includes TRINITY HOSPITAL–ST. JOSEPH'S, 407 3rd Street SE, Minot, North Dakota, Zip 58702–5001, tel. 701/857–2000) (Nonreporting) **A**1 2 3 5 7 10 **S** Trinity Health, Minot, ND
Primary Contact: John M. Kutch, President and Chief Executive Officer
CFO: Jason Hotchkiss, CPA, Chief Financial Officer
CIO: David Wanner, Chief Information Officer
CHR: Paul Simonson, Vice President
Web address: www.trinityhealth.org
Control: Other not–for–profit (including NFP Corporation) **Service**: General medical and surgical

Staffed Beds: 580

UNIMED MEDICAL CENTER See Trinity Hospital–St. Joseph's

NORTHWOOD—Grand Forks County

★ **NORTHWOOD DEACONESS HEALTH CENTER (351312)**, 4 North Park Street, Zip 58267–4102, Mailing Address: P.O. Box 190, Zip 58267–0190; tel. 701/587–6060, (Nonreporting) **A**10 18 **S** Sanford Health, Sioux Falls, SD
Primary Contact: Brock Sherva, Chief Executive Officer
CMO: Jon Berg, M.D., Chief of Staff
CIO: Chad Peterson, Chief Information Officer
Web address: www.ndhc.net
Control: Church operated, Nongovernment, not–for–profit **Service**: General medical and surgical

Staffed Beds: 57

Hospitals, U.S. / NORTH DAKOTA

OAKES—Dickey County

★ **CHI OAKES HOSPITAL (351315)**, 1200 North Seventh Street, Zip 58474–2502; tel. 701/742–3291, (Nonreporting) **A**10 18 **S** CommonSpirit Health, Chicago, IL
Primary Contact: Becki Thompson, President
CFO: Bethany Smith, Director of Finance
CMO: Katie O'Brien–Paradis, M.D., Chief Medical Officer
CHR: Julie Entzminger, Manager Human Resources
CNO: Kimberly A. Ketterling, R.N., Vice President Patient Care Services
Web address: www.oakeshospital.com
Control: Other not–for–profit (including NFP Corporation) **Service**: General medical and surgical

Staffed Beds: 20

PARK RIVER—Walsh County

★ **FIRST CARE HEALTH CENTER (351326)**, 115 Vivian Street, Zip 58270–4540, Mailing Address: PO Box I, Zip 58270–0708; tel. 701/284–7500, (Nonreporting) **A**10 18
Primary Contact: Marcus Lewis, Chief Executive Officer
CFO: Layne Ensrude, Chief Financial Officer
CMO: Joel Johnson, M.D., Chief Medical Staff
CNO: Lori Seim, R.N., Director Nursing Services
Web address: www.firstcarehc.com
Control: Other not–for–profit (including NFP Corporation) **Service**: General medical and surgical

Staffed Beds: 14

ROLLA—Rolette County

PRESENTATION MEDICAL CENTER See SMP Health – St. Kateri

★ **SMP HEALTH – ST. KATERI (351316)**, 213 Second Avenue NE, Zip 58367–7153, Mailing Address: P.O. Box 759, Zip 58367–0759; tel. 701/477–3161, (Nonreporting) **A**10 18 **S** Sisters of Mary of the Presentation Health System, Fargo, ND
Primary Contact: Christopher Albertson, Chief Executive Officer and President
CFO: Paula Wilkie, Chief Financial Officer
CMO: Roy Cordy, M.D., President Medical Staff
Web address: https://smphealth.org/stkateri/
Control: Church operated, Nongovernment, not–for–profit **Service**: General medical and surgical

Staffed Beds: 25

RUGBY—Pierce County

★ **HEART OF AMERICA MEDICAL CENTER (351332)**, 800 Main Avenue South, Zip 58368–2198; tel. 701/776–5261, (Nonreporting) **A**10 18
Primary Contact: Erik Christenson, Chief Executive Officer
CFO: Melissa Shepard, Chief Financial Officer
CIO: Jeremy Schonebery, Director Information Technology
Web address: www.hamc.com
Control: Other not–for–profit (including NFP Corporation) **Service**: General medical and surgical

Staffed Beds: 75

STANLEY—Mountrail County

★ **MOUNTRAIL COUNTY MEDICAL CENTER (351301)**, 615 6th Street SE, Zip 58784–4444, Mailing Address: P.O. Box 399, Zip 58784–0399; tel. 701/628–2424, (Nonreporting) **A**10 18
Primary Contact: Stephanie Everett, Chief Executive Officer
CFO: Eugeniya Griffin, Chief Financial Officer
CMO: Marla Longmuir, M.D., Chief Medical Officer
CIO: Kathy Janssen, Director Medical Records
CHR: Alisha DeBilt, Human Resources Director
CNO: Belinda Moen, R.N., MSN, Interim Director of Nursing
Web address: www.stanleyhealth.org
Control: Other not–for–profit (including NFP Corporation) **Service**: General medical and surgical

Staffed Beds: 11

TIOGA—Williams County

★ **TIOGA MEDICAL CENTER (351300)**, 810 North Welo Street, Zip 58852–7157, Mailing Address: P.O. Box 159, Zip 58852–0159; tel. 701/664–3305, (Nonreporting) **A**10 18
Primary Contact: Jamie Eraas, President and Chief Executive Officer
CFO: Holly Bryant, Chief Financial Officer
CMO: Swami P Gade, M.D., Medical Director
CHR: Mary Ann Holm, Office Clerk
Web address: www.tiogahealth.org
Control: Other not–for–profit (including NFP Corporation) **Service**: General medical and surgical

Staffed Beds: 55

TURTLE LAKE—McLean County

★ **CHI ST. ALEXIUS HEALTH TURTLE LAKE HOSPITAL (351304)**, 220 Fifth Avenue, Zip 58575–4005, Mailing Address: P.O. Box 280, Zip 58575–0280; tel. 701/448–2331, (Nonreporting) **A**10 18 **S** CommonSpirit Health, Chicago, IL
Primary Contact: Adam Maus, Administrator
CFO: Tom Spain, Director Operations Finance
CNO: Jessie Martin, R.N., Chief Nursing Executive
Web address: https://www.chistalexiushealth.org/turtle-lake/facilities/chi-st-alexius-health-turtle-lake-hospital
Control: Church operated, Nongovernment, not–for–profit **Service**: General medical and surgical

Staffed Beds: 25

VALLEY CITY—Barnes County

★ **CHI MERCY HEALTH (351324)**, 570 Chautauqua Boulevard, Zip 58072–3199; tel. 701/845–6400, (Nonreporting) **A**10 18 **S** CommonSpirit Health, Chicago, IL
Primary Contact: D. Ryan. Fowler, President
CFO: Bethany Smith, Vice President Finance
CHR: Nicole Nestler, Division Director Human Resources
Web address: www.mercyhospitalvalleycity.org
Control: Church operated, Nongovernment, not–for–profit **Service**: General medical and surgical

Staffed Beds: 19

WATFORD CITY—Mckenzie County

★ **MCKENZIE COUNTY HEALTHCARE SYSTEM (351302)**, 516 North Main Street, Zip 58854–7310; tel. 701/842–3000, (Nonreporting) **A**10 18
Primary Contact: Peter D. Edis, Chief Executive Officer
COO: Michael Curtis, Chief Administrative Officer
CFO: Kenneth Cox, Interim Chief Financial Officer
CMO: Gary Ramage, M.D., Chief Medical Officer
CIO: Karn Pederson, Manager Health Information Management
CHR: Amy Gonzales, Director of Human Resources
CNO: Cheryl Faulkner, Director of Nursing
Web address: www.mckenziehealth.com
Control: Other not–for–profit (including NFP Corporation) **Service**: General medical and surgical

Staffed Beds: 80

WILLISTON—Williams County

✠ **CHI ST. ALEXIUS HEALTH WILLISTON (351334)**, 1301 15th Avenue West, Zip 58801–3896; tel. 701/774–7400, **A**1 3 10 18 **F**3 11 12 13 15 28 29 30 32 34 35 39 40 43 45 47 50 57 59 63 64 65 70 74 75 76 77 79 81 82 84 85 93 107 108 110 115 118 129 130 131 132 133 134 146 149 150 154 **S** CommonSpirit Health, Chicago, IL
Primary Contact: Garrick Hyde, President
CMO: Brett Vibeto, M.D., Chief of Staff
CIO: Jeff Rust, Information Technology Systems Site Manager
CNO: Lori Hahn, Vice President Nursing Services
Web address: www.mercy-williston.org
Control: Church operated, Nongovernment, not–for–profit **Service**: General medical and surgical

Staffed Beds: 25 **Admissions**: 1569 **Census**: 11

WISHEK—Mcintosh County

★ **SOUTH CENTRAL HEALTH (351321)**, 1007 Fourth Avenue South, Zip 58495–7527, Mailing Address: P.O. Box 647, Zip 58495–0647; tel. 701/452–2326, (Nonreporting) **A**10 18
Primary Contact: Lukas Fischer, R.N., Chief Executive Officer
CFO: Colleen Cannon, Chief Financial Officer
CMO: Joseph Thirumalareddy, M.D., Chief of Staff
CIO: Kari Buchholz, Director Health Information Management
CHR: Shar Bauer, Executive Secretary
Web address: https://schealthnd.com
Control: Other not–for–profit (including NFP Corporation) **Service**: General medical and surgical

Staffed Beds: 19

Hospital, Medicare Provider Number, Address, Telephone, Approval, Facility, and Physician Codes, Health Care System

★ American Hospital Association (AHA) membership
☐ The Joint Commission accreditation
○ Healthcare Facilities Accreditation Program
◇ DNV Healthcare Inc. accreditation
⇑ Center for Improvement in Healthcare Quality Accreditation
△ Commission on Accreditation of Rehabilitation Facilities (CARF) accreditation

Hospitals, U.S. / OHIO

OHIO

AKRON—Summit County

☐ △ **AKRON CHILDREN'S HOSPITAL (363303)**, 1 Perkins Square, Zip 44308–1063; tel. 330/543–1000, (Nonreporting) **A**1 2 3 5 7 8 10
Primary Contact: Christopher A. Gessner, President and Chief Executive Officer
COO: Lisa Aurilio, R.N., MSN, Chief Operating Officer
CFO: Gordon Edwards, Chief Financial Officer
CMO: Robert McGregor, M.D., Chief Medical Officer
CIO: Harun Rashid, Vice President and Chief Information Officer
CHR: Bernett Williams, Interim Chief Human Resource Officer
CNO: Christine Young, R.N., Vice President of Patient Services and Chief Nursing Officer
Web address: www.akronchildrens.org
Control: Other not–for–profit (including NFP Corporation) **Service:** Children's general medical and surgical

Staffed Beds: 466

AKRON CITY HOSPITAL See Summa Akron City Hospital

☒ **CLEVELAND CLINIC AKRON GENERAL (360027)**, 1 Akron General Avenue, Zip 44307–2433; tel. 330/344–6000, **A**1 2 3 5 8 10 19 **F**3 5 8 11 12 13 15 17 18 20 22 24 26 28 29 30 31 33 34 35 36 37 38 40 42 43 44 45 46 47 48 49 50 51 52 53 54 55 56 57 58 59 60 61 62 63 64 65 66 68 70 72 74 75 76 77 78 79 80 81 82 84 85 87 92 93 94 96 97 98 100 101 102 104 105 107 108 110 111 112 114 115 117 118 119 120 121 123 124 126 129 130 131 132 135 145 146 147 148 149 153 154 156 160 161 164 167 169 **S** Cleveland Clinic Health System, Cleveland, OH
Primary Contact: Brian J. Harte, M.D., President
CFO: Dave Frigo, Vice President Financial Planning and Treasury
CIO: David Fiser, Vice President and Chief Information Officer
CHR: Don Corpora, Executive Vice President and Chief Human Resources Officer
CNO: Kelli J. Saucerman–Howard
Web address: www.akrongeneral.org
Control: Other not–for–profit (including NFP Corporation) **Service:** General medical and surgical

Staffed Beds: 485 Admissions: 24754 Census: 322 Outpatient Visits: 738062 Births: 1692 Total Expense ($000): 725153 Payroll Expense ($000): 304319 Personnel: 4114

SAINT THOMAS HOSPITAL See Summa Saint Thomas Hospital

☒ **SELECT SPECIALTY HOSPITAL–AKRON (362027)**, 200 East Market Street, Zip 44308–2015; tel. 330/761–7500, (Nonreporting) **A**1 10 **S** Select Medical Corporation, Mechanicsburg, PA
Primary Contact: Dawne Chaney, Chief Executive Officer
Web address: https://www.selectspecialtyhospitals.com/locations-and-tours/oh/akron/akron/
Control: Corporation, Investor–owned (for–profit) **Service:** Acute long–term care hospital

Staffed Beds: 60

SUMMA AKRON CITY HOSPITAL See Summa Health System – Akron Campus, Akron

SUMMA HEALTH SYSTEM See Summa Health System – Akron Campus

☒ **SUMMA HEALTH SYSTEM – AKRON CAMPUS (360020)**, 525 East Market Street, Zip 44304–1619; tel. 330/375–3000, (Includes SUMMA AKRON CITY HOSPITAL, 525 East Market Street, Akron, Ohio, Zip 44309–2090, P O Box 2090, Zip 44309–2090, tel. 330/375–3000; SUMMA HEALTH SYSTEM BARBERTON HOSPITAL, 155 Fifth Street NE, Barberton, Ohio, Zip 44203–3332, tel. 330/615–3000; SUMMA SAINT THOMAS HOSPITAL, 444 North Main Street, Akron, Ohio, Zip 44310, tel. 330/375–3000) **A**1 2 3 5 8 10 19 **F**3 4 5 8 11 12 13 15 17 18 20 22 24 26 28 29 30 31 34 35 36 37 38 39 40 42 43 44 45 46 47 48 49 50 51 53 54 56 57 58 59 61 64 65 66 70 71 74 75 76 77 78 79 80 81 82 83 84 85 86 87 92 93 97 98 100 101 102 103 104 105 107 110 111 114 115 116 117 118 119 120 121 123 124 126 129 130 131 132 133 135 144 146 147 148 149 153 154 156 157 160 161 162 164 165 166 167 169 **S** Summa Health, Akron, OH
Primary Contact: T. Clifford Deveny, M.D., Chief Executive Officer
CIO: Tanya Authur, Chief Information Officer
CHR: Kyle Klawitter, Vice President Human Resources
Web address: www.summahealth.org
Control: Other not–for–profit (including NFP Corporation) **Service:** General medical and surgical

Staffed Beds: 685 Admissions: 36470 Census: 499 Outpatient Visits: 359780 Births: 4718 Total Expense ($000): 1276424 Payroll Expense ($000): 316228 Personnel: 7166

☐ △ **SUMMA REHAB HOSPITAL (363035)**, 29 North Adams Street, Zip 44304–1641; tel. 330/572–7300, (Nonreporting) **A**1 7 10 **S** Summa Health, Akron, OH
Primary Contact: Janet Hein, Chief Executive Officer
Web address: www.summarehabhospital.com/
Control: Corporation, Investor–owned (for–profit) **Service:** Rehabilitation

Staffed Beds: 60

SUMMA SAINT THOMAS HOSPITAL See Summa Health System – Akron Campus, Akron

ALLIANCE—Stark County

○ **AULTMAN ALLIANCE COMMUNITY HOSPITAL (360131)**, 200 East State Street, Zip 44601–4936; tel. 330/596–6000, (Total facility includes 78 beds in nursing home–type unit) **A**2 5 10 11 **F**3 11 15 28 29 30 31 34 35 36 37 40 41 44 45 50 53 56 57 59 60 61 64 65 68 69 70 71 74 75 77 78 79 81 82 84 85 86 87 89 93 96 98 100 103 107 108 110 111 114 115 118 119 126 128 130 131 132 135 143 146 147 148 149 154 156 157 164 166 167 **P**7 8 **S** Aultman Health Foundation, Canton, OH
Primary Contact: Ryan Jones, Chief Executive Officer
COO: Dale W. Wells, Chief Financial and Operating Officer
CFO: Dale W. Wells, Chief Financial and Operating Officer
CMO: Ashraf Ahmed, M.D., Senior Vice President Physician and Hospital Services
CIO: David W Shroades, Vice President Technology Services
CHR: Nicole L Russ, Director Colleague Relations
CNO: Amy Antonacci, MSN, R.N., Vice President Nursing Services
Web address: https://aultmanalliance.org/
Control: Other not–for–profit (including NFP Corporation) **Service:** General medical and surgical

Staffed Beds: 203 Admissions: 1501 Census: 21 Outpatient Visits: 165521 Births: 0 Total Expense ($000): 102451 Payroll Expense ($000): 40103 Personnel: 636

AMHERST—Lorain County

☐ **SPECIALTY HOSPITAL OF LORAIN (362025)**, 254 Cleveland Avenue, Zip 44001–1620; tel. 440/988–6260, (Nonreporting) **A**1 10
Primary Contact: Susan Adams, Chief Nursing Officer and Chief Operating Officer
COO: Susan Adams, Chief Nursing Officer and Chief Operating Officer
CNO: Susan Adams, Chief Nursing Officer and Chief Operating Officer
Web address: https://specialtyhospitaloflorain.org
Control: Other not–for–profit (including NFP Corporation) **Service:** Acute long–term care hospital

Staffed Beds: 30

ARCHBOLD—Fulton County

ARCHBOLD HOSPITAL See Community Hospitals and Wellness Centers, Bryan

Hospitals, U.S. / OHIO

ASHLAND—Ashland County

★ ⇧ **UNIVERSITY HOSPITALS SAMARITAN MEDICAL CENTER (360002)**, 1025 Center Street, Zip 44805–4011; tel. 419/289–0491, **A**10 21 **F**3 11 15 18 20 22 26 28 29 30 31 34 35 36 38 40 45 47 50 51 54 56 57 59 60 61 64 65 68 70 75 77 78 79 81 82 84 85 86 87 91 93 96 102 107 111 115 116 117 118 119 129 130 131 132 135 144 146 147 148 149 150 154 156 157 162 164 169 **S** University Hospitals, Cleveland, OH
Primary Contact: Sylvia Radziszewski, Chief Operating Officer
CFO: Mary Griest, Vice President Finance and Chief Financial Officer
CMO: Philip Myers, M.D., Vice President Medical Affairs
CIO: Kathleen Metcalf, Chief Information Officer
CHR: Alyce Legg, Vice President Human Resources
CNO: Karin Schwan, Chief Nursing Officer, Vice President Patient Care Services
Web address: https://www.uhhospitals.org/locations/uh-samaritan-medical-center
Control: Other not–for–profit (including NFP Corporation) **Service**: General medical and surgical

Staffed Beds: 28 **Admissions**: 2151 **Census**: 21 **Outpatient Visits**: 94013 **Births**: 104 **Total Expense ($000)**: 92949 **Payroll Expense ($000)**: 26978 **Personnel**: 388

ASHTABULA—Ashtabula County

▨ **ASHTABULA COUNTY MEDICAL CENTER (360125)**, 2420 Lake Avenue, Zip 44004–4954; tel. 440/997–2262, **A**1 5 10 20 **F**3 5 11 15 18 20 28 29 30 31 34 35 38 40 44 45 46 47 50 51 53 57 59 60 62 64 65 68 70 74 75 77 78 79 80 81 82 85 87 89 92 93 97 98 100 101 102 103 104 107 108 110 111 114 115 116 118 119 130 131 132 135 146 147 148 149 153 154 156 157 164 **P**8
Primary Contact: Leonard Stepp, President and Chief Executive Officer
COO: Lewis Hutchison, Vice President Operations and Quality
CFO: Donald L Kepner, Chief Financial Officer
CMO: Jude Cauwenberg, M.D., Chief of Staff
CIO: Jared Swiger, Director Cyber Security
CHR: Jonathan Forbes, Director Human Resources
CNO: Ken Frame, Chief Nursing Officer
Web address: www.acmchealth.org
Control: Other not–for–profit (including NFP Corporation) **Service**: General medical and surgical

Staffed Beds: 130 **Admissions**: 4943 **Census**: 54 **Outpatient Visits**: 240009 **Births**: 0 **Total Expense ($000)**: 123853 **Payroll Expense ($000)**: 41867 **Personnel**: 788

ATHENS—Athens County

☐ **APPALACHIAN BEHAVIORAL HEALTHCARE (364015)**, 100 Hospital Drive, Zip 45701–2301; tel. 740/594–5000, (Nonreporting) **A**1 3 10 **S** Ohio Department of Mental Health, Columbus, OH
Primary Contact: Elaine Crnkovic, Chief Executive Officer
COO: Kelly Sole, Chief Operating Officer
CMO: Todd Jamrose I, Chief Clinical Officer
CHR: Donovan Workman, Director Human Capital Management
CNO: Karen Durniat–Sushrstedt, Nurse Executive
Web address: www.mh.state.oh.us
Control: State, Government, Nonfederal **Service**: Psychiatric

Staffed Beds: 224

O'BLENESS MEMORIAL HOSPITAL See Ohiohealth O'Bleness Hospital

▨ **OHIOHEALTH O'BLENESS HOSPITAL (360014)**, 55 Hospital Drive, Zip 45701–2302; tel. 740/593–5551, (Nonreporting) **A**1 3 5 10 12 13 **S** OhioHealth, Columbus, OH
Primary Contact: LeeAnn Helber, President
CFO: Robert Melaragno, Vice President Finance
CIO: Kristine Barr, Vice President Communication Services
CHR: Sandie Leasure, Senior Vice President Human Resources
CNO: Sandy Wood, MSN, R.N., Vice President Patient Services and Chief Nursing Officer
Web address: www.obleness.org
Control: Other not–for–profit (including NFP Corporation) **Service**: General medical and surgical

Staffed Beds: 67

AVON—Lorain County

▨ **CLEVELAND CLINIC AVON HOSPITAL (360364)**, 33300 Cleveland Clinic Boulevard, Zip 44011; tel. 440/695–5000, **A**1 2 3 10 **F**3 15 18 20 29 30 34 35 36 40 45 49 50 56 59 63 64 68 70 74 75 77 78 79 80 81 82 84 85 86 87 97 100 107 108 110 111 114 115 116 117 119 130 131 146 147 148 149 156 167 **S** Cleveland Clinic Health System, Cleveland, OH
Primary Contact: Rebecca Starck, M.D., Vice President
COO: John Mills, Chief Operating Officer
CFO: Lori Koenig, Assistant Finance Director
CMO: Michael Taylor, M.D., Chief Medical Officer
CNO: Mary R Sauer, R.N., Chief Nursing Officer
Web address: www.my.clevelandclinic.org
Control: Other not–for–profit (including NFP Corporation) **Service**: General medical and surgical

Staffed Beds: 126 **Admissions**: 7759 **Census**: 79 **Outpatient Visits**: 173692 **Births**: 0 **Total Expense ($000)**: 157370 **Payroll Expense ($000)**: 61773 **Personnel**: 688

▨ △ **CLEVELAND CLINIC REHABILITATION HOSPITAL (363038)**, 33355 Health Campus Boulevard, Zip 44011; tel. 440/937–9099, (Includes CLEVELAND CLINIC REHABILITATION HOSPITAL – AKRON, 4389 Medina Road, Copley, Ohio, Zip 44321–1388, tel. 234/815–5100; CLEVELAND CLINIC REHABILITATION HOSPITAL, 3025 Science Park DR, Beachwood, Ohio, Zip 44122–7333, 3025 Science Park Drive, Zip 441122, tel. 216/455–6400; Jessica Daugherty, Chief Executive Officer) **A**1 3 7 10 **F**3 29 30 34 35 38 57 58 59 60 65 68 69 74 75 86 87 90 91 92 94 95 96 97 119 130 132 135 143 148 149 154 156 157 164 167 **S** Select Medical Corporation, Mechanicsburg, PA
Primary Contact: Julie Idoine–Fries, FACHE, Chief Executive Officer
Web address: www.my.clevelandclinic.org
Control: Partnership, Investor–owned (for–profit) **Service**: Rehabilitation

Staffed Beds: 180 **Admissions**: 4305 **Census**: 166 **Outpatient Visits**: 0 **Births**: 0 **Personnel**: 714

☐ △ **UH AVON REHABILITATION HOSPITAL (363039)**, 37900 Chester Road, Zip 44011–1044; tel. 440/695–7100, **A**1 3 7 10 **F**3 28 29 34 35 44 50 57 59 60 65 68 74 75 79 87 90 91 92 95 96 97 119 130 135 148 149 150 154 156 164 **P**6 **S** Kindred Healthcare, Mechanicsburg, PA
Primary Contact: Thomas Stranz, Chief Executive Officer
CFO: Jason DiGuilio, Controller
CHR: Abby Hoag, Director, Human Resources
CNO: Katie Kasper, Chief Clinical Officer
Web address: www.uhhospitals.org/uh-avon-rehabilitation-hospital
Control: Partnership, Investor–owned (for–profit) **Service**: Rehabilitation

Staffed Beds: 40 **Admissions**: 802 **Census**: 30 **Outpatient Visits**: 0 **Births**: 0 **Total Expense ($000)**: 12325 **Payroll Expense ($000)**: 6590 **Personnel**: 93

BARBERTON—Summit County

SUMMA BARBERTON CITIZENS HOSPITAL See Summa Health System Barberton Hospital

BARNESVILLE—Belmont County

▨ **WVU MEDICINE – BARNESVILLE HOSPITAL (361321)**, 639 West Main Street, Zip 43713–1039, Mailing Address: P.O. Box 309, Zip 43713–0309; tel. 740/425–3941, (Nonreporting) **A**1 10 18 **S** West Virginia University Health System, Morgantown, WV
Primary Contact: Stacey Armstrong, Interim President
CFO: Willie Cooper–Lohr, Chief Financial Officer
CMO: David J Hilliard, D.O., Chief of Staff
CHR: Beth K. Brill, Senior Director Human Resources
CNO: Cynthia Touvelle, R.N., Senior Director Care Management and Chief Nursing Officer
Web address: https://wvumedicine.org/barnesville/
Control: Other not–for–profit (including NFP Corporation) **Service**: General medical and surgical

Staffed Beds: 25

Hospital, Medicare Provider Number, Address, Telephone, Approval, Facility, and Physician Codes, Health Care System

★ American Hospital Association (AHA) membership   ◯ Healthcare Facilities Accreditation Program   ⇧ Center for Improvement in Healthcare Quality Accreditation
☐ The Joint Commission accreditation   ◇ DNV Healthcare Inc. accreditation   △ Commission on Accreditation of Rehabilitation Facilities (CARF) accreditation

Hospitals, U.S. / OHIO

BATAVIA—Clermont County

✠ **MERCY HEALTH – CLERMONT HOSPITAL (360236)**, 3000 Hospital Drive, Zip 45103–1921; tel. 513/732–8200, (Nonreporting) **A**1 2 10 **S** Bon Secours Mercy Health, Cincinnati, OH
Primary Contact: Tim Prestridge, President
CFO: Shirley Harper, Chief Financial Officer
CMO: Janice Jones, M.D., Chief of Staff
CHR: Bridget Mentzel, System Director Human Resources
CNO: Sandra Hugueley, Vice President Nursing
Web address: https://www.mercy.com/locations/hospitals/cincinnati/mercy-health-clermont-hospital
Control: Church operated, Nongovernment, not–for–profit **Service**: General medical and surgical

Staffed Beds: 178

BEACHWOOD—Cuyahoga County

⇑ **UH BEACHWOOD MEDICAL CENTER** See University Hospitals Beachwood Medical Center

□ △ **UH REHABILITATION HOSPITAL (363036)**, 23333 Harvard Road, Zip 44122–6232; tel. 216/593–2200, **A**1 3 7 10 **F**3 28 29 34 35 44 50 57 59 60 65 68 75 79 87 90 91 92 95 96 119 130 132 135 148 149 154 156 164 **P**6 **S** Kindred Healthcare, Cincinnati, OH
Web address: https://www.uhhospitals.org/locations/uh-rehabilitation-hospital
Control: Partnership, Investor–owned (for–profit) **Service**: Rehabilitation

Staffed Beds: 46 **Admissions**: 934 **Census**: 27 **Outpatient Visits**: 0
Births: 0 **Total Expense ($000)**: 15103 **Payroll Expense ($000)**: 8643
Personnel: 72

★ ⇑ **UNIVERSITY HOSPITALS AHUJA MEDICAL CENTER (360359)**, 3999 Richmond Road, Zip 44122–6046; tel. 216/593–5500, **A**3 10 21 **F**3 15 18 20 22 24 26 29 30 34 35 36 37 40 45 46 47 48 49 50 51 53 54 55 57 58 59 60 61 62 63 64 65 68 69 70 71 74 75 78 79 80 81 82 84 85 86 87 91 92 93 100 102 107 108 110 111 114 115 119 125 130 131 132 135 145 146 147 148 149 150 154 156 157 160 161 164 165 167 168 **S** University Hospitals, Cleveland, OH
Primary Contact: Alan Papa, President
Web address: https://www.uhhospitals.org/locations/uh-ahuja-medical-center
Control: Other not–for–profit (including NFP Corporation) **Service**: General medical and surgical

Staffed Beds: 144 **Admissions**: 9550 **Census**: 109 **Outpatient Visits**: 211844 **Births**: 0 **Total Expense ($000)**: 285176 **Payroll Expense ($000)**: 83189 **Personnel**: 1120

★ ⇑ **UNIVERSITY HOSPITALS BEACHWOOD MEDICAL CENTER (360367)**, 25501 Chagrin Boulevard, Zip 44122–5603; tel. 216/545–4800, **A**3 10 21 **F**3 29 30 35 38 39 40 50 51 58 68 79 81 82 85 86 87 93 100 102 107 111 119 126 130 131 149 **S** University Hospitals, Cleveland, OH
Primary Contact: Robyn Strosaker, M.D., President and Chief Operating Officer
Web address: https://www.uhhospitals.org/locations/uh-beachwood-medical-center
Control: Other not–for–profit (including NFP Corporation) **Service**: General medical and surgical

Staffed Beds: 24 **Admissions**: 377 **Census**: 4 **Outpatient Visits**: 15787
Births: 0 **Total Expense ($000)**: 64350 **Payroll Expense ($000)**: 11183
Personnel: 153

BEAVERCREEK—Greene County

★ ○ **SOIN MEDICAL CENTER (360360)**, 3535 Pentagon Boulevard, Zip 45431–1705; tel. 937/702–4000, **A**3 10 11 19 **F**3 11 13 15 18 20 22 26 29 30 34 36 40 42 43 44 45 53 54 56 59 64 66 70 73 74 75 76 77 78 79 80 81 82 85 86 87 93 96 102 107 108 109 110 111 114 115 116 117 118 119 120 121 124 126 130 131 135 146 147 148 149 154 157 167 169 **P**3 6 **S** Kettering Health, Dayton, OH
Primary Contact: Daniel Tryon, President
CMO: Michael Caccamo, M.D., Chief Medical Officer
CNO: Belinda Mallett, R.N., MS, Vice President, Patient Care and Clinical Services
Web address: https://www.khnetwork.org/soin
Control: Church operated, Nongovernment, not–for–profit **Service**: General medical and surgical

Staffed Beds: 172 **Admissions**: 9577 **Census**: 110 **Outpatient Visits**: 164214 **Births**: 802 **Total Expense ($000)**: 268442 **Payroll Expense ($000)**: 90013 **Personnel**: 1044

BELLEFONTAINE—Logan County

★ ⇑ **MARY RUTAN HOSPITAL (360197)**, 205 Palmer Avenue, Zip 43311–2281; tel. 937/592–4015, (Nonreporting) **A**5 10 20 21
Primary Contact: Chad A. Ross, President and Chief Executive Officer
CFO: Steven Brown, Vice President Fiscal Affairs
CMO: Grant Varian, M.D., Medical Director
CIO: Robert Reynolds, Director Information Systems
CHR: Vickie L Crumley, Chief Human Resources Officer
CNO: Wendy Rodenberger, Chief Nursing Officer and Vice President, Patient Services
Web address: www.maryrutan.org
Control: Other not–for–profit (including NFP Corporation) **Service**: General medical and surgical

Staffed Beds: 45

BELLEVUE—Sandusky County

✠ **BELLEVUE HOSPITAL, THE (360107)**, 1400 West Main Street, Zip 44811–9088, Mailing Address: P.O. Box 8004, Zip 44811–8004; tel. 419/483–4040, (Nonreporting) **A**1 3 5 10
Primary Contact: Timothy A. Buit, President and Chief Executive Officer
CMO: Corey Fazio, M.D., Chief Medical Officer
CIO: Kim Stults, Director, Information Systems
CHR: Lisa M. Sartain, Vice President, Human Resources
CNO: Sara Brokaw, President and Chief Nursing Officer
Web address: www.bellevuehospital.com
Control: Other not–for–profit (including NFP Corporation) **Service**: General medical and surgical

Staffed Beds: 50

BLUE ASH—Hamilton County

CINCINNATI REHABILITATION HOSPITAL (363047), 4291 Parkview Drive, Zip 45242–5667; tel. 513/788–3313, (Nonreporting) **A**10 22 **S** Nobis Rehabilitation Partners, Allen, TX
Web address: https://www.cincinnati-rehabhospital.com/
Control: Partnership, Investor–owned (for–profit) **Service**: Rehabilitation

Staffed Beds: 40

BLUFFTON—Allen County

✠ **BLUFFTON HOSPITAL (361322)**, 139 Garau Street, Zip 45817–1027; tel. 419/358–9010, (Nonreporting) **A**1 10 18 **S** Blanchard Valley Health System, Findlay, OH
Primary Contact: Myron D. Lewis, Chief Executive Officer
CFO: David Cytlak, Vice President Finance
CMO: William H. Kose, M.D., Vice President Quality and Medical Affairs
CIO: David Cytlak, Vice President Finance
CHR: Ryan Fisher, Director Human Resources
CNO: Barbara J. Pasztor, R.N., Chief Nursing Executive
Web address: www.bvhealthsystem.org/
Control: Other not–for–profit (including NFP Corporation) **Service**: General medical and surgical

Staffed Beds: 25

BOARDMAN—Mahoning County

□ **MERCY HEALTH – ST. ELIZABETH BOARDMAN HOSPITAL (360276)**, 8401 Market Street, Zip 44512–6777; tel. 330/729–2929, (Nonreporting) **A**1 3 5 10 13 **S** Bon Secours Mercy Health, Cincinnati, OH
Primary Contact: Eugenia Aubel, President
CFO: Anthony J. Seminaro, Chief Financial Youngstown
CMO: Heath Dorion, Physician Administrator
CIO: Maureen Kordupel, Director Information Technology Relationship Manager
CNO: Stacie Call, Chief Nursing Officer
Web address: https://www.mercy.com/youngstown
Control: Church operated, Nongovernment, not–for–profit **Service**: General medical and surgical

Staffed Beds: 229

★ **SELECT SPECIALTY HOSPITAL – BOARDMAN (362023)**, 8049 South Avenue, Zip 44512–6154; tel. 330/729–1750, (Includes SELECT SPECIALTY HOSPITAL – TRUMBULL, 1350 East Market Street, 9th Floor, Warren, Ohio, Zip 44483–6608, 1350 E Market Street, 9th Floor, Zip 44483–6608, tel. 330/675–5555; Carl W. Nichols III, Market Chief Executive Officer) (Nonreporting) **A**10 **S** Select Medical Corporation, Mechanicsburg, PA
Primary Contact: Carl W. Nichols III, Chief Executive Officer
Web address: www.selectspecialtyhospitals.com/
Control: Corporation, Investor–owned (for–profit) **Service**: Acute long–term care hospital

Staffed Beds: 24

BOWLING GREEN—Wood County

WOOD COUNTY HOSPITAL (360029), 950 West Wooster Street, Zip 43402–2603; tel. 419/354–8900, **A**1 2 3 5 10 **F**3 11 12 13 15 28 29 32 33 34 35 36 37 40 44 45 50 54 56 57 59 60 64 65 68 69 70 74 75 76 77 78 79 81 82 85 87 89 93 97 107 108 110 111 114 115 118 119 120 121 123 124 126 129 130 131 132 135 144 146 147 148 149 154 156 169 **P**6 8
Primary Contact: Stanley R. Korducki, President
CFO: Karol Bortel, Vice President Financial Services
CMO: Shawn Stansbery, M.D., Chief of Staff
CIO: Joanne White, Chief Information Officer
CHR: Michael Ford, Vice President Patient Services
CNO: Sandra Beidelschies, MSN, R.N., Vice President Patient Services
Web address: www.woodcountyhospital.org
Control: Other not–for–profit (including NFP Corporation) **Service**: General medical and surgical

Staffed Beds: 103 **Admissions**: 2047 **Census**: 17 **Outpatient Visits**: 124978 **Births**: 330 **Total Expense ($000)**: 107282 **Payroll Expense ($000)**: 36433 **Personnel**: 565

BRYAN—Williams County

BRYAN COMMUNITY HOSPITAL See Bryan Hospital

COMMUNITY HOSPITALS AND WELLNESS CENTERS (360121), 433 West High Street, Zip 43506–1679; tel. 419/636–1131, (Includes ARCHBOLD HOSPITAL, 121 Westfield Drive, Archbold, Ohio, Zip 43502, tel. 419/445–4415; BRYAN HOSPITAL, 433 West High Street, Bryan, Ohio, Zip 43506, tel. 419/636–1131; MONTPELIER HOSPITAL, 909 East Snyder Avenue, Montpelier, Ohio, Zip 43543, tel. 419/485–3154) (Nonreporting) **A**1 5 10 19
Primary Contact: Chad Tinkel, Chief Executive Officer
CFO: Leroy P Feather, Vice President Finance
CIO: Greg Slattery, Vice President Information
CHR: Mary Ann Potts, Director Personnel
Web address: www.chwchospital.com
Control: Other not–for–profit (including NFP Corporation) **Service**: General medical and surgical

Staffed Beds: 113

BUCYRUS—Crawford County

BUCYRUS COMMUNITY HOSPITAL (361316), 629 North Sandusky Avenue, Zip 44820–1821; tel. 419/562–4677, (Nonreporting) **A**10 18 21 **S** Avita Health System, Galion, OH
Primary Contact: Jerome Morasko, President and Chief Executive Officer
CMO: Amanda Kovolyan, M.D., Chief Medical Officer
CIO: Alex Reed, Chief Information Officer
CHR: Traci Oswald, Vice President Human Resources
Web address: www.bchonline.org
Control: Other not–for–profit (including NFP Corporation) **Service**: General medical and surgical

Staffed Beds: 25

CADIZ—Harrison County

WVU MEDICINE – HARRISON COMMUNITY HOSPITAL (361311), 951 East Market Street, Zip 43907–9799; tel. 740/942–4631, (Nonreporting) **A**1 10 18 **S** West Virginia University Health System, Morgantown, WV
Primary Contact: Stacey Armstrong, Interim President
CFO: Donald Huelskamp, Interim Chief Financial Officer
CMO: Anandhi Murthy, Chief Medical Officer
CIO: Will Combs, Director Information Technology
CHR: Peter Giordano, Senior Director Human Resources
CNO: Janis Olinski, R.N., Vice President Clinical Services
Web address: www.harrisoncommunity.com
Control: Other not–for–profit (including NFP Corporation) **Service**: General medical and surgical

Staffed Beds: 25

CAMBRIDGE—Guernsey County

OHIOHEALTH SOUTHEASTERN MEDICAL CENTER (360203), 1341 North Clark Street, Zip 43725–9614, Mailing Address: 1341 Clark Street, Zip 43725–0610; tel. 740/439–8000, (Nonreporting) **A**1 2 3 10 20 **S** OhioHealth, Columbus, OH
Primary Contact: Wendy C. Elliott, President
CFO: Timothy R. Evancho, Chief Financial Officer
CMO: E Edwin Conaway, M.D., Vice President Medical Affairs and Chief Medical Officer
CHR: Steven Michael Brooks, Vice President Human Resources
CNO: Gina F. Woods, Chief Nursing Officer
Web address: https://www.ohiohealth.com/locations/hospitals/southeastern-medical-center
Control: Other not–for–profit (including NFP Corporation) **Service**: General medical and surgical

Staffed Beds: 81

CANAL WINCHESTER—Fairfield County

DILEY RIDGE MEDICAL CENTER (360358), 7911 Diley Road, Zip 43110–9653; tel. 614/838–7911, (Nonreporting) **A**1 10 **S** Trinity Health, Livonia, MI
Primary Contact: Stacey Collins, R.N., Site Administrator, Chief Nursing Officer
Web address: www.dileyridgemedicalcenter.com
Control: Other not–for–profit (including NFP Corporation) **Service**: General medical and surgical

Staffed Beds: 10

CANTON—Stark County

ALUTMAN HOSPITAL PEDIATRIC SERVICES See Aultman Hospital Pediatric Services

AULTMAN HOSPITAL (360084), 2600 Sixth Street SW, Zip 44710–1702; tel. 330/452–9911, (Includes AULTMAN HOSPITAL PEDIATRIC SERVICES, 2600 Sixth Street, SW, Canton, Ohio, Zip 44710–1702, tel. 330/363–5455) **A**1 2 3 5 7 8 10 11 13 19 **F**3 7 8 11 12 13 15 17 18 20 22 24 26 28 29 30 31 34 35 39 40 42 43 44 45 48 49 50 51 53 54 55 56 57 58 59 60 61 62 63 64 68 70 71 72 74 75 76 77 78 79 81 82 83 84 85 86 87 89 90 93 96 97 102 104 105 107 108 109 110 111 114 115 116 117 118 119 120 121 123 126 127 128 129 130 131 132 133 134 135 143 144 145 146 147 148 149 150 154 155 156 157 164 166 167 **S** Aultman Health Foundation, Canton, OH
Primary Contact: Anne Gunther, R.N., MSN, President
CFO: Mark Wright, Vice President
CMO: Allison Oprandi, M.D., Chief Medical Officer
CIO: Liz Getz, Chief Information Officer
CHR: Sue Olivera, Vice President
CNO: Nicole Marie Kolacz, R.N., Chief Nursing Officer
Web address: www.aultman.com
Control: Other not–for–profit (including NFP Corporation) **Service**: General medical and surgical

Staffed Beds: 482 **Admissions**: 21946 **Census**: 264 **Outpatient Visits**: 620225 **Births**: 2356 **Total Expense ($000)**: 693947 **Payroll Expense ($000)**: 222302 **Personnel**: 5815

CLEVELAND CLINIC MERCY HOSPITAL (360070), 1320 Mercy Drive NW, Zip 44708–2641; tel. 330/489–1000, **A**1 2 3 5 10 19 **F**3 12 13 15 17 18 20 22 24 26 28 29 30 31 34 35 37 39 40 43 45 48 49 50 51 53 54 55 59 60 61 64 66 68 70 73 74 75 76 77 78 79 80 81 82 84 85 86 87 90 91 92 93 96 97 98 100 102 107 108 110 111 114 115 116 117 118 119 120 121 123 124 126 129 130 131 132 135 144 146 147 148 149 150 154 156 167 169 **S** Cleveland Clinic Health System, Cleveland, OH
Primary Contact: Timothy Crone, M.D., Vice President
CFO: David K Stewart, Senior Vice President and Chief Financial Officer
CMO: David Gormsen, D.O., Senior Vice President and Chief Medical Officer
CIO: Robin Stursa, Vice President, Chief Information Officer
CHR: Patti Bresnahan, Director Human Resources
CNO: Barbara Yingling, R.N., Senior Vice President Patient Care Services and Chief Nursing Officer
Web address: www.cantonmercy.org
Control: Other not–for–profit (including NFP Corporation) **Service**: General medical and surgical

Staffed Beds: 331 **Admissions**: 14972 **Census**: 199 **Outpatient Visits**: 488135 **Births**: 902 **Total Expense ($000)**: 448309 **Payroll Expense ($000)**: 198464 **Personnel**: 2042

Hospital, Medicare Provider Number, Address, Telephone, Approval, Facility, and Physician Codes, Health Care System

★ American Hospital Association (AHA) membership
☐ The Joint Commission accreditation
○ Healthcare Facilities Accreditation Program
◇ DNV Healthcare Inc. accreditation
⇑ Center for Improvement in Healthcare Quality Accreditation
△ Commission on Accreditation of Rehabilitation Facilities (CARF) accreditation

Hospitals, U.S. / OHIO

MERCY MEDICAL CENTER See Cleveland Clinic Mercy Hospital

☒ **SELECT SPECIALTY HOSPITAL–CANTON (362016)**, 1320 Mercy Drive NW, 6th Floor, Zip 44708–2614; tel. 330/489–8189, (Nonreporting) **A**1 10 **S** Select Medical Corporation, Mechanicsburg, PA
Primary Contact: Sheila Tonn–Knopf, Chief Executive Officer
Web address: www.selectspecialtyhospitals.com/company/locations/canton.aspx
Control: Corporation, Investor–owned (for–profit) **Service**: Acute long–term care hospital

Staffed Beds: 30

CHARDON—Geauga County

⇑ **UH REGIONAL HOSPITALS** See University Hospitals Geauga Medical Center

UNIVERSITY HOSPITALS EXTENDED CARE CAMPUS See Heatherhill Care Communities

★ ⇑ **UNIVERSITY HOSPITALS GEAUGA MEDICAL CENTER (360075)**, 13207 Ravenna Road, Zip 44024–7032; tel. 440/269–6000, **A**3 10 21 **F**3 11 12 13 15 18 20 22 26 28 29 30 31 32 34 35 36 38 39 40 41 42 43 44 45 47 48 50 51 54 55 56 57 58 59 60 62 63 64 65 68 70 74 75 76 77 78 79 81 82 84 85 86 87 91 92 93 94 96 98 100 101 102 103 107 108 110 111 114 115 116 117 119 126 129 130 131 132 134 135 143 144 145 146 147 148 149 150 154 157 167 **S** University Hospitals, Cleveland, OH
Primary Contact: Donald DeCarlo, M.D., President
CFO: Paul Amantea, Director Finance
CMO: David Kosnosky, M.D., Chief Medical Officer
CIO: Lou Ciraldo, Information Services Representative
CHR: Danialle Lynce, Manager Human Resources
CNO: Peggy A Kuhar, R.N., MSN, Chief Nursing Officer
Web address: https://www.uhhospitals.org/locations/uh-geauga-medical-center
Control: Other not–for–profit (including NFP Corporation) **Service**: General medical and surgical

Staffed Beds: 120 **Admissions**: 7664 **Census**: 82 **Outpatient Visits**: 174673 **Births**: 1213 **Total Expense ($000)**: 198476 **Payroll Expense ($000)**: 61559 **Personnel**: 879

CHILLICOTHE—Ross County

ADENA MEDICAL CENTER See Adena Regional Medical Center

☒ **ADENA REGIONAL MEDICAL CENTER (360159)**, 272 Hospital Road, Zip 45601–9031; tel. 740/779–7500, (Nonreporting) **A**1 2 3 5 10 19 **S** Adena Health System, Chillicothe, OH
Primary Contact: Jeff Graham, President and Chief Executive Officer
CMO: John Fortney, Senior System Medical Advisor
CIO: Linn Weimer, Chief Information Officer
CHR: Jay D. Justice, Chief Human Resource Officer
Web address: www.adena.org
Control: Other not–for–profit (including NFP Corporation) **Service**: General medical and surgical

Staffed Beds: 246

☒ **CHILLICOTHE VETERANS AFFAIRS MEDICAL CENTER**, 17273 State Route 104, Zip 45601–9718; tel. 740/773–1141, (Nonreporting) **A**1 3 5 **S** Department of Veterans Affairs, Washington, DC
Primary Contact: Kenneth Mortimer, Medical Center Director
COO: Robert Taylor, Associate Medical Center Director
CFO: Rick Deckard, Chief Fiscal Service
CMO: Deborah Meesig, M.D., Chief of Staff
CIO: William Gawler, Chief Information Officer
CHR: Kenneth Clancy, Chief Human Resources Officer
Web address: www.chillicothe.va.gov/
Control: Veterans Affairs, Government, federal **Service**: Psychiatric

Staffed Beds: 295

CINCINNATI—Hamilton County

☒ **BETHESDA NORTH HOSPITAL (360179)**, 10500 Montgomery Road, Zip 45242–4402; tel. 513/865–1111, (Includes BETHESDA BUTLER HOSPITAL, 3125 Hamilton Mason Road, Hamilton, Ohio, Zip 45011–5307, tel. 513/894–8888; Chuck Brown, Administrator) **A**1 3 5 10 **F**3 5 8 9 11 12 13 15 17 18 20 22 24 26 29 30 31 34 35 36 37 38 39 40 41 42 43 44 45 46 47 48 49 50 53 54 55 56 57 58 59 61 62 63 64 65 66 68 70 71 73 74 75 76 77 78 79 81 82 83 84 85 86 87 91 92 93 94 96 97 102 107 110 111 114 115 116 117 118 119 120 121 123 124 126 129 130 131 132 134 135 141 143 144 145 146 147 148 149 152 154 156 160 164 167 169 **P**6 8
Primary Contact: Clint Hutson, President and Chief Operating Officer
COO: Jenny Oliphant, Executive Vice President and Chief Operating Officer
CFO: Michael Crofton, Senior Vice President and Chief Financial Officer
CMO: Georges Feghali, M.D., Senior Vice President Quality and Chief Medical Officer
CIO: Rick Moore, Chief Information Officer
CHR: Walter L McLarty, Chief Human Resources Officer
CNO: Mary Irvin, R.N., MSN, Senior Vice President and Chief Nursing Officer
Web address: https://www.trihealth.com/hospitals-and-practices/bethesda-north-hospital
Control: Other not–for–profit (including NFP Corporation) **Service**: General medical and surgical

Staffed Beds: 465 **Admissions**: 24299 **Census**: 302 **Outpatient Visits**: 407752 **Births**: 3722 **Total Expense ($000)**: 776822 **Payroll Expense ($000)**: 230516 **Personnel**: 3278

☐ **BLUERIDGE VISTA BEHAVIORAL HEALTH (364057)**, 5500 Verulam Avenue, Zip 45213–2418; tel. 513/841–3018, (Nonreporting) **A**1 10
Primary Contact: Ashley Silva, Executive Director
Web address: www.blueridgevista.com
Control: Corporation, Investor–owned (for–profit) **Service**: Psychiatric

Staffed Beds: 44

BLUERIDGE VISTA HEALTH AND WELLNESS See Blueridge Vista Behavioral Health

CHRIST HOSPITAL See The Christ Hospital Health Network

☒ △ **CINCINNATI CHILDREN'S HOSPITAL MEDICAL CENTER (363300)**, 3333 Burnet Avenue MLC 8006, Zip 45229–3039, Mailing Address: 3333 Burnet Avenue, Zip 45229–3039; tel. 513/636–4200, (Includes CHILDREN'S HOSPITAL, 3300 Elland Avenue, Cincinnati, Ohio, Zip 45229–2804, tel. 513/894–8888) **A**1 2 3 5 7 8 10 **F**3 7 8 9 11 12 13 17 18 19 20 21 22 23 24 25 26 27 28 29 30 31 32 34 35 36 37 38 39 40 41 42 43 44 45 46 47 48 49 50 51 54 55 57 58 59 60 61 62 63 64 65 66 68 71 72 74 75 76 77 78 79 81 82 84 85 86 87 88 89 90 91 92 93 94 95 96 97 98 99 100 101 102 104 105 106 107 108 111 112 113 115 117 118 119 120 122 126 129 130 131 132 134 135 136 137 138 139 140 141 142 144 146 148 149 150 153 154 155 157 163 164 165 167 169 **P**8
Primary Contact: Steve Davis, President and Chief Executive Officer
CFO: Paul Jenny, Chief Financial Officer
CIO: Marianne Speight, Vice President Information System and Chief Information Officer
CHR: Nerissa E. Morris, Senior Vice President and Chief Human Resource Officer
CNO: Barbara F. Tofani, R.N., MSN, Senior Vice President and Chief Nursing Officer
Web address: www.cincinnatichildrens.org
Control: Other not–for–profit (including NFP Corporation) **Service**: Children's general medical and surgical

Staffed Beds: 750 **Admissions**: 18643 **Census**: 388 **Outpatient Visits**: 1679357 **Births**: 170 **Total Expense ($000)**: 2999990 **Payroll Expense ($000)**: 1510665 **Personnel**: 16999

☒ **CINCINNATI VETERANS AFFAIRS MEDICAL CENTER**, 3200 Vine Street, Zip 45220–2288; tel. 513/475–6300, (Nonreporting) **A**1 3 5 **S** Department of Veterans Affairs, Washington, DC
Primary Contact: Jane Johnson, MSN, R.N., Executive Medical Center Director
COO: David Ninneman, Associate Director
CFO: Sandra Selvidge, Chief Fiscal Service
CIO: Vique Caro, Chief Information Officer
CHR: Sandra Stenger, Acting Chief Human Resources
Web address: www.cincinnati.va.gov/
Control: Veterans Affairs, Government, federal **Service**: General medical and surgical

Staffed Beds: 212

Hospitals, U.S. / OHIO

☐ **DANIEL DRAKE CENTER FOR POST ACUTE CARE (362004)**, 151 West Galbraith Road, Zip 45216–1015; tel. 513/418–2500, (Nonreporting) **A**1 3 5 10 **S** UC Health, Cincinnati, OH
Primary Contact: Tom Goodwin, Administrator
CFO: Duane Pifko, Interim Director Financial Services
Web address: www.uchealth.com/danieldrakecenter/
Control: Other not–for–profit (including NFP Corporation) **Service:** Acute long–term care hospital

Staffed Beds: 202

⊞ **ENCOMPASS HEALTH REHABILITATION HOSPITAL AT CINCINNATI (363034)**, 151 West Galbraith Road, Zip 45216–1015; tel. 513/418–5600, (Includes HEALTHSOUTH REHABILITATION HOSPITAL OF CINCINNATI AT NORWOOD, 4953 Section Avenue, Cincinnati, Ohio, Zip 45212–2120, tel. 513/712–9200) (Nonreporting) **A**1 3 10 **S** Encompass Health Corporation, Birmingham, AL
Primary Contact: Jason Wessel, Chief Executive Officer
CFO: Scott Corder, Controller
CMO: Mark Goddard, M.D., Medical Director
CHR: Jason Sparks, Director, Human Resources
CNO: Kathy McNally, Chief Nursing Officer
Web address: https://encompasshealth.com/cincinnatirehab
Control: Corporation, Investor–owned (for–profit) **Service:** Rehabilitation

Staffed Beds: 60

⊞ △ **GOOD SAMARITAN HOSPITAL (360134)**, 375 Dixmyth Avenue, Zip 45220–2489; tel. 513/862–1400, (Includes TRIHEALTH GOOD SAMARITAN HOSPITAL AT EVENDALE, 3155 Glendale Milford Road, Cincinnati, Ohio, Zip 45241–3134, tel. 513/454–2222; Jeremiah Kirkland, President and Chief Operating Officer) **A**1 2 3 5 7 8 10 **F**3 5 8 9 11 12 13 15 18 20 22 26 28 29 30 31 34 35 36 38 39 40 41 42 44 45 46 47 48 49 50 53 54 55 56 57 58 59 61 63 64 65 66 68 70 71 72 74 75 76 77 78 79 81 82 83 84 85 86 87 91 92 93 94 96 97 98 100 102 103 105 107 110 111 114 115 116 117 118 119 120 121 123 124 126 129 130 131 132 134 135 136 141 143 144 145 146 147 148 149 152 153 154 156 160 164 167 169 **P**6 8 **S** CommonSpirit Health, Chicago, IL
Primary Contact: Kelvin Hanger, President and Chief Operating Officer
COO: Gerald P Oliphant, Executive Vice President and Chief Operating Officer
CFO: Michael Crofton, Chief Financial Officer
CMO: Georges Feghali, M.D., Senior Vice President Quality and Chief Medical Officer
CIO: Rick Moore, Chief Information Officer
CHR: Walter L McLarty, Chief Human Resources Officer
Web address: www.trihealth.com
Control: Church operated, Nongovernment, not–for–profit **Service:** General medical and surgical

Staffed Beds: 400 **Admissions:** 17989 **Census:** 212 **Outpatient Visits:** 458797 **Births:** 4852 **Total Expense ($000):** 785318 **Payroll Expense ($000):** 227547 **Personnel:** 2920

HEALTHSOUTH REHABILITATION HOSPITAL OF CINCINNATI AT NORWOOD
See Healthsouth Rehabilitation Hospital of Cincinnati At Norwood

⊞ **MERCY HEALTH – ANDERSON HOSPITAL (360001)**, 7500 State Road, Zip 45255–2492; tel. 513/624–4500, **A**1 2 3 10 **F**3 11 13 15 18 20 21 22 24 26 28 29 30 31 34 35 37 38 40 45 46 49 50 51 52 53 54 56 57 58 59 60 64 65 66 68 70 71 73 74 75 76 77 78 79 81 82 84 85 87 90 91 92 93 94 96 97 100 107 108 109 110 111 114 116 117 119 124 126 129 130 131 132 135 143 144 146 147 148 149 150 154 156 164 167 169 **P**6 **S** Bon Secours Mercy Health, Cincinnati, OH
Primary Contact: Kathy Healy–Collier, President
COO: Teresa Ash, Chief Operating Officer
CMO: Jamelle Bowers, M.D., Vice President Medical
CNO: Nicole Barnett, Chief Nursing Officer
Web address: https://www.mercy.com/locations/hospitals/cincinnati/mercy-health-anderson-hospital
Control: Church operated, Nongovernment, not–for–profit **Service:** General medical and surgical

Staffed Beds: 298 **Admissions:** 14432 **Census:** 161 **Outpatient Visits:** 153793 **Births:** 1503 **Total Expense ($000):** 254773 **Payroll Expense ($000):** 82679 **Personnel:** 950

⊞ **MERCY HEALTH – WEST HOSPITAL (360234)**, 3300 Mercy Health Boulevard, Zip 45211–1103; tel. 513/215–5000, (Nonreporting) **A**1 2 10 19 **S** Bon Secours Mercy Health, Cincinnati, OH
Primary Contact: Bradley J. Bertke, President and Chief Operating Officer
COO: Bradley J. Bertke, Chief Operating Officer
CFO: Kyle Klein, Assistant Chief Financial Officer
CMO: Creighton Wright, M.D., Vice President Medical Administration
CHR: Karyn Batdorf, Director Human Resources
Web address: www.e-mercy.com/west-hospital
Control: Church operated, Nongovernment, not–for–profit **Service:** General medical and surgical

Staffed Beds: 250

REGENCY HOSPITAL OF CINCINNATI See Select Specialty Hospital – Cincinnati North

⊞ **SELECT SPECIALTY HOSPITAL–CINCINNATI (362019)**, 2139 Auburn Avenue, 3rd Floor, Zip 45219–2906; tel. 513/572–8720, (Includes SELECT SPECIALTY HOSPITAL – CINCINNATI NORTH, 10500 Montgomery Road, Cincinnati, Ohio, Zip 45242–4402, tel. 513/865–5300; David D Muggli, FACHE, Chief Executive Officer) (Nonreporting) **A**1 10 **S** Select Medical Corporation, Mechanicsburg, PA
CMO: Brian Boster, M.D., Medical Director
CNO: Bobbi Schmidt, Chief Nursing Officer
Web address: www.selectspecialtyhospitals.com/company/locations/cincinnati.aspx
Control: Corporation, Investor–owned (for–profit) **Service:** Acute long–term care hospital

Staffed Beds: 71

⊞ **SUMMIT BEHAVIORAL HEALTHCARE (364035)**, 1101 Summit Road, Zip 45237–2652; tel. 513/948–3600, (Nonreporting) **A**1 3 5 10 **S** Ohio Department of Mental Health, Columbus, OH
Primary Contact: Elizabeth Banks, Chief Executive Officer
COO: Steven Burns, Director Fiscal Services
CFO: Steven Burns, Director Fiscal Services
CMO: Patrick McCullough, M.D., Chief Medical Services
CIO: Eric Bradley, Director Computer Information Services
CHR: Bobbie Carrelli, Director Human Resources
Web address: www.mh.state.oh.us/
Control: State, Government, Nonfederal **Service:** Psychiatric

Staffed Beds: 291

⊞ △ **THE CHRIST HOSPITAL HEALTH NETWORK (360163)**, 2139 Auburn Avenue, Zip 45219–2906; tel. 513/585–2000, (Includes THE CHRIST HOSPITAL MEDICAL CENTER – LIBERTY TOWNSHIP, 6939 Cox Road, Liberty Township, Ohio, Zip 45069–7595, tel. 513/648–7800) **A**1 2 3 5 7 10 **F**3 6 8 9 12 13 15 17 18 20 22 24 26 28 29 30 31 33 34 35 36 37 38 39 40 42 44 45 46 47 48 49 50 51 53 54 55 56 57 58 59 60 64 65 66 68 70 73 74 75 76 77 78 79 80 81 82 83 84 85 86 87 90 92 93 94 96 97 98 100 101 103 104 105 107 108 109 110 111 114 115 116 117 118 119 120 121 123 124 126 129 130 131 132 135 138 141 144 145 146 147 148 149 153 154 156 167 169
Primary Contact: Deborah Hayes, R.N., MS, MSN, President and Chief Executive Officer
COO: Andre A. Boyd, FACHE, Sr, Chief Operating Officer
CMO: Bernard B Gawne, M.D., Vice President and Chief Medical Officer
CIO: Alex Vaillancourt, Chief Information Officer
CHR: Rick Tolson, Chief Administrative Officer and Chief Human Resources Officer
CNO: Julie Holt, R.N., MSN, Chief Nursing Officer
Web address: www.thechristhospital.com
Control: Other not–for–profit (including NFP Corporation) **Service:** General medical and surgical

Staffed Beds: 551 **Admissions:** 23531 **Census:** 301 **Outpatient Visits:** 696458 **Births:** 3812 **Total Expense ($000):** 942345 **Payroll Expense ($000):** 332851 **Personnel:** 4061

⊞ **THE JEWISH HOSPITAL – MERCY HEALTH (360016)**, 4777 East Galbraith Road, Zip 45236–2725; tel. 513/686–3000, (Nonreporting) **A**1 2 3 5 10 **S** Bon Secours Mercy Health, Cincinnati, OH
Primary Contact: Michael Kramer, President
COO: Jack Hill, Chief Operating Officer and Administrator
CFO: Leroy Lopez, Chief Financial Officer
Web address: www.jewishhospitalcincinnati.com/
Control: Other not–for–profit (including NFP Corporation) **Service:** General medical and surgical

Staffed Beds: 162

Hospital, Medicare Provider Number, Address, Telephone, Approval, Facility, and Physician Codes, Health Care System

★ American Hospital Association (AHA) membership ○ Healthcare Facilities Accreditation Program ⇑ Center for Improvement in Healthcare Quality Accreditation
☐ The Joint Commission accreditation ◇ DNV Healthcare Inc. accreditation △ Commission on Accreditation of Rehabilitation Facilities (CARF) accreditation

Hospitals, U.S. / OHIO

☒ △ **TRIHEALTH REHABILITATION HOSPITAL (363041)**, 2155 Dana Avenue, Zip 45207; tel. 513/601-0600, **A**1 5 7 10 **F**29 30 34 35 44 60 68 74 79 84 90 91 95 96 132 148 **S** Select Medical Corporation, Mechanicsburg, PA
Primary Contact: Neil Fedders, Chief Executive Officer
Web address: www.trihealthrehab.com
Control: Corporation, Investor-owned (for-profit) **Service**: Rehabilitation

Staffed Beds: 60 **Admissions**: 1069 **Census**: 44 **Outpatient Visits**: 0 **Births**: 0 **Personnel**: 197

☐ **UNIVERSITY OF CINCINNATI MEDICAL CENTER (360003)**, 234 Goodman Street, Zip 45219-2316; tel. 513/584-1000, **A**1 2 3 5 8 10 19 **F**3 7 9 11 12 13 15 16 17 18 20 22 24 26 29 30 31 34 35 37 38 39 40 41 43 44 45 46 47 48 49 50 51 54 55 56 57 58 59 60 61 63 64 66 68 70 71 72 74 75 76 77 78 79 80 81 82 84 85 86 87 91 92 93 97 98 100 101 102 103 104 107 108 110 111 112 114 115 116 117 118 119 120 121 122 123 124 126 129 130 131 132 134 135 136 137 138 139 141 142 143 145 146 147 148 149 150 154 155 156 157 162 164 165 167 169 **S** UC Health, Cincinnati, OH
Primary Contact: Teri Grau, R.N., Vice President Operations and Chief Nursing Officer
CFO: Matthew Nealon, Vice President, Chief Financial Officer
CMO: Bill Hurford, Chief Medical Officer
CIO: Jay Brown, Vice President and Chief Information Officer
CHR: Clarence Pauley, Senior Vice President and Chief Human Resources Officer
CNO: Teri Grau, R.N., Vice President Operations and Chief Nursing Officer
Web address: www.uchealth.com/university-of-cincinnati-medical-center/
Control: Other not-for-profit (including NFP Corporation) **Service**: General medical and surgical

Staffed Beds: 568 **Admissions**: 23840 **Census**: 462 **Outpatient Visits**: 987438 **Births**: 2645 **Total Expense ($000)**: 1263703 **Payroll Expense ($000)**: 439209 **Personnel**: 4872

CIRCLEVILLE—Pickaway County

☒ **OHIOHEALTH BERGER HOSPITAL (360170)**, 600 North Pickaway Street, Zip 43113-1447; tel. 740/474-2126, (Nonreporting) **A**1 2 3 5 10 **S** OhioHealth, Columbus, OH
Primary Contact: Casey Liddy, President
CFO: Richard Filler, Chief Financial Officer
CMO: Jill Barno, M.D., Chief Medical Officer
CIO: Andy Chileski, Chief Information Officer and Vice President Facilities
CHR: Diane Guglielmi, Vice President, Human Resources
CNO: Kristin Day Gardner, Chief Nursing Officer
Web address: https://www.ohiohealth.com/locations/hospitals/berger-hospital
Control: Other not-for-profit (including NFP Corporation) **Service**: General medical and surgical

Staffed Beds: 56

CLEVELAND—Cuyahoga County

☒ **CLEVELAND CLINIC (360180)**, 9500 Euclid Avenue, Zip 44195-5108; tel. 216/444-2200, (Includes CLEVELAND CLINIC CHILDREN'S HOSPITAL, 9500 Euclid Avenue, Cleveland, Ohio, Zip 44103, tel. 800/223-2273) **A**1 2 3 5 8 10 19 **F**3 6 8 9 12 13 14 15 17 18 19 20 21 22 23 24 25 26 27 28 29 30 31 32 33 34 35 36 37 38 39 40 42 44 45 46 47 48 49 50 51 52 53 54 55 56 57 58 59 60 61 62 63 64 65 66 68 70 71 72 74 75 76 77 78 79 80 81 82 84 85 86 87 88 89 91 92 93 94 95 96 97 100 101 104 107 108 109 110 111 112 113 114 115 116 117 118 119 120 121 123 124 126 129 130 131 132 134 135 136 137 138 139 140 141 142 143 144 145 146 147 148 149 150 154 156 162 163 164 165 167 169 **P**6 **S** Cleveland Clinic Health System, Cleveland, OH
Primary Contact: Scott Steele, M.D., President
CIO: Edward Marx, Chief Information Officer
CNO: K. Kelly Hancock, R.N., Chief Caregiver Officer and Rich Family Chief Caregiver Chair
Web address: www.clevelandclinic.org
Control: Other not-for-profit (including NFP Corporation) **Service**: General medical and surgical

Staffed Beds: 1298 **Admissions**: 53933 **Census**: 1075 **Outpatient Visits**: 7733739 **Births**: 132 **Total Expense ($000)**: 8323996 **Payroll Expense ($000)**: 4256430 **Personnel**: 38457

☒ △ **CLEVELAND CLINIC CHILDREN'S HOSPITAL FOR REHABILITATION (363304)**, 2801 Martin Luther King Jr Drive, Zip 44104-3865; tel. 216/448-6400, **A**1 3 7 10 **F**28 29 30 32 34 35 36 44 50 60 68 74 75 79 82 84 87 90 91 93 94 96 100 130 131 132 143 146 148 149 164 **S** Cleveland Clinic Health System, Cleveland, OH
Primary Contact: Karen Murray, M.D., President
COO: Alec G Kulik, Administrator
CFO: Debra Nyikes, Director Finance and Chief Financial Officer
CMO: Roberta Bauer, M.D., Acting Chair Medical Staff
CIO: C Martin Harris, M.D., Chief Information Officer
CHR: Jan Hlahol, Manager Human Resources
Web address: www.my.clevelandclinic.org/childrens-hospital/default.aspx
Control: Other not-for-profit (including NFP Corporation) **Service**: Children's rehabilitation

Staffed Beds: 25 **Admissions**: 180 **Census**: 16 **Outpatient Visits**: 59368 **Births**: 0 **Total Expense ($000)**: 61282 **Payroll Expense ($000)**: 36171 **Personnel**: 467

☒ **CLEVELAND CLINIC FAIRVIEW HOSPITAL (360077)**, 18101 Lorain Avenue, Zip 44111-5656; tel. 216/476-7000, **A**1 2 3 5 10 19 **F**3 8 11 12 13 15 17 18 20 22 24 26 28 29 30 31 32 34 35 36 40 41 43 45 46 47 50 51 53 55 56 57 58 59 60 63 64 65 66 68 70 72 73 74 75 76 77 78 79 80 81 82 84 85 86 87 89 92 93 97 98 99 100 107 108 110 111 114 115 116 117 118 119 120 121 123 124 126 130 131 132 135 143 146 147 148 149 150 156 160 161 167 169 **S** Cleveland Clinic Health System, Cleveland, OH
Primary Contact: Neil Smith, D.O., President
COO: John C Mills, Senior Vice President Operations
CFO: Ankit Chhabra, Director Finance
CIO: C Martin Harris, M.D., Chief Information Officer
CHR: Ann Beatty, Director Human Resources
Web address: www.fairviewhospital.org
Control: Other not-for-profit (including NFP Corporation) **Service**: General medical and surgical

Staffed Beds: 498 **Admissions**: 28301 **Census**: 339 **Outpatient Visits**: 277441 **Births**: 5616 **Total Expense ($000)**: 551877 **Payroll Expense ($000)**: 222272 **Personnel**: 2418

☒ **CLEVELAND CLINIC HILLCREST HOSPITAL (360230)**, 6780 Mayfield Road, Zip 44124-2203; tel. 440/312-4500, **A**1 2 3 10 19 **F**3 8 12 13 15 17 18 20 22 24 26 28 29 30 31 32 34 35 36 37 38 39 40 41 43 45 46 49 50 51 53 54 55 56 57 59 60 62 63 64 65 68 70 72 74 75 76 77 78 79 81 82 84 85 86 87 89 93 97 100 107 108 110 111 114 115 116 117 118 119 120 121 123 126 129 130 131 132 135 143 145 146 147 148 149 156 167 169 **S** Cleveland Clinic Health System, Cleveland, OH
Primary Contact: Richard Parker, M.D., President
Web address: www.hillcresthospital.org
Control: Other not-for-profit (including NFP Corporation) **Service**: General medical and surgical

Staffed Beds: 496 **Admissions**: 28300 **Census**: 353 **Outpatient Visits**: 323414 **Births**: 4372 **Total Expense ($000)**: 577586 **Payroll Expense ($000)**: 211226 **Personnel**: 2192

☒ **CLEVELAND CLINIC LUTHERAN HOSPITAL (360087)**, 1730 West 25th Street, Zip 44113-3170; tel. 216/696-4300, **A**1 3 10 **F**3 4 5 12 15 18 29 30 31 34 35 37 38 39 40 45 50 53 54 55 56 57 58 59 60 64 65 68 70 74 75 77 78 79 81 82 84 85 86 87 90 93 94 96 98 100 102 103 104 105 107 108 110 111 114 115 119 126 130 131 132 135 143 147 148 149 152 153 156 163 164 169 **S** Cleveland Clinic Health System, Cleveland, OH
Primary Contact: Timothy R. Barnett, M.D., Vice President
COO: Matthew Mattner, Chief Operating Officer
CFO: Don Urbancsik, Director Finance
CMO: Ronald Golovan, M.D., Vice President Medical Operations
CIO: C Martin Harris, M.D., Chief Information Officer
CHR: Judith Santora, Chief Human Resource Officer
CNO: Janet Schuster, Chief Nursing Officer
Web address: www.lutheranhospital.org
Control: Other not-for-profit (including NFP Corporation) **Service**: General medical and surgical

Staffed Beds: 194 **Admissions**: 6914 **Census**: 108 **Outpatient Visits**: 93483 **Births**: 0 **Total Expense ($000)**: 145945 **Payroll Expense ($000)**: 65209 **Personnel**: 659

☐ **GRACE HOSPITAL (362015)**, 2307 West 14th Street, Zip 44113-3698; tel. 216/687-1500, (Nonreporting) **A**1 10
Primary Contact: Michelle Hennis, Interim President and Chief Executive Officer
CFO: Michelle Hennis, Administrative Director Financial Services
CMO: John Nickels, M.D., President Medical Staff
Web address: www.gracehospital.org
Control: Other not-for-profit (including NFP Corporation) **Service**: Acute long-term care hospital

Staffed Beds: 87

HANNA HOUSE See Hanna House Skilled Nursing Facility

HILLCREST HOSPITAL See Cleveland Clinic Hillcrest Hospital

KINDRED HOSPITAL OF CLEVELAND See Select Specialty Hospital – Cleveland Fairhill

LOUIS STOKES CLEVELAND VETERANS AFFAIRS MEDICAL CENTER See Northeast Ohio VA Healthcare System

LUTHERAN HOSPITAL See Cleveland Clinic Lutheran Hospital

MACDONALD HOSPITAL FOR WOMEN See University Macdonald Women's Hospital

METROHEALTH CTR FOR NRSG CARE See Metrohealth Center For Skilled Nursing Care

METROHEALTH MEDICAL CENTER (360059), 2500 MetroHealth Drive, Zip 44109–1998; tel. 216/778–7800, **A**1 2 3 5 7 8 10 **F**3 5 6 7 8 9 11 12 13 15 16 17 18 20 22 24 26 27 28 29 30 31 32 34 35 36 38 39 40 42 43 44 45 46 47 48 49 50 51 52 53 54 55 56 57 58 59 60 61 63 64 65 66 68 70 71 72 73 74 75 76 77 78 79 80 81 82 83 84 85 86 87 88 89 90 91 92 93 94 95 96 97 98 100 104 107 110 111 114 115 116 117 118 119 120 121 123 124 126 129 130 131 135 136 143 144 146 147 148 149 150 153 154 155 156 157 160 162 167 168 169 **P**1
Primary Contact: Airica Steed, Ed.D., R.N., FACHE, President and Chief Executive Officer
COO: Daniel Lewis, Executive Vice President and Chief Operating Officer
CFO: Geoffrey Himes, Interim Chief Financial Officer
CMO: Richard Blinkhorn, Executive Vice President and Chief Physician Executive
CHR: Debbie Warman, Vice President Human Resources
CNO: Melissa Kline, Chief Nursing Officer
Web address: www.metrohealth.org
Control: County, Government, Nonfederal **Service**: General medical and surgical

Staffed Beds: 591 **Admissions**: 22615 **Census**: 391 **Outpatient Visits**: 1321339 **Births**: 2670 **Total Expense ($000)**: 1841317 **Payroll Expense ($000)**: 856993 **Personnel**: 7452

NORTHEAST OHIO VA HEALTHCARE SYSTEM, 10701 East Boulevard, Zip 44106–1702; tel. 216/791–3800, (Nonreporting) **A**1 2 3 5 7 8 **S** Department of Veterans Affairs, Washington, DC
Primary Contact: Jill K. Dietrich Mellon, JD, FACHE, Executive Director, Chief Executive Officer
COO: Andrew Pacyna, Deputy Director
CFO: Michael Pappas, Chief Fiscal Service Officer
CMO: Murray Altose, M.D., Chief of Staff
CIO: Steve Gaj, Facility Chief Information Officer
CHR: Charles Franks, Chief Human Resources
Web address: www.cleveland.va.gov/
Control: Veterans Affairs, Government, federal **Service**: General medical and surgical

Staffed Beds: 617

RAINBOW BABIES AND CHILDREN'S HOSPITAL See University Hospitals Rainbow Babies and Children's

SELECT SPECIALTY HOSPITAL – CLEVELAND FAIRHILL (362026), 11900 Fairhill Road, Zip 44120–1062; tel. 216/983–8030, (Nonreporting) **A**1 **S** Select Medical Corporation, Mechanicsburg, PA
Primary Contact: Jennifer Fess, Chief Executive Officer
Control: Corporation, Investor-owned (for-profit) **Service**: Acute long-term care hospital

Staffed Beds: 50

UNIVERSITY HOSPITALS CLEVELAND MEDICAL CENTER (360137), 11100 Euclid Avenue, Zip 44106–1716; tel. 216/844–1000, (Includes HANNA HOUSE SKILLED NURSING FACILITY, 11100 Euclid Avenue, Cleveland, Ohio, Zip 44106, tel. 800/223–2273; UNIVERSITY MACDONALD WOMEN'S HOSPITAL, 2101 Adelbert Road, Cleveland, Ohio, Zip 44106–2624, tel. 216/844–3911; Patricia DePompei, President) **A**3 5 8 10 19 21 **F**3 5 6 7 8 9 11 12 13 14 15 17 18 19 20 21 22 23 24 25 26 27 28 29 30 31 32 33 34 35 36 37 38 39 40 41 42 43 44 45 46 47 48 49 50 51 52 54 55 56 57 58 59 60 61 62 63 64 65 68 70 71 72 73 74 75 76 77 78 79 80 81 82 83 85 86 87 88 89 91 92 93 94 96 97 100 101 102 104 105 107 108 110 111 112 114 115 116 117 118 119 120 121 122 123 124 126 129 130 131 132 134 135 136 137 138 139 140 141 142 145 146 147 148 149 150 152 153 154 155 156 157 160 161 162 163 164 165 167 168 169 **S** University Hospitals, Cleveland, OH
Primary Contact: Stathis Antoniades, President
COO: Ron Dziedzicki, R.N., Chief Operating Officer
CFO: Sonia Salvino, Vice President Finance
CMO: Gay Wehrli, Chief Medical Officer with University Hospitals/Case Western Reserve University
CIO: Sue Schade, Interim Chief Information Officer
CHR: Julie Chester, Vice President Human Resources
CNO: Jean Blake, Chief Nursing Officer
Web address: https://www.uhhospitals.org/locations/uh-cleveland-medical-center
Control: Other not-for-profit (including NFP Corporation) **Service**: General medical and surgical

Staffed Beds: 983 **Admissions**: 38710 **Census**: 652 **Outpatient Visits**: 1021267 **Births**: 5534 **Total Expense ($000)**: 2424944 **Payroll Expense ($000)**: 696696 **Personnel**: 11090

UNIVERSITY HOSPITALS RAINBOW BABIES AND CHILDREN'S (363302), 2101 Adelbert Road, Zip 44106–2624; tel. 216/844–3911, (Nonreporting) **A**10 21 **S** University Hospitals, Cleveland, OH
Primary Contact: Patricia DePompei, President
Web address: https://www.uhhospitals.org/rainbow
Control: Other not-for-profit (including NFP Corporation) **Service**: Children's general medical and surgical

Staffed Beds: 244

COLDWATER—Mercer County

MERCER HEALTH (360058), 800 West Main Street, Zip 45828–1698; tel. 419/678–2341, **A**1 10 **F**3 7 11 12 13 15 18 28 29 30 31 32 34 35 40 44 45 47 50 51 54 57 59 61 62 64 65 70 75 76 77 78 79 81 82 85 87 92 93 94 95 97 107 108 110 111 114 118 119 126 130 131 132 133 134 135 143 144 145 146 147 148 149 150 154 156 167 169 **P**6
Primary Contact: Lisa R. Klenke, R.N., Chief Executive Officer
CFO: Jon Dingledine, Chief Financial Officer and Chief Operating Officer
CMO: John Terpstra, M.D., Chief Medical Officer
CIO: DeWayne Marsee, Director Information Systems
CHR: Jon Dingledine, Chief Financial Officer and Chief Operating Officer
CNO: Cindy Liette, Vice President Patient Care Services
Web address: www.mercer-health.com
Control: Hospital district or authority, Government, Nonfederal **Service**: General medical and surgical

Staffed Beds: 60 **Admissions**: 2190 **Census**: 16 **Outpatient Visits**: 75211 **Births**: 401 **Total Expense ($000)**: 88536 **Payroll Expense ($000)**: 24916 **Personnel**: 489

COLUMBUS—Franklin County

JAMES CANCER HOSPITAL AND SOLOVE RESEARCH INSTITUTE See The Osuccc – James

MOUNT CARMEL EAST HOSPITAL (364062), 6001 East Broad Street, Zip 43213; tel. 614/234–6000, (Includes MOUNT CARMEL GROVE CITY, 5300 North Meadows Drive, Grove City, Ohio, Zip 43123–2546, tel. 614/234–5000; Sean McKibben, President and Chief Operating Officer) (Nonreporting) **A**1 3 5 10 **S** Trinity Health, Livonia, MI
Primary Contact: Scott Wilber, President and Chief Operating Officer
Web address: https://www.mountcarmelhealth.com/location/mount-carmel-east
Control: Church operated, Nongovernment, not-for-profit **Service**: General medical and surgical

Staffed Beds: 355

Hospitals, U.S. / OHIO

☒ △ **NATIONWIDE CHILDREN'S HOSPITAL (363305)**, 700 Children's Drive, Zip 43205–2664; tel. 614/722–2000, **A**1 2 3 5 7 8 10 **F**3 5 7 8 12 16 17 18 19 20 21 22 23 24 25 26 27 28 29 30 31 32 34 35 36 37 38 39 40 41 42 43 44 45 46 47 48 49 50 51 52 53 54 55 57 58 59 60 61 62 63 64 65 66 68 71 72 73 74 75 76 77 78 79 81 82 83 84 85 86 87 88 89 90 92 93 96 97 98 99 100 101 102 104 105 107 108 111 112 115 116 117 118 119 126 129 130 131 132 134 135 136 137 138 139 140 141 142 143 144 145 146 147 148 149 150 153 154 155 156 157 158 160 161 164 165 166 167 169
Primary Contact: Tim Robinson, Chief Executive Officer
COO: Rick Miller, President and Chief Operating Officer
CMO: Richard Brilli, M.D., Chief Medical Officer
CIO: Denise Zabawski, Vice President Information Services and Chief Information Officer
Web address: www.nationwidechildrens.org
Control: Other not–for–profit (including NFP Corporation) **Service**: Children's general medical and surgical

Staffed Beds: 674 **Admissions**: 16901 **Census**: 458 **Outpatient Visits**: 1790448 **Births**: 4 **Total Expense ($000)**: 1951605 **Payroll Expense ($000)**: 878004 **Personnel**: 9857

☐ **OHIO HOSPITAL FOR PSYCHIATRY (364041)**, 880 Greenlawn Avenue, Zip 43223–2616; tel. 614/449–9664, **A**1 10 **F**98 103 130 153 164 **S** Acadia Healthcare Company, Inc., Franklin, TN
Primary Contact: Natasha Schafer, Chief Executive Officer
COO: Shannon Robbins, Chief Operating Officer
CFO: Steve Snyder, Chief Financial Officer
CMO: Richard Nockowitz, M.D., Medical Director
CNO: Jayne Zink, Director of Nursing
Web address: www.ohiohospitalforpsychiatry.com/
Control: Corporation, Investor–owned (for–profit) **Service**: Psychiatric

Staffed Beds: 130 **Admissions**: 3404 **Census**: 69 **Outpatient Visits**: 2298 **Births**: 0 **Total Expense ($000)**: 21496 **Payroll Expense ($000)**: 11271 **Personnel**: 169

☒ △ **OHIO STATE UNIVERSITY WEXNER MEDICAL CENTER (360085)**, 410 West 10th Avenue, Zip 43210–1240; tel. 614/293–8000, (Includes OHIO STATE UNIVERSITY HOSPITALS EAST, 1492 East Broad Street, Columbus, Ohio, Zip 43205–1546, tel. 614/257–3000) **A**1 3 5 7 8 10 19 **F**3 4 5 6 8 9 11 12 13 15 16 17 18 20 22 24 26 28 29 30 31 33 34 35 36 37 38 39 40 42 43 44 45 46 47 48 49 50 51 52 53 54 55 56 57 58 59 60 61 64 65 66 68 70 71 72 73 74 75 76 77 78 79 80 81 82 84 85 86 87 90 91 92 93 95 96 97 98 100 101 102 103 104 105 107 108 110 111 112 113 114 115 118 119 126 129 130 131 132 134 135 137 138 139 140 141 142 143 145 146 147 148 149 152 153 154 156 157 160 161 162 164 165 166 167 168 169 **S** Ohio State University Health System, Columbus, OH
Primary Contact: John Warner, M.D., Chief Executive Officer
COO: Jay Anderson, Chief Operating Officer
CFO: Vincent Tammaro, Chief Financial Officer and Vice President for Health Sciences
CMO: Andrew Thomas, M.D., Chief Medical Officer
CIO: Tom Bentley, MS, Interim Chief Information Officer
CHR: Kim Shumate, Human Resources Officer
CNO: Deana Sievert, MSN, R.N., Chief Nursing Officer
Web address: https://wexnermedical.osu.edu/
Control: State, Government, Nonfederal **Service**: General medical and surgical

Staffed Beds: 1150 **Admissions**: 46542 **Census**: 920 **Outpatient Visits**: 1327443 **Births**: 5323 **Total Expense ($000)**: 2336942 **Payroll Expense ($000)**: 752668 **Personnel**: 12994

☒ **OHIOHEALTH DOCTORS HOSPITAL (360152)**, 5100 West Broad Street, Zip 43228–1607; tel. 614/544–1000, (Nonreporting) **A**1 2 3 5 10 12 13 **S** OhioHealth, Columbus, OH
Primary Contact: Lindsey Osting, President
CMO: Dean Colwell, D.O., Vice President Medical Affairs
CIO: Michael Krouse, Chief Information Officer
CHR: David Sullivan, Director Human Resources
Web address: www.ohiohealth.com
Control: Church operated, Nongovernment, not–for–profit **Service**: General medical and surgical

Staffed Beds: 206

☒ **OHIOHEALTH GRANT MEDICAL CENTER (360017)**, 111 South Grant Avenue, Zip 43215–1898; tel. 614/566–9000, (Includes OHIOHEALTH GROVE CITY METHODIST HOSPITAL, 1375 Stringtown Road, Grove City, Ohio, Zip 43123–8911, 3830 Olentangy River Road, Blom Administrative Campus, Columbus, Zip 43214–5404, tel. 614/788–0903) (Nonreporting) **A**1 2 3 5 10 **S** OhioHealth, Columbus, OH
Primary Contact: Michael Lawson, President
COO: Kevin Lutz, DPM, Chief Operating Officer, Grant
CFO: Heather Brandon, Vice President of Finance, Grant
CMO: Michael Ezzie, Director of Medical Education and Interim Vice President of Medical Affairs
CIO: Michael Krouse, Chief Information Officer
CHR: Qiana Williams, Director, Human Resource Business Partner, Grant
CNO: Sharon Neenan, Interim Chief Nursing Officer, Grant
Web address: www.ohiohealth.com
Control: Church operated, Nongovernment, not–for–profit **Service**: General medical and surgical

Staffed Beds: 471

☒ △ **OHIOHEALTH REHABILITATION HOSPITAL (363037)**, 1087 Dennison Avenue, 4th Floor, Zip 43201–3201; tel. 614/484–9600, **A**1 7 10 **F**3 29 30 33 34 35 44 50 57 58 59 60 75 90 94 95 96 119 130 132 135 146 148 149 154 **S** Select Medical Corporation, Mechanicsburg, PA
Primary Contact: Matthew Lehn, Chief Executive Officer
CFO: Ted Bolcavage, Vice President Division Controller, Inpatient
CMO: Lisa Lombard, Medical Director
CHR: Josette Alexander, Director, Human Resources
CNO: Graydon Todd Auckerman, Chief Nursing Officer
Web address: www.ohiohealth-rehab.com
Control: Partnership, Investor–owned (for–profit) **Service**: Rehabilitation

Staffed Beds: 74 **Admissions**: 2119 **Census**: 79 **Outpatient Visits**: 0 **Births**: 0 **Personnel**: 397

☒ **OHIOHEALTH RIVERSIDE METHODIST HOSPITAL (360006)**, 3535 Olentangy River Road, Zip 43214–3998; tel. 614/566–5000, (Nonreporting) **A**1 2 3 5.8 10 **S** OhioHealth, Columbus, OH
Primary Contact: Robert J. Cercek, President
CFO: Peter Bury, Vice President Finance
CMO: Thomas Harmon, M.D., Vice President Medical Affairs
CIO: Michael Krouse, Chief Information Officer
CHR: Shereen Solaiman, Vice President Human Resources
CNO: Lisa Gossett, MSN, R.N., Chief Nursing Officer
Web address: www.ohiohealth.com
Control: Church operated, Nongovernment, not–for–profit **Service**: General medical and surgical

Staffed Beds: 880

PARK MEDICAL CENTER See Ohio State University Hospitals East

☒ **REGENCY HOSPITAL OF COLUMBUS (362037)**, 1430 South High Street, Zip 43207–1045; tel. 614/456–0300, (Nonreporting) **A**1 10 **S** Select Medical Corporation, Mechanicsburg, PA
Primary Contact: Ryan Hemmert, Chief Executive Officer
Web address: www.regencyhospital.com/
Control: Corporation, Investor–owned (for–profit) **Service**: Acute long–term care hospital

Staffed Beds: 66

☒ **SELECT SPECIALTY HOSPITAL–COLUMBUS (362022)**, 1087 Dennison Avenue, Zip 43201–3201; tel. 614/458–9000, (Nonreporting) **A**1 10 **S** Select Medical Corporation, Mechanicsburg, PA
Primary Contact: Lisa J. Pettrey, MSN, R.N., Chief Executive Officer
CMO: Victoria Ruff, M.D., Medical Director
CHR: Charles Pankowski, Manager Human Resources
Web address: https://www.selectspecialtyhospitals.com/locations-and-tours/oh/columbus/columbus-victorian-village/
Control: Corporation, Investor–owned (for–profit) **Service**: Acute long–term care hospital

Staffed Beds: 162

☐ **SUN BEHAVIORAL COLUMBUS (364058)**, 900 Dublin Granville Road, Zip 43229–2452; tel. 614/706–2786, (Nonreporting) **A**1 10
Primary Contact: Kent Hess, Chief Executive Officer
Web address: https://www.suncolumbus.com
Control: Corporation, Investor–owned (for–profit) **Service**: Psychiatric

Staffed Beds: 72

Hospitals, U.S. / OHIO

THE OSUCCC – JAMES (360242), 460 West Tenth Avenue, Zip 43210–1240; tel. 614/293–3300, **A**1 2 3 5 10 **F**3 15 29 30 31 32 34 35 36 37 38 39 44 46 47 48 49 50 52 54 55 57 58 59 61 64 65 66 68 70 71 74 75 77 78 79 80 81 82 84 85 86 87 93 97 100 107 108 110 111 112 114 115 116 117 118 119 120 121 122 123 124 126 130 132 134 135 136 141 143 145 146 147 148 149 154 157 160 167 **S** Ohio State University Health System, Columbus, OH
Primary Contact: David Cohn, Interim Chief Executive Officer
CFO: Bell Julian, Associate Executive Director and Chief Financial Officer
CIO: Michael Townsend, Chief Information Officer
CHR: Jill Hannah, Director Human Resources
CNO: Kris M Kipp, Executive Director, Patient Services and Chief Nursing Officer
Web address: https://cancer.osu.edu/
Control: State, Government, Nonfederal **Service**: Cancer

Staffed Beds: 356 **Admissions**: 14171 **Census**: 292 **Outpatient Visits**: 445863 **Births**: 0 **Total Expense ($000)**: 1461175 **Payroll Expense ($000)**: 353612 **Personnel**: 5385

TWIN VALLEY BEHAVIORAL HEALTHCARE (364007), 2200 West Broad Street, Zip 43223–1297; tel. 614/752–0333, (Nonreporting) **A**1 3 10 **S** Ohio Department of Mental Health, Columbus, OH
Primary Contact: Frank Beel, Chief Executive Officer
COO: David Blahnik, Chief Operating Officer
CFO: Tracy Gladen, Chief Financial Officer
CMO: R Alan Freeland, M.D., Chief Clinical Officer
CIO: Missy McGarvey, Chief Information Officer
CHR: Marcia McKeen, Director Human Resources
CNO: Michael Breakwell, R.N., Nurse Executive
Web address: www.mh.state.oh.us/ibhs/bhos/tvbh.html
Control: State, Government, Nonfederal **Service**: Psychiatric

Staffed Beds: 178

CONCORD TOWNSHIP—Lake County

UNIVERSITY HOSPITALSTRIPOINT MEDICAL CENTER See University Hospitals Tripoint Medical Center

CONNEAUT—Ashtabula County

★ ⇑ **UNIVERSITY HOSPITALS CONNEAUT MEDICAL CENTER (361308)**, 158 West Main Road, Zip 44030–2039; tel. 440/593–1131, **A**10 18 21 **F**3 11 15 18 28 29 30 31 34 35 37 40 45 55 56 57 59 62 64 68 70 75 77 78 79 81 82 85 86 87 93 97 107 110 111 115 119 130 132 133 135 146 147 149 150 154 156 157 **S** University Hospitals, Cleveland, OH
Primary Contact: M Steven. Jones, Regional President
COO: Jason Glowczewski, Chief Operating Officer
CFO: Lara Eggleston, Finance Manager
CMO: Abirammy Sundaramoorthy, M.D., Chief Medical Officer
CIO: Kirsten Hale, Coordinator Health Information Services
CHR: Danialle Lynce, Business Partner Human Resources
CNO: Ashley M. Carlucci, R.N., Chief Nursing Officer
Web address: https://www.uhhospitals.org/locations/uh-conneaut-medical-center
Control: Other not–for–profit (including NFP Corporation) **Service**: General medical and surgical

Staffed Beds: 25 **Admissions**: 633 **Census**: 7 **Outpatient Visits**: 24544 **Births**: 0 **Total Expense ($000)**: 32571 **Payroll Expense ($000)**: 10141 **Personnel**: 154

COPLEY—Summit County

EDWIN SHAW REHAB See Cleveland Clinic Rehabiliation Hospital – Akron

COSHOCTON—Coshocton County

COSHOCTON REGIONAL MEDICAL CENTER (360109), 1460 Orange Street, Zip 43812–2229, Mailing Address: P.O. Box 1330, Zip 43812–6330; tel. 740/622–6411, (Nonreporting) **A**1 10 20 **S** Prime Healthcare, Ontario, CA
Primary Contact: Stephanie Conn, Chief Executive Officer
CFO: Dennis Lockard, FACHE, Chief Financial Officer
CMO: Gary J. Carver, M.D., Chief Medical Officer
CIO: Seth Peterson, Director Information Services
CHR: Rick Davis, Chief Operating Officer and Support Services
Web address: https://www.coshoctonhospital.org
Control: Other not–for–profit (including NFP Corporation) **Service**: General medical and surgical

Staffed Beds: 44

CUYAHOGA FALLS—Summit County

○ **WESTERN RESERVE HOSPITAL (360150)**, 1900 23rd Street, Zip 44223–1499; tel. 330/971–7000, **A**3 5 10 11 **F**3 12 15 20 26 29 31 33 34 35 36 38 40 43 44 45 47 49 50 51 54 57 58 59 64 65 66 68 70 74 75 77 78 79 81 82 84 85 86 87 92 93 96 97 107 108 110 111 114 115 119 129 130 131 132 135 144 146 147 148 149 154 **P**6 8
Primary Contact: Robert Kent, D.O., President and Chief Executive Officer
CFO: Jill Hiner, Vice President and Chief Financial Officer
CMO: Charles Feunning, M.D., Chief Medical Officer
CIO: Pamela Banchy, Chief Information Officer
CHR: Heather Milicevic, Vice President and Chief Human Resource Officer
CNO: Carrie Gallo, Chief Nursing Officer
Web address: www.westernreservehospital.org
Control: Partnership, Investor–owned (for–profit) **Service**: General medical and surgical

Staffed Beds: 83 **Admissions**: 3266 **Census**: 35 **Outpatient Visits**: 127902 **Births**: 0 **Total Expense ($000)**: 150928 **Payroll Expense ($000)**: 50033 **Personnel**: 673

DAYTON—Montgomery County

ACCESS HOSPITAL DAYTON (364050), 2611 Wayne Avenue, Zip 45420–1833; tel. 937/256–7801, (Nonreporting) **A**1 10
Primary Contact: Patricia Parsley, Program Director
Web address: www.accesshospital.com/
Control: Corporation, Investor–owned (for–profit) **Service**: Psychiatric

Staffed Beds: 54

DAYTON CHILDREN'S HOSPITAL (363306), 1 Childrens Plaza, Zip 45404–1815, Mailing Address: 1 Children's Plaza, Zip 45404–1815; tel. 937/641–3000, **A**1 2 3 5 10 **F**3 7 8 11 19 29 30 31 32 34 35 37 38 40 41 42 43 44 45 50 53 54 55 57 58 59 60 61 62 63 64 65 66 68 72 74 75 77 78 79 81 82 84 85 86 87 88 89 91 93 96 97 98 99 100 101 102 104 105 107 111 114 115 118 119 129 130 131 132 134 135 144 146 148 149 153 154 156 164 167
Primary Contact: Deborah A. Feldman, President and Chief Executive Officer
COO: Matthew P Graybill, Vice President, Human Resources and Chief Administrative Officer
CFO: Chris Bergman, Chief Financial Officer
CMO: Adam Mezoff, M.D., Vice President and Chief Medical Officer
CIO: Beth Fredette, Chief Information Officer
Web address: www.childrensdayton.org
Control: Other not–for–profit (including NFP Corporation) **Service**: Children's general medical and surgical

Staffed Beds: 181 **Admissions**: 7978 **Census**: 102 **Outpatient Visits**: 601477 **Births**: 0 **Total Expense ($000)**: 656175 **Payroll Expense ($000)**: 354532 **Personnel**: 3793

△ **DAYTON VETERANS AFFAIRS MEDICAL CENTER**, 4100 West Third Street, Zip 45428–9000; tel. 937/268–6511, (Nonreporting) **A**1 3 5 7 **S** Department of Veterans Affairs, Washington, DC
Primary Contact: Jennifer A. Defrancesco, Medical Center Director
CFO: Shannon Rappach, Chief Fiscal Services
CMO: James Hardy, D.O., Chief of Staff
CIO: Susan Sherer, Chief Information Resource Management
CHR: Rolanda Watkins, Chief Human Resources Management Service
Web address: www.dayton.va.gov/
Control: Veterans Affairs, Government, federal **Service**: General medical and surgical

Staffed Beds: 403

HAVEN BEHAVIORAL HOSPITAL OF DAYTON (364048), One Elizabeth Place, Zip 45417–3445; tel. 937/234–0100, (Nonreporting) **A**1 10 **S** Haven Behavioral Healthcare, Nashville, TN
Primary Contact: Jonathan Duckett, Chief Executive Officer
CMO: Amita Patel, M.D., Medical Director
CNO: Cheryl Meyer, MSN, Director of Nursing
Web address: www.havenbehavioraldayton.com/
Control: Corporation, Investor–owned (for–profit) **Service**: Psychiatric

Staffed Beds: 32

HAVEN BEHAVIORAL SENIOR CARE OF DAYTON See Haven Behavioral Hospital of Dayton

HEALTHSOUTH REHABILITATION HOSPITAL OF DAYTON See The Rehabilitation Institute of Ohio

---

Hospital, Medicare Provider Number, Address, Telephone, Approval, Facility, and Physician Codes, Health Care System

★ American Hospital Association (AHA) membership   ○ Healthcare Facilities Accreditation Program   ⇑ Center for Improvement in Healthcare Quality Accreditation
☐ The Joint Commission accreditation   ◇ DNV Healthcare Inc. accreditation   △ Commission on Accreditation of Rehabilitation Facilities (CARF) accreditation

Hospitals, U.S. / OHIO

★ ○ △ **KETTERING HEALTH DAYTON (360133)**, 405 West Grand Avenue, Zip 45405–4796; tel. 937/723–3200, (Includes KETTERING HEALTH WASHINGTON TOWNSHIP, 1997 Miamisburg Centerville RD, Dayton, Ohio, Zip 45459–3800, 1997 Miamisburg–Centerville Road, Zip 45459–3800, tel. 937/401–6000; Erica Schneider, President) **A**2 3 5 7 10 11 12 13 19 **F**3 11 12 13 15 18 20 22 24 26 28 29 30 31 34 36 37 40 42 43 44 45 47 48 49 53 54 56 58 59 61 64 66 70 73 74 75 76 77 78 79 80 81 82 85 86 87 92 93 96 102 107 108 110 111 112 114 115 117 118 119 120 121 123 124 126 129 130 131 132 135 146 147 148 149 154 157 167 169 **P**3 6 **S** Kettering Health, Dayton, OH
Primary Contact: Michael J. Brendel, R.N., President
CMO: Paul Martin, Chief Medical Officer
CHR: Keith Jenkins, Director, Human Resources
CNO: Ronda Brandstater, Vice President Patient Care
Web address: www.ketteringhealth.org/grandview/
Control: Church operated, Nongovernment, not–for–profit **Service**: General medical and surgical

Staffed Beds: 322 **Admissions**: 16550 **Census**: 177 **Outpatient Visits**: 535365 **Births**: 2080 **Total Expense ($000)**: 697300 **Payroll Expense ($000)**: 187626 **Personnel**: 1666

KINDRED HOSPITAL–DAYTON (362033), 707 South Edwin C Moses Boulevard, Zip 45417–3462; tel. 937/222–5963, (Nonreporting) **A**1 10 **S** ScionHealth, Louisville, KY
Primary Contact: Phillip Underwood, Chief Executive Officer
CMO: Felipe Rubio, M.D., Medical Director
Web address: www.khdayton.com
Control: Corporation, Investor–owned (for–profit) **Service**: Acute long–term care hospital

Staffed Beds: 67

MIAMI VALLEY HOSPITAL (360051), 1 Wyoming Sreet, Zip 45409–2722, Mailing Address: 1 Wyoming Street, Zip 45409–2722, tel. 937/208–8000, (Includes MIAMI VALLEY HOSPITAL SOUTH, 2400 Miami Valley Drive, Centerville, Ohio, Zip 45459–4774, tel. 937/438–2400) **A**1 2 3 5 8 10 19 **F**3 7 11 12 13 15 16 17 18 20 22 24 26 28 29 30 31 32 34 35 36 37 38 39 40 41 42 43 44 45 46 47 48 49 50 53 54 55 56 57 58 59 60 61 63 64 68 70 71 72 73 74 75 76 77 78 79 80 81 82 84 85 86 87 91 92 93 94 95 96 98 100 101 102 103 107 108 110 111 114 115 117 118 119 124 126 129 130 131 132 133 134 135 141 145 146 147 148 149 154 155 156 162 164 167 169 **S** Premier Health, Dayton, OH
Primary Contact: Chad Whelan, President
CFO: Thomas M Duncan, Executive Vice President and Chief Financial Officer
CMO: Marc Belcastro, D.O., Chief Medical Officer
Web address: www.miamivalleyhospital.org
Control: Other not–for–profit (including NFP Corporation) **Service**: General medical and surgical

Staffed Beds: 824 **Admissions**: 46573 **Census**: 738 **Outpatient Visits**: 836030 **Births**: 4839 **Total Expense ($000)**: 1425915 **Payroll Expense ($000)**: 439227 **Personnel**: 6866

○ **RIVERVIEW HEALTH INSTITUTE**, 1 Elizabeth Place, Zip 45417–3445; tel. 937/222–5390, (Nonreporting) **A**11
Primary Contact: Azim Shaikh, Chief Executive Officer
COO: Dan Lommer, Vice President, Operations
CMO: Jonathon Paley, Chief Medical Officer
CHR: Cheri Robison, Human Resources Director
CNO: Marcia Dunfee, Chief Nursing Officer
Web address: https://www.riverviewhealthinstitute.com/
Control: Corporation, Investor–owned (for–profit) **Service**: Surgical

Staffed Beds: 10

SHRINERS CHILDREN'S OHIO (363308), One Childrens Plaza, Zip 45404–1873, Mailing Address: One Children's Plaza, Zip 45404–1873; tel. 513/872–6000, (Nonreporting) **A**1 3 5 10 **S** Shriners Hospitals for Children, Tampa, FL
Primary Contact: Randall White, Administrator
CFO: Susan Harris, Director Fiscal Services
CMO: Petra Warner, Chief of Staff
CIO: David Brian, Chief Information Officer
CHR: Gretchen Long, Manager Human Resources
Web address: https://www.shrinershospitalsforchildren.org/ohio
Control: Other not–for–profit (including NFP Corporation) **Service**: Children's other specialty

Staffed Beds: 30

SOUTHVIEW HOSPITAL AND FAMILY HEALTH CENTER See Kettering Health Washington Township

THE REHABILITATION INSTITUTE OF OHIO (363033), 835 South Main Street, Zip 45402–2440; tel. 937/424–8200, **A**1 10 **F**29 36 60 77 82 90 95 96 122 146 148 149 **S** Encompass Health Corporation, Birmingham, AL
Primary Contact: Etene Terrell–Fakorede, Chief Executive Officer
Web address: https://encompasshealth.com/daytonrehab
Control: Individual, Investor–owned (for–profit) **Service**: Rehabilitation

Staffed Beds: 60 **Admissions**: 1541 **Census**: 51 **Outpatient Visits**: 0 **Births**: 0 **Total Expense ($000)**: 24454 **Payroll Expense ($000)**: 15774 **Personnel**: 163

DEFIANCE—Defiance County

MERCY HEALTH – DEFIANCE HOSPITAL (360270), 1404 East Second Street, Zip 43512–2440; tel. 419/782–8444, (Nonreporting) **A**1 10 **S** Bon Secours Mercy Health, Cincinnati, OH
Primary Contact: Sonya Selhorst, R.N., President and Chief Nursing Officer
COO: Kerry Knuth, Chief Operating Officer
CFO: James Puffenberger, Vice President and Chief Financial Officer
CMO: Jeffrey Pruitt, M.D., Chief of Staff
CHR: Susan Pscodna, Director Human Resources
CNO: Sonya Selhorst, R.N., President and Chief Nursing Officer
Web address: https://www.mercy.com/locations/hospitals/toledo/mercy-health-defiance-hospital?utm_source=local-listings&utm_medium=organic&utm_content=website_link
Control: Partnership, Investor–owned (for–profit) **Service**: General medical and surgical

Staffed Beds: 23

MERCY HOSPITAL OF DEFIANCE See Mercy Health – Defiance Hospital

PROMEDICA DEFIANCE REGIONAL HOSPITAL (361328), 1200 Ralston Avenue, Zip 43512–1396; tel. 419/783–6955, **A**1 5 10 18 **F**3 11 13 15 18 20 28 31 32 34 40 43 55 59 64 68 70 75 76 77 78 79 81 82 85 86 87 93 98 100 101 102 104 107 108 110 111 114 118 119 126 129 130 132 133 135 144 146 147 148 153 156 162 169 **S** ProMedica Health System, Toledo, OH
Primary Contact: Keith Burmeister, President
CFO: Ken Swint, Director Finance
CMO: Stanislaw Dajczak, M.D., Chief of Staff
CIO: Patricia Swint, Director Information Management Systems
CHR: Carrie Miller, Director Human Resources
Web address: www.promedica.org
Control: Other not–for–profit (including NFP Corporation) **Service**: General medical and surgical

Staffed Beds: 35 **Admissions**: 1496 **Census**: 14 **Outpatient Visits**: 86523 **Births**: 344 **Total Expense ($000)**: 66127 **Payroll Expense ($000)**: 18948 **Personnel**: 285

DELAWARE—Delaware County

OHIOHEALTH GRADY MEMORIAL HOSPITAL (360210), 561 West Central Avenue, Zip 43015–1410; tel. 740/615–1000, (Nonreporting) **A**1 2 10 **S** OhioHealth, Columbus, OH
Primary Contact: Cherie L. Smith, Ph.D., R.N., President
COO: Anna Hensley, Chief Operating Officer
CFO: David Hensel, Director Financial Operations
CMO: Barbara Evert, M.D., Vice President Medical Affairs
CIO: Michael Krouse, Chief Information Officer Information Services
CNO: Elizabeth Anne Biegler, R.N., Chief Nursing Officer
Web address: https://www.ohiohealth.com/locations/hospitals/grady-memorial-hospital
Control: Church operated, Nongovernment, not–for–profit **Service**: General medical and surgical

Staffed Beds: 61

DENNISON—Tuscarawas County

TRINITY HOSPITAL TWIN CITY (361302), 819 North First Street, Zip 44621–1098; tel. 740/922–2800, (Nonreporting) **A**1 10 18 **S** CommonSpirit Health, Chicago, IL
Primary Contact: Dwayne Richardson, President
CMO: Tim McKnight, M.D., Chief of Staff
CHR: Bianca Love, Assistant Administrator Human Resources
Web address: www.trinitytwincity.org
Control: Church operated, Nongovernment, not–for–profit **Service**: General medical and surgical

Staffed Beds: 12

Hospitals, U.S. / OHIO

DOVER—Tuscarawas County

★ △ ⇑ **CLEVELAND CLINIC UNION HOSPITAL (360010)**, 659 Boulevard Street, Zip 44622-2077; tel. 330/343-3311, **A**5 7 10 19 21 **F**3 11 13 15 18 28 29 30 34 35 40 45 50 51 53 54 57 59 62 64 65 68 69 70 74 75 76 77 78 79 81 82 85 87 90 92 93 100 102 104 105 107 108 110 111 115 118 119 120 121 129 130 131 132 135 144 146 148 149 153 157 167 169 **S** Cleveland Clinic Health System, Cleveland, OH
Primary Contact: Thomas J. Rogers, M.D., Vice President
COO: Jeff Pike, R.N., Chief Operating Officer
CFO: Dave Frigo, Senior Director Financial Operations
CMO: Cody Turner, M.D., Chief Medical Officer
CIO: Butch Sukie, Director, Information Management
CHR: John Aldergate, Director, Human Resources
CNO: John Baker, R.N., Chief Nursing Officer
Web address: www.unionhospital.org
Control: Other not-for-profit (including NFP Corporation) **Service**: General medical and surgical

Staffed Beds: 100 **Admissions**: 4276 **Census**: 44 **Outpatient Visits**: 172452 **Births**: 571 **Total Expense ($000)**: 160044 **Payroll Expense ($000)**: 87313 **Personnel**: 895

DUBLIN—Franklin County

☐ **COLUMBUS SPRINGS DUBLIN (364049)**, 7625 Hospital Drive, Zip 43016-9649; tel. 614/717-1800, (Includes COLUMBUS SPRINGS EAST HOSPITAL, 2085 Citygate Drive, Columbus, Ohio, Zip 43219-3656, tel. 614/412-1772; Jason Staats, Market Chief Executive Officer) (Nonreporting) **A**1 3 10 **S** Springstone, Louisville, KY
Primary Contact: Anthony Guild, Chief Executive Officer
COO: Merissa McKinstry, Chief Operating Officer
CFO: Alexis Barbour, Director Finance
CMO: Mark Blair, M.D., Medical Director
CHR: Tam Wisler, Director Human Resources
Web address: https://columbussprings.com/locations/dublin/
Control: Corporation, Investor-owned (for-profit) **Service**: Psychiatric

Staffed Beds: 144

✠ **OHIOHEALTH DUBLIN METHODIST HOSPITAL (360348)**, 7500 Hospital Drive, Zip 43016-8518; tel. 614/544-8000, (Nonreporting) **A**1 2 3 5 10 **S** OhioHealth, Columbus, OH
Primary Contact: Cherie L. Smith, Ph.D., R.N., President
COO: Anna Hensley, Chief Operating Officer
CFO: Keely Pummel, Director, Financial Operations
CMO: Barbara Evert, M.D., Vice President Medical Affairs
CIO: Michael Krouse, Senior Vice President Chief Information Officer
CNO: Elizabeth Anne Biegler, R.N., Chief Nursing Officer
Web address: www.ohiohealth.com
Control: Church operated, Nongovernment, not-for-profit **Service**: General medical and surgical

Staffed Beds: 113

EAST LIVERPOOL—Columbiana County

☐ **EAST LIVERPOOL CITY HOSPITAL (360096)**, 425 West Fifth Street, Zip 43920-2498; tel. 330/385-7200, (Nonreporting) **A**1 3 5 10 **S** Prime Healthcare, Ontario, CA
Primary Contact: Stephanie Conn, Chief Executive Officer
CFO: Kyle Johnson, Vice President Finance
CMO: Steve LaTulippe, President Medical Staff
CIO: Frank Mader, Director Information Services
CHR: Teri Pasco, Director Human Resources
CNO: Stacie Call, R.N., Vice President Patient Care and Chief Nursing Officer
Web address: www.elch.org
Control: Other not-for-profit (including NFP Corporation) **Service**: General medical and surgical

Staffed Beds: 45

ELYRIA—Lorain County

★ ⇑ **UNIVERSITY HOSPITALS ELYRIA MEDICAL CENTER (360145)**, 630 East River Street, Zip 44035-5902; tel. 440/329-7500, **A**5 10 21 **F**3 11 15 18 20 22 24 26 28 29 30 31 34 35 36 37 40 43 44 45 50 51 53 54 55 57 58 59 60 64 68 70 74 75 78 79 81 85 86 87 92 93 94 98 100 103 107 108 110 111 114 115 116 117 119 126 129 130 131 132 133 135 146 147 148 149 150 154 156 157 164 167 168 **S** University Hospitals, Cleveland, OH
Primary Contact: Todd Harford, Chief Operating Officer
CFO: David A Cook, Vice President and Chief Financial Officer
CHR: Daniel Miller, Vice President Human Resources
CNO: Sandra Jean Kantelas, Chief Nursing Officer
Web address: www.uhhospitals.org/elyria
Control: Other not-for-profit (including NFP Corporation) **Service**: General medical and surgical

Staffed Beds: 175 **Admissions**: 7386 **Census**: 81 **Outpatient Visits**: 239956 **Births**: 0 **Total Expense ($000)**: 227255 **Payroll Expense ($000)**: 70801 **Personnel**: 998

EUCLID—Cuyahoga County

✠ **CLEVELAND CLINIC EUCLID HOSPITAL (360082)**, 18901 Lake Shore Boulevard, Zip 44119-1090; tel. 216/531-9000, (Total facility includes 20 beds in nursing home-type unit) **A**1 3 10 **F**3 8 15 18 28 29 30 34 35 38 40 44 45 50 56 57 59 60 64 68 70 74 75 77 79 81 82 85 87 91 93 94 96 97 98 100 102 103 107 108 111 114 118 119 126 128 130 131 132 135 146 147 148 149 156 167 **S** Cleveland Clinic Health System, Cleveland, OH
Primary Contact: Teresa Dews, M.D., Vice President
COO: Rich Lea, Vice President Operations
CFO: Don Urbancsik, Director Finance
CMO: John Bertsch, M.D., Chief of Staff
Web address: www.euclidhospital.org
Control: Other not-for-profit (including NFP Corporation) **Service**: General medical and surgical

Staffed Beds: 146 **Admissions**: 5334 **Census**: 78 **Outpatient Visits**: 90011 **Births**: 0 **Total Expense ($000)**: 121516 **Payroll Expense ($000)**: 58776 **Personnel**: 584

EUCLID HOSPITAL See Cleveland Clinic Euclid Hospital

FAIRFIELD—Butler County

✠ △ **MERCY HEALTH – FAIRFIELD HOSPITAL (360056)**, 3000 Mack Road, Zip 45014-5335; tel. 513/870-7000, **A**1 2 7 10 19 **F**3 8 11 12 13 15 17 18 20 22 24 26 28 29 30 31 34 35 37 40 45 46 47 48 49 50 51 54 57 59 60 64 68 70 74 76 77 78 79 81 82 84 85 86 87 90 93 96 100 107 108 110 111 114 115 118 119 126 129 130 131 135 146 147 148 149 154 156 167 169 **S** Bon Secours Mercy Health, Cincinnati, OH
Primary Contact: Justin Krueger, FACHE, President
CFO: Liz Mohr, Assistant Chief Financial Officer
CMO: John Kennedy, M.D., Vice President of Medical Affairs
CIO: Rebecca S Sykes, Chief Information Officer
CNO: Ramona Cheek, MS, R.N., Chief Nursing Officer
Web address: https://www.mercy.com
Control: Church operated, Nongovernment, not-for-profit **Service**: General medical and surgical

Staffed Beds: 180 **Admissions**: 13360 **Census**: 146 **Outpatient Visits**: 152922 **Births**: 1008 **Total Expense ($000)**: 289446 **Payroll Expense ($000)**: 89366 **Personnel**: 1065

Hospital, Medicare Provider Number, Address, Telephone, Approval, Facility, and Physician Codes, Health Care System

★ American Hospital Association (AHA) membership ○ Healthcare Facilities Accreditation Program ⇑ Center for Improvement in Healthcare Quality Accreditation
☐ The Joint Commission accreditation ◇ DNV Healthcare Inc. accreditation △ Commission on Accreditation of Rehabilitation Facilities (CARF) accreditation

Hospitals, U.S. / OHIO

FINDLAY—Hancock County

✚ **BLANCHARD VALLEY HOSPITAL (360095)**, 1900 South Main Street, Zip 45840–1214; tel. 419/423–4500, (Includes BLANCHARD VALLEY HOSPITAL, 1900 South Main Street, Findlay, Ohio, Zip 45840, tel. 419/423–4500) **A**1 2 10 19 **F**3 8 11 13 15 17 18 20 22 24 26 28 29 30 31 34 35 40 41 43 44 45 48 49 50 51 54 55 57 58 59 60 64 65 68 70 73 74 76 77 78 79 81 82 85 87 89 91 93 98 100 102 107 108 110 111 114 115 117 118 119 120 121 124 126 129 130 131 132 135 143 146 148 149 154 162 164 165 167 **S** Blanchard Valley Health System, Findlay, OH
Primary Contact: Myron D. Lewis, Chief Executive Officer
CFO: David Cytlak, Chief Financial Officer
CMO: Michael Denike, D.O., Vice President, Medical Affairs
CIO: David Cytlak, Chief Financial Officer
CHR: Ryan Fisher, Director of Human Resources
CNO: Barbara J. Pasztor, R.N., Chief Nursing Executive
Web address: www.bvhealthsystem.org
Control: Other not–for–profit (including NFP Corporation) Service: General medical and surgical

Staffed Beds: 95 Admissions: 7453 Census: 95 Outpatient Visits: 247705 Births: 1001 Total Expense ($000): 264932 Payroll Expense ($000): 103730 Personnel: 1169

BLANCHARD VALLEY REG HLTH CTR See Blanchard Valley Hospital

FOSTORIA—Hancock County

✚ **PROMEDICA FOSTORIA COMMUNITY HOSPITAL (361318)**, 501 Van Buren Street, Zip 44830–1534, Mailing Address: P.O. Box 907, Zip 44830–0907; tel. 419/435–7734, **A**1 10 18 **F**3 11 15 28 29 30 31 34 35 40 45 46 57 59 60 64 70 75 78 79 81 82 85 87 89 93 96 104 107 108 110 111 115 119 128 129 130 131 132 133 135 146 147 148 149 156 157 **S** ProMedica Health System, Toledo, OH
Primary Contact: Jodi Rucker, MSN, R.N., President and Chief Nursing Officer, Vice President of Patient Care Services
COO: Tom Borer, Vice President Operations
CFO: Ken Swint, Vice President Finance and Chief Financial Officer
CMO: Terrence Fondessy, M.D., Vice President Medical Affairs
CIO: Rose Ann Laureto, Chief Information Officer
CNO: Jodi Rucker, MSN, R.N., President and Chief Nursing Officer, Vice President of Patient Care Services
Web address: www.promedica.org
Control: Other not–for–profit (including NFP Corporation) Service: General medical and surgical

Staffed Beds: 25 Admissions: 597 Census: 5 Outpatient Visits: 61511 Births: 0 Total Expense ($000): 42561 Payroll Expense ($000): 10863 Personnel: 150

FREMONT—Sandusky County

✚ **PROMEDICA MEMORIAL HOSPITAL (360156)**, 715 South Taft Avenue, Zip 43420–3237; tel. 419/332–7321, **A**1 3 5 10 **F**3 11 13 15 18 19 28 29 30 31 34 35 38 40 44 45 46 47 48 51 53 56 57 59 64 65 70 74 75 76 77 78 79 81 82 84 85 87 89 93 96 97 107 108 110 111 114 115 119 123 124 129 130 131 132 135 141 142 146 147 148 149 156 157 **P**1 **S** ProMedica Health System, Toledo, OH
Primary Contact: Jodi Rucker, MSN, R.N., President and Chief Nursing Officer, Vice President of Patient Care Services
COO: Corey Leber, R.N., Associate Vice President Operations
CFO: Ken Swint, Adminstrative Director Finance
CMO: John J. Hiestand, M.D., Vice President Medical Affairs
CHR: Warrenette Parthemore, Director Human Resources
CNO: Jodi Rucker, MSN, R.N., President and Chief Nursing Officer, Vice President of Patient Care Services
Web address: https://www.promedica.org
Control: Other not–for–profit (including NFP Corporation) Service: General medical and surgical

Staffed Beds: 43 Admissions: 1404 Census: 11 Outpatient Visits: 80468 Births: 159 Total Expense ($000): 74466 Payroll Expense ($000): 19839 Personnel: 349

GAHANNA—Franklin County

THE WOODS AT PARKSIDE (360247), 349 Olde Ridenour Road, Zip 43230–2528; tel. 614/471–2552, (Nonreporting) **A**10
Primary Contact: Adam Chaffin, Finance and Billing Coordinator
Web address: www.thewoodsatparkside.com
Control: Partnership, Investor–owned (for–profit) Service: Substance Use Disorder

Staffed Beds: 50

GALION—Crawford County

★ ⇧ **GALION COMMUNITY HOSPITAL (361325)**, 269 Portland Way South, Zip 44833–2399; tel. 419/468–4841, (Nonreporting) **A**10 18 21 **S** Avita Health System, Galion, OH
Primary Contact: Jerome Morasko, President and Chief Executive Officer
CFO: D. Eric Draime, Vice President and Chief Financial Officer
CIO: Alex Reed, Chief Information Officer
CHR: Traci L Oswald, Vice President of Human Resources
CNO: Kathy Durflinger, Vice President and Chief Nursing Officer
Web address: www.avitahealth.org
Control: Other not–for–profit (including NFP Corporation) Service: General medical and surgical

Staffed Beds: 35

GALLIPOLIS—Gallia County

✚ △ **HOLZER MEDICAL CENTER (360054)**, 100 Jackson Pike, Zip 45631–1563; tel. 740/446–5000, **A**1 2 3 5 7 10 19 **F**3 8 10 11 13 15 18 20 22 26 28 29 30 33 34 35 37 39 40 42 45 46 47 48 49 50 51 53 54 55 56 57 59 62 63 64 65 70 74 75 76 77 78 79 80 81 82 85 87 89 90 92 93 95 97 98 100 104 107 108 110 111 114 115 116 117 118 119 120 121 123 126 127 129 130 131 133 135 144 145 146 148 149 154 156 157 167 169 **S** Holzer Health System, Jackson, OH
Primary Contact: Rodney Stout, M.D., Chief Executive Officer
CFO: Kenneth G Payne, Chief Financial Officer
CMO: John Viall, M.D., Vice President Medical Affairs
CIO: John Allen, Chief Information Officer
CHR: Lisa B Hackworth, Vice President Human Resources
Web address: www.holzer.org
Control: Other not–for–profit (including NFP Corporation) Service: General medical and surgical

Staffed Beds: 100 Admissions: 4158 Census: 57 Outpatient Visits: 639711 Births: 580 Total Expense ($000): 195477 Payroll Expense ($000): 62950

GARFIELD HEIGHTS—Cuyahoga County

✚ **CLEVELAND CLINIC MARYMOUNT HOSPITAL (360143)**, 12300 McCracken Road, Zip 44125–2975; tel. 216/581–0500, **A**1 3 10 **F**3 8 11 15 18 20 28 29 30 31 34 35 37 38 40 44 45 50 51 53 54 56 57 59 60 62 63 64 65 68 70 71 74 75 77 79 81 82 84 85 86 87 93 96 97 98 100 102 103 104 107 108 110 111 114 115 118 119 126 130 131 132 135 143 146 147 148 149 153 156 157 167 **S** Cleveland Clinic Health System, Cleveland, OH
Primary Contact: Margaret McKenzie, M.D., Vice President
COO: Mark Nussbaum, Vice President Operations
CFO: Mike Stilgenbauer, Director Finance
CMO: Douglas Kohler, M.D., Vice President Medical Operations
CIO: Ralph A Cagna, Director Information Technology Operations, Cleveland Clinic Health System South Market
CHR: Judith Santora, Human Resources Business Partner
CNO: Barbara Zinner, Chief Nursing Officer
Web address: www.marymount.org
Control: Other not–for–profit (including NFP Corporation) Service: General medical and surgical

Staffed Beds: 263 Admissions: 9188 Census: 134 Outpatient Visits: 95889 Births: 0 Total Expense ($000): 197630 Payroll Expense ($000): 80418 Personnel: 844

MARYMOUNT HOSPITAL See Cleveland Clinic Marymount Hospital

GENEVA—Ashtabula County

★ ⇧ **UNIVERSITY HOSPITALS GENEVA MEDICAL CENTER (361307)**, 870 West Main Street, Zip 44041–1295; tel. 440/466–1141, **A**3 10 18 21 **F**3 5 11 15 18 20 29 31 34 35 40 41 51 55 56 57 59 62 64 68 70 75 77 78 79 81 82 84 85 86 87 91 93 97 107 110 111 115 116 117 119 129 130 132 133 135 143 146 147 148 149 150 154 156 157 **S** University Hospitals, Cleveland, OH
Primary Contact: M Steven. Jones, Regional President
COO: Jason Glowczewski, Chief Operating Officer
CFO: Lara Eggleston, Finance Manager
CMO: Amitabh Goel, M.D., Chief Medical Officer
CIO: Kirsten Hale, Coordinator Health Information Systems and Coding
CHR: Danialle Lynce, Business Partner Human Resources
CNO: Ashley M. Carlucci, R.N., Chief Nursing Officer
Web address: https://www.uhhospitals.org/locations/uh-geneva-medical-center
Control: Other not–for–profit (including NFP Corporation) Service: General medical and surgical

Staffed Beds: 25 Admissions: 1563 Census: 15 Outpatient Visits: 53196 Births: 0 Total Expense ($000): 63499 Payroll Expense ($000): 17782 Personnel: 243

Hospitals, U.S. / OHIO

GREENFIELD—Highland County

ADENA GREENFIELD MEDICAL CENTER (361304), 550 Mirabeau Street, Zip 45123-1617; tel. 937/981-9400, (Nonreporting) **A**1 3 7 10 18 **S** Adena Health System, Chillicothe, OH
Primary Contact: Josh McCoy, Senior Operations Executive Officer, Regional Vice President
CFO: Ralph W Sorrell Sr, Chief Financial Officer
CIO: Marcus Bost, Director Information Services and Chief Information Officer
CHR: Brandt Lippert, Vice President Human Resources
Web address: www.adena.org
Control: Other not-for-profit (including NFP Corporation) **Service**: General medical and surgical

Staffed Beds: 25

GREENVILLE—Darke County

★ ○ **WAYNE HEALTHCARE (360044)**, 835 Sweitzer Street, Zip 45331-1077; tel. 937/548-1141, **A**2 3 10 11 **F**3 11 13 15 18 28 29 30 31 34 35 40 41 45 53 57 59 64 65 70 75 76 77 78 79 81 82 84 85 86 87 93 98 107 108 110 111 114 118 119 124 126 129 130 131 132 135 141 146 147 149 154 156 167 169
Primary Contact: Jeffrey R. Subler, President and Chief Executive Officer
COO: Kimberlee Freeman, Vice President of Patient Care Services/Chief Nursing Officer
CFO: Jennifer Williams, Vice President of Finance/Chief Financial Officer
CMO: Safet Hatic, M.D., President Medical Staff
CIO: Shelton Monger, Director Information Technology
CHR: Peggy Schwartz, Vice President Human Resources
CNO: Kimberlee Freeman, Vice President Patient Care Services and Chief Nursing Officer
Web address: www.waynehealthcare.org
Control: Other not-for-profit (including NFP Corporation) **Service**: General medical and surgical

Staffed Beds: 43 **Admissions**: 1097 **Census**: 7 **Outpatient Visits**: 72639 **Births**: 202 **Total Expense ($000)**: 74130 **Payroll Expense ($000)**: 20485 **Personnel**: 430

GROVE CITY—Franklin County

MOUNT CARMEL WEST See Mount Carmel Grove City

HAMILTON—Butler County

BUTLER COUNTY MEDICAL CENTER See Bethesda Butler Hospital

★ ○ **KETTERING HEALTH HAMILTON (360132)**, 630 Eaton Avenue, Zip 45013-2770; tel. 513/867-2000, **A**2 10 11 19 **F**3 11 13 15 18 20 22 26 28 29 30 31 34 36 37 38 40 43 44 45 46 47 48 49 53 54 56 59 62 64 70 73 74 75 76 77 78 79 80 81 82 85 86 87 90 92 93 96 102 107 108 109 110 111 115 116 118 119 120 121 124 126 129 130 131 132 146 147 148 149 154 157 167 169 **S** Kettering Health, Dayton, OH
Primary Contact: Paul Hoover, President
CFO: William Villegas, Vice President Finance
CMO: Marcus Romanello, Chief Medical Officer
CHR: Joseph Geigle, Director Human Resources
CNO: Carol Applegeet, MSN, R.N., Vice President and Chief Nursing Officer
Web address: https://ketteringhealth.org/locations/kettering-health-hamilton-mc001/
Control: Church operated, Nongovernment, not-for-profit **Service**: General medical and surgical

Staffed Beds: 180 **Admissions**: 6358 **Census**: 73 **Outpatient Visits**: 118190 **Births**: 723 **Total Expense ($000)**: 178083 **Payroll Expense ($000)**: 63127 **Personnel**: 792

HIGHLAND HILLS—Cuyahoga County

HIGHLAND SPRINGS HOSPITAL (364053), 4199 Mill Pond Drive, Zip 44122-5731; tel. 602/314-7800, (Nonreporting) **A**1 10 **S** Springstone, Louisville, KY
Primary Contact: Brenda Bailey, Chief Executive Officer
Web address: https://www.highlandspringshealth.com
Control: Corporation, Investor-owned (for-profit) **Service**: Psychiatric

Staffed Beds: 72

HILLSBORO—Highland County

HIGHLAND DISTRICT HOSPITAL (361332), 1275 North High Street, Zip 45133-8273; tel. 937/393-6100, **A**1 3 10 18 **F**3 11 15 29 30 31 34 35 40 44 45 47 49 50 57 59 64 77 78 79 81 82 85 86 87 92 93 94 96 100 104 107 108 110 111 115 118 119 126 127 130 131 132 133 135 146 148 149 153 154 156
Primary Contact: Timothy Parry, R.N., President and Chief Executive Officer
COO: Timothy Parry, R.N., Chief Operating Officer
CMO: Ron Zile, M.D., Chief of Staff
CIO: Tim Bogard, Manager Information Technology
CHR: Melanie Wymer, Director Human Resources
CNO: Pam Barnett, R.N., Director of Nursing
Web address: www.hdh.org
Control: Hospital district or authority, Government, Nonfederal **Service**: General medical and surgical

Staffed Beds: 25 **Admissions**: 878 **Census**: 10 **Outpatient Visits**: 82831 **Births**: 0 **Total Expense ($000)**: 59167 **Payroll Expense ($000)**: 23822 **Personnel**: 416

JACKSON—Jackson County

HOLZER MEDICAL CENTER – JACKSON (361320), 500 Burlington Road, Zip 45640-9360; tel. 740/288-4625, (Nonreporting) **A**1 10 18 **S** Holzer Health System, Jackson, OH
Primary Contact: Kim Wiley. Dulaney, Vice President of Revenue Cycle
CFO: Kevin Yeager, Vice President Fiscal Services
CMO: Nimal Dutla, M.D., Chief Medical Staff
CHR: Sandy Carlisle, Manager Human Resources
Web address: www.holzer.org
Control: Other not-for-profit (including NFP Corporation) **Service**: General medical and surgical

Staffed Beds: 25

KENTON—Hardin County

OHIOHEALTH HARDIN MEMORIAL HOSPITAL (361315), 921 East Franklin Street, Zip 43326-2099; tel. 419/673-0761, (Nonreporting) **A**1 10 18 **S** OhioHealth, Columbus, OH
Primary Contact: Joy Bischoff, MSN, R.N., President
Web address: www.hardinmemorial.org
Control: Other not-for-profit (including NFP Corporation) **Service**: General medical and surgical

Staffed Beds: 25

KETTERING—Montgomery County

★ ○ **KETTERING HEALTH MAIN CAMPUS (360079)**, 3535 Southern Boulevard, Zip 45429-1221; tel. 937/298-4331, **A**2 3 5 8 10 11 19 **F**3 11 13 15 17 18 20 22 24 26 28 29 30 34 36 38 39 40 42 43 44 45 46 47 48 49 54 55 56 58 59 61 62 64 66 70 72 74 75 76 77 78 79 80 81 82 85 86 87 92 93 96 102 107 108 110 111 112 114 115 116 117 118 119 120 121 123 124 126 129 130 131 135 146 147 148 149 154 157 167 169 **P**3 6 **S** Kettering Health, Dayton, OH
Primary Contact: Sharlet M. Briggs, President
CFO: Steven Chavez, Vice President Finance and Operations
CMO: Robert T. Smith, M.D., Chief Medical Officer
CHR: Derek Morgan, Vice President Human Resources
Web address: www.ketteringhealth.org/kettering
Control: Church operated, Nongovernment, not-for-profit **Service**: General medical and surgical

Staffed Beds: 397 **Admissions**: 22608 **Census**: 312 **Outpatient Visits**: 357592 **Births**: 2644 **Total Expense ($000)**: 716371 **Payroll Expense ($000)**: 235607 **Personnel**: 2552

Hospital, Medicare Provider Number, Address, Telephone, Approval, Facility, and Physician Codes, Health Care System

★ American Hospital Association (AHA) membership
□ The Joint Commission accreditation
○ Healthcare Facilities Accreditation Program
◇ DNV Healthcare Inc. accreditation
⇑ Center for Improvement in Healthcare Quality Accreditation
△ Commission on Accreditation of Rehabilitation Facilities (CARF) accreditation

© 2025 AHA Guide

Hospitals, U.S. / OHIO

LANCASTER—Fairfield County

☐ **FAIRFIELD MEDICAL CENTER (360072)**, 401 North Ewing Street, Zip 43130–3371; tel. 740/687–8000, **A**1 2 3 5 10 13 **F**3 8 11 12 13 15 18 20 22 24 26 28 29 30 31 34 35 36 37 38 40 42 44 45 46 47 48 49 50 53 54 57 58 59 64 70 74 75 76 77 78 79 81 82 83 84 85 87 89 92 93 96 97 100 102 104 107 108 110 111 115 118 119 120 121 123 124 126 127 129 130 131 132 135 141 142 144 145 146 147 148 149 154 156 167 169
Primary Contact: John R. Janoso, Chief Executive Officer
CFO: Sky Gettys, Chief Financial Officer
CMO: Renee Wagner, M.D., Chief Medical Officer
CIO: Martha Buckley, Chief Medical Informatics Officer
CHR: Debra L Palmer, MS, R.N., Chief Human Resources Officer and Corporate Compliance Officer
CNO: Helen Harding, Chief Nursing Officer
Web address: www.fmchealth.org
Control: Other not–for–profit (including NFP Corporation) **Service**: General medical and surgical

Staffed Beds: 222 **Admissions**: 8727 **Census**: 97 **Outpatient Visits**: 183900 **Births**: 841 **Total Expense ($000)**: 382643 **Payroll Expense ($000)**: 152892 **Personnel**: 1780

LIMA—Allen County

☐ **INSTITUTE FOR ORTHOPAEDIC SURGERY (360263)**, 801 Medical Drive, Suite B, Zip 45804–4030; tel. 419/224–7586, (Nonreporting) **A**1 10 **S** Bon Secours Mercy Health, Cincinnati, OH
Primary Contact: Chad Stewart, Administrative Director
CMO: Mark McDonald, M.D., President and Chief Executive Officer
CHR: Pat Farmer, Coordinator Human Resources and Safety Officer
Web address: www.ioshospital.com
Control: Partnership, Investor–owned (for–profit) **Service**: Orthopedic

Staffed Beds: 3

✠ **KINDRED HOSPITAL LIMA (362020)**, 730 West Market Street, 6th Floor, Zip 45801–4602; tel. 419/224–1888, (Nonreporting) **A**1 10 **S** ScionHealth, Louisville, KY
Primary Contact: Susan Krinke, Chief Executive Officer
Web address: www.khlima.com
Control: Corporation, Investor–owned (for–profit) **Service**: Acute long–term care hospital

Staffed Beds: 26

✠ △ **LIMA MEMORIAL HEALTH SYSTEM (360009)**, 1001 Bellefontaine Avenue, Zip 45804–2899; tel. 419/228–3335, **A**1 2 7 10 19 **F**3 11 13 15 17 18 20 22 24 26 28 29 30 31 34 35 36 37 40 41 43 45 46 47 48 49 50 54 57 59 60 62 63 64 68 70 73 74 75 76 77 78 79 81 82 84 85 86 87 89 90 93 96 107 108 110 111 114 115 116 119 121 126 129 130 131 132 135 146 147 148 149 154 156 167 169 **P**8
Primary Contact: Michael D. Swick, President and Chief Executive Officer
COO: Robert E. Armstrong, Senior Vice President and Chief Operating Officer
CFO: Eric D. Pohjala, Vice President, Finance and Chief Financial Officer
CIO: Mathew P. Gaug, Executive Director of Information Technology
CHR: Denise G Kiraly, Director, Human Resources and Organization Development
CNO: Ann–Marie J Pohl, Vice President and Chief Nursing Officer
Web address: www.limamemorial.org
Control: Other not–for–profit (including NFP Corporation) **Service**: General medical and surgical

Staffed Beds: 173 **Admissions**: 6343 **Census**: 77 **Outpatient Visits**: 411488 **Births**: 510 **Total Expense ($000)**: 261347 **Payroll Expense ($000)**: 100532 **Personnel**: 1281

☐ △ **MERCY HEALTH – ST. RITA'S MEDICAL CENTER (360066)**, 730 West Market Street, Zip 45801–4602; tel. 419/227–3361, (Nonreporting) **A**1 2 3 5 7 8 10 19 **S** Bon Secours Mercy Health, Cincinnati, OH
Primary Contact: Ronda Lehman, PharmD, President
COO: Ronda Lehman, PharmD, Chief Operating Officer, SRPS
CFO: Tim Rieger, Chief Financial Officer
CMO: Kevin Casey, M.D., Chief Clinical Officer
CHR: Will Cason, Vice President Human Resources
CNO: Jodi Pahl, Chief Nurse Executive
Web address: www.stritas.org
Control: Church operated, Nongovernment, not–for–profit **Service**: General medical and surgical

Staffed Beds: 271

LODI—Medina County

✠ **CLEVELAND CLINIC AKRON GENERAL LODI HOSPITAL (361303)**, 225 Elyria Street, Zip 44254–1096; tel. 330/948–1222, **A**1 10 18 **F**3 15 18 29 30 34 35 40 45 50 56 57 59 64 65 75 79 81 90 93 96 97 104 107 110 111 115 119 128 129 130 133 135 146 147 156 **S** Cleveland Clinic Health System, Cleveland, OH
Primary Contact: Brian J. Harte, M.D., President
COO: Dana Kocsis, Vice President Nursing and Operations
CFO: Dave Frigo, Director Finance and Controller
CIO: Robb Baldauf, Coordinator Information Systems
CHR: Lynn Moraca, Director Human Resources
CNO: Dana Kocsis, Vice President, Nursing and Operations
Web address: www.lodihospital.org
Control: Other not–for–profit (including NFP Corporation) **Service**: General medical and surgical

Staffed Beds: 20 **Admissions**: 403 **Census**: 10 **Outpatient Visits**: 28437 **Births**: 0 **Total Expense ($000)**: 20973 **Payroll Expense ($000)**: 11108 **Personnel**: 116

LOGAN—Hocking County

★ ⇑ **HOCKING VALLEY COMMUNITY HOSPITAL (361330)**, 601 State Route 664 North, Zip 43138–8541, Mailing Address: P.O. Box 966, Zip 43138–0966; tel. 740/380–8000, **A**10 18 21 **F**3 8 11 15 28 29 30 34 40 56 57 59 64 65 70 75 77 79 81 82 85 86 87 93 104 107 111 115 118 119 127 129 130 133 135 143 144 146 147 148 149 154 156 **P**6
Primary Contact: Stacey Gabriel, R.N., President and Chief Executive Officer
CFO: Julie E. Grow, Chief Financial Officer
CMO: Duane Mast, M.D., Medical Director
CIO: John Burgess, Director Information Services
CHR: Robert F Schmidt, Director Human Resources
CNO: Janelle Hicks, R.N., Vice President Patient Services
Web address: www.hvch.org
Control: County, Government, Nonfederal **Service**: General medical and surgical

Staffed Beds: 25 **Admissions**: 564 **Census**: 5 **Outpatient Visits**: 190515 **Births**: 0 **Total Expense ($000)**: 46349 **Payroll Expense ($000)**: 16999 **Personnel**: 308

LONDON—Madison County

✠ **MADISON HEALTH (360189)**, 210 North Main Street, Zip 43140–1115; tel. 740/845–7000, **A**1 10 **F**3 11 15 18 29 31 34 35 40 45 46 50 53 57 59 64 68 70 77 78 79 81 85 87 93 97 107 108 110 111 115 118 119 126 129 130 131 135 141 146 149 154 167 **P**6
Primary Contact: Dana E. Engle, Chief Executive Officer
CFO: Michael Browning, Chief Financial Officer
CMO: Bernard Oppong, D.O., Chief of Staff
CIO: Dennis Vogt, Director Information Technology
CHR: Becky Rozell, Vice President, Human Resources
CNO: Jennifer Piccione, Chief Nursing and Clinical Services Officer
Web address: www.madison-health.com
Control: Other not–for–profit (including NFP Corporation) **Service**: General medical and surgical

Staffed Beds: 37 **Admissions**: 866 **Census**: 9 **Outpatient Visits**: 64270 **Births**: 0 **Total Expense ($000)**: 49937 **Payroll Expense ($000)**: 17696 **Personnel**: 318

LORAIN—Lorain County

☐ **CLEARVISTA HEALTH AND WELLNESS (364052)**, 3364 Kolbe Road, Zip 44053–1628; tel. 440/960–7960, (Nonreporting) **A**1 10
Primary Contact: Colleen Thomas–Phillip, Chief Executive Officer
Web address: www.clearvistahealth.com
Control: Corporation, Investor–owned (for–profit) **Service**: Psychiatric

Staffed Beds: 30

☐ △ **MERCY HEALTH – LORAIN HOSPITAL (360172)**, 3700 Kolbe Road, Zip 44053–1697; tel. 440/960–4000, (Nonreporting) **A**1 2 7 10 **S** Bon Secours Mercy Health, Cincinnati, OH
Primary Contact: John Luellen, M.D., Market President
CMO: Sam El–Dalati, M.D., Chief Medical Officer
CHR: JC Fischer, Director Human Resources
CNO: Catherine Walsh, Interim Nursing Executive
Web address: https://www.mercy.com/locations/hospitals/lorain/mercy-regional-medical-center
Control: Church operated, Nongovernment, not–for–profit **Service**: General medical and surgical

Staffed Beds: 251

MERCY REGIONAL MEDICAL CENTER See Mercy Health – Lorain Hospital

Hospitals, U.S. / OHIO

MANSFIELD—Richland County

MANSFIELD GENERAL HOSPITAL See Mansfield Hospital

OHIOHEALTH MANSFIELD HOSPITAL (360118), 335 Glessner Avenue, Zip 44903-2265; tel. 419/526-8000, (Includes MANSFIELD HOSPITAL, 335 Glessner Avenue, Mansfield, Ohio, Zip 44903-2265, tel. 419/526-8000) (Nonreporting) **A**1 2 3 5 10 19 **S** OhioHealth, Columbus, OH
Primary Contact: Curtis Gingrich, M.D., President
CFO: Joseph Lyren, Chief Financial Officer
CMO: Terry Weston, M.D., Vice President Physician Services
CIO: Cindy Sheets, Vice President Information Systems and Chief Information Officer
CHR: Beth Hildreth, Vice President Human Resources
CNO: Pam Crawford, R.N., Ph.D., Vice President of Nursing and Chief Nursing Officer
Web address: https://www.ohiohealth.com/locations/hospitals/mansfield-hospital
Control: Other not-for-profit (including NFP Corporation) **Service**: General medical and surgical

Staffed Beds: 259

OHIOHEALTH MEDCENTRAL MANSFIELD HOSPITAL See Ohiohealth Mansfield Hospital

MARIETTA—Washington County

★ ○ **MARIETTA MEMORIAL HOSPITAL (360147)**, 401 Matthew Street, Zip 45750-1699; tel. 740/374-1400, (Nonreporting) **A**2 3 5 10 11 19 **S** Memorial Health System, Marietta, OH
Primary Contact: J Scott. Cantley, President and Chief Executive Officer
CFO: Scott Silvestri, Vice President Finance and Chief Financial Officer
CMO: Dan Breece, D.O., Vice President Physician Services and Chief Medical Officer
CIO: Eric Koast, Vice President Information Technology and Chief Information Officer
CHR: Dee Ann Gehlauf, Vice President Business and Organization Development
CNO: Paige L Smith, Vice President Patient Care Services and Chief Nurse Executive
Web address: www.mhsystem.org
Control: Other not-for-profit (including NFP Corporation) **Service**: General medical and surgical

Staffed Beds: 218

★ ○ △ **SELBY GENERAL HOSPITAL (361319)**, 1106 Colegate Drive, Zip 45750-1323; tel. 740/568-2000, (Nonreporting) **A**3 7 10 11 18 **S** Memorial Health System, Marietta, OH
Primary Contact: Jody Bullman, President
CFO: Eric L Young, Chief Financial Officer
CMO: David Spears, D.O., Chief of Staff
CHR: Tricia A Engfehr, Chief Human Resources
CNO: Misti Spencer, Director Inpatient Services
Web address: https://mhsystem.org/selbygeneralhospitalcampus
Control: Other not-for-profit (including NFP Corporation) **Service**: General medical and surgical

Staffed Beds: 35

MARION—Marion County

OHIOHEALTH MARION GENERAL HOSPITAL (360011), 1000 McKinley Park Drive, Zip 43302-6397; tel. 740/383-8400, (Nonreporting) **A**1 2 10 19 **S** OhioHealth, Columbus, OH
Primary Contact: Jim Parobek, President
CIO: Chris King, Director Information Services
CHR: Gianna Ferrarotti, Director Human Resources North Region
Web address: https://www.ohiohealth.com/locations/hospitals/marion-general-hospital
Control: Other not-for-profit (including NFP Corporation) **Service**: General medical and surgical

Staffed Beds: 210

MARYSVILLE—Union County

★ ⇑ **MEMORIAL HEALTH (360092)**, 500 London Avenue, Zip 43040-1594; tel. 937/644-6115, **A**10 21 **F**3 8 11 13 15 18 20 22 26 28 29 30 31 32 34 35 38 40 45 48 49 50 51 53 54 56 57 59 60 62 64 69 74 75 76 77 78 79 81 82 85 86 87 91 92 93 96 100 107 108 110 111 114 115 116 118 119 120 124 129 130 131 132 135 144 145 146 148 149 150 152 156 160 161 167 169
Primary Contact: Olas A. Hubbs III, FACHE, President and Chief Executive Officer
COO: Laurie A Whittington, Chief Operating Officer
CFO: Jeffrey Ehlers, Chief Financial Officer
CMO: Matthew Hazelbaker, M.D., President Medical Staff
CIO: Carl Zani, Chief Technology Director
CHR: Larry C Schleeter, Chief Human Resources Officer
CNO: Robin Slattman, Chief Nursing Officer
Web address: https://memorialohio.com
Control: County, Government, Nonfederal **Service**: General medical and surgical

Staffed Beds: 65 **Admissions**: 2726 **Census**: 22 **Outpatient Visits**: 240945 **Births**: 574 **Total Expense ($000)**: 175544 **Payroll Expense ($000)**: 60225 **Personnel**: 728

MASON—Warren County

LINDNER CENTER OF HOPE (364044), 4075 Old Western Row Road, Zip 45040-3104; tel. 513/536-0311, (Nonreporting) **A**1 3 5 10
Primary Contact: Paul R. Crosby, Chief Executive Officer
COO: Brian Owens, Chief Operating Officer
CFO: David McAdams, Chief Financial Officer
CIO: Cliff McClintick, Chief Information Officer
CHR: Debbie A Strawser, Director Human Resources
Web address: www.lindnercenterofhope.org
Control: Other not-for-profit (including NFP Corporation) **Service**: Psychiatric

Staffed Beds: 64

□ **MERCY HEALTH – KINGS MILLS HOSPITAL (360374)**, 5440 Kings Island Drive, Zip 45040-7931; tel. 513/637-9999, (Nonreporting) **A**1 10 **S** Bon Secours Mercy Health, Cincinnati, OH
Primary Contact: Jason Asic, President
Web address: https://www.mercy.com/locations/hospitals/cincinnati/mercy-health-kings-mills-hospital
Control: Church operated, Nongovernment, not-for-profit **Service**: General medical and surgical

Staffed Beds: 60

MASSILLON—Stark County

□ **HEARTLAND BEHAVIORAL HEALTHCARE (364031)**, 3000 Erie Stree South, Zip 44646-7993, Mailing Address: 3000 Erie Street South, Zip 44646-7976; tel. 330/833-3135, (Nonreporting) **A**1 3 5 10 **S** Ohio Department of Mental Health, Columbus, OH
Primary Contact: Andrea Bucci, Chief Executive Officer
CFO: Patricia Eddleman, Fiscal Officer
CMO: Steven Thomson, M.D., Medical Director
CIO: Robert Hobart, Director Management Information Systems
CHR: Jerald Wilhite, Administrator Human Resources
Web address: https://mha.ohio.gov/about-us/regional-psychiatric-hospitals/healthcare-facilities/heartland/heartland
Control: State, Government, Nonfederal **Service**: Psychiatric

Staffed Beds: 152

MAUMEE—Lucas County

□ **ARROWHEAD BEHAVIORAL HEALTH HOSPITAL (364036)**, 1725 Timber Line Road, Zip 43537-4015; tel. 419/891-9333, (Nonreporting) **A**1 10 **S** Universal Health Services, Inc., King of Prussia, PA
Primary Contact: Norine Wasielewski, R.N., Chief Executive Officer
CFO: Allison Duncan, Chief Financial Officer
CMO: Kenneth Adler, M.D., Medical Director
CIO: Peggy Montgomery, Director Medical Records
CHR: Dawn Bosworth, Director Human Resources
CNO: Anita Zych, Director of Nursing
Web address: www.arrowheadbehavioral.com
Control: Corporation, Investor-owned (for-profit) **Service**: Psychiatric

Staffed Beds: 48

Hospital, Medicare Provider Number, Address, Telephone, Approval, Facility, and Physician Codes, Health Care System

★ American Hospital Association (AHA) membership
□ The Joint Commission accreditation
○ Healthcare Facilities Accreditation Program
◇ DNV Healthcare Inc. accreditation
⇑ Center for Improvement in Healthcare Quality Accreditation
△ Commission on Accreditation of Rehabilitation Facilities (CARF) accreditation

Hospitals, U.S. / OHIO

MEDINA—Medina County

CLEVELAND CLINIC MEDINA HOSPITAL (360091), 1000 East Washington Street, Zip 44256–2170; tel. 330/725–1000, **A**1 3 5 10 **F**3 8 15 18 20 28 29 30 31 34 35 36 37 40 45 47 49 50 51 57 59 60 64 70 74 75 77 78 79 81 82 85 86 93 96 107 111 115 117 119 126 129 130 131 135 167 **S** Cleveland Clinic Health System, Cleveland, OH
Primary Contact: Richard K. Shewbridge, President
COO: Vicky Snyder, Chief Operating Officer
CFO: Becky Molnar, Director of Finance
CMO: Matthew Vrobel, Vice President, Medical Operations
CIO: Frank Longley, Business Partner Information Technology
CHR: Tracie Curtis, Business Partner Human Resources
CNO: Julie Fetto, R.N., Chief Nursing Officer
Web address: www.medinahospital.org
Control: Other not–for–profit (including NFP Corporation) **Service**: General medical and surgical

Staffed Beds: 148 **Admissions**: 7767 **Census**: 93 **Outpatient Visits**: 121659 **Births**: 0 **Total Expense ($000)**: 165296 **Payroll Expense ($000)**: 63329 **Personnel**: 711

MIAMISBURG—Montgomery County

★ ○ **KETTERING HEALTH MIAMISBURG (360239)**, 4000 Miamisburg-Centerville Road, Zip 45342–7615; tel. 937/866–0551, (Includes KETTERING HEALTH BEHAVIORAL MEDICAL CENTER, 5348 Lamme RD, Moraine, Ohio, Zip 45439–3215, 5348 Lamme Road, Zip 45439, tel. 937/534–4600; Jason Brown, Director) **A**3 10 11 19 **F**3 5 11 12 15 18 29 30 34 36 37 38 40 42 44 45 46 49 53 54 56 59 64 70 74 75 77 79 80 81 82 85 86 87 92 93 96 98 100 101 102 104 107 108 110 111 114 115 119 126 129 130 131 135 146 147 148 149 152 153 154 157 160 161 164 165 167 **S** Kettering Health, Dayton, OH
Primary Contact: Erica Schneider, President KH Miamisburg & KH Washington Township
COO: Erica Schneider, Chief Operating Officer
CMO: Robert T. Smith, M.D., Chief Medical Officer
CHR: Derek Morgan, Vice President Human Resources
Web address: https://ketteringhealth.org/locations/kettering-health-miamisburg-mc007/
Control: Church operated, Nongovernment, not–for–profit **Service**: General medical and surgical

Staffed Beds: 168 **Admissions**: 7582 **Census**: 83 **Outpatient Visits**: 146275 **Births**: 0 **Total Expense ($000)**: 182695 **Payroll Expense ($000)**: 64944 **Personnel**: 843

★ **PAM HEALTH REHABILITATION HOSPITAL OF MIAMISBURG (363046)**, 2310 Cross Pointe Drive, Zip 45342–3599; tel. 937/617–0566, (Data for 236 days) **A**10 **F**3 29 30 50 60 64 68 75 85 86 90 91 93 94 96 130 148 **S** PAM Health, Enola, PA
Primary Contact: Amy Broderick, Senior Division President
CFO: Karick Stober, Chief Financial Officer
Web address: www.pamhealth.com
Control: Partnership, Investor–owned (for–profit) **Service**: Rehabilitation

Staffed Beds: 62 **Admissions**: 417 **Census**: 20 **Outpatient Visits**: 101 **Births**: 0 **Total Expense ($000)**: 11935 **Payroll Expense ($000)**: 4995 **Personnel**: 139

PAM SPECIALTY HOSPITAL OF DAYTON (362028), 4000 Miamisburg-Centerville Road, Zip 45342–7615; tel. 937/384–8300, **A**1 10 **F**1 3 12 29 50 57 60 65 154 157 **P**5 **S** PAM Health, Enola, PA
Primary Contact: Susanna Dudley, Director of Operations
CMO: Richard Gregg, M.D., Medical Director
Web address: https://postacutemedical.com
Control: Corporation, Investor–owned (for–profit) **Service**: Acute long–term care hospital

Staffed Beds: 22 **Admissions**: 303 **Census**: 20 **Outpatient Visits**: 0 **Births**: 0 **Total Expense ($000)**: 14202 **Payroll Expense ($000)**: 5839 **Personnel**: 74

MIDDLE POINT—Van Wert County

☐ **RIDGEVIEW BEHAVIORAL HOSPITAL (364047)**, 17872 Lincoln Highway, Zip 45863–9700; tel. 419/968–2950, (Nonreporting) **A**1 10 **S** Oglethorpe Recovery and Behavioral Hospitals, Tampa, FL
Primary Contact: Pat Tracy, Administrator
Web address: www.ridgeviewhospital.net/
Control: Corporation, Investor–owned (for–profit) **Service**: Psychiatric

Staffed Beds: 40

MIDDLEBURG HEIGHTS—Cuyahoga County

⇧ **SOUTHWEST GENERAL HEALTH CENTER (360155)**, 18697 Bagley Road, Zip 44130–3497; tel. 440/816–8000, (Nonreporting) **A**2 3 5 10 21
Primary Contact: William A. Young Jr, President and Chief Executive Officer
COO: Bradley W. Rauh, Vice President, Chief Operating Officer
CFO: Mary Ann Freas, Senior Vice President and Chief Financial Officer
CMO: Marilyn McNamara, M.D., Chief Medical Officer
CIO: Alec Williams, Chief Information Officer
CNO: Martha F. Bauschka, R.N., Vice President and Chief Nursing Officer
Web address: www.swgeneral.com
Control: Other not–for–profit (including NFP Corporation) **Service**: General medical and surgical

Staffed Beds: 252

MIDDLETOWN—Warren County

☐ △ **ATRIUM MEDICAL CENTER (360076)**, One Medical Center Drive, Zip 45005–1066, Mailing Address: 1 Medical Center Drive, Zip 45005–1066; tel. 513/424–2111, **A**1 2 3 7 10 **F**3 8 11 13 15 17 18 20 22 24 26 28 29 30 31 32 34 35 36 37 38 39 40 41 43 44 45 46 47 48 49 50 53 54 55 56 57 59 61 63 64 66 67 68 70 71 73 74 75 76 77 78 79 81 82 84 85 86 87 90 91 92 93 94 96 98 100 102 103 107 108 110 111 114 115 117 118 119 126 129 130 131 132 134 135 141 145 146 147 148 149 154 156 162 164 167 169 **S** Premier Health, Dayton, OH
Primary Contact: Kevin W. Harlan, President
CMO: Matthew Reeves, D.O., Esq, Chief Medical Officer
CHR: Ted Ripperger, Administrative Director Human Resources
CNO: Marquita Turner, Chief Operating Officer and Chief Nursing Officer
Web address: www.PremierHealth.com
Control: Other not–for–profit (including NFP Corporation) **Service**: General medical and surgical

Staffed Beds: 142 **Admissions**: 9962 **Census**: 112 **Outpatient Visits**: 188394 **Births**: 856 **Total Expense ($000)**: 263481 **Payroll Expense ($000)**: 85065 **Personnel**: 1168

MILLERSBURG—Holmes County

POMERENE HOSPITAL (360148), 981 Wooster Road, Zip 44654–1094; tel. 330/674–1015, **A**10 22 **F**3 11 13 15 28 29 30 34 35 36 40 46 48 50 53 54 57 59 62 63 64 65 68 70 71 74 75 76 77 79 81 82 87 93 97 107 108 110 111 112 114 115 119 122 127 128 130 131 133 135 143 144 146 147 149 154 156 157 167 169
Primary Contact: Jason Justus, Chief Executive Officer
CFO: Tia A Cernava, Chief Financial Officer
CMO: Yasser Omran, M.D., President Medical Staff
CIO: Brent Edington, Director Information Services
CHR: Kim Croft, R.N., Executive Director Human Resources
CNO: Fran Lauriha, Chief Nursing Officer
Web address: www.pomerenehospital.org
Control: Other not–for–profit (including NFP Corporation) **Service**: General medical and surgical

Staffed Beds: 71 **Admissions**: 1399 **Census**: 11 **Outpatient Visits**: 47322 **Births**: 679 **Total Expense ($000)**: 37145 **Payroll Expense ($000)**: 14196 **Personnel**: 220

MONTPELIER—Williams County

☐ **COMMUNITY HOSPITALS AND WELLNESS CENTERS–MONTPELIER (361327)**, 909 East Snyder Avenue, Zip 43543–1251; tel. 419/636–1131, (Nonreporting) **A**1 10 18
Primary Contact: Chad Tinkel, President and Chief Executive Officer
Web address: https://www.chwchospital.org
Control: Corporation, Investor–owned (for–profit) **Service**: General medical and surgical

Staffed Beds: 35

MONTPELIER HOSPITAL See Community Hospitals and Wellness Centers, Bryan

WILLIAMS COUNTY GEN HOSPITAL See Montpelier Hospital

MORAINE—Montgomery County

KETTERING BEHAVIORAL MEDICAL CENTER See Kettering Health Behavioral Medical Center

Hospitals, U.S. / OHIO

MOUNT GILEAD—Morrow County

☒ **MORROW COUNTY HOSPITAL (361313)**, 651 West Marion Road, Zip 43338–1027; tel. 419/946–5015, (Nonreporting) **A**1 10 18 **S** OhioHealth, Columbus, OH
Primary Contact: Michael Hyek, President
CFO: Joe Schueler, Chief Financial Officer
Web address: www.morrowcountyhospital.com
Control: County, Government, Nonfederal **Service:** General medical and surgical

Staffed Beds: 22

MOUNT VERNON—Knox County

☒ **KNOX COMMUNITY HOSPITAL (360040)**, 1330 Coshocton Road, Zip 43050–1495; tel. 740/393–9000, (Nonreporting) **A**1 2 3 10 20 **S** Ovation Healthcare, Brentwood, TN
Primary Contact: Bruce D. White, President and Chief Executive Officer
COO: Bruce M Behner, Chief Operating Officer
CFO: Michael Ambrosiani, Chief Financial Officer
CMO: John Hall, Chief Medical Officer
CIO: Kwi Holland, Vice President Information Services
CHR: Lisa Bragg, Vice President Human Resources
CNO: James Middleton, MSN, R.N., Chief Nursing Officer
Web address: www.kch.org
Control: Other not–for–profit (including NFP Corporation) **Service:** General medical and surgical

Staffed Beds: 90

NAPOLEON—Henry County

★ ⇧ **HENRY COUNTY HOSPITAL (361309)**, 1600 East Riverview Avenue, Zip 43545–9399; tel. 419/592–4015, **A**5 10 18 21 **F**3 11 15 28 29 30 31 34 35 36 38 40 45 50 51 53 57 59 64 65 68 70 75 76 77 78 79 81 82 85 86 87 93 97 107 108 110 114 119 130 131 133 135 144 146 147 148 149 154 156 169
Primary Contact: Kristi Barnd, Chief Executive Officer
COO: Kristi Barnd, Chief Operating Officer
CFO: Diane Walther, Controller
CIO: William Grimm, Chief Information Officer
CHR: Jennifer A Fisher, Manager Human Resources
CNO: Patricia Frank, Chief Nursing Officer
Web address: www.henrycountyhospital.org
Control: Other not–for–profit (including NFP Corporation) **Service:** General medical and surgical

Staffed Beds: 25 **Admissions:** 475 **Census:** 6 **Outpatient Visits:** 70354 **Births:** 96 **Total Expense ($000):** 35862 **Payroll Expense ($000):** 14871 **Personnel:** 200

NEW ALBANY—Franklin County

☒ **MOUNT CARMEL NEW ALBANY SURGICAL HOSPITAL (360266)**, 7333 Smith's Mill Road, Zip 43054–9291; tel. 614/775–6600, (Nonreporting) **A**1 3 5 10 **S** Trinity Health, Livonia, MI
Primary Contact: Diane Doucette, R.N., President and Chief Operating Officer
Web address: www.mountcarmelhealth.com
Control: Church operated, Nongovernment, not–for–profit **Service:** General medical and surgical

Staffed Beds: 59

NEWARK—Licking County

☐ ⇧ **LICKING MEMORIAL HOSPITAL (360218)**, 1320 West Main Street, Zip 43055–3699; tel. 740/348–4000, (Includes SHEPHERD HILL HOSPITAL, 200 Messimer Drive, Newark, Ohio, Zip 43055–3627, 1320 West Main Street, Zip 43055–1822, tel. 800/223–6410; Robert A. Montagnese, President and Chief Executive Officer) (Nonreporting) **A**1 2 10 21
Primary Contact: Robert A. Montagnese, President and Chief Executive Officer
CFO: Cynthia Webster, Vice President Financial Services
CMO: Craig Cairns, M.D., Vice President Medical Affairs
CIO: Sallie Arnett, Vice President Information Systems
CHR: Holly D Slaughter, Vice President, Human Resources
Web address: www.lmhealth.org
Control: Other not–for–profit (including NFP Corporation) **Service:** General medical and surgical

Staffed Beds: 159

☒ **SELECT SPECIALTY HOSPITAL OF SOUTHEAST OHIO (362031)**, 2000 Tamarack Road, Zip 43055; tel. 220/564–2600, (Nonreporting) **A**1 10 **S** Select Medical Corporation, Mechanicsburg, PA
Primary Contact: Emily Blevins, Chief Executive Officer
CMO: Armand Bermudez, M.D., Medical Director
CHR: Jacqueline Nezbeth, Human Resources Officer
CNO: Taryn Vierling, Chief Nursing Officer
Web address: www.selectspecialtyhospitals.com/company/locations/zanesville.aspx
Control: Corporation, Investor–owned (for–profit) **Service:** Acute long–term care hospital

Staffed Beds: 35

NORTHFIELD—Summit County

☐ **NORTHCOAST BEHAVIORAL HEALTHCARE (364011)**, 1756 Sagamore Road, Zip 44067–1086; tel. 330/467–7131, (Nonreporting) **A**1 5 10 **S** Ohio Department of Mental Health, Columbus, OH
Primary Contact: Douglas W. Kern, Chief Executive Officer
CIO: Karl Donenwirth, Vice President Information Services
Web address: www.mha.ohio.gov
Control: State, Government, Nonfederal **Service:** Psychiatric

Staffed Beds: 258

NORWALK—Huron County

★ ○ **FISHER–TITUS MEDICAL CENTER (360065)**, 272 Benedict Avenue, Zip 44857–2374; tel. 419/668–8101, (Total facility includes 69 beds in nursing home–type unit) **A**2 5 10 11 19 **F**3 7 10 11 13 15 18 20 22 26 28 29 31 32 34 35 36 37 38 40 41 43 44 45 46 48 49 50 51 54 55 56 57 59 61 62 64 65 68 70 74 75 76 77 78 79 81 85 86 87 89 91 92 93 96 97 107 108 110 111 115 118 119 126 128 129 130 131 132 135 143 145 146 148 149 154 156 164 167 169
Primary Contact: Brent Burkey, M.D., President and Chief Executive Officer
COO: Matthew Mattner, Chief Operations Officer
CFO: Scott Endsley, Chief Financial Officer
CMO: David Levine, Chief Medical Officer
CIO: Linda Stevenson, Chief Information Officer
CHR: Miriam Batke, Interim Chief Human Resource Officer
CNO: Katie Chieda, Chief Nursing Officer
Web address: www.fisher-titus.org
Control: Other not–for–profit (including NFP Corporation) **Service:** General medical and surgical

Staffed Beds: 147 **Admissions:** 3745 **Census:** 88 **Outpatient Visits:** 146433 **Births:** 364 **Total Expense ($000):** 147243 **Payroll Expense ($000):** 62446 **Personnel:** 1052

OBERLIN—Lorain County

MERCY ALLEN HOSPITAL See Mercy Health – Allen Hospital

☐ **MERCY HEALTH – ALLEN HOSPITAL (361306)**, 200 West Lorain Street, Zip 44074–1077; tel. 440/775–1211, (Nonreporting) **A**1 10 18 **S** Bon Secours Mercy Health, Cincinnati, OH
Primary Contact: Carrie Jankowski, President
COO: Ken Hale, Executive Director of Operations
CFO: Cynthia Dennison, Chief Financial Officer
CMO: Rafik Massouh, M.D., Chief of Staff
CHR: Kathy Dolbin, Director of Human Resources
CNO: Cheryl Rieves, Chief Nurse Executive Lorain Region
Web address: https://www.mercy.com/locations/hospitals/lorain/mercy-allen-hospital
Control: Other not–for–profit (including NFP Corporation) **Service:** General medical and surgical

Staffed Beds: 25

Hospital, Medicare Provider Number, Address, Telephone, Approval, Facility, and Physician Codes, Health Care System

★ American Hospital Association (AHA) membership   ○ Healthcare Facilities Accreditation Program   ⇧ Center for Improvement in Healthcare Quality Accreditation
☐ The Joint Commission accreditation   ◇ DNV Healthcare Inc. accreditation   △ Commission on Accreditation of Rehabilitation Facilities (CARF) accreditation

© 2025 AHA Guide

Hospitals, U.S. / OHIO

ONTARIO—Richland County

★ ⇑ **AVITA ONTARIO HOSPITAL (360365)**, 715 Richland Mall, Zip 44906–3802; tel. 567/307–7666, (Nonreporting) **A**10 21 **S** Avita Health System, Galion, OH
Primary Contact: Jerome Morasko, President and Chief Executive Officer
CFO: D. Eric Draime, Vice President and Chief Financial Officer
CIO: Alex Reed, Chief Information Officer
CHR: Traci L Oswald, Vice President, Chief Human Resources
CNO: Kathy Durflinger, Vice President and Chief Nursing Officer
Web address: www.avitahealth.org
Control: Other not–for–profit (including NFP Corporation) **Service**: General medical and surgical

Staffed Beds: 26

OREGON—Lucas County

MERCY ST. CHARLES HOSPITAL See Mercy Health – St. Charles Hospital

⊞ **PROMEDICA BAY PARK HOSPITAL (360259)**, 2801 Bay Park Drive, Zip 43616–4920; tel. 419/690–7900, **A**1 10 **F**3 11 13 15 18 28 29 30 31 34 35 40 45 49 50 53 54 57 59 60 64 68 70 74 75 76 77 78 79 81 82 85 86 92 93 97 107 108 110 111 114 118 119 124 126 129 130 131 132 134 135 143 146 147 148 149 154 156 164 167 **S** ProMedica Health System, Toledo, OH
Primary Contact: Dawn M. Buskey, President, ProMedica Acute Care
COO: Darrell Wachowiak, R.N., Associate Vice President Operations
CFO: Scott Fought, Vice President Finance
CMO: David Lindstrom, M.D., Vice President Medical Affairs
CIO: Rose Ann Laureto, Corporate Vice President Information Resources
CHR: Kara Zimmerly, Manager Human Resources
Web address: www.promedica.org
Control: Other not–for–profit (including NFP Corporation) **Service**: General medical and surgical

Staffed Beds: 56 **Admissions**: 2689 **Census**: 28 **Outpatient Visits**: 115908 **Births**: 456 **Total Expense ($000)**: 96779 **Payroll Expense ($000)**: 27435 **Personnel**: 456

ORRVILLE—Wayne County

⊞ ○ **AULTMAN ORRVILLE HOSPITAL (361323)**, 832 South Main Street, Zip 44667–2208; tel. 330/682–3010, **A**1 10 11 18 **F**3 8 9 11 12 13 14 15 28 29 30 34 35 40 45 49 50 51 53 55 57 59 68 71 75 76 77 79 81 82 85 86 87 93 107 108 110 111 112 114 115 118 119 126 127 129 130 131 132 133 135 143 146 147 152 154 156 157 **S** Aultman Health Foundation, Canton, OH
Primary Contact: Ryan Jones, President
CFO: Adam Luntz, Chief Financial Officer
CIO: Vince Logozzo, Director Information Technology
CNO: Angela McGee, Vice President Nursing Services
Web address: www.aultmanorrville.org
Control: Other not–for–profit (including NFP Corporation) **Service**: General medical and surgical

Staffed Beds: 25 **Admissions**: 1150 **Census**: 9 **Outpatient Visits**: 89025 **Births**: 595 **Total Expense ($000)**: 44770 **Payroll Expense ($000)**: 16331 **Personnel**: 336

OXFORD—Butler County

★ ○ **MCCULLOUGH–HYDE MEMORIAL HOSPITAL/TRIHEALTH (360046)**, 110 North Poplar Street, Zip 45056–1292; tel. 513/523–2111, **A**10 11 **F**3 5 11 13 15 29 30 31 34 35 36 40 41 50 54 57 59 64 68 69 70 75 76 77 78 79 81 82 84 85 86 87 93 94 96 102 107 110 111 115 118 119 129 130 131 132 144 146 147 149 152 154 156 160 164 169 **P**6 8
Primary Contact: Jeremiah Kirkland, President and Chief Operating Officer
CFO: John R Clements, Chief Financial Officer
CMO: Amy Spivey, Chief Medical Officer
CHR: Sharon Hancock, Chief Human Resources Officer
CNO: Pamela Collins, Vice President Chief Patient Services Officer
Web address: www.mhmh.org
Control: Other not–for–profit (including NFP Corporation) **Service**: General medical and surgical

Staffed Beds: 45 **Admissions**: 1491 **Census**: 13 **Outpatient Visits**: 48105 **Births**: 370 **Total Expense ($000)**: 47694 **Payroll Expense ($000)**: 19432 **Personnel**: 275

PARMA—Cuyahoga County

⊞ △ ⇑ **UNIVERSITY HOSPITALS PARMA MEDICAL CENTER (360041)**, 7007 Powers Boulevard, Zip 44129–5495; tel. 440/743–3000, **A**1 3 5 7 10 13 21 **F**3 12 15 17 18 20 22 24 26 28 29 30 31 34 35 36 40 43 44 45 48 49 50 51 54 55 56 57 58 59 60 62 64 65 68 69 70 71 74 75 77 78 79 81 82 84 85 86 87 90 91 92 93 96 97 100 102 107 108 110 111 114 115 116 117 119 120 121 124 126 129 130 131 132 135 145 146 147 148 149 150 154 156 157 164 167 **S** University Hospitals, Cleveland, OH
Primary Contact: James Lee. Hill Sr, M.D., Chief Operating Officer
CMO: Christopher Loyke, Chief Medical Officer
CHR: Daniel Miller, Human Resources Business Partner
Web address: www.uhhospitals.org/parma
Control: Other not–for–profit (including NFP Corporation) **Service**: General medical and surgical

Staffed Beds: 213 **Admissions**: 8584 **Census**: 106 **Outpatient Visits**: 187952 **Births**: 0 **Total Expense ($000)**: 226844 **Payroll Expense ($000)**: 76749 **Personnel**: 1029

PAULDING—Paulding County

⊞ **PAULDING COUNTY HOSPITAL (361300)**, 1035 West Wayne Street, Zip 45879–1544; tel. 419/399–4080, **A**1 10 18 **F**15 28 29 31 32 35 40 45 48 50 53 54 57 59 65 67 68 69 75 77 78 79 81 82 87 92 93 97 107 108 110 111 119 122 130 132 133 146 154 161 169
Primary Contact: Ronald Goedde, Chief Executive Officer
CFO: Rob Goshia, Chief Financial Officer
CMO: Wendell J Spangler, M.D., Chief of Staff
CIO: Dan Kaufman, Director Information Services
CHR: Melanie Rittenour, Director Human Resources
Web address: www.pauldingcountyhospital.com
Control: County, Government, Nonfederal **Service**: General medical and surgical

Staffed Beds: 17 **Admissions**: 329 **Census**: 3 **Outpatient Visits**: 30646 **Births**: 0 **Total Expense ($000)**: 29941 **Payroll Expense ($000)**: 12346 **Personnel**: 190

PORT CLINTON—Ottawa County

⊞ **MAGRUDER MEMORIAL HOSPITAL (361314)**, 615 Fulton Street, Zip 43452–2001; tel. 419/734–3131, (Nonreporting) **A**1 5 10 18
Primary Contact: Nick Marsico, President and Chief Executive Officer
CFO: Julie Georgoff, Vice President of Finance and Chief Financial Officer
CHR: Jason Kraus, Director Human Resources
CNO: Kimberly D Schreiner, MSN, R.N., Vice President of Nursing & Chief Nursing Officer
Web address: www.magruderhospital.com
Control: Other not–for–profit (including NFP Corporation) **Service**: General medical and surgical

Staffed Beds: 25

PORTSMOUTH—Scioto County

⊞ **KING'S DAUGHTERS MEDICAL CENTER OHIO (360361)**, 1901 Argonne Road, Zip 45662–2845, Mailing Address: 2001 Scioto Trail, Zip 45662–2845; tel. 740/991–4000, (Nonreporting) **A**1 10 **S** UK Healthcare, Lexington, KY
Primary Contact: Sara Marks, President and Chief Executive Officer
Web address: www.kdmcohio.com/
Control: Other not–for–profit (including NFP Corporation) **Service**: General medical and surgical

Staffed Beds: 12

⊞ **SOUTHERN OHIO MEDICAL CENTER (360008)**, 1805 27th Street, Zip 45662–2640, Mailing Address: 1805 27th Street,Waller Building Suite B01, Zip 45662–2640; tel. 740/356–5000, **A**1 2 5 10 **F**3 15 17 18 20 22 24 26 28 29 30 31 32 34 35 37 38 40 44 45 46 47 48 49 50 53 54 57 59 62 63 64 65 70 74 75 76 77 78 79 81 82 83 84 85 86 87 90 92 97 100 104 107 108 109 110 111 114 115 116 117 118 119 120 121 122 123 124 129 130 131 132 135 145 146 147 149 152 154 156 157 167 169 **P**3
Primary Contact: Ben Gill, President and Chief Executive Officer
CFO: Dean Wray, Vice President Finance
CMO: Kendall Stewart, M.D., Chief Medical Officer
CIO: Brent Richard, Administrative Director Information Systems
CHR: Vicki Noel, Vice President Human Resources
Web address: www.somc.org
Control: Other not–for–profit (including NFP Corporation) **Service**: General medical and surgical

Staffed Beds: 211 **Admissions**: 10333 **Census**: 128 **Outpatient Visits**: 544225 **Births**: 1008 **Total Expense ($000)**: 448570 **Payroll Expense ($000)**: 169755 **Personnel**: 2823

Hospitals, U.S. / OHIO

PROCTORVILLE—Lawrence County

THREE GABLES SURGERY CENTER (360261), 5897 County Road 107, Zip 45669-8852, Mailing Address: P.O. Box 490, Zip 45669-0490; tel. 740/886-9911, (Nonreporting) **A**3 10
Primary Contact: David Proctor, Administrator
Web address: www.threegablessurgery.com
Control: Partnership, Investor-owned (for-profit) **Service**: Surgical

Staffed Beds: 8

RAVENNA—Portage County

★ ⇑ **UNIVERSITY HOSPITALS PORTAGE MEDICAL CENTER (360078)**, 6847 North Chestnut Street, Zip 44266-3929, Mailing Address: P.O. Box 1204, Zip 44266-1204; tel. 330/297-0811, **A**3 5 10 21 **F**3 11 14 15 18 20 22 26 28 29 30 31 34 35 36 38 40 43 44 45 46 50 51 54 55 56 57 58 59 61 64 65 68 70 74 75 77 78 79 81 82 84 85 86 87 92 93 100 102 107 108 110 111 115 117 118 119 124 129 130 131 135 144 145 146 147 148 149 150 154 156 157 167 **S** University Hospitals, Cleveland, OH
Primary Contact: William Benoit, President
CFO: Jen Hahn, Finance Manager
CMO: Benjamin Prestegaard, Chief Medical Officer
CIO: Rhonda Smith, Applications Support Manager
CHR: Neil Everett, Vice President Human Resources
Web address: www.uhportage.org
Control: Other not-for-profit (including NFP Corporation) **Service**: General medical and surgical

Staffed Beds: 97 **Admissions**: 5379 **Census**: 64 **Outpatient Visits**: 171425
Births: 0 **Total Expense ($000)**: 168840 **Payroll Expense ($000)**: 54612
Personnel: 784

ROCK CREEK—Ashtabula County

GLENBEIGH HOSPITAL AND OUTPATIENT CENTERS (360245), 2863 Route 45, Zip 44084, Mailing Address: P.O. Box 298, Zip 44084-0298; tel. 440/563-3400, (Nonreporting) **A**10
Primary Contact: Patricia Weston-Hall, Chief Executive Officer
CFO: Phil Pawlowski, Chief Financial Officer
CIO: Linda Advey, Manager Information Systems
CHR: Shirley Deary, Director Human Resources
Web address: www.glenbeigh.com
Control: Other not-for-profit (including NFP Corporation) **Service**: Substance Use Disorder

Staffed Beds: 114

SAINT MARYS—Auglaize County

⇑ **GRAND LAKE HEALTH SYSTEM (360032)**, 200 St Clair Street, Zip 45885-2400; tel. 419/394-3335, (Nonreporting) **A**3 10 21
Primary Contact: Cynthia Berning, President and Chief Executive Officer
CFO: Jeffrey W Vossler, Chief Financial Officer
CIO: Joshua Miller, Director Information Systems
CHR: Arthur D Swain, Vice President Support Services
CNO: Debra McKee, R.N., Chief Clinical Officer and Chief Nursing Officer
Web address: www.grandlakehealth.org
Control: Other not-for-profit (including NFP Corporation) **Service**: General medical and surgical

Staffed Beds: 59

SALEM—Columbiana County

⊞ **SALEM REGIONAL MEDICAL CENTER (360185)**, 1995 East State Street, Zip 44460-2423; tel. 330/332-1551, (Nonreporting) **A**1 2 3 5 10
Primary Contact: Anita Hackstedde, M.D., President and Chief Executive Officer
COO: Keith Meredith, Chief Operating Officer
CFO: Mike Giangardella, Vice President Finance and Administration
CMO: Anita Hackstedde, M.D., Vice President Medical Affairs
CIO: Mark L'Italien, Director Information Services
CHR: Barb Hirst, R.N., Vice President Human Resources and Chief Nursing Officer
CNO: Barb Hirst, R.N., Vice President Human Resources and Chief Nursing Officer
Web address: www.salemregional.com
Control: Other not-for-profit (including NFP Corporation) **Service**: General medical and surgical

Staffed Beds: 77

SANDUSKY—Erie County

FIRELANDS COMMUNITY HOSPITAL See Firelands Regional Medical Center – Main Campus

○ **FIRELANDS REGIONAL HEALTH SYSTEM (360025)**, 1111 Hayes Avenue, Zip 44870-3323; tel. 419/557-7400, (Includes FIRELANDS REGIONAL MEDICAL CENTER – MAIN CAMPUS, 1111 Hayes Avenue, Sandusky, Ohio, Zip 44870, tel. 419/557-7400; FIRELANDS REGIONAL MEDICAL CENTER SOUTH CAMPUS, 1912 Hayes Avenue, Sandusky, Ohio, Zip 44870-4736, tel. 419/557-7000) (Nonreporting) **A**2 3 5 10 11 19
Primary Contact: Jeremy Normington-Slay, FACHE, Chief Executive Officer
CFO: Daniel J Moncher, Vice President and Chief Financial Officer
CMO: Brenda Violette, M.D., Director Medical Staff
CIO: Robert Ayres, Director Information Systems
CHR: James Sennish, Vice President Human Resources
Web address: www.firelands.com
Control: Other not-for-profit (including NFP Corporation) **Service**: General medical and surgical

Staffed Beds: 255

PROVIDENCE HOSPITAL See Firelands Regional Medical Center South Campus

SEAMAN—Adams County

☐ **ADAMS COUNTY REGIONAL MEDICAL CENTER (361326)**, 230 Medical Center Drive, Zip 45679-8002; tel. 937/386-3400, (Nonreporting) **A**1 10 18
Primary Contact: Alan Bird, Chief Executive Officer
CFO: Pete Dagenbach, Chief Financial Officer
CHR: Heather Hoop, Human Resources Generalist
CNO: Sharon Ashley, MSN, Chief Nursing Officer
Web address: www.acrmc.com
Control: County, Government, Nonfederal **Service**: General medical and surgical

Staffed Beds: 25

SHELBY—Richland County

OHIOHEALTH MEDCENTRAL SHELBY HOSPITAL See Ohiohealth Shelby Hospital

⊞ **OHIOHEALTH SHELBY HOSPITAL (361324)**, 199 West Main Street, Zip 44875-1490, Mailing Address: 199 West Main Street DOCK, Zip 44875-1490; tel. 419/342-5015, (Nonreporting) **A**1 10 18 **S** OhioHealth, Columbus, OH
Primary Contact: Curtis Gingrich, M.D., President
CNO: Trish DelGreco, Director of Nursing
Web address: https://www.ohiohealth.com/locations/hospitals/shelby-hospital
Control: Other not-for-profit (including NFP Corporation) **Service**: General medical and surgical

Staffed Beds: 25

SIDNEY—Shelby County

★ ○ **WILSON MEMORIAL HOSPITAL (360013)**, 915 West Michigan Street, Zip 45365-2491; tel. 937/498-2311, (Nonreporting) **A**3 10 11
Primary Contact: Mark Klosterman, FACHE, President and Chief Executive Officer
COO: Craig Lannoye, Vice President Operations
CFO: Julie Covault, Vice President Finance
CMO: Robert J McDevitt, M.D., Chief of Staff
CIO: Larry Meyers, Chief Information Officer
CHR: John Eve, Vice President Human Resources and Education
CNO: Linda Maurer, Vice President Patient Care Services
Web address: https://www.wilsonhealth.org
Control: Other not-for-profit (including NFP Corporation) **Service**: General medical and surgical

Staffed Beds: 90

SPRINGFIELD—Clark County

☐ **MENTAL HEALTH SERVICES FOR CLARK AND MADISON COUNTIES (364040)**, 474 North Yellow Springs Street, Zip 45504-2463; tel. 937/399-9500, (Nonreporting) **A**1 10
Primary Contact: Kelly Rigger, Chief Executive Officer
Web address: www.mhscc.org
Control: County, Government, Nonfederal **Service**: Psychiatric

Staffed Beds: 16

Hospital, Medicare Provider Number, Address, Telephone, Approval, Facility, and Physician Codes, Health Care System

★ American Hospital Association (AHA) membership   ○ Healthcare Facilities Accreditation Program   ⇑ Center for Improvement in Healthcare Quality Accreditation
☐ The Joint Commission accreditation   ◇ DNV Healthcare Inc. accreditation   △ Commission on Accreditation of Rehabilitation Facilities (CARF) accreditation

© 2025 AHA Guide

Hospitals, U.S. / OHIO

☐ **MERCY HEALTH – SPRINGFIELD REGIONAL MEDICAL CENTER (360086)**, 100 Medical Center Drive, Zip 45504-2687; tel. 937/523-1000, (Nonreporting) **A**1 2 3 10 19 **S** Bon Secours Mercy Health, Cincinnati, OH
Primary Contact: Adam Groshans, Market President
CFO: William J. Kusnierz, Vice President and Chief Financial Officer
CNO: Elaine Storrs, Chief Nursing Officer
Web address: https://www.mercy.com/locations/hospitals/springfield/springfield-medical-center
Control: Church operated, Nongovernment, not-for-profit **Service**: General medical and surgical
Staffed Beds: 259

☐ **OHIO VALLEY SURGICAL HOSPITAL (360355)**, 100 West Main Street, Zip 45502-1312; tel. 937/521-3900, (Nonreporting) **A**1 10
Primary Contact: William P. Perno, FACHE, Chief Executive Officer
CFO: Amanda martin, Manager Human Resources
CMO: Thales Pavlatos, Medical Director
CIO: Jonathan Bisdorf, Director Information Technology
CNO: Beth Lizza, Chief Nursing Officer
Web address: www.ovsurgical.com/
Control: Partnership, Investor-owned (for-profit) **Service**: Surgical
Staffed Beds: 24

SPRINGFIELD REGIONAL MEDICAL CENTER See Mercy Health – Springfield Regional Medical Center

STEUBENVILLE—Jefferson County

LIFE LINE HOSPITAL (362039), 200 School Street, Zip 43953-9610; tel. 740/346-2600, (Nonreporting) **A**10
Primary Contact: Patricia Cross, Chief Executive Officer
Web address: www.llhospital.com
Control: Partnership, Investor-owned (for-profit) **Service**: Acute long-term care hospital
Staffed Beds: 30

OHIO VALLEY HOSPITAL See Trinity Medical Center East

ST JOHN MEDICAL CENTER See Trinity Medical Center West

✠ **TRINITY HEALTH SYSTEM (360211)**, 380 Summit Avenue, Zip 43952-2699; tel. 740/283-7000, (Includes TRINITY MEDICAL CENTER EAST, 380 Summit Avenue, Steubenville, Ohio, Zip 43952-2699, tel. 740/283-7000; TRINITY MEDICAL CENTER WEST, 4000 Johnson Road, Steubenville, Ohio, Zip 43952-2393, tel. 740/264-8000) (Nonreporting) **A**1 2 3 5 10 19 **S** CommonSpirit Health, Chicago, IL
Primary Contact: Matthew Grimshaw, Market Chief Executive Officer
COO: JoAnn M Mulrooney, R.N., Chief Operating Officer
CFO: Dave Werkin, Vice President Finance and Chief Financial Officer
CMO: Gray Goncz, Vice President of Medical Affairs
CIO: Tom Kiger, Director Information Systems
CHR: Lewis C Musso, Vice President Human Resources
Web address: www.trinityhealth.com
Control: Other not-for-profit (including NFP Corporation) **Service**: General medical and surgical
Staffed Beds: 277

SYLVANIA—Lucas County

FLOWER HOSPITAL See Promedica Flower Hospital

✠ **REGENCY HOSPITAL OF TOLEDO (362036)**, 5220 Alexis Road, Zip 43560-2504; tel. 419/318-5700, (Includes REGENCY HOSPITAL – OREGON, 2600 Navarre Avenue, 5th Foor, Oregon, Ohio, Zip 43616-3207, 2600 Navarre Avenue, 5th Floor, Zip 43616-3207, tel. 419/972-3200) (Nonreporting) **A**1 10 **S** Select Medical Corporation, Mechanicsburg, PA
Primary Contact: Marc Trznadel, Chief Executive Officer
Web address: www.regencyhospital.com
Control: Corporation, Investor-owned (for-profit) **Service**: Acute long-term care hospital
Staffed Beds: 45

TIFFIN—Seneca County

☐ **MERCY HEALTH – TIFFIN HOSPITAL (360089)**, 45 St Lawrence Drive, Zip 44883-8310; tel. 419/455-7000, (Nonreporting) **A**1 2 3 5 10 **S** Bon Secours Mercy Health, Cincinnati, OH
Primary Contact: Andrew Morgan, President
CMO: Steven Bruhl, Chief Medical Officer
CHR: Diana Olson, Director Human Resources
CNO: Anne Zimmerman, Senior Director Patient Care Services and Chief Nursing Officer
Web address: www.mercyweb.org
Control: Church operated, Nongovernment, not-for-profit **Service**: General medical and surgical
Staffed Beds: 45

MERCY TIFFIN HOSPITAL See Mercy Health – Tiffin Hospital

☐ **SOJOURN AT SENECA SENIOR BEHAVIORAL HEALTH (364055)**, 50 St Lawrence Drive, Zip 44883-8310; tel. 567/207-2230, (Nonreporting) **A**1 10
Primary Contact: Patricia Huber, Chief Executive Officer
CNO: Patricia Huber, Chief Nursing Officer
Web address: www.voaseniorliving.org
Control: Other not-for-profit (including NFP Corporation) **Service**: Psychiatric
Staffed Beds: 24

TOLEDO—Lucas County

☐ **ADVANCED SPECIALTY HOSPITAL OF TOLEDO (362038)**, 1015 Garden Lake Parkway, Zip 43614-2779; tel. 419/381-0037, (Nonreporting) **A**1 3 10
Primary Contact: Gary Zaciewski, R.N., Chief Executive Officer
CFO: Troy Holmes, Chief Financial Officer
CMO: B Sarroui, M.D., Chief of Staff
CHR: Lauren Avigdor, Director Human Resources
CNO: Bridgett Mitchell, Chief Clinical Officer
Web address: www.advancedspecialtyhospitals.com
Control: Corporation, Investor-owned (for-profit) **Service**: Acute long-term care hospital
Staffed Beds: 25

✠ **ENCOMPASS HEALTH REHABILITATION HOSPITAL OF TOLEDO (363043)**, 4647 Monroe Street, Zip 43623; tel. 567/290-3500, (Nonreporting) **A**1 10 **S** Encompass Health Corporation, Birmingham, AL
Web address: https://encompasshealth.com/locations/toledorehab
Control: Corporation, Investor-owned (for-profit) **Service**: Rehabilitation
Staffed Beds: 40

☐ △ **MERCY HEALTH – ST. VINCENT MEDICAL CENTER (360112)**, 2213 Cherry Street, Zip 43608-2691; tel. 419/251-3232, (Includes MERCY HEALTH – ST. ANNE HOSPITAL, 3404 West Sylvania Avenue, Toledo, Ohio, Zip 43623-4467, tel. 419/407-2663; Daniel Barbee, Interim President; MERCY HEALTH – ST. CHARLES HOSPITAL, 2600 Navarre Avenue, Oregon, Ohio, Zip 43616-3297, tel. 419/696-7200; Craig Albers, President and Chief Operating Officer) (Nonreporting) **A**1 2 3 5 7 10 13 19 **S** Bon Secours Mercy Health, Cincinnati, OH
Primary Contact: Jeffrey Dempsey, President
CMO: Thomas Welch, M.D., Chief Medical Officer
CHR: Gary George, Senior Vice President Human Resources
CNO: Barbara Martin, Chief Nursing Officer
Web address: www.mercyweb.org
Control: Church operated, Nongovernment, not-for-profit **Service**: General medical and surgical
Staffed Beds: 745

MERCY ST. ANNE HOSPITAL See Mercy Health – St. Anne Hospital

MERCY ST. VINCENT MEDICAL CENTER See Mercy Health – St. Vincent Medical Center

☐ **NATIONWIDE CHILDREN'S HOSPITAL – TOLEDO (363309)**, 2213 Cherry Street, Zip 43608-2603; tel. 567/290-6543, (Nonreporting) **A**1 10
Primary Contact: Rick Miller, President and Chief Operating Officer
COO: Jeff Dempsey, Chief Operating Officer
CFO: Luke Brown, Chief Financial Officer
CMO: Rustin Morse, M.D., Chief Medical Officer
CIO: Denise Zabawski, Chief Information Officer
CHR: Lorina Wise, Chief Human Resources Officer
CNO: Donna Ruedisueli, MSN, R.N., Chief Nursing Officer
Web address: https://www.nationwidechildrens.org/locations/toledo
Control: Other not-for-profit (including NFP Corporation) **Service**: Children's general medical and surgical
Staffed Beds: 76

Hospitals, U.S. / OHIO

☐ **NORTHWEST OHIO PSYCHIATRIC HOSPITAL (364014)**, 930 Detroit Avenue, Zip 43614–2701; tel. 419/381–1881, (Nonreporting) **A**1 3 10 **S** Ohio Department of Mental Health, Columbus, OH
Primary Contact: Charlie Hughes, Chief Executive Officer
COO: Kyle Hurst, Chief Operations Officer
CIO: Michael Carter, Administrator Information Technology
CHR: Ursula Barrera-Richards, Human Resource Director
CNO: Deb Duris, Director of Nursing
Web address: https://mha.ohio.gov/about-us/regional-psychiatric-hospitals/locations/northwest-ohio-psychiatric-hospital
Control: State, Government, Nonfederal **Service**: Psychiatric

Staffed Beds: 112

✣ △ **PROMEDICA TOLEDO HOSPITAL (360068)**, 2142 North Cove Boulevard, Zip 43606–3896; tel. 419/291–4000, (Includes PROMEDICA FLOWER HOSPITAL, 5200 Harroun RD, Sylvania, Ohio, Zip 43560–2196, 5200 Harroun Road, Zip 43560–2196, tel. 419/824–1444; Darrell Wachowiak, R.N., President; PROMEDICA RUSSELL J. EBEID CHILDREN'S HOSPITAL, 2142 North Cove Boulevard, Toledo, Ohio, Zip 43606, tel. 419/291–4000; Dawn M. Buskey, President, Acute Care; PROMEDICA WILDWOOD ORTHOPAEDIC AND SPINE HOSPITAL, 2901 North Reynolds Road, Toledo, Ohio, Zip 43615, tel. 419/578–7700; Thadius Wadsworth, President) **A**1 2 3 5 7 10 19 **F**3 7 8 11 12 13 15 17 18 20 22 24 26 28 29 30 31 32 34 35 36 38 39 40 41 42 43 45 46 47 48 49 50 51 53 54 55 57 58 59 60 64 65 67 68 70 71 72 74 75 76 77 78 79 81 84 85 86 87 88 89 90 91 92 93 94 95 96 97 98 99 100 101 102 103 107 108 109 110 111 113 114 115 116 117 118 119 120 121 123 124 126 129 130 131 132 134 135 143 144 146 147 148 149 150 154 155 157 162 164 165 167 169 **S** ProMedica Health System, Toledo, OH
Primary Contact: Dawn M. Buskey, President, Acute Care
COO: Gary Akenberger, Chief Operating Officer
CFO: Steven Cavanaugh, Chief Financial Officer
CMO: Neeraj Kanwal, M.D., Vice President, Medical Affairs
CIO: Murry Mercier, Chief Information Officer
CHR: Les Thompson, Chief Human Resources Officer
CNO: Corey Leber, R.N., Associate Vice President of Nursing
Web address: www.promedica.org
Control: Other not-for-profit (including NFP Corporation) **Service**: General medical and surgical

Staffed Beds: 834 **Admissions**: 32007 **Census**: 569 **Outpatient Visits**: 902263 **Births**: 4525 **Total Expense ($000)**: 1403502 **Payroll Expense ($000)**: 403996 **Personnel**: 6377

☐ **REHABILITATION HOSPITAL OF NORTHWEST OHIO (363040)**, 1455 West Medical Loop, Zip 43614; tel. 419/214–6600, (Nonreporting) **A**1 3 10 **S** Ernest Health, Inc., Albuquerque, NM
Primary Contact: Andrea Sheehy, Chief Executive Officer
Control: Corporation, Investor-owned (for-profit) **Service**: Rehabilitation

Staffed Beds: 40

✣ **THE UNIVERSITY OF TOLEDO MEDICAL CENTER (360048)**, 3000 Arlington Avenue, Zip 43614–2595; tel. 419/383–4000, (Nonreporting) **A**1 2 3 5 10 19
Primary Contact: Richard P. Swaine, Chief Executive Officer
CMO: Michael Ellis, M.D., Chief Medical Officer
CIO: William McCreary, Vice President and Chief Information Officer
CHR: Wendy Davis, Associate Vice President and Chief Human Resource Officer
CNO: Kurt Kless, Chief Nursing Officer
Web address: www.utoledo.edu
Control: State, Government, Nonfederal **Service**: General medical and surgical

Staffed Beds: 246

TOLEDO CHILDREN'S HOSPITAL See Promedica Russell J. Ebeid Children's Hospital

TROY—Miami County

★ ○ **KETTERING HEALTH TROY (360368)**, 600 W Main Street, Zip 45373–3384; tel. 937/980–7000, **A**10 11 **F**3 11 15 18 29 30 34 36 40 42 44 45 46 54 56 59 64 70 74 75 78 79 81 82 85 87 102 107 108 110 111 114 115 118 119 120 121 124 126 130 135 146 147 148 149 154 157 167 **P**3 6 **S** Kettering Health, Dayton, OH
Primary Contact: Norman Spence, President
Web address: https://ketteringhealth.org/troy
Control: Church operated, Nongovernment, not-for-profit **Service**: General medical and surgical

Staffed Beds: 28 **Admissions**: 1859 **Census**: 15 **Outpatient Visits**: 65466 **Births**: 0 **Total Expense ($000)**: 70357 **Payroll Expense ($000)**: 22405 **Personnel**: 251

☐ △ **UPPER VALLEY MEDICAL CENTER (360174)**, 3130 North County Road 25A, Zip 45373–1309; tel. 937/440–4000, **A**1 2 5 7 10 **F**3 8 11 13 15 18 20 22 26 28 29 30 31 32 34 35 36 37 38 39 40 41 43 44 45 46 49 50 53 54 55 56 57 59 60 61 63 64 68 70 71 73 74 75 76 77 79 80 81 84 85 86 87 90 91 92 93 94 96 98 100 102 103 107 108 110 111 115 117 118 119 126 129 130 131 132 134 135 141 145 146 147 148 149 154 156 162 164 167 169 **S** Premier Health, Dayton, OH
Primary Contact: Kevin W. Harlan, President
CFO: Craig Ganger, Chief Financial Officer
CIO: James Kaiser, Site Director Information Technology
CHR: Kathy Boerger, Director Human Resources
CNO: Terry Fry, R.N., Chief Nursing Officer
Web address: www.uvmc.com
Control: Other not-for-profit (including NFP Corporation) **Service**: General medical and surgical

Staffed Beds: 82 **Admissions**: 6101 **Census**: 67 **Outpatient Visits**: 172718 **Births**: 322 **Total Expense ($000)**: 159716 **Payroll Expense ($000)**: 57712 **Personnel**: 864

UPPER SANDUSKY—Wyandot County

★ **WYANDOT MEMORIAL HOSPITAL (361329)**, 885 North Sandusky Avenue, Zip 43351–1098; tel. 419/294–4991, **A**10 18 **F**3 11 15 17 18 28 29 30 31 34 35 40 45 46 50 53 57 59 62 63 64 65 71 74 75 77 78 79 81 82 84 85 86 87 92 93 97 107 108 110 111 115 116 117 118 119 124 126 127 129 130 131 132 133 135 144 146 147 148 149 154
Primary Contact: Ty Shaull, President and Chief Executive Officer
CFO: Alan H Yeates, Vice President Fiscal Services
CHR: Vickie Underwood, Director Human Resources
CNO: Marty Gray, R.N., Director of Nursing
Web address: www.wyandotmemorial.org
Control: Hospital district or authority, Government, Nonfederal **Service**: General medical and surgical

Staffed Beds: 25 **Admissions**: 602 **Census**: 6 **Outpatient Visits**: 84629 **Births**: 0 **Total Expense ($000)**: 87034 **Payroll Expense ($000)**: 29550 **Personnel**: 311

URBANA—Champaign County

MERCY HEALTH – URBANA HOSPITAL (361312), 904 Scioto Street, Zip 43078–2200; tel. 937/653–5231, (Nonreporting) **A**10 18 **S** Bon Secours Mercy Health, Cincinnati, OH
Primary Contact: Jamie Houseman, President
Web address: www.health-partners.org
Control: Church operated, Nongovernment, not-for-profit **Service**: General medical and surgical

Staffed Beds: 25

MERCY MEMORIAL HOSPITAL See Mercy Health – Urbana Hospital

VAN WERT—Van Wert County

✣ **OHIOHEALTH VAN WERT HOSPITAL (360071)**, 1250 South Washington Street, Zip 45891–2599; tel. 419/238–2390, (Nonreporting) **A**1 5 10 **S** OhioHealth, Columbus, OH
Primary Contact: Joy Bischoff, MSN, R.N., President
CFO: Karen Shadowens, CPA, Chief Financial Officer
CMO: Thomas Conte, M.D., President, Medical Staff
CIO: Brett Taylor, Director Hospital Information Systems
CNO: Elizabeth Neuschwanger, Chief Nursing Officer
Web address: www.vanwerthealth.org
Control: Other not-for-profit (including NFP Corporation) **Service**: General medical and surgical

Staffed Beds: 36

Hospital, Medicare Provider Number, Address, Telephone, Approval, Facility, and Physician Codes, Health Care System

★ American Hospital Association (AHA) membership
☐ The Joint Commission accreditation
○ Healthcare Facilities Accreditation Program
◇ DNV Healthcare Inc. accreditation
⇈ Center for Improvement in Healthcare Quality Accreditation
△ Commission on Accreditation of Rehabilitation Facilities (CARF) accreditation

Hospitals, U.S. / OHIO

WARREN—Trumbull County

△ **HILLSIDE REHABILITATION HOSPITAL (363026)**, 8747 Squires Lane NE, Zip 44484–1649; tel. 330/841–3700, (Nonreporting) A1 5 7 10 **S** Steward Health Care System, LLC, Dallas, TX
Primary Contact: Jeffrey Koontz, Chief Administrator Officer
CMO: Joseph Cerimele, D.O., Medical Director
CIO: Barry Fitts, Chief Information Officer
CHR: Jody Roman, Chief Human Resource Officer
CNO: Susan Joy, Chief Nursing Officer
Web address: https://valleycareofohio.steward.org
Control: Corporation, Investor–owned (for–profit) **Service**: Rehabilitation

Staffed Beds: 65

MERCY HEALTH – ST. JOSEPH WARREN HOSPITAL (360161), 667 Eastland Avenue SE, Zip 44484–4531, Mailing Address: 627 Eastland Avenue, Zip 44484–4531; tel. 330/841–4000, (Nonreporting) A1 2 3 5 10 13 **S** Bon Secours Mercy Health, Cincinnati, OH
Primary Contact: Charlotte Wray, MSN, R.N., President
COO: Donald E. Koenig Jr, Chief Operating Officer
CMO: Nicholas Kreatsoulas, Vice President Medical Affairs
Web address: https://www.mercy.com/locations/hospitals/youngstown/mercy-health-st-joseph-warren-hospital?utm_source=local-listings&utm_medium=organic&utm_content=website_link
Control: Church operated, Nongovernment, not–for–profit **Service**: General medical and surgical

Staffed Beds: 136

TRUMBULL MEMORIAL HOSPITAL See Trumbull Regional Medical Center

TRUMBULL REGIONAL MEDICAL CENTER (360055), 1350 East Market Street, Zip 44483–6628; tel. 330/841–9011, (Nonreporting) A1 3 5 10 19 **S** Steward Health Care System, LLC, Dallas, TX
Primary Contact: Cindy Russo, FACHE, MS, R.N., President
CMO: Thomas L James, M.D., Chief Medical Officer
CIO: Barry Fitts, Chief Information Officer
CHR: Robert Sincich, Vice President Human Resources
CNO: Melissa Bennett, Chief Nursing Officer
Web address: https://trumbullmemorial.org/?_ga=2.209137234.1564767671.1497292183-315051339.1497292183
Control: Corporation, Investor–owned (for–profit) **Service**: General medical and surgical

Staffed Beds: 292

WARRENSVILLE HEIGHTS—Cuyahoga County

CLEVELAND CLINIC SOUTH POINTE HOSPITAL (360144), 20000 Harvard Road, Zip 44122–6805; tel. 216/491–6000, A1 2 3 5 10 13 **F**3 15 18 26 28 29 30 31 33 34 35 36 38 39 40 44 45 48 50 51 55 56 57 58 59 60 61 64 65 66 68 70 74 75 77 78 79 81 82 84 85 86 87 93 97 100 102 107 108 110 111 114 117 119 130 132 143 146 147 148 149 156 167 **S** Cleveland Clinic Health System, Cleveland, OH
Primary Contact: Margaret McKenzie, M.D., Vice President
COO: Andrea Jacobs, Chief Operating Officer
CFO: Lindsay Bird, Director Finance
CMO: Arun Gupta, M.D., Vice President Medical Affairs
CIO: Ralph A Cagna, Director Information Technology
CHR: Doris A. Zajec, Director Human Resources
Web address: www.southpointehospital.org
Control: Other not–for–profit (including NFP Corporation) **Service**: General medical and surgical

Staffed Beds: 172 **Admissions**: 7220 **Census**: 86 **Outpatient Visits**: 98497 **Births**: 0 **Total Expense ($000)**: 154010 **Payroll Expense ($000)**: 71871 **Personnel**: 689

REGENCY NORTH CENTRAL OHIO – CLEVELAND EAST (362029), 4200 Interchange Corporate Center Road, Zip 44128–5631; tel. 216/910–3800, (Includes REGENCY HOSPITAL OF CLEVELAND – WEST, 6990 Engle Road, Middleburg Heights, Ohio, Zip 44130–3420, tel. 440/202–4200; Sherri P. Becker, Chief Executive Officer) (Nonreporting) A1 10 **S** Select Medical Corporation, Mechanicsburg, PA
Primary Contact: Julie Idoine-Fries, FACHE, Chief Executive Officer
Web address: www.regencyhospital.com/
Control: Corporation, Investor–owned (for–profit) **Service**: Acute long–term care hospital

Staffed Beds: 87

SOUTH POINTE HOSPITAL See Cleveland Clinic South Pointe Hospital

WASHINGTON COURT HOUSE—Fayette County

ADENA FAYETTE MEDICAL CENTER (361331), 1430 Columbus Avenue, Zip 43160–1791; tel. 740/335–1210, (Nonreporting) A1 10 18 **S** Adena Health System, Chillicothe, OH
Primary Contact: Josh McCoy, Senior Operations Executive Officer
CFO: Trent Lemle, Chief Financial Officer
CNO: Tammie Wilson, R.N., MSN, Chief Nursing Officer
Web address: www.fcmh.org
Control: Other not–for–profit (including NFP Corporation) **Service**: General medical and surgical

Staffed Beds: 25

WAUSEON—Fulton County

FULTON COUNTY HEALTH CENTER (361333), 725 South Shoop Avenue, Zip 43567–1701; tel. 419/335–2015, (Total facility includes 71 beds in nursing home–type unit) A1 3 5 10 18 **F**3 8 11 12 13 15 18 28 29 31 34 37 40 41 53 56 57 59 61 64 67 69 70 74 75 76 77 78 79 81 85 86 87 89 92 93 97 98 100 101 102 103 104 105 107 108 110 111 114 115 118 119 126 128 130 131 132 135 144 145 146 148 149 153 154 156 160 164 167 169
Primary Contact: Patricia Finn, Chief Executive Officer
COO: Kristine Snyder, Chief Operating Officer
CFO: Jenee Seibert, Chief Finance Officer
CIO: Robbie Daniels, Chief Information Officer
CHR: Rachel Geckle, Chief Human Resource Officer
Web address: www.fultoncountyhealthcenter.org
Control: Other not–for–profit (including NFP Corporation) **Service**: General medical and surgical

Staffed Beds: 106 **Admissions**: 1485 **Census**: 61 **Outpatient Visits**: 110802 **Births**: 296 **Total Expense ($000)**: 83781 **Payroll Expense ($000)**: 30066 **Personnel**: 691

WAVERLY—Pike County

ADENA PIKE MEDICAL CENTER (361334), 100 Dawn Lane, Zip 45690–9138; tel. 740/947–2186, (Nonreporting) A1 10 18 **S** Adena Health System, Chillicothe, OH
Primary Contact: David M. Zanni, Administrator
CFO: Lisa Carlson, Chief Financial Officer
CMO: John Fortney, Chief Medical Officer
CIO: Tom Bialorucki, Chief Information Officer
CHR: Jay D. Justice, Chief Human Resources Officer
Web address: www.adena.org
Control: Other not–for–profit (including NFP Corporation) **Service**: General medical and surgical

Staffed Beds: 25

WEST CHESTER—Butler County

BECKETT SPRINGS (364051), 8614 Shepherd Farm Drive, Zip 45069; tel. 513/942–9500, (Nonreporting) A1 10 **S** Springstone, Louisville, KY
Primary Contact: Loyal Ownes, Chief Executive Officer
Web address: https://beckettsprings.com/
Control: Corporation, Investor–owned (for–profit) **Service**: Psychiatric

Staffed Beds: 96

UNIVERSITY POINTE SURGICAL HOSPITAL See West Chester Hospital Surgical Center

WEST CHESTER HOSPITAL (360354), 7700 University Drive, Zip 45069–2505; tel. 513/298–3000, (Includes WEST CHESTER HOSPITAL SURGICAL CENTER, 7750 University Court, West Chester, Ohio, Zip 45069, tel. 513/475–8300) A1 2 3 5 10 **F**3 7 8 12 13 15 18 20 22 26 29 30 31 34 35 36 37 38 39 40 41 43 44 45 46 47 48 49 50 51 52 54 56 57 58 59 60 61 63 64 65 70 73 74 75 76 77 78 79 80 81 82 84 85 87 92 93 100 101 102 107 108 110 111 114 115 116 117 119 120 126 129 130 131 135 146 147 148 149 150 154 155 156 157 160 161 164 165 167 169 **S** UC Health, Cincinnati, OH
Primary Contact: Jennifer Jackson, R.N., MSN, Vice President of Operations and Chief Nursing Officer
CIO: Jay Brown, Senior Vice President, Chief Information Officer
CHR: Jack Talbot, Director, Human Resources
CNO: Kathie Hays, MSN, R.N., Chief Nursing Officer
Web address: www.uchealth.com/westchesterhospital
Control: Other not–for–profit (including NFP Corporation) **Service**: General medical and surgical

Staffed Beds: 175 **Admissions**: 8947 **Census**: 110 **Outpatient Visits**: 320376 **Births**: 1055 **Total Expense ($000)**: 286231 **Payroll Expense ($000)**: 105607 **Personnel**: 1114

Hospitals, U.S. / OHIO

WESTERVILLE—Delaware County

☒ △ **MOUNT CARMEL REHABILITATION HOSPITAL (363042)**, 597 Executive Campus Drive, Zip 43082–8870; tel. 614/392–3400, (Nonreporting) **A**1 7 10 **S** Encompass Health Corporation, Birmingham, AL
Primary Contact: Angela Bridges, R.N., Chief Executive Officer
CFO: Ibrahima Loume, Controller
CMO: Sarah Grove, M.D., Medical Director
CHR: Merri Foltz, Director of Human Resources
CNO: Jan Bricker, R.N., Chief Nursing Officer
Web address: www.encompasshealth.com
Control: Corporation, Investor–owned (for–profit) **Service**: Rehabilitation

Staffed Beds: 60

WESTERVILLE—Franklin County

☒ **MOUNT CARMEL ST. ANN'S (360012)**, 500 South Cleveland Avenue, Zip 43081–8998; tel. 614/898–4000, (Nonreporting) **A**1 3 5 10 **S** Trinity Health, Livonia, MI
Primary Contact: Diane Doucette, R.N., President and Chief Operating Officer
COO: Diane Doucette, R.N., President and Chief Operating Officer
Web address: www.mountcarmelhealth.com
Control: Church operated, Nongovernment, not–for–profit **Service**: General medical and surgical

Staffed Beds: 304

WESTLAKE—Cuyahoga County

⇑ **UH ST. JOHN MEDICAL CENTER** See University Hospitals St. John Medical Center

★ ⇑ **UNIVERSITY HOSPITALS ST. JOHN MEDICAL CENTER (360123)**, 29000 Center Ridge Road, Zip 44145–5293; tel. 440/835–8000, **A**3 5 10 13 21 **F**3 11 15 18 19 20 22 26 28 29 30 31 34 35 36 39 40 41 43 44 45 46 47 49 50 54 55 56 57 58 59 60 63 64 65 68 70 71 74 75 77 78 79 81 82 84 85 86 87 91 92 93 100 102 107 108 110 111 115 118 119 126 130 131 132 135 146 147 148 149 150 154 156 157 162 164 165 167 **S** University Hospitals, Cleveland, OH
Primary Contact: Jonathan Sague, Chief Operating Officer
CFO: Allen R Tracy, Senior Vice President and Chief Financial Officer
CMO: Michael Dobrovich, M.D., Chief Medical Officer
CIO: James H Carroll, Chief Information Officer
CHR: Gary Lazroff, Vice President Human Resources
Web address: https://www.uhhospitals.org
Control: Other not–for–profit (including NFP Corporation) **Service**: General medical and surgical

Staffed Beds: 124 **Admissions**: 7459 **Census**: 80 **Outpatient Visits**: 141301 **Births**: 0 **Total Expense ($000)**: 206042 **Payroll Expense ($000)**: 66889 **Personnel**: 881

WILLARD—Huron County

☐ **MERCY HEALTH – WILLARD HOSPITAL (361310)**, 1100 Neal Zick Road, Zip 44890–9287; tel. 419/964–5000, (Nonreporting) **A**1 5 10 18 **S** Bon Secours Mercy Health, Cincinnati, OH
Primary Contact: Andrew Morgan, President
CMO: Christopher Bohach, DPM, Chief of Staff
CHR: Diana Olson, Chief Human Resources Officer
Web address: www.mercyweb.org
Control: Church operated, Nongovernment, not–for–profit **Service**: General medical and surgical

Staffed Beds: 25

WILLOUGHBY—Lake County

⇑ **UH LAKE HEALTH MEDICAL CENTER** See University Hospitals Lake Health

★ ⇑ **UNIVERSITY HOSPITALS LAKE HEALTH (360098)**, 36000 Euclid Avenue, Zip 44094–4625; tel. 440/953–9600, (Includes UNIVERSITY HOSPITALS TRIPOINT MEDICAL CENTER, 7590 Auburn RD, Concord Township, Ohio, Zip 44077–9176, 7590 Auburn Road, Zip 44077, tel. 440/375–8100; Robyn Strosaker, M.D., President and Chief Operating Officer) **A**10 21 **F**3 5 9 11 12 13 15 18 20 22 24 26 28 29 30 32 33 34 35 36 38 39 40 43 44 45 46 49 50 51 53 54 55 56 57 58 59 60 61 62 63 64 65 68 70 71 74 75 76 77 78 79 81 82 84 85 86 87 91 92 93 96 97 100 102 107 108 110 111 112 113 114 115 116 117 119 120 121 122 123 124 126 129 130 131 132 135 144 145 146 147 148 149 150 154 156 162 164 165 167 **S** University Hospitals, Cleveland, OH
Primary Contact: Robyn Strosaker, M.D., President and Chief Operating Officer
CFO: Robert B Tracz, CPA, Senior Vice President and Chief Financial Officer
CMO: John Baniewicz, M.D., Chief Medical Officer
CIO: Gerald Peters, Vice President Information Technologies and Chief Information Officer
CHR: Craig J Ghidotti, Vice President Human Resources
Web address: www.lakehealth.org
Control: Other not–for–profit (including NFP Corporation) **Service**: General medical and surgical

Staffed Beds: 308 **Admissions**: 11533 **Census**: 160 **Outpatient Visits**: 344395 **Births**: 878 **Total Expense ($000)**: 428136 **Payroll Expense ($000)**: 117006 **Personnel**: 1615

☐ **WINDSOR–LAURELWOOD CENTER FOR BEHAVIORAL MEDICINE (364029)**, 35900 Euclid Avenue, Zip 44094–4648; tel. 440/953–3000, (Nonreporting) **A**1 10 **S** Universal Health Services, Inc., King of Prussia, PA
Primary Contact: Douglas W. Kern, Chief Executive Officer
CFO: Heather Martn, Chief Financial Officer
CMO: James Psarras, M.D., Chief Medical Officer
CHR: Pam Connell, Manager Human Resources
CNO: Matthew Goodwin, Chief Nursing Officer
Web address: www.windsorlaurelwood.com
Control: Individual, Investor–owned (for–profit) **Service**: Psychiatric

Staffed Beds: 159

WILMINGTON—Clinton County

☒ **CMH REGIONAL HEALTH SYSTEM (360175)**, 610 West Main Street, Zip 45177–2125; tel. 937/382–6611, (Nonreporting) **A**1 2 10 **S** ScionHealth, Louisville, KY
Primary Contact: Tom G. Daskalakis, Chief Executive Officer
CIO: Ray Doherty, Director Information Technology
CHR: Jan Blair, Director Human Resources
CNO: Sheila Martin, Chief Nursing Officer
Web address: www.cmhregional.com
Control: Corporation, Investor–owned (for–profit) **Service**: General medical and surgical

Staffed Beds: 119

WOOSTER—Wayne County

⇑ **WOOSTER COMMUNITY HOSPITAL (360036)**, 1761 Beall Avenue, Zip 44691–2342; tel. 330/263–8100, (Nonreporting) **A**2 3 10 19 21
Primary Contact: William E. Sheron, Chief Executive Officer
Web address: www.woosterhospital.org
Control: City, Government, Nonfederal **Service**: General medical and surgical

Staffed Beds: 152

WRIGHT–PATTERSON AFB—Greene County

☒ **WRIGHT PATTERSON MEDICAL CENTER**, 4881 Sugar Maple Drive, Zip 45433–5529; tel. 937/257–0837, (Nonreporting) **A**1 2 3 5 **S** Department of the Air Force, Washington, DC
Primary Contact: Colonel Dale E. Harrell, Commander, 88th Medical Group, Wright–Patterson AFB
COO: Colonel Brent J Erickson, Administrator
CFO: Major Kelly Lesnick, Resource Manager Flight Commander
CMO: Gregory Sweitzer, Chief Medical Officer
CIO: John Beighle, Flight Chief Medical Information Systems
CHR: Hubert Chatman, Chief Civilian Personnel
CNO: Colonel Daniel Gerke, Chief Nursing Officer
Web address: www.wpafb.af.mil/units/wpmc/
Control: Air Force, Government, federal **Service**: General medical and surgical

Staffed Beds: 62

Hospital, Medicare Provider Number, Address, Telephone, Approval, Facility, and Physician Codes, Health Care System

★ American Hospital Association (AHA) membership   ○ Healthcare Facilities Accreditation Program   ⇑ Center for Improvement in Healthcare Quality Accreditation
☐ The Joint Commission accreditation   ◇ DNV Healthcare Inc. accreditation   △ Commission on Accreditation of Rehabilitation Facilities (CARF) accreditation

© 2025 AHA Guide

Hospitals, U.S. / OHIO

XENIA—Greene County

★ ○ **KETTERING HEALTH GREENE MEMORIAL (360026)**, 1141 North Monroe Drive, Zip 45385–1600; tel. 937/352–2000, **A**10 11 **F**3 11 15 28 29 30 34 40 44 53 54 56 59 64 75 77 93 96 102 107 108 111 115 118 119 127 129 130 135 146 148 149 154 157 **P**3 6 **S** Kettering Health, Dayton, OH
Primary Contact: Daniel Tryon, President
CMO: Michael Caccamo, M.D., Chief Medical Officer
CHR: Jeff Jones, Director Human Resources
Web address: www.ketteringhealth.org/greene
Control: Church operated, Nongovernment, not–for–profit **Service**: General medical and surgical

Staffed Beds: 13 **Admissions**: 649 **Census**: 4 **Outpatient Visits**: 129547 **Births**: 0 **Total Expense ($000)**: 39410 **Payroll Expense ($000)**: 15571 **Personnel**: 137

YOUNGSTOWN—Mahoning County

□ △ **MERCY HEALTH – ST. ELIZABETH YOUNGSTOWN HOSPITAL (360064)**, 1044 Belmont Avenue, Zip 44504–1096, Mailing Address: P.O. Box 1790, Zip 44501–1790; tel. 330/746–7211, (Nonreporting) **A**1 2 3 5 7 10 19 **S** Bon Secours Mercy Health, Cincinnati, OH
Primary Contact: John Luellen, M.D., Market President
COO: Donald E. Koenig Jr, Executive Vice President and Regional Chief Operating Officer, President, St. Elizabeth Youngstown Hospital
CFO: Anthony J. Seminaro, Chief Financial Officer
CIO: Maureen Kordupel, Director Relationship Manager
CNO: Lori DeNiro, Regional Chief Nursing Officer
Web address: www.mercy.com
Control: Church operated, Nongovernment, not–for–profit **Service**: General medical and surgical

Staffed Beds: 375

☒ **SELECT SPECIALTY HOSPITAL–YOUNGSTOWN (362024)**, 1044 Belmont Avenue, Zip 44504–1006; tel. 330/480–2349, (Includes SELECT SPECIALTY HOSPITAL–YOUNGSTOWN, BOARDMAN CAMPUS, 667 Eastland Avenue SE, Warren, Ohio, Zip 44484–4503, tel. 330/729–1700) (Nonreporting) **A**1 2 10 **S** Select Medical Corporation, Mechanicsburg, PA
Primary Contact: Jodi Costello, Chief Executive Officer
Web address: www.selectspecialtyhospitals.com/company/locations/youngstown.aspx
Control: Corporation, Investor–owned (for–profit) **Service**: Acute long–term care hospital

Staffed Beds: 56

□ **SURGICAL HOSPITAL AT SOUTHWOODS (360352)**, 7630 Southern Boulevard, Zip 44512–5633; tel. 330/729–8000, (Nonreporting) **A**1 3 10
Primary Contact: Ed Muransky, Owner
Web address: www.surgeryatsouthwoods.com/
Control: Individual, Investor–owned (for–profit) **Service**: Surgical

Staffed Beds: 12

YOUNGSTOWN—Trumbull County

□ **BELMONT PINES HOSPITAL (364038)**, 615 Churchill–Hubbard Road, Zip 44505–1379; tel. 330/759–2700, (Nonreporting) **A**1 10 **S** Universal Health Services, Inc., King of Prussia, PA
Primary Contact: Eric Kennedy, Chief Executive Officer
CFO: Sylvia Kuppler, Chief Financial Officer
CMO: Phillip G Maiden, M.D., Medical Director
CHR: Deidre L Watson, Director Human Resources
CNO: Tammy Shells, Chief Nursing Officer
Web address: www.belmontpines.com
Control: Corporation, Investor–owned (for–profit) **Service**: Psychiatric

Staffed Beds: 96

ZANESVILLE—Muskingum County

★ ○ **GENESIS HEALTHCARE SYSTEM (360039)**, 2951 Maple Avenue, Zip 43701–1406; tel. 740/454–5000, (Includes BETHESDA HOSPITAL, 2951 Maple Avenue, Zanesville, Ohio, Zip 43701–1465, tel. 614/454–4000; GENESIS BEHAVIORAL HEALTH, 2951 Maple Avenue, Zanesville, Ohio, Zip 43701–1406, tel. 740/454–4000; Matthew J Perry, President and Chief Executive Officer; GOOD SAMARITAN MEDICAL AND REHABILITATION CENTER, 800 Forest Avenue, Zanesville, Ohio, Zip 43701–2881, tel. 614/454–5000) **A**2 3 10 11 **F**3 4 5 7 8 9 11 12 13 15 17 18 20 22 24 26 28 29 30 31 32 34 35 37 40 42 43 44 45 46 47 48 50 51 54 57 58 59 60 63 64 65 68 70 73 74 75 76 77 78 79 81 82 83 84 85 86 87 89 91 92 93 94 96 97 98 99 100 101 102 105 106 107 108 109 110 111 113 114 115 116 117 118 119 120 121 123 124 126 129 130 131 132 135 143 144 146 147 148 151 154 156 157 160 164 167 169 **S** Franciscan Sisters of Christian Charity Sponsored Ministries, Inc., Manitowoc, WI
Primary Contact: Matthew J. Perry, President and Chief Executive Officer
COO: Richard S Helsper, Chief Operating Officer
CFO: Paul Masterson, Chief Financial Officer
CMO: Dan Scheerer, M.D., Chief Medical Officer
CIO: Edmund J Romito, Chief Information Officer
CHR: Dianna LeVeck, Chief Administrative Officer
CNO: Abby Nguyen, R.N., Chief Nursing Officer
Web address: www.genesishcs.org
Control: Other not–for–profit (including NFP Corporation) **Service**: General medical and surgical

Staffed Beds: 316 **Admissions**: 14032 **Census**: 182 **Outpatient Visits**: 611546 **Births**: 1373 **Total Expense ($000)**: 573678 **Payroll Expense ($000)**: 187196 **Personnel**: 3715

OKLAHOMA

ADA—Pontotoc County

✠ **CHICKASAW NATION MEDICAL CENTER (370180)**, 1921 Stonecipher Boulevard, Zip 74820–3439; tel. 580/436–3980, **A**1 3 5 10 13 **F**3 5 7 8 13 15 29 30 32 34 35 38 39 40 41 43 45 50 53 54 57 58 59 64 65 68 69 70 71 75 76 77 79 81 82 85 86 87 89 91 93 97 100 101 102 104 107 110 111 115 119 127 130 132 133 135 143 144 146 147 148 149 150 154 156 157 158 160 164 167 169
Primary Contact: Charles Grim, D.D.S., Secretary of Health
CFO: Marty Wafford, Under Secretary of Support and Programs
CMO: Richard McClain, M.D., Chief Medical Officer
CIO: Desiree Traylor, Chief Information Officer
CHR: Jalinda Kelley, Secretary of Interior Services
CNO: Jerod Waters, Chief Nursing Officer
Web address: www.chickasaw.net
Control: PHS, Indian Service, Government, federal **Service**: General medical and surgical

> **Staffed Beds**: 72 **Admissions**: 2301 **Census**: 16 **Outpatient Visits**: 352971 **Births**: 952 **Total Expense ($000)**: 394477 **Payroll Expense ($000)**: 167066 **Personnel**: 2034

✠ **MERCY HOSPITAL ADA (370020)**, 430 North Monte Vista, Zip 74820–4610; tel. 580/332–2323, **A**1 2 10 **F**3 4 6 7 8 9 11 13 15 18 20 22 26 28 29 30 31 34 35 36 38 40 41 43 44 45 47 48 50 51 53 56 57 58 59 60 64 65 68 69 70 71 72 73 74 75 76 77 78 79 81 82 85 86 87 89 90 91 93 96 98 100 101 102 103 104 107 108 110 111 114 115 118 119 120 121 129 130 131 132 135 143 146 147 148 149 151 153 154 156 160 161 162 164 165 167 169 **S** Mercy, Chesterfield, MO
Primary Contact: Terence Farrell, President
CFO: Mary Garber, Vice President Finance
CMO: Imtiaz Ahmed, Chief of Staff
CHR: Katrina Godfrey, Director Human Resources
CNO: Cynthia Standlee, R.N., Chief Nursing Officer
Web address: https://www.mercy.net/practice/mercy-hospital-ada/
Control: Church operated, Nongovernment, not–for–profit **Service**: General medical and surgical

> **Staffed Beds**: 156 **Admissions**: 4061 **Census**: 50 **Outpatient Visits**: 114890 **Births**: 325 **Total Expense ($000)**: 106233 **Payroll Expense ($000)**: 44845 **Personnel**: 539

☐ **ROLLING HILLS HOSPITAL (374016)**, 1000 Rolling Hills Lane, Zip 74820–9415; tel. 580/436–3600, **A**1 3 10 **F**4 5 38 56 64 98 99 100 102 103 104 105 106 130 149 152 153 164 **S** Acadia Healthcare Company, Inc., Franklin, TN
Primary Contact: Sherri Chandler, Chief Executive Officer
CMO: Robert Morton, M.D., Medical Director
CIO: Sherry Barnes, Director Health Information and Quality Management
CHR: Timothy Blackwell, Manager Human Resources
Web address: www.rollinghillshospital.com
Control: Corporation, Investor–owned (for–profit) **Service**: Psychiatric

> **Staffed Beds**: 112 **Admissions**: 1054 **Census**: 94 **Outpatient Visits**: 1350 **Births**: 0 **Total Expense ($000)**: 20965 **Payroll Expense ($000)**: 11239 **Personnel**: 183

ALTUS—Jackson County

★ ⇧ **JACKSON COUNTY MEMORIAL HOSPITAL (370022)**, 1200 East Pecan Street, Zip 73521–6192, Mailing Address: P.O. Box 8190, Zip 73522–8190; tel. 580/379–5000, **A**10 21 **F**3 10 11 13 15 29 30 34 35 40 45 49 56 57 59 62 63 64 65 70 75 76 77 79 81 82 85 86 87 89 93 100 104 107 110 111 114 115 119 127 129 130 131 132 133 135 146 147 148 149 154 156 162 169 **P**6
Primary Contact: Steve L. Hartgraves, President and Chief Executive Officer
COO: Casey D. Miranda, Executive Vice President and Chief Operating Officer
CFO: Jennifer Combs, Chief Financial Officer
CMO: Julia Rivera, M.D., Chief of Staff
CIO: Mark Driscoll, Chief Information Officer
CHR: Richard Pope, Vice President Human Resources
CNO: Shelley Simmons, Chief Nursing Officer
Web address: www.jcmh.com
Control: Hospital district or authority, Government, Nonfederal **Service**: General medical and surgical

> **Staffed Beds**: 40 **Admissions**: 1786 **Census**: 17 **Outpatient Visits**: 161517 **Births**: 258 **Total Expense ($000)**: 83582 **Payroll Expense ($000)**: 28283 **Personnel**: 649

ALVA—Woods County

⇧ **SHARE MEDICAL CENTER (371341)**, 800 Share Drive, Zip 73717–3618, Mailing Address: P.O. Box 727, Zip 73717–0727; tel. 580/327–2800, **A**10 18 21 **F**3 15 29 40 43 45 59 64 65 68 69 77 81 93 96 97 107 110 114 127 128 130 133 144 149
Primary Contact: Kandice K. Allen, R.N., Chief Executive Officer
CMO: Elizabeth Kinzic, M.D., Chief of Staff
CIO: Alan Vaughan, Director Information Technology
CHR: Mary Herold, Director Human Resources
CNO: Regina Wilson, R.N., Director of Nursing
Web address: www.smcok.com
Control: Hospital district or authority, Government, Nonfederal **Service**: General medical and surgical

> **Staffed Beds**: 21 **Admissions**: 238 **Census**: 2 **Outpatient Visits**: 18877 **Births**: 0 **Total Expense ($000)**: 13567 **Payroll Expense ($000)**: 6179 **Personnel**: 95

ANADARKO—Caddo County

RURAL WELLNESS ANADARKO (371314), 1002 Central Boulevard East, Zip 73005–4496; tel. 405/247–2551, (Nonreporting) **A**10 18 **S** Avem Health Partners, Oklahoma City, OK
Primary Contact: Travis A. Villani, FACHE, Chief Executive Officer and Senior Vice President of Operations
Web address: www.anadarkohospital.com
Control: Partnership, Investor–owned (for–profit) **Service**: General medical and surgical

> **Staffed Beds**: 25

ANTLERS—Pushmataha County

PUSHMATAHA HOSPITAL (370083), 510 East Main Street, Zip 74523–3262, Mailing Address: P.O. Box 518, Zip 74523–0518; tel. 580/298–3341, (Nonreporting) **A**10
Primary Contact: Nick Rowland, Chief Executive Officer
COO: Nick Rowland, Chief Operating Officer
CFO: Rory Ward, Chief Financial Officer
CMO: G Wayne Flatt, D.O., Chief Medical Director
CHR: Paula Schalski, Director Human Resources
CNO: Marla Barnes, Director of Nursing
Web address: www.pushhospital.com
Control: State, Government, Nonfederal **Service**: General medical and surgical

> **Staffed Beds**: 23

Hospital, Medicare Provider Number, Address, Telephone, Approval, Facility, and Physician Codes, Health Care System

★ American Hospital Association (AHA) membership   ◯ Healthcare Facilities Accreditation Program   ⇧ Center for Improvement in Healthcare Quality Accreditation
☐ The Joint Commission accreditation   ◇ DNV Healthcare Inc. accreditation   △ Commission on Accreditation of Rehabilitation Facilities (CARF) accreditation

Hospitals, U.S. / OKLAHOMA

ARDMORE—Carter County

✠ **MERCY HOSPITAL ARDMORE (370047)**, 1011 14th Avenue NW, Zip 73401–1828; tel. 580/223–5400, **A**1 10 **F**3 13 15 18 20 22 28 29 30 31 34 35 40 43 45 47 48 50 51 57 59 60 62 64 67 68 70 74 75 76 77 78 79 81 82 85 87 89 90 93 96 97 98 102 103 107 108 110 111 114 115 117 119 120 121 123 126 129 130 146 148 149 154 156 167 169 **P**6 **S** Mercy, Chesterfield, MO
Primary Contact: Daryle Voss, FACHE, President
CMO: Pam Kimbrough, M.D., Vice President Medical Affairs
CHR: Melinda Sharum, Director Human Resources
CNO: Debra Pender, MS, R.N., Vice President Nursing
Web address: www.mercyok.net
Control: Church operated, Nongovernment, not–for–profit **Service**: General medical and surgical

Staffed Beds: 190 **Admissions**: 6505 **Census**: 78 **Outpatient Visits**: 189327 **Births**: 764 **Total Expense ($000)**: 160365 **Payroll Expense ($000)**: 67707 **Personnel**: 597

ATOKA—Atoka County

★ **ATOKA COUNTY MEDICAL CENTER (371300)**, 1590 West Liberty Road, Zip 74525–1621; tel. 580/364–8205, (Nonreporting) **A**10 18 **S** Carrus Health, Sherman, TX
Primary Contact: Chris Martin, Chief Operating Officer
COO: Chris Martin, Chief Operating Officer
CMO: Ted Rowland, Chief of Medical Staff
CHR: Courtney Jackson, Coordinator Human Resources
CNO: Sally Finch, Chief Nursing Officer
Web address: www.atokamedicalcenter.org
Control: Hospital district or authority, Government, Nonfederal **Service**: General medical and surgical

Staffed Beds: 25

BARTLESVILLE—Washington County

✠ **ASCENSION ST. JOHN JANE PHILLIPS (370018)**, 3500 East Frank Phillips Boulevard, Zip 74006–2411; tel. 918/333–7200, (Nonreporting) **A**1 10 **S** Ascension Healthcare, Saint Louis, MO
Primary Contact: Bryan Cavitt, President
CFO: James Brasel, Chief Financial Officer
CMO: Paul McQuillen, M.D., Chief Medical Officer
CNO: Angie Bidleman, Chief Nursing Officer
Web address: www.jpmc.org
Control: Church operated, Nongovernment, not–for–profit **Service**: General medical and surgical

Staffed Beds: 105

BEAVER—Beaver County

BEAVER COUNTY MEMORIAL HOSPITAL (371322), 212 East Eighth Street, Zip 73932, Mailing Address: P.O. Box 640, Zip 73932–0640; tel. 580/625–4551, (Nonreporting) **A**10 18
Primary Contact: Alissa Schlessman, Administrator
CFO: Cody Gregory, Comptroller
CMO: Gary Mathews, M.D., Medical Doctor
CHR: Karla Leisher, Business Office Manager
CNO: Lyn Sizelove, Director of Nursing
Web address: www.beavercountyhospitalauthority.com
Control: Hospital district or authority, Government, Nonfederal **Service**: General medical and surgical

Staffed Beds: 12

BETHANY—Oklahoma County

○ △ **BETHANY CHILDREN'S HEALTH CENTER (373303)**, 6800 NW 39th Expressway, Zip 73008–2513; tel. 405/789–6711, **A**3 5 7 10 11 **F**1 3 29 30 32 34 35 50 54 57 59 65 68 69 71 74 75 77 86 87 90 91 92 93 95 96 97 100 104 128 130 143 146 148 149 154 158 **P**6
Primary Contact: Nico Gomez, Chief Executive Officer
Web address: https://www.bethanychildrens.org/
Control: Other not–for–profit (including NFP Corporation) **Service**: Children's acute long–term Care

Staffed Beds: 118 **Admissions**: 255 **Census**: 114 **Outpatient Visits**: 21628 **Births**: 0 **Total Expense ($000)**: 90210 **Payroll Expense ($000)**: 53903 **Personnel**: 780

THE CHILDREN'S CENTER REHABILITATION HOSPITAL See Bethany Children's Health Center

BLACKWELL—Kay County

★ **STILLWATER MEDICAL BLACKWELL (370780)**, 710 South 13th Street, Zip 74631–3700; tel. 580/363–2311, **A**10 **F**3 29 40 43 65 67 87 89 90 93 107 119 127 130 135 149 154
Primary Contact: Courtney Kozikuski, President and Chief Financial Officer
CFO: Courtney Kozikuski, Chief Financial Officer
CMO: Jeffery Shuart, M.D., Chief of Staff
CHR: Deb Ellis, Director Human Resource
Web address: https://www.stillwater-medical.org/locations/stillwater-medical-blackwell
Control: Hospital district or authority, Government, Nonfederal

Staffed Beds: 26 **Admissions**: 124 **Census**: 1 **Outpatient Visits**: 21964 **Births**: 0 **Total Expense ($000)**: 8041 **Payroll Expense ($000)**: 3782 **Personnel**: 66

BOISE CITY—Cimarron County

CIMARRON MEMORIAL HOSPITAL (371307), 100 South Ellis Street, Zip 73933, Mailing Address: P.O. Box 1059, Zip 73933–1059; tel. 580/544–2501, (Nonreporting) **A**10 18
Primary Contact: Troye Farmer, Hospital Administrator
CFO: Barbie Miller, Chief Financial Officer
CNO: Barbara Carter, Chief Nursing Officer
Web address: www.cimarronmemorialhospital.org
Control: County, Government, Nonfederal **Service**: General medical and surgical

Staffed Beds: 25

BROKEN ARROW—Tulsa County

✠ **ASCENSION ST. JOHN BROKEN ARROW (370235)**, 1000 West Boise Circle, Zip 74012–4900; tel. 918/994–8100, (Nonreporting) **A**1 10 **S** Ascension Healthcare, Saint Louis, MO
Primary Contact: Matthew Adams, President
CFO: Katie Caughman, Chief Financial Officer
CMO: Jason Lepak, M.D., Medical Director
CNO: Dwan Borens, Chief Nursing Officer
Web address: www.stjohnbrokenarrow.com
Control: Church operated, Nongovernment, not–for–profit **Service**: General medical and surgical

Staffed Beds: 44

✠ **ST. JOHN REHABILITATION HOSPITAL (373034)**, 1200 West Albany Drive, Zip 74012–8146; tel. 918/744–2338, (Nonreporting) **A**1 10 **S** Encompass Health Corporation, Birmingham, AL
Primary Contact: David Nicholas, Chief Executive Officer
Web address: www.stjohnrehab.com
Control: Corporation, Investor–owned (for–profit) **Service**: Rehabilitation

Staffed Beds: 60

BUFFALO—Harper County

★ **HARPER COUNTY COMMUNITY HOSPITAL (370781)**, Highway 64 North, Zip 73834, Mailing Address: P.O. Box 60, Zip 73834–0060; tel. 580/735–2555, (Nonreporting) **A**10
Primary Contact: Kevin O'Brien, Chief Executive Officer
COO: Pam Dodd, Chief Operating Officer
CFO: Lisa Oakley, Chief Financial Officer
CNO: Melissa Madrid, R.N., Chief Nursing Officer
Web address: www.hcchospital.com/
Control: County, Government, Nonfederal

Staffed Beds: 12

CARNEGIE—Caddo County

CARNEGIE TRI–COUNTY MUNICIPAL HOSPITAL (371334), 102 North Broadway, Zip 73015, Mailing Address: P.O. Box 97, Zip 73015–0097; tel. 580/654–1050, (Nonreporting) **A**10 18 **S** Avem Health Partners, Oklahoma City, OK
Primary Contact: Nathan Adam. Richmond, Administrator
Web address: www.carnegiehospital.org/
Control: City, Government, Nonfederal **Service**: General medical and surgical

Staffed Beds: 17

Hospitals, U.S. / OKLAHOMA

CHEYENNE—Roger Mills County

★ **ROGER MILLS MEMORIAL HOSPITAL (371303)**, 501 South L.L. Males, Zip 73628, Mailing Address: P.O. Box 219, Zip 73628; tel. 580/497–3336, (Nonreporting) **A**10 18
Primary Contact: Cynthia Duncan, Chief Executive Officer
Web address: www.rmmhonline.com
Control: Hospital district or authority, Government, Nonfederal **Service:** General medical and surgical

Staffed Beds: 15

CHICKASHA—Grady County

GRADY MEMORIAL HOSPITAL (370054), 2220 West Iowa Avenue, Zip 73018–2738; tel. 405/224–2300, **A**10 **F**3 8 11 15 17 29 30 33 34 35 40 43 45 50 51 54 57 59 64 65 70 79 81 82 85 87 89 91 93 97 107 108 110 111 114 115 119 127 128 130 131 133 144 146 147 148 149 154 167 **P**6
Primary Contact: Warren K. Spellman, Chief Executive Officer
CFO: Jackie McAdoo, Chief Financial Officer
CMO: Mitch Coppedge, M.D., Chief Medical Officer
CIO: Mike Townsend, Interim Director Health Information Systems
CHR: Rebel Rutledge, Director Human Resources
CNO: Cathy Groseclose, Vice President Patient Care Services
Web address: www.gradymem.org
Control: Hospital district or authority, Government, Nonfederal **Service:** General medical and surgical

Staffed Beds: 48 **Admissions:** 1001 **Census:** 10 **Outpatient Visits:** 66836
Births: 0 **Total Expense ($000):** 50775 **Payroll Expense ($000):** 24212
Personnel: 387

CLAREMORE—Rogers County

◇ **CLAREMORE INDIAN HOSPITAL (370173)**, 101 South Moore Avenue, Zip 74017–5091; tel. 918/342–6200, (Nonreporting) **A**1 10 **S** U. S. Indian Health Service, Rockville, MD
Primary Contact: George Valliere, Chief Executive Officer
CFO: LaLana Spears, Supervisor Accounting
CMO: Gary Lang, M.D., Clinical Director
CIO: David Ponder, Information Technology Officer
CHR: Quinn Proctor, Director Human Resources
CNO: Alonna Adair, R.N., MSN, Chief Nurse Executive
Web address: www.ihs.gov
Control: PHS, Indian Service, Government, federal **Service:** General medical and surgical

Staffed Beds: 44

★ ⇑ **HILLCREST HOSPITAL CLAREMORE (370039)**, 1202 North Muskogee Place, Zip 74017–3036; tel. 918/341–2556, **A**10 21 **F**3 4 8 11 13 15 18 20 22 26 28 29 30 34 35 37 40 45 50 51 59 64 65 70 74 75 76 77 79 81 82 85 86 87 93 107 108 110 111 119 127 129 130 131 135 146 147 148 149 154 156 167 169 **S** Ardent Health Services, Nashville, TN
Primary Contact: Jason L. Jones, R.N., Chief Executive Officer
CIO: Celeste Rodden, Chief Information Officer
CHR: Pat Goad, Director Human Resources
CNO: Randy Walker, Chief Nursing Officer
Web address: www.hillcrestclaremore.com
Control: Corporation, Investor–owned (for–profit) **Service:** General medical and surgical

Staffed Beds: 49 **Admissions:** 2305 **Census:** 20 **Outpatient Visits:** 43435
Births: 520 **Total Expense ($000):** 48407 **Payroll Expense ($000):** 17223
Personnel: 283

CLEVELAND—Pawnee County

CLEVELAND AREA HOSPITAL (371320), 1401 West Pawnee Street, Zip 74020–3019; tel. 918/358–2501, (Nonreporting) **A**10 18
Primary Contact: Edred Benton, Chief Executive Officer
COO: Edred Benton, Chief Executive Officer
CMO: Jason Sims, M.D., Chief Medical Officer
CHR: Sherry Brown, Director Human Resources
Web address: www.clevelandareahospital.com
Control: Hospital district or authority, Government, Nonfederal **Service:** General medical and surgical

Staffed Beds: 14

CLINTON—Custer County

○ **CLINTON REGIONAL HOSPITAL (370245)**, 100 North 30, Zip 73601, Mailing Address: PO Box 1567, Zip 73601–1567; tel. 580/547–5128, (Nonreporting) **A**11
Primary Contact: Leonard Lacefield, Chief Executive Officer
CNO: Janae Chittum, Chief Nursing Officer
Control: Other not–for–profit (including NFP Corporation) **Service:** General medical and surgical

Staffed Beds: 22

COALGATE—Coal County

★ **COAL COUNTY GENERAL HOSPITAL (371319)**, 6 North Covington Street, Zip 74538–2002, Mailing Address: P.O. Box 326, Zip 74538–0326; tel. 580/927–2327, (Nonreporting) **A**10 18
Primary Contact: Trent Bourland, Chief Executive Officer
CFO: Diane Downard, Chief Financial Officer
CMO: R.J Helton, D.O., Chief of Staff
CIO: Matt Balliett, Chief Information Officer
CHR: Cyndie Martin, Director
CNO: Farra Ybarra, R.N., Chief Nursing Officer
Web address: www.hillcrest.com
Control: Other not–for–profit (including NFP Corporation) **Service:** General medical and surgical

Staffed Beds: 20

CORDELL—Washita County

★ **CORDELL MEMORIAL HOSPITAL (371325)**, 1220 North Glenn English Street, Zip 73632–2010; tel. 580/832–3339, (Nonreporting) **A**10 18
Primary Contact: Melinda Laird, MS, R.N., Administrator and Director of Nursing
CFO: Sue Kelley, Chief Financial Officer
Web address: www.cordellmemorialhospital.com
Control: City, Government, Nonfederal **Service:** General medical and surgical

Staffed Beds: 14

CUSHING—Payne County

★ **HILLCREST HOSPITAL CUSHING (370099)**, 1027 East Cherry Street, Zip 74023–4101; tel. 918/225–2915, **A**10 **F**11 15 18 29 34 35 39 40 43 44 45 46 50 51 56 57 59 64 68 70 71 75 77 79 81 86 87 93 94 97 107 110 111 114 115 119 129 130 131 143 146 148 149 150 154 157 160 167 **S** Ardent Health Services, Nashville, TN
Primary Contact: Jonathan Schell, R.N., Chief Executive Officer
CFO: Joseph Mendoza, Chief Financial Officer
CHR: Bethany Leininger, Manager Human Resource
CNO: Tina Petersen, Chief Nursing Officer
Web address: www.hillcrestcushing.com/
Control: Corporation, Investor–owned (for–profit) **Service:** General medical and surgical

Staffed Beds: 27 **Admissions:** 507 **Census:** 5 **Outpatient Visits:** 26829
Births: 0 **Total Expense ($000):** 19306 **Payroll Expense ($000):** 6576
Personnel: 78

DRUMRIGHT—Creek County

DRUMRIGHT REGIONAL HOSPITAL (371331), 610 West Bypass, Zip 74030–5957; tel. 918/382–2300, (Nonreporting) **A**10 18
Primary Contact: Cindy West, Chief Executive Officer
CFO: Mark Conrath, Chief Financial Officer
Web address: www.drumrighthospital.com/
Control: Corporation, Investor–owned (for–profit) **Service:** General medical and surgical

Staffed Beds: 15

Hospital, Medicare Provider Number, Address, Telephone, Approval, Facility, and Physician Codes, Health Care System

★ American Hospital Association (AHA) membership
□ The Joint Commission accreditation
○ Healthcare Facilities Accreditation Program
◇ DNV Healthcare Inc. accreditation
⇑ Center for Improvement in Healthcare Quality Accreditation
△ Commission on Accreditation of Rehabilitation Facilities (CARF) accreditation

Hospitals, U.S. / OKLAHOMA

DUNCAN—Stephens County

DUNCAN REGIONAL HOSPITAL (370023), 1407 North Whisenant Drive, Zip 73533–1650, Mailing Address: P.O. Box 2000, Zip 73534–2000; tel. 580/252–5300, (Nonreporting) **A**1 10 20 **S** DRH Health, Duncan, OK
Primary Contact: Jay R. Johnson, FACHE, President and Chief Executive Officer
COO: Roger Neal, Chief Operating Officer
CMO: Krystal Vonfeldt, M.D., Chief of Staff
CHR: Michelle Bivans, Director Human Resources
CNO: Kristen Webb, Chief Nursing Officer
Web address: www.duncanregional.com
Control: Other not–for–profit (including NFP Corporation) **Service**: General medical and surgical

Staffed Beds: 110

DURANT—Bryan County

ALLIANCEHEALTH DURANT (370014), 1800 University Boulevard, Zip 74701–3006, Mailing Address: P.O. Box 1207, Zip 74702–1207; tel. 580/924–3080, **A**1 3 5 10 13 19 **F**3 8 11 13 15 18 20 22 28 29 34 35 40 43 45 54 56 59 60 67 70 74 75 76 79 81 82 85 87 91 107 108 110 111 115 119 126 127 135 144 146 147 149 154 157 167 **S** Community Health Systems, Inc., Franklin, TN
Primary Contact: Shelton Williams, Chief Executive Officer
CFO: Cindy Rios, Chief Financial Officer
CMO: Kevin Gordon, M.D., Chief of Staff
CIO: Katy Stinson, Director Information Services
Web address: www.alliancehealthdurant.com/
Control: Corporation, Investor–owned (for–profit) **Service**: General medical and surgical

Staffed Beds: 138 **Admissions**: 6343 **Census**: 59 **Outpatient Visits**: 50707
Births: 823 **Total Expense ($000)**: 77479 **Payroll Expense ($000)**: 28256
Personnel: 414

EDMOND—Oklahoma County

EDMOND MEDICAL CENTER See OU Medical Center Edmond

INTEGRIS HEALTH EDMOND HOSPITAL (370236), 4801 Integris Parkway, Zip 73034–8864; tel. 405/657–3000, **A**1 5 10 **F**3 11 13 15 18 20 22 28 29 30 34 35 40 43 45 46 47 49 53 54 57 59 60 64 68 70 73 74 76 77 78 79 81 82 85 86 87 90 93 96 97 100 102 107 108 110 111 115 119 130 131 132 135 146 147 148 149 154 167 169 **S** INTEGRIS Health, Oklahoma City, OK
Primary Contact: Jonathan Rule, Chief Hospital Executive
CNO: Angela K Kamermayer, MS, Chief Nursing Officer
Web address: www.integrisok.com/edmond
Control: Other not–for–profit (including NFP Corporation) **Service**: General medical and surgical

Staffed Beds: 99 **Admissions**: 3889 **Census**: 46 **Outpatient Visits**: 78057
Births: 975 **Total Expense ($000)**: 123963 **Payroll Expense ($000)**: 35019
Personnel: 426

OU MEDICAL CENTER EDMOND See OU Health – University of Oklahoma Medical Center, Oklahoma City

★ **SUMMIT MEDICAL CENTER (370225)**, 1800 S Renaissance Boulevard, Zip 73013–3023; tel. 405/359–2400, **A**3 5 10 **F**3 12 29 40 41 45 54 64 70 75 79 81 82 85 107 111 119 129 149 156 164 167
Primary Contact: Curtis Summers, Chief Executive Officer
Web address: www.summitmedcenter.com/
Control: Partnership, Investor–owned (for–profit) **Service**: General medical and surgical

Staffed Beds: 9 **Admissions**: 410 **Census**: 3 **Outpatient Visits**: 14154
Births: 0 **Total Expense ($000)**: 36113 **Payroll Expense ($000)**: 11151
Personnel: 146

ELK CITY—Beckham County

GREAT PLAINS REGIONAL MEDICAL CENTER (370019), 1801 West Third Street, Zip 73644–5145, Mailing Address: P.O. Box 2339, Zip 73648–2339; tel. 580/225–2511, (Nonreporting) **A**1 5 10 20
Primary Contact: Corey Lively, Chief Executive Officer
COO: Jon Gill, Chief Operating Officer
CFO: Monica Scott, Chief Financial Officer
CMO: Craig Phelps, M.D., Chief of Staff
CIO: Terry Price, Director Information Technology
CHR: Misty Carter, Chief Human Resource Officer and Ancillary Services
CNO: Gayle Ann Sturgis, Chief Nursing Officer, Risk Management
Web address: www.gprmc-ok.com
Control: Other not–for–profit (including NFP Corporation) **Service**: General medical and surgical

Staffed Beds: 60

ENID—Garfield County

INTEGRIS BASS BEHAVIORAL HEALTH SYSTEM See Integris Bass Meadowlake

INTEGRIS HEALTH ENID HOSPITAL (370016), 600 South Monroe Street, Zip 73701–7211, Mailing Address: P.O. Box 3168, Zip 73702–3168; tel. 580/233–2300, (Includes INTEGRIS BASS MEADOWLAKE, 2216 South Van Buren Street, Enid, Oklahoma, Zip 73703–8299, tel. 580/234–2220) **A**1 3 10 **F**3 11 13 15 17 18 20 22 26 28 29 30 31 35 40 43 45 49 51 53 56 57 59 62 64 65 67 70 74 75 76 78 79 81 85 89 98 99 107 110 111 114 115 119 120 126 127 129 132 144 146 147 148 149 154 157 167 168 **S** INTEGRIS Health, Oklahoma City, OK
Primary Contact: Keaton Francis, Chief Hospital Executive
CFO: Stacie Mason, Vice President, Regional Chief Financial Officer
CMO: Michael Jackson, M.D., Assistant Chief Medical Officer
CNO: Kenna Wilson, Vice President, Chief Nursing Officer
Web address: https://integrisok.com/locations/hospital/integris-bass-baptist-health-center
Control: Other not–for–profit (including NFP Corporation) **Service**: General medical and surgical

Staffed Beds: 155 **Admissions**: 2958 **Census**: 57 **Outpatient Visits**: 69414
Births: 839 **Total Expense ($000)**: 114660 **Payroll Expense ($000)**: 34996
Personnel: 443

☐ **ST. MARY'S REGIONAL MEDICAL CENTER (370026)**, 305 South Fifth Street, Zip 73701–5899, Mailing Address: P.O. Box 232, Zip 73702–0232; tel. 580/233–6100, **A**1 10 **F**3 11 13 15 18 20 22 28 29 30 31 34 35 37 39 40 43 45 51 56 57 59 60 64 68 70 73 74 75 76 78 79 81 82 85 86 87 89 90 92 93 96 97 98 100 101 107 108 110 111 114 115 118 119 126 129 130 131 132 135 146 147 149 167 169 **S** Universal Health Services, Inc., King of Prussia, PA
Primary Contact: Rex Van Meter, Chief Executive Officer
CFO: David Jamin, Chief Financial Officer
CMO: Michael Pontious, M.D., Chief of Staff
CIO: Tracy Andersen, Chief Information Officer
CHR: David Camp, Director Human Resources
CNO: Douglas W Coffey, R.N., MSN, Chief Nursing Officer
Web address: www.stmarysregional.com
Control: Corporation, Investor–owned (for–profit) **Service**: General medical and surgical

Staffed Beds: 124 **Admissions**: 3811 **Census**: 48 **Outpatient Visits**: 81778
Births: 309 **Total Expense ($000)**: 94368 **Payroll Expense ($000)**: 38896
Personnel: 417

FAIRFAX—Osage County

RURAL WELLNESS FAIRFAX (371318), 40 Hospital Road, Zip 74637–5084; tel. 918/642–3291, (Nonreporting) **A**10 18
Primary Contact: Hunter Thoms, Chief Executive Officer
COO: Linda Thompson, Chief Operating Officer
CMO: Arman Janloo, M.D., Chief Medical Staff
CIO: Lisa Drymon, Manager
CHR: Sharon Binkley, Director Human Resources
Control: Corporation, Investor–owned (for–profit) **Service**: General medical and surgical

Staffed Beds: 15

FAIRVIEW—Major County

FAIRVIEW REGIONAL MEDICAL CENTER (371329), 523 East State Road, Zip 73737–1453, Mailing Address: P.O. Box 548, Zip 73737–0548; tel. 580/227–3721, **A**10 18 **F**3 28 34 35 38 40 43 57 59 64 65 75 77 81 84 93 97 100 107 114 127 128 130 131 132 133 135 148 149 154 164 165 **P**6
Primary Contact: Roger Knak, Administrator and Chief Executive Officer
CMO: John Stephen Price, M.D., Chief of Staff
CIO: Bob Maynard, Chief Information Officer
CHR: Elisabeth Hughes, Director Human Resources and Community Relations
CNO: Tamara Eitzen, Chief Nursing Officer
Web address: www.fairviewregionalmedicalcenter.com
Control: Hospital district or authority, Government, Nonfederal **Service**: General medical and surgical

Staffed Beds: 25 **Admissions**: 148 **Census**: 2 **Outpatient Visits**: 11375
Births: 0 **Total Expense ($000)**: 8133 **Payroll Expense ($000)**: 4638
Personnel: 81

Hospitals, U.S. / OKLAHOMA

GROVE—Delaware County

✠ **INTEGRIS GROVE HOSPITAL (370113)**, 1001 East 18th Street, Zip 74344-2907; tel. 918/786-2243, **A**1 10 20 **F**3 7 11 13 15 18 20 22 29 30 31 34 35 40 43 45 51 54 57 59 64 70 76 77 78 79 81 85 86 91 93 96 107 108 109 110 111 115 119 127 130 131 132 135 143 144 146 147 149 154 167 169 **S** INTEGRIS Health, Oklahoma City, OK
Primary Contact: Jonas Rabel, Chief Hospital Executive
CFO: Stacie Mason, Vice President and Chief Financial Officer
CMO: Kyle Schauf, M.D., President Medical Staff
CNO: Brandi Stewart, R.N., Vice President and Chief Nursing Officer
Web address: https://integrisok.com/locations/hospital/grove-hospital
Control: Other not-for-profit (including NFP Corporation) **Service:** General medical and surgical

Staffed Beds: 58 **Admissions:** 1461 **Census:** 13 **Outpatient Visits:** 41277
Births: 362 **Total Expense ($000):** 61955 **Payroll Expense ($000):** 18399
Personnel: 257

GUTHRIE—Logan County

★ **MERCY HOSPITAL LOGAN COUNTY (371317)**, 200 South Academy Road, Zip 73044-8727, Mailing Address: P.O. Box 1017, Zip 73044-1017; tel. 405/282-6700, **A**10 18 **F**3 15 29 30 35 40 44 50 59 68 75 77 87 93 107 110 111 114 119 127 129 130 133 135 148 149 154 **S** Mercy, Chesterfield, MO
Primary Contact: Bobby Stitt, R.N., Administrator, Rural Facilities
CMO: Jignesh Veragiwala, Chief of Staff
CHR: Mary Jo Messelt, Senior Human Resources Manager
Web address: www.mercy.net
Control: Church operated, Nongovernment, not-for-profit **Service:** General medical and surgical

Staffed Beds: 25 **Admissions:** 475 **Census:** 11 **Outpatient Visits:** 88183
Births: 0 **Total Expense ($000):** 21437 **Payroll Expense ($000):** 13357
Personnel: 104

GUYMON—Texas County

⇧ **MEMORIAL HOSPITAL OF TEXAS COUNTY AUTHORITY (371340)**, 520 Medical Drive, Zip 73942-4438; tel. 580/338-6515, (Nonreporting) **A**10 18 21
Primary Contact: Tracy Johnson, Chief Executive Officer
CFO: Michele Reust, Controller
CIO: Sheldon Spence, Director of Revenue Cycle, IT
CHR: Sarah Wagner, Human Resources Officer
CNO: Dondie Rodgers, Interim Chief Nursing Officer
Web address: www.mhtcguymon.org
Control: County, Government, Nonfederal **Service:** General medical and surgical

Staffed Beds: 7

HEALDTON—Carter County

★ **MERCY HOSPITAL HEALDTON (371310)**, 3462 Hospital Road, Zip 73438-6124, Mailing Address: P.O. Box 928, Zip 73438-0928; tel. 580/229-0701, **A**10 18 **F**3 11 29 30 34 35 40 43 44 50 64 65 68 75 84 86 87 93 96 97 107 115 119 127 133 135 143 146 148 149 154 **S** Mercy, Chesterfield, MO
Primary Contact: Heather Chatham, Administrator
CMO: Mark Newey, D.O., Chief of Staff
CHR: Melinda Sharum, Director Human Resources
Web address: https://www.mercy.net/practice/mercy-hospital-healdton/
Control: Church operated, Nongovernment, not-for-profit **Service:** General medical and surgical

Staffed Beds: 22 **Admissions:** 214 **Census:** 6 **Outpatient Visits:** 13218
Births: 0 **Total Expense ($000):** 7720 **Payroll Expense ($000):** 4601
Personnel: 35

HENRYETTA—Okmulgee County

★ **HILLCREST HOSPITAL HENRYETTA (370183)**, 2401 West Main Street, Zip 74437-3893, Mailing Address: P.O. Box 1269, Zip 74437-1269; tel. 918/650-1100, **A**10 **F**3 15 18 29 34 35 40 41 45 54 57 59 64 65 75 79 81 87 91 93 97 102 107 108 110 111 114 119 127 129 130 131 133 143 148 149 152 154 160 164 **S** Ardent Health Services, Nashville, TN
Primary Contact: Eric Eaton, Chief Executive Officer
CFO: Joseph Mendoza, Chief Financial Officer
CHR: Sheree Snyder, Manager Human Resources
CNO: April Secor, R.N., Chief Nursing Officer
Web address: www.hillcresthenryetta.com
Control: Corporation, Investor-owned (for-profit) **Service:** General medical and surgical

Staffed Beds: 19 **Admissions:** 528 **Census:** 7 **Outpatient Visits:** 67450
Births: 0 **Total Expense ($000):** 20174 **Payroll Expense ($000):** 8274
Personnel: 106

HOBART—Kiowa County

★ **ELKVIEW GENERAL HOSPITAL (370783)**, 429 West Elm Street, Zip 73651-1615; tel. 580/726-1900, **A**10 20 **F**3 15 29 34 40 50 57 59 79 81 85 89 93 107 108 110 111 115 119 127 133 154 **P**6
Primary Contact: Lisa Hart, Chief Executive Officer
CMO: Ross Riddle, D.O., Medical Director
CIO: Dennis Tarver, Director Information Technology
CHR: Sharon Moad, Human Resources Director Health Information Management
CNO: Debbie Norman, MSN, R.N., Chief Nursing Officer
Web address: www.elkviewhospital.com
Control: Hospital district or authority, Government, Nonfederal **Service:** General medical and surgical

Staffed Beds: 12 **Admissions:** 510 **Census:** 6 **Outpatient Visits:** 18065
Births: 0 **Total Expense ($000):** 12412 **Payroll Expense ($000):** 5723
Personnel: 93

HOLDENVILLE—Hughes County

★ **HOLDENVILLE GENERAL HOSPITAL (371321)**, 100 McDougal Drive, Zip 74848-2822; tel. 405/379-4200, (Nonreporting) **A**10 18
Primary Contact: Stephen C. Stewart, Chief Executive Officer
CFO: Drew Johnson, Chief Financial Officer
CMO: Tom Osborn, D.O., Chief Medical Staff
CIO: Mike Combs, Manager Information Technology
CHR: Heather Heard, Director Human Resources
CNO: Jackie Smith, R.N., Chief Nursing Officer
Web address: www.holdenvillehospital.com/
Control: City, Government, Nonfederal **Service:** General medical and surgical

Staffed Beds: 25

HOLLIS—Harmon County

HARMON MEMORIAL HOSPITAL (371338), 400 East Chestnut Street, Zip 73550-2030, Mailing Address: P.O. Box 791, Zip 73550-0791; tel. 580/688-3363, **A**10 18 **F**40 68 75 89 93 107 133 149
Primary Contact: Steve L. Hartgraves, Chief Executive Officer
CFO: Willie Mae Copeland, Chief Financial Officer
CMO: Akram Abraham, M.D., Chief of Staff
CHR: Abbey Welch, Director Human Resources
Web address: www.harmonmemorial.com/
Control: Hospital district or authority, Government, Nonfederal **Service:** General medical and surgical

Staffed Beds: 16 **Admissions:** 123 **Census:** 1 **Outpatient Visits:** 4540
Births: 0 **Total Expense ($000):** 6929 **Payroll Expense ($000):** 2669
Personnel: 52

HUGO—Choctaw County

CHOCTAW MEMORIAL HOSPITAL (370100), 1405 East Kirk Street, Zip 74743-3603; tel. 580/317-9500, (Nonreporting) **A**10
Primary Contact: Nick Rowland, Chief Executive Officer
CIO: Andy Richmond, Director Information Technology
CHR: Darlene Galyon, Director Human Resources
Web address: www.choctawmemorial.com
Control: Hospital district or authority, Government, Nonfederal **Service:** General medical and surgical

Staffed Beds: 34

Hospital, Medicare Provider Number, Address, Telephone, Approval, Facility, and Physician Codes, Health Care System

★ American Hospital Association (AHA) membership   ○ Healthcare Facilities Accreditation Program   ⇧ Center for Improvement in Healthcare Quality Accreditation
☐ The Joint Commission accreditation   ◇ DNV Healthcare Inc. accreditation   △ Commission on Accreditation of Rehabilitation Facilities (CARF) accreditation

Hospitals, U.S. / OKLAHOMA

IDABEL—McCurtain County

⇑ **MCCURTAIN MEMORIAL HOSPITAL (371342)**, 1301 Lincoln Road, Zip 74745–7341; tel. 580/286–7623, (Nonreporting) **A**10 18 21
Primary Contact: Brian Whitfield, Chief Executive Officer
CFO: Kena C Allen, Chief Financial Officer
CMO: Michael C West, M.D., Chief of Staff
CIO: Dana A Stowell, Chief Information Officer
CNO: Pamela Johnson, R.N., Chief Nursing Officer
Web address: www.mmhok.com
Control: Other not–for–profit (including NFP Corporation) **Service**: General medical and surgical

Staffed Beds: 25

KINGFISHER—Kingfisher County

MERCY HOSPITAL KINGFISHER (371313), 1000 Hospital Cirle, Zip 73750–5002, Mailing Address: P.O. Box 59, Zip 73750–0059; tel. 405/375–3141, **A**1 10 18 **F**3 11 15 29 30 34 35 40 41 43 50 59 64 68 75 77 87 93 107 110 111 115 119 129 133 135 146 148 149 154 157 **P**6 **S** Mercy, Chesterfield, MO
Primary Contact: Bobby Stitt, R.N., Administrator, Rural Facilities
CMO: Brett Krablin, M.D., Chief of Staff
CIO: Chad Kliewer, Information Technology Specialist
CHR: Carolyn R Bjerke, Director Human Resources
CNO: Hannah Powell, Chief Nursing Officer
Web address: https://www.mercy.net/practice/mercy-hospital-kingfisher/
Control: Church operated, Nongovernment, not–for–profit **Service**: General medical and surgical

Staffed Beds: 25 **Admissions**: 333 **Census**: 9 **Outpatient Visits**: 15776 **Births**: 0 **Total Expense ($000)**: 14705 **Payroll Expense ($000)**: 8629 **Personnel**: 65

LAWTON—Comanche County

△ **COMANCHE COUNTY MEMORIAL HOSPITAL (370056)**, 3401 West Gore Boulevard, Zip 73505–6332, Mailing Address: P.O. Box 129, Zip 73502–0129; tel. 580/355–8620, (Total facility includes 142 beds in nursing home–type unit) **A**1 3 5 7 10 13 **F**3 5 7 8 11 12 13 15 17 18 20 22 24 26 28 29 30 31 32 34 35 37 39 40 43 45 46 47 48 49 50 51 54 56 57 59 62 63 64 65 66 68 70 72 74 75 76 77 78 79 80 81 82 84 85 86 89 90 91 92 93 96 97 98 101 102 104 107 108 110 111 114 115 116 117 118 119 120 121 126 127 128 129 130 131 132 134 135 143 144 146 147 148 149 154 156 160 161 167 169
Primary Contact: Brent Smith, Chief Executive Officer
CFO: George Kruger, CPA, Chief Financial Officer
CMO: Scott Michener, M.D., Chief Medical Officer
CIO: James Wellman, Senior Director Information Services
CHR: Donna Wade, Senior Director Human Resources
CNO: Melissa Alvillar, MSN, R.N., Chief Nursing Officer
Web address: www.ccmhonline.com
Control: Hospital district or authority, Government, Nonfederal **Service**: General medical and surgical

Staffed Beds: 350 **Admissions**: 10886 **Census**: 217 **Outpatient Visits**: 225052 **Births**: 1333 **Total Expense ($000)**: 332407 **Payroll Expense ($000)**: 129923 **Personnel**: 1608

JIM TALIAFERRO COMMUNITY MENTAL HEALTH CENTER (374008), 602 SW 38th Street, Zip 73505; tel. 580/248–5780, **A**3 10 **F**5 29 34 35 38 44 50 59 66 68 98 100 101 102 104 130 132 134 135 143 146 149 153 154 157 160 164 165
Primary Contact: Terri Lee, Executive Director
Web address: www.odmhsas.org
Control: State, Government, Nonfederal **Service**: Psychiatric

Staffed Beds: 14 **Admissions**: 425 **Census**: 12 **Outpatient Visits**: 0 **Births**: 0

LAWTON INDIAN HOSPITAL (370170), 1515 Lawrie Tatum Road, Zip 73507–3099; tel. 580/353–0350, (Nonreporting) **A**1 10 **S** U. S. Indian Health Service, Rockville, MD
Primary Contact: Brian Wren, Chief Executive Officer
COO: John Bear, Hospital Administrator Officer and Supervisor Human Resources
CFO: Sarabeth Sahmaunt, Supervisory Accountant
CMO: Richard Chadek, M.D., Clinical Director
CIO: William R Harris, Chief Information Officer
CHR: John Bear, Hospital Administrator Officer and Supervisor Human Resources
CNO: Jennifer Wahkinney, Chief Nurse Executive
Web address: www.ihs.gov
Control: PHS, Indian Service, Government, federal **Service**: General medical and surgical

Staffed Beds: 26

△ **SOUTHWESTERN MEDICAL CENTER (370097)**, 5602 SW Lee Boulevard, Zip 73505–9635; tel. 580/531–4700, **A**1 7 10 19 **F**3 8 13 18 20 22 29 30 34 38 40 41 45 47 49 50 51 57 59 60 64 65 67 68 70 74 76 77 79 81 85 87 89 90 91 92 93 98 99 100 101 102 104 106 107 108 111 114 118 119 129 130 131 133 135 146 147 148 164 167 **P**6 **S** ScionHealth, Louisville, KY
Primary Contact: Adam Bracks, Chief Executive Officer
CFO: Wayne Colson, Chief Financial Officer
CMO: Aryan Kadivar, M.D., Chief Medical Officer
CIO: Kent Lewis, Director Information Services
CHR: Danny Hale, Director Human Resources
CNO: Jayne Thomas, Chief Nursing Officer
Web address: www.swmconline.com
Control: Corporation, Investor–owned (for–profit) **Service**: General medical and surgical

Staffed Beds: 165 **Admissions**: 3334 **Census**: 65 **Outpatient Visits**: 58610 **Births**: 463 **Total Expense ($000)**: 84953 **Payroll Expense ($000)**: 31950 **Personnel**: 413

LINDSAY—Garvin County

LINDSAY MUNICIPAL HOSPITAL (370214), Highway 19 West, Zip 73052, Mailing Address: P.O. Box 888, Zip 73052–0888; tel. 405/756–1404, (Nonreporting) **A**10
Primary Contact: Jeff Walraven, Chief Executive Officer
Control: City, Government, Nonfederal **Service**: General medical and surgical

Staffed Beds: 26

MADILL—Marshall County

ALLIANCEHEALTH MADILL (371326), 901 South Fifth Avenue, Zip 73446–3640, Mailing Address: P.O. Box 827, Zip 73446–0827; tel. 580/795–3384, **A**1 10 18 **F**29 35 40 43 45 75 81 93 107 114 119 127 128 133 146 148 154 157 **S** Community Health Systems, Inc., Franklin, TN
Primary Contact: Shelton Williams, Chief Executive Officer
CFO: Thomas Briggs, Chief Financial Officer
CMO: Heidi Haislip, M.D., Chief of Staff
CHR: D.J. Shawn, Director Human Resources
CNO: Carol Wright, Chief Nursing Officer
Web address: www.myalliancehealth.com
Control: Corporation, Investor–owned (for–profit) **Service**: General medical and surgical

Staffed Beds: 25 **Admissions**: 256 **Census**: 7 **Outpatient Visits**: 24164 **Births**: 0 **Total Expense ($000)**: 13158 **Payroll Expense ($000)**: 4824

MANGUM—Greer County

MANGUM REGIONAL MEDICAL CENTER (371330), 1 Wickersham Drive, Zip 73554–9116, Mailing Address: P.O. Box 280, Zip 73554–0280; tel. 580/782–3353, (Nonreporting) **A**10 18
Primary Contact: Kelley Martinez, Hospital Administrator
COO: Gregg Burnam, Chief Financial Officer and Chief Operating Officer
CIO: Gregg Burnam, Chief Information Officer and Manager Business Office
Web address: https://mangumregional.net
Control: City, Government, Nonfederal **Service**: General medical and surgical

Staffed Beds: 18

MARIETTA—Love County

★ **MERCY HEALTH LOVE COUNTY (371306)**, 300 Wanda Street, Zip 73448–1200; tel. 580/276–3347, **A**10 18 **F**3 7 11 29 34 40 43 44 50 57 59 65 77 87 91 107 114 119 127 133 135 146 148 149 **S** Mercy, Chesterfield, MO
Primary Contact: Wesley Scott. Callender, Administrator
CIO: Connie Graham, Public Information Officer
Web address: www.mercyhealthlovecounty.com
Control: Church operated, Nongovernment, not–for–profit **Service**: General medical and surgical

Staffed Beds: 25 **Admissions**: 216 **Census**: 7 **Outpatient Visits**: 28426 **Births**: 0 **Total Expense ($000)**: 17537 **Payroll Expense ($000)**: 10308 **Personnel**: 75

MCALESTER—Pittsburg County

CARL ALBERT COMMUNITY MENTAL HEALTH CENTER (374006), 1101 East Monroe Avenue, Zip 74501–4826; tel. 918/426–7800, (Nonreporting) **A**3 10
Primary Contact: Debbie Moran, Executive Director
CFO: Konnie Taylor, Chief Financial Officer
CMO: William Mings, M.D., Medical Director
CHR: Judy Allen, Human Resource Specialist
Web address: www.odmhsas.org
Control: State, Government, Nonfederal **Service**: Psychiatric

Staffed Beds: 15

Hospitals, U.S. / OKLAHOMA

★ ⁙ **MCALESTER REGIONAL HEALTH CENTER (370034)**, 1 East Clark Bass Boulevard, Zip 74501–4209, Mailing Address: 3473 E Hereford Lane, Zip 74501; tel. 918/426–1800, **A**3 5 10 13 21 **F**3 8 10 11 13 15 18 20 22 26 29 30 34 35 40 43 45 49 50 51 53 54 56 57 59 61 62 63 64 66 68 70 74 75 76 77 79 81 85 86 87 90 91 92 93 98 101 102 103 107 108 109 110 111 114 115 116 117 118 119 125 129 130 131 132 135 144 146 147 148 154 158 167 **P**6
Primary Contact: Julie Powell, Interim Chief Executive Officer
CFO: Darryl Linnington, Chief Financial Officer
CIO: Jason Bray, Chief Information Officer
CHR: Scott Lowe, Director Human Resource
CNO: Kimberly Dawn Stout, Chief Nursing Officer and Chief Operating Officer
Web address: www.mrhcok.com
Control: Hospital district or authority, Government, Nonfederal **Service**: General medical and surgical

Staffed Beds: 209 **Admissions**: 3286 **Census**: 43 **Outpatient Visits**: 103366 **Births**: 408 **Total Expense ($000)**: 105096 **Payroll Expense ($000)**: 44942 **Personnel**: 727

MIAMI—Ottawa County

⌧ **INTEGRIS MIAMI HOSPITAL (370004)**, 200 Second Avenue SW, Zip 74354–6830; tel. 918/542–6611, **A**1 10 20 **F**3 7 11 13 15 28 29 30 34 35 40 43 45 51 53 57 59 62 63 70 75 76 77 79 81 85 89 93 107 108 109 110 111 115 119 127 129 130 131 132 135 144 146 147 148 154 169 **S** INTEGRIS Health, Oklahoma City, OK
Primary Contact: Jonas Rabel, Chief Hospital Executive
CFO: Valerie Reeves, Chief Financial Officer
CMO: Elaine Mader, M.D., Chief of Staff
CHR: Jamil Haynes, Regional Director Human Resources
CNO: Lisa Halstead, Chief Nursing Officer
Web address: www.integrisok.com/miami-hospital
Control: Other not–for–profit (including NFP Corporation) **Service**: General medical and surgical

Staffed Beds: 44 **Admissions**: 1329 **Census**: 12 **Outpatient Visits**: 47401 **Births**: 263 **Total Expense ($000)**: 57169 **Payroll Expense ($000)**: 20023 **Personnel**: 293

★ **WILLOW CREST HOSPITAL (374017)**, 130 'A' Street SW, Zip 74354–6800; tel. 918/542–1836, (Nonreporting) **A**10
Primary Contact: Shari Murphree, Chief Executive Officer
COO: Steven Goodman, Chief Operating Officer
CFO: Cindy Bell, Director Finance
CMO: Mark Elkington, M.D., Chief Medical Officer
CIO: Steven Goodman, Chief Operating Officer
CHR: Kathy Henderson, Director Human Resources
CNO: Kassi Davis, Director Patient Care Services
Web address: www.willowcresthospital.com
Control: Corporation, Investor–owned (for–profit) **Service**: Children's hospital psychiatric

Staffed Beds: 73

MIDWEST CITY—Oklahoma County

☐ **INSPIRE SPECIALTY HOSPITAL (372012)**, 8210 National Avenue, Zip 73110–8518; tel. 405/739–0800, (Nonreporting) **A**1 10
Primary Contact: Bobby Snyder, Chief Executive Officer
CFO: Veronica Scott, Business Office Manager
CHR: Anna Emamghoraishi, Human Resources
CNO: Jason Farris, Chief Nursing Officer
Web address: www.inspirehospital.com
Control: Corporation, Investor–owned (for–profit) **Service**: Acute long–term care hospital

Staffed Beds: 31

⌧ **SSM HEALTH ST. ANTHONY HOSPITAL – MIDWEST (370094)**, 2825 Parklawn Drive, Zip 73110–4258; tel. 405/610–4411, (Nonreporting) **A**1 10 **S** SSM Health, Saint Louis, MO
Primary Contact: Stacy Coleman, MS, President
COO: Lisa Ellis, Chief Operating Officer
CFO: Cynthia Gray, Interim Chief Financial Officer
CMO: Jason Chung, M.D., Vice President, Medical Affairs and Chief Medical Officer
CHR: Dana Leach, Director Human Resources
CNO: Jaconna Joni Tiller, Chief Nursing Officer
Web address: https://www.ssmhealth.com/locations/st-anthony-hospital-midwest
Control: Church operated, Nongovernment, not–for–profit **Service**: General medical and surgical

Staffed Beds: 87

MOORE—Cleveland County

MOORE MEDICAL CENTER See Norman Regional Moore

NORMAN REGIONAL MOORE See Norman Regional Health System, Norman

MUSKOGEE—Muskogee County

★ **CORNERSTONE SPECIALTY HOSPITALS MUSKOGEE (372022)**, 351 South 40th Street, Zip 74401–4916; tel. 918/682–6161, (Includes CORNERSTONE SPECIALTY HOSPITALS BROKEN ARROW, 1000 West Boise Circle, Third Floor, Broken Arrow, Oklahoma, Zip 74012–4900, 1000 West Boise Circle, Zip 74012–4900, tel. 918/994–8300; Craig Koele, Chief Executive Officer) (Nonreporting) **A**10 22 **S** ScionHealth, Louisville, KY
Primary Contact: Denise Benningfield. Crelia, Market Chief Executive Office & Chief Nursing Executive
CMO: Jeremiah Rutherford, Chief Medical Officer
Web address: www.chghospitals.com/muskogee/
Control: Corporation, Investor–owned (for–profit) **Service**: Acute long–term care hospital

Staffed Beds: 41

EASTAR HEALTH SYSTEM, EAST CAMPUS See Saint Francis Hospital Muskogee, Muskogee

EASTERN OKLAHOMA VA HEALTH CARE SYSTEM See Jack C. Montgomery Department of Veterans Affairs Medical Center

⌧ △ **JACK C. MONTGOMERY DEPARTMENT OF VETERANS AFFAIRS MEDICAL CENTER**, 1011 Honor Heights Drive, Zip 74401–1318; tel. 918/577–3000, (Nonreporting) **A**1 3 5 7 **S** Department of Veterans Affairs, Washington, DC
Primary Contact: Kimberly Denning, R.N., Medical Director
CFO: Dwight Beal, Chief Fiscal Services
CMO: Thomas D Schneider, D.O., Chief of Staff
Web address: www.muskogee.va.gov
Control: Veterans Affairs, Government, federal **Service**: General medical and surgical

Staffed Beds: 82

MUSKOGEE COMMUNITY HOSPITAL See Eastar Health System, East Campus

⌧ **SAINT FRANCIS HOSPITAL MUSKOGEE (370025)**, 300 Rockefeller Drive, Zip 74401–5081; tel. 918/682–5501, (Includes EASTAR HEALTH SYSTEM, EAST CAMPUS, 2900 North Main Street, Muskogee, Oklahoma, Zip 74401–4078, tel. 918/687–7777) **A**1 3 10 19 **F**3 8 11 13 15 18 20 22 28 29 30 31 35 37 40 43 45 53 54 56 57 60 64 68 70 74 75 76 78 79 81 82 85 86 87 89 90 92 96 98 100 102 103 107 108 110 111 114 115 119 120 121 123 124 126 129 130 131 141 143 146 147 148 160 162 164 165 **S** Saint Francis Health System, Tulsa, OK
Primary Contact: Michele A. Keeling, President
COO: Tony Capuano, Chief Operating Officer
CFO: Scott Bailey, Chief Financial Officer
CMO: Jay Gregory, M.D., Chief Medical Officer
CIO: James Tolbert, Director Information Systems
CHR: Bill Peterson, Director Human Resources
Web address: https://www.saintfrancis.com/muskogee/Pages/default.aspx
Control: Other not–for–profit (including NFP Corporation) **Service**: General medical and surgical

Staffed Beds: 188 **Admissions**: 10161 **Census**: 131 **Outpatient Visits**: 103944 **Births**: 554 **Total Expense ($000)**: 172116 **Payroll Expense ($000)**: 76614 **Personnel**: 699

NORMAN—Cleveland County

BEHAVIORAL HEALTH CENTER OF PORTER VILLAGE, 506 Wellness Way, Zip 73071, Mailing Address: 3905 Hedgcoxe Road, Unit 250249, Plano, TX, Zip 75025; tel. 405/754–1309, (Nonreporting) **S** Oceans Healthcare, Plano, TX
Primary Contact: William Southwick, Hospital Administrator
CFO: Eric Elliott, Chief Financial Officer
Web address: www.oceanshealthcare.com
Control: Corporation, Investor–owned (for–profit) **Service**: Psychiatric

Staffed Beds: 48

Hospital, Medicare Provider Number, Address, Telephone, Approval, Facility, and Physician Codes, Health Care System

★ American Hospital Association (AHA) membership ◯ Healthcare Facilities Accreditation Program ⁙ Center for Improvement in Healthcare Quality Accreditation
☐ The Joint Commission accreditation ◇ DNV Healthcare Inc. accreditation △ Commission on Accreditation of Rehabilitation Facilities (CARF) accreditation

Hospitals, U.S. / OKLAHOMA

☐ **GRIFFIN MEMORIAL HOSPITAL (374000)**, 900 East Main Street, Zip 73071-5305, Mailing Address: P.O. Box 151, Zip 73070-0151; tel. 405/573-6600, (Nonreporting) **A**1 3 5 10 22 **S** Oklahoma Department of Mental Health and Substance Abuse Services, Oklahoma City, OK
Primary Contact: Henry Hartsell, Ph.D., Executive Director
CFO: Cheryl Cupps, Director Finance
CMO: Clayton Morris, Medical Director
CNO: Mike Abla, Director of Nursing
Web address: www.odmhsas.org
Control: State, Government, Nonfederal **Service:** Psychiatric

Staffed Beds: 120

J. D. MCCARTY CENTER FOR CHILDREN WITH DEVELOPMENTAL DISABILITIES (373300), 2002 East Robinson, Zip 73071-7420; tel. 405/307-2800, (Nonreporting) **A**10
Primary Contact: Michael Powers, Director and Chief Executive Officer
CFO: Erik Paulson, Director of Finance
CMO: Thomas Thurston, M.D., Medical Director
CIO: Jeffery Setzer, Administrator Information Systems
CHR: Tina Martinez, Director Human Resources
Web address: www.jdmc.org
Control: State, Government, Nonfederal **Service:** Children's rehabilitation

Staffed Beds: 36

✠ **NORMAN REGIONAL HEALTH SYSTEM (370008)**, 3300 Healthplex Parkway, Zip 73072-9749, Mailing Address: P.O. Box 1308, Zip 73070-1308; tel. 405/515-1000, (Includes NORMAN REGIONAL HOSPITAL, 3300 Healthplex Parkway, Norman, Oklahoma, Zip 73072-9749, P O Box 1308, Zip 73070-1308, tel. 405/307-1000; Aaron Boyd, M.D., FACHE, Co-Chief Executive Officer; NORMAN REGIONAL MOORE, 700 South Telephone Road, Moore, Oklahoma, Zip 73160, tel. 405/793-9355; Aaron Boyd, M.D., FACHE, Co-Chief Executive Officer) (Nonreporting) **A**1 3 5 10 13
Primary Contact: Aaron Boyd, M.D., FACHE, Co-Chief Executive Officer
COO: John Manfredo, Chief Operating Officer
CFO: Ken Hopkins, Vice President Finance and Chief Financial Officer
CIO: Danny Kelley, Administrative Director, Health Information Technology
CNO: Brittini McGill, MSN, R.N., Chief Nursing Officer
Web address: www.normanregional.com
Control: Hospital district or authority, Government, Nonfederal **Service:** General medical and surgical

Staffed Beds: 387

NOWATA—Nowata County

★ **ASCENSION ST. JOHN NOWATA (371305)**, 237 South Locust Street, Zip 74048-3660; tel. 918/273-3102, (Nonreporting) **A**10 18 **S** Ascension Healthcare, Saint Louis, MO
Primary Contact: Jason McCauley, Administrator
CMO: David Caughell, M.D., Chief of Staff
Web address: www.jpmc.org
Control: Church operated, Nongovernment, not-for-profit **Service:** General medical and surgical

Staffed Beds: 15

OKEENE—Blaine County

★ **OKEENE MUNICIPAL HOSPITAL (371327)**, 207 East 'F' Street, Zip 73763-9441, Mailing Address: P.O. Box 489, Zip 73763-0489; tel. 580/822-4417, (Nonreporting) **A**10 18
Primary Contact: Clark Houser, Chief Executive Officer
COO: Tammi Jantzen, Chief Operating Officer
CFO: Sandra Lamle, Chief Financial Officer
CMO: George S. Stenger, D.O., Chief of Staff
CHR: Barbara Creps, Director Human Resources and Accounting
CNO: Tamara Fischer, Chief Nursing Officer
Web address: www.okeenehospital.com
Control: Hospital district or authority, Government, Nonfederal **Service:** General medical and surgical

Staffed Beds: 17

OKEMAH—Okfuskee County

★ ⇑ **CREEK NATION COMMUNITY HOSPITAL (371333)**, 1800 East Coplin Street, Zip 74859-4642; tel. 918/623-1424, (Nonreporting) **A**10 18 21
Primary Contact: Shawn Terry, Secretary of Health
COO: Rhonda Beaver, Chief Administrative Officer
CFO: Tyler McIntosh, Chief Financial Officer
CMO: Lawrence Vark, M.D., Chief Medical Officer
CIO: Robert Coffee, Chief Information Officer
CHR: Russell B Torbett, Director Human Resources
CNO: Annette James, R.N., MSN, Chief Nursing Officer
Web address: www.creekhealth.org
Control: Other not-for-profit (including NFP Corporation) **Service:** General medical and surgical

Staffed Beds: 25

OKLAHOMA CITY—Cleveland County

⇑ **COMMUNITY HOSPITAL (370203)**, 3100 SW 89th Street, Zip 73159-7900, Mailing Address: 3125 SW 89th Street, Zip 73159-7900; tel. 405/602-8100, (Nonreporting) **A**3 10 21
Primary Contact: Debbie Kearns, Chief Executive Officer
Web address: www.communityhospitalokc.com
Control: Corporation, Investor-owned (for-profit) **Service:** Surgical

Staffed Beds: 45

OKLAHOMA CITY—Oklahoma County

ALLIANCEHEALTH DEACONESS See Integris Baptist Medical Center Portland Avenue

AMG SPECIALTY HOSPITAL – OKLAHOMA CITY (372005), 4300 West Memorial Road, 2nd Floor, Zip 73120-8304; tel. 405/936-5822, (Nonreporting) **A**10 22 **S** AMG Integrated Healthcare Management, Lafayette, LA
Primary Contact: Erick Heflin, R.N., Chief Executive Officer
Web address: https://amgihm.com/locations/oklahoma-city/
Control: Corporation, Investor-owned (for-profit) **Service:** Acute long-term care hospital

Staffed Beds: 30

BONE AND JOINT HOSPITAL See SSM Health Bone and Joint Hospital At St. Anthony

☐ **CEDAR RIDGE (374023)**, 6501 NE 50th Street, Zip 73141-9118; tel. 405/605-6111, (Includes BETHANY BEHAVIORAL HEALTH, 7600 NW 23rd Street, Bethany, Oklahoma, Zip 73008-4944, tel. 405/792-5360) **A**1 10 **F**98 99 105 106 153 **P**6 **S** Universal Health Services, Inc., King of Prussia, PA
Primary Contact: Cesiley Bouseman, Chief Executive Officer
COO: Jackie Baker, Chief Operating Officer
CFO: Benjamin Heath, Chief Financial Officer
Web address: www.cedarridgebhs.com
Control: Corporation, Investor-owned (for-profit) **Service:** Psychiatric

Staffed Beds: 172 **Admissions:** 5060 **Census:** 129 **Outpatient Visits:** 2530 **Births:** 0 **Total Expense ($000):** 29628 **Payroll Expense ($000):** 15882 **Personnel:** 237

CHILDREN'S HOSPITAL OF OKLAHOMA See OU Health – University of Oklahoma Medical Center, Oklahoma City

EVEREST REHABILITATION HOSPITAL OKC See Mercy Rehabilitation Hospital Oklahoma City South

EVERETT TOWER See OU Health – University of Oklahoma Medical Center, Oklahoma City

Hospitals, U.S. / OKLAHOMA

☒ △ **INTEGRIS BAPTIST MEDICAL CENTER (370028)**, 3300 NW Expressway, Zip 73112–4418; tel. 405/949–3011, (Includes INTEGRIS BAPTIST MEDICAL CENTER PORTLAND AVENUE, 5501 North Portland Avenue, Oklahoma City, Oklahoma, Zip 73112–2099, tel. 405/604–6000; Brent Hubbard, FACHE, Interim Chief Executive Officer; INTEGRIS MENTAL HEALTH SYSTEM–SPENCER, 2601 North Spencer Road, Spencer, Oklahoma, Zip 73084–3699, P O Box 11137, Oklahoma City, Zip 73136–0137, tel. 405/717–9800) **A**1 2 3 5 7 10 **F**3 5 11 12 13 15 16 17 18 19 20 22 24 26 28 29 30 31 32 34 35 37 38 39 40 43 44 45 46 47 49 50 51 53 54 55 57 58 59 60 61 62 63 64 65 68 70 71 72 74 75 76 77 78 79 80 81 82 84 85 86 87 88 89 90 92 93 96 97 98 99 100 101 102 104 105 106 107 108 109 110 111 114 115 116 117 118 119 120 121 123 124 126 129 130 131 132 135 137 138 139 140 141 142 146 147 148 149 153 154 156 157 167 169 **S** INTEGRIS Health, Oklahoma City, OK
Primary Contact: Joshua Kemph, Chief Executive Officer
CFO: Cheryl Perry, Chief Financial Officer
CIO: Mark Pasquale, Chief Information Officer
CHR: Jason L Eliot, Vice President Human Resources
CNO: Lewis L. Perkins, R.N., MSN, Jr, Chief Nursing Officer
Web address: www.integrisok.com
Control: Other not–for–profit (including NFP Corporation) **Service:** General medical and surgical

Staffed Beds: 892 **Admissions:** 25160 **Census:** 464 **Outpatient Visits:** 362267 **Births:** 3175 **Total Expense ($000):** 1109827 **Payroll Expense ($000):** 303548 **Personnel:** 2875

⇧ **INTEGRIS HEALTH COMMUNITY HOSPITAL AT COUNCIL CROSSING (370240)**, 9417 North Council Road, Zip 73162–6228; tel. 405/500–3280, (Nonreporting) **A**10 21 **S** Emerus, The Woodlands, TX
Primary Contact: Christopher McAuliffe, R.N., Market Chief Executive Officer
Web address: https://www.integriscommunityhospital.com/locations/council-crossing/
Control: Partnership, Investor–owned (for–profit) **Service:** General medical and surgical

Staffed Beds: 64

☒ **INTEGRIS SOUTHWEST MEDICAL CENTER (370106)**, 4401 South Western, Zip 73109–3413; tel. 405/636–7000, **A**1 2 3 5 10 13 **F**3 11 13 15 18 20 22 24 26 28 29 30 31 34 35 40 43 44 45 47 49 50 51 53 57 58 59 60 64 65 67 68 70 71 74 75 76 77 78 79 81 82 84 85 86 87 89 90 91 92 93 95 96 97 100 107 108 110 111 114 115 118 119 121 123 124 126 129 130 131 135 146 147 148 149 154 156 157 167 168 169 **S** INTEGRIS Health, Oklahoma City, OK
Primary Contact: Phil Harrop, Chief Executive Officer
CFO: Dan Davis, Managing Director and Chief Financial Officer
CMO: Philip Mosca, M.D., President, Medical Staff
CIO: Mark Pasquale, Chief Information Officer
CHR: Lynn Ketch, Regional Director Integris Southwest Medical Center
Web address: https://integrishealth.org/locations/hospital/integris-southwest-medical-center
Control: Other not–for–profit (including NFP Corporation) **Service:** General medical and surgical

Staffed Beds: 257 **Admissions:** 10375 **Census:** 178 **Outpatient Visits:** 165683 **Births:** 1069 **Total Expense ($000):** 303848 **Payroll Expense ($000):** 92830 **Personnel:** 1118

KINDRED HOSPITAL–OKLAHOMA CITY SOUTH See Curahealth Oklahoma

☒ **LAKESIDE WOMEN'S HOSPITAL (370199)**, 11200 North Portland Avenue, Zip 73120–5045; tel. 405/936–1500, **A**1 10 **F**3 13 15 29 30 36 40 45 59 64 73 76 81 85 87 110 119 126 130 147 149 154 **P**2 **S** INTEGRIS Health, Oklahoma City, OK
Primary Contact: Leslie Buford, Chief Hospital Executive
CFO: Darla McCallister, Chief Financial Officer
CMO: Margaret Hall, M.D., Chief Medical Officer
CNO: Stacey L. Decker, MS, R.N., Chief Hospital Executive and Chief Nursing Officer
Web address: https://lakeside-wh.com/
Control: Corporation, Investor–owned (for–profit) **Service:** Obstetrics and gynecology

Staffed Beds: 29 **Admissions:** 1658 **Census:** 10 **Outpatient Visits:** 22169 **Births:** 1580 **Total Expense ($000):** 27557 **Payroll Expense ($000):** 11437 **Personnel:** 128

⇧ **MCBRIDE ORTHOPEDIC HOSPITAL (370222)**, 9600 Broadway Extension, Zip 73114–7408; tel. 405/486–2100, (Nonreporting) **A**3 5 10 21
Primary Contact: Mark Galliart, Chief Executive Officer
CFO: Greg Gisler, Chief Financial Officer
CNO: Krista Reyna, Chief Nursing Officer
Web address: www.mcboh.com
Control: Corporation, Investor–owned (for–profit) **Service:** Orthopedic

Staffed Beds: 60

☒ **MERCY HOSPITAL OKLAHOMA CITY (370013)**, 4300 West Memorial Road, Zip 73120–8362; tel. 405/755–1515, **A**1 2 3 5 10 19 **F**3 8 11 13 15 29 30 31 32 34 35 37 40 42 43 44 45 46 47 48 49 50 53 54 55 57 58 59 60 61 62 63 64 65 68 69 70 72 74 75 76 77 78 79 81 82 83 84 85 86 87 89 91 92 93 94 96 100 101 107 108 110 111 114 115 116 117 118 119 120 121 124 126 129 131 133 134 135 143 146 147 148 149 154 156 162 167 169 **P**6 **S** Mercy, Chesterfield, MO
Primary Contact: Bennett Geister, President, Oklahoma City Communities
COO: Aaron Steffens, Chief Operating Officer
CFO: Jon Vitiello, Senior Vice President, Finance Operations and Analytics
CIO: Ellen Stephens, Vice President Information Services
CHR: Becky J Payton, Vice President Human Resources
Web address: www.mercyok.net
Control: Church operated, Nongovernment, not–for–profit **Service:** General medical and surgical

Staffed Beds: 385 **Admissions:** 17997 **Census:** 217 **Outpatient Visits:** 629838 **Births:** 3881 **Total Expense ($000):** 603364 **Payroll Expense ($000):** 217852 **Personnel:** 2568

☐ △ **MERCY REHABILITATION HOSPITAL OKLAHOMA CITY (373033)**, 5401 West Memorial Rd, Zip 73142–2026; tel. 405/384–5211, **A**1 7 10 **F**3 12 28 29 30 56 74 79 82 90 94 96 122 148 154
Primary Contact: Gina Tess Clemens, PharmD, Market Chief Executive Officer
Web address: https://www.mercy.net/practice/mercy-rehabilitation-hospital-oklahoma-city/
Control: Partnership, Investor–owned (for–profit) **Service:** Rehabilitation

Staffed Beds: 66 **Admissions:** 1270 **Census:** 42 **Outpatient Visits:** 0 **Births:** 0 **Total Expense ($000):** 17316 **Payroll Expense ($000):** 12875 **Personnel:** 175

MERCY REHABILITATION HOSPITAL OKLAHOMA CITY SOUTH (373036), 7900 Mid America Boulevard, Zip 73135; tel. 469/713–1145, **A**10 22 **F**3 12 28 29 30 56 74 79 82 90 94 95 96 119 122 130 135 137 138 139 140 148 154
Primary Contact: Gina Tess Clemens, PharmD, Market Chief Executive Officer
Web address: https://www.mercy.net/practice/mercy-rehabilitation-hospital-oklahoma-city-south/
Control: Partnership, Investor–owned (for–profit) **Service:** Rehabilitation

Staffed Beds: 36 **Admissions:** 664 **Census:** 20 **Outpatient Visits:** 0 **Births:** 0 **Total Expense ($000):** 9717 **Payroll Expense ($000):** 7151 **Personnel:** 95

⇧ **NORTHWEST SURGICAL HOSPITAL (370192)**, 9204 North May Avenue, Zip 73120–4419; tel. 405/848–1918, (Nonreporting) **A**3 5 10 21
Primary Contact: Debbie Kearns, Chief Executive Officer
CFO: Cindy Thompson, Chief Financial Officer
CMO: Jimmy Conway, M.D., President Medical Staff
Web address: www.nwsurgicalokc.com/
Control: Corporation, Investor–owned (for–profit) **Service:** Orthopedic

Staffed Beds: 9

☐ **OAKWOOD SPRINGS (374025)**, 13101 Memorial Springs Court, Zip 73114–2226; tel. 405/438–3000, (Nonreporting) **A**1 10 **S** Springstone, Louisville, KY
Primary Contact: Amir Khan, Chief Executive Officer
Web address: www.oakwoodsprings.com/
Control: Corporation, Investor–owned (for–profit) **Service:** Psychiatric

Staffed Beds: 72

Hospitals, U.S. / OKLAHOMA

☐ **OKLAHOMA CENTER FOR ORTHOPAEDIC AND MULTI-SPECIALTY SURGERY (370212)**, 8100 South Walker, Suite C, Zip 73139-9402, Mailing Address: P.O. Box 890609, Zip 73189-0609; tel. 405/602-6500, (Nonreporting) **A**1 10 **S** United Surgical Partners International, Addison, TX
Primary Contact: Landon Hise, Chief Executive Officer
COO: Jeff Bibb, Chief Operating Officer
CFO: Amy Taylor, Chief Financial Officer
CHR: Emily Phipps, Director Human Resources
CNO: Jolena Wyer, R.N., Chief Nursing Officer
Web address: www.ocomhospital.com
Control: Partnership, Investor-owned (for-profit) **Service**: Orthopedic

Staffed Beds: 9

OKLAHOMA CITY REHABILITATION HOSPITAL (373038), 10240 Broadway Extension, Zip 73114-6309; tel. 405/900-8850, (Nonreporting) **A**10 **S** Nobis Rehabilitation Partners, Allen, TX
Primary Contact: Stacie Goyne, Chief Executive Officer
COO: Christopher Bergh, Chief Operating Officer
CFO: Chester Crouch, Nobis Rehabilitation Partners President and Chief Executive Officer
CHR: April Maldonado, Vice President Human Resources
CNO: Christa M. Lohr, R.N., Chief Clinical Officer
Web address: https://www.oklahomacity-rehab.com/about-okc-rehab
Control: Corporation, Investor-owned (for-profit) **Service**: Rehabilitation

Staffed Beds: 40

✱ △ **OKLAHOMA CITY VA MEDICAL CENTER**, 921 NE 13th Street, Zip 73104-5028; tel. 405/456-1000, (Nonreporting) **A**1 3 5 7 **S** Department of Veterans Affairs, Washington, DC
Primary Contact: Kristopher Wade. Vlosich, Medical Center Director
CFO: Michele Pipgrass, Chief Fiscal Service
CIO: David Buckley, Acting Chief Information Management Services
CHR: Kyle Inhofe, Chief Human Resources Officer
Web address: www.oklahoma.va.gov
Control: Veterans Affairs, Government, federal **Service**: General medical and surgical

Staffed Beds: 198

⇑ **OKLAHOMA HEART HOSPITAL (370215)**, 4050 West Memorial Road, Zip 73120-8382; tel. 405/608-3200, (Nonreporting) **A**3 5 10 21
Primary Contact: John Harvey, M.D., Chief Executive Officer
COO: Peggy Tipton, Chief Operating Officer and Chief Nursing Officer
CFO: Carol Walker, Chief Financial Officer
CMO: John Harvey, M.D., Chief Executive Officer
CIO: Michelle Mullins, Chief Information Officer
CHR: Katherine Wynn, Director Human Resource
Web address: www.okheart.com
Control: Corporation, Investor-owned (for-profit) **Service**: Heart

Staffed Beds: 97

⇑ **OKLAHOMA HEART HOSPITAL SOUTH CAMPUS (370234)**, 5200 East I-240 Service Road, Zip 73135; tel. 405/628-6000, (Nonreporting) **A**10 21
Primary Contact: John Harvey, M.D., Chief Executive Officer
Web address: www.okheart.com
Control: Corporation, Investor-owned (for-profit) **Service**: Heart

Staffed Beds: 44

OKLAHOMA SPINE HOSPITAL (370206), 14101 Parkway Commons Drive, Zip 73134-6012; tel. 405/749-2700, (Nonreporting) **A**10
Primary Contact: Kevin Blaylock, Chief Executive Officer
Web address: www.oklahomaspine.com
Control: Corporation, Investor-owned (for-profit) **Service**: Surgical

Staffed Beds: 12

ONECORE HEALTH (370220), 1044 SW 44th Street, Suite 350, Zip 73109-3609; tel. 405/631-3085, **A**10 **F**3 15 29 40 54 58 74 79 81 82 86 87 107 110 111 114 119 131 148 149
Primary Contact: Steve Hockert, Interim Chief Executive Officer
CMO: Joel L Frazier, M.D., Medical Director
CNO: Teresa Carter, Vice President Patient Care Services
Web address: www.onecorehealth.com
Control: Partnership, Investor-owned (for-profit) **Service**: Orthopedic

Staffed Beds: 7 **Admissions**: 310 **Census**: 2 **Outpatient Visits**: 14596 **Births**: 0 **Total Expense ($000)**: 28166 **Payroll Expense ($000)**: 5538 **Personnel**: 88

✱ **OU HEALTH – UNIVERSITY OF OKLAHOMA MEDICAL CENTER (370093)**, 1200 Everett Drive, Zip 73104-5047, Mailing Address: P.O. Box 26307, Zip 73126-0307; tel. 405/271-3636, (Includes CHILDREN'S HOSPITAL OF OKLAHOMA, 940 NE 13th Street, Oklahoma City, Oklahoma, Zip 73104, P O Box 26307, Zip 73126, tel. 405/271-6165; EVERETT TOWER, 1200 Everett Drive, Oklahoma City, Oklahoma, Zip 73104, tel. 405/271-4700; OU MEDICAL CENTER EDMOND, 1 South Bryant Avenue, Edmond, Oklahoma, Zip 73034-6309, tel. 405/341-6100; PRESBYTERIAN TOWER, 700 NE 13th Street, Oklahoma City, Oklahoma, Zip 73104-5070, tel. 405/271-5100) (Nonreporting) **A**1 2 3 5 8 10 19
Primary Contact: Richard P. Lofgren, M.D., M.P.H., Chief Executive Officer
COO: Jonathan W. Curtright, Chief Operating Officer
CFO: Mike Reese, Chief Financial Officer
CMO: Curt Steinhart, M.D., Chief Medical Officer
CIO: Larry Forsyth, Director Information Services
CHR: Jed M. Liuzza, Chief Human Resources Officer
Web address: https://www.ouhealth.com/find-a-location/ou-health-university-of-oklahoma-medical-center/
Control: Other not-for-profit (including NFP Corporation) **Service**: General medical and surgical

Staffed Beds: 946

★ **PAM HEALTH SPECIALTY HOSPITAL OF OKLAHOMA CITY (372004)**, 1407 North Robinson Avenue, Zip 73103-4823; tel. 405/232-8000, (Includes CURAHEALTH OKLAHOMA, 2129 SW 59th Street, Oklahoma City, Oklahoma, Zip 73119, tel. 405/713-5955) **A**10 22 **F**3 29 30 60 70 130 148 **S** PAM Health, Enola, PA
Primary Contact: Talitha Glosemeyer-Samsel, M.P.H., FACHE, Chief Executive Officer
Web address: https://pamhealth.com/index.php/facilities/find-facility/specialty-hospitals/pam-health-specialty-hospital-oklahoma-city
Control: Individual, Investor-owned (for-profit) **Service**: Acute long-term care hospital

Staffed Beds: 59 **Admissions**: 369 **Census**: 23 **Outpatient Visits**: 0 **Births**: 0 **Total Expense ($000)**: 14893 **Payroll Expense ($000)**: 7034 **Personnel**: 78

PRESBYTERIAN HOSPITAL See Presbyterian Tower

PRESBYTERIAN TOWER See OU Health – University of Oklahoma Medical Center, Oklahoma City

✱ **SELECT SPECIALTY HOSPITAL–OKLAHOMA CITY (372009)**, 3524 NW 56th Street, Zip 73112-4518; tel. 405/606-6700, (Nonreporting) **A**1 10 **S** Select Medical Corporation, Mechanicsburg, PA
Primary Contact: Kelly Duke, Chief Executive Officer
CNO: Lieutenant Autumn Pulis, Chief Nursing Officer
Web address: https://oklahomacity.selectspecialtyhospitals.com/
Control: Corporation, Investor-owned (for-profit) **Service**: Acute long-term care hospital

Staffed Beds: 72

✱ **SSM HEALTH ST. ANTHONY HOSPITAL – OKLAHOMA CITY (370037)**, 1000 North Lee Street, Zip 73102-1080, Mailing Address: P.O. Box 205, Zip 73101-0205; tel. 405/272-7000, (Includes SSM HEALTH BONE AND JOINT HOSPITAL AT ST. ANTHONY, 1111 North Dewey Avenue, Oklahoma City, Oklahoma, Zip 73103-2609, tel. 405/272-9671; Tammy Powell, FACHE, M.P.H., President; SSM HEALTH ST. ANTHONY SOUTH, 2129 SW 59th Street, Oklahoma City, Oklahoma, Zip 73119-7001, tel. 405/713-5700) **A**1 2 3 5 10 12 13 **F**3 4 5 7 8 11 12 13 15 17 18 20 22 24 26 28 30 31 34 35 36 37 38 40 42 43 45 46 47 48 49 50 54 56 57 58 59 64 70 71 72 74 76 77 78 79 81 82 84 85 86 87 90 91 92 93 96 97 98 99 100 101 102 103 104 105 106 107 108 110 111 114 115 118 119 120 121 123 124 126 127 129 130 131 132 144 146 147 148 149 152 153 154 167 **P**4 **S** SSM Health, Saint Louis, MO
Primary Contact: Tammy Powell, FACHE, M.P.H., President
COO: Marti Jourden, FACHE, Chief Quality Officer
CFO: Shasta Manuel, Executive Director Finance
CMO: Kersey Winfree, M.D., Chief Medical Officer
CIO: Kevin Olson, Director Information Systems
CHR: Cynthia Brundise, Vice President Human Resources
Web address: www.saintsok.com
Control: Church operated, Nongovernment, not-for-profit **Service**: General medical and surgical

Staffed Beds: 638 **Admissions**: 21564 **Census**: 388 **Outpatient Visits**: 273547 **Births**: 1167 **Total Expense ($000)**: 703580 **Payroll Expense ($000)**: 206590 **Personnel**: 2291

ST. ANTHONY SOUTH See SSM Health St. Anthony South

Hospitals, U.S. / OKLAHOMA

SURGICAL HOSPITAL OF OKLAHOMA (370201), 100 SE 59th Street, Zip 73129–3616; tel. 405/634–9300, (Nonreporting) **A**3 5 10 22
Primary Contact: Mike Kimzey, Chief Executive Officer
CNO: Cindy Ridge Braly, MAAL, R.N., Chief Nursing Officer
Web address: https://surgicalhospitalok.com/
Control: Partnership, Investor–owned (for–profit) **Service:** Other specialty treatment

Staffed Beds: 12

UNIVERSITY EVERETT TOWER See Everett Tower

VALIR REHABILITATION HOSPITAL (373025), 700 NW Seventh Street, Zip 73102–1212; tel. 405/236–3131, (Nonreporting) **A**1 10
Primary Contact: Joshua Kurtzig, Interim President
COO: Andy Marlette, Chief Operating Officer
CFO: Scott Brown, Chief Financial Officer
CMO: Tonya Washburn, M.D., Medical Director
CIO: Mark Dickey, Director Business Development
CHR: Bill Turner, Vice President Human Resources
Web address: www.valir.com
Control: Corporation, Investor–owned (for–profit) **Service:** Rehabilitation

Staffed Beds: 50

OKMULGEE—Okmulgee County

★ ⇑ **MUSCOGEE CREEK NATION MEDICAL CENTER (370057)**, 1401 Morris Drive, Zip 74447–6429, Mailing Address: P.O. Box 1038, Zip 74447–1038; tel. 918/756–4233, (Nonreporting) **A**3 5 10 21
Primary Contact: Tim Hicks, Administrator
CFO: John W Crawford, Chief Financial Officer
CMO: Michael Sandlin, M.D., Chief of Staff
CHR: Stacey R. Burton, Director Human Resources
Web address: www.creekhealth.org/
Control: Other not–for–profit (including NFP Corporation) **Service:** General medical and surgical

Staffed Beds: 45

⇑ **MUSCOGEE CREEK NATION PHYSICAL REHABILITATION CENTER (372023)**, 1401 Morris Drive, Zip 74447–6429, Mailing Address: P.O. Box 1038, Zip 74447–1938; tel. 918/756–4233, (Nonreporting) **A**10 21
Primary Contact: Tim Hicks, Administrator
Control: Other not–for–profit (including NFP Corporation) **Service:** Acute long–term care hospital

Staffed Beds: 4

OWASSO—Tulsa County

ASCENSION ST. JOHN OWASSO (370227), 12451 East 100th Street North, Zip 74055–4600; tel. 918/274–5000, (Nonreporting) **A**1 10 **S** Ascension Healthcare, Saint Louis, MO
Primary Contact: Mark Clay, President
CFO: Katie Caughman, Chief Financial Officer
CMO: Tim Hepner, M.D., Chief Medical Officer
CIO: Mike Reeves, Chief Information Officer
CNO: Dan Hall, R.N., Chief Operating Officer
Web address: www.stjohnowasso.com
Control: Church operated, Nongovernment, not–for–profit **Service:** General medical and surgical

Staffed Beds: 36

ASCENSION ST. JOHN REHABILITATION HOSPITAL, AN AFFILIATE OF ENCOMPASS HEALTH – OWASSO (373039), 13402 E 86th Street North, Zip 74055–8767; tel. 918/401–3100, (Nonreporting) **S** Encompass Health Corporation, Birmingham, AL
Primary Contact: Harlo McCall, Chief Executive Officer
Web address: https://encompasshealth.com/locations/stjohnrehab-owasso
Control: Corporation, Investor–owned (for–profit) **Service:** Rehabilitation

Staffed Beds: 40

★ ⇑ **BAILEY MEDICAL CENTER (370228)**, 10502 North 110th East Avenue, Zip 74055–6655; tel. 918/376–8000, **A**3 10 21 **F**3 12 13 15 18 29 34 40 45 51 57 64 70 75 76 77 79 81 82 85 93 107 108 110 111 115 119 129 132 146 147 149 154 **S** Ardent Health Services, Nashville, TN
Primary Contact: Scott Lasson, Chief Executive Officer
CFO: Carol Barlow, Chief Financial Officer
CHR: Tandy Groves, Director Human Resources
CNO: Ruby Triplett, Chief Nursing Officer
Web address: www.baileymedicalcenter.com
Control: Corporation, Investor–owned (for–profit) **Service:** General medical and surgical

Staffed Beds: 46 **Admissions:** 1625 **Census:** 10 **Outpatient Visits:** 46550
Births: 644 **Total Expense ($000):** 47934 **Payroll Expense ($000):** 16585
Personnel: 231

ST. JOHN OWASSO See Ascension St. John Owasso

PAULS VALLEY—Garvin County

○ **VALLEY COMMUNITY HOSPITAL (370243)**, 100 Valley Drive, Zip 73075–6613; tel. 405/866–5100, (Nonreporting) **A**10 11
Primary Contact: Cathy Hatton, Interim Chief Hospital Executive
COO: Kinzie Kelley, Chief Operating Officer
CFO: Richard Mathis, Chief Executive Officer
CHR: Val Cothern, Chief Human Resources Officer
Web address: https://spmcghospital.com/
Control: Corporation, Investor–owned (for–profit) **Service:** General medical and surgical

Staffed Beds: 43

PAWHUSKA—Osage County

PAWHUSKA HOSPITAL (371309), 1101 East 15th Street, Zip 74056–1920; tel. 918/287–3232, **A**10 18 **F**2 29 34 35 40 54 57 59 60 64 65 68 77 85 93 97 100 102 107 115 119 127 128 133 148 154 **P**6
Primary Contact: Jason McBride, Chief Executive Officer
CMO: Mike Priest, M.D., Chief of Staff
Web address: https://pawhuskahospital.com/
Control: State, Government, Nonfederal **Service:** General medical and surgical

Staffed Beds: 25 **Admissions:** 297 **Census:** 13 **Outpatient Visits:** 16414
Births: 0 **Total Expense ($000):** 20166 **Payroll Expense ($000):** 7633
Personnel: 107

PERRY—Noble County

★ **STILLWATER MEDICAL PERRY (370779)**, 501 North 14th Street, Zip 73077–5099; tel. 580/336–3541, **A**10 **F**3 11 15 28 29 40 59 81 93 97 107 114 127 146 154
Primary Contact: Courtney Kozikuski, President & Chief Financial Officer
CFO: Courtney Kozikuski, Chief Financial Officer
CMO: Michael Hartwig, M.D., Esq, Chief of Staff
CIO: Jeff Ware, Information Technology Support Technician
CHR: Deb Ellis, Director Human Resources
Web address: https://www.stillwater-medical.org/locations/stillwater-medical-perry
Control: Hospital district or authority, Government, Nonfederal

Staffed Beds: 6 **Admissions:** 1 **Census:** 1 **Outpatient Visits:** 12650
Births: 0 **Total Expense ($000):** 6625 **Payroll Expense ($000):** 2935
Personnel: 45

PONCA CITY—Kay County

INTEGRIS HEALTH PONCA CITY HOSPITAL (370006), 1900 North 14th Street, Zip 74601–2099; tel. 580/765–3321, (Data for 302 days) **A**1 10 **F**3 13 15 18 28 29 30 34 40 43 45 46 50 51 53 57 59 64 70 75 76 79 81 82 85 87 89 93 107 108 110 111 115 119 127 133 146 147 148 149 154 164 167 169 **S** INTEGRIS Health, Oklahoma City, OK
Primary Contact: Christopher Mendoza, Chief Executive Officer
CFO: Sheryl Schmidtberger, Chief Financial Officer
CIO: William Gazaway, Information Technology Security Officer
CHR: Calvin Hodges, Director Human Resources
CNO: Jeanne Stara, R.N., MSN, Chief Nursing Officer
Web address: https://integrisok.com/locations/hospital/ponca-city-hospital
Control: Corporation, Investor–owned (for–profit) **Service:** General medical and surgical

Staffed Beds: 41 **Admissions:** 1691 **Census:** 21 **Outpatient Visits:** 42211
Births: 307 **Total Expense ($000):** 39742 **Payroll Expense ($000):** 12908
Personnel: 246

Hospital, Medicare Provider Number, Address, Telephone, Approval, Facility, and Physician Codes, Health Care System

★ American Hospital Association (AHA) membership ○ Healthcare Facilities Accreditation Program ⇑ Center for Improvement in Healthcare Quality Accreditation
□ The Joint Commission accreditation ◇ DNV Healthcare Inc. accreditation △ Commission on Accreditation of Rehabilitation Facilities (CARF) accreditation

Hospitals, U.S. / OKLAHOMA

POTEAU—Le Flore County

EASTERN OKLAHOMA MEDICAL CENTER (371337), 105 Wall Street, Zip 74953-4433, Mailing Address: P.O. Box 1148, Zip 74953-1148; tel. 918/647-8161, (Nonreporting) **A**10 18
Primary Contact: Tiffany Griffis, Chief Executive Officer
CFO: Shaun Keef, Chief Financial Officer
CMO: Dennis Carter, M.D., Chief of Staff
CIO: Michael C Huggins, Administrator Network System
Web address: www.eomchospital.com
Control: County, Government, Nonfederal **Service:** General medical and surgical

Staffed Beds: 25

PRAGUE—Lincoln County

PRAGUE COMMUNITY HOSPITAL See Prague Regional Memorial Hospital

PRAGUE REGIONAL MEMORIAL HOSPITAL (371301), 1322 Klabzuba Avenue, Zip 74864-9005, Mailing Address: P.O. Box S, Zip 74864-1090; tel. 405/567-4922, (Nonreporting) **A**10 18
Primary Contact: Cheryl Watts, Administrator
COO: Jamal Bandeh, Chief Operating Officer
CFO: Doug Erickson, Chief Financial Officer
CMO: Darryl Jackson, D.O., Chief of Staff
CIO: Rhonda Whitnum, Director Health Improvement Management
CHR: Angie Brezny, Director Human Resources
Web address: https://prague.hospital/
Control: Other not-for-profit (including NFP Corporation) **Service:** General medical and surgical

Staffed Beds: 25

PRYOR—Mayes County

★ ⇑ **HILLCREST HOSPITAL PRYOR (370015)**, 111 North Bailey Street, Zip 74361-4201; tel. 918/825-1600, **A**10 21 **F**3 8 11 15 18 26 29 30 34 35 40 45 50 59 64 65 74 75 77 79 81 82 85 86 87 93 107 108 110 111 114 119 127 131 135 146 147 148 149 154 **S** Ardent Health Services, Nashville, TN
Primary Contact: Jason L. Jones, R.N., Chief Executive Officer
CMO: Jason Joice, M.D., Chief Medical Staff
CHR: Pamela A Guthrie, Chief Human Resources Officer
CNO: Mary Ozment, Chief Nursing Officer
Web address: www.hillcrestpryor.com/
Control: Corporation, Investor-owned (for-profit) **Service:** General medical and surgical

Staffed Beds: 21 **Admissions:** 450 **Census:** 7 **Outpatient Visits:** 34829
Births: 0 **Total Expense ($000):** 23783 **Payroll Expense ($000):** 8339
Personnel: 136

PURCELL—McClain County

PURCELL MUNICIPAL HOSPITAL (370158), 1500 North Green Avenue, Zip 73080-1699, Mailing Address: P.O. Box 511, Zip 73080-0511; tel. 405/527-6524, **A**10 **F**3 11 35 40 45 48 59 64 75 81 86 87 107 119 135 154
Primary Contact: Chris Wright, Chief Executive Officer and Chief Nursing Officer
CFO: Mary Morris, Chief Financial Officer
CMO: David Bryan Dye, M.D., Chief Medical Officer
CIO: Jennifer Coates, Coordinator Information Technology
CHR: Tara Selfridge, Manager Human Resources
CNO: Chris Wright, Chief Executive Officer and Chief Nursing Officer
Web address: www.purcellhospital.com
Control: City, Government, Nonfederal **Service:** General medical and surgical

Staffed Beds: 10 **Admissions:** 256 **Census:** 2 **Outpatient Visits:** 24280
Births: 0 **Total Expense ($000):** 12117 **Payroll Expense ($000):** 3876
Personnel: 79

SALLISAW—Sequoyah County

NORTHEASTERN HEALTH SYSTEM SEQUOYAH (370112), 213 East Redwood Street, Zip 74955-2811, Mailing Address: P.O. Box 505, Zip 74955-0505; tel. 918/774-1100, (Nonreporting) **A**10
Primary Contact: Stephanie Six, Chief Executive Officer
CMO: Jennifer Scoufos, M.D., Chief of Staff
CIO: Gary McClanahan, Chief Information Officer
CHR: Shayna Brooke Roberts, Director Human Resources
CNO: Ozalina Martinez, R.N., Director of Nursing
Web address: https://www.pmtc.ok.gov/sequoyah-memorial-hospital-sallisaw-ok
Control: Hospital district or authority, Government, Nonfederal **Service:** General medical and surgical

Staffed Beds: 41

SAPULPA—Creek County

★ **ASCENSION ST. JOHN SAPULPA (371312)**, 1004 East Bryan Avenue, Zip 74066-4513, Mailing Address: P.O. Box 1368, Zip 74067-1368; tel. 918/224-4280, **A**10 18 **F**3 11 15 28 29 30 34 35 38 40 42 45 48 50 54 56 57 59 64 65 68 75 77 81 87 91 93 94 107 110 111 115 119 126 128 130 133 146 147 148 149 150 153 154 **S** Ascension Healthcare, Saint Louis, MO
Primary Contact: Michael Christian, President
COO: Michael Christian, President
CFO: John W Crawford, Chief Financial Officer
CMO: Jason Lepak, M.D., Medical Director
CNO: Kelly Johnson, R.N., Chief Nursing Officer
Web address: www.stjohnhealthsystem.com/sapulpa
Control: Church operated, Nongovernment, not-for-profit **Service:** General medical and surgical

Staffed Beds: 25 **Admissions:** 525 **Census:** 11 **Outpatient Visits:** 29806
Births: 0 **Total Expense ($000):** 26363 **Payroll Expense ($000):** 8977

ST. JOHN SAPULPA See Ascension St. John Sapulpa

SEILING—Dewey County

SEILING MUNICIPAL HOSPITAL (371332), Highway 60 NE, Zip 73663, Mailing Address: P.O. Box 720, Zip 73663-0720; tel. 580/922-7361, **A**10 18 **F**29 40 93 97 107 114 122 127 128 133
Primary Contact: Rachel Farrow, Administrator
CFO: Nancy Freed, Chief Financial Officer
CMO: Kenneth Duffy, M.D., Medical Director
CHR: Sandy Landreth, Director Human Resources
Web address: www.seilingmunicipalhospital.org/
Control: City, Government, Nonfederal **Service:** General medical and surgical

Staffed Beds: 18 **Admissions:** 174 **Census:** 7 **Outpatient Visits:** 3552
Births: 0

SHATTUCK—Ellis County

NEWMAN MEMORIAL HOSPITAL (371336), 905 South Main Street, Zip 73858-9205; tel. 580/938-2551, (Nonreporting) **A**10 18
Primary Contact: Tom Vasko, Chief Executive Officer
CFO: Steve Brock, Chief Financial Officer
CMO: Danna Stuart, M.D., Chief Medical Officer
CIO: Robert Neal, Manager Information Technology Services
Web address: www.newmanmemorialhospital.org
Control: Other not-for-profit (including NFP Corporation) **Service:** General medical and surgical

Staffed Beds: 25

SHAWNEE—Pottawatomie County

★ **CORNERSTONE SPECIALTY HOSPITALS SHAWNEE (372019)**, 1900 Gordon Cooper Drive, 2nd Floor, Zip 74801-8603, Mailing Address: P.O. Box 1245, Zip 74802-1245; tel. 405/395-5800, (Nonreporting) **A**10 22 **S** ScionHealth, Louisville, KY
Primary Contact: Larissa Trulson, Chief Executive Officer
CMO: Rakesh Shrivastava, M.D., Chief Medical Officer
Web address: www.chghospitals.com/shawnee/
Control: Corporation, Investor-owned (for-profit) **Service:** Acute long-term care hospital

Staffed Beds: 34

SSM HEALTH ST. ANTHONY HOSPITAL – SHAWNEE (370149), 1102 West MacArthur Street, Zip 74804-1744; tel. 405/273-2270, (Includes ALLIANCEHEALTH SEMINOLE, 2401 Wrangler Boulevard, Seminole, Oklahoma, Zip 74868-1917, tel. 405/303-4000; Michael J. Ellis, FACHE, Chief Executive Officer) **A**1 10 19 **F**3 10 11 13 15 18 20 22 29 30 31 34 35 40 43 45 50 57 59 60 62 64 65 68 69 70 76 77 78 79 81 82 84 86 87 94 107 110 111 114 115 116 117 119 120 121 123 129 130 131 132 135 146 147 148 167 168 169 **P**6 **S** SSM Health, Saint Louis, MO
Primary Contact: Angela Mohr, R.N., MS, President
CFO: Jennifer Pierce, Administrative Director of Finance
CMO: Jason Chung, M.D., Vice President, Medical Affairs and Chief Medical Officer
CHR: Michael Spears, Human Resource Leader
Web address: https://www.ssmhealth.com/locations/st-anthony-shawnee-hospital
Control: Other not-for-profit (including NFP Corporation) **Service:** General medical and surgical

Staffed Beds: 70 **Admissions:** 4455 **Census:** 38 **Outpatient Visits:** 84767
Births: 803 **Total Expense ($000):** 124381 **Payroll Expense ($000):** 36934
Personnel: 395

SPENCER—Oklahoma County

INTEGRIS MENTAL HEALTH SYSTEM–SPENCER See Integris Baptist Medical Center, Oklahoma City

WILLOW VIEW MENTAL HLTH SYSTEM See Integris Mental Health System–Spencer

STIGLER—Haskell County

HASKELL REGIONAL HOSPITAL (371335), 401 Northwest 'H' Street, Zip 74462–1625; tel. 918/615-2150, (Nonreporting) **A**10 18
Primary Contact: Michael Gerten, Chief Executive Officer
CMO: Stephen Woodson, D.O., Chief of Staff
CIO: Steve Hurst, Information Technology Specialist
Web address: https://haskellregionalhospital.com/
Control: Other not–for–profit (including NFP Corporation) **Service**: General medical and surgical

Staffed Beds: 20

STILLWATER—Payne County

★ ⇧ **STILLWATER MEDICAL CENTER (370049)**, 1323 West Sixth Avenue, Zip 74074–4399, Mailing Address: P.O. Box 2408, Zip 74076–2408; tel. 405/372-1480, **A**3 10 21 **F**3 13 15 18 20 22 26 28 29 31 32 34 35 37 40 43 44 45 50 53 54 55 59 62 63 64 65 68 70 74 75 76 77 78 79 81 82 85 86 87 89 90 91 92 93 97 100 104 107 108 110 111 115 117 118 119 120 121 124 126 127 130 131 132 135 144 146 147 148 149 154 156 157 160 165 169
Primary Contact: Denise Webber, President and Chief Executive Officer
CFO: Alan Lovelace, Vice President and Chief Financial Officer
CMO: Steve Cummings, M.D., Chief of Medical Staff
CIO: Chris Roark, Chief Information Officer
CHR: Keith Hufnagel, Director Human Resources
CNO: Elizabeth Michael, R.N., MS, Vice President Patient Care Services and Chief Nursing Officer
Web address: www.stillwater-medical.org
Control: Hospital district or authority, Government, Nonfederal **Service**: General medical and surgical

Staffed Beds: 100 **Admissions:** 4731 **Census:** 54 **Outpatient Visits:** 158052 **Births:** 659 **Total Expense ($000):** 297377 **Payroll Expense ($000):** 127058 **Personnel:** 1505

STILWELL—Adair County

MEMORIAL HOSPITAL OF STILWELL (370178), 1401 West Locust, Zip 74960–3275, Mailing Address: P.O. Box 272, Zip 74960–0272; tel. 918/696-3101, (Nonreporting) **A**10
Primary Contact: Jim Causon, President and Chief Executive Officer
COO: Brandy Smith, R.N., Chief Operations Officer
Web address: www.stilwellmemorialhospital.com
Control: Other not–for–profit (including NFP Corporation) **Service**: General medical and surgical

Staffed Beds: 34

STROUD—Lincoln County

RURAL WELLNESS STROUD (371316), Highway 66 West, Zip 74079, Mailing Address: P.O. Box 530, Zip 74079–0530; tel. 918/968-3571, (Nonreporting) **A**10 18
CFO: Richard E Rentsch, President
CMO: Ken Darvin, M.D., Chief of Staff
CIO: Donna Buchanan, Director of Nursing
CHR: Leannette Raffety, Administrative Generalist
Web address: www.stroudhospital.com/
Control: Other not–for–profit (including NFP Corporation) **Service**: General medical and surgical

Staffed Beds: 24

SULPHUR—Murray County

★ **ARBUCKLE MEMORIAL HOSPITAL (371328)**, 2011 West Broadway Street, Zip 73086–4221, Mailing Address: P.O. Box 1109, Zip 73086–8109; tel. 580/622-2161, (Nonreporting) **A**10 18 **S** Mercy, Chesterfield, MO
Primary Contact: Jeremy A. Jones, Administrator
CFO: Denise Welch, Chief Financial Officer
CMO: Ryan Oden, D.O., Chief of Staff
CIO: Tiffany Sands, Manager Health Information
CHR: Sallie Tomlinson, Manager Human Resources
CNO: Sarah Freehill, Chief Nursing Officer
Web address: www.arbucklehospital.com/
Control: County, Government, Nonfederal **Service**: General medical and surgical

Staffed Beds: 17

TAHLEQUAH—Cherokee County

★ ⇧ **CHEROKEE NATION W.W. HASTINGS HOSPITAL (370171)**, W.W. Hastings Hospital, Zip 74464–2512, Mailing Address: 100 South Bliss Avenue, Zip 74464–2512; tel. 918/458-3100, (Nonreporting) **A**3 5 10 21
Primary Contact: Cindy Jo. Martin, Senior Hospital Administrator
COO: Mitchell Thornbrugh, Administrative Officer
CMO: Douglas Nolan, M.D., Medical Director
CIO: Mitchell Thornbrugh, Acting Chief Information Officer
CNO: Valerie J Rogers, Director of Nursing
Web address: https://health.cherokee.org/health-center-and-hospital-locations/inpatient-care/
Control: Public Health Service other than 47, Government, federal **Service**: General medical and surgical

Staffed Beds: 58

★ **NORTHEASTERN HEALTH SYSTEM (370089)**, 1400 East Downing Street, Zip 74464–3324, Mailing Address: P.O. Box 1008, Zip 74465–1008; tel. 918/456-0641, **A**3 5 10 13 20 **F**3 5 7 11 13 15 17 28 29 31 34 35 40 43 45 46 47 48 49 50 51 54 56 57 59 64 65 70 74 75 76 77 78 79 81 82 85 93 97 98 103 107 108 110 111 115 117 119 120 121 123 127 130 131 132 133 144 146 147 149 154 160 167 **P**4 5 7
Primary Contact: James T. Berry, FACHE, Chief Executive Officer
COO: Mark McCroskey, Vice President Operations
CFO: Julie Ward, Vice President Finance
CIO: Julie Ward, Vice President Finance
CHR: Phyllis Smith, Vice President Human Resources
CNO: Donna Dallis, R.N., Vice President Patient Care
Web address: www.nhs-ok.org/
Control: City, Government, Nonfederal **Service**: General medical and surgical

Staffed Beds: 72 **Admissions:** 3778 **Census:** 46 **Outpatient Visits:** 157118 **Births:** 226 **Total Expense ($000):** 150616 **Payroll Expense ($000):** 52984 **Personnel:** 1049

TALIHINA—Latimer County

✚ **CHOCTAW NATION HEALTH CARE CENTER (370172)**, 1 Choctaw Way, Zip 74571–2022; tel. 918/567-7000, (Nonreporting) **A**1 3 10 13
Primary Contact: Todd Hallmark, Executive Officer of Health Operations
COO: Todd Hallmark, Executive Officer of Health Operations
CMO: Jason Hill, M.D., Chief Medical Officer
CIO: Dwane Sorrells, Chief Information Officer
CHR: Jami Beckwith, Director Human Resources
CNO: Lisa Isaac, Chief Nursing Officer
Web address: www.cnhsa.com
Control: Other not–for–profit (including NFP Corporation) **Service**: General medical and surgical

Staffed Beds: 44

TISHOMINGO—Johnston County

★ **MERCY HOSPITAL TISHOMINGO (371304)**, 1000 South Byrd Street, Zip 73460–3299; tel. 580/371-2327, **A**10 18 **F**3 11 29 34 40 43 50 59 64 68 107 114 133 135 143 146 148 154 156 **S** Mercy, Chesterfield, MO
Primary Contact: Lori McMillin, Administrator
CFO: Lisa Dowling, Manager Finance
CHR: Arlita Hummelke, Manager Human Resources
Web address: www.mercy.net/
Control: Church operated, Nongovernment, not–for–profit **Service**: General medical and surgical

Staffed Beds: 12 **Admissions:** 213 **Census:** 7 **Outpatient Visits:** 5988 **Births:** 0 **Total Expense ($000):** 8940 **Payroll Expense ($000):** 5586 **Personnel:** 53

Hospital, Medicare Provider Number, Address, Telephone, Approval, Facility, and Physician Codes, Health Care System

★ American Hospital Association (AHA) membership ○ Healthcare Facilities Accreditation Program ⇧ Center for Improvement in Healthcare Quality Accreditation
□ The Joint Commission accreditation ◇ DNV Healthcare Inc. accreditation △ Commission on Accreditation of Rehabilitation Facilities (CARF) accreditation

Hospitals, U.S. / OKLAHOMA

TULSA—Tulsa County

☒ **ASCENSION ST. JOHN MEDICAL CENTER (370114)**, 1923 South Utica Avenue, Zip 74104-6502; tel. 918/744-2345, (Nonreporting) **A**1 2 3 5 10 19 **S** Ascension Healthcare, Saint Louis, MO
Primary Contact: Bo Beaudry, Chief Executive Officer
CFO: Wayne Walthall, Vice President and Chief Financial Officer
CMO: William Allred, M.D., Vice President Medical Affairs
CIO: Mike Reeves, Vice President
CHR: John Page Bachman, Corporate Vice President
CNO: Pamela Kiser, R.N., MS, Chief Nursing Executive and Vice President of Nursing
Web address: https://healthcare.ascension.org/Locations/Oklahoma/OKTUL/Tulsa-Ascension-St-John-Medical-Center
Control: Church operated, Nongovernment, not-for-profit **Service**: General medical and surgical

Staffed Beds: 523

△ **BROOKHAVEN HOSPITAL (374012)**, 201 South Garnett Road, Zip 74128-1805; tel. 918/438-4257, **A**7 10 **F**29 30 74 75 77 98 101 106 130 164
Primary Contact: Thomas W. Brown, Chief Executive Officer
CFO: Kenneth Pierce, Chief Financial Officer
CMO: Mark Gage, D.O., Medical Director
CHR: Heather Dudley, Director Administrative Services
CNO: Debbie Jones, Director of Nursing
Web address: www.brookhavenhospital.com
Control: Corporation, Investor-owned (for-profit) **Service**: Psychiatric

Staffed Beds: 64 **Admissions**: 22 **Census**: 52 **Outpatient Visits**: 0
Births: 0 **Total Expense ($000)**: 23888 **Payroll Expense ($000)**: 10595
Personnel: 145

⇑ **COUNCIL OAK COMPREHENSIVE HEALTHCARE (370244)**, 10109 East 79th Street, Zip 74133-4564; tel. 918/233-9550, (Nonreporting) **A**21
Primary Contact: Shawn Terry, Secretary of Health
COO: Tim Hicks, Chief Operating Officer, Hospital Services
CFO: Brenda Crawford, Chief Financial Officer
CMO: Joseph Cunningham, Chief Medical Officer
CIO: Brandy Russell, Technology and Analytics Officer
CHR: Jeremy W Smith, Director of Human Resources
CNO: Lindy Bauer, Chief Nursing Officer
Web address: www.creekhealth.org
Control: PHS, Indian Service, Government, federal **Service**: General medical and surgical

Staffed Beds: 40

★ ⇑ **HILLCREST HOSPITAL SOUTH (370202)**, 8801 South 101st East Avenue, Zip 74133-5716; tel. 918/294-4000, **A**3 10 19 21 **F**3 13 15 18 20 22 26 28 29 30 34 35 40 43 45 46 47 48 49 51 57 64 68 70 73 74 76 79 81 82 85 86 87 91 93 107 108 110 111 115 118 119 126 130 146 147 148 167 **S** Ardent Health Services, Nashville, TN
Primary Contact: Kevin J. Gross, FACHE, Interim Chief Executive Officer
COO: Matthew Morgan, Associate Administrator
CFO: Preshie Wilson, Chief Financial Officer
CMO: David L. Pohl, M.D., Chief of Staff
CIO: David Graser, Vice President and Chief Information Officer
CHR: Rachel Steward, Director Human Resources
CNO: Dava Baldridge, R.N., Chief Nursing Officer
Web address: https://hillcrestsouth.com/
Control: Corporation, Investor-owned (for-profit) **Service**: General medical and surgical

Staffed Beds: 175 **Admissions**: 10276 **Census**: 122 **Outpatient Visits**: 123474 **Births**: 1234 **Total Expense ($000)**: 208273 **Payroll Expense ($000)**: 70816 **Personnel**: 755

★ ⇑ **HILLCREST MEDICAL CENTER (370001)**, 1120 South Utica Avenue, Zip 74104-4090; tel. 918/579-1000, **A**3 5 10 19 21 **F**3 11 13 15 16 17 18 20 22 24 26 28 29 30 31 34 37 39 40 43 45 46 49 50 51 53 55 58 59 60 64 68 70 72 73 74 75 76 77 78 79 80 81 83 84 85 86 87 89 90 93 97 100 107 108 110 111 114 115 116 117 119 120 121 123 124 126 129 130 131 135 146 147 148 149 154 156 167 169 **S** Ardent Health Services, Nashville, TN
Primary Contact: Xavier Villarreal, FACHE, Chief Executive Officer
COO: Farron Sneed, Chief Operating Officer
CFO: Joseph Mendoza, Chief Financial Officer
CIO: Richard Gomez, Assistant Vice President Information Technology Division
CHR: Donald Morris, Vice President Human Resources
CNO: Jodi Simmons, Chief Nursing Officer
Web address: www.hillcrestmedicalcenter.com
Control: Corporation, Investor-owned (for-profit) **Service**: General medical and surgical

Staffed Beds: 496 **Admissions**: 21442 **Census**: 338 **Outpatient Visits**: 141532 **Births**: 2011 **Total Expense ($000)**: 613400 **Payroll Expense ($000)**: 165234 **Personnel**: 1769

☒ **LAUREATE PSYCHIATRIC CLINIC AND HOSPITAL (374020)**, 6655 South Yale Avenue, Zip 74136-3329; tel. 918/481-4000, **A**1 3 5 10 **F**4 5 98 99 100 101 102 103 104 105 106 146 151 152 153 160 162 164 165 **S** Saint Francis Health System, Tulsa, OK
Primary Contact: Kenneth Moore, President
CFO: Eric Schick, Senior Vice President, Chief Administrative Officer and Chief Financial Officer
CMO: Reeta Singh, M.D., Chief Medical Officer
Web address: www.laureate.com
Control: Other not-for-profit (including NFP Corporation) **Service**: Psychiatric

Staffed Beds: 90 **Admissions**: 3146 **Census**: 80 **Outpatient Visits**: 9502 **Births**: 0 **Total Expense ($000)**: 45520 **Payroll Expense ($000)**: 27533 **Personnel**: 390

★ ○ **OKLAHOMA STATE UNIVERSITY MEDICAL CENTER (370078)**, 744 West Ninth Street, Zip 74127-9020; tel. 918/599-1000, (Nonreporting) **A**3 5 8 10 11 12 13 19 **S** Saint Francis Health System, Tulsa, OK
Primary Contact: Finny Mathew, President
COO: Jeff Stroup, Chief Operating Officer
CFO: Sara Bradley, Chief Financial Officer
CMO: Damon Baker, D.O., Chief Medical Officer
CIO: Heidi Holmes, Chief Information Officer
Web address: www.osumc.com
Control: City, Government, Nonfederal **Service**: General medical and surgical

Staffed Beds: 118

○ **OKLAHOMA SURGICAL HOSPITAL (370210)**, 2408 East 81st Street, Suite 300, Zip 74137-4215; tel. 918/477-5000, **A**3 5 10 11 **F**3 12 18 20 22 24 26 29 30 37 40 44 45 46 49 50 51 58 64 65 68 70 74 75 77 79 81 82 85 86 87 93 107 108 111 115 118 119 120 121 123 126 130 131 148 149 154 164 167 **P**2
Primary Contact: Rick Ferguson, Chief Executive Officer
CFO: Dub Cleland, Chief Financial Officer
Web address: www.oklahomasurgicalhospital.com
Control: Corporation, Investor-owned (for-profit) **Service**: Surgical

Staffed Beds: 55 **Admissions**: 1840 **Census**: 12 **Outpatient Visits**: 37753 **Births**: 0 **Personnel**: 472

☒ **PAM HEALTH REHABILITATION HOSPITAL OF TULSA (373035)**, 10020 East 91st Street, Zip 74133; tel. 918/893-2400, **A**1 10 **F**3 29 60 64 74 87 90 93 94 95 96 97 148 154 156 167 168 **S** PAM Health, Enola, PA
Primary Contact: Audra Powell, Chief Executive Officer
Web address: www.warmsprings.org/our-facilities/outpatient-rehabilitation
Control: Corporation, Investor-owned (for-profit) **Service**: Rehabilitation

Staffed Beds: 53 **Admissions**: 1478 **Census**: 50 **Outpatient Visits**: 7533 **Births**: 0 **Total Expense ($000)**: 27353 **Payroll Expense ($000)**: 13691 **Personnel**: 197

☒ **PAM HEALTH SPECIALTY HOSPITAL OF TULSA (372018)**, 3219 South 79th East Avenue, Zip 74145-1343; tel. 918/663-8183, **A**1 10 **F**1 3 29 87 107 **P**1 **S** PAM Health, Enola, PA
Primary Contact: Karla Cody, Chief Executive Officer
Web address: www.postacutetulsa.com
Control: Corporation, Investor-owned (for-profit) **Service**: Acute long-term care hospital

Staffed Beds: 60 **Admissions**: 567 **Census**: 30 **Outpatient Visits**: 0 **Births**: 0 **Total Expense ($000)**: 19133 **Payroll Expense ($000)**: 9077 **Personnel**: 130

☐ **PARKSIDE PSYCHIATRIC HOSPITAL AND CLINIC (374021)**, 1619 East 13th Street, Zip 74120-5407; tel. 918/582-2131, (Nonreporting) **A**1 10
Primary Contact: Jim Serratt, Chief Executive Officer
CFO: Saunya Moore, Chief Financial Officer
CMO: Marvin Jin, M.D., Medical Director
CIO: Joe Vitali, Director Information Technology
CHR: David Patterson, Director Human Resources
Web address: www.parksideinc.org
Control: Other not-for-profit (including NFP Corporation) **Service**: Psychiatric

Staffed Beds: 120

POST ACUTE MEDICAL SPECIALTY HOSPITAL OF TULSA See Pam Health Specialty Hospital of Tulsa

SAINT FRANCIS HEART HOSPITAL See Saint Francis Hospital, Tulsa

Hospitals, U.S. / OKLAHOMA

☒ **SAINT FRANCIS HOSPITAL (370091)**, 6161 South Yale Avenue, Zip 74136–1902; tel. 918/494–2200, (Includes CHILDREN'S HOSPITAL AT SAINT FRANCIS, 6161 S Yale Ave, Tulsa, Oklahoma, Zip 74136–1902, 6161 South Yale Avenue, Zip 74136–1902, tel. 918/502–6714; Shannon M. Filosa, Executive Director Women's and Children; SAINT FRANCIS HEART HOSPITAL, 6151 South Yale Avenue, Tulsa, Oklahoma, Zip 74136–1902, tel. 918/494–1817; Douglas Williams, Vice President, Saint Francis Heart Hospital) **A**1 2 3 5 10 19 **F**3 7 8 11 12 13 15 17 18 19 20 21 22 23 24 25 26 27 28 29 30 31 32 34 35 37 38 39 40 41 43 44 45 46 47 48 49 50 51 54 55 56 57 58 59 60 61 62 63 64 66 68 70 72 73 74 75 76 77 78 79 80 81 82 83 84 85 86 87 88 89 90 92 93 95 100 102 107 108 110 111 114 115 116 117 118 119 120 121 123 124 126 128 129 130 131 132 135 136 146 147 148 149 154 156 164 167 169 **P**6 **S** Saint Francis Health System, Tulsa, OK
Primary Contact: Douglas Williams, President
COO: Barry L Steichen, Executive Vice President and Chief Operating Officer, Saint Francis Health System
CFO: Eric Schick, Senior Vice President and Chief Financial Officer, Saint Francis Health System
CMO: Reeta Singh, M.D., Chief Medical Officer
CIO: Meridith Coburn, Vice President Information Services
Web address: www.saintfrancis.com
Control: Other not–for–profit (including NFP Corporation) **Service**: General medical and surgical

Staffed Beds: 910 **Admissions**: 47374 **Census**: 711 **Outpatient Visits**: 535867 **Births**: 4179 **Total Expense ($000)**: 1244519 **Payroll Expense ($000)**: 501549 **Personnel**: 5085

☒ **SAINT FRANCIS HOSPITAL SOUTH (370218)**, 10501 East 91st Street, Zip 74133–5790; tel. 918/307–6010, **A**1 3 10 **F**11 13 15 18 20 22 26 29 30 34 35 37 39 40 42 43 44 48 49 50 51 57 58 60 61 64 68 70 72 75 76 79 80 81 82 85 87 107 108 110 111 114 115 118 119 130 146 148 154 164 **S** Saint Francis Health System, Tulsa, OK
Primary Contact: Todd Schuster, President
COO: Barry L Steichen, Executive Vice President and Chief Operating Officer
CFO: Eric Schick, Chief Financial Officer
CMO: Reeta Singh, M.D., Chief Medical Officer
CIO: Meridith Coburn, Vice President, Information Systems
Web address: www.saintfrancis.com/south/
Control: Other not–for–profit (including NFP Corporation) **Service**: General medical and surgical

Staffed Beds: 110 **Admissions**: 6816 **Census**: 69 **Births**: 888 **Total Expense ($000)**: 128674 **Payroll Expense ($000)**: 54953 **Personnel**: 511

☒ **SELECT SPECIALTY HOSPITAL–TULSA MIDTOWN (372007)**, 744 West 9th Street, 5th Floor, Zip 74127–9907; tel. 918/579–7300, (Nonreporting) **A**1 10 **S** Select Medical Corporation, Mechanicsburg, PA
Primary Contact: Janette Daniels, Chief Executive Officer
CMO: E Joe Schelbar, M.D., Medical Director
CNO: Connie Ryan, Chief Nursing Officer
Web address: www.tulsa.selectspecialtyhospitals.com/
Control: Corporation, Investor–owned (for–profit) **Service**: Acute long–term care hospital

Staffed Beds: 52

THE CHILDREN'S HOSPITAL AT SAINT FRANCIS See Children's Hospital At Saint Francis

☐ **TULSA CENTER FOR BEHAVIORAL HEALTH (374026)**, 2323 South Harvard Ave, Zip 74114–3301; tel. 918/293–2140, (Nonreporting) **A**1 3 5 10
Primary Contact: Autumn Jesse. Nickelson, Executive Director
Web address: https://www.ok.gov/odmhsas/
Control: State, Government, Nonfederal **Service**: Psychiatric

Staffed Beds: 56

TULSA ER & HOSPITAL, 717 West 71st Street, Zip 74132–1824; tel. 918/517–6300, (Nonreporting) **A**22
Primary Contact: Mark Blubaugh, D.O., Medical Director
Web address: https://tulsaer.com/
Control: Partnership, Investor–owned (for–profit) **Service**: General medical and surgical

Staffed Beds: 8

TULSA REHABILITATION HOSPITAL (373037), 7909 South 101st East Avenue, Zip 74133; tel. 918/820–3499, (Nonreporting) **A**10 **S** Nobis Rehabilitation Partners, Allen, TX
Primary Contact: Ian Cooper, Chief Executive Officer
Web address: https://www.tulsa-rehabhospital.com/
Control: Corporation, Investor–owned (for–profit) **Service**: Rehabilitation

Staffed Beds: 40

☒ **TULSA SPINE AND SPECIALTY HOSPITAL (370216)**, 6901 South Olympia Avenue, Zip 74132–1843; tel. 918/388–5701, (Nonreporting) **A**1 3 5 10 **S** Ardent Health Services, Nashville, TN
Primary Contact: Trent Gastineau, Chief Executive Officer
CMO: David Fell, M.D., Chief Medical Officer
Web address: www.tulsaspinehospital.com
Control: Corporation, Investor–owned (for–profit) **Service**: General medical and surgical

Staffed Beds: 38

VINITA—Craig County

OKLAHOMA FORENSIC CENTER, 24800 South 4420 Road, Zip 74301–5544, Mailing Address: P.O. Box 69, Zip 74301–0069; tel. 918/256–7841, **A**3 **F**75 98 100 130 143 154 163 164 **S** Oklahoma Department of Mental Health and Substance Abuse Services, Oklahoma City, OK
Primary Contact: Debbie Moran, Executive Director
CFO: Miriam Harris, Director Finance
CMO: Satwant Tandon, M.D., Director of Clinical Services
CIO: Kevin Marble, Director Information Technology
CHR: Julie Jacobs, Director Human Resources
CNO: Glenda Satterwhite, Director of Nursing
Web address: www.odmhsas.org
Control: State, Government, Nonfederal **Service**: Psychiatric

Staffed Beds: 216 **Admissions**: 210 **Census**: 214 **Outpatient Visits**: 0 **Births**: 0 **Total Expense ($000)**: 22163 **Payroll Expense ($000)**: 11505 **Personnel**: 262

★ ⇑ **SAINT FRANCIS HOSPITAL VINITA (370237)**, 735 North Foreman Street, Zip 74301–1418; tel. 918/256–7551, **A**10 21 **F**3 11 15 18 26 27 28 29 30 34 35 36 40 41 43 45 50 59 64 65 68 74 75 76 77 79 80 82 86 87 93 94 97 98 100 102 103 104 107 108 111 114 115 119 127 129 130 133 143 146 147 148 149 154 160 164 165 **P**6 **S** Saint Francis Health System, Tulsa, OK
Primary Contact: Melinda Culp, Executive Director, Administrator
CMO: Ed Allensworth, M.D., Medical Director
CHR: Darlene R Nolte, Chief Human Resource Officer
CNO: Ann Carr, R.N., Chief Nursing Officer
Web address: https://www.saintfrancis.com/vinita/Pages/default.aspx
Control: Other not–for–profit (including NFP Corporation) **Service**: General medical and surgical

Staffed Beds: 27 **Admissions**: 1218 **Census**: 19 **Outpatient Visits**: 39257 **Births**: 0 **Total Expense ($000)**: 22929 **Payroll Expense ($000)**: 11139 **Personnel**: 125

WAGONER—Wagoner County

WAGONER COMMUNITY HOSPITAL (370166), 1200 West Cherokee Street, Zip 74467–4624, Mailing Address: P.O. Box 407, Zip 74477–0407; tel. 918/485–5514, **A**3 10 **F**3 11 15 18 28 29 34 39 40 41 45 50 51 56 57 59 64 65 70 74 75 79 81 82 85 87 93 98 100 102 107 108 110 111 115 118 119 129 130 131 132 135 146 149 154 156 157
Primary Contact: Jimmy Leopard, FACHE, Chief Executive Officer
COO: Louise Dodson, R.N., Chief Operating Officer and Chief Nursing Officer
CFO: Rebecca Sharp, Chief Financial Officer
CMO: Casey Hanna, M.D., Chief of Staff
CIO: Jim Riley, Director Information Technology
CHR: Barnetta Pofahl, Director Human Resources
CNO: Louise Dodson, R.N., Chief Nursing Officer
Web address: www.wagonerhospital.com
Control: Hospital district or authority, Government, Nonfederal **Service**: General medical and surgical

Staffed Beds: 100 **Admissions**: 1988 **Census**: 28 **Outpatient Visits**: 41627 **Births**: 0 **Total Expense ($000)**: 26469 **Payroll Expense ($000)**: 12343 **Personnel**: 181

Hospital, Medicare Provider Number, Address, Telephone, Approval, Facility, and Physician Codes, Health Care System

★ American Hospital Association (AHA) membership
☐ The Joint Commission accreditation
○ Healthcare Facilities Accreditation Program
◇ DNV Healthcare Inc. accreditation
⇑ Center for Improvement in Healthcare Quality Accreditation
△ Commission on Accreditation of Rehabilitation Facilities (CARF) accreditation

Hospitals, U.S. / OKLAHOMA

WATONGA—Blaine County

★ **MERCY HOSPITAL WATONGA (371302)**, 500 North Clarence Nash Boulevard, Zip 73772–2845, Mailing Address: P.O. Box 370, Zip 73772–0370; tel. 580/623–7211, **A**10 18 **F**3 11 29 30 34 40 43 50 59 64 68 75 77 85 87 93 107 114 119 128 130 132 133 135 149 154 **S** Mercy, Chesterfield, MO
Primary Contact: Bobby Stitt, R.N., Administrator
CHR: Mary Jo Messelt, Manager Human Resources
Web address: www.mercy.net/watongaok/practice/mercy-hospital-watonga
Control: Church operated, Nongovernment, not–for–profit **Service**: General medical and surgical

Staffed Beds: 25 **Admissions**: 181 **Census**: 3 **Outpatient Visits**: 9039
Births: 0 **Total Expense ($000)**: 8042 **Payroll Expense ($000)**: 4737
Personnel: 41

WAURIKA—Jefferson County

★ **JEFFERSON COUNTY HOSPITAL (371311)**, Highway 70 and 81, Zip 73573–3075, Mailing Address: P.O. Box 90, Zip 73573–0090; tel. 580/228–2344, (Nonreporting) **A**10 18 **S** DRH Health, Duncan, OK
Primary Contact: JP Edgar, President
CFO: Richard Tallon, Chief Financial Officer
CMO: Rob Linzman, D.O., Chief of Staff
CIO: Nikki McGahey, Information Officer
Web address: https://www.duncanregional.com/jefferson-county-hospital/
Control: Other not–for–profit (including NFP Corporation) **Service**: General medical and surgical

Staffed Beds: 8

WEATHERFORD—Custer County

★ **WEATHERFORD REGIONAL HOSPITAL (371323)**, 3701 East Main Street, Zip 73096–3309; tel. 580/772–5551, **A**10 18 **F**3 11 15 29 34 40 43 45 59 68 75 76 77 79 81 86 87 89 93 97 107 108 110 111 115 119 129 130 133 135 144 146 147 148 149 168 169 **P**6 **S** SSM Health, Saint Louis, MO
Primary Contact: Darin Farrell, Chief Executive Officer
CFO: Stephanie Helton, Chief Financial Officer
CMO: Jonathan Ray Long, M.D., Chief of Staff
CIO: Amy Outhier, Director Health Information Management
CHR: Tawnya Paden, Director Human Resources
CNO: Delvin Mast, R.N., Director of Nursing
Web address: www.weatherfordhospital.com
Control: Hospital district or authority, Government, Nonfederal **Service**: General medical and surgical

Staffed Beds: 22 **Admissions**: 627 **Census**: 6 **Outpatient Visits**: 41167
Births: 214 **Total Expense ($000)**: 26419 **Payroll Expense ($000)**: 8742
Personnel: 152

WOODWARD—Woodward County

ALLIANCEHEALTH WOODWARD See Integris Health Woodward Hospital

✠ **INTEGRIS HEALTH WOODWARD HOSPITAL (370002)**, 900 17th Street, Zip 73801–2448; tel. 580/256–5511, (Data for 302 days) **A**1 10 20 **F**3 11 13 15 29 30 31 34 40 45 46 48 50 51 54 55 57 59 64 65 68 70 76 77 78 79 81 89 93 96 97 107 108 111 115 118 119 127 129 133 135 144 154 156 169 **S** INTEGRIS Health, Oklahoma City, OK
Primary Contact: Jeff Nowlin, Interim Chief Executive Officer
CFO: Todd Williams, Chief Financial Officer
CIO: Larry Churchill, Director Information Services
CHR: Melinda Brock, Director Human Resources
CNO: Kimberly N Arnold, R.N., Chief Nursing Officer and Interim Chief Quality Officer
Web address: https://integrisok.com/locations/hospital/woodward-hospital
Control: Corporation, Investor–owned (for–profit) **Service**: General medical and surgical

Staffed Beds: 32 **Admissions**: 857 **Census**: 10 **Outpatient Visits**: 32286
Births: 150 **Total Expense ($000)**: 51218 **Payroll Expense ($000)**: 11144
Personnel: 155

NORTHWEST CENTER FOR BEHAVIORAL HEALTH (374001), 1222 10th Street Suite 211, Zip 73801–3156, Mailing Address: 1222 10th Street, Suite 211, Zip 73801–3156; tel. 580/766–2311, **A**3 10 **F**98 101 102 104 130 135 149 153 154 164 **S** Oklahoma Department of Mental Health and Substance Abuse Services, Oklahoma City, OK
Primary Contact: Autumn Jesse. Nickelson, Executive Director
Web address: www.ncbhok.org/
Control: State, Government, Nonfederal **Service**: Psychiatric

Staffed Beds: 24 **Admissions**: 495 **Census**: 16 **Outpatient Visits**: 0
Births: 0 **Total Expense ($000)**: 16026 **Payroll Expense ($000)**: 8702
Personnel: 206

YUKON—Canadian County

✠ **INTEGRIS CANADIAN VALLEY HOSPITAL (370211)**, 1201 Health Center Parkway, Zip 73099–6381; tel. 405/717–6800, **A**1 10 **F**11 13 15 18 29 30 39 40 43 44 45 46 49 60 64 68 70 76 77 79 81 85 87 93 96 107 108 110 111 115 118 119 126 130 135 146 147 149 156 **S** INTEGRIS Health, Oklahoma City, OK
Primary Contact: Teresa Gray, Chief Hospital Executive
COO: Cindy White, CPA, Vice President of Operations
CFO: Errol Mitchell, Chief Financial Officer
CHR: Lynn Ketch, Human Resources Recruiter Generalist
Web address: www.integris-health.com
Control: Other not–for–profit (including NFP Corporation) **Service**: General medical and surgical

Staffed Beds: 82 **Admissions**: 3567 **Census**: 36 **Outpatient Visits**: 69116
Births: 1020 **Total Expense ($000)**: 80973 **Payroll Expense ($000)**: 24675
Personnel: 315

OREGON

ALBANY—Linn County

★ ⇧ **SAMARITAN ALBANY GENERAL HOSPITAL (380022)**, 1046 Sixth Avenue, SW, Zip 97321-1999; tel. 541/812-4000, **A**3 10 21 **F**3 13 15 18 28 29 30 31 34 35 36 37 40 43 44 45 47 49 53 54 57 59 61 63 64 68 70 73 74 75 76 77 78 79 81 84 85 86 87 89 92 93 97 107 108 110 111 114 116 117 119 129 130 131 132 135 144 146 147 148 149 150 154 156 164 169 **P**6 **S** Samaritan Health Services, Corvallis, OR
Primary Contact: Dan Keteri, R.N., Chief Executive Officer
CFO: Daniel B Smith, Vice President Finance
Web address: www.samhealth.org
Control: Other not–for–profit (including NFP Corporation) **Service**: General medical and surgical

Staffed Beds: 67 **Admissions**: 2416 **Census**: 29 **Outpatient Visits**: 310921 **Births**: 455 **Total Expense ($000)**: 251404 **Payroll Expense ($000)**: 105025 **Personnel**: 996

ASHLAND—Jackson County

★ ⇧ **ASANTE ASHLAND COMMUNITY HOSPITAL (380005)**, 280 Maple Street, Zip 97520-1593; tel. 541/201-4000, **A**10 21 **F**3 13 15 29 30 34 35 40 45 48 49 50 55 59 64 65 70 75 76 79 81 84 85 87 93 107 110 111 114 119 130 131 132 135 143 147 148 149 154 169 **P**6 **S** Asante Health System, Medford, OR
Primary Contact: Brandon Mencini, Chief Executive Officer
CFO: Patrick Hocking, Chief Financial Officer
CMO: Bill Steinsick, M.D., Chief Medical Staff
CIO: Mark Hetz, Chief Information Officer
CHR: Gregg Edwards, Vice President Human Resources
CNO: Susan Montgomery, Chief Nursing Officer
Web address: https://www.asante.org/Locations/location-detail/asante-ashland-community-hospital/
Control: Other not–for–profit (including NFP Corporation) **Service**: General medical and surgical

Staffed Beds: 34 **Admissions**: 1322 **Census**: 18 **Outpatient Visits**: 49694 **Births**: 227 **Total Expense ($000)**: 67299 **Payroll Expense ($000)**: 29043 **Personnel**: 189

ASTORIA—Clatsop County

★ ○ **COLUMBIA MEMORIAL HOSPITAL (381320)**, 2111 Exchange Street, Zip 97103-3329; tel. 503/325-4321, **A**2 3 5 10 11 18 **F**3 11 13 15 18 26 28 29 30 31 32 34 35 36 37 40 41 44 45 50 51 57 58 59 62 63 64 65 68 70 75 76 77 78 79 81 85 86 87 89 91 93 97 107 108 110 111 114 115 116 117 119 126 127 130 131 132 133 134 135 143 144 146 147 148 149 154 167 169 **P**5
Primary Contact: Erik Thorsen, President and Chief Executive Officer
COO: Nicole Williams, Chief Operating Officer
CFO: Stephanie D Brenden, Vice President Finance
CMO: Chris Strear, M.D., Chief Medical Officer
CIO: Galina Gandy, Vice President Information Technology
CHR: Lucy G Dupree, Director Human Resources
CNO: Trece Gurrad, Vice President Patient Care Services
Web address: www.columbiamemorial.org
Control: Other not–for–profit (including NFP Corporation) **Service**: General medical and surgical

Staffed Beds: 25 **Admissions**: 1250 **Census**: 10 **Outpatient Visits**: 292664 **Births**: 226 **Total Expense ($000)**: 178184 **Payroll Expense ($000)**: 73103 **Personnel**: 756

BAKER CITY—Baker County

⌧ **SAINT ALPHONSUS MEDICAL CENTER – BAKER CITY (381315)**, 3325 Pocahontas Road, Zip 97814-1464; tel. 541/523-6461, **A**1 10 18 **F**3 13 15 29 30 31 34 35 40 43 44 45 50 57 59 64 68 70 74 75 76 77 78 79 81 83 85 87 93 96 97 107 108 110 111 115 119 127 128 129 130 131 133 143 148 149 154 167 169 **S** Trinity Health, Livonia, MI
Primary Contact: Dina Ellwanger, R.N., President, Eastern Oregon
CFO: Robert D Wehling, Interim Chief Financial Officer
CHR: Jerry Nickell, Vice President Human Resource and Mission
Web address: https://www.saintalphonsus.org/bakercity
Control: Other not–for–profit (including NFP Corporation) **Service**: General medical and surgical

Staffed Beds: 25 **Admissions**: 772 **Census**: 7 **Outpatient Visits**: 29084 **Births**: 84 **Total Expense ($000)**: 37073 **Payroll Expense ($000)**: 14854 **Personnel**: 161

BANDON—Coos County

★ ⇧ **SOUTHERN COOS HOSPITAL AND HEALTH CENTER (381304)**, 900 11th Street SE, Zip 97411-9114; tel. 541/347-2426, **A**10 18 21 **F**3 11 15 29 34 35 40 45 50 57 59 64 65 81 82 85 87 97 107 110 111 115 119 130 133 146 148 149 154 166 **P**6
Primary Contact: Raymond T. Hino, FACHE, Chief Executive Officer
CFO: Alan Dow, Chief Financial Officer
CMO: Megan Holland, Chief Medical Officer and Family Practitioner
CIO: Mandy Calvert, Director Information Systems
CHR: Kalen M Mills, Director Human Resources
CNO: Rachel Beissel, Chief Nursing Officer
Web address: www.southerncoos.org
Control: Hospital district or authority, Government, Nonfederal **Service**: General medical and surgical

Staffed Beds: 17 **Admissions**: 454 **Census**: 8 **Outpatient Visits**: 22276 **Births**: 0 **Total Expense ($000)**: 30256 **Payroll Expense ($000)**: 12848 **Personnel**: 174

BEND—Deschutes County

⌧ **ST. CHARLES BEND (380047)**, 2500 NE Neff Road, Zip 97701-6015; tel. 541/382-4321, **A**1 2 3 5 10 **F**3 8 11 12 13 15 17 18 19 20 21 22 24 26 28 29 31 34 35 36 37 38 40 43 44 45 46 47 49 50 51 53 54 55 58 59 60 62 63 64 65 67 70 72 74 75 76 77 78 79 81 82 84 85 86 87 89 90 91 92 93 97 98 100 101 102 104 106 107 108 109 111 115 119 120 121 123 126 130 132 135 141 146 148 149 154 156 167 169 **S** St. Charles Health System, Inc., Bend, OR
Primary Contact: David Golda, Vice President, Hospital Administrator
CFO: Jennifer Welander, CPA, Senior Vice President Finance and Chief Financial Officer
CMO: Jeffrey Absalon, M.D., Chief Physician Officer
CIO: Jerimiah Brickhouse, Chief Information Officer
CHR: Rebecca Berry, Vice President Human Resources
Web address: www.stcharleshealthcare.org
Control: Other not–for–profit (including NFP Corporation) **Service**: General medical and surgical

Staffed Beds: 308 **Admissions**: 17298 **Census**: 203 **Outpatient Visits**: 202349 **Births**: 2095 **Total Expense ($000)**: 644557 **Payroll Expense ($000)**: 266266 **Personnel**: 2211

Hospital, Medicare Provider Number, Address, Telephone, Approval, Facility, and Physician Codes, Health Care System

★ American Hospital Association (AHA) membership
□ The Joint Commission accreditation
○ Healthcare Facilities Accreditation Program
◇ DNV Healthcare Inc. accreditation
⇧ Center for Improvement in Healthcare Quality Accreditation
△ Commission on Accreditation of Rehabilitation Facilities (CARF) accreditation

Hospitals, U.S. / OREGON

BURNS—Harney County

★ ⇧ **HARNEY DISTRICT HOSPITAL (381307)**, 557 West Washington Street, Zip 97720–1497; tel. 541/573–7281, **A**10 18 21 **F**3 7 13 15 29 31 34 35 40 43 45 50 53 55 57 59 64 65 70 75 76 77 78 79 81 82 85 87 93 97 104 107 111 115 119 126 127 131 132 133 135 146 148 149 154 167 169 **P**6
Primary Contact: Bob Gomes, Chief Executive Officer
CFO: Catherine White, Chief Financial Officer
CMO: Sarah Laiosa, M.D., Chief Medical Staff
CIO: Tanya Strong, Manager Information Technology
CHR: Sammie Masterson, Director Human Resources
CNO: Deana Altman, Interim Chief Nursing Officer
Web address: www.harneydh.com
Control: Hospital district or authority, Government, Nonfederal **Service**: General medical and surgical

Staffed Beds: 25 **Admissions**: 395 **Census**: 5 **Outpatient Visits**: 33295 **Births**: 35 **Total Expense ($000)**: 32160 **Payroll Expense ($000)**: 16248 **Personnel**: 166

CLACKAMAS—Clackamas County

⊞ **KAISER SUNNYSIDE MEDICAL CENTER (380091)**, 10180 SE Sunnyside Road, Zip 97015–8970; tel. 503/652–2880, **A**1 3 5 10 19 **F**3 11 12 13 15 17 18 20 22 24 26 29 30 31 34 35 40 45 46 47 49 51 60 61 64 65 68 70 72 74 75 76 77 78 79 81 85 86 87 89 93 94 97 102 107 108 110 111 114 115 118 119 130 135 141 146 147 148 154 160 162 164 167 168 169 **P**6 **S** Kaiser Foundation Hospitals, Oakland, CA
Primary Contact: Adam Van Den Avyle, Hospital Administrator
CFO: Justin N. Evander, Chief Financial Officer
CMO: Richard Hunt, M.D., Chief Operating Officer
CIO: Mark A Burmester, Vice President Strategy and Communications
CHR: Rich Smith, Vice President Human Resources
CNO: Kathryn Vandewalle, JD, Chief Nurse Executive
Web address: www.kaiserpermanente.org
Control: Other not–for–profit (including NFP Corporation) **Service**: General medical and surgical

Staffed Beds: 302 **Admissions**: 20078 **Census**: 241 **Outpatient Visits**: 71679 **Births**: 2264 **Total Expense ($000)**: 533686 **Payroll Expense ($000)**: 212456 **Personnel**: 1566

COOS BAY—Coos County

⊞ **BAY AREA HOSPITAL (380090)**, 1775 Thompson Road, Zip 97420–2198; tel. 541/269–8111, **A**1 2 3 10 **F**3 11 12 13 15 18 20 22 26 28 29 30 31 34 35 40 43 44 45 50 51 57 58 59 60 64 67 68 70 73 75 76 78 79 81 89 98 99 102 107 108 110 111 115 118 119 120 121 123 124 126 129 130 132 146 147 148 149 154 156 167 169
Primary Contact: Brian Moore, President and Chief Executive Officer
COO: Ben Pfau, Chief Facility and Information Officer
CFO: Sam Patterson, Chief Financial Officer
CMO: Michael van Duren, M.D., Chief Medical Officer
CIO: Bob Adams, Director Information Services
CHR: Suzie Q McDaniel, Chief Human Resource Officer
Web address: www.bayareahospital.org
Control: Hospital district or authority, Government, Nonfederal **Service**: General medical and surgical

Staffed Beds: 132 **Admissions**: 5356 **Census**: 61 **Outpatient Visits**: 139760 **Births**: 575 **Total Expense ($000)**: 242960 **Payroll Expense ($000)**: 109675 **Personnel**: 938

COQUILLE—Coos County

★ **COQUILLE VALLEY HOSPITAL (381312)**, 940 East Fifth Street, Zip 97423–1699; tel. 541/396–3101, **A**10 18 **F**3 11 15 29 30 34 40 43 50 54 56 68 77 79 81 82 107 108 111 114 119 133 135 146 167 **P**6
Primary Contact: Jeff Lang, Chief Executive Officer
CFO: Robert E Fisher, Chief Financial Officer
CMO: James Sinnott, M.D., Chief Medical Staff
CIO: Curt Carpenter, Manager Information Technology
CHR: Monte Johnston, Manager Human Resources
Web address: www.cvhospital.org
Control: Hospital district or authority, Government, Nonfederal **Service**: General medical and surgical

Staffed Beds: 16 **Admissions**: 328 **Census**: 3 **Outpatient Visits**: 30581 **Births**: 0 **Total Expense ($000)**: 36593 **Payroll Expense ($000)**: 14823 **Personnel**: 182

CORVALLIS—Benton County

★ ⇧ **GOOD SAMARITAN REGIONAL MEDICAL CENTER (380014)**, 3600 NW Samaritan Drive, Zip 97330–3737, Mailing Address: P.O. Box 1068, Zip 97339–1068; tel. 541/768–5111, **A**2 3 5 10 12 13 19 21 **F**3 11 12 13 15 17 18 20 22 24 26 28 29 30 31 34 35 36 37 40 43 45 46 47 48 49 53 54 55 56 57 58 59 60 61 64 68 70 71 73 74 76 77 78 79 81 82 85 86 87 89 92 93 97 98 100 101 102 104 105 107 108 110 111 114 115 116 117 118 119 120 121 123 124 126 130 131 132 135 144 146 147 148 149 154 156 164 166 167 169 **P**6 **S** Samaritan Health Services, Corvallis, OR
CFO: Daniel B Smith, Vice President Finance
CIO: Bob Power, Vice President Information Services
CHR: Doug Boysen, Chief Legal Counsel and Vice President Human Resources
CNO: William Howden, Vice President Nursing
Web address: www.samhealth.org
Control: Other not–for–profit (including NFP Corporation) **Service**: General medical and surgical

Staffed Beds: 179 **Admissions**: 8185 **Census**: 110 **Outpatient Visits**: 436883 **Births**: 892 **Total Expense ($000)**: 596797 **Payroll Expense ($000)**: 219121 **Personnel**: 1990

COTTAGE GROVE—Lane County

★ **PEACEHEALTH COTTAGE GROVE COMMUNITY MEDICAL CENTER (381301)**, 1515 Village Drive, Zip 97424–9700; tel. 541/942–0511, **A**10 18 **F**3 11 15 29 30 34 35 40 43 57 59 64 65 75 80 93 97 100 102 104 107 110 111 115 119 130 132 133 135 146 148 149 154 **S** PeaceHealth, Vancouver, WA
Primary Contact: Jason F. Hawkins, Chief Administrative Officer
Web address: www.peacehealth.org
Control: Church operated, Nongovernment, not–for–profit **Service**: General medical and surgical

Staffed Beds: 14 **Admissions**: 142 **Census**: 5 **Outpatient Visits**: 58197 **Births**: 0 **Total Expense ($000)**: 28117 **Payroll Expense ($000)**: 10760 **Personnel**: 117

DALLAS—Polk County

SALEM HEALTH WEST VALLEY (381308), 525 SE Washington Street, Zip 97338–2834, Mailing Address: P.O. Box 378, Zip 97338–0378; tel. 503/623–8301, **A**10 18 **F**3 15 29 35 40 43 44 45 50 59 64 75 79 81 85 87 93 97 107 108 110 111 115 119 131 133 143 146 148 149 154 167 **P**6 **S** Salem Health, Salem, OR
Primary Contact: Cheryl R. Nester Wolfe, R.N., President and Chief Executive Officer
CFO: James Parr, Chief Financial Officer
CMO: Ralph Yates, D.O., Chief Medical Officer
CNO: Sarah Horn, Chief Nursing Officer
Web address: www.salemhealth.org/wvh/
Control: Other not–for–profit (including NFP Corporation) **Service**: General medical and surgical

Staffed Beds: 25 **Admissions**: 493 **Census**: 21 **Outpatient Visits**: 125647 **Births**: 0 **Total Expense ($000)**: 59012 **Payroll Expense ($000)**: 29949 **Personnel**: 203

ENTERPRISE—Wallowa County

★ ⇧ **WALLOWA MEMORIAL HOSPITAL (381306)**, 601 Medical Parkway, Zip 97828–5124; tel. 541/426–3111, **A**3 5 10 18 21 **F**3 7 8 10 11 13 15 29 30 31 34 35 40 43 45 46 50 55 56 57 59 62 64 68 70 75 76 77 78 79 81 82 85 87 93 97 102 104 107 110 115 119 127 128 130 131 132 133 134 135 143 148 149 154 169
Primary Contact: Dan Grigg, Chief Executive Officer
CFO: Daniel Jessup, Chief Financial Officer
CMO: Keith DeYoung, M.D., Chief Medical Staff
CIO: John Straughan, Director Information Technology
CHR: Linda Childers, Director Human Resources
CNO: Jenni Word, R.N., Chief Nursing Officer
Web address: www.wchcd.org
Control: Hospital district or authority, Government, Nonfederal **Service**: General medical and surgical

Staffed Beds: 25 **Admissions**: 474 **Census**: 5 **Outpatient Visits**: 40584 **Births**: 39 **Total Expense ($000)**: 35622 **Payroll Expense ($000)**: 17210 **Personnel**: 181

EUGENE—Lane County

VALLEY WEST HEALTH CENTER See Valley West Health Care Center

Hospitals, U.S. / OREGON

FLORENCE—Lane County

★ ⇑ **PEACEHEALTH PEACE HARBOR MEDICAL CENTER (381316)**, 400 Ninth Street, Zip 97439–7398; tel. 541/997–8412, **A**10 18 21 **F**3 8 13 15 18 28 29 30 34 38 40 43 45 50 57 59 65 68 70 76 77 79 80 81 82 86 87 93 94 96 97 100 104 107 110 111 115 118 119 130 132 133 135 146 147 148 149 154 156 165 169 **S** PeaceHealth, Vancouver, WA
Primary Contact: Jason F. Hawkins, Chief Administrative Officer
CMO: Ron Shearer, M.D., Regional Medical Director
CIO: Ginni Boughal, Director Health Information and Information Technology
CHR: Don Bourland, Vice President Human Resources
Web address: www.peacehealth.org
Control: Church operated, Nongovernment, not–for–profit **Service**: General medical and surgical

Staffed Beds: 21 **Admissions**: 731 **Census**: 7 **Outpatient Visits**: 76604 **Births**: 0 **Total Expense ($000)**: 66318 **Payroll Expense ($000)**: 27337 **Personnel**: 251

FOREST GROVE—Washington County

FOREST GROVE COMM HOSPITAL See Tuality Forest Grove Hospital

TUALITY FOREST GROVE HOSPITAL See Ohsu Health Hillsboro Medical Center, Hillsboro

GOLD BEACH—Curry County

★ ⇑ **CURRY GENERAL HOSPITAL (381322)**, 94220 Fourth Street, Zip 97444–7756; tel. 541/247–3000, **A**10 18 21 **F**3 11 15 28 29 34 40 42 43 44 45 50 51 54 59 64 65 75 81 82 85 87 96 97 107 110 111 115 119 127 130 132 133 135 147 148 149 154 156 169
Primary Contact: Virginia Williams, Chief Executive Officer
CFO: Carl Gerlach, Chief Financial Officer
CMO: Reginald Williams, M.D., Medical Staff President
CIO: Kristina Martin, Chief Information Officer
Web address: www.curryhealthnetwork.com
Control: Hospital district or authority, Government, Nonfederal **Service**: General medical and surgical

Staffed Beds: 12 **Admissions**: 543 **Census**: 7 **Outpatient Visits**: 127359 **Births**: 3 **Total Expense ($000)**: 66081 **Payroll Expense ($000)**: 25981 **Personnel**: 310

GRANTS PASS—Josephine County

★ ⇑ **ASANTE THREE RIVERS MEDICAL CENTER (380002)**, 500 SW Ramsey Avenue, Zip 97527–5554; tel. 541/472–7000, **A**3 5 10 21 **F**3 11 13 15 28 29 30 31 34 40 43 46 48 49 50 53 54 57 59 64 65 70 75 76 78 79 81 85 87 93 94 107 108 110 111 114 115 118 119 120 129 130 132 135 143 144 145 146 147 148 149 154 167 169 **P**6 **S** Asante Health System, Medford, OR
Primary Contact: Patrick Sharp, Chief Executive Officer
CFO: Patrick Hocking, Chief Financial Officer
CMO: Eric Loeliger, Vice President of Medical Affairs
CIO: Mark Hetz, Chief Information Officer
CHR: Gregg Edwards, Chief People Officer
Web address: www.asante.org/trmc/
Control: Other not–for–profit (including NFP Corporation) **Service**: General medical and surgical

Staffed Beds: 123 **Admissions**: 6477 **Census**: 89 **Outpatient Visits**: 305638 **Births**: 707 **Total Expense ($000)**: 275141 **Payroll Expense ($000)**: 105329 **Personnel**: 862

GRESHAM—Multnomah County

⊞ **LEGACY MOUNT HOOD MEDICAL CENTER (380025)**, 24800 SE Stark, Zip 97030–3378; tel. 503/674–1122, **A**1 2 10 **F**3 11 13 15 18 20 22 26 28 29 30 31 32 34 35 38 40 44 45 48 49 50 51 59 60 64 68 70 74 75 76 77 78 79 81 85 86 87 93 100 101 102 107 108 110 111 114 115 118 119 120 121 123 126 129 130 132 146 147 148 149 156 **P**6 **S** Legacy Health, Portland, OR
Primary Contact: James Aberle, President
COO: Michael Newcomb, D.O., Senior Vice President and Chief Operating Officer
CFO: Linda Hoff, Senior Vice President and Chief Financial Officer
CMO: Lewis Low, M.D., Chief Medical Officer
CIO: John Jay Kenagy, Ph.D., Senior Vice President and Chief Information Officer
CHR: Sonja Steves, Senior Vice President Human Resources
Web address: https://www.legacyhealth.org/Doctors-and-Locations/hospitals/legacy-mount-hood-medical-center
Control: Other not–for–profit (including NFP Corporation) **Service**: General medical and surgical

Staffed Beds: 96 **Admissions**: 5185 **Census**: 81 **Outpatient Visits**: 125217 **Births**: 752 **Total Expense ($000)**: 217407 **Payroll Expense ($000)**: 89994 **Personnel**: 677

HEPPNER—Morrow County

PIONEER MEMORIAL HOSPITAL (381310), 564 East Pioneer Drive, Zip 97836–7318, Mailing Address: P.O. Box 9, Zip 97836–0009; tel. 541/676–9133, **A**10 18 **F**3 7 34 35 40 43 50 57 59 62 63 64 66 68 71 75 97 107 119 127 130 133 135 146 147 148 154 **P**6
Primary Contact: Emily Reynolds Roberts, Chief Executive Officer
CFO: Nicole Mahoney, Chief Financial Officer
CIO: Shawn Cutsforth, Information Systems Officer
CHR: Patti Allstott, Administrative Coordinator Human Resources and Grant Writer
Web address: www.morrowcountyhealthdistrict.org
Control: Hospital district or authority, Government, Nonfederal **Service**: General medical and surgical

Staffed Beds: 11 **Admissions**: 83 **Census**: 6 **Outpatient Visits**: 6549 **Births**: 0 **Total Expense ($000)**: 22083 **Payroll Expense ($000)**: 12365 **Personnel**: 160

HERMISTON—Umatilla County

★ ⇑ **GOOD SHEPHERD HEALTH CARE SYSTEM (381325)**, 610 NW 11th Street, Zip 97838–6601; tel. 541/667–3400, **A**10 18 21 **F**3 11 13 15 28 29 30 31 33 34 35 36 37 40 43 44 45 48 50 51 53 54 56 57 59 62 63 64 65 68 70 75 76 77 78 79 81 85 86 87 89 97 107 108 110 111 115 119 126 127 128 129 130 131 132 133 135 143 144 146 147 148 149 154 156 164 169
Primary Contact: Arthur Mathisen, FACHE, Chief Executive Officer
CFO: Jan D Peter, Vice President Fiscal Services and Chief Financial Officer
CMO: Jeremy Anderson, M.D., Medical Staff President
CIO: Rob Rizk, Director Information Technology
CHR: Kelly B. Sanders, Vice President Human Resources
CNO: Theresa Brock, Vice President Nursing
Web address: www.gshealth.org
Control: Other not–for–profit (including NFP Corporation) **Service**: General medical and surgical

Staffed Beds: 25 **Admissions**: 1746 **Census**: 18 **Outpatient Visits**: 125928 **Births**: 395 **Total Expense ($000)**: 145432 **Payroll Expense ($000)**: 51771 **Personnel**: 733

HILLSBORO—Washington County

⊞ **KAISER WESTSIDE MEDICAL CENTER (380103)**, 2875 NE Stucki Avenue, Zip 97124–5806; tel. 971/310–1000, **A**1 10 **F**3 13 15 29 30 31 34 40 45 46 47 49 51 60 61 64 65 68 70 74 75 76 77 79 81 85 86 93 94 96 97 102 107 108 110 111 114 115 118 119 126 130 135 141 146 147 148 149 154 162 164 167 168 169 **P**6 **S** Kaiser Foundation Hospitals, Oakland, CA
Primary Contact: Adam Van Den Avyle, Hospital Administrator
COO: Brantley Dettmer, Chief Operating Officer
CMO: Carol Unitan, M.D., Chief Medical Officer
CIO: Charles Stearns, Area Information Officer
CHR: Rich Smith, Vice President Human Resources
CNO: Janet Lee Reeder, MSN, R.N., Chief Nurse Executive
Web address: www.kp.org
Control: Other not–for–profit (including NFP Corporation) **Service**: General medical and surgical

Staffed Beds: 122 **Admissions**: 8584 **Census**: 87 **Outpatient Visits**: 54781 **Births**: 1338 **Total Expense ($000)**: 230109 **Payroll Expense ($000)**: 88422 **Personnel**: 725

Hospital, Medicare Provider Number, Address, Telephone, Approval, Facility, and Physician Codes, Health Care System

★ American Hospital Association (AHA) membership   ○ Healthcare Facilities Accreditation Program   ⇑ Center for Improvement in Healthcare Quality Accreditation
☐ The Joint Commission accreditation   ◇ DNV Healthcare Inc. accreditation   △ Commission on Accreditation of Rehabilitation Facilities (CARF) accreditation

Hospitals, U.S. / OREGON

★ ⚕ **OHSU HEALTH HILLSBORO MEDICAL CENTER (380021)**, 335 SE Eighth Avenue, Zip 97123–4246; tel. 503/681–1111, (Includes TUALITY COMMUNITY HOSPITAL, 335 SE Eighth Avenue, Hillsboro, Oregon, Zip 97123, P O Box 309, Zip 97123, tel. 503/681–1111; Manuel S Berman, FACHE, President and Chief Executive Officer; TUALITY FOREST GROVE HOSPITAL, 1809 Maple Street, Forest Grove, Oregon, Zip 97116–1995, tel. 503/357–2173; Manuel S Berman, FACHE, President and Chief Executive Officer) **A**3 5 10 21 **F**3 11 12 13 15 18 20 22 24 26 28 29 30 31 32 34 35 40 44 45 47 49 50 53 54 56 57 59 62 64 68 70 71 72 74 75 76 77 78 79 80 81 82 85 86 87 92 93 97 98 100 103 104 107 108 110 111 114 115 118 119 126 129 130 131 132 135 143 144 145 146 147 148 149 154 164 167 **P**1
Primary Contact: Lori James-Nielsen, President
COO: Steven P Krautscheid, Ancillary Services Administrator
CFO: Tim Fleischmann, Chief Financial Officer
CMO: Joe Hardman, M.D., Chief Medical Officer
CHR: Cheryl Gebhart, Chief Human Resources Officer
Web address: www.tuality.org
Control: Other not–for–profit (including NFP Corporation) **Service:** General medical and surgical

Staffed Beds: 127 **Admissions:** 5434 **Census:** 92 **Outpatient Visits:** 242355 **Births:** 775 **Total Expense ($000):** 303555 **Payroll Expense ($000):** 108775 **Personnel:** 1030

HOOD RIVER—Hood River County

⚕ **PROVIDENCE HOOD RIVER MEMORIAL HOSPITAL (381318)**, 810 12th Street, Zip 97031–1587, Mailing Address: P.O. Box 149, Zip 97031–0055; tel. 541/386–3911, **A**1 3 10 18 **F**3 5 9 10 11 12 13 15 29 30 31 34 35 40 43 45 47 48 54 56 57 59 60 64 65 68 70 75 76 77 78 79 81 85 86 92 97 100 101 102 104 107 108 110 111 114 118 119 125 127 130 131 146 147 148 149 154 156 167 169 **P**6 **S** Providence, Renton, WA
Primary Contact: Jeanette Vieira, Chief Executive
CHR: Jami McCaslin, Director Human Resources
Web address: www.providence.org/hoodriver
Control: Church operated, Nongovernment, not–for–profit **Service:** General medical and surgical

Staffed Beds: 25 **Admissions:** 1446 **Census:** 12 **Outpatient Visits:** 108964 **Births:** 320 **Total Expense ($000):** 118242 **Payroll Expense ($000):** 45718 **Personnel:** 460

JOHN DAY—Grant County

★ **BLUE MOUNTAIN HOSPITAL DISTRICT (381305)**, 170 Ford Road, Zip 97845–2009; tel. 541/575–1311, (Total facility includes 21 beds in nursing home–type unit) **A**3 5 10 18 21 **F**3 7 8 11 13 15 29 30 34 35 36 40 41 43 45 50 57 59 62 63 64 65 67 68 70 75 76 77 81 82 85 86 87 93 97 100 107 110 111 114 119 127 130 132 133 134 135 143 145 146 148 149 154 156 169 **P**6
Primary Contact: Cameron M. Marlowe, Chief Executive Officer
CMO: Keith Thomas, M.D., Chief of Staff
CIO: Sean Tsao, Director Information Technology
CHR: Verlene Davis, Director Human Resources
CNO: Les McLeod, Director of Nursing Services
Web address: www.bluemountainhospital.org
Control: Hospital district or authority, Government, Nonfederal **Service:** General medical and surgical

Staffed Beds: 37 **Admissions:** 246 **Census:** 17 **Outpatient Visits:** 24422 **Births:** 36 **Total Expense ($000):** 34540 **Payroll Expense ($000):** 16618 **Personnel:** 155

KLAMATH FALLS—Klamath County

★ ⚕ **SKY LAKES MEDICAL CENTER (380050)**, 2865 Daggett Avenue, Zip 97601–1106; tel. 541/882–6311, **A**3 5 10 21 **F**3 8 11 13 15 18 20 22 29 31 34 35 37 40 43 44 45 46 47 48 50 51 53 54 56 57 59 61 62 64 68 70 71 75 76 77 78 79 81 84 85 86 87 89 92 93 94 96 97 100 102 107 108 110 111 114 115 116 117 118 119 120 121 123 130 131 132 134 135 141 142 143 144 145 146 147 148 149 156 157 167 169 **P**6
Primary Contact: David Cauble, President and Chief Executive Officer
CFO: Richard Rico, Vice President and Chief Financial Officer
CMO: Grant Niskanen, M.D., Vice President Medical Affairs
CIO: John Gaede, Chief Information Officer
CHR: Don York, Vice President and Chief Human Resource Officer
Web address: www.skylakes.org
Control: Other not–for–profit (including NFP Corporation) **Service:** General medical and surgical

Staffed Beds: 117 **Admissions:** 4670 **Census:** 56 **Outpatient Visits:** 374870 **Births:** 669 **Total Expense ($000):** 323006 **Payroll Expense ($000):** 118635 **Personnel:** 1444

LA GRANDE—Union County

⚕ **GRANDE RONDE HOSPITAL (381321)**, 900 Sunset Drive, Zip 97850–1387, Mailing Address: PO Box 3290, Zip 97850–7290; tel. 541/963–8421, **A**1 10 18 **F**3 11 13 15 17 18 29 30 31 32 34 35 37 39 40 43 44 45 50 54 57 59 62 64 66 70 74 75 76 77 78 79 81 82 85 86 87 89 91 92 93 96 97 104 107 108 110 111 115 118 119 127 128 129 130 131 132 133 135 144 146 147 148 149 154 156 162 164 165 167 169 **P**6
Primary Contact: Jeremy P. Davis, President and Chief Executive Officer
CFO: Robert Seymour, Chief Financial Officer/Senior Director Finance
CMO: Stacy Whitaker, M.D., Medical Staff President
CIO: Parhez Sattar, Senior Director Information Technology
CHR: Steve Lyon, Senior Director Human Resources
CNO: Karen Timm, R.N., MSN, Chief Nursing Officer
Web address: www.grh.org
Control: Other not–for–profit (including NFP Corporation) **Service:** General medical and surgical

Staffed Beds: 25 **Admissions:** 1477 **Census:** 13 **Outpatient Visits:** 127743 **Births:** 250 **Total Expense ($000):** 140346 **Payroll Expense ($000):** 67550 **Personnel:** 714

LAKEVIEW—Lake County

★ **LAKE DISTRICT HOSPITAL (381309)**, 700 South 'J' Street, Zip 97630–1679; tel. 541/947–2114, **A**10 18 **F**3 5 7 13 15 28 29 30 31 33 34 35 37 38 40 45 46 57 59 62 63 64 68 75 76 77 78 79 81 82 84 85 87 90 93 97 100 107 111 115 119 127 129 130 132 133 134 135 146 148 149 154 160 164 169 **P**6
Primary Contact: Jim Schlenker, Interim Chief Executive Officer
CFO: Cheryl J Cornwell, Chief Financial Officer
CMO: Stephen Hussey, M.D., Chief of Staff
CIO: Steven Vance, Information Technology Director
CHR: Lesley Hanson, Director Human Resources
CNO: Teresa Squires, R.N., Chief Nursing Officer
Web address: www.lakehealthdistrict.org
Control: Hospital district or authority, Government, Nonfederal **Service:** General medical and surgical

Staffed Beds: 24 **Admissions:** 369 **Census:** 4 **Outpatient Visits:** 55561 **Births:** 66 **Total Expense ($000):** 44485 **Payroll Expense ($000):** 19376 **Personnel:** 313

LEBANON—Linn County

★ ⚕ **SAMARITAN LEBANON COMMUNITY HOSPITAL (381323)**, 525 North Santiam Highway, Zip 97355–4363, Mailing Address: P.O. Box 739, Zip 97355–0739; tel. 541/258–2101, **A**3 10 18 21 **F**3 11 13 15 28 29 30 31 34 35 40 43 44 45 46 47 53 59 64 68 70 75 76 78 79 81 85 86 87 89 92 93 97 107 108 110 111 114 116 117 118 119 127 130 131 132 135 144 146 147 148 149 152 154 156 160 164 169 **P**6 **S** Samaritan Health Services, Corvallis, OR
Primary Contact: Dan Rackham, Chief Executive Officer
CFO: Daniel B Smith, Vice President Finance
CMO: Alan Blake, M.D., President Medical Staff
CIO: Robert Power, Vice President Information Services
CHR: Connie Erwin, Manager
CNO: Wendie Wunderwald, R.N., Vice President Patient Care Services
Web address: www.samhealth.org
Control: Other not–for–profit (including NFP Corporation) **Service:** General medical and surgical

Staffed Beds: 25 **Admissions:** 1441 **Census:** 17 **Outpatient Visits:** 250164 **Births:** 207 **Total Expense ($000):** 158265 **Payroll Expense ($000):** 65959 **Personnel:** 693

LINCOLN CITY—Lincoln County

★ ⚕ **SAMARITAN NORTH LINCOLN HOSPITAL (381302)**, 3043 NE 28th Street, Zip 97367–4518, Mailing Address: P.O. Box 767, Zip 97367–0767; tel. 541/994–3661, **A**3 10 18 21 **F**3 11 13 15 29 30 31 34 35 40 43 44 45 51 57 58 59 64 65 68 75 77 78 79 81 84 85 87 93 97 104 107 110 111 115 116 117 118 119 127 130 132 133 135 144 146 147 148 149 154 156 164 167 **P**6 **S** Samaritan Health Services, Corvallis, OR
Primary Contact: Lesley Ogden, M.D., Chief Executive Officer
CFO: Kathryn Doksum, Director Finance
CMO: Raj Baman, D.O., President Medical Staff
CHR: Gina Tapp, Director Human Resources
CNO: Virginia Riffle, Vice President Patient Care Services
Web address: www.samhealth.org
Control: Other not–for–profit (including NFP Corporation) **Service:** General medical and surgical

Staffed Beds: 12 **Admissions:** 799 **Census:** 9 **Outpatient Visits:** 104047 **Births:** 106 **Total Expense ($000):** 91758 **Payroll Expense ($000):** 35043 **Personnel:** 323

Hospitals, U.S. / OREGON

MADRAS—Jefferson County

★ **ST. CHARLES MADRAS (381324)**, 470 NE 'A' Street, Zip 97741–1844; tel. 541/475–3882, **A**3 5 10 18 **F**3 13 29 30 34 35 40 43 45 59 64 65 70 75 76 77 81 82 85 86 87 90 93 97 119 130 133 135 146 147 148 149 154 167 **S** St. Charles Health System, Inc., Bend, OR
Primary Contact: Todd Shields, Vice President, Hospital Administrator
Web address: www.stcharleshealthcare.org/Our-Locations/Madras
Control: Other not–for–profit (including NFP Corporation) **Service**: General medical and surgical

Staffed Beds: 25 **Admissions**: 738 **Census**: 9 **Outpatient Visits**: 30519 **Births**: 150 **Total Expense ($000)**: 42085 **Payroll Expense ($000)**: 20800 **Personnel**: 168

MCMINNVILLE—Yamhill County

✠ **WILLAMETTE VALLEY MEDICAL CENTER (380071)**, 2700 SE Stratus Avenue, Zip 97128–6255; tel. 503/472–6131, **A**1 2 10 **F**3 11 12 13 15 18 20 24 26 27 28 29 30 31 34 35 40 41 43 45 46 48 50 51 56 57 58 59 60 64 65 70 74 75 76 78 79 81 82 84 85 86 87 91 92 93 98 103 107 108 110 111 114 115 118 119 120 123 124 130 131 132 135 146 147 148 154 156 167 **P**6 **S** Lifepoint Health, Brentwood, TN
Primary Contact: Michael J. Mulkey, Chief Executive Officer
CFO: Chris E. Brooker, Chief Financial Officer
CMO: Timothy Brock, M.D., Chief Medical Officer
CIO: Shawn Thompson, Manager of Information Systems
CHR: Lisa Clark, Director Human Resources
CNO: Karen Reed, Interim Chief Nursing Officer
Web address: www.willamettevalleymedical.com/
Control: Corporation, Investor–owned (for–profit) **Service**: General medical and surgical

Staffed Beds: 60 **Admissions**: 2708 **Census**: 29 **Outpatient Visits**: 103971 **Total Expense ($000)**: 109914 **Payroll Expense ($000)**: 33953 **Personnel**: 426

MEDFORD—Jackson County

★ ⇧ **ASANTE ROGUE REGIONAL MEDICAL CENTER (380018)**, 2825 East Barnett Road, Zip 97504–8332; tel. 541/789–7000, **A**2 3 5 10 19 21 **F**3 11 12 13 15 17 18 20 22 24 26 28 29 30 31 32 34 35 36 37 40 43 45 46 48 49 50 57 58 59 60 61 63 64 65 70 72 74 75 76 78 79 81 85 86 87 89 90 93 96 97 98 102 105 107 108 110 111 112 115 116 117 119 120 121 122 124 126 129 130 132 135 143 145 146 147 148 149 154 162 166 167 169 **P**6 **S** Asante Health System, Medford, OR
Primary Contact: Brandon Mencini, Chief Executive Officer
CFO: Patrick Hocking, Chief Financial Officer
CIO: Mark Hetz, Chief Information Officer
CHR: Gregg Edwards, Chief People Officer
Web address: www.asante.org
Control: Other not–for–profit (including NFP Corporation) **Service**: General medical and surgical

Staffed Beds: 352 **Admissions**: 16177 **Census**: 288 **Outpatient Visits**: 555949 **Births**: 1521 **Total Expense ($000)**: 756717 **Payroll Expense ($000)**: 266142 **Personnel**: 2118

✠ **PROVIDENCE MEDFORD MEDICAL CENTER (380075)**, 1111 Crater Lake Avenue, Zip 97504–6241; tel. 541/732–5000, **A**1 10 19 **F**3 11 13 15 18 20 22 28 29 30 34 35 36 40 43 45 51 54 56 57 58 60 64 68 70 74 75 76 77 78 79 81 82 84 85 90 91 92 93 96 97 102 107 108 110 114 115 118 119 120 121 123 126 129 130 131 132 146 147 148 149 154 167 169 **P**6 **S** Providence, Renton, WA
Primary Contact: Chris Pizzi, Chief Executive Officer
CHR: Julie Levison, Director Human Resources
CNO: Sherri Steele, Chief Nursing Officer
Web address: www.providence.org
Control: Church operated, Nongovernment, not–for–profit **Service**: General medical and surgical

Staffed Beds: 128 **Admissions**: 5505 **Census**: 80 **Outpatient Visits**: 248505 **Births**: 349 **Total Expense ($000)**: 287513 **Payroll Expense ($000)**: 93815 **Personnel**: 923

MILWAUKIE—Clackamas County

✠ **PROVIDENCE MILWAUKIE HOSPITAL (380082)**, 10150 SE 32nd Avenue, Zip 97222–6516; tel. 503/513–8300, **A**1 3 10 **F**3 15 18 29 30 34 35 36 40 44 45 46 50 53 54 56 57 59 63 64 68 70 71 74 75 77 79 81 82 84 85 87 91 92 93 97 98 102 103 104 107 108 110 111 114 115 119 129 130 131 132 133 135 146 147 148 154 167 **P**6 **S** Providence, Renton, WA
Primary Contact: Brad Henry, Interim Chief Executive Officer
COO: Sherri Paris, Chief Operating Officer
CFO: Sheila Waldron, Finance Manager
CHR: Julie Smith, Senior Human Resources Strategic Partner
CNO: Lisa Halvorsen, Chief Nurse Executive
Web address: www.providence.org
Control: Church operated, Nongovernment, not–for–profit **Service**: General medical and surgical

Staffed Beds: 59 **Admissions**: 2972 **Census**: 52 **Outpatient Visits**: 210876 **Births**: 0 **Total Expense ($000)**: 150938 **Payroll Expense ($000)**: 53941

NEWBERG—Yamhill County

✠ **PROVIDENCE NEWBERG MEDICAL CENTER (380037)**, 1001 Providence Drive, Zip 97132–7485; tel. 503/537–1555, **A**1 10 **F**3 11 12 13 15 18 20 28 29 30 34 35 38 40 44 45 46 47 49 50 51 57 59 60 64 70 74 75 76 77 78 79 81 85 87 92 93 100 107 108 110 111 115 119 129 130 146 147 148 149 154 164 167 169 **P**6 **S** Providence, Renton, WA
Primary Contact: Amy Schmitt, M.D., Interim Chief Executive Officer and Chief Medical Officer
CFO: Jack R Sumner, Assistant Administrator Finance
CMO: Amy Schmitt, M.D., Chief Medical Officer
CIO: Laureen O'Brien, Chief Information Officer
CHR: Cheryl Gebhart, Director Human Resources Providence Health Plan and Providence Medical Group
Web address: https://oregon.providence.org/location-directory/p/providence-newberg-medical-center/
Control: Church operated, Nongovernment, not–for–profit **Service**: General medical and surgical

Staffed Beds: 40 **Admissions**: 3069 **Census**: 29 **Outpatient Visits**: 204126 **Births**: 638 **Total Expense ($000)**: 142693 **Payroll Expense ($000)**: 46024

NEWPORT—Lincoln County

★ ⇧ **SAMARITAN PACIFIC COMMUNITIES HOSPITAL (381314)**, 930 SW Abbey Street, Zip 97365–4820, Mailing Address: P.O. Box 945, Zip 97365–0072; tel. 541/265–2244, **A**3 10 18 21 **F**3 11 13 15 26 28 29 30 31 34 35 40 43 44 45 47 53 54 59 64 65 68 70 75 76 77 78 79 81 85 86 87 92 93 97 107 108 110 111 115 116 117 119 126 127 129 130 132 133 135 144 146 147 148 149 154 156 164 165 167 169 **P**6 **S** Samaritan Health Services, Corvallis, OR
Primary Contact: Lesley Ogden, M.D., Chief Executive Officer
CFO: Daniel B Smith, Chief Financial Officer
CIO: Robert Power, Chief Information Officer
CHR: Gina Tapp, Director Human Resources
CNO: Lorie Williams, R.N., Vice President Nursing
Web address: www.samhealth.org
Control: Other not–for–profit (including NFP Corporation) **Service**: General medical and surgical

Staffed Beds: 25 **Admissions**: 1189 **Census**: 12 **Outpatient Visits**: 184039 **Births**: 137 **Total Expense ($000)**: 133536 **Payroll Expense ($000)**: 44203 **Personnel**: 444

ONTARIO—Malheur County

✠ **SAINT ALPHONSUS MEDICAL CENTER – ONTARIO (380052)**, 351 SW Ninth Street, Zip 97914–2693; tel. 541/881–7000, **A**1 5 10 20 **F**3 11 13 15 18 28 29 30 31 34 35 40 43 44 45 50 53 54 56 57 59 63 64 65 68 70 75 76 77 78 79 81 83 84 85 87 89 93 97 107 108 110 111 114 118 119 127 129 130 131 132 135 144 146 147 148 149 154 156 167 169 **S** Trinity Health, Livonia, MI
Primary Contact: Dina Ellwanger, R.N., President and Chief Nursing Officer
CFO: Lannie Checketts, Chief Financial Officer
CMO: Paul Gering, M.D., Vice President Medical Affairs
CHR: Stefanie Thiel, Senior Human Resources Business Partner
Web address: www.saintalphonsus.org/ontario
Control: Other not–for–profit (including NFP Corporation) **Service**: General medical and surgical

Staffed Beds: 35 **Admissions**: 1634 **Census**: 11 **Outpatient Visits**: 92247 **Births**: 286 **Total Expense ($000)**: 76588 **Payroll Expense ($000)**: 29027 **Personnel**: 283

Hospital, Medicare Provider Number, Address, Telephone, Approval, Facility, and Physician Codes, Health Care System

★ American Hospital Association (AHA) membership ○ Healthcare Facilities Accreditation Program ⇧ Center for Improvement in Healthcare Quality Accreditation
□ The Joint Commission accreditation ◇ DNV Healthcare Inc. accreditation △ Commission on Accreditation of Rehabilitation Facilities (CARF) accreditation

Hospitals, U.S. / OREGON

OREGON CITY—Clackamas County

PROVIDENCE WILLAMETTE FALLS MEDICAL CENTER (380038), 1500 Division Street, Zip 97045–1597; tel. 503/656–1631, **A**1 10 **F**3 13 15 28 29 30 34 35 40 45 46 50 53 54 57 59 64 70 74 75 76 77 78 79 81 82 84 85 87 91 92 93 98 99 100 102 104 105 107 108 111 114 119 126 130 131 132 135 146 147 153 167 169 **S** Providence, Renton, WA
Primary Contact: Brad Henry, Chief Executive Officer
COO: Patricia A Markesino, FACHE, Chief Nurse Executive and Chief Operating Officer
CFO: Elizabeth Sublette, Director Finance
CMO: James Watkins, M.D., President Medical Staff
CHR: Joann M Pfister, Director Human Resources
CNO: Jessica Bailey-Oetker, Director Quality and Medical Staff
Web address: www.providence.org/pwfmc
Control: Church operated, Nongovernment, not–for–profit **Service:** General medical and surgical

Staffed Beds: 108 **Admissions:** 4715 **Census:** 63 **Outpatient Visits:** 186074 **Births:** 717 **Total Expense ($000):** 205248 **Payroll Expense ($000):** 66444

PENDLETON—Umatilla County

CHI ST. ANTHONY HOSPITAL (381319), 2801 St Anthony Way, Zip 97801–3800; tel. 541/276–5121, **A**1 10 18 **F**3 11 13 15 29 30 31 35 37 40 43 45 50 53 57 59 64 65 68 70 75 76 77 78 79 81 85 86 87 91 93 97 107 108 110 111 114 118 119 126 127 129 130 131 132 133 134 135 146 147 148 149 156 157 **P**6 **S** CommonSpirit Health, Chicago, IL
Primary Contact: Harold S. Geller, Chief Executive Officer
CMO: John McBee, Chief of Staff
CNO: Joyce Bailey, Vice President Patient Care
Web address: www.sahpendleton.org
Control: Church operated, Nongovernment, not–for–profit **Service:** General medical and surgical

Staffed Beds: 25 **Admissions:** 1167 **Census:** 11 **Outpatient Visits:** 90915 **Births:** 386 **Total Expense ($000):** 93295 **Payroll Expense ($000):** 35409 **Personnel:** 323

PORTLAND—Multnomah County

ADVENTIST HEALTH PORTLAND (380060), 10123 SE Market Street, Zip 97216–2599; tel. 503/257–2500, **A**1 2 3 5 10 **F**3 9 11 12 13 15 17 18 20 22 24 26 28 29 30 34 35 36 37 40 44 45 46 49 50 53 54 59 64 68 70 71 74 75 76 77 78 79 81 84 85 86 87 93 97 107 108 110 111 114 115 117 118 119 120 121 123 126 129 130 131 143 144 146 147 148 149 154 157 167 169 **P**6 **S** Adventist Health, Roseville, CA
Primary Contact: Kyle King, President
CFO: V Mark Perry, Chief Financial Officer
CMO: Wesley E Rippey, M.D., Chief Medical Officer
CHR: Shane Voshell, Director Human Resources
CNO: Ellen Tryon, R.N., Chief Nursing Officer
Web address: https://www.adventisthealth.org/portland/
Control: Church operated, Nongovernment, not–for–profit **Service:** General medical and surgical

Staffed Beds: 163 **Admissions:** 7522 **Census:** 93 **Outpatient Visits:** 516417 **Births:** 600 **Total Expense ($000):** 395262 **Payroll Expense ($000):** 144144 **Personnel:** 1307

GOOD SAMARITAN HOSPITAL AND MEDICAL CENTER See Legacy Good Samaritan Medical Center, Portland

LEGACY EMANUEL CHILDREN'S HOSPITAL See Randall Children's Hospital

LEGACY EMANUEL MEDICAL CENTER (380007), 2801 North Gantenbein Avenue, Zip 97227–1674; tel. 503/413–2200, (Includes RANDALL CHILDREN'S HOSPITAL, 2801 North Gantenbein Avenue, Portland, Oregon, Zip 97221–1623, tel. 503/413–2200) **A**1 2 3 5 7 8 10 **F**3 7 11 13 15 16 17 18 19 20 21 22 23 24 25 26 27 29 30 31 32 34 35 37 38 39 40 41 43 44 45 46 47 48 49 50 51 54 55 56 57 59 60 61 64 65 66 68 72 74 75 76 77 78 79 80 81 83 84 85 86 87 88 89 91 93 97 98 99 100 101 102 103 107 108 110 111 114 115 118 119 126 127 130 131 132 135 144 146 147 148 149 154 169 **P**6 **S** Legacy Health, Portland, OR
Primary Contact: Bahaa Wanly, President
CHR: Sonja Steves, Senior Vice President Human Resources and Marketing
Web address: www.legacyhealth.org
Control: Other not–for–profit (including NFP Corporation) **Service:** General medical and surgical

Staffed Beds: 531 **Admissions:** 19144 **Census:** 444 **Outpatient Visits:** 377513 **Births:** 1750 **Total Expense ($000):** 1209115 **Payroll Expense ($000):** 635924 **Personnel:** 3540

LEGACY GOOD SAMARITAN MEDICAL CENTER (380017), 1015 NW 22nd Avenue, Zip 97210–3099; tel. 503/413–7711, (Includes GOOD SAMARITAN HOSPITAL AND MEDICAL CENTER, 1015 NW 22nd Avenue, Portland, Oregon, Zip 97210, tel. 503/229–7711; REHABILITATION INSTITUTE OF OREGON, 2010 NW Kearney Street, Portland, Oregon, Zip 97209, tel. 503/226–3774) **A**1 2 3 5 7 10 **F**3 8 11 12 15 18 20 22 26 28 29 30 31 33 34 35 38 40 44 45 46 47 48 49 50 51 55 56 57 58 59 60 61 64 65 68 70 74 75 76 77 78 79 80 81 82 83 84 85 86 87 90 91 93 94 95 96 97 107 108 110 111 114 115 116 117 118 119 120 121 123 124 126 129 130 132 135 138 142 143 144 145 146 147 148 149 154 166 167 169 **P**6 **S** Legacy Health, Portland, OR
Primary Contact: Kevin O'Boyle, President
CIO: C Matthew Calais, Senior Vice President and Chief Information Officer
CHR: Sonja Steves, Vice President Marketing
CNO: Cindy Evans, R.N., MS, Chief Nursing Officer
Web address: www.legacyhealth.org
Control: Other not–for–profit (including NFP Corporation) **Service:** General medical and surgical

Staffed Beds: 236 **Admissions:** 8218 **Census:** 159 **Outpatient Visits:** 199446 **Births:** 801 **Total Expense ($000):** 458065 **Payroll Expense ($000):** 178168 **Personnel:** 1331

OHSU HOSPITAL (380009), 3181 SW Sam Jackson Park Road, Zip 97239–3098; tel. 503/494–7451, (Includes DOERNBECHER CHILDREN'S HOSPITAL, 700 SW Campus DR, Portland, Oregon, Zip 97239–3107, 700 SW CAMPUS DRIVE, Zip 97239, tel. 503/494–8811; Timothy Goldfarb, Interim Chief Executive Officer) **A**2 3 5 8 10 19 21 **F**3 4 5 6 8 9 12 13 15 17 18 19 20 21 22 23 24 25 26 27 28 29 30 31 32 33 34 35 36 37 38 39 40 41 43 44 45 46 47 48 49 50 51 52 53 54 55 56 57 58 59 60 61 64 66 67 68 70 71 72 74 75 76 77 78 79 81 82 84 85 86 87 88 89 90 91 92 93 95 96 97 100 101 104 107 108 109 110 111 112 114 115 116 117 118 119 120 121 123 124 126 127 129 130 131 132 136 137 138 139 141 142 144 145 146 147 148 149 153 154 156 158 160 161 162 163 164 165 167 168 169
Primary Contact: John G. Hunter, M.D., FACS, Executive Vice President and Chief Executive Officer
COO: Joe Ness, Chief Operating Officer
CFO: Jennifer Doll, Interim Chief Financial Officer
CMO: Michael Bonazzola, M.D., Interim Chief Medical Officer
CIO: Bridget Barnes, Vice President and Chief Information Officer
CHR: Dan Forbes, Vice President Human Resources
CNO: Brooke Baldwin, R.N., Vice President and Chief Nursing Executive
Web address: www.ohsu.edu
Control: Hospital district or authority, Government, Nonfederal **Service:** General medical and surgical

Staffed Beds: 562 **Admissions:** 27446 **Census:** 487 **Outpatient Visits:** 1217564 **Births:** 2182 **Total Expense ($000):** 2922109 **Payroll Expense ($000):** 989088 **Personnel:** 8742

PORTLAND HCS, 3710 SW U S Veterans Hospital Road, Zip 97239–2964, Mailing Address: 3710 SW US Veterans Hospital Road, Zip 97207–1034; tel. 503/220–8262, (Nonreporting) **A**1 2 3 5 7 8 **S** Department of Veterans Affairs, Washington, DC
Primary Contact: David Holt, Director
CFO: Josh Wiseman, Chief Financial Officer
CMO: Sahana Misra, Acting Chief of Staff
CHR: Karla Azcuy, Acting Chief Human Resources Officer
CNO: Kathleen Chapman Esq, Deputy Director, Patient Care Services
Web address: www.portland.va.gov/
Control: Veterans Affairs, Government, federal **Service:** General medical and surgical

Staffed Beds: 336

PROVIDENCE PORTLAND MEDICAL CENTER (380061), 4805 NE Glisan Street, Zip 97213–2933; tel. 503/215–1111, **A**1 2 3 5 10 **F**3 9 13 15 18 20 22 24 28 29 30 31 34 35 36 37 38 40 44 45 46 49 50 51 54 55 56 57 58 59 60 61 64 70 72 74 75 76 78 79 81 82 84 90 92 93 98 100 101 102 104 105 106 107 108 109 110 111 114 116 117 118 119 120 121 122 123 124 126 129 130 131 132 135 136 146 147 148 149 153 154 167 **P**6 **S** Providence, Renton, WA
Primary Contact: Krista Farnham, Chief Executive
CFO: Eric Olson, Chief Financial Officer
CMO: Robert Wells, M.D., Chief Medical Officer
CIO: Mark Premo, Senior Director HC Intelligence
CHR: Jeannie Mikulic, Director Human Resources
Web address: https://www.providence.org/locations/or/portland-medical-center
Control: Church operated, Nongovernment, not–for–profit **Service:** General medical and surgical

Staffed Beds: 427 **Admissions:** 19208 **Census:** 332 **Outpatient Visits:** 984565 **Births:** 2411 **Total Expense ($000):** 1189832 **Payroll Expense ($000):** 351349

REHABILITATION INSTITUTE OF OREGON See Legacy Good Samaritan Medical Center, Portland

Hospitals, U.S. / OREGON

☐ **SHRINERS HOSPITALS FOR CHILDREN–PORTLAND (383300)**, 3101 SW Sam Jackson Park Road, Zip 97239–3009; tel. 503/241–5090, **A**1 3 5 10 **F**3 29 34 35 37 50 58 64 68 75 79 81 85 86 87 89 91 93 94 100 130 131 132 146 149 154 164 **P**6 **S** Shriners Hospitals for Children, Tampa, FL
Primary Contact: Dereesa Reid, Administrator
CFO: Mark Knudsen, Director Fiscal Services
CMO: Michael Aiona, M.D., Chief of Staff
CIO: Carl Montante, Director Information Systems and Information Technology
CHR: Rhonda Smith, Director Human Resources
CNO: Suzanne Diers, R.N., Director Patient Care Services
Web address: www.shrinershospitalsforchildren.org/portland
Control: Other not–for–profit (including NFP Corporation) **Service:** Children's orthopedic

Staffed Beds: 12 **Admissions:** 339 **Census:** 4 **Outpatient Visits:** 32102 **Births:** 0 **Total Expense ($000):** 42628 **Payroll Expense ($000):** 27840 **Personnel:** 213

✠ **VIBRA SPECIALTY HOSPITAL OF PORTLAND (382004)**, 10300 NE Hancock Street, Zip 97220–3831; tel. 503/257–5500, (Nonreporting) **A**1 10 **S** Vibra Healthcare, Mechanicsburg, PA
Primary Contact: Michael Kerr, Chief Executive Officer
CFO: Stephanie Lawrence, Chief Financial Officer
CMO: Cynthia Wallace, M.D., Medical Director
CHR: Kellie Bernert–Yap, Director Human Resources
CNO: Susan E Brooker, R.N., Chief Clinical Officer
Web address: www.vshportland.com
Control: Corporation, Investor–owned (for–profit) **Service:** Acute long–term care hospital

Staffed Beds: 63

PORTLAND—Washington County

☐ **CEDAR HILLS HOSPITAL (384012)**, 10300 SW Eastridge Street, Zip 97225–5004; tel. 503/944–5000, (Nonreporting) **A**1 10 **S** Universal Health Services, Inc., King of Prussia, PA
Primary Contact: David Melear, Chief Executive Officer
Web address: www.cedarhillshospital.com
Control: Corporation, Investor–owned (for–profit) **Service:** Psychiatric

Staffed Beds: 78

✠ **PROVIDENCE ST. VINCENT MEDICAL CENTER (380004)**, 9205 SW Barnes Road, Zip 97225–6661; tel. 503/216–1234, (Includes CHILDREN AT PROVIDENCE ST. VINCENT, 9205 SW Barnes Road, Portland, Oregon, Zip 97225–6603, tel. 503/216–4400) **A**1 2 3 5 10 **F**3 5 13 15 17 18 20 22 24 26 28 29 30 31 34 35 36 37 38 40 41 44 45 46 47 48 49 50 51 53 54 56 57 58 59 60 61 64 65 70 72 74 75 76 77 78 79 81 82 84 85 86 87 88 89 91 92 93 97 98 100 102 104 105 107 108 109 110 111 112 114 115 116 117 118 119 120 121 123 126 129 130 131 132 135 137 146 147 148 149 153 154 161 164 167 169 **P**6 **S** Providence, Renton, WA
Primary Contact: Jennifer Burrows, R.N., Chief Executive
COO: Nancy Roberts, Chief Operating Officer
CFO: Scott Pfister, Director Finance
Web address: www.providence.org/portland/hospitals
Control: Church operated, Nongovernment, not–for–profit **Service:** General medical and surgical

Staffed Beds: 530 **Admissions:** 23831 **Census:** 378 **Outpatient Visits:** 669310 **Births:** 3029 **Total Expense ($000):** 1129861 **Payroll Expense ($000):** 368152

PRINEVILLE—Crook County

★ **ST. CHARLES PRINEVILLE (381313)**, 384 SE Combs Flat Road, Zip 97754–1206; tel. 541/447–6254, **A**3 5 10 18 **F**3 11 29 30 34 35 40 43 50 53 59 64 65 75 77 81 82 85 86 87 91 93 97 119 127 130 133 135 146 148 149 154 167 **S** St. Charles Health System, Inc., Bend, OR
Primary Contact: Todd Shields, Vice President, Hospital Administrator
CFO: Karen Shepard, Senior Vice President and Chief Financial Officer
CMO: Michel Boileau, M.D., Chief Clinical Officer
CHR: Rebecca Berry, Senior Director Human Resources
Web address: www.stcharleshealthcare.org
Control: Other not–for–profit (including NFP Corporation) **Service:** General medical and surgical

Staffed Beds: 16 **Admissions:** 641 **Census:** 8 **Outpatient Visits:** 64443 **Births:** 0 **Total Expense ($000):** 42413 **Payroll Expense ($000):** 19714 **Personnel:** 147

REDMOND—Deschutes County

✠ **ST. CHARLES REDMOND (380040)**, 1253 NW Canal Boulevard, Zip 97756–1395; tel. 541/548–8131, **A**1 10 **F**3 11 15 26 29 30 31 32 34 35 38 40 43 44 45 50 53 57 59 64 65 70 75 77 78 79 81 82 84 85 87 97 107 111 115 119 126 130 132 135 146 148 149 154 156 167 **S** St. Charles Health System, Inc., Bend, OR
Primary Contact: David Golda, Vice President Hospital and Administrator
CFO: Jennifer Welander, CPA, Senior Vice President Finance and Chief Financial Officer
CMO: Jeffrey Absalon, M.D., Chief Physician Officer
CIO: Jerimiah Brickhouse, Chief Information Officer
CHR: Rebecca Berry, Vice President Human Resources
Web address: www.stcharleshealthcare.org
Control: Other not–for–profit (including NFP Corporation) **Service:** General medical and surgical

Staffed Beds: 36 **Admissions:** 2269 **Census:** 18 **Outpatient Visits:** 69818 **Births:** 0 **Total Expense ($000):** 86976 **Payroll Expense ($000):** 42156 **Personnel:** 337

REEDSPORT—Douglas County

★ **LOWER UMPQUA HOSPITAL DISTRICT (381311)**, 600 Ranch Road, Zip 97467–1795; tel. 541/271–2171, **A**10 18 **F**3 7 15 29 34 35 40 43 45 46 50 57 59 64 65 70 75 77 79 81 82 85 87 93 97 107 108 115 119 127 128 130 131 132 133 135 143 146 148 149 154 **P**6
Primary Contact: John Chivers, Chief Executive Officer
CMO: Ronald Vail, M.D., Chief of Staff
CIO: Timothy Picou, Manager Information Technology
Web address: www.lowerumpquahospital.com
Control: Hospital district or authority, Government, Nonfederal **Service:** General medical and surgical

Staffed Beds: 13 **Admissions:** 460 **Census:** 5 **Outpatient Visits:** 24161 **Births:** 0 **Total Expense ($000):** 37144 **Payroll Expense ($000):** 15219 **Personnel:** 193

ROSEBURG—Douglas County

✠ **MERCY MEDICAL CENTER (380027)**, 2700 Northwest Stewart Parkway, Zip 97471–1281; tel. 541/673–0611, **A**1 3 10 **F**3 8 11 13 15 18 19 20 22 26 28 29 30 35 37 39 40 43 45 50 51 56 59 63 70 76 80 81 84 85 87 89 93 98 100 102 103 107 108 110 111 115 119 126 130 146 148 149 154 157 160 167 169 **P**5 6 7 **S** CommonSpirit Health, Chicago, IL
Primary Contact: Russell Woolley, President and Chief Executive Officer
COO: Debbie Boswell, Chief Operating Officer and Chief Nursing Officer
CFO: Grant L Glines, Vice President Operation Finance
CMO: Jason Gray, M.D., Chief Medical Officer
CIO: Kathleen Nickel, Director Communications
CHR: Debora Lightcap, Director Human Resources
CNO: Debbie Boswell, Chief Operating Officer and Chief Nursing Officer
Web address: www.mercyrose.org
Control: Church operated, Nongovernment, not–for–profit **Service:** General medical and surgical

Staffed Beds: 135 **Admissions:** 6584 **Census:** 70 **Outpatient Visits:** 294240 **Births:** 807 **Total Expense ($000):** 265566 **Payroll Expense ($000):** 98736 **Personnel:** 1185

✠ **ROSEBURG VA MEDICAL CENTER**, 913 NW Garden Valley Boulevard, Zip 97471–6513; tel. 541/440–1000, (Nonreporting) **A**1 3 **S** Department of Veterans Affairs, Washington, DC
Primary Contact: Keith M. Allen, Medical Center Director
CHR: Larry Mentzer, Chief Human Resources Officer
Web address: www.roseburg.va.gov/
Control: Veterans Affairs, Government, federal **Service:** General medical and surgical

Staffed Beds: 13

VETERANS AFFAIRS ROSEBURG HEALTHCARE SYSTEM See Roseburg VA Medical Center

Hospitals, U.S. / OREGON

SALEM—Marion County

☐ **OREGON STATE HOSPITAL (384008)**, 2600 Center Street NE, Zip 97301-2682; tel. 503/945-2870, (Nonreporting) **A**1 3 5 10
Primary Contact: Sara Walker, Interim Superintendent
Web address: www.oregon.gov/OHA/amh/osh/
Control: State, Government, Nonfederal **Service**: Psychiatric

Staffed Beds: 680

REGIONAL REHABILITATION CENTER See Salem Health Rehabilitation Center

✠ **SALEM HOSPITAL (380051)**, 890 Oak Street SE, Zip 97301-3959, Mailing Address: P.O. Box 14001, Zip 97309-5014; tel. 503/561-5200, (Includes PSYCHIATRIC MEDICINE CENTER, 1127 Oak ST SE, Salem, Oregon, Zip 97301-4020, P O Box 14001, Zip 97309-5014, tel. 503/561-5761; SALEM HEALTH REHABILITATION CENTER, 755 Mission ST SE, Salem, Oregon, Zip 97302-6211, P O Box 14001, tel. 503/561-5986) **A**1 2 10 **F**3 5 11 12 13 15 17 18 20 22 24 26 28 29 30 31 34 35 36 37 38 40 43 44 45 46 47 48 49 50 53 54 55 57 58 59 63 64 68 70 72 74 75 76 77 78 79 80 81 82 84 85 86 87 89 90 91 92 93 94 96 97 98 100 101 102 106 107 108 109 110 111 114 115 116 117 118 119 120 121 122 123 124 126 127 129 130 131 132 135 144 145 146 147 148 149 154 156 160 164 167 169 **S** Salem Health, Salem, OR
Primary Contact: Cheryl R. Nester Wolfe, R.N., President and Chief Executive Officer
CFO: James Parr, Chief Financial Officer
CMO: Ralph Yates, D.O., Chief Medical Officer
CIO: Leah Mitchell, R.N., Interim Chief Information Officer
CNO: Sarah Horn, Chief Nursing Officer
Web address: www.salemhealth.org
Control: Other not-for-profit (including NFP Corporation) **Service**: General medical and surgical

Staffed Beds: 567 **Admissions**: 24292 **Census**: 358 **Outpatient Visits**: 545742 **Births**: 2975 **Total Expense ($000)**: 1063867 **Payroll Expense ($000)**: 531090 **Personnel**: 4228

SEASIDE—Clatsop County

✠ **PROVIDENCE SEASIDE HOSPITAL (381303)**, 725 South Wahanna Road, Zip 97138-7735; tel. 503/717-7000, **A**1 3 10 18 **F**3 15 18 29 30 31 32 34 35 40 44 45 46 50 56 57 59 62 64 65 66 70 75 76 78 79 81 84 85 86 87 91 92 93 97 102 104 107 110 111 114 119 127 130 132 133 135 146 147 148 149 156 164 169 **P**6 **S** Providence, Renton, WA
Primary Contact: Rebecca Coplin, Chief Executive Officer
COO: Jason Plamondon, Chief Operating Officer
CFO: Pamela Cooper, Director Finance
CMO: Robert Morse, Chief Medical Officer
CHR: John Anglim, Human Resources Client Manager
CNO: Jason Plamondon, Chief Nursing Officer
Web address: www.providence.org
Control: Church operated, Nongovernment, not-for-profit **Service**: General medical and surgical

Staffed Beds: 24 **Admissions**: 1017 **Census**: 12 **Outpatient Visits**: 82439 **Births**: 54 **Total Expense ($000)**: 92309 **Payroll Expense ($000)**: 43539

SILVERTON—Marion County

✠ **LEGACY SILVERTON MEDICAL CENTER (380029)**, 139 Breyonna Way, Zip 97381, Mailing Address: 342 Fairview Street, Zip 97381-1993; tel. 503/873-1500, **A**1 10 **F**3 11 13 15 28 29 30 34 35 40 43 45 47 50 54 59 64 65 68 70 75 76 77 79 81 85 86 87 93 96 107 108 110 111 114 115 119 124 126 127 130 131 132 135 144 146 147 148 149 154 **P**6 **S** Legacy Health, Portland, OR
Primary Contact: Joseph Yoder, President, Willamette Valley Region
COO: Karen Brady, R.N., MSN, Vice President, Chief Nursing Officer
CFO: Daniel Jessup, Chief Financial Officer
CMO: Joseph Huang, M.D., Chief Medical and Quality Officer
CIO: Karen Brady, R.N., MSN, Vice President, Chief Nursing Officer
CHR: Natalie Britton, Manager Employee Relations
CNO: Karen Brady, R.N., MSN, Vice President, Chief Nursing Officer
Web address: www.legacyhealth.org/locations/hospitals/legacy-silverton-medical-center.aspx
Control: Other not-for-profit (including NFP Corporation) **Service**: General medical and surgical

Staffed Beds: 47 **Admissions**: 2541 **Census**: 20 **Outpatient Visits**: 264344 **Births**: 1212 **Total Expense ($000)**: 137422 **Payroll Expense ($000)**: 62237 **Personnel**: 502

SPRINGFIELD—Lane County

☐ **MCKENZIE–WILLAMETTE MEDICAL CENTER (380020)**, 1460 'G' Street, Zip 97477-4197; tel. 541/726-4400, **A**1 10 **F**3 13 18 20 22 24 26 28 29 34 35 39 40 41 43 45 46 47 49 50 57 59 70 73 76 79 81 82 85 87 89 107 108 111 115 118 119 126 130 132 146 147 148 154 166 167 **P**6 **S** Quorum Health, Brentwood, TN
Primary Contact: David Butler, Chief Executive Officer
CFO: Rosanne Devault, Chief Financial Officer
CIO: David Blomquist, Director Information Technology
CHR: Megan A O'Leary, Vice President Human Resources and Rehabilitation Services
Web address: www.mckweb.com
Control: Corporation, Investor-owned (for-profit) **Service**: General medical and surgical

Staffed Beds: 112 **Admissions**: 7041 **Census**: 76 **Outpatient Visits**: 107433 **Births**: 656 **Total Expense ($000)**: 248884 **Payroll Expense ($000)**: 86957 **Personnel**: 735

★ ⇧ **PEACEHEALTH SACRED HEART MEDICAL CENTER AT RIVERBEND (380102)**, 3333 Riverbend Drive, Zip 97477-8800; tel. 541/222-7300, **A**10 21 **F**3 8 11 12 13 15 18 20 22 24 26 28 29 30 31 32 34 35 37 38 40 43 45 46 47 48 49 50 51 53 54 56 57 58 59 60 65 70 72 74 75 76 77 78 79 81 82 85 87 89 90 91 92 93 94 96 97 98 100 101 102 104 105 107 108 111 115 118 119 120 123 124 126 130 132 135 145 146 147 148 149 153 154 156 167 169 **S** PeaceHealth, Vancouver, WA
Primary Contact: Alicia Beymer, Chief Administrative Officer
COO: Todd Salnas, Chief Operating Officer
CFO: Paul Warda, Chief Financial Officer
CHR: Marie F Stehmer, Senior Director of Human Resources
CNO: Heather Wall, Chief Nursing Officer
Web address: www.peacehealth.org
Control: Church operated, Nongovernment, not-for-profit **Service**: General medical and surgical

Staffed Beds: 416 **Admissions**: 22217 **Census**: 285 **Outpatient Visits**: 191800 **Births**: 2290 **Total Expense ($000)**: 816020 **Payroll Expense ($000)**: 307000 **Personnel**: 2876

STAYTON—Marion County

✠ **SANTIAM HOSPITAL (380056)**, 1401 North 10th Avenue, Zip 97383-1399; tel. 503/769-2175, **A**1 10 **F**3 4 7 11 13 15 16 17 29 30 40 41 43 50 65 70 72 73 76 79 80 81 85 87 88 89 90 98 107 111 115 119 128 130 133 135 143 154 167 169 **P**3
Primary Contact: Maggie Hudson, President and Chief Executive Officer
CFO: Rachael Seeder, Controller
CMO: Scott Hadden, M.D., Medical Staff President
CIO: Trace Jacobs, Director Information Technology
CNO: Sherri Steele, Chief Nursing Officer
Web address: www.santiamhospital.org
Control: Other not-for-profit (including NFP Corporation) **Service**: General medical and surgical

Staffed Beds: 40 **Admissions**: 762 **Census**: 10 **Outpatient Visits**: 54971 **Births**: 144 **Total Expense ($000)**: 112277 **Payroll Expense ($000)**: 52627 **Personnel**: 483

THE DALLES—Wasco County

✠ **ADVENTIST HEALTH COLUMBIA GORGE (380001)**, 1700 East 19th Street, Zip 97058-3317; tel. 541/296-1111, **A**1 10 **F**3 9 11 13 15 18 28 29 30 31 32 34 35 36 40 43 45 46 50 54 57 59 62 64 65 66 70 74 75 76 77 78 79 81 82 85 87 89 90 91 92 93 96 97 100 104 107 108 110 111 114 118 119 120 121 123 126 127 129 130 131 132 135 144 146 147 148 149 154 156 157 160 167 169 **S** Adventist Health, Roseville, CA
Primary Contact: Kyle King, President
COO: Larry Kahl, Chief Operating Officer
CFO: Edwin J Bode, Chief Financial Officer
CMO: Judy Richardson, M.D., President Medical Staff
CIO: Erick Larson, Vice President and Chief Information Officer
CHR: Christine Espy, Division Director
CNO: Felicia M Adams, MS, Chief Nursing Officer
Web address: www.mcmc.net
Control: Other not-for-profit (including NFP Corporation) **Service**: General medical and surgical

Staffed Beds: 43 **Admissions**: 1498 **Census**: 16 **Outpatient Visits**: 198290 **Births**: 183 **Total Expense ($000)**: 140713 **Payroll Expense ($000)**: 66888 **Personnel**: 661

Hospitals, U.S. / OREGON

TILLAMOOK—Tillamook County

ADVENTIST HEALTH TILLAMOOK (381317), 1000 Third Street, Zip 97141–3430; tel. 503/842–4444, **A**1 10 18 **F**2 3 5 7 13 15 18 29 30 31 33 34 35 37 40 43 45 50 59 64 65 68 70 75 76 77 78 79 81 85 86 87 93 94 97 102 104 107 108 110 111 115 119 127 129 130 131 132 133 134 135 144 146 147 148 149 154 156 160 161 167 169 **P**6 **S** Adventist Health, Roseville, CA
Primary Contact: Eric Swanson, President
CFO: Walt Larson, Vice President Finance
CMO: Mark Bowman, M.D., President Medical Staff
CNO: Kathy Saxon, R.N., Vice President Patient Care Services
Web address: https://www.adventisthealth.org/tillamook/
Control: Church operated, Nongovernment, not–for–profit **Service**: General medical and surgical

> **Staffed Beds:** 25 **Admissions:** 922 **Census:** 9 **Outpatient Visits:** 165957 **Births:** 94 **Total Expense ($000):** 106942 **Payroll Expense ($000):** 35643 **Personnel:** 353

TUALATIN—Clackamas County

LEGACY MERIDIAN PARK MEDICAL CENTER (380089), 19300 SW 65th Avenue, Zip 97062–9741; tel. 503/692–1212, **A**1 2 10 **F**3 13 15 18 20 22 28 29 30 31 32 34 35 38 40 44 45 46 49 50 51 56 57 59 60 64 68 70 74 75 76 77 78 79 80 81 85 86 87 91 93 97 100 107 108 110 111 114 115 116 117 118 119 120 121 126 129 130 132 135 145 146 147 148 149 154 167 **P**6 **S** Legacy Health, Portland, OR
Primary Contact: Joseph Yoder, President, Willamette Valley Region
COO: Michael Newcomb, D.O., Senior Vice President and Chief Operating Officer
CMO: Lewis Low, M.D., Senior Vice President and Chief Medical Officer
CIO: John Jay Kenagy, Ph.D., Senior Vice President and Chief Information Officer
CHR: Sonja Steves, Vice President Human Resources and Marketing
Web address: www.legacyhealth.org
Control: Other not–for–profit (including NFP Corporation) **Service**: General medical and surgical

> **Staffed Beds:** 146 **Admissions:** 6538 **Census:** 98 **Outpatient Visits:** 242636 **Births:** 892 **Total Expense ($000):** 266302 **Payroll Expense ($000):** 109777 **Personnel:** 838

WHITE CITY—Jackson County

SOUTHERN OREGON–WHITE CITY VETERANS AFFAIRS REHABILITATION CENTER AND CLINICS See White City, Or Southern Oregon Rehabilitation Center & Clinics

---

Hospital, Medicare Provider Number, Address, Telephone, Approval, Facility, and Physician Codes, Health Care System

★ American Hospital Association (AHA) membership
☐ The Joint Commission accreditation
○ Healthcare Facilities Accreditation Program
◇ DNV Healthcare Inc. accreditation
⇑ Center for Improvement in Healthcare Quality Accreditation
△ Commission on Accreditation of Rehabilitation Facilities (CARF) accreditation

© 2025 AHA Guide

PENNSYLVANIA

ABINGTON—Montgomery County

ABINGTON JEFFERSON HEALTH See Jefferson Abington Health

JEFFERSON ABINGTON HEALTH (390231), 1200 Old York Road, Zip 19001–3720; tel. 215/481–2000, **A**1 2 3 5 10 13 **F**3 4 8 9 11 12 13 15 17 18 20 22 24 26 28 29 30 31 32 34 35 36 37 38 39 40 43 44 45 46 47 48 49 50 52 53 54 55 56 57 58 59 61 63 64 65 66 68 70 72 73 74 75 76 77 78 79 80 81 82 84 85 86 87 89 90 91 92 93 94 96 97 98 100 101 103 104 107 108 110 111 114 115 119 120 121 123 124 126 129 130 131 132 135 145 146 147 148 149 150 154 156 160 162 164 167 169 **P**1 **S** Jefferson Health, Philadelphia, PA
Primary Contact: Brian Sweeney, President, North Region
COO: Alison Ferren, President and Chief Operating Officer
CFO: Michael Walsh, Senior Vice President Finance and Chief Financial Officer
CMO: Gerard M. Cleary, M.D., Senior Vice President, Chief of Staff and Chief Medical Officer
CHR: Meghan Patton, Vice President Human Resources
CNO: Stacey–Ann Okoth, R.N., Senior Vice President and Chief Nursing Officer
Web address: www.abingtonhealth.org
Control: Other not–for–profit (including NFP Corporation) **Service**: General medical and surgical

Staffed Beds: 574 **Admissions**: 28038 **Census**: 454 **Outpatient Visits**: 442612 **Births**: 4503 **Total Expense ($000)**: 987064 **Payroll Expense ($000)**: 402877 **Personnel**: 4720

ALLENTOWN—Lehigh County

ALLENTOWN OSTEOPATHIC MED CTR See St Luke's Hospital – Allentown Campus

△ **GOOD SHEPHERD REHABILITATION NETWORK (393035)**, 850 South 5th Street, Zip 18103–3308; tel. 610/776–3299, **A**1 3 5 7 10 **F**1 10 29 30 34 35 36 53 54 56 57 58 59 64 68 74 75 77 79 82 87 90 91 92 93 94 95 96 107 122 130 131 132 146 147 154 158 **S** Good Shepherd Rehabilitation Network, Allentown, PA
Primary Contact: Michael Spigel, Chief Executive Officer
CFO: Ronald J. Petula, Chief Financial Officer
Web address: www.goodshepherdrehab.org
Control: Other not–for–profit (including NFP Corporation) **Service**: Rehabilitation

Staffed Beds: 94 **Admissions**: 1148 **Census**: 57 **Outpatient Visits**: 249559 **Births**: 0 **Personnel**: 1027

☐ **LEHIGH VALLEY HEALTH NETWORK AT COORDINATED HEALTH (390321)**, 1503 North Cedar Crest Boulevard, Zip 18104–2302; tel. 610/861–8080, (Nonreporting) **A**1 5 10
Primary Contact: James Miller, President of Lehigh Valley Health Muhlenberg and North Hampton Region
Web address: www.coordinatedhealth.com
Control: Other not–for–profit (including NFP Corporation) **Service**: Surgical

Staffed Beds: 20

LEHIGH VALLEY HEALTH NETWORK PEDIATRICS See Lehigh Valley Health Network Pediatrics

LEHIGH VALLEY HOSPITAL–CEDAR CREST (390133), 1200 South Cedar Crest Boulevard, Zip 18103–6248, Mailing Address: P.O. Box 689, Zip 18105–1556; tel. 610/402–8000, (Includes LEHIGH VALLEY HEALTH NETWORK PEDIATRICS, 1200 S Cedar Crest Blvd, Allentown, Pennsylvania, Zip 18103–6202, P.O. Box 689, Zip 18105, tel. 484/862–3131; LEHIGH VALLEY HOSPITAL–MUHLENBERG, 2545 Schoenersville Road, Bethlehem, Pennsylvania, Zip 18017–7300, tel. 484/884–2200; Brian A. Nester, D.O., President and Chief Executive Officer; LEHIGH VALLEY REILLY CHILDREN'S HOSPITAL, 1200 South Cedar Crest Boulevard, Allentown, Pennsylvania, Zip 18103–6202, P.O. Box 689, Zip 18105–1556, tel. 610/402–8000; Anne Baum, President) **A**1 2 3 8 10 13 19 **F**3 6 7 8 9 11 12 13 15 16 17 18 19 20 22 24 26 28 30 31 32 34 35 36 37 38 39 40 41 43 44 45 46 47 48 49 51 53 54 55 56 57 58 59 61 62 63 64 65 68 70 71 72 74 76 77 78 79 80 81 82 84 85 86 87 88 89 90 92 93 94 95 96 97 98 99 100 101 102 104 105 106 107 108 110 111 114 115 116 117 118 119 120 121 123 124 126 128 129 130 131 132 134 135 136 138 141 142 143 144 145 146 147 148 149 150 154 155 160 161 162 164 165 167 169 **P**5 **S** Lehigh Valley Health Network, Allentown, PA
Primary Contact: Robert Begliomini, President, LVH Cedar Crest and Lehigh Region
COO: John Pierro, Executve Vice President and Chief Operating Officer
CFO: Edward O'Dea, Executive Vice President and Chief Financial Officer
CMO: Thomas V. Whalen, M.D., Chief Medical Officer
CIO: Michael N. Minear, Senior Vice President and Chief Information Officer
CNO: Marie Kim Jordan, R.N., Senior Vice President and Chief Nursing Officer
Web address: www.lvhn.org
Control: Other not–for–profit (including NFP Corporation) **Service**: General medical and surgical

Staffed Beds: 1120 **Admissions**: 59155 **Census**: 921 **Outpatient Visits**: 1058500 **Births**: 4557 **Total Expense ($000)**: 3011528 **Payroll Expense ($000)**: 854672 **Personnel**: 11407

SACRED HEART HOSPITAL See St. Luke's Sacred Heart Campus

ST LUKE'S HOSPITAL – ALLENTOWN CAMPUS See St. Luke's University Hospital – Bethlehem Campus, Bethlehem

ALTOONA—Blair County

ENCOMPASS HEALTH REHABILITATION HOSPITAL OF ALTOONA (393040), 2005 Valley View Boulevard, Zip 16602–4598; tel. 814/944–3535, (Nonreporting) **A**1 10 **S** Encompass Health Corporation, Birmingham, AL
Primary Contact: Scott Filler, Chief Executive Officer
CFO: George Berger, Controller
CMO: Rakesh Patel, D.O., Medical Director
CIO: Kathleen Edwards, Manager Information Systems Operation
CHR: Christine Filer, Director Human Resources
CNO: Mary Gen Boyles, Chief Nursing Officer
Web address: www.healthsouthaltoona.com
Control: Corporation, Investor–owned (for–profit) **Service**: Rehabilitation

Staffed Beds: 80

JAMES E. VAN ZANDT VETERANS AFFAIRS MEDICAL CENTER, 2907 Pleasant Valley Boulevard, Zip 16602–4305; tel. 814/943–8164, (Nonreporting) **A**1 3 **S** Department of Veterans Affairs, Washington, DC
Primary Contact: Derek Coughenour, DPT, CLD, Medical Center Director
CFO: Carl Parrish, Chief Fiscal Service
CIO: Michael Hynoski, Chief Information Resource Management
CHR: Gina Dunio, Chief Human Resources
Web address: www.altoona.va.gov/
Control: Veterans Affairs, Government, federal **Service**: General medical and surgical

Staffed Beds: 89

UPMC ALTOONA (390073), 620 Howard Avenue, Zip 16601–4804; tel. 814/889–2011, **A**1 2 3 5 10 12 13 20 **F**3 8 12 13 15 17 18 20 22 24 26 28 29 30 31 34 35 37 38 39 40 43 44 45 47 48 49 50 51 56 57 59 60 61 64 65 66 68 70 73 74 75 76 77 78 79 81 83 84 85 86 87 89 97 98 100 101 102 103 107 108 110 111 114 115 117 118 119 120 121 123 126 129 130 131 132 135 146 147 148 149 154 155 156 163 165 167 169 **P**6 **S** UPMC, Pittsburgh, PA
Primary Contact: Michael Corso, President and Chief Executive Officer, UPMC Altoona/Bedford
COO: Ron McConnell, Chief Operating Officer
CFO: Monica Klatt, Chief Financial Officer
CMO: Linnane Batzel, M.D., Senior Vice President Quality and Medical Affairs and Chief Medical Officer
CIO: Dale Fuller, Vice President and Chief Information Officer
CHR: Michelle A Speck, Vice President Human Resources
CNO: Chris Rickens, R.N., MS, Senior Vice President and Chief Nursing Officer
Web address: www.altoonaregional.org
Control: Other not–for–profit (including NFP Corporation) **Service**: General medical and surgical

Staffed Beds: 346 **Admissions**: 15065 **Census**: 221 **Outpatient Visits**: 373381 **Births**: 1571 **Total Expense ($000)**: 587096 **Payroll Expense ($000)**: 181499 **Personnel**: 1666

AMBLER—Montgomery County

☐ **THE HORSHAM CLINIC (394034)**, 722 East Butler Pike, Zip 19002–2310; tel. 215/643–7800, **A**1 3 5 10 **F**4 98 99 105 **S** Universal Health Services, Inc., King of Prussia, PA
Primary Contact: Kim Whitelock, Chief Executive Officer
CMO: James B Congdon, M.D., Medical Director
CIO: Suzanne Scholz, Director Medical Records
CHR: Kathleen Nichelson, Director Human Resources
CNO: Calvin Litka, R.N., Director of Nursing
Web address: www.horshamclinic.com
Control: Corporation, Investor–owned (for–profit) **Service**: Psychiatric

Staffed Beds: 206 **Admissions**: 4306 **Census**: 189 **Outpatient Visits**: 0 **Births**: 0 **Total Expense ($000)**: 65149 **Payroll Expense ($000)**: 31158 **Personnel**: 457

Hospitals, U.S. / PENNSYLVANIA

BEAVER—Beaver County

☐ **HERITAGE VALLEY BEAVER (390036)**, 1000 Dutch Ridge Road, Zip 15009–9727; tel. 724/728–7000, (Nonreporting) **A**1 3 5 10 13 **S** Heritage Valley Health System, Beaver, PA
Primary Contact: Norman F. Mitry, President and Chief Executive Officer
COO: John Luellen, M.D., Chief Operating Officer
CFO: Robert Rosenberger, Chief Financial Officer
CMO: Michael Cratty, M.D., Chief Medical Officer
CIO: David Carleton, Chief Information Officer
CHR: Bruce Edwards, Vice President Human Resources
CNO: Linda Homyk, Chief Nursing Officer
Web address: https://www.heritagevalley.org/locations/heritage-valley-beaver/
Control: Other not–for–profit (including NFP Corporation) **Service**: General medical and surgical

Staffed Beds: 285

★ **PAM HEALTH SPECIALTY HOSPITAL OF HERITAGE VALLEY (392043)**, 1000 Dutch Ridge Road, Zip 15009–9727; tel. 724/773–8480, **A**10 22 **F**1 148 **S** PAM Health, Enola, PA
Primary Contact: Emily Hensh, Chief Executive Officer
CFO: Chad Deardorff, Chief Financial Officer
CMO: Jeffrey Erukhimou, M.D., Medical Director
CNO: Geri Reichenbach, Nurse Executive
Web address: https://pamhealth.com/index.php/facilities/find-facility/specialty-hospitals/pam-health-specialty-hospital-heritage-valley
Control: Corporation, Investor–owned (for–profit) **Service**: Acute long–term care hospital

Staffed Beds: 35 **Admissions**: 294 **Census**: 18 **Outpatient Visits**: 0 **Births**: 0 **Total Expense ($000)**: 10541 **Payroll Expense ($000)**: 5346 **Personnel**: 78

BENSALEM—Bucks County

LIVENGRIN FOUNDATION, 4833 Hulmeville Road, Zip 19020–3099; tel. 215/638–5200, (Nonreporting)
Primary Contact: David Blenk, President and Chief Executive Officer
CFO: Hai H. Nguyen, CPA, Vice President Finance
CMO: James W. Cornish, M.D., Medical Director
CIO: William Miller, Coordinator Management Information Systems
Web address: www.livengrin.org
Control: Other not–for–profit (including NFP Corporation) **Service**: Substance Use Disorder

Staffed Beds: 76

☐ **ROTHMAN ORTHOPAEDIC SPECIALTY HOSPITAL (390322)**, 3300 Tillman Drive, Zip 19020–2071; tel. 215/244–7400, (Nonreporting) **A**1 3 10
Primary Contact: Kelly Doyle, Chief Executive Officer
Web address: www.rothmanspecialtyhospital.com/
Control: Partnership, Investor–owned (for–profit) **Service**: Orthopedic

Staffed Beds: 24

BERWICK—Columbia County

BERWICK HOSPITAL CENTER (394058), 701 East 16th Street, Zip 18603–2397; tel. 570/759–5000, (Nonreporting) **A**10
Primary Contact: Priyam Sharma, Chief Executive Officer
CFO: Whitney Holloway, Chief Financial Officer
CMO: John A. Guerriero, D.O., III, Chief of Staff
CIO: Kerry Yeager, Director Information Technology
CHR: Gail Kauffman, Director Human Resources
Web address: https://berwickhospitalcenter.com/
Control: Corporation, Investor–owned (for–profit) **Service**: Psychiatric

Staffed Beds: 101

BETHLEHEM—Lehigh County

☐ △ **GOOD SHEPHERD SPECIALTY HOSPITAL (392033)**, 2545 Schoenersville Road, Zip 18017–7300; tel. 484/884–5056, (Nonreporting) **A**1 7 10 **S** Good Shepherd Rehabilitation Network, Allentown, PA
Primary Contact: Michael Spigel, Chief Executive Officer
CFO: Ronald J. Petula, Chief Financial Officer
CIO: Michael Cirba, Chief Information Officer
CHR: Kristen Melan, Director Human Resources Administration
CNO: Samuel Miranda Jr, Chief Nursing Officer
Web address: www.goodshepherdrehab.org
Control: Other not–for–profit (including NFP Corporation) **Service**: Acute long–term care hospital

Staffed Beds: 32

MUHLENBERG HOSPITAL CENTER See Lehigh Valley Hospital–Muhlenberg

☐ △ **ST. LUKE'S UNIVERSITY HOSPITAL – BETHLEHEM CAMPUS (390049)**, 801 Ostrum Street, Zip 18015–1065; tel. 484/526–4000, (Includes ST LUKE'S HOSPITAL – ALLENTOWN CAMPUS, 1736 Hamilton Street, Allentown, Pennsylvania, Zip 18104–5656, tel. 610/628–8300; William Moyer, President; ST. LUKE'S LEHIGHTON CAMPUS, 211 North 12th Street, Lehighton, Pennsylvania, Zip 18235–1138, tel. 610/377–1300; John L Nespoli, President; ST. LUKE'S SACRED HEART CAMPUS, 421 West Chew Street, Allentown, Pennsylvania, Zip 18102–3490, tel. 610/776–4500; Frank Ford, President) (Nonreporting) **A**1 2 3 5 7 8 10 12 13 19 **S** St. Luke's University Health Network, Bethlehem, PA
Primary Contact: Carol Kuplen, R.N., MSN, President
CFO: Tom Lichtenwalner, Vice President Finance
CMO: Jeffrey Jahre, M.D., Vice President Medical and Academic Affairs
CIO: Chad Brisendine, Chief Information Officer
CHR: Robert Zimmel, Senior Vice President Human Resources
Web address: https://www.slhn.org/bethlehem
Control: Other not–for–profit (including NFP Corporation) **Service**: General medical and surgical

Staffed Beds: 959

BLOOMSBURG—Columbia County

★ **GEISINGER–BLOOMSBURG HOSPITAL (390003)**, 549 Fair Street, Zip 17815–1419; tel. 570/387–2100, **A**3 5 10 **F**3 11 13 15 26 28 29 30 34 35 38 40 44 45 50 51 55 56 57 59 62 63 65 68 74 75 76 81 85 86 87 89 91 92 93 98 100 101 102 104 107 108 110 111 115 119 130 132 135 144 146 147 148 149 150 154 156 160 164 **P**1 5 8 **S** Geisinger, Danville, PA
Primary Contact: Megan M. Brosious, Chief Administrative Officer, Central Region
COO: Joseph M DeVito, Vice President Finance and Chief Operating Officer
CFO: Joseph M DeVito, Vice President Finance and Chief Operating Officer
CMO: James Joseph, M.D., President Medical Staff
CIO: Thomas Wray, Director Information
Web address: https://www.geisinger.org/patient-care/find-a-location/geisinger-bloomsburg-hospital
Control: Other not–for–profit (including NFP Corporation) **Service**: General medical and surgical

Staffed Beds: 60 **Admissions**: 2800 **Census**: 35 **Outpatient Visits**: 102008 **Births**: 381 **Total Expense ($000)**: 72711 **Payroll Expense ($000)**: 31690 **Personnel**: 421

BRADFORD—Mckean County

BRADFORD HOSPITAL See Bradford Regional Medical Center

BRISTOL—Bucks County

☐ **LOWER BUCKS HOSPITAL (390070)**, 501 Bath Road, Zip 19007–3190; tel. 215/785–9200, (Nonreporting) **A**1 3 5 10 13 **S** Prime Healthcare, Ontario, CA
Primary Contact: Michael J. Motte, Chief Executive Officer
CFO: David Lim, Chief Financial Officer
CMO: Sanjay Bhatia, Chief Medical Officer
CIO: Steve Kane, Director Information Technology
CNO: Pat Bain, Chief Nursing Officer
Web address: www.lowerbuckshosp.com
Control: Other not–for–profit (including NFP Corporation) **Service**: General medical and surgical

Staffed Beds: 100

BROOKVILLE—Jefferson County

PENN HIGHLANDS BROOKVILLE (391312), 100 Hospital Road, Zip 15825–1367; tel. 814/849–2312, (Nonreporting) **A**3 10 18
Primary Contact: Julianne Peer, President
CFO: Jessica Park, Director Accounting
CMO: Timothy Pendleton, M.D., President Medical Staff
CIO: Thomas Johnson, Director Information Systems
CHR: Rebecca Edwards, Chief Human Resources Officer
CNO: Debra A. Thomas, Vice President of Patient Care Services and Chief Nursing Officer
Web address: www.phhealthcare.org/
Control: Other not–for–profit (including NFP Corporation) **Service**: General medical and surgical

Staffed Beds: 35

Hospital, Medicare Provider Number, Address, Telephone, Approval, Facility, and Physician Codes, Health Care System

★ American Hospital Association (AHA) membership   ○ Healthcare Facilities Accreditation Program   ⇧ Center for Improvement in Healthcare Quality Accreditation
☐ The Joint Commission accreditation   ◇ DNV Healthcare Inc. accreditation   △ Commission on Accreditation of Rehabilitation Facilities (CARF) accreditation

© 2025 AHA Guide

Hospitals, U.S. / PENNSYLVANIA

BRYN MAWR—Montgomery County

✠ **BRYN MAWR HOSPITAL (390139)**, 130 South Bryn Mawr Avenue, Zip 19010-3160; tel. 484/337-3000, **A**1 2 3 5 10 13 19 **F**3 11 12 13 15 18 20 22 26 28 29 30 31 32 34 35 36 38 39 40 41 45 49 54 55 56 57 58 59 61 63 64 65 66 69 70 72 74 75 76 77 78 79 80 81 82 84 85 86 87 89 93 98 100 102 104 105 107 108 110 111 114 115 119 120 121 123 124 126 129 130 131 132 134 135 145 146 148 149 153 154 157 162 164 167 169 **S** Main Line Health, Ontario, CA
Primary Contact: John T. Schwarz, President
CFO: Michael J Buongiorno, Executive Vice President Finance and Chief Financial Officer
CMO: Andrew J Norton, M.D., Chief Medical Officer
CIO: Kay Carr, Chief Information Officer
CHR: Terry Dougherty, Director Human Resources
CNO: Barbara A Wadsworth, MSN, R.N., FACHE, DNP, RN, Chief Nursing Officer
Web address: www.brynmawrhospital.org
Control: Other not-for-profit (including NFP Corporation) **Service**: General medical and surgical

Staffed Beds: 284 **Admissions**: 16317 **Census**: 193 **Outpatient Visits**: 255758 **Births**: 2001 **Total Expense ($000)**: 442473 **Payroll Expense ($000)**: 135575 **Personnel**: 1740

BUTLER—Butler County

★ **BUTLER MEMORIAL HOSPITAL (390168)**, 1 Hospital Way, Zip 16001-4697; tel. 724/283-6666, **A**3 10 **F**3 4 5 11 12 13 15 18 20 22 24 26 28 29 30 31 32 35 40 45 49 57 59 63 64 70 74 75 76 77 79 81 82 84 85 87 92 93 98 100 102 103 105 107 108 111 114 115 118 119 124 125 129 130 131 132 135 146 147 148 149 152 154 160 167 **P**2 6 8 **S** Independence Health System, Butler, PA
Primary Contact: Karen A. Allen, R.N., President, Butler & Clarion Hospitals
COO: Jason R. Sciarro, Chief Operating Officer
CFO: Eric Huss, Chief Financial Officer
CMO: David Rottinghaus, M.D., Director
CIO: Roger Lutz, Chief Information Officer
CHR: Thomas A Genevro, Vice President Human Resources
Web address: www.butlerhealthsystem.org
Control: Other not-for-profit (including NFP Corporation) **Service**: General medical and surgical

Staffed Beds: 261 **Admissions**: 9195 **Census**: 140 **Outpatient Visits**: 441075 **Births**: 542 **Total Expense ($000)**: 294093 **Payroll Expense ($000)**: 119040 **Personnel**: 1484

CAMP HILL—Cumberland County

✠ **PENN STATE HEALTH HOLY SPIRIT MEDICAL CENTER (390004)**, 503 North 21st Street, Zip 17011-2204; tel. 717/763-2100, **A**1 3 5 10 **F**3 14 15 17 18 20 22 24 26 28 29 30 37 38 40 43 44 45 46 47 48 49 50 54 57 58 59 64 65 66 70 74 77 78 79 81 84 85 86 87 98 100 101 102 104 105 107 108 110 111 114 115 118 119 120 121 123 124 126 129 130 131 132 134 135 145 146 147 148 149 153 154 156 162 164 165 167 **S** Penn State Health, Hershey, PA
Primary Contact: Kyle C. Snyder, President
CMO: J. Bret DeLone, M.D., Vice President, Medical Affairs
CNO: Gloria Santos, Vice President, Nursing
Web address: www.pennstatehealth.org
Control: Other not-for-profit (including NFP Corporation) **Service**: General medical and surgical

Staffed Beds: 188 **Admissions**: 8745 **Census**: 149 **Outpatient Visits**: 208541 **Births**: 0 **Total Expense ($000)**: 298038 **Payroll Expense ($000)**: 93731 **Personnel**: 1272

✠ **SELECT SPECIALTY HOSPITAL–CAMP HILL (392039)**, 503 North 21st Street, 5th Floor, Zip 17011-2204; tel. 717/972-4575, (Includes SELECT SPECIALTY HOSPITAL–HARRISBURG, 111 S Front ST Bldg 5th, Alex Grass Building, 5Th Floor, Harrisburg, Pennsylvania, Zip 17101-2010, 111 South Front Street, Zip 17101, tel. 717/724-6610; John E. Simodejka, Market Chief Executive Officer; SELECT SPECIALTY HOSPITAL–YORK, 1701 Innovation Drive, 5th Floor, York, Pennsylvania, Zip 17408-8815, tel. 717/851-2661; Gregory P. Toot, Chief Executive Officer) (Nonreporting) **A**1 10 **S** Select Medical Corporation, Mechanicsburg, PA
Primary Contact: Adam Beck, Market Chief Executive Officer
CNO: Courtney Morse, Chief Nursing Officer
Web address: www.camphill.selectspecialtyhospitals.com/
Control: Corporation, Investor-owned (for-profit) **Service**: Acute long-term care hospital

Staffed Beds: 92

STATE CORRECTIONAL INSTITUTION AT CAMP HILL, 2500 Lisburn Road, Zip 17011-8005, Mailing Address: P.O. Box 200, Zip 17001-0200; tel. 717/737-4531, (Nonreporting)
Primary Contact: Beth Herb, Administrator
Web address: www.cor.state.pa.us/
Control: State, Government, Nonfederal **Service**: Hospital unit of an institution (prison hospital, college infirmary, etc.)

Staffed Beds: 34

CANONSBURG—Washington County

✠ **CANONSBURG HOSPITAL (390160)**, 100 Medical Boulevard, Zip 15317-9762; tel. 724/745-6100, **A**1 10 **F**3 7 8 11 15 18 28 29 34 35 40 44 45 46 47 50 54 57 59 65 70 74 75 77 78 79 81 82 85 86 87 90 92 93 96 107 108 110 111 114 115 118 119 129 130 132 135 141 146 148 149 154 167 169 **S** Allegheny Health Network, Pittsburgh, PA
Primary Contact: Chong S. Park, M.D., Chief Executive Officer
COO: Kelly Kassab, Chief Operating Officer
CMO: Thomas B Corkery, D.O., Chief Medical Officer
CIO: David Vincent, Director Information Systems
CHR: Martha L Clister, Director Human Resources
Web address: www.wpahs.org
Control: Other not-for-profit (including NFP Corporation) **Service**: General medical and surgical

Staffed Beds: 64 **Admissions**: 1610 **Census**: 26 **Outpatient Visits**: 93596 **Births**: 0 **Total Expense ($000)**: 66267 **Payroll Expense ($000)**: 24934 **Personnel**: 351

CARLISLE—Cumberland County

✠ **UPMC CARLISLE (390058)**, 361 Alexander Spring Road, Zip 17015-6940; tel. 717/249-1212, **A**1 3 10 **F**3 8 14 15 18 20 29 30 31 34 35 37 38 40 44 45 46 48 49 50 51 54 55 57 59 60 64 65 68 70 72 75 76 77 78 79 81 84 85 87 90 96 102 107 108 109 110 111 114 115 117 118 119 120 121 123 126 129 130 132 146 147 148 149 154 164 167 169 **S** UPMC, Pittsburgh, PA
Primary Contact: Jarrod G. Johnson, FACHE, President
CFO: Alison Bernhardt, Chief Financial Officer
CMO: Ivan' Sola', President Medical Staff
CHR: Sylvia Rockwood, Director Human Resources
Web address: https://www.upmc.com/locations/hospitals/carlisle
Control: Other not-for-profit (including NFP Corporation) **Service**: General medical and surgical

Staffed Beds: 86 **Admissions**: 5109 **Census**: 72 **Outpatient Visits**: 184826 **Total Expense ($000)**: 152848 **Payroll Expense ($000)**: 45606 **Personnel**: 752

CENTRE HALL—Centre County

✠ **THE MEADOWS PSYCHIATRIC CENTER (394040)**, 132 The Meadows Drive, Zip 16828-9231; tel. 814/364-2161, (Nonreporting) **A**1 10 **S** Universal Health Services, Inc., King of Prussia, PA
Primary Contact: Rodney Kornrumpf, Chief Executive Officer
CFO: Stephen DelRossi, Chief Financial Officer
CMO: Orlando Davis, M.D., Medical Director
CHR: Mary Jane Schreffler, Director Human Resources
CNO: Tara Kunkel, R.N., MSN, Chief Nursing Officer
Web address: www.themeadows.net
Control: Corporation, Investor-owned (for-profit) **Service**: Psychiatric

Staffed Beds: 119

CHAMBERSBURG—Franklin County

★ ⇑ **WELLSPAN CHAMBERSBURG HOSPITAL (390151)**, 112 North Seventh Street, Zip 17201-1720; tel. 717/267-3000, **A**2 3 5 10 19 21 **F**3 11 12 13 15 17 18 20 22 26 28 29 30 40 44 49 50 59 68 70 72 74 75 76 79 81 84 85 86 87 90 93 96 98 100 102 104 107 108 110 111 114 115 119 126 129 130 131 146 148 149 154 167 **S** WellSpan Health, York, PA
Primary Contact: John P. Massimilla, FACHE, WSH Vice President and President of Wellspan Chambersburg
CFO: Kimberly Rzomp, Vice President and Chief Financial Officer
CMO: Thomas Anderson, M.D., Vice President Medical Affairs
CIO: Michele Zeigler, Vice President and Chief Information Officer
CNO: Elyse Fisler, Chief Nursing Officer
Web address: https://www.wellspan.org/offices-locations/wellspan-chambersburg-hospital/
Control: Other not-for-profit (including NFP Corporation) **Service**: General medical and surgical

Staffed Beds: 286 **Admissions**: 11450 **Census**: 242 **Outpatient Visits**: 268604 **Births**: 1562 **Total Expense ($000)**: 412370 **Payroll Expense ($000)**: 120100 **Personnel**: 4455

CLARION—Clarion County

☐ **CLARION HOSPITAL (390093)**, 1 Hospital Drive, Zip 16214–8501;
tel. 814/226–9500, **A**1 3 5 10 12 13 **F**3 7 15 18 28 29 31 34 35 40 44 45 46
47 48 49 51 57 59 63 65 68 70 78 81 82 85 87 91 96 107 108 110 111 116
117 119 120 121 122 123 128 129 130 132 133 143 146 149 154 156 167 **S**
Independence Health System, Butler, PA
Primary Contact: Karen A. Allen, R.N., President
CFO: Will Grant, Interim Chief Financial Officer
CMO: Anie Perard, M.D., President, Medical Staff
CIO: James Confer, Manager Information Systems
CHR: Brooke N. Divins, Director Human Resources
CNO: Leslie Walters, MSN, Chief Nursing Officer
Web address: www.clarionhospital.org
Control: Other not–for–profit (including NFP Corporation) **Service**: General medical and surgical

Staffed Beds: 67 **Admissions**: 974 **Census**: 13 **Outpatient Visits**: 117530
Births: 0 **Total Expense ($000)**: 49927 **Payroll Expense ($000)**: 23106
Personnel: 277

CLARION PSYCHIATRIC CENTER (394043), 2 Hospital Drive,
Zip 16214–8502; tel. 814/226–9545, (Nonreporting) **A**10 **S** Universal Health Services, Inc., King of Prussia, PA
Primary Contact: Jessica Hansford, Chief Executive Officer
CFO: Shelly Rhoades, Chief Financial Officer
CMO: Jeffrey Moll, M.D., Medical Director
CHR: Dianne C Bilunka, Director Human Resources
CNO: Rhonda Massa, Director of Nursing
Web address: www.clarioncenter.com
Control: Corporation, Investor–owned (for–profit) **Service**: Psychiatric

Staffed Beds: 96

CLARKS SUMMIT—Lackawanna County

CLARKS SUMMIT STATE HOSPITAL (394012), 1451 Hillside Drive,
Zip 18411–9504; tel. 570/586–2011, **A**10 **F**29 39 56 57 65 75 98 101 130 146 156
Primary Contact: Monica Bradbury, Chief Executive Officer
COO: Gordon Weber, Chief Operating Officer
CMO: David Waibel, M.D., Medical Director
CHR: William Abda, Chief Human Resources Officer
Web address: www.dpw.state.pa.us/
Control: State, Government, Nonfederal **Service**: Psychiatric

Staffed Beds: 203 **Admissions**: 33 **Census**: 137 **Outpatient Visits**: 0
Births: 0 **Total Expense ($000)**: 56938 **Payroll Expense ($000)**: 24222
Personnel: 274

CLEARFIELD—Clearfield County

CLEARFIELD HOSPITAL See Penn Highlands Clearfield

COAL TOWNSHIP—Northumberland County

GEISINGER SHAMOKIN AREA COMMUNITY HOSPITAL See Geisinger–Shamokin Area Community Hospital

COALDALE—Schuylkill County

☐ **ST. LUKE'S HOSPITAL–MINERS CAMPUS (390183)**, 360 West Ruddle Street,
Zip 18218–1027; tel. 570/645–2131, (Nonreporting) **A**1 3 10 **S** St. Luke's University Health Network, Bethlehem, PA
Primary Contact: Diane Laquintz, President
COO: Joel Fagerstrom, Executive Vice President and Chief Operating Officer
CFO: Michele Levitz, Director Finance
CIO: Chad Brisendine, Vice President and Chief Information Officer
CHR: Susan Van Why, Director Human Resources
CNO: Kimberly Sargent, Vice President Patient Services
Web address: https://www.slhn.org/locations/stlukes-hospital-miners-campus
Control: Other not–for–profit (including NFP Corporation) **Service**: General medical and surgical

Staffed Beds: 97

COATESVILLE—Chester County

✠ **COATESVILLE VETERANS AFFAIRS MEDICAL CENTER**, 1400 Black Horse Hill Road, Zip 19320–2040; tel. 610/384–7711, (Nonreporting) **A**1 3 5 **S** Department of Veterans Affairs, Washington, DC
Primary Contact: Jennifer Harkins, Executive Director
CFO: Tony Wolfgang, Chief Financial Officer
CMO: Sheila Chellappa, M.D., Chief of Staff
CIO: Ryan McGettigan, Chief Information Officer
CHR: Andrew Sutton, Chief Human Resources Officer
CNO: Nancy A Schmid, R.N., MS, Associate Director Patient Care Services
Web address: www.coatesville.va.gov/
Control: Veterans Affairs, Government, federal **Service**: Substance Use Disorder

Staffed Beds: 302

CONNELLSVILLE—Fayette County

HIGHLANDS HOSPITAL See Penn Highlands Connellsville

PENN HIGHLANDS CONNELLSVILLE (390184), 401 East Murphy Avenue,
Zip 15425–2700; tel. 724/628–1500, (Nonreporting) **A**10
Primary Contact: Peter J. Adamo, Regional Market President, SW Region/President, Penn Highlands Mon Valley
CMO: Paul Means, M.D., President Medical Staff
CHR: Mary June Krosoff, Chief Human Resources Officer
CNO: Vicki Rough, Chief Nursing Officer
Web address: www.highlandshospital.org
Control: Other not–for–profit (including NFP Corporation) **Service**: General medical and surgical

Staffed Beds: 61

CORRY—Erie County

LECOM HEALTH CORRY MEMORIAL HOSPITAL (391308), 965 Shamrock Lane, Zip 16407; tel. 814/664–4641, (Nonreporting) **A**3 10 18
Primary Contact: Dan Grolemund, Chief Executive Officer
CFO: Michael Heller, Chief Financial Officer
CMO: Paul McGeehan, M.D., Chief Medical Staff
CHR: Brenda Cooper, Director Quality and Human Resources
CNO: Patty White, R.N., Director Patient Care Services
Web address: www.corryhospital.com
Control: Other not–for–profit (including NFP Corporation) **Service**: General medical and surgical

Staffed Beds: 25

COUDERSPORT—Potter County

✠ **UPMC COLE (391313)**, 1001 East Second Street, Zip 16915–8161;
tel. 814/274–9300, (Total facility includes 44 beds in nursing home–type unit) **A**1
3 10 18 **F**3 10 13 15 18 28 29 30 31 32 34 35 39 40 44 45 47 49 50 53 57
59 62 63 64 68 70 75 76 77 78 79 81 82 84 85 86 87 89 90 93 96 97 107
108 110 111 115 117 118 119 127 128 130 131 132 133 146 147 148 149
154 156 157 169 **P**6 **S** UPMC, Pittsburgh, PA
Primary Contact: Janie Marie. Hilfiger, R.N., President
CFO: Ronald Rapp, Vice President Finance
CMO: Brenda Wahlers, M.D., Chief of Staff
CHR: James Evens, Executive Director, Human Resources and General Services
CNO: Emily Ann Bunnell, Chief Nurse Executive, Senior Director of Acute Care
Web address: www.colememorial.org/
Control: Other not–for–profit (including NFP Corporation) **Service**: General medical and surgical

Staffed Beds: 69 **Admissions**: 1184 **Census**: 40 **Outpatient Visits**: 257629
Births: 189 **Total Expense ($000)**: 96134 **Payroll Expense ($000)**: 45227
Personnel: 374

CRANBERRY TOWNSHIP—Butler County

ST FRANCIS HOSPITAL CRANBERRY See UPMC Passavant Cranberry

UPMC PASSAVANT CRANBERRY See UPMC Passavant, Pittsburgh

Hospital, Medicare Provider Number, Address, Telephone, Approval, Facility, and Physician Codes, Health Care System

★ American Hospital Association (AHA) membership
☐ The Joint Commission accreditation
○ Healthcare Facilities Accreditation Program
◇ DNV Healthcare Inc. accreditation
⇧ Center for Improvement in Healthcare Quality Accreditation
△ Commission on Accreditation of Rehabilitation Facilities (CARF) accreditation

Hospitals, U.S. / PENNSYLVANIA

DANVILLE—Montour County

DANVILLE STATE HOSPITAL (394004), 200 State Hospital Drive, Zip 17821–9198; tel. 570/271–4500, (Nonreporting) **A**10
Primary Contact: Theresa Long, Chief Executive Officer
COO: Thomas J Burk, Chief Operating Officer
CFO: Patricia Riegert, Director Fiscal Services
CMO: Vikrant Mittal, M.D., Chief Medical Officer
CHR: Thomas J Burk, Chief Operating Officer
CNO: Brenda Lahout, Chief Nurse Executive
Web address: www.dpw.state.pa.us/foradults/statehospitals/danvillestatehospital/index.htm
Control: State, Government, Nonfederal **Service**: Psychiatric

Staffed Beds: 161

GEISINGER ENCOMPASS HEALTH REHABILITATION HOSPITAL (393047), 64 Rehab Lane, Zip 17821–8498; tel. 570/271–6733, (Nonreporting) **A**1 3 10 **S** Encompass Health Corporation, Birmingham, AL
Primary Contact: Lorie Dillon, Chief Executive Officer
CMO: Greg Burke, M.D., Medical Director
CHR: Christian Shirley, Director Human Resources
Web address: www.geisingerhealthsouth.com
Control: Corporation, Investor–owned (for–profit) **Service**: Rehabilitation

Staffed Beds: 42

GEISINGER MEDICAL CENTER (390006), 100 North Academy Avenue, Zip 17822–2201; tel. 570/271–6211, (Includes GEISINGER–SHAMOKIN AREA COMMUNITY HOSPITAL, 4200 Hospital Road, Coal Township, Pennsylvania, Zip 17866–9697, tel. 570/644–4200) **A**1 2 3 5 8 10 13 19 **F**1 3 4 5 7 8 9 11 12 13 14 15 17 18 19 20 21 22 23 24 25 26 27 28 29 30 31 32 34 35 36 37 39 40 41 43 44 45 46 47 48 49 50 51 52 53 54 55 56 57 58 59 60 61 62 63 64 65 66 68 70 71 72 74 75 76 77 79 81 82 83 84 85 86 87 88 89 91 92 93 94 96 97 98 100 101 102 104 107 108 110 111 114 115 116 117 118 119 120 121 123 124 126 129 130 131 132 134 135 136 138 139 141 143 145 146 147 148 149 150 153 154 155 156 160 162 164 166 167 **P**1 5 8 **S** Geisinger, Danville, PA
Primary Contact: Megan M. Brosious, Chief Administrative Officer, Central Region
CFO: Kevin Lanciotti, Chief Financial Officer, Vice President Finance
CIO: Frank Richards, Chief Information Officer
CHR: Amy Brayford, Chief Human Resources Officer
Web address: www.geisinger.org
Control: Other not–for–profit (including NFP Corporation) **Service**: General medical and surgical

Staffed Beds: 553 **Admissions**: 29593 **Census**: 437 **Outpatient Visits**: 1147984 **Births**: 1946 **Total Expense ($000)**: 1606191 **Payroll Expense ($000)**: 560721 **Personnel**: 6765

DARBY—Delaware County

FITZGERALD MERCY HOSPITAL See Mercy Fitzgerald Hospital

MERCY FITZGERALD HOSPITAL (390156), 1500 Lansdowne Avenue, Zip 19023–1200; tel. 610/237–4000, (Includes MERCY FITZGERALD HOSPITAL, 1500 South Lansdowne Avenue, Darby, Pennsylvania, Zip 19023, tel. 610/237–4000) **A**1 2 3 5 6 **F**3 11 12 15 18 21 22 24 26 28 29 30 31 34 35 40 45 46 49 50 51 54 57 59 61 64 66 70 74 75 77 78 79 81 82 85 86 87 90 91 92 93 97 98 100 101 102 107 108 110 111 114 115 118 119 120 121 123 124 126 130 131 132 135 145 146 147 148 149 150 154 164 167 **S** Trinity Health, Livonia, MI
Primary Contact: Marlow Levy, President
COO: Ruth Thomas, Chief Operating Officer
CFO: Don Snenk, Chief Financial Officer
CMO: Jeff Komins, M.D., Chief Medical Officer
CIO: Jeff Byda, Vice President Information Technology
CNO: Sharon Urban, R.N., Chief Nursing Officer
Web address: https://www.trinityhealthma.org/location/mcmc-mercy-fitzgerald
Control: Other not–for–profit (including NFP Corporation) **Service**: General medical and surgical

Staffed Beds: 104 **Admissions**: 7076 **Census**: 99 **Outpatient Visits**: 108171 **Births**: 0 **Total Expense ($000)**: 215284 **Payroll Expense ($000)**: 74508 **Personnel**: 584

DOWNINGTOWN—Chester County

★ **SAINT JOHN VIANNEY HOSPITAL**, 151 Woodbine Road, Zip 19335–3057; tel. 610/269–2600, **F**4 29 38 75 77 98 100 106 135 154 **P**6
Primary Contact: David Shellenberger, President
CMO: James MacFadyen, M.D., Medical Director
CHR: Linda Rava Esq, Director Human Resources
CNO: Diana Karanja, R.N., Director of Nursing
Web address: www.sjvcenter.org
Control: Other not–for–profit (including NFP Corporation) **Service**: Psychiatric

Staffed Beds: 50 **Admissions**: 160 **Census**: 37 **Outpatient Visits**: 415 **Births**: 0 **Total Expense ($000)**: 11054 **Payroll Expense ($000)**: 3762 **Personnel**: 80

DOYLESTOWN—Bucks County

△ **DOYLESTOWN HEALTH (390203)**, 595 West State Street, Zip 18901–2597; tel. 215/345–2200, **A**1 2 3 5 7 10 **F**3 13 15 17 18 20 22 24 26 28 29 30 31 32 34 35 40 45 46 47 49 50 54 55 56 57 58 59 62 63 64 65 70 73 74 75 76 77 78 79 80 81 84 85 86 87 92 93 94 96 107 108 110 111 115 118 119 124 126 130 131 132 134 135 145 146 147 148 149 154 156 164 167 169
Primary Contact: James L. Brexler, FACHE, President and Chief Executive Officer
COO: Eleanor Wilson, R.N., MSN, Vice President and Chief Operating Officer
CFO: Daniel Upton, Vice President and Chief Financial Officer
CMO: Scott S Levy, M.D., Vice President and Chief Medical Officer
CIO: Richard Lang, Ed.D., Vice President and Chief Information Officer
CHR: Barbara Hebel, Vice President Human Resources
CNO: Patricia A Stover, Administrator Nursing
Web address: www.doylestownhealth.org
Control: Other not–for–profit (including NFP Corporation) **Service**: General medical and surgical

Staffed Beds: 247 **Admissions**: 13769 **Census**: 158 **Outpatient Visits**: 293755 **Births**: 1367 **Total Expense ($000)**: 351317 **Payroll Expense ($000)**: 146196 **Personnel**: 2311

☐ **FOUNDATIONS BEHAVIORAL HEALTH (394038)**, 833 East Butler Avenue, Zip 18901–2280; tel. 215/345–0444, (Nonreporting) **A**1 10 **S** Universal Health Services, Inc., King of Prussia, PA
Primary Contact: Amy Smith, Interim Chief Executive Officer
Web address: www.fbh.com
Control: Other not–for–profit (including NFP Corporation) **Service**: Children's hospital psychiatric

Staffed Beds: 58

DUBOIS—Clearfield County

⇑ **PENN HIGHLANDS DUBOIS (390086)**, 100 Hospital Avenue, Zip 15801–1440, Mailing Address: P.O. Box 447, Zip 15801–0447; tel. 814/371–2200, (Includes PENN HIGHLANDS CLEARFIELD, 809 Turnpike Avenue, Clearfield, Pennsylvania, Zip 16830–1232, P O Box 992, Zip 16830–0992, tel. 814/765–5341; Rhonda Halstead, President) (Nonreporting) **A**3 5 10 13 21
Primary Contact: William A. Chinn, President
CFO: Brian S Kline, Vice President and Chief Financial Officer
CMO: Gary Dugan, M.D., Vice President Medical Affairs
CHR: Jake Maijala, Chief Human Resource Officer
Web address: www.drmc.org
Control: Other not–for–profit (including NFP Corporation) **Service**: General medical and surgical

Staffed Beds: 259

EAGLEVILLE—Montgomery County

★ **EAGLEVILLE HOSPITAL (390278)**, 100 Eagleville Road, Zip 19403–1829, Mailing Address: P.O. Box 45, Zip 19408–0045; tel. 610/539–6000, (Nonreporting) **A**5 10
Primary Contact: Eugene J. Ott Jr, Chief Executive Officer
CFO: Alfred P Salvitti, Chief Financial Officer
CMO: Robert Wilson, D.O., Director Medical Services
CIO: Richard R Mitchell, Director Information Technology
CHR: Zoe Yousaitis, Director Human Resources
Web address: https://www.eagleville.org/
Control: Other not–for–profit (including NFP Corporation) **Service**: Substance Use Disorder

Staffed Beds: 83

EAST NORRITON—Montgomery County

EINSTEIN MEDICAL CENTER MONTGOMERY See Jefferson Einstein Montgomery Hospital

☐ **JEFFERSON EINSTEIN MONTGOMERY HOSPITAL (390329)**, 559 West Germantown Pike, Zip 19403–4250; tel. 484/622–1000, **A**1 2 3 5 10 **F**3 4 8 11 12 13 15 18 20 22 24 26 29 30 31 34 35 40 45 46 49 54 55 57 59 63 64 68 70 72 74 75 76 78 79 80 81 82 85 87 92 107 108 110 111 115 117 119 120 121 123 126 129 130 131 132 135 146 147 148 149 167 169 **P**6 **S** Jefferson Health, Philadelphia, PA
Primary Contact: Brian Sweeney, President, North Region
COO: Beth Duffy, President and Chief Operating Officer
CFO: Gerard Blaney, Vice President, Finance
CMO: Angela Nicholas, Vice President, Medical Affairs
CIO: Mary Carroll Ford, Chief Information Officer
CNO: AnnMarie Papa, R.N., Vice President and Chief Nursing Officer
Web address: https://www.einstein.edu/einstein-medical-center-montgomery
Control: Other not–for–profit (including NFP Corporation) **Service**: General medical and surgical

Staffed Beds: 195 **Admissions**: 10671 **Census**: 141 **Outpatient Visits**: 128984 **Births**: 1888 **Total Expense ($000)**: 256160 **Payroll Expense ($000)**: 94421 **Personnel**: 1552

Hospitals, U.S. / PENNSYLVANIA

☐ **SUBURBAN COMMUNITY HOSPITAL (390116)**, 2701 Dekalb Pike, Zip 19401-1820; tel. 610/278-2000, (Nonreporting) **A**1 3 5 10 12 13 **S** Prime Healthcare, Ontario, CA
Primary Contact: Michael J. Motte, Chief Executive Officer
COO: Joseph Schofield, Chief Operating Officer
CFO: Joseph Marino, Chief Financial Officer
CMO: Andrea D Pedano, D.O., Chief Medical Officer
CIO: Jason Wayne, Network Administrator
CHR: Gretchen Pendleton, Director Human Resources
CNO: Mary Ellen Rauner, R.N., Chief Nursing Officer
Web address: www.suburbanhosp.org
Control: Other not-for-profit (including NFP Corporation) **Service**: General medical and surgical

Staffed Beds: 126

EAST STROUDSBURG—Monroe County

✚ **LEHIGH VALLEY HOSPITAL – POCONO (390201)**, 206 East Brown Street, Zip 18301-3006; tel. 570/421-4000, **A**1 2 10 **F**3 11 12 13 15 17 18 20 22 24 26 28 29 31 35 38 39 40 43 44 45 46 49 50 54 55 59 63 64 65 68 70 72 74 75 76 78 79 80 81 84 85 87 89 90 94 96 98 100 102 107 108 109 111 115 116 117 118 119 120 121 123 124 128 130 132 135 144 146 149 154 160 161 164 167 169 **P**6 **S** Lehigh Valley Health Network, Allentown, PA
Primary Contact: Cornelio R. Catena, FACHE, President
COO: Kim Jordan, Chief Operating officer
CMO: William K. Cors, M.D., Senior Medical Director
CIO: Ferd Feola, Chief Information Officer
CHR: Lynn Lansdowne, Vice President Labor Relations and Human Resources
CNO: Michele Roberts, Vice President, Patient Care Services
Web address: www.pmchealthsystem.org
Control: Other not-for-profit (including NFP Corporation) **Service**: General medical and surgical

Staffed Beds: 249 **Admissions**: 8833 **Census**: 100 **Outpatient Visits**: 252545 **Births**: 681 **Total Expense ($000)**: 234024 **Payroll Expense ($000)**: 78296 **Personnel**: 1498

EASTON—Northampton County

☐ **ST. LUKE'S ANDERSON CAMPUS (390326)**, 1872 Riverside Circle, Zip 18045-5669; tel. 484/503-3000, (Nonreporting) **A**1 2 3 5 10 **S** St. Luke's University Health Network, Bethlehem, PA
Primary Contact: Edward Nawrocki, President
CMO: Justin P Psaila, M.D., Vice President Medical Affairs
CNO: Darla Frack, MSN, Vice President, Patient Services
Web address: www.mystlukesonline.org
Control: Other not-for-profit (including NFP Corporation) **Service**: General medical and surgical

Staffed Beds: 199

☐ **ST. LUKE'S EASTON CAMPUS (390162)**, 250 South 21st Street, Zip 18042-3892; tel. 610/250-4000, (Nonreporting) **A**1 3 5 10 19 **S** St. Luke's University Health Network, Bethlehem, PA
Primary Contact: Linda J. Grass, President
COO: Ronald Ziobro, Chief Operating Officer
CFO: Arthur Comito, Chief Financial Officer
CMO: Roman Tuma, Chief Medical Officer
CIO: Don Lutz, Director Information Technology
CHR: Tanya Segal, Director
CNO: Karen Vadyak, Chief Nursing Officer
Web address: https://www.easton-hospital.org/
Control: Other not-for-profit (including NFP Corporation) **Service**: General medical and surgical

Staffed Beds: 23

ELKINS PARK—Montgomery County

MOSS REHAB, EINSTEIN AT ELKINS PARK See Einstein Medical Center Elkins Park

ENOLA—Cumberland County

✚ **PENN STATE HEALTH HAMPDEN MEDICAL CENTER (390336)**, 2200 Good Hope Road, Zip 17025-1210; tel. 787/981-9000, **A**1 **F**3 13 15 18 29 30 34 35 37 40 44 45 47 49 50 57 59 60 65 70 72 74 76 77 79 80 81 84 85 86 87 102 107 108 110 111 115 119 126 130 135 146 147 149 150 154 167 169 **S** Penn State Health, Hershey, PA
Primary Contact: Kyle C. Snyder, President
COO: Deborah Addo, Executive Vice Preisdent and Chief Operating Officer
CMO: James Learning, M.D., Interim Vice President Medical Affairs and Staff Development
CIO: Cletis Earle, Senior Vice President and Chief Information Officer
CHR: David Swift, Senior Vice President and Chief Human Resource Officer
CNO: Hirsch–Lanute Hirsch–Lanute, Interim Vice President and Chief Nursing Officer
Web address: www.pennstatehealth.org/
Control: Other not-for-profit (including NFP Corporation) **Service**: General medical and surgical

Staffed Beds: 47 **Admissions**: 3179 **Census**: 35 **Outpatient Visits**: 33427 **Births**: 528 **Total Expense ($000)**: 137338 **Payroll Expense ($000)**: 36278 **Personnel**: 452

EPHRATA—Lancaster County

★ ⇑ **WELLSPAN EPHRATA COMMUNITY HOSPITAL (390225)**, 169 Martin Avenue, Zip 17522-1724, Mailing Address: P.O. Box 1002, Zip 17522-1002; tel. 717/733-0311, **A**2 3 10 19 21 **F**3 7 12 13 15 18 20 22 26 28 29 30 31 40 44 46 49 50 51 54 60 64 68 70 72 74 75 76 77 78 79 80 81 82 84 85 86 87 90 92 98 100 107 108 110 111 114 115 116 117 118 119 120 121 123 126 129 130 131 132 146 147 148 149 154 155 167 169 **S** WellSpan Health, York, PA
Primary Contact: Tina Citro, R.N., President and Vice President Operations
CFO: David Kreider, Controller
CMO: Mark Jacobson, D.O., Vice President Medical Affairs
CIO: Leon John Jabour, Regional Chief Information Officer
CHR: Jana Salaki, Regional Director Human Resources
CNO: Orie Chambers Jr, Vice President Patient Care Services and Chief Nursing Officer
Web address: https://www.wellspan.org/locations/wellspan-ephrata-community-hospital-loc0000169489
Control: Other not-for-profit (including NFP Corporation) **Service**: General medical and surgical

Staffed Beds: 141 **Admissions**: 5712 **Census**: 131 **Outpatient Visits**: 78333 **Births**: 763 **Total Expense ($000)**: 279607 **Payroll Expense ($000)**: 59742 **Personnel**: 653

ERIE—Erie County

✚ **ENCOMPASS HEALTH REHABILITATION HOSPITAL OF ERIE (393046)**, 143 East Second Street, Zip 16507-1501; tel. 814/878-1200, (Nonreporting) **A**1 10 **S** Encompass Health Corporation, Birmingham, AL
Primary Contact: Janet Hein, Chief Executive Officer
CFO: Lori Gibbens, Controller
CMO: Douglas Grisier, D.O., Medical Director
CIO: Sharon Zielinski, Manager Health Information
CHR: William Robinson, Director Human Resources
Web address: www.healthsoutherie.com
Control: Corporation, Investor–owned (for–profit) **Service**: Rehabilitation

Staffed Beds: 108

✚ **ERIE VETERANS AFFAIRS MEDICAL CENTER**, 135 East 38th Street, Zip 16504-1559; tel. 814/860-2576, (Nonreporting) **A**1 **S** Department of Veterans Affairs, Washington, DC
Primary Contact: John Gennaro, FACHE, Director
CFO: Joann Pritchard, Chief Financial Officer
CMO: Anthony Behm, D.O., Chief of Staff
CIO: Jonathan Seale, Chief Information Officer
CHR: Lynn Nies, Human Resources Officer
CNO: Dorene M. Sommers, Associate Director Patient Care Services
Web address: www.erie.va.gov/
Control: Veterans Affairs, Government, federal **Service**: General medical and surgical

Staffed Beds: 75

Hospitals, U.S. / PENNSYLVANIA

○ **LECOM HEALTH MILLCREEK COMMUNITY HOSPITAL (390198)**, 5515 Peach Street, Zip 16509-2695; tel. 814/864-4031, (Nonreporting) **A**3 5 10 11 12 13
Primary Contact: Mary L. Eckert, President and Chief Executive Officer
CFO: Richard P Olinger, Chief Financial Officer
CMO: James Y Lin, D.O., Chief of Staff
CIO: Cheryl Girardier, Director Information Technology
CHR: Polly Momeyer, Manager Human Resources
CNO: Katie Agresti, R.N., Director Patient Care Services
Web address: www.millcreekcommunityhospital.com
Control: Other not-for-profit (including NFP Corporation) **Service**: General medical and surgical

Staffed Beds: 171

SAINT VINCENT HOSPITAL (390009), 232 West 25th Street, Zip 16544-0002; tel. 814/452-5000, **A**1 2 3 5 10 12 13 19 **F**3 8 11 12 13 15 17 18 19 20 21 22 24 26 28 29 30 31 34 35 37 39 40 44 45 46 47 48 49 50 54 56 57 58 59 60 61 64 65 70 71 72 74 75 76 77 78 79 80 81 82 84 85 86 87 89 90 92 93 94 96 97 98 100 101 102 103 107 108 110 111 115 116 117 118 119 120 121 122 123 124 126 130 131 132 133 141 146 147 148 149 154 167 169 **S** Allegheny Health Network, Pittsburgh, PA
Primary Contact: Christopher Clark, D.O., President
COO: Karen Surkala, Chief Operating Officer
CFO: Randolph Levis, Chief Financial Officer
CIO: Richard B Ong, Chief Information Officer
CHR: Johnie M Atkinson, Chief Human Resources Officer
Web address: www.svhs.org
Control: Other not-for-profit (including NFP Corporation) **Service**: General medical and surgical

Staffed Beds: 375 **Admissions**: 11685 **Census**: 180 **Outpatient Visits**: 184351 **Births**: 1233 **Total Expense ($000)**: 442436 **Payroll Expense ($000)**: 136907 **Personnel**: 1818

SELECT SPECIALTY HOSPITAL-ERIE (392037), 252 West 11th Street, Zip 16501-1702; tel. 814/874-5300, (Nonreporting) **A**1 10 **S** Select Medical Corporation, Mechanicsburg, PA
Primary Contact: Michael A. Post, Chief Executive Officer
CNO: Keith Christiansen, Chief Nursing Officer
Web address: www.erie.selectspecialtyhospitals.com/
Control: Corporation, Investor-owned (for-profit) **Service**: Acute long-term care hospital

Staffed Beds: 30

TWINBROOK NURSING & CONV HOME See Twinbrook Medical Center

UPMC HAMOT (390063), 201 State Street, Zip 16550-0002; tel. 814/877-6000, **A**1 2 3 5 10 19 **F**3 9 12 13 15 17 18 20 22 24 26 28 29 30 31 34 35 36 37 38 39 40 43 44 45 46 47 48 49 50 51 54 56 57 58 59 60 61 64 65 66 68 70 72 74 75 76 77 78 79 80 81 82 84 85 86 87 89 91 92 93 96 97 100 101 102 107 108 109 110 111 114 115 118 119 124 126 129 130 131 132 134 135 138 141 147 148 149 150 154 157 160 166 167 169 **P**6 **S** UPMC, Pittsburgh, PA
Primary Contact: Brian Durniok, President
CFO: Bradley Dinger, Chief Financial Officer
CMO: Richard Long, M.D., Chief Medical Officer
CIO: Lisa D McChesney, R.N., Senior Director Information Systems
CNO: James E Donnelly, Chief Nursing Officer and Vice President Patient Care Services
Web address: www.upmc.com/locations/hospitals/hamot
Control: Other not-for-profit (including NFP Corporation) **Service**: General medical and surgical

Staffed Beds: 343 **Admissions**: 17331 **Census**: 279 **Outpatient Visits**: 240986 **Births**: 1963 **Total Expense ($000)**: 551029 **Payroll Expense ($000)**: 174095 **Personnel**: 2168

EVERETT—Bedford County

UPMC BEDFORD (390117), 10455 Lincoln Highway, Zip 15537-7046; tel. 814/623-6161, **A**1 10 20 **F**3 8 15 18 28 29 30 34 35 36 38 40 45 50 51 56 57 59 61 64 65 68 74 75 77 79 81 85 86 87 102 107 108 110 111 114 119 129 130 131 132 135 146 147 148 149 154 156 167 **P**6 **S** UPMC, Pittsburgh, PA
Primary Contact: Michael Corso, President & Chief Executive Officer
CFO: Monica Klatt, Chief Financial Officer
CIO: Mark Wiley, Manager Information Systems Development
CHR: Michelle A Speck, Vice President Human Resources
CNO: Paula Thomas, Vice President Patient Services
Web address: www.upmcbedfordmemorial.com
Control: Other not-for-profit (including NFP Corporation) **Service**: General medical and surgical

Staffed Beds: 24 **Admissions**: 1240 **Census**: 11 **Outpatient Visits**: 99940 **Births**: 0 **Total Expense ($000)**: 48305 **Payroll Expense ($000)**: 15580 **Personnel**: 222

FARRELL—Mercer County

SHENANGO VALLEY CAMPUS See UPMC Horizon, Farrell

SHENANGO VALLEY MEDICAL CENTER See Shenango Valley Campus

UPMC HORIZON (390178), 2200 Memorial Drive, Zip 16121-1357; tel. 724/588-2100, (Includes GREENVILLE CAMPUS, 110 North Main Street, Greenville, Pennsylvania, Zip 16125-1795, tel. 724/588-2100; SHENANGO VALLEY CAMPUS, 2200 Memorial Drive, Farrell, Pennsylvania, Zip 16121-1398, tel. 724/981-3500) **A**1 3 5 10 13 **F**3 11 13 15 18 26 28 29 30 31 32 34 35 40 44 45 46 49 50 51 54 57 59 64 65 68 73 74 75 76 77 78 79 81 82 85 86 87 92 93 100 107 108 110 111 114 115 116 118 119 120 121 123 129 130 132 133 135 146 147 148 149 154 156 157 160 164 169 **S** UPMC, Pittsburgh, PA
Primary Contact: David J. Patton, President
CFO: Brian Fritz, Chief Financial Officer
CMO: Samuel Daisley, D.O., Vice President Medical Affairs
CHR: Connie Mayle, Vice President Administrative Services
Web address: www.upmc.com
Control: Other not-for-profit (including NFP Corporation) **Service**: General medical and surgical

Staffed Beds: 69 **Admissions**: 3488 **Census**: 32 **Outpatient Visits**: 249824 **Births**: 1002 **Total Expense ($000)**: 165922 **Payroll Expense ($000)**: 44496 **Personnel**: 568

FORT WASHINGTON—Montgomery County

□ **BROOKE GLEN BEHAVIORAL HOSPITAL (394049)**, 7170 Lafayette Avenue, Zip 19034-2301; tel. 215/641-5300, (Nonreporting) **A**1 10 **S** Universal Health Services, Inc., King of Prussia, PA
Primary Contact: Neil Callahan, Chief Executive Officer
COO: William R Mason, Chief Operating Officer
CFO: Robert Zagerman, Chief Financial Officer
CMO: Chand Nair, M.D., Medical Director
CHR: Dawn Kownacki, Director Human Resources
Web address: www.brookeglenhospital.com
Control: Corporation, Investor-owned (for-profit) **Service**: Psychiatric

Staffed Beds: 146

GETTYSBURG—Adams County

★ ⇧ **WELLSPAN GETTYSBURG HOSPITAL (390065)**, 147 Gettys Street, Zip 17325-2534; tel. 717/334-2121, **A**2 3 10 21 **F**3 8 11 13 15 18 20 22 26 28 29 30 31 38 40 44 45 46 50 51 54 59 60 64 68 70 74 75 76 77 78 79 81 82 84 85 86 87 91 92 93 94 96 102 107 108 110 111 115 118 119 120 121 123 126 129 130 131 132 135 144 145 146 147 148 149 154 160 164 167 169 **S** WellSpan Health, York, PA
Primary Contact: Michael Cogliano Sr, President
COO: Joseph H Edgar, Senior Vice President Operations
CMO: Charles Marley, D.O., Vice President Medical Affairs
CIO: Robin Kimple, Director Information Services
Web address: www.wellspan.org
Control: Other not-for-profit (including NFP Corporation) **Service**: General medical and surgical

Staffed Beds: 76 **Admissions**: 4617 **Census**: 74 **Outpatient Visits**: 127421 **Births**: 410 **Total Expense ($000)**: 278520 **Payroll Expense ($000)**: 53685 **Personnel**: 612

GREENSBURG—Westmoreland County

⇧ **AHN HEMPFIELD NEIGHBORHOOD HOSPITAL (390333)**, 6321 State Route 30, Zip 15601-9703; tel. 878/295-4735, (Includes AHN EMERUS NEIGHBORHOOD HOSPITALS – BRENTWOOD, 3290 Saw Mill Run Boulevard, Brentwood, Pennsylvania, Zip 15227-2318, tel. 412/437-2600; Cynthia M. Dorundo, Chief Executive Officer; AHN EMERUS NEIGHBORHOOD HOSPITALS – HARMAR, 2501 Freeport Road, Pittsburgh, Pennsylvania, Zip 15238-1409, tel. 412/550-5550; Cynthia M. Dorundo, Chief Executive Officer; AHN EMERUS NEIGHBORHOOD HOSPITALS – MCCANDLESS, 8950 Duncan Avenue, Pittsburgh, Pennsylvania, Zip 15237-5803, tel. 878/999-9035; Cynthia M. Dorundo, Chief Executive Officer) **A**10 21 **F**3 29 35 40 41 65 68 100 107 114 119 130 154 **S** Allegheny Health Network, Pittsburgh, PA
Primary Contact: Cynthia M. Dorundo, Market Chief Executive Officer
Web address: www.AHNneighborhood.org
Control: Corporation, Investor-owned (for-profit) **Service**: General medical and surgical

Staffed Beds: 20 **Admissions**: 380 **Census**: 2 **Outpatient Visits**: 60696 **Births**: 0 **Total Expense ($000)**: 45465 **Payroll Expense ($000)**: 14114 **Personnel**: 157

Hospitals, U.S. / PENNSYLVANIA

☐ **EXCELA HEALTH WESTMORELAND HOSPITAL (390145)**, 532 West Pittsburgh Street, Zip 15601–2282; tel. 724/832–4000, (Nonreporting) **A**1 3 10 **S** Independence Health System, Butler, PA
Primary Contact: Brian Fritz, President, Westmoreland, Latrobe, Frick Hospitals
COO: Jeffrey Tiesi, Executive Vice President and Chief Operating Officer
CFO: Jeffrey T Curry, Executive Vice President and Chief Financial Officer
CMO: Jerome Granato, M.D., Senior Vice President and Chief Medical Officer
CIO: Vasanth Balu, Senior Vice Prssident and Chief Information Officer
CHR: John Caverno, Chief Human Resources Officer
CNO: Helen K Burns, Ph.D., R.N., Senior Vice President and Chief Nursing Officer
Web address: www.excelahealth.org
Control: Other not–for–profit (including NFP Corporation) **Service:** General medical and surgical

Staffed Beds: 272

GREENVILLE—Mercer County

GREENVILLE REGIONAL HOSPITAL See Greenville Campus

GROVE CITY—Mercer County

★ **AHN GROVE CITY (390266)**, 631 North Broad Street Extension, Zip 16127–4603; tel. 724/450–7000, **A**10 **F**3 8 15 20 28 29 31 35 40 43 45 64 65 70 75 77 78 79 81 85 87 92 93 107 108 110 111 115 118 119 129 130 131 145 146 148 154 167 **S** Allegheny Health Network, Pittsburgh, PA
Primary Contact: Christopher Clark, D.O., President
COO: Jason Roeback, Chief Operating Officer
CFO: Richard W Fries, Vice President Finance
CMO: Daniel Ferguson, Chief of Staff
CIO: Philip Swartwood, Director Information Systems
CHR: David Poland, Interim Chief Human Resource Officer
CNO: Anthony Bono Jr, Chief Nursing Officer
Web address: www.gcmcpa.org
Control: Other not–for–profit (including NFP Corporation) **Service:** General medical and surgical

Staffed Beds: 36 **Admissions:** 836 **Census:** 6 **Outpatient Visits:** 87025 **Births:** 0 **Total Expense ($000):** 61327 **Payroll Expense ($000):** 16225 **Personnel:** 246

HANOVER—York County

✠ **UPMC HANOVER (390233)**, 300 Highland Avenue, Zip 17331–2297; tel. 717/316–3711, **A**1 3 10 **F**3 11 13 15 18 20 22 26 28 29 30 31 34 35 40 44 45 49 50 51 53 54 59 60 64 68 74 75 76 77 78 79 81 84 85 87 89 93 96 102 107 108 110 111 114 115 118 119 126 129 130 132 135 141 143 146 147 148 149 167 **S** UPMC, Pittsburgh, PA
Primary Contact: Michael W. Gaskins, President
COO: Michael A. Hockenberry, Senior Vice President and Chief Operating Officer
CFO: Donna L. Muller, Vice President Finance, Southern Region
CMO: Michael H Ader, M.D., Vice President Medical Affairs
CIO: William C. Tandy, Chief Information Officer
CHR: Christine Miller, General Counsel and Vice President Human Resources
CNO: M Patricia Saunders, R.N., MS, Vice President Nursing
Web address: www.hanoverhospital.org
Control: Other not–for–profit (including NFP Corporation) **Service:** General medical and surgical

Staffed Beds: 81 **Admissions:** 5420 **Census:** 64 **Outpatient Visits:** 247823 **Births:** 473 **Total Expense ($000):** 191923 **Payroll Expense ($000):** 60479 **Personnel:** 1234

HARRISBURG—Dauphin County

✠ **HELEN M. SIMPSON REHABILITATION HOSPITAL (393056)**, 4300 Londonderry Road, Zip 17109–5317; tel. 717/920–4300, **A**1 10 13 **F**29 44 58 60 68 74 77 86 87 90 91 92 93 94 95 96 100 130 132 135 148 149 156 157 **S** Select Medical Corporation, Mechanicsburg, PA
Primary Contact: Brett D. McChesney, Chief Executive Officer
Web address: www.simpson-rehab.com/
Control: Partnership, Investor–owned (for–profit) **Service:** Rehabilitation

Staffed Beds: 55 **Admissions:** 1255 **Census:** 44 **Outpatient Visits:** 0 **Births:** 0 **Personnel:** 153

☐ **PENNSYLVANIA PSYCHIATRIC INSTITUTE (394051)**, 2501 North Third Street, Zip 17110–1904; tel. 717/782–6420, (Nonreporting) **A**1 3 5 10
Primary Contact: Kimberly Feeman, President
CFO: Robert Fotter, Chief Financial Officer
CMO: Elisabeth J. Kunkel, M.D., Professor, Pennsylvania State College of Medicine
CHR: Wanda Geesey, Director Human Resources
CNO: Teresa Terry–Williams, R.N., Chief Nursing Officer
Web address: www.ppimhs.org/
Control: Other not–for–profit (including NFP Corporation) **Service:** Psychiatric

Staffed Beds: 84

PINNACLEHEALTH AT COMMUNITY GENERAL OSTEOPATHIC HOSPITAL See UPMC Community Osteopathic

SELECT SPECIALTY HOSPITAL–HARRISBURG See Select Specialty Hospital–Camp Hill, Camp Hill

UPMC COMMUNITY OSTEOPATHIC See UPMC Harrisburg, Harrisburg

✠ **UPMC HARRISBURG (390067)**, 111 South Front Street, Zip 17101–2010, Mailing Address: P.O. Box 8700, Zip 17105–8700; tel. 717/231–8900, (Includes UPMC COMMUNITY OSTEOPATHIC, 4300 Londonderry Road, Harrisburg, Pennsylvania, Zip 17109–5397, P O Box 3000, Zip 17105–3000, tel. 717/652–3000; UPMC WEST SHORE, 1995 Technology Parkway, Mechanicsburg, Pennsylvania, Zip 17050–8522, tel. 717/791–2600; Lou Baverso, Chief Operating Officer President, Central Pennsylvania Region) **A**1 2 3 5 10 12 19 **F**3 7 8 11 12 13 14 15 17 18 19 20 22 24 26 27 28 29 30 31 32 34 35 36 37 38 39 40 44 45 46 47 48 49 50 51 52 53 54 55 56 57 58 59 60 61 64 65 66 68 70 72 74 75 76 77 78 79 81 82 84 85 86 87 88 89 93 96 97 100 102 107 108 109 110 111 114 115 116 117 118 119 120 121 123 124 126 129 130 131 132 134 138 141 142 143 144 145 146 147 148 149 150 154 156 157 167 169 **P**6 **S** UPMC, Pittsburgh, PA
Primary Contact: Elizabeth Ritter, President
CFO: Alison Bernhardt, Chief Financial Officer
CMO: Nirmal Joshi, M.D., Senior Vice President Medical Affairs and Chief Medical Officer
CHR: Ann H Gormley, Senior Vice President Human Resources
CNO: Susan Comp, Senior Vice President and Chief Nursing Officer
Web address: www.pinnaclehealth.org
Control: Other not–for–profit (including NFP Corporation) **Service:** General medical and surgical

Staffed Beds: 741 **Admissions:** 32199 **Census:** 456 **Outpatient Visits:** 1111354 **Births:** 3592 **Total Expense ($000):** 1419599 **Payroll Expense ($000):** 367129 **Personnel:** 5453

HASTINGS—Cambria County

✠ **CONEMAUGH MINERS MEDICAL CENTER (391317)**, 290 Haida Avenue, Zip 16646–5610, Mailing Address: P.O. Box 689, Zip 16646–0689; tel. 814/247–3100, (Nonreporting) **A**1 10 18 **S** Lifepoint Health, Brentwood, TN
Primary Contact: Timothy Harclerode, R.N., FACHE, Chief Executive Officer
CFO: Linda Fanale, Chief Financial Officer
CMO: Susan Williams, M.D., Chief Medical Officer
CIO: Joe Dado, Chief Information Officer
CNO: Jessica Svidergol–Peterman, MSN, R.N., Chief Nursing Officer
Web address: www.conemaugh.org
Control: Corporation, Investor–owned (for–profit) **Service:** General medical and surgical

Staffed Beds: 25

HAZLETON—Luzerne County

★ ○ **LEHIGH VALLEY HOSPITAL – HAZLETON (390185)**, 700 East Broad Street, Zip 18201–6897; tel. 570/501–4000, **A**10 11 **F**3 7 8 11 12 13 15 18 28 29 30 31 32 34 35 40 43 44 45 50 53 54 57 60 62 63 64 65 68 69 70 74 75 76 77 78 79 81 82 83 84 85 87 89 90 92 93 107 108 110 111 114 115 118 119 120 121 124 126 129 130 132 135 143 146 148 149 150 154 155 157 164 167 169 **P**5 6 **S** Lehigh Valley Health Network, Allentown, PA
Primary Contact: Tammy Torres, President
CFO: William Bauer, Vice President Finance and Chief Financial Officer
CMO: Anthony Valente, M.D., Vice President Medical Affairs
CIO: Carl Shoener, Chief Information Officer
CHR: Lynn Lansdowne, Vice President Labor Relations and Human Resources
Web address: www.lvhn.org/hazleton/
Control: Other not–for–profit (including NFP Corporation) **Service:** General medical and surgical

Staffed Beds: 111 **Admissions:** 4436 **Census:** 60 **Outpatient Visits:** 127188 **Births:** 625 **Total Expense ($000):** 125765 **Payroll Expense ($000):** 37619 **Personnel:** 570

Hospital, Medicare Provider Number, Address, Telephone, Approval, Facility, and Physician Codes, Health Care System

★ American Hospital Association (AHA) membership
☐ The Joint Commission accreditation
○ Healthcare Facilities Accreditation Program
◇ DNV Healthcare Inc. accreditation
✠ Center for Improvement in Healthcare Quality Accreditation
△ Commission on Accreditation of Rehabilitation Facilities (CARF) accreditation

Hospitals, U.S. / PENNSYLVANIA

HERSHEY—Dauphin County

✠ **PENN STATE MILTON S. HERSHEY MEDICAL CENTER (390256)**, 500 University Drive, Zip 17033–2360, Mailing Address: P.O. Box 850, Zip 17033–0850; tel. 717/531–8521, (Includes PENN STATE CHILDREN'S HOSPITAL, 600 University Drive, Hershey, Pennsylvania, Zip 17033–2360, tel. 717/531–8521; Stephen M. Massini, Chief Executive Officer, Penn State Health) **A**1 2 3 5 8 10 19 **F**3 6 7 8 9 11 12 13 14 15 17 18 19 20 21 22 23 24 25 26 27 28 29 30 31 32 34 35 36 37 38 39 40 41 43 44 45 46 47 48 49 50 51 52 53 54 55 56 57 58 59 60 61 64 65 66 68 70 71 72 74 75 76 77 78 79 80 81 82 84 85 86 87 88 89 91 92 93 96 97 100 101 102 104 105 107 108 110 111 114 115 116 117 118 119 120 121 123 124 126 127 129 130 131 132 134 135 136 137 138 139 141 142 143 145 146 147 148 149 150 154 155 156 157 160 162 164 166 167 169 **P**6 **S** Penn State Health, Hershey, PA
Primary Contact: Donald McKenna, President
CMO: Thomas Tracy Jr, Chief Medical Officer
CHR: Jane Mannon, Vice President Human Resources
CNO: Michele Szkolnicki, R.N., Senior Vice President and Chief Nursing Officer
Web address: www.pennstatehershey.org/
Control: Other not-for-profit (including NFP Corporation) **Service**: General medical and surgical

Staffed Beds: 601 **Admissions**: 26199 **Census**: 506 **Outpatient Visits**: 1281346 **Births**: 2246 **Total Expense ($000)**: 2129550 **Payroll Expense ($000)**: 573073 **Personnel**: 9488

HONESDALE—Wayne County

★ **WAYNE MEMORIAL HOSPITAL (390125)**, 601 Park Street, Zip 18431–1498; tel. 570/253–8100, **A**10 20 **F**3 13 15 18 20 22 26 28 29 34 35 39 40 43 46 57 59 63 70 74 75 76 77 78 79 81 85 86 89 90 92 93 100 107 108 110 111 119 128 129 130 132 133 135 146 148 149 154 156 169
Primary Contact: James Pettinato, R.N., Chief Executive Officer
COO: John Conte, Director Facility Services and Real Estate
CFO: Michael J Clifford, Director Finance
CMO: Sean McVeigh, M.D., Chief of Medical Staff
CIO: Tom Hoffman, Manager Information Systems
CHR: Elizabeth McDonald, Director Human Resources
Web address: www.wmh.org
Control: Other not-for-profit (including NFP Corporation) **Service**: General medical and surgical

Staffed Beds: 75 **Admissions**: 2896 **Census**: 40 **Outpatient Visits**: 168584 **Births**: 437 **Total Expense ($000)**: 117099 **Payroll Expense ($000)**: 43419 **Personnel**: 682

HUMMELSTOWN—Dauphin County

✠ △ **PENN STATE HEALTH REHABILITATION HOSPITAL (393053)**, 1135 Old West Chocolate Avenue, Zip 17036; tel. 717/832–2600, **A**1 3 5 7 10 **F**3 29 44 58 60 69 74 75 77 86 87 90 91 92 93 94 95 96 100 130 132 143 148 149 157 **S** Select Medical Corporation, Mechanicsburg, PA
Primary Contact: Mark Freeburn, Chief Executive Officer
CMO: Brenda Mallory, M.D., Medical Director
Web address: www.psh-rehab.com
Control: Corporation, Investor-owned (for-profit) **Service**: Rehabilitation

Staffed Beds: 98 **Admissions**: 1692 **Census**: 70 **Births**: 0 **Personnel**: 240

PENN STATE HERSHEY REHABILITATION HOSPITAL See Penn State Health Rehabilitation Hospital

HUNTINGDON—Huntingdon County

☐ **PENN HIGHLANDS HUNTINGDON (390056)**, 1225 Warm Springs Avenue, Zip 16652–2398; tel. 814/643–2290, (Nonreporting) **A**1 10 20
Primary Contact: Rhonda Halstead, Region President, Huntingdon & Tyrone
COO: Adam Dimm, Chief Executive Officer
CMO: James Hayden, M.D., Chief Medical Officer
CIO: Armen Arakelian, Chief Information Officer
CHR: Susan Hess, Director Human Resources
CNO: Joye Gingrich, Director Patient Care Services and Chief Nursing Officer
Web address: www.jcblair.org
Control: Other not-for-profit (including NFP Corporation) **Service**: General medical and surgical

Staffed Beds: 59

INDIANA—Indiana County

★ **INDIANA REGIONAL MEDICAL CENTER (390173)**, 835 Hospital Road, Zip 15701–3629, Mailing Address: P.O. Box 788, Zip 15701–0788; tel. 724/357–7000, (Nonreporting) **A**2 3 10 20 22
Primary Contact: Stephen A. Wolfe, President and Chief Executive Officer
COO: Dominic Paccapaniccia, Chief Operating Officer
CFO: Robert Gongaware, Chief Financial Officer
CMO: Bruce A. Bush, M.D., Interim Chief Medical Officer
CIO: Mark Volovic, Chief Information Officer
CHR: James W. Kinneer, Chief Human Resource Officer
CNO: Wendy Haislip, Chief Nursing Officer
Web address: www.indianarmc.org
Control: Other not-for-profit (including NFP Corporation) **Service**: General medical and surgical

Staffed Beds: 166

JEFFERSON HILLS—Allegheny County

✠ **JEFFERSON HOSPITAL (390265)**, 565 Coal Valley Road, Zip 15025–3703, Mailing Address: Box 18119, Pittsburgh, Zip 15236–0119; tel. 412/469–5000, **A**1 2 3 10 **F**3 5 11 12 13 15 17 18 20 22 24 26 28 29 30 31 34 35 40 44 45 46 47 48 49 50 54 59 60 64 65 70 73 74 75 76 77 78 79 80 81 82 84 85 86 87 90 92 93 96 98 100 102 104 107 108 110 111 114 115 117 118 119 120 121 123 124 126 129 130 131 132 135 146 147 148 149 153 154 162 164 167 169 **S** Allegheny Health Network, Pittsburgh, PA
Primary Contact: Chong S. Park, M.D., Chief Executive Officer
COO: Kelly Kassab, Chief Operating Officer
CMO: Richard F Collins, M.D., Executive Vice President and Chief Medical Officer
CIO: James Witenske, Chief Information Officer
CNO: Kimberley Finnerty, MSN, R.N., Chief Nursing Officer
Web address: www.jeffersonregional.com
Control: Other not-for-profit (including NFP Corporation) **Service**: General medical and surgical

Staffed Beds: 305 **Admissions**: 11023 **Census**: 160 **Outpatient Visits**: 355865 **Births**: 1142 **Total Expense ($000)**: 335265 **Payroll Expense ($000)**: 102768 **Personnel**: 1473

JERSEY SHORE—Lycoming County

✠ **GEISINGER JERSEY SHORE HOSPITAL (391300)**, 1020 Thompson Street, Zip 17740–1794; tel. 570/398–0100, **A**1 3 5 10 18 **F**3 5 12 15 18 28 29 34 35 40 45 50 57 59 65 68 75 79 81 85 93 97 107 110 111 115 119 129 130 132 133 135 147 149 154 156 160 164 **P**1 5 8 **S** Geisinger, Danville, PA
Primary Contact: Tammy Anderer, Ph.D., Vice President of Clinical Operations for the North Central Region
CFO: Mark Rice, CPA, Chief Financial Officer
CMO: Stephen Goykovich, D.O., Chief Medical Officer
CIO: Christine Haas, Chief Information Officer
CHR: Joan Rounsley, Director Human Resources
CNO: Paulette Nish, Chief Nursing Officer
Web address: https://www.geisinger.org/
Control: Other not-for-profit (including NFP Corporation) **Service**: General medical and surgical

Staffed Beds: 25 **Admissions**: 1572 **Census**: 11 **Outpatient Visits**: 41003 **Births**: 0 **Total Expense ($000)**: 40242 **Payroll Expense ($000)**: 18538 **Personnel**: 264

JOHNSTOWN—Cambria County

✠ **CONEMAUGH MEMORIAL MEDICAL CENTER (390110)**, 1086 Franklin Street, Zip 15905–4398; tel. 814/534–9000, (Includes MEMORIAL MEDICAL CENTER – LEE CAMPUS, 320 Main Street, Johnstown, Pennsylvania, Zip 15901–1601, tel. 814/533–0123) (Nonreporting) **A**1 3 5 10 13 **S** Lifepoint Health, Brentwood, TN
Primary Contact: Rodney Reider, Chief Executive Officer
COO: Timothy Harclerode, R.N., FACHE, Chief Operating Officer
CFO: Lynn Kennington, Chief Financial Officer
CMO: Susan Williams, M.D., Chief Medical Officer
CIO: Joe Dado, Chief Information Officer
CNO: Claudia Rager, R.N., Vice President Patient Care Services
Web address: www.conemaugh.org
Control: Corporation, Investor-owned (for-profit) **Service**: General medical and surgical

Staffed Beds: 510

Hospitals, U.S. / PENNSYLVANIA

MEM MED CTR LEE CAMPUS See Memorial Medical Center – Lee Campus

MEMORIAL MEDICAL CENTER – LEE CAMPUS See Conemaugh Memorial Medical Center, Johnstown

☒ **SELECT SPECIALTY HOSPITAL–JOHNSTOWN (392031)**, 320 Main Street, 3rd Floor, Zip 15901–1601; tel. 814/534–7360, (Nonreporting) **A**1 10 **S** Select Medical Corporation, Mechanicsburg, PA
Primary Contact: Kelly Blake, Chief Executive Officer
CMO: Gary Davidson, M.D., Medical Director
Web address: www.selectspecialtyhospitals.com/company/locations/johnstown.aspx
Control: Corporation, Investor–owned (for–profit) **Service**: Acute long–term care hospital

Staffed Beds: 39

KANE—Mckean County

★ ○ **UPMC KANE (390104)**, 4372 Route 6, Zip 16735–3060; tel. 814/837–8585, **A**10 11 20 **F**3 11 15 18 28 29 30 34 35 40 45 46 50 57 59 64 65 75 77 79 81 82 85 93 97 100 107 108 110 111 115 118 119 130 131 132 133 135 147 149 154 156 167 **P**4 **S** UPMC, Pittsburgh, PA
Primary Contact: Mark Papalia, President
CFO: Bradley Dinger, Chief Financial Officer
CMO: Linda Rettger, M.D., President Medical Staff
CIO: Deano Cherry, Chief Information Officer
CHR: Marsha Keller, Director Human Resources
CNO: Pam Bray, Director of Nursing and Director Inpatient Services
Web address: www.kanehosp.org
Control: Other not–for–profit (including NFP Corporation) **Service**: General medical and surgical

Staffed Beds: 14 **Admissions**: 231 **Census**: 2 **Outpatient Visits**: 63463 **Births**: 0 **Total Expense ($000)**: 22699 **Payroll Expense ($000)**: 10679 **Personnel**: 139

KITTANNING—Armstrong County

⇧ **ACMH HOSPITAL (390163)**, One Nolte Drive, Zip 16201–7111, Mailing Address: 1 Nolte Drive, Zip 16201–7111; tel. 724/543–8500, (Total facility includes 17 beds in nursing home–type unit) **A**10 19 21 **F**3 11 13 15 17 18 20 22 26 28 29 30 31 34 35 40 45 47 48 49 54 59 65 70 75 76 77 78 79 81 82 85 93 98 100 102 107 108 110 111 114 119 120 121 126 127 128 129 130 132 135 146 148 149 154 156 160 161 164 167 169
Primary Contact: Nichole Geraci, President and Chief Executive Officer
COO: Nichole Geraci, Chief Operating Officer
CFO: Patrick Burns, Vice President Finance
CMO: Harold Altman, M.D., Chief Medical Officer
CIO: Dianne Emminger, Vice President Information Services
CHR: Anne Remaley, Vice President Human Resources
Web address: www.acmh.org
Control: Other not–for–profit (including NFP Corporation) **Service**: General medical and surgical

Staffed Beds: 112 **Admissions**: 3201 **Census**: 52 **Outpatient Visits**: 244054 **Births**: 305 **Total Expense ($000)**: 135173 **Payroll Expense ($000)**: 49003 **Personnel**: 796

LANCASTER—Armstrong County

☐ **LANCASTER BEHAVIORAL HEALTH HOSPITAL (394055)**, 333 Harrisburg Avenue, Zip 17603; tel. 717/740–4100, (Nonreporting) **A**1 10 **S** University of Pennsylvania Health System, Philadelphia, PA
Primary Contact: Ryan Tatu, Chief Executive Officer
Web address: https://lancasterbehavioral.org/
Control: Corporation, Investor–owned (for–profit) **Service**: Psychiatric

Staffed Beds: 126

LANCASTER—Lancaster County

☐ △ **LANCASTER REHABILITATION HOSPITAL (393054)**, 675 Good Drive, Zip 17601–2426; tel. 717/406–3000, **A**1 7 10 **F**29 90 122 130 132 135 148 149
Primary Contact: Amy Teal, Chief Executive Officer
CFO: David Stark, Chief Financial Officer
CHR: Lisa Andrews, Director Human Resources
Web address: www.lancastergeneral.org
Control: Corporation, Investor–owned (for–profit) **Service**: Rehabilitation

Staffed Beds: 59 **Admissions**: 1371 **Census**: 45 **Outpatient Visits**: 0 **Births**: 0 **Total Expense ($000)**: 20708 **Payroll Expense ($000)**: 11260 **Personnel**: 156

☒ **PENN MEDICINE LANCASTER GENERAL HEALTH (390100)**, 555 North Duke Street, Zip 17602–2250; tel. 717/544–5511, **A**1 2 3 5 10 19 **F**3 8 12 13 14 15 17 18 20 22 24 26 28 29 30 31 32 34 35 36 37 38 39 40 41 43 44 45 46 47 48 49 50 51 52 54 55 56 57 58 59 60 61 63 64 65 66 68 70 72 73 74 75 76 77 78 79 80 81 82 84 85 86 87 89 91 92 93 94 95 96 97 100 101 102 107 108 110 114 115 118 119 120 121 122 123 124 126 129 130 132 134 135 141 142 145 146 147 148 149 150 154 156 157 160 161 162 164 167 169 **P**6 **S** University of Pennsylvania Health System, Philadelphia, PA
Primary Contact: John J. Herman, FACHE, Chief Executive Officer
COO: Steven G Littleson, FACHE, Chief Operating and Integration Officer
CFO: Joseph Byorick, Senior Vice President and Chief Financial Officer
CMO: Lee M Duke, M.D., II, Senior Vice President and Chief Physician Executive
CIO: Gary Davidson, Senior Vice President and Chief Information Officer
CHR: Regina Mingle, Senior Vice President and Chief Leadership Officer
CNO: Lanyce Roldan, Chief Nursing Officer
Web address: https://lancastergeneralhealth.org/patient-and-visitor-information/find-a-location/lancaster-general-hospital
Control: Other not–for–profit (including NFP Corporation) **Service**: General medical and surgical

Staffed Beds: 620 **Admissions**: 27971 **Census**: 417 **Outpatient Visits**: 1851942 **Births**: 4217 **Total Expense ($000)**: 1362689 **Payroll Expense ($000)**: 517320 **Personnel**: 6112

PENN MEDICINE LANCASTER GENERAL HOSPITAL See Penn Medicine Lancaster General Health

☒ **PENN STATE HEALTH LANCASTER MEDICAL CENTER (390339)**, 2160 State Road, Zip 17601–1812; tel. 610/378–2300, **A**1 **F**3 13 18 20 22 26 29 30 36 40 45 46 48 49 51 60 64 68 70 74 76 77 78 79 81 82 84 85 87 100 102 107 108 111 114 115 118 119 126 130 146 148 149 154 167 169 **S** Penn State Health, Hershey, PA
Primary Contact: Joseph Frank, Regional Hospital President, East Region
COO: Claire Bradley Mooney, R.N., Senior Vice President an Chief Executive Officer
CFO: Edward Chabalowski, Vice President, Finance and Chief Financial Officer, East Region
CHR: Scott Mengle, Vice President, Human Resources, East Region
Web address: https://www.pennstatehealth.org/locations/penn-state-health-lancaster-medical-center
Control: Other not–for–profit (including NFP Corporation) **Service**: General medical and surgical

Staffed Beds: 108 **Admissions**: 2616 **Census**: 34 **Outpatient Visits**: 28497 **Births**: 33 **Total Expense ($000)**: 141666 **Payroll Expense ($000)**: 45370 **Personnel**: 638

LANGHORNE—Bucks County

BUCK COUNTY CAMPUS See Bucks County Campus

BUCKS COUNTY CAMPUS See Jefferson Health Northeast, Philadelphia

☒ △ **ST. MARY MEDICAL CENTER (390258)**, 1201 Langhorne–Newtown Road, Zip 19047–1201; tel. 215/710–2000, **A**1 2 3 5 7 10 19 **F**3 12 15 17 18 20 22 24 26 28 29 30 31 32 34 35 36 37 39 40 41 43 44 45 46 49 50 51 53 54 56 57 58 59 63 64 70 72 74 75 76 77 78 79 81 82 84 85 86 87 89 91 92 93 94 96 107 108 110 111 112 114 115 116 117 118 119 120 121 123 124 126 130 131 132 135 146 147 148 149 154 156 160 167 169 **S** Trinity Health, Livonia, MI
Primary Contact: Michael Magro Jr, D.O., President
COO: Jeffrey N Yarmel, Chief Operating Officer
CFO: Daniel Confalone, Chief Financial Officer and Vice President Finance
CMO: Edward O'Dell, D.O., Chief Medical Officer
CIO: Bonnie J. Buehler, Chief Information Officer
CNO: Sharon Brown, Vice President Patient Care and Chief Nursing Officer
Web address: www.stmaryhealthcare.org
Control: Other not–for–profit (including NFP Corporation) **Service**: General medical and surgical

Staffed Beds: 373 **Admissions**: 16267 **Census**: 217 **Outpatient Visits**: 170396 **Births**: 1159 **Total Expense ($000)**: 399076 **Payroll Expense ($000)**: 148282 **Personnel**: 1765

☐ △ **ST. MARY REHABILITATION HOSPITAL (393055)**, 1208 Langhorne Newtown Road, Zip 19047–1234; tel. 267/560–1111, (Nonreporting) **A**1 7 10 **S** Trinity Health, Livonia, MI
Primary Contact: Lisa Haney, Chief Executive Officer
Web address: www.stmaryhealthcare.org
Control: Church operated, Nongovernment, not–for–profit **Service**: Rehabilitation

Staffed Beds: 50

Hospital, Medicare Provider Number, Address, Telephone, Approval, Facility, and Physician Codes, Health Care System

★ American Hospital Association (AHA) membership ○ Healthcare Facilities Accreditation Program ⇧ Center for Improvement in Healthcare Quality Accreditation
☐ The Joint Commission accreditation ◇ DNV Healthcare Inc. accreditation △ Commission on Accreditation of Rehabilitation Facilities (CARF) accreditation

© 2025 AHA Guide   Hospitals **A543**

Hospitals, U.S. / PENNSYLVANIA

LANSDALE—Montgomery County

ABINGTON–LANSDALE HOSPITAL JEFFERSON HEALTH See Jefferson Lansdale Hospital

JEFFERSON LANSDALE HOSPITAL (390012), 100 Medical Campus Drive, Zip 19446-1200; tel. 215/368-2100, **A**1 3 10 **F**2 3 4 11 15 18 28 29 30 32 34 35 36 37 38 40 44 45 49 50 53 56 57 59 64 65 66 68 70 74 75 77 78 79 81 82 84 85 86 87 93 96 97 107 108 110 111 114 115 119 126 129 130 131 132 135 146 147 148 149 150 154 156 160 164 167 **S** Jefferson Health, Philadelphia, PA
Primary Contact: Brian Sweeney, President, North Region
CFO: Michael Walsh, Senior Vice President Finance and Chief Financial Officer
CMO: Jonathan Sternlieb, M.D., Chief Medical Officer
CHR: Meghan Patton, Vice President Human Resources
CNO: Kelly Cummings, Chief Nursing Officer
Web address: www.abingtonhealth.org/find-a-location/abington-lansdale-hospital/#.V5dyVVL9yk4
Control: Other not–for–profit (including NFP Corporation) **Service**: General medical and surgical

Staffed Beds: 99 **Admissions**: 5179 **Census**: 70 **Outpatient Visits**: 75934 **Births**: 0 **Total Expense ($000)**: 100126 **Payroll Expense ($000)**: 36800 **Personnel**: 572

LATROBE—Westmoreland County

☐ **EXCELA HEALTH LATROBE HOSPITAL (390219)**, 1 Mellon Way, Zip 15650-1096; tel. 724/537-1000, (Nonreporting) **A**1 3 5 10 13 19 **S** Independence Health System, Butler, PA
Primary Contact: Brian Fritz, President
COO: Jeffrey Tiesi, Executive Vice President and Chief Operating Officer
CMO: Carol J. Fox, M.D., Senior Vice President and Chief Medical Officer
CIO: Vasanth Balu, Senior Vice Prssident and Chief Information Officer
CHR: Laurie English, Senior Vice President and Chief Human Resource Officer
CNO: Helen K Burns, Ph.D., R.N., Senior Vice President and Chief Nursing Officer
Web address: www.excelahealth.org
Control: Other not–for–profit (including NFP Corporation) **Service**: General medical and surgical

Staffed Beds: 122

SELECT SPECIALTY HOSPITAL – LAUREL HIGHLANDS (392036), 1 Mellon Way, Zip 15650-1197; tel. 724/539-3870, (Nonreporting) **A**1 10 **S** Select Medical Corporation, Mechanicsburg, PA
Primary Contact: Stacy Carson, President
Web address: www.laurelhighlands.selectspecialtyhospitals.com/
Control: Corporation, Investor-owned (for-profit) **Service**: Acute long-term care hospital

Staffed Beds: 40

LEBANON—Lebanon County

LEBANON VETERANS AFFAIRS MEDICAL CENTER, 1700 South Lincoln Avenue, Zip 17042-7529; tel. 717/272-6621, (Nonreporting) **A**1 3 5 **S** Department of Veterans Affairs, Washington, DC
Primary Contact: Jeffrey A. Beiler II, Director
CFO: Geoffrey Smith, Chief Financial Officer
CMO: Kanan Chatterjee, M.D., Chief of Staff
CIO: Andru Ditzler, Chief Information Officer
CHR: Cindy Shiner, Manager Human Resources
Web address: www.lebanon.va.gov
Control: Veterans Affairs, Government, federal **Service**: General medical and surgical

Staffed Beds: 187

★ ⇧ **WELLSPAN GOOD SAMARITAN HOSPITAL (390066)**, 252 South 4th Street, Zip 17042-1281, Mailing Address: 169 Martin Ave, Ephrata, Zip 17522-1724; tel. 717/270-7500, **A**2 3 10 13 19 21 **F**3 8 11 13 14 15 17 18 20 22 24 26 28 29 30 31 34 35 40 44 45 49 50 51 54 55 56 57 59 60 61 64 65 68 70 74 75 76 78 79 80 81 82 84 85 87 90 91 92 93 96 100 107 108 110 111 114 115 116 118 119 120 121 124 126 129 130 146 148 149 154 156 167 169 **S** WellSpan Health, York, PA
Primary Contact: Patricia F. Donley, R.N., MSN, President
COO: Kimberly Feeman, Senior Vice President and Chief Operating Officer
CMO: Robert D Shaver, M.D., Vice President Medical Affairs
CIO: Leon John Jabour, Regional Chief Information Officer
CHR: Denise M Garman, Director Human Resources
CNO: Jacquelyn M Gould, MS, R.N., Vice President Patient Care Services and Chief Nursing Officer
Web address: www.gshleb.org
Control: Other not–for–profit (including NFP Corporation) **Service**: General medical and surgical

Staffed Beds: 163 **Admissions**: 6778 **Census**: 156 **Outpatient Visits**: 71261 **Births**: 646 **Total Expense ($000)**: 282212 **Payroll Expense ($000)**: 59610 **Personnel**: 593

LEHIGHTON—Carbon County

LUKE'S HOSPITAL – CARBON CAMPUS See St. Luke's Carbon Campus

☐ **ST. LUKE'S CARBON CAMPUS (390335)**, 500 St. Luke's Drive, Zip 18235; tel. 484/464-9000, (Nonreporting) **A**1 10 **S** St. Luke's University Health Network, Bethlehem, PA
Primary Contact: John L. Nespoli, President
Web address: www.slhn.org/carbon
Control: Other not-for-profit (including NFP Corporation) **Service**: General medical and surgical

Staffed Beds: 40

LEWISBURG—Union County

EVANGELICAL COMMUNITY HOSPITAL (390013), 1 Hospital Drive, Zip 17837-9350; tel. 570/522-2000, **A**2 10 19 **F**3 7 8 12 13 15 18 20 22 28 29 30 34 35 40 43 45 50 51 54 57 59 63 64 65 70 71 74 75 76 77 78 79 81 82 84 85 86 87 90 91 92 93 96 97 107 108 110 111 114 115 116 117 118 119 129 130 131 132 135 143 144 146 147 148 149 154 156 157 164 167 169 **P**7
Primary Contact: Kendra A. Aucker, Senior Vice President, WellSpan North Region/President, WellSpan Evangelical Community Hosp.
COO: Kendra A. Aucker, Vice President Operations
CFO: Jim Stopper, CPA, Chief Financial Officer
CIO: Dale Moyer, Vice President Information Systems
CHR: Angela Hummel, Vice President Human Resources
CNO: Tamara Fetchina Persing, Chief Nursing Officer
Web address: www.evanhospital.com
Control: Other not-for-profit (including NFP Corporation) **Service**: General medical and surgical

Staffed Beds: 131 **Admissions**: 5159 **Census**: 58 **Outpatient Visits**: 199233 **Births**: 632 **Total Expense ($000)**: 212170 **Payroll Expense ($000)**: 80591 **Personnel**: 1678

U. S. PENITENTIARY INFIRMARY, Route 7, Zip 17837-9303; tel. 570/523-1251, (Nonreporting)
Primary Contact: Steve Brown, Health Services Director
Control: Department of Justice, Government, federal **Service**: Hospital unit of an institution (prison hospital, college infirmary, etc.)

Staffed Beds: 17

LEWISTOWN—Mifflin County

GEISINGER LEWISTOWN HOSPITAL (390048), 400 Highland Avenue, Zip 17044-1198; tel. 717/248-5411, **A**1 2 3 5 10 **F**3 8 11 13 15 18 26 28 29 30 31 34 35 40 43 45 46 48 49 50 51 54 57 59 60 64 65 68 70 71 74 75 76 77 78 79 81 82 84 85 86 87 92 98 100 101 102 103 107 108 110 111 114 115 116 117 118 119 120 121 123 124 126 129 130 132 135 146 147 148 149 154 156 157 164 167 **S** Geisinger, Danville, PA
Primary Contact: Tammy Anderer, Ph.D., Chief Administrative Officer
COO: Aaron Hartsock, Associate Vice President, Clinical Operations, Western Region
CFO: Kristy Hine, Associate Vice President Finance
CMO: Michael T Hegstrom, M.D., Chief Medical Officer
CIO: Ronald M Cowan, Vice President Information Systems
CNO: Stacey M. Osborne, Chief Nursing Officer
Web address: www.geisinger.org
Control: Other not-for-profit (including NFP Corporation) **Service**: General medical and surgical

Staffed Beds: 133 **Admissions**: 5312 **Census**: 55 **Outpatient Visits**: 189587 **Births**: 473 **Total Expense ($000)**: 196318 **Payroll Expense ($000)**: 73698 **Personnel**: 1036

LITITZ—Lancaster County

UPMC LITITZ (390068), 1500 Highlands Drive, Zip 17543-7694; tel. 717/625-5000, **A**1 3 5 10 13 **F**3 13 15 18 22 26 28 29 30 31 34 35 37 38 40 44 45 49 50 51 57 58 59 60 64 65 68 70 72 74 75 76 77 78 79 81 82 84 85 87 93 102 107 108 110 111 114 115 119 126 129 130 135 146 147 148 149 154 160 167 169 **S** UPMC, Pittsburgh, PA
Primary Contact: Deborah J. Willwerth, R.N., MSN, President
CIO: David Fisher, Director Information Systems
CNO: Barry Mitchneck, Chief Nursing Officer, Director of Patient Care Services
Web address: https://www.upmc.com/campaigns/southcentral-pa
Control: Other not-for-profit (including NFP Corporation) **Service**: General medical and surgical

Staffed Beds: 60 **Admissions**: 3566 **Census**: 36 **Outpatient Visits**: 145066 **Total Expense ($000)**: 132841 **Payroll Expense ($000)**: 36238 **Personnel**: 670

Hospitals, U.S. / PENNSYLVANIA

MALVERN—Chester County

✠ △ **BRYN MAWR REHABILITATION HOSPITAL (393025)**, 414 Paoli Pike, Zip 19355–3300, Mailing Address: P.O. Box 3007, Zip 19355–0707; tel. 484/596–5400, **A**1 3 7 10 **F**3 11 29 30 34 35 36 44 54 58 64 82 84 86 87 90 91 93 95 96 119 130 131 132 146 148 149 154 157 **P**5 **S** Main Line Health, Pittsburgh, PA
Primary Contact: Donna Phillips, President
CFO: Dave Schmotzer, Chief Financial Officer
CMO: John Kraus, M.D., Chief Medical Officer
CIO: Kay Carr, Chief Information Officer
Web address: www.brynmawrrehab.org
Control: Other not–for–profit (including NFP Corporation) **Service**: Rehabilitation

Staffed Beds: 148 **Admissions**: 2067 **Census**: 96 **Outpatient Visits**: 99070 **Births**: 0 **Total Expense ($000)**: 85992 **Payroll Expense ($000)**: 43039 **Personnel**: 620

DEVEREUX CHILDREN'S BEHAVIORAL HEALTH CENTER, 655 Sugartown Road, Zip 19355–3303, Mailing Address: 655 Sugartown Rd, Zip 19355–3303; tel. 800/345–1292, (Nonreporting) **S** Devereux, Villanova, PA
Primary Contact: Patricia Hillis-Clark, Executive Director
CFO: Tim Evans, Assistant Financial Director
CMO: Jacquelyn Zavodnick, M.D., Medical Director
CIO: MaryLou Hettinger, Director Quality Management
CHR: Sean Maher, Director Human Resources
CNO: Deanna Reiss, Hospital Director of Nursing
Web address: www.devereux.org
Control: Other not–for–profit (including NFP Corporation) **Service**: Children's hospital psychiatric

Staffed Beds: 48

MALVERN INSTITUTE, 940 King Road, Zip 19355–3166; tel. 610/647–0330, (Nonreporting)
Primary Contact: Geoff Botak, Chief Executive Officer
CFO: Janet Corley, Accountant
Web address: www.malverninstitute.com
Control: Corporation, Investor–owned (for–profit) **Service**: Substance Use Disorder

Staffed Beds: 175

MC CONNELLSBURG—Fulton County

★ **FULTON COUNTY MEDICAL CENTER (391303)**, 214 Peach Orchard Road, Zip 17233–8559, Mailing Address: McConnellsburg, tel. 717/485–3155, (Nonreporting) **A**10 18
Primary Contact: Michael D. Makosky, Chief Executive Officer
COO: Kim Slee, Chief Operating Officer
CFO: Deborah A Shughart, Chief Financial Officer
CMO: Sharon E Martin, M.D., Ph.D., President Medical Staff
CIO: Armen Arakelian, Chief Information Officer
CHR: Cheryl Rose, Human Resources Director
Web address: www.fcmcpa.org
Control: Other not–for–profit (including NFP Corporation) **Service**: General medical and surgical

Staffed Beds: 88

MCKEES ROCKS—Allegheny County

☐ **HERITAGE VALLEY KENNEDY (390157)**, 25 Heckel Road, Zip 15136–1694; tel. 412/777–6161, (Nonreporting) **A**1 10 **S** Heritage Valley Health System, Beaver, PA
Primary Contact: Norman F. Mitry, President and Chief Executive Officer
CFO: Jack Nelson, Vice President Finance and Chief Financial Officer
CHR: Erin J Frohnhofer, Vice President Human Resources
CNO: Paulette Bingham, Director Nursing Services
Web address: www.ohiovalleyhospital.org
Control: Other not–for–profit (including NFP Corporation) **Service**: General medical and surgical

Staffed Beds: 124

MCKEESPORT—Allegheny County

✠ **SELECT SPECIALTY HOSPITAL–MCKEESPORT (392045)**, 1500 Fifth Avenue, 6th Floor, Zip 15132–2422; tel. 412/664–2900, (Nonreporting) **A**1 10 **S** Select Medical Corporation, Mechanicsburg, PA
Primary Contact: Louise Urban, R.N., Chief Operating Officer
Web address: www.mckeesport.selectspecialtyhospitals.com/
Control: Corporation, Investor–owned (for–profit) **Service**: Acute long–term care hospital

Staffed Beds: 30

✠ **UPMC MCKEESPORT (390002)**, 1500 Fifth Avenue, Zip 15132–2422; tel. 412/664–2000, **A**1 3 5 10 13 **F**3 4 18 20 28 29 30 31 34 35 40 49 50 54 56 57 59 60 62 64 65 68 74 75 77 78 79 81 82 83 84 85 86 87 90 96 98 100 101 102 107 108 111 114 115 119 130 132 135 143 146 148 154 156 157 160 161 167 **S** UPMC, Pittsburgh, PA
Primary Contact: Mark O'Hern, President
COO: Amy Bush, R.N., Vice President Operations
CFO: Laurene Timmons, Chief Financial Officer
CMO: R Curtis Waligura, D.O., Vice President Medical Affairs, Chief Medical Officer
CIO: Terri Keeling, Vice President Information Systems
CHR: Kelli Reale, Vice President Human Resources
Web address: www.mckeesport.upmc.com
Control: Other not–for–profit (including NFP Corporation) **Service**: General medical and surgical

Staffed Beds: 136 **Admissions**: 4378 **Census**: 92 **Outpatient Visits**: 97742 **Births**: 0 **Total Expense ($000)**: 161944 **Payroll Expense ($000)**: 52830 **Personnel**: 607

MEADOWBROOK—Montgomery County

⇑ **HOLY REDEEMER HOSPITAL (390097)**, 1648 Huntingdon Pike, Zip 19046–8001; tel. 215/947–3000, (Nonreporting) **A**2 3 5 10 21
Primary Contact: Gregory Wozniak, President and Chief Operating Officer
COO: Gregory Wozniak, President and Chief Operating Officer
CFO: Russell R Wagner, Executive Vice President and Chief Financial Officer
CMO: Henry D. Unger, M.D., Senior Vice President and Chief Medical Officer
CIO: Donald F. Friel, Executive Vice President
CHR: Joseph J Cassidy, Vice President
CNO: Anne Catino, MS, R.N., Vice President and Chief Nursing Officer
Web address: www.holyredeemer.com
Control: Other not–for–profit (including NFP Corporation) **Service**: General medical and surgical

Staffed Beds: 263

MEADVILLE—Crawford County

★ ⇑ **MEADVILLE MEDICAL CENTER (390113)**, 751 Liberty Street, Zip 16335–2559; tel. 814/333–5000, (Nonreporting) **A**3 5 10 12 13 21 **S** Meadville Medical Center, Meadville, PA
Primary Contact: Philip E. Pandolph, FACHE, President and Chief Executive Officer
CFO: Renato Suntay, Chief Financial Officer
CMO: Denise Johnson, M.D., Medical Director
CHR: Greg Maras, Vice President Human Resources
CNO: MaryAnn Hewston, R.N., Chief Nurse Executive
Web address: www.mmchs.org
Control: Other not–for–profit (including NFP Corporation) **Service**: General medical and surgical

Staffed Beds: 232

MECHANICSBURG—Cumberland County

✠ **ENCOMPASS HEALTH REHABILITATION HOSPITAL OF MECHANICSBURG (393031)**, 175 Lancaster Boulevard, Zip 17055–3562; tel. 717/691–3700, (Nonreporting) **A**1 10 **S** Encompass Health Corporation, Birmingham, AL
Primary Contact: Kristen Turner, Chief Executive Officer
CMO: Michael Lupinacci, M.D., Medical Director
CHR: David Staskin, Director Human Resources
Web address: www.healthsouthpa.com
Control: Corporation, Investor–owned (for–profit) **Service**: Rehabilitation

Staffed Beds: 75

Hospital, Medicare Provider Number, Address, Telephone, Approval, Facility, and Physician Codes, Health Care System

★ American Hospital Association (AHA) membership
☐ The Joint Commission accreditation
○ Healthcare Facilities Accreditation Program
◇ DNV Healthcare Inc. accreditation
⇑ Center for Improvement in Healthcare Quality Accreditation
△ Commission on Accreditation of Rehabilitation Facilities (CARF) accreditation

Hospitals, U.S. / PENNSYLVANIA

MEDIA—Delaware County

✠ **RIDDLE HOSPITAL (390222)**, 1068 West Baltimore Pike, Zip 19063–5177; tel. 484/227-9400, **A**1 2 3 10 **F**3 7 11 13 15 18 20 22 26 28 29 30 31 34 35 36 38 39 40 41 45 49 50 51 53 54 55 56 57 58 59 63 64 65 70 72 74 75 76 78 79 80 81 82 84 85 86 87 93 96 100 102 107 108 110 111 114 115 118 119 120 121 123 124 126 128 129 130 131 132 135 141 146 148 149 154 157 164 167 169 **S** Main Line Health, Birmingham, AL
Primary Contact: Shelly Buck, President
CFO: Ed McKillip, Vice President Finance
CMO: David Thomas, President Medical Staff
CHR: Mary Louise Ciciretti, Director Human Resources
Web address: www.riddlehospital.org
Control: Other not–for–profit (including NFP Corporation) **Service**: General medical and surgical

Staffed Beds: 182 **Admissions**: 10433 **Census**: 124 **Outpatient Visits**: 218478 **Births**: 1071 **Total Expense ($000)**: 266877 **Payroll Expense ($000)**: 93714 **Personnel**: 1072

MEYERSDALE—Somerset County

✠ **CONEMAUGH MEYERSDALE MEDICAL CENTER (391302)**, 200 Hospital Drive, Zip 15552–1249; tel. 814/634-5911, (Nonreporting) **A**1 10 18 **S** Lifepoint Health, Brentwood, TN
Primary Contact: Timothy Harclerode, R.N., FACHE, Chief Executive Officer
CMO: Dwayne Platt, M.D., Chief Medical Officer
CNO: Jessica Svidergol–Peterman, MSN, R.N., Chief Nursing Officer
Web address: https://www.conemaugh.org/meyersdale
Control: Corporation, Investor–owned (for–profit) **Service**: General medical and surgical

Staffed Beds: 20

MONONGAHELA—Washington County

MONONGAHELA VALLEY HOSPITAL See Penn Highlands Mon Valley

☐ **PENN HIGHLANDS MON VALLEY (390147)**, 1163 Country Club Road, Zip 15063–1095; tel. 724/258-1000, (Nonreporting) **A**1 10
Primary Contact: Peter J. Adamo, Regional Market President, SW Region/President, Penn Highlands Mon Valley
COO: Patrick J Alberts, Senior Vice President and Chief Operating Officer
CFO: Daniel F Simmons, Senior Vice President and Treasurer
CMO: L. Douglas Pepper, M.D., President, Medical Staff
CIO: Matt Rashilla, Chief Information and Application Officer
CHR: Christopher Kovski, Senior Vice President Human Resources
Web address: www.monvalleyhospital.com
Control: Other not–for–profit (including NFP Corporation) **Service**: General medical and surgical

Staffed Beds: 200

MONROEVILLE—Allegheny County

✠ **FORBES HOSPITAL (390267)**, 2570 Haymaker Road, Zip 15146–3513; tel. 412/858-2000, **A**1 2 3 10 **F**3 8 11 15 15 17 18 20 22 24 26 28 29 30 31 34 35 36 37 38 40 43 44 45 46 47 48 49 50 54 55 57 58 59 64 65 69 70 73 74 75 76 77 78 79 80 81 82 84 85 86 87 90 92 96 98 100 101 102 107 108 110 111 115 117 118 119 120 121 123 126 130 131 132 135 141 145 146 147 148 149 154 155 167 169 **S** Allegheny Health Network, Pittsburgh, PA
Primary Contact: Mark Rubino, M.D., President
COO: Krista A. Bragg, MSN, Chief Operating Officer
CFO: Tom Hipkiss, Vice President Finance
CIO: Sharon Lewis, Director Information Systems
CHR: Georgia Redding, Director Human Resources
Web address: www.ahn.org
Control: Other not–for–profit (including NFP Corporation) **Service**: General medical and surgical

Staffed Beds: 314 **Admissions**: 12016 **Census**: 202 **Outpatient Visits**: 173575 **Births**: 1141 **Total Expense ($000)**: 350534 **Payroll Expense ($000)**: 119545 **Personnel**: 1387

✠ **UPMC EAST (390328)**, 2775 Mosside Boulevard, Zip 15146–2760; tel. 412/357-3000, **A**1 2 3 10 **F**3 18 20 22 29 30 34 35 40 45 47 49 50 57 59 60 62 65 68 70 74 75 77 78 79 81 82 84 85 87 90 96 100 107 108 111 115 119 120 121 123 132 135 146 148 154 156 157 167 **S** UPMC, Pittsburgh, PA
Primary Contact: Mark O'Hern, President
CFO: Laurene Timmons, Chief Financial Officer
CNO: Tamra Minton, R.N., MSN, Vice President Patient Care Services and Chief Nursing Officer
Web address: www.upmc.com/locations/hospitals/east/Pages/default.aspx
Control: Other not–for–profit (including NFP Corporation) **Service**: General medical and surgical

Staffed Beds: 155 **Admissions**: 7275 **Census**: 129 **Outpatient Visits**: 89682 **Births**: 0 **Total Expense ($000)**: 232917 **Payroll Expense ($000)**: 69529 **Personnel**: 929

MONTROSE—Susquehanna County

ENDLESS MOUNTAINS HEALTH SYSTEMS (391306), 100 Hospital Drive, Zip 18801–6402; tel. 570/278-3801, (Nonreporting) **A**10 18
Primary Contact: Loren Stone, Chief Executive Officer
CIO: Gary Passmore, Chief Information Officer
CHR: Paula Anderson, Administrative Director Human Resources
Web address: www.endlesscare.org
Control: Other not–for–profit (including NFP Corporation) **Service**: General medical and surgical

Staffed Beds: 25

MOUNT GRETNA—Lebanon County

★ ⇑ **WELLSPAN PHILHAVEN (394020)**, 283 Butler Road, Zip 17064, Mailing Address: P.O. Box 550, Zip 17064–0550; tel. 717/273-8871, **A**3 10 21 **F**29 30 44 98 99 100 101 102 103 104 105 130 149 153 154 164 **S** WellSpan Health, York, PA
Primary Contact: Mantah Kotsalos, VP & President, WellSpan Philhaven
COO: Philip D. Hess, President
CFO: Matt Rogers, Chief Financial Officer
CMO: Francis D. Sparrow, M.D., Medical Director
CHR: Janelle Greenawalt, Director Human Resources
CNO: Heidi McMullan, R.N., Chief Nursing Officer
Web address: https://www.wellspanphilhaven.org/Locations/Lebanon-County/Mt-Gretna
Control: Other not–for–profit (including NFP Corporation) **Service**: Psychiatric

Staffed Beds: 140 **Admissions**: 1609 **Census**: 197 **Outpatient Visits**: 0 **Births**: 0 **Total Expense ($000)**: 95992 **Payroll Expense ($000)**: 41370 **Personnel**: 637

MOUNT PLEASANT—Westmoreland County

☐ **EXCELA FRICK HOSPITAL (390217)**, 508 South Church Street, Zip 15666–1790; tel. 724/547-1500, (Nonreporting) **A**1 10 **S** Independence Health System, Butler, PA
Primary Contact: Brian Fritz, President
COO: Jeffrey Tiesi, Executive Vice President and Chief Operating Officer
CFO: Jeffrey T Curry, Executive Vice President and Chief Financial Officer
CMO: Jerome Granato, M.D., Senior Vice President and Chief Medical Officer
CIO: Vasanth Balu, Senior Vice President and Chief Information Officer
CHR: John Caverno, Chief Human Resources Officer
CNO: Helen K Burns, Ph.D., R.N., Senior Vice President and Chief Nursing Officer
Web address: www.excelahealth.org/PatientsandVisitors/HospitalsFacilities/Hospitals/Frick.aspx
Control: Other not–for–profit (including NFP Corporation) **Service**: General medical and surgical

Staffed Beds: 33

MUNCY—Lycoming County

★ **GEISINGER MEDICAL CENTER MUNCY (390337)**, 255 Route 220 Highway, Zip 17756–7569; tel. 570/271-6211, **A**10 **F**3 5 12 15 18 28 29 34 35 40 45 50 57 59 65 68 75 79 81 85 93 97 107 110 111 115 119 126 130 132 135 147 149 154 156 160 164 **S** Geisinger, Danville, PA
Primary Contact: Tammy Anderer, Ph.D., Vice President of Clinical Operations for the North Central Region
CFO: Kristy Hine, Chief Financial Officer
CMO: Jason Schauer, M.D., Chief Medical Officer
CIO: Frank Richards, Chief Information Officer
CHR: Amy Brayford, Chief Human Resources Officer
CNO: Wendy Batschelet, MSN, R.N., Chief Nursing Officer
Web address: www.geisinger.org
Control: Other not–for–profit (including NFP Corporation) **Service**: General medical and surgical

Staffed Beds: 20 **Admissions**: 1275 **Census**: 10 **Outpatient Visits**: 102157 **Births**: 0 **Total Expense ($000)**: 68663 **Payroll Expense ($000)**: 15565 **Personnel**: 330

✠ **UPMC MUNCY (391301)**, 215 East Water Street, Zip 17756–8700; tel. 570/546-8282, (Total facility includes 138 beds in nursing home–type unit) **A**1 10 18 **F**6 11 15 29 30 34 35 40 44 45 46 50 56 57 59 64 67 68 77 81 86 87 90 93 96 97 107 108 110 114 115 118 119 128 130 131 132 133 146 147 149 154 157 **S** UPMC, Pittsburgh, PA
Primary Contact: Ronald J. Reynolds, President
CIO: Timothy E Schoener, Chief Information Officer
CHR: Dawn Wright, Vice President Human Resources
CNO: C Cynthia Whipple, Director of Nursing
Web address: www.susquehannahealth.org
Control: Other not–for–profit (including NFP Corporation) **Service**: General medical and surgical

Staffed Beds: 154 **Admissions**: 770 **Census**: 103 **Outpatient Visits**: 36786 **Births**: 0 **Total Expense ($000)**: 54302 **Payroll Expense ($000)**: 24403 **Personnel**: 196

NATRONA HEIGHTS—Allegheny County

ALLE KISKI MEDICAL CENTER See Select Specialty Hospital – Alle Kiski

ALLEGHENY VALLEY HOSPITAL (390032), 1301 Carlisle Street, Zip 15065–1152; tel. 724/224–5100, **A**1 2 3 10 **F**3 11 15 17 18 28 29 30 31 34 35 36 37 38 39 40 44 45 47 49 50 54 56 57 58 59 64 65 70 74 75 77 78 79 80 81 82 84 85 86 87 90 92 93 96 98 100 101 102 103 107 108 110 111 115 118 119 120 121 123 126 129 130 131 132 135 136 141 145 146 149 154 155 167 168 **S** Allegheny Health Network, Pittsburgh, PA
Primary Contact: Mark Rubino, M.D., President
COO: Krista A. Bragg, MSN, Chief Operating Officer
CFO: James A Kanuch, Vice President Finance
CMO: Suzanne M. Labriola, D.O., Chief Medical Officer
CIO: Linda Fergus, Manager Information Technology
CHR: Cindy Moser, Director Human Resources
Web address: www.wpahs.org
Control: Other not–for–profit (including NFP Corporation) **Service:** General medical and surgical

Staffed Beds: 111 **Admissions:** 3228 **Census:** 49 **Outpatient Visits:** 154277 **Births:** 0 **Total Expense ($000):** 129969 **Payroll Expense ($000):** 46843 **Personnel:** 645

NEW CASTLE—Lawrence County

UPMC JAMESON (390016), 1211 Wilmington Avenue, Zip 16105–2516; tel. 724/658–9001, **A**1 3 10 19 **F**3 12 15 18 20 28 29 30 34 35 40 45 46 49 50 57 59 64 65 68 70 74 75 77 79 81 82 85 86 87 90 92 93 96 100 105 107 108 110 111 114 115 118 119 126 130 135 146 147 148 149 154 156 157 164 **S** UPMC, Pittsburgh, PA
Primary Contact: David J. Patton, President
COO: Albert Boland, Vice President Operations
CFO: Brian Fritz, Chief Financial Officer
CIO: Charles M. Rudek, Chief Information Officer
CHR: Eric D. McIntosh, Vice President Human Resources
CNO: Marianna Stoneburner, R.N., Chief Nursing Officer
Web address: www.upmcjameson.com
Control: Other not–for–profit (including NFP Corporation) **Service:** General medical and surgical

Staffed Beds: 91 **Admissions:** 4981 **Census:** 70 **Outpatient Visits:** 144239 **Births:** 0 **Total Expense ($000):** 137626 **Payroll Expense ($000):** 52143 **Personnel:** 742

NORRISTOWN—Montgomery County

MONTGOMERY COUNTY EMERGENCY SERVICE (394033), 50 Beech Drive, Zip 19403–5421; tel. 610/279–6100, **A**1 10 **F**7 50 98 102 106 122 130 161 164
Primary Contact: William Myers, Chief Executive Officer
CFO: Wendy Wait, Chief Financial Officer
CMO: Marina Cooney, Medical Director
CHR: Byanka Meacham, Director Human Resources
CNO: Naomi Finkel, Nurse Executive
Web address: www.mces.org
Control: Other not–for–profit (including NFP Corporation) **Service:** Psychiatric

Staffed Beds: 58 **Admissions:** 1049 **Census:** 43 **Outpatient Visits:** 0 **Births:** 0 **Personnel:** 160

NORRISTOWN STATE HOSPITAL (394001), 1001 Sterigere Street, Zip 19401–5300; tel. 610/270–1000, (Nonreporting) **A**10
Primary Contact: Jessica Keith, Chief Executive Officer
COO: Gary Raisner, Chief Operating Officer
CMO: Mia Marcovici, M.D., Chief Medical Officer
CHR: Richard Szczurowski, Director Human Resources
CNO: Taryn Mason-Jones, Chief Nurse Executive
Control: State, Government, Nonfederal **Service:** Psychiatric

Staffed Beds: 374

VALLEY FORGE MEDICAL CENTER (390272), 1033 West Germantown Pike, Zip 19403–3905; tel. 610/539–8500, (Nonreporting) **A**1 10 22
Primary Contact: Gregg Y. Slocum, Chief Executive Officer
CMO: Robert E Colcher, M.D., Medical Director
CHR: Frederick D Jackes, Assistant Administrator and Director Human Resources
Web address: www.vfmc.net
Control: Corporation, Investor–owned (for–profit) **Service:** Substance Use Disorder

Staffed Beds: 86

OAKDALE—Allegheny County

★ **PAM HEALTH SPECIALTY HOSPITAL OF PITTSBURGH (392028)**, 7777 Steubenville Pike, Zip 15071–3409; tel. 412/494–5500, **A**10 22 **F**1 3 29 60 148 **S** PAM Health, Enola, PA
Primary Contact: Carli Chakamba, Chief Executive Officer
CFO: Kevin Varley, Chief Financial Officer
CMO: Ravi Alagar, M.D., Medical Director
Web address: https://pamhealth.com/index.php/facilities/find-facility/specialty-hospitals/pam-health-specialty-hospital-oakdale
Control: Corporation, Investor–owned (for–profit) **Service:** Acute long–term care hospital

Staffed Beds: 31 **Admissions:** 275 **Census:** 20 **Outpatient Visits:** 0 **Births:** 0 **Total Expense ($000):** 13114 **Payroll Expense ($000):** 6118 **Personnel:** 97

OREFIELD—Lehigh County

KIDSPEACE CHILDREN'S HOSPITAL (394047), 5300 Kids Peace Drive, Zip 18069–2044; tel. 610/799–8000, (Nonreporting) **A**3 10
Primary Contact: Michael W. Slack, President and Chief Executive Officer
CFO: Michael Callan, Executive Vice President and Chief Financial Officer
CMO: Matthew Koval, M.D., Vice President Medical Affairs
CIO: Joan Lesko, Director Technical Support and Services
CHR: Sheila Rulli, Director Human Resources
CNO: Tamara Wasilick, Director Operations
Web address: www.kidspeace.org
Control: Other not–for–profit (including NFP Corporation) **Service:** Children's hospital psychiatric

Staffed Beds: 120

ORWIGSBURG—Schuylkill County

GEISINGER ST. LUKE'S HOSPITAL (390332), 100 Paramount Boulevard, Zip 17961–2202; tel. 272/639–1000, (Nonreporting) **A**1 3 10 **S** St. Luke's University Health Network, Bethlehem, PA
Primary Contact: Gabriel Kamarousky, President
Web address: https://www.geisingerstlukes.org/
Control: Other not–for–profit (including NFP Corporation) **Service:** General medical and surgical

Staffed Beds: 40

PALMERTON—Carbon County

BLUE MOUNTAIN HOSPITAL PALMERTON CAMPUS See St. Luke's – Palmerton Campus

PAOLI—Chester County

PAOLI HOSPITAL (390153), 255 West Lancaster Avenue, Zip 19301–1763; tel. 484/565–1000, **A**1 2 3 5 10 **F**3 11 13 15 18 20 22 26 28 29 30 31 32 34 35 36 38 39 40 41 43 44 45 49 51 54 55 56 57 58 59 61 63 64 65 70 72 74 75 76 78 79 80 81 82 84 85 86 87 93 100 102 107 108 110 111 114 115 119 120 121 123 124 126 129 130 131 132 135 141 145 146 148 149 154 156 164 167 169 **S** Main Line Health, Bethlehem, PA
Primary Contact: James Paradis, President
CFO: John Doyle, Vice President Finance
CMO: Andrew J Norton, M.D., Chief Medical Officer
CIO: Kay Carr, Senior Vice President and Chief Information Officer
CHR: Deborah Fedora, Director Human Resources
Web address: www.mainlinehealth.org
Control: Other not–for–profit (including NFP Corporation) **Service:** General medical and surgical

Staffed Beds: 249 **Admissions:** 15702 **Census:** 189 **Outpatient Visits:** 284023 **Births:** 2122 **Total Expense ($000):** 411976 **Payroll Expense ($000):** 128233 **Personnel:** 1394

Hospitals, U.S. / PENNSYLVANIA

PHILADELPHIA—Philadelphia County

☐ **BEHAVIORAL WELLNESS CENTER AT GIRARD, THE**, 801 West Girard Ave, Zip 19122–4212, Mailing Address: 801 West Girard Avenue, Zip 19122–4212; tel. 215/787–9000, (Includes GIRARD MEDICAL CENTER, Girard Avenue at Eighth Street, Philadelphia, Pennsylvania, Zip 19122, tel. 215/787–2000; Gerri H. Walker, President and Chief Executive Officer) (Nonreporting) **A**1 10
Primary Contact: Gerri H. Walker, President and Chief Executive Officer
CFO: Ronald Kaplan, Chief Financial Officer
CIO: Tony Iero, Director Management Information Systems
CHR: James Gloner, Senior Vice President
Web address: www.nphs.com
Control: Other not-for-profit (including NFP Corporation) **Service**: Psychiatric

Staffed Beds: 175

☐ **BELMONT BEHAVIORAL HEALTH SYSTEM (394023)**, 4200 Monument Road, Zip 19131–1625; tel. 215/877–2000, (Nonreporting) **A**1 3 5 10 **S** Acadia Healthcare Company, Inc., Franklin, TN
Primary Contact: Laura Longstreet, Chief Executive Officer
CFO: Guy Romaniello, Director Fiscal Services
CMO: Richard Jaffe, M.D., Medical Director
CHR: Jenna Pacini, Human Resources Specialist
CNO: Nona Fain, Ph.D., R.N., Director of Nursing
Web address: https://www.belmontbehavioral.com/
Control: Corporation, Investor-owned (for-profit) **Service**: Psychiatric

Staffed Beds: 224

☐ **CHILDREN'S HOSPITAL OF PHILADELPHIA (393303)**, 3401 Civic Center Boulevard, Zip 19104–4319; tel. 215/590–1000, **A**1 3 5 8 10 **F**3 5 8 9 11 12 13 14 17 18 19 20 21 22 23 24 25 26 27 28 29 30 31 32 33 34 35 36 37 38 39 40 41 43 44 45 46 48 49 50 53 54 55 57 58 59 60 61 62 64 65 66 68 69 71 72 74 75 76 77 78 79 81 82 83 84 85 86 87 88 89 90 91 92 93 95 96 97 100 101 102 104 105 107 108 111 113 114 115 116 117 118 119 126 129 130 131 132 134 135 136 137 138 139 140 141 142 143 144 146 148 149 150 153 154 156 157 160 161 162 163 164 165 167 169 **P**6
Primary Contact: Madeline Bell, President and Chief Executive Officer
COO: Douglas G Hock, Executive Vice President and Chief Operating Officer
CFO: Sophia G. Holder, Executive Vice President and Chief Financial Officer
CMO: Jan Boswinkel, M.D., Vice President Medical Operations and Chief Safety Officer
CHR: Robert Croner, Senior Vice President and Chief Human Resources Officer
CNO: Paula M Agosto, R.N., MSN, Senior Vice President and Chief Nursing Officer
Web address: www.chop.edu
Control: Other not-for-profit (including NFP Corporation) **Service**: Children's general medical and surgical

Staffed Beds: 664 **Admissions:** 33681 **Census:** 552 **Outpatient Visits:** 1577311 **Births:** 485 **Total Expense ($000):** 3427531 **Payroll Expense ($000):** 1643321 **Personnel:** 16000

☐ △ **EINSTEIN MEDICAL CENTER PHILADELPHIA (390142)**, 5501 Old York Road, Zip 19141–3098; tel. 215/456–7890, (Includes EINSTEIN MEDICAL CENTER ELKINS PARK, 60 Township Line Road, Elkins Park, Pennsylvania, Zip 19027–2220, tel. 215/663–6000; Kenneth Levitan, President and Chief Executive Officer) (Total facility includes 44 beds in nursing home-type unit) **A**1 2 3 5 7 8 10 **F**3 5 8 11 12 13 15 17 18 20 22 24 26 28 29 30 31 34 35 36 37 38 39 40 43 44 45 46 47 48 49 50 54 55 56 57 58 59 61 64 65 66 68 70 72 73 74 75 76 77 78 79 80 81 82 83 84 85 86 87 90 91 92 93 94 95 96 97 98 100 101 102 103 104 106 107 108 110 111 114 115 119 120 121 123 124 125 128 129 130 131 132 138 139 142 143 145 146 147 148 149 150 154 156 157 158 160 161 162 164 167 169 **P**6 **S** Jefferson Health, Philadelphia, PA
Primary Contact: Dixieanne James, President and Chief Operating Officer, Central Region
COO: Ruth Lefton, Chief Operating Officer
CFO: Gerard Blaney, Vice President Finance and Interim Chief Financial Officer
CMO: Steven Sivak, M.D., Chief Medical Officer, Einstein Physicians Philadelphia
CIO: Brenda West, Vice President, Information Services and Interim Chief Information Officer
CHR: Lynne R Kornblatt, Chief Human Resources Officer
CNO: Jill Stunkard, R.N., MSN, Associate Chief Nurse Executive and Interim Chief Nursing Officer
Web address: www.einstein.edu
Control: Other not-for-profit (including NFP Corporation) **Service**: General medical and surgical

Staffed Beds: 496 **Admissions:** 23508 **Census:** 466 **Outpatient Visits:** 534274 **Births:** 2578 **Total Expense ($000):** 1039073 **Payroll Expense ($000):** 326065 **Personnel:** 5661

EPISCOPAL HOSPITAL See Temple University Hospital – Episcopal Division

☐ **FAIRMOUNT BEHAVIORAL HEALTH SYSTEM (394027)**, 561 Fairthorne Avenue, Zip 19128–2499; tel. 215/487–4000, (Nonreporting) **A**1 10 **S** Universal Health Services, Inc., King of Prussia, PA
Primary Contact: Vernetta Simmons, Interim Chief Executive Officer
CFO: Anthony Tortella, Chief Financial Officer
CMO: Silvia Gratz, D.O., Chief Medical Officer
CIO: Anthony Tortella, Chief Financial Officer
CHR: Brendan Aurand, Director, Human Resources
CNO: Wanda Nolasco, Chief Nursing Officer
Web address: www.fairmountbhs.com
Control: Corporation, Investor-owned (for-profit) **Service**: Psychiatric

Staffed Beds: 235

✠ **FOX CHASE CANCER CENTER (390196)**, 333 Cottman Avenue, Zip 19111–2434; tel. 215/728–6900, **A**1 2 3 5 10 **F**11 15 29 30 31 34 35 36 45 46 47 49 50 55 57 58 59 64 68 70 71 75 77 78 79 81 82 84 85 86 87 93 100 104 107 108 109 110 111 114 115 116 117 118 119 120 121 123 124 126 130 132 135 145 146 147 148 149 154 157 164 167 **S** Temple University Health System, Philadelphia, PA
Primary Contact: Robert Uzzo, M.D., President and Chief Executive Officer
COO: Joel Helmke, Chief Operating Officer
CFO: Jarred Matchett, Chief Financial Officer
CMO: James Helstrom, M.D., Chief Medical Officer
CIO: Michael Sweeney, Chief Information Officer
CNO: Anna Liza Rodriguez, Chief Nursing Officer
Web address: https://www.foxchase.org
Control: Other not-for-profit (including NFP Corporation) **Service**: Cancer

Staffed Beds: 60 **Admissions:** 3554 **Census:** 59 **Outpatient Visits:** 173366 **Births:** 0 **Total Expense ($000):** 255453 **Payroll Expense ($000):** 96466 **Personnel:** 1480

☐ **FRIENDS HOSPITAL (394008)**, 4641 Roosevelt Boulevard, Zip 19124–2343; tel. 215/831–4600, (Nonreporting) **A**1 3 10 **S** Universal Health Services, Inc., King of Prussia, PA
Primary Contact: Angela Cantwell, R.N., MSN, Chief Executive Officer
COO: Diane Carugati, Chief Operating Officer
CFO: Michael Terwilliger, Chief Financial Officer
CMO: Marc Rothman, M.D., Medical Director
CIO: John Healy, Manager Information Technology
CHR: Paul Cavanaugh, Director Human Resources
Web address: www.friendshospital.com
Control: Corporation, Investor-owned (for-profit) **Service**: Psychiatric

Staffed Beds: 192

☐ △ **GOOD SHEPHERD PENN PARTNERS (392050)**, 1800 Lombard Street, Zip 19146–1414; tel. 215/893–2541, **A**1 7 10 **F**1 3 29 34 50 56 58 68 74 75 85 86 87 93 94 95 96 130 131 132 143 146 148 149 154
Primary Contact: Jessica Cooper, Executive Director
CFO: Ronald J. Petula, Vice President Finance
CMO: Michael Grippi, M.D., Chief Medical Officer
CHR: Mark Sneff, Vice President Human Resources
CNO: Jean Romano, Chief Nursing Officer
Web address: www.phillyrehab.com
Control: Other not-for-profit (including NFP Corporation) **Service**: Acute long-term care hospital

Staffed Beds: 18 **Admissions:** 143 **Census:** 15 **Outpatient Visits:** 287863 **Births:** 0 **Total Expense ($000):** 62337 **Payroll Expense ($000):** 29593 **Personnel:** 394

☐ **HAVEN BEHAVIORAL HOSPITAL OF PHILADELPHIA (394053)**, 3300 Henry Avenue, Four Falls Building, Suite 100, Zip 19129–1141; tel. 215/475–3400, (Nonreporting) **A**1 10 **S** Haven Behavioral Healthcare, Nashville, TN
Primary Contact: Maurice Washington, Chief Executive Officer
Web address: https://philadelphia.havenbehavioral.com
Control: Corporation, Investor-owned (for-profit) **Service**: Psychiatric

Staffed Beds: 36

Hospitals, U.S. / PENNSYLVANIA

✣ **HOSPITAL OF THE UNIVERSITY OF PENNSYLVANIA (390111)**, 3400 Spruce Street, Zip 19104–4206; tel. 215/662–4000, (Includes SCHEIE EYE INSTITUTE OF THE HOSPITAL OF THE UNIVERSITY OF PENNSYLVANIA, 3400 Civic Center Blvd FL 3, West Pavilion, 3rd Floor, Philadelphia, Pennsylvania, Zip 19104–5127, tel. 215/662–8100; Sheara Hollin, Chief Operating Officer) **A**1 2 3 5 8 10 19 **F**3 4 6 7 9 11 12 13 15 17 18 20 22 24 26 29 30 31 34 35 36 38 39 40 41 44 45 46 47 48 49 50 51 52 53 54 55 56 57 58 59 60 61 62 63 64 65 66 68 69 70 72 73 74 75 76 77 78 79 80 81 82 84 85 86 87 90 91 92 93 94 95 96 97 98 100 102 104 107 108 110 111 112 113 115 116 117 118 119 120 121 122 123 124 126 129 130 131 132 135 136 137 138 139 140 141 142 145 146 147 148 149 150 154 155 157 160 161 162 164 167 169 **P**6 **S** University of Pennsylvania Health System, Philadelphia, PA
Primary Contact: Regina Cunningham, Ph.D., R.N., Chief Executive Officer
CFO: Joseph M Huber, Chief Financial Officer
CMO: Patrick J Brennan, M.D., Senior Vice President and Chief Medical Officer
CIO: Michael Restuccia, Chief Information Officer
CHR: Denise J. Mariotti, Chief Human Resource Officer
Web address: www.pennmedicine.org
Control: Other not-for-profit (including NFP Corporation) **Service:** General medical and surgical

Staffed Beds: 1038 **Admissions:** 39360 **Census:** 835 **Outpatient Visits:** 3150986 **Births:** 4085 **Total Expense ($000):** 4160428 **Payroll Expense ($000):** 1540281 **Personnel:** 19152

✣ △ **JEFFERSON HEALTH NORTHEAST (390115)**, 10800 Knights Road, Zip 19114–4200; tel. 215/612–4000, (Includes BUCKS COUNTY CAMPUS, 380 North Oxford Valley Road, Langhorne, Pennsylvania, Zip 19047–8399, tel. 215/949–5000; FRANKFORD CAMPUS, 4900 Frankford Avenue, Philadelphia, Pennsylvania, Zip 19124–2618, tel. 215/831–2000) **A**1 2 3 5 7 10 **F**3 4 11 12 15 17 18 20 22 24 26 28 29 30 31 34 35 39 40 43 44 45 46 49 50 53 54 55 57 58 59 64 65 68 70 74 75 77 78 79 80 81 82 84 85 86 87 92 93 96 100 107 108 110 111 114 115 117 118 119 120 121 123 124 126 129 130 131 132 135 144 146 147 148 149 154 156 160 161 164 166 167 **P**8 **S** Jefferson Health, Philadelphia, PA
Primary Contact: Richard Galup, President
COO: Richard Galup, Chief Operating Officer
CFO: William Degnan, Vice President Finance
CMO: Stanton Segal, M.D., Chief Medical Officer
CHR: Dorinda Carolina, Chief Human Resources Officer
CNO: Michelle E Conley, R.N., Chief Nursing Officer
Web address: https://www.jeffersonhealth.org/locations/torresdale-hospital
Control: Other not-for-profit (including NFP Corporation) **Service:** General medical and surgical

Staffed Beds: 457 **Admissions:** 22468 **Census:** 347 **Outpatient Visits:** 225781 **Births:** 0 **Total Expense ($000):** 587905 **Payroll Expense ($000):** 209158 **Personnel:** 3423

JEFFERSON METHODIST HOSPITAL See Thomas Jefferson University Hospital, Philadelphia

☐ **KENSINGTON HOSPITAL (390025)**, 136 West Diamond Street, Zip 19122–1721; tel. 215/426–8100, (Nonreporting) **A**1 10
Primary Contact: Kathleen Lalli, Chief Executive Officer
CFO: Kenneth Biddle, Controller
CMO: Luis F Vera, M.D., Medical Director
CNO: Aleyamma John, R.N., Director of Nursing
Control: State, Government, Nonfederal **Service:** General medical and surgical

Staffed Beds: 33

✣ **KINDRED HOSPITAL PHILADELPHIA (392027)**, 6129 Palmetto Street, Zip 19111–5729; tel. 215/722–8555, (Includes KINDRED HOSPITAL PHILADELPHIA – HAVERTOWN, 2000 Old West Chester Pike, Havertown, Pennsylvania, Zip 19083–2712, tel. 610/536–2100; Margaret M Murphy, Chief Executive Officer) (Nonreporting) **A**1 10 **S** ScionHealth, Louisville, KY
Primary Contact: Andrew P. Donet, Market Chief Executive Officer
CFO: Kathy Andrews, Chief Financial Officer
CNO: Erin McCullough, Chief Clinical Officer
Web address: www.kindredphila.com/
Control: Corporation, Investor-owned (for-profit) **Service:** Acute long-term care hospital

Staffed Beds: 86

✣ △ **MAGEE REHABILITATION (393038)**, 1513 Race Street, Zip 19102–1177; tel. 215/587–3000, **A**1 3 5 7 10 **F**29 30 38 44 50 58 59 60 64 68 74 75 90 91 93 94 95 96 119 130 132 146 148 149 150 154 **P**6 **S** Jefferson Health, Philadelphia, PA
Primary Contact: Dixieanne James, President and Chief Operating Officer
COO: Dixieanne James, President and Chief Operating Officer
CFO: Stephen DeStefano, Chief Financial Officer
CMO: Guy Fried, M.D., Chief Medical Officer
CIO: Shawna White, Chief Information Officer
CHR: Cindy Tobin–Payne, Director
Web address: www.mageerehab.org
Control: Other not-for-profit (including NFP Corporation) **Service:** Rehabilitation

Staffed Beds: 83 **Admissions:** 1021 **Census:** 72 **Outpatient Visits:** 36326 **Births:** 0 **Total Expense ($000):** 81163 **Payroll Expense ($000):** 42800 **Personnel:** 595

METHODIST HOSPITAL See Jefferson Methodist Hospital

✣ **NAZARETH HOSPITAL (390204)**, 2601 Holme Avenue, Zip 19152–2096; tel. 215/335–6000, (Total facility includes 19 beds in nursing home–type unit) **A**1 3 5 10 **F**3 12 15 18 20 22 26 28 29 30 31 34 35 37 39 40 44 45 46 49 50 53 56 57 58 59 64 65 70 74 75 77 78 79 81 82 84 85 86 87 90 93 96 97 100 107 108 110 111 114 118 119 120 121 126 128 130 131 132 146 147 148 149 154 157 167 **S** Trinity Health, Livonia, MI
Primary Contact: Michael Magro Jr, D.O., President
CFO: David Wajda, Chief Financial Officer
CMO: Edward O'Dell, D.O., Chief Medical Officer
CIO: Bonnie J. Buehler, Chief Information Technology
CHR: Kathleen M. Pries, Director Human Resources
Web address: www.nazarethhospital.org
Control: Other not-for-profit (including NFP Corporation) **Service:** General medical and surgical

Staffed Beds: 147 **Admissions:** 6754 **Census:** 107 **Outpatient Visits:** 69552 **Births:** 0 **Total Expense ($000):** 167882 **Payroll Expense ($000):** 67951 **Personnel:** 870

NORTH PHILADELPHIA HEALTH SYST See Girard Medical Center

✣ **PENN PRESBYTERIAN MEDICAL CENTER (390223)**, 51 North 39th Street, Zip 19104–2699; tel. 215/662–8000, (Total facility includes 19 beds in nursing home–type unit) **A**1 2 3 5 10 19 **F**3 4 5 8 9 11 12 15 17 18 20 22 24 26 29 30 31 32 34 35 37 38 39 40 41 43 44 45 46 47 48 49 50 51 52 54 55 56 57 58 59 60 61 62 63 64 65 66 68 70 71 74 75 77 78 79 81 82 84 85 86 87 92 93 94 96 97 98 100 101 104 107 108 110 111 115 118 119 121 126 129 130 131 132 134 135 141 142 145 146 147 148 149 150 153 154 156 157 160 161 162 164 167 **S** University of Pennsylvania Health System, Philadelphia, PA
Primary Contact: Robert J. Russell, MS, FACHE, Chief Executive Officer
CFO: Anthony Zumpano, Chief Financial Officer
CMO: Kevin Fosnocht, M.D., Chief Medical Officer and Associate Executive Director
CIO: Theresa Hiltunen, Entity Information Officer
CHR: Margorie Michele, Chief Human Resources Officer
CNO: James R Ballinghoff, MSN, R.N., DNP, RN, Chief Nursing Officer and Associate Executive Director
Web address: www.pennmedicine.org/pmc/
Control: Other not-for-profit (including NFP Corporation) **Service:** General medical and surgical

Staffed Beds: 399 **Admissions:** 18182 **Census:** 356 **Outpatient Visits:** 370213 **Births:** 0 **Total Expense ($000):** 1015787 **Payroll Expense ($000):** 334772 **Personnel:** 3352

✣ **PENNSYLVANIA HOSPITAL (390226)**, 800 Spruce Street, Zip 19107–6192; tel. 215/829–3000, **A**1 2 3 5 10 13 19 **F**3 8 12 13 15 17 18 20 22 26 28 29 30 31 34 35 36 37 38 39 40 41 44 45 46 49 50 51 52 54 55 56 57 58 59 60 61 63 64 65 66 68 70 72 74 75 76 77 78 79 80 81 82 84 85 86 87 93 94 96 97 98 100 101 102 103 104 107 108 110 111 115 116 117 119 120 121 123 124 126 129 130 131 132 134 135 141 145 146 148 149 154 156 164 165 167 168 169 **P**6 **S** University of Pennsylvania Health System, Philadelphia, PA
Primary Contact: Alicia Gresham, Chief Executive Officer
COO: Daniel Wilson, R.N., Chief Operating Officer
CFO: Frank Anastasi, Chief Financial Officer
CMO: Daniel Feinberg, M.D., Chief Medical Officer
CIO: Kwon Lee, Chief Information Officer
Web address: www.pahosp.com
Control: Other not-for-profit (including NFP Corporation) **Service:** General medical and surgical

Staffed Beds: 503 **Admissions:** 18959 **Census:** 278 **Outpatient Visits:** 376828 **Births:** 5245 **Total Expense ($000):** 804237 **Payroll Expense ($000):** 281437 **Personnel:** 4085

Hospitals, U.S. / PENNSYLVANIA

PHILADELPHIA VETERANS AFFAIRS MEDICAL CENTER, 3900 Woodland Avenue, Zip 19104–4594; tel. 215/823–5800, (Nonreporting) **A**1 3 5 7 **S** Department of Veterans Affairs, Washington, DC
Primary Contact: Karen Ann. Flaherty–Oxler, MSN, R.N., Medical Center Director
CMO: Dave Oslin, M.D., Chief of Staff
CIO: Adrienne Ficchi, Vice President Information Management
CHR: Gerald Morelli, Director Human Resources
Web address: www.philadelphia.va.gov/
Control: Veterans Affairs, Government, federal **Service**: General medical and surgical

Staffed Beds: 279

PHILADELPHIA VETERANS AFFAIRS MEDICAL CENTER See Philadelphia Veterans Affairs Medical Center

ROXBOROUGH MEMORIAL HOSPITAL (390304), 5800 Ridge Avenue, Zip 19128–1737; tel. 215/483–9900, (Nonreporting) **A**1 3 5 10 **S** Prime Healthcare, Ontario, CA
Primary Contact: Darshan Shawn. Parekh, PharmD, FACHE, Chief Executive Officer
CFO: Thomas Reinboth, Chief Financial Officer
CHR: Michael Henrici, Associate Administrator
Web address: www.roxboroughmemorial.com
Control: Corporation, Investor–owned (for–profit) **Service**: General medical and surgical

Staffed Beds: 72

SCHEIE INSTITUTE OF THE HOSPITAL OF THE UNIVERSITY OF PENNSYLVANIA See Scheie Eye Institute of The Hospital of The University of Pennsylvania

SHRINERS CHILDREN'S PHILADELPHIA (393309), 3551 North Broad Street, Zip 19140–4160; tel. 215/430–4000, (Nonreporting) **A**1 3 5 10 **S** Shriners Hospitals for Children, Tampa, FL
Primary Contact: Gregory Passanante, Hospital Administrator
CFO: Mario Salvati, Director Fiscal Services
CMO: Scott Kozin, M.D., Chief of Staff
CHR: Megan Hauser, Director Human Resources
CNO: Krista Miller, R.N., Chief Nursing Officer
Web address: https://www.shrinerschildrens.org/en/locations/philadelphia
Control: Other not–for–profit (including NFP Corporation) **Service**: Children's orthopedic

Staffed Beds: 39

ST. CHRISTOPHER'S HOSPITAL FOR CHILDREN (393307), 3601 A Street, Zip 19134–1043, Mailing Address: 160 E. Erie Avenue, Zip 19134–1011; tel. 215/427–5000, **A**1 3 5 10 **F**3 12 19 21 23 25 27 29 30 31 34 35 39 40 41 43 45 48 50 55 58 60 61 64 65 68 72 74 75 77 78 79 80 81 82 85 88 89 93 107 108 111 115 119 129 130 131 132 134 136 138 144 146 148 149 154 167 **P**6
Primary Contact: Robert M. Brooks, FACHE, President and Chief Operating Officer
CMO: Mary Moran, M.D., Pediatrician In Chief
CIO: Robert Taylor, Director Information Services
CHR: Kellie T. Pearson, Chief Human Resource Officer
CNO: Joanna Horst, MSN, R.N., Chief Nursing Officer
Web address: www.stchristophershospital.com
Control: Other not–for–profit (including NFP Corporation) **Service**: Children's general medical and surgical

Staffed Beds: 100 **Admissions**: 4861 **Census**: 60 **Outpatient Visits**: 107851 **Births**: 0 **Total Expense ($000)**: 334815 **Payroll Expense ($000)**: 147659 **Personnel**: 1631

TEMPLE HEALTH–CHESTNUT HILL HOSPITAL (390026), 8835 Germantown Avenue, Zip 19118–2718; tel. 215/248–8200, (Nonreporting) **A**1 3 5 10 **S** Temple University Health System, Philadelphia, PA
Primary Contact: Richard Newell, President and Chief Executive Officer
CFO: Gerald P Oetzel, Chief Financial Officer
CMO: James Helstrom, M.D., Interim Chief Medical Officer
CHR: Marilyn DiCicco, Director Human Resources
CNO: Margaret Collazo, MSN, R.N., Chief Nursing Officer
Web address: www.chhealthsystem.com
Control: Other not–for–profit (including NFP Corporation) **Service**: General medical and surgical

Staffed Beds: 212

TEMPLE UNIVERSITY HOSPITAL (390027), 3401 North Broad Street, Zip 19140–5103; tel. 215/707–2000, (Includes TEMPLE UNIVERSITY HOSPITAL – EPISCOPAL DIVISION, 100 East Lehigh Avenue, Philadelphia, Pennsylvania, Zip 19125–1098, tel. 215/427–7000; Kathleen Barron, Executive Director; TEMPLE UNIVERSITY HOSPITAL – JEANES CAMPUS, 7600 Central Avenue, Philadelphia, Pennsylvania, Zip 19111–2499, tel. 215/728–2000; Marc P. Hurowitz, D.O., Chief Executive Officer) **A**1 2 3 5 8 10 19 **F**3 6 8 11 12 13 15 16 17 18 20 22 24 26 28 29 30 31 34 35 37 38 40 43 44 45 46 47 48 49 50 51 55 56 57 58 59 60 61 64 65 68 70 72 73 74 75 76 77 78 79 81 82 83 84 85 86 87 91 92 93 94 96 97 98 100 101 102 107 108 110 111 112 114 115 117 118 119 120 121 124 126 129 130 132 135 136 137 138 139 140 141 142 145 146 147 148 149 150 154 156 157 160 164 165 167 **S** Temple University Health System, Philadelphia, PA
Primary Contact: Abhinav Rastogi, President and Chief Executive Officer
CMO: Carl Sirio, M.D., Chief Medical Officer
CHR: John Lasky Jr, Vice President, Chief Human Resources Officer
CNO: Angelo Venditti, R.N., Chief Nursing Executive, Co–Chair Patient Experience
Web address: www.tuh.templehealth.org/content/default.htm
Control: Other not–for–profit (including NFP Corporation) **Service**: General medical and surgical

Staffed Beds: 879 **Admissions**: 44398 **Census**: 716 **Outpatient Visits**: 599613 **Births**: 2031 **Total Expense ($000)**: 1911238 **Payroll Expense ($000)**: 592198 **Personnel**: 6057

TEMPLE UNIVERSITYHOSPITAL – JEANES CAMPUS See Temple University Hospital – Jeanes Campus

THOMAS JEFFERSON UNIVERSITY HOSPITAL (390174), 111 South 11th Street, Zip 19107–5084; tel. 215/955–6000, (Includes JEFFERSON METHODIST HOSPITAL, 2301 South Broad Street, Philadelphia, Pennsylvania, Zip 19148, tel. 215/952–9000; Joseph Cacchione, M.D., Chief Executive Officer) **A**1 2 3 5 8 10 **F**3 4 5 6 7 8 9 11 12 13 14 15 16 17 18 20 22 24 26 28 29 30 31 34 35 36 37 38 39 40 43 44 45 46 47 48 49 50 51 54 55 56 57 58 59 61 64 65 66 68 70 71 72 74 76 77 78 79 80 81 82 84 85 86 87 92 93 96 97 98 100 101 103 104 107 108 110 111 114 115 118 119 120 121 123 124 126 129 131 132 134 135 136 137 138 139 141 142 143 144 145 146 147 148 149 150 151 153 154 155 156 160 162 164 165 167 169 **P**6 **S** Jefferson Health, Philadelphia, PA
Primary Contact: Dixieanne James, President and Chief Operating Officer
COO: Christopher Cullom, FACHE, Chief Operating Officer, Thomas Jefferson University Hospitals
CFO: Neil Lubarsky, Senior Vice President, Finance and Chief Financial Officer
CMO: Edmund A. Pribitkin, M.D., Chief Medical Officer
CIO: Nassar Nizami, Chief Information Officer
CHR: Jeffrey Stevens, Executive Vice President and Chief Human Resource Officer
CNO: Mary Ann McGinley, Ph.D., Senior Vice President, Patient Services and Chief Nursing Officer
Web address: www.jefferson.edu
Control: Other not–for–profit (including NFP Corporation) **Service**: General medical and surgical

Staffed Beds: 882 **Admissions**: 34599 **Census**: 650 **Outpatient Visits**: 446040 **Births**: 2774 **Total Expense ($000)**: 2246841 **Payroll Expense ($000)**: 620686 **Personnel**: 9099

WILLS EYE HOSPITAL (390331), 840 Walnut Street, Zip 19107–5109; tel. 215/928–3000, **A**3 5 11 **F**3 58 81 130
Primary Contact: Joseph P. Bilson, Chief Executive Officer
CFO: Jeri Mogle, Assistant Executive Director Finance
CMO: William Tasman, M.D., Ophthalmologist in Chief
CIO: William Romano, Director Information Systems and Privacy
CHR: Cynthia Farano, Director Human Resources and Compliance Officer
Web address: www.willseye.org
Control: City, Government, Nonfederal **Service**: Eye, ear, nose and throat

Staffed Beds: 4 **Admissions**: 275 **Census**: 2 **Outpatient Visits**: 11580 **Births**: 0 **Total Expense ($000)**: 54026 **Payroll Expense ($000)**: 16756 **Personnel**: 133

PHOENIXVILLE—Chester County

PHOENIXVILLE HOSPITAL (390127), 140 Nutt Road, Zip 19460–3900, Mailing Address: P.O. Box 3001, Zip 19460–0916; tel. 610/983–1000, **A**1 2 3 7 10 19 **F**3 8 13 15 18 20 22 24 26 28 29 30 31 34 35 40 45 50 51 55 57 58 59 61 64 68 69 70 72 74 75 76 78 79 81 84 85 86 87 90 91 92 96 100 107 108 111 114 115 117 118 119 126 130 132 134 135 146 147 148 149 154 156 167 169 **S** Tower Health, West Reading, PA
Primary Contact: Richard McLaughlin, M.D., President and Chief Executive Officer
CIO: Terry Murphy, Director Information Services
CHR: Denise Chiolo, Chief Human Resources Officer
CNO: Sarah Strzelecki, Ed.D., R.N., Chief Nursing Officer
Web address: https://phoenixville.towerhealth.org
Control: Other not–for–profit (including NFP Corporation) **Service**: General medical and surgical

Staffed Beds: 144 **Admissions**: 7412 **Census**: 90 **Outpatient Visits**: 95116 **Births**: 995 **Total Expense ($000)**: 195210 **Payroll Expense ($000)**: 64845 **Personnel**: 782

PITTSBURGH—Allegheny County

ALLEGHENY GENERAL HOSPITAL (390050), 320 East North Avenue, Zip 15212–4756; tel. 412/359–3131, **A**1 2 3 5 10 12 **F**3 5 6 11 12 15 17 18 20 22 24 26 28 29 30 31 34 35 36 37 38 39 40 43 44 45 46 47 48 49 50 53 54 56 57 58 59 60 61 64 65 66 70 74 75 77 78 79 81 82 84 85 86 87 89 92 93 96 100 102 104 105 107 108 110 111 114 115 117 118 119 120 121 123 124 126 130 131 132 135 137 138 139 140 141 142 143 146 147 148 149 150 152 153 154 155 162 164 167 **P**6 **S** Allegheny Health Network, Pittsburgh, PA
Primary Contact: Imran Qadeer, President
COO: Duke Rupert, Chief Operating Officer
CFO: Richard W Fries, Vice President Finance
CMO: Tony Farah, M.D., President Medical Staff
CIO: John Foley, Chief Information Officer
Web address: www.wpahs.org/locations/allegheny-general-hospital
Control: Other not–for–profit (including NFP Corporation) **Service**: General medical and surgical

Staffed Beds: 350 **Admissions**: 20733 **Census**: 355 **Outpatient Visits**: 337318 **Births**: 0 **Total Expense ($000)**: 942965 **Payroll Expense ($000)**: 286816 **Personnel**: 2996

ENCOMPASS HEALTH REHABILITATION HOSPITAL OF HARMARVILLE (393027), 320 Guys Run Road, Zip 15238–0460, Mailing Address: P.O. Box 11460, Zip 15238–0460; tel. 412/828–1300, (Nonreporting) **A**1 10 **S** Encompass Health Corporation, Birmingham, AL
Primary Contact: Michelle P. Cunningham, Chief Executive Officer
CFO: Daniel A Vrana, Controller
CMO: James Kreshon, M.D., Medical Director
CHR: Kathy Grills, Director Human Resources
CNO: Eileen Skalski, Chief Nursing Officer
Web address: https://encompasshealth.com/Harmarvillerehab
Control: Corporation, Investor–owned (for–profit) **Service**: Rehabilitation

Staffed Beds: 42

EYE AND EAR HOSPITAL OF PITTSBURGH See UPMC Presbyterian, Pittsburgh

MONTEFIORE HOSPITAL See UPMC Montefiore

SELECT SPECIALTY HOSPITAL–PITTSBURGH/UPMC (392044), 200 Lothrop Street, E824, Zip 15213–2536, Mailing Address: 3459 5th Avenue, MUH S872, Zip 15213; tel. 412/586–9819, (Includes SELECT SPECIALTY HOSPITAL – ALLE KISKI, 1301 Carlisle Street, Natrona Heights, Pennsylvania, Zip 15065–1152, tel. 724/226–7312; Shantel Platt, Chief Executive Officer) (Nonreporting) **A**1 10 **S** Select Medical Corporation, Mechanicsburg, PA
Primary Contact: John Duemmel, Chief Executive Officer
CMO: Michael Donahue, M.D., Medical Director
CHR: Prudence Sloan, Coordinator Human Resources
CNO: Eli Babich, Chief Nursing Officer
Web address: www.pittsburghupmc.selectspecialtyhospitals.com/
Control: Corporation, Investor–owned (for–profit) **Service**: Acute long–term care hospital

Staffed Beds: 32

SHADYSIDE HOSPITAL See UPMC Shadyside

SOUTHWOOD PSYCHIATRIC HOSPITAL, 2575 Boyce Plaza Road, Zip 15241–3925; tel. 412/257–2290, (Nonreporting) **A**1 **S** Acadia Healthcare Company, Inc., Franklin, TN
Primary Contact: Kim Lira, Chief Executive Officer
CFO: Frank Urban, Chief Financial Officer
CMO: Allan W Clark, M.D., Medical Director
CHR: Erin J Frohnhofer, Director Human Resources
Web address: www.southwoodhospital.com
Control: Corporation, Investor–owned (for–profit) **Service**: Children's hospital psychiatric

Staffed Beds: 74

ST. CLAIR HEALTH (390228), 1000 Bower Hill Road, Zip 15243–1873; tel. 412/942–4000, **A**1 2 3 10 **F**3 13 15 17 18 20 22 24 26 28 29 31 40 44 45 46 47 48 49 50 51 53 54 58 60 64 70 71 73 74 75 76 77 78 79 80 81 85 86 87 89 93 96 98 100 101 102 107 108 110 111 114 115 117 118 119 120 121 123 126 129 130 132 135 143 144 146 148 149 153 154 157 164 167 169
Primary Contact: Michael J. Flanagan, President and Chief Executive Officer
COO: Marion A. McGowan, Senior Vice President and Chief Operating Officer
CFO: Eric Luttringer, Vice President, Finance and Chief Financial Officer
CMO: John Sullivan, M.D., Chief Medical Officer
CIO: Richard Schaeffer, Vice President Information Systems and Chief Information Officer
CHR: Andrea Kalina, Vice President External Affairs and Chief Human Resources Officer
CNO: Joan Massella, Administrative Vice President and Chief Nursing Officer
Web address: www.stclair.org
Control: Other not–for–profit (including NFP Corporation) **Service**: General medical and surgical

Staffed Beds: 289 **Admissions**: 14456 **Census**: 190 **Outpatient Visits**: 285995 **Births**: 1215 **Total Expense ($000)**: 380700 **Payroll Expense ($000)**: 126882 **Personnel**: 1493

THE CHILDREN'S HOME OF PITTSBURGH (393304), 5324 Penn Avenue, Zip 15224–1733; tel. 412/441–4884, (Nonreporting) **A**10
COO: Stacy Schesler, Chief Operating Officer
CFO: Kimberly A Phillips, Chief Financial Officer
CMO: Frederick C Sherman, M.D., Chief Medical Officer
Web address: www.childrenshomepgh.org
Control: Other not–for–profit (including NFP Corporation) **Service**: Children's general medical and surgical

Staffed Beds: 30

THE CHILDREN'S INSTITUTE OF PITTSBURGH (393308), 1405 Shady Avenue, Zip 15217–1350; tel. 412/420–2400, (Nonreporting) **A**10
Primary Contact: Wendy Ann. Pardee, President and Chief Executive Officer
COO: Stacey Vaccaro, Chief Operating Officer
CFO: John Jubas, Vice President Finance
CMO: Matthew Masiello, M.D., Chief Medical Officer
CIO: Sharon Dorogy, Chief Information Officer
CHR: Linda M Allen, Vice President Human Resources
Web address: www.amazingkids.org
Control: Other not–for–profit (including NFP Corporation) **Service**: Children's rehabilitation

Staffed Beds: 62

UPMC CHILDREN'S HOSPITAL OF PITTSBURGH (393302), 1 Childrens Hospital DR, Zip 15224–1529; tel. 412/692–5325, **A**1 3 5 7 10 **F**3 8 12 17 18 19 20 21 22 23 24 25 26 27 28 29 30 31 32 34 35 36 37 38 39 40 41 43 45 46 48 49 50 53 54 55 57 58 59 60 61 64 65 66 68 71 72 74 75 77 78 79 81 82 84 86 87 88 89 90 91 92 93 94 97 100 107 108 111 112 114 115 116 117 118 119 120 121 123 124 126 127 129 130 131 132 134 135 136 137 138 139 140 141 142 143 144 146 148 150 154 156 164 167 **S** UPMC, Pittsburgh, PA
Primary Contact: Diane Hupp, R.N., President
CFO: Mario Wilfong, Chief Financial Officer
CMO: Brian Martin, Vice President Medical Affairs
CIO: Srinivasan Suresh, M.D., Chief Medical Information Officer
CHR: Rhonda Larimore, Vice President, Human Resources
Web address: www.chp.edu
Control: Other not–for–profit (including NFP Corporation) **Service**: Children's general medical and surgical

Staffed Beds: 307 **Admissions**: 14678 **Census**: 250 **Outpatient Visits**: 350369 **Births**: 0 **Total Expense ($000)**: 890533 **Payroll Expense ($000)**: 210959 **Personnel**: 2708

UPMC MAGEE–WOMENS HOSPITAL (390114), 300 Halket Street, Zip 15213–3108; tel. 412/641–1000, (Total facility includes 15 beds in nursing home–type unit) **A**1 3 5 10 **F**3 8 11 12 13 15 18 29 30 31 34 35 36 40 44 45 46 50 52 54 55 56 57 58 59 60 64 65 66 68 70 72 74 75 76 77 78 79 80 81 82 84 85 86 87 91 97 100 107 108 110 111 115 117 119 120 121 123 126 129 130 132 134 135 146 147 148 149 150 154 156 160 162 167 169 **S** UPMC, Pittsburgh, PA
Primary Contact: Richard Beigi, M.D., President and Professor UPSOM
CFO: Jared Weiner, Chief Financial Officer
CMO: Dennis English, M.D., Vice President Medical Affairs
CHR: Rhonda Larimore, Vice President Human Resources
Web address: www.magee.edu
Control: Other not–for–profit (including NFP Corporation) **Service**: Obstetrics and gynecology

Staffed Beds: 339 **Admissions**: 18556 **Census**: 256 **Outpatient Visits**: 654899 **Births**: 9789 **Total Expense ($000)**: 1293346 **Payroll Expense ($000)**: 201718 **Personnel**: 3747

Hospital, Medicare Provider Number, Address, Telephone, Approval, Facility, and Physician Codes, Health Care System

★ American Hospital Association (AHA) membership
☐ The Joint Commission accreditation
○ Healthcare Facilities Accreditation Program
◇ DNV Healthcare Inc. accreditation
⇧ Center for Improvement in Healthcare Quality Accreditation
△ Commission on Accreditation of Rehabilitation Facilities (CARF) accreditation

Hospitals, U.S. / PENNSYLVANIA

UPMC MERCY (390028), 1400 Locust Street, Zip 15219–5166; tel. 412/232–8111, **A**1 3 5 10 13 **F**3 4 16 17 18 20 22 24 26 28 29 30 31 34 35 36 39 40 43 44 45 46 47 48 49 50 51 54 56 57 58 59 60 61 64 65 66 68 70 74 75 77 78 79 81 82 84 85 86 87 90 91 92 93 94 95 96 97 100 101 102 107 108 111 114 115 116 118 119 126 129 130 131 132 135 141 142 146 148 154 156 157 160 161 167 **S** UPMC, Pittsburgh, PA
Primary Contact: Richard Beigi, M.D., President and Professor
COO: Julie Hecker, Vice President, Operations
CFO: Jared Weiner, Chief Financial Officer
CIO: Kevin Conway, Chief Information Officer
CHR: Tracey Stange–Kolo, Vice President, Human Resources
Web address: www.upmc.com/HospitalsFacilities/HFHome/Hospitals/Mercy/
Control: Other not–for–profit (including NFP Corporation) **Service**: General medical and surgical

Staffed Beds: 297 **Admissions:** 11904 **Census:** 261 **Outpatient Visits:** 139262 **Births:** 0 **Total Expense ($000):** 517045 **Payroll Expense ($000):** 176915 **Personnel:** 2261

UPMC MONTEFIORE See UPMC Presbyterian, Pittsburgh

UPMC PASSAVANT (390107), 9100 Babcock Boulevard, Zip 15237–5815; tel. 412/748–6700, (Includes UPMC PASSAVANT CRANBERRY, 1 Saint Francis Way, Cranberry Township, Pennsylvania, Zip 16066–5119, 1 St Francis Way, Cranberry, Zip 16066, tel. 724/772–5300; Teresa G Petrick, President) **A**1 2 3 5 10 **F**3 8 9 11 15 17 18 20 22 24 26 28 29 30 31 34 35 40 44 45 46 47 48 49 51 54 56 57 58 59 60 61 63 64 65 68 70 74 75 77 78 79 81 82 84 85 86 87 90 96 97 100 107 108 111 114 115 117 118 119 120 121 123 126 129 130 131 132 135 143 146 147 148 154 156 157 167 **S** UPMC, Pittsburgh, PA
Primary Contact: Elizabeth A. Piccione, M.D., President
CFO: Brian Fritz, Chief Financial Officer
CMO: James W Boyle, M.D., Chief Medical Officer
CNO: Susan E Hoolahan, R.N., MSN, Vice President Patient Care Services and Chief Nursing Officer
Web address: https://www.upmc.com/locations/hospitals/passavant
Control: Other not–for–profit (including NFP Corporation) **Service**: General medical and surgical

Staffed Beds: 316 **Admissions:** 12830 **Census:** 217 **Outpatient Visits:** 297394 **Births:** 0 **Total Expense ($000):** 474537 **Payroll Expense ($000):** 142126 **Personnel:** 1693

UPMC PRESBYTERIAN (390164), 200 Lothrop Street, Zip 15213–2536; tel. 412/647–2345, (Includes EYE AND EAR HOSPITAL OF PITTSBURGH, 200 Lothrop Street, Pittsburgh, Pennsylvania, Zip 15213–2592, tel. 412/647–2345; UPMC MONTEFIORE, 3459 Fifth Avenue, Pittsburgh, Pennsylvania, Zip 15213, tel. 412/647–2345; Sandra Rader, R.N., President, UPMC Presbyterian; UPMC PRESBYTERIAN HOSPITAL, 200 Lothrop Street, Pittsburgh, Pennsylvania, Zip 15213, tel. 412/647–2345; UPMC SHADYSIDE, 5230 Centre Avenue, Pittsburgh, Pennsylvania, Zip 15232–1381, tel. 412/623–2121; Sandra Rader, R.N., President; WESTERN PSYCHIATRIC INSTITUTE AND CLINIC, 3811 Ohara ST, Pittsburgh, Pennsylvania, Zip 15213–2561, 3811 O'Hara Street, Zip 15213–2593, tel. 412/624–2100; Deborah Brodine, President) **A**1 2 3 5 8 10 19 **F**3 4 5 6 8 9 11 12 14 17 18 20 22 24 26 28 29 30 31 34 35 36 37 38 39 40 43 44 45 46 47 48 49 50 51 54 55 56 57 58 59 60 61 63 64 65 66 68 70 71 74 75 77 78 79 81 82 84 85 86 87 90 91 92 93 94 95 96 97 98 99 100 101 102 103 104 105 106 107 108 111 113 114 115 116 117 118 119 120 121 123 124 126 129 130 131 132 135 136 137 138 139 140 141 142 145 146 148 149 151 153 154 156 157 158 160 161 162 164 165 166 167 168 169 **S** UPMC, Pittsburgh, PA
Primary Contact: Sandra Rader, R.N., President
CFO: Jared Weiner, Chief Financial Officer
CMO: Margaret Reidy, M.D., Vice President Medical Affairs
CHR: Kathryn Devine, Vice President Human Resources
CNO: Brandy Hershberger, CNO, VP Patient Care Services
Web address: https://www.upmc.com/locations/hospitals/presbyterian/
Control: Other not–for–profit (including NFP Corporation) **Service**: General medical and surgical

Staffed Beds: 1412 **Admissions:** 43826 **Census:** 1053 **Outpatient Visits:** 998639 **Births:** 0 **Total Expense ($000):** 2615639 **Payroll Expense ($000):** 725802 **Personnel:** 11654

UPMC ST. MARGARET (390102), 815 Freeport Road, Zip 15215–3301; tel. 412/784–4000, **A**1 3 5 10 13 **F**3 8 9 11 15 18 20 26 29 30 31 34 35 40 44 45 49 51 54 56 57 58 59 60 61 63 64 65 68 70 74 75 77 78 79 81 82 84 85 86 87 90 96 97 100 107 108 111 114 115 119 120 121 123 126 129 130 131 132 135 143 146 147 148 154 156 157 167 **S** UPMC, Pittsburgh, PA
Primary Contact: Andrew Ritchie, President
COO: Merle Taylor, Vice President Operations
CFO: Brian Fritz, Chief Financial Officer
CMO: John Lagnese, M.D., Vice President Medical Affairs
CIO: Charles M. Rudek, Chief Information Officer
CHR: Tracey Stange–Kolo, Vice President Human Resources
CNO: Marianna Stoneburner, R.N., Vice President, Patient Care Services and Chief Nursing Officer
Web address: www.upmc.com/locations/hospitals/st-margaret/Pages/default.aspx
Control: Other not–for–profit (including NFP Corporation) **Service**: General medical and surgical

Staffed Beds: 181 **Admissions:** 7780 **Census:** 122 **Outpatient Visits:** 159689 **Births:** 0 **Total Expense ($000):** 286433 **Payroll Expense ($000):** 85122 **Personnel:** 1142

UPMC–PRESBYTERIAN HOSPITAL See UPMC Presbyterian Hospital

VETERANS ADM MEDICAL CENTER See Veterans Affairs Medical Center

VETERANS AFF MEDICAL CENTER See Veterans Affairs Medical Center

△ **VETERANS AFFAIRS PITTSBURGH HEALTHCARE SYSTEM**, University Drive C, Zip 15240; tel. 866/482–7488, (Includes VETERANS AFFAIRS MEDICAL CENTER, 7180 Highland Drive, Pittsburgh, Pennsylvania, Zip 15206–1297, tel. 412/365–4900; VETERANS AFFAIRS MEDICAL CENTER, University Drive 'c', Pittsburgh, Pennsylvania, Zip 15240, tel. 412/688–6000) (Nonreporting) **A**1 2 3 5 7 8 **S** Department of Veterans Affairs, Washington, DC
Primary Contact: Donald E. Koenig, Director
CMO: Ali Sonel, M.D., Chief of Staff
CIO: John Kovac, Facility Chief Information Officer
CHR: Amber Mesoras, Chief Human Resources Officer
CNO: Ira Richmond, Associate Director Patient Care Services
Web address: www.pittsburgh.va.gov/
Control: Veterans Affairs, Government, federal **Service**: Psychiatric

Staffed Beds: 532

WEST PENN HOSPITAL (390090), 4800 Friendship Avenue, Zip 15224–1722; tel. 412/578–5000, **A**1 2 3 5 10 **F**3 11 12 15 16 17 18 20 22 26 29 30 31 34 35 36 37 40 41 44 45 46 47 48 49 50 51 54 55 57 58 59 64 66 70 72 73 74 75 76 77 78 79 80 81 82 84 85 86 87 90 96 102 107 108 110 111 115 117 118 119 120 121 123 126 129 130 132 135 136 141 142 145 146 147 148 149 154 160 167 169 **S** Allegheny Health Network, Pittsburgh, PA
Primary Contact: Brian Johnson, President and Chief Executive Officer
CFO: James A Kanuch, Vice President Finance
CMO: I William Goldfarb, Chief Medical Officer
CIO: Jacqueline Dailey, Chief Information Officer
CHR: Sally Carozza, Director Human Resources
CNO: Paula A Lacher, MSN, R.N., Chief Nursing Officer
Web address: www.wpahs.org
Control: Other not–for–profit (including NFP Corporation) **Service**: General medical and surgical

Staffed Beds: 239 **Admissions:** 11200 **Census:** 203 **Outpatient Visits:** 207460 **Births:** 3582 **Total Expense ($000):** 726268 **Payroll Expense ($000):** 154866 **Personnel:** 1728

WESTERN PSYCHIATRIC INSTITUTE AND CLINIC See UPMC Presbyterian, Pittsburgh

PLEASANT GAP—Centre County

ENCOMPASS HEALTH REHABILITATION HOSPITAL OF NITTANY VALLEY (393039), 550 West College Avenue, Zip 16823–7401; tel. 814/359–3421, (Nonreporting) **A**1 10 **S** Encompass Health Corporation, Birmingham, AL
Primary Contact: Amy Lynn. Adams, Chief Executive Officer
CFO: Alan M Phillips, Controller
CMO: Richard Allatt, M.D., Medical Director
CHR: Michelle Katz, Director Human Resources
CNO: Penny Frownfelter, Chief Nursing Officer
Web address: www.nittanyvalleyrehab.com
Control: Corporation, Investor–owned (for–profit) **Service**: Rehabilitation

Staffed Beds: 73

Hospitals, U.S. / PENNSYLVANIA

POTTSTOWN—Montgomery County

✖ **POTTSTOWN HOSPITAL (390123)**, 1600 East High Street, Zip 19464–5093; tel. 610/327–7000, **A**1 2 3 10 **F**3 15 18 29 30 31 34 35 38 40 44 49 50 59 60 64 65 70 74 75 77 78 79 80 81 82 85 87 92 93 97 98 100 102 103 107 108 111 114 115 116 117 118 119 120 121 123 130 131 146 149 154 156 157 160 164 165 167 **S** Tower Health, West Reading, PA
Primary Contact: Richard McLaughlin, M.D., President and Chief Executive Officer
COO: Bryce Sillyman, Chief Operating Officer
CFO: Debbie Konarski, Chief Financial Officer
CIO: Chad Paine, Director Client Services
CHR: Kimberly Schneider, Director Human Resources
CNO: Ann Blankenhorn, Chief Nursing Officer
Web address: https://pottstown.towerhealth.org/
Control: Other not–for–profit (including NFP Corporation) **Service**: General medical and surgical

Staffed Beds: 213 **Admissions**: 6772 **Census**: 92 **Outpatient Visits**: 99281 **Births**: 0 **Total Expense ($000)**: 183030 **Payroll Expense ($000)**: 53531 **Personnel**: 692

POTTSVILLE—Schuylkill County

✖ **LEHIGH VALLEY HOSPITAL – SCHUYLKILL (390030)**, 700 East Norwegian Street, Zip 17901–2710; tel. 570/621–5000, (Includes LEHIGH VALLEY HOSPITAL – SCHUYLKILL EAST NORWEGIAN STREET, 700 East Norwegian Street, Pottsville, Pennsylvania, Zip 17901–2710, tel. 570/621–4000; Terrence J. Purcell, President) **A**1 10 19 **F**3 5 11 13 15 18 19 28 29 30 31 34 35 40 43 45 47 49 56 57 59 60 62 64 70 74 75 76 77 78 79 81 82 84 85 86 90 92 93 95 96 98 99 100 101 102 103 107 108 110 111 114 117 118 119 126 130 132 135 146 148 149 154 156 167 169 **P**8 **S** Lehigh Valley Health Network, Allentown, PA
Primary Contact: Terrence J. Purcell, President
CFO: Diane Boris, Chief Financial Officer
CIO: Tina Zanis, Director Information Systems
CHR: Lynn Lansdowne, Vice President Labor Relations and Human Resources
CNO: Darnell F Furer, MS, R.N., Vice President Patient Care Services and Chief Nursing Officer
Web address: www.schuylkillhealth.com
Control: Other not–for–profit (including NFP Corporation) **Service**: General medical and surgical

Staffed Beds: 186 **Admissions**: 5196 **Census**: 109 **Outpatient Visits**: 93590 **Births**: 577 **Total Expense ($000)**: 137555 **Payroll Expense ($000)**: 57294 **Personnel**: 833

SCHUYLKILL MEDICAL CENTER – EAST NORWEGIAN STREET See Lehigh Valley Hospital – Schuylkill East Norwegian Street

PUNXSUTAWNEY—Jefferson County

PUNXSUTAWNEY AREA HOSPITAL (390199), 81 Hillcrest Drive, Zip 15767–2616; tel. 814/938–1800, **A**10 20 **F**3 13 15 26 29 30 31 34 35 40 44 45 46 48 50 51 59 62 64 65 70 74 75 76 77 78 79 81 82 85 86 87 92 93 97 100 104 107 108 110 111 115 118 119 124 130 132 133 146 147 148 149 154 167 169
Primary Contact: Jack G. Sisk, President
CMO: Dajani Zuhd, M.D., President Medical Staff
CIO: Chuck States, Director Information Systems
CHR: Barbara Kostok, Manager Human Resources
CNO: Paula Spack, R.N., MSN, Vice President Nursing
Web address: www.pah.org
Control: Other not–for–profit (including NFP Corporation) **Service**: General medical and surgical

Staffed Beds: 49 **Admissions**: 1129 **Census**: 15 **Outpatient Visits**: 106014 **Births**: 160 **Total Expense ($000)**: 55504 **Payroll Expense ($000)**: 27766 **Personnel**: 363

QUAKERTOWN—Bucks County

☐ **ST. LUKE'S QUAKERTOWN CAMPUS (390035)**, 1021 Park Avenue, Zip 18951–1573; tel. 215/538–4500, (Includes ST. LUKE's HOSPITAL UPPER BUCKS CAMPUS, 3000 St. Luke's Drive, Quakertown, Pennsylvania, Zip 18951–1696, tel. 267/985–1000; Dennis Pfleiger, President) (Nonreporting) **A**1 3 10 **S** St. Luke's University Health Network, Bethlehem, PA
Primary Contact: Dennis Pfleiger, President
CFO: Theresa Corrado, Director Finance
CMO: Thomas Filipowicz, M.D., Medical Director
CIO: Chad Brisendine, Chief Information Officer
CHR: Shelley Maley, Director Human Resources
Web address: https://www.slhn.org/quakertown
Control: Other not–for–profit (including NFP Corporation) **Service**: General medical and surgical

Staffed Beds: 79

READING—Berks County

✖ **ENCOMPASS HEALTH REHABILITATION HOSPITAL OF READING (393026)**, 1623 Morgantown Road, Zip 19607–9455; tel. 610/796–6000, (Nonreporting) **A**1 10 **S** Encompass Health Corporation, Birmingham, AL
Primary Contact: Judy Parker, Chief Executive Officer
CFO: Jason Pulaski, Controller
CMO: Suzanne Adam, D.O., Medical Director
CHR: Kelly Kozik, Director Human Resources
Web address: https://www.encompasshealth.com/readingrehab
Control: Corporation, Investor–owned (for–profit) **Service**: Rehabilitation

Staffed Beds: 48

☐ **HAVEN BEHAVIORAL HOSPITAL OF EASTERN PENNSYLVANIA (394052)**, 145 North 6th Street, 3rd Floor, Zip 19601–3096; tel. 610/406–4340, **A**1 10 **F**98 104 105 **S** Haven Behavioral Healthcare, Nashville, TN
Primary Contact: Kathryn Schane, Chief Executive Officer
CMO: Mark Putnam, M.D., Medical Director
CHR: Kathy Copenhaver, Director Human Resources
Web address: https://www.havenreading.com/
Control: Corporation, Investor–owned (for–profit) **Service**: Psychiatric

Staffed Beds: 86 **Admissions**: 1946 **Census**: 82 **Outpatient Visits**: 196 **Births**: 0

✖ **PENN STATE HEALTH ST. JOSEPH (390096)**, 2500 Bernville Road, Zip 19605–9453, Mailing Address: P.O. Box 316, Zip 19603–0316; tel. 610/378–2000, (Includes PENN STATE HEALTH ST. JOSEPH – DOWNTOWN CAMPUS, 145 North Sixth Street, Reading, Pennsylvania, Zip 19601, P O Box 316, Zip 19603–0316, tel. 610/378–2000; Joseph Frank, Interim President) **A**1 2 3 5 10 13 19 **F**3 12 13 15 18 20 22 24 26 28 29 30 31 32 34 35 39 40 44 45 46 47 49 50 51 54 55 57 58 59 64 66 68 70 72 74 75 76 77 78 79 80 81 82 84 87 89 92 93 97 107 108 110 111 113 114 115 116 117 118 119 120 121 126 130 132 135 144 146 147 148 149 154 156 157 164 167 169 **S** Penn State Health, Hershey, PA
Primary Contact: Joseph Frank, Regional Hospital President, East Region
CMO: Jeffrey Held, M.D., Vice President, Medical Affairs
CIO: Amanda Klopp, Director, Innovation and Clinical Integration
CHR: Scott Mengle, Vice President Human Resources
CNO: Maria Lariccia Brennan, R.N., Chief Nursing Officer
Web address: www.thefutureofhealthcare.org
Control: Other not–for–profit (including NFP Corporation) **Service**: General medical and surgical

Staffed Beds: 128 **Admissions**: 7155 **Census**: 87 **Outpatient Visits**: 209408 **Births**: 749 **Total Expense ($000)**: 285478 **Payroll Expense ($000)**: 95536 **Personnel**: 1296

ST. JOSEPH MEDICAL CENTER–DOWNTOWN READING See Penn State Health St. Joseph – Downtown Campus

RENOVO—Clinton County

BUCKTAIL MEDICAL CENTER (391304), 1001 Pine Street, Zip 17764–1620; tel. 570/923–1000, (Nonreporting) **A**10 18
Primary Contact: Laura Murnyack, Interim Chief Executive Officer
CFO: Wendy Janerella, Controller
CMO: Alvin Berlot, M.D., Medical Director
Web address: https://bucktailmedicalcenter.org/
Control: Other not–for–profit (including NFP Corporation) **Service**: General medical and surgical

Staffed Beds: 59

RIDLEY PARK—Delaware County

TAYLOR HOSPITAL See Crozer–Chester Medical Center, Upland

ROARING SPRING—Blair County

✖ **CONEMAUGH NASON MEDICAL CENTER (390062)**, 105 Nason Drive, Zip 16673–1202; tel. 814/224–2141, (Nonreporting) **A**1 10 **S** Lifepoint Health, Brentwood, TN
Primary Contact: Timothy Harclerode, R.N., FACHE, Chief Executive Officer
CFO: Kimberly Semelsberger, CPA, Chief Financial Officer
CHR: Lorie Smith, Director Human Resources
Web address: www.nasonhospital.com
Control: Corporation, Investor–owned (for–profit) **Service**: General medical and surgical

Staffed Beds: 45

Hospital, Medicare Provider Number, Address, Telephone, Approval, Facility, and Physician Codes, Health Care System

★ American Hospital Association (AHA) membership
☐ The Joint Commission accreditation
○ Healthcare Facilities Accreditation Program
◇ DNV Healthcare Inc. accreditation
⇑ Center for Improvement in Healthcare Quality Accreditation
△ Commission on Accreditation of Rehabilitation Facilities (CARF) accreditation

© 2025 AHA Guide

Hospitals, U.S. / PENNSYLVANIA

ROYERSFORD—Montgomery County

⇑ **PHYSICIANS CARE SURGICAL HOSPITAL (390324)**, 454 Enterprise Drive, Zip 19468-1200; tel. 610/495-3330, (Nonreporting) **A**10 21
Primary Contact: Kristin L. Thompson, Campus Administrator
Web address: www.phycarehospital.com
Control: Partnership, Investor-owned (for-profit) **Service:** Surgical

Staffed Beds: 12

SAINT MARYS—Elk County

PENN HIGHLANDS ELK (391315), 763 Johnsonburg Road, Zip 15857-3498; tel. 814/788-8000, (Nonreporting) **A**3 10 18
Primary Contact: Julianne Peer, President
CFO: Laurie MacDonald, Vice President Finance
CMO: David Johe, M.D., President Medical Staff
CIO: Mary Ann Schwabenbauer, Director Information Technology
CHR: Seanna D'Amore, Director Human Resources
Web address: www.phhealthcare.org
Control: Other not-for-profit (including NFP Corporation) **Service:** General medical and surgical

Staffed Beds: 173

SAYRE—Bradford County

☐ **GUTHRIE ROBERT PACKER HOSPITAL (390079)**, 1 Guthrie Square, Zip 18840-1698; tel. 570/888-6666, (Includes GUTHRIE ROBERT PACKER HOSPITAL, TOWANDA CAMPUS, 91 Hospital Drive, Towanda, Pennsylvania, Zip 18848-9702, tel. 570/265-2191; Felissa Koernig, President and Chief Operating Officer) (Nonreporting) **A**1 2 3 5 10 13 19 **S** Guthrie Clinic, Sayre, PA
Primary Contact: Joseph T. Sawyer Jr, President and Chief Operating Officer
CMO: Brian Fillipo, M.D., Chief Medical Officer
CIO: Burt Robles, Vice President Information Services
CHR: John R. Petrov, Senior Vice President, Chief Human Resource Officer
CNO: Patricia Vassell, Senior Vice President, Nursing Services and Chief Nursing Officer
Web address: https://www.guthrie.org/location/robert-packer-hospital
Control: Other not-for-profit (including NFP Corporation) **Service:** General medical and surgical

Staffed Beds: 338

SCRANTON—Lackawanna County

☐ **ALLIED SERVICES SCRANTON REHABILITATION HOSPITAL (393030)**, 475 Morgan Highway, Zip 18508-2605, Mailing Address: P.O. Box 1103, Zip 18501-1103; tel. 570/348-1300, (Nonreporting) **A**1 3 10
Primary Contact: William P. Conaboy, Chief Executive Officer
CFO: Michael Avvisato, Senior Vice President and Chief Financial Officer
CMO: Gregory Basting, M.D., Vice President Medical Affairs
CIO: John Regula, Chief Information Officer
CHR: Judy P Oprisko, Vice President
CNO: Jeana Sluck, R.N., Executive Director Nursing Clinical Inpatient Departments
Web address: www.allied-services.org
Control: Other not-for-profit (including NFP Corporation) **Service:** Rehabilitation

Staffed Beds: 97

✠ **GEISINGER COMMUNITY MEDICAL CENTER (390001)**, 1800 Mulberry Street, Zip 18510-2369; tel. 570/703-8000, **A**1 2 3 5 10 19 **F**1 3 4 12 15 16 17 18 20 22 24 26 28 29 30 31 34 35 37 39 40 43 44 45 46 47 49 53 54 56 58 59 61 64 65 67 68 70 72 73 74 75 76 77 78 79 80 81 82 84 85 86 87 88 89 90 91 92 93 94 97 98 102 107 108 110 111 114 115 117 118 119 126 128 129 130 131 132 135 145 146 147 148 149 154 156 160 164 166 167 **P**1 5 8 **S** Geisinger, Danville, PA
Primary Contact: Ronald R. Beer, FACHE, Chief Administrative Officer
CHR: Lois Wolfe, Director Human Resources
Web address: www.geisinger.org/for-patients/locations-directions/gcmc/
Control: Other not-for-profit (including NFP Corporation) **Service:** General medical and surgical

Staffed Beds: 318 **Admissions:** 22409 **Census:** 207 **Outpatient Visits:** 400162 **Births:** 785 **Total Expense ($000):** 470896 **Payroll Expense ($000):** 170112 **Personnel:** 1774

✠ **REGIONAL HOSPITAL OF SCRANTON (390237)**, 746 Jefferson Avenue, Zip 18510-1624; tel. 570/348-7100, (Includes MOSES TAYLOR HOSPITAL, 700 Quincy Avenue, Scranton, Pennsylvania, Zip 18510-1724, tel. 570/770-5000; Michael Curran, Chief Executive Officer) **A**1 3 10 19 **F**8 11 12 15 17 18 20 22 24 26 28 29 31 34 35 39 40 44 45 46 47 48 49 50 51 53 54 57 58 59 60 61 64 65 66 68 70 74 75 77 78 79 81 82 85 86 87 91 92 93 97 100 107 108 109 110 111 112 113 114 115 116 117 118 119 120 121 122 123 124 126 130 132 143 144 145 146 147 148 149 154 157 167 **S** Community Health Systems, Inc., Franklin, TN
Primary Contact: Michael Curran, Chief Executive Officer
CFO: Stephen Franko, Vice President Finance and Chief Financial Officer
CMO: Anthony Yanni, M.D., Vice President Medical Affairs
CIO: Jorge Coronel, Chief Information Officer
Web address: www.regionalhospitalofscranton.net
Control: Corporation, Investor-owned (for-profit) **Service:** General medical and surgical

Staffed Beds: 186 **Admissions:** 7732 **Census:** 113 **Outpatient Visits:** 65798 **Births:** 0 **Total Expense ($000):** 207601 **Payroll Expense ($000):** 65204 **Personnel:** 724

SELLERSVILLE—Bucks County

✠ **GRAND VIEW HEALTH (390057)**, 700 Lawn Avenue, Zip 18960-1548, Mailing Address: P.O. Box 902, Zip 18960-0902; tel. 215/453-4000, **A**1 2 3 5 10 **F**3 7 11 12 13 15 18 20 22 26 28 29 30 34 35 37 38 40 41 43 45 46 50 51 54 55 56 57 59 60 62 63 64 70 72 75 76 77 78 79 81 82 83 85 86 87 89 90 93 97 107 108 110 111 115 116 117 119 120 121 123 126 129 130 131 132 135 143 144 145 146 147 148 149 154 156 157 164 167 169 **P**1 6
Primary Contact: Douglas Hughes, R.N., President and Chief Executive Officer
COO: J Mark Horne, Senior Vice President, Ambulatory Services and Chief Operating Officer
CFO: Arthur Anderson, Chief Financial Officer
CMO: Michael Prasto, M.D., Vice President and Chief Medical Officer
CIO: Jane Doll Loveless, Vice President, Chief Information Officer
Web address: www.gvh.org
Control: Other not-for-profit (including NFP Corporation) **Service:** General medical and surgical

Staffed Beds: 194 **Admissions:** 7502 **Census:** 99 **Outpatient Visits:** 384671 **Births:** 732 **Total Expense ($000):** 293869 **Payroll Expense ($000):** 141844 **Personnel:** 1609

SENECA—Venango County

✠ **UPMC NORTHWEST (390091)**, 100 Fairfield Drive, Zip 16346-2130; tel. 814/676-7600, (Total facility includes 16 beds in nursing home-type unit) **A**1 3 10 19 **F**3 11 13 15 18 28 29 30 31 34 35 40 44 45 46 50 57 59 60 64 67 68 70 74 75 76 78 79 81 82 83 84 85 87 90 91 92 93 94 96 98 103 107 108 110 111 114 115 119 120 121 128 130 132 135 146 148 149 154 156 167 **S** UPMC, Pittsburgh, PA
Primary Contact: Brian Durniok, President
COO: Brian Durniok, Vice President Operations
CFO: Bradley Dinger, Chief Financial Officer
CMO: David McCandless, Vice President Medical Affairs
CHR: Brian Durniok, President
Web address: www.upmc.com/locations/hospitals/northwest/Pages/default.aspx
Control: Other not-for-profit (including NFP Corporation) **Service:** General medical and surgical

Staffed Beds: 167 **Admissions:** 5141 **Census:** 79 **Outpatient Visits:** 157547 **Births:** 542 **Total Expense ($000):** 158828 **Payroll Expense ($000):** 43352 **Personnel:** 612

SEWICKLEY—Allegheny County

✠ **ENCOMPASS HEALTH REHABILITATION HOSPITAL OF SEWICKLEY (393045)**, 351 Camp Meeting Road, Zip 15143-8322; tel. 412/741-9500, (Nonreporting) **A**1 10 **S** Encompass Health Corporation, Birmingham, AL
Primary Contact: Leah Laffey, R.N., Chief Executive Officer
CFO: Daniel A Vrana, Area Controller
CMO: Shelana Gibbs-McElvy, M.D., Medical Director
CIO: Jamie Smith, Supervisor Health Information Management Systems
CHR: Melissa Coleman, Director Human Resources
CNO: Christie Ryan, Chief Nursing Officer
Web address: www.healthsouthsewickley.com
Control: Corporation, Investor-owned (for-profit) **Service:** Rehabilitation

Staffed Beds: 67

Hospitals, U.S. / PENNSYLVANIA

☐ **SEWICKLEY VALLEY HOSPITAL, (A DIVISION OF VALLEY MEDICAL FACILITIES) (390037)**, 720 Blackburn Road, Zip 15143-1459; tel. 412/741-6600, (Nonreporting) **A**1 3 10 **S** Heritage Valley Health System, Beaver, PA
Primary Contact: Norman F. Mitry, President and Chief Executive Officer
COO: John Luellen, M.D., Chief Operating Officer
CFO: Robert Rosenberger, Chief Financial Officer
CMO: Michael Cratty, M.D., Chief Medical Officer
CIO: David Carleton, Chief Information Officer
CHR: Bruce Edwards, Vice President Human Resources
CNO: Linda Homyk, Chief Nursing Officer
Web address: www.heritagevalley.org
Control: Other not-for-profit (including NFP Corporation) **Service:** General medical and surgical

Staffed Beds: 179

SHARON—Mercer County

☐ **SHARON REGIONAL MEDICAL CENTER (390211)**, 740 East State Street, Zip 16146-3395; tel. 724/983-3911, (Nonreporting) **A**1 3 10 19 **S** Steward Health Care System, LLC, Dallas, TX
Primary Contact: Robert Rogalski, President
Web address: https://www.sharonregionalmedical.org
Control: Corporation, Investor-owned (for-profit) **Service:** General medical and surgical

Staffed Beds: 218

SHICKSHINNY—Luzerne County

HUNTINGTON CREEK RECOVERY CENTER, 890 Bethel Road, Zip 18655; tel. 570/864-3116, (Nonreporting)
Primary Contact: Tom Cain, Chief Executive Officer
Web address: https://www.huntingtoncreekrecovery.com/?utm_source=GMB&utm_medium=organic&utm_campaign=listing&utm_term=brand
Control: Other not-for-profit (including NFP Corporation) **Service:** Substance Use Disorder

Staffed Beds: 65

SHIPPENSBURG—Franklin County

☐ **ROXBURY TREATMENT CENTER (394050)**, 601 Roxbury Road, Zip 17257-9302; tel. 888/829-9974, (Nonreporting) **A**1 10 **S** Universal Health Services, Inc., King of Prussia, PA
Primary Contact: Shauna Mogerman, Chief Executive Officer
Web address: www.roxburyhospital.com
Control: Corporation, Investor-owned (for-profit) **Service:** Psychiatric

Staffed Beds: 112

SOMERSET—Somerset County

⊞ **UPMC SOMERSET (390039)**, 225 South Center Avenue, Zip 15501-2088; tel. 814/443-5000, **A**1 10 20 **F**3 15 17 18 20 22 26 28 29 30 31 32 34 35 39 40 45 49 50 53 57 59 62 63 64 65 66 68 75 77 81 82 85 86 87 89 97 98 100 102 107 108 110 111 115 119 129 130 131 132 133 135 146 149 154 156 160 167 **S** UPMC, Pittsburgh, PA
Primary Contact: Andrew G. Rush, President
CFO: Monica Klatt, Chief Financial Officer
CIO: Dale Fuller, Vice President, Chief Information Officer
CHR: Tracey Stange-Kolo, Vice President Human Resources
Web address: www.somersethospital.com
Control: Other not-for-profit (including NFP Corporation) **Service:** General medical and surgical

Staffed Beds: 56 **Admissions:** 2289 **Census:** 33 **Outpatient Visits:** 113257
Births: 0 **Total Expense ($000):** 85032 **Payroll Expense ($000):** 33443
Personnel: 478

SPRINGFIELD—Delaware County

METRO HOSP-SPRINGFIELD DIV See Springfield Hospital

SPRINGFIELD HOSPITAL See Crozer-Chester Medical Center, Upland

STATE COLLEGE—Centre County

⊞ **MOUNT NITTANY MEDICAL CENTER (390268)**, 1800 East Park Avenue, Zip 16803-6797; tel. 814/231-7000, (Nonreporting) **A**1 2 3 5 10 20
Primary Contact: Kathleen Rhine, President and Chief Executive Officer
CFO: Bryan Roach, Executive Vice President and Chief Financial Officer
CMO: Nirmal Joshi, M.D., System Chief Medical Officer
CIO: Michael Martz, Senior Vice President and Chief Information Officer
CNO: Tiffany Cabibbo, Executive Vice President and Chief Nursing Officer
Web address: www.mountnittany.org
Control: Other not-for-profit (including NFP Corporation) **Service:** General medical and surgical

Staffed Beds: 260

STROUDSBURG—Monroe County

☐ **ST. LUKE'S MONROE CAMPUS (390330)**, 100 St. Lukes Lane, Zip 18360-6217, Mailing Address: 100 St. Luke's Lane, Zip 18360; tel. 484/526-2116, (Nonreporting) **A**1 3 10 **S** St. Luke's University Health Network, Bethlehem, PA
Primary Contact: Donald Seiple, President
Web address: www.slhn.org/Choose/choose-monroe
Control: Other not-for-profit (including NFP Corporation) **Service:** General medical and surgical

Staffed Beds: 98

SUSQUEHANNA—Susquehanna County

BARNES-KASSON COUNTY HOSPITAL (391309), 2872 Turnpike Street, Zip 18847-2771; tel. 570/853-3135, (Nonreporting) **A**10 18
Primary Contact: Sara F. Adornato, Chief Executive Officer
CFO: Kelli R Kane, Director of Finance
CMO: Pravinchandra Patel, M.D., Chief Medical Officer
CIO: Eric Detwiler, Director Information Technology
Web address: www.barnes-kasson.org
Control: Other not-for-profit (including NFP Corporation) **Service:** General medical and surgical

Staffed Beds: 83

TITUSVILLE—Crawford County

★ **TITUSVILLE AREA HOSPITAL (391314)**, 406 West Oak Street, Zip 16354-1404; tel. 814/827-1851, (Nonreporting) **A**10 18 **S** Meadville Medical Center, Meadville, PA
Primary Contact: Lee M. Clinton, FACHE, President and Chief Executive Officer
CFO: Jill Neely, Chief Financial Officer
CMO: William Sonnenberg, M.D., President Medical Staff
CIO: Karen Humes, Chief Information Officer
CHR: Jeffrey Saintz, Vice President Human Resources
CNO: Brenda Burnett, R.N., Vice President Patient Care Services and Chief Nursing Officer
Web address: www.titusvillehospital.org
Control: Other not-for-profit (including NFP Corporation) **Service:** General medical and surgical

Staffed Beds: 25

TORRANCE—Westmoreland County

TORRANCE STATE HOSPITAL (394026), Torrance Road, Zip 15779-0111, Mailing Address: P.O. Box 111, Zip 15779-0111; tel. 724/459-8000, **A**10 **F**39 65 75 77 98 100 101 130 135 146 147 148 154
Primary Contact: Stacey Keilman, Chief Executive Officer
COO: John O'Donnell, Chief Operating Officer
CFO: Cathy Palmer, Chief Financial Officer
CMO: Brent Ednie, M.D., Chief Medical Officer
Web address: www.dpw.state.pa.us
Control: State, Government, Nonfederal **Service:** Psychiatric

Staffed Beds: 357 **Admissions:** 334 **Census:** 285 **Outpatient Visits:** 0 **Births:** 0
Total Expense ($000): 96603 **Payroll Expense ($000):** 46556 **Personnel:** 688

TRANSFER—Mercer County

EDGEWOOD SURGICAL HOSPITAL (390307), 239 Edgewood Drive Extension, Zip 16154-1817; tel. 724/646-0400, (Nonreporting) **A**10
Primary Contact: Kevin Gramley, Chief Executive Officer
Web address: www.edgewoodsurgical.com
Control: Corporation, Investor-owned (for-profit) **Service:** Surgical

Staffed Beds: 10

Hospital, Medicare Provider Number, Address, Telephone, Approval, Facility, and Physician Codes, Health Care System

★ American Hospital Association (AHA) membership ○ Healthcare Facilities Accreditation Program ⇧ Center for Improvement in Healthcare Quality Accreditation
☐ The Joint Commission accreditation ◇ DNV Healthcare Inc. accreditation △ Commission on Accreditation of Rehabilitation Facilities (CARF) accreditation

Hospitals, U.S. / PENNSYLVANIA

TROY—Bradford County

○ **GUTHRIE TROY COMMUNITY HOSPITAL (391305)**, 275 Guthrie Drive, Zip 16947; tel. 570/297-2121, (Nonreporting) **A**3 10 11 18 **S** Guthrie Clinic, Sayre, PA
Primary Contact: Paul VerValin, Executive Vice President and Chief Operating Officer
CFO: Bernie Smith, Chief Financial Officer
CMO: Vance A Good, M.D., Chief Medical Staff
CHR: John R. Petrov, Senior Vice President, Chief Human Resource Officer
Web address: www.guthrie.org
Control: Other not-for-profit (including NFP Corporation) **Service**: General medical and surgical

Staffed Beds: 25

TYRONE—Blair County

PENN HIGHLANDS TYRONE (391307), 187 Hospital Drive, Zip 16686-1808; tel. 814/684-1255, (Nonreporting) **A**10 18
Primary Contact: Rhonda Halstead, Region President for Huntington and Tyrone
CMO: Kelly Biggs, M.D., Chief Medical Officer
CHR: Rosemary Jorden Best, Director Human Resources
CNO: Sharon Fisher, R.N., Chief Nursing Officer
Web address: www.tyronehospital.org
Control: Other not-for-profit (including NFP Corporation) **Service**: General medical and surgical

Staffed Beds: 25

UNIONTOWN—Fayette County

✠ **WVU MEDICINE UNIONTOWN HOSPITAL (390041)**, 500 West Berkeley Street, Zip 15401-5596; tel. 724/430-5000, (Nonreporting) **A**1 3 10 **S** West Virginia University Health System, Morgantown, WV
Primary Contact: Carrie Willetts, President & Chief Executive Officer
CHR: James Proud, Vice President Human Resources and Marketing
CNO: Betty Ann Rock, Vice President Nursing and Chief Nursing Officer
Web address: www.uniontownhospital.com
Control: Other not-for-profit (including NFP Corporation) **Service**: General medical and surgical

Staffed Beds: 145

UPLAND—Delaware County

☐ **CROZER-CHESTER MEDICAL CENTER (390180)**, 1 Medical Center Boulevard, Zip 19013-3995; tel. 610/447-2000, (Includes SPRINGFIELD HOSPITAL, 190 West Sproul Road, Springfield, Pennsylvania, Zip 19064-2097, tel. 610/328-8700; TAYLOR HOSPITAL, 175 East Chester Pike, Ridley Park, Pennsylvania, Zip 19078-2212, tel. 610/595-6000) (Nonreporting) **A**1 2 3 5 8 10 12 13 **S** Prospect Medical Holdings, Los Angeles, CA
Primary Contact: Anthony Esposito, President
CFO: Arthur Anderson, Chief Financial Officer
CMO: Sat Arora, M.D., President Medical and Dental Staff
CIO: Robert E Wilson, Vice President and Chief Information Officer
Web address: www.crozer.org
Control: Other not-for-profit (including NFP Corporation) **Service**: General medical and surgical

Staffed Beds: 313

WARREN—Warren County

WARREN GENERAL HOSPITAL (390146), 2 West Crescent Park, Zip 16365-2111, Mailing Address: P.O. Box 68, Zip 16365-0068; tel. 814/723-4973, **A**10 **F**4 11 13 15 18 26 27 28 29 31 34 35 40 44 45 47 48 50 51 59 62 64 68 70 75 76 77 78 79 81 85 87 89 92 93 97 98 100 101 102 107 108 109 110 111 114 115 116 117 118 119 120 121 123 130 133 145 146 148 149 157
Primary Contact: Richard Allen, Chief Executive Officer
COO: Randy California, Chief Operating Officer
CFO: Mark Cye, Chief Financial Officer
CMO: John Maljovec, M.D., Medical Director
CIO: Helen Rosequist, Manager Information Systems
CHR: Matthew Franklin, Director Human Resources
CNO: Joe Akif, Chief Clinical Officer and Chief Nursing Officer
Web address: www.wgh.org
Control: Other not-for-profit (including NFP Corporation) **Service**: General medical and surgical

Staffed Beds: 76 **Admissions**: 2317 **Census**: 31 **Outpatient Visits**: 21731 **Births**: 175 **Total Expense ($000)**: 98842 **Payroll Expense ($000)**: 36471 **Personnel**: 501

WARREN STATE HOSPITAL (394016), 33 Main Drive, Zip 16365-5001; tel. 814/723-5500, (Nonreporting) **A**10
Primary Contact: Charlotte M. Uber, Chief Executive Officer
COO: Ronnie Cropper, Chief Operating Officer
CFO: Terry Crambes, Manager Finance
CMO: Andrea J. Richard, M.D., Chief Medical Officer
CIO: Karen Byler, Information Technology Generalist
CNO: Sara Flasher, Chief Nurse Executive
Web address: https://www.dhs.pa.gov/Services/Assistance/Pages/Warren-State-Hospital.aspx
Control: State, Government, Nonfederal **Service**: Psychiatric

Staffed Beds: 152

WASHINGTON—Washington County

☐ **ADVANCED SURGICAL HOSPITAL (390323)**, 100 Trich Drive Suite 1, Zip 15301-5990; tel. 724/884-0710, (Nonreporting) **A**1 10
Primary Contact: Anne S. Hast, R.N., Chief Executive Officer
Web address: www.ashospital.net
Control: Partnership, Investor-owned (for-profit) **Service**: Orthopedic

Staffed Beds: 14

✠ **UPMC WASHINGTON (390042)**, 155 Wilson Avenue, Zip 15301-3398; tel. 724/225-7000, **A**1 3 5 10 13 19 **F**3 5 11 12 13 15 18 20 22 24 26 28 29 30 31 32 34 35 36 38 39 40 44 45 46 49 50 51 53 54 56 57 59 60 64 65 70 73 74 75 76 77 78 79 81 82 84 85 86 87 89 91 92 93 94 96 97 98 100 101 102 103 107 108 110 111 114 115 118 119 126 127 130 131 132 135 146 147 148 149 154 156 167 169 **S** UPMC, Pittsburgh, PA
Primary Contact: Brook Ward, President and Chief Executive Officer
COO: Rodney Louk, Chief Operating Officer
CFO: Alisa Rucker, Vice President Finance and Chief Financial Officer
CHR: Barbara A McCullough, Vice President Human Resources
CNO: Karen A Bray, R.N., MSN, Vice President Patient Care Services
Web address: https://whs.org/
Control: Other not-for-profit (including NFP Corporation) **Service**: General medical and surgical

Staffed Beds: 172 **Admissions**: 8198 **Census**: 104 **Outpatient Visits**: 557720 **Births**: 615 **Total Expense ($000)**: 265643 **Payroll Expense ($000)**: 115032 **Personnel**: 1422

WAYNESBORO—Franklin County

★ ⇧ **WELLSPAN WAYNESBORO HOSPITAL (390138)**, 501 East Main Street, Zip 17268-2394; tel. 717/765-4000, **A**10 19 21 **F**3 11 15 17 18 26 29 30 40 44 45 47 48 50 60 64 68 70 74 79 81 82 84 85 86 87 93 97 100 107 108 110 111 115 119 124 126 130 131 133 135 146 148 149 154 167 **S** WellSpan Health, York, PA
Primary Contact: Melissa Dubrow, Vice President Wellspan Health and President WellSpan Waynesboro Hospital
CFO: Kimberly Rzomp, Vice President Finance
CMO: Thomas Anderson, M.D., Vice President Medical Affairs
CIO: Michele Zeigler, Vice President Information Services
CHR: Jennifer Knight, Manager Human Resources
CNO: Elyse Fisler, Chief Nursing Officer
Web address: https://www.wellspan.org/offices-locations/wellspan-waynesboro-hospital/
Control: Other not-for-profit (including NFP Corporation) **Service**: General medical and surgical

Staffed Beds: 53 **Admissions**: 1761 **Census**: 20 **Outpatient Visits**: 92777 **Births**: 0 **Total Expense ($000)**: 71337 **Payroll Expense ($000)**: 20051 **Personnel**: 195

WAYNESBURG—Greene County

★ **UPMC GREENE (390150)**, 350 Bonar Avenue, Zip 15370-1608; tel. 724/627-3101, **A**3 5 10 **F**3 11 15 29 40 64 107 108 110 111 115 119 130 133 146 164 **S** UPMC, Pittsburgh, PA
Primary Contact: Terry Wiltrout, President
COO: Janel Mudry, Chief Operating Officer
CMO: Jamie Boris, M.D., President Medical Staff
CIO: Leslie Hayhurst, Director Information Systems
CHR: Patricia Marshall, Assistant Administrator Human Resources
Web address: www.southwestregionalmedical.com/
Control: Other not-for-profit (including NFP Corporation) **Service**: General medical and surgical

Staffed Beds: 18 **Admissions**: 380 **Census**: 4 **Outpatient Visits**: 31628 **Births**: 0 **Total Expense ($000)**: 20585 **Payroll Expense ($000)**: 8809 **Personnel**: 112

Hospitals, U.S. / PENNSYLVANIA

WELLSBORO—Tioga County

UPMC WELLSBORO (391316), 32 Central Avenue, Zip 16901–1899; tel. 570/723–7764, **A**1 3 10 18 **F**3 7 11 13 15 17 28 29 30 31 32 34 35 40 41 45 46 50 54 57 59 60 62 63 68 70 75 76 77 78 79 81 84 86 87 89 90 93 96 97 107 108 110 111 115 118 119 129 130 131 132 146 147 154 156 157 169 **P**6 **S** UPMC, Pittsburgh, PA
Primary Contact: Daniel Glunk, M.D., Chief Quality Officer
CMO: Walter Laibinis, M.D., Chief Medical Officer
CIO: Timothy E Schoener, Senior Vice President and Chief Information Officer
CHR: Dawn Wright, Vice President Human Resources
CNO: Matt Romania, Director of Nursing
Web address: www.susquehannahealth.org
Control: Other not–for–profit (including NFP Corporation) **Service**: General medical and surgical

Staffed Beds: 39 **Admissions**: 1517 **Census**: 19 **Outpatient Visits**: 62261 **Births**: 108 **Total Expense ($000)**: 91177 **Payroll Expense ($000)**: 36985 **Personnel**: 427

WERNERSVILLE—Berks County

WERNERSVILLE STATE HOSPITAL (394014), 160 Main Street, Zip 19565–9490; tel. 610/678–3411, (Nonreporting) **A**10
Primary Contact: Shirley Sowizral, Chief Executive Officer
COO: Cheryl Benson, Chief Operating Officer
CMO: Dale K Adair, M.D., Chief Medical Officer
CIO: William Edwards, Information Technology Generalist
CHR: Melvin McMinn, Director Human Resources
Web address: www.dhs.pa.gov/citizens/statehospitals/wernersvillestatehospital/
Control: State, Government, Nonfederal **Service**: Psychiatric

Staffed Beds: 266

WEST CHESTER—Chester County

PENN MEDICINE CHESTER COUNTY HOSPITAL (390179), 701 East Marshall Street, Zip 19380–4412; tel. 610/431–5000, **A**1 2 3 5 10 19 **F**3 11 12 13 15 17 18 20 22 24 26 28 29 30 31 32 34 35 36 37 39 40 41 44 45 46 49 50 51 54 55 56 57 58 59 60 63 64 65 66 68 69 70 72 74 75 76 77 78 79 81 84 85 86 87 89 92 93 96 102 107 108 110 111 115 116 117 118 119 120 121 126 130 131 132 135 141 142 146 147 148 149 150 154 156 164 167 169 **S** University of Pennsylvania Health System, Philadelphia, PA
Primary Contact: Michael J. Duncan, President and Chief Executive Officer
COO: Michael Barber, Chief Operating Officer
CFO: Kenneth E Flickinger, Chief Financial Officer
CMO: Richard D Donze, D.O., Senior Vice President Medical Affairs
CIO: Karen Pinsky, M.D., Chief Medical Information Officer
CHR: Jacqueline Felicetti, Chief Human Resource Officer
CNO: Angela R. Coladonato, R.N., MSN, Chief Nursing Officer
Web address: www.chestercountyhospital.org
Control: Other not–for–profit (including NFP Corporation) **Service**: General medical and surgical

Staffed Beds: 329 **Admissions**: 17759 **Census**: 203 **Outpatient Visits**: 353339 **Births**: 3181 **Total Expense ($000)**: 502490 **Payroll Expense ($000)**: 190437 **Personnel**: 2397

WEST READING—Berks County

READING HOSPITAL (390044), 420 South Fifth Avenue, Zip 19611–2143, Mailing Address: P.O. Box 16052, Zip 19612–6052; tel. 610/988–8000, **A**1 2 3 5 10 13 19 **F**3 5 8 9 11 12 13 14 15 17 18 20 22 24 26 28 29 30 31 32 34 35 37 38 39 40 41 43 44 45 46 47 48 49 50 51 53 54 55 56 57 58 59 60 61 62 63 64 65 66 68 70 71 72 73 74 75 76 78 79 80 81 82 83 84 85 86 87 89 90 92 93 95 96 101 102 104 107 108 110 111 114 115 116 117 118 119 120 121 123 124 126 128 129 130 132 134 135 144 145 146 147 148 149 150 152 154 156 157 160 161 162 165 167 169 **S** Tower Health, West Reading, PA
Primary Contact: Charles Barbera, M.D., President and Chief Executive Officer
COO: Michelle Trupp, Chief Operating Officer
CFO: Mark Reyngoudt, Chief Financial Officer
CMO: Ron Nutting, M.D., Chief Medical Officer
CIO: Jayashree Raman, Vice President and Chief Information Officer
CNO: Barbara Romig DNP, RN, Chief Nursing Officer
Web address: www.readinghospital.org
Control: Other not–for–profit (including NFP Corporation) **Service**: General medical and surgical

Staffed Beds: 650 **Admissions**: 35593 **Census**: 548 **Outpatient Visits**: 941964 **Births**: 2861 **Total Expense ($000)**: 1079481 **Payroll Expense ($000)**: 461897 **Personnel**: 5459

WEXFORD—Allegheny County

AHN WEXFORD HOSPITAL (390334), 12351 Perry Highway, Zip 15090–8344; tel. 724/939–3673, **A**1 3 10 **F**3 7 12 13 18 20 22 29 32 34 35 36 37 38 39 40 41 44 45 46 49 50 51 53 56 57 59 61 64 65 66 70 73 74 75 76 77 79 81 82 84 85 86 87 89 93 96 100 102 107 108 110 111 112 114 115 118 119 122 126 130 131 132 135 145 146 147 148 149 154 156 160 162 164 167 168 169 **S** Allegheny Health Network, Pittsburgh, PA
Primary Contact: Allan Klapper, M.D., President
COO: Amy Cashdollar, Chief Operating Officer and Chief Innovation Officer
CMO: Katie Farah, M.D., Chief Medical Officer
CIO: John Lee, M.D., Chief Information Officer
CHR: Donna Bologna, Manager, Human Resources
CNO: Lisa Graper, R.N., MSN, Chief Nursing Officer
Control: Other not–for–profit (including NFP Corporation) **Service**: General medical and surgical

Staffed Beds: 105 **Admissions**: 5754 **Census**: 62 **Outpatient Visits**: 131405 **Births**: 1398 **Total Expense ($000)**: 175340 **Payroll Expense ($000)**: 52074 **Personnel**: 753

WILKES BARRE—Luzerne County

GEISINGER WYOMING VALLEY MEDICAL CENTER (390270), 1000 East Mountain Boulevard, Zip 18711–0027; tel. 570/808–7300, **A**1 2 3 5 10 13 19 **F**3 6 8 9 11 12 13 15 17 18 19 20 22 24 26 28 29 30 31 32 34 35 39 40 43 44 45 46 47 48 49 52 53 54 56 57 58 59 61 64 65 68 70 71 72 74 75 76 77 78 79 80 81 82 84 85 86 87 89 91 92 93 94 96 97 107 108 110 111 114 115 116 117 118 119 120 121 123 124 126 129 130 131 132 133 135 144 145 146 147 148 149 154 156 160 162 164 167 169 **P**1 5 8 **S** Geisinger, Danville, PA
Primary Contact: Ronald R. Beer, FACHE, Chief Administrative Officer
CFO: Thomas A Bielecki, Chief Financial Officer
CMO: Steven Pierdon, M.D., Executive Vice President and Chief Medical Officer
CIO: Frank Richards, Chief Information Officer
CHR: Margaret Heffers, Assistant Vice President Human Resources
Web address: https://www.geisinger.org/patient-care/find-a-location/geisinger-wyoming-valley-medical-center
Control: Other not–for–profit (including NFP Corporation) **Service**: General medical and surgical

Staffed Beds: 351 **Admissions**: 24003 **Census**: 253 **Outpatient Visits**: 608499 **Births**: 1898 **Total Expense ($000)**: 779325 **Payroll Expense ($000)**: 257696 **Personnel**: 3083

PAM HEALTH SPECIALTY HOSPITAL OF WILKES–BARRE (392025), 575 North River Street, 7th Floor, Zip 18702–2634; tel. 570/208–3310, **A**1 10 **F**1 3 29 34 60 68 77 79 82 100 101 148 **S** PAM Health, Enola, PA
Primary Contact: David Long, Chief Executive Officer
Web address: https://postacutemedical.com
Control: Corporation, Investor–owned (for–profit) **Service**: Acute long–term care hospital

Staffed Beds: 36 **Admissions**: 208 **Census**: 17 **Outpatient Visits**: 0 **Births**: 0 **Total Expense ($000)**: 11973 **Payroll Expense ($000)**: 5218 **Personnel**: 59

WILKES–BARRE—Luzerne County

JOHN HEINZ INSTITUTE OF REHABILITATION MEDICINE (393036), 150 Mundy Street, Zip 18702–6830; tel. 570/826–3800, (Nonreporting) **A**1 3 10
Primary Contact: Karen Kearney, Vice President Inpatient Rehabilitation Services
CFO: Mike Avvisato, Vice President and Chief Financial Officer
CMO: Gregory Basting, M.D., Vice President Medical Affairs
CIO: John Regula, Chief Information Officer
CNO: Maria Berlyn, Assistant Vice President Nursing Services
Web address: www.allied-services.org
Control: Other not–for–profit (including NFP Corporation) **Service**: Rehabilitation

Staffed Beds: 92

Hospital, Medicare Provider Number, Address, Telephone, Approval, Facility, and Physician Codes, Health Care System

★ American Hospital Association (AHA) membership
□ The Joint Commission accreditation
○ Healthcare Facilities Accreditation Program
◇ DNV Healthcare Inc. accreditation
⇑ Center for Improvement in Healthcare Quality Accreditation
△ Commission on Accreditation of Rehabilitation Facilities (CARF) accreditation

© 2025 AHA Guide

Hospitals, U.S. / PENNSYLVANIA

✠ △ **WILKES–BARRE GENERAL HOSPITAL (390137)**, 575 North River Street, Zip 18764–0001; tel. 570/829–8111, (Includes WILKES–BARRE GENERAL HOSPITAL, 575 North River Street, Wilkes–Barre, Pennsylvania, Zip 18764, tel. 570/829–8111) **A**1 3 5 7 10 19 **F**3 8 12 15 17 18 20 22 24 26 28 29 30 31 34 40 44 45 46 47 48 49 50 51 54 56 57 59 60 61 64 66 70 74 75 78 79 81 82 83 84 85 86 87 90 92 93 96 107 108 110 111 112 114 115 116 117 118 119 120 121 123 124 126 129 130 145 146 149 154 167 **S** Community Health Systems, Inc., Franklin, TN
Primary Contact: Christopher L. Howe, R.N., Interim Chief Executive Officer
COO: Robert Stiekes, Chief Operating Officer
CFO: Roy Boyd, Chief Financial Officer
CMO: Jennifer Price Goldstein, Chief Medical Officer
CIO: Denis Tucker, Chief Information Officer
CHR: James Carmody, Vice President Human Resources
CNO: Robert P Hoffman, R.N., Chief Nursing Officer
Web address: https://www.commonwealthhealth.net/
Control: Corporation, Investor–owned (for–profit) **Service**: General medical and surgical

Staffed Beds: 160 **Admissions**: 7893 **Census**: 101 **Births**: 219

✠ **WILKES–BARRE VETERANS AFFAIRS MEDICAL CENTER**, 1111 East End Boulevard, Zip 18711–0030; tel. 570/824–3521, (Total facility includes 100 beds in nursing home–type unit) **A**1 2 3 5 **F**1 3 4 5 8 9 10 11 12 15 18 20 22 24 26 28 29 30 31 33 34 35 36 37 38 39 40 44 45 46 48 50 52 53 54 55 56 57 58 59 60 61 62 63 64 65 66 67 70 71 74 75 77 78 79 81 82 83 84 86 87 90 91 92 93 94 96 97 98 100 101 102 104 105 106 107 108 110 111 114 115 117 118 119 120 124 126 127 128 130 131 132 135 137 138 139 143 145 146 147 148 149 150 152 153 154 156 157 158 160 161 162 163 164 165 167 168 169 **S** Department of Veterans Affairs, Washington, DC
Primary Contact: Russell E. Lloyd, Medical Center Director
COO: Joesph P. Sharon, Associate Director
CFO: Donald E Foote, Fiscal Officer
CMO: Mirza Z Ali, M.D., Chief of Staff
CIO: David Longmore, Chief Information Officer
CHR: Dawn P DeMorrow, Chief Human Resources Service
Web address: www.va.gov/vamcwb
Control: Veterans Affairs, Government, federal **Service**: General medical and surgical

Staffed Beds: 156 **Admissions**: 2728 **Census**: 92 **Outpatient Visits**: 421084 **Births**: 0 **Total Expense ($000)**: 339055 **Payroll Expense ($000)**: 151081 **Personnel**: 1491

WILLIAMSPORT—Lycoming County

UPMC SUSQUEHANNA DIVINE PROVIDENCE See UPMC Susquehanna Divine Providence Campus

✠ **UPMC WILLIAMSPORT (390045)**, 700 High Street, Zip 17701–3100; tel. 570/321–1000, (Includes UPMC SUSQUEHANNA DIVINE PROVIDENCE CAMPUS, 1100 Grampian Boulevard, Williamsport, Pennsylvania, Zip 17701–1995, tel. 570/326–8000; Robert E. Kane, President) **A**1 2 3 5 10 13 19 **F**3 7 11 13 15 18 20 22 24 26 28 29 30 31 32 34 35 38 40 42 43 44 45 46 47 48 49 50 54 55 56 57 59 60 61 62 63 64 70 73 74 75 76 77 78 79 80 81 82 84 85 86 87 89 90 91 92 93 96 97 98 100 104 107 108 110 111 114 115 117 118 119 120 121 123 124 126 129 130 131 132 134 135 138 139 143 146 147 148 149 150 154 156 157 167 169 **S** UPMC, Pittsburgh, PA
Primary Contact: Patti Jackson–Gehris, President
CIO: Timothy E Schoener, Vice President and Chief Information Officer
CHR: Donald Wilver Jr, Vice President Human Resources
CNO: Lori A Beucler, MSN, RN, BS–NE, FACHE, R.N., Vice President and Chief Nursing Officer
Web address: www.susquehannahealth.org
Control: Other not–for–profit (including NFP Corporation) **Service**: General medical and surgical

Staffed Beds: 226 **Admissions**: 10346 **Census**: 171 **Outpatient Visits**: 330098 **Births**: 971 **Total Expense ($000)**: 391951 **Payroll Expense ($000)**: 157467 **Personnel**: 2106

WINDBER—Somerset County

★ **CHAN SOON–SHIONG MEDICAL CENTER AT WINDBER (390112)**, 600 Somerset Avenue, Zip 15963–1331; tel. 814/467–3000, **A**10 **F**3 11 12 15 18 20 22 26 28 29 30 34 35 36 40 44 45 48 53 55 56 57 58 59 62 63 70 75 77 79 81 83 84 85 93 107 108 110 111 114 119 130 131 132 135 145 146 147 154
Primary Contact: Thomas M. Kurtz, President and Chief Executive Officer
CFO: Richard Sukenik, CPA, Vice President Finance and Chief Financial Officer
CIO: Renee Adams, Director Information Technology
CHR: Jamie Brock, Vice President Human Resources
CNO: Michelle Hamula, Director of Nursing and Quality
Web address: www.windbercare.org
Control: Other not–for–profit (including NFP Corporation) **Service**: General medical and surgical

Staffed Beds: 54 **Admissions**: 1073 **Census**: 8 **Outpatient Visits**: 109879 **Births**: 0 **Total Expense ($000)**: 60253 **Payroll Expense ($000)**: 25617 **Personnel**: 378

WYNNEWOOD—Montgomery County

✠ **LANKENAU MEDICAL CENTER (390195)**, 100 East Lancaster Avenue, Zip 19096–3411; tel. 484/476–2000, **A**1 2 3 5 8 10 12 13 19 **F**3 11 13 15 17 18 20 22 24 26 28 29 30 31 32 34 35 36 38 39 40 41 43 45 46 47 48 49 54 55 57 58 59 61 64 65 66 69 70 72 73 74 75 76 78 79 80 81 82 84 85 86 87 91 93 96 97 100 102 107 108 110 111 114 115 118 119 120 121 123 124 126 129 130 131 132 135 138 141 145 146 148 149 150 154 157 164 167 169 **S** Main Line Health, Pittsburgh, PA
Primary Contact: Kathleen B. Galbraith, FACHE, President
CFO: Michael J Buongiorno, Vice President Finance
CMO: Robert Benz, M.D., Chief Medical Officer
CIO: Kay Carr, Chief Information Officer
CHR: Paul Yakulis, MS, R.N., Senior Vice President Human Resources
Web address: https://www.mainlinehealth.org/locations/lankenau-medical-center
Control: Other not–for–profit (including NFP Corporation) **Service**: General medical and surgical

Staffed Beds: 370 **Admissions**: 19578 **Census**: 280 **Outpatient Visits**: 358731 **Births**: 2872 **Total Expense ($000)**: 723578 **Payroll Expense ($000)**: 199292 **Personnel**: 2272

WYOMISSING—Berks County

□ △ **READING HOSPITAL REHABILITATION AT WYOMISSING**, 2802 Papermill Road, Zip 19610–1065; tel. 484/628–2388, (Nonreporting) **A**1 7
Primary Contact: Brittany M. Blose, Director of Nursing
Web address: https://towerhealth.org/locations/reading-hospital-rehabilitation-wyomissing
Control: Other not–for–profit (including NFP Corporation) **Service**: Rehabilitation

Staffed Beds: 112

✠ **SURGICAL INSTITUTE OF READING (390316)**, 2752 Century Boulevard, Zip 19610–3345; tel. 610/378–8800, (Nonreporting) **A**1 10
Primary Contact: Lorri Wildi, Chief Executive Officer
CFO: Cheryl Peterson, Business Office Manager
CHR: Megan Schaffer, Administrative Assistant
Web address: www.sireading.com
Control: Partnership, Investor–owned (for–profit) **Service**: Surgical

Staffed Beds: 15

YORK—York County

✠ **ENCOMPASS HEALTH REHABILITATION HOSPITAL OF YORK (393037)**, 1850 Normandie Drive, Zip 17408–1534; tel. 717/767–6941, (Nonreporting) **A**1 10 **S** Encompass Health Corporation, Birmingham, AL
Primary Contact: Josette Meyers, Chief Executive Officer
CFO: Joyce Henry, Controller
CMO: Bruce Sicilia, M.D., Medical Director
CIO: Laura Emig, Director Marketing Operations
CHR: Bradley Teahl, Director Human Resources
CNO: Julie Scott, Chief Nursing Officer
Web address: https://www.encompasshealth.com/yorkrehab
Control: Corporation, Investor–owned (for–profit) **Service**: Rehabilitation

Staffed Beds: 90

□ **OSS HEALTH (390325)**, 1861 Powder Mill Road, Zip 17402–4723; tel. 717/718–2000, (Nonreporting) **A**1 10
Primary Contact: Shawn M. Lovelady, Chief Executive Officer
CFO: Dale Bushey, Chief Financial Officer
CMO: Todd A. Curran, M.D., President Medical Staff
CIO: Tricia Wolf, Director Information Technology
CHR: Maureen M Putnam, Director Human Resources
CNO: Debra Garton, R.N., Chief Nursing Officer
Web address: www.osshealth.com
Control: Partnership, Investor–owned (for–profit) **Service**: Orthopedic

Staffed Beds: 26

Hospitals, U.S. / PENNSYLVANIA

SELECT SPECIALTY HOSP – YORK See Select Specialty Hospital–York

SELECT SPECIALTY HOSPITAL–YORK See Select Specialty Hospital–Camp Hill, Camp Hill

✠ **UPMC MEMORIAL (390101)**, 1701 Innovation Drive, Zip 17408–8815, Mailing Address: P.O. Box 15118, Zip 17405–7118; tel. 717/843–8623, **A**1 3 10 13 **F**3 13 15 18 20 22 26 29 30 31 34 35 37 38 40 44 47 48 49 50 51 54 55 56 57 58 59 60 65 68 70 72 74 75 76 77 78 79 81 84 85 87 89 92 97 102 107 108 109 110 111 114 115 116 117 118 119 120 121 126 129 130 132 135 141 144 145 146 147 148 149 150 154 156 157 160 161 167 **S** UPMC, Pittsburgh, PA
Primary Contact: Michelle Del Pizzo, President
COO: Joseph Iandolo, Vice President, Operations
CFO: Donna L. Muller, Vice President Finance, Southern Region
CMO: Michael Spangler, D.O., Vice President, Medical Affairs
CIO: Timothy E Schoener, Chief Information Officer
CHR: Corey Hudak, Director, Human Resources
CNO: Tracy Miller, Chief Nursing Officer, Vice President, Patient Care Services
Web address: www.mhyork.org
Control: Other not–for–profit (including NFP Corporation) **Service**: General medical and surgical

Staffed Beds: 79 **Admissions**: 5110 **Census**: 64 **Outpatient Visits**: 180461 **Births**: 523 **Total Expense ($000)**: 160390 **Payroll Expense ($000)**: 56927 **Personnel**: 962

△ ⇑ **WELLSPAN SURGERY AND REHABILITATION HOSPITAL (390327)**, 55 Monument Road, Zip 17403–5023; tel. 717/812–6100, **A**3 7 10 21 **F**3 29 30 44 50 57 60 68 71 74 75 79 81 85 90 91 93 96 100 107 110 112 114 115 119 130 132 146 148 154 **S** WellSpan Health, York, PA
Primary Contact: Carol Smith, President
Web address: www.wellspan.org
Control: Other not–for–profit (including NFP Corporation) **Service**: Rehabilitation

Staffed Beds: 73 **Admissions**: 1253 **Census**: 59 **Outpatient Visits**: 16782 **Births**: 0 **Total Expense ($000)**: 116019 **Payroll Expense ($000)**: 24973 **Personnel**: 298

✠ **WELLSPAN YORK HOSPITAL (390046)**, 1001 South George Street, Zip 17403–3645; tel. 717/851–2345, **A**1 2 3 5 8 10 12 13 19 **F**3 11 12 13 14 15 17 18 20 22 24 26 28 29 30 31 35 38 39 40 43 44 45 46 47 48 49 50 51 58 60 63 64 67 68 70 71 72 74 75 76 77 78 79 81 82 84 85 86 87 89 92 98 100 103 107 108 109 110 111 112 114 115 116 117 118 119 120 121 122 123 124 126 129 130 146 148 149 154 167 168 **S** WellSpan Health, York, PA
Primary Contact: Alyssa Moyer, President
COO: Raymond Rosen, FACHE, Vice President Operations
CFO: Laura Buczkowski, Senior Vice President and Chief Financial Officer
CMO: Peter M Hartmann, M.D., Vice President Medical Affairs
CIO: R Hal Baker, M.D., Vice President and Chief Information Officer
CNO: Astrid Davis, R.N., Chief Nursing Officer
Web address: www.wellspan.org
Control: Other not–for–profit (including NFP Corporation) **Service**: General medical and surgical

Staffed Beds: 593 **Admissions**: 26690 **Census**: 672 **Outpatient Visits**: 844648 **Births**: 2992 **Total Expense ($000)**: 1322847 **Payroll Expense ($000)**: 296452 **Personnel**: 3406

Hospital, Medicare Provider Number, Address, Telephone, Approval, Facility, and Physician Codes, Health Care System

★ American Hospital Association (AHA) membership ○ Healthcare Facilities Accreditation Program ⇑ Center for Improvement in Healthcare Quality Accreditation
□ The Joint Commission accreditation ◇ DNV Healthcare Inc. accreditation △ Commission on Accreditation of Rehabilitation Facilities (CARF) accreditation

© 2025 AHA Guide

RHODE ISLAND

CRANSTON—Providence County

☐ **ELEANOR SLATER HOSPITAL (412001)**, 111 Howard Avenue, Zip 02920–0269, Mailing Address: P.O. Box 8269, Zip 02920–0269; tel. 401/462–3085, (Nonreporting) **A**1 3 10
Primary Contact: Brett Johnson, Chief Executive Officer
COO: Chris Feisthamel, Chief Operating Officer
CMO: Sue Ferranti, M.D., Interim Chief Medical Officer
CHR: Genevieve Simard, Program Administrator, Human Resources
CNO: Anne Mongeau, Chief Nursing Officer
Web address: https://bhddh.ri.gov/eleanor-slater-hospital
Control: State, Government, Nonfederal **Service**: Acute long–term care hospital

Staffed Beds: 284

EAST PROVIDENCE—Providence County

☐ **EMMA PENDLETON BRADLEY HOSPITAL (414003)**, 1011 Veterans Memorial Parkway, Zip 02915–5099; tel. 401/432–1000, **A**1 3 5 10 **F**5 29 30 35 55 75 98 99 101 104 105 106 130 132 152 153 154 160 161 164 **P**7 **S** Lifespan Corporation, Providence, RI
Primary Contact: Henry T. Sachs III, M.D., President
CFO: Mamie Wakefield, Vice President Finance and Chief Financial Officer
CIO: Carole Cotter, Senior Vice President and Chief Information Officer
CHR: Rob Duval, Chief Human Resources Officer
CNO: Vareen O'Keefe Domaleski, MS, R.N., Vice Patient Care Services and Chief Nursing Officer
Web address: www.lifespan.org
Control: Other not–for–profit (including NFP Corporation) **Service**: Children's hospital psychiatric

Staffed Beds: 70 **Admissions**: 780 **Census**: 67 **Outpatient Visits**: 2622
Births: 0 **Total Expense ($000)**: 103042 **Payroll Expense ($000)**: 64651
Personnel: 692

NEWPORT—Newport County

☐ △ **NEWPORT HOSPITAL (410006)**, 11 Friendship Street, Zip 02840–2299; tel. 401/846–6400, **A**1 2 3 5 7 10 **F**3 8 9 13 15 18 20 28 29 30 31 34 35 36 37 40 45 50 51 53 56 57 59 60 64 65 68 70 74 75 76 77 78 79 81 82 85 86 87 90 91 92 93 94 96 97 98 100 102 104 105 107 108 110 111 114 118 119 130 131 132 135 143 146 147 148 154 156 157 158 160 161 167 169 **S** Lifespan Corporation, Providence, RI
Primary Contact: Crista F. Durand, President
CFO: Frank J Byrne, Vice President Finance
CMO: Jeffrey Gaines, M.D., Vice President and Chief Medical Officer
CHR: Barbara J. Arcangeli, Vice President Human Resources
CNO: Orla Brandos, Vice President of Patient Care Services and Chief Nursing Officer
Web address: www.newporthospital.org
Control: Other not–for–profit (including NFP Corporation) **Service**: General medical and surgical

Staffed Beds: 109 **Admissions**: 4947 **Census**: 80 **Outpatient Visits**: 86401
Births: 421 **Total Expense ($000)**: 138342 **Payroll Expense ($000)**: 67499
Personnel: 704

NORTH PROVIDENCE—Providence County

☐ △ **ST. JOSEPH HEALTH SERVICES OF RHODE ISLAND (410005)**, 200 High Service Avenue, Zip 02904–5199; tel. 401/456–3000, (Includes OUR LADY OF FATIMA HOSPITAL, 200 High Service Ave, North Providence, Rhode Island, Zip 02904–5113, 200 High Service Avenue, Zip 02904, tel. 401/456–3000; Thomas Hughes, President; ST. JOSEPH HOSPITAL FOR SPECIALTY CARE, 21 Peace ST, Providence, Rhode Island, Zip 02907–1510, 21 Peace Street, Zip 02907, tel. 401/456–3000) (Nonreporting) **A**1 3 7 10 **S** Prospect Medical Holdings, Los Angeles, CA
Primary Contact: Jeffrey H. Liebman, Chief Executive Officer
CFO: Michael E Conklin Jr, Chief Financial Officer
CIO: Susan Cerrone Abely, Chief Information Officer
CHR: Darlene Souza, Vice President
CNO: Patricia A Nadle, R.N., Chief Nursing Officer
Web address: www.saintjosephri.com
Control: Other not–for–profit (including NFP Corporation) **Service**: General medical and surgical

Staffed Beds: 125

NORTH SMITHFIELD—Providence County

LANDMARK MEDICAL CENTER–FOGARTY UNIT See Landmark Medical Center, Woonsocket

☐ **REHABILITATION HOSPITAL OF RHODE ISLAND (413025)**, 116 Eddie Dowling Highway, Zip 02896–7327; tel. 401/766–0800, (Nonreporting) **A**1 10 **S** Prime Healthcare, Ontario, CA
Primary Contact: Sheri Godfrin, Chief Executive Officer
COO: Demetra Ouellette, Chief Operating Officer
CFO: Thomas Klessens, Chief Financial Officer
CMO: Khin Yin, Medical Director
CIO: Vincent Larosa, Director of Information Technology Services
CHR: Gail Gosselin, Director Human Resources
CNO: Kathy Keeling, Director of Nursing
Web address: https://www.rehabhospitalri.com/
Control: Other not–for–profit (including NFP Corporation) **Service**: Rehabilitation

Staffed Beds: 70

PROVIDENCE—Providence County

✠ **BUTLER HOSPITAL (414000)**, 345 Blackstone Boulevard, Zip 02906–4829; tel. 401/455–6200, (Nonreporting) **A**1 3 5 10 **S** Care New England Health System, Providence, RI
Primary Contact: Mary Marran, MS, President and Chief Operating Officer; Interim President, The Providence Center
CFO: Bonnie Baker, Vice President Finance and Chief Financial Officer
CMO: James Sullivan, M.D., Chief Medical Officer
CIO: Summa Gaddam, Chief Information Officer
CHR: Timothy Bigelow, Director Human Resources
CNO: Mary Leveillee, Senior Vice President Patient Care Services and Chief Nursing Officer
Web address: www.butler.org
Control: Other not–for–profit (including NFP Corporation) **Service**: Psychiatric

Staffed Beds: 143

☐ **MIRIAM HOSPITAL (410012)**, 164 Summit Avenue, Zip 02906–2853; tel. 401/793–2500, **A**1 2 3 5 8 10 **F**3 8 9 12 15 18 20 22 26 28 29 30 31 34 35 36 37 40 44 45 46 47 48 49 50 51 55 56 57 58 59 61 64 65 66 67 68 70 74 75 77 78 79 81 82 84 85 86 87 91 92 93 97 100 101 102 104 107 108 110 111 114 115 118 119 126 130 132 135 146 147 148 149 156 157 160 161 162 164 165 167 **S** Lifespan Corporation, Providence, RI
Primary Contact: Maria Ducharme, R.N., President
COO: Maria Ducharme, R.N., Senior Vice President Patient Care Services and Chief Nursing Officer
CFO: Mamie Wakefield, Chief Financial Officer
CMO: G. Dean Roye, M.D., Senior Vice President of Medical Affairs and Chief Medical Officer
CIO: Carole Cotter, Vice President and Chief Information Officer
CHR: Nancy McMahon, Vice President Human Resources
Web address: www.lifespan.org
Control: Other not–for–profit (including NFP Corporation) **Service**: General medical and surgical

Staffed Beds: 247 **Admissions**: 16383 **Census**: 196 **Outpatient Visits**: 291320 **Births**: 0 **Total Expense ($000)**: 602656 **Payroll Expense ($000)**: 260890 **Personnel**: 2850

✠ **PROVIDENCE VETERANS AFFAIRS MEDICAL CENTER**, 830 Chalkstone Avenue, Zip 02908–4799; tel. 401/273–7100, (Nonreporting) **A**1 2 3 5 **S** Department of Veterans Affairs, Washington, DC
Primary Contact: Lawrence B. Connell, Medical Center Director
COO: Erin Clare Sears, Associate Director of Operations
CMO: Satish C Sharma, M.D., Chief of Staff
Web address: www.providence.va.gov/
Control: Veterans Affairs, Government, federal **Service**: General medical and surgical

Staffed Beds: 106

Hospitals, U.S. / RHODE ISLAND

☐ **RHODE ISLAND HOSPITAL (410007)**, 593 Eddy Street, Zip 02903–4900; tel. 401/444–4000, (Includes HASBRO CHILDREN'S HOSPITAL, 593 Eddy Street, Providence, Rhode Island, Zip 02903–4923, tel. 401/444–4000) **A**1 2 3 5 8 10 **F**3 6 7 8 11 15 16 17 18 19 20 21 22 23 24 26 29 30 31 32 34 35 36 38 39 40 41 43 44 45 46 47 48 49 50 51 54 55 56 57 58 59 60 61 64 65 67 68 70 71 74 75 77 78 79 81 82 83 84 85 86 87 88 89 91 92 93 94 96 97 98 99 100 101 102 103 104 105 107 108 110 111 114 115 116 117 118 119 120 121 122 123 124 126 129 130 131 132 135 138 143 145 146 147 148 149 154 156 157 160 161 166 167 **S** Lifespan Corporation, Providence, RI
Primary Contact: Sarah Frost, Chief, Lifespan Hospital Operations, and President, Rhode Island Hospital and Hasbro Children's Hosp
COO: Fredrick Macri, Executive Vice President
CFO: Mamie Wakefield, Senior Vice President and Chief Financial Officer
CMO: John B Murphy, M.D., Vice President Medical Affairs and Chief Medical Officer
CIO: Carole Cotter, Senior Vice President and Chief Information Officer
CHR: Louis J Sperling, Vice President Human Resources
Web address: www.rhodeislandhospital.org/
Control: Other not–for–profit (including NFP Corporation) **Service**: General medical and surgical

Staffed Beds: 638 **Admissions**: 32008 **Census**: 554 **Outpatient Visits**: 537683 **Births**: 0 **Total Expense ($000)**: 1896030 **Payroll Expense ($000)**: 775831 **Personnel**: 6772

☐ **ROGER WILLIAMS MEDICAL CENTER (410004)**, 825 Chalkstone Avenue, Zip 02908–4735; tel. 401/456–2000, (Nonreporting) **A**1 2 3 5 10 **S** Prospect Medical Holdings, Los Angeles, CA
Primary Contact: Jeffrey H. Liebman, Chief Executive Officer
CFO: Addy Kane, Chief Financial Officer
CMO: Elaine Jones, M.D., President Medical Staff
CIO: Susan Cerrone Abely, Vice President and Chief Information Officer
Web address: www.rwmc.org/
Control: Other not–for–profit (including NFP Corporation) **Service**: General medical and surgical

Staffed Beds: 86

ST. JOSEPH HOSPITAL FOR SPECIALTY CARE See St. Joseph Health Services of Rhode Island, North Providence

⊞ **WOMEN & INFANTS HOSPITAL OF RHODE ISLAND (410010)**, 101 Dudley Street, Zip 02905–2499; tel. 401/274–1100, (Nonreporting) **A**1 2 3 5 8 10 **S** Care New England Health System, Providence, RI
Primary Contact: Shannon Sullivan, President and Chief Operating Officer
CFO: Robert W Pacheco, Vice President Finance
CMO: Raymond Powrie, M.D., Senior Vice President Quality and Clinical Effectiveness
CHR: Paul F Heffernan, Vice President Human Resources
Web address: www.womenandinfants.org
Control: Other not–for–profit (including NFP Corporation) **Service**: Obstetrics and gynecology

Staffed Beds: 247

WAKEFIELD—Washington County

☐ **SOUTH COUNTY HOSPITAL (410008)**, 100 Kenyon Avenue, Zip 02879–4299; tel. 401/782–8000, (Nonreporting) **A**1 2 10
Primary Contact: Aaron Robinson, President and Chief Executive Officer
CFO: Thomas Breen, Vice President and Chief Financial Officer
CMO: John Russell Corcoran, Vice President Medical Affairs
CIO: Gary Croteau, Assistant Vice President and Chief Information Officer
CHR: Maggie Thomas, Vice President Human Resources and Practice Management
Web address: https://www.southcountyhealth.org/
Control: Other not–for–profit (including NFP Corporation) **Service**: General medical and surgical

Staffed Beds: 97

WARWICK—Kent County

KENT COUNTY MEMORIAL HOSPITAL See Kent Hospital

⊞ **KENT HOSPITAL (410009)**, 455 Tollgate Road, Zip 02886–2770; tel. 401/737–7000, (Nonreporting) **A**1 2 3 5 10 13 **S** Care New England Health System, Providence, RI
Primary Contact: Paari Gopalakrishnan, M.D., President and Chief Operating Officer
CFO: James M. Burke, Vice President Finance, Chief Nursing Executive Medical Surgical Hospitals
CMO: Paari Gopalakrishnan, M.D., Chief Medical Officer
CIO: Sumalatha Gaddam, Senior Vice President and Chief Information Officer
CHR: Marilyn J Walsh, Vice President Human Resources
CNO: Rebecca Burke, R.N., MS, Senior Vice President and Chief Nursing Officer
Web address: www.kentri.org
Control: Other not–for–profit (including NFP Corporation) **Service**: General medical and surgical

Staffed Beds: 309

WESTERLY—Washington County

⊞ **WESTERLY HOSPITAL (410013)**, 25 Wells Street, Zip 02891–2934; tel. 401/596–6000, **A**1 10 **F**3 11 15 18 20 26 28 29 30 31 34 35 40 44 45 47 48 49 51 54 56 57 59 63 64 68 70 75 77 78 79 81 82 84 85 86 87 91 93 94 98 101 103 107 108 110 111 115 119 126 130 132 135 146 148 149 154 164 167 **S** Yale New Haven Health, New Haven, CT
Primary Contact: Richard Lisitano, President
CMO: Oliver Mayorga, M.D., Chief Medical Officer
CHR: Donna Epps, Vice President, Chief Human Resource Officer
Web address: www.westerlyhospital.org
Control: Other not–for–profit (including NFP Corporation) **Service**: General medical and surgical

Staffed Beds: 87 **Admissions**: 3241 **Census**: 53 **Outpatient Visits**: 135465 **Births**: 0 **Total Expense ($000)**: 146000 **Payroll Expense ($000)**: 50429 **Personnel**: 584

WOONSOCKET—Providence County

⊞ **LANDMARK MEDICAL CENTER (410011)**, 115 Cass Avenue, Zip 02895–4731; tel. 401/769–4100, (Includes LANDMARK MEDICAL CENTER–FOGARTY UNIT, 116 Eddie Dowling Highway, North Smithfield, Rhode Island, Zip 02896–7327, tel. 401/766–0800; LANDMARK MEDICAL CENTER–WOONSOCKET UNIT, 115 Cass Ave, Woonsocket, Rhode Island, Zip 02895–4705, 115 Cass Avenue, Zip 02895, tel. 401/769–4100) (Nonreporting) **A**1 3 5 10 **S** Prime Healthcare, Ontario, CA
Primary Contact: Michael Souza, Chief Executive Officer
CFO: Thomas Klessens, Chief Financial Officer
CMO: Glenn Fort, Chief Medical Officer
CIO: Vincent Larosa, Director of Information Systems
CHR: Gail Gosselin, Director Human Resources
Web address: www.landmarkmedcenter.com
Control: Other not–for–profit (including NFP Corporation) **Service**: General medical and surgical

Staffed Beds: 140

Hospital, Medicare Provider Number, Address, Telephone, Approval, Facility, and Physician Codes, Health Care System

★ American Hospital Association (AHA) membership
☐ The Joint Commission accreditation
○ Healthcare Facilities Accreditation Program
◇ DNV Healthcare Inc. accreditation
⇑ Center for Improvement in Healthcare Quality Accreditation
△ Commission on Accreditation of Rehabilitation Facilities (CARF) accreditation

SOUTH CAROLINA

ABBEVILLE—Abbeville County

★ ⇑ **ABBEVILLE AREA MEDICAL CENTER (421301)**, 420 Thomson Circle, Zip 29620–5656, Mailing Address: P.O. Box 887, Zip 29620–0887; tel. 864/366–5011, (Nonreporting) **A**10 18 21 **S** Ovation Healthcare, Brentwood, TN
Primary Contact: Will Gordon, Vice President and Chief Administrative Officer
CFO: Timothy Wren, Chief Financial Officer
CMO: Christopher Ceraldi, M.D., Chief of Staff
CIO: Tim Stewart, Chief Information Officer
CHR: Alice Rigney, Chief Human Resources Officer
CNO: Ernest Shock, Chief Nursing Officer
Web address: www.abbevilleareamc.com
Control: County, Government, Nonfederal **Service**: General medical and surgical

Staffed Beds: 18

AIKEN—Aiken County

☐ **AIKEN REGIONAL MEDICAL CENTERS (420082)**, 302 University Parkway, Zip 29801–6302; tel. 803/641–5000, (Includes AURORA PAVILION, 655 Medical Park Drive, Aiken, South Carolina, Zip 29801, tel. 803/641–5900) **A**1 3 5 10 **F**1 3 4 8 11 13 15 18 20 22 24 29 30 31 34 35 40 42 46 49 54 56 57 58 59 64 70 73 74 76 77 78 79 81 85 86 87 89 90 94 96 98 99 100 101 102 103 104 107 108 110 111 114 115 119 121 123 126 128 129 130 131 132 135 146 147 148 149 **S** Universal Health Services, Inc., King of Prussia, PA
Primary Contact: Matthew Merrifield, Chief Executive Officer
Web address: www.aikenregional.com
Control: Corporation, Investor–owned (for–profit) **Service**: General medical and surgical

Staffed Beds: 281 **Admissions**: 13305 **Census**: 163 **Outpatient Visits**: 100412 **Births**: 1116 **Personnel**: 881

ANDERSON—Anderson County

⇑ **ANMED HEALTH MEDICAL CENTER** See Anmed Medical Center

ANMED HEALTH REHABILITATION HOSPITAL See Anmed Rehabilitation Hospital

★ ⇑ **ANMED MEDICAL CENTER (420027)**, 800 North Fant Street, Zip 29621–5793; tel. 864/512–1000, (Includes ANMED HEALTH WOMEN'S AND CHILDREN'S HOSPITAL, 2000 East Greenville Street, Anderson, South Carolina, Zip 29621, tel. 864/512–1000; William A Kenley, FACHE, Chief Executive Officer) **A**2 3 5 10 20 21 **F**1 3 4 8 11 12 15 17 18 20 22 24 26 28 29 30 31 34 35 37 38 39 40 43 45 46 47 49 50 51 53 54 56 57 58 59 60 62 64 65 68 70 71 73 74 75 76 77 78 79 81 84 85 86 87 89 90 91 94 97 98 100 101 102 103 104 107 108 110 111 112 114 115 117 118 119 120 121 123 126 127 128 129 130 131 132 144 146 147 148 149 157 **S** AnMed Health, Anderson, SC
Primary Contact: William A. Kenley, FACHE, Chief Executive Officer
COO: Tina M. Jury, R.N., Chief Hospital Operations
CFO: Christine Pearson, Chief Financial Officer
CMO: Thomas Kayrouz, M.D., Chief Medical Officer
CIO: Marty Stewart, Chief Information Officer
CNO: Shaunda Trotter, R.N., Chief Nursing Officer
Web address: www.anmedhealth.org
Control: Other not–for–profit (including NFP Corporation) **Service**: General medical and surgical

Staffed Beds: 365 **Admissions**: 22363 **Census**: 265 **Outpatient Visits**: 287048 **Births**: 1397 **Total Expense ($000)**: 627036 **Payroll Expense ($000)**: 273941 **Personnel**: 3626

✠ **ANMED REHABILITATION HOSPITAL (423029)**, 1 Spring Back Way, Zip 29621–2676; tel. 864/716–2600, **A**1 10 **F**1 3 29 56 57 60 68 74 75 79 90 91 93 96 128 130 148 149 **S** Encompass Health Corporation, Birmingham, AL
Primary Contact: Denise R. Murray, Chief Executive Officer
CFO: Julie Harris, Controller
CMO: William Vogentiz, M.D., Medical Director
CHR: Morgan Clements, Director of Human Resources
CNO: Kelly Davis, Chief Nursing Officer
Web address: www.anmedrehab.com
Control: Corporation, Investor–owned (for–profit) **Service**: Rehabilitation

Staffed Beds: 60 **Admissions**: 1437 **Census**: 44 **Personnel**: 160

☐ **PATRICK B. HARRIS PSYCHIATRIC HOSPITAL (424011)**, 130 Highway 252, Zip 29621–5054; tel. 864/231–2600, (Nonreporting) **A**1 3 5 10
Primary Contact: Allen McEniry, Executive Director
Web address: www.patrickbharris.com/
Control: State, Government, Nonfederal **Service**: Psychiatric

Staffed Beds: 131

BEAUFORT—Beaufort County

✠ **BEAUFORT MEMORIAL HOSPITAL (420067)**, 955 Ribaut Road, Zip 29902–5441; tel. 843/522–5200, **A**1 2 10 **F**1 3 11 12 13 15 18 20 22 28 29 30 31 32 34 35 37 40 45 46 48 49 50 51 53 54 55 57 59 60 62 64 65 69 70 71 73 74 75 76 77 78 79 81 85 86 87 89 90 91 93 94 96 97 98 100 101 102 103 104 107 108 110 111 114 115 118 119 120 121 126 127 128 130 132 134 145 146 147 148 149
Primary Contact: Edmond Russell. Baxley III, President and Chief Executive Officer
CFO: Ken Miller, Chief Financial Officer
CMO: Kurt Gambla, D.O., Chief Medical Officer
CIO: Edward Ricks, Vice President and Chief Information Officer
CHR: Brian Hoffman, Chief Human
CNO: Karen Manuel Carroll, R.N., Vice President Patient Care Services
Web address: www.bmhsc.org
Control: County, Government, Nonfederal **Service**: General medical and surgical

Staffed Beds: 207 **Admissions**: 8482 **Census**: 99 **Outpatient Visits**: 221058 **Births**: 1147 **Personnel**: 1946

✠ **NAVAL HOSPITAL BEAUFORT**, 1 Pinckney Boulevard, Zip 29902–6122; tel. 843/228–5301, (Nonreporting) **A**1 **S** Bureau of Medicine and Surgery, Department of the Navy, Falls Church, VA
Primary Contact: Captain Raymond R. Batz, Commanding Officer
Web address: https://beaufort.tricare.mil/
Control: Navy, Government, federal **Service**: General medical and surgical

Staffed Beds: 20

BLUFFTON—Beaufort County

✠ **ENCOMPASS HEALTH REHABILITATION HOSPITAL OF BLUFFTON (423032)**, 107 Seagrass Station Road, Zip 29910–9549; tel. 843/836–8200, **A**1 10 **F**1 3 29 30 34 56 57 60 68 74 75 79 90 91 93 96 128 130 132 146 148 149 **S** Encompass Health Corporation, Birmingham, AL
Primary Contact: Wayne B. Boutwell Jr, Chief Executive Officer
CFO: Jennifer Griffey, Chief Financial Officer
CMO: Vincent Somaio, M.D., Medical Director
CHR: LaFreda Doctor, Director, Human Resources
CNO: Nancy L Kendall, Chief Nursing Officer
Web address: https://encompasshealth.com/blufftonrehab
Control: Corporation, Investor–owned (for–profit) **Service**: Rehabilitation

Staffed Beds: 38 **Admissions**: 1014 **Census**: 33 **Total Expense ($000)**: 18699 **Payroll Expense ($000)**: 9764 **Personnel**: 180

CADES—Williamsburg County

✠ **MUSC HEALTH BLACK RIVER MEDICAL CENTER**, 3555 North Williamsburg County Highway, Zip 29518–3008; tel. 843/210–5000, (Nonreporting) **A**1 **S** MUSC Health, Charleston, SC
Primary Contact: Allen Abernethy, Chief Executive Officer
COO: Jason Cox, Chief Operating Officer
CFO: Steven Downs, Chief Financial Officer
CMO: Ramy Zebian, M.D., Chief Medical Officer
CHR: Kay Douglas, Executive Director
CNO: Costa King Cockfield, Chief Nursing Officer
Web address: https://muschealth.org/black-river-medical-center
Control: State, Government, Nonfederal **Service**: General medical and surgical

Staffed Beds: 25

CAMDEN—Kershaw County

✠ **MUSC HEALTH KERSHAW MEDICAL CENTER (420048)**, 1315 Roberts Street, Zip 29020–3737, Mailing Address: P.O. Box 7003, Zip 29021–7003; tel. 803/432–4311, **A**1 10 **F**1 3 11 13 15 18 20 24 28 29 30 31 32 34 35 40 44 45 49 50 51 54 57 59 61 62 63 64 66 68 70 75 76 77 78 79 81 85 86 87 89 90 94 97 98 100 103 107 108 110 111 114 115 118 119 128 129 130 132 135 144 146 147 148 154 **S** MUSC Health, Charleston, SC
Primary Contact: Matthew Littlejohn, FACHE, Chief Executive Officer
CFO: Holt Smith, Chief Financial Officer
CMO: Tallulah Holmstrom, M.D., Chief Medical Officer
CIO: Diane Arrants, Chief Information Officer
CHR: Angela F Nettles, Vice President, Human Resources and Support Services
Web address: www.kershawhealth.org
Control: Hospital district or authority, Government, Nonfederal **Service**: General medical and surgical

Staffed Beds: 72 **Admissions**: 3664 **Census**: 49 **Outpatient Visits**: 119290 **Births**: 324 **Personnel**: 1173

Hospitals, U.S. / SOUTH CAROLINA

CHARLESTON—Charleston County

BON SECOURS ST. FRANCIS HOSPITAL (420065), 2095 Henry Tecklenburg Drive, Zip 29414-5733; tel. 843/402-1000, **A**1 10 **F**1 3 7 12 13 15 29 30 31 34 35 40 45 46 47 48 49 50 51 54 56 57 59 63 64 67 68 70 73 74 75 76 77 78 79 80 81 82 84 85 86 87 90 93 94 100 102 107 108 110 111 114 115 117 118 119 120 121 123 124 126 128 130 131 132 145 146 147 148 149 154 **S** Bon Secours Mercy Health, Cincinnati, OH
Primary Contact: Matthew Desmond, Regional President, Bon Secours St. Francis and Mount Pleasant Hospitals & Vice President of Operati
CIO: Michael Taylor, Chief Information Officer
CNO: Pennie Peralta, R.N., VP, Nursing & Chief Nursing Officer
Web address: www.rsfh.com/
Control: Other not-for-profit (including NFP Corporation) **Service**: General medical and surgical

Staffed Beds: 136 **Admissions**: 9633 **Census**: 101 **Outpatient Visits**: 237072 **Births**: 2317 **Total Expense ($000)**: 477342 **Payroll Expense ($000)**: 86710 **Personnel**: 1063

MUSC CHILDREN'S HOSPITAL See Children's Hospital of South Carolina At Musc

MUSC HEALTH OF MEDICAL UNIVERSITY OF SOUTH CAROLINA See Musc Health University Medical Center

MUSC HEALTH REHABILITATION HOSPITAL, AN AFFILIATE OF ENCOMPASS HEALTH (423027), 9181 Medcom Street, Zip 29406-9168; tel. 843/820-7777, (Includes MUSC REHABILITATION HOSPITAL AN AFFILIATE OF ENCOMPASS HEALTH, 9181 Medcom Street, North Charleston, South Carolina, Zip 29406-9168, tel. 843/820-7777; Richard C. Hundorfean, Chief Executive Officer) **A**1 10 **F**1 90 96 128 148 149 **P**5 **S** Encompass Health Corporation, Birmingham, AL
Primary Contact: Richard C. Hundorfean, Chief Executive Officer
CFO: Tricia Nelson, Chief Financial Officer
CMO: Heather Walker, M.D., Chief Medical Officer
CHR: Susan Trantham, Director Human Resources
Web address: www.healthsouthcharleston.com
Control: Corporation, Investor-owned (for-profit) **Service**: Rehabilitation

Staffed Beds: 49 **Admissions**: 1233 **Census**: 40 **Outpatient Visits**: 0 **Births**: 0 **Personnel**: 124

MUSC HEALTH UNIVERSITY MEDICAL CENTER (420004), 169 Ashley Avenue, Zip 29425-8905; tel. 843/792-2300, (Includes CHILDREN'S HOSPITAL OF SOUTH CAROLINA AT MUSC, 171 Ashley Avenue, Charleston, South Carolina, Zip 29425-8908, tel. 843/792-1414; Patrick J. Cawley, M.D., FACHE, Chief Executive Officer, MUSC Health and Vice President for Health Affairs, University; SHAWN JENKINS CHILDREN'S HOSPITAL, 10 Mcclennan Banks Drive, Charleston, South Carolina, Zip 29401-1164, tel. 843/792-1414; David William Zaas, M.D., Chief Executive Officer) **A**1 2 3 5 8 10 19 **F**1 3 4 5 6 7 8 9 11 12 13 14 15 16 17 18 19 20 21 22 23 24 25 26 27 28 29 30 31 32 34 35 36 37 38 39 40 41 43 44 45 46 47 48 49 50 51 52 53 54 55 56 57 58 59 60 61 62 63 64 66 67 68 70 71 72 73 74 75 76 77 78 79 80 81 82 84 85 86 87 88 89 91 92 93 94 97 98 99 100 101 102 103 104 105 107 108 109 110 111 114 115 116 117 118 119 120 121 123 124 126 128 129 130 131 132 134 135 136 137 138 139 140 141 142 144 145 146 147 148 149 150 151 152 153 154 155 156 157 **S** MUSC Health, Charleston, SC
Primary Contact: Saju Joy, M.D., Chief Executive Officer
CFO: Lisa Goodlett, Administrator Finance and Support Services
CIO: Mark W McMath, Chief Information Officer
CHR: Darrick Paul, Chief People Officer
Web address: www.muschealth.com
Control: Hospital district or authority, Government, Nonfederal **Service**: General medical and surgical

Staffed Beds: 843 **Admissions**: 38424 **Census**: 752 **Outpatient Visits**: 1312233 **Births**: 3324 **Personnel**: 10095

PALMETTO LOWCOUNTRY BEHAVIORAL HEALTH (424006), 2777 Speissegger Drive, Zip 29405-8229; tel. 843/747-5830, **A**1 10 **F**1 4 5 98 99 102 103 104 105 128 153 154 **S** Universal Health Services, Inc., King of Prussia, PA
Primary Contact: Patrick McDaniel, Chief Executive Officer
CFO: Stan Markowski, Chief Financial Officer
CMO: Steven Lopez, M.D., Chief Medical Officer
CHR: Sheila Simpson, Vice President Human Resources
CNO: Jo Good, Director of Nursing
Web address: www.palmettobehavioralhealth.com
Control: Corporation, Investor-owned (for-profit) **Service**: Psychiatric

Staffed Beds: 103 **Admissions**: 2650 **Census**: 58 **Outpatient Visits**: 8963 **Personnel**: 148

RALPH H. JOHNSON VETERANS AFFAIRS MEDICAL CENTER, 109 Bee Street, Zip 29401-5799; tel. 843/577-5011, (Nonreporting) **A**1 2 3 5 8 **S** Department of Veterans Affairs, Washington, DC
Primary Contact: Scott R. Isaacks, FACHE, Director and Chief Executive Officer
CFO: Cassandra Helfer, Chief Financial Officer
CMO: Florence N. Hutchison, M.D., Chief of Staff
CIO: LaBon Hardy, Chief Information Officer
CHR: Renae A. Jacobson, Human Resources Officer
CNO: Garett E. Schreier, R.N., Associate Director, Nursing and Patient Care Services
Web address: www.charleston.va.gov/
Control: Veterans Affairs, Government, federal **Service**: General medical and surgical

Staffed Beds: 128

ROPER HOSPITAL (420087), 316 Calhoun Street, Zip 29401-1125; tel. 843/724-2000, **A**1 2 3 5 7 10 **F**1 3 7 8 9 15 17 18 20 22 24 26 28 29 30 31 34 35 37 40 42 45 49 50 51 53 54 55 56 57 58 59 60 61 62 63 64 65 67 68 70 74 75 77 78 79 80 81 82 84 85 86 87 90 92 93 94 95 96 102 107 108 110 111 115 118 119 120 121 123 126 128 129 130 131 132 135 136 143 146 147 148 149 **S** Bon Secours Mercy Health, Cincinnati, OH
Primary Contact: Troy Powell, Regional President, Roper Hospital and Berkeley Hospital
CHR: Melanie Stith, Vice President Human Resources
Web address: https://www.rsfh.com/roper-hospital
Control: Other not-for-profit (including NFP Corporation) **Service**: General medical and surgical

Staffed Beds: 300 **Admissions**: 12736 **Census**: 207 **Outpatient Visits**: 135640 **Births**: 0 **Total Expense ($000)**: 418465 **Payroll Expense ($000)**: 131145 **Personnel**: 1729

TRIDENT MEDICAL CENTER (420079), 9330 Medical Plaza Drive, Zip 29406-9195; tel. 843/797-7000, (Includes LIVE OAK MENTAL HEALTH AND WELLNESS, 3445 Ingleside Boulevard, Ladson, South Carolina, Zip 29456-4142, tel. 843/797-4200; MONCKS CORNER MEDICAL CENTER, 401 North Live Oak Drive, Highway 17A, Moncks Corner, South Carolina, Zip 29461-5603, tel. 843/761-8721; SUMMERVILLE MEDICAL CENTER, 295 Midland Parkway, Summerville, South Carolina, Zip 29485-8104, tel. 843/832-5000; Stephen Chandler, Chief Executive Officer) **A**1 2 3 5 10 **F**1 3 8 15 17 18 20 22 24 26 29 30 31 34 35 40 42 43 45 46 48 49 50 54 55 56 59 60 61 64 70 74 75 77 78 79 81 84 85 86 87 89 90 93 94 98 100 102 104 107 108 110 111 114 115 116 117 118 119 120 121 123 126 128 130 131 132 145 146 147 148 **S** HCA Healthcare, Nashville, TN
Primary Contact: Jeff Wilson, Chief Executive Officer
COO: Scott Weiskittel, Chief Operating Officer
CFO: Andy Miller, Chief Financial Officer
CMO: Jane Appleby, M.D., Chief Medical Officer
CHR: Vickie Cummings, Vice President of Human Resources
CNO: Jenn Freund, MSN, R.N., Chief Nursing Officer
Web address: www.tridenthealthsystem.com
Control: Corporation, Investor-owned (for-profit) **Service**: General medical and surgical

Staffed Beds: 398 **Admissions**: 27483 **Census**: 342 **Outpatient Visits**: 213202 **Births**: 2717 **Personnel**: 1326

CHERAW—Chesterfield County

MCLEOD HEALTH CHERAW (420107), 711 Chesterfield Highway, Zip 29520-7002; tel. 843/537-7881, **A**3 10 21 **F**1 3 11 15 28 29 30 34 35 38 40 44 45 50 57 59 60 62 63 64 65 68 70 75 79 80 81 85 87 97 102 107 108 110 111 114 119 126 127 128 130 133 135 143 145 146 148 149 154 **P**3 6 **S** McLeod Health, Florence, SC
Primary Contact: Bren T. Lowe, Chief Executive Officer, Vice President, McLeod Health
CFO: Louis Anderson, Chief Financial Officer
CMO: David Bersinger, M.D., Chief of Staff
CIO: Jim Spencer, Director Information System
Web address: https://www.mcleodhealth.org/locations/mcleod-cheraw/
Control: Other not-for-profit (including NFP Corporation) **Service**: General medical and surgical

Staffed Beds: 31 **Admissions**: 1839 **Census**: 22 **Outpatient Visits**: 44855 **Births**: 0 **Total Expense ($000)**: 56940 **Payroll Expense ($000)**: 23136 **Personnel**: 604

Hospital, Medicare Provider Number, Address, Telephone, Approval, Facility, and Physician Codes, Health Care System

★ American Hospital Association (AHA) membership
☐ The Joint Commission accreditation
○ Healthcare Facilities Accreditation Program
◇ DNV Healthcare Inc. accreditation
⇑ Center for Improvement in Healthcare Quality Accreditation
△ Commission on Accreditation of Rehabilitation Facilities (CARF) accreditation

Hospitals, U.S. / SOUTH CAROLINA

CHESTER—Chester County

MUSC HEALTH CHESTER MEDICAL CENTER (420019), 1 Medical Park Drive, Zip 29706–9769; tel. 803/581–3151, **A**1 10 **F**1 3 15 18 29 34 35 40 45 50 56 57 59 74 75 77 79 81 84 85 87 90 102 107 108 110 111 114 119 127 128 130 131 132 135 149 154 157 **S** MUSC Health, Charleston, SC
Primary Contact: Joseph Scott. Broome, M.P.H., FACHE, Chief Executive Officer
CFO: Tracey Claxton, Chief Financial Officer
CMO: Terry Dodge, M.D., Chief of Staff
CIO: Shaw Laird, Chief Information Officer
CHR: Karen Chapman, Director Human Resources
CNO: Betty Griffin, Interim Chief Nursing Officer
Web address: www.muschealth.org/locations/chester-medical-center
Control: Hospital district or authority, Government, Nonfederal **Service**: General medical and surgical

Staffed Beds: 43 **Admissions**: 852 **Census**: 11 **Outpatient Visits**: 35709 **Births**: 0 **Personnel**: 470

CLINTON—Laurens County

BAILEY MEMORIAL HOSPITAL See GHS – Laurens County Memorial Hospital

PRISMA HEALTH LAURENS COUNTY HOSPITAL (420038), 22725 Highway 76 East, Zip 29325–7527, Mailing Address: P O Drawer 976, Zip 29325–0976; tel. 864/833–9100, (Includes GHS – LAURENS COUNTY MEMORIAL HOSPITAL, 22725 Highway 76 E, Po Drawer 976, Clinton, South Carolina, Zip 29325–7527, PO Box 976, Zip 29325–0976, tel. 803/833–9100; Justin Benfield, Southern Region Chief Operating Officer) **A**1 5 10 20 **F**1 3 13 15 18 28 29 40 45 46 59 67 70 76 80 81 84 87 94 97 107 110 111 114 115 119 127 128 129 130 131 132 146 147 149 **S** Prisma Health – Midlands, Columbia, SC
Primary Contact: Justin Benfield, Chief Executive Officer
CFO: Michael Norrick, Director of Campus Operations
CMO: Vincent Green, Medical Director
CIO: Kathleen Anderson, Director, Acute Clinical Systems
CHR: Cathy M Rogers, Manager Human Resources
CNO: Kay Swisher, Chief Nursing Officer
Web address: https://prismahealth.org/locations/hospitals/laurens-county-hospital
Control: Other not–for–profit (including NFP Corporation) **Service**: General medical and surgical

Staffed Beds: 76 **Admissions**: 2894 **Census**: 37 **Outpatient Visits**: 67060 **Births**: 236 **Total Expense ($000)**: 71958 **Payroll Expense ($000)**: 24586 **Personnel**: 276

COLUMBIA—Lexington County

PRISMA HEALTH BAPTIST PARKRIDGE HOSPITAL (420106), 400 Palmetto Health Parkway, Zip 29212–1760, Mailing Address: P.O. Box 2266, Zip 29202–2266; tel. 803/907–7000, **A**1 3 5 10 **F**1 3 8 11 13 15 18 29 30 34 35 40 50 57 59 64 70 73 75 76 77 79 80 81 85 86 87 107 110 111 115 119 128 130 132 146 147 149 **P**6 **S** Prisma Health – Midlands, Columbia, SC
Primary Contact: Michael N. Bundy, Chief Executive Officer
COO: Emilie Keene, FACHE, Interim Chief Operating Officer
Web address: https://www.prismahealth.org/locations/hospitals/baptist-parkridge-hospital
Control: Other not–for–profit (including NFP Corporation) **Service**: General medical and surgical

Staffed Beds: 72 **Admissions**: 5308 **Census**: 57 **Outpatient Visits**: 85893 **Births**: 1128 **Total Expense ($000)**: 140873 **Payroll Expense ($000)**: 35769 **Personnel**: 428

COLUMBIA—Richland County

COLUMBIA VA HEALTH CARE SYSTEM, 6439 Garners Ferry Road, Zip 29209–1639; tel. 803/776–4000, (Nonreporting) **A**1 3 5 **S** Department of Veterans Affairs, Washington, DC
Primary Contact: Rebecca Strini, Acting Director
CMO: Bernard L. DeKoning, M.D., Chief of Staff
CIO: Steve Chalphant, Director Information Management Service Line
CHR: Phyllis Jones, Chief Human Resources
CNO: Ruth Mustard, R.N., MSN, Suffix, Associate Director Nursing and Patient Services
Web address: www.columbiasc.va.gov/
Control: Veterans Affairs, Government, federal **Service**: General medical and surgical

Staffed Beds: 112

★ **CONTINUECARE HOSPITAL AT PALMETTO HEALTH BAPTIST (422006)**, Taylor at Marion Street, Zip 29220, Mailing Address: PO BOX 11069, Zip 29211–1069; tel. 803/296–3757, (Nonreporting) **A**2 10 22 **S** Community Hospital Corporation, Plano, TX
Primary Contact: Holly Powell, Interim Chief Executive Officer
Web address: www.continuecare.org/palmetto//
Control: Other not–for–profit (including NFP Corporation) **Service**: Acute long-term care hospital

Staffed Beds: 35

ENCOMPASS HEALTH REHABILITATION HOSPITAL OF COLUMBIA (423025), 2935 Colonial Drive, Zip 29203–6811; tel. 803/254–7777, **A**1 10 **F**1 29 30 34 50 53 60 68 74 75 77 79 90 91 93 96 128 148 149 **S** Encompass Health Corporation, Birmingham, AL
Primary Contact: Nicole Smith. Hendricks Woods, FACHE, Chief Executive Officer
CFO: Jessica Burriss, Chief Financial Officer
CMO: Devin Troyer, M.D., Medical Director
CHR: Luanne Burton, Director Human Resources
CNO: April Brooks, Chief Nursing Officer
Web address: www.healthsouthcolumbia.com
Control: Corporation, Investor–owned (for–profit) **Service**: Rehabilitation

Staffed Beds: 96 **Admissions**: 2063 **Census**: 67 **Outpatient Visits**: 0 **Births**: 0 **Personnel**: 277

G. WERBER BRYAN PSYCHIATRIC HOSPITAL (424005), 220 Faison Drive, Zip 29203–3210; tel. 803/935–7140, **A**1 3 10 **F**1 4 30 50 74 75 97 98 99 101 103 128 130 132 135 146
Primary Contact: Allen McEniry, Interim Director
COO: Jaclyn Upfield, Chief Operating Officer
CIO: Sam Livingston, Information Resource Consultant
CHR: Kim Church, Manager Human Resources
Web address: www.scdmh.org
Control: State, Government, Nonfederal **Service**: Psychiatric

Staffed Beds: 157 **Admissions**: 326 **Census**: 128 **Personnel**: 585

MORRIS VILLAGE ALCOHOL AND DRUG ADDICTION TREATMENT CENTER, 610 Faison Drive, Zip 29203–3218; tel. 803/935–7100, **F**1 4 29 39 53 61 67 74 75 87 98 128 130 132 146
Primary Contact: George McConnell, Director
Web address: www.state.sc.us/dmh/morrisvillage/home.html
Control: State, Government, Nonfederal **Service**: Substance Use Disorder

Staffed Beds: 45 **Admissions**: 776 **Census**: 52 **Personnel**: 152

MUSC HEALTH COLUMBIA MEDICAL CENTER DOWNTOWN (420026), 2435 Forest Drive, Zip 29204–2098; tel. 803/865–4500, (Includes MUSC HEALTH COLUMBIA MEDICAL CENTER NORTHEAST, 120 Gateway Corporate Boulevard, Columbia, South Carolina, Zip 29203–9611, tel. 803/865–4500; Matthew Littlejohn, FACHE, Chief Executive Officer) **A**1 10 19 **F**1 3 11 15 17 18 20 22 24 26 28 29 30 34 35 38 40 42 44 45 49 50 53 54 57 58 59 60 63 64 70 74 75 77 79 81 84 85 86 87 90 93 100 107 108 110 111 115 119 128 129 130 132 135 141 146 148 **S** MUSC Health, Charleston, SC
Primary Contact: Matthew Littlejohn, FACHE, Chief Executive Officer
CFO: Holt Smith, Chief Financial Officer
CIO: Daniel King, Director, Information Systems
CHR: Jill Anelli, Director, Human Resources
CNO: Maria Calloway, Chief Nursing Officer
Web address: https://muschealth.org/columbia-medical-center-downtown
Control: Hospital district or authority, Government, Nonfederal **Service**: General medical and surgical

Staffed Beds: 199 **Admissions**: 8224 **Census**: 99 **Outpatient Visits**: 187402 **Births**: 0 **Personnel**: 1786

MUSC HEALTH COLUMBIA MEDICAL CENTER NORTHEAST See Musc Health Columbia Medical Center Downtown, Columbia

PALMETTO HEALTH CHILDREN'S HOSPITAL See Prisma Health Children's Hospital

Hospitals, U.S. / SOUTH CAROLINA

☐ **PRISMA HEALTH BAPTIST HOSPITAL (420086)**, Taylor at Marion Street, Zip 29220–0001; tel. 803/296–5010, **A**1 2 3 5 10 **F**1 3 5 11 12 13 15 18 29 30 31 34 35 37 38 40 45 46 47 48 49 57 59 61 63 64 70 72 73 74 75 76 77 78 79 80 81 84 85 86 87 98 99 100 101 102 103 104 105 107 108 110 111 115 117 118 119 126 128 130 132 146 147 149 152 153 **P**6 **S** Prisma Health – Midlands, Columbia, SC
Primary Contact: Michael N. Bundy, Chief Executive Officer
COO: James M Bridges, Executive Vice President and Chief Operating Officer
CFO: Paul K Duane, Chief Financial Officer and Office of Health Reform
CMO: Mark J Mayson, M.D., Medical Director
CIO: Michelle Edwards, Executive Vice President Information Technology
CHR: Trip Gregory, Senior Vice President Human Resources
Web address: www.palmettohealth.org
Control: Other not-for-profit (including NFP Corporation) **Service**: General medical and surgical

Staffed Beds: 232 **Admissions**: 11309 **Census**: 161 **Outpatient Visits**: 119266 **Births**: 2129 **Total Expense ($000)**: 248641 **Payroll Expense ($000)**: 74338 **Personnel**: 984

☐ **PRISMA HEALTH RICHLAND HOSPITAL (420018)**, 5 Richland Medical Park Drive, Zip 29203–6897; tel. 803/434–7000, (Includes PRISMA HEALTH CHILDREN'S HOSPITAL, Five Richland Medical Park Drive, Columbia, South Carolina, Zip 29203–6863, Five Richland Medical Park Dr, Zip 29203–6863, tel. 803/434–6882) **A**1 2 3 5 8 10 19 **F**1 3 7 11 13 15 16 17 18 19 20 22 24 26 28 29 30 31 32 34 35 38 39 40 41 43 45 46 47 48 49 50 52 53 54 55 56 57 58 59 61 63 64 65 66 70 72 73 74 75 76 77 78 79 80 81 84 85 86 87 88 89 92 93 94 97 98 100 101 102 107 110 111 114 115 119 124 126 128 129 130 131 132 134 146 147 148 149 150 154 156 **P**6 **S** Prisma Health – Midlands, Columbia, SC
Primary Contact: Michael N. Bundy, Chief Executive Officer
CFO: Paul K Duane, Chief Financial Officer and Office of Health Reform
CMO: Eric Brown, M.D., Physician Executive
CNO: Carole A Siegfried, MSN, R.N., Campus Nurse Executive
Web address: https://prismahealth.org/hospitals/richland-hospital
Control: Other not-for-profit (including NFP Corporation) **Service**: General medical and surgical

Staffed Beds: 598 **Admissions**: 28168 **Census**: 527 **Outpatient Visits**: 523514 **Births**: 2232 **Total Expense ($000)**: 933351 **Payroll Expense ($000)**: 260026 **Personnel**: 3060

SOUTH CAROLINA DEPARTMENT OF CORRECTIONS HOSPITAL, 4344 Broad River Road, Zip 29210–4098; tel. 803/896–8567, (Nonreporting) **A**3
Primary Contact: John Solomon, M.D., Director
Web address: www.doc.sc.gov/
Control: State, Government, Nonfederal **Service**: Hospital unit of an institution (prison hospital, college infirmary, etc.)

Staffed Beds: 70

WILLIAM S. HALL PSYCHIATRIC INSTITUTE (424003), 1800 Colonial Drive, Zip 29203–6827; tel. 803/898–1693, (Nonreporting) **A**10
Primary Contact: Mary Jane Hicks, Hospital Director
COO: Doug Glover, Controller
CFO: Doug Glover, Controller
CMO: Phyllis Bryant–Mobley, M.D., Director Medical Services
CIO: Mesa Foard, Director Information technology
CHR: Kim Church, Manager Human Resources
Web address: www.scdmh.org
Control: State, Government, Nonfederal **Service**: Psychiatric

Staffed Beds: 37

CONWAY—Horry County

★ ⇑ **CONWAY MEDICAL CENTER (420049)**, 300 Singleton Ridge Road, Zip 29526–9142; tel. 843/347–7111, **A**3 5 10 21 **F**1 3 8 9 11 12 13 15 18 20 22 26 28 29 30 31 34 35 37 40 43 45 46 47 49 50 51 53 54 57 59 60 61 63 64 68 70 71 73 74 75 76 77 78 79 81 82 84 85 86 87 89 90 93 94 97 102 107 108 110 111 114 115 118 119 126 127 128 129 130 131 132 135 146 147 148 149 150 154 156 **P**6
Primary Contact: Brian Argo, Chief Executive Officer
CMO: Paul McKinley Richardson Jr, Chief Medical Officer
CIO: David Crutchfield, Vice President, Information Services & Chief Information Officer
CHR: Matthew J. Securro, Vice President, Human Resources
CNO: Tony L. Minshew, Vice President, Patient Care Services
Web address: www.conwaymedicalcenter.com
Control: Other not-for-profit (including NFP Corporation) **Service**: General medical and surgical

Staffed Beds: 178 **Admissions**: 8646 **Census**: 135 **Outpatient Visits**: 478679 **Births**: 1509 **Personnel**: 1669

☐ **LIGHTHOUSE BEHAVIORAL HEALTH HOSPITAL (424002)**, 152 Waccamaw Medical Park Drive, Zip 29526–8901; tel. 843/347–8871, **A**1 3 10 **F**1 4 5 98 99 101 102 103 104 128 153 154 **P**5 **S** Universal Health Services, Inc., King of Prussia, PA
Primary Contact: Julie Parker, Chief Executive Officer
CFO: Gabrielle Gale, Chief Financial Officer
CMO: Adedapo Oduwole, M.D., Medical Director
CIO: Gabrielle Gale, Chief Financial Officer
CHR: Lois Woodall, Director Human Resources
Web address: www.lighthousecarecenterofconway.com/
Control: Corporation, Investor–owned (for–profit) **Service**: Psychiatric

Staffed Beds: 105 **Admissions**: 2940 **Census**: 66 **Personnel**: 149

DILLON—Dillon County

⇑ **MCLEOD HEALTH DILLON (420005)**, 301 East Jackson Street, Zip 29536–2509, Mailing Address: P.O. Box 1327, Zip 29536–1327; tel. 843/774–4111, **A**10 21 **F**1 3 11 13 15 28 29 30 34 35 38 40 44 45 50 57 59 62 63 64 65 68 70 74 75 76 79 80 81 85 87 89 102 107 108 110 111 114 119 126 127 128 130 133 134 135 145 146 148 149 154 **P**3 6 **S** McLeod Health, Florence, SC
Primary Contact: Jenny Hardee, MSN, Chief Executive Officer
CMO: Catherine Rabon, M.D., Regional Chief Medical Officer
CHR: Cynthia Causey, Associate Administrator Human and Mission Services
CNO: Esther Marcia Wilds, Vice President and Chief Nursing Officer
Web address: https://www.mcleodhealth.org/locations/mcleod-dillon/
Control: Other not-for-profit (including NFP Corporation) **Service**: General medical and surgical

Staffed Beds: 40 **Admissions**: 1770 **Census**: 19 **Outpatient Visits**: 58279 **Births**: 238 **Total Expense ($000)**: 52043 **Payroll Expense ($000)**: 17375 **Personnel**: 271

EASLEY—Pickens County

☐ **PRISMA HEALTH BAPTIST EASLEY HOSPITAL (420015)**, 200 Fleetwood Drive, Zip 29640–2022, Mailing Address: P.O. Box 2129, Zip 29641–2129; tel. 864/442–7200, **A**1 3 5 10 **F**1 3 11 15 18 28 29 30 34 35 40 45 56 57 59 64 70 74 75 77 79 80 81 84 85 87 89 94 107 111 114 115 119 128 129 130 132 146 147
Primary Contact: Hunter Kome, Chief Operations Executive
CFO: Kathleen Stapleton, Chief Financial Officer
CIO: Cynthia Ellenburg, Director Health Information Services
CHR: Richard B Posey, Director Human Resources
CNO: Mary Ann Hunter, Director Nursing Services
Web address: https://www.ghs.org/locations/baptist-easley-medical-campus/
Control: Other not-for-profit (including NFP Corporation) **Service**: General medical and surgical

Staffed Beds: 90 **Admissions**: 4829 **Census**: 54 **Outpatient Visits**: 114581 **Births**: 0 **Total Expense ($000)**: 100513 **Payroll Expense ($000)**: 32802 **Personnel**: 394

EDGEFIELD—Edgefield County

EDGEFIELD COUNTY HEALTHCARE (421304), 300 Ridge Medical Plaza, Zip 29824–4525, Mailing Address: PO Box 590, Zip 29824–4525; tel. 803/637–3174, (Nonreporting) **A**10 18
Primary Contact: Will Gordon, Vice President and Chief Administrative Officer
CFO: Lori Jacobs, Chief Financial Officer
CMO: Tami Massey, M.D., Chief of Medical Staff
CIO: Juli Corley, Chief Information Officer
CHR: Theresa Stover, Chief Human Resource Officer
CNO: Cheryl Faust, Chief Nursing Officer
Web address: https://www.selfregional.org/edgefield-county-healthcare/
Control: County, Government, Nonfederal **Service**: General medical and surgical

Staffed Beds: 25

ELGIN—Kershaw County

☐ **MIDLANDS REGIONAL REHABILITATION HOSPITAL (423034)**, 20 Pinnacle Parkway, Zip 29045–8389; tel. 803/438–8890, **A**1 10 **F**1 3 75 90 128 148 **S** Ernest Health, Inc., Albuquerque, NM
Primary Contact: Rebecca Cartright, FACHE, Chief Executive Officer
Web address: www.mrrh.ernesthealth.com
Control: Corporation, Investor–owned (for–profit) **Service**: Rehabilitation

Staffed Beds: 40 **Admissions**: 693 **Census**: 27 **Personnel**: 76

Hospital, Medicare Provider Number, Address, Telephone, Approval, Facility, and Physician Codes, Health Care System

★ American Hospital Association (AHA) membership   ◯ Healthcare Facilities Accreditation Program   ⇑ Center for Improvement in Healthcare Quality Accreditation
☐ The Joint Commission accreditation   ◇ DNV Healthcare Inc. accreditation   △ Commission on Accreditation of Rehabilitation Facilities (CARF) accreditation

Hospitals, U.S. / SOUTH CAROLINA

FAIRFAX—Allendale County

★ **ALLENDALE COUNTY HOSPITAL (421300)**, 1787 Allendale Fairfax Highway, Zip 29827–9133, Mailing Address: P.O. Box 218, Zip 29827–0218; tel. 803/632–3311, **A**10 18 **F**1 3 15 34 35 40 56 57 59 61 64 67 68 77 90 92 94 97 107 110 114 119 127 128 133 147
Primary Contact: Lari Gooding, Chief Executive Officer
CFO: Teresa Hicks, Chief Financial Officer
CIO: Tammy Smith, Director
CHR: Tammy Smith, Director
CNO: Becky Rowell, R.N., Director
Web address: www.achospital.org
Control: County, Government, Nonfederal **Service**: General medical and surgical

Staffed Beds: 25 **Admissions**: 111 **Census**: 1 **Outpatient Visits**: 18068 **Births**: 0 **Personnel**: 121

FLORENCE—Florence County

✠ **ENCOMPASS HEALTH REHABILITATION HOSPITAL OF FLORENCE (423026)**, 900 East Cheves Street, Zip 29506–2704; tel. 843/679–9000, **A**1 10 **F**1 9 28 29 34 35 56 57 59 60 75 77 82 86 87 90 91 92 93 95 96 128 148 149 **S** Encompass Health Corporation, Birmingham, AL
Primary Contact: John Jones, Chief Executive Officer
CFO: Robert Wheeler, Controller
CMO: Adora Matthews, M.D., Medical Director
CHR: Susan Trantham, Director Human Resources
CNO: Amanda Lusk Kidd, Chief Nursing Officer
Web address: https://encompasshealth.com/florencerehab
Control: Corporation, Investor–owned (for–profit) **Service**: Rehabilitation

Staffed Beds: 88 **Admissions**: 1216 **Census**: 40 **Outpatient Visits**: 0 **Births**: 0 **Personnel**: 149

★ ⇑ **MCLEOD REGIONAL MEDICAL CENTER (420051)**, 555 East Cheves Street, Zip 29506–2617, Mailing Address: P.O. Box 100551, Zip 29502–0551; tel. 843/777–2000, (Includes MCLEOD HEALTH DARLINGTON, 701 Cashua Ferry Road, Darlington, South Carolina, Zip 29532–8488, P O Box 1859, Zip 29540, tel. 843/395–1100; John Will McLeod, Chief Executive Officer) **A**2 3 5 10 19 21 **F**1 3 11 13 15 17 18 19 20 21 22 24 26 28 29 30 31 32 34 35 38 39 40 43 44 45 46 47 48 49 50 51 53 54 56 57 58 59 60 61 62 63 64 65 66 68 70 72 73 74 75 76 78 79 80 81 84 85 87 88 89 94 97 98 100 102 103 107 108 110 111 115 117 119 120 121 123 124 126 127 128 129 130 131 132 134 135 144 145 146 147 148 149 150 154 **P**3 6 **S** McLeod Health, Florence, SC
Primary Contact: John Will. McLeod, Chief Executive Officer
COO: Michelle Logan–Owens, Ph.D., R.N., Chief Operating Officer
CMO: Clifford Dale Lusk, M.D., Senior Vice President of Corporate Quality and Safety and Executive Medical Officer
CNO: Tony Derrick, MSN, R.N., Vice President and Chief Nursing Officer
Web address: https://www.mcleodhealth.org/locations/mcleod-regional-medical-center-florence/
Control: Other not–for–profit (including NFP Corporation) **Service**: General medical and surgical

Staffed Beds: 551 **Admissions**: 23190 **Census**: 407 **Outpatient Visits**: 250278 **Births**: 1879 **Total Expense ($000)**: 870327 **Payroll Expense ($000)**: 250542 **Personnel**: 3370

✠ △ **MUSC HEALTH FLORENCE MEDICAL CENTER (420091)**, 805 Pamplico Highway, Zip 29505–6050, Mailing Address: P.O. Box 100550, Zip 29502–0550; tel. 843/674–5000, **A**1 3 7 10 19 **F**1 3 4 8 11 15 17 18 20 22 24 26 28 29 31 34 35 40 43 45 46 47 49 53 56 57 59 64 67 70 74 75 77 78 79 81 82 87 89 94 107 108 110 111 115 117 119 120 121 126 128 129 130 131 132 135 146 148 149 157 **S** MUSC Health, Charleston, SC
Primary Contact: Jay Hinesley, FACHE, Chief Executive Officer
COO: Kyle Baxter, Chief Operating Officer
CFO: Loren Rials, Chief Financial Officer
CIO: Lynn Northcutt, Chief Information Officer
CHR: Kay Douglas, Human Resources Director
CNO: Costa King Cockfield, Chief Nursing Officer
Web address: www.carolinashospital.com
Control: Hospital district or authority, Government, Nonfederal **Service**: General medical and surgical

Staffed Beds: 183 **Admissions**: 9040 **Census**: 131 **Outpatient Visits**: 198189 **Personnel**: 1739

✠ **REGENCY HOSPITAL OF FLORENCE (422007)**, 805 Pamplico Highway, 2nd and 3rd Floors, South Tower, Zip 29505–6047, Mailing Address: 805 Pamplico Highway 2nd and 3rd Floors, South Tower, Zip 29505–6047; tel. 843/661–3471, **A**1 10 **F**1 3 29 34 35 57 58 77 80 85 90 100 128 130 148 **S** Select Medical Corporation, Mechanicsburg, PA
Primary Contact: Amy Metz, MSN, R.N., Chief Executive Officer
CMO: Stephen Dersch, M.D., President Medical Staff
CHR: Tina Stokes, Manager Human Resources
Web address: www.regencyhospital.com
Control: Corporation, Investor–owned (for–profit) **Service**: Acute long–term care hospital

Staffed Beds: 44 **Admissions**: 510 **Census**: 37 **Outpatient Visits**: 0 **Births**: 0 **Personnel**: 136

FORT JACKSON—Richland County

★ **MONCRIEF ARMY COMMUNITY HOSPITAL**, 4500 Stuart Street, Zip 29207–5700; tel. 803/751–2160, (Nonreporting) **A**5 **S** Department of the Army, Office of the Surgeon General, Falls Church, VA
Primary Contact: Colonel Tara Hall, Commander
Web address: https://moncrief.tricare.mil/
Control: Army, Government, federal **Service**: General medical and surgical

Staffed Beds: 60

GAFFNEY—Cherokee County

★ ⇑ **CHEROKEE MEDICAL CENTER (420043)**, 1530 North Limestone Street, Zip 29340–4738; tel. 864/487–4271, **A**10 21 **F**1 3 15 18 29 34 35 40 45 46 53 57 59 63 64 70 75 79 80 81 85 86 87 107 108 110 111 115 119 127 128 129 130 131 132 149 154 **S** Spartanburg Regional Healthcare System, Spartanburg, SC
Primary Contact: Cody Butts, President
CFO: Christine Poplawski, Chief Financial Officer
CMO: Frank Phillips, M.D., Chief of Staff
CIO: John Odonell, Director Information Systems
CHR: Angie Benfield, Director Human Resources
CNO: Mychelle Ross, R.N., Chief Nursing Officer
Web address: www.maryblackgaffney.com/mary-black-gaffney/home.aspx
Control: Hospital district or authority, Government, Nonfederal **Service**: General medical and surgical

Staffed Beds: 31 **Admissions**: 1210 **Census**: 18 **Births**: 0 **Personnel**: 546

GEORGETOWN—Georgetown County

✠ **TIDELANDS GEORGETOWN MEMORIAL HOSPITAL (420020)**, 606 Black River Road, Zip 29440–3368, Mailing Address: P.O. Box 421718, Zip 29442–4203; tel. 843/527–7000, **A**1 5 10 19 **F**1 3 12 15 17 18 20 22 26 28 29 30 31 32 34 35 40 45 46 49 50 53 56 57 59 60 61 64 65 68 70 74 75 77 78 79 81 82 84 85 86 87 89 90 93 94 100 102 107 108 110 111 115 118 119 128 129 130 131 132 133 135 146 147 148 **S** Tidelands Health, Murrells Inlet, SC
Primary Contact: Bruce P. Bailey, President & Chief Executive Officer
COO: Gayle L Resetar, Executive Vice President and Chief Operating Officer
CFO: Elizabeth S. Ward, Chief Financial Officer
CHR: James F Harper, Senior Vice President and Chief Human Resources Officer
Web address: www.tidelandshealth.org
Control: Other not–for–profit (including NFP Corporation) **Service**: General medical and surgical

Staffed Beds: 69 **Admissions**: 3441 **Census**: 45 **Outpatient Visits**: 204799 **Births**: 0 **Total Expense ($000)**: 189668 **Payroll Expense ($000)**: 66254 **Personnel**: 847

GREENVILLE—Greenville County

BON SECOURS ST. FRANCIS EASTSIDE See St. Francis Eastside

✠ △ **BON SECOURS ST. FRANCIS HEALTH SYSTEM (420023)**, 1 Saint Francis Drive, Zip 29601–3955; tel. 864/255–1000, (Includes ST. FRANCIS EASTSIDE, 125 Commonwealth Drive, Greenville, South Carolina, Zip 29615–4812, tel. 864/675–4000) **A**1 2 7 10 **F**1 3 8 17 18 20 22 24 26 28 29 30 31 34 35 37 40 44 45 46 47 48 49 50 51 57 59 60 62 64 68 70 71 74 75 77 78 79 81 82 84 85 86 87 89 90 92 94 96 97 107 108 111 114 115 118 119 121 124 126 128 129 130 132 135 136 141 146 148 149 154 **S** Bon Secours Mercy Health, Cincinnati, OH
Primary Contact: Matthew T. Caldwell, Market President
COO: Jennifer Wehrs, Market Chief Operating Officer– Greenville Market
CFO: Ronnie Hyatt, Senior Vice President Finance and Chief Financial Officer
CIO: Rita Hooker, Administrative Director Information Services
CHR: Fernando Fleites, Senior Vice President Human Resources
CNO: Teri Ficicchy, R.N., MSN, Chief Nursing Officer
Web address: https://www.bonsecours.com/locations/hospitals-medical-centers/greenville/st-francis-downtown
Control: Other not–for–profit (including NFP Corporation) **Service**: General medical and surgical

Staffed Beds: 248 **Admissions**: 19743 **Census**: 195 **Outpatient Visits**: 87463 **Total Expense ($000)**: 395766 **Payroll Expense ($000)**: 103028

Hospitals, U.S. / SOUTH CAROLINA

CHILDREN'S HOSPITAL See GHS Children's Hospital

✠ **ENCOMPASS HEALTH REHABILITATION HOSPITAL OF GREENVILLE (423035)**, 3372 Laurens Road, Zip 29607; tel. 864/537-4600, (Nonreporting) **A**1 10 **S** Encompass Health Corporation, Birmingham, AL
Primary Contact: Joshua Trout, Chief Executive Officer
CFO: Stephanie Johnson, Controller
CMO: Angelica Soberon-Cassar, M.D., Chief Medical Officer
CHR: Tara Myers, Director, Human Resources
CNO: Cheryl Fieldhouse, Chief Nursing Officer
Web address: www.encompasshealth.com/greenvillerehab
Control: Corporation, Investor-owned (for-profit) **Service**: Rehabilitation

Staffed Beds: 40

☐ △ **PRISMA HEALTH GREENVILLE MEMORIAL HOSPITAL (420078)**, 701 Grove Road, Zip 29605-4295; tel. 864/455-7000, (Includes GHS CHILDREN'S HOSPITAL, 701 Grove Road, Greenville, South Carolina, Zip 29605-5611, tel. 864/455-7000; MARSHALL I. PICKENS HOSPITAL, 701 Grove Road, Greenville, South Carolina, Zip 29605-5601, tel. 864/455-8988; ROGER C. PEACE REHABILITATION HOSPITAL, 701 Grove Road, Greenville, South Carolina, Zip 29605-4295, tel. 864/455-7000) **A**1 2 3 5 7 8 10 19 **F**1 3 11 13 15 17 18 19 20 22 24 26 27 28 29 30 31 32 34 35 36 38 39 40 41 43 44 45 46 47 48 49 50 51 52 53 54 56 57 58 59 61 64 65 66 68 70 72 73 74 75 76 77 78 79 80 81 82 84 85 86 87 88 89 90 91 92 93 94 96 97 98 99 100 101 102 103 104 105 107 108 110 111 114 115 116 117 118 119 120 121 123 124 125 128 129 130 132 134 136 138 141 142 145 146 147 148 149 153 154 **S** Prisma Health - Midlands, Columbia, SC
Primary Contact: Tim Brookshire, FACHE, Chief Operations Executive
COO: Greg Rusnak, Executive Vice President and Chief Operating Officer
CFO: Terri T. Newsom, Vice President of Finance and Chief Financial Officer
CMO: Angelo Sinopoli, M.D., Vice President Clinical Integration and Chief Medical Officer
CIO: Rich Rogers, Vice President Information Services
CHR: Doug Dorman, Vice President Human Resources
CNO: Michelle T Smith, R.N., MSN, FACHE, Vice President Nursing Chief Nursing Officer Chief Experience Officer
Web address: www.ghs.org
Control: Other not-for-profit (including NFP Corporation) **Service**: General medical and surgical

Staffed Beds: 846 **Admissions:** 42410 **Census:** 706 **Outpatient Visits:** 789191 **Births:** 4421 **Total Expense ($000):** 1363229 **Payroll Expense ($000):** 340192 **Personnel:** 4935

☐ **PRISMA HEALTH PATEWOOD HOSPITAL (420102)**, 175 Patewood Drive, Zip 29615-3570; tel. 864/797-1000, **A**1 3 5 10 **F**1 3 11 13 18 26 29 30 35 37 45 50 64 73 74 76 77 79 80 81 82 85 86 116 117 128 130 131 146 147 149 **S** Prisma Health - Midlands, Columbia, SC
Primary Contact: Todd Walker, Chief Executive Officer
Web address: https://prismahealth.org/locations/hospitals/patewood-hospital
Control: Other not-for-profit (including NFP Corporation) **Service**: Surgical

Staffed Beds: 76 **Admissions:** 3704 **Census:** 22 **Outpatient Visits:** 137641 **Births:** 3194 **Total Expense ($000):** 159722 **Payroll Expense ($000):** 35694 **Personnel:** 341

✠ **REGENCY HOSPITAL OF GREENVILLE (422009)**, 1 Saint Francis Drive, Zip 29601-3955, Mailing Address: 1 St Francis Drive, Zip 29601-3955; tel. 864/255-1438, **A**1 10 **F**1 3 29 56 75 85 128 148 149 **S** Select Medical Corporation, Mechanicsburg, PA
Primary Contact: Tammy Ratliff, Chief Executive Officer
Web address: www.regencyhospital.com
Control: Corporation, Investor-owned (for-profit) **Service**: Acute long-term care hospital

Staffed Beds: 32 **Admissions:** 269 **Census:** 19 **Outpatient Visits:** 0 **Births:** 0 **Personnel:** 94

☐ **SHRINERS HOSPITALS FOR CHILDREN-GREENVILLE (423300)**, 950 West Faris Road, Zip 29605-4277; tel. 864/271-3444, (Nonreporting) **A**1 3 10 **S** Shriners Hospitals for Children, Tampa, FL
Primary Contact: William Munley, Administrator
CFO: John Conti, Director Finance
CMO: J. Michael Wattenbarger, M.D., Chief of Staff
CHR: Willis E Tisdale, Director Human Resources
CNO: Allison Leigh Windas, Director of Patient Care Services-Nurse Executive
Web address: www.greenvilleshrinershospital.org
Control: Other not-for-profit (including NFP Corporation) **Service**: Children's orthopedic

Staffed Beds: 15

GREENWOOD—Greenwood County

☐ **GREENWOOD REGIONAL REHABILITATION HOSPITAL (423030)**, 1530 Parkway, Zip 29646-4027; tel. 864/330-1800, **A**1 10 **F**1 3 75 90 128 143 148 **S** Ernest Health, Inc., Albuquerque, NM
Primary Contact: Kristin Manske, Chief Executive Officer
CFO: Charity Martin, Controller and Regional Business Officer Manager
CMO: Cam Monda, D.O., Medical Director
CHR: Michelle Watkins, Human Resources Manager
CNO: Jessica Lawson, Director of Nursing
Web address: www.grrh.ernesthealth.com
Control: Corporation, Investor-owned (for-profit) **Service**: Rehabilitation

Staffed Beds: 42 **Admissions:** 663 **Census:** 28 **Outpatient Visits:** 0 **Births:** 0 **Personnel:** 85

★ ⇑ **SELF REGIONAL HEALTHCARE (420071)**, 1325 Spring Street, Zip 29646-3860; tel. 864/725-4111, **A**2 3 5 10 21 **F**1 3 4 8 11 13 15 17 18 19 20 22 24 26 28 29 30 31 34 35 37 39 40 43 44 45 46 48 49 50 51 55 57 58 59 60 61 62 64 65 68 70 71 72 73 74 75 76 77 78 79 80 81 82 85 86 87 89 90 91 94 96 97 98 100 102 103 107 108 110 111 114 115 117 118 119 120 121 123 124 126 127 128 129 130 132 134 135 146 147 148 149 154
Primary Contact: Matthew T. Logan, M.D., President and Chief Executive Officer
CFO: Timothy Evans, Vice President and Chief Financial Officer
CMO: Priya Kumar, Chief Medical Officer and Vice President of Medical Affairs
CIO: Andy Hartung, Assistant Vice President of Information Systems and Chief Information Officer
CHR: Brent Parris, Vice President of Human Resources
CNO: Carol Stefaniuk, Chief Nursing Officer, Vice President, Long Term Acute Care
Web address: www.selfregional.org
Control: State, Government, Nonfederal **Service**: General medical and surgical

Staffed Beds: 322 **Admissions:** 10153 **Census:** 161 **Outpatient Visits:** 554636 **Births:** 1126 **Personnel:** 2202

GREER—Greenville County

☐ **CAROLINA CENTER FOR BEHAVIORAL HEALTH (424010)**, 2700 East Phillips Road, Zip 29650-4816; tel. 864/235-2335, (Nonreporting) **A**1 10 **S** Universal Health Services, Inc., King of Prussia, PA
Primary Contact: John Willingham, Division Vice President
CFO: James P Boynton Jr, Chief Financial Officer
CMO: Gergana Dimitrova, M.D., Medical Director
CHR: Ginny Savage, Director of Human Resources
CNO: Jennifer Daigle, R.N., Director of Nursing and Utilization Review
Web address: www.thecarolinacenter.com
Control: Corporation, Investor-owned (for-profit) **Service**: Psychiatric

Staffed Beds: 138

☐ **PRISMA HEALTH GREER MEMORIAL HOSPITAL (420033)**, 830 South Buncombe Road, Zip 29650-2400; tel. 864/797-8000, **A**1 3 5 10 **F**1 3 11 13 15 18 28 29 30 34 35 40 44 45 46 49 50 51 57 59 64 65 68 69 70 73 76 77 79 80 81 84 85 87 89 94 107 108 110 111 115 119 126 128 130 146 147 148 149 **S** Prisma Health - Midlands, Columbia, SC
Primary Contact: Todd Walker, Chief Executive Officer
Web address: https://prismahealth.org/locations/hospitals/greer-memorial-hospital
Control: Other not-for-profit (including NFP Corporation) **Service**: General medical and surgical

Staffed Beds: 83 **Admissions:** 5516 **Census:** 64 **Outpatient Visits:** 109953 **Births:** 915 **Total Expense ($000):** 116611 **Payroll Expense ($000):** 36032 **Personnel:** 449

GREER—Spartanburg County

★ ⇑ **PELHAM MEDICAL CENTER (420103)**, 250 Westmoreland Road, Zip 29651-9013; tel. 864/530-6000, **A**10 21 **F**1 3 11 15 18 20 26 29 30 34 35 37 40 45 49 50 54 57 59 64 68 70 74 75 77 79 80 81 82 84 85 86 87 90 94 96 107 108 110 111 114 115 117 118 119 126 128 130 146 148 149 154 **S** Spartanburg Regional Healthcare System, Spartanburg, SC
Primary Contact: Anthony Kouskolekas, FACHE, President
CNO: Myra C Whiten, Chief Nursing Officer
Web address: www.pelhammedicalcenter.com
Control: Hospital district or authority, Government, Nonfederal **Service**: General medical and surgical

Staffed Beds: 48 **Admissions:** 2937 **Census:** 33 **Births:** 0 **Total Expense ($000):** 122681 **Payroll Expense ($000):** 32807 **Personnel:** 526

Hospital, Medicare Provider Number, Address, Telephone, Approval, Facility, and Physician Codes, Health Care System

★ American Hospital Association (AHA) membership ○ Healthcare Facilities Accreditation Program ⇑ Center for Improvement in Healthcare Quality Accreditation
☐ The Joint Commission accreditation ◇ DNV Healthcare Inc. accreditation △ Commission on Accreditation of Rehabilitation Facilities (CARF) accreditation

Hospitals, U.S. / SOUTH CAROLINA

HARDEEVILLE—Jasper County

COASTAL CAROLINA HOSPITAL (420101), 1000 Medical Center Drive, Zip 29927-3446; tel. 843/784-8000, **A**1 10 **F**1 3 11 13 15 28 29 30 34 35 40 42 45 46 47 48 57 59 64 65 70 74 75 76 77 79 81 82 85 90 93 94 107 108 110 111 115 119 126 128 132 146 147 148 154 **S** Novant Health, Winston Salem, NC
Primary Contact: Ryan D. Lee, FACHE, Chief Executive Officer
COO: Christopher Borgstrom, Associate Administrator
CFO: Ronald J. Groteluschen, Chief Financial Officer
CIO: Cheryl Grant, Director Information Systems
CHR: Darlene E. Nester, Market Chief Human Resources Officer
CNO: Christina Brzezinski, Chief Nursing Officer
Web address: www.coastalhospital.com
Control: Corporation, Investor-owned (for-profit) **Service:** General medical and surgical

Staffed Beds: 35 Admissions: 3622 Census: 25 Outpatient Visits: 62798
Births: 788 Total Expense ($000): 75146 Payroll Expense ($000): 22739
Personnel: 281

HARTSVILLE—Darlington County

CAROLINA PINES REGIONAL MEDICAL CENTER (420010), 1304 West Bobo Newsom Highway, Zip 29550-4710; tel. 843/339-2100, **A**1 10 19 **F**1 3 13 15 20 29 30 34 35 37 40 46 49 57 64 70 73 75 76 79 80 81 82 85 86 87 89 90 93 107 108 110 111 119 126 128 129 131 132 135 146 147 148 **S** ScionHealth, Louisville, KY
Primary Contact: William Little, Chief Executive Officer
CFO: Rodney VanDonkelaar, Chief Financial Officer
CMO: Tallulah Holmstrom, M.D., Chief Medical Officer
CIO: Denise Barefoot, Director of Information Technology
CHR: Charlotte Adams, Director of Human Resources
CNO: Christy Moody, R.N., Chief Nursing Officer
Web address: www.cprmc.com
Control: Corporation, Investor-owned (for-profit) **Service:** General medical and surgical

Staffed Beds: 116 Admissions: 3180 Census: 29 Outpatient Visits: 60298
Births: 593 Personnel: 469

HILTON HEAD ISLAND—Beaufort County

HILTON HEAD HOSPITAL (420080), 25 Hospital Center Boulevard, Zip 29926-2738; tel. 843/681-6122, **A**1 10 20 **F**1 3 11 13 15 17 18 20 22 24 26 28 29 30 34 35 37 40 45 46 48 50 54 56 57 59 64 65 67 70 74 76 77 78 79 81 85 86 89 94 96 107 108 110 111 114 115 119 126 128 130 131 132 146 147 148 154 **S** Novant Health, Winston Salem, NC
Primary Contact: Joel C. Taylor, Market Chief Executive Officer
CMO: Glenn Neil Love, M.D., Medical Director
CIO: Stephen Brendler, Director Information Systems
CHR: Darlene E. Nester, Chief Human Resources Officer
Web address: www.hiltonheadregional.com
Control: Partnership, Investor-owned (for-profit) **Service:** General medical and surgical

Staffed Beds: 93 Admissions: 5549 Census: 55 Outpatient Visits: 73830
Births: 222 Total Expense ($000): 115376 Payroll Expense ($000): 29118
Personnel: 356

LANCASTER—Lancaster County

MUSC HEALTH LANCASTER MEDICAL CENTER (420036), 800 West Meeting Street, Zip 29720-2298; tel. 803/286-1214, **A**1 5 10 **F**1 3 11 13 15 17 18 20 29 34 35 40 45 47 48 49 53 54 57 59 60 64 70 73 74 75 76 77 78 79 81 85 87 90 94 98 100 102 107 108 110 111 114 115 117 118 119 126 128 129 130 131 132 135 138 146 147 148 149 154 157 **S** MUSC Health, Charleston, SC
Primary Contact: Joseph Scott. Broome, M.P.H., FACHE, Chief Executive Officer
COO: Richard Warrin, Chief Operating Officer
CFO: Holt Smith, Chief Financial Officer
CMO: Douglas Tiedt, M.D., Chief of Staff
CIO: Chrys Steele, Director Information Systems
CHR: Karen Chapman, Human Resources Director
CNO: Karen Martin, Chief Nursing Officer
Web address: www.springsmemorial.com
Control: Hospital district or authority, Government, Nonfederal **Service:** General medical and surgical

Staffed Beds: 93 Admissions: 4390 Census: 66 Outpatient Visits: 107409
Births: 442 Personnel: 921

☐ **REBOUND BEHAVIORAL HEALTH (424014)**, 134 East Rebound Road, Zip 29720-7712; tel. 855/999-9501, **A**1 10 **F**1 4 98 102 105 128 152 154 **S** Acadia Healthcare Company, Inc., Franklin, TN
Primary Contact: Alli Marion, Chief Executive Officer
Web address: www.reboundbehavioralhealth.com
Control: Corporation, Investor-owned (for-profit) **Service:** Psychiatric

Staffed Beds: 63 Admissions: 2497 Census: 51 Outpatient Visits: 3089
Personnel: 230

LORIS—Horry County

MCLEOD HEALTH LORIS (420105), 3655 Mitchell Street, Zip 29569-2827; tel. 843/716-7000, (Includes MCLEOD SEACOAST, 4000 Highway 9 East, Little River, South Carolina, Zip 29566-7833, tel. 843/390-8100; Monica Vehige, Chief Executive Officer) **A**10 21 **F**1 3 11 13 15 28 29 30 34 35 40 42 44 45 50 51 53 57 59 60 62 63 64 65 68 70 74 75 76 80 81 85 87 89 102 103 107 108 110 111 115 119 128 130 132 134 135 145 146 147 148 149 154 **P**3 6 **S** McLeod Health, Florence, SC
Primary Contact: Michael Scott. Montgomery, Chief Executive Officer, Vice President, McLeod Health
CMO: Matthew Weeks, Chief Medical Officer
CNO: Nancy Barnes, MSN, Vice President and Chief Nursing Officer
Web address: www.mcleodhealth.org
Control: Other not-for-profit (including NFP Corporation) **Service:** General medical and surgical

Staffed Beds: 50 Admissions: 2763 Census: 32 Outpatient Visits: 58849
Births: 457 Total Expense ($000): 270105 Payroll Expense ($000): 89428
Personnel: 365

MANNING—Clarendon County

MCLEOD HEALTH CLARENDON (420109), 10 Hospital Street, Zip 29102-3153, Mailing Address: P.O. Box 550, Zip 29102-0550; tel. 803/433-3000, **A**3 10 21 **F**1 3 11 13 15 28 29 30 34 35 40 44 45 50 53 57 59 63 64 65 68 70 75 76 79 80 81 85 87 89 102 107 108 110 111 114 119 126 127 128 130 132 133 135 145 146 147 148 149 154 **P**3 6 **S** McLeod Health, Florence, SC
Primary Contact: Rachel Gainey, Chief Executive Officer, Vice President McLeod Health
CMO: Catherine Rabon, M.D., Regional Chief Medical Officer
CNO: Kimberly Jolly, Vice President and Chief Nursing Officer
Web address: https://www.mcleodhealth.org/locations/mcleod-clarendon/
Control: Other not-for-profit (including NFP Corporation) **Service:** General medical and surgical

Staffed Beds: 36 Admissions: 1829 Census: 23 Outpatient Visits: 50905
Births: 281 Total Expense ($000): 59469 Payroll Expense ($000): 24838
Personnel: 368

MONCKS CORNER—Berkeley County

BERKELEY REGIONAL MEDICAL CENTER See Moncks Corner Medical Center

MOUNT PLEASANT—Charleston County

EAST COOPER MEDICAL CENTER (420089), 2000 Hospital Drive, Zip 29464-3764; tel. 843/881-0100, **A**1 3 5 10 **F**1 3 13 15 18 20 29 31 34 35 37 40 43 45 46 49 50 51 59 60 64 68 70 73 74 75 76 77 78 79 80 81 82 84 85 86 90 92 93 94 96 100 102 107 108 110 111 114 115 119 126 128 129 130 131 132 135 141 142 146 147 148 149 **S** Novant Health, Winston Salem, NC
Primary Contact: Tyler Sherrill, Chief Executive Officer
CFO: Patrick C Bolander, Chief Financial Officer
CMO: Kevin Keenan, M.D., Physician Advisor
CIO: Michael Foster, Director Information Systems
CHR: Tracy Hunter, Chief Human Resources Officer
CNO: Patrick Beaver, MSN, R.N., Chief Nursing Officer
Web address: www.eastcoopermedctr.com
Control: Corporation, Investor-owned (for-profit) **Service:** General medical and surgical

Staffed Beds: 140 Admissions: 4992 Census: 47 Outpatient Visits: 49362
Births: 1760 Total Expense ($000): 151683 Payroll Expense ($000): 38466 Personnel: 542

ROPER ST. FRANCIS MOUNT PLEASANT HOSPITAL (420104), 3500 Highway 17 North, Zip 29466-9123, Mailing Address: 3500 North Highway 17, Zip 29466-9123; tel. 843/606-7000, **A**1 10 **F**1 3 7 15 28 29 30 34 40 45 46 49 54 59 63 67 68 70 75 77 79 81 84 85 86 87 90 94 102 107 108 110 111 115 118 119 126 128 129 143 146 148 149 154 **S** Bon Secours Mercy Health, Cincinnati, OH
Primary Contact: Ashleigh Wiedemann, Chief Administrative Officer
CMO: Mitchell Siegan, M.D., Chief Medical Officer
CIO: Laishy Williams-Carlson, Chief Information Officer
CHR: Melanie Stith, Vice President Human Resources
CNO: Happy Everett, Chief Nursing Officer
Web address: www.rsfh.com/mount-pleasant-hospital
Control: Other not-for-profit (including NFP Corporation) **Service:** General medical and surgical

Staffed Beds: 52 Admissions: 2994 Census: 33 Outpatient Visits: 64193
Births: 0 Total Expense ($000): 98439 Payroll Expense ($000): 25235
Personnel: 285

Hospitals, U.S. / SOUTH CAROLINA

MT. PLEASANT—Mt. Pleasant County

☒ **VIBRA HOSPITAL OF CHARLESTON (422005)**, 1200 Hospital Drive, Zip 29464; tel. 843/375-4000, **A**1 10 **F**1 3 29 60 75 77 82 85 90 107 114 128 148 **S** Vibra Healthcare, Mechanicsburg, PA
Primary Contact: Tamra Hennis, Chief Executive Officer
CFO: Julia Smith, Chief Financial Officer
CMO: Athena Beldecos, M.D., Medical Director
CHR: Julia Taylor, Area Director Human Resources
Web address: www.vhcharleston.com
Control: Corporation, Investor-owned (for-profit) **Service**: Acute long-term care hospital

Staffed Beds: 42 **Admissions**: 343 **Census**: 33

MULLINS—Marion County

☒ **MUSC HEALTH MARION MEDICAL CENTER (420055)**, 2829 East Highway 76, Zip 29574-6035, Mailing Address: P O Drawer 1150, Marion, Zip 29571-1150; tel. 843/431-2000, **A**1 10 **F**1 3 15 18 29 34 35 40 45 46 53 57 59 70 75 77 79 81 82 87 94 107 108 110 111 115 119 128 130 131 133 135 146 148 149 157 **S** MUSC Health, Charleston, SC
Primary Contact: Jay Hinesley, FACHE, Chief Executive Officer
CFO: Loren Rials, Chief Financial Officer
CMO: Robert DeGrood, M.D., Chief Medical Staff
CIO: Charlie Grantham, Manager Information Systems
CHR: Christi Meggs, Director
CNO: Linda Parnell, Chief Nursing Officer
Web address: https://muschealth.org/locations/marion-medical-center
Control: Hospital district or authority, Government, Nonfederal **Service**: General medical and surgical

Staffed Beds: 56 **Admissions**: 1316 **Census**: 17 **Outpatient Visits**: 56094 **Births**: 0 **Personnel**: 519

MURRELLS INLET—Georgetown County

TIDELANDS HEALTH REHABILITATION HOSPITAL, AN AFFILIATE OF ENCOMPASS HEALTH (423033), 4070 Highway 17 Bypass South, 4th Floor, Zip 29576-5033; tel. 843/652-1415, (Nonreporting) **S** Encompass Health Corporation, Birmingham, AL
Primary Contact: Carey Swanson, Chief Executive Officer
Web address: https://encompasshealth.com/locations/tidelandshealth-murrellsinlet
Control: Corporation, Investor-owned (for-profit) **Service**: Rehabilitation

Staffed Beds: 29

☒ **TIDELANDS WACCAMAW COMMUNITY HOSPITAL (420098)**, 4070 Highway 17 Bypass, Zip 29576-5033, Mailing Address: P.O. Box 421718, Georgetown, Zip 29442-4203; tel. 843/652-1000, **A**1 2 3 10 19 **F**1 3 12 13 15 17 18 28 29 31 32 35 37 40 45 50 56 60 61 64 65 68 70 73 74 75 76 77 78 79 81 82 84 85 86 87 89 90 93 94 100 102 107 108 110 111 115 118 119 128 130 131 146 147 148 **S** Tidelands Health, Murrells Inlet, SC
Primary Contact: Bruce P. Bailey, President & Chief Executive Officer
CFO: Elizabeth S. Ward, Chief Financial Officer
Web address: www.tidelandswaccamawcommunity.org
Control: Other not-for-profit (including NFP Corporation) **Service**: General medical and surgical

Staffed Beds: 126 **Admissions**: 7439 **Census**: 80 **Outpatient Visits**: 119427 **Births**: 843 **Total Expense ($000)**: 177271 **Payroll Expense ($000)**: 43900 **Personnel**: 600

MYRTLE BEACH—Horry County

☒ **GRAND STRAND MEDICAL CENTER (420085)**, 809 82nd Parkway, Zip 29572-4607; tel. 843/692-1000, **A**1 3 5 10 19 **F**1 3 11 12 13 15 17 18 20 22 24 26 28 29 30 34 35 37 38 39 40 41 42 43 45 49 50 54 57 58 59 60 64 67 70 73 74 75 76 77 79 80 81 84 85 86 87 88 89 90 96 98 101 102 104 105 107 108 110 111 114 115 119 120 121 123 124 126 128 130 132 135 146 147 149 153 154 **S** HCA Healthcare, Nashville, TN
Primary Contact: Mark E. Sims, Chief Executive Officer
CFO: Turner Wortham, Chief Financial Officer
Web address: www.grandstrandmed.com
Control: Corporation, Investor-owned (for-profit) **Service**: General medical and surgical

Staffed Beds: 405 **Admissions**: 24513 **Census**: 338 **Outpatient Visits**: 88104 **Births**: 646 **Personnel**: 219

NEWBERRY—Newberry County

☒ **NEWBERRY COUNTY MEMORIAL HOSPITAL (420053)**, 2669 Kinard Street, Zip 29108-2911, Mailing Address: P.O. Box 497, Zip 29108-0497; tel. 803/276-7570, **A**1 10 20 **F**1 3 7 13 15 28 29 30 31 32 34 35 37 40 45 47 53 56 57 59 64 68 70 75 76 77 78 79 81 82 85 86 87 89 90 94 107 108 110 111 115 119 128 130 133 135 143 146 148 149 **P**6 **S** Ovation Healthcare, Brentwood, TN
Primary Contact: John Snow, Chief Executive Officer
CFO: Jeffrey Mullis, Interim Chief Financial Officer
CMO: Mark Davis, M.D., Chief of Staff
CIO: David Wolff, Director Information Technology
CHR: Dyan Bowman, Director Human Resources
Web address: www.newberryhospital.org
Control: County, Government, Nonfederal **Service**: General medical and surgical

Staffed Beds: 54 **Admissions**: 1559 **Census**: 15 **Outpatient Visits**: 37686 **Births**: 220 **Total Expense ($000)**: 57301 **Payroll Expense ($000)**: 20765 **Personnel**: 367

ORANGEBURG—Orangeburg County

☒ **MUSC HEALTH – ORANGEBURG (420068)**, 3000 St Matthews Road, Zip 29118-1442; tel. 803/395-2200, **A**1 2 3 10 **F**1 3 11 12 13 14 15 17 18 20 28 29 30 31 34 35 40 42 43 44 45 46 47 48 49 50 53 57 58 59 60 61 62 64 65 66 68 70 71 73 76 77 78 79 81 82 84 85 86 87 89 90 93 94 97 98 100 101 102 103 104 107 108 110 111 114 115 119 120 121 123 124 127 128 129 130 131 132 135 144 146 147 149 157 **S** MUSC Health, Charleston, SC
Primary Contact: Walter Bennett III, FACHE, Chief Executive Officer
COO: Sem Ganthier, FACHE, Director, Operations
CFO: Anthony B. Sands, Associate Chief Financial Officer
CMO: Nazir A. Adam, M.D., Chief Medical Officer
CIO: Michelle E. Edwards, Interim DCIO of Operations
CHR: Tara M. Morris, Interim Director, Human Resources
CNO: Karrie S. Powell, MSN, R.N., Chief Nursing Officer
Web address: https://muschealth.org/orangeburg/
Control: Hospital district or authority, Government, Nonfederal **Service**: General medical and surgical

Staffed Beds: 204 **Admissions**: 6665 **Census**: 94 **Outpatient Visits**: 230496 **Births**: 451 **Personnel**: 1535

☐ **WILLIAM J. MCCORD ADOLESCENT TREATMENT FACILITY (424013)**, 910 Cook Road, Zip 29118-2124, Mailing Address: P.O. Box 1166, Zip 29116-1166; tel. 803/534-2328, (Nonreporting) **A**1 10
Primary Contact: Michael Dennis, Executive Director
CFO: Laura Murdaugh, Finance Director
CMO: Dorothy Kendall, Medical Director
CNO: Linda Mitchum, Director of Nursing
Web address: www.tccada.com
Control: Other not-for-profit (including NFP Corporation) **Service**: Substance Use Disorder

Staffed Beds: 15

PICKENS—Pickens County

★ ⇧ **ANMED CANNON (420011)**, 123 W G Acker Drive, Zip 29671-2739, Mailing Address: P.O. Box 188, Zip 29671-0188; tel. 864/878-4791, **A**10 21 **F**1 3 11 15 29 34 40 45 50 56 57 59 64 70 75 79 81 85 97 107 108 110 111 114 119 127 128 135 146 149 **P**6 **S** AnMed Health, Anderson, SC
Primary Contact: Michael Cunningham, Vice President for Advancement
CFO: Shon Herron, Director, Finance
CMO: Daniel J. Dahlhausen, M.D., Chief, Medical Staff
Web address: https://anmed.org/locations/anmed-cannon
Control: Other not-for-profit (including NFP Corporation) **Service**: General medical and surgical

Staffed Beds: 24 **Admissions**: 668 **Census**: 7 **Total Expense ($000)**: 25477 **Payroll Expense ($000)**: 11298 **Personnel**: 192

⇧ **ANMED HEALTH CANNON** See Anmed Cannon

ROCK HILL—York County

☒ **ENCOMPASS HEALTH REHABILITATION HOSPITAL OF ROCK HILL (423028)**, 1795 Dr. Frank Gaston Boulevard, Zip 29732-1190; tel. 803/326-3500, (Nonreporting) **A**1 10 **S** Encompass Health Corporation, Birmingham, AL
Primary Contact: Michelle Von Arx, MS, Chief Executive Officer
Web address: https://encompasshealth.com/locations/rockhillrehab
Control: Corporation, Investor-owned (for-profit) **Service**: Rehabilitation

Staffed Beds: 50

Hospital, Medicare Provider Number, Address, Telephone, Approval, Facility, and Physician Codes, Health Care System

★ American Hospital Association (AHA) membership   ○ Healthcare Facilities Accreditation Program   ⇧ Center for Improvement in Healthcare Quality Accreditation
☐ The Joint Commission accreditation   ◇ DNV Healthcare Inc. accreditation   △ Commission on Accreditation of Rehabilitation Facilities (CARF) accreditation

© 2025 AHA Guide

Hospitals, U.S. / SOUTH CAROLINA

☒ **PIEDMONT MEDICAL CENTER (420002)**, 222 Herlong Avenue, Zip 29732; tel. 803/329-1234, **A**1 5 10 **F**1 3 7 11 12 13 15 17 18 20 22 24 26 28 29 30 31 34 35 40 43 45 49 50 57 59 60 64 67 70 72 73 74 75 76 77 78 79 81 82 85 86 89 90 91 93 98 100 102 103 107 108 110 111 114 115 118 119 126 128 130 132 135 146 147 148 **S** TENET Healthcare Corporation, Dallas, TX
Primary Contact: Teresa C. Urquhart, Market Chief Executive Officer
COO: Matthew Hinkle, R.N., Chief Operating Officer
CFO: Stephen Gilmore, Chief Financial Officer
CIO: Joel Dean, Director Information Services
CHR: Elizabeth Elich, Chief Human Resources Officer
CNO: Elaine Hastings, MSN, R.N., Chief Nursing Officer
Web address: www.piedmontmedicalcenter.com
Control: Corporation, Investor-owned (for-profit) **Service:** General medical and surgical

Staffed Beds: 394 **Admissions:** 15824 **Census:** 229 **Outpatient Visits:** 135915 **Births:** 1315 **Total Expense ($000):** 375002 **Payroll Expense ($000):** 119940 **Personnel:** 2300

SENECA—Oconee County

☐ **PRISMA HEALTH OCONEE MEMORIAL HOSPITAL (420009)**, 298 Memorial Drive, Zip 29672-9499; tel. 864/882-3351, **A**1 3 5 10 20 **F**1 3 7 11 13 15 17 18 20 28 29 30 34 35 39 40 51 57 59 60 64 65 70 74 75 76 77 79 80 81 82 84 85 87 89 90 94 97 107 108 110 111 115 116 117 119 124 126 128 130 132 135 143 146 149 **S** Prisma Health – Midlands, Columbia, SC
Primary Contact: Hunter Kome, Chief Operations Executive
CMO: Conrad K Shuler, M.D., Chief Medical Officer
CIO: Jay Hansen, Director Information Services
CNO: Patricia Smith, Chief Nursing Officer
Web address: https://prismahealth.org/locations/hospitals/oconee-memorial-hospital
Control: Other not-for-profit (including NFP Corporation) **Service:** General medical and surgical

Staffed Beds: 169 **Admissions:** 6998 **Census:** 87 **Outpatient Visits:** 137606 **Births:** 496 **Total Expense ($000):** 157581 **Payroll Expense ($000):** 51315 **Personnel:** 640

SIMPSONVILLE—Greenville County

☐ **PRISMA HEALTH HILLCREST HOSPITAL (420037)**, 729 SE Main Street, Zip 29681-3280; tel. 864/454-6100, **A**1 3 5 10 **F**1 3 11 12 15 18 29 34 35 40 44 45 50 57 59 64 67 68 70 79 80 81 84 85 86 90 107 108 110 111 115 119 126 128 129 130 132 146 149 **S** Prisma Health – Midlands, Columbia, SC
Primary Contact: Justin Benfield, Chief Operations Executive
Web address: https://prismahealth.org/locations/hospitals/hillcrest-hospital
Control: Other not-for-profit (including NFP Corporation) **Service:** General medical and surgical

Staffed Beds: 43 **Admissions:** 3024 **Census:** 29 **Outpatient Visits:** 84062 **Births:** 0 **Total Expense ($000):** 77159 **Payroll Expense ($000):** 24536 **Personnel:** 272

SPARTANBURG—Spartanburg County

★ **SPARTANBURG HOSPITAL FOR RESTORATIVE CARE (422004)**, 389 Serpentine Drive, Zip 29303-3026; tel. 864/560-3280, **A**10 **F**1 3 29 30 31 35 70 75 77 79 80 82 85 87 90 119 128 130 148 149 **S** Spartanburg Regional Healthcare System, Spartanburg, SC
Primary Contact: Jill Jolley Greene, MSN, R.N., President
Web address: https://www.spartanburgregional.com/locations/spartanburg-hospital-for-restorative-care/restorative-care-medical-staff
Control: Hospital district or authority, Government, Nonfederal **Service:** Acute long-term care hospital

Staffed Beds: 68 **Admissions:** 323 **Census:** 30 **Outpatient Visits:** 0 **Births:** 0 **Total Expense ($000):** 26369 **Payroll Expense ($000):** 12819 **Personnel:** 442

★ ⚕ **SPARTANBURG MEDICAL CENTER – CHURCH STREET CAMPUS (420007)**, 101 East Wood Street, Zip 29303-3040; tel. 864/560-6000, (Includes SPARTANBURG MEDICAL CENTER – MARY BLACK, 1700 Skylyn Drive, Spartanburg, South Carolina, Zip 29307-1061, P O Box 3217, Zip 29304-3217, tel. 864/573-3000; J Philip Feisal, Preident) **A**2 3 5 10 21 **F**1 3 7 11 12 13 15 17 18 20 22 24 26 28 29 30 31 34 35 36 37 38 39 40 43 44 45 46 47 48 49 50 53 54 56 57 58 59 60 61 62 63 64 65 66 68 70 71 72 73 74 75 76 77 78 79 80 81 82 83 84 85 86 87 88 89 90 94 97 98 99 100 101 102 103 104 107 108 110 111 114 115 117 118 119 120 123 124 126 128 129 131 132 143 144 145 146 147 148 149 154 **S** Spartanburg Regional Healthcare System, Spartanburg, SC
Primary Contact: J Philip. Feisal, President and Chief Executive Officer
COO: Mark Aycock, Chief Operating Officer
CMO: Charles Morrow, M.D., Chief Medical Officer
CIO: Harold Moore, Chief Information Technology Officer
CHR: Kathy Sinclair, Vice President Human Resources
Web address: www.spartanburgregional.com
Control: Hospital district or authority, Government, Nonfederal **Service:** General medical and surgical

Staffed Beds: 673 **Admissions:** 29786 **Census:** 511 **Outpatient Visits:** 376983 **Births:** 3839 **Total Expense ($000):** 1150409 **Payroll Expense ($000):** 364537 **Personnel:** 5519

☐ **SPARTANBURG REHABILITATION INSTITUTE (423031)**, 160 Harold Fleming Court, Zip 29303-4226; tel. 864/594-9600, **A**1 10 **F**1 29 75 90 94 128 148 149 **S** Ernest Health, Inc., Albuquerque, NM
Primary Contact: Richard Schulz, Chief Executive Officer
Web address: www.sri.ernesthealth.com
Control: Corporation, Investor-owned (for-profit) **Service:** Rehabilitation

Staffed Beds: 40 **Admissions:** 799 **Census:** 33 **Outpatient Visits:** 4267 **Births:** 0 **Total Expense ($000):** 17581 **Payroll Expense ($000):** 8753 **Personnel:** 123

SUMMERVILLE—Berkeley County

☒ **ROPER ST. FRANCIS BERKELEY HOSPITAL (420110)**, 100 Callen Boulevard, Zip 29486-2807; tel. 854/529-3100, **A**1 10 **F**1 3 7 13 15 18 20 29 30 35 40 45 51 64 67 68 70 76 78 79 81 82 84 94 102 107 108 110 111 115 118 119 126 128 146 148 149 **S** Bon Secours Mercy Health, Cincinnati, OH
Primary Contact: Patrick Bosse, Chief Administrative Officer
CMO: Robert Oliverio, M.D., Vice President and Chief Medical Officer, Ambulatory Care and Population Health
Web address: https://www.rsfh.com/berkeley-hospital/
Control: Other not-for-profit (including NFP Corporation) **Service:** General medical and surgical

Staffed Beds: 50 **Admissions:** 4125 **Census:** 36 **Outpatient Visits:** 87850 **Births:** 887 **Total Expense ($000):** 104039 **Payroll Expense ($000):** 31406 **Personnel:** 387

ROPER ST. FRANCIS HOSPITAL–BERKELEY See Roper St. Francis Berkeley Hospital

SUMMERVILLE—Dorchester County

SUMMERVILLE MEDICAL CENTER See Summerville Medical Center

SUMTER—Sumter County

☐ **PRISMA HEALTH TUOMEY HOSPITAL (420070)**, 129 North Washington Street, Zip 29150-4983; tel. 803/774-9000, **A**1 3 5 10 19 **F**1 3 11 13 15 18 20 28 29 30 31 32 34 35 40 47 48 49 50 51 54 56 59 63 64 70 71 73 75 76 77 78 79 80 81 82 84 85 86 87 89 90 94 102 107 108 110 111 114 119 120 121 126 128 130 131 132 135 146 147 148 149 **P**6 **S** Prisma Health – Midlands, Columbia, SC
Primary Contact: Michael N. Bundy, Chief Executive Officer
CFO: Mark Lovell, Vice President and Chief Financial Officer
CMO: Gene Dickerson, M.D., Vice President Medical Affairs
CIO: Cheryl Martin, Chief Information Officer
CHR: Letitia Pringle-Miller, Administrative Director
CNO: Levi Campbell, R.N., Interim Chief Nursing Officer
Web address: https://prismahealth.org/locations/hospitals/tuomey-hospital
Control: Other not-for-profit (including NFP Corporation) **Service:** General medical and surgical

Staffed Beds: 173 **Admissions:** 8725 **Census:** 123 **Outpatient Visits:** 181466 **Births:** 1029 **Total Expense ($000):** 223523 **Payroll Expense ($000):** 69029 **Personnel:** 860

Hospitals, U.S. / SOUTH CAROLINA

TRAVELERS REST—Greenville County

☐ △ **PRISMA HEALTH NORTH GREENVILLE HOSPITAL (422008)**, 807 North Main Street, Zip 29690–1551; tel. 864/455–9206, **A**1 5 7 10 **F**1 3 15 29 30 34 35 40 44 50 75 79 80 85 86 87 107 110 111 115 119 128 130 146 148 **S** Prisma Health – Midlands, Columbia, SC
Primary Contact: Tim Brookshire, FACHE, Chief Operations Executive
CMO: Amy Treece, M.D., Medical Director
CHR: Carol Bish, Human Resources Coordinator
CNO: Marian Lorraine McVey, Chief Nursing Officer
Web address: https://prismahealth.org/locations/hospitals/north-greenville-hospital
Control: Other not–for–profit (including NFP Corporation) **Service**: Acute long-term care hospital

Staffed Beds: 44 **Admissions**: 294 **Census**: 33 **Outpatient Visits**: 21802 **Births**: 0 **Total Expense ($000)**: 31338 **Payroll Expense ($000)**: 12096 **Personnel**: 134

☐ **SPRINGBROOK BEHAVIORAL HEALTH (424007)**, 1 Havenwood Lane, Zip 29690–9680, Mailing Address: P.O. Box 1005, Zip 29690–1005; tel. 864/834–8013, **A**1 3 10 **F**1 4 98 99 103 128
Primary Contact: Mike Rowley, Chief Executive Officer
COO: Mary Ann Bennett, Chief Operating Officer and Chief Nursing Officer
CFO: Bart Bennett, Chief Financial Officer
CMO: Mathew Fisher, M.D., Medical Director
CIO: Bart Bennett, Chief Information Technology Officer
CHR: Robin B Callas, Human Resource Director
CNO: Mary Ann Bennett, Director of Nursing
Web address: www.springbrookbehavioral.com
Control: Corporation, Investor–owned (for–profit) **Service**: Psychiatric

Staffed Beds: 62 **Admissions**: 1007 **Census**: 36 **Personnel**: 149

UNION—Union County

★ ⇑ **UNION MEDICAL CENTER (420108)**, 322 West South Street, Zip 29379–2857, Mailing Address: P.O. Box 789, Zip 29379–0789; tel. 864/301–2000, **A**10 21 **F**1 3 18 29 30 34 35 40 57 59 64 75 80 107 111 115 119 127 128 130 146 149 154 **S** Spartanburg Regional Healthcare System, Spartanburg, SC
Primary Contact: Paul R. Newhouse, President
CFO: Cindy L. Gault, Chief Financial Officer
CHR: Angie Benfield, Human Resources Generalist
CNO: Beth Lawson, Chief Nursing Officer
Web address: https://www.spartanburgregional.com/locations/union-medical-center/
Control: Hospital district or authority, Government, Nonfederal **Service**: General medical and surgical

Staffed Beds: 15 **Admissions**: 369 **Census**: 4 **Births**: 0 **Total Expense ($000)**: 31566 **Payroll Expense ($000)**: 13892 **Personnel**: 338

VARNVILLE—Hampton County

★ **HAMPTON REGIONAL MEDICAL CENTER (420072)**, 503 West Carolina Avenue, Zip 29944–4735, Mailing Address: P.O. Box 338, Zip 29944–0338; tel. 803/943–2771, **A**10 20 **F**1 3 15 17 18 24 28 29 31 32 34 40 57 59 65 67 70 75 77 78 79 81 90 93 94 102 107 108 110 111 115 119 127 128 133 154
Primary Contact: Dave H. Hamill, President and Chief Executive Officer
Web address: www.hamptonregional.com
Control: Other not–for–profit (including NFP Corporation) **Service**: General medical and surgical

Staffed Beds: 24 **Admissions**: 546 **Census**: 6 **Outpatient Visits**: 13256 **Births**: 1 **Total Expense ($000)**: 29173 **Payroll Expense ($000)**: 14533 **Personnel**: 205

WALTERBORO—Colleton County

✠ **COLLETON MEDICAL CENTER (420030)**, 501 Robertson Boulevard, Zip 29488–5714; tel. 843/782–2000, **A**1 3 10 20 **F**1 3 11 13 15 18 26 29 30 32 34 35 36 40 41 45 47 49 56 57 59 60 64 65 68 70 75 76 77 79 81 82 85 86 87 89 90 93 94 96 98 102 107 108 110 111 114 115 119 128 130 131 132 146 147 148 149 **S** HCA Healthcare, Nashville, TN
Primary Contact: Jimmy O. Hiott III, Chief Executive Officer
CFO: Cassie Ball, Chief Financial Officer
CMO: Mark Greenslit, M.D., Chief Medical Staff
CIO: Phil Gansz, Director Information Technology
CHR: Robert Valenca, Director, Human Resources
Web address: www.colletonmedical.com
Control: Corporation, Investor–owned (for–profit) **Service**: General medical and surgical

Staffed Beds: 131 **Admissions**: 3899 **Census**: 48 **Births**: 283 **Total Expense ($000)**: 75829 **Payroll Expense ($000)**: 23600 **Personnel**: 321

WEST COLUMBIA—Lexington County

★ ⇑ **LEXINGTON MEDICAL CENTER (420073)**, 2720 Sunset Boulevard, Zip 29169–4810; **A**2 3 5 10 21 **F**1 3 8 11 12 13 15 18 20 22 24 26 28 29 30 31 32 34 35 38 39 40 43 44 45 46 48 49 50 51 53 54 57 58 59 60 61 64 68 70 73 74 75 76 77 78 79 80 81 82 84 85 86 87 90 92 93 94 96 102 107 108 110 111 114 115 117 118 119 120 121 123 124 126 127 128 129 130 131 132 135 141 142 144 145 146 147 148 **P**6
Primary Contact: Tod Augsburger, FACHE, President and Chief Executive Officer
CFO: Melinda Kruzner, Chief Financial Officer
CMO: Brent Powers, M.D., Vice President/Chief Medical Officer
CIO: Kathleen R Herald, Vice President and Chief Information Officer
CHR: Brian Smith, Vice President Human Resources
CNO: Melissa Taylor, R.N., MSN, Chief Nursing Officer
Web address: www.lexmed.com
Control: Other not–for–profit (including NFP Corporation) **Service**: General medical and surgical

Staffed Beds: 561 **Admissions**: 29848 **Census**: 425 **Outpatient Visits**: 203677 **Births**: 3771 **Total Expense ($000)**: 962454 **Payroll Expense ($000)**: 372124 **Personnel**: 4266

☐ **THREE RIVERS BEHAVIORAL HEALTH (424008)**, 2900 Sunset Boulevard, Zip 29169–3422; tel. 803/796–9911, **A**1 10 **F**1 4 98 99 100 101 103 104 128 **S** Universal Health Services, Inc., King of Prussia, PA
Primary Contact: Shannon Marcus, Chief Executive Officer
CFO: Christopher Jensen, Chief Financial Officer
CMO: Christina Lynn, M.D., Medical Director
CHR: Nita Sundberg, Director Human Resources
CNO: Lilly Wing, Chief Nursing Officer
Web address: www.threeriversbehavioral.org
Control: Corporation, Investor–owned (for–profit) **Service**: Psychiatric

Staffed Beds: 129 **Admissions**: 4586 **Census**: 102 **Outpatient Visits**: 0 **Births**: 0 **Personnel**: 200

Hospital, Medicare Provider Number, Address, Telephone, Approval, Facility, and Physician Codes, Health Care System

★ American Hospital Association (AHA) membership
☐ The Joint Commission accreditation
○ Healthcare Facilities Accreditation Program
◇ DNV Healthcare Inc. accreditation
⇑ Center for Improvement in Healthcare Quality Accreditation
△ Commission on Accreditation of Rehabilitation Facilities (CARF) accreditation

© 2025 AHA Guide

Hospitals, U.S. / SOUTH DAKOTA

SOUTH DAKOTA

ABERDEEN—Brown County

✣ **AVERA ST. LUKE'S HOSPITAL (430014)**, 305 South State Street, Zip 57401–4527; tel. 605/622–5000, (Total facility includes 137 beds in nursing home–type unit) **A**1 2 10 19 **F**2 3 5 10 11 13 15 18 20 21 28 29 30 31 32 34 35 36 39 40 43 45 46 47 48 50 53 56 57 59 60 61 64 65 70 71 74 75 76 77 78 79 81 82 84 85 87 89 91 92 93 96 97 98 99 100 101 102 103 104 107 108 110 111 114 115 116 117 118 119 120 121 125 126 127 128 129 130 131 132 133 135 144 145 146 147 148 149 150 154 155 156 157 162 164 167 169 **P**6 **S** Avera Health, Sioux Falls, SD
Primary Contact: Dan Bjerknes, Chief Executive Officer, Regional President
CFO: Geoff Durst, Vice President Finance
CMO: Shahid Chaudhary, M.D., Chief Medical Officer
CIO: Julie Kusler, Manager Information Services
CHR: Tracy L Olson, Human Resource Officer
CNO: Jan Patterson, Chief Nursing Officer
Web address: www.avera.org/st-lukes-hospital/
Control: Church operated, Nongovernment, not–for–profit **Service**: General medical and surgical

Staffed Beds: 197 **Admissions:** 3514 **Census:** 160 **Outpatient Visits:** 154782 **Births:** 355 **Total Expense ($000):** 219636 **Payroll Expense ($000):** 98363 **Personnel:** 930

★ **SANFORD ABERDEEN MEDICAL CENTER (430097)**, 2905 3rd Avenue SE, Zip 57401–5420; tel. 605/626–4200, (Nonreporting) **A**10 **S** Sanford Health, Sioux Falls, SD
Primary Contact: Kila LeGrand, Executive Director
CFO: Jeffrey Poppen, Chief Financial Officer
CMO: Samuel Nyamu, M.D., Chief Medical Officer
CHR: Katie Palmer, Manager Human Resources
CNO: KaSara Sutton, Director of Nursing and Clinical Services
Web address: https://www.sanfordhealth.org/locations/sanford-aberdeen-medical-center
Control: Other not–for–profit (including NFP Corporation) **Service**: General medical and surgical

Staffed Beds: 48

ARMOUR—Douglas County

DOUGLAS COUNTY MEMORIAL HOSPITAL (431305), 708 Eighth Street, Zip 57313–2102; tel. 605/724–2159, (Nonreporting) **A**10 18
Primary Contact: Heath Brouwer, Administrator
CFO: Dorothy Spease, Manager Business Office
Web address: www.dcmhsd.org
Control: Other not–for–profit (including NFP Corporation) **Service**: General medical and surgical

Staffed Beds: 11

BOWDLE—Edmunds County

★ **BOWDLE HOSPITAL (431318)**, 8001 West Fifth Street, Zip 57428, Mailing Address: P.O. Box 556, Zip 57428–0556; tel. 605/285–6146, (Nonreporting) **A**10 18
Primary Contact: Kirby Kleffman, Chief Executive Officer
CFO: Brooke Heilman, Chief Financial Officer
CMO: John Ottenbacher, Chief of Staff
CNO: Bobbi Noess, Director of Nursing
Web address: www.bowdlehc.com
Control: City, Government, Nonfederal **Service**: General medical and surgical

Staffed Beds: 50

BRITTON—Marshall County

★ **MARSHALL COUNTY HEALTHCARE CENTER AVERA (431312)**, 413 Ninth Street, Zip 57430–2274; tel. 605/448–2253, (Nonreporting) **A**10 18 **S** Avera Health, Sioux Falls, SD
Primary Contact: Nick Fosness, Chief Executive Officer
Web address: www.avera.org
Control: Other not–for–profit (including NFP Corporation) **Service**: General medical and surgical

Staffed Beds: 18

BROOKINGS—Brookings County

★ **BROOKINGS HEALTH SYSTEM (430008)**, 300 22nd Avenue, Zip 57006–2496; tel. 605/696–9000, (Nonreporting) **A**10 20
Primary Contact: Jason R. Merkley, Chief Executive Officer
CFO: Melissa Wagner, Chief Financial Officer
CMO: Shelby Eischens, Chief Medical Officer
CHR: September Bessler, Director, Human Resources
CNO: Tammy Hillestad, Chief Nursing Officer
Web address: www.brookingshealth.org
Control: City, Government, Nonfederal **Service**: General medical and surgical

Staffed Beds: 128

BURKE—Gregory County

★ **COMMUNITY MEMORIAL HOSPITAL (431309)**, 809 Jackson Street, Zip 57523–2065, Mailing Address: P.O. Box 319, Zip 57523–0319; tel. 605/775–2621, (Nonreporting) **A**10 18 **S** Sanford Health, Sioux Falls, SD
Primary Contact: Mistie Drey, Chief Executive Officer
CMO: Megan Smith, M.D., Chief Medical Staff
CHR: Tami Lyon, Director Human Resources
Web address: www.sanfordhealth.org
Control: Other not–for–profit (including NFP Corporation) **Service**: General medical and surgical

Staffed Beds: 16

CANTON—Lincoln County

★ **SANFORD CANTON–INWOOD MEDICAL CENTER (431333)**, 440 North Hiawatha Drive, Zip 57013–5800; tel. 605/764–1400, (Nonreporting) **A**10 18 **S** Sanford Health, Sioux Falls, SD
Primary Contact: Scott C. Larson, Chief Executive Officer
CFO: Paul Gerhart, Chief Financial Officer
Web address: www.sanfordcantoninwood.org
Control: Other not–for–profit (including NFP Corporation) **Service**: General medical and surgical

Staffed Beds: 11

CHAMBERLAIN—Brule County

★ **SANFORD CHAMBERLAIN MEDICAL CENTER (431329)**, 300 South Byron Boulevard, Zip 57325–9741; tel. 605/234–5511, (Nonreporting) **A**10 18 **S** Sanford Health, Sioux Falls, SD
Primary Contact: Erica Peterson, Chief Executive Officer
COO: Paul Miller, Director of Operations
CFO: Erica Peterson, Chief Executive Officer and Chief Financial Officer
CMO: Lacey Olson, M.D., Chief Medical Staff
CHR: Dorothy Hieb, Director Human Resources
CNO: Sarah Talbott, Chief Nursing Officer
Web address: www.sanfordchamberlain.org
Control: Other not–for–profit (including NFP Corporation) **Service**: General medical and surgical

Staffed Beds: 60

CLEAR LAKE—Deuel County

★ **SANFORD CLEAR LAKE MEDICAL CENTER (431307)**, 701 Third Avenue South, Zip 57226–2016; tel. 605/874–2141, (Nonreporting) **A**10 18 **S** Sanford Health, Sioux Falls, SD
Primary Contact: Lori Sisk, R.N., Chief Executive Officer
CFO: Allison Nelson, Chief Financial Officer
CMO: Terrance Smith, M.D., Chairman Medical Staff
CNO: Stephanie Dobbs, Chief Nursing Officer
Web address: www.sanforddeuelcounty.org
Control: Other not–for–profit (including NFP Corporation) **Service**: General medical and surgical

Staffed Beds: 10

Hospitals, U.S. / SOUTH DAKOTA

CUSTER—Custer County

★ **MONUMENT HEALTH CUSTER HOSPITAL (431323)**, 1220 Montgomery Street, Zip 57730–1705; tel. 605/673–2229, (Nonreporting) **A**10 18 **S** Monument Health, Rapid City, SD
Primary Contact: Barbara K. Hespen, R.N., President
Web address: www.regionalhealth.com
Control: Other not–for–profit (including NFP Corporation) **Service:** General medical and surgical

Staffed Beds: 67

DAKOTA DUNES—Union County

☐ **DUNES SURGICAL HOSPITAL (430089)**, 600 North Sioux Point Road, Zip 57049–5000; tel. 605/232–3332, (Nonreporting) **A**1 10
Primary Contact: Robert Monical, Chief Executive Officer
Web address: www.dunessurgicalhospital.com
Control: Corporation, Investor–owned (for–profit) **Service:** Surgical

Staffed Beds: 40

DE SMET—Kingsbury County

★ **AVERA DE SMET MEMORIAL HOSPITAL (431332)**, 306 Prairie Avenue SW, Zip 57231–2285, Mailing Address: P.O. Box 160, Zip 57231–0160; tel. 605/854–6100, **A**10 18 **F**3 15 28 34 35 40 59 68 93 107 133 154 164 **P**6 **S** Avera Health, Sioux Falls, SD
Primary Contact: Stephanie Reasy, Administrator and Chief Executive Officer
Web address: www.avera.org
Control: Other not–for–profit (including NFP Corporation) **Service:** General medical and surgical

Staffed Beds: 6 **Admissions:** 93 **Census:** 1 **Outpatient Visits:** 9909
Births: 0 **Total Expense ($000):** 6494 **Payroll Expense ($000):** 3305
Personnel: 37

DEADWOOD—Lawrence County

★ **MONUMENT HEALTH LEAD–DEADWOOD HOSPITAL (431320)**, 61 Charles Street, Zip 57732–1303; tel. 605/717–6000, (Nonreporting) **A**10 18 **S** Monument Health, Rapid City, SD
Primary Contact: Mark C. Schmidt, President
CMO: Elizabeth Sayler, M.D., Chief of Staff
CHR: Kathryn L Shockey, Director Human Resources
Web address: www.regionalhealth.com
Control: State, Government, Nonfederal **Service:** General medical and surgical

Staffed Beds: 18

DELL RAPIDS—Minnehaha County

★ **AVERA DELLS AREA HOSPITAL (431331)**, 909 North Iowa Avenue, Zip 57022–1231; tel. 605/428–5431, **A**10 18 **F**3 15 28 34 35 40 41 45 53 57 59 64 65 75 81 86 92 93 94 97 107 110 129 132 133 134 144 148 154 **P**6 **S** Avera Health, Sioux Falls, SD
Primary Contact: Bryan Breitling, Chief Executive Officer
CFO: Kory Holt, Division Controller Network Operations
CMO: Valerie Larson, M.D., Chief Medical Officer
CIO: Val Witham, Director of Health Information
CHR: Nikki Tiff, Regional Manager Human Resources
CNO: Karla Carstensen, Director Patient Care
Web address: https://www.avera.org/locations/profile/avera-dells-area-hospital/
Control: Other not–for–profit (including NFP Corporation) **Service:** General medical and surgical

Staffed Beds: 23 **Admissions:** 140 **Census:** 2 **Outpatient Visits:** 9491
Births: 0 **Total Expense ($000):** 10390 **Payroll Expense ($000):** 5048
Personnel: 74

EAGLE BUTTE—Dewey County

⊞ **U. S. PUBLIC HEALTH SERVICE INDIAN HOSPITAL (430083)**, 317 Main Street, Zip 57625–1012, Mailing Address: P.O. Box 1012, Zip 57625–1012; tel. 605/964–7724, (Nonreporting) **A**1 10 **S** U. S. Indian Health Service, Rockville, MD
Primary Contact: Charles Fisher, Chief Executive Officer
CFO: Lisa Deal, Budget Analyst
Web address: www.ihs.gov
Control: PHS, Indian Service, Government, federal **Service:** General medical and surgical

Staffed Beds: 8

EUREKA—Mcpherson County

★ **EUREKA COMMUNITY HEALTH SERVICES AVERA (431308)**, 410 Ninth Street, Zip 57437–2182, Mailing Address: P.O. Box 517, Zip 57437–0517; tel. 605/284–2661, (Nonreporting) **A**10 18 **S** Avera Health, Sioux Falls, SD
Primary Contact: Carmen Weber, Administrator
CFO: Joyce Schwingler, Chief Financial Officer
Web address: www.avera.org
Control: Other not–for–profit (including NFP Corporation) **Service:** General medical and surgical

Staffed Beds: 4

FAULKTON—Faulk County

FAULKTON AREA MEDICAL CENTER (431301), 1300 Oak Street, Zip 57438–2149, Mailing Address: P.O. Box 100, Zip 57438–0100; tel. 605/598–6262, (Nonreporting) **A**10 18
Primary Contact: Heather Bode, Chief Executive Officer
COO: Jay A Jahnig, Chief Executive Officer
CFO: Susan Miller, Financial Administrator
CMO: K A Bartholomew, M.D., Medical Director
CIO: Cheryl Bue, Health Information Transcriptionist
CHR: Blythe Smith, Administrative Assistant
CNO: Shannon Stuwe, Director of Nursing
Web address: www.faulktonmedical.org
Control: Other not–for–profit (including NFP Corporation) **Service:** General medical and surgical

Staffed Beds: 12

FLANDREAU—Moody County

★ **AVERA FLANDREAU HOSPITAL (431310)**, 214 North Prairie Street, Zip 57028–1243; tel. 605/997–2433, **A**10 18 **F**3 28 34 35 40 41 45 57 59 64 65 75 81 86 92 93 97 107 127 129 133 134 144 146 148 154 **P**6 **S** Avera Health, Sioux Falls, SD
Primary Contact: Bryan Breitling, Chief Executive Officer
CFO: Kory Holt, Assistant Vice President for Financial Integration
CIO: Val Witham, Director Health Information
CHR: Nikki Tiff, Human Resources Analyst
CNO: Heather Hubbell, Director of Patient Care
Web address: www.avera.org/flandreau-medical/
Control: Other not–for–profit (including NFP Corporation) **Service:** General medical and surgical

Staffed Beds: 18 **Admissions:** 140 **Census:** 2 **Outpatient Visits:** 8443
Births: 0 **Total Expense ($000):** 8957 **Payroll Expense ($000):** 4597
Personnel: 60

FORT MEADE—Meade County

⊞ **BLACK HILLS HCS**, 113 Comanche Road, Zip 57741–1099; tel. 605/347–2511, (Includes VETERANS AFFAIRS MEDICAL CENTER HOT SPRINGS CAMPUS, 500 North Fifth Street, Hot Springs, South Dakota, Zip 57747, tel. 605/745–2052) (Nonreporting) **A**1 5 **S** Department of Veterans Affairs, Washington, DC
CFO: Joseph Ferris, Chief Financial Officer
CHR: Denis Sullivan, Chief Human Resources Management
Web address: www.blackhills.va.gov/
Control: Veterans Affairs, Government, federal **Service:** General medical and surgical

Staffed Beds: 133

VETERANS AFFAIRS BLACK HILLS HEALTH CARE SYSTEM See Black Hills HCS

FREEMAN—Hutchinson County

★ **FREEMAN REGIONAL HEALTH SERVICES (431313)**, 510 East Eighth Street, Zip 57029–2086, Mailing Address: P.O. Box 370, Zip 57029–0370; tel. 605/925–4000, (Nonreporting) **A**10 18
Primary Contact: Phillip Husher, Interim Co–Chief Executive Officer
CFO: Phillip Husher, Chief Financial Officer
CNO: Courtney Unruh, Chief Nursing Officer
Web address: www.freemanregional.com
Control: Other not–for–profit (including NFP Corporation) **Service:** General medical and surgical

Staffed Beds: 63

Hospital, Medicare Provider Number, Address, Telephone, Approval, Facility, and Physician Codes, Health Care System
★ American Hospital Association (AHA) membership   ○ Healthcare Facilities Accreditation Program   ⇑ Center for Improvement in Healthcare Quality Accreditation
☐ The Joint Commission accreditation   ◇ DNV Healthcare Inc. accreditation   △ Commission on Accreditation of Rehabilitation Facilities (CARF) accreditation

© 2025 AHA Guide

Hospitals, U.S. / SOUTH DAKOTA

GETTYSBURG—Potter County

★ **AVERA MISSOURI RIVER HEALTH CENTER (431302)**, 606 East Garfield Avenue, Zip 57442–1398; tel. 605/765–2488, (Total facility includes 53 beds in nursing home–type unit) **A**10 18 **F**2 3 6 11 29 30 31 34 35 36 40 41 43 44 50 53 56 59 64 65 68 81 82 83 85 86 87 97 107 119 125 130 133 135 146 148 149 154 157 **S** Avera Health, Sioux Falls, SD
Primary Contact: Rena Robbennolt, Interim Administrator
Web address: https://www.avera.org/locations/profile/avera-missouri-river-health-center/
Control: Church operated, Nongovernment, not–for–profit **Service**: General medical and surgical

Staffed Beds: 60 **Admissions**: 152 **Census**: 33 **Outpatient Visits**: 5390
Births: 0 **Total Expense ($000)**: 12770 **Payroll Expense ($000)**: 6667
Personnel: 78

GREGORY—Gregory County

★ **AVERA GREGORY HOSPITAL (431338)**, 400 Park Avenue, Zip 57533–1302, Mailing Address: P.O. Box 408, Zip 57533–0408; tel. 605/835–8394, (Total facility includes 30 beds in nursing home–type unit) **A**10 18 **F**28 29 30 31 34 35 40 43 45 54 56 59 60 65 77 81 93 97 107 110 111 127 128 133 154 **P**6 **S** Avera Health, Sioux Falls, SD
Primary Contact: Anthony Timanus, Chief Executive Officer
CFO: Trish Keiser, Comptroller
CMO: Rich Kafka, M.D., Chief Medical Officer
CIO: Justin Keegan, Director Support Services
CHR: Carol Postulka, Administrative Coordinator
Web address: www.gregoryhealthcare.org
Control: Church operated, Nongovernment, not–for–profit **Service**: General medical and surgical

Staffed Beds: 43 **Admissions**: 346 **Census**: 32 **Outpatient Visits**: 9489
Births: 0 **Total Expense ($000)**: 21572 **Payroll Expense ($000)**: 10289
Personnel: 154

HOT SPRINGS—Fall River County

★ **FALL RIVER HEALTH SERVICES (431322)**, 1201 Highway 71 South, Zip 57747–8800; tel. 605/745–3159, (Total facility includes 59 beds in nursing home–type unit) **A**10 18 **F**5 28 29 34 35 40 45 47 48 56 57 59 64 65 66 68 77 81 93 97 99 100 103 104 107 115 119 127 128 129 130 131 133 135 146 148 154 164 165 169
Primary Contact: Jeremy Schultes, Chief Executive Officer
CFO: Jesse Naze, Chief Financial Officer
CMO: Ami Garrigan, M.D., Chief of Staff
CIO: Dustin Kleinsasser, Manager, Information Technology
CHR: Barb Lutz, Director of Human Resources, Compliance and Informatics
CNO: Alicia Kunz, Director of Acute Care
Web address: www.frhssd.org
Control: Other not–for–profit (including NFP Corporation) **Service**: General medical and surgical

Staffed Beds: 84 **Admissions**: 303 **Census**: 57 **Outpatient Visits**: 39611
Births: 0 **Total Expense ($000)**: 30101 **Payroll Expense ($000)**: 12837
Personnel: 181

FALL RIVER HOSPITAL See Fall River Health Services

VETERANS AFFAIRS MEDICAL CENTER See Veterans Affairs Medical Center Hot Springs Campus

VETERANS AFFAIRS MEDICAL CENTER HOT SPRINGS CAMPUS See Black Hills HCS, Fort Meade

HURON—Beadle County

★ **HURON REGIONAL MEDICAL CENTER (431335)**, 172 Fourth Street SE, Zip 57350–2590; tel. 605/353–6200, (Nonreporting) **A**10 18 **S** Ovation Healthcare, Brentwood, TN
Primary Contact: Erick J. Larson, President and Chief Executive Officer
CFO: Marcia Zwanziger, Vice President Finance
CMO: Bill Miner, M.D., Chief of Staff
CHR: Rhonda Hanson, Director Human Resources
CNO: Gail Robeson, Vice President Patient Services
Web address: www.huronregional.org
Control: Other not–for–profit (including NFP Corporation) **Service**: General medical and surgical

Staffed Beds: 30

MADISON—Lake County

★ **MADISON REGIONAL HEALTH SYSTEM (431300)**, 323 SW 10th Street, Zip 57042–3200; tel. 605/256–6551, **A**10 18 **F**7 13 15 28 29 31 34 35 40 41 43 50 57 59 64 65 70 75 76 77 81 82 85 87 89 93 97 107 110 111 115 119 129 130 132 133 135 146 148 154 156 169 **P**6
Primary Contact: Tamara Miller, FACHE, Chief Executive Officer and Administrator
CFO: Teresa Mallett, Chief Financial Officer
CNO: Charlotte Charles, Director Acute Patient Services
Web address: www.madisonregionalhealth.org
Control: Other not–for–profit (including NFP Corporation) **Service**: General medical and surgical

Staffed Beds: 22 **Admissions**: 689 **Census**: 12 **Outpatient Visits**: 29348
Births: 50 **Total Expense ($000)**: 34275 **Payroll Expense ($000)**: 17156
Personnel: 248

MARTIN—Bennett County

★ **BENNETT COUNTY HOSPITAL AND NURSING HOME (431314)**, 102 Major Allen Street, Zip 57551–6005, Mailing Address: P.O. Box 70, Zip 57551–0070; tel. 605/685–6622, (Nonreporting) **A**10 18
Primary Contact: Michael Christensen, Chief Executive Officer
CFO: Jean Kirk, Chief Financial Officer
CMO: Peter Knowles–Smith, M.D., Medical Director
CIO: Jean Kirk, Chief Financial Officer
CHR: T J Porter, Director Human Resources
Web address: www.bennettcountyhospital.com/
Control: Other not–for–profit (including NFP Corporation) **Service**: General medical and surgical

Staffed Beds: 62

MILBANK—Grant County

★ **MILBANK AREA HOSPITAL AVERA (431326)**, 301 Flynn Drive, Zip 57252–1508; tel. 605/432–4538, **A**10 18 **F**3 15 28 31 34 35 40 43 45 57 59 60 64 65 75 81 86 97 107 110 111 115 119 127 129 130 132 133 144 146 148 154 169 **P**6 **S** Avera Health, Sioux Falls, SD
Primary Contact: Natalie Gauer, Administrator
CMO: Kevin Bjordahl, M.D., Chief Medical Officer
CHR: Mona Schafer, Regional Manager Human Resources
Web address: www.averamilbank.org
Control: Church operated, Nongovernment, not–for–profit **Service**: General medical and surgical

Staffed Beds: 25 **Admissions**: 434 **Census**: 4 **Outpatient Visits**: 18521
Births: 48 **Total Expense ($000)**: 20697 **Payroll Expense ($000)**: 8122
Personnel: 110

MILLER—Hand County

★ **AVERA HAND COUNTY MEMORIAL HOSPITAL (431337)**, 300 West Fifth Street, Zip 57362–1238; tel. 605/853–2421, **A**10 18 **F**3 15 34 35 40 41 45 57 59 64 65 75 81 86 92 93 97 107 129 133 134 146 148 154 **P**6 **S** Avera Health, Sioux Falls, SD
Primary Contact: Matthew Campion, Administrator
CFO: Debbie Pullman, Director Finance
CMO: John Hopkins, M.D., Chief of Staff
CIO: Janice Purrington, Coordinator Medical Records
CNO: Sarah DeHaai, R.N., Director of Nursing
Web address: www.avera.org
Control: Other not–for–profit (including NFP Corporation) **Service**: General medical and surgical

Staffed Beds: 25 **Admissions**: 260 **Census**: 3 **Outpatient Visits**: 9686
Births: 0 **Total Expense ($000)**: 9072 **Payroll Expense ($000)**: 4195
Personnel: 61

Hospitals, U.S. / SOUTH DAKOTA

MITCHELL—Davison County

☒ **AVERA QUEEN OF PEACE HOSPITAL (431340)**, 525 North Foster, Zip 57301-2999; tel. 605/995-2000, (Total facility includes 84 beds in nursing home–type unit) **A**1 2 10 18 **F**3 10 13 15 28 29 30 31 34 40 43 45 48 50 51 53 54 57 59 64 69 70 71 75 76 77 78 79 81 82 84 85 86 93 94 96 104 107 108 110 111 114 117 118 119 121 123 127 128 129 130 131 132 133 135 146 147 148 154 155 156 164 169 **P**6 **S** Avera Health, Sioux Falls, SD
Primary Contact: Douglas R. Ekeren, FACHE, Regional President and Chief Executive Officer
CFO: Will Flett, Vice President Finance and Chief Financial Officer
CMO: David Balt, D.O., Chief Medical Officer
CIO: Jim Hanson, Director Information Systems
CHR: Rita Lemon, Director Human Resources
CNO: Rochelle Reider, Vice President Patient Care
Web address: www.averaqueenofpeace.org
Control: Church operated, Nongovernment, not–for–profit **Service**: General medical and surgical

Staffed Beds: 109 **Admissions**: 1874 **Census**: 85 **Outpatient Visits**: 91776 **Births**: 399 **Total Expense ($000)**: 118784 **Payroll Expense ($000)**: 53586 **Personnel**: 601

MOBRIDGE—Walworth County

★ **MOBRIDGE REGIONAL HOSPITAL (431325)**, 1401 Tenth Avenue West, Zip 57601-1106, Mailing Address: P.O. Box 580, Zip 57601-0580; tel. 605/845-3692, (Nonreporting) **A**10 18
Primary Contact: John J. Ayoub, FACHE, Chief Executive Officer
COO: Beth Jensen, Director Clinic Operations
CFO: Renae Tisdall, Chief Financial, Compliance and Security Officer
CMO: Travis Henderson, M.D., Chief of Staff
CIO: Lewus Morgan, Director, Information Technology
CHR: Keri Wientjes, Director Human Resources
CNO: Kristi Voller, Director of Nursing
Web address: www.mobridgehospital.org
Control: Other not–for–profit (including NFP Corporation) **Service**: General medical and surgical

Staffed Beds: 25

PARKSTON—Hutchinson County

★ **AVERA ST. BENEDICT HEALTH CENTER (431330)**, 401 West Glynn Drive, Zip 57366-9605; tel. 605/928-3311, (Total facility includes 49 beds in nursing home–type unit) **A**10 18 **F**2 3 8 10 13 15 28 29 30 31 32 34 35 38 40 45 53 56 57 59 62 64 65 69 71 75 76 81 82 83 85 86 87 89 107 110 111 115 116 119 127 129 130 131 132 133 135 146 147 148 154 156 169 **P**6 **S** Avera Health, Sioux Falls, SD
Primary Contact: Lindsay Weber, President and Chief Executive Officer
CMO: Antoinette VanderPol, Chief of Staff
CIO: Adam Popp, Director Information Systems
CHR: Phyllis Ehler, Director Human Resources
CNO: Denise Muntefering, Vice President Patient Care Services
Web address: www.averastbenedict.org
Control: Church operated, Nongovernment, not–for–profit **Service**: General medical and surgical

Staffed Beds: 74 **Admissions**: 564 **Census**: 53 **Outpatient Visits**: 20585 **Births**: 52 **Total Expense ($000)**: 23181 **Payroll Expense ($000)**: 11421 **Personnel**: 151

PHILIP—Haakon County

★ **PHILIP HEALTH SERVICES (431319)**, 503 West Pine Street, Zip 57567-3300, Mailing Address: P.O. Box 790, Zip 57567-0790; tel. 605/859-2511, (Nonreporting) **A**10 18 **S** Monument Health, Rapid City, SD
Primary Contact: Jeremy S. Schultes, Administrator and Chief Executive Officer
Web address: www.philiphealthservices.com/
Control: Other not–for–profit (including NFP Corporation) **Service**: General medical and surgical

Staffed Beds: 50

PIERRE—Hughes County

☒ **AVERA ST. MARY'S HOSPITAL (430015)**, 801 East Sioux Avenue, Zip 57501-3323; tel. 605/224-3100, (Total facility includes 80 beds in nursing home–type unit) **A**1 2 3 10 20 **F**3 8 10 13 15 18 28 29 30 31 40 43 45 51 59 60 64 65 68 70 75 76 78 79 81 82 85 93 97 107 108 110 111 115 119 120 121 128 129 130 132 133 146 147 154 156 167 169 **P**6 **S** Avera Health, Sioux Falls, SD
Primary Contact: Shantel Krebs, Chief Executive Officer
CFO: Tom Wagner, Interim Vice President Finance
CMO: Denise Hanisch, M.D., Chief of Staff
CIO: Jamie Raske, Information Technology Lead
CHR: Paul Marso, Vice President Human Resources
Web address: www.avera.org/st-marys-pierre/
Control: Church operated, Nongovernment, not–for–profit **Service**: General medical and surgical

Staffed Beds: 130 **Admissions**: 2266 **Census**: 68 **Outpatient Visits**: 58782 **Births**: 430 **Total Expense ($000)**: 116154 **Payroll Expense ($000)**: 53872 **Personnel**: 470

PINE RIDGE—Shannon County

☒ **U. S. PUBLIC HEALTH SERVICE INDIAN HOSPITAL (430098)**, East Highway 18, Zip 57770, Mailing Address: P.O. Box 1201, Zip 57770-1201; tel. 605/867-5131, (Nonreporting) **A**1 10 **S** U. S. Indian Health Service, Rockville, MD
Primary Contact: Travis Scott, Service Unit Director
CFO: Sophia Conny, Deputy Administrative Officer
CMO: Jan Colton, M.D., Acting Clinical Director
CHR: Annabelle Blackbear, Human Resources Specialist
Web address: www.ihs.gov
Control: PHS, Indian Service, Government, federal **Service**: General medical and surgical

Staffed Beds: 45

PLATTE—Charles Mix County

★ **PLATTE HEALTH CENTER AVERA (431306)**, 601 East Seventh, Zip 57369-2123, Mailing Address: P.O. Box 200, Zip 57369-0200; tel. 605/337-3364, (Nonreporting) **A**10 18 **S** Avera Health, Sioux Falls, SD
Primary Contact: Mark Burket, Chief Executive Officer
CFO: Jerry Hoffman, Chief Financial Officer
Web address: www.phcavera.org
Control: Other not–for–profit (including NFP Corporation) **Service**: General medical and surgical

Staffed Beds: 17

RAPID CITY—Pennington County

BLACK HILLS SURGICAL HOSPITAL (430091), 216 Anamaria Drive, Zip 57701-7366, Mailing Address: 1868 Lombardy Drive, Zip 57703-4130; tel. 605/721-4900, (Nonreporting) **A**10 22
Primary Contact: Jack Kaup, Chief Executive Officer
COO: Greg Loos, Chief Operating Officer
Web address: www.bhsc.com
Control: Partnership, Investor–owned (for–profit) **Service**: Surgical

Staffed Beds: 26

INDIAN HEALTH SERVICE HOSPITAL (430082), 3200 Canyon Lake Drive, Zip 57702-8197; tel. 605/355-2280, (Nonreporting) **A**10 **S** U. S. Indian Health Service, Rockville, MD
Primary Contact: Kevin J. Stiffarm, Chief Executive Officer
Web address: www.ihs.gov
Control: PHS, Indian Service, Government, federal **Service**: General medical and surgical

Staffed Beds: 9

Hospital, Medicare Provider Number, Address, Telephone, Approval, Facility, and Physician Codes, Health Care System

★ American Hospital Association (AHA) membership
☐ The Joint Commission accreditation
○ Healthcare Facilities Accreditation Program
◇ DNV Healthcare Inc. accreditation
⇑ Center for Improvement in Healthcare Quality Accreditation
△ Commission on Accreditation of Rehabilitation Facilities (CARF) accreditation

Hospitals, U.S. / SOUTH DAKOTA

☒ **MONUMENT HEALTH RAPID CITY HOSPITAL (430077)**, 353 Fairmont Boulevard, Zip 57701–7393, Mailing Address: P.O. Box 6000, Zip 57709–6000; tel. 605/755–1000, **A**1 3 5 10 **F**3 11 12 13 15 17 18 20 22 24 26 28 29 30 31 34 35 40 43 45 46 48 49 50 51 53 54 56 57 58 59 60 61 62 63 64 70 72 74 75 76 77 78 79 81 82 84 85 87 89 90 92 93 97 98 99 100 102 104 107 108 111 115 118 119 120 121 124 126 127 129 130 131 132 144 146 148 149 154 156 157 160 162 164 165 167 **S** Monument Health, Rapid City, SD
Primary Contact: John Pierce, President
COO: Mark Schulte, FACHE, Vice President of Operations
CFO: Mark Thompson, Vice President Financial Services
CMO: David Houser, M.D., Vice President Medical Affairs
CHR: Maureen Henson, Vice President Human Resources
Web address: https://directory.monument.health/facility/sd/rapid-city/353-fairmont-boulevard-6671503
Control: Other not–for–profit (including NFP Corporation) **Service:** General medical and surgical

Staffed Beds: 431 **Admissions:** 20131 **Census:** 287 **Outpatient Visits:** 601902 **Births:** 1957 **Total Expense ($000):** 843421 **Payroll Expense ($000):** 305877 **Personnel:** 4507

SAME DAY SURGERY CENTER (430093), 651 Cathedral Drive, Zip 57701–7368; tel. 605/755–9900, (Nonreporting) **A**10
Primary Contact: Doris Fritts, R.N., Executive Director
Web address: www.samedaysurgerycenter.org
Control: Corporation, Investor–owned (for–profit) **Service:** Surgical

Staffed Beds: 8

REDFIELD—Spink County

COMMUNITY MEMORIAL HOSPITAL (431316), 110 West Tenth Avenue, Zip 57469–1520, Mailing Address: P.O. Box 420, Zip 57469–0420; tel. 605/472–1110, (Nonreporting) **A**10 18
Primary Contact: Karen Sjurseth, Chief Executive Officer
CMO: Kristine Wren, M.D., Chief Medical Director
CHR: Rhonda Stroh, Chief Human Resources Officer
CNO: Tena Kolda, Director of Nursing
Web address: www.redfieldcmh.org/
Control: City, Government, Nonfederal **Service:** General medical and surgical

Staffed Beds: 25

ROSEBUD—Todd County

☒ **U. S. PUBLIC HEALTH SERVICE INDIAN HOSPITAL (430084)**, Highway 18, Soldier Creek Road, Zip 57570; tel. 605/747–2231, (Nonreporting) **A**1 10 **S** U. S. Indian Health Service, Rockville, MD
Primary Contact: Melody Price–Yonts, Chief Executive Officer
COO: Romeo Vivit, Chief Surgeon
CMO: Valerie Parker, M.D., Clinical Director
CHR: Michelle Zephier, Human Resource Specialist
Web address: www.ihs.gov
Control: PHS, Indian Service, Government, federal **Service:** General medical and surgical

Staffed Beds: 35

SCOTLAND—Bon Homme County

★ **LANDMANN–JUNGMAN MEMORIAL HOSPITAL AVERA (431317)**, 600 Billars Street, Zip 57059–2026; tel. 605/583–2226, (Nonreporting) **A**10 18 **S** Avera Health, Sioux Falls, SD
Primary Contact: Melissa Gale, Chief Executive Officer
CFO: Darcy Permann, Manager Business Office
Web address: www.ljmh.org
Control: Other not–for–profit (including NFP Corporation) **Service:** General medical and surgical

Staffed Beds: 10

SIOUX FALLS—Lincoln County

☐ **AVERA HEART HOSPITAL OF SOUTH DAKOTA (430095)**, 4500 West 69th Street, Zip 57108–8148; tel. 605/977–7000, **A**1 5 10 **F**3 17 18 19 20 21 22 23 24 26 28 29 30 34 40 41 43 50 57 58 59 60 64 68 74 75 81 84 85 87 102 107 108 111 115 118 119 135 154 157 **P**2 **S** Avera Health, Sioux Falls, SD
Primary Contact: Michael Gibbs, President
CFO: Jean White, Vice President Finance
Web address: www.avera.org/heart-hospital
Control: Corporation, Investor–owned (for–profit) **Service:** Heart

Staffed Beds: 53 **Admissions:** 2603 **Census:** 25 **Outpatient Visits:** 13370 **Births:** 0 **Total Expense ($000):** 132831 **Payroll Expense ($000):** 41635 **Personnel:** 555

☒ **ENCOMPASS HEALTH REHABILITATION HOSPITAL OF SIOUX FALLS (433027)**, 4700 W 69th Street, Zip 57108–8757; tel. 605/305–5600, (Nonreporting) **A**1 10 **S** Encompass Health Corporation, Birmingham, AL
Primary Contact: Kristina Schroder, Chief Executive Officer
Web address: www.encompasshealth.com/siouxfallsrehab
Control: Corporation, Investor–owned (for–profit) **Service:** Rehabilitation

Staffed Beds: 40

SIOUX FALLS—Minnehaha County

☒ △ **AVERA MCKENNAN HOSPITAL AND UNIVERSITY HEALTH CENTER (430016)**, 1325 South Cliff Avenue, Zip 57105–1007, Mailing Address: P.O. Box 5045, Zip 57117–5045; tel. 605/322–8000, (Includes AVERA BEHAVIORAL HEALTH CENTER, 4400 West 69th Street, Sioux Falls, South Dakota, Zip 57108–8170, tel. 605/322–4065; Steve Lindquist, Assistant Vice President, Behavioral Health; AVERA CHILDREN'S HOSPITAL, 1325 South Cliff Avenue, Sioux Falls, South Dakota, Zip 57105–1016, PO Box 5045, Zip 57117–5045, tel. 605/322–5437) (Total facility includes 114 beds in nursing home–type unit) **A**1 2 3 5 7 10 19 **F**3 4 5 8 11 12 13 15 16 18 19 20 21 22 23 24 28 29 31 32 34 35 36 38 39 40 41 42 43 44 45 46 47 48 49 50 53 54 55 56 57 58 60 61 64 65 66 68 70 71 72 74 75 76 77 78 79 81 82 83 84 85 86 87 88 89 90 91 92 93 94 96 97 98 99 100 101 102 103 104 105 107 108 109 110 111 112 114 115 116 117 118 119 120 121 123 124 126 127 128 129 130 131 132 134 135 136 138 139 141 142 143 144 145 146 147 148 149 152 153 154 155 156 157 160 162 163 164 165 167 168 169 **P**6 **S** Avera Health, Sioux Falls, SD
Primary Contact: Lieutenant General Ronald J. Place, M.D., President and Chief Executive Officer
COO: Judy Blauwet, M.P.H., R.N., Senior Vice President Operations
CFO: Julie Lautt, CPA, Vice President, Operational Finance
CMO: Michael Elliott, M.D., Chief Medical Officer and Senior Vice President of Medical Affairs
CIO: Kristin Gross, Director Information Technology Center
CHR: Lynne D Hagen, SHRM–CP, Human Resources Officer
CNO: Tamera J Larsen–Engelkes, Chief Nursing Officer
Web address: www.averamckennan.org
Control: Church operated, Nongovernment, not–for–profit **Service:** General medical and surgical

Staffed Beds: 705 **Admissions:** 25849 **Census:** 517 **Outpatient Visits:** 448336 **Births:** 2274 **Total Expense ($000):** 1466640 **Payroll Expense ($000):** 595928 **Personnel:** 6831

LIFESCAPE (433300), 2501 West 26th Street, Zip 57105–2498; tel. 605/444–9500, (Nonreporting) **A**10
Primary Contact: Steve Watkins, Chief Executive Officer
CFO: Stephan A. Wilson, Chief Financial Officer
CMO: Christiane Maroun, M.D., Chief of Staff
CHR: Tiffany Reilly, Director Human Resources
Web address: www.cchs.org
Control: Other not–for–profit (including NFP Corporation) **Service:** Children's rehabilitation

Staffed Beds: 114

☒ **ROYAL C. JOHNSON VETERANS' MEMORIAL HOSPITAL**, 2501 West 22nd Street, Zip 57105–1305, Mailing Address: P.O. Box 5046, Zip 57117–5046; tel. 605/336–3230, (Nonreporting) **A**1 3 5 **S** Department of Veterans Affairs, Washington, DC
Primary Contact: Sara Ackert, Executive Director and Chief Executive Officer
CFO: Daniel Hubbard, Chief Financial Officer
CMO: John M Wempe, M.D., Chief of Staff
CIO: Eric Heiser, Chief Information Resource Management
CHR: Betsy Geiver, Chief Human Resources Officer
CNO: Barbara Teal, R.N., Associate Director Patient Care Services and Nurse Executive
Web address: www.siouxfalls.va.gov
Control: Veterans Affairs, Government, federal **Service:** General medical and surgical

Staffed Beds: 175

SANFORD CHILDREN'S HOSPITAL See Sanford Children's Hospital Sioux Falls

Hospitals, U.S. / SOUTH DAKOTA

✦ △ **SANFORD USD MEDICAL CENTER (430027)**, 1305 West 18th Street, Zip 57105–0496, Mailing Address: P.O. Box 5039, Zip 57117–5039; tel. 605/333–1000, (Includes SANFORD CHILDREN'S HOSPITAL SIOUX FALLS, 1600 West 22nd Street, Sioux Falls, South Dakota, Zip 57105–1521, PO Box 5039, Zip 57117–5039, tel. 605/333–1000) **A**1 2 3 5 7 8 10 19 **F**3 5 7 8 9 11 12 13 14 15 17 18 19 20 21 22 23 24 25 26 27 28 29 30 31 32 34 35 36 37 38 40 43 44 45 46 47 48 49 50 51 52 53 54 55 56 57 58 59 60 61 62 63 64 65 66 67 68 69 70 71 72 73 74 75 76 77 78 79 80 81 82 83 84 85 86 87 88 89 90 91 92 93 94 96 97 99 100 101 102 103 104 105 106 107 108 110 111 114 115 116 117 118 119 120 121 123 124 125 126 129 130 131 132 134 135 138 141 142 143 144 146 147 148 149 150 151 152 153 154 155 156 157 160 162 163 164 165 167 169 **P**6 **S** Sanford Health, Sioux Falls, SD
Primary Contact: Paul A. Hanson, FACHE, President
COO: Brad J. Schipper, Chief Operating Officer
CFO: Merrilee Schultz, Chief Finance
CMO: Michael Wilde, M.D., Vice President Medical Officer
CIO: Arlyn Broekhuis, Vice President and Chief Information Officer
CHR: Evan Burkett, Chief Human Resource Officer
Web address: https://www.sanfordhealth.org/locations/sanford-usd-medical-center
Control: Other not–for–profit (including NFP Corporation) **Service:** General medical and surgical

Staffed Beds: 410 **Admissions:** 23336 **Census:** 292 **Outpatient Visits:** 502332 **Births:** 3229 **Total Expense ($000):** 1331708 **Payroll Expense ($000):** 545476 **Personnel:** 5728

✦ **SELECT SPECIALTY HOSPITAL–SIOUX FALLS (432002)**, 1305 West 18th Street, Zip 57105–0401; tel. 605/312–9500, (Nonreporting) **A**1 10 **S** Select Medical Corporation, Mechanicsburg, PA
Primary Contact: Scott James. Hargens, Chief Executive Officer
CNO: Alison Anderson, Chief Nursing Officer
Web address: www.selectspecialtyhospitals.com/company/locations/siouxfalls.aspx
Control: Corporation, Investor–owned (for–profit) **Service:** Acute long–term care hospital

Staffed Beds: 24

○ **SIOUX FALLS SPECIALTY HOSPITAL (430090)**, 910 East 20th Street, Zip 57105–1012; tel. 605/334–6730, (Nonreporting) **A**10 11
Primary Contact: R Blake. Curd, M.D., Chief Executive Officer
CFO: Kyle Goldammer, Chief Financial Officer
Web address: www.sfsurgical.com
Control: Partnership, Investor–owned (for–profit) **Service:** Surgical

Staffed Beds: 35

SIOUX FALLS VAMC See Royal C. Johnson Veterans' Memorial Hospital

SISSETON—Roberts County

★ **COTEAU DES PRAIRIES HOSPITAL (431339)**, 205 Orchard Drive, Zip 57262–2398; tel. 605/698–7647, (Nonreporting) **A**10 18 **S** Sanford Health, Sioux Falls, SD
Primary Contact: Craig A. Kantos, Chief Executive Officer
CFO: Larry Moen, Chief Financial Officer
CMO: David Staub, M.D., Chief of Staff
CIO: Cheryl Kaufman, Information Technology Technician
CHR: Leslie Hendrickson, Director Human Resources
Web address: www.cdphospital.com
Control: Other not–for–profit (including NFP Corporation) **Service:** General medical and surgical

Staffed Beds: 25

SPEARFISH—Lawrence County

★ **MONUMENT HEALTH SPEARFISH HOSPITAL (430048)**, 1440 North Main Street, Zip 57783–1504; tel. 605/644–4000, (Includes SPEARFISH REGIONAL SURGERY CENTER, 1316 N 10th St, Spearfish, South Dakota, Zip 57783–1530, 1316 North 10th Street, Zip 57783–1530, tel. 605/642–3113) **A**10 20 **F**3 12 13 15 18 28 29 30 31 34 37 40 43 45 48 49 56 57 59 64 68 70 75 76 79 81 82 83 84 85 89 93 94 97 107 108 110 111 115 119 126 127 129 131 132 144 147 148 149 154 156 169 **P**6 **S** Monument Health, Rapid City, SD
Primary Contact: Thomas Worsley, Chief Executive Officer
CFO: Marcia Olson, Director Finance and Controller
CMO: Christopher Gasbarre, D.O., Community Medical Director
CHR: Patsy Aiken, Coordinator Human Resource
CNO: Suzanne Campbell, R.N., Director Patient Services
Web address: www.regionalhealth.com/Our-Locations/Regional-Hospitals/Spearfish-Regional-Hospital.aspx
Control: Other not–for–profit (including NFP Corporation) **Service:** General medical and surgical

Staffed Beds: 35 **Admissions:** 1410 **Census:** 10 **Outpatient Visits:** 284964 **Births:** 458 **Total Expense ($000):** 113943 **Payroll Expense ($000):** 51330 **Personnel:** 466

SPEARFISH SURGERY CENTER See Spearfish Regional Surgery Center

STURGIS—Meade County

★ **MONUMENT HEALTH STURGIS HOSPITAL (431321)**, 2140 Junction Avenue, Zip 57785–2452; tel. 605/720–2400, (Nonreporting) **A**10 18 **S** Monument Health, Rapid City, SD
Primary Contact: Mark C. Schmidt, President
CFO: Jodie Mitchell, Facility Financial Director
CMO: Constance Stock, M.D., Chief Medical Officer
CHR: Ginger Chord, Coordinator Human Resources
CNO: Rikki Plaggemeyer, Director Acute Care Nursing
Web address: https://directory.monument.health/facility/sd/sturgis/2140-junction-avenue-6671505
Control: Other not–for–profit (including NFP Corporation) **Service:** General medical and surgical

Staffed Beds: 109

TYNDALL—Bon Homme County

★ **ST. MICHAEL'S HOSPITAL AVERA (431327)**, 410 West 16th Avenue, Zip 57066–2318; tel. 605/589–2100, (Nonreporting) **A**10 18 **S** Avera Health, Sioux Falls, SD
Primary Contact: Ashli Danilko, Chief Executive Officer
CFO: Lisa Ronke, Director Finance
CMO: Melvin Wallinga, M.D., Medical Director
Web address: www.stmichaels-bhfp.org
Control: Church operated, Nongovernment, not–for–profit **Service:** General medical and surgical

Staffed Beds: 25

VERMILLION—Clay County

★ **SANFORD VERMILLION MEDICAL CENTER (431336)**, 20 South Plum Street, Zip 57069–3346; tel. 605/677–3500, (Nonreporting) **A**10 18 **S** Sanford Health, Sioux Falls, SD
Primary Contact: Timothy J. Tracy, Senior Director
CFO: Valerie Osterberg, Chief Financial Officer
CMO: Roy Mortinsen, M.D., Chief of Staff
CIO: Mary C Merrigan, Manager Public Relations
CHR: Cindy Benzel, Manager Human Resources
CNO: Jeff Berens, MS, Chief Nursing Officer
Web address: www.sanfordvermillion.org
Control: Other not–for–profit (including NFP Corporation) **Service:** General medical and surgical

Staffed Beds: 88

Hospital, Medicare Provider Number, Address, Telephone, Approval, Facility, and Physician Codes, Health Care System

★ American Hospital Association (AHA) membership   ◇ Healthcare Facilities Accreditation Program   ⇧ Center for Improvement in Healthcare Quality Accreditation
□ The Joint Commission accreditation   ◊ DNV Healthcare Inc. accreditation   △ Commission on Accreditation of Rehabilitation Facilities (CARF) accreditation

Hospitals, U.S. / SOUTH DAKOTA

VIBORG—Turner County

★ **PIONEER MEMORIAL HOSPITAL AND HEALTH SERVICES (431328)**, 315 North Washington Street, Zip 57070–2002, Mailing Address: P.O. Box 368, Zip 57070–0368; tel. 605/326–5161, (Nonreporting) **A**10 18 **S** Sanford Health, Sioux Falls, SD
Primary Contact: Isaac Gerdes, Chief Executive Officer
CFO: Anne Christiansen, Chief Financial Officer
CMO: Syed Shah, M.D., Chief of Staff
Web address: www.pioneermemorial.org
Control: Other not–for–profit (including NFP Corporation) **Service**: General medical and surgical

Staffed Beds: 55

WAGNER—Charles Mix County

★ **U. S. PUBLIC HEALTH SERVICE INDIAN HOSPITAL (430086)**, 111 Washington Avenue Northwest, Zip 57380–4300, Mailing Address: Box 490, Zip 57380–4090; tel. 605/384–3621, (Nonreporting) **A**10 **S** U. S. Indian Health Service, Rockville, MD
Primary Contact: Michael Horned Eagle, Chief Executive Officer
Control: PHS, Indian Service, Government, federal **Service**: Other specialty treatment

Staffed Beds: 23

★ **WAGNER COMMUNITY MEMORIAL HOSPITAL AVERA (431315)**, 513 Third Street SW, Zip 57380–9675, Mailing Address: P.O. Box 280, Zip 57380–0280; tel. 605/384–3611, (Nonreporting) **A**10 18 **S** Avera Health, Sioux Falls, SD
Primary Contact: Bryan Slaba, Chief Executive Officer
CFO: Lisa Weisser, Controller
CHR: Marcia Podzimek, Chief Human Resources Officer
Web address: www.avera.org/wagnerhospital
Control: Other not–for–profit (including NFP Corporation) **Service**: General medical and surgical

Staffed Beds: 20

WATERTOWN—Codington County

★ **PRAIRIE LAKES HEALTHCARE SYSTEM (430005)**, 401 9th Avenue NW, Zip 57201–1548, Mailing Address: 401 9th Ave NW, Zip 57201–1548; tel. 605/882–7000, **A**10 20 **F**3 8 12 13 18 20 22 28 29 30 31 34 35 40 41 43 47 49 50 57 58 59 60 62 63 64 75 76 77 78 79 80 81 82 85 86 89 91 93 97 111 114 115 118 119 120 121 123 130 131 132 146 148 154 169
Primary Contact: John Allen, President and Chief Executive Officer
COO: Traci Rabine, Vice President Clinic Operations
CFO: Lynn Severson, Chief Financial Officer
CMO: Leighton Singh, M.D., Chief of Staff
CIO: Grant Tillett, Chief Information Officer
CHR: Nathan Lake, Vice President Human Resources
CNO: Shelly Turbak, R.N., Chief Nursing Officer
Web address: www.prairielakes.com
Control: Other not–for–profit (including NFP Corporation) **Service**: General medical and surgical

Staffed Beds: 58 **Admissions**: 2412 **Census**: 23 **Outpatient Visits**: 115819 **Births**: 572 **Total Expense ($000)**: 139557 **Payroll Expense ($000)**: 64921 **Personnel**: 604

WEBSTER—Day County

★ **SANFORD WEBSTER MEDICAL CENTER (431311)**, 1401 West 1st Street, Zip 57274–1054, Mailing Address: P.O. Box 489, Zip 57274–0489; tel. 605/345–3336, (Nonreporting) **A**10 18 **S** Sanford Health, Sioux Falls, SD
Primary Contact: Isaac Gerdes, Chief Executive Officer
CFO: Sheryl L Pappas, Chief Financial Officer
Web address: https://www.sanfordhealth.org/locations/sanford-webster-medical-center
Control: Other not–for–profit (including NFP Corporation) **Service**: General medical and surgical

Staffed Beds: 20

WESSINGTON SPRINGS—Jerauld County

★ **AVERA WESKOTA MEMORIAL HOSPITAL (431324)**, 604 First Street NE, Zip 57382–2166; tel. 605/539–1201, **A**10 18 **F**3 15 28 34 35 40 53 57 59 64 75 77 85 93 107 114 119 130 131 133 **S** Avera Health, Sioux Falls, SD
Primary Contact: Stephanie Reasy, Administrator and Chief Executive Officer
CFO: Linda Jager, Director Finance
CMO: Thomas Dean, M.D., Chief of Staff
CNO: JoAnn Hettinger, R.N., Director of Patient Care Services
Web address: www.aveaweskota.org
Control: Other not–for–profit (including NFP Corporation) **Service**: General medical and surgical

Staffed Beds: 16 **Admissions**: 103 **Census**: 2 **Outpatient Visits**: 4856 **Births**: 0 **Total Expense ($000)**: 4680 **Payroll Expense ($000)**: 2112 **Personnel**: 21

WINNER—Tripp County

★ **WINNER REGIONAL HEALTHCARE CENTER (431334)**, 745 East Eighth Street, Zip 57580–2631; tel. 605/842–7100, (Nonreporting) **A**10 18 **S** Sanford Health, Sioux Falls, SD
Primary Contact: Brian Williams, Chief Executive Officer
COO: Debra K. Davis, Director of Operations
CFO: Earl Pierce, Chief Financial Officer
CMO: Tony L. Berg, M.D., Chief of Staff
CIO: Gary Burrus, Director Information Technology
CHR: Susan Hughes, Interim Director Human Resources
CNO: Julie Hennebold, R.N., Interim Chief Nursing Officer
Web address: www.winnerregional.org
Control: Other not–for–profit (including NFP Corporation) **Service**: General medical and surgical

Staffed Beds: 104

YANKTON—Yankton County

✠ **AVERA SACRED HEART HOSPITAL (430012)**, 501 Summit Avenue, Zip 57078–3855; tel. 605/668–8000, (Includes AVERA FOX RUN HEALTH CAMPUS, 2601 Fox Run Parkway, Yankton, South Dakota, Zip 57078–5341; tel. 605/665–5100; Douglas Doorn, Chief Executive Officer) (Total facility includes 187 beds in nursing home–type unit) **A**1 2 3 5 10 **F**2 3 6 8 10 13 15 18 20 28 29 30 31 34 35 39 40 43 45 46 47 48 53 57 59 60 63 64 70 71 75 76 77 78 79 81 82 84 85 86 87 89 91 93 96 97 100 104 107 108 110 111 114 115 118 119 120 121 125 128 129 130 131 132 133 146 147 148 154 156 167 169 **P**6 **S** Avera Health, Sioux Falls, SD
Primary Contact: Douglas R. Ekeren, FACHE, Regional President and Chief Executive Officer, Administration
CFO: Jamie Schaefer, Vice President Finance
CIO: Kathy Quinlivan, Director Management Information Systems
CHR: Jane E. Miller, Human Resources Officer
Web address: www.averasacredheart.com
Control: Church operated, Nongovernment, not–for–profit **Service**: General medical and surgical

Staffed Beds: 229 **Admissions**: 3217 **Census**: 200 **Outpatient Visits**: 90308 **Births**: 486 **Total Expense ($000)**: 124770 **Payroll Expense ($000)**: 52574 **Personnel**: 752

TENNESSEE

ASHLAND CITY—Cheatham County

TRISTAR ASHLAND CITY MEDICAL CENTER (440779), 313 North Main Street, Zip 37015–1347; tel. 615/792–3030, (Nonreporting) **S** HCA Healthcare, Nashville, TN
Primary Contact: Timothy McPherson, Emergency Room Director
Web address: https://www.tristarhealth.com/locations/tristar-ashland-city-medical-center
Control: Corporation, Investor–owned (for–profit)

Staffed Beds: 12

ATHENS—Mcminn County

STARR REGIONAL MEDICAL CENTER (440068), 1114 West Madison Avenue, Zip 37303–4150, Mailing Address: P.O. Box 250, Zip 37371–0250; tel. 423/745–1411, (Nonreporting) **A**1 3 10 **S** Lifepoint Health, Brentwood, TN
Primary Contact: John R. McLain, Chief Executive Officer
COO: Michael Herr, Chief Operating Officer
CFO: David Alley, Chief Financial Officer
Web address: www.starrregional.com
Control: Corporation, Investor–owned (for–profit) **Service:** General medical and surgical

Staffed Beds: 63

BARTLETT—Shelby County

SAINT FRANCIS HOSPITAL–BARTLETT (440228), 2986 Kate Bond Road, Zip 38133–4003; tel. 901/820–7000, (Nonreporting) **A**1 10 **S** TENET Healthcare Corporation, Dallas, TX
Primary Contact: Sherwin Stewart, Chief Executive Officer
COO: Gwen Bonner, Chief Operating Officer
CFO: Tina Kovacs, Chief Financial Officer
CMO: David Schwartz, M.D., Chief Medical Officer
CIO: Mark Lawrence, Director Information Systems
CHR: Adrienne Huntley, Chief Human Resources Officer
CNO: Jacquelyn Whobrey, MSN, R.N., Chief Nursing Officer
Web address: www.saintfrancisbartlett.com
Control: Corporation, Investor–owned (for–profit) **Service:** General medical and surgical

Staffed Beds: 196

BOLIVAR—Hardeman County

WEST TENNESSEE HEALTHCARE BOLIVAR HOSPITAL (441320), 650 Nuckolls Road, Zip 38008–1532, Mailing Address: PO Box 509, Zip 38008–0509; tel. 731/658–3100, **A**1 10 18 **F**3 15 29 30 35 40 44 57 59 64 75 87 93 107 119 129 130 132 133 146 149 **S** West Tennessee Healthcare, Jackson, TN
Primary Contact: Ruby Kirby, Chief Executive Officer
CFO: Dana Lawrence, Controller
CMO: Felix Nnaji, Chief Medical Staff
Web address: www.wth.net
Control: Hospital district or authority, Government, Nonfederal **Service:** General medical and surgical

Staffed Beds: 17 **Admissions:** 95 **Census:** 1 **Outpatient Visits:** 15307
Births: 1 **Total Expense ($000):** 8381 **Payroll Expense ($000):** 3966
Personnel: 58

WESTERN MENTAL HEALTH INSTITUTE (444008), 11100 Old Highway 64, West, Zip 38008–1554; tel. 731/228–2000, **A**1 10 **F**98 100 130 154 164
Primary Contact: Josh Carter, Chief Executive Officer
CFO: Richard Taylor, Chief Financial Officer
CMO: Doug King, M.D., Director Clinical Services
CIO: Earl Bates, Director Information Technology
CHR: Barry Young, Director Human Resources
Web address: https://www.tn.gov/behavioral-health/hospitals/western.html
Control: State, Government, Nonfederal **Service:** Psychiatric

Staffed Beds: 150 **Admissions:** 548 **Census:** 128 **Outpatient Visits:** 0
Births: 0 **Total Expense ($000):** 41337 **Payroll Expense ($000):** 23763
Personnel: 423

BRISTOL—Sullivan County

BRISTOL REGIONAL MEDICAL CENTER (440012), 1 Medical Park Boulevard, Zip 37620–7430; tel. 423/844–1121, (Nonreporting) **A**1 2 3 5 10 19 **S** Ballad Health, Johnson City, TN
Primary Contact: John Jeter, Chief Executive Officer
COO: Christopher Brian Hobson, Chief Operating Officer
CFO: Bob Bender, Vice–President Hospital Finance and Operations, Northeast Market
CIO: Pam Austin, Senior Vice–President, Chief Information Officer
CHR: Deborah L Dover, Senior Vice–President of Human Resources
CNO: Bobbie Murphy, R.N., Chief Nursing Officer
Web address: https://www.balladhealth.org/locations/hospitals/bristol-regional
Control: Other not–for–profit (including NFP Corporation) **Service:** General medical and surgical

Staffed Beds: 296

SELECT SPECIALTY HOSPITAL–TRI CITIES (442016), 1 Medical Park Boulevard, Zip 37620–8964; tel. 423/844–5900, (Nonreporting) **A**1 10 **S** Select Medical Corporation, Mechanicsburg, PA
Primary Contact: Jeffery Wright, Chief Executive Officer
CMO: John Byers, M.D., Medical Director
CHR: William G Ison, Human Resources Manager
CNO: Valerie Anderson, Chief Nursing Officer
Web address: www.tricities.selectspecialtyhospitals.com/
Control: Corporation, Investor–owned (for–profit) **Service:** Acute long–term care hospital

Staffed Beds: 33

CAMDEN—Benton County

WEST TENNESSEE HEALTHCARE CAMDEN HOSPITAL (441316), 175 Hospital Drive, Zip 38320–1617; tel. 731/593–6300, **A**1 10 18 **F**3 15 29 30 35 40 44 57 59 64 75 79 85 87 93 107 111 119 130 132 133 146 149 **S** West Tennessee Healthcare, Jackson, TN
Primary Contact: Ruby Kirby, Chief Executive Officer
CFO: Terry Swindell, Chief Financial Officer
CMO: Jon R. Winter, D.O., Chief of Staff
CIO: Jeff Frieling, Vice President Information Systems
CHR: Barry Phillips, Executive Director Human Resources
Web address: www.wth.net
Control: Hospital district or authority, Government, Nonfederal **Service:** General medical and surgical

Staffed Beds: 15 **Admissions:** 177 **Census:** 3 **Outpatient Visits:** 11821
Births: 0 **Total Expense ($000):** 9545 **Payroll Expense ($000):** 4466
Personnel: 67

CARTHAGE—Smith County

RIVERVIEW REGIONAL MEDICAL CENTER (441307), 158 Hospital Drive, Zip 37030–1096; tel. 615/735–1560, (Nonreporting) **A**1 10 18 **S** Lifepoint Health, Brentwood, TN
Primary Contact: Rod Harkleroad, R.N., Chief Executive Officer
CFO: Amanda Pruitt, Chief Financial Officer
CHR: Gina Anderson, Human Resources Officer
CNO: Angela Pruett, Chief Nursing Officer
Web address: www.myriverviewmedical.com/
Control: Corporation, Investor–owned (for–profit) **Service:** General medical and surgical

Staffed Beds: 35

Hospitals, U.S. / TENNESSEE

CENTERVILLE—Hickman County

☒ **ASCENSION SAINT THOMAS HICKMAN (441300)**, 135 East Swan Street, Zip 37033–1417; tel. 931/729–4271, **A**1 10 18 **F**3 15 18 29 30 34 35 40 45 46 48 50 57 59 64 65 66 75 77 86 93 97 100 101 104 107 111 114 119 127 130 131 132 133 135 148 149 150 153 154 156 164 165 **S** Ascension Healthcare, Saint Louis, MO
Primary Contact: Kevin Campbell, Chief Executive Officer
COO: Robin Crowell, Chief Nursing Officer and Chief Operating Officer
CMO: Zachary Hutchens, M.D., Chief Medical Officer
CHR: Patty Matney, Human Resources Consultant
CNO: Robin Crowell, Chief Nursing Officer and Chief Operating Officer
Web address: https://healthcare.ascension.org/Locations/Tennessee/TNNAS/Centerville-Ascension-Saint-Thomas-Hickman/Visitor-Information
Control: Other not–for–profit (including NFP Corporation) **Service**: General medical and surgical

Staffed Beds: 8 **Admissions**: 121 **Census**: 4 **Outpatient Visits**: 33412 **Births**: 0 **Total Expense ($000)**: 19885 **Payroll Expense ($000)**: 9507 **Personnel**: 104

CHATTANOOGA—Hamilton County

☒ **CHI MEMORIAL (440091)**, 2525 De Sales Avenue, Zip 37404–1161; tel. 423/495–2525, (Includes MEMORIAL HOSPITAL HIXSON, 2051 Hamill Road, Hixson, Tennessee, Zip 37343–4026, tel. 423/495–7100; Janelle Reilly, Market Chief Executive Officer) **A**1 2 3 5 10 **F**3 7 8 11 12 15 17 18 20 22 24 26 28 29 30 31 34 35 36 37 40 44 45 46 47 48 49 50 53 54 55 56 57 58 59 60 64 67 70 71 74 75 77 78 79 81 82 85 86 87 93 100 102 107 108 109 110 111 114 115 116 117 118 119 120 121 124 126 129 130 132 135 143 145 146 147 148 149 150 154 156 167 **P**3 6 7 8 **S** CommonSpirit Health, Chicago, IL
Primary Contact: Janelle Reilly, Market Chief Executive Officer
COO: Rhonda Adams Scott, Ph.D., R.N., Market Chief Operating Officer and President
CFO: Michael Sutton, Chief Financial Officer
CHR: Brad W Pope, Vice President Human Resources
CNO: Rhonda Hatfield, Chief Nursing Officer and Vice President of Clinical Operations
Web address: www.memorial.org
Control: Church operated, Nongovernment, not–for–profit **Service**: General medical and surgical

Staffed Beds: 423 **Admissions**: 19556 **Census**: 277 **Outpatient Visits**: 356420 **Births**: 0 **Total Expense ($000)**: 496117 **Payroll Expense ($000)**: 202843 **Personnel**: 2250

☒ **ENCOMPASS HEALTH REHABILITATION HOSPITAL OF CHATTANOOGA (443032)**, 2412 McCallie Avenue, Zip 37404–3398; tel. 423/698–0221, (Nonreporting) **A**1 2 10 **S** Encompass Health Corporation, Birmingham, AL
Primary Contact: Matthew Pearson, Chief Executive Officer
COO: Scott Rowe, Chief Executive Officer
CFO: Karen Klassen, Controller
CMO: Amjad Munir, M.D., Medical Director
CIO: Denise Smith, Director Health Information
CHR: Rebekah McNair, Director Human Resources
CNO: Cinthia Campbell, Chief Nursing Officer
Web address: www.healthsouthchattanooga.com
Control: Corporation, Investor–owned (for–profit) **Service**: Rehabilitation

Staffed Beds: 50

☐ **ERLANGER BEHAVIORAL HOSPITAL (444026)**, 804 North Holtzclaw Avenue, Zip 37404–1235; tel. 423/834–7176, (Nonreporting) **A**1 10
Primary Contact: Tyler Davis, Chief Executive Officer
Web address: https://www.erlangerbh.com/
Control: Corporation, Investor–owned (for–profit) **Service**: Psychiatric

Staffed Beds: 96

★ ⇑ **ERLANGER MEDICAL CENTER (440104)**, 975 East Third Street, Zip 37403–2147; tel. 423/778–7000, (Includes CHILDREN'S HOSPITAL AT ERLANGER, 910 Blackford Street, Chattanooga, Tennessee, Zip 37403–1405, tel. 423/778–6011; ERLANGER EAST HOSPITAL, 1755 Gunbarrel Road, Chattanooga, Tennessee, Zip 37421, tel. 423/680–8000; Tyler Winks, Chief Executive Officer; ERLANGER NORTH HOSPITAL, 632 Morrison Springs Road, Chattanooga, Tennessee, Zip 37415, tel. 423/778–3300; Tyler Winks, Chief Executive Officer; T. C. THOMPSON CHILDREN'S HOSPITAL, 910 Blackford Street, Chattanooga, Tennessee, Zip 37403, tel. 615/778–6011; WILLIE D. MILLER EYE CENTER, 975 East Third Street, Chattanooga, Tennessee, Zip 37403, tel. 615/778–6011) **A**2 3 5 10 19 21 **F**3 8 11 12 13 14 15 17 18 19 20 21 22 23 24 25 26 27 28 29 30 31 32 34 35 37 38 39 40 41 43 44 45 46 47 48 49 50 51 52 53 54 55 56 57 58 59 60 61 64 65 66 68 70 72 73 74 75 76 77 78 79 81 82 84 85 86 87 88 89 92 93 96 97 100 101 102 107 108 109 110 111 112 114 115 116 117 118 119 120 121 123 124 126 129 130 131 132 134 135 138 141 144 146 147 148 149 150 154 155 156 157 164 165 167 169 **P**6 **S** Erlanger Health System, Chattanooga, TN
Primary Contact: Jim Coleman Jr, Chief Executive Officer
CMO: Douglas Brewer, M.D., Chief Medical Officer
CIO: David Peterson, Senior Vice President, Chief Technology Officer
CHR: Floyd Chasse, Vice President Human Resources
Web address: www.erlanger.org
Control: Hospital district or authority, Government, Nonfederal **Service**: General medical and surgical

Staffed Beds: 697 **Admissions**: 31400 **Census**: 429 **Outpatient Visits**: 1048845 **Births**: 5538 **Total Expense ($000)**: 1169642 **Payroll Expense ($000)**: 461012 **Personnel**: 5053

ERLANGER WOMEN'S EAST HOSPITAL See Erlanger East Hospital

☒ **KINDRED HOSPITAL–CHATTANOOGA (442007)**, 709 Walnut Street, Zip 37402–1916; tel. 423/266–7721, (Nonreporting) **A**1 10 **S** ScionHealth, Louisville, KY
Primary Contact: Andrea White, Chief Executive Officer
COO: Rick Rheinheimer, Chief Clinical Officer
CFO: Julia Smith, Chief Financial Officer
CMO: Randy Heisser, M.D., Medical Director
CHR: Kellie McCampbell, Coordinator Human Resources
CNO: Gigi Johnson, Chief Nursing Officer
Web address: www.kindredchattanooga.com/
Control: Corporation, Investor–owned (for–profit) **Service**: Acute long–term care hospital

Staffed Beds: 39

☐ **MOCCASIN BEND MENTAL HEALTH INSTITUTE (444002)**, 100 Moccasin Bend Road, Zip 37405–4415; tel. 423/265–2271, (Nonreporting) **A**1 10
Primary Contact: Mary C. Young, Chief Executive Officer
CFO: Sylvia Harris, Fiscal Director
CMO: Terry R Holmes, M.D., Clinical Director
CIO: Mickey Williams, Manager Information Technology
CHR: Cynthia Honeycutt, Director Human Resources
CNO: Charlynne Parson, Nurse Executive
Web address: www.state.tn.us/mental/mhs/mbhmhi/moc.htm
Control: State, Government, Nonfederal **Service**: Psychiatric

Staffed Beds: 165

☒ **PARKRIDGE MEDICAL CENTER (440156)**, 2333 McCallie Avenue, Zip 37404–3258; tel. 423/698–6061, (Includes EAST RIDGE HOSPITAL, 941 Spring Creek Road, East Ridge, Tennessee, Zip 37412, P O Box 91229, Zip 37412–6229, tel. 423/855–3500; PARKRIDGE EAST HOSPITAL, 941 Spring Creek Road, Chattanooga, Tennessee, Zip 37412–3909, tel. 423/894–7870; William Windham, Chief Executive Officer; PARKRIDGE VALLEY CHILD AND ADOLESCENT CAMPUS, 2200 Morris Hill Road, Chattanooga, Tennessee, Zip 37421, tel. 423/894–4220; Melissa Arkin, Chief Executive Officer; PARKRIDGE WEST HOSPITAL, 1000 Highway 28, Jasper, Tennessee, Zip 37347–3638, tel. 423/837–9500; Shirley K Scarlatti, Associate Chief Nursing Officer) (Nonreporting) **A**1 2 3 5 10 **S** HCA Healthcare, Nashville, TN
Primary Contact: Christopher Cosby, President and Chief Executive Officer
CMO: Timothy M. Grant, M.D., Chief Medical Officer
CIO: David Cornelius, Director Information Systems
CNO: Jerri C Underwood, R.N., Chief Nursing Officer
Web address: www.parkridgemedicalcenter.com
Control: Corporation, Investor–owned (for–profit) **Service**: General medical and surgical

Staffed Beds: 645

PARKRIDGE VALLEY HOSPTIAL See Parkridge Valley Child and Adolescent Campus

Hospitals, U.S. / TENNESSEE

★ △ **SISKIN HOSPITAL FOR PHYSICAL REHABILITATION (443025)**, 1 Siskin Plaza, Zip 37403–1306; tel. 423/634–1200, (Total facility includes 39 beds in nursing home–type unit) **A**7 10 22 **F**29 34 35 44 53 54 57 64 74 75 90 91 93 96 128 130 132 148 157
Primary Contact: Matthew Gibson, Ph.D., FACHE, Chief Executive Officer
CFO: Carol Arnhart, Vice President Finance and Chief Financial Officer
CMO: David N Bowers, M.D., Medical Director
CIO: Shane Pilcher, Administrative Director Information Systems
CHR: Kristi Delaney, Director, Human Resources
CNO: Tracy Collings Reed, Vice President Patient Care Services, Chief Nursing Officer
Web address: www.siskinrehab.org
Control: Other not–for–profit (including NFP Corporation) **Service**: Rehabilitation

Staffed Beds: 135 **Admissions**: 2487 **Census**: 116 **Outpatient Visits**: 34673 **Births**: 0 **Total Expense ($000)**: 49180 **Payroll Expense ($000)**: 28080 **Personnel**: 304

T. C. THOMPSON CHILDREN'S HOSPITAL See Erlanger Medical Center, Chattanooga

CLARKSVILLE—Montgomery County

✠ **TENNOVA HEALTHCARE–CLARKSVILLE (440035)**, 651 Dunlop Lane, Zip 37040–5015, Mailing Address: P.O. Box 31629, Zip 37040–0028; tel. 931/502–1000, (Nonreporting) **A**1 10 **S** Community Health Systems, Inc., Franklin, TN
Primary Contact: Andrew Emery, Chief Executive Officer
CFO: Valerie Bryant, Chief Financial Officer
CMO: David Price, M.D., Chief Medical Advisor
CIO: Scott Greene, Chief Information Officer
CHR: Liza Edmunds, Director Human Resources
CNO: Michelle Dickerson, Chief Nursing Officer
Web address: www.tennova.com/
Control: Partnership, Investor–owned (for–profit) **Service**: General medical and surgical

Staffed Beds: 270

UNITY PSYCHIATRIC CARE–CLARKSVILLE (444019), 930 Professional Park Drive, Zip 37040–5136; tel. 931/538–6420, (Nonreporting) **A**10 **S** Tennessee Health Management, Parsons, TN
Primary Contact: Jessica Thurston, Administrator
CMO: Michael McGhee, M.D., Medical Director
CNO: Chrissy Myers, R.N., Director of Nursing
Web address: www.unitypsych.com
Control: Partnership, Investor–owned (for–profit) **Service**: Psychiatric

Staffed Beds: 26

CLEVELAND—Bradley County

CLEVELAND COMMUNITY HOSPITAL See Skyridge Medical Center – Westside Campus

✠ **TENNOVA HEALTHCARE – CLEVELAND (440185)**, 2305 Chambliss Avenue NW, Zip 37311–3847, Mailing Address: P.O. Box 3060, Zip 37320–3060; tel. 423/559–6000, (Includes SKYRIDGE MEDICAL CENTER – WESTSIDE CAMPUS, 2800 Westside Drive NW, Cleveland, Tennessee, Zip 37312–3599, tel. 423/339–4100; R Coleman Foss, Chief Executive Officer) (Nonreporting) **A**1 10 19
Primary Contact: Lisa Lovelace, Chief Executive Officer
CMO: William F Johnson, Chief Medical Officer
CHR: Kristine Godfrey, Director Human Resources
Web address: https://www.tennovacleveland.com/
Control: Corporation, Investor–owned (for–profit) **Service**: General medical and surgical

Staffed Beds: 183

COLLIERVILLE—Shelby County

★ **BAPTIST MEMORIAL HOSPITAL–COLLIERVILLE (440217)**, 1500 West Poplar Avenue, Zip 38017–0601; tel. 901/861–9400, **A**5 10 **F**3 7 8 12 15 18 29 30 34 35 36 38 40 41 45 46 47 48 49 50 53 57 58 59 60 61 64 65 70 74 75 77 79 80 81 84 85 87 91 92 93 96 107 108 109 110 111 114 115 119 120 126 129 130 132 135 146 147 148 149 154 **S** Baptist Memorial Health Care Corporation, Memphis, TN
Primary Contact: Lindsay Stencel, Chief Executive Officer and Administrator
CFO: Terri Seago, Chief Financial Officer
CIO: Doug Reiselt, Vice President and Chief Information Officer
CHR: Brenda Johnson, Director Human Resources
CNO: Denise Ferguson, Chief Nursing Officer
Web address: www.baptistonline.org/collierville/
Control: Other not–for–profit (including NFP Corporation) **Service**: General medical and surgical

Staffed Beds: 81 **Admissions**: 4145 **Census**: 56 **Outpatient Visits**: 51811 **Births**: 0 **Total Expense ($000)**: 78501 **Payroll Expense ($000)**: 32073 **Personnel**: 379

COLUMBIA—Maury County

✠ **MAURY REGIONAL MEDICAL CENTER (440073)**, 1224 Trotwood Avenue, Zip 38401–4802; tel. 931/381–1111, **A**1 2 10 19 **F**3 7 8 11 13 15 18 20 22 26 28 29 30 31 34 35 37 38 40 41 44 45 46 47 48 49 50 51 53 54 55 57 58 59 60 62 64 68 70 71 73 74 75 76 77 78 79 80 81 82 84 85 86 87 89 91 92 93 96 102 107 108 110 111 114 115 116 117 118 119 120 121 123 124 126 129 130 131 132 135 146 147 149 154 167 169 **S** Maury Regional Health System, Columbia, TN
Primary Contact: Martin Chaney, M.D., Chief Executive Officer
COO: Deborah Lumpkins, MSN, Chief Operating Officer
CFO: Charles Brinkley III, Chief Financial Officer
CHR: Kaye Brewer, Chief Human Resources Officer
Web address: www.mauryregional.com
Control: County, Government, Nonfederal **Service**: General medical and surgical

Staffed Beds: 208 **Admissions**: 11700 **Census**: 133 **Outpatient Visits**: 246799 **Births**: 1736 **Total Expense ($000)**: 373564 **Payroll Expense ($000)**: 146319 **Personnel**: 1948

✠ **PINEWOOD SPRINGS (444029)**, 1001 North James M. Campbell Boulevard, Zip 38401, Mailing Address: 1001 North James M Campbell Boulevard, Zip 38401; tel. 931/777–6000, (Nonreporting) **A**1 10 **S** HCA Healthcare, Nashville, TN
Primary Contact: Jake Golich, Interim Chief Executive Officer
Web address: www.pinewoodsprings.com/
Control: Corporation, Investor–owned (for–profit) **Service**: Psychiatric

Staffed Beds: 60

UNITY PSYCHIATRIC CARE–COLUMBIA (444021), 1400 Rosewood Drive, Zip 38401–4878; tel. 931/388–6573, (Nonreporting) **A**10 **S** Tennessee Health Management, Parsons, TN
Primary Contact: Morgan Reddix, Administrator
CMO: Rodney Poling, M.D., Medical Director
CHR: Pam Brown, Human Resources Manager
CNO: Sheila Ridner, R.N., Director of Nursing
Web address: www.unitypsych.com
Control: Partnership, Investor–owned (for–profit) **Service**: Psychiatric

Staffed Beds: 16

Hospitals, U.S. / TENNESSEE

COOKEVILLE—Putnam County

☒ **COOKEVILLE REGIONAL MEDICAL CENTER (440059)**, 1 Medical Center Boulevard, Zip 38501–4294; tel. 931/783–2000, **A**1 10 **F**7 11 12 15 17 18 20 22 24 26 28 29 30 31 32 33 34 35 38 40 41 44 45 46 47 48 49 50 51 53 54 56 57 59 60 61 62 68 70 74 75 76 77 78 79 81 86 87 90 92 96 97 100 102 108 110 111 114 115 117 119 120 126 128 129 130 131 135 144 146 147 148 149 154 156 158 164 167 169 **P**7
Primary Contact: Buffy Key, Chief Executive Officer
COO: Buffy Key, Chief Operating Officer
CMO: Jeffrey J Gleason, M.D., Chief Medical Officer
CIO: Les Bernstein, Chief Information Officer
CHR: Angela Lewis, Senior Vice President Administration
CNO: Linda Crawford, R.N., MSN, Chief Nursing Officer
Web address: www.crmchealth.org
Control: Hospital district or authority, Government, Nonfederal **Service:** General medical and surgical

Staffed Beds: 245 **Admissions:** 12272 **Census:** 168 **Outpatient Visits:** 203809 **Births:** 1450 **Total Expense ($000):** 388597 **Payroll Expense ($000):** 117343 **Personnel:** 1572

COVINGTON—Tipton County

☒ **BAPTIST MEMORIAL HOSPITAL–TIPTON (440131)**, 1995 Highway 51 South, Zip 38019–3635; tel. 901/476–2621, **A**1 2 10 **F**3 11 15 29 30 31 34 35 40 45 55 58 59 65 70 74 75 76 78 79 81 84 85 87 89 93 107 108 110 111 114 115 119 120 121 130 135 146 148 149 154 **S** Baptist Memorial Health Care Corporation, Memphis, TN
Primary Contact: Parker Harris, Chief Executive Officer and Administrator
CFO: Monique Hart, Chief Financial Officer
CMO: Kenneth Afenya, M.D., Chief of Staff
CHR: Myra Cousar, Director Human Resources
Web address: www.baptistonline.org/tipton/
Control: Other not–for–profit (including NFP Corporation) **Service:** General medical and surgical

Staffed Beds: 36 **Admissions:** 1333 **Census:** 10 **Outpatient Visits:** 115516 **Births:** 326 **Total Expense ($000):** 206639 **Payroll Expense ($000):** 29744 **Personnel:** 403

CROSSVILLE—Cumberland County

☐ **CUMBERLAND MEDICAL CENTER (440009)**, 421 South Main Street, Zip 38555–5031; tel. 931/484–9511, **A**1 10 20 **F**3 11 13 15 18 20 22 28 29 30 31 34 35 38 39 40 44 45 47 48 49 51 53 57 58 59 61 64 65 67 70 74 75 76 77 78 79 81 82 85 86 87 93 94 101 102 107 108 110 111 114 115 117 119 120 121 129 130 132 135 141 146 147 148 149 154 163 167 169 **S** Covenant Health, Knoxville, TN
Primary Contact: Randy Davis, Chief Executive Officer
CFO: April VonAchen, Chief Financial Officer and Vice President Financial Services
CIO: Joe Lowe, Director Management Information Systems
CHR: Charles Sexton, Manager Human Resources
CNO: Rebecca Foster, MSN, R.N., Chief Nursing Officer
Web address: www.cmchealthcare.org
Control: Other not–for–profit (including NFP Corporation) **Service:** General medical and surgical

Staffed Beds: 84 **Admissions:** 4736 **Census:** 55 **Outpatient Visits:** 96540 **Births:** 719 **Total Expense ($000):** 97343 **Payroll Expense ($000):** 36045 **Personnel:** 516

DAYTON—Rhea County

★ ⇑ **RHEA MEDICAL CENTER (441310)**, 9400 Rhea County Highway, Zip 37321–7922; tel. 423/775–1121, (Nonreporting) **A**3 10 18 21 **S** Ovation Healthcare, Brentwood, TN
Primary Contact: Horace Whitt, Chief Executive Officer
CFO: Harv Sanders, Chief Financial Officer
CMO: Benjamin Kellogg, M.D., Chief of Staff
CNO: Samantha Bryant, Chief Nursing Officer
Web address: www.rheamedical.org
Control: County, Government, Nonfederal **Service:** General medical and surgical

Staffed Beds: 25

DICKSON—Dickson County

☒ **TRISTAR HORIZON MEDICAL CENTER (440046)**, 111 Highway 70 East, Zip 37055–2080; tel. 615/446–0446, (Nonreporting) **A**1 2 3 10 **S** HCA Healthcare, Nashville, TN
Primary Contact: Cindy Bergmeier, Chief Executive Officer
CFO: Lauren Sligh, Chief Financial Officer
CIO: Rick Stoker, Director Management Information Systems
CHR: Sheila Kight, Director Human Resources
CNO: Gina Bullington, Chief Nursing Officer
Web address: www.horizonmedicalcenter.com
Control: Corporation, Investor–owned (for–profit) **Service:** General medical and surgical

Staffed Beds: 157

DYERSBURG—Dyer County

☒ **WEST TENNESSEE HEALTHCARE DYERSBURG HOSPITAL (440072)**, 400 East Tickle Street, Zip 38024–3120; tel. 731/285–2410, **A**1 10 20 **F**3 7 8 11 13 15 18 20 22 26 28 29 30 34 35 39 40 44 45 46 47 48 49 50 51 57 59 60 70 76 79 81 82 85 87 92 93 97 107 108 110 111 115 119 120 121 124 129 130 145 146 147 148 149 157 167 169 **S** West Tennessee Healthcare, Jackson, TN
Primary Contact: Scott Barber, Chief Executive Officer
CFO: Meredith Malone, Chief Financial Officer
CMO: Darren Johnson, M.D., Chief of Staff
CIO: Russ Shephard, Senior Systems Analyst
CHR: Beverly Ray, Director Human Resources
CNO: Jan Leann Zimmer, R.N., MSN, R.N., MS, Chief Nursing Officer
Web address: www.wth.org/locations/west-tennessee-healthcare-dyersburg-hospital
Control: Hospital district or authority, Government, Nonfederal **Service:** General medical and surgical

Staffed Beds: 115 **Admissions:** 2788 **Census:** 35 **Outpatient Visits:** 46314 **Births:** 468 **Total Expense ($000):** 62038 **Payroll Expense ($000):** 24900 **Personnel:** 357

EAST RIDGE—Hamilton County

COLUMBIA EAST RIDGE HOSPITAL See East Ridge Hospital

EAST RIDGE HOSPITAL See Parkridge Medical Center, Chattanooga

ELIZABETHTON—Carter County

☐ **SYCAMORE SHOALS HOSPITAL (440018)**, 1501 West Elk Avenue, Zip 37643–2874; tel. 423/542–1300, (Nonreporting) **A**1 10 **S** Ballad Health, Johnson City, TN
Primary Contact: Dwayne Taylor, Chief Executive Officer, Southeast Market
COO: Melanie Stanton, R.N., Chief Nursing Officer
CFO: Chase Wilson, Chief Financial Officer
CMO: Morris H Seligman, M.D., Chief Medical Officer and Chief Medical Information Officer
CIO: Paul Merrywell, Chief Information Officer
CHR: Sharon Sheppard, Manager Human Resources
Web address: www.msha.com
Control: Other not–for–profit (including NFP Corporation) **Service:** General medical and surgical

Staffed Beds: 74

ERIN—Houston County

⇑ **HOUSTON COUNTY COMMUNITY HOSPITAL (441322)**, 5001 East Main Street, Zip 37061–4115, Mailing Address: P.O. Box 489, Zip 37061–0489; tel. 931/289–4211, (Nonreporting) **A**10 18 21
Primary Contact: William Lomax, Chief Executive Officer
CFO: Alisha Harvey, Director of Finance
CMO: Michael Carter, M.D., Chief Medical Officer
CIO: Richard Christy, Information Technology Manager
CHR: Leslie Booth, Human Resources Director
CNO: Donna Jackson, Chief Nursing Officer
Web address: https://shamrock.health/home
Control: County, Government, Nonfederal **Service:** General medical and surgical

Staffed Beds: 15

Hospitals, U.S. / TENNESSEE

ERWIN—Unicoi County

★ **UNICOI COUNTY HOSPITAL (440001)**, 2030 Temple Hill Road, Zip 37650–8721; tel. 423/735–4700, (Nonreporting) **A**1 10 **S** Ballad Health, Johnson City, TN
Primary Contact: Loveland Hobson, Chief Executive Office
CFO: Toni Buchanan, Chief Financial Officer
CMO: Jose Picaza, M.D., Chief of Staff
CIO: Maggie Tipton, Chief Information Officer
CHR: Susan Broyles, Director Human Resources and Safety
CNO: Melanie Stanton, R.N., Chief Nursing Officer
Web address: https://www.balladhealth.org/hospitals/unicoi-county-hospital-erwin
Control: Other not–for–profit (including NFP Corporation) **Service:** General medical and surgical

Staffed Beds: 50

FAYETTEVILLE—Lincoln County

☐ **LINCOLN COUNTY HEALTH SYSTEM (440102)**, 106 Medical Center Boulevard, Zip 37334–2684, Mailing Address: PO Box 637, Zip 37334–2684; tel. 931/438–1100, (Nonreporting) **A**1 10
Primary Contact: Mary Beth Seals, President
CIO: John Kenneth Lavender, Chief Information Officer
CHR: Wendy Nogler, Director Human Resources
CNO: Paul Davis, Chief Nursing Officer
Web address: www.lchealthsystem.com
Control: County, Government, Nonfederal **Service:** General medical and surgical

Staffed Beds: 313

FRANKLIN—Williamson County

★ **ENCOMPASS HEALTH REHABILITATION HOSPITAL OF FRANKLIN (443035)**, 1000 Physicians Way, Zip 37067–1471; tel. 615/721–4000, (Nonreporting) **A**1 10 **S** Encompass Health Corporation, Birmingham, AL
Primary Contact: Scott J. Peterson, Chief Executive Officer
CFO: Patricia Huffman, Controller
CMO: Scott Craig, M.D., Medical Director
CHR: Dawn McMaster, Human Resources Director
CNO: Valerie Shoulders, R.N., Chief Nursing Officer
Web address: https://encompasshealth.com/franklinrehab
Control: Corporation, Investor–owned (for–profit) **Service:** Rehabilitation

Staffed Beds: 40

☐ **ROLLING HILLS HOSPITAL (444007)**, 2014 Quail Hollow Circle, Zip 37067–5967; tel. 615/628–5700, (Nonreporting) **A**1 10 **S** Universal Health Services, Inc., King of Prussia, PA
Primary Contact: James Miller, Chief Executive Officer
COO: Laurel Roberts, R.N., MSN, Chief Operating Officer
CFO: Ray Brocato, Chief Financial Officer
CMO: James Hart, M.D., Medical Director
CHR: Lisa Hodge, Director, Human Resources
CNO: Hilary Gipson, Director of Nursing
Web address: www.RollingHillsHospital.org/
Control: Corporation, Investor–owned (for–profit) **Service:** Psychiatric

Staffed Beds: 130

☐ **WILLIAMSON MEDICAL CENTER (440029)**, 4321 Carothers Parkway, Zip 37067–8542; tel. 615/435–5000, **A**1 2 3 5 10 **F**3 7 8 11 12 13 15 18 20 22 24 28 29 30 31 34 35 37 40 41 45 46 50 51 54 56 57 59 64 65 68 70 72 74 75 76 77 78 79 81 82 84 85 86 87 89 93 94 96 97 102 107 108 110 111 114 115 118 119 122 126 130 131 132 135 141 143 146 147 148 149 154 155 156 167 169
Primary Contact: Phillip J. Mazzuca, Chief Executive Officer
COO: Julie Miller, Chief Operating Officer
CFO: Paul Bolin, Chief Financial Officer
CMO: Starling C Evins, M.D., Chief of Staff
CIO: Jeff Goad, Chief Information Officer
CHR: Phyllis Molyneux, Associate Administrator Human Resources and Education
Web address: www.williamsonmedicalcenter.org
Control: County, Government, Nonfederal **Service:** General medical and surgical

Staffed Beds: 203 **Admissions:** 9950 **Census:** 98 **Outpatient Visits:** 97829 **Births:** 1743 **Total Expense ($000):** 280299 **Payroll Expense ($000):** 120510 **Personnel:** 1494

GALLATIN—Sumner County

★ **SUMNER REGIONAL MEDICAL CENTER (440003)**, 555 Hartsville Pike, Zip 37066–2400, Mailing Address: P.O. Box 1558, Zip 37066–1558; tel. 615/452–4210, (Nonreporting) **A**1 2 3 10 **S** Lifepoint Health, Brentwood, TN
Primary Contact: Rod Harkleroad, R.N., Chief Executive Officer
CMO: Geoffrey Lifferth, M.D., Chief Medical Officer
CIO: Vickie Carter, Information Systems Director
Web address: www.mysumnermedical.com
Control: Corporation, Investor–owned (for–profit) **Service:** General medical and surgical

Staffed Beds: 120

GERMANTOWN—Shelby County

☐ △ **BAPTIST MEMORIAL REHABILITATION HOSPITAL (443034)**, 1240 South Germantown Road, Zip 38138–2226; tel. 901/275–3300, (Nonreporting) **A**1 3 7 10 **S** Baptist Memorial Health Care Corporation, Memphis, TN
Primary Contact: Christopher L. Bariola, Chief Executive Officer
CFO: Carlos Mendoza, Controller
CHR: Stacie Schroeppel, Director of Human Resources
CNO: Donna Hale, Director of Nursing
Web address: www.baptistrehab.com
Control: Partnership, Investor–owned (for–profit) **Service:** Rehabilitation

Staffed Beds: 49

METHODIST HLTHCARE–GERMANTOWN See Methodist Le Bonheur Germantown Hospital

METHODIST LE BONHEUR GERMANTOWN HOSPITAL See Methodist Healthcare Memphis Hospitals, Memphis

GREENEVILLE—Greene County

GREENEVILLE COMMUNITY HOSPITAL EAST (440050), 1420 Tusculum Boulevard, Zip 37745–5825; tel. 423/787–5000, (Nonreporting) **A**2 10 **S** Ballad Health, Johnson City, TN
Primary Contact: Eric Carroll, Chief Executive Officer
CFO: Mark Compton, Chief Financial Officer
CMO: Mark Patterson, M.D., Chief Medical Officer
CIO: Eric L Garrison, Chief Information Officer
CNO: Brenda Cannon, R.N., Director of Nursing
Web address: www.balladhealth.org/hospitals/laughlin-memorial-greeneville
Control: Other not–for–profit (including NFP Corporation) **Service:** General medical and surgical

Staffed Beds: 121

HARRIMAN—Roane County

☐ **ROANE MEDICAL CENTER (440031)**, 8045 Roane Medical Center Drive, Zip 37748–8333; tel. 865/316–1000, **A**1 10 **F**3 11 15 18 20 28 29 30 34 35 38 40 44 45 46 50 57 58 59 61 64 65 69 70 74 75 77 78 79 81 82 85 86 87 92 93 94 96 101 102 107 108 110 111 115 118 119 129 130 132 135 146 147 148 149 154 163 167 **S** Covenant Health, Knoxville, TN
Primary Contact: Jason B. Pilant, President and Chief Administrative Officer
CFO: Julie Utterback, Chief Financial Officer
CMO: Mark Browne, M.D., Chief Medical Officer
CIO: Mike Ward, Senior Vice President Chief Information Officer
CHR: Randall Carr, Director Human Resources
CNO: Carolyn Shipley, R.N., Chief Nursing Officer
Web address: www.roanemedical.com
Control: Other not–for–profit (including NFP Corporation) **Service:** General medical and surgical

Staffed Beds: 52 **Admissions:** 2781 **Census:** 28 **Outpatient Visits:** 61967 **Births:** 0 **Total Expense ($000):** 43660 **Payroll Expense ($000):** 17023 **Personnel:** 253

Hospital, Medicare Provider Number, Address, Telephone, Approval, Facility, and Physician Codes, Health Care System

★ American Hospital Association (AHA) membership   ○ Healthcare Facilities Accreditation Program   ⇑ Center for Improvement in Healthcare Quality Accreditation
☐ The Joint Commission accreditation   ◇ DNV Healthcare Inc. accreditation   △ Commission on Accreditation of Rehabilitation Facilities (CARF) accreditation

Hospitals, U.S. / TENNESSEE

HARTSVILLE—Trousdale County

TROUSDALE MEDICAL CENTER (441301), 500 Church Street, Zip 37074-1744; tel. 615/374-2221, (Nonreporting) **A**1 10 18 **S** Lifepoint Health, Brentwood, TN
Primary Contact: Carolyn Sparks, Chief Executive Officer
CFO: Amanda Pruitt, Chief Financial Officer
CHR: Amy Overstreet, Director Human Resources
CNO: Angela Pruett, Chief Nursing Officer
Web address: www.mytrousdalemedical.com
Control: Corporation, Investor-owned (for-profit) **Service**: General medical and surgical

Staffed Beds: 25

HENDERSONVILLE—Sumner County

TRISTAR HENDERSONVILLE MEDICAL CENTER (440194), 355 New Shackle Island Road, Zip 37075-2479; tel. 615/338-1000, (Nonreporting) **A**1 2 10 **S** HCA Healthcare, Nashville, TN
Primary Contact: Justin Coury, Chief Executive Officer
CFO: Stephen Bearden, Chief Financial Officer
CMO: Keith Campbell, Chief Medical Officer
CIO: Hal Schultheis, Director Information Systems
CHR: Amy L Hobdy, Vice President of Human Resources
CNO: Lisa Hochstetler, R.N., Chief Nursing Officer
Web address: www.hendersonvillemedicalcenter.com
Control: Corporation, Investor-owned (for-profit) **Service**: General medical and surgical

Staffed Beds: 125

HERMITAGE—Davidson County

TRISTAR SUMMIT MEDICAL CENTER (440150), 5655 Frist Boulevard, Zip 37076-2053; tel. 615/316-3000, (Nonreporting) **A**1 2 3 10 **S** HCA Healthcare, Nashville, TN
Primary Contact: Daphne David, Chief Executive Officer
COO: Andrew Tyrer, Chief Operating Officer
CFO: Bryan Shephard, Chief Financial Officer
CMO: Kevin M. Hamilton, M.D., Chief Medical Officer
CIO: Joel Bain, Director Information Services
CHR: Emily Dye, Vice President Human Resources
CNO: Mary Ann Angle, R.N., FACHE, Chief Nursing Officer
Web address: www.summitmedctr.com
Control: Corporation, Investor-owned (for-profit) **Service**: General medical and surgical

Staffed Beds: 218

HIXSON—Hamilton County

MEMORIAL NORTH PARK HOSPITAL See Memorial Hospital Hixson

HUNTINGDON—Carroll County

BAPTIST MEMORIAL HOSPITAL-CARROLL COUNTY (440016), 631 R.B. Wilson Drive, Zip 38344-1727; tel. 731/986-4461, **A**1 3 10 **F**3 11 12 15 18 22 29 30 34 35 40 44 50 54 56 57 59 61 64 65 66 70 75 77 79 81 85 86 87 93 97 98 101 102 103 104 107 108 110 111 115 118 119 127 129 130 131 132 133 134 135 146 148 149 154 156 **S** Baptist Memorial Health Care Corporation, Memphis, TN
Primary Contact: Susan M. Breeden, Chief Executive Officer and Administrator
CFO: Sharron Holland, Chief Financial Officer
CHR: Kim King, Director Human Resources and Public Relations
CNO: Kimberly Sanders, Chief Nursing Officer
Web address: www.baptistonline.org/huntingdon/
Control: Other not-for-profit (including NFP Corporation) **Service**: General medical and surgical

Staffed Beds: 53 **Admissions**: 1071 **Census**: 13 **Outpatient Visits**: 26453 **Births**: 1 **Total Expense ($000)**: 28260 **Payroll Expense ($000)**: 11361 **Personnel**: 188

JACKSON—Madison County

★ **PATHWAYS OF TENNESSEE (444010)**, 238 Summar Drive, Zip 38301-3906; tel. 731/541-8200, **A**10 **F**3 5 29 35 38 44 57 59 71 98 99 100 101 102 103 104 132 134 135 149 150 153 154 157 160 161 162 164 165 **S** West Tennessee Healthcare, Jackson, TN
Primary Contact: Pam Henson, Executive Director
CFO: Jeff Blankenship, CPA, Chief Financial Officer
CMO: Kevin Turner, M.D., Medical Director
CIO: Jeff Frieling, Chief Information Officer
CHR: Wendy Carlson, Director Human Resources
CNO: Angela Hensley, Director of Nursing
Web address: www.wth.net/pathways
Control: Hospital district or authority, Government, Nonfederal **Service**: Psychiatric

Staffed Beds: 25 **Admissions**: 1191 **Census**: 16 **Outpatient Visits**: 3728 **Births**: 0 **Total Expense ($000)**: 26013 **Payroll Expense ($000)**: 13841 **Personnel**: 260

☐ **PERIMETER BEHAVIORAL HOSPITAL OF JACKSON (444023)**, 49 Old Hickory Boulevard, Zip 38305-4551; tel. 731/668-7073, (Nonreporting) **A**1 10 **S** Perimeter Healthcare, Alpharetta, GA
Primary Contact: Forrest Blue. Summers, Chief Executive Officer
Web address: https://www.perimeterhealthcare.com/facilities/perimeter-behavioral-hospital-of-jackson/
Control: Corporation, Investor-owned (for-profit) **Service**: Psychiatric

Staffed Beds: 45

★ **SELECT SPECIALTY HOSPITAL – WEST TENNESSEE (442018)**, 620 Skyline Drive, Zip 38301-3923; tel. 731/437-2500, (Nonreporting) **S** Select Medical Corporation, Mechanicsburg, PA
Primary Contact: Anupam Lahiri, Chief Executive Officer
Web address: https://www.selectspecialtyhospitals.com/locations-and-tours/tn/jackson/west-tennessee/?ty=xt
Control: Corporation, Investor-owned (for-profit) **Service**: Acute long-term care hospital

Staffed Beds: 50

TENNOVA HEALTHCARE REGIONAL HOSPITAL OF JACKSON See West Tennessee Healthcare North Hospital

WEST TENNESSEE HEALTHCARE REHABILITATION HOSPITAL JACKSON, A PARTNERSHIP WITH ENCOMPASS HEALTH (443036), 616 West Forest Avenue, Zip 38301-3902; tel. 731/574-3000, (Nonreporting) **A**1 10 **S** Encompass Health Corporation, Birmingham, AL
Primary Contact: Julie Taylor, Chief Executive Officer
Web address: https://encompasshealth.com/locations/jacksonrehab/
Control: Corporation, Investor-owned (for-profit) **Service**: Rehabilitation

Staffed Beds: 48

JASPER—Marion County

GRANDVIEW MEDICAL CENTER See Parkridge West Hospital

JEFFERSON CITY—Jefferson County

TENNOVA HEALTHCARE–JEFFERSON MEMORIAL HOSPITAL (440056), 110 Hospital Drive, Zip 37760-5281; tel. 865/471-2500, (Nonreporting) **A**1 10 **S** Community Health Systems, Inc., Franklin, TN
Primary Contact: Benjamin Ridder, Chief Executive Officer
CFO: Roseann M Devault, Chief Financial Officer
CMO: Richard Carter, M.D., Chief of Staff
Web address: www.tennova.com/
Control: Corporation, Investor-owned (for-profit) **Service**: General medical and surgical

Staffed Beds: 58

JOHNSON CITY—Washington County

☐ **FRANKLIN WOODS COMMUNITY HOSPITAL (440184)**, 300 MedTech Parkway, Zip 37604-2277; tel. 423/302-1000, (Nonreporting) **A**1 3 10 **S** Ballad Health, Johnson City, TN
Primary Contact: Melanie Steagall. Stanton, Chief Executive Officer
CFO: Andrew R. Wampler, Chief Financial Officer
CHR: Brooke Graham, Human Resources Manager
CNO: Rhonda Mann, Chief Nursing Officer
Web address: www.msha.com
Control: Other not-for-profit (including NFP Corporation) **Service**: General medical and surgical

Staffed Beds: 102

Hospitals, U.S. / TENNESSEE

☒ **JAMES H. QUILLEN DEPARTMENT OF VETERANS AFFAIRS MEDICAL CENTER**, 809 Lamont Street, Zip 37604–5453, Mailing Address: P.O. Box 4000, Mountain Home, Zip 37684–4000; tel. 423/926–1171, (Nonreporting) **A**1 3 5 **S** Department of Veterans Affairs, Washington, DC
Primary Contact: Dean B. Borsos, Medical Center Director
CFO: Sandra Nash, Chief Fiscal Service
CMO: David Hecht, M.D., Chief of Staff
CIO: Karen Perry, Chief Information Resource Management Services
CHR: John Henderson, Chief Human Resources Management
CNO: Linda M McConnell, R.N., MSN, FACHE, Associate Medical Center Director Patient Care Services
Web address: www.mountainhome.va.gov/
Control: Veterans Affairs, Government, federal **Service**: General medical and surgical

Staffed Beds: 218

☒ **JOHNSON CITY MEDICAL CENTER (440063)**, 400 North State of Franklin Road, Zip 37604–6094; tel. 423/431–6111, (Includes NISWONGER CHILDREN'S HOSPITAL, 400 North State of Franklin Road, Johnson City, Tennessee, Zip 37604–6035, tel. 423/431–6111; Christopher Jett, Chief Executive Officer; WOODRIDGE HOSPITAL, 403 State of Franklin Road, Johnson City, Tennessee, Zip 37604–6034, tel. 423/431–7111) **A**1 2 3 5 8 10 19 **F**3 9 11 12 13 15 17 18 19 20 21 22 24 26 28 29 30 41 43 45 46 47 48 49 51 53 57 59 60 64 68 70 72 73 74 75 76 77 78 79 81 83 84 87 88 89 97 98 99 100 101 102 103 104 106 107 108 109 110 111 114 115 117 118 119 120 123 129 130 131 135 146 147 148 149 150 154 156 157 164 169 **S** Ballad Health, Johnson City, TN
Primary Contact: Kenny Shafer, Chief Executive Officer
COO: Kenny Shafer, Chief Operating Officer
CFO: Richard Boone, Chief Financial Officer
CMO: Clay Runnels, Vice President Chief Medical Officer Washington County
CHR: Barry Tourigny, Human Resources Director
CNO: Dru Michele Malcolm, MSN, R.N., Vice President and Chief Nursing Officer
Web address: https://www.balladhealth.org/hospitals/johnson-city-medical-center
Control: Other not–for–profit (including NFP Corporation) **Service**: General medical and surgical

Staffed Beds: 581 **Admissions**: 26057 **Census**: 405 **Outpatient Visits**: 221051 **Births**: 1158 **Total Expense ($000)**: 590848 **Payroll Expense ($000)**: 179076 **Personnel**: 2011

MOUNTAIN HOME See James H. Quillen Department of Veterans Affairs Medical Center

☒ **QUILLEN REHABILITATION HOSPITAL, A JOINT VENTURE OF BALLAD HEALTH AND ENCOMPASS HEALTH (443033)**, 2511 Wesley Street, Zip 37601–1723; tel. 423/952–1700, **A**1 10 **F**29 60 75 90 130 132 135 148 149 150 154 **S** Encompass Health Corporation, Birmingham, AL
Primary Contact: Rob Adams, Chief Executive Officer
CFO: Debbie Wyse, Controller
CHR: Penny Lawson, Human Resource Director
CNO: Lynn Langan, Chief Nursing Officer
Web address: www.quillenrehabilitationhospital.com/
Control: Corporation, Investor–owned (for–profit) **Service**: Rehabilitation

Staffed Beds: 36 **Admissions**: 927 **Census**: 32 **Outpatient Visits**: 0 **Births**: 0 **Total Expense ($000)**: 15268 **Payroll Expense ($000)**: 7510 **Personnel**: 116

KINGSPORT—Sullivan County

☐ **CREEKSIDE BEHAVIORAL HEALTH (444027)**, 1025 Executive Park Boulevard, Zip 37660–4620; tel. 423/830–8110, (Nonreporting) **A**1 10
Primary Contact: Ric McAllister, Chief Executive Officer
Web address: www.creeksidebh.com
Control: Corporation, Investor–owned (for–profit) **Service**: Psychiatric

Staffed Beds: 72

☒ **ENCOMPASS HEALTH REHABILITATION HOSPITAL OF KINGSPORT (443027)**, 113 Cassel Drive, Zip 37660–3775; tel. 423/246–7240, (Nonreporting) **A**1 10 **S** Encompass Health Corporation, Birmingham, AL
Primary Contact: Troy Clark, Chief Executive Officer
CFO: Natalie Tilson, Controller
CMO: James P Little, M.D., Medical Director
CIO: Natalie Tilson, Controller
CHR: Joyce Jones, Director Human Resources
CNO: Debra Smith, Chief Nursing Officer
Web address: www.healthsouthkingsport.com
Control: Corporation, Investor–owned (for–profit) **Service**: Rehabilitation

Staffed Beds: 50

☐ **HOLSTON VALLEY MEDICAL CENTER (440017)**, 130 West Ravine Street, Zip 37660–3837, Mailing Address: P.O. Box 238, Zip 37662–0238; tel. 423/224–4000, (Nonreporting) **A**1 2 3 5 10 13 19 **S** Ballad Health, Johnson City, TN
Primary Contact: Rebecca Beck, Chief Executive Officer
COO: Robert Kennedy, Chief Operating Officer
CFO: Dale Poe, Vice President Finance and Operations
CMO: Daniel Carlson, M.D., Chief Medical Officer
CHR: Hamlin J Wilson, Senior Vice President Human Resources
CNO: Adnan Brka, Chief Nursing Officer
Web address: https://www.balladhealth.org/hospitals/holston-valley-medical-center
Control: Other not–for–profit (including NFP Corporation) **Service**: General medical and surgical

Staffed Beds: 336

☐ **INDIAN PATH COMMUNITY HOSPITAL (440176)**, 2000 Brookside Drive, Zip 37660–4627; tel. 423/857–7000, (Nonreporting) **A**1 2 5 10 **S** Ballad Health, Johnson City, TN
Primary Contact: Rebecca Beck, Chief Executive Officer
COO: Dwight Owens, Chief Operating Officer
CFO: Andrew R. Wampler, Vice President, Operational Excellence
CMO: Herbert D. Ladley, M.D., Chief Medical Officer
CIO: Randy F. Hart, Manager, Information Technology Regional Operations
CHR: Rowena L. Lyons, Human Resource Manager
CNO: Stephanie L. Rhoton, Director, Patient Care Services
Web address: https://www.balladhealth.org/locations/hospitals/indian-path
Control: Other not–for–profit (including NFP Corporation) **Service**: General medical and surgical

Staffed Beds: 117

KNOXVILLE—Knox County

☐ **EAST TENNESSEE CHILDREN'S HOSPITAL (443303)**, 2018 Clinch Avenue, Zip 37916–2393, Mailing Address: P.O. Box 15010, Zip 37901–5010; tel. 865/541–8000, (Nonreporting) **A**1 3 5 10
Primary Contact: Matthew Schaefer, President and Chief Executive Officer
COO: Steven Godbold, Vice President Operations and Chief Operating Officer
CFO: Caryn Hawthorne, Vice President Finance and Chief Finance Officer
CIO: John Hanks, Director Information Systems
CHR: Sue Wilburn, Vice President Human Resources and Organizational Development
CNO: Hella Ewing, R.N., Vice President Patient Care Services and Chief Nursing Officer
Web address: www.etch.com
Control: Other not–for–profit (including NFP Corporation) **Service**: Children's general medical and surgical

Staffed Beds: 152

☐ △ **FORT SANDERS REGIONAL MEDICAL CENTER (440125)**, 1901 West Clinch Avenue, Zip 37916–2307; tel. 865/541–1111, **A**1 3 7 10 19 **F**3 11 12 13 15 17 18 20 22 24 26 28 29 30 31 34 35 37 38 39 40 44 45 46 47 49 50 51 55 57 58 59 60 61 63 64 65 70 74 75 76 77 78 79 80 81 82 84 85 86 87 91 92 93 94 96 101 102 107 108 110 111 114 115 116 117 118 119 120 121 123 124 126 128 129 130 132 135 146 147 148 149 154 163 167 168 169 **S** Covenant Health, Knoxville, TN
Primary Contact: Keith Altshuler, President and Chief Administrative Officer
CNO: Lynda Watts, Vice President, Chief Nursing Officer
Web address: www.covenanthealth.com
Control: Other not–for–profit (including NFP Corporation) **Service**: General medical and surgical

Staffed Beds: 365 **Admissions**: 19151 **Census**: 267 **Outpatient Visits**: 181554 **Births**: 3661 **Total Expense ($000)**: 398006 **Payroll Expense ($000)**: 115460 **Personnel**: 1519

Hospital, Medicare Provider Number, Address, Telephone, Approval, Facility, and Physician Codes, Health Care System

★ American Hospital Association (AHA) membership ◯ Healthcare Facilities Accreditation Program ⇑ Center for Improvement in Healthcare Quality Accreditation
☐ The Joint Commission accreditation ◇ DNV Healthcare Inc. accreditation △ Commission on Accreditation of Rehabilitation Facilities (CARF) accreditation

© 2025 AHA Guide

Hospitals, U.S. / TENNESSEE

☒ **PARKWEST MEDICAL CENTER (440173)**, 9352 Park West Boulevard, Zip 37923-4325, Mailing Address: P.O. Box 22993, Zip 37933-0993; tel. 865/373-1000, (Includes PENINSULA HOSPITAL, 2347 Jones Bend Road, Louisville, Tennessee, Zip 37777-5213, P O Box 2000, Zip 37777-2000, tel. 865/970-9800; Elizabeth P Clary, Vice President Behavioral Health) **A**1 2 10 **F**3 11 12 13 15 17 18 20 22 24 26 28 29 30 31 34 35 37 38 39 40 44 45 46 48 49 50 51 56 57 58 59 60 61 63 64 65 70 74 75 76 77 78 79 80 81 82 84 85 86 87 92 93 94 96 98 99 100 101 102 103 104 107 108 110 111 114 115 116 117 118 119 120 121 123 126 129 130 132 135 146 147 148 149 153 154 160 161 163 164 165 167 168 **S** Covenant Health, Knoxville, TN
Primary Contact: James VanderSteeg, Acting Chief Executive Officer
COO: Jason Draper, Vice President and Chief Support Officer
CFO: Scott Hamilton, Vice President and Chief Financial Officer
CHR: Stephen Wilder, Director Human Resources
CNO: Lynn Cagle, Chief Nursing Officer
Web address: https://www.covenanthealth.com/parkwest/
Control: Other not-for-profit (including NFP Corporation) **Service**: General medical and surgical

Staffed Beds: 412 **Admissions**: 19838 **Census**: 261 **Outpatient Visits**: 257440 **Births**: 1828 **Total Expense ($000)**: 428391 **Payroll Expense ($000)**: 122105 **Personnel**: 1621

PATRICIA NEAL REHABILITATION HOSPITAL (443039), 101 Fort Sanders West Boulevard, Zip 37922-3342; tel. 865/895-3000, (Nonreporting) **S** Encompass Health Corporation, Birmingham, AL
Primary Contact: Jennifer Steely, Chief Executive Officer
Web address: https://encompasshealth.com/knoxvillerehab
Control: Corporation, Investor-owned (for-profit) **Service**: Rehabilitation

Staffed Beds: 51

TURKEY CREEK MEDICAL CENTER See Tennova Turkey Creek Medical Center

☒ **UNIVERSITY OF TENNESSEE MEDICAL CENTER (440015)**, 1924 Alcoa Highway, Zip 37920-6900; tel. 865/305-9000, **A**1 2 3 5 8 10 19 **F**3 6 8 9 11 12 13 15 17 18 20 22 24 26 28 29 30 31 34 35 36 37 39 40 41 42 43 44 45 46 47 48 49 50 51 53 54 55 56 57 58 59 60 61 64 65 68 69 70 71 72 74 75 76 77 78 79 80 81 82 83 84 85 86 87 88 91 92 93 94 96 97 100 102 105 107 108 109 110 111 114 115 116 117 118 119 120 121 123 124 126 127 129 130 131 132 135 136 138 141 144 145 146 147 148 149 150 152 154 156 157 160 161 164 165 166 167 169 **P**5 6
Primary Contact: Keith Gray, M.D., FACS, President and Chief Executive Officer
COO: David Hall, Senior Vice President and Chief Operating Officer
CFO: Thomas Fisher, Senior Vice President and Chief Financial Officer
CIO: Michael Saad, Vice President and Chief Information Officer
CHR: Julie Simpson, Vice President Human Resources
CNO: Janell Cecil, R.N., MSN, Senior Vice President and Chief Nursing Officer
Web address: www.utmedicalcenter.org
Control: Other not-for-profit (including NFP Corporation) **Service**: General medical and surgical

Staffed Beds: 710 **Admissions**: 31699 **Census**: 516 **Outpatient Visits**: 390911 **Births**: 4672 **Total Expense ($000)**: 1428045 **Payroll Expense ($000)**: 522418 **Personnel**: 5025

LA FOLLETTE—Campbell County

☒ **TENNOVA HEALTHCARE–LAFOLLETTE MEDICAL CENTER (440033)**, 923 East Central Avenue, Zip 37766-2768, Mailing Address: P.O. Box 1301, Zip 37766-1301; tel. 423/907-1200, (Nonreporting) **A**1 10 20 **S** Community Health Systems, Inc., Franklin, TN
Primary Contact: Mark Cain, Chief Executive Officer
COO: Sara Heatherly-Lloyd, Chief Operating Officer
CFO: Michael Cherry, Chief Financial Officer
CMO: George O'Neal Vinsant, M.D., Chief Medical Officer
CIO: Dillon Ward, Management Information Systems Specialist
CHR: Bess Stout, Director Human Resources
CNO: Kathy R Myers, MS, R.N., Chief Nursing Officer
Web address: www.tennova.com
Control: Corporation, Investor-owned (for-profit) **Service**: General medical and surgical

Staffed Beds: 164

LAFAYETTE—Macon County

★ ⇑ **MACON COMMUNITY HOSPITAL (441305)**, 305 West Locust Street, Zip 37083-1712, Mailing Address: P.O. Box 378, Zip 37083-0378; tel. 615/666-2147, **A**10 18 21 **F**3 8 15 18 20 26 28 29 30 34 35 40 48 56 57 59 64 65 68 75 77 79 81 86 87 92 93 96 107 110 111 114 119 122 128 130 132 133 135 143 146 147 156 165 167 **S** Ovation Healthcare, Brentwood, TN
Primary Contact: Scott A. Tongate, Chief Executive Officer
CFO: Paul Merklin, Assistant Administrator, Chief Financial Officer
CHR: Kelly Morris, Director of Human Resources
CNO: Leanne Bilbrey, Chief Nursing Officer, Director of Quality
Web address: https://maconcommunityhospital.com/
Control: Other not-for-profit (including NFP Corporation) **Service**: General medical and surgical

Staffed Beds: 25 **Admissions**: 699 **Census**: 9 **Outpatient Visits**: 42029 **Births**: 0 **Total Expense ($000)**: 19928 **Payroll Expense ($000)**: 9471 **Personnel**: 179

LAWRENCEBURG—Lawrence County

☒ **SOUTHERN TENNESSEE REGIONAL HEALTH SYSTEM–LAWRENCEBURG (440175)**, 1607 South Locust Avenue, Zip 38464-4011, Mailing Address: P.O. Box 847, Zip 38464-0847; tel. 931/762-6571, (Nonreporting) **A**1 10 **S** Lifepoint Health, Brentwood, TN
Primary Contact: Michael Howard, Chief Executive Officer
CFO: Kristie Taylor, Chief Financial Officer
CIO: Jason Weaver, Director Information Systems
CHR: Robert Augustin, Director Human Resources
CNO: Marcia Patterson, MSN, R.N., Chief Nursing Officer
Web address: www.crocketthospital.com
Control: Corporation, Investor-owned (for-profit) **Service**: General medical and surgical

Staffed Beds: 80

LEBANON—Wilson County

TENNOVA HEALTHCARE–LEBANON MCFARLAND CAMPUS See Vanderbilt Wilson County Hospital–Mcfarland Hospital

☒ **VANDERBILT WILSON COUNTY HOSPITAL (440193)**, 1411 Baddour Parkway, Zip 37087-2513; tel. 615/444-8262, (Includes VANDERBILT WILSON COUNTY HOSPITAL–MCFARLAND HOSPITAL, 500 Park Avenue, Lebanon, Tennessee, Zip 37087-3720, tel. 615/449-0500) **A**1 10 **F**3 8 12 13 15 18 20 22 26 28 29 30 31 34 35 37 40 45 49 54 57 59 64 68 70 74 75 76 77 78 79 81 82 84 85 86 87 93 96 97 107 108 110 111 115 118 119 120 121 123 124 126 129 130 131 132 135 141 146 147 148 149 154 164 167 169 **S** Vanderbilt Health, Nashville, TN
Primary Contact: Scott McCarver, President
COO: Scott McCarver, Chief Operating Officer
CMO: Andrew Jordan, M.D., Chief of Staff
CIO: Adrian Fung, Director Information Systems
Web address: https://www.vanderbiltwilsoncountyhospital.com
Control: Other not-for-profit (including NFP Corporation) **Service**: General medical and surgical

Staffed Beds: 119 **Admissions**: 6797 **Census**: 87 **Outpatient Visits**: 94419 **Births**: 674 **Total Expense ($000)**: 170058 **Payroll Expense ($000)**: 79223 **Personnel**: 641

LENOIR CITY—Loudon County

☐ **FORT LOUDOUN MEDICAL CENTER (440110)**, 550 Fort Loudoun Medical Center Drive, Zip 37772-5673; tel. 865/271-6000, **A**1 10 **F**3 11 15 18 28 29 30 34 35 38 40 44 45 46 47 48 50 57 58 59 61 63 64 65 70 74 75 77 78 79 81 82 85 86 87 92 93 94 96 101 102 107 108 110 111 115 118 119 130 132 135 146 147 148 149 154 163 **S** Covenant Health, Knoxville, TN
Primary Contact: Connie Martin, President and Chief Administrative Officer
CNO: Teresa Fisher, R.N., Chief Nursing Officer
Web address: www.covenanthealth.com
Control: Other not-for-profit (including NFP Corporation) **Service**: General medical and surgical

Staffed Beds: 30 **Admissions**: 2261 **Census**: 28 **Outpatient Visits**: 61007 **Births**: 0 **Total Expense ($000)**: 39838 **Payroll Expense ($000)**: 16482 **Personnel**: 237

Hospitals, U.S. / TENNESSEE

LEWISBURG—Marshall County

MARSHALL MEDICAL CENTER (441309), 1080 North Ellington Parkway, Zip 37091-2227, Mailing Address: P.O. Box 1609, Zip 37091-1609; tel. 931/359-6241, **A** 1 5 10 18 **F** 3 11 15 29 30 34 40 45 50 59 68 75 77 81 85 86 92 93 104 107 108 110 111 114 119 127 129 130 131 132 133 135 146 149 154 167 **S** Maury Regional Health System, Columbia, TN
Primary Contact: Phyllis Brown, Chief Executive Officer
CFO: Kyle Jones, Chief Financial Officer
CMO: Tim Nash, M.D., Chief of Staff, Board Vice Chairman
CHR: Jeff M Pierce, Chief Human Resource Officer
CNO: Karen Martin, R.N., MSN, Chief Nursing Officer
Web address: www.mauryregional.com
Control: County, Government, Nonfederal **Service**: General medical and surgical

Staffed Beds: 17 **Admissions**: 256 **Census**: 5 **Outpatient Visits**: 128254
Births: 0 **Total Expense ($000)**: 37685 **Payroll Expense ($000)**: 19471
Personnel: 257

LEXINGTON—Henderson County

⇑ **HENDERSON COUNTY COMMUNITY HOSPITAL (440008)**, 200 West Church Street, Zip 38351-2038; tel. 731/968-3646, **A** 10 21 **F** 3 8 11 12 15 18 20 22 24 28 29 30 31 34 35 37 38 40 44 45 46 47 48 49 50 53 54 56 57 58 59 60 61 62 63 65 66 68 69 70 71 74 75 76 77 78 79 81 82 83 84 85 86 87 89 97 98 100 101 102 105 107 109 110 111 118 119 126 129 130 131 132 134 135 144 146 147 148 149 150 152 154 156 157 164 167 169 **P** 6
Primary Contact: Gary Stewart, Chief Executive Officer
CHR: Linda Durham, Director Human Resources
CNO: Charlene Morgan, Chief Nursing Officer
Web address: www.hendersoncchospital.com
Control: County, Government, Nonfederal **Service**: General medical and surgical

Staffed Beds: 158 **Admissions**: 7473 **Census**: 85 **Outpatient Visits**: 117248 **Births**: 375 **Total Expense ($000)**: 360463 **Payroll Expense ($000)**: 139463 **Personnel**: 1807

LIVINGSTON—Overton County

LIVINGSTON REGIONAL HOSPITAL (440187), 315 Oak Street, Zip 38570-1728, Mailing Address: P.O. Box 550, Zip 38570-0550; tel. 931/823-5611, **A** 1 10 **F** 3 8 13 15 18 29 30 34 35 40 50 56 57 60 76 79 81 87 90 93 98 103 107 108 110 111 115 119 122 130 131 133 164 167 **S** ScionHealth, Louisville, KY
Primary Contact: Timothy W. McGill, Chief Executive Officer
CMO: Christopher Nahm, M.D., Chief Medical Officer
CIO: Mark Hambridge, Director Information Systems
CNO: Penny V Kirby, MSN, Chief Nursing Officer
Web address: www.MyLivingstonHospital.com
Control: Corporation, Investor-owned (for-profit) **Service**: General medical and surgical

Staffed Beds: 89 **Admissions**: 1959 **Census**: 29 **Outpatient Visits**: 15424
Births: 429 **Personnel**: 235

MADISON—Davidson County

SKYLINE MADISON CAMPUS See Tristar Skyline Madison Campus

MANCHESTER—Coffee County

★ ⇑ **UNITY MEDICAL CENTER (440007)**, 481 Interstate Drive, Zip 37355-2455, Mailing Address: P.O. Box 1079, Zip 37349-1079; tel. 931/728-3586, (Nonreporting) **A** 10 21
Primary Contact: Martha Henley, Chief Executive Officer
CFO: Pam Jernigan, Chief Financial Officer
CMO: James Van Winkle, M.D., Chief of Staff
CIO: Matt Burks, Director Information Technology
CHR: Sherry Holt, Director Human Resources
CNO: Stephanie Byars, Chief Nursing Officer
Web address: www.unitymedicalmanchester.com
Control: Other not-for-profit (including NFP Corporation) **Service**: General medical and surgical

Staffed Beds: 36

MARTIN—Weakley County

UNITY PSYCHIATRIC CARE-MARTIN (444005), 458 Hannings Lane, Zip 38237-3308; tel. 731/588-2830, (Nonreporting) **A** 10 **S** Tennessee Health Management, Parsons, TN
Primary Contact: Carrie Brawley, Administrator
Web address: www.unitypsych.com
Control: Partnership, Investor-owned (for-profit) **Service**: Psychiatric

Staffed Beds: 16

WEST TENNESSEE HEALTHCARE REHABILITATION HOSPITAL CANE CREEK, A PARTNERSHIP WITH ENCOMPASS HEALTH (443030), 180 Mount Pelia Road, Zip 38237-3812; tel. 731/587-4231, (Nonreporting) **A** 1 10 **S** Encompass Health Corporation, Birmingham, AL
Primary Contact: Jonathan McAnulty, Chief Executive Officer
CFO: Bethany Smith, Controller
CMO: Belinda Merritt, M.D., Medical Director
CIO: Jan Trowhill, Director Health Information Management Systems
CHR: Sharon Shihady, Director Human Resources
CNO: Lindsey Rotger, Chief Nursing Officer
Web address: https://www.encompasshealth.com/locations/canecreekrehab
Control: Corporation, Investor-owned (for-profit) **Service**: Rehabilitation

Staffed Beds: 40

WEST TENNESSEE HEALTHCARE VOLUNTEER HOSPITAL (440061), 161 Mount Pelia Road, Zip 38237-3811; tel. 731/587-4261, **A** 1 10 **F** 3 11 13 15 18 28 29 34 35 40 45 50 53 57 59 68 70 76 79 81 85 91 93 107 108 110 111 115 119 127 129 130 133 135 148 154 **S** West Tennessee Healthcare, Jackson, TN
Primary Contact: William (Kevin) Decker, Chief Executive Officer
CFO: Jason Draper, Chief Financial Officer
CMO: Elizabeth Lund, M.D., Chief of Staff
CHR: Tammie Bell, Director Human Resources
CNO: Donna Barfield, Chief Nursing Officer
Web address: www.wth.org/
Control: Hospital district or authority, Government, Nonfederal **Service**: General medical and surgical

Staffed Beds: 22 **Admissions**: 971 **Census**: 8 **Outpatient Visits**: 56605
Births: 227 **Total Expense ($000)**: 28735 **Payroll Expense ($000)**: 13895
Personnel: 206

MARYVILLE—Blount County

BLOUNT MEMORIAL HOSPITAL (440011), 907 East Lamar Alexander Parkway, Zip 37804-5016; tel. 865/983-7211, (Nonreporting) **A** 1 2 10 19
Primary Contact: Jonathan Smith, Interim Chief Executive Officer
CFO: Brian Hollomon, Chief Financial Officer
CMO: Jane Souther, M.D., Chief Medical Officer
CHR: Chris Wilkes, MS, Chief Human Resources
CNO: Joe Newsome, Chief Nursing Officer
Web address: www.blountmemorial.org
Control: County, Government, Nonfederal **Service**: General medical and surgical

Staffed Beds: 274

MC MINNVILLE—Warren County

ASCENSION SAINT THOMAS RIVER PARK (440151), 1559 Sparta Street, Zip 37110-1316; tel. 931/815-4000, **A** 1 10 **F** 3 15 28 29 30 40 51 53 64 66 70 75 76 77 79 81 90 93 98 103 107 110 111 115 119 126 130 135 147 149 167 169 **S** Ascension Healthcare, Saint Louis, MO
Primary Contact: Robert Dale. Humphrey, Chief Executive Officer
CFO: Christina Patterson, Chief Financial Officer
CMO: Randal D Rampp, M.D., Chief Medical Officer
CIO: Jeff Johnson, Director Information Systems
CHR: Deeann Johnson, Director Human Resources
Web address: https://healthcare.ascension.org/Locations/Tennessee/TNNAS/McMinnville-Ascension-Saint-Thomas-River-Park/Visitor-Information
Control: Other not-for-profit (including NFP Corporation) **Service**: General medical and surgical

Staffed Beds: 63 **Admissions**: 2253 **Census**: 31 **Outpatient Visits**: 43723
Births: 347 **Total Expense ($000)**: 59988 **Payroll Expense ($000)**: 18741
Personnel: 283

Hospital, Medicare Provider Number, Address, Telephone, Approval, Facility, and Physician Codes, Health Care System

★ American Hospital Association (AHA) membership ○ Healthcare Facilities Accreditation Program ⇑ Center for Improvement in Healthcare Quality Accreditation
☐ The Joint Commission accreditation ◇ DNV Healthcare Inc. accreditation △ Commission on Accreditation of Rehabilitation Facilities (CARF) accreditation

Hospitals, U.S. / TENNESSEE

MEDINA—Madison County

☒ **JACKSON–MADISON COUNTY GENERAL HOSPITAL (440002)**, 620 Skyline Drive, Zip 38355, Mailing Address: Jackson, tel. 731/541-5000, (Includes WEST TENNESSEE HEALTHCARE NORTH HOSPITAL, 367 Hospital Boulevard, Jackson, Tennessee, Zip 38305-2080, tel. 731/661-2000; James E. Ross, President and Chief Executive Officer) **A**1 2 3 5 10 **F**3 7 8 11 13 15 17 18 20 22 24 26 28 29 30 31 34 35 37 38 39 40 44 45 46 47 48 49 51 53 55 56 57 58 59 60 63 64 65 68 70 72 74 75 76 77 78 79 80 81 82 84 85 86 87 92 93 94 96 97 107 108 109 110 111 114 115 116 117 118 119 120 121 124 126 129 130 131 132 135 145 146 147 148 149 154 156 157 167 169 **S** West Tennessee Healthcare, Jackson, TN
Primary Contact: Deann Thelen, Vice President and Chief Executive Officer
COO: Tina Prescott, Executive Vice President and Chief Operating Officer
CFO: Jeff Blankenship, CPA, Vice President and Chief Financial Officer
CMO: David Roberts, M.D., Chief Medical Officer
CIO: Jeff Frieling, Vice President and Chief Information Officer
CHR: Wendie Carlson, Chief Human Resources Officer
Web address: https://www.wth.org/locations/jackson-madison-co-general/
Control: Hospital district or authority, Government, Nonfederal **Service**: General medical and surgical

Staffed Beds: 580 **Admissions**: 28173 **Census**: 433 **Outpatient Visits**: 233448 **Births**: 3367 **Total Expense ($000)**: 801240 **Payroll Expense ($000)**: 300539 **Personnel**: 3917

MEMPHIS—Shelby County

☒ **BAPTIST MEMORIAL HOSPITAL – MEMPHIS (440048)**, 6019 Walnut Grove Road, Zip 38120-2173; tel. 901/226-5000, **A**1 2 8 10 **F**3 6 8 12 17 18 20 22 26 27 28 29 30 31 34 35 36 40 41 45 46 47 48 49 50 53 54 56 57 58 59 60 63 64 65 68 70 74 75 77 78 79 80 81 82 84 85 86 87 91 92 93 102 107 108 109 111 112 114 115 116 118 119 120 121 122 123 124 126 130 132 135 136 137 143 146 148 154 157 167 **S** Baptist Memorial Health Care Corporation, Memphis, TN
Primary Contact: Paul Cade, Chief Executive Officer and Administrator
CFO: Cyndi Pittman, Chief Financial Officer
CMO: Christian C Patrick, M.D., Chief Medical Officer
CIO: Doug Reiselt, Vice President and Chief Information Officer
CHR: Jerry Barbaree, Director Human Resources
CNO: Dana Dye, R.N., Vice President
Web address: www.baptistonline.org/memphis/
Control: Other not-for-profit (including NFP Corporation) **Service**: General medical and surgical

Staffed Beds: 547 **Admissions**: 25735 **Census**: 480 **Outpatient Visits**: 134631 **Births**: 2 **Total Expense ($000)**: 666059 **Payroll Expense ($000)**: 245217 **Personnel**: 2470

★ **BAPTIST MEMORIAL HOSPITAL FOR WOMEN (440222)**, 6225 Humphreys Boulevard, Zip 38120-2373; tel. 901/227-9000, **A**3 5 10 **F**3 7 12 13 15 19 29 30 32 34 35 38 41 45 46 47 48 49 54 55 56 57 58 59 64 65 68 70 71 72 73 74 75 76 77 78 79 81 82 85 86 87 88 89 107 108 109 110 111 115 119 124 126 130 132 135 146 147 148 154 169 **S** Baptist Memorial Health Care Corporation, Memphis, TN
Primary Contact: Allison Bosse, Chief Executive Officer and Administrator
CFO: Margaret Williams, Chief Financial Officer
CMO: Judi Carney, M.D., President Medical Staff
CIO: Melissa Nelson, Assistant Administrator
CHR: Karen Ingram, Director Human Resources
CNO: Carol Thetford, Chief Nursing Officer
Web address: www.baptistonline.org/womens/
Control: Other not-for-profit (including NFP Corporation) **Service**: Obstetrics and gynecology

Staffed Beds: 140 **Admissions**: 6833 **Census**: 47 **Outpatient Visits**: 73452 **Births**: 5439 **Total Expense ($000)**: 137358 **Payroll Expense ($000)**: 59645 **Personnel**: 692

☒ **BAPTIST MEMORIAL RESTORATIVE CARE HOSPITAL (442010)**, 6019 Walnut Grove Road, Zip 38120-2113; tel. 901/226-4200, (Nonreporting) **A**1 10 **S** Baptist Memorial Health Care Corporation, Memphis, TN
Primary Contact: Mark Kelly, Chief Executive Officer
Web address: www.baptistonline.org/restorative-care/
Control: Other not-for-profit (including NFP Corporation) **Service**: Acute long-term care hospital

Staffed Beds: 30

☐ **CRESTWYN BEHAVIORAL HEALTH (444025)**, 9485 Crestwyn Hills Cove, Zip 38125-8515; tel. 901/248-1500, (Nonreporting) **A**1 10 **S** Acadia Healthcare Company, Inc., Franklin, TN
Primary Contact: Lindsey Blevins, Chief Executive Officer
Web address: www.crestwynbh.com
Control: Corporation, Investor-owned (for-profit) **Service**: Psychiatric

Staffed Beds: 80

☐ **DELTA SPECIALTY HOSPITAL (440159)**, 3000 Getwell Road, Zip 38118-2299; tel. 901/369-8100, (Nonreporting) **A**1 10 **S** Acadia Healthcare Company, Inc., Franklin, TN
Primary Contact: Stephanie Reese, Chief Executive Officer
CFO: Mike Reynolds, Chief Financial Officer
CMO: David Richardson, M.D., Chief of Staff
CIO: Patrick Duffee, Director Medical Information Systems
CHR: Karyn Erickson, Director Human Resources
CNO: Donna Lanier, R.N., Chief Nursing Officer
Web address: www.deltaspecialtyhospital.com
Control: Corporation, Investor-owned (for-profit) **Service**: General medical and surgical

Staffed Beds: 164

☒ **ENCOMPASS HEALTH REHABILITATION HOSPITAL OF MEMPHIS, A PARTNER OF METHODIST HEALTHCARE (443029)**, 1282 Union Avenue, Zip 38104-3414; tel. 901/722-2000, (Nonreporting) **A**1 10 **S** Encompass Health Corporation, Birmingham, AL
Primary Contact: Toni Wackerfuss, Chief Executive Officer
CFO: Eric Gray, Chief Financial Officer
CMO: Jonathan D Ellen, M.D., Medical Director
CHR: Sandra Milburn, Director Human Resources
CNO: Jennifer Ferrell, Chief Nursing Officer
Web address: www.healthsouthmemphis.com
Control: Partnership, Investor-owned (for-profit) **Service**: Rehabilitation

Staffed Beds: 72

☒ **ENCOMPASS HEALTH REHABILITATION HOSPITAL OF NORTH MEMPHIS, A PARTNER OF METHODIST HEALTHCARE (443031)**, 4100 Austin Peay Highway, Zip 38128-2502; tel. 901/213-5400, (Nonreporting) **A**1 10 **S** Encompass Health Corporation, Birmingham, AL
Primary Contact: Yolanda Motley, Chief Executive Officer
CFO: Thaddeus Williams, Controller
CMO: Donald Sullivan, M.D., Medical Director
CHR: Adrienne Huntley, Director Human Resources
CNO: Charlotte Boyce, Chief Nursing Officer
Web address: https://encompasshealth.com/
Control: Corporation, Investor-owned (for-profit) **Service**: Rehabilitation

Staffed Beds: 50

☒ **LAKESIDE BEHAVIORAL HEALTH SYSTEM (444004)**, 2911 Brunswick Road, Zip 38133-4199; tel. 901/377-4700, (Nonreporting) **A**1 3 5 10 **S** Universal Health Services, Inc., King of Prussia, PA
Primary Contact: Joy Golden, Chief Executive Officer
CFO: Heather N. Tuck, Chief Financial Officer
CMO: C Hal Brunt, M.D., Medical Director
CIO: Jacob Arnett, Chief Information Technology Officer
CHR: Terri Starling, Director of Human Resources
CNO: Robert Edwards, Chief Nursing Officer
Web address: www.lakesidebhs.com
Control: Corporation, Investor-owned (for-profit) **Service**: Psychiatric

Staffed Beds: 345

LE BONHEUR CHILDREN'S HOSPITAL See Methodist Healthcare Memphis Hospitals, Memphis

LE BONHEUR CHILDREN'S MEDICAL CENTER See Le Bonheur Children's Hospital

☒ △ **LT. COL. LUKE WEATHERS, JR. VA MEDICAL CENTER**, 1030 Jefferson Avenue, Zip 38104-2193; tel. 901/523-8990, (Nonreporting) **A**1 3 5 7 **S** Department of Veterans Affairs, Washington, DC
Primary Contact: Joseph Vaughn, FACHE, Medical Center Director
CFO: Kristi Depperman, Chief Financial Officer
CMO: Christopher Marino, M.D., Chief of Staff
CIO: Robert Page III, Chief Information and Technology Officer
CHR: Natalie Brown, Chief Human Resources Management Services
CNO: Karen Gillette, Associate Director Patient Care Services
Web address: www.memphis.va.gov/
Control: Veterans Affairs, Government, federal **Service**: General medical and surgical

Staffed Beds: 177

☐ **MEMPHIS MENTAL HEALTH INSTITUTE (444001)**, 951 Court Ave, Zip 38103-2813, Mailing Address: P.O. Box 63656, Zip 38163-3656; tel. 901/577-1800, (Nonreporting) **A**1 3 5 10
Primary Contact: Jeff Coons, Chief Executive Officer
CFO: Donny Hornsby, Director Fiscal Services
CHR: Claudette Seymour, Director Personnel
Web address: www.memphis-institute.edan.io/
Control: State, Government, Nonfederal **Service**: Psychiatric

Staffed Beds: 55

Hospitals, U.S. / TENNESSEE

MEMPHIS VAMC See Lt. Col. Luke Weathers, Jr. VA Medical Center

METH HEALTHCARE – SOUTH HOSP See Methodist Healthcare–South Hospital

★ ⇧ **METHODIST HEALTHCARE MEMPHIS HOSPITALS (440049)**, 1265 Union Avenue, Zip 38104–3415; tel. 901/516–7000, (Includes LE BONHEUR CHILDREN'S HOSPITAL, 848 Adams Avenue, Memphis, Tennessee, Zip 38103, tel. 901/287–5437; Trey Eubanks, M.D., President; METHODIST HEALTHCARE–NORTH HOSPITAL, 3960 New Covington Pike, Memphis, Tennessee, Zip 38128, tel. 901/516–5200; Florence Jones, President; METHODIST HEALTHCARE–SOUTH HOSPITAL, 1300 Wesley Drive, Memphis, Tennessee, Zip 38116, tel. 901/516–3700; Jessie Lee Tucker III, Ph.D., Chief Executive Officer; METHODIST LE BONHEUR GERMANTOWN HOSPITAL, 7691 Poplar Avenue, Germantown, Tennessee, Zip 38138, tel. 901/516–6000; Rebecca Cullison, President) **A** 2 3 5 8 10 21 **F** 3 7 8 9 11 12 13 15 17 18 19 20 21 22 23 24 25 26 27 28 29 30 31 32 34 35 37 38 39 40 41 43 44 45 46 47 48 49 50 54 55 56 57 58 59 60 61 64 65 68 70 71 72 73 74 75 76 78 79 80 81 82 84 85 86 87 88 89 91 92 93 94 96 97 98 100 101 102 103 104 107 108 110 111 112 113 114 115 116 117 118 119 120 121 123 126 129 130 131 132 134 135 136 137 138 139 141 142 143 144 146 147 148 149 150 154 156 160 164 167 169 **S** Methodist Le Bonheur Healthcare, Memphis, TN
Primary Contact: Michael Ugwueke Sr, FACHE, President and Chief Executive Officer
CFO: Chris McLean, Chief Administrative Officer
CHR: Sarah Colley, Senior Vice President and Chief Human Resource Officer
CNO: Nikki S Polis, Ph.D., Chief Nurse Executive
Web address: www.methodisthealth.org
Control: Other not–for–profit (including NFP Corporation) **Service**: General medical and surgical

Staffed Beds: 1348 **Admissions**: 52922 **Census**: 950 **Outpatient Visits**: 692075 **Births**: 4646 **Total Expense ($000)**: 1733189 **Payroll Expense ($000)**: 589845 **Personnel**: 6888

METHODIST NORTH–J HARRIS HSP See Methodist Healthcare–North Hospital

⊞ **REGIONAL ONE HEALTH (440152)**, 877 Jefferson Avenue, Zip 38103–2897; tel. 901/545–7100, (Nonreporting) **A** 1 3 5 10
Primary Contact: Reginald W. Coopwood, M.D., President and Chief Executive Officer
COO: Rob Sumter, Executive Vice President and Chief Operating Officer
CFO: Rick Wagers, Senior Executive Vice President and Chief Financial Officer
CMO: Martin Croce, M.D., Senior Vice President and Chief Medical Officer
CIO: Rob Sumter, Executive Vice President and Chief Operation Officer
CHR: Sarah Colley, Senior Vice President Human Resources
CNO: Pam Castleman, MSN, Chief Nursing Officer
Web address: www.regionalonehealth.org
Control: Other not–for–profit (including NFP Corporation) **Service**: General medical and surgical

Staffed Beds: 382

△ **REGIONAL ONE HEALTH EXTENDED CARE HOSPITAL (442017)**, 890 Madison Avenue, Turner Tower, Zip 38103–3409; tel. 901/515–3000, (Nonreporting) **A** 7 10 22
Primary Contact: Phillip Underwood, Chief Executive Officer
CNO: Paula Harrell, Chief Nursing Officer
Web address: www.regionalonehealth.org/extended-care-hospital/
Control: Other not–for–profit (including NFP Corporation) **Service**: Acute long–term care hospital

Staffed Beds: 21

⊞ **SAINT FRANCIS HOSPITAL (440183)**, 5959 Park Avenue, Zip 38119–5198; tel. 901/765–1000, (Nonreporting) **A** 1 3 5 10 **S** TENET Healthcare Corporation, Dallas, TX
Primary Contact: Scott M. Smith, Market Chief Executive Officer
COO: Manoucheka Thermitus, Chief Operating Officer
CFO: Tina Kovacs, Chief Financial Officer
CMO: David Schwartz, M.D., Chief Medical Officer
CIO: Keith Scarbrough, Director, Information Systems
CHR: Marty Keith, Chief Human Resources Officer
CNO: Jennifer Chiusano, R.N., Chief Nursing Officer
Web address: www.saintfrancishosp.com
Control: Corporation, Investor–owned (for–profit) **Service**: General medical and surgical

Staffed Beds: 479

⊞ **SELECT SPECIALTY HOSPITAL–MEMPHIS (442014)**, 1265 Union Avenue, 10th Floor, Zip 38104–3415; tel. 901/765–1245, (Nonreporting) **A** 1 10 **S** Select Medical Corporation, Mechanicsburg, PA
Primary Contact: Marcia Taylor, Chief Executive Officer
Web address: www.selectspecialtyhospitals.com/company/locations/memphis.aspx
Control: Corporation, Investor–owned (for–profit) **Service**: Acute long–term care hospital

Staffed Beds: 39

★ ⇧ **ST. JUDE CHILDREN'S RESEARCH HOSPITAL (443302)**, 262 Danny Thomas Place, Zip 38105–3678; tel. 901/595–3300, **A** 3 5 10 21 **F** 14 30 31 39 50 52 53 55 64 68 75 77 78 79 80 81 82 84 86 87 88 93 94 107 108 111 114 117 118 119 120 121 122 123 124 130 136 141 142 146 149 154 167
Primary Contact: James R. Downing, M.D., Chief Executive Officer
COO: Mary Anna Quinn, Executive Vice President, Chief Administrative Officer
CFO: Abed Abdo, Chief Financial Officer
CMO: Ellis Neufeld, M.D., Chief Medical Officer
CIO: Darrin Keith Perry, Chief Information Officer and Senior Vice President
CHR: Dana Bottenfield, Vice President Human Resources
Web address: www.stjude.org
Control: Other not–for–profit (including NFP Corporation)

Staffed Beds: 73 **Admissions**: 3285 **Census**: 51 **Outpatient Visits**: 77222 **Births**: 0 **Total Expense ($000)**: 1519049 **Payroll Expense ($000)**: 601582 **Personnel**: 6044

UNITY PSYCH CARE–MEMPHIS (444024), 1505 North Second Street, Zip 38107–1003; tel. 901/791–0600, (Nonreporting) **A** 10
Primary Contact: Robert Edwards, Administrator
Web address: https://www.unitypsych.com/memphis
Control: Corporation, Investor–owned (for–profit) **Service**: Psychiatric

Staffed Beds: 16

MILAN—Gibson County

⊞ **WEST TENNESSEE HEALTHCARE MILAN HOSPITAL (440060)**, 4039 Highland Street, Zip 38358–3483; tel. 731/686–1591, **A** 1 10 **F** 3 15 28 29 30 34 35 40 44 45 57 59 64 68 70 81 87 107 110 114 119 129 130 132 133 135 146 149 154 **S** West Tennessee Healthcare, Jackson, TN
Primary Contact: Sherry Scruggs, Chief Executive Officer
CMO: Joe Appleton, M.D., Chief of Surgery
CNO: Carolyn Drake, Director of Nursing
Web address: www.wth.org
Control: Hospital district or authority, Government, Nonfederal **Service**: General medical and surgical

Staffed Beds: 25 **Admissions**: 397 **Census**: 4 **Outpatient Visits**: 21418 **Births**: 0 **Total Expense ($000)**: 15824 **Payroll Expense ($000)**: 6405 **Personnel**: 101

MORRISTOWN—Hamblen County

□ **MORRISTOWN–HAMBLEN HEALTHCARE SYSTEM (440030)**, 908 West Fourth North Street, Zip 37814–3894, Mailing Address: P.O. Box 1178, Zip 37816–1178; tel. 423/492–9000, **A** 1 3 5 10 **F** 3 11 13 15 18 20 22 26 28 29 30 31 34 35 37 38 39 40 42 44 45 46 49 50 51 54 56 57 58 59 60 61 64 65 74 75 76 77 78 79 80 81 82 85 86 87 93 94 96 98 101 102 103 107 108 110 111 114 115 117 118 119 120 121 123 126 130 131 132 135 146 147 148 149 154 163 167 169 **S** Covenant Health, Knoxville, TN
Primary Contact: Gordon Lintz, President and Chief Administrative Officer
CFO: Amy Herndon, Chief Finance Officer
CIO: Mike Ward, Chief Information Officer
CNO: Wilma Hart–Flynn, Ph.D., R.N., Chief Nursing Officer
Web address: www.morristownhamblen.com
Control: Other not–for–profit (including NFP Corporation) **Service**: General medical and surgical

Staffed Beds: 121 **Admissions**: 7167 **Census**: 95 **Outpatient Visits**: 109660 **Births**: 835 **Total Expense ($000)**: 117686 **Payroll Expense ($000)**: 46312 **Personnel**: 653

Hospital, Medicare Provider Number, Address, Telephone, Approval, Facility, and Physician Codes, Health Care System

★ American Hospital Association (AHA) membership ○ Healthcare Facilities Accreditation Program ⇧ Center for Improvement in Healthcare Quality Accreditation
□ The Joint Commission accreditation ◇ DNV Healthcare Inc. accreditation △ Commission on Accreditation of Rehabilitation Facilities (CARF) accreditation

Hospitals, U.S. / TENNESSEE

MOUNTAIN CITY—Johnson County

JOHNSON COUNTY COMMUNITY HOSPITAL (441304), 1901 South Shady Street, Zip 37683–2271; tel. 423/727–1100, (Nonreporting) **A**10 18 **S** Ballad Health, Johnson City, TN
Primary Contact: Chastity Trivette, Administrator
CNO: Charmaine Crowe, Team Manager, Nursing and Infection Prevention
Web address: https://www.balladhealth.org/hospitals/johnson-county-community
Control: Other not–for–profit (including NFP Corporation) **Service**: General medical and surgical

Staffed Beds: 2

MURFREESBORO—Rutherford County

ALVIN C. YORK CAMPUS See Tennessee Valley HCS – Nashville and Murfreesboro, Nashville

ALVIN C. YORK VETERANS AFFAIRS MEDICAL CENTER See Alvin C. York Campus

ASCENSION SAINT THOMAS RUTHERFORD (440053), 1700 Medical Center Parkway, Zip 37129–2245; tel. 615/396–4100, **A**1 2 3 5 10 **F**3 12 18 20 22 24 26 28 29 30 31 34 37 40 44 45 46 47 49 50 51 53 54 57 59 64 65 66 70 71 72 74 75 76 77 78 79 81 84 85 86 87 89 91 92 97 107 111 115 118 119 120 121 124 126 130 131 135 146 147 148 149 154 157 160 164 167 169 **S** Ascension Healthcare, Saint Louis, MO
Primary Contact: Gordon B. Ferguson, President and Chief Executive Officer
COO: Thomas Roddy, Chief Operating Officer
CFO: Bailey Pratt, Chief Financial Officer
CMO: Richard Rogers, M.D., Chief Medical Officer
CHR: Carol Bragdon, Director Human Resources
Web address: https://healthcare.ascension.org/Locations/Tennessee/TNNAS/Murfreesboro-Ascension-Saint-Thomas-Rutherford
Control: Other not–for–profit (including NFP Corporation) **Service**: General medical and surgical

Staffed Beds: 368 Admissions: 20527 Census: 297 Outpatient Visits: 105818 Births: 3627 Total Expense ($000): 443191 Payroll Expense ($000): 126208 Personnel: 1518

TRUSTPOINT HOSPITAL (440231), 1009 North Thompson Lane, Zip 37129–4351; tel. 615/867–1111, (Nonreporting) **A**1 10 **S** Acadia Healthcare Company, Inc., Franklin, TN
Primary Contact: Holly Russell, Chief Executive Officer
Web address: www.trustpointhospital.com
Control: Corporation, Investor–owned (for–profit) **Service**: Rehabilitation

Staffed Beds: 155

NASHVILLE—Davidson County

ASCENSION SAINT THOMAS BEHAVIORAL HEALTH HOSPITAL (444030), 300 Great Circle Road, Zip 37228–1752; tel. 615/813–1880, (Nonreporting) **A**1 10 **S** Ascension Healthcare, Saint Louis, MO
Primary Contact: Jared Roe, Chief Executive Officer
Web address: www.saintthomasbehavioral.com
Control: Corporation, Investor–owned (for–profit) **Service**: Psychiatric

Staffed Beds: 76

ASCENSION SAINT THOMAS HOSPITAL (443038), 4220 Harding Pike, Zip 37205–2095, Mailing Address: P.O. Box 380, Zip 37202–0380; tel. 615/222–2111, (Includes ASCENSION SAINT THOMAS HOSPITAL MIDTOWN, 2000 Church Street, Nashville, Tennessee, Zip 37236–0002, tel. 615/284–5555; Shubhada Jagasia, President and Chief Executive Officer) **A**1 2 3 5 10 **F**3 12 13 15 17 18 20 22 24 26 28 29 30 31 34 36 37 39 40 44 45 46 47 48 49 50 51 53 54 55 57 58 59 64 65 66 70 71 72 73 74 75 76 77 78 79 80 81 84 85 86 87 91 92 93 96 97 107 110 111 112 115 116 118 119 120 121 123 124 126 130 131 135 137 138 141 145 147 148 149 154 157 164 167 169 **S** Ascension Healthcare, Saint Louis, MO
Primary Contact: Shubhada Jagasia, President and Chief Executive Officer
COO: Harrison Kiser, Chief Operating Officer
CFO: Pamela Hess, Chief Financial Officer
CMO: Dale Batchelor, M.D., Chief Medical Officer
CHR: Bud Wood, Chief Human Resources Officer
CNO: Sam Straton, Chief Nursing Officer
Web address: https://healthcare.ascension.org/Locations/Tennessee/TNNAS/Nashville-Ascension-Saint-Thomas-Hospital
Control: Other not–for–profit (including NFP Corporation) **Service**: General medical and surgical

Staffed Beds: 864 Admissions: 36489 Census: 536 Outpatient Visits: 207926 Births: 6781 Total Expense ($000): 1022823 Payroll Expense ($000): 258720 Personnel: 3108

★ **ASCENSION SAINT THOMAS HOSPITAL FOR SPECIALTY SURGERY (440218)**, 2011 Murphy Avenue, Suite 400, Zip 37203–2065; tel. 615/341–7500, (Nonreporting) **A**10 **S** Ascension Healthcare, Saint Louis, MO
Primary Contact: Ryan Walker, Chief Executive Officer
COO: Kathy Watson, R.N., Administrator and Chief Nursing Officer
CFO: Angie Crow, Director Finance
CMO: Carl Hampf, M.D., Chief Medical Officer
CNO: Kathy Watson, R.N., Administrator and Chief Nursing Officer
Web address: https://healthcare.ascension.org/Locations/Tennessee/TNNAS/Nashville-Saint-Thomas-Hospital-for-Specialty-Surgery
Control: Partnership, Investor–owned (for–profit) **Service**: General medical and surgical

Staffed Beds: 23

MIDDLE TENNESSEE MENTAL HEALTH INSTITUTE (444014), 221 Stewarts Ferry Pike, Zip 37214–3325; tel. 615/902–7400, (Nonreporting) **A**1 3 5 10
Primary Contact: Eric Doxy, Administrator
CFO: Mark Stanley, Director Fiscal Services
CMO: Mohammad S Jahan, M.D., Clinical Director
CHR: Margie Dunn, Director Human Resources
Web address: https://www.tn.gov/behavioral-health/hospitals/middle-tennessee.html
Control: State, Government, Nonfederal **Service**: Psychiatric

Staffed Beds: 207

MONROE CARELL JR. CHILDREN'S HOSPITAL AT VANDERBILT See Vanderbilt University Medical Center, Nashville

NASHVILLE GENERAL HOSPITAL (440111), 1818 Albion Street, Zip 37208–2918; tel. 615/341–4000, (Nonreporting) **A**1 2 3 5 10
Primary Contact: Joseph Webb, FACHE, Chief Executive Officer
CMO: Deann Bullock, M.D., Chief Medical Officer
CIO: Chris Whorley, Chief Information Officer
CHR: Diana Wohlfardt, Director Human Resources
CNO: Leonora Collins, Chief Nursing Officer
Web address: www.nashvillegeneral.org/
Control: City–county, Government, Nonfederal **Service**: General medical and surgical

Staffed Beds: 114

PSYCHIATRIC HOSPITAL AT VANDERBILT See Vanderbilt Psychiatric Hospital

SAINT THOMAS MIDTOWN HOSPITAL See Ascension Saint Thomas Hospital Midtown

SELECT SPECIALTY HOSPITAL NASHVILLE (442011), 2000 Hayes Street, Suite 1502, Zip 37203–2318; tel. 615/284–4599, (Includes SELECT SPECIALTY HOSPITAL–NASHVILLE WEST, 4220 Harding Pike, Nashville, Tennessee, Zip 37205–2005, tel. 629/253–2300; James Bills, Chief Executive Officer) (Nonreporting) **A**1 10 **S** Select Medical Corporation, Mechanicsburg, PA
Primary Contact: Jordan McClure, Chief Executive Officer
CNO: Karen Cagle, Chief Nursing Officer
Web address: https://www.selectspecialtyhospitals.com/locations-and-tours/tn/nashville/nashville/?utm_source=gmb&utm_medium=organic
Control: Corporation, Investor–owned (for–profit) **Service**: Acute long–term care hospital

Staffed Beds: 70

TENNESSEE VALLEY HCS – NASHVILLE AND MURFREESBORO, 1310 24th Avenue South, Zip 37212–2637; tel. 615/327–4751, (Includes ALVIN C. YORK CAMPUS, 3400 Lebanon Pike, Murfreesboro, Tennessee, Zip 37129–1236, tel. 615/867–6000; NASHVILLE CAMPUS, 1310 24th Avenue South, Nashville, Tennessee, Zip 37212–2637, tel. 615/327–4751) (Nonreporting) **A**1 3 5 **S** Department of Veterans Affairs, Washington, DC
Primary Contact: Michael B. Renfrow, Medical Center Director
COO: Suzanne L. Jene, Chief Operating Officer
CFO: Lynn Menthcoast, Chief Fiscal Service
CMO: Roger Jones, M.D., Interim Chief of Staff
CIO: Paul Mardy, Chief Information Technology Officer
CHR: Shirley F Pettite, Chief Human Resources Officer
CNO: Janice M Cobb, R.N., Chief Nursing Officer
Web address: www.tennesseevalley.va.gov
Control: Veterans Affairs, Government, federal **Service**: General medical and surgical

Staffed Beds: 361

TENNESSEE VALLEY HEALTHCARE SYSTEM See Tennessee Valley HCS – Nashville and Murfreesboro

Hospitals, U.S. / TENNESSEE

TRISTAR CENTENNIAL MEDICAL CENTER (440161), 2300 Patterson Street, Zip 37203–1528; tel. 615/342–1000; (Includes TRISTAR CENTENNIAL WOMEN'S & CHILDREN'S, 2221 Murphy Avenue, Nashville, Tennessee, Zip 37203, tel. 615/342–1000; Mitchell C. Edgeworth, President) (Nonreporting) **A**1 2 3 5 10 **S** HCA Healthcare, Nashville, TN
Primary Contact: Thomas H. Ozburn, FACHE, President and Chief Executive Officer
CFO: Tom Jackson, Chief Financial Officer
CHR: Tammy Kaminski, Vice President, Human Resources
Web address: www.tristarcentennial.com
Control: Corporation, Investor–owned (for–profit) **Service:** General medical and surgical

Staffed Beds: 735

TRISTAR SKYLINE MEDICAL CENTER (440006), 3441 Dickerson Pike, Zip 37207–2539; tel. 615/769–2000, (Includes TRISTAR SKYLINE MADISON CAMPUS, 500 Hospital Drive, Madison, Tennessee, Zip 37115–5032, tel. 615/769–5000) (Nonreporting) **A**1 2 3 7 10 **S** HCA Healthcare, Nashville, TN
Primary Contact: Mark Miller, FACHE, Chief Executive Officer
COO: Nick Howald, Chief Operating Officer
CFO: Michael Morrison, Chief Financial Officer
CMO: Christopher Conley, M.D., President of the Medical Staff
CIO: Troy Sypien, Director Information Technology and Systems
CHR: Robert A Hooper, Director Human Resources
CNO: Christine Staigl, Chief Nursing Officer
Web address: www.tristarskyline.com
Control: Corporation, Investor–owned (for–profit) **Service:** General medical and surgical

Staffed Beds: 407

TRISTAR SOUTHERN HILLS MEDICAL CENTER (440197), 391 Wallace Road, Zip 37211–4859; tel. 615/781–4000, (Nonreporting) **A**1 2 3 10 **S** HCA Healthcare, Nashville, TN
Primary Contact: Nick Howald, Chief Executive Officer
COO: Joe White, Chief Operating Officer
CFO: John Porada, Chief Financial Officer
CMO: Eric Schuck, M.D., Chief Medical Officer
CIO: Ronnie Gannon, Director Information Services
CHR: Gary Briggs, Vice President Human Resources
Web address: www.tristarsouthernhills.com
Control: Corporation, Investor–owned (for–profit) **Service:** General medical and surgical

Staffed Beds: 87

VANDERBILT PSYCHIATRIC HOSPITAL See Vanderbilt University Medical Center, Nashville

VANDERBILT STALLWORTH REHABILITATION HOSPITAL (443028), 2201 Childrens Way, Zip 37212–3165; tel. 615/320–7600, **A**1 3 5 10 **F**29 65 68 90 96 143 148 149 164 **S** Encompass Health Corporation, Birmingham, AL
Primary Contact: Jeffrey Palmucci, Chief Executive Officer
CFO: Christine Campbell, Controller
CMO: Jeffery Johns, M.D., Medical Director
CHR: Ruth Beasley, Director Human Resources
CNO: Karen Lasher, Chief Nursing Officer
Web address: www.vanderbiltstallworthrehab.com
Control: Partnership, Investor–owned (for–profit) **Service:** Rehabilitation

Staffed Beds: 80 **Admissions:** 1264 **Census:** 45 **Outpatient Visits:** 0 **Births:** 0 **Total Expense ($000):** 24386 **Payroll Expense ($000):** 11931 **Personnel:** 185

VANDERBILT UNIVERSITY MEDICAL CENTER (440039), 1211 Medical Center Drive, Zip 37232–2102; tel. 615/322–5000, (Includes MONROE CARELL JR. CHILDREN'S HOSPITAL AT VANDERBILT, 2200 Childrens Way, Nashville, Tennessee, Zip 37232–0005, 2200 Children's Way, Zip 37232, tel. 615/936–1000; Meg Rush, M.D., Interim President; VANDERBILT PSYCHIATRIC HOSPITAL, 1601 23rd Avenue South, Nashville, Tennessee, Zip 37212–3198, tel. 615/320–7770) **A**1 2 3 5 8 10 **F**3 4 5 6 7 8 9 11 12 13 15 16 17 18 19 20 21 22 23 24 25 26 27 28 29 30 31 32 34 35 36 37 38 39 40 41 43 44 45 46 47 48 49 50 51 52 53 54 55 56 57 58 59 60 61 62 63 65 66 68 69 70 71 72 74 75 76 77 78 79 80 81 82 83 84 85 86 87 88 89 90 91 92 93 94 96 97 98 99 100 101 102 103 104 105 107 108 109 110 111 114 115 116 117 118 119 120 121 123 124 126 127 129 130 131 132 134 135 136 137 138 139 140 141 142 143 144 146 147 148 149 150 151 152 153 154 156 157 160 161 162 163 164 165 166 167 168 169 **P**1 2 6 **S** Vanderbilt Health, Nashville, TN
Primary Contact: Jeffrey R. Balser, M.D., Ph.D., President and Chief Executive Officer Vanderbilt Medical Center and Dean, Vanderbilt University Scho
CFO: Cecelia B Moore, CPA, Associate Vice Chancellor Finance
CMO: Paul Sternberg, M.D., Professor and Chairman
CIO: William Stead, Associate Vice Chancellor Health Affairs, Director Informatics Center and Chief Strategy and Information Officer
CHR: Traci Nordberg, Chief Human Resources Officer
Web address: https://search.vanderbilthealth.com/locations/vanderbilt-university-medical-center
Control: Other not–for–profit (including NFP Corporation) **Service:** General medical and surgical

Staffed Beds: 1202 **Admissions:** 60814 **Census:** 1096 **Outpatient Visits:** 3323634 **Births:** 5255 **Total Expense ($000):** 5307850 **Payroll Expense ($000):** 1992474 **Personnel:** 28104

VETERANS ADM MEDICAL CENTER See Nashville Campus

NEWPORT—Cocke County

TENNOVA NEWPORT MEDICAL CENTER (440153), 435 Second Street, Zip 37821–3799; tel. 423/625–2200, (Nonreporting) **A**1 10 **S** Community Health Systems, Inc., Franklin, TN
Primary Contact: Scott Williams, Chief Executive Officer
CFO: Jon Richards, Chief Financial Officer
CMO: Larry Mathers, M.D., Chief of Staff
Web address: www.tennova.com
Control: Corporation, Investor–owned (for–profit) **Service:** General medical and surgical

Staffed Beds: 130

OAK RIDGE—Anderson County

METHODIST MEDICAL CENTER OF OAK RIDGE (440034), 990 Oak Ridge Turnpike, Zip 37830–6976, Mailing Address: P.O. Box 2529, Zip 37831–2529; tel. 865/835–1000, **A**1 3 5 10 **F**3 11 13 15 17 18 20 22 24 26 28 29 30 31 34 35 37 38 39 40 44 45 46 49 50 51 54 57 58 59 60 61 63 64 65 70 74 75 76 77 78 79 81 82 84 85 86 87 92 93 94 96 101 102 107 108 110 111 115 118 119 120 121 123 126 129 130 132 135 146 147 148 149 154 163 167 169 **S** Covenant Health, Knoxville, TN
Primary Contact: Jeremy Biggs, President and Chief Administrative Officer
COO: Connie Martin, Vice President and Chief Support Officer
CFO: Rick Carringer, Vice President and Chief Financial Officer
CMO: Mark Browne, M.D., Covenant Health, Senior Vice President and Chief Medical Officer
CIO: Mike Ward, Covenant Health, Senior Vice President and Chief Information Officer
CHR: Rick Akens, Director Human Resources and Labor Relations
CNO: Mike P. Cavacos, MSN, Chief Nursing Officer
Web address: www.mmcoakridge.com
Control: Other not–for–profit (including NFP Corporation) **Service:** General medical and surgical

Staffed Beds: 176 **Admissions:** 8579 **Census:** 119 **Outpatient Visits:** 142134 **Births:** 503 **Total Expense ($000):** 179347 **Payroll Expense ($000):** 59107 **Personnel:** 716

RIDGEVIEW PSYCHIATRIC HOSPITAL AND CENTER (444003), 240 West Tyrone Road, Zip 37830–6571; tel. 865/482–1076, (Nonreporting) **A**10
Primary Contact: Brian Buuck, Chief Executive Officer
CFO: Mary Claire Duff, CPA, Chief Financial Officer
CMO: Renu Bhateja, M.D., President Medical Staff
CHR: Julie M Wright, Director Human Resources
Web address: www.ridgeviewresources.com
Control: Other not–for–profit (including NFP Corporation) **Service:** Psychiatric

Staffed Beds: 20

Hospital, Medicare Provider Number, Address, Telephone, Approval, Facility, and Physician Codes, Health Care System

★ American Hospital Association (AHA) membership
☐ The Joint Commission accreditation
○ Healthcare Facilities Accreditation Program
◇ DNV Healthcare Inc. accreditation
⇑ Center for Improvement in Healthcare Quality Accreditation
△ Commission on Accreditation of Rehabilitation Facilities (CARF) accreditation

Hospitals, U.S. / TENNESSEE

ONEIDA—Scott County

BIG SOUTH FORK MEDICAL CENTER (441323), 18797 Alberta Street, Zip 37841–2127; tel. 423/286–5500, (Nonreporting) **A**10 18
Primary Contact: Hal W. Leftwich, FACHE, Chief Executive Officer
Web address: www.bsfmedical.com
Control: Other not–for–profit (including NFP Corporation) **Service**: General medical and surgical

Staffed Beds: 25

PARIS—Henry County

HENRY COUNTY MEDICAL CENTER (440132), 301 Tyson Avenue, Zip 38242–4544, Mailing Address: P.O. Box 1030, Zip 38242–1030; tel. 731/642–1220, (Total facility includes 70 beds in nursing home–type unit) **A**1 10 **F**3 7 11 13 15 18 20 28 29 30 32 34 35 37 40 44 50 51 53 56 57 59 62 63 64 65 67 68 70 71 76 77 79 81 85 86 87 89 93 98 100 102 103 107 108 110 111 114 115 118 119 126 127 128 129 130 131 132 133 135 143 146 147 148 154 156 165 **P**6
Primary Contact: John Tucker, Chief Executive Officer
CFO: Brad Bloemer, Chief Financial Officer
CIO: Pam Ridley, Director Information Systems
CHR: Edwin L Ledden, Assistant Administrator and Director Human Resources
Web address: www.hcmc-tn.org
Control: Hospital district or authority, Government, Nonfederal **Service**: General medical and surgical

Staffed Beds: 119 **Admissions**: 2601 **Census**: 92 **Outpatient Visits**: 161486 **Births**: 431 **Total Expense ($000)**: 103120 **Payroll Expense ($000)**: 42301 **Personnel**: 575

PIKEVILLE—Bledsoe County

ERLANGER BLEDSOE HOSPITAL (441306), 71 Wheelertown Avenue, Zip 37367–5246, Mailing Address: P.O. Box 699, Zip 37367–0699; tel. 423/447–2112, **A**10 18 21 **F**3 11 15 18 29 30 34 35 38 40 42 44 50 54 56 57 58 59 61 64 65 66 68 74 75 77 78 79 82 84 85 86 87 91 92 93 96 97 100 101 102 107 110 114 119 127 130 131 132 133 134 135 146 147 148 149 150 154 156 157 164 167 169 **P**6 **S** Erlanger Health System, Chattanooga, TN
Primary Contact: Stephanie Boynton, Administrator
CMO: Arturo L Quito, M.D., Chief of Staff
CIO: Debbie Rains, Coordinator Health Information Management
CHR: Patsy Brown, Site Coordinator Human Resources
Web address: www.erlanger.org
Control: Hospital district or authority, Government, Nonfederal **Service**: General medical and surgical

Staffed Beds: 25 **Admissions**: 179 **Census**: 4 **Outpatient Visits**: 26588 **Births**: 0 **Total Expense ($000)**: 17078 **Payroll Expense ($000)**: 7670 **Personnel**: 93

POWELL—Knox County

SELECT SPECIALTY HOSPITAL–NORTH KNOXVILLE (442015), 7557B Dannaher Drive, Suite 145, Zip 37849–3568; tel. 865/512–2450, (Includes SELECT SPECIALTY HOSPITAL–KNOXVILLE, 1901 Clinch Avenue, 4th Floor North, Knoxville, Tennessee, Zip 37916–2307, tel. 865/541–2615; Stacey Naughton, Chief Executive Officer) (Nonreporting) **A**1 10 **S** Select Medical Corporation, Mechanicsburg, PA
Primary Contact: Steve Plumlee, Chief Executive Officer
CFO: David Elledge, Controller
CMO: Jeff Summers, M.D., Medical Director
CIO: Steve Plumlee, Chief Executive Officer
CHR: Mallory Wilson, Administrative Assistant and Human Resources Coordinator
CNO: Nancy Johnson, Chief Nursing Officer
Web address: www.northknoxville.selectspecialtyhospitals.com/
Control: Corporation, Investor–owned (for–profit) **Service**: Acute long–term care hospital

Staffed Beds: 33

TENNOVA NORTH KNOXVILLE MEDICAL CENTER (440120), 7565 Dannaher Way, Zip 37849–4029; tel. 865/859–8000, (Includes TENNOVA TURKEY CREEK MEDICAL CENTER, 10820 Parkside Drive, Knoxville, Tennessee, Zip 37934–1956, tel. 865/218–7092; Ben Youree, Chief Executive Officer) (Nonreporting) **A**1 2 10 19 **S** Community Health Systems, Inc., Franklin, TN
Primary Contact: Bill Rich, Chief Executive Officer
COO: Drew Grey, Chief Operating Officer
Web address: https://www.tennovanorthknoxville.com/
Control: Corporation, Investor–owned (for–profit) **Service**: General medical and surgical

Staffed Beds: 116

PULASKI—Giles County

SOUTHERN TENNESSEE REGIONAL HEALTH SYSTEM–PULASKI (440020), 1265 East College Street, Zip 38478–4541; tel. 931/363–7531, (Nonreporting) **A**1 10 **S** Lifepoint Health, Brentwood, TN
Primary Contact: Jason Russell. Fugleberg, R.N., Chief Executive Officer
CFO: Donald Gavin, Chief Financial Officer
CMO: J Michael Windland, M.D., Chief of Staff
CIO: Mitzi Foster, Director Information Services
CHR: Jane Petty, Director Human Resources
CNO: Verno Davidson, R.N., Interim Chief Nursing Officer
Web address: www.southerntnpulaski.com/
Control: Corporation, Investor–owned (for–profit) **Service**: General medical and surgical

Staffed Beds: 32

RIPLEY—Lauderdale County

LAUDERDALE COMMUNITY HOSPITAL (441314), 326 Asbury Avenue, Zip 38063–5577; tel. 731/221–2200, (Nonreporting) **A**10 18
Primary Contact: Tracy P. Byers, FACHE, Chief Executive Officer
CFO: T J Sheehan, Chief Financial Officer
CMO: Syed A. Zaidi, M.D., Chief of Staff
CIO: Jim Vaden, Director Information Systems
CHR: Joan W. Simpson, Manager Human Resources
CNO: Michelle Simpson, Chief Nursing Officer and Quality Leader
Web address: www.lauderdalehospital.org
Control: Corporation, Investor–owned (for–profit) **Service**: General medical and surgical

Staffed Beds: 25

ROCKY TOP—Anderson County

BEHAVIORAL HEALTH OF ROCKY TOP (444028), 210 Industrial Park Lane, Zip 37769–2301; tel. 865/630–9200, (Nonreporting) **A**10
Primary Contact: Richard H. Lawrence, Administrator
CNO: Keisha Carroll, Chief Nursing Officer
Web address: https://www.behavioralhealthofrockytop.com/
Control: Corporation, Investor–owned (for–profit) **Service**: Psychiatric

Staffed Beds: 18

ROGERSVILLE—Hawkins County

HAWKINS COUNTY MEMORIAL HOSPITAL (440032), 851 Locust Street, Zip 37857–2407, Mailing Address: P.O. Box 130, Zip 37857–0130; tel. 423/921–7000, (Nonreporting) **A**1 10 **S** Ballad Health, Johnson City, TN
Primary Contact: Hunter Hamilton, Chief Executive Officer
CFO: Dale Poe, Vice President and Chief Financial Officer
CMO: Daniel Lewis, Chief Medical Officer
CHR: Robin Poteete, Manager Human Resources
Web address: www.wellmont.org
Control: Other not–for–profit (including NFP Corporation) **Service**: General medical and surgical

Staffed Beds: 16

SAVANNAH—Hardin County

HARDIN MEDICAL CENTER (440109), 935 Wayne Road, Zip 38372–1904, Mailing Address: 5045 HWY 226, Zip 38372; tel. 731/926–8000, (Nonreporting) **A**10 21
Primary Contact: James H. Edmondson, Chief Executive Officer
CFO: Leigh Ann Hughes, Chief Financial Officer
CMO: Gilbert M. Thayer, M.D., Chief Medical Staff
CIO: Jacob Bomar, Director Information Technology
CNO: Jesse Wint, Director of Nursing
Web address: www.hardinmedicalcenter.org
Control: County, Government, Nonfederal **Service**: General medical and surgical

Staffed Beds: 122

Hospitals, U.S. / TENNESSEE

SEVIERVILLE—Sevier County

☐ **LECONTE MEDICAL CENTER (440081)**, 742 Middle Creek Road, Zip 37862-5019, Mailing Address: P.O. Box 8005, Zip 37864-8005; tel. 865/446-7000, **A**1 10 **F**3 11 13 15 18 20 28 29 30 31 34 35 38 40 44 45 46 50 51 53 57 58 59 60 61 64 65 70 74 75 76 77 78 79 80 81 82 85 86 87 92 93 94 96 101 102 107 108 110 111 114 115 116 117 118 119 120 121 123 124 130 131 132 133 135 146 147 148 149 154 163 167 169 **S** Covenant Health, Knoxville, TN
Primary Contact: Aaron Burns, President and Chief Executive Officer
COO: Michael Hatmaker, Vice President Support Services and Admin Nursing Home
CFO: Jacqueline Hounshell, Chief Financial Officer
CMO: William Clifford Cole, M.D., Chief of Staff
Web address: www.lecontemedicalcenter.com
Control: Other not-for-profit (including NFP Corporation) **Service**: General medical and surgical

Staffed Beds: 79 **Admissions**: 4117 **Census**: 46 **Outpatient Visits**: 134520
Births: 696 **Total Expense ($000)**: 113322 **Payroll Expense ($000)**: 34636
Personnel: 466

SEWANEE—Franklin County

EMERALD-HODGSON HOSPITAL See Southern Tennessee Regional Health System–Sewanee

SOUTHERN TENNESSEE REGIONAL HEALTH SYSTEM-SEWANEE See Southern Tennessee Regional Health System–Winchester, Winchester

SHELBYVILLE—Bedford County

✠ **VANDERBILT BEDFORD HOSPITAL (440137)**, 2835 Highway 231 North, Zip 37160-7327; tel. 931/685-5433, **A**1 10 **F**3 11 12 15 18 29 34 35 40 45 50 57 59 64 65 68 70 74 75 77 79 81 85 86 87 93 97 107 108 109 110 111 115 119 127 129 130 131 133 135 141 142 144 147 148 149 154 164 167 **S** Vanderbilt Health, Nashville, TN
Primary Contact: Travis Capers, FACHE, Chief Executive Officer, Regional Community Hospitals
CFO: Tammy Cobb, Chief Financial Officer
CIO: Jonathon Willis, Director Information Services
CHR: Charisse Parker, Director Human Resources
CNO: Vickie Vaughn, Chief Nursing Officer
Web address: www.Tennova.com
Control: Other not-for-profit (including NFP Corporation) **Service**: General medical and surgical

Staffed Beds: 32 **Admissions**: 1149 **Census**: 12 **Outpatient Visits**: 58322
Births: 0 **Total Expense ($000)**: 49040 **Payroll Expense ($000)**: 21952
Personnel: 283

SMITHVILLE—Dekalb County

✠ **ASCENSION SAINT THOMAS DEKALB (440148)**, 520 West Main Street, Zip 37166-1138, Mailing Address: P.O. Box 640, Zip 37166-0640; tel. 615/215-5000, **A**1 10 **F**3 18 28 29 30 40 75 79 81 93 107 110 111 115 119 130 135 149 154 167 **S** Ascension Healthcare, Saint Louis, MO
Primary Contact: Raymond Johnson, Chief Administrative Officer
CFO: Alan Sharp, Chief Financial Officer
CMO: Kimberly Collins, M.D., Chief of Staff
CNO: Emily Elrod, R.N., Chief Nursing Officer
Web address: https://healthcare.ascension.org/Locations/Tennessee/TNNAS/Smithville-Ascension-Saint-Thomas-Dekalb
Control: Other not-for-profit (including NFP Corporation) **Service**: General medical and surgical

Staffed Beds: 12 **Admissions**: 385 **Census**: 4 **Outpatient Visits**: 13074
Births: 0 **Total Expense ($000)**: 14317 **Payroll Expense ($000)**: 4387
Personnel: 69

SMYRNA—Rutherford County

✠ **TRISTAR STONECREST MEDICAL CENTER (440227)**, 200 StoneCrest Boulevard, Zip 37167-6810; tel. 615/768-2000, (Nonreporting) **A**1 2 3 10 **S** HCA Healthcare, Nashville, TN
Primary Contact: Louis Caputo, Chief Executive Officer
CFO: Joseph E Bowman, Chief Financial Officer
CMO: William Mayfield, M.D., Chief of Staff
CHR: Cynthia Adams, Vice President Human Resources
CNO: Amy Cason, MSN, Chief Nursing Officer
Web address: www.stonecrestmedical.com
Control: Corporation, Investor-owned (for-profit) **Service**: General medical and surgical

Staffed Beds: 101

SNEEDVILLE—Hancock County

HANCOCK COUNTY HOSPITAL (441313), 1519 Main Street, Zip 37869-3657; tel. 423/733-5000, (Nonreporting) **A**10 18 **S** Ballad Health, Johnson City, TN
Primary Contact: Hunter Hamilton, Chief Executive Officer/Administrator
COO: Eric Deaton, Executive Vice President, Chief Operating Officer and Corporate Operating
CFO: Regina Day, Director of Finance
CMO: Daniel Lewis, Chief Medical Officer
CIO: Martha O'Regan Chill, Interim Chief Information Officer
CHR: Denise Adams, Human Resources Generalist
CNO: Phyllis Dossett, Director of Clinical Services
Web address: https://www.balladhealth.org/hospitals/hancock-county-sneedville
Control: Other not-for-profit (including NFP Corporation) **Service**: General medical and surgical

Staffed Beds: 10

SPARTA—White County

✠ **ASCENSION SAINT THOMAS HIGHLANDS (440192)**, 401 Sewell Road, Zip 38583-1299; tel. 931/738-9211, **A**1 10 **F**3 15 29 30 40 75 79 81 93 98 103 107 110 111 115 119 130 149 167 **S** Ascension Healthcare, Saint Louis, MO
Primary Contact: Robert Peglow, Chief Administrative Officer
CFO: Rodney VanDonkelaar, Chief Financial Officer
CMO: Robert Knowles, M.D., Chief of Staff
CIO: Glenn Wade, Director Information Systems
CHR: Kent Frisbee, Director Human Resources
CNO: Gearline Copeland, R.N., Chief Nursing Officer
Web address: https://healthcare.ascension.org/Locations/Tennessee/TNNAS/Sparta-Ascension-Saint-Thomas-Highlands
Control: Other not-for-profit (including NFP Corporation) **Service**: General medical and surgical

Staffed Beds: 26 **Admissions**: 613 **Census**: 12 **Outpatient Visits**: 24047
Births: 0 **Total Expense ($000)**: 24055 **Payroll Expense ($000)**: 7702
Personnel: 111

SPRINGFIELD—Robertson County

NORTHCREST MEDICAL CENTER See Tristar Northcrest Medical Center

✠ **TRISTAR NORTHCREST MEDICAL CENTER (440065)**, 100 Northcrest Drive, Zip 37172-3961; tel. 615/384-2411, (Nonreporting) **A**1 3 10 **S** HCA Healthcare, Nashville, TN
Primary Contact: Sean Patterson, Chief Executive Officer
CFO: Sam Williamson, Chief Financial Officer
CHR: Scott Mayeaux, Director of Human Resources
CNO: Bri O'Neill, Chief Nursing Officer
Web address: https://www.tristarhealth.com/locations/tristar-northcrest-medical-center
Control: Other not-for-profit (including NFP Corporation) **Service**: General medical and surgical

Staffed Beds: 90

Hospital, Medicare Provider Number, Address, Telephone, Approval, Facility, and Physician Codes, Health Care System

★ American Hospital Association (AHA) membership ○ Healthcare Facilities Accreditation Program ⇧ Center for Improvement in Healthcare Quality Accreditation
☐ The Joint Commission accreditation ◇ DNV Healthcare Inc. accreditation △ Commission on Accreditation of Rehabilitation Facilities (CARF) accreditation

Hospitals, U.S. / TENNESSEE

SWEETWATER—Monroe County

☒ **SWEETWATER HOSPITAL (440084)**, 304 Wright Street, Zip 37874–2823; tel. 865/213–8200, (Nonreporting) **A**1 10
Primary Contact: Andrea Henry, Chief Executive Officer
CFO: Debbie Thompson, Chief Financial Officer
CMO: David Norris, Chief Medical Staff
CIO: Tony Sharp, Supervisor Information System
CHR: Lucretia Allen, Director Human Resources
CNO: Andrea Henry, Director of Nursing
Web address: www.sweetwaterhospital.org
Control: Other not–for–profit (including NFP Corporation) **Service**: General medical and surgical

Staffed Beds: 59

TAZEWELL—Claiborne County

☐ **CLAIBORNE MEDICAL CENTER (440057)**, 1850 Old Knoxville Road, Zip 37879–3625; tel. 423/626–4211, (Total facility includes 85 beds in nursing home–type unit) **A**1 3 10 **F**3 7 11 15 18 28 29 30 34 35 38 40 45 50 56 57 58 59 61 64 65 70 74 75 77 79 81 85 86 87 93 94 96 101 102 107 108 115 119 128 130 132 143 146 147 148 149 154 163 **S** Covenant Health, Knoxville, TN
Primary Contact: Patricia P. Ketterman, R.N., President and Chief Administrative Officer
CFO: Tracee McFarland, Chief Financial Officer
CHR: Susan Stone, Director Human Resources
Web address: www.clairbornehospital.org
Control: Other not–for–profit (including NFP Corporation) **Service**: General medical and surgical

Staffed Beds: 111 **Admissions**: 1298 **Census**: 81 **Outpatient Visits**: 36721
Births: 0 **Total Expense ($000)**: 34488 **Payroll Expense ($000)**: 17315
Personnel: 304

TULLAHOMA—Coffee County

☒ **VANDERBILT TULLAHOMA HARTON HOSPITAL (440144)**, 1801 North Jackson Street, Zip 37388–8259; tel. 931/393–3000, **A**1 10 19 **F**3 13 15 18 20 22 28 29 30 34 35 38 40 45 50 51 57 59 64 68 70 72 74 75 76 77 79 80 81 85 86 87 93 107 108 109 110 111 114 115 119 124 129 130 131 135 147 148 149 154 157 164 167 169 **S** Vanderbilt Health, Nashville, TN
Primary Contact: Richard Ellis, President
CFO: Mitchell Frank, Chief Financial Officer
CHR: Charisse Parker, Director Human Resources
CNO: Marilyn Smith, Chief Nursing Officer
Web address: www.hartonmedicalcenter.com
Control: Other not–for–profit (including NFP Corporation) **Service**: General medical and surgical

Staffed Beds: 91 **Admissions**: 3570 **Census**: 44 **Outpatient Visits**: 32641
Births: 458 **Total Expense ($000)**: 85983 **Payroll Expense ($000)**: 38116
Personnel: 425

UNION CITY—Obion County

☒ **BAPTIST MEMORIAL HOSPITAL–UNION CITY (440130)**, 1201 Bishop Street, Zip 38261–5403, Mailing Address: P.O. Box 310, Zip 38281–0310; tel. 731/885–2410, **A**1 2 3 10 **F**11 13 15 18 20 26 28 29 30 34 35 40 45 48 50 51 57 59 63 64 70 75 76 77 78 79 81 82 84 85 86 87 89 91 93 100 107 108 109 110 111 115 118 119 121 124 130 132 135 146 156 **S** Baptist Memorial Health Care Corporation, Memphis, TN
Primary Contact: Barry Bondurant, Chief Executive Officer and Administrator
CFO: Mike Perryman, Chief Financial Officer
CMO: Kofi Nuako, M.D., President Medical Staff
CIO: David Mercer, Coordinator Information Systems
CHR: Nicky Thomas, Director Human Resources
CNO: Lori Brown, Chief Nursing Officer
Web address: www.baptistonline.org/union-city/
Control: Other not–for–profit (including NFP Corporation) **Service**: General medical and surgical

Staffed Beds: 63 **Admissions**: 2152 **Census**: 20 **Outpatient Visits**: 53342
Births: 667 **Total Expense ($000)**: 54295 **Payroll Expense ($000)**: 18068
Personnel: 291

WAVERLY—Humphreys County

★ **ASCENSION ST. THOMAS THREE RIVERS (441303)**, 451 Highway 13 South, Zip 37185–2109, Mailing Address: P.O. Box 437, Zip 37185–0437; tel. 931/296–4203, **A**10 18 **F**3 15 18 28 29 30 40 75 77 93 107 110 114 119 127 130 133 135 149 167 **S** Ascension Healthcare, Saint Louis, MO
Primary Contact: Freda Russell, R.N., Administrator
CFO: Shannon Allison, Finance Manager
CMO: George Mathai, M.D., Chief of Staff
CIO: Joe Hildreth, Technician, Desktop Support
CHR: Linda Rawlings, Director Human Resources and Personnel
CNO: Alana Peters, Nurse Manager
Web address: https://healthcare.ascension.org/locations/tennessee/tnnas/waverly-ascension-saint-thomas-three-rivers?intent_source=location_title&result_position=3
Control: Other not–for–profit (including NFP Corporation) **Service**: General medical and surgical

Staffed Beds: 14 **Admissions**: 321 **Census**: 7 **Outpatient Visits**: 27165
Births: 0 **Total Expense ($000)**: 11574 **Payroll Expense ($000)**: 4718
Personnel: 81

THREE RIVERS HOSPITAL See Ascension St. Thomas Three Rivers

WAYNESBORO—Wayne County

☒ **WAYNE MEDICAL CENTER (440010)**, 103 J V Mangubat Drive, Zip 38485–2440, Mailing Address: P.O. Box 580, Zip 38485–0580; tel. 931/722–5411, **A**1 10 20 **F**3 7 15 29 34 35 40 41 45 50 59 68 75 77 81 85 86 93 102 107 110 111 114 119 129 130 133 135 149 **S** Maury Regional Health System, Columbia, TN
Primary Contact: Phyllis Brown, Chief Executive Officer
CMO: Harish Veeramachaneni, M.D., Chief of Staff
CHR: Jeff M Pierce, Manager Human Resources
CNO: Madora Bevis, R.N., Chief Nursing Officer
Web address: https://www.mauryregional.com/wayne-medical-center/wayne-medical-center
Control: County, Government, Nonfederal **Service**: General medical and surgical

Staffed Beds: 18 **Admissions**: 455 **Census**: 8 **Outpatient Visits**: 24342
Births: 0 **Total Expense ($000)**: 15505 **Payroll Expense ($000)**: 7462
Personnel: 132

WINCHESTER—Franklin County

☒ **SOUTHERN TENNESSEE REGIONAL HEALTH SYSTEM–WINCHESTER (440058)**, 185 Hospital Road, Zip 37398–2404; tel. 931/967–8200, (Includes SOUTHERN TENNESSEE REGIONAL HEALTH SYSTEM–SEWANEE, 1260 University Avenue, Sewanee, Tennessee, Zip 37375–2303, tel. 931/598–5691; Adam Martin, Chief Executive Officer) (Nonreporting) **A**1 10 **S** Lifepoint Health, Brentwood, TN
Primary Contact: Adam Martin, Chief Executive Officer
CFO: Shaun Adams, Chief Financial Officer
CIO: James Payne, Director Information Systems
CHR: Linda Tipps, Director Human Resources
Web address: https://www.southerntnwinchester.com/
Control: Corporation, Investor–owned (for–profit) **Service**: General medical and surgical

Staffed Beds: 190

WOODBURY—Cannon County

☒ **ASCENSION SAINT THOMAS STONES RIVER (440200)**, 324 Doolittle Road, Zip 37190–1139; tel. 615/563–4001, **A**1 10 **F**3 29 30 40 75 93 98 103 107 110 115 119 130 135 149 154 167 **S** Ascension Healthcare, Saint Louis, MO
Primary Contact: Raymond Johnson, Chief Administrative Officer
CFO: Alan Sharp, Chief Financial Officer
CMO: James Spurlock, D.O., Chief of Staff
CNO: Emily Elrod, R.N., Director of Nursing
Web address: https://healthcare.ascension.org/Locations/Tennessee/TNNAS/Woodbury-Ascension-Saint-Thomas-Stones-River
Control: Other not–for–profit (including NFP Corporation) **Service**: General medical and surgical

Staffed Beds: 36 **Admissions**: 793 **Census**: 20 **Outpatient Visits**: 7131
Births: 0 **Total Expense ($000)**: 12812 **Payroll Expense ($000)**: 4953
Personnel: 78

TEXAS

ABILENE—Taylor County

ABILENE REGIONAL MEDICAL CENTER See Hendrick Medical Center South

★ **CONTINUECARE HOSPITAL AT HENDRICK MEDICAL CENTER (452029)**, 1900 Pine Street, Zip 79601-2432; tel. 325/670-6251, **A**10 22 **F**1 3 29 35 148 149 **S** Community Hospital Corporation, Plano, TX
Primary Contact: Anna Rojas, Chief Executive Officer
CFO: Lisa Young, CPA, Chief Financial Officer
CHR: Trisha Kane, Director Human Resources
CNO: Sherry Hendricksen, R.N., MSN, Chief Nursing Officer
Web address: https://hendrick.continuecare.org/
Control: Other not-for-profit (including NFP Corporation) **Service:** Acute long-term care hospital

Staffed Beds: 23 **Admissions:** 290 **Census:** 18 **Outpatient Visits:** 0 **Births:** 0 **Total Expense ($000):** 9643 **Payroll Expense ($000):** 4490 **Personnel:** 29

✠ **ENCOMPASS HEALTH REHABILITATION HOSPITAL OF ABILENE (673039)**, 6401 Directors Parkway, Zip 79606-5869; tel. 325/691-1600, **A**1 10 **F**3 29 57 59 74 75 77 90 96 130 143 148 149 **S** Encompass Health Corporation, Birmingham, AL
Primary Contact: Boyd Davis III, Chief Executive Officer
Web address: https://encompasshealth.com/locations/abilenerehab/our-programs
Control: Corporation, Investor-owned (for-profit) **Service:** Rehabilitation

Staffed Beds: 60 **Admissions:** 1369 **Census:** 46 **Outpatient Visits:** 0 **Births:** 0 **Total Expense ($000):** 24130 **Payroll Expense ($000):** 12157 **Personnel:** 150

✠ **HENDRICK MEDICAL CENTER (450229)**, 1900 Pine Street, Zip 79601-2432; tel. 325/670-2000, (Includes HENDRICK MEDICAL CENTER SOUTH, 6250 US Highway 83/84, Abilene, Texas, Zip 79606-5299, tel. 325/428-1000; Krista Baty, R.N., Chief Executive Officer) (Total facility includes 20 beds in nursing home-type unit) **A**1 10 **F**2 3 8 11 12 13 14 15 17 18 20 22 24 26 28 29 30 31 34 35 38 39 40 42 43 44 45 46 49 50 51 53 54 55 56 57 58 59 60 61 62 63 64 68 70 71 72 74 75 76 77 78 79 80 81 82 84 85 86 87 88 89 90 91 92 93 96 97 102 107 108 110 111 114 115 119 120 121 123 124 126 128 129 130 131 146 147 148 149 156 167 168 169 **P**6 8 **S** Hendrick Health System, Abilene, TX
Primary Contact: Brad D. Holland, President and Chief Executive Officer
COO: Michael D. Murphy, FACHE, Chief Operaitng Officer
CFO: Jeremy Tyler Walker, Vice President and Chief Financial Officer
CMO: Rob Wiley, M.D., Chief Medical Officer
CIO: Mike Hart, System Assistant Vice President, Information Systems
CNO: Susan Greenwood, R.N., Chief Nursing Officer
Web address: www.ehendrick.org
Control: Church operated, Nongovernment, not-for-profit **Service:** General medical and surgical

Staffed Beds: 673 **Admissions:** 22186 **Census:** 287 **Outpatient Visits:** 415998 **Births:** 2654 **Total Expense ($000):** 676008 **Payroll Expense ($000):** 244183 **Personnel:** 5400

☐ **OCEANS BEHAVIORAL HOSPITAL ABILENE (454122)**, 4225 Woods Place, Zip 79602-7991; tel. 325/691-0030, **A**1 3 10 **F**29 34 35 98 99 100 101 103 104 130 132 149 153 154 **P**6 **S** Oceans Healthcare, Plano, TX
Primary Contact: Stacy Sanford, Administrator
Web address: www.oceansabilene.com
Control: Corporation, Investor-owned (for-profit) **Service:** Psychiatric

Staffed Beds: 90 **Admissions:** 2276 **Census:** 63 **Outpatient Visits:** 37441 **Births:** 0 **Total Expense ($000):** 17734 **Payroll Expense ($000):** 9241 **Personnel:** 157

ADDISON—Dallas County

⇑ **METHODIST HOSPITAL FOR SURGERY (670073)**, 17101 North Dallas Parkway, Zip 75001-7103; tel. 469/248-3900, **A**10 21 **F**3 29 37 40 64 68 70 75 79 81 85 93 107 111 114 119 146 148 149
Primary Contact: Trey Klawiter, President
CFO: Edward Sopiarz, Chief Financial Officer
CMO: Robert Fischer, M.D., Medical Director
CHR: Erik Leopard, Manager Human Resource
CNO: Patti Griffith, R.N., MS, Chief Nursing Officer
Web address: www.methodisthospitalforsurgery.com/
Control: Partnership, Investor-owned (for-profit) **Service:** Surgical

Staffed Beds: 32 **Admissions:** 1507 **Census:** 12 **Outpatient Visits:** 76290 **Births:** 0 **Total Expense ($000):** 142071 **Payroll Expense ($000):** 24016 **Personnel:** 241

ALICE—Jim Wells County

✠ **CHRISTUS SPOHN HOSPITAL ALICE (450828)**, 2500 East Main Street, Zip 78332-4169; tel. 361/661-8000, **A**1 10 20 **F**3 13 18 20 22 28 29 30 40 43 45 46 50 65 70 76 77 81 87 107 111 119 127 130 146 167 **S** CHRISTUS Health, Irving, TX
Primary Contact: Richard Morin, R.N., President CHRISTUS Spohn Hospital – Alice/Kleberg
CFO: Michael Guajardo, Director Finance
CMO: Jerry Liles, D.O., Chief Medical Officer
CHR: Mindy Soliz, Director Human Resources
CNO: Margot Rios, R.N., Chief Nursing Officer
Web address: https://www.christushealth.org/spohn/alice
Control: Church operated, Nongovernment, not-for-profit **Service:** General medical and surgical

Staffed Beds: 42 **Admissions:** 2025 **Census:** 19 **Outpatient Visits:** 73187 **Births:** 118 **Total Expense ($000):** 56342 **Payroll Expense ($000):** 16692 **Personnel:** 202

ALLEN—Collin County

✠ **PAM REHABILITATION HOSPITAL OF ALLEN (673025)**, 1001 Raintree Circle, Zip 75013-4912; tel. 972/908-2015, (Includes PAM HEALTH REHABILITATION HOSPITAL OF RICHARDSON, 401 West Campbell Road, Richardson, Texas, Zip 75080-3416, tel. 210/941-4886; Tracy Penny, Interim Chief Executive Officer) **A**1 10 **F**3 29 34 56 60 64 68 74 75 77 82 87 90 93 94 96 132 148 **S** PAM Health, Enola, PA
Primary Contact: Kyron J. Kooken, MS, Chief Executive Officer
Web address: www.warmsprings.org
Control: Partnership, Investor-owned (for-profit) **Service:** Rehabilitation

Staffed Beds: 56 **Admissions:** 1593 **Census:** 35 **Outpatient Visits:** 8914 **Births:** 0 **Total Expense ($000):** 26364 **Payroll Expense ($000):** 12875 **Personnel:** 143

✠ **TEXAS HEALTH PRESBYTERIAN HOSPITAL ALLEN (450840)**, 1105 Central Expressway North, Suite 140, Zip 75013-6103; tel. 972/747-1000, **A**1 10 **F**3 4 13 15 18 20 22 26 28 29 30 34 35 37 40 45 49 51 57 58 59 64 65 68 70 72 73 74 75 76 77 79 81 84 85 86 87 91 93 98 102 107 108 110 111 114 115 118 119 126 130 131 146 147 149 150 154 167 169 **S** Texas Health Resources, Arlington, TX
Primary Contact: Amanda Thrash, FACHE, President
COO: Crispin P Hocate, Professional and Support Services Officer
CFO: Lisa Gildon, Group Financial Officer
CMO: Bob Schwab, M.D., Chief Medical Officer
CHR: Sharon Chisholm, Entity Human Resource Officer
Web address: https://www.texashealth.org/Locations/Texas-Health-Allen
Control: Other not-for-profit (including NFP Corporation) **Service:** General medical and surgical

Staffed Beds: 68 **Admissions:** 3758 **Census:** 32 **Outpatient Visits:** 46459 **Births:** 454 **Total Expense ($000):** 121845 **Payroll Expense ($000):** 41318 **Personnel:** 372

Hospital, Medicare Provider Number, Address, Telephone, Approval, Facility, and Physician Codes, Health Care System

★ American Hospital Association (AHA) membership
☐ The Joint Commission accreditation
○ Healthcare Facilities Accreditation Program
◇ DNV Healthcare Inc. accreditation
⇑ Center for Improvement in Healthcare Quality Accreditation
△ Commission on Accreditation of Rehabilitation Facilities (CARF) accreditation

Hospitals, U.S. / TEXAS

ALPINE—Brewster County

☐ **BIG BEND REGIONAL MEDICAL CENTER (451378)**, 2600 North State Highway 118, Zip 79830–2002; tel. 432/837–3447, **A**1 3 10 18 **F**3 11 13 29 34 40 43 45 50 56 59 64 65 68 70 75 76 77 81 82 84 85 93 97 107 111 115 119 127 131 132 133 135 146 147 148 149 154 165 169 **P**6 **S** Quorum Health, Brentwood, TN
Primary Contact: Rick Flores, Chief Executive Officer
CNO: Keith Ellison, Chief Nursing Officer
Web address: www.bigbendhealthcare.com
Control: Corporation, Investor–owned (for-profit) **Service**: General medical and surgical

Staffed Beds: 25 **Admissions**: 492 **Census**: 6 **Outpatient Visits**: 17635 **Births**: 99 **Total Expense ($000)**: 26426 **Payroll Expense ($000)**: 10410 **Personnel**: 132

ALVIN—Brazoria County

ALVIN DIAGNOSTIC AND URGENT CARE CENTER See HCA Houston Healthcare Clear Lake, Webster

ALVIN MEDICAL CENTER See Alvin Diagnostic and Urgent Care Center

AMARILLO—Potter County

AMARILLO HCS See Thomas E. Creek Department of Veterans Affairs Medical Center

★ ⇑ **BSA HOSPITAL, LLC (450231)**, 1600 Wallace Boulevard, Zip 79106–1799; tel. 806/212–2000, **A**2 3 5 10 19 21 **F**3 7 8 11 12 13 15 17 18 20 22 24 26 28 29 30 31 34 35 40 43 45 46 47 48 49 51 53 54 56 57 58 59 64 70 71 72 74 75 76 77 78 79 81 82 84 86 87 88 89 90 91 92 93 96 107 108 109 110 111 114 115 116 117 118 119 120 121 123 124 125 126 129 130 143 145 146 147 148 154 167 169 **S** Ardent Health Services, Nashville, TN
Primary Contact: Michael Cruz, Chief Executive Officer
CFO: Lorenzo Olivarez, Senior Vice President and Chief Financial Officer
CMO: Mike Lamanteer, M.D., Senior Vice President Medical Affairs
CIO: Lewis Brown, Director Information Technology
CHR: Mona Tucker, Vice President Human Resources
CNO: Belinda D Gibson, R.N., Senior Vice President Patient Services
Web address: www.bsahs.org
Control: Corporation, Investor–owned (for-profit) **Service**: General medical and surgical

Staffed Beds: 379 **Admissions**: 21675 **Census**: 242 **Outpatient Visits**: 174141 **Births**: 1666 **Total Expense ($000)**: 460028 **Payroll Expense ($000)**: 147086 **Personnel**: 1766

BSA–PANHANDLE SURGICAL HOSP See Physicians Surgical Hospital – Panhandle Campus

⊞ **KPC PROMISE HOSPITAL OF AMARILLO (452060)**, 1540 Research Street, Zip 79124–1109; tel. 806/639–8670, (Nonreporting) **A**1 10
Primary Contact: Melany McCarty, R.N., Chief Executive Officer
CFO: Carlene Wright, Chief Financial Officer
CMO: Pablo Rodrigues, M.D., Medical Director
CNO: Melany McCarty, R.N., Chief Clinical Officer
Web address: www.amarillo.kpcph.com/
Control: Corporation, Investor–owned (for-profit) **Service**: Acute long-term care hospital

Staffed Beds: 37

☐ **NORTHWEST TEXAS HEALTHCARE SYSTEM (450209)**, 1501 South Coulter Avenue, Zip 79106–1770, Mailing Address: P.O. Box 1110, Zip 79105–1110; tel. 806/354–1000, (Includes NORTHWEST CHILDREN'S HOSPITAL, 1501 South Coulter Street, Amarillo, Texas, Zip 79106–1770, tel. 806/354–1000; NORTHWEST PAVILION, 7201 Evans ST, Amarillo, Texas, Zip 79106–1707, P O Box 1110, Zip 79105–1110, tel. 806/354–1000; Jason Barrett, Chief Executive Officer; NORTHWEST TEXAS SURGERY CENTER, 3501 South Soncy Road Suite 118, Amarillo, Texas, Zip 79119–6405, tel. 806/359–7999; Jason Barrett, Chief Executive Officer) **A**1 3 5 10 19 **F**3 4 5 8 11 12 13 15 17 18 20 22 24 26 28 29 30 31 32 35 37 38 39 40 42 43 44 45 46 49 50 54 56 57 59 60 61 64 65 66 68 70 72 74 75 76 77 78 79 81 82 84 85 86 87 88 89 90 92 93 94 96 97 98 99 100 101 102 103 104 105 107 108 110 111 115 118 119 126 129 130 132 135 144 146 147 148 151 152 153 154 162 164 165 169 **S** Universal Health Services, Inc., King of Prussia, PA
Primary Contact: Jason Barrett, Chief Executive Officer
COO: John McDonald, FACHE, Chief Operating Officer
CFO: Divya Matai, Chief Financial Officer
CMO: Brian Weis, M.D., Chief Medical Officer
CIO: Bach Nguyen, Director Information Systems
CHR: Samuel Lynn, Director Human Resources
Web address: www.nwtexashealthcare.com
Control: Corporation, Investor–owned (for-profit) **Service**: General medical and surgical

Staffed Beds: 428 **Admissions**: 16983 **Census**: 257 **Outpatient Visits**: 225492 **Births**: 2470 **Total Expense ($000)**: 312240 **Payroll Expense ($000)**: 124097 **Personnel**: 1827

OCEANS BEHAVIORAL HOSPITAL OF AMARILLO (454154), 7501 Wallace Boulevard, Suite 200, Zip 79124–2150, Mailing Address: 3905 Hedgcoxe Road, Unit 250249, Plano, Zip 75025–0840; tel. 806/310–2205, (Nonreporting) **S** Oceans Healthcare, Plano, TX
Primary Contact: Heather Duby, Administrator
CFO: Eric Elliott, Chief Financial Officer
Web address: www.oceanshealthcare.com
Control: Corporation, Investor–owned (for-profit) **Service**: Psychiatric

Staffed Beds: 28

★ ⇑ **PHYSICIANS SURGICAL HOSPITAL – QUAIL CREEK (450875)**, 6819 Plum Creek, Zip 79124–1602; tel. 806/354–6100, (Includes PHYSICIANS SURGICAL HOSPITAL – PANHANDLE CAMPUS, 7100 West 9th Avenue, Amarillo, Texas, Zip 79106–1704, tel. 806/212–0247; Todd Greene, Chief Executive Officer) **A**10 21 **F**3 29 30 37 40 62 64 68 79 81 93 107 111 115 119 126 130 131 149 154 **S** Ardent Health Services, Nashville, TN
Primary Contact: Bryan S. Bateman, Chief Executive Officer
CFO: Natalia Ballew, Chief Financial Officer
CMO: Robert Crabtree, M.D., Chief of Staff and Medical Director
CNO: Debbie Inman, Chief Nursing Officer
Web address: www.physurg.com
Control: Partnership, Investor–owned (for-profit) **Service**: Surgical

Staffed Beds: 40 **Admissions**: 700 **Census**: 3 **Outpatient Visits**: 10414 **Births**: 0 **Total Expense ($000)**: 67986 **Payroll Expense ($000)**: 17436 **Personnel**: 221

THE CHILDREN'S HOSPITAL See Northwest Children's Hospital

⊞ **THOMAS E. CREEK DEPARTMENT OF VETERANS AFFAIRS MEDICAL CENTER**, 6010 West Amarillo Boulevard, Zip 79106–1992; tel. 806/355–9703, (Nonreporting) **A**1 2 3 5 **S** Department of Veterans Affairs, Washington, DC
Primary Contact: Rodney Gonzalez, M.D., Medical Center Director
CHR: Ken Creamer, Chief Human Resource
Web address: www.amarillo.va.gov/
Control: Veterans Affairs, Government, federal **Service**: General medical and surgical

Staffed Beds: 38

⊞ △ **VIBRA REHABILITATION HOSPITAL OF AMARILLO (453096)**, 7200 West 9th Avenue, Zip 79106–1703; tel. 806/468–2900, **A**1 7 10 **F**3 29 34 86 87 90 96 97 130 148 149
Primary Contact: Tammie Tabor, Chief Executive Officer
Web address: www.vrhamarillo.com
Control: Corporation, Investor–owned (for-profit) **Service**: Rehabilitation

Staffed Beds: 44 **Admissions**: 707 **Census**: 23 **Outpatient Visits**: 0 **Births**: 0 **Total Expense ($000)**: 13609 **Payroll Expense ($000)**: 7257 **Personnel**: 93

Hospitals, U.S. / TEXAS

ANAHUAC—Chambers County

BAYSIDE COMMUNITY HOSPITAL See Chambers Health

★ **CHAMBERS HEALTH (451320)**, 200 Hospital Drive, Zip 77514, Mailing Address: P.O. Box 398, Zip 77514–0398; tel. 409/267–3143, **A**10 18 **F**11 29 34 35 40 41 45 50 53 54 56 57 59 64 86 107 119 130 133 **P**3
Primary Contact: Ann Newton, Chief Executive Officer
COO: Paul Aslin, Chief Operating Officer
CFO: Jay Hodges, Chief Financial Officer
CMO: Anthony Capili, M.D., Chief of Staff
CIO: David Odom, Director, Information Technology
CHR: Natalie Vazquez Clarke, Director Human Resources
CNO: Christi Morris, Director of Nursing
Web address: https://chambershealth.org/
Control: Hospital district or authority, Government, Nonfederal **Service:** General medical and surgical

Staffed Beds: 14 **Admissions:** 81 **Census:** 1 **Outpatient Visits:** 36071
Births: 0 **Total Expense ($000):** 26752 **Payroll Expense ($000):** 6228
Personnel: 104

ANDREWS—Andrews County

★ ⇑ **PERMIAN REGIONAL MEDICAL CENTER (450144)**, 720 Hospital Drive, Zip 79714–3617, Mailing Address: P.O. Box 2108, Zip 79714–2108; tel. 432/523–2200, (Total facility includes 93 beds in nursing home–type unit) **A**10 20 21 **F**3 11 13 15 28 29 34 35 36 40 43 44 48 49 50 53 54 55 56 57 59 62 63 64 65 68 75 76 77 81 82 84 85 86 87 93 97 107 108 110 111 115 119 125 127 128 129 130 131 132 133 135 145 146 148 **P**6
Primary Contact: Donny Booth, Chief Executive Officer
CFO: Sandra Cox, Controller
CIO: Dan Smart, Chief Information Management Officer
CHR: Pam McCormick, Director Human Resources
Web address: www.permianregional.com
Control: Hospital district or authority, Government, Nonfederal **Service:** General medical and surgical

Staffed Beds: 125 **Admissions:** 831 **Census:** 57 **Outpatient Visits:** 56405
Births: 240 **Total Expense ($000):** 66702 **Payroll Expense ($000):** 29945
Personnel: 248

ANGLETON—Brazoria County

ANGLETON DANBURY MEDICAL CENTER See Angleton Danbury Campus

ANSON—Jones County

ANSON GENERAL HOSPITAL (670781), 101 Avenue 'J', Zip 79501–2198; tel. 325/823–3231, **A**10 **F**11 29 40 75 77 93 107 114 115 127 **P**8
Primary Contact: Ted D. Matthews, Chief Executive Officer
CIO: Lynna B Cox, Director Health Information Services
Web address: https://www.ansongeneralhospital.com/
Control: Hospital district or authority, Government, Nonfederal **Service:** General medical and surgical

Staffed Beds: 7 **Admissions:** 88 **Census:** 1 **Outpatient Visits:** 17618
Births: 0 **Total Expense ($000):** 7514 **Payroll Expense ($000):** 4026
Personnel: 54

ARLINGTON—Tarrant County

☐ **BAYLOR ORTHOPEDIC AND SPINE HOSPITAL AT ARLINGTON (670067)**, 707 Highlander Boulevard, Zip 76015–4319; tel. 817/583–7100, **A**1 3 10 **F**29 37 40 79 81 82 97 107 111 114 119 126 131
Primary Contact: Allan Beck, Chief Executive Officer
Web address: www.baylorarlington.com/
Control: Partnership, Investor–owned (for–profit) **Service:** General medical and surgical

Staffed Beds: 20 **Admissions:** 1713 **Census:** 9 **Outpatient Visits:** 19737
Births: 0 **Total Expense ($000):** 80414 **Payroll Expense ($000):** 17158
Personnel: 211

✠ **ENCOMPASS HEALTH REHABILITATION HOSPITAL OF ARLINGTON (453040)**, 3200 Matlock Road, Zip 76015–2911; tel. 817/468–4000, **A**1 10 **F**29 34 60 74 75 77 79 90 91 95 96 130 148 154 **S** Encompass Health Corporation, Birmingham, AL
Primary Contact: Ashley Donahoe, Chief Executive Officer
CFO: Kathy Dickerson, Chief Financial Officer
CMO: Todd Daniels, M.D., Medical Director
CHR: Nancy Rosiles, Director Human Resources
Web address: https://encompasshealth.com/arlingtonrehab
Control: Corporation, Investor–owned (for–profit) **Service:** Rehabilitation

Staffed Beds: 85 **Admissions:** 1661 **Census:** 62 **Outpatient Visits:** 0
Births: 0 **Total Expense ($000):** 34250 **Payroll Expense ($000):** 16079
Personnel: 228

✠ **KINDRED HOSPITAL TARRANT COUNTY–ARLINGTON (452028)**, 1000 North Cooper Street, Zip 76011–5540; tel. 817/548–3400, (Includes KINDRED HOSPITAL TARRANT COUNTY–FORT WORTH SOUTHWEST, 7800 Oakmont Boulevard, Fort Worth, Texas, Zip 76132–4299, tel. 817/346–0094; Susan Schaetti, Chief Executive Officer) **A**1 10 **F**1 3 29 45 56 60 75 77 80 82 119 130 148 **S** ScionHealth, Louisville, KY
Primary Contact: Christina Richard, Chief Executive Officer
CFO: Jennifer Penland, Controller
CMO: Bernard A McGowen, M.D., Medical Director
Web address: www.kindredhospitalarl.com/
Control: Corporation, Investor–owned (for–profit) **Service:** Acute long–term care hospital

Staffed Beds: 68 **Admissions:** 319 **Census:** 30 **Outpatient Visits:** 0
Births: 0 **Total Expense ($000):** 23624 **Payroll Expense ($000):** 10453
Personnel: 122

✠ **MEDICAL CITY ARLINGTON (450675)**, 3301 Matlock Road, Zip 76015–2908; tel. 817/465–3241, **A**1 2 3 10 **F**3 11 12 13 17 18 20 22 24 26 29 30 31 34 35 37 39 40 41 42 43 45 46 49 50 51 57 59 60 64 70 72 74 75 76 78 79 81 84 85 86 87 90 93 96 107 108 111 114 115 118 119 126 130 131 132 135 146 147 148 149 167 **S** HCA Healthcare, Nashville, TN
Primary Contact: LaSharndra Barbarin, Chief Executive Officer
CFO: Jeff Ardemagni, Chief Financial Officer
CMO: Eric Benink, M.D., Chief Medical Officer
CIO: Craig Santangelo, Director Information Services
Web address: www.medicalcenterarlington.com
Control: Partnership, Investor–owned (for–profit) **Service:** General medical and surgical

Staffed Beds: 379 **Admissions:** 20773 **Census:** 259 **Outpatient Visits:** 139922 **Births:** 3446 **Total Expense ($000):** 323303 **Payroll Expense ($000):** 134686 **Personnel:** 1313

☐ **MILLWOOD HOSPITAL (454012)**, 1011 North Cooper Street, Zip 76011–5517; tel. 817/261–3121, **A**1 10 **F**4 5 29 30 35 75 87 98 99 100 101 102 103 104 105 130 132 143 148 152 153 154 160 164 **S** Universal Health Services, Inc., King of Prussia, PA
Primary Contact: Loren Fouch, Chief Executive Officer
CFO: Jeff Epperson, Chief Financial Officer
CMO: Robert Bennett, M.D., Medical Director
CIO: Morgan Wilson, Director Health Information Management
CHR: Yolanda Ross, Director Human Resources
CNO: Stacy Jacobs, Chief Nursing Officer
Web address: www.millwoodhospital.com
Control: Partnership, Investor–owned (for–profit) **Service:** Psychiatric

Staffed Beds: 134 **Admissions:** 5052 **Census:** 98 **Outpatient Visits:** 22513
Births: 0 **Total Expense ($000):** 28035 **Payroll Expense ($000):** 17397
Personnel: 272

☐ **PERIMETER BEHAVIORAL HOSPITAL OF ARLINGTON (454148)**, 7000 US Highway 287 South, Zip 76001; tel. 817/662–6342, **A**1 10 **F**98 99 101 102 130 154 164 **P**5 **S** Perimeter Healthcare, Alpharetta, GA
Primary Contact: Michelle Work, Chief Executive Officer
Web address: https://www.perimeterhealthcare.com/facilities/perimeter-behavioral-hospital-of-arlington/
Control: Partnership, Investor–owned (for–profit) **Service:** Psychiatric

Staffed Beds: 116 **Admissions:** 2492 **Census:** 63 **Outpatient Visits:** 0
Births: 0 **Total Expense ($000):** 17759 **Payroll Expense ($000):** 9862
Personnel: 147

Hospital, Medicare Provider Number, Address, Telephone, Approval, Facility, and Physician Codes, Health Care System

★ American Hospital Association (AHA) membership   ◯ Healthcare Facilities Accreditation Program   ⇑ Center for Improvement in Healthcare Quality Accreditation
☐ The Joint Commission accreditation   ◇ DNV Healthcare Inc. accreditation   △ Commission on Accreditation of Rehabilitation Facilities (CARF) accreditation

Hospitals, U.S. / TEXAS

REUNION REHABILITATION HOSPITAL ARLINGTON (673081), 4351 Centreway Place, Zip 76018; tel. 682/339-1400, (Data for 251 days) **A**22 **F**3 28 29 74 75 79 82 90 95 96 132 148 149 **S** Nobis Rehabilitation Partners, Allen, TX
Primary Contact: Tyrrell Taplin, Chief Executive Officer
CMO: Tanisha Toaston, Medical Director
CHR: Bianca Vargas, Human Resources Manager
CNO: Genia Wetsel, Chief Nursing Officer
Web address: https://reunionrehabhospital.com/locations/arlington/
Control: Partnership, Investor-owned (for-profit) **Service**: Rehabilitation

Staffed Beds: 40 **Admissions**: 343 **Census**: 17 **Outpatient Visits**: 0 **Births**: 0 **Total Expense ($000)**: 9307 **Payroll Expense ($000)**: 4361 **Personnel**: 95

TEXAS HEALTH ARLINGTON MEMORIAL HOSPITAL (450064), 800 West Randol Mill Road, Zip 76012-2503; tel. 817/548-6100, **A**1 2 5 10 **F**3 13 15 18 28 29 30 31 34 35 38 40 41 43 45 46 47 48 49 50 51 56 57 58 59 60 61 64 65 66 68 70 72 74 76 77 78 79 80 81 82 83 84 85 86 87 93 94 98 99 101 102 103 104 105 107 110 111 114 115 118 119 120 124 126 130 131 132 135 145 146 147 148 149 153 154 156 157 164 167 169 **S** Texas Health Resources, Arlington, TX
Primary Contact: Blake Kretz, FACHE, President
CMO: Robert N Cluck, M.D., Vice President and Medical Director
CHR: Yvonne Kyler, Director Human Resources
Web address: www.arlingtonmemorial.org
Control: Other not-for-profit (including NFP Corporation) **Service**: General medical and surgical

Staffed Beds: 245 **Admissions**: 13904 **Census**: 187 **Outpatient Visits**: 99844 **Births**: 1537 **Total Expense ($000)**: 327910 **Payroll Expense ($000)**: 127441 **Personnel**: 1339

TEXAS HEALTH HEART & VASCULAR HOSPITAL ARLINGTON (670071), 811 Wright Street, Zip 76012-4708; tel. 817/960-3500, **A**1 10 **F**3 17 18 20 22 24 26 29 30 34 44 64 65 68 81 85 119 130 149 167
Primary Contact: Vijay Jayachandran, M.D., President
COO: Sherri Leigh Emerson, Chief Operating Officer
CFO: Kay Mason, Chief Financial Officer
CMO: Baron L Hamman, M.D., Chief Medical Officer
CHR: Yvonne Kyler, Director Human Resources
Web address: www.texashealthheartandvascular.org/
Control: Partnership, Investor-owned (for-profit) **Service**: Heart

Staffed Beds: 26 **Admissions**: 1047 **Census**: 12 **Outpatient Visits**: 2275 **Births**: 0 **Total Expense ($000)**: 60194 **Payroll Expense ($000)**: 14252 **Personnel**: 115

TEXAS REHABILITATION HOSPITAL OF ARLINGTON (673060), 900 W Arbrook Blvd, Zip 76015; tel. 682/304-6000, **A**1 3 7 10 **F**3 29 34 35 90 95 96 130 132 135 148 149 156
Primary Contact: Teresa Huffman, Chief Executive Officer
CFO: Debbie Horn, Controller
CMO: Camelia Mitchell, M.D., Medical Director
CHR: Stanley Coleman, Director Human Resources
Web address: www.texasrehabarlington.com
Control: Corporation, Investor-owned (for-profit) **Service**: Rehabilitation

Staffed Beds: 40 **Admissions**: 899 **Census**: 31 **Outpatient Visits**: 0 **Births**: 0 **Total Expense ($000)**: 16513 **Payroll Expense ($000)**: 9135 **Personnel**: 106

USMD HOSPITAL AT ARLINGTON (450872), 801 West Interstate 20, Zip 76017-5851; tel. 817/472-3400, **A**1 5 10 **F**3 12 29 34 35 36 39 40 45 46 49 50 51 57 59 64 70 74 75 78 79 81 82 85 86 87 107 108 111 114 115 119 126 132 **S** USMD Health System, Irving, TX
Primary Contact: Marcia Crim, MSN, R.N., Chief Executive Officer & Chief Nursing Officer
CFO: Tonya Smith, Chief Financial Officer
CMO: Christopher Spikes, M.D., President, Medical Staff
CIO: Bob Rick, Vice President Information Technology
CHR: Jill Housand, Director Human Resources
Web address: www.usmdarlington.com
Control: Partnership, Investor-owned (for-profit) **Service**: General medical and surgical

Staffed Beds: 34 **Admissions**: 497 **Census**: 4 **Outpatient Visits**: 14709 **Births**: 0 **Total Expense ($000)**: 69086 **Payroll Expense ($000)**: 21147 **Personnel**: 286

ASPERMONT—Stonewall County

STONEWALL MEMORIAL HOSPITAL (451318), 821 North Broadway, Zip 79502-2029, Mailing Address: P.O. Box 'C', Zip 79502-0902; tel. 940/989-3551, **A**10 18 **F**3 29 34 35 40 41 56 57 59 64 93 97 107 114 119 127 133 148 **P**5
Primary Contact: Michael Moorhead, Chief Executive Officer
CMO: Frederic K Passmann, M.D., Chief of Staff
CNO: Jan Harris, R.N., Director of Nursing
Web address: www.smhdhealth.org/
Control: Hospital district or authority, Government, Nonfederal **Service**: General medical and surgical

Staffed Beds: 20 **Admissions**: 92 **Census**: 4 **Outpatient Visits**: 6871 **Births**: 0 **Total Expense ($000)**: 14314 **Payroll Expense ($000)**: 6899 **Personnel**: 54

ATHENS—Henderson County

UT HEALTH ATHENS (450389), 2000 South Palestine Street, Zip 75751-5610; tel. 903/676-1000, **A**1 2 3 10 **F**3 11 13 15 18 29 34 40 42 43 45 49 50 57 68 70 74 75 76 78 79 81 82 85 87 107 108 110 111 114 115 118 119 130 132 145 146 148 156 169 **S** Ardent Health Services, Nashville, TN
Primary Contact: Buddy Daniels, Chief Executive Officer
CFO: Wesley Knight, Chief Financial Officer
CHR: Jennifer Rummel, Director Human Resources
CNO: Kevin M Jablonski, Chief Nursing Officer
Web address: https://uthealthathens.com/
Control: Corporation, Investor-owned (for-profit) **Service**: General medical and surgical

Staffed Beds: 90 **Admissions**: 4552 **Census**: 47 **Outpatient Visits**: 85798 **Births**: 562 **Total Expense ($000)**: 99648 **Payroll Expense ($000)**: 31811 **Personnel**: 441

ATLANTA—Cass County

CHRISTUS ST. MICHAEL'S HEALTH SYSTEM See Christus St. Michael Hospital-Atlanta

AUBREY—Denton County

BAYLOR SCOTT & WHITE EMERGENCY HOSPITALS-AUBREY (670062), 26791 Highway 380, Zip 76227; tel. 972/347-2525, (Includes BAYLOR EMERGENCY MEDICAL CENTER MURPHY, 511 FM 544, Suite 100, Plano, Texas, Zip 75094, tel. 214/294-6150; Victor Schmerbeck, Chief Executive Officer; BAYLOR EMERGENCY MEDICAL CENTERS – COLLEYVILLE, 5500 Colleyville Boulevard, Colleyville, Texas, Zip 76034-5835, tel. 214/294-6350; Victor Schmerbeck, Chief Executive Officer; BAYLOR EMERGENCY MEDICAL CENTERS – KELLER, 620 S Main Street, Suite 100, Keller, Texas, Zip 76248-4960, tel. 214/294-6100; Victor Schmerbeck, Chief Executive Officer; BAYLOR SCOTT & WHITE EMERGENCY HOSPITAL – ROCKWALL, 1975 Alpha Drive Suite 100, Rockwall, Texas, Zip 75087-4951, tel. 214/294-6200; Victor Schmerbeck, Chief Executive Officer) **A**10 21 **F**3 29 40 107 130 148 149 154 **S** Emerus, The Woodlands, TX
Primary Contact: Letemia Medina, Administrator
CMO: Amynah Kara, M.D., Chief Medical Officer
CIO: Trang Dawson, Chief Information Officer
CHR: Larry Guillory, Chief Human Resources Officer
Web address: www.bemcataubrey.com
Control: Corporation, Investor-owned (for-profit) **Service**: General medical and surgical

Staffed Beds: 32 **Admissions**: 344 **Census**: 2 **Births**: 2 **Total Expense ($000)**: 45120 **Payroll Expense ($000)**: 11707 **Personnel**: 154

AUSTIN—Travis County

ARISE AUSTIN MEDICAL CENTER (450871), 3003 Bee Caves Road, Zip 78746-5542; tel. 512/314-3800, (Nonreporting) **A**1 10
Primary Contact: Jerry Jasper, Interim Chief Executive Officer
CFO: Lawrence Oldham, Chief Financial Officer
CMO: Robert Wills, M.D., Chief Medical Officer
CHR: Marilyn Jennings, Director Human Resources
Web address: https://www.arisemedicalcenter.com/
Control: Partnership, Investor-owned (for-profit) **Service**: Orthopedic

Staffed Beds: 19

Hospitals, U.S. / TEXAS

ASCENSION SETON MEDICAL CENTER AUSTIN (450056), 1201 West 38th Street, Zip 78705–1006; tel. 512/324–1000, **A**1 2 3 5 10 **F**3 7 8 12 13 15 17 18 20 22 24 26 28 29 30 31 35 37 40 43 44 45 46 47 48 49 50 54 55 59 60 62 64 65 66 68 69 70 72 74 75 76 77 78 79 80 81 82 83 84 85 86 87 90 91 93 96 97 100 107 108 111 112 114 115 119 120 121 126 130 133 135 137 141 142 143 146 147 148 149 150 154 155 156 157 164 167 169 **S** Ascension Healthcare, Saint Louis, MO
Primary Contact: Wesley Tidwell, President
COO: Tad Hatton, Vice President Chief Operating Officer
CFO: Robert Scott Herndon, Vice President Chief Financial Officer
CMO: David W Martin, M.D., Vice President Chief Medical Officer
CIO: Michael H. Minks, Chief Information Officer VI
CHR: Joe Canales, Vice President Human Resources
CNO: Coleen Elizabeth Backus, Chief Nursing Officer
Web address: https://healthcare.ascension.org/locations/texas/txaus/austin-ascension-seton-medical-center-austin
Control: Church operated, Nongovernment, not–for–profit **Service**: General medical and surgical

> **Staffed Beds**: 390 **Admissions**: 19578 **Census**: 302 **Outpatient Visits**: 123963 **Births**: 5900 **Total Expense ($000)**: 638822 **Payroll Expense ($000)**: 179079 **Personnel**: 1820

ASCENSION SETON NORTHWEST (450867), 11113 Research Boulevard, Zip 78759–5236; tel. 512/324–6000, **A**1 3 5 10 **F**3 11 13 29 30 34 35 37 40 41 45 47 49 51 57 59 70 72 75 76 79 80 81 85 86 87 107 108 111 114 115 117 119 126 130 132 146 147 154 164 **S** Ascension Healthcare, Saint Louis, MO
Primary Contact: Steven Brockman–Weber, President Seton Southwest & Northwest
COO: Tony DeDominico, Chief Operating Officer
CFO: Scott Herndon, FACHE, Chief Financial Officer, Texas Market
CMO: Jason Martin, M.D., Medical Director
CIO: Michael H. Minks, Chief Information Officer
CHR: Joe Canales, Vice President, Ascension and Human Resources Officer, Texas Market
Web address: www.seton.net
Control: Church operated, Nongovernment, not–for–profit **Service**: General medical and surgical

> **Staffed Beds**: 98 **Admissions**: 4783 **Census**: 50 **Outpatient Visits**: 51621 **Births**: 876 **Total Expense ($000)**: 123895 **Payroll Expense ($000)**: 37492 **Personnel**: 348

ASCENSION SETON SHOAL CREEK (454029), 3501 Mills Avenue, Zip 78731–6391; tel. 512/324–2000, **A**1 3 5 10 **F**4 5 29 30 98 100 101 130 132 135 149 153 154 160 162 **S** Ascension Healthcare, Saint Louis, MO
Primary Contact: Sam Cunningham, Director Ascension Seton Shoal Creek
COO: William Henricks, Ph.D., Vice President and Chief Operating Officer
CFO: Robert Scott Herndon, Chief Financial Officer
CMO: Amy E. Walton, M.D., Chief Medical Officer
CIO: Michael H. Minks, Chief Information Officer
CHR: Joe Canales, Director Human Resources
Web address: https://healthcare.ascension.org/locations/texas/txaus/austin-ascension-seton-shoal-creek
Control: Church operated, Nongovernment, not–for–profit **Service**: Psychiatric

> **Staffed Beds**: 62 **Admissions**: 1350 **Census**: 32 **Outpatient Visits**: 16136 **Births**: 0 **Total Expense ($000)**: 23213 **Payroll Expense ($000)**: 9984 **Personnel**: 124

ASCENSION SETON SOUTHWEST (450865), 7900 F M 1826, Building 1, Zip 78737–1407; tel. 512/324–9000, **A**1 10 **F**3 11 28 29 30 40 41 45 50 57 64 79 81 85 87 107 111 119 126 130 131 135 146 **S** Ascension Healthcare, Saint Louis, MO
Primary Contact: Steven Brockman–Weber, President Seton Southwest & Northwest
Web address: https://healthcare.ascension.org/locations/texas/txaus/austin-ascension-seton-southwest
Control: Church operated, Nongovernment, not–for–profit **Service**: General medical and surgical

> **Staffed Beds**: 11 **Admissions**: 375 **Census**: 3 **Outpatient Visits**: 30010 **Births**: 0 **Total Expense ($000)**: 32142 **Payroll Expense ($000)**: 9592 **Personnel**: 81

AUSTIN OAKS HOSPITAL (454121), 1407 West Stassney Lane, Zip 78745–2947; tel. 512/440–4800, **A**1 10 **F**5 29 30 38 64 98 99 100 101 103 104 105 130 147 153 154 160 162 164 **S** Universal Health Services, Inc., King of Prussia, PA
Primary Contact: Steve Kelly, Chief Executive Officer
COO: Meg Haden, Chief Operating Officer
CFO: Margo Wilhelm, Chief Financial Officer
Web address: www.austinoakshospital.com
Control: Partnership, Investor–owned (for–profit) **Service**: Psychiatric

> **Staffed Beds**: 80 **Admissions**: 2809 **Census**: 51 **Outpatient Visits**: 13640 **Births**: 0 **Total Expense ($000)**: 17359 **Payroll Expense ($000)**: 9360 **Personnel**: 192

AUSTIN STATE HOSPITAL (454084), 4110 Guadalupe Street, Zip 78751–4296; tel. 512/452–0381, **A**1 3 5 10 **F**29 30 50 56 75 77 86 91 97 98 99 103 130 132 135 143 146 148 149 156 163 164 165 **P**1 **S** Texas Department of State Health Services, Austin, TX
Primary Contact: Stacey Thompson, Superintendent
CMO: Ross Taylor, M.D., Clinical Director
CIO: Cindy Reed, Director Community Relations
Web address: www.dshs.state.tx.us/mhhospitals/austinsh/default.shtm
Control: State, Government, Nonfederal **Service**: Psychiatric

> **Staffed Beds**: 263 **Admissions**: 185 **Census**: 166 **Outpatient Visits**: 0 **Births**: 0 **Total Expense ($000)**: 84825 **Payroll Expense ($000)**: 45671 **Personnel**: 676

BAYLOR SCOTT & WHITE MEDICAL CENTER – AUSTIN (670136), 5245 West US Highway 290 Service Road, Zip 78735, Mailing Address: 5251 West US Highway 290, Zip 78735; tel. 512/654–2100, **A**1 10 **F**15 29 30 31 35 37 40 44 45 48 49 50 57 65 70 77 78 79 81 85 87 91 93 97 102 107 110 111 114 119 126 130 146 147 148 149 154 157 **S** Baylor Scott & White Health, Dallas, TX
Primary Contact: Jay Fox, FACHE, President
Web address: https://www.bswhealth.com/locations/austin-medical-center/pages/default.aspx
Control: Other not–for–profit (including NFP Corporation) **Service**: General medical and surgical

> **Staffed Beds**: 17 **Admissions**: 575 **Census**: 5 **Outpatient Visits**: 24370 **Births**: 0 **Total Expense ($000)**: 39454 **Payroll Expense ($000)**: 12720 **Personnel**: 119

CENTRAL TEXAS REHABILITATION HOSPITAL (673027), 700 West 45th Street, Zip 78751–2800; tel. 512/407–2111, **A**1 3 5 10 **F**3 29 68 90 91 95 96 130 148
Primary Contact: Trent Pierce, R.N., Regional Vice President, HCA Rehabilitation Division
CFO: Lisa Donnely, Controller II
CMO: Christopher Garrison, M.D., Medical Director
CHR: Trena Robinson, Director, Human Resources
CNO: Lauren Brandt, Chief Clinical Officer
Web address: www.khrehabcentraltexas.com/
Control: Corporation, Investor–owned (for–profit) **Service**: Rehabilitation

> **Staffed Beds**: 50 **Admissions**: 706 **Census**: 23 **Outpatient Visits**: 0 **Births**: 0 **Total Expense ($000)**: 12844 **Payroll Expense ($000)**: 7890 **Personnel**: 132

★ **CORNERSTONE SPECIALTY HOSPITALS AUSTIN ROUND ROCK** (452034), 4207 Burnet Road, Zip 78756–3396; tel. 512/706–1900, (Includes CORNERSTONE HOSPITAL OF AUSTIN, 1005 East 32nd Street, Austin, Texas, Zip 78705, tel. 512/867–5822; Edward J Sherwood, M.D., Chief Executive Officer; CORNERSTONE HOSPITAL OF ROUND ROCK, 4681 College Park DR, Round Rock, Texas, Zip 78665–1526, 4681 College Park Drive, Zip 78655, tel. 512/533–2525; Edward L Dyer, Chief Executive Officer) **A**10 22 **F**1 3 29 30 45 64 70 75 77 87 107 148 **S** ScionHealth, Louisville, KY
Primary Contact: Curt L. Roberts, Market Chief Executive Officer
CMO: David F. Pohl, M.D., Chief of Staff
Web address: www.chghospitals.com/austin/
Control: Corporation, Investor–owned (for–profit) **Service**: Acute long–term care hospital

> **Staffed Beds**: 96 **Admissions**: 1008 **Census**: 67 **Outpatient Visits**: 4526 **Births**: 0 **Total Expense ($000)**: 38534 **Payroll Expense ($000)**: 19065 **Personnel**: 178

Hospital, Medicare Provider Number, Address, Telephone, Approval, Facility, and Physician Codes, Health Care System

★ American Hospital Association (AHA) membership ○ Healthcare Facilities Accreditation Program ⇑ Center for Improvement in Healthcare Quality Accreditation
☐ The Joint Commission accreditation ◇ DNV Healthcare Inc. accreditation △ Commission on Accreditation of Rehabilitation Facilities (CARF) accreditation

© 2025 AHA Guide

Hospitals, U.S. / TEXAS

☒ **CROSS CREEK HOSPITAL (454133)**, 8402 Cross Park Drive, Zip 78754; tel. 512/215–3900, **A**1 10 **F**4 98 99 103 105 153 154 **S** Acadia Healthcare Company, Inc., Franklin, TN
Primary Contact: Kay McKennery, Chief Executive Officer
COO: Michael Russell, Chief Operations Officer
CHR: Debbie Belcher, Director, Human Resources
Web address: www.cornerstonehealthcaregroup.com
Control: Corporation, Investor–owned (for–profit) **Service**: Psychiatric

Staffed Beds: 90 Admissions: 3898 Census: 80 Outpatient Visits: 3486 Births: 0 Total Expense ($000): 20948 Payroll Expense ($000): 12024 Personnel: 157

☒ **DELL CHILDREN'S MEDICAL CENTER OF CENTRAL TEXAS (453310)**, 4900 Mueller Boulevard, Zip 78723–3079; tel. 512/324–0000, **A**1 2 3 5 10 **F**3 11 13 17 19 20 21 22 23 24 25 26 27 28 29 30 31 32 34 35 39 40 41 43 44 46 49 50 54 55 57 58 59 60 61 62 63 64 65 66 67 72 74 75 76 77 78 79 81 82 84 85 86 87 88 89 90 92 93 96 97 98 99 100 101 102 104 105 107 108 111 112 113 114 115 118 119 126 129 130 131 132 137 143 146 148 149 150 153 154 156 162 167 169 **S** Ascension Healthcare, Saint Louis, MO
Primary Contact: Michael Wiggins, President
CMO: Z. Leah Harris, M.D., Chief Physician
CNO: Elizabeth Fredeboelling, Chief Nursing Officer
Web address: https://healthcare.ascension.org/locations/texas/txaus/dcmc/our-locations/austin-dell-childrens-medical-center
Control: Church operated, Nongovernment, not–for–profit **Service**: Children's general medical and surgical

Staffed Beds: 299 Admissions: 8526 Census: 166 Outpatient Visits: 127859 Births: 216 Total Expense ($000): 985440 Payroll Expense ($000): 277607 Personnel: 1768

☒ **DELL SETON MEDICAL CENTER AT THE UNIVERSITY OF TEXAS (450124)**, 1500 Red River Street, Zip 78701; tel. 512/324–7000, **A**1 2 3 5 10 19 **F**3 11 16 18 20 22 29 30 31 34 35 37 38 39 40 43 44 45 46 47 48 49 51 57 58 59 64 65 66 70 71 74 75 77 78 79 81 82 84 85 87 91 100 102 107 108 110 111 114 115 118 119 124 126 130 132 135 137 143 146 148 154 156 160 167 **S** Ascension Healthcare, Saint Louis, MO
Primary Contact: Adam Messer, President
CFO: Scott Herndon, FACHE, Chief Financial Officer, Ministry Market Texas
CMO: Tom Caven, M.D., Vice President, Medical Director
CIO: Michael H. Minks, Chief Information Officer VI
CHR: Joe Canales, Vice President Human Resources, Ministry Market Texas
Web address: www.seton.net/locations/dell-seton/
Control: Church operated, Nongovernment, not–for–profit **Service**: General medical and surgical

Staffed Beds: 320 Admissions: 10267 Census: 212 Outpatient Visits: 82747 Births: 1 Total Expense ($000): 915019 Payroll Expense ($000): 334286 Personnel: 1306

☒ **ENCOMPASS HEALTH REHABILITATION HOSPITAL OF AUSTIN (673054)**, 330 West Ben White Boulevard, Zip 78704; tel. 512/730–4800, **A**1 10 **F**3 29 60 90 91 **S** Encompass Health Corporation, Birmingham, AL
Primary Contact: Lauren Suarez, Chief Executive Officer
CFO: Pamela McLaughlin, Chief Financial Officer
CMO: Johnny Shane Ross, Executive Medical Director
Web address: www.healthsouthaustin.com
Control: Corporation, Investor–owned (for–profit) **Service**: Rehabilitation

Staffed Beds: 60 Admissions: 1170 Census: 40 Outpatient Visits: 0 Births: 0 Total Expense ($000): 28310 Payroll Expense ($000): 12739 Personnel: 179

☐ **NORTHWEST HILLS SURGICAL HOSPITAL (450808)**, 6818 Austin Center Boulevard, Suite 100, Zip 78731–3199; tel. 512/346–1994, (Nonreporting) **A**1 10
Primary Contact: Cullen Scott, Acting Chief Executive Officer and Director of Operations for Surgical Care Affiliates
CFO: Jenny Salome, Chief Financial Officer and Assistant Administrator
Web address: www.northwesthillssurgical.com
Control: Partnership, Investor–owned (for–profit) **Service**: Surgical

Staffed Beds: 8

ST David's REHAB HOSPITAL See St. David's Rehabilitation Center

☒ **ST. David's MEDICAL CENTER (450431)**, 919 East 32nd Street, Zip 78705–2709, Mailing Address: P.O. Box 4039, Zip 78765–4039; tel. 512/476–7111, (Includes HEART HOSPITAL OF AUSTIN, 3801 North Lamar Boulevard, Austin, Texas, Zip 78756–4080, tel. 512/407–7000; Brett Matens, FACHE, Chief Executive Officer; ST. David's GEORGETOWN HOSPITAL, 2000 Scenic Drive, Georgetown, Texas, Zip 78626–7726, tel. 512/943–3000; Hugh Brown, Chief Executive Officer; ST. David's REHABILITATION CENTER, 1005 East 32nd Street, Austin, Texas, Zip 78705–2713, P O Box 4270, Zip 78765–4270, tel. 512/544–5100; Diane Owens, Assistant Administrator) **A**1 2 3 5 10 **F**3 8 11 13 15 17 18 20 22 24 26 27 28 29 30 31 34 35 36 37 39 40 43 45 46 47 48 49 53 57 58 59 60 61 64 70 72 73 74 75 76 77 78 79 80 81 82 83 84 85 86 87 90 93 95 96 107 108 110 111 114 115 116 118 119 126 129 130 131 132 135 144 146 147 148 149 154 167 169 **P**3 6 **S** HCA Healthcare, Nashville, TN
Primary Contact: Todd E. Steward, FACHE, Chief Executive Officer
COO: Esther Chung, Chief Operating Officer
CFO: Daniel Huffine, Chief Financial Officer
CMO: John Marietta, M.D., Chief Medical Officer
CIO: Richard Lear, Director Information Systems
CHR: Julie Hajek, Director Human Resources
Web address: www.stdavids.com
Control: Other not–for–profit (including NFP Corporation) **Service**: General medical and surgical

Staffed Beds: 482 Admissions: 29338 Census: 424 Outpatient Visits: 123464 Births: 4750 Total Expense ($000): 688363 Payroll Expense ($000): 205526 Personnel: 2232

☒ **ST. David's NORTH AUSTIN MEDICAL CENTER (450809)**, 12221 North MoPac Expressway, Zip 78758–2496; tel. 512/901–1000, **A**1 2 3 10 **F**3 8 12 13 18 20 22 24 26 28 29 30 31 34 35 37 40 41 42 43 45 46 47 48 49 51 54 55 57 58 59 60 64 67 70 71 72 74 75 76 77 78 79 81 84 85 86 87 88 89 90 91 92 93 96 107 108 111 114 115 118 119 126 129 130 138 146 147 148 149 154 157 167 169 **P**3 6 **S** HCA Healthcare, Nashville, TN
Primary Contact: Jeremy Barclay, FACHE, Chief Executive Officer
COO: Becky Barnes, Chief Operating Officer
CFO: Natalie Pack, Chief Financial Officer
CMO: Ryan Charbeneau, M.D., Chief Medical Officer
CIO: Marshall Pearson, Director Management Information Systems
CHR: Laura Light, Director Human Resources
Web address: www.northaustin.com
Control: Other not–for–profit (including NFP Corporation) **Service**: General medical and surgical

Staffed Beds: 476 Admissions: 25434 Census: 328 Outpatient Visits: 172853 Births: 9552 Total Expense ($000): 466151 Payroll Expense ($000): 146329 Personnel: 1552

☒ **ST. David's SOUTH AUSTIN MEDICAL CENTER (450713)**, 901 West Ben White Boulevard, Zip 78704–6903; tel. 512/447–2211, **A**1 2 3 10 **F**3 8 11 13 15 17 18 20 22 24 26 28 29 30 31 35 37 40 42 43 45 46 47 49 58 59 60 64 70 73 74 75 76 77 78 79 80 81 85 87 107 108 110 111 115 119 126 130 136 146 147 148 149 154 167 169 **P**3 6 **S** HCA Healthcare, Nashville, TN
Primary Contact: Charles Laird, Chief Executive Officer
COO: Kyle Landry, Chief Operating Officer
CFO: Wesley D Fountain, Chief Financial Officer
CMO: DeVry Anderson, Chief Medical Officer
CIO: Richard Lear, Director Information Systems
CHR: Lisa Talbot, Director Human Resources
CNO: Sally A Gillam, R.N., Chief Nursing Officer
Web address: https://stdavids.com/locations/st-davids-south-austin-medical-center/
Control: Other not–for–profit (including NFP Corporation) **Service**: General medical and surgical

Staffed Beds: 331 Admissions: 22199 Census: 279 Outpatient Visits: 138030 Births: 2416 Total Expense ($000): 415369 Payroll Expense ($000): 148294 Personnel: 1183

★ **TEXAS NEUROREHAB CENTER (452038)**, 1106 West Dittmar Road, Building 9, Zip 78745–6328, Mailing Address: P.O. Box 150459, Zip 78715–0459; tel. 512/444–4835, (Includes TEXAS NEUROREHAB CENTER, 1106 West Dittmar Road, Austin, Texas, Zip 78745–6328, tel. 512/444–4835; Edgar E. Prettyman, PsyD, Chief Executive Officer) **A**10 **F**1 3 29 30 54 74 75 77 79 93 108 130 148 **P**5 **S** Universal Health Services, Inc., King of Prussia, PA
Primary Contact: Edgar E. Prettyman, PsyD, Chief Executive Officer
COO: Janet Bitner, Chief Operating Officer
CFO: Omar Correa, Chief Financial Officer
CMO: James Boysen, M.D., Executive Medical Director
CHR: Colleen Lewis, Director Human Resources
Web address: www.texasneurorehab.com
Control: Partnership, Investor–owned (for–profit) **Service**: Acute long–term care hospital

Staffed Beds: 47 **Admissions**: 487 **Census**: 37 **Outpatient Visits**: 5737
Births: 0 **Total Expense ($000)**: 23326 **Payroll Expense ($000)**: 14594
Personnel: 286

AUSTIN—Williamson County

☐ **TEXAS CHILDREN'S HOSPITAL NORTH AUSTIN CAMPUS**, 9835 North Lake Creek Parkway, Zip 78717; tel. 737/229–2000, (Nonreporting) **A**1
Primary Contact: Mark A. Wallace, FACHE, Chief Executive Officer
CFO: Weldon Gage, Executive Vice President, Chief Financial Officer
Web address: https://www.texaschildrens.org/austin
Control: Other not–for–profit (including NFP Corporation) **Service**: Children's general medical and surgical

Staffed Beds: 52

AZLE—Tarrant County

✠ **TEXAS HEALTH HARRIS METHODIST HOSPITAL AZLE (450419)**, 108 Denver Trail, Zip 76020–3614; tel. 817/444–8600, **A**1 10 **F**3 11 15 18 29 30 34 35 40 43 45 57 59 64 70 75 77 79 81 85 93 107 110 114 119 130 135 146 148 149 150 154 156 **S** Texas Health Resources, Arlington, TX
Primary Contact: Tonya Sosebee, MSN, R.N., Chief Operating and Nursing Officer
COO: Tonya Sosebee, MSN, R.N., Chief Operating and Nursing Officer
CFO: Brian Blessing, Chief Financial Officer
CMO: Judy Laviolette, M.D., Chief Medical Officer
CIO: Patricia Johnston, Vice President Information Services
CHR: Lance Waring, Director Human Resources
CNO: Tonya Sosebee, MSN, R.N., Chief Operating and Nursing Officer
Web address: www.texashealth.org/Azle
Control: Other not–for–profit (including NFP Corporation) **Service**: General medical and surgical

Staffed Beds: 31 **Admissions**: 1347 **Census**: 12 **Outpatient Visits**: 31877
Births: 0 **Total Expense ($000)**: 44714 **Payroll Expense ($000)**: 19374
Personnel: 187

BALLINGER—Runnels County

★ **BALLINGER MEMORIAL HOSPITAL (451310)**, 608 Avenue 'B', Zip 76821–2499, Mailing Address: P.O. Box 617, Zip 76821–0617; tel. 325/365–2531, **A**10 18 **F**3 7 11 15 29 34 35 40 43 53 64 65 68 77 93 107 111 114 119 127 130 133 135 148 154 156
Primary Contact: Rhett D. Fricke, Chief Executive Officer/Administrator
CFO: Josilyn Peterson, Chief Financial Officer
CHR: Roselyn Hudgens, Director Human Resources
Web address: www.ballingerhospital.org
Control: Hospital district or authority, Government, Nonfederal **Service**: General medical and surgical

Staffed Beds: 16 **Admissions**: 169 **Census**: 7 **Outpatient Visits**: 39549
Births: 0 **Total Expense ($000)**: 23499 **Payroll Expense ($000)**: 7732
Personnel: 160

BASTROP—Bastrop County

✠ **ASCENSION SETON BASTROP (670143)**, 630 TX–71 West, Zip 78602–4234; tel. 737/881–7400, **A**1 10 **F**3 11 15 29 30 35 40 50 57 77 85 87 97 107 110 111 114 119 127 130 143 147 149 165 **S** Ascension Healthcare, Saint Louis, MO
Primary Contact: Jace Jones, Chief Administrative Officer
CNO: Steven Brockman–Weber, System Chief Nursing Officer
Web address: https://healthcare.ascension.org/Locations/Texas/TXAUS/Bastrop-Ascension-Seton-Bastrop
Control: Church operated, Nongovernment, not–for–profit **Service**: General medical and surgical

Staffed Beds: 7 **Admissions**: 110 **Census**: 1 **Outpatient Visits**: 33148
Births: 0 **Total Expense ($000)**: 14860 **Payroll Expense ($000)**: 5495
Personnel: 60

BAY CITY—Matagorda County

✠ **MATAGORDA REGIONAL MEDICAL CENTER (450465)**, 104 7th Street, Zip 77414–4853; tel. 979/245–6383, **A**1 10 20 **F**3 11 13 15 18 20 22 28 29 30 34 38 39 40 43 45 46 47 50 51 53 57 59 64 65 66 68 70 75 76 77 79 81 82 85 86 89 93 107 108 110 111 114 129 130 132 135 146 147 148 154 156 167 **S** Ovation Healthcare, Brentwood, TN
Primary Contact: James Warren. Robicheaux, FACHE, Chief Executive Officer
CFO: Bryan Prochnow, Chief Financial Officer
CIO: Beverly Trombatore, R.N., Director Managed Information Systems
CHR: Cindy Krebs, District Director Human Resources
CNO: Mike Lee, R.N., Chief Nursing Officer
Web address: www.matagordaregional.org
Control: Hospital district or authority, Government, Nonfederal **Service**: General medical and surgical

Staffed Beds: 46 **Admissions**: 1605 **Census**: 13 **Outpatient Visits**: 54087
Births: 378 **Total Expense ($000)**: 67480 **Payroll Expense ($000)**: 26862
Personnel: 306

BAYTOWN—Harris County

BMC BAYTOWN (670109), 1626 West Baker Road, Zip 77521–2271; tel. 281/837–7600, (Nonreporting) **A**10 22
Primary Contact: Don Vickers, Chief Executive Officer
Web address: https://altushospitals.org/
Control: Corporation, Investor–owned (for–profit) **Service**: General medical and surgical

Staffed Beds: 10

★ ⇑ **HOUSTON METHODIST BAYTOWN HOSPITAL (450424)**, 4401 Garth Road, Zip 77521–2122; tel. 281/420–8600, **A**2 3 10 21 **F**3 8 11 12 13 15 18 20 22 24 26 28 29 30 31 34 35 38 40 41 44 45 49 50 51 53 55 56 57 59 60 61 63 64 65 68 70 73 74 75 76 77 78 79 81 82 84 85 86 87 91 93 94 96 102 107 108 110 111 115 117 118 119 120 121 123 126 129 130 131 132 146 147 148 149 154 156 164 167 169 **P**5 6 **S** Houston Methodist, Houston, TX
Primary Contact: Adrienne Joseph, Ph.D., Chief Executive Officer
CFO: Jonathan Sturgis, Chief Financial Officer
CMO: Klaus Thaler, FACS, M.D., Chief Medical Officer
CHR: Courtney Lewis, Director Human Resources
CNO: Rebecca Chalupa, MSN, R.N., Chief Nursing Officer
Web address: www.houstonmethodist.org
Control: Other not–for–profit (including NFP Corporation) **Service**: General medical and surgical

Staffed Beds: 285 **Admissions**: 14953 **Census**: 190 **Outpatient Visits**: 192037 **Births**: 1831 **Total Expense ($000)**: 434595 **Payroll Expense ($000)**: 151635 **Personnel**: 1835

Hospitals, U.S. / TEXAS

BEAUMONT—Jefferson County

★ **BAPTIST HOSPITALS OF SOUTHEAST TEXAS (450346)**, 3080 College Street, Zip 77701–4689, Mailing Address: P.O. Box 1591, Zip 77704–1591; tel. 409/212–5000, (Includes BAPTIST BEAUMONT HOSPITAL, 3080 College, Beaumont, Texas, Zip 77701, Box 5817, Zip 77726–5817, tel. 409/833–1411; BAPTIST HOSPITALS OF SOUTHEAST TEXAS FANNIN BEHAVIORAL HEALTH CENTER, 3250 Fannin Street, Beaumont, Texas, Zip 77701, tel. 409/212–7000; Justin Doss, Chief Executive Officer) **A**2 3 5 10 19 22 **F**3 8 11 12 13 15 17 18 20 22 24 26 28 29 30 31 34 35 40 41 43 45 46 48 49 50 51 54 57 58 59 60 61 64 68 70 72 73 76 78 79 81 85 87 89 90 93 98 99 100 102 103 107 108 110 111 114 115 117 118 119 120 121 123 126 129 130 146 148 153 154 157 167 169 **S** Community Hospital Corporation, Plano, TX
Primary Contact: Justin Doss, Chief Executive Officer
CFO: Gary Troutman, CPA, Chief Financial Officer
CMO: Shariq Ahmad, M.D., Chief of Staff
CIO: William Toon, Chief Information Officer
CHR: Hannah Schiesler, Interim Assistant Director Human Resources
CNO: Karen Garcia, MSN, R.N., Chief Nursing Officer
Web address: www.bhset.net
Control: Other not–for–profit (including NFP Corporation) **Service**: General medical and surgical

Staffed Beds: 315 **Admissions**: 13751 **Census**: 188 **Outpatient Visits**: 195767 **Births**: 1276 **Total Expense ($000)**: 342174 **Payroll Expense ($000)**: 110548 **Personnel**: 1631

BEAUMONT EMERGENCY HOSPITAL, 4004 College Street, Zip 77707–4004; tel. 409/840–4004, **A**22 **F**3 29 34 40 57 59 68 107 114 119 135 149
Primary Contact: James P. Frazier III, Chief Executive Officer
Web address: www.beaumonteh.com
Control: Corporation, Investor–owned (for–profit) **Service**: General medical and surgical

Staffed Beds: 4 **Admissions**: 36 **Census**: 1 **Outpatient Visits**: 9979 **Births**: 0 **Total Expense ($000)**: 11677 **Payroll Expense ($000)**: 3749 **Personnel**: 52

BEAUMONT REGIONAL MEDICAL CENTER See Baptist Beaumont Hospital

☐ **CHRISTUS DUBUIS HOSPITAL OF BEAUMONT (452042)**, 2830 Calder Avenue, 4th Floor, Zip 77702–1809; tel. 409/899–7680, (Includes CHRISTUS DUBUIS HOSPITAL OF PORT ARTHUR, 3600 Gates Boulevard, 3rd Floor West, Port Arthur, Texas, Zip 77642–3858, tel. 409/989–5300) **A**1 10 **F**1 3 18 29 31 75 148 154 **S** LHC Group, Lafayette, LA
Primary Contact: Jason Baker, Administrator
Web address: www.christusdubuis.org/BeaumontandPortArthurSystem-CHRISTUSDubuisHospitalofBeaumont
Control: Corporation, Investor–owned (for–profit) **Service**: Acute long–term care hospital

Staffed Beds: 33 **Admissions**: 298 **Census**: 17 **Outpatient Visits**: 0 **Births**: 0 **Total Expense ($000)**: 9505 **Payroll Expense ($000)**: 4744 **Personnel**: 64

✠ **CHRISTUS SOUTHEAST TEXAS HOSPITAL – ST. ELIZABETH (450034)**, 2830 Calder Avenue, Zip 77702–1809, Mailing Address: P.O. Box 5405, Zip 77726–5405; tel. 409/892–7171, **A**1 5 10 19 **F**3 11 12 13 15 17 18 20 22 24 26 28 29 30 31 34 35 36 38 40 42 43 44 45 46 49 50 51 54 57 59 60 63 64 70 72 74 75 76 77 78 79 81 82 84 85 86 87 88 89 93 94 107 108 110 111 114 118 119 126 130 131 132 144 146 147 148 149 156 169 **P**8 **S** CHRISTUS Health, Irving, TX
Primary Contact: Paul Trevino, President and Chief Executive Officer
CFO: Shawn Adams, Chief Financial Officer
CMO: Rick Tyler, M.D., Vice President Medical Affairs
CIO: Robert Jacobs, Regional Director Information Management
CHR: Charles Foster, Regional Director Human Resources
Web address: www.christushospital.org
Control: Church operated, Nongovernment, not–for–profit **Service**: General medical and surgical

Staffed Beds: 375 **Admissions**: 15857 **Census**: 180 **Outpatient Visits**: 423836 **Births**: 3020 **Total Expense ($000)**: 390767 **Payroll Expense ($000)**: 125464 **Personnel**: 2187

CHRISTUS SOUTHEAST TEXAS ORTHOPEDIC SPECIALTY CENTER (670007), 3650 Laurel Street, Zip 77707–2216; tel. 409/838–0346, (Nonreporting) **A**10
Primary Contact: William Klamfoth, Administrator
Web address: www.orthodoc.aaos.org/bbji/
Control: Partnership, Investor–owned (for–profit) **Service**: General medical and surgical

Staffed Beds: 6

☐ **KATE DISHMAN REHABILITATION HOSPITAL (673030)**, 2830 Calder Street, 6th Floor, Zip 77702–1809; tel. 409/899–8380, (Nonreporting) **A**1 10 **S** CHRISTUS Health, Irving, TX
Primary Contact: Patrick Flannery, Chief Executive Officer and Administrator
Web address: https://katedishmanrehab.com/
Control: Partnership, Investor–owned (for–profit) **Service**: Rehabilitation

Staffed Beds: 27

MEMORIAL HERMANN BAPTIST FANNIN BEHAVIORAL HEALTH CENTER See Baptist Hospitals of Southeast Texas Fannin Behavioral Health Center

MID–JEFFERSON EXTENDED CARE HOSPITAL OF BEAUMONT (452083), 860 South 8th Street, Zip 77701–4626; tel. 409/363–5800, (Includes MID–JEFFERSON EXTENDED CARE HOSPITAL, 2600 Highway 365, Nederland, Texas, Zip 77627–6237, tel. 409/726–8700; Mark J. Rice, Chief Executive Officer) (Nonreporting)
Primary Contact: Candice Hill, Chief Executive Officer
Web address: www.midjeffextendedcare.com
Control: Corporation, Investor–owned (for–profit) **Service**: Acute long–term care hospital

Staffed Beds: 78

✠ **PAM REHABILITATION HOSPITAL OF BEAUMONT (453048)**, 3340 Plaza 10 Boulevard, Zip 77707–2551; tel. 409/835–0835, **A**1 10 **F**3 28 29 34 35 57 59 60 64 68 74 75 77 82 90 91 93 135 148 149 154 **S** PAM Health, Enola, PA
Primary Contact: Randy Thompson, FACHE, Chief Executive Officer
CHR: Joanna Donica, Director Human Resource
CNO: Barbara Morris, R.N., Chief Nursing Officer
Web address: www.postacutemedical.com/our-facilities/outpatient-rehabilitation/rehabilitation-hospital-beaumont/
Control: Partnership, Investor–owned (for–profit) **Service**: Rehabilitation

Staffed Beds: 31 **Admissions**: 551 **Census**: 22 **Outpatient Visits**: 10482 **Births**: 0 **Total Expense ($000)**: 14712 **Payroll Expense ($000)**: 7550 **Personnel**: 97

BEDFORD—Tarrant County

✠ **ENCOMPASS HEALTH REHABILITATION HOSPITAL OF THE MID–CITIES (673044)**, 2304 State Highway 121, Zip 76021–5985; tel. 817/684–2000, **A**1 10 **F**3 29 34 75 77 82 87 90 91 96 148 149 154 164 **P**6 **S** Encompass Health Corporation, Birmingham, AL
Primary Contact: Ashley Donahoe, Chief Executive Officer
CFO: Mary Mwaniki, Chief Financial Officer
CMO: Toni Willis, M.D., Medical Director
CHR: Frances Fuentes, Human Resources Director
Web address: https://encompasshealth.com/midcitiesrehab
Control: Corporation, Investor–owned (for–profit) **Service**: Rehabilitation

Staffed Beds: 60 **Admissions**: 1582 **Census**: 53 **Outpatient Visits**: 0 **Births**: 0 **Total Expense ($000)**: 30350 **Payroll Expense ($000)**: 14302 **Personnel**: 214

✠ **TEXAS HEALTH HARRIS METHODIST HOSPITAL HURST–EULESS–BEDFORD (450639)**, 1600 Hospital Parkway, Zip 76022–6913; tel. 817/685–4000, (Includes TEXAS HEALTH SPRINGWOOD BEHAVIORAL HEALTH HOSPITAL, 1608 Hospital Parkway, Bedford, Texas, Zip 76022, tel. 817/355–7700; Jay Frayser, MSN, R.N., Administrator) **A**1 5 10 **F**3 11 13 18 20 22 24 26 28 29 30 31 34 40 43 45 46 47 48 49 50 60 64 70 72 74 76 77 78 79 80 81 84 85 93 107 108 111 114 115 119 124 126 130 135 145 146 148 149 167 **S** Texas Health Resources, Arlington, TX
Primary Contact: Jared Shelton, FACHE, President
COO: Alice Landers, Administrative Director Operations
CFO: Jaime James, Entity Finance Officer
CMO: Susann Land, M.D., Chief Medical Officer
CHR: Lee Mulvey, Human Resource Officer
CNO: Ray Kelly, R.N., MSN, Vice President Chief Nursing Officer
Web address: www.texashealth.org
Control: Other not–for–profit (including NFP Corporation) **Service**: General medical and surgical

Staffed Beds: 209 **Admissions**: 15461 **Census**: 178 **Outpatient Visits**: 73332 **Births**: 2542 **Total Expense ($000)**: 310761 **Payroll Expense ($000)**: 118381 **Personnel**: 1205

TEXAS HEALTH SPRINGWOOD See Texas Health Springwood Behavioral Health Hospital

Hospitals, U.S. / TEXAS

BEEVILLE—Bee County

☒ **CHRISTUS SPOHN HOSPITAL BEEVILLE (450082)**, 1500 East Houston Street, Zip 78102–5312; tel. 361/354–2000, **A**1 10 20 **F**3 11 13 15 18 29 30 34 35 40 43 45 50 53 57 59 64 68 70 74 76 77 81 85 87 93 97 107 108 110 111 114 115 119 127 130 146 147 148 149 154 **S** CHRISTUS Health, Irving, TX
Primary Contact: Richard Morin, R.N., President CHRISTUS Spohn Hospital – Alice/Kleberg
Web address: www.christusspohn.org
Control: Church operated, Nongovernment, not–for–profit **Service:** General medical and surgical

Staffed Beds: 49 **Admissions:** 1183 **Census:** 9 **Outpatient Visits:** 50937
Births: 56 **Total Expense ($000):** 39015 **Payroll Expense ($000):** 12324
Personnel: 172

BELLAIRE—Harris County

⇧ **FIRST SURGICAL HOSPITAL (670029)**, 4801 Bissonnet Street, Zip 77401–4028; tel. 713/275–1111, **A**10 21 **F**8 12 29 37 40 45 48 77 79 81 85 107 149
Primary Contact: James L. Alexander, R.N., Chief Nursing Officer/Operating Chief Executive Officer
CNO: James L. Alexander, R.N., Chief Nursing Officer
Web address: https://firstsurgical.com/
Control: Corporation, Investor–owned (for–profit) **Service:** Surgical

Staffed Beds: 19 **Admissions:** 518 **Census:** 3 **Outpatient Visits:** 1858
Births: 0 **Total Expense ($000):** 20970 **Payroll Expense ($000):** 7416
Personnel: 116

⇧ **HARRIS HEALTH SYSTEM (450289)**, 4800 Fournace Place, Zip 77401–2324; tel. 713/634–1000, (Includes BEN TAUB HOSPITAL, 1504 Taub Loop, Houston, Texas, Zip 77030, tel. 713/873–2000; Glorimar Medina, M.D., Executive Vice President and Administrator; LYNDON B JOHNSON GENERAL HOSPITAL, 5656 Kelley, Houston, Texas, Zip 77026, tel. 713/566–5000; Colonel Patricia Darnauer, Administrator; QUENTIN MEASE HOSPITAL, 3601 North MacGregor, Houston, Texas, Zip 77004, tel. 713/873–3700; Jeffrey Webster, Administrator) **A**2 3 5 10 21 **F**3 5 7 8 13 15 17 18 20 22 24 26 28 29 30 31 32 34 35 38 40 43 44 45 46 49 50 51 53 54 55 56 57 58 59 60 61 64 65 66 68 70 71 72 73 74 75 76 77 78 79 81 82 84 85 86 87 91 92 93 94 97 98 100 101 102 104 107 108 110 111 114 115 118 119 120 121 124 126 129 130 132 134 135 143 146 147 148 149 150 153 154 156 157 163 165 167 169
Primary Contact: Esmaeil Porsa, M.D., President and Chief Executive Officer
CFO: Victoria Nikitin, Chief Financial Officer
CMO: Steven Brass, Chief Medical Officer
CIO: Ronald Fuschillo, Chief Information Officer
CNO: Jacqueline Dawn Brock, Chief Nursing Officer
Web address: https://www.harrishealth.org
Control: Hospital district or authority, Government, Nonfederal **Service:** General medical and surgical

Staffed Beds: 694 **Admissions:** 31530 **Census:** 539 **Outpatient Visits:** 1488887 **Births:** 5494 **Total Expense ($000):** 2279927 **Payroll Expense ($000):** 799435 **Personnel:** 10114

MEMORIAL HERMANN HOUSTON ORTHOPEDIC AND SPINE HOSPITAL See Memorial Hermann Orthopedic and Spine Hospital

BELLVILLE—Austin County

BELLVILLE MEDICAL CENTER See Midcoast Medical Center – Bellville

○ **MIDCOAST MEDICAL CENTER – BELLVILLE (450253)**, 44 North Cummings Street, Zip 77418–1347, Mailing Address: P.O. Box 977, Zip 77418–0977; tel. 979/413–7400, **A**10 11 **F**3 11 15 29 34 35 40 42 43 45 50 53 57 59 64 65 68 75 77 79 81 87 91 93 97 107 110 111 114 119 131 133 146 154 157 **P**6
Primary Contact: James A. Lee Jr, Administrator
CMO: Christophe Gay, M.D., Chief of Staff
CHR: Jacqueline McEuen, Coordinator Human Resources
Web address: https://bellvillemidcoasthospital.org/
Control: Other not–for–profit (including NFP Corporation) **Service:** General medical and surgical

Staffed Beds: 10 **Admissions:** 64 **Census:** 1 **Outpatient Visits:** 25662
Births: 0 **Total Expense ($000):** 14541 **Payroll Expense ($000):** 5280
Personnel: 75

BELTON—Bell County

☒ **CEDAR CREST HOSPITAL AND RESIDENTIAL TREATMENT CENTER (454114)**, 3500 I–35 South, Zip 76513; tel. 254/939–2100, **A**1 10 **F**4 29 34 35 59 68 86 87 98 99 100 101 103 104 105 106 130 143 153 154
Primary Contact: Brady Serafin, Chief Executive Officer
CFO: Melissa West, Chief Financial Officer
CMO: Alejandro Munoz, M.D., Chief Medical Officer
CIO: Cesar Osorio, Specialist Information Technology
CHR: Allison Liston, Director, Human Resources
Web address: www.cedarcresthospital.com
Control: Corporation, Investor–owned (for–profit) **Service:** Psychiatric

Staffed Beds: 68 **Admissions:** 2424 **Census:** 51 **Outpatient Visits:** 2220
Births: 0 **Total Expense ($000):** 14355 **Payroll Expense ($000):** 8057
Personnel: 268

BIG LAKE—Reagan County

★ **REAGAN MEMORIAL HOSPITAL (451301)**, 1300 North Main, Zip 76932–3938; tel. 325/884–2561, **A**10 18 **F**40 43 53 57 93 107 114 115 130 133 143 154 156 157 **P**5
Primary Contact: Jonathon Voelkel, Chief Executive Officer
CMO: Joseph Sudolcan, M.D., Medical Director
Web address: www.reaganhealth.com/getpage.php?name=index
Control: Hospital district or authority, Government, Nonfederal **Service:** General medical and surgical

Staffed Beds: 7 **Admissions:** 16 **Census:** 1 **Outpatient Visits:** 5246
Births: 0 **Total Expense ($000):** 17702 **Payroll Expense ($000):** 6912
Personnel: 100

BIG SPRING—Howard County

☐ **BIG SPRING STATE HOSPITAL (454000)**, 1901 North Highway 87, Zip 79720–0283; tel. 432/267–8216, **A**1 3 5 10 **F**3 30 50 56 59 61 75 77 86 87 97 98 101 103 130 135 146 154 158 163 164 **P**6 **S** Texas Department of State Health Services, Austin, TX
Primary Contact: Deborah Young, Superintendent
CFO: Adrienne Bides, Assistant Chief Financial Officer and Budget Analyst
CMO: Guido Spangher, M.D., Clinical Director
CIO: Elizabeth Correa, Director Information Management
CNO: Stormy Ward, Chief Nurse Executive
Web address: www.dshs.state.tx.us/mhhospitals/BigSpringSH/default.shtm
Control: State, Government, Nonfederal **Service:** Psychiatric

Staffed Beds: 144 **Admissions:** 138 **Census:** 136 **Outpatient Visits:** 0
Births: 0 **Total Expense ($000):** 52398 **Payroll Expense ($000):** 28280
Personnel: 503

⇧ **SCENIC MOUNTAIN MEDICAL CENTER (450653)**, 1601 West 11th Place, Zip 79720–4198; tel. 432/263–1211, **A**10 20 21 **F**3 13 15 18 20 29 30 34 35 40 43 47 50 57 59 64 69 70 75 76 77 79 81 85 86 87 93 98 100 105 107 108 110 111 115 119 129 130 146 147 148 156 169 **S** Steward Health Care System, LLC, Dallas, TX
Primary Contact: Stacey L. Brown, President
CFO: Rodger W Bowen, M.P.H., Chief Financial Officer
CMO: Keith Ledford, M.D., Chief of Staff
CIO: Gene Mills, Director Information Technology
CHR: Deborah Elder, Director Human Resources
CNO: Judy Roever, MSN, R.N., Chief Nursing Officer
Web address: www.smmccares.com
Control: Corporation, Investor–owned (for–profit) **Service:** General medical and surgical

Staffed Beds: 80 **Admissions:** 1507 **Census:** 14 **Outpatient Visits:** 28947
Births: 198 **Total Expense ($000):** 45161 **Payroll Expense ($000):** 13922
Personnel: 229

Hospital, Medicare Provider Number, Address, Telephone, Approval, Facility, and Physician Codes, Health Care System

★ American Hospital Association (AHA) membership ○ Healthcare Facilities Accreditation Program ⇧ Center for Improvement in Healthcare Quality Accreditation
☐ The Joint Commission accreditation ◇ DNV Healthcare Inc. accreditation △ Commission on Accreditation of Rehabilitation Facilities (CARF) accreditation

Hospitals, U.S. / TEXAS

★ **WEST TEXAS VA HEALTH CARE SYSTEM**, 300 Veterans Boulevard, Zip 79720–5500, Mailing Address: Big Springs, tel. 432/263–7361, (Nonreporting) **A**3 5 **S** Department of Veterans Affairs, Washington, DC
Primary Contact: Keith Bass, Medical Center Director
CFO: Ray Olivas, Chief Fiscal Service
CMO: Martin Schnier, D.O., Chief of Staff
CIO: Mike McKinley, Information Security Officer
CHR: Anna Osborne, Chief Human Resources Management Service
Web address: https://www.va.gov/west-texas-health-care/locations/george-h-obrien-jr-department-of-veterans-affairs-medical-center/
Control: Veterans Affairs, Government, federal **Service:** General medical and surgical

Staffed Beds: 149

WEST TEXAS VETERANS AFFAIRS HEALTH CARE SYSTEM See West Texas VA Health Care System

BONHAM—Fannin County

SAM RAYBURN MEMORIAL VETERANS CENTER See Dallas VA North Texas HCS, Dallas

★ **TMC BONHAM HOSPITAL (451370)**, 504 Lipscomb Street, Zip 75418–4028; tel. 903/583–8585, **A**10 18 **F**3 11 15 28 29 30 34 35 40 43 45 50 57 59 64 65 75 77 81 87 93 107 108 110 111 119 129 130 133 135 148 154 **P**6
Primary Contact: Christopher Zeringue, Chief Executive Officer
CMO: Michael Brown, D.O., Chief of Staff
CIO: Jack Farguson, Director Information Technology
CHR: Brenda Bagley, Director Human Resources
CNO: William Kiefer, Chief Nursing Officer
Web address: https://tmcbonham.com/
Control: Hospital district or authority, Government, Nonfederal **Service:** General medical and surgical

Staffed Beds: 25 **Admissions:** 523 **Census:** 13 **Outpatient Visits:** 18988 **Births:** 0 **Total Expense ($000):** 22531 **Payroll Expense ($000):** 10870 **Personnel:** 115

BORGER—Hutchinson County

GOLDEN PLAINS COMMUNITY HOSPITAL (451369), 100 Medical Drive, Zip 79007–7579; tel. 806/467–5700, **A**10 18 **F**11 13 15 29 30 34 35 40 43 45 50 54 56 57 59 64 65 66 68 70 75 76 77 79 81 85 86 87 93 107 108 110 115 119 127 130 131 132 133 143 146 147 148 153 154 156 164 169 **P**6
Primary Contact: Don Bates, Chief Executive Officer
COO: Melody Lynn Henderson, Ph.D., R.N., Chief Operating Officer and Chief Nursing Officer
CFO: Dina Hermes, Chief Financial Officer
CMO: Tanay M. Patel, M.D., Chief of Staff
CHR: Jennifer Harvey, Director Human Resources
Web address: www.goldenplains.org
Control: Other not–for–profit (including NFP Corporation) **Service:** General medical and surgical

Staffed Beds: 17 **Admissions:** 358 **Census:** 3 **Outpatient Visits:** 47708 **Births:** 175 **Total Expense ($000):** 36215 **Payroll Expense ($000):** 10136 **Personnel:** 178

BRADY—Mcculloch County

HEART OF TEXAS HEALTHCARE SYSTEM (451348), 2008 Nine Road, Zip 76825–7210, Mailing Address: P.O. Box 1150, Zip 76825–1150; tel. 325/597–2901, **A**10 18 **F**15 28 40 43 45 64 81 93 107 111 114 119 127 133 152 154 156 157 **P**4
Primary Contact: Tim Jones, Chief Executive Officer
CFO: Brad Burnett, Chief Financial Officer
CMO: Pete Castro, D.O., Chief of Staff
Web address: https://www.heartoftexashealthcare.org/
Control: Other not–for–profit (including NFP Corporation) **Service:** General medical and surgical

Staffed Beds: 14 **Admissions:** 193 **Census:** 2 **Outpatient Visits:** 23696 **Births:** 0 **Total Expense ($000):** 17722 **Payroll Expense ($000):** 4679 **Personnel:** 97

HEART OF TEXAS MEMORIAL HOSPITAL See Heart of Texas Healthcare System

BRECKENRIDGE—Stephens County

★ **STEPHENS MEMORIAL HOSPITAL (450498)**, 200 South Geneva Street, Zip 76424–4799; tel. 254/559–2242, **A**10 20 **F**3 8 11 15 28 29 30 34 35 40 43 45 50 53 54 56 57 59 63 64 68 69 81 85 87 89 93 97 107 114 127 130 133 144 146 154 **P**6
Primary Contact: Brian Roland, Chief Executive Officer
CFO: Doug Smith, Chief Financial Officer
CMO: Cynthia Perry, M.D., Chief of Staff
CIO: Bobby Thompson, Director Information Technology
CHR: Michelle Funderburg, Director Human Resources
CNO: Alicia Whitt, R.N., Chief Nursing Officer
Web address: www.smhtx.com
Control: Hospital district or authority, Government, Nonfederal **Service:** General medical and surgical

Staffed Beds: 40 **Admissions:** 97 **Census:** 2 **Outpatient Visits:** 14952 **Births:** 0 **Total Expense ($000):** 15177 **Payroll Expense ($000):** 6633 **Personnel:** 54

BRENHAM—Washington County

✠ **BAYLOR SCOTT & WHITE MEDICAL CENTER – BRENHAM (451397)**, 700 Medical Parkway, Zip 77833–5498; tel. 979/337–5000, **A**1 10 18 **F**3 13 18 28 29 30 34 35 40 45 50 51 54 56 59 64 68 75 76 77 81 82 85 87 93 102 107 114 115 119 127 130 135 146 147 149 154 156 164 169 **S** Baylor Scott & White Health, Dallas, TX
Primary Contact: Jason Jennings, FACHE, President
CFO: Jane Wellmann, Chief Financial Officer
CMO: Michael Schlabach, M.D., Chief Medical Officer
CIO: Sharon Schwartz, Director Medical Records
CHR: Virginia Counts, Manager Human Resources
Web address: https://www.bswhealth.com/locations/brenham-hospital
Control: Other not–for–profit (including NFP Corporation) **Service:** General medical and surgical

Staffed Beds: 25 **Admissions:** 1260 **Census:** 9 **Outpatient Visits:** 72647 **Births:** 370 **Total Expense ($000):** 38842 **Payroll Expense ($000):** 14942 **Personnel:** 156

BROWNFIELD—Terry County

★ **BROWNFIELD REGIONAL MEDICAL CENTER (450399)**, 705 East Felt Street, Zip 79316–3439; tel. 806/637–3551, **A**10 20 **F**3 7 11 13 28 29 30 34 40 43 45 50 53 57 59 62 64 65 68 75 76 80 81 85 86 87 93 97 102 107 111 114 119 127 130 135 148 149 154 169 **P**6
Primary Contact: Charles Norris, Interim Chief Executive Officer
CFO: Grady Paul Gafford, Chief Financial Officer
CIO: Edgar Rivera, Chief Information Officer
CHR: Kelly Barnett, Human Resource Officer
CNO: Chris Beard, Chief Nursing Officer
Web address: www.brownfield-rmc.org
Control: Hospital district or authority, Government, Nonfederal **Service:** General medical and surgical

Staffed Beds: 26 **Admissions:** 292 **Census:** 4 **Outpatient Visits:** 34559 **Births:** 146 **Total Expense ($000):** 20298 **Payroll Expense ($000):** 9231 **Personnel:** 151

BROWNSVILLE—Cameron County

SOLARA HOSPITAL HARLINGEN–BROWNSVILLE CAMPUS See Solara Specialty Hospitals Harlingen–Brownsville

★ **SOLARA SPECIALTY HOSPITALS HARLINGEN–BROWNSVILLE (452101)**, 333 Lorenaly Drive, Zip 78526–4333; tel. 956/546–0808, (Includes SOLARA SPECIALTY HOSPITALS HARLINGEN–BROWNSVILLE, 508 Victoria Lane, Harlingen, Texas, Zip 78550–3225, tel. 956/425–9600; Alberto Sanchez, Chief Executive Officer) (Nonreporting) **S** ScionHealth, Louisville, KY
Primary Contact: Cynthia Issacs, Chief Executive Officer
Web address: www.chghospitals.com/brownsville/
Control: Corporation, Investor–owned (for–profit) **Service:** Acute long–term care hospital

Staffed Beds: 41

Hospitals, U.S. / TEXAS

☐ **SOUTH TEXAS REHABILITATION HOSPITAL (453092)**, 425 East Alton Gloor Boulevard, Zip 78526–3361; tel. 956/554–6000, **A**1 10 **F**3 28 29 34 35 59 64 68 75 77 86 87 90 93 94 96 130 132 148 149 **S** Ernest Health, Inc., Albuquerque, NM
Primary Contact: Leo Garza, Chief Executive Officer
CFO: Ernest Nash, Chief Financial Officer
CMO: Christopher Wilson, M.D., Inpatient Medical Director
CIO: Deborah Alcocer, Chief Information Officer
CHR: Tony Rodriguez, Director Human Resources
CNO: Aaron Cepeda, Director Nursing Operations
Web address: www.strh.ernesthealth.com
Control: Partnership, Investor-owned (for-profit) Service: Rehabilitation

Staffed Beds: 40 **Admissions:** 692 **Census:** 29 **Outpatient Visits:** 10285 **Births:** 0 **Total Expense ($000):** 15338 **Payroll Expense ($000):** 7378 **Personnel:** 128

✠ **VALLEY BAPTIST MEDICAL CENTER–BROWNSVILLE (450028)**, 1040 West Jefferson Street, Zip 78520–6338, Mailing Address: P.O. Box 3590, Zip 78523–3590; tel. 956/698–5400, **A**1 5 10 **F**3 11 12 13 15 18 20 22 24 29 30 34 35 37 40 42 43 44 45 49 50 51 54 56 57 59 60 63 64 65 68 70 72 74 75 76 77 79 81 82 84 85 86 87 89 93 107 108 110 111 114 115 118 119 126 129 130 132 146 147 148 149 154 157 167 169 **S** TENET Healthcare Corporation, Dallas, TX
Primary Contact: Leslie Bingham, Senior Vice President and Chief Executive Officer
COO: Marisa Aguilar, Chief Operating Officer
CFO: Edwin Cordero, Chief Financial Officer
CMO: Jose L Ayala, M.D., Chief Medical Officer
CNO: Marisa Aguilar, Interim Chief Nursing Officer
Web address: https://www.valleybaptist.net/location/detail/vbmc-brownsville
Control: Corporation, Investor-owned (for-profit) Service: General medical and surgical

Staffed Beds: 225 **Admissions:** 10177 **Census:** 128 **Outpatient Visits:** 82482 **Births:** 2257 **Total Expense ($000):** 163717 **Payroll Expense ($000):** 67471 **Personnel:** 655

✠ **VALLEY REGIONAL MEDICAL CENTER (450662)**, 100A Alton Gloor Boulevard, Zip 78526–3354; tel. 956/350–7101, **A**1 3 10 **F**3 12 13 15 18 20 22 24 26 28 29 30 31 34 35 40 43 44 45 47 49 50 57 59 60 61 64 65 68 70 72 73 74 75 76 77 78 79 81 82 84 85 86 87 89 93 107 108 110 111 115 118 119 124 126 130 132 147 148 149 154 156 167 **S** HCA Healthcare, Nashville, TN
Primary Contact: David Irizarry, Chief Executive Officer
COO: Steven C Hoelscher, Chief Operating Officer
CIO: Carlos Leal, Director Information Technology
CHR: Vicky Kahl, Director Human Resources
Web address: www.valleyregionalmedicalcenter.com
Control: Partnership, Investor-owned (for-profit) Service: General medical and surgical

Staffed Beds: 214 **Admissions:** 10461 **Census:** 120 **Outpatient Visits:** 74002 **Births:** 1871 **Total Expense ($000):** 100693 **Payroll Expense ($000):** 61288 **Personnel:** 725

BROWNWOOD—Brown County

BROWNWOOD REGIONAL MEDICAL CENTER See Hendrick Medical Center Brownwood

✠ **HENDRICK MEDICAL CENTER BROWNWOOD (450587)**, 1501 Burnet Road, Zip 76801–8520; tel. 325/649–3302, **A**1 10 20 **F**3 11 13 15 18 20 22 26 28 29 30 31 34 35 37 39 40 41 43 45 46 47 48 50 51 53 54 55 56 57 59 64 68 70 71 73 74 75 76 77 78 79 81 86 87 93 94 107 108 110 111 115 117 118 119 120 121 123 126 129 130 131 135 144 146 148 149 154 167 168 169 **S** Hendrick Health System, Abilene, TX
Primary Contact: Krista Baty, R.N., Chief Administrative & Nursing Officer
COO: Brett Emmett, Chief Operating Officer
CFO: Erich Wallschaleger, Chief Financial Officer
CNO: Krista Baty, R.N., Chief Administrative & Nursing Officer
Web address: https://www.hendrickhealth.org/
Control: Church operated, Nongovernment, not-for-profit Service: General medical and surgical

Staffed Beds: 68 **Admissions:** 2734 **Census:** 31 **Outpatient Visits:** 72136 **Births:** 543 **Total Expense ($000):** 96620 **Payroll Expense ($000):** 31284 **Personnel:** 535

BRYAN—Brazos County

CAPROCK HOSPITAL (670259), 3134 Briarcrest Drive, Zip 77802–3014; tel. 979/314–2323, **A**10 22 **F**3 29 34 40 41 42 44 57 59 68 82 107 114 115 149
Primary Contact: Brenda Davis, Chief Executive Officer
Control: Partnership, Investor-owned (for-profit) Service: General medical and surgical

Staffed Beds: 6 **Admissions:** 224 **Census:** 1 **Births:** 0 **Total Expense ($000):** 9312 **Payroll Expense ($000):** 2362 **Personnel:** 50

✠ **CHI ST. JOSEPH HEALTH REHABILITATION HOSPITAL, AN AFFILIATE OF ENCOMPASS HEALTH (673065)**, 1600 Joseph Drive, Suite 2000, Zip 77802–1502; tel. 979/213–4300, **A**1 10 **F**3 9 28 29 77 90 91 96 130 148 149 **S** Encompass Health Corporation, Birmingham, AL
Primary Contact: Amy Gray, Chief Executive Officer
CFO: Kris Smith, Controller
Web address: www.encompasshealth.com/locations/stjrehab
Control: Partnership, Investor-owned (for-profit) Service: Rehabilitation

Staffed Beds: 61 **Admissions:** 1595 **Census:** 54 **Outpatient Visits:** 0 **Births:** 0 **Total Expense ($000):** 24952 **Payroll Expense ($000):** 13525 **Personnel:** 151

✠ **CHI ST. JOSEPH REGIONAL HEALTH CENTER (450011)**, 2801 Franciscan Drive, Zip 77802–2599; tel. 979/776–3777, (Includes ST. JOSEPH HEALTH COLLEGE STATION HOSPITAL, 1604 Rock Prairie Road, College Station, Texas, Zip 77845–8345, tel. 979/764–5100; Kimberly Shaw, FACHE, President and Chief Executive Officer) **A**1 2 3 5 10 19 **F**3 7 11 12 15 17 18 20 22 24 28 29 30 31 32 34 35 37 40 43 44 45 46 48 49 50 53 54 57 59 64 65 68 70 74 75 77 78 79 80 81 82 84 85 86 87 93 96 107 110 111 114 118 119 121 123 124 126 129 130 131 132 135 143 144 146 148 167 **S** CommonSpirit Health, Chicago, IL
Primary Contact: Kimberly Shaw, FACHE, St. Joseph Market President
CFO: Lisa McNair, CPA, Senior Vice President and Chief Financial Officer
CMO: Kia Parsi, M.D., Chief Medical Officer
CIO: John Phillips, Vice President Information Services
CHR: Michael G Costa, Vice President Human Resources
Web address: https://stjoseph.stlukeshealth.org/locations/chi-st-joseph-health-regional-hospital
Control: Church operated, Nongovernment, not-for-profit Service: General medical and surgical

Staffed Beds: 189 **Admissions:** 11451 **Census:** 142 **Outpatient Visits:** 288437 **Births:** 0 **Total Expense ($000):** 358229 **Payroll Expense ($000):** 103208 **Personnel:** 1176

☐ **THE PHYSICIANS CENTRE HOSPITAL (450834)**, 3131 University Drive East, Zip 77802–3473; tel. 979/731–3100, **A**1 3 10 **F**3 12 29 40 45 64 75 79 81 82 85 107 111 115 119 126 141 147 149 157 167
Primary Contact: Harold Engle, R.N., Chief Executive Officer
CFO: Paul Tannos, Chief Financial Officer
CMO: Barry Solcher, M.D., Chief of Staff
CIO: Shawn Clark, Director Information Systems
CHR: LeeAnn Ford, Director Human Resources and Imaging
CNO: Robert Raymond Lemay, R.N., Chief Nursing Officer
Web address: www.thephysicianscentre.com
Control: Corporation, Investor-owned (for-profit) Service: Surgical

Staffed Beds: 16 **Admissions:** 450 **Census:** 2 **Outpatient Visits:** 12736 **Births:** 0 **Total Expense ($000):** 23923 **Payroll Expense ($000):** 6103 **Personnel:** 119

BUDA—Hays County

✠ **BAYLOR SCOTT & WHITE MEDICAL CENTER – BUDA (670131)**, 5330 Overpass Road, Zip 78610–2300, Mailing Address: 5330 Overpass Drive, Zip 78610–2300; tel. 737/999–6200, **A**1 10 **F**3 29 40 45 46 50 70 79 81 85 97 107 111 114 119 130 154 **S** Baylor Scott & White Health, Dallas, TX
Primary Contact: Jay Fox, FACHE, President
Web address: https://www.bswhealth.com/locations/buda/Pages/default.aspx
Control: Other not-for-profit (including NFP Corporation) Service: General medical and surgical

Staffed Beds: 15 **Admissions:** 346 **Census:** 3 **Outpatient Visits:** 22702 **Births:** 0 **Total Expense ($000):** 29603 **Payroll Expense ($000):** 11211 **Personnel:** 107

Hospital, Medicare Provider Number, Address, Telephone, Approval, Facility, and Physician Codes, Health Care System

★ American Hospital Association (AHA) membership
☐ The Joint Commission accreditation
○ Healthcare Facilities Accreditation Program
◇ DNV Healthcare Inc. accreditation
⇧ Center for Improvement in Healthcare Quality Accreditation
△ Commission on Accreditation of Rehabilitation Facilities (CARF) accreditation

Hospitals, U.S. / TEXAS

BURLESON—Tarrant County

BAYLOR SCOTT & WHITE EMERGENCY HOSPITAL – BURLESON (670107), 12500 South Freeway Suite 100, Zip 76028-7128; tel. 214/294-6250, (Includes BAYLOR EMERGENCY MEDICAL CENTERS – MANSFIELD, 1776 US 287, Suite 100, Mansfield, Texas, Zip 76063, tel. 214/294-6300; Victor Schmerbeck, Chief Executive Officer; BAYLOR SCOTT & WHITE EMERGENCY HOSPITAL – GRAND PRAIRIE, 3095 Kingswood Boulevard, Grand Prairie, Texas, Zip 75052-4512, tel. 972/854-0009; Victor Schmerbeck, Chief Executive Officer) **A**10 21 **F**2 3 29 40 107 130 148 149 154 **S** Emerus, The Woodlands, TX
Primary Contact: Victor Schmerbeck, Chief Executive Officer
Web address: www.bayloremc.com/burleson
Control: Corporation, Investor-owned (for-profit) **Service**: General medical and surgical

Staffed Beds: 24 **Admissions**: 254 **Census**: 1 **Outpatient Visits**: 37411 **Births**: 0 **Total Expense ($000)**: 31639 **Payroll Expense ($000)**: 7689 **Personnel**: 112

TEXAS HEALTH HUGULEY HOSPITAL FORT WORTH SOUTH (450677), 11801 South Freeway, Zip 76028-7021, Mailing Address: P.O. Box 6337, Fort Worth, Zip 76115-0337; tel. 817/293-9110, **A**1 10 **F**3 4 5 11 13 15 17 18 20 22 24 26 28 29 30 31 32 34 35 37 38 40 41 43 45 46 48 49 50 51 53 54 56 57 59 60 64 65 66 68 70 71 73 74 75 76 77 78 79 80 81 82 84 85 86 87 91 93 98 100 101 102 103 104 105 107 108 110 111 115 118 119 126 130 131 132 135 146 147 148 151 152 153 154 156 160 162 164 167 169 **P**6 **S** AdventHealth, Altamonte Springs, FL
Primary Contact: Penny Johnson, Chief Executive Officer
CFO: Jesse Sutton, Senior Vice President and Chief Financial Officer
CIO: John Delano, Chief Information Officer, Southwest Region
CHR: Amber Owen, Regional Vice President, Human Resources
CNO: Tammy Ellis, FACHE, R.N., Vice President Patient Services
Web address: www.TexasHealthHuguley.org
Control: Church operated, Nongovernment, not-for-profit **Service**: General medical and surgical

Staffed Beds: 228 **Admissions**: 12053 **Census**: 147 **Outpatient Visits**: 136729 **Births**: 1408 **Total Expense ($000)**: 259963 **Payroll Expense ($000)**: 103891 **Personnel**: 1530

BURNET—Burnet County

ASCENSION SETON HIGHLAND LAKES (451365), 3201 South Water Street, Zip 78611-4510, Mailing Address: P.O. Box 1219, Zip 78611-7219; tel. 512/715-3000, **A**1 3 5 10 18 **F**3 11 15 18 28 29 30 34 35 40 43 45 50 57 59 64 71 74 79 81 85 87 92 93 97 107 108 110 111 115 118 119 124 126 127 130 132 133 146 154 165 **S** Ascension Healthcare, Saint Louis, MO
Primary Contact: Karen Christine. Litterer, R.N., MSN, Chief Administrator and Chief Nursing Officer
COO: Karen Christine Litterer, R.N., MSN, Administrator and Chief Operating Officer
CFO: Douglas D Waite, Senior Vice President and Chief Financial Officer
CNO: Steven Brockman-Weber, System Chief Nursing Officer
Web address: https://healthcare.ascension.org/locations/texas/txaus/burnet-ascension-seton-highland-lakes
Control: Church operated, Nongovernment, not-for-profit **Service**: General medical and surgical

Staffed Beds: 19 **Admissions**: 518 **Census**: 8 **Outpatient Visits**: 103432 **Births**: 0 **Total Expense ($000)**: 53783 **Payroll Expense ($000)**: 16207 **Personnel**: 188

CALDWELL—Burleson County

CHI ST. JOSEPH HEALTH BURLESON HOSPITAL (451305), 1101 Woodson Drive, Zip 77836-1052, Mailing Address: P.O. Box 360, Zip 77836-0360; tel. 979/567-3245, **A**1 10 18 **F**3 11 28 29 30 34 40 43 50 57 59 64 93 119 130 133 146 148 167 **S** CommonSpirit Health, Chicago, IL
Primary Contact: Kyle Sims, Division Vice President
CFO: Austin Jones, CPA, Chief Financial Officer
CMO: Kristel Leubner, D.O., Chief of Staff
CHR: Jackie Stradtman, Director Human Resources
CNO: Heather Page, MSN, Director of Nursing
Web address: https://stjoseph-locations.stlukeshealth.org/location/chi-st-joseph-health-burleson-hospital
Control: Church operated, Nongovernment, not-for-profit **Service**: General medical and surgical

Staffed Beds: 15 **Admissions**: 193 **Census**: 6 **Outpatient Visits**: 13636 **Births**: 0 **Total Expense ($000)**: 13151 **Payroll Expense ($000)**: 5421 **Personnel**: 50

CANADIAN—Hemphill County

HEMPHILL COUNTY HOSPITAL DISTRICT (450578), 1020 South Fourth Street, Zip 79014-3315; tel. 806/323-6422, (Total facility includes 48 beds in nursing home-type unit) **A**10 21 **F**2 3 7 10 29 34 35 40 45 56 57 59 62 63 64 65 68 69 77 87 89 93 97 102 104 107 108 119 127 128 129 130 131 133 146 147 148 154 **P**6
Primary Contact: Kelsey Haley, Chief Executive Officer
CFO: Bob Ericson, Chief Financial Officer
CMO: G. Anthony Cook, M.D., Medical Director
CIO: Brian Goza, Chief Information Officer
CHR: David G Troublefield, Director, Human Resources
CNO: Debra Sappenfield, R.N., Chief Nursing Officer
Web address: www.hchdst.org
Control: Hospital district or authority, Government, Nonfederal **Service**: General medical and surgical

Staffed Beds: 67 **Admissions**: 431 **Census**: 44 **Outpatient Visits**: 36141 **Births**: 0 **Total Expense ($000)**: 35149 **Payroll Expense ($000)**: 11685 **Personnel**: 160

CARRIZO SPRINGS—Dimmit County

DIMMIT REGIONAL HOSPITAL (451390), 704 Hospital Drive, Zip 78834-3836, Mailing Address: P.O. Box 1016, Zip 78834-7016; tel. 830/876-2424, **A**10 18 **F**13 15 40 43 57 64 81 93 107 115 119 133 148 154
Primary Contact: Andres Duran, Chief Executive Officer
CFO: Alma Melendez, Controller
CNO: Carmen P Esquivel, R.N., Chief Nursing Officer
Web address: www.dimmitregionalhospital.com/
Control: Other not-for-profit (including NFP Corporation) **Service**: General medical and surgical

Staffed Beds: 25 **Admissions**: 468 **Census**: 6 **Outpatient Visits**: 18446 **Births**: 92 **Total Expense ($000)**: 28741 **Payroll Expense ($000)**: 11401 **Personnel**: 178

CARROLLTON—Denton County

CARROLLTON REGIONAL MEDICAL CENTER (450730), 4343 North Josey Lane, Zip 75010-4691; tel. 972/492-1010, **A**1 10 **F**3 11 14 15 18 20 22 29 30 31 34 35 40 41 45 46 47 48 49 50 51 54 56 57 59 60 64 66 68 70 74 75 78 79 80 81 84 85 93 107 108 109 110 111 112 113 114 115 116 117 118 119 126 129 130 132 134 146 148 154
Primary Contact: Caleb F. O'Rear, Chief Executive Officer
CFO: John Keefe, Chief Financial Officer
CMO: Matthew Smith, M.D., Vice President Medical Affairs and Chief Medical Officer
CIO: Paul Ratcliff, Director Information Services
CHR: Erica Calime, Director Human Resources
CNO: Barbara Vaughn, R.N., Chief Nursing Officer
Web address: https://www.crmc.health/
Control: Other not-for-profit (including NFP Corporation) **Service**: General medical and surgical

Staffed Beds: 89 **Admissions**: 3040 **Census**: 31 **Births**: 0 **Total Expense ($000)**: 86854 **Payroll Expense ($000)**: 35121 **Personnel**: 553

CARROLLTON SPRINGS (454119), 2225 Parker Road, Zip 75010-4711; tel. 972/242-4114, **A**1 10 **F**4 5 98 103 104 105 151 152 153 154 **S** Springstone, Louisville, KY
Primary Contact: John Fisher, Interim Chief Executive Officer
Web address: www.carrolltonsprings.com
Control: Corporation, Investor-owned (for-profit) **Service**: Psychiatric

Staffed Beds: 78 **Admissions**: 2705 **Census**: 66 **Outpatient Visits**: 40118 **Births**: 0 **Total Expense ($000)**: 27472 **Payroll Expense ($000)**: 15362 **Personnel**: 178

LEGENT ORTHOPEDIC HOSPITAL CARROLLTON (670265), 1401 East Trinity Mills Road, Zip 75006; tel. 972/810-0700, **A**10 **F**3 29 37 40 58 64 68 70 74 75 79 81 85 87 107 126 131 149 157 164
Primary Contact: Terri LeBlanc, Chief Executive and Nursing Officer
Web address: https://www.psnaffiliates.com/
Control: Partnership, Investor-owned (for-profit) **Service**: Surgical

Staffed Beds: 18 **Admissions**: 695 **Census**: 3 **Outpatient Visits**: 4079 **Births**: 0 **Total Expense ($000)**: 41569 **Payroll Expense ($000)**: 10159 **Personnel**: 96

Hospitals, U.S. / TEXAS

CARTHAGE—Panola County

☒ **UT HEALTH CARTHAGE (450210)**, 409 Cottage Road, Zip 75633–1466; tel. 903/693–3841, **A**1 10 20 **F**3 18 28 29 30 34 35 40 43 45 50 57 59 64 65 75 107 108 110 111 115 119 127 129 145 149 154 156 157 169 **S** Ardent Health Services, Nashville, TN
Primary Contact: Mark Leitner, FACHE, Chief Executive Officer
CMO: Salah Almohammed, Chief of Staff
CIO: Renee Lawhorn, Director Medical Records
CHR: Amber Cox, Director Human Resources
CNO: Judy Peterson, R.N., Chief Nursing Officer
Web address: https://uthealthcarthage.com/
Control: Corporation, Investor–owned (for–profit) **Service**: General medical and surgical

Staffed Beds: 23 **Admissions**: 314 **Census**: 3 **Outpatient Visits**: 55306
Births: 0 **Total Expense ($000)**: 21840 **Payroll Expense ($000)**: 7393
Personnel: 91

CEDAR PARK—Williamson County

BAYLOR SCOTT & WHITE EMERGENCY MEDICAL CENTER– CEDAR PARK (670087), 900 East Whitestone Boulevard, Zip 78613–9093; tel. 512/684–4911, (Nonreporting) **A**10
Primary Contact: Jay Fox, FACHE, President BSWH Austin Area
Web address: www.sweh.org
Control: Other not–for–profit (including NFP Corporation) **Service**: General medical and surgical

Staffed Beds: 8

☒ **CEDAR PARK REGIONAL MEDICAL CENTER (670043)**, 1401 Medical Parkway, Zip 78613–7763; tel. 512/528–7000, **A**1 10 **F**3 12 13 15 18 20 22 29 30 34 35 37 40 42 43 45 46 47 49 50 51 54 57 59 60 64 70 73 74 75 76 77 78 79 81 82 85 87 89 93 107 108 110 111 114 115 116 118 119 126 129 130 132 135 146 147 148 154 167 169 **S** Community Health Systems, Inc., Franklin, TN
Primary Contact: Sean Tinney, FACHE, Chief Executive Officer
COO: Joseph Warburton, Chief Operating Officer
CFO: Erich Wallschlaeger, Chief Financial Officer
CIO: Brad Hoar, Director Information and Technology
CHR: Jeffery Ward, Director Human Resources
Web address: www.cedarparkregional.com
Control: Corporation, Investor–owned (for–profit) **Service**: General medical and surgical

Staffed Beds: 126 **Admissions**: 6789 **Census**: 62 **Outpatient Visits**: 81577
Births: 1566 **Total Expense ($000)**: 134201 **Payroll Expense ($000)**: 44249 **Personnel**: 539

CHILDRESS—Childress County

★ **CHILDRESS REGIONAL MEDICAL CENTER (450369)**, 901 Highway 83 North, Zip 79201–5800, Mailing Address: P.O. Box 1030, Zip 79201–1030; tel. 940/937–6371, **A**10 20 **F**3 7 8 13 15 29 31 32 34 35 40 43 45 50 56 57 59 60 61 62 63 64 65 66 68 76 77 78 79 81 84 91 92 93 107 108 111 114 119 126 127 129 130 133 154 157 **P**6
Primary Contact: Holly Holcomb, R.N., Chief Executive Officer
COO: LaDonna Willis, Chief Operating Officer
CFO: Emilee Stratton, Chief Financial Officer
CMO: Dustin Pratt, M.D., Chief of Staff
CHR: Gayle Cannon, Director Human Resources
CNO: Sulynn Mester, R.N., Chief Nursing Officer
Web address: www.childresshospital.com
Control: Hospital district or authority, Government, Nonfederal **Service**: General medical and surgical

Staffed Beds: 37 **Admissions**: 517 **Census**: 6 **Outpatient Visits**: 250604
Births: 141 **Total Expense ($000)**: 39461 **Payroll Expense ($000)**: 19602
Personnel: 221

CLEBURNE—Johnson County

☒ **TEXAS HEALTH HARRIS METHODIST HOSPITAL CLEBURNE (450148)**, 201 Walls Drive, Zip 76033–4007; tel. 817/641–2551, **A**1 10 **F**3 11 13 15 18 29 30 34 35 40 43 50 57 59 60 64 66 68 70 75 76 79 81 85 87 93 107 108 110 114 119 126 146 147 148 149 154 169 **S** Texas Health Resources, Arlington, TX
Primary Contact: Christopher Leu, President
CFO: Shelly Miland, Group Finance Officer
CMO: Judy Laviolette, M.D., Chief Medical Officer
CIO: Brenda Taylor, Director Information Systems
CHR: Marsha Adams, Interim Director Human Resources
CNO: Vicki Brockman, R.N., Chief Nursing Officer
Web address: www.texashealth.org
Control: Other not–for–profit (including NFP Corporation) **Service**: General medical and surgical

Staffed Beds: 69 **Admissions**: 3299 **Census**: 33 **Outpatient Visits**: 40929
Births: 369 **Total Expense ($000)**: 81826 **Payroll Expense ($000)**: 32367
Personnel: 308

CLIFTON—Bosque County

★ ⇧ **GOODALL–WITCHER HOSPITAL (451385)**, 101 Posey Avenue, Zip 76634–1289, Mailing Address: P.O. Box 549, Zip 76634–0549; tel. 254/675–8322, **A**10 18 21 **F**3 11 13 15 28 29 30 34 35 36 40 43 45 50 53 56 57 59 62 64 65 68 76 77 81 87 93 97 100 102 104 107 108 110 115 119 127 129 130 131 132 133 143 148 154 156 165 169 **P**6
Primary Contact: Adam Willmann, President and Chief Executive Officer
CFO: Jerry Lynn Pickett, Chief Financial Officer
CMO: Kevin Blanton, D.O., Chief of Staff
CHR: Jennie Oldham, Director Human Resources
CNO: Donna Nichols, R.N., Chief Nursing Officer
Web address: www.gwhf.org
Control: Hospital district or authority, Government, Nonfederal **Service**: General medical and surgical

Staffed Beds: 25 **Admissions**: 324 **Census**: 6 **Outpatient Visits**: 87845
Births: 66 **Total Expense ($000)**: 37515 **Payroll Expense ($000)**: 15998
Personnel: 228

COLEMAN—Coleman County

COLEMAN COUNTY MEDICAL CENTER (451347), 310 South Pecos Street, Zip 76834–4159; tel. 325/625–2135, **A**10 18 **F**3 11 13 28 29 32 34 35 40 43 44 45 50 56 57 59 64 65 68 81 84 86 87 93 97 107 114 119 127 133 147 148 149 154 169 **S** Preferred Management Corporation, Shawnee, OK
Primary Contact: Clay Vogel, Administrator
CMO: Paul Reynolds, M.D., Medical Director
CIO: Harvey Ramirez, Chief Information Officer
CNO: Melissa Ereman, R.N., Chief Nursing Officer
Web address: https://colemancountymc.com/
Control: Corporation, Investor–owned (for–profit) **Service**: General medical and surgical

Staffed Beds: 25 **Admissions**: 336 **Census**: 6 **Outpatient Visits**: 21126
Births: 20 **Total Expense ($000)**: 12869 **Payroll Expense ($000)**: 5820
Personnel: 109

COLLEGE STATION—Brazos County

☒ **BAYLOR SCOTT & WHITE HOSPITAL MEDICAL CENTER – COLLEGE STATION (670088)**, 700 Scott & White Drive, Zip 77845; tel. 979/207–0100, **A**1 2 5 10 19 **F**3 12 13 14 15 18 20 22 24 26 28 29 30 31 34 35 40 43 45 46 47 48 49 50 51 56 57 59 61 64 65 70 72 74 75 76 77 78 79 80 81 82 83 84 85 87 93 97 101 102 104 107 108 110 111 115 118 119 120 121 122 123 124 126 127 129 130 131 135 142 145 146 147 148 149 154 157 162 165 167 169 **S** Baylor Scott & White Health, Dallas, TX
Primary Contact: Jason Jennings, FACHE, President
COO: Geoffrey Christian, Chief Operating Officer
Web address: www.sw.org/location/college-station-hospital
Control: Other not–for–profit (including NFP Corporation) **Service**: General medical and surgical

Staffed Beds: 142 **Admissions**: 9356 **Census**: 97 **Outpatient Visits**: 533506 **Births**: 1720 **Total Expense ($000)**: 274947 **Payroll Expense ($000)**: 77856 **Personnel**: 1063

CHI ST. JOSEPH COLLEGE STATION HOSPITAL See St. Joseph Health College Station Hospital

---

Hospital, Medicare Provider Number, Address, Telephone, Approval, Facility, and Physician Codes, Health Care System

★ American Hospital Association (AHA) membership
☐ The Joint Commission accreditation
○ Healthcare Facilities Accreditation Program
◇ DNV Healthcare Inc. accreditation
⇧ Center for Improvement in Healthcare Quality Accreditation
△ Commission on Accreditation of Rehabilitation Facilities (CARF) accreditation

Hospitals, U.S. / TEXAS

COLORADO CITY—Mitchell County

★ **MITCHELL COUNTY HOSPITAL (451342)**, 997 West Interstate 20, Zip 79512-2685; tel. 325/728-3431, **A**10 18 **F**3 7 11 28 29 34 35 40 43 45 50 53 57 59 64 65 68 71 81 82 86 87 93 107 108 109 114 119 127 133 135 146 154 166 167 **P**6
Primary Contact: Michelle Gafford, Chief Executive Officer
CMO: Dee A Roach, M.D., Chief of Staff
CHR: Deana Overton, Director Human Resources
CNO: Donna Goebel, M.D., Chief Nursing Officer
Web address: www.mitchellcountyhospital.com
Control: Hospital district or authority, Government, Nonfederal **Service**: General medical and surgical

> **Staffed Beds**: 17 **Admissions**: 207 **Census**: 4 **Outpatient Visits**: 14404 **Total Expense ($000)**: 22441 **Payroll Expense ($000)**: 11455 **Personnel**: 158

COLUMBUS—Colorado County

COLUMBUS COMMUNITY HOSPITAL (450370), 110 Shult Drive, Zip 78934-3010; tel. 979/732-2371, **A**5 10 20 **F**3 11 13 15 29 34 35 40 43 57 68 76 77 79 81 93 107 108 110 111 114 119 127 130 133 148 149 154 156 169
Primary Contact: James Vanek, Chief Executive Officer
CFO: Regina Wicke, Chief Financial Officer
CMO: Robert Katz, M.D., Chief of Staff
CIO: Ashley Mathis, Privacy Officer
CHR: Janie Hammonds, Human Resources Officer
CNO: Jeno Hargrove, R.N., Director of Nursing
Web address: www.columbusch.com
Control: Other not-for-profit (including NFP Corporation) **Service**: General medical and surgical

> **Staffed Beds**: 40 **Admissions**: 768 **Census**: 5 **Outpatient Visits**: 99390 **Births**: 385 **Total Expense ($000)**: 36680 **Payroll Expense ($000)**: 10261 **Personnel**: 161

COMANCHE—Comanche County

★ **COMANCHE COUNTY MEDICAL CENTER (451382)**, 10201 Highway 16, Zip 76442-4462; tel. 254/879-4900, **A**10 18 **F**3 11 15 28 29 30 34 35 40 43 45 50 53 54 59 64 65 71 75 77 79 81 85 86 87 93 97 104 107 108 110 111 115 119 127 130 131 133 135 145 146 147 148 154 156 157 164 **P**6
Primary Contact: Larry Troxell, Chief Executive Officer
CFO: Hong Wade, Chief Financial Officer
CMO: Guyle Donham, M.D., Chief of Staff
CIO: Ismelda Garza, Director Information Systems
CHR: Karen DeLavan, Interim Director Human Resources
CNO: Colleen Jedlicka, R.N., JD, Chief Nursing Officer
Web address: www.comanchecmc.org
Control: Other not-for-profit (including NFP Corporation) **Service**: General medical and surgical

> **Staffed Beds**: 23 **Admissions**: 477 **Census**: 6 **Outpatient Visits**: 44354 **Births**: 0 **Total Expense ($000)**: 49635 **Payroll Expense ($000)**: 16360 **Personnel**: 284

CONROE—Montgomery County

★ **ASPIRE HOSPITAL (670093)**, 2006 South Loop 336 West, Suite 500, Zip 77304-3315; tel. 936/647-3500, **A**10 22 **F**3 5 77 78 93 98 100 103 105 107 111 114 115 119 120 121 124 135 149 152 153 154 162 164
Primary Contact: Jose Silvas, Vice President of Operations
CFO: Bob Gray, Chief Financial Officer
CIO: John Heemann, Vice President and Chief Information Officer
Web address: www.aspirehospital.com
Control: Partnership, Investor-owned (for-profit) **Service**: Psychiatric

> **Staffed Beds**: 30 **Admissions**: 582 **Census**: 13 **Outpatient Visits**: 39520 **Births**: 0 **Total Expense ($000)**: 16480 **Payroll Expense ($000)**: 5160 **Personnel**: 95

★ **CORNERSTONE SPECIALTY HOSPITALS CONROE (452107)**, 1500 Grand Lake Drive, Zip 77304-2891; tel. 936/523-1800, **A**10 22 **F**1 3 26 29 56 65 69 74 75 82 85 86 87 107 148 **S** ScionHealth, Louisville, KY
Primary Contact: Suzanne Kretschmer, Chief Executive Officer
Web address: www.chghospitals.com/conroe/
Control: Partnership, Investor-owned (for-profit) **Service**: Acute long-term care hospital

> **Staffed Beds**: 41 **Admissions**: 403 **Census**: 26 **Outpatient Visits**: 0 **Births**: 0 **Total Expense ($000)**: 18439 **Payroll Expense ($000)**: 7340 **Personnel**: 100

ENCOMPASS HEALTH REHABILITATION HOSPITAL OF THE WOODLANDS (453059), 18550 'IH' 45 South, Zip 77384; tel. 281/364-2000, **A**1 10 **F**3 28 29 34 35 44 59 60 74 75 77 79 82 86 87 90 91 95 96 130 148 149 **S** Encompass Health Corporation, Birmingham, AL
Primary Contact: Angela L. Simmons, Chief Executive Officer
CMO: Ben Agana, M.D., Medical Director
CHR: Valerie Wells, Manager Human Resources
Web address: www.healthsouththewoodlands.com
Control: Corporation, Investor-owned (for-profit) **Service**: Rehabilitation

> **Staffed Beds**: 40 **Admissions**: 861 **Census**: 29 **Outpatient Visits**: 0 **Births**: 0 **Total Expense ($000)**: 18786 **Payroll Expense ($000)**: 9132 **Personnel**: 135

HCA HOUSTON HEALTHCARE CONROE (450222), 504 Medical Boulevard, Zip 77304, Mailing Address: P.O. Box 1538, Zip 77305-1538; tel. 936/539-1111, **A**1 3 10 **F**3 7 12 13 17 18 20 22 24 26 28 29 34 40 43 45 46 47 48 49 51 53 54 57 59 60 64 70 72 74 75 76 77 78 79 81 82 85 90 91 93 107 108 111 114 115 116 117 118 119 126 129 130 131 135 142 147 148 157 167 169 **S** HCA Healthcare, Nashville, TN
Primary Contact: Matt Davis, FACHE, Chief Executive Officer
CFO: Brandon Frazier, Chief Financial Officer
CMO: Mujtaba Ali-Khan, D.O., Chief Medical Officer
CIO: Jeremy Fuller, Director Information Systems
CHR: Diana Howell, Director Human Resources
Web address: www.conroeregional.com/
Control: Partnership, Investor-owned (for-profit) **Service**: General medical and surgical

> **Staffed Beds**: 304 **Admissions**: 14511 **Census**: 182 **Outpatient Visits**: 89705 **Births**: 1650 **Total Expense ($000)**: 209452 **Payroll Expense ($000)**: 90381 **Personnel**: 1063

☐ **WOODLAND SPRINGS HOSPITAL (454144)**, 15680 Old Conroe Road, Zip 77384; tel. 936/270-7520, **A**1 10 **F**5 87 98 99 104 105 152 153 154 164 **S** Springstone, Louisville, KY
Primary Contact: Dustin Davis, Chief Executive Officer
Web address: https://www.woodlandspringshealth.com
Control: Corporation, Investor-owned (for-profit) **Service**: Psychiatric

> **Staffed Beds**: 96 **Admissions**: 3059 **Census**: 73 **Outpatient Visits**: 9666 **Births**: 0 **Total Expense ($000)**: 26701 **Payroll Expense ($000)**: 12725 **Personnel**: 171

CORPUS CHRISTI—Nueces County

ADA WILSON HOSP OF PHYS MED See Ada Wilson Children's Center For Rehabilitation

CHRISTUS SPOHN HOSP SHORELINE See Christus Spohn Hospital Corpus Christi Shoreline

★ **CHRISTUS SPOHN HOSPITAL CORPUS CHRISTI SHORELINE (450046)**, 600 Elizabeth Street, Zip 78404-2235; tel. 361/881-3000, (Includes CHRISTUS SPOHN HOSPITAL CORPUS CHRISTI SOUTH, 5950 Saratoga, Corpus Christi, Texas, Zip 78414-4100, tel. 361/985-5000; LaNell Scott, President) (Nonreporting) **S** CHRISTUS Health, Irving, TX
Primary Contact: Raymond Acebo, M.D., Administrator/Chief Medical Officer
Web address: www.christusspohn.org
Control: Church operated, Nongovernment, not-for-profit **Service**: General medical and surgical

> **Staffed Beds**: 368

☐ **CHRISTUS SURGICAL HOSPITAL (670061)**, 6130 Parkway Drive, Zip 78414-2455; tel. 361/993-2000, (Nonreporting) **A**1 10 **S** National Surgical Healthcare, Chicago, IL
Primary Contact: Steven Daniel, Chief Executive Officer
CFO: Julie Wittwer, Chief Financial Officer
CMO: Michael Mintz, M.D., Chief Medical Officer
CHR: Lory Beth Smith, Manager Human Resource
CNO: Jan O'Donnell, Chief Nursing Officer
Web address: www.southtexassurgicalhospital.com
Control: Partnership, Investor-owned (for-profit) **Service**: Surgical

> **Staffed Beds**: 20

Hospitals, U.S. / TEXAS

☒ **CORPUS CHRISTI MEDICAL CENTER – DOCTORS REGIONAL (450788)**, 3315 South Alameda Street, Zip 78411-1883, Mailing Address: P.O. Box 8991, Zip 78468-8991; tel. 361/761-1400, (Includes CORPUS CHRISTI MEDICAL CENTER – BAYVIEW BEHAVIORAL HOSPITAL, 6629 Wooldridge Road, Corpus Christi, Texas, Zip 78414, tel. 361/986-9444; CORPUS CHRISTI MEDICAL CENTER – THE HEART HOSPITAL, 7002 Williams Drive, Corpus Christi, Texas, Zip 78412-4911, tel. 361/761-1000; Eric Evans, Chief Executive Officer; CORPUS CHRISTI MEDICAL CENTER BAY AREA, 7101 South Padre Island Drive, Corpus Christi, Texas, Zip 78412-4999, tel. 361/985-1200; Eric Evans, Chief Executive Officer) **A**1 3 5 10 13 **F**3 5 11 12 13 15 17 18 20 22 24 26 28 29 31 34 35 37 38 40 42 43 44 47 49 50 53 55 56 57 58 59 64 70 72 73 74 75 76 77 78 79 81 82 85 86 87 90 93 97 98 99 100 103 104 105 107 111 114 115 119 120 121 123 124 126 130 131 132 146 147 148 149 150 152 153 154 156 157 167 169 **P**8 **S** HCA Healthcare, Nashville, TN
Primary Contact: David Irizarry, Chief Executive Officer
CFO: Chris Nicosia, Chief Financial Officer
CHR: Michael Conwill, Director Human Resources
CNO: Kathleen A Rubano, MSN, R.N., Chief Nursing Officer
Web address: www.ccmedicalcenter.com
Control: Partnership, Investor-owned (for-profit) Service: General medical and surgical

Staffed Beds: 424 **Admissions**: 23785 **Census**: 310 **Outpatient Visits**: 151333 **Births**: 3934 **Total Expense ($000)**: 353782 **Payroll Expense ($000)**: 134506 **Personnel**: 1439

☐ **CORPUS CHRISTI REHABILITATION HOSPITAL (673053)**, 5726 Esplanade Drive, Zip 78414; tel. 361/906-3700, **A**1 10 **F**3 28 29 34 35 44 56 59 74 75 77 79 82 90 96 130 132 148 149 **S** Ernest Health, Inc., Albuquerque, NM
Primary Contact: Michael L. Pierce, Chief Executive Officer
Web address: www.ccrh.ernesthealth.com
Control: Corporation, Investor-owned (for-profit) Service: Rehabilitation

Staffed Beds: 35 **Admissions**: 873 **Census**: 31 **Outpatient Visits**: 5195 **Births**: 0 **Total Expense ($000)**: 14818 **Payroll Expense ($000)**: 7896 **Personnel**: 135

CORPUS CHRUSTI MEDICAL CENTER See Corpus Christi Medical Center Bay Area

☐ △ **DRISCOLL CHILDREN'S HOSPITAL (453301)**, 3533 South Alameda Street, Zip 78411-1785, Mailing Address: P.O. Box 6530, Zip 78466-6530; tel. 361/694-5000, **A**1 3 5 7 10 **F**3 7 11 12 19 21 23 25 27 29 30 31 32 34 35 37 38 39 40 41 43 45 48 50 54 55 57 58 59 60 61 64 65 68 72 73 74 75 77 78 79 81 82 85 86 87 88 89 91 93 96 100 104 107 108 111 115 118 119 129 130 131 132 134 138 143 144 145 146 148 149 150 153 154 155 156 157 164 167
Primary Contact: Eric Hamon, President and Chief Executive Officer
COO: Mary Peterson, M.D., Executive Vice President and Chief Operating Officer
CFO: Eric Hamon, Executive Vice President and Chief Financial Officer
CIO: Miguel Perez, III, Chief Information Officer
CHR: Bill Larsen, Vice President Human Resources
CNO: Julie A. Pina, Assistant Vice President Patient Care Services and Chief Nursing Officer
Web address: www.driscollchildrens.org
Control: Other not-for-profit (including NFP Corporation) Service: Children's general medical and surgical

Staffed Beds: 170 **Admissions**: 3479 **Census**: 103 **Outpatient Visits**: 235138 **Births**: 0 **Total Expense ($000)**: 520526 **Payroll Expense ($000)**: 169348 **Personnel**: 3291

☐ **OCEANS BEHAVIORAL HOSPITAL OF CORPUS CHRISTI (454155)**, 600 Elizabeth Street, Building B, 5th Floor, Zip 78404-2235, Mailing Address: 3905 Hedgcoxe Road Unit 250249, Plano, Zip 75025; tel. 361/371-8933, **A**1 10 **F**29 34 35 64 68 98 100 101 103 104 130 132 149 153 154 164 **S** Oceans Healthcare, Plano, TX
Primary Contact: Michelle C. Lozano, Chief Executive Officer and Hospital Administrator
CMO: John Lusins, M.D., Medical Director
CHR: Rebekah Poklandik, Human Resources Director
CNO: Philip Valadez, Director of Nursing
Web address: https://oceanshealthcare.com/ohc-location/corpus-christi/
Control: Corporation, Investor-owned (for-profit) Service: Psychiatric

Staffed Beds: 42 **Admissions**: 1396 **Census**: 37 **Outpatient Visits**: 1042 **Births**: 0 **Total Expense ($000)**: 10279 **Payroll Expense ($000)**: 4936 **Personnel**: 69

PADRE BEHAVIORAL HOSPITAL See Corpus Christi Medical Center – Bayview Behavioral Hospital

☒ **PAM REHABILITATION HOSPITAL OF CORPUS CHRISTI (673067)**, 345 South Water Street, Zip 78401-2819; tel. 361/500-0600, **A**1 10 **F**3 28 29 34 60 64 90 91 93 96 132 **S** PAM Health, Enola, PA
Primary Contact: Hector Bernal, Chief Executive Officer
Web address: www.postacutemedical.com
Control: Corporation, Investor-owned (for-profit) Service: Rehabilitation

Staffed Beds: 40 **Admissions**: 1059 **Census**: 35 **Outpatient Visits**: 19973 **Births**: 0 **Total Expense ($000)**: 22437 **Payroll Expense ($000)**: 10537 **Personnel**: 225

☒ **POST ACUTE MEDICAL SPECIALTY HOSPITAL OF CORPUS CHRISTI – NORTH (452086)**, 600 Elizabeth Street, 3rd Floor, Zip 78404-2235; tel. 361/881-3223, (Includes PAM SPECIALTY HOSPITAL OF CORPUS CHRISTI BAYFRONT, 345 South Water Street, Corpus Christi, Texas, Zip 78401-2819, tel. 361/500-0600; Hector Bernal, Chief Executive Officer) **A**1 10 **F**1 3 29 75 85 148 **S** PAM Health, Enola, PA
Primary Contact: Hector Bernal, Chief Executive Officer
Web address: www.postacutemedical.com/our-facilities/hospitals/post-acute-medical-specialty-hospital-corpus-christi/
Control: Corporation, Investor-owned (for-profit) Service: Acute long-term care hospital

Staffed Beds: 43 **Admissions**: 548 **Census**: 35 **Outpatient Visits**: 0 **Births**: 0 **Total Expense ($000)**: 19965 **Payroll Expense ($000)**: 9029 **Personnel**: 108

SOUTH TEXAS SURGICAL HOSPITAL See Christus Surgical Hospital

CORSICANA—Navarro County

☒ **NAVARRO REGIONAL HOSPITAL (450447)**, 3201 West State Highway 22, Zip 75110-2469; tel. 903/654-6800, **A**1 10 19 **F**3 11 13 18 20 22 28 29 30 34 35 39 40 43 45 46 50 51 54 60 64 68 70 75 76 79 81 82 85 89 93 107 111 114 115 119 127 135 146 149 154 167 **S** Community Health Systems, Inc., Franklin, TN
Primary Contact: John Manolakis, Chief Executive Officer
CFO: Shea C. Brock, Chief Financial Officer
CIO: Bryan Chilton, Director Information Systems
CHR: Melodee Pugh, Director Human Resources
CNO: Dona E Townsend, Chief Nursing Officer
Web address: www.navarrohospital.com
Control: Partnership, Investor-owned (for-profit) Service: General medical and surgical

Staffed Beds: 49 **Admissions**: 2318 **Census**: 19 **Outpatient Visits**: 95206 **Births**: 580 **Total Expense ($000)**: 59290 **Payroll Expense ($000)**: 20142 **Personnel**: 331

CRANE—Crane County

★ **CRANE MEMORIAL HOSPITAL (451353)**, 1310 South Alford Street, Zip 79731-3899; tel. 432/558-3555, **A**10 18 **F**3 29 32 34 40 57 59 64 65 68 75 81 86 97 107 114 119 127 133 147 148 154 **P**6
Primary Contact: Laci Harris, MSN, R.N., Chief Executive Officer
CFO: Daniel Ibarra, Chief Financial Officer
CMO: Sixta Gumato, M.D., Chief Medical Officer
CHR: Becky Esparza, Human Resources
CNO: Pat Touchstone, Chief Nursing Officer
Web address: www.cranememorial.org
Control: Hospital district or authority, Government, Nonfederal Service: General medical and surgical

Staffed Beds: 10 **Admissions**: 57 **Census**: 2 **Outpatient Visits**: 12017 **Births**: 0 **Total Expense ($000)**: 9210 **Payroll Expense ($000)**: 3977 **Personnel**: 57

CROCKETT—Houston County

⇑ **CROCKETT MEDICAL CENTER** See Midcoast Medical Center – Crockett

⇑ **MIDCOAST MEDICAL CENTER – CROCKETT (451393)**, 1100 East Loop 304, Zip 75835-1810; tel. 936/546-3891, **A**5 10 18 21 **F**3 15 29 32 40 45 59 65 66 75 79 81 85 87 93 96 97 102 107 110 111 115 119 127 131 133 135 146 149 154
Primary Contact: Ashley Solis, DON Interim Administrator
Web address: https://crockettmidcoasthospital.com/
Control: Corporation, Investor-owned (for-profit) Service: General medical and surgical

Staffed Beds: 15 **Admissions**: 127 **Census**: 1 **Outpatient Visits**: 21029 **Births**: 0 **Total Expense ($000)**: 17051 **Payroll Expense ($000)**: 7958 **Personnel**: 68

Hospital, Medicare Provider Number, Address, Telephone, Approval, Facility, and Physician Codes, Health Care System

★ American Hospital Association (AHA) membership ○ Healthcare Facilities Accreditation Program ⇑ Center for Improvement in Healthcare Quality Accreditation
☐ The Joint Commission accreditation ◇ DNV Healthcare Inc. accreditation △ Commission on Accreditation of Rehabilitation Facilities (CARF) accreditation

Hospitals, U.S. / TEXAS

CROSBYTON—Crosby County

CROSBYTON CLINIC HOSPITAL (670779), 710 West Main Street, Zip 79322–2143; tel. 806/675–2382, **A**10 **F**7 40 68 93
Primary Contact: Debra Miller, Administrator
CFO: Cherie Parkhill, Chief Financial Officer
CMO: Steve B Alley, M.D., Chief of Staff
CHR: Janie Cantu, Director Human Resources
CNO: Freda Bartlett, Director of Nursing
Web address: www.crosbytonclinichospital.com
Control: Other not–for–profit (including NFP Corporation)

Staffed Beds: 2 **Admissions**: 0 **Census**: 1 **Outpatient Visits**: 4437 **Births**: 0
Total Expense ($000): 4929 **Payroll Expense ($000)**: 1940 **Personnel**: 50

CUERO—Dewitt County

★ **CUERO REGIONAL HOSPITAL (450597)**, 2550 North Esplanade Street, Zip 77954–4716; tel. 361/275–6191, **A**3 10 **F**3 7 11 13 15 28 29 34 40 43 45 53 57 59 62 64 68 70 75 76 79 81 85 86 107 108 110 111 115 118 119 126 127 129 130 131 146 147 148 149 154 169 **P**6
Primary Contact: Lynn Falcone, Chief Executive Officer
CFO: Greg Pritchett, Chief Financial Officer
CMO: Michael McLeod, M.D., Chief Medical Officer
CIO: Ismelda Garza, Chief Information Officer
CHR: Wanda S Kolodziejcyk, Director Human Resources
CNO: Judith Krupala, R.N., Chief Nursing Officer
Web address: www.cuerohospital.org
Control: Hospital district or authority, Government, Nonfederal **Service**: General medical and surgical

Staffed Beds: 24 **Admissions**: 612 **Census**: 5 **Outpatient Visits**: 117345
Births: 172 **Total Expense ($000)**: 47354 **Payroll Expense ($000)**: 19204
Personnel: 248

CYPRESS—Harris County

☐ **LONE STAR BEHAVIORAL HEALTH (454118)**, 16303 Grant Road, Zip 77429–1253; tel. 281/516–6200, **A**1 10 **F**98 100 102 104 105 153 164
Primary Contact: Nathan Daniel. Ingram, Chief Executive Officer and Owner
Web address: www.lonestarbehavioralhealth.com
Control: Corporation, Investor–owned (for–profit) **Service**: Psychiatric

Staffed Beds: 24 **Admissions**: 545 **Census**: 15 **Outpatient Visits**: 36201
Births: 0 **Total Expense ($000)**: 6203 **Payroll Expense ($000)**: 3735
Personnel: 78

MEMORIAL HERMAN HOSPITAL CYPRESS See Memorial Herman Cypress

NORTH CYPRESS MEDICAL CENTER See HCA Houston Healthcare North Cypress

DALHART—Hartley County

COON MEMORIAL HOSPITAL (451331), 1411 Denver Avenue, Zip 79022–4809, Mailing Address: P.O. Box 2014, Zip 79022–6014; tel. 806/244–4571, **A**10 18 **F**3 7 10 11 13 30 34 35 40 43 45 50 53 57 59 62 63 64 65 68 69 71 76 77 79 81 82 83 85 93 97 103 107 114 119 125 127 131 133 143 144 146 148 167 **P**5
Primary Contact: Melissa Bundy, Chief Executive Officer
CFO: Donny Pettit, Chief Financial Officer
CMO: Randy Herring, M.D., Chief of Staff
CIO: Anthony Lovato, Director Information Technology
CHR: Dee Dawn McCormick, Director Personnel and Human Resources
Web address: www.dhchd.org/
Control: Hospital district or authority, Government, Nonfederal **Service**: General medical and surgical

Staffed Beds: 21 **Admissions**: 353 **Census**: 6 **Outpatient Visits**: 23341
Births: 181 **Total Expense ($000)**: 26751 **Payroll Expense ($000)**: 7827
Personnel: 109

DALLAS—Dallas County

⊞ **BAYLOR SCOTT & WHITE HEART & VASCULAR HOSPITAL–DALLAS (450851)**, 621 North Hall Street, Suite 150, Zip 75226–1339; tel. 214/820–0600, **A**1 5 10 **F**3 11 17 18 20 22 24 26 28 29 30 34 35 44 50 57 58 59 60 63 64 65 68 75 77 81 84 85 86 87 100 107 111 115 119 130 132 135 146 149 154 156
Primary Contact: Nancy Vish, Ph.D., FACHE, R.N., President and Chief Nursing Officer
CFO: Julius Wicke III, Vice President Finance and Hospital Financial Officer
CMO: Kevin Wheelan, M.D., Medical Director
CHR: Kim Krause, Director Human Resources
Web address: www.baylorhearthospital.com
Control: Partnership, Investor–owned (for–profit) **Service**: General medical and surgical

Staffed Beds: 53 **Admissions**: 2998 **Census**: 27 **Outpatient Visits**: 48756
Births: 0 **Total Expense ($000)**: 191188 **Payroll Expense ($000)**: 49527
Personnel: 460

⊞ **BAYLOR SCOTT & WHITE INSTITUTE FOR REHABILITATION – DALLAS (453036)**, 909 North Washington Avenue, Zip 75246–1520; tel. 214/820–9300, **A**1 3 10 **F**3 28 29 30 34 35 38 44 58 59 62 64 65 74 75 77 78 79 85 86 87 90 91 92 93 94 95 96 100 130 131 132 135 143 148 149 154 156 157 164 **S** Select Medical Corporation, Mechanicsburg, PA
Primary Contact: David Smith, Chief Executive Officer
CMO: Amy Wilson, M.D., Medical Director
CHR: Karen Hill, Director Human Resources
CNO: Beth Hudson, Chief Nursing Officer
Web address: https://www.bswrehab.com/locations-and-tours/bswir-dallas/
Control: Partnership, Investor–owned (for–profit) **Service**: Rehabilitation

Staffed Beds: 90 **Admissions**: 1606 **Census**: 82 **Outpatient Visits**: 23100
Births: 0 **Total Expense ($000)**: 100242 **Payroll Expense ($000)**: 61001
Personnel: 343

☐ **BAYLOR SCOTT & WHITE MEDICAL CENTER–UPTOWN (450422)**, 2727 East Lemmon Avenue, Zip 75204–2895; tel. 214/443–3000, **A**1 3 5 10 **F**29 34 40 79 81 85 107 111 114 126 130 **P**2 5 **S** United Surgical Partners International, Addison, TX
Primary Contact: Kyle Armstrong, President Central Region of BSW Health
CFO: Colene Fielding, Manager Business Office
CMO: Mark Armstrong, M.D., Medical Director
CIO: Javier Vela, Director Information Technology
CHR: Emalie Sanchez, Director Human Resources
CNO: Verette Neeb, R.N., MSN, Chief Nursing Officer
Web address: https://bayloruptown.com/
Control: Partnership, Investor–owned (for–profit) **Service**: Surgical

Staffed Beds: 24 **Admissions**: 433 **Census**: 3 **Outpatient Visits**: 9265
Births: 0 **Total Expense ($000)**: 61418 **Payroll Expense ($000)**: 14278
Personnel: 211

⊞ **BAYLOR UNIVERSITY MEDICAL CENTER (450021)**, 3500 Gaston Avenue, Zip 75246–2088; tel. 214/820–0111, (Includes A. WEBB ROBERTS HOSPITAL, 3500 Gaston Avenue, Dallas, Texas, Zip 75246–2017, tel. 361/500–0600; ERIK AND MARGARET JONSSON HOSPITAL, 3500 Gaston Avenue, Dallas, Texas, Zip 75246–2017, tel. 361/500–0600; GEORGE W. TRUETT MEMORIAL HOSPITAL, 3500 Gaston Avenue, Dallas, Texas, Zip 75246, tel. 361/500–0600; KARL AND ESTHER HOBLITZELLE MEMORIAL HOSPITAL, 3500 Gaston Avenue, Dallas, Texas, Zip 75246, tel. 361/500–0600) **A**1 2 3 5 8 10 **F**3 6 8 9 11 12 13 14 15 17 18 19 20 21 22 24 26 29 30 31 34 35 36 37 38 39 40 41 43 44 45 46 47 48 49 50 51 52 53 54 55 56 57 58 59 60 61 63 64 65 66 68 70 71 72 74 75 76 77 78 79 80 81 82 83 84 85 86 87 97 100 101 102 107 108 110 111 112 114 115 116 117 118 119 120 121 122 123 124 126 129 130 131 132 135 136 137 138 139 140 141 142 144 145 146 147 148 149 150 154 156 157 162 163 164 165 166 167 169 **S** Baylor Scott & White Health, Dallas, TX
Primary Contact: Kyle Armstrong, President Central Region of BSW Health
COO: Kyle Armstrong, Chief Operating Officer
CFO: Jay Whitfield, Chief Financial Officer
CMO: Brad Lembcke, M.D., Vice President Medical Staff Affairs
CHR: Julie Strittmatter, Director Human Resources
Web address: www.baylorhealth.com/PhysiciansLocations/Dallas/Pages/Default.aspx
Control: Other not–for–profit (including NFP Corporation) **Service**: General medical and surgical

Staffed Beds: 812 **Admissions**: 38479 **Census**: 696 **Outpatient Visits**: 221594 **Births**: 5248 **Total Expense ($000)**: 1291381 **Payroll Expense ($000)**: 401542 **Personnel**: 4029

✠ **CHILDREN'S MEDICAL CENTER DALLAS (453302)**, 1935 Medical District Drive, Zip 75235–7701; tel. 214/456–7000, **A**1 3 5 8 10 **F**3 5 7 8 11 12 17 18 19 20 21 22 23 24 25 26 27 28 29 30 31 32 34 35 36 38 39 40 41 43 44 45 46 48 49 50 51 54 55 57 58 59 60 61 62 64 65 66 68 72 74 75 77 78 79 81 82 84 85 86 87 88 89 91 92 93 94 96 97 100 101 102 104 105 107 108 111 115 116 117 118 119 126 127 129 130 131 132 134 136 137 138 139 141 142 143 145 146 148 152 153 154 155 164 165 167 169 **S** Children's Health, Dallas, TX
Primary Contact: Christopher J. Durovich, President and Chief Executive Officer
CFO: Richard P. Goode, Executive Vice President and Chief Financial Officer
CMO: W. Robert Morrow, M.D., Executive Vice President and Chief Medical Officer
CIO: Pamela Arora, Senior Vice President Information Systems
CHR: Kim Besse, Executive Vice President and Chief Human Resource Officer
CNO: Mary Stowe, Senior Vice President and Chief Nursing Officer
Web address: www.childrens.com
Control: Other not–for–profit (including NFP Corporation) **Service:** Children's general medical and surgical

Staffed Beds: 401 **Admissions:** 13341 **Census:** 278 **Outpatient Visits:** 492407 **Births:** 0 **Total Expense ($000):** 1683604 **Payroll Expense ($000):** 538837 **Personnel:** 5300

CITY HOSPITAL AT WHITE ROCK See White Rock Medical Center

☐ **DALLAS MEDICAL CENTER (450379)**, 7 Medical Parkway, Zip 75234–7823, Mailing Address: P.O. Box 819094, Zip 75381–9094; tel. 972/247–1000, **A**1 10 **F**3 8 12 15 18 20 22 26 28 29 30 34 40 43 44 45 46 49 50 59 60 64 68 70 74 75 77 79 81 82 84 85 86 93 97 107 108 110 111 114 115 116 119 130 131 141 142 144 146 147 148 149 154 167 **P**6 **S** Prime Healthcare, Ontario, CA
Primary Contact: Ruben Garza, Chief Executive Officer
CHR: Sheila K Richards, Human Resources Director
Web address: www.dallasmedcenter.com
Control: Corporation, Investor–owned (for–profit) **Service:** General medical and surgical

Staffed Beds: 80 **Admissions:** 3265 **Census:** 37 **Outpatient Visits:** 25645 **Births:** 0 **Total Expense ($000):** 61368 **Payroll Expense ($000):** 20551 **Personnel:** 372

✠ △ **DALLAS VA NORTH TEXAS HCS**, 4500 South Lancaster Road, Zip 75216–7167; tel. 214/742–8387, (Includes SAM RAYBURN MEMORIAL VETERANS CENTER, 1201 East Ninth Street, Bonham, Texas, Zip 75418–4091, tel. 903/583–2111; Elizabeth Dannel, Administrator, Operations Manager) (Nonreporting) **A**1 2 3 7 **S** Department of Veterans Affairs, Washington, DC
Primary Contact: Jason Cave, JD, Executive Medical Center Director
CFO: Alton McKinley, Chief Financial Officer
CIO: Lucy Rogers, Chief Information Resource Management Systems
Web address: www.northtexas.va.gov/
Control: Veterans Affairs, Government, federal **Service:** General medical and surgical

Staffed Beds: 467

✠ **ENCOMPASS HEALTH REHABILITATION HOSPITAL OF DALLAS (673043)**, 7930 Northaven Road, Zip 75230–3331; tel. 214/706–8200, **A**1 10 **F**3 29 90 95 96 130 148 149 164 **S** Encompass Health Corporation, Birmingham, AL
Primary Contact: Sharon Garrett, Chief Executive Officer
CFO: Elizabeth Robertson, Area Controller
CMO: Anna Freed–Sigurdsson, M.D., Medical Director
CHR: Lindsay Battles, Director Human Resources
CNO: Elysia Clay, Chief Nursing Officer
Web address: www.healthsouthdallas.com
Control: Corporation, Investor–owned (for–profit) **Service:** Rehabilitation

Staffed Beds: 60 **Admissions:** 1434 **Census:** 51 **Outpatient Visits:** 0 **Births:** 0 **Total Expense ($000):** 30704 **Payroll Expense ($000):** 15607 **Personnel:** 158

☐ **FIRST BAPTIST MEDICAL CENTER**, 8111 Meadow Road, Zip 75231; tel. 469/329–3700, **A**1 **F**3 12 29 40 45 64 70 79 81 82 85 86 87 107 114 119 130 149
Primary Contact: Aaron Miller, Chief Executive Officer/Chief Operating Officer
Web address: www.fbmcdallas.com
Control: Corporation, Investor–owned (for–profit) **Service:** Surgical

Staffed Beds: 18 **Admissions:** 326 **Census:** 4 **Outpatient Visits:** 2584 **Births:** 0 **Total Expense ($000):** 22257 **Payroll Expense ($000):** 7681 **Personnel:** 112

✠ **KINDRED HOSPITAL DALLAS CENTRAL (452108)**, 8050 Meadow Road, Zip 75231–3406; tel. 469/232–6500, **A**1 10 **F**1 3 29 60 75 77 85 87 96 107 114 148 **S** ScionHealth, Louisville, KY
Primary Contact: Abiola Anyebe, Market Chief Executive Officer
CFO: Robin Fry, CPA, Market Controller
CNO: Traci Brewer, R.N., Chief Clinical Officer
Web address: www.khdallascentral.com/
Control: Individual, Investor–owned (for–profit) **Service:** Acute long–term care hospital

Staffed Beds: 54 **Admissions:** 591 **Census:** 39 **Outpatient Visits:** 0 **Births:** 0 **Total Expense ($000):** 31715 **Payroll Expense ($000):** 13530 **Personnel:** 154

☐ **KPC PROMISE HOSPITAL OF DALLAS (452067)**, 7955 Harry Hines Boulevard, Zip 75235–3305; tel. 214/637–0000, (Nonreporting) **A**1 10 **S** KPC Healthcare, Inc., Santa Ana, CA
Primary Contact: Rachel Bailey, Chief Executive Officer
CFO: Diana B Smith, Chief Financial Officer
CMO: Gary E. Goff, M.D., Medical Director
CHR: Ginger Davenport, Director Human Resources
Web address: www.dallas.kpcph.com/
Control: Corporation, Investor–owned (for–profit) **Service:** Acute long–term care hospital

Staffed Beds: 66

✠ **MEDICAL CITY DALLAS (450647)**, 7777 Forest Lane, Zip 75230–2598; tel. 972/566–7000, (Includes MEDICAL CITY CHILDREN'S HOSPITAL, 7777 Forest Lane, Dallas, Texas, Zip 75230–2505, tel. 972/566–7000; Jay deVenny, FACHE, Chief Executive Officer; MEDICAL CITY HEART HOSPITAL, 11970 North Central Expressway, Dallas, Texas, Zip 75243–3768, tel. 972/940–8000; Josh Kempf, Chief Operating Officer; MEDICAL CITY SPINE HOSPITAL, 11970 North Central Expressway, Dallas, Texas, Zip 75243–3768, tel. 972/940–8000; Jay deVenny, FACHE, Chief Executive Officer) **A**1 2 3 5 10 **F**3 8 11 12 13 17 18 19 20 21 22 23 24 25 26 27 28 29 31 35 37 40 41 43 44 45 46 47 48 49 50 51 55 56 57 58 59 60 64 65 68 70 72 73 74 75 76 77 78 79 81 82 84 85 86 87 88 89 90 91 93 96 107 108 111 114 115 116 117 118 119 124 126 130 132 135 136 137 138 139 141 142 143 146 147 148 149 154 157 167 169 **S** HCA Healthcare, Nashville, TN
Primary Contact: Jay deVenny, FACHE, Chief Executive Officer
CFO: Mark Atchley, Vice President and Chief Financial Officer
CMO: Joseph Parra, M.D., Division Chief Medical Officer
CIO: Troy Sypien, Director Information Technology and Systems
CHR: Jenifer K Tertel, Director Human Resources
CNO: Joyce Soule, R.N., MSN, Chief Nursing Officer
Web address: https://medicalcityhealthcare.com/locations/medical-city-dallas/
Control: Corporation, Investor–owned (for–profit) **Service:** General medical and surgical

Staffed Beds: 896 **Admissions:** 34944 **Census:** 576 **Outpatient Visits:** 194699 **Births:** 5251 **Total Expense ($000):** 653024 **Payroll Expense ($000):** 308486 **Personnel:** 2760

✠ **MEDICAL CITY GREEN OAKS HOSPITAL (454094)**, 7808 Clodus Fields Drive, Zip 75251–2206; tel. 972/991–9504, **A**1 5 10 **F**4 5 29 30 68 87 98 99 101 102 103 104 105 130 132 135 149 152 153 154 160 162 164 165 **S** HCA Healthcare, Nashville, TN
Primary Contact: Krysla Karlix, Chief Executive Officer
COO: Pam Whitley, R.N., Chief Operating Officer and Chief Nursing Officer
CMO: Joel Holiner, M.D., Executive Medical Director
CIO: Richard Fontenault, Director Information Systems
CHR: Kevin Adkins, Director Human Resources
CNO: Pam Whitley, R.N., Chief Nursing Officer and Chief Operating Officer
Web address: https://medicalcitygreenoaks.com/
Control: Corporation, Investor–owned (for–profit) **Service:** Psychiatric

Staffed Beds: 124 **Admissions:** 5913 **Census:** 102 **Outpatient Visits:** 17855 **Births:** 0 **Total Expense ($000):** 42547 **Payroll Expense ($000):** 18571 **Personnel:** 224

Hospital, Medicare Provider Number, Address, Telephone, Approval, Facility, and Physician Codes, Health Care System

★ American Hospital Association (AHA) membership
☐ The Joint Commission accreditation
○ Healthcare Facilities Accreditation Program
◇ DNV Healthcare Inc. accreditation
⇑ Center for Improvement in Healthcare Quality Accreditation
△ Commission on Accreditation of Rehabilitation Facilities (CARF) accreditation

Hospitals, U.S. / TEXAS

◼ **METHODIST CHARLTON MEDICAL CENTER (450723)**, 3500 West Wheatland Road, Zip 75237–3460, Mailing Address: P.O. Box 225357, Zip 75222–5357; tel. 214/947–7777, **A**1 2 3 5 10 **F**3 11 13 15 18 20 22 24 28 29 30 31 34 35 40 43 44 45 46 47 49 50 53 58 59 60 64 66 68 70 74 76 78 79 81 82 84 85 86 87 97 107 108 110 111 114 115 118 119 126 130 131 132 146 148 156 167 **P**5 6 **S** Methodist Health System, Dallas, TX
Primary Contact: Michael K. Stewart, President
COO: Pamela Stoyanoff, President and Chief Operating Officer
CFO: Craig Bjerke, Executive Vice President and Chief Financial Officer
CIO: Pamela McNutt, Vice President Information Systems
CHR: Merridth Simpson, Director Human Resources
CNO: Teresa Kay Land, R.N., Chief Nursing Officer, Vice President Nursing
Web address: www.methodisthealthsystem.org/charlton
Control: Other not–for–profit (including NFP Corporation) **Service**: General medical and surgical

Staffed Beds: 291 **Admissions**: 12467 **Census**: 203 **Outpatient Visits**: 143428 **Births**: 1258 **Total Expense ($000)**: 322553 **Payroll Expense ($000)**: 140493 **Personnel**: 1357

◼ **METHODIST DALLAS MEDICAL CENTER (450051)**, 1441 North Beckley Avenue, Zip 75203–1201, Mailing Address: P.O. Box 655999, Zip 75265–5999; tel. 214/947–8181, **A**1 2 3 5 10 **F**3 11 12 13 15 18 20 22 24 26 28 29 30 31 34 35 37 40 43 45 46 47 48 49 50 53 54 58 59 60 64 66 68 70 72 74 76 78 79 81 82 84 85 87 92 93 97 107 108 110 111 114 115 118 119 126 130 132 138 139 142 146 148 149 150 156 167 169 **P**5 6 **S** Methodist Health System, Dallas, TX
Primary Contact: John E. Phillips, FACHE, President
COO: Pamela Stoyanoff, Executive Vice President and Chief Operating Officer
CFO: Randy Walker, Vice President
CMO: Leslie Cler, M.D., Chief Medical Officer
CIO: Pamela McNutt, Senior Vice President and Chief Information Officer
CHR: Jackie Middleton, Vice President Human Resources
Web address: www.methodisthealthsystem.org/Dallas
Control: Other not–for–profit (including NFP Corporation) **Service**: General medical and surgical

Staffed Beds: 375 **Admissions**: 14453 **Census**: 276 **Outpatient Visits**: 179037 **Births**: 2005 **Total Expense ($000)**: 583274 **Payroll Expense ($000)**: 217054 **Personnel**: 2005

△ **METHODIST REHABILITATION HOSPITAL (673031)**, 3020 West Wheatland Road, Zip 75237–3537; tel. 972/708–8600, **A**7 10 22 **F**3 29 50 90 91 95 96 130
Primary Contact: Shari Moore, Chief Executive Officer
CFO: Darline Kennemer, Controller
Web address: www.methodist-rehab.com
Control: Partnership, Investor–owned (for–profit) **Service**: Rehabilitation

Staffed Beds: 50 **Admissions**: 1319 **Census**: 43 **Outpatient Visits**: 0 **Births**: 0 **Total Expense ($000)**: 20971 **Payroll Expense ($000)**: 10730 **Personnel**: 143

☐ **NORTH CENTRAL SURGICAL CENTER (670049)**, 9301 North Central Expressway, Suite 100, Zip 75231–0802; tel. 214/265–2810, **A**1 3 10 **F**3 8 29 37 40 45 46 51 64 68 79 81 82 85 107 111 115 119 126 130 131 149 167 **P**2
Primary Contact: Leigh Patterson, Chief Executive Officer
COO: Leigh Patterson, Chief Operating Officer
CFO: Leigh Patterson, Chief Financial Officer
CMO: Stuart Simon, M.D., Medical Director
CNO: Trisha Fitzgerald, Chief Nursing Officer
Web address: www.northcentralsurgical.com
Control: Partnership, Investor–owned (for–profit) **Service**: Surgical

Staffed Beds: 23 **Admissions**: 911 **Census**: 6 **Outpatient Visits**: 20128 **Births**: 0 **Total Expense ($000)**: 99258 **Payroll Expense ($000)**: 20862 **Personnel**: 274

☐ **PARKLAND HEALTH (450015)**, 2370 Victory Avenue, Zip 75219, Mailing Address: 5200 Harry Hines Boulevard, Zip 75235–7708; tel. 214/590–8000, **A**1 2 3 5 10 19 **F**3 5 8 9 11 16 17 18 20 22 24 26 28 29 30 31 33 34 35 36 37 38 39 40 43 44 45 46 47 48 49 50 51 54 55 56 57 58 59 60 61 62 64 65 66 68 70 71 72 74 75 76 77 78 79 81 82 84 85 86 87 90 91 92 93 94 96 97 98 100 101 102 104 107 108 109 110 111 112 113 114 115 116 117 118 119 120 121 122 123 124 126 127 129 130 131 132 135 138 141 144 145 146 147 148 149 150 153 154 156 157 160 161 162 163 164 165 167 168 169
Primary Contact: Fred Cerise, M.D., Chief Executive Officer
COO: Edmundo Castañeda, Executive Vice President and Chief Operating Officer
CFO: Richard Humphrey, Executive Vice President and Chief Financial Officer
CIO: Joseph Longo, Chief Information Officer
CHR: Corey D. Jackson, Executive Vice President and Chief Talent Officer
Web address: https://www.parklandhealth.org/home
Control: Hospital district or authority, Government, Nonfederal **Service**: General medical and surgical

Staffed Beds: 841 **Admissions**: 41903 **Census**: 653 **Outpatient Visits**: 1441991 **Births**: 13072 **Total Expense ($000)**: 2703037 **Payroll Expense ($000)**: 1211295 **Personnel**: 13204

◼ **SCOTTISH RITE FOR CHILDREN (453314)**, 2222 Welborn Street, Zip 75219–3924; tel. 214/559–5000, **A**1 3 5 10 **F**3 8 9 11 29 32 34 35 39 50 53 54 57 58 59 64 68 74 75 77 79 81 82 85 86 87 89 90 92 93 94 107 111 115 119 130 131 132 146 148 149 154 157 164 **P**6
Primary Contact: Robert L. Walker, FACHE, President and Chief Executive Officer
CFO: William R Huston, Senior Vice President and Chief Financial Officer
CMO: Daniel J Sucato, M.D., MS, Chief of Staff
CIO: Les Clonch, Chief Information Officer
CHR: Connie Wright, Vice President Human Resources
CNO: Debbie A Sayles, R.N., Vice President and Chief Nursing Officer
Web address: https://scottishriteforchildren.org/
Control: Other not–for–profit (including NFP Corporation) **Service**: Children's orthopedic

Staffed Beds: 52 **Admissions**: 514 **Census**: 10 **Outpatient Visits**: 84201 **Births**: 0 **Total Expense ($000)**: 224185 **Payroll Expense ($000)**: 104456 **Personnel**: 862

◼ △ **TEXAS HEALTH PRESBYTERIAN HOSPITAL DALLAS (450462)**, 8200 Walnut Hill Lane, Zip 75231–4426; tel. 214/345–6789, **A**1 2 3 5 7 10 **F**3 5 12 13 15 17 18 20 22 24 26 28 29 30 31 34 35 37 38 39 40 43 44 45 46 47 49 50 51 55 56 57 58 59 60 61 64 65 66 68 69 70 72 73 74 75 76 77 78 79 81 84 85 86 87 90 92 93 96 97 98 100 101 102 104 105 107 108 110 111 112 114 115 118 119 126 132 135 141 143 146 148 149 152 153 154 156 157 160 161 162 164 167 169 **S** Texas Health Resources, Arlington, TX
Primary Contact: Christopher York, FACHE, President
CFO: Brian Craft, Group Finance Officer
CMO: Aurora Estevez, M.D., Chief Medical Officer
CIO: Tammy Phillips, Director, Information Systems
CHR: Stacy Miller, Entity Human Resources Officer
Web address: https://www.texashealth.org/Locations/Texas-Health-Dallas
Control: Other not–for–profit (including NFP Corporation) **Service**: General medical and surgical

Staffed Beds: 595 **Admissions**: 26519 **Census**: 389 **Outpatient Visits**: 108184 **Births**: 4058 **Total Expense ($000)**: 761499 **Payroll Expense ($000)**: 257562 **Personnel**: 2631

TEXAS INSTITUTE FOR SURGERY AT TEXAS HEALTH PRESBYTERIAN DALLAS (450889), 7115 Greenville Avenue, Suite 100, Zip 75231–5100; tel. 214/647–5300, **A**10 22 **F**40 51 64 79 81 82 107 114 115 119
Primary Contact: John S. Croley, Chief Executive Officer and Chief Financial Officer
CFO: John S. Croley, Chief Executive Officer and Chief Financial Officer
CMO: Presley Mock, M.D., Chief of Staff
CHR: Jennifer C. Levy, Director Human Resources
CNO: Tammy Jarvis, Vice President Clinical Services and Chief Nursing Officer
Web address: www.texasinstituteforsurgery.com
Control: Partnership, Investor–owned (for–profit) **Service**: General medical and surgical

Staffed Beds: 9 **Admissions**: 317 **Census**: 2 **Outpatient Visits**: 7600 **Births**: 0 **Total Expense ($000)**: 61308 **Payroll Expense ($000)**: 14635 **Personnel**: 180

TEXAS SCOTTISH RITE HOSPITAL FOR CHILDREN See Scottish Rite For Children

◼ △ **UNIVERSITY OF TEXAS SOUTHWESTERN MEDICAL CENTER (450044)**, 5323 Harry Hines Boulevard, Zip 75390–9265; tel. 214/648–3111, (Includes UNIVERSITY OF TEXAS SOUTHWESTERN MEDICAL CENTER – ZALE LIPSHY, 5151 Harry Hines Boulevard, Dallas, Zip 75390–9265, tel. 214/645–8300; Daniel Podolsky, M.D., President; WILLIAM P. CLEMENTS, JR. UNIVERSITY HOSPITAL, 6201 Harry Hines Boulevard, Dallas, Texas, Zip 75235–5202, tel. 214/633–5555; Daniel Podolsky, M.D., President) **A**1 2 3 5 7 8 10 19 **F**2 3 5 6 8 9 11 12 13 14 15 17 18 19 20 21 22 23 24 25 26 27 28 29 30 31 33 34 35 36 37 38 39 40 41 44 45 46 47 48 49 50 52 53 54 55 56 57 58 59 60 61 62 63 64 65 68 70 71 72 74 75 76 77 78 79 80 81 82 83 84 85 86 90 91 92 93 94 95 96 97 98 100 101 102 103 104 107 108 109 110 111 112 113 114 115 116 117 118 119 120 121 123 124 126 127 129 130 131 132 134 135 136 137 138 139 140 141 142 143 145 146 147 148 149 150 153 154 156 157 160 161 162 163 164 165 167 169 **P**6
Primary Contact: Daniel Podolsky, M.D., President and Professor, Department of Internal Medicine
COO: Becky McCulley, Chief Operations Officer
CIO: Marc E. Milstein, Vice President Information Resources
CHR: Ivan Thompson, Vice President, Chief Human Resource Officer
CNO: Susan Hernandez, R.N., Chief Nurse Executive
Web address: www.utsouthwestern.edu
Control: State, Government, Nonfederal **Service**: General medical and surgical

Staffed Beds: 825 **Admissions**: 32528 **Census**: 621 **Outpatient Visits**: 737332 **Births**: 2226 **Total Expense ($000)**: 2349656 **Payroll Expense ($000)**: 922595 **Personnel**: 10182

VETERANS AFFAIRS NORTH TEXAS HEALTH CARE SYSTEM See Dallas VA North Texas HCS

Hospitals, U.S. / TEXAS

☒ **WHITE ROCK MEDICAL CENTER (450678)**, 9440 Poppy Drive, Zip 75218-3694; tel. 214/324-6100, **A**1 10 **F**3 8 12 17 18 20 22 24 26 29 30 34 35 40 42 45 47 49 50 51 53 56 57 59 64 74 75 77 78 79 81 85 93 107 108 110 111 114 115 119 120 124 126 129 130 131 135 167 **S** Pipeline Health, El Segundo, CA
Primary Contact: Mirza N. Baig, M.D., Ph.D., Chief Executive Officer
CFO: Lana Adams, Chief Financial Officer
CMO: John Meyers, M.D., Chief Medical Officer
CNO: Jenny Humpal, Chief Nursing Officer
Web address: https://www.whiterockmedicalcenter.com/
Control: Partnership, Investor-owned (for-profit) **Service:** General medical and surgical

Staffed Beds: 65 **Admissions:** 4371 **Census:** 44 **Outpatient Visits:** 38049 **Births:** 499 **Total Expense ($000):** 103997 **Payroll Expense ($000):** 35877 **Personnel:** 257

ZALE LIPSHY UNIV HOSPITAL See University of Texas Southwestern Medical Center – Zale Lipshy

DECATUR—Wise County

☒ **MEDICAL CITY DECATUR (450271)**, 609 Medical Center Drive, Zip 76234-3836; tel. 940/627-5921, (Includes MEDICAL CITY DECATUR, 2000 South Fm 51, Decatur, Texas, Zip 76234-3702, tel. 940/627-5921; Jason Wren, FACHE, Chief Executive Officer) **A**1 2 10 **F**3 11 12 13 15 17 18 20 22 24 26 28 29 30 31 32 34 38 40 43 45 47 49 51 53 54 56 57 59 60 64 70 74 75 76 77 78 79 81 82 85 87 89 90 93 96 97 98 103 104 107 108 110 111 114 115 117 118 119 121 124 126 129 130 131 132 135 147 148 149 154 156 164 167 169 **S** HCA Healthcare, Nashville, TN
Primary Contact: Jason Wren, FACHE, President and Chief Executive Officer
COO: Leon Fuqua, Chief Operating Officer
CFO: Todd Scroggins, Chief Financial Officer
CMO: Jon W. Walker, M.D., Chief Medical Officer
CIO: Joe Arispe, Director Information Systems
CHR: Mike McQuiston, Administrative Director Human Resources
Web address: https://www.wisehealthsystem.com/
Control: Hospital district or authority, Government, Nonfederal **Service:** General medical and surgical

Staffed Beds: 133 **Admissions:** 4575 **Census:** 60 **Outpatient Visits:** 351659 **Births:** 436 **Total Expense ($000):** 274985 **Payroll Expense ($000):** 84641 **Personnel:** 1197

DEL RIO—Val Verde County

★ **VAL VERDE REGIONAL MEDICAL CENTER (450154)**, 801 Bedell Avenue, Zip 78840-4112, Mailing Address: 801 North Bedell Avenue, Zip 78840-4112; tel. 830/775-8566, **A**10 20 22 **F**3 7 11 13 15 17 18 20 22 28 29 30 34 35 40 43 46 48 54 56 57 59 63 64 73 75 76 77 79 81 82 84 85 87 89 93 96 101 104 107 108 110 111 114 119 127 129 130 131 132 133 146 147 149 153 154 155 156
Primary Contact: Jorge I. Jurado, Interim Chief Executive Officer
CFO: Eddie Read, Interim Chief Financial Officer
CMO: Mohamed Shafiu, M.D., Chief of Staff
CIO: Val King, Chief Information Officer
CNO: Kathy Fletcher, R.N., MSN, Interim Chief Nursing Officer
Web address: www.vvrmc.org
Control: Hospital district or authority, Government, Nonfederal **Service:** General medical and surgical

Staffed Beds: 80 **Admissions:** 2184 **Census:** 15 **Outpatient Visits:** 92080 **Births:** 776 **Total Expense ($000):** 85843 **Payroll Expense ($000):** 33469 **Personnel:** 677

DENISON—Grayson County

☐ **TEXOMA MEDICAL CENTER (450324)**, 5016 South US Highway 75, Zip 75020-4584, Mailing Address: P.O. Box 890, Zip 75021-0890; tel. 903/416-4000, (Includes TMC BEHAVIORAL HEALTH CENTER, 2601 North Cornerstone Drive, Sherman, Texas, Zip 75092-2551, tel. 903/416-3000; Harry Lemming, Interim Chief Executive Officer) **A**1 3 5 10 13 19 **F**3 11 12 13 15 17 18 20 22 24 28 29 30 31 34 35 37 40 42 43 45 46 47 48 49 50 53 54 56 57 59 62 64 70 72 74 75 76 77 78 79 80 81 82 85 86 87 89 90 91 93 96 98 99 100 101 102 103 104 107 108 110 111 115 118 119 126 129 130 144 145 146 147 148 149 150 153 156 164 167 169 **S** Universal Health Services, Inc., King of Prussia, PA
Primary Contact: Sean T. Dardeau, FACHE, Chief Executive Officer
CMO: Robert Sanders, M.D., Chief Medical Officer
CIO: Lisa Engle, Director Information Technology
CHR: Bill Heinzmann, Director Human Resources
CNO: Andrea Brenn, R.N., Chief Nursing Officer
Web address: www.texomamedicalcenter.net
Control: Corporation, Investor-owned (for-profit) **Service:** General medical and surgical

Staffed Beds: 414 **Admissions:** 22488 **Census:** 324 **Outpatient Visits:** 163210 **Births:** 1269 **Total Expense ($000):** 410630 **Payroll Expense ($000):** 176504 **Personnel:** 1957

DENTON—Denton County

☒ **BAYLOR SCOTT & WHITE THE HEART HOSPITAL DENTON (450893)**, 2801 South Mayhill Road, Zip 76208-5910, Mailing Address: 2891 South Mayhill Road, Zip 76208; tel. 469/814-3278, **A**1 3 10 **F**3 17 18 20 22 24 26 28 29 30 34 35 38 40 50 53 54 57 59 60 64 68 70 75 77 81 82 84 85 87 90 107 115 119 129 130 132 135 146 148 149 154 157 164
Primary Contact: Mark Valentine, President
COO: Brad D. McCall, Vice President Operations
CFO: Bryan Nichols, Chief Financial Officer
CMO: Trent Pettijohn, M.D., Esq, Chief Medical Officer
CHR: Anna Gemeny, Regional Director Human Resources
CNO: Susan K. Moats, R.N., Chief Nursing Officer
Web address: https://denton.thehearthospitalbaylor.com
Control: Partnership, Investor-owned (for-profit) **Service:** Heart

Staffed Beds: 31 **Admissions:** 1046 **Census:** 12 **Outpatient Visits:** 17397 **Births:** 0 **Total Expense ($000):** 60841 **Payroll Expense ($000):** 19635 **Personnel:** 177

☒ **DENTON REHAB (673036)**, 2620 Scripture Street, Zip 76201-4315; tel. 940/297-6500, **A**1 10 **F**3 29 34 35 44 58 64 68 74 75 77 79 82 86 87 90 91 93 95 96 130 131 132 135 148 149 157 **S** Select Medical Corporation, Mechanicsburg, PA
Primary Contact: Andrew Carlson, Chief Executive Officer
CFO: Doug Selsor, Director Finance
CHR: Patsy Martin, Manager Human Resources
CNO: Lee Ann Elliott, R.N., Director of Nursing
Web address: www.selectrehab-denton.com/
Control: Corporation, Investor-owned (for-profit) **Service:** Rehabilitation

Staffed Beds: 44 **Admissions:** 1043 **Census:** 35 **Outpatient Visits:** 10783 **Births:** 0 **Total Expense ($000):** 20349 **Payroll Expense ($000):** 11948 **Personnel:** 181

☐ **HORIZON MEDICAL CENTER, LLC (452111)**, 2813 South Mayhill Road, Zip 76208-5910; tel. 940/565-8580, **A**1 10 **F**1 3 8 29 64 75 81 90 148 **P**3
Primary Contact: Dennise Erwin, Chief Executive Officer
CNO: Tonia Torregrossa, Chief Nursing Officer
Web address: https://www.horizonmedcenter.com/
Control: Partnership, Investor-owned (for-profit) **Service:** Acute long-term care hospital

Staffed Beds: 32 **Admissions:** 234 **Census:** 8 **Outpatient Visits:** 7924 **Births:** 0 **Total Expense ($000):** 48917 **Payroll Expense ($000):** 8751 **Personnel:** 130

Hospitals, U.S. / TEXAS

☐ **MAYHILL HOSPITAL (670010)**, 2809 South Mayhill Road, Zip 76208–5910; tel. 940/239–3000, **A**1 10 **F**3 4 5 29 30 40 44 56 57 59 64 86 87 98 100 101 102 103 104 105 130 135 152 153 154 164 **S** Universal Health Services, Inc., King of Prussia, PA
Primary Contact: Holly Doherty, Chief Executive Officer
CFO: Emmy Adams, Chief Financial Officer
CMO: Asad Islam, M.D., Chief Medical Officer
CIO: Kyle Murphy, Director Information Technology
CHR: Patricia Gloria–Barraza, Coordinator Human Resources
Web address: www.mayhillhospital.com
Control: Partnership, Investor–owned (for–profit) **Service**: Psychiatric

Staffed Beds: 59 **Admissions**: 1711 **Census**: 44 **Outpatient Visits**: 937
Births: 0 **Total Expense ($000)**: 15259 **Payroll Expense ($000)**: 8470
Personnel: 143

✠ **MEDICAL CITY DENTON (450634)**, 3535 South I–35 East, Zip 76210; tel. 940/384–3535, (Includes MEDICAL CITY ARGYLE, 7218 Crawford RD, Argyle, Texas, Zip 76226–2579, 7218 Crawford Road, Zip 76226, tel. 940/293–2885; Jason Wren, FACHE, President and Chief Executive Officer) **A**1 3 10 **F**3 12 15 18 20 22 24 26 28 29 30 34 35 40 41 42 43 45 46 47 49 50 57 64 70 74 75 77 78 79 80 81 82 84 85 86 87 93 107 108 110 111 114 115 118 119 126 130 132 146 148 149 154 167 **S** HCA Healthcare, Nashville, TN
Primary Contact: Steven Edgar, FACHE, President and Chief Executive Officer
CFO: Todd Gibson, Chief Financial Officer
CMO: Howard Shaw, M.D., Chief Medical Officer
CHR: Stacey Bravo, Vice President Human Resources
CNO: Brandy H Farrer, R.N., Chief Nursing Officer
Web address: www.dentonregional.com
Control: Partnership, Investor–owned (for–profit) **Service**: General medical and surgical

Staffed Beds: 184 **Admissions**: 11937 **Census**: 151 **Outpatient Visits**: 92540 **Births**: 0 **Total Expense ($000)**: 204722 **Payroll Expense ($000)**: 82510 **Personnel**: 945

SELECT REHABILITATION HOSPITAL OF DENTON See Denton Rehab

✠ **TEXAS HEALTH PRESBYTERIAN HOSPITAL DENTON (450743)**, 3000 North I–35, Zip 76201–5119; tel. 940/898–7000, **A**1 3 10 **F**3 12 13 15 18 20 22 24 26 28 29 30 31 34 35 40 43 46 47 48 49 57 59 65 66 68 70 72 74 75 76 78 79 81 83 84 85 86 87 93 107 108 110 111 115 118 119 126 130 132 135 146 147 148 149 156 167 169 **S** Texas Health Resources, Arlington, TX
Primary Contact: Jeff Reecer, FACHE, President
CFO: David B Meltzer, Chief Financial Officer
CMO: Timothy Harris, M.D., Chief Quality Officer
CIO: Melissa Smart, Communication ad Public Relations Specialist
CHR: Kathy Hardcastle, Director Human Resources
CNO: Deborah Bostic, R.N., Chief Nursing Officer
Web address: www.dentonhospital.com
Control: Other not–for–profit (including NFP Corporation) **Service**: General medical and surgical

Staffed Beds: 239 **Admissions**: 11530 **Census**: 136 **Outpatient Visits**: 70636 **Births**: 1761 **Total Expense ($000)**: 268689 **Payroll Expense ($000)**: 93773 **Personnel**: 900

✠ **UNIVERSITY BEHAVIORAL HEALTH OF DENTON (454104)**, 2026 West University Drive, Zip 76201–0644; tel. 940/320–8100, **A**1 10 **F**4 5 68 98 100 101 104 105 106 132 134 135 143 152 153 154 160 161 164 165 **S** Universal Health Services, Inc., King of Prussia, PA
Primary Contact: Matthew Bertagnole, Chief Executive Officer
CMO: Atique Khan, M.D., Medical Director
CIO: Marsh Smith, Manager Health Information
CHR: Dorie Atherton, Manager Human Resources
CNO: Vicki Stoker, Chief Nursing Officer
Web address: www.ubhdenton.com
Control: Partnership, Investor–owned (for–profit) **Service**: Psychiatric

Staffed Beds: 104 **Admissions**: 3158 **Census**: 57 **Outpatient Visits**: 6927
Births: 0 **Total Expense ($000)**: 27595 **Payroll Expense ($000)**: 12260
Personnel: 167

DENVER CITY—Yoakum County

★ **YOAKUM COUNTY HOSPITAL (451308)**, 412 Mustang Avenue, Zip 79323–2762, Mailing Address: P.O. Box 1130, Zip 79323–1130; tel. 806/592–2121, **A**10 18 **F**3 11 13 28 34 35 40 41 43 45 50 53 57 59 60 64 70 76 81 87 89 93 107 114 119 127 129 133 149 169 **P**6
Primary Contact: Collin McLarty, Chief Executive Officer
CFO: Suann Parrish, Chief Financial Officer
CMO: Dan Khan, M.D., Chief Medical Officer
CIO: Todd Carrillo, Chief Information Officer
CHR: Teresa Howard, Manager Human Resources
Web address: www.ych.us
Control: County, Government, Nonfederal **Service**: General medical and surgical

Staffed Beds: 22 **Admissions**: 425 **Census**: 4 **Outpatient Visits**: 48917
Births: 273 **Total Expense ($000)**: 32659 **Payroll Expense ($000)**: 10989
Personnel: 188

DESOTO—Dallas County

☐ **DALLAS BEHAVIORAL HEALTHCARE HOSPITAL (454126)**, 800 Kirnwood Drive, Zip 75115–2000; tel. 855/982–0897, **A**1 10 **F**5 29 56 87 98 99 100 101 103 104 105 130 152 153 154 **S** Signature Healthcare Services, Corona, CA
Primary Contact: Matthew Matusiak, Chief Executive Officer
CFO: Nabil Zaiour, Chief Financial Officer
CMO: Rahim Haqqani, M.D., Medical Director
CHR: Henry In, Director Human Resources
CNO: Susie Edler, R.N., Chief Nursing Officer
Web address: www.dallasbehavioral.com
Control: Individual, Investor–owned (for–profit) **Service**: Psychiatric

Staffed Beds: 116 **Admissions**: 3365 **Census**: 77 **Outpatient Visits**: 5521
Births: 0 **Total Expense ($000)**: 25910 **Payroll Expense ($000)**: 13647
Personnel: 204

☐ **HICKORY TRAIL HOSPITAL (454065)**, 2000 Old Hickory Trail, Zip 75115–2242; tel. 972/298–7323, **A**1 10 **F**3 5 29 38 98 100 101 103 105 130 152 153 154 164 **S** Universal Health Services, Inc., King of Prussia, PA
Primary Contact: Jeff Baker, Chief Executive Officer
CFO: Terri Logsdon, Chief Financial Officer
CMO: Manoochehr Khatami, M.D., Medical Director
CHR: Sarah Warren, Coordinator Human Resources
Web address: www.hickorytrail.com
Control: Corporation, Investor–owned (for–profit) **Service**: Psychiatric

Staffed Beds: 58 **Admissions**: 2856 **Census**: 64 **Outpatient Visits**: 5945
Births: 0 **Total Expense ($000)**: 22094 **Payroll Expense ($000)**: 12456
Personnel: 162

★ **SELECT SPECIALTY HOSPITAL – DALLAS DOWNTOWN (452119)**, 2700 Walker Way, Zip 75115–2088; tel. 469/801–4500, **A**10 **F**1 3 29 74 77 85 86 87 91 96 148 **S** Select Medical Corporation, Mechanicsburg, PA
Primary Contact: Tremayne Myles, Chief Executive Officer
Web address: https://www.selectspecialtyhospitals.com/locations-and-tours/tx/dallas/dallas-downtown/
Control: Corporation, Investor–owned (for–profit) **Service**: Acute long–term care hospital

Staffed Beds: 40 **Admissions**: 235 **Census**: 23 **Outpatient Visits**: 0
Births: 0 **Total Expense ($000)**: 19890 **Payroll Expense ($000)**: 8469
Personnel: 128

DIMMITT—Castro County

PLAINS MEMORIAL HOSPITAL (451350), 310 West Halsell Street, Zip 79027–1846, Mailing Address: P.O. Box 278, Zip 79027–0278; tel. 806/647–2191, **A**10 18 **F**3 7 11 32 34 35 40 43 53 57 59 64 65 69 74 75 77 85 86 87 93 97 107 114 115 119 127 130 133 135 149 154 156
Primary Contact: Elisha Rosier, Chief Executive Officer
CFO: Terri Martinez, Chief Financial Officer
CMO: Gary R Hardee, M.D., Medical Director
CIO: Terry Young, Chief Information Officer
CHR: Debbie Underwood, Manager Human Resources
CNO: Renee Castillo, Chief Nursing Officer
Web address: www.plainsmemorial.com
Control: Hospital district or authority, Government, Nonfederal **Service**: General medical and surgical

Staffed Beds: 17 **Admissions**: 160 **Census**: 3 **Outpatient Visits**: 13699
Births: 0 **Total Expense ($000)**: 13855 **Payroll Expense ($000)**: 5374
Personnel: 94

Hospitals, U.S. / TEXAS

DUMAS—Moore County

MOORE COUNTY HOSPITAL DISTRICT (451386), 224 East Second Street, Zip 79029–3808; tel. 806/935–7171, **A**10 18 22 **F**3 7 11 13 15 28 34 35 40 43 46 50 51 57 59 62 63 70 75 79 81 85 86 91 93 107 110 111 115 119 127 130 131 132 133 135 146 147 148 154 167
Primary Contact: Jeff Turner, FACHE, Chief Executive Officer
COO: Ashleigh Wiswell, Chief Operations Officer
CFO: John E. Bailey, Chief Financial Officer
CHR: Kathie Fuston, Director Human Resources
CNO: Ronda Crow, Chief Nursing Officer
Web address: www.mchd.net
Control: Hospital district or authority, Government, Nonfederal **Service**: General medical and surgical

> **Staffed Beds**: 19 **Admissions**: 1172 **Census**: 6 **Outpatient Visits**: 31573
> **Births**: 192 **Total Expense ($000)**: 55435 **Payroll Expense ($000)**: 26324
> **Personnel**: 336

EAGLE LAKE—Colorado County

RICE MEDICAL CENTER (451312), 600 South Austin Road, Zip 77434–3298, Mailing Address: P.O. Box 277, Zip 77434–0277; tel. 979/234–5571, **A**10 18 **F**3 11 15 29 34 35 40 43 56 59 64 65 75 77 79 80 81 85 101 104 107 111 114 119 127 133 153 154 156 **P**6
Primary Contact: Kurt Sunderman, Chief Executive Officer
CMO: Russell Thomas, M.D., Chief of Staff
CHR: Velma Loya, Administrative Human Resource Coordinator
CNO: Susan Hernandez, R.N., Chief Nursing Officer
Web address: https://ricemedicalcenter.net/
Control: Other not-for-profit (including NFP Corporation) **Service**: General medical and surgical

> **Staffed Beds**: 15 **Admissions**: 216 **Census**: 3 **Outpatient Visits**: 28115
> **Births**: 0 **Total Expense ($000)**: 18208 **Payroll Expense ($000)**: 4384
> **Personnel**: 101

EAGLE PASS—Maverick County

☐ **FORT DUNCAN REGIONAL MEDICAL CENTER (450092)**, 3333 North Foster Maldonado Boulevard, Zip 78852–5893; tel. 830/773–5321, **A**1 10 20 **F**3 11 12 13 15 18 20 22 29 34 35 40 43 45 46 51 57 59 60 70 76 79 81 85 87 89 90 93 96 107 111 114 115 119 130 146 147 148 149 156 169 **S** Universal Health Services, Inc., King of Prussia, PA
Primary Contact: Eladio Montalvo, Chief Executive Officer
COO: Alan Gonzalez, Chief Operating Officer
CFO: Joel Morales, Chief Financial Officer
CMO: Ruben de los Santos, M.D., Chief Medical Officer
CIO: Jose Elias, Director Information Technology
CHR: Daisy Rodriquez, Director Human Resources
CNO: Scott Lethi, R.N., FACHE, Chief Nursing Officer
Web address: www.fortduncanmedicalcenter.com
Control: Partnership, Investor–owned (for-profit) **Service**: General medical and surgical

> **Staffed Beds**: 60 **Admissions**: 4109 **Census**: 39 **Outpatient Visits**: 52720
> **Births**: 1037 **Total Expense ($000)**: 60017 **Payroll Expense ($000)**: 26078
> **Personnel**: 319

EASTLAND—Eastland County

EASTLAND MEMORIAL HOSPITAL (450411), 304 South Daugherty Street, Zip 76448–2609, Mailing Address: P.O. Box 897, Zip 76448–0897; tel. 254/629–2601, **A**10 20 **F**7 11 12 15 28 29 30 34 35 40 43 45 50 53 57 59 60 64 68 77 81 85 86 87 93 107 110 114 115 127 130 131 133 146 148 154
Primary Contact: Joe Wright, Chief Executive Officer
CFO: Jamie Hayden, Chief Financial Officer
CHR: Leisha Hodges, Human Resources Officer
Web address: www.eastlandmemorial.com
Control: Hospital district or authority, Government, Nonfederal **Service**: General medical and surgical

> **Staffed Beds**: 19 **Admissions**: 684 **Census**: 6 **Outpatient Visits**: 44245
> **Births**: 0 **Total Expense ($000)**: 21715 **Payroll Expense ($000)**: 8560
> **Personnel**: 146

EDEN—Concho County

★ **CONCHO COUNTY HOSPITAL (451325)**, 614 Eaker Street, Zip 76837–0359, Mailing Address: P.O. Box 987, Zip 76837–0987; tel. 325/869–5911, **A**10 18 **F**3 40 43 50 57 59 77 87 107 115 127 129 133 146
Primary Contact: Melissa Wilson, Administrator and Chief Executive Officer
CFO: Jerry Lynn Pickett, Interim Chief Financial Officer
CNO: Toby Lehn, Director of Nurses
Web address: https://www.conchocounty.hospital/
Control: Hospital district or authority, Government, Nonfederal **Service**: General medical and surgical

> **Staffed Beds**: 16 **Admissions**: 52 **Census**: 1 **Outpatient Visits**: 4663
> **Births**: 0 **Total Expense ($000)**: 11710 **Payroll Expense ($000)**: 3282
> **Personnel**: 55

EDINBURG—Hidalgo County

⊞ **CORNERSTONE REGIONAL HOSPITAL (450825)**, 2302 Cornerstone Boulevard, Zip 78539–8471; tel. 956/618–4444, **A**1 10 **F**3 8 29 34 35 37 39 40 45 46 47 57 59 68 74 79 81 82 85 87 111 119 126 **S** Universal Health Services, Inc., King of Prussia, PA
Primary Contact: Rance Ramsey, Chief Executive Officer
CFO: Janie Alvarez, Accounting Director
CMO: Omar Gomez, M.D., Chief of Staff
CHR: Erika Betancourt, Coordinator Human Resources
CNO: Roxanne Reyes, Director of Nursing
Web address: www.cornerstoneregional.com
Control: Partnership, Investor–owned (for–profit) **Service**: General medical and surgical

> **Staffed Beds**: 14 **Admissions**: 167 **Census**: 1 **Outpatient Visits**: 4567
> **Births**: 0 **Total Expense ($000)**: 25088 **Payroll Expense ($000)**: 6056
> **Personnel**: 132

☐ △ **DOCTOR'S HOSPITAL AT RENAISSANCE (450869)**, 5501 South McColl Road, Zip 78539–9152; tel. 956/362–7360, **A**1 2 3 5 7 8 10 **F**3 5 8 9 12 13 14 15 17 18 19 20 21 22 23 24 25 26 27 28 29 30 31 34 35 37 38 40 41 42 43 44 45 46 47 48 49 50 51 54 55 56 57 58 59 60 63 64 65 66 68 70 71 72 73 74 75 76 77 78 79 80 81 82 83 84 85 86 87 88 89 90 91 92 93 94 95 96 97 98 99 100 101 102 103 104 107 108 109 110 111 114 115 117 118 119 120 121 122 123 124 126 127 130 131 132 135 138 139 144 145 146 147 148 149 150 154 156 157 167 169 **P**1 3 6
Primary Contact: Manish Singh, M.D., Chief Executive Officer
COO: Marissa Castaneda, Chief Operating Officer and Director Marketing
Web address: www.dhr-rgv.com
Control: Partnership, Investor–owned (for-profit) **Service**: General medical and surgical

> **Staffed Beds**: 518 **Admissions**: 36438 **Census**: 400 **Outpatient Visits**: 555312 **Births**: 7892 **Total Expense ($000)**: 896091 **Payroll Expense ($000)**: 286076 **Personnel**: 6765

EDINBURG REGIONAL HOSPITAL See Edinburg Regional Medical Center

☐ **SOUTH TEXAS HEALTH SYSTEM (450119)**, 1400 West Trenton Road, Zip 78539–9105, Mailing Address: 1102 West Trenton Road, Zip 78539–9105; tel. 956/388–6000, (Includes EDINBURG CHILDREN'S HOSPITAL, 1400 West Trenton Road, Edinburg, Texas, Zip 78539, tel. 956/388–8000; EDINBURG REGIONAL MEDICAL CENTER, 1102 West Trenton Road, Edinburg, Texas, Zip 78539–6199, tel. 956/388–6000; Lance Ames, Interim Chief Executive Officer; MCALLEN HEART HOSPITAL, 1900 South D Street, McAllen, Texas, Zip 78503, tel. 956/994–2000; Dan Caldwell, Chief Executive Officer; SOUTH TEXAS BEHAVIORAL HEALTH CENTER, 2101 West Trenton Road, Edinburg, Texas, Zip 78539, tel. 956/388–1300; Sharon Pendlebury, Chief Executive Officer; SOUTH TEXAS HEALTH SYSTEM MCALLEN, 301 West Expressway 83, McAllen, Texas, Zip 78503–3045, tel. 956/632–4000) **A**1 3 5 10 19 **F**3 4 11 12 15 17 18 19 20 22 24 25 26 28 29 30 31 34 35 40 41 42 43 45 46 54 56 57 58 59 64 70 72 73 74 76 79 81 82 88 89 90 92 93 96 98 99 101 102 103 107 108 110 111 115 118 119 130 146 148 149 154 164 167 **S** Universal Health Services, Inc., King of Prussia, PA
Primary Contact: Lance Ames, Chief Executive Officer
CFO: Carlos Guajardo, Chief Financial Officer
CMO: Yuri Bermudez, M.D., Chief of Staff
CIO: Rosie L Mendiola–Balderas, Director Information Systems
CHR: Patricia Mcclelland, Director Human Resources
Web address: https://www.edinburgregional.com/
Control: Partnership, Investor–owned (for-profit) **Service**: General medical and surgical

> **Staffed Beds**: 919 **Admissions**: 34395 **Census**: 505 **Outpatient Visits**: 300873 **Births**: 2227 **Total Expense ($000)**: 572672 **Payroll Expense ($000)**: 219459 **Personnel**: 2924

Hospital, Medicare Provider Number, Address, Telephone, Approval, Facility, and Physician Codes, Health Care System

★ American Hospital Association (AHA) membership
☐ The Joint Commission accreditation
○ Healthcare Facilities Accreditation Program
◇ DNV Healthcare Inc. accreditation
⇑ Center for Improvement in Healthcare Quality Accreditation
△ Commission on Accreditation of Rehabilitation Facilities (CARF) accreditation

© 2025 AHA Guide

Hospitals, U.S. / TEXAS

EDNA—Jackson County

★ **JACKSON COUNTY HOSPITAL DISTRICT (451363)**, 1013 South Wells Street, Zip 77957-4098; tel. 361/782-7800, **A**10 18 22 **F**3 7 15 29 34 35 40 43 44 45 50 53 57 59 62 64 65 68 75 81 87 97 102 107 110 114 119 127 130 133 143 146 156 157 **P**8
Primary Contact: Lance Smiga, Chief Executive Officer, Chief Financial Officer
CFO: Lance Smiga, Chief Executive Officer, Chief Financial Officer
CMO: Francisco Ortiz, M.D., Chief of Staff
CIO: Jeff Prukop, Director Professional Services
CHR: Donna Coleman, Coordinator Human Resources
CNO: Tammy Zajicek, Director of Nursing
Web address: www.jchd.org
Control: Hospital district or authority, Government, Nonfederal **Service**: General medical and surgical

Staffed Beds: 17 **Admissions**: 155 **Census**: 3 **Outpatient Visits**: 47455 **Births**: 0 **Total Expense ($000)**: 26175 **Payroll Expense ($000)**: 10821 **Personnel**: 169

EL CAMPO—Wharton County

★ **EL CAMPO MEMORIAL HOSPITAL (450694)**, 303 Sandy Corner Road, Zip 77437-9535; tel. 979/543-6251, **A**10 20 **F**3 11 15 18 20 28 29 30 32 34 35 40 45 54 57 59 60 64 65 66 68 70 77 79 81 85 86 91 92 93 97 107 108 110 111 112 114 119 127 129 130 133 135 147 148 154 **P**6
Primary Contact: Brett Kirkham, Chief Executive Officer
CFO: David Mak, Chief Financial Officer
CMO: Thai Huynh, M.D., Chief of Medical Staff
CIO: Bill Eller, Director Information Technology
CHR: Ginger Andreas, Coordinator Personnel and Credentialing
CNO: Desiree Cernoch, Director of Nurses
Web address: www.ecmh.org
Control: Other not-for-profit (including NFP Corporation) **Service**: General medical and surgical

Staffed Beds: 29 **Admissions**: 824 **Census**: 9 **Outpatient Visits**: 137344 **Births**: 0 **Total Expense ($000)**: 50469 **Payroll Expense ($000)**: 21482 **Personnel**: 392

EL PASO—El Paso County

CHILDREN'S HOSPITAL AT PROVIDENCE See Providence Children's Hospital

COLUMBIA MEDICAL CENTER-EAST See Del Sol Medical Center

DEL SOL REHABILITATION HOSPITAL See Las Palmas Rehabilitation Hospital

☐ **EL PASO BEHAVIORAL HEALTH SYSTEM (454109)**, 1900 Denver Avenue, Zip 79902-3008; tel. 915/544-4000, **A**1 5 10 **F**3 4 5 29 34 56 57 75 86 87 98 99 100 101 102 103 104 105 130 135 149 150 152 153 154 164 **S** Universal Health Services, Inc., King of Prussia, PA
Primary Contact: Jennifer Castaneda, Interim Chief Executive Officer
CFO: Phillip Sosa, Chief Financial Officer
CMO: Arthur L. Ramirez, M.D., Medical Director
CIO: Victor Torres, Information Technology Specialist Administrator
CHR: Brenda Holguin, Manager Human Resources
CNO: Susan Brown, Chief Nursing Officer
Web address: www.ubhelpaso.com/
Control: Corporation, Investor-owned (for-profit) **Service**: Psychiatric

Staffed Beds: 166 **Admissions**: 6576 **Census**: 147 **Outpatient Visits**: 24072 **Births**: 0 **Total Expense ($000)**: 46367 **Payroll Expense ($000)**: 17262 **Personnel**: 258

☐ **EL PASO CHILDREN'S HOSPITAL (453313)**, 4845 Alameda Avenue, Zip 79905-2705; tel. 915/242-8614, **A**1 3 5 10 **F**3 19 27 29 30 31 32 34 35 38 39 40 41 44 45 48 49 50 57 58 59 61 64 65 68 72 73 74 75 78 79 81 82 85 86 87 88 89 93 96 99 104 108 111 119 130 132 146 148 149 150 154 156 **P**5
Primary Contact: Cindy Stout, R.N., President and Chief Executive Officer
CMO: Bradley Fuhrman, M.D., Physician in Chief
CIO: Janina Prada, Director Information Technology
CNO: Ranae M Thompson, R.N., MSN, Vice President & Chief Nursing Officer
Web address: www.elpasochildrens.org
Control: Other not-for-profit (including NFP Corporation) **Service**: Children's general medical and surgical

Staffed Beds: 73 **Admissions**: 4442 **Census**: 73 **Outpatient Visits**: 107300 **Births**: 0 **Total Expense ($000)**: 169604 **Payroll Expense ($000)**: 63489 **Personnel**: 794

EL PASO LTAC HOSPITAL (452122), 1221 North Cotton Street, 3rd Floor, Zip 79902-3015; tel. 915/546-5822, **A**10 22 **F**1 3 29 30 34 57 60 75 77 82 84 85 86 87 100 119 130 148
Primary Contact: Elias Velez, Chief Executive Officer
CFO: Eddie Martinez, Chief Financial Officer
Web address: https://el-paso-ltac-hospital.business.site/
Control: Partnership, Investor-owned (for-profit) **Service**: Acute long-term care hospital

Staffed Beds: 33 **Admissions**: 123 **Census**: 11 **Outpatient Visits**: 0 **Births**: 0 **Total Expense ($000)**: 7065 **Payroll Expense ($000)**: 4389 **Personnel**: 79

☐ **EL PASO PSYCHIATRIC CENTER (454100)**, 4615 Alameda Avenue, Zip 79905-2702; tel. 915/532-2202, **A**1 3 5 10 **F**29 98 103 130 135 149 163 **P**6 **S** Texas Department of State Health Services, Austin, TX
Primary Contact: Zulema Carrillo, Superintendent
CFO: David Osterhout, Assistant Superintendent and Chief Financial Officer
CNO: Raul D. Luna, Chief Nurse Executive
Web address: www.dshs.state.tx.us/mhhospitals/ElPasoPC/default.shtm
Control: State, Government, Nonfederal **Service**: Psychiatric

Staffed Beds: 74 **Admissions**: 505 **Census**: 52 **Outpatient Visits**: 0 **Births**: 0 **Total Expense ($000)**: 19039 **Payroll Expense ($000)**: 13463 **Personnel**: 266

EVEREST REHABILITATION HOSPITAL OF EL PASO, 2230 Joe Battle Boulevard, Zip 79938; tel. 915/910-6042, (Data for 236 days) **A**22 **F**3 29 44 60 74 77 79 82 86 87 90 91 92 96 101 119 148 149 164 **S** Everest Rehabilitation Hospitals, LLC, Dallas, TX
Primary Contact: Jose Huerta, Chief Executive Officer
Web address: https://everestrehab.com/hospitals/el-paso-tx/
Control: Corporation, Investor-owned (for-profit) **Service**: Rehabilitation

Staffed Beds: 36 **Admissions**: 112 **Census**: 3 **Outpatient Visits**: 0 **Births**: 0 **Total Expense ($000)**: 1017 **Payroll Expense ($000)**: 716 **Personnel**: 27

✠ **KINDRED HOSPITAL EL PASO (452079)**, 1740 Curie Drive, Zip 79902-2901; tel. 915/351-9044, **A**1 10 **F**1 3 29 45 46 60 70 75 77 85 91 148 149 150 154 **S** ScionHealth, Louisville, KY
Primary Contact: America Jones, R.N., Chief Executive Officer
CFO: Melissa Campa, Controller
CMO: Edward Juarez, M.D., Chief Medical Officer
CHR: Laura Anchondo, Administrator Human Resources
Web address: www.khelpaso.com
Control: Corporation, Investor-owned (for-profit) **Service**: Acute long-term care hospital

Staffed Beds: 42 **Admissions**: 417 **Census**: 30 **Outpatient Visits**: 0 **Births**: 0 **Total Expense ($000)**: 19673 **Payroll Expense ($000)**: 10392 **Personnel**: 113

✠ △ **LAS PALMAS MEDICAL CENTER (450107)**, 1801 North Oregon Street, Zip 79902-3591; tel. 915/521-1200, (Includes DEL SOL MEDICAL CENTER, 10301 Gateway Boulevard West, El Paso, Texas, Zip 79925-7798, tel. 915/595-9000; Art Garza, FACHE, Chief Executive Officer; HIGHLANDS REHABILITATION HOSPITAL, 1395 George Dieter Drive, El Paso, Texas, Zip 79936-7410, tel. 915/298-7222; Diana Schultz, Chief Executive Officer; LAS PALMAS REHABILITATION HOSPITAL, 300 Waymore Drive, El Paso, Texas, Zip 79902-1628, tel. 915/577-2600; Don Karl, Interim Chief Executive Officer) **A**1 3 5 7 10 **F**3 12 13 15 17 18 20 22 24 26 29 30 31 33 35 37 40 42 43 45 46 47 48 49 50 51 54 55 56 59 60 64 67 68 70 72 73 74 75 76 77 79 80 81 84 85 87 88 89 90 92 93 96 97 107 108 109 110 111 112 114 116 117 118 119 121 122 124 126 130 134 143 144 145 146 147 148 157 167 169 **P**3 6 **S** HCA Healthcare, Nashville, TN
Primary Contact: Don Karl, Chief Executive Officer
COO: Don Karl, Chief Operating Officer
CMO: Oscar Vega, M.D., Chief Medical Officer
CNO: Christine Walker, Chief Nursing Officer
Web address: www.laspalmashealth.com
Control: Partnership, Investor-owned (for-profit) **Service**: General medical and surgical

Staffed Beds: 585 **Admissions**: 30406 **Census**: 403 **Outpatient Visits**: 197087 **Births**: 5698 **Total Expense ($000)**: 363568 **Payroll Expense ($000)**: 162545 **Personnel**: 2093

Hospitals, U.S. / TEXAS

★ **PAM HEALTH REHABILITATION HOSPITAL OF EL PASO (673075)**, 1600 East Cliff Drive, Zip 79902–5130; tel. 915/975–8630, **A**22 **F**3 29 60 64 74 75 77 79 90 91 93 96 143 148 149 156 164 **P**5 **S** PAM Health, Enola, PA
Primary Contact: Jarrod McGee, Chief Executive Officer
Web address: https://pamhealth.com/index.php/facilities/find-facility/rehabilitation-hospitals/pam-health-rehabilitation-hospital-el-paso
Control: Corporation, Investor–owned (for–profit) **Service**: Rehabilitation

Staffed Beds: 42 **Admissions**: 817 **Census**: 15 **Outpatient Visits**: 0 **Births**: 0 **Total Expense ($000)**: 17291 **Payroll Expense ($000)**: 8431 **Personnel**: 154

☐ **PREMIER SPECIALTY HOSPITAL OF EL PASO (452035)**, 2311 North Oregon Street, 5th Floor, Zip 79902–3216; tel. 915/545–1823, (Nonreporting) **A**1 10
Primary Contact: Frank Rivera, Chief Executive Officer
COO: Elena Pino, Chief Operating Officer and Chief Nursing Officer
CFO: Priscilla Carter, Chief Financial Officer
Web address: www.specialtyhospitalmesahills.com/
Control: Corporation, Investor–owned (for–profit) **Service**: Acute long–term care hospital

Staffed Beds: 32

⊞ **RIO VISTA BEHAVIORAL HEALTH (454146)**, 1390 Northwestern Drive, Zip 79912–8003; tel. 915/209–4513, **A**1 3 5 10 **F**5 98 99 103 104 105 152 153 154 160 **S** Acadia Healthcare Company, Inc., Franklin, TN
Primary Contact: Marie Alvarez, Chief Executive Officer
Web address: https://www.riovistabehavioral.com/
Control: Corporation, Investor–owned (for–profit) **Service**: Psychiatric

Staffed Beds: 132 **Admissions**: 2806 **Census**: 93 **Outpatient Visits**: 16033 **Births**: 0 **Total Expense ($000)**: 22925 **Payroll Expense ($000)**: 12160 **Personnel**: 174

⊞ **THE HOSPITALS OF PROVIDENCE EAST CAMPUS – TENET HEALTHCARE (670047)**, 3280 Joe Battle Boulevard, Zip 79938–2622; tel. 915/832–2000, **A**1 10 **F**3 12 13 15 18 20 22 26 28 29 30 31 34 35 39 40 41 42 43 45 49 50 51 57 58 59 60 64 70 72 73 74 75 76 77 78 79 81 84 85 86 87 93 107 108 110 111 114 115 119 126 130 134 135 146 147 148 149 154 156 164 166 167 **S** TENET Healthcare Corporation, Dallas, TX
Primary Contact: Tasha Hopper, MSN, R.N., FACHE, Chief Executive Officer
Web address: www.sphn.com
Control: Partnership, Investor–owned (for–profit) **Service**: General medical and surgical

Staffed Beds: 218 **Admissions**: 14080 **Census**: 190 **Outpatient Visits**: 112758 **Births**: 2181 **Total Expense ($000)**: 255410 **Payroll Expense ($000)**: 89788 **Personnel**: 842

⊞ **THE HOSPITALS OF PROVIDENCE MEMORIAL CAMPUS – TENET HEALTHCARE (450002)**, 2001 North Oregon Street, Zip 79902–3368; tel. 915/577–6625, (Includes PROVIDENCE CHILDREN'S HOSPITAL, 2001 North Oregon Street, El Paso, Texas, Zip 79902–3320, tel. 915/577–7746) **A**1 2 3 10 **F**3 8 11 12 13 14 15 18 19 20 21 22 23 26 29 30 31 32 34 35 37 40 41 42 43 45 46 48 49 50 54 55 56 57 58 59 60 64 65 70 71 72 74 75 76 77 78 79 80 81 84 85 86 87 88 89 93 97 98 100 101 102 103 105 107 110 111 115 119 126 130 132 134 141 143 145 146 147 148 149 150 154 157 169 **P**5 **S** TENET Healthcare Corporation, Dallas, TX
Primary Contact: Rob J. Anderson, Chief Executive Officer
COO: Roddex Barlow, Chief Operating Officer
CFO: Charles Handley, Chief Financial Officer
CIO: Vince Randazzo, Texas Regional Director Information Systems, Tenet Account
CHR: Stephanie S. Talley, Market Chief Human Resource Officer
CNO: Mark Phillips, Chief Nursing Officer
Web address: www.thehospitalsofprovidence.com
Control: Partnership, Investor–owned (for–profit) **Service**: General medical and surgical

Staffed Beds: 289 **Admissions**: 12114 **Census**: 150 **Outpatient Visits**: 85784 **Births**: 2131 **Total Expense ($000)**: 241120 **Payroll Expense ($000)**: 79730 **Personnel**: 927

⊞ △ **THE HOSPITALS OF PROVIDENCE SIERRA CAMPUS – TENET HEALTHCARE (450668)**, 1625 Medical Center Drive, Zip 79902–5005; tel. 915/747–4000, (Includes THE HOSPITALS OF PROVIDENCE SPECIALTY CAMPUS – TENET HEALTHCARE, 1755 Curie Drive, El Paso, Texas, Zip 79902–2919, tel. 915/747–1311; Erik Cazares, Chief Executive Officer) **A**1 5 7 11 **F**11 15 18 20 22 24 26 28 29 34 40 43 46 47 49 50 54 57 59 60 61 64 70 74 77 78 79 80 81 85 90 92 93 96 107 108 109 110 111 114 115 119 126 130 132 146 148 149 154 157 **S** TENET Healthcare Corporation, Dallas, TX
Primary Contact: Tasha Hopper, MSN, R.N., FACHE, Chief Executive Officer
COO: Sereka Barlow, Chief Operating Officer
CFO: Charles Handley, Chief Financial Officer
CIO: Charlie Ortega, Administrative Director Information Systems
CHR: Stephanie S. Talley, Chief Human Resource Officer
CNO: Carlos Castillo, R.N., Chief Nursing Officer
Web address: www.thehospitalsofprovidence.com
Control: Partnership, Investor–owned (for–profit) **Service**: General medical and surgical

Staffed Beds: 306 **Admissions**: 8260 **Census**: 132 **Outpatient Visits**: 59701 **Births**: 0 **Total Expense ($000)**: 230466 **Payroll Expense ($000)**: 67665 **Personnel**: 674

⊞ **THE HOSPITALS OF PROVIDENCE TRANSMOUNTAIN CAMPUS – TENET HEALTHCARE (670120)**, 2000 Transmountain Road, Zip 79911; tel. 915/877–8300, **A**1 3 8 10 **F**3 11 13 18 20 22 26 29 30 34 35 40 41 43 44 45 46 47 48 49 50 51 57 59 60 64 68 70 72 74 75 76 77 78 79 81 85 92 93 97 107 108 111 114 115 118 119 126 130 146 148 149 154 167 169 **S** TENET Healthcare Corporation, Dallas, TX
Primary Contact: David T. Byrd, Chief Executive Officer
CMO: Gustavo Martell, M.D., Chief Medical Officer
CIO: Vince Randazzo, Interim Chief Information Officer
CHR: Stephanie S. Talley, Chief Human Resource Officer
CNO: Linda B. Lawson, Chief Nursing Officer
Web address: https://www.thehospitalsofprovidence.com/our-locations/transmountain
Control: Partnership, Investor–owned (for–profit) **Service**: General medical and surgical

Staffed Beds: 108 **Admissions**: 6108 **Census**: 66 **Outpatient Visits**: 48186 **Births**: 408 **Total Expense ($000)**: 133067 **Payroll Expense ($000)**: 45066 **Personnel**: 399

⊞ **UNIVERSITY MEDICAL CENTER OF EL PASO (450024)**, 4815 Alameda Avenue, Zip 79905–2794; tel. 915/544–1200, **A**1 2 3 5 10 19 **F**3 8 13 15 17 18 20 22 24 26 29 31 34 35 37 40 41 42 43 45 46 47 48 49 50 54 56 57 59 64 65 70 71 74 75 76 78 79 80 81 82 84 85 87 93 97 107 108 110 111 115 119 126 127 130 146 148 149 154 167 169
Primary Contact: Jacob Cintron, FACHE, President and Chief Executive Officer
COO: Maria Zampini, Chief Operating Officer
CFO: Michael Nunez, Chief Financial Officer
CMO: Joel Hendryx, M.D., Chief Medical Officer
CIO: Janina Prada, Director Information Services
CHR: Janice M Harris, Director Human Resources
CNO: Amyra Daher, MSN, R.N., Chief Nursing Officer
Web address: https://www.umcelpaso.org/
Control: Hospital district or authority, Government, Nonfederal **Service**: General medical and surgical

Staffed Beds: 308 **Admissions**: 16855 **Census**: 264 **Outpatient Visits**: 1001734 **Births**: 3007 **Total Expense ($000)**: 835835 **Payroll Expense ($000)**: 292402 **Personnel**: 3874

VIBRA HIGHLANDS REHABILITATION HOSPITAL OF EL PASO See Highlands Rehabilitation Hospital

⊞ **WILLIAM BEAUMONT ARMY MEDICAL CENTER**, 18511 Highlander Medics Street, Zip 79918; tel. 915/742–7777, (Nonreporting) **A**1 2 3 5 **S** Department of the Army, Office of the Surgeon General, Falls Church, VA
Primary Contact: Colonel Brett H. Venable, FACHE, Commander
CIO: Major Rion Koon, Chief Information Management Division
Web address: https://www.wbamc.amedd.army.mil/NewPersonnel/CDR.aspx
Control: Army, Government, federal **Service**: General medical and surgical

Staffed Beds: 209

Hospital, Medicare Provider Number, Address, Telephone, Approval, Facility, and Physician Codes, Health Care System

★ American Hospital Association (AHA) membership ○ Healthcare Facilities Accreditation Program ⇑ Center for Improvement in Healthcare Quality Accreditation
☐ The Joint Commission accreditation ◇ DNV Healthcare Inc. accreditation △ Commission on Accreditation of Rehabilitation Facilities (CARF) accreditation

Hospitals, U.S. / TEXAS

ELDORADO—Schleicher County

SCHLEICHER COUNTY MEDICAL CENTER (451304), 102 North US Highway 277, Zip 76936–4010; tel. 325/853–2507, **A**10 18 **F**34 40 43 57 59 64 65 68 87 93 97 107 114 127 133 154 **S** Preferred Management Corporation, Shawnee, OK
Primary Contact: Billie Petterson-Carter, Administrator
CFO: Larry Stephens, Chief Financial Officer
CMO: Gordy Day, M.D., Medical Director
CHR: Beverly Minor, Chief Human Resources
Web address: www.scmc.us
Control: Corporation, Investor-owned (for-profit) **Service**: General medical and surgical

Staffed Beds: 14 **Admissions**: 84 **Census**: 2 **Outpatient Visits**: 6757 **Births**: 0 **Total Expense ($000)**: 6327 **Payroll Expense ($000)**: 3200 **Personnel**: 48

ELECTRA—Wichita County

★ **ELECTRA MEMORIAL HOSPITAL (451343)**, 1207 South Bailey Street, Zip 76360–3221, Mailing Address: P.O. Box 1112, Zip 76360–1112; tel. 940/495–3981, **A**10 18 **F**3 7 11 28 29 34 35 40 43 53 57 59 62 64 65 66 75 77 86 93 97 107 114 119 127 129 130 131 133 141 143 147 148 149 154 160
Primary Contact: Rebecca J. McCain, Chief Executive Officer
CFO: Ginnie Holmes, Chief Financial Officer
CIO: Brandon Huffstutler, Chief Information Officer
CNO: Kim Gilbert, R.N., Chief Nursing Officer
Web address: www.electrahospital.com
Control: Hospital district or authority, Government, Nonfederal **Service**: General medical and surgical

Staffed Beds: 19 **Admissions**: 287 **Census**: 6 **Outpatient Visits**: 55787 **Births**: 0 **Total Expense ($000)**: 32323 **Payroll Expense ($000)**: 16224 **Personnel**: 156

ENNIS—Ellis County

✠ **ENNIS REGIONAL MEDICAL CENTER (450833)**, 2201 West Lampasas Street, Zip 75119–5644; tel. 972/875–0900, **A**1 10 **F**3 11 15 28 29 30 34 35 40 43 45 50 51 57 59 64 65 70 75 77 79 81 82 91 93 107 108 110 111 119 146 152 157 **S** ScionHealth, Louisville, KY
Primary Contact: Doug Holzbog, Market Chief Executive Officer
CFO: Jack Wilcox, Chief Financial Officer
CMO: John M. Sullivan, M.D., Chief of Staff
CHR: Selena Cryer, Director Human Resources
CNO: Cynthia Dry, MSN, Chief Nursing Officer
Web address: www.ennisregional.com
Control: Partnership, Investor-owned (for-profit) **Service**: General medical and surgical

Staffed Beds: 58 **Admissions**: 366 **Census**: 3 **Outpatient Visits**: 24986 **Births**: 0 **Total Expense ($000)**: 19172 **Payroll Expense ($000)**: 7516 **Personnel**: 139

FAIRFIELD—Freestone County

★ **FREESTONE MEDICAL CENTER (450658)**, 125 Newman Street, Zip 75840–1499; tel. 903/389–2121, **A**10 22 **F**3 29 34 40 43 45 50 57 59 64 68 75 79 80 81 107 108 110 111 115 119 127 133 134 135 149 **P**6 **S** Community Hospital Corporation, Plano, TX
Primary Contact: Melissa Wilson, Chief Executive Officer
CMO: Darryl White, M.D., Chief of Staff
CHR: Jennifer Rummel, Director Human Resources
CNO: Tonya Basque, Chief Nursing Officer
Web address: www.freestonemc.com/
Control: Hospital district or authority, Government, Nonfederal **Service**: General medical and surgical

Staffed Beds: 10 **Admissions**: 335 **Census**: 2 **Outpatient Visits**: 28312 **Births**: 0 **Total Expense ($000)**: 14903 **Payroll Expense ($000)**: 5312 **Personnel**: 166

FLORESVILLE—Wilson County

CONNALLY MEMORIAL MEDICAL CENTER (450108), 499 10th Street, Zip 78114–3175; tel. 830/393–1300, **A**10 **F**3 15 18 29 34 35 40 43 45 47 49 54 57 59 62 64 70 75 81 82 85 86 87 91 93 107 108 110 111 114 119 130 132 133 144 146 148 154 156 **P**6
Primary Contact: Bob Gillespie, Chief Executive Officer
COO: Bob Gillespie, Chief Operating Officer
CFO: Curtis Rojas, Interim Chief Financial Officer
CMO: Wade Krause, M.D., Chief Medical Officer
CHR: Loretta Y Morgan, Director Human Resources
CNO: Sue Tackitt, Chief Nursing Officer
Web address: www.connallymmc.org
Control: Hospital district or authority, Government, Nonfederal **Service**: General medical and surgical

Staffed Beds: 26 **Admissions**: 623 **Census**: 6 **Outpatient Visits**: 161687 **Total Expense ($000)**: 43732 **Payroll Expense ($000)**: 19644 **Personnel**: 358

FLOWER MOUND—Denton County

☐ **CLEARSKY REHABILITATION HOSPITAL OF FLOWER MOUND (673076)**, 3100 Peters Colony Road, Zip 75022–2949; tel. 469/933–2855, **A**1 **F**3 29 82 90 93 96 130 143 148 149 **S** ClearSky Health, West Lake Hills, TX
Primary Contact: Brian Abraham, Regional Chief Executive Officer
Web address: https://www.clearskyhealth.com/flowermound/
Control: Partnership, Investor-owned (for-profit) **Service**: Rehabilitation

Staffed Beds: 29 **Admissions**: 652 **Census**: 23 **Outpatient Visits**: 314 **Births**: 0 **Total Expense ($000)**: 12019 **Payroll Expense ($000)**: 5446 **Personnel**: 67

ICARE REHABILITATION HOSPITAL (673064), 650 Parker Square Road, Zip 75028; tel. 214/513–0333, (Nonreporting) **A**10
Primary Contact: Gina Tomaseski, Chief Executive Officer
Web address: https://www.icarerehabilitation.com/
Control: Corporation, Investor-owned (for-profit) **Service**: Rehabilitation

Staffed Beds: 41

☐ **TEXAS HEALTH PRESBYTERIAN HOSPITAL FLOWER MOUND (670068)**, 4400 Long Prairie Road, Zip 75028–1892; tel. 469/322–7000, **A**1 10 **F**3 12 13 15 20 22 29 30 31 40 45 46 47 49 51 70 73 74 75 76 77 78 79 80 81 82 85 86 87 93 107 108 110 111 114 115 119 126 130 146 147 148 149 167
Primary Contact: John J. Klitsch, President
COO: Shelley R Tobey, R.N., MS, Chief Operating Officer
CFO: Tom Howard, Chief Financial Officer
CHR: Nicole Schweigert, Director Human Resources
CNO: Sandip Gill, R.N., Chief Nursing Officer
Web address: www.texashealthflowermound.com/
Control: Partnership, Investor-owned (for-profit) **Service**: General medical and surgical

Staffed Beds: 99 **Admissions**: 5899 **Census**: 55 **Outpatient Visits**: 47581 **Births**: 1434 **Total Expense ($000)**: 163631 **Payroll Expense ($000)**: 54761 **Personnel**: 617

FORT HOOD—Coryell County

✠ **CARL R. DARNALL ARMY MEDICAL CENTER**, 36065 Santa Fe Avenue, Zip 76544–5060; tel. 254/288–8000, (Nonreporting) **A**1 3 5 **S** Department of the Army, Office of the Surgeon General, Falls Church, VA
Primary Contact: Colonel Daniel J. Moore, CRDAMC Commander
CHR: Charles Burton, Chief Human Resources
Web address: https://www.crdamc.amedd.army.mil/Default.aspx
Control: Army, Government, federal **Service**: General medical and surgical

Staffed Beds: 109

FORT SAM HOUSTON—Bexar County

✠ **BROOKE ARMY MEDICAL CENTER**, 3551 Roger Brooke Drive, Zip 78234–4501; tel. 210/916–4141, (Nonreporting) **A**1 2 3 5 **S** Department of the Army, Office of the Surgeon General, Falls Church, VA
Primary Contact: Colonel Mark Stackle, Commanding Officer and Chief Executive Officer
CMO: Colonel Joseph P Chozinski, M.D., Deputy Commander Clinical Services
CHR: Rose Juarez, Chief Civilian Personnel Branch
CNO: Colonel Sheri Howell, Deputy Commander Nursing
Web address: https://bamc.tricare.mil
Control: Army, Government, federal **Service**: General medical and surgical

Staffed Beds: 483

Hospitals, U.S. / TEXAS

FORT STOCKTON—Pecos County

★ **PECOS COUNTY MEMORIAL HOSPITAL (451389)**, 387 West I H–10, Zip 79735–8912, Mailing Address: P.O. Box 1648, Zip 79735–1648; tel. 432/336–2004, **A**3 10 18 **F**3 11 13 29 34 35 40 43 45 46 50 53 57 59 62 63 64 65 75 76 81 93 107 111 119 127 130 133 144 146 148 167 169 **P**6
Primary Contact: Betsy Briscoe, Chief Executive Officer
COO: Margaret Davis, Chief Operating Officer
CFO: Sharon Hunt, Interim Chief Financial Officer
CMO: Subodh Mallik, M.D., Chief of Staff
CHR: Malissa Trevino, Director Human Resources
CNO: Gina Kalka, R.N., Chief Nursing Officer
Web address: www.pcmhfs.com
Control: County, Government, Nonfederal **Service**: General medical and surgical

Staffed Beds: 25 **Admissions**: 388 **Census**: 3 **Outpatient Visits**: 22510
Births: 95 **Total Expense ($000)**: 28933 **Payroll Expense ($000)**: 11767
Personnel: 244

FORT WORTH—Tarrant County

☒ **BAYLOR SCOTT & WHITE ALL SAINTS MEDICAL CENTER – FORT WORTH (450137)**, 1400 Eighth Avenue, Zip 76104–4192; tel. 817/926–2544, **A**1 2 3 5 10 **F**3 11 13 15 17 18 20 22 24 26 28 29 30 31 34 35 36 37 38 39 40 41 43 44 45 46 47 48 49 51 53 54 55 56 57 59 60 61 63 64 70 72 73 74 75 76 77 78 79 80 81 82 84 85 86 87 100 107 108 109 110 111 114 115 118 119 120 121 124 126 130 132 135 138 139 141 142 143 145 146 147 148 149 150 154 156 162 164 167 169 **S** Baylor Scott & White Health, Dallas, TX
Primary Contact: Charles E. Williams, President DFW – West Region
CFO: Lucy Catala, Vice President Finance
CMO: Dahlia Hassani, Vice President of Medical Affairs
CIO: Sandy Vaughn, Director Information Services
CHR: Tracy Stanford, Director Human Resources
Web address: https://www.bswhealth.com/locations/fort-worth-hospital
Control: Other not–for–profit (including NFP Corporation) **Service**: General medical and surgical

Staffed Beds: 400 **Admissions**: 23258 **Census**: 288 **Outpatient Visits**: 85836 **Births**: 6481 **Total Expense ($000)**: 534759 **Payroll Expense ($000)**: 183527 **Personnel**: 1724

☒ △ **BAYLOR SCOTT & WHITE INSTITUTE FOR REHABILITATION–FORT WORTH (673035)**, 6601 Harris Parkway, Zip 76132–6108; tel. 817/433–9600, **A**1 3 7 10 **F**3 28 29 30 44 64 68 71 74 75 86 87 90 91 92 93 94 95 96 100 130 131 132 135 148 149 154 157 164 **S** Select Medical Corporation, Mechanicsburg, PA
Primary Contact: J. Michael DeLeon, FACHE, Chief Executive Officer
CMO: Asher Light, M.D., Medical Director
CHR: Nissi Dalton, Manager Human Resources
CNO: Catherine Ewing, M.D., Chief Nursing Officer
Web address: https://www.bswrehab.com/locations-and-tours/bswir-fort-worth/
Control: Partnership, Investor–owned (for–profit) **Service**: Rehabilitation

Staffed Beds: 42 **Admissions**: 768 **Census**: 27 **Outpatient Visits**: 6169
Births: 0 **Total Expense ($000)**: 23020 **Payroll Expense ($000)**: 11786
Personnel: 126

☐ **BAYLOR SCOTT & WHITE SURGICAL HOSPITAL FORT WORTH (450880)**, 1800 Park Place Avenue, Zip 76110–1302; tel. 682/703–5600, **A**1 3 5 10 **F**3 29 30 37 40 68 70 79 81 85 107 111 119 126 **P**2
Primary Contact: Sally Stutes, Chief Nursing Officer/Interim Chief Operating Officer
COO: Sally Stutes, Interim Chief Operating Officer
CMO: Daud Ashai, M.D., Chief Medical Officer
CNO: Sally Stutes, Chief Nursing Officer
Web address: https://bshfw.com/
Control: Partnership, Investor–owned (for–profit) **Service**: General medical and surgical

Staffed Beds: 29 **Admissions**: 1334 **Census**: 8 **Outpatient Visits**: 10351
Births: 0 **Total Expense ($000)**: 100728 **Payroll Expense ($000)**: 21855
Personnel: 296

☒ **COOK CHILDREN'S MEDICAL CENTER (453300)**, 801 Seventh Avenue, Zip 76104–2796; tel. 682/885–4000, **A**1 2 3 5 10 **F**3 7 8 17 19 21 23 25 27 29 30 31 32 34 35 37 38 39 40 41 43 44 45 46 47 49 50 53 54 55 57 58 59 60 61 62 64 65 66 68 72 74 75 77 78 79 80 81 82 84 85 86 87 88 89 90 91 92 93 94 95 97 98 99 100 101 102 104 105 107 108 111 112 113 114 118 119 126 129 130 131 132 136 138 141 143 144 146 148 149 150 154 155 164 166 167 **P**6
Primary Contact: Rick W. Merrill, System President and Chief Executive Officer
CFO: Stephen Kimmel, Chief Financial Officer
CMO: James C Cunningham, M.D., Chief Medical Officer
CIO: Theresa Meadows, Chief Information Officer
CNO: Cheryl Petersen, Vice President and Chief Nursing Officer
Web address: www.cookchildrens.org
Control: Other not–for–profit (including NFP Corporation) **Service**: Children's general medical and surgical

Staffed Beds: 447 **Admissions**: 10258 **Census**: 241 **Outpatient Visits**: 355045 **Births**: 0 **Total Expense ($000)**: 1449814 **Payroll Expense ($000)**: 404247 **Personnel**: 4668

☒ **ENCOMPASS HEALTH REHABILITATION HOSPITAL OF CITY VIEW (453042)**, 6701 Oakmont Boulevard, Zip 76132–2957; tel. 817/370–4700, **A**1 10 **F**3 29 75 77 90 91 94 95 96 130 148 154 **S** Encompass Health Corporation, Birmingham, AL
Primary Contact: Kyllan Cody, Chief Executive Officer
Web address: https://encompasshealth.com/cityviewrehab
Control: Corporation, Investor–owned (for–profit) **Service**: Rehabilitation

Staffed Beds: 77 **Admissions**: 1734 **Census**: 57 **Outpatient Visits**: 0
Births: 0 **Total Expense ($000)**: 30815 **Payroll Expense ($000)**: 15511
Personnel: 226

FOREST PARK MEDICAL CENTER See Texas Health Hospital Clearfork

JOHN PETER SMITH HOSPITAL See JPS Health Network, Fort Worth

☒ **JPS HEALTH NETWORK (450039)**, 1500 South Main Street, Zip 76104–4917; tel. 817/921–3431, (Includes JOHN PETER SMITH HOSPITAL, 1500 South Main Street, Fort Worth, Texas, Zip 76104, tel. 817/921–3431; TRINITY SPRINGS PAVILION, 1500 South Main Street, Fort Worth, Texas, Zip 76104–4917, tel. 817/927–3636; Lily Wong, Director Psychiatry) **A**1 2 3 8 10 19 **F**3 8 11 13 18 20 22 24 26 28 29 30 31 32 34 35 36 39 40 43 44 45 46 47 49 50 54 56 57 58 59 60 61 64 65 66 68 70 71 72 74 75 76 77 78 79 80 81 82 84 85 86 87 91 92 93 97 98 100 101 102 104 105 107 108 110 111 114 115 118 119 121 123 124 126 130 131 132 135 141 143 144 146 147 148 149 153 154 156 160 164 165 167 169
Primary Contact: Karen Duncan, President and Chief Executive Officer
CIO: Melinda Custin, Chief Information Officer
CHR: Ashley M. Ridgeway–Washington, Senior Vice President, Chief Human Resources Officer
CNO: Wanda V. Peebles, Chief Nursing Officer
Web address: www.jpshealthnet.org
Control: Hospital district or authority, Government, Nonfederal **Service**: General medical and surgical

Staffed Beds: 639 **Admissions**: 29967 **Census**: 518 **Outpatient Visits**: 1082815 **Births**: 4408 **Total Expense ($000)**: 1395006 **Payroll Expense ($000)**: 596688 **Personnel**: 6843

KINDRED HOSPITAL–FORT WORTH SW See Kindred Hospital Tarrant County–Fort Worth Southwest

LIFECARE HOSPITALS OF NORTH TEXAS–FORT WORTH See Lifecare Hospitals of Fort Worth

☒ **MEDICAL CITY ALLIANCE (670103)**, 3101 North Tarrant Parkway, Zip 76177; tel. 817/639–1000, (Includes MEDICAL CITY SURGICAL HOSPITAL ALLIANCE, 3200 North Tarrant Parkway, Fort Worth, Texas, Zip 76177–8611, tel. 817/502–7300; Jason Wren, FACHE, Chief Executive Officer) **A**1 3 10 **F**3 12 13 18 20 22 26 29 34 40 42 43 45 47 49 50 51 57 60 64 70 72 74 75 76 77 79 81 85 86 87 107 108 110 111 114 115 119 126 130 132 135 146 147 148 149 154 156 167 169 **S** HCA Healthcare, Nashville, TN
Primary Contact: Glenn Wallace, Chief Executive Officer
Web address: https://www.bswrehab.com/locations-and-tours/bswir-fort-worth/
Control: Corporation, Investor–owned (for–profit) **Service**: General medical and surgical

Staffed Beds: 123 **Admissions**: 7247 **Census**: 73 **Outpatient Visits**: 95486
Births: 1057 **Total Expense ($000)**: 124555 **Payroll Expense ($000)**: 48532 **Personnel**: 596

Hospital, Medicare Provider Number, Address, Telephone, Approval, Facility, and Physician Codes, Health Care System

★ American Hospital Association (AHA) membership
☐ The Joint Commission accreditation
○ Healthcare Facilities Accreditation Program
◇ DNV Healthcare Inc. accreditation
⇧ Center for Improvement in Healthcare Quality Accreditation
△ Commission on Accreditation of Rehabilitation Facilities (CARF) accreditation

Hospitals, U.S. / TEXAS

- **MEDICAL CITY FORT WORTH (450672)**, 900 Eighth Avenue, Zip 76104-3902; tel. 817/336-2100, **A**1 2 3 5 10 **F**3 11 12 17 18 20 22 24 26 28 29 30 31 37 40 42 45 46 47 48 49 50 56 58 64 70 74 77 78 79 81 85 87 90 91 93 107 108 111 114 115 119 126 130 138 142 145 146 148 154 **S** HCA Healthcare, Nashville, TN
  Primary Contact: John Hoover, Chief Executive Officer
  CFO: Andrew Lane, Chief Financial Officer
  CMO: Terry Loftus, M.D., Chief Medical Officer
  CIO: Kelley Fredrickson, Director Information Services
  CHR: Cyndi Roberts, Director Human Resources
  CNO: Ulondia D. Lee, R.N., MSN, Chief Nursing Officer
  Web address: www.medicalcityfortworth.com/about/
  Control: Partnership, Investor-owned (for-profit) **Service:** General medical and surgical

  Staffed Beds: 257 **Admissions:** 13636 **Census:** 188 **Outpatient Visits:** 60066 **Births:** 0 **Total Expense ($000):** 304754 **Payroll Expense ($000):** 108437 **Personnel:** 1225

- **MESA SPRINGS (454124)**, 5560 Mesa Springs Drive, Zip 76123; tel. 817/292-4600, **A**1 5 10 **F**5 98 101 104 105 152 153 154 **S** Springstone, Louisville, KY
  Primary Contact: Andrew Carlton, Chief Executive Officer
  CFO: Kent Ashley, Chief Financial Officer
  CMO: Stewart Keller, M.D., Medical Director
  CNO: Ana Ramirez, Director of Nursing
  Web address: https://mesasprings.com/
  Control: Corporation, Investor-owned (for-profit) **Service:** Psychiatric

  Staffed Beds: 72 **Admissions:** 3124 **Census:** 62 **Outpatient Visits:** 34152 **Births:** 0 **Total Expense ($000):** 28357 **Payroll Expense ($000):** 14799 **Personnel:** 196

- **TEXAS HEALTH HARRIS METHODIST HOSPITAL ALLIANCE (670085)**, 10864 Texas Health Trail, Zip 76244-4897; tel. 682/212-2000, **A**1 5 10 **F**3 11 12 13 15 18 20 22 24 26 28 29 30 34 35 40 43 45 48 49 50 64 70 72 74 75 76 79 80 81 84 85 86 93 107 110 111 114 115 118 119 126 130 131 146 148 149 **S** Texas Health Resources, Arlington, TX
  Primary Contact: Clint Abernathy, President
  Web address: https://www.texashealth.org/alliance/Pages/default.aspx
  Control: Other not-for-profit (including NFP Corporation) **Service:** General medical and surgical

  Staffed Beds: 125 **Admissions:** 7760 **Census:** 71 **Outpatient Visits:** 49075 **Births:** 2016 **Total Expense ($000):** 162826 **Payroll Expense ($000):** 59680 **Personnel:** 591

- **TEXAS HEALTH HARRIS METHODIST HOSPITAL FORT WORTH (450135)**, 1301 Pennsylvania Avenue, Zip 76104-2122; tel. 817/250-2000, **A**1 2 3 5 10 19 **F**3 8 11 13 15 16 17 18 20 22 24 26 28 29 30 31 34 35 36 38 40 42 43 44 45 46 47 48 49 51 53 54 55 56 57 58 59 60 61 63 64 65 66 67 70 72 73 74 75 76 78 79 81 82 83 84 85 87 93 107 108 110 111 114 115 117 118 119 126 130 131 132 135 138 146 147 148 149 154 156 164 167 169 **S** Texas Health Resources, Arlington, TX
  Primary Contact: Jared Shelton, FACHE, President
  CFO: Shelly Miland, Group Financial Officer
  CMO: Joseph Prosser, M.D., Chief Medical Officer
  CHR: Ginger Morrow, Entity Human Resources Officer
  CNO: Elaine Nelson, R.N., MSN, Chief Nursing Officer
  Web address: www.texashealth.org
  Control: Other not-for-profit (including NFP Corporation) **Service:** General medical and surgical

  Staffed Beds: 764 **Admissions:** 42060 **Census:** 684 **Outpatient Visits:** 189659 **Births:** 3033 **Total Expense ($000):** 1135946 **Payroll Expense ($000):** 380802 **Personnel:** 4088

- **TEXAS HEALTH HARRIS METHODIST HOSPITAL SOUTHWEST FORT WORTH (450779)**, 6100 Harris Parkway, Zip 76132-4199; tel. 817/433-5000, (Includes TEXAS HEALTH HOSPITAL CLEARFORK, 5400 Clearfork Main Street, Fort Worth, Texas, Zip 76109-3553, tel. 682/703-5000; Ajith Pai, PharmD, FACHE, Chief Executive Officer) **A**1 5 10 **F**3 11 13 15 18 20 22 28 29 30 35 36 37 40 43 45 46 47 48 49 50 57 59 60 64 70 72 75 76 77 78 79 80 81 84 85 86 87 93 102 107 110 111 114 115 119 126 130 131 146 147 149 154 169 **S** Texas Health Resources, Arlington, TX
  Primary Contact: Ajith Pai, PharmD, FACHE, President
  CFO: Charlotte Ward, Entity Financial Officer
  CMO: Mark Montgomery, M.D., Chief Medical Officer
  CHR: Leanna W Nalley, Director Human Resources
  CNO: Mary Robinson, Chief Nursing Officer and Vice President Patient Care Services
  Web address: www.texashealth.org
  Control: Other not-for-profit (including NFP Corporation) **Service:** General medical and surgical

  Staffed Beds: 233 **Admissions:** 15733 **Census:** 168 **Outpatient Visits:** 92493 **Births:** 3291 **Total Expense ($000):** 351959 **Payroll Expense ($000):** 118182 **Personnel:** 1138

- **TEXAS HEALTH SPECIALTY HOSPITAL (452018)**, 1301 Pennsylvania Avenue, 4th Floor, Zip 76104-2190; tel. 817/250-5500, **A**1 10 **F**1 3 87 130 148 149 **S** Texas Health Resources, Arlington, TX
  Primary Contact: Pamela Duffey, R.N., Vice President/Chief Operating Office/Chief Nursing Officer
  COO: Pamela Duffey, R.N., Chief Operating Officer and Chief Nursing Officer
  CFO: Shelly Miland, Chief Financial Officer
  CMO: Michael Thornsberry, M.D., Chief Medical Officer
  CNO: Pamela Duffey, R.N., Chief Nursing Officer
  Web address: https://www.texashealth.org/texas-health-specialty-hospital/
  Control: Other not-for-profit (including NFP Corporation) **Service:** Acute long-term care hospital

  Staffed Beds: 10 **Admissions:** 64 **Census:** 9 **Outpatient Visits:** 0 **Births:** 0 **Total Expense ($000):** 9732 **Payroll Expense ($000):** 4112 **Personnel:** 34

- △ **TEXAS REHABILITATION HOSPITAL OF FORT WORTH (673048)**, 425 Alabama Avenue, Zip 76104-1022; tel. 817/820-3400, **A**5 7 10 22 **F**3 29 30 34 57 68 74 79 90 91 96 130 132 148 156 157 **P**1 2 3 4 5 6 7 8 **S** Lifepoint Health, Brentwood, TN
  Primary Contact: Jake Daggett, Market Chief Executive Officer
  CFO: Oscar Sanchez, Chief Financial Officer
  CMO: William Bridges, M.D., Chief Medical Officer
  CIO: Oscar Sanchez, Chief Financial Officer
  CHR: Mackenzi Fry
  CNO: Lana Galer, Chief Nursing Officer
  Web address: www.texasrehabhospital.com/
  Control: Corporation, Investor-owned (for-profit) **Service:** Rehabilitation

  Staffed Beds: 66 **Admissions:** 1404 **Census:** 49 **Outpatient Visits:** 0 **Births:** 0 **Total Expense ($000):** 21706 **Payroll Expense ($000):** 11867 **Personnel:** 174

  TRINITY SPRINGS PAVILION-EAST See Trinity Springs Pavilion

- ☐ **WELLBRIDGE HEALTHCARE OF FORT WORTH (454128)**, 6200 Overton Ridge Boulevard, Zip 76132-3614; tel. 817/361-1991, **A**1 10 **F**98 135 153
  Primary Contact: Soni Helmicki, Chief Executive Officer
  Web address: www.oceanshealthcare.com
  Control: Corporation, Investor-owned (for-profit) **Service:** Psychiatric

  Staffed Beds: 48 **Admissions:** 1412 **Census:** 39 **Outpatient Visits:** 565 **Births:** 0 **Total Expense ($000):** 10419 **Payroll Expense ($000):** 6105 **Personnel:** 85

FREDERICKSBURG—Gillespie County

HILL COUNTRY MEMORIAL HOSPITAL See Methodist Hospital Hill Country

- **METHODIST HOSPITAL HILL COUNTRY (450604)**, 1020 South State Highway 16, Zip 78624-4471, Mailing Address: P.O. Box 835, Zip 78624-0835; tel. 830/997-4353, **A**1 10 **F**3 11 13 15 18 20 28 29 30 34 35 37 40 43 45 49 50 51 57 59 62 63 64 68 70 74 75 76 77 78 79 81 82 85 86 87 93 96 97 107 108 110 111 114 115 119 124 126 129 130 131 132 135 144 146 148 149 167 **P**6 **S** HCA Healthcare, Nashville, TN
  Primary Contact: Clint Kotal, Chief Executive Officer
  COO: Mike Reno, Chief Operating Officer
  CFO: Mark Jones, Chief Financial Officer
  CMO: James R Partin, M.D., Chief Medical Director
  CIO: John Mason, Chief Information Officer
  CHR: Alysha Metzger, Director Human Resources
  CNO: Maureen Polivka, Chief Nursing Officer
  Web address: www.hillcountrymemorial.org
  Control: Partnership, Investor-owned (for-profit) **Service:** General medical and surgical

  Staffed Beds: 58 **Admissions:** 1934 **Census:** 16 **Outpatient Visits:** 46973 **Births:** 384 **Total Expense ($000):** 85781 **Payroll Expense ($000):** 26294 **Personnel:** 275

FRIONA—Parmer County

- **PARMER MEDICAL CENTER (451300)**, 1307 Cleveland Street, Zip 79035-1121; tel. 806/250-2754, **A**10 18 **F**11 30 34 35 40 57 64 75 77 93 107 119 127 130 133 154 **S** Preferred Management Corporation, Shawnee, OK
  Primary Contact: Gayla Quillin, Administrator
  Web address: www.parmermedicalcenter.com
  Control: Other not-for-profit (including NFP Corporation) **Service:** General medical and surgical

  Staffed Beds: 25 **Admissions:** 151 **Census:** 3 **Outpatient Visits:** 20274 **Births:** 0 **Total Expense ($000):** 12301 **Payroll Expense ($000):** 4823 **Personnel:** 86

Hospitals, U.S. / TEXAS

FRISCO—Collin County

■ △ **BAYLOR SCOTT & WHITE INSTITUTE FOR REHABILITATION–FRISCO (673046)**, 2990 Legacy Drive, Zip 75034–6066; tel. 469/888–5100, **A**1 7 10 **F**3 11 29 30 34 35 36 44 54 56 57 58 60 62 64 68 74 75 77 79 82 86 90 91 92 93 94 95 96 100 104 119 130 132 134 135 143 148 149 154 156 157 164 **S** Select Medical Corporation, Mechanicsburg, PA
Primary Contact: Katharine Powers, MS, Chief Executive Officer
Web address: https://www.bswrehab.com/locations-and-tours/bswir-frisco/
Control: Partnership, Investor–owned (for–profit) **Service**: Rehabilitation

Staffed Beds: 44 **Admissions:** 1086 **Census:** 42 **Outpatient Visits:** 11008 **Births:** 0 **Total Expense ($000):** 31606 **Payroll Expense ($000):** 16088 **Personnel:** 174	

■ **BAYLOR SCOTT & WHITE MEDICAL CENTER – CENTENNIAL (450885)**, 12505 Lebanon Road, Zip 75035–8298; tel. 972/963–3333, **A**1 10 **F**3 11 13 17 18 20 22 24 26 29 30 34 35 37 40 43 45 46 49 50 56 57 59 60 70 72 74 75 76 77 78 79 81 84 85 87 100 102 107 108 111 114 115 116 119 126 130 146 148 154 156 167 **S** Baylor Scott & White Health, Dallas, TX
Primary Contact: Ryan Gebhart, FACHE, President
CIO: Dianne Yarborough, Director of Information Technology
CHR: Stephanie S. Talley, Director Human Resources
CNO: Calee Travis, R.N., Chief Nursing Officer
Web address: https://www.bswhealth.com/
Control: Other not–for–profit (including NFP Corporation) **Service**: General medical and surgical

Staffed Beds: 106 **Admissions:** 5140 **Census:** 55 **Outpatient Visits:** 27481 **Births:** 1416 **Total Expense ($000):** 119257 **Payroll Expense ($000):** 43693 **Personnel:** 366

□ **BAYLOR SCOTT & WHITE MEDICAL CENTER–FRISCO (450853)**, 5601 Warren Parkway, Zip 75034–4069; tel. 214/407–5000, **A**1 3 5 10 **F**3 13 29 34 37 40 45 51 54 64 68 72 76 79 81 85 86 87 107 108 111 115 119 126 129 130 144 167 **S** United Surgical Partners International, Addison, TX
Primary Contact: Eli Smith, FACHE, Chief Executive Officere
COO: Kevin Coats, Chief Operating Officer and Chief Financial Officer
CFO: Kevin Coats, Chief Financial Officer
CMO: Jimmy Laferney, M.D., Vice President Medical Staff Affairs
CIO: Rick Barry, Director Information Systems
CHR: Margaret Garcia, Manager Human Resources
CNO: Randi Elliott, MSN, Chief Nursing Officer
Web address: www.bmcf.com
Control: Partnership, Investor–owned (for–profit) **Service**: Surgical

Staffed Beds: 68 **Admissions:** 3260 **Census:** 27 **Outpatient Visits:** 32058 **Births:** 2187 **Total Expense ($000):** 137189 **Payroll Expense ($000):** 46894 **Personnel:** 457

MEDICAL CENTER FRISCO See Medical City Frisco

□ **MEDICAL CITY MENTAL HEALTH & WELLNESS CENTER – FRISCO (454161)**, 5680 Frisco Square Boulevard, Suite 3000, Zip 75034–3300; tel. 469/353–2219, **A**1 10 **F**98 99 103 130 153 **P**5 **S** Haven Behavioral Healthcare, Nashville, TN
Primary Contact: Jon Lasell, Chief Executive Officer
Web address: www.frisco.havenbehavioral.com/
Control: Corporation, Investor–owned (for–profit) **Service**: Psychiatric

Staffed Beds: 70 **Admissions:** 2609 **Census:** 55 **Outpatient Visits:** 796 **Births:** 0 **Total Expense ($000):** 18509 **Payroll Expense ($000):** 8331 **Personnel:** 119

TEXAS HEALTH FRISCO See Texas Health Hospital Frisco

■ **TEXAS HEALTH HOSPITAL FRISCO (670260)**, 12400 Dallas Parkway, Zip 75033–4224; tel. 469/495–2000, **A**1 3 10 **F**3 12 13 18 20 22 29 30 34 35 40 45 46 47 48 49 51 58 64 70 72 74 75 76 77 79 81 82 84 85 86 87 107 111 115 118 119 126 130 146 148 149 167 **S** Texas Health Resources, Arlington, TX
Primary Contact: Brett D. Lee, President
Web address: https://www.texashealth.org/locations/texas-health-frisco
Control: Other not–for–profit (including NFP Corporation) **Service**: General medical and surgical

Staffed Beds: 77 **Admissions:** 4853 **Census:** 46 **Outpatient Visits:** 32023 **Births:** 974 **Total Expense ($000):** 151344 **Payroll Expense ($000):** 48808 **Personnel:** 445

GAINESVILLE—Cooke County

★ **NORTH TEXAS MEDICAL CENTER (450090)**, 1900 Hospital Boulevard, Zip 76240–2002; tel. 940/665–1751, **A**10 20 22 **F**3 11 12 13 15 28 29 34 35 40 43 45 50 57 59 64 65 66 70 75 76 77 79 81 85 87 93 107 108 110 111 115 119 127 129 146 147 149 154 169 **P**6 **S** Community Hospital Corporation, Plano, TX
Primary Contact: Thomas Sledge, Chief Executive Officer
CFO: Melissa Walker, CPA, Chief Financial Officer
CHR: Teresa Westover, Director Human Resources
CNO: Becky Small, Chief Nursing Officer
Web address: www.ntmconline.net
Control: Other not–for–profit (including NFP Corporation) **Service**: General medical and surgical

Staffed Beds: 48 **Admissions:** 1539 **Census:** 18 **Outpatient Visits:** 51035 **Births:** 329 **Total Expense ($000):** 45096 **Payroll Expense ($000):** 19209 **Personnel:** 268

GALVESTON—Galveston County

□ **SHRINERS HOSPITALS FOR CHILDREN (453311)**, 815 Market Street, Zip 77550–2725; tel. 409/770–6600, **A**1 3 5 10 **F**3 11 16 29 34 35 50 64 68 75 77 79 81 82 85 86 89 93 94 100 119 130 132 146 148 154 **S** Shriners Hospitals for Children, Tampa, FL
Primary Contact: Mary Glendening, FACHE, Administrator
CFO: Michael B Schimming, Director Financial Services
CMO: Steven Wolf, D.O., Chief of Staff
CIO: Michael Lyons, Regional Director Information Services
CHR: Robert A Magee, Director Human Resources
CNO: Jeannie Keith, R.N., Nurse Executive
Web address: www.shrinershospitalsforchildren.org/Hospitals/Locations/Galveston.aspx
Control: Other not–for–profit (including NFP Corporation) **Service**: Children's other specialty

Staffed Beds: 30 **Admissions:** 261 **Census:** 10 **Outpatient Visits:** 12792 **Births:** 0 **Total Expense ($000):** 59602 **Payroll Expense ($000):** 21599 **Personnel:** 328

■ **UNIVERSITY OF TEXAS MEDICAL BRANCH (450018)**, 301 University Boulevard, Zip 77555–0128; tel. 409/772–1011, (Includes ANGLETON DANBURY CAMPUS, 132 E Hospital DR, Angleton, Texas, Zip 77515–4112, 132 East Hospital Drive, Angleton, Texas, Zip 77515–4112, tel. 979/849–7721; Elizabeth Meagan Reimschissel, Administrator and Associate Chief Nursing Officer; LEAGUE CITY CAMPUS, 2240 Gulf Freeway South, League City, Texas, Zip 77573–5143, tel. 409/772–1011) **A**1 2 3 5 10 **F**3 5 11 12 13 15 16 18 19 20 22 24 26 28 29 30 31 34 35 36 37 38 39 40 41 43 44 46 47 48 49 50 51 52 53 54 55 56 57 58 59 60 61 62 63 64 65 66 68 70 71 72 73 74 75 76 77 78 79 81 82 84 85 86 87 88 89 92 93 96 97 100 101 104 107 108 110 111 112 114 115 116 117 118 119 120 121 123 124 126 129 130 131 132 134 135 137 138 141 142 144 145 146 147 148 149 150 154 156 161 162 163 164 166 167 169 **S** University of Texas System, Austin, TX
Primary Contact: Jochen Reiser, President and Chief Executive Officer
COO: Deborah A McGrew, Vice President and Chief Operating Officer
CFO: Cheryl A Sadro, Executive Vice President Chief Business and Finance Officer
CIO: Todd Leach, Vice President and Chief Information Officer
CHR: Ronald McKinley, Ph.D., Vice President Human Resources and Employee Services
CNO: Merry Philip, M.D., Chief Nursing Officer
Web address: www.utmb.edu
Control: State, Government, Nonfederal **Service**: General medical and surgical

Staffed Beds: 562 **Admissions:** 38396 **Census:** 532 **Outpatient Visits:** 1537060 **Births:** 6701 **Total Expense ($000):** 1509111 **Payroll Expense ($000):** 535530 **Personnel:** 5699

GARLAND—Dallas County

□ ⇧ **PERIMETER BEHAVIORAL HOSPITAL OF DALLAS (454149)**, 2696 West Walnut Street, Zip 75042–6441; tel. 972/370–5517, **A**1 10 21 **F**98 99 103 **P**5 **S** Perimeter Healthcare, Alpharetta, GA
Primary Contact: Susan Somers, Chief Executive Officer
Web address: https://www.perimeterhealthcare.com/facilities/perimeter-behavioral-hospital-of-dallas/
Control: Partnership, Investor–owned (for–profit) **Service**: Psychiatric

Staffed Beds: 100 **Admissions:** 2143 **Census:** 54 **Outpatient Visits:** 0 **Births:** 0 **Total Expense ($000):** 16702 **Payroll Expense ($000):** 10662 **Personnel:** 162

Hospital, Medicare Provider Number, Address, Telephone, Approval, Facility, and Physician Codes, Health Care System

★ American Hospital Association (AHA) membership
□ The Joint Commission accreditation
○ Healthcare Facilities Accreditation Program
◇ DNV Healthcare Inc. accreditation
⇧ Center for Improvement in Healthcare Quality Accreditation
△ Commission on Accreditation of Rehabilitation Facilities (CARF) accreditation

Hospitals, U.S. / TEXAS

GATESVILLE—Coryell County

☐ **CORYELL HEALTH (451379)**, 1507 West Main Street, Zip 76528–1098; tel. 254/865–8251, **A**1 10 18 **F**3 7 10 11 12 15 18 20 22 24 28 29 32 34 35 37 40 43 45 50 55 57 58 59 60 62 64 65 68 70 74 75 77 78 79 81 82 84 86 87 93 97 100 102 104 107 108 110 111 114 115 116 117 119 125 126 127 129 130 131 133 146 148 154 156 158 167 169
Primary Contact: David Byrom, Chief Executive Officer
COO: David Byrom, Chief Executive Officer
CFO: Carol Jones, Controller and Manager Business Office
CMO: Diedra Wuenschel, D.O., President Medical Staff
CIO: Mike Huckabee, Network Administrator
CHR: Paula Smithhart, Director Human Resources
CNO: Jeanne Griffith, Chief Nursing Officer
Web address: www.cmhos.org
Control: Hospital district or authority, Government, Nonfederal **Service**: General medical and surgical

Staffed Beds: 25 **Admissions**: 694 **Census**: 8 **Outpatient Visits**: 120987 **Births**: 0 **Total Expense ($000)**: 84985 **Payroll Expense ($000)**: 28946 **Personnel**: 627

GEORGETOWN—Williamson County

☐ **GEORGETOWN BEHAVIORAL HEALTH INSTITUTE (454129)**, 3101 South Austin Avenue, Zip 78626–7541; tel. 512/819–1100, **A**1 10 **F**4 5 98 99 100 104 105 130 132 135 151 152 153 154 164 **S** Signature Healthcare Services, Corona, CA
Primary Contact: Brittney Sky Dick, Chief Executive Officer
COO: Ellen Payne, Chief Operating Officer
CFO: Shelli Surcouf, Chief Financial Officer
CHR: Kristi Hynes, Director Human Resources
CNO: Nini Perry, Chief Nursing Officer
Web address: www.georgetownbehavioral.com
Control: Corporation, Investor–owned (for–profit) **Service**: Psychiatric

Staffed Beds: 118 **Admissions**: 3951 **Census**: 76 **Outpatient Visits**: 2913 **Births**: 0 **Total Expense ($000)**: 23663 **Payroll Expense ($000)**: 11108 **Personnel**: 195

GEORGETOWN HEALTHCARE SYSTEM See St. David's Georgetown Hospital

⊞ **ROCK SPRINGS (454127)**, 700 Southeast Inner Loop, Zip 78626; tel. 512/819–9400, **A**1 10 **F**4 5 54 80 98 99 100 105 151 152 153 **P**6 **S** Springstone, Louisville, KY
Primary Contact: Erin Basalay, PsyD, Chief Executive Officer
CFO: Amy Jordan, Chief Financial Officer
CHR: Sharon McMurray, Director, Human Resources
CNO: Jennifer Cooley, Director of Nursing
Web address: www.rockspringshealth.com/
Control: Corporation, Investor–owned (for–profit) **Service**: Psychiatric

Staffed Beds: 72 **Admissions**: 2416 **Census**: 63 **Outpatient Visits**: 15789 **Births**: 0 **Total Expense ($000)**: 25502 **Payroll Expense ($000)**: 12900 **Personnel**: 192

GLEN ROSE—Somervell County

☐ **GLEN ROSE MEDICAL CENTER (450451)**, 1021 Holden Street, Zip 76043–4937, Mailing Address: P.O. Box 2099, Zip 76043–2099; tel. 254/897–2215, **A**1 10 **F**3 15 28 29 34 40 45 48 53 54 56 57 59 65 68 71 81 93 97 103 104 107 110 114 119 126 128 133 135 141 146 149 154 164 167
Primary Contact: Michael Honea, Chief Executive Officer
CHR: Ladonna Green, Director Human Resources
Web address: www.glenrosemedicalcenter.com
Control: Hospital district or authority, Government, Nonfederal **Service**: General medical and surgical

Staffed Beds: 10 **Admissions**: 327 **Census**: 4 **Outpatient Visits**: 47157 **Total Expense ($000)**: 34599 **Payroll Expense ($000)**: 14169 **Personnel**: 181

GONZALES—Gonzales County

★ **GONZALES HEALTHCARE SYSTEMS (450235)**, 1110 Sarah Dewitt Drive, Zip 78629–3311, Mailing Address: P.O. Box 587, Zip 78629–0587; tel. 830/672–7581, **A**10 20 **F**3 11 13 15 34 40 53 57 59 62 64 65 75 76 77 79 81 85 87 93 97 107 110 111 114 115 119 127 130 148 149 169 **S** Ovation Healthcare, Brentwood, TN
Primary Contact: Brandon Anzaldua, Chief Executive Officer
CMO: Commie Hisey, D.O., Chief of Staff
CHR: Joni Leland, Director Human Resources
CNO: Lori Parker, Chief Nursing Officer
Web address: www.gonzaleshealthcare.com
Control: Hospital district or authority, Government, Nonfederal **Service**: General medical and surgical

Staffed Beds: 33 **Admissions**: 514 **Census**: 4 **Outpatient Visits**: 33653 **Births**: 147 **Total Expense ($000)**: 63060 **Payroll Expense ($000)**: 15990 **Personnel**: 313

GRAHAM—Young County

⇧ **GRAHAM REGIONAL MEDICAL CENTER (450085)**, 1301 Montgomery Road, Zip 76450–4240, Mailing Address: P.O. Box 1390, Zip 76450–1390; tel. 940/549–3400, **A**10 21 **F**3 7 11 12 15 28 29 40 45 50 53 57 59 79 81 85 87 93 97 107 110 111 115 119 127 130 135 154
Primary Contact: Shane Kernell, Chief Executive Officer
CIO: Jeff Clark, Director Information Systems
Web address: www.grahamrmc.com
Control: Hospital district or authority, Government, Nonfederal **Service**: General medical and surgical

Staffed Beds: 17 **Admissions**: 130 **Census**: 1 **Outpatient Visits**: 50164 **Births**: 0 **Total Expense ($000)**: 24406 **Payroll Expense ($000)**: 9513 **Personnel**: 248

GRANBURY—Hood County

⊞ **LAKE GRANBURY MEDICAL CENTER (450596)**, 1310 Paluxy Road, Zip 76048–5655; tel. 817/573–2273, **A**1 3 10 **F**3 8 11 12 13 15 18 20 22 26 28 29 30 34 37 40 43 45 49 53 57 59 64 68 70 74 75 76 77 79 81 82 85 86 93 107 108 110 111 114 118 119 129 146 147 148 149 154 157 167 **S** Community Health Systems, Inc., Franklin, TN
Primary Contact: Curt M. Junkins, Chief Executive Officer
CFO: Noe Gutierrez, Chief Financial Officer
CIO: Kevin Myers, Director Information Systems
CHR: Brooke Montoya, Director Human Resources
CNO: Abigail Kendall, Chief Nursing Officer
Web address: www.lakegranburymedicalcenter.com
Control: Corporation, Investor–owned (for–profit) **Service**: General medical and surgical

Staffed Beds: 73 **Admissions**: 3266 **Census**: 33 **Outpatient Visits**: 82038 **Births**: 549 **Total Expense ($000)**: 63442 **Payroll Expense ($000)**: 31280 **Personnel**: 341

GRAPEVINE—Tarrant County

⊞ **BAYLOR SCOTT & WHITE MEDICAL CENTER – GRAPEVINE (450563)**, 1650 West College Street, Zip 76051–3565; tel. 817/481–1588, **A**1 2 3 5 10 **F**3 12 13 15 18 20 22 26 28 29 30 31 34 35 40 43 45 46 47 48 49 56 57 59 60 63 64 65 70 72 74 76 77 78 79 80 81 82 84 85 86 87 90 107 108 110 111 115 118 119 126 130 131 132 145 146 147 148 149 154 167 169 **S** Baylor Scott & White Health, Dallas, TX
Primary Contact: Naman Mahajan, Chief Executive Officer
COO: Melissa Winter, R.N., MSN, Chief Operating Officer and Chief Nursing Officer
CFO: Terri Foster, Hospital Finance Officer
CMO: Ron Jensen, D.O., Chief Medical Officer and Vice President
CIO: Sandy Vaughn, Director Information Systems
CHR: Donna Stark, Director Human Resources
CNO: Melissa Winter, R.N., MSN, Regional Chief Nursing Officer
Web address: https://www.bswhealth.com/locations/grapevine/?utm_source=google-mybusiness&utm_medium=organic&utm_campaign=9488
Control: Other not–for–profit (including NFP Corporation) **Service**: General medical and surgical

Staffed Beds: 286 **Admissions**: 14537 **Census**: 182 **Outpatient Visits**: 88810 **Births**: 2183 **Total Expense ($000)**: 300066 **Payroll Expense ($000)**: 114080 **Personnel**: 989

Hospitals, U.S. / TEXAS

GREENVILLE—Hunt County

✠ **GLEN OAKS HOSPITAL (454050)**, 301 Division Street, Zip 75401–4101; tel. 903/454–6000, **A**1 10 **F**29 34 35 98 100 101 102 104 105 153 **S** Universal Health Services, Inc., King of Prussia, PA
Primary Contact: Harry Lemming, Chief Executive Officer
Web address: www.glenoakshospital.com
Control: Corporation, Investor-owned (for-profit) **Service:** Psychiatric

> **Staffed Beds:** 54 **Admissions:** 2566 **Census:** 49 **Outpatient Visits:** 2571
> **Births:** 0 **Total Expense ($000):** 13373 **Payroll Expense ($000):** 7617
> **Personnel:** 143

☐ **HUNT REGIONAL MEDICAL CENTER (450352)**, 4215 Joe Ramsey Boulevard East, Zip 75401–7899, Mailing Address: P.O. Box 1059, Zip 75403–1059; tel. 903/408–5000, **A**1 10 **F**3 12 13 15 28 29 30 34 35 37 38 40 42 43 45 46 47 48 49 51 54 56 57 59 60 61 62 64 65 68 70 72 74 75 76 77 79 81 82 85 87 90 93 97 102 104 107 108 109 110 111 115 119 126 127 129 130 131 132 135 144 146 147 148 149 154 156 164 167 169 **P**6
Primary Contact: Steven Lee. Boles, Chief Executive Officer
CMO: James H Sandin, M.D., Assistant Administrator Medical Affairs
CIO: Richard Montanye, Director Information Systems
CNO: Deborah Clack, Chief Nursing Officer
Web address: www.huntregional.org
Control: Hospital district or authority, Government, Nonfederal **Service:** General medical and surgical

> **Staffed Beds:** 173 **Admissions:** 8700 **Census:** 119 **Outpatient Visits:** 177819 **Births:** 1310 **Total Expense ($000):** 250161 **Payroll Expense ($000):** 104703 **Personnel:** 1565

GROESBECK—Limestone County

LIMESTONE MEDICAL CENTER (451303), 701 McClintic Drive, Zip 76642–2128; tel. 254/729–3281, **A**10 18 **F**3 7 11 28 29 32 34 35 40 41 43 45 57 62 64 65 68 75 77 84 85 93 96 97 104 107 111 115 119 127 129 130 133 135 146 148 153 165 **P**6
Primary Contact: Larry Price, Chief Executive Officer
CFO: Michael F. Williams, Chief Financial Officer
CMO: Jeffrey Rettig, D.O., Chief of Staff
CIO: Byong Lee, Chief Information Officer
CHR: Jean Koester, Manager Human Resources
CNO: Jean Wragge, Chief Nursing Officer
Web address: www.lmchospital.com
Control: Hospital district or authority, Government, Nonfederal **Service:** General medical and surgical

> **Staffed Beds:** 20 **Admissions:** 209 **Census:** 7 **Outpatient Visits:** 31571
> **Births:** 0 **Total Expense ($000):** 26934 **Payroll Expense ($000):** 13678
> **Personnel:** 239

HALLETTSVILLE—Lavaca County

LAVACA MEDICAL CENTER (451376), 1400 North Texana Street, Zip 77964–2099; tel. 361/798–3671, **A**10 18 **F**3 11 15 18 28 29 34 40 41 43 45 47 53 56 57 59 64 65 68 75 77 81 82 85 86 87 93 107 108 110 111 114 118 119 127 133 135 146 148 149 154
Primary Contact: Stephen Bowen, Chief Executive Officer
Web address: https://www.lavacamedcen.com/
Control: Hospital district or authority, Government, Nonfederal **Service:** General medical and surgical

> **Staffed Beds:** 25 **Admissions:** 403 **Census:** 6 **Outpatient Visits:** 21240
> **Births:** 0 **Total Expense ($000):** 22179 **Payroll Expense ($000):** 8303
> **Personnel:** 160

HAMILTON—Hamilton County

★ ⇑ **HAMILTON GENERAL HOSPITAL (451392)**, 400 North Brown Street, Zip 76531–1518; tel. 254/386–1600, **A**10 18 21 **F**3 7 11 15 28 29 34 35 40 43 44 45 50 53 57 59 64 65 68 75 79 81 82 85 86 87 93 97 104 107 108 110 111 115 119 127 129 130 131 133 148 149 154 156 157
Primary Contact: Grady A. Hooper, Chief Executive Officer
CMO: James R Lee, M.D., Chief of Staff
CIO: Chad Reinert, Chief Information Officer
CHR: Keela Payne, Director Human Resources
CNO: Debra Martin, Chief Nursing Officer
Web address: www.hamiltonhospital.org
Control: Hospital district or authority, Government, Nonfederal **Service:** General medical and surgical

> **Staffed Beds:** 25 **Admissions:** 396 **Census:** 4 **Outpatient Visits:** 84028
> **Births:** 0 **Total Expense ($000):** 51886 **Payroll Expense ($000):** 24814
> **Personnel:** 456

HARKER HEIGHTS—Bell County

✠ **SETON MEDICAL CENTER HARKER HEIGHTS (670080)**, 850 West Central Texas Expressway, Zip 76548–1890; tel. 254/690–0900, **A**1 10 **F**3 13 15 18 20 22 26 28 29 30 34 35 40 43 45 49 50 51 57 59 60 70 76 79 81 91 93 107 108 110 111 115 119 130 131 146 147 148 149 154 **S** Ardent Health Services, Nashville, TN
Primary Contact: Patrick Swindle, Chief Executive Officer
CFO: Shanna Cameron, Chief Financial Officer
CNO: Pamela Craig, R.N., Chief Nursing Officer
Web address: www.setonharkerheights.net
Control: Partnership, Investor-owned (for-profit) **Service:** General medical and surgical

> **Staffed Beds:** 83 **Admissions:** 3814 **Census:** 29 **Outpatient Visits:** 74514
> **Births:** 493 **Total Expense ($000):** 103433 **Payroll Expense ($000):** 31350
> **Personnel:** 357

HARLINGEN—Cameron County

☐ **HARLINGEN MEDICAL CENTER (450855)**, 5501 South Expressway 77, Zip 78550–3213; tel. 956/365–1000, **A**1 3 10 **F**3 12 15 17 18 20 22 24 26 29 34 35 40 43 49 50 57 59 60 64 68 70 74 75 76 79 81 85 86 107 108 110 111 114 115 118 119 129 130 146 147 148 **S** Prime Healthcare, Ontario, CA
Primary Contact: Candi Constantine–Castillo, DHA, DNP, MSN, R.N., Chief Executive Officer
CFO: Michael Bergstrom, Chief Financial Officer
CMO: Elizabeth Juarez, M.D., Chief Medical Officer
CHR: Emmett Craig, Director Human Resources
CNO: Deborah Meeks, Chief Nursing Officer
Web address: www.harlingenmedicalcenter.com
Control: Partnership, Investor-owned (for-profit) **Service:** General medical and surgical

> **Staffed Beds:** 88 **Admissions:** 6448 **Census:** 82 **Outpatient Visits:** 66477
> **Births:** 640 **Total Expense ($000):** 115114 **Payroll Expense ($000):** 42349
> **Personnel:** 532

☐ **RIO GRANDE STATE CENTER/SOUTH TEXAS HEALTH CARE SYSTEM (454088)**, 1401 South Rangerville Road, Zip 78552–7638; tel. 956/364–8000, (Includes RIO GRANDE STATE CENTER, 1401 South Rangerville Road, Harlingen, Texas, Zip 78552–7638, tel. 956/364–8000; SOUTH TEXAS HEALTH CARE SYSTEM, 1401 Rangerville Road, Harlingen, Texas, Zip 78552–7609, tel. 956/364–8000) **A**1 3 5 10 **F**3 65 66 68 75 87 97 98 101 119 130 132 135 143 146 147 154 156 163 164 167 **S** Texas Department of State Health Services, Austin, TX
Primary Contact: Sonia Hernandez–Keeble, Superintendent
CFO: Tom Garza, Director Fiscal and Support
CMO: David Moron, M.D., Clinical Director
CIO: Blas Ortiz Jr, Assistant Superintendent and Public Information Officer
CHR: Irma Garcia, Job Coordinator
CNO: Maia Baker, MSN, Chief Nurse Executive
Web address: www.dshs.state.tx.us/mhhospitals/RioGrandeSC/default.shtm
Control: State, Government, Nonfederal **Service:** Psychiatric

> **Staffed Beds:** 55 **Admissions:** 396 **Census:** 53 **Outpatient Visits:** 0
> **Births:** 0 **Total Expense ($000):** 23406 **Payroll Expense ($000):** 11929
> **Personnel:** 255

SOUTH TEXAS HOSPITAL See South Texas Health Care System

Hospital, Medicare Provider Number, Address, Telephone, Approval, Facility, and Physician Codes, Health Care System

★ American Hospital Association (AHA) membership
☐ The Joint Commission accreditation
◯ Healthcare Facilities Accreditation Program
◇ DNV Healthcare Inc. accreditation
⇑ Center for Improvement in Healthcare Quality Accreditation
△ Commission on Accreditation of Rehabilitation Facilities (CARF) accreditation

Hospitals, U.S. / TEXAS

★ **VA TEXAS VALLEY COASTAL HCS**, 2601 Veterans Drive, Zip 78550–8942; tel. 956/291–9000, (Nonreporting) **S** Department of Veterans Affairs, Washington, DC
Primary Contact: Homero S. Martinez III, Director
Control: Veterans Affairs, Government, federal **Service**: General medical and surgical

Staffed Beds: 25

✠ **VALLEY BAPTIST MEDICAL CENTER–HARLINGEN (450033)**, 2101 Pease Street, Zip 78550–8307, Mailing Address: P O Drawer 2588, Zip 78551–2588; tel. 956/389–1100, **A**1 3 5 10 **F**3 11 12 13 14 15 17 18 20 22 24 26 28 29 30 31 34 35 39 40 41 42 43 44 45 46 47 48 49 50 54 56 57 58 59 60 63 64 65 68 70 72 73 74 75 76 77 78 79 80 81 82 84 85 86 87 88 89 90 92 93 94 98 100 101 102 103 104 105 107 108 110 111 112 114 115 119 126 129 130 132 146 147 148 156 157 164 167 169 **S** TENET Healthcare Corporation, Dallas, TX
Primary Contact: Michael Cline, Chief Executive Officer
COO: Archie Drake, Chief Operating Officer
CNO: Stephen Hill, Vice President and Chief Nursing Officer
Web address: https://www.valleybaptist.net/locations/detail/vbmc-harlingen/
Control: Corporation, Investor–owned (for–profit) **Service**: General medical and surgical

Staffed Beds: 423 **Admissions**: 19830 **Census**: 290 **Outpatient Visits**: 144439 **Births**: 1719 **Total Expense ($000)**: 332329 **Payroll Expense ($000)**: 128821 **Personnel**: 1186

HASKELL—Haskell County

HASKELL MEMORIAL HOSPITAL (451341), 1 North Avenue 'N', Zip 79521–5499, Mailing Address: P.O. Box 1117, Zip 79521–1117; tel. 940/864–2621, **A**10 18 **F**11 28 29 30 34 35 40 53 57 59 64 68 75 77 86 87 93 97 107 111 119 127 129 130 131 133 146 148 154 **P**1 6
Primary Contact: Michelle Stevens, Chief Executive Officer
CHR: Emily Moore, Director Human Resources and Information Technology
CNO: Teri Turner, Chief Nursing Officer
Web address: www.haskellmemorialhospital.com/
Control: Hospital district or authority, Government, Nonfederal **Service**: General medical and surgical

Staffed Beds: 9 **Admissions**: 102 **Census**: 2 **Outpatient Visits**: 8135 **Births**: 1 **Total Expense ($000)**: 13336 **Payroll Expense ($000)**: 6302 **Personnel**: 88

HEMPHILL—Sabine County

SABINE COUNTY HOSPITAL (451361), 2301 Worth Street, Zip 75948–7216, Mailing Address: P.O. Box 750, Zip 75948–0750; tel. 409/787–3300, **A**10 18 **F**3 35 40 43 59 65 93 97 107 114 119 127 133 148 154 **S** Preferred Management Corporation, Shawnee, OK
Primary Contact: Kaylee McDaniel, Administrator
COO: Mike Easley, Vice President and Chief Operating Officer
CFO: Larry Stephens, Chief Financial Officer
CMO: Vera Luther, M.D., Chief of Staff
CIO: Margaret Moore, Director Business Office
CHR: Laura Simpson, Director Human Resources
CNO: Margie Watson MSN, RN–B, Chief Nursing Officer
Web address: www.sabinecountyhospital.com/
Control: Corporation, Investor–owned (for–profit) **Service**: General medical and surgical

Staffed Beds: 25 **Admissions**: 99 **Census**: 1 **Outpatient Visits**: 19541 **Births**: 0 **Total Expense ($000)**: 10974 **Payroll Expense ($000)**: 4788 **Personnel**: 78

HENDERSON—Rusk County

✠ **UT HEALTH HENDERSON (450475)**, 300 Wilson Street, Zip 75652–5956; tel. 903/657–7541, **A**1 10 **F**3 13 15 18 28 29 30 34 35 37 40 43 45 50 57 59 64 65 75 76 79 81 82 87 107 108 110 111 115 119 127 129 131 135 145 146 147 148 149 154 156 169 **S** Ardent Health Services, Nashville, TN
Primary Contact: Mark Leitner, FACHE, Administrator
CFO: Wesley Knight, Chief Financial Officer
CHR: William Henry, Director Human Resources
CNO: Donna K Stanley, R.N., Chief Nursing Officer
Web address: https://uthealthhenderson.com/
Control: Corporation, Investor–owned (for–profit) **Service**: General medical and surgical

Staffed Beds: 42 **Admissions**: 989 **Census**: 8 **Outpatient Visits**: 59656 **Births**: 218 **Total Expense ($000)**: 40989 **Payroll Expense ($000)**: 12360 **Personnel**: 168

HENRIETTA—Clay County

CLAY COUNTY MEMORIAL HOSPITAL (451362), 310 West South Street, Zip 76365–3346; tel. 940/538–5621, **A**10 18 **F**7 8 11 28 34 35 40 50 53 57 62 68 75 80 81 82 90 93 107 111 119 130 132 133 144 146
Primary Contact: James E. Koulovatos, Chief Executive Officer
CFO: Debra Haehn, Chief Financial Officer
CMO: Lexi Mitchell Sanchez, D.O., Chief of Staff
CNO: Kelley McMillion, Chief Nursing Officer
Web address: www.ccmhospital.com
Control: County, Government, Nonfederal **Service**: General medical and surgical

Staffed Beds: 25 **Admissions**: 147 **Census**: 1 **Outpatient Visits**: 15449 **Births**: 0 **Total Expense ($000)**: 11309 **Payroll Expense ($000)**: 5280 **Personnel**: 81

HEREFORD—Deaf Smith County

HEREFORD REGIONAL MEDICAL CENTER (450155), 540 West 15th Street, Zip 79045–2820; tel. 806/364–2141, **A**3 10 **F**3 7 11 13 15 29 35 40 43 50 57 59 65 70 76 77 81 85 93 100 102 107 111 115 119 127 130 133 147 148 156 164 169 **P**6
Primary Contact: Candice Smith, MSN, Chief Executive Officer
CFO: Sharon Hunt, Chief Financial Officer
CIO: Laura Garza, Manager Information Technology
CHR: Patsy Smith, Director Human Resources
CNO: Candice Smith, MSN, Chief Nursing Officer
Web address: www.dschd.org
Control: Hospital district or authority, Government, Nonfederal **Service**: General medical and surgical

Staffed Beds: 24 **Admissions**: 491 **Census**: 4 **Outpatient Visits**: 60093 **Births**: 236 **Total Expense ($000)**: 31233 **Payroll Expense ($000)**: 11923 **Personnel**: 184

HILLSBORO—Hill County

✠ **HILL REGIONAL HOSPITAL (451395)**, 101 Circle Drive, Zip 76645–2670; tel. 254/580–8500, **A**1 10 18 **F**3 13 15 29 34 35 40 43 45 57 59 64 65 68 75 76 78 79 81 86 87 93 107 111 114 118 119 133 146 147 149 154 169
Primary Contact: Raji Kumar, Managing Partner and Chief Executive Officer
CFO: Susan Popp, Chief Financial Officer
CHR: Rachael Esparza, Human Resource Coordinator
CNO: Catana Villarreal, Chief Nursing Officer
Web address: https://www.hillregionalhospital.com/
Control: Partnership, Investor–owned (for–profit) **Service**: General medical and surgical

Staffed Beds: 25 **Admissions**: 1437 **Census**: 13 **Outpatient Visits**: 21748 **Births**: 173 **Total Expense ($000)**: 35565 **Payroll Expense ($000)**: 10696 **Personnel**: 191

HONDO—Medina County

MEDINA REGIONAL HOSPITAL (451330), 3100 Avenue E, Zip 78861–3599; tel. 830/426–7700, **A**10 18 **F**3 11 13 15 28 29 30 35 40 43 45 50 56 59 64 65 68 75 76 77 79 81 82 84 85 87 91 92 93 107 110 111 115 119 127 130 133 135 146 147 148 149 154 156 157 167 169 **P**4
Primary Contact: Billie Bell, R.N., Chief Executive Officer
CFO: Kevin Frosch, Chief Financial Officer
CMO: Matthew Windrow, M.D., Chief of Staff
CIO: Ken Gallegos, Director Support Services and Information Technology
CHR: Sharon Garcia, Human Resources Representative
Web address: www.medinahospital.net
Control: Hospital district or authority, Government, Nonfederal **Service**: General medical and surgical

Staffed Beds: 25 **Admissions**: 676 **Census**: 10 **Outpatient Visits**: 46714 **Births**: 138 **Total Expense ($000)**: 37861 **Payroll Expense ($000)**: 15435 **Personnel**: 286

HORIZON CITY—El Paso County

⇧ **THE HOSPITALS OF PROVIDENCE HORIZON CITY CAMPUS (670124)**, 13600 Horizon Boulevard, Zip 79928; tel. 915/407–7878, **A**21 **F**3 29 40 42 102 107 114 149 **S** Emerus, The Woodlands, TX
Primary Contact: Catherine Lozano, Chief Executive Officer
Control: Corporation, Investor–owned (for–profit) **Service**: General medical and surgical

Staffed Beds: 16 **Admissions**: 548 **Census**: 3 **Births**: 2 **Total Expense ($000)**: 41342 **Payroll Expense ($000)**: 12382 **Personnel**: 110

Hospitals, U.S. / TEXAS

HOUSTON—Harris County

ADVANCED DIAGNOSTICS HOSPITAL See East Houston Hospitals & Clinics

⇧ **BAYLOR ST. LUKE'S MEDICAL CENTER** See Chi St Luke's Health – Baylor St Luke's Medical Center

☒ **BEHAVIORAL HOSPITAL OF BELLAIRE (454107)**, 5314 Dashwood Drive, Zip 77081–4603; tel. 713/600–9500, **A**1 10 **F**4 5 29 98 99 100 101 103 105 130 152 153 154 162 163 164 165 **S** Universal Health Services, Inc., King of Prussia, PA
Primary Contact: Amanda Tejeda–Blanco, Chief Executive Officer
CFO: Autumn Crouse, Chief Financial Officer
Web address: www.bhbhospital.com
Control: Corporation, Investor–owned (for–profit) **Service**: Psychiatric

Staffed Beds: 122 **Admissions**: 4651 **Census**: 101 **Outpatient Visits**: 6716
Births: 0 **Total Expense ($000)**: 25881 **Payroll Expense ($000)**: 14731
Personnel: 226

BEN TAUB GENERAL HOSPITAL See Ben Taub Hospital

★ ⇧ **CHI ST LUKE'S HEALTH – BAYLOR ST LUKE'S MEDICAL CENTER (450193)**, 6720 Bertner Avenue, Zip 77030–2697, Mailing Address: P.O. Box 20269, Zip 77225–0269; tel. 832/355–1000, (Includes BAYLOR ST. LUKE'S MEDICAL CENTER MCNAIR CAMPUS, 7200 Cambridge Street, Houston, Texas, Zip 77030–4202, tel. 713/798–4951; T. Douglas Lawson, Ph.D., FACHE, Chief Executive Officer) **A**2 3 5 8 10 21 **F**3 6 8 11 12 14 15 17 18 20 22 24 26 28 29 30 31 34 35 36 37 39 40 42 45 46 47 48 49 50 51 52 54 55 56 57 58 59 60 61 63 64 65 66 68 70 74 75 77 78 79 80 81 82 84 85 86 87 90 91 92 93 100 107 108 109 110 111 112 113 114 115 116 117 118 119 120 121 122 123 124 126 129 130 131 132 137 138 139 140 141 146 148 149 154 156 167 **S** CommonSpirit Health, Chicago, IL
Primary Contact: Bradley T. Lembcke, M.D., President
CMO: John Byrne, M.D., Vice President and Chief Medical Officer
CIO: James Albin, Chief Information Officer
CHR: Susan Bailey–Newell, Vice President Human Resources
CNO: Loretta Lee, Acting Chief Nursing Officer
Web address: https://locations.stlukeshealth.org/location/baylor-st-lukes-medical-center
Control: Church operated, Nongovernment, not–for–profit **Service**: General medical and surgical

Staffed Beds: 651 **Admissions**: 21695 **Census**: 435 **Outpatient Visits**: 173195 **Births**: 0 **Total Expense ($000)**: 1206063 **Payroll Expense ($000)**: 354707 **Personnel**: 3251

CHI ST. LUKE'S HOSPITAL – THE VINTAGE HOSPITAL See St. Luke's Health – The Vintage Hospital

CORNERSTONE SPECIALTY HOSPITAL HOUSTON MEDICAL CENTER See Vibra Hospital of Houston

☐ **CYPRESS CREEK HOSPITAL (454108)**, 17750 Cali Drive, Zip 77090–2700; tel. 281/586–7600, **A**1 3 10 **F**4 5 40 64 75 87 98 100 102 103 104 105 130 132 152 153 154 **S** Universal Health Services, Inc., King of Prussia, PA
Primary Contact: Amanda Vail, Chief Executive Officer
CFO: Stephen Copeland, Chief Financial Officer
CMO: Marshall Lucas, M.D., Medical Director
CIO: James Harmon, Information Technology
CHR: Brenda Dominguez, Director Human Resources
CNO: Michael Smith, Director of Nursing
Web address: www.cypresscreekhospital.com
Control: Corporation, Investor–owned (for–profit) **Service**: Psychiatric

Staffed Beds: 128 **Admissions**: 4251 **Census**: 98 **Outpatient Visits**: 8731
Births: 0 **Total Expense ($000)**: 24914 **Payroll Expense ($000)**: 15866
Personnel: 228

CYPRESS FAIRBANKS MEDICAL CENTER See HCA Houston Healthcare Cypress Fairbanks

☐ **EAST HOUSTON HOSPITALS & CLINICS (670102)**, 12950 East Freeway, Zip 77015–5710; tel. 713/330–3887, (Includes ADVANCED DALLAS HOSPITAL AND CLINICS, 7502 Greenville Avenue, Dallas, Texas, Zip 75231–3802, tel. 469/221–6000; Thomas Alexander, Chief Executive Officer; RIVER OAKS HOSPITALS & CLINICS, 4200 Twelve Oaks Drive, Houston, Texas, Zip 77027–6812, tel. 713/980–7900; Robert A Turner, Chief Executive Officer) **A**1 10 22 **F**12 15 29 35 40 45 54 59 64 68 70 75 77 79 81 82 85 86 87 93 97 100 102 107 110 111 114 115 119 131 148 149 154 156
Primary Contact: Rubin Shah, Chief Executive Officer
CFO: Carol Files, Chief Financial Officer
CMO: Ian Reynolds, Chief Medical Officer
CIO: Yobi Kasper, Chief Information Officer
CHR: Gabby Myers, Human Resources Director
CNO: David Gonzalez, Chief Clinical Officer
Web address: www.adhealthcare.com
Control: Individual, Investor–owned (for–profit) **Service**: General medical and surgical

Staffed Beds: 34 **Admissions**: 1899 **Census**: 19 **Outpatient Visits**: 51842
Births: 0 **Total Expense ($000)**: 68428 **Payroll Expense ($000)**: 23010
Personnel: 377

☒ **ENCOMPASS HEALTH REHABILITATION HOSPITAL OF CYPRESS (673050)**, 13031 Wortham Center Drive, Zip 77065–5662; tel. 832/280–2500, **A**1 10 **F**3 29 34 57 59 75 77 82 86 87 90 91 96 130 132 148 149 156 **S** Encompass Health Corporation, Birmingham, AL
Primary Contact: Katy Reed, Chief Executive Officer
CFO: Melissa Haddox, Controller
CMO: Ignazio LaChina, M.D., Medical Director
CNO: Roshonda Henry, Chief Nursing Officer
Web address: www.healthsouthcypress.com
Control: Corporation, Investor–owned (for–profit) **Service**: Rehabilitation

Staffed Beds: 60 **Admissions**: 1132 **Census**: 42 **Outpatient Visits**: 0
Births: 0 **Total Expense ($000)**: 23452 **Payroll Expense ($000)**: 12103
Personnel: 170

☒ **ENCOMPASS HEALTH REHABILITATION HOSPITAL THE VINTAGE (673052)**, 20180 Chasewood Park Drive, Zip 77070–1436; tel. 281/205–5100, **A**1 10 **F**3 28 29 65 90 91 96 130 132 148 149 154 **S** Encompass Health Corporation, Birmingham, AL
Primary Contact: Krista Uselman, Chief Executive Officer
CNO: Stanley F Kiebzak, R.N., Chief Nursing Officer
Web address: www.reliantnwhouston.com
Control: Corporation, Investor–owned (for–profit) **Service**: Rehabilitation

Staffed Beds: 60 **Admissions**: 1358 **Census**: 46 **Outpatient Visits**: 0
Births: 0 **Total Expense ($000)**: 27756 **Payroll Expense ($000)**: 13165
Personnel: 178

☒ **HCA HOUSTON HEALTHCARE MEDICAL CENTER (450659)**, 1313 Hermann Drive, Zip 77004–7092; tel. 713/527–5000, **A**1 3 5 10 **F**3 12 17 18 20 22 24 26 29 30 37 40 46 49 50 58 60 70 74 75 79 81 85 86 92 107 108 110 111 114 115 118 119 120 121 123 126 130 146 148 167 **S** HCA Healthcare, Nashville, TN
Primary Contact: Chris Osentowski, Chief Executive Officer
COO: Mary Jo Goodman, Chief Operating Officer
CFO: Melissa Mendoza, Chief Financial Officer
CIO: Terry Janis, Assistant Vice President
CHR: Melanie R Webb, Vice President Human Resources
Web address: https://hcahoustonhealthcare.com/locations/medical-center/
Control: Corporation, Investor–owned (for–profit) **Service**: General medical and surgical

Staffed Beds: 136 **Admissions**: 4592 **Census**: 70 **Outpatient Visits**: 20704
Births: 0 **Total Expense ($000)**: 203547 **Payroll Expense ($000)**: 54747
Personnel: 411

Hospital, Medicare Provider Number, Address, Telephone, Approval, Facility, and Physician Codes, Health Care System

★ American Hospital Association (AHA) membership   ○ Healthcare Facilities Accreditation Program   ⇧ Center for Improvement in Healthcare Quality Accreditation
☐ The Joint Commission accreditation   ◇ DNV Healthcare Inc. accreditation   △ Commission on Accreditation of Rehabilitation Facilities (CARF) accreditation

Hospitals, U.S. / TEXAS

☒ **HCA HOUSTON HEALTHCARE NORTHWEST (450638)**, 710 Cypress Creek Parkway, Zip 77090–3402; tel. 281/440–1000, **A**1 3 5 10 **F**3 11 12 13 18 20 22 24 26 28 29 30 31 34 35 40 42 43 45 46 47 48 49 50 57 59 60 64 65 70 72 74 75 76 77 78 79 80 81 82 84 85 86 87 90 92 93 107 108 111 115 119 126 129 130 132 135 146 147 148 149 154 167 **S** HCA Healthcare, Nashville, TN
Primary Contact: Tricia Mcgusty, Interim Chief Executive Officer
CFO: Cameron Pophan, Chief Financial Officer
CMO: Arabinda Pani, Chief Medical Officer
CIO: Ed Roberson, Director Information Systems
CHR: Melanie R Webb, Vice President Human Resources
CNO: Cindy Henning, R.N., Chief Nursing Officer
Web address: www.hnmc.com
Control: Partnership, Investor–owned (for–profit) **Service**: General medical and surgical

Staffed Beds: 316 **Admissions**: 16248 **Census**: 219 **Outpatient Visits**: 86480 **Births**: 3103 **Total Expense ($000)**: 362016 **Payroll Expense ($000)**: 121321 **Personnel**: 1321

☒ **HCA HOUSTON HEALTHCARE WEST (450644)**, 12141 Richmond Avenue, Zip 77082–2499; tel. 281/558–3444, **A**1 3 5 10 **F**3 11 12 13 15 18 20 22 24 26 28 29 31 39 40 45 46 47 48 49 50 51 54 56 57 59 60 64 65 70 73 74 75 76 77 78 79 80 81 82 85 87 90 93 96 102 107 108 110 111 114 115 116 117 118 119 121 124 126 129 130 132 135 145 146 147 148 149 167 169 **S** HCA Healthcare, Nashville, TN
Primary Contact: Megan Marietta, Chief Executive Officer
COO: Justin Brewer, Chief Operating Officer
CFO: Stanley K Nord, Chief Financial Officer
CMO: Magdy Rizk, M.D., Chief of Staff
CIO: Sergio Almeida, Director Information Systems
CHR: Carol Melville, Director Human Resources
Web address: https://hcahoustonhealthcare.com/locations/west/
Control: Partnership, Investor–owned (for–profit) **Service**: General medical and surgical

Staffed Beds: 251 **Admissions**: 10839 **Census**: 123 **Outpatient Visits**: 104300 **Births**: 1489 **Total Expense ($000)**: 228618 **Payroll Expense ($000)**: 77302 **Personnel**: 665

☐ **HOUSTON BEHAVIORAL HEALTHCARE HOSPITAL (454135)**, 2801 Gessner Road, Zip 77080–2503; tel. 832/834–7710, **A**1 10 **F**5 29 35 56 98 99 103 104 105 130 152 153 154 160 161 164 **S** Signature Healthcare Services, Corona, CA
Primary Contact: Adrian Flores, Chief Executive Officer
Web address: www.houstonbehavioralhealth.com/
Control: Individual, Investor–owned (for–profit) **Service**: Psychiatric

Staffed Beds: 163 **Admissions**: 5835 **Census**: 137 **Outpatient Visits**: 7409 **Births**: 0 **Total Expense ($000)**: 35149 **Payroll Expense ($000)**: 18779 **Personnel**: 251

★ ⇧ **HOUSTON METHODIST CLEAR LAKE HOSPITAL (450709)**, 18300 Houston Methodist Drive, Zip 77058–6302; tel. 281/333–5503, **A**2 3 5 10 21 **F**3 8 11 12 13 15 18 20 22 24 26 29 30 31 34 35 39 40 41 42 44 45 46 48 49 50 51 53 54 57 59 60 63 64 65 68 70 72 74 75 76 77 78 79 81 82 84 85 86 87 93 94 96 102 107 108 110 111 115 118 119 120 121 123 126 130 131 132 135 146 147 148 149 150 154 167 169 **P**5 6 **S** Houston Methodist, Houston, TX
Primary Contact: Carl Little, Chief Executive Officer
CFO: David A Witt, Vice President Finances
CHR: Becky A Merritt, Director Human Resources
Web address: https://www.houstonmethodist.org/locations/clear-lake/
Control: Other not–for–profit (including NFP Corporation) **Service**: General medical and surgical

Staffed Beds: 134 **Admissions**: 6843 **Census**: 80 **Outpatient Visits**: 240457 **Births**: 570 **Total Expense ($000)**: 273100 **Payroll Expense ($000)**: 99369 **Personnel**: 938

★ △ ⇧ **HOUSTON METHODIST HOSPITAL (450358)**, 6565 Fannin Street, D200, Zip 77030–2707; tel. 713/790–3311, (Total facility includes 18 beds in nursing home–type unit) **A**2 3 5 7 8 10 21 **F**3 5 6 7 8 9 11 12 13 14 15 17 18 20 22 24 26 28 29 30 31 34 35 36 37 38 39 40 41 42 44 45 46 47 48 49 50 51 52 53 54 55 56 57 58 59 60 61 63 64 65 66 68 70 73 74 75 76 77 78 79 80 81 82 84 85 86 87 90 91 92 93 95 96 97 98 100 101 102 103 104 107 108 110 111 112 114 115 117 118 119 120 121 123 124 126 128 129 130 131 132 135 136 137 138 139 140 141 142 143 145 146 147 148 149 150 153 154 156 160 162 164 167 169 **P**5 6 **S** Houston Methodist, Houston, TX
Primary Contact: Roberta Schwartz, Ph.D., Executive Vice President
CMO: Robert Phillips, M.D., Ph.D., FACC, Executive Vice President and Chief Medical Officer
CNO: Katherine Walsh, MS, R.N., Dr.PH, Vice President and Chief Nursing Officer
Web address: www.methodisthealth.com
Control: Other not–for–profit (including NFP Corporation) **Service**: General medical and surgical

Staffed Beds: 963 **Admissions**: 41177 **Census**: 835 **Outpatient Visits**: 544502 **Births**: 1562 **Total Expense ($000)**: 2726380 **Payroll Expense ($000)**: 723297 **Personnel**: 12749

★ ⇧ **HOUSTON METHODIST WEST HOSPITAL (670077)**, 18500 Katy Freeway, Zip 77094–1110; tel. 832/522–1000, **A**2 10 21 **F**3 11 12 13 15 17 18 20 22 24 26 28 29 30 31 34 35 36 37 38 39 40 41 42 44 45 46 48 49 50 51 53 54 55 56 57 58 59 60 61 63 64 68 70 72 74 75 76 77 78 79 81 82 84 85 86 87 92 93 94 97 102 107 108 110 111 114 115 117 118 119 120 121 123 124 126 130 131 132 135 146 147 148 149 150 154 156 160 164 167 169 **P**5 6 **S** Houston Methodist, Houston, TX
Primary Contact: Wayne M. Voss, Chief Executive Officer
CNO: Victoria Brownewell, Chief Nursing Officer
Web address: www.methodisthealth.com
Control: Other not–for–profit (including NFP Corporation) **Service**: General medical and surgical

Staffed Beds: 271 **Admissions**: 16196 **Census**: 178 **Outpatient Visits**: 223054 **Births**: 2714 **Total Expense ($000)**: 516106 **Payroll Expense ($000)**: 175989 **Personnel**: 2016

★ ⇧ **HOUSTON METHODIST WILLOWBROOK HOSPITAL (450844)**, 18220 Tomball Pkwy, Zip 77070–4347, Mailing Address: 18220 Tomball Pwy, Zip 77070–4347; tel. 281/477–1000, **A**3 10 21 **F**3 8 11 12 13 15 18 20 22 24 26 28 29 30 31 34 35 36 37 40 42 44 45 49 50 53 54 57 59 64 65 70 72 73 74 75 76 77 78 79 81 82 84 85 86 87 93 97 100 102 107 108 110 111 112 115 119 120 121 123 124 126 130 131 132 135 146 147 148 149 150 154 156 167 169 **P**5 6 **S** Houston Methodist, Houston, TX
Primary Contact: Keith Barber, CPA, Chief Executive Officer
CHR: Elizabeth Acevedo, Director Human Resources
CNO: Nancy C Keenan, R.N., Senior Vice President and Chief Nursing Officer
Web address: www.houstonmethodist.org/locations/willowbrook/
Control: Other not–for–profit (including NFP Corporation) **Service**: General medical and surgical

Staffed Beds: 358 **Admissions**: 24273 **Census**: 296 **Outpatient Visits**: 291333 **Births**: 3770 **Total Expense ($000)**: 673031 **Payroll Expense ($000)**: 237462 **Personnel**: 2399

JEFFERSON DAVIS HOSPITAL See Lyndon B Johnson General Hospital

☒ **KINDRED HOSPITAL HOUSTON MEDICAL CENTER (452023)**, 6441 Main Street, Zip 77030–1596; tel. 713/790–0500, **A**1 3 5 10 **F**3 1 29 30 60 70 75 77 90 107 130 148 167 **S** ScionHealth, Louisville, KY
Primary Contact: Laura Rodriguez, Chief Executive Officer
CFO: Sara Langlitz, Controller
Web address: www.khhouston.com/
Control: Corporation, Investor–owned (for–profit) **Service**: Acute long–term care hospital

Staffed Beds: 84 **Admissions**: 807 **Census**: 60 **Outpatient Visits**: 0 **Births**: 0 **Total Expense ($000)**: 47816 **Payroll Expense ($000)**: 20961 **Personnel**: 211

☒ **KINDRED HOSPITAL–HOUSTON NORTHWEST (452039)**, 11297 Fallbrook Drive, Zip 77065–4292; tel. 281/897–8114, **A**1 10 **F**1 3 29 30 49 57 60 64 70 77 85 87 107 130 148 **S** ScionHealth, Louisville, KY
Primary Contact: Tracy Kohler, Chief Executive Officer
Web address: https://www.kindredhospitals.com/locations/ltac/kindred-hospital-houston-northwest
Control: Corporation, Investor–owned (for–profit) **Service**: Acute long–term care hospital

Staffed Beds: 84 **Admissions**: 549 **Census**: 46 **Outpatient Visits**: 28 **Births**: 0 **Total Expense ($000)**: 34930 **Payroll Expense ($000)**: 15482 **Personnel**: 226

LYNDON B JOHNSON GENERAL HOSPITAL See Harris Health System, Bellaire

MEM HERMANN CHILDREN'S HOSP See Children's Memorial Hermann Hospital

Hospitals, U.S. / TEXAS

◻ △ **MEMORIAL HERMANN – TEXAS MEDICAL CENTER (450068)**, 6411 Fannin Street, Zip 77030–1501; tel. 713/704–4000, (Includes CHILDREN'S MEMORIAL HERMANN HOSPITAL, 6411 Fannin, Houston, Texas, Zip 77030, tel. 713/704–5437; MEMORIAL HERMAN CYPRESS, 27700 Highway 290 Ste 380, Cypress, Texas, Zip 77433–8029, 27700 NW Freeway, Suite 380, Zip 77433, tel. 832/658–3102; Jerry Ashworth, Senior Vice President and Chief Executive Officer; MEMORIAL HERMANN ORTHOPEDIC AND SPINE HOSPITAL, 5410 West Loop South, Bellaire, Texas, Zip 77401–2103, tel. 713/314–4500; Gregory Haralson, FACHE, Senior Vice President and Chief Executive Officer) **A**1 2 3 5 7 8 10 19 **F**3 6 7 8 9 11 12 13 15 16 17 18 19 20 21 22 23 24 25 26 27 28 29 30 31 32 34 35 36 37 39 40 41 43 44 45 46 47 48 49 50 52 53 54 55 56 57 58 59 60 61 62 63 64 65 66 68 69 70 71 72 74 75 76 77 78 79 80 81 82 83 84 85 86 87 88 89 90 92 93 97 100 102 107 108 109 110 111 112 113 114 115 116 117 118 119 120 121 122 123 124 126 128 129 130 131 134 137 138 139 140 141 142 143 144 145 146 147 148 149 150 154 155 157 167 169 **S** Memorial Hermann Health System, Houston, TX
Primary Contact: Jason Glover, Chief Executive Officer
CFO: William Pack, Chief Financial Officer
CMO: Jeffrey Katz, M.D., Chief Medical Officer
CIO: David Bradshaw, Chief Information Officer
Web address: www.mhhs.org
Control: Other not–for–profit (including NFP Corporation) **Service:** General medical and surgical

Staffed Beds: 1234 **Admissions:** 45868 **Census:** 860 **Outpatient Visits:** 333146 **Births:** 6630 **Total Expense ($000):** 2566832 **Payroll Expense ($000):** 738782 **Personnel:** 7586

◻ △ **MEMORIAL HERMANN GREATER HEIGHTS HOSPITAL (450184)**, 1635 North Loop West, Zip 77008–1532; tel. 713/867–3380, (Includes MEMORIAL HERMANN PEARLAND MEDICAL CENTER, 16100 South Freeway, Pearland, Texas, Zip 77584–1895, tel. 713/413–5000; Colonel Noel J. Cardenas, FACHE, Senior Vice President and Chief Executive Officer; MEMORIAL HERMANN SOUTHEAST HOSPITAL, 11800 Astoria Boulevard, Houston, Texas, Zip 77089–6041, tel. 281/929–6100; Colonel Noel J. Cardenas, FACHE, Senior Vice President and Chief Executive Officer; MEMORIAL HERMANN SOUTHWEST HOSPITAL, 7600 Beechnut, Houston, Texas, Zip 77074–1850, tel. 713/456–5000; Malisha Patel, Senior Vice President and Chief Executive Officer; MEMORIAL HERMANN THE WOODLANDS HOSPITAL, 9250 Pinecroft Drive, The Woodlands, Texas, Zip 77380–3225, tel. 281/364–2300; Justin Kendrick, Senior Vice President and Chief Executive Officer) **A**1 2 3 5 7 8 10 **F**3 11 12 13 15 17 18 20 22 24 26 28 29 30 31 33 34 35 36 37 40 41 42 43 44 45 46 47 48 49 50 51 54 55 56 57 58 59 60 62 63 64 65 70 72 73 74 75 76 77 78 79 80 81 82 84 85 86 87 89 90 91 92 93 94 96 107 108 109 110 111 112 113 114 115 116 117 118 119 120 121 123 124 126 129 130 131 132 135 143 144 146 147 148 149 154 155 156 167 **P**5 6 **S** Memorial Hermann Health System, Houston, TX
Primary Contact: Paul O'Sullivan, FACHE, Chief Executive Officer
CFO: James R Shallock, Chief Financial Officer
CMO: Maurice Leibman, M.D., Chief Medical Officer
CIO: David Bradshaw, Chief Information Officer
CNO: Ann Szapor, Vice President and Chief Nursing Officer
Web address: www.memorialhermann.org
Control: Other not–for–profit (including NFP Corporation) **Service:** General medical and surgical

Staffed Beds: 1465 **Admissions:** 72709 **Census:** 1032 **Outpatient Visits:** 657772 **Births:** 11416 **Total Expense ($000):** 1989399 **Payroll Expense ($000):** 695352 **Personnel:** 7395

◻ **MEMORIAL HERMANN MEMORIAL CITY MEDICAL CENTER (450610)**, 921 Gessner Road, Zip 77024–2501; tel. 713/242–3000, **A**1 2 3 5 10 **F**3 12 13 15 18 20 22 24 26 28 29 30 31 34 35 37 40 41 43 44 45 46 47 49 50 51 56 57 59 60 65 70 72 74 75 76 77 78 79 80 81 82 84 85 86 87 89 107 108 110 111 114 115 117 118 119 120 121 123 124 126 129 130 131 132 135 146 147 148 149 156 164 167 169 **S** Memorial Hermann Health System, Houston, TX
Primary Contact: Paul O'Sullivan, FACHE, Chief Executive Officer
COO: Allen Tseng, Chief Operations Officer
CFO: Lisa Kendler, Chief Financial Officer
CMO: Harold Gottlieb, M.D., Chief Medical Officer
CIO: David Bradshaw, Chief Information, Planning and Marketing Officer
CHR: Suzanne S Meier, System Director, Compensation and Human Resources Technology
CNO: Dan Kelly, R.N., Chief Nursing Officer
Web address: www.memorialhermann.org
Control: Other not–for–profit (including NFP Corporation) **Service:** General medical and surgical

Staffed Beds: 444 **Admissions:** 20369 **Census:** 258 **Outpatient Visits:** 172406 **Births:** 4427 **Total Expense ($000):** 646329 **Payroll Expense ($000):** 187741 **Personnel:** 2110

MEMORIAL HERMANN SOUTHEAST See Memorial Hermann Southeast Hospital

MEMORIAL HERMANN SOUTHEAST HOSPITAL See Memorial Hermann Greater Heights Hospital, Houston

MEMORIAL HERMANN SOUTHWEST HOSPITAL See Memorial Hermann Greater Heights Hospital, Houston

MEMORIAL HOSPITAL SOUTHWEST See Memorial Hermann Southwest Hospital

◻ **MENNINGER CLINIC**, 12301 Main Street, Zip 77035–6207; tel. 713/275–5000, **A**1 3 5 **F**5 30 35 62 74 98 99 101 104 105 129 130 132 152 153 154 160 161 163 165 169
Primary Contact: Armando Colombo, Chief Executive Officer
CFO: Anthony Gaglio, CPA, Senior Vice President and Chief Financial Officer
CIO: M. Justin Coffey, Vice President and Chief Information Officer, Medical Director Center for Brain Stimulation
CHR: Andrea Preisinger, Director Human Resources
Web address: www.menningerclinic.com
Control: Other not–for–profit (including NFP Corporation) **Service:** Psychiatric

Staffed Beds: 120 **Admissions:** 728 **Census:** 58 **Outpatient Visits:** 8535 **Births:** 0 **Total Expense ($000):** 72573 **Payroll Expense ($000):** 31123 **Personnel:** 448

◻ △ **MICHAEL E. DEBAKEY DEPARTMENT OF VETERANS AFFAIRS MEDICAL CENTER**, 2002 Holcombe Boulevard, Zip 77030–4298; tel. 713/791–1414, (Nonreporting) **A**1 2 3 5 7 **S** Department of Veterans Affairs, Washington, DC
Primary Contact: Francisco Vazquez, Director
CFO: Alisa Cooper, Manager Financial Resources
CMO: Jagadeesh S Kalavar, M.D., Chief of Staff
CIO: Kevin Lenamond, Information Management Service Line Executive
CHR: Mark Muhammad, Manager Human Resources
CNO: Kelly Ann Irving MSN, RN–B, Associate Director for Patient Care Services
Web address: www.houston.va.gov
Control: Veterans Affairs, Government, federal **Service:** General medical and surgical

Staffed Beds: 357

MICHAEL E. DEBAKEY VA MEDICAL CENTER See Michael E. Debakey Department of Veterans Affairs Medical Center

⇧ **NEXUS CHILDREN'S HOSPITAL HOUSTON (453309)**, 2929 Woodland Park Drive, Zip 77082–2687; tel. 281/293–7774, **A**5 10 21 **F**3 12 29 64 74 75 79 85 87 89 91 93 100 130 146 148 164 **P**5 **S** Nexus Health Systems, Houston, TX
Primary Contact: Roger Caron, Chief Executive Officer
CMO: Hailey Bennion, Chief Clinical Officer
CHR: Guy Murdock, Vice President Human Resources
Web address: https://www.nexuscontinuum.com/services/childrens-hospital/
Control: Partnership, Investor–owned (for–profit) **Service:** Children's other specialty

Staffed Beds: 111 **Admissions:** 154 **Census:** 35 **Outpatient Visits:** 563 **Births:** 0 **Total Expense ($000):** 36203 **Payroll Expense ($000):** 15720 **Personnel:** 356

★ **PAM HEALTH REHABILITATION HOSPITAL OF HOUSTON HEIGHTS (673072)**, 1917 Ashland Street, 4th Floor, Zip 77008–3907; tel. 713/814–9100, **A**22 **F**3 12 29 56 60 68 90 91 94 107 111 114 115 119 130 **S** PAM Health, Enola, PA
Primary Contact: Micheal Simpson, Interim Chief Executive Officer
Web address: https://pamhealth.com/index.php/facilities/find-facility/rehabilitation-hospitals/pam-health-rehabilitation-hospital-houston-heights
Control: Corporation, Investor–owned (for–profit) **Service:** Rehabilitation

Staffed Beds: 35 **Admissions:** 742 **Census:** 27 **Outpatient Visits:** 0 **Births:** 0 **Total Expense ($000):** 16228 **Payroll Expense ($000):** 7495 **Personnel:** 113

SPECIALTY HOSPITAL OF HOUSTON See Cornerstone Hospital of Houston – Bellaire

---

Hospital, Medicare Provider Number, Address, Telephone, Approval, Facility, and Physician Codes, Health Care System

★ American Hospital Association (AHA) membership ◯ Healthcare Facilities Accreditation Program ⇧ Center for Improvement in Healthcare Quality Accreditation
◻ The Joint Commission accreditation ◇ DNV Healthcare Inc. accreditation △ Commission on Accreditation of Rehabilitation Facilities (CARF) accreditation

Hospitals, U.S. / TEXAS

⇧ **ST. JOSEPH MEDICAL CENTER (450035)**, 1401 St Joseph Parkway, Zip 77002–8301; tel. 713/757–1000, **A**3 5 10 21 **F**3 12 13 15 18 20 22 24 26 29 30 34 38 40 43 45 49 50 51 57 59 60 64 68 70 72 74 75 76 77 78 79 81 82 84 85 86 87 93 101 102 107 108 110 111 114 115 116 117 118 119 121 123 124 126 130 131 148 149 154 156 164 167 169 **S** Steward Health Care System, LLC, Dallas, TX
Primary Contact: Scott Flowers, Interim President and Chief Operating Officer
COO: Laura Fortin, R.N., Chief Operating Officer
CFO: Mark Hartman, Interim Chief Financial Officer
CHR: Kris Clatanoff, Director Human Resources
Web address: www.sjmctx.com
Control: Partnership, Investor–owned (for–profit) **Service:** General medical and surgical

> **Staffed Beds:** 216 **Admissions:** 10096 **Census:** 118 **Outpatient Visits:** 74887 **Births:** 2983 **Total Expense ($000):** 234230 **Payroll Expense ($000):** 81631 **Personnel:** 831

ST. LUKE'S HEALTH – THE VINTAGE HOSPITAL (670075), 20171 Chasewood Park Drive, Zip 77070–1437; tel. 832/534–5000, **A**1 10 **F**3 13 15 18 20 22 24 26 29 30 34 35 40 44 45 46 49 50 57 59 64 68 70 72 74 76 77 79 81 85 86 87 107 108 110 111 114 115 118 119 130 146 149 167 **S** CommonSpirit Health, Chicago, IL
Primary Contact: Mario J. Garner, Ed.D., FACHE, Chief Executive Officer
Web address: https://locations.stlukeshealth.org/location/vintage-hospital
Control: Church operated, Nongovernment, not–for–profit **Service:** General medical and surgical

> **Staffed Beds:** 94 **Admissions:** 5946 **Census:** 64 **Outpatient Visits:** 35231 **Births:** 953 **Total Expense ($000):** 113904 **Payroll Expense ($000):** 43425 **Personnel:** 447

SUN BEHAVIORAL HOUSTON (454139), 7601 Fannin Street, Zip 77054–1905; tel. 713/796–2273, **A**1 5 10 **F**5 98 99 100 101 102 103 104 105 106 132 134 135 149 150 152 153 154 162 163 164 165
Primary Contact: Brennan Francois, Chief Executive Officer
CMO: Vernon Walling, M.D., Chief Medical Officer
Web address: www.sunhouston.com
Control: Corporation, Investor–owned (for–profit) **Service:** Psychiatric

> **Staffed Beds:** 148 **Admissions:** 5327 **Census:** 120 **Outpatient Visits:** 10920 **Births:** 0 **Total Expense ($000):** 34095 **Payroll Expense ($000):** 18158 **Personnel:** 275

△ **TEXAS CHILDREN'S HOSPITAL (453304)**, 6621 Fannin Street, Zip 77030–2399, Mailing Address: Box 300630, Zip 77230–0630; tel. 832/824–1000, (Includes TEXAS CHILDREN'S HOSPITAL THE WOODLANDS, 17600 Interstate 45 South, The Woodlands, Texas, Zip 77384–5148, tel. 936/267–5000; Ketrese White, R.N., Senior Vice President; TEXAS CHILDREN'S HOSPITAL WEST CAMPUS, 18200 Katy Freeway, Houston, Texas, Zip 77094–1285, tel. 832/227–1000; Ketrese White, R.N., Senior Vice President) **A**1 3 5 7 8 10 **F**3 7 11 12 13 17 19 20 21 22 23 24 25 26 27 29 30 31 32 34 35 37 38 39 40 41 43 45 46 48 49 50 51 52 54 55 57 58 59 60 61 63 64 65 66 68 71 72 73 74 75 76 77 78 79 80 81 82 84 85 86 87 88 89 90 92 93 94 95 96 97 100 101 102 104 107 108 111 112 113 114 115 116 117 118 119 122 124 126 129 130 131 132 134 136 137 138 139 140 146 147 148 149 150 153 154 155 156 162 164 165 166 167 169
Primary Contact: Mark A. Wallace, FACHE, Chief Executive Officer
CMO: Jim Versalovic, M.D., Ph.D., Interim Physican–in–Chief
CIO: Myra Davis, Senior Vice President and Chief Information Officer
CHR: Linda W Aldred, Senior Vice President
CNO: Jacqueline Ward, MSN, R.N., Chief Nursing Officer
Web address: www.texaschildrens.org
Control: Other not–for–profit (including NFP Corporation) **Service:** Children's general medical and surgical

> **Staffed Beds:** 905 **Admissions:** 30922 **Census:** 656 **Outpatient Visits:** 1872588 **Births:** 6688 **Total Expense ($000):** 3638037 **Payroll Expense ($000):** 1186473 **Personnel:** 12312

TEXAS ORTHOPEDIC HOSPITAL (450804), 7401 South Main Street, Zip 77030–4509; tel. 713/799–8600, **A**1 3 5 10 **F**3 29 30 34 35 37 40 50 53 58 59 64 68 70 79 81 82 85 86 87 93 94 97 107 111 119 126 131 141 149 154 157 164 167 **P**2 **S** HCA Healthcare, Nashville, TN
Primary Contact: Eric Becker, Chief Executive Officer
CFO: Blair Callaway, Chief Financial Officer
CMO: Gregory Stocks, M.D., Chief of Staff
CNO: Troy Sarver, R.N., Chief Nursing Officer
Web address: www.texasorthopedic.com
Control: Partnership, Investor–owned (for–profit) **Service:** Orthopedic

> **Staffed Beds:** 42 **Admissions:** 2493 **Census:** 16 **Outpatient Visits:** 45495 **Births:** 0 **Total Expense ($000):** 148497 **Payroll Expense ($000):** 39792 **Personnel:** 470

△ **TIRR MEMORIAL HERMANN (453025)**, 1333 Moursund Street, Zip 77030–3405; tel. 713/799–5000, **A**1 3 5 7 10 **F**3 11 29 30 34 35 44 45 50 54 58 59 64 65 68 74 75 77 79 82 86 87 90 91 92 93 95 96 97 100 104 107 114 119 129 130 131 132 135 143 146 148 149 154 157 **S** Memorial Hermann Health System, Houston, TX
Primary Contact: Rhonda Abbott, Senior Vice President and Chief Executive Officer
CFO: Wayne Gordon, Chief Financial Officer
CMO: Gerard E Francisco, M.D., Chief Medical Officer
CIO: Gina Tripp, Director Information Systems
CNO: Nicole Harrison, R.N., CNO
Web address: www.memorialhermann.org/locations/tirr.html
Control: Other not–for–profit (including NFP Corporation) **Service:** Rehabilitation

> **Staffed Beds:** 134 **Admissions:** 1619 **Census:** 103 **Outpatient Visits:** 34743 **Births:** 0 **Total Expense ($000):** 156705 **Payroll Expense ($000):** 76775 **Personnel:** 998

TOPS SURGICAL SPECIALTY HOSPITAL (450774), 17080 Red Oak Drive, Zip 77090–2602; tel. 281/539–2900, **A**1 10 **F**3 15 18 20 29 34 45 48 51 64 79 81 82 86 87 108 109 110 119 124 131 132 148 149 167 **P**2 **S** United Surgical Partners International, Addison, TX
Primary Contact: Grant Magness, Chief Executive Officer
CFO: Daniel Smith, Chief Financial Officer
CMO: Thomas Barton, M.D., Medical Director
CIO: Maud Jones, Manager Medical Records
CHR: Ashley Monzingo, Human Resources, Accounts Payable and Payroll
CNO: Andrea Wappelhorst, Chief Nursing Officer
Web address: www.tops-hospital.com
Control: Partnership, Investor–owned (for–profit) **Service:** Surgical

> **Staffed Beds:** 15 **Admissions:** 433 **Census:** 2 **Outpatient Visits:** 49456 **Births:** 0 **Total Expense ($000):** 46234 **Payroll Expense ($000):** 10158 **Personnel:** 112

UNIVERSITY OF TEXAS M.D. ANDERSON CANCER CENTER (450076), 1515 Holcombe Boulevard Unit 1495, Zip 77030–4000, Mailing Address: 1515 Holcombe Boulevard, Unit 1495, Zip 77030–4000; tel. 713/792–2121, **A**1 2 3 5 8 10 **F**3 11 14 15 18 20 26 30 31 32 34 35 36 37 38 39 40 41 44 45 46 47 48 49 50 51 54 55 56 57 58 59 64 68 70 71 74 75 77 78 79 80 81 82 83 84 85 86 87 88 89 90 91 92 93 94 96 97 100 102 104 107 108 110 111 112 114 115 116 117 118 119 120 121 122 123 124 126 129 130 132 134 135 136 141 142 145 146 147 148 149 150 154 157 164 167 **P**6 **S** University of Texas System, Austin, TX
Primary Contact: Peter Pisters, M.D., President and Chief Executive Officer
COO: Stephen Hahn, Deputy to the President and Chief Operating Officer
CFO: Omer Sulta, Chief Financial Officer
CHR: Shibu Varghese, Vice President Human Resources
CNO: Barbara L. Summers, Ph.D., R.N., Vice President Nursing Practice and Chief Nursing Officer
Web address: www.mdanderson.org
Control: State, Government, Nonfederal **Service:** Cancer

> **Staffed Beds:** 721 **Admissions:** 29256 **Census:** 629 **Outpatient Visits:** 1654046 **Births:** 0 **Total Expense ($000):** 6585408 **Payroll Expense ($000):** 2586776 **Personnel:** 24079

UTHEALTH HARRIS COUNTY PSYCHIATRIC CENTER (454076), 2800 South MacGregor Way, Zip 77021–1000; tel. 713/741–7870, **A**1 3 5 10 **F**29 30 34 35 57 58 68 75 86 87 98 99 100 101 103 104 130 146 **P**6 **S** University of Texas System, Austin, TX
Primary Contact: Jair C. Soares, M.D., Executive Director
COO: Stephen Glazier, Chief Operating Officer
CFO: Lois K. Pierson, Chief Financial Officer
CMO: R Andrew Harper, M.D., Medical Director
CNO: Margaret Pung, R.N., Chief Nursing Officer
Web address: https://hcpc.uth.edu/
Control: State, Government, Nonfederal **Service:** Psychiatric

> **Staffed Beds:** 537 **Admissions:** 8015 **Census:** 331 **Outpatient Visits:** 1102 **Births:** 0 **Total Expense ($000):** 111771 **Payroll Expense ($000):** 71386 **Personnel:** 954

VIBRA HOSPITAL OF HOUSTON (452046), 1300 Binz Street, Zip 77004–7016; tel. 713/285–1000, **A**10 22 **F**1 3 29 35 85 87 **P**4
Primary Contact: Guido J. Cubellis, Chief Executive Officer
CFO: Charles Handley, Chief Financial Officer
CMO: Wasae S Tabibi, M.D., President Medical Staff
CIO: Michael Turner, Chief Information Officer
Web address: https://vhhouston.com/
Control: Corporation, Investor–owned (for–profit) **Service:** Acute long–term care hospital

> **Staffed Beds:** 46 **Admissions:** 334 **Census:** 25 **Outpatient Visits:** 0 **Births:** 0 **Total Expense ($000):** 19255 **Payroll Expense ($000):** 9694 **Personnel:** 96

Hospitals, U.S. / TEXAS

WEST CHASE HOUSTON HOSPITAL (670135), 6011 West Sam Houston Parkway South, Zip 77072-1646; tel. 713/773-0556, (Nonreporting) **A**10 22
Primary Contact: Don Vickers, Chief Executive Officer
Web address: https://altushospital.org
Control: Partnership, Investor-owned (for-profit) **Service**: General medical and surgical

Staffed Beds: 10

✠ **WEST OAKS HOSPITAL (454026)**, 6500 Hornwood Drive, Zip 77074-5095; tel. 713/995-0909, **A**1 5 10 **F**4 5 29 54 56 64 68 98 99 101 104 105 132 152 153 164 **S** Universal Health Services, Inc., King of Prussia, PA
Primary Contact: Phuong Cardoza, Chief Executive Officer
CFO: Paul Veillon, CPA, Chief Finanial Officer
CMO: Vernon Walling, M.D., Executive Medical Director
CIO: James Harmon, Network Administrator
CHR: Janice Webster, Director Human Resources
CNO: Israel Ahaine, Chief Nursing Officer
Web address: www.westoakshospital.com
Control: Corporation, Investor-owned (for-profit) **Service**: Psychiatric

Staffed Beds: 160 **Admissions**: 6198 **Census**: 148 **Outpatient Visits**: 12739 **Births**: 0 **Total Expense ($000)**: 34345 **Payroll Expense ($000)**: 21734 **Personnel**: 301

✠ **WOMAN'S HOSPITAL OF TEXAS (450674)**, 7600 Fannin Street, Zip 77054-1906; tel. 713/790-1234, **A**1 3 5 10 **F**3 13 19 29 30 34 35 40 41 43 45 46 50 54 55 58 64 65 68 70 72 73 75 76 78 79 81 84 85 86 87 88 89 93 100 107 108 111 114 119 126 130 146 147 149 154 156 162 169 **S** HCA Healthcare, Nashville, TN
Primary Contact: Jeanna Bamburg, FACHE, Chief Executive Officer
CFO: Scott Bentley, Chief Financial Officer
CMO: Eberhard Lotze, M.D., Chief Medical Officer
CIO: Emily Le, Director Information Technology and Services
CHR: Arnita Crawford, Director Human Resources
CNO: Holley Tyler, R.N., Chief Nursing Officer
Web address: www.womanshospital.com
Control: Corporation, Investor-owned (for-profit) **Service**: Obstetrics and gynecology

Staffed Beds: 403 **Admissions**: 15479 **Census**: 218 **Outpatient Visits**: 53169 **Births**: 10191 **Total Expense ($000)**: 274091 **Payroll Expense ($000)**: 108226 **Personnel**: 980

HOUSTON—UNITED STATES County

MEDICAL BEHAVIORAL HOSPITAL OF CLEAR LAKE (454151), 16850 Buccaneer Lane, Zip 77058; tel. 833/971-2356, **A**10 **F**98 100 101 103 **S** NeuroPsychiatric Hospitals, Mishawaka, IN
Primary Contact: Richard Remley, Chief Executive Officer
COO: Christy Gilbert, President and Chief Operating Officer
CFO: Carlos Missagia, Chief Financial Officer
CHR: Becky Holloway, Vice President, Human Resources
Web address: https://www.neuropsychiatrichospitals.net/
Control: Corporation, Investor-owned (for-profit) **Service**: Psychiatric

Staffed Beds: 92 **Admissions**: 1468 **Census**: 48 **Outpatient Visits**: 0 **Births**: 0 **Total Expense ($000)**: 19328 **Payroll Expense ($000)**: 7608 **Personnel**: 122

HUMBLE—Harris County

CLEVELAND EMERGENCY HOSPITAL (670115), 8901 FM 1960 Bypass Road West, Zip 77338-4018; tel. 281/964-2900, (Includes TEXAS EMERGENCY HOSPITAL, 300 East Crockett Street, Cleveland, Texas, Zip 77327-4029, tel. 281/592-5410; Michael T. Adkins, Chief Executive Officer) **F**3 18 20 22 29 34 40 42 45 46 47 50 57 79 81 82 87 107 108 109 111 114 115 119 127 149
Primary Contact: Michael T. Adkins, Chief Executive Officer
COO: Patti Foster, Chief Operations Officer
CFO: Antonio Canales, Chief Financial Officer
CMO: Param Maewal, M.D., Chief Medical Officer
CIO: Brenda Ewing, Chief Information Officer
CHR: Robin Mason, Chief Human Resources Officer
CNO: Cassie Kavanaugh, Chief Nursing Officer
Web address: www.emergencyhospitals.care
Control: Partnership, Investor-owned (for-profit) **Service**: General medical and surgical

Staffed Beds: 4 **Admissions**: 59 **Census**: 1 **Outpatient Visits**: 11670 **Births**: 0 **Total Expense ($000)**: 34418 **Payroll Expense ($000)**: 12208 **Personnel**: 149

✠ **ENCOMPASS HEALTH REHABILITATION HOSPITAL OF HUMBLE (453029)**, 19002 McKay Drive, Zip 77338-5701; tel. 281/446-6148, **A**1 10 **F**29 56 75 77 78 79 82 86 87 90 91 92 95 96 130 132 143 148 149 **P**5 **S** Encompass Health Corporation, Birmingham, AL
Primary Contact: Jonathan Strader, Chief Executive Officer
CFO: Sheila Shepard, Controller
CMO: Emile Mathurin, M.D., Jr, Medical Director
CHR: Christy Dixon, Chief Human Resources Officer
CNO: Christie Griffin-Jones, R.N., Chief Nursing Officer
Web address: https://encompasshealth.com/locations/houston/humblerehab
Control: Corporation, Investor-owned (for-profit) **Service**: Rehabilitation

Staffed Beds: 76 **Admissions**: 1142 **Census**: 40 **Outpatient Visits**: 0 **Births**: 0 **Total Expense ($000)**: 20950 **Payroll Expense ($000)**: 12331 **Personnel**: 167

✠ **MEMORIAL HERMANN NORTHEAST (450684)**, 18951 North Memorial Drive, Zip 77338-4297; tel. 281/540-7700, **A**1 2 3 5 10 **F**3 11 13 15 18 20 22 24 26 29 30 31 34 35 40 42 44 45 46 47 48 49 53 54 57 59 64 65 68 70 72 74 75 76 77 78 79 80 81 84 85 87 91 93 100 107 108 111 115 119 120 121 126 129 130 131 132 135 146 147 148 149 154 157 167 169 **S** Memorial Hermann Health System, Houston, TX
Primary Contact: Justin Kendrick, Senior Vice President and Chief Executive Officer
CFO: Rebecca Tucker, Chief Financial Officer
CMO: Giridhar Vedala, M.D., Regional Chief Medical Officer
CHR: Monica Baisden, Director Human Resources
CNO: Linda Stephens, R.N., Chief Nursing Officer
Web address: www.memorialhermann.org/locations/northeast/
Control: Other not-for-profit (including NFP Corporation) **Service**: General medical and surgical

Staffed Beds: 227 **Admissions**: 14752 **Census**: 202 **Outpatient Visits**: 163444 **Births**: 1139 **Total Expense ($000)**: 364791 **Payroll Expense ($000)**: 137111 **Personnel**: 1421

✠ **PAM REHABILITATION HOSPITAL OF HUMBLE (673061)**, 18839 McKay Drive, Zip 77338-5721; tel. 281/446-3655, (Nonreporting) **A**1 10 **S** PAM Health, Enola, PA
Primary Contact: Ivan Besa, Chief Executive Officer
Web address: https://postacutemedical.com/facilities/find-facility/rehabilitation-hospitals/PAM-Rehabilitation-Hospital-of-Humble
Control: Corporation, Investor-owned (for-profit) **Service**: Rehabilitation

Staffed Beds: 46

TOWNSEN MEMORIAL HOSPITAL (670266), 1475 FM 1960 Bypass Road East, Zip 77338-3909; tel. 281/369-9001, (Nonreporting)
Primary Contact: Steve Winnett, Chief Executive Officer
COO: James Brown, Chief Operating Officer
Web address: www.townsenmemorialhospital.com
Control: Individual, Investor-owned (for-profit) **Service**: General medical and surgical

Staffed Beds: 5

HUNTSVILLE—Walker County

★ **HUNTSVILLE MEMORIAL HOSPITAL (450347)**, 110 Memorial Hospital Drive, Zip 77340-4940, Mailing Address: P.O. Box 4001, Zip 77342-4001; tel. 936/291-3411, **A**3 10 22 **F**3 11 12 13 15 18 20 22 26 28 29 34 35 40 43 45 46 47 50 57 59 60 64 65 66 70 75 76 77 79 81 84 85 86 87 90 92 93 96 97 102 107 108 110 111 114 115 119 127 130 131 132 135 146 147 148 149 150 154 167 **S** Community Hospital Corporation, Plano, TX
Primary Contact: Patrick Shannon, Chief Executive Officer
CFO: Jim Jenkins, Chief Financial Officer
CHR: Bonnie Bowen, Director Human Resources
CNO: Linda Kathryn Lawson, Chief Nursing Officer
Web address: www.huntsvillememorial.com
Control: Other not-for-profit (including NFP Corporation) **Service**: General medical and surgical

Staffed Beds: 77 **Admissions**: 3734 **Census**: 51 **Outpatient Visits**: 66803 **Births**: 241 **Total Expense ($000)**: 90174 **Payroll Expense ($000)**: 35083 **Personnel**: 502

Hospital, Medicare Provider Number, Address, Telephone, Approval, Facility, and Physician Codes, Health Care System

★ American Hospital Association (AHA) membership   ○ Healthcare Facilities Accreditation Program   ⇑ Center for Improvement in Healthcare Quality Accreditation
☐ The Joint Commission accreditation   ◇ DNV Healthcare Inc. accreditation   △ Commission on Accreditation of Rehabilitation Facilities (CARF) accreditation

Hospitals, U.S. / TEXAS

IRAAN—Pecos County

★ **IRAAN GENERAL HOSPITAL (451307)**, 600 349 North, Zip 79744, Mailing Address: P.O. Box 665, Zip 79744–0665; tel. 432/639–2871, **A**10 18 **F**28 34 40 43 50 53 56 57 59 64 65 75 77 82 86 93 107 119 127 130 131 133 135 154
Primary Contact: William Nall, Interim Chief Executive Officer
CFO: Nelia Hernandez, Chief Financial Officer
CMO: Robert W Garcia, M.D., Chief Medical Officer
CHR: Cathy Tucker, Director Human Resources
CNO: William Nall, Chief Nursing Officer
Web address: www.igh-hospital.com
Control: Hospital district or authority, Government, Nonfederal **Service**: General medical and surgical

Staffed Beds: 14 **Admissions**: 31 **Census**: 1 **Outpatient Visits**: 3898 **Births**: 0 **Total Expense ($000)**: 8398 **Payroll Expense ($000)**: 4211 **Personnel**: 43

IRVING—Dallas County

✠ **BAYLOR SCOTT & WHITE MEDICAL CENTER–IRVING (450079)**, 1901 North MacArthur Boulevard, Zip 75061–2220; tel. 972/579–8100, **A**1 2 3 5 10 **F**3 11 13 15 17 18 20 22 24 26 28 29 30 31 34 35 40 45 46 47 49 54 55 57 58 59 61 64 65 66 70 72 74 75 76 77 78 79 80 81 82 84 85 86 87 90 92 93 94 100 107 108 110 111 114 115 116 117 118 119 120 121 123 124 126 130 141 143 146 147 148 149 150 154 156 164 167 169 **S** Baylor Scott & White Health, Dallas, TX
Primary Contact: Cindy K. Schamp, FACHE, President
CFO: Steve Roussel, Vice President Finance
CMO: Jeffrey Embrey, M.D., Chief Medical Officer
CIO: Tim Huffman, Western Region Director, Information Systems Business Relationships
CHR: Vonetta Fuller–Williams, Director Human Resources Strategic and Business Services
Web address: www.bswhealth.com
Control: Other not–for–profit (including NFP Corporation) **Service**: General medical and surgical

Staffed Beds: 247 **Admissions**: 12952 **Census**: 154 **Outpatient Visits**: 109179 **Births**: 2651 **Total Expense ($000)**: 281604 **Payroll Expense ($000)**: 100651 **Personnel**: 850

☐ **BAYLOR SURGICAL HOSPITAL AT LAS COLINAS (450874)**, 400 West Lyndon B Johnson Freeway, Zip 75063–3718; tel. 972/868–4000, **A**1 10 **F**3 29 40 51 79 81 119 126 **S** United Surgical Partners International, Addison, TX
Primary Contact: Josiah De La Garza, Chief Executive Officer
CFO: Gabrielle Holland, Chief Financial Officer
CMO: Scott McGraw, M.D., Medical Director
CNO: Jessica Doll, Chief Nursing Officer
Web address: www.baylorhealth.com/About/Community/Assessments/West/ICSH/Pages/Default.aspx
Control: Partnership, Investor–owned (for–profit) **Service**: General medical and surgical

Staffed Beds: 12 **Admissions**: 656 **Census**: 3 **Births**: 0 **Total Expense ($000)**: 53360 **Payroll Expense ($000)**: 11928 **Personnel**: 168

✠ **MEDICAL CITY LAS COLINAS (450822)**, 6800 North MacArthur Boulevard, Zip 75039–2422; tel. 972/969–2000, **A**1 10 **F**3 12 13 15 18 20 22 24 26 29 34 35 37 40 43 45 46 47 48 49 50 53 57 59 60 64 68 72 74 75 76 77 79 80 81 85 87 100 102 107 108 110 111 114 118 119 126 130 147 148 149 167 169 **S** HCA Healthcare, Nashville, TN
Primary Contact: Jessica O'Neal, Chief Executive Officer
COO: Marcus Jackson, Chief Operating Officer
CFO: Nick Galt, Chief Financial Officer
CMO: Miguel Benet, M.D., Chief Medical Officer
Web address: www.lascolinasmedical.com
Control: Corporation, Investor–owned (for–profit) **Service**: General medical and surgical

Staffed Beds: 80 **Admissions**: 4616 **Census**: 45 **Outpatient Visits**: 56912 **Births**: 791 **Total Expense ($000)**: 97459 **Payroll Expense ($000)**: 34852 **Personnel**: 428

JACKSBORO—Jack County

FAITH COMMUNITY HOSPITAL (450241), 215 Chisholm Trail, Zip 76458–1111; tel. 940/567–6633, **A**10 20 **F**7 11 13 28 34 35 40 42 43 45 53 57 59 65 66 68 75 76 77 79 81 93 97 107 114 119 127 130 133 135 148 149 154 169 **P**6
Primary Contact: Frank Beaman, Chief Executive Officer
COO: Kim Lee, Chief Operating Officer
CFO: Bonnie Blevins, R.N., Chief Financial Officer
CMO: Robert Cooper, M.D., Chief Medical Officer
CIO: Troy McKenzie, Chief information Officer
CHR: Deborah White, Human Resource Coordinator
CNO: Joy Henry, R.N., Chief of Nursing
Web address: www.fchtexas.com
Control: Hospital district or authority, Government, Nonfederal **Service**: General medical and surgical

Staffed Beds: 17 **Admissions**: 191 **Census**: 2 **Outpatient Visits**: 90078 **Births**: 125 **Total Expense ($000)**: 57272 **Payroll Expense ($000)**: 15316 **Personnel**: 190

JACKSONVILLE—Cherokee County

✠ **CHRISTUS MOTHER FRANCES HOSPITAL – JACKSONVILLE (451319)**, 2026 South Jackson, Zip 75766–5822; tel. 903/541–4500, **A**1 10 18 **F**3 7 8 11 15 18 26 29 30 32 34 35 40 43 45 50 53 56 57 59 66 68 79 81 82 85 93 97 107 108 110 111 114 119 129 133 145 146 147 148 154 155 **S** CHRISTUS Health, Irving, TX
Primary Contact: Barry D. Lofquist, Chief Executive Officer
CFO: Elizabeth Pulliam, Chief Financial Officer
CMO: Peter Sirianni, M.D., President Medical Staff
CNO: Jamie Maddox, Chief Nursing Officer
Web address: www.tmfhs.org/jacksonville
Control: Church operated, Nongovernment, not–for–profit **Service**: General medical and surgical

Staffed Beds: 23 **Admissions**: 712 **Census**: 11 **Outpatient Visits**: 77623 **Births**: 0 **Total Expense ($000)**: 74534 **Payroll Expense ($000)**: 18317 **Personnel**: 293

✠ **UT HEALTH JACKSONVILLE (450194)**, 501 South Ragsdale Street, Zip 75766–2413; tel. 903/541–5000, **A**1 10 20 **F**3 13 15 18 29 34 35 40 43 45 57 59 64 65 70 75 76 79 81 82 87 97 100 107 108 110 111 115 118 119 127 129 131 147 148 149 154 169 **S** Ardent Health Services, Nashville, TN
Primary Contact: DeLeigh Haley, Chief Executive Officer
CMO: Todd Parrish, M.D., Chief of Staff
CHR: Elysia Epperson, Director Human Resources
CNO: Jana Bateman, R.N., Chief Nursing Officer
Web address: https://uthealthjacksonville.com/
Control: Corporation, Investor–owned (for–profit) **Service**: General medical and surgical

Staffed Beds: 38 **Admissions**: 1273 **Census**: 11 **Outpatient Visits**: 80426 **Births**: 329 **Total Expense ($000)**: 47981 **Payroll Expense ($000)**: 13871 **Personnel**: 191

JASPER—Jasper County

✠ **CHRISTUS SOUTHEAST TEXAS JASPER MEMORIAL (450573)**, 1275 Marvin Hancock Drive, Zip 75951–4995; tel. 409/384–5461, **A**1 10 20 **F**3 11 15 29 30 34 40 43 50 51 57 59 64 70 77 79 81 82 107 110 111 114 119 127 130 135 146 149 **P**8 **S** CHRISTUS Health, Irving, TX
Primary Contact: Crystal Goode, President/Chief Nursing Officer
COO: Mark Durand, Assistant Administrator Operations
CFO: Nikki Martin, Chief Financial Officer
CIO: Robert Jacobs, Regional Information Management Executive
CHR: Kay Powell, Director Human Resources
Web address: https://www.christushealth.org/locations/southeast-texas-jasper
Control: Church operated, Nongovernment, not–for–profit **Service**: General medical and surgical

Staffed Beds: 33 **Admissions**: 542 **Census**: 5 **Outpatient Visits**: 59353 **Births**: 0 **Total Expense ($000)**: 28698 **Payroll Expense ($000)**: 9490 **Personnel**: 175

Hospitals, U.S. / TEXAS

JOURDANTON—Atascosa County

METHODIST HOSPITAL SOUTH (450165), 1905 Highway 97 East, Zip 78026–1504; tel. 830/769–3515, **A**1 10 20 **F**3 15 18 29 30 34 35 39 40 43 45 49 59 60 63 64 68 70 74 75 77 79 81 85 93 107 108 110 111 115 119 129 130 154 **S** HCA Healthcare, Nashville, TN
Primary Contact: Gregory A. Seiler, Chief Executive Officer
COO: Pamela Guillory, Chief Operating Officer and Chief Nursing Officer
CFO: Joe Vazquez, Chief Financial Officer
CIO: Rita S Castillo, R.N., Vice President, Quality, Risk and Safety
CNO: Pamela Guillory, Chief Operating Officer and Chief Nursing Officer
Web address: https://sahealth.com/locations/methodist-hospital-atascosa/
Control: Partnership, Investor–owned (for–profit) **Service**: General medical and surgical

Staffed Beds: 59 **Admissions:** 1534 **Census:** 12 **Outpatient Visits:** 44274 **Births:** 4 **Total Expense ($000):** 39300 **Payroll Expense ($000):** 11541 **Personnel:** 169

JUNCTION—Kimble County

KIMBLE HOSPITAL (451306), 349 Reid Road, Zip 76849–3049; tel. 325/446–3321, **A**10 18 **F**3 40 43 45 57 59 65 68 93 97 107 114 119 127 133 135 154 **S** Preferred Management Corporation, Shawnee, OK
Primary Contact: Susan Parker, Chief Executive Officer
COO: Teena Hagood, Chief Nursing Officer
CFO: Larry Stephens, Chief Financial Officer
CMO: Ben Udall, M.D., Chief of Staff
CIO: Anna Henry, Chief Information Officer
CHR: Hope Lamb, Manager Human Resources
Web address: www.kimblehospital.org/
Control: Corporation, Investor–owned (for–profit) **Service**: General medical and surgical

Staffed Beds: 15 **Admissions:** 108 **Census:** 1 **Outpatient Visits:** 13810 **Births:** 0 **Total Expense ($000):** 8669 **Payroll Expense ($000):** 3559 **Personnel:** 61

KATY—Fort Bend County

ENCOMPASS HEALTH REHABILITATION HOSPITAL OF KATY (673071), 23331 Grand Reserve Drive, Zip 77494–4850; tel. 281/505–3500, **A**1 **F**3 28 29 90 91 148 149 **S** Encompass Health Corporation, Birmingham, AL
Primary Contact: Nicholas Hardin, FACHE, Chief Executive Officer
Web address: https://www.encompasshealth.com/katyrehab
Control: Corporation, Investor–owned (for–profit) **Service**: Rehabilitation

Staffed Beds: 60 **Admissions:** 1403 **Census:** 47 **Outpatient Visits:** 0 **Births:** 0 **Total Expense ($000):** 30768 **Payroll Expense ($000):** 14013 **Personnel:** 182

KATY—Harris County

★ ⇧ **HOUSTON METHODIST CONTINUING CARE HOSPITAL (452118)**, 701 Fry Road, Zip 77450–2255; tel. 281/599–5700, **A**10 21 **F**1 65 68 75 82 84 86 87 107 149 150 **S** Houston Methodist, Houston, TX
Primary Contact: Gary L. Kempf, R.N., Chief Executive Officer
CFO: Nancy Brock, Chief Financial Officer
CHR: James A Fitch, Director Human Resources
Web address: www.houstonmethodist.org/katy-st-catherine-hospital
Control: Other not–for–profit (including NFP Corporation) **Service**: Acute long-term care hospital

Staffed Beds: 145 **Admissions:** 599 **Census:** 53 **Outpatient Visits:** 0 **Births:** 0 **Total Expense ($000):** 85490 **Payroll Expense ($000):** 34175 **Personnel:** 373

MEMORIAL HERMANN KATY HOSPITAL (450847), 23900 Katy Freeway, Zip 77494–1323; tel. 281/644–8453, **A**1 2 3 5 10 **F**3 11 13 15 18 20 22 26 29 30 31 34 35 37 39 40 41 42 43 45 46 49 50 51 54 57 59 61 64 65 68 70 72 73 74 75 76 77 78 79 80 81 84 85 87 89 93 102 107 108 110 111 114 119 126 130 131 132 144 145 146 147 149 154 167 **S** Memorial Hermann Health System, Houston, TX
Primary Contact: Jerry Ashworth, Senior Vice President and Chief Executive Officer
CFO: Linda Kulhanek, Chief Financial Officer
Web address: www.memorialhermann.org/locations/katy/
Control: Other not–for–profit (including NFP Corporation) **Service**: General medical and surgical

Staffed Beds: 290 **Admissions:** 13963 **Census:** 153 **Outpatient Visits:** 158875 **Births:** 2347 **Total Expense ($000):** 352918 **Payroll Expense ($000):** 130941 **Personnel:** 1510

△ **MEMORIAL HERMANN REHABILITATION HOSPITAL – KATY (673038)**, 21720 Kingsland Boulevard, 2nd Floor, Zip 77450–2550; tel. 800/447–3422, **A**1 7 10 **F**3 29 30 64 74 75 77 79 90 92 93 96 100 107 111 114 119 129 130 131 132 135 146 148 149 154 **S** Memorial Hermann Health System, Houston, TX
Primary Contact: Rhonda Abbott, Senior Vice President and Chief Executive Officer
COO: Mary Ann Euliarte, R.N., Chief Operating Officer
CFO: Wayne Gordon, Chief Financial Officer
CMO: Shalin Patel, M.D., Chief Medical Officer
CHR: Joyce Williams, Consultant Human Resources and Organizational Development
CNO: Mary Ann Euliarte, R.N., Chief Nursing Officer
Web address: www.memorialhermann.org/locations/katy-rehab/
Control: Partnership, Investor–owned (for–profit) **Service**: Rehabilitation

Staffed Beds: 35 **Admissions:** 672 **Census:** 24 **Outpatient Visits:** 15431 **Births:** 0 **Total Expense ($000):** 27238 **Payroll Expense ($000):** 14309 **Personnel:** 166

☐ **OCEANS BEHAVIORAL HOSPITAL KATY (454136)**, 455 Park Grove Lane, Zip 77450–1572; tel. 281/492–8888, **A**1 10 **F**29 34 35 64 98 100 101 103 104 149 153 154 164 **S** Oceans Healthcare, Plano, TX
Primary Contact: Shannon Brown, Hospital Administrator
Web address: www.memorialhermann.org/locations/katy-rehab/
Control: Corporation, Investor–owned (for–profit) **Service**: Psychiatric

Staffed Beds: 48 **Admissions:** 1070 **Census:** 37 **Outpatient Visits:** 18729 **Births:** 0 **Total Expense ($000):** 11978 **Payroll Expense ($000):** 5725 **Personnel:** 80

KAUFMAN—Kaufman County

TEXAS HEALTH PRESBYTERIAN HOSPITAL KAUFMAN (450292), 850 Ed Hall Drive, Zip 75142–1861, Mailing Address: 850 Ed Hall Dr, Zip 75142; tel. 972/932–7200, **A**1 10 **F**3 15 29 30 34 35 40 45 57 59 64 65 70 75 81 82 85 86 87 93 102 107 108 110 111 114 115 119 130 141 143 146 149 154 156 157 **S** Texas Health Resources, Arlington, TX
Primary Contact: Toya White, JD, MSN, Chief Operating Officer & Chief Nursing Officer
COO: Toya White, JD, MSN, Chief Operating Officer
CMO: Benjamin Bradshaw, M.D., President Medical Staff
CHR: Mark J Rainey, Director Human Resources
CNO: Toya White, JD, MSN, Chief Nursing Officer
Web address: www.texashealth.org/Kaufman
Control: Other not–for–profit (including NFP Corporation) **Service**: General medical and surgical

Staffed Beds: 42 **Admissions:** 1003 **Census:** 7 **Outpatient Visits:** 33157 **Births:** 0 **Total Expense ($000):** 41908 **Payroll Expense ($000):** 16110 **Personnel:** 156

Hospital, Medicare Provider Number, Address, Telephone, Approval, Facility, and Physician Codes, Health Care System

★ American Hospital Association (AHA) membership
☐ The Joint Commission accreditation
○ Healthcare Facilities Accreditation Program
◇ DNV Healthcare Inc. accreditation
⇧ Center for Improvement in Healthcare Quality Accreditation
△ Commission on Accreditation of Rehabilitation Facilities (CARF) accreditation

Hospitals, U.S. / TEXAS

KELLER—Tarrant County

TEXAS REHABILITATION HOSPITAL OF KELLER (673077), 791 South Main Street, Zip 76248–4905; tel. 817/898–6900, **A**10 22 **F**3 29 34 57 68 74 77 79 90 91 95 96 130 132 148 157 **P**1 2 3 4 5 6 7 8 **S** Lifepoint Health, Brentwood, TN
Primary Contact: Jake Daggett, Market Chief Executive Officer
COO: Oscar Sanchez, Chief Financial Officer
Web address: www.texasrehabkeller.com
Control: Corporation, Investor–owned (for–profit) **Service**: Rehabilitation

Staffed Beds: 36 **Admissions**: 802 **Census**: 25 **Outpatient Visits**: 0 **Births**: 0 **Total Expense ($000)**: 11236 **Payroll Expense ($000)**: 6200 **Personnel**: 69

KENEDY—Karnes County

★ **OTTO KAISER MEMORIAL HOSPITAL (451364)**, 3349 South Highway 181, Zip 78119–5247; tel. 830/583–3401, **A**10 18 **F**3 11 15 29 30 34 40 43 45 46 53 57 59 62 64 68 77 81 93 107 111 115 119 132 133 135 148 154
Primary Contact: David Lee, Chief Executive Officer
CIO: Joseph Wiatrek, Director Information Technology
CHR: Christina Benavides, Director Employee Services
CNO: Vincent Sowell, Chief Nursing Officer
Web address: www.okmh.org/
Control: Hospital district or authority, Government, Nonfederal **Service**: General medical and surgical

Staffed Beds: 25 **Admissions**: 168 **Census**: 3 **Outpatient Visits**: 25666 **Births**: 0 **Total Expense ($000)**: 33988 **Payroll Expense ($000)**: 11813 **Personnel**: 176

KERMIT—Winkler County

WINKLER COUNTY MEMORIAL HOSPITAL (451314), 821 Jeffee Drive, Zip 79745–4696, Mailing Address: P.O. Box H, Zip 79745–6008; tel. 432/586–5864, **A**10 18 **F**3 34 40 57 59 64 65 69 93 107 119 127 133 135 154
Primary Contact: Lorenzo Serrano, Chief Executive Officer
CFO: Wannah Hartley, Controller
CMO: K Pham, M.D., Chief of Staff
CIO: Keith Palmer, Assistant Administrator
Control: Hospital district or authority, Government, Nonfederal **Service**: General medical and surgical

Staffed Beds: 19 **Admissions**: 87 **Census**: 2 **Outpatient Visits**: 168408 **Births**: 0 **Total Expense ($000)**: 17039 **Payroll Expense ($000)**: 6675 **Personnel**: 120

KERRVILLE—Kerr County

KERRVILLE DIVISION See South Texas Veterans Healthcare System Audie L Murphy, San Antonio

☐ **KERRVILLE STATE HOSPITAL (454014)**, 721 Thompson Drive, Zip 78028–5154; tel. 830/896–2211, **A**1 10 **F**9 30 39 59 68 75 77 86 87 91 98 100 101 130 132 135 146 154 163 **S** Texas Department of State Health Services, Austin, TX
Primary Contact: Leigh Ann Fitzpatrick, Superintendent
CFO: Laurie Harris, Chief Accountant
CMO: Matthew Faubion, M.D., Clinical Director
CNO: Amanda McDonald, MSN, Chief Nurse Executive
Web address: www.dshs.state.tx.us/mhhospitals/KerrvilleSH/default.shtm
Control: State, Government, Nonfederal **Service**: Psychiatric

Staffed Beds: 290 **Admissions**: 58 **Census**: 165 **Outpatient Visits**: 0 **Births**: 0 **Total Expense ($000)**: 64424 **Payroll Expense ($000)**: 34174 **Personnel**: 630

★ ⇑ **PETERSON HEALTH (450007)**, 551 Hill Country Drive, Zip 78028–6085; tel. 830/896–4200, **A**10 19 21 **F**3 8 11 13 15 18 20 22 26 28 29 30 31 34 35 39 40 43 44 45 47 49 51 57 59 62 63 64 65 68 70 74 75 76 77 78 79 81 82 84 85 86 87 90 93 96 97 107 108 109 110 111 114 115 118 119 126 127 130 135 145 146 147 148 149 154 156 157 167 168 169 **P**8
Primary Contact: Cory Edmondson, President and Chief Executive Officer
CFO: Lisa Medovich, Chief Financial Officer
CMO: Al Roschmann, M.D., Chief of Staff
CIO: Brian Robicheaux, Chief Information Officer
CHR: Buddy Volpe, Director Human Resources
CNO: Kaeli Dressler, R.N., MSN, Chief Nursing Officer
Web address: www.petersonhealth.com
Control: Other not–for–profit (including NFP Corporation) **Service**: General medical and surgical

Staffed Beds: 124 **Admissions**: 4920 **Census**: 57 **Outpatient Visits**: 180475 **Births**: 481 **Total Expense ($000)**: 172150 **Payroll Expense ($000)**: 80842 **Personnel**: 1228

VETERANS AFFAIRS MED CENTER See Kerrville Division

KILLEEN—Bell County

✠ **ADVENTHEALTH CENTRAL TEXAS (450152)**, 2201 South Clear Creek Road, Zip 76549–4110; tel. 254/526–7523, (Includes METROPLEX BEHAVIORAL HEALTH CENTER, 2201 South Clear Creek Road, Killeen, Texas, Zip 76549–4110, tel. 254/628–1000; Kevin A. Roberts, FACHE, President and Chief Executive Officer) **A**1 3 10 **F**3 8 11 12 13 15 18 20 22 26 28 29 30 34 35 39 40 43 45 46 48 49 54 57 59 65 68 70 71 72 74 75 76 77 78 79 81 82 83 85 86 87 91 93 98 99 100 101 102 104 107 108 110 111 114 115 118 119 129 130 131 132 135 146 147 148 154 156 169 **P**6 **S** AdventHealth, Altamonte Springs, FL
Primary Contact: Kevin A. Roberts, FACHE, President and Chief Executive Officer
CMO: Erin Bird, M.D., Chief Medical Officer
CHR: Brenda Coley, Executive Director
CNO: Tammy Rodriguez, Vice President Patient Care Services
Web address: www.mplex.org
Control: Church operated, Nongovernment, not–for–profit **Service**: General medical and surgical

Staffed Beds: 183 **Admissions**: 7722 **Census**: 77 **Outpatient Visits**: 110720 **Births**: 1476 **Total Expense ($000)**: 156568 **Payroll Expense ($000)**: 67274 **Personnel**: 803

KINGSVILLE—Kleberg County

✠ **CHRISTUS SPOHN HOSPITAL KLEBERG (450163)**, 1311 General Cavazos Boulevard, Zip 78363–7130; tel. 361/595–1661, **A**1 10 20 **F**3 8 13 15 18 28 29 30 38 40 41 43 45 50 53 64 65 68 70 74 75 76 77 81 83 84 85 87 92 93 97 102 107 110 111 114 115 119 130 135 146 147 148 149 154 157 **S** CHRISTUS Health, Irving, TX
Primary Contact: Richard Morin, R.N., President CHRISTUS Spohn Hospital – Alice/Kleberg
COO: David LeMonte, Vice President and Chief Operating Officer
CFO: Jessica Pena, Manager Finance
CHR: Mindy Soliz, Director Human Resource Strategy
CNO: Lieutenant Laci Lasater, R.N., Chief Nursing Officer
Web address: www.christusspohn.org
Control: Church operated, Nongovernment, not–for–profit **Service**: General medical and surgical

Staffed Beds: 50 **Admissions**: 1839 **Census**: 18 **Outpatient Visits**: 62870 **Births**: 286 **Total Expense ($000)**: 45096 **Payroll Expense ($000)**: 14923 **Personnel**: 194

KINGWOOD—Harris County

ELITE HOSPITAL KINGWOOD (670285), 23330 US 59 North, Zip 77339–3043; tel. 832/777–6165, **A**22 **F**3 34 40 57 64 107 115
Primary Contact: Jeremy M. Brynes, Chief Executive Officer
Control: Partnership, Investor–owned (for–profit) **Service**: General medical and surgical

Staffed Beds: 6 **Admissions**: 149 **Census**: 1 **Outpatient Visits**: 11762 **Births**: 0 **Total Expense ($000)**: 14298 **Payroll Expense ($000)**: 4524 **Personnel**: 52

KINGWOOD EMERGENCY HOSPITAL See Elite Hospital Kingwood

✠ **KINGWOOD PINES HOSPITAL (454103)**, 2001 Ladbrook Drive, Zip 77339–3004; tel. 281/404–1001, **A**1 10 **F**4 75 86 87 98 99 101 102 104 105 130 135 149 153 154 160 161 164 **S** Universal Health Services, Inc., King of Prussia, PA
Primary Contact: Kristin Williams, Chief Executive Officer
COO: Beryl Shorter, Chief Operating Officer, Director Performance Improvement
CFO: Sharon Corum, Chief Financial Officer
CMO: Bharath Raj, M.D., Medical Director
CHR: Robert Fontenot, Director Human Resources
CNO: Barbara Vasquez, Chief Nursing Officer
Web address: www.kingwoodpines.com
Control: Corporation, Investor–owned (for–profit) **Service**: Psychiatric

Staffed Beds: 93 **Admissions**: 3912 **Census**: 86 **Outpatient Visits**: 4622 **Births**: 0 **Total Expense ($000)**: 24327 **Payroll Expense ($000)**: 14657 **Personnel**: 178

KINGWOOD—Montgomery County

HCA HOUSTON HEALTHCARE KINGWOOD (450775), 22999 US Highway 59 North, Zip 77339; tel. 281/348–8000, (Includes HCA HOUSTON HEALTHCARE NORTH CYPRESS, 21214 Northwest Freeway, Cypress, Texas, Zip 77429–3373, tel. 832/912–3500; Jim Brown, Chief Executive Officer) **A**1 2 3 10 **F**3 12 13 18 19 20 22 24 26 28 29 34 35 40 41 42 43 45 46 47 49 57 58 59 70 72 74 75 76 77 79 80 81 84 85 89 90 96 102 107 108 111 114 115 118 119 126 146 148 154 167 169 **S** HCA Healthcare, Nashville, TN
Primary Contact: John Corbeil, Chief Executive Officer
CFO: Daniel E Davis, Chief Financial Officer
CMO: Eugene Ogrod, M.D., Chief Medical Officer
Web address: www.kingwoodmedical.com
Control: Corporation, Investor–owned (for–profit) **Service**: General medical and surgical

Staffed Beds: 563 **Admissions**: 37480 **Census**: 481 **Outpatient Visits**: 274219 **Births**: 2553 **Total Expense ($000)**: 701967 **Payroll Expense ($000)**: 257593 **Personnel**: 2694

MEMORIAL HERMANN SURGICAL HOSPITAL KINGWOOD (670005), 300 Kingwood Medical Drive, Zip 77339–6400; tel. 281/312–4000, **A**1 10 **F**3 29 34 45 79 81 82 85 111 119 126 131 149 **P**2
Primary Contact: Melinda Eller, Chief Executive Officer
CFO: Jay Michael Gomez, Chief Financial Officer
CNO: Shawna Fugler, R.N., Chief Nursing Officer
Web address: www.memorialhermannkingwood.com
Control: Partnership, Investor–owned (for–profit) **Service**: Surgical

Staffed Beds: 10 **Admissions**: 289 **Census**: 2 **Outpatient Visits**: 7345 **Births**: 0 **Total Expense ($000)**: 28485 **Payroll Expense ($000)**: 6097 **Personnel**: 82

KNOX CITY—Knox County

KNOX COUNTY HOSPITAL (451394), 701 South Fifth Street, Zip 79529–2107, Mailing Address: P.O. Box 608, Zip 79529–0608; tel. 940/657–3535, **A**10 18 **F**3 7 11 28 33 35 40 43 57 59 62 107 127 130 133 149 154 169 **P**6
Primary Contact: Stephen A. Kuehler, Administrator and Chief Executive Officer
CFO: Dan Offutt, Manager Finance
CMO: Ezekiel Duke, M.D., Chief of Staff
CNO: Sheila Kuehler, R.N., Director of Nursing
Web address: www.knoxcountyhospital-texas.com
Control: Hospital district or authority, Government, Nonfederal **Service**: General medical and surgical

Staffed Beds: 14 **Admissions**: 83 **Census**: 2 **Outpatient Visits**: 18395 **Births**: 0 **Total Expense ($000)**: 16703 **Payroll Expense ($000)**: 7667 **Personnel**: 84

KYLE—Hays County

ASCENSION SETON HAYS (670056), 6001 Kyle Parkway, Zip 78640–6112; tel. 512/504–5000, **A**1 3 5 10 **F**3 11 13 15 17 18 20 22 24 28 29 30 34 35 37 40 41 43 45 46 47 48 49 50 53 54 56 57 59 62 64 70 72 74 76 78 79 81 82 84 85 87 93 100 107 108 110 111 115 119 126 129 130 131 132 135 143 145 146 154 156 162 164 167 169 **S** Ascension Healthcare, Saint Louis, MO
Primary Contact: Joan Ross, President
Web address: www.seton.net/locations/seton_medical_center_hays/
Control: Church operated, Nongovernment, not–for–profit **Service**: General medical and surgical

Staffed Beds: 154 **Admissions**: 9940 **Census**: 121 **Outpatient Visits**: 81011 **Births**: 1651 **Total Expense ($000)**: 231812 **Payroll Expense ($000)**: 75747 **Personnel**: 713

WARM SPRINGS REHABILITATION HOSPITAL OF KYLE (673057), 5980 Kyle Parkway, Zip 78640–2400; tel. 512/262–0821, **A**1 10 **F**3 29 60 74 75 79 90 93 95 96 130 131 132 148 154 169 **S** PAM Health, Enola, PA
Primary Contact: Shawn Todd, Interim Chief Executive Officer
Web address: www.warmsprings.org/our-facilities/outpatient-rehabilitation/warm-springs-rehabilitation-center-kyle/
Control: Partnership, Investor–owned (for–profit) **Service**: Rehabilitation

Staffed Beds: 40 **Admissions**: 1067 **Census**: 38 **Outpatient Visits**: 12469 **Births**: 0 **Total Expense ($000)**: 20291 **Payroll Expense ($000)**: 10417 **Personnel**: 223

LAKE JACKSON—Brazoria County

CHI ST. LUKE'S HEALTH BRAZOSPORT (450072), 100 Medical Drive, Zip 77566–5674; tel. 979/297–4411, **A**1 10 **F**3 8 11 15 18 20 22 28 29 30 31 34 37 40 45 47 48 49 50 51 59 60 64 65 70 74 75 78 79 81 82 85 86 87 90 91 93 94 100 102 107 108 110 111 114 115 117 118 119 120 121 123 130 131 132 146 149 154 164 167 **P**8 **S** CommonSpirit Health, Chicago, IL
Primary Contact: Robert J. Trautman, President
CFO: Chuck Jeffress, Vice President Fiscal Services
CMO: Michael Gilliand, M.D., Chief of Staff
CIO: Todd Edwards, Director Information Management Systems
CHR: Christopher Calia, Vice President Human Resources
CNO: Shannon Haltom, Vice President, Patient Care Services
Web address: www.chistlukesbrazosport.org
Control: Church operated, Nongovernment, not–for–profit **Service**: General medical and surgical

Staffed Beds: 93 **Admissions**: 3576 **Census**: 40 **Outpatient Visits**: 63114 **Births**: 68 **Total Expense ($000)**: 91930 **Payroll Expense ($000)**: 35333 **Personnel**: 405

LAKEWAY—Travis County

BAYLOR SCOTT & WHITE INSTITUTE FOR REHABILITATION – LAKEWAY (673058), 2000 Medical Drive, Zip 78734–4200; tel. 512/263–4500, **A**1 7 10 **F**3 29 34 35 44 74 75 77 86 87 90 91 93 96 130 132 148 149 154 157 164 **S** Select Medical Corporation, Mechanicsburg, PA
Primary Contact: Sarah North, Chief Executive Officer
CMO: Maria Elena Arizmendez, M.D., Medical Director
CHR: Debbie Belcher, Director Human Resource
CNO: Ramon Austria, R.N., Chief Nursing Officer
Web address: https://www.bswrehab.com/locations-and-tours/bswir-lakeway/
Control: Partnership, Investor–owned (for–profit) **Service**: Rehabilitation

Staffed Beds: 36 **Admissions**: 588 **Census**: 20 **Outpatient Visits**: 8528 **Births**: 0 **Total Expense ($000)**: 23921 **Payroll Expense ($000)**: 8237 **Personnel**: 98

LAKEWAY REGIONAL MEDICAL CENTER See Baylor Scott & White Medical Center – Lakeway

LAMESA—Dawson County

MEDICAL ARTS HOSPITAL (450489), 2200 North Bryan Avenue, Zip 79331–2451; tel. 806/872–2183, **A**10 11 20 **F**3 7 11 29 30 35 40 43 50 57 59 64 75 87 97 107 111 115 119 127 130 133 146 148 166 167 **P**6
Primary Contact: Freddy Olivarez, Chief Executive Officer
COO: Jo Beth Smith, Chief Operating Officer
CMO: Michael Sprys, D.O., Chief of Staff
CHR: Traci Brown, Director Human Resources
CNO: Diane Sherrill, R.N., Director of Nursing
Web address: www.medicalartshospital.org
Control: Hospital district or authority, Government, Nonfederal **Service**: General medical and surgical

Staffed Beds: 22 **Admissions**: 564 **Census**: 5 **Outpatient Visits**: 40717 **Births**: 0 **Total Expense ($000)**: 19589 **Payroll Expense ($000)**: 8107 **Personnel**: 122

LAMPASAS—Lampasas County

ADVENTHEALTH ROLLINS BROOK (451323), 608 North Key Avenue, Zip 76550–1106, Mailing Address: P.O. Box 589, Zip 76550–0032; tel. 512/556–3682, **A**1 10 18 **F**3 15 29 35 40 43 45 46 61 81 85 87 93 97 107 110 111 114 133 146 **P**6 **S** AdventHealth, Altamonte Springs, FL
Primary Contact: Kevin A. Roberts, FACHE, President and Chief Executive Officer
CFO: Robert Brock, Chief Financial Officer and Vice President
CMO: Erin Bird, M.D., Chief Medical Officer
CIO: Carl Elkins, Director Information Technology
CHR: Brenda Coley, Executive Director
Web address: https://www.adventhealth.com/hospital/adventhealth-rollins-brook
Control: Church operated, Nongovernment, not–for–profit **Service**: General medical and surgical

Staffed Beds: 18 **Admissions**: 419 **Census**: 6 **Outpatient Visits**: 18068 **Births**: 0 **Total Expense ($000)**: 20226 **Payroll Expense ($000)**: 6035 **Personnel**: 84

Hospitals, U.S. / TEXAS

LANCASTER—Dallas County

⇧ **CRESCENT MEDICAL CENTER LANCASTER (670090)**, 2600 West Pleasant Run Road, Zip 75146–1114; tel. 972/230–8888, **A**10 21 **F**3 18 20 22 24 29 34 40 49 51 57 59 60 64 68 70 74 77 79 81 82 85 93 107 108 111 115 119 130 143 148 149 154 167
Primary Contact: Raji Kumar, Managing Partner and Chief Executive Officer
CFO: Becky Speight, Chief Financial Officer and Administrator
Web address: www.cmcl.us/
Control: Partnership, Investor–owned (for–profit) **Service**: General medical and surgical

Staffed Beds: 43 **Admissions**: 863 **Census**: 9 **Outpatient Visits**: 39932 **Births**: 0 **Total Expense ($000)**: 36114 **Payroll Expense ($000)**: 15487 **Personnel**: 308

LAREDO—Webb County

☐ **DOCTORS HOSPITAL OF LAREDO (450643)**, 10700 McPherson Road, Zip 78045–6268; tel. 956/523–2000, **A**1 2 10 19 **F**3 13 15 18 20 24 28 29 31 34 35 37 40 42 43 45 48 49 50 54 57 59 60 63 64 70 72 74 75 76 77 78 79 81 85 89 90 91 93 107 108 110 111 114 115 118 119 121 126 129 130 131 146 147 148 154 167 169 **P**5 **S** Universal Health Services, Inc., King of Prussia, PA
Primary Contact: Andrew Wilson, Chief Executive Officer
COO: Victor Le Gloahec, Chief Operating Officer
CMO: Santiago Gutierrez, M.D., Chief Medical Officer
CIO: Maribel Mata, Director Information Services
CHR: Roseann Figueroa, Director Human Resources
CNO: Daman Mott, MSN, Chief Nursing Officer
Web address: www.doctorshosplaredo.com
Control: Partnership, Investor–owned (for–profit) **Service**: General medical and surgical

Staffed Beds: 183 **Admissions**: 8054 **Census**: 88 **Outpatient Visits**: 160089 **Births**: 2108 **Total Expense ($000)**: 148190 **Payroll Expense ($000)**: 57078 **Personnel**: 726

✠ **LAREDO MEDICAL CENTER (450029)**, 1700 East Saunders Avenue, Zip 78041–5474, Mailing Address: P.O. Box 2068, Zip 78044–2068; tel. 956/796–5000, (Total facility includes 18 beds in nursing home–type unit) **A**1 3 10 19 **F**3 8 11 12 13 15 18 20 22 24 26 28 29 30 31 34 35 40 42 43 45 46 49 50 51 54 57 59 60 64 65 68 70 72 74 75 76 77 78 79 81 85 86 87 89 91 92 93 94 97 107 108 110 111 114 115 119 120 121 123 126 128 129 144 147 148 154 167 169 **S** Community Health Systems, Inc., Franklin, TN
Primary Contact: Jorge E. Leal, FACHE, Chief Executive Officer
CIO: Joe Rivera, Chief Information Technology Officer
Web address: www.laredomedical.com
Control: Corporation, Investor–owned (for–profit) **Service**: General medical and surgical

Staffed Beds: 326 **Admissions**: 14222 **Census**: 201 **Outpatient Visits**: 157695 **Births**: 2840 **Total Expense ($000)**: 214536 **Payroll Expense ($000)**: 74925 **Personnel**: 1001

☐ **LAREDO REHABILITATION HOSPITAL (673059)**, 2005a East Bustamante Street, Zip 78041; tel. 956/764–8555, **A**1 10 **F**3 29 75 90 93 96 149 **S** Ernest Health, Inc., Albuquerque, NM
Primary Contact: Hanna Huang, Administrator and Chief Operating Officer
Web address: www.lrh.ernesthealth.com
Control: Corporation, Investor–owned (for–profit) **Service**: Rehabilitation

Staffed Beds: 21 **Admissions**: 421 **Census**: 18 **Outpatient Visits**: 5449 **Births**: 0 **Total Expense ($000)**: 8128 **Payroll Expense ($000)**: 4296 **Personnel**: 47

☐ **LAREDO SPECIALTY HOSPITAL (452096)**, 2005 Bustamente Street, Zip 78041–5470; tel. 956/753–5353, **A**1 10 **F**1 3 29 75 85 96 130 149 **S** Ernest Health, Inc., Albuquerque, NM
Primary Contact: Hanna Huang, Administrator and Chief Operating Officer
CFO: Robert Voss, Chief Financial Officer
CMO: Marisa Guerrero, Director Human Resources
Web address: https://lsh.ernesthealth.com/
Control: Partnership, Investor–owned (for–profit) **Service**: Acute long–term care hospital

Staffed Beds: 40 **Admissions**: 272 **Census**: 15 **Outpatient Visits**: 0 **Births**: 0 **Total Expense ($000)**: 11501 **Payroll Expense ($000)**: 4111 **Personnel**: 92

LEAGUE CITY—Galveston County

ELITECARE EMERGENCY HOSPITAL, 2530 Gulf Freeway S, Zip 77573–6743; tel. 281/337–7500, (Nonreporting)
Primary Contact: Chad Bush, Managing Director
Web address: www.elite24er.com
Control: Partnership, Investor–owned (for–profit) **Service**: General medical and surgical

Staffed Beds: 4

LEVELLAND—Hockley County

★ **COVENANT HOSPITAL–LEVELLAND (450755)**, 1900 College Avenue, Zip 79336–6508; tel. 806/894–4963, **A**10 **F**3 7 11 13 15 29 30 34 40 43 45 57 59 64 65 68 75 76 77 81 85 87 97 107 110 115 119 127 135 149 **P**3 **S** Providence, Renton, WA
Primary Contact: Newman Wheeler, Chief Executive Officer
CMO: Harry Weaver, M.D., Chief of Staff
CIO: Kevin Elmore, Chief Information Officer
CHR: Tammy Franklin, Manager Personnel and Marketing
CNO: Connie Thomman, Director of Nursing
Web address: https://www.covenanthealth.org/contact-us/locations/covenant-health-levelland2/
Control: Church operated, Nongovernment, not–for–profit **Service**: General medical and surgical

Staffed Beds: 21 **Admissions**: 341 **Census**: 2 **Outpatient Visits**: 47443 **Births**: 176 **Total Expense ($000)**: 32807 **Payroll Expense ($000)**: 11069 **Personnel**: 164

LEWISVILLE—Denton County

✠ **MEDICAL CITY LEWISVILLE (450669)**, 500 West Main, Zip 75057–3699; tel. 972/420–1000, **A**1 3 10 **F**3 12 13 18 20 22 24 26 28 29 30 34 35 37 40 41 42 43 45 46 47 49 50 56 57 59 60 63 65 68 70 72 74 75 76 77 78 79 81 82 84 87 90 91 92 93 96 97 107 108 110 111 114 119 126 129 130 132 146 147 148 149 154 167 **S** HCA Healthcare, Nashville, TN
Primary Contact: John Walker, Chief Executive Officer
COO: Allen Marsh, Chief Operating Officer
CFO: Lisa Brodbeck, Chief Financial Officer
CIO: Shirley Archambeault, Chief Information Officer
CHR: Dara Biegert, Vice President Human Resources
CNO: Lynn O'Neill, R.N., Chief Nursing Officer
Web address: www.lewisvillemedical.com
Control: Corporation, Investor–owned (for–profit) **Service**: General medical and surgical

Staffed Beds: 128 **Admissions**: 8345 **Census**: 103 **Outpatient Visits**: 72712 **Births**: 1898 **Total Expense ($000)**: 165571 **Payroll Expense ($000)**: 61920 **Personnel**: 584

LIBERTY—Liberty County

LIBERTY DAYTON REGIONAL MEDICAL CENTER (451375), 1353 North Travis, Zip 77575–3549; tel. 936/336–7316, **A**10 18 **F**3 29 40 59 64 89 93 107 115 119 127 130 133 154
Primary Contact: Rhonda Campbell, Chief Executive Officer
CFO: Hal Mayo, Chief Financial Officer
CMO: Don Callens, M.D., Chief Medical Officer
CNO: Cindy Griffin, Chief Nursing Officer
Web address: www.libertydaytonrmc.com
Control: Hospital district or authority, Government, Nonfederal **Service**: General medical and surgical

Staffed Beds: 15 **Admissions**: 90 **Census**: 1 **Outpatient Visits**: 18994 **Births**: 0 **Total Expense ($000)**: 10222 **Payroll Expense ($000)**: 7258 **Personnel**: 120

LITTLEFIELD—Lamb County

LAMB HEALTHCARE CENTER (450698), 1500 South Sunset, Zip 79339–4899; tel. 806/385–6411, **A**10 20 **F**13 35 40 43 50 57 59 64 66 75 76 81 86 87 107 114 119 127 132 133 134 146 147 149 156
Primary Contact: Mike McNutt, Chief Executive Officer
CMO: Isabel Molina, M.D., Chief Medical Officer
CHR: Joan Williams, Administrative Assistant/Human Resources
CNO: Stacie Styron, Chief Nursing Officer
Web address: www.littlefieldtexas.net/index.php/our-community/lamb-healthcare-center
Control: County, Government, Nonfederal **Service**: General medical and surgical

Staffed Beds: 42 **Admissions**: 219 **Census**: 2 **Outpatient Visits**: 22879 **Births**: 76 **Total Expense ($000)**: 14685 **Payroll Expense ($000)**: 5164 **Personnel**: 116

Hospitals, U.S. / TEXAS

LIVE OAK—Bexar County

NORTHEAST METHODIST HOSPITAL See Methodist Hospital Northeast

LIVINGSTON—Polk County

CHI ST. LUKE'S HEALTH MEMORIAL LIVINGSTON See St. Luke's Health – Memorial Livingston

ST. LUKE'S HEALTH – MEMORIAL LIVINGSTON (450395), 1717 Highway 59 Loop North, Zip 77351–5710, Mailing Address: P.O. Box 1257, Zip 77351–0022; tel. 936/329–8700, **A**1 10 20 **F**3 11 13 15 29 34 35 40 42 43 45 46 50 57 59 64 68 70 74 75 76 79 81 85 87 89 107 108 110 111 114 119 129 130 132 146 149 156 167 **S** CommonSpirit Health, Chicago, IL
Primary Contact: Kristi Froese, R.N., Vice President Clinical Operations
CMO: Verner Nellsch, M.D., Chief of Staff
CIO: Kathy DeFiguieredo, Director, Information Technology
CHR: Heather Jordan, Director Human Resources
CNO: Kristi Froese, R.N., Chief Nursing Officer
Web address: https://www.chistlukeshealthmemorial.org/centers/livingston
Control: Other not–for–profit (including NFP Corporation) Service: General medical and surgical

Staffed Beds: 52 Admissions: 1390 Census: 13 Outpatient Visits: 48240 Births: 207 Total Expense ($000): 51612 Payroll Expense ($000): 15718 Personnel: 145

LLANO—Llano County

★ ○ MIDCOAST CENTRAL – LLANO (451396), 200 West Ollie Street, Zip 78643–2628; tel. 325/247–5040, **A**10 11 18 **F**3 29 40 90 93 107 111 115 119 128 133 154
Primary Contact: Hatch Cummings Smith Jr, Administrator
COO: Royce Bramer Owens, Chief Operating Officer
CFO: Jennie Campbell, Chief Financial Officer
CMO: Paul Cook, M.D., Chief Medical Officer
CIO: Rodney Lott, Director Management Information Systems and Facility Operations
CHR: Jane Frasure, Human Resources
Web address: https://midcoasthealthsystem.org/midcoast-medical-center-central/
Control: Other not–for–profit (including NFP Corporation) Service: General medical and surgical

Staffed Beds: 10 Admissions: 149 Census: 4 Outpatient Visits: 5812 Births: 0 Total Expense ($000): 8768 Payroll Expense ($000): 2423 Personnel: 37

MIDCOAST MEDICAL CENTER – CENTRAL See Midcoast Central – Llano

LOCKNEY—Floyd County

★ W. J. MANGOLD MEMORIAL HOSPITAL (451337), 320 North Main Street, Zip 79241–0037, Mailing Address: Box 37, Zip 79241–0037; tel. 806/652–3373, **A**10 18 **F**3 29 35 40 45 53 59 64 65 68 81 85 93 97 107 115 127 133 145 148 149 154 157 **P**6
Primary Contact: Vincent DiFranco, Chief Executive Officer
CFO: Alyssa McCarter, Chief Financial Officer
CMO: Kevin T Stennett, M.D., Chief of Staff
CIO: David Green, Manager Information Technology
CNO: Billie Hendrix, R.N., Director of Nursing
Web address: www.mangoldmemorial.org
Control: Hospital district or authority, Government, Nonfederal Service: General medical and surgical

Staffed Beds: 25 Admissions: 154 Census: 2 Outpatient Visits: 20148 Births: 0 Total Expense ($000): 11670 Payroll Expense ($000): 6550 Personnel: 93

LONGVIEW—Gregg County

EVEREST REHABILITATION HOSPITAL LONGVIEW See Longview Rehabilitation Hospital

GOOD SHEPHERD MEDICAL CENTER See Christus Good Shepherd Medical Center

LONGVIEW REGIONAL MEDICAL CENTER (450702), 2901 North Fourth Street, Zip 75605–5191, Mailing Address: P.O. Box 14000, Zip 75607–4000; tel. 903/758–1818, **A**1 3 10 19 **F**3 8 11 13 15 18 20 22 24 26 28 29 30 31 34 35 37 40 42 43 45 46 47 49 50 51 57 59 60 61 64 65 70 72 74 75 76 77 78 79 81 85 87 89 90 91 107 108 110 111 114 115 118 119 120 124 126 130 135 148 149 154 167 **P**8 **S** Community Health Systems, Inc., Franklin, TN
Primary Contact: Steve Gordon, Chief Executive Officer
COO: Roy Finch, Chief Operating Officer
CFO: Todd Johnson, Chief Financial Officer
CMO: Kenneth McClure, M.D., Chief of Staff
CIO: Keith Jarvis, Director Information Systems
CHR: Terry Hardan, Director Human Resources
CNO: Stephanie Foster, MSN, R.N., Chief Nursing Officer
Web address: www.longviewregional.com
Control: Partnership, Investor–owned (for–profit) Service: General medical and surgical

Staffed Beds: 224 Admissions: 11910 Census: 130 Outpatient Visits: 89182 Births: 2291 Total Expense ($000): 252486 Payroll Expense ($000): 74317 Personnel: 966

LONGVIEW REHABILITATION HOSPITAL (673073), 701 East Loop 281, Zip 75605–5006; tel. 430/240–4600, **A**10 22 **F**3 77 90 91 92 93 95 96 130 132 149 **S** Everest Rehabilitation Hospitals, LLC, Dallas, TX
Primary Contact: Toyia Urbaniak, Chief Executive Officer
Web address: https://everestrehab.com/hospitals/longview-tx/
Control: Corporation, Investor–owned (for–profit) Service: Rehabilitation

Staffed Beds: 36 Admissions: 655 Census: 16 Outpatient Visits: 0 Births: 0 Total Expense ($000): 8346 Payroll Expense ($000): 4573 Personnel: 63

☐ OCEANS BEHAVIORAL HOSPITAL LONGVIEW (454117), 615 Clinic Drive, Zip 75605–5172; tel. 903/212–3105, **A**1 10 **F**29 64 98 100 101 103 104 130 132 149 153 154 164 **P**6 **S** Oceans Healthcare, Plano, TX
Primary Contact: Ben Kellogg, Administrator
Web address: https://oceanshealthcare.com/ohc-location/longview/
Control: Corporation, Investor–owned (for–profit) Service: Psychiatric

Staffed Beds: 24 Admissions: 558 Census: 18 Outpatient Visits: 23188 Births: 0 Total Expense ($000): 6903 Payroll Expense ($000): 3247 Personnel: 57

LUBBOCK—Lubbock County

COVENANT CHILDREN'S HOSPITAL (453306), 4015 22nd Place, Zip 79410; tel. 806/725–1011, **A**1 3 5 10 **F**3 11 13 15 19 21 23 25 27 29 30 31 32 35 39 40 41 43 45 58 59 70 72 76 78 79 80 81 88 89 93 102 104 107 119 126 146 147 148 154 169 **S** Providence, Renton, WA
Primary Contact: Amy Thompson, M.D., Chief Executive Officer
COO: Clay Taylor, Chief Operating Officer
CMO: Craig Rhyne, M.D., FACS, Chief Medical Officer
CIO: Jim Reid, Vice President and Chief Information Officer
CHR: Chris Shaver, Vice President Human Resources
Web address: www.covenanthealth.org/About-Us/Facilities/Childrens-Hospital.aspx
Control: Other not–for–profit (including NFP Corporation) Service: Children's general medical and surgical

Staffed Beds: 181 Admissions: 4538 Census: 67 Outpatient Visits: 207364 Births: 2405 Total Expense ($000): 362737 Payroll Expense ($000): 67189 Personnel: 768

Hospital, Medicare Provider Number, Address, Telephone, Approval, Facility, and Physician Codes, Health Care System

★ American Hospital Association (AHA) membership ○ Healthcare Facilities Accreditation Program ⇑ Center for Improvement in Healthcare Quality Accreditation
☐ The Joint Commission accreditation ◇ DNV Healthcare Inc. accreditation △ Commission on Accreditation of Rehabilitation Facilities (CARF) accreditation

Hospitals, U.S. / TEXAS

✠ **COVENANT MEDICAL CENTER (450040)**, 3615 19th Street, Zip 79410–1203, Mailing Address: P.O. Box 1201, Zip 79408–1201; tel. 806/725–0000, (Includes COVENANT MEDICAL CENTER–LAKESIDE, 4000 24th Street, Lubbock, Texas, Zip 79410–1894, tel. 806/725–0000) **A**1 3 5 10 19 **F**5 7 8 12 15 17 18 19 20 22 23 26 27 28 30 34 35 37 39 40 42 43 46 47 48 49 50 51 53 54 55 57 58 59 60 61 63 64 65 68 70 71 74 75 77 78 79 80 81 82 83 84 85 86 87 91 92 93 94 107 108 109 111 114 115 116 117 119 120 121 123 129 130 131 132 135 143 144 146 147 148 **S** Providence, Renton, WA
Primary Contact: Amy Thompson, M.D., Chief Executive Officer
CFO: John A Grigson, Vice President and Chief Financial Officer
CMO: Craig Rhyne, M.D., FACS, Chief Medical Officer
CIO: Troy Pratt, Information Technology Site Director
CHR: Chris Shaver, Vice President Human Resources
CNO: Karen Baggerly, Chief Nursing Officer and Vice President
Web address: www.covenanthealth.org
Control: Other not–for–profit (including NFP Corporation) **Service**: General medical and surgical

| **Staffed Beds**: 360 **Admissions**: 14901 **Census**: 237 **Outpatient Visits**: 346666 **Births**: 11 **Total Expense ($000)**: 582349 **Payroll Expense ($000)**: 141351 **Personnel**: 1933 |

★ **COVENANT SPECIALTY HOSPITAL (452102)**, 3815 20th Street, Zip 79410–1235; tel. 806/725–9200, **A**10 **F**1 3 29 30 31 60 63 68 75 77 78 79 87 119 130 143 148 **S** Providence, Renton, WA
Primary Contact: Ely Perea, Director & Chief Executive Officer
CFO: John Carigson, Chief Financial Officer
CMO: Naidu Chekuru, M.D., Chief Medical Officer
CHR: Chris Shaver, Vice President Human Resources
Web address: www.covenanthealth.org/view/Facilities/Specialty_Hospital
Control: Other not–for–profit (including NFP Corporation) **Service**: Acute long–term care hospital

| **Staffed Beds**: 56 **Admissions**: 215 **Census**: 14 **Outpatient Visits**: 0 **Births**: 0 **Total Expense ($000)**: 14135 **Payroll Expense ($000)**: 5727 **Personnel**: 80 |

GRACE MEDICAL CENTER See Grace Surgical Hospital

✠ **GRACE SURGICAL HOSPITAL (450162)**, 7509 Marsha Sharp Freeway, Zip 79407–8202; tel. 806/788–4100, **A**1 5 10 **F**3 8 11 12 15 29 34 35 37 40 45 47 50 51 54 55 59 64 65 66 75 79 81 82 85 87 107 108 110 111 114 115 118 119 130 135 149 157 164 **S** Providence, Renton, WA
Primary Contact: Vanessa Reasoner, Chief Executive Officer
CMO: Howard Beck, M.D., Chief of Staff
CIO: Jason Derouen, Director Management Information Systems
CHR: Sally Charles, Coordinator Human Resources
Web address: https://www.providence.org/locations/covenant-health/grace-surgical-hospital
Control: Other not–for–profit (including NFP Corporation) **Service**: Surgical

| **Staffed Beds**: 32 **Admissions**: 209 **Census**: 1 **Outpatient Visits**: 119703 **Births**: 0 **Total Expense ($000)**: 102204 **Payroll Expense ($000)**: 11940 **Personnel**: 187 |

LUBBOCK HEART & SURGICAL HOSPITAL (450876), 4810 North Loop 289, Zip 79416–3025; tel. 806/687–7777, **A**5 10 **F**3 8 12 17 18 20 22 24 25 26 29 34 37 40 45 47 49 51 54 57 59 60 70 75 77 79 81 82 85 100 107 108 115 126 130 131 148 149 164 167
Primary Contact: Cameron Lewis, Chief Executive Officer
Web address: https://lubbockheart.com/
Control: Partnership, Investor–owned (for–profit) **Service**: Surgical

| **Staffed Beds**: 60 **Admissions**: 1588 **Census**: 15 **Outpatient Visits**: 44316 **Births**: 0 **Total Expense ($000)**: 96190 **Payroll Expense ($000)**: 25734 **Personnel**: 382 |

OCEANS BEHAVIORAL HOSPITAL OF LUBBOCK (454157), 4202 Princeton Street, Zip 79415, Mailing Address: 3905 Hedgcoxe Road, Unit 250249, Plano, Zip 75025–0840; tel. 806/516–1190, (Data for 335 days) **F**29 34 35 64 98 100 101 103 104 130 132 149 153 154 164 **S** Oceans Healthcare, Plano, TX
Primary Contact: Marybeth Moran Murphy, Hospital Chief Executive Officer
CFO: Eric Elliott, Chief Financial Officer
CMO: Ashot Azatian, M.D., Medical Director
CNO: Jennifer Manner, Director of Nursing
Web address: https://oceanshealthcare.com/ohc-location/lubbock/
Control: Corporation, Investor–owned (for–profit) **Service**: Psychiatric

| **Staffed Beds**: 32 **Admissions**: 521 **Census**: 17 **Outpatient Visits**: 4438 **Births**: 0 **Total Expense ($000)**: 8091 **Payroll Expense ($000)**: 3840 **Personnel**: 57 |

✠ **SOUTH PLAINS REHABILITATION HOSPITAL, AN AFFILIATE OF UMC AND ENCOMPASS HEALTH (673070)**, 5406 Colgate Street, Zip 79416; tel. 806/507–3500, **A**1 10 **F**3 29 50 56 60 74 75 77 79 82 87 90 96 100 130 132 148 149 154 **S** Encompass Health Corporation, Birmingham, AL
Primary Contact: Beth Elder, Chief Executive Officer
CFO: Mark Proctor, Chief Financial Officer
Web address: https://www.encompasshealth.com/locations/southplainsrehab
Control: Partnership, Investor–owned (for–profit) **Service**: Rehabilitation

| **Staffed Beds**: 66 **Admissions**: 1838 **Census**: 64 **Outpatient Visits**: 0 **Births**: 0 **Total Expense ($000)**: 29817 **Payroll Expense ($000)**: 15845 **Personnel**: 209 |

ST MARY OF THE PLAINS HOSPITAL See Covenant Medical Center–Lakeside

☐ **SUNRISE CANYON HOSPITAL (454093)**, 1950 Aspen Ave, Zip 79404–1211, Mailing Address: P.O. Box 2828, Zip 79408–2828; tel. 806/740–1420, **A**1 10 **F**35 38 98 101 130 135 149 154 160 164 **P**6
Primary Contact: Beth Lawson, Chief Executive Officer
CFO: Jerome Flores, Chief Financial Officer
CMO: Dana Butler, M.D., Medical Director
CIO: Wendy Potitadkul, Chief Information Officer
CHR: Barbara McCann, Director Human Resources
Web address: www.starcarelubbock.org
Control: Other not–for–profit (including NFP Corporation) **Service**: Psychiatric

| **Staffed Beds**: 30 **Admissions**: 769 **Census**: 18 **Outpatient Visits**: 0 **Births**: 0 **Total Expense ($000)**: 9468 **Payroll Expense ($000)**: 4148 **Personnel**: 63 |

☐ **TRUSTPOINT REHABILITATION HOSPITAL OF LUBBOCK (673063)**, 4302A Princeton Street, Zip 79415–1304; tel. 806/749–2222, **A**1 3 5 10 **F**3 29 90 93 95 96 **S** Ernest Health, Inc., Albuquerque, NM
Primary Contact: Craig Bragg, Chief Executive Officer
CFO: Crystal Roach, Chief Financial Officer
CNO: John Parsons, R.N., Chief Nursing Officer
Web address: www.trustpointhospital.com/
Control: Partnership, Investor–owned (for–profit) **Service**: Rehabilitation

| **Staffed Beds**: 72 **Admissions**: 1548 **Census**: 69 **Outpatient Visits**: 11355 **Births**: 0 **Total Expense ($000)**: 31579 **Payroll Expense ($000)**: 15345 **Personnel**: 264 |

⇑ **UNIVERSITY MEDICAL CENTER (450686)**, 602 Indiana Avenue, Zip 79415–3364, Mailing Address: P.O. Box 5980, Zip 79408–5980; tel. 806/775–8200, **A**2 3 5 8 10 19 21 **F**3 7 8 11 12 13 15 16 17 18 19 20 22 24 26 28 29 30 31 34 35 36 38 40 41 42 43 45 46 47 48 49 50 53 54 55 56 57 59 64 65 68 70 72 74 75 76 77 78 79 81 83 84 85 86 87 88 89 93 96 97 102 107 108 110 111 114 115 116 117 118 119 120 121 122 123 124 126 130 131 132 135 141 142 143 144 146 147 148 149 150 154 156 167 169
Primary Contact: Mark Funderburk, President and Chief Executive Officer
CFO: Jeff Dane, Executive Vice President and Chief Financial Officer
CMO: Michael Ragain, M.D., Chief Medical Officer and Senior Vice President
CIO: Bill Eubanks, Senior Vice President and Chief Information Officer
CHR: Adrienne Cozart, Senior Vice President Human Resources
CNO: Timothy W. Howell, R.N., Senior Vice President, Patient Care Services
Web address: www.umchealthsystem.com
Control: Hospital district or authority, Government, Nonfederal **Service**: General medical and surgical

| **Staffed Beds**: 472 **Admissions**: 34081 **Census**: 388 **Outpatient Visits**: 241719 **Births**: 3154 **Total Expense ($000)**: 801378 **Payroll Expense ($000)**: 309416 **Personnel**: 4402 |

LUFKIN—Angelina County

✠ **CHI ST. LUKE'S HEALTH MEMORIAL LUFKIN (450211)**, 1201 West Frank Avenue, Zip 75904–3357, Mailing Address: P.O. Box 1447, Zip 75902–1447; tel. 936/634–8111, **A**1 3 5 10 19 **F**3 11 12 13 14 15 17 18 20 21 22 23 24 26 28 29 30 31 34 35 37 38 40 42 43 44 45 46 47 48 49 50 51 56 57 59 60 61 64 68 70 71 72 74 75 76 77 78 79 81 82 83 84 85 86 87 90 91 92 93 97 100 101 102 107 108 110 111 112 114 116 117 119 121 126 129 130 132 135 143 144 146 147 148 149 156 167 **S** CommonSpirit Health, Chicago, IL
Primary Contact: Monte J. Bostwick, Market Chief Executive Officer
CFO: Kristi Gay, Chief Financial Officer
CHR: Tanya Tyler, Vice President Human Resources
Web address: www.memorialhealth.us/centers/lufkin
Control: Other not–for–profit (including NFP Corporation) **Service**: General medical and surgical

| **Staffed Beds**: 159 **Admissions**: 5829 **Census**: 72 **Outpatient Visits**: 81038 **Births**: 572 **Total Expense ($000)**: 178408 **Payroll Expense ($000)**: 56297 **Personnel**: 651 |

Hospitals, U.S. / TEXAS

☐ **OCEANS BEHAVIORAL HOSPITAL LUFKIN (454123)**, 302 Gobblers Knob Road, Zip 75904–5419; tel. 936/632–2276, **A**1 10 **F**29 35 64 98 100 101 103 104 130 153 154 164 **P**6 **S** Oceans Healthcare, Plano, TX
Primary Contact: Laci Laird, Administrator
Web address: www.oceanslufkin.com/ **Service**: Psychiatric
Control: Corporation, Investor–owned (for–profit) **Service**: Psychiatric

Staffed Beds: 24 **Admissions**: 630 **Census**: 21 **Outpatient Visits**: 17413
Births: 0 **Total Expense ($000)**: 7348 **Payroll Expense ($000)**: 3669
Personnel: 60

✠ **WOODLAND HEIGHTS MEDICAL CENTER (450484)**, 505 South John Redditt Drive, Zip 75904–3157, Mailing Address: P.O. Box 150610, Zip 75904; tel. 936/634–8311, **A**1 10 19 **F**8 11 12 13 15 18 20 22 24 26 28 29 34 35 40 41 45 46 49 50 51 53 57 59 60 64 68 70 72 74 75 76 77 78 79 81 82 85 86 87 93 102 107 108 111 114 115 118 119 126 129 130 131 146 147 148 154 156 167 **S** Community Health Systems, Inc., Franklin, TN
Primary Contact: Jose A. Echavarria, Chief Executive Officer
COO: Conner Hickey, Chief Operating Officer
CFO: William Whiddon, Chief Financial Officer
CMO: Imran Nazeer, M.D., Chief of Staff
CIO: Kalvin Buckley, Director Information Systems
CHR: Emilie Hobbs, Director Human Resources
Web address: www.woodlandheights.net
Control: Partnership, Investor–owned (for–profit) **Service**: General medical and surgical

Staffed Beds: 131 **Admissions**: 7180 **Census**: 77 **Outpatient Visits**: 61010
Births: 841 **Total Expense ($000)**: 108551 **Payroll Expense ($000)**: 36464
Personnel: 544

LULING—Caldwell County

✠ **ASCENSION SETON EDGAR B. DAVIS HOSPITAL (451371)**, 130 Hays Street, Zip 78648–3207; tel. 830/875–7000, **A**1 10 18 **F**3 11 15 28 29 30 35 40 43 44 45 46 50 56 57 59 64 65 66 71 81 85 97 103 104 107 110 111 115 119 127 130 133 135 146 150 165 **S** Ascension Healthcare, Saint Louis, MO
Primary Contact: Jace Jones, Chief Administrative Officer
CMO: Arjun Mohandas, M.D., Chief of Staff
CIO: Michael H. Minks, Chief Information Officer
CHR: Joe Canales, Director Human Resources
CNO: Steven Brockman–Weber, System Chief Nursing Officer
Web address: https://healthcare.ascension.org/locations/texas/txaus/luling-ascension-seton-edgar-b-davis
Control: Church operated, Nongovernment, not–for–profit **Service**: General medical and surgical

Staffed Beds: 15 **Admissions**: 527 **Census**: 7 **Outpatient Visits**: 81106
Births: 0 **Total Expense ($000)**: 33095 **Payroll Expense ($000)**: 12277
Personnel: 134

✠ **PAM SPECIALTY HOSPITAL OF LULING (452062)**, 200 Memorial Drive, Zip 78648–3213; tel. 830/875–8400, **A**1 10 **F**1 3 29 53 64 90 93 96 130 148 **S** PAM Health, Enola, PA
Primary Contact: Jana Kuykendall, Chief Executive Officer
Web address: www.warmsprings.org
Control: Partnership, Investor–owned (for–profit) **Service**: Acute long–term care hospital

Staffed Beds: 34 **Admissions**: 670 **Census**: 26 **Outpatient Visits**: 19997
Births: 0 **Total Expense ($000)**: 18724 **Payroll Expense ($000)**: 9788
Personnel: 168

LUMBERTON—Hardin County

ALTUS LUMBERTON HOSPITAL (670134), 137 North LHS Drive, Zip 77657–8620; tel. 409/755–2273, **A**10 22 **F**3 40 41 42 75 107 115 119 154 157
Primary Contact: Jason Lisovicz, President/Chief Executive Officer
Web address: www.altuslumbertonhospital.org
Control: Partnership, Investor–owned (for–profit) **Service**: General medical and surgical

Staffed Beds: 4 **Admissions**: 195 **Census**: 1 **Outpatient Visits**: 11577
Births: 0 **Total Expense ($000)**: 11304 **Payroll Expense ($000)**: 4337
Personnel: 58

MADISONVILLE—Madison County

✠ **CHI ST. JOSEPH HEALTH MADISON HOSPITAL (451316)**, 100 West Cross Street, Zip 77864–2432, Mailing Address: Box 698, Zip 77864–0698; tel. 936/348–2631, **A**1 10 18 **F**3 7 11 15 29 34 40 43 50 57 59 64 75 77 93 102 107 111 119 130 133 146 148 167 **S** CommonSpirit Health, Chicago, IL
Primary Contact: Kyle Sims, Division Vice President
CMO: Grover Hubley, M.D., President Medical Staff
CIO: Maurita Turner, Team Leader Health Information Systems Services
CNO: Roxanne Hass, Director of Nursing
Web address: https://stjoseph.stlukeshealth.org/locations/chi-st-joseph-health-madison-hospital
Control: Church operated, Nongovernment, not–for–profit **Service**: General medical and surgical

Staffed Beds: 15 **Admissions**: 165 **Census**: 7 **Outpatient Visits**: 14290
Births: 0 **Total Expense ($000)**: 13424 **Payroll Expense ($000)**: 5491
Personnel: 63

MANSFIELD—Johnson County

✠ **TEXAS HEALTH HOSPITAL MANSFIELD (670309)**, 2300 Lone Star Road, Zip 76063–8744; tel. 682/341–5019, **A**1 **F**3 12 13 15 18 20 22 26 29 30 34 35 37 40 45 50 57 59 64 68 70 75 76 79 80 81 85 87 93 100 107 108 110 111 115 118 119 126 130 131 146 147 149 154 156 157 167 169 **S** AdventHealth, Altamonte Springs, FL
Primary Contact: Eulanie Lashley, President and Chief Executive Officer
CMO: Edward Arthur Laue, M.D., Chief Medical Officer
Web address: https://www.texashealth.org/locations/texas-health-mansfield
Control: Church operated, Nongovernment, not–for–profit **Service**: General medical and surgical

Staffed Beds: 59 **Admissions**: 1925 **Census**: 14 **Outpatient Visits**: 26454
Births: 685 **Total Expense ($000)**: 77964 **Payroll Expense ($000)**: 26761
Personnel: 297

MANSFIELD—Tarrant County

✠ **METHODIST MANSFIELD MEDICAL CENTER (670023)**, 2700 East Broad Street, Zip 76063–5899; tel. 682/622–2000, **A**1 3 5 10 **F**3 11 13 15 18 20 22 24 29 30 31 34 35 37 40 43 45 46 48 49 50 58 59 60 64 68 70 72 74 76 78 79 81 82 85 87 93 97 107 108 110 111 115 118 119 126 130 132 146 148 156 167 **P**5 6 **S** Methodist Health System, Dallas, TX
Primary Contact: Juan Fresquez, President
CFO: Jary M. Ganske, Chief Financial Officer
CIO: Pamela McNutt, Senior Vice President and Chief Information Officer
CNO: Nora Frasier, R.N., FACHE, Chief Nursing Officer
Web address: https://www.methodisthealthsystem.org/methodist-mansfield-medical-center/
Control: Other not–for–profit (including NFP Corporation) **Service**: General medical and surgical

Staffed Beds: 262 **Admissions**: 12324 **Census**: 182 **Outpatient Visits**: 113490 **Births**: 2124 **Total Expense ($000)**: 287569 **Payroll Expense ($000)**: 128146 **Personnel**: 1261

MARBLE FALLS—Burnet County

✠ **BAYLOR SCOTT & WHITE MEDICAL CENTER – MARBLE FALLS (670108)**, 800 West Highway 71, Zip 78654; tel. 830/201–8000, **A**1 10 20 **F**3 13 15 18 20 22 26 29 30 31 34 35 37 40 43 45 49 65 68 70 74 75 76 77 78 79 81 82 85 86 87 93 97 107 110 111 115 117 119 126 127 129 130 131 144 146 147 149 154 167 169 **S** Baylor Scott & White Health, Dallas, TX
Primary Contact: Timothy A. Ols, FACHE, President
Web address: www.sw.org/location/marble-falls-hospital
Control: Other not–for–profit (including NFP Corporation) **Service**: General medical and surgical

Staffed Beds: 46 **Admissions**: 2784 **Census**: 26 **Outpatient Visits**: 198015
Births: 399 **Total Expense ($000)**: 126329 **Payroll Expense ($000)**: 43351
Personnel: 440

Hospital, Medicare Provider Number, Address, Telephone, Approval, Facility, and Physician Codes, Health Care System

★ American Hospital Association (AHA) membership
☐ The Joint Commission accreditation
◯ Healthcare Facilities Accreditation Program
◇ DNV Healthcare Inc. accreditation
⇑ Center for Improvement in Healthcare Quality Accreditation
△ Commission on Accreditation of Rehabilitation Facilities (CARF) accreditation

Hospitals, U.S. / TEXAS

MARLIN—Falls County

FALLS COMMUNITY HOSPITAL AND CLINIC (670780), 322 Coleman Street, Zip 76661–2358, Mailing Address: P.O. Box 60, Zip 76661–0060; tel. 254/803–3561, **A**10 **F**3 11 18 32 33 34 35 40 56 57 59 64 65 66 68 75 87 97 100 102 104 107 115 119 127 147 154
Primary Contact: Jessica Ford, Interim Chief Executive Officer
COO: Becca Brewer, Chief Operations Officer
CMO: James Scott Crockett, M.D., Chief of Staff
CIO: Chris Smith, Chief Information Officer
CHR: Peggy Polster, Manager Personnel and Administrative Assistant
CNO: Tasha Burnett, Director of Nursing
Web address: www.fallshospital.com
Control: Other not–for–profit (including NFP Corporation)

> **Staffed Beds**: 32 **Admissions**: 22 **Census**: 1 **Outpatient Visits**: 52730
> **Births**: 0 **Total Expense ($000)**: 11817 **Payroll Expense ($000)**: 5297
> **Personnel**: 89

MARSHALL—Harrison County

✠ **CHRISTUS GOOD SHEPHERD MEDICAL CENTER–MARSHALL (450032)**, 811 South Washington Avenue, Zip 75670–5336, Mailing Address: P.O. Box 1599, Zip 75671–1599; tel. 903/927–6000, (Includes CHRISTUS GOOD SHEPHERD MEDICAL CENTER, 700 East Marshall Avenue, Longview, Texas, Zip 75601–5580, tel. 903/315–1800; Todd Hancock, President) **A**1 3 5 10 19 **F**3 8 11 12 13 15 18 20 22 24 26 28 29 30 31 34 35 38 40 42 43 44 45 46 47 48 49 50 51 53 56 57 59 60 61 64 65 67 68 70 71 72 73 74 75 76 77 78 79 81 82 84 85 86 87 89 90 93 97 100 101 102 104 107 110 111 114 115 119 129 130 131 132 135 143 145 146 147 148 149 150 154 156 162 163 164 165 167 **S** CHRISTUS Health, Irving, TX
Primary Contact: Todd Hancock, Market President and Chief Executive Officer
COO: Keith Creel, Vice President Operations
CFO: Michael Cheek, Chief Financial Officer
CMO: Larry Verfurth, D.O., Executive Vice President and Chief Medical Officer
CIO: Walter Grimes, Director Information Technology
CNO: Kathleen A. Redler, Chief Nursing Officer
Web address: https://www.christushealth.org/good-shepherd/marshall
Control: Church operated, Nongovernment, not–for–profit **Service**: General medical and surgical

> **Staffed Beds**: 574 **Admissions**: 15259 **Census**: 226 **Outpatient Visits**: 364159 **Births**: 1259 **Total Expense ($000)**: 533165 **Payroll Expense ($000)**: 163610 **Personnel**: 1993

MCALLEN—Hidalgo County

MCALLEN MEDICAL CENTER See South Texas Health System Mcallen

✠ **RIO GRANDE REGIONAL HOSPITAL (450711)**, 101 East Ridge Road, Zip 78503–1299; tel. 956/632–6000, **A**1 3 10 19 **S** 3 8 12 13 15 18 19 20 21 22 23 24 25 26 27 29 30 31 34 35 39 40 41 42 43 45 46 47 49 50 51 54 56 57 59 60 63 64 65 66 68 70 72 73 74 75 76 77 78 79 81 82 84 85 87 88 89 90 93 97 107 108 110 111 114 118 119 126 130 132 143 144 147 148 149 154 156 157 167 169 **S** HCA Healthcare, Nashville, TN
Primary Contact: Laura Disque, MSN, R.N., Chief Executive Officer
CFO: William Saller, Chief Financial Officer
CHR: Marjorie Whittemore, Director Human Resources
Web address: www.riohealth.com
Control: Partnership, Investor–owned (for–profit) **Service**: General medical and surgical

> **Staffed Beds**: 279 **Admissions**: 14326 **Census**: 164 **Outpatient Visits**: 148780 **Births**: 2010 **Total Expense ($000)**: 182174 **Payroll Expense ($000)**: 86756 **Personnel**: 729

★ **SOLARA SPECIALTY HOSPITALS MCALLEN (452095)**, 301 West Expressway 83, 8th Floor, Zip 78503–3045; tel. 956/632–4880, **A**10 22 **F**1 3 29 30 56 70 75 77 82 86 87 91 100 130 148 149 164 **S** ScionHealth, Louisville, KY
Primary Contact: Alberto Sanchez, Chief Executive Officer
Web address: www.chghospitals.com/mcallen/
Control: Corporation, Investor–owned (for–profit) **Service**: Acute long–term care hospital

> **Staffed Beds**: 53 **Admissions**: 605 **Census**: 46 **Outpatient Visits**: 0 **Total Expense ($000)**: 20598 **Payroll Expense ($000)**: 10485 **Personnel**: 172

MCCAMEY—Upton County

★ **MCCAMEY COUNTY HOSPITAL DISTRICT (451309)**, 2500 Highway 305 South, Zip 79752, Mailing Address: P.O. Box 1200, Zip 79752–1200; tel. 432/652–8626, (Total facility includes 30 beds in nursing home–type unit) **A**10 18 **F**3 40 53 59 64 65 66 93 127 128 133
Primary Contact: Jason J. Menefee, Chief Executive Officer
CFO: Jason J Menefee, Chief Financial Officer
CMO: John Bruce Addison, D.O., Chief Medical Officer
CIO: Larry Rollins, Supervisor Information Technology
CHR: Ashley Johnson, Director Human Resource
CNO: Erin Mann, R.N., Chief Nursing Officer
Web address: www.mccameyhospitaldistrict.org
Control: Hospital district or authority, Government, Nonfederal **Service**: General medical and surgical

> **Staffed Beds**: 41 **Admissions**: 55 **Census**: 31 **Outpatient Visits**: 7927
> **Births**: 0 **Total Expense ($000)**: 17991 **Payroll Expense ($000)**: 7014
> **Personnel**: 71

MCKINNEY—Collin County

✠ **BAYLOR SCOTT & WHITE MEDICAL CENTER AT – MCKINNEY (670082)**, 5252 West University Drive, Zip 75071–7822; tel. 469/764–1000, **A**1 2 10 **F**3 11 13 15 29 30 31 34 35 40 43 45 46 47 48 49 50 51 55 57 59 60 70 72 73 74 75 76 77 78 79 81 82 84 85 87 107 110 111 114 115 116 119 126 130 131 145 146 147 148 149 154 162 167 169 **S** Baylor Scott & White Health, Dallas, TX
Primary Contact: Tim Bowen, FACHE, President
COO: Melissa Winter, R.N., MSN, Chief Operating Officer and Chief Nursing Officer
CFO: Steve Roussel, Chief Financial Officer
Web address: www.baylorhealth.com/PhysiciansLocations/McKinney/Pages/Default.aspx
Control: Other not–for–profit (including NFP Corporation) **Service**: General medical and surgical

> **Staffed Beds**: 192 **Admissions**: 11527 **Census**: 137 **Outpatient Visits**: 78126 **Births**: 2476 **Total Expense ($000)**: 252828 **Payroll Expense ($000)**: 90896 **Personnel**: 771

✠ **MEDICAL CITY MCKINNEY (450403)**, 4500 Medical Center Drive, Zip 75069–1650; tel. 972/547–8000, **A**1 10 **F**3 4 11 13 18 20 22 24 26 28 29 30 34 37 40 42 43 45 49 50 56 57 59 60 64 68 70 72 74 75 76 77 78 79 81 82 84 85 87 90 91 92 93 94 96 97 98 100 101 102 103 104 105 107 108 109 111 114 115 119 126 130 131 132 135 146 147 148 149 153 164 167 168 169 **S** HCA Healthcare, Nashville, TN
Primary Contact: Mark S. Deno, FACHE, Chief Executive Officer
COO: Andrew Zenger, Chief Operating Officer
CFO: Anthony Villigran, Chief Financial Officer
CMO: Jaya Kumar, M.D., Chief Medical Officer
CIO: Kevin Fletcher, Director Information Systems
CHR: Alayne Sewick, Vice President Human Resources
CNO: Cassidi Summers, Chief Nursing Officer
Web address: www.medicalcenterofmckinney.com
Control: Partnership, Investor–owned (for–profit) **Service**: General medical and surgical

> **Staffed Beds**: 306 **Admissions**: 18707 **Census**: 231 **Outpatient Visits**: 94968 **Births**: 2537 **Total Expense ($000)**: 306289 **Payroll Expense ($000)**: 97595 **Personnel**: 1070

☐ **METHODIST MCKINNEY HOSPITAL (670069)**, 8000 West Eldorado Parkway, Zip 75070–5940; tel. 972/569–2700, **A**1 10 **F**3 8 29 34 35 37 40 44 45 51 57 64 68 75 79 81 82 84 85 93 107 111 115 119 126 130 131 148 149 157
Primary Contact: James C. Evely, President
CFO: Mike Conroy, Chief Financial Officer
CIO: Sharon Stark, R.N., Manager Clinical Information Systems
CHR: Diana Hume, Manager Human Resources
CNO: Robin Elwell Winebar, Chief Nursing Officer
Web address: www.methodistmckinneyhospital.com
Control: Partnership, Investor–owned (for–profit) **Service**: Surgical

> **Staffed Beds**: 23 **Admissions**: 504 **Census**: 4 **Outpatient Visits**: 105284
> **Births**: 0 **Total Expense ($000)**: 73552 **Payroll Expense ($000)**: 16194
> **Personnel**: 213

Hospitals, U.S. / TEXAS

MESQUITE—Dallas County

☐ **DALLAS REGIONAL MEDICAL CENTER (450688)**, 1011 North Galloway Avenue, Zip 75149–2433; tel. 214/320–7000, **A**1 10 **F**3 12 13 15 18 20 22 24 26 29 30 34 35 37 40 41 43 45 46 49 50 54 56 57 58 59 64 65 70 74 75 76 78 79 81 85 86 87 93 102 105 107 108 110 111 115 118 119 130 134 135 146 147 148 149 154 157 164 167 169 **S** Prime Healthcare, Ontario, CA
Primary Contact: Glenda Matchett, Chief Executive Officer
CMO: Srinivas Gunukula, M.D., Chief of Staff
Web address: www.dallasregionalmedicalcenter.com
Control: Individual, Investor–owned (for–profit) **Service:** General medical and surgical

Staffed Beds: 127 **Admissions:** 6944 **Census:** 74 **Outpatient Visits:** 45886 **Births:** 1381 **Total Expense ($000):** 104507 **Payroll Expense ($000):** 44288 **Personnel:** 474

☐ **MESQUITE REHABILITATION INSTITUTE (673045)**, 1023 North Belt Line Road, Zip 75149–1788; tel. 972/216–2400, **A**1 10 **F**3 28 29 34 90 93 96 130 132 148 149 **S** Ernest Health, Inc., Albuquerque, NM
Primary Contact: Diana Schultz, Chief Executive Officer
Web address: https://mri.ernesthealth.com/
Control: Corporation, Investor–owned (for–profit) **Service:** Rehabilitation

Staffed Beds: 30 **Admissions:** 627 **Census:** 27 **Outpatient Visits:** 4153 **Births:** 0 **Total Expense ($000):** 13268 **Payroll Expense ($000):** 7269 **Personnel:** 70

☐ **MESQUITE SPECIALTY HOSPITAL (452100)**, 1024 North Galloway Avenue, Zip 75149–2434; tel. 972/216–2300, **A**1 10 **F**1 3 29 75 148 149 154 **S** Ernest Health, Inc., Albuquerque, NM
Primary Contact: Diana Schultz, Chief Executive Officer
Web address: https://msh.ernesthealth.com/
Control: Partnership, Investor–owned (for–profit) **Service:** Acute long–term care hospital

Staffed Beds: 40 **Admissions:** 247 **Census:** 18 **Outpatient Visits:** 0 **Births:** 0 **Total Expense ($000):** 15428 **Payroll Expense ($000):** 6880 **Personnel:** 115

MEXIA—Limestone County

✠ **PARKVIEW REGIONAL HOSPITAL (450400)**, 600 South Bonham, Zip 76667–3603; tel. 254/562–5332, **A**1 10 **F**3 11 15 29 30 34 35 40 43 45 51 53 56 57 59 64 65 70 75 77 78 79 81 85 86 87 93 97 98 103 107 108 110 111 114 119 127 130 132 133 146 **S** ScionHealth, Louisville, KY
Primary Contact: Doug Holzbog, Market Chief Executive Officer
COO: R. Austin Wratchford, Chief Operating Officer
CFO: Jack Wilcox, Chief Financial Officer
CNO: Cynthia Dry, MSN, Chief Nursing Officer
Web address: www.parkviewregional.com
Control: Partnership, Investor–owned (for–profit) **Service:** General medical and surgical

Staffed Beds: 58 **Admissions:** 449 **Census:** 4 **Outpatient Visits:** 18973 **Births:** 0 **Total Expense ($000):** 19685 **Payroll Expense ($000):** 6740 **Personnel:** 119

MIDLAND—Midland County

✠ **ENCOMPASS HEALTH REHABILITATION HOSPITAL OF MIDLAND ODESSA (453057)**, 1800 Heritage Boulevard, Zip 79707–9750; tel. 432/520–1600, **A**1 10 **F**3 29 34 57 65 75 77 82 90 91 96 130 143 148 154 **S** Encompass Health Corporation, Birmingham, AL
Primary Contact: Boyd Davis III, Interim Chief Executive Officer
CFO: Vivian Irwin, Chief Financial Officer and Controller
CMO: Mark A Fredrickson, M.D., Medical Director
CHR: Tina Parker, Director Human Resources
Web address: www.healthsouthmidland.com
Control: Corporation, Investor–owned (for–profit) **Service:** Rehabilitation

Staffed Beds: 85 **Admissions:** 2223 **Census:** 75 **Outpatient Visits:** 0 **Births:** 0 **Total Expense ($000):** 41779 **Payroll Expense ($000):** 21264 **Personnel:** 268

MIDLAND MEM HOSP WEST CAMPUS See Midland Memorial Hospital

★ ⇧ **MIDLAND MEMORIAL HOSPITAL (450133)**, 400 Rosalind Redfern Grover Parkway, Zip 79701–6499; tel. 432/221–1111, (Includes MIDLAND MEMORIAL HOSPITAL, 400 Rosalind Redfern Grover Pkwy, Midland, Texas, Zip 79701–5846, tel. 432/221–1111; Stephen Bowerman, President and Chief Executive Officer) **A**3 5 10 19 21 **F**3 8 11 12 13 15 17 18 20 22 24 26 28 29 30 32 34 35 37 40 43 45 49 50 53 56 57 59 61 62 64 68 70 73 74 75 76 77 78 79 80 81 82 84 85 86 87 88 89 93 97 107 108 110 111 114 115 116 117 118 119 124 126 129 130 131 132 135 145 146 147 148 154 156 167 **P**8
Primary Contact: Stephen Bowerman, President and Chief Executive Officer
CFO: Marie Castro, Chief Financial Officer
CMO: Lawrence Wilson, M.D., Vice President, Chief Medical Officer
CIO: Taylor Weems, Vice President, Chief Information Officer
CHR: Roberta SoloRio, Vice President, Chief Human Resource Officer
Web address: https://www.midlandhealth.org/
Control: Hospital district or authority, Government, Nonfederal **Service:** General medical and surgical

Staffed Beds: 300 **Admissions:** 11882 **Census:** 145 **Outpatient Visits:** 183139 **Births:** 2595 **Total Expense ($000):** 350375 **Payroll Expense ($000):** 132229 **Personnel:** 1860

☐ **OCEANS BEHAVIORAL HEALTH CENTER PERMIAN BASIN (454110)**, 3300 South FM 1788, Zip 79706–2601; tel. 432/561–5915, **A**1 3 10 **F**29 34 35 64 68 98 99 100 101 103 104 132 153 154 164 **P**6 **S** Oceans Healthcare, Plano, TX
Primary Contact: Emileh Flitton, Administrator
Web address: www.oceanspermianbasin.com/
Control: Corporation, Investor–owned (for–profit) **Service:** Psychiatric

Staffed Beds: 62 **Admissions:** 1749 **Census:** 38 **Outpatient Visits:** 12667 **Births:** 0 **Total Expense ($000):** 11243 **Payroll Expense ($000):** 5941 **Personnel:** 90

MIDLOTHIAN—Ellis County

✠ **METHODIST MIDLOTHIAN MEDICAL CENTER (670300)**, 1201 East US Highway 287, Zip 76065–4107; tel. 469/846–2000, **A**1 10 **F**3 13 15 18 29 30 34 35 40 56 57 70 74 76 79 81 84 85 87 107 111 115 119 126 130 146 147 148 149 154 **P**5 6 **S** Methodist Health System, Dallas, TX
Primary Contact: Jary M. Ganske, Chief Executive Officer and VP of Finance
Web address: www.methodisthealthsystem.org
Control: Other not–for–profit (including NFP Corporation) **Service:** General medical and surgical

Staffed Beds: 46 **Admissions:** 1905 **Census:** 21 **Outpatient Visits:** 31917 **Births:** 175 **Total Expense ($000):** 71346 **Payroll Expense ($000):** 29136 **Personnel:** 292

MINERAL WELLS—Palo Pinto County

✠ **PALO PINTO GENERAL HOSPITAL (450565)**, 400 SW 25th Avenue, Zip 76067–8246; tel. 940/325–7891, **A**1 10 **F**11 13 15 18 28 29 34 35 40 43 45 46 51 53 54 57 59 64 65 66 68 69 70 71 74 75 76 77 78 79 81 82 86 87 91 93 107 108 110 111 114 119 127 129 130 131 133 135 146 147 148 154
Primary Contact: Ross Korkmas, Chief Executive Officer
COO: Shane Coleman, Chief Operating Officer
CFO: Daniel Smith, Chief Financial Officer
CMO: George Thomas, M.D., Chief of Staff
CHR: Mary B Braddock, Director Human Resources
CNO: Tina Linton, Chief Nursing Officer
Web address: www.ppgh.com
Control: Hospital district or authority, Government, Nonfederal **Service:** General medical and surgical

Staffed Beds: 54 **Admissions:** 1450 **Census:** 16 **Outpatient Visits:** 35613 **Births:** 292 **Total Expense ($000):** 64633 **Payroll Expense ($000):** 26644 **Personnel:** 248

Hospitals, U.S. / TEXAS

MISSION—Hidalgo County

☐ △ **MISSION REGIONAL MEDICAL CENTER (450176)**, 900 South Bryan Road, Zip 78572–6613; tel. 956/323–9103, **A**1 7 10 19 **F**3 11 12 13 15 18 20 22 29 34 35 40 43 45 46 49 50 51 57 59 60 64 65 66 68 70 72 74 75 76 77 79 81 85 87 89 90 93 96 107 108 110 111 115 118 119 130 132 146 147 148 149 154 167 169 **S** Prime Healthcare, Ontario, CA
Primary Contact: Kane A. Dawson, Chief Executive Officer
CFO: Lester Surrock, Chief Financial Officer
CMO: Humberto F. Nunez, M.D., Chief Medical Officer
CNO: Kennetha Foster, Chief Nursing Officer
Web address: www.missionrmc.org
Control: Other not–for–profit (including NFP Corporation) **Service**: General medical and surgical

Staffed Beds: 228 **Admissions**: 8658 **Census**: 111 **Outpatient Visits**: 90477 **Births**: 1815 **Total Expense ($000)**: 132258 **Payroll Expense ($000)**: 51787 **Personnel**: 873

MONAHANS—Ward County

★ **WARD MEMORIAL HOSPITAL (451373)**, 406 South Gary Street, Zip 79756–4798, Mailing Address: P.O. Box 40, Zip 79756–0040; tel. 432/943–2511, **A**10 18 **F**3 11 28 29 40 43 45 57 64 65 66 81 82 89 93 107 114 119 127 131 133 148 154 169 **P**6
Primary Contact: Leticia Rodriguez, Chief Executive Officer
CFO: Alison Cooper, Chief Financial Officer
CMO: Htin Thaung, M.D., Chief Medical Officer
CIO: David Hargrave, Chief Information Officer
CHR: Corina Subia, Director Human Resources
CNO: Jason Harbin, Director of Nursing
Web address: www.wardmemorial.com
Control: County, Government, Nonfederal **Service**: General medical and surgical

Staffed Beds: 25 **Admissions**: 303 **Census**: 5 **Outpatient Visits**: 45554 **Births**: 0 **Total Expense ($000)**: 21046 **Payroll Expense ($000)**: 9534 **Personnel**: 145

MORTON—Cochran County

COCHRAN MEMORIAL HOSPITAL (451366), 201 East Grant Street, Zip 79346–3444; tel. 806/266–5565, **A**10 18 **F**7 40 57 59 65 127 149 **P**6
Primary Contact: Kody Kitchens, Chief Executive Officer
CFO: Maggie Ramon, Chief Financial Officer
CIO: David Turney, Chief Information Officer
CHR: Amanda Turney, Director Human Resources
CNO: Rosemary Franco, Chief Nursing Officer
Web address: https://www.cochranmemorial.com/
Control: Hospital district or authority, Government, Nonfederal **Service**: General medical and surgical

Staffed Beds: 4 **Admissions**: 9 **Census**: 1 **Outpatient Visits**: 5503 **Births**: 0 **Total Expense ($000)**: 4693 **Payroll Expense ($000)**: 2306 **Personnel**: 48

MOUNT PLEASANT—Titus County

✠ **TITUS REGIONAL MEDICAL CENTER (450080)**, 2001 North Jefferson Avenue, Zip 75455–2398; tel. 903/577–6000, **A**1 10 **F**3 7 11 12 13 15 18 20 22 24 28 29 30 31 34 35 39 40 43 45 47 50 51 53 54 56 57 58 59 64 68 70 73 74 75 76 77 78 79 81 82 85 87 89 90 93 97 98 103 107 108 110 111 114 115 117 118 119 121 123 126 127 129 130 131 132 135 147 148 149 154 156 167 169
Primary Contact: Terry Scoggin, Chief Executive Officer
CMO: Chris Burling, M.D., Chief of Staff
CIO: Kevin Harris, Director Information Systems
CHR: Tony Piazza, Director Human Resources
CNO: Carol Slider, Chief Nursing Officer
Web address: www.titusregional.com
Control: Hospital district or authority, Government, Nonfederal **Service**: General medical and surgical

Staffed Beds: 73 **Admissions**: 3161 **Census**: 33 **Outpatient Visits**: 236860 **Births**: 874 **Total Expense ($000)**: 126944 **Payroll Expense ($000)**: 51663 **Personnel**: 604

MUENSTER—Cooke County

MUENSTER MEMORIAL HOSPITAL (451335), 605 North Maple Street, Zip 76252–2424, Mailing Address: P.O. Box 370, Zip 76252–0370; tel. 940/759–2271, **A**10 18 **F**11 35 40 43 45 53 57 59 64 65 75 77 93 107 114 119 127 130 133 146 **P**8
Primary Contact: Marion Bruce, Chief Executive Officer
CFO: Julie Williams, Chief Financial Officer
CNO: Tiffany Lutkenhaus, Chief Nursing Officer
Web address: www.muensterhospital.com
Control: Hospital district or authority, Government, Nonfederal **Service**: General medical and surgical

Staffed Beds: 18 **Admissions**: 26 **Census**: 9 **Outpatient Visits**: 7521 **Births**: 0 **Total Expense ($000)**: 13667 **Payroll Expense ($000)**: 5798 **Personnel**: 94

MULESHOE—Bailey County

MULESHOE AREA MEDICAL CENTER (451372), 708 South First Street, Zip 79347–3627; tel. 806/272–4524, **A**10 18 **F**40 93 97 107 119 127 133 154 **S** Preferred Management Corporation, Shawnee, OK
Primary Contact: Dennis Fleenor, R.N., Administrator
CMO: Bruce Purdy, M.D., Chief of Staff
CHR: Suzanne Nichols, Director Human Resources
Web address: www.mahdtx.org
Control: Corporation, Investor–owned (for–profit) **Service**: General medical and surgical

Staffed Beds: 25 **Admissions**: 47 **Census**: 1 **Outpatient Visits**: 13252 **Births**: 0 **Total Expense ($000)**: 9246 **Payroll Expense ($000)**: 3394 **Personnel**: 64

NACOGDOCHES—Nacogdoches County

✠ **NACOGDOCHES MEDICAL CENTER (450656)**, 4920 NE Stallings Drive, Zip 75965–1200; tel. 936/569–9481, **A**1 10 19 **F**3 12 13 15 18 20 22 29 31 34 35 40 42 43 45 46 50 54 56 57 59 64 65 68 70 72 74 76 77 78 79 81 85 87 93 96 97 100 102 107 108 110 111 114 115 118 119 120 121 122 123 126 129 130 131 132 135 146 147 154 167 169 **S** TENET Healthcare Corporation, Dallas, TX
Primary Contact: Jeff Patterson, Chief Executive Officer
CFO: Randy Slack, Chief Financial Officer
CMO: Charles Thompson, M.D., Chief Medical Officer
CIO: Teresa Simon, Director Information Systems
CHR: Teresa Farrell, Chief Human Resources Officer
CNO: Patti Bennett, Chief Nursing Officer
Web address: www.nacmedicalcenter.com
Control: Partnership, Investor–owned (for–profit) **Service**: General medical and surgical

Staffed Beds: 109 **Admissions**: 5042 **Census**: 55 **Outpatient Visits**: 79995 **Births**: 922 **Total Expense ($000)**: 96171 **Payroll Expense ($000)**: 34306 **Personnel**: 382

☐ **NACOGDOCHES MEMORIAL HOSPITAL (450508)**, 1204 North Mound Street, Zip 75961–4061; tel. 936/564–4611, **A**1 10 19 **F**3 8 13 15 17 18 19 20 22 28 29 35 40 41 43 44 45 48 49 50 55 59 60 64 65 68 70 72 73 74 75 76 77 78 79 80 81 82 85 87 89 90 93 96 97 105 107 108 110 111 114 115 119 126 127 130 147 148 167 **P**6
Primary Contact: Rhonda McCabe, Chief Executive Officer
CFO: Jane Ann Bridges, Chief Financial Officer
CNO: Beth Knight, Chief Nursing Officer
Web address: www.nacmem.org
Control: Partnership, Investor–owned (for–profit) **Service**: General medical and surgical

Staffed Beds: 131 **Admissions**: 2816 **Census**: 34 **Outpatient Visits**: 77709 **Births**: 489 **Total Expense ($000)**: 73588 **Payroll Expense ($000)**: 25700 **Personnel**: 539

NAVASOTA—Grimes County

✠ **CHI ST. JOSEPH HEALTH GRIMES HOSPITAL (451322)**, 210 South Judson Street, Zip 77868-3704; tel. 936/825-6585, **A**1 10 18 **F**3 28 29 34 40 43 56 57 59 75 77 93 107 119 130 132 133 135 146 167 **S** CommonSpirit Health, Chicago, IL
Primary Contact: Kyle Sims, Division Vice President
CFO: Austin Jones, CPA, Chief Financial Officer
CMO: Luke P Scamardo, M.D., II, Chief of Staff
CIO: Mike Russo, Vice President Information Systems
CHR: Kristina Lee, Director Human Resources
CNO: Cesar Lopez, R.N., Director of Nurses
Web address: https://stjoseph.stlukeshealth.org/locations/chi-st-joseph-health-grimes-hospital
Control: Church operated, Nongovernment, not-for-profit **Service**: General medical and surgical

Staffed Beds: 15 **Admissions**: 182 **Census**: 7 **Outpatient Visits**: 12296 **Births**: 0 **Total Expense ($000)**: 13694 **Payroll Expense ($000)**: 5070 **Personnel**: 60

NEDERLAND—Jefferson County

PROMISE SPECIALTY HOSPITAL OF SOUTHEAST TEXAS See Mid-Jefferson Extended Care Hospital

NEW BRAUNFELS—Comal County

CHRISTUS SANTA ROSA HOSPITAL – NEW BRAUNFELS See Christus Santa Rosa Hospital – New Braunfels

NEW BRAUNFELS ER & HOSPITAL, 3221 Commercial Cirle, Zip 78132-4447; tel. 830/402-2170, **A**22 **F**3 40 107 114 119
Primary Contact: Tom Vo, M.D., Chief Executive Officer, NuTex Corporation
COO: David Heitzman, Chief Administrative Officer and Chief Nursing Officer
CFO: David Heitzman, Chief Administrative Officer and Chief Nursing Officer
CMO: Scott Knepper, M.D., Chief Medical Officer
CIO: David Heitzman, Chief Administrative Officer and Chief Nursing Officer
CHR: Elizabeth Hall, Chief Human Resources Officer
CNO: David Heitzman, Chief Administrative Officer and Chief Nursing Officer
Web address: www.nberhospital.com
Control: Partnership, Investor-owned (for-profit) **Service**: General medical and surgical

Staffed Beds: 4 **Admissions**: 214 **Census**: 2 **Outpatient Visits**: 3767 **Births**: 0 **Total Expense ($000)**: 6977 **Payroll Expense ($000)**: 1991 **Personnel**: 31

☐ **NEW BRAUNFELS REGIONAL REHABILITATION HOSPITAL (673049)**, 2041 Sundance Parkway, Zip 78130-2779; tel. 830/625-6700, **A**1 10 **F**3 29 34 57 64 90 93 96 130 132 148 **S** Ernest Health, Inc., Albuquerque, NM
Primary Contact: Nicholas Nilest, Chief Executive Officer
CFO: Sue Thomsen, Chief Financial Officer
CMO: Maria R Lomba, Medical Director
CHR: Cheryl Smith, Manager Human Resources
CNO: Peggy Schmits, Director, Nursing Operations
Web address: www.nbrrh.ernesthealth.com
Control: Corporation, Investor-owned (for-profit) **Service**: Rehabilitation

Staffed Beds: 40 **Admissions**: 826 **Census**: 35 **Outpatient Visits**: 18619 **Total Expense ($000)**: 17592 **Payroll Expense ($000)**: 9245 **Personnel**: 133

✠ **PAM SPECIALTY HOSPITAL OF NEW BRAUNFELS (452106)**, 1445 Hanz Drive, Zip 78130-2567; tel. 830/627-7600, **A**1 10 **F**1 3 28 29 30 60 85 90 130 148 **S** PAM Health, Enola, PA
Primary Contact: Greg Wuchter, Chief Executive Officer
Web address: www.warmsprings.org/locations/hos/h1/
Control: Partnership, Investor-owned (for-profit) **Service**: Acute long-term care hospital

Staffed Beds: 32 **Admissions**: 767 **Census**: 30 **Outpatient Visits**: 0 **Births**: 0 **Total Expense ($000)**: 17481 **Payroll Expense ($000)**: 8170 **Personnel**: 116

RESOLUTE HEALTH (670098), 555 Creekside Crossing, Zip 78130-2594; tel. 830/500-6000, **A**1 10 **F**3 13 15 18 20 22 29 30 34 35 40 45 48 49 50 60 64 65 70 72 74 75 76 77 79 81 85 87 107 108 111 114 115 119 120 126 130 146 147 148 149 156 167 **S** TENET Healthcare Corporation, Dallas, TX
Primary Contact: Mark L. Bernard, Chief Executive Officer
Web address: www.resolutehealth.com
Control: Corporation, Investor-owned (for-profit) **Service**: General medical and surgical

Staffed Beds: 128 **Admissions**: 5842 **Census**: 53 **Outpatient Visits**: 37707 **Births**: 1278 **Total Expense ($000)**: 95716 **Payroll Expense ($000)**: 34569 **Personnel**: 368

NOCONA—Montague County

NOCONA GENERAL HOSPITAL (450641), 100 Park Road, Zip 76255-3616; tel. 940/825-3235, **A**10 20 **F**3 7 28 29 30 34 35 40 45 50 53 57 59 62 64 75 81 82 86 87 93 97 100 107 108 115 119 127 130 146 148 154
Primary Contact: Lance Meekins, Chief Executive Officer
CFO: Lance Meekins, Chief Executive Officer
CMO: Chance Dingler, M.D., Chief Medical Officer
CHR: Paula Clark, Administrative Assistant and Director Human Resources
Web address: www.noconageneral.com/
Control: Hospital district or authority, Government, Nonfederal **Service**: General medical and surgical

Staffed Beds: 18 **Admissions**: 354 **Census**: 3 **Outpatient Visits**: 11713 **Births**: 0 **Total Expense ($000)**: 12397 **Payroll Expense ($000)**: 5594 **Personnel**: 121

NORTH RICHLAND HILLS—Tarrant County

✠ **MEDICAL CITY NORTH HILLS (450087)**, 4401 Booth Calloway Road, Zip 76180-7399; tel. 817/255-1000, **A**1 3 10 **F**3 12 17 18 20 22 24 26 29 34 35 37 39 40 43 45 46 49 50 51 57 60 64 70 74 75 79 81 85 86 87 107 108 111 115 118 119 126 130 132 135 146 148 149 154 167 **S** HCA Healthcare, Nashville, TN
Primary Contact: Mark S. Deno, FACHE, Chief Executive Officer
COO: Nancy L Hill, R.N., MSN, Chief Operating Officer
CFO: Nick Galt, Chief Financial Officer
CMO: John McDonald, M.D., Chief Medical Officer
CIO: Jason Sims, Facility Information Security Officer
CNO: John Marker, MSN, R.N., Chief Nursing Officer
Web address: www.northhillshospital.com
Control: Partnership, Investor-owned (for-profit) **Service**: General medical and surgical

Staffed Beds: 142 **Admissions**: 8264 **Census**: 92 **Outpatient Visits**: 48512 **Births**: 0 **Total Expense ($000)**: 123641 **Payroll Expense ($000)**: 49601 **Personnel**: 596

ODESSA—Ector County

★ **CONTINUECARE HOSPITAL AT MEDICAL CENTER (ODESSA) (452121)**, 500 West Fourth Street, 4th Floor, Zip 79761-5001; tel. 432/640-4380, **A**10 22 **F**1 3 29 34 35 85 87 **S** Community Hospital Corporation, Plano, TX
Primary Contact: Adebola Awino, Chief Nursing Officer/Interim Chief Executive Offier
CNO: Ade Adelekan, Chief Nursing Officer
Web address: https://odessa.continuecare.org/
Control: Other not-for-profit (including NFP Corporation) **Service**: Acute long-term care hospital

Staffed Beds: 25 **Admissions**: 240 **Census**: 19 **Outpatient Visits**: 0 **Births**: 0 **Total Expense ($000)**: 10068 **Payroll Expense ($000)**: 5354 **Personnel**: 60

Hospitals, U.S. / TEXAS

★ ⇑ **MEDICAL CENTER HEALTH SYSTEM (450132)**, 500 West Fourth Street, Zip 79761-5059, Mailing Address: P O Drawer 7239, Zip 79760-7239; tel. 432/640-4000, **A**3 5 10 19 21 **F**3 8 11 12 13 15 17 18 20 22 24 26 28 29 30 31 34 35 37 40 41 43 44 45 46 47 48 49 50 51 53 54 57 59 60 64 65 66 68 70 72 74 75 76 77 78 79 81 82 85 87 89 93 97 100 107 110 111 115 117 118 119 126 130 131 132 135 144 146 147 148 149 154 156 157 167 169 **P**1 6 7
Primary Contact: Russell Tippin, President and Chief Executive Officer
COO: Tony Ruiz, Senior Vice President, Chief Operating Officer
CFO: Steven Ewing, Chief Financial Officer
CMO: Sari A. Nabulshi, M.D., Chief Medical Officer
CIO: Gary Barnes, Senior Vice President, Chief Information Officer
CHR: Robbi Banks, Vice President, Human Resources
CNO: Chad Dunavan, R.N., Vice President, Chief Nursing Officer
Web address: www.mchodessa.com
Control: Hospital district or authority, Government, Nonfederal **Service**: General medical and surgical

Staffed Beds: 361 **Admissions**: 13073 **Census**: 183 **Outpatient Visits**: 358853 **Births**: 2051 **Total Expense ($000)**: 350467 **Payroll Expense ($000)**: 121302 **Personnel**: 1740

⇑ **ODESSA REGIONAL MEDICAL CENTER (450661)**, 520 East Sixth Street, Zip 79761-4565, Mailing Address: P.O. Box 4859, Zip 79760-4859; tel. 432/582-8000, **A**3 5 10 19 21 **F**3 12 13 15 17 18 20 22 24 29 34 35 40 43 46 49 50 51 55 57 59 60 64 66 70 72 74 75 76 79 81 82 85 86 87 89 107 108 111 115 119 124 126 130 132 146 147 148 154 167 169 **S** Steward Health Care System, LLC, Dallas, TX
Primary Contact: Stacey L. Brown, Chief Executive Officer
CIO: Jimmy Diaz, Director Information Technology
CHR: Jill Sparkman, Director Human Resources
CNO: Levi Ross Stone, R.N., Chief Nursing Officer and Chief Operating Officer
Web address: https://www.odessaregionalmedicalcenter.org/
Control: Partnership, Investor-owned (for-profit) **Service**: General medical and surgical

Staffed Beds: 112 **Admissions**: 5832 **Census**: 72 **Outpatient Visits**: 50638 **Births**: 1912 **Total Expense ($000)**: 150041 **Payroll Expense ($000)**: 43489 **Personnel**: 768

OLNEY—Young County

HAMILTON HOSPITAL See Olney Hamilton Hospital

★ **OLNEY HAMILTON HOSPITAL (451354)**, 901 West Hamilton Street, Zip 76374-1725, Mailing Address: P.O. Box 158, Zip 76374-0158; tel. 940/564-5521, **A**10 18 **F**7 11 13 28 29 30 34 40 43 53 57 76 77 81 86 89 93 107 114 127 129 130 133 146 169
Primary Contact: Michael H. Huff, Chief Executive Officer
CFO: Coy Noles, Chief Financial Officer Consultant
CMO: Mark L Mankins, M.D., Chief of Staff
CIO: Rick Oliver, Information Technology
CHR: Amy Moore, Human Resources
CNO: Samantha Isbell, R.N., Chief Nursing Officer
Web address: www.olneyhamiltonhospital.com
Control: Hospital district or authority, Government, Nonfederal **Service**: General medical and surgical

Staffed Beds: 25 **Admissions**: 199 **Census**: 7 **Outpatient Visits**: 17493 **Births**: 40 **Total Expense ($000)**: 19110 **Payroll Expense ($000)**: 7379 **Personnel**: 137

PALACIOS—Matagorda County

★ **PALACIOS COMMUNITY MEDICAL CENTER (451332)**, 311 Green Street, Zip 77465-3213; tel. 361/972-2511, **A**10 18 **F**3 29 34 35 40 50 57 59 64 65 87 91 93 96 107 119 128 133 146 148
Primary Contact: Huyen Tran, Administrator
COO: Lisa Henderson, Chief Operating Officer
CFO: Claude Manning, Chief Financial Officer
CIO: Angela Yeager, Director Information Technology
CHR: Lisa Henderson, Chief Operations Officer
CNO: Susan Easter, Chief Nursing Officer
Web address: www.palacioshospital.net/
Control: Other not-for-profit (including NFP Corporation) **Service**: General medical and surgical

Staffed Beds: 15 **Admissions**: 143 **Census**: 3 **Outpatient Visits**: 4966 **Births**: 0 **Total Expense ($000)**: 5668 **Payroll Expense ($000)**: 1687 **Personnel**: 31

PALESTINE—Anderson County

✠ **PALESTINE REGIONAL MEDICAL CENTER–EAST (450747)**, 2900 South Loop 256, Zip 75801-6958; tel. 903/731-1000, (Includes PALESTINE REGIONAL MEDICAL CENTER, 2900 S Loop 256, Palestine, Texas, Zip 75801-6958, tel. 903/731-1000; Doug Holzbog, Market Chief Executive Officer) **A**1 5 10 **F**3 7 13 15 18 20 22 26 28 29 31 34 40 43 44 47 48 49 50 51 56 57 59 60 70 76 79 81 82 85 86 87 89 90 93 96 97 98 100 107 108 110 111 114 118 119 129 130 131 146 147 148 154 163 164 167 169 **P**6 **S** ScionHealth, Louisville, KY
Primary Contact: Doug Holzbog, Market Chief Executive Officer
CFO: Celena Brim, Chief Financial Officer
CIO: Rebecca Chou, Director Information Systems
CHR: Rhonda Beard, Director Human Resources
Web address: www.palestineregional.com
Control: Partnership, Investor-owned (for-profit) **Service**: General medical and surgical

Staffed Beds: 160 **Admissions**: 2830 **Census**: 63 **Outpatient Visits**: 61628 **Births**: 498 **Total Expense ($000)**: 82657 **Payroll Expense ($000)**: 35339 **Personnel**: 468

PALESTINE REGIONAL REHABILITATION CENTER See Palestine Regional Medical Center

PAMPA—Gray County

○ **PAMPA REGIONAL MEDICAL CENTER (450099)**, 1 Medical Plaza, Zip 79065; tel. 806/665-3721, **A**10 11 **F**3 11 15 18 20 22 29 34 35 40 41 44 45 46 50 57 59 60 64 65 67 70 77 79 81 85 87 91 92 93 96 97 99 107 108 110 111 115 119 130 133 143 144 146 147 148 149 154 167 **S** Prime Healthcare, Ontario, CA
Primary Contact: Jonathan Gill, Chief Executive Officer
CFO: Ronald Collins, Chief Financial Officer
CMO: James Hall, M.D., Chief Medical Officer
CIO: Joy Patton, Director Information Technology
CHR: Debbie Dixon, Director Human Resources
CNO: Twilla Thomas, Chief Nursing Officer
Web address: www.prmctx.com
Control: Other not-for-profit (including NFP Corporation) **Service**: General medical and surgical

Staffed Beds: 25 **Admissions**: 924 **Census**: 10 **Outpatient Visits**: 28305 **Births**: 0 **Total Expense ($000)**: 42183 **Payroll Expense ($000)**: 14692 **Personnel**: 185

PARIS—Lamar County

CHRISTUS ST JOSEPH HOSPITAL NORTH See Paris Regional Medical Center

✠ **PARIS REGIONAL MEDICAL CENTER (450196)**, 865 Deshong Drive, Zip 75460-9313, Mailing Address: P.O. Box 9070, Zip 75461-9070; tel. 903/785-4521, (Includes PARIS REGIONAL MEDICAL CENTER, 865 Deshong Drive, Paris, Texas, Zip 75462-2097, tel. 903/785-4521) **A**1 10 **F**3 11 13 15 17 18 20 22 24 26 28 29 30 31 34 35 36 40 43 45 49 50 51 57 59 60 64 70 74 75 76 77 78 79 81 85 86 87 89 90 91 93 97 102 107 108 110 111 115 118 119 126 127 129 131 135 145 146 147 148 149 154 167 **P**5 7 **S** Lifepoint Health, Brentwood, TN
Primary Contact: Steve Hyde, Chief Executive Officer
COO: Scott B. Avery, Chief Operating Officer
CFO: Donald E McDaniel III, Chief Financial Officer
CMO: Richard Bercher, M.D., Chief Medical Officer
CHR: Cheryl Perry, Executive Director Human Resources
CNO: Debra Taylor, Chief Nursing Officer
Web address: https://parisregionalmedical.com/
Control: Partnership, Investor-owned (for-profit) **Service**: General medical and surgical

Staffed Beds: 154 **Admissions**: 7344 **Census**: 84 **Outpatient Visits**: 71863 **Births**: 906 **Total Expense ($000)**: 123551 **Payroll Expense ($000)**: 39848 **Personnel**: 640

PASADENA—Harris County

⇑ **CHI ST. LUKE'S HEALTH – PATIENTS MEDICAL CENTER** See St. Luke's Health – Patients Medical Center

Hospitals, U.S. / TEXAS

☒ **HCA HOUSTON HEALTHCARE SOUTHEAST (450097)**, 4000 Spencer Highway, Zip 77504–1202; tel. 713/359–2000, **A**1 10 **F**3 11 12 13 18 20 22 24 26 28 29 31 34 35 40 42 43 45 49 50 51 57 59 60 64 70 72 74 75 76 77 79 81 82 84 85 90 91 92 93 96 100 102 107 108 111 114 115 118 119 126 128 129 130 131 146 167 **S** HCA Healthcare, Nashville, TN
Primary Contact: Yasmene McDaniel, Chief Executive Officer
CFO: John Armour, Chief Financial Officer
CIO: Clifford Ferguson, Director Information Technology and Systems
CNO: Gurvir K Saini MSN, RN, Chief Nursing Officer
Web address: https://hcahoustonhealthcare.com/locations/southeast/
Control: Partnership, Investor–owned (for–profit) **Service**: General medical and surgical

Staffed Beds: 278 **Admissions**: 15029 **Census**: 212 **Outpatient Visits**: 149195 **Births**: 2594 **Total Expense ($000)**: 264249 **Payroll Expense ($000)**: 111441 **Personnel**: 1152

☐ **OCEANS BEHAVIORAL HOSPITAL OF PASADENA (454147)**, 4001 Preston Drive, Zip 77505–2069; tel. 832/619–8836, (Nonreporting) **A**1 **S** Oceans Healthcare, Plano, TX
Primary Contact: Shamieka Thomas, Administrator
Web address: https://oceanshealthcare.com/pasadena
Control: Corporation, Investor–owned (for–profit) **Service**: Psychiatric

Staffed Beds: 22

★ ⇧ **ST. LUKE'S HEALTH – PATIENTS MEDICAL CENTER (670031)**, 4600 East Sam Houston Parkway South, Zip 77505–3948; tel. 713/948–7000, **A**10 21 **F**12 15 18 20 22 24 26 28 29 30 35 40 42 44 45 46 54 59 64 70 74 77 79 81 82 86 87 91 93 94 107 108 111 114 115 116 119 130 145 146 148 149 157 **S** CommonSpirit Health, Chicago, IL
Primary Contact: Steven Foster, President and Chief Executive Officer
CNO: Jane Stirrup, Vice President, Patient Care Services and Chief Nursing Officer
Web address: https://locations.stlukeshealth.org/location/patients-medical-center
Control: Partnership, Investor–owned (for–profit) **Service**: General medical and surgical

Staffed Beds: 61 **Admissions**: 3075 **Census**: 37 **Outpatient Visits**: 32375 **Births**: 0 **Total Expense ($000)**: 78976 **Payroll Expense ($000)**: 34495 **Personnel**: 417

○ **SURGERY SPECIALTY HOSPITALS OF AMERICA (450831)**, 4301B Vista Road, Zip 77504; tel. 713/378–3000, **A**10 11 **F**3 12 29 40 79 81 82 107 111 119 130 131
Primary Contact: Eric Chan, M.D., Chief Executive Officer
COO: Hemant Khemka, Chief Operating Officer
CFO: Hemant Khemka, Chief Financial Officer
CMO: Xiao H. Li, M.D., Chief of Staff
CIO: Ringo Cheng, Director Information Technology
Web address: www.surgeryspecialty.com/
Control: Partnership, Investor–owned (for–profit) **Service**: General medical and surgical

Staffed Beds: 10 **Admissions**: 35 **Census**: 1 **Outpatient Visits**: 3446 **Births**: 0 **Total Expense ($000)**: 16512 **Payroll Expense ($000)**: 5512 **Personnel**: 77

PEARLAND—Brazoria County

☒ **ENCOMPASS HEALTH REHABILITATION HOSPITAL OF PEARLAND (673066)**, 2121 Business Center Drive, Zip 77584–2153; tel. 346/907–3000, **A**1 10 **F**3 29 90 96 130 132 **S** Encompass Health Corporation, Birmingham, AL
Primary Contact: Michael Cabiro, Chief Executive Officer
CFO: Carol Neilson, CPA, Area Controller
Web address: https://www.encompasshealth.com/locations/pearlandrehab
Control: Corporation, Investor–owned (for–profit) **Service**: Rehabilitation

Staffed Beds: 60 **Admissions**: 1255 **Census**: 46 **Outpatient Visits**: 0 **Births**: 0 **Total Expense ($000)**: 25166 **Payroll Expense ($000)**: 13852 **Personnel**: 160

☒ **HCA HOUSTON HEALTHCARE PEARLAND (670106)**, 11100 Shadow Creek Parkway, Zip 77584–7285; tel. 713/770–7000, **A**1 10 **F**3 18 20 22 26 29 31 34 35 37 40 41 45 49 50 51 57 59 68 70 74 75 77 78 79 81 82 85 86 87 107 108 110 111 114 119 126 130 143 146 148 157 168 **S** HCA Healthcare, Nashville, TN
Primary Contact: Justin Brewer, Interim Chief Executive Officer
CNO: Jeanette Pennick, Chief Nursing Officer
Web address: www.pearlandmc.com
Control: Partnership, Investor–owned (for–profit) **Service**: General medical and surgical

Staffed Beds: 48 **Admissions**: 4298 **Census**: 58 **Outpatient Visits**: 43254 **Births**: 0 **Total Expense ($000)**: 106892 **Payroll Expense ($000)**: 34593 **Personnel**: 317

PEARSALL—Frio County

★ **FRIO REGIONAL HOSPITAL (451391)**, 200 South I H 35, Zip 78061–3998; tel. 830/334–3617, **A**10 18 **F**3 13 15 29 34 35 40 43 45 57 59 62 64 76 77 79 81 84 87 93 96 107 110 115 119 127 130 133 146 147 148 **P**6
Primary Contact: John R. Hughson, Chief Executive Officer
CMO: Samer Arab, M.D., Chief Medical Officer
CHR: Nancy Ortiz, Director Human Resource and Marketing
CNO: Louisa Martinez, Director of Nursing
Web address: www.frioregionalhospital.com
Control: Other not–for–profit (including NFP Corporation) **Service**: General medical and surgical

Staffed Beds: 22 **Admissions**: 525 **Census**: 9 **Outpatient Visits**: 41274 **Births**: 92 **Total Expense ($000)**: 26331 **Payroll Expense ($000)**: 10958 **Personnel**: 166

PECOS—Reeves County

REEVES COUNTY HOSPITAL DISTRICT See Reeves Regional Health

★ **REEVES REGIONAL HEALTH (451377)**, 2349 Medical Drive, Zip 79772–2251; tel. 432/447–3551, **A**10 18 **F**3 11 13 15 35 40 43 57 60 62 64 68 70 76 81 87 89 93 107 109 110 111 114 119 127 130 131 133 146 147 148 154
Primary Contact: Brenda McKinney, Chief Executive Officer
COO: Yvette Riker, Chief Operating Officer
CFO: Bomi Bharucha, Chief Financial Officer
CMO: Deitrick Gorman, M.D., Chief of Staff
CHR: Nadine Smith, Director Human Resources
CNO: Faye Lease, Chief Nursing Officer
Web address: www.reevesregional.com
Control: Hospital district or authority, Government, Nonfederal **Service**: General medical and surgical

Staffed Beds: 25 **Admissions**: 639 **Census**: 7 **Outpatient Visits**: 87535 **Births**: 138 **Total Expense ($000)**: 63388 **Payroll Expense ($000)**: 23697 **Personnel**: 284

PERRYTON—Ochiltree County

⇧ **OCHILTREE GENERAL HOSPITAL (451359)**, 3101 Garrett Drive, Zip 79070–5323; tel. 806/435–3606, **A**10 18 21 **F**3 10 11 13 15 29 30 34 35 40 43 45 50 57 59 62 63 64 65 69 76 79 81 85 89 93 97 104 107 108 110 119 127 129 130 133 135 143 144 146 147 148 149 154 167 169 **P**1
Primary Contact: Kelly Paige. Judice, Interim Chief Executive Officer
CFO: Debbie Blodgett, Director Fiscal Services
CMO: Rex Mann, M.D., Chief Medical Officer
CIO: Dyan Harrison, Manager Health Information
CHR: Debbie Beck, Manager Human Resource and Payroll
Web address: www.ochiltreehospital.com
Control: Hospital district or authority, Government, Nonfederal **Service**: General medical and surgical

Staffed Beds: 25 **Admissions**: 378 **Census**: 3 **Outpatient Visits**: 39063 **Births**: 115 **Total Expense ($000)**: 27823 **Payroll Expense ($000)**: 12380 **Personnel**: 196

Hospital, Medicare Provider Number, Address, Telephone, Approval, Facility, and Physician Codes, Health Care System

★ American Hospital Association (AHA) membership
☐ The Joint Commission accreditation
○ Healthcare Facilities Accreditation Program
◇ DNV Healthcare Inc. accreditation
⇧ Center for Improvement in Healthcare Quality Accreditation
△ Commission on Accreditation of Rehabilitation Facilities (CARF) accreditation

Hospitals, U.S. / TEXAS

PFLUGERVILLE—Travis County

☒ **BAYLOR SCOTT & WHITE MEDICAL CENTER – PFLUGERVILLE (670128)**, 2600 East Pflugerville Parkway, Zip 78660–5998; tel. 512/654–6100, **A**1 10 **F**3 4 8 12 15 29 30 34 35 40 45 46 49 50 54 56 64 65 68 70 74 75 79 81 84 85 87 90 97 100 101 102 103 107 110 111 114 119 126 130 135 141 146 147 148 149 154 157 **S** Baylor Scott & White Health, Dallas, TX
Primary Contact: Jay Fox, FACHE, President
Web address: https://www.bswhealth.com/locations/pflugerville-mc
Control: Other not–for–profit (including NFP Corporation) **Service:** General medical and surgical

Staffed Beds: 25 **Admissions:** 1116 **Census:** 11 **Outpatient Visits:** 41175 **Births:** 0 **Total Expense ($000):** 42025 **Payroll Expense ($000):** 15758 **Personnel:** 137

PITTSBURG—Camp County

☒ **UT HEALTH PITTSBURG (451367)**, 2701 Highway 271 North, Zip 75686–1032; tel. 903/946–5000, **A**1 3 10 18 **F**3 12 28 29 34 35 40 43 45 50 57 59 64 65 75 77 79 81 82 84 85 87 92 93 97 107 108 111 114 119 127 129 130 133 146 147 149 154 156 **S** Ardent Health Services, Nashville, TN
Primary Contact: Guybertho Cayo, Chief Executive Officer
CFO: Shawna Shacklett, Chief Financial Officer
CMO: W R Christensen, M.D., Chief of Staff
CIO: Paula Anthony, Vice President Information Services
CHR: Kathy Shelton, Director Human Resources
CNO: Casey Mayben, Chief Nursing Officer
Web address: https://uthealthpittsburg.com/
Control: Partnership, Investor–owned (for–profit) **Service:** General medical and surgical

Staffed Beds: 25 **Admissions:** 741 **Census:** 8 **Outpatient Visits:** 67260 **Births:** 0 **Total Expense ($000):** 32780 **Payroll Expense ($000):** 10348 **Personnel:** 155

PLAINVIEW—Hale County

ALLEGIANCE BEHAVIORAL HEALTH CENTER OF PLAINVIEW (454101), 2601 Dimmit Road, Suite 400, Zip 79072–1833; tel. 806/296–9191, **A**10 **F**29 35 56 64 98 101 103 104 164 **S** Allegiance Health Management, Shreveport, LA
Primary Contact: William E. Ernst Jr, Chief Executive Officer
CMO: Victor A Gutierrez, M.D., Medical Director
CIO: Joe Monsour, Chief Information Officer
CHR: Danny J. Wagner, Chief Human Resource Officer
Web address: www.ahmgt.com
Control: Corporation, Investor–owned (for–profit) **Service:** Psychiatric

Staffed Beds: 20 **Admissions:** 245 **Census:** 11 **Outpatient Visits:** 0 **Births:** 0 **Total Expense ($000):** 4578 **Payroll Expense ($000):** 1599 **Personnel:** 40

☒ **COVENANT HOSPITAL PLAINVIEW (450539)**, 2601 Dimmitt Road, Zip 79072–1833; tel. 806/296–5531, **A**1 10 20 **F**3 11 13 15 18 29 30 32 34 35 38 40 43 45 48 57 59 64 65 68 70 75 76 77 79 80 81 85 86 87 97 107 108 110 111 114 119 126 127 129 130 131 132 135 146 147 148 149 154 167 **P**3 **S** Providence, Renton, WA
Primary Contact: Cassie Mogg, Chief Executive Officer
COO: Mike McNutt, Assistant Administrator
CMO: Sergio Lara, M.D., Chief Medical Officer
CNO: Leslie Hackett, Chief Nursing Officer
Web address: www.covenantplainview.org
Control: Other not–for–profit (including NFP Corporation) **Service:** General medical and surgical

Staffed Beds: 49 **Admissions:** 1110 **Census:** 8 **Outpatient Visits:** 153015 **Births:** 378 **Total Expense ($000):** 79276 **Payroll Expense ($000):** 21274 **Personnel:** 369

PLANO—Collin County

☒ **BAYLOR SCOTT & WHITE MEDICAL CENTER – PLANO (450890)**, 4700 Alliance Boulevard, Zip 75093–5323; tel. 469/814–2000, **A**1 2 3 5 10 **F**3 12 15 18 29 30 31 34 35 37 40 45 46 47 48 49 50 51 54 57 58 59 60 63 64 65 66 68 70 74 75 77 78 79 80 81 82 84 85 86 87 97 107 108 110 111 114 115 119 126 130 132 135 146 147 148 149 154 167 **S** Baylor Scott & White Health, Dallas, TX
Primary Contact: Jerri Garison, R.N., President
COO: Joseph C. Brown, Vice President Operations
CFO: Deanne Kindred, Vice President Finance
CMO: John Marcucci, M.D., Vice President Medical Affairs
CHR: Kriss Gamez, Director Human Resources
Web address: www.baylorhealth.com/PhysiciansLocations/Plano/Pages/Default.aspx
Control: Other not–for–profit (including NFP Corporation) **Service:** General medical and surgical

Staffed Beds: 160 **Admissions:** 7388 **Census:** 97 **Outpatient Visits:** 85100 **Births:** 0 **Total Expense ($000):** 244006 **Payroll Expense ($000):** 76776 **Personnel:** 662

☒ **BAYLOR SCOTT & WHITE THE HEART HOSPITAL PLANO (670025)**, 1100 Allied Drive, Zip 75093–5348; tel. 469/814–3278, **A**1 3 5 10 **F**3 17 18 20 22 24 26 28 29 30 34 35 38 40 46 53 54 55 56 57 58 59 60 64 68 74 75 77 81 82 84 85 86 87 90 107 108 111 112 115 119 126 129 130 132 135 146 148 149 154 157 164 **S** Baylor Scott & White Health, Dallas, TX
Primary Contact: Mark Valentine, President
COO: Brad D. McCall, Vice President Operations
CFO: Bryan Nichols, Chief Financial Officer
CMO: Trent Pettijohn, M.D., Esq, Chief Medical Officer
CHR: Anna Gemeny, Regional Director Human Resources
CNO: Susan K. Moats, R.N., Vice President Patient Care Services and Chief Nursing Officer
Web address: https://www.bswhealth.com/the-heart-hospital/locations/plano
Control: Partnership, Investor–owned (for–profit) **Service:** Heart

Staffed Beds: 109 **Admissions:** 6680 **Census:** 97 **Outpatient Visits:** 66899 **Births:** 0 **Total Expense ($000):** 373063 **Payroll Expense ($000):** 110742 **Personnel:** 1004

☐ **CHILDREN'S MEDICAL CENTER PLANO (453316)**, 7601 Preston Road, Zip 75024–3214; tel. 469/303–7000, **A**1 3 5 10 **F**3 19 21 23 29 30 31 34 39 40 41 43 53 54 59 64 68 74 75 77 78 79 81 82 85 86 87 88 89 93 97 98 99 104 105 107 108 111 114 115 118 126 129 130 131 146 148 153 154 156 164 167 **S** Children's Health, Dallas, TX
Primary Contact: Jeremiah Radandt, Executive Vice President Northern Market/Administrator
CIO: Pamela Arora, Senior Vice President and Chief Information Officer
CHR: Kim Besse, Executive Vice President and Chief Human Resource Officer
CNO: Mary Stowe, Senior Vice President and Chief Nursing Officer
Web address: https://www.childrens.com/location-landing/locations-and-directions/childrens-health-plano
Control: Other not–for–profit (including NFP Corporation) **Service:** Children's general medical and surgical

Staffed Beds: 72 **Admissions:** 4123 **Census:** 47 **Outpatient Visits:** 74569 **Births:** 0 **Total Expense ($000):** 325217 **Payroll Expense ($000):** 108190 **Personnel:** 1176

☒ **ENCOMPASS HEALTH REHABILITATION HOSPITAL OF PLANO (453047)**, 2800 West 15th Street, Zip 75075–7526; tel. 972/612–9000, **A**1 10 **F**34 57 59 90 93 95 96 130 132 148 149 **S** Encompass Health Corporation, Birmingham, AL
Primary Contact: Wray Borland, Chief Executive Officer
CFO: Catrina Madkins, Controller and Chief Financial Officer
CMO: Omar Colon, M.D., Medical Director
Web address: https://encompasshealth.com/locations/planorehab
Control: Corporation, Investor–owned (for–profit) **Service:** Rehabilitation

Staffed Beds: 83 **Admissions:** 1728 **Census:** 61 **Outpatient Visits:** 0 **Births:** 0 **Total Expense ($000):** 27006 **Payroll Expense ($000):** 15438 **Personnel:** 218

☐ **LEGENT HOSPITAL FOR SPECIAL SURGERY (670322)**, 4100 Mapleshade Lane, Zip 75093–0012; tel. 972/265–1050, **A**1 **F**3 29 40 64 68 74 75 79 81 85 87 149 157 164
Primary Contact: Cole Schmitz, Chief Executive Officer
Web address: https://www.legenthealth.com/
Control: Partnership, Investor–owned (for–profit) **Service:** Surgical

Staffed Beds: 7 **Admissions:** 202 **Census:** 1 **Outpatient Visits:** 735 **Births:** 0 **Total Expense ($000):** 25474 **Payroll Expense ($000):** 5816 **Personnel:** 47

LIFECARE HOSPITALS OF PLANO See Lifecare Hospital of Plano

Hospitals, U.S. / TEXAS

☒ **MEDICAL CITY PLANO (450651)**, 3901 West 15th Street, Zip 75075–7738; tel. 972/596–6800, (Includes MEDICAL CITY FRISCO, 5500 Frisco Square Boulevard, Frisco, Texas, Zip 75034–3305, tel. 214/618–0500; Christina Mathis, Chief Executive Officer) **A**1 2 3 10 **F**3 12 13 15 18 19 20 22 24 26 28 29 30 31 34 35 40 41 43 45 46 47 48 49 51 55 57 58 59 60 64 70 72 73 74 75 76 78 79 81 82 84 85 86 87 90 93 107 108 110 111 112 114 115 117 118 119 124 126 130 132 135 145 146 147 148 157 167 169 **S** HCA Healthcare, Nashville, TN
Primary Contact: Ben Coogan, Chief Executive Officer
COO: Cameron Howard, Chief Operating Officer
CFO: Brad Stein, Chief Financial Officer
CMO: Ann Arnold, M.D., Medical Director
CIO: Michael Gfeller, Director Information Systems
CHR: Shanna Warren, Director Human Resources
CNO: Damita Williams, Ed.D., R.N., MSN, Chief Nursing Officer
Web address: www.medicalcenterplano.com
Control: Partnership, Investor–owned (for–profit) **Service**: General medical and surgical

Staffed Beds: 621 **Admissions**: 30995 **Census**: 453 **Outpatient Visits**: 160601 **Births**: 3901 **Total Expense ($000)**: 531756 **Payroll Expense ($000)**: 236622 **Personnel**: 2190

REUNION REHABILITATION HOSPITAL PLANO, 3600 Mapleshade Lane, Zip 75075; tel. 469/830–2350, (Data for 221 days) **A**22 **F**3 28 29 74 75 79 82 90 95 96 132 148 149 **S** Nobis Rehabilitation Partners, Allen, TX
Primary Contact: Ty Burgess, Chief Executive Officer
Web address: https://reunionrehabhospital.com/locations/plano/
Control: Partnership, Investor–owned (for–profit) **Service**: Rehabilitation

Staffed Beds: 48 **Admissions**: 381 **Census**: 21 **Outpatient Visits**: 0 **Births**: 0 **Total Expense ($000)**: 9927 **Payroll Expense ($000)**: 5019 **Personnel**: 137

☒ **SELECT SPECIALTY HOSPITAL–DALLAS (452022)**, 1100 Allied Drive, Zip 75093–5348; tel. 469/892–1400, (Nonreporting) **A**1 10 **S** Select Medical Corporation, Mechanicsburg, PA
Primary Contact: Misti Varnell, Chief Executive Officer
Web address: https://www.selectspecialtyhospitals.com/locations-and-tours/tx/plano/dallas-plano/
Control: Corporation, Investor–owned (for–profit) **Service**: Acute long–term care hospital

Staffed Beds: 60

☐ **TEXAS HEALTH CENTER FOR DIAGNOSTIC & SURGERY (450891)**, 6020 West Parker Road, Suite 100, Zip 75093–8171; tel. 972/403–2700, **A**1 10 **F**3 29 37 38 40 41 45 51 54 64 79 81 82 85 86 87 107 111 115 119 126 129 149 164
Primary Contact: Mitchell Mulvehill, President
CFO: Douglas Browning, Chief Financial Officer
CHR: Cookie Tedder, Human Resources Manager
CNO: Ellen Baldwin, R.N., Chief Nursing Officer
Web address: www.thcds.com
Control: Partnership, Investor–owned (for–profit) **Service**: General medical and surgical

Staffed Beds: 18 **Admissions**: 367 **Census**: 2 **Outpatient Visits**: 14972 **Births**: 0 **Total Expense ($000)**: 65969 **Payroll Expense ($000)**: 17885 **Personnel**: 165

☒ **TEXAS HEALTH PRESBYTERIAN HOSPITAL PLANO (450771)**, 6200 West Parker Road, Zip 75093–8185; tel. 972/981–8000, **A**1 2 3 10 **F**3 12 13 15 18 19 20 22 24 26 28 29 30 31 34 35 37 38 40 42 43 44 45 46 47 49 50 54 57 58 59 64 70 72 74 75 76 78 79 81 85 92 93 96 100 107 108 110 111 115 119 126 130 132 135 146 147 149 167 169 **S** Texas Health Resources, Arlington, TX
Primary Contact: Fraser Hay, FACHE, President
CFO: Lisa Gildon, Vice President and Chief Financial Officer
CMO: Gwen Webster, M.D., President Medical Staff
CIO: Susan Anderson, Director Information Systems
CHR: Kelly K. Martin, Vice President, Human Resources
Web address: www.texashealth.org
Control: Other not–for–profit (including NFP Corporation) **Service**: General medical and surgical

Staffed Beds: 327 **Admissions**: 19671 **Census**: 280 **Outpatient Visits**: 93001 **Births**: 3276 **Total Expense ($000)**: 451759 **Payroll Expense ($000)**: 157964 **Personnel**: 1536

☐ **WELLBRIDGE HEALTHCARE GREATER DALLAS (454130)**, 4301 Mapleshade Lane, Zip 75093–0010; tel. 972/596–5445, **A**1 10 **F**64 98 101 102 103 104 105 130 132 153 164 165
Primary Contact: Daniel Martinez–Torres, Chief Executive Officer
Web address: www.wellbridgedallas.com/
Control: Corporation, Investor–owned (for–profit) **Service**: Psychiatric

Staffed Beds: 48 **Admissions**: 1229 **Census**: 36 **Outpatient Visits**: 177 **Births**: 0 **Total Expense ($000)**: 12445 **Payroll Expense ($000)**: 5825 **Personnel**: 86

PLANO—Denton County

ACUTE REHABILITATION HOSPITAL OF PLANO. (673055), 2301 Marsh Lane, #200, Zip 75093–8497; tel. 972/899–5510, **A**10 22 **F**3 29 90 96 130 132
Primary Contact: Marla C. Wilson, Chief Executive Officer
Web address: www.accelrehab.com
Control: Partnership, Investor–owned (for–profit) **Service**: Rehabilitation

Staffed Beds: 36 **Admissions**: 658 **Census**: 21 **Outpatient Visits**: 1028 **Births**: 0 **Total Expense ($000)**: 12488 **Payroll Expense ($000)**: 4809 **Personnel**: 81

TEXAS SURGICAL HOSPITAL, 2301 Marsh Lane, Zip 75093–8497; tel. 972/820–2600, **F**3 12 45 48 79 81 82 85 107 167 **P**2
Primary Contact: Thomas M. Dunning, Chief Executive Officer
CFO: Muhtar Dhanjy, Comptroller
Web address: https://txsurgical.com/
Control: Partnership, Investor–owned (for–profit) **Service**: General medical and surgical

Staffed Beds: 26 **Admissions**: 94 **Census**: 1 **Outpatient Visits**: 2275 **Births**: 0 **Total Expense ($000)**: 8461 **Payroll Expense ($000)**: 5674 **Personnel**: 112

PORT ARTHUR—Jefferson County

CHRISTUS DUBUIS HOSPITAL OF PORT ARTHUR See Christus Dubuis Hospital of Port Arthur

⇑ **THE MEDICAL CENTER OF SOUTHEAST TEXAS (450518)**, 2555 Jimmy Johnson Boulevard, Zip 77640–2007; tel. 409/724–7389, **A**10 21 **F**3 13 15 17 18 20 22 26 29 34 39 40 43 44 45 47 49 56 57 59 60 64 70 72 75 76 77 79 81 82 85 86 87 91 93 96 104 107 108 110 111 114 115 119 126 130 132 147 149 153 167 169 **S** Steward Health Care System, LLC, Dallas, TX
Primary Contact: Brent A. Cope, President
COO: Chris McMahon, Chief Operating Officer
CFO: Jason R. Miller, Chief Financial Officer
CMO: Ryan McHugh, M.D., Chief of Staff
CIO: Bryan Hebert, Director Information Systems
CHR: Carol Hebert, Director Human Resources
CNO: Debbie Vaughn, Chief Nursing Officer
Web address: https://www.medicalcentersetexas.org/
Control: Partnership, Investor–owned (for–profit) **Service**: General medical and surgical

Staffed Beds: 184 **Admissions**: 4704 **Census**: 52 **Outpatient Visits**: 72572 **Births**: 569 **Total Expense ($000)**: 153646 **Payroll Expense ($000)**: 38290 **Personnel**: 491

PORT LAVACA—Calhoun County

★ **MEMORIAL MEDICAL CENTER (451356)**, 815 North Virginia Street, Zip 77979–3025, Mailing Address: P.O. Box 25, Zip 77979–0025; tel. 361/552–6713, **A**10 18 **F**3 11 13 15 18 28 29 34 35 40 43 45 49 50 56 57 59 65 70 75 76 77 81 82 84 85 87 93 97 104 107 108 110 111 115 119 127 129 130 131 132 133 147 148 153 154 **P**6
Primary Contact: Erin R. Clevenger, Interim Chief Executive Officer
COO: Roshanda Gray, Assistant Administrator
CFO: Diane C. Moore, Chief Financial Officer
CMO: Jeannine Griffin, M.D., Chief of Staff
CIO: Adam Besio, Chief Information Officer
CNO: Erin R. Clevenger, Chief Nursing Officer
Web address: www.mmcportlavaca.com
Control: County, Government, Nonfederal **Service**: General medical and surgical

Staffed Beds: 25 **Admissions**: 672 **Census**: 5 **Outpatient Visits**: 36228 **Births**: 118 **Total Expense ($000)**: 25778 **Payroll Expense ($000)**: 14255 **Personnel**: 230

Hospital, Medicare Provider Number, Address, Telephone, Approval, Facility, and Physician Codes, Health Care System

★ American Hospital Association (AHA) membership
☐ The Joint Commission accreditation
○ Healthcare Facilities Accreditation Program
◇ DNV Healthcare Inc. accreditation
⇑ Center for Improvement in Healthcare Quality Accreditation
△ Commission on Accreditation of Rehabilitation Facilities (CARF) accreditation

Hospitals, U.S. / TEXAS

PROSPER—Denton County

COOK CHILDREN'S MEDICAL CENTER – PROSPER (453317), 4100 W University Drive, Zip 75078–3123, Mailing Address: PO Box 730108, Dallas, Zip 75373–0108; tel. 682/885–4000, (Nonreporting)
Primary Contact: Rick W. Merrill, Chief Executive Officer
COO: Stan Davis, FACHE, Senior Vice President and Chief Operating Officer
CFO: Cory Rhoades, Chief Financial Officer
CMO: Anthony Anani, Chief Medical Officer
CHR: Keith M Holtz, Chief Administrative Office
CNO: Cheryl Petersen, Chief Nursing Officer
Web address: www.cookchildrens.org/medical-center/prosper
Control: Other not–for–profit (including NFP Corporation) **Service**: Children's general medical and surgical

Staffed Beds: 24

QUANAH—Hardeman County

HARDEMAN COUNTY MEMORIAL HOSPITAL (451352), 402 Mercer Street, Zip 79252–4026, Mailing Address: P.O. Box 90, Zip 79252–0090; tel. 940/663–2795, **A**10 18 **F**28 29 34 40 43 50 56 57 59 64 65 75 93 94 100 101 104 107 127 130 133 148 149 153 154 **P**5
Primary Contact: Dennis Thomas, Chief Executive Officer
CFO: Tracy Betts, Chief Financial Officer
CMO: Kevin Lane, D.O., Chief of Staff
Web address: www.hcmhosp.net/
Control: Hospital district or authority, Government, Nonfederal **Service**: General medical and surgical

Staffed Beds: 18 **Admissions**: 145 **Census**: 2 **Outpatient Visits**: 16288
Births: 0 **Total Expense ($000)**: 11783 **Payroll Expense ($000)**: 5216
Personnel: 90

QUITMAN—Wood County

✣ **UT HEALTH QUITMAN (451380)**, 117 Winnsboro Street, Zip 75783–2144, Mailing Address: P.O. Box 1000, Zip 75783–1000; tel. 903/763–6300, **A**1 3 10 18 **F**3 28 29 30 34 35 40 43 45 50 57 59 64 65 77 79 81 82 84 85 87 107 108 111 115 119 126 127 129 130 133 144 146 148 149 154 **S** Ardent Health Services, Nashville, TN
Primary Contact: Jared Smith, Chief Executive Officer
CFO: Janet Andersen, Chief Financial Officer
CHR: William Henry, Director Human Resources
CNO: Allicia Settles, Chief Nursing Officer
Web address: https://uthealthquitman.com/
Control: Partnership, Investor–owned (for–profit) **Service**: General medical and surgical

Staffed Beds: 25 **Admissions**: 914 **Census**: 11 **Outpatient Visits**: 82067
Births: 0 **Total Expense ($000)**: 35699 **Payroll Expense ($000)**: 12421
Personnel: 173

RANKIN—Upton County

★ **RANKIN COUNTY HOSPITAL DISTRICT (451329)**, 1105 Elizabeth Street, Zip 79778, Mailing Address: P.O. Box 327, Zip 79778–0327; tel. 432/693–2443, **A**10 18 **F**3 34 35 40 53 54 55 56 57 59 64 65 66 68 75 86 87 93 97 102 107 115 119 127 130 131 133 135 147 148 156 **P**6
Primary Contact: Jim Horton, Chief Executive Officer
CFO: Tami Burks, Comptroller
CMO: Thomas J Curvin, M.D., Chief of Staff
Web address: www.rankincountyhospital.com/
Control: Hospital district or authority, Government, Nonfederal **Service**: General medical and surgical

Staffed Beds: 14 **Admissions**: 43 **Census**: 2 **Outpatient Visits**: 12712
Births: 0 **Total Expense ($000)**: 18070 **Payroll Expense ($000)**: 8876
Personnel: 81

REFUGIO—Refugio County

REFUGIO COUNTY MEMORIAL HOSPITAL (451317), 107 Swift Street, Zip 78377–2425; tel. 361/526–2321, **A**10 18 **F**3 7 29 40 43 57 61 64 75 81 86 87 93 97 107 119 127 133 **P**6
Primary Contact: Corey Wasicek, Chief Executive Officer
Web address: www.refugiohospital.com/
Control: Hospital district or authority, Government, Nonfederal **Service**: General medical and surgical

Staffed Beds: 20 **Admissions**: 115 **Census**: 3 **Outpatient Visits**: 40654
Births: 0 **Total Expense ($000)**: 18777 **Payroll Expense ($000)**: 7504
Personnel: 121

RICHARDSON—Collin County

⇑ **EMINENT MEDICAL CENTER**, 1351 West President George Bush Hwy, Zip 75080; tel. 469/910–8800, **A**21 **F**3 29 37 40 75 77 79 81 82 85 86 87 111 119 126 149
Primary Contact: Rhonda Lopp, Chief Executive Officer
CNO: Erin Baker, Chief Nursing Officer
Web address: www.eminentmedicalcenter.com
Control: Partnership, Investor–owned (for–profit) **Service**: Surgical

Staffed Beds: 5 **Admissions**: 151 **Census**: 1 **Outpatient Visits**: 3253
Births: 0 **Total Expense ($000)**: 36402 **Payroll Expense ($000)**: 5565
Personnel: 81

✣ **ENCOMPASS HEALTH REHABILITATION HOSPITAL OF RICHARDSON (673029)**, 3351 Waterview Parkway, Zip 75080–1449; tel. 972/398–5700, **A**1 10 **F**3 29 30 90 96 132 148 149 **S** Encompass Health Corporation, Birmingham, AL
Primary Contact: Meagan Bailey, Chief Executive Officer
CMO: Richard Jones, M.D., Medical Director
CNO: Pam Smith, Chief Nursing Officer
Web address: www.relianthcp.com
Control: Corporation, Investor–owned (for–profit) **Service**: Rehabilitation

Staffed Beds: 50 **Admissions**: 1397 **Census**: 48 **Outpatient Visits**: 0
Births: 0 **Total Expense ($000)**: 21169 **Payroll Expense ($000)**: 13110
Personnel: 175

✣ **METHODIST RICHARDSON MEDICAL CENTER (450537)**, 2831 East President George Bush Hwy, Zip 75082–3561; tel. 469/204–1000, **A**1 2 3 5 10 **F**3 5 11 13 15 18 20 22 24 29 30 31 34 35 38 40 43 45 46 49 54 55 56 57 59 64 65 68 70 72 74 75 76 77 78 79 81 82 85 86 87 93 97 98 100 101 102 103 104 105 107 108 109 110 111 112 115 116 117 119 120 121 123 124 126 129 130 131 132 135 146 147 148 153 156 160 162 165 167 **P**5 6 **S** Methodist Health System, Dallas, TX
Primary Contact: E. Kenneth. Hutchenrider Jr, FACHE, President
COO: Robert Simpson, Vice President Operations
CFO: Ed Abbott, Vice President Finance
CMO: Mark Smith, M.D., Chief Medical Officer
CIO: Pamela McNutt, Senior Vice President and Chief Information Officer
CHR: Chris Loyd, Director Human Resources
CNO: Irene T Strejc, M.P.H., R.N., Vice President, Nursing
Web address: https://www.methodisthealthsystem.org/methodist-richardson-medical-center/
Control: Other not–for–profit (including NFP Corporation) **Service**: General medical and surgical

Staffed Beds: 312 **Admissions**: 14764 **Census**: 243 **Outpatient Visits**: 149605 **Births**: 2150 **Total Expense ($000)**: 389204 **Payroll Expense ($000)**: 159661 **Personnel**: 1467

RICHMOND—Fort Bend County

☐ **OAKBEND MEDICAL CENTER (450330)**, 1705 Jackson Street, Zip 77469–3289; tel. 281/341–3000, (Includes HOSPITAL FOR SURGICAL EXCELLENCE, 1211 Highway 6, Suite 70, Sugar Land, Texas, Zip 77478–4940, tel. 281/238–3900; Joe Freudenberger, Chief Executive Officer; OAKBEND MEDICAL CENTER WILLIAMS WAY CAMPUS, 22003 Southwest Freeway, Richmond, Texas, Zip 77469–7003, tel. 281/341–2000; Joe Freudenberger, Chief Executive Officer) (Total facility includes 36 beds in nursing home–type unit) **A**1 10 **F**3 8 13 15 18 20 22 24 26 28 29 30 34 35 40 43 45 46 48 49 50 51 53 56 57 59 64 70 72 74 75 76 77 78 79 81 85 87 93 97 98 103 107 108 110 111 114 115 119 128 129 130 131 146 147 148 154 167 169 **P**6
Primary Contact: Joe Freudenberger, Chief Executive Officer
CFO: Rodney Lenfant, Chief Financial Officer
CMO: Douglas Thibodeaux, M.D., Chief Medical Officer
CIO: Tim McCarty, Chief Information Officer
CHR: Eileen Gamboa, Vice President Human Resources, HCA Houston Healthcare Southeast
Web address: www.oakbendmedcenter.org
Control: Hospital district or authority, Government, Nonfederal **Service**: General medical and surgical

Staffed Beds: 237 **Admissions**: 3439 **Census**: 60 **Outpatient Visits**: 76840
Births: 563 **Total Expense ($000)**: 152255 **Payroll Expense ($000)**: 49823
Personnel: 741

☐ **WESTPARK SPRINGS (454131)**, 6902 South Peek Road, Zip 77407; tel. 832/532–8107, **A**1 10 **F**4 5 64 68 98 99 101 102 105 106 130 151 152 153 154 160 162 164 **S** Springstone, Louisville, KY
Primary Contact: Shaun Fenton, Chief Executive Officer
Web address: www.westparksprings.com/why-westpark-springs/
Control: Corporation, Investor–owned (for–profit) **Service**: Psychiatric

Staffed Beds: 72 **Admissions**: 2578 **Census**: 62 **Outpatient Visits**: 11215
Births: 0 **Total Expense ($000)**: 22661 **Payroll Expense ($000)**: 11577
Personnel: 150

Hospitals, U.S. / TEXAS

RIO GRANDE CITY—Starr County

★ **STARR COUNTY MEMORIAL HOSPITAL (450654)**, 128 N FM 3167, Zip 78582–6211, Mailing Address: P.O. Box 78, Zip 78582–0078; tel. 956/487–5561, **A**10 20 **F**7 11 13 15 29 34 35 40 43 45 46 50 57 59 64 65 66 68 75 76 81 89 97 107 110 111 115 119 127 130 135 145 146 147 148 154 **P**5
Primary Contact: Thalia H. Munoz, R.N., MS, Chief Executive Officer
CFO: Rafael Olivares, Controller
CHR: Amaro Salinas, Assistant Administrator and Human Resource Officer
CNO: Mario Segura, Director of Nursing
Web address: www.starrcountyhospital.com
Control: Hospital district or authority, Government, Nonfederal **Service**: General medical and surgical

Staffed Beds: 47 **Admissions**: 956 **Census**: 9 **Outpatient Visits**: 53956 **Births**: 262 **Total Expense ($000)**: 41188 **Payroll Expense ($000)**: 17301 **Personnel**: 297

ROBINSON—Mclennan County

☐ **ENCOMPASS HEALTH REHABILITATION HOSPITAL OF WACO (673079)**, 3600 S Loop 340 Highway, Zip 76706–4828; tel. 254/523–2200, (Nonreporting) **A**1 **S** Encompass Health Corporation, Birmingham, AL
Primary Contact: Donna Harris, Chief Executive Officer
Web address: https://encompasshealth.com/locations/wacorehab
Control: Corporation, Investor–owned (for–profit) **Service**: Rehabilitation

Staffed Beds: 40

ROCKWALL—Rockwall County

✠ **TEXAS HEALTH HOSPITAL ROCKWALL (670044)**, 3150 Horizon Road, Zip 75032–7805; tel. 469/698–1000, **A**1 10 **F**3 11 12 13 15 18 22 28 29 30 34 35 40 45 46 47 49 50 51 68 70 72 75 76 77 79 81 82 85 87 90 107 108 110 111 112 115 118 119 126 130 131 146 147 148 149 154 164 169
Primary Contact: Jason Linscott, CPA, President
CMO: Gary Bonacquisti, M.D., Chief Medical Officer
CHR: Candy Marie Stewart, Vice President People and Culture, Chief Human Resouces Officer
CNO: Tami Hawkins, R.N., MSN, Vice President Patient Care and Chief Nursing Officer
Web address: https://www.texashealth.org/Locations/texas-health-rockwall#
Control: Partnership, Investor–owned (for–profit) **Service**: General medical and surgical

Staffed Beds: 104 **Admissions**: 3777 **Census**: 36 **Outpatient Visits**: 51920 **Births**: 515 **Total Expense ($000)**: 130178 **Payroll Expense ($000)**: 44794 **Personnel**: 512

TEXAS HEALTH PRESBYTERIAN HOSPITAL OF ROCKWALL See Texas Health Hospital Rockwall

ROTAN—Fisher County

★ **FISHER COUNTY HOSPITAL DISTRICT (451313)**, 774 State Highway 70 North, Zip 79546–6918, Mailing Address: P O Drawer 'F', Zip 79546–4019; tel. 325/735–2256, **A**10 18 **F**7 28 32 34 35 40 43 50 53 56 57 59 64 66 75 93 97 107 119 127 133 155 **P**6
Primary Contact: Leanne Martinez, Chief Executive Officer and Administrator
CFO: Debbie Hull, Chief Financial Officer
CMO: Joseph Lampley, D.O., Chief of Staff
CHR: Teresa Terry, Director Human Resource, Payroll
CNO: D'Linda Benham, Director of Nursing
Web address: www.fishercountyhospital.com
Control: Hospital district or authority, Government, Nonfederal **Service**: General medical and surgical

Staffed Beds: 14 **Admissions**: 25 **Census**: 2 **Outpatient Visits**: 9775 **Births**: 0 **Total Expense ($000)**: 11209 **Payroll Expense ($000)**: 5382 **Personnel**: 65

ROUND ROCK—Williamson County

✠ **ASCENSION SETON WILLIAMSON (670041)**, 201 Seton Parkway, Zip 78665–8000; tel. 512/324–4000, **A**1 3 5 10 **F**3 11 12 13 18 20 22 24 26 28 29 30 34 35 37 40 41 43 44 45 46 47 48 49 64 70 72 74 76 77 79 81 85 87 92 100 107 108 111 114 115 116 119 120 126 129 130 131 132 146 148 154 164 167 **S** Ascension Healthcare, Saint Louis, MO
Primary Contact: Andrew Gnann, President
CFO: Douglas D Waite, Senior Vice President and Chief Financial Officer
CMO: Hugh V Gilmore, M.D., Vice President Medical Affairs
CHR: Thomas Wilken, Vice President Human Resources
Web address: https://healthcare.ascension.org/locations/texas/txaus/round-rock-ascension-seton-williamson
Control: Church operated, Nongovernment, not–for–profit **Service**: General medical and surgical

Staffed Beds: 181 **Admissions**: 9082 **Census**: 138 **Outpatient Visits**: 61258 **Births**: 610 **Total Expense ($000)**: 236631 **Payroll Expense ($000)**: 71940 **Personnel**: 712

✠ **BAYLOR SCOTT & WHITE MEDICAL CENTER – ROUND ROCK (670034)**, 300 University Boulevard, Zip 78665–1032; tel. 512/509–0100, (Includes BAYLOR SCOTT & WHITE MEDICAL CENTER – LAKEWAY, 100 Medical Parkway, Lakeway, Texas, Zip 78738–5621, tel. 512/571–5000; Philippe Bochaton, President) **A**1 2 3 5 10 **F**3 11 13 15 17 18 20 22 24 26 28 29 30 31 33 34 35 36 37 40 42 45 46 47 49 50 51 54 57 59 60 65 68 70 74 75 76 77 78 79 81 82 84 85 87 91 92 93 97 100 107 110 111 114 115 116 117 118 119 126 129 130 131 132 135 144 146 147 148 149 154 167 169 **S** Baylor Scott & White Health, Dallas, TX
Primary Contact: Jay Fox, FACHE, President
COO: Joseph C. Brown, Vice President Operations
CFO: Jason Cole, Regional Chief Financial Officer
CMO: Rob Watson, M.D., Chief Medical Officer
CIO: Matthew Chambers, Chief Information Officer
CHR: Mark A. Sherry, Regional Director Human Resource Strategic Services, Austin/Round Rock Region
CNO: Leslie Gembol, MSN, R.N., Chief Nursing Officer
Web address: www.sw.org
Control: Other not–for–profit (including NFP Corporation) **Service**: General medical and surgical

Staffed Beds: 175 **Admissions**: 11221 **Census**: 121 **Outpatient Visits**: 850435 **Births**: 1117 **Total Expense ($000)**: 451051 **Payroll Expense ($000)**: 134310 **Personnel**: 1655

BRUSHY CREEK FAMILY HOSPITAL (670326), 230 Deer Ridge Drive, Zip 78681–5515; tel. 512/766–1400, **F**3 40 42 64 68 79 81 87 102 107 115 119 149 **P**2
Primary Contact: Henry Higgins, M.D., Chief Executive Officer
Web address: https://familyhospitalsystems.com/locations/family-hosptial-at-brushy-creek/
Control: Partnership, Investor–owned (for–profit) **Service**: General medical and surgical

Staffed Beds: 4 **Admissions**: 128 **Census**: 1 **Outpatient Visits**: 2241 **Births**: 0 **Total Expense ($000)**: 9678 **Payroll Expense ($000)**: 3281 **Personnel**: 26

✠ **ENCOMPASS HEALTH REHABILITATION HOSPITAL OF ROUND ROCK (673032)**, 1400 Hesters Crossing Road, Zip 78681–8025; tel. 512/244–4400, **A**1 3 10 **F**3 29 35 60 74 75 79 90 96 130 132 148 149 **S** Encompass Health Corporation, Birmingham, AL
Primary Contact: Tarra Washington, Chief Executive Officer
CHR: Amelia Leudecke, Director Human Resources
CNO: Randi Cruz, Chief Nursing Officer
Web address: https://www.encompasshealth.com/roundrockrehab
Control: Corporation, Investor–owned (for–profit) **Service**: Rehabilitation

Staffed Beds: 75 **Admissions**: 1816 **Census**: 67 **Outpatient Visits**: 0 **Births**: 0 **Total Expense ($000)**: 33549 **Payroll Expense ($000)**: 17247 **Personnel**: 214

✠ **PAM REHABILITATION HOSPITAL OF ROUND ROCK (673069)**, 351 Seton Parkway, Zip 78665–8001; tel. 737/708–9800, **A**1 10 **F**29 77 90 91 93 96 148 154 **S** PAM Health, Enola, PA
Primary Contact: Duke Saldivar, FACHE, Interim Chief Executive Officer
Web address: www.postacutemedical.com
Control: Individual, Investor–owned (for–profit) **Service**: Rehabilitation

Staffed Beds: 40 **Admissions**: 905 **Census**: 30 **Outpatient Visits**: 7351 **Births**: 0 **Total Expense ($000)**: 18635 **Payroll Expense ($000)**: 9658 **Personnel**: 126

Hospital, Medicare Provider Number, Address, Telephone, Approval, Facility, and Physician Codes, Health Care System

★ American Hospital Association (AHA) membership ○ Healthcare Facilities Accreditation Program ⇑ Center for Improvement in Healthcare Quality Accreditation
☐ The Joint Commission accreditation ◇ DNV Healthcare Inc. accreditation △ Commission on Accreditation of Rehabilitation Facilities (CARF) accreditation

Hospitals, U.S. / TEXAS

✠ **ST. David's ROUND ROCK MEDICAL CENTER (450718)**, 2400 Round Rock Avenue, Zip 78681-4097; tel. 512/341-1000, **A**1 2 3 10 **F**3 12 13 15 18 20 22 24 26 28 29 30 31 34 35 40 42 43 45 49 58 59 64 70 72 74 76 78 79 81 84 85 87 90 93 102 107 108 110 111 114 115 116 117 119 124 126 130 131 132 135 146 147 148 149 154 157 167 169 **P**3 6 **S** HCA Healthcare, Nashville, TN
Primary Contact: Laura Wiess, Interim Chief Executive Officer
COO: Katie Lattanzi, Chief Operating Officer
CFO: Cindy Sexton, Chief Financial Officer
CHR: Amy Noak, Director Human Resources
Web address: www.stdavids.com
Control: Other not-for-profit (including NFP Corporation) **Service**: General medical and surgical

> **Staffed Beds**: 173 **Admissions**: 12056 **Census**: 157 **Outpatient Visits**: 83936 **Births**: 1602 **Total Expense ($000)**: 240277 **Payroll Expense ($000)**: 72552 **Personnel**: 729

ROWLETT—Rockwall County

✠ **BAYLOR SCOTT & WHITE MEDICAL CENTER - LAKE POINTE (450742)**, 6800 Scenic Drive, Zip 75088-4552, Mailing Address: P.O. Box 1550, Zip 75030-1550; tel. 972/412-2273, **A**1 10 **F**3 13 15 18 20 22 26 28 29 30 34 35 37 40 42 43 45 46 47 49 50 59 60 64 70 72 73 74 75 76 77 79 81 82 84 85 86 87 93 97 100 107 108 110 111 115 116 117 118 119 126 129 130 146 147 148 149 154 164 167 169 **S** Baylor Scott & White Health, Dallas, TX
Primary Contact: Donas Cole, FACHE, President
COO: Benson Chacko, Vice President, Operations
Web address: https://www.bswhealth.com/locations/lake-pointe/
Control: Other not-for-profit (including NFP Corporation) **Service**: General medical and surgical

> **Staffed Beds**: 157 **Admissions**: 9935 **Census**: 104 **Outpatient Visits**: 121734 **Births**: 2294 **Total Expense ($000)**: 227888 **Payroll Expense ($000)**: 82621 **Personnel**: 715

RUSK—Cherokee County

☐ **RUSK STATE HOSPITAL (454009)**, 805 North Dickinson, Zip 75785-2333, Mailing Address: P.O. Box 318, Zip 75785-0318; tel. 903/683-3421, **A**1 3 5 10 **F**3 29 30 39 68 86 87 98 100 103 106 130 135 143 146 149 163 **P**6 **S** Texas Department of State Health Services, Austin, TX
Primary Contact: Brenda Slaton, Superintendent
COO: Lynda Roberson, Senior Program Director
CFO: Rhonda Transier, Financial Officer
CMO: Joe Bates, M.D., Clinical Director
CHR: Kendra Brown, Job Requisition Coordinator
Web address: www.dshs.state.tx.us/mhhospitals/RuskSH/default.shtm
Control: State, Government, Nonfederal **Service**: Psychiatric

> **Staffed Beds**: 288 **Admissions**: 127 **Census**: 169 **Outpatient Visits**: 0 **Births**: 0 **Total Expense ($000)**: 85054 **Payroll Expense ($000)**: 44417 **Personnel**: 1023

SAN ANGELO—Tom Green County

COLUMBIA MEDICAL CENTER See Shannon South

CONCHO VALLEY REGIONAL HOSP See Shannon Medical Center- St. John's Campus

☐ **RIVER CREST HOSPITAL (454064)**, 1636 Hunters Glen Road, Zip 76901-5016; tel. 325/949-5722, **A**1 3 10 **F**4 5 29 64 87 98 99 100 101 103 104 105 130 132 151 152 153 161 **P**5 **S** Universal Health Services, Inc., King of Prussia, PA
Primary Contact: Patricia A Spatz, Chief Executive Officer
CMO: Raymond Mays, M.D., Medical Director
CHR: Lydia Cardenas, Director Human Resources
CNO: Debra Millsap, Director of Nursing
Web address: www.rivercresthospital.com
Control: Corporation, Investor-owned (for-profit) **Service**: Psychiatric

> **Staffed Beds**: 62 **Admissions**: 2382 **Census**: 42 **Outpatient Visits**: 3017 **Births**: 0 **Total Expense ($000)**: 13771 **Payroll Expense ($000)**: 7564 **Personnel**: 129

★ **SHANNON MEDICAL CENTER (450571)**, 120 East Harris Street, Zip 76903-5976, Mailing Address: P.O. Box 1879, Zip 76902-1879; tel. 325/653-6741, (Includes SHANNON MEDICAL CENTER- ST. JOHN'S CAMPUS, 2018 Pulliam Street, San Angelo, Texas, Zip 76905-5197, tel. 325/659-7100; Bryan Horner, President and Chief Executive Officer; SHANNON SOUTH, 3501 Knickerbocker Road, San Angelo, Texas, Zip 76904-7698, tel. 325/949-9511; Rodney Schumacher, Administrative Director) (Total facility includes 21 beds in nursing home-type unit) **A**3 5 10 22 **F**3 8 11 12 13 15 18 20 22 24 26 28 29 30 31 32 34 35 37 38 40 43 44 45 47 48 49 50 51 53 54 56 57 58 59 60 61 62 64 68 70 71 72 73 74 75 76 77 78 79 80 81 82 84 85 86 87 89 92 93 94 96 98 100 101 102 107 108 110 111 114 115 117 119 120 121 123 124 126 128 130 132 145 146 147 148 149 154 155 167
Primary Contact: Shane Plymell, Chief Executive Officer
COO: Pamela Bradshaw, R.N., Vice President, Chief Operating Officer and Chief Nursing Officer
CFO: Staci Wetz, Chief Financial Officer
CMO: Irvin Zeitler, D.O., Vice President Medical Affairs
CIO: Tom Perkins, Chief Information Officer
CNO: Pamela Bradshaw, R.N., Vice President, Chief Operating Officer and Chief Nursing Officer
Web address: www.shannonhealth.com
Control: Other not-for-profit (including NFP Corporation) **Service**: General medical and surgical

> **Staffed Beds**: 375 **Admissions**: 17449 **Census**: 234 **Outpatient Visits**: 305303 **Births**: 1856 **Total Expense ($000)**: 513925 **Payroll Expense ($000)**: 187184 **Personnel**: 2162

☐ **SHANNON REHABILITATION HOSPITAL, AN AFFILIATE OF ENCOMPASS HEALTH (673078)**, 6102 Appaloosa Trail, Zip 76901; tel. 325/284-4000, (Nonreporting) **A**1 **S** Encompass Health Corporation, Birmingham, AL
Primary Contact: Bill Perkins, Chief Executive Officer
Web address: https://encompasshealth.com/locations/sanangelorehab
Control: Corporation, Investor-owned (for-profit) **Service**: Rehabilitation

> **Staffed Beds**: 40

SAN ANTONIO—Bexar County

AUDIE L MURPHY MEM HOSPITAL See San Antonio Division

⇑ **BAPTIST EMERGENCY HOSPITAL** See Baptist Neighborhood Hospital At Thousand Oaks

✠ △ **BAPTIST MEDICAL CENTER (450058)**, 111 Dallas Street, Zip 78205-1230; tel. 210/297-7000, (Includes MISSION TRAIL BAPTIST HOSPITAL, 3333 Research Plaza, San Antonio, Texas, Zip 78235-5154, tel. 210/297-3000; Michael Cline, Chief Executive Officer; NORTH CENTRAL BAPTIST HOSPITAL, 520 Madison Oak Drive, San Antonio, Texas, Zip 78258-3912, tel. 210/297-4000; NORTHEAST BAPTIST HOSPITAL, 8811 Village Drive, San Antonio, Texas, Zip 78217-5440, tel. 210/297-2000; J Phillip Young, FACHE, Chief Executive Officer; ST. LUKE'S BAPTIST HOSPITAL, 7930 Floyd Curl Drive, San Antonio, Texas, Zip 78229-0100, tel. 210/297-5000; Vicki Gulczewski, Chief Executive Officer) **A**1 2 3 5 7 10 **F**3 12 13 18 19 20 22 24 26 28 29 30 31 34 35 37 40 41 43 44 45 46 47 48 49 50 53 54 55 56 59 60 64 65 68 70 72 73 74 75 76 77 78 79 81 82 84 85 86 87 88 89 90 93 96 98 100 101 103 107 108 111 114 115 119 124 126 129 130 131 132 135 145 146 147 148 149 154 162 164 167 169 **S** TENET Healthcare Corporation, Dallas, TX
Primary Contact: Thomas McKinney, FACHE, Chief Executive Officer
COO: Sandy Ethridge, Interim Chief Operating Officer
CIO: Gary Davis, Vice President Information Systems
Web address: www.baptisthealthsystem.com
Control: Partnership, Investor-owned (for-profit) **Service**: General medical and surgical

> **Staffed Beds**: 1292 **Admissions**: 58345 **Census**: 824 **Outpatient Visits**: 241641 **Births**: 9589 **Total Expense ($000)**: 1030639 **Payroll Expense ($000)**: 425097 **Personnel**: 4864

Hospitals, U.S. / TEXAS

⇑ **BAPTIST NEIGHBORHOOD HOSPITAL AT THOUSAND OAKS (670078)**, 16088 San Pedro, Zip 78232–2249; tel. 210/402–4092, (Includes BAPTIST EMERGENCY HOSPITAL – HAUSMAN, 8230 North 1604 West, San Antonio, Texas, Zip 78249, tel. 210/572–8885; Shannon Crinion, Chief Executive Officer; BAPTIST EMERGENCY HOSPITAL – OVERLOOK, 25615 US Highway 281 North, San Antonio, Texas, Zip 78258–7135, tel. 210/572–2911; Shannon Crinion, Chief Executive Officer; BAPTIST EMERGENCY HOSPITAL – SCHERTZ, 16977 Interstate 35 North, Schertz, Texas, Zip 78154–1466, tel. 210/572–8400; Shannon Crinion, Chief Executive Officer; BAPTIST EMERGENCY HOSPITAL – WESTOVER HILLS, 10811 Town Center Drive, San Antonio, Texas, Zip 78251–4585, tel. 210/572–0911; Shannon Crinion, Chief Executive Officer) **A**10 21 **F**3 29 40 42 87 107 130 154 **S** Emerus, The Woodlands, TX
Primary Contact: Shannon Crinion, Chief Executive Officer
CNO: David Mitchell, Vice President Nursing
Web address: www.baptistemergencyhospital.com
Control: Corporation, Investor–owned (for–profit) **Service**: General medical and surgical

Staffed Beds: 41 **Admissions**: 1472 **Census**: 9 **Births**: 2 **Total Expense ($000)**: 94600 **Payroll Expense ($000)**: 27757 **Personnel**: 339

BRADY–GREEN COMM HEALTH CENTER See University Health Center – Downtown

CHILDREN'S HOSPITAL OF SAN ANTONIO See Christus Children's

✣ **CHRISTUS CHILDREN'S (453315)**, 333 North Santa Rosa Street, Zip 78207; tel. 210/704–2011, **A**1 3 5 10 **F**3 8 11 13 19 21 23 25 27 28 29 30 31 32 34 37 39 40 41 42 43 45 46 48 49 54 55 58 59 60 64 65 68 70 71 72 73 74 75 76 77 78 79 80 81 82 84 85 86 87 88 89 93 97 107 108 111 114 115 117 118 119 126 129 130 131 132 136 144 146 147 148 149 154 156 157 167 **S** CHRISTUS Health, Irving, TX
Primary Contact: Cris Daskevich, FACHE, Senior Vice President, Maternal Services and Chief Executive Officer
Web address: www.chofsa.org/
Control: Church operated, Nongovernment, not–for–profit **Service**: Children's general medical and surgical

Staffed Beds: 215 **Admissions**: 5388 **Census**: 98 **Outpatient Visits**: 286930 **Births**: 951 **Total Expense ($000)**: 387015 **Payroll Expense ($000)**: 109256 **Personnel**: 1154

✣ **CHRISTUS SANTA ROSA HEALTH SYSTEM (450237)**, 333 North Santa Rosa Street, Zip 78207–3108, Mailing Address: 100 NE Loop 410 Suite 800, Zip 78216–4749; tel. 210/704–2000, (Includes CHRISTUS SANTA ROSA HOSPITAL – ALAMO HEIGHTS, 403 Treeline Park Building, San Antonio, Texas, Zip 78209–2042, tel. 210/294–8000; Sherry Fraser, Administrator; CHRISTUS SANTA ROSA HOSPITAL – NEW BRAUNFELS, 600 North Union Avenue, New Braunfels, Texas, Zip 78130–4191, tel. 830/606–9111; Nikki Rivers, R.N., Chief Nursing Officer and Interim Chief Executive Officer; CHRISTUS SANTA ROSA–MEDICAL CENTER, 2827 Babcock Road, San Antonio, Texas, Zip 78229–4813, tel. 210/705–6300; Ian Thompson Jr, M.D., President) (Nonreporting) **A**1 3 5 10 19 **S** CHRISTUS Health, Irving, TX
Primary Contact: Cris Daskevich, FACHE, Chief Executive Officer Children's Hosp SA & SVP Maternal Svces CHRISTUS Health
CFO: Linda Kirks, Vice President and Chief Financial Officer
CMO: Kenneth Davis, M.D., Chief Medical Officer
CHR: Crystal H Kohanke, Group Vice President, Human Resources
CNO: Patty Toney, R.N., MSN, Chief Nurse Executive
Web address: www.christussantarosa.org
Control: Church operated, Nongovernment, not–for–profit **Service**: General medical and surgical

Staffed Beds: 403

CHRISTUS SANTA ROSA REHABILITATION HOSPITAL See Christus Santa Rosa–Medical Center

☐ **CLARITY CHILD GUIDANCE CENTER**, 8535 Tom Slick, Zip 78229–3363; tel. 210/616–0300, **A**1 3 5 **F**29 34 35 68 98 99 101 102 104 105 146 154 164
Primary Contact: Jessica Knudsen, Chief Executive Officer
CFO: Michael Bernick, Executive Vice President and Chief Financial Officer
CMO: Soad Michelson, M.D., Senior Medical Director
CHR: Gina Massey, Vice President Human Resources
CNO: Carol Carver, MSN, R.N., Vice President Patient Services
Web address: www.claritycgc.org
Control: Other not–for–profit (including NFP Corporation) **Service**: Children's hospital psychiatric

Staffed Beds: 66 **Admissions**: 3424 **Census**: 53 **Outpatient Visits**: 12273 **Births**: 0 **Total Expense ($000)**: 29556 **Payroll Expense ($000)**: 16066 **Personnel**: 277

✣ **ENCOMPASS HEALTH REHABILITATION HOSPITAL OF SAN ANTONIO (453031)**, 9119 Cinnamon Hill, Zip 78240–5401; tel. 210/691–0737, **A**1 10 **F**29 60 90 91 96 130 148 **S** Encompass Health Corporation, Birmingham, AL
Primary Contact: Andrew Meade, Chief Executive Officer
CFO: Larry Floyd Spriggs, CPA, Controller
CMO: Chaula Rana, M.D., Medical Director
CHR: Vanessa Tejada, Director Human Resources
CNO: Matthew D'Ambrosio, MSN, R.N., Chief Nursing Officer
Web address: www.hsriosa.com
Control: Corporation, Investor–owned (for–profit) **Service**: Rehabilitation

Staffed Beds: 96 **Admissions**: 1469 **Census**: 52 **Outpatient Visits**: 0 **Births**: 0 **Total Expense ($000)**: 29735 **Payroll Expense ($000)**: 15170 **Personnel**: 185

⇑ **FOUNDATION SURGICAL HOSPITAL OF SAN ANTONIO (670054)**, 9522 Huebner Road, Zip 78240–1548; tel. 210/478–5400, **A**3 5 10 21 **F**3 12 29 40 58 68 74 75 77 79 81 82 85 87 107 126 132 149
Primary Contact: Jill Finke, FACHE, Interim Chief Executive Officer
CNO: Beckie Leonard, R.N., Chief Nursing Officer
Web address: https://www.fshsanantonio.com/
Control: Corporation, Investor–owned (for–profit) **Service**: Surgical

Staffed Beds: 20 **Admissions**: 901 **Census**: 4 **Births**: 0 **Total Expense ($000)**: 36195 **Payroll Expense ($000)**: 7159 **Personnel**: 87

GLOBALREHAB HOSPITAL – SAN ANTONIO See Methodist Hospital Stone Oak Rehabilitation Center

✣ **KINDRED HOSPITAL SAN ANTONIO CENTRAL (452073)**, 111 Dallas Street, 4th Floor, Zip 78205–1201; tel. 210/297–7185, **A**1 10 **F**1 3 29 60 75 77 87 91 130 148 154 157 **S** ScionHealth, Louisville, KY
Primary Contact: Bo Bowman, Chief Executive Officer
Web address: www.kindredsanantoniocentral.com/
Control: Corporation, Investor–owned (for–profit) **Service**: Acute long–term care hospital

Staffed Beds: 44 **Admissions**: 376 **Census**: 25 **Outpatient Visits**: 0 **Births**: 0 **Total Expense ($000)**: 17174 **Payroll Expense ($000)**: 8818 **Personnel**: 113

✣ **KINDRED HOSPITAL–SAN ANTONIO (452016)**, 3636 Medical Drive, Zip 78229–2183; tel. 210/616–0616, **A**1 10 **F**1 3 29 30 60 70 75 77 85 87 91 107 130 148 **S** ScionHealth, Louisville, KY
Primary Contact: Lana Bamiro, Chief Executive Officer and Chief Operating Officer
COO: Lana Bamiro, Chief Executive Officer and Chief Operating Officer
CFO: Erin Russell, Controller
CMO: Charles Duncan, M.D., Medical Director
CHR: Stanley Richardson, Coordinator Human Resources and Payroll Benefits
Web address: https://www.kindredhospitals.com/locations/ltac/kindred-hospital-san-antonio
Control: Corporation, Investor–owned (for–profit) **Service**: Acute long–term care hospital

Staffed Beds: 59 **Admissions**: 382 **Census**: 26 **Outpatient Visits**: 0 **Births**: 0 **Total Expense ($000)**: 20364 **Payroll Expense ($000)**: 9584 **Personnel**: 112

Hospitals, U.S. / TEXAS

LAUREL RIDGE TREATMENT CENTER (454060), 17720 Corporate Woods Drive, Zip 78259–3500; tel. 210/491–9400, **A**1 5 10 **F**4 5 29 35 38 75 87 98 99 100 101 102 103 105 106 130 132 135 151 152 153 154 160 162 164 **S** Universal Health Services, Inc., King of Prussia, PA
Primary Contact: Ashley Sacriste, Chief Executive Officer
CFO: Chris Barela, Chief Financial Officer
CMO: Benigno J Fernandez, M.D., Executive Medical Director
CHR: Brenda Frederick, Director Human Resources
CNO: Kathy Rosetta, Chief Nursing Officer
Web address: www.laurelridgetc.com
Control: Partnership, Investor–owned (for–profit) **Service**: Psychiatric

Staffed Beds: 288 **Admissions**: 9758 **Census**: 270 **Outpatient Visits**: 29657 **Births**: 0 **Total Expense ($000)**: 81109 **Payroll Expense ($000)**: 33417 **Personnel**: 605

LEGENT ORTHOPEDIC + SPINE HOSPITAL (670112), 5330 North Loop 1604 West, Zip 78249; tel. 210/877–8000, **A**1 10 **F**3 29 37 40 64 65 67 74 75 79 81 107 141
Primary Contact: Terri LeBlanc, Chief Executive and Nursing Officer
CNO: Lisa Kuopus, Chief Nursing Officer
Web address: https://www.legenthealth.com/
Control: Partnership, Investor–owned (for–profit) **Service**: Surgical

Staffed Beds: 25 **Admissions**: 754 **Census**: 5 **Outpatient Visits**: 7578 **Births**: 0 **Total Expense ($000)**: 78132 **Payroll Expense ($000)**: 12503 **Personnel**: 161

MEDICAL CENTER HOSPITAL See University Hospital

METHODIST HOSPITAL (450388), 7700 Floyd Curl Drive, Zip 78229–3993; tel. 210/575–4000, (Includes METHODIST CHILDREN'S HOSPITAL, 7700 Floyd Curl Drive, San Antonio, Texas, Zip 78229–3383, tel. 210/575–7000; Robert Lenza, Chief Executive Officer; METHODIST HOSPITAL LANDMARK, 5510 Presidio Parkway, San Antonio, Texas, Zip 78249–3192, tel. 210/583–7200; METHODIST HOSPITAL NORTHEAST, 12412 Judson Road, Live Oak, Texas, Zip 78233–3255, tel. 210/757–5000; Jerrica George, FACHE, Chief Executive Officer; METHODIST SPECIALTY AND TRANSPLANT HOSPITAL, 8026 Floyd Curl Drive, San Antonio, Texas, Zip 78229–3915, tel. 210/575–8090; Kevin Scoggin, Chief Executive Officer; METHODIST TEXSAN HOSPITAL, 6700 W Interstate 10, San Antonio, Texas, Zip 78201–2009, 6700 IH–10 West, Zip 78201, tel. 210/736–6700; Scott Rausch, Chief Executive Officer; METROPOLITAN METHODIST HOSPITAL, 1310 McCullough Avenue, San Antonio, Texas, Zip 78212–2617, tel. 210/757–2909; Gregory A Seiler, Chief Executive Officer) **A**1 2 3 5 10 19 **F**3 5 8 11 12 13 15 16 17 18 19 20 21 22 23 24 25 26 27 28 29 30 31 34 35 38 40 41 42 43 44 45 46 47 48 49 51 53 54 56 57 58 59 60 62 64 65 68 70 72 74 75 76 77 78 79 80 81 82 84 85 86 87 88 89 90 93 95 96 98 100 101 102 103 104 105 107 108 111 112 114 115 118 119 120 121 124 126 127 129 130 132 135 136 137 138 139 140 142 143 144 145 146 147 148 152 153 154 156 164 167 **P**7 **S** HCA Healthcare, Nashville, TN
Primary Contact: Ryan Simpson, Chief Executive Officer
CFO: Enrique Bernal, Chief Financial Officer
CMO: Russell Woodward, M.D., Chief Medical Officer
CIO: Eddie Cuellar, Vice President Information Systems
CHR: Nancy Edgar, Vice President Human Resources
CNO: Lori Townsend, Chief Nursing Officer
Web address: www.sahealth.com
Control: Partnership, Investor–owned (for–profit) **Service**: General medical and surgical

Staffed Beds: 1765 **Admissions**: 106299 **Census**: 1511 **Outpatient Visits**: 630317 **Births**: 9779 **Total Expense ($000)**: 2013286 **Payroll Expense ($000)**: 676715 **Personnel**: 8068

METHODIST STONE OAK HOSPITAL (670055), 1139 E Sonterra Boulevard, Zip 78258–4347, Mailing Address: 1139 East Sonterra Boulevard, Zip 78258–4347; tel. 210/638–2100, (Includes METHODIST HOSPITAL STONE OAK REHABILITATION CENTER, 19126 Stonehue Road, San Antonio, Texas, Zip 78258–3490, tel. 210/482–3400; John Deleon, Chief Executive Officer) **A**1 3 5 10 19 **F**3 13 15 18 20 22 24 28 29 30 31 34 35 38 40 41 43 44 45 46 47 49 56 57 59 60 65 68 70 72 74 75 76 77 78 79 80 81 82 84 85 87 90 102 107 108 111 115 119 126 130 146 147 148 149 154 **P**7 **S** HCA Healthcare, Nashville, TN
Primary Contact: Michael D. Beaver, Chief Executive Officer
CFO: Gabriel Marrufo, Chief Financial Officer
CMO: Peter DeYoung, M.D., Chief Medical Officer
CNO: Ann M Winn, M.D., R.N., FACHE, Chief Nursing Officer
Web address: www.sahealth.com/locations/methodist-stone-oak-hospital/
Control: Partnership, Investor–owned (for–profit) **Service**: General medical and surgical

Staffed Beds: 284 **Admissions**: 18288 **Census**: 247 **Outpatient Visits**: 66052 **Births**: 1965 **Total Expense ($000)**: 298833 **Payroll Expense ($000)**: 98736 **Personnel**: 1160

METHODIST WOMEN'S & CHILD HOSP See Methodist Children's Hospital

METROPOLITAN HOSPITAL See Metropolitan Methodist Hospital

PAM SPECIALTY HOSPITAL OF SAN ANTONIO CENTER (452059), 8902 Floyd Curl Drive, Zip 78240–1681; tel. 210/690–7000, **A**1 10 **F**1 3 29 30 60 70 77 82 87 107 114 130 148 **S** PAM Health, Enola, PA
Primary Contact: Greg Lessard, Chief Executive Officer
CMO: Randall C Bell, M.D., Medical Director
Web address: www.lifecare-hospitals.com
Control: Partnership, Investor–owned (for–profit) **Service**: Acute long–term care hospital

Staffed Beds: 62 **Admissions**: 695 **Census**: 44 **Outpatient Visits**: 0 **Births**: 0 **Total Expense ($000)**: 29359 **Payroll Expense ($000)**: 12856 **Personnel**: 178

POST ACUTE/WARM SPRINGS SPECIALTY HOSPITAL OF SAN ANTONIO (452090), 5418 North Loop 1604 W, Zip 78247; tel. 210/921–3550, **A**1 10 **F**1 3 29 30 60 74 75 77 82 85 86 87 148 149 154 **S** PAM Health, Enola, PA
Primary Contact: Kristen Lowe, Chief Executive Officer
CNO: Carrie Nims, Director of Nursing
Web address: www.postacutemedical.com
Control: Partnership, Investor–owned (for–profit) **Service**: Acute long–term care hospital

Staffed Beds: 26 **Admissions**: 363 **Census**: 23 **Outpatient Visits**: 0 **Births**: 0 **Total Expense ($000)**: 14949 **Payroll Expense ($000)**: 6622 **Personnel**: 98

SAN ANTONIO BEHAVIORAL HEALTHCARE HOSPITAL (454132), 8550 Huebner Road, Zip 78240–1803; tel. 210/541–5300, **A**1 10 **F**5 87 98 99 100 101 103 104 105 132 152 153 154 **S** Signature Healthcare Services, Corona, CA
Primary Contact: Camillia McKinney, Chief Executive Officer
CFO: Sam Silberman, Chief Financial Officer
CMO: Joseph Hernandez, M.D., Medical Director
CNO: Shawn Larabie, Chief Nursing Officer
Web address: www.sanantoniobehavioral.com
Control: Individual, Investor–owned (for–profit) **Service**: Psychiatric

Staffed Beds: 198 **Admissions**: 8025 **Census**: 154 **Outpatient Visits**: 9951 **Births**: 0 **Total Expense ($000)**: 42638 **Payroll Expense ($000)**: 21772 **Personnel**: 309

SAN ANTONIO COMMUNITY HOSPITAL See Methodist Specialty and Transplant Hospital

SAN ANTONIO REHABILITATION HOSPITAL, 8903 Floyd Curl Drive, Zip 78240; tel. 726/201–5501, (Data for 305 days) **A**22 **F**3 28 29 34 35 57 60 68 74 77 82 86 87 90 91 95 96 130 132 148 **S** Nobis Rehabilitation Partners, Allen, TX
Primary Contact: Claudia Torres, Interim Chief Executive Officer
Web address: https://www.sanantonio-rehabhospital.com/
Control: Partnership, Investor–owned (for–profit) **Service**: Rehabilitation

Staffed Beds: 48 **Admissions**: 50 **Census**: 10 **Births**: 0 **Total Expense ($000)**: 12090 **Payroll Expense ($000)**: 8170

SAN ANTONIO STATE HOSPITAL (454011), 6711 South New Braunfels, Suite 100, Zip 78223–3006; tel. 210/531–7711, **A**1 3 5 10 **F**30 39 53 56 57 59 68 75 77 86 87 91 98 100 101 103 130 132 135 146 154 163 **P**1 **S** Texas Department of State Health Services, Austin, TX
Primary Contact: Robert C. Arizpe, Superintendent
CFO: Janie Rabago, Chief Accountant
CMO: Terresa Stallworth, M.D., Clinical Director
CIO: Chris Stanush, Director Information Management
CHR: Renee Bourland, Human Resources Specialist
CNO: Maria DC Ostrander, R.N., MSN, Chief Nurse Executive
Web address: www.dshs.state.tx.us/mhhospitals/SanAntonioSH/default.shtm
Control: State, Government, Nonfederal **Service**: Psychiatric

Staffed Beds: 262 **Admissions**: 315 **Census**: 196 **Outpatient Visits**: 0 **Births**: 0 **Total Expense ($000)**: 84412 **Payroll Expense ($000)**: 46123 **Personnel**: 866

Hospitals, U.S. / TEXAS

☐ **SOUTH TEXAS SPINE AND SURGICAL HOSPITAL (450856)**, 18600 Hardy Oak Boulevard, Zip 78258–4206; tel. 210/507–4090, **A**1 5 10 **F**3 8 18 24 29 34 40 54 58 64 79 81 82 131 149 **S** National Surgical Healthcare, Chicago, IL
Primary Contact: Angie Kauffman, Chief Executive Officer
CFO: Sylvia Garcia, Chief Accounting Officer
CHR: Sally Hall, Manager Human Resources
CNO: Jennifer West, R.N., Chief Nursing Officer
Web address: www.southtexassurgical.com
Control: Partnership, Investor–owned (for–profit) **Service**: Orthopedic

Staffed Beds: 32 **Admissions**: 1496 **Census**: 10 **Outpatient Visits**: 2679 **Births**: 0 **Total Expense ($000)**: 62492 **Payroll Expense ($000)**: 12510 **Personnel**: 174

SOUTH TEXAS VETERANS HCS See South Texas Veterans Healthcare System Audie L Murphy

✠ △ **SOUTH TEXAS VETERANS HEALTHCARE SYSTEM AUDIE L MURPHY**, 7400 Merton Minter Boulevard, Zip 78229–4404; tel. 210/617–5300, (Includes KERRVILLE DIVISION, 3600 Memorial Boulevard, Kerrville, Texas, Zip 78028, tel. 210/896–2020; SAN ANTONIO DIVISION, 7400 Merton Minter Boulevard, San Antonio, Texas, Zip 78284–5799, tel. 210/617–5300) (Nonreporting) **A**1 2 3 5 7 8 **S** Department of Veterans Affairs, Washington, DC
Primary Contact: Julianne Flynn, M.D., Executive Director
COO: Joe Perez, Associate Director
CFO: Eloisa Salazar, Chief Financial Officer
CIO: Simon Willett, Director Administrative Operations
CHR: Jeffrey Young, Chief Human Resource Officer
CNO: Sharon Millican, Associate Director, Patient Care Services
Web address: www.southtexas.va.gov/
Control: Veterans Affairs, Government, federal **Service**: General medical and surgical

Staffed Beds: 235

SOUTHEAST BAPTIST HOSPITAL See Mission Trail Baptist Hospital

ST LUKE'S LUTHERAN HOSPITAL See St. Luke's Baptist Hospital

ST. LUKE'S BAPTIST HOSPITAL See Baptist Medical Center, San Antonio

☐ **TEXAS CENTER FOR INFECTIOUS DISEASE (670125)**, 2303 SE Military Drive, Zip 78223–3597; tel. 210/534–8857, **A**1 3 5 10 **F**3 29 30 35 50 53 57 58 59 61 64 65 68 75 80 86 87 130 132 135 143 146 149 164 167 **S** Texas Department of State Health Services, Austin, TX
Primary Contact: James N. Elkins, FACHE, Director
CFO: Glenda Armstrong–Huff, Assistant Superintendent
CMO: David Griffith, M.D., Medical Director
CIO: Andre Avant, Facility Automation Manager
CHR: Gerald Shackelford, Staff Support Specialist
CNO: Rebecca Sanchez, R.N., M.P.H., Director of Nursing
Web address: www.dshs.state.tx.us/tcid/default.shtm
Control: State, Government, Nonfederal **Service**: Tuberculosis and other respiratory diseases

Staffed Beds: 50 **Admissions**: 69 **Census**: 28 **Outpatient Visits**: 305 **Births**: 0 **Total Expense ($000)**: 18618 **Payroll Expense ($000)**: 7450 **Personnel**: 166

TEXSAN HEART HOSPITAL See Methodist Texsan Hospital

✠ **UNIVERSITY HEALTH (450213)**, 4502 Medical Drive, Zip 78229–4493; tel. 210/358–2000, (Includes UNIVERSITY HEALTH CENTER – DOWNTOWN, 4502 Medical Drive, San Antonio, Texas, Zip 78229–4493, tel. 210/358–3400; UNIVERSITY HOSPITAL, 4502 Medical Drive, San Antonio, Texas, Zip 78229–4493, tel. 210/358–4000; Michael Roussos, Administrator) **A**1 2 3 5 8 10 19 **F**3 4 8 12 13 14 15 16 17 18 19 20 21 22 23 24 25 26 27 28 29 30 31 32 34 35 36 37 38 39 40 41 43 44 45 46 47 48 49 50 51 53 54 55 56 57 58 59 60 61 64 65 66 68 70 71 72 73 74 75 76 77 78 79 81 82 84 85 86 87 88 89 90 92 93 95 96 97 98 100 101 102 104 107 108 110 111 112 115 118 119 126 129 130 131 132 134 135 138 139 140 141 142 144 145 146 147 148 149 154 156 162 164 167 168 169 **P**5 6
Primary Contact: Edward Banos, President and Chief Executive Officer
CFO: Peggy Deming, Executive Vice President and Chief Financial Officer
CMO: Bryan Alsip, M.D., Executive Vice President, Chief Medical Officer
CIO: Bill Phillips, Vice President Information Services
CHR: Theresa Scepanski, Vice President People and Organizational Development
CNO: Tommye Austin, Ph.D., R.N., MSN, Chief Nursing Executive
Web address: www.universityhealthsystem.com
Control: Hospital district or authority, Government, Nonfederal **Service**: General medical and surgical

Staffed Beds: 741 **Admissions**: 34406 **Census**: 635 **Outpatient Visits**: 1809780 **Births**: 4307 **Total Expense ($000)**: 2118399 **Payroll Expense ($000)**: 786642 **Personnel**: 9810

✠ **WARM SPRINGS REHABILITATION HOSPITAL OF SAN ANTONIO (453035)**, 5101 Medical Drive, Zip 78229–4801; tel. 210/616–0100, (Includes PAM HEALTH REHABILITATION HOSPITAL NORTHEAST SAN ANTONIO, 11407 Wayland Way, San Antonio, Texas, Zip 78233, tel. 210/581–5300; Kyle Sinclair, Chief Executive Officer; WARM SPRINGS REHABILITATION HOSPITAL OF WESTOVER HILLS, 10323 State Highway 151, San Antonio, Texas, Zip 78251–4557, tel. 210/581–5306; Brian Lidiak, Chief Executive Officer) **A**1 3 5 10 **F**3 11 29 30 34 57 64 68 74 75 77 79 82 90 93 94 95 96 100 130 132 146 148 149 154 **S** PAM Health, Enola, PA
Primary Contact: Kyle Sinclair, Chief Executive Officer
CIO: Rick Marek, Vice President Medical Information Systems
Web address: www.postacutemedical.com/our-facilities/hospitals/warm-springs-rehabilitation-hospital-san-antonio/
Control: Partnership, Investor–owned (for–profit) **Service**: Rehabilitation

Staffed Beds: 145 **Admissions**: 3592 **Census**: 112 **Outpatient Visits**: 37960 **Births**: 0 **Total Expense ($000)**: 66169 **Payroll Expense ($000)**: 32583 **Personnel**: 487

SAN AUGUSTINE—San Augustine County

★ **CHI ST. LUKE'S HEALTH MEMORIAL SAN AUGUSTINE (670783)**, 511 East Hospital Street, Zip 75972–2121, Mailing Address: P.O. Box 658, Zip 75972–0658; tel. 936/275–3446, **A**10 **F**3 29 30 35 40 57 59 64 102 107 119 132 133 149 **S** CommonSpirit Health, Chicago, IL
Primary Contact: Ashley London, R.N., Administrator
CFO: Kristi Gay, Chief Financial Officer
Web address: https://locations.stlukeshealth.org/location/memorial-san-augustine-hospital
Control: Other not–for–profit (including NFP Corporation)

Staffed Beds: 9 **Admissions**: 75 **Census**: 1 **Outpatient Visits**: 10585 **Births**: 0 **Total Expense ($000)**: 10952 **Payroll Expense ($000)**: 3262 **Personnel**: 35

SAN MARCOS—Hays County

✠ **CHRISTUS SANTA ROSA HOSPITAL – SAN MARCOS (450272)**, 1301 Wonder World Drive, Zip 78666–7544; tel. 512/353–8979, **A**1 10 **F**3 11 12 13 15 18 20 22 24 26 28 29 30 34 35 40 41 43 45 46 50 57 59 60 63 64 68 70 72 74 75 76 77 79 80 81 82 83 84 85 87 91 93 97 100 102 107 108 109 110 111 114 116 117 118 119 124 126 129 130 143 146 147 148 154 156 157 167 **S** CHRISTUS Health, Irving, TX
Primary Contact: Robert Honeycutt, President
CFO: Rick Villarreal, Vice President Finance
CMO: Lee Johannsen, M.D., Vice President and Chief Medical Officer
CHR: Debbie D. Cox, Administrative Director Human Resources
CNO: William Micah Johnson, MSN, R.N., Chief Nursing Officer
Web address: https://www.christushealth.org/santa-rosa/san-marcos
Control: Church operated, Nongovernment, not–for–profit **Service**: General medical and surgical

Staffed Beds: 139 **Admissions**: 2820 **Census**: 34 **Outpatient Visits**: 68808 **Births**: 679 **Total Expense ($000)**: 108503 **Payroll Expense ($000)**: 40736 **Personnel**: 362

Hospital, Medicare Provider Number, Address, Telephone, Approval, Facility, and Physician Codes, Health Care System

★ American Hospital Association (AHA) membership ◯ Healthcare Facilities Accreditation Program ⇑ Center for Improvement in Healthcare Quality Accreditation
☐ The Joint Commission accreditation ◇ DNV Healthcare Inc. accreditation △ Commission on Accreditation of Rehabilitation Facilities (CARF) accreditation

Hospitals, U.S. / TEXAS

SEGUIN—Guadalupe County

GUADALUPE REGIONAL MEDICAL CENTER (450104), 1215 East Court Street, Zip 78155–5189; tel. 830/379–2411, **A**1 10 **F**3 5 11 13 15 18 20 22 24 26 29 30 31 34 35 38 39 40 43 45 46 49 50 51 53 57 58 59 60 63 66 68 70 74 75 76 77 78 79 81 82 84 85 90 93 96 104 107 110 111 114 115 119 126 132 135 143 144 146 147 148 149 150 154 156 167 **P**8
Primary Contact: Robert Gerard. Haynes, FACHE, Chief Executive Officer
COO: Sheri Williams, Chief Operating Officer
CFO: Penny Wallace, Chief Financial Officer
CMO: Robert Ryan, M.D., Chief Medical Officer
CIO: Steve Ratliff, Director Information Technology
CHR: Fay Bennett, Vice President Employee Services
CNO: Daphne Blake, R.N., MSN, Chief Nursing Officer
Web address: www.grmedcenter.com
Control: City–county, Government, Nonfederal **Service**: General medical and surgical

Staffed Beds: 90 **Admissions**: 4004 **Census**: 37 **Outpatient Visits**: 151925
Births: 716 **Total Expense ($000)**: 131116 **Payroll Expense ($000)**: 49246
Personnel: 804

SEMINOLE—Gaines County

MEMORIAL HOSPITAL (451358), 209 NW Eighth Street, Zip 79360–3447; tel. 432/758–5811, (Total facility includes 16 beds in nursing home–type unit) **A**10 18 **F**3 10 11 13 28 29 30 32 34 35 40 43 45 53 56 57 59 62 63 64 65 75 76 81 87 93 97 102 107 111 114 119 127 129 130 131 132 133 143 146 147 148
Primary Contact: Albert Pilkington, Chief Executive Officer
COO: Heath Mitchell, Chief Operating Officer
CFO: Traci Anderson, Chief Financial Officer
CMO: Michael Watson, M.D., Chief of Staff
Web address: www.seminolehospitaldistrict.com
Control: Hospital district or authority, Government, Nonfederal **Service**: General medical and surgical

Staffed Beds: 41 **Admissions**: 167 **Census**: 4 **Outpatient Visits**: 23617
Births: 642 **Total Expense ($000)**: 80181 **Payroll Expense ($000)**: 20157
Personnel: 293

SEYMOUR—Baylor County

SEYMOUR HOSPITAL (451399), 200 Stadium Drive, Zip 76380–2344; tel. 940/889–5572, **A**10 18 21 **F**7 11 13 28 29 34 40 45 50 53 56 57 59 62 64 65 68 70 75 76 81 85 86 87 93 103 107 111 119 127 130 133 135 146 147 148 154 **P**1
Primary Contact: Leslie Hardin, Chief Executive Officer and Chief Financial Officer
CFO: Leslie Hardin, Chief Executive Officer and Chief Financial Officer
CMO: Kory Lann Martin, M.D., Chief of Staff
CHR: Linda Moore, Manager Human Resources
CNO: Julie Smajstrla, Director Nursing
Web address: www.seymourhospital.com/
Control: Hospital district or authority, Government, Nonfederal **Service**: General medical and surgical

Staffed Beds: 25 **Admissions**: 304 **Census**: 4 **Outpatient Visits**: 23900
Births: 32 **Total Expense ($000)**: 18564 **Payroll Expense ($000)**: 7733
Personnel: 123

SHAMROCK—Wheeler County

SHAMROCK GENERAL HOSPITAL (451340), 1000 South Main Street, Zip 79079–2896, Mailing Address: P.O. Box 511, Zip 79079–0511; tel. 806/256–2114, **A**10 18 **F**7 11 29 34 35 40 43 65 68 93 107 119 127 133
Primary Contact: Paul Burke, Administrator
CHR: Cecille Williams, Assistant Administrator
CNO: Jeanne Crossland, Director of Nursing
Web address: https://shamrockhospital.com/
Control: Corporation, Investor–owned (for–profit) **Service**: General medical and surgical

Staffed Beds: 25 **Admissions**: 48 **Census**: 1 **Outpatient Visits**: 7142
Births: 0 **Total Expense ($000)**: 7763 **Payroll Expense ($000)**: 3222
Personnel: 59

SHENANDOAH—Montgomery County

ENCOMPASS HEALTH REHABILITATION HOSPITAL VISION PARK (673034), 117 Vision Park Boulevard, Zip 77384–3001; tel. 936/444–1700, **A**1 10 **F**3 28 29 34 35 44 57 59 65 68 74 75 77 78 79 82 86 87 90 91 95 96 130 132 148 149 164 **S** Encompass Health Corporation, Birmingham, AL
Primary Contact: Angela Simmons, Chief Executive Officer
CFO: Terri Weiss, Chief Financial Officer
Web address: www.healthsouthvisionpark.com/
Control: Corporation, Investor–owned (for–profit) **Service**: Rehabilitation

Staffed Beds: 60 **Admissions**: 1517 **Census**: 50 **Outpatient Visits**: 0
Births: 0 **Total Expense ($000)**: 22210 **Payroll Expense ($000)**: 13905
Personnel: 158

NEXUS SPECIALTY HOSPITAL, 123 Vision Park Boulevard, Zip 77384–3001; tel. 281/364–0317, (Nonreporting) **S** Nexus Health Systems, Houston, TX
Primary Contact: James R. Resendez, FACHE, Chief Executive Officer
CFO: David Strickler, Chief Financial Officer
CMO: Ather Siddiqi, M.D., Medical Director
CIO: Noe Salinas, Vice President Information Technology
CHR: Kevin McAndrews, Vice President Human Resources
CNO: Rhena Anderson, Chief Nursing Officer
Web address: www.nexusspecialty.com
Control: Partnership, Investor–owned (for–profit) **Service**: General medical and surgical

Staffed Beds: 55

SHERMAN—Grayson County

AHS SHERMAN MEDICAL CENTER (450469), 500 North Highland Avenue, Zip 75092–7354; tel. 903/870–4611, **A**1 10 **F**3 12 13 18 20 22 24 28 29 30 34 35 40 41 43 45 47 49 53 56 57 58 59 64 70 74 75 76 77 79 81 83 84 85 87 91 92 93 96 98 103 107 108 111 119 130 132 135 146 147 148 149 154 156 157 169 **S** Alecto Healthcare, Irvine, CA
Primary Contact: Julie Stumbers, Chief Executive Officer
CFO: Andrea Lane, Chief Financial Officer
CMO: Michael Benson, M.D., President Medical Staff
CIO: Prabhu Bollu, Director Information Technology
CHR: Bill Barrett, Manager Human Resources
CNO: Mandy Dick MSN, RN, Chief Nursing Officer
Web address: www.wnj.org
Control: Corporation, Investor–owned (for–profit) **Service**: General medical and surgical

Staffed Beds: 109 **Admissions**: 2106 **Census**: 28 **Outpatient Visits**: 14664
Births: 32 **Total Expense ($000)**: 43869 **Payroll Expense ($000)**: 19466
Personnel: 327

BAYLOR SCOTT & WHITE SURGICAL HOSPITAL–SHERMAN (670076), 3601 North Calais Street, Zip 75090–1785; tel. 903/870–0999, **A**10 21 **F**3 8 18 29 37 39 40 45 47 64 79 81 82 85 107 111 119 126 145 **S** Baylor Scott & White Health, Dallas, TX
Primary Contact: Nikole Best, Chief Executive Officer
CMO: Curtis Holbrook, M.D., Chief Medical Officer
CIO: Grant Hulsey, Director Information Technology
CHR: Terrie Langford, Director Human Resources
CNO: Teresa Dutton, R.N., Chief Nursing Officer
Web address: https://baylorsherman.com
Control: Partnership, Investor–owned (for–profit) **Service**: General medical and surgical

Staffed Beds: 12 **Admissions**: 318 **Census**: 2 **Outpatient Visits**: 18323
Births: 0 **Total Expense ($000)**: 45872 **Payroll Expense ($000)**: 11736
Personnel: 161

CARRUS BEHAVIORAL HOSPITAL (454153), 1724 West U.S. Highway 82, Suite 200, Zip 75092–7037, Mailing Address: 1810 West U.S. Highway 82, Zip 75092–7069; tel. 903/870–1200, **A**1 10 **F**29 38 44 75 77 87 98 99 100 101 104 105 130 134 153 160 161 164 **S** Carrus Health, Sherman, TX
Primary Contact: Anbu Nachimuthu, Chief Executive Officer and Chairman
Web address: https://www.carrushealth.com/inpatient-services/behavioral-health-coming-soon/
Control: Corporation, Investor–owned (for–profit) **Service**: Psychiatric

Staffed Beds: 28 **Admissions**: 919 **Census**: 22 **Outpatient Visits**: 3968
Births: 0 **Total Expense ($000)**: 8270 **Payroll Expense ($000)**: 4313
Personnel: 102

☐ **CARRUS REHABILITATION HOSPITAL (673041)**, 1810 West US Highway 82, Suite 100, Zip 75092–7069; tel. 903/870–2600, **A**1 10 **F**3 29 40 41 44 65 74 75 77 79 85 86 87 90 91 96 130 **S** Carrus Health, Sherman, TX
Primary Contact: Anbu Nachimuthu, Chief Executive Officer and Chairman
CFO: Michael Exline, Chief Financial Officer
CMO: Jose Matus, M.D., Director Medical
CIO: Gary Glenn, Director Information Technology
CHR: Charlene Shupert, Director Staff Services
CNO: Marie Johnson, Chief Nursing Officer
Web address: www.carrushospital.com
Control: Corporation, Investor–owned (for–profit) **Service**: Rehabilitation

Staffed Beds: 24 **Admissions**: 667 **Census**: 23 **Outpatient Visits**: 0
Births: 0 **Total Expense ($000)**: 10802 **Payroll Expense ($000)**: 4715
Personnel: 86

☐ **CARRUS SPECIALTY HOSPITAL (452041)**, 1810 West US Highway 82, Zip 75092–7069; tel. 903/870–2600, **A**1 10 **F**1 3 29 40 41 44 56 65 74 75 77 78 79 82 83 85 86 87 91 102 107 115 119 129 130 148 167 **S** Carrus Health, Sherman, TX
Primary Contact: Jon Michael. Rains, President and Chief Operating Officer
CFO: Michael Exline, Chief Financial Officer
CMO: Nathan Watson, M.D., Jr, Chief of Staff
CIO: Gary Glenn, Director Information Technology
CHR: Charlene Shupert, Director Staff Services
CNO: Marie Johnson, Chief Nursing Officer
Web address: www.carrushospital.com
Control: Corporation, Investor–owned (for–profit) **Service**: Acute long–term care hospital

Staffed Beds: 33 **Admissions**: 377 **Census**: 24 **Outpatient Visits**: 1846
Births: 0 **Total Expense ($000)**: 15625 **Payroll Expense ($000)**: 7291
Personnel: 129

SMITHVILLE—Bastrop County

✣ **ASCENSION SETON SMITHVILLE (450143)**, 1201 Hill Road, Zip 78957; tel. 512/237–3214, **A**1 10 **F**3 11 15 29 30 34 35 40 45 50 57 68 79 81 85 87 92 93 97 107 110 111 114 119 127 130 143 146 147 149 154 165 **S** Ascension Healthcare, Saint Louis, MO
Primary Contact: Jace Jones, Chief Executive Officer and Administrator
CFO: Melissa Nordyke, Chief Financial Officer
CHR: Sara Rodriguez, Human Resources
CNO: Christine Laflamme, R.N., MSN, Chief Nursing Officer
Web address: https://healthcare.ascension.org/Locations/Texas/TXAUS/Smithville-Ascension-Seton-Smithville
Control: Church operated, Nongovernment, not–for–profit **Service**: General medical and surgical

Staffed Beds: 8 **Admissions**: 207 **Census**: 5 **Outpatient Visits**: 32538
Births: 0 **Total Expense ($000)**: 18196 **Payroll Expense ($000)**: 7096
Personnel: 82

SNYDER—Scurry County

⇑ **COGDELL MEMORIAL HOSPITAL (451384)**, 1700 Cogdell Boulevard, Zip 79549–6198; tel. 325/573–6374, **A**10 18 21 **F**3 8 11 12 13 15 18 19 29 30 34 35 40 43 45 46 47 48 49 50 53 56 57 59 62 63 64 65 66 68 75 76 77 79 81 83 84 85 86 87 91 92 93 97 105 107 110 111 115 119 127 130 131 132 133 145 146 147 148 149 154 156 157 169
Primary Contact: Ella Raye. Helms, Chief Executive Officer
CFO: John Everett, Chief Financial Officer
CMO: Robert Rakov, M.D., Chief Medical Officer
CHR: Linda Warren, Director Human Resources
Web address: www.cogdellhospital.com
Control: Hospital district or authority, Government, Nonfederal **Service**: General medical and surgical

Staffed Beds: 25 **Admissions**: 672 **Census**: 6 **Outpatient Visits**: 98494
Births: 140 **Total Expense ($000)**: 52656 **Payroll Expense ($000)**: 22341
Personnel: 310

SONORA—Sutton County

LILLIAN M. HUDSPETH MEMORIAL HOSPITAL (451324), 308 Hudspeth Avenue, Zip 76950–8003, Mailing Address: P.O. Box 455, Zip 76950–0455; tel. 325/387–2521, **A**10 18 **F**3 7 15 26 28 29 30 34 35 40 41 43 50 53 57 59 63 64 65 66 68 75 79 86 87 90 93 96 97 107 110 111 115 119 127 128 131 133 135 154
Primary Contact: Joe Marshall, Chief Executive Officer
COO: Joe Marshall, Chief Operating Officer
CFO: Michelle Schaefer, Chief Financial Officer
CNO: Lara Ellen Teague, R.N., Chief Nursing Officer
Web address: www.sonora-hospital.org
Control: Hospital district or authority, Government, Nonfederal **Service**: General medical and surgical

Staffed Beds: 13 **Admissions**: 47 **Census**: 2 **Outpatient Visits**: 6568
Births: 0 **Total Expense ($000)**: 12311 **Payroll Expense ($000)**: 5610
Personnel: 80

SOUTHLAKE—Tarrant County

✣ **METHODIST SOUTHLAKE HOSPITAL (670132)**, 421 East State Highway 114, Zip 76092; tel. 817/865–4400, **A**1 **F**3 12 29 40 45 49 50 51 68 70 75 79 81 82 85 107 111 115 119 124 126 130 135 149 **P**5 6 **S** Methodist Health System, Dallas, TX
Primary Contact: Benson Chacko, President
Web address: https://www.methodisthealthsystem.org/methodist-southlake-medical-center/
Control: Other not–for–profit (including NFP Corporation) **Service**: General medical and surgical

Staffed Beds: 22 **Admissions**: 413 **Census**: 4 **Outpatient Visits**: 11460
Births: 0 **Total Expense ($000)**: 63019 **Payroll Expense ($000)**: 16938
Personnel: 166

☐ **TEXAS HEALTH HARRIS METHODIST HOSPITAL SOUTHLAKE (450888)**, 1545 East Southlake Boulevard, Zip 76092–6422; tel. 817/748–8700, **A**1 10 **F**3 29 30 34 40 57 64 65 68 74 75 78 79 81 82 85 93 107 111 115 119 126 130 149
Primary Contact: Traci Bernard, R.N., President, Chief Executive Officer and Chief Operating Officer
CFO: Mitchell Mulvehill, Group Financial Officer
CMO: David Taunton, M.D., Chief of Staff
CHR: Tasha Sledge, Director Human Resources
CNO: Debra Ennis, Vice President and Chief Nursing Officer
Web address: www.texashealthsouthlake.com
Control: Partnership, Investor–owned (for–profit) **Service**: Surgical

Staffed Beds: 17 **Admissions**: 340 **Census**: 2 **Outpatient Visits**: 13245
Births: 0 **Total Expense ($000)**: 64784 **Payroll Expense ($000)**: 11531
Personnel: 134

SPEARMAN—Hansford County

⇑ **HANSFORD HOSPITAL (451344)**, 707 South Roland Street, Zip 79081–3441; tel. 806/659–2535, **A**10 18 21 **F**3 7 11 32 34 35 40 43 56 57 59 62 63 64 65 68 69 77 93 107 127 130 133 148 **P**6
Primary Contact: Jonathan D. Bailey, Chief Executive Officer and Administrator
CFO: Scott Beedy, Chief Financial Officer
CMO: Mark Garnett, M.D., Chief of Staff
CHR: Jackie Nelson, Director Human Resources
Web address: www.hchd.net
Control: Hospital district or authority, Government, Nonfederal **Service**: General medical and surgical

Staffed Beds: 14 **Admissions**: 128 **Census**: 2 **Outpatient Visits**: 22256
Births: 0 **Total Expense ($000)**: 25037 **Payroll Expense ($000)**: 9475
Personnel: 104

Hospital, Medicare Provider Number, Address, Telephone, Approval, Facility, and Physician Codes, Health Care System

★ American Hospital Association (AHA) membership   ◯ Healthcare Facilities Accreditation Program   ⇑ Center for Improvement in Healthcare Quality Accreditation
☐ The Joint Commission accreditation   ◇ DNV Healthcare Inc. accreditation   △ Commission on Accreditation of Rehabilitation Facilities (CARF) accreditation

Hospitals, U.S. / TEXAS

SPRING—Harris County

NORTH HOUSTON SURGICAL HOSPITAL See Spring Hospital

SPRING HOSPITAL (670280), 20635 Kuykendahl Road, Zip 77379-3533; tel. 832/844-3746, (Includes THE HEIGHTS HOSPITAL, 1917 Ashland Street, Houston, Texas, Zip 77008-3907, tel. 346/396-1314; Syed Barkaat, Chief Executive Officer) **A**10 22 **F**3 29 40 45 49 50 56 81 85 107 135 149 157
Primary Contact: Syed Rashid, Chief Executive Officer
COO: Sana Farooqui, Chief Operating Officer
CFO: Will Simpson, Chief Financial Officer
CIO: Mohsin Kamal, Chief Information Officer
CHR: Talbert Davis, Human Resources Manager
CNO: Heather Anderson, Chief Nursing Officer
Web address: https://www.springheights.care/
Control: Corporation, Investor-owned (for-profit) **Service**: General medical and surgical

Staffed Beds: 12 **Admissions:** 228 **Census:** 1 **Outpatient Visits:** 3767 **Births:** 0 **Total Expense ($000):** 54825 **Payroll Expense ($000):** 22075 **Personnel:** 250

STAFFORD—Fort Bend County

ATRIUM MEDICAL CENTER (452114), 11929 West Airport Boulevard, Zip 77477-2451; tel. 281/207-8200, **A**10 22 **F**1 3 28 29 34 40 45 50 56 57 59 60 64 65 68 70 74 75 77 82 83 84 85 91 100 107 114 119 130 148 156
Primary Contact: Ahmad Zaid, Chief Executive Officer
COO: Rachid Al Rayes, Chief Operating Officer
CFO: Gloria Carrion, Chief Financial Offricer
CMO: Shatish Patel, M.D., Chief Medical Officer
CNO: Vivian Bradly, Chief Nursing Officer
Web address: www.atriummedicalcenter.com
Control: Partnership, Investor-owned (for-profit) **Service**: Acute long-term care hospital

Staffed Beds: 68 **Admissions:** 160 **Census:** 11 **Outpatient Visits:** 0 **Births:** 0 **Total Expense ($000):** 11119 **Payroll Expense ($000):** 1682 **Personnel:** 46

STANTON—Martin County

MARTIN COUNTY HOSPITAL DISTRICT (451333), 600 Interstate 20E, Zip 79782, Mailing Address: P.O. Box 640, Zip 79782-0640; tel. 432/607-3200, **A**10 18 **F**3 7 29 34 35 39 40 45 53 57 59 62 63 64 65 75 77 81 82 87 93 107 112 114 119 127 133 154 157 167 **P**6
Primary Contact: Nancy Cooke, Chief Executive Officer
CFO: Michele Cathey, Interim Chief Financial officer
CIO: Freddy Oliveras, Chief Information Officer
CHR: Paula Dority, Director Human Resources
CNO: Brandi Avila, Chief Nursing Officer
Web address: www.martincountyhospital.org/
Control: Hospital district or authority, Government, Nonfederal **Service**: General medical and surgical

Staffed Beds: 18 **Admissions:** 205 **Census:** 3 **Outpatient Visits:** 31568 **Births:** 0 **Total Expense ($000):** 36481 **Payroll Expense ($000):** 15983 **Personnel:** 185

STEPHENVILLE—Erath County

TEXAS HEALTH HARRIS METHODIST HOSPITAL STEPHENVILLE (450351), 411 North Belknap Street, Zip 76401-3415; tel. 254/965-1500, **A**1 10 20 **F**3 13 15 28 29 30 34 35 39 40 43 45 50 57 59 63 64 65 68 70 75 76 77 79 81 85 86 87 89 107 110 111 114 117 119 130 146 147 148 149 154 156 169 **S** Texas Health Resources, Arlington, TX
Primary Contact: Claudia A. Eisenmann, FACHE, President
CMO: Marilyn Brister, M.D., Chief of Staff
CHR: Kimberly Leondar, Director Human Resources
CNO: Cynthia L McCarthy, Chief Nursing Officer
Web address: www.texashealth.org/landing.cfm?id=108
Control: Other not-for-profit (including NFP Corporation) **Service**: General medical and surgical

Staffed Beds: 47 **Admissions:** 1579 **Census:** 11 **Outpatient Visits:** 27971 **Births:** 283 **Total Expense ($000):** 61223 **Payroll Expense ($000):** 22237 **Personnel:** 201

SUGAR LAND—Fort Bend County

ENCOMPASS HEALTH REHABILITATION HOSPITAL OF SUGAR LAND (673042), 1325 Highway 6, Zip 77478-4906; tel. 281/276-7574, **A**1 10 **F**3 29 30 34 75 87 90 91 95 96 130 132 146 148 149 154 **S** Encompass Health Corporation, Birmingham, AL
Primary Contact: Bindu Varghese, R.N., Chief Executive Officer
CNO: Steve Midgett, R.N., Chief Nursing Officer
Web address: www.healthsouthsugarland.com
Control: Corporation, Investor-owned (for-profit) **Service**: Rehabilitation

Staffed Beds: 50 **Admissions:** 1267 **Census:** 45 **Outpatient Visits:** 0 **Births:** 0 **Total Expense ($000):** 24801 **Payroll Expense ($000):** 13297 **Personnel:** 187

★ **HOUSTON METHODIST SUGAR LAND HOSPITAL (450820)**, 16655 SW Freeway, Zip 77479-2329; tel. 281/274-7000, **A**2 3 5 10 21 **F**3 12 13 15 18 20 22 24 26 28 29 30 31 33 34 35 36 37 38 40 41 42 44 45 48 49 50 51 53 55 57 58 59 60 61 63 64 65 68 70 73 74 75 76 77 78 79 80 81 82 84 85 86 87 91 92 93 94 96 100 102 107 108 110 111 112 114 115 117 118 119 120 121 123 124 126 130 131 132 135 146 147 148 149 150 154 156 164 167 169 **P**5 6 **S** Houston Methodist, Houston, TX
Primary Contact: Michael Garcia, Chief Executive Officer
CMO: Jeffrey Jackson, M.D., Medical Director
CHR: Luis Mario Garcia Jr, Director Human Resources
Web address: www.methodisthealth.com
Control: Other not-for-profit (including NFP Corporation) **Service**: General medical and surgical

Staffed Beds: 339 **Admissions:** 20321 **Census:** 252 **Outpatient Visits:** 349991 **Births:** 2254 **Total Expense ($000):** 672567 **Payroll Expense ($000):** 223693 **Personnel:** 2561

KINDRED HOSPITAL SUGAR LAND (452080), 1550 First Colony Boulevard, Zip 77479-4000; tel. 281/275-6000, **A**1 10 **F**1 3 29 30 60 64 75 77 82 84 87 90 96 107 130 146 148 167 **S** ScionHealth, Louisville, KY
Primary Contact: Hala Alameddine, Chief Executive Officer
CFO: Sara Rodriguez, Chief Financial Officer
CMO: Subodh Bhuchar, M.D., Chief of Staff
CIO: Feisal Ndomea, Director Case Management
CHR: Lupe Delgado, Coordinator Human Resources
CNO: Hala Alameddine, Chief Nursing Executive
Web address: www.kindred.com
Control: Corporation, Investor-owned (for-profit) **Service**: Acute long-term care hospital

Staffed Beds: 91 **Admissions:** 468 **Census:** 36 **Outpatient Visits:** 359 **Births:** 0 **Total Expense ($000):** 29725 **Payroll Expense ($000):** 13537 **Personnel:** 186

MEMORIAL HERMANN SUGAR LAND HOSPITAL (450848), 17500 West Grand Parkway South, Zip 77479-2562; tel. 281/725-5000, **A**1 3 5 10 **F**3 8 11 12 13 15 18 20 22 26 29 30 34 35 37 40 41 43 44 45 46 47 48 49 50 51 55 56 57 58 59 64 65 68 70 72 74 75 76 77 78 79 80 81 82 85 86 87 89 91 107 108 109 110 111 112 114 119 126 129 130 131 146 147 148 154 167 169 **S** Memorial Hermann Health System, Houston, TX
Primary Contact: Malisha Patel, Senior Vice President and Chief Executive Officer
CFO: Lisa Kendler, Chief Financial Officer
CMO: William Riley, M.D., Jr, Chief of Staff
CHR: Robert Blake, Chief Human Resources Officer Southwest Market
Web address: www.memorialhermann.org
Control: Other not-for-profit (including NFP Corporation) **Service**: General medical and surgical

Staffed Beds: 179 **Admissions:** 11348 **Census:** 118 **Outpatient Visits:** 133993 **Births:** 2556 **Total Expense ($000):** 274377 **Payroll Expense ($000):** 97576 **Personnel:** 1069

☐ **MEMORIAL HERMANN SURGICAL HOSPITAL–FIRST COLONY (450860)**, 16906 Southwest Freeway, Zip 77479-2350; tel. 281/243-1000, **A**1 10 **F**3 29 37 45 47 77 81 85 107 111 119 126 145 **P**2 **S** Memorial Hermann Health System, Houston, TX
Primary Contact: Daniel Smith, Chief Executive Officer
CFO: Raquel Hebert, Business Manager
CMO: Ken Thomson, M.D., Medical Director
Web address: www.memorialhermannfirstcolony.com
Control: Partnership, Investor-owned (for-profit) **Service**: Surgical

Staffed Beds: 6 **Admissions:** 264 **Census:** 2 **Outpatient Visits:** 9129 **Births:** 0 **Total Expense ($000):** 44120 **Payroll Expense ($000):** 7633 **Personnel:** 124

Hospitals, U.S. / TEXAS

☒ **ST. LUKE'S HEALTH – SUGAR LAND HOSPITAL (670053)**, 1317 Lake Pointe Parkway, Zip 77478–3997; tel. 281/637–7000, **A**1 10 **F**3 13 15 18 20 22 26 29 30 34 35 37 40 41 43 44 45 46 49 51 53 54 57 59 60 64 68 70 72 74 75 76 79 81 82 85 87 107 108 110 111 114 115 119 126 130 146 148 149 157 167 **S** CommonSpirit Health, Chicago, IL
Primary Contact: Steven Foster, President and Chief Executive Officer
CFO: Bill Beauchamp, Chief Financial Officer
CNO: Wes Garrison
Web address: https://www.chistlukeshealth.org/locations/sugar-land-hospital?utm_source=local-listing&utm_medium=organic&utm_campaign=website-link
Control: Church operated, Nongovernment, not–for–profit **Service:** General medical and surgical

Staffed Beds: 100 **Admissions:** 4885 **Census:** 55 **Outpatient Visits:** 27414 **Births:** 1036 **Total Expense ($000):** 105102 **Payroll Expense ($000):** 41120 **Personnel:** 333

ST. LUKE'S SUGAR LAND HOSPITAL See St. Luke's Health – Sugar Land Hospital

ST. MICHAEL'S ELITE HOSPITAL (670314), 16000 Southwest Freeway, Zip 77479–2673; tel. 281/980–4357, **A**22 **F**3 29 34 35 40 41 56 57 59 65 75 85 86 87 102 107 111 114 119 149 **P**5
Primary Contact: Diane Hutchings, R.N., MS, Interim Chief Executive Officer
CFO: Brian Orsak, Chief Financial Officer
CMO: Shannon Orsak, Chief Medical Officer
CNO: Autumn Norsworthy, Director of Nursing
Web address: https://www.24hrer.com/
Control: Partnership, Investor–owned (for–profit) **Service:** General medical and surgical

Staffed Beds: 6 **Admissions:** 26 **Census:** 1 **Outpatient Visits:** 5109 **Births:** 0 **Total Expense ($000):** 7959 **Payroll Expense ($000):** 2739 **Personnel:** 37

SULPHUR SPRINGS—Hopkins County

☒ **CHRISTUS MOTHER FRANCES HOSPITAL – SULPHUR SPRINGS (450236)**, 115 Airport Road, Zip 75482–2105; tel. 903/885–7671, **A**1 10 20 **F**1 3 11 13 15 28 29 30 34 35 37 40 43 45 49 51 53 57 59 60 64 70 72 76 79 80 81 82 84 85 92 93 96 97 107 108 110 111 114 115 119 126 129 130 131 146 147 148 154 167 **S** CHRISTUS Health, Irving, TX
Primary Contact: Paul Harvey, President/Chief Executive Officer
COO: Donna Geiken Wallace, Chief Operating Officer and Chief Financial Officer
CFO: Donna Geiken Wallace, Chief Operating Officer and Chief Financial Officer
CMO: Chris Gallagher, M.D., Chief Medical Officer
CHR: Donna Rudzik, Director Human Resources
Web address: www.tmfhc.org/maps-and-locations-locations-profile/?id=72&searchId=8bcb329f-a152-e611-b37f-2c768a4e1b84&sort=11&page=1&pageSize=10
Control: Church operated, Nongovernment, not–for–profit **Service:** General medical and surgical

Staffed Beds: 62 **Admissions:** 3303 **Census:** 36 **Outpatient Visits:** 94430 **Births:** 593 **Total Expense ($000):** 109498 **Payroll Expense ($000):** 29391 **Personnel:** 493

SUNNYVALE—Dallas County

☒ **BAYLOR SCOTT & WHITE MEDICAL CENTER – SUNNYVALE (670060)**, 231 South Collins Road, Zip 75182–4624; tel. 972/892–3000, **A**1 10 **F**3 15 18 20 24 26 28 29 40 45 49 70 74 77 79 80 81 82 85 87 93 107 108 110 111 115 119 130 148 149 167 **S** United Surgical Partners International, Addison, TX
Primary Contact: Jon Duckert, FACHE, Chief Executive Officer
CMO: William G. Jones, M.D., Chief Medical Officer
CNO: Deborah A Moeller, R.N., MS, Interim Chief Nursing Officer
Web address: www.BaylorScottandWhite.com/Sunnyvale
Control: Partnership, Investor–owned (for–profit) **Service:** General medical and surgical

Staffed Beds: 70 **Admissions:** 3735 **Census:** 47 **Outpatient Visits:** 32450 **Births:** 0 **Total Expense ($000):** 86774 **Payroll Expense ($000):** 27049 **Personnel:** 391

SWEENY—Brazoria County

SWEENY COMMUNITY HOSPITAL (451311), 305 North McKinney Street, Zip 77480–2895; tel. 979/548–1500, **A**10 18 **F**7 10 11 15 29 40 43 53 59 64 69 75 81 85 93 107 110 114 119 127 133 148 149 154 **P**6
Primary Contact: Kelly Park, R.N., Chief Executive Officer
CFO: Hong Wade, Chief Financial Officer
CMO: Fabio Aglieco, D.O., Chief of Staff
CIO: Stuart Butler, Director Information Technology
CHR: Dana Quintanilla, Director Human Resources
CNO: Kelly Park, R.N., Chief Nursing Officer
Web address: www.sweenyhospital.org
Control: Hospital district or authority, Government, Nonfederal **Service:** General medical and surgical

Staffed Beds: 12 **Admissions:** 286 **Census:** 6 **Outpatient Visits:** 39687 **Births:** 0 **Total Expense ($000):** 70933 **Payroll Expense ($000):** 11747 **Personnel:** 189

SWEETWATER—Nolan County

★ ⇑ **ROLLING PLAINS MEMORIAL HOSPITAL (450055)**, 200 East Arizona Street, Zip 79556–7199, Mailing Address: P.O. Box 690, Zip 79556–0690; tel. 325/235–1701, **A**3 10 20 21 **F**3 11 13 15 28 29 34 40 43 45 53 57 59 62 70 76 77 79 81 85 89 93 107 108 114 119 127 130 131 133 135 146 148 156 169 **P**6
Primary Contact: Doug Dippel, R.N., MSN, Chief Executive Officer
COO: Rhonda Guelker, Senior Director Finance
CFO: Rhonda Guelker, Senior Director Finance
CIO: Rhonda Guelker, Senior Director Finance
CHR: Ame Monroe, Director Human Resources
CNO: Maxine Montano, R.N., Chief Nursing Officer
Web address: www.rpmh.net
Control: Hospital district or authority, Government, Nonfederal **Service:** General medical and surgical

Staffed Beds: 57 **Admissions:** 832 **Census:** 9 **Outpatient Visits:** 68436 **Births:** 187 **Total Expense ($000):** 46657 **Payroll Expense ($000):** 22470 **Personnel:** 299

TAHOKA—Lynn County

★ **LYNN COUNTY HOSPITAL DISTRICT (451351)**, 2600 Lockwood, Zip 79373–4118; tel. 806/998–4533, **A**10 18 **F**3 7 10 28 29 30 32 34 35 40 44 53 54 56 57 59 64 65 66 75 84 86 87 93 97 107 111 114 115 119 127 133 135 144 147 148 149 154 **P**5
Primary Contact: Melanie Richburg, Chief Executive Officer
CMO: Donald Freitag, M.D., Chief Medical Officer
CIO: Jim Brown, Director Information Technology
CHR: Jill Stone, Manager Human Resources
CNO: Angie Jalomo, Chief Nursing Officer
Web address: www.lchdhealthcare.org
Control: Hospital district or authority, Government, Nonfederal **Service:** General medical and surgical

Staffed Beds: 24 **Admissions:** 114 **Census:** 5 **Outpatient Visits:** 12095 **Births:** 0 **Total Expense ($000):** 19786 **Payroll Expense ($000):** 11143 **Personnel:** 192

TAYLOR—Williamson County

☒ **BAYLOR SCOTT & WHITE MEDICAL CENTER – TAYLOR (451374)**, 305 Mallard Lane, Zip 76574–1208; tel. 512/352–7611, **A**1 10 18 **F**3 15 18 29 30 34 35 40 45 50 56 59 64 65 68 75 77 79 81 82 84 85 87 93 96 97 107 108 110 115 119 129 130 133 146 147 148 149 154 **S** Baylor Scott & White Health, Dallas, TX
Primary Contact: Jay Fox, FACHE, President
Web address: https://www.bswhealth.com/locations/taylor/pages/default.aspx?utm_source=BSWHealth.com-Taylor&utm_medium=offline&utm_campaign=BSWHealth.com&utm_term=BSWHealth.com-Taylor&utm_content=redirect
Control: Other not–for–profit (including NFP Corporation) **Service:** General medical and surgical

Staffed Beds: 15 **Admissions:** 368 **Census:** 6 **Outpatient Visits:** 73340 **Births:** 0 **Total Expense ($000):** 31553 **Payroll Expense ($000):** 12449 **Personnel:** 123

Hospital, Medicare Provider Number, Address, Telephone, Approval, Facility, and Physician Codes, Health Care System

★ American Hospital Association (AHA) membership
☐ The Joint Commission accreditation
○ Healthcare Facilities Accreditation Program
◇ DNV Healthcare Inc. accreditation
⇑ Center for Improvement in Healthcare Quality Accreditation
△ Commission on Accreditation of Rehabilitation Facilities (CARF) accreditation

Hospitals, U.S. / TEXAS

TEMPLE—Bell County

BAYLOR SCOTT & WHITE CONTINUING CARE HOSPITAL–TEMPLE (452105), 546 North Kegley Road, Zip 76502–4069; tel. 254/215–0900, (Total facility includes 23 beds in nursing home–type unit) **A**1 10 **F**1 3 29 30 60 68 107 119 128 130 148 149 **S** Baylor Scott & White Health, Dallas, TX
Primary Contact: Candice Gourley, President
CMO: David P Ciceri, M.D., Chief Medical Officer
CNO: Robert Pisicotta, Chief Nursing Officer
Web address: www.sw.org/location/temple-cch
Control: Other not–for–profit (including NFP Corporation) **Service**: Acute long–term care hospital

> **Staffed Beds**: 48 **Admissions**: 591 **Census**: 44 **Outpatient Visits**: 274 **Births**: 0 **Total Expense ($000)**: 23301 **Payroll Expense ($000)**: 12589 **Personnel**: 111

BAYLOR SCOTT & WHITE MEDICAL CENTER – TEMPLE (450054), 2401 South 31st Street, Zip 76508–0002; tel. 254/724–2111, (Includes MCLANE CHILDREN'S HOSPITAL SCOTT & WHITE, 1901 SW H K Dodgen Loop, Temple, Texas, Zip 76502–1896, tel. 254/771–8600; Shahin Motakef, FACHE, Chief Executive Officer; MCLANE CHILDREN'S HOSPITAL SCOTT & WHITE, 2401 South 31st Street, Temple, Texas, Zip 76508–0001, tel. 877/724–5437; Shahin Motakef, FACHE, President) **A**1 2 3 5 8 10 **F**3 5 7 8 11 12 13 14 15 17 18 19 20 22 24 26 28 29 30 31 32 34 35 37 38 39 40 41 43 44 45 46 47 48 49 50 51 52 54 55 56 57 58 59 60 61 63 64 65 68 70 72 73 74 76 77 78 79 80 81 82 83 84 85 86 87 88 89 91 92 93 96 97 100 101 104 107 108 110 111 115 116 117 118 119 120 121 123 124 126 127 129 130 131 135 137 138 141 142 144 145 146 147 148 149 150 154 156 157 160 161 162 164 167 168 169 **S** Baylor Scott & White Health, Dallas, TX
Primary Contact: Gregory Haralson, FACHE, President
CFO: Alita Prosser, Chief Financial Officer
CMO: Stephen Sibbitt, M.D., Chief Medical Officer
CIO: Matthew Chambers, Chief Information Officer
CHR: Pat Balz, Vice President Operations Human Resources
Web address: https://www.bswhealth.com/locations/temple/Pages/default.aspx
Control: Other not–for–profit (including NFP Corporation) **Service**: General medical and surgical

> **Staffed Beds**: 625 **Admissions**: 33890 **Census**: 502 **Outpatient Visits**: 2173640 **Births**: 2998 **Total Expense ($000)**: 1377573 **Payroll Expense ($000)**: 428074 **Personnel**: 6247

☐ **CANYON CREEK BEHAVIORAL HEALTH (454152)**, 1201 Canyon Creek Drive, Zip 76502; tel. 254/410–5100, **A**1 3 10 **F**98 99 105 130 153 154 **S** Universal Health Services, Inc., King of Prussia, PA
Primary Contact: Jennifer Card, Chief Executive Officer
CFO: Denise Curran, Chief Financial Officer
Web address: https://canyoncreekbh.com/
Control: Corporation, Investor–owned (for–profit) **Service**: Psychiatric

> **Staffed Beds**: 102 **Admissions**: 2904 **Census**: 53 **Outpatient Visits**: 3707 **Births**: 0 **Total Expense ($000)**: 21890 **Payroll Expense ($000)**: 9391 **Personnel**: 135

CENTRAL TEXAS VETERANS AFFAIRS HEALTH CARE SYSTEM, OLIN E. TEAGUE VETERANS CENTER See Central Texas Veterans Affairs Health Care System, Olin E. Teague Veterans Medical Center

CENTRAL TEXAS VETERANS AFFAIRS HEALTH CARE SYSTEM, OLIN E. TEAGUE VETERANS MEDICAL CENTER See Central Texas Veterans HCS/Temple Tx, Temple

CENTRAL TEXAS VETERANS HCS/TEMPLE TX, 1901 Veterans Memorial Drive, Zip 76504–7445; tel. 254/778–4811, (Includes CENTRAL TEXAS VETERANS AFFAIRS HEALTH CARE SYSTEM, OLIN E. TEAGUE VETERANS MEDICAL CENTER, 1901 Veterans Memorial Drive, Temple, Texas, Zip 76504, tel. 254/778–4811; Colonel Michael L Kiefer, FACHE, Director; CENTRAL TEXAS VETERANS HEALTH CARE SYSTEM, DORIS MILLER VETERANS MEDICAL CENTER, 4800 Memorial Drive, Waco, Texas, Zip 76711–1397, tel. 254/752–6581; Colonel Michael L Kiefer, FACHE, Director) (Nonreporting) **A**1 5 8 **S** Department of Veterans Affairs, Washington, DC
Primary Contact: Colonel Michael L. Kiefer, FACHE, Medical Center Director
CFO: Rosey Anzures, Acting Chief Financial Officer
CMO: Olawale Fashina, M.D., Chief of Staff
CIO: Victor Vitolas, Acting Chief Information Technology Services
CHR: Mary P. Doerfler, Chief Human Resources Officer
Web address: www.centraltexas.va.gov/
Control: Veterans Affairs, Government, federal **Service**: General medical and surgical

> **Staffed Beds**: 141

CENTRAL TEXAS VETERANS HEALTH CARE SYSTEM See Central Texas Veterans HCS/Temple Tx

CHILDREN'S HOSPITAL AT SCOTT & WHITE See Mclane Children's Hospital Scott & White

KING'S DAUGHTERS HOSPITAL See Mclane Children's Hospital Scott & White

MCLANE CHILDREN'S HOSPITAL SCOTT & WHITE See Baylor Scott & White Medical Center – Temple, Temple

TEMPLE REHABILITATION HOSPITAL (673074), 23621 SE H. K. Dodgen Loop, Zip 76504–8664, Mailing Address: 23621 SE H.K. Dodgen Loop, Zip 76504–8664; tel. 254/410–0555, **A**10 22 **F**3 28 29 31 68 86 87 90 91 96 148 149 **S** Everest Rehabilitation Hospitals, LLC, Dallas, TX
Primary Contact: Michael Hutka, Chief Executive Officer
Web address: https://everestrehab.com/hospitals/temple-tx/
Control: Corporation, Investor–owned (for–profit) **Service**: Rehabilitation

> **Staffed Beds**: 36 **Admissions**: 485 **Census**: 14 **Outpatient Visits**: 0 **Births**: 0 **Total Expense ($000)**: 8570 **Payroll Expense ($000)**: 4559 **Personnel**: 78

TERRELL—Kaufman County

COLONIAL HOSPITAL See Terrell Community Hospital, Colonial Campus

☐ **TERRELL STATE HOSPITAL (454006)**, 1200 East Brin Street, Zip 75160–2938, Mailing Address: P.O. Box 70, Zip 75160–9000; tel. 972/524–6452, **A**1 3 5 10 **F**3 30 34 39 57 75 86 87 98 99 100 101 103 130 132 135 146 164 **P**6 **S** Texas Department of State Health Services, Austin, TX
Primary Contact: Mark Messer, D.O., Interim Superintendent
CFO: David R. Teel, Financial Officer
CMO: Mark Messer, D.O., Clinical Director
CIO: Sims Anderson, Manager Facility Automation
CNO: Kathryn Griffin, Chief Nurse Executive
Web address: www.dshs.state.tx.us/mhhospitals/terrellsh
Control: State, Government, Nonfederal **Service**: Psychiatric

> **Staffed Beds**: 305 **Admissions**: 1310 **Census**: 197 **Outpatient Visits**: 0 **Births**: 0 **Total Expense ($000)**: 88616 **Payroll Expense ($000)**: 50141 **Personnel**: 989

TEXARKANA—Bowie County

CHRISTUS ST. MICHAEL HEALTH SYSTEM (450801), 2600 St Michael Drive, Zip 75503–5220; tel. 903/614–1000, (Includes CHRISTUS ST. MICHAEL HOSPITAL–ATLANTA, 1007 South William Street, Atlanta, Texas, Zip 75551–3245, tel. 903/799–3000; Jason Adams, Preisdent) **A**1 10 19 **F**3 11 13 15 17 18 20 22 24 26 28 29 30 31 34 35 37 40 41 43 45 48 49 50 51 55 56 57 59 60 64 65 68 70 71 72 73 74 75 76 77 78 79 80 81 82 84 85 86 87 89 90 92 102 107 108 109 110 111 114 115 118 119 120 121 122 123 124 126 129 130 131 132 135 146 147 148 149 154 156 167 **S** CHRISTUS Health, Irving, TX
Primary Contact: Jason Adams, President
COO: Jennifer Wright, Vice President Operations
CFO: Glen Boles, Vice President and Chief Financial Officer
CMO: Loren Robinson, M.D., Chief Medical Officer
CIO: Stephen DeLoach, Regional Information Management Executive
CHR: Wendy Chandler, Vice President Human Resources
CNO: Louise Thornell, Ph.D., R.N., Chief Nursing Officer
Web address: www.christusstmichael.org
Control: Church operated, Nongovernment, not–for–profit **Service**: General medical and surgical

> **Staffed Beds**: 341 **Admissions**: 13539 **Census**: 191 **Outpatient Visits**: 272755 **Births**: 1543 **Total Expense ($000)**: 392361 **Payroll Expense ($000)**: 111845 **Personnel**: 1699

△ **CHRISTUS ST. MICHAEL REHABILITATION HOSPITAL (453065)**, 2400 St Michael Drive, Zip 75503–2374; tel. 903/614–4000, (Nonreporting) **A**1 7 10 **S** CHRISTUS Health, Irving, TX
Primary Contact: Kristine Bell, Administrator
CFO: Glen Boles, Vice President and Chief Financial Officer
CMO: Richard Sharp, M.D., Medical Director
CIO: Alana Higgins, Regional Information Management Executive
CHR: Jennifer Wright, Vice President Human Resources
CNO: Stacey Breedlove, Chief Nursing Officer
Web address: www.christusstmichael.org/rehab
Control: Church operated, Nongovernment, not–for–profit **Service**: Rehabilitation

> **Staffed Beds**: 50

Hospitals, U.S. / TEXAS

☒ **ENCOMPASS HEALTH REHABILITATION HOSPITAL OF TEXARKANA (453053)**, 515 West 12th Street, Zip 75501–4416; tel. 903/735–5000, **A**1 10 **F**3 28 29 74 77 79 90 91 96 130 143 148 149 **S** Encompass Health Corporation, Birmingham, AL
Primary Contact: Todd Wallace, Chief Executive Officer
CFO: Kathy Dickerson, Interim Controller
CMO: Mark A Wren, M.D., Medical Director
CHR: Ann R Clapp, Director Human Resources
CNO: Lorri Oglesby, Chief Nursing Officer
Web address: https://encompasshealth.com/locations/texarkanarehab
Control: Corporation, Investor–owned (for–profit) Service: Rehabilitation

Staffed Beds: 60 Admissions: 1015 Census: 35 Outpatient Visits: 0 Births: 0 Total Expense ($000): 21423 Payroll Expense ($000): 10373 Personnel: 165

☒ **POST ACUTE MEDICAL SPECIALTY HOSPITAL OF TEXARKANA – NORTH (452061)**, 2400 St Michael Drive, 2nd Floor, Zip 75503–2372; tel. 903/614–7600, **A**1 10 **F**1 3 29 60 68 85 148 154 **S** PAM Health, Enola, PA
Primary Contact: Greg Lessard, Chief Executive Officer
Web address: www.postacutemedical.com
Control: Corporation, Investor–owned (for–profit) Service: Acute long–term care hospital

Staffed Beds: 30 Admissions: 330 Census: 21 Outpatient Visits: 0 Births: 0 Total Expense ($000): 12331 Payroll Expense ($000): 5376 Personnel: 71

TEXARKANA EMERGENCY CENTER & HOSPITAL, 4646 Cowhorn Creek Road, Zip 75503–2572, Mailing Address: 6030 South Rice Ave, Houston, Zip 77081–2943; tel. 903/838–8000, (Nonreporting) **A**22
Primary Contact: Tom Vo, M.D., Chief Executive Officer
COO: Amy Tankersley, Director of Operations
CMO: Matthew S. Young, Chief Medical Officer
CNO: Kyndel Griffith, Chief Nursing Officer
Web address: www.texarkanaemergencycenter.com
Control: Corporation, Investor–owned (for–profit) Service: General medical and surgical

Staffed Beds: 4

⇧ **WADLEY REGIONAL MEDICAL CENTER (450200)**, 1000 Pine Street, Zip 75501–5170; tel. 903/798–8000, **A**3 5 10 19 21 **F**3 11 13 15 18 20 22 28 29 30 31 34 35 40 43 45 49 50 56 57 59 60 64 65 70 71 72 74 75 76 77 78 79 81 85 86 87 89 93 107 108 110 111 114 115 119 126 130 146 147 148 149 154 167 169 **S** Steward Health Care System, LLC, Dallas, TX
Primary Contact: Thomas D. Gilbert, FACHE, Chief Executive Officer
CFO: Bonny Sorensen, Chief Financial Officer
CIO: Matt Kesterson, Director Information Services
CHR: Debby Butler, Director Human Resources
CNO: Shelly Strayhorn, R.N., Chief Nursing Officer
Web address: https://www.wadleyhealth.org/contact-us
Control: Corporation, Investor–owned (for–profit) Service: General medical and surgical

Staffed Beds: 163 Admissions: 7227 Census: 61 Outpatient Visits: 63896 Births: 914 Total Expense ($000): 107774 Payroll Expense ($000): 39423 Personnel: 440

TEXAS CITY—Galveston County

MAINLAND MEDICAL CENTER See HCA Houston Healthcare Mainland

THE COLONY—Denton County

THE COLONY ER HOSPITAL, 4780 State Highway 121, Zip 75056–2913; tel. 214/469–1119, **F**3 40 41 42 54 107 115 119 149
Primary Contact: Russell Kaiser, Interim Chief Executive Officer and Chief Nursing Officer
Web address: https://thecolonyer.com/
Control: Individual, Investor–owned (for–profit) Service: General medical and surgical

Staffed Beds: 8 Admissions: 11 Census: 1 Outpatient Visits: 14817 Births: 1 Total Expense ($000): 26351 Payroll Expense ($000): 7405 Personnel: 93

THE WOODLANDS—Montgomery County

CHI ST. LUKE'S HEALTH–LAKESIDE HOSPITAL See St. Luke's Health – Lakeside Hospital

CHI ST. LUKE'S HEALTH–THE WOODLANDS HOSPITAL See St. Luke's Health – The Woodlands Hospital

★ ⇧ **HOUSTON METHODIST THE WOODLANDS HOSPITAL (670122)**, 17201 Interstate 45 South, Zip 77385; tel. 713/790–3333, **A**2 3 10 21 **F**3 11 12 13 15 18 20 22 24 26 28 29 30 31 34 35 36 37 40 41 42 44 45 46 47 48 49 50 51 53 54 57 59 64 65 68 70 72 74 75 76 77 78 79 81 82 84 85 86 87 93 95 96 97 102 107 108 110 111 115 117 118 119 120 121 123 124 126 129 130 131 132 135 146 147 148 149 154 167 169 **P**5 6 **S** Houston Methodist, Houston, TX
Primary Contact: David P. Bernard, FACHE, Chief Executive Officer
CNO: Kerrie Guerrero, R.N., MSN, Vice President and Chief Nursing Officer
Web address: www.houstonmethodist.org/locations/the-woodlands/
Control: Other not–for–profit (including NFP Corporation) Service: General medical and surgical

Staffed Beds: 277 Admissions: 17449 Census: 191 Outpatient Visits: 249834 Births: 2335 Total Expense ($000): 533365 Payroll Expense ($000): 171186 Personnel: 1982

MEMORIAL HERMANN THE WOODLANDS HOSPITAL See Memorial Hermann Greater Heights Hospital, Houston

MEMORIAL HOSPITAL See Memorial Hermann The Woodlands Hospital

NEXUS SPECIALITY HOSPITAL – THE WOODLANDS CAMPUS (670267), 9182 Six Pines Drive, Zip 77380–3670, Mailing Address: 25540 I–45 North, Suite 100, Spring, Zip 77380–3670; tel. 281/602–8160, **A**22 **F**3 18 20 22 26 29 40 45 46 47 48 49 50 80 81 82 107 108 109 111 115 118 119 120 149
Primary Contact: Roger Caron, Chief Executive Officer
CFO: Virginia de Bond, Chief Financial Officer
Web address: www.woodlandsspecialtyhospital.com/
Control: Individual, Investor–owned (for–profit) Service: General medical and surgical

Staffed Beds: 8 Admissions: 282 Census: 1 Outpatient Visits: 3920 Births: 0 Total Expense ($000): 29460 Payroll Expense ($000): 8932 Personnel: 91

⇧ **NEXUS SPECIALTY HOSPITAL THE WOODLANDS (452057)**, 9182 Six Pines Drive, Zip 77380–3670; tel. 281/364–0317, (Nonreporting) **A**10 21
Primary Contact: Roger Caron, Chief Executive Officer
CFO: David Strickler, Chief Financial Officer
CMO: Ather Siddiqi, M.D., Medical Director
CIO: Noe Salinas, Vice President Information Technology
CHR: Kevin McAndrews, Vice President, Human Resources
CNO: Rhena Anderson, Chief Nursing Officer
Web address: www.nexusspecialty.com
Control: Partnership, Investor–owned (for–profit) Service: Acute long–term care hospital

Staffed Beds: 21

☒ **ST. LUKE'S HEALTH – LAKESIDE HOSPITAL (670059)**, 17400 St. Luke's Way, Zip 77384–8036; tel. 936/266–9000, **A**1 10 **F**3 18 20 22 26 29 30 34 35 40 57 59 64 68 75 79 81 87 94 107 111 115 119 130 131 135 157 **S** CommonSpirit Health, Chicago, IL
Primary Contact: James Parisi, Chief Executive Officer
CHR: Debra Roberts, Director of Human Resources
CNO: Diane Freeman, R.N., Assistant Vice President and Chief Nursing Officer
Web address: www.stlukeslakeside.com/
Control: Corporation, Investor–owned (for–profit) Service: Surgical

Staffed Beds: 8 Admissions: 551 Census: 4 Outpatient Visits: 14777 Births: 0 Total Expense ($000): 42029 Payroll Expense ($000): 10628 Personnel: 133

Hospital, Medicare Provider Number, Address, Telephone, Approval, Facility, and Physician Codes, Health Care System

★ American Hospital Association (AHA) membership
☐ The Joint Commission accreditation
○ Healthcare Facilities Accreditation Program
◇ DNV Healthcare Inc. accreditation
⇧ Center for Improvement in Healthcare Quality Accreditation
△ Commission on Accreditation of Rehabilitation Facilities (CARF) accreditation

© 2025 AHA Guide

Hospitals, U.S. / TEXAS

✠ **ST. LUKE'S HEALTH – THE WOODLANDS HOSPITAL (450862)**, 17200 St. Luke's Way, Zip 77384-8007; tel. 936/266-2000, **A**1 3 5 10 **F**3 11 12 13 15 18 20 22 24 26 28 29 30 31 34 35 38 40 41 42 45 49 50 57 58 59 64 70 72 74 75 76 78 79 81 82 85 86 87 90 93 107 108 109 110 111 114 118 119 124 126 129 130 131 135 145 146 147 148 149 167 169 **S** CommonSpirit Health, Chicago, IL
Primary Contact: James Parisi, Chief Executive Officer
CMO: Charles Sims, M.D., Chief of Staff
CNO: Ellen Pitcher, Senior Vice President Patient Care Services and Chief Nursing Officer
Web address: https://locations.stlukeshealth.org/location/woodlands-hospital
Control: Church operated, Nongovernment, not-for-profit **Service**: General medical and surgical

Staffed Beds: 238 **Admissions**: 12758 **Census**: 150 **Outpatient Visits**: 98906 **Births**: 1677 **Total Expense ($000)**: 318829 **Payroll Expense ($000)**: 103597 **Personnel**: 1092

THROCKMORTON—Throckmorton County

THROCKMORTON COUNTY MEMORIAL HOSPITAL (451339), 802 North Minter Avenue, Zip 76483-5357, Mailing Address: P.O. Box 729, Zip 76483-0729; tel. 940/849-2151, **A**10 18 **F**1 7 34 40 41 43 44 50 59 61 64 65 68 77 79 87 97 102 127 128 130 133 148 **P**6
Primary Contact: Kirby Gober, Chief Executive Officer
CMO: Craig Beasley, M.D., Chief Medical Officer
CHR: Karla Benson, Executive Assistant
CNO: Kinsi Voss, R.N., Chief Nursing Officer
Web address: www.throckmortonhospital.com
Control: County, Government, Nonfederal **Service**: General medical and surgical

Staffed Beds: 14 **Admissions**: 56 **Census**: 1 **Outpatient Visits**: 13669 **Births**: 0 **Total Expense ($000)**: 5774 **Payroll Expense ($000)**: 2260 **Personnel**: 54

TOMBALL—Harris County

✠ **HCA HOUSTON HEALTHCARE TOMBALL (450670)**, 605 Holderrieth Street, Zip 77375-6445; tel. 281/401-7500, (Includes HCA HOUSTON HEALTHCARE CYPRESS FAIRBANKS, 10655 Steepletop Drive, Houston, Texas, Zip 77065-4297, tel. 281/890-4285; Robert Marmerstein, Chief Executive Officer) **A**1 10 **F**3 8 12 13 15 18 20 22 24 26 28 29 30 31 34 35 40 42 43 44 45 46 47 48 49 50 51 53 54 57 59 60 64 65 70 72 74 75 76 77 78 79 80 81 82 85 86 87 90 91 93 94 96 98 103 107 108 111 119 124 126 129 130 131 132 144 145 146 147 148 149 154 167 169 **S** HCA Healthcare, Nashville, TN
Primary Contact: Robert Marmerstein, Chief Executive Officer
COO: Adrian Moreno, Chief Operating Officer
CFO: Richard Ervin, Chief Financial Officer
CMO: Mauricio Pinto, M.D., Chief Medical Officer
CIO: Marisa Smith, Director
CHR: Vanessa Hunt, Director Human Resources
Web address: www.tomballregionalmedicalcenter.com
Control: Corporation, Investor-owned (for-profit) **Service**: General medical and surgical

Staffed Beds: 261 **Admissions**: 8967 **Census**: 129 **Outpatient Visits**: 93254 **Births**: 1394 **Total Expense ($000)**: 217280 **Payroll Expense ($000)**: 73751 **Personnel**: 867

LEGENT NORTH HOUSTON SURGICAL HOSPITAL, 24429 State Highway 249, Zip 77375-8214; tel. 346/766-0880, **F**3 29 37 40 64 79 81 82 87 135 149 164 **P**2
Primary Contact: Cole Schmitz, Chief Executive Officer
COO: Kim Hale, R.N., Chief Nursing and Operating Officer
CFO: Ryan King, Chief Financial Officer
CHR: Alysia White, Vice President, Human Resources
CNO: Kim Hale, R.N., Chief Nursing and Operating Officer
Web address: https://www.legenthealth.com
Control: Partnership, Investor-owned (for-profit) **Service**: Surgical

Staffed Beds: 5 **Admissions**: 34 **Census**: 1 **Outpatient Visits**: 1821 **Births**: 0 **Total Expense ($000)**: 13459 **Payroll Expense ($000)**: 4346 **Personnel**: 63

TRINITY—Trinity County

MID COAST MEDICAL CENTER – TRINITY, 317 Prospect Drive, Zip 75862-6202; tel. 936/337-4111, (Nonreporting)
Primary Contact: Kent Waters, Administrator
Web address: https://trinitymidcoasthospital.org/
Control: Other not-for-profit (including NFP Corporation) **Service**: General medical and surgical

Staffed Beds: 10

TROPHY CLUB—Denton County

☐ **BAYLOR SCOTT & WHITE MEDICAL CENTER – TROPHY CLUB (450883)**, 2850 East State Highway 114, Zip 76262-5302; tel. 817/837-4600, **A**1 10 **F**3 29 40 70 75 79 81 85 87 107 108 111 114 121 123 126 141 167
Primary Contact: Jonathan Saunders, Chief Executive Officer
CMO: Mike Stanton, D.O., Medical Director
CIO: Scot Bradford, Chief Information Officer
CHR: Donna Irvin, Director Human Resources
Web address: www.baylortrophyclub.com
Control: Partnership, Investor-owned (for-profit) **Service**: General medical and surgical

Staffed Beds: 21 **Admissions**: 537 **Census**: 4 **Outpatient Visits**: 8541 **Births**: 0 **Total Expense ($000)**: 56245 **Payroll Expense ($000)**: 12660 **Personnel**: 224

TULIA—Swisher County

★ **SWISHER MEMORIAL HEALTHCARE SYSTEM (451349)**, 539 Southeast Second, Zip 79088-2400, Mailing Address: P.O. Box 808, Zip 79088-0808; tel. 806/995-3581, **A**10 18 **F**3 7 10 11 29 33 34 35 36 40 43 50 53 57 59 64 65 68 75 77 93 107 114 127 130 133 135 148 154 **P**4
Primary Contact: Luke Brewer, Chief Executive Officer
CFO: Connie Wilhelm, Chief Financial Officer
CIO: Brad Roberts, Network Administrator
Web address: www.swisherhospital.com
Control: Other not-for-profit (including NFP Corporation) **Service**: General medical and surgical

Staffed Beds: 20 **Admissions**: 64 **Census**: 3 **Outpatient Visits**: 13283 **Births**: 0 **Total Expense ($000)**: 11721 **Payroll Expense ($000)**: 5155 **Personnel**: 83

TYLER—Smith County

✠ **BAYLOR SCOTT & WHITE TEXAS SPINE & JOINT HOSPITAL-TYLER (450864)**, 1814 Roseland Boulevard, Suite 100, Zip 75701-4262; tel. 903/525-3300, **A**1 10 **F**39 40 53 77 79 81 82 107 111 119 126 131 144 154 **P**5
Primary Contact: Tony Wahl, Chief Executive Officer
CFO: Tiffinie Garner, Chief Financial Officer
CMO: Kim Foreman, M.D., Chief of Staff
CNO: Aaron Fleet, R.N., Chief Nursing Officer
Web address: www.tsjh.org
Control: Partnership, Investor-owned (for-profit) **Service**: Orthopedic

Staffed Beds: 20 **Admissions**: 1482 **Census**: 10 **Outpatient Visits**: 35623 **Births**: 0 **Total Expense ($000)**: 106779 **Payroll Expense ($000)**: 28129 **Personnel**: 460

✠ **CHRISTUS MOTHER FRANCES HOSPITAL – TYLER (450102)**, 800 East Dawson Street, Zip 75701-2036; tel. 903/593-8441, (Includes LOUIS & PEACHES OWEN HEART HOSPITAL, 703 South Fleishel Avenue, Tyler, Texas, Zip 75701-2015, tel. 903/606-3000; John McGreevy, FACHE, Chief Executive Officer) **A**1 2 3 10 19 **F**3 8 11 12 13 15 17 18 20 22 24 26 28 29 30 31 34 35 37 40 41 42 43 45 46 47 48 49 51 53 54 56 57 60 64 68 70 71 72 74 75 76 79 80 81 82 85 86 87 89 93 107 108 109 110 111 113 114 115 119 126 129 130 131 144 145 146 147 148 154 157 167 **S** CHRISTUS Health, Irving, TX
Primary Contact: Jason J. Proctor, President
COO: Jason J Proctor, President
CFO: Joyce Hester, CPA, Senior Vice President and Chief Financial Officer
CMO: Fadi Nasrallah, M.D., Vice President Medical Affairs
CIO: Jeff Pearson, Vice President and Chief Information Officer
CHR: Thomas Wilken, Senior Vice President and Chief Human Resources Officer
Web address: www.tmfhc.org
Control: Church operated, Nongovernment, not-for-profit **Service**: General medical and surgical

Staffed Beds: 495 **Admissions**: 25924 **Census**: 381 **Outpatient Visits**: 647912 **Births**: 3564 **Total Expense ($000)**: 1136690 **Payroll Expense ($000)**: 263981 **Personnel**: 3399

✠ **CHRISTUS TRINITY MOTHER FRANCES REHABILITATION HOSPITAL, A PARTNER OF ENCOMPASS HEALTH (453056)**, 3131 Troup Highway, Zip 75701-8352; tel. 903/510-7000, **A**1 10 **F**3 9 12 28 29 56 74 75 77 79 82 87 90 91 96 130 132 143 148 149 154 156 157 **S** Encompass Health Corporation, Birmingham, AL
Primary Contact: Sharla Anderson, Chief Executive Officer
CFO: Michael G Treadway, Controller
CMO: Bradley Merritt, M.D., Medical Director
Web address: www.tmfrehabhospital.com
Control: Partnership, Investor-owned (for-profit) **Service**: Rehabilitation

Staffed Beds: 94 **Admissions**: 2227 **Census**: 73 **Outpatient Visits**: 0 **Births**: 0 **Total Expense ($000)**: 32337 **Payroll Expense ($000)**: 16193 **Personnel**: 243

★ **TYLER CONTINUECARE HOSPITAL (452091)**, 800 East Dawson, 4th Floor, Zip 75701–2036; tel. 903/531–4080, **A**10 22 **F**1 3 29 34 57 59 85 86 130 148 **P**4 **S** Community Hospital Corporation, Plano, TX
Primary Contact: Stephanie Hyde, R.N., MSN, Chief Executive Officer
Web address: www.continuecare.org
Control: Other not-for-profit (including NFP Corporation) **Service**: Acute long-term care hospital

Staffed Beds: 51 **Admissions**: 450 **Census**: 34 **Outpatient Visits**: 0
Births: 0 **Total Expense ($000)**: 19961 **Payroll Expense ($000)**: 8090
Personnel: 90

UT HEALTH EAST TEXAS REHABILITATION HOSPITAL (453072), 701 Olympic Plaza Circle, Zip 75701–1950, Mailing Address: P.O. Box 7530, Zip 75711–7530; tel. 903/596–3000, **A**1 2 10 **F**3 28 29 34 53 57 74 75 79 86 90 91 93 96 130 131 148 **S** Ardent Health Services, Nashville, TN
Primary Contact: Tracy Vinciguerra, MS, Chief Executive Officer
CFO: James Blanton, Chief Financial Officer
CMO: Perry Wallach, M.D., Chief Medical Officer
CIO: Paul Campbell, Director Technology Support and Operations
CHR: Wes Griffin, Division Human Resources Manager
CNO: Laurie Lehnhof-Watts, Administrator and Chief Nursing Officer
Web address: https://uthealthrehab.com/
Control: Corporation, Investor-owned (for-profit) **Service**: Rehabilitation

Staffed Beds: 42 **Admissions**: 856 **Census**: 32 **Outpatient Visits**: 103487
Births: 0 **Total Expense ($000)**: 34636 **Payroll Expense ($000)**: 16601
Personnel: 201

UT HEALTH NORTH CAMPUS TYLER (450690), 11937 Highway 271, Zip 75708–3154; tel. 903/877–7777, **A**1 2 8 10 **F**3 5 11 15 18 26 28 29 30 31 32 34 35 39 40 43 45 46 47 49 50 53 54 55 56 57 58 59 64 65 70 71 75 77 78 79 84 85 86 87 93 97 98 100 101 102 103 104 105 106 107 108 110 111 114 115 116 117 118 119 120 121 123 127 128 129 130 132 135 143 146 147 148 153 156 160 162 **S** University of Texas System, Austin, TX
Primary Contact: Zachary K. Dietze, Chief Executive Officer
COO: Joe Woelkers, Executive Vice President and Chief Staff
CFO: Juie Krc, Chief Financial Officer
CMO: Steven Cox, M.D., Chief Medical Officer
CHR: Jesse Gomez, Vice President Human Resources
CNO: Don Hunt, M.D., Vice President Patient Centered Care and Chief Nursing Officer
Web address: https://uthealthnorth.com/
Control: State, Government, Nonfederal **Service**: General medical and surgical

Staffed Beds: 130 **Admissions**: 2149 **Census**: 72 **Outpatient Visits**: 121951 **Births**: 0 **Total Expense ($000)**: 178570 **Payroll Expense ($000)**: 64606 **Personnel**: 1175

UT HEALTH TYLER (450083), 1000 South Beckham Street, Zip 75701–1908, Mailing Address: Box 6400, Zip 75711–6400; tel. 903/597–0351, **A**1 2 3 5 10 **F**3 5 8 11 12 13 15 17 18 20 22 24 26 28 29 30 31 34 35 37 38 40 42 43 44 45 46 47 48 49 51 56 58 59 60 61 64 65 68 70 71 72 74 75 76 78 79 81 82 84 85 86 87 89 93 100 101 102 107 110 111 115 117 118 119 126 129 130 132 141 145 146 147 148 149 150 152 156 160 164 167 **S** Ardent Health Services, Nashville, TN
Primary Contact: Zachary K. Dietze, Chief Executive Officer
CFO: Daniel Goggin, Chief Financial Officer
CMO: John Andrews, M.D., Chief of Staff
CIO: Paula Anthony, Vice President Information Services
CHR: Mike Gray, Corporate Vice President Human Resources
CNO: Mariarose Kulma, R.N., Vice President Patient Services
Web address: https://uthealthtylerhospital.com/
Control: Individual, Investor-owned (for-profit) **Service**: General medical and surgical

Staffed Beds: 432 **Admissions**: 20927 **Census**: 300 **Outpatient Visits**: 212442 **Births**: 727 **Total Expense ($000)**: 517384 **Payroll Expense ($000)**: 139856 **Personnel**: 2141

UVALDE—Uvalde County

UVALDE MEMORIAL HOSPITAL (451387), 1025 Garner Field Road, Zip 78801–4809; tel. 830/278–6251, **A**1 10 18 **F**3 11 13 15 18 29 30 34 39 40 43 45 46 57 59 63 64 70 76 79 81 84 85 86 87 93 104 107 108 110 111 115 118 119 127 130 132 133 146 147 148 149 165 **P**3
Primary Contact: Adam Apolinar, Chief Executive Officer
CFO: Valerie Lopez, CPA, Chief Financial Officer
CMO: Jared Reading, M.D., Chief of Staff
CIO: Blake Eaker, Interim Director Information Services
CHR: Charla Garcia, Human Resource Officer
Web address: www.umhtx.org
Control: Hospital district or authority, Government, Nonfederal **Service**: General medical and surgical

Staffed Beds: 25 **Admissions**: 1409 **Census**: 19 **Outpatient Visits**: 84218
Births: 481 **Total Expense ($000)**: 87888 **Payroll Expense ($000)**: 33864
Personnel: 436

VAN HORN—Culberson County

CULBERSON HOSPITAL (451338), Eisenhower–Farm Market Road 2185, Zip 79855, Mailing Address: P.O. Box 609, Zip 79855–0609; tel. 432/283–2760, **A**10 18 **F**3 7 40 43 93 107 114 119 127 133 154 **S** Preferred Management Corporation, Shawnee, OK
Primary Contact: John O'Hearn, Interim Chief Executive Officer
CMO: John Garner, D.O., Medical Director
Web address: www.culbersonhospital.org
Control: Corporation, Investor-owned (for-profit) **Service**: General medical and surgical

Staffed Beds: 14 **Admissions**: 30 **Census**: 1 **Outpatient Visits**: 10201
Births: 0 **Total Expense ($000)**: 9284 **Payroll Expense ($000)**: 4090
Personnel: 61

VERNON—Wilbarger County

☐ **NORTH TEXAS STATE HOSPITAL**, 4730 College Drive, Zip 76384–4009, Mailing Address: P.O. Box 2231, Zip 76385–2231; tel. 940/552–9901, **A**1 **F**30 39 50 56 57 68 75 87 96 97 98 99 100 101 103 130 132 135 143 146 149 154 **P**6 **S** Texas Department of State Health Services, Austin, TX
Primary Contact: Albert Ragland, Superintendent
CFO: Robin Moreno, Financial Officer
CIO: Chad Hughes, Information Officer
Web address: https://www.hhs.texas.gov/services/mental-health-substance-use/state-hospitals/north-texas-state-hospital
Control: State, Government, Nonfederal **Service**: Psychiatric

Staffed Beds: 530 **Admissions**: 922 **Census**: 340 **Outpatient Visits**: 0
Births: 0 **Total Expense ($000)**: 155657 **Payroll Expense ($000)**: 84025
Personnel: 1972

★ **WILBARGER GENERAL HOSPITAL (450584)**, 920 Hillcrest Drive, Zip 76384–3196; tel. 940/552–9351, **A**10 20 **F**3 11 15 28 29 30 34 35 40 43 45 57 59 60 64 65 74 75 77 79 81 82 84 85 86 93 97 100 107 108 110 111 114 119 130 133 146 148 149 154 157 **P**6 **S** Ovation Healthcare, Brentwood, TN
Primary Contact: Tom Siemers, Chief Executive Officer
CFO: Chris Dover, CPA, Chief Financial Officer
CMO: Travis Lehman, M.D., Medical Director
CHR: Alisha Nix, Director Human Resources
CNO: Tonya Price, Chief Nursing Officer
Web address: www.wghospital.com
Control: Hospital district or authority, Government, Nonfederal **Service**: General medical and surgical

Staffed Beds: 28 **Admissions**: 654 **Census**: 8 **Outpatient Visits**: 33325
Births: 0 **Total Expense ($000)**: 28582 **Payroll Expense ($000)**: 13811
Personnel: 186

Hospitals, U.S. / TEXAS

VICTORIA—Victoria County

★ ⇪ **CITIZENS MEDICAL CENTER (450023)**, 2701 Hospital Drive, Zip 77901–5749; tel. 361/573–9181, (Total facility includes 20 beds in nursing home–type unit) **A**10 19 21 **F**3 11 12 13 15 18 20 22 24 26 28 29 30 31 34 35 40 41 43 45 46 49 50 51 53 54 56 57 59 62 64 65 70 72 74 75 76 78 79 81 82 85 86 87 89 93 97 107 108 109 110 111 113 114 115 116 117 118 119 120 121 123 126 128 129 130 131 132 135 146 147 148 149 154 167 169
Primary Contact: Michael R. Olson, Chief Executive Officer
CFO: Carolyn Zafereo, Chief Accounting Officer
CMO: Daniel Cano, M.D., Chief Medical Officer
CIO: Russell Witte, Director Information Technology
CHR: Kathleen C Mosmeyer, Director Human Resources
Web address: www.citizensmedicalcenter.org
Control: County, Government, Nonfederal **Service**: General medical and surgical

> **Staffed Beds**: 265 **Admissions**: 7557 **Census**: 100 **Outpatient Visits**: 126738 **Births**: 878 **Total Expense ($000)**: 201871 **Payroll Expense ($000)**: 95523 **Personnel**: 1235

DETAR HEALTHCARE SYSTEM (450147), 506 East San Antonio Street, Zip 77901–6060, Mailing Address: P.O. Box 2089, Zip 77902–2089; tel. 361/575–7441, (Includes DETAR HOSPITAL NORTH, 101 Medical Drive, Victoria, Texas, Zip 77904–3198, tel. 361/573–6100; Bernard Leger, Chief Executive Officer) **A**1 3 5 10 19 **F**3 12 13 15 18 20 22 24 26 28 29 30 31 34 39 40 41 43 45 47 49 50 51 53 56 64 70 72 74 75 76 77 78 81 82 85 86 87 89 90 93 107 108 110 111 114 118 119 126 130 132 146 147 148 149 156 167 169 **P**5 **S** Community Health Systems, Inc., Franklin, TN
Primary Contact: Bernard Leger, Chief Executive Officer
COO: George N Parsley, Chief Operating Officer
CFO: Donald E Hagan, Chief Financial Officer
CMO: Conde Nevin Anderson, M.D., Chief of Staff
CIO: Kim Tompkins, Director Information Services
CHR: Dwight Linton, Director Human Resources
CNO: Sammie Drehr, Chief Nursing Officer
Web address: www.detar.com
Control: Corporation, Investor–owned (for–profit) **Service**: General medical and surgical

> **Staffed Beds**: 235 **Admissions**: 7667 **Census**: 90 **Outpatient Visits**: 198487 **Births**: 1066 **Total Expense ($000)**: 184204 **Payroll Expense ($000)**: 57677 **Personnel**: 926

PAM REHABILITATION HOSPITAL OF VICTORIA (673056), 101 James Coleman Drive, Zip 77904–3147; tel. 361/220–7900, **A**1 10 **F**3 29 74 75 90 **S** PAM Health, Enola, PA
Primary Contact: Tommy Beyer, Director of Operations
Web address: www.warmsprings.org/our-facilities/outpatient-rehabilitation/warm-springs-rehabilitation-center-victoria/
Control: Corporation, Investor–owned (for–profit) **Service**: Rehabilitation

> **Staffed Beds**: 26 **Admissions**: 801 **Census**: 22 **Outpatient Visits**: 0 **Births**: 0 **Total Expense ($000)**: 13436 **Payroll Expense ($000)**: 6531 **Personnel**: 118

PAM SPECIALTY HOSPITAL OF VICTORIA NORTH (452094), 102 Medical Drive, Zip 77904–3101; tel. 361/576–6200, (Includes PAM SPECIALTY HOSPITAL OF VICTORIA SOUTHEAST, 2701 Hospital Drive, 6th Floor, Victoria, Texas, Zip 77901–5748, tel. 361/237–1957; Christina Adrean, Chief Executive Officer) **A**1 10 **F**1 3 29 64 75 77 85 93 94 **S** PAM Health, Enola, PA
Primary Contact: Jason Dan. Hudson, R.N., Chief Executive Officer
CMO: Adam Burick, M.D., Chief Medical Officer
Web address: https://pamhealth.com/facilities/find-facility/specialty-hospitals/PAM-Specialty-Hospital-Victoria-North/about
Control: Corporation, Investor–owned (for–profit) **Service**: Acute long–term care hospital

> **Staffed Beds**: 42 **Admissions**: 739 **Census**: 35 **Outpatient Visits**: 11533 **Births**: 0 **Total Expense ($000)**: 25595 **Payroll Expense ($000)**: 10337 **Personnel**: 148

REGIONAL MEDICAL CENTER See Detar Hospital North

WACO—McLennan County

ASCENSION PROVIDENCE (450042), 6901 Medical Parkway, Zip 76712–7998, Mailing Address: P.O. Box 2589, Zip 76702–2589; tel. 254/751–4000, (Includes DEPAUL CENTER, 301 Londonderry Drive, Waco, Texas, Zip 76712, tel. 254/776–5970; Vicky Campbell, Vice President Mental Health and Support Services) **A**1 2 10 19 **F**3 11 13 15 18 20 22 24 26 28 29 30 31 34 35 37 38 40 41 43 45 46 47 49 50 54 57 58 59 61 64 70 74 75 76 77 78 79 81 82 84 85 87 93 96 97 100 102 104 107 108 110 111 114 115 119 126 129 130 131 132 135 146 149 154 164 167 169 **S** Ascension Healthcare, Saint Louis, MO
Primary Contact: Philip A. Patterson, President Providence Health Center/Network
CFO: Karen K. Richardson, Senior Vice President and Chief Financial Officer
CMO: Brian Becker, Vice President Medical Affairs and Chief Medical Officer
CIO: Jay Scherler, Vice President Finance and Chief Information Officer
CNO: Cyndy Dunlap, R.N., FACHE, Chief Nursing Officer
Web address: https://healthcare.ascension.org/locations/texas/txwac/waco-ascension-providence
Control: Church operated, Nongovernment, not–for–profit **Service**: General medical and surgical

> **Staffed Beds**: 285 **Admissions**: 14011 **Census**: 175 **Outpatient Visits**: 216355 **Births**: 1449 **Total Expense ($000)**: 302655 **Payroll Expense ($000)**: 100445 **Personnel**: 980

△ **BAYLOR SCOTT & WHITE MEDICAL CENTER – HILLCREST (450101)**, 100 Hillcrest Medical Boulevard, Zip 76712–8897; tel. 254/202–2000, **A**1 2 3 7 10 19 **F**3 8 13 15 17 18 20 22 24 26 28 29 30 31 34 35 37 38 40 43 44 45 46 49 50 51 54 55 56 57 58 59 68 70 72 74 75 76 77 78 79 80 81 82 83 84 85 86 89 90 92 93 94 96 97 102 107 108 110 111 115 118 119 120 121 123 126 129 130 131 132 135 144 146 147 148 149 154 156 167 169 **S** Baylor Scott & White Health, Dallas, TX
Primary Contact: Chris Lancaster, President
COO: David Blackwell, Vice President Operations
CFO: Richard Perkins, Chief Financial Officer
CMO: J. E. Morrison, M.D., M.P.H., Chief Medical Officer
CNO: Rebecca Kay Hardie, Chief Nursing Officer
Web address: www.sw.org/hillcrest-medical-center
Control: Other not–for–profit (including NFP Corporation) **Service**: General medical and surgical

> **Staffed Beds**: 260 **Admissions**: 16417 **Census**: 197 **Outpatient Visits**: 214742 **Births**: 2780 **Total Expense ($000)**: 400951 **Payroll Expense ($000)**: 125686 **Personnel**: 1233

CENTRAL TEXAS VETERANS HEALTH CARE SYSTEM, DORIS MILLER VETERANS MEDICAL CENTER See Central Texas Veterans HCS/Temple Tx, Temple

☐ **OCEANS BEHAVIORAL HEALTH OF WACO (454150)**, 5931 Crosslake Parkway, Zip 76712–6986; tel. 254/870–4874, **A**1 10 **F**29 34 35 64 98 100 101 103 104 130 132 149 153 154 164 **P**6 **S** Oceans Healthcare, Plano, TX
Primary Contact: Stuart Archer, Chief Executive Officer
Web address: https://oceanshealthcare.com/
Control: Corporation, Investor–owned (for–profit) **Service**: Psychiatric

> **Staffed Beds**: 48 **Admissions**: 1032 **Census**: 37 **Outpatient Visits**: 16691 **Births**: 0 **Total Expense ($000)**: 11811 **Payroll Expense ($000)**: 5885 **Personnel**: 83

WACO VETERANS AFFAIRS HOSPITAL See Central Texas Veterans Health Care System, Doris Miller Veterans Medical Center

WAXAHACHIE—Ellis County

BAYLOR SCOTT & WHITE MEDICAL CENTER–WAXAHACHIE (450372), 2400 North I–35E, Zip 75165; tel. 469/843–4000, **A**1 2 3 10 **F**3 8 11 12 13 15 18 20 22 28 29 30 31 34 35 37 40 43 45 46 47 48 49 50 51 56 58 59 60 64 65 68 70 73 74 75 76 77 78 79 80 81 84 85 93 96 100 102 107 108 110 111 114 115 116 117 118 119 120 121 123 126 129 130 131 132 135 145 146 147 148 149 154 164 167 168 169 **S** Baylor Scott & White Health, Dallas, TX
Primary Contact: Will Turner, Chief Executive Officer
COO: Cindy Murray, R.N., Chief Nursing Officer and Chief Operating Officer
CFO: Cheryl McMullan, Chief Financial Officer
CMO: Thomas Glenn Ledbetter, M.D., Chief Medical Officer
CNO: Cindy Murray, R.N., Chief Nursing Officer and Chief Operating Officer
Web address: www.baylorhealth.com/PhysiciansLocations/Waxahachie/Pages/Default.aspx
Control: Other not–for–profit (including NFP Corporation) **Service**: General medical and surgical

> **Staffed Beds**: 128 **Admissions**: 8685 **Census**: 103 **Outpatient Visits**: 111533 **Births**: 1249 **Total Expense ($000)**: 233449 **Payroll Expense ($000)**: 71231 **Personnel**: 708

Hospitals, U.S. / TEXAS

WEATHERFORD—Parker County

☐ **CLEARSKY REHABILITATION HOSPITAL OF WEATHERFORD (673062)**, 703 Eureka Street, Zip 76086-6547; tel. 682/803-0100, **A**1 10 **F**3 29 90 93 96 143 149 **S** ClearSky Health, West Lake Hills, TX
Primary Contact: Aaron Lee. Lopez, Chief Executive Officer
Web address: https://www.clearskyhealth.com/Weatherford/
Control: Partnership, Investor-owned (for-profit) **Service**: Rehabilitation

Staffed Beds: 26 **Admissions:** 678 **Census:** 21 **Outpatient Visits:** 435
Births: 0 **Total Expense ($000):** 10313 **Payroll Expense ($000):** 5063
Personnel: 73

✠ **MEDICAL CITY WEATHERFORD (450203)**, 713 East Anderson Street, Zip 76086-5705; tel. 682/582-1000, **A**1 3 5 10 **F**3 13 15 18 20 22 24 26 28 29 34 40 43 45 46 47 48 49 50 57 59 64 70 74 75 76 77 79 81 82 85 93 107 110 111 114 119 126 130 146 147 148 167 **S** HCA Healthcare, Nashville, TN
Primary Contact: Sean Kamber, Chief Executive Officer
CMO: Sanjeeb Shrestha, M.D., Chief Medical Staff
CIO: Brett Cates, Director Information Services
CNO: Donna Boone, MS, R.N., Chief Nursing Officer
Web address: www.weatherfordregional.com
Control: Partnership, Investor-owned (for-profit) **Service**: General medical and surgical

Staffed Beds: 96 **Admissions:** 6519 **Census:** 71 **Outpatient Visits:** 69487
Births: 703 **Total Expense ($000):** 113730 **Payroll Expense ($000):** 42151
Personnel: 522

WEBSTER—Harris County

COLUMBIA CLEAR LAKE MED CTR See Clear Lake Regional Medical Center

CORNERSTONE HOSPITAL OF HOUSTON AT CLEARLAKE See Vibra Hospital of Clear Lake

✠ **HCA HOUSTON HEALTHCARE CLEAR LAKE (450617)**, 500 W Medical Center Boulevard, Zip 77598-4220, Mailing Address: 500 West Medical Center Boulevard, Zip 77598-4220; tel. 281/332-2511, (Includes ALVIN DIAGNOSTIC AND URGENT CARE CENTER, 301 Medic Lane, Alvin, Texas, Zip 77511-5597, tel. 281/331-6141; CLEAR LAKE REGIONAL MEDICAL CENTER, 500 Medical Center Boulevard, Webster, Texas, Zip 77598-4286, tel. 281/338-3110; HCA HOUSTON HEALTHCARE MAINLAND, 6801 Emmett F Lowry Expy, Texas City, Texas, Zip 77591-2500, 6801 'E' 'F' Lowry Expressway, Zip 77591, tel. 409/938-5000; Tripp Montalbo, Chief Executive Officer) **A**1 2 3 5 10 **F**3 11 12 13 17 18 19 20 22 24 26 28 29 30 31 34 35 40 41 42 43 44 45 46 47 49 50 51 56 57 59 60 64 69 70 72 74 75 76 78 79 81 85 86 87 88 89 90 91 93 96 100 107 108 111 114 115 119 124 126 130 132 146 147 148 149 154 167 169 **S** HCA Healthcare, Nashville, TN
Primary Contact: Todd Caliva, FACHE, Chief Executive Officer
CFO: Chase Redden, Chief Financial Officer
CMO: William Killinger, M.D., Chief Medical Officer
CIO: Ley Samson, Director Management Information Systems
CHR: Brad Horst, Director Human Resources
Web address: www.clearlakermc.com
Control: Partnership, Investor-owned (for-profit) **Service**: General medical and surgical

Staffed Beds: 596 **Admissions:** 30837 **Census:** 424 **Outpatient Visits:** 175156 **Births:** 4054 **Total Expense ($000):** 463947 **Payroll Expense ($000):** 218601 **Personnel:** 2015

⇑ **HOUSTON PHYSICIANS HOSPITAL (670008)**, 333 North Texas Avenue, Suite 1000, Zip 77598-4966; tel. 281/557-5620, **A**10 21 **F**3 18 24 26 29 37 40 45 51 64 74 79 81 82 85 86 91 93 107 111 114 126 141 149 167
Primary Contact: Heather Womack, Chief Executive Officer
Web address: www.houstonphysianshospital.com
Control: Corporation, Investor-owned (for-profit) **Service**: Surgical

Staffed Beds: 15 **Admissions:** 682 **Census:** 4 **Outpatient Visits:** 130004
Births: 0 **Total Expense ($000):** 94226 **Payroll Expense ($000):** 23631
Personnel: 353

✠ **KINDRED HOSPITAL CLEAR LAKE (452075)**, 350 Blossom Street, Zip 77598; tel. 281/316-7800, **A**1 10 **F**1 3 29 30 45 57 60 64 75 77 84 85 91 95 96 107 130 148 **S** ScionHealth, Louisville, KY
Primary Contact: Angel Gradney, Chief Executive Officer
Web address: www.khclearlake.com
Control: Corporation, Investor-owned (for-profit) **Service**: Acute long-term care hospital

Staffed Beds: 110 **Admissions:** 617 **Census:** 48 **Outpatient Visits:** 3077
Births: 0 **Total Expense ($000):** 33576 **Payroll Expense ($000):** 16692
Personnel: 215

✠ **PAM REHABILITATION HOSPITAL OF CLEAR LAKE (453052)**, 110 East Medical Center Boulevard, Zip 77598-4301; tel. 832/224-9500, (Includes PAM REHABILITATION HOSPITAL OF CLEAR LAKE – NORTH, 655 East Medical Center Boulevard, Webster, Texas, Zip 77598-4328, tel. 281/286-1500; Johnny Bellew, Chief Executive Officer) **A**1 10 **F**3 29 90 91 93 95 96 130 148 154 **S** PAM Health, Enola, PA
Primary Contact: Claudia Hauser, Chief Executive Officer
Web address: https://postacutemedical.com
Control: Partnership, Investor-owned (for-profit) **Service**: Rehabilitation

Staffed Beds: 151 **Admissions:** 3282 **Census:** 110 **Outpatient Visits:** 44380 **Births:** 0 **Total Expense ($000):** 67304 **Payroll Expense ($000):** 32975 **Personnel:** 393

PAM REHABILITATION HOSPITAL OF CLEAR LAKE See Pam Rehabilitation Hospital of Clear Lake – North

VIBRA HOSPITAL OF CLEAR LAKE (452032), 709 Medical Center Boulevard, Zip 77598; tel. 281/332-3322, (Includes CORNERSTONE HOSPITAL OF HOUSTON – BELLAIRE, 5314 Dashwood, Houston, Texas, Zip 77081-4603, tel. 713/295-5300; Austin B. Cleveland, Chief Executive Officer) (Nonreporting) **A**10 22
Primary Contact: Amy Rodriguez, Chief Executive Officer
COO: Brenda Lucero, Chief Clinical Officer
CFO: A Shane Wells, Chief Financial Officer
CMO: Mark Barlow, M.D., Chief Medical Officer and President Medical Staff
CIO: Jerald Harris, Chief Information Officer
CHR: Yolanda Jacobs, Coordinator Human Resources
Web address: https://vhclearlake.com/
Control: Partnership, Investor-owned (for-profit) **Service**: Acute long-term care hospital

Staffed Beds: 74

WELLINGTON—Collingsworth County

COLLINGSWORTH GENERAL HOSPITAL (451355), 1013 15th Street, Zip 79095-3703, Mailing Address: P.O. Box 1112, Zip 79095-1112; tel. 806/447-2521, **A**10 18 **F**3 40 57 59 64 65 68 93 96 97 107 114 127 133 154 **S** Preferred Management Corporation, Shawnee, OK
Primary Contact: Candy Powell, Administrator
CFO: Larry Stephens, Chief Financial Officer
CMO: Wesley Nickens, M.D., Chief of Staff
CIO: Thomas T. Ng, Chief Information Officer
CHR: April Wright, Human Resources Officer
CNO: Vikki Barton, R.N., Chief Nursing Officer
Web address: www.collingsworthgeneral.net
Control: Corporation, Investor-owned (for-profit) **Service**: General medical and surgical

Staffed Beds: 13 **Admissions:** 82 **Census:** 2 **Outpatient Visits:** 9235
Births: 0 **Total Expense ($000):** 8255 **Payroll Expense ($000):** 3846
Personnel: 64

Hospital, Medicare Provider Number, Address, Telephone, Approval, Facility, and Physician Codes, Health Care System

★ American Hospital Association (AHA) membership ◯ Healthcare Facilities Accreditation Program ⇑ Center for Improvement in Healthcare Quality Accreditation
☐ The Joint Commission accreditation ◇ DNV Healthcare Inc. accreditation △ Commission on Accreditation of Rehabilitation Facilities (CARF) accreditation

Hospitals, U.S. / TEXAS

WESLACO—Hidalgo County

☐ **KNAPP MEDICAL CENTER (450128)**, 1401 East Eighth Street, Zip 78596–6640, Mailing Address: P.O. Box 1110, Zip 78599–1110; tel. 956/968–8567, **A**1 3 5 10 **F**3 11 13 15 18 19 20 26 29 30 31 34 35 38 39 40 43 44 46 49 50 51 56 57 59 60 64 70 73 74 75 76 77 78 79 81 82 84 85 86 87 89 93 107 108 110 111 114 115 119 130 131 132 134 135 146 147 148 149 151 154 156 167 169 **P**8 **S** Prime Healthcare, Ontario, CA
Primary Contact: Rene Lopez, Chief Executive Officer
CFO: Dinah L. Gonzalez, Chief Financial Officer
CIO: Teri Garza, Director Health Information Services
CHR: Emmett Craig, Chief Human Resources Officer
CNO: Anna Hinojosa, MSN, R.N., Interim Chief Nursing Officer
Web address: www.knappmed.org
Control: Other not–for–profit (including NFP Corporation) **Service**: General medical and surgical

Staffed Beds: 154 **Admissions**: 5996 **Census**: 65 **Outpatient Visits**: 56532 **Births**: 1317 **Total Expense ($000)**: 101431 **Payroll Expense ($000)**: 36845 **Personnel**: 476

☐ **WESLACO REGIONAL REHABILITATION HOSPITAL (453091)**, 906 South James Street, Zip 78596–9840; tel. 956/969–2222, **A**1 10 **F**3 29 34 35 68 82 86 87 90 96 130 132 148 149 154 **S** Ernest Health, Inc., Albuquerque, NM
Primary Contact: Diana Schultz, Chief Executive Officer
CFO: Ernest Nash, Chief Financial Officer
CMO: Daisy Arce, President Medical Staff
CHR: Debbie Pemelton, Director Human Resources
CNO: Rita Mata–Guerrero, Director of Nursing
Web address: www.wrrh.ernesthealth.com
Control: Corporation, Investor–owned (for–profit) **Service**: Rehabilitation

Staffed Beds: 32 **Admissions**: 454 **Census**: 17 **Outpatient Visits**: 4982 **Births**: 0 **Total Expense ($000)**: 9881 **Payroll Expense ($000)**: 5071 **Personnel**: 78

WEST LAKE HILLS—Travis County

⇑ **THE HOSPITAL AT WESTLAKE MEDICAL CENTER (670006)**, 5656 Bee Caves Road, Suite M302, Zip 78746–5814; tel. 512/327–0000, (Nonreporting) **A**10 21
Primary Contact: Jerry Jasper, Interim Chief Executive Officer
CFO: Devon Culbert, Controller
CMO: Tom Burns, M.D., Chief of Staff
CHR: Kellie Bryson, Director Human Resources
Web address: www.westlakemedical.com
Control: Partnership, Investor–owned (for–profit) **Service**: General medical and surgical

Staffed Beds: 23

WHEELER—Wheeler County

★ **PARKVIEW HOSPITAL (451334)**, 901 Sweetwater Street, Zip 79096–2421, Mailing Address: P.O. Box 1030, Zip 79096–1030; tel. 806/826–5581, (Total facility includes 2 beds in nursing home–type unit) **A**10 18 **F**3 7 10 40 43 59 62 64 65 68 91 93 107 114 127 128 130 133 148
Primary Contact: Cecil W. Gaither, Interim Chief Executive Officer
CFO: Jace Henderson, Chief Financial Officer
CMO: John P. Lavelle, M.D., Chief Medical Officer
CNO: Melisa Scales, Director of Nursing
Web address: www.parkviewhosp.org
Control: Hospital district or authority, Government, Nonfederal **Service**: General medical and surgical

Staffed Beds: 16 **Admissions**: 44 **Census**: 1 **Outpatient Visits**: 5386 **Births**: 0 **Total Expense ($000)**: 10913 **Payroll Expense ($000)**: 4907 **Personnel**: 112

WICHITA FALLS—Wichita County

BETHANIA REGIONAL HEALTH CNTR See United Regional Health Care System–Eleventh Street Campus

⊞ **ENCOMPASS HEALTH REHABILITATION HOSPITAL OF WICHITA FALLS (453054)**, 3901 Armory Road, Zip 76302–2204; tel. 940/720–5700, **A**1 10 **F**3 28 29 68 74 75 77 79 86 87 90 91 94 95 96 130 132 **S** Encompass Health Corporation, Birmingham, AL
Primary Contact: Jody Gregory, Chief Executive Officer
CMO: Virgil Frardo, M.D., Medical Director
CIO: Mary Walker, Manager Information Technology
CHR: Kathleen Pirtle, Director Human Resources
CNO: Jody S Gregory, R.N., Chief Nursing Officer
Web address: www.healthsouthwichitafalls.com
Control: Partnership, Investor–owned (for–profit) **Service**: Rehabilitation

Staffed Beds: 63 **Admissions**: 1622 **Census**: 58 **Outpatient Visits**: 0 **Births**: 0 **Total Expense ($000)**: 22214 **Payroll Expense ($000)**: 13054 **Personnel**: 185

KELL WEST REGIONAL HOSPITAL (450827), 5420 Kell West Boulevard, Zip 76310–1610; tel. 940/692–5888, **A**10 22 **F**3 29 37 39 40 51 54 59 65 74 75 79 81 85 87 97 102 107 108 114 119 126 129 130 131 135 149 154 167
Primary Contact: Jerry Myers, M.D., Chief Executive Officer and Medical Director
CFO: Fran Lindemann, Director Finance
Web address: www.kellwest.com
Control: Partnership, Investor–owned (for–profit) **Service**: General medical and surgical

Staffed Beds: 15 **Admissions**: 626 **Census**: 4 **Outpatient Visits**: 27858 **Total Expense ($000)**: 31592 **Payroll Expense ($000)**: 10559 **Personnel**: 236

☐ **KPC PROMISE HOSPITAL OF WICHITA FALLS (452068)**, 1103 Grace Street, Zip 76301–4414; tel. 940/720–6633, **A**1 10 **F**1 3 29 75 100 119 135 148 **S** KPC Healthcare, Inc., Santa Ana, CA
Primary Contact: Rachel Bailey, Chief Executive Officer
CFO: Debbie Herder, Controller
CMO: Robert McBroom, M.D., Medical Director
CIO: Gail McIlroy, Director Medical Records
CNO: Deanna Dowling, R.N., Chief Nursing Officer
Web address: www.wichitafalls.kpcph.com/
Control: Corporation, Investor–owned (for–profit) **Service**: Acute long–term care hospital

Staffed Beds: 31 **Admissions**: 261 **Census**: 15 **Outpatient Visits**: 0 **Births**: 0 **Total Expense ($000)**: 8535 **Payroll Expense ($000)**: 4100 **Personnel**: 92

☐ **NORTH TEXAS STATE HOSPITAL, WICHITA FALLS CAMPUS (454008)**, 6515 Lake Road, Zip 76308–5419, Mailing Address: Box 300, Zip 76307–0300; tel. 940/692–1220, (Nonreporting) **A**1 3 10
Primary Contact: Albert Ragland, Superintendent
CFO: Robin Moreno, Chief Financial Officer
CMO: Eulon Ross Taylor, Clinical Director
CIO: Chad Hughes, Chief Information Officer
Web address: www.online.dshs.state.tx.us/northtexassh/default.htm
Control: State, Government, Nonfederal **Service**: Psychiatric

Staffed Beds: 640

☐ **RED RIVER HOSPITAL, LLC (454018)**, 1505 Eighth Street, Zip 76301–3106; tel. 940/322–3171, **A**1 10 **F**4 5 29 38 50 86 87 98 99 100 101 102 103 104 105 130 135 143 149 152 153 157 160 164 165 **S** Acadia Healthcare Company, Inc., Franklin, TN
Primary Contact: Nelson Alexander. Wanee, Chief Executive Officer
CFO: Bruce Porter, Chief Financial Officer
CMO: Harvey C Martin, M.D., Medical Director
CIO: Fay Helton, Director Medical Records
CHR: Kimberley Pellegrin, Director, Human Resources
CNO: Glenda Lawrence, R.N., Chief Nursing Officer
Web address: www.redriverhospital.com
Control: Corporation, Investor–owned (for–profit) **Service**: Psychiatric

Staffed Beds: 96 **Admissions**: 2121 **Census**: 72 **Outpatient Visits**: 3777 **Births**: 0 **Total Expense ($000)**: 19043 **Payroll Expense ($000)**: 10267 **Personnel**: 165

Hospitals, U.S. / TEXAS

⊞ **UNITED REGIONAL HEALTH CARE SYSTEM (450010)**, 1600 11th Street, Zip 76301–4300; tel. 940/764–7000, (Includes UNITED REGIONAL HEALTH CARE SYSTEM–ELEVENTH STREET CAMPUS, 1600 11th Street, Wichita Falls, Texas, Zip 76301–9988, tel. 940/764–7000) **A**1 10 20 **F**3 11 12 13 15 17 18 20 21 22 24 26 28 29 30 31 32 34 35 37 39 40 43 44 45 46 47 48 49 50 51 53 57 59 60 61 64 65 68 70 71 73 74 75 76 77 78 79 80 81 82 84 85 86 87 89 91 92 93 102 107 108 110 111 114 115 118 119 126 130 131 132 134 146 147 148 149 154 156 167 169
Primary Contact: Phyllis A. Cowling, CPA, President and Chief Executive Officer
CFO: Robert M Pert, Vice President Finance and Chief Financial Officer
CIO: Stephanie McDonell, Vice President and Chief Information Officer
CHR: Kristi Faulkner, Vice President Organizational Growth
Web address: www.unitedregional.org
Control: Other not–for–profit (including NFP Corporation) **Service**: General medical and surgical

Staffed Beds: 293 **Admissions**: 16083 **Census**: 176 **Outpatient Visits**: 133062 **Births**: 1849 **Total Expense ($000)**: 389980 **Payroll Expense ($000)**: 162141 **Personnel**: 1887

WINNIE—Chambers County

RICELAND MEDICAL CENTER (451328), 538 Broadway, Zip 77665–7600; tel. 409/296–6000, **A**10 18 **F**3 8 15 29 34 40 54 57 59 64 65 81 82 93 105 107 110 111 114 119 127 133 146 154
Primary Contact: Suggie Daigle, Administrator
CFO: Julie Harris, Chief Financial Officer
CMO: Leonidas Andres, M.D., Chief of Staff
CHR: Anha Simon, Director Human Resources
Web address: www.energis.in/index.html
Control: Partnership, Investor–owned (for–profit) **Service**: General medical and surgical

Staffed Beds: 25 **Admissions**: 300 **Census**: 3 **Outpatient Visits**: 72787 **Births**: 0 **Total Expense ($000)**: 37890 **Payroll Expense ($000)**: 15696 **Personnel**: 290

WINNSBORO—Wood County

⊞ **CHRISTUS MOTHER FRANCES HOSPITAL – WINNSBORO (451381)**, 719 West Coke Road, Zip 75494–3011; tel. 903/342–5227, **A**1 10 18 **F**3 8 29 30 34 35 40 43 56 77 81 85 87 93 107 115 119 133 149 156 **S** CHRISTUS Health, Irving, TX
Primary Contact: Paul Harvey, President and Chief Executive Officer
CFO: Glenn Peltier, Chief Financial Officer
CNO: Kevin Jablonski, Chief Nursing Officer
Web address: www.tmfhs.org
Control: Church operated, Nongovernment, not–for–profit **Service**: General medical and surgical

Staffed Beds: 14 **Admissions**: 353 **Census**: 8 **Outpatient Visits**: 25036 **Births**: 0 **Total Expense ($000)**: 20589 **Payroll Expense ($000)**: 6668 **Personnel**: 111

WINTERS—Runnels County

NORTH RUNNELS HOSPITAL (451315), 7821 State Highway 153, Zip 79567–7345, Mailing Address: P.O. Box 185, Zip 79567–0185; tel. 325/754–4553, **A**10 18 **F**7 11 29 40 54 57 59 62 65 66 68 69 93 97 107 119 127 133 154
Primary Contact: Trace George, Chief Financial Officer
CFO: Benny Helm, Chief Financial Officer
CMO: Mark McKinnon, M.D., Chief of Staff
CNO: Bobbie Collom, Nursing Director
Web address: https://northrunnelsmedicalcenter.com/
Control: Hospital district or authority, Government, Nonfederal **Service**: General medical and surgical

Staffed Beds: 15 **Admissions**: 153 **Census**: 2 **Outpatient Visits**: 11749 **Births**: 0 **Total Expense ($000)**: 12762 **Payroll Expense ($000)**: 6296 **Personnel**: 79

WOODVILLE—Tyler County

★ **TYLER COUNTY HOSPITAL (450460)**, 1100 West Bluff Street, Zip 75979–4799, Mailing Address: P.O. Box 549, Zip 75979–0549; tel. 409/283–8141, **A**10 20 **F**3 11 30 35 40 43 57 59 64 75 107 114 119 127 146 149
Primary Contact: Sondra D. Williams, R.N., MSN, Chief Executive Officer
CFO: Scott Elton McCluskey, Chief Financial Officer
CMO: Paula Lajean Denson, M.D., President
CIO: Rachel Joy Haygood, Director Information Technology
CHR: Kenneth Lynn Jobe, Director Human Resources
Web address: www.tchospital.us
Control: County, Government, Nonfederal **Service**: General medical and surgical

Staffed Beds: 25 **Admissions**: 202 **Census**: 2 **Outpatient Visits**: 22086 **Births**: 0 **Total Expense ($000)**: 15140 **Payroll Expense ($000)**: 5398 **Personnel**: 130

YOAKUM—Lavaca County

★ **YOAKUM COMMUNITY HOSPITAL (451346)**, 1200 Carl Ramert Drive, Zip 77995–4868; tel. 361/293–2321, **A**10 18 **F**3 11 15 28 29 34 35 40 43 56 57 59 64 70 79 81 85 86 93 104 107 108 111 114 119 129 132 133 134 146 148 153 **S** Community Hospital Corporation, Plano, TX
Primary Contact: Tiffany Miller, Chief Executive Officer
CFO: Robert Foret, Chief Financial Officer
CMO: Timothy Wagner, M.D., Chief Medical Staff
CIO: Barbara Vasek, Director Information Technology
CHR: Karen Roznovsky, Director Human Resources
CNO: Jennifer Franklin, R.N., Chief Clinical Officer
Web address: www.yoakumhospital.org
Control: Other not–for–profit (including NFP Corporation) **Service**: General medical and surgical

Staffed Beds: 23 **Admissions**: 520 **Census**: 8 **Outpatient Visits**: 22101 **Births**: 0 **Total Expense ($000)**: 23347 **Payroll Expense ($000)**: 9579 **Personnel**: 143

Hospitals, U.S. / UTAH

UTAH

AMERICAN FORK—Utah County

✠ **AMERICAN FORK HOSPITAL (460023)**, 170 North 1100 East, Zip 84003–2096; tel. 801/855–3300, **A**1 10 **F**3 9 13 15 18 28 29 31 34 35 38 40 41 42 43 44 45 48 49 50 53 54 57 59 60 63 64 68 70 73 75 76 77 78 79 81 82 84 85 86 87 90 93 100 101 102 104 107 108 110 111 115 117 118 119 120 121 123 124 126 129 130 131 132 135 141 145 146 147 148 149 150 154 157 164 167 169 **S** Intermountain Health, Salt Lake City, UT
Primary Contact: Jason Wilson, President
CFO: Craig Carrier, Chief Financial Officer
CMO: Scott Van Wagoner, M.D., Chief Medical Officer
CIO: Mary Gathers, Manager Information Systems
CHR: Scott Walker, Chief Human Resource Officer
Web address: https://intermountainhealthcare.org/locations/american-fork-hospital/
Control: Other not–for–profit (including NFP Corporation) **Service**: General medical and surgical

Staffed Beds: 68 **Admissions:** 6170 **Census:** 48 **Outpatient Visits:** 291511 **Births:** 2953 **Total Expense ($000):** 189948 **Payroll Expense ($000):** 55699 **Personnel:** 676

BEAVER—Beaver County

BEAVER VALLEY HOSPITAL (461335), 1109 North 100 West, Zip 84713, Mailing Address: P.O. Box 1670, Zip 84713–1670; tel. 435/438–7100, (Nonreporting) **A**10 18
Primary Contact: Scott Langford, Administrator
Web address: www.bvhospital.com/
Control: City, Government, Nonfederal **Service**: General medical and surgical

Staffed Beds: 27

BLANDING—San Juan County

★ **BLUE MOUNTAIN HOSPITAL (461310)**, 802 South 200 West, Suite A, Zip 84511–3910; tel. 435/678–3993, **A**3 10 18 **F**3 8 12 13 15 29 34 35 38 39 40 41 44 45 47 50 60 64 65 68 75 76 78 79 81 87 100 102 107 109 110 111 114 119 131 133 146 148 154 169 **P**6
Primary Contact: Jeremy Lyman, Chief Executive Officer
CFO: Jimmy Johnson, Chief Financial Officer
CMO: Mahana Fisher, M.D., Medical Director
CIO: Anthony Torres, Manager Information Technology
CHR: Gail M. Northern, Director Human Resources
CNO: Derrill Kent Turek, R.N., Chief Nursing Officer
Web address: www.bmhutah.org/
Control: Other not–for–profit (including NFP Corporation) **Service**: General medical and surgical

Staffed Beds: 11 **Admissions:** 479 **Census:** 3 **Outpatient Visits:** 6922 **Births:** 87 **Total Expense ($000):** 19715 **Payroll Expense ($000):** 7045

BOUNTIFUL—Davis County

✠ **LAKEVIEW HOSPITAL (460042)**, 630 East Medical Drive, Zip 84010–4908; tel. 801/299–2200, (Nonreporting) **A**1 10 **S** HCA Healthcare, Nashville, TN
Primary Contact: Troy Wood, Chief Executive Officer
CFO: Wayne Dalton, Chief Financial Officer
CMO: Michael Hess, M.D., Chief Medical Officer
CIO: Mark Ellis, Director Information Technology
CHR: Julie Isom, Director Human Resources
CNO: Marilyn Mariani, R.N., Chief Nursing Officer
Web address: www.lakeviewhospital.com
Control: Corporation, Investor–owned (for–profit) **Service**: General medical and surgical

Staffed Beds: 119

SOUTH DAVIS COMMUNITY HOSPITAL (462003), 401 South 400 East, Zip 84010–4933; tel. 801/295–2361, (Nonreporting) **A**10
Primary Contact: Mechelle Wiggill, Chief Executive Officer
CMO: Scott Southworth, M.D., Medical Director
CHR: Jamey Sulser, Director Human Resources
Web address: www.sdch.com
Control: Other not–for–profit (including NFP Corporation) **Service**: Acute long–term care hospital

Staffed Beds: 176

BRIGHAM CITY—Box Elder County

✠ **BRIGHAM CITY COMMUNITY HOSPITAL (460017)**, 950 South Medical Drive, Zip 84302–4724; tel. 435/734–9471, (Nonreporting) **A**1 10 **S** HCA Healthcare, Nashville, TN
Primary Contact: Richard Spuhler, Chief Executive Officer
CMO: Derrick Walker, M.D., Chief Medical Officer
CIO: Steve Reichard, Manager Information Systems
CHR: Tracie Greene, Director Human Resources
CNO: Jerry Bushman, Chief Nursing Officer
Web address: www.brighamcityhospital.com
Control: Corporation, Investor–owned (for–profit) **Service**: General medical and surgical

Staffed Beds: 40

CEDAR CITY—Iron County

✠ **CEDAR CITY HOSPITAL (460007)**, 1303 North Main Street, Zip 84721–9746; tel. 435/868–5000, **A**1 10 20 **F**3 9 13 15 18 28 29 31 34 35 38 39 40 41 43 44 45 50 51 54 57 59 60 64 68 70 75 76 77 78 79 81 82 84 85 86 87 89 90 93 97 100 101 102 104 107 108 110 111 115 117 118 119 120 121 123 124 130 131 132 135 141 146 147 148 149 150 154 155 156 157 164 168 169 **S** Intermountain Health, Salt Lake City, UT
Primary Contact: Eric Packer, President
CFO: Craig Corry, Chief Financial Officer
CMO: Gerald Rowland, M.D., Chief Medical Officer
CIO: Becki Bronson, Chief Information Officer
CHR: Amy Martin, Chief Human Resource Officer
CNO: Cyndi Wallace, R.N., MSN, Chief Nursing Officer
Web address: https://intermountainhealthcare.org/locations/cedar-city-hospital/
Control: Other not–for–profit (including NFP Corporation) **Service**: General medical and surgical

Staffed Beds: 48 **Admissions:** 2054 **Census:** 12 **Outpatient Visits:** 193269 **Births:** 787 **Total Expense ($000):** 111516 **Payroll Expense ($000):** 29593 **Personnel:** 365

DELTA—Millard County

★ **DELTA COMMUNITY MEDICAL CENTER (461300)**, 126 South White Sage Avenue, Zip 84624–8937; tel. 435/864–5591, **A**10 18 **F**1 3 13 15 29 34 35 38 40 41 43 45 50 54 59 64 65 68 75 76 81 84 85 86 87 97 100 101 102 104 107 110 111 115 119 128 129 130 133 135 147 148 149 150 154 157 164 169 **S** Intermountain Health, Salt Lake City, UT
Primary Contact: Kurt Forsyth, President
CFO: Vince Donohue, Chief Financial Officer
CHR: Mathias Moyano, Chief Human Resource Officer
CNO: Ches Jacobson, Chief Nursing Officer
Web address: https://intermountainhealthcare.org/locations/delta-community-hospital/
Control: Other not–for–profit (including NFP Corporation) **Service**: General medical and surgical

Staffed Beds: 15 **Admissions:** 186 **Census:** 1 **Outpatient Visits:** 20257 **Births:** 77 **Total Expense ($000):** 16733 **Payroll Expense ($000):** 6273 **Personnel:** 63

Hospitals, U.S. / UTAH

DRAPER—Salt Lake County

✠ **LONE PEAK HOSPITAL (460060)**, 1925 South State Street, Zip 84020; tel. 801/545–8000, (Nonreporting) **A**1 10 **S** HCA Healthcare, Nashville, TN
Primary Contact: Brian Lines, Chief Executive Officer
CFO: Braden Tibbitts, Chief Financial Officer
CMO: Julie Fox, M.D., Chief Medical Officer
CNO: Melinda Patterson, MSN, R.N., Chief Nursing Officer
Web address: www.lonepeakhospital.com
Control: Corporation, Investor–owned (for–profit) **Service:** General medical and surgical

Staffed Beds: 32

FILLMORE—Millard County

★ **FILLMORE COMMUNITY HOSPITAL (461301)**, 674 South Highway 99, Zip 84631–5013; tel. 435/743–5591, **A**10 18 **F**3 13 15 29 31 34 35 38 40 41 43 44 45 50 54 57 59 64 65 68 75 76 81 84 85 86 87 97 100 101 102 104 107 110 111 115 119 128 129 130 132 133 135 146 147 148 149 150 154 157 164 169 **S** Intermountain Health, Salt Lake City, UT
Primary Contact: Kurt Forsyth, President
CFO: Vince Donohue, Chief Financial Officer
CHR: Mathias Moyano, Chief Human Resource Officer
CNO: Andrea Wardle, Chief Nursing Officer
Web address: www.ihc.com
Control: Other not–for–profit (including NFP Corporation) **Service:** General medical and surgical

Staffed Beds: 7 **Admissions:** 241 **Census:** 2 **Outpatient Visits:** 13146
Births: 38 **Total Expense ($000):** 13771 **Payroll Expense ($000):** 5471
Personnel: 53

GUNNISON—Sanpete County

★ **GUNNISON VALLEY HOSPITAL (461306)**, 64 East 100 North, Zip 84634, Mailing Address: P.O. Box 759, Zip 84634–0759; tel. 435/528–7246, (Nonreporting) **A**10 18
Primary Contact: Brenda Bartholomew, Chief Executive Officer
CFO: Brian Murray, Chief Financial Officer
CIO: Mike Ryan, Director of Information Services
CNO: Brenda Bartholomew, Chief Nursing Officer
Web address: www.gvhospital.org
Control: County, Government, Nonfederal **Service:** General medical and surgical

Staffed Beds: 119

HEBER CITY—Wasatch County

★ **HEBER VALLEY HOSPITAL (461307)**, 1485 South Highway 40, Zip 84032–3522; tel. 435/654–2500, **A**10 18 **F**3 9 13 15 18 29 31 34 35 36 38 40 41 43 44 45 50 51 53 54 57 59 60 63 64 68 75 76 77 79 81 84 85 86 87 89 90 93 100 101 102 104 107 110 111 115 119 128 129 130 131 133 135 146 147 148 149 150 154 157 164 169 **S** Intermountain Health, Salt Lake City, UT
Primary Contact: Si William. Hutt, President
CFO: Jennilyn Ferry, Chief Financial Officer
CMO: Stanton B McDonald, M.D., Medical Director
CIO: Dennis De Melo, Chief Information Officer
CHR: Bruce Dent, Human Resources Director
CNO: Jill Teuscher, Chief Nursing Officer
Web address: https://intermountainhealthcare.org/locations/heber-valley-hospital/
Control: Other not–for–profit (including NFP Corporation) **Service:** General medical and surgical

Staffed Beds: 19 **Admissions:** 708 **Census:** 4 **Outpatient Visits:** 78050
Births: 229 **Total Expense ($000):** 55788 **Payroll Expense ($000):** 17204
Personnel: 147

KANAB—Kane County

KANE COUNTY HOSPITAL (461309), 355 North Main Street, Zip 84741–3260; tel. 435/644–5811, **A**10 18 **F**7 11 13 29 40 57 59 64 75 76 79 81 107 111 115 119 128 130 131 132 133 154 167
Primary Contact: Kurt Loveless, Chief Executive Officer
CFO: Stephen Howells, Chief Financial Officer
CMO: Darin Ott, D.O., Chief of Staff
CHR: Laurali Noteman, Director Human Resources
Web address: https://kchosp.net/
Control: Hospital district or authority, Government, Nonfederal **Service:** General medical and surgical

Staffed Beds: 25 **Admissions:** 121 **Census:** 1 **Outpatient Visits:** 13111
Births: 22 **Total Expense ($000):** 18620 **Payroll Expense ($000):** 6882

LAYTON—Davis County

★ ⇧ **HOLY CROSS HOSPITAL – DAVIS (460041)**, 1600 West Antelope Drive, Zip 84041–1142; tel. 801/807–1000, **A**10 21 **F**3 8 13 15 20 22 29 30 34 35 38 40 42 43 45 46 47 48 49 50 51 54 57 59 60 63 64 65 68 70 72 74 75 76 77 78 79 80 81 85 86 87 89 91 92 93 98 101 102 105 107 108 109 110 111 114 115 116 117 118 119 120 121 123 124 126 129 130 135 146 147 148 154 156 164 167 **S** CommonSpirit Health, Chicago, IL
Primary Contact: Kyle J. Brostrom, Chief Executive Officer
COO: Jared Spackman, Chief Operating Officer
CFO: Jared Spackman, Chief Financial Officer
CMO: Les Greenwood, M.D., President, Medical Staff
CIO: Shane Williams, Director Information Systems
CHR: Tara Figgins, Director Human Resources
CNO: J Christopher Johnson, Chief Nursing Officer
Web address: https://www.centura.org/location/holy-cross-hospital-davis/hc
Control: Other not–for–profit (including NFP Corporation) **Service:** General medical and surgical

Staffed Beds: 220 **Admissions:** 4836 **Census:** 55 **Outpatient Visits:** 94434
Births: 1407 **Total Expense ($000):** 186314 **Payroll Expense ($000):** 50579 **Personnel:** 625

✠ **LAYTON HOSPITAL (460061)**, 201 West Layton Parkway, Zip 84041–3692; tel. 801/543–6000, **A**1 10 **F**3 8 13 18 19 28 29 31 34 35 38 40 41 43 44 45 49 50 51 53 59 60 63 64 68 70 73 75 76 77 78 79 81 82 84 85 86 87 90 93 100 101 102 104 107 108 110 111 115 118 119 126 129 130 135 141 146 147 148 149 150 154 156 157 164 169 **S** Intermountain Health, Salt Lake City, UT
Primary Contact: Kelly L. Duffin, President
CFO: Trever Porter, Chief Financial Officer
CMO: Glen Morrell, M.D., Chief Medical Officer
CHR: Jennifer L. Jensen, Chief Human Resource Officer
Web address: https://intermountainhealthcare.org/locations/layton-hospital/medical-services/
Control: Other not–for–profit (including NFP Corporation) **Service:** General medical and surgical

Staffed Beds: 37 **Admissions:** 3052 **Census:** 21 **Outpatient Visits:** 178172
Births: 1464 **Total Expense ($000):** 127249 **Payroll Expense ($000):** 32112 **Personnel:** 389

LOGAN—Cache County

✠ **LOGAN REGIONAL HOSPITAL (460015)**, 1400 North 500 East, Zip 84341–2455; tel. 435/716–1000, **A**1 10 19 **F**3 5 9 13 15 18 19 20 22 28 29 31 34 35 37 38 39 40 41 43 44 45 49 50 51 54 56 57 59 60 63 64 68 70 73 75 76 77 78 79 81 84 85 86 87 90 93 97 98 100 101 102 104 107 108 110 111 115 117 118 119 120 121 123 124 126 128 129 130 131 132 134 135 141 146 147 148 149 150 154 157 160 161 162 164 167 168 169 **S** Intermountain Health, Salt Lake City, UT
Primary Contact: Brandon McBride, President
COO: Brandon McBride, Operations Officer
CFO: Justin Wiser, Chief Financial Officer
CMO: Todd A Brown, M.D., Medical Director
CIO: Dave Felts, Chief Information Systems
CHR: Jolene Clonts, Director Human Resources
CNO: Neil C Perkes, Operations Officer
Web address: www.loganregionalhospital.org
Control: Other not–for–profit (including NFP Corporation) **Service:** General medical and surgical

Staffed Beds: 139 **Admissions:** 6057 **Census:** 51 **Outpatient Visits:** 399098 **Births:** 1927 **Total Expense ($000):** 260599 **Payroll Expense ($000):** 67266 **Personnel:** 816

MILFORD—Beaver County

★ **MILFORD VALLEY MEMORIAL HOSPITAL (461305)**, 850 North Main Street, Zip 84751–0640, Mailing Address: P.O. Box 640, Zip 84751–0640; tel. 435/387–2411, (Nonreporting) **A**10 18
Primary Contact: Scott Langford, Administrator
COO: Michelle Barton, Chief Operating Officer
CFO: Tyler Moss, Chief Financial Officer
CNO: Amy Contreras Esq, Chief Nursing Officer
Web address: www.milfordmemorialhospital.org
Control: Hospital district or authority, Government, Nonfederal **Service:** General medical and surgical

Staffed Beds: 25

Hospital, Medicare Provider Number, Address, Telephone, Approval, Facility, and Physician Codes, Health Care System

★ American Hospital Association (AHA) membership
☐ The Joint Commission accreditation
◯ Healthcare Facilities Accreditation Program
◇ DNV Healthcare Inc. accreditation
⇧ Center for Improvement in Healthcare Quality Accreditation
△ Commission on Accreditation of Rehabilitation Facilities (CARF) accreditation

© 2025 AHA Guide

Hospitals, U.S. / UTAH

MOAB—Grand County

★ **MOAB REGIONAL HOSPITAL (461302)**, 450 West Williams Way, Zip 84532-2065, Mailing Address: P.O. Box 998, Zip 84532-0998; tel. 435/719-3500, (Nonreporting) **A** 3 10 18
Primary Contact: Jennifer Sadoff, Chief Executive Officer
COO: Vicki Gigliotti, Chief Clinical Officer
CFO: Craig M Daniels, Chief Financial Officer
CMO: Dylan Cole, Chief Medical Officer
CIO: Mike Foster, Manager Information Systems
CHR: Katherine Sullivan, Director, Human Resources
Web address: www.mrhmoab.org
Control: Other not-for-profit (including NFP Corporation) **Service**: General medical and surgical

Staffed Beds: 17

MONTICELLO—San Juan County

★ **SAN JUAN HEALTH SERVICE DISTRICT (461308)**, 380 West 100 North, Zip 84535, Mailing Address: P.O. Box 308, Zip 84535-0308; tel. 435/587-2116, (Nonreporting) **A** 10 18
Primary Contact: Clayton Holt, Chief Executive Officer
CFO: Lyman Duncan, Chief Financial Officer
CMO: Kelly Jeppesen, Chief Medical Officer
CIO: Julie Bingham, IT Supervisor
CHR: Deana Dalton, Human Resources
CNO: Ashley Reynolds, Chief Nursing Officer
Web address: www.sanjuanhealthservices.org/
Control: County, Government, Nonfederal **Service**: General medical and surgical

Staffed Beds: 25

MOUNT PLEASANT—Sanpete County

★ **SANPETE VALLEY HOSPITAL (461303)**, 1100 South Medical Drive, Zip 84647-2222; tel. 435/462-2441, **A** 10 18 **F** 3 13 15 29 31 34 35 38 39 40 41 43 44 45 50 57 59 63 64 65 68 75 76 77 78 79 81 84 85 86 87 100 101 102 104 107 110 111 115 119 129 130 131 132 133 135 141 146 147 148 149 150 154 157 164 167 169 **S** Intermountain Health, Salt Lake City, UT
Primary Contact: Aaron C. Wood, President
COO: Kristina Skinner, Director Quality
CFO: Vince Donohue, Chief Financial Officer
CMO: Robert Armstrong, M.D., Chief Medical Officer
CIO: Michael Ence, Computer Specialist
CHR: Katey Nelson, Chief Human Resource Officer
CNO: Ryan Robison, Chief Nursing Officer
Web address: www.intermountainhealthcare.com
Control: Other not-for-profit (including NFP Corporation) **Service**: General medical and surgical

Staffed Beds: 14 **Admissions**: 412 **Census**: 3 **Outpatient Visits**: 42141 **Births**: 134 **Total Expense ($000)**: 30541 **Payroll Expense ($000)**: 10167 **Personnel**: 103

MURRAY—Salt Lake County

▣ △ **INTERMOUNTAIN MEDICAL CENTER (460010)**, 5121 South Cottonwood Street, Zip 84107-5701; tel. 801/507-7000, **A** 1 2 3 5 7 10 19 **F** 3 11 13 15 17 18 19 20 22 24 26 28 29 30 31 34 35 37 38 39 40 41 43 44 45 46 47 48 49 50 51 52 53 54 55 56 57 58 59 60 61 63 64 68 70 72 74 75 76 77 78 79 81 82 83 84 85 86 87 90 91 92 93 94 95 96 97 100 101 102 104 107 108 110 111 115 117 118 119 120 121 123 124 126 129 130 131 132 135 137 138 139 141 142 146 147 148 149 150 154 156 157 162 164 166 167 169 **S** Intermountain Health, Salt Lake City, UT
Primary Contact: Ralph Jean-Mary, Chief Executive Officer
COO: Kelly L Duffin, Operations Officer
CFO: Royce Stephens, Director Finance
CMO: Mark Ott, M.D., Regional Chief Medical Director
CIO: Heather Romualdo, Chief Information Officer
CHR: Cammie Cable, Chief Human Resource Officer
CNO: Suzanne P. Anderson, Nurse Administrator
Web address: https://intermountainhealthcare.org/locations/intermountain-medical-center/
Control: Other not-for-profit (including NFP Corporation) **Service**: General medical and surgical

Staffed Beds: 510 **Admissions**: 27861 **Census**: 379 **Outpatient Visits**: 709003 **Births**: 3518 **Total Expense ($000)**: 1230395 **Payroll Expense ($000)**: 355345 **Personnel**: 3887

NEPHI—Juab County

★ **CENTRAL VALLEY MEDICAL CENTER (461304)**, 48 West 1500 North, Zip 84648-8900; tel. 435/623-3000, **A** 10 18 **F** 3 8 13 15 29 31 34 35 36 40 43 45 50 57 59 62 63 64 65 68 75 76 77 78 81 82 85 86 87 93 97 101 102 104 107 110 111 115 119 126 129 130 131 133 146 147 148 156
Primary Contact: Mark R. Stoddard, Chief Executive Officer
COO: Randy Cuff, Chief Operating Officer
CFO: Brent Davis, Chief Financial Officer
CMO: Mark Oveson, M.D., Chief Medical Staff
CIO: Ken Richens, Chief Information Officer
CHR: Brian Allsop, Director Human Resources
CNO: Randy Allinson, R.N., Chief Nursing Officer
Web address: www.cvmed.net
Control: Other not-for-profit (including NFP Corporation) **Service**: General medical and surgical

Staffed Beds: 25 **Admissions**: 610 **Census**: 7

NORTH LOGAN—Cache County

▣ **CACHE VALLEY HOSPITAL (460054)**, 2380 North 400 East, Zip 84341-6000; tel. 435/713-9700, (Nonreporting) **A** 1 5 10 **S** HCA Healthcare, Nashville, TN
Primary Contact: Blake Rose, Chief Executive Officer
CFO: David S Geary, Chief Financial Officer
CMO: Jess Jewett, Chief Medical Officer
Web address: www.cachevalleyhospital.com/
Control: Corporation, Investor-owned (for-profit) **Service**: General medical and surgical

Staffed Beds: 28

OGDEN—Weber County

▣ △ **MCKAY-DEE HOSPITAL (460004)**, 4401 Harrison Boulevard, Zip 84403-3195; tel. 801/387-2800, **A** 1 2 3 5 7 10 19 **F** 3 9 13 15 17 18 20 22 24 26 28 29 30 31 34 35 36 37 38 39 40 41 43 44 45 48 49 50 51 53 54 57 59 60 61 63 64 65 68 70 72 74 75 76 77 78 79 80 81 82 83 84 85 86 87 89 90 91 92 93 94 95 96 97 98 99 100 101 102 104 107 108 110 111 115 117 118 119 120 121 123 124 126 129 130 131 132 135 141 146 147 148 149 150 154 156 157 162 164 167 169 **S** Intermountain Health, Salt Lake City, UT
Primary Contact: Judy Williamson, R.N., President
CFO: Trever Porter, Chief Financial Officer
CMO: Masood Safaee Semiromi, M.D., Chief Medical Officer
CIO: Mary Gathers, Director Information Systems
CHR: Christopher Saling, Chief Human Resource Officer
CNO: Donna Lynn Chapman, R.N., Chief Nursing Officer
Web address: www.mckay-dee.org
Control: Other not-for-profit (including NFP Corporation) **Service**: General medical and surgical

Staffed Beds: 307 **Admissions**: 17495 **Census**: 201 **Outpatient Visits**: 509788 **Births**: 2324 **Total Expense ($000)**: 571939 **Payroll Expense ($000)**: 167240 **Personnel**: 2017

▣ **OGDEN REGIONAL MEDICAL CENTER (460005)**, 5475 South 500 East, Zip 84405-6905; tel. 801/479-2111, (Nonreporting) **A** 1 2 10 13 **S** HCA Healthcare, Nashville, TN
Primary Contact: Mark B. Adams, Chief Executive Officer
COO: Brian Lines, Chief Operating Officer
CMO: Jeffrey Abel, M.D., Chief Medical Officer
CIO: Eric Peterson, Director
CHR: Chris Bissenden, Director Human Resources
Web address: www.ogdenregional.com
Control: Corporation, Investor-owned (for-profit) **Service**: General medical and surgical

Staffed Beds: 232

OREM—Utah County

☐ **ASPEN GROVE BEHAVIORAL HOSPITAL (464014)**, 1350 East 750 North, Zip 84097-4345; tel. 801/852-2273, (Nonreporting) **A** 1 10 **S** Universal Health Services, Inc., King of Prussia, PA
Primary Contact: Jeremy Cottle, Ph.D., Chief Executive Officer
CFO: Emmy Adams, Chief Financial Officer
CHR: Diann Decker, Chief Human Resource Officer
Web address: https://aspengrovehospital.com/
Control: Corporation, Investor-owned (for-profit) **Service**: Psychiatric

Staffed Beds: 80

Hospitals, U.S. / UTAH

OREM COMMUNITY HOSPITAL (460043), 331 North 400 West, Zip 84057–1999; tel. 801/224–4080, **A**1 10 **F**3 13 15 29 34 35 38 40 41 44 50 57 59 64 68 75 76 77 78 79 81 82 84 85 86 87 93 97 100 101 102 104 107 110 111 115 119 130 135 141 146 147 149 150 154 157 164 169 **S** Intermountain Health, Salt Lake City, UT
Primary Contact: Lenny Lyons, President
CFO: Craig Carrier, Chief Financial Officer
CMO: Tracy Hill, M.D., Chief Medical Officer
CHR: Jeremy H Rogers, Chief Human Resource Officer
CNO: Amber Iverson, Chief Nursing Officer
Web address: www.intermountainhealthcare.org
Control: Other not–for–profit (including NFP Corporation) **Service**: General medical and surgical

Staffed Beds: 24 **Admissions**: 709 **Census**: 3 **Outpatient Visits**: 46657 **Births**: 691 **Total Expense ($000)**: 33606 **Payroll Expense ($000)**: 11805 **Personnel**: 130

PROVO CANYON BEHAVIORAL HOSPITAL See Aspen Grove Behavioral Hospital

TIMPANOGOS REGIONAL HOSPITAL (460052), 750 West 800 North, Zip 84057–3660; tel. 801/714–6000, (Nonreporting) **A**1 5 10 **S** HCA Healthcare, Nashville, TN
Primary Contact: Austin Manning, Chief Executive Officer
COO: Ryan LeMasters, Chief Operating Officer
CFO: Jody S Dial, Chief Financial Officer
CMO: Randle L Likes, M.D., Chief Medical Officer
CIO: Richard Neilson, Director of Information Services
CHR: Tim Black, Director Human Resources
CNO: Sandy Ewell, Chief Nursing Officer
Web address: www.timpanogosregionalhospital.com
Control: Corporation, Investor–owned (for–profit) **Service**: General medical and surgical

Staffed Beds: 106

PANGUITCH—Garfield County

★ **GARFIELD MEMORIAL HOSPITAL (461333)**, 200 North 400 East, Zip 84759, Mailing Address: P.O. Box 389, Zip 84759–0389; tel. 435/676–8811, **A**10 18 **F**3 13 15 29 34 35 38 40 41 43 44 45 50 56 59 64 65 68 71 75 76 77 81 84 85 86 87 89 97 100 101 102 104 107 110 115 119 128 130 133 135 148 149 150 154 157 164 169 **S** Intermountain Health, Salt Lake City, UT
Primary Contact: DeAnn Brown, Administrator
CFO: Craig Corry, Chief Financial Officer
CMO: Mitchell Miller, M.D., Chief Medical Officer
CHR: Carla Ramsay, Chief Human Resource Officer
Web address: https://intermountainhealthcare.org/locations/garfield-memorial-hospital/
Control: County, Government, Nonfederal **Service**: General medical and surgical

Staffed Beds: 15 **Admissions**: 289 **Census**: 3 **Outpatient Visits**: 33746 **Births**: 34 **Total Expense ($000)**: 15091 **Payroll Expense ($000)**: 8378 **Personnel**: 101

PARK CITY—Summit County

PARK CITY HOSPITAL (460057), 900 Round Valley Drive, Zip 84060–7552; tel. 435/658–7000, **A**1 10 **F**3 9 13 15 18 23 28 29 31 34 35 36 38 40 41 43 45 50 51 52 53 57 59 63 64 65 68 70 75 76 77 78 79 81 82 84 85 86 87 90 93 97 100 101 102 104 107 108 110 111 115 117 118 119 126 129 130 132 135 141 146 147 148 149 150 154 157 164 169 **S** Intermountain Health, Salt Lake City, UT
Primary Contact: Lori Weston, President
CFO: Jennilyn Ferry, Chief Financial Officer
CMO: Wing Province, M.D., Chief Medical Officer
CHR: Celene Roberts, Chief Human Resource Officer
CNO: Dan Davis, MSN, R.N., Nurse Administrator
Web address: www.intermountainhealthcare.org
Control: Other not–for–profit (including NFP Corporation) **Service**: General medical and surgical

Staffed Beds: 37 **Admissions**: 1213 **Census**: 7 **Outpatient Visits**: 138421 **Births**: 269 **Total Expense ($000)**: 113879 **Payroll Expense ($000)**: 33926 **Personnel**: 330

PAYSON—Utah County

MOUNTAIN VIEW HOSPITAL (460013), 1000 East 100 North, Zip 84651–1600; tel. 801/465–7000, (Nonreporting) **A**1 10 **S** HCA Healthcare, Nashville, TN
Primary Contact: Kevin Johnson, Chief Executive Officer
COO: Ric Johnson, Associate Administrator
CFO: Steven R Schramm, Chief Financial Officer
CMO: Jeffrey Wallentine, Chief of Staff
CIO: Cindy Mecham, Health Information Director
CHR: Wally Trotter, Director Human Resources
CNO: Katie King, R.N., Chief Nursing Officer
Web address: www.mvhpayson.com
Control: Corporation, Investor–owned (for–profit) **Service**: General medical and surgical

Staffed Beds: 124

PRICE—Carbon County

CASTLEVIEW HOSPITAL (460011), 300 North Hospital Drive, Zip 84501–4200; tel. 435/637–4800, **A**1 10 20 **F**3 4 5 8 11 12 13 15 18 29 31 34 39 40 41 43 45 50 51 54 56 57 59 64 65 68 70 75 76 77 78 79 81 82 84 86 87 89 92 93 97 107 108 110 111 115 119 126 127 130 131 133 144 146 147 148 149 154 156 157 160 167 **P**8 **S** Lifepoint Health, Brentwood, TN
Primary Contact: Greg Cook, Chief Executive Officer
CFO: Ryan Pugh, Chief Financial Officer
CMO: Glen T. Etzel, M.D., Chief of Staff
CIO: Fiore Wilson, Director Information Systems
CHR: Misty Birch, Director Human Resources
CNO: Lindsey Metelko, Chief Nursing Officer
Web address: www.castleviewhospital.net
Control: Corporation, Investor–owned (for–profit) **Service**: General medical and surgical

Staffed Beds: 51 **Admissions**: 1694 **Census**: 11 **Outpatient Visits**: 56140 **Births**: 237 **Total Expense ($000)**: 48615 **Payroll Expense ($000)**: 16863

PROVO—Utah County

☐ **UTAH STATE HOSPITAL (464001)**, 1300 East Center Street, Zip 84606–3554, Mailing Address: P.O. Box 270, Zip 84603–0270; tel. 801/344–4400, **A**1 5 10 **F**29 30 39 77 98 99 103 130 146 149 154 157 163 164 **P**6
Primary Contact: Dallas Earnshaw, Superintendent
COO: Dallas Earnshaw, Superintendent
CFO: Robert Burton, Manager Finance
CMO: Madhu Gundlapalli, M.D., Clinical Director
CIO: Jill Hill, Director Information Technology
CHR: Devin Patrick, Manager Human Resources
CNO: Chris Metcalf, Director of Nursing
Web address: www.ush.utah.gov
Control: State, Government, Nonfederal **Service**: Psychiatric

Staffed Beds: 348 **Admissions**: 274 **Census**: 290 **Outpatient Visits**: 0 **Births**: 0 **Total Expense ($000)**: 89091 **Payroll Expense ($000)**: 46770 **Personnel**: 876

△ **UTAH VALLEY HOSPITAL (460001)**, 1034 North 500 West, Zip 84604–3337; tel. 801/357–7850, **A**1 2 3 5 7 10 19 **F**3 5 8 9 11 12 13 15 17 18 19 20 22 24 26 28 29 30 31 34 35 36 37 38 40 41 43 44 45 46 47 48 49 50 51 53 54 56 57 59 60 61 63 64 65 68 70 72 74 75 76 77 78 79 81 82 84 85 86 87 88 89 90 91 92 93 94 95 96 98 100 101 102 104 107 108 110 111 115 117 118 119 120 121 123 124 126 129 130 131 132 135 141 145 146 147 148 149 150 154 157 162 164 167 168 169 **S** Intermountain Health, Salt Lake City, UT
Primary Contact: Kyle A. Hansen, President
CFO: Nathan Empey, Chief Finanial Officer
CMO: Tracy Hill, M.D., Chief Medical Officer
CIO: Mary Gathers, Director Information Systems
CHR: Brady Anderson, Chief Human Resource Officer
CNO: Maria Black, Chief Nursing Officer
Web address: https://intermountainhealthcare.org/locations/utah-valley-hospital/
Control: Other not–for–profit (including NFP Corporation) **Service**: General medical and surgical

Staffed Beds: 398 **Admissions**: 19460 **Census**: 246 **Outpatient Visits**: 549739 **Births**: 3041 **Total Expense ($000)**: 691858 **Payroll Expense ($000)**: 194356 **Personnel**: 2376

Hospital, Medicare Provider Number, Address, Telephone, Approval, Facility, and Physician Codes, Health Care System

★ American Hospital Association (AHA) membership
☐ The Joint Commission accreditation
○ Healthcare Facilities Accreditation Program
◇ DNV Healthcare Inc. accreditation
⇧ Center for Improvement in Healthcare Quality Accreditation
△ Commission on Accreditation of Rehabilitation Facilities (CARF) accreditation

Hospitals, U.S. / UTAH

☐ **UTAH VALLEY SPECIALTY HOSPITAL (462005)**, 306 River Bend Lane, Zip 84604–5625; tel. 801/226–8880, (Nonreporting) **A**1 10 **S** Ernest Health, Inc., Albuquerque, NM
Primary Contact: Reuben Jessop, Chief Executive Officer
Web address: www.uvsh.ernesthealth.com
Control: Corporation, Investor–owned (for–profit) **Service**: Acute long–term care hospital

Staffed Beds: 40

RICHFIELD—Sevier County

✣ **SEVIER VALLEY HOSPITAL (460026)**, 1000 North Main Street, Zip 84701–1857; tel. 435/893–4100, **A**1 10 20 **F**3 9 12 13 15 18 29 31 34 35 38 39 40 41 43 44 45 50 51 56 57 59 60 64 65 68 75 76 77 78 79 81 84 85 86 87 89 100 101 102 104 107 108 110 111 115 118 119 129 130 131 132 135 141 146 147 148 149 150 154 155 157 164 169 **S** Intermountain Health, Salt Lake City, UT
Primary Contact: Brent Schmidt, President
CFO: Bert Zimmerli, Executive Vice President and Chief Financial Officer
CMO: Justin Abbott, M.D., Medical Director
CHR: Katey Nelson, Director Human Resources
CNO: Cami Blackham, R.N., Nurse Administrator
Web address: www.sevierhospital.org
Control: Other not–for–profit (including NFP Corporation) **Service**: General medical and surgical

Staffed Beds: 24 **Admissions**: 743 **Census**: 5 **Outpatient Visits**: 81012 **Births**: 231 **Total Expense ($000)**: 57819 **Payroll Expense ($000)**: 14300 **Personnel**: 165

RIVERTON—Salt Lake County

✣ **RIVERTON HOSPITAL (460058)**, 3741 West 12600 South, Zip 84065–7215; tel. 801/285–4000, **A**1 3 5 10 **F**3 9 13 15 18 29 31 34 35 38 39 40 41 43 44 45 49 50 59 68 70 73 75 76 77 78 79 81 82 84 85 86 87 89 90 93 100 101 102 104 107 108 110 111 115 117 118 119 120 121 124 126 129 130 131 132 135 141 144 146 147 148 149 150 154 156 157 164 168 169 **S** Intermountain Health, Salt Lake City, UT
Primary Contact: Todd Neubert, President
CFO: Andrew Ozmun, Chief Financial Officer
CMO: Dean Mayer, M.D., Chief Medical Officer
CIO: Susan Hanks, Chief Information Officer
CHR: Kimberly Dansie, Chief Human Resource Officer
CNO: Brian Pendleton, Chief Nursing Officer
Web address: www.intermountainhealthcare.org/
Control: Other not–for–profit (including NFP Corporation) **Service**: General medical and surgical

Staffed Beds: 97 **Admissions**: 5702 **Census**: 40 **Outpatient Visits**: 271096 **Births**: 2396 **Total Expense ($000)**: 182769 **Payroll Expense ($000)**: 51049 **Personnel**: 579

ROOSEVELT—Duchesne County

★ **UINTAH BASIN MEDICAL CENTER (460019)**, 250 West 300 North, 75–2, Zip 84066–2336; tel. 435/722–6163, **A**10 20 **F**6 7 11 13 15 17 35 40 45 50 52 53 54 57 59 60 62 63 70 73 74 79 81 82 84 85 87 89 93 107 108 110 111 115 119 126 127 129 130 131 132 135 146 147 148 154 155 156
Primary Contact: James I. Marshall, President and Chief Executive Officer
CFO: Brent Hales, Chief Financial Officer
CMO: Gary B White, M.D., Chief Medical Staff
CHR: Randall Bennett, Assistant Administrator
Web address: www.ubmc.org
Control: Other not–for–profit (including NFP Corporation) **Service**: General medical and surgical

Staffed Beds: 49 **Admissions**: 1239 **Census**: 8

SAINT GEORGE—Washington County

✣ △ **ST. GEORGE REGIONAL HOSPITAL (460021)**, 1380 East Medical Center Drive, Zip 84790–2123; tel. 435/251–1000, (Includes DIXIE REGIONAL MEDICAL CENTER, 544 South 400 East, St George, Utah, Zip 84770, tel. 940/764–7000) **A**1 2 7 10 **F**3 8 9 12 13 15 17 18 19 20 22 24 26 28 29 30 31 34 35 36 37 38 39 40 41 42 43 44 45 48 49 50 51 52 53 54 56 57 59 60 61 63 64 65 67 68 70 72 74 75 76 77 78 79 80 81 82 83 84 85 86 87 89 90 91 92 93 94 95 96 97 98 100 101 102 104 107 108 110 111 112 115 117 118 119 120 121 123 124 126 129 130 131 132 135 141 144 146 147 148 149 150 154 156 157 162 164 167 169 **S** Intermountain Health, Salt Lake City, UT
Primary Contact: Natalie Ashby, President
CFO: Don Cannon, Chief Financial Officer
CMO: Patrick Carroll, M.D., Chief Medical Officer
CIO: Kenley Brinkerhoff, Chief Information Officer
CHR: Colette Eppley, Chief Human Resource Officer
CNO: Natalie Ashby, Chief Nursing Officer
Web address: https://intermountainhealthcare.org/locations/st-george-regional-hospital/
Control: Other not–for–profit (including NFP Corporation) **Service**: General medical and surgical

Staffed Beds: 300 **Admissions**: 19400 **Census**: 202 **Outpatient Visits**: 861199 **Births**: 2783 **Total Expense ($000)**: 768843 **Payroll Expense ($000)**: 189732 **Personnel**: 2304

SALT LAKE CITY—Salt Lake County

✣ △ **GEORGE E. WAHLEN DEPARTMENT OF VETERANS AFFAIRS MEDICAL CENTER**, 500 Foothill Drive, Zip 84148–0002; tel. 801/582–1565, (Nonreporting) **A**1 3 5 7 **S** Department of Veterans Affairs, Washington, DC
Primary Contact: Angela Williams, PharmD, MS, Medical Center Director
CFO: Val Martin, Director Financial Management Services Center
CMO: Ronald J Gebhart, M.D., Chief of Staff
CIO: Lisa Leonelis, Chief Information Officer
CHR: Lisa Porter, Director Human Resources, Leadership and Education
Web address: www.saltlakecity.va.gov/
Control: Veterans Affairs, Government, federal **Service**: General medical and surgical

Staffed Beds: 127

★ ⇑ **HOLY CROSS HOSPITAL – SALT LAKE (460003)**, 1050 East South Temple, Zip 84102–1507; tel. 801/350–4111, **A**3 5 10 21 **F**3 12 15 17 18 20 22 24 26 28 29 30 34 35 37 38 40 45 46 47 48 49 50 51 56 57 59 60 65 68 74 75 77 79 80 81 82 85 86 87 91 92 93 102 103 107 108 110 111 114 119 126 130 131 132 135 147 148 154 156 164 167 **S** CommonSpirit Health, Chicago, IL
Primary Contact: Jeremy Bradshaw, Market President
CFO: Brian Ebright, Chief Financial Officer
CMO: Blake Johnson, M.D., Chief of Staff
CIO: Mark Runyan, Director Information Services
CHR: Carolyn Livingston, Director Human Resources
CNO: Terron Arbon, R.N., Chief Nursing Officer
Web address: https://www.mountain.commonspirit.org/location/holy-cross-hospital-salt-lake
Control: Other not–for–profit (including NFP Corporation) **Service**: General medical and surgical

Staffed Beds: 97 **Admissions**: 1742 **Census**: 20 **Outpatient Visits**: 24984 **Total Expense ($000)**: 98772 **Payroll Expense ($000)**: 30645

KPC PROMISE HOSPITAL OF SALT LAKE (462004), 8 Avenue, C Street, Zip 84143; tel. 385/425–0050, (Nonreporting) **A**10 **S** KPC Healthcare, Inc., Santa Ana, CA
Primary Contact: Kenny Peterson, Chief Executive Officer
CMO: Geoff Harding, Chief Clinical Officer
Web address: www.saltlake.kpcph.com/
Control: Corporation, Investor–owned (for–profit) **Service**: Acute long–term care hospital

Staffed Beds: 41

Hospitals, U.S. / UTAH

✚ **LDS HOSPITAL (460006)**, Eighth Avenue and 'C' Street, Zip 84143–0001; tel. 801/408–1100, **A**1 3 5 10 19 **F**3 4 5 8 9 12 13 15 18 29 34 35 36 37 38 40 41 43 44 45 46 47 48 49 50 53 54 55 56 57 58 59 60 61 63 64 65 68 70 73 74 75 76 77 78 79 81 82 84 85 86 87 90 93 97 98 100 101 102 104 107 108 110 111 115 117 118 119 120 121 123 124 126 129 130 131 132 135 136 141 146 147 148 149 150 154 157 158 160 161 162 164 165 167 168 169 **S** Intermountain Health, Salt Lake City, UT
Primary Contact: Heather Wall, President
CFO: Mike Demotte, Chief Financial Officer
CMO: Kerry Fisher, M.D., Medical Director
CIO: David Baird, Chief Information Officer
CHR: Andy Lawson, Chief Human Resource Officer
Web address: https://intermountainhealthcare.org/locations/lds-hospital/
Control: Other not–for–profit (including NFP Corporation) **Service:** General medical and surgical

Staffed Beds: 252 **Admissions:** 9670 **Census:** 118 **Outpatient Visits:** 211541 **Births:** 1683 **Total Expense ($000):** 350894 **Payroll Expense ($000):** 100951 **Personnel:** 1122

✚ **MARIAN CENTER (464012)**, 451 East Bishop Federal Lane, Zip 84115–2357; tel. 801/487–7557, **A**1 10 **F**98 100 103 130
Primary Contact: Lee Kilpack, Chief Executive Officer
Web address: www.stjosephvilla.com
Control: Corporation, Investor–owned (for–profit) **Service:** Psychiatric

Staffed Beds: 14 **Admissions:** 221 **Census:** 10 **Outpatient Visits:** 0 **Births:** 0 **Total Expense ($000):** 3117 **Payroll Expense ($000):** 1855 **Personnel:** 30

✚ △ **PRIMARY CHILDREN'S HOSPITAL (463301)**, 100 North Mario Capecchi Drive, Zip 84113–1100; tel. 801/662–1000, **A**1 3 5 7 10 **F**3 8 17 19 20 21 23 25 29 30 31 32 34 35 36 38 39 40 41 43 44 45 46 48 49 50 51 53 54 57 59 60 61 63 64 65 68 71 72 74 75 77 78 79 80 81 82 83 84 85 86 87 88 89 90 91 92 93 94 95 96 98 99 100 101 102 104 105 106 107 108 111 112 115 117 118 119 126 129 130 131 132 134 136 137 138 139 141 146 148 149 150 153 154 157 164 167 **S** Intermountain Health, Salt Lake City, UT
Primary Contact: Katy Welkie MBA, R.N., Chief Executive Officer
CFO: Sidney P. Norton, Chief Financial Officer
CMO: Angelo Giardino, M.D., Chief Medical Officer
CIO: Joe Hales, Chief Information Officer
CHR: Ben Buckworth, Human Resources Administrative Director
CNO: Angie Scartezina, Chief Nursing Officer
Web address: www.intermountainhealthcare.org
Control: Other not–for–profit (including NFP Corporation) **Service:** Children's general medical and surgical

Staffed Beds: 287 **Admissions:** 13469 **Census:** 227 **Outpatient Visits:** 411030 **Births:** 0 **Total Expense ($000):** 933767 **Payroll Expense ($000):** 287258 **Personnel:** 3207

□ **SALT LAKE BEHAVIORAL HEALTH (464013)**, 3802 South 700 East, Zip 84106–1182; tel. 801/264–6000, **A**1 10 **F**5 29 38 75 98 104 130 135 151 155 **S** Universal Health Services, Inc., King of Prussia, PA
Primary Contact: Kreg Gillman, Chief Executive Officer
CFO: Daren Woolstenhulme, Chief Financial Officer
CMO: Monica Polk, M.D., Chief Medical Officer
CHR: Robyn Holsten, Human Resources Director
CNO: Suzanne Nelson, R.N., Director of Nursing
Web address: www.saltlakebehavioralhealth.com
Control: Corporation, Investor–owned (for–profit) **Service:** Psychiatric

Staffed Beds: 118 **Admissions:** 2023 **Census:** 75 **Births:** 0

SALT LAKE CITY HCS See George E. Wahlen Department of Veterans Affairs Medical Center

SHRINERS HOSPITALS FOR CHILDREN–SALT LAKE CITY (463302), 1275 East Fairfax Road, Zip 84103–4399; tel. 801/536–3500, (Nonreporting) **A**3 5 10 **S** Shriners Hospitals for Children, Tampa, FL
Primary Contact: Kevin Martin, M.P.H., R.N., FACHE, Administrator
CFO: Heath Braby, Director Fiscal Services
CMO: Kristen Carroll, M.D., Chief of Staff
CIO: Mike Allen, Director Information Technology
CHR: Kris Goldman, Director Human Resources
CNO: Gail McGuill, R.N., MSN, Chief Nursing Officer and Administrative Director of Patient Care Services
Web address: www.shrinershospitalsforchildren.org/Hospitals/Locations/SaltLakeCity.aspx
Control: Other not–for–profit (including NFP Corporation) **Service:** Children's orthopedic

Staffed Beds: 12

✚ **ST. MARK'S HOSPITAL (460047)**, 1200 East 3900 South, Zip 84124–1390; tel. 801/268–7111, (Nonreporting) **A**1 2 3 5 10 **S** HCA Healthcare, Nashville, TN
Primary Contact: Matthew Steven. Hasbrouck, Chief Executive Officer
CFO: Michael Herron, Chief Financial Officer
CMO: J Eric Vanderhooft, M.D., President Medical Staff
CIO: Jesse Trujillo, Chief Information Officer
CHR: Robyn Opheikens, Assistant Administrator Human Resources
CNO: Nicki Roderman, Chief Nursing Officer
Web address: www.stmarkshospital.com
Control: Corporation, Investor–owned (for–profit) **Service:** General medical and surgical

Staffed Beds: 298

★ △ ⇑ **UNIVERSITY OF UTAH HEALTH (460009)**, 50 North Medical Drive, Zip 84132–0002; tel. 801/953–3198, (Includes UNIVERSITY OF UTAH HUNTSMAN MENTAL HEALTH INSTITUTE, 501 South Chipeta Way, Salt Lake City, Utah, Zip 84108–1222, tel. 801/583–2500; Ross Van Vranken, Executive Director) **A**2 3 5 7 8 10 19 21 **F**3 4 5 6 7 8 9 11 12 13 14 15 16 17 18 20 22 24 26 28 29 30 31 34 35 36 37 38 39 40 42 43 44 45 46 47 48 49 50 51 52 53 54 55 56 57 58 59 60 61 62 64 65 68 70 71 72 73 74 75 76 77 78 79 80 81 82 83 84 85 86 87 90 91 92 93 94 95 96 97 98 99 100 101 102 103 104 105 106 107 108 109 110 111 112 114 115 116 117 118 119 120 121 122 124 126 129 130 131 132 134 135 136 137 138 139 140 141 142 143 144 145 146 147 148 149 150 151 152 153 154 155 156 157 160 161 162 163 164 165 167 168 169
Primary Contact: Dan Lundergan, Chief Executive Officer
COO: Gina Hawley, Dr.PH, Chief Operating Officer
CFO: Charlton Gordon Park, Chief Financial Officer and Chief Analytics Officer
CMO: Thomas Miller, M.D., Medical Director
CIO: Donna Roach, MS, Chief Information Officer
Web address: www.uuhsc.utah.edu
Control: State, Government, Nonfederal **Service:** General medical and surgical

Staffed Beds: 927 **Admissions:** 36313 **Census:** 661 **Outpatient Visits:** 1868451 **Births:** 4890 **Total Expense ($000):** 2863807 **Payroll Expense ($000):** 1049814 **Personnel:** 13151

UTAH NEUROPSYCHIATRIC INST See University of Utah Huntsman Mental Health Institute

SANDY—Salt Lake County

✚ **ALTA VIEW HOSPITAL (460044)**, 9660 South 1300 East, Zip 84094–3793; tel. 801/501–2600, **A**1 10 **F**3 9 13 15 18 29 31 34 35 38 39 40 41 43 44 45 49 50 51 54 57 59 63 64 68 70 75 76 77 78 79 81 82 84 85 86 87 90 93 100 101 102 104 107 108 110 111 115 118 119 126 129 130 131 132 135 141 146 147 148 149 150 154 157 164 167 168 169 **S** Intermountain Health, Salt Lake City, UT
Primary Contact: Scott Roberson, President
CFO: Andrew Ozmun, Chief Financial Officer
CMO: Laurie Niederee, M.D., Chief Medical Officer
CHR: Marissa Johnson, Chief Human Resource Officer
CNO: David Hurst, Chief Nursing Officer
Web address: www.intermountainhealthcare.org
Control: Other not–for–profit (including NFP Corporation) **Service:** General medical and surgical

Staffed Beds: 68 **Admissions:** 2879 **Census:** 21 **Outpatient Visits:** 181476 **Births:** 959 **Total Expense ($000):** 137500 **Payroll Expense ($000):** 38619 **Personnel:** 451

✚ **ENCOMPASS HEALTH REHABILITATION HOSPITAL OF UTAH (463025)**, 8074 South 1300 East, Zip 84094–0743; tel. 801/561–3400, **A**1 10 **F**28 29 30 60 77 90 91 95 100 130 149 154 **S** Encompass Health Corporation, Birmingham, AL
Primary Contact: Charles Smith, Chief Executive Officer
CMO: Joseph VickRoy, M.D., Medical Director
CHR: Troy Jensen, Director Human Resources
Web address: https://www.encompasshealth.com/utahrehab
Control: Corporation, Investor–owned (for–profit) **Service:** Rehabilitation

Staffed Beds: 53 **Admissions:** 999 **Census:** 37 **Outpatient Visits:** 0 **Births:** 0 **Total Expense ($000):** 21239 **Payroll Expense ($000):** 11391

Hospital, Medicare Provider Number, Address, Telephone, Approval, Facility, and Physician Codes, Health Care System

★ American Hospital Association (AHA) membership   ○ Healthcare Facilities Accreditation Program   ⇑ Center for Improvement in Healthcare Quality Accreditation
□ The Joint Commission accreditation   ◇ DNV Healthcare Inc. accreditation   △ Commission on Accreditation of Rehabilitation Facilities (CARF) accreditation

Hospitals, U.S. / UTAH

SOUTH OGDEN—Weber County

☐ **NORTHERN UTAH REHABILITATION HOSPITAL (463027)**, 5825 Harrison Boulevard, Zip 84403-4316; tel. 801/475-5254, (Nonreporting) **A**1 10 **S** Ernest Health, Inc., Albuquerque, NM
Primary Contact: Reuben Jessop, Chief Executive Officer
CFO: Daniel J Foster, Chief Financial Officer
CNO: Terina Chapman, Director of Nursing
Web address: www.ernesthealth.com/gallery-item/northern-utah-rehabilitation-hospital/
Control: Other not-for-profit (including NFP Corporation) **Service:** Rehabilitation

Staffed Beds: 20

SPANISH FORK—Utah County

✠ **INTERMOUNTAIN SPANISH FORK HOSPITAL (460062)**, 765 East Market Place Drive, Zip 84660-1396; tel. 385/344-5000, **A**1 10 **F**3 13 15 18 29 31 34 35 38 40 41 43 44 45 49 50 53 57 59 61 63 64 65 68 70 75 76 77 78 79 81 82 84 85 86 87 90 93 97 100 101 102 107 110 111 115 119 126 130 131 135 141 146 147 148 149 150 154 157 160 161 164 169 **S** Intermountain Health, Salt Lake City, UT
Primary Contact: Megan Elizabeth. Johnson, President
Web address: https://intermountainhealthcare.org/locations/spanish-fork-hospital/
Control: Other not-for-profit (including NFP Corporation) **Service:** General medical and surgical

Staffed Beds: 33 **Admissions:** 1654 **Census:** 9 **Outpatient Visits:** 124301 **Births:** 740 **Total Expense ($000):** 78626 **Payroll Expense ($000):** 22071 **Personnel:** 274

TOOELE—Tooele County

☐ **MOUNTAIN WEST MEDICAL CENTER (460014)**, 2055 North Main Street, Zip 84074-9819; tel. 435/843-3600, (Nonreporting) **A**1 10 **S** Quorum Health, Brentwood, TN
Primary Contact: Philip Eaton, Chief Executive Officer
CMO: James Antinori, M.D., Chief of Staff
CIO: Marc Taylor, IS Director
CHR: Matthew Flygare, Director Human Resources
CNO: Yvonne Nielson, Chief Nursing Officer, Director Quality Management and Regulatory Compliance
Web address: www.mountainwestmc.com
Control: Corporation, Investor-owned (for-profit) **Service:** General medical and surgical

Staffed Beds: 44

TREMONTON—Box Elder County

★ **BEAR RIVER VALLEY HOSPITAL (460039)**, 905 North 1000 West, Zip 84337-2497; tel. 435/207-4500, **A**10 **F**3 9 13 15 28 29 34 35 38 40 41 43 44 45 50 59 63 65 68 75 76 77 79 81 84 85 86 87 90 93 100 101 102 104 107 110 111 115 119 129 130 131 132 135 146 148 149 150 154 157 164 169 **S** Intermountain Health, Salt Lake City, UT
Primary Contact: Brandon Vonk, President
CFO: Justin Wiser, Chief Financial Officer
CMO: Brett Nance, M.D., Chief Medical Officer
CHR: Joy Sadler, Director Human Resources
CNO: James Montgomery, Chief Nursing Officer
Web address: https://intermountainhealthcare.org/locations/bear-river-valley-hospital/
Control: Other not-for-profit (including NFP Corporation) **Service:** General medical and surgical

Staffed Beds: 16 **Admissions:** 339 **Census:** 2 **Outpatient Visits:** 58355 **Births:** 106 **Total Expense ($000):** 32601 **Payroll Expense ($000):** 11601 **Personnel:** 115

VERNAL—Uintah County

✠ **ASHLEY REGIONAL MEDICAL CENTER (460030)**, 150 West 100 North, Zip 84078-2036; tel. 435/789-3342, (Nonreporting) **A**1 10 20 **S** Lifepoint Health, Brentwood, TN
Primary Contact: Alan C. Olive, Chief Executive Officer
CFO: Ryan Pugh, Chief Financial Officer
CMO: Dennis Lewis, M.D., Chief of Staff
CIO: Cameron Winn, Director Information Services
CHR: Deena Mansfield, Director Human Resources
Web address: www.ashleyregional.com
Control: Corporation, Investor-owned (for-profit) **Service:** General medical and surgical

Staffed Beds: 39

WEST JORDAN—Salt Lake County

★ ⇧ **HOLY CROSS HOSPITAL – JORDAN VALLEY (460051)**, 3580 West 9000 South, Zip 84088-8812; tel. 801/561-8888, (Includes HOLY CROSS HOSPITAL – JORDAN VALLEY WEST, 3460 South Pioneer Parkway, West Valley City, Utah, Zip 84120-2049, tel. 801/561-8888; Christine McSweeney, FACHE, Chief Executive Officer; HOLY CROSS HOSPITAL – MOUNTAIN POINT, 3000 North Triumph Boulevard, Lehi, Utah, Zip 84043-4999, tel. 385/345-3000; Chris Stines, Chief Executive Officer) **A**5 10 21 **F**3 12 13 15 18 20 22 28 29 30 31 34 35 37 38 40 43 45 48 49 50 51 54 55 57 58 59 60 64 68 70 72 74 75 76 77 78 79 81 82 85 86 87 90 91 92 93 96 98 100 102 104 107 108 109 110 111 114 115 116 117 119 120 124 126 129 130 147 148 149 154 156 167 169 **S** CommonSpirit Health, Chicago, IL
Primary Contact: Christine McSweeney, FACHE, Chief Executive Officer
CFO: Kurt Shipley, Chief Financial Officer
CMO: B Dee Allred, M.D., President Medical Staff
Web address: https://www.centura.org/location/holy-cross-hospital-jordan-valley/hc
Control: Church operated, Nongovernment, not-for-profit **Service:** General medical and surgical

Staffed Beds: 189 **Admissions:** 9459 **Census:** 101 **Outpatient Visits:** 120230 **Births:** 1925 **Total Expense ($000):** 260311 **Payroll Expense ($000):** 85002 **Personnel:** 1053

VERMONT

BENNINGTON—Bennington County

⊞ **SOUTHWESTERN VERMONT MEDICAL CENTER (470012)**, 100 Hospital Drive, Zip 05201-5004; tel. 802/442-6361, **A**1 5 10 **F**3 4 5 11 13 15 18 28 29 30 31 32 34 35 37 38 39 40 44 45 46 47 48 49 50 51 54 57 58 59 60 61 62 63 64 65 68 69 70 74 75 76 77 78 79 81 82 83 84 85 87 89 91 92 93 94 97 107 108 109 110 112 115 119 120 121 122 123 126 127 129 130 131 132 133 135 144 146 147 148 149 151 154 156 157 160 161 167 169 **P**6 **S** Dartmouth Health, Lebanon, NH
Primary Contact: Thomas A. Dee, President and Chief Executive Officer
CFO: Stephen D Majetich, CPA, Chief Financial Officer
CMO: Trey Dobson, M.D., Chief Medical Officer
CIO: Richard Ogilvie, Chief Information Officer
CHR: Rudolph D Weaver, Vice President Human Resources
CNO: Pamela Duchene, R.N., Vice President Patient Care Services, Chief Nursing Officer
Web address: www.svhealthcare.org
Control: Other not-for-profit (including NFP Corporation) **Service:** General medical and surgical

Staffed Beds: 56 **Admissions:** 2823 **Census:** 32 **Outpatient Visits:** 305402 **Births:** 363 **Total Expense ($000):** 204149 **Payroll Expense ($000):** 62188 **Personnel:** 920

BERLIN—Washington County

⊞ **THE UNIVERSITY OF VERMONT HEALTH NETWORK CENTRAL VERMONT MEDICAL CENTER (470001)**, 130 Fisher Road, Zip 05602-9516, Mailing Address: P.O. Box 547, Barre, Zip 05641-0547; tel. 802/371-4100, (Total facility includes 153 beds in nursing home-type unit) **A**1 3 5 10 **F**3 5 13 15 18 28 29 30 31 34 35 36 37 40 44 50 51 54 59 63 64 65 68 70 74 75 76 77 78 79 81 82 84 85 86 87 92 93 94 96 97 98 100 102 104 107 108 110 111 114 115 118 119 120 121 123 128 130 131 132 135 141 143 144 147 148 149 154 160 161 165 169 **P**6 **S** The University of Vermont Health Network, Burlington, VT
Primary Contact: Anna T. Noonan, President and Chief Operating Officer
CMO: Philip Brown, D.O., Vice President Medical Affairs
CHR: Robert Patterson, Vice President Human Resources and Rehabilitation Services
CNO: Matthew Choate, Chief Nursing Officer
Web address: www.cvmc.org/
Control: Other not-for-profit (including NFP Corporation) **Service:** General medical and surgical

Staffed Beds: 251 **Admissions:** 4582 **Census:** 176 **Outpatient Visits:** 180601 **Births:** 216 **Total Expense ($000):** 219822 **Payroll Expense ($000):** 94236 **Personnel:** 1351

☐ **VERMONT PSYCHIATRIC CARE HOSPITAL (474004)**, 350 Fisher Road, Zip 05602; tel. 802/828-3300, (Nonreporting) **A**1 10
Primary Contact: Sarah Squirrell, Commissioner of Vermont Department of Mental Health
Web address: www.mentalhealth.vermont.gov/Vermont-psychiatric-care-hospital
Control: State, Government, Nonfederal **Service:** Psychiatric

Staffed Beds: 25

BRATTLEBORO—Windham County

★ **BRATTLEBORO MEMORIAL HOSPITAL (470011)**, 17 Belmont Avenue, Zip 05301-3498; tel. 802/257-0341, **A**5 10 **F**3 11 13 15 18 28 29 30 31 34 35 37 40 44 45 50 51 53 55 59 61 64 68 71 74 75 76 78 79 81 85 87 93 97 107 108 110 111 115 118 119 126 131 132 135 146 147 148 149 154 169 **P**6
Primary Contact: Christopher J. Dougherty, President and Chief Executive Officer
CFO: Jennifer Griffey, Chief Financial Officer
CMO: Kathleen McGraw, M.D., Chief Medical Officer
CIO: Jonathan Farina, Chief Information Officer
CHR: William Norwood, Vice President, Human Resources
CNO: Mary Urquhart, R.N., Vice President Patient Care
Web address: www.bmhvt.org
Control: Other not-for-profit (including NFP Corporation) **Service:** General medical and surgical

Staffed Beds: 40 **Admissions:** 1769 **Census:** 19 **Outpatient Visits:** 93729 **Births:** 320 **Total Expense ($000):** 112706 **Payroll Expense ($000):** 47407 **Personnel:** 565

⊞ **BRATTLEBORO RETREAT (474001)**, 1 Anna Marsh Lane, Zip 05301, Mailing Address: P.O. Box 803, Zip 05302-0803; tel. 802/257-7785, **A**1 3 10 **F**29 34 35 44 50 68 75 87 98 99 100 101 102 104 105 106 132 135 149 152 153 154 162 163 164 165 **P**6
Primary Contact: Steve Cummings, Interim President & Chief Executive Officer
COO: Gerri Cote, Chief Operating Officer
CFO: Steven Monette, Chief Financial Officer
CMO: Frederick Engstrom, M.D., Chief Medical Officer
CHR: Jeffrey T. Corrigan, Vice President Human Resources
CNO: Katharine Bak, Chief Nursing Office and Vice President of Patient Care Services
Web address: www.brattlebororetreat.org
Control: Other not-for-profit (including NFP Corporation) **Service:** Psychiatric

Staffed Beds: 119 **Admissions:** 1778 **Census:** 91 **Outpatient Visits:** 31777 **Births:** 0 **Total Expense ($000):** 90751 **Payroll Expense ($000):** 35154 **Personnel:** 398

BURLINGTON—Chittenden County

⊞ **UNIVERSITY OF VERMONT MEDICAL CENTER (470003)**, 111 Colchester Avenue, Zip 05401-1473; tel. 802/847-5630, (Includes FANNY ALLEN CAMPUS, 101 College Parkway, Colchester, Vermont, Zip 05446-3035, tel. 802/847-0000; MEDICAL CENTER HOSPITAL CAMPUS, 111 Colchester Ave, Burlington, Vermont, Zip 05401-1473, 111 Colchester Avenue, Zip 05401, tel. 802/847-2345; VERMONT CHILDREN'S HOSPITAL, 111 Colchester Avenue, Burlington, Vermont, Zip 05401-1473, tel. 802/847-0000) **A**1 2 3 5 8 10 **F**3 4 5 6 7 9 11 12 13 15 17 18 19 20 21 22 23 24 25 26 28 29 30 31 32 34 35 36 37 39 40 43 44 45 46 47 48 49 50 51 52 54 55 56 57 58 59 60 61 63 64 65 66 68 70 72 73 74 75 76 77 78 79 81 82 84 85 86 87 88 89 90 91 92 93 94 96 97 98 99 100 101 102 103 104 105 107 108 110 111 114 115 116 117 118 119 120 121 123 124 126 129 130 131 132 135 136 138 141 142 143 144 145 146 147 148 149 152 153 154 155 160 162 164 167 169 **P**6 **S** The University of Vermont Health Network, Burlington, VT
Primary Contact: Stephen Leffler, M.D., President and Chief Operating Officer
CFO: Todd Keating, Chief Financial Officer
CMO: Isabelle Desjardins, M.D., Chief Medical Officer
CHR: Jerald Novak, Chief People Officer
CNO: Margaret Gagne, R.N., MS, Chief Nursing Officer
Web address: www.uvmhealth.org/medcenter/Pages/default.aspx
Control: Other not-for-profit (including NFP Corporation) **Service:** General medical and surgical

Staffed Beds: 537 **Admissions:** 20797 **Census:** 390 **Outpatient Visits:** 1349214 **Births:** 2213 **Total Expense ($000):** 2003412 **Payroll Expense ($000):** 914600 **Personnel:** 8178

COLCHESTER—Chittenden County

FANNY ALLEN CAMPUS See University of Vermont Medical Center, Burlington

MIDDLEBURY—Addison County

PORTER MEDICAL CENTER See The University of Vermont Health Network Porter Medical Center

★ **THE UNIVERSITY OF VERMONT HEALTH NETWORK PORTER MEDICAL CENTER (471307)**, 115 Porter Drive, Zip 05753-8423; tel. 802/388-4701, (Nonreporting) **A**3 10 18 **S** The University of Vermont Health Network, Burlington, VT
Primary Contact: Robert Ortmyer, President & Chief Operating Officer
CMO: Fred Kniffin, M.D., Chief Medical Officer
CIO: Rebecca Woods, Chief Information Officer
CHR: David Fuller, Vice President of Human Resources
CNO: Lorraina Smith-Zuba, R.N., MSN, Chief Nursing Officer
Web address: www.portermedical.org
Control: Other not-for-profit (including NFP Corporation) **Service:** General medical and surgical

Staffed Beds: 29

Hospitals, U.S. / VERMONT

MORRISVILLE—Lamoille County

★ **COPLEY HOSPITAL (471305)**, 528 Washington Highway, Zip 05661–8973; tel. 802/888–8888, (Nonreporting) **A**5 10 18
Primary Contact: Joseph L. Woodin, President and Chief Executive Officer
COO: Vera A. Jones, Chief Operating Officer
CFO: Alan House, Interim Chief Financial Officer
CMO: Joel Silverstein, M.D., Chief Medical Officer
CIO: Randy Chesley, Director Information Technology
CHR: Amy Fitzgerald, Human Resources Manager
Web address: www.copleyvt.org
Control: Other not–for–profit (including NFP Corporation) **Service:** General medical and surgical

Staffed Beds: 25

NEWPORT—Orleans County

⚕ ⇑ **NORTH COUNTRY HOSPITAL AND HEALTH CENTER (471304)**, 189 Prouty Drive, Zip 05855–9326; tel. 802/334–7331, **A**1 10 18 21 **F**11 15 18 28 29 34 35 40 45 46 50 53 57 70 75 76 79 81 82 84 85 87 89 93 97 104 107 108 110 111 115 117 118 119 127 130 133 135 146 147 148 154 156 157 167 169
Primary Contact: Thomas Frank, President & Chief Executive Officer
CFO: Kyle Kovacevich, Chief Financial Officer
CHR: William Perket, Vice President Human Resources
CNO: Avril Cochran, R.N., Vice President Patient Care Services
Web address: www.nchsi.org
Control: Other not–for–profit (including NFP Corporation) **Service:** General medical and surgical

Staffed Beds: 25 **Admissions:** 1331 **Census:** 16 **Outpatient Visits:** 68828 **Births:** 122 **Total Expense ($000):** 108072 **Payroll Expense ($000):** 46686 **Personnel:** 429

RANDOLPH—Orange County

★ **GIFFORD MEDICAL CENTER (471301)**, 44 South Main Street, Zip 05060–1381, Mailing Address: P.O. Box 2000, Zip 05060–2000; tel. 802/728–7000, (Nonreporting) **A**5 10 18
Primary Contact: Michael Costa, President and Chief Executive Officer
CFO: Stephen Conti, Controller
CMO: Joshua Plavin, M.D., Medical Director Medicine Division
CIO: Sean Patrick, Director Information Systems
CHR: Janice Davis, Interim Director Human Resources
CNO: Linda Minsinger, Vice President Hospital Division
Web address: www.giffordmed.org
Control: Other not–for–profit (including NFP Corporation) **Service:** General medical and surgical

Staffed Beds: 52

RUTLAND—Rutland County

⚕ **RUTLAND REGIONAL MEDICAL CENTER (470005)**, 160 Allen Street, Zip 05701–4595; tel. 802/775–7111, **A**1 2 3 5 10 **F**3 5 13 15 18 28 29 31 34 37 40 44 45 50 55 57 59 64 65 70 74 76 78 79 81 82 83 84 85 87 92 93 98 100 101 102 104 107 108 109 110 111 115 117 118 119 120 121 123 124 129 130 133 135 146 147 148 149 154 156 157 160 164 167 169
Primary Contact: Judi Kennedy. Fox, President and Chief Executive Officer
CMO: Philip Lapp, Vice President of Medical Affairs, Medical Director, Endocrinology
CNO: Kelly Watson, R.N., FACHE, Vice President and Chief Nursing Officer
Web address: www.rrmc.org
Control: Other not–for–profit (including NFP Corporation) **Service:** General medical and surgical

Staffed Beds: 128 **Admissions:** 6350 **Census:** 86 **Outpatient Visits:** 276065 **Births:** 292 **Total Expense ($000):** 209537 **Payroll Expense ($000):** 159247 **Personnel:** 1356

SAINT ALBANS—Franklin County

⚕ **NORTHWESTERN MEDICAL CENTER (470024)**, 133 Fairfield Street, Zip 05478–1726; tel. 802/524–5911, **A**1 2 5 10 20 **F**3 11 13 15 29 34 35 40 44 45 57 59 64 68 70 75 76 79 81 85 87 89 93 107 108 110 111 114 115 118 119 129 131 135 144 145 146 148 149 154 156 167 169 **S** Ovation Healthcare, Brentwood, TN
Primary Contact: Peter J. Wright, FACHE, Chief Executive Officer
COO: Jonathan E Billings, Chief Operating Officer
CFO: Stephanie Breault, Chief Financial Officer
CMO: John Minadeo, M.D., Chief Medical Quality Officer
CIO: Joel Benware, Vice President Information Technology and Compliance
CHR: Ryan Hamel, Chief People Officer
CNO: Anneke Merritt, R.N., Chief Nursing Officer
Web address: www.northwesternmedicalcenter.org
Control: Other not–for–profit (including NFP Corporation) **Service:** General medical and surgical

Staffed Beds: 51 **Admissions:** 2421 **Census:** 31 **Outpatient Visits:** 166589 **Births:** 325 **Total Expense ($000):** 131465 **Payroll Expense ($000):** 52930 **Personnel:** 614

SAINT JOHNSBURY—Caledonia County

★ **NORTHEASTERN VERMONT REGIONAL HOSPITAL (471303)**, 1315 Hospital Drive, Zip 05819–9210, Mailing Address: PO Box 905, Zip 05819–0905; tel. 802/748–8141, **A**5 10 18 22 **F**3 8 11 13 15 18 28 29 30 34 35 40 45 50 54 57 59 61 64 65 68 70 74 75 76 77 79 81 82 84 85 86 87 93 94 97 100 107 108 110 111 115 118 119 127 130 131 132 133 135 144 146 147 148 149 150 154 156 157 160 161 164 169
Primary Contact: Shawn Tester, Chief Executive Officer
CFO: Andre Bissonnette, Chief Financial Officer
CMO: Michael Rousse, M.D., Chief Medical Officer
CIO: Shawn Burroughs, Director of Information Services
CHR: Elizabeth Gwatkin, Vice President Human Resources
Web address: www.nvrh.org
Control: Other not–for–profit (including NFP Corporation) **Service:** General medical and surgical

Staffed Beds: 25 **Admissions:** 1513 **Census:** 16 **Outpatient Visits:** 96766 **Births:** 217 **Total Expense ($000):** 120954 **Payroll Expense ($000):** 54955 **Personnel:** 527

SPRINGFIELD—Windsor County

★ **SPRINGFIELD HOSPITAL (471306)**, 25 Ridgewood Road, Zip 05156–3050, Mailing Address: 25 Ridgewood Rd, Zip 05156–3050; tel. 802/885–2151, (Nonreporting) **A**5 10 18
Primary Contact: Robert S. Adcock, FACHE, President and Chief Executive Officer
COO: Lori Profota, Chief Operating Officer/Chief Nursing Officer
CFO: Scott Whittemore, Chief Financial Officer and Chief of Ancillary Services
CMO: Richard Marasa, M.D., President Medical Staff
CIO: Kyle Peoples, Director Technology Management Services
CHR: Janet Lyle, Chief Human Resources and Allied Health Services
CNO: Lori Profota, Chief Operating Officer/Chief Nursing Officer
Web address: https://springfieldhospital.org/
Control: Other not–for–profit (including NFP Corporation) **Service:** General medical and surgical

Staffed Beds: 35

TOWNSHEND—Windham County

★ **GRACE COTTAGE HOSPITAL (471300)**, 185 Grafton Road, Zip 05353–0216, Mailing Address: P.O. Box 216, Zip 05353–0216; tel. 802/365–7357, **A**10 18 **F**3 29 34 35 40 50 59 64 65 68 77 85 87 93 96 97 104 107 115 119 127 130 132 133 135 146 147 149 154 156 160
Primary Contact: Olivia Sweetnam, President & Chief Executive Officer
CFO: Stephen A Brown, Chief Financial Officer
CMO: George Terwilliger, Chief Medical Officer
CIO: Christopher Paul Boucher, Director of Information Services
CHR: Jennifer Newman, Director of Human Resources
CNO: Lisa J. Eaton, R.N., Chief Nursing Officer
Web address: www.gracecottage.org
Control: Other not–for–profit (including NFP Corporation) **Service:** General medical and surgical

Staffed Beds: 19 **Admissions:** 361 **Census:** 10

WHITE RIVER JUNCTION—Windsor County

⚕ **WHITE RIVER JUNCTION VETERANS AFFAIRS MEDICAL CENTER**, 215 North Main Street, Zip 05009–0001; tel. 802/295–9363, (Nonreporting) **A**1 3 5 8 **S** Department of Veterans Affairs, Washington, DC
Primary Contact: Brett Rusch, M.D., Executive Director
CFO: Joan Wilmot, Chief Finance Officer
CMO: M. Ganga Hematillake, M.D., Chief of Staff
CIO: Matthew Rafus, Chief Information Officer
CHR: Barbara Nadeau, Chief Human Resources Management Service
Web address: www.whiteriver.va.gov/
Control: Veterans Affairs, Government, federal **Service:** General medical and surgical

Staffed Beds: 57

WINDSOR—Windsor County

★ △ **MT. ASCUTNEY HOSPITAL AND HEALTH CENTER (471302)**, 289 County Road, Zip 05089–9000; tel. 802/674–6711, **A**3 5 7 10 18 **F**3 10 11 15 18 24 26 28 29 30 31 32 34 35 38 40 44 45 50 51 54 64 65 68 69 70 77 78 81 85 90 91 92 93 94 95 96 97 104 107 110 115 119 130 133 135 146 148 149 154 157 160 164 167 **P**6 **S** Dartmouth Health, Lebanon, NH
Primary Contact: Jocelyn Caple, Interim CEO
COO: Hannah Bianchi, Chief Operating Officer
CFO: David Sanville, Chief Financial Officer
CMO: Joseph L. Perras, M.D., Chief Medical Officer
CHR: Jean Martaniuk, Director Human Resources
CNO: Amy Visser Lynch, Chief Nursing Officer
Web address: www.mtascutneyhospital.org
Control: Other not–for–profit (including NFP Corporation) **Service:** General medical and surgical

Staffed Beds: 35 **Admissions:** 951 **Census:** 27 **Outpatient Visits:** 76922 **Births:** 0 **Total Expense ($000):** 68442 **Payroll Expense ($000):** 28991 **Personnel:** 271

VIRGINIA

ABINGDON—Washington County

☐ **JOHNSTON MEMORIAL HOSPITAL (490053)**, 16000 Johnston Memorial Drive, Zip 24211-7659; tel. 276/258-1000, (Nonreporting) **A**1 2 3 5 10 13 **S** Ballad Health, Johnson City, TN
Primary Contact: John Jeter, Chief Executive Officer
COO: Bryan Mullins, Chief Operating Officer
CMO: Brian Condit, M.D., Chief Medical Officer
CIO: Jackson Dale, Director Management Information Services
CHR: Jackie G Phipps, Director Human Resources
Web address: www.jmh.org
Control: Other not-for-profit (including NFP Corporation) **Service**: General medical and surgical

Staffed Beds: 116

ALDIE—Loudoun County

⊞ **ENCOMPASS HEALTH REHABILITATION HOSPITAL OF NORTHERN VIRGINIA (493033)**, 24430 Millstream Drive, Zip 20105-3098; tel. 703/957-2000, (Nonreporting) **A**1 10 **S** Encompass Health Corporation, Birmingham, AL
Primary Contact: Vidhya Kannan, Chief Executive Officer
Web address: https://encompasshealth.com/northernvirginiarehab
Control: Corporation, Investor-owned (for-profit) **Service**: Rehabilitation

Staffed Beds: 60

ALEXANDRIA—Alexandria City County

⊞ **INOVA ALEXANDRIA HOSPITAL (490040)**, 4320 Seminary Road, Zip 22304-1535; tel. 703/504-3167, **A**1 2 3 10 **F**3 11 13 14 15 18 20 22 26 28 29 30 31 34 35 38 39 40 42 44 45 46 47 48 49 50 54 55 56 57 58 59 60 61 63 64 65 67 68 70 72 74 75 76 77 78 79 81 82 84 85 86 87 91 92 93 100 101 102 107 110 111 114 115 118 119 120 121 123 124 126 129 130 131 132 135 145 146 147 148 149 154 156 157 167 169 **P**6 **S** Inova Health System, Fairfax, VA
Primary Contact: Rina Bansal, M.D., President
CFO: Todd Lockcuff, Chief Financial Officer
CMO: William L Jackson, Chief Medical Officer
CHR: Hugo Aguas, Vice President Human Resources
Web address: www.inova.org
Control: Other not-for-profit (including NFP Corporation) **Service**: General medical and surgical

Staffed Beds: 336 **Admissions**: 14029 **Census**: 183 **Outpatient Visits**: 215735 **Births**: 3115 **Total Expense ($000)**: 452052 **Payroll Expense ($000)**: 151999 **Personnel**: 1779

ALEXANDRIA—Fairfax County

⊞ **INOVA MOUNT VERNON HOSPITAL (490122)**, 2501 Parker's Lane, Zip 22306-3209; tel. 703/664-7000, **A**1 3 10 **F**3 11 14 15 18 28 29 30 31 34 35 37 38 40 42 44 45 48 49 50 51 53 54 55 56 57 58 59 60 61 63 64 65 68 70 74 75 77 78 79 81 82 84 85 86 87 90 91 92 93 94 95 96 98 100 101 102 104 107 108 110 111 115 118 119 126 130 131 132 135 146 147 148 149 154 156 157 167 169 **P**6 **S** Inova Health System, Fairfax, VA
Primary Contact: Roberta Tinch, President
CHR: Bev Sugar, Associate Administrator and Director Human Resources
Web address: www.inova.org
Control: Other not-for-profit (including NFP Corporation) **Service**: General medical and surgical

Staffed Beds: 225 **Admissions**: 7142 **Census**: 146 **Outpatient Visits**: 132241 **Births**: 0 **Total Expense ($000)**: 293651 **Payroll Expense ($000)**: 107727 **Personnel**: 1250

★ **INOVA SPECIALTY HOSPITAL (492012)**, 2501 Parkers Lane, Zip 22306-3209; tel. 571/547-3600, (Nonreporting) **S** Select Medical Corporation, Mechanicsburg, PA
Primary Contact: Karan Patel, Chief Executive Officer
Web address: https://www.selectspecialtyhospitals.com/locations-and-tours/va/alexandria/inova/?ty=xt
Control: Corporation, Investor-owned (for-profit) **Service**: Acute long-term care hospital

Staffed Beds: 32

ARLINGTON—Arlington County

CAPITAL CARING (490129), 4715 15th Street North, Zip 22205-2640; tel. 703/538-2065, (Nonreporting) **A**10
Primary Contact: Tom Koutsoumpas, President and Chief Executive Officer
CFO: David Schwind, Chief Financial Officer
CIO: Diane Rigsby, Chief Information Officer
Web address: https://www.capitalcaring.org/get-help/our-locations/advanced-illness-management-arlington-va-halquist-center/
Control: Other not-for-profit (including NFP Corporation) **Service**: Other specialty treatment

Staffed Beds: 15

⊞ △ **VHC HEALTH (490050)**, 1701 North George Mason Drive, Zip 22205-3698; tel. 703/558-5000, (Nonreporting) **A**1 2 3 5 7 10
Primary Contact: Christopher Lane, President and Chief Executive Officer
CFO: John Zabrowski, Senior Vice President and Chief Financial Officer
CIO: Michael Mistretta, Vice President and Chief Information Officer
CHR: Michael Malone, Vice President and Chief Human Resources Officer
CNO: Melody Dickerson, R.N., MSN, Senior Vice President, Chief Nursing Officer
Web address: www.virginiahospitalcenter.com
Control: Other not-for-profit (including NFP Corporation) **Service**: General medical and surgical

Staffed Beds: 407

BEDFORD—Bedford City County

⊞ **CENTRA BEDFORD MEMORIAL HOSPITAL (490088)**, 1613 Oakwood Street, Zip 24523-1213; tel. 540/586-2441, **A**1 5 10 **F**2 3 11 15 28 29 30 34 35 40 45 46 53 57 59 63 64 70 81 84 86 87 107 110 115 119 130 143 146 148 149 154 **S** Centra Health, Inc., Lynchburg, VA
Primary Contact: Stacey L. Vaught, MSN, President
CFO: Donald E Lorton, Executive Vice President
CMO: E Allen Joslyn, M.D., Chief Medical Officer
Web address: https://www.centrahealth.com/locations/centra-bedford-memorial-hospital
Control: Other not-for-profit (including NFP Corporation) **Service**: General medical and surgical

Staffed Beds: 33 **Admissions**: 1407 **Census**: 14 **Outpatient Visits**: 41800 **Births**: 0 **Total Expense ($000)**: 44901 **Payroll Expense ($000)**: 18023 **Personnel**: 279

BIG STONE GAP—Wise County

☐ **LONESOME PINE HOSPITAL (490114)**, 1990 Holton Avenue East, Zip 24219-3350; tel. 276/523-3111, (Nonreporting) **A**1 2 3 5 10 13 20 **S** Ballad Health, Johnson City, TN
Primary Contact: Cindy Elkins, Chief Executive Officer
CFO: Regina Day, Executive Vice President of Finance
CMO: Michael Ketcham, President, Medical Staff
CHR: Bobby Collins, Director Human Resources
Web address: https://www.balladhealth.org/locations/hospitals/lonesome-pine
Control: Other not-for-profit (including NFP Corporation) **Service**: General medical and surgical

Staffed Beds: 60

BLACKSBURG—Montgomery County

⊞ **LEWISGALE HOSPITAL MONTGOMERY (490110)**, 3700 South Main Street, Zip 24060-7081, Mailing Address: P.O. Box 90004, Zip 24062-9004; tel. 540/951-1111, (Nonreporting) **A**1 3 5 10 12 13 **S** HCA Healthcare, Nashville, TN
Primary Contact: Lauren Dudley, Chief Executive Officer
COO: Devin Tobin, Chief Operating Officer
CFO: Timothy W Haasken, Chief Financial Officer
CIO: Diron Lane, Director Information Systems
CNO: Ellen Y Linkenhoker, Chief Nursing Officer
Web address: https://www.hcavirginia.com/locations/lewisgale-hospital-montgomery
Control: Corporation, Investor-owned (for-profit) **Service**: General medical and surgical

Staffed Beds: 146

Hospital, Medicare Provider Number, Address, Telephone, Approval, Facility, and Physician Codes, Health Care System

★ American Hospital Association (AHA) membership
☐ The Joint Commission accreditation
◯ Healthcare Facilities Accreditation Program
◇ DNV Healthcare Inc. accreditation
⇑ Center for Improvement in Healthcare Quality Accreditation
△ Commission on Accreditation of Rehabilitation Facilities (CARF) accreditation

© 2025 AHA Guide

Hospitals, U.S. / VIRGINIA

BOONES MILL—Salem City County

☒ **LEWISGALE MEDICAL CENTER (490048)**, 8633 Grassy Hill Rd, Zip 24065, Mailing Address: 1900 Electric Road, Salem, Zip 24153-7494; tel. 540/776-4000, (Includes LEWIS-GALE PAVILION, 1902 Braeburn Drive, Salem, Virginia, Zip 24153-7391, tel. 703/772-2800) (Nonreporting) **A**1 2 3 5 10 **S** HCA Healthcare, Nashville, TN
Primary Contact: Alan J. Fabian, Chief Executive Officer
COO: Andrew Welcome, Chief Operating Officer
CFO: Angela D Reynolds, Chief Financial Officer
CMO: Joseph Nelson, M.D., President Medical Staff
CIO: Beth Cole, Director Information Services
CHR: Dale Beaudoin, Vice President Human Resources
Web address: https://www.hcavirginia.com/locations/lewisgale-medical-center
Control: Corporation, Investor-owned (for-profit) **Service**: General medical and surgical

Staffed Beds: 506

BRISTOL—Bristol City County

☒ **REHABILITATION HOSPITAL OF BRISTOL (493034)**, 103 North Street, Zip 24201-3201; tel. 276/642-7900, (Nonreporting) **A**1 3 10 **S** Encompass Health Corporation, Birmingham, AL
Primary Contact: Britta Milhorn, Chief Executive Officer
Web address: www.rehabilitationhospitalswvirginia.com
Control: Corporation, Investor-owned (for-profit) **Service**: Rehabilitation

Staffed Beds: 25

BURKEVILLE—Nottoway County

☐ **PIEDMONT GERIATRIC HOSPITAL (490134)**, 5001 East Patrick Henry Hwy, Zip 23922-3460, Mailing Address: P.O. Box 427, Zip 23922-0427; tel. 434/767-4401, (Nonreporting) **A**1 10 **S** Virginia Department of Mental Health, Richmond, VA
Primary Contact: Emma L. Lowry, M.D., Acting Facility Director, Chief Executive Officer
COO: Jarvis T. Griffin, Assistant Director Administration and Chief Operating Officer
CFO: Cynthia Arthur, Fiscal Director
CMO: Ramesh Chaudry, M.D., Medical Director
CHR: Michelle Wingo, Director Human Resources
CNO: Regina E. Johnson, Chief Nurse Executive
Web address: www.pgh.dmhmrsas.virginia.gov
Control: State, Government, Nonfederal **Service**: Other specialty treatment

Staffed Beds: 135

CATAWBA—Roanoke County

☐ **CATAWBA HOSPITAL (494033)**, 5525 Catawba Hospital Drive, Zip 24070-2115, Mailing Address: P.O. Box 200, Zip 24070-0200; tel. 540/375-4200, **A**1 3 5 10 **F**39 44 68 77 98 101 103 130 143 146 149 154 163 **S** Virginia Department of Mental Health, Richmond, VA
Primary Contact: Charles Law, Ph.D., Facility Director
CFO: Cecil Hardin, CPA, Chief Financial Officer
CMO: Yad Jabbarpour, M.D., Chief of Staff
CHR: Patricia Ebbett, Chief Human Resources Officer
CNO: Vicky Fisher, Ph.D., R.N., Chief Nurse Executive
Web address: www.catawba.dbhds.virginia.gov
Control: State, Government, Nonfederal **Service**: Psychiatric

Staffed Beds: 110 **Admissions:** 586 **Census:** 99 **Outpatient Visits:** 0 **Births:** 0 **Total Expense ($000):** 34353 **Payroll Expense ($000):** 20576 **Personnel:** 287

CHARLOTTESVILLE—Albemarle County

☒ **UVA ENCOMPASS HEALTH REHABILITATION HOSPITAL (493029)**, 515 Ray C Hunt Drive, Zip 22903-2981; tel. 434/244-2000, (Nonreporting) **A**1 3 5 10 **S** Encompass Health Corporation, Birmingham, AL
Primary Contact: Vivian White, Chief Executive Officer
CFO: Dianna Gomez, Controller
CMO: Alan Alfano, M.D., Medical Director
CIO: Michael Vanhoy, Director of Quality
CHR: Tonya Loving, Director of Human Resources
CNO: Sherry Herring, Chief Nursing Officer
Web address: www.uvahealthsouth.com
Control: Partnership, Investor-owned (for-profit) **Service**: Rehabilitation

Staffed Beds: 50

★ **UVA HEALTH UNIVERSITY MEDICAL CENTER IVY (492011)**, 2965 Ivy Rd (250 West), Zip 22903-9330; tel. 434/924-8245, (Nonreporting) **A**10 **S** UVA Health, Charlottesville, VA
Primary Contact: Wendy Michelle. Horton, PharmD, FACHE, Chief Executive Officer
Web address: www.uvahealth.com/services/transitional-care-hospital
Control: State, Government, Nonfederal **Service**: Acute long-term care hospital

Staffed Beds: 18

CHARLOTTESVILLE—Charlottesville City County

★ ⇧ **SENTARA MARTHA JEFFERSON HOSPITAL (490077)**, 500 Martha Jefferson Drive, Zip 22911-4668; tel. 434/654-7000, **A**10 19 21 **F**3 8 12 13 15 18 20 22 26 28 29 30 31 34 35 36 40 41 42 44 45 46 47 48 49 50 51 53 54 55 57 58 59 60 61 64 65 66 68 70 71 74 75 76 77 78 79 80 81 82 84 85 86 87 91 92 93 94 97 100 102 107 108 110 111 114 115 116 117 118 119 120 121 123 126 129 130 131 132 145 146 147 148 149 154 156 162 164 167 169 **P**7 8 **S** Sentara Health, Virginia Beach, VA
Primary Contact: Rita A. Bunch, M.P.H., FACHE, Division President
COO: Amy Black, R.N., MSN, Chief Operating Officer
CFO: Stewart R Nelson, Vice President and Chief Financial Officer
CMO: F Michael Ashby, M.D., Vice President and Medical Director
CIO: Marijo Lecker, Vice President
CHR: Debbie Desmond, Director Human Resources
Web address: www.marthajefferson.org
Control: Other not-for-profit (including NFP Corporation) **Service**: General medical and surgical

Staffed Beds: 135 **Admissions:** 7582 **Census:** 83 **Outpatient Visits:** 217891 **Births:** 1262 **Total Expense ($000):** 353022 **Payroll Expense ($000):** 83218 **Personnel:** 754

☒ **UVA HEALTH UNIVERSITY MEDICAL CENTER (490009)**, 1215 Lee Street, Zip 22908-0001, Mailing Address: P.O. Box 800809, Zip 22908-0809; tel. 434/924-0211, (Includes UNIVERSITY OF VIRGINIA CHILDREN'S HOSPITAL, 1215 Lee Street, Charlottesville, Virginia, Zip 22908-0816, PO Box 800566, Zip 22908, tel. 434/243-5500) **A**1 2 3 5 8 10 19 **F**3 5 6 7 8 9 11 12 13 15 16 17 18 19 20 21 22 23 24 25 26 27 28 29 30 31 32 34 35 36 37 38 39 40 41 43 44 45 46 47 48 49 50 51 52 54 55 56 57 58 59 60 61 62 63 64 65 66 68 70 71 72 73 74 76 77 78 79 80 81 82 83 84 85 86 87 88 89 90 91 92 93 94 97 98 99 100 101 102 103 104 107 108 109 110 111 112 113 114 115 116 117 118 119 120 121 123 124 126 127 129 130 131 132 134 135 136 137 138 139 140 141 142 143 145 146 147 148 149 154 155 156 157 160 162 163 164 166 167 169 **S** UVA Health, Charlottesville, VA
Primary Contact: Wendy Michelle. Horton, PharmD, FACHE, Chief Executive Officer
COO: Min Y. Lee, PharmD, Chief Operating Officer
CFO: Nick Mendyka, Chief Financial Officer
CIO: Richard Skinner, Chief Information Technology Officer
CHR: John Boswell, Chief Human Resources Officer
CNO: Mary E. Dixon, MSN, R.N., Interim Chief Nursing Officer
Web address: www.healthsystem.virginia.edu
Control: State, Government, Nonfederal **Service**: General medical and surgical

Staffed Beds: 659 **Admissions:** 26410 **Census:** 534 **Outpatient Visits:** 2291470 **Births:** 2312 **Total Expense ($000):** 2384445 **Payroll Expense ($000):** 700032 **Personnel:** 8340

CHESAPEAKE—Chesapeake City County

★ ○ **CHESAPEAKE REGIONAL MEDICAL CENTER (490120)**, 736 Battlefield Boulevard North, Zip 23320-4941, Mailing Address: P.O. Box 2028, Zip 23327-2028; tel. 757/312-8121, (Nonreporting) **A**2 3 10 11 19
Primary Contact: Reese Jackson, President and Chief Executive Officer
COO: Amber Egyud, R.N., Chief Nursing Officer and Chief Operating Officer
CFO: Stephen C McDonnell, Chief Financial Officer
CMO: Raymond McCue, M.D., Vice President, Medical Affairs and Chief Medical Officer
CIO: Maurice Bastarache, Chief Information Officer
CHR: Deborah L Rosenburg, Vice President Human Resources
CNO: Amber Egyud, R.N., Chief Nursing Officer and Chief Operating Officer
Web address: www.chesapeakeregional.com
Control: Hospital district or authority, Government, Nonfederal **Service**: General medical and surgical

Staffed Beds: 315

Hospitals, U.S. / VIRGINIA

CHRISTIANSBURG—Montgomery County

✠ **CARILION NEW RIVER VALLEY MEDICAL CENTER (490042)**, 2900 Lamb Circle, Zip 24073–6344, Mailing Address: P.O. Box 5, Radford, Zip 24143–0005; tel. 540/731–2000, (Includes CARILION CLINIC SAINT ALBANS HOSPITAL, 2900 Lamb Circle, Christiansburg, Virginia, Zip 24073–6344, tel. 540/731–2000) **A**1 3 5 10 19 **F**3 5 8 12 13 15 18 20 22 24 26 28 29 30 31 34 35 36 40 43 45 47 48 49 50 51 53 57 59 60 62 63 64 65 68 70 74 75 76 77 79 81 82 84 85 86 87 89 91 92 93 96 98 99 102 103 104 105 107 108 110 111 114 115 118 119 126 129 130 131 135 146 147 148 149 154 156 160 164 165 169 **S** Carilion Clinic, Roanoke, VA
Primary Contact: William Flattery, Vice President and Administrator Western Division
CMO: Dennis Means, M.D., Vice President Medical Affairs
CIO: Daniel Borchi, Chief Information Officer
Web address: www.carilionclinic.org/Carilion/cnrv
Control: Other not–for–profit (including NFP Corporation) **Service:** General medical and surgical

Staffed Beds: 95 **Admissions:** 7189 **Census:** 93 **Outpatient Visits:** 128291 **Births:** 771 **Total Expense ($000):** 257932 **Payroll Expense ($000):** 92501 **Personnel:** 1137

CARILION SAINT ALBANS HOSPITAL See Carilion Clinic Saint Albans Hospital

CLINTWOOD—Dickenson County

☐ **DICKENSON COMMUNITY HOSPITAL (491303)**, 312 Hospital Drive, Zip 24228, Mailing Address: P.O. Box 1440, Zip 24228–1440; tel. 276/926–0300, (Nonreporting) **A**1 10 18 **S** Ballad Health, Johnson City, TN
Primary Contact: Terri Roop, Assistant Vice President and Administrator
CFO: Kevin Morrison, Chief Financial Officer
CMO: Erin Mullins, D.O., Chief Medical Staff
CHR: Valeri J Colyer, Director Human Resources
CNO: Terri Roop, Director Patient Care Services
Web address: www.msha.com/dch
Control: Other not–for–profit (including NFP Corporation) **Service:** General medical and surgical

Staffed Beds: 11

CULPEPER—Culpeper County

✠ **UVA HEALTH CULPEPER MEDICAL CENTER (490019)**, 501 Sunset Lane, Zip 22701–3917, Mailing Address: P.O. Box 592, Zip 22701–0500; tel. 540/829–4100, (Nonreporting) **A**1 3 5 10 **S** UVA Health, Charlottesville, VA
Primary Contact: Erik Shannon, Chief Executive Officer
CFO: David J Plaviak, Interim Chief Financial Officer
CMO: Morton Chiles, M.D., Chief Medical Officer
CIO: Steven Speelman, Director Information Systems
CHR: Susan Edwards, Vice President Human Resources
Web address: https://uvahealth.com/locations/Culpeper-Medical-Center-5597271
Control: Other not–for–profit (including NFP Corporation) **Service:** General medical and surgical

Staffed Beds: 68

DANVILLE—Danville City County

☐ **SOUTHERN VIRGINIA MENTAL HEALTH INSTITUTE (494017)**, 382 Taylor Drive, Zip 24541–4023; tel. 434/799–6220, (Nonreporting) **A**1 10 **S** Virginia Department of Mental Health, Richmond, VA
Primary Contact: William Cook, Director
CFO: Wayne Peters, Administrator
CMO: Pravin Patel, M.D., Acting President and Chief Executive Officer
CIO: Larry Hays, Director Information Technology
CHR: Stephanie Haywood, Director Human Resources
CNO: Kathy M Dodd, Director of Nursing
Web address: www.svmhi.dbhds.virginia.gov
Control: State, Government, Nonfederal **Service:** Psychiatric

Staffed Beds: 72

✠ **SOVAH HEALTH–DANVILLE (490075)**, 142 South Main Street, Zip 24541–2922; tel. 434/799–2100, (Nonreporting) **A**1 2 3 5 10 13 19 **S** Lifepoint Health, Brentwood, TN
Primary Contact: Steve Heatherly, Chief Executive Officer
COO: Tory Shepherd, Market Chief Operating Officer
CFO: Mark T Anderson, Chief Financial Officer
CMO: James F Starling, M.D., Chief Medical Officer
CIO: David Cartwright, Director Management Information Systems
CNO: Lindsay Barker Crumpton, Market Chief Nursing Officer
Web address: https://www.sovahhealth.com/danville
Control: Other not–for–profit (including NFP Corporation) **Service:** General medical and surgical

Staffed Beds: 250

DULLES—Loudoun County

✠ **STONESPRINGS HOSPITAL CENTER (490145)**, 24440 Stone Spring Boulevard, Zip 20166–2247; tel. 571/349–4000, (Nonreporting) **A**1 10 **S** HCA Healthcare, Nashville, TN
Primary Contact: Tammy Razmic, Chief Executive Officer
CMO: Walter R Zolkiwsky, M.D., Chief Medical Officer
CHR: Tiffani Smith, Chief Human Resources Officer
CNO: Michelle L. Epps, MSN, R.N., Chief Nursing Officer
Web address: https://www.hcavirginia.com/locations/stonesprings-hospital-center
Control: Corporation, Investor–owned (for–profit) **Service:** General medical and surgical

Staffed Beds: 71

EMPORIA—Emporia City County

☐ **BON SECOURS – SOUTHERN VIRGINIA MEDICAL CENTER (490097)**, 727 North Main Street, Zip 23847–1274; tel. 434/348–4400, (Nonreporting) **A**1 10 **S** Bon Secours Mercy Health, Cincinnati, OH
Primary Contact: Brenda Woodcock, President
CFO: Jim Porter, Chief Financial Officer
CMO: Fitzgerald Marcelin, M.D., Chief of Staff
CIO: Larry Gold, Vice President, Information Services
CHR: Becky Parrish, Director Human Resources
Web address: www.svrmc.com
Control: Corporation, Investor–owned (for–profit) **Service:** General medical and surgical

Staffed Beds: 80

FAIRFAX—Fairfax County

✠ **INOVA FAIR OAKS HOSPITAL (490101)**, 3600 Joseph Siewick Drive, Zip 22033–1798; tel. 703/391–3600, **A**1 2 3 5 10 **F**3 11 12 13 14 15 18 28 29 30 31 34 35 37 38 39 40 41 44 45 47 48 49 50 51 54 55 56 57 58 59 60 61 63 64 65 68 70 72 74 75 76 77 78 79 80 81 82 84 85 86 87 91 92 93 100 101 102 107 108 110 111 114 115 118 119 120 121 123 124 126 129 130 131 132 135 145 146 147 148 149 154 156 157 167 169 **P**6 **S** Inova Health System, Fairfax, VA
Primary Contact: Raj Chand, M.D., President
CFO: Jerry Seager, Assistant Vice President and Chief Financial Officer
CMO: G Michael Lynch, M.D., Chief Medical Officer
CIO: Marshall Ruffin, Chief Information Officer
CHR: Jeanne Robinson, Director Human Resources
Web address: www.inova.org
Control: Other not–for–profit (including NFP Corporation) **Service:** General medical and surgical

Staffed Beds: 223 **Admissions:** 11670 **Census:** 122 **Outpatient Visits:** 120143 **Births:** 3771 **Total Expense ($000):** 374211 **Payroll Expense ($000):** 115178 **Personnel:** 1441

FALLS CHURCH—Fairfax County

✠ **DOMINION HOSPITAL (494023)**, 2960 Sleepy Hollow Road, Zip 22044–2030; tel. 703/536–2000, (Nonreporting) **A**1 3 10 **S** HCA Healthcare, Nashville, TN
Primary Contact: Benjamin Brown, Chief Executive Officer
CMO: Gary Litovitz, M.D., Medical Director
CIO: Leslie Gilliam, Director Health Information Management
CHR: Lesley Channell, Vice President Human Resources
Web address: www.dominionhospital.com
Control: Corporation, Investor–owned (for–profit) **Service:** Psychiatric

Staffed Beds: 116

Hospital, Medicare Provider Number, Address, Telephone, Approval, Facility, and Physician Codes, Health Care System

★ American Hospital Association (AHA) membership   ○ Healthcare Facilities Accreditation Program   ⇧ Center for Improvement in Healthcare Quality Accreditation
☐ The Joint Commission accreditation   ◇ DNV Healthcare Inc. accreditation   △ Commission on Accreditation of Rehabilitation Facilities (CARF) accreditation

Hospitals, U.S. / VIRGINIA

INOVA FAIRFAX HOSPITAL See Inova Fairfax Medical Campus

INOVA FAIRFAX MEDICAL CAMPUS (490063), 3300 Gallows Road, Zip 22042-3300; tel. 703/776-4001, (Includes INOVA FAIRFAX HOSPITAL FOR CHILDREN, 3300 Gallows Road, Falls Church, Virginia, Zip 22042-3307, tel. 703/776-4002) **A**1 2 3 5 10 **F**3 4 5 8 11 13 14 15 17 18 19 20 21 22 23 24 25 26 27 28 29 30 31 32 34 35 36 37 38 39 40 41 42 43 44 45 46 47 48 49 50 51 53 54 55 56 57 58 59 60 61 63 64 65 67 68 70 72 74 75 76 77 78 79 81 82 83 84 85 86 87 88 89 90 91 92 93 94 96 98 99 101 102 103 104 105 107 108 109 110 111 114 115 118 119 120 121 122 123 124 126 129 130 131 132 135 137 138 140 141 142 145 146 147 148 149 150 152 153 154 156 157 160 162 164 165 167 169 **P**6 **S** Inova Health System, Fairfax, VA
Primary Contact: Steve Narang, M.D., President and President, Pediatric Service Line
CFO: Ronald Ewald, Chief Financial Officer
CMO: Joseph Hallal, M.D., Chief Medical Officer
CIO: Geoffrey Brown, Vice President Information Systems
CHR: Ken Hull, Director Human Resources
Web address: https://www.inova.org/locations/inova-fairfax-medical-campus
Control: Other not-for-profit (including NFP Corporation) **Service**: General medical and surgical

Staffed Beds: 1036 **Admissions**: 52527 **Census**: 868 **Outpatient Visits**: 709543 **Births**: 9269 **Total Expense ($000)**: 2590122 **Payroll Expense ($000)**: 778229 **Personnel**: 14339

NORTHERN VIRGINIA MENTAL HEALTH INSTITUTE (494010), 3302 Gallows Road, Zip 22042-3398; tel. 703/207-7100, (Nonreporting) **A**1 3 5 10 **S** Virginia Department of Mental Health, Richmond, VA
Primary Contact: Amy Smiley, Chief Executive Officer
CFO: John Poffenbarger, Director Fiscal Services
CMO: R Maximilien del Rio, M.D., Medical Director
CHR: Cynthia Lott, Director Human Resources
Web address: www.nvmhi.dbhds.virginia.gov
Control: State, Government, Nonfederal **Service**: Psychiatric

Staffed Beds: 134

FARMVILLE—Prince Edward County

CENTRA SOUTHSIDE COMMUNITY HOSPITAL (490090), 800 Oak Street, Zip 23901-1199; tel. 434/392-8811, **A**1 10 20 **F**3 11 13 15 18 20 22 26 28 29 30 31 34 35 40 44 45 49 50 57 59 62 63 64 70 74 75 76 77 78 79 80 81 82 84 87 107 108 110 111 115 118 119 126 129 130 132 146 147 149 154 **S** Centra Health, Inc., Lynchburg, VA
Primary Contact: Thomas Angelo, Chief Executive Officer
Web address: www.sch.centrahealth.com/
Control: Other not-for-profit (including NFP Corporation) **Service**: General medical and surgical

Staffed Beds: 86 **Admissions**: 2811 **Census**: 32 **Outpatient Visits**: 83893 **Births**: 281 **Total Expense ($000)**: 105684 **Payroll Expense ($000)**: 31179 **Personnel**: 465

FISHERSVILLE—Augusta County

★ **AUGUSTA HEALTH (490018)**, 78 Medical Center Drive, Zip 22939-2332, Mailing Address: P.O. Box 1000, Zip 22939-1000; tel. 540/932-4000, **A**2 3 5 10 **F**3 7 11 12 13 15 17 18 20 22 24 26 28 29 30 31 32 34 35 36 40 41 44 45 46 49 50 51 53 54 55 56 57 58 59 61 62 63 64 65 66 68 69 70 71 74 75 76 77 78 79 81 82 83 84 85 86 87 89 90 92 93 96 97 98 100 101 102 103 104 107 108 110 111 114 115 118 119 120 121 123 124 126 127 128 129 130 131 132 135 143 144 146 147 148 154 156 157 160 164 167 169 **P**6
Primary Contact: Mary N. Mannix, FACHE, President and Chief Executive Officer
COO: Crystal Farmer, MSN, R.N., FACHE, Chief Operating Officer and Chief Nursing Officer
CFO: Joe Meador, Chief financial Officer
CMO: Richard Embrey, M.D., Chief Medical Officer
CIO: Michael Canfield, Chief Information Officer
CHR: Sue Krzastek, Vice President Human Resources
CNO: Crystal Farmer, MSN, R.N., FACHE, Chief Operating Officer and Chief Nursing Officer
Web address: www.augustahealth.com
Control: Other not-for-profit (including NFP Corporation) **Service**: General medical and surgical

Staffed Beds: 213 **Admissions**: 10067 **Census**: 125 **Outpatient Visits**: 903599 **Births**: 1118 **Total Expense ($000)**: 533185 **Payroll Expense ($000)**: 218870 **Personnel**: 2335

FORT BELVOIR—Fairfax County

FORT BELVOIR COMMUNITY HOSPITAL, 9300 Dewitt Loop, Zip 22060-5285; tel. 571/231-3224, (Nonreporting) **A**1 2 5 **S** Department of the Army, Office of the Surgeon General, Falls Church, VA
Primary Contact: Colonel Kathy Spangler, Director
CMO: Lieutenant Colonel Mark D Harris, Deputy Commander Clinical Services
CIO: Terrance Branch, Chief Information Management
Web address: https://belvoirhospital.tricare.mil/
Control: Army, Government, federal **Service**: General medical and surgical

Staffed Beds: 46

FRANKLIN—Franklin City County

BON SECOURS – SOUTHAMPTON MEDICAL CENTER (490092), 100 Fairview Drive, Zip 23851-1238, Mailing Address: P.O. Box 817, Zip 23851-0817; tel. 757/569-6100, (Nonreporting) **A**1 10 20 **S** Bon Secours Mercy Health, Cincinnati, OH
Primary Contact: Kimberly W. Marks, President
CFO: Steve Ramey, Chief Financial Officer
CMO: Donald Bowling, M.D., Chief Medical Staff
CIO: Kristie Howell, System Information Technology Director
CHR: Loretha Ricks, Human Resources Supervisor
CNO: Laurie Ross, Chief Nursing Officer
Web address: https://www.bonsecours.com/locations/hospitals-medical-centers/hampton-roads/southampton-memorial-hospital
Control: Corporation, Investor-owned (for-profit) **Service**: General medical and surgical

Staffed Beds: 206

BON SECOURS – SOUTHAMPTON MEMORIAL HOSPITAL See Bon Secours – Southampton Medical Center

FREDERICKSBURG—Fredericksburg City County

ENCOMPASS HEALTH REHABILITATION HOSPITAL OF FREDERICKSBURG (493032), 300 Park Hill Drive, Zip 22401-3387; tel. 540/368-7300, (Nonreporting) **A**1 10 **S** Encompass Health Corporation, Birmingham, AL
Primary Contact: Anand Murthy, FACHE, Interim Chief Executive Officer
Web address: www.fredericksburgrehabhospital.com
Control: Corporation, Investor-owned (for-profit) **Service**: Rehabilitation

Staffed Beds: 40

MARY WASHINGTON HOSPITAL (490022), 1001 Sam Perry Boulevard, Zip 22401-3354; tel. 540/741-1100, (Includes SNOWDEN AT FREDERICKSBURG, 1200 Sam Perry Boulevard, Fredericksburg, Virginia, Zip 22401-4456, tel. 540/741-3900; Charles Scercy, Corporate Director) **A**1 2 3 5 10 **F**3 5 12 13 18 20 22 24 26 29 30 31 34 35 36 37 40 42 43 44 45 46 47 48 49 50 54 55 57 58 59 61 62 64 70 72 74 75 76 77 78 79 81 83 84 85 86 87 89 92 93 96 98 99 100 101 102 104 105 107 108 111 114 115 118 119 120 121 124 126 129 130 131 132 135 143 146 147 148 152 153 154 156 166 167 **S** Mary Washington Healthcare, Fredericksburg, VA
Primary Contact: Michael P. McDermott, M.D., President and Chief Executive Officer
COO: Thomas Gettinger, Executive Vice President and Chief Operating Officer
CFO: Sean Barden, Executive Vice President and Chief Financial Officer
CMO: Rebecca Bigoney, Executive Vice President and Chief Medical Officer
CIO: Justin K. Box, Senior Vice President & Chief Information Officer
CHR: Kathryn S Wall, Executive Vice President, Human Resources and Organizational Development
CNO: Eileen L Dohmann, R.N., Senior Vice President and Chief Nursing Officer
Web address: https://www.marywashingtonhealthcare.com/locations/mary-washington-hospital/
Control: Other not-for-profit (including NFP Corporation) **Service**: General medical and surgical

Staffed Beds: 471 **Admissions**: 20649 **Census**: 295 **Outpatient Visits**: 372117 **Births**: 2261 **Total Expense ($000)**: 589614 **Payroll Expense ($000)**: 167806 **Personnel**: 1998

FREDERICKSBURG—Spotsylvania County

SPOTSYLVANIA REGIONAL MEDICAL CENTER (490141), 4600 Spotsylvania Parkway, Zip 22408-7762; tel. 540/498-4000, **A**1 5 10 **F**3 4 11 13 14 15 18 20 22 26 29 30 37 40 42 45 46 51 56 60 61 63 64 68 70 72 74 76 77 78 79 80 81 82 91 93 98 100 102 104 107 108 111 115 119 126 130 146 147 148 149 154 155 167 169 **S** HCA Healthcare, Nashville, TN
Primary Contact: Ryan DeWeese, Chief Executive Officer
Web address: https://www.hcavirginia.com/locations/spotsylvania-regional-medical-center
Control: Corporation, Investor-owned (for-profit) **Service**: General medical and surgical

Staffed Beds: 137 **Admissions**: 8286 **Census**: 88 **Outpatient Visits**: 79915 **Births**: 1021 **Personnel**: 539

Hospitals, U.S. / VIRGINIA

FRONT ROYAL—Warren County

☒ **VALLEY HEALTH – WARREN MEMORIAL HOSPITAL (490033)**, 351 Valley Health Way, Zip 22630; tel. 540/636–0300, **A**1 3 5 10 **F**3 11 15 18 20 22 28 29 30 34 35 36 40 50 53 54 56 57 59 64 65 75 77 79 81 82 85 86 87 93 96 107 108 111 114 118 119 130 132 135 144 146 147 148 154 156 **P**6 **S** Valley Health System, Winchester, VA
Primary Contact: Jennifer Coello, Vice President, Operations and Administrator
CFO: Phillip Graybeal, CPA, Chief Financial Officer
CMO: Robert Meltvedt, M.D., Jr, Vice President Medical Affairs
CNO: Terri A Mayes, Vice President and Chief Nursing Officer
Web address: www.valleyhealthlink.com/WMH
Control: Other not-for-profit (including NFP Corporation) **Service**: General medical and surgical

Staffed Beds: 36 **Admissions**: 2163 **Census**: 18 **Outpatient Visits**: 159546 **Births**: 0 **Total Expense ($000)**: 102704 **Payroll Expense ($000)**: 30018 **Personnel**: 311

GALAX—Galax City County

☒ **TWIN COUNTY REGIONAL HEALTHCARE (490115)**, 200 Hospital Drive, Zip 24333–2227; tel. 276/236–8181, (Nonreporting) **A**1 5 10 20 **S** Lifepoint Health, Brentwood, TN
Primary Contact: Sudandra Ratnasamy,FACHE, R.N., FACHE, Chief Executive Officer
CFO: David Munton, Chief Financial Officer
CHR: Kristal Herrington, Senior Director, Human Resources
CNO: William Alley, Chief Nursing Officer
Web address: www.tcrh.org
Control: Partnership, Investor-owned (for-profit) **Service**: General medical and surgical

Staffed Beds: 45

GLOUCESTER—Gloucester County

⇧ **RIVERSIDE WALTER REED HOSPITAL (490130)**, 7547 Hospital Drive, Zip 23061–4178, Mailing Address: P.O. Box 1130, Zip 23061–1130; tel. 804/693–8800, **A**2 10 21 **F**3 15 28 29 30 34 35 40 44 45 50 51 57 59 60 63 64 70 74 75 78 79 81 84 85 86 87 92 93 96 100 107 108 110 111 114 115 116 118 119 120 121 123 130 132 146 147 148 149 154 167 **S** Riverside Health System, Newport News, VA
Primary Contact: Shelly Johnson, Administrator and President
CHR: Tabetha Holt, Director of Human Resources
CNO: Ivan Pierce, MSN, R.N., Chief Nursing Officer
Web address: www.riversideonline.com
Control: Other not-for-profit (including NFP Corporation) **Service**: General medical and surgical

Staffed Beds: 23 **Admissions**: 2229 **Census**: 22 **Outpatient Visits**: 124354 **Births**: 0 **Total Expense ($000)**: 88391 **Payroll Expense ($000)**: 28235 **Personnel**: 305

GRUNDY—Buchanan County

☒ **BUCHANAN GENERAL HOSPITAL (490127)**, 1535 Slate Creek Road, Zip 24614–6974; tel. 276/935–1000, (Nonreporting) **A**1 10 20
Primary Contact: Robert D. Ruchti, Chief Executive Officer
CFO: Kim Boyd, Chief Financial Officer
CIO: Rita Ramey, Director Information Systems
CHR: Wanda B. Stiltner, Director Human Resources
CNO: Patty Dorton, Director of Nursing
Web address: www.bgh.org
Control: Other not-for-profit (including NFP Corporation) **Service**: General medical and surgical

Staffed Beds: 49

HAMPTON—Hampton City County

☒ **HAMPTON VETERANS AFFAIRS MEDICAL CENTER**, 100 Emancipation Drive, Zip 23667–0001; tel. 757/722–9961, (Nonreporting) **A**1 3 5 **S** Department of Veterans Affairs, Washington, DC
Primary Contact: Taquisa Simmons, Ph.D., Executive Director
COO: Lorraine B Price, Associate Director
CFO: Terry Grew, Chief Business Office
CMO: Val Gibberman, M.D., Acting Chief of Staff
CIO: Cary Parks, Chief Information Resource Management
Web address: www.hampton.va.gov/
Control: Veterans Affairs, Government, federal **Service**: General medical and surgical

Staffed Beds: 213

PENINSULA BEHAVIORAL CENTER See Riverside Behavioral Health Center

★ ⇧ **SENTARA CAREPLEX HOSPITAL (490093)**, 3000 Coliseum Drive, Zip 23666–5963; tel. 757/736–1000, **A**2 3 5 10 19 21 **F**3 8 12 13 15 18 20 22 26 28 29 30 31 34 35 36 37 40 41 42 44 45 46 47 48 49 50 51 54 57 58 59 60 61 64 65 66 70 73 74 75 76 77 78 79 80 81 82 84 85 86 87 91 92 93 96 97 100 102 107 110 111 115 118 119 120 121 126 129 130 131 132 141 146 147 148 149 154 156 157 162 164 167 169 **S** Sentara Health, Virginia Beach, VA
Primary Contact: Kirkpatrick Conley, Senior Vice President, Regional President, Central
COO: Rita A. Bunch, M.P.H., FACHE, Vice President of Operations
CFO: Cheryl Larner, Chief Financial Officer
CMO: Arthur Greene, M.D., Vice President Medical Affairs
CIO: Thomas Ewing, Director Information Technology
CHR: David Kidd, Manager Human Resources
Web address: www.sentara.com
Control: Other not-for-profit (including NFP Corporation) **Service**: General medical and surgical

Staffed Beds: 140 **Admissions**: 6909 **Census**: 90 **Outpatient Visits**: 292436 **Births**: 482 **Total Expense ($000)**: 297187 **Payroll Expense ($000)**: 91190 **Personnel**: 795

★ **U. S. AIR FORCE HOSPITAL**, 77 Nealy Avenue, Zip 23665–2040; tel. 757/764–6969, (Nonreporting) **A**3 **S** Department of the Air Force, Washington, DC
Primary Contact: Colonel Gregory Beaulieu, Commander
COO: Colonel Michael Dietz, Administrator
CFO: Major Steven Dadd, Flight Commander Resource Management
CMO: Lieutenant Brian B. Glodt, Chief of Medical Staff
CIO: Major Merlinda Vergonio, Chief Information Management and Technology
CHR: Major Steven Dadd, Flight Commander Resource Management
CNO: Colonel Marlene Kerchenski, Chief Nurse
Web address: https://langleyeustis.tricare.mil/
Control: Air Force, Government, federal **Service**: General medical and surgical

Staffed Beds: 60

HARRISONBURG—Harrisonburg City County

★ ⇧ **SENTARA RMH MEDICAL CENTER (490004)**, 2010 Health Campus Drive, Zip 22801–3293; tel. 540/689–1000, **A**2 10 21 **F**3 5 9 12 13 15 17 18 20 22 24 26 29 30 31 32 34 35 36 37 40 41 44 45 46 47 48 49 50 51 53 54 55 57 58 59 60 61 64 65 68 70 71 73 74 75 76 77 78 79 80 81 82 84 85 86 87 91 92 93 94 97 98 100 102 104 105 107 108 110 111 115 116 117 118 119 120 121 123 124 126 129 130 131 132 135 141 143 146 147 148 149 150 152 154 156 162 164 165 167 169 **S** Sentara Health, Virginia Beach, VA
Primary Contact: Douglas J. Moyer, Division President
COO: Richard L Haushalter, Senior Vice President Operations and Chief Operating Officer
CFO: Stewart R Nelson, Vice President and Chief Financial Officer
CMO: Susan McDonald, Vice President, Medical Affairs
Web address: www.rmhonline.com
Control: Other not-for-profit (including NFP Corporation) **Service**: General medical and surgical

Staffed Beds: 214 **Admissions**: 10965 **Census**: 123 **Outpatient Visits**: 268799 **Births**: 1539 **Total Expense ($000)**: 476824 **Payroll Expense ($000)**: 116821 **Personnel**: 1214

HAYMARKET—Prince William County

☒ **UVA HEALTH HAYMARKET MEDICAL CENTER (490144)**, 15225 Heathcote Boulevard, Zip 20155–4023, Mailing Address: 14535 John Marshall Hwy, Gainesville, Zip 20155–4023; tel. 571/284–1000, (Nonreporting) **A**1 2 10 **S** UVA Health, Charlottesville, VA
Primary Contact: Erik Shannon, Chief Executive Officer
CFO: Charles Coder, Vice President
CMO: Doug Wall, M.D., Vice President of Medical Affairs
CIO: David B Garrett, Senior Vice President and Chief Information Officer
CHR: Tracy Bowers, Vice President Human Resources and Administrative Services
CNO: Maggie C Conklin, M.P.H., Interim Chief Nursing Officer
Web address: www.novanthealth.org
Control: Other not-for-profit (including NFP Corporation) **Service**: General medical and surgical

Staffed Beds: 18

Hospital, Medicare Provider Number, Address, Telephone, Approval, Facility, and Physician Codes, Health Care System

★ American Hospital Association (AHA) membership   ○ Healthcare Facilities Accreditation Program   ⇧ Center for Improvement in Healthcare Quality Accreditation
☐ The Joint Commission accreditation   ◇ DNV Healthcare Inc. accreditation   △ Commission on Accreditation of Rehabilitation Facilities (CARF) accreditation

Hospitals, U.S. / VIRGINIA

HOPEWELL—Hopewell City County

JOHN RANDOLPH MEDICAL CENTER See Tricities Hospital

TRICITIES HOSPITAL (490020), 411 West Randolph Road, Zip 23860–2938; tel. 804/541–1600, (Nonreporting) **A**1 5 10 **S** HCA Healthcare, Nashville, TN
Primary Contact: Joseph Mazzo, Chief Executive Officer
CFO: Jennifer Honaker, Chief Financial Officer
CHR: MaDena DuChemin, Assistant Administrator Human Resources
Web address: https://www.hcavirginia.com/locations/tricities-hospital
Control: Corporation, Investor–owned (for–profit) **Service:** General medical and surgical

Staffed Beds: 147

HOT SPRINGS—Bath County

★ ⇑ **BATH COMMUNITY HOSPITAL (491300)**, 106 Park Drive, Zip 24445–2921, Mailing Address: P.O. Box Z, Zip 24445–0750; tel. 540/839–7000, (Nonreporting) **A**10 18 21
Primary Contact: Jeffrey Lingerfelt, Chief Executive Officer
COO: Mitzi Grey, Chief Operating Officer
CMO: James Redington, M.D., Chief of Staff
CIO: Tracy Bartley, Manager Information Technology
CHR: Patricia Foutz, Director Human Resources
CNO: Kyna Moore, R.N., Director of Nursing
Web address: https://bathhospital.org
Control: Other not–for–profit (including NFP Corporation) **Service:** General medical and surgical

Staffed Beds: 25

KILMARNOCK—Lancaster County

BON SECOURS RAPPAHANNOCK GENERAL HOSPITAL (491308), 101 Harris Drive, Zip 22482–3880, Mailing Address: P.O. Box 1449, Zip 22482–1449; tel. 804/435–8000, (Nonreporting) **A**1 10 18 **S** Bon Secours Mercy Health, Cincinnati, OH
Primary Contact: John Emery, President
Web address: https://www.bonsecours.com/locations/imaging-radiology/richmond/rappahannock-general-hospital
Control: Other not–for–profit (including NFP Corporation) **Service:** General medical and surgical

Staffed Beds: 35

RAPPAHANNOCK GENERAL HOSPITAL See Bon Secours Rappahannock General Hospital

LEBANON—Russell County

RUSSELL COUNTY MEDICAL CENTER (490002), 58 Carroll Street, Zip 24266, Mailing Address: P.O. Box 3600, Zip 24266–0200; tel. 276/883–8000, (Nonreporting) **A**1 10 **S** Ballad Health, Johnson City, TN
Primary Contact: Greta M. Morrison, Administrator, Assistant Vice President and Chief Nursing Officer
CMO: Brian Condit, M.D., Vice President Chief Medical Officer, Virginia Operations Medical Staff Services
CHR: Beth Hill, Director Human Resources
Web address: www.mountainstateshealth.com/rcmc
Control: Other not–for–profit (including NFP Corporation) **Service:** General medical and surgical

Staffed Beds: 78

LEESBURG—Loudoun County

INOVA LOUDOUN HOSPITAL (490043), 44045 Riverside Parkway, Zip 20176–5101, Mailing Address: P.O. Box 6000, Zip 20177–0600; tel. 703/858–6000, **A**1 2 3 5 10 **F**3 11 13 14 15 18 20 22 26 28 29 30 31 34 35 37 38 39 40 41 42 43 44 45 46 47 48 49 50 54 55 56 57 58 59 60 61 63 64 65 68 70 72 74 75 76 77 78 79 80 81 82 84 85 86 87 89 91 92 93 94 96 98 100 101 102 104 105 107 108 110 111 114 115 118 119 120 121 123 124 126 130 131 132 135 145 146 147 148 149 154 156 157 167 169 **P**6 **S** Inova Health System, Fairfax, VA
Primary Contact: Susan T. Carroll, FACHE, President
CFO: William Bane, Chief Financial Officer
CMO: Christopher Chiantella, M.D., Chief Medical Officer
CHR: Sarah Pavik, Director Human Resources and Guest Services
CNO: Elizabeth Dugan, Ph.D., R.N., MSN, Chief Nursing Officer
Web address: www.inova.org
Control: Other not–for–profit (including NFP Corporation) **Service:** General medical and surgical

Staffed Beds: 271 **Admissions:** 14579 **Census:** 175 **Outpatient Visits:** 234549 **Births:** 2625 **Total Expense ($000):** 457305 **Payroll Expense ($000):** 155780 **Personnel:** 2090

LEXINGTON—Lexington City County

CARILION ROCKBRIDGE COMMUNITY HOSPITAL (491304), 1 Health Circle, Zip 24450–2492; tel. 540/458–3300, **A**1 3 10 18 **F**3 8 15 18 28 29 34 35 40 45 53 56 57 59 65 68 70 75 77 79 81 85 87 91 93 94 97 107 108 110 111 115 119 127 129 130 131 133 135 148 149 154 160 **S** Carilion Clinic, Roanoke, VA
Primary Contact: Greg T. Madsen, Vice President, Hospital Administrator Carilion Rockbridge Community Hospital
CMO: Lyle McClung, M.D., Chief of Staff
Web address: www.carilionclinic.org
Control: Other not–for–profit (including NFP Corporation) **Service:** General medical and surgical

Staffed Beds: 14 **Admissions:** 1255 **Census:** 14 **Outpatient Visits:** 124253 **Births:** 0 **Total Expense ($000):** 65562 **Payroll Expense ($000):** 26992 **Personnel:** 279

CARILION STONEWALL JACKSON HOSPITAL See Carilion Rockbridge Community Hospital

LOW MOOR—Alleghany County

LEWISGALE HOSPITAL ALLEGHANY (490126), 1 Arh Lane, Zip 24457, Mailing Address: P.O. Box 7, Zip 24457–0007; tel. 540/862–6011, (Nonreporting) **A**1 10 20 **S** HCA Healthcare, Nashville, TN
Primary Contact: Lee Higginbotham, Chief Executive Officer
CMO: Michele Ballou, M.D., Chief Medical Staff
CIO: Jeffrey Steelman, Director Information Systems
CHR: Bernard M Campbell, Administrator Human Resources
CNO: Robin Broughman, R.N., Ph.D., Chief Nursing Officer
Web address: www.alleghanyregional.com
Control: Corporation, Investor–owned (for–profit) **Service:** General medical and surgical

Staffed Beds: 205

LURAY—Page County

VALLEY HEALTH – PAGE MEMORIAL HOSPITAL (491307), 200 Memorial Drive, Zip 22835–1005; tel. 540/743–4561, **A**1 10 18 **F**3 7 8 11 15 28 29 30 34 35 40 53 56 57 59 60 64 66 68 69 74 75 77 79 81 85 93 107 108 110 111 114 119 127 129 130 133 135 143 146 148 154 155 156 **P**2 **S** Valley Health System, Winchester, VA
Primary Contact: N. Travis. Clark, President
CFO: Phillip Graybeal, CPA, Chief Financial Officer
Web address: www.valleyhealthlink.com/page
Control: Other not–for–profit (including NFP Corporation) **Service:** General medical and surgical

Staffed Beds: 25 **Admissions:** 849 **Census:** 12 **Outpatient Visits:** 82139 **Births:** 0 **Total Expense ($000):** 44196 **Payroll Expense ($000):** 14631 **Personnel:** 174

LYNCHBURG—Lynchburg City County

CENTRA LYNCHBURG GENERAL HOSPITAL (490021), 1901 Tate Springs Road, Zip 24501–1109; tel. 434/200–4700, (Includes CENTRA VIRGINIA BAPTIST HOSPITAL, 3300 Rivermont Avenue, Lynchburg, Virginia, Zip 24503–2053, tel. 434/200–4000; Tabitha Culbertson, President; LYNCHBURG GENERAL HOSPITAL, 1901 Tate Springs Road, Lynchburg, Virginia, Zip 24501–1167, tel. 434/200–3000) **A**1 2 3 5 10 **F**3 4 5 7 11 12 13 15 17 18 19 20 22 24 26 28 29 30 31 34 35 38 40 41 42 43 44 45 46 47 48 49 50 53 54 55 56 57 59 62 63 64 70 71 72 73 74 75 76 77 78 79 80 81 82 84 86 87 89 90 93 96 98 99 100 101 102 103 104 105 106 107 108 109 110 111 114 115 116 117 118 119 120 121 123 124 126 127 129 130 131 132 135 143 144 146 147 148 149 152 153 154 155 156 162 164 167 **S** Centra Health, Inc., Lynchburg, VA
Primary Contact: Tabitha Culbertson, President
COO: Georgia Harrington, Senior Vice President and Chief Operations Officer
CFO: Lewis C Addison, Senior Vice President and Chief Financial Officer
CMO: Chalmers Nunn, M.D., Chief Medical Officer and Senior Vice President
CIO: Ben Clark, Vice President and Chief Information Officer
CHR: Jan Walker, Director Human Resources
Web address: https://www.centrahealth.com/locations/centra-lynchburg-general-hospital
Control: Other not–for–profit (including NFP Corporation) **Service:** General medical and surgical

Staffed Beds: 582 **Admissions:** 25298 **Census:** 391 **Outpatient Visits:** 520660 **Births:** 2539 **Total Expense ($000):** 854733 **Payroll Expense ($000):** 359763 **Personnel:** 4326

Hospitals, U.S. / VIRGINIA

☐ **CENTRA SPECIALTY HOSPITAL (492010)**, 3300 Rivermont Avenue, Zip 24503-2030; tel. 434/200-1799, (Nonreporting) **A**1 5 10 **S** Centra Health, Inc., Lynchburg, VA
Primary Contact: Kay Bowling, Chief Executive Officer
Control: Other not-for-profit (including NFP Corporation) **Service**: Acute long-term care hospital

Staffed Beds: 28

VIRGINIA BAPTIST HOSPITAL See Centra Virginia Baptist Hospital

MANASSAS—Manassas City County

✠ **UVA HEALTH PRINCE WILLIAM MEDICAL CENTER (490045)**, 8700 Sudley Road, Zip 20110-4418, Mailing Address: P.O. Box 2610, Zip 20108-0867; tel. 703/369-8000, (Nonreporting) **A**1 2 3 5 10 **S** UVA Health, Charlottesville, VA
Primary Contact: Erik Shannon, Chief Executive Officer
CFO: Charles Coder, Vice President
CMO: Doug Wall, M.D., Vice President Medical Affairs
CIO: David B Garrett, Senior Vice President and Chief Information Officer
CHR: Tracy Bowers, Vice President Human Resources and Administrative Services
CNO: Maggie C Conklin, M.P.H., Interim Chief Nurse Officer
Web address: https://uvahealth.com/locations/Prince-William-Medical-Center-5597282
Control: Other not-for-profit (including NFP Corporation) **Service**: General medical and surgical

Staffed Beds: 87

MARION—Smyth County

☐ **SMYTH COUNTY COMMUNITY HOSPITAL (490038)**, 245 Medical Park Drive, Zip 24354, Mailing Address: P.O. Box 880, Zip 24354-0880; tel. 276/378-1000, (Nonreporting) **A**1 10 **S** Ballad Health, Johnson City, TN
Primary Contact: Dale M. Clark, Vice President and Chief Executive Officer
CHR: Sue Henderson, Human Resource Manager
CNO: Ethan Collins, R.N., Chief Nursing Officer
Web address: www.msha.com/scch
Control: Other not-for-profit (including NFP Corporation) **Service**: General medical and surgical

Staffed Beds: 153

☐ **SOUTHWESTERN VIRGINIA MENTAL HEALTH INSTITUTE (494029)**, 340 Bagley Circle, Zip 24354-3390; tel. 276/783-1200, (Nonreporting) **A**1 10 **S** Virginia Department of Mental Health, Richmond, VA
Primary Contact: Cynthia McClaskey, Ph.D., Director
CIO: Kim Ratliff, Director Health Information Management
Web address: www.swvmhi.dmhmrsas.virginia.gov/
Control: State, Government, Nonfederal **Service**: Psychiatric

Staffed Beds: 166

MARTINSVILLE—Martinsville City County

✠ **SOVAH HEALTH–MARTINSVILLE (490079)**, 320 Hospital Drive, Zip 24112-1981, Mailing Address: P.O. Box 4788, Zip 24115-4788; tel. 276/666-7200, (Nonreporting) **A**1 5 10 **S** Lifepoint Health, Brentwood, TN
Primary Contact: Steve Heatherly, Chief Executive Officer
COO: Tory Shepherd, Market Chief Operating Officer
CFO: Brandy Hanners, Chief Financial Officer
CIO: Jeff Butker, Chief Information Officer
CHR: Sherry Schofield, Director Human Resources
CNO: Lindsay Barker Crumpton, Market Chief Nursing Officer
Web address: https://www.sovahhealth.com/patients-visitors/about-us/sovah-health-martinsville
Control: Corporation, Investor-owned (for-profit) **Service**: General medical and surgical

Staffed Beds: 150

MECHANICSVILLE—Hanover County

☐ **BON SECOURS MEMORIAL REGIONAL MEDICAL CENTER (490069)**, 8260 Atlee Road, Zip 23116-1844; tel. 804/764-6000, (Nonreporting) **A**1 2 3 5 10 19 **S** Bon Secours Mercy Health, Cincinnati, OH
Primary Contact: John Emery, President
COO: Eric Young, Chief Operating Officer
CMO: Sunil K. Sinha, M.D., FACHE, Chief Medical Officer
CIO: Gwen Harding, Site Manager Information Systems
CHR: Rebecca Kamguia, Administrative Director Human Resources
CNO: Jill M Kennedy, R.N., Chief Nursing Executive, Providence Group
Web address: www.bonsecours.com
Control: Church operated, Nongovernment, not-for-profit **Service**: General medical and surgical

Staffed Beds: 251

MIDLOTHIAN—Chesterfield County

☐ **BON SECOURS ST. FRANCIS MEDICAL CENTER (490136)**, 13710 St Francis Boulevard, Zip 23114-3267; tel. 804/594-7300, (Nonreporting) **A**1 2 3 5 10 **S** Bon Secours Mercy Health, Cincinnati, OH
Primary Contact: Joseph Wilkins, President
COO: Bridget Fitzpatrick, Chief Operating Officer
CMO: Michael Menen, M.D., Chief Medical Officer
CIO: Terri Spence, Vice President and Regional Chief Information Officer
Web address: www.bonsecours.com/sfmc/default.asp
Control: Other not-for-profit (including NFP Corporation) **Service**: General medical and surgical

Staffed Beds: 130

☐ **SHELTERING ARMS INSTITUTE (493030)**, 13700 St. Francis Boulevard, Suite 400, Zip 23114-3222; tel. 804/764-1000, (Nonreporting) **A**10
Primary Contact: Alan Lombardo, Chief Executive Officer
CFO: James Litsinger, CPA, Chief Operating Officer
CMO: Timothy Silver, M.D., Medical Director, SAH-S
CIO: Chris Sorenson, Chief Health Information Officer
CHR: Ellen B Vance, Chief Human Resources Officer
CNO: Sandra Eyler, MS, Chief Nursing Officer
Web address: https://shelteringarmsinstitute.com/
Control: Other not-for-profit (including NFP Corporation) **Service**: Rehabilitation

Staffed Beds: 28

NEW KENT—New Kent County

☐ **CUMBERLAND HOSPITAL FOR CHILDREN AND ADOLESCENTS (493300)**, 9407 Cumberland Road, Zip 23124-2029; tel. 804/966-2242, (Nonreporting) **A**1 10 **S** Universal Health Services, Inc., King of Prussia, PA
Primary Contact: Garrett Hamilton, Chief Executive Officer
CFO: Joanne Rial, Chief Financial Officer
CMO: Daniel N Davidow, M.D., Medical Director
CIO: Leslie Bowery, Director of Standards and Compliance
CHR: Kim Ivey, Director of Human Resources
CNO: Paula Roberts, Chief Nursing Officer
Web address: www.cumberlandhospital.com
Control: Corporation, Investor-owned (for-profit) **Service**: Children's rehabilitation

Staffed Beds: 74

NEWPORT NEWS—Newport News City County

☐ **BON SECOURS MARY IMMACULATE HOSPITAL (490041)**, 2 Bernardine Drive, Zip 23602-4499; tel. 757/886-6000, (Nonreporting) **A**1 10 **S** Bon Secours Mercy Health, Cincinnati, OH
Primary Contact: Alan E. George, President
CIO: Terri Spence, Vice President Information Services
CHR: Vickie Witcher Humphries, Vice President Human Resources
Web address: https://www.bonsecours.com/locations/hospitals-medical-centers/hampton-roads/bon-secours-mary-immaculate-hospital
Control: Other not-for-profit (including NFP Corporation) **Service**: General medical and surgical

Staffed Beds: 238

Hospital, Medicare Provider Number, Address, Telephone, Approval, Facility, and Physician Codes, Health Care System

★ American Hospital Association (AHA) membership   ○ Healthcare Facilities Accreditation Program   ⇧ Center for Improvement in Healthcare Quality Accreditation
☐ The Joint Commission accreditation   ◇ DNV Healthcare Inc. accreditation   △ Commission on Accreditation of Rehabilitation Facilities (CARF) accreditation

Hospitals, U.S. / VIRGINIA

NEWPORT NEWS BEHAVIORAL HEALTH CENTER (494031), 17579 Warwick Boulevard, Zip 23603–1343; tel. 757/888–0400, (Nonreporting) **A**10
Primary Contact: Thomas Whinnett, Chief Executive Officer
CFO: Holly Hernandez, Chief Financial Officer
CMO: Avtar Dhillon, M.D., Medical Director
CIO: Terry Rethamel, Director of Support Services
CHR: Kristine Pierce, Director Human Resources
CNO: Karen Bruce, Director of Nursing
Web address: www.newportnewsbhc.com/
Control: Corporation, Investor–owned (for–profit) **Service**: Psychiatric

Staffed Beds: 132

⇑ **RIVERSIDE REGIONAL MEDICAL CENTER (490052)**, 500 J Clyde Morris Boulevard, Zip 23601–1929; tel. 757/594–2000, (Includes RIVERSIDE BEHAVIORAL HEALTH CENTER, 2244 Executive Drive, Hampton, Virginia, Zip 23666–2430, tel. 757/827–1001; Debra Campbell, R.N., Administrator) (Nonreporting) **A**2 3 5 10 19 21 **S** Riverside Health System, Newport News, VA
Primary Contact: Michael Oshiki, M.D., MS, FACHE, President
COO: John Peterman, Vice President and Chief Operating Officer
CFO: Wade Broughman, Executive Vice President and Chief Financial Officer
CMO: Barry L Gross, M.D., Executive Vice President and Chief Medical Officer
CIO: Dennis Loftis, Senior Vice President and Chief Information Officer
CHR: Sally Hartman, Senior Vice President
CNO: Candice R. Carroll, Nurse Executive
Web address: https://www.riversideonline.com/rrmc/index.cfm
Control: Other not–for–profit (including NFP Corporation) **Service**: General medical and surgical

Staffed Beds: 307

★ ⇑ **SELECT SPECIALTY HOSPITAL HAMPTON ROADS (492008)**, 500 J. Clyde Morris Boulevard, 4 East/4 Annex, Zip 23601–1929, Mailing Address: 500 J. Clyde Morris Boulevard, 4 East/4Annex, Zip 23601–1929; tel. 757/534–5000, (Nonreporting) **A**10 21 **S** Select Medical Corporation, Mechanicsburg, PA
Primary Contact: Will Aycock, Chief Executive Officer
Web address: www.hamptonroadsspecialtyhospital.com
Control: Corporation, Investor–owned (for–profit) **Service**: Acute long–term care hospital

Staffed Beds: 50

NORFOLK—Norfolk City County

⇑ **CHILDREN'S HOSPITAL OF THE KING'S DAUGHTERS (493301)**, 601 Children's Lane, Zip 23507–1910; tel. 757/668–7000, **A**3 5 10 21 **F**3 7 8 9 12 16 17 19 21 23 25 27 29 30 31 32 34 35 39 40 41 43 44 45 48 49 50 55 57 58 59 60 61 63 64 65 66 68 72 73 74 75 77 78 79 81 82 84 85 86 87 88 89 90 91 92 93 96 97 98 99 100 101 102 104 105 107 108 111 115 116 117 118 119 129 130 131 132 134 138 144 145 146 148 149 150 153 154 156 160 161 162 163 164 165 166 167
Primary Contact: Amy Sampson, President and Chief Executive Officer
CFO: Dennis Ryan, Senior Vice President and Chief Financial Officer
CMO: Chris Foley, Chief of Medicine
CIO: Deborah Barnes, Vice President and Chief Information Officer
CHR: Paul J Morlock, FACHE, Vice President Human Resources and Occupational Health
CNO: Karen Mitchell, Vice President Patient Care Services
Web address: www.chkd.org
Control: Other not–for–profit (including NFP Corporation) **Service**: Children's general medical and surgical

Staffed Beds: 213 **Admissions:** 5372 **Census:** 142 **Outpatient Visits:** 483353 **Births:** 0 **Total Expense ($000):** 600039 **Payroll Expense ($000):** 266569 **Personnel:** 3111

HOSPITAL FOR EXTENDED RECOVERY (492007), 600 Gresham Drive, Suite 700, Zip 23507–1904; tel. 757/388–1700, (Nonreporting) **A**10
Primary Contact: Aimee Vergara, Chief Executive Officer
Control: Other not–for–profit (including NFP Corporation) **Service**: Acute long–term care hospital

Staffed Beds: 25

☐ **KEMPSVILLE CENTER FOR BEHAVIORAL HEALTH (494011)**, 860 Kempsville Road, Zip 23502–3980; tel. 757/461–4565, (Nonreporting) **A**1 10
Primary Contact: Jaime Fernandez, Chief Executive Officer
Control: Corporation, Investor–owned (for–profit) **Service**: Psychiatric

Staffed Beds: 77

LAKE TAYLOR TRANSITIONAL CARE HOSPITAL (492001), 1309 Kempsville Road, Zip 23502–2286; tel. 757/461–5001, (Nonreporting) **A**3 5 10
Primary Contact: Thomas J. Orsini, President and Chief Executive Officer
CFO: Robert W Fogg, Director Finance
CMO: Kevin Murray, M.D., Director Medical Services
CIO: Mark Davis, Director Information Systems
CHR: LeeAnn Lowman, Director Human Resources
Web address: www.laketaylor.org
Control: Hospital district or authority, Government, Nonfederal **Service**: Acute long–term care hospital

Staffed Beds: 296

★ ⇑ **SENTARA LEIGH HOSPITAL (490046)**, 830 Kempsville Road, Zip 23502–3920; tel. 757/261–6000, **A**2 3 5 10 19 21 **F**3 13 15 18 20 22 26 28 29 30 31 34 35 36 37 40 41 44 45 46 47 48 49 50 53 54 57 58 59 60 61 64 65 68 70 71 74 75 76 77 78 79 80 81 84 85 86 87 91 92 93 94 96 97 100 102 107 108 110 111 114 115 116 117 118 119 126 130 131 132 141 146 147 148 149 154 156 157 162 164 167 169 **S** Sentara Health, Virginia Beach, VA
Primary Contact: Joanne Inman, Division President
CFO: Robert Broermann, Senior Vice President and Chief Financial Officer
CMO: Terry Gilliland, M.D., Chief Medical Officer
CIO: Bert Reese, Chief Information Officer
CHR: Michael V Taylor, Senior Vice President Human Resources
CNO: Genemarie McGee, R.N., MS, Chief Nursing Officer
Web address: www.sentara.com
Control: Other not–for–profit (including NFP Corporation) **Service**: General medical and surgical

Staffed Beds: 274 **Admissions:** 17235 **Census:** 226 **Outpatient Visits:** 330819 **Births:** 3094 **Total Expense ($000):** 483895 **Payroll Expense ($000):** 150468 **Personnel:** 1455

★ ⇑ **SENTARA NORFOLK GENERAL HOSPITAL (490007)**, 600 Gresham Drive, Zip 23507–1904; tel. 757/388–3000, **A**2 3 5 8 10 19 21 **F**3 12 13 15 16 17 18 20 22 24 25 26 28 29 30 31 33 34 35 36 37 38 40 41 43 44 45 46 47 48 49 50 51 53 54 55 57 58 59 60 61 64 65 66 68 70 72 74 75 76 77 78 79 80 81 82 83 84 85 86 87 90 91 92 93 94 96 97 98 100 101 102 107 108 110 111 112 114 115 116 117 118 119 120 121 123 124 126 129 130 131 132 135 136 137 138 141 142 143 145 146 147 148 149 150 154 155 156 157 162 164 167 168 169 **S** Sentara Health, Virginia Beach, VA
Primary Contact: Liisa Ortegon, R.N., Division President
CFO: Robert Broermann, Senior Vice President and Chief Financial Officer
CIO: Bert Reese, Chief Information Officer
Web address: www.sentara.com
Control: Other not–for–profit (including NFP Corporation) **Service**: General medical and surgical

Staffed Beds: 587 **Admissions:** 26652 **Census:** 461 **Outpatient Visits:** 288183 **Births:** 3245 **Total Expense ($000):** 1407138 **Payroll Expense ($000):** 316329 **Personnel:** 2939

NORTH CHESTERFIELD—Chesterfield County

HCA JOHNSTON–WILLIS HOSPITAL See Johnston–Willis Hospital

JOHNSTON–WILLIS HOSPITAL See CJW Medical Center, Richmond

NORTON—Norton City County

☐ **NORTON COMMUNITY HOSPITAL (490001)**, 100 15th Street NW, Zip 24273–1616; tel. 276/679–9600, (Nonreporting) **A**1 3 5 10 13 **S** Ballad Health, Johnson City, TN
Primary Contact: Shannon Showalter, Vice President and Chief Executive Officer
CFO: Stephen Sawyer, Chief Financial Officer
CMO: Allen Mullens, M.D., Chief Medical Staff
CIO: Judy Lawson, Director Information Services
CHR: Valeri J Colyer, Director Human Resources
Web address: www.msha.com/nch
Control: Other not–for–profit (including NFP Corporation) **Service**: General medical and surgical

Staffed Beds: 66

ONANCOCK—Accomack County

★ ⇧ **RIVERSIDE SHORE MEMORIAL HOSPITAL (490037)**, 20480 Market Street, Zip 23417-4309, Mailing Address: P.O. Box 430, Zip 23417; tel. 757/302-2100, **A**2 3 10 20 21 **F**3 13 15 28 29 30 31 34 35 40 44 45 50 51 54 55 57 59 60 63 64 70 74 75 76 78 79 81 84 85 86 87 92 93 96 107 108 110 111 114 115 118 119 120 121 129 130 132 135 146 147 149 154 156 167 169 **S** Riverside Health System, Newport News, VA
Primary Contact: Nicolas Chuquin, President
CFO: W William Austin Jr, Senior Vice President Finance
CMO: David Jones, Service Chief
CHR: Nicole Miller, Director Human Resources
Web address: www.riversideonline.com
Control: Other not-for-profit (including NFP Corporation) **Service**: General medical and surgical

Staffed Beds: 20 **Admissions**: 2107 **Census**: 18 **Outpatient Visits**: 94986 **Births**: 331 **Total Expense ($000)**: 86267 **Payroll Expense ($000)**: 27695 **Personnel**: 270

PEARISBURG—Giles County

✠ **CARILION GILES COMMUNITY HOSPITAL (491302)**, 159 Hartley Way, Zip 24134-2471; tel. 540/921-6000, **A**1 5 10 18 **F**3 11 15 18 28 29 30 34 35 36 40 45 50 53 54 57 59 64 65 68 70 75 77 79 81 85 86 87 91 93 96 107 108 110 111 115 118 119 127 130 133 135 146 147 148 149 154 156 **S** Carilion Clinic, Roanoke, VA
Primary Contact: Kristie Williams, Vice President and Hospital Administrator
CMO: John Tamminen, M.D., President Medical Staff
CHR: Carrie Boggess, Human Resource Generalist
CNO: Veronica Stump, Director of Nursing
Web address: https://www.carilionclinic.org
Control: Other not-for-profit (including NFP Corporation) **Service**: General medical and surgical

Staffed Beds: 17 **Admissions**: 1071 **Census**: 16 **Outpatient Visits**: 322228 **Births**: 0 **Total Expense ($000)**: 94238 **Payroll Expense ($000)**: 42564 **Personnel**: 458

PETERSBURG—Petersburg City County

☐ **BON SECOURS - SOUTHSIDE MEDICAL CENTER (490067)**, 200 Medical Park Boulevard, Zip 23805-9274; tel. 804/765-5000, (Nonreporting) **A**1 2 5 10 **S** Bon Secours Mercy Health, Cincinnati, OH
Primary Contact: Brenda Woodcock, President
CMO: Boyd Wickizer, M.D., Jr, Chief Medical Officer
CIO: Eric Synnestvedt, Director Information Technology
CHR: Irene Buskey, Director Human Resources
CNO: Beverly Bzdek Smith, Chief Nursing Officer
Web address: www.srmconline.com
Control: Church operated, Nongovernment, not-for-profit **Service**: General medical and surgical

Staffed Beds: 294

☐ **CENTRAL STATE HOSPITAL**, 26317 West Washington Street, Zip 23803-2727, Mailing Address: P.O. Box 4030, Zip 23803-0030; tel. 804/524-7000, (Nonreporting) **A**1 **S** Virginia Department of Mental Health, Richmond, VA
Primary Contact: Brandi Justice, Interim Director
COO: Ann Bailey, Assistant Director Administration
CFO: Robert Kaufman, Director Financial Services
CMO: Ronald O Forbes, M.D., Medical Director
CIO: Jonathan Baber, Director Information Technology
CHR: Tracy Salisbury, Regional Manager Human Resources
CNO: Eva Parham, R.N., Chief Nurse Executive
Web address: www.csh.dbhds.virginia.gov
Control: State, Government, Nonfederal **Service**: Psychiatric

Staffed Beds: 277

✠ **ENCOMPASS HEALTH REHABILITATION HOSPITAL OF PETERSBURG (493031)**, 95 Medical Park Boulevard, Zip 23805-9233; tel. 804/504-8100, (Nonreporting) **A**1 10 **S** Encompass Health Corporation, Birmingham, AL
Primary Contact: John Laurenzana, Chief Executive Officer
Web address: https://www.encompasshealth.com
Control: Corporation, Investor-owned (for-profit) **Service**: Rehabilitation

Staffed Beds: 53

☐ **HIRAM W. DAVIS MEDICAL CENTER (490104)**, 26317 West Washington Street, Zip 23803-2727, Mailing Address: P.O. Box 4030, Zip 23803-0030; tel. 804/524-7420, (Nonreporting) **A**1 10 **S** Virginia Department of Mental Health, Richmond, VA
Primary Contact: Jarvis T. Griffin, Chief Executive Officer, Facility Director
CFO: Robert Kaufman, Fiscal Officer
CHR: Tracy Salisbury, Director Human Resources
Control: State, Government, Nonfederal **Service**: Other specialty treatment

Staffed Beds: 96

✠ **POPLAR SPRINGS HOSPITAL (494022)**, 350 Poplar Drive, Zip 23805-9367; tel. 804/733-6874, **A**1 10 **F**4 5 29 38 87 98 99 100 104 105 106 130 132 134 151 152 153 154 160 162 164 165 **P**6 **S** Universal Health Services, Inc., King of Prussia, PA
Primary Contact: Michael S. Triggs, Group Chief Executive Officer and Managing Director
COO: Rachel Beal, Chief Operating Officer
CFO: Michael Felice, Chief Financial Officer
CMO: Thresa Simon, M.D., Medical Director
CHR: Morris Mitchell, Director Human Resources
Web address: www.poplarsprings.com
Control: Corporation, Investor-owned (for-profit) **Service**: Psychiatric

Staffed Beds: 208 **Admissions**: 3311 **Census**: 130 **Outpatient Visits**: 5242 **Births**: 0 **Total Expense ($000)**: 31565 **Payroll Expense ($000)**: 20877 **Personnel**: 293

PORTSMOUTH—Portsmouth City County

☐ **BON SECOURS MARYVIEW MEDICAL CENTER (490017)**, 3636 High Street, Zip 23707-3270; tel. 757/398-2200, (Nonreporting) **A**1 3 5 10 **S** Bon Secours Mercy Health, Cincinnati, OH
Primary Contact: Shane Knisley, President
CFO: Ernest C Padden, Chief Financial Officer
CMO: Warren Austin, M.D., Vice President Medical Affairs
CIO: Terri Spence, Chief Information Officer
CHR: Vickie Witcher Humphries, Director Human Resources
Web address: https://www.bonsecours.com/locations/hospitals-medical-centers/hampton-roads/bon-secours-maryview-medical-center
Control: Other not-for-profit (including NFP Corporation) **Service**: General medical and surgical

Staffed Beds: 466

✠ **NAVAL MEDICAL CENTER**, 620 John Paul Jones Circle, Zip 23708-2197; tel. 757/953-1980, (Nonreporting) **A**1 2 3 5 **S** Bureau of Medicine and Surgery, Department of the Navy, Falls Church, VA
Primary Contact: Captain Brian Feldman, Commanding Officer
CMO: Captain Cynthia J Gantt, Chief of Staff
CIO: Lieutenant Colonel Karen Albany, Chief Information Officer
Web address: https://www.med.navy.mil/sites/nmcp/SitePages/home.aspx
Control: Navy, Government, federal **Service**: General medical and surgical

Staffed Beds: 177

PULASKI—Pulaski County

✠ **LEWISGALE HOSPITAL PULASKI (490116)**, 2400 Lee Highway, Zip 24301-2326, Mailing Address: P.O. Box 759, Zip 24301-0759; tel. 540/994-8100, (Nonreporting) **A**1 2 10 **S** HCA Healthcare, Nashville, TN
Primary Contact: Sean Pressman, Chief Executive Officer
CFO: Jeff Kurcab, Chief Financial Officer
CMO: Karanita Ojomo, M.D., Chief of Staff
CIO: Diron Lane, Director Information Systems
CHR: Jana Beckner, Director Human Resources
Web address: www.lewisgale.com/
Control: Corporation, Investor-owned (for-profit) **Service**: General medical and surgical

Staffed Beds: 147

Hospitals, U.S. / VIRGINIA

RESTON—Fairfax County

RESTON HOSPITAL CENTER (490107), 1850 Town Center Parkway, Zip 20190–3219; tel. 703/689–9000, (Nonreporting) **A**1 2 10 **S** HCA Healthcare, Nashville, TN
Primary Contact: John A. Deardorff, President and Chief Executive, Northern Virginia Market
COO: Jane Raymond, Vice President and Chief Operating Officer
CMO: Walter R Zolkiwsky, M.D., Chief Medical Officer
CIO: Paresh Shah, Director Information Systems
CHR: Lesley Channell, Vice President Human Resources
CNO: Cynthia Glover, R.N., Vice President and Chief Nursing Officer
Web address: https://hcavirginia.com/locations/reston-hospital-center/
Control: Corporation, Investor–owned (for–profit) **Service**: General medical and surgical

Staffed Beds: 245

RICHLANDS—Tazewell County

CLINCH VALLEY MEDICAL CENTER (490060), 6801 Governor G C Peery Highway, Zip 24641–2194; tel. 276/596–6000, (Nonreporting) **A**1 5 10 **S** Lifepoint Health, Brentwood, TN
Primary Contact: Peter Mulkey, Chief Executive Officer
CFO: Jason Schmiedt, Chief Financial Officer
CMO: George Farrell, M.D., Chief Medical Officer
CIO: Chris Perkins, Director Information Services
CHR: John Knowles, Director Human Resources
Web address: www.clinchvalleymedicalcenter.com
Control: Corporation, Investor–owned (for–profit) **Service**: General medical and surgical

Staffed Beds: 75

RICHMOND—Goochland County

★ **SHELTERING ARMS INSTITUTE (493036)**, 2000 Wilkes Ridge Drive, Zip 23233–7632; tel. 804/877–4002, **A**3 10 21 **F**3 29 30 34 35 36 44 50 54 58 60 65 68 74 75 77 79 82 85 86 87 90 91 93 94 95 96 119 132 146 148 149 154 164
Primary Contact: Alan Lombardo, Chief Executive Officer
Web address: https://shelteringarmsinstitute.com
Control: Other not–for–profit (including NFP Corporation) **Service**: Rehabilitation

Staffed Beds: 114 **Admissions:** 2362 **Census:** 100 **Outpatient Visits:** 108352 **Births:** 0 **Total Expense ($000):** 83861 **Payroll Expense ($000):** 44130 **Personnel:** 613

RICHMOND—Henrico County

BON SECOURS ST. MARY'S HOSPITAL (490059), 5801 Bremo Road, Zip 23226–1907; tel. 804/285–2011, (Includes BON SECOURS ST. MARY'S CHILDREN'S SERVICES, 5801 Bremo Road, Richmond, Virginia, Zip 23226–1907, tel. 804/285–2011) (Nonreporting) **A**1 2 3 5 10 19 **S** Bon Secours Mercy Health, Cincinnati, OH
Primary Contact: W. Bryan. Lee, President
CMO: Khiet Trinh, M.D., Chief Medical Officer
CIO: Terri Spence, Chief Information Officer
CHR: Kishah White, Director Human Resources
CNO: Jody A. Bishop, Chief Nursing Officer
Web address: www.bonsecours.com
Control: Church operated, Nongovernment, not–for–profit **Service**: General medical and surgical

Staffed Beds: 391

ENCOMPASS HEALTH REHABILITATION HOSPITAL OF RICHMOND (493028), 5700 Fitzhugh Avenue, Zip 23226–1800; tel. 804/288–5700, **A**1 10 **F**60 90 132 148 149 154 **S** Encompass Health Corporation, Birmingham, AL
Primary Contact: James Miller, Chief Executive Officer
CMO: Roger Giordano, M.D., Medical Director
CIO: Faye Encke, Director Information Management
CHR: Tonya Ferguson, Director Human Resources
CNO: Michelle Anthony, Chief Nursing Officer
Web address: https://www.encompasshealth.com
Control: Corporation, Investor–owned (for–profit) **Service**: Rehabilitation

Staffed Beds: 40 **Admissions:** 1144 **Census:** 34 **Outpatient Visits:** 0 **Births:** 0

HEALTHSOUTH MEDICAL CENTER See Henrico Doctors' Hospital – Parham

HENRICO DOCTOR'S HOSPITAL See Henrico Doctors' Hospital – Forest

HENRICO DOCTORS' HOSPITAL (490118), 1602 Skipwith Road, Zip 23229–5205; tel. 804/289–4500, (Includes HENRICO DOCTORS' HOSPITAL – FOREST, 1602 Skipwith Road, Richmond, Virginia, Zip 23229–5298, tel. 804/289–4500; HENRICO DOCTORS' HOSPITAL – PARHAM, 7700 East Parham Road, Richmond, Virginia, Zip 23294–4301, tel. 804/747–5600; Allyssa Tobitt, Chief Executive Officer; HENRICO DOCTORS' HOSPITAL – RETREAT CAMPUS, 2621 Grove Avenue, Richmond, Virginia, Zip 23220–4308, tel. 804/254–5100; Elizabeth Matish, Chief Executive Officer) **A**1 2 10 **F**3 5 8 12 13 15 17 18 20 22 24 26 28 29 30 31 33 34 35 36 37 38 40 41 42 43 44 45 46 47 48 49 50 51 54 55 56 57 59 60 64 65 68 70 72 73 74 75 76 77 78 79 81 85 86 87 90 92 93 96 97 98 100 102 104 105 107 108 109 110 111 112 114 115 116 117 119 120 121 123 124 126 129 130 131 132 135 138 141 146 147 148 149 150 152 153 154 157 162 164 167 169 **S** HCA Healthcare, Nashville, TN
Primary Contact: Ryan Jensen, Chief Executive Officer
COO: Zachary Reed, Chief Operating Officer
CFO: Christopher Denton, Chief Financial Officer
CIO: Daniel Patton, Director Information Systems
CHR: Steven Burgess, Administrator Human Resources
Web address: www.henricodoctorshospital.com
Control: Corporation, Investor–owned (for–profit) **Service**: General medical and surgical

Staffed Beds: 574 **Admissions:** 24491 **Census:** 336 **Outpatient Visits:** 277421 **Births:** 4284 **Personnel:** 1496

SELECT SPECIALTY HOSPITAL – RICHMOND (492009), 2220 Edward Holland Drive, Zip 23230–2519; tel. 804/678–7000, (Nonreporting) **A**1 10 **S** Select Medical Corporation, Mechanicsburg, PA
Primary Contact: Shirley Martell, Chief Executive Officer
CMO: Gerard Weeden, Chief Medical Officer
CHR: Jonnitra Peeples, Chief Human Resource Officer
CNO: Crystal Richardson, Chief Nursing Officer
Web address: https://www.selectspecialtyhospitals.com/locations-and-tours/va/richmond/richmond/
Control: Corporation, Investor–owned (for–profit) **Service**: Acute long–term care hospital

Staffed Beds: 50

VIBRA HOSPITAL OF RICHMOND See Select Specialty Hospital – Richmond

RICHMOND—Richmond City County

BON SECOURS RICHMOND COMMUNITY HOSPITAL (490094), 1500 North 28th Street, Zip 23223–5396, Mailing Address: P.O. Box 27184, Zip 23261–7184; tel. 804/225–1700, (Nonreporting) **A**1 10 **S** Bon Secours Mercy Health, Cincinnati, OH
Primary Contact: W. Bryan Lee, President
CIO: Jeff Burke, Chief Information Officer
CHR: Shelia White, Director Human Resources
Web address: www.bonsecours.com
Control: Church operated, Nongovernment, not–for–profit **Service**: General medical and surgical

Staffed Beds: 96

BON SECOURS–RICHMOND COMMUNITY HOSPITAL See Bon Secours Richmond Community Hospital

★ **CHILDREN'S HOSPITAL OF RICHMOND AT VCU (493302)**, 2924 Brook Road, Zip 23220–1298, Mailing Address: 1000 E. Broad Street, Zip 23219; tel. 804/321–7474, (Nonreporting) **A**3 5 10 **S** VCU Health System, Richmond, VA
Primary Contact: Elias Neujahr, President
CFO: James A Deyarmin, Controller
CMO: Eugene A Monasterio, M.D., Medical Director
CIO: Tim Gibbs, Director of Information Technology, Information Security Officer
CNO: Sharon Darby, R.N., FACHE, Vice President, Clinical Operations
Web address: www.chrichmond.org
Control: Other not–for–profit (including NFP Corporation) **Service**: Children's rehabilitation

Staffed Beds: 36

Hospitals, U.S. / VIRGINIA

☒ **CJW MEDICAL CENTER (490112)**, 7101 Jahnke Road, Zip 23225–4044; tel. 804/483–0000, (Includes CHIPPENHAM MEDICAL CENTER, 7101 Jahnke Road, Richmond, Virginia, Zip 23225, tel. 804/320–3911; JOHNSTON–WILLIS HOSPITAL, 1401 Johnston Willis DR, North Chesterfield, Virginia, Zip 23235–4730, 1401 Johnston–Willis Drive, Richmond, Virginia, Zip 23235, tel. 804/330–2000; Lance Jones, Chief Executive Officer) (Nonreporting) **A**1 2 3 5 10 19 **S** HCA Healthcare, Nashville, TN
Primary Contact: Lance Jones, Chief Executive Officer
CFO: Lynn Strader, Chief Financial Officer
CMO: Georgean DeBlois, M.D., Chairman Medical Staff
CIO: Tracy Hechler, Healthcare Director Information Services
CHR: Kris Lukish, Human Resources Officer
Web address: www.cjwmedical.com
Control: Corporation, Investor–owned (for–profit) **Service**: General medical and surgical

Staffed Beds: 673

HCA CHIPPENHAM MEDICAL CENTER See Chippenham Medical Center

☒ △ **HUNTER HOLMES MCGUIRE VETERANS AFFAIRS MEDICAL CENTER– RICHMOND**, 1201 Broad Rock Boulevard, Zip 23249–0002; tel. 804/675–5000, (Nonreporting) **A**1 3 5 7 8 **S** Department of Veterans Affairs, Washington, DC
Primary Contact: J. Ronald. Johnson, Medical Center Director
CFO: Tanza Westry, Chief Financial Officer
CMO: Julie Beales, M.D., Chief of Staff
CIO: David Dahlstrand, Chief, OI&T
CHR: Adriana H Hamilton, Chief Human Resources Officer
CNO: Marjorie Lyne, Associate Director for Patient Care Services
Web address: www.richmond.va.gov/
Control: Veterans Affairs, Government, federal **Service**: General medical and surgical

Staffed Beds: 143

RETREAT DOCTORS' HOSPITAL See Henrico Doctors' Hospital – Retreat Campus

VCU HEALTH SYSTEM CHILDREN'S MEDICAL CENTER See Children's Hospital of Richmond At Vcu

☒ **VCU MEDICAL CENTER (490032)**, 1250 East Marshall Street, Zip 23298–5051, Mailing Address: P.O. Box 980510, Zip 23298–0510; tel. 804/828–9000, (Includes CHILDREN'S HOSPITAL OF RICHMOND AT VCU, 1000 East Broad Street, Richmond, Virginia, Zip 23219–1918, PO Box 980646, Zip 23298–0646, tel. 804/828–2467; Elias Neujahr, Chief Executive Officer) **A**1 2 3 5 8 10 19 **F**2 3 5 8 9 11 12 13 15 16 17 18 19 20 21 22 23 24 25 26 27 28 29 30 31 32 34 35 36 37 38 39 40 41 42 43 44 45 46 47 48 49 50 51 52 54 55 56 57 58 59 60 61 62 64 65 66 68 70 72 73 74 75 76 78 79 80 81 82 83 84 85 86 87 88 89 91 92 93 95 96 97 98 99 100 101 102 103 104 107 108 109 110 111 114 115 116 117 118 119 120 121 123 124 126 129 130 131 132 134 135 136 137 138 139 141 142 143 145 146 147 148 149 150 153 154 156 160 162 164 165 166 167 168 169 **P**6 **S** VCU Health System, Richmond, VA
Primary Contact: Michael Roussos, President
COO: James Willis, Chief Operating Officer
CMO: Ron Clark, M.D., Vice President Clinical Activities and Chief Medical Officer
CIO: Susan Steagall, Vice President Information Services
CHR: Maria Curran, Vice President Human Resources
CNO: Tina Mammone, Ph.D., R.N., Chief Nursing Officer
Web address: www.vcuhealth.org
Control: Hospital district or authority, Government, Nonfederal **Service**: General medical and surgical

Staffed Beds: 823 **Admissions:** 37648 **Census:** 664 **Outpatient Visits:** 1913720 **Births:** 2826 **Total Expense ($000):** 2268930 **Payroll Expense ($000):** 820295 **Personnel:** 9722

ROANOKE—Roanoke City County

CARILION ROANOKE COMM HOSP See Carilion Roanoke Community Hospital

☒ **CARILION ROANOKE MEMORIAL HOSPITAL (490024)**, 1906 Belleview Avenue Southeast, Zip 24014–1838, Mailing Address: P.O. Box 13367, Zip 24033–3367; tel. 540/981–7000, (Includes CARILION CLINIC CHILDREN'S HOSPITAL, 1906 Belleview Avenue, SE, Roanoke, Virginia, Zip 24014–1838, tel. 540/981–7000; CARILION ROANOKE COMMUNITY HOSPITAL, 101 Elm Avenue SE, Roanoke, Virginia, Zip 24013–2230, P O Box 12946, Zip 24029–2946, tel. 540/985–8000; ROANOKE MEMORIAL REHABILITATION CENTER, South Jefferson and McClanahan Streets, Roanoke, Virginia, Zip 24014, P O Box 13367, Zip 24033, tel. 703/342–4541) **A**1 2 3 5 8 10 13 **F**3 4 5 7 8 9 11 12 13 15 17 18 19 20 22 24 26 28 29 30 31 32 33 34 35 36 37 38 39 40 41 43 44 45 46 47 48 49 50 51 52 53 54 55 56 57 58 59 60 61 62 63 64 65 66 68 70 71 72 73 74 75 76 77 78 79 81 82 83 84 85 86 87 88 89 90 91 92 93 95 96 97 98 99 100 101 102 103 104 106 107 108 110 111 113 114 115 116 117 118 119 120 121 124 126 129 130 131 132 134 135 143 144 146 147 148 149 150 151 154 155 156 157 160 162 163 164 165 167 168 169 **S** Carilion Clinic, Roanoke, VA
Primary Contact: Steven C. Arner, President and Chief Operating Officer, Hospital Administrator
COO: Steven C. Arner, President and Chief Operating Officer, Hospital Administrator
CFO: Donald B Halliwill, Executive Vice President and Chief Financial Officer
CHR: Heather S Shepardson, Vice President Human Resources
Web address: www.carilionclinic.org
Control: Other not–for–profit (including NFP Corporation) **Service**: General medical and surgical

Staffed Beds: 598 **Admissions:** 32195 **Census:** 532 **Outpatient Visits:** 1735104 **Births:** 3062 **Total Expense ($000):** 1701735 **Payroll Expense ($000):** 740224 **Personnel:** 7216

ROCKY MOUNT—Franklin County

☒ **CARILION FRANKLIN MEMORIAL HOSPITAL (490089)**, 180 Floyd Avenue, Zip 24151–1389; tel. 540/483–5277, **A**1 3 5 10 **F**3 11 15 18 28 29 30 34 35 40 45 50 53 57 59 62 63 65 68 70 75 81 82 84 85 93 96 107 110 111 115 119 130 132 146 148 149 154 **S** Carilion Clinic, Roanoke, VA
Primary Contact: Carl T. Cline, Vice President, Carilion Clinic and Hospital Administrator
COO: Steven C. Arner, President and Chief Operating Officer
CFO: Donald B Halliwill, Chief Financial Officer
CMO: Patrice M. Weiss, M.D., Chief Medical Officer
CIO: Robert Keith Perry, Senior Vice President, Chief Information Officer
CHR: Paul C. Hudgins, Senior Vice President
Web address: www.carilionclinic.org/CFMH
Control: Other not–for–profit (including NFP Corporation) **Service**: General medical and surgical

Staffed Beds: 20 **Admissions:** 1718 **Census:** 19 **Outpatient Visits:** 53339 **Births:** 0 **Total Expense ($000):** 67150 **Payroll Expense ($000):** 25398 **Personnel:** 367

SALEM—Roanoke County

LEWIS–GALE PSYCHIATRIC CENTER See Lewis–Gale Pavilion

SALEM—Salem City County

☒ **SALEM VETERANS AFFAIRS MEDICAL CENTER**, 1970 Roanoke Boulevard, Zip 24153–6478; tel. 540/982–2463, (Nonreporting) **A**1 3 5 8 **S** Department of Veterans Affairs, Washington, DC
Primary Contact: Rebecca J. Stackhouse, FACHE, Executive Director
CFO: Codie Walker, Chief Financial Officer
CMO: Anne Hutchins, M.D., Chief of Staff
CIO: Sharon Collins, Chief Information Officer
CHR: Brian Zeman, Chief Human Resources
CNO: Teresa England, R.N., Ph.D., Nurse Executive
Web address: www.salem.va.gov
Control: Veterans Affairs, Government, federal **Service**: General medical and surgical

Staffed Beds: 176

Hospital, Medicare Provider Number, Address, Telephone, Approval, Facility, and Physician Codes, Health Care System

★ American Hospital Association (AHA) membership
☐ The Joint Commission accreditation
○ Healthcare Facilities Accreditation Program
◇ DNV Healthcare Inc. accreditation
⇑ Center for Improvement in Healthcare Quality Accreditation
△ Commission on Accreditation of Rehabilitation Facilities (CARF) accreditation

Hospitals, U.S. / VIRGINIA

SOUTH BOSTON—Halifax County

★ ⇧ **SENTARA HALIFAX REGIONAL HOSPITAL (490013)**, 2204 Wilborn Avenue, Zip 24592–1638; tel. 434/517–3100, **A**5 10 21 **F**3 5 15 18 20 28 29 30 31 34 35 36 38 40 41 44 45 46 47 48 50 54 57 59 60 61 64 65 66 68 70 75 77 78 79 81 86 87 91 92 93 97 100 102 104 105 107 108 110 111 114 115 119 127 129 130 131 132 145 146 147 148 149 152 153 154 156 162 164 165 167 **P**4 **S** Sentara Health, Virginia Beach, VA
Primary Contact: Brian Zwoyer, R.N., Division President
CFO: Stewart R Nelson, Vice President and Chief Financial Officer
CMO: Said Iskandar, M.D., Chief Medical Officer
CIO: William Zirkle, Manager Information Systems
CHR: Catherine Howard, Director Human Resources
CNO: Patricia F Thomas, Chief Nursing Officer
Web address: https://www.sentara.com/halifax-southern-virginia/hospitalslocations/locations/sentara-halifax-regional-hospital/directions-parking.aspx
Control: Other not–for–profit (including NFP Corporation) **Service:** General medical and surgical

Staffed Beds: 44 **Admissions:** 2521 **Census:** 27 **Outpatient Visits:** 83671 **Births:** 126 **Total Expense ($000):** 131001 **Payroll Expense ($000):** 36027 **Personnel:** 295

SOUTH HILL—Mecklenburg County

⊞ **VCU HEALTH COMMUNITY MEMORIAL HOSPITAL (490098)**, 125 Buena Vista Circle, Zip 23970–1431, Mailing Address: P.O. Box 90, Zip 23970–0090; tel. 434/447–3151, (Total facility includes 136 beds in nursing home–type unit) **A**1 2 3 10 20 **F**3 11 13 15 18 20 29 30 31 34 35 39 40 45 46 49 50 54 57 59 62 63 64 65 70 74 75 76 77 78 79 81 82 84 85 86 87 93 97 100 104 107 108 110 111 115 118 119 120 121 123 126 128 130 131 132 133 135 146 147 148 149 154 166 169 **S** VCU Health System, Richmond, VA
Primary Contact: Sheldon Barr, President
CFO: Kenneth Libby, Vice President Finance
CMO: Manhal Saleeby, M.D., Chief of Staff
CIO: Brian Rock, Director of Information Systems
CHR: Maria Stephens, Director Human Resources, Education and Occupational Health and Wellness
CNO: Ursula N Butts, FACHE, Vice President of Patient Care Services
Web address: www.cmh-sh.org
Control: Other not–for–profit (including NFP Corporation) **Service:** General medical and surgical

Staffed Beds: 210 **Admissions:** 3208 **Census:** 123 **Outpatient Visits:** 203242 **Births:** 224 **Total Expense ($000):** 138368 **Payroll Expense ($000):** 52837 **Personnel:** 629

STAFFORD—Stafford County

⊞ **STAFFORD HOSPITAL (490140)**, 101 Hospital Center Boulevard, Zip 22554–6200; tel. 540/741–9000, **A**1 3 10 **F**3 13 15 18 20 22 26 29 30 31 34 35 36 40 44 45 46 47 48 49 50 54 57 58 59 64 70 73 74 75 76 77 78 79 81 84 85 86 87 92 93 96 102 107 108 110 111 115 118 119 120 121 129 130 131 132 135 146 147 148 156 167 **P**6 **S** Mary Washington Healthcare, Fredericksburg, VA
Primary Contact: Debra Marinari, Associate Vice President Hospital Operations
COO: Thomas Gettinger, Executive Vice President and Chief Operating Officer
CFO: Sean Barden, Executive Vice President and Chief Financial Officer
CMO: Rebecca Bigoney, Executive Vice President and Chief Medical Officer
CIO: Justin K. Box, Senior Vice President and Chief Information Officer
CHR: Kathryn S Wall, Executive Vice President Human Resources and Organizational Development
CNO: Eileen L Dohmann, R.N., Senior Vice President and Chief Nursing Officer
Web address: www.mwhc.com
Control: Other not–for–profit (including NFP Corporation) **Service:** General medical and surgical

Staffed Beds: 100 **Admissions:** 4320 **Census:** 38 **Outpatient Visits:** 78063 **Births:** 1053 **Total Expense ($000):** 126504 **Payroll Expense ($000):** 35981 **Personnel:** 378

STAUNTON—Staunton City County

☐ **COMMONWEALTH CENTER FOR CHILDREN AND ADOLESCENTS**, 1355 Richmond Road, Zip 24401–9146, Mailing Address: Box 4000, Zip 24402–4000; tel. 540/332–2100, (Nonreporting) **A**1 5 **S** Virginia Department of Mental Health, Richmond, VA
Primary Contact: George Newsome, Director
Web address: www.ccca.dbhds.virginia.gov
Control: State, Government, Nonfederal **Service:** Children's hospital psychiatric

Staffed Beds: 60

☐ **WESTERN STATE HOSPITAL (494021)**, 103 Valley Center Drive, Zip 24401–9146, Mailing Address: P.O. Box 2500, Zip 24402–2500; tel. 540/332–8000, (Nonreporting) **A**1 3 5 10 **S** Virginia Department of Mental Health, Richmond, VA
Primary Contact: Mary Clare. Smith, Director
CFO: Jon Chapman, Fiscal Officer
CMO: Jonathan Anderson, Medical Director
CIO: Sharon Johnson, Director Health Information Management
CNO: Diane Pavalonis, Chief Nurse Executive
Web address: www.dbhds.virginia.gov
Control: State, Government, Nonfederal **Service:** Psychiatric

Staffed Beds: 246

SUFFOLK—Suffolk City County

★ ⇧ **SENTARA OBICI HOSPITAL (490044)**, 2800 Godwin Boulevard, Zip 23434–8038; tel. 757/934–4000, **A**2 3 5 10 19 21 **F**3 8 11 12 13 15 18 20 22 26 28 29 30 31 33 34 35 36 37 40 41 42 44 45 46 47 48 49 50 51 54 57 58 59 60 61 64 65 68 70 74 75 76 77 78 79 80 81 84 85 86 87 91 92 93 94 96 97 98 100 102 107 108 110 111 114 115 118 119 120 121 123 124 126 129 130 131 132 141 145 146 147 148 149 154 156 160 161 162 164 167 169 **S** Sentara Health, Virginia Beach, VA
Primary Contact: David J. Masterson, Division President
CFO: Mike Mounie, Director Finance
CMO: Steve Julian, M.D., Vice President Medical Affairs
CIO: Alice Oxton, Director Information Technology
CHR: Deborah Ferguson, Human Resources Consultant
Web address: www.sentara.com
Control: Other not–for–profit (including NFP Corporation) **Service:** General medical and surgical

Staffed Beds: 175 **Admissions:** 11176 **Census:** 136 **Outpatient Visits:** 261489 **Births:** 1162 **Total Expense ($000):** 308416 **Payroll Expense ($000):** 102179 **Personnel:** 925

TAPPAHANNOCK—Essex County

★ ⇧ **VCU HEALTH TAPPAHANNOCK HOSPITAL (490084)**, 618 Hospital Road, Zip 22560–5000; tel. 804/443–3311, (Nonreporting) **A**10 20 21 **S** VCU Health System, Richmond, VA
Primary Contact: Elizabeth J. Martin, Hospital President
CFO: Jeri Sibley, Director Revenue Cycle
CMO: Robert Culley, D.O., Chief Medical Officer
CHR: Lindsey Custer, Director Human Resources
CNO: Judith Matthews, Nurse Executive
Web address: https://www.riversideonline.com
Control: Other not–for–profit (including NFP Corporation) **Service:** General medical and surgical

Staffed Beds: 16

TAZEWELL—Tazewell County

⊞ **CARILION TAZEWELL COMMUNITY HOSPITAL (490117)**, 388 Ben Bolt Avenue, Zip 24651–9700; tel. 276/988–8700, **A**1 5 10 **F**3 11 15 29 30 34 40 50 57 59 62 64 65 68 75 77 85 87 91 93 107 111 114 119 133 135 146 149 **P**6 **S** Carilion Clinic, Roanoke, VA
Primary Contact: Kristie Williams, Vice President and Hospital Administrator
CMO: Michael Rorrer, M.D., Chief of Medical Staff
CHR: Carrie Boggess, Human Resources Generalist
CNO: Alicia Bales, Senior Director, Chief Executive Officer and Chief Nursing Officer
Web address: www.carilionclinic.org
Control: Other not–for–profit (including NFP Corporation) **Service:** General medical and surgical

Staffed Beds: 8 **Admissions:** 569 **Census:** 8 **Outpatient Visits:** 17191 **Births:** 0 **Total Expense ($000):** 26307 **Payroll Expense ($000):** 9120 **Personnel:** 132

VIRGINIA BEACH—Virginia Beach City County

★ ⇧ **SENTARA PRINCESS ANNE HOSPITAL (490119)**, 2025 Glenn Mitchell Drive, Zip 23456–0178; tel. 757/507–1000, **A**2 3 5 10 19 21 **F**3 11 13 15 18 20 22 26 28 29 30 31 33 34 35 36 37 40 41 44 45 46 47 48 49 50 51 53 54 55 57 58 59 60 61 64 65 68 70 74 75 76 77 78 79 80 81 82 84 85 86 87 91 92 93 94 96 97 100 102 107 108 110 111 114 115 118 119 126 129 130 131 132 141 146 147 148 149 154 156 162 164 167 169 **S** Sentara Health, Virginia Beach, VA
Primary Contact: Dana Weston Graves, Division President
CFO: Robert Broermann, Senior Vice President and Chief Financial Officer
CMO: Terry Gilliland, M.D., Senior Vice President and Chief Medical Officer
CIO: Bert Reese, Chief Information Officer
CHR: Michael V Taylor, Vice President Human Resources
CNO: Grace Myers, MSN, Vice President, Nurse Executive
Web address: www.sentara.com
Control: Other not–for–profit (including NFP Corporation) **Service:** General medical and surgical

Staffed Beds: 174 **Admissions:** 12317 **Census:** 154 **Outpatient Visits:** 232135 **Births:** 2049 **Total Expense ($000):** 356658 **Payroll Expense ($000):** 110809 **Personnel:** 1046

★ ⇑ **SENTARA VIRGINIA BEACH GENERAL HOSPITAL (490057)**, 1060 First Colonial Road, Zip 23454–3002; tel. 757/395–8000, **A**2 3 5 10 19 21 **F**3 4 5 8 11 15 17 18 20 22 26 28 29 30 31 34 35 36 37 40 41 42 43 44 45 46 47 48 49 50 51 53 54 55 57 58 59 60 61 62 64 65 68 70 74 75 77 78 79 80 81 82 83 84 85 86 87 90 91 92 93 94 96 97 98 100 102 104 105 107 108 110 111 114 115 118 119 120 121 123 126 129 130 131 141 145 146 147 148 149 152 153 154 156 160 161 162 164 165 167 **S** Sentara Health, Virginia Beach, VA
Primary Contact: Elwood Bernard. Boone III, FACHE, Division President
CFO: Marley Nacey, Director Finance
CHR: Michelle Meekins, Manager Human Resources
CNO: Peggy Braun, R.N., Vice President Patient Care Services and Chief Nurse Executive
Web address: www.sentara.com
Control: Other not–for–profit (including NFP Corporation) **Service:** General medical and surgical

Staffed Beds: 273 **Admissions:** 14191 **Census:** 228 **Outpatient Visits:** 273082 **Births:** 0 **Total Expense ($000):** 412717 **Payroll Expense ($000):** 128627 **Personnel:** 1280

☐ **VIRGINIA BEACH PSYCHIATRIC CENTER (494025)**, 1100 First Colonial Road, Zip 23454–2403; tel. 757/496–6000, (Nonreporting) **A**1 10 **S** Universal Health Services, Inc., King of Prussia, PA
Primary Contact: Kurtis Hooks, Chief Executive Officer
Web address: www.vbpcweb.com
Control: Corporation, Investor–owned (for–profit) **Service:** Psychiatric

Staffed Beds: 100

WARRENTON—Fauquier County

✠ **FAUQUIER HOSPITAL (490023)**, 500 Hospital Drive, Zip 20186–3099; tel. 540/316–5000, (Nonreporting) **A**1 10 **S** Lifepoint Health, Brentwood, TN
Primary Contact: Rebecca Segal, FACHE, President and Chief Executive Officer
CFO: Lionel J Phillips, Vice President Financial Services
CIO: Donna Staton, Chief Information Officer
CHR: Katy Reeves, Vice President Human Resources
CNO: Linda Sharkey, R.N., MSN, Vice President Patient Care Services and Chief Nurse Executive
Web address: www.fauquierhealth.org/
Control: Other not–for–profit (including NFP Corporation) **Service:** General medical and surgical

Staffed Beds: 210

WILLIAMSBURG—James City County

☐ **EASTERN STATE HOSPITAL (490109)**, 4601 Ironbound Road, Zip 23188–2652; tel. 757/253–5161, (Nonreporting) **A**1 5 10 **S** Virginia Department of Mental Health, Richmond, VA
Primary Contact: Donna Moore, PsyD, Director
CFO: E Clifford Love, Director Fiscal Services
CMO: Guillermo Schrader, M.D., Acting Medical Director
CIO: Barbara Lambert, Director Healthcare Compliance
CHR: Edie Rogan, Manager Human Resources
Web address: www.esh.dmhmrsas.virginia.gov/
Control: State, Government, Nonfederal **Service:** Psychiatric

Staffed Beds: 300

⇑ **RIVERSIDE DOCTORS' HOSPITAL WILLIAMSBURG (490143)**, 1500 Commonwealth Avenue, Zip 23185–5229; tel. 757/585–2200, **A**3 10 21 **F**3 28 29 30 34 35 40 44 45 50 54 57 59 60 64 70 74 75 78 79 81 82 84 85 86 87 92 93 107 108 111 114 115 119 120 121 123 130 132 146 147 148 149 154 **S** Riverside Health System, Newport News, VA
Primary Contact: Adria Vanhoozier, President
CNO: Arlene Messina, R.N., MSN, Director of Nursing
Web address: www.riversideonline.com/rdhw
Control: Other not–for–profit (including NFP Corporation) **Service:** General medical and surgical

Staffed Beds: 24 **Admissions:** 2152 **Census:** 20 **Outpatient Visits:** 26383 **Births:** 0 **Total Expense ($000):** 70384 **Payroll Expense ($000):** 24868 **Personnel:** 253

WILLIAMSBURG—York County

★ ⇑ **SENTARA WILLIAMSBURG REGIONAL MEDICAL CENTER (490066)**, 100 Sentara Circle, Zip 23188–5713; tel. 757/984–6000, **A**2 10 19 21 **F**3 8 13 15 18 20 22 26 28 29 30 31 34 35 36 37 39 40 41 44 45 46 47 48 49 50 51 57 58 59 60 61 64 65 68 70 74 75 76 77 78 79 81 84 85 86 87 89 90 91 92 93 96 97 100 102 107 110 111 115 119 126 129 130 131 132 141 146 147 148 149 154 156 157 162 164 166 167 169 **S** Sentara Health, Virginia Beach, VA
Primary Contact: Amber Price, Division President
CFO: Andreas Roehrle, Director Finance
CMO: Joe Robbins, M.D., Vice President Medical Affairs
CIO: Mike Freeman, Director Information Technology
CHR: Lois B Demerich, Director Human Resources
CNO: Donna Wilmoth, Vice President Patient Care Services and Chief Nursing Officer
Web address: www.sentara.com
Control: Other not–for–profit (including NFP Corporation) **Service:** General medical and surgical

Staffed Beds: 128 **Admissions:** 9699 **Census:** 120 **Outpatient Visits:** 137056 **Births:** 670 **Total Expense ($000):** 212222 **Payroll Expense ($000):** 64592 **Personnel:** 600

☐ **THE PAVILION AT WILLIAMSBURG PLACE (494032)**, 5483 Mooretown Road, Zip 23188–2108; tel. 757/767–5111, (Nonreporting) **A**1 10
Primary Contact: Angela Pasley–Rich, Chief Executive Officer
CMO: Avtar Dhillon, M.D., Medical Director
CNO: Nicole K. Beer, Chief Nursing Officer
Web address: www.pavilionwp.com
Control: Corporation, Investor–owned (for–profit) **Service:** Psychiatric

Staffed Beds: 66

WINCHESTER—Winchester City County

✠ **VALLEY HEALTH – WINCHESTER MEDICAL CENTER (490005)**, 1840 Amherst Street, Zip 22601–2808, Mailing Address: P.O. Box 3340, Zip 22604–2540; tel. 540/536–8000, **A**1 2 3 5 10 20 **F**3 5 8 11 12 13 15 17 18 20 22 24 26 28 29 30 31 34 35 36 38 40 41 43 44 45 46 47 49 50 51 54 55 56 57 58 59 61 62 64 65 66 68 70 71 72 74 75 76 77 78 79 80 81 82 84 85 86 87 89 90 91 92 93 97 98 100 101 102 103 104 107 108 110 111 114 115 116 117 118 119 120 121 123 124 126 129 130 131 132 135 136 146 147 148 149 153 154 156 169 **P**6 **S** Valley Health System, Winchester, VA
Primary Contact: Tonya Smith, President
CFO: Robert Amos, Vice President and Chief Financial Officer
CMO: Nicolas Restrepo, M.D., Vice President Medical Affairs
CHR: Elizabeth Savage, Senior Vice President and Chief Human Resource Officer and Vice President Community Health and Wellness
CNO: Anne Whiteside, Vice President Nursing
Web address: www.valleyhealthlink.com/WMC
Control: Other not–for–profit (including NFP Corporation) **Service:** General medical and surgical

Staffed Beds: 541 **Admissions:** 24642 **Census:** 335 **Outpatient Visits:** 448044 **Births:** 2442 **Total Expense ($000):** 790438 **Payroll Expense ($000):** 218285 **Personnel:** 2362

WOODBRIDGE—Prince William County

★ ⇑ **SENTARA NORTHERN VIRGINIA MEDICAL CENTER (490113)**, 2300 Opitz Boulevard, Zip 22191–3399; tel. 703/523–1000, **A**2 10 19 21 **F**3 8 12 13 15 18 20 22 26 28 29 30 31 33 34 35 36 40 41 42 43 44 45 46 47 48 49 50 51 53 54 55 57 58 59 60 61 64 65 66 68 70 72 74 75 76 77 78 79 81 84 85 86 87 91 92 93 94 96 97 100 102 107 108 110 111 114 115 118 119 121 126 130 131 132 135 141 143 144 145 147 148 149 150 154 156 162 164 167 169 **S** Sentara Health, Virginia Beach, VA
Primary Contact: Jeff Joyner, FACHE, Division President
COO: Heather Causseaux, Vice President of Operations
CMO: Debra Lee, Chief Medical Officer
CIO: Thomas Ewing, Director Information Technology
CHR: Brett Willsie, Vice President Human Resources
CNO: Valerie E Keane, FACHE, Chief Nursing Executive
Web address: www.sentara.com/northernvirginia
Control: Other not–for–profit (including NFP Corporation) **Service:** General medical and surgical

Staffed Beds: 183 **Admissions:** 9699 **Census:** 120 **Outpatient Visits:** 186002 **Births:** 1630 **Total Expense ($000):** 311282 **Payroll Expense ($000):** 103845 **Personnel:** 886

Hospital, Medicare Provider Number, Address, Telephone, Approval, Facility, and Physician Codes, Health Care System

★ American Hospital Association (AHA) membership
☐ The Joint Commission accreditation
○ Healthcare Facilities Accreditation Program
◇ DNV Healthcare Inc. accreditation
⇑ Center for Improvement in Healthcare Quality Accreditation
△ Commission on Accreditation of Rehabilitation Facilities (CARF) accreditation

Hospitals, U.S. / VIRGINIA

WOODSTOCK—Shenandoah County

VALLEY HEALTH – SHENANDOAH MEMORIAL HOSPITAL (491305), 759 South Main Street, Zip 22664–1127; tel. 540/459–1100, **A**1 10 18 **F**3 11 15 18 28 29 30 35 40 45 50 53 57 59 64 65 68 69 70 75 77 79 81 82 87 92 93 97 104 107 108 110 111 114 118 119 127 129 130 132 133 135 146 147 148 153 154 155 156 **P**6 **S** Valley Health System, Winchester, VA
Primary Contact: N. Travis. Clark, President
CFO: Phillip Graybeal, CPA, Vice President, Finance
CMO: Greg Byrd, Vice President Medical Affairs
CIO: James Burton, Vice President and Chief Information Officer, Valley Health
CHR: Abbey Rembold, Manager, Human Resource Business Partnerships
CNO: April McClain–Clower, Director of Patient Care
Web address: www.valleyhealthlink.com/shenandoah
Control: Other not–for–profit (including NFP Corporation) **Service**: General medical and surgical

> **Staffed Beds**: 25 **Admissions**: 1487 **Census**: 19 **Outpatient Visits**: 145618
> **Births**: 0 **Total Expense ($000)**: 75222 **Payroll Expense ($000)**: 28625
> **Personnel**: 318

WYTHEVILLE—Wythe County

WYTHE COUNTY COMMUNITY HOSPITAL (490111), 600 West Ridge Road, Zip 24382–1099; tel. 276/228–0200, (Nonreporting) **A**1 5 10 20 **S** Lifepoint Health, Brentwood, TN
Primary Contact: Vicki Parks, Chief Executive Officer
CFO: Donald Hayes, Chief Financial Officer
CIO: Andrea Harless, Director Information Services
CHR: Kristie E Walker, M.P.H., Director Human Resources
CNO: Theresa Dix, MSN, R.N., Chief Nursing Officer
Web address: www.wcchcares.com
Control: Corporation, Investor–owned (for–profit) **Service**: General medical and surgical

> **Staffed Beds**: 70

YORKTOWN—York County

COASTAL VIRGINIA REHABILITATION (493027), 250 Josephs Drive, Zip 23693–3405; tel. 757/928–8000, **A**1 10 **F**3 29 30 35 44 60 68 74 75 77 82 86 87 90 93 94 95 96 130 132 143 148 149 154 157 **S** Select Medical Corporation, Mechanicsburg, PA
Primary Contact: Daniel Ballin, Administrator
CFO: Bill Austin, Senior Vice President of Finance
CMO: C Renee Moss, M.D., Chief Medical Officer
CIO: Dennis Loftis, Senior Vice President of Information Systems
CHR: Rob Cuthrell, Director of Human Resources
CNO: Debbie Outlaw, R.N., Director Patient Care Services
Web address: www.riversideonline.com/rri/index.cfm
Control: Corporation, Investor–owned (for–profit) **Service**: Rehabilitation

> **Staffed Beds**: 50 **Admissions**: 1289 **Census**: 44 **Outpatient Visits**: 0
> **Births**: 0 **Personnel**: 196

WASHINGTON

ABERDEEN—Grays Harbor County

⇧ **GRAYS HARBOR COMMUNITY HOSPITAL** See Harbor Regional Health

⇧ **HARBOR REGIONAL HEALTH (500031)**, 915 Anderson Drive, Zip 98520–1006; tel. 360/532-8330, (Nonreporting) **A**10 20 21
Primary Contact: Tom Jensen, Chief Executive Officer
CMO: Anne Marie Wong, M.D., Chief Medical Officer
CIO: Brad Wallace, Director Information Services
CHR: Julie Feller, Executive Director Human Resources
CNO: Melanie Brandt Esq, Chief Nursing Officer
Web address: www.ghcares.org
Control: Other not–for–profit (including NFP Corporation) **Service:** General medical and surgical

Staffed Beds: 105

ANACORTES—Skagit County

★ ⇧ **ISLAND HEALTH (500007)**, 1211 24th Street, Zip 98221–2562; tel. 360/299-1300, **A**10 21 **F**13 15 28 29 30 31 34 35 40 43 44 45 50 53 54 56 57 59 64 65 68 70 75 76 77 78 79 81 82 87 89 91 93 97 100 101 104 107 110 111 112 126 127 130 131 132 135 143 144 146 147 148 149 154 156 157 164 169
Primary Contact: Elise Cutter, FACHE, Chief Executive Officer, Superintendent
CIO: Tom Bluhm, Director Information Systems
CNO: Carol Northup, R.N., Chief Nursing Officer
Web address: www.islandhospital.org
Control: Hospital district or authority, Government, Nonfederal **Service:** General medical and surgical

Staffed Beds: 43 **Admissions:** 2178 **Census:** 17 **Outpatient Visits:** 140573 **Births:** 457 **Total Expense ($000):** 118995 **Payroll Expense ($000):** 53063 **Personnel:** 538

⇧ **ISLAND HOSPITAL** See Island Health

ARLINGTON—Snohomish County

⇧ **CASCADE VALLEY HOSPITAL (500060)**, 330 South Stillaguamish Avenue, Zip 98223–1642; tel. 360/435-2133, (Nonreporting) **A**10 21 **S** Skagit Regional Health, Mount Vernon, WA
Primary Contact: Brian K. Ivie, President and Chief Executive Officer
COO: Danny Vera, PharmD, Regional Vice President and Chief Operating Officer
CFO: Paul Ishizuka, Regional Vice President and Chief Financial Officer
CMO: James Fletcher, M.D., Medical Staff President
CIO: Lisa Buller, Regional Vice President and Chief Information Officer
CHR: Deborah Martin, Regional Vice President Human Resources
Web address: www.cascadevalley.org
Control: Hospital district or authority, Government, Nonfederal **Service:** General medical and surgical

Staffed Beds: 36

AUBURN—King County

⊞ **MULTICARE AUBURN MEDICAL CENTER (500015)**, 202 North Division, Plaza One, Zip 98001–4908; tel. 253/833-7711, **A**1 3 10 **F**3 13 18 20 22 28 29 30 34 35 40 43 45 49 50 51 56 57 64 65 68 70 73 74 75 76 77 79 81 84 85 87 90 93 96 98 102 103 107 108 111 114 115 119 126 129 130 132 135 146 147 148 149 164 167 **S** MultiCare Health System, Tacoma, WA
Primary Contact: June Altaras, R.N., President and Market Leader
CMO: Chad Krilich, M.D., Chief Med Officer–AMC/CMC
CHR: Kevin B Dull, Senior Vice President Human Potential
Web address: https://www.multicare.org/auburn-medical-center/
Control: Other not–for–profit (including NFP Corporation) **Service:** General medical and surgical

Staffed Beds: 167 **Admissions:** 7422 **Census:** 140 **Outpatient Visits:** 81817 **Births:** 1274 **Total Expense ($000):** 255360 **Payroll Expense ($000):** 111354 **Personnel:** 785

BELLEVUE—King County

⊞ **OVERLAKE MEDICAL CENTER AND CLINICS (500051)**, 1035 116th Avenue NE, Zip 98004–4604; tel. 425/688-5000, **A**1 2 3 10 **F**3 5 8 12 13 15 17 18 20 22 24 26 28 29 30 31 34 35 36 37 38 40 41 43 45 46 47 48 49 50 51 54 55 56 57 58 59 60 61 64 67 72 73 74 75 76 77 78 79 81 82 84 85 86 87 92 93 96 97 98 100 101 102 103 104 107 108 110 111 114 115 117 118 119 120 121 123 124 126 129 130 131 132 135 144 146 147 148 149 153 154 156 160 164 165 167 169 **P**6
Primary Contact: J. Michael. Marsh, President and Chief Executive Officer
COO: Thomas DeBord, Chief Operating Officer
CFO: Andrew Tokar, Chief Financial Officer
CMO: David Knoepfler, M.D., Chief Medical Officer
CHR: Lisa M Brock, Chief Human Resource Officer
Web address: www.overlakehospital.org
Control: Other not–for–profit (including NFP Corporation) **Service:** General medical and surgical

Staffed Beds: 310 **Admissions:** 14894 **Census:** 218 **Outpatient Visits:** 356648 **Births:** 3260 **Total Expense ($000):** 771876 **Payroll Expense ($000):** 344769 **Personnel:** 2838

BELLINGHAM—Whatcom County

★ ⇧ **PEACEHEALTH ST. JOSEPH MEDICAL CENTER (500030)**, 2901 Squalicum Parkway, Zip 98225–1851; tel. 360/734-5400, **A**2 5 10 20 21 **F**3 11 13 17 18 20 22 24 26 28 29 30 31 34 35 36 39 40 43 45 47 48 49 50 51 57 58 63 64 67 68 70 73 75 76 77 80 81 85 87 89 93 98 100 102 107 108 111 115 119 120 121 123 124 126 132 146 148 149 154 167 **S** PeaceHealth, Vancouver, WA
Primary Contact: Charles Prosper, Chief Executive, PeaceHealth Northwest
COO: Misty Parris, Vice President Operations, PHMG Northwest
CFO: Krista Touros, Chief Financial Officer, Northwest
CMO: Sudhakar Karlapudi, Chief Medical Officer and Patient Safety Officer, Northwest
CIO: Kelly Lundy, Chief Information Officer
CHR: Cindy C Klein, Vice President Human Resources
CNO: Roseanna Bell, Chief Nursing Officer
Web address: www.peacehealth.org
Control: Church operated, Nongovernment, not–for–profit **Service:** General medical and surgical

Staffed Beds: 274 **Admissions:** 14821 **Census:** 196 **Outpatient Visits:** 185009 **Births:** 1859 **Total Expense ($000):** 539767 **Payroll Expense ($000):** 189769 **Personnel:** 2010

BREMERTON—Kitsap County

⊞ **NAVAL HOSPITAL BREMERTON**, 1 Boone Road, Zip 98312–1898; tel. 360/475-4000, (Nonreporting) **A**1 3 5 **S** Bureau of Medicine and Surgery, Department of the Navy, Falls Church, VA
Primary Contact: Captain Patrick J. Fitzpatrick, Commanding Officer
CFO: Judith Hogan, Comptroller and Director Resources and Logistics
CIO: Patrick Flaherty, Director Management Information
Web address: https://bremerton.tricare.mil/
Control: Navy, Government, federal **Service:** General medical and surgical

Staffed Beds: 23

BREWSTER—Okanogan County

★ **THREE RIVERS HOSPITAL (501324)**, 507 Hospital Way, Zip 98812–0577, Mailing Address: P.O. Box 577, Zip 98812–0577; tel. 509/689-2517, (Nonreporting) **A**10 18
Primary Contact: Scott Graham, Chief Executive Officer
CFO: Jennifer Munson, Chief Financial Officer
CMO: Gordon Tagge, M.D., President Medical Staff
CIO: Edgar Alejandro Arellano, Chief Information Technologist
CHR: Anita Fisk, Director Human Resources
CNO: Gretchen Aguilar, Director Patient Care and Chief Nursing Officer
Web address: www.threerivershospital.net
Control: Hospital district or authority, Government, Nonfederal **Service:** General medical and surgical

Staffed Beds: 20

Hospitals, U.S. / WASHINGTON

BURIEN—King County

☩ **ST. ANNE HOSPITAL (500011)**, 16251 Sylvester Road SW, Zip 98166–3052; tel. 206/244–9970, **A**1 2 10 **F**3 11 13 15 18 28 29 30 31 34 35 40 45 49 50 51 57 59 60 64 70 73 74 75 76 77 78 79 80 81 85 86 87 92 93 107 108 110 111 114 115 117 119 126 129 130 131 132 135 136 146 147 148 149 164 167 **P**6 **S** CommonSpirit Health, Chicago, IL
Primary Contact: Deepak Devasthali, Chief Operating Officer
CMO: Dennis De Leon, M.D., Associate Chief Medical Officer and Vice President Medical Affairs
CNO: Kim Baisch, R.N., Associate Vice President Patient Care Services
Web address: https://www.vmfh.org/our-hospitals/st-anne-hospital
Control: Church operated, Nongovernment, not–for–profit **Service**: General medical and surgical

Staffed Beds: 115 Admissions: 6582 Census: 79 Outpatient Visits: 104188 Births: 971 Total Expense ($000): 230268 Payroll Expense ($000): 82005 Personnel: 664

CENTRALIA—Lewis County

☩ **PROVIDENCE CENTRALIA HOSPITAL (500019)**, 914 S Scheuber RD, Zip 98531–9027, Mailing Address: 914 South Scheuber Road, Zip 98531–9027; tel. 360/736–2803, **A**1 3 10 20 **F**3 11 13 15 29 30 32 34 35 40 43 44 45 46 50 51 54 56 57 58 59 62 63 64 65 68 70 73 74 75 76 77 78 79 80 81 82 84 85 86 87 89 91 93 94 96 100 101 102 107 108 110 111 114 115 118 119 120 121 123 124 130 146 148 149 150 154 157 164 169 **S** Providence, Renton, WA
Primary Contact: Darin Goss, FACHE, Chief Executive Officer
CFO: Denise Marroni, Chief Financial Officer
CMO: Kevin Caserta, M.D., Chief Medical Officer
CIO: Kerry Miles, Site Director
CHR: Dana Vandewege, Director Human Resources
Web address: https://www.providence.org/locations/wa/centralia-hospital
Control: Other not–for–profit (including NFP Corporation) **Service**: General medical and surgical

Staffed Beds: 132 Admissions: 4267 Census: 59 Outpatient Visits: 256582 Births: 644 Total Expense ($000): 257273 Payroll Expense ($000): 80324 Personnel: 763

CHELAN—Chelan County

★ ⋔ **LAKE CHELAN HEALTH (501334)**, 503 East Highland Avenue, Zip 98816–8631, Mailing Address: P.O. Box 908, Zip 98816–0908; tel. 509/682–3300, (Nonreporting) **A**3 10 18 21
Primary Contact: Aaron Edwards, Chief Executive Officer
COO: Brad Hankins, Chief Operating Quality Officer
CFO: Mike Ellis, Chief Financial Officer
CMO: Ty Witt, M.D., Chief Medical Officer
CIO: Ross Hurd, Chief Information Officer
CHR: DeLynn K Barnett, Director Human Resources
Web address: https://lakechelanhealth.org/
Control: Hospital district or authority, Government, Nonfederal **Service**: General medical and surgical

Staffed Beds: 25

CHEWELAH—Stevens County

☩ **PROVIDENCE ST. JOSEPH'S HOSPITAL (501309)**, 500 East Webster Street, Zip 99109–9523; tel. 509/935–8211, (Nonreporting) **A**1 10 18 **S** Providence, Renton, WA
Primary Contact: Ronald G. Rehn, Chief Executive Officer
CFO: Helen Andrus, Chief Financial Officer
CMO: Jeff Collins, Chief Medical Officer
CNO: Deborah Watson, R.N., Chief Nursing Officer
Web address: www.washington.providence.org/hospitals/st-josephs-hospital/
Control: Church operated, Nongovernment, not–for–profit **Service**: General medical and surgical

Staffed Beds: 15

CLARKSTON—Asotin County

★ ⋔ **TRI–STATE MEMORIAL HOSPITAL (501332)**, 1221 Highland Avenue, Zip 99403–2829, Mailing Address: P.O. Box 189, Zip 99403–0189; tel. 509/758–5511, (Nonreporting) **A**10 18 21
Primary Contact: Kym Clift, FACHE, Chief Executive Officer
CFO: Alex Town, Vice President Finance
CMO: Don Greggain, M.D., Physician Network Director
CIO: Joleen Carper, Vice President Quality and Risk
CHR: Regana Davis, Vice President Human Resources
CNO: Rhonda Mason, Vice President of Patient Care Services
Web address: https://tristatehospital.org/
Control: Other not–for–profit (including NFP Corporation) **Service**: General medical and surgical

Staffed Beds: 25

COLFAX—Whitman County

★ **WHITMAN HOSPITAL AND MEDICAL CENTER (501327)**, 1200 West Fairview Street, Zip 99111–9579; tel. 509/397–3435, **A**10 18 **F**3 13 15 28 29 34 35 36 40 43 45 50 53 56 64 68 75 76 77 79 81 82 84 85 87 93 97 107 110 111 114 115 119 130 131 133 148 154 167 169
Primary Contact: Hank Hanigan, FACHE, Chief Executive Officer
CFO: Hank Hanigan, FACHE, Interim Chief Financial Officer
CMO: Bryan N Johnson, M.D., Chief Medical Officer
CHR: Michelle Ellis, Director Human Resources
CNO: Pam Akin, R.N., MSN, Chief Nursing Officer
Web address: www.whitmanhospital.org
Control: Hospital district or authority, Government, Nonfederal **Service**: General medical and surgical

Staffed Beds: 21 Admissions: 689 Census: 6 Outpatient Visits: 57042 Births: 43 Total Expense ($000): 55399 Payroll Expense ($000): 22575 Personnel: 241

COLVILLE—Stevens County

☩ **PROVIDENCE MOUNT CARMEL HOSPITAL (501326)**, 982 East Columbia Avenue, Zip 99114–3352; tel. 509/685–5100, (Nonreporting) **A**1 3 10 18 **S** Providence, Renton, WA
Primary Contact: Ronald G. Rehn, Chief Administrative Officer
CFO: Helen Andrus, Chief Financial Officer
CNO: Deborah Watson, R.N., Chief Nursing Officer
Web address: www.mtcarmelhospital.org
Control: Church operated, Nongovernment, not–for–profit **Service**: General medical and surgical

Staffed Beds: 25

COUPEVILLE—Island County

★ ⋔ **WHIDBEYHEALTH (501339)**, 101 North Main Street, Zip 98239–3413; tel. 360/678–5151, (Nonreporting) **A**2 10 18 21 **S** HealthTech Management Services, Plano, TX
Primary Contact: Nathan Staggs, Chief Executive Officer
CMO: Gabe Barrio, M.D., Chief of Staff
CNO: Linda Stephens Gipson, MSN, Ph.D., Chief Nursing Officer
Web address: https://whidbeyhealth.org/
Control: Hospital district or authority, Government, Nonfederal **Service**: General medical and surgical

Staffed Beds: 25

COVINGTON—King County

☩ **MULTICARE COVINGTON MEDICAL CENTER (500154)**, 17700 SE 272nd Street, Zip 98042–4951; tel. 253/372–6500, **A**1 **F**3 8 12 29 30 34 35 40 50 56 57 68 81 85 87 96 102 107 111 114 115 119 130 146 148 149 **S** MultiCare Health System, Tacoma, WA
Primary Contact: June Altaras, R.N., President and Market Leader
Control: Other not–for–profit (including NFP Corporation) **Service**: General medical and surgical

Staffed Beds: 38 Admissions: 2260 Census: 24 Outpatient Visits: 65982 Births: 0 Total Expense ($000): 95509 Payroll Expense ($000): 34168 Personnel: 288

DAVENPORT—Lincoln County

★ **LINCOLN HOSPITAL (501305)**, 10 Nicholls Street, Zip 99122–9729; tel. 509/725–7101, (Nonreporting) **A**10 18
Primary Contact: Tyson Lacy, Chief Executive Officer and Superintendent
CFO: Tim O'Connell, Chief Financial Officer
CMO: Fred Reed, M.D., Chief of Staff
CIO: Elliott Donson, Chief Information Specialist
CHR: Becky Bailey, Director Human Resources
CNO: Jennifer Larmer, R.N., Chief Clinical Officer
Web address: www.lincolnhosp.org
Control: Hospital district or authority, Government, Nonfederal **Service**: General medical and surgical

Staffed Beds: 50

DAYTON—Columbia County

★ ⇧ **COLUMBIA COUNTY HEALTH SYSTEM (501302)**, 1012 South Third Street, Zip 99328–1696; tel. 509/382–2531, **A**10 18 21 **F**3 29 35 36 40 43 64 65 77 87 93 107 115 119 133 135 148 149 152 154 160 161 167 **P**6
Primary Contact: Shane A. McGuire, Chief Executive Officer
CHR: Steven J Stahl, Director Human Resources
CNO: Stephanie Carpenter, Director of Nursing Services
Web address: www.cchd-wa.org
Control: Hospital district or authority, Government, Nonfederal **Service:** General medical and surgical

Staffed Beds: 25 **Admissions:** 270 **Census:** 7 **Outpatient Visits:** 12878 **Births:** 1 **Total Expense ($000):** 37239 **Payroll Expense ($000):** 16439 **Personnel:** 256

EDMONDS—Snohomish County

★ ⇧ **PROVIDENCE SWEDISH EDMONDS (500026)**, 21601 76th Avenue West, Zip 98026–7506; tel. 425/640–4000, **A**2 3 10 21 **F**3 8 11 13 15 17 18 20 22 24 26 29 30 31 34 35 38 40 43 45 49 57 58 59 64 65 68 70 72 73 74 75 76 77 78 79 80 81 82 85 87 98 100 101 102 104 105 107 108 110 111 114 115 116 117 119 120 121 123 124 130 132 135 141 146 149 164 167 169 **S** Swedish Health Services, Seattle, WA
Primary Contact: Kristy Carrington, R.N., Chief Executive Officer
CMO: Sandeep Sachdeva, M.D., Vice President Medical Affairs
CNO: Jean Doerge, R.N., MSN, Nurse Executive
Web address: www.swedish.org
Control: Other not–for–profit (including NFP Corporation) **Service:** General medical and surgical

Staffed Beds: 271 **Admissions:** 8666 **Census:** 145 **Outpatient Visits:** 291353 **Births:** 1195 **Total Expense ($000):** 348075 **Payroll Expense ($000):** 141135 **Personnel:** 1210

⇧ **SWEDISH EDMONDS** See Providence Swedish Edmonds

ELLENSBURG—Kittitas County

★ ⇧ **KITTITAS VALLEY HEALTHCARE (501333)**, 603 South Chestnut Street, Zip 98926–3875; tel. 509/962–7302, **A**3 10 18 21 **F**3 5 13 15 29 30 34 35 37 40 41 43 44 45 46 50 56 57 59 62 63 64 65 68 70 73 74 75 76 77 79 81 85 87 89 93 96 107 110 111 115 119 127 130 131 132 133 144 146 147 148 149 154 156 160 167 168 169
Primary Contact: Julie Petersen, CPA, Chief Executive Officer
CFO: Libby Allgood, Chief Financial Officer
CMO: Don Solberg, M.D., Chief Medical Officer
CIO: Jack Schwartz, Director Information Technology
CHR: Carrie Youngblood, Director of Human Resources
CNO: Vicky Machorro, R.N., Chief Nursing Officer
Web address: www.kvhealthcare.org
Control: Hospital district or authority, Government, Nonfederal **Service:** General medical and surgical

Staffed Beds: 25 **Admissions:** 887 **Census:** 10 **Outpatient Visits:** 131863 **Births:** 226 **Total Expense ($000):** 128032 **Payroll Expense ($000):** 59535 **Personnel:** 642

ELMA—Grays Harbor County

★ ⇧ **SUMMIT PACIFIC MEDICAL CENTER (501304)**, 600 East Main Street, Zip 98541–9560; tel. 360/346–2222, (Nonreporting) **A**3 10 18 21
Primary Contact: Josh Martin, Chief Executive Officer
COO: Josh Martin, Chief Executive Officer
CFO: James Hansen, Chief Financial Officer
CMO: Ken Dietrich, Chief Medical Officer
CIO: Jeff Painter, Network Administrator, Information Technology
CHR: Mindy Portchy, Manager Human Resources
CNO: Tori Louise Bernier, Chief Nursing Officer
Web address: www.markreed.org
Control: Hospital district or authority, Government, Nonfederal **Service:** General medical and surgical

Staffed Beds: 10

ENUMCLAW—King County

★ **ST. ELIZABETH HOSPITAL (501335)**, 1455 Battersby Avenue, Zip 98022–3634, Mailing Address: P.O. Box 218, Zip 98022–0218; tel. 360/802–8800, **A**10 18 **F**3 13 15 18 29 30 35 40 44 45 50 59 64 70 74 75 76 79 81 85 87 93 107 108 110 111 114 115 119 130 132 133 135 146 147 149 154 164 **P**6 **S** CommonSpirit Health, Chicago, IL
Primary Contact: Danna Shaner, President
COO: Deepak Devasthali, Chief Operating Officer, Vice President
CFO: Philip Hjembo, Chief Financial Officer
CHR: Jerilyn Ray, Manager Human Resources
Web address: https://www.vmfh.org/our-hospitals/st-elizabeth-hospital
Control: Church operated, Nongovernment, not–for–profit **Service:** General medical and surgical

Staffed Beds: 25 **Admissions:** 1842 **Census:** 14 **Outpatient Visits:** 37224 **Births:** 406 **Total Expense ($000):** 62236 **Payroll Expense ($000):** 26300 **Personnel:** 255

EPHRATA—Grant County

★ **COLUMBIA BASIN HOSPITAL (501317)**, 200 Nat Washington Way, Zip 98823–1982; tel. 509/754–4631, **A**10 18 **F**3 10 11 15 29 30 32 34 35 40 56 59 65 77 84 91 93 97 107 110 114 119 127 130 132 133 146 147 154
Primary Contact: Rosalinda Kibby, Superintendent and Administrator
CFO: Rhonda Handley, Chief Financial Officer
CMO: Lowell C Allred, M.D., Chief of Staff
CHR: Suzanne Little, Human Resources Specialist
Web address: www.columbiabasinhospital.org
Control: Hospital district or authority, Government, Nonfederal **Service:** General medical and surgical

Staffed Beds: 69 **Admissions:** 320 **Census:** 25 **Outpatient Visits:** 42107 **Births:** 0 **Total Expense ($000):** 22983 **Payroll Expense ($000):** 11067 **Personnel:** 144

EVERETT—Snohomish County

PROVIDENCE GENERAL MEDICAL CTR See Providence Everett Medical Center – Pacific Campus

PROVIDENCE GENERAL MEDICAL CTR See Providence Everett Medical Center – Colby Campus

⊞ △ **PROVIDENCE REGIONAL MEDICAL CENTER EVERETT (500014)**, 1700 13th Street, Zip 98201–1689, Mailing Address: P.O. Box 1147, Zip 98206–1147; tel. 425/261–2000, (Includes PROVIDENCE EVERETT MEDICAL CENTER – COLBY CAMPUS, 1321 Colby Avenue, Everett, Washington, Zip 98206, P O Box 1147, Zip 98206, tel. 425/261–2000; PROVIDENCE EVERETT MEDICAL CENTER – PACIFIC CAMPUS, 916 Pacific Avenue, Everett, Washington, Zip 98201–4147, P O Box 1067, Zip 98206–1067, tel. 206/258–7123) **A**1 2 3 5 7 10 **F**3 4 5 11 12 13 15 17 18 20 22 24 26 28 29 30 31 32 34 35 36 37 38 40 43 44 45 46 47 48 49 50 53 55 57 58 59 60 61 64 68 70 72 73 74 75 76 77 78 79 81 84 85 86 87 89 90 93 96 98 100 107 108 109 110 111 114 115 116 117 118 119 120 121 123 124 126 129 130 132 135 146 147 148 149 150 154 156 157 160 166 167 169 **S** Providence, Renton, WA
Primary Contact: Kristy Carrington, R.N., Chief Executive Officer
CFO: Scott Combs, NWSA Chief Financial Officer
CMO: James Cook, PRMCE Chief Medical Officer
CIO: Matt Wonser, Director, Information Services
CHR: Kathleen Groen, Chief Human Resources Officer
CNO: Barbara M Hyland-Hill, R.N., Chief Nursing Officer
Web address: www.providence.org
Control: Other not–for–profit (including NFP Corporation) **Service:** General medical and surgical

Staffed Beds: 595 **Admissions:** 26002 **Census:** 483 **Outpatient Visits:** 388301 **Births:** 4040 **Total Expense ($000):** 987958 **Payroll Expense ($000):** 363624 **Personnel:** 3146

Hospitals, U.S. / WASHINGTON

FEDERAL WAY—King County

☒ **ST. FRANCIS HOSPITAL (500141)**, 34515 Ninth Avenue South, Zip 98003-6799; tel. 253/944-8100, **A**1 2 3 5 10 **F**3 8 11 12 13 15 18 20 22 26 28 29 30 31 35 37 38 40 43 44 45 46 47 48 49 50 51 60 63 64 70 73 74 75 76 78 79 80 81 82 84 85 87 92 93 102 107 108 110 111 114 115 117 119 126 129 130 135 146 147 149 154 164 167 **S** CommonSpirit Health, Chicago, IL
Primary Contact: Dino Johnson, R.N., Interim Chief Operating Officer
CFO: Mike Fitzgerald, Chief Financial Officer
CMO: Dennis deLeon, M.D., Chief Medical Officer, King Region
CIO: Rand Strobel, Regional Chief Information Officer
CHR: Les Soltis, Director – Human Resources
Web address: https://www.vmfh.org/our-hospitals/st-francis-hospital
Control: Church operated, Nongovernment, not-for-profit **Service**: General medical and surgical

Staffed Beds: 124 **Admissions**: 9740 **Census**: 110 **Outpatient Visits**: 124554 **Births**: 1523 **Total Expense ($000)**: 291940 **Payroll Expense ($000)**: 105904 **Personnel**: 984

FORKS—Clallam County

⇧ **FORKS COMMUNITY HOSPITAL (501325)**, 530 Bogachiel Way, Zip 98331-9120; tel. 360/374-6271, (Nonreporting) **A**10 18 21
Primary Contact: Heidi Anderson, Chief Executive Officer
CFO: Joe Bradick, Chief Financial Officer
CIO: Andrea Perkins-Peppers, Chief Information Officer
CHR: Cindy Paget, Chief Human Resources Officer
CNO: Laura Kripinski, Chief Nursing Officer
Web address: www.forkshospital.org
Control: Hospital district or authority, Government, Nonfederal **Service**: General medical and surgical

Staffed Beds: 45

FRIDAY HARBOR—San Juan County

★ ⇧ **PEACEHEALTH PEACE ISLAND MEDICAL CENTER (501340)**, 1117 Spring Street, Zip 98250-9782; tel. 360/378-2141, **A**5 10 18 21 **F**29 30 31 34 40 59 64 65 68 75 78 79 81 97 100 102 104 107 115 119 130 132 135 146 149 154 **S** PeaceHealth, Vancouver, WA
Primary Contact: Jack Estrada, Chief Administrative Officer
CFO: Carolyn Foster, Chief Financial Officer
CMO: Michael Sullivan, M.D., Medical Director Emergency Services
CHR: Lorraine Allison, Human Resource Partner
CNO: Sheryl Murphy, Chief Nursing Officer and Director of Clinical Services
Web address: www.peacehealth.org
Control: Church operated, Nongovernment, not-for-profit **Service**: General medical and surgical

Staffed Beds: 10 **Admissions**: 83 **Census**: 1 **Outpatient Visits**: 26941 **Births**: 0 **Total Expense ($000)**: 22339 **Payroll Expense ($000)**: 9055 **Personnel**: 77

GIG HARBOR—Pierce County

☒ **ST. ANTHONY HOSPITAL (500151)**, 11567 Canterwood Boulevard NW, Zip 98332-5812; tel. 253/530-2000, **A**1 3 10 **F**3 11 15 18 20 29 30 31 34 38 40 44 45 49 50 51 59 60 64 70 74 75 77 78 79 80 81 85 86 87 92 93 107 108 110 111 114 115 118 119 126 129 130 131 135 146 147 154 164 **P**6 **S** CommonSpirit Health, Chicago, IL
Primary Contact: Dino Johnson, R.N., Chief Operating Officer
Web address: https://www.vmfh.org/our-hospitals/st-anthony-hospital
Control: Church operated, Nongovernment, not-for-profit **Service**: General medical and surgical

Staffed Beds: 112 **Admissions**: 7486 **Census**: 95 **Outpatient Visits**: 97470 **Births**: 0 **Total Expense ($000)**: 223259 **Payroll Expense ($000)**: 82088 **Personnel**: 761

GOLDENDALE—Klickitat County

KLICKITAT VALLEY HEALTH (501316), 310 South Roosevelt Avenue, Zip 98620-9201; tel. 509/773-4022, (Nonreporting) **A**10 18
Primary Contact: Jonathan Hatfield, Chief Executive Officer
CFO: Jamie Eldred, Controller
CMO: Rod Krehbiel, M.D., Chief of Staff
CIO: Jonathan Hatfield, Supervisor Information Technology
CHR: Herbert Hill, Director Human Resources
CNO: Gwen Cox, Director Nursing Services
Web address: www.kvhealth.net
Control: Hospital district or authority, Government, Nonfederal **Service**: General medical and surgical

Staffed Beds: 16

GRAND COULEE—Grant County

★ ⇧ **COULEE MEDICAL CENTER (501308)**, 411 Fortuyn Road, Zip 99133-8718; tel. 509/633-1753, **A**10 18 21 **F**13 15 29 40 43 50 57 64 75 81 93 97 104 107 114 119 122 127 132 133 146 148 149 154 156 160 167 169
Primary Contact: Kelly Hughes, Chief Executive Officer
CFO: Kelly Hughes, Chief Financial Officer
CMO: Sam Hsieh, M.D., FACS, Chief of Staff and Chief Medical Officer
CHR: Heather McCleary, Director Human Resources
CNO: Marlene L Elliott, MSN, R.N., Chief Nursing Officer
Web address: www.cmccares.org
Control: County, Government, Nonfederal **Service**: General medical and surgical

Staffed Beds: 25 **Admissions**: 328 **Census**: 3 **Outpatient Visits**: 34945 **Births**: 52 **Total Expense ($000)**: 38072 **Payroll Expense ($000)**: 17808 **Personnel**: 210

ILWACO—Pacific County

★ **OCEAN BEACH HOSPITAL AND MEDICAL CLINICS (501314)**, 174 First Avenue North, Zip 98624-9137, Mailing Address: P.O. Box H, Zip 98624-0258; tel. 360/244-2184, **A**3 10 18 **F**3 11 15 29 30 34 35 40 43 45 55 56 57 59 68 75 77 81 86 87 89 93 97 107 108 110 115 119 127 128 130 132 133 135 149 154 156 166 **P**6
Primary Contact: Merry-Ann Keane, MSN, FACHE, Chief Executive Officer
CFO: Kathy Hubbard, Controller
CMO: Patty Malone, M.D., Chief Medical Officer
CIO: Julie P Oakes, R.N., Manager Risk and Quality
CHR: Beth Whitton, Director Human Resources
CNO: Linda Kaino, Chief Nursing Officer
Web address: www.oceanbeachhospital.com
Control: Hospital district or authority, Government, Nonfederal **Service**: General medical and surgical

Staffed Beds: 21 **Admissions**: 398 **Census**: 6 **Outpatient Visits**: 58357 **Births**: 0 **Total Expense ($000)**: 37975 **Payroll Expense ($000)**: 17078 **Personnel**: 109

ISSAQUAH—King County

★ ⇧ **SWEDISH ISSAQUAH (500152)**, 751 NE Blakely Drive, Zip 98029-6201; tel. 425/313-4000, **A**3 10 21 **F**3 8 9 12 14 15 18 20 29 30 31 34 35 37 38 40 45 46 47 48 49 57 58 59 60 61 64 65 68 70 73 74 75 76 77 78 79 80 81 82 85 87 102 107 108 110 111 115 116 117 119 120 121 123 124 126 130 132 135 142 146 149 156 164 167 169 **S** Swedish Health Services, Seattle, WA
Primary Contact: Elizabeth Wako, M.D., Chief Executive
Web address: www.swedish.org/issaquah
Control: Other not-for-profit (including NFP Corporation) **Service**: General medical and surgical

Staffed Beds: 144 **Admissions**: 7248 **Census**: 81 **Outpatient Visits**: 186342 **Births**: 1912 **Total Expense ($000)**: 317667 **Payroll Expense ($000)**: 103175 **Personnel**: 921

KENNEWICK—Benton County

☒ **TRIOS HEALTH (500053)**, 900 South Auburn Street, Zip 99336-5621, Mailing Address: P.O. Box 6128, Zip 99336-0128; tel. 509/221-6339, (Includes TRIOS SOUTHRIDGE HOSPITAL, 3810 Plaza Way, Kennewick, Washington, Zip 99338-2722, tel. 509/221-6339) (Nonreporting) **A**1 3 5 10 13 **S** Lifepoint Health, Brentwood, TN
Primary Contact: David Elgarico, Chief Executive Officer
COO: Terry Olinger, Interim Chief Operating Officer
CIO: Michael Cloutier, Director Information Services
CHR: Russ Keefer, Chief Human Resources Officer
CNO: Dena Putnam-Gilchrist, Chief Nursing Officer
Web address: www.trioshealth.org
Control: Hospital district or authority, Government, Nonfederal **Service**: General medical and surgical

Staffed Beds: 109

Hospitals, U.S. / WASHINGTON

KIRKLAND—King County

✚ **EVERGREENHEALTH (500124)**, 12040 NE 128th Street, Zip 98034-3013; tel. 425/899-1000, **A**1 2 3 5 10 **F**3 8 12 13 15 18 20 22 26 28 29 30 34 35 36 37 38 40 42 43 44 45 46 49 50 51 54 55 56 57 58 59 61 62 63 64 65 68 70 71 72 73 74 75 76 78 79 80 81 82 84 85 86 87 89 90 91 92 93 94 95 96 97 100 101 104 107 108 110 111 114 115 118 119 120 121 123 124 126 129 130 131 132 134 135 142 144 146 147 148 149 154 156 162 164 167 169 **P**4 6
Primary Contact: Ettore Palazzo, Chief Executive Officer
COO: Christopher Bredeson, Chief Operating Officer
CFO: Frank Hemeon, Interim Chief Financial Officer
CIO: Tom Martin, Senior Vice President, Strategy and Information Technology Officer
CHR: Bob Sampson, Senior Vice President, Human Resources
CNO: Mary Shepler, R.N., Senior Vice President, Chief Nursing Officer
Web address: www.evergreenhealth.com
Control: Hospital district or authority, Government, Nonfederal **Service**: General medical and surgical

Staffed Beds: 354 **Admissions:** 16590 **Census:** 240 **Outpatient Visits:** 1783673 **Births:** 4475 **Total Expense ($000):** 1035045 **Payroll Expense ($000):** 551154 **Personnel:** 4076

✚ **FAIRFAX BEHAVIORAL HEALTH (504002)**, 10200 NE 132nd Street, Zip 98034-2899; tel. 425/821-2000, (Includes FAIRFAX BEHAVIORAL HEALTH EVERETT, 916 Pacific Avenue, Everett, Washington, Zip 98201-4147, tel. 425/821-2000) (Nonreporting) **A**1 10 **S** Universal Health Services, Inc., King of Prussia, PA
Primary Contact: Sascha Hughes, Chief Executive Officer
COO: Todd Thama, Chief Operating Officer
CFO: Pam Rhoads, Chief Financial Officer
CMO: Samir Aziz, M.D., Medical Director
CHR: Anne Schreiber, Manager Human Resources
Web address: www.fairfaxhospital.com
Control: Corporation, Investor-owned (for-profit) **Service**: Psychiatric

Staffed Beds: 221

LAKEWOOD—Pierce County

✚ **ST. CLARE HOSPITAL (500021)**, 11315 Bridgeport Way SW, Zip 98499-3004; tel. 253/985-1711, **A**1 2 10 **F**3 11 18 29 30 31 34 35 37 40 49 50 60 64 70 74 75 77 78 79 80 81 84 85 86 87 107 108 109 111 115 119 129 130 131 146 147 149 154 164 167 **P**6 **S** CommonSpirit Health, Chicago, IL
Primary Contact: Matthew Metsker, President
CFO: Mike Fitzgerald, Chief Financial Officer
CIO: Bruce Elkington, Regional Chief Information Officer
CHR: David C. Lawson, Senior Vice President Human Resources
Web address: https://www.vmfh.org/our-hospitals/st-clare-hospital
Control: Church operated, Nongovernment, not-for-profit **Service**: General medical and surgical

Staffed Beds: 104 **Admissions:** 5892 **Census:** 86 **Outpatient Visits:** 68962 **Births:** 0 **Total Expense ($000):** 185930 **Payroll Expense ($000):** 69053 **Personnel:** 639

LEAVENWORTH—Chelan County

★ **CASCADE MEDICAL (501313)**, 817 Commercial Street, Zip 98826-1316; tel. 509/548-5815, (Nonreporting) **A**5 10 18
Primary Contact: Diane Blake, Chief Executive Officer
COO: Pat Songer, Chief Operations Officer
CFO: Marianne Vincent, Chief Financial Officer
CMO: Jerome Jerome, M.D., Clinic Medical Director
CIO: Charles Amstutz, Director of Information Technology
CHR: Reyne Boik, Director Human Resources
CNO: Shawn Ottley, R.N., Chief Clinical Officer
Web address: www.cascademedical.org
Control: Hospital district or authority, Government, Nonfederal **Service**: General medical and surgical

Staffed Beds: 9

LONGVIEW—Cowlitz County

★ ⇧ **PEACEHEALTH ST. JOHN MEDICAL CENTER (500041)**, 1615 Delaware Street, Zip 98632-2367, Mailing Address: P.O. Box 3002, Zip 98632-0302; tel. 360/414-2000, **A**2 10 21 **F**3 11 13 15 18 20 22 26 28 29 30 31 34 35 40 43 45 59 68 70 75 76 78 79 81 82 84 93 98 100 104 107 108 110 111 115 117 118 119 120 121 123 124 129 130 132 145 146 148 154 167 **S** PeaceHealth, Vancouver, WA
Primary Contact: Kendall Sawa, R.N., Chief Hospital Executive
CMO: Sheila Lynam, M.D., Chief Medical Officer
CHR: Kelley Frengle, Director, Human Resources
Web address: www.peacehealth.org
Control: Church operated, Nongovernment, not-for-profit **Service**: General medical and surgical

Staffed Beds: 180 **Admissions:** 6425 **Census:** 85 **Outpatient Visits:** 158406 **Births:** 746 **Total Expense ($000):** 253660 **Payroll Expense ($000):** 97434 **Personnel:** 1128

MARYSVILLE—Snohomish County

☐ **SMOKEY POINT BEHAVIORAL HOSPITAL (504012)**, 3955 156th Street Northeast, Zip 98271; tel. 844/202-5555, (Nonreporting) **A**1 10
Primary Contact: Gerald M. Cholewa, MSN, R.N., Interim Chief Executive Officer
Web address: www.smokeypointbehavioralhospital.com
Control: Other not-for-profit (including NFP Corporation) **Service**: Psychiatric

Staffed Beds: 115

MEDICAL LAKE—Spokane County

☐ **EASTERN STATE HOSPITAL (504004)**, Maple Street, Zip 99022-0045, Mailing Address: P.O. Box 800, Zip 99022-0800; tel. 509/565-4705, (Nonreporting) **A**1 3 10
Primary Contact: Eric Carpenter, Chief Executive Officer
COO: Ronda Kenney, Chief Operating Officer
CMO: Kamal Floura, M.D., Medical Director
CNO: Chet Roshetko, Chief Nursing Officer
Web address: www.dshs.wa.gov/bha/division-state-hospitals/eastern-state-hospital-overview
Control: State, Government, Nonfederal **Service**: Psychiatric

Staffed Beds: 342

MONROE—Snohomish County

★ ⇧ **EVERGREENHEALTH MONROE (500084)**, 14701 179th SE, Zip 98272-1108, Mailing Address: P.O. Box 646, Zip 98272-0646; tel. 360/794-7497, **A**10 21 **F**3 4 5 15 18 19 29 34 35 40 43 44 45 56 57 70 75 77 79 81 82 85 93 107 111 114 115 119 126 130 132 146 148 149 152 154
Primary Contact: Lisa LaPlante, Chief Administrative Officer
CFO: Scott Olander, Chief Financial Officer
CMO: Jack Handley, M.D., Chief Medical Officer
CIO: John Gepford, Director Information Systems
CHR: Kathryn Rothberg, Director Human Resources
CNO: Brenda West, R.N., MSN, Chief Nursing Officer
Web address: www.evergreenhealthmonroe.com
Control: Hospital district or authority, Government, Nonfederal **Service**: General medical and surgical

Staffed Beds: 27 **Admissions:** 963 **Census:** 11 **Outpatient Visits:** 27785 **Births:** 0 **Total Expense ($000):** 59285 **Payroll Expense ($000):** 26280 **Personnel:** 191

MORTON—Lewis County

★ ⇧ **ARBOR HEALTH, MORTON HOSPITAL (501319)**, 521 Adams Avenue ATTN: Tina Clevenger, Zip 98356-9323, Mailing Address: P.O. Box 1138, Zip 98356-0019; tel. 360/496-5112, **A**10 18 21 **F**3 15 29 34 40 45 50 57 59 64 65 68 69 75 77 81 87 93 94 96 97 107 110 111 115 119 127 129 130 133 135 144 147 148 149 154 **P**6
Primary Contact: Robert Mach, FACHE, Chief Executive Officer
CFO: Geoff Hamilton, Interim Chief Financial Officer
CIO: Randy Nielsen, Director Information Technology
CHR: Shannon Kelly, Director Human Resources
CNO: Heidi Anderson, Chief Nursing Officer
Web address: https://www.myarborhealth.org/
Control: Hospital district or authority, Government, Nonfederal **Service**: General medical and surgical

Staffed Beds: 25 **Admissions:** 190 **Census:** 4 **Outpatient Visits:** 46704 **Births:** 0 **Total Expense ($000):** 40734 **Payroll Expense ($000):** 22538 **Personnel:** 175

Hospital, Medicare Provider Number, Address, Telephone, Approval, Facility, and Physician Codes, Health Care System

★ American Hospital Association (AHA) membership
☐ The Joint Commission accreditation
○ Healthcare Facilities Accreditation Program
◇ DNV Healthcare Inc. accreditation
⇧ Center for Improvement in Healthcare Quality Accreditation
△ Commission on Accreditation of Rehabilitation Facilities (CARF) accreditation

Hospitals, U.S. / WASHINGTON

MOSES LAKE—Grant County

★ ⚕ **SAMARITAN HEALTHCARE (500033)**, 801 East Wheeler Road, Zip 98837-1899; tel. 509/765-5606, (Nonreporting) **A**10 20 21
Primary Contact: Theresa Sullivan, Chief Executive Officer
COO: Kris Neff, Chief Operating Officer
CFO: Alex Town, Chief Financial Officer
CMO: Andrea Carter, M.D., Chief Medical Officer
CNO: Jan Sternberg, Chief of Patient Care Services/Chief Nursing Officer
Web address: www.samaritanhealthcare.com
Control: Hospital district or authority, Government, Nonfederal **Service**: General medical and surgical

Staffed Beds: 50

MOUNT VERNON—Skagit County

★ ⚕ **SKAGIT VALLEY HOSPITAL (500003)**, 300 Hospital Parkway, Zip 98273, Mailing Address: P.O. Box 1376, Zip 98273-1376; tel. 360/424-4111, (Nonreporting) **A**2 3 5 10 13 19 21 **S** Skagit Regional Health, Mount Vernon, WA
Primary Contact: Brian K. Ivie, President and Chief Executive Officer
COO: Jim Geist, Executive Vice President and Chief Operating Officer
CFO: Paul Ishizuka, Chief Financial Officer
CMO: Jeffrey S. Gibbs, M.D., Regional Vice President Medical Affairs
CIO: John Dwight, Regional Vice President and Chief Information Officer
CHR: Deborah Martin, Regional Vice President Human Resources
CNO: Roxanne Olason, R.N., FACHE, Vice President and Chief Nursing Officer
Web address: www.skagitregionalhealth.org
Control: Hospital district or authority, Government, Nonfederal **Service**: General medical and surgical

Staffed Beds: 137

NEWPORT—Pend Oreille County

⚕ **NEWPORT HOSPITAL AND HEALTH SERVICES (501310)**, 714 West Pine Street, Zip 99156-9046; tel. 509/447-2441, (Nonreporting) **A**10 18 21
Primary Contact: Kim Manus, Interim CEO/CFO
CFO: Kim Manus, Chief Financial Officer
CMO: Aaron Reinke, M.D., Chief of Medical Staff
CNO: Theresa Hollinger, Chief Nursing Officer
Web address: www.newporthospitalandhealth.org
Control: Hospital district or authority, Government, Nonfederal **Service**: General medical and surgical

Staffed Beds: 74

ODESSA—Lincoln County

★ **ODESSA MEMORIAL HEALTHCARE CENTER (501307)**, 502 East Amende Drive, Zip 99159-7003, Mailing Address: P.O. Box 368, Zip 99159-0368; tel. 509/982-2611, (Nonreporting) **A**10 18
Primary Contact: Brett Antczak, Chief Executive Officer
CFO: Annette Edwards, Chief Financial Officer
CMO: Linda J Powel, M.D., Medical Director
CHR: Jodi J Bailey, Human Resources Director
CNO: Megan Shepard, Director Clinical Services
Web address: www.omhc.org
Control: Hospital district or authority, Government, Nonfederal **Service**: General medical and surgical

Staffed Beds: 13

OLYMPIA—Thurston County

CAPITAL MEDICAL CENTER See Multicare Capital Medical Center

✠ **MULTICARE CAPITAL MEDICAL CENTER (500139)**, 3900 Capital Mall Drive SW, Zip 98502-5026; tel. 360/754-5858, **A**1 10 **F**3 12 13 15 18 20 22 24 28 29 31 34 35 37 40 42 46 47 48 50 59 60 64 70 74 75 76 77 78 79 80 81 85 86 87 93 107 108 110 111 114 115 119 120 121 122 123 124 126 130 146 147 148 149 154 **S** MultiCare Health System, Tacoma, WA
Primary Contact: William Callicoat, President
COO: D Christopher Sloan, Chief Operating Officer
CFO: Jennifer Weldon, Chief Financial Officer
CMO: Rojesh Sharangpani, M.D., Chief of Staff
CIO: Renee Crotty, Coordinator Marketing and Public Relations
CHR: Dana Vandewege, Director Human Resources
CNO: Verno Davidson, R.N., Interim Chief Nursing Officer
Web address: www.capitalmedical.com
Control: Other not-for-profit (including NFP Corporation) **Service**: General medical and surgical

Staffed Beds: 69 **Admissions**: 4444 **Census**: 42 **Outpatient Visits**: 60431 **Births**: 372 **Total Expense ($000)**: 157767 **Payroll Expense ($000)**: 58087 **Personnel**: 543

✠ **PROVIDENCE ST. PETER HOSPITAL (500024)**, 413 Lilly Road NE, Zip 98506-5166; tel. 360/491-9480, **A**1 3 5 10 19 **F**3 5 8 11 13 17 18 20 22 24 26 28 29 30 31 32 34 35 37 39 40 43 44 45 46 47 48 49 50 51 53 54 56 57 58 59 60 62 63 64 65 66 68 69 70 71 73 74 75 76 77 78 79 80 81 82 84 85 86 87 89 91 93 94 96 98 100 101 102 104 105 107 108 111 114 115 118 119 126 129 130 132 135 146 148 149 150 152 153 154 157 160 161 164 165 167 168 169 **S** Providence, Renton, WA
Primary Contact: Darin Goss, FACHE, Chief Executive Officer
CFO: Denise Marroni, Chief Financial Officer
CMO: Kevin Caserta, M.D., Chief Medical Officer
CIO: Kerry Miles, Chief Information Officer
CHR: Susan Meenk, Vice President Human Resources
Web address: https://www.providence.org/locations/wa/st-peter-hospital
Control: Other not-for-profit (including NFP Corporation) **Service**: General medical and surgical

Staffed Beds: 449 **Admissions**: 16775 **Census**: 312 **Outpatient Visits**: 327080 **Births**: 1954 **Total Expense ($000)**: 682023 **Payroll Expense ($000)**: 263709 **Personnel**: 2369

OMAK—Okanogan County

⚕ **MID-VALLEY HOSPITAL AND CLINICS (501328)**, 810 Jasmine, Zip 98841-9578; tel. 509/826-1760, (Nonreporting) **A**3 5 10 18 21
Primary Contact: Holly Stanley, Co-Chief Executive Officer
COO: Christina Wagar, Chief Operating Officer
CFO: Holly Stanley, Chief Financial Officer
CMO: Jennifer Thill, Chief of Staff
CIO: Ethan Harris, Manager Information Systems
CHR: Randy Coffell, Manager Human Resources
CNO: Rebecca Christoph, Director Nursing and Patient Care Services
Web address: www.mvhealth.org
Control: Hospital district or authority, Government, Nonfederal **Service**: General medical and surgical

Staffed Beds: 25

OTHELLO—Adams County

★ **OTHELLO COMMUNITY HOSPITAL (501318)**, 315 North 14th Avenue, Zip 99344-1297; tel. 509/488-2636, (Nonreporting) **A**10 18
Primary Contact: Connie Agenbroad, Chief Executive Officer
CFO: Mark Bunch, Director Finance
CHR: Mindy Gonzales, Chief Human Resources Officer
CNO: Tina Bernsen, Chief Nursing Officer
Web address: www.othellocommunityhospital.org
Control: Hospital district or authority, Government, Nonfederal **Service**: General medical and surgical

Staffed Beds: 25

PASCO—Franklin County

✠ △ **LOURDES HEALTH (501337)**, 520 North Fourth Avenue, Zip 99301-5257; tel. 509/547-7704, (Nonreporting) **A**1 3 7 10 18 **S** Lifepoint Health, Brentwood, TN
Primary Contact: Mark C. Holyoak, FACHE, Chief Executive Officer
CFO: Erika Wier, Chief Financial Officer
CMO: Venkataraman Sambasivan, M.D., Chief Medical Officer
CIO: Deb Carpenter, Director Information Technology
CHR: Barbara Blood, Executive Director Human Resources
CNO: Kena Chase, Chief Nursing Officer
Web address: https://www.yourlourdes.com/
Control: Corporation, Investor-owned (for-profit) **Service**: General medical and surgical

Staffed Beds: 53

POMEROY—Garfield County

★ **GARFIELD COUNTY PUBLIC HOSPITAL DISTRICT (501301)**, 66 North 6th Street, Zip 99347-9705; tel. 509/843-1591, (Nonreporting) **A**10 18
Primary Contact: Jayd Keener, Co-Chief Executive Officer
CMO: Glenn Jefferson, Chief Medical Officer
CHR: Alicia Scharnhorst, Human Resources and Administrative Assistant
CNO: Barbara DeHerrera, Chief Nursing Officer
Web address: www.pomeroymd.com
Control: Hospital district or authority, Government, Nonfederal **Service**: General medical and surgical

Staffed Beds: 45

Hospitals, U.S. / WASHINGTON

PORT ANGELES—Clallam County

★ ⇑ **OLYMPIC MEDICAL CENTER (500072)**, 939 Caroline Street, Zip 98362-3997; tel. 360/417-7000, **A**2 3 10 21 **F**3 13 15 18 28 29 30 31 34 37 40 43 44 45 46 50 54 58 62 64 65 70 74 75 76 77 78 79 81 82 85 87 91 93 97 102 104 107 108 110 111 114 115 119 120 121 123 124 127 129 130 131 132 144 147 148 149 154 156 160 163 164 165
Primary Contact: Darryl Wolfe, Chief Executive Officer
COO: Darryl Wolfe, Chief Operating Officer
CFO: Lorraine Cannon, Chief Financial Officer
CMO: R. Scott Kennedy, M.D., Chief Medical Officer and Safety Officer
CHR: Jennifer Burkhardt, Chief Human Resources Officer
Web address: www.olympicmedical.org
Control: Hospital district or authority, Government, Nonfederal **Service:** General medical and surgical

Staffed Beds: 67 **Admissions:** 3334 **Census:** 38 **Outpatient Visits:** 494037 **Births:** 398 **Total Expense ($000):** 265691 **Payroll Expense ($000):** 119275 **Personnel:** 1718

PORT TOWNSEND—Jefferson County

★ ⇑ **JEFFERSON HEALTHCARE (501323)**, 834 Sheridan Street, Zip 98368-2443; tel. 360/385-2200, (Nonreporting) **A**2 10 18 21
Primary Contact: Mike Glenn, Chief Executive Officer
COO: Paula Dowdle, Chief Operating Officer
CFO: Hilary Whittington, Chief Financial Officer
CMO: Joe Mattern, M.D., Chief Medical Officer
CHR: Heather Bailey, Chief Human Resources Officer
CNO: Tina Toner, Chief Nursing Officer
Web address: www.jeffersonhealthcare.org
Control: Hospital district or authority, Government, Nonfederal **Service:** General medical and surgical

Staffed Beds: 25

PROSSER—Benton County

★ **PROSSER MEMORIAL HEALTH (501312)**, 723 Memorial Street, Zip 99350-1524; tel. 509/786-2222, **A**3 10 18 **F**3 7 11 12 13 15 29 30 34 35 37 40 43 44 45 46 47 48 49 50 54 57 59 65 66 68 75 76 77 79 81 82 85 87 89 91 93 97 107 108 109 110 111 114 115 119 127 128 130 131 132 133 135 143 146 147 148 149 154 169
Primary Contact: Craig J. Marks, FACHE, Chief Executive Officer
CFO: Tim Cooper, Chief Financial Officer
CIO: Jim Zoesch, Information Technology Director
CNO: Marla Davis, Interim Chief Nursing Officer
Web address: www.pmhmedicalcenter.com/
Control: Hospital district or authority, Government, Nonfederal **Service:** General medical and surgical

Staffed Beds: 25 **Admissions:** 1309 **Census:** 13 **Outpatient Visits:** 128885 **Births:** 629 **Total Expense ($000):** 106328 **Payroll Expense ($000):** 46314 **Personnel:** 497

PULLMAN—Whitman County

⇑ **PULLMAN REGIONAL HOSPITAL (501331)**, 835 SE Bishop Boulevard, Zip 99163-5512; tel. 509/332-2541, (Nonreporting) **A**3 10 18 21
Primary Contact: Matthew Forge, Chief Executive Officer
CFO: Steven Febus, Chief Financial Officer
CMO: Gerald L Early, M.D., Chief Medical Officer
CHR: Bernadette Berney, Director Human Resources
Web address: www.pullmanhospital.org
Control: Hospital district or authority, Government, Nonfederal **Service:** General medical and surgical

Staffed Beds: 25

PUYALLUP—Pierce County

✚ △ **MULTICARE GOOD SAMARITAN HOSPITAL (500079)**, 401 15th Avenue SE, Zip 98372-3770, Mailing Address: P.O. Box 1247, Zip 98371-0192; tel. 253/697-4000, **A**1 2 3 7 10 **F**3 7 11 13 17 18 20 22 24 28 29 30 31 34 35 38 40 41 42 43 45 47 49 50 51 55 56 57 58 59 60 61 64 65 66 68 70 73 74 75 76 78 79 80 81 82 83 84 85 87 90 91 93 96 97 101 108 111 114 115 116 117 118 119 126 129 130 132 146 147 148 149 154 156 167 168 169 **S** MultiCare Health System, Tacoma, WA
Primary Contact: Tim Holmes, Interim President
CMO: Walter Fink, Chief Medical Officer
CHR: Kevin B Dull, Senior Vice President Human Potential
CNO: Lucy Norris, Administrator Interim Chief Nursing Officer
Web address: www.multicare.org/good-samaritan-hospital/
Control: Other not-for-profit (including NFP Corporation) **Service:** General medical and surgical

Staffed Beds: 333 **Admissions:** 20110 **Census:** 328 **Outpatient Visits:** 235038 **Births:** 2441 **Total Expense ($000):** 668338 **Payroll Expense ($000):** 272671 **Personnel:** 2042

QUINCY—Grant County

QUINCY VALLEY MEDICAL CENTER (501320), 908 10th Avenue SW, Zip 98848-1376; tel. 509/787-3531, (Nonreporting) **A**10 18
Primary Contact: Glenda Bishop, Interim Chief Executive Officer
CFO: Dean Taplett, Controller
CMO: Mark Vance, M.D., Chief Medical Officer
CIO: Ruth Vance, Director Information Systems
CHR: Alene Walker, Director Human Resources
Web address: www.quincyhospital.org
Control: County, Government, Nonfederal **Service:** General medical and surgical

Staffed Beds: 25

RENTON—King County

✚ **UW MEDICINE/VALLEY MEDICAL CENTER (500088)**, 400 South 43rd Street, Zip 98055-5714, Mailing Address: P.O. Box 50010, Zip 98058-5010; tel. 425/228-3450, **A**1 2 3 5 10 **F**3 8 11 13 15 18 19 20 22 26 28 29 30 31 32 34 35 36 37 38 40 43 44 45 48 49 50 51 53 54 55 56 57 58 59 60 63 64 65 66 68 70 72 74 75 76 77 78 79 81 82 83 84 85 86 87 89 91 92 93 94 96 97 100 101 102 104 107 110 111 114 115 118 119 120 121 123 124 126 129 130 131 132 135 144 146 147 148 149 153 154 156 167 169 **P**6 **S** UW Medicine, Seattle, WA
Primary Contact: Jeannine M. Grinnell, Interim Chief Executive Officer
CFO: Larry Smith, Senior Vice President and Chief Financial Officer
CMO: Kathryn Beattie, M.D., Senior Vice President and Chief Medical Officer
CHR: Barbara Mitchell, Senior Vice President Marketing and Human Resources
CNO: Scott Alleman, Senior Vice President Patient Care Services and Chief Nursing Officer
Web address: www.valleymed.org
Control: Hospital district or authority, Government, Nonfederal **Service:** General medical and surgical

Staffed Beds: 325 **Admissions:** 16350 **Census:** 233 **Outpatient Visits:** 835494 **Births:** 2507 **Total Expense ($000):** 945579 **Payroll Expense ($000):** 481811 **Personnel:** 3610

REPUBLIC—Ferry County

★ **FERRY COUNTY MEMORIAL HOSPITAL (501322)**, 36 Klondike Road, Zip 99166-9701; tel. 509/775-3333, (Nonreporting) **A**10 18
Primary Contact: Jennifer Reed, Chief Executive Officer
CFO: Kelly Leslie, Chief Financial Officer
CMO: Farhad H Alrashedy, M.D., Chief Medical Officer
CIO: James Davidson, Director of Information Services
CHR: Michelle Loftis, Human Resources Officer
CNO: Thomas Durham, Chief Nursing Officer
Web address: www.fcphd.org
Control: Hospital district or authority, Government, Nonfederal **Service:** General medical and surgical

Staffed Beds: 25

Hospital, Medicare Provider Number, Address, Telephone, Approval, Facility, and Physician Codes, Health Care System

★ American Hospital Association (AHA) membership   ○ Healthcare Facilities Accreditation Program   ⇑ Center for Improvement in Healthcare Quality Accreditation
☐ The Joint Commission accreditation   ◇ DNV Healthcare Inc. accreditation   △ Commission on Accreditation of Rehabilitation Facilities (CARF) accreditation

Hospitals, U.S. / WASHINGTON

RICHLAND—Benton County

KADLEC REGIONAL MEDICAL CENTER (500058), 888 Swift Boulevard, Zip 99352-3514; tel. 509/946-4611, **A**1 2 3 5 10 19 **F**13 15 18 20 22 24 26 28 29 31 34 40 42 43 45 49 51 52 54 55 56 59 60 65 67 68 70 72 74 75 76 77 78 79 81 82 83 84 86 89 92 93 97 107 108 111 114 116 119 130 131 132 146 147 148 149 154 164 167 169 **P**6 **S** Providence, Renton, WA
Primary Contact: Reza Kaleel, Chief Executive
CFO: Spencer Harris, Chief Financial Officer
CMO: Kevin Pieper, Chief Medical Officer
CHR: Angela N Mager, Director, Human Resources
CNO: Kirk Harper, R.N., Chief Nursing Officer
Web address: https://www.kadlec.org
Control: Other not-for-profit (including NFP Corporation) **Service**: General medical and surgical

Staffed Beds: 305 **Admissions**: 15614 **Census**: 212 **Outpatient Visits**: 1198087 **Total Expense ($000)**: 669431 **Payroll Expense ($000)**: 360346 **Personnel**: 4070

LOURDES COUNSELING CENTER (504008), 1175 Carondelet Drive, Zip 99354-3300; tel. 509/943-9104, (Nonreporting) **A**1 3 10 **S** Lifepoint Health, Brentwood, TN
Primary Contact: Mark C. Holyoak, FACHE, Chief Executive Officer
CIO: Jared Fleming, Director, Information Services
CHR: Barbara Blood, Director Human Resources
Web address: https://www.yourlourdes.com/locations/lourdes-counseling-center
Control: Corporation, Investor-owned (for-profit) **Service**: Psychiatric

Staffed Beds: 20

RITZVILLE—Adams County

★ **EAST ADAMS RURAL HEALTHCARE (501311)**, 903 South Adams Street, Zip 99169-2298; tel. 509/659-1200, (Nonreporting) **A**10 18
Primary Contact: Corey J. Fedie, Chief Executive Officer
COO: Dina McBride, Chief Operating Officer and Director Human Resources
CMO: Charles Sackmann, M.D., Chief of Staff
CIO: Kellie Ottmar, Manager Information Services
CHR: Dina McBride, Chief Operating Officer and Director Human Resources
CNO: Brenda Herr, Chief Nursing Officer
Web address: www.earh.com
Control: Hospital district or authority, Government, Nonfederal **Service**: General medical and surgical

Staffed Beds: 20

SEATTLE—King County

BALLARD COMMUNITY HOSPITAL See Swedish Medical Center–Ballard

FRED HUTCHINSON CANCER CENTER (500138), 825 Eastlake Avenue East, Zip 98109-4405, Mailing Address: P.O. Box 19023, Zip 98109-1023; tel. 206/288-1400, **A**1 2 3 5 10 **F**3 5 14 15 29 30 31 34 35 36 38 39 44 45 46 50 54 55 57 58 59 64 65 68 75 77 78 80 81 82 84 86 87 93 94 100 101 104 107 110 111 115 116 117 118 119 120 121 122 123 130 132 135 136 143 146 147 148 149 154 160 164 167
Primary Contact: Thomas Lynch, President and Director
CFO: Jonathan Tingstad, Vice President and Chief Financial Officer
CMO: Marc Stewart, M.D., Vice President and Medical Director
CIO: David Ackerson, Chief Information Officer
CHR: Han Nachtrieb, Vice President Human Resources
Web address: www.seattlecca.org
Control: Other not-for-profit (including NFP Corporation) **Service**: Cancer

Staffed Beds: 20 **Admissions**: 530 **Census**: 19 **Outpatient Visits**: 130457 **Births**: 0 **Total Expense ($000)**: 1083048 **Payroll Expense ($000)**: 204997 **Personnel**: 2049

KINDRED HOSPITAL SEATTLE–FIRST HILL (502002), 1334 Terry Avenue, Zip 98101-2747; tel. 206/682-2661, (Nonreporting) **A**1 10 **S** ScionHealth, Louisville, KY
Primary Contact: Brian Nall, Chief Executive Officer
Web address: www.khseattlefirsthill.com
Control: Corporation, Investor-owned (for-profit) **Service**: Acute long-term care hospital

Staffed Beds: 10

☐ **NAVOS (504009)**, 2600 SW Holden Street, Zip 98126-3505; tel. 206/933-7299, **A**1 10 **F**68 98 106 162 164 **S** MultiCare Health System, Tacoma, WA
Primary Contact: Tim Holmes, Chief Executive Officer
COO: Cassie Undlin, Chief Operating Officer
CIO: Mary Sellers, Chief Information Officer
CHR: Karen White, Interim Vice President of Human Resources
CNO: Angela Naylor, Inpatient Chief Operating Executive and Chief Nursing Executive of Behavioral Health Network
Web address: www.navos.org
Control: Other not-for-profit (including NFP Corporation) **Service**: Psychiatric

Staffed Beds: 70 **Admissions**: 659 **Census**: 66 **Outpatient Visits**: 0 **Births**: 0 **Total Expense ($000)**: 25678 **Payroll Expense ($000)**: 14405 **Personnel**: 98

NORTHWEST HOSPITAL & MEDICAL CENTER See UW Medicine/Northwest Hospital & Medical Center

★ △ ⇧ **PROVIDENCE SWEDISH CHERRY HILL (500025)**, 500 17th Avenue, Zip 98122-5711; tel. 206/320-2000, **A**3 7 10 19 21 **F**3 8 11 17 18 20 22 24 26 28 29 30 34 35 37 38 40 45 53 57 58 59 60 61 64 65 68 70 74 75 77 80 81 82 85 87 90 93 102 107 108 111 115 120 121 123 124 126 129 130 132 135 141 146 148 149 154 156 164 167 **S** Swedish Health Services, Seattle, WA
Primary Contact: Elizabeth Wako, M.D., Chief Executive
CFO: Jeffrey Veilleux, Senior Vice President and Chief Financial Officer
CIO: Janice Newell, Chief Information Officer
Web address: https://www.swedish.org/locations/cherry-hill-campus
Control: Other not-for-profit (including NFP Corporation) **Service**: General medical and surgical

Staffed Beds: 211 **Admissions**: 8860 **Census**: 150 **Outpatient Visits**: 141604 **Births**: 0 **Total Expense ($000)**: 526326 **Payroll Expense ($000)**: 175095 **Personnel**: 1466

★ ⇧ **PROVIDENCE SWEDISH FIRST HILL (500027)**, 747 Broadway, Zip 98122-4307; tel. 206/386-6000, (Includes SWEDISH MEDICAL CENTER–BALLARD, 5300 Tallman Avenue NW, Seattle, Washington, Zip 98107-3932, tel. 206/782-2700; Elizabeth Wako, M.D., Chief Executive) **A**2 3 5 10 19 21 **F**3 4 5 7 8 11 12 13 15 17 18 19 20 21 22 23 24 25 26 29 30 31 32 34 35 37 38 39 40 42 45 46 47 48 49 52 54 55 57 58 59 60 61 64 65 68 70 71 72 73 74 75 76 77 78 79 80 81 82 85 86 87 88 89 98 102 105 107 108 109 110 111 114 115 116 118 119 120 121 123 124 126 129 130 132 134 135 138 139 141 142 146 147 148 149 152 154 156 162 164 167 169 **S** Swedish Health Services, Seattle, WA
Primary Contact: Elizabeth Wako, M.D., Chief Executive
CFO: Jeffrey Veilleux, Executive Vice President and Chief Financial Officer
CIO: Janice Newell, Chief Information Officer
Web address: https://www.swedish.org/locations/first-hill-campus
Control: Other not-for-profit (including NFP Corporation) **Service**: General medical and surgical

Staffed Beds: 581 **Admissions**: 24293 **Census**: 405 **Outpatient Visits**: 477811 **Births**: 6545 **Total Expense ($000)**: 1657601 **Payroll Expense ($000)**: 544492 **Personnel**: 4005

△ ⇧ **SEATTLE CHILDREN'S HOSPITAL (503300)**, 4800 Sand Point Way NE, Zip 98105-3901, Mailing Address: P.O. Box 5371, Zip 98145-5005; tel. 206/987-2000, (Nonreporting) **A**3 5 7 10 21
Primary Contact: Jeff Sperring, M.D., Chief Executive Officer
COO: Cindy Gazecki, Senior Vice President, Hospital Operations
CFO: Suzanne Beitel, Senior Vice President and Chief Financial Officer
CMO: Ruth A. McDonald, M.D., Chief Medical Officer
CIO: Zafar Chaudry, M.D., Senior Vice President and Chief Information Officer
CHR: Steven Hurwitz, Senior Vice President Shared Services
CNO: Susan Heath, R.N., Senior Vice President and Chief Nursing Officer
Web address: www.seattlechildrens.org
Control: Other not-for-profit (including NFP Corporation) **Service**: Children's general medical and surgical

Staffed Beds: 316

SEATTLE, WA PUGET SOUND HCS See VA Puget Sound Healthcare System – Seattle

⇧ **SWEDISH MEDICAL CENTER–FIRST HILL** See Providence Swedish First Hill

Hospitals, U.S. / WASHINGTON

✠ △ **UW MEDICINE/HARBORVIEW MEDICAL CENTER (500064)**, 325 Ninth Avenue, Zip 98104–2499; tel. 206/744-3000; **A**1 3 5 7 8 10 19 **F**3 5 6 9 11 16 17 18 20 22 24 26 29 30 31 32 34 35 36 37 38 40 41 43 44 45 46 47 48 49 50 51 56 57 58 59 60 61 64 65 66 68 70 71 74 75 77 78 79 81 82 84 85 86 87 90 91 92 93 94 95 96 97 98 100 101 102 103 104 107 108 111 114 115 118 119 124 129 130 131 132 134 135 141 142 145 146 147 148 149 150 154 156 160 161 163 164 165 167 169 **S** UW Medicine, Seattle, WA
Primary Contact: Sommer Kleweno–Walley, Chief Executive Officer
CFO: Kera Dennis, Assistant Administrator, Finance
CMO: J. Richard Goss, M.D., M.P.H., Medical Director
CIO: Joy Grosser, Chief Information Officer
CHR: Nicki McCraw, Assistant Vice President Human Resources
Web address: www.uwmedicine.org/Patient-Care/Locations/HMC/Pages/default.aspx
Control: County, Government, Nonfederal **Service**: General medical and surgical

Staffed Beds: 463 **Admissions**: 16024 **Census**: 474 **Outpatient Visits**: 268144 **Births**: 0 **Total Expense ($000)**: 1373794 **Payroll Expense ($000)**: 559661 **Personnel**: 5884

✠ △ **UW MEDICINE/UNIVERSITY OF WASHINGTON MEDICAL CENTER (500008)**, 1959 NE Pacific Street, Zip 98195–6151; tel. 206/598-3300, (Includes UW MEDICINE/NORTHWEST HOSPITAL & MEDICAL CENTER, 1550 North 115th Street, Seattle, Washington, Zip 98133–8401, tel. 206/364–0500; Cynthia Hecker, R.N., Chief Executive Officer, UW Medical Center) **A**1 2 3 5 7 8 10 19 **F**3 5 9 11 12 13 15 17 18 20 22 24 26 28 29 30 31 34 35 36 37 43 44 45 46 47 48 49 50 51 52 54 55 56 57 58 59 60 61 64 65 68 70 72 73 74 75 76 77 78 79 80 81 82 84 85 86 87 90 91 92 93 95 96 97 98 100 101 102 104 107 108 110 111 115 116 117 118 119 120 121 123 124 126 130 131 132 135 136 137 138 139 140 141 142 145 146 147 148 149 154 156 160 161 162 164 167 169 **P**6 **S** UW Medicine, Seattle, WA
Primary Contact: Cynthia Hecker, R.N., Chief Executive Officer
COO: Geoff Austin, Chief Operating Officer
CFO: Jacque Cabe, Chief Financial Officer
CMO: Tom Staiger, Medical Director
CIO: Joy Grosser, Chief Information Officer
CHR: Jennifer J Petritz, Director Human Resources
CNO: Cindy Sayre, Ph.D., R.N., Chief Nursing Officer
Web address: www.uwmedicine.org/uw-medical-center
Control: State, Government, Nonfederal **Service**: General medical and surgical

Staffed Beds: 688 **Admissions**: 29001 **Census**: 576 **Outpatient Visits**: 627760 **Births**: 3809 **Total Expense ($000)**: 2334538 **Payroll Expense ($000)**: 782079 **Personnel**: 8605

✠ △ **VA PUGET SOUND HEALTHCARE SYSTEM – SEATTLE**, 1660 South Columbian Way, Zip 98108–1597; tel. 206/762–1010, (Includes VETERANS AFFAIRS PUGET SOUND HEALTH CARE SYSTEM–AMERICAN LAKE DIVISION, 9600 Veterans Drive, Tacoma, Washington, Zip 98493–0003, tel. 253/582–8440) (Nonreporting) **A**1 2 3 5 7 **S** Department of Veterans Affairs, Washington, DC
Primary Contact: Colonel Thomas S. Bundt, Ph.D., FACHE, Executive Director
CFO: Kenneth J Hudson, Chief Financial Officer
CMO: Gordon Starkebaum, M.D., Chief of Staff
CIO: Glenn Zwinger, Manager Information Systems Services
Web address: www.pugetsound.va.gov/
Control: Veterans Affairs, Government, federal **Service**: General medical and surgical

Staffed Beds: 316

✠ **VIRGINIA MASON MEDICAL CENTER (500005)**, 1100 Ninth Avenue, Zip 98101–2756, Mailing Address: P.O. Box 900, Zip 98111–0900; tel. 206/223–6600, **A**1 2 3 5 10 19 **F**3 8 9 11 12 13 15 18 20 22 24 26 28 29 30 31 32 34 35 36 37 40 44 45 46 47 48 49 50 51 54 55 56 57 58 59 60 61 63 64 65 70 73 74 75 76 77 78 79 80 81 82 83 84 85 86 87 90 91 92 93 94 96 97 100 101 102 104 107 108 110 111 112 114 115 117 118 119 120 121 123 124 126 128 129 130 131 132 135 138 141 142 144 145 146 147 148 154 156 160 162 163 167 169 **P**6 **S** CommonSpirit Health, Chicago, IL
Primary Contact: Monica Hilt, President
CFO: Craig Goodrich, Chief Financial Officer
CMO: Michael Glenn, M.D., Chief Medical Officer
CIO: Bill Poppy, Chief Information Officer
CHR: Kathy J. Shingleton, Ed.D., Vice President, Human Resources
CNO: Charleen Tachibana, R.N., Senior Vice President and Chief Nursing Officer
Web address: www.VirginiaMason.org
Control: Church operated, Nongovernment, not–for–profit **Service**: General medical and surgical

Staffed Beds: 218 **Admissions**: 12839 **Census**: 173 **Outpatient Visits**: 233080 **Births**: 483 **Total Expense ($000)**: 1269277 **Payroll Expense ($000)**: 653968 **Personnel**: 4691

SEDRO-WOOLLEY—Skagit County

★ △ ⇑ **PEACEHEALTH UNITED GENERAL MEDICAL CENTER (501329)**, 2000 Hospital Drive, Zip 98284–4327; tel. 360/856–6021, **A**2 7 10 18 21 **F**3 11 15 29 30 31 34 35 40 43 45 50 57 64 68 70 77 78 79 81 85 92 93 107 108 110 115 118 119 120 121 123 129 130 132 133 143 146 148 149 167 **S** PeaceHealth, Vancouver, WA
Primary Contact: Christopher Johnston, Chief Administrative Officer
CFO: Carolyn Haupt, Chief Financial Officer
CHR: Tracie Skrinde, Senior Human Resources Partner
Web address: www.peacehealth.org/united-general
Control: Church operated, Nongovernment, not–for–profit **Service**: General medical and surgical

Staffed Beds: 25 **Admissions**: 854 **Census**: 14 **Outpatient Visits**: 47654 **Births**: 0 **Total Expense ($000)**: 69971 **Payroll Expense ($000)**: 26615 **Personnel**: 314

SHELTON—Mason County

★ ⇑ **MASON HEALTH (501336)**, 901 Mountain View Drive, Zip 98584–4401, Mailing Address: P.O. Box 1668, Zip 98584–5001; tel. 360/426–1611, (Nonreporting) **A**10 18 21
Primary Contact: Eric Moll, Chief Executive Officer
COO: Mark Batty, Chief Operating Officer
CFO: Rick Smith, Chief Financial Officer
CMO: Dean Gushee, M.D., Medical Director
CIO: Tom Hornburg, Director Information Systems
CNO: Melissa D Strong, Chief Nursing Officer
Web address: www.masongeneral.com
Control: Hospital district or authority, Government, Nonfederal **Service**: General medical and surgical

Staffed Beds: 25

SILVERDALE—Kitsap County

CHI FRANCISCAN ST. MICHAEL MEDICAL CENTER See St. Michael Medical Center

✠ **ST. MICHAEL MEDICAL CENTER (500039)**, 1800 Northwest Myhre Road, Zip 98383–7663; tel. 564/240–1000, **A**1 3 10 19 **F**3 11 12 13 15 18 20 22 24 26 28 29 30 31 34 35 38 40 43 44 45 46 49 50 57 59 60 64 70 73 74 75 76 77 78 79 80 81 82 84 85 86 87 93 94 107 108 110 111 114 115 117 118 119 120 121 124 126 129 130 132 135 144 146 147 148 149 154 164 **P**6 **S** CommonSpirit Health, Chicago, IL
Primary Contact: Chad Melton, President
COO: Matthew Wheelus, Vice President, Chief Operating Officer
CFO: Mike Fitzgerald, Chief Financial Officer
CMO: David Weiss, M.D., Vice President, Medical Operations, Peninsula Region
CIO: Rand Strobel, Regional Chief Information Officer, Information Technology Services
CHR: Vickie Lackman, Human Resource Director, Peninsula Region
Web address: https://www.vmfh.org/our-hospitals/st-michael-medical-center.html
Control: Church operated, Nongovernment, not–for–profit **Service**: General medical and surgical

Staffed Beds: 248 **Admissions**: 15084 **Census**: 221 **Outpatient Visits**: 425796 **Births**: 1908 **Total Expense ($000)**: 664445 **Payroll Expense ($000)**: 211599 **Personnel**: 1889

SNOQUALMIE—King County

SNOQUALMIE VALLEY HEALTH (501338), 9801 Frontier Avenue SE, Zip 98065–9577; tel. 425/831–2300, (Nonreporting) **A**10 18
Primary Contact: Renee K. Jensen, Chief Executive Officer
CMO: Kimberly Witkop, M.D., Chief Medical Officer
Web address: www.snoqualmiehospital.org/
Control: Hospital district or authority, Government, Nonfederal **Service**: General medical and surgical

Staffed Beds: 25

SNOQUALMIE VALLEY HOSPITAL DISTRICT See Snoqualmie Valley Health

---

Hospital, Medicare Provider Number, Address, Telephone, Approval, Facility, and Physician Codes, Health Care System

★ American Hospital Association (AHA) membership ◯ Healthcare Facilities Accreditation Program ⇑ Center for Improvement in Healthcare Quality Accreditation
☐ The Joint Commission accreditation ◇ DNV Healthcare Inc. accreditation △ Commission on Accreditation of Rehabilitation Facilities (CARF) accreditation

Hospitals, U.S. / WASHINGTON

SOUTH BEND—Pacific County

⇑ **WILLAPA HARBOR HOSPITAL (501303)**, 800 Alder Street, Zip 98586–4900, Mailing Address: P.O. Box 438, Zip 98586–0438; tel. 360/875–5526, **A**10 18 21 **F**3 11 15 28 29 34 35 40 41 43 45 47 48 50 54 56 59 65 68 77 81 87 97 102 107 114 115 119 127 133 148 149 154 156 157 **P**6
Primary Contact: Matthew Kempton, Chief Executive Officer
CFO: Terry Stone, Chief Financial Officer and Chief Information Officer
CIO: Terry Stone, Chief Financial Officer and Chief Information Officer
CHR: Krisy L Funkhouser, Manager Human Resources
Web address: www.willapaharborhospital.com
Control: Hospital district or authority, Government, Nonfederal **Service:** General medical and surgical

Staffed Beds: 10 Admissions: 198 Census: 2 Outpatient Visits: 30746 Births: 1 Total Expense ($000): 28635 Payroll Expense ($000): 14322 Personnel: 158

SPOKANE—Spokane County

☐ **INLAND NORTHWEST BEHAVIORAL HEALTH (504014)**, 104 West 5th Avenue, Zip 99204–4820; tel. 509/992–1888, (Nonreporting) **A**1 10
Primary Contact: Rlynn Wickel, President and Chief Executive Officer
Web address: https://inlandnorthwestbh.com/
Control: Corporation, Investor–owned (for–profit) **Service:** Psychiatric

Staffed Beds: 100

MANN–GRANDSTAFF DEPARTMENT OF VETERANS AFFAIRS MEDICAL CENTER, 4815 North Assembly Street, Zip 99205–6197; tel. 509/434–7000, (Nonreporting) **A**1 3 5 **S** Department of Veterans Affairs, Washington, DC
Primary Contact: Robert Fischer, M.D., Medical Center Director
COO: Perry Klein, Chief Engineering
CFO: Michael Stuhlmiller, Chief Financial Officer
CIO: Rob Fortenberry, Chief Information Officer
CHR: Jacqueline Ross, Chief Human Resources Officer
CNO: Nancy Benton, Assistant Director Patient Care Services
Web address: www.spokane.va.gov/
Control: Veterans Affairs, Government, federal **Service:** General medical and surgical

Staffed Beds: 67

MULTICARE DEACONESS HOSPITAL (500044), 800 West Fifth Avenue, Zip 99204–2803, Mailing Address: P.O. Box 248, Zip 99210–0248; tel. 509/458–5800, **A**1 3 5 10 **F**3 12 13 15 17 18 20 22 24 26 28 29 30 31 35 40 42 43 45 46 47 48 49 50 51 53 60 64 65 68 70 72 73 74 76 77 78 79 81 82 84 85 86 87 91 92 94 100 102 107 108 109 110 111 114 115 116 117 118 119 120 121 124 126 129 130 131 132 146 147 148 149 154 160 161 167 **P**6 **S** MultiCare Health System, Tacoma, WA
Primary Contact: Gregory George. Repetti III, FACHE, President
CFO: Rodney Higgins, Chief Financial Officer
CMO: David Chen, M.D., Chief Medical Officer
CIO: Richard DeRoche, Manager Information Technology
CHR: Melinda Moore, Director Human Resources
CNO: Jennifer Petrik, Interim Chief Nursing Officer
Web address: https://www.multicare.org/deaconess-hospital/
Control: Other not–for–profit (including NFP Corporation) **Service:** General medical and surgical

Staffed Beds: 279 Admissions: 11509 Census: 156 Outpatient Visits: 127239 Births: 1524 Total Expense ($000): 520516 Payroll Expense ($000): 167483 Personnel: 1427

PROVIDENCE HOLY FAMILY HOSPITAL (500077), 5633 North Lidgerwood Street, Zip 99208–1224; tel. 509/482–0111, (Nonreporting) **A**1 2 3 5 10 **S** Providence, Renton, WA
Primary Contact: Susan Scott, Chief Operating Officer
COO: Cathy J Simchuk, Chief Operating Officer
CFO: Shelby Stokoe, Chief Financial Officer
CMO: Dean Martz, Chief Medical Officer
CIO: Mark Vogelsang, Director Information Services
CHR: Mark Smith, Director Human Resources
CNO: Sharon Hershman, R.N., Chief Nursing Officer
Web address: https://www.providence.org/locations/wa/holy-family-hospital
Control: Church operated, Nongovernment, not–for–profit **Service:** General medical and surgical

Staffed Beds: 191

PROVIDENCE SACRED HEART MEDICAL CENTER & CHILDREN'S HOSPITAL (500054), 101 West Eighth Avenue, Zip 99204–2364, Mailing Address: P.O. Box 2555, Zip 99220–2555; tel. 509/474–3131, (Includes SACRED HEART CHILDREN'S HOSPITAL, 101 W 8th Ave, Spokane, Washington, Zip 99204–2307, PO Box 2555, Zip 99220–2555, tel. 509/474–4841; Keith Georgeson, M.D., Chief Executive) (Nonreporting) **A**1 2 3 5 10 19 **S** Providence, Renton, WA
Primary Contact: Susan Stacey, R.N., Chief Executive
CFO: Shelby Stokoe, Senior Director Finance
CMO: Dean Martz, Chief Medical Officer
CHR: Mark Smith, Director Human Resources
Web address: www.shmc.org
Control: Church operated, Nongovernment, not–for–profit **Service:** General medical and surgical

Staffed Beds: 665

PROVIDENCE ST. LUKE'S REHABILITATION INSTITUTE See Providence St. Luke's Rehabilitation Medical Center

△ **PROVIDENCE ST. LUKE'S REHABILITATION MEDICAL CENTER (503025)**, 711 South Cowley Street, Zip 99202–1388; tel. 509/473–6000, (Nonreporting) **A**1 3 7 10 **S** Providence, Renton, WA
Primary Contact: Nancy Webster, Administrator and Chief Operating Officer
CFO: Helen Andrus, Chief Financial Officer
CMO: Gregory Carter, M.D., Chief Medical Officer
CIO: Fred Galusha, Chief Information Officer
CHR: Staci Franz, Director Human Resources
CNO: Kimberly J Ward, Chief Nurse Officer
Web address: www.st-lukes.org
Control: Other not–for–profit (including NFP Corporation) **Service:** Rehabilitation

Staffed Beds: 72

SACRED HEART CHILDEN'S HOSPITAL See Sacred Heart Children's Hospital

☐ **SHRINERS HOSPITALS FOR CHILDREN–SPOKANE (503302)**, 911 West Fifth Avenue, Zip 99204–2901, Mailing Address: P.O. Box 2472, Zip 99210–2472; tel. 509/455–7844, (Nonreporting) **A**1 3 5 10 **S** Shriners Hospitals for Children, Tampa, FL
Primary Contact: Peter G. Brewer, Administrator
CFO: Monica Hickman, Director Fiscal Services
CMO: Glen Baird, M.D., Chief of Staff
CIO: Mike Allen, Director Information Services
CHR: Karen Mattern, Director of Human Resources
CNO: Lynda Vilanova, Director Patient Care Services
Web address: www.shrinershospitalsforchildren.org/Hospitals/Locations/Spokane.aspx
Control: Other not–for–profit (including NFP Corporation) **Service:** Children's orthopedic

Staffed Beds: 30

SPOKANE VAMC See Mann–Grandstaff Department of Veterans Affairs Medical Center

SPOKANE VALLEY—Spokane County

MULTICARE VALLEY HOSPITAL (500119), 12606 East Mission Avenue, Zip 99216–1090; tel. 509/924–6650, **A**1 3 10 **F**3 13 20 26 29 30 40 43 45 46 49 50 60 68 70 74 75 76 77 79 81 85 87 107 108 111 114 115 119 124 130 131 146 147 167 **S** MultiCare Health System, Tacoma, WA
Primary Contact: Gregory George. Repetti III, FACHE, President
COO: David Martin, Assistant Administrator
CFO: Justin Voelker, Chief Financial Officer
CMO: David Chen, M.D., Chief Medical Officer
CIO: Brain Jones, Director of Information Technology
CHR: Jamie Caine, Director of Human Resources
CNO: Shannon S. Holland, R.N., MSN, Chief Nursing Officer
Web address: https://www.multicare.org/location/valley-hospital/
Control: Other not–for–profit (including NFP Corporation) **Service:** General medical and surgical

Staffed Beds: 123 Admissions: 4934 Census: 63 Outpatient Visits: 63105 Births: 629 Total Expense ($000): 175416 Payroll Expense ($000): 70562 Personnel: 603

SUNNYSIDE—Yakima County

★ **ASTRIA SUNNYSIDE HOSPITAL (501330)**, 1016 Tacoma Avenue, Zip 98944–2263, Mailing Address: P.O. Box 719, Zip 98944–0719; tel. 509/837–1500, (Nonreporting) **A**3 10 18 **S** Astria Health, Sunnyside, WA
Primary Contact: Brian P. Gibbons, Chief Executive Officer
CFO: Cary Rowan, Chief Financial Officer
CIO: John Andersen, Manager Information Systems
CHR: Elaina Wagner, Director Human Resources
CNO: Winnie R Adams, Chief Nursing Officer
Web address: https://www.astria.health/locations/astria-sunnyside-hospital
Control: Other not–for–profit (including NFP Corporation) **Service:** General medical and surgical

Staffed Beds: 37

Hospitals, U.S. / WASHINGTON

TACOMA—Pierce County

ALLENMORE HOSPITAL See Multicare Tacoma General Hospital, Tacoma

☐ **CHI FRANCISCAN REHABILITATION (503026)**, 815 S Vassault Street, Zip 98465-2008; tel. 253/444-3320, (Nonreporting) **A**1 **S** Kindred Healthcare, Sunnyside, WA
Primary Contact: Alex Seymour, Chief Executive Officer
Web address: https://www.chifranciscan.org/rehabilitation-hospital.html
Control: Corporation, Investor-owned (for-profit) **Service:** Rehabilitation

Staffed Beds: 60

HUMANA HOSPITAL-TACOMA See Allenmore Hospital

✠ **MADIGAN ARMY MEDICAL CENTER**, 9040 Jackson Avenue, Zip 98431-1100; tel. 253/968-1110, (Nonreporting) **A**1 2 3 5 **S** Department of the Army, Office of the Surgeon General, Falls Church, VA
Primary Contact: Colonel Hope M. Williamson-Younce, Commander
CFO: Lieutenant Colonel Nolan Brandt, Chief Finance Officer
CMO: Colonel George Leonard, M.D., Chief Medical Officer
CIO: Colonel James A Morrison, Chief Information Officer
CHR: Anthony Munoz, Chief, Civilian Human Resources Branch
CNO: Colonel Louis Stout, Chief Nursing Officer and Deputy Commander Health Readiness
Web address: https://madigan.tricare.mil/
Control: Army, Government, federal **Service:** General medical and surgical

Staffed Beds: 203

✠ **MULTICARE MARY BRIDGE CHILDREN'S HOSPITAL AND HEALTH CENTER (503301)**, 317 Martin Luther King Jr Way, Zip 98405-4234, Mailing Address: P.O. Box 5299, Zip 98415-0299; tel. 253/403-1400, **A**1 3 5 10 19 21 23 25 27 29 30 31 32 34 35 38 40 41 43 45 46 48 53 54 55 57 58 59 60 61 62 64 65 66 68 71 72 73 74 75 78 79 81 82 84 85 86 87 88 89 91 92 93 94 96 97 100 104 107 108 111 114 115 119 120 121 123 124 126 129 130 131 132 143 144 146 148 149 150 153 154 156 158 164 167 **S** MultiCare Health System, Tacoma, WA
Primary Contact: Jeffrey S. Poltawsky, President and Market Leader
COO: Ben Whitworth, Chief Operating Officer
CMO: Vanessa Carroll, Chief Medical Officer
CHR: Kevin B Dull, Senior Vice President Human Potential
CNO: Jodi Gragg, Interim Chief Nursing Executive
Web address: www.multicare.org/marybridge
Control: Other not-for-profit (including NFP Corporation) **Service:** Children's general medical and surgical

Staffed Beds: 152 **Admissions:** 4617 **Census:** 47 **Outpatient Visits:** 157467 **Births:** 0 **Total Expense ($000):** 395460 **Payroll Expense ($000):** 160917 **Personnel:** 1271

✠ **MULTICARE TACOMA GENERAL HOSPITAL (500129)**, 315 Martin Luther King Jr Way, Zip 98405-4234, Mailing Address: P.O. Box 5299, Zip 98415-0299; tel. 253/403-1000, (Includes ALLENMORE HOSPITAL, 1901 S Union Ave, Tacoma, Washington, Zip 98405-1702, P O Box 11414, Zip 98411-0414, tel. 253/459-6633; Eddie Bratko, President) **A**1 2 3 5 10 **F**3 8 12 13 15 17 18 20 22 24 26 28 29 30 31 34 35 36 40 42 43 44 45 46 47 48 49 50 51 53 54 55 57 58 59 64 70 74 75 76 78 79 80 81 82 84 85 87 98 99 100 102 105 107 108 109 111 114 115 116 117 119 120 121 123 124 126 129 130 131 132 135 146 147 148 149 154 157 167 168 169 **P**6 **S** MultiCare Health System, Tacoma, WA
Primary Contact: Eddie Bratko, President
COO: Julia Truman, Chief Operating Officer
CHR: Kevin B Dull, Senior Vice President Human Potential
CNO: Anita Wolfe, Chief Nurse Executive
Web address: www.multicare.org
Control: Other not-for-profit (including NFP Corporation) **Service:** General medical and surgical

Staffed Beds: 381 **Admissions:** 24655 **Census:** 384 **Outpatient Visits:** 301038 **Births:** 3225 **Total Expense ($000):** 1262008 **Payroll Expense ($000):** 421843 **Personnel:** 3054

✠ **ST. JOSEPH MEDICAL CENTER (500108)**, 1717 South 'J' Street, Zip 98405-3004, Mailing Address: P.O. Box 2197, Zip 98401-2197; tel. 253/426-4101, **A**1 2 3 5 10 **F**3 11 13 18 20 22 24 26 28 29 30 31 35 40 43 45 46 47 48 49 50 51 59 64 65 68 70 72 74 75 76 77 78 79 80 81 84 85 87 102 107 108 109 111 114 115 118 119 126 130 136 146 148 154 157 164 167 **P**2 6 **S** CommonSpirit Health, Chicago, IL
Primary Contact: Syd Bersante, R.N., Interim President
CFO: Mike Fitzgerald, Chief Financial Officer
CMO: Michael Anderson, M.D., Chief Medical Officer
CIO: Shawn Shuffield, Interim Chief Information Officer
CNO: Ruth Flint, Chief Nursing Officer
Web address: https://www.vmfh.org/our-hospitals/st-joseph-medical-center
Control: Church operated, Nongovernment, not-for-profit **Service:** General medical and surgical

Staffed Beds: 353 **Admissions:** 21223 **Census:** 344 **Outpatient Visits:** 184800 **Births:** 4127 **Total Expense ($000):** 828289 **Payroll Expense ($000):** 294407 **Personnel:** 2651

VETERANS AFFAIRS MED CENTER See Veterans Affairs Puget Sound Health Care System–American Lake Division

VETERANS AFFAIRS PUGET SOUND HEALTH CARE SYSTEM–AMERICAN LAKE DIVISION See VA Puget Sound Healthcare System – Seattle, Seattle

✠ **WELLFOUND BEHAVIORAL HEALTH HOSPITAL (504016)**, 3402 South 19th Street, Zip 98405-2487; tel. 253/301-5400, **A**1 10 **F**38 98 102 130 149 164 **S** CommonSpirit Health, Chicago, IL
Primary Contact: Angela Naylor, Interim Chief Executive Officer
Web address: https://www.wellfound.org/
Control: Other not-for-profit (including NFP Corporation) **Service:** Psychiatric

Staffed Beds: 84 **Admissions:** 2176 **Census:** 68 **Outpatient Visits:** 0 **Births:** 0 **Total Expense ($000):** 41797 **Payroll Expense ($000):** 25629 **Personnel:** 215

WESTERN STATE HOSPITAL (504003), 9601 Steilacom Boulevard SW, Zip 98498-7213; tel. 253/582-8900, (Nonreporting) **A**10
Primary Contact: Charles Southerland, Chief Executive Officer
CFO: Sue Breen, Chief Financial Officer
CHR: Lori Manning, Administrator Human Resources
Web address: www.dshs.wa.gov/bhsia/division-state-hospitals/western-state-hospital
Control: State, Government, Nonfederal **Service:** Psychiatric

Staffed Beds: 837

TONASKET—Okanogan County

★ **NORTH VALLEY HOSPITAL (501321)**, 203 South Western Avenue, Zip 98855-8803; tel. 509/486-2151, (Nonreporting) **A**10 18
Primary Contact: John McReynolds, Chief Executive Officer
CFO: Matthew Matthiessen, Chief Financial Officer
CMO: Paul Lacey, M.D., Chief Medical Staff
CIO: Kelly Cariker, Chief Information Officer
CHR: Jan Gonzales, Director Human Resources
Web address: www.nvhospital.org
Control: Hospital district or authority, Government, Nonfederal **Service:** General medical and surgical

Staffed Beds: 67

TOPPENISH—Yakima County

☐ **ASTRIA TOPPENISH HOSPITAL (500037)**, 502 West Fourth Avenue, Zip 98948-1616, Mailing Address: P.O. Box 672, Zip 98948-0672; tel. 509/865-3105, (Nonreporting) **A**1 10 **S** Astria Health, Sunnyside, WA
Primary Contact: Cathy Bambrick, Administrator
CHR: Rosa Solorzano, Interim Director Human Resources
Web address: https://www.astria.health/locations/astria-toppenish-hospital
Control: Other not-for-profit (including NFP Corporation) **Service:** General medical and surgical

Staffed Beds: 48

Hospitals, U.S. / WASHINGTON

VANCOUVER—Clark County

✠ **LEGACY SALMON CREEK MEDICAL CENTER (500150)**, 2211 NE 139th Street, Zip 98686–2742; tel. 360/487–1000, **A**1 2 3 5 10 **F**3 11 13 15 18 20 22 26 28 29 30 31 32 34 35 37 38 39 40 41 44 45 46 47 49 50 51 55 57 59 60 65 68 69 70 72 74 75 76 77 78 79 81 82 84 85 87 93 94 96 97 107 108 110 111 114 115 116 117 118 119 120 121 126 130 132 135 146 147 148 149 150 154 167 **P**6 **S** Legacy Health, Portland, OR
Primary Contact: Jon Hersen, President
COO: Michael Newcomb, D.O., Senior Vice President and Chief Operating Officer
CMO: Lewis Low, M.D., Senior Vice President and Chief Medical Officer
CHR: Sonja Steves, Senior Vice President Human Resources
Web address: www.legacyhealth.org
Control: Other not–for–profit (including NFP Corporation) **Service**: General medical and surgical

Staffed Beds: 212 **Admissions**: 13020 **Census**: 188 **Outpatient Visits**: 173277 **Births**: 3395 **Total Expense ($000)**: 503388 **Payroll Expense ($000)**: 249334 **Personnel**: 1948

★ △ ✠ **PEACEHEALTH SOUTHWEST MEDICAL CENTER (500050)**, 400 NE Mother Joseph Place, Zip 98664–3200, Mailing Address: P.O. Box 1600, Zip 98668–1600; tel. 360/256–2000, (Includes VANCOUVER MEMORIAL CAMPUS, 3400 Main Street, Vancouver, Washington, Zip 98663, tel. 360/514–2000; Sean Gregory, Chief Executive, Columbia Network) **A**2 3 5 7 10 21 **F**3 11 12 13 15 17 18 20 22 24 26 28 29 30 31 34 35 40 42 43 44 45 46 49 50 51 54 57 58 59 60 61 62 63 64 65 68 70 72 73 74 75 76 77 78 79 81 82 84 85 86 87 89 90 92 93 96 97 100 101 102 104 105 107 108 109 110 111 114 115 116 117 119 120 121 122 124 126 129 130 131 132 135 144 146 147 148 149 153 154 156 167 **S** PeaceHealth, Vancouver, WA
Primary Contact: Cherelle Montanye–Ireland, Chief Hospital Executive
COO: Gary Foster, R.N., Chief Operating Officer
CFO: Tracey Fernandez, Chief Financial Officer
CMO: Lawrence Neville, Chief Medical Officer
CIO: Donn McMillan, Senior Director, IST Client Liaison
CHR: Kelley Frengle, Senior Director, Human Resources
CNO: Tanya Shanks–Connors, R.N., MSN, Chief Nursing Officer
Web address: https://www.peacehealth.org/phmg/vancouver
Control: Church operated, Nongovernment, not–for–profit **Service**: General medical and surgical

Staffed Beds: 399 **Admissions**: 19222 **Census**: 308 **Outpatient Visits**: 258675 **Births**: 1792 **Total Expense ($000)**: 677940 **Payroll Expense ($000)**: 258603 **Personnel**: 2861

☐ **RAINIER SPRINGS HOSPITAL (504013)**, 2805 Northeast 129th Street, Zip 98686–3324; tel. 360/356–1890, (Nonreporting) **A**1 10 **S** Springstone, Louisville, KY
Primary Contact: Beckie Shauinger, Interim Chief Executive Officer
Web address: https://www.rainiersprings.com
Control: Corporation, Investor–owned (for–profit) **Service**: Psychiatric

Staffed Beds: 72

VANCOUVER MEMORIAL HOSPITAL See Vancouver Memorial Campus

WALLA WALLA—Walla Walla County

✠ △ **PROVIDENCE ST. MARY MEDICAL CENTER (500002)**, 401 W Poplar Street, Zip 99362–2846, Mailing Address: P.O. Box 1477, Zip 99362–0312; tel. 509/897–3320, **A**1 7 10 **F**2 3 8 13 15 18 20 22 28 29 30 31 34 35 37 38 40 43 45 46 47 49 50 51 58 59 60 62 64 65 66 67 68 70 71 73 74 75 76 77 78 79 81 82 84 85 87 90 93 94 96 97 107 108 109 110 111 114 115 116 117 118 119 121 123 124 129 130 131 132 135 144 146 147 148 149 154 155 156 167 169 **P**6 **S** Providence, Renton, WA
Primary Contact: Reza Kaleel, Chief Executive
COO: Susan Blackburn, Chief Operating Officer
CMO: Joel Wassermann, Chief Medical Officer
CIO: Martin Manny, Director, I.S.
CNO: Yvonne M Strader, Chief Nursing Officer
Web address: www.washington.providence.org/hospitals/st-mary/
Control: Church operated, Nongovernment, not–for–profit **Service**: General medical and surgical

Staffed Beds: 129 **Admissions**: 4677 **Census**: 61 **Outpatient Visits**: 181334 **Births**: 601 **Total Expense ($000)**: 158627 **Payroll Expense ($000)**: 77234 **Personnel**: 866

STATE PENITENTIARY HOSPITAL, 1313 North 13th Street, Zip 99362–8817; tel. 509/525–3610, (Nonreporting)
Primary Contact: Donald Holbrook, Chief Executive Officer
Control: State, Government, Nonfederal **Service**: Hospital unit of an institution (prison hospital, college infirmary, etc.)

Staffed Beds: 36

WENATCHEE—Chelan County

★ ✠ **CONFLUENCE HEALTH HOSPITAL – CENTRAL CAMPUS (500016)**, 1201 South Miller Street, Zip 98801–3201, Mailing Address: P.O. Box 1887, Zip 98807–1887; tel. 509/662–1511, (Nonreporting) **A**3 10 21
Primary Contact: Andrew Jones, M.D., Chief Executive Officer
COO: Vikki Noyes, Executive Vice President and Chief Operating Officer
CFO: John Doyle, Chief Financial Officer
CMO: Stuart Freed, M.D., Chief Medical Officer
CIO: Robert Pageler, Chief Information Officer
CHR: Jim Wood, Chief Administrative Officer
Web address: www.cwhs.com
Control: Other not–for–profit (including NFP Corporation) **Service**: General medical and surgical

Staffed Beds: 176

△ **CONFLUENCE HEALTH HOSPITAL – MARES CAMPUS (500148)**, 820 North Chelan Avenue, Zip 98801–2028; tel. 509/663–8711, (Nonreporting) **A**3 7 10
Primary Contact: Andrew Jones, M.D., Chief Executive Officer
COO: Kevin Gilbert, R.N., Vice President
CFO: John Doyle, Chief Financial Officer
CMO: Stuart Freed, M.D., Medical Director
CIO: Robert Pageler, Chief Information Officer
CHR: Jim Wood, Chief Human Resources Officer
Web address: www.confluencehealth.org
Control: Other not–for–profit (including NFP Corporation) **Service**: General medical and surgical

Staffed Beds: 20

✠ **CONFLUENCE HEALTH/CENTRAL WASHINGTON HOSPITAL** See Confluence Health Hospital – Central Campus

CONFLUENCE HEALTH/WENATCHEE VALLEY HOSPITAL See Confluence Health Hospital – Mares Campus

WHITE SALMON—Klickitat County

SKYLINE HEALTH (501315), 211 Skyline Drive, Zip 98672–1918, Mailing Address: P.O. Box 99, Zip 98672–0099; tel. 509/493–1101, (Nonreporting) **A**10 18
Primary Contact: Matt Kollman, Chief Executive Officer
CFO: Brenda Schneider, Chief Financial Officer
CMO: Christopher Samuels, Chief of Staff
CIO: Steve Opbroek, Manager Information Technology
CHR: Jessie Ramos, Manager Human Resources
CNO: Stefanie Boen, Chief Nursing Officer
Web address: www.skylinehospital.org
Control: Hospital district or authority, Government, Nonfederal **Service**: General medical and surgical

Staffed Beds: 14

SKYLINE HOSPITAL See Skyline Health

YAKIMA—Yakima County

✠ **MULTICARE YAKIMA MEMORIAL HOSPITAL (500036)**, 2811 Tieton Drive, Zip 98902–3761; tel. 509/575–8000, **A**1 2 3 5 10 20 **F**3 8 13 15 17 18 20 22 26 28 29 30 31 32 34 35 40 41 43 44 47 48 49 50 51 54 55 57 58 59 62 63 64 68 70 72 73 75 76 77 78 79 81 82 84 85 86 87 89 91 92 93 96 97 98 100 102 103 107 108 110 111 114 115 116 117 118 119 120 121 123 124 126 129 130 131 132 135 146 147 148 149 154 156 160 162 167 **P**6 **S** MultiCare Health System, Tacoma, WA
Primary Contact: Tammy K. Buyok, President
COO: Diane Patterson, Senior Vice President, Chief Operating Officer and Chief Nursing Officer
CFO: Tim Reed, Vice President and Chief Financial Officer
CMO: Marty Brueggemann, Chief Medical Officer
CIO: Jeff Yamada, Vice President
CNO: Diane Patterson, Senior Vice President, Chief Operating Officer and Chief Nursing Officer
Web address: www.yakimamemorial.org
Control: Other not–for–profit (including NFP Corporation) **Service**: General medical and surgical

Staffed Beds: 259 **Admissions**: 12136 **Census**: 135 **Outpatient Visits**: 302839 **Births**: 2376 **Total Expense ($000)**: 566109 **Payroll Expense ($000)**: 236787 **Personnel**: 2425

WEST VIRGINIA

BECKLEY—Raleigh County

⇧ **BECKLEY ARH HOSPITAL (510062)**, 306 Stanaford Road, Zip 25801-3142; tel. 304/255-3000, **A**10 19 21 **F**3 11 15 18 20 22 26 28 29 30 31 34 35 38 39 40 43 45 46 49 50 57 59 60 61 65 70 74 75 76 77 78 79 81 84 85 86 87 89 93 96 97 98 99 100 101 102 103 107 108 110 111 114 115 119 126 129 130 131 132 134 135 141 147 148 149 154 160 161 162 164 **S** Appalachian Regional Healthcare, Inc., Lexington, KY
Primary Contact: Todd Howell, Chief Executive Officer
CMO: Ahmad Khiami, Chief of Staff
CHR: Sue Thomas, Manager Human Resources
CNO: Angela Rivera, Chief Nursing Officer
Web address: www.arh.org
Control: Other not-for-profit (including NFP Corporation) **Service**: General medical and surgical

Staffed Beds: 109 **Admissions**: 5710 **Census**: 94 **Outpatient Visits**: 71335 **Births**: 0 **Total Expense ($000)**: 134753 **Payroll Expense ($000)**: 30299

✠ **BECKLEY VETERANS AFFAIRS MEDICAL CENTER**, 200 Veterans Avenue, Zip 25801-6499; tel. 304/255-2121, (Nonreporting) **A**1 3 5 **S** Department of Veterans Affairs, Washington, DC
Primary Contact: Brett Vess, Medical Center Director
CFO: Terry Massey, Chief Fiscal Services
CMO: John David Berryman, M.D., Chief of Staff
CIO: Sherry Gregg, Chief Information Technology Officer
CNO: Debra Lynn Legg, Associate Director Patient Care Services and Nurse Executive
Web address: www.beckley.va.gov/
Control: Veterans Affairs, Government, federal **Service**: General medical and surgical

Staffed Beds: 23

✠ **RALEIGH GENERAL HOSPITAL (510070)**, 1710 Harper Road, Zip 25801-3397; tel. 304/256-4100, **A**1 3 5 10 19 **F**3 13 15 17 18 20 22 29 30 31 34 35 40 43 45 49 50 57 59 60 64 70 74 75 76 77 79 81 85 87 89 107 108 110 111 114 115 116 117 119 120 126 130 132 146 147 148 149 156 167 **S** Lifepoint Health, Brentwood, TN
Primary Contact: David V. Bunch, Chief Executive Officer
COO: Rhonda Mann, Chief Operating Officer
CFO: Randy Harrison, Chief Financial Officer
CMO: Syed Siddiqi, M.D., President Medical Staff
CIO: Kevin Sexton, Director Information Systems
CHR: Chris T Beebe, Director Human Resources
CNO: Alene Lewis, R.N., Chief Nursing Officer
Web address: https://www.raleighgeneral.com/
Control: Corporation, Investor-owned (for-profit) **Service**: General medical and surgical

Staffed Beds: 229 **Admissions**: 9640 **Census**: 121 **Outpatient Visits**: 56955 **Births**: 725 **Total Expense ($000)**: 179765 **Payroll Expense ($000)**: 59576 **Personnel**: 890

BERKELEY SPRINGS—Morgan County

✠ **VALLEY HEALTH - WAR MEMORIAL HOSPITAL (511309)**, 1 Healthy Way, Zip 25411-7463; tel. 304/258-1234, (Total facility includes 16 beds in nursing home-type unit) **A**1 10 18 **F**3 11 15 18 28 29 30 34 35 40 45 50 53 54 57 59 64 65 75 77 79 81 85 86 87 93 97 107 110 114 119 129 130 132 133 135 147 155 156 **S** Valley Health System, Winchester, VA
Primary Contact: Heather Sigel, Vice President, Operations
CFO: Kathryn Morales, Director of Finance
CMO: Gerald Bechamps, M.D., Vice President Medical Affairs
CHR: Abbey Rembold, Human Resources Senior Generalist
Web address: www.valleyhealthlink.com/war
Control: Other not-for-profit (including NFP Corporation) **Service**: General medical and surgical

Staffed Beds: 41 **Admissions**: 644 **Census**: 25 **Outpatient Visits**: 50993 **Births**: 0 **Total Expense ($000)**: 33172 **Payroll Expense ($000)**: 12279 **Personnel**: 131

BRIDGEPORT—Harrison County

✠ **UNITED HOSPITAL CENTER (510006)**, 327 Medical Park Drive, Zip 26330-9006; tel. 681/342-1000, **A**1 2 3 5 10 12 13 **F**3 11 12 13 15 17 18 20 22 26 28 29 30 31 34 35 36 37 39 40 44 45 46 47 48 49 50 51 54 55 57 58 59 60 64 65 68 70 74 75 76 77 78 79 80 81 82 84 85 86 87 89 92 93 96 97 98 100 104 107 108 110 111 115 117 118 119 120 121 126 128 129 130 131 132 135 146 147 148 149 150 154 156 160 167 169 **P**6 **S** West Virginia University Health System, Morgantown, WV
Primary Contact: David F. Hess, M.D., President and Chief Executive Officer
COO: John Fernandez, Chief Operating Officer
CFO: Jim Rutkowski, Chief Financial Officer
CMO: Eric Radcliffe, M.D., Medical Director
CIO: Brian Cottrill, Chief Information Officer
CHR: Timothy M Allen, Vice President Human Resources
CNO: Stephanie Smart, Chief Nursing Officer
Web address: https://wvumedicine.org/united-hospital-center/
Control: Other not-for-profit (including NFP Corporation) **Service**: General medical and surgical

Staffed Beds: 264 **Admissions**: 12488 **Census**: 186 **Outpatient Visits**: 478769 **Births**: 763 **Total Expense ($000)**: 537220 **Payroll Expense ($000)**: 170123 **Personnel**: 2388

BUCKEYE—Pocahontas County

★ **POCAHONTAS MEMORIAL HOSPITAL (511314)**, 150 Duncan Road, Zip 24924; tel. 304/799-7400, (Nonreporting) **A**10 18
Primary Contact: Michelle Deeds, Chief Executive Officer
COO: Terry Wagner, R.N., Chief Operating Officer
CFO: Rebecca J Hammer, Chief Financial Officer
CMO: Jeffrey Pilney, Chief Medical Officer
CIO: Samuel Walker, Director of IT
CHR: Katie Brown, Coordinator Human Resources
CNO: Kyna Moore, R.N., Chief Nursing Officer
Web address: www.pmhwv.org/
Control: County, Government, Nonfederal **Service**: General medical and surgical

Staffed Beds: 24

BUCKHANNON—Upshur County

✠ △ **ST. JOSEPH'S HOSPITAL (511321)**, 1 Amalia Drive, Zip 26201-2276; tel. 304/473-2000, (Total facility includes 16 beds in nursing home-type unit) **A**1 7 10 18 **F**3 11 13 15 18 28 30 31 34 35 40 43 44 45 50 57 59 64 65 70 75 76 77 81 83 84 85 87 89 107 110 111 115 119 126 127 128 130 132 133 144 146 147 148 149 156 169 **P**6 **S** West Virginia University Health System, Morgantown, WV
Primary Contact: Skip Gjolberg Jr, FACHE, President and Chief Executive Officer
CFO: Russell J Plywaczynski, CPA, Director of Finance
CMO: Bartley Brown, D.O., Chief of Staff
CIO: Brian Williams, Web Services and Information Technology Manager
CHR: Anissa J Hite Davis, Vice President Human Resources
CNO: Annamarie Chidester, R.N., Vice President, Patient Care Services
Web address: www.stj.net
Control: Other not-for-profit (including NFP Corporation) **Service**: General medical and surgical

Staffed Beds: 41 **Admissions**: 1277 **Census**: 25 **Outpatient Visits**: 93578 **Births**: 351 **Total Expense ($000)**: 96548 **Payroll Expense ($000)**: 33263 **Personnel**: 463

CHARLESTON—Kanawha County

CAMC MEMORIAL HOSPITAL See Charleston Area Medical Center, Charleston

CAMC WOMEN AND CHILDREN'S HOSPITAL See Charleston Area Medical Center, Charleston

---

Hospital, Medicare Provider Number, Address, Telephone, Approval, Facility, and Physician Codes, Health Care System

★ American Hospital Association (AHA) membership
□ The Joint Commission accreditation
○ Healthcare Facilities Accreditation Program
◇ DNV Healthcare Inc. accreditation
⇧ Center for Improvement in Healthcare Quality Accreditation
△ Commission on Accreditation of Rehabilitation Facilities (CARF) accreditation

Hospitals, U.S. / WEST VIRGINIA

★ △ ⇑ **CHARLESTON AREA MEDICAL CENTER (510022)**, 501 Morris Street, Zip 25301–1300, Mailing Address: P.O. Box 1547, Zip 25326–1547; tel. 304/388–5432, (Includes CAMC MEMORIAL HOSPITAL, 3200 MacCorkle Avenue SE, Charleston, West Virginia, Zip 25304, PO Box 2069, Zip 25327, tel. 304/388–5973; Jeffrey L. Oskin, Vice President and Administrator; CAMC TEAYS VALLEY HOSPITAL, 1400 Hospital Drive, Hurricane, West Virginia, Zip 25526–9202, tel. 304/757–1700; Randall H Hodges, FACHE, Vice President and Administrator; CAMC WOMEN AND CHILDREN'S HOSPITAL, 800 Pennsylvania Avenue, Charleston, West Virginia, Zip 25302, P O Box 6669, Zip 25362, tel. 304/388–5432; Andrew Weber, Vice President and Administrator; GENERAL HOSPITAL, 501 Morris ST, Charleston, West Virginia, Zip 25301–1326, Box 1393, Zip 25325, tel. 304/388–5432; Michael D Williams, Vice President and Administrator) **A**2 3 5 7 8 10 19 21 **F**3 7 8 11 12 13 15 17 18 19 20 22 24 26 28 29 30 31 32 34 35 37 38 39 40 41 43 44 45 46 47 48 49 50 51 52 54 55 56 57 59 60 61 64 65 68 70 71 72 74 75 76 77 78 79 81 82 84 85 86 87 88 89 90 91 92 93 94 95 96 97 98 100 101 102 104 107 108 110 111 114 115 116 117 118 119 120 121 123 124 126 129 130 131 132 134 135 138 143 144 145 146 147 148 149 150 154 156 157 167 169 **P**6 **S** Vandalia Health, Charleston, WV
Primary Contact: Glenn Crotty Jr, M.D., President and Chief Executive Officer
COO: Jeffrey L. Oskin, Senior Vice President and Chief Operating Officer
CFO: Jeff D Sandene, Executive Vice President and Chief Financial Officer
CMO: T Pinckney McIlwain, M.D., Vice President and Chief Medical Officer
CHR: Kristi Snyder, Vice President Human Resources
CNO: Heidi Edwards, Chief Nursing Officer
Web address: www.camc.org
Control: Other not–for–profit (including NFP Corporation) **Service**: General medical and surgical

Staffed Beds: 859 **Admissions**: 33738 **Census**: 580 **Outpatient Visits**: 889272 **Births**: 2662 **Total Expense ($000)**: 1643820 **Payroll Expense ($000)**: 617261 **Personnel**: 8573

CHARLESTON GENERAL HOSPITAL See General Hospital

☐ **CHARLESTON SURGICAL HOSPITAL (510091)**, 1306 Kanawha Boulevard East, Zip 25301–3001, Mailing Address: P.O. Box 2271, Zip 25328–2271; tel. 304/343–4371, (Nonreporting) **A**1 10
Primary Contact: Christina Arvon, Administrator and Chief Executive Officer
CMO: James W Candill, M.D., President Medical Staff
Web address: https://charlestonsurgicalhospital.com/
Control: Corporation, Investor–owned (for–profit) **Service**: Surgical

Staffed Beds: 6

GENERAL HOSPITAL See Charleston Area Medical Center, Charleston

☐ **HIGHLAND HOSPITAL (514001)**, 300 56th Street SE, Zip 25304–2361, Mailing Address: P.O. Box 4107, Zip 25364–4107; tel. 304/926–1600, (Nonreporting) **A**1 10
Primary Contact: Nadine Dexter, R.N., MSN, Chief Executive Officer
COO: Rick Rucker, Chief Operating Officer
CFO: Chris K. Miller, Chief Financial Officer
CMO: Kiran S. Devaraj, Chief Medical Officer and Chief Clinical Officer
CIO: Damon Carradine, Director Information Technology
CNO: Leigh Dalton, Director of Nursing and Patient Care Services
Web address: www.highlandhosp.com
Control: Other not–for–profit (including NFP Corporation) **Service**: Psychiatric

Staffed Beds: 115

MEMORIAL DIVISION See CAMC Memorial Hospital

⊠ **SELECT SPECIALTY HOSPITAL–CHARLESTON (512002)**, 333 Laidley Street, 3rd Floor East, Zip 25301–1614; tel. 304/720–7234, (Nonreporting) **A**1 10 **S** Select Medical Corporation, Mechanicsburg, PA
Primary Contact: Frank Weber, Chief Executive Officer
CHR: Sabrina White, Coordinator Human Resources
Web address: www.selectspecialtyhospitals.com/company/locations/charleston.aspx
Control: Corporation, Investor–owned (for–profit) **Service**: Acute long–term care hospital

Staffed Beds: 32

WOMEN AND CHILDREN'S HOSP See CAMC Women and Children's Hospital

CLARKSBURG—Harrison County

☐ **HIGHLAND–CLARKSBURG HOSPITAL (514011)**, 3 Hospital Plaza, Zip 26301–9316; tel. 304/969–3100, (Nonreporting) **A**1 10
Primary Contact: Victoria Jones, Chief Executive Officer
CFO: Shelly Giaguinto, Chief Financial Officer
CMO: Christi Cooper–Lehki, Chief Clinical Officer
CIO: Kimberly Samuelson, Director of Information Management
CHR: Vanessa Defazio, Chief Human Resources Officer
CNO: Melissa Hitt, Director of Nursing
Web address: www.highlandhosp.com
Control: Other not–for–profit (including NFP Corporation) **Service**: Psychiatric

Staffed Beds: 115

⊠ **LOUIS A. JOHNSON VETERANS AFFAIRS MEDICAL CENTER**, 1 Medical Center Drive, Zip 26301–4199; tel. 304/623–3461, (Nonreporting) **A**1 3 5 **S** Department of Veterans Affairs, Washington, DC
Primary Contact: Barbara Forsha, Interim Medical Center Director
CMO: Glenn R Snider, M.D., Chief of Staff
CIO: Michael Matthey, Facility Chief Information Officer
CHR: Ian Jacobs, Chief, Human Resource Management Service
Web address: www.clarksburg.va.gov
Control: Veterans Affairs, Government, federal **Service**: General medical and surgical

Staffed Beds: 48

ELKINS—Randolph County

⊠ **DAVIS MEDICAL CENTER (510030)**, 812 Gorman Avenue, Zip 26241–3181, Mailing Address: P.O. Box 1484, Zip 26241–1484; tel. 304/636–3300, **A**1 10 20 **F**11 13 15 28 29 30 31 32 34 35 40 49 50 51 54 56 57 59 64 68 69 70 71 75 76 78 79 81 82 84 85 86 87 89 92 94 97 98 103 107 108 109 110 111 115 116 117 118 119 121 123 129 130 132 135 146 147 148 154 169 **S** Vandalia Health, Charleston, WV
Primary Contact: Mark Doak, Interim President
CFO: Melanie Dempsey, Vice President and Chief Financial Officer
CIO: Steve Crowl, Director of Information Services
Web address: https://www.davishealthsystem.org/index
Control: Other not–for–profit (including NFP Corporation) **Service**: General medical and surgical

Staffed Beds: 80 **Admissions**: 1894 **Census**: 30 **Outpatient Visits**: 114489 **Births**: 196 **Total Expense ($000)**: 130352 **Payroll Expense ($000)**: 59432 **Personnel**: 816

GASSAWAY—Braxton County

★ **BRAXTON COUNTY MEMORIAL HOSPITAL (511308)**, 100 Hoylman DR, Zip 26624–9318, Mailing Address: 100 Hoylman Drive, Zip 26624–9318; tel. 304/364–5156, **A**10 18 **F**3 8 11 15 29 30 32 34 35 40 43 45 57 59 64 65 75 79 81 93 97 105 107 108 114 119 127 130 133 146 147 149 154 156 158 **P**6 **S** West Virginia University Health System, Morgantown, WV
Primary Contact: John C. Forester, Interim President
CFO: Kimber Knight, Chief Financial Officer
CMO: Russell L Stewart, D.O., Medical Director
CNO: Julia Rose, R.N., Director of Nursing
Web address: https://wvumedicine.org/braxton/
Control: Other not–for–profit (including NFP Corporation) **Service**: General medical and surgical

Staffed Beds: 25 **Admissions**: 420 **Census**: 4 **Outpatient Visits**: 17459 **Births**: 0 **Total Expense ($000)**: 26223 **Payroll Expense ($000)**: 8661 **Personnel**: 140

GLEN DALE—Marshall County

⊠ **REYNOLDS MEMORIAL HOSPITAL (510013)**, 800 Wheeling Avenue, Zip 26038–1697; tel. 304/845–3211, **A**1 10 **F**3 11 13 15 18 19 20 28 29 30 31 35 38 40 45 46 49 50 59 64 65 70 74 75 76 77 78 79 80 81 82 85 86 87 89 91 92 93 94 96 97 98 100 101 102 103 104 107 108 110 111 115 119 124 127 130 131 132 135 144 146 147 148 149 150 154 156 160 161 164 165 167 169 **P**6 **S** West Virginia University Health System, Morgantown, WV
Primary Contact: Tony Martinelli, PharmD, President and Chief Executive Officer
COO: Kevin Britt, Chief Operating Officer
CFO: William Robert Hunt, Chief Financial Officer
CIO: Warren Kelley, Chief Information Officer
CHR: R. Craig Madden, Director Employee Relations
CNO: Carol R Miller, R.N., Chief Nursing Officer
Web address: https://wvumedicine.org/reynolds-memorial/
Control: Other not–for–profit (including NFP Corporation) **Service**: General medical and surgical

Staffed Beds: 94 **Admissions**: 3525 **Census**: 35 **Outpatient Visits**: 106730 **Births**: 316 **Total Expense ($000)**: 136807 **Payroll Expense ($000)**: 57411

GRAFTON—Taylor County

GRAFTON CITY HOSPITAL (511307), 1 Hospital Plaza, Zip 26354–1283; tel. 304/265–0400, **A**10 18 **F**5 8 11 15 29 32 34 40 45 48 50 53 56 57 59 64 65 68 80 81 83 84 87 89 93 97 105 107 110 114 119 127 129 130 132 133 146 149 152 154 157 160 161 **P**6
Primary Contact: Melissa Lockwood, Chief Administration Officer
CFO: Kevin M. Gessler, Interim Chief Financial Officer
CMO: David B Bender, M.D., Chief Medical Staff
CIO: Jim Harris, Director Information Technology
CHR: Missey Kimbrew, Director Human Resources
CNO: Violet Shaw, R.N., Director of Nursing
Web address: www.graftonhospital.com
Control: City–county, Government, Nonfederal **Service**: General medical and surgical

Staffed Beds: 25 **Admissions**: 246 **Census**: 4 **Outpatient Visits**: 22134 **Births**: 1

GRANTSVILLE—Calhoun County

★ **MINNIE HAMILTON HEALTHCARE CENTER (511303)**, 186 Hospital Drive, Zip 26147–7100; tel. 304/354–9244, (Nonreporting) **A**10 18
Primary Contact: Steve Whited, Chief Executive Officer
CMO: Suresh Balasubramony, M.D., Chief Medical Officer
CIO: Brent Barr, Chief Information Officer
CHR: Sheila Gherke, Director Human Resources
CNO: Kim Houchin, Chief Nursing Officer
Web address: www.mhhcc.org
Control: Other not–for–profit (including NFP Corporation) **Service**: General medical and surgical

Staffed Beds: 42

HINTON—Summers County

⇑ **SUMMERS COUNTY ARH HOSPITAL (511310)**, 115 Summers Hospital Road, Zip 25951–5172, Mailing Address: P.O. Box 940, Zip 25951–0940; tel. 304/466–1000, (Nonreporting) **A**10 18 21 **S** Appalachian Regional Healthcare, Inc., Lexington, KY
Primary Contact: Joseph Preast, Chief Executive Officer
CMO: Waheed Khan, M.D., President Medical Staff
CIO: Brent Styer, Chief Information Officer
CHR: Beth Elswick, Administrative Assistant
CNO: Sharon Milburn, Chief Nursing Officer
Web address: www.arh.org
Control: Other not–for–profit (including NFP Corporation) **Service**: General medical and surgical

Staffed Beds: 25

HUNTINGTON—Cabell County

✠ **CABELL HUNTINGTON HOSPITAL (510055)**, 1340 Hal Greer Boulevard, Zip 25701–0195; tel. 304/526–2000, (Includes HOOPS FAMILY CHILDREN'S HOSPITAL, 1340 Hal Greer Boulevard, Huntington, West Virginia, Zip 25701–3800, tel. 304/399–4667; Melanie Akers, R.N., Vice President Women's and Children's Services) **A**1 2 3 5 8 10 19 **F**3 5 8 11 12 13 15 16 20 22 28 29 30 31 34 35 37 38 40 41 43 44 45 46 47 48 49 50 51 52 54 55 56 57 58 59 61 64 65 70 72 73 74 75 76 77 78 79 81 82 83 84 85 86 87 88 89 91 92 93 94 96 97 104 107 108 110 111 114 115 116 117 118 119 120 121 123 124 126 129 130 132 134 135 143 144 145 146 147 148 149 150 154 156 157 160 167 169 **S** Marshall Health Network, Huntington, WV
Primary Contact: Tim Martin, Chief Operating Officer
CFO: David M Ward, Chief Financial Officer and Chief Acquisition Officer
CMO: Hoyt J. Burdick, M.D., Vice President Medical Affairs
CIO: Dennis Lee, Vice President and Chief Information Officer
CHR: Barry Tourigny, Vice President Human Resources and Organizational Development
CNO: Joy S Pelfrey, R.N., MSN, Vice President and Chief Nursing Officer
Web address: www.cabellhuntington.org
Control: Other not–for–profit (including NFP Corporation) **Service**: General medical and surgical

Staffed Beds: 347 **Admissions**: 16004 **Census**: 251 **Outpatient Visits**: 568994 **Births**: 2647 **Total Expense ($000)**: 747718 **Payroll Expense ($000)**: 199377 **Personnel**: 2559

✠ **CORNERSTONE SPECIALTY HOSPITALS HUNTINGTON (512003)**, 2900 First Avenue, Two East, Zip 25702–1241; tel. 304/399–2600, **A**1 10 **F**1 3 29 130 148 **S** ScionHealth, Louisville, KY
Primary Contact: Rodney Midkiff, Chief Executive Officer
CFO: Carla Jeffs, Chief Financial Officer
CMO: William Beam, M.D., Chief of Staff
Web address: www.chghospitals.com
Control: Corporation, Investor–owned (for–profit) **Service**: Acute long–term care hospital

Staffed Beds: 32 **Admissions**: 343 **Census**: 26 **Outpatient Visits**: 0 **Births**: 0 **Total Expense ($000)**: 13994 **Payroll Expense ($000)**: 5768 **Personnel**: 85

✠ **ENCOMPASS HEALTH REHABILITATION HOSPITAL OF HUNTINGTON (513028)**, 6900 West Country Club Drive, Zip 25705–2000; tel. 304/733–1060, (Nonreporting) **A**1 10 **S** Encompass Health Corporation, Birmingham, AL
Primary Contact: Michael E. Zuliani, Chief Executive Officer
CHR: Helen Arigan, Director Human Resources
CNO: Lisa Caldwell, Chief Nursing Officer
Web address: https://www.encompasshealth.com/huntingtonrehab
Control: Corporation, Investor–owned (for–profit) **Service**: Rehabilitation

Staffed Beds: 60

☐ **MILDRED MITCHELL–BATEMAN HOSPITAL (514009)**, 1530 Norway Avenue, Zip 25705–1358, Mailing Address: P.O. Box 448, Zip 25709–0448; tel. 304/525–7801, (Nonreporting) **A**1 3 5 10
Primary Contact: Craig A. Richards, Chief Executive Officer
CFO: Lucille Gedies, Chief Financial Officer
CMO: Shahid Masood, M.D., Clinical Director
CIO: Elias Majdalani, Director Management Information Systems
CHR: Kieth Anne Worden, Director Human Resources
CNO: Patricia Hamilton, R.N., Director of Nursing
Web address: www.batemanhospital.org
Control: State, Government, Nonfederal **Service**: Psychiatric

Staffed Beds: 110

☐ **RIVER PARK HOSPITAL (514008)**, 1230 Sixth Avenue, Zip 25701–2312, Mailing Address: P.O. Box 1875, Zip 25719–1875; tel. 304/526–9111, (Nonreporting) **A**1 3 5 10 **S** Universal Health Services, Inc., King of Prussia, PA
Primary Contact: Steve Kuhn, Chief Executive Officer
CMO: Mark A. Hughes, M.D., Medical Director
CIO: James Martin, Chief Information Officer
CHR: Mary Stratton, Director Human Resources
CNO: Michelle Gilliland, Director of Nursing
Web address: www.riverparkhospital.net
Control: Corporation, Investor–owned (for–profit) **Service**: Psychiatric

Staffed Beds: 175

✠ △ **ST. MARY'S MEDICAL CENTER (510007)**, 2900 First Avenue, Zip 25702–1272; tel. 304/526–1234, (Total facility includes 19 beds in nursing home–type unit) **A**1 2 3 5 7 10 19 **F**3 11 12 15 17 18 20 22 24 26 28 29 30 31 32 34 35 36 37 38 39 40 42 43 44 45 46 47 48 49 50 51 53 54 55 56 57 58 59 60 61 62 64 65 66 67 68 70 74 75 77 78 79 81 82 83 84 85 86 87 91 92 93 97 98 100 102 105 107 108 110 111 114 115 116 117 118 119 120 121 123 124 126 128 129 130 131 132 135 144 146 147 149 154 156 157 160 161 162 163 164 165 167 **S** Marshall Health Network, Huntington, WV
Primary Contact: Angela Swearingen, Chief Operating Officer
COO: Angela Swearingen, Chief Operating Officer
CMO: Ernest Lee Taylor, M.D., Vice President Medical Affairs
CIO: David Wendell, Manager, Information Systems
CHR: Susan Beth Robinson, Vice President Human Resources
CNO: Elizabeth Bosley, R.N., FACHE, Vice President Patient Services and Chief Nursing Officer
Web address: www.st-marys.org
Control: Other not–for–profit (including NFP Corporation) **Service**: General medical and surgical

Staffed Beds: 393 **Admissions**: 14582 **Census**: 272 **Outpatient Visits**: 382599 **Births**: 39 **Total Expense ($000)**: 560253 **Payroll Expense ($000)**: 194095 **Personnel**: 3318

Hospitals, U.S. / WEST VIRGINIA

HUNTINGTON—Wayne County

☒ **HUNTINGTON VETERANS AFFAIRS MEDICAL CENTER**, 1540 Spring Valley Drive, Zip 25704–9300; tel. 304/429–6741, (Nonreporting) **A**1 3 5 **S** Department of Veterans Affairs, Washington, DC
Primary Contact: Brian Nimmo, Medical Center Director
CIO: Gary Henderson, Chief Information Resources Management Services
Web address: www.huntington.va.gov/
Control: Veterans Affairs, Government, federal **Service**: General medical and surgical

Staffed Beds: 75

HURRICANE—Putnam County

TEAYS VALLEY HOSPITAL See CAMC Teays Valley Hospital

KEYSER—Mineral County

☒ **WVU MEDICINE POTOMAC VALLEY HOSPITAL (511315)**, 100 Pin Oak Lane, Zip 26726–5908; tel. 304/597–3500, **A**1 10 18 **F**3 15 18 28 29 31 34 35 40 44 45 50 54 57 59 64 65 66 68 70 71 74 75 77 78 79 81 82 85 86 87 92 93 97 104 107 108 110 111 114 119 127 130 131 132 133 135 143 146 148 149 154 156 **P**6 **S** West Virginia University Health System, Morgantown, WV
Primary Contact: Mark G. Boucot, FACHE, President and Chief Executive Officer
CFO: Marian Cardwell, Chief Financial Officer
CMO: Charles Bess, M.D., Medical Director
CIO: Micah Reel, Director of Bio–Med
CHR: Dianne Smith, Director Personnel and Human Resources
CNO: Mary Ann Billings, Director of Nursing
Web address: https://wvumedicine.org/potomac-valley-hospital/
Control: Other not–for–profit (including NFP Corporation) **Service**: General medical and surgical

Staffed Beds: 25 **Admissions**: 1085 **Census**: 12 **Outpatient Visits**: 76878 **Births**: 0 **Total Expense ($000)**: 71414 **Payroll Expense ($000)**: 26061 **Personnel**: 337

KINGWOOD—Preston County

★ **MON HEALTH PRESTON MEMORIAL HOSPITAL (511312)**, 150 Memorial Drive, Zip 26537–1495; tel. 304/329–1400, **A**10 18 **F**3 5 18 28 29 30 31 34 35 40 43 45 47 48 50 53 55 57 59 64 65 68 70 74 75 77 78 79 81 92 93 97 107 108 110 111 114 119 126 127 132 133 135 144 146 147 148 154 160 161 162 163 164 165 167 169 **P**6 **S** Vandalia Health, Charleston, WV
Primary Contact: Melissa Lockwood, Chief Executive Officer
CFO: Kevin M. Gessler, Chief Financial Officer
CIO: Beth Horne, System Administrator Information Technology
CHR: Michele Batiste, Director Human Resources
Web address: https://www.monhealth.com/preston-memorial
Control: Other not–for–profit (including NFP Corporation) **Service**: General medical and surgical

Staffed Beds: 25 **Admissions**: 454 **Census**: 6 **Outpatient Visits**: 76155 **Births**: 0 **Total Expense ($000)**: 52932 **Payroll Expense ($000)**: 21582 **Personnel**: 313

LOGAN—Logan County

☒ **LOGAN REGIONAL MEDICAL CENTER (510048)**, 20 Hospital Drive, Zip 25601–3452; tel. 304/831–1101, **A**1 3 10 20 **F**3 11 13 15 18 20 28 29 30 31 34 35 38 40 43 45 46 48 49 51 54 57 59 60 64 65 68 70 74 75 76 77 78 79 81 82 84 85 86 87 89 90 91 92 93 97 107 108 110 111 115 118 119 126 129 130 131 133 135 145 146 147 148 149 154 156 167 169 **S** ScionHealth, Louisville, KY
Primary Contact: David L. Brash, Chief Executive Officer
CFO: Tim Matney, Chief Financial Officer
CMO: Kathy Harvey, D.O., Chief Medical Officer
CIO: Barry Hensley, Director Information Systems
CHR: Jessica Martin, Director Human Resources
CNO: Karen Barnes, Interim Chief Nursing Officer
Web address: www.loganregionalmedicalcenter.com
Control: Corporation, Investor–owned (for–profit) **Service**: General medical and surgical

Staffed Beds: 140 **Admissions**: 3984 **Census**: 53 **Outpatient Visits**: 68053 **Births**: 193 **Total Expense ($000)**: 84094 **Payroll Expense ($000)**: 29950 **Personnel**: 578

MADISON—Boone County

☒ **BOONE MEMORIAL HOSPITAL (511313)**, 701 Madison Avenue, Zip 25130–1699; tel. 304/369–1230, **A**1 10 18 **F**3 5 11 15 18 28 29 30 34 35 38 40 43 45 47 48 50 53 55 59 64 65 75 77 79 81 82 84 86 87 93 97 100 104 107 108 110 111 114 118 119 127 129 130 131 133 135 144 146 149 154 156 160 165 **P**6
Primary Contact: Virgil Underwood, Chief Executive Officer
CFO: Cole Malcolm, Chief Financial Officer
CMO: Ziad Chanaa, M.D., Chief of Staff
CIO: Susan Shreve, Executive Director Information Technology
CHR: Sheliah Cook, Director Human Resources
CNO: Teresa Meade, R.N., Chief Nursing Officer
Web address: www.bmh.org
Control: Other not–for–profit (including NFP Corporation) **Service**: General medical and surgical

Staffed Beds: 25 **Admissions**: 2213 **Census**: 21 **Outpatient Visits**: 102743 **Births**: 0 **Total Expense ($000)**: 69135 **Payroll Expense ($000)**: 31197 **Personnel**: 388

MARTINSBURG—Berkeley County

☒ **BERKELEY MEDICAL CENTER (510008)**, 2500 Hospital Drive, Zip 25401–3402; tel. 304/264–1000, **A**1 2 3 5 10 19 **F**3 5 8 11 12 13 15 17 18 20 22 28 29 30 31 34 35 37 38 40 43 44 45 47 49 51 54 56 57 59 61 62 64 70 72 74 75 76 77 78 79 81 82 84 85 86 87 89 92 93 98 100 102 104 107 108 110 111 114 115 118 119 124 126 129 130 131 132 135 143 145 146 147 148 152 154 156 157 160 164 165 167 **P**8 **S** West Virginia University Health System, Morgantown, WV
Primary Contact: Dean Thomas, FACHE, President and Chief Executive Officer
CFO: Zach Kerns, Vice President, Finance
CIO: James Venturella, Vice President, Information Technology
CHR: Justin Ruble, Director, Human Resources
CNO: Samantha M Richards, MSN, Vice President Patient Care Services and Chief Nursing Officer
Web address: https://wvumedicine.org/berkeley/
Control: Other not–for–profit (including NFP Corporation) **Service**: General medical and surgical

Staffed Beds: 190 **Admissions**: 7955 **Census**: 121 **Outpatient Visits**: 295547 **Births**: 1015 **Total Expense ($000)**: 342567 **Payroll Expense ($000)**: 80222 **Personnel**: 1115

☒ **MARTINSBURG VETERANS AFFAIRS MEDICAL CENTER**, 510 Butler Avenue, Zip 25405–9990; tel. 304/263–0811, (Nonreporting) **A**1 3 5 **S** Department of Veterans Affairs, Washington, DC
Primary Contact: Kenneth W. Allensworth, FACHE, Medical Center Director
CMO: Jonathan Fierer, M.D., Chief of Staff
CIO: Mary Ann Creel, Chief Information Resource Management
CHR: Brenda Byrd–Pelaez, Chief Human Resources Management Office
CNO: Susan George, R.N., M.P.H., Associate Director Patient Care Services
Web address: https://www.martinsburg.va.gov/locations/directions.asp
Control: Veterans Affairs, Government, federal **Service**: General medical and surgical

Staffed Beds: 201

MONTGOMERY—Fayette County

★ **MONTGOMERY GENERAL HOSPITAL (511318)**, 401 Sixth Avenue, Zip 25136–2116, Mailing Address: P.O. Box 270, Zip 25136–0270; tel. 304/442–5151, (Total facility includes 44 beds in nursing home–type unit) **A**10 18 **F**3 11 15 29 30 32 34 35 40 45 46 50 53 56 57 59 64 67 68 77 79 81 84 86 87 96 97 100 104 107 108 110 111 114 119 127 128 129 130 131 132 133 135 143 146 165 **P**6
Primary Contact: Deborah Ann. Hill, Chief Executive Officer
CFO: Sherri Murray, Chief Financial Officer
CMO: Traci Acklin, M.D., Chief of Staff
CIO: Denzil Blevins, Director Information Systems
CHR: Kelly D Frye, Director Human Resources
Web address: www.mghwv.com
Control: Other not–for–profit (including NFP Corporation) **Service**: General medical and surgical

Staffed Beds: 69 **Admissions**: 360 **Census**: 37 **Outpatient Visits**: 53344 **Births**: 0 **Total Expense ($000)**: 33485 **Payroll Expense ($000)**: 15463 **Personnel**: 222

MORGANTOWN—Monongalia County

CHESTNUT RIDGE HOSPITAL See West Virginia University Hospitals, Morgantown

ENCOMPASS HEALTH REHABILITATION HOSPITAL OF MORGANTOWN (513030), 1160 Van Voorhis Road, Zip 26505-3437; tel. 304/598-1100, (Nonreporting) **A**1 10 **S** Encompass Health Corporation, Birmingham, AL
Primary Contact: Ashley Black, Chief Executive Officer
CFO: Jason Gizzi, Controller
CMO: Govind Patel, M.D., Medical Director
CIO: Robin Wherry, Risk Manager and Director Quality Assurance and Health Information Management
CHR: Shannon Hyde, Director Human Resources
CNO: Stacy Jones, Chief Nursing Officer
Web address: https://encompasshealth.com/morgantownrehab
Control: Corporation, Investor-owned (for-profit) **Service**: Rehabilitation

Staffed Beds: 96

MON HEALTH MEDICAL CENTER (510024), 1200 J D Anderson Drive, Zip 26505-3486; tel. 304/598-1200, (Nonreporting) **A**1 2 3 10 19 **S** Vandalia Health, Charleston, WV
Primary Contact: David Goldberg, President and Chief Executive Officer, Mon Health System, Executive Vice President, Vandalia Health
CMO: Matthew P Darmelio, Chief of Staff
CIO: Steve Carter, Chief Information Officer
CHR: Melissa Shreves Shahnam, Director Human Resources
Web address: www.mongeneral.com
Control: Other not-for-profit (including NFP Corporation) **Service**: General medical and surgical

Staffed Beds: 160

★ **SELECT SPECIALTY HOSPITAL – MORGANTOWN (512004)**, 1200 J D Anderson Drive, 4th Floor, Zip 26505-3494; tel. 304/285-2235, (Nonreporting) **A**3 **S** Select Medical Corporation, Mechanicsburg, PA
Primary Contact: Daniel C. Dunmyer, Chief Executive Officer
Web address: https://www.selectspecialtyhospitals.com/morgantown/
Control: Partnership, Investor-owned (for-profit) **Service**: Acute long-term care hospital

Staffed Beds: 25

WEST VIRGINIA UNIVERSITY HOSPITALS (510001), 1 Medical Center Drive, Zip 26506-4749; tel. 304/598-4000, (Includes CHESTNUT RIDGE HOSPITAL, 930 Chestnut Ridge Road, Morgantown, West Virginia, Zip 26505-2854, tel. 304/293-4000; WEST VIRGINIA UNIVERSITY CHILDREN'S HOSPITAL, 1 Medical Center DR, Morgantown, West Virginia, Zip 26506-1200, 1 Medical Center Drive, Zip 26506-8111, tel. 304/598-1111; Amy Bush, R.N., Chief Administrative Officer) **A**1 2 3 5 8 10 19 **F**1 3 4 5 11 12 13 15 16 17 18 19 20 21 22 23 24 25 26 27 28 29 30 31 32 33 34 35 36 37 38 39 40 41 42 43 45 46 47 48 49 50 51 52 53 54 55 56 57 58 59 60 61 62 63 65 67 68 70 71 72 73 74 75 76 77 78 79 80 81 82 84 85 87 88 89 90 91 92 93 94 95 97 98 100 101 102 104 105 106 107 108 109 110 111 112 113 114 115 116 117 118 119 120 121 122 123 124 126 127 128 129 130 131 132 133 135 136 137 138 141 142 143 144 145 146 147 148 149 152 153 154 156 157 160 161 164 165 166 167 169 **S** West Virginia University Health System, Morgantown, WV
Primary Contact: Michael Grace, Ed.D., FACHE, President
COO: Ron Pellegrino, Chief Operating Officer
CFO: Melissa McCoy, Vice President and Chief Financial Officer
CMO: Judie Charlton, M.D., Chief Medical Officer
CNO: Douglas W Mitchell, Vice President and Chief Nursing Officer
Web address: www.health.wvu.edu
Control: Other not-for-profit (including NFP Corporation) **Service**: General medical and surgical

Staffed Beds: 851 **Admissions:** 38670 **Census:** 592 **Outpatient Visits:** 1907892 **Births:** 2611 **Total Expense ($000):** 2002880 **Payroll Expense ($000):** 508847 **Personnel:** 8097

NEW MARTINSVILLE—Wetzel County

WETZEL COUNTY HOSPITAL (510072), 3 East Benjamin Drive, Zip 26155-2758; tel. 304/455-8000, (Nonreporting) **A**1 10 20 **S** West Virginia University Health System, Morgantown, WV
Primary Contact: Tony Martinelli, PharmD, President and Chief Executive Officer
CFO: Edwin Szewczyk, Chief Financial Officer
CMO: Donald A. Blum, M.D., Chief of Staff
CIO: Amy Frazier, Supervisor Management Information Systems
CHR: Sarah Boley, Director Human Resources
Web address: www.wetzelcountyhospital.com
Control: County, Government, Nonfederal **Service**: General medical and surgical

Staffed Beds: 58

OAK HILL—Fayette County

CAMC PLATEAU MEDICAL CENTER (511317), 430 Main Street, Zip 25901-3455; tel. 304/469-8600, **A**1 3 10 18 **F**3 11 15 18 29 34 40 45 46 50 57 68 70 75 77 79 81 87 93 104 107 108 110 111 115 118 119 124 126 129 133 146 149 151 154 167 **S** Vandalia Health, Charleston, WV
Primary Contact: Justus Smith, Chief Executive Officer
CFO: Heather Hylton, Vice President, Finance
CMO: Jacob McNeel, D.O., Chief of Staff
CIO: Nick Stover, Director Information Systems
CHR: Tammie Chinn, Director Marketing and Public Relations
CNO: Randell Thompson, Chief Nursing Officer
Web address: www.plateaumedicalcenter.com
Control: Other not-for-profit (including NFP Corporation) **Service**: General medical and surgical

Staffed Beds: 25 **Admissions:** 794 **Census:** 10 **Outpatient Visits:** 33217 **Births:** 0 **Total Expense ($000):** 41475 **Payroll Expense ($000):** 12283 **Personnel:** 226

PLATEAU MEDICAL CENTER See CAMC Plateau Medical Center

PARKERSBURG—Wood County

CAMDEN CLARK MEDICAL CENTER (510058), 800 Garfield Avenue, Zip 26101-5378, Mailing Address: P.O. Box 718, Zip 26102-0718; tel. 304/424-2111, (Nonreporting) **A**1 2 3 5 10 19 **S** West Virginia University Health System, Morgantown, WV
Primary Contact: Sean Smith, President and Chief Executive Officer
CFO: Carolyn Allen, Vice President and Chief Financial Officer
CMO: Walter Kerschl, Chief Medical Officer
CIO: Josh Woods, Director Information Systems
CHR: Tom Heller, Vice President Operations and Human Resources
Web address: https://wvumedicine.org/camden-clark/
Control: Other not-for-profit (including NFP Corporation) **Service**: General medical and surgical

Staffed Beds: 284

ENCOMPASS HEALTH REHABILITATION HOSPITAL OF PARKERSBURG (513027), 3 Western Hills Drive, Zip 26105-8122; tel. 304/420-1300, (Nonreporting) **A**1 10 **S** Encompass Health Corporation, Birmingham, AL
Primary Contact: Nathan Ford, Chief Executive Officer
CFO: Jessica Gum, Controller
CMO: Kalapala Rao, M.D., Medical Director
CHR: Olivia Morrison, Human Resource Manager
Control: Corporation, Investor-owned (for-profit) **Service**: Rehabilitation

Staffed Beds: 40

PETERSBURG—Grant County

★ **GRANT MEMORIAL HOSPITAL (511316)**, 117 Hospital Drive, Zip 26847-9566, Mailing Address: P.O. Box 1019, Zip 26847-1019; tel. 304/257-1026, **A**10 18 **F**3 11 13 15 28 29 31 34 35 40 45 50 57 59 64 65 70 75 76 77 78 79 81 87 93 107 108 110 111 114 118 119 131 132 133 135 146 147 148 149 156 157 **S** West Virginia University Health System, Morgantown, WV
Primary Contact: John B. Sylvia, President and Chief Executive Officer
COO: Kari Evans, Chief Operating Officer
CFO: David Applewood, Chief Financial Officer
CMO: Caroline Armstrong, D.O., M.D., Chief of Staff
CIO: Derek Nesselrodt, Director Information Systems
CHR: Ronnie Arbaugh, Director Human Resources
CNO: Kelley M. Scott, Interim Chief Nursing Officer
Web address: www.grantmemorial.com
Control: County, Government, Nonfederal **Service**: General medical and surgical

Staffed Beds: 25 **Admissions:** 997 **Census:** 16 **Outpatient Visits:** 38689 **Births:** 227 **Total Expense ($000):** 48860 **Payroll Expense ($000):** 19918 **Personnel:** 305

Hospitals, U.S. / WEST VIRGINIA

PHILIPPI—Barbour County

★ **BROADDUS HOSPITAL (511300)**, 1 Healthcare Drive, Zip 26416-9405, Mailing Address: P.O. Box 930, Zip 26416-0930; tel. 304/457-1760, (Total facility includes 60 beds in nursing home-type unit) **A**10 18 **F**3 15 29 30 34 35 40 57 59 64 75 85 87 107 110 115 119 128 130 133 135 143 146 148 **S** Vandalia Health, Charleston, WV
Primary Contact: Dana L. Gould, Chief Executive Officer
CHR: Penny D. Brown, Human Resource Representative
CNO: Lesa Corley, Director of Nursing
Web address: www.davishealthsystem.org/
Control: Other not-for-profit (including NFP Corporation) **Service**: General medical and surgical

> Staffed Beds: 72 Admissions: 198 Census: 55 Outpatient Visits: 18521
> Births: 0 Total Expense ($000): 22800 Payroll Expense ($000): 10719
> Personnel: 181

POINT PLEASANT—Mason County

PLEASANT VALLEY HOSPITAL See Rivers Health

⊞ **RIVERS HEALTH (510012)**, 2520 Valley Drive, Zip 25550-2031; tel. 304/675-4340, **A**1 10 **F**3 11 15 18 26 28 29 30 31 34 35 40 43 45 46 47 48 50 53 56 57 59 64 65 70 71 74 75 77 78 79 80 81 85 86 87 93 96 97 107 108 110 111 114 115 118 119 127 129 130 131 132 133 135 143 144 146 147 148 149 152 154 156 164 **P**6 **S** Marshall Health Network, Huntington, WV
Primary Contact: Justin Turner, Chief Operating Officer
COO: Keith Biddle, Chief Operating Officer
CMO: Agnes Enrico-Simon, M.D., President Medical Staff
CIO: Paula Brooker, Director Information Services
CNO: Amber Findley, Senior Director Nursing Services and NRC Administrator
Web address: https://rivershealth.org/
Control: Other not-for-profit (including NFP Corporation) **Service**: General medical and surgical

> Staffed Beds: 53 Admissions: 1100 Census: 18 Outpatient Visits: 81177
> Births: 0 Total Expense ($000): 62518 Payroll Expense ($000): 24034
> Personnel: 375

PRINCETON—Mercer County

⊞ **ENCOMPASS HEALTH REHABILITATION HOSPITAL OF PRINCETON (513026)**, 120 Twelfth Street, Zip 24740-2352; tel. 304/487-8000, (Nonreporting) **A**1 10 **S** Encompass Health Corporation, Birmingham, AL
Primary Contact: Robert Williams, Chief Executive Officer
CFO: Amy Flowers, Controller
CMO: Robert Walker, M.D., Medical Director
CIO: Brian Bales, Director Plant Operations
CHR: Jan Thibodeau, Director Human Resources
CNO: Lisa Lester, Chief Nursing Officer
Web address: www.healthsouthsouthernhills.com
Control: Corporation, Investor-owned (for-profit) **Service**: Rehabilitation

> Staffed Beds: 45

★ ⇈ **PRINCETON COMMUNITY HOSPITAL (510046)**, 122 12th Street, Zip 24740-2352, Mailing Address: P.O. Box 1369, Zip 24740-1369; tel. 304/487-7000, (Nonreporting) **A**2 10 21 **S** West Virginia University Health System, Morgantown, WV
Primary Contact: Karen L. Bowling, MSN, R.N., President and Chief Executive Officer
CFO: Frank J Sinicrope Jr, Vice President Financial Services
CMO: Wesley Asbury, M.D., President Medical Staff
CIO: Stephen A Curry, Director Information Services
CHR: Heather Poff, Director Human Resources
CNO: Rose Morgan, MS, R.N., Vice President Patient Care Services
Web address: www.pchonline.org
Control: City, Government, Nonfederal **Service**: General medical and surgical

> Staffed Beds: 164

RANSON—Jefferson County

⊞ **JEFFERSON MEDICAL CENTER (511319)**, 300 South Preston Street, Zip 25438-1631; tel. 304/728-1600, (Nonreporting) **A**1 3 5 10 18 **S** West Virginia University Health System, Morgantown, WV
Primary Contact: Dean Thomas, FACHE, President and Chief Executive Officer
CFO: Zach Kerns, Vice President, Finance
CIO: James Venturella, Vice President, Information Technology
CHR: Justin Ruble, Director Human Resources
CNO: Samantha M Richards, MSN, Vice President Patient Care Services and Chief Nursing Officer
Web address: https://wvumedicine.org/jefferson/
Control: Other not-for-profit (including NFP Corporation) **Service**: General medical and surgical

> Staffed Beds: 25

RIPLEY—Jackson County

★ **JACKSON GENERAL HOSPITAL (511320)**, 122 Pinnell Street, Zip 25271-9101, Mailing Address: P.O. Box 720, Zip 25271-0720; tel. 304/372-2731, (Nonreporting) **A**10 18 **S** West Virginia University Health System, Morgantown, WV
Primary Contact: Candace N. Miller, President and Chief Executive Officer
CFO: Angela Frame, Chief Financial Officer
CMO: James G Gaal, M.D., Chief of Medical Staff
CIO: John Manley, Director Information Systems
CHR: Jeffrey Tabor, Director Human Resources
Web address: https://wvumedicine.org/jackson-general-hospital/
Control: Other not-for-profit (including NFP Corporation) **Service**: General medical and surgical

> Staffed Beds: 25

WVU MEDICINE JACKSON GENERAL HOSPITAL See Jackson General Hospital

ROMNEY—Hampshire County

⊞ **VALLEY HEALTH - HAMPSHIRE MEMORIAL HOSPITAL (511311)**, 363 Sunrise Boulevard, Zip 26757-4607; tel. 304/822-4561, (Total facility includes 30 beds in nursing home-type unit) **A**1 10 18 **F**3 15 18 29 30 40 45 50 54 59 64 65 71 77 79 81 85 86 93 97 107 110 115 119 127 128 129 130 133 148 154 155 156 157 **S** Valley Health System, Winchester, VA
Primary Contact: Heather Sigel, Vice President Operations
CFO: Kathryn Morales, Director of Finance
CMO: Gerald Bechamps, M.D., Vice President Medical Affairs
CHR: Abbey Rembold, Human Resources Senior Generalist
CNO: Mary Sas, Vice President
Web address: www.valleyhealthlink.com/hampshire
Control: Other not-for-profit (including NFP Corporation) **Service**: General medical and surgical

> Staffed Beds: 44 Admissions: 503 Census: 35 Outpatient Visits: 52921
> Births: 0 Total Expense ($000): 35547 Payroll Expense ($000): 13951
> Personnel: 159

RONCEVERTE—Greenbrier County

★ ○ **CAMC GREENBRIER VALLEY MEDICAL CENTER (510002)**, 202 Maplewood Avenue, Zip 24970-1334, Mailing Address: P.O. Box 497, Zip 24970-0497; tel. 304/647-4411, **A**3 5 10 11 12 13 **F**3 13 15 29 40 51 60 70 76 79 81 89 97 107 108 109 110 111 114 115 117 119 128 129 133 146 154 167 169 **S** Vandalia Health, Charleston, WV
Primary Contact: Rebecca Harless, Chief Executive Officer
CFO: Paige Adkins, Chief Financial Officer
CMO: John Johnson, M.D., Chief of Staff
CIO: Matt Turley, Interim Director Information Systems
CHR: Melissa Wickline, Director Marketing
CNO: Charlene Warren, R.N., Chief Nursing Officer
Web address: www.gvmc.com
Control: Other not-for-profit (including NFP Corporation) **Service**: General medical and surgical

> Staffed Beds: 78 Admissions: 2133 Census: 27 Outpatient Visits: 42698
> Births: 338 Total Expense ($000): 103707 Payroll Expense ($000): 38950
> Personnel: 527

SISTERSVILLE—Tyler County

★ **SISTERSVILLE GENERAL HOSPITAL (511304)**, 314 South Wells Street, Zip 26175-1098; tel. 304/652-2611, (Nonreporting) **A**10 18
Primary Contact: Dan Breece, D.O., President
COO: Brandon Chadock, Chief Administrative Officer
CMO: Dan Breece, D.O., Chief Medical Officer
CIO: Casey Tuttle, Supervisor Information Technology
CNO: Stephen Todd Strickler, Clinical Nurse Manager
Web address: www.sistersvillehospital.com
Control: Other not-for-profit (including NFP Corporation) **Service**: General medical and surgical

> Staffed Beds: 7

Hospitals, U.S. / WEST VIRGINIA

SOUTH CHARLESTON—Kanawha County

THOMAS MEMORIAL HOSPITAL (510029), 4605 MacCorkle Avenue SW, Zip 25309–1398; tel. 304/766–3600, (Includes SAINT FRANCIS HOSPITAL, 333 Laidley Street, Charleston, West Virginia, Zip 25301–1628, P O Box 471, Zip 25322–0471, tel. 304/347–6500; J. Gregory Rosencrance, M.D., President and Chief Executive Officer) (Nonreporting) **A**1 5 10 **S** West Virginia University Health System, Morgantown, WV
Primary Contact: J. Gregory. Rosencrance, M.D., President and Chief Executive Officer
CFO: Timothy Skeldon, Chief Financial Officer
CMO: Matthew Upton, M.D., Chief Medical Officer
CHR: Patrick Rawlings, Human Resources Director
CNO: Rebecca Brannon, R.N., Chief Nursing Officer
Web address: www.thomashealth.org
Control: Other not-for-profit (including NFP Corporation) **Service**: General medical and surgical

Staffed Beds: 254

SPENCER—Roane County

ROANE GENERAL HOSPITAL (511306), 200 Hospital Drive, Zip 25276–1050; tel. 304/927–4444, (Total facility includes 35 beds in nursing home-type unit) **A**1 10 18 **F**3 7 11 15 18 28 29 31 34 35 40 43 45 53 57 59 64 65 67 68 75 78 81 82 85 90 93 97 107 108 110 114 119 127 128 129 130 132 133 135 143 148 154 156 **P**6
Primary Contact: Douglas E. Bentz, Chief Executive Officer
CFO: Kyle A. Pierson, Chief Financial Officer
CMO: Hong-Kin Ng, M.D., Chief Medical Officer
CIO: Tony Keaton, Director Information Systems
CHR: Jeffery B Hunt, Vice President, Business Development and Support Services
CNO: Julie R. Carr, Chief Nursing Officer
Web address: www.roanegeneralhospital.com
Control: Other not-for-profit (including NFP Corporation) **Service**: General medical and surgical

Staffed Beds: 60 **Admissions:** 202 **Census:** 36 **Outpatient Visits:** 53499 **Births:** 0 **Total Expense ($000):** 59665 **Payroll Expense ($000):** 22721 **Personnel:** 326

SUMMERSVILLE—Nicholas County

★ **SUMMERSVILLE REGIONAL MEDICAL CENTER (511322)**, 400 Fairview Heights Road, Zip 26651–9308; tel. 304/872–2891, **A**10 18 **F**3 15 28 29 34 40 43 45 57 59 64 65 70 74 75 77 79 81 85 97 107 108 110 111 115 119 127 130 133 154 **P**6 **S** West Virginia University Health System, Morgantown, WV
Primary Contact: John C. Forester, Interim President
CFO: Brian Kelbaugh, Chief Financial Officer
CMO: Bandy Mullins, M.D., Chief of Staff
CIO: Mike Ellison, Information Systems Lead
CHR: David M Henderson, Director Human Resources
CNO: Jennifer McCue, Director Patient Care
Web address: https://www.summersvilleregional.org/
Control: Other not-for-profit (including NFP Corporation) **Service**: General medical and surgical

Staffed Beds: 25 **Admissions:** 1832 **Census:** 18 **Outpatient Visits:** 40613 **Births:** 0 **Total Expense ($000):** 68651 **Payroll Expense ($000):** 27192 **Personnel:** 407

WEBSTER SPRINGS—Webster County

★ **WEBSTER COUNTY MEMORIAL HOSPITAL (511301)**, 324 Miller Mountain Drive, Zip 26288–1087, Mailing Address: P.O. Box 312, Zip 26288–0312; tel. 304/847–5682, (Nonreporting) **A**10 18 **S** Vandalia Health, Charleston, WV
Primary Contact: William J. Dempsey, Chief Executive Officer
CFO: Kenneth Chad Wright, Chief Financial Officer
CIO: Jeannie Fisher, Coordinator Information Technology
CHR: Michelle Holcomb, Human Resources
Web address: www.wcmhwv.org
Control: Other not-for-profit (including NFP Corporation) **Service**: General medical and surgical

Staffed Beds: 15

WEIRTON—Brooke County

ACUITY SPECIALTY HOSPITAL–OHIO VALLEY AT WEIRTON (512005), 601 Colliers Way, Zip 26062–5014; tel. 304/919–4300, (Includes SELECT SPECIALTY HOSPITAL – WHEELING, 500 Medical Park, 2nd Floor, Wheeling, West Virginia, Zip 26003–7600, tel. 304/238–5750; Christopher Heilman, Chief Executive Officer) **A**1 10 **F**1 3 18 60 100 148 149 **S** Select Medical Corporation, Mechanicsburg, PA
Primary Contact: Dusty A. Bowers, Chief Executive Officer
COO: Richard L. Cassady, CPA, Executive Vice–President and Chief Operating Officer
CFO: Sara Lane, Chief Financial Officer
CMO: Melvin Saludes, M.D., Medical Officer
CIO: Kevin Williams, Vice President, Information Technology
CHR: Melissa Milliron, Regional Director of Human Resources
CNO: Christine Smalley, Chief Clinical Officer
Web address: https://acuityhealthcare.net
Control: Corporation, Investor-owned (for-profit) **Service**: General medical and surgical

Staffed Beds: 20 **Admissions:** 257 **Census:** 19 **Outpatient Visits:** 0 **Births:** 0

WEIRTON MEDICAL CENTER (510023), 601 Colliers Way, Zip 26062–5091; tel. 304/797–6000, (Total facility includes 33 beds in nursing home-type unit) **A**1 10 19 **F**3 9 11 13 15 17 18 20 22 28 29 30 32 34 35 37 40 41 43 45 46 47 48 49 50 51 54 56 57 59 60 61 62 64 68 70 74 75 76 77 79 81 82 85 86 87 89 90 92 93 96 97 100 102 107 108 110 111 114 115 116 118 119 124 126 128 129 130 131 132 135 143 145 146 147 148 149 154 167 169 **P**6
Primary Contact: John C. Frankovitch, President and Chief Executive Officer
COO: David S Artman, Chief Operating Officer
CFO: Eugene Trout, Chief Financial Officer
CMO: Atul Shetty, Chief of Staff
CIO: Cristen Nopwaskey, Chief Information Officer
CHR: Gabe D'Ortenzio, Director of Human Resources
CNO: Denise P Westwood, Chief Nursing Officer
Web address: www.weirtonmedical.com
Control: Other not-for-profit (including NFP Corporation) **Service**: General medical and surgical

Staffed Beds: 167 **Admissions:** 6370 **Census:** 89 **Outpatient Visits:** 499463 **Births:** 505 **Total Expense ($000):** 217025 **Payroll Expense ($000):** 96386 **Personnel:** 1111

WELCH—Mcdowell County

WELCH COMMUNITY HOSPITAL (510086), 454 McDowell Street, Zip 24801–2097; tel. 304/436–8461, (Nonreporting) **A**10 20
Primary Contact: Mark Simpson, Chief Executive Officer
COO: Heather Smith, Chief Operating Officer
CFO: Johnny Brant, Chief Financial Officer
CMO: Chandra Sharma, M.D., Chief of Staff
CHR: Diana Blankenship, Director Human Resources
Web address: https://dhhr.wv.gov/officeofhealthfacilities/Pages/Welch-Community-Hospital.aspx
Control: State, Government, Nonfederal **Service**: General medical and surgical

Staffed Beds: 75

WESTON—Lewis County

★ ⇧ **MON HEALTH STONEWALL JACKSON MEMORIAL HOSPITAL (510038)**, 230 Hospital Plaza, Zip 26452–8558; tel. 304/269–8000, **A**10 21 **F**3 5 11 13 15 28 29 30 31 34 35 40 43 45 48 50 53 56 57 59 64 68 70 76 78 79 81 87 92 93 97 107 108 111 112 114 118 119 127 129 130 131 132 135 145 146 147 148 151 152 154 157 160 161 169 **P**6 **S** Vandalia Health, Charleston, WV
Primary Contact: Kevin P. Stalnaker, CPA, Chief Executive Officer
CFO: Daris Rosencrance, Chief Financial Officer
CMO: Doyle R. Sickles, M.D., Chief of Medical Staff
CIO: Kay Butcher, Director Health Information Management
CHR: Rhonda K. Mitchell, Director Human Resources
CNO: Carole Norton, Chief Nursing Officer
Web address: https://www.monhealth.com/main/locations/mon-health-stonewall-jackson-memorial-hospital-36
Control: Other not-for-profit (including NFP Corporation) **Service**: General medical and surgical

Staffed Beds: 70 **Admissions:** 1097 **Census:** 11 **Outpatient Visits:** 73658 **Births:** 117 **Total Expense ($000):** 53509 **Payroll Expense ($000):** 21604 **Personnel:** 276

Hospital, Medicare Provider Number, Address, Telephone, Approval, Facility, and Physician Codes, Health Care System

★ American Hospital Association (AHA) membership ○ Healthcare Facilities Accreditation Program ⇧ Center for Improvement in Healthcare Quality Accreditation
☐ The Joint Commission accreditation ◇ DNV Healthcare Inc. accreditation △ Commission on Accreditation of Rehabilitation Facilities (CARF) accreditation

Hospitals, U.S. / WEST VIRGINIA

☐ **WILLIAM R. SHARPE, JR. HOSPITAL (514012)**, 936 Sharpe Hospital Road, Zip 26452–8550; tel. 304/269–1210, **A**1 3 5 10 **F**3 11 30 50 53 56 68 75 86 87 98 100 101 103 130 132 143 146 157 160 163 165 **P**6
Primary Contact: Patrick Ryan, Chief Executive Officer
COO: Terry L. Small, Assistant Chief Executive Officer
CFO: Robert J. Kimble, Chief Financial Officer
CIO: Pam Lewis, Chief Compliance Officer
CNO: Cheryl France, M.D., Chief Medical Officer
Web address: www.wvdhhr.org/sharpe
Control: State, Government, Nonfederal **Service**: Psychiatric

Staffed Beds: 200 **Admissions:** 1012 **Census:** 196 **Outpatient Visits:** 0
Births: 0 **Total Expense ($000):** 115810 **Payroll Expense ($000):** 15854
Personnel: 336

WHEELING—Ohio County

ACUITY SPECIALTY HOSPITAL–OHIO VALLEY AT WHEELING See Select Specialty Hospital – Wheeling

★ **PETERSON HEALTHCARE AND REHABILITATION HOSPITAL (513025)**, 20 Homestead Avenue, Zip 26003–6638; tel. 304/234–0500, (Nonreporting) **A**10
Primary Contact: Melanie Torok, Administrator
CFO: Tammy Bortz, Director of Finance
CMO: William Mercer, M.D., Director
CIO: Hope Miller, Director of Medical Records
CHR: Spencer McIlvain, Director of Human Resources
CNO: Charlene Jones, Chief Nursing Officer
Web address: https://guardianeldercare.com/locations/peterson/
Control: Corporation, Investor–owned (for–profit) **Service**: Rehabilitation

Staffed Beds: 172

✣ **WHEELING HOSPITAL (510050)**, 1 Medical Park, Zip 26003–6379; tel. 304/243–3000, **A**1 2 3 5 10 19 **F**3 8 9 11 12 13 15 17 18 20 22 24 26 28 29 30 31 32 33 34 35 36 40 43 44 45 46 47 48 49 50 51 53 54 55 56 57 58 59 60 61 64 65 66 68 70 71 72 74 75 76 77 78 79 80 81 82 84 85 86 87 89 91 92 93 96 97 100 107 108 110 111 114 115 116 117 118 119 120 121 123 126 129 130 131 132 135 136 143 144 146 147 148 149 150 154 156 162 164 167 169 **S** West Virginia University Health System, Morgantown, WV
Primary Contact: Douglass Harrison, Chief Executive Officer
COO: David D. Phillips, Chief Operating Officer
CFO: James B. Murdy, Chief Financial Officer
CMO: Angelo Georges, M.D., President Medical and Dental Staff
CIO: David Rapp, Chief Information Officer
CHR: Kareen Simon, Vice President of Operations
CNO: Kathy Stahl, Chief Nursing Officer
Web address: www.wheelinghospital.org
Control: Other not–for–profit (including NFP Corporation) **Service**: General medical and surgical

Staffed Beds: 223 **Admissions:** 11678 **Census:** 135 **Outpatient Visits:** 586859 **Births:** 876 **Total Expense ($000):** 485641 **Payroll Expense ($000):** 201763 **Personnel:** 2188

WHITE HALL—Marion County

⇑ **MON HEALTH MARION NEIGHBORHOOD HOSPITAL (510093)**, 140 Middletown Loop, Zip 26554–8701; tel. 304/333–1150, (Nonreporting) **A**10 21 **S** Vandalia Health, Charleston, WV
Primary Contact: Carla Hamner, Hospital Administrator
Web address: https://www.monhealth.com/mhmh/mhmh-home
Control: Other not–for–profit (including NFP Corporation) **Service**: General medical and surgical

Staffed Beds: 10

WISCONSIN

ALTOONA—Eau Claire County

☐ **OAKLEAF SURGICAL HOSPITAL (520196)**, 1000 OakLeaf Way, Zip 54701–3016; tel. 715/831–8130, **A**1 10 **F**51 64 75 80 81 82 107 111 119 130 **S** National Surgical Healthcare, Chicago, IL
Primary Contact: Jim Nemeth, FACHE, Chief Executive Officer
COO: Erma Radke, Director of Operations
CFO: Denise Freid–Scheppke, Chief Accounting Officer
CHR: Nikki Yankton, Director Human Resources
CNO: Jacquelyn Maki, Chief Nursing Officer
Web address: www.oakleafmedical.com
Control: Corporation, Investor–owned (for–profit) **Service:** General medical and surgical

Staffed Beds: 13 **Admissions:** 309 **Census:** 2 **Outpatient Visits:** 13466 **Births:** 0 **Total Expense ($000):** 77200 **Payroll Expense ($000):** 21332 **Personnel:** 250

AMERY—Polk County

☒ **AMERY HOSPITAL AND CLINIC (521308)**, 265 Griffin Street East, Zip 54001–1439; tel. 715/268–8000, **A**1 3 5 10 18 **F**6 11 13 15 28 29 34 36 38 40 53 54 56 64 75 76 77 78 80 81 82 86 87 89 93 98 99 100 103 104 107 108 111 119 130 131 144 146 **P**6 **S** HealthPartners, Bloomington, MN
Primary Contact: Debra Rudquist, FACHE, President and Chief Executive Officer
CMO: James Quenan, M.D., Chief Medical Officer
CIO: Patrice P Wolff, Director Management Information Systems
CHR: Joanne Jackson, Administrator Human Resources, Community Relations and Quality Improvement
Web address: www.amerymedicalcenter.org
Control: Other not–for–profit (including NFP Corporation) **Service:** General medical and surgical

Staffed Beds: 19 **Admissions:** 1202 **Census:** 14 **Outpatient Visits:** 93884 **Births:** 95 **Total Expense ($000):** 74252 **Payroll Expense ($000):** 41155 **Personnel:** 272

ANTIGO—Langlade County

☒ **ASPIRUS LANGLADE HOSPITAL (521350)**, 112 East Fifth Avenue, Zip 54409–2796; tel. 715/623–2331, **A**1 3 10 18 **F**3 11 13 15 28 29 30 31 34 35 36 40 43 53 56 57 59 64 65 66 68 69 70 75 76 77 78 79 81 82 84 85 86 87 89 92 93 95 96 97 107 108 110 111 115 118 119 121 127 129 130 132 133 135 143 144 146 148 154 156 160 168 169 **P**8 **S** Aspirus, Inc., Wausau, WI
Primary Contact: Sherry Bunten, R.N., FACHE, President
CFO: Pat Tincher, Director Finance
CHR: Janelle K. Markgraf, SHRM–SCP, SPHR, Director Human Resources and Off Campus Services
CNO: Sherry Bunten, R.N., FACHE, Director Patient Care Services
Web address: https://www.aspirus.org/find-a-location/aspirus-langlade-hospital-283
Control: Church operated, Nongovernment, not–for–profit **Service:** General medical and surgical

Staffed Beds: 18 **Admissions:** 972 **Census:** 9 **Outpatient Visits:** 59968 **Births:** 156 **Total Expense ($000):** 94837 **Payroll Expense ($000):** 33901 **Personnel:** 223

APPLETON—Outagamie County

☒ △ **ASCENSION NORTHEAST WISCONSIN ST. ELIZABETH HOSPITAL (520009)**, 1506 South Oneida Street, Zip 54915–1305; tel. 920/738–2000, **A**1 2 3 5 7 10 **F**4 5 9 12 13 15 17 20 22 24 28 29 34 40 43 53 54 56 60 64 70 72 75 76 78 80 81 86 87 89 93 98 99 100 101 102 103 104 107 108 111 116 118 119 130 131 144 147 154 **P**6 **S** Ascension Healthcare, Saint Louis, MO
Primary Contact: Michael Bergmann, President
CFO: Jeff Badger, Chief Financial Officer
CMO: Lawrence Donatelle, M.D., Vice President Medical Affairs
CIO: Will Weider, Chief Information Officer
CHR: Vince Gallucci, Senior Vice President Human Resources
Web address: https://healthcare.ascension.org/locations/wisconsin/wiapa/appleton-ascension-ne-wisconsin-st-elizabeth-campus
Control: Church operated, Nongovernment, not–for–profit **Service:** General medical and surgical

Staffed Beds: 114 **Admissions:** 7736 **Census:** 102 **Outpatient Visits:** 285683 **Births:** 1172 **Total Expense ($000):** 256058 **Payroll Expense ($000):** 64162 **Personnel:** 839

☒ **THEDACARE REGIONAL MEDICAL CENTER–APPLETON (520160)**, 1818 North Meade Street, Zip 54911–3496; tel. 920/731–4101, **A**1 2 3 5 10 **F**4 9 13 15 17 20 24 28 29 34 40 51 54 64 70 75 76 78 80 81 82 86 88 89 100 107 108 111 118 119 130 154 **S** Froedtert ThedaCare Health, Inc., Milwaukee, WI
Primary Contact: Dale Gisi, President
CFO: Tim Olson, Senior Vice President Finance
CMO: Gregory L Long, M.D., Chief Medical Officer
CIO: Keith Livingston, Senior Vice President and Chief Information Officer
Web address: https://directory.thedacare.org/location/thedacare-regional-medical-center-appleton
Control: Other not–for–profit (including NFP Corporation) **Service:** General medical and surgical

Staffed Beds: 143 **Admissions:** 7780 **Census:** 80 **Outpatient Visits:** 190266 **Births:** 777 **Total Expense ($000):** 292491 **Payroll Expense ($000):** 82808 **Personnel:** 931

ASHLAND—Ashland County

★ ⇑ **TAMARACK HEALTH ASHLAND MEDICAL CENTER (521359)**, 1615 Maple Lane, Zip 54806–3689; tel. 715/685–5500, **A**2 5 10 18 21 **F**5 13 15 29 34 40 64 75 76 78 81 82 86 93 98 99 100 101 102 103 104 107 108 111 118 119 130 131 144 147 154 **S** Tamarack Health, Ashland, WI
Primary Contact: Luke Beirl, PharmD, Interim Chief Executive Officer
COO: Karen Hansen, Vice President and Chief Operating Officer
CFO: Kent Dumonseau, Vice President Finance and Information Services
CIO: Todd Reynolds, Chief Information Officer
CHR: Diane Lulich, Director Human Resources
CNO: Kathryn Tuttle, R.N., Director of Nursing
Web address: https://www.tamarackhealth.org/
Control: Other not–for–profit (including NFP Corporation) **Service:** General medical and surgical

Staffed Beds: 35 **Admissions:** 2028 **Census:** 27 **Outpatient Visits:** 92158 **Births:** 203 **Total Expense ($000):** 137311 **Payroll Expense ($000):** 49686 **Personnel:** 543

BALDWIN—St. Croix County

★ **WESTERN WISCONSIN HEALTH (521347)**, 1100 Bergslien Street, Zip 54002–2600; tel. 715/684–3311, **A**10 18 **F**3 11 13 15 28 29 31 32 34 36 37 40 41 43 45 46 47 48 53 55 56 64 68 75 76 77 78 79 80 81 85 86 89 90 93 107 108 109 110 111 115 119 126 131 133 146 147 154 **P**6
Primary Contact: Eilidh Pederson, Chief Executive Officer
CIO: Kendra Shaw, Chief Information Officer
CHR: Chris Riba, Director Human Resources
Web address: https://www.wwhealth.org
Control: Other not–for–profit (including NFP Corporation) **Service:** General medical and surgical

Staffed Beds: 14 **Admissions:** 887 **Census:** 8 **Outpatient Visits:** 115467 **Births:** 303 **Total Expense ($000):** 63024 **Payroll Expense ($000):** 29255 **Personnel:** 304

BARABOO—Sauk County

☒ **SSM HEALTH ST. CLARE HOSPITAL–BARABOO (520057)**, 707 14th Street, Zip 53913–1597; tel. 608/356–1400, **A**1 3 5 10 **F**11 13 15 28 29 34 40 56 64 69 70 75 76 78 80 81 82 86 89 93 107 108 118 119 130 131 144 146 154 **S** SSM Health, Saint Louis, MO
Primary Contact: DeAnn Thurmer, President and Chief Nursing Officer
CFO: Troy Walker, Director Finance
CMO: Maureen Murphy, M.D., Director of Medical Affairs
CIO: Heather Stephens, Director of Information Health Technology
CHR: Jason Stelzer, Director Human Resources
CNO: Ginger Selle, Vice President Patient Care Services
Web address: www.stclare.com
Control: Church operated, Nongovernment, not–for–profit **Service:** General medical and surgical

Staffed Beds: 43 **Admissions:** 1827 **Census:** 16 **Outpatient Visits:** 102910 **Births:** 196 **Total Expense ($000):** 62251 **Payroll Expense ($000):** 23776 **Personnel:** 278

Hospital, Medicare Provider Number, Address, Telephone, Approval, Facility, and Physician Codes, Health Care System

★ American Hospital Association (AHA) membership ◯ Healthcare Facilities Accreditation Program ⇑ Center for Improvement in Healthcare Quality Accreditation
☐ The Joint Commission accreditation ◇ DNV Healthcare Inc. accreditation △ Commission on Accreditation of Rehabilitation Facilities (CARF) accreditation

Hospitals, U.S. / WISCONSIN

BARRON—Barron County

☐ **MAYO CLINIC HEALTH SYSTEM – NORTHLAND IN BARRON (521315)**, 1222 East Woodland Avenue, Zip 54812–1798; tel. 715/537–3186, **A**1 10 18 **F**15 28 29 34 38 40 43 54 55 56 60 64 77 78 79 81 82 86 87 89 90 93 100 104 107 111 130 131 144 147 154 **P**6 **S** Mayo Clinic, Rochester, MN
Primary Contact: Richard Helmers, M.D., Regional Vice President
COO: Karolyn Bartlett, Assistant Administrator
CFO: Paul Bammel, Vice President
CMO: Richard Nagler, M.D., Chief of Staff
CIO: Todd Muden, Section Head Information Management
CHR: Blythe Rinaldi, Vice President
CNO: Patricia Keller, MSN, R.N., Nurse Administrator
Web address: www.luthermidelfortnorthland.org
Control: Other not–for–profit (including NFP Corporation) **Service**: General medical and surgical

Staffed Beds: 15 **Admissions**: 934 **Census**: 11 **Outpatient Visits**: 79998 **Births**: 0 **Total Expense ($000)**: 72663 **Payroll Expense ($000)**: 26407 **Personnel**: 272

BEAVER DAM—Dodge County

✠ **MARSHFIELD MEDICAL CENTER – BEAVER DAM (520076)**, 707 South University Avenue, Zip 53916–3089; tel. 920/887–7181, **A**1 10 19 **S** Marshfield Clinic Health System, Marshfield, WI
Primary Contact: Angelia Foster, Chief Administrative Officer
CMO: Jason Smith, Chief Medical Officer
CHR: Melanie Bruins, Chief Talent Officer
CNO: Carolyn Catton, Interim Chief Patient Care Officer
Web address: www.bdch.com
Control: Other not–for–profit (including NFP Corporation) **Service**: General medical and surgical

Staffed Beds: 163 **Admissions**: 1137 **Census**: 69 **Outpatient Visits**: 115814 **Births**: 156 **Total Expense ($000)**: 89902 **Payroll Expense ($000)**: 33255 **Personnel**: 494

BELOIT—Rock County

☐ **BELOIT HEALTH SYSTEM (520100)**, 1969 West Hart Road, Zip 53511–2299; tel. 608/364–5011, **A**1 3 10 **F**3 5 6 8 9 10 11 12 13 15 17 18 20 22 24 28 29 31 34 35 36 38 40 41 43 45 50 51 53 54 56 57 58 60 62 63 65 71 74 75 76 77 78 79 80 81 82 84 85 86 87 89 93 97 99 100 101 102 103 104 108 110 111 114 115 116 117 118 119 120 121 126 129 130 131 132 144 146 147 148 153 154 156 157 161 162 165 167 169
Primary Contact: Timothy M. McKevett, President and Chief Executive Officer
CFO: William E Groeper, Vice President Finance
CMO: Kenneth Klein, M.D., Vice President Medical Affairs
CHR: Thomas J McCawley, Vice President
CNO: Doris Mulder, Vice President Nursing
Web address: www.beloithealthsystem.org
Control: Other not–for–profit (including NFP Corporation) **Service**: General medical and surgical

Staffed Beds: 97 **Admissions**: 4187 **Census**: 52 **Outpatient Visits**: 383111 **Births**: 308 **Total Expense ($000)**: 296100 **Payroll Expense ($000)**: 113206 **Personnel**: 1205

BERLIN—Green Lake County

✠ **THEDACARE MEDICAL CENTER–BERLIN (521355)**, 225 Memorial Drive, Zip 54923–1295; tel. 920/361–1313, **A**1 10 18 **F**11 13 15 17 28 29 34 40 43 51 64 70 75 76 78 80 81 86 88 89 90 93 107 108 111 118 119 130 144 146 154 **S** Froedtert ThedaCare Health, Inc., Milwaukee, WI
Primary Contact: Tammy Bending, Vice President, Critical Access Hospital
CFO: Thomas P Krystowiak, Chief Financial Officer
Web address: www.chnwi.org
Control: Other not–for–profit (including NFP Corporation) **Service**: General medical and surgical

Staffed Beds: 25 **Admissions**: 857 **Census**: 8 **Outpatient Visits**: 50793 **Births**: 108 **Total Expense ($000)**: 55626 **Payroll Expense ($000)**: 20802 **Personnel**: 188

BLACK RIVER FALLS—Jackson County

☐ **BLACK RIVER MEMORIAL HOSPITAL (521333)**, 711 West Adams Street, Zip 54615–9113; tel. 715/284–5361, **A**1 10 18 **F**3 8 11 13 29 30 31 34 35 40 50 53 56 57 59 62 63 64 65 69 75 76 79 81 85 86 87 89 93 97 104 107 111 114 115 116 118 119 127 129 130 131 132 133 135 144 146 148 154 156
Primary Contact: Carl Selvick, President and Chief Executive Officer
COO: Holly Winn, FACHE, Chief Operating Officer
CFO: Robert Daley, CPA, Chief Financial Officer
CMO: Esteban Miller, Chief Medical Officer
CIO: Robert Daley, CPA, Vice President Fiscal and Information Technology Services
CNO: Melissa Erickson, R.N., Chief Nursing Officer
Web address: www.brmh.net
Control: Other not–for–profit (including NFP Corporation) **Service**: General medical and surgical

Staffed Beds: 25 **Admissions**: 598 **Census**: 9 **Outpatient Visits**: 20564 **Births**: 104 **Total Expense ($000)**: 58391 **Payroll Expense ($000)**: 25983 **Personnel**: 269

BLOOMER—Chippewa County

☐ **MAYO CLINIC HEALTH SYSTEM – CHIPPEWA VALLEY IN BLOOMER (521314)**, 1501 Thompson Street, Zip 54724–1299; tel. 715/568–2000, **A**1 10 18 **F**15 28 29 34 38 40 43 54 56 64 77 80 81 86 87 89 90 93 104 107 130 131 144 147 154 **P**6 **S** Mayo Clinic, Rochester, MN
Primary Contact: Richard Helmers, M.D., Regional Vice President
Web address: www.bloomermedicalcenter.org
Control: Other not–for–profit (including NFP Corporation) **Service**: General medical and surgical

Staffed Beds: 22 **Admissions**: 489 **Census**: 13 **Outpatient Visits**: 53792 **Births**: 0 **Total Expense ($000)**: 37195 **Payroll Expense ($000)**: 16358 **Personnel**: 168

BOSCOBEL—Grant County

★ **GUNDERSEN BOSCOBEL AREA HOSPITAL AND CLINICS (521344)**, 205 Parker Street, Zip 53805–1698; tel. 608/375–4112, **A**10 18 **F**11 15 28 29 34 40 43 53 56 62 64 75 77 78 81 82 86 93 99 100 101 104 107 108 111 118 119 130 144 146 154
Primary Contact: Theresa Lynn. Braudt, Administrator
CFO: Melissa Uselman, Chief Financial Officer
CIO: Tonia Midtlien, Information Systems Support Specialist
CHR: Jennifer Dax, Director Human Resources
CNO: Theresa Lynn Braudt, Chief Nursing Officer
Web address: www.gundersenhealth.org/boscobel
Control: Other not–for–profit (including NFP Corporation) **Service**: General medical and surgical

Staffed Beds: 8 **Admissions**: 205 **Census**: 4 **Outpatient Visits**: 45104 **Births**: 0 **Total Expense ($000)**: 24539 **Payroll Expense ($000)**: 9747 **Personnel**: 135

BROOKFIELD—Waukesha County

★ **ASCENSION SOUTHEAST WISCONSIN HOSPITAL – ELMBROOK CAMPUS (520170)**, 19333 West North Avenue, Zip 53045–4198; tel. 262/785–2000, **A**5 10 **F**11 12 13 15 20 22 28 29 34 36 40 43 51 54 56 64 76 77 78 80 81 82 86 87 90 93 100 107 108 111 116 118 119 130 131 144 146 154 **P**6 **S** Ascension Healthcare, Saint Louis, MO
Primary Contact: Kurt Schley, President
CFO: Michael Petitt, Director of Finance
CMO: Rita Hanson, M.D., Vice President Medical Affairs
CIO: Andrew Donovan, Director Information Technology
CHR: Christopher Morris, Director Human Resources
Web address: https://healthcare.ascension.org/locations/wisconsin/wiwhe/brookfield-ascension-se-wisconsin-hospital-elmbrook-campus
Control: Church operated, Nongovernment, not–for–profit **Service**: General medical and surgical

Staffed Beds: 46 **Admissions**: 3566 **Census**: 46 **Outpatient Visits**: 159043 **Births**: 352 **Total Expense ($000)**: 155655 **Payroll Expense ($000)**: 38540 **Personnel**: 470

BROWN DEER—Milwaukee County

CHARTER NORTHBROOKE BEHAVIORAL HEALTH SYSTEM OF MILWAUKEE/BROWN DEER See Rogers Memorial Hospital–Brown Deer

Hospitals, U.S. / WISCONSIN

BURLINGTON—Racine County

★ ⇑ **AURORA MEDICAL CENTER BURLINGTON (520059)**, 252 McHenry Street, Zip 53105–1828; tel. 262/767–6000, **A**2 10 21 **F**3 8 11 15 17 18 20 26 28 29 30 34 35 36 40 43 44 46 49 50 51 57 59 60 64 68 70 74 75 79 80 81 82 84 85 86 87 89 93 94 96 100 107 108 110 111 115 116 118 119 130 131 132 134 135 146 148 167 **S** Advocate Aurora Health, Downers Grove, IL
Primary Contact: Darrick Minzey, Vice President Finance
CFO: Stuart Arnett, Vice President Finance and Chief Financial Officer
CIO: Jean Chase, Regional Manager Information Services
CHR: Gene Krauklis, Regional Vice President Human Resources
Web address: https://www.aurorahealthcare.org/locations/hospital/aurora-medical-center-burlington/
Control: Other not–for–profit (including NFP Corporation) **Service**: General medical and surgical

Staffed Beds: 43 **Admissions**: 2215 **Census**: 26 **Outpatient Visits**: 103730 **Births**: 0 **Total Expense ($000)**: 96814 **Payroll Expense ($000)**: 31223 **Personnel**: 353

CHILTON—Calumet County

ASCENSION CALUMET HOSPITAL (521317), 614 Memorial Drive, Zip 53014–1597; tel. 920/849–2386, **A**1 10 18 **F**5 7 15 28 29 34 40 53 56 64 75 78 80 81 82 86 87 93 104 107 108 111 116 118 119 130 131 144 147 154 **P**6 **S** Ascension Healthcare, Saint Louis, MO
Primary Contact: Michael Bergmann, President
CFO: Jeff Badger, Chief Financial Officer
CMO: Mark W Kehrberg, M.D., Chief Medical Officer
CIO: Will Weider, Chief Information Officer
Web address: https://healthcare.ascension.org/locations/wisconsin/wiapa/chilton-ascension-calumet-hospital
Control: Church operated, Nongovernment, not–for–profit **Service**: General medical and surgical

Staffed Beds: 12 **Admissions**: 248 **Census**: 4 **Outpatient Visits**: 81961 **Births**: 0 **Total Expense ($000)**: 29458 **Payroll Expense ($000)**: 7084 **Personnel**: 87

COLUMBUS—Columbia County

PRAIRIE RIDGE HEALTH, INC. (521338), 1515 Park Avenue, Zip 53925–2402; tel. 920/623–2200, **A**1 10 18 **F**3 5 7 8 13 15 16 17 18 28 29 34 35 36 40 45 47 50 51 54 56 57 59 64 70 75 79 80 81 85 86 88 93 97 100 101 104 107 110 115 119 130 131 132 133 135 144 147 154 156 161 167 169 **P**6
Primary Contact: John D. Russell, President and Chief Executive Officer
CFO: Melissa Mangan, Vice President of Finance and Chief Financial Officer
CMO: Matthew Niesen, M.D., Chief of the Medical Staff
CIO: Melissa Mangan, Vice President of Finance and Chief Financial Officer
CHR: Ann Roundy, Vice President of Employee and Support Services
CNO: Jamie Hendrix, Vice President Patient Care Services
Web address: www.prairieridge.health
Control: Other not–for–profit (including NFP Corporation) **Service**: General medical and surgical

Staffed Beds: 25 **Admissions**: 806 **Census**: 8 **Outpatient Visits**: 84292 **Births**: 138 **Total Expense ($000)**: 65179 **Payroll Expense ($000)**: 27975 **Personnel**: 277

CUBA CITY—Grant County

CUBA CITY MEDICAL CENTER See Southwest Health Center Nursing Home

SOUTHWEST HEALTH CENTER NURSING HOME See Southwest Health, Platteville

CUDAHY—Milwaukee County

AURORA ST. LUKE'S SOUTH SHORE See Aurora St. Luke's Medical Center, Milwaukee

ST LUKE'S SOUTH SHORE See Aurora St. Luke's South Shore

CUMBERLAND—Barron County

☐ **CUMBERLAND HEALTHCARE (521353)**, 1110 Seventh Avenue, Zip 54829–9138; tel. 715/822–2741, **A**1 10 18 **F**11 15 28 29 34 40 43 53 54 56 64 75 77 78 81 82 86 87 89 93 99 100 101 102 103 104 107 130 131 144 146 154
Primary Contact: Emily Dilley, Chief Executive Officer
COO: Bob Lindberg, Chief Operating Officer
CFO: Angela Martens, Chief Financial Officer
CMO: Tom Lingen, M.D., Chief of Staff
CIO: Jason Morse, Director Information Technology
CHR: Hilary Butzler, Director Human Resources
Web address: www.cumberlandhealthcare.com
Control: Other not–for–profit (including NFP Corporation) **Service**: General medical and surgical

Staffed Beds: 9 **Admissions**: 295 **Census**: 4 **Outpatient Visits**: 18167 **Births**: 0 **Total Expense ($000)**: 32873 **Payroll Expense ($000)**: 13803 **Personnel**: 180

DARLINGTON—Lafayette County

★ **MEMORIAL HOSPITAL OF LAFAYETTE COUNTY (521312)**, 800 Clay Street, Zip 53530–1228, Mailing Address: P.O. Box 70, Zip 53530–0070; tel. 608/776–4466, **A**10 18 **F**1 11 15 28 29 34 40 54 56 64 75 80 81 82 86 90 93 102 107 111 116 119 130 131 144 146 147 154
Primary Contact: Kathleen Kuepers, Chief Executive Officer
CFO: Marie Wamsley, Chief Financial Officer
Web address: www.memorialhospitaloflafayettecounty.org
Control: County, Government, Nonfederal **Service**: General medical and surgical

Staffed Beds: 25 **Admissions**: 270 **Census**: 3 **Outpatient Visits**: 33507 **Births**: 0 **Total Expense ($000)**: 31891 **Payroll Expense ($000)**: 11480 **Personnel**: 151

DODGEVILLE—Iowa County

☐ **UPLAND HILLS HEALTH (521352)**, 800 Compassion Way, Zip 53533–1956, Mailing Address: P.O. Box 800, Zip 53533–0800; tel. 608/930–8000, (Total facility includes 44 beds in nursing home–type unit) **A**1 3 10 18 **F**11 13 15 17 28 29 34 36 40 43 53 54 56 62 63 64 67 70 75 76 77 80 81 82 86 87 88 89 90 93 107 111 119 128 130 131 144 146 147
Primary Contact: Lisa W. Schnedler, FACHE, President and Chief Executive Officer
CFO: Karl Pustina, Vice President Finance
CIO: Karen Thuli, Information Systems Coordinator
CHR: Troy Marx, Human Resources Director
CNO: Lynn Hebgen, MSN, R.N., Vice President of Nursing
Web address: www.uplandhillshealth.org
Control: Other not–for–profit (including NFP Corporation) **Service**: General medical and surgical

Staffed Beds: 69 **Admissions**: 960 **Census**: 41 **Outpatient Visits**: 87150 **Births**: 234 **Total Expense ($000)**: 72523 **Payroll Expense ($000)**: 32038 **Personnel**: 361

DURAND—Pepin County

★ **ADVENTHEALTH DURAND (521307)**, 1220 Third Avenue West, Zip 54736–1600, Mailing Address: P.O. Box 224, Zip 54736–0224; tel. 715/672–4211, **A**10 18 **F**15 28 29 34 40 43 56 64 75 81 86 87 107 130 154 **S** AdventHealth, Altamonte Springs, FL
Primary Contact: Douglas R. Peterson, President and Chief Executive Officer
Web address: https://www.adventhealth.com/hospital/adventhealth-durand
Control: Church operated, Nongovernment, not–for–profit **Service**: General medical and surgical

Staffed Beds: 25 **Admissions**: 139 **Census**: 1 **Outpatient Visits**: 20518 **Births**: 0 **Total Expense ($000)**: 15436 **Payroll Expense ($000)**: 5828 **Personnel**: 74

Hospital, Medicare Provider Number, Address, Telephone, Approval, Facility, and Physician Codes, Health Care System

★ American Hospital Association (AHA) membership ○ Healthcare Facilities Accreditation Program ⇑ Center for Improvement in Healthcare Quality Accreditation
☐ The Joint Commission accreditation ◇ DNV Healthcare Inc. accreditation △ Commission on Accreditation of Rehabilitation Facilities (CARF) accreditation

Hospitals, U.S. / WISCONSIN

EAGLE RIVER—Vilas County

★ **ASPIRUS EAGLE RIVER HOSPITAL (521300)**, 201 Hospital Road, Zip 54521–8835; tel. 715/479–7411, **A**10 18 **F**3 6 7 11 12 13 15 20 22 24 28 29 34 36 40 43 51 53 54 55 56 59 60 64 65 68 69 75 77 78 82 83 84 85 86 87 89 93 97 99 100 102 103 104 107 111 116 118 119 127 130 133 144 146 147 154 **P**8 **S** Aspirus, Inc., Wausau, WI
Primary Contact: Teresa Theiler, President
COO: Laurie Oungst, Vice President, Operations
CFO: Jamon Lamers, Director Finance
CMO: Roderick Brodhead, Chief Medical Officer
CIO: Howard Dobizl, Director Information Technology Services
CHR: Michelle Cornelius, Director Human Resources for Northern Region
CNO: Jacqualyn Monge, Director of Nursing
Web address: https://www.aspirus.org/find-a-location/aspirus-eagle-river-hospital-533
Control: Other not–for–profit (including NFP Corporation) **Service**: General medical and surgical

Staffed Beds: 11 **Admissions**: 321 **Census**: 7 **Outpatient Visits**: 22129
Births: 0 **Total Expense ($000)**: 16264 **Payroll Expense ($000)**: 7441
Personnel: 69

EAGLE RIVER HOSPITAL See Aspirus Eagle River Hospital

EAU CLAIRE—Eau Claire County

✠ **MARSHFIELD MEDICAL CENTER – EAU CLAIRE HOSPITAL (520210)**, 2310 Craig Road, Zip 54701–6128; tel. 715/858–8100, **A**1 **F**3 6 11 12 13 14 15 17 20 22 26 28 29 30 31 32 34 37 40 43 45 49 51 56 59 64 65 68 70 75 76 77 78 79 80 81 82 85 86 87 89 91 92 93 96 97 107 108 111 116 118 119 126 129 130 131 135 144 146 147 153 154 156 157 164 165 167 169 **P**6 **S** Marshfield Clinic Health System, Marshfield, WI
Primary Contact: Bradley D. Groseth, President – West Market
Web address: https://www.marshfieldclinic.org
Control: Other not–for–profit (including NFP Corporation) **Service**: General medical and surgical

Staffed Beds: 44 **Admissions**: 2308 **Census**: 32 **Outpatient Visits**: 202209
Births: 446 **Total Expense ($000)**: 240985 **Payroll Expense ($000)**: 82030
Personnel: 1012

☐ **MAYO CLINIC HEALTH SYSTEM IN EAU CLAIRE (520070)**, 1221 Whipple Street, Zip 54703–5270, Mailing Address: P.O. Box 4105, Zip 54702; tel. 715/838–3311, **A**1 2 3 5 10 19 **F**3 4 5 6 12 13 15 17 18 20 22 24 26 28 29 30 31 32 34 35 37 38 40 43 44 45 46 49 50 55 56 57 58 59 60 61 64 65 66 68 70 72 74 76 77 78 79 80 81 82 85 86 87 89 90 92 93 94 96 97 98 99 100 101 102 103 104 105 107 108 110 111 115 116 117 118 119 120 121 123 124 126 129 130 131 132 133 134 135 144 145 147 148 152 153 154 156 157 160 161 162 164 165 167 168 169 **P**6 **S** Mayo Clinic, Rochester, MN
Primary Contact: Richard Helmers, M.D., Regional Vice President
COO: John M Dickey, Chief Administrative Officer
CFO: Denise Mattison, Director Finance and Accounting Services
CMO: Robert C Peck, M.D., Chief Medical Officer
CHR: Kenneth Lee, Division Chair, Human Resource Advisory
CNO: Pamela K. White, R.N., MSN, Chief Nursing Officer
Web address: https://www.mayoclinichealthsystem.org/locations/eau-claire
Control: Other not–for–profit (including NFP Corporation) **Service**: General medical and surgical

Staffed Beds: 190 **Admissions**: 11253 **Census**: 146 **Outpatient Visits**: 458102 **Births**: 1141 **Total Expense ($000)**: 739451 **Payroll Expense ($000)**: 351547 **Personnel**: 3107

REHABILITATION HOSPITAL OF WESTERN WISCONSIN (523030), 900 W Clairemont Avenue, 8th Floor, Zip 54701–6122; tel. 715/717–2828, (Nonreporting) **S** Encompass Health Corporation, Birmingham, AL
Primary Contact: Anne Sadowska, Chief Executive Officer
Web address: https://encompasshealth.com/locations/eauclairerehab
Control: Corporation, Investor–owned (for–profit) **Service**: Rehabilitation

Staffed Beds: 36

EDGERTON—Rock County

★ **EDGERTON HOSPITAL AND HEALTH SERVICES (521319)**, 11101 North Sherman Road, Zip 53534–9002; tel. 608/884–3441, **A**10 18 **F**11 15 28 34 40 43 64 75 77 80 81 82 86 90 93 107 108 111 119 130 144 146 154
Primary Contact: Marc Augsburger, R.N., President and Chief Executive Officer
CFO: Charles Roader, Vice President Finance
CMO: Brian Stubitsch, M.D., Chief Medical Officer
CIO: JT Johrendt, Information Technology Network Specialist
CHR: Mark Kindschi, Director Human Resources
CNO: Susan Alwin–Popp, R.N., Vice President of Clinical Services/Chief Clinical Officer
Web address: www.edgertonhospital.com
Control: Other not–for–profit (including NFP Corporation) **Service**: General medical and surgical

Staffed Beds: 13 **Admissions**: 307 **Census**: 7 **Outpatient Visits**: 33036
Births: 0 **Total Expense ($000)**: 29948 **Payroll Expense ($000)**: 12289
Personnel: 167

ELK MOUND—Dunn County

VERNON MEMORIAL HEALTHCARE (521348), E8270 660th Ave, Zip 54739–4401, Mailing Address: 507 South Main Street, Viroqua, Zip 54665–2096; tel. 608/637–2101, **A**10 18 **F**5 13 15 28 29 34 36 40 43 56 64 75 76 77 80 81 82 86 87 89 93 99 100 103 104 107 119 130 131 144 **P**6
Primary Contact: David Hartberg, Chief Executive Officer
COO: Kristy Wiltrout, R.N., Chief Operating Officer
CFO: Mary Koenig, Chief Financial Officer
CIO: Scott Adkins, Manager Information Technology
CHR: Kay Starr, Manager Human Resources
Web address: www.vmh.org
Control: Other not–for–profit (including NFP Corporation) **Service**: General medical and surgical

Staffed Beds: 25 **Admissions**: 773 **Census**: 7 **Outpatient Visits**: 132870
Births: 117 **Total Expense ($000)**: 76853 **Payroll Expense ($000)**: 34087
Personnel: 360

ELKHORN—Walworth County

★ ⇧ **AURORA LAKELAND MEDICAL CENTER (520102)**, W3985 County Road NN, Zip 53121–4389; tel. 262/741–2000, **A**2 3 10 21 **F**3 11 13 17 18 29 30 34 35 36 40 43 44 50 51 57 59 60 64 68 70 74 75 76 79 80 81 82 84 85 86 87 89 93 94 96 107 108 111 115 118 119 126 127 129 130 131 132 135 146 148 169 **S** Advocate Aurora Health, Downers Grove, IL
Primary Contact: Darrick Minzey, Vice President Finance
CFO: Stuart Arnett, Regional Vice President Finance
CMO: Greg Gerber, M.D., Chief Medical Officer
CIO: Jean Chase, Regional Manager Information Services
CHR: Gene Krauklis, Regional Vice President Human Resources
Web address: https://www.aurorahealthcare.org/locations/hospital/aurora-lakeland-medical-center/
Control: Other not–for–profit (including NFP Corporation) **Service**: General medical and surgical

Staffed Beds: 62 **Admissions**: 2778 **Census**: 28 **Outpatient Visits**: 81893
Births: 659 **Total Expense ($000)**: 69261 **Payroll Expense ($000)**: 25922
Personnel: 434

FOND DU LAC—Fond Du Lac County

FOND DU LAC COUNTY MENTAL HEALTH CENTER (524025), 459 East First Street, Zip 54935–4599; tel. 920/929–3502, **A**10 **F**4 38 98 102 103 130 **P**6
Primary Contact: J.R. Musunuru, M.D., Executive Director
Web address: www.fdlco.wi.gov
Control: County, Government, Nonfederal **Service**: Psychiatric

Staffed Beds: 16 **Admissions**: 518 **Census**: 9 **Outpatient Visits**: 0 **Births**: 0
Personnel: 38

✠ **SSM HEALTH ST. AGNES HOSPITAL – FOND DU LAC (520088)**, 430 East Division Street, Zip 54935–4560, Mailing Address: P.O. Box 385, Zip 54936–0385; tel. 920/929–2300, **A**1 2 10 20 **F**2 5 6 11 13 15 20 22 24 28 29 34 38 40 43 51 53 54 56 60 62 63 64 69 75 76 78 80 81 82 86 87 89 90 93 98 99 100 101 102 103 104 107 108 111 118 119 130 131 146 147 154 **P**3 6 8 **S** SSM Health, Saint Louis, MO
Primary Contact: Katherine Vergos, FACHE, President
CFO: Bonnie Schmitz, Vice President and Chief Financial Officer
CMO: Derek Colmenares, M.D., Chief Medical Officer
CIO: Nancy Birschbach, Vice President and Chief Information Officer
CHR: Sue Edminster, Vice President Human Resources
CNO: Tami Schattschneider, Chief Nursing Officer
Web address: https://www.ssmhealth.com/
Control: Church operated, Nongovernment, not–for–profit **Service**: General medical and surgical

Staffed Beds: 127 **Admissions**: 7004 **Census**: 79 **Outpatient Visits**: 190343 **Births**: 823 **Total Expense ($000)**: 254358 **Payroll Expense ($000)**: 98783 **Personnel**: 992

ST. AGNES HOSPITAL See SSM Health St. Agnes Hospital – Fond Du Lac

FORT ATKINSON—Jefferson County

✠ **FORT HEALTHCARE (520071)**, 611 Sherman Avenue East, Zip 53538–1998; tel. 920/568–5000, **A**1 10 **F**3 8 11 13 15 18 28 29 32 34 35 37 40 41 44 45 47 48 50 53 55 56 57 59 65 68 75 76 77 79 80 81 82 85 86 87 89 90 93 94 96 99 100 104 107 108 110 111 115 118 119 127 130 132 135 144 146 147 148 154 156 160 161 164 169 **P**5 8
Primary Contact: Michael Anderson, President/Chief Executive Officer
CFO: James J Nelson, Senior Vice President Finance and Strategic Planning
CMO: William Cannon, M.D., Medical Director
CIO: Jennifer Winter, Chief Medical Information Officer
CHR: Nancy Alstad, Director Human Resources
CNO: Marie Wiesmann, Vice President of Nursing and Chief Nursing Officer
Web address: www.forthealthcare.com
Control: Other not–for–profit (including NFP Corporation) **Service**: General medical and surgical

Staffed Beds: 25 **Admissions**: 1462 **Census**: 13 **Outpatient Visits**: 266767 **Births**: 335 **Total Expense ($000)**: 142821 **Payroll Expense ($000)**: 61483 **Personnel**: 674

FRANKLIN—Milwaukee County

★ **ASCENSION SOUTHEAST WISCONSIN HOSPITAL – FRANKLIN CAMPUS (520204)**, 10101 South 27th Street, Zip 53132–7209; tel. 414/325–4700, **A**10 **F**15 17 20 22 29 34 40 43 51 64 70 77 80 81 86 87 93 107 108 111 119 130 147 **P**6 **S** Ascension Healthcare, Saint Louis, MO
Primary Contact: Jonathon Matuszewski, Hospital Administrator
CFO: Aaron Bridgeland, Director Finance
CMO: Michelle Graham, M.D., Vice President Medical Affairs
CIO: Gregory Smith, Senior Vice President and Chief Information Officer
CNO: Sheila Gansemer, R.N., Vice President Patient Care Services and Chief Nursing Officer
Web address: https://healthcare.ascension.org/locations/wisconsin/wiwhe/franklin-ascension-se-wisconsin-hospital-franklin-campus?utm_campaign=gmb&utm_medium=organic&utm_source=local
Control: Church operated, Nongovernment, not–for–profit **Service**: General medical and surgical

Staffed Beds: 33 **Admissions**: 2605 **Census**: 36 **Outpatient Visits**: 78775 **Births**: 0 **Total Expense ($000)**: 82001 **Payroll Expense ($000)**: 24510 **Personnel**: 282

✠ **MIDWEST ORTHOPEDIC SPECIALTY HOSPITAL (520205)**, 10101 South 27th Street, 2nd Floor, Zip 53132–7209; tel. 414/817–5800, **A**1 3 10 **F**29 34 64 80 81 82 86 130 131 **P**8 **S** Ascension Healthcare, Saint Louis, MO
CFO: Aaron Bridgeland, Director Finance
CMO: Daniel Guehlstorf, M.D., Chief of Staff
CIO: Gregory Smith, Senior Vice President and Chief Information Officer
Web address: www.mymosh.com/
Control: Partnership, Investor–owned (for–profit) **Service**: General medical and surgical

Staffed Beds: 16 **Admissions**: 567 **Census**: 3 **Outpatient Visits**: 68801 **Births**: 0 **Total Expense ($000)**: 52972 **Payroll Expense ($000)**: 14302 **Personnel**: 161

FRIENDSHIP—Adams County

★ **GUNDERSEN MOUNDVIEW HOSPITAL & CLINICS (521309)**, 402 West Lake Street, Zip 53934–9699, Mailing Address: P.O. Box 40, Zip 53934–0040; tel. 608/339–3331, **A**10 18 **F**6 11 15 28 29 34 36 40 53 56 64 77 81 82 86 87 93 107 108 111 119 130 131 146 154
Primary Contact: Francisco Perez-Guerra, Administrator
Web address: www.moundview.org
Control: Other not–for–profit (including NFP Corporation) **Service**: General medical and surgical

Staffed Beds: 25 **Admissions**: 193 **Census**: 4 **Outpatient Visits**: 26781 **Births**: 0 **Total Expense ($000)**: 32287 **Payroll Expense ($000)**: 9059 **Personnel**: 120

GLENDALE—Milwaukee County

ORTHOPAEDIC HOSPITAL OF WISCONSIN (520194), 475 West River Woods Parkway, Zip 53212–1081; tel. 414/961–6800, **A**10 **F**29 34 38 53 64 80 81 82 86 93 107 111 119 130 131
Primary Contact: Brandon Goldbeck, Chief Executive Officer
CFO: Tom Swiderski, Chief Financial Officer
CMO: Rory Wright, M.D., President Medical Staff
CIO: Todd Heikkinen, Manager Sports Medicine and Rehabilitation Services
CNO: Nanette Johnson, Chief Nursing Officer
Web address: www.ohow.org
Control: Partnership, Investor–owned (for–profit) **Service**: General medical and surgical

Staffed Beds: 30 **Admissions**: 922 **Census**: 4 **Outpatient Visits**: 64572 **Births**: 0 **Total Expense ($000)**: 56240 **Payroll Expense ($000)**: 19640 **Personnel**: 253

GRAFTON—Ozaukee County

★ ⇧ **AURORA MEDICAL CENTER GRAFTON (520207)**, 975 Port Washington Road, Zip 53024–9201; tel. 262/329–1000, **A**2 3 5 10 21 **F**3 8 11 12 13 15 17 18 20 22 24 26 28 29 30 31 34 35 36 40 41 43 44 45 46 47 49 50 51 53 57 59 60 64 65 68 70 72 74 75 76 79 80 81 82 84 85 86 87 89 92 93 94 107 108 110 111 114 115 116 117 118 119 120 121 124 126 130 131 135 146 147 148 154 156 167 169 **S** Advocate Aurora Health, Downers Grove, IL
Primary Contact: Carla Lafever, President
CMO: Doug McManus, Chief Medical Officer
Web address: www.aurorahealthcare.com
Control: Other not–for–profit (including NFP Corporation) **Service**: General medical and surgical

Staffed Beds: 132 **Admissions**: 7119 **Census**: 85 **Outpatient Visits**: 165889 **Births**: 1023 **Total Expense ($000)**: 251481 **Payroll Expense ($000)**: 80912 **Personnel**: 1390

GRANTSBURG—Burnett County

★ **BURNETT MEDICAL CENTER (521331)**, 257 West St George Avenue, Zip 54840–7827; tel. 715/463–5353, (Total facility includes 50 beds in nursing home–type unit) **A**10 18 **F**2 15 28 29 34 40 43 56 64 75 77 78 80 81 82 86 87 89 90 93 107 128 130 131 144 154 **P**6
Primary Contact: Gordon Lewis, Chief Executive Officer
CFO: Gordy Forbort, Interim Chief Financial Officer
CMO: Hans Rechsteiner, M.D., Chief of Staff
CIO: Andy Douglas, Manager Information Technology
CHR: Sandy Hinrichs, Director Human Resources
Web address: www.burnettmedicalcenter.com
Control: Other not–for–profit (including NFP Corporation) **Service**: General medical and surgical

Staffed Beds: 67 **Admissions**: 269 **Census**: 39 **Outpatient Visits**: 26645 **Births**: 0 **Total Expense ($000)**: 20474 **Payroll Expense ($000)**: 8061 **Personnel**: 124

Hospitals, U.S. / WISCONSIN

GREEN BAY—Brown County

★ ⇧ **AURORA BAYCARE MEDICAL CENTER (520193)**, 2845 Greenbrier Road, Zip 54311-6519, Mailing Address: P.O. Box 8900, Zip 54308-8900; tel. 920/288-8000, **A**2 3 10 21 **F**3 11 12 13 15 17 18 20 22 24 26 28 29 30 31 34 35 36 37 40 43 45 46 47 48 49 53 54 57 58 60 64 68 70 72 74 75 76 78 79 80 81 82 84 85 86 87 89 90 91 92 93 94 97 107 108 110 111 114 115 116 117 118 119 120 121 123 124 126 129 130 131 132 134 135 144 146 147 148 154 167 169 **S** Advocate Aurora Health, Downers Grove, IL
Primary Contact: Thomas Miller, President
COO: Daniel T Meyer, President
CFO: Gwen Christensen, Vice President, Finance
CMO: Brian Johnson, M.D., Chief Medical Officer
CIO: Chuck Geurts, Manager Information Technology Client Services
CNO: Heather Schroeder, R.N., Vice President Nursing
Web address: www.aurorabaycare.com
Control: Partnership, Investor-owned (for-profit) **Service**: General medical and surgical

Staffed Beds: 183 **Admissions**: 8193 **Census**: 115 **Outpatient Visits**: 482748 **Births**: 1393 **Total Expense ($000)**: 454591 **Payroll Expense ($000)**: 140509 **Personnel**: 1826

★ ⇧ **BELLIN HOSPITAL (520049)**, 744 South Webster Avenue, Zip 54301-3581, Mailing Address: P.O. Box 23400, Zip 54305-3400; tel. 920/433-3500, **A**2 10 19 21 **F**3 12 13 15 17 18 20 22 24 26 28 29 30 31 34 35 36 37 40 41 43 45 46 47 48 49 51 53 54 58 62 64 72 75 76 77 78 80 81 82 86 87 89 90 91 92 96 97 107 108 110 111 115 116 117 118 119 123 124 126 127 129 130 131 132 144 145 148 154 156 167 **P**6
Primary Contact: Chris Woleske, President and Chief Executive Officer
CMO: Cynthia Lasecki, M.D., Chief Medical Officer
CIO: John Rocheleau, Vice President Business Support and Information Technology
CHR: Troy L Koebke, Director Human Resources Management
CNO: Laura Hieb, R.N., Chief Nursing Officer
Web address: www.bellin.org
Control: Other not-for-profit (including NFP Corporation) **Service**: General medical and surgical

Staffed Beds: 189 **Admissions**: 8436 **Census**: 103 **Outpatient Visits**: 1181906 **Births**: 1625 **Total Expense ($000)**: 664957 **Payroll Expense ($000)**: 337692 **Personnel**: 3660

⇧ **BELLIN PSYCHIATRIC CENTER (524038)**, 301 East St Joseph Street, Zip 54301, Mailing Address: P.O. Box 23725, Zip 54305-3725; tel. 920/433-3630, **A**3 5 10 21 **F**4 5 6 29 34 36 38 53 54 56 64 75 86 87 98 99 100 101 102 103 104 105 106 115 117 123 124 126 127 129 130 132 135 145 148 152 154 160 161 162 163 164 165 167 **P**6
Primary Contact: Sharla Baenen, MSN, R.N., President Mental Well Being, Vice President Emergency Medicine, Hospitalists & Medical Subspecialist
CFO: Kevin McGurk, Controller
CIO: Troy Schiesl, Director Information Services
CHR: Troy L Koebke, Director Human Resources
CNO: Crystal Malakar, Team Leader Inpatient Nursing
Web address: www.bellin.org
Control: Other not-for-profit (including NFP Corporation) **Service**: Psychiatric

Staffed Beds: 45 **Admissions**: 1781 **Census**: 24 **Outpatient Visits**: 94889 **Births**: 0 **Total Expense ($000)**: 30771 **Payroll Expense ($000)**: 19779 **Personnel**: 201

BROWN COUNTY COMMUNITY TREATMENT CENTER (524014), 3150 Gershwin Drive, Zip 54311-5899; tel. 920/391-4700, **A**3 5 10 **F**98 102 130
Primary Contact: Roberta Morschauser, Administrator
CFO: Margaret Hoff, Account Manager
CMO: Yogesh Pareek, M.D., Clinical Director
CIO: Dawn LaPlant, Manager Health Information Management
CHR: Brent R Miller, Manager Human Resources
Web address: www.co.brown.wi.us/
Control: County, Government, Nonfederal **Service**: Psychiatric

Staffed Beds: 16 **Admissions**: 546 **Census**: 10 **Outpatient Visits**: 0 **Births**: 0 **Total Expense ($000)**: 4062 **Payroll Expense ($000)**: 2945 **Personnel**: 33

⊞ **HSHS ST. MARY'S HOSPITAL MEDICAL CENTER (520097)**, 1726 Shawano Avenue, Zip 54303-3282; tel. 920/498-4200, **A**1 2 10 **F**3 13 15 17 18 20 22 26 28 29 30 31 34 35 40 43 44 45 46 47 48 49 50 51 53 55 57 59 64 65 70 74 75 77 78 79 80 82 84 85 86 87 92 94 96 102 107 108 110 111 114 115 116 117 118 119 131 132 142 143 145 148 154 167 **S** HSHS Hospital Sisters Health System, Springfield, IL
Primary Contact: Robert J. Erickson, Market President and Chief Executive Officer and President and Chief Executive Officer
COO: Lawrence J Connors, Chief Operating Officer
CFO: Greg Simia, Chief Financial Officer
CMO: Ken Johnson, Chief Physician Executive
CIO: Shane Miller, Chief Information Officer
CHR: Christine Jensema, Chief People Officer
CNO: Paula Hafeman, Chief Nursing Officer
Web address: https://www.hshs.org/st-marys-green-bay
Control: Church operated, Nongovernment, not-for-profit **Service**: General medical and surgical

Staffed Beds: 72 **Admissions**: 3164 **Census**: 38 **Outpatient Visits**: 91023 **Births**: 0 **Total Expense ($000)**: 125427 **Payroll Expense ($000)**: 28977 **Personnel**: 374

⊞ **HSHS ST. VINCENT HOSPITAL (520075)**, 835 South Van Buren Street, Zip 54301-3526, Mailing Address: P.O. Box 13508, Zip 54307-3508; tel. 920/433-0111, **A**1 2 3 10 **F**3 5 9 11 12 13 15 17 18 19 20 22 24 26 29 30 31 32 34 36 37 40 43 44 45 49 50 51 56 57 58 59 62 64 65 70 72 74 75 76 77 78 79 80 81 83 84 85 86 87 88 89 90 91 92 94 96 100 108 110 111 114 115 116 117 118 119 120 121 123 124 126 129 130 132 135 143 144 146 147 148 154 160 161 167 169 **S** HSHS Hospital Sisters Health System, Springfield, IL
Primary Contact: Robert J. Erickson, Market President and Chief Executive Officer and President and Chief Executive Officer
CFO: Greg Simia, Chief Financial Officer
CMO: Ken Johnson, Chief Physician Executive
CIO: Shane Miller, Chief Information Officer
CHR: Christine Jensema, Chief Human Resources Officer
CNO: Kenneth E Nelson, R.N., III, Chief Nursing Officer
Web address: www.stvincenthospital.org
Control: Church operated, Nongovernment, not-for-profit **Service**: General medical and surgical

Staffed Beds: 224 **Admissions**: 9178 **Census**: 154 **Outpatient Visits**: 206315 **Births**: 1415 **Total Expense ($000)**: 361038 **Payroll Expense ($000)**: 98776 **Personnel**: 1113

☐ **WILLOW CREEK BEHAVIORAL HEALTH (524041)**, 1351 Ontario Road, Zip 54311-8302; tel. 920/328-1220, **A**1 10 **F**4 5 29 34 64 75 86 87 98 99 101 103 104 130 154 **S** Strategic Behavioral Health, LLC, Memphis, TN
Primary Contact: Alison Denil, Chief Executive Officer
Web address: www.willowcreekbh.com
Control: Corporation, Investor-owned (for-profit) **Service**: Psychiatric

Staffed Beds: 39 **Admissions**: 2370 **Census**: 53 **Outpatient Visits**: 3634 **Births**: 0 **Total Expense ($000)**: 18430 **Payroll Expense ($000)**: 11781 **Personnel**: 135

HARTFORD—Washington County

★ ⇧ **AURORA MEDICAL CENTER IN WASHINGTON COUNTY (520038)**, 1032 East Sumner Street, Zip 53027-1698; tel. 262/673-2300, **A**2 10 21 **F**3 8 11 15 28 29 30 34 35 36 40 41 43 44 45 46 47 48 49 50 53 54 56 57 59 60 64 65 68 75 77 79 80 81 82 84 85 86 87 89 90 91 92 93 94 95 96 107 108 111 112 113 114 118 119 129 130 132 135 146 148 157 167 **S** Advocate Aurora Health, Downers Grove, IL
Primary Contact: Jessica Bauer, President
CIO: John Sipek, Supervisor Client Services
CNO: Terry Kabitzke-Groth, R.N., Chief Nursing Officer
Web address: www.aurorahealthcare.org
Control: Other not-for-profit (including NFP Corporation) **Service**: General medical and surgical

Staffed Beds: 35 **Admissions**: 1199 **Census**: 11 **Outpatient Visits**: 96342 **Births**: 0 **Total Expense ($000)**: 59908 **Payroll Expense ($000)**: 22293 **Personnel**: 303

Hospitals, U.S. / WISCONSIN

HAYWARD—Sawyer County

★ ⇧ **TAMARACK HEALTH HAYWARD MEDICAL CENTER (521336)**, 11040 North State Road 77, Zip 54843-6391; tel. 715/934-4321, (Total facility includes 90 beds in nursing home-type unit) **A**10 18 21 **F**10 11 13 15 29 34 40 43 51 53 64 75 76 78 81 82 86 93 107 108 111 119 125 128 130 131 146 147 154 **S** Tamarack Health, Ashland, WI
Primary Contact: Luke Beirl, PharmD, Chief Executive Officer
CFO: Kent Dumonseau, Vice President Finance and Information Services
CHR: Rose Gates, Director Human Resources
Web address: https://www.tamarackhealth.org/
Control: Other not-for-profit (including NFP Corporation) **Service**: General medical and surgical

Staffed Beds: 115 **Admissions**: 928 **Census**: 90 **Outpatient Visits**: 47840
Births: 116 **Total Expense ($000)**: 66571 **Payroll Expense ($000)**: 29542
Personnel: 327

HILLSBORO—Vernon County

★ **GUNDERSEN ST. JOSEPH'S HOSPITAL AND CLINICS (521304)**, 400 Water Avenue, Zip 54634-9054, Mailing Address: P.O. Box 527, Zip 54634-0527; tel. 608/489-8000, **A**10 18 **F**15 28 29 34 36 38 40 43 53 56 64 69 75 77 80 81 82 86 87 89 90 93 99 100 101 103 104 107 108 130 131 144 147 154
Primary Contact: Kristie McCoic, Administrator
CFO: Robin Nelson, Chief Financial Officer
CMO: William Cooke, M.D., Chief of Staff
CIO: Danial Phetteplace, Director Information Technology
CHR: Kristie McCoic, Clinic Operations Officer and Director Human Resources
Web address: www.gundersenhealth.org/st-josephs
Control: Other not-for-profit (including NFP Corporation) **Service**: General medical and surgical

Staffed Beds: 13 **Admissions**: 261 **Census**: 5 **Outpatient Visits**: 41675
Births: 0 **Total Expense ($000)**: 33259 **Payroll Expense ($000)**: 11732
Personnel: 170

HUDSON—St. Croix County

☐ **HUDSON HOSPITAL AND CLINIC (521335)**, 405 Stageline Road, Zip 54016-7848; tel. 715/531-6000, **A**1 3 10 18 **F**5 13 15 28 29 34 38 40 43 53 54 56 64 75 76 80 81 86 87 89 93 107 108 111 119 130 141 154 **P**2 **S** HealthPartners, Bloomington, MN
Primary Contact: Thomas Borowski, FACHE, President
CFO: Douglas E Johnson, Vice President, Chief Financial Officer
CMO: Levon O'hAodha, Chief of Staff
CHR: Kristen Novak, Director, Human Resources
CNO: Kristy Yaeger, Vice President, Patient Care Services and Chief Nursing Officer
Web address: www.hudsonhospital.org
Control: Other not-for-profit (including NFP Corporation) **Service**: General medical and surgical

Staffed Beds: 24 **Admissions**: 1384 **Census**: 13 **Outpatient Visits**: 44575
Births: 508 **Total Expense ($000)**: 70164 **Payroll Expense ($000)**: 25989
Personnel: 267

JANESVILLE—Rock County

✠ **MERCYHEALTH HOSPITAL AND TRAUMA CENTER – JANESVILLE (520066)**, 1000 Mineral Point Avenue, Zip 53548-2982; tel. 608/756-6000, (Total facility includes 20 beds in nursing home-type unit) **A**1 2 3 5 10 19 **F**11 13 15 17 28 29 34 38 40 43 56 64 70 75 76 77 78 80 81 82 86 87 89 93 98 101 102 103 104 107 108 111 118 119 128 130 131 144 146 147 154 **P**6 **S** Mercy Health System, Janesville, WI
Primary Contact: Javon R. Bea, President and Chief Executive Officer
CFO: John Cook, Vice President and Chief Financial Officer
CMO: Mark L. Goelzer, M.D., Director Medical Affairs
CHR: Kathy Harris, Vice President
Web address: www.mercyhealthsystem.org
Control: Other not-for-profit (including NFP Corporation) **Service**: General medical and surgical

Staffed Beds: 140 **Admissions**: 6219 **Census**: 90 **Outpatient Visits**: 883562 **Births**: 686 **Total Expense ($000)**: 494587 **Payroll Expense ($000)**: 164451 **Personnel**: 1049

✠ **SSM HEALTH ST. MARY'S HOSPITAL JANESVILLE (520208)**, 3400 East Racine Street, Zip 53546-2344, Mailing Address: 3400 East Racine Steeet, Zip 53546-2344; tel. 608/373-8000, **A**1 10 **F**13 28 29 34 38 40 43 64 70 75 76 80 81 86 87 89 90 107 108 111 119 130 154 **S** SSM Health, Saint Louis, MO
Primary Contact: Jane Curran-Meuli, President
Web address: www.stmarysjanesville.com
Control: Church operated, Nongovernment, not-for-profit **Service**: General medical and surgical

Staffed Beds: 50 **Admissions**: 2585 **Census**: 24 **Outpatient Visits**: 65871
Births: 454 **Total Expense ($000)**: 65907 **Payroll Expense ($000)**: 22384
Personnel: 291

KENOSHA—Kenosha County

★ ⇧ **AURORA MEDICAL CENTER KENOSHA (520189)**, 10400 75th Street, Zip 53142-7884; tel. 262/948-5600, (Includes AURORA MEDICAL CENTER MOUNT PLEASANT, 13250 Washington Avenue, Mount Pleasant, Wisconsin, Zip 53177-1516, tel. 262/799-8700; Lisa Just, Patient Service Area President South Wisconsin, President, Aurora Medical Center Mount Pleasant) **A**2 3 10 21 **F**3 8 11 13 15 17 18 19 20 22 26 28 29 30 31 34 35 36 37 40 43 44 45 46 47 48 49 50 51 54 57 59 60 64 68 70 72 74 75 76 79 80 81 82 83 85 86 87 89 93 94 96 100 107 108 111 114 115 116 118 119 126 129 130 131 132 135 146 147 148 154 167 169 **S** Advocate Aurora Health, Downers Grove, IL
Primary Contact: Donna F. Jamieson, Ph.D., R.N., President
COO: Linda A. Gump, Chief Clinical Services Officer
CFO: Laurie B. Yake, Vice President Finance
CMO: James Santarelli, M.D., President Medical Staff
CIO: Debora R. Chapdelaine, Manager Information Technology
CHR: Kellie Nelson, Director Human Resources
CNO: Kristie A Geil, Vice President and Chief Nursing Officer
Web address: www.aurorahealthcare.org
Control: Other not-for-profit (including NFP Corporation) **Service**: General medical and surgical

Staffed Beds: 193 **Admissions**: 10120 **Census**: 123 **Outpatient Visits**: 320481 **Births**: 1201 **Total Expense ($000)**: 340635 **Payroll Expense ($000)**: 114816 **Personnel**: 2128

☐ **FROEDTERT SOUTH – KENOSHA MEDICAL CENTER (520021)**, 6308 Eighth Avenue, Zip 53143-5082; tel. 262/656-2011, (Includes FROEDTERT PLEASANT PRAIRIE HOSPIITAL, 9555 76th Street, Pleasant Prairie, Wisconsin, Zip 53158-1984, 6308 Eighth Avenue, Kenosha, Zip 53143-5082, tel. 262/577-8000; Richard O Schmidt Jr, President and Chief Executive Officer) **A**1 2 10 19 **F**11 12 13 15 17 20 22 24 28 29 34 38 40 43 51 53 54 60 64 70 72 75 76 78 80 81 86 87 89 93 100 102 107 108 111 116 118 119 130 146 147 **S** Froedtert ThedaCare Health, Inc., Milwaukee, WI
Primary Contact: Richard O. Schmidt Jr, President and Chief Executive Officer
CFO: Thomas J. Kelley, Executive Vice President and Chief Financial Officer
Web address: www.froedtertsouth.com
Control: Other not-for-profit (including NFP Corporation) **Service**: General medical and surgical

Staffed Beds: 95 **Admissions**: 5099 **Census**: 72 **Outpatient Visits**: 501618
Births: 553 **Total Expense ($000)**: 349160 **Payroll Expense ($000)**: 151682 **Personnel**: 1608

LA CROSSE—La Crosse County

✠ △ **GUNDERSEN LUTHERAN MEDICAL CENTER (520087)**, 1900 South Avenue, Zip 54601-5467; tel. 608/782-7300, **A**1 2 3 5 7 8 10 19 **F**4 5 6 9 12 13 15 20 22 24 28 29 34 36 38 40 43 51 54 55 56 60 61 63 64 72 75 76 77 78 80 81 82 86 87 88 89 90 93 98 99 100 101 102 103 104 107 111 116 118 119 130 131 144 147
Primary Contact: Scott W. Rathgaber, M.D., Chief Executive Officer
COO: Heather Schimmers, Chief Operating Officer and Chief Nursing Officer
CMO: Mike Dolan, Executive Vice President and Medical Chief Operating Officer
CIO: Praveen Chopra, Chief Information Officer
CHR: Mary Ellen McCartney, Chief Human Resource Officer
Web address: www.gundluth.org
Control: Other not-for-profit (including NFP Corporation) **Service**: General medical and surgical

Staffed Beds: 307 **Admissions**: 15511 **Census**: 202 **Outpatient Visits**: 765926 **Births**: 1709 **Total Expense ($000)**: 1402868 **Payroll Expense ($000)**: 575303 **Personnel**: 3003

Hospital, Medicare Provider Number, Address, Telephone, Approval, Facility, and Physician Codes, Health Care System

★ American Hospital Association (AHA) membership
☐ The Joint Commission accreditation
○ Healthcare Facilities Accreditation Program
◇ DNV Healthcare Inc. accreditation
⇧ Center for Improvement in Healthcare Quality Accreditation
△ Commission on Accreditation of Rehabilitation Facilities (CARF) accreditation

Hospitals, U.S. / WISCONSIN

MAYO CLINIC HEALTH SYSTEM – FRANCISCAN HEALTHCARE IN LA CROSSE See Mayo Clinic Health System In La Crosse

MAYO CLINIC HEALTH SYSTEM IN LA CROSSE (520004), 700 West Avenue South, Zip 54601–4783; tel. 608/785–0940, **A** 1 2 3 5 10 19 **F** 3 6 11 12 13 15 17 18 20 22 26 28 29 30 31 32 34 35 38 40 43 44 45 46 47 48 49 50 52 55 56 57 58 59 60 63 64 65 66 68 69 70 72 74 76 77 78 79 80 81 82 84 85 86 87 89 90 92 93 94 96 97 99 100 101 104 107 108 110 111 115 116 117 118 119 120 121 123 126 129 130 131 134 135 144 145 146 147 148 153 154 156 157 160 161 162 164 165 167 169 **P** 6 **S** Mayo Clinic, Rochester, MN
Primary Contact: Richard Helmers, M.D., Chief Executive Officer
CFO: Tom Tiggelaar, Vice President Finance
CMO: David Rushlow, Vice President Medical Affairs
CIO: Neal Sanger, Vice President Information Services
Web address: https://www.mayoclinichealthsystem.org/locations/la-crosse
Control: Other not–for–profit (including NFP Corporation) **Service**: General medical and surgical

Staffed Beds: 92 **Admissions**: 4440 **Census**: 50 **Outpatient Visits**: 368857 **Births**: 560 **Total Expense ($000)**: 450906 **Payroll Expense ($000)**: 212568 **Personnel**: 2059

LADYSMITH—Rusk County

★ **MARSHFIELD MEDICAL CENTER – LADYSMITH (521328)**, 900 College Avenue West, Zip 54848–2116; tel. 715/532–5561, **A** 10 18 **S** Marshfield Clinic Health System, Marshfield, WI
Primary Contact: Bradley D. Groseth, President
CFO: David Kuehn, Chief Financial Officer
CMO: Ganesh Pawar, M.D., Chief of Staff
CHR: Rita Telitz, Chief Administrative Officer
Web address: https://www.marshfieldclinic.org/locations/centers/Ladysmith%20-%20Marshfield%20Medical%20Center
Control: Other not–for–profit (including NFP Corporation) **Service**: General medical and surgical

Staffed Beds: 25 **Admissions**: 207 **Census**: 3 **Outpatient Visits**: 36643 **Births**: 0 **Total Expense ($000)**: 33352 **Payroll Expense ($000)**: 11730 **Personnel**: 106

LAKE GENEVA—Walworth County

☐ **MERCYHEALTH HOSPITAL AND MEDICAL CENTER – WALWORTH (521357)**, N2950 State Road 67, Zip 53147–2655; tel. 262/245–0535, **A** 1 3 10 18 **F** 9 11 13 15 17 28 29 34 38 40 43 56 64 70 75 76 77 78 80 81 82 85 86 87 89 93 101 103 104 107 108 111 118 119 130 131 144 146 147 154 **P** 6 **S** Mercy Health System, Janesville, WI
Primary Contact: Javon R. Bea, President and Chief Executive Officer
COO: Jennifer Hallatt, Vice President
CNO: Caryn Lynn Oleston, FACHE, MSN, R.N., Chief Nursing Officer
Web address: www.mercyhealthsystem.org
Control: Other not–for–profit (including NFP Corporation) **Service**: General medical and surgical

Staffed Beds: 18 **Admissions**: 1158 **Census**: 8 **Outpatient Visits**: 165585 **Births**: 139 **Total Expense ($000)**: 90700 **Payroll Expense ($000)**: 21829 **Personnel**: 345

LANCASTER—Grant County

GRANT REGIONAL HEALTH CENTER (521322), 507 South Monroe Street, Zip 53813–2054; tel. 608/723–2143, **A** 1 10 18 **F** 11 13 15 28 29 32 34 35 36 40 43 44 45 50 53 54 57 59 64 65 66 69 74 75 76 77 79 81 86 87 91 92 93 97 107 110 111 112 115 119 127 130 131 133 135 144 146 148 154 156 157 167 169
Primary Contact: Tami Chambers, President and Chief Executive Officer
CFO: Dawn Bandy, Chief Financial Officer
CMO: Jessica Varnam, Chief of Staff
CIO: Ken Kaiser, Coordinator Information Systems
CHR: Stacy L Martin, Director Human Resources
CNO: Jennifer Rutkowski, R.N., MSN, Vice President Professional Services
Web address: www.grantregional.com
Control: Other not–for–profit (including NFP Corporation) **Service**: General medical and surgical

Staffed Beds: 21 **Admissions**: 507 **Census**: 6 **Outpatient Visits**: 55352 **Births**: 149 **Total Expense ($000)**: 47857 **Payroll Expense ($000)**: 22233 **Personnel**: 230

MADISON—Dane County

MADISON VAH See William S. Middleton Memorial Veterans' Hospital

☐ **MENDOTA MENTAL HEALTH INSTITUTE (524008)**, 301 Troy Drive, Zip 53704–1599; tel. 608/301–1000, **A** 1 3 5 10 **F** 6 29 34 38 56 75 82 86 87 98 100 101 103 104 130 154
Primary Contact: Greg Van Rybroek, Chief Executive Officer
CFO: Stacie Schiereck, Director Management Services
CMO: Molli Martha Rolli, M.D., Medical Director
CNO: Jane Walters, Director of Nursing
Web address: www.dhfs.state.wi.us
Control: State, Government, Nonfederal **Service**: Psychiatric

Staffed Beds: 319 **Admissions**: 622 **Census**: 273 **Outpatient Visits**: 0 **Births**: 0 **Total Expense ($000)**: 123306 **Payroll Expense ($000)**: 73132 **Personnel**: 813

SELECT SPECIALTY HOSPITAL–MADISON (522008), 801 Braxton Place, Zip 53715–1415; tel. 608/260–2700, **A** 1 10 **F** 1 29 34 60 75 82 86 107 119 130 154 **P** 3 5 7 **S** Select Medical Corporation, Mechanicsburg, PA
Primary Contact: Marc Trznadel, Chief Executive Officer
CHR: Mallary Stramowski, Chief Human Resources Officer
CNO: Dana McKinney, Chief Nursing Officer
Web address: www.madison.selectspecialtyhospitals.com
Control: Corporation, Investor–owned (for–profit) **Service**: Acute long–term care hospital

Staffed Beds: 58 **Admissions**: 373 **Census**: 30 **Outpatient Visits**: 0 **Births**: 0 **Total Expense ($000)**: 27122 **Payroll Expense ($000)**: 12086 **Personnel**: 148

SSM HEALTH ST. MARY'S HOSPITAL (520083), 700 South Park Street, Zip 53715–1830; tel. 608/251–6100, **A** 1 3 5 10 19 **F** 9 11 13 15 17 20 22 24 28 29 34 40 43 53 56 64 70 72 76 77 78 80 81 82 85 86 89 90 98 100 101 102 103 107 108 111 116 118 119 130 141 146 154 **S** SSM Health, Saint Louis, MO
Primary Contact: Eric Thornton, President
CFO: Steve Caldwell, Vice President Finance and Chief Financial Officer
CHR: Linda Taplin Statz, System Director, Employee Experience
CNO: Ginger Malone MSN, RN-B, Chief Nursing Officer
Web address: https://www.ssmhealth.com/locations/st-marys-hospital-madison
Control: Church operated, Nongovernment, not–for–profit **Service**: General medical and surgical

Staffed Beds: 374 **Admissions**: 18099 **Census**: 257 **Outpatient Visits**: 95831 **Births**: 1888 **Total Expense ($000)**: 440862 **Payroll Expense ($000)**: 141295 **Personnel**: 1447

⇧ **UNITYPOINT HEALTH MERITER (520089)**, 202 South Park Street, Zip 53715–1507; tel. 608/417–6000, **A** 1 3 5 10 19 21 **S** UnityPoint Health, West Des Moines, IA
Primary Contact: James Arnett, Market President–Madison
CFO: Beth Erdman, Chief Financial Officer
CMO: Pam Wetzel, M.D., Market Chief Medical Officer
CIO: Denise Gomez, Assistant Vice President Information Systems
CNO: Sherry Casali, R.N., Market Chief Nursing Officer
Web address: www.meriter.com
Control: Other not–for–profit (including NFP Corporation) **Service**: General medical and surgical

Staffed Beds: 249 **Admissions**: 17155 **Census**: 227 **Outpatient Visits**: 360302 **Births**: 4589 **Total Expense ($000)**: 561918 **Payroll Expense ($000)**: 221352 **Personnel**: 2263

UNIVERSITY HOSPITAL (520098), 600 Highland Avenue, Zip 53792–0002; tel. 608/263–6400, (Includes AMERICAN FAMILY CHILDREN'S HOSPITAL, 1675 Highland Avenue, Madison, Wisconsin, Zip 53705, tel. 608/890–5437; Jeffrey S Poltawsky, Senior Vice President) **A** 1 2 3 5 8 10 19 **F** 7 12 15 16 17 20 22 24 28 29 34 36 40 43 51 53 54 56 60 61 64 70 72 77 78 80 81 82 86 87 88 89 93 98 100 102 103 104 107 108 111 116 118 119 130 131 136 137 138 140 141 147 154 **S** UW Health, Madison, WI
Primary Contact: Alan Kaplan, M.D., Chief Executive Officer
COO: Ron Sliwinski, Chief of Hospital Division
CFO: Robert Flannery, Chief Financial Officer
CMO: Peter Newcomer, M.D., Chief Medical Officer
CIO: Jocelyn DeWitt, Ph.D., Vice President and Chief Information Officer
Web address: www.uwhealth.org
Control: State, Government, Nonfederal **Service**: General medical and surgical

Staffed Beds: 675 **Admissions**: 29865 **Census**: 511 **Outpatient Visits**: 1203614 **Births**: 9 **Total Expense ($000)**: 2537049 **Payroll Expense ($000)**: 834562 **Personnel**: 10536

Hospitals, U.S. / WISCONSIN

☐ **UW HEALTH REHABILITATION HOSPITAL (523028)**, 5115 North Biltmore Lane, Zip 53718–2161; tel. 608/592–8100, **A**1 3 10 **F**29 34 75 86 90 **P**3 **S** UW Health, Madison, WI
Primary Contact: Kenneth Bowman, Chief Executive Officer
CFO: Karen Bindl, CPA, Controller
Web address: www.uwhealth.org
Control: Partnership, Investor–owned (for–profit) **Service**: Rehabilitation

Staffed Beds: 50 **Admissions**: 1281 **Census**: 46 **Outpatient Visits**: 0 **Births**: 0 **Total Expense ($000)**: 21665 **Payroll Expense ($000)**: 10400 **Personnel**: 138

✠ **WILLIAM S. MIDDLETON MEMORIAL VETERANS' HOSPITAL**, 2500 Overlook Terrace, Zip 53705–2286; tel. 608/256–1901, (Nonreporting) **A**1 3 5 **S** Department of Veterans Affairs, Washington, DC
Primary Contact: Christine Kleckner, Medical Center Director
CFO: Evarista Mikell, Assistant Finance Officer
CMO: Alan J Bridges, M.D., Chief of Staff
CIO: Randall Margenau, Chief Information Officer
CHR: Stuart Souders, Chief, Human Resources
CNO: Rebecca Kordahl, R.N., Associate Director, Patient Care Services
Web address: www.madison.va.gov
Control: Veterans Affairs, Government, federal **Service**: General medical and surgical

Staffed Beds: 98

MANITOWOC—Manitowoc County

✠ **HOLY FAMILY MEMORIAL (520107)**, 2300 Western Avenue, Zip 54220–3712, Mailing Address: P.O. Box 1450, Zip 54221–1450; tel. 920/320–2011, **A**1 2 10 **S** Froedtert ThedaCare Health, Inc., Milwaukee, WI
Primary Contact: Ryan T. Neville, FACHE, President Northeast Market
CFO: Patricia Huettl, Vice President Finance and Chief Financial Officer
CMO: Steve Driggers, M.D., Chief Medical Officer
CIO: Theron Pappas, Director Management Information Systems
CHR: Laura M Fielding, Administrative Director Organizational Development
CNO: Bonny Range, MSN, Chief Nursing Officer
Web address: www.hfmhealth.org
Control: Church operated, Nongovernment, not–for–profit **Service**: General medical and surgical

Staffed Beds: 58 **Admissions**: 1784 **Census**: 4 **Outpatient Visits**: 118220 **Births**: 94 **Total Expense ($000)**: 102526 **Payroll Expense ($000)**: 37920 **Personnel**: 393

MARINETTE—Marinette County

★ ⇧ **AURORA MEDICAL CENTER – BAY AREA (520113)**, 3003 University Drive, Zip 54143–4110; tel. 715/735–4200, **A**2 10 20 21 **F**3 7 11 13 15 17 28 29 30 31 34 36 40 43 44 45 50 51 54 57 59 65 70 71 74 75 76 78 79 80 81 82 85 86 87 89 92 93 94 96 107 108 109 110 111 113 114 115 119 120 121 123 124 130 131 135 143 146 147 148 167 169 **S** Advocate Aurora Health, Downers Grove, IL
Primary Contact: Edward A. Harding, FACHE, President
CFO: Daniel Cook, Director of Finance
CMO: Syed Ali, M.D., Chief Medical Officer
CNO: Nicole Swanson, Vice President of Nursing
Web address: www.bamc.org
Control: Other not–for–profit (including NFP Corporation) **Service**: General medical and surgical

Staffed Beds: 55 **Admissions**: 2221 **Census**: 23 **Outpatient Visits**: 100447 **Births**: 196 **Total Expense ($000)**: 97359 **Payroll Expense ($000)**: 34366 **Personnel**: 515

MARSHFIELD—Wood County

✠ △ **MARSHFIELD MEDICAL CENTER (520037)**, 611 St Joseph Avenue, Zip 54449–1898; tel. 715/387–1713, (Includes MARSHFIELD CHILDEN'S HOSPITAL, 611 Saint Joseph Avenue, Marshfield, Wisconsin, Zip 54449–1832, tel. 715/387–1713) **A**1 2 3 5 7 10 20 **S** Marshfield Clinic Health System, Marshfield, WI
Primary Contact: Robert S. Chaloner, President, Central Region
CFO: William J Hinner, Vice President Financial Analysis and Planning Ministry Health Care
CIO: Will Weider, Chief Information Officer
CHR: Cheryl F Zima, Vice President Human Resources Ministry Health Care
CNO: Robin Kretschman, MSN, R.N., Vice President Patient Care Services
Web address: www.stjosephs-marshfield.org
Control: Other not–for–profit (including NFP Corporation) **Service**: General medical and surgical

Staffed Beds: 205 **Admissions**: 11990 **Census**: 182 **Outpatient Visits**: 460430 **Births**: 967 **Total Expense ($000)**: 911555 **Payroll Expense ($000)**: 281522 **Personnel**: 3411

NORWOOD HEALTH CENTER (524019), 1600 North Chestnut Avenue, Zip 54449–1499; tel. 715/384–2188, (Total facility includes 32 beds in nursing home–type unit) **A**3 10 **F**3 30 50 69 75 98 99 100 101 102 103 106 128 130 143 148 154 **P**6
Primary Contact: Jordan Bruce, Administrator
CFO: Jo Timmerman, Manager Accounting
CHR: Larry Shear, Administrative Assistant
Web address: www.co.wood.wi.us/norwood/index.htm
Control: County, Government, Nonfederal **Service**: Psychiatric

Staffed Beds: 48 **Admissions**: 333 **Census**: 31 **Outpatient Visits**: 0 **Births**: 0 **Total Expense ($000)**: 9451 **Payroll Expense ($000)**: 3732 **Personnel**: 32

SAINT JOSEPH'S CHILDREN'S HOSPITAL See Marshfield Children's Hospital

MAUSTON—Juneau County

☐ **MILE BLUFF MEDICAL CENTER (520109)**, 1050 Division Street, Zip 53948–1997; tel. 608/847–6161, (Total facility includes 74 beds in nursing home–type unit) **A**1 10 20 **F**10 11 13 15 28 29 34 36 40 43 54 56 60 64 69 75 76 77 78 80 81 82 86 87 89 93 107 108 111 118 119 125 128 130 131 144 146 154 **P**2
Primary Contact: Dara Bartels, Chief Executive Officer
CFO: Francis James Fish, Vice President and Chief Financial Officer
CMO: Tim Bjelland Esq, Physician
CHR: Sue Wafle, Director, Human Resources
CNO: Jean Surguy, Vice President, Chief Nursing Officer
Web address: www.milebluff.com
Control: Other not–for–profit (including NFP Corporation) **Service**: General medical and surgical

Staffed Beds: 92 **Admissions**: 1069 **Census**: 97 **Outpatient Visits**: 183131 **Births**: 168 **Total Expense ($000)**: 121548 **Payroll Expense ($000)**: 40338 **Personnel**: 544

MEDFORD—Taylor County

✠ **ASPIRUS MEDFORD HOSPITAL & CLINICS (521324)**, 135 South Gibson Street, Zip 54451; tel. 715/748–8100, (Total facility includes 33 beds in nursing home–type unit) **A**1 3 10 18 **F**3 8 10 11 13 15 18 26 28 29 31 34 35 36 37 40 43 45 46 47 48 49 53 55 56 59 60 64 65 68 74 75 76 77 78 79 81 82 83 84 85 86 89 92 93 96 97 107 109 110 111 113 114 115 117 118 119 120 121 123 124 125 126 127 128 129 130 131 132 133 134 135 143 144 145 146 147 148 156 167 169 **P**8 **S** Aspirus, Inc., Wausau, WI
Primary Contact: Jason Troxell, President
CFO: Greg Shaw, Vice President, Finance
CMO: Clint Semrau, President Medical Staff
CIO: Todd Richardson, Chief Information Officer
CHR: Julie Zeps, Vice President Human Resources
CNO: Barb Lato, Chief Nursing Officer
Web address: www.aspirus.org
Control: Other not–for–profit (including NFP Corporation) **Service**: General medical and surgical

Staffed Beds: 54 **Admissions**: 936 **Census**: 44 **Outpatient Visits**: 72991 **Births**: 145 **Total Expense ($000)**: 86473 **Payroll Expense ($000)**: 27419 **Personnel**: 197

MENOMONEE FALLS—Waukesha County

★ ⇧ **ASCENSION WISCONSIN HOSPITAL – MENOMONEE FALLS CAMPUS (520214)**, N88W14275 Main Street Suite 100, Zip 53051–2315; tel. 262/415–2001, (Includes ASCENSION WISCONSIN HOSPITAL – GREENFIELD CAMPUS, 4935 South 76th Street Suite 100, Milwaukee, Wisconsin, Zip 53220–4305, tel. 414/567–3211; Daniel Gell, MSN, Market Chief Executive Officer; ASCENSION WISCONSIN HOSPITAL – WAUKESHA CAMPUS, 2325 Fox Run Boulevard Suite 100, Waukesha, Wisconsin, Zip 53188–6602, tel. 262/732–3865; Daniel Gell, MSN, Market Chief Executive Officer) **A**10 21 **F**3 34 59 65 86 114 119 157 **S** Ascension Healthcare, Saint Louis, MO
Primary Contact: Daniel Gell, MSN, Market Chief Executive Officer
COO: Vanessa Smith, Chief Operating Officer
CFO: Mark Kopser, Interim Chief Financial Officer
CMO: Dan Middlebrook, Chief Medical Officer
CIO: Ashwin Rego, Chief Information Officer
CHR: Carole King, Chief Human Resources Officer
CNO: Daniel Gell, MSN, Regional Chief Nursing Officer
Web address: www.ascensionwisconhospital.org
Control: Corporation, Investor–owned (for–profit) **Service**: General medical and surgical

Staffed Beds: 24 **Admissions**: 620 **Census**: 3 **Outpatient Visits**: 23338 **Births**: 0 **Total Expense ($000)**: 25001 **Payroll Expense ($000)**: 8075 **Personnel**: 30

Hospital, Medicare Provider Number, Address, Telephone, Approval, Facility, and Physician Codes, Health Care System

★ American Hospital Association (AHA) membership ○ Healthcare Facilities Accreditation Program ⇧ Center for Improvement in Healthcare Quality Accreditation
☐ The Joint Commission accreditation ◇ DNV Healthcare Inc. accreditation △ Commission on Accreditation of Rehabilitation Facilities (CARF) accreditation

Hospitals, U.S. / WISCONSIN

☒ **FROEDTERT MENOMONEE FALLS HOSPITAL (520103)**, W180 N8085 Town Hall Road, Zip 53051–3518, Mailing Address: P.O. Box 408, Zip 53052–0408; tel. 262/251–1000, **A**1 3 5 10 **S** Froedtert ThedaCare Health, Inc., Milwaukee, WI
Primary Contact: Teresa M. Lux, President and Chief Operating Officer
COO: Allen Ericson, Chief Operating Officer, Community Hospital Division and President, St. Joseph's Hospital
CFO: Scott Hawig, Senior Vice President of Finance, Chief Financial Officer and Treasurer
CMO: David Goldberg, M.D., Vice President Medical Affairs and Chief Medical Officer
CHR: Keith Allen, Senior Vice President and Chief Human Resources Officer
Web address: https://www.froedtert.com
Control: Other not–for–profit (including NFP Corporation) **Service**: General medical and surgical

> **Staffed Beds**: 202 **Admissions**: 8366 **Census**: 99 **Outpatient Visits**: 97302 **Births**: 733 **Total Expense ($000)**: 271128 **Payroll Expense ($000)**: 89760 **Personnel**: 974

MENOMONIE—Dunn County

☐ **MAYO CLINIC HEALTH SYSTEM – RED CEDAR IN MENOMONIE (521340)**, 2321 Stout Road, Zip 54751–2397; tel. 715/235–5531, **A**1 3 5 10 18 **F**15 28 29 34 38 40 43 54 55 56 60 64 77 78 80 81 82 86 87 89 90 93 99 100 101 102 103 104 107 108 111 119 130 131 144 147 154 **P**6 **S** Mayo Clinic, Rochester, MN
Primary Contact: Richard Helmers, M.D., Regional Vice President
CFO: Jeanie Lubinsky, Chief Financial Officer
CMO: Mark Deyo Svendsen, M.D., Medical Director
CIO: Frank Wrogg, Director Information Technology
CHR: Leann Wurtzel, Director Human Resources
Web address: www.rcmc-mhs.org
Control: Other not–for–profit (including NFP Corporation) **Service**: General medical and surgical

> **Staffed Beds**: 20 **Admissions**: 1082 **Census**: 15 **Outpatient Visits**: 133966 **Births**: 0 **Total Expense ($000)**: 96616 **Payroll Expense ($000)**: 39227 **Personnel**: 416

MEQUON—Ozaukee County

☒ **ASCENSION SACRED HEART REHABILITATION HOSPITAL (523025)**, 13111 North Port Washington Road, Zip 53097–2416; tel. 262/292–0400, **A**1 10 **F**9 29 34 56 64 77 86 90 93 100 102 103 130 131 **P**6 **S** Ascension Healthcare, Saint Louis, MO
Primary Contact: Julie Jolitz, Administrator
CFO: Matthew Hanselman, Chief Financial Officer
CMO: Rick Shimp, M.D., Chief Medical Officer
CIO: Gagan Singh, Chief Information Officer
CHR: Olivia Locklier, Vice President Organizational Effectiveness
CNO: Marlly Cadavid, Chief Nursing Officer
Web address: https://healthcare.ascension.org/locations/wisconsin/wimil/milwaukee-ascension-sacred-heart-rehabilitation-hospital
Control: Church operated, Nongovernment, not–for–profit **Service**: Rehabilitation

> **Staffed Beds**: 15 **Admissions**: 229 **Census**: 10 **Outpatient Visits**: 4973 **Births**: 0 **Total Expense ($000)**: 7803 **Payroll Expense ($000)**: 3869 **Personnel**: 54

MERRILL—Lincoln County

☒ **ASPIRUS MERRILL HOSPITAL & CLINICS, INC. (521339)**, 601 South Center Avenue, Zip 54452–3404; tel. 715/536–5511, **A**1 10 18 **F**8 15 30 34 40 43 64 68 71 74 77 79 81 84 85 86 87 89 92 93 107 108 111 119 127 130 133 143 144 147 154 **P**8 **S** Aspirus, Inc., Wausau, WI
Primary Contact: Jeffrey Wicklander, President
CFO: David Jirovec, Director Finance
CHR: Nancy Kwiesielewicz, Human Resources Manager
CNO: Kristine McGarigle, R.N., Vice President Patient Care
Web address: https://www.aspirus.org/find-a-location/aspirus-merrill-hospital-536
Control: Other not–for–profit (including NFP Corporation) **Service**: General medical and surgical

> **Staffed Beds**: 18 **Admissions**: 467 **Census**: 5 **Outpatient Visits**: 15530 **Births**: 0 **Total Expense ($000)**: 22949 **Payroll Expense ($000)**: 8852 **Personnel**: 124

GOOD SAMARITAN HOSPITAL See Aspirus Merrill Hospital & Clinics, Inc.

MILWAUKEE—Milwaukee County

☒ **ASCENSION COLUMBIA ST. MARY'S HOSPITAL MILWAUKEE (520051)**, 2301 North Lake Drive, Zip 53211–4508; tel. 414/291–1000, (Includes ASCENSION COLUMBIA ST. MARY'S HOSPITAL OZAUKEE, 13111 North Port Washington Road, Mequon, Wisconsin, Zip 53097–2416, tel. 262/243–7300; John Joyce, President; ASCENSION COLUMBIA ST. MARY'S WOMEN'S MEDICAL CENTER, 2323 North Lake Drive, Milwaukee, Wisconsin, Zip 53211–9682, P O Box 503, Zip 53201–0503, tel. 414/291–1000; Andre Storey, President; COLUMBIA ST. MARY'S COLUMBIA HOSPITAL, 2025 East Newport Avenue, Milwaukee, Wisconsin, Zip 53211–2990, tel. 414/961–3300) **A**1 2 3 5 10 19 **F**5 9 12 13 15 16 17 20 22 24 28 29 34 36 38 40 43 51 53 54 56 64 70 72 76 77 78 80 81 86 87 89 93 100 102 103 104 107 108 111 116 118 119 130 144 147 **P**6 **S** Ascension Healthcare, Saint Louis, MO
Primary Contact: Andre Storey, President
COO: Duke Walker, Interim Chief Operating Officer
CFO: Rhonda Anderson, Executive Vice President Finance and Chief Financial Officer
CMO: David Shapiro, M.D., Vice President Medical Affairs and Chief Medical Officer
CIO: Mary Paul, Chief Information Officer
CHR: Cheryl Hill, Vice President Human Resources
CNO: Sheila Johnson, Chief Nursing Officer
Web address: https://healthcare.ascension.org/locations/wisconsin/wimil/milwaukee-ascension-columbia-st-marys-hospital-milwaukee/
Control: Church operated, Nongovernment, not–for–profit **Service**: General medical and surgical

> **Staffed Beds**: 230 **Admissions**: 13293 **Census**: 218 **Outpatient Visits**: 909938 **Births**: 2419 **Total Expense ($000)**: 760829 **Payroll Expense ($000)**: 130853 **Personnel**: 2267

☒ **ASCENSION SOUTHEAST WISCONSIN HOSPITAL – ST. JOSEPH'S CAMPUS (520136)**, 5000 West Chambers Street, Zip 53210–1650; tel. 414/447–2000, **A**1 2 3 5 10 **F**4 5 6 11 13 15 17 20 22 29 34 40 43 53 54 56 64 70 72 76 77 78 80 81 86 87 89 93 100 107 108 111 118 119 130 131 144 146 147 154 **P**6 **S** Ascension Healthcare, Saint Louis, MO
Primary Contact: Peter Stamas, M.D., Chief Administrative Officer
CFO: Michael Petitt, Director of Finance
CMO: Rita Hanson, M.D., Vice President Medical Affairs
CIO: Andrew Donovan, Regional Director Information Services
CHR: Christopher Morris, Senior Director, Human Resources
Web address: www.mywheaton.org/stjoseph
Control: Church operated, Nongovernment, not–for–profit **Service**: General medical and surgical

> **Staffed Beds**: 59 **Admissions**: 4297 **Census**: 61 **Outpatient Visits**: 136543 **Births**: 1484 **Total Expense ($000)**: 129619 **Payroll Expense ($000)**: 40273 **Personnel**: 486

☒ **ASCENSION ST. FRANCIS HOSPITAL (520078)**, 3237 South 16th Street, Zip 53215; tel. 414/647–5000, **A**1 2 10 **F**4 5 11 13 15 17 20 22 28 29 34 38 40 43 54 56 61 64 70 77 78 80 81 82 86 87 93 98 100 101 102 103 104 107 108 111 118 119 130 131 146 147 154 **P**6 **S** Ascension Healthcare, Saint Louis, MO
Primary Contact: Jonathon Matuszewski, Hospital Administrator
CFO: Aaron Bridgeland, Director Finance
CMO: Michelle Graham, M.D., Vice President Medical Affairs
CIO: Gregory Smith, Senior Vice President and Chief Information Officer
Web address: https://healthcare.ascension.org/locations/wisconsin/wiwhe/milwaukee-ascension-st-francis-hospital
Control: Church operated, Nongovernment, not–for–profit **Service**: General medical and surgical

> **Staffed Beds**: 26 **Admissions**: 2642 **Census**: 39 **Outpatient Visits**: 133031 **Births**: 104 **Total Expense ($000)**: 136377 **Payroll Expense ($000)**: 32041 **Personnel**: 353

Hospitals, U.S. / WISCONSIN

★ △ ⇑ **AURORA ST. LUKE'S MEDICAL CENTER (520138)**, 2900 West Oklahoma Avenue, Zip 53215–4330, Mailing Address: P.O. Box 2901, Zip 53201–2901; tel. 414/649–6000, (Includes AURORA SINAI MEDICAL CENTER, 945 North 12th Street, Milwaukee, Wisconsin, Zip 53233–1337, P O Box 342, Zip 53201–0342, tel. 414/219–2000; Nkem Iroegbu, M.D., M.P.H., President; AURORA ST. LUKE'S SOUTH SHORE, 5900 South Lake Drive, Cudahy, Wisconsin, Zip 53110–8903, tel. 414/769–9000; Nkem Iroegbu, M.D., M.P.H., President) **A**2 3 5 7 8 10 19 21 **F**1 3 4 11 12 15 17 18 20 22 24 26 28 29 30 31 34 35 36 37 38 40 41 43 44 45 46 47 48 49 50 51 54 56 57 58 59 60 64 65 68 70 74 75 78 79 80 81 82 84 85 86 87 89 90 91 92 93 94 95 96 102 103 107 108 109 110 111 115 116 117 118 119 120 121 123 124 126 129 130 131 132 135 136 137 138 139 140 142 145 146 148 154 167 **S** Advocate Aurora Health, Downers Grove, IL
Primary Contact: Jennifer Schomburg, President
CFO: Nan Nelson, Senior Vice President Finance
CIO: Philip Loftus, Ph.D., Vice President and Chief Information Officer
CHR: Thomas C Ter Horst, Vice President Human Resources
CNO: Faye Zwieg, R.N., Vice President and Chief Nursing Officer
Web address: https://www.aurorahealthcare.org/locations/hospital/aurora-st-lukes-medical-center/
Control: Other not–for–profit (including NFP Corporation) **Service**: General medical and surgical

Staffed Beds: 633 **Admissions**: 25139 **Census**: 493 **Outpatient Visits**: 515083 **Births**: 0 **Total Expense ($000)**: 1445767 **Payroll Expense ($000)**: 372964 **Personnel**: 6375

CHILDREN'S HOSPITAL OF WISCONSIN See Children's Wisconsin

⊞ **CHILDREN'S WISCONSIN (523300)**, 8915 West Connell Avenue, Zip 53226–3067, Mailing Address: P.O. Box 1997, Zip 53201–1997; tel. 414/266–2000, **A**1 3 5 10 **F**12 20 22 24 28 29 34 36 38 40 43 51 54 60 61 64 72 75 77 78 81 82 86 87 88 89 93 99 100 102 104 107 108 111 116 118 119 130 131 136 137 138 140 141 **S** Children's Wisconsin, Milwaukee, WI
Primary Contact: Peggy N. Troy, President and Chief Executive Officer
CFO: Marc Cadieux, Corporate Vice President and Chief Financial Officer
CMO: Michael Gutzeit, M.D., Chief Medical Officer
CIO: Michael B Nauman, Chief Information Officer
CHR: Thomas Shanahan, Vice President, Human Resources
CNO: Nancy K Korom, Chief Nursing Officer and Vice President
Web address: www.chw.org
Control: Other not–for–profit (including NFP Corporation) **Service**: Children's general medical and surgical

Staffed Beds: 192 **Admissions**: 9938 **Census**: 186 **Outpatient Visits**: 446404 **Births**: 0 **Total Expense ($000)**: 805478 **Payroll Expense ($000)**: 252384 **Personnel**: 3045

⊞ △ **CLEMENT J. ZABLOCKI VETERANS' ADMINISTRATION MEDICAL CENTER**, 5000 West National Avenue, Zip 53295–0001; tel. 414/384–2000, (Nonreporting) **A**1 2 3 5 7 **S** Department of Veterans Affairs, Washington, DC
Primary Contact: James D. McLain, Executive Director
COO: James McClain, Deputy Director
CFO: John Lasota, Assistant Finance Officer
CMO: Michael Erdmann, M.D., Chief of Staff
CIO: Bryan Vail, Chief Information Officer
CHR: Kay Schwieger, Chief Human Resources Officer
CNO: Mary E. Brunn, R.N., Acting Associate Director Nursing
Web address: www.milwaukee.va.gov/
Control: Veterans Affairs, Government, federal **Service**: General medical and surgical

Staffed Beds: 265

COLUMBIA ST MARY'S–COLUMBIA See Columbia St. Mary's Columbia Hospital

COLUMBIA ST MARY'S–MILWAUKEE See Ascension Columbia St. Mary's Women's Medical Center

⊞ △ **FROEDTERT AND THE MEDICAL COLLEGE OF WISCONSIN FROEDTERT HOSPITAL (520177)**, 9200 West Wisconsin Avenue, Zip 53226–3596, Mailing Address: P.O. Box 26099, Zip 53226–0099; tel. 414/805–3000, **A**1 2 3 5 7 8 10 19 **S** Froedtert ThedaCare Health, Inc., Milwaukee, WI
Primary Contact: Eric Conley, President
CFO: Scott Hawig, Senior Vice President Finance, Chief Financial Officer and Treasurer
CMO: Lee Biblo, M.D., Chief Medical Officer
CHR: Keith Allen, Senior Vice President and Chief Human Resources Officer
CNO: Kathleen Bechtel, MSN, R.N., Vice President Patient Care Services and Chief Nursing Officer
Web address: www.froedtert.com
Control: Other not–for–profit (including NFP Corporation) **Service**: General medical and surgical

Staffed Beds: 717 **Admissions**: 37160 **Census**: 592 **Outpatient Visits**: 966125 **Births**: 3554 **Total Expense ($000)**: 2249837 **Payroll Expense ($000)**: 526973 **Personnel**: 6302

⇑ **MENTAL HEALTH EMERGENCY CENTER (524044)**, 1525 North 12th Street, Zip 53205–2591; tel. 414/966–3030, **A**10 21 **F**4 29 34 64 75 86 87 98 99 102 103 130
Web address: www.mentalhealthmke.org
Control: Other not–for–profit (including NFP Corporation) **Service**: Psychiatric

Staffed Beds: 6 **Admissions**: 96 **Census**: 1 **Births**: 0 **Total Expense ($000)**: 16469 **Payroll Expense ($000)**: 12251 **Personnel**: 74

MILWAUKEE REHABILITATION HOSPITAL AT GREENFIELD (523029), 3200 South 103rd Street, Zip 53227–4104; tel. 414/441–0500, **F**29 34 60 75 77 86 90 **P**2 **S** Nobis Rehabilitation Partners, Allen, TX
Primary Contact: Shelley Stubbendeck, Chief Executive Officer
Web address: https://www.milwaukee-rehabhospital.com/
Control: Partnership, Investor–owned (for–profit) **Service**: Rehabilitation

Staffed Beds: 35 **Admissions**: 724 **Census**: 27 **Outpatient Visits**: 0 **Births**: 0 **Total Expense ($000)**: 16735 **Payroll Expense ($000)**: 6341 **Personnel**: 85

MILWAUKEE VAMC See Clement J. Zablocki Veterans' Administration Medical Center

⊞ **SELECT SPECIALTY HOSPITAL–MILWAUKEE (522006)**, 8901 West Lincoln Avenue, 2nd Floor, Zip 53227–2409, Mailing Address: West Allis, tel. 414/328–7700, (Includes SELECT SPECIALTY HOSPITAL–MILWAUKEE, ST. LUKE'S CAMPUS, 2900 West Oklahoma Avenue, Milwaukee, Wisconsin, Zip 53215–4330, tel. 414/647–3995; Shital Tipnis, Chief Executive Officer) **A**1 10 **F**1 29 38 60 130 **S** Select Medical Corporation, Mechanicsburg, PA
Primary Contact: Brandon James. Weiland, Chief Executive Officer
CMO: Matt Mathai, M.D., Medical Director
CHR: Chris Froh, Senior Coordinator Human Resources
CNO: Jane Cerra, Market Nurse Executive and Chief Nursing Officer
Web address: https://www.selectspecialtyhospitals.com/locations-and-tours/wi/west-allis/milwaukee-west-allis/
Control: Corporation, Investor–owned (for–profit) **Service**: Acute long–term care hospital

Staffed Beds: 34 **Admissions**: 258 **Census**: 22 **Outpatient Visits**: 0 **Births**: 0 **Total Expense ($000)**: 18101 **Payroll Expense ($000)**: 7391 **Personnel**: 110

SELECT SPECIALTY HOSPITAL–MILWAUKEE, ST. LUKE'S CAMPUS See Select Specialty Hospital–Milwaukee, Milwaukee

MINOCQUA—Oneida County

⊞ **MARSHFIELD MEDICAL CENTER – MINOCQUA (520212)**, 9576 State Highway 70, Zip 54548; tel. 715/358–1710, **A**1 10 **S** Marshfield Clinic Health System, Marshfield, WI
Primary Contact: Ty Erickson, Chief Administrative Officer
Web address: www.marshfieldclinic.org
Control: Other not–for–profit (including NFP Corporation) **Service**: General medical and surgical

Staffed Beds: 19 **Admissions**: 1103 **Census**: 11 **Outpatient Visits**: 110765 **Births**: 221 **Total Expense ($000)**: 110187 **Payroll Expense ($000)**: 33367 **Personnel**: 446

MONROE—Green County

MONROE CLINIC See SSM Health Monroe Clinic

Hospital, Medicare Provider Number, Address, Telephone, Approval, Facility, and Physician Codes, Health Care System

★ American Hospital Association (AHA) membership
□ The Joint Commission accreditation
○ Healthcare Facilities Accreditation Program
◇ DNV Healthcare Inc. accreditation
⇑ Center for Improvement in Healthcare Quality Accreditation
△ Commission on Accreditation of Rehabilitation Facilities (CARF) accreditation

Hospitals, U.S. / WISCONSIN

☒ **SSM HEALTH MONROE CLINIC (520028)**, 515 22nd Avenue, Zip 53566–1598; tel. 608/324–2000, **A**1 3 5 10 13 **F**6 9 13 15 17 20 22 28 29 34 38 40 43 51 55 56 60 62 63 70 75 76 77 78 80 81 82 86 89 90 93 99 100 101 102 103 104 107 108 111 119 130 131 144 147 154 **S** SSM Health, Saint Louis, MO
Primary Contact: Jane Curran-Meuli, President
CMO: Darren Pipp, M.D., Chief Medical Officer
CHR: Jane Monahan, Vice President Ministry, Spiritual Care and Human Resources
Web address: www.monroeclinic.org
Control: Other not–for–profit (including NFP Corporation) **Service**: General medical and surgical

> **Staffed Beds**: 58 **Admissions**: 2255 **Census**: 25 **Outpatient Visits**: 364008 **Births**: 461 **Total Expense ($000)**: 203808 **Payroll Expense ($000)**: 86317 **Personnel**: 791

NEENAH—Winnebago County

☐ **CHILDREN'S HOSPITAL OF WISCONSIN–FOX VALLEY (523302)**, 130 Second Street, Zip 54956–2883; tel. 920/969–7900, **A**1 10 **F**34 72 75 86 89 93 130 154 **P**6 **S** Children's Wisconsin, Milwaukee, WI
Primary Contact: Peggy N. Troy, President and Chief Executive Officer
COO: Debra Franckowiak, Executive Director
CFO: Marc Cadieux, Corporate Vice President and Chief Financial Officer
CMO: Paul Myers, M.D., Neonatologist and Chief Medical Officer
CIO: Michael B Nauman, Chief Information Officer and Corporate Vice President
CHR: Thomas Shanahan, Vice President, Human Resources
CNO: Nancy K Korom, Chief Nursing Officer and Vice President
Web address: www.chw.org
Control: Other not–for–profit (including NFP Corporation) **Service**: Children's general medical and surgical

> **Staffed Beds**: 21 **Admissions**: 612 **Census**: 16 **Outpatient Visits**: 4248 **Births**: 0 **Total Expense ($000)**: 32482 **Payroll Expense ($000)**: 14727 **Personnel**: 112

☒ **THEDACARE REGIONAL MEDICAL CENTER–NEENAH (520045)**, 130 Second Street, Zip 54956–2883, Mailing Address: P.O. Box 2021, Zip 54957–2021; tel. 920/729–3100, **A**1 3 5 10 19 **F**4 5 9 12 13 15 17 20 28 29 34 40 43 51 64 70 75 76 78 80 81 82 86 88 90 98 100 107 108 111 118 119 130 147 154 **S** Froedtert ThedaCare Health, Inc., Milwaukee, WI
Primary Contact: Lynn Detterman, Senior Vice President, President, ThedaCare South Region
CFO: Tim Olson, Senior Vice President Finance
CMO: Gregory L Long, M.D., Chief Medical Officer
CIO: Keith Livingston, Senior Vice President and Chief Information Officer
Web address: www.thedacare.org
Control: Other not–for–profit (including NFP Corporation) **Service**: General medical and surgical

> **Staffed Beds**: 160 **Admissions**: 8499 **Census**: 95 **Outpatient Visits**: 116995 **Births**: 1659 **Total Expense ($000)**: 223029 **Payroll Expense ($000)**: 73784 **Personnel**: 876

NEILLSVILLE—Clark County

★ **MARSHFIELD MEDICAL CENTER – NEILSVILLE (521323)**, N3708 River Avenue, Zip 54456–7218; tel. 715/743–3101, **A**10 18 **S** Marshfield Clinic Health System, Marshfield, WI
Primary Contact: Robert S. Chaloner, President, Central Region
CMO: Timothy Meyer, M.D., Chief of Staff
CIO: Derrick Longdo, Director Information Systems
CHR: Tamie Zarak, Director Human Resources
Web address: www.memorialmedcenter.org
Control: Other not–for–profit (including NFP Corporation) **Service**: General medical and surgical

> **Staffed Beds**: 10 **Admissions**: 211 **Census**: 3 **Outpatient Visits**: 30678 **Births**: 0 **Total Expense ($000)**: 28030 **Payroll Expense ($000)**: 10503 **Personnel**: 150

NEW BERLIN—Waukesha County

★ ⇧ **FROEDTERT COMMUNITY HOSPITAL – NEW BERLIN (520213)**, 4805 South Moorland Road, Zip 53151–7401; tel. 262/796–0001, (Includes FROEDTERT COMMUNITY HOSPITAL – PEWAUKEE, 209 Pewaukee Road, Pewaukee, Wisconsin, Zip 53072, tel. 262/956–6150; Allen Ericson, President) **A**21 **S** Froedtert ThedaCare Health, Inc., Milwaukee, WI
Primary Contact: Allen Ericson, Chief Executive Officer
CFO: Scott Hawig, Senior Vice President Finance, Chief Financial Officer and Treasurer
CMO: David Goldberg, M.D., Board Vice Chair and Chief Clinical Officer
CIO: Sony Jacob, Senior Vice President, Chief Information Officer
CHR: Eric Humphrey, Senior Vice President Human Resources
Web address: https://www.froedtert.com/locations/hospital/froedtert-community-hospital-new-berlin
Control: Other not–for–profit (including NFP Corporation) **Service**: General medical and surgical

> **Staffed Beds**: 8 **Admissions**: 154 **Census**: 1 **Outpatient Visits**: 11808 **Births**: 0 **Total Expense ($000)**: 6738 **Payroll Expense ($000)**: 2987 **Personnel**: 27

NEW LONDON—Outagamie County

☒ **THEDACARE MEDICAL CENTER–NEW LONDON (521326)**, 1405 Mill Street, Zip 54961–0307, Mailing Address: P.O. Box 307, Zip 54961–0307; tel. 920/531–2000, **A**1 10 18 **F**11 15 28 29 34 40 43 64 75 78 80 81 82 86 89 90 93 107 108 111 119 130 146 154 **S** Froedtert ThedaCare Health, Inc., Milwaukee, WI
Primary Contact: Kellie Diedrick, Vice President
CFO: Betty Gehring, Finance Director, Operations
CMO: Paul Hoell, M.D., President Medical Staff
CNO: Peggy School, Director of Nursing
Web address: www.thedacare.org
Control: Other not–for–profit (including NFP Corporation) **Service**: General medical and surgical

> **Staffed Beds**: 25 **Admissions**: 632 **Census**: 8 **Outpatient Visits**: 55648 **Births**: 0 **Total Expense ($000)**: 32012 **Payroll Expense ($000)**: 14667 **Personnel**: 140

NEW RICHMOND—St. Croix County

☒ **WESTFIELDS HOSPITAL AND CLINIC (521345)**, 535 Hospital Road, Zip 54017–1449; tel. 715/243–2600, **A**1 3 10 18 **F**5 13 15 28 29 34 38 40 43 56 64 75 76 77 78 80 81 86 87 89 93 104 107 111 119 130 131 144 154 **P**8 **S** HealthPartners, Bloomington, MN
Primary Contact: Steven Massey, President and Chief Executive Officer
CFO: Jason J. Luhrs, Vice President Fiscal Services
CMO: David O DeGear, M.D., Vice President Medical Affairs
CIO: Patrice P Wolff, Director Information Services
CHR: Chad P Engstrom, Director Human Resources
Web address: www.westfieldshospital.com
Control: Other not–for–profit (including NFP Corporation) **Service**: General medical and surgical

> **Staffed Beds**: 25 **Admissions**: 967 **Census**: 10 **Outpatient Visits**: 118491 **Births**: 99 **Total Expense ($000)**: 86120 **Payroll Expense ($000)**: 26789 **Personnel**: 295

OCONOMOWOC—Waukesha County

OCONOMOWOC MEMORIAL HOSPITAL See Prohealth Oconomowoc Memorial Hospital

☒ **PROHEALTH OCONOMOWOC MEMORIAL HOSPITAL (520062)**, 791 Summit Avenue, Zip 53066–3896; tel. 262/569–9400, **A**1 2 10 **F**11 13 15 20 22 29 40 43 54 56 64 70 72 75 76 77 78 81 87 89 100 107 108 111 119 130 131 146 154 **S** ProHealth Care, Inc., Waukesha, WI
Primary Contact: Susan A. Edwards, President and Chief Executive Officer
COO: Mary Jo O'Malley, R.N., MS, Vice President Diagnostics and Support Services
CMO: Brian Lipman, M.D., Medical Director and Medical Staff Services
CIO: Christine Bessler, Vice President Information Services
CHR: Edward Malindzak, Chief Human Resources Officer
Web address: https://www.prohealthcare.org/locations/profile/hospital-oconomowoc/
Control: Other not–for–profit (including NFP Corporation) **Service**: General medical and surgical

> **Staffed Beds**: 63 **Admissions**: 2773 **Census**: 24 **Outpatient Visits**: 85554 **Births**: 433 **Total Expense ($000)**: 122650 **Payroll Expense ($000)**: 34085 **Personnel**: 279

☒ **ROGERS BEHAVIORAL HEALTH (524018)**, 34700 Valley Road, Zip 53066–4599; tel. 262/646–4411, (Includes ROGERS MEMORIAL HOSPITAL–BROWN DEER, 4600 West Schroeder Drive, Brown Deer, Wisconsin, Zip 53223, tel. 414/865–2500; Jim Kubicek, Vice President, Operations; ROGERS MEMORIAL HOSPITAL–WEST ALLIS, 11101 West Lincoln Avenue, West Allis, Wisconsin, Zip 53227, tel. 414/327–3000; T Orvin Fillman, Dr.PH, Vice President, Operations) **A**1 3 10 **F**4 5 29 34 38 53 54 75 86 87 98 99 100 101 102 103 104 130 154
Primary Contact: Cindy Meyer, Chief Executive Officer
COO: Ashley Muchnick, Chief Operating Officer
CFO: Gerald A Noll, Chief Financial Officer
CMO: Peter M Lake, M.D., Chief Medical Officer
CIO: Wayne Mattson, Management Information Systems Specialist
CHR: Stacy Bably, Chief Human Resources
CNO: Teresa L Schultz, R.N., Vice President, Patient Care
Web address: www.rogershospital.org
Control: Other not–for–profit (including NFP Corporation) **Service**: Psychiatric

> **Staffed Beds**: 202 **Admissions**: 8916 **Census**: 162 **Outpatient Visits**: 91858 **Births**: 0 **Total Expense ($000)**: 228735 **Payroll Expense ($000)**: 106647 **Personnel**: 1398

OCONTO—Oconto County

⇧ **BELLIN HEALTH OCONTO HOSPITAL (521356)**, 820 Arbutus Avenue, Zip 54153–2004, Mailing Address: PO Box 23400, Green Bay, Zip 54305–3400; tel. 920/835–1100, **A**10 18 21 **F**15 18 26 29 30 31 35 40 43 45 46 47 48 49 51 64 78 80 81 82 90 91 92 96 99 100 101 107 110 111 115 117 119 123 124 127 129 130 134 144 145 148 154 156 167 169 **P**6
Primary Contact: Julie Bieber, Vice President
CHR: Troy L Koebke, Human Resource Director
Web address: www.bellin.org/facilities_amenities/oconto_hospital_medical_center/
Control: Other not–for–profit (including NFP Corporation) **Service:** General medical and surgical

Staffed Beds: 10 **Admissions:** 160 **Census:** 5 **Outpatient Visits:** 24651 **Births:** 0 **Total Expense ($000):** 79805 **Payroll Expense ($000):** 33321 **Personnel:** 361

OCONTO FALLS—Oconto County

★ **HSHS ST. CLARE MEMORIAL HOSPITAL (521310)**, 855 South Main Street, Zip 54154–1296; tel. 920/846–3444, **A**10 18 **F**3 11 15 28 29 30 34 35 40 43 44 50 56 57 59 64 65 75 77 79 80 81 85 86 87 89 90 94 96 107 108 110 111 114 119 127 129 130 132 133 144 146 148 **S** HSHS Hospital Sisters Health System, Springfield, IL
Primary Contact: Christopher Brabant, President and Chief Executive Officer
CFO: Greg Simia, Chief Financial Officer
CMO: Richard Cooley, M.D., Chief Physician Executive
CIO: Shane Miller, Chief Information Officer
CHR: Christine Jensema, Chief Human Resources Officer
CNO: Paula Hafeman, Chief Nursing Officer
Web address: www.stclarememorial.org
Control: Church operated, Nongovernment, not–for–profit **Service:** General medical and surgical

Staffed Beds: 22 **Admissions:** 368 **Census:** 2 **Outpatient Visits:** 19238 **Births:** 0 **Total Expense ($000):** 32806 **Payroll Expense ($000):** 8787 **Personnel:** 103

OSCEOLA—Polk County

★ **OSCEOLA MEDICAL CENTER (521318)**, 2600 65th Avenue, Zip 54020–4370, Mailing Address: P.O. Box 218, Zip 54020–0218; tel. 715/294–2111, **A**10 18 **F**11 13 15 28 29 34 40 43 56 64 70 75 76 77 78 81 82 86 87 93 107 111 119 146
Primary Contact: Kelly Macken–Marble, Chief Executive Officer
CMO: Rene Milner, Chief Medical Officer
CIO: Shawn Kammerud, Manager Information Services
CHR: Margie Evenson, Manager Human Resources
Web address: www.osceolamedicalcenter.com
Control: Other not–for–profit (including NFP Corporation) **Service:** General medical and surgical

Staffed Beds: 13 **Admissions:** 383 **Census:** 5 **Outpatient Visits:** 34667 **Births:** 76 **Total Expense ($000):** 47499 **Payroll Expense ($000):** 17878 **Personnel:** 209

OSHKOSH—Winnebago County

★ **ASCENSION NORTHEAST WISCONSIN MERCY HOSPITAL (520048)**, 500 South Oakwood Road, Zip 54904–7944; tel. 920/223–2000, **A**2 10 **F**4 5 9 13 15 17 20 22 28 29 34 40 43 53 56 60 64 70 75 76 78 80 81 86 87 90 93 98 100 101 102 103 104 107 108 111 116 118 119 130 131 144 147 154 **P**6 **S** Ascension Healthcare, Saint Louis, MO
Primary Contact: Shane Carter, R.N., President
CFO: Jeff Badger, Chief Financial Officer
CMO: Mark W Kehrberg, M.D., Senior Vice President and Chief Medical Officer
CIO: Will Weider, Chief Information Officer
CHR: Vince Gallucci, Senior Vice President Human Resources
Web address: www.affinityhealth.org
Control: Church operated, Nongovernment, not–for–profit **Service:** General medical and surgical

Staffed Beds: 41 **Admissions:** 3219 **Census:** 41 **Outpatient Visits:** 114661 **Births:** 223 **Total Expense ($000):** 93246 **Payroll Expense ($000):** 26101 **Personnel:** 303

★ ⇧ **AURORA MEDICAL CENTER OF OSHKOSH (520198)**, 855 North Westhaven Drive, Zip 54904–7668; tel. 920/456–6000, **A**2 10 19 21 **F**3 8 11 12 13 15 17 18 20 22 26 28 29 30 31 34 36 37 40 43 47 49 53 54 60 64 68 70 71 72 74 75 76 78 79 80 81 82 85 86 87 89 92 93 94 107 108 109 110 111 113 114 115 117 118 119 120 121 123 124 126 129 130 131 135 145 146 147 148 154 160 161 167 169 **S** Advocate Aurora Health, Downers Grove, IL
Primary Contact: Jeffrey Bard, President
CFO: Brian McGinnis, Director Finance
CIO: Philip Loftus, Ph.D., Vice President and Chief Information Officer
CHR: Russ Haase, Director Human Resources
CNO: Mary Beth Kingston, Ph.D., R.N., MSN, Executive Vice President and Chief Nursing Officer
Web address: www.aurorahealthcare.com
Control: Other not–for–profit (including NFP Corporation) **Service:** General medical and surgical

Staffed Beds: 83 **Admissions:** 3632 **Census:** 40 **Outpatient Visits:** 195366 **Births:** 762 **Total Expense ($000):** 189454 **Payroll Expense ($000):** 51992 **Personnel:** 1300

OSSEO—Trempealeau County

☐ **MAYO CLINIC HEALTH SYSTEM – OAKRIDGE IN OSSEO (521302)**, 13025 Eighth Street, Zip 54758–7634, Mailing Address: P.O. Box 70, Zip 54758–0070; tel. 715/597–3121, **A**1 10 18 **F**15 28 29 34 38 40 43 54 56 64 77 80 86 87 89 90 93 107 130 144 154 **P**6 **S** Mayo Clinic, Rochester, MN
Primary Contact: Richard Helmers, M.D., Regional Vice President
Web address: www.mayoclinichealthsystem.org/locations/osseo
Control: Other not–for–profit (including NFP Corporation) **Service:** General medical and surgical

Staffed Beds: 13 **Admissions:** 482 **Census:** 11 **Outpatient Visits:** 37744 **Births:** 0 **Total Expense ($000):** 32454 **Payroll Expense ($000):** 13690 **Personnel:** 134

PARK FALLS—Price County

FLAMBEAU HOSPITAL See Marshfield Medical Center – Park Falls

★ **MARSHFIELD MEDICAL CENTER – PARK FALLS (FORMERLY FLAMBEAU HOSPITAL) (521325)**, 98 Sherry Avenue, Zip 54552–1467, Mailing Address: P.O. Box 310, Zip 54552–0310; tel. 715/762–2484, **A**10 18 **S** Marshfield Clinic Health System, Marshfield, WI
Primary Contact: Ty Erickson, Chief Administrative Officer
CMO: Yusuf Kasirye, M.D., Chief of Staff
CHR: Elizabeth Harrop, Director, Human Resources
CNO: Elizabeth Schreiber, R.N., Director Patient Care Services
Web address: https://www.marshfieldclinic.org/locations/centers/park%20 falls%20-%20marshfield%20medical%20center
Control: Other not–for–profit (including NFP Corporation) **Service:** General medical and surgical

Staffed Beds: 25 **Admissions:** 344 **Census:** 5 **Outpatient Visits:** 33567 **Births:** 0 **Total Expense ($000):** 27020 **Payroll Expense ($000):** 10554 **Personnel:** 133

PLATTEVILLE—Grant County

◇ **SOUTHWEST HEALTH (521354)**, 1400 Eastside Road, Zip 53818–9800; tel. 608/348–2331, (Includes SOUTHWEST HEALTH CENTER NURSING HOME, 808 South Washington Street, Cuba City, Wisconsin, Zip 53807, tel. 608/744–2161) **A**1 10 18 **F**6 7 13 15 28 29 34 36 40 43 56 64 75 76 77 80 81 82 86 87 93 98 100 101 102 103 104 107 111 130 131 144 147 154 **P**2
Primary Contact: Dan D. Rohrbach, President
CFO: Matthew Streeter, Chief Financial Officer
CMO: Andrew Klann, D.O., Chief of Staff
CIO: Todd Lull, Director Information Technology
CHR: Holly Beehn, Director Human Resources
CNO: Suzi Okey, Director of Nursing
Web address: www.southwesthealth.org
Control: Other not–for–profit (including NFP Corporation) **Service:** General medical and surgical

Staffed Beds: 35 **Admissions:** 1234 **Census:** 11 **Outpatient Visits:** 106598 **Births:** 243 **Total Expense ($000):** 90142 **Payroll Expense ($000):** 42588 **Personnel:** 490

Hospitals, U.S. / WISCONSIN

PLEASANT PRAIRIE—Kenosha County

FROEDTERT SOUTH – ST. CATHERINE'S MEDICAL CENTER See Froedtert Pleasant Prairie Hospital

PORTAGE—Columbia County

ASPIRUS DIVINE SAVIOR HOSPITAL & CLINICS (520041), 2817 New Pinery Road, Zip 53901-9240, Mailing Address: P.O. Box 387, Zip 53901-0387; tel. 608/742-4131, **A**1 10 **F**3 8 13 15 26 28 30 31 34 40 43 45 46 53 54 59 60 62 64 65 70 76 77 79 80 81 82 86 87 89 90 93 96 107 108 110 111 114 118 119 124 127 131 132 135 144 145 147 148 154 167 169 **P**8 **S** Aspirus, Inc., Wausau, WI
Primary Contact: Chris Squire, Regional President
CFO: Marlin Pete Nelson, Vice President Fiscal Services
CMO: Elizabeth Strabel, M.D., Chief Medical Staff
CHR: Carol J Bank, Vice President Human Resources
Web address: www.dshealthcare.com
Control: Other not–for–profit (including NFP Corporation) **Service:** General medical and surgical

Staffed Beds: 46 **Admissions:** 1077 **Census:** 11 **Outpatient Visits:** 83538
Births: 109 **Total Expense ($000):** 80534 **Payroll Expense ($000):** 28533
Personnel: 212

PRAIRIE DU CHIEN—Crawford County

CROSSING RIVERS HEALTH (521330), 37868 US Highway 18, Zip 53821-8416; tel. 608/357-2000, **A**1 10 18 **F**11 13 15 28 29 34 36 40 43 53 56 63 64 75 76 77 78 81 82 86 87 93 99 104 107 111 119 130 131 144 146 147 154
Primary Contact: Christopher Brophy, Chief Executive Officer
CFO: Dave Breitbach, Chief Financial Officer
CMO: Steven Bush, Chief Medical Officer
CIO: John Daane, Information Systems Officer
CHR: Samantha Donahue, Director Human Resources
Web address: www.crossingrivers.org
Control: Other not–for–profit (including NFP Corporation) **Service:** General medical and surgical

Staffed Beds: 25 **Admissions:** 639 **Census:** 5 **Outpatient Visits:** 12334
Births: 135 **Total Expense ($000):** 67020 **Payroll Expense ($000):** 26480
Personnel: 305

PRAIRIE DU SAC—Sauk County

SAUK PRAIRIE HEALTHCARE (520095), 260 26th Street, Zip 53578-1599; tel. 608/643-3311, **A**3 5 10 11 **F**11 13 15 28 29 34 36 38 40 43 53 54 55 56 69 75 76 77 80 81 82 86 89 90 93 102 107 108 111 118 119 130 131 144 146 147 154 **P**7
Primary Contact: Shawn Lerch, Chief Executive Officer
CFO: James Dregney, Vice President Finance and Operations, Chief Financial Officer
CMO: Todd Schad, M.D., Medical Director
CIO: Richard C Bonjour, Chief Information Officer
CHR: Robbi E Bos, Vice President Human Resources
CNO: Lisa Pickarts, Vice President Patient Services
Web address: www.saukprairiehealthcare.org/
Control: Other not–for–profit (including NFP Corporation) **Service:** General medical and surgical

Staffed Beds: 36 **Admissions:** 1230 **Census:** 9 **Outpatient Visits:** 129537
Births: 427 **Total Expense ($000):** 115506 **Payroll Expense ($000):** 56465
Personnel: 566

RACINE—Racine County

ASCENSION ALL SAINTS (520096), 3801 Spring Street, Zip 53405-1690; tel. 262/687-4011, **A**1 2 5 7 10 19 **F**4 5 6 13 15 17 20 22 28 29 34 38 40 51 53 56 64 70 72 76 77 78 80 81 82 86 87 90 98 99 100 101 102 103 104 107 108 111 118 119 130 131 144 147 **P**6 **S** Ascension Healthcare, Saint Louis, MO
Primary Contact: Kristin McManmon, President
CFO: Jeanne Gramza, Director Finance
CMO: Jerry Hardacre, M.D., Chief of Staff
CIO: Joanne Bisterfeldt, Chief Information Officer
CHR: Mary Jo Wodicka, Vice President Human Resources
Web address: www.allsaintshealth.com
Control: Church operated, Nongovernment, not–for–profit **Service:** General medical and surgical

Staffed Beds: 124 **Admissions:** 8200 **Census:** 119 **Outpatient Visits:** 421333 **Births:** 1211 **Total Expense ($000):** 324134 **Payroll Expense ($000):** 79683 **Personnel:** 1123

REEDSBURG—Sauk County

REEDSBURG AREA MEDICAL CENTER (521351), 2000 North Dewey Street, Zip 53959-1097; tel. 608/524-6487, **A**1 10 18 **F**11 12 13 15 17 28 29 34 36 40 43 51 53 64 70 75 76 78 80 81 82 86 87 88 89 93 107 108 111 130 131 146 147
Primary Contact: Robert Van Meeteren, President and Chief Executive Officer
COO: Dale Turner, Chief Operating Officer
CFO: Barry Borchert, Vice President Finance
Web address: www.ramchealth.com
Control: Other not–for–profit (including NFP Corporation) **Service:** General medical and surgical

Staffed Beds: 19 **Admissions:** 952 **Census:** 9 **Outpatient Visits:** 111059
Births: 206 **Total Expense ($000):** 100557 **Payroll Expense ($000):** 41890
Personnel: 502

RHINELANDER—Oneida County

ASPIRUS RHINELANDER HOSPITAL (520019), 2251 North Shore Drive, Zip 54501-6710; tel. 715/361-2000, (Includes ST. MARY'S HOSPITAL, 1044 Kabel Avenue, Rhinelander, Wisconsin, Zip 54501, tel. 715/369-6600) **A**1 3 5 10 20 **F**3 4 8 13 15 18 29 30 31 34 40 45 54 64 65 68 70 74 75 76 78 79 80 81 82 84 85 86 87 89 93 97 98 100 102 103 107 108 110 111 115 116 119 120 121 123 126 127 130 132 135 143 144 148 154 156 162 164 165 167 169 **P**8 **S** Aspirus, Inc., Wausau, WI
Primary Contact: Teresa Theiler, President – North Region
CFO: Jamon Lamers, Director Finance
CMO: Mark Banas, M.D., Chief Medical Officer
CIO: Howard Dobizl, Director Information Services for the Northern Region
CHR: Michelle Cornelius, Director Human Resources for the Northern Region
CNO: Christine Krebs, Director or Nursing
Web address: https://www.aspirus.org/find-a-location/aspirus-rhinelander-hospital-535
Control: Other not–for–profit (including NFP Corporation) **Service:** General medical and surgical

Staffed Beds: 49 **Admissions:** 2548 **Census:** 32 **Outpatient Visits:** 87002
Births: 229 **Total Expense ($000):** 221997 **Payroll Expense ($000):** 89164
Personnel: 299

ST. MARY'S HOSPITAL See Aspirus Rhinelander Hospital

RICE LAKE—Barron County

MARSHFIELD MEDICAL CENTER – RICE LAKE (520011), 1700 West Stout Street, Zip 54868-5000; tel. 715/234-1515, **A**1 10 20 **S** Marshfield Clinic Health System, Marshfield, WI
Primary Contact: Bradley D. Groseth, Chief Administrative Officer
COO: Cindy Arts-Strenke, R.N., Chief Operating Officer and Chief Nursing Officer
CFO: Jacqueline Klein, Chief Financial Officer
CMO: John L. Olson, M.D., Medical Director
CIO: Brad Gerrits, Director Information Systems
CHR: Kathy Mitchell, Director Human Resources
Web address: www.lakeviewmedical.com
Control: Other not–for–profit (including NFP Corporation) **Service:** General medical and surgical

Staffed Beds: 40 **Admissions:** 1532 **Census:** 14 **Outpatient Visits:** 83222
Births: 348 **Total Expense ($000):** 120132 **Payroll Expense ($000):** 34553
Personnel: 379

RICHLAND CENTER—Richland County

RICHLAND HOSPITAL (521341), 333 East Second Street, Zip 53581-1914; tel. 608/647-6321, **A**5 10 18 21 **F**3 8 12 13 15 28 30 34 35 40 46 56 57 59 64 65 68 70 75 76 78 79 80 81 82 85 87 89 93 96 97 107 114 119 127 129 130 131 133 134 135 144 148 154 156 157 160
Primary Contact: Bruce E. Roesler, FACHE, Chief Executive Officer
CFO: Jeffery Longbrake, Interim Vice President, Chief Financial Officer
CMO: Christine Richards, Chief of Staff
CIO: Jerry Cooper, Director, Information Technology
CHR: Rhonda Sutton, Director Human Resources
CNO: Charles Burnley, Vice President, Chief Nursing Officer
Web address: www.richlandhospital.com
Control: Other not–for–profit (including NFP Corporation) **Service:** General medical and surgical

Staffed Beds: 25 **Admissions:** 932 **Census:** 9 **Outpatient Visits:** 61098
Births: 132 **Total Expense ($000):** 71081 **Payroll Expense ($000):** 32643
Personnel: 364

Hospitals, U.S. / WISCONSIN

RIPON—Fond Du Lac County

RIPON MEDICAL CENTER See SSM Health Ripon Community Hospital

☒ **SSM HEALTH RIPON COMMUNITY HOSPITAL (521321)**, 845 Parkside Street, Zip 54971–8505, Mailing Address: P.O. Box 390, Zip 54971–0390; tel. 920/748–3101, **A**1 10 18 **F**5 11 15 28 29 40 43 53 64 69 70 75 77 78 80 81 82 87 90 93 101 104 107 108 111 118 119 130 131 144 146 154 **P**3 6 8 **S** SSM Health, Saint Louis, MO
Primary Contact: DeAnn Thurmer, President and Chief Nursing Officer
CFO: Bonnie Schmitz, Chief Financial Officer
CMO: Derek Colmenares, M.D., Chief Medical Officer
CIO: Nancy Birschbach, Vice President and Chief Information Officer
CHR: Sue Edminster, Vice President Human Resources
CNO: DeAnn Thurmer, President and Chief Nursing Officer
Web address: https://www.ssmhealth.com/
Control: Church operated, Nongovernment, not-for-profit **Service:** General medical and surgical

Staffed Beds: 16 **Admissions:** 436 **Census:** 5 **Outpatient Visits:** 22919 **Births:** 0 **Total Expense ($000):** 34420 **Payroll Expense ($000):** 13141 **Personnel:** 118

RIVER FALLS—St. Croix County

☒ **RIVER FALLS AREA HOSPITAL (521349)**, 1629 East Division Street, Zip 54022–1571; tel. 715/425–6155, **A**1 2 10 18 **F**11 15 28 29 34 40 43 51 54 56 64 75 78 80 81 82 86 87 90 93 102 107 111 119 130 131 146 147 154 **P**6 **S** Allina Health, Minneapolis, MN
Primary Contact: Jill Ostrem, President
COO: William Frommelt, Director Operations and Finance
CFO: William Frommelt, Director Operations and Finance
CHR: Kristen Novak, Manager Human Resources
Web address: www.allina.com
Control: Other not-for-profit (including NFP Corporation) **Service:** General medical and surgical

Staffed Beds: 18 **Admissions:** 479 **Census:** 7 **Outpatient Visits:** 20862 **Births:** 0 **Total Expense ($000):** 39967 **Payroll Expense ($000):** 13444 **Personnel:** 104

SHAWANO—Shawano County

☒ **THEDACARE MEDICAL CENTER-SHAWANO (521346)**, 100 County Road B, Zip 54166–2127; tel. 715/526–2111, **A**1 10 18 **F**11 13 15 28 29 34 40 64 75 76 77 78 80 81 82 86 89 90 107 108 111 118 119 130 146 154 **S** Froedtert ThedaCare Health, Inc., Milwaukee, WI
Primary Contact: Kellie Diedrick, Interim Vice President
CFO: Kerry Lee Blanke, Chief Financial Officer
CMO: Mindy Frimodig, D.O., President Medical Staff ThedaCare Physicians Shawano
CIO: Jennifer Quinn, Quality and Safety Coordinator
CNO: Patricia A Angelucci, MS, R.N., Director Patient Care Services
Web address: https://directory.thedacare.org/location/thedacare-medical-center-shawano
Control: Other not-for-profit (including NFP Corporation) **Service:** General medical and surgical

Staffed Beds: 23 **Admissions:** 1263 **Census:** 11 **Outpatient Visits:** 96628 **Births:** 206 **Total Expense ($000):** 75258 **Payroll Expense ($000):** 33356 **Personnel:** 252

SHEBOYGAN—Sheboygan County

★ ⇑ **AURORA MEDICAL CENTER – SHEBOYGAN COUNTY (520035)**, 3400 Union Avenue, Zip 53081–8426; tel. 920/451–5000, **A**2 10 19 21 **F**3 4 5 11 13 17 18 20 22 26 28 29 30 31 32 34 35 36 40 41 43 44 45 49 50 53 56 57 58 59 60 64 65 68 70 72 74 75 76 78 79 80 81 82 84 85 86 87 89 92 93 94 98 99 100 102 103 104 105 107 108 111 112 114 115 117 118 119 120 121 123 126 129 130 131 132 135 143 146 147 148 152 153 154 160 161 167 169 **S** Advocate Aurora Health, Downers Grove, IL
Primary Contact: Aric Kinney, President
CFO: Pamela Ott, Vice President Finance
CIO: Steve Serketich, Manager Information Services
CHR: Stacie A Schneider, Director Human Resources
CNO: Lori Knitt, Chief Nursing Officer
Web address: https://www.aurorahealthcare.org/locations/hospital/aurora-medical-center-sheboygan-county/
Control: Other not-for-profit (including NFP Corporation) **Service:** General medical and surgical

Staffed Beds: 124 **Admissions:** 6061 **Census:** 70 **Outpatient Visits:** 117855 **Births:** 839 **Total Expense ($000):** 208115 **Payroll Expense ($000):** 60075 **Personnel:** 999

⇑ **AURORA SHEBOYGAN MEMORIAL MEDICAL CENTER** See Aurora Medical Center – Sheboygan County

☒ **HSHS ST. NICHOLAS HOSPITAL (520044)**, 3100 Superior Avenue, Zip 53081–1948; tel. 920/459–8300, **A**1 2 10 **F**3 8 11 13 15 17 18 20 22 28 29 30 31 34 35 36 38 40 43 44 45 47 50 53 54 57 59 60 62 63 64 65 70 71 74 75 76 77 79 80 81 84 85 86 87 89 90 93 107 108 110 111 114 115 116 117 118 119 120 126 129 130 132 146 148 154 167 **S** HSHS Hospital Sisters Health System, Springfield, IL
Primary Contact: Justin Selle, Chief Executive Officer
CFO: Greg Simia, Chief Financial Officer
CMO: Richard Cooley, M.D., Chief Physician Executive
CIO: Shane Miller, Chief Information Officer
CHR: Christine Jensema, Chief People Officer
Web address: www.stnicholashospital.org
Control: Church operated, Nongovernment, not-for-profit **Service:** General medical and surgical

Staffed Beds: 49 **Admissions:** 1605 **Census:** 16 **Outpatient Visits:** 74641 **Births:** 239 **Total Expense ($000):** 80948 **Payroll Expense ($000):** 18658 **Personnel:** 226

SHELL LAKE—Washburn County

☐ **INDIANHEAD MEDICAL CENTER (521342)**, 113 Fourth Avenue, Zip 54871–4457, Mailing Address: P.O. Box 300, Zip 54871–0300; tel. 715/468–7833, **A**1 10 18 **F**15 28 34 40 43 56 62 64 80 81 86 89 93 107 119 130 144 **P**5
Primary Contact: Shannon Jack, Administrator
CFO: Michael Elliott, Controller
CMO: Allan Haesemeyer, M.D., Chief of Staff
CHR: Gwen Nielsen, Manager Human Resources
Web address: www.indianheadmedicalcenter.com
Control: Other not-for-profit (including NFP Corporation) **Service:** General medical and surgical

Staffed Beds: 10 **Admissions:** 167 **Census:** 2 **Outpatient Visits:** 19291 **Births:** 0 **Total Expense ($000):** 13340 **Payroll Expense ($000):** 5011 **Personnel:** 83

SPARTA—Monroe County

MAYO CLINIC HEALTH SYSTEM – FRANCISCAN HEALTHCARE IN SPARTA See Mayo Clinic Health System In Sparta

☒ **MAYO CLINIC HEALTH SYSTEM IN SPARTA (521305)**, 310 West Main Street, Zip 54656–2171; tel. 608/269–2132, **A**1 10 18 **F**6 11 15 28 29 34 40 43 52 55 56 64 77 81 86 87 93 107 119 130 131 146 154 **P**6 **S** Mayo Clinic, Rochester, MN
Primary Contact: Richard Helmers, M.D., Chief Executive Officer
CFO: Julie S Hansen, Chief Financial Officer
CMO: Tracy Warsing, M.D., Site Leader Chief of Staff
CHR: Cathryn H. Fraser, Chief Human Resources Officer
Web address: https://www.mayoclinichealthsystem.org/locations/sparta
Control: Other not-for-profit (including NFP Corporation) **Service:** General medical and surgical

Staffed Beds: 14 **Admissions:** 314 **Census:** 9 **Outpatient Visits:** 57679 **Births:** 0 **Total Expense ($000):** 37515 **Payroll Expense ($000):** 16372 **Personnel:** 172

SPOONER—Washburn County

★ **SPOONER HEALTH (521332)**, 1280 Chandler Drive, Zip 54801–1299; tel. 715/635–2111, **A**10 18 **F**3 11 15 29 30 31 34 35 40 43 45 50 56 57 59 62 64 65 68 75 78 79 80 81 82 85 86 87 89 93 107 108 111 119 129 130 132 133 146 148 **S** HealthTech Management Services, Plano, TX
Primary Contact: Michael Schafer, Chief Executive Officer and Administrator
CFO: Rebecca Busch, Chief Financial Officer
CMO: Mark Van Etten, M.D., Chief of Staff
CHR: Cindy Rouzer, Director Human Resources
CNO: Clint Miller, Chief Nursing Officer
Web address: www.spoonerhealth.com
Control: Other not-for-profit (including NFP Corporation) **Service:** General medical and surgical

Staffed Beds: 20 **Admissions:** 381 **Census:** 6 **Outpatient Visits:** 31218 **Births:** 0 **Total Expense ($000):** 32417 **Payroll Expense ($000):** 9483 **Personnel:** 119

Hospital, Medicare Provider Number, Address, Telephone, Approval, Facility, and Physician Codes, Health Care System

★ American Hospital Association (AHA) membership
☐ The Joint Commission accreditation
◯ Healthcare Facilities Accreditation Program
◇ DNV Healthcare Inc. accreditation
⇑ Center for Improvement in Healthcare Quality Accreditation
△ Commission on Accreditation of Rehabilitation Facilities (CARF) accreditation

Hospitals, U.S. / WISCONSIN

ST CROIX FALLS—Polk County

★ **ST. CROIX REGIONAL MEDICAL CENTER (521337)**, 235 State Street, Zip 54024-4117; tel. 715/483-3261, **A**10 18 **F**6 9 13 15 28 29 34 36 40 43 51 54 55 56 64 70 75 76 77 78 81 82 86 87 93 99 100 101 104 107 108 111 116 118 119 130 131 147 154 **P**6
Primary Contact: Michael Youso, Interim Chief Executive Officer and Chief Financial Officer
CFO: Michael Youso, Chief Financial Officer
CMO: Talha Khan, Vice President Medical Affairs
CIO: Brent McCurdy, Director Management Information
CHR: Betsy Nordby, Director of Human Resources
CNO: Andrea Olson, Vice President Patient Care
Web address: www.scrmc.org
Control: Other not-for-profit (including NFP Corporation) **Service**: General medical and surgical

> **Staffed Beds**: 25 **Admissions**: 1290 **Census**: 13 **Outpatient Visits**: 172258 **Births**: 219 **Total Expense ($000)**: 142239 **Payroll Expense ($000)**: 58013 **Personnel**: 425

STANLEY—Chippewa County

★ **ASPIRUS STANLEY HOSPITAL & CLINICS, INC. (521311)**, 1120 Pine Street, Zip 54768-1297; tel. 715/644-5571, **A**10 18 **F**3 8 15 31 35 37 40 43 45 46 47 48 49 64 65 68 69 71 74 75 79 81 83 84 85 87 89 93 96 97 107 109 110 113 114 115 117 120 121 123 124 127 129 130 133 135 144 147 148 154 156 167 169 **P**8 **S** Aspirus, Inc., Wausau, WI
Primary Contact: Dale Hustedt, President
CFO: Terri Lewandowski, Director Financial Services
Web address: https://www.aspirus.org/find-a-location/aspirus-stanley-clinic-559
Control: Other not-for-profit (including NFP Corporation) **Service**: General medical and surgical

> **Staffed Beds**: 13 **Admissions**: 213 **Census**: 2 **Outpatient Visits**: 16178 **Births**: 0 **Total Expense ($000)**: 20651 **Payroll Expense ($000)**: 7012 **Personnel**: 61

OUR LADY OF VICTORY HOSPITAL See Aspirus Stanley Hospital & Clinics, Inc.

STEVENS POINT—Portage County

✠ **ASPIRUS STEVEN's POINT HOSPITAL & CLINICS, INC. (520002)**, 900 Illinois Avenue, Zip 54481-3196; tel. 715/346-5000, **A**1 3 5 10 19 **F**3 4 5 8 13 15 17 18 20 22 26 28 31 34 40 43 44 51 54 64 70 72 74 76 77 78 79 80 81 83 84 85 86 87 89 93 98 99 100 102 103 104 107 108 110 111 113 114 115 117 118 119 120 121 123 126 127 129 130 131 144 147 148 154 156 160 161 162 169 **P**8 **S** Aspirus, Inc., Wausau, WI
Primary Contact: Teresa Theiler, Chief Administrative Officer
CFO: William J Hinner, Vice President Financial Analysis and Planning
CIO: Will Weider, Chief Information Officer
CHR: Celia Shaunessy, Vice President Human Resources
CNO: Tom Veeser, Chief Nursing Officer
Web address: https://www.aspirus.org/find-a-location/aspirus-stevens-point-hospital-539
Control: Other not-for-profit (including NFP Corporation) **Service**: General medical and surgical

> **Staffed Beds**: 71 **Admissions**: 2704 **Census**: 30 **Outpatient Visits**: 114501 **Births**: 299 **Total Expense ($000)**: 142259 **Payroll Expense ($000)**: 45870 **Personnel**: 414

✠ **MARSHFIELD MEDICAL CENTER – RIVER REGION (520215)**, 4100 State Highway 66, Zip 54482-8410; tel. 715/997-6000, **A**1 10 **F**11 15 34 40 43 64 78 82 86 87 93 107 111 116 119 130 131 144 146 147 154 **P**2 6 **S** Marshfield Clinic Health System, Marshfield, WI
Primary Contact: Christopher Soska, President, Marshfield Medical Center, Weston, Wisconsin Rapids, Stevens Point
Web address: https://www.marshfieldclinic.org/locations/centers/Stevens%20Point%20-%20Marshfield%20Medical%20Center-River%20Region
Control: Other not-for-profit (including NFP Corporation) **Service**: General medical and surgical

> **Staffed Beds**: 5 **Admissions**: 197 **Census**: 2 **Outpatient Visits**: 62371 **Births**: 0 **Total Expense ($000)**: 48682 **Payroll Expense ($000)**: 13244 **Personnel**: 174

ST. MICHAEL'S HOSPITAL See Aspirus Steven's Point Hospital & Clinics, Inc.

STOUGHTON—Dane County

★ ⇑ **STOUGHTON HEALTH (521343)**, 900 Ridge Street, Zip 53589-1864; tel. 608/873-6611, **A**5 10 18 21 **F**4 6 15 28 29 34 40 43 54 56 62 64 70 75 77 80 81 86 87 89 90 93 98 100 103 107 130 131 144 147 154
Primary Contact: Daniel DeGroot, President and Chief Executive Officer
CFO: Michelle Abey, Chief Financial Officer
CHR: Christopher Schmitz, Associate Vice President, Director Human Resources
CNO: Teresa Lindfors, Vice President Growth and Development
Web address: https://stoughtonhealth.com/
Control: Other not-for-profit (including NFP Corporation) **Service**: General medical and surgical

> **Staffed Beds**: 27 **Admissions**: 685 **Census**: 11 **Outpatient Visits**: 83391 **Births**: 0 **Total Expense ($000)**: 55735 **Payroll Expense ($000)**: 21896 **Personnel**: 248

STURGEON BAY—Door County

★ **DOOR COUNTY MEDICAL CENTER (521358)**, 323 South 18th Avenue, Zip 54235-1495; tel. 920/743-5566, (Total facility includes 30 beds in nursing home-type unit) **A**10 18 **F**3 6 8 11 13 15 17 28 29 30 32 34 35 36 40 43 44 45 47 50 54 56 57 59 61 64 65 66 70 75 76 79 80 81 84 85 86 87 89 90 93 96 97 101 107 108 110 111 115 118 119 126 127 128 129 130 131 132 133 135 144 145 146 147 148 154 156 160 161 167 169 **P**6
Primary Contact: Brian Stephens, President and Chief Executive Officer
CFO: Andrew LaLuzerne, Chief Financial Officer
CMO: James Heise, Chief Medical Officer
CIO: Mary Lopas, Chief Information Officer
CHR: Kelli Bowling, Chief Culture Officer
CNO: Christa Krause, Chief Nursing Officer
Web address: www.dcmedical.org
Control: Church operated, Nongovernment, not-for-profit **Service**: General medical and surgical

> **Staffed Beds**: 50 **Admissions**: 1104 **Census**: 41 **Outpatient Visits**: 194666 **Births**: 126 **Total Expense ($000)**: 104169 **Payroll Expense ($000)**: 50573 **Personnel**: 585

SUMMIT—Waukesha County

★ ⇑ **AURORA MEDICAL CENTER SUMMIT (520206)**, 36500 Aurora Drive, Zip 53066-4899; tel. 262/434-1000, **A**2 3 10 19 21 **F**3 8 11 12 13 15 17 18 20 22 26 28 29 30 31 34 35 36 40 41 43 44 47 48 49 50 53 54 58 59 60 64 68 70 72 74 75 76 79 80 81 82 85 86 87 89 90 93 94 96 102 107 108 110 111 114 115 116 117 118 119 120 121 123 126 129 130 131 132 135 146 147 148 154 157 167 **S** Advocate Aurora Health, Downers Grove, IL
Primary Contact: Jessica Bauer, President
Web address: www.aurorahealthcare.org
Control: Other not-for-profit (including NFP Corporation) **Service**: General medical and surgical

> **Staffed Beds**: 117 **Admissions**: 4927 **Census**: 59 **Outpatient Visits**: 130221 **Births**: 503 **Total Expense ($000)**: 165840 **Payroll Expense ($000)**: 53138 **Personnel**: 1205

SUPERIOR—Douglas County

✠ **ESSENTIA HEALTH ST. MARY'S HOSPITAL OF SUPERIOR (521329)**, 3500 Tower Avenue, Zip 54880-5395; tel. 715/817-7000, **A**1 10 18 **F**11 15 28 29 34 40 56 75 77 78 80 81 82 86 87 90 93 99 104 107 119 130 146 **S** Essentia Health, Duluth, MN
Primary Contact: Kim Renee. Pearson, Administrator
CFO: Scott Nigon, Finance Senior Manager
CNO: Kim Renee Pearson, Nursing Director
Web address: www.essentiahealth.org/EssentiaHealthStMarysHospitalofSuperiorFoundation/overview.aspx
Control: Other not-for-profit (including NFP Corporation) **Service**: General medical and surgical

> **Staffed Beds**: 25 **Admissions**: 482 **Census**: 11 **Outpatient Visits**: 67925 **Births**: 0 **Total Expense ($000)**: 75732 **Payroll Expense ($000)**: 36077 **Personnel**: 324

Hospitals, U.S. / WISCONSIN

TOMAH—Monroe County

☒ **TOMAH HEALTH (521320)**, 501 Gopher Drive, Zip 54660–4513; tel. 608/372–2181, **A**1 10 18 **F**12 13 28 34 40 43 54 63 64 76 77 80 81 82 86 87 89 90 93 107 108 111 119 130 144 147 154 **P**5 6 **S** HealthTech Management Services, Plano, TX
Primary Contact: Derek Daly, Chief Executive Officer
CFO: Joseph Zeps, Chief Financial Officer
CIO: Heather Laudon, Director Information Technology Services
CHR: Brenda Reinert, Director Human Resources
CNO: Tracy Myhre, R.N., MSN, Chief Nursing Officer
Web address: www.tomahhospital.org
Control: Other not-for-profit (including NFP Corporation) **Service:** General medical and surgical

Staffed Beds: 25 **Admissions:** 818 **Census:** 8 **Outpatient Visits:** 62376
Births: 239 **Total Expense ($000):** 76023 **Payroll Expense ($000):** 29215
Personnel: 362

☒ **TOMAH VA MEDICAL CENTER**, 500 East Veterans Street, Zip 54660–3105; tel. 608/372–3971, (Nonreporting) **A**1 3 5 **S** Department of Veterans Affairs, Washington, DC
Primary Contact: Karen K. Long, Medical Center Director
CFO: Jane Mashak–Ekern, Fiscal Officer
CMO: David Houlihan, M.D., Chief of Staff
CIO: Edward Hensel, Chief Information Officer
CHR: David Dechant, Chief Human Resources Officer
Web address: www.tomah.va.gov
Control: Veterans Affairs, Government, federal **Service:** General medical and surgical

Staffed Beds: 36

TOMAH VAMC See Tomah VA Medical Center

TOMAHAWK—Lincoln County

★ **ASPIRUS TOMAHAWK HOSPITAL (521313)**, 401 West Mohawk Drive, Zip 54487–2274; tel. 715/453–7700, **A**10 18 **F**3 7 11 12 13 15 20 22 24 28 29 34 36 40 43 51 53 55 56 59 60 64 65 68 69 75 77 78 80 82 83 84 85 86 87 89 93 97 99 100 102 103 104 107 108 119 127 130 133 136 137 140 144 146 147 154 **P**8 **S** Aspirus, Inc., Wausau, WI
Primary Contact: Laurie Oungst, Chief Administrative Officer
CFO: Jamon Lamers, Director Finance
CMO: Russ Sudbury, M.D., President Medical Staff
CIO: Howard Dobizl, Director Information Technology Services
CHR: Michelle Cornelius, Director Human Resources
CNO: Christine Krebs, Director of Nursing
Web address: https://www.aspirus.org/find-a-location/aspirus-tomahawk-hospital-537
Control: Other not-for-profit (including NFP Corporation) **Service:** General medical and surgical

Staffed Beds: 12 **Admissions:** 225 **Census:** 4 **Outpatient Visits:** 24239
Births: 0 **Total Expense ($000):** 13607 **Payroll Expense ($000):** 5565
Personnel: 53

SACRED HEART HOSPITAL See Aspirus Tomahawk Hospital

TWO RIVERS—Manitowoc County

★ ⇑ **AURORA MEDICAL CENTER – MANITOWOC COUNTY (520034)**, 5000 Memorial Drive, Zip 54241–3900; tel. 920/794–5000, **A**2 10 21 **F**3 8 11 13 28 29 30 33 34 35 36 40 41 43 46 48 49 57 58 59 60 64 65 75 76 78 79 80 81 82 86 87 89 91 93 94 96 97 107 108 109 110 111 112 115 117 118 119 120 121 123 124 129 130 131 132 135 146 147 148 154 156 169 **S** Advocate Aurora Health, Downers Grove, IL
Primary Contact: Cathie A. Kocourek, President
CFO: Joyce Nwatuobi, Vice President Finance
CMO: Scott Voskuil, M.D., Chief Medical Officer
CIO: Bobbie Byrne, M.D., Chief Information Officer
CHR: Elizabeth A Kirby, Senior Director Human Resources
CNO: Natalie Weber, R.N., Nurse Manager
Web address: www.aurorahealthcare.org
Control: Other not-for-profit (including NFP Corporation) **Service:** General medical and surgical

Staffed Beds: 49 **Admissions:** 1985 **Census:** 17 **Outpatient Visits:** 102367
Births: 410 **Total Expense ($000):** 73472 **Payroll Expense ($000):** 22979
Personnel: 375

WATERFORD—Racine County

☐ **LAKEVIEW SPECIALTY HOSPITAL AND REHAB (522005)**, 1701 Sharp Road, Zip 53185–5214; tel. 262/534–7297, **A**1 10 **F**1 29 34 38 53 60 64 75 86 87 90 93 130 **P**6
Primary Contact: Andy Olivares, Chief Executive Officer
Web address: www.lakeviewsystem.com
Control: Corporation, Investor–owned (for–profit) **Service:** Acute long–term care hospital

Staffed Beds: 55 **Admissions:** 299 **Census:** 29 **Outpatient Visits:** 3188
Births: 0 **Total Expense ($000):** 24856 **Payroll Expense ($000):** 11105
Personnel: 117

WATERTOWN—Dodge County

☒ **WATERTOWN REGIONAL MEDICAL CENTER (520116)**, 125 Hospital Drive, Zip 53098–3303; tel. 920/261–4210, **A**1 10 **F**10 11 13 15 20 22 28 29 34 36 40 53 54 56 64 69 75 76 77 80 81 82 86 87 89 90 93 98 103 104 107 108 111 118 119 125 130 131 144 146 147 154 **P**8 **S** ScionHealth, Louisville, KY
Primary Contact: Richard Keddington, Chief Executive Officer
COO: John P Kosanovich, President
CFO: John Graf, Senior Vice President
CMO: David Parkins, M.D., Chief of Staff
CIO: Jennifer Laughlin, Chief Information Officer
CHR: Duane Floyd, Vice President Human Resources and Professional Services
Web address: www.watertownregional.com/Main/Home.aspx
Control: Corporation, Investor–owned (for–profit) **Service:** General medical and surgical

Staffed Beds: 64 **Admissions:** 2246 **Census:** 26 **Outpatient Visits:** 78525
Births: 180 **Total Expense ($000):** 99848 **Payroll Expense ($000):** 43972
Personnel: 478

WAUKESHA—Waukesha County

☐ △ **PROHEALTH REHABILITATION HOSPITAL OF WISCONSIN (523027)**, 1625 Coldwater Creek Drive, Zip 53188–8028; tel. 262/521–8800, **A**1 7 10 **F**28 29 34 64 75 86 90 93 100 130 **S** Kindred Healthcare, Louisville, KY
Primary Contact: Ben Mallon, Chief Executive Officer
CFO: Kim Stoltz, Controller
CMO: Tim McAvoy, M.D., Medical Director
CHR: Katelyn Gonyo, Director of Human Resources
CNO: Vanessa Plante, Chief Clinical Officer
Web address: www.rehabhospitalwi.com
Control: Partnership, Investor–owned (for–profit) **Service:** Rehabilitation

Staffed Beds: 27 **Admissions:** 1016 **Census:** 33 **Outpatient Visits:** 8287
Births: 0 **Total Expense ($000):** 17088 **Payroll Expense ($000):** 9116
Personnel: 115

☒ **PROHEALTH WAUKESHA MEMORIAL HOSPITAL (520008)**, 725 American Avenue, Zip 53188–5099; tel. 262/928–1000, **A**1 2 3 5 10 **F**4 5 11 12 13 15 20 22 24 28 29 34 40 43 51 55 56 60 64 72 75 76 77 78 80 81 82 86 87 89 93 98 100 101 102 103 104 107 108 111 118 119 130 131 146 147 154 **S** ProHealth Care, Inc., Waukesha, WI
Primary Contact: Susan A. Edwards, President and Chief Executive Officer
CMO: James D Gardner, M.D., Vice President and Chief Medical Officer
CIO: Rodney Dykehouse, Senior Vice President Information Services
CHR: Nadine T Guirl, Senior Vice President Human Resources
Web address: https://www.prohealthcare.org/locations/profile/hospital-waukesha/
Control: Other not-for-profit (including NFP Corporation) **Service:** General medical and surgical

Staffed Beds: 258 **Admissions:** 10599 **Census:** 136 **Outpatient Visits:** 351104 **Births:** 1548 **Total Expense ($000):** 482906 **Payroll Expense ($000):** 135503 **Personnel:** 1598

REHABILITATION HOSPITAL OF WISCONSIN See Prohealth Rehabilitation Hospital of Wisconsin

WAUKESHA COUNTY MENTAL HEALTH CENTER (524026), 1501 Airport Road, Zip 53188; tel. 262/548–7950, **A**10 **F**4 29 34 35 44 50 59 68 87 98 103 130 132 135 154 160 161 162 163 164 165
Primary Contact: Jeff Lewis, Administrator
CFO: Randy R Setzer, Financial Services Manager
Web address: www.waukeshacounty.gov/
Control: County, Government, Nonfederal **Service:** Psychiatric

Staffed Beds: 14 **Admissions:** 489 **Census:** 10 **Outpatient Visits:** 0
Births: 0 **Total Expense ($000):** 7760 **Payroll Expense ($000):** 3423
Personnel: 41

Hospital, Medicare Provider Number, Address, Telephone, Approval, Facility, and Physician Codes, Health Care System

★ American Hospital Association (AHA) membership ○ Healthcare Facilities Accreditation Program ⇑ Center for Improvement in Healthcare Quality Accreditation
☐ The Joint Commission accreditation ◇ DNV Healthcare Inc. accreditation △ Commission on Accreditation of Rehabilitation Facilities (CARF) accreditation

Hospitals, U.S. / WISCONSIN

WAUKESHA MEMORIAL HOSPITAL See Prohealth Waukesha Memorial Hospital

WAUPACA—Waupaca County

THEDACARE MEDICAL CENTER–WAUPACA (521334), 800 Riverside Drive, Zip 54981-1999; tel. 715/258-1000, **A**1 10 18 **F**11 13 17 28 29 34 40 64 70 75 76 78 80 81 82 86 88 89 90 107 111 119 130 144 146 147 **S** Froedtert ThedaCare Health, Inc., Milwaukee, WI
Primary Contact: Kellie Diedrick, Vice President
CFO: Kerry Lee Blanke, Director Financial Services
CMO: James Williams, M.D., Chief of Staff
CHR: Kevin J Gossens, Director Human Resources
Web address: https://directory.thedacare.org/location/thedacare-medical-center-waupaca
Control: Other not–for–profit (including NFP Corporation) Service: General medical and surgical

> **Staffed Beds:** 25 **Admissions:** 918 **Census:** 9 **Outpatient Visits:** 77713 **Births:** 124 **Total Expense ($000):** 44087 **Payroll Expense ($000):** 17150 **Personnel:** 180

WAUPUN—Dodge County

SSM HEALTH WAUPUN MEMORIAL HOSPITAL (521327), 620 West Brown Street, Zip 53963-1799; tel. 920/324-5581, **A**1 10 18 **F**5 13 15 28 29 40 43 60 64 69 70 75 76 77 78 80 81 82 90 93 104 107 108 111 118 119 144 154 **P**3 6 8 **S** SSM Health, Saint Louis, MO
Primary Contact: DeAnn Thurmer, President and Chief Nursing Officer
CFO: Bonnie Schmitz, Chief Financial Officer
CMO: Derek Colmenares, M.D., Chief Medical Officer
CIO: Nancy Birschbach, Vice President and Chief Information Officer
CHR: Sue Edminster, Vice President Human Resources
CNO: DeAnn Thurmer, President and Chief Nursing Officer
Web address: https://www.ssmhealth.com/
Control: Church operated, Nongovernment, not–for–profit Service: General medical and surgical

> **Staffed Beds:** 25 **Admissions:** 843 **Census:** 7 **Outpatient Visits:** 59969 **Births:** 135 **Total Expense ($000):** 50957 **Payroll Expense ($000):** 19241 **Personnel:** 184

WAUPUN MEMORIAL HOSPITAL See SSM Health Waupun Memorial Hospital

WAUSAU—Marathon County

ASPIRUS WAUSAU HOSPITAL, INC. (520030), 333 Pine Ridge Boulevard, Zip 54401-4187, Mailing Address: 1900 Westwood Drive, Zip 54402; tel. 715/847-2121, (Includes ASPIRUS PLOVER HOSPITAL, 5409 Vern Holmes Drive, Stevens Point, Wisconsin, Zip 54482-8853, tel. 715/344-1600; Matthew Heywood, President and Chief Executive Officer) **A**1 2 3 5 7 10 19 **S** Aspirus, Inc., Wausau, WI
Primary Contact: Jeffrey Wicklander, President
CFO: Sidney C Sczygelski, Senior Vice President Finance and Chief Financial Officer
CMO: Ryan Andrews, M.D., Chief Medical Officer
CNO: Jeannine Nosko, Vice President Patient Care
Web address: www.aspirus.org
Control: Other not–for–profit (including NFP Corporation) Service: General medical and surgical

> **Staffed Beds:** 260 **Admissions:** 13066 **Census:** 207 **Outpatient Visits:** 226478 **Births:** 1326 **Total Expense ($000):** 620852 **Payroll Expense ($000):** 170500 **Personnel:** 3697

NORTH CENTRAL HEALTH CARE (524017), 1100 Lake View Drive, Zip 54403-6785; tel. 715/848-4600, (Total facility includes 126 beds in nursing home–type unit) **A**1 3 5 10 **F**4 5 11 29 75 77 80 87 93 98 99 102 103 104 128 130 146 154
Primary Contact: Gary Olson, Executive Director
COO: Jarret Nickel, Operations Executive
CMO: Robert Gouthro, M.D., Chief Medical Officer
CIO: Thomas Boutain, Information Services Executive
Web address: www.norcen.org
Control: County, Government, Nonfederal Service: Psychiatric

> **Staffed Beds:** 190 **Admissions:** 1126 **Census:** 126 **Outpatient Visits:** 104097 **Births:** 0 **Total Expense ($000):** 58268 **Payroll Expense ($000):** 23652 **Personnel:** 66

WAUWATOSA—Milwaukee County

★ **AURORA PSYCHIATRIC HOSPITAL (524000)**, 1220 Dewey Avenue, Zip 53213-2598; tel. 414/454-6600, **A**3 5 10 21 **F**4 5 11 29 30 32 34 35 36 38 44 50 54 64 68 75 86 87 98 99 103 104 105 106 130 132 134 135 146 152 153 154 158 160 161 **S** Advocate Aurora Health, Downers Grove, IL
Primary Contact: Jessica Small, President
CFO: Susan Dwyer, Vice President Finance
CMO: Anthony Meyer, M.D., Medical Director
CIO: Philip Loftus, Ph.D., Vice President and Chief Information Officer
CHR: Pamela Gamb, Manager Human Resources
CNO: Jamie Lewiston, R.N., MSN, Chief Nursing Officer
Web address: www.aurorahealthcare.org
Control: Other not–for–profit (including NFP Corporation) Service: Psychiatric

> **Staffed Beds:** 74 **Admissions:** 4675 **Census:** 56 **Outpatient Visits:** 51082 **Births:** 0 **Total Expense ($000):** 48035 **Payroll Expense ($000):** 23257 **Personnel:** 472

WEST ALLIS—Milwaukee County

★ **AURORA WEST ALLIS MEDICAL CENTER (520139)**, 8901 West Lincoln Avenue, Zip 53227-2409, Mailing Address: P.O. Box 27901, Zip 53227-0901; tel. 414/328-6000, **A**2 3 10 21 **F**3 11 12 13 15 17 28 29 30 31 32 34 35 36 37 38 40 43 44 45 46 49 50 51 52 54 55 56 57 59 64 65 68 70 72 74 75 76 78 79 80 81 82 84 85 86 87 89 91 93 94 95 96 97 107 108 110 111 114 115 116 117 118 119 120 121 123 126 130 132 134 135 146 147 148 154 167 169 **S** Advocate Aurora Health, Downers Grove, IL
Primary Contact: Holly Schmidtke, FACHE, R.N., President
COO: Gerard Colman, Chief Operating Officer
CFO: Chris Hemmer, Director Finance
CMO: Andrew McDonagh, M.D., Chief Medical Officer
CIO: Philip Loftus, Ph.D., Chief Information Officer
CHR: Shannon Christenson, Director Human Resources
CNO: Kathy Becker, Ph.D., R.N., Vice President and Chief Nursing Officer
Web address: www.aurorahealthcare.org
Control: Other not–for–profit (including NFP Corporation) Service: General medical and surgical

> **Staffed Beds:** 220 **Admissions:** 8591 **Census:** 91 **Outpatient Visits:** 169921 **Births:** 3372 **Total Expense ($000):** 246974 **Payroll Expense ($000):** 86144 **Personnel:** 2074

CHARTER BEHAVIORAL HEALTH SYSTEM OF MILWAUKEE/WEST ALLIS See Rogers Memorial Hospital–West Allis

GRANITE HILLS HOSPITAL (524043), 1706 South 68th Street, Zip 53214-4949; tel. 414/667-4800, **A**1 10 **F**75 98 99 130 154 **S** Universal Health Services, Inc., King of Prussia, PA
Primary Contact: Angela Sanders, Chief Executive Officer
CFO: Keith Degner, Chief Financial Officer
Web address: https://granitehillshospital.com/
Control: Partnership, Investor–owned (for–profit) Service: Psychiatric

> **Staffed Beds:** 48 **Admissions:** 1445 **Census:** 32 **Outpatient Visits:** 0 **Births:** 0 **Total Expense ($000):** 17430 **Payroll Expense ($000):** 7526 **Personnel:** 105

WEST BEND—Washington County

FROEDTERT WEST BEND HOSPITAL (520063), 3200 Pleasant Valley Road, Zip 53095-9274; tel. 262/836-5533, **A**1 3 5 10 **S** Froedtert ThedaCare Health, Inc., Milwaukee, WI
Primary Contact: Allen Ericson, President
COO: Teresa M Lux, President and Chief Operating Officer
CFO: Scott Hawig, Senior Vice President of Finance, Chief Financial Officer and Treasurer
CMO: Patrick Gardner, M.D., Associate Vice President, Medical Affairs, St. Joseph's Hospital
CIO: Kathryn McClellan, Senior Vice President and Chief Information Officer
CHR: Eric Humphrey, Senior Vice President, Chief Human Resources Officer
CNO: Shelly Waala, Vice President Patient Care Services and Chief Nursing Officer
Web address: www.froedtert.com
Control: Other not–for–profit (including NFP Corporation) Service: General medical and surgical

> **Staffed Beds:** 70 **Admissions:** 4042 **Census:** 43 **Outpatient Visits:** 96679 **Births:** 740 **Total Expense ($000):** 142126 **Payroll Expense ($000):** 45213 **Personnel:** 470

WESTON—Marathon County

✠ **MARSHFIELD MEDICAL CENTER – WESTON (520202)**, 3400 Ministry Parkway, Zip 54476–5220; tel. 715/393–3000, **A**1 10 **F**3 8 11 13 17 18 20 22 24 26 28 29 30 31 32 34 35 40 41 43 44 46 47 49 50 57 59 64 68 70 74 76 78 79 80 81 82 84 85 86 87 89 93 97 107 108 111 114 116 117 118 119 120 121 123 126 129 130 131 132 135 142 144 146 147 148 154 156 162 164 167 169 **P**2 6 **S** Marshfield Clinic Health System, Marshfield, WI
Primary Contact: Christopher Soska, President of MMC_Weston,Wisconsin Rapids and Stevens Point
CFO: Charlotte Esselman, Director Finance
CIO: Tammy Hawkey, Manager Information Technology Client Services
CHR: Nancy Kwiesielewicz, Human Resources Manager
CNO: Sally E. Zillman, Interim Vice President, Patient Care Services
Web address: https://www.marshfieldclinic.org/locations/centers/Weston%20-%20Marshfield%20Medical%20Center/
Control: Other not–for–profit (including NFP Corporation) **Service:** General medical and surgical

Staffed Beds: 36 **Admissions:** 3861 **Census:** 49 **Outpatient Visits:** 121943 **Births:** 424 **Total Expense ($000):** 142508 **Payroll Expense ($000):** 65836 **Personnel:** 793

WHITEHALL—Trempealeau County

★ **GUNDERSEN TRI-COUNTY HOSPITAL AND CLINICS (521316)**, 18601 Lincoln Street, Zip 54773–8605; tel. 715/538–4361, (Total facility includes 35 beds in nursing home–type unit) **A**10 18 **F**6 7 10 11 15 28 34 40 43 53 54 56 64 75 78 81 82 86 87 93 99 100 103 104 107 108 130 144 146 154 **P**6
Primary Contact: Joni Olson, Chief Executive Officer
CFO: Roxane K Schliech, Chief Financial Officer
CMO: Kim B Breidenbach, Medical Director
CIO: John Waldera, Director Information Technology
CHR: Jill Wesener Dieck, Human Resources Operations Manager
CNO: Kelsey N Underwood, Director of Nursing
Web address: www.gundersenhealth.org/tri-county
Control: Other not–for–profit (including NFP Corporation) **Service:** General medical and surgical

Staffed Beds: 50 **Admissions:** 305 **Census:** 16 **Outpatient Visits:** 32272 **Births:** 0 **Total Expense ($000):** 32107 **Payroll Expense ($000):** 12425 **Personnel:** 167

WILD ROSE—Waushara County

★ **THEDA CARE MEDICAL CENTER – WILD ROSE (521303)**, 601 Grove Avenue, Zip 54984–6903, Mailing Address: P.O. Box 243, Zip 54984–0243; tel. 920/622–3257, **A**10 18 **F**11 15 28 29 34 40 43 54 64 75 77 80 81 86 89 90 93 107 111 119 131 144 146 147 **S** Froedtert ThedaCare Health, Inc., Milwaukee, WI
Primary Contact: Tammy Bending, Vice President
CFO: Joanne Horvath, Vice President Finance
CMO: Chandler Caves, M.D., Chief Medical Officer
CIO: James Albin, Chief Information Officer
CHR: Maggie A. Lund, Chief Human Resources Officer
Web address: https://www.thedacare.org
Control: Other not–for–profit (including NFP Corporation) **Service:** General medical and surgical

Staffed Beds: 12 **Admissions:** 233 **Census:** 4 **Outpatient Visits:** 18200 **Births:** 0 **Total Expense ($000):** 12327 **Payroll Expense ($000):** 7245 **Personnel:** 60

WINNEBAGO—Winnebago County

☐ **WINNEBAGO MENTAL HEALTH INSTITUTE (524002)**, 1300 South Drive, Zip 54985, Mailing Address: Box 9, Zip 54985–0009; tel. 920/235–4910, **A**1 3 10 **F**4 29 34 75 82 86 87 98 99 103 130 **P**6
Primary Contact: Byran Bartow, Director
COO: Chris Craggs, Deputy Director
CFO: Lisa Spanbauer, Financial Program Supervisor
CMO: Randy Kerswill, M.D., Medical Director
CIO: Terrance J. Sweet, Director Information Technology
CHR: Mary Howard, Director Human Resources
CNO: Lori Monroe, Director of Nursing
Web address: www.dhfs.state.wi.us/mh_winnebago
Control: State, Government, Nonfederal **Service:** Psychiatric

Staffed Beds: 184 **Admissions:** 3752 **Census:** 175 **Outpatient Visits:** 0 **Births:** 0 **Total Expense ($000):** 111339 **Payroll Expense ($000):** 45352 **Personnel:** 456

WISCONSIN RAPIDS—Wood County

✠ **ASPIRUS RIVERVIEW HOSPITAL AND CLINICS, INC. (520033)**, 410 Dewey Street, Zip 54494–4715, Mailing Address: P.O. Box 8080, Zip 54495–8080; tel. 715/423–6060, **A**1 3 10 **F**3 4 8 13 15 17 18 26 28 30 31 34 37 40 43 44 45 47 49 54 64 65 68 69 70 74 76 77 78 79 80 81 82 83 84 85 86 87 88 89 90 92 93 96 98 104 107 108 109 110 111 113 114 115 117 118 119 120 121 123 124 126 129 131 132 134 135 143 144 145 147 148 154 156 157 167 169 **P**8 **S** Aspirus, Inc., Wausau, WI
Primary Contact: Brian Kief, President
CFO: Nancy Roth–Mallek, Vice President of Finance
CHR: Jessica Fox, Director of Human Resources
CNO: Kimberly A Johnson, R.N., MSN, Vice President Patient Care and Chief Nursing Officer
Web address: www.aspirus.org
Control: Other not–for–profit (including NFP Corporation) **Service:** General medical and surgical

Staffed Beds: 52 **Admissions:** 2477 **Census:** 27 **Outpatient Visits:** 81561 **Births:** 503 **Total Expense ($000):** 137277 **Payroll Expense ($000):** 48300 **Personnel:** 262

WOODRUFF—Oneida County

HOWARD YOUNG MEDICAL CENTER See Howard Young Medical Center, Inc.

✠ **HOWARD YOUNG MEDICAL CENTER, INC. (520091)**, 240 Maple Street, Zip 54568–9190, Mailing Address: P.O. Box 470, Zip 54568–0470; tel. 715/356–8000, **A**1 10 20 **F**3 8 11 15 18 26 28 29 30 34 40 43 45 46 51 56 64 65 68 70 75 79 80 81 82 84 85 86 87 88 89 93 96 97 107 110 111 115 119 129 130 132 134 135 143 146 148 154 **P**8 **S** Aspirus, Inc., Wausau, WI
Primary Contact: Teresa Theiler, President – North Region
CFO: Jamon Lamers, Director Finance
CMO: John Crump, M.D., Medical Staff President
CIO: Howard Dobizl, Director Information Technology Services
CHR: Michelle Cornelius, Director Human Resources
CNO: Jacqualyn Monge, Director of Nursing
Web address: https://www.aspirus.org/find-a-location/howard-young-medical-center-538
Control: Other not–for–profit (including NFP Corporation) **Service:** General medical and surgical

Staffed Beds: 17 **Admissions:** 933 **Census:** 12 **Outpatient Visits:** 37453 **Births:** 0 **Total Expense ($000):** 36807 **Payroll Expense ($000):** 14361 **Personnel:** 144

Hospitals, U.S. / WYOMING

WYOMING

AFTON—Lincoln County

★ **STAR VALLEY HEALTH (531313)**, 901 Adams Street, Zip 83110–9621, Mailing Address: P.O. Box 579, Zip 83110–0579; tel. 307/885–5800, (Nonreporting) **A**10 18
Primary Contact: Daniel Ordyna, Chief Executive Officer
COO: Mike Hunsaker, Chief Operating Officer
CFO: Chad Turner, Chief Financial Officer
CMO: Donald Kirk, M.D., Chief of Staff
CIO: Amy R Johnson, R.N., Quality Improvement Safety Officer
CHR: Trevor Merritt, Director Human Resources
CNO: Derek Greenwald, Chief Nursing Officer
Web address: https://starvalleyhealth.org/
Control: Hospital district or authority, Government, Nonfederal **Service**: General medical and surgical

Staffed Beds: 22

BASIN—Big Horn County

SOUTH BIG HORN COUNTY HOSPITAL See Three Rivers Health

★ **THREE RIVERS HEALTH (531301)**, 388 South US Highway 20, Zip 82410–8902; tel. 307/568–3311, (Nonreporting) **A**10 18
Primary Contact: Joel Jackson, Chief Executive Officer
Web address: https://www.trhealth.com/
Control: Hospital district or authority, Government, Nonfederal **Service**: General medical and surgical

Staffed Beds: 47

BUFFALO—Johnson County

JOHNSON COUNTY HEALTHCARE CENTER (531308), 497 West Lott Street, Zip 82834–1691; tel. 307/684–5521, (Nonreporting) **A**10 18
Primary Contact: Luke Senden, Chief Executive Officer
CMO: Blaine Ruby, M.D., Chief of Staff
CIO: Laurie Hansen, Director of Administration
CHR: Karen Ferguson, Director Human Resources
CNO: Mary Whaley, Director of Acute Care
Web address: www.jchealthcare.com
Control: Hospital district or authority, Government, Nonfederal **Service**: General medical and surgical

Staffed Beds: 15

CASPER—Natrona County

☐ **ELKHORN VALLEY REHABILITATION HOSPITAL (533027)**, 5715 East 2nd Street, Zip 82609–4322; tel. 307/265–0005, (Nonreporting) **A**1 10 **S** Ernest Health, Inc., Albuquerque, NM
Primary Contact: Connie Longwell, Chief Executive Officer
Web address: www.evrh.ernesthealth.com/
Control: Corporation, Investor–owned (for–profit) **Service**: Rehabilitation

Staffed Beds: 41

☐ ⇧ **SUMMIT MEDICAL CENTER (530034)**, 6350 East 2nd Street, Zip 82609–4264; tel. 307/232–6600, (Nonreporting) **A**1 10 21
Primary Contact: Raymond Vucetic, Chief Executive Officer
COO: Mindi L. Pile, Chief Operations Officer
CFO: Calvin Carey, Chief Financial Officer
CMO: Joseph Vigneri, M.D., Chief Medical Officer
CNO: Vanessa Sorensen, Chief Nursing Officer
Web address: www.summitmedicalcasper.com/
Control: Corporation, Investor–owned (for–profit) **Service**: General medical and surgical

Staffed Beds: 16

☐ **WYOMING BEHAVIORAL INSTITUTE (534004)**, 2521 East 15th Street, Zip 82609–4126; tel. 307/237–7444, (Nonreporting) **A**1 10 **S** Universal Health Services, Inc., King of Prussia, PA
Primary Contact: Mike Phillips, Chief Executive Officer
CFO: Carmel Bickford, Chief Financial Officer
CMO: Steven Brown, M.D., Medical Director
CHR: Jon Barra, Director Human Resources
Web address: www.wbihelp.com
Control: Corporation, Investor–owned (for–profit) **Service**: Psychiatric

Staffed Beds: 114

☒ **WYOMING MEDICAL CENTER (530012)**, 1233 East Second Street, Zip 82601–2988; tel. 307/577–7201, **A**1 3 5 10 20 **F**3 7 13 20 22 24 28 29 30 40 41 43 45 46 47 48 49 51 53 58 68 70 75 76 77 79 81 85 89 107 108 114 115 118 119 126 129 130 146 148 149 154 167 169 **S** Banner Health, Phoenix, AZ
Primary Contact: Lance Porter, President and Chief Executive Officer
COO: Rachel Bryant, Chief Operating Officer
CNO: Connie Coleman, R.N., Chief Nursing Officer
Web address: https://wyomingmedicalcenter.org/
Control: Other not–for–profit (including NFP Corporation) **Service**: General medical and surgical

Staffed Beds: 249 **Admissions**: 8122 **Census**: 100 **Outpatient Visits**: 93248 **Births**: 812 **Total Expense ($000)**: 240171 **Payroll Expense ($000)**: 75028 **Personnel**: 877

CHEYENNE—Laramie County

☒ △ **CHEYENNE REGIONAL MEDICAL CENTER (530014)**, 214 East 23rd Street, Zip 82001–3790; tel. 307/634–2273, **A**1 3 5 7 10 20 **F**3 5 8 11 12 13 15 18 20 22 24 26 28 29 30 31 32 34 35 37 38 40 43 44 45 46 47 48 49 50 51 55 56 59 60 61 62 63 64 65 68 70 72 73 74 75 76 77 78 79 81 82 83 84 85 86 87 89 90 91 92 93 96 97 98 100 101 102 104 107 108 111 115 116 117 118 119 120 121 122 123 124 126 130 131 135 143 146 147 148 149 153 154 156 157 162 164 165 167 169
Primary Contact: Timothy Thornell, FACHE, President and Chief Executive Officer
COO: Robin Roling, FACHE, MS, R.N., Chief Operating Officer
CFO: Neil W Bertrand, Interim Chief Financial Officer
CMO: Jeffrey Chapman, M.D., Chief Medical Officer
CNO: Tracy Garcia, MS, Chief Nursing Officer
Web address: www.cheyenneregional.org/
Control: County, Government, Nonfederal **Service**: General medical and surgical

Staffed Beds: 209 **Admissions**: 9252 **Census**: 102 **Outpatient Visits**: 164070 **Births**: 1041 **Total Expense ($000)**: 355514 **Payroll Expense ($000)**: 165635 **Personnel**: 1717

☒ **CHEYENNE VA MEDICAL CENTER**, 2360 East Pershing Boulevard, Zip 82001–5392; tel. 307/778–7550, (Nonreporting) **A**1 3 **S** Department of Veterans Affairs, Washington, DC
Primary Contact: Paul L. Roberts, Director
CFO: Melvin Cranford, Chief Fiscal Services
CMO: Roger Johnson, M.D., Chief of Staff
CIO: Liz McCulloch, Chief Information Resource Management Systems
CHR: Ron Lester, Chief Human Resources
Web address: www.cheyenne.va.gov/
Control: Veterans Affairs, Government, federal **Service**: General medical and surgical

Staffed Beds: 32

CODY—Park County

★ **CODY REGIONAL HEALTH (531312)**, 707 Sheridan Avenue, Zip 82414–3409; tel. 307/527–7501, (Total facility includes 94 beds in nursing home–type unit) **A**1 10 18 **F**3 4 5 7 11 13 15 18 20 28 29 30 31 34 35 40 41 43 45 55 56 57 59 60 62 63 64 68 70 76 78 79 81 84 85 87 89 93 97 100 101 102 104 107 108 109 110 111 115 119 120 121 124 127 128 130 131 132 133 146 147 148 149 151 152 153 154 156 160 167 **P**6 **S** Ovation Healthcare, Brentwood, TN
Primary Contact: Douglas A. McMillan, Administrator and Chief Executive Officer
CFO: Patrick G McConnell, Chief Financial Officer
CMO: Gary Hart, M.D., Chief Medical Officer
CHR: Dick Smith, Director Human Resources
Web address: www.westparkhospital.org
Control: Hospital district or authority, Government, Nonfederal **Service**: General medical and surgical

Staffed Beds: 112 **Admissions**: 1400 **Census**: 70

DOUGLAS—Converse County

★ **MEMORIAL HOSPITAL OF CONVERSE COUNTY (531302)**, 111 South Fifth Street, Zip 82633-2434, Mailing Address: P.O. Box 1450, Zip 82633-1450; tel. 307/358-2122, (Nonreporting) **A**10 18
Primary Contact: Matt Dammeyer, Ph.D., Chief Executive Officer
CFO: Curtis R. Dugger, Chief Financial Officer
CMO: James Morgan, M.D., Chief Medical Officer
CIO: Dave Patterson, Chief Information Officer
CHR: Linda York, Director Human Resource
CNO: Cristy Dicklich-Cobb, Chief Nursing Officer
Web address: www.conversehospital.com
Control: County, Government, Nonfederal **Service**: General medical and surgical

Staffed Beds: 25

EVANSTON—Uinta County

✠ **EVANSTON REGIONAL HOSPITAL (530032)**, 190 Arrowhead Drive, Zip 82930-9266; tel. 307/789-3636, (Nonreporting) **A**1 10 20 **S** Quorum Health, Brentwood, TN
Primary Contact: Cheri Willard, MSN, R.N., Chief Executive Officer
CHR: Joshua Jones, Director Human Resources
CNO: Angie Foster, Chief Nursing Officer
Web address: www.evanstonregionalhospital.com
Control: Corporation, Investor-owned (for-profit) **Service**: General medical and surgical

Staffed Beds: 42

WYOMING STATE HOSPITAL (534001), 830 Highway 150 South, Zip 82931-5341, Mailing Address: P.O. Box 177, Zip 82931-0177; tel. 307/789-3464, (Nonreporting) **A**10
Primary Contact: Kristi Barker, Administrator
CIO: Steve Baldwin, Manager Information Technology
Web address: https://health.wyo.gov/behavioralhealth/statehospital/
Control: State, Government, Nonfederal **Service**: Psychiatric

Staffed Beds: 104

GILLETTE—Campbell County

★ ⇑ **CAMPBELL COUNTY HEALTH (530002)**, 501 South Burma Avenue, Zip 82716-3426, Mailing Address: P.O. Box 3011, Zip 82717-3011; tel. 307/682-8811, (Nonreporting) **A**10 20 21
Primary Contact: Matthew Shahan, Chief Executive Officer
CFO: Dalton Huber, Chief Financial Officer
CIO: Chris Harrison, Manager Information Systems
CHR: John A Fitch, Vice President Human Resources
CNO: Deb L Tonn, Vice President Patient Care
Web address: https://www.cchwyo.org/
Control: Hospital district or authority, Government, Nonfederal **Service**: General medical and surgical

Staffed Beds: 217

JACKSON—Teton County

★ ⇑ **ST. JOHN'S HEALTH (530015)**, 625 East Broadway Street, Zip 83001-8642, Mailing Address: P.O. Box 428, Zip 83001-0428; tel. 307/733-3636, (Total facility includes 57 beds in nursing home-type unit) **A**5 10 20 21 **F**3 11 13 15 18 19 26 28 29 30 31 32 34 35 36 37 38 40 43 44 45 46 47 48 49 50 51 53 54 56 57 59 61 62 63 64 65 68 70 74 75 76 77 78 79 81 82 84 85 86 87 90 93 94 97 100 101 104 107 108 110 111 114 115 118 119 120 126 128 129 130 131 132 133 135 143 144 146 147 148 149 154 156 157 160
Primary Contact: Jeff Sollis, Chief Executive Officer
CIO: Lance Spranger, Chief Information Officer
CHR: Thomas Kinney, Chief Human Resource Officer
Web address: www.tetonhospital.org
Control: Hospital district or authority, Government, Nonfederal **Service**: General medical and surgical

Staffed Beds: 120 **Admissions**: 1849 **Census**: 60 **Outpatient Visits**: 121511 **Births**: 367 **Total Expense ($000)**: 163225 **Payroll Expense ($000)**: 79424 **Personnel**: 789

KEMMERER—Lincoln County

★ **SOUTH LINCOLN MEDICAL CENTER (531315)**, 711 Onyx Street, Zip 83101-3214; tel. 307/877-4401, (Nonreporting) **A**10 18
Primary Contact: Dave Ryerse, Chief Executive Officer
CFO: Curtis Nielson, Chief Financial Officer
CMO: G Christopher Krell, M.D., Chief of Staff
CNO: Kathi Parks, Director of Nursing
Web address: www.southlincolnmedical.com
Control: Hospital district or authority, Government, Nonfederal **Service**: General medical and surgical

Staffed Beds: 28

LANDER—Fremont County

SAGEWEST HEALTHCARE–LANDER See Sagewest Health Care At Lander

LARAMIE—Albany County

✠ **IVINSON MEMORIAL HOSPITAL (530025)**, 255 North 30th Street, Zip 82072-5140; tel. 307/742-2141, **A**1 3 10 20 **F**3 11 13 15 28 29 31 32 34 35 36 38 40 43 45 46 51 56 57 59 60 64 65 68 70 75 76 77 78 79 81 84 85 87 89 93 97 98 99 100 103 107 108 111 115 119 120 121 123 124 126 129 130 132 133 135 144 146 147 148 149 154 164 169
Primary Contact: Doug Faus, FACHE, Chief Executive Officer
COO: Terry Moss, Chief Operating Officer
CFO: Karl Vilums, Chief Financial Officer
CMO: John Ullrich, M.D., Chief of Staff
CIO: Brandon Lewis, Director of Information Technology
CHR: Kayla Parry, Manager Human Resources
CNO: Nicole Roonery, Chief Nursing Officer
Web address: www.ivinsonhospital.org
Control: Other not-for-profit (including NFP Corporation) **Service**: General medical and surgical

Staffed Beds: 50 **Admissions**: 1726 **Census**: 18 **Outpatient Visits**: 84936 **Births**: 398 **Total Expense ($000)**: 116999 **Payroll Expense ($000)**: 42541 **Personnel**: 511

LOVELL—Big Horn County

★ **NORTH BIG HORN HOSPITAL DISTRICT (531309)**, 1115 Lane 12, Zip 82431-9537; tel. 307/548-5200, (Nonreporting) **A**10 18
Primary Contact: Eric Connell, Chief Executive Officer
CFO: Lori Smith, Chief Financial Officer
CMO: Richard Jay, D.O., Chief of Staff
CIO: Lisa Strom, Director Information Systems
CHR: Barbara Shumway, Director Human Resources
Web address: www.nbhh.com
Control: Hospital district or authority, Government, Nonfederal **Service**: General medical and surgical

Staffed Beds: 109

LUSK—Niobrara County

★ **NIOBRARA COMMUNITY HOSPITAL (531314)**, 921 Ballencee Avenue, Zip 82225, Mailing Address: P.O. Box 780, Zip 82225-0780; tel. 307/334-4000, (Nonreporting) **A**10 18
Primary Contact: Dana Gilleland, Chief Executive Officer, Chief Financial Officer
Web address: www.niobrarahospital.com
Control: Hospital district or authority, Government, Nonfederal **Service**: General medical and surgical

Staffed Beds: 24

NEWCASTLE—Weston County

★ **WESTON COUNTY HEALTH SERVICES (531303)**, 1124 Washington Boulevard, Zip 82701-2972; tel. 307/746-4491, (Nonreporting) **A**10 18 **S** Monument Health, Rapid City, SD
Primary Contact: Randy L. Lindauer, Ph.D., FACHE, Chief Executive Officer
COO: Piper Allard, Chief Operating Officer
CFO: Lynn Moller, Chief Financial Officer
CMO: Chuck Franklin, M.D., Chief Medical Staff
CIO: Terri Frye, Information Technology Officer
CHR: Julie A Sindlinger, Director of Human Resources
Web address: www.wchs-wy.org
Control: Hospital district or authority, Government, Nonfederal **Service**: General medical and surgical

Staffed Beds: 70

Hospitals, U.S. / WYOMING

POWELL—Park County

★ **POWELL VALLEY HEALTH CARE (531310)**, 777 Avenue 'H', Zip 82435–2296; tel. 307/754–2267, (Total facility includes 100 beds in nursing home–type unit) **A**10 18 **F**3 7 10 11 13 14 15 18 28 29 31 34 35 40 43 45 50 56 59 65 67 68 70 75 76 78 79 81 85 87 89 97 100 107 110 111 115 119 130 131 133 135 146 147 149 154 156 169
Primary Contact: Joy Coulston, Chief Executive Officer
CMO: Valerie Lengfelder, M.D., Chief of Staff
CIO: Joshua Baxter, Director, Information Systems
CHR: Cassie Tinsley, Director, Human Resources
CNO: Arleen Campeau, R.N., Vice President Patient Care Services, Chief Nursing Officer
Web address: www.pvhc.org
Control: Hospital district or authority, Government, Nonfederal **Service**: General medical and surgical

Staffed Beds: 125 **Admissions**: 658 **Census**: 56 **Outpatient Visits**: 28552 **Births**: 153 **Total Expense ($000)**: 72190 **Payroll Expense ($000)**: 27491 **Personnel**: 404

RAWLINS—Carbon County

★ **MEMORIAL HOSPITAL OF CARBON COUNTY (531316)**, 2221 West Elm Street, Zip 82301–5108, Mailing Address: P.O. Box 460, Zip 82301–0460; tel. 307/324–2221, **A**10 18 **F**3 7 11 15 29 30 40 41 43 44 45 50 57 59 64 65 68 70 75 79 81 85 87 89 102 105 107 110 111 115 126 129 130 133 143 146 148 154 155 157 166 167 **S** Ovation Healthcare, Brentwood, TN
CMO: David Cesko, M.D., Chief of Staff
CIO: Toby Schaef, Director Information Technology
Web address: www.imhcc.com
Control: County, Government, Nonfederal **Service**: General medical and surgical

Staffed Beds: 25 **Admissions**: 1701 **Census**: 9 **Outpatient Visits**: 11281 **Births**: 33 **Personnel**: 163

RIVERTON—Fremont County

⊞ **SAGEWEST HEALTH CARE (530008)**, 2100 West Sunset Drive, Zip 82501–2274; tel. 307/856–4161, (Includes SAGEWEST HEALTH CARE AT LANDER, 1320 Bishop Randall Drive, Lander, Wyoming, Zip 82520–3996, tel. 307/332–4420; Stephen M Erixon, Chief Executive Officer) (Nonreporting) **A**1 10 20 **S** ScionHealth, Louisville, KY
Primary Contact: John Whiteside, Chief Executive Officer
CFO: Jennifer Hamilton, Chief Financial Officer
CMO: Cielette Karn, M.D., Chief of Staff
CIO: Linda Tice, Director Information Systems
CHR: Dawn Nelson, Director Human Resources
CNO: Charlene Falgout, Chief Nursing Officer
Web address: www.sagewesthealthcare.com
Control: Corporation, Investor–owned (for–profit) **Service**: General medical and surgical

Staffed Beds: 145

ROCK SPRINGS—Sweetwater County

⇑ **ASPEN MOUNTAIN MEDICAL CENTER (530035)**, 4401 College Drive, Zip 82901–3507; tel. 307/352–8900, (Nonreporting) **A**10 21
Primary Contact: Melissa Anderson, MSN, R.N., Acting Chief Executive Officer
Web address: www.aspenmountainmc.com
Control: Partnership, Investor–owned (for–profit) **Service**: General medical and surgical

Staffed Beds: 16

⊞ **MEMORIAL HOSPITAL OF SWEETWATER COUNTY (530011)**, 1200 College Drive, Zip 82901–5868, Mailing Address: P.O. Box 1359, Zip 82902–1359; tel. 307/362–3711, **A**1 10 20 **F**3 11 13 15 28 30 31 34 35 37 40 43 44 48 50 51 55 56 57 59 60 64 68 70 71 74 75 76 77 78 79 81 82 87 93 96 97 107 110 111 114 115 118 119 120 121 122 123 126 129 130 131 132 134 135 146 147 148 149 154 167 169 **P**6
Primary Contact: Irene Richardson, Chief Executive Officer
COO: Mandeep Gill, Chief Operating Officer
CFO: Tami Love, Chief Financial Officer
CMO: Sigsbee Duck, M.D., President, Medical Staff
CHR: Amber Fisk, Director Human Resources
CNO: Kallie Mikkelsen, Vice President Nursing
Web address: www.sweetwatermemorial.com/default.aspx
Control: County, Government, Nonfederal **Service**: General medical and surgical

Staffed Beds: 58 **Admissions**: 1437 **Census**: 14 **Outpatient Visits**: 179348 **Births**: 397 **Total Expense ($000)**: 117309 **Payroll Expense ($000)**: 46103 **Personnel**: 516

SARATOGA—Carbon County

⇑ **NORTH PLATTE VALLEY MEDICAL CENTER (530037)**, 1300 West Bridge Avenue, Zip 82331, Mailing Address: PO Box 549, Zip 82331–0549; tel. 307/326–3169, (Nonreporting) **A**21
Primary Contact: Jeffrey Mincy, Chief Executive Officer
COO: EvaMarie Popelka, Chief Operating Officer
CFO: Donna Pratt, Controller
CMO: Brendan Fitzsimmons, Medical Director
CHR: Rachel Blumenthal, Human Resources Generalist
CNO: Tamara Hobson, Director of Nursing
Web address: www.npvmc.org
Control: Other not–for–profit (including NFP Corporation) **Service**: General medical and surgical

Staffed Beds: 25

SHERIDAN—Sheridan County

⊞ **SHERIDAN MEMORIAL HOSPITAL (530006)**, 1401 West Fifth Street, Zip 82801–2799; tel. 307/672–1000, (Nonreporting) **A**1 5 10 20
Primary Contact: Michael McCafferty, Chief Executive Officer
CMO: John Addlesperger, D.O., Chief Medical Officer
CIO: Nyle Morgan, Chief Information Officer
CHR: Len Gross, Chief Human Resources Officer
Web address: www.sheridanhospital.org
Control: County, Government, Nonfederal **Service**: General medical and surgical

Staffed Beds: 88

⊞ **SHERIDAN VA MEDICAL CENTER**, 1898 Fort Road, Zip 82801–8320; tel. 307/672–3473, (Nonreporting) **A**1 **S** Department of Veterans Affairs, Washington, DC
Primary Contact: Pamela Crowell, Director
COO: Chandra Lake, Associate Director
CFO: Donna Fuerstenberg, Fiscal Chief
CMO: Wendell Robison, M.D., Chief of Staff
CIO: Anthony Giljum, Chief Information Officer
CHR: James Hardin, Human Resources Officer
Web address: www.sheridan.va.gov/
Control: Veterans Affairs, Government, federal **Service**: Psychiatric

Staffed Beds: 31

SUNDANCE—Crook County

★ **CROOK COUNTY MEDICAL SERVICES DISTRICT (531311)**, 713 Oak Street, Zip 82729, Mailing Address: P.O. Box 517, Zip 82729–0517; tel. 307/283–3501, (Total facility includes 20 beds in nursing home–type unit) **A**10 18 **F**7 29 32 34 40 41 56 57 59 64 65 67 68 75 89 97 107 111 115 119 127 128 133 147 148 154 169
Primary Contact: Micki Lyons, Chief Executive Officer
CFO: Betty Meyers, Chief Financial Officer
CMO: Jeremi Villano, M.D., Chief of Staff
CHR: Patricia Feist, Manager Human Resources
Web address: www.ccmsd.org/
Control: Hospital district or authority, Government, Nonfederal **Service**: General medical and surgical

Staffed Beds: 28 **Admissions**: 179 **Census**: 27 **Outpatient Visits**: 9291 **Births**: 0

THERMOPOLIS—Hot Springs County

★ **HOT SPRINGS COUNTY HOSPITAL DISTRICT (531304)**, 150 East Arapahoe Street, Zip 82443–2498; tel. 307/864–3121, (Nonreporting) **A**3 10 18 **S** HealthTech Management Services, Plano, TX
Primary Contact: Scott Alwin, Chief Executive Officer
CFO: Shelly Larson, Chief Financial Officer
CHR: Patti Jeunehomme, Director Human Resources
CNO: Sarah Aliff, Ph.D., Chief Nursing Officer
Web address: www.hscmh.org
Control: County, Government, Nonfederal **Service**: General medical and surgical

Staffed Beds: 15

Hospitals, U.S. / WYOMING

TORRINGTON—Goshen County

☒ **COMMUNITY HOSPITAL (531307)**, 2000 Campbell Drive, Zip 82240–1597; tel. 307/532–4181, **A**1 10 18 **F**3 13 15 18 28 29 30 34 35 40 43 45 55 56 57 59 65 68 70 75 76 79 81 85 89 90 93 94 97 102 104 107 110 115 119 127 128 130 131 133 143 146 147 148 149 153 154 157 169 **S** Banner Health, Phoenix, AZ
Primary Contact: Ingrid Long, Chief Executive Officer and Chief Nursing Officer
CFO: Jennifer McMillan, Chief Financial Officer
CIO: Rod Miller, Chief Information Technology
CNO: Ingrid Long, Chief Executive Officer and Chief Nursing Officer
Web address: https://www.bannerhealth.com/locations/torrington/community-hospital
Control: Other not–for–profit (including NFP Corporation) **Service**: General medical and surgical

> **Staffed Beds**: 25 **Admissions**: 717 **Census**: 8 **Outpatient Visits**: 21561
> **Births**: 64 **Total Expense ($000)**: 42170 **Payroll Expense ($000)**: 15561
> **Personnel**: 151

WHEATLAND—Platte County

☒ **PLATTE COUNTY MEMORIAL HOSPITAL (531305)**, 201 14th Street, Zip 82201–3201, Mailing Address: P.O. Box 848, Zip 82201–0848; tel. 307/322–3636, **A**1 10 18 **F**3 7 13 15 28 29 30 32 34 35 40 45 46 47 48 50 56 57 59 65 68 70 75 76 77 79 81 85 89 93 102 107 108 110 115 119 127 133 135 146 147 148 149 150 154 156 169 **S** Banner Health, Phoenix, AZ
Primary Contact: Sandy Dugger, Chief Executive Officer
CFO: Jennifer McMillan, Chief Financial Officer
CIO: Robin May, Director Information Systems
CNO: Ingrid Long, Chief Nursing Officer
Web address: https://www.bannerhealth.com/locations/wheatland/platte-county-memorial-hospital
Control: Other not–for–profit (including NFP Corporation) **Service**: General medical and surgical

> **Staffed Beds**: 25 **Admissions**: 407 **Census**: 5 **Outpatient Visits**: 13631
> **Births**: 33 **Total Expense ($000)**: 28324 **Payroll Expense ($000)**: 12730
> **Personnel**: 160

WORLAND—Washakie County

★ **WASHAKIE MEDICAL CENTER (531306)**, 400 South 15th Street, Zip 82401–3531, Mailing Address: P.O. Box 700, Zip 82401–0700; tel. 307/347–3221, **A**10 18 **F**3 8 11 13 15 28 29 31 34 40 43 45 59 64 68 70 75 76 77 78 79 81 85 93 107 110 111 115 119 133 145 146 148 149 154 167 **S** Banner Health, Phoenix, AZ
Primary Contact: Jay Stallings, Chief Executive Officer
CFO: Jennifer McMillan, Chief Financial Officer
CHR: Jerry Clipp, Manager Human Resources
CNO: Lisa Van Brunt, Chief Nursing Officer
Web address: https://www.bannerhealth.com/locations/worland/washakie-medical-center
Control: Other not–for–profit (including NFP Corporation) **Service**: General medical and surgical

> **Staffed Beds**: 18 **Admissions**: 389 **Census**: 4 **Outpatient Visits**: 16966
> **Births**: 23 **Total Expense ($000)**: 29938 **Payroll Expense ($000)**: 10366
> **Personnel**: 122

Hospital, Medicare Provider Number, Address, Telephone, Approval, Facility, and Physician Codes, Health Care System

★ American Hospital Association (AHA) membership
☐ The Joint Commission accreditation
○ Healthcare Facilities Accreditation Program
◇ DNV Healthcare Inc. accreditation
⇑ Center for Improvement in Healthcare Quality Accreditation
△ Commission on Accreditation of Rehabilitation Facilities (CARF) accreditation

Hospitals in Areas Associated with the United States by Area

AMERICAN SAMOA

PAGO PAGO—Washakie County

★ **LYNDON B. JOHNSON TROPICAL MEDICAL CENTER (640001)**, Faga'alu Village, Zip 96799, Mailing Address: P.O. Box LBJ, Zip 96799; tel. 684/633-1222, (Nonreporting) **A**10
Primary Contact: Akapusi Ledua, Chief Executive Officer
Web address: https://lbjtmc.org/
Control: State, Government, Nonfederal **Service**: General medical and surgical

Staffed Beds: 144

GUAM

AGANA—Guam County

⊞ **U. S. NAVAL HOSPITAL GUAM**, Building #50 Farenholt Avenue, Zip 96910, Mailing Address: PSC 490, Box 208, FPO, Zip 96540; tel. 671/344-9340, (Nonreporting) **A**1 **S** Bureau of Medicine and Surgery, Department of the Navy, Falls Church, VA
Primary Contact: Captain Daniel Cornwell, Command Officer
Web address: www.med.navy.mil/sites/usnhguam/Pages/default.aspx
Control: Navy, Government, federal **Service**: General medical and surgical

Staffed Beds: 55

DEDEDO—Guam County

☐ **GUAM REGIONAL MEDICAL CITY (650003)**, 133 Route 3, Zip 96932, Mailing Address: P.O. Box 3830, Hagatna, Zip 96932; tel. 671/483-8046, (Nonreporting) **A**1 10
Primary Contact: Alan V. Funtanilla, Executive Vice President, Chief Operating Officer
Web address: www.grmc.gu/
Control: Corporation, Investor-owned (for-profit) **Service**: General medical and surgical

Staffed Beds: 130

TAMUNING—Guam County

GUAM MEMORIAL HOSPITAL AUTHORITY (650001), 850 Governor Carlos G Camacho Road, Zip 96913; tel. 671/647-2108, (Nonreporting) **A**10
Primary Contact: Lillian Posadas, Hospital Administrator, Chief Executive Officer
CFO: Alan Ulrich, Chief Financial Officer
CMO: James J Stadler, M.D., Associate Administrator Medical Services
CIO: Vince Quichocho, Manager Information Systems
CHR: Elizabeth Claros, Administrator Personnel Services
Web address: www.gmha.org
Control: Hospital district or authority, Government, Nonfederal **Service**: General medical and surgical

Staffed Beds: 104

MARIANA ISLANDS

SAIPAN—Guam County

★ **COMMONWEALTH HEALTH CENTER (660001)**, Navy Hill Road, Zip 96950, Mailing Address: P.O. Box 500409, Zip 96950; tel. 670/234-8950, (Nonreporting) **A**10
Primary Contact: Esther L. Muna, FACHE, Chief Executive Officer
CFO: Perlita Santos, Chief Financial Officer
CMO: John M. Tudela, M.D., Chief Medical Officer
CIO: Anthony Reyes, Information Technology Director
CHR: Clarinda Ngiraisui, Director, Human Resources
CNO: Leslie Camacho, R.N., Director of Nursing
Web address: www.chcc.gov.mp
Control: Corporation, Investor-owned (for-profit) **Service**: General medical and surgical

Staffed Beds: 86

MARSHALL ISLANDS

KWAJALEIN ATOLL—Guam County

KWAJALEIN HOSPITAL, U S Army Kwajalein Atoll, Zip 96555, Mailing Address: Ocean Road, P.O. Box 1607, APO AP, Zip 96555-5000; tel. 805/355-2225, (Nonreporting) **S** Department of the Army, Office of the Surgeon General, Falls Church, VA
Primary Contact: Elaine McMahon, Administrator
Control: Army, Government, federal **Service**: General medical and surgical

Staffed Beds: 14

PUERTO RICO

AGUADILLA—Aguadilla County

⊞ **HOSPITAL BUEN SAMARITANO (400079)**, Carr #2 Km 141-1 Ave Severiano Cuevas, Zip 00603, Mailing Address: P.O. Box 4055, Zip 00605-4055; tel. 787/658-0000, (Nonreporting) **A**1 10
Primary Contact: Giselle K. Van Derdys Arroyo, Chief Executive Officer
CFO: Edwin Orama Acevedo, Financial Supervisor
CMO: Arturo Cedeno Llorens, M.D., Medical Director
CHR: Jose Garcia Rivera, Director Human Resources
CNO: Eneida Alicea Perez, Interim Nursing Director
Web address: www.hbspr.org
Control: Other not-for-profit (including NFP Corporation) **Service**: General medical and surgical

Staffed Beds: 145

Hospitals, U.S. / PUERTO RICO

AIBONITO—Aibonito County

CENTRO DE SALUD CONDUCTUAL MENONITA–CIMA (404009), Carretera Estatal 14 Interior, Zip 00705, Mailing Address: PO Box 871, Zip 00705; tel. 787/714–2462, **A**1 3 10 **F**3 5 29 30 38 98 101 102 104 105 127 130 132 135 149 152 153 154 160 161 162 164 165 **P**5
Primary Contact: Marie Cruz, Administrator
Web address: www.menonitacima.org
Control: Other not–for–profit (including NFP Corporation) Service: Psychiatric

Staffed Beds: 61 Admissions: 3353 Census: 50 Outpatient Visits: 0 Births: 0 Total Expense ($000): 19039 Payroll Expense ($000): 6044 Personnel: 218

MENNONITE GENERAL HOSPITAL (400018), Calle Jose C Vasquez, Zip 00705, Mailing Address: P.O. Box 372800, Cayey, Zip 00737–2800; tel. 787/316–3200, **A**1 5 10 **F**3 13 15 30 34 40 41 45 46 57 59 60 64 65 66 68 70 75 76 78 79 81 82 89 107 110 111 114 115 119 130 145 146 147 148 149 157 169
Primary Contact: Maribel Toro, Chief Executive Officer
COO: Marta R Mercado Suro, Chief Operating Officer
CFO: Jose E Solivan, Chief Financial Officer
CMO: Victor Hernandez Miranda, M.D., Chief of Staff
CIO: Daniza Morales, Manager Information System
CHR: Evelyn Padilla Ortiz, Director Human Resources
CNO: Gloria Mercado, Director of Nursing
Web address: www.hospitalmenonita.com
Control: Other not–for–profit (including NFP Corporation) Service: General medical and surgical

Staffed Beds: 137 Admissions: 5916 Census: 77 Outpatient Visits: 129317 Births: 126 Total Expense ($000): 84983 Payroll Expense ($000): 25521 Personnel: 788

ARECIBO—Arecibo County

HOSPITAL METROPOLITANO DR. SUSONI (400117), Calle Palma #55, Zip 00612, Mailing Address: P.O. Box 145200, Zip 00614; tel. 787/650–1030, (Nonreporting) **A**1 10
Primary Contact: Humberto Perez-Pola, Executive Director
CFO: Francisco Silva, Financial Director
CMO: Ada S Miranda, M.D., Medical Director
CIO: Mayra Montano, Director Information Systems
CHR: Janira Hernandez, Coordinator Human Resources
CNO: Damaris Rios, Executive Nursing Director
Web address: www.metropavia.com/DrSusoni.cfm
Control: Corporation, Investor–owned (for–profit) Service: General medical and surgical

Staffed Beds: 119

HOSPITAL PAVIA ARECIBO (400087), 129 San Luis Avenue, Zip 00612, Mailing Address: P.O. Box 659, Zip 00613; tel. 787/650–7272, (Nonreporting) **A**1 3 10
Primary Contact: Adrin Gonzlez Figueroa, Executive Director
COO: Jamie Rivera, Chief Financial Officer
CFO: Agustin Gonzalez, Director Finance
CMO: Antoine Pavia, M.D., Medical Director
CIO: David Valle, Chief Information Officer
CHR: Yesenia Natal, Coordinator Human Resources
CNO: Iris Toledo, Chief Nursing Officer
Web address: www.cayetano@xsn.net
Control: Corporation, Investor–owned (for–profit) Service: General medical and surgical

Staffed Beds: 184

BAYAMON—Bayamon County

BAYAMON MEDICAL CENTER (400032), Route 2, KM 11–7, Zip 00960, Mailing Address: P.O. Box 306, Zip 00960; tel. 787/620–8181, (Includes PUERTO RICO WOMEN AND CHILDREN'S HOSPITAL, P O Box 1999, Bayamon, Puerto Rico, Zip 00960, tel. 787/474–1378; Jose Samuel Rosado, Chief Executive Officer) (Nonreporting) **A**1 3 5 10
Primary Contact: Jose Samuel. Rosado, Chief Executive Officer
CFO: Luz D Medina, Controller
CMO: Norma Ortiz, M.D., Medical Director
CIO: Leticia Santana, Administrator Medical Records
Web address: www.hospitalhermanosmelendez.net
Control: Corporation, Investor–owned (for–profit) Service: General medical and surgical

Staffed Beds: 211

★ **DOCTOR'S CENTER OF BAYAMON (400102)**, Extension Hermanas Davila, Zip 00960, Mailing Address: P.O. Box 2957, Zip 00960; tel. 787/622–5420, (Nonreporting) **A**10
Primary Contact: Maria Marte, Administrator
Web address: https://www.tuhospitalfamiliar.com
Control: Corporation, Investor–owned (for–profit) Service: General medical and surgical

Staffed Beds: 91

HOSPITAL SAN PABLO (400109), Calle Santa Cruz 70, Zip 00961–7020, Mailing Address: P.O. Box 236, Zip 00960–0236; tel. 787/740–4747, (Nonreporting) **A**1 3 5 10
Primary Contact: Annabelle Irizarry Morales, Administrator
Web address: www.sanpablo.com
Control: Corporation, Investor–owned (for–profit) Service: General medical and surgical

Staffed Beds: 313

HOSPITAL UNIVERSITARIO DR. RAMON RUIZ ARNAU (400105), Avenue Laurel #100, Santa Juanita, Zip 00956; tel. 787/787–5151, (Nonreporting) **A**1 3 5 10 **S** Puerto Rico Department of Health, San Juan, PR
Primary Contact: Victor L. Medina Cruz, M.D., Executive Director
CFO: Elsie Morales, Chief Financial Officer
CMO: Hector Cintron Principe, M.D., Director
CIO: Irma Duprey, Administrator Medical Records
CHR: Aurea De Leon, Chief Human Resources Officer
Web address: www.salud.gov.pr/Dept-de-Salud/Pages/Nuestros-Hospitales.aspx
Control: State, Government, Nonfederal Service: General medical and surgical

Staffed Beds: 101

PUERTO RICO CHILDREN'S HOSPITAL See Puerto Rico Women and Children's Hospital

CABO ROJO—Cabo Rojo County

HOSPITAL PSIQUIATRICO METROPOLITANO (404007), 108 Munoz Rivera Street, Zip 00623–4060, Mailing Address: P.O. Box 910, Zip 00623–0910; tel. 787/851–2025, (Nonreporting) **A**1 10
Primary Contact: Giovanni Ortiz, Executive Director
Web address: www.metropavia.com/CaboRojo.cfm
Control: Other not–for–profit (including NFP Corporation) Service: Psychiatric

Staffed Beds: 43

CAGUAS—Caguas County

HIMA SAN PABLO CAGUAS (400120), Avenida Munoz Marin, Zip 00726, Mailing Address: P.O. Box 4980, Zip 00726; tel. 787/653–3434, (Nonreporting) **A**1 2 3 10
Primary Contact: Andre Rodriguez, Administrator
CFO: Luis A Arroyo, Chief Financial Officer
CMO: Ivan E Del Toro, M.D., Medical Director
CIO: Giovanni Piereschi, Vice President Enterprise Information and Chief Information Officer
CHR: Elena Robinson, Chief Human Resources Officer
CNO: Elenia Berrios, Chief Nursing Officer
Web address: www.himasanpablo.com
Control: Partnership, Investor–owned (for–profit) Service: General medical and surgical

Staffed Beds: 415

HOSPITAL MENONITA DE CAGUAS (400104), P.O. Box 6660, Zip 00726–6660; tel. 787/653–0550, (Nonreporting) **A**1 3 5 10
Primary Contact: Jose Guillermo. Pastrana, Executive Director
Web address: www.sistemamenonita.com
Control: Other not–for–profit (including NFP Corporation) Service: General medical and surgical

Staffed Beds: 200

Hospital, Medicare Provider Number, Address, Telephone, Approval, Facility, and Physician Codes, Health Care System

★ American Hospital Association (AHA) membership
☐ The Joint Commission accreditation
○ Healthcare Facilities Accreditation Program
◇ DNV Healthcare Inc. accreditation
⇑ Center for Improvement in Healthcare Quality Accreditation
△ Commission on Accreditation of Rehabilitation Facilities (CARF) accreditation

© 2025 AHA Guide

Hospitals, U.S. / PUERTO RICO

CAROLINA—Carolina County

- **HOSPITAL DE LA UNIVERSIDAD DE PUERTO RICO/DR. FEDERICO TRILLA (400112)**, 65th Infanteria, KM 8 3, Zip 00984, Mailing Address: P.O. Box 6021, Zip 00984; tel. 787/757-1800, (Nonreporting) **A**1 3 5 10
  Primary Contact: Yelitza Sanchez Rodriguez, Chief Executive Officer
  CFO: Yolanda Quinonez, Chief Financial Officer
  CMO: Marina Roman, M.D., Medical Director
  CIO: Francisco Perez, Manager Management Information Systems
  CHR: Betzaida Jimenez, Director Human Resources
  Web address: www.hospitalupr.org
  Control: Corporation, Investor-owned (for-profit) **Service**: General medical and surgical

  Staffed Beds: 250

CASTANER—Lares County

- ★ **CASTANER GENERAL HOSPITAL (400010)**, KM 64-2, Route 135, Zip 00631, Mailing Address: P.O. Box 1003, Zip 00631; tel. 787/829-5010, (Nonreporting) **A**5 10
  Primary Contact: Robin Russell, Executive Director
  COO: Agustin Ponce, Supervisor Maintenance
  CFO: Guillermo Jimenez, Director Finance
  CMO: Jose O Rodriguez, M.D., Medical Director
  CHR: Nydimar Salcedo, Chief Human Resources Officer
  CNO: Margarita Rentas, R.N., Nursing Director
  Web address: www.hospitalcastaner.com
  Control: Other not-for-profit (including NFP Corporation) **Service**: General medical and surgical

  Staffed Beds: 24

CAYEY—Cayey County

- **HOSPITAL MENONITA DE CAYEY (400013)**, 4 H Mendoza Street, Zip 00736-3801, Mailing Address: P.O. Box 373130, Zip 00737-3130; tel. 787/263-1001, (Nonreporting) **A**1 5 10
  Primary Contact: Maria del Mar Torres Hernandez, Administrator
  COO: Leda Marta R Mercado, Chief Operating Officer
  CFO: Jose E Solivan, Chief Financial Officer
  CMO: Luis J Rodriquez Saenz, M.D., Medical Director
  CIO: Daniza Morales, Chief Information Officer
  CHR: Evelyn Padilla Ortiz, Director Human Resources
  Web address: www.hospitalmenonita.com
  Control: Other not-for-profit (including NFP Corporation) **Service**: General medical and surgical

  Staffed Beds: 225

CIDRA—Cidra County

- **FIRST HOSPITAL PANAMERICANO (404004)**, State Road 787 KM 1 5, Zip 00739, Mailing Address: P.O. Box 1400, Zip 00739; tel. 787/739-5555, (Nonreporting) **A**1 3 5 10 **S** Universal Health Services, Inc., King of Prussia, PA
  Primary Contact: Astro Munoz, Executive Director
  COO: Tim McCarthy, President Puerto Rico Division
  CFO: Arthur Fernandez, Chief Financial Officer
  CMO: William Almodavar, M.D., Director Medical
  CIO: Tomas Rodriguez, Chief Information Technology Officer
  CHR: Shirley Ayala, Director Human Resources
  Web address: www.hospitalpanamericano.com
  Control: Corporation, Investor-owned (for-profit) **Service**: Psychiatric

  Staffed Beds: 153

COTO LAUREL—Ponce County

- ★ **HOSPITAL MENONITA PONCE (400113)**, 506 Carr Road, Zip 00780; tel. 787/848-2100, **A**3 10 **F**3 13 15 18 20 22 29 30 38 45 47 49 51 70 72 74 75 76 77 79 81 89 107 108 110 111 114 118 119 130 148 149 157 164
  Primary Contact: Alexander Reyes Meléndez, Executive Director
  CFO: Marian Collazo, Director Finance
  CMO: Ramon Rodriguez Rivas, M.D., Medical Director
  CIO: Ramon Acevedo, Supervisor Information Systems
  CHR: Candie Rodriguez, Director Human Resources
  Web address: https://www.sistemamenonita.com/nuevo-hospital-menonita-ponce
  Control: Other not-for-profit (including NFP Corporation) **Service**: General medical and surgical

  Staffed Beds: 135 **Admissions**: 4808 **Census**: 72 **Births**: 392 **Total Expense ($000)**: 39642 **Payroll Expense ($000)**: 12714 **Personnel**: 430

HOSPITAL SAN CRISTOBAL See Hospital Menonita Ponce

FAJARDO—Fajardo County

- **CARIBBEAN MEDICAL CENTER (400131)**, 151 Avenue Osvaldo Molina, Zip 00738-4013, Mailing Address: Call Box 70006, Zip 00738-7006; tel. 787/801-0081, (Nonreporting) **A**1 10
  Primary Contact: Ana Oliveras Laguna, Administrator
  CMO: Miguel Rodriguez, Medical Director
  Web address: www.caribbeanmedicalcenter.com
  Control: Other not-for-profit (including NFP Corporation) **Service**: General medical and surgical

  Staffed Beds: 39

- ★ **HOSPITAL SAN PABLO DEL ESTE HIMA FAJARDO (400125)**, Avenida General Valero, 404, Zip 00738, Mailing Address: P.O. Box 1028, Zip 00738-1028; tel. 787/863-0505, (Nonreporting) **A**10
  Primary Contact: Orlando Rivera, Executive Director
  CFO: Luis A Arroyo, Chief Financial Officer
  CMO: Manuel Navas, M.D., Medical Director
  CHR: Vilma Rodriguez, Director Human Resources
  Web address: www.sanpablo.com
  Control: Corporation, Investor-owned (for-profit) **Service**: General medical and surgical

  Staffed Beds: 72

GUAYAMA—Guayama County

- **HOSPITAL MENONITA GUAYAMA (400048)**, Avenue Pedro Albizu Campos, Zip 00784, Mailing Address: PO Box 10011, Zip 00785-1006; tel. 787/864-4300, **A**1 5 10 **F**3 13 15 18 29 30 31 34 35 40 41 45 51 57 59 60 65 70 75 76 78 79 81 87 89 93 96 97 107 110 111 114 115 119 130 145 146 147 148 149 154 157 164
  Primary Contact: Rogelio Diaz Garcia, Executive Director
  COO: Arnaldo Rodriguez Sanchez, M.D., Chief Operating Officer
  CFO: Rosemary De La Cruz, Chief Financial Officer
  CMO: Gerson Jimenez, M.D., Medical Director
  CHR: Ivette Lacot, Director Human Resources
  Web address: www.ssepr.com
  Control: Other not-for-profit (including NFP Corporation) **Service**: General medical and surgical

  Staffed Beds: 155 **Admissions**: 7086 **Census**: 95 **Outpatient Visits**: 65165 **Births**: 419 **Total Expense ($000)**: 65615 **Payroll Expense ($000)**: 14522 **Personnel**: 444

GUAYNABO—Guaynabo County

- **PROFESSIONAL HOSPITAL GUAYNABO (400122)**, Carretera 199 Km 1.2 Avenue, Zip 00969, Mailing Address: PO Box 1609, Zip 00970; tel. 787/708-6560, (Nonreporting) **A**10
  Primary Contact: Edwin Sueiro, Chief Executive Officer
  Web address: www.professionalhospital.com
  Control: Other not-for-profit (including NFP Corporation) **Service**: Psychiatric

  Staffed Beds: 54

HATO REY—San Juan County

- **I. GONZALEZ MARTINEZ ONCOLOGIC HOSPITAL (400012)**, Puerto Rico Medical Center, Zip 00935, Mailing Address: P.O. Box 191811, Zip 00919-1811; tel. 787/765-2382, **A**1 2 3 5 10 **F**3 8 15 29 30 31 55 59 70 75 77 78 79 81 87 90 91 93 96 107 110 111 114 119 130 148
  Primary Contact: Yarisis Centeno, Executive Director
  COO: Felix Ortiz Baez, Administrator
  CFO: Yolanda Quinones, Director Finance
  CMO: Carlos Chevere, M.D., Medical Director
  CHR: Luz Maria Hernandez, Director Human Resources
  Control: Other not-for-profit (including NFP Corporation)

  Staffed Beds: 66 **Admissions**: 1310 **Census**: 20 **Outpatient Visits**: 51171 **Births**: 0 **Total Expense ($000)**: 22501 **Payroll Expense ($000)**: 7391 **Personnel**: 221

Hospitals, U.S. / PUERTO RICO

HUMACAO—Humacao County

☒ **HOSPITAL HIMA DE HUMACAO (400005)**, 3 Font Martelo Street, Zip 00791–3342, Mailing Address: P.O. Box 639, Zip 00792–0639; tel. 787/656–2424, (Nonreporting) **A**1 10
Primary Contact: Maria E. Jacobo, Executive Director
COO: Carlos M Pineiro, President
CFO: Luis A Arroyo, Chief Financial Officer
CMO: Francisco R. Carballo, M.D., Medical Director
CIO: Giovanni Piereschi, Vice President Management Information Systems
CHR: Iris Abreu, Supervisor Human Resources
Web address: www.himasanpablo.com
Control: Corporation, Investor–owned (for–profit) **Service**: General medical and surgical

Staffed Beds: 49

★ **HOSPITAL MENONITA HUMACAO (400011)**, 300 Font Martelo Street, Zip 00791–3230, Mailing Address: P.O. Box 8630, Zip 00792–0699; tel. 787/852–0505, **A**10 **F**3 8 30 35 40 41 45 64 70 74 75 77 79 81 86 87 89 107 114 119 130 145 146 148 149 157
Primary Contact: Pedro Diaz Vazquez, Administrator
CFO: Ivonne Rivera–Santos, Director Finance
CMO: Carmelo Herrero, M.D., Medical Director
CHR: Ivonne Lopez, Director Human Resources
Control: Other not–for–profit (including NFP Corporation) **Service**: General medical and surgical

Staffed Beds: 73 **Admissions:** 4412 **Census:** 64 **Births:** 0 **Total Expense ($000):** 36491 **Payroll Expense ($000):** 9175 **Personnel:** 270

★ **RYDER MEMORIAL HOSPITAL (400007)**, 355 Font Martelo Street, Zip 00791–3249, Mailing Address: P.O. Box 859, Zip 00792–0859; tel. 787/852–0768, (Nonreporting) **A**5 10
Primary Contact: Carmen Colon, Chief Executive Officer
CFO: Jose O Ortiz, Chief Financial Officer
CMO: Raul Ramos Pereira, M.D., Medical Director
CIO: Joseph V Cruz, Chief Information Officer
CHR: Maria Figueroa, Director Human Resources
CNO: Aurelis Burgus, Nursing Director
Web address: www.hryder@prtc.net
Control: Other not–for–profit (including NFP Corporation) **Service**: General medical and surgical

Staffed Beds: 179

MANATI—Manati County

☒ **DOCTORS CENTER MANATI (400118)**, KM 47-7, Zip 00674, Mailing Address: P.O. Box 30532, Zip 00674; tel. 787/854–3322, (Nonreporting) **A**1 3 5 10
Primary Contact: Obdulia Medina Rivera, Executive Director
Web address: https://www.tuhospitalfamiliar.com
Control: Corporation, Investor–owned (for–profit) **Service**: General medical and surgical

Staffed Beds: 238

★ **ENCOMPASS HEALTH REHABILITATION HOSPITAL OF MANATI (403026)**, Carretera 2, Kilometro 47 7, Zip 00674; tel. 787/621–3800, (Nonreporting) **A**10 **S** Encompass Health Corporation, Birmingham, AL
Primary Contact: Ruthmaris Nieves Martinez, Chief Executive Officer
CFO: Jesus M Corazon, Controller
CMO: Jamie L Marrero, M.D., Medical Director
CHR: Erika Landrau, Director Human Resources
CNO: Evelyn Diaz, R.N., Chief Nursing Officer
Web address: www.healthsouth.com
Control: Corporation, Investor–owned (for–profit) **Service**: Rehabilitation

Staffed Beds: 40

☒ **HOSPITAL MANATI MEDICAL CENTER (400114)**, Calle Hernandez, Carrion 668, Zip 00674, Mailing Address: P.O. Box 1142, Zip 00674–1142; tel. 787/621–3700, (Nonreporting) **A**1 3 5 10
Primary Contact: Ildefonso Vargas, Executive Director
CMO: Luis R Rosa–Toledo, M.D., Medical Director
CIO: Alberto Medina, Information Technology Senior Consultant
CHR: Nilda Paravisini, Director Human Resources
Web address: www.manatimedical.com
Control: Corporation, Investor–owned (for–profit) **Service**: General medical and surgical

Staffed Beds: 235

MAYAGUEZ—Mayaguez County

☒ **BELLA VISTA HOSPITAL (400014)**, State Road 349, Zip 00680, Mailing Address: P.O. Box 1750, Zip 00681; tel. 787/834–6000, (Nonreporting) **A**1 3 5 10
Primary Contact: Mara Marrero Gonzalez, Executive Director
CFO: Enrique Rivera, Chief Financial Officer
CMO: Miguel Cruz, M.D., Medical Director
CHR: Benjamin Astacio, Director Human Resources
Web address: www.bvhpr.org
Control: Church operated, Nongovernment, not–for–profit **Service**: General medical and surgical

Staffed Beds: 157

DR. RAMON E. BETANCES HOSPITAL–MAYAGUEZ MEDICAL CENTER BRANCH See Mayaguez Medical Center

★ **HOSPITAL PEREA (400123)**, 15 Basora Street, Zip 00681, Mailing Address: P.O. Box 170, Zip 00681; tel. 787/834–0101, (Nonreporting) **A**3 10 **S** United Medical Corporation, Windermere, FL
Primary Contact: Marco A. Reyes Concepcion, Executive Director
CFO: Joannie Garcia, CPA, Director Finance
CMO: Humberto Olivencia, M.D., Medical Director
Web address: www.paviahealth.com/perea_hospital.htm
Control: Corporation, Investor–owned (for–profit) **Service**: General medical and surgical

Staffed Beds: 103

☒ **MAYAGUEZ MEDICAL CENTER (400103)**, 410 Hostos Avenue, Zip 00680–1501, Mailing Address: P.O. Box 600, Zip 00681–0600; tel. 787/652–9200, (Nonreporting) **A**1 3 5 10
Primary Contact: Jaime Maestre, Executive Director
CMO: Milton D Carrero, M.D., Medical Director
CHR: Betsmari Medina, Director Human Resources
Web address: www.mayaguezmedical.com
Control: State, Government, Nonfederal **Service**: General medical and surgical

Staffed Beds: 189

MAYAGUEZ—Mataguez County

★ **HOSPITAL SAN ANTONIO (018487)**, Calle Dr Ramon Emeterio Betances N #18, Zip 00680, Mailing Address: PO Box 546, Zip 00681–0546; tel. 787/834–0050, (Nonreporting) **A**3 10
Primary Contact: Francisco Martinez, Executive Director
Web address: www.hsaipr.com/
Control: Other not–for–profit (including NFP Corporation) **Service**: General medical and surgical

Staffed Beds: 25

MOCA—Moca County

★ **HOSPITAL SAN CARLOS BORROMEO (400111)**, 550 Concepcion Vera Ayala, Zip 00676, Mailing Address: PO Box 68, Zip 00676; tel. 787/877–8000, (Nonreporting) **A**10
Primary Contact: Sarah I. Villanueva Cabrera, Acting Executive Director
CFO: Irma Cabrera, Finance Director
CMO: Erick Nieves, M.D., Medical Director
CIO: Juan Carlos Soto, Director Information Systems
CHR: Migdalia Ortiz, Director Human Resources
CNO: Luz M Velez, Director–Administration of Nursing Services
Web address: www.hscbpr.org
Control: Other not–for–profit (including NFP Corporation) **Service**: General medical and surgical

Staffed Beds: 108

PONCE—Ponce County

☒ **DR. PILA'S HOSPITAL (400003)**, Avenida Las Americas, Zip 00731, Mailing Address: P.O. Box 1910, Zip 00733–1910; tel. 787/848–5600, (Nonreporting) **A**1 10
Primary Contact: Rafael Alvarado, Chief Executive Officer
Web address: www.drpila.com
Control: Other not–for–profit (including NFP Corporation) **Service**: General medical and surgical

Staffed Beds: 143

Hospital, Medicare Provider Number, Address, Telephone, Approval, Facility, and Physician Codes, Health Care System

★ American Hospital Association (AHA) membership ○ Healthcare Facilities Accreditation Program ⇑ Center for Improvement in Healthcare Quality Accreditation
☐ The Joint Commission accreditation ◇ DNV Healthcare Inc. accreditation △ Commission on Accreditation of Rehabilitation Facilities (CARF) accreditation

Hospitals, U.S. / PUERTO RICO

☒ **HOSPITAL DE DAMAS (400022)**, 2213 Ponce Bypass, Zip 00717;
tel. 787/840–8686, **A**1 3 5 10 **F**3 12 13 14 17 18 20 22 24 26 29 30 34 40 45 49 50 54 56 57 64 68 70 72 74 75 76 77 79 81 82 85 86 87 89 97 98 102 103 107 114 115 116 119 126 128 129 130 145 148 157 **P**6
Primary Contact: Maria Mercedes Torres. Bernal, Administrator
CFO: Julio Colon, Financial Director
CMO: Pedro Benitez, M.D., Medical Director
CIO: Bienvenido Ortiz, Coordinator Information Systems
CHR: Gilberto Cuevas, Director Human Resources
CNO: Sandra Dominicci, Nursing Director
Web address: www.hospitaldamas.com/
Control: Other not–for–profit (including NFP Corporation) **Service**: General medical and surgical

Staffed Beds: 201 **Admissions**: 5806 **Census**: 90 **Outpatient Visits**: 58849 **Births**: 452 **Total Expense ($000)**: 77195 **Payroll Expense ($000)**: 23132 **Personnel**: 661

HOSPITAL DE PSIQUIATRIA FORENSE, Road 14, Zip 00731;
tel. 787/844–0210, (Nonreporting)
Primary Contact: Luz M. Torres Rios, Chief Executive Officer
Web address: https://hospitalespr.org/2019/10/04/hospital-psiquiatrico-forense-de-ponce/
Control: State, Government, Nonfederal **Service**: Psychiatric

Staffed Beds: 25

☒ **ST. LUKE'S EPISCOPAL HOSPITAL (400044)**, 917 Tito Castro Avenue, Zip 00731–4717, Mailing Address: P.O. Box 336810, Zip 00733–6810;
tel. 787/844–2080, (Nonreporting) **A**1 3 10
Primary Contact: Elyonel Ponton–Cruz, Executive Director
CFO: Carlos Valentin, Chief Financial Officer
CMO: Jesus Cruz Correa, Chief Medical Officer
CIO: Jose Abrams, Chief Information Officer
CHR: Hector Troche Garcin, Human Resources Director
CNO: Zoraida Vega, MSN, R.N., Chief Nursing Officer
Web address: www.sanlucaspr.com
Control: Church operated, Nongovernment, not–for–profit **Service**: General medical and surgical

Staffed Beds: 380

RIO PIEDRAS—San Juan County

☒ **UNIVERSITY PEDIATRIC HOSPITAL (403301)**, Barrio Monacenno, Carretera 22, Zip 00935, Mailing Address: P.O. Box 191079, San Juan, Zip 00910–1070;
tel. 787/777–3535, (Nonreporting) **A**1 3 5 10 **S** Puerto Rico Department of Health, San Juan, PR
Primary Contact: Victor Diaz Guzman, Executive Director
CMO: Myrna Quinones Feliciano, M.D., Medical Director
Web address: www.md.rcm.upr.edu/pediatrics/university_pediatric_hospital.php
Control: State, Government, Nonfederal **Service**: Children's general medical and surgical

Staffed Beds: 145

SAN GERMAN—San German County

☒ **HOSPITAL DE LA CONCEPCION (400021)**, Carr 2, Km 173, Bo Cain Alto, Zip 00683–3920, Mailing Address: P.O. Box 285, Zip 00683–0285;
tel. 787/892–1860, **A**1 3 5 10 **F**3 13 15 18 20 26 29 30 34 35 39 40 45 46 56 57 59 60 64 65 69 70 72 74 75 76 77 78 79 81 87 90 91 93 96 97 107 110 111 115 119 128 130 144 145 148 149 157 167 169
Primary Contact: Felicita Bonilla, Administrator
COO: Gustavo Almodovar, Executive Director
CFO: Lizmari Calderon, Director Finance
CMO: Ivan Acosta, M.D., Medical Director
CIO: Daniel Ferreira, Director Management Information Systems
CHR: Ada Bermudez, Director Human Resources
CNO: Amanda Caraballo, Nursing Director
Web address: www.hospitalconcepcion.org
Control: Church operated, Nongovernment, not–for–profit **Service**: General medical and surgical

Staffed Beds: 217 **Admissions**: 8366 **Census**: 128 **Outpatient Visits**: 85869 **Births**: 212 **Total Expense ($000)**: 96112 **Payroll Expense ($000)**: 34211 **Personnel**: 874

★ **HOSPITAL METROPOLITANO SAN GERMAN (400126)**, Calle Javilla Al Costado Parque de Bombas, Zip 00683, Mailing Address: PO Box 63, Zip 00683; tel. 787/892–5300, (Nonreporting) **A**10
Primary Contact: Winston Ramirez Delgado, Executive Director
Control: Corporation, Investor–owned (for–profit) **Service**: Other specialty treatment

Staffed Beds: 76

SAN JUAN—San Juan County (Mailing Addresses – Hato Rey, Rio Piedras)

☒ **ASHFORD PRESBYTERIAN COMMUNITY HOSPITAL (400001)**, 1451 Avenue Ashford, Zip 00907–1511, Mailing Address: P.O. Box 9020032, Zip 00902–0032;
tel. 787/721–2160, (Nonreporting) **A**1 3 10
Primary Contact: Itza Soto, MSN, Chief Executive Officer
COO: Obdulia Medina, MSN, MSN, Associate Director for Administrative Support, Clinical Management and Ambulatory Care
CFO: Mayra Torres, CPA, Chief Financial Officer
CMO: Rafael Gonzalez, M.D., Medical Director
CIO: Sigfredo Irizarry, Information Technology Director
CHR: Irma Carrillo, Director Human Resources
CNO: Berenice Perez, Chief Nursing Officer
Web address: www.presbypr.com
Control: Other not–for–profit (including NFP Corporation) **Service**: General medical and surgical

Staffed Beds: 171

☒ **AUXILIO MUTUO HOSPITAL (400016)**, Ponce De Leon Avenue, Zip 00918–1000, Mailing Address: P.O. Box 191227, Zip 00919–1227;
tel. 787/758–2000, (Nonreporting) **A**1 3 5 10
Primary Contact: Jorge L Matta. Serrano, Administrator
COO: Carmen Martin, Associate Administrator
CFO: Maria L Marti, Director Fiscal Services
CMO: Jose Isado, M.D., Medical Director
CIO: Edgardo Rodriguez, Director Management Information Systems
CHR: Maria Vega, Director Human Resources
Web address: www.auxiliomutuo.com
Control: Other not–for–profit (including NFP Corporation) **Service**: General medical and surgical

Staffed Beds: 408

☒ **CARDIOVASCULAR CENTER OF PUERTO RICO AND THE CARIBBEAN (400124)**, Americo Miranda Centro Medico, Zip 00936, Mailing Address: P.O. Box 366528, Zip 00936–6528; tel. 787/754–8500, (Nonreporting) **A**1 3 5 10 **S** Puerto Rico Department of Health, San Juan, PR
Primary Contact: Javier Marrero. Marrero, Executive Director
COO: Wilfredo Rabelo Millan, Chief Operating Officer
CFO: Arthur J Fernandez del Valle, Chief Financial Officer
CMO: Jose E Novoa Loyola, M.D., Medical Director
CIO: Eugenio Torres Ayala, Director Information Systems
CHR: Myriam T Rodriguez Schmidt, Director Human Resources
CNO: Pedro Laureano Cantre, Chief Nursing Officer
Web address: www.cardiovascular.gobierno.pr
Control: State, Government, Nonfederal **Service**: General medical and surgical

Staffed Beds: 164

★ **DOCTORS' CENTER HOSPITAL SAN JUAN (400006)**, 1395 San Rafael Street, Zip 00909–2518, Mailing Address: Box 11338, Santurce Station, Zip 00910–3428; tel. 787/999–7620, (Nonreporting) **A**10
Primary Contact: Belinda L. Toro Palacios, President and Chief Executive Officer
CFO: Alejandro Santiago, Director Finance
CMO: Ubaldo Santiago, M.D., Chairman
CIO: Luis Alicea, Chief Information Officer
CHR: Carmen Perez, Director Human Resources
CNO: Lesbia Lopez, Chief Nursing Officer
Web address: www.tuhospitalfamiliar.com
Control: Corporation, Investor–owned (for–profit) **Service**: General medical and surgical

Staffed Beds: 133

Hospitals, U.S. / PUERTO RICO

★ **ENCOMPASS HEALTH REHABILITATION HOSPITAL OF SAN JUAN (403025)**, University Hospital, 3rd Floor, Zip 00923, Mailing Address: PMB #340 P.O. Box 70344, Zip 00923; tel. 787/274-5100, (Nonreporting) **A**3 5 10 **S** Encompass Health Corporation, Birmingham, AL
Primary Contact: Daniel Del Castillo, Chief Executive Officer
CFO: Jesus M Corazon, Controller
CMO: Eduardo Ramos, M.D., Medical Director
CNO: Zamarys Rivera, R.N., Chief Nursing Officer
Web address: www.healthsouthsanjuan.com
Control: Corporation, Investor-owned (for-profit) **Service**: Rehabilitation

Staffed Beds: 32

⇧ **HOSPITAL CENTRO COMPRENSIVO DE CANCER, UNIVERSIDAD DE PUERTO RICO (400135)**, Carr. PR-21 Int. PR-18 Bo. Monacillo Urbano, Zip 00927, Mailing Address: P.O. Box 363027, Zip 00936-3027; tel. 787/772-8300, (Nonreporting) **A**10 21 **S** Puerto Rico Department of Health, San Juan, PR
Primary Contact: Marcia Cruz Correa, Administrator
Web address: www.cccupr.org
Control: State, Government, Nonfederal **Service**: Other specialty treatment

Staffed Beds: 29

HOSPITAL DE PSIQUIATRIA (404006), Dr. Ramon Fernandez Marina, P O Box 2100, Zip 00936; tel. 787/766-4646, (Nonreporting) **A**1 5 10
Primary Contact: Carmen Bonet, Executive Director
CMO: Brunilda Vazquez, Medical Director
CHR: Idalia Garcia, Chief Human Resources Officer
Control: State, Government, Nonfederal **Service**: Psychiatric

Staffed Beds: 141

HOSPITAL DEL MAESTRO (400004), 550 Sergio Cuevas, Zip 00918-3741, Mailing Address: P.O. Box 364708, Zip 00936-4708; tel. 787/758-8383, **A**1 5 10 **F**3 15 20 22 29 40 41 45 46 69 70 75 78 79 81 85 87 89 91 92 93 107 110 111 114 115 119 130 146 147 148 154 157 167
Primary Contact: Yarimir Rodriguez Diaz, Executive Director
CFO: Marisol Vargas, Director Finance
CMO: Jose Montalvo, M.D., Medical Director
CIO: Laura Rodriguez, Director Medical Records
CHR: Orlando Santiago, Human Resources Officer
Web address: www.hospitaldelmaestro.org
Control: Other not-for-profit (including NFP Corporation) **Service**: General medical and surgical

Staffed Beds: 125 **Admissions**: 1949 **Census**: 35 **Outpatient Visits**: 11083 **Births**: 0 **Total Expense ($000)**: 20307 **Payroll Expense ($000)**: 7147

★ **HOSPITAL EPISCOPAL SAN LUCAS METRO (400121)**, 138 Avenue Winston Churchill, Zip 00926-6013; tel. 787/761-8383, (Nonreporting) **A**10
Primary Contact: Yelitza Lucena Quiles, Chief Executive Officer
CFO: Ivonne Rivera-Santos, Chief Financial Officer
Web address: https://hospitales.cybo.com/PR-biz/hospital-san-gerardo_2P
Control: Other not-for-profit (including NFP Corporation) **Service**: Chronic disease

Staffed Beds: 60

HOSPITAL HIMA CUPEY See Hospital Episcopal San Lucas Metro

HOSPITAL METROPOLITANO (400106), 1785 Carr 21, Zip 00921-3399, Mailing Address: P.O. Box 11981, Zip 00922; tel. 787/782-9999, **A**1 3 5 10 **F**13 15 18 34 40 41 45 59 65 70 73 75 76 89 93 97 110 111 114 115 119 122 128 130 148 157
Primary Contact: José M. Talavera Reyes, Executive Director
CFO: Maritza Rodriguez, Chief Financial Officer
CMO: Maria de los Angeles Correa, M.D., Medical Director
CIO: Manuel Santiago, Chief Information Officer
Control: State, Government, Nonfederal **Service**: General medical and surgical

Staffed Beds: 122 **Admissions**: 3594 **Census**: 81 **Outpatient Visits**: 88898 **Births**: 66 **Total Expense ($000)**: 35524 **Payroll Expense ($000)**: 12370 **Personnel**: 385

HOSPITAL PAVIA-HATO REY (400128), 435 Ponce De Leon Avenue, Zip 00917-3428, Mailing Address: PO Box 190828, Zip 00917-3428; tel. 787/641-2323, (Nonreporting) **A**1 5 10 **S** United Medical Corporation, Windermere, FL
Primary Contact: Carlos Santiago Rosario, Executive Director
Web address: www.paviahealth.com
Control: Corporation, Investor-owned (for-profit) **Service**: General medical and surgical

Staffed Beds: 180

HOSPITAL PAVIA-SANTURCE (400019), 1462 Asia Street, Zip 00909-2143, Mailing Address: Box 11137, Santurce Station, Zip 00910-1137; tel. 787/727-6060, (Nonreporting) **A**1 3 10 **S** United Medical Corporation, Windermere, FL
Primary Contact: Domingo Cruz-Vivaldi, Executive Director
CFO: Francisco Espina, Director Finance
Web address: www.paviahealth.com
Control: Corporation, Investor-owned (for-profit) **Service**: General medical and surgical

Staffed Beds: 155

★ **HOSPITAL PSIQUIATRICO CORRECCIONAL**, PMB 302 P O Box 70344, Zip 00936; tel. 939/225-2400, (Nonreporting)
Primary Contact: Felicita E. Alvarado, Administrator
Web address: www.www2.pr.gov/Directorios/Pages/InfoAgencia.aspx?PRIFA=220
Control: State, Government, Nonfederal **Service**: General medical and surgical

Staffed Beds: 25

HOSPITAL SAN FRANCISCO (400098), 371 Avenida De Diego, Zip 00923-1711, Mailing Address: P.O. Box 29025, Zip 00929-0025; tel. 787/767-5100, (Nonreporting) **A**1 10 **S** United Medical Corporation, Windermere, FL
Primary Contact: Dominao Cruz Vivaldi, Executive Director
CFO: Aristides Castro, Director Finance
CMO: Hector L Cotto, M.D., Medical Director
CIO: Deborah Nieves, Director Management Information Systems
CHR: Sugehi Santiago, Director
Web address: www.metropavia.com/SanFrancisco.cfm
Control: Corporation, Investor-owned (for-profit) **Service**: General medical and surgical

Staffed Beds: 133

★ **INDUSTRIAL HOSPITAL**, Puerto Rico Medical Center, Zip 00936, Mailing Address: P.O. Box 365028, Zip 00936; tel. 787/754-2525, (Nonreporting)
Primary Contact: Ernesto Santiago, Executive Director
CFO: Robert Bernier Casanova, Chief Financial Officer
CMO: Carmen Carrasquillo, M.D., Medical Director
CHR: Sonia M Lebron, Human Resources Specialist
Control: State, Government, Nonfederal **Service**: General medical and surgical

Staffed Beds: 108

MULTY MEDICAL REHABILITATION HOSPITAL SAN JUAN (403027), #402 Muñoz Rivera Avenue, El Vedado, Zip 00918-3310, Mailing Address: PO Box 194000 PMB196, Zip 00919; tel. 787/705-8677, (Nonreporting) **A**10 22
Primary Contact: Tania Conde Sterling, President
COO: Roberto Hernandez, Administrator and Executive Director
CFO: Jose Luis Suarez, Comptroller
CMO: Rafael Sein, M.D., Medical Director
CIO: Hector Tapia, Manager, Information Technology
CHR: Moises Rivera, Interim Human Resource Director
CNO: Maria Lugo, Director of Nurses
Web address: www.multymedical.com
Control: Corporation, Investor-owned (for-profit) **Service**: Rehabilitation

Staffed Beds: 61

SAN JUAN CAPESTRANO HOSPITAL (404005), Rural Route 2, Box 11, Zip 00926; tel. 787/625-2900, (Nonreporting) **A**1 5 10 **S** Acadia Healthcare Company, Inc., Franklin, TN
Primary Contact: Marta Rivera. Plaza, Chief Executive Officer and Managing Director
CFO: Julia Cruz, Chief Financial Officer
CMO: Jose' Alonso, M.D., Medical Director
CIO: Ana Morandeira, Director Marketing
CHR: Luis Rivera, Director Human Resources
Web address: www.sjcapestrano.com
Control: Corporation, Investor-owned (for-profit) **Service**: Psychiatric

Staffed Beds: 158

Hospital, Medicare Provider Number, Address, Telephone, Approval, Facility, and Physician Codes, Health Care System

★ American Hospital Association (AHA) membership   ○ Healthcare Facilities Accreditation Program   ⇧ Center for Improvement in Healthcare Quality Accreditation
□ The Joint Commission accreditation   ◇ DNV Healthcare Inc. accreditation   △ Commission on Accreditation of Rehabilitation Facilities (CARF) accreditation

© 2025 AHA Guide

Hospitals, U.S. / VIRGIN ISLANDS

SAN JUAN CITY HOSPITAL (400015), Puerto Rico Medical Center, Zip 00928, Mailing Address: PMB 79, P O Box 70344, Zip 00936-8344; tel. 787/766-2222, (Nonreporting) **A**1 3 5 10
Primary Contact: Juan Benitez, Chief Executive Office and Executive Director
COO: Carmen Guede, Chief Operating Officer
CFO: Jaime Rodriguez, Chief Financial Officer
CMO: Raul Reyes, M.D., Medical Director
CIO: Gustavo Mesa, Chief Information Officer
CHR: Jose Garcia, Chief Human Resources Officer
Web address: www.massalud.com
Control: City, Government, Nonfederal **Service**: General medical and surgical

Staffed Beds: 267

UNIVERSITY HOSPITAL (400061), Nineyas 869 Rio Piedras, Zip 00922, Mailing Address: P.O. Box 2116, Zip 00922; tel. 787/754-0101, (Nonreporting) **A**1 3 5 10 **S** Puerto Rico Department of Health, San Juan, PR
Primary Contact: Jorge Matta. Gonzalez, Executive Director
CFO: Janet Baez, Director
CMO: Ricardo Moscoso, M.D., Medical Director
CIO: Josue Martinez, Coordinator Information Systems
CHR: Ramomita Navarro, Director Human Resources
Control: State, Government, Nonfederal **Service**: General medical and surgical

Staffed Beds: 220

△ **VETERANS AFFAIRS CARIBBEAN HEALTHCARE SYSTEM**, 10 Casia Street, Zip 00921-3201; tel. 787/641-7582, (Nonreporting) **A**1 2 3 5 7 8 **S** Department of Veterans Affairs, Washington, DC
Primary Contact: Carlos R. Escobar, FACHE, Director
CFO: Oscar Rodriguez, Chief Fiscal Officer
CIO: Manuel Negron, Chief Information Technology Service
CHR: Omar Ahmed, Acting Manager Human Resources
CNO: Kathleen Ruiz, M.D., Associate Director Patient Care Services
Web address: www.caribbean.va.gov/
Control: Veterans Affairs, Government, federal **Service**: General medical and surgical

Staffed Beds: 321

SAN JUAN—Moca County

HOSPITAL CUIDADO AGUDO ESPECIALIZADO EN PACIENTES POLITRAUMATIZADOS (400127), Carr. Num. 22 BO. Monacillos, Centro Medico, Zip 00922-2129, Mailing Address: PO Box 2129, Zip 00922-2129; tel. 787/777-3535, (Nonreporting) **A**10
Primary Contact: Victor L. Medina Cruz, M.D., Executive Director
Web address: www.asempr.org
Control: Other not-for-profit (including NFP Corporation) **Service**: General medical and surgical

Staffed Beds: 25

SANTURCE—San Juan County

★ ⇧ **SAN JORGE CHILDREN'S AND WOMEN HOSPITAL (400134)**, 258 San Jorge Street, Santurce, Zip 00912-3310, Mailing Address: PO Box 6308, San Juan, Zip 00912-3310; tel. 787/727-1000, (Nonreporting) **A**3 5 10 21 **S** United Medical Corporation, Windermere, FL
Primary Contact: Jose Luis. Rodriguez, Executive Director
CFO: Jose Marrero, Director Finance
CMO: Luis Clavell, M.D., Medical Director
CIO: Rogelio Caballero, Chief Information Systems
CHR: Odette Burgos, Supervisor Human Resources
CNO: Leticia Fuentes, Nursing Director
Web address: www.sanjorgechildrenshospital.com
Control: Corporation, Investor-owned (for-profit) **Service**: Children's general medical and surgical

Staffed Beds: 167

UTUADO—Utuado County

★ **METROPOLITANO DE LA MONTANA (400130)**, Calle Issac Gonzalez Martinez, Zip 00641, Mailing Address: P.O. Box 2600, Zip 00641; tel. 787/933-1100, (Nonreporting) **A**3 5 10
Primary Contact: Janice Cruz, Executive Director
Web address: www.metropavia.com/DeLaMontana.cfm
Control: Corporation, Investor-owned (for-profit) **Service**: General medical and surgical

Staffed Beds: 25

VEGA BAJA—Vega Alta County

★ **WILMA N. VAZQUEZ MEDICAL CENTER (400115)**, KM 39 1/2 Road 2, Call Box 7001, Zip 00694; tel. 787/858-1580, (Nonreporting) **A**10
Primary Contact: José M. Talavera Reyes, Administrator
COO: Jose O Pabon, Director Operations
CFO: Youdie Reynolds-Gossette, Controller
CMO: Jorge Feria, M.D., President Medical Staff
CIO: Miguel Aponte, Supervisor Management Information Systems
CHR: Aymette Garcia, Manager Human Resources
Control: Corporation, Investor-owned (for-profit) **Service**: General medical and surgical

Staffed Beds: 92

YAUCO—Yauco County

HOSPITAL PAVIA YAUCO (400110), Carretera 128 KM 1.0, Zip 00698, Mailing Address: P.O. Box 5643, Zip 00698; tel. 787/856-1000, (Nonreporting) **A**1 10
Primary Contact: Dinorah Hernandez Esq, Executive Director
CFO: Elizabeth Gonzalez, CPA, Financial Director
CMO: Juan Pillot, M.D., Esq, Medical Director
CIO: Edson Ortiz, Chief Information Officer
Web address: https://metropavia.com/hospital-pavia-yauco/
Control: Corporation, Investor-owned (for-profit) **Service**: General medical and surgical

Staffed Beds: 115

VIRGIN ISLANDS

CHRISTIANSTED—St. Croix County

GOVERNOR JUAN F. LUIS HOSPITAL (480002), 4007 Estate Diamond Ruby, Zip 00820-4421; tel. 340/778-6311, (Nonreporting) **A**10
Primary Contact: Douglas Edward. Koch, Chief Executive Officer
CFO: Rosalie Javois, Chief Financial Officer
CMO: Robert Centeno, M.D., Chief Medical Officer
CIO: Reuben D Molloy, Chief Information Officer
CHR: Joan Jean-Baptiste, Vice President Human Resources
Web address: www.jflusvi.org
Control: State, Government, Nonfederal **Service**: General medical and surgical

Staffed Beds: 165

SAINT THOMAS—St. Thomas County

☐ **SCHNEIDER REGIONAL MEDICAL CENTER (480001)**, 9048 Sugar Estate, Charlotte Amalie, Zip 00802; tel. 340/776-8311, (Nonreporting) **A**1 10
Primary Contact: Tina A. Comissiong Esq, Chief Executive Officer
CMO: Thelma Ruth Watson, M.D., Medical Director
CIO: J C Creque, Director Management Information Systems
CHR: Marlene J Adams, Director Human Resources
Web address: www.rlshospital.org
Control: State, Government, Nonfederal **Service**: General medical and surgical

Staffed Beds: 86

U.S. Government Hospitals Outside the United States, by Area

GERMANY
Heidelberg: ★ Heidelberg Army Community Hospital, APO, CMR 242, AE 09042

Landstuhl: ★ Landstuhl Army Regional Medical Center, APO, CMR 402, AE 09180

Wuerzburg: ★ Wuerzburg Army Community Hospital, APO, USAMEDDAC Wuerzburg, Ut 26610, AE 09244

ITALY
Naples: ★ U. S. Naval Hospital, FPO, none, AE 09619

JAPAN
Yokosuka: ★ U. S. Naval Hospital, PSC 475, Box 1, FPO, AP, 96350-1600

SOUTH KOREA
Seoul: ★ Brian Allgood Army Community Hospital, 121st General Hospital, UNIT 96205

SPAIN
Rota: ★ U. S. Naval Hospital, Rota, FPO, PSC 819, Box 18, AE 09645–2500

TAIWAN
Taipei: ★ U. S. Naval Hospital Taipei, No 300 Shin–Pai Road, Sec 2

Index of Hospitals

This section is an index of all hospitals in alphabetical order by hospital name, followed by the city, state, and page reference to the hospital's listing in Section A.

A

ABBEVILLE AREA MEDICAL CENTER, ABBEVILLE, SC, p. A562
ABBEVILLE GENERAL HOSPITAL, ABBEVILLE, LA, p. A276
ABBOTT NORTHWESTERN HOSPITAL, MINNEAPOLIS, MN, p. A350
ABILENE REGIONAL MEDICAL CENTER, ABILENE, TX, p. A595
ABINGTON JEFFERSON HEALTH, ABINGTON, PA, p. A534
ABINGTON–LANSDALE HOSPITAL JEFFERSON HEALTH, LANSDALE, PA, p. A544
ABRAHAM LINCOLN MEMORIAL HOSPITAL, LINCOLN, IL, p. A200
ABRAZO ARROWHEAD CAMPUS, GLENDALE, AZ, p. A32
ABRAZO CENTRAL CAMPUS, PHOENIX, AZ, p. A35
ABRAZO SCOTTSDALE CAMPUS, PHOENIX, AZ, p. A35
ABRAZO WEST CAMPUS, GOODYEAR, AZ, p. A32
ACADIA–ST. LANDRY HOSPITAL, CHURCH POINT, LA, p. A280
ACADIAN MEDICAL CENTER, EUNICE, LA, p. A281
ACADIANA REHABILITATION, LAFAYETTE, LA, p. A285
ACCESS HOSPITAL DAYTON, DAYTON, OH, p. A493
ACCORD REHABILITATION HOSPITAL, PLAQUEMINE, LA, p. A291
ACMH HOSPITAL, KITTANNING, PA, p. A543
ACOMA–CANONCITO–LAGUNA HOSPITAL, ACOMA, NM, p. A432
ACUITY SPECIALTY HOSPITAL OF NEW JERSEY, ATLANTIC CITY, NJ, p. A418
ACUITY SPECIALTY HOSPITAL OF SOUTHERN NEW JERSEY, WILLINGBORO, NJ, p. A430
ACUITY SPECIALTY HOSPITAL–OHIO VALLEY AT WEIRTON, WEIRTON, WV, p. A705
ACUITY SPECIALTY HOSPITAL–OHIO VALLEY AT WHEELING, WHEELING, WV, p. A706
ACUTE REHABILITATION HOSPITAL OF PLANO., PLANO, TX, p. A645
ADA WILSON HOSP OF PHYS MED, CORPUS CHRISTI, TX, p. A608
ADAIR COUNTY HEALTH SYSTEM, GREENFIELD, IA, p. A236
ADAMS COUNTY REGIONAL MEDICAL CENTER, SEAMAN, OH, p. A503
ADAMS MEMORIAL HOSPITAL, DECATUR, IN, p. A215
ADCARE HOSPITAL OF WORCESTER, WORCESTER, MA, p. A320
ADDISON GILBERT HOSPITAL, GLOUCESTER, MA, p. A314
ADENA FAYETTE MEDICAL CENTER, WASHINGTON COURT HOUSE, OH, p. A506
ADENA GREENFIELD MEDICAL CENTER, GREENFIELD, OH, p. A497
ADENA MEDICAL CENTER, CHILLICOTHE, OH, p. A488
ADENA PIKE MEDICAL CENTER, WAVERLY, OH, p. A506
ADENA REGIONAL MEDICAL CENTER, CHILLICOTHE, OH, p. A488
ADIRONDACK HEALTH, SARANAC LAKE, NY, p. A458
ADVANCED CARE HOSPITAL OF MONTANA, BILLINGS, MT, p. A389
ADVANCED CARE HOSPITAL OF SOUTHERN NEW MEXICO, LAS CRUCES, NM, p. A435
ADVANCED CARE HOSPITAL OF WHITE COUNTY, SEARCY, AR, p. A53
ADVANCED DIAGNOSTICS HOSPITAL, HOUSTON, TX, p. A625
ADVANCED SPECIALTY HOSPITAL OF TOLEDO, TOLEDO, OH, p. A504
ADVANCED SURGICAL HOSPITAL, WASHINGTON, PA, p. A556
ADVENTHEALTH ALTAMONTE SPRINGS, ALTAMONTE SPRINGS, FL, p. A125
ADVENTHEALTH APOPKA, APOPKA, FL, p. A125
ADVENTHEALTH AVISTA, LOUISVILLE, CO, p. A111
ADVENTHEALTH BOLINGBROOK, BOLINGBROOK, IL, p. A186
ADVENTHEALTH CARROLLWOOD, TAMPA, FL, p. A151
ADVENTHEALTH CASTLE ROCK, CASTLE ROCK, CO, p. A104
ADVENTHEALTH CELEBRATION, CELEBRATION, FL, p. A127
ADVENTHEALTH CENTRAL TEXAS, KILLEEN, TX, p. A632
ADVENTHEALTH CONNERTON, LAND O'LAKES, FL, p. A137
ADVENTHEALTH DADE CITY, DADE CITY, FL, p. A129

ADVENTHEALTH DAYTONA BEACH, DAYTONA BEACH, FL, p. A129
ADVENTHEALTH DELAND, DELAND, FL, p. A130
ADVENTHEALTH DURAND, DURAND, WI, p. A709
ADVENTHEALTH FISH MEMORIAL, ORANGE CITY, FL, p. A143
ADVENTHEALTH GLENOAKS, GLENDALE HEIGHTS, IL, p. A196
ADVENTHEALTH GORDON, CALHOUN, GA, p. A160
ADVENTHEALTH HEART OF FLORIDA, DAVENPORT, FL, p. A129
ADVENTHEALTH HENDERSONVILLE, HENDERSONVILLE, NC, p. A470
ADVENTHEALTH HINSDALE, HINSDALE, IL, p. A198
ADVENTHEALTH KISSIMMEE, KISSIMMEE, FL, p. A136
ADVENTHEALTH LA GRANGE, LA GRANGE, IL, p. A199
ADVENTHEALTH LAKE WALES, LAKE WALES, FL, p. A136
ADVENTHEALTH LITTLETON, LITTLETON, CO, p. A111
ADVENTHEALTH MANCHESTER, MANCHESTER, KY, p. A271
ADVENTHEALTH MURRAY, CHATSWORTH, GA, p. A160
ADVENTHEALTH NEW SMYRNA BEACH, NEW SMYRNA BEACH, FL, p. A142
ADVENTHEALTH NORTH PINELLAS, TARPON SPRINGS, FL, p. A153
ADVENTHEALTH OCALA, OCALA, FL, p. A143
ADVENTHEALTH ORLANDO, ORLANDO, FL, p. A144
ADVENTHEALTH OTTAWA, OTTAWA, KS, p. A256
ADVENTHEALTH PALM COAST, PALM COAST, FL, p. A145
ADVENTHEALTH PALM COAST PARKWAY, PALM COAST, FL, p. A145
ADVENTHEALTH PARKER, PARKER, CO, p. A112
ADVENTHEALTH PORTER, DENVER, CO, p. A106
ADVENTHEALTH REDMOND, ROME, GA, p. A170
ADVENTHEALTH ROLLINS BROOK, LAMPASAS, TX, p. A633
ADVENTHEALTH SEBRING, SEBRING, FL, p. A150
ADVENTHEALTH SHAWNEE MISSION, MERRIAM, KS, p. A255
ADVENTHEALTH SOUTH OVERLAND PARK, OVERLAND PARK, KS, p. A257
ADVENTHEALTH TAMPA, TAMPA, FL, p. A152
ADVENTHEALTH WATERMAN, TAVARES, FL, p. A153
ADVENTHEALTH WAUCHULA, WAUCHULA, FL, p. A154
ADVENTHEALTH WESLEY CHAPEL, WESLEY CHAPEL, FL, p. A154
ADVENTHEALTH WINTER PARK, WINTER PARK, FL, p. A155
ADVENTHEALTH ZEPHYRHILLS, ZEPHYRHILLS, FL, p. A155
ADVENTIST BEHAVIORAL HEALTH ROCKVILLE, ROCKVILLE, MD, p. A306
ADVENTIST HEALTH – TULARE, TULARE, CA, p. A98
ADVENTIST HEALTH AND RIDEOUT, MARYSVILLE, CA, p. A77
ADVENTIST HEALTH BAKERSFIELD, BAKERSFIELD, CA, p. A56
ADVENTIST HEALTH CASTLE, KAILUA, HI, p. A176
ADVENTIST HEALTH CLEAR LAKE, CLEARLAKE, CA, p. A59
ADVENTIST HEALTH COLUMBIA GORGE, THE DALLES, OR, p. A532
ADVENTIST HEALTH DELANO, DELANO, CA, p. A61
ADVENTIST HEALTH GLENDALE, GLENDALE, CA, p. A66
ADVENTIST HEALTH HANFORD, HANFORD, CA, p. A66
ADVENTIST HEALTH HOWARD MEMORIAL, WILLITS, CA, p. A101
ADVENTIST HEALTH LODI MEMORIAL, LODI, CA, p. A70
ADVENTIST HEALTH MENDOCINO COAST, FORT BRAGG, CA, p. A63
ADVENTIST HEALTH PORTLAND, PORTLAND, OR, p. A530
ADVENTIST HEALTH REEDLEY, REEDLEY, CA, p. A85
ADVENTIST HEALTH SIMI VALLEY, SIMI VALLEY, CA, p. A96
ADVENTIST HEALTH SONORA, SONORA, CA, p. A96
ADVENTIST HEALTH ST. HELENA, SAINT HELENA, CA, p. A88
ADVENTIST HEALTH TEHACHAPI VALLEY, TEHACHAPI, CA, p. A97
ADVENTIST HEALTH TILLAMOOK, TILLAMOOK, OR, p. A533
ADVENTIST HEALTH UKIAH VALLEY, UKIAH, CA, p. A99
ADVENTIST HEALTH VALLEJO – CENTER FOR BEHAVIORAL HEALTH, VALLEJO, CA, p. A99
ADVENTIST HEALTH VALLEJO, VALLEJO, CA, p. A99
ADVENTIST HEALTH WHITE MEMORIAL, LOS ANGELES, CA, p. A71
ADVENTIST HEALTH WHITE MEMORIAL MONTEBELLO, MONTEBELLO, CA, p. A78
ADVENTIST HEALTHCARE FORT WASHINGTON MEDICAL CENTER, FORT WASHINGTON, MD, p. A304

ADVENTIST HEALTHCARE REHABILITATION, ROCKVILLE, MD, p. A306
ADVENTIST HEALTHCARE SHADY GROVE MEDICAL CENTER, ROCKVILLE, MD, p. A306
ADVENTIST HEALTHCARE WHITE OAK MEDICAL CENTER, SILVER SPRING, MD, p. A307
ADVOCATE BETHANY HOSPITAL, CHICAGO, IL, p. A188
ADVOCATE CHRIST MEDICAL CENTER, OAK LAWN, IL, p. A204
ADVOCATE CONDELL MEDICAL CENTER, LIBERTYVILLE, IL, p. A200
ADVOCATE GOOD SAMARITAN HOSPITAL, DOWNERS GROVE, IL, p. A193
ADVOCATE GOOD SHEPHERD HOSPITAL, BARRINGTON, IL, p. A186
ADVOCATE ILLINOIS MASONIC MEDICAL CENTER, CHICAGO, IL, p. A188
ADVOCATE LUTHERAN GENERAL HOSPITAL, PARK RIDGE, IL, p. A205
ADVOCATE SHERMAN HOSPITAL, ELGIN, IL, p. A194
ADVOCATE SOUTH SUBURBAN HOSPITAL, HAZEL CREST, IL, p. A197
ADVOCATE TRINITY HOSPITAL, CHICAGO, IL, p. A188
AHMC ANAHEIM REGIONAL MEDICAL CENTER, ANAHEIM, CA, p. A55
AHMC SETON MEDICAL CENTER, DALY CITY, CA, p. A61
AHN GROVE CITY, GROVE CITY, PA, p. A541
AHN HEMPFIELD NEIGHBORHOOD HOSPITAL, GREENSBURG, PA, p. A540
AHN WEXFORD HOSPITAL, WEXFORD, PA, p. A557
AHS SHERMAN MEDICAL CENTER, SHERMAN, TX, p. A652
AIKEN REGIONAL MEDICAL CENTERS, AIKEN, SC, p. A562
AKRON CHILDREN'S HOSPITAL, AKRON, OH, p. A484
AKRON CITY HOSPITAL, AKRON, OH, p. A484
ALAMEDA COUNTY MEDICAL CENTER–FAIRMONT CAMPUS, SAN LEANDRO, CA, p. A92
ALAMEDA HOSPITAL, ALAMEDA, CA, p. A55
ALASKA NATIVE MEDICAL CENTER, ANCHORAGE, AK, p. A27
ALASKA PSYCHIATRIC INSTITUTE, ANCHORAGE, AK, p. A27
ALASKA REGIONAL HOSPITAL, ANCHORAGE, AK, p. A27
ALBANY MEDICAL CENTER, ALBANY, NY, p. A438
ALBANY STRATTON VETERANS AFFAIRS MEDICAL CENTER, ALBANY, NY, p. A438
ALBERT J. SOLNIT CHILDREN'S CENTER, MIDDLETOWN, CT, p. A116
ALCOHOLISM TREATMENT CENTER, WINFIELD, IL, p. A210
ALEDA E. LUTZ DEPARTMENT OF VETERANS AFFAIRS MEDICAL CENTER, SAGINAW, MI, p. A336
ALEXANDRIA VA MEDICAL CENTER, PINEVILLE, LA, p. A291
ALEXIAN BROTHERS WOMEN & CHILDREN'S HOSPITAL, HOFFMAN ESTATES, IL, p. A198
ALEXIAN REHABILITATION HOSPITAL, ELK GROVE VILLAGE, IL, p. A194
ALFRED I. DUPONT HOSPITAL FOR CHILDREN, WILMINGTON, DE, p. A122
ALHAMBRA HOSPITAL MEDICAL CENTER, ALHAMBRA, CA, p. A55
ALICE PECK DAY MEMORIAL HOSPITAL, LEBANON, NH, p. A415
ALLE KISKI MEDICAL CENTER, NATRONA HEIGHTS, PA, p. A547
ALLEGHANY HEALTH, SPARTA, NC, p. A476
ALLEGHANY MEMORIAL HOSPITAL, SPARTA, NC, p. A476
ALLEGHENY GENERAL HOSPITAL, PITTSBURGH, PA, p. A551
ALLEGHENY VALLEY HOSPITAL, NATRONA HEIGHTS, PA, p. A547
ALLEGIANCE BEHAVIORAL HEALTH CENTER OF PLAINVIEW, PLAINVIEW, TX, p. A644
ALLEGIANCE BEHAVIORAL HEALTH CENTERS, MONROE, LA, p. A288
ALLEGIANCE SPECIALTY HOSPITAL OF GREENVILLE, GREENVILLE, MS, p. A362
ALLEN COUNTY REGIONAL HOSPITAL, IOLA, KS, p. A251
ALLEN PARISH COMMUNITY HEALTHCARE, KINDER, LA, p. A285
ALLENDALE COUNTY HOSPITAL, FAIRFAX, SC, p. A566
ALLENMORE HOSPITAL, TACOMA, WA, p. A697
ALLENTOWN OSTEOPATHIC MED CTR, ALLENTOWN, PA, p. A534
ALLIANCE HEALTH CENTER, MERIDIAN, MS, p. A366

ALLIANCE HEALTHCARE SYSTEM, HOLLY SPRINGS, MS, p. A363
ALLIANCEHEALTH DEACONESS, OKLAHOMA CITY, OK, p. A516
ALLIANCEHEALTH DURANT, DURANT, OK, p. A512
ALLIANCEHEALTH MADILL, MADILL, OK, p. A514
ALLIANCEHEALTH WOODWARD, WOODWARD, OK, p. A524
ALLIED SERVICES SCRANTON REHABILITATION HOSPITAL, SCRANTON, PA, p. A554
ALLINA HEALTH FARIBAULT MEDICAL CENTER, FARIBAULT, MN, p. A346
ALOMERE HEALTH, ALEXANDRIA, MN, p. A342
ALTA BATES SUMMIT MEDICAL CENTER – SUMMIT CAMPUS, OAKLAND, CA, p. A80
ALTA BATES SUMMIT MEDICAL CENTER–ALTA BATES CAMPUS, BERKELEY, CA, p. A57
ALTA VIEW HOSPITAL, SANDY, UT, p. A669
ALTA VISTA REGIONAL HOSPITAL, LAS VEGAS, NM, p. A435
ALTON MEMORIAL HOSPITAL, ALTON, IL, p. A185
ALTON MENTAL HEALTH CENTER, ALTON, IL, p. A185
ALTRU HEALTH SYSTEM, GRAND FORKS, ND, p. A481
ALTRU REHAB CENTER, GRAND FORKS, ND, p. A481
ALTRU REHABILITATION HOSPITAL, GRAND FORKS, ND, p. A481
ALTUS LUMBERTON HOSPITAL, LUMBERTON, TX, p. A637
ALUTMAN HOSPITAL PEDIATRIC SERVICES, CANTON, OH, p. A487
ALVARADO PARKWAY INSTITUTE BEHAVIORAL HEALTH SYSTEM, LA MESA, CA, p. A68
ALVIN C. YORK CAMPUS, MURFREESBORO, TN, p. A590
ALVIN C. YORK VETERANS AFFAIRS MEDICAL CENTER, MURFREESBORO, TN, p. A590
ALVIN DIAGNOSTIC AND URGENT CARE CENTER, ALVIN, TX, p. A596
ALVIN MEDICAL CENTER, ALVIN, TX, p. A596
AMARILLO HCS, AMARILLO, TX, p. A596
AMBERWELL HEALTH, ATCHISON, KS, p. A246
AMBERWELL HIAWATHA, HIAWATHA, KS, p. A250
AMERICAN FORK HOSPITAL, AMERICAN FORK, UT, p. A664
AMERY HOSPITAL AND CLINIC, AMERY, WI, p. A707
AMG PHYSICAL REHABILITATION HOSPITAL, COVINGTON, LA, p. A280
AMG SPECIALTY HOSPITAL – LAS VEGAS, LAS VEGAS, NV, p. A409
AMG SPECIALTY HOSPITAL – OKLAHOMA CITY, OKLAHOMA CITY, OK, p. A516
AMG SPECIALTY HOSPITAL NORTHWEST INDIANA, CROWN POINT, IN, p. A214
AMG SPECIALTY HOSPITAL–ALBUQUERQUE, ALBUQUERQUE, NM, p. A432
AMG SPECIALTY HOSPITAL–HOUMA, HOUMA, LA, p. A283
AMG SPECIALTY HOSPITAL–LAFAYETTE, LAFAYETTE, LA, p. A285
AMG SPECIALTY HOSPITAL–ZACHARY, ZACHARY, LA, p. A294
AMI ARROYO GRANDE COMM HOSP, ARROYO GRANDE, CA, p. A56
AMITA HEALTH ALEXIAN BROTHERS BEHAVIORAL HEALTH HOSPITAL, HOFFMAN ESTATES, IL, p. A198
AMITA HEALTH ALEXIAN BROTHERS MEDICAL CENTER ELK GROVE VILLAGE, ELK GROVE VILLAGE, IL, p. A194
AMITA HEALTH HOLY FAMILY MEDICAL CENTER, DES PLAINES, IL, p. A193
AMITA HEALTH MERCY MEDICAL CENTER, AURORA, IL, p. A185
AMITA HEALTH RESURRECTION MEDICAL CENTER, CHICAGO, IL, p. A188
AMITA HEALTH SAINT FRANCIS HOSPITAL EVANSTON, EVANSTON, IL, p. A194
AMITA HEALTH SAINT JOSEPH HOSPITAL, ELGIN, IL, p. A194
AMITA HEALTH SAINT JOSEPH MEDICAL CENTER, JOLIET, IL, p. A199
AMITA HEALTH SAINTS MARY & ELIZABETH MEDICAL CENTER, CHICAGO, IL, p. A188
AMITA HEALTH ST. ALEXIUS MEDICAL CENTER HOFFMAN ESTATES, HOFFMAN ESTATES, IL, p. A198
AMITA HEALTH ST. MARY'S HOSPITAL, KANKAKEE, IL, p. A199
ANAHEIM GLOBAL MEDICAL CENTER, ANAHEIM, CA, p. A55
ANCHOR HOSPITAL, ATLANTA, GA, p. A156
ANCORA PSYCHIATRIC HOSPITAL, HAMMONTON, NJ, p. A422
ANDALUSIA HEALTH, ANDALUSIA, AL, p. A15
ANDERSON COUNTY HOSPITAL, GARNETT, KS, p. A249
ANDERSON HOSPITAL, MARYVILLE, IL, p. A201
ANDERSON REGIONAL HEALTH SYSTEM, MERIDIAN, MS, p. A366
ANDERSON REGIONAL HEALTH SYSTEM SOUTH, MERIDIAN, MS, p. A366
ANDERSON REHABILITATION INSTITUTE, EDWARDSVILLE, IL, p. A193
ANDREW MCFARLAND MENTAL HEALTH CENTER, SPRINGFIELD, IL, p. A208
ANDROSCOGGIN VALLEY HOSPITAL, BERLIN, NH, p. A414
ANDRUS PAVILION, YONKERS, NY, p. A462
ANGEL MEDICAL CENTER, FRANKLIN, NC, p. A468
ANGLETON DANBURY MEDICAL CENTER, ANGLETON, TX, p. A597
ANIMAS SURGICAL HOSPITAL, DURANGO, CO, p. A107
ANMED CANNON, PICKENS, SC, p. A569
ANMED HEALTH CANNON, PICKENS, SC, p. A569
ANMED HEALTH MEDICAL CENTER, ANDERSON, SC, p. A562
ANMED HEALTH REHABILITATION HOSPITAL, ANDERSON, SC, p. A562
ANMED MEDICAL CENTER, ANDERSON, SC, p. A562
ANMED REHABILITATION HOSPITAL, ANDERSON, SC, p. A562
ANN & ROBERT H. LURIE CHILDREN'S HOSPITAL OF CHICAGO, CHICAGO, IL, p. A188
ANNA JAQUES HOSPITAL, NEWBURYPORT, MA, p. A316
ANNE ARUNDEL MEDICAL CENTER, ANNAPOLIS, MD, p. A300
ANNIE JEFFREY MEMORIAL COUNTY HEALTH CENTER, OSCEOLA, NE, p. A405
ANNIE PENN HOSPITAL, REIDSVILLE, NC, p. A475
ANNIE PENN MEMORIAL HOSPITAL, REIDSVILLE, NC, p. A475
ANOKA METRO REGIONAL TREATMENT CENTER, ANOKA, MN, p. A342
ANSON GENERAL HOSPITAL, ANSON, TX, p. A597
ANTELOPE MEMORIAL HOSPITAL, NELIGH, NE, p. A403
ANTELOPE VALLEY MEDICAL CENTER, LANCASTER, CA, p. A69
APOLLO BEHAVIORAL HEALTH HOSPITAL, BATON ROUGE, LA, p. A277
APPALACHIAN BEHAVIORAL HEALTHCARE, ATHENS, OH, p. A485
APPALACHIAN REGIONAL BEHAVIORAL HEALTH, LINVILLE, NC, p. A472
APPLETON AREA HEALTH, APPLETON, MN, p. A342
APPLING HEALTHCARE SYSTEM, BAXLEY, GA, p. A159
ARBOR HEALTH, MORTON HOSPITAL, MORTON, WA, p. A691
ARBOUR H. R. I. HOSPITAL, BROOKLINE, MA, p. A312
ARBOUR HOSPITAL, BOSTON, MA, p. A309
ARBOUR-FULLER HOSPITAL, ATTLEBORO, MA, p. A309
ARBUCKLE MEMORIAL HOSPITAL, SULPHUR, OK, p. A521
ARCHBOLD BROOKS, QUITMAN, GA, p. A169
ARCHBOLD GRADY, CAIRO, GA, p. A159
ARCHBOLD HOSPITAL, ARCHBOLD, OH, p. A484
ARCHBOLD MEDICAL CENTER, THOMASVILLE, GA, p. A172
ARCHBOLD MITCHELL, CAMILLA, GA, p. A160
ARH OUR LADY OF THE WAY, MARTIN, KY, p. A271
ARISE AUSTIN MEDICAL CENTER, AUSTIN, TX, p. A598
ARIZONA CHILDREN'S CENTER MARICOPA MEDICAL CENTER, PHOENIX, AZ, p. A35
ARIZONA HEART HOSPITAL, PHOENIX, AZ, p. A35
ARIZONA ORTHOPEDIC SURGICAL HOSPITAL, CHANDLER, AZ, p. A30
ARIZONA SPINE AND JOINT HOSPITAL, MESA, AZ, p. A33
ARIZONA STATE HOSPITAL, PHOENIX, AZ, p. A35
ARKANSAS CHILDREN'S HOSPITAL, LITTLE ROCK, AR, p. A49
ARKANSAS CHILDREN'S NORTHWEST, SPRINGDALE, AR, p. A53
ARKANSAS CONTINUED CARE HOSPITAL, JONESBORO, AR, p. A48
ARKANSAS CONTINUED CARE HOSPITAL OF JONESBORO, JONESBORO, AR, p. A48
ARKANSAS HEART HOSPITAL, LITTLE ROCK, AR, p. A49
ARKANSAS METHODIST MEDICAL CENTER, PARAGOULD, AR, p. A52
ARKANSAS STATE HOSPITAL, LITTLE ROCK, AR, p. A49
ARKANSAS SURGICAL HOSPITAL, NORTH LITTLE ROCK, AR, p. A51
ARKANSAS VALLEY REGIONAL MEDICAL CENTER, LA JUNTA, CO, p. A110
ARMS ACRES, CARMEL, NY, p. A441
ARNOLD PALMER CHILDREN'S HOSPITAL, ORLANDO, FL, p. A144
ARNOLD PALMER HOSPITAL FOR CHILDREN, ORLANDO, FL, p. A144
ARNOT OGDEN MEDICAL CENTER, ELMIRA, NY, p. A442
AROOSTOOK HEALTH CENTER, MARS HILL, ME, p. A298
ARROWHEAD BEHAVIORAL HEALTH HOSPITAL, MAUMEE, OH, p. A499
ARROWHEAD REGIONAL MEDICAL CENTER, COLTON, CA, p. A60
ARTESIA GENERAL HOSPITAL, ARTESIA, NM, p. A433
ASANTE ASHLAND COMMUNITY HOSPITAL, ASHLAND, OR, p. A525
ASANTE ROGUE REGIONAL MEDICAL CENTER, MEDFORD, OR, p. A527
ASANTE THREE RIVERS MEDICAL CENTER, GRANTS PASS, OR, p. A527
ASBURY–SALINA REG MEDICAL CTR, SALINA, KS, p. A259
ASCENSION ALEXIAN BROTHERS, ELK GROVE VILLAGE, IL, p. A194
ASCENSION ALEXIAN BROTHERS BEHAVIORAL HEALTH HOSPITAL, HOFFMAN ESTATES, IL, p. A198
ASCENSION ALL SAINTS, RACINE, WI, p. A720
ASCENSION ALLEGAN HOSPITAL, ALLEGAN, MI, p. A321
ASCENSION BORGESS ALLEGAN HOSPITAL, ALLEGAN, MI, p. A321
ASCENSION BORGESS HOSPITAL, KALAMAZOO, MI, p. A331
ASCENSION BORGESS–LEE HOSPITAL, DOWAGIAC, MI, p. A326
ASCENSION BRIGHTON CENTER FOR RECOVERY, BRIGHTON, MI, p. A323
ASCENSION CALUMET HOSPITAL, CHILTON, WI, p. A709
ASCENSION COLUMBIA ST. MARY'S HOSPITAL MILWAUKEE, MILWAUKEE, WI, p. A716
ASCENSION GENESYS HOSPITAL, GRAND BLANC, MI, p. A327
ASCENSION GONZALES REHABILITATION HOSPITAL, GONZALES, LA, p. A282
ASCENSION HOLY FAMILY, DES PLAINES, IL, p. A193
ASCENSION MACOMB–OAKLAND HOSPITAL, WARREN, MI, p. A339
ASCENSION MACOMB–OAKLAND HOSPITAL, WARREN CAMPUS, WARREN, MI, p. A340
ASCENSION MERCY, AURORA, IL, p. A185
ASCENSION NORTHEAST WISCONSIN MERCY HOSPITAL, OSHKOSH, WI, p. A719
ASCENSION NORTHEAST WISCONSIN ST. ELIZABETH HOSPITAL, APPLETON, WI, p. A707
ASCENSION PROVIDENCE, WACO, TX, p. A660
ASCENSION PROVIDENCE HOSPITAL, SOUTHFIELD CAMPUS, SOUTHFIELD, MI, p. A338
ASCENSION PROVIDENCE ROCHESTER HOSPITAL, ROCHESTER, MI, p. A336
ASCENSION RESURRECTION, CHICAGO, IL, p. A188
ASCENSION RIVER DISTRICT HOSPITAL, EAST CHINA, MI, p. A326
ASCENSION SACRED HEART BAY, PANAMA CITY, FL, p. A145
ASCENSION SACRED HEART EMERALD COAST, MIRAMAR BEACH, FL, p. A141
ASCENSION SACRED HEART GULF, PORT ST JOE, FL, p. A147
ASCENSION SACRED HEART PENSACOLA, PENSACOLA, FL, p. A146
ASCENSION SACRED HEART REHABILITATION HOSPITAL, MEQUON, WI, p. A716
ASCENSION SAINT AGNES, BALTIMORE, MD, p. A300
ASCENSION SAINT FRANCIS, EVANSTON, IL, p. A194
ASCENSION SAINT JOSEPH – CHICAGO, CHICAGO, IL, p. A188
ASCENSION SAINT JOSEPH – ELGIN, ELGIN, IL, p. A194
ASCENSION SAINT JOSEPH – JOLIET, JOLIET, IL, p. A199
ASCENSION SAINT MARY – CHICAGO, CHICAGO, IL, p. A188
ASCENSION SAINT THOMAS BEHAVIORAL HEALTH HOSPITAL, NASHVILLE, TN, p. A590
ASCENSION SAINT THOMAS DEKALB, SMITHVILLE, TN, p. A593
ASCENSION SAINT THOMAS HICKMAN, CENTERVILLE, TN, p. A580
ASCENSION SAINT THOMAS HIGHLANDS, SPARTA, TN, p. A593
ASCENSION SAINT THOMAS HOSPITAL, NASHVILLE, TN, p. A590
ASCENSION SAINT THOMAS HOSPITAL FOR SPECIALTY SURGERY, NASHVILLE, TN, p. A590
ASCENSION SAINT THOMAS RIVER PARK, MC MINNVILLE, TN, p. A587
ASCENSION SAINT THOMAS RUTHERFORD, MURFREESBORO, TN, p. A590
ASCENSION SAINT THOMAS STONES RIVER, WOODBURY, TN, p. A594
ASCENSION SETON BASTROP, BASTROP, TX, p. A601
ASCENSION SETON EDGAR B. DAVIS HOSPITAL, LULING, TX, p. A637
ASCENSION SETON HAYS, KYLE, TX, p. A633
ASCENSION SETON HIGHLAND LAKES, BURNET, TX, p. A606
ASCENSION SETON MEDICAL CENTER AUSTIN, AUSTIN, TX, p. A599
ASCENSION SETON NORTHWEST, AUSTIN, TX, p. A599
ASCENSION SETON SHOAL CREEK, AUSTIN, TX, p. A599
ASCENSION SETON SMITHVILLE, SMITHVILLE, TX, p. A653
ASCENSION SETON SOUTHWEST, AUSTIN, TX, p. A599
ASCENSION SETON WILLIAMSON, ROUND ROCK, TX, p. A647
ASCENSION SOUTHEAST WISCONSIN HOSPITAL – ELMBROOK CAMPUS, BROOKFIELD, WI, p. A708
ASCENSION SOUTHEAST WISCONSIN HOSPITAL – FRANKLIN CAMPUS, FRANKLIN, WI, p. A711

Index of Hospitals / Ascension Southeast Wisconsin Hospital – St. Joseph's Campus

ASCENSION SOUTHEAST WISCONSIN HOSPITAL – ST. JOSEPH'S CAMPUS, MILWAUKEE, WI, p. A716
ASCENSION ST. ALEXIUS, HOFFMAN ESTATES, IL, p. A198
ASCENSION ST. FRANCIS HOSPITAL, MILWAUKEE, WI, p. A716
ASCENSION ST. JOHN BROKEN ARROW, BROKEN ARROW, OK, p. A510
ASCENSION ST. JOHN HOSPITAL, DETROIT, MI, p. A325
ASCENSION ST. JOHN JANE PHILLIPS, BARTLESVILLE, OK, p. A510
ASCENSION ST. JOHN MEDICAL CENTER, TULSA, OK, p. A522
ASCENSION ST. JOHN NOWATA, NOWATA, OK, p. A516
ASCENSION ST. JOHN OWASSO, OWASSO, OK, p. A519
ASCENSION ST. JOHN REHABILITATION HOSPITAL, AN AFFILIATE OF ENCOMPASS HEALTH – OWASSO, OWASSO, OK, p. A519
ASCENSION ST. JOHN SAPULPA, SAPULPA, OK, p. A520
ASCENSION ST. MARY – KANKAKEE, KANKAKEE, IL, p. A199
ASCENSION ST. THOMAS THREE RIVERS, WAVERLY, TN, p. A594
ASCENSION ST. VINCENT ANDERSON, ANDERSON, IN, p. A212
ASCENSION ST. VINCENT CARMEL HOSPITAL, CARMEL, IN, p. A213
ASCENSION ST. VINCENT CLAY HOSPITAL, BRAZIL, IN, p. A213
ASCENSION ST. VINCENT EVANSVILLE, EVANSVILLE, IN, p. A216
ASCENSION ST. VINCENT FISHERS, FISHERS, IN, p. A216
ASCENSION ST. VINCENT HEART CENTER, INDIANAPOLIS, IN, p. A218
ASCENSION ST. VINCENT INDIANAPOLIS HOSPITAL, INDIANAPOLIS, IN, p. A219
ASCENSION ST. VINCENT JENNINGS, NORTH VERNON, IN, p. A225
ASCENSION ST. VINCENT KOKOMO, KOKOMO, IN, p. A221
ASCENSION ST. VINCENT MERCY, ELWOOD, IN, p. A215
ASCENSION ST. VINCENT RANDOLPH, WINCHESTER, IN, p. A229
ASCENSION ST. VINCENT SALEM, SALEM, IN, p. A227
ASCENSION ST. VINCENT SETON SPECIALTY HOSPITAL, INDIANAPOLIS, IN, p. A219
ASCENSION ST. VINCENT WARRICK, BOONVILLE, IN, p. A213
ASCENSION ST. VINCENT WILLIAMSPORT, WILLIAMSPORT, IN, p. A229
ASCENSION ST. VINCENT'S BIRMINGHAM, BIRMINGHAM, AL, p. A16
ASCENSION ST. VINCENT'S BLOUNT, ONEONTA, AL, p. A23
ASCENSION ST. VINCENT'S CHILTON, CLANTON, AL, p. A18
ASCENSION ST. VINCENT'S CLAY COUNTY, MIDDLEBURG, FL, p. A141
ASCENSION ST. VINCENT'S EAST, BIRMINGHAM, AL, p. A16
ASCENSION ST. VINCENT'S RIVERSIDE, JACKSONVILLE, FL, p. A134
ASCENSION ST. VINCENT'S SOUTHSIDE, JACKSONVILLE, FL, p. A134
ASCENSION ST. VINCENT'S ST. CLAIR, PELL CITY, AL, p. A23
ASCENSION ST. VINCENT's ST. JOHNS COUNTY, SAINT JOHNS, FL, p. A148
ASCENSION VIA CHRISTI HOSPITAL ON ST. TERESA, WICHITA, KS, p. A261
ASCENSION VIA CHRISTI HOSPITAL ST. FRANCIS, WICHITA, KS, p. A261
ASCENSION VIA CHRISTI HOSPITAL, MANHATTAN, MANHATTAN, KS, p. A254
ASCENSION VIA CHRISTI REHABILITATION HOSPITAL, WICHITA, KS, p. A261
ASCENSION VIA CHRISTI ST. FRANCIS, MULVANE, KS, p. A255
ASCENSION WISCONSIN HOSPITAL – MENOMONEE FALLS CAMPUS, MENOMONEE FALLS, WI, p. A715
ASHE MEMORIAL HOSPITAL, JEFFERSON, NC, p. A471
ASHEVILLE SPECIALTY HOSPITAL, ASHEVILLE, NC, p. A463
ASHFORD PRESBYTERIAN COMMUNITY HOSPITAL, SAN JUAN, PR, p. A734
ASHLAND HEALTH CENTER, ASHLAND, KS, p. A246
ASHLEY COUNTY MEDICAL CENTER, CROSSETT, AR, p. A45
ASHLEY MEDICAL CENTER, ASHLEY, ND, p. A479
ASHLEY REGIONAL MEDICAL CENTER, VERNAL, UT, p. A670
ASHTABULA COUNTY MEDICAL CENTER, ASHTABULA, OH, p. A485
ASPEN GROVE BEHAVIORAL HOSPITAL, OREM, UT, p. A666
ASPEN MOUNTAIN MEDICAL CENTER, ROCK SPRINGS, WY, p. A728
ASPEN VALLEY HOSPITAL, ASPEN, CO, p. A103
ASPIRE HEALTH PARTNERS, ORLANDO, FL, p. A144
ASPIRE HOSPITAL, CONROE, TX, p. A608
ASPIRUS DIVINE SAVIOR HOSPITAL & CLINICS, PORTAGE, WI, p. A720
ASPIRUS EAGLE RIVER HOSPITAL, EAGLE RIVER, WI, p. A710

ASPIRUS IRON RIVER HOSPITAL, IRON RIVER, MI, p. A330
ASPIRUS IRON RIVER HOSPITALS & CLINICS, INC., IRON RIVER, MI, p. A330
ASPIRUS IRONWOOD HOSPITAL & CLINICS, INC., IRONWOOD, MI, p. A330
ASPIRUS IRONWOOD HOSPITAL, IRONWOOD, MI, p. A330
ASPIRUS KEWEENAW HOSPITAL, LAURIUM, MI, p. A332
ASPIRUS LAKE VIEW HOSPITAL, TWO HARBORS, MN, p. A356
ASPIRUS LANGLADE HOSPITAL, ANTIGO, WI, p. A707
ASPIRUS MEDFORD HOSPITAL & CLINICS, MEDFORD, WI, p. A715
ASPIRUS MERRILL HOSPITAL & CLINICS, INC., MERRILL, WI, p. A716
ASPIRUS RHINELANDER HOSPITAL, RHINELANDER, WI, p. A720
ASPIRUS RIVERVIEW HOSPITAL AND CLINICS, INC., WISCONSIN RAPIDS, WI, p. A725
ASPIRUS ST. LUKE's HOSPITAL, DULUTH, MN, p. A346
ASPIRUS STANLEY HOSPITAL & CLINICS, INC., STANLEY, WI, p. A722
ASPIRUS STEVEN's POINT HOSPITAL & CLINICS, INC., STEVENS POINT, WI, p. A722
ASPIRUS TOMAHAWK HOSPITAL, TOMAHAWK, WI, p. A723
ASPIRUS WAUSAU HOSPITAL, INC., WAUSAU, WI, p. A724
ASSUMPTION COMMUNITY HOSPITAL, NAPOLEONVILLE, LA, p. A289
ASTERA HEALTH, WADENA, MN, p. A356
ASTRIA SUNNYSIDE HOSPITAL, SUNNYSIDE, WA, p. A696
ASTRIA TOPPENISH HOSPITAL, TOPPENISH, WA, p. A697
ATASCADERO STATE HOSPITAL, ATASCADERO, CA, p. A56
ATHENS–LIMESTONE HOSPITAL, ATHENS, AL, p. A15
ATHOL HOSPITAL, ATHOL, MA, p. A309
ATLANTA VETERANS AFFAIRS MEDICAL CENTER, DECATUR, GA, p. A162
ATLANTIC GENERAL HOSPITAL, BERLIN, MD, p. A302
ATLANTIC REHABILITATION INSTITUTE, MADISON, NJ, p. A423
ATLANTICARE REGIONAL MEDICAL CENTER, ATLANTIC CITY, NJ, p. A418
ATLANTICARE REGIONAL MEDICAL CENTER–MAINLAND DIVISION, POMONA, NJ, p. A427
ATLANTICARE REGIONAL MEDICAL CENTER, ATLANTIC CAMPUS, ATLANTIC CITY, NJ, p. A418
ATLANTICARE REGIONAL MEDICAL CENTER, MAINLAND CAMPUS, POMONA, NJ, p. A427
ATMORE COMMUNITY HOSPITAL, ATMORE, AL, p. A15
ATOKA COUNTY MEDICAL CENTER, ATOKA, OK, p. A510
ATRIUM HEALTH ANSON, WADESBORO, NC, p. A477
ATRIUM HEALTH CABARRUS, CONCORD, NC, p. A466
ATRIUM HEALTH CLEVELAND, SHELBY, NC, p. A476
ATRIUM HEALTH FLOYD CHEROKEE MEDICAL CENTER, CENTRE, AL, p. A17
ATRIUM HEALTH FLOYD MEDICAL CENTER, ROME, GA, p. A170
ATRIUM HEALTH FLOYD POLK MEDICAL CENTER, CEDARTOWN, GA, p. A160
ATRIUM HEALTH LINCOLN, LINCOLNTON, NC, p. A472
ATRIUM HEALTH NAVICENT BALDWIN, MILLEDGEVILLE, GA, p. A168
ATRIUM HEALTH NAVICENT PEACH, MACON, GA, p. A167
ATRIUM HEALTH NAVICENT REHABILITATION HOSPITAL, MACON, GA, p. A167
ATRIUM HEALTH NAVICENT THE MEDICAL CENTER, MACON, GA, p. A167
ATRIUM HEALTH PINEVILLE, CHARLOTTE, NC, p. A465
ATRIUM HEALTH STANLY, ALBEMARLE, NC, p. A463
ATRIUM HEALTH UNION, MONROE, NC, p. A472
ATRIUM HEALTH UNIVERSITY CITY, CHARLOTTE, NC, p. A465
ATRIUM HEALTH WAKE FOREST BAPTIST, WINSTON–SALEM, NC, p. A478
ATRIUM HEALTH WAKE FOREST BAPTIST DAVIE MEDICAL CENTER, BERMUDA RUN, NC, p. A463
ATRIUM HEALTH WAKE FOREST BAPTIST LEXINGTON MEDICAL CENTER, LEXINGTON, NC, p. A472
ATRIUM HEALTH WAKE FOREST BAPTIST WILKES MEDICAL CENTER, NORTH WILKESBORO, NC, p. A474
ATRIUM HEALTH WAKE FORET BAPTIST HIGH POINT MEDICAL CENTER, HIGH POINT, NC, p. A470
ATRIUM HEALTH'S CAROLINAS MEDICAL CENTER, CHARLOTTE, NC, p. A465
ATRIUM MEDICAL CENTER, MIDDLETOWN, OH, p. A500
ATRIUM MEDICAL CENTER, STAFFORD, TX, p. A654
AUBURN COMMUNITY HOSPITAL, AUBURN, NY, p. A438
AUDIE L MURPHY MEM HOSPITAL, SAN ANTONIO, TX, p. A648
AUDUBON COUNTY MEMORIAL HOSPITAL AND CLINICS, AUDUBON, IA, p. A230
AUDUBON HOSPITAL, LOUISVILLE, KY, p. A269
AUGUSTA HEALTH, FISHERSVILLE, VA, p. A676
AULTMAN ALLIANCE COMMUNITY HOSPITAL, ALLIANCE, OH, p. A484
AULTMAN HOSPITAL, CANTON, OH, p. A487
AULTMAN ORRVILLE HOSPITAL, ORRVILLE, OH, p. A502

AURELIA OSBORN FOX MEMORIAL HOSPITAL, ONEONTA, NY, p. A455
AURORA BAYCARE MEDICAL CENTER, GREEN BAY, WI, p. A712
AURORA BEHAVIORAL HEALTH SYSTEM EAST, TEMPE, AZ, p. A39
AURORA BEHAVIORAL HEALTH SYSTEM WEST, GLENDALE, AZ, p. A32
AURORA BEHAVIORAL HEALTHCARE SAN DIEGO, SAN DIEGO, CA, p. A88
AURORA CHARTER OAK HOSPITAL, COVINA, CA, p. A60
AURORA LAKELAND MEDICAL CENTER, ELKHORN, WI, p. A710
AURORA MEDICAL CENTER – BAY AREA, MARINETTE, WI, p. A715
AURORA MEDICAL CENTER – MANITOWOC COUNTY, TWO RIVERS, WI, p. A723
AURORA MEDICAL CENTER – SHEBOYGAN COUNTY, SHEBOYGAN, WI, p. A721
AURORA MEDICAL CENTER BURLINGTON, BURLINGTON, WI, p. A709
AURORA MEDICAL CENTER GRAFTON, GRAFTON, WI, p. A711
AURORA MEDICAL CENTER IN WASHINGTON COUNTY, HARTFORD, WI, p. A712
AURORA MEDICAL CENTER KENOSHA, KENOSHA, WI, p. A713
AURORA MEDICAL CENTER OF OSHKOSH, OSHKOSH, WI, p. A719
AURORA MEDICAL CENTER SUMMIT, SUMMIT, WI, p. A722
AURORA PSYCHIATRIC HOSPITAL, WAUWATOSA, WI, p. A724
AURORA REGIONAL MEDICAL CENTER, AURORA, CO, p. A103
AURORA SANTA ROSA HOSPITAL, SANTA ROSA, CA, p. A95
AURORA SHEBOYGAN MEMORIAL MEDICAL CENTER, SHEBOYGAN, WI, p. A721
AURORA ST. LUKE'S MEDICAL CENTER, MILWAUKEE, WI, p. A717
AURORA ST. LUKE'S SOUTH SHORE, CUDAHY, WI, p. A709
AURORA WEST ALLIS MEDICAL CENTER, WEST ALLIS, WI, p. A724
AUSTEN RIGGS CENTER, STOCKBRIDGE, MA, p. A318
AUSTIN OAKS HOSPITAL, AUSTIN, TX, p. A599
AUSTIN STATE HOSPITAL, AUSTIN, TX, p. A599
AUXILIO MUTUO HOSPITAL, SAN JUAN, PR, p. A734
AVALA, COVINGTON, LA, p. A280
AVENIR BEHAVIORAL HEALTH CENTER, SURPRISE, AZ, p. A39
AVENTURA HOSPITAL AND MEDICAL CENTER, AVENTURA, FL, p. A125
AVERA CREIGHTON HOSPITAL, CREIGHTON, NE, p. A399
AVERA DE SMET MEMORIAL HOSPITAL, DE SMET, SD, p. A573
AVERA DELLS AREA HOSPITAL, DELL RAPIDS, SD, p. A573
AVERA FLANDREAU HOSPITAL, FLANDREAU, SD, p. A573
AVERA GRANITE FALLS, GRANITE FALLS, MN, p. A348
AVERA GREGORY HOSPITAL, GREGORY, SD, p. A574
AVERA HAND COUNTY MEMORIAL HOSPITAL, MILLER, SD, p. A574
AVERA HEART HOSPITAL OF SOUTH DAKOTA, SIOUX FALLS, SD, p. A576
AVERA HOLY FAMILY HOSPITAL, ESTHERVILLE, IA, p. A236
AVERA MARSHALL REGIONAL MEDICAL CENTER, MARSHALL, MN, p. A350
AVERA MCKENNAN HOSPITAL AND UNIVERSITY HEALTH CENTER, SIOUX FALLS, SD, p. A576
AVERA MERRILL PIONEER HOSPITAL, ROCK RAPIDS, IA, p. A242
AVERA MISSOURI RIVER HEALTH CENTER, GETTYSBURG, SD, p. A574
AVERA QUEEN OF PEACE HOSPITAL, MITCHELL, SD, p. A575
AVERA SACRED HEART HOSPITAL, YANKTON, SD, p. A578
AVERA ST. ANTHONY'S HOSPITAL, O'NEILL, NE, p. A403
AVERA ST. BENEDICT HEALTH CENTER, PARKSTON, SD, p. A575
AVERA ST. LUKE'S HOSPITAL, ABERDEEN, SD, p. A572
AVERA ST. MARY'S HOSPITAL, PIERRE, SD, p. A575
AVERA TYLER, TYLER, MN, p. A356
AVERA WESKOTA MEMORIAL HOSPITAL, WESSINGTON SPRINGS, SD, p. A578
AVISTA ADVENTIST HOSPITAL, LOUISVILLE, CO, p. A112
AVITA ONTARIO HOSPITAL, ONTARIO, OH, p. A502
AVOYELLES HOSPITAL, MARKSVILLE, LA, p. A288

B

BACON COUNTY HOSPITAL AND HEALTH SYSTEM, ALMA, GA, p. A156
BAILEY MEDICAL CENTER, OWASSO, OK, p. A519

Index of Hospitals / Baylor Scott & White Medical Center – Temple

BAILEY MEMORIAL HOSPITAL, CLINTON, SC, p. A564
BAKERSFIELD BEHAVIORAL HEALTHCARE HOSPITAL, BAKERSFIELD, CA, p. A56
BAKERSFIELD HEART HOSPITAL, BAKERSFIELD, CA, p. A56
BAKERSFIELD MEMORIAL HOSPITAL, BAKERSFIELD, CA, p. A56
BAKERSFIELD REHABILITATION HOSPITAL, BAKERSFIELD, CA, p. A57
BALDPATE HOSPITAL, GEORGETOWN, MA, p. A314
BALLARD COMMUNITY HOSPITAL, SEATTLE, WA, p. A694
BALLARD REHABILITATION HOSPITAL, SAN BERNARDINO, CA, p. A88
BALLINGER MEMORIAL HOSPITAL, BALLINGER, TX, p. A601
BANNER – UNIVERSITY MEDICAL CENTER PHOENIX, PHOENIX, AZ, p. A35
BANNER – UNIVERSITY MEDICAL CENTER SOUTH, TUCSON, AZ, p. A40
BANNER – UNIVERSITY MEDICAL CENTER TUCSON, TUCSON, AZ, p. A40
BANNER BAYWOOD MEDICAL CENTER, MESA, AZ, p. A33
BANNER BEHAVIORAL HEALTH HOSPITAL – SCOTTSDALE, SCOTTSDALE, AZ, p. A38
BANNER BOSWELL MEDICAL CENTER, SUN CITY, AZ, p. A39
BANNER CASA GRANDE MEDICAL CENTER, CASA GRANDE, AZ, p. A30
BANNER CHILDREN'S HOSPITAL, MESA, AZ, p. A33
BANNER CHURCHILL COMMUNITY HOSPITAL, FALLON, NV, p. A408
BANNER DEL E. WEBB MEDICAL CENTER, SUN CITY WEST, AZ, p. A39
BANNER DESERT MEDICAL CENTER, MESA, AZ, p. A33
BANNER ESTRELLA MEDICAL CENTER, PHOENIX, AZ, p. A35
BANNER FORT COLLINS MEDICAL CENTER, FORT COLLINS, CO, p. A108
BANNER GATEWAY MEDICAL CENTER, GILBERT, AZ, p. A31
BANNER GOLDFIELD MEDICAL CENTER, APACHE JUNCTION, AZ, p. A30
BANNER HEART HOSPITAL, MESA, AZ, p. A33
BANNER IRONWOOD MEDICAL CENTER, SAN TAN VALLEY, AZ, p. A38
BANNER LASSEN MEDICAL CENTER, SUSANVILLE, CA, p. A97
BANNER MCKEE MEDICAL CENTER, LOVELAND, CO, p. A112
BANNER NORTH COLORADO MEDICAL CENTERNORTH COLORADO MEDICAL CENTER, GREELEY, CO, p. A109
BANNER OCOTILLO MEDICAL CENTER, CHANDLER, AZ, p. A30
BANNER PAYSON MEDICAL CENTER, PAYSON, AZ, p. A34
BANNER REHABILITATION HOSPITAL PHOENIX, PHOENIX, AZ, p. A35
BANNER THUNDERBIRD MEDICAL CENTER, GLENDALE, AZ, p. A32
BAPTIST ANDERSON REGIONAL MEDICAL CENTER – SOUTH, MERIDIAN, MS, p. A366
BAPTIST ANDERSON REGIONAL MEDICAL CENTER, MERIDIAN, MS, p. A366
BAPTIST EMERGENCY HOSPITAL, SAN ANTONIO, TX, p. A648
BAPTIST HEALTH – VAN BUREN, VAN BUREN, AR, p. A54
BAPTIST HEALTH CORBIN, CORBIN, KY, p. A264
BAPTIST HEALTH DEACONESS MADISONVILLE, INC., MADISONVILLE, KY, p. A271
BAPTIST HEALTH EXTENDED CARE HOSPITAL, LITTLE ROCK, AR, p. A49
BAPTIST HEALTH FLOYD, NEW ALBANY, IN, p. A225
BAPTIST HEALTH–FORT SMITH, FORT SMITH, AR, p. A46
BAPTIST HEALTH HARDIN, ELIZABETHTOWN, KY, p. A265
BAPTIST HEALTH LA GRANGE, LA GRANGE, KY, p. A268
BAPTIST HEALTH LEXINGTON, LEXINGTON, KY, p. A268
BAPTIST HEALTH LOUISVILLE, LOUISVILLE, KY, p. A269
BAPTIST HEALTH MADISONVILLE, MADISONVILLE, KY, p. A271
BAPTIST HEALTH MEDICAL CENTER – CONWAY, CONWAY, AR, p. A44
BAPTIST HEALTH MEDICAL CENTER – DREW COUNTY, MONTICELLO, AR, p. A50
BAPTIST HEALTH MEDICAL CENTER – NORTH LITTLE ROCK, NORTH LITTLE ROCK, AR, p. A51
BAPTIST HEALTH MEDICAL CENTER–ARKADELPHIA, ARKADELPHIA, AR, p. A43
BAPTIST HEALTH MEDICAL CENTER–HEBER SPRINGS, HEBER SPRINGS, AR, p. A47
BAPTIST HEALTH MEDICAL CENTER–HOT SPRING COUNTY, MALVERN, AR, p. A50
BAPTIST HEALTH MEDICAL CENTER–LITTLE ROCK, LITTLE ROCK, AR, p. A49
BAPTIST HEALTH MEDICAL CENTER–STUTTGART, STUTTGART, AR, p. A54
BAPTIST HEALTH PADUCAH, PADUCAH, KY, p. A272
BAPTIST HEALTH REHABILITATION INSTITUTE, LITTLE ROCK, AR, p. A49

BAPTIST HEALTH RICHMOND, RICHMOND, KY, p. A273
BAPTIST HEALTH SOUTH FLORIDA, BAPTIST HOSPITAL OF MIAMI, MIAMI, FL, p. A139
BAPTIST HEALTH SOUTH FLORIDA, DOCTORS HOSPITAL, CORAL GABLES, FL, p. A128
BAPTIST HEALTH SOUTH FLORIDA, HOMESTEAD HOSPITAL, HOMESTEAD, FL, p. A134
BAPTIST HEALTH SOUTH FLORIDA, MARINERS HOSPITAL, TAVERNIER, FL, p. A153
BAPTIST HEALTH SOUTH FLORIDA, SOUTH MIAMI HOSPITAL, MIAMI, FL, p. A139
BAPTIST HEALTH SOUTH FLORIDA, WEST KENDALL BAPTIST HOSPITAL, MIAMI, FL, p. A139
BAPTIST HOSPITAL, PENSACOLA, FL, p. A146
BAPTIST HOSPITALS OF SOUTHEAST TEXAS, BEAUMONT, TX, p. A602
BAPTIST MEDICAL CENTER – ATTALA, KOSCIUSKO, MS, p. A365
BAPTIST MEDICAL CENTER – LEAKE, CARTHAGE, MS, p. A360
BAPTIST MEDICAL CENTER – YAZOO, YAZOO CITY, MS, p. A370
BAPTIST MEDICAL CENTER, SAN ANTONIO, TX, p. A648
BAPTIST MEDICAL CENTER BEACHES, JACKSONVILLE BEACH, FL, p. A135
BAPTIST MEDICAL CENTER EAST, MONTGOMERY, AL, p. A22
BAPTIST MEDICAL CENTER JACKSONVILLE, JACKSONVILLE, FL, p. A134
BAPTIST MEDICAL CENTER NASSAU, FERNANDINA BEACH, FL, p. A131
BAPTIST MEDICAL CENTER SOUTH, MONTGOMERY, AL, p. A22
BAPTIST MEMORIAL HOSPITAL – CALHOUN, CALHOUN CITY, MS, p. A360
BAPTIST MEMORIAL HOSPITAL – MEMPHIS, MEMPHIS, TN, p. A588
BAPTIST MEMORIAL HOSPITAL FOR WOMEN, MEMPHIS, TN, p. A588
BAPTIST MEMORIAL HOSPITAL–BOONEVILLE, BOONEVILLE, MS, p. A360
BAPTIST MEMORIAL HOSPITAL–CARROLL COUNTY, HUNTINGDON, TN, p. A584
BAPTIST MEMORIAL HOSPITAL–COLLIERVILLE, COLLIERVILLE, TN, p. A581
BAPTIST MEMORIAL HOSPITAL–CRITTENDEN, WEST MEMPHIS, AR, p. A54
BAPTIST MEMORIAL HOSPITAL–DESOTO, SOUTHAVEN, MS, p. A369
BAPTIST MEMORIAL HOSPITAL–GOLDEN TRIANGLE, COLUMBUS, MS, p. A361
BAPTIST MEMORIAL HOSPITAL–NORTH MISSISSIPPI, OXFORD, MS, p. A367
BAPTIST MEMORIAL HOSPITAL–TIPTON, COVINGTON, TN, p. A582
BAPTIST MEMORIAL HOSPITAL–UNION CITY, UNION CITY, TN, p. A594
BAPTIST MEMORIAL HOSPITAL–UNION COUNTY, NEW ALBANY, MS, p. A367
BAPTIST MEMORIAL REHABILITATION HOSPITAL, GERMANTOWN, TN, p. A583
BAPTIST MEMORIAL RESTORATIVE CARE HOSPITAL, MEMPHIS, TN, p. A588
BAPTIST NEIGHBORHOOD HOSPITAL AT THOUSAND OAKS, SAN ANTONIO, TX, p. A649
BARAGA COUNTY MEMORIAL HOSPITAL, L'ANSE, MI, p. A331
BARBOURVILLE ARH HOSPITAL, BARBOURVILLE, KY, p. A263
BARLOW RESPIRATORY HOSPITAL, LOS ANGELES, CA, p. A71
BARNES–JEWISH HOSPITAL, SAINT LOUIS, MO, p. A383
BARNES–JEWISH ST. PETERS HOSPITAL, SAINT PETERS, MO, p. A386
BARNES–JEWISH WEST COUNTY HOSPITAL, SAINT LOUIS, MO, p. A384
BARNES–KASSON COUNTY HOSPITAL, SUSQUEHANNA, PA, p. A555
BARRETT HOSPITAL & HEALTHCARE, DILLON, MT, p. A391
BARSTOW COMMUNITY HOSPITAL, BARSTOW, CA, p. A57
BARTLETT REGIONAL HOSPITAL, JUNEAU, AK, p. A28
BARTON MEMORIAL HOSPITAL, SOUTH LAKE TAHOE, CA, p. A96
BARTOW REGIONAL MEDICAL CENTER, BARTOW, FL, p. A125
BASSETT ARMY COMMUNITY HOSPITAL, FORT WAINWRIGHT, AK, p. A28
BASSETT MEDICAL CENTER, COOPERSTOWN, NY, p. A441
BATES COUNTY MEMORIAL HOSPITAL, BUTLER, MO, p. A372
BATES MEDICAL CENTER, BENTONVILLE, AR, p. A43
BATH COMMUNITY HOSPITAL, HOT SPRINGS, VA, p. A678
BATH VETERANS AFFAIRS MEDICAL CENTER, BATH, NY, p. A439

BATON ROUGE BEHAVIORAL HOSPITAL, BATON ROUGE, LA, p. A277
BATON ROUGE GEN HEALTH CENTER, BATON ROUGE, LA, p. A277
BATON ROUGE GENERAL MEDICAL CENTER, BATON ROUGE, LA, p. A277
BATON ROUGE REHABILITATION HOSPITAL, BATON ROUGE, LA, p. A277
BATTLE CREEK ADVENTIST HOSP, BATTLE CREEK, MI, p. A322
BATTLE CREEK VETERANS AFFAIRS MEDICAL CENTER, BATTLE CREEK, MI, p. A322
BATTLE MOUNTAIN GENERAL HOSPITAL, BATTLE MOUNTAIN, NV, p. A408
BAXTER HEALTH, MOUNTAIN HOME, AR, p. A51
BAXTER REGIONAL MEDICAL CENTER, MOUNTAIN HOME, AR, p. A51
BAY AREA HOSPITAL, COOS BAY, OR, p. A526
BAY PINES VETERANS AFFAIRS HEALTHCARE SYSTEM, BAY PINES, FL, p. A125
BAY REGIONAL MEDICAL CENTER–WEST CAMPUS, BAY CITY, MI, p. A322
BAYAMON MEDICAL CENTER, BAYAMON, PR, p. A731
BAYCARE ALLIANT HOSPITAL, DUNEDIN, FL, p. A130
BAYCARE HOSPITAL WESLEY CHAPEL, WESLEY CHAPEL, FL, p. A154
BAYFRONT HEALTH BROOKSVILLE, BROOKSVILLE, FL, p. A127
BAYFRONT HEALTH SEVEN RIVERS, CRYSTAL RIVER, FL, p. A129
BAYFRONT HEALTH SPRING HILL, SPRING HILL, FL, p. A150
BAYFRONT HEALTH ST. PETERSBURG, SAINT PETERSBURG, FL, p. A148
BAYHEALTH, DOVER, DE, p. A121
BAYHEALTH MEDICAL CENTER, DOVER, DE, p. A121
BAYHEALTH MEDICAL CENTER, MILFORD MEMORIAL HOSPITAL, MILFORD, DE, p. A121
BAYLOR ORTHOPEDIC AND SPINE HOSPITAL AT ARLINGTON, ARLINGTON, TX, p. A597
BAYLOR SCOTT & WHITE ALL SAINTS MEDICAL CENTER – FORT WORTH, FORT WORTH, TX, p. A619
BAYLOR SCOTT & WHITE CONTINUING CARE HOSPITAL–TEMPLE, TEMPLE, TX, p. A656
BAYLOR SCOTT & WHITE EMERGENCY HOSPITAL – BURLESON, BURLESON, TX, p. A606
BAYLOR SCOTT & WHITE EMERGENCY HOSPITALS–AUBREY, AUBREY, TX, p. A598
BAYLOR SCOTT & WHITE EMERGENCY MEDICAL CENTER–CEDAR PARK, CEDAR PARK, TX, p. A607
BAYLOR SCOTT & WHITE HEART & VASCULAR HOSPITAL–DALLAS, DALLAS, TX, p. A610
BAYLOR SCOTT & WHITE HOSPITAL MEDICAL CENTER – COLLEGE STATION, COLLEGE STATION, TX, p. A607
BAYLOR SCOTT & WHITE INSTITUTE FOR REHABILITATION – DALLAS, DALLAS, TX, p. A610
BAYLOR SCOTT & WHITE INSTITUTE FOR REHABILITATION – LAKEWAY, LAKEWAY, TX, p. A633
BAYLOR SCOTT & WHITE INSTITUTE FOR REHABILITATION–FORT WORTH, FORT WORTH, TX, p. A619
BAYLOR SCOTT & WHITE INSTITUTE FOR REHABILITATION–FRISCO, FRISCO, TX, p. A621
BAYLOR SCOTT & WHITE MEDICAL CENTER – AUSTIN, AUSTIN, TX, p. A599
BAYLOR SCOTT & WHITE MEDICAL CENTER – BRENHAM, BRENHAM, TX, p. A604
BAYLOR SCOTT & WHITE MEDICAL CENTER – BUDA, BUDA, TX, p. A605
BAYLOR SCOTT & WHITE MEDICAL CENTER – CENTENNIAL, FRISCO, TX, p. A621
BAYLOR SCOTT & WHITE MEDICAL CENTER – GRAPEVINE, GRAPEVINE, TX, p. A622
BAYLOR SCOTT & WHITE MEDICAL CENTER – HILLCREST, WACO, TX, p. A660
BAYLOR SCOTT & WHITE MEDICAL CENTER – LAKE POINTE, ROWLETT, TX, p. A648
BAYLOR SCOTT & WHITE MEDICAL CENTER – MARBLE FALLS, MARBLE FALLS, TX, p. A637
BAYLOR SCOTT & WHITE MEDICAL CENTER – PFLUGERVILLE, PFLUGERVILLE, TX, p. A644
BAYLOR SCOTT & WHITE MEDICAL CENTER – PLANO, PLANO, TX, p. A644
BAYLOR SCOTT & WHITE MEDICAL CENTER – ROUND ROCK, ROUND ROCK, TX, p. A647
BAYLOR SCOTT & WHITE MEDICAL CENTER – SUNNYVALE, SUNNYVALE, TX, p. A655
BAYLOR SCOTT & WHITE MEDICAL CENTER – TAYLOR, TAYLOR, TX, p. A655
BAYLOR SCOTT & WHITE MEDICAL CENTER – TEMPLE, TEMPLE, TX, p. A656

© 2025 AHA Guide

Index of Hospitals / Baylor Scott & White Medical Center – Trophy Club

BAYLOR SCOTT & WHITE MEDICAL CENTER – TROPHY CLUB, TROPHY CLUB, TX, p. A658
BAYLOR SCOTT & WHITE MEDICAL CENTER AT – MCKINNEY, MCKINNEY, TX, p. A638
BAYLOR SCOTT & WHITE MEDICAL CENTER–FRISCO, FRISCO, TX, p. A621
BAYLOR SCOTT & WHITE MEDICAL CENTER–IRVING, IRVING, TX, p. A630
BAYLOR SCOTT & WHITE MEDICAL CENTER–UPTOWN, DALLAS, TX, p. A610
BAYLOR SCOTT & WHITE MEDICAL CENTER–WAXAHACHIE, WAXAHACHIE, TX, p. A660
BAYLOR SCOTT & WHITE SURGICAL HOSPITAL FORT WORTH, FORT WORTH, TX, p. A619
BAYLOR SCOTT & WHITE SURGICAL HOSPITAL–SHERMAN, SHERMAN, TX, p. A652
BAYLOR SCOTT & WHITE TEXAS SPINE & JOINT HOSPITAL–TYLER, TYLER, TX, p. A658
BAYLOR SCOTT & WHITE THE HEART HOSPITAL DENTON, DENTON, TX, p. A613
BAYLOR SCOTT & WHITE THE HEART HOSPITAL PLANO, PLANO, TX, p. A644
BAYLOR ST. LUKE'S MEDICAL CENTER, HOUSTON, TX, p. A625
BAYLOR SURGICAL HOSPITAL AT LAS COLINAS, IRVING, TX, p. A630
BAYLOR UNIVERSITY MEDICAL CENTER, DALLAS, TX, p. A610
BAYNE–JONES ARMY COMMUNITY HOSPITAL, FORT POLK, LA, p. A282
BAYOU BEND HEALTH SYSTEM, FRANKLIN, LA, p. A282
BAYPOINTE BEHAVIORAL HEALTH, MOBILE, AL, p. A21
BAYSIDE COMMUNITY HOSPITAL, ANAHUAC, TX, p. A597
BAYSTATE FRANKLIN MEDICAL CENTER, GREENFIELD, MA, p. A314
BAYSTATE MEDICAL CENTER, SPRINGFIELD, MA, p. A318
BAYSTATE NOBLE HOSPITAL, WESTFIELD, MA, p. A319
BAYSTATE WING HOSPITAL, PALMER, MA, p. A317
BAYVIEW HOSP & MENTAL SYSTEM, CHULA VISTA, CA, p. A59
BCA STONECREST CENTER, DETROIT, MI, p. A325
BEACHAM MEMORIAL HOSPITAL, MAGNOLIA, MS, p. A365
BEACON BEHAVIORAL HOSPITAL – NEW ORLEANS, NEW ORLEANS, LA, p. A290
BEACON BEHAVIORAL HOSPITAL – NORTHSHORE, LACOMBE, LA, p. A285
BEACON BEHAVIORAL HOSPITAL, BUNKIE, LA, p. A279
BEACON BEHAVIORAL HOSPITAL, LUTCHER, LA, p. A287
BEACON BEHAVIORAL HOSPITAL, LUVERNE, AL, p. A21
BEACON CHILDREN'S HOSPITAL, LUVERNE, AL, p. A21
BEACON HEALTH SYSTEM – THREE RIVERS HEALTH SYSTEM, INC., THREE RIVERS, MI, p. A339
BEAR LAKE MEMORIAL HOSPITAL, MONTPELIER, ID, p. A182
BEAR RIVER VALLEY HOSPITAL, TREMONTON, UT, p. A670
BEAR VALLEY COMMUNITY HOSPITAL, BIG BEAR LAKE, CA, p. A58
BEARTOOTH BILLINGS CLINIC, RED LODGE, MT, p. A395
BEATRICE COMMUNITY HOSPITAL AND HEALTH CENTER, BEATRICE, NE, p. A398
BEAUFORT MEMORIAL HOSPITAL, BEAUFORT, SC, p. A562
BEAUMONT EMERGENCY HOSPITAL, BEAUMONT, TX, p. A602
BEAUMONT REGIONAL MEDICAL CENTER, BEAUMONT, TX, p. A602
BEAUREGARD HEALTH SYSTEM, DE RIDDER, LA, p. A281
BEAVER COUNTY MEMORIAL HOSPITAL, BEAVER, OK, p. A510
BEAVER VALLEY HOSPITAL, BEAVER, UT, p. A664
BECKETT SPRINGS, WEST CHESTER, OH, p. A506
BECKLEY ARH HOSPITAL, BECKLEY, WV, p. A699
BECKLEY VETERANS AFFAIRS MEDICAL CENTER, BECKLEY, WV, p. A699
BEDFORD VAMC, BEDFORD, MA, p. A309
BEDFORD VETERANS AFFAIRS MEDICAL CENTER, EDITH NOURSE ROGERS MEMORIAL VETERANS HOSPITAL, BEDFORD, MA, p. A309
BEEBE HEALTHCARE, LEWES, DE, p. A121
BEHAVIORAL CENTER OF MICHIGAN, WARREN, MI, p. A340
BEHAVIORAL HEALTH CENTER OF PORTER VILLAGE, NORMAN, OK, p. A515
BEHAVIORAL HEALTH OF ROCKY TOP, ROCKY TOP, TN, p. A592
BEHAVIORAL HOSPITAL OF BELLAIRE, HOUSTON, TX, p. A625
BEHAVIORAL WELLNESS CENTER AT GIRARD, THE, PHILADELPHIA, PA, p. A548
BELLA VISTA HOSPITAL, MAYAGUEZ, PR, p. A733
BELLEVUE HOSPITAL, THE, BELLEVUE, OH, p. A486
BELLEVUE WOMAN'S HOSPITAL, SCHENECTADY, NY, p. A458
BELLIN HEALTH OCONTO HOSPITAL, OCONTO, WI, p. A719

BELLIN HOSPITAL, GREEN BAY, WI, p. A712
BELLIN PSYCHIATRIC CENTER, GREEN BAY, WI, p. A712
BELLVILLE MEDICAL CENTER, BELLVILLE, TX, p. A603
BELMONT BEHAVIORAL HEALTH SYSTEM, PHILADELPHIA, PA, p. A548
BELMONT PINES HOSPITAL, YOUNGSTOWN, OH, p. A508
BELOIT HEALTH SYSTEM, BELOIT, WI, p. A708
BELTON REGIONAL MEDICAL CENTER, BELTON, MO, p. A371
BEN TAUB GENERAL HOSPITAL, HOUSTON, TX, p. A625
BENEFIS HEALTH CARE–EAST CAMP, GREAT FALLS, MT, p. A392
BENEFIS HEALTH CARE–WEST CAMP, GREAT FALLS, MT, p. A392
BENEFIS HEALTH SYSTEM, GREAT FALLS, MT, p. A392
BENEFIS TETON MEDICAL CENTER, CHOTEAU, MT, p. A390
BENEWAH COMMUNITY HOSPITAL, SAINT MARIES, ID, p. A183
BENNETT COUNTY HOSPITAL AND NURSING HOME, MARTIN, SD, p. A574
BENNING MARTIN ARMY COMMUNITY HOSPITAL, FORT BENNING, GA, p. A164
BENSON HOSPITAL, BENSON, AZ, p. A30
BERGEN NEW BRIDGE MEDICAL CENTER, PARAMUS, NJ, p. A426
BERKELEY MEDICAL CENTER, MARTINSBURG, WV, p. A702
BERKELEY REGIONAL MEDICAL CENTER, MONCKS CORNER, SC, p. A568
BERKSHIRE MEDICAL CENTER, PITTSFIELD, MA, p. A317
BERNARD MITCHELL HOSPITAL, CHICAGO, IL, p. A188
BERTRAND CHAFFEE HOSPITAL, SPRINGVILLE, NY, p. A459
BERWICK HOSPITAL CENTER, BERWICK, PA, p. A535
BETH ABRAHAM HOSPITAL, NEW YORK, NY, p. A447
BETH ISRAEL DEACONESS HOSPITAL–MILTON, MILTON, MA, p. A316
BETH ISRAEL DEACONESS HOSPITAL–NEEDHAM, NEEDHAM, MA, p. A316
BETH ISRAEL DEACONESS HOSPITAL–PLYMOUTH, PLYMOUTH, MA, p. A317
BETH ISRAEL DEACONESS MEDICAL CENTER, BOSTON, MA, p. A309
BETH ISRAEL MEDICAL CENTER–KINGS HIGHWAY DIVISION, NEW YORK, NY, p. A447
BETHANIA REGIONAL HEALTH CNTR, WICHITA FALLS, TX, p. A662
BETHANY CHILDREN'S HEALTH CENTER, BETHANY, OK, p. A510
BETHESDA HOSPITAL EAST, BOYNTON BEACH, FL, p. A126
BETHESDA NORTH HOSPITAL, CINCINNATI, OH, p. A488
BETHESDA REHABILITATION HOSPITAL, BATON ROUGE, LA, p. A277
BEVERLY HOSPITAL, BEVERLY, MA, p. A309
BHC ALHAMBRA HOSPITAL, ROSEMEAD, CA, p. A86
BIBB MEDICAL CENTER, CENTREVILLE, AL, p. A17
BIENVILLE MEDICAL CENTER, ARCADIA, LA, p. A277
BIG BEND REGIONAL MEDICAL CENTER, ALPINE, TX, p. A596
BIG HORN HOSPITAL, HARDIN, MT, p. A392
BIG SANDY MEDICAL CENTER, BIG SANDY, MT, p. A389
BIG SOUTH FORK MEDICAL CENTER, ONEIDA, TN, p. A592
BIG SPRING STATE HOSPITAL, BIG SPRING, TX, p. A603
BIGFORK VALLEY HOSPITAL, BIGFORK, MN, p. A343
BILLINGS CLINIC, BILLINGS, MT, p. A389
BILLINGS CLINIC BROADWATER, TOWNSEND, MT, p. A396
BILOXI VA MEDICAL CENTER, BILOXI, MS, p. A359
BINGHAM MEMORIAL HOSPITAL, BLACKFOOT, ID, p. A179
BINGHAMTON GENERAL HOSPITAL, BINGHAMTON, NY, p. A439
BIRMINGHAM VA MEDICAL CENTER, BIRMINGHAM, AL, p. A16
BIRMINGHAM VAMC, BIRMINGHAM, AL, p. A16
BITTERROOT HEALTH – DALY HOSPITAL, HAMILTON, MT, p. A392
BLACK HILLS HCS, FORT MEADE, SD, p. A573
BLACK HILLS SURGICAL HOSPITAL, RAPID CITY, SD, p. A575
BLACK RIVER MEMORIAL HOSPITAL, BLACK RIVER FALLS, WI, p. A708
BLACKFEET COMMUNITY HOSPITAL, SAINT MARY, MT, p. A395
BLAKE MEDICAL CENTER, BRADENTON, FL, p. A126
BLANCHARD VALLEY HOSPITAL, FINDLAY, OH, p. A496
BLANCHARD VALLEY REG HLTH CTR, FINDLAY, OH, p. A496
BLANK CHILDREN'S HOSPITAL, DES MOINES, IA, p. A234
BLECKLEY MEMORIAL HOSPITAL, COCHRAN, GA, p. A160
BLESSING HOSPITAL, QUINCY, IL, p. A206
BLIANT SPECIALTY HOSPITAL, NEW ORLEANS, LA, p. A290
BLOOMINGTON MEADOWS HOSPITAL, BLOOMINGTON, IN, p. A212
BLOOMINGTON REGIONAL REHABILITATION HOSPITAL, BLOOMINGTON, IN, p. A213
BLOUNT MEMORIAL HOSPITAL, MARYVILLE, TN, p. A587
BLOWING ROCK HOSPITAL, BLOWING ROCK, NC, p. A464
BLUE MOUNTAIN HOSPITAL, BLANDING, UT, p. A664

BLUE MOUNTAIN HOSPITAL DISTRICT, JOHN DAY, OR, p. A528
BLUE MOUNTAIN HOSPITAL PALMERTON CAMPUS, PALMERTON, PA, p. A547
BLUE RIDGE MEDICAL CENTER, BLUE RIDGE, GA, p. A159
BLUE RIDGE REGIONAL HOSPITAL, SPRUCE PINE, NC, p. A476
BLUEGRASS COMMUNITY HOSPITAL, VERSAILLES, KY, p. A274
BLUERIDGE VISTA BEHAVIORAL HEALTH, CINCINNATI, OH, p. A488
BLUERIDGE VISTA HEALTH AND WELLNESS, CINCINNATI, OH, p. A488
BLUFFTON HOSPITAL, BLUFFTON, OH, p. A486
BLUFFTON REGIONAL MEDICAL CENTER, BLUFFTON, IN, p. A213
BLYTHEDALE CHILDREN'S HOSPITAL, VALHALLA, NY, p. A460
BMC BAYTOWN, BAYTOWN, TX, p. A601
BOB STUMP DEPARTMENT OF VETERANS AFFAIRS MEDICAL CENTER, PRESCOTT, AZ, p. A37
BOB WILSON MEMORIAL GRANT COUNTY HOSPITAL, ULYSSES, KS, p. A261
BOCA RATON REGIONAL HOSPITAL, BOCA RATON, FL, p. A126
BOISE VA MEDICAL CENTER, BOISE, ID, p. A179
BOLIVAR MEDICAL CENTER, CLEVELAND, MS, p. A361
BON SECOURS – SOUTHAMPTON MEDICAL CENTER, FRANKLIN, VA, p. A676
BON SECOURS – SOUTHAMPTON MEMORIAL HOSPITAL, FRANKLIN, VA, p. A676
BON SECOURS – SOUTHERN VIRGINIA MEDICAL CENTER, EMPORIA, VA, p. A675
BON SECOURS – SOUTHSIDE MEDICAL CENTER, PETERSBURG, VA, p. A681
BON SECOURS COMMUNITY HOSPITAL, PORT JERVIS, NY, p. A456
BON SECOURS MARY IMMACULATE HOSPITAL, NEWPORT NEWS, VA, p. A679
BON SECOURS MARYVIEW MEDICAL CENTER, PORTSMOUTH, VA, p. A681
BON SECOURS MEMORIAL REGIONAL MEDICAL CENTER, MECHANICSVILLE, VA, p. A679
BON SECOURS RAPPAHANNOCK GENERAL HOSPITAL, KILMARNOCK, VA, p. A678
BON SECOURS RICHMOND COMMUNITY HOSPITAL, RICHMOND, VA, p. A682
BON SECOURS ST. FRANCIS EASTSIDE, GREENVILLE, SC, p. A566
BON SECOURS ST. FRANCIS HEALTH SYSTEM, GREENVILLE, SC, p. A566
BON SECOURS ST. FRANCIS HOSPITAL, CHARLESTON, SC, p. A563
BON SECOURS ST. FRANCIS MEDICAL CENTER, MIDLOTHIAN, VA, p. A679
BON SECOURS ST. MARY'S HOSPITAL, RICHMOND, VA, p. A682
BON SECOURS–RICHMOND COMMUNITY HOSPITAL, RICHMOND, VA, p. A682
BONE AND JOINT HOSPITAL, OKLAHOMA CITY, OK, p. A516
BONNER GENERAL HEALTH, SANDPOINT, ID, p. A184
BOONE COUNTY HEALTH CENTER, ALBION, NE, p. A397
BOONE COUNTY HOSPITAL, BOONE, IA, p. A231
BOONE HOSPITAL CENTER, COLUMBIA, MO, p. A374
BOONE MEMORIAL HOSPITAL, MADISON, WV, p. A702
BORGESS-PIPP HOSPITAL, PLAINWELL, MI, p. A335
BOSTON CHILDREN'S HOSPITAL, BOSTON, MA, p. A310
BOSTON MEDICAL CENTER, BOSTON, MA, p. A310
BOTHWELL REGIONAL HEALTH CENTER, SEDALIA, MO, p. A386
BOULDER CITY HOSPITAL, BOULDER CITY, NV, p. A408
BOULDER COMMUNITY HEALTH, BOULDER, CO, p. A104
BOUNDARY COMMUNITY HOSPITAL, BONNERS FERRY, ID, p. A180
BOURBON COMMUNITY HOSPITAL, PARIS, KY, p. A273
BOURNEWOOD HEALTH SYSTEMS, BROOKLINE, MA, p. A312
BOWDLE HOSPITAL, BOWDLE, SD, p. A572
BOX BUTTE GENERAL HOSPITAL, ALLIANCE, NE, p. A397
BOYS TOWN NATIONAL RESEARCH HOSPITAL, OMAHA, NE, p. A403
BOZEMAN HEALTH, BOZEMAN, MT, p. A390
BOZEMAN HEALTH BIG SKY MEDICAL CENTER, BIG SKY, MT, p. A389
BOZEMAN HEALTH DEACONESS REGIONAL MEDICAL CENTER, BOZEMAN, MT, p. A390
BRADFORD HEALTH SERVICES AT HUNTSVILLE, MADISON, AL, p. A21
BRADFORD HEALTH SERVICES AT WARRIOR LODGE, WARRIOR, AL, p. A26
BRADFORD HOSPITAL, BRADFORD, PA, p. A535
BRADLEY CENTER, COLUMBUS, GA, p. A161

BRADLEY CENTER OF ST. FRANCIS, COLUMBUS, GA, p. A161
BRADLEY COUNTY MEDICAL CENTER, WARREN, AR, p. A54
BRADLEY MEMORIAL, SOUTHINGTON, CT, p. A119
BRADLEY MEMORIAL HOSPITAL AND HEALTH CENTER, SOUTHINGTON, CT, p. A119
BRADY–GREEN COMM HEALTH CENTER, SAN ANTONIO, TX, p. A649
BRATTLEBORO MEMORIAL HOSPITAL, BRATTLEBORO, VT, p. A671
BRATTLEBORO RETREAT, BRATTLEBORO, VT, p. A671
BRAXTON COUNTY MEMORIAL HOSPITAL, GASSAWAY, WV, p. A700
BRECKINRIDGE MEMORIAL HOSPITAL, HARDINSBURG, KY, p. A266
BRENNER CHILDREN'S HOSPITAL & HEALTH SERVICES, WINSTON SALEM, NC, p. A478
BRENTWOOD BEHAVIORAL HEALTHCARE OF MISSISSIPPI, FLOWOOD, MS, p. A361
BRENTWOOD HOSPITAL, SHREVEPORT, LA, p. A292
BRENTWOOD SPRINGS, NEWBURGH, IN, p. A225
BRIDGEPOINT CONTINUING CARE HOSPITAL – CAPITOL HILL, WASHINGTON, DC, p. A123
BRIDGEPOINT CONTINUING CARE HOSPITAL – NATIONAL HARBORSIDE, WASHINGTON, DC, p. A123
BRIDGEPOINT CONTINUING CARE HOSPITAL, MARRERO, LA, p. A288
BRIDGEPOINT HOSPITAL CAPITOL HILL, WASHINGTON, DC, p. A123
BRIDGEPORT HOSPITAL, BRIDGEPORT, CT, p. A115
BRIDGETON HEALTH CENTER, BRIDGETON, NJ, p. A419
BRIDGETON HOSPITAL, BRIDGETON, NJ, p. A419
BRIDGEWATER STATE HOSPITAL, BRIDGEWATER, MA, p. A311
BRIDGTON HOSPITAL, BRIDGTON, ME, p. A296
BRIGHAM AND WOMEN'S FAULKNER HOSPITAL, BOSTON, MA, p. A310
BRIGHAM AND WOMEN'S HOSPITAL, BOSTON, MA, p. A310
BRIGHAM CITY COMMUNITY HOSPITAL, BRIGHAM CITY, UT, p. A664
BRIGHTON CAMPUS–MAINE MED CTR, PORTLAND, ME, p. A298
BRISTOL BAY AREA HEALTH CORPORATION, DILLINGHAM, AK, p. A28
BRISTOL HEALTH, BRISTOL, CT, p. A115
BRISTOL REGIONAL MEDICAL CENTER, BRISTOL, TN, p. A579
BROADDUS HOSPITAL, PHILIPPI, WV, p. A704
BROADLAWNS MEDICAL CENTER, DES MOINES, IA, p. A234
BROADWATER HEALTH CENTER, TOWNSEND, MT, p. A396
BRODSTONE MEMORIAL HOSPITAL, SUPERIOR, NE, p. A406
BROMENN REGIONAL MEDICAL CENTER, NORMAL, IL, p. A203
BRONSON BATTLE CREEK HOSPITAL, BATTLE CREEK, MI, p. A322
BRONSON LAKEVIEW HOSPITAL, PAW PAW, MI, p. A335
BRONSON METHODIST HOSPITAL, KALAMAZOO, MI, p. A331
BRONSON SOUTH HAVEN HOSPITAL, SOUTH HAVEN, MI, p. A338
BRONX PSYCHIATRIC CENTER, NEW YORK, NY, p. A447
BRONXCARE HEALTH SYSTEM, NEW YORK, NY, p. A447
BROOK LANE, HAGERSTOWN, MD, p. A304
BROOK LANE HEALTH SERVICES, HAGERSTOWN, MD, p. A304
BROOKDALE HOSPITAL MEDICAL CENTER, NEW YORK, NY, p. A447
BROOKE ARMY MEDICAL CENTER, FORT SAM HOUSTON, TX, p. A618
BROOKE GLEN BEHAVIORAL HOSPITAL, FORT WASHINGTON, PA, p. A540
BROOKHAVEN HOSPITAL, TULSA, OK, p. A522
BROOKINGS HEALTH SYSTEM, BROOKINGS, SD, p. A572
BROOKLYN HOSPITAL CENTER, NEW YORK, NY, p. A447
BROOKS REHABILITATION HOSPITAL, JACKSONVILLE, FL, p. A134
BROOKS-TLC HOSPITAL SYSTEM, INC., DUNKIRK, NY, p. A442
BROOKWOOD BAPTIST MEDICAL CENTER, BIRMINGHAM, AL, p. A16
BROUGHTON HOSPITAL, MORGANTON, NC, p. A473
BROWARD HEALTH CORAL SPRINGS, CORAL SPRINGS, FL, p. A129
BROWARD HEALTH IMPERIAL POINT, FORT LAUDERDALE, FL, p. A131
BROWARD HEALTH MEDICAL CENTER, FORT LAUDERDALE, FL, p. A131
BROWARD HEALTH NORTH, DEERFIELD BEACH, FL, p. A130
BROWN COUNTY COMMUNITY TREATMENT CENTER, GREEN BAY, WI, p. A712
BROWN COUNTY HOSPITAL, AINSWORTH, NE, p. A397

BROWNFIELD REGIONAL MEDICAL CENTER, BROWNFIELD, TX, p. A604
BROWNWOOD REGIONAL MEDICAL CENTER, BROWNWOOD, TX, p. A605
BRUNSWICK PSYCH CENTER, AMITYVILLE, NY, p. A438
BRUSHY CREEK FAMILY HOSPITAL, ROUND ROCK, TX, p. A647
BRYAN COMMUNITY HOSPITAL, BRYAN, OH, p. A487
BRYAN MEDICAL CENTER, LINCOLN, NE, p. A401
BRYAN W. WHITFIELD MEMORIAL HOSPITAL, DEMOPOLIS, AL, p. A18
BRYANLGH MEDICAL CENTER-EAST, LINCOLN, NE, p. A401
BRYANLGH MEDICAL CENTER-WEST, LINCOLN, NE, p. A401
BRYCE HOSPITAL, TUSCALOOSA, AL, p. A25
BRYLIN HOSPITALS, BUFFALO, NY, p. A440
BRYN MAWR HOSPITAL, BRYN MAWR, PA, p. A536
BRYN MAWR REHABILITATION HOSPITAL, MALVERN, PA, p. A545
BRYNN MARR HOSPITAL, JACKSONVILLE, NC, p. A471
BSA HOSPITAL, LLC, AMARILLO, TX, p. A596
BSA-PANHANDLE SURGICAL HOSP, AMARILLO, TX, p. A596
BUCHANAN COUNTY HEALTH CENTER, INDEPENDENCE, IA, p. A238
BUCHANAN GENERAL HOSPITAL, GRUNDY, VA, p. A677
BUCK COUNTY CAMPUS, LANGHORNE, PA, p. A543
BUCKS COUNTY CAMPUS, LANGHORNE, PA, p. A543
BUCKTAIL MEDICAL CENTER, RENOVO, PA, p. A553
BUCYRUS COMMUNITY HOSPITAL, BUCYRUS, OH, p. A487
BUENA VISTA REGIONAL MEDICAL CENTER, STORM LAKE, IA, p. A244
BUFFALO HOSPITAL, BUFFALO, MN, p. A344
BUFFALO PSYCHIATRIC CENTER, BUFFALO, NY, p. A440
BULLOCK COUNTY HOSPITAL, UNION SPRINGS, AL, p. A25
BUNKIE GENERAL HOSPITAL, BUNKIE, LA, p. A279
BURDETT BIRTH CENTER, TROY, NY, p. A460
BURGESS HEALTH CENTER, ONAWA, IA, p. A241
BURKE MEDICAL CENTER, WAYNESBORO, GA, p. A174
BURKE REHABILITATION HOSPITAL, WHITE PLAINS, NY, p. A462
BURNETT MEDICAL CENTER, GRANTSBURG, WI, p. A711
BUTLER COUNTY HEALTH CARE CENTER, DAVID CITY, NE, p. A399
BUTLER COUNTY MEDICAL CENTER, HAMILTON, OH, p. A497
BUTLER HOSPITAL, PROVIDENCE, RI, p. A560
BUTLER MEMORIAL HOSPITAL, BUTLER, PA, p. A536
BUTTONWOOD HOSPITAL OF BURLINGTON, NEW LISBON, NJ, p. A425
BYRD REGIONAL HOSPITAL, LEESVILLE, LA, p. A287

C

CABELL HUNTINGTON HOSPITAL, HUNTINGTON, WV, p. A701
CABINET PEAKS MEDICAL CENTER, LIBBY, MT, p. A394
CACHE VALLEY HOSPITAL, NORTH LOGAN, UT, p. A666
CALAIS COMMUNITY HOSPITAL, CALAIS, ME, p. A296
CALDWELL MEDICAL CENTER, PRINCETON, KY, p. A273
CALDWELL MEMORIAL HOSPITAL, COLUMBIA, LA, p. A280
CALDWELL REGIONAL MEDICAL CENTER, CALDWELL, KS, p. A247
CALDWELL UNC HEALTH CARE, LENOIR, NC, p. A471
CALHOUN LIBERTY HOSPITAL, BLOUNTSTOWN, FL, p. A126
CALIFORNIA HEART AND SURGICAL HOSPITAL, LOMA LINDA, CA, p. A70
CALIFORNIA HOSPITAL MEDICAL CENTER, LOS ANGELES, CA, p. A72
CALIFORNIA MEDICAL FACILITY, VACAVILLE, CA, p. A99
CALIFORNIA MENS COLONY CORRECTIONAL TREATMENT CENTER, SAN LUIS OBISPO, CA, p. A92
CALIFORNIA PACIFIC MEDICAL CENTER, SAN FRANCISCO, CA, p. A90
CALIFORNIA PACIFIC MEDICAL CENTER–DAVIES CAMPUS, SAN FRANCISCO, CA, p. A90
CALIFORNIA PACIFIC MEDICAL CENTER–MISSION BERNAL CAMPUS, SAN FRANCISCO, CA, p. A90
CALIFORNIA PACIFIC MEDICAL CENTER–ST. LUKE'S CAMPUS, SAN FRANCISCO, CA, p. A90
CALIFORNIA PACIFIC MEDICAL CENTER–VAN NESS CAMPUS, SAN FRANCISCO, CA, p. A90
CALIFORNIA REHABILITATION INSTITUTE, LOS ANGELES, CA, p. A72
CALLAWAY DISTRICT HOSPITAL, CALLAWAY, NE, p. A398
CALVARY HOSPITAL, NEW YORK, NY, p. A447
CALVERTHEALTH MEDICAL CENTER, PRINCE FREDERICK, MD, p. A306
CAMBRIDGE HEALTH ALLIANCE, CAMBRIDGE, MA, p. A312

CAMBRIDGE MEDICAL CENTER, CAMBRIDGE, MN, p. A344
CAMC GREENBRIER VALLEY MEDICAL CENTER, RONCEVERTE, WV, p. A704
CAMC MEMORIAL HOSPITAL, CHARLESTON, WV, p. A699
CAMC PLATEAU MEDICAL CENTER, OAK HILL, WV, p. A703
CAMC WOMEN AND CHILDREN'S HOSPITAL, CHARLESTON, WV, p. A699
CAMDEN CLARK MEDICAL CENTER, PARKERSBURG, WV, p. A703
CAMERON MEMORIAL COMMUNITY HOSPITAL, ANGOLA, IN, p. A212
CAMERON REGIONAL MEDICAL CENTER, CAMERON, MO, p. A372
CAMPBELL COUNTY HEALTH, GILLETTE, WY, p. A727
CANDLER COUNTY HOSPITAL, METTER, GA, p. A168
CANDLER HOSPITAL-SAVANNAH, SAVANNAH, GA, p. A170
CANONSBURG HOSPITAL, CANONSBURG, PA, p. A536
CANYON CREEK BEHAVIORAL HEALTH, TEMPLE, TX, p. A656
CANTON–POTSDAM HOSPITAL, POTSDAM, NY, p. A456
CANYON RIDGE HOSPITAL, CHINO, CA, p. A59
CANYON VISTA MEDICAL CENTER, SIERRA VISTA, AZ, p. A39
CAPE COD HOSPITAL, HYANNIS, MA, p. A314
CAPE CORAL HOSPITAL, CAPE CORAL, FL, p. A127
CAPE FEAR MEMORIAL HOSPITAL, WILMINGTON, NC, p. A477
CAPE FEAR VALLEY BLADEN COUNTY HOSPITAL, ELIZABETHTOWN, NC, p. A468
CAPE FEAR VALLEY MEDICAL CENTER, FAYETTEVILLE, NC, p. A468
CAPITAL CARING, ARLINGTON, VA, p. A673
CAPITAL DISTRICT PSYCHIATRIC CENTER, ALBANY, NY, p. A438
CAPITAL HEALTH MEDICAL CENTER–HOPEWELL, PENNINGTON, NJ, p. A427
CAPITAL HEALTH REGIONAL MEDICAL CENTER, TRENTON, NJ, p. A429
CAPITAL MEDICAL CENTER, OLYMPIA, WA, p. A692
CAPITAL REGION MEDICAL CENTER, JEFFERSON CITY, MO, p. A376
CAPITAL REGIONAL MEDICAL CENTER, TALLAHASSEE, FL, p. A151
CAPROCK HOSPITAL, BRYAN, TX, p. A605
CAPTAIN JAMES A. LOVELL FEDERAL HEALTH CARE CENTER, NORTH CHICAGO, IL, p. A203
CARDINAL CUSHING GEN HOSPITAL, BROCKTON, MA, p. A311
CARDIOVASCULAR CENTER OF PUERTO RICO AND THE CARIBBEAN, SAN JUAN, PR, p. A734
CARDON CHILDREN'S MEDICAL CENTER, MESA, AZ, p. A33
CAREONE AT HACKSENSACK UNIVERSITY MEDICAL CENTER AT PASCACK VALLEY, WESTWOOD, NJ, p. A430
CAREONE AT TRINITAS REGIONAL MEDICAL CENTER, ELIZABETH, NJ, p. A420
CAREPARTNERS REHABILITATION HOSPITAL, ASHEVILLE, NC, p. A463
CAREPOINT HEALTH BAYONNE MEDICAL CENTER, BAYONNE, NJ, p. A418
CAREPOINT HEALTH CHRIST HOSPITAL, JERSEY CITY, NJ, p. A422
CAREPOINT HEALTH HOBOKEN UNIVERSITY MEDICAL CENTER, HOBOKEN, NJ, p. A422
CAREWELL HEALTH MEDICAL CENTER, EAST ORANGE, NJ, p. A420
CARIBBEAN MEDICAL CENTER, FAJARDO, PR, p. A732
CARIBOU MEDICAL CENTER, SODA SPRINGS, ID, p. A184
CARIBOU MEMORIAL HOSPITAL AND LIVING CENTER, SODA SPRINGS, ID, p. A184
CARILION FRANKLIN MEMORIAL HOSPITAL, ROCKY MOUNT, VA, p. A683
CARILION GILES COMMUNITY HOSPITAL, PEARISBURG, VA, p. A681
CARILION NEW RIVER VALLEY MEDICAL CENTER, CHRISTIANSBURG, VA, p. A675
CARILION ROANOKE COMM HOSP, ROANOKE, VA, p. A683
CARILION ROANOKE MEMORIAL HOSPITAL, ROANOKE, VA, p. A683
CARILION ROCKBRIDGE COMMUNITY HOSPITAL, LEXINGTON, VA, p. A678
CARILION SAINT ALBANS HOSPITAL, CHRISTIANSBURG, VA, p. A675
CARILION STONEWALL JACKSON HOSPITAL, LEXINGTON, VA, p. A678
CARILION TAZEWELL COMMUNITY HOSPITAL, TAZEWELL, VA, p. A684
CARL ALBERT COMMUNITY MENTAL HEALTH CENTER, MCALESTER, OK, p. A514
CARL R. DARNALL ARMY MEDICAL CENTER, FORT HOOD, TX, p. A618
CARL T. HAYDEN VETERANS' ADMINISTRATION MEDICAL CENTER, PHOENIX, AZ, p. A35

Index of Hospitals / Carl Vinson Veterans Affairs Medical Center

CARL VINSON VETERANS AFFAIRS MEDICAL CENTER, DUBLIN, GA, p. A163
CARLE BROMENN MEDICAL CENTER, NORMAL, IL, p. A203
CARLE EUREKA HOSPITAL, EUREKA, IL, p. A194
CARLE FOUNDATION HOSPITAL, URBANA, IL, p. A210
CARLE HEALTH METHODIST HOSPITAL, PEORIA, IL, p. A205
CARLE HEALTH PEKIN HOSPITAL, PEKIN, IL, p. A205
CARLE HEALTH PROCTOR HOSPITAL, PEORIA, IL, p. A206
CARLE HOOPESTON REGIONAL HEALTH CENTER, HOOPESTON, IL, p. A198
CARLE RICHLAND MEMORIAL HOSPITAL, OLNEY, IL, p. A204
CARLINVILLE AREA HOSPITAL, CARLINVILLE, IL, p. A187
CARLSBAD MEDICAL CENTER, CARLSBAD, NM, p. A433
CARNEGIE TRI–COUNTY MUNICIPAL HOSPITAL, CARNEGIE, OK, p. A510
CARO CENTER, CARO, MI, p. A323
CAROLINA CENTER FOR BEHAVIORAL HEALTH, GREER, SC, p. A567
CAROLINA DUNES BEHAVIORAL HEALTH, LELAND, NC, p. A471
CAROLINA PINES REGIONAL MEDICAL CENTER, HARTSVILLE, SC, p. A568
CAROLINAEAST HEALTH SYSTEM, NEW BERN, NC, p. A473
CAROLINAS CONTINUECARE HOSPITAL AT PINEVILLE, CHARLOTTE, NC, p. A465
CAROLINAS HEALTHCARE SYSTEM – BLUE RIDGE – MORGANTON, MORGANTON, NC, p. A473
CAROLINAS HEALTHCARE SYSTEM – BLUE RIDGE – VALDESE CAMPUS, VALDESE, NC, p. A477
CAROLINAS HEALTHCARE SYSTEM KINGS MOUNTAIN, KINGS MOUNTAIN, NC, p. A471
CAROLINAS MED CENTER–PINEVILLE, CHARLOTTE, NC, p. A465
CAROLINAS REHABILITATION, CHARLOTTE, NC, p. A465
CAROMONT REGIONAL MEDICAL CENTER, GASTONIA, NC, p. A469
CARONDELET HOLY CROSS HOSPITAL, NOGALES, AZ, p. A34
CARONDELET ST. JOSEPH'S HOSPITAL, TUCSON, AZ, p. A40
CARONDELET ST. MARY'S HOSPITAL, TUCSON, AZ, p. A40
CARRIS HEALTH – REDWOOD, REDWOOD FALLS, MN, p. A353
CARROLL COUNTY MEMORIAL HOSPITAL, CARROLLTON, KY, p. 264
CARROLL COUNTY MEMORIAL HOSPITAL, CARROLLTON, MO, p. A373
CARROLL HOSPITAL, WESTMINSTER, MD, p. A308
CARROLL HOSPITAL CENTER, WESTMINSTER, MD, p. A308
CARROLLTON REGIONAL MEDICAL CENTER, CARROLLTON, TX, p. A606
CARROLLTON SPRINGS, CARROLLTON, TX, p. A606
CARRUS BEHAVIORAL HOSPITAL, SHERMAN, TX, p. A652
CARRUS REHABILITATION HOSPITAL, SHERMAN, TX, p. A653
CARRUS SPECIALTY HOSPITAL, SHERMAN, TX, p. A653
CARSON TAHOE HEALTH, CARSON CITY, NV, p. A408
CARSON VALLEY MEDICAL CENTER, GARDNERVILLE, NV, p. A408
CARTERET HEALTH CARE, MOREHEAD CITY, NC, p. A473
CARTERSVILLE MEDICAL CENTER, CARTERSVILLE, GA, p. A160
CARTHAGE AREA HOSPITAL, CARTHAGE, NY, p. A441
CARY MEDICAL CENTER, CARIBOU, ME, p. A296
CASA COLINA HOSPITAL AND CENTERS FOR HEALTHCARE, POMONA, CA, p. A84
CASCADE MEDICAL, LEAVENWORTH, WA, p. A691
CASCADE MEDICAL CENTER, CASCADE, ID, p. A180
CASCADE VALLEY HOSPITAL, ARLINGTON, WA, p. A687
CASEY COUNTY HOSPITAL, LIBERTY, KY, p. A269
CASS COUNTY HEALTH SYSTEM, ATLANTIC, IA, p. A230
CASS HEALTH, ATLANTIC, IA, p. A230
CASS REGIONAL MEDICAL CENTER, HARRISONVILLE, MO, p. A376
CASSIA REGIONAL HOSPITAL, BURLEY, ID, p. A180
CASTANER GENERAL HOSPITAL, CASTANER, PR, p. A732
CASTLE ROCK ADVENTIST HOSPITAL, CASTLE ROCK, CO, p. A104
CASTLEVIEW HOSPITAL, PRICE, UT, p. A667
CATALINA ISLAND MEDICAL CENTER, AVALON, CA, p. A56
CATAWBA HOSPITAL, CATAWBA, VA, p. A674
CATAWBA VALLEY MEDICAL CENTER, HICKORY, NC, p. A470
CATHERINE MCAULEY MANOR, KENMORE, NY, p. A444
CATHOLIC MEDICAL CENTER, MANCHESTER, NH, p. A416
CAVALIER COUNTY MEMORIAL HOSPITAL AND CLINICS, LANGDON, ND, p. A482
CAYUGA MEDICAL CENTER AT ITHACA, ITHACA, NY, p. A444
CCC AT PINEVIEW HOSPITAL, LAKESIDE, AZ, p. A33
CCM HEALTH, MONTEVIDEO, MN, p. A351
CEDAR CITY HOSPITAL, CEDAR CITY, UT, p. A664
CEDAR COUNTY MEMORIAL HOSPITAL, EL DORADO SPRINGS, MO, p. A374

CEDAR CREEK HOSPITAL OF MICHIGAN, SAINT JOHNS, MI, p. A337
CEDAR CREST HOSPITAL AND RESIDENTIAL TREATMENT CENTER, BELTON, TX, p. A603
CEDAR HILLS HOSPITAL, PORTLAND, OR, p. A531
CEDAR PARK REGIONAL MEDICAL CENTER, CEDAR PARK, TX, p. A607
CEDAR RIDGE, OKLAHOMA CITY, OK, p. A516
CEDAR SPRINGS HOSPITAL, COLORADO SPRINGS, CO, p. A104
CEDARS MEDICAL CENTER, MIAMI, FL, p. A139
CEDARS–SINAI MARINA DEL REY HOSPITAL, MARINA DEL REY, CA, p. A76
CEDARS–SINAI MEDICAL CENTER, LOS ANGELES, CA, p. A72
CENTEGRA HOSPITAL – HUNTLEY, HUNTLEY, IL, p. A198
CENTENNIAL HILLS HOSPITAL MEDICAL CENTER, LAS VEGAS, NV, p. A409
CENTENNIAL PEAKS HOSPITAL, LOUISVILLE, CO, p. A112
CENTER FOR BEHAVIORAL HEALTH MARYLAND HEIGHTS, MARYLAND HEIGHTS, MO, p. A380
CENTER FOR BEHAVIORAL MEDICINE, KANSAS CITY, MO, p. A377
CENTER FOR FORENSIC PSYCHIATRY, SALINE, MI, p. A337
CENTERPOINT MEDICAL CENTER, INDEPENDENCE, MO, p. A376
CENTERPOINTE HOSPITAL, SAINT CHARLES, MO, p. A383
CENTERPOINTE HOSPITAL OF COLUMBIA, COLUMBIA, MO, p. A374
CENTERSTONE HOSPITAL, BRADENTON, FL, p. A126
CENTINELA HOSPITAL MEDICAL CENTER, INGLEWOOD, CA, p. A67
CENTRA BEDFORD MEMORIAL HOSPITAL, BEDFORD, VA, p. A673
CENTRA LYNCHBURG GENERAL HOSPITAL, LYNCHBURG, VA, p. A678
CENTRA SOUTHSIDE COMMUNITY HOSPITAL, FARMVILLE, VA, p. A676
CENTRA SPECIALTY HOSPITAL, LYNCHBURG, VA, p. A679
CENTRACARE – BENSON, BENSON, MN, p. A343
CENTRACARE – LONG PRAIRIE, LONG PRAIRIE, MN, p. A349
CENTRACARE – MELROSE, MELROSE, MN, p. A350
CENTRACARE – MONTICELLO, MONTICELLO, MN, p. A351
CENTRACARE – PAYNESVILLE, PAYNESVILLE, MN, p. A352
CENTRACARE – REDWOOD, REDWOOD FALLS, MN, p. A353
CENTRACARE – RICE MEMORIAL HOSPITAL, WILLMAR, MN, p. A357
CENTRACARE – SAUK CENTRE, SAUK CENTRE, MN, p. A355
CENTRACARE – ST. CLOUD HOSPITAL, SAINT CLOUD, MN, p. A354
CENTRAL ALABAMA HCS, MONTGOMERY, AL, p. A22
CENTRAL ALABAMA VA HEALTH CARE SYSTEM–MONTGOMERY DIVISION, MONTGOMERY, AL, p. A22
CENTRAL ALABAMA VA MEDICAL CENTER–MONTGOMERY, MONTGOMERY, AL, p. A22
CENTRAL ALABAMA VETERANS AFFAIRS HEALTH CARE SYSTEM–TUSKEGEE DIVISION, TUSKEGEE, AL, p. A25
CENTRAL ARKANSAS VETERANS AFFAIRS HEALTHCARE SYSTEM, EUGENE TOWBIN HEALTHCARE CENTER, NORTH LITTLE ROCK, AR, p. A51
CENTRAL ARKANSAS VETERANS HEALTHCARE SYSTEM, LITTLE ROCK, AR, p. A49
CENTRAL CALIFORNIA HCS, FRESNO, CA, p. A64
CENTRAL CAROLINA HOSPITAL, SANFORD, NC, p. A476
CENTRAL DESERT BEHAVIORAL HEALTH HOSPITAL, ALBUQUERQUE, NM, p. A432
CENTRAL FLORIDA BEHAVIORAL HOSPITAL, ORLANDO, FL, p. A144
CENTRAL FLORIDA REGIONAL HOSPITAL, SANFORD, FL, p. A149
CENTRAL INDIANA AMG SPECIALTY HOSPITAL, MUNCIE, IN, p. A224
CENTRAL LOUISIANA STATE HOSPITAL, PINEVILLE, LA, p. A291
CENTRAL LOUISIANA SURGICAL HOSPITAL, ALEXANDRIA, LA, p. A276
CENTRAL MAINE MEDICAL CENTER, LEWISTON, ME, p. A297
CENTRAL MONTANA MEDICAL CENTER, LEWISTOWN, MT, p. A393
CENTRAL NEW YORK PSYCHIATRIC CENTER, MARCY, NY, p. A446
CENTRAL PENINSULA HOSPITAL, SOLDOTNA, AK, p. A29
CENTRAL PRISON HOSPITAL, RALEIGH, NC, p. A474
CENTRAL REGIONAL HOSPITAL, BUTNER, NC, p. A464
CENTRAL STATE HOSPITAL, LOUISVILLE, KY, p. A269
CENTRAL STATE HOSPITAL, MILLEDGEVILLE, GA, p. A168
CENTRAL STATE HOSPITAL, PETERSBURG, VA, p. A681
CENTRAL TEXAS REHABILITATION HOSPITAL, AUSTIN, TX, p. A599

CENTRAL TEXAS VETERANS AFFAIRS HEALTH CARE SYSTEM, OLIN E. TEAGUE VETERANS CENTER, TEMPLE, TX, p. A656
CENTRAL TEXAS VETERANS AFFAIRS HEALTH CARE SYSTEM, OLIN E. TEAGUE VETERANS MEDICAL CENTER, TEMPLE, TX, p. A656
CENTRAL TEXAS VETERANS HCS/TEMPLE TX, TEMPLE, TX, p. A656
CENTRAL TEXAS VETERANS HEALTH CARE SYSTEM, TEMPLE, TX, p. A656
CENTRAL TEXAS VETERANS HEALTH CARE SYSTEM, DORIS MILLER VETERANS MEDICAL CENTER, WACO, TX, p. A660
CENTRAL VALLEY MEDICAL CENTER, NEPHI, UT, p. A666
CENTRAL VALLEY SPECIALTY HOSPITAL, MODESTO, CA, p. A77
CENTRASTATE HEALTHCARE SYSTEM, FREEHOLD, NJ, p. A421
CENTRO DE SALUD CONDUCTUAL MENONITA–CIMA, AIBONITO, PR, p. A731
CGH MEDICAL CENTER, STERLING, IL, p. A209
CHA HOLLYWOOD PRESBYTERIAN MEDICAL CENTER, LOS ANGELES, CA, p. A72
CHADRON COMMUNITY HOSPITAL AND HEALTH SERVICES, CHADRON, NE, p. A398
CHAMBERS HEALTH, ANAHUAC, TX, p. A597
CHAMBERS MEMORIAL HOSPITAL, DANVILLE, AR, p. A45
CHAN SOON–SHIONG MEDICAL CENTER AT WINDBER, WINDBER, PA, p. A558
CHANDLER REGIONAL MEDICAL CENTER, CHANDLER, AZ, p. A30
CHAPMAN GLOBAL MEDICAL CENTER, ORANGE, CA, p. A81
CHARLES A. CANNON JR. MEMORIAL HOSPITAL, NEWLAND, NC, p. A473
CHARLES GEORGE VETERANS AFFAIRS MEDICAL CENTER, ASHEVILLE, NC, p. A463
CHARLESTON AREA MEDICAL CENTER, CHARLESTON, WV, p. A700
CHARLESTON GENERAL HOSPITAL, CHARLESTON, WV, p. A700
CHARLESTON SURGICAL HOSPITAL, CHARLESTON, WV, p. A700
CHARLIE NORWOOD VETERANS AFFAIRS MEDICAL CENTER, AUGUSTA, GA, p. A158
CHARLOTTE HUNGERFORD HOSPITAL, TORRINGTON, CT, p. A119
CHARLTON MEMORIAL HOSPITAL, FALL RIVER, MA, p. A313
CHARTER BEHAVIORAL HEALTH SYSTEM OF MILWAUKEE/WEST ALLIS, WEST ALLIS, WI, p. A724
CHARTER GREENSBORO HEALTH SYST, GREENSBORO, NC, p. A469
CHARTER NORTHBROOKE BEHAVIORAL HEALTH SYSTEM OF MILWAUKEE/BROWN DEER, BROWN DEER, WI, p. A708
CHASE COUNTY COMMUNITY HOSPITAL, IMPERIAL, NE, p. A401
CHATUGE REGIONAL HOSPITAL AND NURSING HOME, HIAWASSEE, GA, p. A165
CHELSEA HOSPITAL, CHELSEA, MI, p. A324
CHEROKEE INDIAN HOSPITAL, CHEROKEE, NC, p. A466
CHEROKEE MEDICAL CENTER, GAFFNEY, SC, p. A566
CHEROKEE MENTAL HEALTH INSTITUTE, CHEROKEE, IA, p. A232
CHEROKEE NATION W.W. HASTINGS HOSPITAL, TAHLEQUAH, OK, p. A521
CHEROKEE REGIONAL MEDICAL CENTER, CHEROKEE, IA, p. A232
CHERRY COUNTY HOSPITAL, VALENTINE, NE, p. A406
CHERRY HOSPITAL, GOLDSBORO, NC, p. A469
CHESAPEAKE REGIONAL MEDICAL CENTER, CHESAPEAKE, VA, p. A674
CHESHIRE MEDICAL CENTER, KEENE, NH, p. A415
CHESTER MENTAL HEALTH CENTER, CHESTER, IL, p. A188
CHESTNUT RIDGE HOSPITAL, MORGANTOWN, WV, p. A703
CHEYENNE COUNTY HOSPITAL, SAINT FRANCIS, KS, p. A259
CHEYENNE REGIONAL MEDICAL CENTER, CHEYENNE, WY, p. A726
CHEYENNE VA MEDICAL CENTER, CHEYENNE, WY, p. A726
CHI FLAGET MEMORIAL HOSPITAL, BARDSTOWN, KY, p. 263
CHI FRANCISCAN REHABILITATION, TACOMA, WA, p. A697
CHI FRANCISCAN ST. MICHAEL MEDICAL CENTER, SILVERDALE, WA, p. A695
CHI HEALTH CREIGHTON UNIVERSITY MEDICAL CENTER – BERGAN MERCY, OMAHA, NE, p. A403
CHI HEALTH GOOD SAMARITAN, KEARNEY, NE, p. A401
CHI HEALTH IMMANUEL, OMAHA, NE, p. A403
CHI HEALTH LAKESIDE, OMAHA, NE, p. A403
CHI HEALTH MERCY CORNING, CORNING, IA, p. A233
CHI HEALTH MERCY COUNCIL BLUFFS, COUNCIL BLUFFS, IA, p. A233
CHI HEALTH MIDLANDS, PAPILLION, NE, p. A405

Index of Hospitals / Cincinnati Veterans Affairs Medical Center

CHI HEALTH MISSOURI VALLEY, MISSOURI VALLEY, IA, p. A240
CHI HEALTH NEBRASKA HEART, LINCOLN, NE, p. A401
CHI HEALTH PLAINVIEW, PLAINVIEW, NE, p. A405
CHI HEALTH SAINT FRANCIS, GRAND ISLAND, NE, p. A400
CHI HEALTH SCHUYLER, SCHUYLER, NE, p. A405
CHI HEALTH ST ELIZABETH, LINCOLN, NE, p. A402
CHI HEALTH ST. MARY'S, NEBRASKA CITY, NE, p. A402
CHI LAKEWOOD HEALTH, BAUDETTE, MN, p. A343
CHI LISBON HEALTH, LISBON, ND, p. A482
CHI MEMORIAL, CHATTANOOGA, TN, p. A580
CHI MEMORIAL HOSPITAL – GEORGIA, FORT OGLETHORPE, GA, p. A164
CHI MERCY HEALTH, VALLEY CITY, ND, p. A483
CHI OAKES HOSPITAL, OAKES, ND, p. A483
CHI SAINT JOSEPH BEREA, BEREA, KY, p. A263
CHI SAINT JOSEPH EAST, LEXINGTON, KY, p. A268
CHI SAINT JOSEPH HEALTH – FLAGET MEMORIAL HOSPITAL, BARDSTOWN, KY, p. A263
CHI SAINT JOSEPH HEALTH – SAINT JOSEPH BEREA, BEREA, KY, p. A263
CHI SAINT JOSEPH HEALTH – SAINT JOSEPH EAST, LEXINGTON, KY, p. A268
CHI SAINT JOSEPH HEALTH – SAINT JOSEPH LONDON, LONDON, KY, p. A269
CHI SAINT JOSEPH HEALTH – SAINT JOSEPH MOUNT STERLING, MOUNT STERLING, KY, p. A272
CHI SAINT JOSEPH HEALTH, LEXINGTON, KY, p. A268
CHI SAINT JOSEPH LONDON, LONDON, KY, p. A269
CHI ST ALEXIUS HEALTH CARRINGTON, CARRINGTON, ND, p. A479
CHI ST. LUKE'S HEALTH – BAYLOR ST LUKE'S MEDICAL CENTER, HOUSTON, TX, p. A625
CHI ST. ALEXIUS HEALTH, BISMARCK, ND, p. A479
CHI ST. ALEXIUS HEALTH BISMARCK, BISMARCK, ND, p. A479
CHI ST. ALEXIUS HEALTH DEVILS LAKE, DEVILS LAKE, ND, p. A480
CHI ST. ALEXIUS HEALTH DICKINSON, DICKINSON, ND, p. A480
CHI ST. ALEXIUS HEALTH GARRISON, GARRISON, ND, p. A481
CHI ST. ALEXIUS HEALTH TURTLE LAKE HOSPITAL, TURTLE LAKE, ND, p. A483
CHI ST. ALEXIUS HEALTH WILLISTON, WILLISTON, ND, p. A483
CHI ST. ALEXIUS HEALTH–GARRISON MEMORIAL HOSPITAL, GARRISON, ND, p. A481
CHI ST. ANTHONY HOSPITAL, PENDLETON, OR, p. A530
CHI ST. FRANCIS HEALTH, BRECKENRIDGE, MN, p. A344
CHI ST. GABRIEL'S HEALTH, LITTLE FALLS, MN, p. A349
CHI ST. JOSEPH COLLEGE STATION HOSPITAL, COLLEGE STATION, TX, p. A607
CHI ST. JOSEPH HEALTH BURLESON HOSPITAL, CALDWELL, TX, p. A606
CHI ST. JOSEPH HEALTH GRIMES HOSPITAL, NAVASOTA, TX, p. A641
CHI ST. JOSEPH HEALTH MADISON HOSPITAL, MADISONVILLE, TX, p. A637
CHI ST. JOSEPH HEALTH REHABILITATION HOSPITAL, AN AFFILIATE OF ENCOMPASS HEALTH, BRYAN, TX, p. A605
CHI ST. JOSEPH REGIONAL HEALTH CENTER, BRYAN, TX, p. A605
CHI ST. JOSEPH'S HEALTH, PARK RAPIDS, MN, p. A352
CHI ST. LUKE'S HEALTH – PATIENTS MEDICAL CENTER, PASADENA, TX, p. A642
CHI ST. LUKE'S HEALTH BRAZOSPORT, LAKE JACKSON, TX, p. A633
CHI ST. LUKE'S HEALTH–LAKESIDE HOSPITAL, THE WOODLANDS, TX, p. A657
CHI ST. LUKE'S HEALTH MEMORIAL LIVINGSTON, LIVINGSTON, TX, p. A635
CHI ST. LUKE'S HEALTH MEMORIAL LUFKIN, LUFKIN, TX, p. A636
CHI ST. LUKE'S HEALTH MEMORIAL SAN AUGUSTINE, SAN AUGUSTINE, TX, p. A651
CHI ST. LUKE'S HEALTH–THE WOODLANDS HOSPITAL, THE WOODLANDS, TX, p. A657
CHI ST. LUKE'S HOSPITAL – THE VINTAGE HOSPITAL, HOUSTON, TX, p. A625
CHI ST. VINCENT HOT SPRINGS, HOT SPRINGS, AR, p. A48
CHI ST. VINCENT HOT SPRINGS REHABILITATION HOSPITAL, A PARTNER OF ENCOMPASS HEALTH, HOT SPRINGS, AR, p. A48
CHI ST. VINCENT INFIRMARY, LITTLE ROCK, AR, p. A49
CHI ST. VINCENT MORRILTON, MORRILTON, AR, p. A51
CHI ST. VINCENT NORTH, SHERWOOD, AR, p. A53
CHI ST. VINCENT SHERWOOD REHABILITATION HOSPITAL, A PARTNER OF ENCOMPASS HEALTH, SHERWOOD, AR, p. A53

CHICAGO BEHAVIORAL HOSPITAL, DES PLAINES, IL, p. 193
CHICAGO LYING–IN (CLI), CHICAGO, IL, p. A188
CHICAGO LYING–IN HOSPITAL, CHICAGO, IL, p. A188
CHICAGO–READ MENTAL HEALTH CENTER, CHICAGO, IL, p. A189
CHICKASAW NATION MEDICAL CENTER, ADA, OK, p. A509
CHICO COMMUNITY HOSPITAL, CHICO, CA, p. A59
CHICOT MEMORIAL MEDICAL CENTER, LAKE VILLAGE, AR, p. A49
CHILD AND ADOLESCENT BEHAVIORAL HEALTH SERVICES, WILLMAR, MN, p. A357
CHILD'S HOSPITAL, ALBANY, NY, p. A438
CHILDREN'S CENTER AT WESLEY, WICHITA, KS, p. A261
CHILDREN'S HEALTH CARE, MINNEAPOLIS, MN, p. A350
CHILDREN'S HEALTH CENTER ST. JOSEPH'S HOSPITAL AND MEDICAL CENTER, PHOENIX, AZ, p. A35
CHILDREN'S HEALTHCARE OF ATLANTA, ATLANTA, GA, p. A157
CHILDREN'S HOSP OF NEW YORK, NEW YORK, NY, p. A448
CHILDREN'S HOSP OF SF, SAN FRANCISCO, CA, p. A90
CHILDREN'S HOSPITAL & CLINICS, SAINT PAUL, MN, p. A354
CHILDREN'S HOSPITAL, BUFFALO, NY, p. A440
CHILDREN'S HOSPITAL, GREENVILLE, SC, p. A567
CHILDREN'S HOSPITAL, MACON, GA, p. A167
CHILDREN'S HOSPITAL AT DARTMOUTH, LEBANON, NH, p. A415
CHILDREN'S HOSPITAL AT PROVIDENCE, EL PASO, TX, p. A616
CHILDREN'S HOSPITAL AT SCOTT & WHITE, TEMPLE, TX, p. A656
CHILDREN'S HOSPITAL AT ST. MARY'S MEDICAL CENTER, WEST PALM BEACH, FL, p. A154
CHILDREN'S HOSPITAL COLORADO – COLORADO SPRINGS, COLORADO SPRINGS, CO, p. A105
CHILDREN'S HOSPITAL COLORADO, AURORA, CO, p. A103
CHILDREN'S HOSPITAL LOS ANGELES, LOS ANGELES, CA, p. A72
CHILDREN'S HOSPITAL NEW ORLEANS, NEW ORLEANS, LA, p. A290
CHILDREN'S HOSPITAL OF OKLAHOMA, OKLAHOMA CITY, OK, p. A516
CHILDREN'S HOSPITAL OF ORANGE COUNTY, ORANGE, CA, p. A81
CHILDREN'S HOSPITAL OF PHILADELPHIA, PHILADELPHIA, PA, p. A548
CHILDREN'S HOSPITAL OF RICHMOND AT VCU, RICHMOND, VA, p. A682
CHILDREN'S HOSPITAL OF SAN ANTONIO, SAN ANTONIO, TX, p. A649
CHILDREN'S HOSPITAL OF SOUTHWEST FLORIDA, FORT MYERS, FL, p. A131
CHILDREN'S HOSPITAL OF THE KING'S DAUGHTERS, NORFOLK, VA, p. A680
CHILDREN'S HOSPITAL OF WISCONSIN, MILWAUKEE, WI, p. A717
CHILDREN'S HOSPITAL OF WISCONSIN–FOX VALLEY, NEENAH, WI, p. A718
CHILDREN'S HOSPITALS AND CLINICS OF MINNESOTA, MINNEAPOLIS, MN, p. A350
CHILDREN'S MEDICAL CENTER AT WINTHROP UNIVERSITY HOSPITAL, MINEOLA, NY, p. A446
CHILDREN'S MEDICAL CENTER DALLAS, DALLAS, TX, p. A611
CHILDREN'S MEDICAL CENTER PLANO, PLANO, TX, p. A644
CHILDREN'S MERCY HOSPITAL KANSAS, OVERLAND PARK, KS, p. A257
CHILDREN'S MERCY KANSAS CITY, KANSAS CITY, MO, p. A377
CHILDREN'S MINNESOTA, MINNEAPOLIS, MN, p. A350
CHILDREN'S NATIONAL HOSPITAL, WASHINGTON, DC, p. A123
CHILDREN'S NEBRASKA, OMAHA, NE, p. A404
CHILDREN'S OF ALABAMA, BIRMINGHAM, AL, p. A16
CHILDREN'S SPECIALIZED HOSPITAL, NEW BRUNSWICK, NJ, p. A424
CHILDREN'S WISCONSIN, MILWAUKEE, WI, p. A717
CHILDRESS REGIONAL MEDICAL CENTER, CHILDRESS, TX, p. A607
CHILLICOTHE VETERANS AFFAIRS MEDICAL CENTER, CHILLICOTHE, OH, p. A488
CHILTON MEDICAL CENTER, POMPTON PLAINS, NJ, p. A427
CHINESE HOSPITAL, SAN FRANCISCO, CA, p. A90
CHINLE COMPREHENSIVE HEALTH CARE FACILITY, CHINLE, AZ, p. A31
CHINO VALLEY MEDICAL CENTER, CHINO, CA, p. A59
CHOATE MENTAL HEALTH CENTER, ANNA, IL, p. A185
CHOC CHILDREN'S AT MISSION HOSPITAL, MISSION VIEJO, CA, p. A77
CHOCTAW GENERAL HOSPITAL, BUTLER, AL, p. A17
CHOCTAW HEALTH CENTER, PHILADELPHIA, MS, p. A367

CHOCTAW MEMORIAL HOSPITAL, HUGO, OK, p. A513
CHOCTAW NATION HEALTH CARE CENTER, TALIHINA, OK, p. A521
CHOCTAW REGIONAL MEDICAL CENTER, ACKERMAN, MS, p. A359
CHOWCHILLA DISTRICT MEMORIAL HOSPITAL, CHOWCHILLA, CA, p. A59
CHRIST HOSPITAL, CINCINNATI, OH, p. A488
CHRISTIAN HEALTH, WYCKOFF, NJ, p. A431
CHRISTIAN HOSPITAL, SAINT LOUIS, MO, p. A385
CHRISTIANACARE, NEWARK, DE, p. A122
CHRISTIANACARE, UNION HOSPITAL, ELKTON, MD, p. A304
CHRISTUS CHILDREN'S, SAN ANTONIO, TX, p. A649
CHRISTUS COUSHATTA HEALTH CARE CENTER, COUSHATTA, LA, p. A280
CHRISTUS DUBUIS HOSPITAL OF ALEXANDRIA, ALEXANDRIA, LA, p. A276
CHRISTUS DUBUIS HOSPITAL OF BEAUMONT, BEAUMONT, TX, p. A602
CHRISTUS DUBUIS HOSPITAL OF FORT SMITH, FORT SMITH, AR, p. A46
CHRISTUS DUBUIS HOSPITAL OF HOT SPRINGS, HOT SPRINGS NATIONAL PARK, AR, p. A48
CHRISTUS DUBUIS HOSPITAL OF PORT ARTHUR, PORT ARTHUR, TX, p. A645
CHRISTUS GOOD SHEPHERD MEDICAL CENTER–MARSHALL, MARSHALL, TX, p. A638
CHRISTUS HEALTH SHREVEPORT–BOSSIER, SHREVEPORT, LA, p. A292
CHRISTUS MOTHER FRANCES HOSPITAL – JACKSONVILLE, JACKSONVILLE, TX, p. A630
CHRISTUS MOTHER FRANCES HOSPITAL – SULPHUR SPRINGS, SULPHUR SPRINGS, TX, p. A655
CHRISTUS MOTHER FRANCES HOSPITAL – TYLER, TYLER, TX, p. A658
CHRISTUS MOTHER FRANCES HOSPITAL – WINNSBORO, WINNSBORO, TX, p. A663
CHRISTUS OCHSNER LAKE AREA HOSPITAL, LAKE CHARLES, LA, p. A286
CHRISTUS OCHSNER ST. PATRICK, LAKE CHARLES, LA, p. A286
CHRISTUS SANTA ROSA HEALTH SYSTEM, SAN ANTONIO, TX, p. A649
CHRISTUS SANTA ROSA HOSPITAL – NEW BRAUNFELS, NEW BRAUNFELS, TX, p. A641
CHRISTUS SANTA ROSA HOSPITAL – SAN MARCOS, SAN MARCOS, TX, p. A651
CHRISTUS SANTA ROSA REHABILITATION HOSPITAL, SAN ANTONIO, TX, p. A649
CHRISTUS SCHUMPERT HIGHLAND, SHREVEPORT, LA, p. A292
CHRISTUS SOUTHEAST TEXAS HOSPITAL – ST. ELIZABETH, BEAUMONT, TX, p. A602
CHRISTUS SOUTHEAST TEXAS JASPER MEMORIAL, JASPER, TX, p. A630
CHRISTUS SOUTHEAST TEXAS ORTHOPEDIC SPECIALTY CENTER, BEAUMONT, TX, p. A602
CHRISTUS SPOHN HOSP SHORELINE, CORPUS CHRISTI, TX, p. A608
CHRISTUS SPOHN HOSPITAL ALICE, ALICE, TX, p. A595
CHRISTUS SPOHN HOSPITAL BEEVILLE, BEEVILLE, TX, p. A603
CHRISTUS SPOHN HOSPITAL CORPUS CHRISTI SHORELINE, CORPUS CHRISTI, TX, p. A608
CHRISTUS SPOHN HOSPITAL KLEBERG, KINGSVILLE, TX, p. A632
CHRISTUS ST JOSEPH HOSP NORTH, PARIS, TX, p. A642
CHRISTUS ST. FRANCES CABRINI HOSPITAL, ALEXANDRIA, LA, p. A276
CHRISTUS ST. MICHAEL HEALTH SYSTEM, TEXARKANA, TX, p. A656
CHRISTUS ST. MICHAEL REHABILITATION HOSPITAL, TEXARKANA, TX, p. A656
CHRISTUS ST. MICHAEL'S HEALTH SYSTEM, ATLANTA, TX, p. A598
CHRISTUS ST. VINCENT REGIONAL MEDICAL CENTER, SANTA FE, NM, p. A436
CHRISTUS SURGICAL HOSPITAL, CORPUS CHRISTI, TX, p. A608
CHRISTUS TRINITY MOTHER FRANCES REHABILITATION HOSPITAL, A PARTNER OF ENCOMPASS HEALTH, TYLER, TX, p. A658
CIBOLA GENERAL HOSPITAL, GRANTS, NM, p. A434
CIMARRON MEMORIAL HOSPITAL, BOISE CITY, OK, p. A510
CINCINNATI CHILDREN'S HOSPITAL MEDICAL CENTER, CINCINNATI, OH, p. A488
CINCINNATI REHABILITATION HOSPITAL, BLUE ASH, OH, p. A486
CINCINNATI VETERANS AFFAIRS MEDICAL CENTER, CINCINNATI, OH, p. A488

Index of Hospitals / Circle City Medical Center

CIRCLE CITY MEDICAL CENTER, CORONA, CA, p. A60
CIRCLES OF CARE, MELBOURNE, FL, p. A138
CITIZENS BAPTIST MEDICAL CENTER, TALLADEGA, AL, p. A24
CITIZENS MEDICAL CENTER, COLBY, KS, p. A247
CITIZENS MEDICAL CENTER, COLUMBIA, LA, p. A280
CITIZENS MEDICAL CENTER, VICTORIA, TX, p. A660
CITIZENS MEMORIAL HOSPITAL, BOLIVAR, MO, p. A371
CITRUS MEMORIAL HEALTH SYSTEM, INVERNESS, FL, p. A134
CITRUS VALLEY MEDICAL CENTER–INTER–COMMUNITY CAMPUS, COVINA, CA, p. A60
CITRUS VALLEY MEDICAL CENTER–QUEEN OF THE VALLEY CAMPUS, WEST COVINA, CA, p. A101
CITY HOSPITAL AT WHITE ROCK, DALLAS, TX, p. A611
CITY OF HOPE ATLANTA, NEWNAN, GA, p. A169
CITY OF HOPE CHICAGO, ZION, IL, p. A211
CITY OF HOPE PHOENIX, GOODYEAR, AZ, p. A32
CITY OF HOPE'S HELFORD CLINICAL RESEARCH HOSPITAL, DUARTE, CA, p. A62
CJW MEDICAL CENTER, RICHMOND, VA, p. A683
CLAIBORNE COUNTY MEDICAL CENTER, PORT GIBSON, MS, p. A368
CLAIBORNE MEDICAL CENTER, TAZEWELL, TN, p. A594
CLAIBORNE MEMORIAL MEDICAL CENTER, HOMER, LA, p. A283
CLARA BARTON HOSPITAL, HOISINGTON, KS, p. A250
CLARA BARTON MEDICAL CENTER, HOISINGTON, KS, p. A250
CLARA MAASS MEDICAL CENTER, BELLEVILLE, NJ, p. A418
CLAREMORE INDIAN HOSPITAL, CLAREMORE, OK, p. A511
CLARINDA REGIONAL HEALTH CENTER, CLARINDA, IA, p. A232
CLARION HOSPITAL, CLARION, PA, p. A537
CLARION PSYCHIATRIC CENTER, CLARION, PA, p. A537
CLARITY CHILD GUIDANCE CENTER, SAN ANTONIO, TX, p. A649
CLARK FORK VALLEY HOSPITAL, PLAINS, MT, p. A394
CLARK REGIONAL MEDICAL CENTER, WINCHESTER, KY, p. A275
CLARKE COUNTY HOSPITAL, OSCEOLA, IA, p. A241
CLARKS SUMMIT STATE HOSPITAL, CLARKS SUMMIT, PA, p. A537
CLAXTON–HEPBURN MEDICAL CENTER, OGDENSBURG, NY, p. A455
CLAY COUNTY HOSPITAL, ASHLAND, AL, p. A15
CLAY COUNTY HOSPITAL, FLORA, IL, p. A195
CLAY COUNTY MEDICAL CENTER, CLAY CENTER, KS, p. A247
CLAY COUNTY MEMORIAL HOSPITAL, HENRIETTA, TX, p. A624
CLEARFIELD HOSPITAL, CLEARFIELD, PA, p. A537
CLEARSKY REHABILITATION HOSPITAL OF FLOWER MOUND, FLOWER MOUND, TX, p. A618
CLEARSKY REHABILITATION HOSPITAL OF LEESVILLE, LEESVILLE, LA, p. A287
CLEARSKY REHABILITATION HOSPITAL OF RIO RANCHO, RIO RANCHO, NM, p. A436
CLEARSKY REHABILITATION HOSPITAL OF ROSEPINE, LEESVILLE, LA, p. A287
CLEARSKY REHABILITATION HOSPITAL OF WEATHERFORD, WEATHERFORD, TX, p. A661
CLEARVISTA HEALTH AND WELLNESS, LORAIN, OH, p. A498
CLEARWATER VALLEY HEALTH, OROFINO, ID, p. A183
CLEMENT J. ZABLOCKI VETERANS' ADMINISTRATION MEDICAL CENTER, MILWAUKEE, WI, p. A717
CLEVELAND AREA HOSPITAL, CLEVELAND, OK, p. A511
CLEVELAND CLINIC, CLEVELAND, OH, p. A490
CLEVELAND CLINIC AKRON GENERAL, AKRON, OH, p. A484
CLEVELAND CLINIC AKRON GENERAL LODI HOSPITAL, LODI, OH, p. A498
CLEVELAND CLINIC AVON HOSPITAL, AVON, OH, p. A485
CLEVELAND CLINIC CHILDREN'S HOSPITAL FOR REHABILITATION, CLEVELAND, OH, p. A490
CLEVELAND CLINIC EUCLID HOSPITAL, EUCLID, OH, p. A495
CLEVELAND CLINIC FAIRVIEW HOSPITAL, CLEVELAND, OH, p. A490
CLEVELAND CLINIC FLORIDA, WESTON, FL, p. A155
CLEVELAND CLINIC HILLCREST HOSPITAL, CLEVELAND, OH, p. A490
CLEVELAND CLINIC INDIAN RIVER HOSPITAL, VERO BEACH, FL, p. A154
CLEVELAND CLINIC LUTHERAN HOSPITAL, CLEVELAND, OH, p. A490
CLEVELAND CLINIC MARTIN NORTH HOSPITAL, STUART, FL, p. A150
CLEVELAND CLINIC MARYMOUNT HOSPITAL, GARFIELD HEIGHTS, OH, p. A496
CLEVELAND CLINIC MEDINA HOSPITAL, MEDINA, OH, p. A500
CLEVELAND CLINIC MERCY HOSPITAL, CANTON, OH, p. A487
CLEVELAND CLINIC REHABILITATION HOSPITAL, AVON, OH, p. A485
CLEVELAND CLINIC SOUTH POINTE HOSPITAL, WARRENSVILLE HEIGHTS, OH, p. A506
CLEVELAND CLINIC UNION HOSPITAL, DOVER, OH, p. A495
CLEVELAND COMMUNITY HOSPITAL, CLEVELAND, TN, p. A581
CLEVELAND EMERGENCY HOSPITAL, HUMBLE, TX, p. A629
CLIFTON–FINE HOSPITAL, STAR LAKE, NY, p. A459
CLIFTON SPRINGS HOSPITAL AND CLINIC, CLIFTON SPRINGS, NY, p. A441
CLIFTON T. PERKINS HOSPITAL CENTER, JESSUP, MD, p. A305
CLINCH MEMORIAL HOSPITAL, HOMERVILLE, GA, p. A165
CLINCH VALLEY MEDICAL CENTER, RICHLANDS, VA, p. A682
CLINTON HOSPITAL, CLINTON, MA, p. A312
CLINTON REGIONAL HOSPITAL, CLINTON, OK, p. A511
CLIVE BEHAVIORAL HEALTH, CLIVE, IA, p. A233
CLOUD COUNTY HEALTH CENTER, CONCORDIA, KS, p. A248
CLOVIS COMMUNITY MEDICAL CENTER, CLOVIS, CA, p. A60
CMH REGIONAL HEALTH SYSTEM, WILMINGTON, OH, p. A507
COAL COUNTY GENERAL HOSPITAL, COALGATE, OK, p. A511
COAST PLAZA HOSPITAL, NORWALK, CA, p. A80
COASTAL CAROLINA HOSPITAL, HARDEEVILLE, SC, p. A568
COASTAL HARBOR TREATMENT CENTER, SAVANNAH, GA, p. A171
COASTAL VIRGINIA REHABILITATION, YORKTOWN, VA, p. A686
COATESVILLE VETERANS AFFAIRS MEDICAL CENTER, COATESVILLE, PA, p. A537
COBALT REHABILITATION HOSPITAL OF NEW ORLEANS, NEW ORLEANS, LA, p. A290
COBLESKILL REGIONAL HOSPITAL, COBLESKILL, NY, p. A441
COBRE VALLEY REGIONAL MEDICAL CENTER, GLOBE, AZ, p. A32
COCHRAN MEMORIAL HOSPITAL, MORTON, TX, p. A640
CODY REGIONAL HEALTH, CODY, WY, p. A726
COFFEE REGIONAL MEDICAL CENTER, DOUGLAS, GA, p. A163
COFFEY COUNTY HOSPITAL, BURLINGTON, KS, p. A247
COFFEYVILLE REGIONAL MEDICAL CENTER, COFFEYVILLE, KS, p. A247
COGDELL MEMORIAL HOSPITAL, SNYDER, TX, p. A653
COLEMAN COUNTY MEDICAL CENTER, COLEMAN, TX, p. A607
COLER MEMORIAL HOSPITAL, NEW YORK, NY, p. A448
COLISEUM MEDICAL CENTERS, MACON, GA, p. A167
COLISEUM NORTHSIDE HOSPITAL, MACON, GA, p. A167
COLISEUM PSYCHIATRIC CENTER, MACON, GA, p. A167
COLLEGE HOSPITAL CERRITOS, CERRITOS, CA, p. A59
COLLEGE HOSPITAL COSTA MESA, COSTA MESA, CA, p. A60
COLLEGE MEDICAL CENTER, LONG BEACH, CA, p. A70
COLLETON MEDICAL CENTER, WALTERBORO, SC, p. A571
COLLINGSWORTH GENERAL HOSPITAL, WELLINGTON, TX, p. A661
COLMERY–O'NEIL VETERANS AFFAIRS MEDICAL CENTER, TOPEKA, KS, p. A260
COLONEL FLORENCE A. BLANCHFIELD ARMY COMMUNITY HOSPITAL, FORT CAMPBELL, KY, p. A265
COLONIAL HOSPITAL, TERRELL, TX, p. A656
COLORADO CANYONS HOSPITAL AND MEDICAL CENTER, FRUITA, CO, p. A108
COLORADO MENTAL HEALTH INSTITUTE AT FORT LOGAN, DENVER, CO, p. A106
COLORADO MENTAL HEALTH INSTITUTE AT PUEBLO, PUEBLO, CO, p. A112
COLORADO PLAINS MEDICAL CENTER, FORT MORGAN, CO, p. A108
COLORADO RIVER MEDICAL CENTER, NEEDLES, CA, p. A80
COLQUITT REGIONAL MEDICAL CENTER, MOULTRIE, GA, p. A169
COLUMBIA BASIN HOSPITAL, EPHRATA, WA, p. A689
COLUMBIA CLEAR LAKE MED CTR, WEBSTER, TX, p. A661
COLUMBIA COUNTY HEALTH SYSTEM, DAYTON, WA, p. A689
COLUMBIA EAST RIDGE HOSPITAL, EAST RIDGE, TN, p. A582
COLUMBIA–GREENE LONG TERM CARE, CATSKILL, NY, p. A441
COLUMBIA MEDICAL CENTER, SAN ANGELO, TX, p. A648
COLUMBIA MEDICAL CENTER–EAST, EL PASO, TX, p. A616
COLUMBIA MEMORIAL HOSPITAL, ASTORIA, OR, p. A525
COLUMBIA MEMORIAL HOSPITAL, HUDSON, NY, p. A444
COLUMBIA PRESBYTERIAN MED CTR, AURORA, CO, p. A103
COLUMBIA PRESBYTERIAN MED CTR, NEW YORK, NY, p. A448
COLUMBIA REGIONAL HOSPITAL, COLUMBIA, MO, p. A374
COLUMBIA ST MARY'S–COLUMBIA, MILWAUKEE, WI, p. A717
COLUMBIA ST MARY'S–MILWAUKEE, MILWAUKEE, WI, p. A717
COLUMBIA VA HEALTH CARE SYSTEM, COLUMBIA, SC, p. A564
COLUMBIA VAMC, COLUMBIA, MO, p. A374
COLUMBUS COMMUNITY HOSPITAL, COLUMBUS, NE, p. A399
COLUMBUS COMMUNITY HOSPITAL, COLUMBUS, TX, p. A608
COLUMBUS HOSPITAL LTACH, NEWARK, NJ, p. A425
COLUMBUS REGIONAL HEALTHCARE SYSTEM, WHITEVILLE, NC, p. A477
COLUMBUS REGIONAL HOSPITAL, COLUMBUS, IN, p. A214
COLUMBUS SPECIALTY HOSPITAL, COLUMBUS, GA, p. A161
COLUMBUS SPRINGS DUBLIN, DUBLIN, OH, p. A495
COMANCHE COUNTY HOSPITAL, COLDWATER, KS, p. A247
COMANCHE COUNTY MEDICAL CENTER, COMANCHE, TX, p. A608
COMANCHE COUNTY MEMORIAL HOSPITAL, LAWTON, OK, p. A514
COMER CHILDREN'S HOSPITAL, CHICAGO, IL, p. A189
COMMON SPIRIT ST. ELIZABETH HOSPITAL, FORT MORGAN, CO, p. A108
COMMONSPIRIT – MERCY HOSPITAL, DURANGO, CO, p. A107
COMMONSPIRIT – ST. ANTHONY SUMMIT MEDICAL CENTER, FRISCO, CO, p. A108
COMMONSPIRIT – ST. MARY-CORWIN HOSPITAL, PUEBLO, CO, p. A112
COMMONWEALTH CENTER FOR CHILDREN AND ADOLESCENTS, STAUNTON, VA, p. A684
COMMONWEALTH HEALTH CENTER, SAIPAN, MARIANA ISLANDS, p. A730
COMMONWEALTH REGIONAL SPECIALTY HOSPITAL, BOWLING GREEN, KY, p. A263
COMMUNITY BEHAVIORAL HEALTH CENTER, FRESNO, CA, p. A64
COMMUNITY BEHAVIORAL HEALTH HOSPITAL – ALEXANDRIA, ALEXANDRIA, MN, p. A342
COMMUNITY BEHAVIORAL HEALTH HOSPITAL – ANNANDALE, ANNANDALE, MN, p. A342
COMMUNITY BEHAVIORAL HEALTH HOSPITAL – BAXTER, BAXTER, MN, p. A343
COMMUNITY BEHAVIORAL HEALTH HOSPITAL – BEMIDJI, BEMIDJI, MN, p. A343
COMMUNITY BEHAVIORAL HEALTH HOSPITAL – FERGUS FALLS, FERGUS FALLS, MN, p. A346
COMMUNITY BEHAVIORAL HEALTH HOSPITAL – ROCHESTER, ROCHESTER, MN, p. A353
COMMUNITY CARE HOSPITAL, NEW ORLEANS, LA, p. A290
COMMUNITY FAIRBANKS RECOVERY CENTER, INDIANAPOLIS, IN, p. A219
COMMUNITY FIRST MEDICAL CENTER, CHICAGO, IL, p. A189
COMMUNITY GENERAL HEALTH CENTER, FORT FAIRFIELD, ME, p. A297
COMMUNITY GENERAL HOSPITAL, FORT FAIRFIELD, ME, p. A297
COMMUNITY–GENERAL HOSPITAL OF GREATER SYRACUSE, SYRACUSE, NY, p. A459
COMMUNITY HEALTHCARE SYSTEM, ONAGA, KS, p. A256
COMMUNITY HOSPITAL, GRAND JUNCTION, CO, p. A108
COMMUNITY HOSPITAL, MCCOOK, NE, p. A402
COMMUNITY HOSPITAL, MUNSTER, IN, p. A224
COMMUNITY HOSPITAL, OKLAHOMA CITY, OK, p. A516
COMMUNITY HOSPITAL, TALLASSEE, AL, p. A25
COMMUNITY HOSPITAL, TORRINGTON, WY, p. A729
COMMUNITY HOSPITAL ANDERSON, ANDERSON, IN, p. A212
COMMUNITY HOSPITAL AT DOBBS FERRY, DOBBS FERRY, NY, p. A442
COMMUNITY HOSPITAL EAST, INDIANAPOLIS, IN, p. A219
COMMUNITY HOSPITAL NORTH, INDIANAPOLIS, IN, p. A219
COMMUNITY HOSPITAL OF ANACONDA, ANACONDA, MT, p. A389
COMMUNITY HOSPITAL OF BREMEN, BREMEN, IN, p. A213
COMMUNITY HOSPITAL OF HUNTINGTON PARK, HUNTINGTON PARK, CA, p. A67
COMMUNITY HOSPITAL OF LOS GATOS, LOS GATOS, CA, p. A76
COMMUNITY HOSPITAL OF SAN BERNARDINO, SAN BERNARDINO, CA, p. A88
COMMUNITY HOSPITAL OF STAUNTON, STAUNTON, IL, p. A209
COMMUNITY HOSPITAL OF THE MONTEREY PENINSULA, MONTEREY, CA, p. A78
COMMUNITY HOSPITAL SOUTH, INDIANAPOLIS, IN, p. A219
COMMUNITY HOSPITAL–FAIRFAX, FAIRFAX, MO, p. A375
COMMUNITY HOSPITALS AND WELLNESS CENTERS, BRYAN, OH, p. A487

COMMUNITY HOSPITALS AND WELLNESS CENTERS–
  MONTPELIER, MONTPELIER, OH, p. A500
COMMUNITY HOWARD REGIONAL HEALTH, KOKOMO, IN,
  p. A221
COMMUNITY MEDICAL CENTER, MISSOULA, MT, p. A394
COMMUNITY MEDICAL CENTER, TOMS RIVER, NJ, p. A429
COMMUNITY MEDICAL CENTER, INC., FALLS CITY, NE,
  p. A399
COMMUNITY MEMORIAL HEALTHCARE, MARYSVILLE, KS,
  p. A254
COMMUNITY MEMORIAL HOSPITAL – VENTURA, VENTURA,
  CA, p. A100
COMMUNITY MEMORIAL HOSPITAL, BURKE, SD, p. A572
COMMUNITY MEMORIAL HOSPITAL, CLOQUET, MN, p. A345
COMMUNITY MEMORIAL HOSPITAL, HAMILTON, NY, p. A444
COMMUNITY MEMORIAL HOSPITAL, REDFIELD, SD, p. A576
COMMUNITY MEMORIAL HOSPITAL, SUMNER, IA, p. A244
COMMUNITY MENTAL HEALTH CENTER, LAWRENCEBURG,
  IN, p. A222
COMMUNITY REGIONAL MEDICAL CENTER, FRESNO, CA,
  p. A64
COMMUNITY REHABILITATION HOSPITAL NORTH,
  INDIANAPOLIS, IN, p. A219
COMMUNITY REHABILITATION HOSPITAL SOUTH,
  GREENWOOD, IN, p. A218
COMPASS BEHAVIORAL CENTER OF ALEXANDRIA,
  ALEXANDRIA, LA, p. A276
COMPASS BEHAVIORAL CENTER OF HOUMA, HOUMA, LA,
  p. A283
COMPASS BEHAVIORAL CENTER OF LAFAYETTE, LAFAYETTE,
  LA, p. A285
COMPASS BEHAVIORAL CENTER OF MARKSVILLE,
  MARKSVILLE, LA, p. A288
COMPASS MEMORIAL HEALTHCARE, MARENGO, IA, p. A239
CONCHO COUNTY HOSPITAL, EDEN, TX, p. A615
CONCHO VALLEY REGIONAL HOSP, SAN ANGELO, TX,
  p. A648
CONCORD HOSPITAL – FRANKLIN, FRANKLIN, NH, p. A415
CONCORD HOSPITAL – LACONIA, LACONIA, NH, p. A415
CONCORD HOSPITAL, CONCORD, NH, p. A414
CONCOURSE DIVISION, NEW YORK, NY, p. A448
CONCOURSE NURSING HOME, NEW YORK, NY, p. A448
CONE HEALTH ALAMANCE REGIONAL MEDICAL CENTER,
  BURLINGTON, NC, p. A464
CONE HEALTH MOSES CONE HOSPITAL, GREENSBORO, NC,
  p. A469
CONEMAUGH MEMORIAL MEDICAL CENTER, JOHNSTOWN,
  PA, p. A542
CONEMAUGH MEYERSDALE MEDICAL CENTER,
  MEYERSDALE, PA, p. A546
CONEMAUGH MINERS MEDICAL CENTER, HASTINGS, PA,
  p. A541
CONEMAUGH NASON MEDICAL CENTER, ROARING SPRING,
  PA, p. A553
CONFLUENCE HEALTH HOSPITAL – CENTRAL CAMPUS,
  WENATCHEE, WA, p. A698
CONFLUENCE HEALTH HOSPITAL – MARES CAMPUS,
  WENATCHEE, WA, p. A698
CONFLUENCE HEALTH/CENTRAL WASHINGTON HOSPITAL,
  WENATCHEE, WA, p. A698
CONFLUENCE HEALTH/WENATCHEE VALLEY HOSPITAL,
  WENATCHEE, WA, p. A698
CONIFER PARK, GLENVILLE, NY, p. A443
CONNALLY MEMORIAL MEDICAL CENTER, FLORESVILLE, TX,
  p. A618
CONNECTICUT CHILDREN'S, HARTFORD, CT, p. A116
CONNECTICUT DEPARTMENT OF CORRECTION'S HOSPITAL,
  SOMERS, CT, p. A118
CONNECTICUT MENTAL HEALTH CENTER, NEW HAVEN, CT,
  p. A117
CONNECTICUT VALLEY HOSPITAL, MIDDLETOWN, CT,
  p. A117
CONNECTICUT VETERANS HOME AND HOSPITAL, ROCKY
  HILL, CT, p. A118
CONTINUECARE HOSPITAL AT BAPTIST HEALTH CORBIN,
  CORBIN, KY, p. A264
CONTINUECARE HOSPITAL AT BAPTIST HEALTH PADUCAH,
  PADUCAH, KY, p. A273
CONTINUECARE HOSPITAL AT HENDRICK MEDICAL CENTER,
  ABILENE, TX, p. A595
CONTINUECARE HOSPITAL AT MADISONVILLE,
  MADISONVILLE, KY, p. A271
CONTINUECARE HOSPITAL AT MEDICAL CENTER (ODESSA),
  ODESSA, TX, p. A641
CONTINUECARE HOSPITAL AT PALMETTO HEALTH BAPTIST,
  COLUMBIA, SC, p. A564
CONTINUING CARE HOSPITAL, LEXINGTON, KY, p. A268
CONTRA COSTA REGIONAL MEDICAL CENTER, MARTINEZ,
  CA, p. A76
CONWAY BEHAVIORAL HEALTH, CONWAY, AR, p. A44
CONWAY MEDICAL CENTER, CONWAY, SC, p. A565
CONWAY REGIONAL HEALTH SYSTEM, CONWAY, AR, p. A44
CONWAY REGIONAL REHABILITATION HOSPITAL, CONWAY,
  AR, p. A44
COOK CHILDREN'S MEDICAL CENTER – PROSPER, PROSPER,
  TX, p. A646
COOK CHILDREN'S MEDICAL CENTER, FORT WORTH, TX,
  p. A619
COOK HOSPITAL & CARE CENTER, COOK, MN, p. A345
COOKEVILLE REGIONAL MEDICAL CENTER, COOKEVILLE,
  TN, p. A582
COOLEY DICKINSON HOSPITAL, NORTHAMPTON, MA,
  p. A316
COON MEMORIAL HOSPITAL, DALHART, TX, p. A610
COOPER UNIVERSITY HEALTH CARE, CAMDEN, NJ, p. A419
COOPER UNIVERSITY HOSPITAL CAPE REGIONAL, CAPE MAY
  COURT HOUSE, NJ, p. A419
COOPERMAN BARNABAS MEDICAL CENTER, LIVINGSTON,
  NJ, p. A423
COOPERSTOWN MEDICAL CENTER, COOPERSTOWN, ND,
  p. A480
COOSA VALLEY MEDICAL CENTER, SYLACAUGA, AL, p. A24
COPIAH COUNTY MEDICAL CENTER, HAZLEHURST, MS,
  p. A363
COPLEY HOSPITAL, MORRISVILLE, VT, p. A672
COPPER QUEEN COMMUNITY HOSPITAL, BISBEE, AZ, p. A30
COPPER SPRINGS HOSPITAL, AVONDALE, AZ, p. A30
COQUILLE VALLEY HOSPITAL, COQUILLE, OR, p. A526
CORAL GABLES HOSPITAL, CORAL GABLES, FL, p. A128
CORDELL MEMORIAL HOSPITAL, CORDELL, OK, p. A511
CORDOVA COMMUNITY MEDICAL CENTER, CORDOVA, AK,
  p. A28
COREWELL HEALTH BEAUMONT GROSSE POINTE HOSPITAL,
  GROSSE POINTE, MI, p. A329
COREWELL HEALTH BEAUMONT TROY HOSPITAL, TROY, MI,
  p. A339
COREWELL HEALTH BIG RAPIDS HOSPITAL, BIG RAPIDS, MI,
  p. A322
COREWELL HEALTH BUTTERWORTH HOSPITAL, GRAND
  RAPIDS, MI, p. A328
COREWELL HEALTH DEARBORN HOSPITAL, DEARBORN, MI,
  p. A324
COREWELL HEALTH FARMINGTON HILLS HOSPITAL,
  FARMINGTON HILLS, MI, p. A326
COREWELL HEALTH GERBER HOSPITAL, FREMONT, MI,
  p. A327
COREWELL HEALTH GREENVILLE HOSPITAL, GREENVILLE,
  MI, p. A329
COREWELL HEALTH LAKELAND HOSPITAL, SAINT JOSEPH,
  MI, p. A337
COREWELL HEALTH LAKELAND HOSPITALS, SAINT JOSEPH,
  MI, p. A337
COREWELL HEALTH LUDINGTON HOSPITAL, LUDINGTON,
  MI, p. A332
COREWELL HEALTH PENNOCK HOSPITAL, HASTINGS, MI,
  p. A329
COREWELL HEALTH REED CITY HOSPITAL, REED CITY, MI,
  p. A336
COREWELL HEALTH TAYLOR HOSPITAL, TAYLOR, MI, p. A339
COREWELL HEALTH TRENTON HOSPITAL, TRENTON, MI,
  p. A339
COREWELL HEALTH WATERVLIET HOSPITAL, WATERVLIET,
  MI, p. A340
COREWELL HEALTH WAYNE HOSPITAL, WAYNE, MI, p. A340
COREWELL HEALTH WILLIAM BEAUMONT UNIVERSITY
  HOSPITAL, ROYAL OAK, MI, p. A336
COREWELL HEALTH ZEELAND HOSPITAL, ZEELAND, MI,
  p. A341
COREWELL HEALTH'S BEAUMONT HOSPITAL, DEARBORN,
  DEARBORN, MI, p. A324
COREWELL HEALTH'S BEAUMONT HOSPITAL, FARMINGTON
  HILLS, FARMINGTON HILLS, MI, p. A326
COREWELL HEALTH'S BEAUMONT HOSPITAL, TAYLOR,
  TAYLOR, MI, p. A339
COREWELL HEALTH'S BEAUMONT HOSPITAL, TRENTON,
  TRENTON, MI, p. A339
COREWELL HEALTH'S BEAUMONT HOSPITAL, TROY, TROY,
  MI, p. A339
COREWELL HEALTH'S BEAUMONT HOSPITAL, WAYNE,
  WAYNE, MI, p. A340
CORNERSTONE BEHAVIORAL HEALTH HOSPITAL OF UNION
  COUNTY, BERKELEY HEIGHTS, NJ, p. A418
CORNERSTONE HOSPITAL OF HOUSTON AT CLEARLAKE,
  WEBSTER, TX, p. A661
CORNERSTONE OF MEDICAL ARTS CENTER HOSPITAL,
  FRESH MEADOWS, NY, p. A443
CORNERSTONE REGIONAL HOSPITAL, EDINBURG, TX,
  p. A615
CORNERSTONE SPECIALTY HOSPITAL HOUSTON MEDICAL
  CENTER, HOUSTON, TX, p. A625
CORNERSTONE SPECIALTY HOSPITALS AUSTIN ROUND
  ROCK, AUSTIN, TX, p. A599
CORNERSTONE SPECIALTY HOSPITALS BOSSIER CITY,
  BOSSIER CITY, LA, p. A279
CORNERSTONE SPECIALTY HOSPITALS CONROE, CONROE,
  TX, p. A608
CORNERSTONE SPECIALTY HOSPITALS HUNTINGTON,
  HUNTINGTON, WV, p. A701
CORNERSTONE SPECIALTY HOSPITALS LITTLE ROCK, LITTLE
  ROCK, AR, p. A50
CORNERSTONE SPECIALTY HOSPITALS MUSKOGEE,
  MUSKOGEE, OK, p. A515
CORNERSTONE SPECIALTY HOSPITALS SHAWNEE,
  SHAWNEE, OK, p. A520
CORNERSTONE SPECIALTY HOSPITALS SOUTHWEST
  LOUISIANA, LAKE CHARLES, LA, p. A286
CORNERSTONE SPECIALTY HOSPITALS TUCSON, TUCSON,
  AZ, p. A40
CORNERSTONE SPECIALTY HOSPITALS WEST MONROE,
  WEST MONROE, LA, p. A294
CORNWALL HOSPITAL, CORNWALL, NY, p. A441
CORONA REGIONAL MEDICAL CENTER, CORONA, CA, p. A60
CORPUS CHRISTI MEDICAL CENTER – DOCTORS REGIONAL,
  CORPUS CHRISTI, TX, p. A609
CORPUS CHRISTI REHABILITATION HOSPITAL, CORPUS
  CHRISTI, TX, p. A609
CORPUS CHRUSTI MEDICAL CENTER, CORPUS CHRISTI, TX,
  p. A609
CORYELL HEALTH, GATESVILLE, TX, p. A622
COSHOCTON REGIONAL MEDICAL CENTER, COSHOCTON,
  OH, p. A493
COTEAU DES PRAIRIES HOSPITAL, SISSETON, SD, p. A577
COTTAGE HOSPITAL, WOODSVILLE, NH, p. A417
COTTAGE REHABILITATION HOSPITAL, SANTA BARBARA, CA,
  p. A93
COTTONWOOD CREEK BEHAVIORAL HOSPITAL, MERIDIAN,
  ID, p. A182
COTTONWOOD SPRINGS HOSPITAL, OLATHE, KS, p. A256
COULEE MEDICAL CENTER, GRAND COULEE, WA, p. A690
COUNCIL OAK COMPREHENSIVE HEALTHCARE, TULSA, OK,
  p. A522
COVENANT CHILDREN'S HOSPITAL, LUBBOCK, TX, p. A635
COVENANT HEALTH HOBBS HOSPITAL, HOBBS, NM, p. A435
COVENANT HEALTHCARE, SAGINAW, MI, p. A336
COVENANT HOSPITAL PLAINVIEW, PLAINVIEW, TX, p. A644
COVENANT HOSPITAL–LEVELLAND, LEVELLAND, TX, p. A634
COVENANT MEDICAL CENTER, LUBBOCK, TX, p. A636
COVENANT SPECIALTY HOSPITAL, LUBBOCK, TX, p. A636
COVINGTON BEHAVIORAL HEALTH, COVINGTON, LA, p. A280
COVINGTON COUNTY HOSPITAL, COLLINS, MS, p. A361
COVINGTON TRACE ER & HOSPITAL, MANDEVILLE, LA,
  p. A287
COX BARTON COUNTY MEMORIAL HOSPITAL, LAMAR, MO,
  p. A379
COX MEDICAL CENTER BRANSON, BRANSON, MO, p. A372
COX MEDICAL CENTERS, SPRINGFIELD, MO, p. A386
COX MONETT HOSPITAL, INC, MONETT, MO, p. A380
COX NORTH HOSPITAL, SPRINGFIELD, MO, p. A386
COZAD COMMUNITY HEALTH SYSTEM, COZAD, NE, p. A399
CRAIG HOSPITAL, ENGLEWOOD, CO, p. A107
CRANE MEMORIAL HOSPITAL, CRANE, TX, p. A609
CRANFORD HEALTH AND EC CENTER, CRANFORD, NJ,
  p. A419
CRAWFORD COUNTY MEMORIAL HOSPITAL, DENISON, IA,
  p. A234
CRAWFORD MEMORIAL HOSPITAL, ROBINSON, IL, p. A207
CREEDMOOR PSYCHIATRIC CENTER, NEW YORK, NY,
  p. A448
CREEK NATION COMMUNITY HOSPITAL, OKEMAH, OK,
  p. A516
CREEKSIDE BEHAVIORAL HEALTH, KINGSPORT, TN, p. A585
CRENSHAW COMMUNITY HOSPITAL, LUVERNE, AL, p. A21
CRESCENT MEDICAL CENTER LANCASTER, LANCASTER,
  TX, p. A634
CRESTWOOD MEDICAL CENTER, HUNTSVILLE, AL, p. A20
CRESTWYN BEHAVIORAL HEALTH, MEMPHIS, TN, p. A588
CRETE AREA MEDICAL CENTER, CRETE, NE, p. A399
CRISP REGIONAL HOSPITAL, CORDELE, GA, p. A161
CRITTENDEN COMMUNITY HOSPITAL, MARION, KY, p. A271
CRITTENDEN COUNTY HOSPITAL, MARION, KY, p. A271
CRITTENTON CHILDREN'S CENTER, KANSAS CITY, MO,
  p. A377
CROCKETT MEDICAL CENTER, CROCKETT, TX, p. A609
CROOK COUNTY MEDICAL SERVICES DISTRICT, SUNDANCE,
  WY, p. A728
CROSBYTON CLINIC HOSPITAL, CROSBYTON, TX, p. A610
CROSS CREEK HOSPITAL, AUSTIN, TX, p. A600
CROSSING RIVERS HEALTH, PRAIRIE DU CHIEN, WI, p. A720
CROSSRIDGE COMMUNITY HOSPITAL, WYNNE, AR, p. A54
CROUSE HEALTH, SYRACUSE, NY, p. A460

Index of Hospitals / Crow/Northern Cheyenne Hospital

CROW/NORTHERN CHEYENNE HOSPITAL, CROW AGENCY, MT, p. A391
CROZER–CHESTER MEDICAL CENTER, UPLAND, PA, p. A556
C.S. MOTT CHILDREN'S HOSPITAL, ANN ARBOR, MI, p. A321
CUBA CITY MEDICAL CENTER, CUBA CITY, WI, p. A709
CUBA MEMORIAL HOSPITAL, CUBA, NY, p. A442
CUERO REGIONAL HOSPITAL, CUERO, TX, p. A610
CULBERSON HOSPITAL, VAN HORN, TX, p. A659
CULLMAN REGIONAL MEDICAL CENTER, CULLMAN, AL, p. A18
CUMBERLAND COUNTY HOSPITAL, BURKESVILLE, KY, p. A264
CUMBERLAND HALL HOSPITAL, HOPKINSVILLE, KY, p. A267
CUMBERLAND HEALTHCARE, CUMBERLAND, WI, p. A709
CUMBERLAND HOSPITAL, FAYETTEVILLE, NC, p. A468
CUMBERLAND HOSPITAL FOR CHILDREN AND ADOLESCENTS, NEW KENT, VA, p. A679
CUMBERLAND MEDICAL CENTER, CROSSVILLE, TN, p. A582
CURAHEALTH TUCSON, TUCSON, AZ, p. A40
CURRY GENERAL HOSPITAL, GOLD BEACH, OR, p. A527
CUYUNA REGIONAL MEDICAL CENTER, CROSBY, MN, p. A345
CYPRESS CREEK HOSPITAL, HOUSTON, TX, p. A625
CYPRESS FAIRBANKS MEDICAL CENTER, HOUSTON, TX, p. A625
CYPRESS GROVE BEHAVIORAL HEALTH, BASTROP, LA, p. A277
CYPRESS POINTE SURGICAL HOSPITAL, HAMMOND, LA, p. A282

D

DAHL MEMORIAL HEALTHCARE ASSOCIATION, EKALAKA, MT, p. A391
DAKOTA REGIONAL MEDICAL CENTER, COOPERSTOWN, ND, p. A480
DALE MEDICAL CENTER, OZARK, AL, p. A23
DALLAS BEHAVIORAL HEALTHCARE HOSPITAL, DESOTO, TX, p. A614
DALLAS COUNTY HOSPITAL, PERRY, IA, p. A242
DALLAS COUNTY MEDICAL CENTER, FORDYCE, AR, p. A46
DALLAS MEDICAL CENTER, DALLAS, TX, p. A611
DALLAS REGIONAL MEDICAL CENTER, MESQUITE, TX, p. A639
DALLAS VA NORTH TEXAS HCS, DALLAS, TX, p. A611
DAMERON HOSPITAL, STOCKTON, CA, p. A96
DANA-FARBER CANCER INSTITUTE, BOSTON, MA, p. A310
DANBURY HOSPITAL, DANBURY, CT, p. A115
DANIEL DRAKE CENTER FOR POST ACUTE CARE, CINCINNATI, OH, p. A489
DANIELS MEMORIAL HEALTHCARE CENTER, SCOBEY, MT, p. A395
DANVILLE STATE HOSPITAL, DANVILLE, PA, p. A538
DARDANELLE REGIONAL MEDICAL CENTER, DARDANELLE, AR, p. A45
DARTMOUTH–HITCHCOCK MEDICAL CENTER, LEBANON, NH, p. A416
DAVID GRANT USAF MEDICAL CENTER, TRAVIS AIR FORCE BASE, CA, p. A98
DAVIESS COMMUNITY HOSPITAL, WASHINGTON, IN, p. A229
DAVIS COUNTY HOSPITAL AND CLINICS, BLOOMFIELD, IA, p. A231
DAVIS MEDICAL CENTER, ELKINS, WV, p. A700
DAVIS REGIONAL MEDICAL CENTER, STATESVILLE, NC, p. A477
DAY KIMBALL HOSPITAL, PUTNAM, CT, p. A118
DAYTON CHILDREN'S HOSPITAL, DAYTON, OH, p. A493
DAYTON VETERANS AFFAIRS MEDICAL CENTER, DAYTON, OH, p. A493
DCH REGIONAL MEDICAL CENTER, TUSCALOOSA, AL, p. A25
DE GRAFF MEDICAL PARK, NORTH TONAWANDA, NY, p. A454
DE SOTO REGIONAL HEALTH SYSTEM, MANSFIELD, LA, p. A288
DEACONESS GIBSON HOSPITAL, PRINCETON, IN, p. A226
DEACONESS HENDERSON HOSPITAL, HENDERSON, KY, p. A267
DEACONESS ILLINOIS CROSSROADS, MOUNT VERNON, IL, p. A202
DEACONESS ILLINOIS MEDICAL CENTER, MARION, IL, p. A200
DEACONESS ILLINOIS UNION COUNTY, ANNA, IL, p. A185
DEACONESS MIDTOWN HOSPITAL, EVANSVILLE, IN, p. A216

DEACONESS UNION COUNTY HOSPITAL, MORGANFIELD, KY, p. A272
DEBORAH HEART AND LUNG CENTER, BROWNS MILLS, NJ, p. A419
DECATUR COUNTY HOSPITAL, LEON, IA, p. A239
DECATUR COUNTY MEMORIAL HOSPITAL, GREENSBURG, IN, p. A218
DECATUR GENERAL HOSPITAL–WEST, DECATUR, AL, p. A18
DECATUR HEALTH SYSTEMS, OBERLIN, KS, p. A256
DECATUR MEMORIAL HOSPITAL, DECATUR, IL, p. A192
DECATUR MORGAN HOSPITAL, DECATUR, AL, p. A18
DECKERVILLE COMMUNITY HOSPITAL, DECKERVILLE, MI, p. A324
DEER LODGE MEDICAL CENTER, DEER LODGE, MT, p. A391
DEER'S HEAD HOSPITAL CENTER, SALISBURY, MD, p. A307
DEKALB REGIONAL MEDICAL CENTER, FORT PAYNE, AL, p. A19
DEL AMO BEHAVIORAL HEALTH SYSTEM, TORRANCE, CA, p. A98
DEL AMO HOSPITAL, TORRANCE, CA, p. A98
DEL SOL REHABILITATION HOSP, EL PASO, TX, p. A616
DELAWARE PSYCHIATRIC CENTER, NEW CASTLE, DE, p. A121
DELHI HOSPITAL, DELHI, LA, p. A281
DELL CHILDREN'S MEDICAL CENTER OF CENTRAL TEXAS, AUSTIN, TX, p. A600
DELL SETON MEDICAL CENTER AT THE UNIVERSITY OF TEXAS, AUSTIN, TX, p. A600
DELRAY MEDICAL CENTER, DELRAY BEACH, FL, p. A130
DELTA COMMUNITY MEDICAL CENTER, DELTA, UT, p. A664
DELTA COUNTY MEMORIAL HOSPITAL, DELTA, CO, p. A106
DELTA HEALTH – NORTHWEST REGIONAL, CLARKSDALE, MS, p. A360
DELTA HEALTH, DELTA, CO, p. A106
DELTA HEALTH SYSTEM, DUMAS, AR, p. A45
DELTA HEALTH–THE MEDICAL CENTER, GREENVILLE, MS, p. A362
DELTA MEMORIAL HOSPITAL, DUMAS, AR, p. A45
DELTA SPECIALTY HOSPITAL, MEMPHIS, TN, p. A588
DENTON REHAB, DENTON, TX, p. A613
DENVER HEALTH, DENVER, CO, p. A106
DENVER REGIONAL REHABILITATION HOSPITAL, THORNTON, CO, p. A113
DENVER SPRINGS, ENGLEWOOD, CO, p. A107
DEPT OF VETERANS AFF MED CTR, DES MOINES, IA, p. A235
DEPT OF VETERANS AFF MED CTR, KNOXVILLE, IA, p. A239
DEQUINCY MEMORIAL HOSPITAL, DEQUINCY, LA, p. A281
DES MOINES DIVISION, DES MOINES, IA, p. A235
DESERT PARKWAY BEHAVIORAL HEALTHCARE HOSPITAL, LAS VEGAS, NV, p. A409
DESERT REGIONAL MEDICAL CENTER, PALM SPRINGS, CA, p. A82
DESERT VALLEY HOSPITAL, VICTORVILLE, CA, p. A100
DESERT VIEW HOSPITAL, PAHRUMP, NV, p. A412
DESERT WILLOW TREATMENT CENTER, LAS VEGAS, NV, p. A410
DESERT WINDS HOSPITAL, LAS VEGAS, NV, p. A410
DESOTO MEMORIAL HOSPITAL, ARCADIA, FL, p. A125
DETAR HEALTHCARE SYSTEM, VICTORIA, TX, p. A660
DEVEREUX ADVANCED BEHAVIORAL HEALTH GEORGIA, KENNESAW, GA, p. A166
DEVEREUX CHILDREN'S BEHAVIORAL HEALTH CENTER, MALVERN, PA, p. A545
DEVEREUX HOSPITAL AND CHILDREN'S CENTER OF FLORIDA, MELBOURNE, FL, p. A138
DEWITT HOSPITAL & NURSING HOME, DEWITT, AR, p. A45
DEWITT HOSPITAL, DEWITT, AR, p. A45
DICKENSON COMMUNITY HOSPITAL, CLINTWOOD, VA, p. A675
DIGNITY HEALTH ARIZONA GENERAL HOSPITAL, LAVEEN, AZ, p. A33
DIGNITY HEALTH ARIZONA GENERAL HOSPITAL MESA, LLC, MESA, AZ, p. A33
DIGNITY HEALTH EAST VALLEY REHABILITATION HOSPITAL – GILBERT, GILBERT, AZ, p. A32
DIGNITY HEALTH EAST VALLEY REHABILITATION HOSPITAL, CHANDLER, AZ, p. A30
DIGNITY HEALTH REHABILITATION HOSPITAL, HENDERSON, NV, p. A409
DIGNITY HEALTH YAVAPAI REGIONAL MEDICAL CENTER, PRESCOTT, AZ, p. A37
DIGNITY ST. ROSE – CRAIG RANCH, NORTH LAS VEGAS, NV, p. A411
DILEY RIDGE MEDICAL CENTER, CANAL WINCHESTER, OH, p. A487
DIMMIT REGIONAL HOSPITAL, CARRIZO SPRINGS, TX, p. A606
DISTRICT ONE HOSPITAL, FARIBAULT, MN, p. A346

DMC CHILDREN'S HOSPITAL OF MICHIGAN, DETROIT, MI, p. A325
DMC DETROIT RECEIVING HOSPITAL & UNIVERSITY HEALTH CENTER, DETROIT, MI, p. A325
DMC HARPER UNIVERSITY HOSPITAL, DETROIT, MI, p. A325
DMC HURON VALLEY–SINAI HOSPITAL, COMMERCE TOWNSHIP, MI, p. A324
DMC REHABILITATION INSTITUTE OF MICHIGAN, DETROIT, MI, p. A325
DMC SINAI-GRACE HOSPITAL, DETROIT, MI, p. A325
DOCS SURGICAL HOSPITAL, LOS ANGELES, CA, p. A72
DOCTOR'S CENTER OF BAYAMON, BAYAMON, PR, p. A731
DOCTOR'S HOSPITAL, LEAWOOD, KS, p. A253
DOCTOR'S HOSPITAL AT RENAISSANCE, EDINBURG, TX, p. A615
DOCTORS CENTER MANATI, MANATI, PR, p. A733
DOCTORS HOSP OF JEFFERSON, METAIRIE, LA, p. A288
DOCTORS HOSPITAL, AUGUSTA, GA, p. A158
DOCTORS HOSPITAL OF LAREDO, LAREDO, TX, p. A634
DOCTORS HOSPITAL OF LODI, LODI, CA, p. A70
DOCTORS HOSPITAL OF MANTECA, MANTECA, CA, p. A76
DOCTORS HOSPITAL OF SARASOTA, SARASOTA, FL, p. A149
DOCTORS MEDICAL CENTER OF MODESTO, MODESTO, CA, p. A77
DOCTORS MEMORIAL HOSPITAL, BONIFAY, FL, p. A126
DOCTORS NEUROPSYCHIATRIC HOSPITAL, BREMEN, IN, p. A213
DOCTORS SPECIALTY HOSPITAL, COLUMBUS, GA, p. A161
DOCTORS' CENTER HOSPITAL SAN JUAN, SAN JUAN, PR, p. A734
DOCTORS' MEMORIAL HOSPITAL, PERRY, FL, p. A147
DODGE COUNTY HOSPITAL, EASTMAN, GA, p. A163
DOMINICAN HOSPITAL, SANTA CRUZ, CA, p. A94
DOMINION HOSPITAL, FALLS CHURCH, VA, p. A675
DONALSONVILLE HOSPITAL, DONALSONVILLE, GA, p. A163
DOOR COUNTY MEDICAL CENTER, STURGEON BAY, WI, p. A722
DOR-A-LIN OF SOUTH BEND, SOUTH BEND, IN, p. A227
DORMINY MEDICAL CENTER, FITZGERALD, GA, p. A164
DOROTHEA DIX PSYCHIATRIC CENTER, BANGOR, ME, p. A295
DOSHER MEMORIAL HOSPITAL, SOUTHPORT, NC, p. A476
DOUGLAS COUNTY COMMUNITY MENTAL HEALTH CENTER, OMAHA, NE, p. A404
DOUGLAS COUNTY MEMORIAL HOSPITAL, ARMOUR, SD, p. A572
DOVER BEHAVIORAL HEALTH SYSTEM, DOVER, DE, p. A121
DOWN EAST COMMUNITY HOSPITAL, MACHIAS, ME, p. A298
DOYLESTOWN HEALTH, DOYLESTOWN, PA, p. A538
DR. DAN C. TRIGG MEMORIAL HOSPITAL, TUCUMCARI, NM, p. A437
DR. J. CORRIGAN MENTAL HEALTH CENTER, FALL RIVER, MA, p. A313
DR. PILA'S HOSPITAL, PONCE, PR, p. A733
DR. RAMON E. BETANCES HOSPITAL–MAYAGUEZ MEDICAL CENTER BRANCH, MAYAGUEZ, PR, p. A733
DR. SOLOMON CARTER FULLER MENTAL HEALTH CENTER, BOSTON, MA, p. A310
DRISCOLL CHILDREN'S HOSPITAL, CORPUS CHRISTI, TX, p. A609
DRUMRIGHT REGIONAL HOSPITAL, DRUMRIGHT, OK, p. A511
DSH METROPOLITAN, NORWALK, CA, p. A80
DSH PATTON, PATTON, CA, p. A83
DUANE L. WATERS HOSPITAL, JACKSON, MI, p. A330
DUKE RALEIGH HOSPITAL, RALEIGH, NC, p. A474
DUKE REGIONAL HOSPITAL, DURHAM, NC, p. A467
DUKE UNIVERSITY HOSPITAL, DURHAM, NC, p. A467
DUKES MEMORIAL HOSPITAL, PERU, IN, p. A226
DUNCAN REGIONAL HOSPITAL, DUNCAN, OK, p. A512
DUNDY COUNTY HOSPITAL, BENKELMAN, NE, p. A398
DUNES SURGICAL HOSPITAL, DAKOTA DUNES, SD, p. A573
DUPONT HOSPITAL, FORT WAYNE, IN, p. A216
DURHAM VA HEALTH CARE SYSTEM, DURHAM, NC, p. A467
DWIGHT D. EISENHOWER VETERANS AFFAIRS MEDICAL CENTER, LEAVENWORTH, KS, p. A253
DWIGHT DAVID EISENHOWER ARMY MEDICAL CENTER, FORT GORDON, GA, p. A164
D. W. MCMILLAN MEMORIAL HOSPITAL, BREWTON, AL, p. A17

E

EAGLE RIVER HOSPITAL, EAGLE RIVER, WI, p. A710
EAGLE VIEW BEHAVIORAL HEALTH, BETTENDORF, IA, p. A230
EAGLEVILLE HOSPITAL, EAGLEVILLE, PA, p. A538

Index of Hospitals / Encompass Health Rehabilitation Hospital of Morgantown

EARLY MEDICAL CENTER, BLAKELY, GA, p. A159
EAST ADAMS RURAL HEALTHCARE, RITZVILLE, WA, p. A694
EAST ALABAMA MEDICAL CENTER, OPELIKA, AL, p. A23
EAST CARROLL PARISH HOSPITAL, LAKE PROVIDENCE, LA, p. A287
EAST CENTRAL REGIONAL HOSPITAL, AUGUSTA, GA, p. A158
EAST CENTRAL REGIONAL HOSPITAL, GRACEWOOD, GA, p. A164
EAST COOPER MEDICAL CENTER, MOUNT PLEASANT, SC, p. A568
EAST GEORGIA REGIONAL MEDICAL CENTER, STATESBORO, GA, p. A171
EAST HOUSTON HOSPITALS & CLINICS, HOUSTON, TX, p. A625
EAST JEFFERSON GENERAL HOSPITAL, METAIRIE, LA, p. A288
EAST LIVERPOOL CITY HOSPITAL, EAST LIVERPOOL, OH, p. A495
EAST LOS ANGELES DOCTORS HOSPITAL, LOS ANGELES, CA, p. A72
EAST MISSISSIPPI STATE HOSPITAL, MERIDIAN, MS, p. A366
EAST MORGAN COUNTY HOSPITAL, BRUSH, CO, p. A104
EAST ORANGE GENERAL HOSPITAL, EAST ORANGE, NJ, p. A420
EAST RIDGE HOSPITAL, EAST RIDGE, TN, p. A582
EAST TENNESSEE CHILDREN'S HOSPITAL, KNOXVILLE, TN, p. A585
EASTAR HEALTH SYSTEM, EAST CAMPUS, MUSKOGEE, OK, p. A515
EASTERN COLORADO HCS, AURORA, CO, p. A103
EASTERN IDAHO REGIONAL MEDICAL CENTER, IDAHO FALLS, ID, p. A181
EASTERN IOWA REHABILITATION HOSPITAL, CORALVILLE, IA, p. A233
EASTERN KANSAS HCS, TOPEKA, KS, p. A260
EASTERN LONG ISLAND HOSPITAL, GREENPORT, NY, p. A443
EASTERN LOUISIANA MENTAL HEALTH SYSTEM, JACKSON, LA, p. A283
EASTERN NEW MEXICO MEDICAL CENTER, ROSWELL, NM, p. A436
EASTERN OKLAHOMA MEDICAL CENTER, POTEAU, OK, p. A520
EASTERN OKLAHOMA VA HEALTH CARE SYSTEM, MUSKOGEE, OK, p. A515
EASTERN PLUMAS HEALTH CARE, PORTOLA, CA, p. A84
EASTERN SHORE HOSPITAL CENTER, CAMBRIDGE, MD, p. A303
EASTERN STATE HOSPITAL, LEXINGTON, KY, p. A268
EASTERN STATE HOSPITAL, MEDICAL LAKE, WA, p. A691
EASTERN STATE HOSPITAL, WILLIAMSBURG, VA, p. A685
EASTLAND MEMORIAL HOSPITAL, EASTLAND, TX, p. A615
EASTPOINTE HOSPITAL, DAPHNE, AL, p. A18
EASTSIDE PSYCHIATRIC HOSPITAL, TALLAHASSEE, FL, p. A151
EATON RAPIDS MEDICAL CENTER, EATON RAPIDS, MI, p. A326
ECU HEALTH BERTIE HOSPITAL, WINDSOR, NC, p. A478
ECU HEALTH CHOWAN HOSPITAL, EDENTON, NC, p. A467
ECU HEALTH DUPLIN HOSPITAL, KENANSVILLE, NC, p. A471
ECU HEALTH EDGECOMBE HOSPITAL, TARBORO, NC, p. A477
ECU HEALTH MEDICAL CENTER, GREENVILLE, NC, p. A470
ECU HEALTH NORTH HOSPITAL, ROANOKE RAPIDS, NC, p. A475
ECU HEALTH ROANOKE-CHOWAN HOSPITAL, AHOSKIE, NC, p. A463
ED FRASER MEMORIAL HOSPITAL, MACCLENNY, FL, p. A138
EDEN MEDICAL CENTER, CASTRO VALLEY, CA, p. A59
EDGEFIELD COUNTY HEALTHCARE, EDGEFIELD, SC, p. A565
EDGERTON HOSPITAL AND HEALTH SERVICES, EDGERTON, WI, p. A710
EDGEWOOD SURGICAL HOSPITAL, TRANSFER, PA, p. A555
EDINBURG REGIONAL HOSPITAL, EDINBURG, TX, p. A615
EDMOND MEDICAL CENTER, EDMOND, OK, p. A512
EDWARD HINES, JR. VETERANS AFFAIRS HOSPITAL, HINES, IL, p. A198
EDWARDS COUNTY MEDICAL CENTER, KINSLEY, KS, p. A252
EDWIN SHAW REHAB, COPLEY, OH, p. A493
EFFINGHAM HEALTH SYSTEM, SPRINGFIELD, GA, p. A171
EGLESTON CHILDREN'S HOSPITAL, ATLANTA, GA, p. A157
EINSTEIN MEDICAL CENTER MONTGOMERY, EAST NORRITON, PA, p. A538
EINSTEIN MEDICAL CENTER PHILADELPHIA, PHILADELPHIA, PA, p. A548
EINSTEIN-WEILER HOSPITAL, NEW YORK, NY, p. A448
EISENHOWER HEALTH, RANCHO MIRAGE, CA, p. A84
EL CAMINO HEALTH, MOUNTAIN VIEW, CA, p. A79
EL CAMINO HOSPITAL, MOUNTAIN VIEW, CA, p. A79

EL CAMPO MEMORIAL HOSPITAL, EL CAMPO, TX, p. A616
EL CENTRO REGIONAL MEDICAL CENTER, EL CENTRO, CA, p. A62
EL PASO BEHAVIORAL HEALTH SYSTEM, EL PASO, TX, p. A616
EL PASO CHILDREN'S HOSPITAL, EL PASO, TX, p. A616
EL PASO LTAC HOSPITAL, EL PASO, TX, p. A616
EL PASO PSYCHIATRIC CENTER, EL PASO, TX, p. A616
ELBERT MEMORIAL HOSPITAL, ELBERTON, GA, p. A163
ELBOW LAKE MEDICAL CENTER, ELBOW LAKE, MN, p. A346
ELEANOR SLATER HOSPITAL, CRANSTON, RI, p. A560
ELECTRA MEMORIAL HOSPITAL, ELECTRA, TX, p. A618
ELGIN MENTAL HEALTH CENTER, ELGIN, IL, p. A194
ELITE HOSPITAL KINGWOOD, KINGWOOD, TX, p. A632
ELITECARE EMERGENCY HOSPITAL, LEAGUE CITY, TX, p. A634
ELIZABETH PARSONS WARE PACKARD MENTAL HEALTH CENTER, SPRINGFIELD, IL, p. A209
ELIZABETH SETON PEDIATRIC CENTER, YONKERS, NY, p. A462
ELKHART GENERAL HOSPITAL, ELKHART, IN, p. A215
ELKHORN VALLEY REHABILITATION HOSPITAL, CASPER, WY, p. A726
ELKVIEW GENERAL HOSPITAL, HOBART, OK, p. A513
ELLENVILLE REGIONAL HOSPITAL, ELLENVILLE, NY, p. A442
ELLETT MEMORIAL HOSPITAL, APPLETON CITY, MO, p. A371
ELLINWOOD DISTRICT HOSPITAL, ELLINWOOD, KS, p. A248
ELLIOT HOSPITAL, MANCHESTER, NH, p. A416
ELLIS FISCHEL CANCER CENTER, COLUMBIA, MO, p. A374
ELLIS FISCHEL CANCER CTR, COLUMBIA, MO, p. A374
ELLIS HOSPITAL HEALTH CENTER, SCHENECTADY, NY, p. A458
ELLIS HOSPITAL MCCLELLAN CAMPUS, SCHENECTADY, NY, p. A458
ELLIS MEDICINE, SCHENECTADY, NY, p. A458
ELLSWORTH COUNTY MEDICAL CENTER, ELLSWORTH, KS, p. A249
ELMHURST HOSPITAL, ELMHURST, IL, p. A194
ELMIRA PSYCHIATRIC CENTER, ELMIRA, NY, p. A443
ELMORE COMMUNITY HOSPITAL, WETUMPKA, AL, p. A26
ELY-BLOOMENSON COMMUNITY HOSPITAL, ELY, MN, p. A346
EMANATE HEALTH FOOTHILL PRESBYTERIAN HOSPITAL, GLENDORA, CA, p. A66
EMANATE HEALTH INTER-COMMUNITY HOSPITAL, COVINA, CA, p. A61
EMANUEL MEDICAL CENTER, SWAINSBORO, GA, p. A172
EMANUEL MEDICAL CENTER, TURLOCK, CA, p. A98
EMERALD COAST BEHAVIORAL HOSPITAL, PANAMA CITY, FL, p. A145
EMERALD-HODGSON HOSPITAL, SEWANEE, TN, p. A593
EMERSON HOSPITAL, CONCORD, MA, p. A313
EMINENT MEDICAL CENTER, RICHARDSON, TX, p. A646
EMMA PENDLETON BRADLEY HOSPITAL, EAST PROVIDENCE, RI, p. A560
EMORY DECATUR HOSPITAL, DECATUR, GA, p. A162
EMORY HILLANDALE HOSPITAL, LITHONIA, GA, p. A166
EMORY JOHNS CREEK HOSPITAL, JOHNS CREEK, GA, p. A166
EMORY LONG-TERM ACUTE CARE, DECATUR, GA, p. A162
EMORY REHABILITATION HOSPITAL, ATLANTA, GA, p. A157
EMORY SAINT JOSEPH'S HOSPITAL, ATLANTA, GA, p. A157
EMORY UNIVERSITY HOSPITAL, ATLANTA, GA, p. A157
EMORY UNIVERSITY HOSPITAL MIDTOWN, ATLANTA, GA, p. A157
ENCINO HOSPITAL MEDICAL CENTER, ENCINO, CA, p. A62
ENCOMPASS HEALTH CARDINAL HILL REHABILITATION HOSPITAL, LEXINGTON, KY, p. A268
ENCOMPASS HEALTH DEACONESS REHABILITATION HOSPITAL, NEWBURGH, IN, p. A225
ENCOMPASS HEALTH LAKESHORE REHABILITATION HOSPITAL, BIRMINGHAM, AL, p. A16
ENCOMPASS HEALTH REHABILITATION HOSPITAL, SHREVEPORT, LA, p. A292
ENCOMPASS HEALTH REHABILITATION HOSPITAL AT CINCINNATI, CINCINNATI, OH, p. A489
ENCOMPASS HEALTH REHABILITATION HOSPITAL OF ABILENE, ABILENE, TX, p. A595
ENCOMPASS HEALTH REHABILITATION HOSPITAL OF ALBUQUERQUE, ALBUQUERQUE, NM, p. A432
ENCOMPASS HEALTH REHABILITATION HOSPITAL OF ALEXANDRIA, ALEXANDRIA, LA, p. A276
ENCOMPASS HEALTH REHABILITATION HOSPITAL OF ALTAMONTE SPRINGS, ALTAMONTE SPRINGS, FL, p. A125
ENCOMPASS HEALTH REHABILITATION HOSPITAL OF ALTOONA, ALTOONA, PA, p. A534
ENCOMPASS HEALTH REHABILITATION HOSPITAL OF ARLINGTON, ARLINGTON, TX, p. A597
ENCOMPASS HEALTH REHABILITATION HOSPITAL OF AUSTIN, AUSTIN, TX, p. A600

ENCOMPASS HEALTH REHABILITATION HOSPITAL OF BAKERSFIELD, BAKERSFIELD, CA, p. A57
ENCOMPASS HEALTH REHABILITATION HOSPITAL OF BLUFFTON, BLUFFTON, SC, p. A562
ENCOMPASS HEALTH REHABILITATION HOSPITAL OF BRAINTREE, BRAINTREE, MA, p. A311
ENCOMPASS HEALTH REHABILITATION HOSPITAL OF CAPE CORAL, CAPE CORAL, FL, p. A127
ENCOMPASS HEALTH REHABILITATION HOSPITAL OF CHATTANOOGA, CHATTANOOGA, TN, p. A580
ENCOMPASS HEALTH REHABILITATION HOSPITAL OF CITY VIEW, FORT WORTH, TX, p. A619
ENCOMPASS HEALTH REHABILITATION HOSPITAL OF CLERMONT, CLERMONT, FL, p. A128
ENCOMPASS HEALTH REHABILITATION HOSPITAL OF COLORADO SPRINGS, COLORADO SPRINGS, CO, p. A105
ENCOMPASS HEALTH REHABILITATION HOSPITAL OF COLUMBIA, COLUMBIA, SC, p. A564
ENCOMPASS HEALTH REHABILITATION HOSPITAL OF CONCORD, CONCORD, NH, p. A414
ENCOMPASS HEALTH REHABILITATION HOSPITAL OF CUMMING, CUMMING, GA, p. A162
ENCOMPASS HEALTH REHABILITATION HOSPITAL OF CYPRESS, HOUSTON, TX, p. A625
ENCOMPASS HEALTH REHABILITATION HOSPITAL OF DALLAS, DALLAS, TX, p. A611
ENCOMPASS HEALTH REHABILITATION HOSPITAL OF DESERT CANYON, LAS VEGAS, NV, p. A410
ENCOMPASS HEALTH REHABILITATION HOSPITAL OF DOTHAN, DOTHAN, AL, p. A18
ENCOMPASS HEALTH REHABILITATION HOSPITAL OF EAST VALLEY, MESA, AZ, p. A33
ENCOMPASS HEALTH REHABILITATION HOSPITAL OF ERIE, ERIE, PA, p. A539
ENCOMPASS HEALTH REHABILITATION HOSPITAL OF FLORENCE, FLORENCE, SC, p. A566
ENCOMPASS HEALTH REHABILITATION HOSPITAL OF FRANKLIN, FRANKLIN, TN, p. A583
ENCOMPASS HEALTH REHABILITATION HOSPITAL OF FREDERICKSBURG, FREDERICKSBURG, VA, p. A676
ENCOMPASS HEALTH REHABILITATION HOSPITAL OF GADSDEN, GADSDEN, AL, p. A19
ENCOMPASS HEALTH REHABILITATION HOSPITAL OF GREENVILLE, GREENVILLE, SC, p. A567
ENCOMPASS HEALTH REHABILITATION HOSPITAL OF HARMARVILLE, PITTSBURGH, PA, p. A551
ENCOMPASS HEALTH REHABILITATION HOSPITAL OF HENDERSON, HENDERSON, NV, p. A409
ENCOMPASS HEALTH REHABILITATION HOSPITAL OF HUMBLE, HUMBLE, TX, p. A629
ENCOMPASS HEALTH REHABILITATION HOSPITAL OF HUNTINGTON, HUNTINGTON, WV, p. A701
ENCOMPASS HEALTH REHABILITATION HOSPITAL OF JACKSONVILLE, JACKSONVILLE, FL, p. A134
ENCOMPASS HEALTH REHABILITATION HOSPITAL OF JONESBORO, JONESBORO, AR, p. A48
ENCOMPASS HEALTH REHABILITATION HOSPITAL OF KATY, KATY, TX, p. A631
ENCOMPASS HEALTH REHABILITATION HOSPITAL OF KINGSPORT, KINGSPORT, TN, p. A585
ENCOMPASS HEALTH REHABILITATION HOSPITAL OF LAKELAND, LAKELAND, FL, p. A136
ENCOMPASS HEALTH REHABILITATION HOSPITAL OF LAKEVIEW, ELIZABETHTOWN, KY, p. A265
ENCOMPASS HEALTH REHABILITATION HOSPITAL OF LARGO, LARGO, FL, p. A137
ENCOMPASS HEALTH REHABILITATION HOSPITAL OF LAS VEGAS, LAS VEGAS, NV, p. A410
ENCOMPASS HEALTH REHABILITATION HOSPITAL OF LITTLETON, LITTLETON, CO, p. A111
ENCOMPASS HEALTH REHABILITATION HOSPITAL OF MANATI, MANATI, PR, p. A733
ENCOMPASS HEALTH REHABILITATION HOSPITAL OF MECHANICSBURG, MECHANICSBURG, PA, p. A545
ENCOMPASS HEALTH REHABILITATION HOSPITAL OF MEMPHIS, A PARTNER OF METHODIST HEALTHCARE, MEMPHIS, TN, p. A588
ENCOMPASS HEALTH REHABILITATION HOSPITAL OF MIAMI, CUTLER BAY, FL, p. A129
ENCOMPASS HEALTH REHABILITATION HOSPITAL OF MIDDLETOWN, MIDDLETOWN, DE, p. A121
ENCOMPASS HEALTH REHABILITATION HOSPITAL OF MIDLAND ODESSA, MIDLAND, TX, p. A639
ENCOMPASS HEALTH REHABILITATION HOSPITAL OF MODESTO, MODESTO, CA, p. A77
ENCOMPASS HEALTH REHABILITATION HOSPITAL OF MONTGOMERY, MONTGOMERY, AL, p. A22
ENCOMPASS HEALTH REHABILITATION HOSPITAL OF MORGANTOWN, MORGANTOWN, WV, p. A703

Index of Hospitals / Encompass Health Rehabilitation Hospital of Murrieta

ENCOMPASS HEALTH REHABILITATION HOSPITAL OF MURRIETA, MURRIETA, CA, p. A79
ENCOMPASS HEALTH REHABILITATION HOSPITAL OF NEW ENGLAND, WOBURN, MA, p. A320
ENCOMPASS HEALTH REHABILITATION HOSPITAL OF NEWNAN, NEWNAN, GA, p. A169
ENCOMPASS HEALTH REHABILITATION HOSPITAL OF NITTANY VALLEY, PLEASANT GAP, PA, p. A552
ENCOMPASS HEALTH REHABILITATION HOSPITAL OF NORTH ALABAMA, HUNTSVILLE, AL, p. A20
ENCOMPASS HEALTH REHABILITATION HOSPITAL OF NORTH MEMPHIS, A PARTNER OF METHODIST HEALTHCARE, MEMPHIS, TN, p. A588
ENCOMPASS HEALTH REHABILITATION HOSPITAL OF NORTH TAMPA, LUTZ, FL, p. A138
ENCOMPASS HEALTH REHABILITATION HOSPITAL OF NORTHERN KENTUCKY, EDGEWOOD, KY, p. A265
ENCOMPASS HEALTH REHABILITATION HOSPITAL OF NORTHERN VIRGINIA, ALDIE, VA, p. A673
ENCOMPASS HEALTH REHABILITATION HOSPITAL OF NORTHWEST TUCSON, TUCSON, AZ, p. A40
ENCOMPASS HEALTH REHABILITATION HOSPITAL OF OCALA, OCALA, FL, p. A143
ENCOMPASS HEALTH REHABILITATION HOSPITAL OF PANAMA CITY, PANAMA CITY, FL, p. A146
ENCOMPASS HEALTH REHABILITATION HOSPITAL OF PARKERSBURG, PARKERSBURG, WV, p. A703
ENCOMPASS HEALTH REHABILITATION HOSPITAL OF PEARLAND, PEARLAND, TX, p. A643
ENCOMPASS HEALTH REHABILITATION HOSPITAL OF PENSACOLA, PENSACOLA, FL, p. A146
ENCOMPASS HEALTH REHABILITATION HOSPITAL OF PETERSBURG, PETERSBURG, VA, p. A681
ENCOMPASS HEALTH REHABILITATION HOSPITAL OF PLANO, PLANO, TX, p. A644
ENCOMPASS HEALTH REHABILITATION HOSPITAL OF PRINCETON, PRINCETON, WV, p. A704
ENCOMPASS HEALTH REHABILITATION HOSPITAL OF READING, READING, PA, p. A553
ENCOMPASS HEALTH REHABILITATION HOSPITAL OF RICHARDSON, RICHARDSON, TX, p. A646
ENCOMPASS HEALTH REHABILITATION HOSPITAL OF RICHMOND, RICHMOND, VA, p. A682
ENCOMPASS HEALTH REHABILITATION HOSPITAL OF ROCK HILL, ROCK HILL, SC, p. A569
ENCOMPASS HEALTH REHABILITATION HOSPITAL OF ROUND ROCK, ROUND ROCK, TX, p. A647
ENCOMPASS HEALTH REHABILITATION HOSPITAL OF SALISBURY, SALISBURY, MD, p. A307
ENCOMPASS HEALTH REHABILITATION HOSPITAL OF SAN ANTONIO, SAN ANTONIO, TX, p. A649
ENCOMPASS HEALTH REHABILITATION HOSPITAL OF SAN JUAN, SAN JUAN, PR, p. A735
ENCOMPASS HEALTH REHABILITATION HOSPITAL OF SARASOTA, SARASOTA, FL, p. A149
ENCOMPASS HEALTH REHABILITATION HOSPITAL OF SAVANNAH, SAVANNAH, GA, p. A171
ENCOMPASS HEALTH REHABILITATION HOSPITAL OF SCOTTSDALE, SCOTTSDALE, AZ, p. A38
ENCOMPASS HEALTH REHABILITATION HOSPITAL OF SEWICKLEY, SEWICKLEY, PA, p. A554
ENCOMPASS HEALTH REHABILITATION HOSPITAL OF SHELBY COUNTY, PELHAM, AL, p. A23
ENCOMPASS HEALTH REHABILITATION HOSPITAL OF SIOUX FALLS, SIOUX FALLS, SD, p. A576
ENCOMPASS HEALTH REHABILITATION HOSPITAL OF SPRING HILL, BROOKSVILLE, FL, p. A127
ENCOMPASS HEALTH REHABILITATION HOSPITAL OF ST. AUGUSTINE, ST AUGUSTINE, FL, p. A150
ENCOMPASS HEALTH REHABILITATION HOSPITAL OF SUGAR LAND, SUGAR LAND, TX, p. A654
ENCOMPASS HEALTH REHABILITATION HOSPITAL OF SUNRISE, SUNRISE, FL, p. A151
ENCOMPASS HEALTH REHABILITATION HOSPITAL OF TALLAHASSEE, TALLAHASSEE, FL, p. A151
ENCOMPASS HEALTH REHABILITATION HOSPITAL OF TEXARKANA, TEXARKANA, TX, p. A657
ENCOMPASS HEALTH REHABILITATION HOSPITAL OF THE MID–CITIES, BEDFORD, TX, p. A602
ENCOMPASS HEALTH REHABILITATION HOSPITAL OF THE WOODLANDS, CONROE, TX, p. A608
ENCOMPASS HEALTH REHABILITATION HOSPITAL OF TINTON FALLS, A JOINT VENTURE WITH MONMOUTH MEDICAL CENTER, TINTON FALLS, NJ, p. A429
ENCOMPASS HEALTH REHABILITATION HOSPITAL OF TOLEDO, TOLEDO, OH, p. A504
ENCOMPASS HEALTH REHABILITATION HOSPITAL OF TOMS RIVER, TOMS RIVER, NJ, p. A429
ENCOMPASS HEALTH REHABILITATION HOSPITAL OF TREASURE COAST, VERO BEACH, FL, p. A154
ENCOMPASS HEALTH REHABILITATION HOSPITAL OF TUSTIN, TUSTIN, CA, p. A99
ENCOMPASS HEALTH REHABILITATION HOSPITAL OF UTAH, SANDY, UT, p. A669
ENCOMPASS HEALTH REHABILITATION HOSPITAL OF VINELAND, VINELAND, NJ, p. A429
ENCOMPASS HEALTH REHABILITATION HOSPITAL OF WACO, ROBINSON, TX, p. A647
ENCOMPASS HEALTH REHABILITATION HOSPITAL OF WESTERN MASSACHUSETTS, LUDLOW, MA, p. A315
ENCOMPASS HEALTH REHABILITATION HOSPITAL OF WICHITA FALLS, WICHITA FALLS, TX, p. A662
ENCOMPASS HEALTH REHABILITATION HOSPITAL OF YORK, YORK, PA, p. A558
ENCOMPASS HEALTH REHABILITATION HOSPITAL THE VINTAGE, HOUSTON, TX, p. A625
ENCOMPASS HEALTH REHABILITATION HOSPITAL VISION PARK, SHENANDOAH, TX, p. A652
ENCOMPASS HEALTH REHABILITATION HOSPITAL, A PARTNER OF MEMORIAL HOSPITAL AT GULFPORT, GULFPORT, MS, p. A362
ENCOMPASS HEALTH REHABILITATION HOSPITAL, A PARTNER OF WASHINGTON REGIONAL, FAYETTEVILLE, AR, p. A46
ENCOMPASS HEALTH REHABILITATION HOSPITAL, AN AFFILIATE OF MARTIN HEALTH, STUART, FL, p. A150
ENCOMPASS HEALTH REHABILITATION INSTITUTE OF LIBERTYVILLE, LIBERTYVILLE, IL, p. A200
ENCOMPASS HEALTH REHABILITATION INSTITUTE OF TUCSON, TUCSON, AZ, p. A40
ENCOMPASS HEALTH VALLEY OF THE SUN REHABILITATION HOSPITAL, GLENDALE, AZ, p. A32
ENCOMPASSS HEALTH REHABILITATION HOSPITAL OF FORT SMITH, FORT SMITH, AR, p. A47
ENDEAVOR HEALTH EDWARD HOSPITAL, NAPERVILLE, IL, p. A203
ENDEAVOR HEALTH ELMHURST HOSPITAL, ELMHURST, IL, p. A194
ENDEAVOR HEALTH EVANSTON HOSPITAL, EVANSTON, IL, p. A195
ENDEAVOR HEALTH LINDEN OAKS HOSPITAL, NAPERVILLE, IL, p. A203
ENDEAVOR HEALTH NORTHWEST COMMUNITY HOSPITAL, ARLINGTON HEIGHTS, IL, p. A185
ENDEAVOR HEALTH SWEDISH HOSPITAL, CHICAGO, IL, p. A189
ENDLESS MOUNTAINS HEALTH SYSTEMS, MONTROSE, PA, p. A546
ENGLEWOOD COMMUNITY HOSPITAL, ENGLEWOOD, FL, p. A131
ENGLEWOOD HEALTH, ENGLEWOOD, NJ, p. A421
ENLOE HEALTH, CHICO, CA, p. A59
ENLOE MEDICAL CENTER, CHICO, CA, p. A59
ENNIS REGIONAL MEDICAL CENTER, ENNIS, TX, p. A618
EPHRAIM MCDOWELL FORT LOGAN HOSPITAL, STANFORD, KY, p. A274
EPHRAIM MCDOWELL JAMES B. HAGGIN MEMORIAL HOSPITAL, HARRODSBURG, KY, p. A266
EPHRAIM MCDOWELL REGIONAL MEDICAL CENTER, DANVILLE, KY, p. A264
EPISCOPAL HOSPITAL, PHILADELPHIA, PA, p. A548
ERIE COUNTY MEDICAL CENTER, BUFFALO, NY, p. A440
ERIE VETERANS AFFAIRS MEDICAL CENTER, ERIE, PA, p. A539
ERLANGER BEHAVIORAL HOSPITAL, CHATTANOOGA, TN, p. A580
ERLANGER BLEDSOE HOSPITAL, PIKEVILLE, TN, p. A592
ERLANGER MEDICAL CENTER, CHATTANOOGA, TN, p. A580
ERLANGER WESTERN CAROLINA HOSPITAL, MURPHY, NC, p. A473
ERLANGER WOMEN'S EAST HOSPITAL, CHATTANOOGA, TN, p. A580
ESKENAZI HEALTH, INDIANAPOLIS, IN, p. A219
ESSENTIA HEALTH–ADA, ADA, MN, p. A342
ESSENTIA HEALTH–DEER RIVER, DEER RIVER, MN, p. A345
ESSENTIA HEALTH DULUTH, DULUTH, MN, p. A346
ESSENTIA HEALTH FARGO, FARGO, ND, p. A480
ESSENTIA HEALTH–FOSSTON, FOSSTON, MN, p. A347
ESSENTIA HEALTH–GRACEVILLE, GRACEVILLE, MN, p. A347
ESSENTIA HEALTH MOOSE LAKE, MOOSE LAKE, MN, p. A351
ESSENTIA HEALTH NORTHERN PINES, AURORA, MN, p. A343
ESSENTIA HEALTH SANDSTONE, SANDSTONE, MN, p. A355
ESSENTIA HEALTH–ST. JOSEPH'S MEDICAL CENTER, BRAINERD, MN, p. A344
ESSENTIA HEALTH ST. MARY'S – DETROIT LAKES, DETROIT LAKES, MN, p. A345
ESSENTIA HEALTH ST. MARY'S HOSPITAL OF SUPERIOR, SUPERIOR, WI, p. A722
ESSENTIA HEALTH ST. MARY'S MEDICAL CENTER, DULUTH, MN, p. A346
ESSENTIA HEALTH–VIRGINIA, VIRGINIA, MN, p. A356
ESSEX COUNTY HOSPITAL CENTER, CEDAR GROVE, NJ, p. A419
ESTES PARK HEALTH, ESTES PARK, CO, p. A107
ESTES PARK MEDICAL CENTER, ESTES PARK, CO, p. A107
EUCLID HOSPITAL, EUCLID, OH, p. A495
EUREKA COMMUNITY HEALTH SERVICES AVERA, EUREKA, SD, p. A573
EUREKA SPRINGS HOSPITAL, EUREKA SPRINGS, AR, p. A45
EVANGELICAL COMMUNITY HOSPITAL, LEWISBURG, PA, p. A544
EVANS MEMORIAL HOSPITAL, CLAXTON, GA, p. A160
EVANS U. S. ARMY COMMUNITY HOSPITAL, FORT CARSON, CO, p. A107
EVANSTON HOSPITAL, EVANSTON, IL, p. A195
EVANSTON REGIONAL HOSPITAL, EVANSTON, WY, p. A727
EVANSVILLE PSYCHIATRIC CHILDREN CENTER, EVANSVILLE, IN, p. A216
EVANSVILLE STATE HOSPITAL, EVANSVILLE, IN, p. A216
EVEREST REHABILITATION HOSPITAL LONGVIEW, LONGVIEW, TX, p. A635
EVEREST REHABILITATION HOSPITAL OF EL PASO, EL PASO, TX, p. A616
EVEREST REHABILITATION HOSPITAL OF ROGERS, ROGERS, AR, p. A52
EVEREST REHABILITATION HOSPITAL OKC, OKLAHOMA CITY, OK, p. A516
EVERETT TOWER, OKLAHOMA CITY, OK, p. A516
EVERGREEN MEDICAL CENTER, EVERGREEN, AL, p. A19
EVERGREENHEALTH, KIRKLAND, WA, p. A691
EVERGREENHEALTH MONROE, MONROE, WA, p. A691
EXCELA FRICK HOSPITAL, MOUNT PLEASANT, PA, p. A546
EXCELA HEALTH LATROBE, LATROBE, PA, p. A544
EXCELA HEALTH WESTMORELAND HOSPITAL, GREENSBURG, PA, p. A541
EXCELSIOR SPRINGS HOSPITAL, EXCELSIOR SPRINGS, MO, p. A374
EXCEPTIONAL COMMUNITY HOSPITAL MARICOPA, MARICOPA, AZ, p. A33
EXCEPTIONAL COMMUNITY HOSPITAL YUMA, YUMA, AZ, p. A41
EXETER HOSPITAL, EXETER, NH, p. A415
EYE AND EAR HOSPITAL OF PITTSBURGH, PITTSBURGH, PA, p. A551

F

FAIR OAKS HOSPITAL, DELRAY BEACH, FL, p. A130
FAIRBANKS, INDIANAPOLIS, IN, p. A219
FAIRBANKS MEMORIAL HOSPITAL, FAIRBANKS, AK, p. A28
FAIRCHILD MEDICAL CENTER, YREKA, CA, p. A102
FAIRFAX BEHAVIORAL HEALTH, KIRKLAND, WA, p. A691
FAIRFIELD MEDICAL CENTER, LANCASTER, OH, p. A498
FAIRFIELD MEMORIAL HOSPITAL, FAIRFIELD, IL, p. A195
FAIRLAWN REHABILITATION HOSPITAL, WORCESTER, MA, p. A320
FAIRMONT HOSPITAL, SAN LEANDRO, CA, p. A92
FAIRMOUNT BEHAVIORAL HEALTH SYSTEM, PHILADELPHIA, PA, p. A548
FAIRVIEW HOSPITAL, GREAT BARRINGTON, MA, p. A314
FAIRVIEW PARK HOSPITAL, DUBLIN, GA, p. A163
FAIRVIEW RANGE, HIBBING, MN, p. A348
FAIRVIEW REGIONAL MEDICAL CENTER, FAIRVIEW, OK, p. A512
FAIRVIEW RIVERSIDE HOSPITAL, MINNEAPOLIS, MN, p. A350
FAITH COMMUNITY HOSPITAL, JACKSBORO, TX, p. A630
FAITH REGIONAL HEALTH SERVICES, NORFOLK, NE, p. A403
FALL RIVER HEALTH SERVICES, HOT SPRINGS, SD, p. A574
FALL RIVER HOSPITAL, HOT SPRINGS, SD, p. A574
FALLON MEDICAL COMPLEX, BAKER, MT, p. A389
FALLS COMMUNITY HOSPITAL AND CLINIC, MARLIN, TX, p. A638
FALMOUTH HOSPITAL, FALMOUTH, MA, p. A313
FAMILY HEALTH WEST, FRUITA, CO, p. A108
FANNIN REGIONAL HOSPITAL, BLUE RIDGE, GA, p. A159
FANNY ALLEN CAMPUS, COLCHESTER, VT, p. A671
FARGO NURSING HOME, FARGO, ND, p. A480
FARGO VA MEDICAL CENTER, FARGO, ND, p. A480
FARGO VAMC, FARGO, ND, p. A480
FARREN MEMORIAL HOSPITAL, TURNERS FALLS, MA, p. A319
FAULKTON AREA MEDICAL CENTER, FAULKTON, SD, p. A573
FAUQUIER HOSPITAL, WARRENTON, VA, p. A685

Index of Hospitals / George E. Weems Memorial Hospital

FAWCETT MEMORIAL HOSPITAL, PORT CHARLOTTE, FL, p. A147
FAXTON–ST LUKE'S HEALTHCARE, UTICA, NY, p. A460
FAYETTE COUNTY HOSPITAL, VANDALIA, IL, p. A210
FAYETTE MEDICAL CENTER, FAYETTE, AL, p. A19
FAYETTEVILLE VETERANS AFFAIRS MEDICAL CENTER, FAYETTEVILLE, NC, p. A468
FEDERAL CORRECTIONAL INSTITUTE HOSPITAL, LITTLETON, CO, p. A111
FEDERAL MEDICAL CENTER, LEXINGTON, KY, p. A268
FERRELL HOSPITAL, ELDORADO, IL, p. A194
FERRY COUNTY MEMORIAL HOSPITAL, REPUBLIC, WA, p. A693
F. F. THOMPSON HOSPITAL, CANANDAIGUA, NY, p. A440
FHN MEMORIAL HOSPITAL, FREEPORT, IL, p. A195
FIELD MEMORIAL COMMUNITY HOSPITAL, CENTREVILLE, MS, p. A360
FILLMORE COMMUNITY HOSPITAL, FILLMORE, UT, p. A665
FILLMORE COUNTY HOSPITAL, GENEVA, NE, p. A400
FIRELANDS COMMUNITY HOSPITAL, SANDUSKY, OH, p. A503
FIRELANDS REGIONAL HEALTH SYSTEM, SANDUSKY, OH, p. A503
FIRST BAPTIST MEDICAL CENTER, DALLAS, TX, p. A611
FIRST CARE HEALTH CENTER, PARK RIVER, ND, p. A483
FIRST HOSPITAL PANAMERICANO, CIDRA, PR, p. A732
FIRST SURGICAL HOSPITAL, BELLAIRE, TX, p. A603
FIRSTHEALTH MONTGOMERY MEMORIAL HOSPITAL, TROY, NC, p. A477
FIRSTHEALTH MOORE REGIONAL HOSPITAL, PINEHURST, NC, p. A474
FIRSTHEALTH RICHMOND MEMORIAL HOSPITAL, ROCKINGHAM, NC, p. A475
FISHER COUNTY HOSPITAL DISTRICT, ROTAN, TX, p. A647
FISHER–TITUS MEDICAL CENTER, NORWALK, OH, p. A501
FISHERMEN'S HOSPITAL, MARATHON, FL, p. A138
FITZGERALD MERCY HOSPITAL, DARBY, PA, p. A538
FITZGIBBON HOSPITAL, MARSHALL, MO, p. A380
FLAGSTAFF MEDICAL CENTER, FLAGSTAFF, AZ, p. A31
FLAMBEAU HOSPITAL, PARK FALLS, WI, p. A719
FLEMING COUNTY HOSPITAL, FLEMINGSBURG, KY, p. A265
FLINT RIVER HOSPITAL, MONTEZUMA, GA, p. A168
FLORIDA HOSPITAL CELEBRATION HEALTH, CELEBRATION, FL, p. A127
FLORIDA HOSPITAL EAST ORLANDO, ORLANDO, FL, p. A144
FLORIDA HOSPITAL FOR CHILDREN–WALT DISNEY PAVILION, ORLANDO, FL, p. A144
FLORIDA HOSPITAL KISSIMMEE, KISSIMMEE, FL, p. A136
FLORIDA HOSPITAL–ALTAMONTE, ALTAMONTE SPRINGS, FL, p. A125
FLORIDA HOSPITAL–APOPKA, APOPKA, FL, p. A125
FLORIDA STATE HOSPITAL, CHATTAHOOCHEE, FL, p. A127
FLOWER HOSPITAL, SYLVANIA, OH, p. A504
FLOWERS HOSPITAL, DOTHAN, AL, p. A18
FLOYD COUNTY MEDICAL CENTER, CHARLES CITY, IA, p. A232
FLOYD MEDICAL CENTER, ROME, GA, p. A170
FLOYD VALLEY HEALTHCARE, LE MARS, IA, p. A239
FLUSHING HOSPITAL MEDICAL CENTER, NEW YORK, NY, p. A448
FOND DU LAC COUNTY MENTAL HEALTH CENTER, FOND DU LAC, WI, p. A710
FOOTHILL REGIONAL MEDICAL CENTER, TUSTIN, CA, p. A99
FORBES HOSPITAL, MONROEVILLE, PA, p. A546
FOREST GROVE COMM HOSPITAL, FOREST GROVE, OR, p. A527
FOREST HEALTH MEDICAL CENTER, YPSILANTI, MI, p. A341
FOREST HILLS HOSPITAL, NEW YORK, NY, p. A448
FOREST PARK MEDICAL CENTER, FORT WORTH, TX, p. A619
FOREST VIEW PSYCHIATRIC HOSPITAL, GRAND RAPIDS, MI, p. A328
FORKS COMMUNITY HOSPITAL, FORKS, WA, p. A690
FORREST CITY MEDICAL CENTER, FORREST CITY, AR, p. A46
FORREST GENERAL HOSPITAL, HATTIESBURG, MS, p. A363
FORT BELKNAP SERVICE UNIT, HARLEM, MT, p. A393
FORT BELVOIR COMMUNITY HOSPITAL, FORT BELVOIR, VA, p. A676
FORT DUNCAN REGIONAL MEDICAL CENTER, EAGLE PASS, TX, p. A615
FORT HARRISON VA MEDICAL CENTER, FORT HARRISON, MT, p. A392
FORT HEALTHCARE, FORT ATKINSON, WI, p. A711
FORT LAUDERDALE BEHAVIORAL HEALTH CENTER, OAKLAND PARK, FL, p. A143
FORT LOUDOUN MEDICAL CENTER, LENOIR CITY, TN, p. A586
FORT MADISON COMMUNITY HOSPITAL, FORT MADISON, IA, p. A236
FORT SANDERS REGIONAL MEDICAL CENTER, KNOXVILLE, TN, p. A585

FOUNDATION SURGICAL HOSPITAL OF SAN ANTONIO, SAN ANTONIO, TX, p. A649
FOUNDATIONS BEHAVIORAL HEALTH, DOYLESTOWN, PA, p. A538
FOUNTAIN VALLEY REGIONAL HOSPITAL AND MEDICAL CENTER, FOUNTAIN VALLEY, CA, p. A64
4C HEALTH, LOGANSPORT, IN, p. A222
FOUR COUNTY COUNSELING CENTER, LOGANSPORT, IN, p. A222
FOUR WINDS HOSPITAL, KATONAH, NY, p. A444
FOUR WINDS HOSPITAL, SARATOGA SPRINGS, NY, p. A458
FOX CHASE CANCER CENTER, PHILADELPHIA, PA, p. A548
FRAMINGTON UNION HOSPITAL, FRAMINGHAM, MA, p. A313
FRANCES MAHON DEACONESS HOSPITAL, GLASGOW, MT, p. A392
FRANCISCAN CHILDREN'S, BRIGHTON, MA, p. A311
FRANCISCAN HEALTH – LAFAYETTE CENTRAL, LAFAYETTE, IN, p. A221
FRANCISCAN HEALTH CARMEL, CARMEL, IN, p. A213
FRANCISCAN HEALTH CRAWFORDSVILLE, CRAWFORDSVILLE, IN, p. A214
FRANCISCAN HEALTH CROWN POINT, CROWN POINT, IN, p. A214
FRANCISCAN HEALTH DYER, DYER, IN, p. A215
FRANCISCAN HEALTH HAMMOND, HAMMOND, IN, p. A218
FRANCISCAN HEALTH INDIANAPOLIS, INDIANAPOLIS, IN, p. A219
FRANCISCAN HEALTH LAFAYETTE EAST, LAFAYETTE, IN, p. A221
FRANCISCAN HEALTH MICHIGAN CITY, MICHIGAN CITY, IN, p. A223
FRANCISCAN HEALTH MOORESVILLE, MOORESVILLE, IN, p. A224
FRANCISCAN HEALTH OLYMPIA FIELDS, OLYMPIA FIELDS, IL, p. A204
FRANCISCAN HEALTH RENSSELEAR, RENSSELAER, IN, p. A226
FRANCISCAN HEALTHCARE, WEST POINT, NE, p. A407
FRANCISCAN HEALTHCARE MUNSTER, MUNSTER, IN, p. A224
FRANKFORT REGIONAL MEDICAL CENTER, FRANKFORT, KY, p. A266
FRANKLIN COUNTY MEDICAL CENTER, PRESTON, ID, p. A183
FRANKLIN COUNTY MEMORIAL HOSPITAL, FRANKLIN, NE, p. A399
FRANKLIN COUNTY MEMORIAL HOSPITAL, MEADVILLE, MS, p. A366
FRANKLIN FOUNDATION HOSPITAL, FRANKLIN, LA, p. A282
FRANKLIN GENERAL HOSPITAL, HAMPTON, IA, p. A237
FRANKLIN HOSPITAL, VALLEY STREAM, NY, p. A461
FRANKLIN HOSPITAL DISTRICT, BENTON, IL, p. A186
FRANKLIN MEDICAL CENTER, WINNSBORO, LA, p. A294
FRANKLIN MEMORIAL HOSPITAL, FARMINGTON, ME, p. A297
FRANKLIN WOODS COMMUNITY HOSPITAL, JOHNSON CITY, TN, p. A584
FRAZIER INSTITUTE, LOUISVILLE, KY, p. A269
FRED HUTCHINSON CANCER CENTER, SEATTLE, WA, p. A694
FREDERICK HEALTH, FREDERICK, MD, p. A304
FREDONIA REGIONAL HOSPITAL, FREDONIA, KS, p. A249
FREEMAN HEALTH SYSTEM, JOPLIN, MO, p. A377
FREEMAN NEOSHO HOSPITAL, NEOSHO, MO, p. A381
FREEMAN REGIONAL HEALTH SERVICES, FREEMAN, SD, p. A573
FREESTONE MEDICAL CENTER, FAIRFIELD, TX, p. A618
FREMONT HOSPITAL, FREMONT, CA, p. A64
FREMONT MEDICAL CENTER, YUBA CITY, CA, p. A102
FRENCH HOSPITAL MEDICAL CENTER, SAN LUIS OBISPO, CA, p. A93
FRESNO HEART AND SURGICAL HOSPITAL, FRESNO, CA, p. A64
FRESNO SURGICAL HOSPITAL, FRESNO, CA, p. A64
FRIEND COMMUNITY HEALTHCARE SYSTEM, FRIEND, NE, p. A400
FRIENDS HOSPITAL, PHILADELPHIA, PA, p. A548
FRIO REGIONAL HOSPITAL, PEARSALL, TX, p. A643
FRISBIE MEMORIAL HOSPITAL, ROCHESTER, NH, p. A417
FROEDTERT AND THE MEDICAL COLLEGE OF WISCONSIN FROEDTERT HOSPITAL, MILWAUKEE, WI, p. A717
FROEDTERT COMMUNITY HOSPITAL – NEW BERLIN, NEW BERLIN, WI, p. A718
FROEDTERT MENOMONEE FALLS HOSPITAL, MENOMONEE FALLS, WI, p. A716
FROEDTERT SOUTH – KENOSHA MEDICAL CENTER, KENOSHA, WI, p. A713
FROEDTERT SOUTH – ST. CATHERINE'S MEDICAL CENTER, PLEASANT PRAIRIE, WI, p. A720
FROEDTERT WEST BEND HOSPITAL, WEST BEND, WI, p. A724

FRYE REGIONAL MEDICAL CENTER, HICKORY, NC, p. A470
FULTON COUNTY HEALTH CENTER, WAUSEON, OH, p. A506
FULTON COUNTY HOSPITAL, SALEM, AR, p. A53
FULTON COUNTY MEDICAL CENTER, MC CONNELLSBURG, PA, p. A545
FULTON DIVISION, NEW YORK, NY, p. A448
FULTON STATE HOSPITAL, FULTON, MO, p. A375
F. W. HUSTON MEDICAL CENTER, WINCHESTER, KS, p. A262

G

GADSDEN REGIONAL MEDICAL CENTER, GADSDEN, AL, p. A20
GALICHIA HEART HOSPITAL, WICHITA, KS, p. A261
GALION COMMUNITY HOSPITAL, GALION, OH, p. A496
GALLUP INDIAN MEDICAL CENTER, GALLUP, NM, p. A434
GARDEN CITY HOSPITAL, GARDEN CITY, MI, p. A327
GARDEN GROVE HOSPITAL AND MEDICAL CENTER, GARDEN GROVE, CA, p. A65
GARFIELD COUNTY HEALTH CENTER, JORDAN, MT, p. A393
GARFIELD COUNTY PUBLIC HOSPITAL DISTRICT, POMEROY, WA, p. A692
GARFIELD MEDICAL CENTER, MONTEREY PARK, CA, p. A78
GARFIELD MEMORIAL HOSPITAL, PANGUITCH, UT, p. A667
GARFIELD PARK BEHAVIORAL HOSPITAL, CHICAGO, IL, p. A189
GARFIELD PARK HOSPITAL, CHICAGO, IL, p. A189
GARNET HEALTH MEDICAL CENTER – CATSKILLS, CALLICOON CAMPUS, CALLICOON, NY, p. A440
GARNET HEALTH MEDICAL CENTER – CATSKILLS, HARRIS CAMPUS, HARRIS, NY, p. A444
GARNET HEALTH MEDICAL CENTER, MIDDLETOWN, NY, p. A446
GARRETT REGIONAL MEDICAL CENTER, OAKLAND, MD, p. A306
GATEWAY REGIONAL MEDICAL CENTER, GRANITE CITY, IL, p. A196
GATEWAY REHABILITATION HOSPITAL, FLORENCE, KY, p. A265
GATEWAYS HOSPITAL AND MENTAL HEALTH CENTER, LOS ANGELES, CA, p. A72
GAYLORD SPECIALTY HEALTHCARE, WALLINGFORD, CT, p. A119
GBMC HEALTHCARE, BALTIMORE, MD, p. A302
GEISINGER COMMUNITY MEDICAL CENTER, SCRANTON, PA, p. A554
GEISINGER ENCOMPASS HEALTH REHABILITATION HOSPITAL, DANVILLE, PA, p. A538
GEISINGER JERSEY SHORE HOSPITAL, JERSEY SHORE, PA, p. A542
GEISINGER LEWISTOWN HOSPITAL, LEWISTOWN, PA, p. A544
GEISINGER MEDICAL CENTER, DANVILLE, PA, p. A538
GEISINGER MEDICAL CENTER MUNCY, MUNCY, PA, p. A546
GEISINGER SHAMOKIN AREA COMMUNITY HOSPITAL, COAL TOWNSHIP, PA, p. A537
GEISINGER ST. LUKE'S HOSPITAL, ORWIGSBURG, PA, p. A547
GEISINGER WYOMING VALLEY MEDICAL CENTER, WILKES BARRE, PA, p. A557
GEISINGER–BLOOMSBURG HOSPITAL, BLOOMSBURG, PA, p. A535
GENERAL HOSPITAL, CHARLESTON, WV, p. A700
GENERAL LEONARD WOOD ARMY COMMUNITY HOSPITAL, FORT LEONARD WOOD, MO, p. A375
GENESEE MEMORIAL HOSPITAL, BATAVIA, NY, p. A438
GENESIS BEHAVIORAL HOSPITAL, BREAUX BRIDGE, LA, p. A279
GENESIS HEALTHCARE SYSTEM, ZANESVILLE, OH, p. A508
GENESIS MEDICAL CENTER – DAVENPORT, DAVENPORT, IA, p. A234
GENESIS MEDICAL CENTER-ALEDO, ALEDO, IL, p. A185
GENESIS MEDICAL CENTER, DEWITT, DE WITT, IA, p. A234
GENESIS MEDICAL CENTER, SILVIS, SILVIS, IL, p. A208
GENEVA GENERAL HOSPITAL, GENEVA, NY, p. A443
GENOA MEDICAL FACILITIES, GENOA, NE, p. A400
GEORGE AND MARIE BACKUS CHILDREN'S HOSPITAL, SAVANNAH, GA, p. A171
GEORGE C. GRAPE COMMUNITY HOSPITAL, HAMBURG, IA, p. A237
GEORGE E. WAHLEN DEPARTMENT OF VETERANS AFFAIRS MEDICAL CENTER, SALT LAKE CITY, UT, p. A668
GEORGE E. WEEMS MEMORIAL HOSPITAL, APALACHICOLA, FL, p. A125

© 2025 AHA Guide

Index of Hospitals / George L. Mee Memorial Hospital

GEORGE L. MEE MEMORIAL HOSPITAL, KING CITY, CA, p. A68
GEORGE REGIONAL HOSPITAL, LUCEDALE, MS, p. A365
GEORGE WASHINGTON UNIVERSITY HOSPITAL, WASHINGTON, DC, p. A123
GEORGETOWN BEHAVIORAL HEALTH INSTITUTE, GEORGETOWN, TX, p. A622
GEORGETOWN COMMUNITY HOSPITAL, GEORGETOWN, KY, p. A266
GEORGETOWN HEALTHCARE SYSTEM, GEORGETOWN, TX, p. A622
GEORGIA REGIONAL HOSPITAL AT ATLANTA, DECATUR, GA, p. A162
GEORGIA REGIONAL HOSPITAL AT SAVANNAH, SAVANNAH, GA, p. A171
GERALD CHAMPION REGIONAL MEDICAL CENTER, ALAMOGORDO, NM, p. A432
GIBSON AREA HOSPITAL AND HEALTH SERVICES, GIBSON CITY, IL, p. A196
GIFFORD MEDICAL CENTER, RANDOLPH, VT, p. A672
GILA REGIONAL MEDICAL CENTER, SILVER CITY, NM, p. A437
GILLETTE CHILDREN'S SPECIALTY HEALTHCARE, SAINT PAUL, MN, p. A354
GIRARD MEDICAL CENTER, GIRARD, KS, p. A249
GLACIAL RIDGE HEALTH SYSTEM, GLENWOOD, MN, p. A347
GLACIER VIEW HOSPITAL, KALISPELL, MT, p. A393
GLEN COVE HOSPITAL, GLEN COVE, NY, p. A443
GLEN OAKS HOSPITAL, GREENVILLE, TX, p. A623
GLEN ROSE MEDICAL CENTER, GLEN ROSE, TX, p. A622
GLENBEIGH HOSPITAL AND OUTPATIENT CENTERS, ROCK CREEK, OH, p. A503
GLENCOE REGIONAL HEALTH, GLENCOE, MN, p. A347
GLENDALE MEMORIAL HOSPITAL AND HEALTH CENTER, GLENDALE, CA, p. A66
GLENDIVE MEDICAL CENTER, GLENDIVE, MT, p. A392
GLENDORA HOSPITAL, GLENDORA, CA, p. A66
GLENDORA OAKS BEHAVIORAL HEALTH HOSPITAL, GLENDORA, CA, p. A66
GLENMORE FOUNDATION, CROOKSTON, MN, p. A345
GLENN MEDICAL CENTER, WILLOWS, CA, p. A101
GLENS FALLS HOSPITAL, GLENS FALLS, NY, p. A443
GLENWOOD REGIONAL MEDICAL CENTER, WEST MONROE, LA, p. A294
GLOBALREHAB HOSPITAL – SAN ANTONIO, SAN ANTONIO, TX, p. A649
GOLDEN PLAINS COMMUNITY HOSPITAL, BORGER, TX, p. A604
GOLDEN VALLEY MEMORIAL HEALTHCARE, CLINTON, MO, p. A373
GOLDWATER MEMORIAL HOSPITAL, NEW YORK, NY, p. A448
GOLETA VALLEY COTTAGE HOSPITAL, SANTA BARBARA, CA, p. A94
GOLISANO CHILDREN'S HOSPITAL OF SOUTHWEST FLORIDA, FORT MYERS, FL, p. A131
GONZALES HEALTHCARE SYSTEMS, GONZALES, TX, p. A622
GOOD SAMARITAN HOSPITAL – SAN JOSE, SAN JOSE, CA, p. A92
GOOD SAMARITAN HOSPITAL, BAKERSFIELD, CA, p. A57
GOOD SAMARITAN HOSPITAL, CINCINNATI, OH, p. A489
GOOD SAMARITAN HOSPITAL, MERRILL, WI, p. A716
GOOD SAMARITAN HOSPITAL, VINCENNES, IN, p. A228
GOOD SAMARITAN HOSPITAL AND MEDICAL CENTER, PORTLAND, OR, p. A530
GOOD SAMARITAN HOSPITAL MEDICAL CENTER, WEST ISLIP, NY, p. A461
GOOD SAMARITAN MEDICAL CENTER, BROCKTON, MA, p. A311
GOOD SAMARITAN MEDICAL CENTER, LAFAYETTE, CO, p. A110
GOOD SAMARITAN MEDICAL CENTER, WEST PALM BEACH, FL, p. A154
GOOD SAMARITAN REGIONAL MEDICAL CENTER, CORVALLIS, OR, p. A526
GOOD SAMARITAN REGIONAL MEDICAL CENTER, SUFFERN, NY, p. A459
GOOD SHEPHERD HEALTH CARE SYSTEM, HERMISTON, OR, p. A527
GOOD SHEPHERD MEDICAL CENTER, LONGVIEW, TX, p. A635
GOOD SHEPHERD PENN PARTNERS, PHILADELPHIA, PA, p. A548
GOOD SHEPHERD REHABILITATION NETWORK, ALLENTOWN, PA, p. A534
GOOD SHEPHERD SPECIALTY HOSPITAL, BETHLEHEM, PA, p. A535
GOODALL–WITCHER HOSPITAL, CLIFTON, TX, p. A607
GOODLAND REGIONAL MEDICAL CENTER, GOODLAND, KS, p. A250
GORDON MEMORIAL HEALTH SERVICES, GORDON, NE, p. A400

GOSHEN HEALTH, GOSHEN, IN, p. A217
GOTHENBURG HEALTH, GOTHENBURG, NE, p. A400
GOTTLIEB MEMORIAL HOSPITAL, MELROSE PARK, IL, p. A201
GOUVERNEUR HOSPITAL, GOUVERNEUR, NY, p. A443
GOUVERNEUR HOSPITAL, NEW YORK, NY, p. A448
GOVE COUNTY MEDICAL CENTER, QUINTER, KS, p. A258
GOVERNOR JUAN F. LUIS HOSPITAL, CHRISTIANSTED, VI, p. A736
GRACE COTTAGE HOSPITAL, TOWNSHEND, VT, p. A672
GRACE HOSPITAL, CLEVELAND, OH, p. A490
GRACE MEDICAL CENTER, LUBBOCK, TX, p. A636
GRACE SURGICAL HOSPITAL, LUBBOCK, TX, p. A636
GRACIE SQUARE HOSPITAL, NEW YORK, NY, p. A448
GRADY HEALTH SYSTEM, ATLANTA, GA, p. A157
GRADY MEMORIAL HOSPITAL, ATLANTA, GA, p. A157
GRADY MEMORIAL HOSPITAL, CHICKASHA, OK, p. A511
GRAFTON CITY HOSPITAL, GRAFTON, WV, p. A701
GRAHAM COUNTY HOSPITAL, HILL CITY, KS, p. A250
GRAHAM HOSPITAL, CANTON, IL, p. A187
GRAHAM HOSPITAL ASSOCIATION, CANTON, IL, p. A187
GRAHAM REGIONAL MEDICAL CENTER, GRAHAM, TX, p. A622
GRAND ISLAND REGIONAL MEDICAL CENTER, GRAND ISLAND, NE, p. A400
GRAND ITASCA CLINIC AND HOSPITAL, GRAND RAPIDS, MN, p. A347
GRAND JUNCTION VA MEDICAL CENTER, GRAND JUNCTION, CO, p. A108
GRAND LAKE HEALTH SYSTEM, SAINT MARYS, OH, p. A503
GRAND RIVER HOSPITAL DISTRICT, RIFLE, CO, p. A113
GRAND STRAND MEDICAL CENTER, MYRTLE BEACH, SC, p. A569
GRAND VALLEY NURSING CENTRE, GRAND RAPIDS, MI, p. A328
GRAND VIEW HEALTH, SELLERSVILLE, PA, p. A554
GRANDE RONDE HOSPITAL, LA GRANDE, OR, p. A528
GRANDVIEW MEDICAL CENTER, BIRMINGHAM, AL, p. A16
GRANDVIEW MEDICAL CENTER, JASPER, TN, p. A584
GRANITE COUNTY MEDICAL CENTER, PHILIPSBURG, MT, p. A394
GRANITE HILLS HOSPITAL, WEST ALLIS, WI, p. A724
GRANT–BLACKFORD MENTAL HEALTH CENTER, MARION, IN, p. A223
GRANT MEMORIAL HOSPITAL, PETERSBURG, WV, p. A703
GRANT REGIONAL HEALTH CENTER, LANCASTER, WI, p. A714
GRANVILLE HEALTH SYSTEM, OXFORD, NC, p. A474
GRAYS HARBOR COMMUNITY HOSPITAL, ABERDEEN, WA, p. A687
GREAT FALLS CLINIC HOSPITAL, GREAT FALLS, MT, p. A392
GREAT PLAINS HEALTH, NORTH PLATTE, NE, p. A403
GREAT PLAINS REGIONAL MEDICAL CENTER, ELK CITY, OK, p. A512
GREAT RIVER MEDICAL CENTER, BLYTHEVILLE, AR, p. A43
GREAT RIVER MEDICAL CENTER, WEST BURLINGTON, IA, p. A245
GREATER BALTIMORE MEDICAL CENTER, BALTIMORE, MD, p. A302
GREATER BINGHAMTON HEALTH CENTER, BINGHAMTON, NY, p. A439
GREATER EL MONTE COMMUNITY HOSPITAL, SOUTH EL MONTE, CA, p. A96
GREATER LOS ANGELES HCS, LOS ANGELES, CA, p. A72
GREATER REGIONAL HEALTH, CRESTON, IA, p. A234
GREELEY COUNTY HEALTH SERVICES, TRIBUNE, KS, p. A261
GREENE COUNTY GENERAL HOSPITAL, LINTON, IN, p. A222
GREENE COUNTY HEALTH SYSTEM, EUTAW, AL, p. A19
GREENE COUNTY HOSPITAL, LEAKESVILLE, MS, p. A365
GREENE COUNTY MEDICAL CENTER, JEFFERSON, IA, p. A238
GREENEVILLE COMMUNITY HOSPITAL EAST, GREENEVILLE, TN, p. A583
GREENLEAF BEHAVIORAL HEALTH HOSPITAL, VALDOSTA, GA, p. A173
GREENSBORO HOSPITAL, GREENSBORO, NC, p. A469
GREENVILLE REGIONAL HOSPITAL, GREENVILLE, PA, p. A541
GREENWICH HOSPITAL, GREENWICH, CT, p. A116
GREENWOOD COUNTY HOSPITAL, EUREKA, KS, p. A249
GREENWOOD LEFLORE HOSPITAL, GREENWOOD, MS, p. A362
GREENWOOD REGIONAL REHABILITATION HOSPITAL, GREENWOOD, SC, p. A567
GREYSTONE PARK PSYCHIATRIC HOSPITAL, MORRIS PLAINS, NJ, p. A424
GRIFFIN HEALTH, DERBY, CT, p. A115
GRIFFIN MEMORIAL HOSPITAL, NORMAN, OK, p. A516
GRISELL MEMORIAL HOSPITAL DISTRICT ONE, RANSOM, KS, p. A258
GRITMAN MEDICAL CENTER, MOSCOW, ID, p. A182

GROTTA CENTER FOR SENIOR CARE, WEST ORANGE, NJ, p. A430
GROVE CREEK MEDICAL CENTER, BLACKFOOT, ID, p. A179
GROVE HILL MEMORIAL HOSPITAL, GROVE HILL, AL, p. A20
GROVER C. DILS MEDICAL CENTER, CALIENTE, NV, p. A408
GRUNDY COUNTY MEMORIAL HOSPITAL, GRUNDY CENTER, IA, p. A236
GUADALUPE COUNTY HOSPITAL, SANTA ROSA, NM, p. A437
GUADALUPE REGIONAL MEDICAL CENTER, SEGUIN, TX, p. A652
GUAM MEMORIAL HOSPITAL AUTHORITY, TAMUNING, GU, p. A730
GUAM REGIONAL MEDICAL CITY, DEDEDO, GU, p. A730
GUIDANCE CENTER, FLAGSTAFF, AZ, p. A31
GULF BREEZE HOSPITAL, GULF BREEZE, FL, p. A133
GULF COAST HCS, BILOXI, MS, p. A359
GULF COAST MEDICAL CENTER, FORT MYERS, FL, p. A131
GULF COAST REGIONAL MEDICAL CENTER, PANAMA CITY, FL, p. A146
GULFPORT BEHAVIORAL HEALTH SYSTEM, GULFPORT, MS, p. A362
GUMMERVILLE MEDICAL CENTER, SUMMERVILLE, SC, p. A570
GUNDERSEN BOSCOBEL AREA HOSPITAL AND CLINICS, BOSCOBEL, WI, p. A708
GUNDERSEN LUTHERAN MEDICAL CENTER, LA CROSSE, WI, p. A713
GUNDERSEN MOUNDVIEW HOSPITAL & CLINICS, FRIENDSHIP, WI, p. A711
GUNDERSEN PALMER LUTHERAN HOSPITAL AND CLINICS, WEST UNION, IA, p. A245
GUNDERSEN SAINT ELIZABETH'S HOSPITAL & CLINICS, WABASHA, MN, p. A356
GUNDERSEN ST. JOSEPH'S HOSPITAL AND CLINICS, HILLSBORO, WI, p. A713
GUNDERSEN TRI–COUNTY HOSPITAL AND CLINICS, WHITEHALL, WI, p. A725
GUNNISON VALLEY HEALTH, GUNNISON, CO, p. A109
GUNNISON VALLEY HOSPITAL, GUNNISON, CO, p. A109
GUNNISON VALLEY HOSPITAL, GUNNISON, UT, p. A665
GUTHRIE CORNING HOSPITAL, CORNING, NY, p. A441
GUTHRIE CORTLAND REGIONAL MEDICAL CENTER, CORTLAND, NY, p. A441
GUTHRIE COUNTY HOSPITAL, GUTHRIE CENTER, IA, p. A237
GUTHRIE LOURDES HOSPITAL, BINGHAMTON, NY, p. A439
GUTHRIE ROBERT PACKER HOSPITAL, SAYRE, PA, p. A554
GUTHRIE TROY COMMUNITY HOSPITAL, TROY, PA, p. A556
GUTTENBERG MUNICIPAL HOSPITAL AND CLINICS, GUTTENBERG, IA, p. A237
G.V. (SONNY) MONTGOMERY DEPARTMENT OF VETERANS AFFAIRS MEDICAL CENTER, JACKSON, MS, p. A364
G. WERBER BRYAN PSYCHIATRIC HOSPITAL, COLUMBIA, SC, p. A564
GWINNETT MEDICAL CENTER–DULUTH, DULUTH, GA, p. A163

H

HACKENSACK MERIDIAN HEALTH BAYSHORE COMMUNITY HOSPITAL, HOLMDEL, NJ, p. A422
HACKENSACK MERIDIAN HEALTH CARRIER CLINIC, BELLE MEAD, NJ, p. A418
HACKENSACK MERIDIAN HEALTH HACKENSACK UNIVERSITY MEDICAL CENTER, HACKENSACK, NJ, p. A421
HACKENSACK MERIDIAN HEALTH JERSEY SHORE UNIVERSITY MEDICAL CENTER, NEPTUNE, NJ, p. A424
HACKENSACK MERIDIAN HEALTH JFK MEDICAL CENTER, EDISON, NJ, p. A420
HACKENSACK MERIDIAN HEALTH OCEAN UNIVERSITY MEDICAL CENTER, BRICK TOWNSHIP, NJ, p. A419
HACKENSACK MERIDIAN HEALTH PALISADES MEDICAL CENTER, NORTH BERGEN, NJ, p. A426
HACKENSACK MERIDIAN HEALTH PASCACK VALLEY MEDICAL CENTER, WESTWOOD, NJ, p. A430
HACKENSACK MERIDIAN HEALTH RARITAN BAY MEDICAL CENTER, PERTH AMBOY, NJ, p. A427
HACKENSACK MERIDIAN HEALTH RIVERVIEW MEDICAL CENTER, RED BANK, NJ, p. A428
HACKENSACK MERIDIAN HEALTH SHORE REHABILITATION INSTITUTE, BRICK, NJ, p. A418
HACKENSACK MERIDIAN HEALTH SOUTHERN OCEAN MEDICAL CENTER, MANAHAWKIN, NJ, p. A423
HACKENSACK MERIDIAN MOUNTAINSIDE MEDICAL CENTER, MONTCLAIR, NJ, p. A424

HACKETTSTOWN MEDICAL CENTER, HACKETTSTOWN, NJ, p. A421
HALE COUNTY HOSPITAL, GREENSBORO, AL, p. A20
HALE HO'OLA HAMAKUA, HONOKAA, HI, p. A175
HALE MAKUA, KAHULUI, HI, p. A176
HALIFAX BEHAVIORAL CENTER, DAYTONA BEACH, FL, p. A129
HALIFAX HEALTH MEDICAL CENTER OF DAYTONA BEACH, DAYTONA BEACH, FL, p. A130
HALIFAX HEALTH/UF HEALTH MEDICAL CENTER OF DELTONA, DELTONA, FL, p. A130
HALIFAX HOSPITAL PORT ORANGE, PORT ORANGE, FL, p. A147
HALL–BROOKE HOSPITAL, A DIVISION OF HALL–BROOKE BEHAVIORAL HEALTH SERVICES, WESTPORT, CT, p. A120
HAMILTON CENTER, TERRE HAUTE, IN, p. A228
HAMILTON COUNTY HOSPITAL, SYRACUSE, KS, p. A260
HAMILTON GENERAL HOSPITAL, HAMILTON, TX, p. A623
HAMILTON HOSPITAL, OLNEY, TX, p. A642
HAMILTON MEDICAL CENTER, DALTON, GA, p. A162
HAMILTON MEMORIAL HOSPITAL DISTRICT, MCLEANSBORO, IL, p. A201
HAMMOND–HENRY HOSPITAL, GENESEO, IL, p. A196
HAMPSTEAD HOSPITAL & RESIDENTIAL TREATMENT FACILITY, HAMPSTEAD, NH, p. A415
HAMPTON BEHAVIORAL HEALTH CENTER, WESTAMPTON, NJ, p. A430
HAMPTON REGIONAL MEDICAL CENTER, VARNVILLE, SC, p. A571
HAMPTON VETERANS AFFAIRS MEDICAL CENTER, HAMPTON, VA, p. A677
HANCOCK COUNTY HEALTH SYSTEM, BRITT, IA, p. A231
HANCOCK COUNTY HOSPITAL, SNEEDVILLE, TN, p. A593
HANCOCK REGIONAL HOSPITAL, GREENFIELD, IN, p. A218
HANNA HOUSE, CLEVELAND, OH, p. A491
HANNIBAL REGIONAL HOSPITAL, HANNIBAL, MO, p. A376
HANOVER HOSPITAL, HANOVER, KS, p. A250
HANSEN FAMILY HOSPITAL, IOWA FALLS, IA, p. A238
HANSFORD HOSPITAL, SPEARMAN, TX, p. A653
HARBOR BEACH COMMUNITY HOSPITAL, HARBOR BEACH, MI, p. A329
HARBOR BEACH COMMUNITY HOSPITAL INC., HARBOR BEACH, MI, p. A329
HARBOR OAKS HOSPITAL, NEW BALTIMORE, MI, p. A334
HARBOR REGIONAL HEALTH, ABERDEEN, WA, p. A687
HARBOR–UCLA MEDICAL CENTER, TORRANCE, CA, p. A98
HARBOUR SHORES OF LAWNWOOD, FORT PIERCE, FL, p. A132
HARDEMAN COUNTY MEMORIAL HOSPITAL, QUANAH, TX, p. A646
HARDIN COUNTY GENERAL HOSPITAL, ROSICLARE, IL, p. A208
HARDIN MEDICAL CENTER, SAVANNAH, TN, p. A592
HARDTNER MEDICAL CENTER, OLLA, LA, p. A291
HARLAN ARH HOSPITAL, HARLAN, KY, p. A266
HARLAN COUNTY HEALTH SYSTEM, ALMA, NE, p. A397
HARLINGEN MEDICAL CENTER, HARLINGEN, TX, p. A623
HARMON MEDICAL AND REHABILITATION HOSPITAL, LAS VEGAS, NV, p. A410
HARMON MEMORIAL HOSPITAL, HOLLIS, OK, p. A513
HARNETT HEALTH SYSTEM, DUNN, NC, p. A467
HARNEY DISTRICT HOSPITAL, BURNS, OR, p. A526
HARPER COUNTY COMMUNITY HOSPITAL, BUFFALO, OK, p. A510
HARRINGTON HOSPITAL, SOUTHBRIDGE, MA, p. A318
HARRIS HEALTH SYSTEM, BELLAIRE, TX, p. A603
HARRIS REGIONAL HOSPITAL, SYLVA, NC, p. A477
HARRISBURG MEDICAL CENTER, HARRISBURG, IL, p. A197
HARRISON COUNTY COMMUNITY HOSPITAL, BETHANY, MO, p. A371
HARRISON COUNTY HOSPITAL, CORYDON, IN, p. A214
HARRISON MEMORIAL HOSPITAL, CYNTHIANA, KY, p. A264
HARRY S. TRUMAN MEMORIAL VETERANS' HOSPITAL, COLUMBIA, MO, p. A374
HARSHA BEHAVIORAL CENTER, TERRE HAUTE, IN, p. A228
HARTFORD HOSPITAL, HARTFORD, CT, p. A116
HARTGROVE BEHAVIORAL HEALTH SYSTEM, CHICAGO, IL, p. A189
HARTGROVE HOSPITAL, CHICAGO, IL, p. A189
HASKELL MEMORIAL HOSPITAL, HASKELL, TX, p. A624
HASKELL REGIONAL HOSPITAL, STIGLER, OK, p. A521
HAVASU REGIONAL MEDICAL CENTER, LAKE HAVASU CITY, AZ, p. A32
HAVEN BEHAVIORAL HOSPITAL OF DAYTON, DAYTON, OH, p. A493
HAVEN BEHAVIORAL HOSPITAL OF EASTERN PENNSYLVANIA, READING, PA, p. A553
HAVEN BEHAVIORAL HOSPITAL OF PHILADELPHIA, PHILADELPHIA, PA, p. A548
HAVEN BEHAVIORAL HOSPITAL OF PHOENIX, PHOENIX, AZ, p. A35

HAVEN BEHAVIORAL SENIOR CARE OF ALBUQUERQUE, ALBUQUERQUE, NM, p. A432
HAVEN BEHAVIORAL SENIOR CARE OF DAYTON, DAYTON, OH, p. A493
HAVENWYCK HOSPITAL, AUBURN HILLS, MI, p. A321
HAVENWYCK HOSPITAL, INC., AUBURN HILLS, MI, p. A322
HAWAII MEDICAL CENTER–WEST, EWA BEACH, HI, p. A175
HAWAII STATE HOSPITAL, KANEOHE, HI, p. A177
HAWARDEN REGIONAL HEALTHCARE, HAWARDEN, IA, p. A237
HAWKINS COUNTY MEMORIAL HOSPITAL, ROGERSVILLE, TN, p. A592
HAWTHORN CENTER, NORTHVILLE, MI, p. A334
HAWTHORN CHILDREN PSYCHIATRIC HOSPITAL, SAINT LOUIS, MO, p. A385
HAXTUN HOSPITAL DISTRICT, HAXTUN, CO, p. A109
HAYS MEDICAL CENTER, HAYS, KS, p. A250
HAYWOOD REGIONAL MEDICAL CENTER, CLYDE, NC, p. A466
HAZARD ARH REGIONAL MEDICAL CENTER, HAZARD, KY, p. A267
HAZEL HAWKINS MEMORIAL HOSPITAL, HOLLISTER, CA, p. A67
H. C. WATKINS MEMORIAL HOSPITAL, QUITMAN, MS, p. A368
HCA CHIPPENHAM MEDICAL CENTER, RICHMOND, VA, p. A683
HCA FLORIDA AVENTURA HOSPITAL, AVENTURA, FL, p. A125
HCA FLORIDA BAYONET POINT HOSPITAL, HUDSON, FL, p. A134
HCA FLORIDA BLAKE HOSPITAL, BRADENTON, FL, p. A126
HCA FLORIDA BRANDON HOSPITAL, BRANDON, FL, p. A127
HCA FLORIDA CAPITAL HOSPITAL, TALLAHASSEE, FL, p. A151
HCA FLORIDA CITRUS HOSPITAL, INVERNESS, FL, p. A134
HCA FLORIDA ENGLEWOOD HOSPITAL, ENGLEWOOD, FL, p. A131
HCA FLORIDA FAWCETT HOSPITAL, PORT CHARLOTTE, FL, p. A147
HCA FLORIDA FORT WALTON–DESTIN HOSPITAL, FORT WALTON BEACH, FL, p. A132
HCA FLORIDA GULF COAST HOSPITAL, PANAMA CITY, FL, p. A146
HCA FLORIDA HIGHLANDS HOSPITAL, SEBRING, FL, p. A150
HCA FLORIDA JFK HOSPITAL, ATLANTIS, FL, p. A125
HCA FLORIDA KENDALL HOSPITAL, MIAMI, FL, p. A139
HCA FLORIDA LAKE CITY HOSPITAL, LAKE CITY, FL, p. A136
HCA FLORIDA LAKE MONROE HOSPITAL, SANFORD, FL, p. A149
HCA FLORIDA LARGO HOSPITAL, LARGO, FL, p. A137
HCA FLORIDA LAWNWOOD HOSPITAL, FORT PIERCE, FL, p. A132
HCA FLORIDA MEMORIAL HOSPITAL, JACKSONVILLE, FL, p. A134
HCA FLORIDA MERCY HOSPITAL, MIAMI, FL, p. A140
HCA FLORIDA NORTH FLORIDA HOSPITAL, GAINESVILLE, FL, p. A132
HCA FLORIDA NORTHSIDE HOSPITAL, SAINT PETERSBURG, FL, p. A149
HCA FLORIDA NORTHWEST HOSPITAL, MARGATE, FL, p. A138
HCA FLORIDA OAK HILL HOSPITAL, BROOKSVILLE, FL, p. A127
HCA FLORIDA OCALA HOSPITAL, OCALA, FL, p. A143
HCA FLORIDA ORANGE PARK HOSPITAL, ORANGE PARK, FL, p. A144
HCA FLORIDA OSCEOLA HOSPITAL, KISSIMMEE, FL, p. A136
HCA FLORIDA PALMS WEST HOSPITAL, LOXAHATCHEE, FL, p. A138
HCA FLORIDA PASADENA HOSPITAL, SAINT PETERSBURG, FL, p. A149
HCA FLORIDA POINCIANA HOSPITAL, KISSIMMEE, FL, p. A136
HCA FLORIDA PUTNAM HOSPITAL, PALATKA, FL, p. A145
HCA FLORIDA RAULERSON HOSPITAL, OKEECHOBEE, FL, p. A143
HCA FLORIDA SARASOTA DOCTORS HOSPITAL, SARASOTA, FL, p. A149
HCA FLORIDA SOUTH SHORE HOSPITAL, SUN CITY CENTER, FL, p. A151
HCA FLORIDA ST. LUCIE HOSPITAL, PORT ST LUCIE, FL, p. A147
HCA FLORIDA ST. PETERSBURG HOSPITAL, SAINT PETERSBURG, FL, p. A149
HCA FLORIDA TRINITY HOSPITAL, TRINITY, FL, p. A153
HCA FLORIDA TWIN CITIES HOSPITAL, NICEVILLE, FL, p. A142
HCA FLORIDA UNIVERSITY HOSPITAL, DAVIE, FL, p. A129
HCA FLORIDA WEST HOSPITAL, PENSACOLA, FL, p. A146
HCA FLORIDA WEST TAMPA HOSPITAL, TAMPA, FL, p. A152

HCA FLORIDA WESTSIDE HOSPITAL, PLANTATION, FL, p. A147
HCA FLORIDA WOODMONT HOSPITAL, TAMARAC, FL, p. A151
HCA FORT WALTON–DESTIN HOSPITAL, FORT WALTON BEACH, FL, p. A132
HCA HOUSTON HEALTHCARE CLEAR LAKE, WEBSTER, TX, p. A661
HCA HOUSTON HEALTHCARE CONROE, CONROE, TX, p. A608
HCA HOUSTON HEALTHCARE KINGWOOD, KINGWOOD, TX, p. A633
HCA HOUSTON HEALTHCARE MEDICAL CENTER, HOUSTON, TX, p. A625
HCA HOUSTON HEALTHCARE NORTHWEST, HOUSTON, TX, p. A626
HCA HOUSTON HEALTHCARE PEARLAND, PEARLAND, TX, p. A643
HCA HOUSTON HEALTHCARE SOUTHEAST, PASADENA, TX, p. A643
HCA HOUSTON HEALTHCARE TOMBALL, TOMBALL, TX, p. A658
HCA HOUSTON HEALTHCARE WEST, HOUSTON, TX, p. A626
HCA JOHNSTON–WILLIS HOSPITAL, NORTH CHESTERFIELD, VA, p. A680
HEALDSBURG DISTRICT HOSPITAL, HEALDSBURG, CA, p. A67
HEALDSBURG HOSPITAL, HEALDSBURG, CA, p. A67
HEALTH ALLIANCE HOSPITAL – BROADWAY CAMPUS, KINGSTON, NY, p. A445
HEALTH ALLIANCE HOSPITAL – MARY'S AVENUE CAMPUS, KINGSTON, NY, p. A445
HEALTH FIRST CAPE CANAVERAL HOSPITAL, COCOA BEACH, FL, p. A128
HEALTH FIRST HOLMES REGIONAL MEDICAL CENTER, MELBOURNE, FL, p. A139
HEALTH FIRST PALM BAY HOSPITAL, PALM BAY, FL, p. A145
HEALTH FIRST VIERA HOSPITAL, MELBOURNE, FL, p. A139
HEALTHBRIDGE CHILDREN'S HOSPITAL, ORANGE, CA, p. A81
HEALTHPARTNERS OLIVIA HOSPITAL & CLINIC, OLIVIA, MN, p. A352
HEALTHSOURCE SAGINAW INC., SAGINAW, MI, p. A337
HEALTHSOURCE SAGINAW, INC., SAGINAW, MI, p. A337
HEALTHSOUTH MEDICAL CENTER, BIRMINGHAM, AL, p. A16
HEALTHSOUTH MEDICAL CENTER, RICHMOND, VA, p. A682
HEALTHSOUTH REHABILITATION HOSPITAL OF CINCINNATI AT NORWOOD, CINCINNATI, OH, p. A489
HEALTHSOUTH REHABILITATION HOSPITAL OF DAYTON, DAYTON, OH, p. A493
HEART HOSPITAL OF LAFAYETTE, LAFAYETTE, LA, p. A285
HEART OF AMERICA MEDICAL CENTER, RUGBY, ND, p. A483
HEART OF TEXAS HEALTHCARE SYSTEM, BRADY, TX, p. A604
HEART OF TEXAS MEMORIAL HOSPITAL, BRADY, TX, p. A604
HEART OF THE ROCKIES REGIONAL MEDICAL CENTER, SALIDA, CO, p. A113
HEARTLAND BEHAVIORAL HEALTH SERVICES, NEVADA, MO, p. A381
HEARTLAND BEHAVIORAL HEALTHCARE, MASSILLON, OH, p. A499
HEARTLAND SURGICAL SPECIALTY HOSPITAL, OVERLAND PARK, KS, p. A257
HEBER VALLEY HOSPITAL, HEBER CITY, UT, p. A665
HEBREW HOME FOR AGED–RIVERDALE, NEW YORK, NY, p. A448
HEBREW HOSP FOR CHRONIC SICK, NEW YORK, NY, p. A448
HEBREW REHABILITATION CENTER, ROSLINDALE, MA, p. A317
HEDRICK MEDICAL CENTER, CHILLICOTHE, MO, p. A373
HEGG HEALTH CENTER AVERA, ROCK VALLEY, IA, p. A242
HELEN DEVOS CHILDREN'S HOSPITAL, GRAND RAPIDS, MI, p. A328
HELEN HAYES HOSPITAL, WEST HAVERSTRAW, NY, p. A461
HELEN KELLER HOSPITAL, SHEFFIELD, AL, p. A24
HELEN M. SIMPSON REHABILITATION HOSPITAL, HARRISBURG, PA, p. A541
HELEN NEWBERRY JOY HOSPITAL & HEALTHCARE CENTER, NEWBERRY, MI, p. A334
HELENA REGIONAL MEDICAL CENTER, HELENA, AR, p. A47
HEMET GLOBAL MEDICAL CENTER, HEMET, CA, p. A67
HEMPHILL COUNTY HOSPITAL DISTRICT, CANADIAN, TX, p. A606
HENDERSON COUNTY COMMUNITY HOSPITAL, LEXINGTON, TN, p. A587
HENDERSON HEALTH CARE SERVICES, HENDERSON, NE, p. A401
HENDERSON HOSPITAL, HENDERSON, NV, p. A409
HENDRICK MEDICAL CENTER, ABILENE, TX, p. A595
HENDRICK MEDICAL CENTER BROWNWOOD, BROWNWOOD, TX, p. A605

Index of Hospitals / Hendricks Community Hospital Association

HENDRICKS COMMUNITY HOSPITAL ASSOCIATION, HENDRICKS, MN, p. A348
HENDRICKS REGIONAL HEALTH, DANVILLE, IN, p. A215
HENDRY REGIONAL MEDICAL CENTER, CLEWISTON, FL, p. A128
HENNEPIN HEALTHCARE, MINNEAPOLIS, MN, p. A350
HENRICO DOCTOR'S HOSPITAL, RICHMOND, VA, p. A682
HENRICO DOCTORS' HOSPITAL, RICHMOND, VA, p. A682
HENRY COMMUNITY HEALTH, NEW CASTLE, IN, p. A225
HENRY COUNTY HEALTH CENTER, MOUNT PLEASANT, IA, p. A240
HENRY COUNTY HOSPITAL, NAPOLEON, OH, p. A501
HENRY COUNTY MEDICAL CENTER, PARIS, TN, p. A592
HENRY FORD HOSPITAL, DETROIT, MI, p. A325
HENRY FORD JACKSON HOSPITAL, JACKSON, MI, p. A331
HENRY FORD KINGSWOOD HOSPITAL, FERNDALE, MI, p. A326
HENRY FORD MACOMB HOSPITAL, CLINTON TOWNSHIP, MI, p. A324
HENRY FORD WEST BLOOMFIELD HOSPITAL, WEST BLOOMFIELD, MI, p. A340
HENRY FORD WYANDOTTE HOSPITAL, WYANDOTTE, MI, p. A341
HENRY J. CARTER SPECIALTY HOSPITAL & NURSING FACILITY, NEW YORK, NY, p. A448
HENRY MAYO NEWHALL HOSPITAL, VALENCIA, CA, p. A99
HEREFORD REGIONAL MEDICAL CENTER, HEREFORD, TX, p. A624
HERITAGE OAKS HOSPITAL, SACRAMENTO, CA, p. A86
HERITAGE VALLEY BEAVER, BEAVER, PA, p. A535
HERITAGE VALLEY KENNEDY, MCKEES ROCKS, PA, p. A545
HERMANN AREA DISTRICT HOSPITAL, HERMANN, MO, p. A376
HERRICK HOSPITAL & HLTH CENTER, BERKELEY, CA, p. A57
HERRIN HOSPITAL, HERRIN, IL, p. A197
HEYWOOD HOSPITAL, GARDNER, MA, p. A314
HI-DESERT MEDICAL CENTER, JOSHUA TREE, CA, p. A68
HIALEAH HOSPITAL, HIALEAH, FL, p. A133
HIAWATHA COMMUNITY HOSPITAL, HIAWATHA, KS, p. A250
HICKORY TRAIL HOSPITAL, DESOTO, TX, p. A614
HIGGINS GENERAL HOSPITAL, BREMEN, GA, p. A159
HIGHLAND COMMUNITY HOSPITAL, PICAYUNE, MS, p. A368
HIGHLAND DISTRICT HOSPITAL, HILLSBORO, OH, p. A497
HIGHLAND HILLS MEDICAL CENTER, SENATOBIA, MS, p. A369
HIGHLAND HOSPITAL, CHARLESTON, WV, p. A700
HIGHLAND HOSPITAL, OAKLAND, CA, p. A80
HIGHLAND HOSPITAL, ROCHESTER, NY, p. A457
HIGHLAND PARK HOSPITAL, MIAMI, FL, p. A140
HIGHLAND SPRINGS HOSPITAL, HIGHLAND HILLS, OH, p. A497
HIGHLAND–CLARKSBURG HOSPITAL, CLARKSBURG, WV, p. A700
HIGHLANDS ARH REGIONAL MEDICAL CENTER, PRESTONSBURG, KY, p. A273
HIGHLANDS BEHAVIORAL HEALTH SYSTEM, LITTLETON, CO, p. A111
HIGHLANDS HOSPITAL, CONNELLSVILLE, PA, p. A537
HIGHLANDS MEDICAL CENTER, SCOTTSBORO, AL, p. A24
HIGHLANDS–CASHIERS HOSPITAL, HIGHLANDS, NC, p. A470
HIGHSMITH–RAINEY SPECIALTY HOSPITAL, FAYETTEVILLE, NC, p. A468
HILL COUNTRY MEMORIAL HOSPITAL, FREDERICKSBURG, TX, p. A620
HILL CREST BEHAVIORAL HEALTH SERVICES, BIRMINGHAM, AL, p. A17
HILL HOSPITAL OF SUMTER COUNTY, YORK, AL, p. A26
HILL REGIONAL HOSPITAL, HILLSBORO, TX, p. A624
HILLCREST HOSPITAL, CLEVELAND, OH, p. A491
HILLCREST HOSPITAL CLAREMORE, CLAREMORE, OK, p. A511
HILLCREST HOSPITAL CUSHING, CUSHING, OK, p. A511
HILLCREST HOSPITAL HENRYETTA, HENRYETTA, OK, p. A513
HILLCREST HOSPITAL PRYOR, PRYOR, OK, p. A520
HILLCREST HOSPITAL SOUTH, TULSA, OK, p. A522
HILLCREST MEDICAL CENTER, TULSA, OK, p. A522
HILLS & DALES HEALTHCARE, CASS CITY, MI, p. A323
HILLSBORO AREA HOSPITAL, HILLSBORO, IL, p. A198
HILLSBORO COMMUNITY HOSPITAL, HILLSBORO, KS, p. A250
HILLSBORO NURSING HOME, HILLSBORO, ND, p. A481
HILLSDALE HOSPITAL, HILLSDALE, MI, p. A329
HILLSIDE REHABILITATION HOSPITAL, WARREN, OH, p. A506
HILO MEDICAL CENTER, HILO, HI, p. A175
HILTON HEAD HOSPITAL, HILTON HEAD ISLAND, SC, p. A568
HIMA SAN PABLO CAGUAS, CAGUAS, PR, p. A731
HIRAM W. DAVIS MEDICAL CENTER, PETERSBURG, VA, p. A681
H. LEE MOFFITT CANCER CENTER AND RESEARCH INSTITUTE, TAMPA, FL, p. A152

HOAG MEMORIAL HOSPITAL PRESBYTERIAN, NEWPORT BEACH, CA, p. A80
HOAG ORTHOPEDIC INSTITUTE, IRVINE, CA, p. A67
HOBBS HOSPITAL, HOBBS, NM, p. A435
HOCKING VALLEY COMMUNITY HOSPITAL, LOGAN, OH, p. A498
HODGEMAN COUNTY HEALTH CENTER, JETMORE, KS, p. A251
HOKE HOSPITAL, RAEFORD, NC, p. A474
HOLDENVILLE GENERAL HOSPITAL, HOLDENVILLE, OK, p. A513
HOLLAND HOSPITAL, HOLLAND, MI, p. A330
HOLLY HILL HOSPITAL, RALEIGH, NC, p. A474
HOLLYWOOD COMMUNITY HOSPITAL OF VAN NUYS, LOS ANGELES, CA, p. A72
HOLLYWOOD MEDICAL CENTER, HOLLYWOOD, FL, p. A133
HOLLYWOOD PRESBYTERIAN MEDICAL CENTER, LOS ANGELES, CA, p. A72
HOLSTON VALLEY MEDICAL CENTER, KINGSPORT, TN, p. A585
HOLTON COMMUNITY HOSPITAL, HOLTON, KS, p. A250
HOLTZ CHILDREN'S HOSPITAL JACKSON MEMORIAL HOSPITAL, MIAMI, FL, p. A140
HOLY CROSS GERMANTOWN HOSPITAL, GERMANTOWN, MD, p. A304
HOLY CROSS HOSPITAL – DAVIS, LAYTON, UT, p. A665
HOLY CROSS HOSPITAL – JORDAN VALLEY, WEST JORDAN, UT, p. A670
HOLY CROSS HOSPITAL – SALT LAKE, SALT LAKE CITY, UT, p. A668
HOLY CROSS HOSPITAL, CHICAGO, IL, p. A189
HOLY CROSS HOSPITAL, FORT LAUDERDALE, FL, p. A131
HOLY CROSS HOSPITAL, SILVER SPRING, MD, p. A307
HOLY CROSS HOSPITAL, TAOS, NM, p. A437
HOLY FAMILY HOME FOR THE AGED, NEW YORK, NY, p. A448
HOLY FAMILY HOPSITAL AT MERRIMACK VALLEY, HAVERHILL, MA, p. A314
HOLY FAMILY HOSPITAL, METHUEN, MA, p. A316
HOLY FAMILY MEMORIAL, MANITOWOC, WI, p. A715
HOLY NAME MEDICAL CENTER, TEANECK, NJ, p. A429
HOLY REDEEMER HOSPITAL, MEADOWBROOK, PA, p. A545
HOLY ROSARY HEALTHCARE, MILES CITY, MT, p. A394
HOLYOKE MEDICAL CENTER, HOLYOKE, MA, p. A314
HOLZER MEDICAL CENTER – JACKSON, JACKSON, OH, p. A497
HOLZER MEDICAL CENTER, GALLIPOLIS, OH, p. A496
HONORHEALTH DEER VALLEY MEDICAL CENTER, PHOENIX, AZ, p. A35
HONORHEALTH JOHN C. LINCOLN MEDICAL CENTER, PHOENIX, AZ, p. A36
HONORHEALTH REHABILITATION HOSPITAL, SCOTTSDALE, AZ, p. A38
HONORHEALTH SCOTTSDALE OSBORN MEDICAL CENTER, SCOTTSDALE, AZ, p. A38
HONORHEALTH SCOTTSDALE SHEA MEDICAL CENTER, SCOTTSDALE, AZ, p. A38
HONORHEALTH SCOTTSDALE THOMPSON PEAK MEDICAL CENTER, SCOTTSDALE, AZ, p. A38
HONORHEALTH SONORAN CROSSING MEDICAL CENTER, PHOENIX, AZ, p. A36
HOOD MEMORIAL HOSPITAL, AMITE, LA, p. A276
HOPEDALE MEDICAL COMPLEX, HOPEDALE, IL, p. A198
HOPI HEALTH CARE CENTER, KEAMS CANYON, AZ, p. A32
HORIZON MEDICAL CENTER, LLC, DENTON, TX, p. A613
HORIZON SPECIALTY HOSPITAL, LAS VEGAS, NV, p. A410
HORN MEMORIAL HOSPITAL, IDA GROVE, IA, p. A237
HOSPITAL BUEN SAMARITANO, AGUADILLA, PR, p. A730
HOSPITAL CENTRO COMPRENSIVO DE CANCER, UNIVERSIDAD DE PUERTO RICO, SAN JUAN, PR, p. A735
HOSPITAL CUIDADO AGUDO ESPECIALIZADO EN PACIENTES POLITRAUMATIZADOS, SAN JUAN, PR, p. A736
HOSPITAL DE DAMAS, PONCE, PR, p. A734
HOSPITAL DE LA CONCEPCION, SAN GERMAN, PR, p. A734
HOSPITAL DE LA UNIVERSIDAD DE PUERTO RICO/DR. FEDERICO TRILLA, CAROLINA, PR, p. A732
HOSPITAL DE PSIQUIATRIA, SAN JUAN, PR, p. A735
HOSPITAL DE PSIQUIATRIA FORENSE, PONCE, PR, p. A734
HOSPITAL DEL MAESTRO, SAN JUAN, PR, p. A735
HOSPITAL DISTRICT 6 – PATTERSON HEALTH CENTER, ANTHONY, KS, p. A246
HOSPITAL DISTRICT NO 1 OF RICE COUNTY, LYONS, KS, p. A254
HOSPITAL EPISCOPAL SAN LUCAS METRO, SAN JUAN, PR, p. A735
HOSPITAL FOR BEHAVIORAL MEDICINE, WORCESTER, MA, p. A320
HOSPITAL FOR EXTENDED RECOVERY, NORFOLK, VA, p. A680
HOSPITAL FOR SPECIAL CARE, NEW BRITAIN, CT, p. A117
HOSPITAL FOR SPECIAL SURGERY, NEW YORK, NY, p. A448

HOSPITAL HIMA CUPEY, SAN JUAN, PR, p. A735
HOSPITAL HIMA DE HUMACAO, HUMACAO, PR, p. A733
HOSPITAL MANATI MEDICAL CENTER, MANATI, PR, p. A733
HOSPITAL MENONITA DE CAGUAS, CAGUAS, PR, p. A731
HOSPITAL MENONITA DE CAYEY, CAYEY, PR, p. A732
HOSPITAL MENONITA GUAYAMA, GUAYAMA, PR, p. A732
HOSPITAL MENONITA HUMACAO, HUMACAO, PR, p. A733
HOSPITAL MENONITA PONCE, COTO LAUREL, PR, p. A732
HOSPITAL METROPOLITANO, SAN JUAN, PR, p. A735
HOSPITAL METROPOLITANO DR. SUSONI, ARECIBO, PR, p. A731
HOSPITAL METROPOLITANO SAN GERMAN, SAN GERMAN, PR, p. A734
HOSPITAL OF SAINT RAPHAEL, NEW HAVEN, CT, p. A117
HOSPITAL OF THE UNIVERSITY OF PENNSYLVANIA, PHILADELPHIA, PA, p. A549
HOSPITAL PAVIA ARECIBO, ARECIBO, PR, p. A731
HOSPITAL PAVIA YAUCO, YAUCO, PR, p. A736
HOSPITAL PAVIA–HATO REY, SAN JUAN, PR, p. A735
HOSPITAL PAVIA–SANTURCE, SAN JUAN, PR, p. A735
HOSPITAL PEREA, MAYAGUEZ, PR, p. A733
HOSPITAL PSIQUIATRICO CORRECCIONAL, SAN JUAN, PR, p. A735
HOSPITAL PSIQUIATRICO METROPOLITANO, CABO ROJO, PR, p. A731
HOSPITAL SAN ANTONIO, MAYAGUEZ, PR, p. A733
HOSPITAL SAN CARLOS BORROMEO, MOCA, PR, p. A733
HOSPITAL SAN CRISTOBAL, COTO LAUREL, PR, p. A732
HOSPITAL SAN FRANCISCO, SAN JUAN, PR, p. A735
HOSPITAL SAN PABLO, BAYAMON, PR, p. A731
HOSPITAL SAN PABLO DEL ESTE HIMA FAJARDO, FAJARDO, PR, p. A732
HOSPITAL UNIVERSITARIO DR. RAMON RUIZ ARNAU, BAYAMON, PR, p. A731
HOT SPRINGS COUNTY HOSPITAL DISTRICT, THERMOPOLIS, WY, p. A728
HOULTON REGIONAL HOSPITAL, HOULTON, ME, p. A297
HOUSTON BEHAVIORAL HEALTHCARE HOSPITAL, HOUSTON, TX, p. A626
HOUSTON COUNTY COMMUNITY HOSPITAL, ERIN, TN, p. A582
HOUSTON MEDICAL CENTER, WARNER ROBINS, GA, p. A173
HOUSTON METHODIST BAYTOWN HOSPITAL, BAYTOWN, TX, p. A601
HOUSTON METHODIST CLEAR LAKE HOSPITAL, HOUSTON, TX, p. A626
HOUSTON METHODIST CONTINUING CARE HOSPITAL, KATY, TX, p. A631
HOUSTON METHODIST HOSPITAL, HOUSTON, TX, p. A626
HOUSTON METHODIST SUGAR LAND HOSPITAL, SUGAR LAND, TX, p. A654
HOUSTON METHODIST THE WOODLANDS HOSPITAL, THE WOODLANDS, TX, p. A657
HOUSTON METHODIST WEST HOSPITAL, HOUSTON, TX, p. A626
HOUSTON METHODIST WILLOWBROOK HOSPITAL, HOUSTON, TX, p. A626
HOUSTON PHYSICIANS' HOSPITAL, WEBSTER, TX, p. A661
HOWARD COUNTY GENERAL HOSPITAL, COLUMBIA, MD, p. A303
HOWARD COUNTY MEDICAL CENTER, SAINT PAUL, NE, p. A405
HOWARD MEMORIAL HOSPITAL, NASHVILLE, AR, p. A51
HOWARD UNIVERSITY HOSPITAL, WASHINGTON, DC, p. A123
HOWARD YOUNG MEDICAL CENTER, WOODRUFF, WI, p. A725
HOWARD YOUNG MEDICAL CENTER, INC., WOODRUFF, WI, p. A725
HSHS GOOD SHEPHERD HOSPITAL, SHELBYVILLE, IL, p. A208
HSHS HOLY FAMILY HOSPITAL IN GREENVILLE, GREENVILLE, IL, p. A196
HSHS ST. ANTHONY'S MEMORIAL HOSPITAL, EFFINGHAM, IL, p. A194
HSHS ST. CLARE MEMORIAL HOSPITAL, OCONTO FALLS, WI, p. A719
HSHS ST. ELIZABETH'S HOSPITAL, O FALLON, IL, p. A204
HSHS ST. FRANCIS HOSPITAL, LITCHFIELD, IL, p. A200
HSHS ST. JOHN'S HOSPITAL, SPRINGFIELD, IL, p. A209
HSHS ST. JOSEPH'S HOSPITAL, BREESE, IL, p. A186
HSHS ST. JOSEPH'S HOSPITAL, HIGHLAND, IL, p. A197
HSHS ST. JOSEPH'S HOSPITAL BREESE, BREESE, IL, p. A187
HSHS ST. JOSEPH'S HOSPITAL HIGHLAND, HIGHLAND, IL, p. A197
HSHS ST. MARY'S HOSPITAL, DECATUR, IL, p. A193
HSHS ST. MARY'S HOSPITAL MEDICAL CENTER, GREEN BAY, WI, p. A712
HSHS ST. NICHOLAS HOSPITAL, SHEBOYGAN, WI, p. A721
HSHS ST. VINCENT HOSPITAL, GREEN BAY, WI, p. A712

HUDSON COUNTY MEADOWVIEW PSYCHIATRIC HOSPITAL, SECAUCUS, NJ, p. A428
HUDSON HOSPITAL AND CLINIC, HUDSON, WI, p. A713
HUDSON REGIONAL HOSPITAL, SECAUCUS, NJ, p. A428
HUGGINS HOSPITAL, WOLFEBORO, NH, p. A417
HUGH CHATHAM HEALTH, ELKIN, NC, p. A468
HUGH CHATHAM MEMORIAL HOSPITAL, ELKIN, NC, p. A468
HUHUKAM MEMORIAL HOSPITAL, SACATON, AZ, p. A37
HUMANA HOSPITAL–TACOMA, TACOMA, WA, p. A697
HUMBOLDT COUNTY MEMORIAL HOSPITAL, HUMBOLDT, IA, p. A237
HUMBOLDT COUNTY MENTAL HEALTH, EUREKA, CA, p. A62
HUMBOLDT GENERAL HOSPITAL, WINNEMUCCA, NV, p. A413
HUMBOLDT PARK HEALTH, CHICAGO, IL, p. A189
HUNT REGIONAL MEDICAL CENTER, GREENVILLE, TX, p. A623
HUNTER HOLMES MCGUIRE VETERANS AFFAIRS MEDICAL CENTER–RICHMOND, RICHMOND, VA, p. A683
HUNTERDON HEALTHCARE, FLEMINGTON, NJ, p. A421
HUNTINGTON BEACH HOSPITAL, HUNTINGTON BEACH, CA, p. A67
HUNTINGTON CREEK RECOVERY CENTER, SHICKSHINNY, PA, p. A555
HUNTINGTON HEALTH, PASADENA, CA, p. A83
HUNTINGTON HOSPITAL, HUNTINGTON, NY, p. A444
HUNTINGTON HOSPITAL, PASADENA, CA, p. A83
HUNTINGTON VETERANS AFFAIRS MEDICAL CENTER, HUNTINGTON, WV, p. A702
HUNTSVILLE HOSPITAL, HUNTSVILLE, AL, p. A21
HUNTSVILLE HOSPITAL EAST, HUNTSVILLE, AL, p. A21
HUNTSVILLE MEMORIAL HOSPITAL, HUNTSVILLE, TX, p. A629
HURLEY MEDICAL CENTER, FLINT, MI, p. A326
HURON REGIONAL MEDICAL CENTER, HURON, SD, p. A574
HUTCHINSON HEALTH, HUTCHINSON, MN, p. A348
HUTCHINSON REGIONAL MEDICAL CENTER, HUTCHINSON, KS, p. A251
HUTZEL WOMEN'S HOSPITAL, DETROIT, MI, p. A325

I

IBERIA MEDICAL CENTER, NEW IBERIA, LA, p. A289
IBERIA REHABILITATION HOSPITAL, LAFAYETTE, LA, p. A285
ICARE REHABILITATION HOSPITAL, FLOWER MOUND, TX, p. A618
IDAHO FALLS COMMUNITY HOSPITAL, IDAHO FALLS, ID, p. A181
I. GONZALEZ MARTINEZ ONCOLOGIC HOSPITAL, HATO REY, PR, p. A732
ILLINI COMMUNITY HOSPITAL, PITTSFIELD, IL, p. A206
INCLINE VILLAGE COMMUNITY HOSPITAL, INCLINE VILLAGE, NV, p. A409
INCOMPASS HEALTHCARE, LAWRENCEBURG, IN, p. A222
INDEPENDENCE MENTAL HEALTH INSTITUTE, INDEPENDENCE, IA, p. A238
INDIAN HEALTH SERVICE HOSPITAL, RAPID CITY, SD, p. A575
INDIAN PATH COMMUNITY HOSPITAL, KINGSPORT, TN, p. A585
INDIANA HEART HOSPITAL, INDIANAPOLIS, IN, p. A219
INDIANA REGIONAL MEDICAL CENTER, INDIANA, PA, p. A542
INDIANA SPINE HOSPITAL, CARMEL, IN, p. A214
INDIANA UNIVERSITY HEALTH ARNETT HOSPITAL, LAFAYETTE, IN, p. A222
INDIANA UNIVERSITY HEALTH BALL MEMORIAL HOSPITAL, MUNCIE, IN, p. A224
INDIANA UNIVERSITY HEALTH BEDFORD HOSPITAL, BEDFORD, IN, p. A212
INDIANA UNIVERSITY HEALTH BLOOMINGTON HOSPITAL, BLOOMINGTON, IN, p. A213
INDIANA UNIVERSITY HEALTH FRANKFORT, FRANKFORT, IN, p. A217
INDIANA UNIVERSITY HEALTH JAY HOSPITAL, PORTLAND, IN, p. A226
INDIANA UNIVERSITY HEALTH METHODIST HOSPITAL, FRANKFORT, IN, p. A217
INDIANA UNIVERSITY HEALTH NORTH HOSPITAL, CARMEL, IN, p. A214
INDIANA UNIVERSITY HEALTH PAOLI HOSPITAL, PAOLI, IN, p. A226
INDIANA UNIVERSITY HEALTH TIPTON HOSPITAL, TIPTON, IN, p. A228
INDIANA UNIVERSITY HEALTH UNIVERSITY HOSPITAL, INDIANAPOLIS, IN, p. A220
INDIANA UNIVERSITY HEALTH WEST HOSPITAL, AVON, IN, p. A212
INDIANA UNIVERSITY HEALTH WHITE MEMORIAL HOSPITAL, MONTICELLO, IN, p. A224
INDIANA UNIVERSITY HOSPITAL, INDIANAPOLIS, IN, p. A220
INDIANA UNIVERSITY MED CENTER, INDIANAPOLIS, IN, p. A220
INDIANAPOLIS REHABILITATION HOSPITAL, CARMEL, IN, p. A214
INDIANHEAD MEDICAL CENTER, SHELL LAKE, WI, p. A721
INDUSTRIAL HOSPITAL, SAN JUAN, PR, p. A735
INFIRMARY LONG TERM ACUTE CARE HOSPITAL, MOBILE, AL, p. A21
INGALLS MEMORIAL HOSPITAL, HARVEY, IL, p. A197
INGHAM REGIONAL MEDICAL CENTER, GREENLAWN CAMPUS, LANSING, MI, p. A331
INGHAM REGIONAL ORTHOPEDIC HOSPITAL, PENNSYLVANIA CAMPUS, LANSING, MI, p. A331
INLAND NORTHWEST BEHAVIORAL HEALTH, SPOKANE, WA, p. A696
INLAND VALLEY REG MEDICAL CTR, WILDOMAR, CA, p. A101
INOVA ALEXANDRIA HOSPITAL, ALEXANDRIA, VA, p. A673
INOVA FAIR OAKS HOSPITAL, FAIRFAX, VA, p. A675
INOVA FAIRFAX HOSPITAL, FALLS CHURCH, VA, p. A676
INOVA FAIRFAX MEDICAL CAMPUS, FALLS CHURCH, VA, p. A676
INOVA LOUDOUN HOSPITAL, LEESBURG, VA, p. A678
INOVA MOUNT VERNON HOSPITAL, ALEXANDRIA, VA, p. A673
INOVA SPECIALTY HOSPITAL, ALEXANDRIA, VA, p. A673
INSIGHT HOSPITAL AND MEDICAL CENTER, CHICAGO, IL, p. A189
INSIGHT SURGICAL HOSPITAL, WARREN, MI, p. A340
INSPIRA MEDICAL CENTER MULLICA HILL, MULLICA HILL, NJ, p. A424
INSPIRA MEDICAL CENTER–VINELAND, VINELAND, NJ, p. A430
INSPIRE SPECIALTY HOSPITAL, MIDWEST CITY, OK, p. A515
INSTITUTE FOR ORTHOPAEDIC SURGERY, LIMA, OH, p. A498
INSTITUTE OF PSYCHIATRY, CHICAGO, IL, p. A189
INTEGRIS BAPTIST MEDICAL CENTER, OKLAHOMA CITY, OK, p. A517
INTEGRIS BASS BEHAVIORAL HEALTH SYSTEM, ENID, OK, p. A512
INTEGRIS CANADIAN VALLEY HOSPITAL, YUKON, OK, p. A524
INTEGRIS GROVE HOSPITAL, GROVE, OK, p. A513
INTEGRIS HEALTH COMMUNITY HOSPITAL AT COUNCIL CROSSING, OKLAHOMA CITY, OK, p. A517
INTEGRIS HEALTH EDMOND HOSPITAL, EDMOND, OK, p. A512
INTEGRIS HEALTH ENID HOSPITAL, ENID, OK, p. A512
INTEGRIS HEALTH PONCA CITY HOSPITAL, PONCA CITY, OK, p. A519
INTEGRIS HEALTH WOODWARD HOSPITAL, WOODWARD, OK, p. A524
INTEGRIS MENTAL HEALTH SYSTEM–SPENCER, SPENCER, OK, p. A521
INTEGRIS MIAMI HOSPITAL, MIAMI, OK, p. A515
INTEGRIS SOUTHWEST MEDICAL CENTER, OKLAHOMA CITY, OK, p. A517
INTENSIVE SPECIALTY HOSPITAL – SHREVEPORT CAMPUS, SHREVEPORT, LA, p. A292
INTERFAITH MEDICAL CENTER, NEW YORK, NY, p. A448
INTERMOUNTAIN HEALTH PLATTE VALLEY HOSPITAL, BRIGHTON, CO, p. A104
INTERMOUNTAIN HEALTH SAINT JOSEPH HOSPITAL, DENVER, CO, p. A106
INTERMOUNTAIN HEALTH ST. MARY'S REGIONAL HOSPITAL, GRAND JUNCTION, CO, p. A109
INTERMOUNTAIN HOSPITAL, BOISE, ID, p. A179
INTERMOUNTAIN MEDICAL CENTER, MURRAY, UT, p. A666
INTERMOUNTAIN SPANISH FORK HOSPITAL, SPANISH FORK, UT, p. A670
IOANNIS A. LOUGARIS VETERANS' ADMINISTRATION MEDICAL CENTER, RENO, NV, p. A412
IOWA CITY VA HEALTH SYSTEM, IOWA CITY, IA, p. A238
IOWA MEDICAL AND CLASSIFICATION CENTER, CORALVILLE, IA, p. A233
IOWA SPECIALTY HOSPITAL–BELMOND, BELMOND, IA, p. A230
IOWA SPECIALTY HOSPITAL–CLARION, CLARION, IA, p. A232
IRA DAVENPORT MEMORIAL HOSPITAL, BATH, NY, p. A439
IRAAN GENERAL HOSPITAL, IRAAN, TX, p. A630
IREDELL HEALTH SYSTEM, STATESVILLE, NC, p. A477
IRON COUNTY MEDICAL CENTER, PILOT KNOB, MO, p. A382
IRON MOUNTAIN VAMC, IRON MOUNTAIN, MI, p. A330
IROQUOIS MEMORIAL HOSPITAL AND RESIDENT HOME, WATSEKA, IL, p. A210
IRWIN ARMY COMMUNITY HOSPITAL, JUNCTION CITY, KS, p. A251
IRWIN COUNTY HOSPITAL, OCILLA, GA, p. A169
ISLAND HEALTH, ANACORTES, WA, p. A687
ISLAND HOSPITAL, ANACORTES, WA, p. A687
IU HEALTH SAXONY HOSPITAL, FISHERS, IN, p. A216
IVINSON MEMORIAL HOSPITAL, LARAMIE, WY, p. A727
IZARD COUNTY MEDICAL CENTER, CALICO ROCK, AR, p. A44

J

JACK C. MONTGOMERY DEPARTMENT OF VETERANS AFFAIRS MEDICAL CENTER, MUSKOGEE, OK, p. A515
JACK D WEILER HOSPITAL OF ALBERT EINSTEIN COLLEGE OF MEDICINE, NEW YORK, NY, p. A448
JACK HUGHSTON MEMORIAL HOSPITAL, PHENIX CITY, AL, p. A24
JACKSON BEHAVIORAL HEALTH HOSPITAL, MIAMI, FL, p. A140
JACKSON COUNTY HOSPITAL DISTRICT, EDNA, TX, p. A616
JACKSON COUNTY MEMORIAL HOSPITAL, ALTUS, OK, p. A509
JACKSON COUNTY REGIONAL HEALTH CENTER, MAQUOKETA, IA, p. A239
JACKSON GENERAL HOSPITAL, RIPLEY, WV, p. A704
JACKSON HEALTH SYSTEM, MIAMI, FL, p. A140
JACKSON HOSPITAL, MARIANNA, FL, p. A138
JACKSON HOSPITAL AND CLINIC, MONTGOMERY, AL, p. A22
JACKSON MEDICAL CENTER, JACKSON, AL, p. A21
JACKSON NORTH MEDICAL CENTER, NORTH MIAMI BEACH, FL, p. A142
JACKSON PARISH HOSPITAL, JONESBORO, LA, p. A284
JACKSON PARK HOSPITAL AND MEDICAL CENTER, CHICAGO, IL, p. A189
JACKSON PURCHASE MEDICAL CENTER, MAYFIELD, KY, p. A271
JACKSON SOUTH COMMUNITY HOSPITAL, MIAMI, FL, p. A140
JACKSON SOUTH MEDICAL CENTER, MIAMI, FL, p. A140
JACKSON–MADISON COUNTY GENERAL HOSPITAL, MEDINA, TN, p. A588
JACKSONVILLE MEMORIAL HOSPITAL, JACKSONVILLE, IL, p. A199
JACOBSON MEMORIAL HOSPITAL CARE CENTER, ELGIN, ND, p. A480
JAMAICA HOSPITAL MEDICAL CENTER, NEW YORK, NY, p. A448
JAMES A. HALEY VETERANS' HOSPITAL–TAMPA, TAMPA, FL, p. A152
JAMES CANCER HOSPITAL AND SOLOVE RESEARCH INSTITUTE, COLUMBUS, OH, p. A491
JAMES E. VAN ZANDT VETERANS AFFAIRS MEDICAL CENTER, ALTOONA, PA, p. A534
JAMES H. QUILLEN DEPARTMENT OF VETERANS AFFAIRS MEDICAL CENTER, JOHNSON CITY, TN, p. A585
JAMES J. PETERS VETERANS AFFAIRS MEDICAL CENTER, NEW YORK, NY, p. A448
JAMES M JACKSON MEMORIAL HOSP, MIAMI, FL, p. A140
JAMESTOWN REGIONAL MEDICAL CENTER, JAMESTOWN, ND, p. A482
JANE TODD CRAWFORD HOSPITAL, GREENSBURG, KY, p. A266
JASPER GENERAL HOSPITAL, BAY SPRINGS, MS, p. A359
JASPER MEMORIAL HOSPITAL, MONTICELLO, GA, p. A168
JAY HOSPITAL, JAY, FL, p. A135
J. D. MCCARTY CENTER FOR CHILDREN WITH DEVELOPMENTAL DISABILITIES, NORMAN, OK, p. A516
JEFF DAVIS HOSPITAL, HAZLEHURST, GA, p. A165
JEFFERSON ABINGTON HEALTH, ABINGTON, PA, p. A534
JEFFERSON COMMUNITY HEALTH AND LIFE, FAIRBURY, NE, p. A399
JEFFERSON COUNTY HEALTH CENTER, FAIRFIELD, IA, p. A236
JEFFERSON COUNTY HOSPITAL, FAYETTE, MS, p. A361
JEFFERSON COUNTY HOSPITAL, WAURIKA, OK, p. A524
JEFFERSON DAVIS COMMUNITY HOSPITAL, PRENTISS, MS, p. A368
JEFFERSON DAVIS HOSPITAL, HOUSTON, TX, p. A626
JEFFERSON EINSTEIN MONTGOMERY HOSPITAL, EAST NORRITON, PA, p. A538
JEFFERSON HEALTH NORTHEAST, PHILADELPHIA, PA, p. A549
JEFFERSON HEALTHCARE, PORT TOWNSEND, WA, p. A693
JEFFERSON HOSPITAL, JEFFERSON HILLS, PA, p. A542
JEFFERSON HOSPITAL, LOUISVILLE, GA, p. A166
JEFFERSON LANSDALE HOSPITAL, LANSDALE, PA, p. A544
JEFFERSON MEDICAL CENTER, RANSON, WV, p. A704
JEFFERSON METHODIST HOSPITAL, PHILADELPHIA, PA, p. A549

Index of Hospitals / Jefferson Regional

JEFFERSON REGIONAL, PINE BLUFF, AR, p. A52
JEFFERSON STRATFORD HOSPITAL, STRATFORD, NJ, p. A428
JEFFERSON WASHINGTON TOWNSHIP HOSPITAL, TURNERSVILLE, NJ, p. A429
JENKINS COUNTY MEDICAL CENTER, MILLEN, GA, p. A168
JENNIE M. MELHAM MEMORIAL MEDICAL CENTER, BROKEN BOW, NE, p. A398
JENNIE STUART MEDICAL CENTER, HOPKINSVILLE, KY, p. A267
JENNIFER MORENO DEPARTMENT OF VETERANS AFFAIRS MEDICAL CENTER, SAN DIEGO, CA, p. A88
JENNINGS SENIOR CARE HOSPITAL, JENNINGS, LA, p. A284
JEROLD PHELPS COMMUNITY HOSPITAL, GARBERVILLE, CA, p. A65
JERRY L. PETTIS MEMORIAL VETERANS' HOSPITAL, LOMA LINDA, CA, p. A70
JERSEY CITY MEDICAL CENTER, JERSEY CITY, NJ, p. A422
JERSEY COMMUNITY HOSPITAL, JERSEYVILLE, IL, p. A199
JESSE BROWN VA MEDICAL CENTER, CHICAGO, IL, p. A189
JESSE BROWN VETERANS AFFAIRS MEDICAL CENTER, CHICAGO, IL, p. A189
JEWELL COUNTY HOSPITAL, MANKATO, KS, p. A254
JEWISH HOME FOR THE AGED, LONGMEADOW, MA, p. A315
JEWISH HOME OF SAN FRANCISCO, SAN FRANCISCO, CA, p. A90
JFK JOHNSON REHABILITATION INSTITUTE AT HACKENSACK MERIDIAN HEALTH, EDISON, NJ, p. A420
JFK MEDICAL CENTER, ATLANTIS, FL, p. A125
JFK MEDICAL CENTER NORTH CAMPUS, WEST PALM BEACH, FL, p. A154
JFK MEMORIAL HOSPITAL, INDIO, CA, p. A67
JIM TALIAFERRO COMMUNITY MENTAL HEALTH CENTER, LAWTON, OK, p. A514
JOHN C. FREMONT HEALTHCARE DISTRICT, MARIPOSA, CA, p. A76
JOHN C. STENNIS MEMORIAL HOSPITAL, DE KALB, MS, p. A361
JOHN D. ARCHBOLD MEMORIAL HOSPITAL, THOMASVILLE, GA, p. A172
JOHN D. DINGELL DEPARTMENT OF VETERANS AFFAIRS MEDICAL CENTER, DETROIT, MI, p. A325
JOHN H. STROGER JR. HOSPITAL OF COOK COUNTY, CHICAGO, IL, p. A190
JOHN HEINZ INSTITUTE OF REHABILITATION MEDICINE, WILKES-BARRE, PA, p. A557
JOHN J. MADDEN MENTAL HEALTH CENTER, HINES, IL, p. A198
JOHN J. PERSHING VETERANS' ADMINISTRATION MEDICAL CENTER, POPLAR BLUFF, MO, p. A382
JOHN L. MCCLELLAN MEMORIAL VETERANS' HOSPITAL, LITTLE ROCK, AR, p. A50
JOHN MUIR BEHAVIORAL HEALTH CENTER, CONCORD, CA, p. A60
JOHN MUIR HEALTH, CONCORD MEDICAL CENTER, CONCORD, CA, p. A60
JOHN MUIR MEDICAL CENTER, WALNUT CREEK, WALNUT CREEK, CA, p. A100
JOHN PETER SMITH HOSPITAL, FORT WORTH, TX, p. A619
JOHN RANDOLPH MEDICAL CENTER, HOPEWELL, VA, p. A678
JOHN STODDARD CANCER CENTER, DES MOINES, IA, p. A235
JOHNS HOPKINS ALL CHILDREN'S HOSPITAL, SAINT PETERSBURG, FL, p. A149
JOHNS HOPKINS BAYVIEW MEDICAL CENTER, BALTIMORE, MD, p. A300
JOHNS HOPKINS HOSPITAL, BALTIMORE, MD, p. A300
JOHNS HOPKINS HOWARD COUNTY MEDICAL CENTER, COLUMBIA, MD, p. A303
JOHNSON CITY MEDICAL CENTER, JOHNSON CITY, TN, p. A585
JOHNSON COUNTY COMMUNITY HOSPITAL, MOUNTAIN CITY, TN, p. A590
JOHNSON COUNTY HEALTHCARE CENTER, BUFFALO, WY, p. A726
JOHNSON COUNTY HOSPITAL, TECUMSEH, NE, p. A406
JOHNSON COUNTY REHABILITATION HOSPITAL, OVERLAND PARK, KS, p. A257
JOHNSON MEMORIAL HEALTH SERVICES, DAWSON, MN, p. A345
JOHNSON MEMORIAL HOSPITAL, FRANKLIN, IN, p. A217
JOHNSON MEMORIAL HOSPITAL, STAFFORD SPRINGS, CT, p. A119
JOHNSON REGIONAL MEDICAL CENTER, CLARKSVILLE, AR, p. A44
JOHNSON REHABILITATION INSTITUTE AT HACKENSACK MERIDIAN HEALTH OCEAN MEDICAL CENTER, BRICK, NJ, p. A418
JOHNSTON MEMORIAL HOSPITAL, ABINGDON, VA, p. A673
JOHNSTON R. BOWMAN HEALTH CENTER, CHICAGO, IL, p. A190
JOHNSTON-WILLIS HOSPITAL, NORTH CHESTERFIELD, VA, p. A680
JONES MEMORIAL HOSPITAL, WELLSVILLE, NY, p. A461
JOSEPH'S HOSPITAL SOUTH, RIVERVIEW, FL, p. A148
JOSEPH'S HOSPITAL-NORTH, LUTZ, FL, p. A138
JOYCE EISENBERG-KEEFER MEDICAL CENTER, RESEDA, CA, p. A85
JPS HEALTH NETWORK, FORT WORTH, TX, p. A619
JULIAN F. KEITH ALCOHOL AND DRUG ABUSE TREATMENT CENTER, BLACK MOUNTAIN, NC, p. A464
JUPITER MEDICAL CENTER, JUPITER, FL, p. A136

K

KADLEC REGIONAL MEDICAL CENTER, RICHLAND, WA, p. A694
KAHUKU MEDICAL CENTER, KAHUKU, HI, p. A176
KAISER FOUNDATION HOSPITAL - ORANGE COUNTY, IRVINE, CA, p. A67
KAISER FOUNDATION HOSPITAL - SAN MARCOS, SAN MARCOS, CA, p. A93
KAISER FOUNDATION HOSPITAL, MARTINEZ, CA, p. A77
KAISER FOUNDATION HOSPITAL, MODESTO, CA, p. A77
KAISER FOUNDATION MENTAL HEALTH CENTER, LOS ANGELES, CA, p. A72
KAISER PERMANENTE ANTIOCH MEDICAL CENTER, ANTIOCH, CA, p. A55
KAISER PERMANENTE BALDWIN PARK MEDICAL CENTER, BALDWIN PARK, CA, p. A57
KAISER PERMANENTE DOWNEY MEDICAL CENTER, DOWNEY, CA, p. A61
KAISER PERMANENTE FONTANA MEDICAL CENTER, FONTANA, CA, p. A63
KAISER PERMANENTE FREMONT MEDICAL CENTER, FREMONT, CA, p. A64
KAISER PERMANENTE FRESNO MEDICAL CENTER, FRESNO, CA, p. A65
KAISER PERMANENTE LOS ANGELES MEDICAL CENTER, LOS ANGELES, CA, p. A73
KAISER PERMANENTE MANTECA MEDICAL CENTER, MANTECA, CA, p. A76
KAISER PERMANENTE MEDICAL CENTER, HONOLULU, HI, p. A175
KAISER PERMANENTE MEDICAL CNTR, MARTINEZ, CA, p. A77
KAISER PERMANENTE MORENO VALLEY MEDICAL CENTER, MORENO VALLEY, CA, p. A78
KAISER PERMANENTE OAKLAND MEDICAL CENTER, OAKLAND, CA, p. A81
KAISER PERMANENTE ORANGE COUNTY ANAHEIM MEDICAL CENTER, ANAHEIM, CA, p. A55
KAISER PERMANENTE PANORAMA CITY MEDICAL CENTER, LOS ANGELES, CA, p. A73
KAISER PERMANENTE REDWOOD CITY MEDICAL CENTER, REDWOOD CITY, CA, p. A85
KAISER PERMANENTE RICHMOND MEDICAL CENTER, RICHMOND, CA, p. A86
KAISER PERMANENTE RIVERSIDE MEDICAL CENTER, RIVERSIDE, CA, p. A86
KAISER PERMANENTE ROSEVILLE MEDICAL CENTER, ROSEVILLE, CA, p. A86
KAISER PERMANENTE SACRAMENTO MEDICAL CENTER, SACRAMENTO, CA, p. A86
KAISER PERMANENTE SAN FRANCISCO MEDICAL CENTER, SAN FRANCISCO, CA, p. A91
KAISER PERMANENTE SAN JOSE MEDICAL CENTER, SAN JOSE, CA, p. A92
KAISER PERMANENTE SAN LEANDRO MEDICAL CENTER, SAN LEANDRO, CA, p. A92
KAISER PERMANENTE SAN RAFAEL MEDICAL CENTER, SAN RAFAEL, CA, p. A93
KAISER PERMANENTE SANTA CLARA MEDICAL CENTER, SANTA CLARA, CA, p. A94
KAISER PERMANENTE SANTA ROSA MEDICAL CENTER, SANTA ROSA, CA, p. A95
KAISER PERMANENTE SOUTH BAY MEDICAL CENTER, LOS ANGELES, CA, p. A73
KAISER PERMANENTE SOUTH SACRAMENTO MEDICAL CENTER, SACRAMENTO, CA, p. A87
KAISER PERMANENTE SOUTH SAN FRANCISCO MEDICAL CENTER, SOUTH SAN FRANCISCO, CA, p. A96
KAISER PERMANENTE VACAVILLE MEDICAL CENTER, VACAVILLE, CA, p. A99
KAISER PERMANENTE VALLEJO MEDICAL CENTER, VALLEJO, CA, p. A99
KAISER PERMANENTE WALNUT CREEK MEDICAL CENTER, WALNUT CREEK, CA, p. A100
KAISER PERMANENTE WEST LOS ANGELES MEDICAL CENTER, LOS ANGELES, CA, p. A73
KAISER PERMANENTE WOODLAND HILLS MEDICAL CENTER, LOS ANGELES, CA, p. A73
KAISER PERMANENTE ZION MEDICAL CENTER, SAN DIEGO, CA, p. A89
KAISER SUNNYSIDE MEDICAL CENTER, CLACKAMAS, OR, p. A526
KAISER WESTSIDE MEDICAL CENTER, HILLSBORO, OR, p. A527
KALAMAZOO PSYCHIATRIC HOSPITAL, KALAMAZOO, MI, p. A331
KALEIDA HEALTH, BUFFALO, NY, p. A440
KALKASKA MEMORIAL HEALTH CENTER, KALKASKA, MI, p. A331
KANE COUNTY HOSPITAL, KANAB, UT, p. A665
KANSAS CITY ORTHOPAEDIC INSTITUTE, LEAWOOD, KS, p. A253
KANSAS CITY VA MEDICAL CENTER, KANSAS CITY, MO, p. A377
KANSAS CITY VAMC, KANSAS CITY, MO, p. A377
KANSAS HEART HOSPITAL, WICHITA, KS, p. A261
KANSAS MEDICAL CENTER, ANDOVER, KS, p. A246
KANSAS NEUROLOGICAL INSTITUTE, TOPEKA, KS, p. A260
KANSAS REHABILITATION HOSPITAL, TOPEKA, KS, p. A260
KANSAS SPINE & SPECIALTY HOSPITAL, WICHITA, KS, p. A262
KANSAS SURGERY AND RECOVERY CENTER, WICHITA, KS, p. A262
KAPIOLANI MEDICAL CENTER FOR WOMEN & CHILDREN, HONOLULU, HI, p. A175
KARMANOS CANCER CENTER, DETROIT, MI, p. A326
KASEMAN PRESBYTERIAN HOSPITAL, ALBUQUERQUE, NM, p. A432
KATE DISHMAN REHABILITATION HOSPITAL, BEAUMONT, TX, p. A602
KATHERINE SHAW BETHEA HOSPITAL, DIXON, IL, p. A193
KA'U HOSPITAL, PAHALA, HI, p. A177
KAUAI VETERANS MEMORIAL HOSPITAL, WAIMEA, HI, p. A178
KAWEAH HEALTH MEDICAL CENTER, VISALIA, CA, p. A100
KEARNEY COUNTY HEALTH SERVICES, MINDEN, NE, p. A402
KEARNEY REGIONAL MEDICAL CENTER, KEARNEY, NE, p. A401
KEARNY COUNTY HOSPITAL, LAKIN, KS, p. A252
KECK HOSPITAL OF USC, LOS ANGELES, CA, p. A73
KEDREN COMMUNITY HEALTH CENTER, LOS ANGELES, CA, p. A73
KEDREN COMMUNITY MENTAL HEALTH CENTER, LOS ANGELES, CA, p. A73
KEEFE MEMORIAL HOSPITAL, CHEYENNE WELLS, CO, p. A104
KELL WEST REGIONAL HOSPITAL, WICHITA FALLS, TX, p. A662
KELLER ARMY COMMUNITY HOSPITAL, WEST POINT, NY, p. A462
KEMPSVILLE CENTER FOR BEHAVIORAL HEALTH, NORFOLK, VA, p. A680
KENDALL REGIONAL MEDICAL CENTER, MIAMI, FL, p. A140
KENMORE MERCY HOSPITAL, KENMORE, NY, p. A444
KENNEDY KRIEGER INSTITUTE, BALTIMORE, MD, p. A300
KENNEDY UNIVERSITY HOSPITAL - STRATFORD, STRATFORD, NJ, p. A428
KENNEDY UNIVERSITY HOSPITAL - WASHINGTON TOWNSHIP, TURNERSVILLE, NJ, p. A429
KENSINGTON HOSPITAL, PHILADELPHIA, PA, p. A549
KENT COUNTY MEMORIAL HOSPITAL, WARWICK, RI, p. A561
KENT GENERAL HOSPITAL, DOVER, DE, p. A121
KENT HOSPITAL, WARWICK, RI, p. A561
KENTFIELD HOSPITAL, KENTFIELD, CA, p. A68
KENTUCKY RIVER MEDICAL CENTER, JACKSON, KY, p. A267
KEOKUK COUNTY HOSPITAL & CLINICS, SIGOURNEY, IA, p. A243
KERALTY HOSPITAL MIAMI, MIAMI, FL, p. A140
KERN MEDICAL, BAKERSFIELD, CA, p. A57
KERN VALLEY HEALTHCARE DISTRICT, LAKE ISABELLA, CA, p. A69
KERRVILLE DIVISION, KERRVILLE, TX, p. A632
KERRVILLE STATE HOSPITAL, KERRVILLE, TX, p. A632
KESSLER INSTITUTE FOR REHABILITATION, CHESTER, NJ, p. A419
KESSLER INSTITUTE FOR REHABILITATION, SADDLE BROOK, NJ, p. A428
KESSLER INSTITUTE FOR REHABILITATION, WEST ORANGE, NJ, p. A430
KESSLER MARLTON REHABILITATION, MARLTON, NJ, p. A423

KESWICK–HOME FOR INCURABLES, BALTIMORE, MD, p. A300
KETTERING BEHAVIORAL MEDICAL CENTER, MORAINE, OH, p. A500
KETTERING HEALTH DAYTON, DAYTON, OH, p. A494
KETTERING HEALTH GREENE MEMORIAL, XENIA, OH, p. A508
KETTERING HEALTH HAMILTON, HAMILTON, OH, p. A497
KETTERING HEALTH MAIN CAMPUS, KETTERING, OH, p. A497
KETTERING HEALTH MIAMISBURG, MIAMISBURG, OH, p. A500
KETTERING HEALTH TROY, TROY, OH, p. A505
KIDSPEACE CHILDREN'S HOSPITAL, OREFIELD, PA, p. A547
KIMBALL HEALTH SERVICES, KIMBALL, NE, p. A401
KIMBLE HOSPITAL, JUNCTION, TX, p. A631
KINDRED CHICAGO LAKESHORE, CHICAGO, IL, p. A190
KINDRED HOSP–FORT WORTH SW, FORT WORTH, TX, p. A619
KINDRED HOSPITAL ARIZONA–NORTHWEST PHOENIX, PEORIA, AZ, p. A34
KINDRED HOSPITAL BAY AREA, SAINT PETERSBURG, FL, p. A149
KINDRED HOSPITAL BAY AREA–TAMPA, TAMPA, FL, p. A152
KINDRED HOSPITAL CENTRAL TAMPA, TAMPA, FL, p. A152
KINDRED HOSPITAL CHICAGO–NORTHLAKE, NORTHLAKE, IL, p. A204
KINDRED HOSPITAL CLEAR LAKE, WEBSTER, TX, p. A661
KINDRED HOSPITAL DALLAS CENTRAL, DALLAS, TX, p. A611
KINDRED HOSPITAL EAST NEW JERSEY, PASSAIC, NJ, p. A426
KINDRED HOSPITAL EL PASO, EL PASO, TX, p. A616
KINDRED HOSPITAL HOUSTON MEDICAL CENTER, HOUSTON, TX, p. A626
KINDRED HOSPITAL INDIANAPOLIS NORTH, INDIANAPOLIS, IN, p. A220
KINDRED HOSPITAL LAS VEGAS–SAHARA, HENDERSON, NV, p. A409
KINDRED HOSPITAL LIMA, LIMA, OH, p. A498
KINDRED HOSPITAL LOUISVILLE AT JEWISH HOSPITAL, LOUISVILLE, KY, p. A269
KINDRED HOSPITAL MELBOURNE, MELBOURNE, FL, p. A139
KINDRED HOSPITAL NEW JERSEY – RAHWAY, RAHWAY, NJ, p. A427
KINDRED HOSPITAL NEW JERSEY – WAYNE, PASSAIC, NJ, p. A426
KINDRED HOSPITAL NORTH FLORIDA, GREEN COVE SPRINGS, FL, p. A133
KINDRED HOSPITAL NORTHLAND, KANSAS CITY, MO, p. A377
KINDRED HOSPITAL OCALA, OCALA, FL, p. A143
KINDRED HOSPITAL OF CLEVELAND, CLEVELAND, OH, p. A491
KINDRED HOSPITAL PARAMOUNT, PARAMOUNT, CA, p. A82
KINDRED HOSPITAL PARK VIEW–CENTRAL MASSACHUSETTS, ROCHDALE, MA, p. A317
KINDRED HOSPITAL PEORIA, PEORIA, IL, p. A206
KINDRED HOSPITAL PHILADELPHIA, PHILADELPHIA, PA, p. A549
KINDRED HOSPITAL RANCHO, RANCHO CUCAMONGA, CA, p. A84
KINDRED HOSPITAL RIVERSIDE, PERRIS, CA, p. A83
KINDRED HOSPITAL SAN ANTONIO CENTRAL, SAN ANTONIO, TX, p. A649
KINDRED HOSPITAL SEATTLE–FIRST HILL, SEATTLE, WA, p. A694
KINDRED HOSPITAL SOUTH BAY, GARDENA, CA, p. A65
KINDRED HOSPITAL SOUTH FLORIDA–FORT LAUDERDALE, FORT LAUDERDALE, FL, p. A131
KINDRED HOSPITAL ST. LOUIS–ST. ANTHONY'S, SAINT LOUIS, MO, p. A385
KINDRED HOSPITAL SUGAR LAND, SUGAR LAND, TX, p. A654
KINDRED HOSPITAL TARRANT COUNTY–ARLINGTON, ARLINGTON, TX, p. A597
KINDRED HOSPITAL THE PALM BEACHES, RIVIERA BEACH, FL, p. A148
KINDRED HOSPITAL–ALBUQUERQUE, ALBUQUERQUE, NM, p. A432
KINDRED HOSPITAL–AURORA, AURORA, CO, p. A103
KINDRED HOSPITAL–BALDWIN PARK, BALDWIN PARK, CA, p. A57
KINDRED HOSPITAL–BREA, BREA, CA, p. A58
KINDRED HOSPITAL–CHATTANOOGA, CHATTANOOGA, TN, p. A580
KINDRED HOSPITAL–CHICAGO NORTH, CHICAGO, IL, p. A190
KINDRED HOSPITAL–DAYTON, DAYTON, OH, p. A494
KINDRED HOSPITAL–DENVER, DENVER, CO, p. A106
KINDRED HOSPITAL–GREENSBORO, GREENSBORO, NC, p. A469
KINDRED HOSPITAL–HOLLYWOOD, HOLLYWOOD, FL, p. A133
KINDRED HOSPITAL–HOUSTON NORTHWEST, HOUSTON, TX, p. A626
KINDRED HOSPITAL–INDIANAPOLIS, INDIANAPOLIS, IN, p. A220
KINDRED HOSPITAL–LA MIRADA, LA MIRADA, CA, p. A68
KINDRED HOSPITAL–LOS ANGELES, LOS ANGELES, CA, p. A73
KINDRED HOSPITAL–LOUISVILLE, LOUISVILLE, KY, p. A269
KINDRED HOSPITAL–NEW JERSEY MORRIS COUNTY, DOVER, NJ, p. A420
KINDRED HOSPITAL–OKLAHOMA CITY SOUTH, OKLAHOMA CITY, OK, p. A517
KINDRED HOSPITAL–ONTARIO, ONTARIO, CA, p. A81
KINDRED HOSPITAL–SAN ANTONIO, SAN ANTONIO, TX, p. A649
KINDRED HOSPITAL–SAN DIEGO, SAN DIEGO, CA, p. A89
KINDRED HOSPITAL–SAN FRANCISCO BAY AREA, SAN LEANDRO, CA, p. A92
KINDRED HOSPITAL–ST. LOUIS, SAINT LOUIS, MO, p. A383
KINDRED HOSPITAL–SYCAMORE, SYCAMORE, IL, p. A209
KINDRED HOSPITAL–WESTMINSTER, WESTMINSTER, CA, p. A101
KING'S DAUGHTERS HOSPITAL, TEMPLE, TX, p. A656
KING'S DAUGHTERS MEDICAL CENTER, ASHLAND, KY, p. A263
KING'S DAUGHTERS MEDICAL CENTER, BROOKHAVEN, MS, p. A360
KING'S DAUGHTERS MEDICAL CENTER OHIO, PORTSMOUTH, OH, p. A502
KING'S DAUGHTERS' HEALTH, MADISON, IN, p. A223
KINGMAN COMMUNITY HOSPITAL, KINGMAN, KS, p. A252
KINGMAN REGIONAL MEDICAL CENTER, KINGMAN, AZ, p. A32
KINGSBORO PSYCHIATRIC CENTER, NEW YORK, NY, p. A448
KINGWOOD EMERGENCY HOSPITAL, KINGWOOD, TX, p. A632
KINGWOOD PINES HOSPITAL, KINGWOOD, TX, p. A632
KIOWA COUNTY MEMORIAL HOSPITAL, GREENSBURG, KS, p. A250
KIOWA DISTRICT HEALTHCARE, KIOWA, KS, p. A252
KIRBY FORENSIC PSYCHIATRIC CENTER, NEW YORK, NY, p. A448
KIRBY MEDICAL CENTER, MONTICELLO, IL, p. A202
KIT CARSON COUNTY HEALTH SERVICE DISTRICT, BURLINGTON, CO, p. A104
KIT CARSON COUNTY MEMORIAL HOSPITAL, BURLINGTON, CO, p. A104
KITTITAS VALLEY HEALTHCARE, ELLENSBURG, WA, p. A689
KITTSON HEALTHCARE, HALLOCK, MN, p. A348
KITTSON MEMORIAL HEALTHCARE CENTER, HALLOCK, MN, p. A348
KLICKITAT VALLEY HEALTH, GOLDENDALE, WA, p. A690
KNAPP MEDICAL CENTER, WESLACO, TX, p. A662
KNOX COMMUNITY HOSPITAL, MOUNT VERNON, OH, p. A501
KNOX COUNTY HOSPITAL, KNOX CITY, TX, p. A633
KNOXVILLE DIVISION, KNOXVILLE, IA, p. A239
KNOXVILLE HOSPITAL & CLINICS, KNOXVILLE, IA, p. A239
KOHALA HOSPITAL, KOHALA, HI, p. A177
KONA COMMUNITY HOSPITAL, KEALAKEKUA, HI, p. A177
KOOTENAI HEALTH, COEUR D'ALENE, ID, p. A180
KOSCIUSKO COMMUNITY HOSPITAL, WARSAW, IN, p. A229
KOSSUTH REGIONAL HEALTH CENTER, ALGONA, IA, p. A230
KPC PROMISE HOSPITAL OF AMARILLO, AMARILLO, TX, p. A596
KPC PROMISE HOSPITAL OF BATON ROUGE, BATON ROUGE, LA, p. A277
KPC PROMISE HOSPITAL OF DALLAS, DALLAS, TX, p. A611
KPC PROMISE HOSPITAL OF OVERLAND PARK, OVERLAND PARK, KS, p. A257
KPC PROMISE HOSPITAL OF PHOENIX, MESA, AZ, p. A34
KPC PROMISE HOSPITAL OF SALT LAKE, SALT LAKE CITY, UT, p. A668
KPC PROMISE HOSPITAL OF WICHITA FALLS, WICHITA FALLS, TX, p. A662
KUAKINI MEDICAL CENTER, HONOLULU, HI, p. A175
KULA HOSPITAL, KULA, HI, p. A177
KVC PRAIRIE RIDGE PSYCHIATRIC HOSPITAL, KANSAS CITY, KS, p. A251
KWAJALEIN HOSPITAL, KWAJALEIN ATOLL, MARSHALL ISLANDS, p. A730

L

LA DOWNTOWN MEDICAL CENTER, LLC, LOS ANGELES, CA, p. A73
LA PALMA INTERCOMMUNITY HOSPITAL, LA PALMA, CA, p. A69
LA PAZ REGIONAL HOSPITAL, PARKER, AZ, p. A34
LA RABIDA CHILDREN'S HOSPITAL, CHICAGO, IL, p. A190
LABETTE HEALTH, PARSONS, KS, p. A258
LAC–OLIVE VIEW–UCLA MEDICAL CENTER, LOS ANGELES, CA, p. A74
LAC+USC MEDICAL CENTER, LOS ANGELES, CA, p. A74
LACKEY MEMORIAL HOSPITAL, FOREST, MS, p. A362
LADY OF THE SEA GENERAL HOSPITAL, CUT OFF, LA, p. A281
LAFAYETTE GENERAL SOUTHWEST, LAFAYETTE, LA, p. A285
LAFAYETTE GENERAL SURGICAL HOSPITAL, LAFAYETTE, LA, p. A285
LAFAYETTE PHYSICAL REHABILITATION HOSPITAL, LAFAYETTE, LA, p. A285
LAFAYETTE REGIONAL HEALTH CENTER, LEXINGTON, MO, p. A379
LAFAYETTE REGIONAL REHABILITATION HOSPITAL, LAFAYETTE, IN, p. A222
LAGUNA HONDA HOSPITAL AND REHABILITATION CENTER, SAN FRANCISCO, CA, p. A91
LAHEY HOSPITAL & MEDICAL CENTER, BURLINGTON, MA, p. A312
LAIRD HOSPITAL, UNION, MS, p. A369
LAKE BEHAVIORAL HOSPITAL, WAUKEGAN, IL, p. A210
LAKE BUTLER HOSPITAL, LAKE BUTLER, FL, p. A136
LAKE CHARLES MEMORIAL HOSPITAL, LAKE CHARLES, LA, p. A286
LAKE CHELAN HEALTH, CHELAN, WA, p. A688
LAKE CITY MEDICAL CENTER, LAKE CITY, FL, p. A136
LAKE CUMBERLAND REGIONAL HOSPITAL, SOMERSET, KY, p. A274
LAKE DISTRICT HOSPITAL, LAKEVIEW, OR, p. A528
LAKE GRANBURY MEDICAL CENTER, GRANBURY, TX, p. A622
LAKE HURON MEDICAL CENTER, PORT HURON, MI, p. A336
LAKE MARTIN COMMUNITY HOSPITAL, DADEVILLE, AL, p. A18
LAKE NORMAN REGIONAL MEDICAL CENTER, MOORESVILLE, NC, p. A472
LAKE REGION HEALTHCARE CORPORATION, FERGUS FALLS, MN, p. A347
LAKE REGIONAL HEALTH SYSTEM, OSAGE BEACH, MO, p. A381
LAKE TAYLOR TRANSITIONAL CARE HOSPITAL, NORFOLK, VA, p. A680
LAKE VIEW HOSPITAL, TWO HARBORS, MN, p. A356
LAKELAND BEHAVIORAL HEALTH SYSTEM, SPRINGFIELD, MO, p. A386
LAKELAND COMMUNITY HOSPITAL, HALEYVILLE, AL, p. A20
LAKELAND HOSPITAL, NILES, NILES, MI, p. A334
LAKELAND REGIONAL HEALTH MEDICAL CENTER, LAKELAND, FL, p. A137
LAKES REGIONAL HEALTHCARE, SPIRIT LAKE, IA, p. A244
LAKESIDE BEHAVIORAL HEALTH SYSTEM, MEMPHIS, TN, p. A588
LAKESIDE MEDICAL CENTER, BELLE GLADE, FL, p. A125
LAKESIDE WOMEN'S HOSPITAL, OKLAHOMA CITY, OK, p. A517
LAKEVIEW BEHAVIORAL HEALTH, NORCROSS, GA, p. A169
LAKEVIEW HOSPITAL, BOUNTIFUL, UT, p. A664
LAKEVIEW HOSPITAL, STILLWATER, MN, p. A355
LAKEVIEW REGIONAL MEDICAL CENTER, COVINGTON, LA, p. A280
LAKEVIEW SPECIALTY HOSPITAL AND REHAB, WATERFORD, WI, p. A723
LAKEWAY REGIONAL MEDICAL CENTER, LAKEWAY, TX, p. A633
LAKEWOOD HEALTH SYSTEM, STAPLES, MN, p. A355
LAKEWOOD RANCH MEDICAL CENTER, BRADENTON, FL, p. A126
LAKEWOOD REGIONAL MEDICAL CENTER, LAKEWOOD, CA, p. A69
LALLIE KEMP MEDICAL CENTER, INDEPENDENCE, LA, p. A283
LAMB HEALTHCARE CENTER, LITTLEFIELD, TX, p. A634
LANAI COMMUNITY HOSPITAL, LANAI CITY, HI, p. A177
LANCASTER BEHAVIORAL HEALTH HOSPITAL, LANCASTER, PA, p. A543
LANCASTER REHABILITATION HOSPITAL, LANCASTER, PA, p. A543
LANDMANN–JUNGMAN MEMORIAL HOSPITAL AVERA, SCOTLAND, SD, p. A576
LANDMARK HOSPITAL OF ATHENS, ATHENS, GA, p. A156
LANDMARK HOSPITAL OF CAPE GIRARDEAU, CAPE GIRARDEAU, MO, p. A372
LANDMARK HOSPITAL OF COLUMBIA, COLUMBIA, MO, p. A374
LANDMARK HOSPITAL OF JOPLIN, JOPLIN, MO, p. A377
LANDMARK HOSPITAL OF SAVANNAH, SAVANNAH, GA, p. A171
LANDMARK HOSPITAL OF SOUTHWEST FLORIDA, NAPLES, FL, p. A141

Index of Hospitals / Landmark Medical Center

LANDMARK MEDICAL CENTER, WOONSOCKET, RI, p. A561
LANDMARK MEDICAL CENTER–FOGARTY UNIT, NORTH SMITHFIELD, RI, p. A560
LANE COUNTY HOSPITAL, DIGHTON, KS, p. A248
LANE REGIONAL MEDICAL CENTER, ZACHARY, LA, p. A294
LANGDON PRAIRIE HEALTH, LANGDON, ND, p. A482
LANIER HEALTH SERVICES, VALLEY, AL, p. A25
LANKENAU MEDICAL CENTER, WYNNEWOOD, PA, p. A558
LAREDO MEDICAL CENTER, LAREDO, TX, p. A634
LAREDO REHABILITATION HOSPITAL, LAREDO, TX, p. A634
LAREDO SPECIALTY HOSPITAL, LAREDO, TX, p. A634
LARKIN COMMUNITY HOSPITAL BEHAVIORAL HEALTH SERVICES, HOLLYWOOD, FL, p. A133
LARKIN COMMUNITY HOSPITAL–PALM SPRINGS CAMPUS, HIALEAH, FL, p. A133
LARKIN COMMUNITY HOSPITAL–SOUTH MIAMI CAMPUS, SOUTH MIAMI, FL, p. A150
LARNED STATE HOSPITAL, LARNED, KS, p. A252
LARRY B. ZIEVERINK, SR. ALCOHOLISM TREATMENT CENTER, RALEIGH, NC, p. A474
LAS ENCINAS HOSPITAL, PASADENA, CA, p. A83
LAS PALMAS MEDICAL CENTER, EL PASO, TX, p. A616
LASALLE GENERAL HOSPITAL, JENA, LA, p. A284
LAUDERDALE COMMUNITY HOSPITAL, RIPLEY, TN, p. A592
LAUREATE PSYCHIATRIC CLINIC AND HOSPITAL, TULSA, OK, p. A522
LAUREL OAKS BEHAVIORAL HEALTH CENTER, DOTHAN, AL, p. A18
LAUREL RIDGE TREATMENT CENTER, SAN ANTONIO, TX, p. A650
LAVACA MEDICAL CENTER, HALLETTSVILLE, TX, p. A623
LAWRENCE + MEMORIAL HOSPITAL, NEW LONDON, CT, p. A118
LAWRENCE COUNTY HOSPITAL, MONTICELLO, MS, p. A366
LAWRENCE COUNTY MEMORIAL HOSPITAL, LAWRENCEVILLE, IL, p. A200
LAWRENCE GENERAL HOSPITAL, LAWRENCE, MA, p. A314
LAWRENCE HOSPITAL CENTER, BRONXVILLE, NY, p. A440
LAWRENCE MEDICAL CENTER, MOULTON, AL, p. A23
LAWRENCE MEMORIAL HOSPITAL, WALNUT RIDGE, AR, p. A54
LAWRENCE MEMORIAL HOSPITAL OF MEDFORD, MEDFORD, MA, p. A315
LAWTON INDIAN HOSPITAL, LAWTON, OK, p. A514
LAYTON HOSPITAL, LAYTON, UT, p. A665
LDS HOSPITAL, SALT LAKE CITY, UT, p. A669
LE BONHEUR CHILDREN'S HOSPITAL, MEMPHIS, TN, p. A588
LE BONHEUR CHILDREN'S MEDICAL CENTER, MEMPHIS, TN, p. A588
LEAHI HOSPITAL, HONOLULU, HI, p. A175
LEBANON VETERANS AFFAIRS MEDICAL CENTER, LEBANON, PA, p. A544
LECOM HEALTH CORRY MEMORIAL HOSPITAL, CORRY, PA, p. A537
LECOM HEALTH MILLCREEK COMMUNITY HOSPITAL, ERIE, PA, p. A540
LECONTE MEDICAL CENTER, SEVIERVILLE, TN, p. A593
LEE MEMORIAL HOSPITAL, FORT MYERS, FL, p. A132
LEE'S SUMMIT MEDICAL CENTER, LEE'S SUMMIT, MO, p. A379
LEESBURG REGIONAL MEDICAL CENTER, LEESBURG, FL, p. A137
LEGACY EMANUEL CHILDREN'S HOSPITAL, PORTLAND, OR, p. A530
LEGACY EMANUEL MEDICAL CENTER, PORTLAND, OR, p. A530
LEGACY GOOD SAMARITAN MEDICAL CENTER, PORTLAND, OR, p. A530
LEGACY MERIDIAN PARK MEDICAL CENTER, TUALATIN, OR, p. A533
LEGACY MOUNT HOOD MEDICAL CENTER, GRESHAM, OR, p. A527
LEGACY SALMON CREEK MEDICAL CENTER, VANCOUVER, WA, p. A698
LEGACY SILVERTON MEDICAL CENTER, SILVERTON, OR, p. A532
LEGENT HOSPITAL FOR SPECIAL SURGERY, PLANO, TX, p. A644
LEGENT NORTH HOUSTON SURGICAL HOSPITAL, TOMBALL, TX, p. A658
LEGENT ORTHOPEDIC + SPINE HOSPITAL, SAN ANTONIO, TX, p. A650
LEGENT ORTHOPEDIC HOSPITAL CARROLLTON, CARROLLTON, TX, p. A606
LEHIGH REGIONAL MEDICAL CENTER, LEHIGH ACRES, FL, p. A137
LEHIGH VALLEY HEALTH NETWORK AT COORDINATED HEALTH, ALLENTOWN, PA, p. A534
LEHIGH VALLEY HEALTH NETWORK PEDIATRICS, ALLENTOWN, PA, p. A534

LEHIGH VALLEY HOSPITAL – HAZLETON, HAZLETON, PA, p. A541
LEHIGH VALLEY HOSPITAL – POCONO, EAST STROUDSBURG, PA, p. A539
LEHIGH VALLEY HOSPITAL – SCHUYLKILL, POTTSVILLE, PA, p. A553
LEHIGH VALLEY HOSPITAL–CEDAR CREST, ALLENTOWN, PA, p. A534
LEMUEL SHATTUCK HOSPITAL, JAMAICA PLAIN, MA, p. A314
LENOX HILL HOSPITAL, NEW YORK, NY, p. A449
LEONARD J. CHABERT MEDICAL CENTER, HOUMA, LA, p. A283
LESTER E. COX MEDICAL CENTER NORTH, SPRINGFIELD, MO, p. A386
LESTER E. COX MEDICAL CENTER SOUTH, SPRINGFIELD, MO, p. A386
LEVI HOSPITAL, HOT SPRINGS NATIONAL PARK, AR, p. A48
LEVINDALE HEBREW GERIATRIC CENTER AND HOSPITAL, BALTIMORE, MD, p. A300
LEVINDALE HEBREW HOSPITAL AND NURSING, BALTIMORE, MD, p. A300
LEWIS COUNTY GENERAL HOSPITAL, LOWVILLE, NY, p. A445
LEWIS–GALE PSYCHIATRIC CENTER, SALEM, VA, p. A683
LEWISGALE HOSPITAL ALLEGHANY, LOW MOOR, VA, p. A678
LEWISGALE HOSPITAL MONTGOMERY, BLACKSBURG, VA, p. A673
LEWISGALE HOSPITAL PULASKI, PULASKI, VA, p. A681
LEWISGALE MEDICAL CENTER, BOONES MILL, VA, p. A674
LEXINGTON MEDICAL CENTER, WEST COLUMBIA, SC, p. A571
LEXINGTON REGIONAL HEALTH CENTER, LEXINGTON, NE, p. A401
LEXINGTON VAMC, LEXINGTON, KY, p. A268
LHC GROUP – HOME HEALTHCARE, LAFAYETTE, LA, p. A285
LI JEWISH–HILLSIDE MED CENTER, NEW YORK, NY, p. A449
LIBERTY DAYTON REGIONAL MEDICAL CENTER, LIBERTY, TX, p. A634
LIBERTY HOSPITAL, LIBERTY, MO, p. A379
LIBERTY REGIONAL MEDICAL CENTER, HINESVILLE, GA, p. A165
LICKING MEMORIAL HOSPITAL, NEWARK, OH, p. A501
LIFE LINE HOSPITAL, STEUBENVILLE, OH, p. A504
LIFEBRITE COMMUNITY HOSPITAL OF STOKES, DANBURY, NC, p. A466
LIFECARE HOSPITALS OF NORTH TEXAS–FORT WORTH, FORT WORTH, TX, p. A619
LIFECARE HOSPITALS OF PLANO, PLANO, TX, p. A644
LIFECARE MEDICAL CENTER, ROSEAU, MN, p. A354
LIFECOURSE REHABILITATION HOSP, FARMINGTON, NM, p. A434
LIFESCAPE, SIOUX FALLS, SD, p. A576
LIFESTREAM BEHAVIORAL CENTER, LEESBURG, FL, p. A137
LIFEWAYS BEHAVIORAL HOSPITAL, BOISE, ID, p. A179
LIGHTHOUSE BEHAVIORAL HEALTH HOSPITAL, CONWAY, SC, p. A565
LILLIAN M. HUDSPETH MEMORIAL HOSPITAL, SONORA, TX, p. A653
LIMA MEMORIAL HEALTH SYSTEM, LIMA, OH, p. A498
LIMESTONE MEDICAL CENTER, GROESBECK, TX, p. A623
LINCOLN COMMUNITY HOSPITAL AND NURSING HOME, HUGO, CO, p. A109
LINCOLN COUNTY HEALTH SYSTEM, FAYETTEVILLE, TN, p. A583
LINCOLN COUNTY HOSPITAL, LINCOLN, KS, p. A253
LINCOLN COUNTY MEDICAL CENTER, RUIDOSO, NM, p. A436
LINCOLN DIVISION, LINCOLN, NE, p. A402
LINCOLN HEALTH, HUGO, CO, p. A110
LINCOLN HOSPITAL, DAVENPORT, WA, p. A688
LINCOLN MEMORIAL HOSPITAL, LINCOLN, IL, p. A200
LINCOLN PRAIRIE BEHAVIORAL HEALTH CENTER, SPRINGFIELD, IL, p. A209
LINCOLN REGIONAL CENTER, LINCOLN, NE, p. A402
LINCOLN SURGICAL HOSPITAL, LINCOLN, NE, p. A402
LINCOLN TRAIL BEHAVIORAL HEALTH SYSTEM, RADCLIFF, KY, p. A273
LINCOLNHEALTH, DAMARISCOTTA, ME, p. A296
LINDEN OAKS HOSPITAL, NAPERVILLE, IL, p. A203
LINDNER CENTER OF HOPE, MASON, OH, p. A499
LINDSAY MUNICIPAL HOSPITAL, LINDSAY, OK, p. A514
LINDSBORG COMMUNITY HOSPITAL, LINDSBORG, KS, p. A253
LINTON REGIONAL MEDICAL CENTER, LINTON, ND, p. A482
LITTLE COLORADO MEDICAL CENTER, WINSLOW, AZ, p. A41
LITTLE FALLS HOSPITAL, LITTLE FALLS, NY, p. A445
LITTLE RIVER MEDICAL CENTER, INC., ASHDOWN, AR, p. A43
LITTLE RIVER MEMORIAL HOSPITAL, ASHDOWN, AR, p. A43
LITTLETON ADVENTIST HOSPITAL, LITTLETON, CO, p. A111

LITTLETON REGIONAL HEALTHCARE, LITTLETON, NH, p. A416
LIVENGRIN FOUNDATION, BENSALEM, PA, p. A535
LIVINGSTON HEALTHCARE, LIVINGSTON, MT, p. A394
LIVINGSTON HOSPITAL AND HEALTHCARE SERVICES, SALEM, KY, p. A274
LIVINGSTON REGIONAL HOSPITAL, LIVINGSTON, TN, p. A587
LMH HEALTH, LAWRENCE, KS, p. A253
LOCKPORT MEMORIAL HOSPITAL, LOCKPORT, NY, p. A445
LOGAN COUNTY HOSPITAL, OAKLEY, KS, p. A256
LOGAN HEALTH – CONRAD, CONRAD, MT, p. A390
LOGAN HEALTH – CUT BANK, CUT BANK, MT, p. A391
LOGAN HEALTH – WHITEFISH, WHITEFISH, MT, p. A396
LOGAN HEALTH, KALISPELL, MT, p. A393
LOGAN HEALTH CHESTER, CHESTER, MT, p. A390
LOGAN HEALTH SHELBY, SHELBY, MT, p. A395
LOGAN MEMORIAL HOSPITAL, RUSSELLVILLE, KY, p. A274
LOGAN REGIONAL HOSPITAL, LOGAN, UT, p. A665
LOGAN REGIONAL MEDICAL CENTER, LOGAN, WV, p. A702
LOGANSPORT MEMORIAL HOSPITAL, LOGANSPORT, IN, p. A223
LOGANSPORT STATE HOSPITAL, LOGANSPORT, IN, p. A223
LOMA LINDA UNIV COMM MED CTR, LOMA LINDA, CA, p. A70
LOMA LINDA UNIVERSITY CHILDREN'S HOSPITAL, LOMA LINDA, CA, p. A70
LOMA LINDA UNIVERSITY HEART & SURGICAL HOSPITAL, LOMA LINDA, CA, p. A70
LOMA LINDA UNIVERSITY MEDICAL CENTER, LOMA LINDA, CA, p. A70
LOMA LINDA UNIVERSITY MEDICAL CENTER–MURRIETA, MURRIETA, CA, p. A79
LOMPOC VALLEY MEDICAL CENTER, LOMPOC, CA, p. A70
LONE PEAK HOSPITAL, DRAPER, UT, p. A665
LONE STAR BEHAVIORAL HEALTH, CYPRESS, TX, p. A610
LONESOME PINE HOSPITAL, BIG STONE GAP, VA, p. A673
LONG BEACH MEDICAL CENTER, LONG BEACH, CA, p. A71
LONG ISLAND COMMUNITY HOSPITAL, PATCHOGUE, NY, p. A455
LONG ISLAND JEWISH MEDICAL CENTER, NEW HYDE PARK, NY, p. A447
LONG–TERM ACUTE CARE HOSPITAL, MOSAIC LIFE CARE AT ST. JOSEPH, SAINT JOSEPH, MO, p. A383
LONGLEAF HOSPITAL, ALEXANDRIA, LA, p. A276
LONGMONT UNITED HOSPITAL, LONGMONT, CO, p. A111
LONGVIEW REGIONAL MEDICAL CENTER, LONGVIEW, TX, p. A635
LONGVIEW REHABILITATION HOSPITAL, LONGVIEW, TX, p. A635
LORETTO HOSPITAL, CHICAGO, IL, p. A190
LORING HOSPITAL, SAC CITY, IA, p. A242
LOS ALAMITOS MEDICAL CENTER, LOS ALAMITOS, CA, p. A71
LOS ALAMOS MEDICAL CENTER, LOS ALAMOS, NM, p. A435
LOS ANGELES COMMUNITY HOSPITAL AT LOS ANGELES, LOS ANGELES, CA, p. A74
LOS ANGELES COMMUNITY HOSPITAL OF NORWALK, NORWALK, CA, p. A80
LOS ANGELES COUNTY CENTRAL JAIL HOSPITAL, LOS ANGELES, CA, p. A74
LOS ANGELES GENERAL MEDICAL CENTER, LOS ANGELES, CA, p. A74
LOS ROBLES HEALTH SYSTEM, THOUSAND OAKS, CA, p. A97
LOS ROBLES HOSPITAL AND MEDICAL CENTER, THOUSAND OAKS, CA, p. A97
LOST RIVERS MEDICAL CENTER, ARCO, ID, p. A179
LOUIS A. JOHNSON VETERANS AFFAIRS MEDICAL CENTER, CLARKSBURG, WV, p. A700
LOUIS A. WEISS MEMORIAL HOSPITAL, CHICAGO, IL, p. A190
LOUIS STOKES CLEVELAND VETERANS AFFAIRS MEDICAL CENTER, CLEVELAND, OH, p. A491
LOUISIANA BEHAVIORAL HEALTH, SHREVEPORT, LA, p. A292
LOUISIANA EXTENDED CARE HOSPITAL OF LAFAYETTE, LAFAYETTE, LA, p. A285
LOUISIANA EXTENDED CARE HOSPITAL OF NATCHITOCHES, NATCHITOCHES, LA, p. A289
LOUISVILLE VAMC, LOUISVILLE, KY, p. A269
LOURDES COUNSELING CENTER, RICHLAND, WA, p. A694
LOURDES HEALTH, PASCO, WA, p. A692
LOURDES HOSPITAL, PADUCAH, KY, p. A273
LOVELACE MEDICAL CENTER, ALBUQUERQUE, NM, p. A432
LOVELACE REGIONAL HOSPITAL – ROSWELL, ROSWELL, NM, p. A436
LOVELACE UNM REHABILITATION HOSPITAL, ALBUQUERQUE, NM, p. A432
LOVELACE WESTSIDE HOSPITAL, ALBUQUERQUE, NM, p. A432
LOVELACE WOMEN'S HOSPITAL, ALBUQUERQUE, NM, p. A433
LOWELL GENERAL HOSPITAL, LOWELL, MA, p. A315

Index of Hospitals / McCready Foundation

LOWER BUCKS HOSPITAL, BRISTOL, PA, p. A535
LOWER KEYS MEDICAL CENTER, KEY WEST, FL, p. A136
LOWER UMPQUA HOSPITAL DISTRICT, REEDSPORT, OR, p. A531
LOYOLA UNIVERSITY MEDICAL CENTER, MAYWOOD, IL, p. A201
LT. COL. LUKE WEATHERS, JR. VA MEDICAL CENTER, MEMPHIS, TN, p. A588
LUBBOCK HEART & SURGICAL HOSPITAL, LUBBOCK, TX, p. A636
LUCAS COUNTY HEALTH CENTER, CHARITON, IA, p. A232
LUCILE PACKARD CHILDREN'S HOSPITAL STANFORD, PALO ALTO, CA, p. A82
LUKE'S HOSPITAL – CARBON CAMPUS, LEHIGHTON, PA, p. A544
LUMINIS HEALTH ANNE ARUNDEL MEDICAL CENTER, ANNAPOLIS, MD, p. A300
LUMINIS HEALTH DOCTORS COMMUNITY MEDICAL CENTER, LANHAM, MD, p. A305
LUTHERAN DOWNTOWN HOSPITAL, FORT WAYNE, IN, p. A216
LUTHERAN HOSPITAL, CLEVELAND, OH, p. A491
LUTHERAN HOSPITAL OF INDIANA, FORT WAYNE, IN, p. A216
LUTHERAN KOSCIUSKO HOSPITAL, WARSAW, IN, p. A229
LUTHERAN MEDICAL CENTER, WHEAT RIDGE, CO, p. A114
LYNDON B JOHNSON GENERAL HOSPITAL, HOUSTON, TX, p. A626
LYNDON B. JOHNSON TROPICAL MEDICAL CENTER, PAGO PAGO, AMERICAN SAMOA, p. A730
LYNN COUNTY HOSPITAL DISTRICT, TAHOKA, TX, p. A655
LYONS DIVISION, LYONS, NJ, p. A423

M

MACDONALD HOSPITAL FOR WOMEN, CLEVELAND, OH, p. A491
MACKINAC STRAITS HEALTH SYSTEM, INC., SAINT IGNACE, MI, p. A337
MACNEAL HOSPITAL, BERWYN, IL, p. A186
MACON COMMUNITY HOSPITAL, LAFAYETTE, TN, p. A586
MAD RIVER COMMUNITY HOSPITAL, ARCATA, CA, p. A56
MADELIA COMMUNITY HOSPITAL, MADELIA, MN, p. A349
MADELIA HEALTH, MADELIA, MN, p. A349
MADIGAN ARMY MEDICAL CENTER, TACOMA, WA, p. A697
MADISON COUNTY HEALTH CARE SYSTEM, WINTERSET, IA, p. A245
MADISON COUNTY MEMORIAL HOSPITAL, MADISON, FL, p. A138
MADISON HEALTH, LONDON, OH, p. A498
MADISON HEALTHCARE SERVICES, MADISON, MN, p. A349
MADISON MEDICAL CENTER, FREDERICKTOWN, MO, p. A375
MADISON MEMORIAL HOSPITAL, REXBURG, ID, p. A183
MADISON PARISH HOSPITAL, TALLULAH, LA, p. A293
MADISON REGIONAL HEALTH SYSTEM, MADISON, SD, p. A574
MADISON STATE HOSPITAL, MADISON, IN, p. A223
MADISON VAH, MADISON, WI, p. A714
MADISON VALLEY MEDICAL CENTER, ENNIS, MT, p. A391
MADISONHEALTH, REXBURG, ID, p. A183
MADONNA REHABILITATION HOSPITAL, LINCOLN, NE, p. A402
MADONNA REHABILITATION SPECIALTY HOSPITAL LINCOLN, LINCOLN, NE, p. A402
MADONNA REHABILITATION SPECIALTY HOSPITAL OMAHA, OMAHA, NE, p. A404
MAGEE GENERAL HOSPITAL, MAGEE, MS, p. A365
MAGEE REHABILITATION, PHILADELPHIA, PA, p. A549
MAGNOLIA REGIONAL HEALTH CENTER, CORINTH, MS, p. A361
MAGNOLIA REGIONAL MEDICAL CENTER, MAGNOLIA, AR, p. A50
MAGRUDER MEMORIAL HOSPITAL, PORT CLINTON, OH, p. A502
MAHASKA HEALTH, OSKALOOSA, IA, p. A241
MAHNOMEN HEALTH, MAHNOMEN, MN, p. A349
MAHNOMEN HEALTH CENTER, MAHNOMEN, MN, p. A349
MAIMONIDES MEDICAL CENTER, NEW YORK, NY, p. A449
MAINE VETERANS AFFAIRS MEDICAL CENTER, AUGUSTA, ME, p. A295
MAINEGENERAL MEDICAL CENTER, AUGUSTA, ME, p. A295
MAINEGENERAL MEDICAL CENTER–AUGUSTA CAMPUS, AUGUSTA, ME, p. A295
MAINEHEALTH BEHAVIORAL HEALTH AT SPRING HARBOR, WESTBROOK, ME, p. A299

MAINEHEALTH MAINE MEDICAL CENTER, PORTLAND, ME, p. A298
MAINEHEALTH PEN BAY MEDICAL CENTER, ROCKPORT, ME, p. A299
MAINEHEALTH STEPHENS HOSPITAL, NORWAY, ME, p. A298
MAINLAND MEDICAL CENTER, TEXAS CITY, TX, p. A657
MAJOR HOSPITAL, SHELBYVILLE, IN, p. A227
MALCOM RANDALL VETERANS AFFAIRS MEDICAL CENTER, GAINESVILLE, FL, p. A132
MALVERN INSTITUTE, MALVERN, PA, p. A545
MAMMOTH HOSPITAL, MAMMOTH LAKES, CA, p. A76
MANATEE MEMORIAL HOSPITAL, BRADENTON, FL, p. A126
MANCHESTER MEMORIAL HOSPITAL, MANCHESTER, CT, p. A116
MANCHESTER VETERANS AFFAIRS MEDICAL CENTER, MANCHESTER, NH, p. A416
MANGUM REGIONAL MEDICAL CENTER, MANGUM, OK, p. A514
MANHASSET AMBULATORY CARE CTR, MANHASSET, NY, p. A445
MANHATTAN EET HOSPITAL, NEW YORK, NY, p. A449
MANHATTAN PSYCHIATRIC CENTER–WARD'S ISLAND, NEW YORK, NY, p. A449
MANHATTAN SURGICAL, MANHATTAN, KS, p. A254
MANIILAQ HEALTH CENTER, KOTZEBUE, AK, p. A29
MANN–GRANDSTAFF DEPARTMENT OF VETERANS AFFAIRS MEDICAL CENTER, SPOKANE, WA, p. A696
MANNING REGIONAL HEALTHCARE CENTER, MANNING, IA, p. A239
MANSFIELD GENERAL HOSPITAL, MANSFIELD, OH, p. A499
MAPLE GROVE HOSPITAL, MAPLE GROVE, MN, p. A349
MARCUS DALY MEMORIAL HOSPITAL, HAMILTON, MT, p. A392
MARGARET MARY HEALTH, BATESVILLE, IN, p. A212
MARGARET TIETZ CNTR FOR NRSG, NEW YORK, NY, p. A449
MARGARETVILLE HOSPITAL, MARGARETVILLE, NY, p. A446
MARIA PARHAM HEALTH, DUKE LIFEPOINT HEALTHCARE, HENDERSON, NC, p. A470
MARIAN CENTER, SALT LAKE CITY, UT, p. A669
MARIAN REGIONAL MEDICAL CENTER, SANTA MARIA, CA, p. A94
MARIETTA MEMORIAL HOSPITAL, MARIETTA, OH, p. A499
MARINHEALTH MEDICAL CENTER, GREENBRAE, CA, p. A66
MARION GENERAL HOSPITAL, COLUMBIA, MS, p. A361
MARION GENERAL HOSPITAL, MARION, IN, p. A223
MARION HEALTH, MARION, IN, p. A223
MARION MEMORIAL HOSPITAL, BUENA VISTA, GA, p. A159
MARION VETERANS AFFAIRS MEDICAL CENTER, MARION, IL, p. A200
MARK TWAIN MEDICAL CENTER, SAN ANDREAS, CA, p. A88
MARLETTE REGIONAL HOSPITAL, MARLETTE, MI, p. A333
MARSHALL BROWNING HOSPITAL, DU QUOIN, IL, p. A193
MARSHALL COUNTY HEALTHCARE CENTER AVERA, BRITTON, SD, p. A572
MARSHALL COUNTY HOSPITAL, BENTON, KY, p. A263
MARSHALL MEDICAL CENTER, LEWISBURG, TN, p. A587
MARSHALL MEDICAL CENTER, PLACERVILLE, CA, p. A83
MARSHALL MEDICAL CENTER NORTH, GUNTERSVILLE, AL, p. A20
MARSHALL MEDICAL CENTER SOUTH, BOAZ, AL, p. A17
MARSHFIELD MEDICAL CENTER – BEAVER DAM, BEAVER DAM, WI, p. A708
MARSHFIELD MEDICAL CENTER – DICKINSON, IRON MOUNTAIN, MI, p. A330
MARSHFIELD MEDICAL CENTER – EAU CLAIRE HOSPITAL, EAU CLAIRE, WI, p. A710
MARSHFIELD MEDICAL CENTER – LADYSMITH, LADYSMITH, WI, p. A714
MARSHFIELD MEDICAL CENTER – MINOCQUA, MINOCQUA, WI, p. A717
MARSHFIELD MEDICAL CENTER – NEILSVILLE, NEILLSVILLE, WI, p. A718
MARSHFIELD MEDICAL CENTER – PARK FALLS, PARK FALLS, WI, p. A719
MARSHFIELD MEDICAL CENTER – RICE LAKE, RICE LAKE, WI, p. A720
MARSHFIELD MEDICAL CENTER – RIVER REGION, STEVENS POINT, WI, p. A722
MARSHFIELD MEDICAL CENTER – WESTON, WESTON, WI, p. A725
MARSHFIELD MEDICAL CENTER, MARSHFIELD, WI, p. A715
MARTHA'S VINEYARD HOSPITAL, OAK BLUFFS, MA, p. A317
MARTIN ARMY COMMUNITY HOSPITAL, FORT BENNING, GA, p. A164
MARTIN COUNTY HOSPITAL DISTRICT, STANTON, TX, p. A654
MARTIN LUTHER KING, JR. COMMUNITY HOSPITAL, LOS ANGELES, CA, p. A74
MARTIN MEMORIAL HOSPITAL SOUTH, STUART, FL, p. A150

MARTINSBURG VETERANS AFFAIRS MEDICAL CENTER, MARTINSBURG, WV, p. A702
MARWOOD MANOR, PORT HURON, MI, p. A336
MARY BRECKINRIDGE ARH HOSPITAL, HYDEN, KY, p. A267
MARY FREE BED REHABILITATION HOSPITAL, GRAND RAPIDS, MI, p. A328
MARY GREELEY MEDICAL CENTER, AMES, IA, p. A230
MARY LANNING HEALTHCARE, HASTINGS, NE, p. A400
MARY RUTAN HOSPITAL, BELLEFONTAINE, OH, p. A486
MARY WASHINGTON HOSPITAL, FREDERICKSBURG, VA, p. A676
MARY'S HARPER GERIATRIC PSYCHIATRY CENTER, TUSCALOOSA, AL, p. A25
MARYMOUNT HOSPITAL, GARFIELD HEIGHTS, OH, p. A496
MASON DISTRICT HOSPITAL, HAVANA, IL, p. A197
MASON HEALTH, SHELTON, WA, p. A695
MASONICARE HEALTH CENTER, WALLINGFORD, CT, p. A119
MASSAC MEMORIAL HOSPITAL, METROPOLIS, IL, p. A202
MASSACHUSETTS EYE AND EAR, BOSTON, MA, p. A310
MASSACHUSETTS GENERAL HOSPITAL, BOSTON, MA, p. A310
MASSENA HOSPITAL, INC., MASSENA, NY, p. A446
MAT–SU REGIONAL MEDICAL CENTER, PALMER, AK, p. A29
MATAGORDA REGIONAL MEDICAL CENTER, BAY CITY, TX, p. A601
MATHENY MEDICAL AND EDUCATIONAL CENTER, PEAPACK, NJ, p. A426
MATHER HOSPITAL, PORT JEFFERSON, NY, p. A456
MAUI MEMORIAL MEDICAL CENTER, WAILUKU, HI, p. A177
MAURY REGIONAL MEDICAL CENTER, COLUMBIA, TN, p. A581
MAYAGUEZ MEDICAL CENTER, MAYAGUEZ, PR, p. A733
MAYERS MEMORIAL HOSPITAL DISTRICT, FALL RIVER MILLS, CA, p. A63
MAYHILL HOSPITAL, DENTON, TX, p. A614
MAYO CLINIC – SAINT MARYS HOSPITAL, ROCHESTER, MN, p. A353
MAYO CLINIC HEALTH SYSTEM – ALBERT LEA AND AUSTIN, ALBERT LEA, MN, p. A342
MAYO CLINIC HEALTH SYSTEM – CHIPPEWA VALLEY IN BLOOMER, BLOOMER, WI, p. A708
MAYO CLINIC HEALTH SYSTEM – FRANCISCAN HEALTHCARE IN LA CROSSE, LA CROSSE, WI, p. A714
MAYO CLINIC HEALTH SYSTEM – FRANCISCAN HEALTHCARE IN SPARTA, SPARTA, WI, p. A721
MAYO CLINIC HEALTH SYSTEM – NORTHLAND IN BARRON, BARRON, WI, p. A708
MAYO CLINIC HEALTH SYSTEM – OAKRIDGE IN OSSEO, OSSEO, WI, p. A719
MAYO CLINIC HEALTH SYSTEM – RED CEDAR IN MENOMONIE, MENOMONIE, WI, p. A716
MAYO CLINIC HEALTH SYSTEM IN CANNON FALLS, CANNON FALLS, MN, p. A344
MAYO CLINIC HEALTH SYSTEM IN EAU CLAIRE, EAU CLAIRE, WI, p. A710
MAYO CLINIC HEALTH SYSTEM IN FAIRMONT, FAIRMONT, MN, p. A346
MAYO CLINIC HEALTH SYSTEM IN LA CROSSE, LA CROSSE, WI, p. A714
MAYO CLINIC HEALTH SYSTEM IN LAKE CITY, LAKE CITY, MN, p. A348
MAYO CLINIC HEALTH SYSTEM IN MANKATO, MANKATO, MN, p. A349
MAYO CLINIC HEALTH SYSTEM IN NEW PRAGUE, NEW PRAGUE, MN, p. A351
MAYO CLINIC HEALTH SYSTEM IN RED WING, RED WING, MN, p. A353
MAYO CLINIC HEALTH SYSTEM IN SAINT JAMES, SAINT JAMES, MN, p. A354
MAYO CLINIC HEALTH SYSTEM IN SPARTA, SPARTA, WI, p. A721
MAYO CLINIC HEALTH SYSTEM IN WASECA, WASECA, MN, p. A357
MAYO CLINIC HEALTH SYSTEM–ALBERT LEA AND AUSTIN, AUSTIN, MN, p. A343
MAYO CLINIC HOSPITAL – ROCHESTER, ROCHESTER, MN, p. A353
MAYO CLINIC HOSPITAL IN ARIZONA, PHOENIX, AZ, p. A36
MAYO CLINIC HOSPITAL IN FLORIDA, JACKSONVILLE, FL, p. A135
MCALESTER REGIONAL HEALTH CENTER, MCALESTER, OK, p. A515
MCALLEN MEDICAL CENTER, MCALLEN, TX, p. A638
MCBRIDE ORTHOPEDIC HOSPITAL, OKLAHOMA CITY, OK, p. A517
MCCAMEY COUNTY HOSPITAL DISTRICT, MCCAMEY, TX, p. A638
MCCONE COUNTY HEALTH CENTER, CIRCLE, MT, p. A390
MCCREADY FOUNDATION, CRISFIELD, MD, p. A303

Index of Hospitals / McCullough–Hyde Memorial Hospital/Trihealth

MCCULLOUGH–HYDE MEMORIAL HOSPITAL/TRIHEALTH, OXFORD, OH, p. A502
MCCURTAIN MEMORIAL HOSPITAL, IDABEL, OK, p. A514
MCDONOUGH DISTRICT HOSPITAL, MACOMB, IL, p. A200
MCDOWELL ARH HOSPITAL, MCDOWELL, KY, p. A271
MCG CHILDREN'S MEDICAL CENTER, AUGUSTA, GA, p. A158
MCGEHEE HOSPITAL, MCGEHEE, AR, p. A50
MCKAY–DEE HOSPITAL, OGDEN, UT, p. A666
MCKEE MEDICAL CENTER, LOVELAND, CO, p. A112
MCKENZIE COUNTY HEALTHCARE SYSTEM, WATFORD CITY, ND, p. A483
MCKENZIE HEALTH SYSTEM, SANDUSKY, MI, p. A337
MCKENZIE–WILLAMETTE MEDICAL CENTER, SPRINGFIELD, OR, p. A532
MCLANE CHILDREN'S HOSPITAL SCOTT & WHITE, TEMPLE, TX, p. A656
MCLAREN BAY REGION, BAY CITY, MI, p. A322
MCLAREN BAY SPECIAL CARE, BAY CITY, MI, p. A322
MCLAREN CARO REGION, CARO, MI, p. A323
MCLAREN CENTRAL MICHIGAN, MOUNT PLEASANT, MI, p. A334
MCLAREN FLINT, FLINT, MI, p. A327
MCLAREN GREATER LANSING, LANSING, MI, p. A331
MCLAREN LAPEER REGION, LAPEER, MI, p. A332
MCLAREN MACOMB, MOUNT CLEMENS, MI, p. A333
MCLAREN NORTHERN MICHIGAN, PETOSKEY, MI, p. A335
MCLAREN OAKLAND, PONTIAC, MI, p. A335
MCLAREN PORT HURON, PORT HURON, MI, p. A336
MCLAREN THUMB REGION, BAD AXE, MI, p. A322
MCLEAN HOSPITAL, BELMONT, MA, p. A309
MCLEOD HEALTH CHERAW, CHERAW, SC, p. A563
MCLEOD HEALTH CLARENDON, MANNING, SC, p. A568
MCLEOD HEALTH DILLON, DILLON, SC, p. A565
MCLEOD HEALTH LORIS, LORIS, SC, p. A568
MCLEOD REGIONAL MEDICAL CENTER, FLORENCE, SC, p. A566
MCPHERSON HOSPITAL, INC., MCPHERSON, KS, p. A254
MEADE DISTRICT HOSPITAL, MEADE, KS, p. A254
MEADOW WOOD BEHAVIORAL HEALTH SYSTEM, NEW CASTLE, DE, p. A122
MEADOWBROOK REHABILITATION HOSPITAL, GARDNER, KS, p. A249
MEADOWCREST HOSPITAL, GRETNA, LA, p. A282
MEADOWVIEW REGIONAL MEDICAL CENTER, MAYSVILLE, KY, p. A271
MEADVILLE MEDICAL CENTER, MEADVILLE, PA, p. A545
MEASE COUNTRYSIDE HOSPITAL, SAFETY HARBOR, FL, p. A148
MEASE DUNEDIN HOSPITAL, DUNEDIN, FL, p. A130
MEDICAL ARTS HOSPITAL, LAMESA, TX, p. A633
MEDICAL BEHAVIORAL HOSPITAL OF CLEAR LAKE, HOUSTON, TX, p. A629
MEDICAL BEHAVIORAL HOSPITAL OF MISHAWAKA, MISHAWAKA, IN, p. A223
MEDICAL BEHAVIORAL HOSPITAL OF NORTHERN ARIZONA, PRESCOTT, AZ, p. A37
MEDICAL CENTER AT FRANKLIN, FRANKLIN, KY, p. A266
MEDICAL CENTER AT SCOTTSVILLE, SCOTTSVILLE, KY, p. A274
MEDICAL CENTER BARBOUR, EUFAULA, AL, p. A19
MEDICAL CENTER ENTERPRISE, ENTERPRISE, AL, p. A19
MEDICAL CENTER FRISCO, FRISCO, TX, p. A621
MEDICAL CENTER HEALTH SYSTEM, ODESSA, TX, p. A642
MEDICAL CENTER HOSPITAL, SAN ANTONIO, TX, p. A650
MEDICAL CENTER OF AURORA, AURORA, CO, p. A103
MEDICAL CENTER OF PEACH COUNTY, NAVICENT HEALTH, MACON, GA, p. A167
MEDICAL CENTER OF SOUTH ARKANSAS, EL DORADO, AR, p. A45
MEDICAL CENTER OF TRINITY, TRINITY, FL, p. A153
MEDICAL CITY ALLIANCE, FORT WORTH, TX, p. A619
MEDICAL CITY ARLINGTON, ARLINGTON, TX, p. A597
MEDICAL CITY DALLAS, DALLAS, TX, p. A611
MEDICAL CITY DECATUR, DECATUR, TX, p. A613
MEDICAL CITY DENTON, DENTON, TX, p. A614
MEDICAL CITY FORT WORTH, FORT WORTH, TX, p. A620
MEDICAL CITY GREEN OAKS HOSPITAL, DALLAS, TX, p. A611
MEDICAL CITY LAS COLINAS, IRVING, TX, p. A630
MEDICAL CITY LEWISVILLE, LEWISVILLE, TX, p. A634
MEDICAL CITY MCKINNEY, MCKINNEY, TX, p. A638
MEDICAL CITY MENTAL HEALTH & WELLNESS CENTER – FRISCO, FRISCO, TX, p. A621
MEDICAL CITY NORTH HILLS, NORTH RICHLAND HILLS, TX, p. A641
MEDICAL CITY PLANO, PLANO, TX, p. A645
MEDICAL CITY WEATHERFORD, WEATHERFORD, TX, p. A661
MEDICAL WEST, BESSEMER, AL, p. A16
MEDICINE LODGE MEMORIAL HOSPITAL, MEDICINE LODGE, KS, p. A254
MEDINA REGIONAL HOSPITAL, HONDO, TX, p. A624
MEDSTAR FRANKLIN SQUARE MEDICAL CENTER, BALTIMORE, MD, p. A302
MEDSTAR GEORGETOWN UNIVERSITY HOSPITAL, WASHINGTON, DC, p. A123
MEDSTAR GOOD SAMARITAN HOSPITAL, BALTIMORE, MD, p. A300
MEDSTAR HARBOR HOSPITAL, BALTIMORE, MD, p. A301
MEDSTAR MONTGOMERY MEDICAL CENTER, OLNEY, MD, p. A306
MEDSTAR NATIONAL REHABILITATION HOSPITAL, WASHINGTON, DC, p. A123
MEDSTAR SOUTHERN MARYLAND HOSPITAL CENTER, CLINTON, MD, p. A303
MEDSTAR ST. MARY'S HOSPITAL, LEONARDTOWN, MD, p. A305
MEDSTAR UNION MEMORIAL HOSPITAL, BALTIMORE, MD, p. A301
MEDSTAR WASHINGTON HOSPITAL CENTER, WASHINGTON, DC, p. A124
MEEKER MEMORIAL HOSPITAL AND CLINICS, LITCHFIELD, MN, p. A348
MELBOURNE REGIONAL MEDICAL CENTER, MELBOURNE, FL, p. A139
MELISSA MEMORIAL HOSPITAL, HOLYOKE, CO, p. A109
MELROSEWAKEFIELD HEALTHCARE, MELROSE, MA, p. A315
MEM HERMANN CHILDREN'S HOSP, HOUSTON, TX, p. A626
MEM MED CTR LEE CAMPUS, JOHNSTOWN, PA, p. A543
MEMORIAL CHILDREN'S HOSPITAL, SOUTH BEND, IN, p. A227
MEMORIAL COMMUNITY HEALTH, AURORA, NE, p. A397
MEMORIAL COMMUNITY HOSPITAL AND HEALTH SYSTEM, BLAIR, NE, p. A398
MEMORIAL DIVISION, CHARLESTON, WV, p. A700
MEMORIAL HEALTH, MARYSVILLE, OH, p. A499
MEMORIAL HEALTH, SAVANNAH, GA, p. A171
MEMORIAL HEALTH CARE SYSTEMS, SEWARD, NE, p. A406
MEMORIAL HEALTH MEADOWS HOSPITAL, VIDALIA, GA, p. A173
MEMORIAL HEALTH SYSTEM, ABILENE, KS, p. A246
MEMORIAL HEALTH UNIVERSITY MEDICAL CENTER, SAVANNAH, GA, p. A171
MEMORIAL HEALTHCARE, OWOSSO, MI, p. A334
MEMORIAL HERMAN HOSPITAL CYPRESS, CYPRESS, TX, p. A610
MEMORIAL HERMANN – TEXAS MEDICAL CENTER, HOUSTON, TX, p. A627
MEMORIAL HERMANN BAPTIST FANNIN BEHAVIORAL HEALTH CENTER, BEAUMONT, TX, p. A602
MEMORIAL HERMANN GREATER HEIGHTS HOSPITAL, HOUSTON, TX, p. A627
MEMORIAL HERMANN HOUSTON ORTHOPEDIC AND SPINE HOSPITAL, BELLAIRE, TX, p. A603
MEMORIAL HERMANN KATY HOSPITAL, KATY, TX, p. A631
MEMORIAL HERMANN MEMORIAL CITY MEDICAL CENTER, HOUSTON, TX, p. A627
MEMORIAL HERMANN NORTHEAST, HUMBLE, TX, p. A629
MEMORIAL HERMANN REHABILITATION HOSPITAL – KATY, KATY, TX, p. A631
MEMORIAL HERMANN SOUTHEAST, HOUSTON, TX, p. A627
MEMORIAL HERMANN SOUTHEAST HOSPITAL, HOUSTON, TX, p. A627
MEMORIAL HERMANN SOUTHWEST HOSPITAL, HOUSTON, TX, p. A627
MEMORIAL HERMANN SUGAR LAND HOSPITAL, SUGAR LAND, TX, p. A654
MEMORIAL HERMANN SURGICAL HOSPITAL KINGWOOD, KINGWOOD, TX, p. A633
MEMORIAL HERMANN SURGICAL HOSPITAL–FIRST COLONY, SUGAR LAND, TX, p. A654
MEMORIAL HERMANN THE WOODLANDS HOSPITAL, THE WOODLANDS, TX, p. A657
MEMORIAL HOSPITAL, ALBANY, NY, p. A438
MEMORIAL HOSPITAL, BELLEVILLE, IL, p. A186
MEMORIAL HOSPITAL, CHESTER, IL, p. A188
MEMORIAL HOSPITAL, NORTH CONWAY, NH, p. A417
MEMORIAL HOSPITAL, SEMINOLE, TX, p. A652
MEMORIAL HOSPITAL, THE WOODLANDS, TX, p. A657
MEMORIAL HOSPITAL AND HEALTH CARE CENTER, JASPER, IN, p. A220
MEMORIAL HOSPITAL AND MANOR, BAINBRIDGE, GA, p. A159
MEMORIAL HOSPITAL ASSOCIATION, CARTHAGE, IL, p. A187
MEMORIAL HOSPITAL AT GULFPORT, GULFPORT, MS, p. A362
MEMORIAL HOSPITAL AT STONE COUNTY, WIGGINS, MS, p. A370
MEMORIAL HOSPITAL BELLEVILLE, BELLEVILLE, IL, p. A186
MEMORIAL HOSPITAL FOR CHILDREN, COLORADO SPRINGS, CO, p. A105
MEMORIAL HOSPITAL JACKSONVILLE, JACKSONVILLE, FL, p. A135
MEMORIAL HOSPITAL LOS BANOS, LOS BANOS, CA, p. A76
MEMORIAL HOSPITAL MIRAMAR, MIRAMAR, FL, p. A141
MEMORIAL HOSPITAL NORTH, COLORADO SPRINGS, CO, p. A105
MEMORIAL HOSPITAL OF CARBON COUNTY, RAWLINS, WY, p. A728
MEMORIAL HOSPITAL OF CARBONDALE, CARBONDALE, IL, p. A187
MEMORIAL HOSPITAL OF CONVERSE COUNTY, DOUGLAS, WY, p. A727
MEMORIAL HOSPITAL OF GARDENA, GARDENA, CA, p. A65
MEMORIAL HOSPITAL OF LAFAYETTE COUNTY, DARLINGTON, WI, p. A709
MEMORIAL HOSPITAL OF SOUTH BEND, SOUTH BEND, IN, p. A227
MEMORIAL HOSPITAL OF STILWELL, STILWELL, OK, p. A521
MEMORIAL HOSPITAL OF SWEETWATER COUNTY, ROCK SPRINGS, WY, p. A728
MEMORIAL HOSPITAL OF TEXAS COUNTY AUTHORITY, GUYMON, OK, p. A513
MEMORIAL HOSPITAL PEMBROKE, PEMBROKE PINES, FL, p. A146
MEMORIAL HOSPITAL SOUTHWEST, HOUSTON, TX, p. A627
MEMORIAL HOSPITAL WEST, PEMBROKE PINES, FL, p. A146
MEMORIAL MEDICAL CENTER – LEE CAMPUS, JOHNSTOWN, PA, p. A543
MEMORIAL MEDICAL CENTER, LAS CRUCES, NM, p. A435
MEMORIAL MEDICAL CENTER, MODESTO, CA, p. A78
MEMORIAL MEDICAL CENTER, NEW ORLEANS, LA, p. A290
MEMORIAL MEDICAL CENTER, PORT LAVACA, TX, p. A645
MEMORIAL MEDICAL CENTER, SPRINGFIELD, IL, p. A209
MEMORIAL MISSION HOSPITAL, ASHEVILLE, NC, p. A463
MEMORIAL NORTH PARK HOSPITAL, HIXSON, TN, p. A584
MEMORIAL REGIONAL HEALTH, CRAIG, CO, p. A105
MEMORIAL REGIONAL HEALTH, HOLLYWOOD, FL, p. A133
MEMORIAL SATILLA HEALTH, WAYCROSS, GA, p. A174
MEMORIAL SLOAN KETTERING CANCER CENTER, NEW YORK, NY, p. A449
MEMPHIS MENTAL HEALTH INSTITUTE, MEMPHIS, TN, p. A588
MEMPHIS VAMC, MEMPHIS, TN, p. A589
MENA REGIONAL HEALTH SYSTEM, MENA, AR, p. A50
MENDOTA MENTAL HEALTH INSTITUTE, MADISON, WI, p. A714
MENIFEE GLOBAL MEDICAL CENTER, SUN CITY, CA, p. A97
MENIFEE VALLEY MEDICAL CENTER, SUN CITY, CA, p. A97
MENNINGER CLINIC, HOUSTON, TX, p. A627
MENNONITE GENERAL HOSPITAL, AIBONITO, PR, p. A731
MENORAH MEDICAL CENTER, OVERLAND PARK, KS, p. A257
MENTAL HEALTH EMERGENCY CENTER, MILWAUKEE, WI, p. A717
MENTAL HEALTH SERVICES FOR CLARK AND MADISON COUNTIES, SPRINGFIELD, OH, p. A503
MERCER HEALTH, COLDWATER, OH, p. A491
MERCY ALLEN HOSPITAL, OBERLIN, OH, p. A501
MERCY BEHAVIORAL HOSPITAL LLC, LECOMPTE, LA, p. A287
MERCY CARE CENTER, OMAHA, NE, p. A404
MERCY CRYSTAL LAKE HOSPITAL AND MEDICAL CENTER, CRYSTAL LAKE, IL, p. A192
MERCY FITZGERALD HOSPITAL, DARBY, PA, p. A538
MERCY GENERAL HOSPITAL, SACRAMENTO, CA, p. A87
MERCY GILBERT MEDICAL CENTER, GILBERT, AZ, p. A32
MERCY HEALTH – ALLEN HOSPITAL, OBERLIN, OH, p. A501
MERCY HEALTH – ANDERSON HOSPITAL, CINCINNATI, OH, p. A489
MERCY HEALTH – CLERMONT HOSPITAL, BATAVIA, OH, p. A486
MERCY HEALTH – DEFIANCE HOSPITAL, DEFIANCE, OH, p. A494
MERCY HEALTH – FAIRFIELD HOSPITAL, FAIRFIELD, OH, p. A495
MERCY HEALTH – KINGS MILLS HOSPITAL, MASON, OH, p. A499
MERCY HEALTH – LORAIN HOSPITAL, LORAIN, OH, p. A498
MERCY HEALTH – LOURDES HOSPITAL, PADUCAH, KY, p. A273
MERCY HEALTH – MARCUM AND WALLACE, IRVINE, KY, p. A267
MERCY HEALTH – SPRINGFIELD REGIONAL MEDICAL CENTER, SPRINGFIELD, OH, p. A504
MERCY HEALTH – ST. ELIZABETH BOARDMAN HOSPITAL, BOARDMAN, OH, p. A486
MERCY HEALTH – ST. ELIZABETH YOUNGSTOWN HOSPITAL, YOUNGSTOWN, OH, p. A508
MERCY HEALTH – ST. JOSEPH WARREN HOSPITAL, WARREN, OH, p. A506

MERCY HEALTH – ST. RITA'S MEDICAL CENTER, LIMA, OH, p. A498
MERCY HEALTH – ST. VINCENT MEDICAL CENTER, TOLEDO, OH, p. A504
MERCY HEALTH – TIFFIN HOSPITAL, TIFFIN, OH, p. A504
MERCY HEALTH – URBANA HOSPITAL, URBANA, OH, p. A505
MERCY HEALTH – WEST HOSPITAL, CINCINNATI, OH, p. A489
MERCY HEALTH – WILLARD HOSPITAL, WILLARD, OH, p. A507
MERCY HEALTH LOVE COUNTY, MARIETTA, OK, p. A514
MERCY HEALTH, LAKESHORE CAMPUS, SHELBY, MI, p. A338
MERCY HOSPITAL, BUFFALO, NY, p. A440
MERCY HOSPITAL, COON RAPIDS, MN, p. A345
MERCY HOSPITAL, DAVENPORT, IA, p. A234
MERCY HOSPITAL, MIAMI, FL, p. A140
MERCY HOSPITAL, OWENSBORO, KY, p. A272
MERCY HOSPITAL ADA, ADA, OK, p. A509
MERCY HOSPITAL AND MEDICAL CENTER, CHICAGO, IL, p. A190
MERCY HOSPITAL ARDMORE, ARDMORE, OK, p. A510
MERCY HOSPITAL AURORA, AURORA, MO, p. A371
MERCY HOSPITAL BERRYVILLE, BERRYVILLE, AR, p. A43
MERCY HOSPITAL BOONEVILLE, BOONEVILLE, AR, p. A44
MERCY HOSPITAL CARTHAGE, CARTHAGE, MO, p. A373
MERCY HOSPITAL CASSVILLE, CASSVILLE, MO, p. A373
MERCY HOSPITAL COLUMBUS, COLUMBUS, KS, p. A248
MERCY HOSPITAL DOWNTOWN, BAKERSFIELD, CA, p. A57
MERCY HOSPITAL FORT SMITH, FORT SMITH, AR, p. A47
MERCY HOSPITAL HEALDTON, HEALDTON, OK, p. A513
MERCY HOSPITAL INC., MOUNDRIDGE, KS, p. A255
MERCY HOSPITAL JEFFERSON, FESTUS, MO, p. A375
MERCY HOSPITAL JOPLIN, JOPLIN, MO, p. A377
MERCY HOSPITAL KINGFISHER, KINGFISHER, OK, p. A514
MERCY HOSPITAL LEBANON, LEBANON, MO, p. A379
MERCY HOSPITAL LINCOLN, TROY, MO, p. A387
MERCY HOSPITAL LOGAN COUNTY, GUTHRIE, OK, p. A513
MERCY HOSPITAL NORTHWEST ARKANSAS, ROGERS, AR, p. A52
MERCY HOSPITAL OF DEFIANCE, DEFIANCE, OH, p. A494
MERCY HOSPITAL OF FOLSOM, FOLSOM, CA, p. A63
MERCY HOSPITAL OKLAHOMA CITY, OKLAHOMA CITY, OK, p. A517
MERCY HOSPITAL OZARK, OZARK, AR, p. A52
MERCY HOSPITAL PARIS, PARIS, AR, p. A52
MERCY HOSPITAL PERRY, PERRYVILLE, MO, p. A382
MERCY HOSPITAL PITTSBURG, PITTSBURG, KS, p. A258
MERCY HOSPITAL SOUTH, SAINT LOUIS, MO, p. A385
MERCY HOSPITAL SOUTHEAST, CAPE GIRARDEAU, MO, p. A372
MERCY HOSPITAL SPRINGFIELD, SPRINGFIELD, MO, p. A387
MERCY HOSPITAL ST. LOUIS, SAINT LOUIS, MO, p. A385
MERCY HOSPITAL STODDARD, DEXTER, MO, p. A374
MERCY HOSPITAL TISHOMINGO, TISHOMINGO, OK, p. A521
MERCY HOSPITAL WALDRON, WALDRON, AR, p. A54
MERCY HOSPITAL WASHINGTON, WASHINGTON, MO, p. A388
MERCY HOSPITAL WATONGA, WATONGA, OK, p. A524
MERCY HOSPITALS OF BAKERSFIELD, BAKERSFIELD, CA, p. A57
MERCY IOWA CITY REHABILITATION HOSPITAL, CORALVILLE, IA, p. A233
MERCY MEDICAL CENTER – CEDAR RAPIDS, CEDAR RAPIDS, IA, p. A231
MERCY MEDICAL CENTER – WEST LAKES, WEST DES MOINES, IA, p. A245
MERCY MEDICAL CENTER, BALTIMORE, MD, p. A301
MERCY MEDICAL CENTER, CANTON, OH, p. A488
MERCY MEDICAL CENTER, ROCKVILLE CENTRE, NY, p. A458
MERCY MEDICAL CENTER, ROSEBURG, OR, p. A531
MERCY MEDICAL CENTER, SPRINGFIELD, MA, p. A318
MERCY MEDICAL CENTER MERCED, MERCED, CA, p. A77
MERCY MEDICAL CENTER MOUNT SHASTA, MOUNT SHASTA, CA, p. A79
MERCY MEDICAL CENTER REDDING, REDDING, CA, p. A85
MERCY MEMORIAL HOSPITAL, URBANA, OH, p. A505
MERCY REGIONAL MEDICAL CENTER, LORAIN, OH, p. A498
MERCY REGIONAL MEDICAL CENTER, VILLE PLATTE, LA, p. A294
MERCY REHABILITATION HOSPITAL FORT SMITH, FORT SMITH, AR, p. A47
MERCY REHABILITATION HOSPITAL OKLAHOMA CITY, OKLAHOMA CITY, OK, p. A517
MERCY REHABILITATION HOSPITAL OKLAHOMA CITY SOUTH, OKLAHOMA CITY, OK, p. A517
MERCY REHABILITATION HOSPITAL SOUTH, SAINT LOUIS, MO, p. A385
MERCY REHABILITATION HOSPITAL ST. LOUIS, CHESTERFIELD, MO, p. A373
MERCY REHABILITION HOSPITAL SPRINGFIELD, SPRINGFIELD, MO, p. A387

MERCY SAN JUAN MEDICAL CENTER, CARMICHAEL, CA, p. A58
MERCY SPECIALTY HOSPITAL SOUTHEAST KANSAS, GALENA, KS, p. A249
MERCY ST. ANNE HOSPITAL, TOLEDO, OH, p. A504
MERCY ST. CHARLES HOSPITAL, OREGON, OH, p. A502
MERCY ST. FRANCIS HOSPITAL, MOUNTAIN VIEW, MO, p. A381
MERCY ST. VINCENT MEDICAL CENTER, TOLEDO, OH, p. A504
MERCY TIFFIN HOSPITAL, TIFFIN, OH, p. A504
MERCYHEALTH HOSPITAL – ROCKTON AVENUE, ROCKFORD, IL, p. A207
MERCYHEALTH HOSPITAL AND MEDICAL CENTER – HARVARD, HARVARD, IL, p. A197
MERCYHEALTH HOSPITAL AND MEDICAL CENTER – WALWORTH, LAKE GENEVA, WI, p. A714
MERCYHEALTH HOSPITAL AND PHYSICIAN CLINIC–CRYSTAL LAKE, CRYSTAL LAKE, IL, p. A192
MERCYHEALTH HOSPITAL AND TRAUMA CENTER – JANESVILLE, JANESVILLE, WI, p. A713
MERCYHEALTH JAVON BEA HOSPITAL – RIVERSIDE CAMPUS, ROCKFORD, IL, p. A207
MERCYONE CEDAR FALLS MEDICAL CENTER, CEDAR FALLS, IA, p. A231
MERCYONE CENTERVILLE MEDICAL CENTER, CENTERVILLE, IA, p. A232
MERCYONE CLINTON MEDICAL CENTER, CLINTON, IA, p. A233
MERCYONE CLIVE REHABILITATION HOSPITAL, CLIVE, IA, p. A233
MERCYONE DES MOINES MEDICAL CENTER, DES MOINES, IA, p. A235
MERCYONE DUBUQUE MEDICAL CENTER, DUBUQUE, IA, p. A235
MERCYONE DYERSVILLE MEDICAL CENTER, DYERSVILLE, IA, p. A236
MERCYONE ELKADER MEDICAL CENTER, ELKADER, IA, p. A236
MERCYONE IOWA CITY, IOWA CITY, IA, p. A238
MERCYONE NEW HAMPTON MEDICAL CENTER, NEW HAMPTON, IA, p. A240
MERCYONE NEWTON MEDICAL CENTER, NEWTON, IA, p. A241
MERCYONE NORTH IOWA MEDICAL CENTER, MASON CITY, IA, p. A240
MERCYONE OELWEIN MEDICAL CENTER, OELWEIN, IA, p. A241
MERCYONE PRIMGHAR MEDICAL CENTER, PRIMGHAR, IA, p. A242
MERCYONE SIOUXLAND MEDICAL CENTER, SIOUX CITY, IA, p. A243
MERCYONE WATERLOO MEDICAL CENTER, WATERLOO, IA, p. A244
MERIDIAN HEALTH SERVICES, MUNCIE, IN, p. A224
MERIT HEALTH BILOXI, BILOXI, MS, p. A359
MERIT HEALTH CENTRAL, JACKSON, MS, p. A364
MERIT HEALTH MADISON, CANTON, MS, p. A360
MERIT HEALTH NATCHEZ, NATCHEZ, MS, p. A367
MERIT HEALTH RANKIN, BRANDON, MS, p. A360
MERIT HEALTH RIVER OAKS, FLOWOOD, MS, p. A362
MERIT HEALTH RIVER REGION, VICKSBURG, MS, p. A369
MERIT HEALTH WESLEY, HATTIESBURG, MS, p. A363
MERIT HEALTH WOMAN'S HOSPITAL, FLOWOOD, MS, p. A362
MERITCARE SOUTH UNIVERSITY, FARGO, ND, p. A480
MERITUS HEALTH, HAGERSTOWN, MD, p. A305
MERITUS MEDICAL CENTER, HAGERSTOWN, MD, p. A305
MERRICK MEDICAL CENTER, CENTRAL CITY, NE, p. A398
MESA SPRINGS, FORT WORTH, TX, p. A620
MESA VIEW REGIONAL HOSPITAL, MESQUITE, NV, p. A411
MESCALERO PUBLIC HEALTH SERVICE INDIAN HOSPITAL, MESCALERO, NM, p. A436
MESILLA VALLEY HOSPITAL, LAS CRUCES, NM, p. A435
MESQUITE REHABILITATION INSTITUTE, MESQUITE, TX, p. A639
MESQUITE SPECIALTY HOSPITAL, MESQUITE, TX, p. A639
METH HEALTHCARE – SOUTH HOSP, MEMPHIS, TN, p. A589
METHODIST BEHAVIORAL HOSPITAL, MAUMELLE, AR, p. A50
METHODIST CHARLTON MEDICAL CENTER, DALLAS, TX, p. A612
METHODIST DALLAS MEDICAL CENTER, DALLAS, TX, p. A612
METHODIST FREMONT HEALTH, FREMONT, NE, p. A400
METHODIST HEALTHCARE MEMPHIS HOSPITALS, MEMPHIS, TN, p. A589
METHODIST HEALTHCARE OLIVE BRANCH HOSPITAL, OLIVE BRANCH, MS, p. A367
METHODIST HLTHCARE–GERMANTOWN, GERMANTOWN, TN, p. A583
METHODIST HOSPITAL, FRANKFORT, IN, p. A217

METHODIST HOSPITAL, PHILADELPHIA, PA, p. A549
METHODIST HOSPITAL, SAN ANTONIO, TX, p. A650
METHODIST HOSPITAL FOR SURGERY, ADDISON, TX, p. A595
METHODIST HOSPITAL HILL COUNTRY, FREDERICKSBURG, TX, p. A620
METHODIST HOSPITAL OF CHICAGO, CHICAGO, IL, p. A190
METHODIST HOSPITAL OF SACRAMENTO, SACRAMENTO, CA, p. A87
METHODIST HOSPITAL SOUTH, JOURDANTON, TX, p. A631
METHODIST HOSPITAL UNION COUNTY, MORGANFIELD, KY, p. A272
METHODIST HOSPITALS, GARY, IN, p. A217
METHODIST JENNIE EDMUNDSON HOSPITAL, COUNCIL BLUFFS, IA, p. A234
METHODIST LE BONHEUR GERMANTOWN HOSPITAL, GERMANTOWN, TN, p. A583
METHODIST MANSFIELD MEDICAL CENTER, MANSFIELD, TX, p. A637
METHODIST MCKINNEY HOSPITAL, MCKINNEY, TX, p. A638
METHODIST MEDICAL CENTER OF OAK RIDGE, OAK RIDGE, TN, p. A591
METHODIST MIDLOTHIAN MEDICAL CENTER, MIDLOTHIAN, TX, p. A639
METHODIST NORTH–J HARRIS HSP, MEMPHIS, TN, p. A589
METHODIST REHABILITATION CENTER, JACKSON, MS, p. A364
METHODIST REHABILITATION HOSPITAL, DALLAS, TX, p. A612
METHODIST RICHARDSON MEDICAL CENTER, RICHARDSON, TX, p. A646
METHODIST SOUTHLAKE HOSPITAL, SOUTHLAKE, TX, p. A653
METHODIST STONE OAK HOSPITAL, SAN ANTONIO, TX, p. A650
METHODIST WEST HOSPITAL, WEST DES MOINES, IA, p. A245
METHODIST WOMEN'S & CHILD HOSP, SAN ANTONIO, TX, p. A650
METHODIST WOMEN'S HOSPITAL, ELKHORN, NE, p. A399
METRO HEALTH – UNIVERSITY OF MICHIGAN HEALTH, WYOMING, MI, p. A341
METRO HOSP–SPRINGFIELD DIV, SPRINGFIELD, PA, p. A555
METROHEALTH CTR FOR NRSG CARE, CLEVELAND, OH, p. A491
METROHEALTH MEDICAL CENTER, CLEVELAND, OH, p. A491
METROPOLITAN HOSPITAL, SAN ANTONIO, TX, p. A650
METROPOLITANO DE LA MONTANA, UTUADO, PR, p. A736
METROWEST MEDICAL CENTER, FRAMINGHAM, MA, p. A313
M HEALTH FAIRVIEW BETHESDA HOSPITAL, SAINT PAUL, MN, p. A354
M HEALTH FAIRVIEW LAKES MEDICAL CENTER, WYOMING, MN, p. A358
M HEALTH FAIRVIEW NORTHLAND MEDICAL CENTER, PRINCETON, MN, p. A353
M HEALTH FAIRVIEW RIDGES HOSPITAL, BURNSVILLE, MN, p. A344
M HEALTH FAIRVIEW SOUTHDALE HOSPITAL, EDINA, MN, p. A346
M HEALTH FAIRVIEW ST. JOHN'S HOSPITAL, MAPLEWOOD, MN, p. A349
M HEALTH FAIRVIEW UNIVERSITY OF MINNESOTA MEDICAL CENTER, MINNEAPOLIS, MN, p. A350
M HEALTH FAIRVIEW WOODWINDS HOSPITAL, WOODBURY, MN, p. A357
MIAMI COUNTY MEDICAL CENTER, PAOLA, KS, p. A257
MIAMI HEART CAMPUS AT MOUNT SINAI MEDICAL CENTER, MIAMI BEACH, FL, p. A141
MIAMI HEART INST & MED CTR, MIAMI BEACH, FL, p. A141
MIAMI JEWISH HEALTH, MIAMI, FL, p. A140
MIAMI VALLEY HOSPITAL, DAYTON, OH, p. A494
MIAMI VETERANS AFFAIRS HEALTHCARE SYSTEM, MIAMI, FL, p. A140
MICHAEL E. DEBAKEY DEPARTMENT OF VETERANS AFFAIRS MEDICAL CENTER, HOUSTON, TX, p. A627
MICHAEL E. DEBAKEY VA MEDICAL CENTER, HOUSTON, TX, p. A627
MICHIANA BEHAVIORAL HEALTH CENTER, PLYMOUTH, IN, p. A226
MID COAST HOSPITAL, BRUNSWICK, ME, p. A296
MID COAST MEDICAL CENTER – TRINITY, TRINITY, TX, p. A658
MID–AMERICA REHABILITATION HOSPITAL, SHAWNEE MISSION, KS, p. A260
MIDCOAST CENTRAL – LLANO, LLANO, TX, p. A635
MIDCOAST MEDICAL CENTER – BELLVILLE, BELLVILLE, TX, p. A603
MIDCOAST MEDICAL CENTER – CENTRAL, LLANO, TX, p. A635
MIDCOAST MEDICAL CENTER – CROCKETT, CROCKETT, TX, p. A609

Index of Hospitals / Middle Park Health–Kremmling

MIDDLE PARK HEALTH–KREMMLING, KREMMLING, CO, p. A110
MIDDLE TENNESSEE MENTAL HEALTH INSTITUTE, NASHVILLE, TN, p. A590
MIDDLESBORO ARH HOSPITAL, MIDDLESBORO, KY, p. A271
MIDDLESEX HEALTH, MIDDLETOWN, CT, p. A117
MIDDLESEX HOSPITAL, MIDDLETOWN, CT, p. A117
MID–HUDSON FORENSIC PSYCHIATRIC CENTER, NEW HAMPTON, NY, p. A446
MID–JEFFERSON EXTENDED CARE HOSPITAL OF BEAUMONT, BEAUMONT, TX, p. A602
MIDLAND MEM HOSP WEST CAMPUS, MIDLAND, TX, p. A639
MIDLAND MEMORIAL HOSPITAL, MIDLAND, TX, p. A639
MIDLANDS REGIONAL REHABILITATION HOSPITAL, ELGIN, SC, p. A565
MID–MAINE GENERAL MEDICAL CTR, AUGUSTA, ME, p. A295
MIDMICHIGAN MEDICAL CENTER – ALPENA, ALPENA, MI, p. A321
MIDMICHIGAN MEDICAL CENTER – WEST BRANCH, WEST BRANCH, MI, p. A340
MIDMICHIGAN MEDICAL CENTER–GLADWIN, GLADWIN, MI, p. A327
MIDMICHIGAN MEDICAL CENTER–MIDLAND, MIDLAND, MI, p. A333
MIDSTATE MEDICAL CENTER, MERIDEN, CT, p. A116
MID–VALLEY HOSPITAL AND CLINICS, OMAK, WA, p. A692
MIDWEST MEDICAL CENTER, GALENA, IL, p. A195
MIDWEST ORTHOPEDIC SPECIALTY HOSPITAL, FRANKLIN, WI, p. A711
MIDWEST SURGICAL HOSPITAL, OMAHA, NE, p. A404
MIKE O'CALLAGHAN FEDERAL HOSPITAL, NELLIS AFB, NV, p. A411
MILBANK AREA HOSPITAL AVERA, MILBANK, SD, p. A574
MILDRED MITCHELL–BATEMAN HOSPITAL, HUNTINGTON, WV, p. A701
MILE BLUFF MEDICAL CENTER, MAUSTON, WI, p. A715
MILFORD MEMORIAL HOSPITAL, MILFORD, DE, p. A121
MILFORD REGIONAL MEDICAL CENTER, MILFORD, MA, p. A316
MILFORD VALLEY MEMORIAL HOSPITAL, MILFORD, UT, p. A665
MILLARD FILLMORE SUBURBAN HOSPITAL, WILLIAMSVILLE, NY, p. A462
MILLE LACS HEALTH SYSTEM, ONAMIA, MN, p. A352
MILLER CHILDREN'S & WOMEN'S HOSPITAL LONG BEACH, LONG BEACH, CA, p. A71
MILLER COUNTY HOSPITAL, COLQUITT, GA, p. A161
MILLINOCKET REGIONAL HOSPITAL, MILLINOCKET, ME, p. A298
MILLS HEALTH CENTER, SAN MATEO, CA, p. A93
MILLS HOSPITAL, SAN MATEO, CA, p. A93
MILLS–PENINSULA HEALTH SERVICES, BURLINGAME, CA, p. A58
MILLS–PENINSULA MEDICAL CENTER, BURLINGAME, CA, p. A58
MILLWOOD HOSPITAL, ARLINGTON, TX, p. A597
MILWAUKEE REHABILITATION HOSPITAL AT GREENFIELD, MILWAUKEE, WI, p. A717
MILWAUKEE VAMC, MILWAUKEE, WI, p. A717
MIMBRES MEMORIAL HOSPITAL, DEMING, NM, p. A434
MINDEN MEDICAL CENTER, MINDEN, LA, p. A288
MINERAL COMMUNITY HOSPITAL, SUPERIOR, MT, p. A396
MINERS' COLFAX MEDICAL CENTER, RATON, NM, p. A436
MINERS' HOSPITAL OF NEW MEXICO, RATON, NM, p. A436
MINIDOKA MEMORIAL HOSPITAL, RUPERT, ID, p. A183
MINIMALLY INVASIVE SURGERY HOSPITAL, LENEXA, KS, p. A253
MINNEAPOLIS VA HEALTH CARE SYSTEM, MINNEAPOLIS, MN, p. A351
MINNEAPOLIS VAMC, MINNEAPOLIS, MN, p. A351
MINNEOLA DISTRICT HOSPITAL, MINNEOLA, KS, p. A255
MINNIE HAMILTON HEALTHCARE CENTER, GRANTSVILLE, WV, p. A701
MIRACARE BEHAVIORAL HEALTH CARE, TINLEY PARK, IL, p. A210
MIRAVISTA BEHAVIORAL HEALTH CENTER, HOLYOKE, MA, p. A314
MIRIAM HOSPITAL, PROVIDENCE, RI, p. A560
MISSION COMMUNITY HOSPITAL, LOS ANGELES, CA, p. A74
MISSION HOSPITAL, ASHEVILLE, NC, p. A463
MISSION HOSPITAL MCDOWELL, MARION, NC, p. A472
MISSION HOSPITAL MISSION VIEJO, MISSION VIEJO, CA, p. A77
MISSION REGIONAL MEDICAL CENTER, MISSION, TX, p. A640
MISSISSIPPI BAPTIST MEDICAL CENTER, JACKSON, MS, p. A364
MISSISSIPPI STATE HOSPITAL, WHITFIELD, MS, p. A370
MISSOURI BAPTIST MEDICAL CENTER, SAINT LOUIS, MO, p. A385

MISSOURI BAPTIST SULLIVAN HOSPITAL, SULLIVAN, MO, p. A387
MISSOURI DELTA MEDICAL CENTER, SIKESTON, MO, p. A386
MISSOURI RIVER MEDICAL CENTER, FORT BENTON, MT, p. A392
MITCHELL COUNTY HOSPITAL, COLORADO CITY, TX, p. A608
MITCHELL COUNTY HOSPITAL HEALTH SYSTEMS, BELOIT, KS, p. A247
MITCHELL COUNTY REGIONAL HEALTH CENTER, OSAGE, IA, p. A241
MIZELL MEMORIAL HOSPITAL, OPP, AL, p. A23
MLK COMMUNITY HEALTHCARE, LOS ANGELES, CA, p. A74
MOAB REGIONAL HOSPITAL, MOAB, UT, p. A666
MOBERLY REGIONAL MEDICAL CENTER, MOBERLY, MO, p. A380
MOBILE INFIRMARY MEDICAL CENTER, MOBILE, AL, p. A21
MOBRIDGE REGIONAL HOSPITAL, MOBRIDGE, SD, p. A575
MOCCASIN BEND MENTAL HEALTH INSTITUTE, CHATTANOOGA, TN, p. A580
MODESTO MEDICAL CENTER, MODESTO, CA, p. A78
MODOC MEDICAL CENTER, ALTURAS, CA, p. A55
MOHAWK VALLEY PSYCHIATRIC CENTER, UTICA, NY, p. A460
MOLOKAI GENERAL HOSPITAL, KAUNAKAKAI, HI, p. A177
MON HEALTH MARION NEIGHBORHOOD HOSPITAL, WHITE HALL, WV, p. A706
MON HEALTH MEDICAL CENTER, MORGANTOWN, WV, p. A703
MON HEALTH PRESTON MEMORIAL HOSPITAL, KINGWOOD, WV, p. A702
MON HEALTH STONEWALL JACKSON MEMORIAL HOSPITAL, WESTON, WV, p. A705
MONADNOCK COMMUNITY HOSPITAL, PETERBOROUGH, NH, p. A417
MONCRIEF ARMY COMMUNITY HOSPITAL, FORT JACKSON, SC, p. A566
MONMOUTH MEDICAL CENTER, LONG BRANCH CAMPUS, LONG BRANCH, NJ, p. A423
MONMOUTH MEDICAL CENTER, SOUTHERN CAMPUS, LAKEWOOD, NJ, p. A422
MONONGAHELA VALLEY HOSPITAL, MONONGAHELA, PA, p. A546
MONROE CARELL JR. CHILDREN'S HOSPITAL AT VANDERBILT, NASHVILLE, TN, p. A590
MONROE CLINIC, MONROE, WI, p. A717
MONROE COUNTY HOSPITAL, FORSYTH, GA, p. A164
MONROE COUNTY HOSPITAL, MONROEVILLE, AL, p. A22
MONROE COUNTY HOSPITAL AND CLINICS, ALBIA, IA, p. A230
MONROE COUNTY MEDICAL CENTER, TOMPKINSVILLE, KY, p. A274
MONROE HOSPITAL, BLOOMINGTON, IN, p. A213
MONROE REGIONAL HOSPITAL, ABERDEEN, MS, p. A359
MONROE SURGICAL HOSPITAL, MONROE, LA, p. A288
MONROVIA MEMORIAL HOSPITAL, MONROVIA, CA, p. A78
MONTANA HCS, FORT HARRISON, MT, p. A392
MONTANA STATE HOSPITAL, WARM SPRINGS, MT, p. A396
MONTCLAIR HOSPITAL MEDICAL CENTER, MONTCLAIR, CA, p. A78
MONTEFIORE HOSPITAL, PITTSBURGH, PA, p. A551
MONTEFIORE MEDICAL CENTER, NEW YORK, NY, p. A449
MONTEFIORE MOUNT VERNON, MOUNT VERNON, NY, p. A446
MONTEFIORE NEW ROCHELLE, NEW ROCHELLE, NY, p. A447
MONTEFIORE NYACK HOSPITAL, NYACK, NY, p. A454
MONTEFIORE ST. LUKE'S CORNWALL, NEWBURGH, NY, p. A454
MONTEREY PARK HOSPITAL, MONTEREY PARK, CA, p. A78
MONTGOMERY COUNTY EMERGENCY SERVICE, NORRISTOWN, PA, p. A547
MONTGOMERY COUNTY MEMORIAL HOSPITAL, RED OAK, IA, p. A242
MONTGOMERY DIVISION, MONTGOMERY, AL, p. A23
MONTGOMERY GENERAL HOSPITAL, MONTGOMERY, WV, p. A702
MONTPELIER HOSPITAL, MONTPELIER, OH, p. A500
MONTROSE BEHAVIORAL HEALTH HOSPITAL, CHICAGO, IL, p. A190
MONTROSE MEMORIAL HOSPITAL, MONTROSE, CO, p. A112
MONTROSE REGIONAL HEALTH, MONTROSE, CO, p. A112
MONUMENT HEALTH CUSTER HOSPITAL, CUSTER, SD, p. A573
MONUMENT HEALTH LEAD–DEADWOOD HOSPITAL, DEADWOOD, SD, p. A573
MONUMENT HEALTH RAPID CITY HOSPITAL, RAPID CITY, SD, p. A576
MONUMENT HEALTH SPEARFISH HOSPITAL, SPEARFISH, SD, p. A577
MONUMENT HEALTH STURGIS HOSPITAL, STURGIS, SD, p. A577
MOORE COUNTY HOSPITAL DISTRICT, DUMAS, TX, p. A615

MOORE MEDICAL CENTER, MOORE, OK, p. A515
MOREHOUSE GENERAL HOSPITAL, BASTROP, LA, p. A277
MORGAN COUNTY ARH HOSPITAL, WEST LIBERTY, KY, p. A275
MORGAN MEDICAL CENTER, MADISON, GA, p. A167
MORGAN MEMORIAL HOSPITAL, MADISON, GA, p. A167
MORGAN STANLEY CHILDREN'S HOSPITAL OF NEW YORK–PRESBYTERIAN, NEW YORK, NY, p. A449
MORRILL COUNTY COMMUNITY HOSPITAL, BRIDGEPORT, NE, p. A398
MORRIS COUNTY HOSPITAL, COUNCIL GROVE, KS, p. A248
MORRIS HOSPITAL & HEALTHCARE CENTERS, MORRIS, IL, p. A202
MORRIS VILLAGE ALCOHOL AND DRUG ADDICTION TREATMENT CENTER, COLUMBIA, SC, p. A564
MORRISON COMMUNITY HOSPITAL, MORRISON, IL, p. A202
MORRISTOWN MEDICAL CENTER, MORRISTOWN, NJ, p. A424
MORRISTOWN–HAMBLEN HEALTHCARE SYSTEM, MORRISTOWN, TN, p. A589
MORROW COUNTY HOSPITAL, MOUNT GILEAD, OH, p. A501
MORTON COUNTY HEALTH SYSTEM, ELKHART, KS, p. A248
MORTON HOSPITAL AND MEDICAL CENTER, TAUNTON, MA, p. A319
MORTON PLANT HOSPITAL, CLEARWATER, FL, p. A128
MORTON PLANT NORTH BAY HOSPITAL, NEW PORT RICHEY, FL, p. A142
MORTON PLANT REHAB & NRSG CNTR, BELLEAIR, FL, p. A125
MOSAIC LIFE CARE AT ST. JOSEPH – MEDICAL CENTER, SAINT JOSEPH, MO, p. A383
MOSAIC MEDICAL CENTER – ALBANY, ALBANY, MO, p. A371
MOSAIC MEDICAL CENTER – MARYVILLE, MARYVILLE, MO, p. A380
MOSES H. CONE MEMORIAL HOSPITAL, GREENSBORO, NC, p. A469
MOSES LUDINGTON HOSPITAL, TICONDEROGA, NY, p. A460
MOSS REHAB, EINSTEIN AT ELKINS PARK, ELKINS PARK, PA, p. A539
MOTION PICTURE AND TELEVISION FUND HOSPITAL AND RESIDENTIAL SERVICES, LOS ANGELES, CA, p. A74
MOUNT AUBURN HOSPITAL, CAMBRIDGE, MA, p. A312
MOUNT CARMEL EAST HOSPITAL, COLUMBUS, OH, p. A491
MOUNT CARMEL NEW ALBANY SURGICAL HOSPITAL, NEW ALBANY, OH, p. A501
MOUNT CARMEL REHABILITATION HOSPITAL, WESTERVILLE, OH, p. A507
MOUNT CARMEL ST. ANN'S, WESTERVILLE, OH, p. A507
MOUNT CARMEL WEST, GROVE CITY, OH, p. A497
MOUNT DESERT ISLAND HOSPITAL, BAR HARBOR, ME, p. A295
MOUNT GRANT GENERAL HOSPITAL, HAWTHORNE, NV, p. A409
MOUNT NITTANY MEDICAL CENTER, STATE COLLEGE, PA, p. A555
MOUNT SINAI BETH ISRAEL, NEW YORK, NY, p. A449
MOUNT SINAI HOSPITAL, CHICAGO, IL, p. A190
MOUNT SINAI HOSPITAL OF QUEENS, NEW YORK, NY, p. A449
MOUNT SINAI MEDICAL CENTER, MIAMI BEACH, FL, p. A141
MOUNT SINAI MORNINGSIDE, NEW YORK, NY, p. A449
MOUNT SINAI REHABILITATION HOSPITAL, HARTFORD, CT, p. A116
MOUNT SINAI ROOSEVELT HOSPITAL, NEW YORK, NY, p. A450
MOUNT SINAI SOUTH NASSAU, OCEANSIDE, NY, p. A454
MOUNT SINAI WEST HOSPITAL, NEW YORK, NY, p. A450
MOUNT ST. MARY'S HOSPITAL AND HEALTH CENTER, LEWISTON, NY, p. A445
MOUNTAIN HOME, JOHNSON CITY, TN, p. A585
MOUNTAIN LAKES MEDICAL CENTER, CLAYTON, GA, p. A160
MOUNTAIN VALLEY REGIONAL REHABILITATION HOSPITAL, PRESCOTT VALLEY, AZ, p. A37
MOUNTAIN VIEW HOSPITAL, GADSDEN, AL, p. A20
MOUNTAIN VIEW HOSPITAL, IDAHO FALLS, ID, p. A181
MOUNTAIN VIEW HOSPITAL, PAYSON, UT, p. A667
MOUNTAIN VISTA MEDICAL CENTER, MESA, AZ, p. A34
MOUNTAIN WEST MEDICAL CENTER, TOOELE, UT, p. A670
MOUNTAINVIEW HOSPITAL, LAS VEGAS, NV, p. A410
MOUNTAINVIEW MEDICAL CENTER, WHITE SULPHUR SPRINGS, MT, p. A396
MOUNTAINVIEW REGIONAL MEDICAL CENTER, LAS CRUCES, NM, p. A435
MOUNTRAIL COUNTY MEDICAL CENTER, STANLEY, ND, p. A483
MPTF/MOTION PICTURE & TELEVISION FUND, LOS ANGELES, CA, p. A74
MT. ASCUTNEY HOSPITAL AND HEALTH CENTER, WINDSOR, VT, p. A672

MT. GRAHAM REGIONAL MEDICAL CENTER, SAFFORD, AZ, p. A38
MT. SAN RAFAEL HOSPITAL, TRINIDAD, CO, p. A114
MT. WASHINGTON PEDIATRIC HOSPITAL, BALTIMORE, MD, p. A301
MUENSTER MEMORIAL HOSPITAL, MUENSTER, TX, p. A640
MUHLENBERG HOSPITAL CENTER, BETHLEHEM, PA, p. A535
MULESHOE AREA MEDICAL CENTER, MULESHOE, TX, p. A640
MULTICARE AUBURN MEDICAL CENTER, AUBURN, WA, p. A687
MULTICARE CAPITAL MEDICAL CENTER, OLYMPIA, WA, p. A692
MULTICARE COVINGTON MEDICAL CENTER, COVINGTON, WA, p. A688
MULTICARE DEACONESS HOSPITAL, SPOKANE, WA, p. A696
MULTICARE GOOD SAMARITAN HOSPITAL, PUYALLUP, WA, p. A693
MULTICARE MARY BRIDGE CHILDREN'S HOSPITAL AND HEALTH CENTER, TACOMA, WA, p. A697
MULTICARE TACOMA GENERAL HOSPITAL, TACOMA, WA, p. A697
MULTICARE VALLEY HOSPITAL, SPOKANE VALLEY, WA, p. A696
MULTICARE YAKIMA MEMORIAL HOSPITAL, YAKIMA, WA, p. A698
MULTY MEDICAL REHABILITATION HOSPITAL SAN JUAN, SAN JUAN, PR, p. A735
MUNISING MEMORIAL HOSPITAL, MUNISING, MI, p. A334
MUNSON HEALTHCARE CADILLAC HOSPITAL, CADILLAC, MI, p. A323
MUNSON HEALTHCARE CHARLEVOIX HOSPITAL, CHARLEVOIX, MI, p. A323
MUNSON HEALTHCARE GRAYLING HOSPITAL, GRAYLING, MI, p. A329
MUNSON HEALTHCARE MANISTEE HOSPITAL, MANISTEE, MI, p. A332
MUNSON HEALTHCARE OTSEGO MEMORIAL HOSPITAL, GAYLORD, MI, p. A327
MUNSON HEALTHCARE PAUL OLIVER MEMORIAL HOSPITAL, FRANKFORT, MI, p. A327
MUNSON MEDICAL CENTER, TRAVERSE CITY, MI, p. A339
MURRAY COUNTY MEDICAL CENTER, SLAYTON, MN, p. A355
MURRAY–CALLOWAY COUNTY HOSPITAL, MURRAY, KY, p. A272
MUSC CHILDREN'S HOSPITAL, CHARLESTON, SC, p. A563
MUSC HEALTH – ORANGEBURG, ORANGEBURG, SC, p. A569
MUSC HEALTH BLACK RIVER MEDICAL CENTER, CADES, SC, p. A562
MUSC HEALTH CHESTER MEDICAL CENTER, CHESTER, SC, p. A564
MUSC HEALTH COLUMBIA MEDICAL CENTER DOWNTOWN, COLUMBIA, SC, p. A564
MUSC HEALTH COLUMBIA MEDICAL CENTER NORTHEAST, COLUMBIA, SC, p. A564
MUSC HEALTH FLORENCE MEDICAL CENTER, FLORENCE, SC, p. A566
MUSC HEALTH KERSHAW MEDICAL CENTER, CAMDEN, SC, p. A562
MUSC HEALTH LANCASTER MEDICAL CENTER, LANCASTER, SC, p. A568
MUSC HEALTH MARION MEDICAL CENTER, MULLINS, SC, p. A569
MUSC HEALTH OF MEDICAL UNIVERSITY OF SOUTH CAROLINA, CHARLESTON, SC, p. A563
MUSC HEALTH REHABILITATION HOSPITAL, AN AFFILIATE OF ENCOMPASS HEALTH, CHARLESTON, SC, p. A563
MUSC HEALTH UNIVERSITY MEDICAL CENTER, CHARLESTON, SC, p. A563
MUSCOGEE CREEK NATION MEDICAL CENTER, OKMULGEE, OK, p. A519
MUSCOGEE CREEK NATION PHYSICAL REHABILITATION CENTER, OKMULGEE, OK, p. A519
MUSKOGEE COMMUNITY HOSPITAL, MUSKOGEE, OK, p. A515
MYMICHIGAN MEDICAL CENTER ALMA, ALMA, MI, p. A321
MYMICHIGAN MEDICAL CENTER ALPENA, ALPENA, MI, p. A321
MYMICHIGAN MEDICAL CENTER CLARE, CLARE, MI, p. A324
MYMICHIGAN MEDICAL CENTER GLADWIN, GLADWIN, MI, p. A327
MYMICHIGAN MEDICAL CENTER MIDLAND, MIDLAND, MI, p. A333
MYMICHIGAN MEDICAL CENTER SAGINAW, SAGINAW, MI, p. A337
MYMICHIGAN MEDICAL CENTER SAULT, SAULT SAINTE MARIE, MI, p. A338
MYMICHIGAN MEDICAL CENTER STANDISH, STANDISH, MI, p. A338
MYMICHIGAN MEDICAL CENTER TAWAS, TAWAS CITY, MI, p. A339
MYMICHIGAN MEDICAL CENTER WEST BRANCH, WEST BRANCH, MI, p. A340
MYMICHIGAN MEDICAL CENTER–CLARE, CLARE, MI, p. A324
MYMICHIGAN MEDICAL CENTER–GRATIOT, ALMA, MI, p. A321
MYRTUE MEDICAL CENTER, HARLAN, IA, p. A237

N

NACOGDOCHES MEDICAL CENTER, NACOGDOCHES, TX, p. A640
NACOGDOCHES MEMORIAL HOSPITAL, NACOGDOCHES, TX, p. A640
NANTUCKET COTTAGE HOSPITAL, NANTUCKET, MA, p. A316
NAPA STATE HOSPITAL, NAPA, CA, p. A79
NASHVILLE GENERAL HOSPITAL, NASHVILLE, TN, p. A590
NASSAU UNIVERSITY MEDICAL CENTER, EAST MEADOW, NY, p. A442
NATCHAUG HOSPITAL, MANSFIELD CENTER, CT, p. A116
NATCHITOCHES REGIONAL MEDICAL CENTER, NATCHITOCHES, LA, p. A289
NATHAN LITTAUER HOSPITAL AND NURSING HOME, GLOVERSVILLE, NY, p. A443
NATIONAL INSTITUTES OF HEALTH CLINICAL CENTER, BETHESDA, MD, p. A302
NATIONAL JEWISH HEALTH, DENVER, CO, p. A106
NATIONAL PARK MEDICAL CENTER, HOT SPRINGS, AR, p. A48
NATIONWIDE CHILDREN'S HOSPITAL – TOLEDO, TOLEDO, OH, p. A504
NATIONWIDE CHILDREN'S HOSPITAL, COLUMBUS, OH, p. A492
NATIVIDAD, SALINAS, CA, p. A88
NATIVIDAD MEDICAL CENTER, SALINAS, CA, p. A88
NAVAJO HEALTH FOUNDATION – SAGE MEMORIAL HOSPITAL, GANADO, AZ, p. A31
NAVAL HOSPITAL BEAUFORT, BEAUFORT, SC, p. A562
NAVAL HOSPITAL BREMERTON, BREMERTON, WA, p. A687
NAVAL HOSPITAL CAMP LEJEUNE, CAMP LEJEUNE, NC, p. A464
NAVAL HOSPITAL CAMP PENDLETON, CAMP PENDLETON, CA, p. A58
NAVAL HOSPITAL JACKSONVILLE, JACKSONVILLE, FL, p. A135
NAVAL HOSPITAL PENSACOLA, PENSACOLA, FL, p. A146
NAVAL MEDICAL CENTER, PORTSMOUTH, VA, p. A681
NAVAL MEDICAL CENTER SAN DIEGO, SAN DIEGO, CA, p. A89
NAVARRO REGIONAL HOSPITAL, CORSICANA, TX, p. A609
NAVOS, SEATTLE, WA, p. A694
NAZARETH HOSPITAL, PHILADELPHIA, PA, p. A549
NAZARETH NURSING HOME, BUFFALO, NY, p. A440
NCH BAKER HOSPITAL, NAPLES, FL, p. A142
NEA BAPTIST MEMORIAL HOSPITAL, JONESBORO, AR, p. A48
NEBRASKA MEDICINE – BELLEVUE, BELLEVUE, NE, p. A398
NEBRASKA MEDICINE – NEBRASKA MEDICAL CENTER, OMAHA, NE, p. A404
NEBRASKA METHODIST HOSPITAL, OMAHA, NE, p. A404
NEBRASKA PENAL AND CORRECTIONAL HOSPITAL, LINCOLN, NE, p. A402
NEBRASKA SPINE HOSPITAL, OMAHA, NE, p. A404
NEBRASKA–WESTERN IOWA HCS, OMAHA, NE, p. A404
NELL J. REDFIELD MEMORIAL HOSPITAL, MALAD CITY, ID, p. A182
NELSON COUNTY HEALTH SYSTEM, MCVILLE, ND, p. A482
NEMAHA COUNTY HOSPITAL, AUBURN, NE, p. A397
NEMAHA VALLEY COMMUNITY HOSPITAL, SENECA, KS, p. A260
NEMOURS CHILDREN'S HOSPITAL, ORLANDO, FL, p. A144
NEMOURS CHILDREN'S HOSPITAL, DELAWARE, WILMINGTON, DE, p. A122
NEOSHO MEMORIAL REGIONAL MEDICAL CENTER, CHANUTE, KS, p. A247
NESHOBA GENERAL, PHILADELPHIA, MS, p. A367
NESS COUNTY HOSPITAL DISTRICT NO 2, NESS CITY, KS, p. A255
NEUROBEHAVIORAL HOSPITAL OF NW INDIANA/GREATER CHICAGO, CROWN POINT, IN, p. A215
NEURODIAGNOSTIC INSTITUTE AND ADVANCED TREATMENT CENTER, INDIANAPOLIS, IN, p. A220
NEUROPSYCHIATRIC HOSPITAL OF INDIANAPOLIS, INDIANAPOLIS, IN, p. A220
NEVADA REGIONAL MEDICAL CENTER, NEVADA, MO, p. A381
NEW BRAUNFELS ER & HOSPITAL, NEW BRAUNFELS, TX, p. A641
NEW BRAUNFELS REGIONAL REHABILITATION HOSPITAL, NEW BRAUNFELS, TX, p. A641
NEW BRITAIN GENERAL HOSPITAL, NEW BRITAIN, CT, p. A117
NEW ENGLAND BAPTIST HOSPITAL, BOSTON, MA, p. A311
NEW ENGLAND REHABILITATION HOSPITAL OF PORTLAND, PORTLAND, ME, p. A298
NEW HAMPSHIRE HOSPITAL, CONCORD, NH, p. A414
NEW LONDON HOSPITAL, NEW LONDON, NH, p. A416
NEW MEXICO BEHAVIORAL HEALTH INSTITUTE AT LAS VEGAS, LAS VEGAS, NM, p. A435
NEW MEXICO HCS, ALBUQUERQUE, NM, p. A433
NEW MEXICO REHABILITATION CENTER, ROSWELL, NM, p. A436
NEW ORLEANS EAST HOSPITAL, NEW ORLEANS, LA, p. A290
NEW ULM MEDICAL CENTER, NEW ULM, MN, p. A352
NEW YORK CITY CHILDREN'S CENTER, NEW YORK, NY, p. A450
NEW YORK COMMUNITY HOSPITAL, NEW YORK, NY, p. A450
NEW YORK DOWNTOWN HOSPITAL, NEW YORK, NY, p. A450
NEW YORK EYE AND EAR INFIRMARY OF MOUNT SINAI, NEW YORK, NY, p. A450
NEW YORK FOUNDLING HOSPITAL, NEW YORK, NY, p. A450
NEW YORK STATE PSYCHIATRIC INSTITUTE, NEW YORK, NY, p. A450
NEW YORK WEILL CORNELL MED CTR, NEW YORK, NY, p. A450
NEW YORK–PRESBYTERIAN HOSPITAL, NEW YORK, NY, p. A450
NEW YORK–PRESBYTERIAN HOSPITAL, WESTCHESTER DIVISION, WHITE PLAINS, NY, p. A462
NEW YORK–PRESBYTERIAN QUEENS, NEW YORK, NY, p. A450
NEW YORK–PRESBYTERIAN/HUDSON VALLEY HOSPITAL, CORTLANDT MANOR, NY, p. A442
NEWARK BETH ISRAEL MEDICAL CENTER, NEWARK, NJ, p. A425
NEWARK–WAYNE COMMUNITY HOSPITAL, NEWARK, NY, p. A454
NEWBERRY COUNTY MEMORIAL HOSPITAL, NEWBERRY, SC, p. A569
NEWMAN MEMORIAL HOSPITAL, SHATTUCK, OK, p. A520
NEWMAN REGIONAL HEALTH, EMPORIA, KS, p. A249
NEWPORT HOSPITAL, NEWPORT, RI, p. A560
NEWPORT HOSPITAL AND HEALTH SERVICES, NEWPORT, WA, p. A692
NEWPORT NEWS BEHAVIORAL HEALTH CENTER, NEWPORT NEWS, VA, p. A680
NEWTON MEDICAL CENTER, NEWTON, NJ, p. A426
NEWTON–WELLESLEY HOSPITAL, NEWTON LOWER FALLS, MA, p. A316
NEXUS CHILDREN'S HOSPITAL HOUSTON, HOUSTON, TX, p. A627
NEXUS SPECIALITY HOSPITAL – THE WOODLANDS CAMPUS, THE WOODLANDS, TX, p. A657
NEXUS SPECIALTY HOSPITAL, SHENANDOAH, TX, p. A652
NEXUS SPECIALTY HOSPITAL THE WOODLANDS, THE WOODLANDS, TX, p. A657
NIAGARA FALLS MEMORIAL MEDICAL CENTER, NIAGARA FALLS, NY, p. A454
NICHOLAS H. NOYES MEMORIAL HOSPITAL, DANSVILLE, NY, p. A442
NICKLAUS CHILDREN'S HOSPITAL, MIAMI, FL, p. A140
NIH CLINICAL CENTER, BETHESDA, MD, p. A302
NIOBRARA COMMUNITY HOSPITAL, LUSK, WY, p. A727
NIOBRARA VALLEY HOSPITAL, LYNCH, NE, p. A402
NMC HEALTH, NEWTON, KS, p. A255
NOCONA GENERAL HOSPITAL, NOCONA, TX, p. A641
NOLAND HOSPITAL ANNISTON, ANNISTON, AL, p. A15
NOLAND HOSPITAL BIRMINGHAM, BIRMINGHAM, AL, p. A17
NOLAND HOSPITAL DOTHAN, DOTHAN, AL, p. A18
NOLAND HOSPITAL MONTGOMERY, MONTGOMERY, AL, p. A23
NOLAND HOSPITAL SHELBY, ALABASTER, AL, p. A15
NOLAND HOSPITAL TUSCALOOSA, TUSCALOOSA, AL, p. A25
NOR–LEA HOSPITAL DISTRICT, LOVINGTON, NM, p. A435
NORMAN REGIONAL HEALTH SYSTEM, NORMAN, OK, p. A516
NORMAN REGIONAL MOORE, MOORE, OK, p. A515
NORRISTOWN STATE HOSPITAL, NORRISTOWN, PA, p. A547
NORTH ALABAMA MEDICAL CENTER, FLORENCE, AL, p. A19
NORTH ALABAMA SHOALS HOSPITAL, MUSCLE SHOALS, AL, p. A23
NORTH ALABAMA SPECIALTY HOSPITAL, ATHENS, AL, p. A15
NORTH ARKANSAS REGIONAL MEDICAL CENTER, HARRISON, AR, p. A47
NORTH BALDWIN INFIRMARY, BAY MINETTE, AL, p. A16
NORTH BIG HORN HOSPITAL DISTRICT, LOVELL, WY, p. A727

Index of Hospitals / North Caddo Medical Center

NORTH CADDO MEDICAL CENTER, VIVIAN, LA, p. A294
NORTH CANYON MEDICAL CENTER, GOODING, ID, p. A181
NORTH CAROLINA SPECIALTY HOSPITAL, DURHAM, NC, p. A467
NORTH CENTRAL BRONX HOSPITAL, NEW YORK, NY, p. A450
NORTH CENTRAL HEALTH CARE, WAUSAU, WI, p. A724
NORTH CENTRAL KANSAS MEDICAL CENTER, CONCORDIA, KS, p. A248
NORTH CENTRAL SURGICAL CENTER, DALLAS, TX, p. A612
NORTH COUNTRY HOSPITAL AND HEALTH CENTER, NEWPORT, VT, p. A672
NORTH CYPRESS MEDICAL CENTER, CYPRESS, TX, p. A610
NORTH DAKOTA STATE HOSPITAL, JAMESTOWN, ND, p. A482
NORTH FLORIDA/SOUTH GEORGIA VETERAN'S HEALTH SYSTEM, GAINESVILLE, FL, p. A132
NORTH HOUSTON SURGICAL HOSPITAL, SPRING, TX, p. A654
NORTH IDAHO BEHAVIORAL HEALTH, DIVISION OF KOOTENAI MEDICAL CENTER, COEUR D ALENE, ID, p. A180
NORTH KANSAS CITY HOSPITAL, NORTH KANSAS CITY, MO, p. A381
NORTH LAS VEGAS VA MEDICAL CENTER, NORTH LAS VEGAS, NV, p. A412
NORTH LITTLE ROCK DIVISION, NORTH LITTLE ROCK, AR, p. A51
NORTH MEMORIAL HEALTH HOSPITAL, ROBBINSDALE, MN, p. A353
NORTH MISSISSIPPI MEDICAL CENTER – TUPELO, TUPELO, MS, p. A369
NORTH MISSISSIPPI MEDICAL CENTER GILMORE–AMORY, AMORY, MS, p. A359
NORTH MISSISSIPPI MEDICAL CENTER–EUPORA, EUPORA, MS, p. A361
NORTH MISSISSIPPI MEDICAL CENTER–HAMILTON, HAMILTON, AL, p. A20
NORTH MISSISSIPPI MEDICAL CENTER-IUKA, IUKA, MS, p. A363
NORTH MISSISSIPPI MEDICAL CENTER–PONTOTOC, PONTOTOC, MS, p. A368
NORTH MISSISSIPPI MEDICAL CENTER–WEST POINT, WEST POINT, MS, p. A370
NORTH MISSISSIPPI STATE HOSPITAL, TUPELO, MS, p. A369
NORTH OAKS MEDICAL CENTER, HAMMOND, LA, p. A282
NORTH OAKS REHABILITATION HOSPITAL, HAMMOND, LA, p. A282
NORTH OKALOOSA MEDICAL CENTER, CRESTVIEW, FL, p. A129
NORTH OTTAWA COMMUNITY HOSPITAL, GRAND HAVEN, MI, p. A328
NORTH PHILADELPHIA HEALTH SYST, PHILADELPHIA, PA, p. A549
NORTH PLATTE VALLEY MEDICAL CENTER, SARATOGA, WY, p. A728
NORTH RUNNELS HOSPITAL, WINTERS, TX, p. A663
NORTH SHORE CHILDREN'S HOSPITAL, SALEM, MA, p. A317
NORTH SHORE HEALTH, GRAND MARAIS, MN, p. A347
NORTH SHORE MEDICAL CENTER, MIAMI, FL, p. A140
NORTH SHORE MEDICAL CENTER, SALEM, MA, p. A317
NORTH SHORE MEDICAL CENTER, FLORIDA MEDICAL CENTER CAMPUS, FORT LAUDERDALE, FL, p. A131
NORTH SHORE UNIVERSITY HOSPITAL, MANHASSET, NY, p. A445
NORTH SHORE UNIVERSITY HOSPITAL AT SYOSSET, SYOSSET, NY, p. A459
NORTH STAR BEHAVIORAL HEALTH SYSTEM, ANCHORAGE, AK, p. A27
NORTH STAR HLTH SYST, ANCHORAGE, AK, p. A27
NORTH SUBURBAN MEDICAL CENTER, THORNTON, CO, p. A113
NORTH SUNFLOWER MEDICAL CENTER, RULEVILLE, MS, p. A368
NORTH TAMPA BEHAVIORAL HEALTH, WESLEY CHAPEL, FL, p. A154
NORTH TEXAS MEDICAL CENTER, GAINESVILLE, TX, p. A621
NORTH TEXAS STATE HOSPITAL, VERNON, TX, p. A659
NORTH TEXAS STATE HOSPITAL, WICHITA FALLS CAMPUS, WICHITA FALLS, TX, p. A662
NORTH VALLEY HEALTH CENTER, WARREN, MN, p. A357
NORTH VALLEY HOSPITAL, TONASKET, WA, p. A697
NORTH VALLEY HOSPITAL, WHITEFISH, MT, p. A396
NORTH VISTA HOSPITAL, NORTH LAS VEGAS, NV, p. A412
NORTHBAY MEDICAL CENTER, FAIRFIELD, CA, p. A63
NORTHBAY VACAVALLEY HOSPITAL, VACAVILLE, CA, p. A99
NORTHBROOK BEHAVIORAL HEALTH HOSPITAL, BLACKWOOD, NJ, p. A418
NORTHCOAST BEHAVIORAL HEALTHCARE, NORTHFIELD, OH, p. A501
NORTHCREST MEDICAL CENTER, SPRINGFIELD, TN, p. A593
NORTHEAST FLORIDA STATE HOSPITAL, MACCLENNY, FL, p. A138
NORTHEAST GEORGIA MEDICAL CENTER, GAINESVILLE, GA, p. A164
NORTHEAST GEORGIA MEDICAL CENTER BARROW, WINDER, GA, p. A174
NORTHEAST GEORGIA MEDICAL CENTER HABERSHAM, DEMOREST, GA, p. A162
NORTHEAST GEORGIA MEDICAL CENTER LUMPKIN, DAHLONEGA, GA, p. A162
NORTHEAST METHODIST HOSPITAL, LIVE OAK, TX, p. A635
NORTHEAST OHIO VA HEALTHCARE SYSTEM, CLEVELAND, OH, p. A491
NORTHEAST REGIONAL MEDICAL CENTER, KIRKSVILLE, MO, p. A378
NORTHEAST REHABILITATION HOSPITAL, SALEM, NH, p. A417
NORTHEASTERN CENTER, AUBURN, IN, p. A212
NORTHEASTERN HEALTH SYSTEM, TAHLEQUAH, OK, p. A521
NORTHEASTERN HEALTH SYSTEM SEQUOYAH, SALLISAW, OK, p. A520
NORTHEASTERN NEVADA REGIONAL HOSPITAL, ELKO, NV, p. A408
NORTHEASTERN VERMONT REGIONAL HOSPITAL, SAINT JOHNSBURY, VT, p. A672
NORTHERN ARIZONA HCS, PRESCOTT, AZ, p. A37
NORTHERN COCHISE COMMUNITY HOSPITAL, WILLCOX, AZ, p. A41
NORTHERN COLORADO LONG TERM ACUTE HOSPITAL, JOHNSTOWN, CO, p. A110
NORTHERN COLORADO REHABILITATION HOSPITAL, JOHNSTOWN, CO, p. A110
NORTHERN DUTCHESS HOSPITAL, RHINEBECK, NY, p. A457
NORTHERN IDAHO ADVANCED CARE HOSPITAL, POST FALLS, ID, p. A183
NORTHERN INYO HOSPITAL, BISHOP, CA, p. A58
NORTHERN LIGHT BLUE HILL HOSPITAL, BLUE HILL, ME, p. A296
NORTHERN LIGHT CA DEAN HOSPITAL, GREENVILLE, ME, p. A297
NORTHERN LIGHT EASTERN MAINE MEDICAL CENTER, BANGOR, ME, p. A295
NORTHERN LIGHT INLAND HOSPITAL, WATERVILLE, ME, p. A299
NORTHERN LIGHT MAINE COAST HOSPITAL, ELLSWORTH, ME, p. A297
NORTHERN LIGHT MAYO HOSPITAL, DOVER–FOXCROFT, ME, p. A297
NORTHERN LIGHT MERCY HOSPITAL, PORTLAND, ME, p. A298
NORTHERN LIGHT SEBASTICOOK VALLEY HOSPITAL, PITTSFIELD, ME, p. A298
NORTHERN LOUISIANA MEDICAL CENTER, RUSTON, LA, p. A291
NORTHERN MAINE MEDICAL CENTER, FORT KENT, ME, p. A297
NORTHERN MONTANA HOSPITAL, HAVRE, MT, p. A393
NORTHERN NAVAJO MEDICAL CENTER, SHIPROCK, NM, p. A437
NORTHERN NEVADA ADULT MENTAL HEALTH SERVICES, SPARKS, NV, p. A413
NORTHERN NEVADA MEDICAL CENTER, SPARKS, NV, p. A413
NORTHERN REGIONAL HOSPITAL, MOUNT AIRY, NC, p. A473
NORTHERN UTAH REHABILITATION HOSPITAL, SOUTH OGDEN, UT, p. A670
NORTHERN VIRGINIA MENTAL HEALTH INSTITUTE, FALLS CHURCH, VA, p. A676
NORTHERN WESTCHESTER HOSPITAL, MOUNT KISCO, NY, p. A446
NORTHFIELD HOSPITAL AND CLINICS, NORTHFIELD, MN, p. A352
NORTHLAKE BEHAVIORAL HEALTH SYSTEM, MANDEVILLE, LA, p. A287
NORTHPORT HOSPITAL–DCH, NORTHPORT, AL, p. A23
NORTHPORT VETERANS AFFAIRS MEDICAL CENTER, NORTHPORT, NY, p. A454
NORTHRIDGE HOSPITAL MEDICAL CENTER, LOS ANGELES, CA, p. A74
NORTHSHORE GLENBROOK HOSPITAL, GLENVIEW, IL, p. A196
NORTHSHORE HIGHLAND PARK HOSPITAL, HIGHLAND PARK, IL, p. A197
NORTHSHORE REHABILITATION HOSPITAL, LACOMBE, LA, p. A285
NORTHSHORE SKOKIE HOSPITAL, SKOKIE, IL, p. A208
NORTHSHORE UNIVERSITY HEALTHSYSTEM–GLENBROOK HOSPITAL, GLENVIEW, IL, p. A196
NORTHSHORE UNIVERSITY HEALTHSYSTEM–HIGHLAND PARK HOSPITAL, HIGHLAND PARK, IL, p. A197
NORTHSIDE HOSPITAL – DULUTH, DULUTH, GA, p. A163
NORTHSIDE HOSPITAL, ATLANTA, GA, p. A157
NORTHSIDE HOSPITAL CHEROKEE, CANTON, GA, p. A160
NORTHSIDE HOSPITAL FORSYTH, CUMMING, GA, p. A162
NORTHSIDE HOSPITAL GWINNETT/DULUTH, LAWRENCEVILLE, GA, p. A166
NORTHWEST CENTER FOR BEHAVIORAL HEALTH, WOODWARD, OK, p. A524
NORTHWEST COMMUNITY HEALTHCARE, ARLINGTON HEIGHTS, IL, p. A185
NORTHWEST FLORIDA COMMUNITY HOSPITAL, CHIPLEY, FL, p. A128
NORTHWEST HEALTH – LA PORTE, LA PORTE, IN, p. A221
NORTHWEST HEALTH – PORTER, VALPARAISO, IN, p. A228
NORTHWEST HEALTH – STARKE, KNOX, IN, p. A221
NORTHWEST HEALTH PHYSICIANS' SPECIALTY HOSPITAL, FAYETTEVILLE, AR, p. A46
NORTHWEST HILLS SURGICAL HOSPITAL, AUSTIN, TX, p. A600
NORTHWEST HOSPITAL & MEDICAL CENTER, SEATTLE, WA, p. A694
NORTHWEST HOSPITAL, RANDALLSTOWN, MD, p. A306
NORTHWEST MEDICAL CENTER – SPRINGDALE, SPRINGDALE, AR, p. A53
NORTHWEST MEDICAL CENTER, MARGATE, FL, p. A138
NORTHWEST MEDICAL CENTER, TUCSON, AZ, p. A40
NORTHWEST MEDICAL CENTER, WINFIELD, AL, p. A26
NORTHWEST MEDICAL CENTER SAHUARITA, SAHUARITA, AZ, p. A38
NORTHWEST MISSOURI PSYCHIATRIC REHABILITATION CENTER, SAINT JOSEPH, MO, p. A383
NORTHWEST OHIO PSYCHIATRIC HOSPITAL, TOLEDO, OH, p. A505
NORTHWEST SPECIALTY HOSPITAL, POST FALLS, ID, p. A183
NORTHWEST SURGICAL HOSPITAL, OKLAHOMA CITY, OK, p. A517
NORTHWEST TEXAS HEALTHCARE SYSTEM, AMARILLO, TX, p. A596
NORTHWESTERN MEDICAL CENTER, SAINT ALBANS, VT, p. A672
NORTHWESTERN MEDICINE CENTRAL DUPAGE HOSPITAL, WINFIELD, IL, p. A211
NORTHWESTERN MEDICINE DELNOR HOSPITAL, GENEVA, IL, p. A196
NORTHWESTERN MEDICINE KISHWAUKEE HOSPITAL, DEKALB, IL, p. A193
NORTHWESTERN MEDICINE LAKE FOREST HOSPITAL, LAKE FOREST, IL, p. A200
NORTHWESTERN MEDICINE MARIANJOY REHABILITATION HOSPITAL, WHEATON, IL, p. A210
NORTHWESTERN MEDICINE MCHENRY, MCHENRY, IL, p. A201
NORTHWESTERN MEDICINE PALOS HOSPITAL, PALOS HEIGHTS, IL, p. A205
NORTHWESTERN MEDICINE VALLEY WEST HOSPITAL, SANDWICH, IL, p. A208
NORTHWESTERN MEMORIAL HOSPITAL, CHICAGO, IL, p. A190
NORTHWESTERN WOODSTOCK, WOODSTOCK, IL, p. A211
NORTHWOOD DEACONESS HEALTH CENTER, NORTHWOOD, ND, p. A482
NORTON CHILDREN'S HOSPITAL, LOUISVILLE, KY, p. A269
NORTON CLARK HOSPITAL, JEFFERSONVILLE, IN, p. A221
NORTON COMMUNITY HOSPITAL, NORTON, VA, p. A680
NORTON COUNTY HOSPITAL, NORTON, KS, p. A256
NORTON HEALTHCARE PAVILION, LOUISVILLE, KY, p. A269
NORTON HOSPITAL, LOUISVILLE, KY, p. A270
NORTON KING'S DAUGHTERS' HEALTH, MADISON, IN, p. A223
NORTON MEDICAL PAVILION, LOUISVILLE, KY, p. A270
NORTON SCOTT HOSPITAL, SCOTTSBURG, IN, p. A227
NORTON SOUND REGIONAL HOSPITAL, NOME, AK, p. A29
NORTON SOUTHWEST HOSPITAL, LOUISVILLE, KY, p. A270
NORTON WOMEN'S AND KOSAIR CHILDREN'S HOSPITAL, LOUISVILLE, KY, p. A270
NORWALK COMMUNITY HOSPITAL, NORWALK, CA, p. A80
NORWALK HOSPITAL, NORWALK, CT, p. A118
NORWOOD HEALTH CENTER, MARSHFIELD, WI, p. A715
NOVANT HEALTH BALLANTYNE MEDICAL CENTER, CHARLOTTE, NC, p. A465
NOVANT HEALTH BRUNSWICK MEDICAL CENTER, BOLIVIA, NC, p. A464
NOVANT HEALTH CHARLOTTE ORTHOPAEDIC HOSPITAL, CHARLOTTE, NC, p. A466
NOVANT HEALTH FORSYTH MEDICAL CENTER, WINSTON–SALEM, NC, p. A478
NOVANT HEALTH HUNTERSVILLE MEDICAL CENTER, HUNTERSVILLE, NC, p. A470

Index of Hospitals / Orlando Regional South Seminole Hospital

NOVANT HEALTH MATTHEWS MEDICAL CENTER, MATTHEWS, NC, p. A472
NOVANT HEALTH MEDICAL PARK HOSPITAL, WINSTON-SALEM, NC, p. A478
NOVANT HEALTH MINT HILL MEDICAL CENTER, CHARLOTTE, NC, p. A466
NOVANT HEALTH NEW HANOVER REGIONAL MEDICAL CENTER, WILMINGTON, NC, p. A478
NOVANT HEALTH PENDER MEDICAL CENTER, BURGAW, NC, p. A464
NOVANT HEALTH PRESBYTERIAN MEDICAL CENTER, CHARLOTTE, NC, p. A466
NOVANT HEALTH REHABILITATION HOSPITAL, AN AFFILIATE OF ENCOMPASS HEALTH, WINSTON SALEM, NC, p. A478
NOVANT HEALTH ROWAN MEDICAL CENTER, SALISBURY, NC, p. A475
NOVANT HEALTH THOMASVILLE MEDICAL CENTER, THOMASVILLE, NC, p. A477
NOVATO COMMUNITY HOSPITAL, NOVATO, CA, p. A80
NOXUBEE GENERAL HOSPITAL, MACON, MS, p. A365
NYC HEALTH + HOSPITALS/BELLEVUE, NEW YORK, NY, p. A450
NYC HEALTH + HOSPITALS/CONEY ISLAND, NEW YORK, NY, p. A450
NYC HEALTH + HOSPITALS/ELMHURST, NEW YORK, NY, p. A451
NYC HEALTH + HOSPITALS/HARLEM, NEW YORK, NY, p. A451
NYC HEALTH + HOSPITALS/HENRY J CARTER SPECIALTY HOSPITAL AND MEDICAL CENTER, NEW YORK, NY, p. A451
NYC HEALTH + HOSPITALS/JACOBI, NEW YORK, NY, p. A451
NYC HEALTH + HOSPITALS/KINGS COUNTY, NEW YORK, NY, p. A451
NYC HEALTH + HOSPITALS/LINCOLN, NEW YORK, NY, p. A451
NYC HEALTH + HOSPITALS/METROPOLITAN, NEW YORK, NY, p. A451
NYC HEALTH + HOSPITALS/QUEENS, NEW YORK, NY, p. A451
NYC HEALTH + HOSPITALS/SOUTH BROOKLYN HEALTH, NEW YORK, NY, p. A452
NYC HEALTH + HOSPITALS/WOODHULL, NEW YORK, NY, p. A452
NYU CHILDREN'S HOSPITAL, NEW YORK, NY, p. A452
NYU LANGONE HOSPITALS, NEW YORK, NY, p. A452
NYU LANGONE MEDICAL CENTER'S HOSPITAL FOR JOINT DISEASES, NEW YORK, NY, p. A452
NYU LUTHERAN (NYU HOSPITALS CENTER), NEW YORK, NY, p. A452
NYU WINTHROP HOSPITAL, MINEOLA, NY, p. A446

O

OAK HILL HOSPITAL, BROOKSVILLE, FL, p. A127
OAK HILL HOSPITAL, JOPLIN, MO, p. A377
OAK VALLEY HOSPITAL, OAKDALE, CA, p. A80
OAKBEND MEDICAL CENTER, RICHMOND, TX, p. A646
OAKDALE COMMUNITY HOSPITAL, OAKDALE, LA, p. A290
OAKLAWN HOSPITAL, MARSHALL, MI, p. A333
OAKLAWN PSYCHIATRIC CENTER, GOSHEN, IN, p. A218
OAKLEAF SURGICAL HOSPITAL, ALTOONA, WI, p. A707
OAKWOOD SPRINGS, OKLAHOMA CITY, OK, p. A517
OASIS BEHAVIORAL HEALTH – CHANDLER, CHANDLER, AZ, p. A31
OASIS HOSPITAL, PHOENIX, AZ, p. A36
O'BLENESS MEMORIAL HOSPITAL, ATHENS, OH, p. A485
OCALA REGIONAL MEDICAL CENTER, OCALA, FL, p. A143
OCEAN BEACH HOSPITAL AND MEDICAL CLINICS, ILWACO, WA, p. A690
OCEAN SPRINGS HOSPITAL, OCEAN SPRINGS, MS, p. A367
OCEANS BEHAVIORAL HEALTH CENTER PERMIAN BASIN, MIDLAND, TX, p. A639
OCEANS BEHAVIORAL HEALTH OF WACO, WACO, TX, p. A660
OCEANS BEHAVIORAL HOSPITAL ABILENE, ABILENE, TX, p. A595
OCEANS BEHAVIORAL HOSPITAL BILOXI, BILOXI, MS, p. A359
OCEANS BEHAVIORAL HOSPITAL KATY, KATY, TX, p. A631
OCEANS BEHAVIORAL HOSPITAL LONGVIEW, LONGVIEW, TX, p. A635
OCEANS BEHAVIORAL HOSPITAL LUFKIN, LUFKIN, TX, p. A637
OCEANS BEHAVIORAL HOSPITAL OF ALEXANDRIA, ALEXANDRIA, LA, p. A276
OCEANS BEHAVIORAL HOSPITAL OF AMARILLO, AMARILLO, TX, p. A596
OCEANS BEHAVIORAL HOSPITAL OF BATON ROUGE – SOUTH, BATON ROUGE, LA, p. A277
OCEANS BEHAVIORAL HOSPITAL OF BROUSSARD, BROUSSARD, LA, p. A279
OCEANS BEHAVIORAL HOSPITAL OF CORPUS CHRISTI, CORPUS CHRISTI, TX, p. A609
OCEANS BEHAVIORAL HOSPITAL OF DERIDDER, DERIDDER, LA, p. A281
OCEANS BEHAVIORAL HOSPITAL OF GREATER NEW ORLEANS, KENNER, LA, p. A284
OCEANS BEHAVIORAL HOSPITAL OF LAKE CHARLES, LAKE CHARLES, LA, p. A286
OCEANS BEHAVIORAL HOSPITAL OF LUBBOCK, LUBBOCK, TX, p. A636
OCEANS BEHAVIORAL HOSPITAL OF OPELOUSAS, OPELOUSAS, LA, p. A291
OCEANS BEHAVIORAL HOSPITAL OF PASADENA, PASADENA, TX, p. A643
OCEANS BEHAVIORAL HOSPITAL OF TUPELO, TUPELO, MS, p. A369
OCH REGIONAL MEDICAL CENTER, STARKVILLE, MS, p. A369
OCHILTREE GENERAL HOSPITAL, PERRYTON, TX, p. A643
OCHSNER ABROM KAPLAN MEMORIAL HOSPITAL, KAPLAN, LA, p. A284
OCHSNER ACADIA GENERAL HOSPITAL, CROWLEY, LA, p. A280
OCHSNER AMERICAN LEGION HOSPITAL, JENNINGS, LA, p. A284
OCHSNER CHOCTAW GENERAL, BUTLER, AL, p. A17
OCHSNER EXTENDED CARE HOSPITAL, NEW ORLEANS, LA, p. A289
OCHSNER LAFAYETTE GENERAL MEDICAL CENTER, LAFAYETTE, LA, p. A285
OCHSNER LAIRD HOSPITAL, UNION, MS, p. A369
OCHSNER LSU HEALTH SHREVEPORT – ACADEMIC MEDICAL CENTER, SHREVEPORT, LA, p. A292
OCHSNER LSU HEALTH SHREVEPORT – MONROE MEDICAL CENTER, MONROE, LA, p. A288
OCHSNER LSU HEALTH SHREVEPORT – ST. MARY MEDICAL CENTER, LLC, SHREVEPORT, LA, p. A292
OCHSNER MEDICAL CENTER – BATON ROUGE, BATON ROUGE, LA, p. A278
OCHSNER MEDICAL CENTER – HANCOCK, BAY SAINT LOUIS, MS, p. A359
OCHSNER MEDICAL CENTER – KENNER, KENNER, LA, p. A284
OCHSNER MEDICAL CENTER – NORTH SHORE, SLIDELL, LA, p. A293
OCHSNER MEDICAL CENTER, NEW ORLEANS, LA, p. A289
OCHSNER REHABILITATON HOSPITAL WEST CAMPUS, JEFFERSON, LA, p. A284
OCHSNER RUSH MEDICAL CENTER, MERIDIAN, MS, p. A366
OCHSNER SCOTT REGIONAL, MORTON, MS, p. A367
OCHSNER SPECIALTY HOSPITAL, MERIDIAN, MS, p. A366
OCHSNER ST. ANNE GENERAL HOSPITAL, RACELAND, LA, p. A291
OCHSNER ST. MARTIN HOSPITAL, BREAUX BRIDGE, LA, p. A279
OCHSNER ST. MARY, MORGAN CITY, LA, p. A289
OCHSNER STENNIS HOSPITAL, DE KALB, MS, p. A361
OCHSNER UNIVERSITY HOSPITAL & CLINICS, LAFAYETTE, LA, p. A286
OCHSNER WATKINS HOSPITAL, QUITMAN, MS, p. A368
OCONOMOWOC MEMORIAL HOSPITAL, OCONOMOWOC, WI, p. A718
O'CONNOR HOSPITAL, DELHI, NY, p. A442
O'CONNOR HOSPITAL, SAN JOSE, CA, p. A92
ODESSA MEMORIAL HEALTHCARE CENTER, ODESSA, WA, p. A692
ODESSA REGIONAL MEDICAL CENTER, ODESSA, TX, p. A642
OGALLALA COMMUNITY HOSPITAL, OGALLALA, NE, p. A403
OGDEN REGIONAL MEDICAL CENTER, OGDEN, UT, p. A666
OHIO COUNTY HOSPITAL, HARTFORD, KY, p. A267
OHIO HOSPITAL FOR PSYCHIATRY, COLUMBUS, OH, p. A492
OHIO STATE UNIVERSITY WEXNER MEDICAL CENTER, COLUMBUS, OH, p. A492
OHIO VALLEY HOSPITAL, STEUBENVILLE, OH, p. A504
OHIO VALLEY SURGICAL HOSPITAL, SPRINGFIELD, OH, p. A504
OHIOHEALTH BERGER HOSPITAL, CIRCLEVILLE, OH, p. A490
OHIOHEALTH DOCTORS HOSPITAL, COLUMBUS, OH, p. A492
OHIOHEALTH DUBLIN METHODIST HOSPITAL, DUBLIN, OH, p. A495
OHIOHEALTH GRADY MEMORIAL HOSPITAL, DELAWARE, OH, p. A494
OHIOHEALTH GRANT MEDICAL CENTER, COLUMBUS, OH, p. A492
OHIOHEALTH HARDIN MEMORIAL HOSPITAL, KENTON, OH, p. A497
OHIOHEALTH MANSFIELD HOSPITAL, MANSFIELD, OH, p. A499
OHIOHEALTH MARION GENERAL HOSPITAL, MARION, OH, p. A499
OHIOHEALTH MEDCENTRAL MANSFIELD HOSPITAL, MANSFIELD, OH, p. A499
OHIOHEALTH MEDCENTRAL SHELBY HOSPITAL, SHELBY, OH, p. A503
OHIOHEALTH O'BLENESS HOSPITAL, ATHENS, OH, p. A485
OHIOHEALTH REHABILITATION HOSPITAL, COLUMBUS, OH, p. A492
OHIOHEALTH RIVERSIDE METHODIST HOSPITAL, COLUMBUS, OH, p. A492
OHIOHEALTH SHELBY HOSPITAL, SHELBY, OH, p. A503
OHIOHEALTH SOUTHEASTERN MEDICAL CENTER, CAMBRIDGE, OH, p. A487
OHIOHEALTH VAN WERT HOSPITAL, VAN WERT, OH, p. A505
OHSU HEALTH HILLSBORO MEDICAL CENTER, HILLSBORO, OR, p. A528
OHSU HOSPITAL, PORTLAND, OR, p. A530
OJAI VALLEY COMMUNITY HOSPITAL, OJAI, CA, p. A81
OKEENE MUNICIPAL HOSPITAL, OKEENE, OK, p. A516
OKLAHOMA CENTER FOR ORTHOPAEDIC AND MULTI-SPECIALTY SURGERY, OKLAHOMA CITY, OK, p. A518
OKLAHOMA CITY REHABILITATION HOSPITAL, OKLAHOMA CITY, OK, p. A518
OKLAHOMA CITY VA MEDICAL CENTER, OKLAHOMA CITY, OK, p. A518
OKLAHOMA FORENSIC CENTER, VINITA, OK, p. A523
OKLAHOMA HEART HOSPITAL, OKLAHOMA CITY, OK, p. A518
OKLAHOMA HEART HOSPITAL SOUTH CAMPUS, OKLAHOMA CITY, OK, p. A518
OKLAHOMA SPINE HOSPITAL, OKLAHOMA CITY, OK, p. A518
OKLAHOMA STATE UNIVERSITY MEDICAL CENTER, TULSA, OK, p. A522
OKLAHOMA SURGICAL HOSPITAL, TULSA, OK, p. A522
OLATHE MEDICAL CENTER, OLATHE, KS, p. A256
OLD BRIDGE DIVISION, OLD BRIDGE, NJ, p. A426
OLD VINEYARD BEHAVIORAL HEALTH SERVICES, WINSTON-SALEM, NC, p. A478
OLEAN GENERAL HOSPITAL, OLEAN, NY, p. A455
OLIVE VIEW–UCLA MEDICAL CENTER, LOS ANGELES, CA, p. A74
OLMSTED MEDICAL CENTER, ROCHESTER, MN, p. A354
OLNEY HAMILTON HOSPITAL, OLNEY, TX, p. A642
OLYMPIC MEDICAL CENTER, PORT ANGELES, WA, p. A693
OMAHA VA MEDICAL CENTER, OMAHA, NE, p. A404
ONECORE HEALTH, OKLAHOMA CITY, OK, p. A518
ONEIDA HEALTHCARE, ONEIDA, NY, p. A455
ONSLOW MEMORIAL HOSPITAL, JACKSONVILLE, NC, p. A471
ONTARIO MEDICAL CENTER, ONTARIO, CA, p. A81
OPELOUSAS GENERAL HEALTH STSTEM–SOUTH CAMPUS, OPELOUSAS, LA, p. A291
OPELOUSAS GENERAL HEALTH SYSTEM, OPELOUSAS, LA, p. A291
OPTIM MEDICAL CENTER – SCREVEN, SYLVANIA, GA, p. A172
OPTIM MEDICAL CENTER – TATTNALL, REIDSVILLE, GA, p. A169
OPTIONS BEHAVIORAL HEALTH SYSTEM, INDIANAPOLIS, IN, p. A220
ORANGE CITY AREA HEALTH SYSTEM, ORANGE CITY, IA, p. A241
ORANGE COAST MEDICAL CENTER, FOUNTAIN VALLEY, CA, p. A64
ORANGE COUNTY GLOBAL MEDICAL CENTER, INC., SANTA ANA, CA, p. A93
ORANGE COUNTY IRVINE MEDICAL CENTER, IRVINE, CA, p. A67
ORANGE PARK MEDICAL CENTER, ORANGE PARK, FL, p. A144
ORCHARD HOSPITAL, GRIDLEY, CA, p. A66
ORCHARD PARK NURSING HOME, ORCHARD PARK, NY, p. A455
OREGON STATE HOSPITAL, SALEM, OR, p. A532
OREM COMMUNITY HOSPITAL, OREM, UT, p. A667
ORLANDO HEALTH – HEALTH CENTRAL HOSPITAL, OCOEE, FL, p. A143
ORLANDO HEALTH ORLANDO REGIONAL MEDICAL CENTER, ORLANDO, FL, p. A144
ORLANDO HEALTH SOUTH LAKE HOSPITAL, CLERMONT, FL, p. A128
ORLANDO HEALTH ST. CLOUD HOSPITAL, SAINT CLOUD, FL, p. A148
ORLANDO REG SAND LAKE HOSP, ORLANDO, FL, p. A144
ORLANDO REGIONAL SOUTH SEMINOLE HOSPITAL, LONGWOOD, FL, p. A137

Index of Hospitals / Orlando Rehabilitation Hospital

ORLANDO REHABILITATION HOSPITAL, ALTAMONTE SPRINGS, FL, p. A125
ORLANDO VA MEDICAL CENTER, ORLANDO, FL, p. A144
ORLEANS COMMUNITY HEALTH, MEDINA, NY, p. A446
ORO VALLEY HOSPITAL, ORO VALLEY, AZ, p. A34
OROVILLE HOSPITAL, OROVILLE, CA, p. A82
ORTHOCOLORADO HOSPITAL, LAKEWOOD, CO, p. A110
ORTHOINDY HOSPITAL, INDIANAPOLIS, IN, p. A220
ORTHONEBRASKA HOSPITAL, OMAHA, NE, p. A404
ORTHOPAEDIC HOSPITAL OF LUTHERAN HEALTH NETWORK, FORT WAYNE, IN, p. A216
ORTHOPAEDIC HOSPITAL OF WISCONSIN, GLENDALE, WI, p. A711
ORTHOPEDIC SPECIALTY HOSPITAL OF NEVADA, LAS VEGAS, NV, p. A410
ORTONVILLE AREA HEALTH SERVICES, ORTONVILLE, MN, p. A352
OSAGE BEACH CENTER FOR BEHAVIORAL HEALTH, LLC, OSAGE BEACH, MO, p. A381
OSAWATOMIE STATE HOSPITAL AT ADAIR ACUTE CARE, OSAWATOMIE, KS, p. A256
OSBORNE COUNTY MEMORIAL HOSPITAL, OSBORNE, KS, p. A256
OSCAR G. JOHNSON DEPARTMENT OF VETERANS AFFAIRS MEDICAL FACILITY, IRON MOUNTAIN, MI, p. A330
OSCEOLA MEDICAL CENTER, OSCEOLA, WI, p. A719
OSCEOLA REGIONAL HEALTH CENTER, SIBLEY, IA, p. A243
OSF HEALTHCARE LITTLE COMPANY OF MARY MEDICAL CENTER, EVERGREEN PARK, IL, p. A195
OSF HEALTHCARE SAINT ANTHONY'S HEALTH CENTER, ALTON, IL, p. A185
OSF HEART OF MARY MEDICAL CENTER, URBANA, IL, p. A210
OSF HOLY FAMILY MEDICAL CENTER, MONMOUTH, IL, p. A202
OSF SACRED HEART MEDICAL CENTER, DANVILLE, IL, p. A192
OSF SAINT ANTHONY MEDICAL CENTER, ROCKFORD, IL, p. A207
OSF SAINT CLARE MEDICAL CENTER, PRINCETON, IL, p. A206
OSF SAINT CLARE'S HOSPITAL, ALTON, IL, p. A185
OSF SAINT ELIZABETH MEDICAL CENTER, OTTAWA, IL, p. A204
OSF SAINT FRANCIS MEDICAL CENTER, PEORIA, IL, p. A206
OSF SAINT JAMES – JOHN W. ALBRECHT MEDICAL CENTER, PONTIAC, IL, p. A206
OSF SAINT LUKE MEDICAL CENTER, KEWANEE, IL, p. A199
OSF SAINT PAUL MEDICAL CENTER, MENDOTA, IL, p. A201
OSF ST. FRANCIS HOSPITAL AND MEDICAL GROUP, ESCANABA, MI, p. A326
OSF ST. JOSEPH MEDICAL CENTER, BLOOMINGTON, IL, p. A186
OSF ST. MARY MEDICAL CENTER, GALESBURG, IL, p. A196
OSF TRANSITIONAL CARE HOSPITAL, PEORIA, IL, p. A206
OSMOND GENERAL HOSPITAL, OSMOND, NE, p. A405
OSS HEALTH, YORK, PA, p. A558
OSSINING CORRECTIONAL FACILITIES HOSPITAL, OSSINING, NY, p. A455
OSWEGO HOSPITAL, OSWEGO, NY, p. A455
OTHELLO COMMUNITY HOSPITAL, OTHELLO, WA, p. A692
OTIS R. BOWEN CENTER FOR HUMAN SERVICES, WARSAW, IN, p. A229
OTTAWA COUNTY HEALTH CENTER, MINNEAPOLIS, KS, p. A255
OTTO KAISER MEMORIAL HOSPITAL, KENEDY, TX, p. A632
OTTUMWA REGIONAL HEALTH CENTER, OTTUMWA, IA, p. A241
OU HEALTH – UNIVERSITY OF OKLAHOMA MEDICAL CENTER, OKLAHOMA CITY, OK, p. A518
OU MEDICAL CENTER EDMOND, EDMOND, OK, p. A512
OUACHITA COMMUNITY HOSPITAL, WEST MONROE, LA, p. A294
OUACHITA COUNTY MEDICAL CENTER, CAMDEN, AR, p. A44
OUR LADY OF LOURDES REGIONAL MEDICAL CENTER, LAFAYETTE, LA, p. A286
OUR LADY OF MERCY MED CENTER, NEW YORK, NY, p. A452
OUR LADY OF THE ANGELS HOSPITAL, BOGALUSA, LA, p. A279
OUR LADY OF THE LAKE ASSUMPTION COMMUNITY HOSPITAL, NAPOLEONVILLE, LA, p. A289
OUR LADY OF THE LAKE REGIONAL MEDICAL CENTER, BATON ROUGE, LA, p. A278
OUR LADY OF VICTORY HOSPITAL, STANLEY, WI, p. A722
OVERLAKE MEDICAL CENTER AND CLINICS, BELLEVUE, WA, p. A687
OVERLAND PARK REGIONAL MEDICAL CENTER, OVERLAND PARK, KS, p. A257
OVERLOOK MEDICAL CENTER, SUMMIT, NJ, p. A428

OVERTON BROOKS VETERANS' ADMINISTRATION MEDICAL CENTER, SHREVEPORT, LA, p. A292
OVIEDO MEDICAL CENTER, OVIEDO, FL, p. A145
OWATONNA HOSPITAL, OWATONNA, MN, p. A352
OWENSBORO HEALTH MUHLENBERG COMMUNITY HOSPITAL, GREENVILLE, KY, p. A266
OWENSBORO HEALTH REGIONAL HOSPITAL, OWENSBORO, KY, p. A272
OWENSBORO HEALTH TWIN LAKES REGIONAL MEDICAL CENTER, LEITCHFIELD, KY, p. A268
OZARK HEALTH MEDICAL CENTER, CLINTON, AR, p. A44
OZARKS COMMUNITY HOSPITAL, GRAVETTE, AR, p. A47
OZARKS HEALTHCARE, WEST PLAINS, MO, p. A388

P

PACIFIC GROVE HOSPITAL, RIVERSIDE, CA, p. A86
PACIFICA HOSPITAL OF THE VALLEY, LOS ANGELES, CA, p. A74
PADRE BEHAVIORAL HOSPITAL, CORPUS CHRISTI, TX, p. A609
PAGE HOSPITAL, PAGE, AZ, p. A34
PAGOSA SPRINGS MEDICAL CENTER, PAGOSA SPRINGS, CO, p. A112
PAINTSVILLE ARH HOSPITAL, PAINTSVILLE, KY, p. A273
PALACIOS COMMUNITY MEDICAL CENTER, PALACIOS, TX, p. A642
PALESTINE REGIONAL MEDICAL CENTER–EAST, PALESTINE, TX, p. A642
PALESTINE REGIONAL REHABILITATION CENTER, PALESTINE, TX, p. A642
PALI MOMI MEDICAL CENTER, AIEA, HI, p. A175
PALM BEACH GARDENS MEDICAL CENTER, PALM BEACH GARDENS, FL, p. A145
PALM POINT BEHAVIORAL HEALTH, TITUSVILLE, FL, p. A153
PALMDALE REGIONAL MEDICAL CENTER, PALMDALE, CA, p. A82
PALMETTO GENERAL HOSPITAL, HIALEAH, FL, p. A133
PALMETTO HEALTH CHILDREN'S HOSPITAL, COLUMBIA, SC, p. A564
PALMETTO LOWCOUNTRY BEHAVIORAL HEALTH, CHARLESTON, SC, p. A563
PALMS OF PASADENA HOSPITAL, SAINT PETERSBURG, FL, p. A149
PALMS WEST HOSPITAL, LOXAHATCHEE, FL, p. A138
PALMYRA MEDICAL CENTERS, ALBANY, GA, p. A156
PALO ALTO COUNTY HEALTH SYSTEM, EMMETSBURG, IA, p. A236
PALO PINTO GENERAL HOSPITAL, MINERAL WELLS, TX, p. A639
PALO VERDE BEHAVIORAL HEALTH, TUCSON, AZ, p. A40
PALO VERDE HOSPITAL, BLYTHE, CA, p. A58
PALOMAR HEALTH REHABILITATION INSTITUTE, ESCONDIDO, CA, p. A62
PALOMAR MEDICAL CENTER ESCONDIDO, ESCONDIDO, CA, p. A62
PALOMAR MEDICAL CENTER POWAY, POWAY, CA, p. A84
PAM HEALTH REHABILITATION HOSPITAL OF EL PASO, EL PASO, TX, p. A617
PAM HEALTH REHABILITATION HOSPITAL OF GEORGETOWN, GEORGETOWN, DE, p. A121
PAM HEALTH REHABILITATION HOSPITAL OF GREATER INDIANA, CLARKSVILLE, IN, p. A214
PAM HEALTH REHABILITATION HOSPITAL OF HOUSTON HEIGHTS, HOUSTON, TX, p. A627
PAM HEALTH REHABILITATION HOSPITAL OF MIAMISBURG, MIAMISBURG, OH, p. A500
PAM HEALTH REHABILITATION HOSPITAL OF SURPRISE, SURPRISE, AZ, p. A39
PAM HEALTH REHABILITATION HOSPITAL OF TULSA, TULSA, OK, p. A522
PAM HEALTH REHABILITATION HOSPITAL OF WESTMINSTER, WESTMINSTER, CO, p. A114
PAM HEALTH SPECIALTY HOSPITAL OF DENVER, DENVER, CO, p. A106
PAM HEALTH SPECIALTY HOSPITAL OF HERITAGE VALLEY, BEAVER, PA, p. A535
PAM HEALTH SPECIALTY HOSPITAL OF JACKSONVILLE, JACKSONVILLE, FL, p. A135
PAM HEALTH SPECIALTY HOSPITAL OF OKLAHOMA CITY, OKLAHOMA CITY, OK, p. A518
PAM HEALTH SPECIALTY HOSPITAL OF PITTSBURGH, OAKDALE, PA, p. A547
PAM HEALTH SPECIALTY HOSPITAL OF STOUGHTON, STOUGHTON, MA, p. A319

PAM HEALTH SPECIALTY HOSPITAL OF TULSA, TULSA, OK, p. A522
PAM HEALTH SPECIALTY HOSPITAL OF WILKES–BARRE, WILKES BARRE, PA, p. A557
PAM REHABILITATION HOSPITAL OF ALLEN, ALLEN, TX, p. A595
PAM REHABILITATION HOSPITAL OF BEAUMONT, BEAUMONT, TX, p. A602
PAM REHABILITATION HOSPITAL OF CENTENNIAL HILLS, LAS VEGAS, NV, p. A410
PAM REHABILITATION HOSPITAL OF CLEAR LAKE, WEBSTER, TX, p. A661
PAM REHABILITATION HOSPITAL OF CORPUS CHRISTI, CORPUS CHRISTI, TX, p. A609
PAM REHABILITATION HOSPITAL OF DOVER, DOVER, DE, p. A121
PAM REHABILITATION HOSPITAL OF FARGO, FARGO, ND, p. A480
PAM REHABILITATION HOSPITAL OF HUMBLE, HUMBLE, TX, p. A629
PAM REHABILITATION HOSPITAL OF JUPITER, JUPITER, FL, p. A136
PAM REHABILITATION HOSPITAL OF ROUND ROCK, ROUND ROCK, TX, p. A647
PAM REHABILITATION HOSPITAL OF TAVARES, TAVARES, FL, p. A153
PAM REHABILITATION HOSPITAL OF VICTORIA, VICTORIA, TX, p. A660
PAM SPECIALTY HOSPITAL OF COVINGTON, COVINGTON, LA, p. A280
PAM SPECIALTY HOSPITAL OF DAYTON, MIAMISBURG, OH, p. A500
PAM SPECIALTY HOSPITAL OF HAMMOND, HAMMOND, LA, p. A283
PAM SPECIALTY HOSPITAL OF LAS VEGAS, LAS VEGAS, NV, p. A410
PAM SPECIALTY HOSPITAL OF LULING, LULING, TX, p. A637
PAM SPECIALTY HOSPITAL OF NEW BRAUNFELS, NEW BRAUNFELS, TX, p. A641
PAM SPECIALTY HOSPITAL OF RENO, SPARKS, NV, p. A413
PAM SPECIALTY HOSPITAL OF ROCKY MOUNT, ROCKY MOUNT, NC, p. A475
PAM SPECIALTY HOSPITAL OF SAN ANTONIO CENTER, SAN ANTONIO, TX, p. A650
PAM SPECIALTY HOSPITAL OF SARASOTA, SARASOTA, FL, p. A150
PAM SPECIALTY HOSPITAL OF SHREVEPORT, SHREVEPORT, LA, p. A292
PAM SPECIALTY HOSPITAL OF VICTORIA NORTH, VICTORIA, TX, p. A660
PAMPA REGIONAL MEDICAL CENTER, PAMPA, TX, p. A642
PANA COMMUNITY HOSPITAL, PANA, IL, p. A205
PANOLA MEDICAL CENTER, BATESVILLE, MS, p. A359
PAOLI HOSPITAL, PAOLI, PA, p. A547
PAPPAS REHABILITATION HOSPITAL FOR CHILDREN, CANTON, MA, p. A312
PARADISE VALLEY HOSPITAL, NATIONAL CITY, CA, p. A79
PARIS COMMUNITY HOSPITAL, PARIS, IL, p. A205
PARIS REGIONAL MEDICAL CENTER, PARIS, TX, p. A642
PARK CITY HOSPITAL, PARK CITY, UT, p. A667
PARK MEDICAL CENTER, COLUMBUS, OH, p. A492
PARK NICOLLET METHODIST HOSPITAL, SAINT LOUIS PARK, MN, p. A354
PARK PLACE SURGICAL HOSPITAL, LAFAYETTE, LA, p. A286
PARK ROYAL HOSPITAL, FORT MYERS, FL, p. A132
PARKER ADVENTIST HOSPITAL, PARKER, CO, p. A112
PARKLAND HEALTH, DALLAS, TX, p. A612
PARKLAND HEALTH CENTER – FARMINGTON COMMUNITY, FARMINGTON, MO, p. A375
PARKLAND HEALTH CENTER–BONNE TERRE, BONNE TERRE, MO, p. A371
PARKLAND MEDICAL CENTER, DERRY, NH, p. A414
PARKRIDGE MEDICAL CENTER, CHATTANOOGA, TN, p. A580
PARKRIDGE VALLEY HOSPTIAL, CHATTANOOGA, TN, p. A580
PARKSIDE PSYCHIATRIC HOSPITAL AND CLINIC, TULSA, OK, p. A522
PARKVIEW COMMUNITY HOSPITAL MEDICAL CENTER, RIVERSIDE, CA, p. A86
PARKVIEW DEKALB HOSPITAL, AUBURN, IN, p. A212
PARKVIEW HOSPITAL, FORT WAYNE, IN, p. A216
PARKVIEW HOSPITAL, WHEELER, TX, p. A662
PARKVIEW HUNTINGTON HOSPITAL, HUNTINGTON, IN, p. A218
PARKVIEW LAGRANGE HOSPITAL, LAGRANGE, IN, p. A222
PARKVIEW NOBLE HOSPITAL, KENDALLVILLE, IN, p. A221
PARKVIEW NORTH HOSPITAL, FORT WAYNE, IN, p. A216
PARKVIEW ORTHO HOSPITAL, FORT WAYNE, IN, p. A217
PARKVIEW REGIONAL HOSPITAL, MEXIA, TX, p. A639
PARKVIEW REGIONAL MEDICAL CENTER, FORT WAYNE, IN, p. A217

Index of Hospitals / Port St. Lucie Hospital

PARKVIEW WABASH HOSPITAL, WABASH, IN, p. A228
PARKVIEW WHITLEY HOSPITAL, COLUMBIA CITY, IN, p. A214
PARKWAY REGIONAL MED CENTER, NORTH MIAMI BEACH, FL, p. A142
PARKWEST MEDICAL CENTER, KNOXVILLE, TN, p. A586
PARKWOOD BEHAVIORAL HEALTH SYSTEM, OLIVE BRANCH, MS, p. A367
PARMER MEDICAL CENTER, FRIONA, TX, p. A620
PARRISH MEDICAL CENTER, TITUSVILLE, FL, p. A153
PARSONS STATE HOSPITAL AND TRAINING CENTER, PARSONS, KS, p. A258
PASSAVANT AREA HOSPITAL, JACKSONVILLE, IL, p. A199
PATHWAY REHABILITATION HOSPITAL OF BOSSIER, BOSSIER CITY, LA, p. A279
PATHWAYS OF TENNESSEE, JACKSON, TN, p. A584
PATIENTS CHOICE MEDICAL CENTER OF SMITH COUNTY, RALEIGH, MS, p. A368
PATIENTS' HOSPITAL OF REDDING, REDDING, CA, p. A85
PATRICIA NEAL REHABILITATION HOSPITAL, KNOXVILLE, TN, p. A586
PATRICK B. HARRIS PSYCHIATRIC HOSPITAL, ANDERSON, SC, p. A562
PATTERSON HEALTH CENTER, ANTHONY, KS, p. A246
PAUL B. HALL REGIONAL MEDICAL CENTER, PAINTSVILLE, KY, p. A273
PAUL OLIVER MEMORIAL HOSPITAL, FRANKFORT, MI, p. A327
PAULDING COUNTY HOSPITAL, PAULDING, OH, p. A502
PAWHUSKA HOSPITAL, PAWHUSKA, OK, p. A519
PAWNEE COUNTY MEMORIAL HOSPITAL AND RURAL HEALTH CLINIC, PAWNEE CITY, NE, p. A405
PAWNEE VALLEY COMMUNITY HOSPITAL, LARNED, KS, p. A253
PAYNE WHITNEY PSYCHIATRIC CLINIC, NEW YORK, NY, p. A452
PEACEHEALTH COTTAGE GROVE COMMUNITY MEDICAL CENTER, COTTAGE GROVE, OR, p. A526
PEACEHEALTH KETCHIKAN MEDICAL CENTER, KETCHIKAN, AK, p. A28
PEACEHEALTH PEACE HARBOR MEDICAL CENTER, FLORENCE, OR, p. A527
PEACEHEALTH PEACE ISLAND MEDICAL CENTER, FRIDAY HARBOR, WA, p. A690
PEACEHEALTH SACRED HEART MEDICAL CENTER AT RIVERBEND, SPRINGFIELD, OR, p. A532
PEACEHEALTH SOUTHWEST MEDICAL CENTER, VANCOUVER, WA, p. A698
PEACEHEALTH ST. JOHN MEDICAL CENTER, LONGVIEW, WA, p. A691
PEACEHEALTH ST. JOSEPH MEDICAL CENTER, BELLINGHAM, WA, p. A687
PEACEHEALTH UNITED GENERAL MEDICAL CENTER, SEDRO-WOOLLEY, WA, p. A695
PEACHFORD BEHAVIORAL HEALTH SYSTEM, ATLANTA, GA, p. A157
PEAK BEHAVIORAL HEALTH SERVICES, SANTA TERESA, NM, p. A437
PEAK VIEW BEHAVIORAL HEALTH, COLORADO SPRINGS, CO, p. A105
PEARL RIVER COUNTY HOSPITAL, POPLARVILLE, MS, p. A368
PECONIC BAY MEDICAL CENTER, RIVERHEAD, NY, p. A457
PECOS COUNTY MEMORIAL HOSPITAL, FORT STOCKTON, TX, p. A619
PELHAM MEDICAL CENTER, GREER, SC, p. A567
PELLA REGIONAL HEALTH CENTER, PELLA, IA, p. A242
PEMBINA COUNTY MEMORIAL HOSPITAL AND WEDGEWOOD MANOR, CAVALIER, ND, p. A480
PEMBROKE HOSPITAL, PEMBROKE, MA, p. A317
PEMISCOT MEMORIAL HEALTH SYSTEM, HAYTI, MO, p. A376
PENDER COMMUNITY HOSPITAL, PENDER, NE, p. A405
PENINSULA BEHAVIORAL CENTER, HAMPTON, VA, p. A677
PENINSULA HOSPITAL, BURLINGAME, CA, p. A58
PENN HIGHLANDS BROOKVILLE, BROOKVILLE, PA, p. A535
PENN HIGHLANDS CONNELLSVILLE, CONNELLSVILLE, PA, p. A537
PENN HIGHLANDS DUBOIS, DUBOIS, PA, p. A538
PENN HIGHLANDS ELK, SAINT MARYS, PA, p. A554
PENN HIGHLANDS HUNTINGDON, HUNTINGDON, PA, p. A542
PENN HIGHLANDS MON VALLEY, MONONGAHELA, PA, p. A546
PENN HIGHLANDS TYRONE, TYRONE, PA, p. A556
PENN MEDICINE CHESTER COUNTY HOSPITAL, WEST CHESTER, PA, p. A557
PENN MEDICINE LANCASTER GENERAL HEALTH, LANCASTER, PA, p. A543
PENN MEDICINE LANCASTER GENERAL HOSPITAL, LANCASTER, PA, p. A543
PENN MEDICINE PRINCETON MEDICAL CENTER, PLAINSBORO, NJ, p. A427

PENN PRESBYTERIAN MEDICAL CENTER, PHILADELPHIA, PA, p. A549
PENN STATE HEALTH HAMPDEN MEDICAL CENTER, ENOLA, PA, p. A539
PENN STATE HEALTH HOLY SPIRIT MEDICAL CENTER, CAMP HILL, PA, p. A536
PENN STATE HEALTH LANCASTER MEDICAL CENTER, LANCASTER, PA, p. A543
PENN STATE HEALTH REHABILITATION HOSPITAL, HUMMELSTOWN, PA, p. A542
PENN STATE HEALTH ST. JOSEPH, READING, PA, p. A553
PENN STATE HERSHEY REHABILITATION HOSPITAL, HUMMELSTOWN, PA, p. A542
PENN STATE MILTON S. HERSHEY MEDICAL CENTER, HERSHEY, PA, p. A542
PENNSYLVANIA HOSPITAL, PHILADELPHIA, PA, p. A549
PENNSYLVANIA PSYCHIATRIC INSTITUTE, HARRISBURG, PA, p. A541
PENOBSCOT VALLEY HOSPITAL, LINCOLN, ME, p. A298
PENROSE HOSPITALS, COLORADO SPRINGS, CO, p. A105
PENROSE-ST. FRANCIS HEALTH SERVICES, COLORADO SPRINGS, CO, p. A105
PERHAM HEALTH, PERHAM, MN, p. A352
PERIMETER BEHAVIORAL HOSPITAL OF ARLINGTON, ARLINGTON, TX, p. A597
PERIMETER BEHAVIORAL HOSPITAL OF DALLAS, GARLAND, TX, p. A621
PERIMETER BEHAVIORAL HOSPITAL OF JACKSON, JACKSON, TN, p. A584
PERIMETER BEHAVIORAL HOSPITAL OF NEW ORLEANS, KENNER, LA, p. A284
PERIMETER BEHAVIORAL HOSPITAL OF SPRINGFIELD, SPRINGFIELD, MO, p. A387
PERIMETER BEHAVIORAL HOSPITAL OF WEST MEMPHIS, WEST MEMPHIS, AR, p. A54
PERKINS COUNTY HEALTH SERVICES, GRANT, NE, p. A400
PERMIAN REGIONAL MEDICAL CENTER, ANDREWS, TX, p. A597
PERRY COUNTY GENERAL HOSPITAL, RICHTON, MS, p. A368
PERRY COUNTY MEMORIAL HOSPITAL, PERRYVILLE, MO, p. A382
PERRY COUNTY MEMORIAL HOSPITAL, TELL CITY, IN, p. A227
PERRY MEMORIAL HOSPITAL, PRINCETON, IL, p. A206
PERSHING GENERAL HOSPITAL, LOVELOCK, NV, p. A411
PERSHING MEMORIAL HOSPITAL, BROOKFIELD, MO, p. A372
PERSON MEMORIAL HOSPITAL, ROXBORO, NC, p. A475
PERTH AMBOY DIVISION, PERTH AMBOY, NJ, p. A427
PETALUMA VALLEY HOSPITAL, PETALUMA, CA, p. A83
PETERSBURG MEDICAL CENTER, PETERSBURG, AK, p. A29
PETERSON HEALTH, KERRVILLE, TX, p. A632
PETERSON HEALTHCARE AND REHABILITATION HOSPITAL, WHEELING, WV, p. A706
PHELPS HEALTH, ROLLA, MO, p. A382
PHELPS MEMORIAL HEALTH CENTER, HOLDREGE, NE, p. A401
PHELPS MEMORIAL HOSPITAL CENTER, SLEEPY HOLLOW, NY, p. A459
PHILADELPHIA VETERANS AFFAIRS MEDICAL CENTER, PHILADELPHIA, PA, p. A550
PHILIP HEALTH SERVICES, PHILIP, SD, p. A575
PHILLIPS COUNTY HEALTH SYSTEMS, PHILLIPSBURG, KS, p. A258
PHILLIPS COUNTY HOSPITAL, MALTA, MT, p. A394
PHOEBE PUTNEY MEMORIAL HOSPITAL, ALBANY, GA, p. A156
PHOEBE SUMTER MEDICAL CENTER, AMERICUS, GA, p. A156
PHOEBE WORTH MEDICAL CENTER, SYLVESTER, GA, p. A172
PHOENIX CHILDREN'S, PHOENIX, AZ, p. A36
PHOENIX HCS, PHOENIX, AZ, p. A36
PHOENIX MEDICAL PSYCHIATRIC HOSPITAL, PHOENIX, AZ, p. A36
PHOENIXVILLE HOSPITAL, PHOENIXVILLE, PA, p. A550
PHS SANTA FE INDIAN HOSPITAL, SANTA FE, NM, p. A436
PHYSICIANS BEHAVIORAL HOSPITAL, SHREVEPORT, LA, p. A292
PHYSICIANS CARE SURGICAL HOSPITAL, ROYERSFORD, PA, p. A554
PHYSICIANS MEDICAL CENTER, HOUMA, LA, p. A283
PHYSICIANS MEDICAL CENTER OF SANTA FE HOSPITAL, SANTA FE, NM, p. A436
PHYSICIANS REGIONAL - PINE RIDGE, NAPLES, FL, p. A142
PHYSICIANS REGIONAL MEDICAL CENTER, NAPLES, FL, p. A142
PHYSICIANS SURGICAL HOSPITAL - QUAIL CREEK, AMARILLO, TX, p. A596
PHYSICIANS' MEDICAL CENTER, NEW ALBANY, IN, p. A225

PIEDMONT ATHENS REGIONAL MEDICAL CENTER, ATHENS, GA, p. A156
PIEDMONT ATLANTA HOSPITAL, ATLANTA, GA, p. A158
PIEDMONT AUGUSTA, AUGUSTA, GA, p. A158
PIEDMONT CARTERSVILLE, CARTERSVILLE, GA, p. A160
PIEDMONT COLUMBUS REGIONAL MIDTOWN, COLUMBUS, GA, p. A161
PIEDMONT COLUMBUS REGIONAL NORTHSIDE, COLUMBUS, GA, p. A161
PIEDMONT EASTSIDE MEDICAL CENTER, SNELLVILLE, GA, p. A171
PIEDMONT FAYETTE HOSPITAL, FAYETTEVILLE, GA, p. A164
PIEDMONT GERIATRIC HOSPITAL, BURKEVILLE, VA, p. A674
PIEDMONT HENRY HOSPITAL, STOCKBRIDGE, GA, p. A172
PIEDMONT HOSPITAL, ATLANTA, GA, p. A158
PIEDMONT MACON, MACON, GA, p. A167
PIEDMONT MACON NORTH, MACON, GA, p. A167
PIEDMONT MCDUFFIE, THOMSON, GA, p. A172
PIEDMONT MEDICAL CENTER, ROCK HILL, SC, p. A570
PIEDMONT MOUNTAINSIDE HOSPITAL, JASPER, GA, p. A165
PIEDMONT NEWNAN HOSPITAL, NEWNAN, GA, p. A169
PIEDMONT NEWTON HOSPITAL, COVINGTON, GA, p. A162
PIEDMONT ROCKDALE HOSPITAL, CONYERS, GA, p. A161
PIEDMONT WALTON HOSPITAL, MONROE, GA, p. A168
PIGGOTT COMMUNITY HOSPITAL, PIGGOTT, AR, p. A52
PIGGOTT HEALTH SYSTEM, PIGGOTT, AR, p. A52
PIH HEALTH DOWNEY HOSPITAL, DOWNEY, CA, p. A61
PIH HEALTH GOOD SAMARITAN HOSPITAL, LOS ANGELES, CA, p. A74
PIH HEALTH HOSPITAL - DOWNEY, DOWNEY, CA, p. A61
PIH HEALTH HOSPITAL - WHITTIER, WHITTIER, CA, p. A101
PIH HEALTH WHITTIER HOSPITAL, WHITTIER, CA, p. A101
PIKE COUNTY MEMORIAL HOSPITAL, LOUISIANA, MO, p. A379
PIKEVILLE MEDICAL CENTER, PIKEVILLE, KY, p. A273
PILGRIM PSYCHIATRIC CENTER, BRENTWOOD, NY, p. A439
PINCKNEYVILLE COMMUNITY HOSPITAL, PINCKNEYVILLE, IL, p. A206
PINE REST CHRISTIAN MENTAL HEALTH SERVICES, GRAND RAPIDS, MI, p. A328
PINEVILLE COMMUNITY HEALTH CENTER, PINEVILLE, KY, p. A273
PINEWOOD SPRINGS, COLUMBIA, TN, p. A581
PINNACLE HOSPITAL, CROWN POINT, IN, p. A215
PINNACLE POINTE BEHAVIORAL HEALTHCARE SYSTEM, LITTLE ROCK, AR, p. A50
PINNACLEHEALTH AT COMMUNITY GENERAL OSTEOPATHIC HOSPITAL, HARRISBURG, PA, p. A541
PIONEER MEDICAL CENTER, BIG TIMBER, MT, p. A389
PIONEER MEMORIAL HOSPITAL, HEPPNER, OR, p. A527
PIONEER MEMORIAL HOSPITAL AND HEALTH SERVICES, VIBORG, SD, p. A578
PIONEER SPECIALTY HOSPITAL, PONTIAC, MI, p. A335
PIONEERS MEDICAL CENTER, MEEKER, CO, p. A112
PIONEERS MEMORIAL HEALTHCARE DISTRICT, BRAWLEY, CA, p. A58
PIPESTONE COUNTY MEDICAL CENTER, PIPESTONE, MN, p. A352
PLACENTIA-LINDA HOSPITAL, PLACENTIA, CA, p. A83
PLAINS MEMORIAL HOSPITAL, DIMMITT, TX, p. A614
PLAINS REGIONAL MEDICAL CENTER, CLOVIS, NM, p. A434
PLAINVIEW HOSPITAL, PLAINVIEW, NY, p. A456
PLATEAU MEDICAL CENTER, OAK HILL, WV, p. A703
PLATTE COUNTY MEMORIAL HOSPITAL, WHEATLAND, WY, p. A729
PLATTE HEALTH CENTER AVERA, PLATTE, SD, p. A575
PLEASANT VALLEY HOSPITAL, POINT PLEASANT, WV, p. A704
PLUMAS DISTRICT HOSPITAL, QUINCY, CA, p. A84
PLYMOUTH MEDICAL CENTER, PLYMOUTH, IN, p. A226
POCAHONTAS COMMUNITY HOSPITAL, POCAHONTAS, IA, p. A242
POCAHONTAS MEMORIAL HOSPITAL, BUCKEYE, WV, p. A699
POCASSET MENTAL HEALTH CENTER, POCASSET, MA, p. A317
POINTE COUPEE GENERAL HOSPITAL, NEW ROADS, LA, p. A290
POLARA HEALTH, PRESCOTT VALLEY, AZ, p. A37
POLK MEDICAL CENTER, CEDARTOWN, GA, p. A160
POMERENE HOSPITAL, MILLERSBURG, OH, p. A500
POMONA VALLEY HOSPITAL MEDICAL CENTER, POMONA, CA, p. A84
PONDERA MEDICAL CENTER, CONRAD, MT, p. A390
PONTIAC GENERAL HOSPITAL, PONTIAC, MI, p. A335
POPLAR BLUFF REGIONAL MEDICAL CENTER, POPLAR BLUFF, MO, p. A382
POPLAR BLUFF VAMC, POPLAR BLUFF, MO, p. A382
POPLAR COMMUNITY HOSPITAL, POPLAR, MT, p. A395
POPLAR SPRINGS HOSPITAL, PETERSBURG, VA, p. A681
PORT ST. LUCIE HOSPITAL, PORT ST LUCIE, FL, p. A147

© 2025 AHA Guide

Index of Hospitals / Porter Adventist Hospital

PORTER ADVENTIST HOSPITAL, DENVER, CO, p. A106
PORTER MEDICAL CENTER, MIDDLEBURY, VT, p. A671
PORTER-STARKE SERVICES, VALPARAISO, IN, p. A228
PORTERVILLE DEVELOPMENTAL CENTER, PORTERVILLE, CA, p. A84
PORTLAND HCS, PORTLAND, OR, p. A530
PORTNEUF MEDICAL CENTER, POCATELLO, ID, p. A183
PORTSMOUTH REGIONAL HOSPITAL, PORTSMOUTH, NH, p. A417
POST ACUTE MEDICAL SPECIALTY HOSPITAL OF CORPUS CHRISTI – NORTH, CORPUS CHRISTI, TX, p. A609
POST ACUTE MEDICAL SPECIALTY HOSPITAL OF TEXARKANA – NORTH, TEXARKANA, TX, p. A657
POST ACUTE MEDICAL SPECIALTY HOSPITAL OF TULSA, TULSA, OK, p. A522
POST ACUTE/WARM SPRINGS SPECIALTY HOSPITAL OF SAN ANTONIO, SAN ANTONIO, TX, p. A650
POTTSTOWN HOSPITAL, POTTSTOWN, PA, p. A553
POWELL VALLEY HEALTH CARE, POWELL, WY, p. A728
POWER COUNTY HOSPITAL DISTRICT, AMERICAN FALLS, ID, p. A179
PRAGUE COMMUNITY HOSPITAL, PRAGUE, OK, p. A520
PRAGUE REGIONAL MEMORIAL HOSPITAL, PRAGUE, OK, p. A520
PRAIRE RIDGE HEALTHCARE, ELBOW LAKE, MN, p. A346
PRAIRIE COUNTY HOSPITAL DISTRICT, TERRY, MT, p. A396
PRAIRIE LAKES HEALTHCARE SYSTEM, WATERTOWN, SD, p. A578
PRAIRIE RIDGE HEALTH, INC., COLUMBUS, WI, p. A709
PRAIRIE ST. JOHN'S, FARGO, ND, p. A480
PRAIRIE VIEW, NEWTON, KS, p. A256
PRAIRIECARE BROOKLYN PARK, BROOKLYN PARK, MN, p. A344
PRATT REGIONAL MEDICAL CENTER, PRATT, KS, p. A258
PRATTVILLE BAPTIST HOSPITAL, PRATTVILLE, AL, p. A24
PREMIER SPECIALTY HOSPITAL OF EL PASO, EL PASO, TX, p. A617
PRENTICE WOMEN'S HOSPITAL, CHICAGO, IL, p. A190
PRESBYTERIAN ESPANOLA HOSPITAL, ESPANOLA, NM, p. A434
PRESBYTERIAN HOSPITAL, ALBUQUERQUE, NM, p. A433
PRESBYTERIAN HOSPITAL, OKLAHOMA CITY, OK, p. A518
PRESBYTERIAN SANTA FE MEDICAL CENTER, SANTA FE, NM, p. A437
PRESBYTERIAN TOWER, OKLAHOMA CITY, OK, p. A518
PRESBYTERIAN/ST. LUKE'S MEDICAL CENTER, DENVER, CO, p. A106
PRESENTATION MEDICAL CENTER, ROLLA, ND, p. A483
PREVOST MEMORIAL HOSPITAL, DONALDSONVILLE, LA, p. A281
PRIMARY CHILDREN'S HOSPITAL, SALT LAKE CITY, UT, p. A669
PRINCETON BAPTIST MEDICAL CENTER, BIRMINGHAM, AL, p. A17
PRINCETON COMMUNITY HOSPITAL, PRINCETON, WV, p. A704
PRISMA HEALTH BAPTIST EASLEY HOSPITAL, EASLEY, SC, p. A565
PRISMA HEALTH BAPTIST HOSPITAL, COLUMBIA, SC, p. A565
PRISMA HEALTH BAPTIST PARKRIDGE HOSPITAL, COLUMBIA, SC, p. A564
PRISMA HEALTH GREENVILLE MEMORIAL HOSPITAL, GREENVILLE, SC, p. A567
PRISMA HEALTH GREER MEMORIAL HOSPITAL, GREER, SC, p. A567
PRISMA HEALTH HILLCREST HOSPITAL, SIMPSONVILLE, SC, p. A570
PRISMA HEALTH LAURENS COUNTY HOSPITAL, CLINTON, SC, p. A564
PRISMA HEALTH NORTH GREENVILLE HOSPITAL, TRAVELERS REST, SC, p. A571
PRISMA HEALTH OCONEE MEMORIAL HOSPITAL, SENECA, SC, p. A570
PRISMA HEALTH PATEWOOD HOSPITAL, GREENVILLE, SC, p. A567
PRISMA HEALTH RICHLAND HOSPITAL, COLUMBIA, SC, p. A565
PRISMA HEALTH TUOMEY HOSPITAL, SUMTER, SC, p. A570
PROFESSIONAL HOSPITAL GUAYNABO, GUAYNABO, PR, p. A732
PROGRESS WEST HOSPITAL, O FALLON, MO, p. A381
PROHEALTH OCONOMOWOC MEMORIAL HOSPITAL, OCONOMOWOC, WI, p. A718
PROHEALTH REHABILITATION HOSPITAL OF WISCONSIN, WAUKESHA, WI, p. A723
PROHEALTH WAUKESHA MEMORIAL HOSPITAL, WAUKESHA, WI, p. A723
PROMEDICA BAY PARK HOSPITAL, OREGON, OH, p. A502
PROMEDICA CHARLES AND VIRGINIA HICKMAN HOSPITAL, ADRIAN, MI, p. A321
PROMEDICA COLDWATER REGIONAL HOSPITAL, COLDWATER, MI, p. A324
PROMEDICA DEFIANCE REGIONAL HOSPITAL, DEFIANCE, OH, p. A494
PROMEDICA FOSTORIA COMMUNITY HOSPITAL, FOSTORIA, OH, p. A496
PROMEDICA MEMORIAL HOSPITAL, FREMONT, OH, p. A496
PROMEDICA MONROE REGIONAL HOSPITAL, MONROE, MI, p. A333
PROMEDICA TOLEDO HOSPITAL, TOLEDO, OH, p. A505
PROMISE HOSPITAL OF BOSSIER CITY, BOSSIER CITY, LA, p. A279
PROMISE HOSPITAL OF LOUISIANA – SHREVEPORT CAMPUS, SHREVEPORT, LA, p. A293
PROMISE SPECIALTY HOSPITAL OF SOUTHEAST TEXAS, NEDERLAND, TX, p. A641
PROSSER MEMORIAL HEALTH, PROSSER, WA, p. A693
PROVIDENCE – PROVIDENCE PARK HOSPITAL, NOVI CAMPUS, NOVI, MI, p. A334
PROVIDENCE ALASKA MEDICAL CENTER, ANCHORAGE, AK, p. A27
PROVIDENCE CEDARS-SINAI TARZANA MEDICAL CENTER, LOS ANGELES, CA, p. A74
PROVIDENCE CENTRALIA HOSPITAL, CENTRALIA, WA, p. A688
PROVIDENCE GENERAL MEDICAL CTR, EVERETT, WA, p. A689
PROVIDENCE HOLY CROSS MEDICAL CENTER, LOS ANGELES, CA, p. A75
PROVIDENCE HOLY FAMILY HOSPITAL, SPOKANE, WA, p. A696
PROVIDENCE HOOD RIVER MEMORIAL HOSPITAL, HOOD RIVER, OR, p. A528
PROVIDENCE HOSPITAL, MOBILE, AL, p. A21
PROVIDENCE HOSPITAL, SANDUSKY, OH, p. A503
PROVIDENCE KODIAK ISLAND MEDICAL CENTER, KODIAK, AK, p. A28
PROVIDENCE LITTLE COMPANY OF MARY MEDICAL CENTER – TORRANCE, TORRANCE, CA, p. A98
PROVIDENCE LITTLE COMPANY OF MARY MEDICAL CENTER SAN PEDRO, LOS ANGELES, CA, p. A75
PROVIDENCE MEDFORD MEDICAL CENTER, MEDFORD, OR, p. A529
PROVIDENCE MEDICAL CENTER, KANSAS CITY, KS, p. A252
PROVIDENCE MEDICAL CENTER, WAYNE, NE, p. A406
PROVIDENCE MILWAUKIE HOSPITAL, MILWAUKIE, OR, p. A529
PROVIDENCE MISSION HOSPITAL MISSION VIEJO, MISSION VIEJO, CA, p. A77
PROVIDENCE MOUNT CARMEL HOSPITAL, COLVILLE, WA, p. A688
PROVIDENCE NEWBERG MEDICAL CENTER, NEWBERG, OR, p. A529
PROVIDENCE PARK HOSPITAL, NOVI, MI, p. A334
PROVIDENCE PORTLAND MEDICAL CENTER, PORTLAND, OR, p. A530
PROVIDENCE QUEEN OF THE VALLEY MEDICAL CENTER, NAPA, CA, p. A79
PROVIDENCE REDWOOD MEMORIAL HOSPITAL, FORTUNA, CA, p. A63
PROVIDENCE REGIONAL MEDICAL CENTER EVERETT, EVERETT, WA, p. A689
PROVIDENCE SACRED HEART MEDICAL CENTER & CHILDREN'S HOSPITAL, SPOKANE, WA, p. A696
PROVIDENCE SAINT JOHN'S HEALTH CENTER, SANTA MONICA, CA, p. A95
PROVIDENCE SAINT JOSEPH MEDICAL CENTER, BURBANK, CA, p. A58
PROVIDENCE SANTA ROSA MEMORIAL HOSPITAL, SANTA ROSA, CA, p. A95
PROVIDENCE SEASIDE HOSPITAL, SEASIDE, OR, p. A532
PROVIDENCE SEWARD MEDICAL CENTER, SEWARD, AK, p. A29
PROVIDENCE ST. ELIAS SPECIALTY HOSPITAL, ANCHORAGE, AK, p. A27
PROVIDENCE ST. JOSEPH HOSPITAL EUREKA, EUREKA, CA, p. A62
PROVIDENCE ST. JOSEPH HOSPITAL ORANGE, ORANGE, CA, p. A81
PROVIDENCE ST. JOSEPH MEDICAL CENTER, POLSON, MT, p. A395
PROVIDENCE ST. JOSEPH'S HOSPITAL, CHEWELAH, WA, p. A688
PROVIDENCE ST. JUDE MEDICAL CENTER, FULLERTON, CA, p. A65
PROVIDENCE ST. LUKE'S REHABILITATION INSTITUTE, SPOKANE, WA, p. A696
PROVIDENCE ST. LUKE'S REHABILITATION MEDICAL CENTER, SPOKANE, WA, p. A696
PROVIDENCE ST. MARY MEDICAL CENTER, APPLE VALLEY, CA, p. A56
PROVIDENCE ST. MARY MEDICAL CENTER, WALLA WALLA, WA, p. A698
PROVIDENCE ST. PATRICK HOSPITAL, MISSOULA, MT, p. A394
PROVIDENCE ST. PETER HOSPITAL, OLYMPIA, WA, p. A692
PROVIDENCE ST. VINCENT MEDICAL CENTER, PORTLAND, OR, p. A531
PROVIDENCE SWEDISH CHERRY HILL, SEATTLE, WA, p. A694
PROVIDENCE SWEDISH EDMONDS, EDMONDS, WA, p. A689
PROVIDENCE SWEDISH FIRST HILL, SEATTLE, WA, p. A694
PROVIDENCE TARZANA MEDICAL CENTER, LOS ANGELES, CA, p. A75
PROVIDENCE VALDEZ MEDICAL CENTER, VALDEZ, AK, p. A29
PROVIDENCE VETERANS AFFAIRS MEDICAL CENTER, PROVIDENCE, RI, p. A560
PROVIDENCE WILLAMETTE FALLS MEDICAL CENTER, OREGON CITY, OR, p. A530
PROVIDENT HOSPITAL OF COOK COUNTY, CHICAGO, IL, p. A190
PROVO CANYON BEHAVIORAL HOSPITAL, OREM, UT, p. A667
PROWERS MEDICAL CENTER, LAMAR, CO, p. A111
PSYCHIATRIC HOSPITAL AT VANDERBILT, NASHVILLE, TN, p. A590
PSYCHIATRIC INSTITUTE OF WASHINGTON, WASHINGTON, DC, p. A124
PUERTO RICO CHILDREN'S HOSPITAL, BAYAMON, PR, p. A731
PULASKI MEMORIAL HOSPITAL, WINAMAC, IN, p. A229
PULLMAN REGIONAL HOSPITAL, PULLMAN, WA, p. A693
PUNXSUTAWNEY AREA HOSPITAL, PUNXSUTAWNEY, PA, p. A553
PURCELL MUNICIPAL HOSPITAL, PURCELL, OK, p. A520
PUSHMATAHA HOSPITAL, ANTLERS, OK, p. A509
PUTNAM COMMUNITY MEDICAL CENTER, PALATKA, FL, p. A145
PUTNAM COUNTY HOSPITAL, GREENCASTLE, IN, p. A218
PUTNAM COUNTY MEMORIAL HOSPITAL, UNIONVILLE, MO, p. A388
PUTNAM GENERAL HOSPITAL, EATONTON, GA, p. A163
PUTNAM HOSPITAL, CARMEL, NY, p. A441
PUTNAM HOSPITAL CENTER, CARMEL, NY, p. A441

Q

QUAD CITIES REHABILITATION INSTITUTE, THE, MOLINE, IL, p. A202
QUAIL RUN BEHAVIORAL HEALTH, PHOENIX, AZ, p. A36
QUEEN OF THE VALLEY MEDICAL CENTER, NAPA, CA, p. A79
QUEEN'S NORTH HAWAII COMMUNITY HOSPITAL, KAMUELA, HI, p. A176
QUENTIN N. BURDICK MEMORIAL HEALTHCARE FACILITY, BELCOURT, ND, p. A479
QUILLEN REHABILITATION HOSPITAL, A JOINT VENTURE OF BALLAD HEALTH AND ENCOMPASS HEALTH, JOHNSON CITY, TN, p. A585
QUINCY VALLEY MEDICAL CENTER, QUINCY, WA, p. A693

R

RADIANT HEALTH, MARION, IN, p. A223
RADY CHILDREN'S HOSPITAL – SAN DIEGO, SAN DIEGO, CA, p. A89
RAINBOW BABIES AND CHILDREN'S HOSPITAL, CLEVELAND, OH, p. A491
RAINIER SPRINGS HOSPITAL, VANCOUVER, WA, p. A698
RAINY LAKE MEDICAL CENTER, INTERNATIONAL FALLS, MN, p. A348
RALEIGH GENERAL HOSPITAL, BECKLEY, WV, p. A699
RALPH H. JOHNSON VETERANS AFFAIRS MEDICAL CENTER, CHARLESTON, SC, p. A563
RANCHO LOS AMIGOS NATIONAL REHABILITATION CENTER, DOWNEY, CA, p. A62
RANDOLPH HEALTH, ASHEBORO, NC, p. A463
RANGELY DISTRICT HOSPITAL, RANGELY, CO, p. A113

Index of Hospitals / Rochelle Community Hospital

RANKEN JORDAN PEDIATRIC BRIDGE HOSPITAL, MARYLAND HEIGHTS, MO, p. A380
RANKIN COUNTY HOSPITAL DISTRICT, RANKIN, TX, p. A646
RAPIDES REGIONAL MEDICAL CENTER, ALEXANDRIA, LA, p. A276
RAPPAHANNOCK GENERAL HOSPITAL, KILMARNOCK, VA, p. A678
RAWLINS COUNTY HEALTH CENTER, ATWOOD, KS, p. A246
RAY COUNTY HOSPITAL AND HEALTHCARE, RICHMOND, MO, p. A382
RAYMOND G. MURPHY DEPARTMENT OF VETERANS AFFAIRS MEDICAL CENTER, ALBUQUERQUE, NM, p. A433
READING HOSPITAL, WEST READING, PA, p. A557
READING HOSPITAL REHABILITATION AT WYOMISSING, WYOMISSING, PA, p. A558
REAGAN MEMORIAL HOSPITAL, BIG LAKE, TX, p. A603
REBOUND BEHAVIORAL HEALTH, LANCASTER, SC, p. A568
RECEPTION AND MEDICAL CENTER, LAKE BUTLER, FL, p. A136
RED BAY HOSPITAL, RED BAY, AL, p. A24
RED BUD REGIONAL HOSPITAL, RED BUD, IL, p. A207
RED LAKE INDIAN HEALTH SERVICE HOSPITAL, RED LAKE, MN, p. A353
RED RIVER BEHAVIORAL CENTER, BOSSIER CITY, LA, p. A279
RED RIVER HOSPITAL, LLC, WICHITA FALLS, TX, p. A662
REDINGTON-FAIRVIEW GENERAL HOSPITAL, SKOWHEGAN, ME, p. A299
REDLANDS COMMUNITY HOSPITAL, REDLANDS, CA, p. A85
REDMOND REGIONAL MEDICAL CENTER, ROME, GA, p. A170
REDWOOD MEMORIAL HOSPITAL, FORTUNA, CA, p. A63
REEDSBURG AREA MEDICAL CENTER, REEDSBURG, WI, p. A720
REEVES COUNTY HOSPITAL DISTRICT, PECOS, TX, p. A643
REEVES MEMORIAL MEDICAL CENTER, BERNICE, LA, p. A278
REEVES REGIONAL HEALTH, PECOS, TX, p. A643
REFUGIO COUNTY MEMORIAL HOSPITAL, REFUGIO, TX, p. A646
REGENCY HOSPITAL – MACON, MACON, GA, p. A167
REGENCY HOSPITAL OF CENTRAL GEORGIA, MACON, GA, p. A167
REGENCY HOSPITAL OF CINCINNATI, CINCINNATI, OH, p. A489
REGENCY HOSPITAL OF COLUMBUS, COLUMBUS, OH, p. A492
REGENCY HOSPITAL OF FLORENCE, FLORENCE, SC, p. A566
REGENCY HOSPITAL OF GREENVILLE, GREENVILLE, SC, p. A567
REGENCY HOSPITAL OF MERIDIAN, MERIDIAN, MS, p. A366
REGENCY HOSPITAL OF MINNEAPOLIS, GOLDEN VALLEY, MN, p. A347
REGENCY HOSPITAL OF NORTHWEST ARKANSAS - SPRINGDALE, SPRINGDALE, AR, p. A53
REGENCY HOSPITAL OF NORTHWEST INDIANA, EAST CHICAGO, IN, p. A215
REGENCY HOSPITAL OF TOLEDO, SYLVANIA, OH, p. A504
REGENCY NORTH CENTRAL OHIO – CLEVELAND EAST, WARRENSVILLE HEIGHTS, OH, p. A506
REGIONAL HEALTH SERVICES OF HOWARD COUNTY, CRESCO, IA, p. A234
REGIONAL HOSPITAL OF SCRANTON, SCRANTON, PA, p. A554
REGIONAL MEDICAL CENTER, MANCHESTER, IA, p. A239
REGIONAL MEDICAL CENTER, VICTORIA, TX, p. A660
REGIONAL MEDICAL CENTER BAYONET POINT, HUDSON, FL, p. A134
REGIONAL MEDICAL CENTER OF CENTRAL ALABAMA, GREENVILLE, AL, p. A20
REGIONAL MEDICAL CENTER OF SAN JOSE, SAN JOSE, CA, p. A92
REGIONAL MENTAL HEALTH CENTER, MERRILLVILLE, IN, p. A223
REGIONAL ONE HEALTH, MEMPHIS, TN, p. A589
REGIONAL ONE HEALTH EXTENDED CARE HOSPITAL, MEMPHIS, TN, p. A589
REGIONAL REHABILITATION CENTER, SALEM, OR, p. A532
REGIONAL REHABILITATION HOSPITAL, PHENIX CITY, AL, p. A24
REGIONAL WEST GARDEN COUNTY, OSHKOSH, NE, p. A405
REGIONAL WEST MEDICAL CENTER, SCOTTSBLUFF, NE, p. A406
REGIONS BEHAVIORAL HOSPITAL, BATON ROUGE, LA, p. A278
REGIONS HOSPITAL, SAINT PAUL, MN, p. A354
REHAB INST AT SANTA BARBARA, SANTA BARBARA, CA, p. A94
REHABILITATION HOSPITAL OF BOWIE, BOWIE, MD, p. A303
REHABILITATION HOSPITAL OF BRISTOL, BRISTOL, VA, p. A674

REHABILITATION HOSPITAL OF FORT WAYNE, FORT WAYNE, IN, p. A217
REHABILITATION HOSPITAL OF HENRY, MCDONOUGH, GA, p. A168
REHABILITATION HOSPITAL OF INDIANA, INDIANAPOLIS, IN, p. A220
REHABILITATION HOSPITAL OF JENNINGS, JENNINGS, LA, p. A284
REHABILITATION HOSPITAL OF NAPLES, NAPLES, FL, p. A142
REHABILITATION HOSPITAL OF NORTHERN ARIZONA, FLAGSTAFF, AZ, p. A31
REHABILITATION HOSPITAL OF NORTHERN INDIANA, MISHAWAKA, IN, p. A224
REHABILITATION HOSPITAL OF NORTHWEST OHIO, TOLEDO, OH, p. A505
REHABILITATION HOSPITAL OF OVERLAND PARK, OVERLAND PARK, KS, p. A257
REHABILITATION HOSPITAL OF RHODE ISLAND, NORTH SMITHFIELD, RI, p. A560
REHABILITATION HOSPITAL OF SOUTHERN CALIFORNIA, RANCHO MIRAGE, CA, p. A84
REHABILITATION HOSPITAL OF SOUTHERN NEW MEXICO, LAS CRUCES, NM, p. A435
REHABILITATION HOSPITAL OF THE NORTHWEST, POST FALLS, ID, p. A183
REHABILITATION HOSPITAL OF THE PACIFIC, HONOLULU, HI, p. A176
REHABILITATION HOSPITAL OF WESTERN WISCONSIN, EAU CLAIRE, WI, p. A710
REHABILITATION HOSPITAL OF WISCONSIN, WAUKESHA, WI, p. A723
REHABILITATION HOSPITAL, NAVICENT HEALTH, MACON, GA, p. A167
REHABILITATION INSTITUTE OF OREGON, PORTLAND, OR, p. A530
REHABILITATION INSTITUTE OF SOUTHERN ILLINOIS, LLC, THE, SHILOH, IL, p. A208
REHABILITATION INSTITUTE OF WEST FLORIDA, PENSACOLA, FL, p. A147
REHOBOTH MCKINLEY CHRISTIAN HEALTH CARE SERVICES, GALLUP, NM, p. A434
REID HEALTH, RICHMOND, IN, p. A226
RENO BEHAVIORAL HEALTHCARE HOSPITAL, RENO, NV, p. A412
RENOWN REGIONAL MEDICAL CENTER, RENO, NV, p. A412
RENOWN REHABILITATION HOSPITAL, RENO, NV, p. A412
RENOWN SOUTH MEADOWS MEDICAL CENTER, RENO, NV, p. A412
REPUBLIC COUNTY HOSPITAL, BELLEVILLE, KS, p. A246
RESEARCH MEDICAL CENTER, KANSAS CITY, MO, p. A378
RESOLUTE HEALTH, NEW BRAUNFELS, TX, p. A641
RESTON HOSPITAL CENTER, RESTON, VA, p. A682
RETREAT DOCTORS' HOSPITAL, RICHMOND, VA, p. A683
REUNION REHABILITATION HOSPITAL ARLINGTON, ARLINGTON, TX, p. A598
REUNION REHABILITATION HOSPITAL DENVER, DENVER, CO, p. A107
REUNION REHABILITATION HOSPITAL INVERNESS, ENGLEWOOD, CO, p. A107
REUNION REHABILITATION HOSPITAL PEORIA, PEORIA, AZ, p. A34
REUNION REHABILITATION HOSPITAL PHOENIX, PHOENIX, AZ, p. A36
REUNION REHABILITATION HOSPITAL PLANO, PLANO, TX, p. A645
REYNOLDS MEMORIAL HOSPITAL, GLEN DALE, WV, p. A700
RHEA MEDICAL CENTER, DAYTON, TN, p. A582
RHODE ISLAND HOSPITAL, PROVIDENCE, RI, p. A561
RICE MEDICAL CENTER, EAGLE LAKE, TX, p. A615
RICELAND MEDICAL CENTER, WINNIE, TX, p. A663
RICHARD H. HUTCHINGS PSYCHIATRIC CENTER, SYRACUSE, NY, p. A460
RICHARD H. YOUNG HOSPITAL, KEARNEY, NE, p. A401
RICHARD L. ROUDEBUSH VETERANS AFFAIRS MEDICAL CENTER, INDIANAPOLIS, IN, p. A220
RICHARDSON MEDICAL CENTER, RAYVILLE, LA, p. A291
RICHLAND HOSPITAL, RICHLAND CENTER, WI, p. A720
RICHLAND PARISH HOSPITAL–DELHI, DELHI, LA, p. A281
RICHMOND MEDICAL CENTER, RICHMOND, CA, p. A86
RICHMOND STATE HOSPITAL, RICHMOND, IN, p. A226
RICHMOND UNIVERSITY MEDICAL CENTER, NEW YORK, NY, p. A452
RIDDLE HOSPITAL, MEDIA, PA, p. A546
RIDGE BEHAVIORAL HEALTH SYSTEM, LEXINGTON, KY, p. A269
RIDGECREST REGIONAL HOSPITAL, RIDGECREST, CA, p. A86
RIDGEVIEW BEHAVIORAL HOSPITAL, MIDDLE POINT, OH, p. A500

RIDGEVIEW INSTITUTE – MONROE, MONROE, GA, p. A168
RIDGEVIEW INSTITUTE – SMYRNA, SMYRNA, GA, p. A171
RIDGEVIEW LE SUEUR MEDICAL CENTER, LE SUEUR, MN, p. A348
RIDGEVIEW MEDICAL CENTER, WACONIA, MN, p. A356
RIDGEVIEW PSYCHIATRIC HOSPITAL AND CENTER, OAK RIDGE, TN, p. A591
RIDGEVIEW SIBLEY MEDICAL CENTER, ARLINGTON, MN, p. A342
RILEY HOSPITAL FOR CHILDREN, INDIANAPOLIS, IN, p. A220
RILEY HOSPITAL FOR CHILDREN AT INDIANA UNIVERSITY HEALTH, INDIANAPOLIS, IN, p. A220
RINGGOLD COUNTY HOSPITAL, MOUNT AYR, IA, p. A240
RIO GRANDE HOSPITAL, DEL NORTE, CO, p. A106
RIO GRANDE REGIONAL HOSPITAL, MCALLEN, TX, p. A638
RIO GRANDE STATE CENTER/SOUTH TEXAS HEALTH CARE SYSTEM, HARLINGEN, TX, p. A623
RIO VISTA BEHAVIORAL HEALTH, EL PASO, TX, p. A617
RIPON MEDICAL CENTER, RIPON, WI, p. A721
RIVENDELL BEHAVIORAL HEALTH HOSPITAL, BOWLING GREEN, KY, p. A263
RIVENDELL BEHAVIORAL HEALTH SERVICES, BENTON, AR, p. A43
RIVER BEND HOSPITAL, WEST LAFAYETTE, IN, p. A229
RIVER CREST HOSPITAL, SAN ANGELO, TX, p. A648
RIVER FALLS AREA HOSPITAL, RIVER FALLS, WI, p. A721
RIVER HOSPITAL, ALEXANDRIA BAY, NY, p. A438
RIVER OAKS HOSPITAL, NEW ORLEANS, LA, p. A290
RIVER PARK HOSPITAL, HUNTINGTON, WV, p. A701
RIVER PLACE BEHAVIORAL HEALTH, LA PLACE, LA, p. A285
RIVER POINT BEHAVIORAL HEALTH, JACKSONVILLE, FL, p. A135
RIVER'S EDGE HOSPITAL AND CLINIC, SAINT PETER, MN, p. A355
RIVERBEND REHABILITATION HOSPITAL, BASTROP, LA, p. A277
RIVERBRIDGE SPECIALTY HOSPITAL, VIDALIA, LA, p. A294
RIVEREDGE HOSPITAL, FOREST PARK, IL, p. A195
RIVERS HEALTH, POINT PLEASANT, WV, p. A704
RIVERSIDE COMMUNITY HOSPITAL, RIVERSIDE, CA, p. A86
RIVERSIDE DOCTORS' HOSPITAL WILLIAMSBURG, WILLIAMSBURG, VA, p. A685
RIVERSIDE HOSP – SKILLED CARE, RENO, NV, p. A412
RIVERSIDE HOSPITAL, ALEXANDRIA, LA, p. A276
RIVERSIDE MEDICAL CENTER, FRANKLINTON, LA, p. A282
RIVERSIDE MEDICAL CENTER, KANKAKEE, IL, p. A199
RIVERSIDE REGIONAL MEDICAL CENTER, NEWPORT NEWS, VA, p. A680
RIVERSIDE SHORE MEMORIAL HOSPITAL, ONANCOCK, VA, p. A681
RIVERSIDE UNIVERSITY HEALTH SYSTEM–MEDICAL CENTER, MORENO VALLEY, CA, p. A78
RIVERSIDE WALTER REED HOSPITAL, GLOUCESTER, VA, p. A677
RIVERTON HOSPITAL, RIVERTON, UT, p. A668
RIVERVALLEY BEHAVIORAL HEALTH HOSPITAL, OWENSBORO, KY, p. A272
RIVERVIEW BEHAVIORAL HEALTH, TEXARKANA, AR, p. A54
RIVERVIEW HEALTH, CROOKSTON, MN, p. A345
RIVERVIEW HEALTH, NOBLESVILLE, IN, p. A225
RIVERVIEW HEALTH INSTITUTE, DAYTON, OH, p. A494
RIVERVIEW PSYCHIATRIC CENTER, AUGUSTA, ME, p. A295
RIVERVIEW REGIONAL MEDICAL CENTER, CARTHAGE, TN, p. A579
RIVERVIEW REGIONAL MEDICAL CENTER, GADSDEN, AL, p. A20
RIVERWOOD HEALTHCARE CENTER, AITKIN, MN, p. A342
RIVERWOODS BEHAVIORAL HEALTH SYSTEM, RIVERDALE, GA, p. A170
RMC ANNISTON, ANNISTON, AL, p. A15
RML SPECIALTY HOSPITAL, HINSDALE, IL, p. A198
ROANE GENERAL HOSPITAL, SPENCER, WV, p. A705
ROANE MEDICAL CENTER, HARRIMAN, TN, p. A583
ROBERT E. BUSH NAVAL HOSPITAL, TWENTYNINE PALMS, CA, p. A99
ROBERT J. DOLE DEPARTMENT OF VETERANS AFFAIRS MEDICAL AND REGIONAL OFFICE CENTER, WICHITA, KS, p. A262
ROBERT WOOD JOHNSON UNIVERSITY HOSPITAL, NEW BRUNSWICK, NJ, p. A425
ROBERT WOOD JOHNSON UNIVERSITY HOSPITAL AT HAMILTON, HAMILTON, NJ, p. A422
ROBERT WOOD JOHNSON UNIVERSITY HOSPITAL RAHWAY, RAHWAY, NJ, p. A427
ROBERT WOOD JOHNSON UNIVERSITY HOSPITAL SOMERSET, SOMERVILLE, NJ, p. A428
ROBLEY REX DEPARTMENT OF VETERANS AFFAIRS MEDICAL CENTER, LOUISVILLE, KY, p. A270
ROCHELLE COMMUNITY HOSPITAL, ROCHELLE, IL, p. A207

ROCHESTER GENERAL HOSPITAL, ROCHESTER, NY, p. A457
ROCHESTER METHODIST HOSPITAL, ROCHESTER, MN, p. A354
ROCHESTER PSYCHIATRIC CENTER, ROCHESTER, NY, p. A457
ROCK COUNTY HOSPITAL, BASSETT, NE, p. A397
ROCK REGIONAL HOSPITAL, DERBY, KS, p. A248
ROCK SPRINGS, GEORGETOWN, TX, p. A622
ROCKCASTLE REGIONAL HOSPITAL AND RESPIRATORY CARE CENTER, MOUNT VERNON, KY, p. A272
ROCKEFELLER UNIVERSITY HOSPITAL, NEW YORK, NY, p. A452
ROCKFORD CENTER, NEWARK, DE, p. A122
ROCKLAND CHILDREN'S PSYCHIATRIC CENTER, ORANGEBURG, NY, p. A455
ROCKLAND PSYCHIATRIC CENTER, ORANGEBURG, NY, p. A455
ROCKLEDGE REGIONAL MEDICAL CENTER, ROCKLEDGE, FL, p. A148
ROCKVILLE GENERAL HOSPITAL, VERNON, CT, p. A119
ROCKY MOUNTAIN REGIONAL VA MEDICAL CENTER, AURORA, CO, p. A103
ROGER MILLS MEMORIAL HOSPITAL, CHEYENNE, OK, p. A511
ROGER WILLIAMS MEDICAL CENTER, PROVIDENCE, RI, p. A561
ROGERS BEHAVIORAL HEALTH, OCONOMOWOC, WI, p. A718
ROLLING HILLS HOSPITAL, ADA, OK, p. A509
ROLLING HILLS HOSPITAL, FRANKLIN, TN, p. A583
ROLLING PLAINS MEMORIAL HOSPITAL, SWEETWATER, TX, p. A655
ROME HEALTH, ROME, NY, p. A458
RONALD REAGAN UCLA MEDICAL CENTER, LOS ANGELES, CA, p. A75
ROOKS COUNTY HEALTH CENTER, PLAINVILLE, KS, p. A258
ROOSEVELT GENERAL HOSPITAL, PORTALES, NM, p. A436
ROOSEVELT HOSPITAL, EDISON, NJ, p. A420
ROOSEVELT MEDICAL CENTER, CULBERTSON, MT, p. A391
ROOSEVELT WARM SPRINGS LONG TERM ACUTE CARE HOSPITAL, WARM SPRINGS, GA, p. A173
ROOSEVELT WARM SPRINGS REHABILITATION AND SPECIALTY HOSPITALS, WARM SPRINGS, GA, p. A173
ROOSEVELT WARM SPRINGS REHABILITATION HOSPITAL, WARM SPRINGS, GA, p. A173
ROPER HOSPITAL, CHARLESTON, SC, p. A563
ROPER ST. FRANCIS BERKELEY HOSPITAL, SUMMERVILLE, SC, p. A570
ROPER ST. FRANCIS HOSPITAL-BERKELEY, SUMMERVILLE, SC, p. A570
ROPER ST. FRANCIS MOUNT PLEASANT HOSPITAL, MOUNT PLEASANT, SC, p. A568
ROSE MEDICAL CENTER, DENVER, CO, p. A107
ROSEBUD HEALTH CARE CENTER, FORSYTH, MT, p. A391
ROSEBURG VA MEDICAL CENTER, ROSEBURG, OR, p. A531
ROSELAND COMMUNITY HOSPITAL, CHICAGO, IL, p. A190
ROSWELL PARK COMPREHENSIVE CANCER CENTER, BUFFALO, NY, p. A440
ROTARY REHABILITATION HOSPITAL, MOBILE, AL, p. A21
ROTHMAN ORTHOPAEDIC SPECIALTY HOSPITAL, BENSALEM, PA, p. A535
ROUNDUP MEMORIAL HEALTHCARE, ROUNDUP, MT, p. A395
ROXBOROUGH MEMORIAL HOSPITAL, PHILADELPHIA, PA, p. A550
ROXBURY TREATMENT CENTER, SHIPPENSBURG, PA, p. A555
ROYAL C. JOHNSON VETERANS' MEMORIAL HOSPITAL, SIOUX FALLS, SD, p. A576
ROYAL OAKS HOSPITAL, WINDSOR, MO, p. A388
RUBY VALLEY MEDICAL CENTER, SHERIDAN, MT, p. A396
RUMFORD HOSPITAL, RUMFORD, ME, p. A299
RUNNELLS SPECIALIZED HOSPITAL OF UNION COUNTY, BERKELEY HEIGHTS, NJ, p. A418
RURAL WELLNESS ANADARKO, ANADARKO, OK, p. A509
RURAL WELLNESS FAIRFAX, FAIRFAX, OK, p. A512
RURAL WELLNESS STROUD, STROUD, OK, p. A521
RUSH-COPLEY MEDICAL CENTER, AURORA, IL, p. A186
RUSH COUNTY MEMORIAL HOSPITAL, LA CROSSE, KS, p. A252
RUSH MEMORIAL HOSPITAL, RUSHVILLE, IN, p. A227
RUSH OAK PARK HOSPITAL, OAK PARK, IL, p. A204
RUSH SPECIALTY HOSPITAL, CHICAGO, IL, p. A190
RUSH UNIVERSITY MEDICAL CENTER, CHICAGO, IL, p. A191
RUSK INSTITUTE, NEW YORK, NY, p. A452
RUSK REHABILITATION HOSPITAL, COLUMBIA, MO, p. A374
RUSK STATE HOSPITAL, RUSK, TX, p. A648
RUSSELL COUNTY HOSPITAL, RUSSELL SPRINGS, KY, p. A274
RUSSELL COUNTY MEDICAL CENTER, LEBANON, VA, p. A678
RUSSELL MEDICAL, ALEXANDER CITY, AL, p. A15

RUSSELL REGIONAL HOSPITAL, RUSSELL, KS, p. A258
RUSSELLVILLE HOSPITAL, RUSSELLVILLE, AL, p. A24
RUSTON REGIONAL SPECIALTY HOSPITAL, RUSTON, LA, p. A291
RUTGERS UNIVERSITY BEHAVIORAL HEALTHCARE, PISCATAWAY, NJ, p. A427
RUTHERFORD REGIONAL HEALTH SYSTEM, RUTHERFORDTON, NC, p. A475
RUTLAND REGIONAL MEDICAL CENTER, RUTLAND, VT, p. A672
RWJBARNABAS HEALTH BEHAVIORAL HEALTH CENTER, TOMS RIVER, NJ, p. A429
RYDER MEMORIAL HOSPITAL, HUMACAO, PR, p. A733

S

SABETHA COMMUNITY HOSPITAL, SABETHA, KS, p. A259
SABINE COUNTY HOSPITAL, HEMPHILL, TX, p. A624
SABINE MEDICAL CENTER, MANY, LA, p. A288
SACRAMENTO REHABILITATION HOSPITAL, LLC, SACRAMENTO, CA, p. A87
SACRED HEART CHILDEN'S HOSPITAL, SPOKANE, WA, p. A696
SACRED HEART HOSP & CNTR, HANFORD, CA, p. A66
SACRED HEART HOSPITAL, ALLENTOWN, PA, p. A534
SACRED HEART HOSPITAL, TOMAHAWK, WI, p. A723
SADDLEBACK MEDICAL CENTER, LAGUNA HILLS, CA, p. A69
SAGAMORE CHILDREN'S PSYCHIATRIC CENTER, DIX HILLS, NY, p. A442
SAGE REHABILITATION HOSPITAL, BATON ROUGE, LA, p. A278
SAGE SPECIALTY HOSPITAL (LTAC), DENHAM SPRINGS, LA, p. A281
SAGEWEST HEALTH CARE, RIVERTON, WY, p. A728
SAGEWEST HEALTHCARE-LANDER, LANDER, WY, p. A727
SAGINAW GENERAL HOSPITAL, SAGINAW, MI, p. A337
SAINT AGNES MEDICAL CENTER, FRESNO, CA, p. A65
SAINT ALPHONSUS MEDICAL CENTER – BAKER CITY, BAKER CITY, OR, p. A525
SAINT ALPHONSUS MEDICAL CENTER – NAMPA, NAMPA, ID, p. A182
SAINT ALPHONSUS MEDICAL CENTER – ONTARIO, ONTARIO, OR, p. A529
SAINT ALPHONSUS REGIONAL MEDICAL CENTER, BOISE, ID, p. A179
SAINT ALPHONSUS REGIONAL REHABILITATION HOSPITAL, AN AFFILIATE OF ENCOMPASS HEALTH, BOISE, ID, p. A179
SAINT ANNE'S HOSPITAL, FALL RIVER, MA, p. A313
SAINT ANTHONY HOSPITAL, CHICAGO, IL, p. A191
SAINT BARNABAS MEDICAL CENTER, LIVINGSTON, NJ, p. A423
SAINT CLAIRE HOME, PEORIA HEIGHTS, IL, p. A206
SAINT CLARE'S DENVILLE HOSPITAL, DENVILLE, NJ, p. A420
SAINT CLARE'S HOSPITAL/BOONTON TOWNSHIP, BOONTON TOWNSHIP, NJ, p. A418
SAINT CLARE'S HOSPITAL/DENVILLE, DENVILLE, NJ, p. A420
SAINT ELIZABETH HOSPITAL, CHICAGO, IL, p. A191
SAINT ELIZABETHS HOSPITAL, WASHINGTON, DC, p. A124
SAINT FRANCIS HEART HOSPITAL, TULSA, OK, p. A522
SAINT FRANCIS HOSPITAL, HARTFORD, CT, p. A116
SAINT FRANCIS HOSPITAL, MEMPHIS, TN, p. A589
SAINT FRANCIS HOSPITAL, TULSA, OK, p. A523
SAINT FRANCIS HOSPITAL AND HEALTH CENTERS, POUGHKEEPSIE, NY, p. A456
SAINT FRANCIS HOSPITAL MUSKOGEE, MUSKOGEE, OK, p. A515
SAINT FRANCIS HOSPITAL SOUTH, TULSA, OK, p. A523
SAINT FRANCIS HOSPITAL VINITA, VINITA, OK, p. A523
SAINT FRANCIS HOSPITAL-BARTLETT, BARTLETT, TN, p. A579
SAINT FRANCIS MEDICAL CENTER, CAPE GIRARDEAU, MO, p. A372
SAINT FRANCIS MEMORIAL HEALTH CENTER, GRAND ISLAND, NE, p. A400
SAINT JOHN HOSPITAL, LEAVENWORTH, KS, p. A253
SAINT JOHN VIANNEY HOSPITAL, DOWNINGTOWN, PA, p. A538
SAINT JOSEPH HEALTH SYSTEM, MISHAWAKA, IN, p. A224
SAINT JOSEPH MOUNT STERLING, MOUNT STERLING, KY, p. A272
SAINT JOSEPH'S CHILDEN'S HOSPITAL, MARSHFIELD, WI, p. A715
SAINT JOSEPH'S MEDICAL CENTER, YONKERS, NY, p. A462
SAINT LUKE INSTITUTE, SILVER SPRING, MD, p. A307
SAINT LUKE'S EAST HOSPITAL, LEE'S SUMMIT, MO, p. A379

SAINT LUKE'S HOSPITAL OF KANSAS CITY, KANSAS CITY, MO, p. A378
SAINT LUKE'S NORTH HOSPITAL – BARRY ROAD, KANSAS CITY, MO, p. A378
SAINT LUKE'S NORTHLAND HOSPITAL-SMITHVILLE CAMPUS, SMITHVILLE, MO, p. A386
SAINT LUKE'S SOUTH HOSPITAL, OVERLAND PARK, KS, p. A257
SAINT MARGARET HOSP & HLTH CTR, HAMMOND, IN, p. A218
SAINT MARY'S HOSPITAL, WATERBURY, CT, p. A119
SAINT MARY'S REGIONAL MEDICAL CENTER, RENO, NV, p. A412
SAINT MARY'S REGIONAL MEDICAL CENTER, RUSSELLVILLE, AR, p. A53
SAINT MICHAEL'S MEDICAL CENTER, NEWARK, NJ, p. A425
SAINT PETER'S HEALTHCARE SYSTEM, NEW BRUNSWICK, NJ, p. A425
SAINT PETER'S UNIVERSITY HOSPITAL, NEW BRUNSWICK, NJ, p. A425
SAINT SIMONS BY-THE-SEA HOSPITAL, SAINT SIMONS ISLAND, GA, p. A170
SAINT THOMAS HOSPITAL, AKRON, OH, p. A484
SAINT THOMAS MIDTOWN HOSPITAL, NASHVILLE, TN, p. A590
SAINT VINCENT HOSPITAL, ERIE, PA, p. A540
SAINT VINCENT HOSPITAL, WORCESTER, MA, p. A320
SAINTS MEDICAL CENTER, LOWELL, MA, p. A315
SAKAKAWEA MEDICAL CENTER, HAZEN, ND, p. A481
SALEM HEALTH WEST VALLEY, DALLAS, OR, p. A526
SALEM HOSPITAL, SALEM, MA, p. A318
SALEM HOSPITAL, SALEM, OR, p. A532
SALEM MEMORIAL DISTRICT HOSPITAL, SALEM, MO, p. A386
SALEM REGIONAL MEDICAL CENTER, SALEM, OH, p. A503
SALEM TOWNSHIP HOSPITAL, SALEM, IL, p. A208
SALEM VETERANS AFFAIRS MEDICAL CENTER, SALEM, VA, p. A683
SALINA REGIONAL HEALTH CENTER, SALINA, KS, p. A259
SALINA SURGICAL HOSPITAL, SALINA, KS, p. A259
SALINAS VALLEY HEALTH, SALINAS, CA, p. A88
SALINAS VALLEY MEMORIAL HEALTHCARE SYSTEM, SALINAS, CA, p. A88
SALINE MEMORIAL HOSPITAL, BENTON, AR, p. A43
SALT LAKE BEHAVIORAL HEALTH, SALT LAKE CITY, UT, p. A669
SALT LAKE CITY HCS, SALT LAKE CITY, UT, p. A669
SAM RAYBURN MEMORIAL VETERANS CENTER, BONHAM, TX, p. A604
SAMARITAN ALBANY GENERAL HOSPITAL, ALBANY, OR, p. A525
SAMARITAN BEHAVELBACK HOSPITAL, MESA, AZ, p. A34
SAMARITAN BEHAVIORAL HEALTH CENTER-DESERT SAMARITAN MEDICAL CENTER, MESA, AZ, p. A34
SAMARITAN BEHAVIORAL HLTH CTR, GLENDALE, AZ, p. A32
SAMARITAN HEALTHCARE, MOSES LAKE, WA, p. A692
SAMARITAN HOSPITAL – MAIN CAMPUS, TROY, NY, p. A460
SAMARITAN HOSPITAL, MACON, MO, p. A380
SAMARITAN LEBANON COMMUNITY HOSPITAL, LEBANON, OR, p. A528
SAMARITAN MEDICAL CENTER, WATERTOWN, NY, p. A461
SAMARITAN NORTH LINCOLN HOSPITAL, LINCOLN CITY, OR, p. A528
SAMARITAN PACIFIC COMMUNITIES HOSPITAL, NEWPORT, OR, p. A529
SAMARITAN SERVICES FOR AGING, CLINTON, IA, p. A233
SAME DAY SURGERY CENTER, RAPID CITY, SD, p. A576
SAMPSON REGIONAL MEDICAL CENTER, CLINTON, NC, p. A466
SAMUEL MAHELONA MEMORIAL HOSPITAL, KAPAA, HI, p. A177
SAMUEL SIMMONDS MEMORIAL HOSPITAL, BARROW, AK, p. A27
SAN ANTONIO BEHAVIORAL HEALTHCARE HOSPITAL, SAN ANTONIO, TX, p. A650
SAN ANTONIO COMMUNITY HOSPITAL, SAN ANTONIO, TX, p. A650
SAN ANTONIO REGIONAL HOSPITAL, UPLAND, CA, p. A99
SAN ANTONIO REHABILITATION HOSPITAL, SAN ANTONIO, TX, p. A650
SAN ANTONIO STATE HOSPITAL, SAN ANTONIO, TX, p. A650
SAN BERNARDINO MOUNTAINS COMMUNITY HOSPITAL, LAKE ARROWHEAD, CA, p. A69
SAN CARLOS APACHE HEALTHCARE CORPORATION, PERIDOT, AZ, p. A34
SAN DIEGO COUNTY PSYCHIATRIC HOSPITAL, SAN DIEGO, CA, p. A89
SAN DIEGO HCS, SAN DIEGO, CA, p. A89
SAN DIMAS COMMUNITY HOSPITAL, SAN DIMAS, CA, p. A90
SAN FRANCISCO CAMPUS FOR JEWISH LIVING, SAN FRANCISCO, CA, p. A91

SAN FRANCISCO VA HEALTH CARE SYSTEM, SAN FRANCISCO, CA, p. A91
SAN GABRIEL VALLEY MEDICAL CENTER, SAN GABRIEL, CA, p. A91
SAN GORGONIO MEMORIAL HOSPITAL, BANNING, CA, p. A57
SAN JOAQUIN GENERAL HOSPITAL, FRENCH CAMP, CA, p. A64
SAN JOAQUIN VALLEY REHABILITATION HOSPITAL, FRESNO, CA, p. A65
SAN JORGE CHILDREN'S AND WOMEN HOSPITAL, SANTURCE, PR, p. A736
SAN JOSE BEHAVORIAL HEALTH, SAN JOSE, CA, p. A92
SAN JUAN CAPESTRANO HOSPITAL, SAN JUAN, PR, p. A735
SAN JUAN CITY HOSPITAL, SAN JUAN, PR, p. A736
SAN JUAN HEALTH SERVICE DISTRICT, MONTICELLO, UT, p. A666
SAN JUAN REGIONAL MEDICAL CENTER, FARMINGTON, NM, p. A434
SAN LUIS VALLEY HEALTH, ALAMOSA, CO, p. A103
SAN LUIS VALLEY HEALTH CONEJOS COUNTY HOSPITAL, LA JARA, CO, p. A110
SAN MATEO MEDICAL CENTER, SAN MATEO, CA, p. A93
SAN RAMON REGIONAL MEDICAL CENTER, SAN RAMON, CA, p. A93
SANFORD ABERDEEN MEDICAL CENTER, ABERDEEN, SD, p. A572
SANFORD BAGLEY MEDICAL CENTER, BAGLEY, MN, p. A343
SANFORD BEHAVIORAL HEALTH CENTER, THIEF RIVER FALLS, MN, p. A356
SANFORD BEMIDJI MEDICAL CENTER, BEMIDJI, MN, p. A343
SANFORD CANBY MEDICAL CENTER, CANBY, MN, p. A344
SANFORD CANTON–INWOOD MEDICAL CENTER, CANTON, SD, p. A572
SANFORD CHAMBERLAIN MEDICAL CENTER, CHAMBERLAIN, SD, p. A572
SANFORD CHILDREN'S HOSPITAL, SIOUX FALLS, SD, p. A576
SANFORD CLEAR LAKE MEDICAL CENTER, CLEAR LAKE, SD, p. A572
SANFORD HILLSBORO MEDICAL CENTER, HILLSBORO, ND, p. A482
SANFORD JACKSON MEDICAL CENTER, JACKSON, MN, p. A348
SANFORD LUVERNE MEDICAL CENTER, LUVERNE, MN, p. A349
SANFORD MAYVILLE MEDICAL CENTER, MAYVILLE, ND, p. A482
SANFORD MEDICAL CENTER BISMARCK, BISMARCK, ND, p. A479
SANFORD MEDICAL CENTER FARGO, FARGO, ND, p. A481
SANFORD SHELDON MEDICAL CENTER, SHELDON, IA, p. A243
SANFORD THIEF RIVER FALLS MEDICAL CENTER, THIEF RIVER FALLS, MN, p. A356
SANFORD TRACY MEDICAL CENTER, TRACY, MN, p. A356
SANFORD USD MEDICAL CENTER, SIOUX FALLS, SD, p. A577
SANFORD VERMILLION MEDICAL CENTER, VERMILLION, SD, p. A577
SANFORD WEBSTER MEDICAL CENTER, WEBSTER, SD, p. A578
SANFORD WESTBROOK MEDICAL CENTER, WESTBROOK, MN, p. A357
SANFORD WHEATON MEDICAL CENTER, WHEATON, MN, p. A357
SANFORD WORTHINGTON MEDICAL CENTER, WORTHINGTON, MN, p. A358
SANPETE VALLEY HOSPITAL, MOUNT PLEASANT, UT, p. A666
SANTA BARBARA COTTAGE HOSPITAL, SANTA BARBARA, CA, p. A94
SANTA BARBARA COUNTY PSYCHIATRIC HEALTH FACILITY, SANTA BARBARA, CA, p. A94
SANTA CLARA VALLEY MEDICAL CENTER, SAN JOSE, CA, p. A92
SANTA CRUZ COUNTY PSYCHIATRIC HEALTH FACILITY, SANTA CRUZ, CA, p. A94
SANTA ROSA BEHAVIORAL HEALTHCARE HOSPITAL, SANTA ROSA, CA, p. A95
SANTA ROSA MEDICAL CENTER, MILTON, FL, p. A141
SANTA ROSA MEMORIAL HOSPITAL, SANTA ROSA, CA, p. A95
SANTA YNEZ VALLEY COTTAGE HOSPITAL, SOLVANG, CA, p. A96
SANTIAM HOSPITAL, STAYTON, OR, p. A532
SARAH BUSH LINCOLN HEALTH CENTER, MATTOON, IL, p. A201
SARAH D. CULBERTSON MEMORIAL HOSPITAL, RUSHVILLE, IL, p. A208
SARASOTA MEMORIAL HOSPITAL – SARASOTA, SARASOTA, FL, p. A150

SARASOTA MEMORIAL HOSPITAL – VENICE, NORTH VENICE, FL, p. A142
SARASOTA MEMORIAL HOSPITAL, SARASOTA, FL, p. A150
SARATOGA HOSPITAL, SARATOGA SPRINGS, NY, p. A458
SATANTA DISTRICT HOSPITAL AND LONG TERM CARE, SATANTA, KS, p. A259
SAUK PRAIRIE HEALTHCARE, PRAIRIE DU SAC, WI, p. A720
SAUNDERS MEDICAL CENTER, WAHOO, NE, p. A406
SAVOY MEDICAL CENTER, MAMOU, LA, p. A287
SBL FAYETTE COUNTY HOSPITAL AND LONG TERM CARE, VANDALIA, IL, p. A210
SCENIC MOUNTAIN MEDICAL CENTER, BIG SPRING, TX, p. A603
SCHEIE INSTITUTE OF THE HOSPITAL OF THE UNIVERSITY OF PENNSYLVANIA, PHILADELPHIA, PA, p. A550
SCHEURER HEALTH, PIGEON, MI, p. A335
SCHLEICHER COUNTY MEDICAL CENTER, ELDORADO, TX, p. A618
SCHNECK MEDICAL CENTER, SEYMOUR, IN, p. A227
SCHNEIDER REGIONAL MEDICAL CENTER, SAINT THOMAS, VI, p. A736
SCHOOLCRAFT MEMORIAL HOSPITAL, MANISTIQUE, MI, p. A333
SCHUYLER HOSPITAL, MONTOUR FALLS, NY, p. A446
SCHUYLKILL MEDICAL CENTER – EAST NORWEGIAN STREET, POTTSVILLE, PA, p. A553
SCHWAB REHABILITATION HOSPITAL, CHICAGO, IL, p. A191
SCL HEALTH – ST. VINCENT HEALTHCARE, BILLINGS, MT, p. A389
SCL HEALTH MT – ST. JAMES HEALTHCARE, BUTTE, MT, p. A390
SCL HEALTH MT – ST. VINCENT HEALTHCARE, BILLINGS, MT, p. A390
SCOTLAND COUNTY HOSPITAL, MEMPHIS, MO, p. A380
SCOTLAND HEALTH CARE SYSTEM, LAURINBURG, NC, p. A471
SCOTT COUNTY HOSPITAL, SCOTT CITY, KS, p. A259
SCOTT REGIONAL HOSPITAL, MORTON, MS, p. A367
SCOTTISH RITE CHILDREN'S CTR, ATLANTA, GA, p. A158
SCOTTISH RITE FOR CHILDREN, DALLAS, TX, p. A612
SCRIPPS GREEN HOSPITAL, LA JOLLA, CA, p. A68
SCRIPPS MEMORIAL HOSPITAL, CHULA VISTA, CA, p. A59
SCRIPPS MEMORIAL HOSPITAL–ENCINITAS, ENCINITAS, CA, p. A62
SCRIPPS MEMORIAL HOSPITAL–LA JOLLA, LA JOLLA, CA, p. A68
SCRIPPS MERCY HOSPITAL, SAN DIEGO, CA, p. A89
SCRIPPS MERCY HOSPITAL CHULA VISTA, CHULA VISTA, CA, p. A59
SCRIPPS OCEANVIEW CONV HOSP, ENCINITAS, CA, p. A62
SCRIPPS TORREY PINES CONV HOSP, LA JOLLA, CA, p. A68
SEA PINES REHABILITATION HOSPITAL, AN AFFILIATE OF ENCOMPASS HEALTH, MELBOURNE, FL, p. A139
SEA VIEW HOSPITAL REHABILITATION CENTER AND HOME, NEW YORK, NY, p. A452
SEARHC MT. EDGECUMBE HOSPITAL, SITKA, AK, p. A29
SEASIDE HEALTH SYSTEM – BATON ROUGE, BATON ROUGE, LA, p. A278
SEATTLE CHILDREN'S HOSPITAL, SEATTLE, WA, p. A694
SEATTLE, WA PUGET SOUND HCS, SEATTLE, WA, p. A694
SEBASTIAN RIVER MEDICAL CENTER, SEBASTIAN, FL, p. A150
SEDAN CITY HOSPITAL, SEDAN, KS, p. A259
SEDGWICK COUNTY HEALTH CENTER, JULESBURG, CO, p. A110
SEILING MUNICIPAL HOSPITAL, SEILING, OK, p. A520
SELBY GENERAL HOSPITAL, MARIETTA, OH, p. A499
SELECT REHABILITATION HOSPITAL OF DENTON, DENTON, TX, p. A614
SELECT SPECIALTY HOSP – YORK, YORK, PA, p. A559
SELECT SPECIALTY HOSPITAL – ANN ARBOR, YPSILANTI, MI, p. A341
SELECT SPECIALTY HOSPITAL – ATLANTIC CITY, ATLANTIC CITY, NJ, p. A418
SELECT SPECIALTY HOSPITAL – BATTLE CREEK, BATTLE CREEK, MI, p. A322
SELECT SPECIALTY HOSPITAL – BELHAVEN, JACKSON, MS, p. A364
SELECT SPECIALTY HOSPITAL – BOARDMAN, BOARDMAN, OH, p. A486
SELECT SPECIALTY HOSPITAL – CLEVELAND FAIRHILL, CLEVELAND, OH, p. A491
SELECT SPECIALTY HOSPITAL – COREWELL HEALTH GRAND RAPIDS, GRAND RAPIDS, MI, p. A328
SELECT SPECIALTY HOSPITAL – DALLAS DOWNTOWN, DESOTO, TX, p. A614
SELECT SPECIALTY HOSPITAL – DOWNRIVER, WYANDOTTE, MI, p. A341
SELECT SPECIALTY HOSPITAL – FLINT, FLINT, MI, p. A327

SELECT SPECIALTY HOSPITAL – LAUREL HIGHLANDS, LATROBE, PA, p. A544
SELECT SPECIALTY HOSPITAL – MACOMB COUNTY, MOUNT CLEMENS, MI, p. A334
SELECT SPECIALTY HOSPITAL – MORGANTOWN, MORGANTOWN, WV, p. A703
SELECT SPECIALTY HOSPITAL – RICHMOND, RICHMOND, VA, p. A682
SELECT SPECIALTY HOSPITAL – SAGINAW, SAGINAW, MI, p. A337
SELECT SPECIALTY HOSPITAL – SAN DIEGO, SAN DIEGO, CA, p. A89
SELECT SPECIALTY HOSPITAL – TUCSON, TUCSON, AZ, p. A41
SELECT SPECIALTY HOSPITAL – WEST TENNESSEE, JACKSON, TN, p. A584
SELECT SPECIALTY HOSPITAL – WILLINGBORO, WILLINGBORO, NJ, p. A430
SELECT SPECIALTY HOSPITAL DAYTONA BEACH, DAYTONA BEACH, FL, p. A130
SELECT SPECIALTY HOSPITAL HAMPTON ROADS, NEWPORT NEWS, VA, p. A680
SELECT SPECIALTY HOSPITAL MIDTOWN ATLANTA, ATLANTA, GA, p. A158
SELECT SPECIALTY HOSPITAL NASHVILLE, NASHVILLE, TN, p. A590
SELECT SPECIALTY HOSPITAL OF SOUTHEAST OHIO, NEWARK, OH, p. A501
SELECT SPECIALTY HOSPITAL–AKRON, AKRON, OH, p. A484
SELECT SPECIALTY HOSPITAL–AUGUSTA, AUGUSTA, GA, p. A158
SELECT SPECIALTY HOSPITAL–BATTLE CREEK, BATTLE CREEK, MI, p. A322
SELECT SPECIALTY HOSPITAL–BIRMINGHAM, BIRMINGHAM, AL, p. A17
SELECT SPECIALTY HOSPITAL–CAMP HILL, CAMP HILL, PA, p. A536
SELECT SPECIALTY HOSPITAL–CANTON, CANTON, OH, p. A488
SELECT SPECIALTY HOSPITAL–CENTRAL KENTUCKY, DANVILLE, KY, p. A265
SELECT SPECIALTY HOSPITAL–CHARLESTON, CHARLESTON, WV, p. A700
SELECT SPECIALTY HOSPITAL–CINCINNATI, CINCINNATI, OH, p. A489
SELECT SPECIALTY HOSPITAL–COLUMBUS, COLUMBUS, OH, p. A492
SELECT SPECIALTY HOSPITAL–DALLAS, PLANO, TX, p. A645
SELECT SPECIALTY HOSPITAL–DES MOINES, DES MOINES, IA, p. A235
SELECT SPECIALTY HOSPITAL–DOWNRIVER, WYANDOTTE, MI, p. A341
SELECT SPECIALTY HOSPITAL–DURHAM, DURHAM, NC, p. A467
SELECT SPECIALTY HOSPITAL–ERIE, ERIE, PA, p. A540
SELECT SPECIALTY HOSPITAL–EVANSVILLE, EVANSVILLE, IN, p. A216
SELECT SPECIALTY HOSPITAL–FLINT, FLINT, MI, p. A327
SELECT SPECIALTY HOSPITAL–FORT MYERS, FORT MYERS, FL, p. A132
SELECT SPECIALTY HOSPITAL–FORT SMITH, FORT SMITH, AR, p. A47
SELECT SPECIALTY HOSPITAL–GAINESVILLE, GAINESVILLE, FL, p. A132
SELECT SPECIALTY HOSPITAL–GREENSBORO, GREENSBORO, NC, p. A469
SELECT SPECIALTY HOSPITAL–GULFPORT, GULFPORT, MS, p. A363
SELECT SPECIALTY HOSPITAL–HARRISBURG, HARRISBURG, PA, p. A541
SELECT SPECIALTY HOSPITAL–JACKSON, JACKSON, MS, p. A364
SELECT SPECIALTY HOSPITAL–JOHNSTOWN, JOHNSTOWN, PA, p. A543
SELECT SPECIALTY HOSPITAL–KANSAS CITY, KANSAS CITY, KS, p. A252
SELECT SPECIALTY HOSPITAL–MACOMB COUNTY, MOUNT CLEMENS, MI, p. A334
SELECT SPECIALTY HOSPITAL–MADISON, MADISON, WI, p. A714
SELECT SPECIALTY HOSPITAL–MCKEESPORT, MCKEESPORT, PA, p. A545
SELECT SPECIALTY HOSPITAL–MEMPHIS, MEMPHIS, TN, p. A589
SELECT SPECIALTY HOSPITAL–MIAMI, MIAMI, FL, p. A140
SELECT SPECIALTY HOSPITAL–MIAMI LAKES, MIAMI LAKES, FL, p. A141
SELECT SPECIALTY HOSPITAL–MILWAUKEE, MILWAUKEE, WI, p. A717

Index of Hospitals / Select Specialty Hospital–Milwaukee

SELECT SPECIALTY HOSPITAL–MILWAUKEE, ST. LUKE'S CAMPUS, MILWAUKEE, WI, p. A717
SELECT SPECIALTY HOSPITAL–NORTH KNOXVILLE, POWELL, TN, p. A592
SELECT SPECIALTY HOSPITAL–NORTHEAST NEW JERSEY, ROCHELLE PARK, NJ, p. A428
SELECT SPECIALTY HOSPITAL–NORTHERN KENTUCKY, FORT THOMAS, KY, p. A265
SELECT SPECIALTY HOSPITAL–OKLAHOMA CITY, OKLAHOMA CITY, OK, p. A518
SELECT SPECIALTY HOSPITAL–OMAHA, OMAHA, NE, p. A404
SELECT SPECIALTY HOSPITAL–ORLANDO, ORLANDO, FL, p. A144
SELECT SPECIALTY HOSPITAL–ORLANDO NORTH, ORLANDO, FL, p. A144
SELECT SPECIALTY HOSPITAL–PALM BEACH, LAKE WORTH, FL, p. A136
SELECT SPECIALTY HOSPITAL–PANAMA CITY, PANAMA CITY, FL, p. A146
SELECT SPECIALTY HOSPITAL–PENSACOLA, PENSACOLA, FL, p. A147
SELECT SPECIALTY HOSPITAL–PHOENIX, PHOENIX, AZ, p. A36
SELECT SPECIALTY HOSPITAL–PHOENIX DOWNTOWN, PHOENIX, AZ, p. A36
SELECT SPECIALTY HOSPITAL–PITTSBURGH/UPMC, PITTSBURGH, PA, p. A551
SELECT SPECIALTY HOSPITAL–QUAD CITIES, DAVENPORT, IA, p. A234
SELECT SPECIALTY HOSPITAL–SAGINAW, SAGINAW, MI, p. A337
SELECT SPECIALTY HOSPITAL–SAVANNAH, SAVANNAH, GA, p. A171
SELECT SPECIALTY HOSPITAL–SIOUX FALLS, SIOUX FALLS, SD, p. A577
SELECT SPECIALTY HOSPITAL–SPRINGFIELD, SPRINGFIELD, MO, p. A387
SELECT SPECIALTY HOSPITAL–ST. LOUIS, SAINT CHARLES, MO, p. A383
SELECT SPECIALTY HOSPITAL–TALLAHASSEE, TALLAHASSEE, FL, p. A151
SELECT SPECIALTY HOSPITAL–THE VILLAGES, OXFORD, FL, p. A145
SELECT SPECIALTY HOSPITAL–TRI CITIES, BRISTOL, TN, p. A579
SELECT SPECIALTY HOSPITAL–TULSA MIDTOWN, TULSA, OK, p. A523
SELECT SPECIALTY HOSPITAL–WICHITA, WICHITA, KS, p. A262
SELECT SPECIALTY HOSPITAL–WILMINGTON, WILMINGTON, DE, p. A122
SELECT SPECIALTY HOSPITAL–YORK, YORK, PA, p. A559
SELECT SPECIALTY HOSPITAL–YOUNGSTOWN, YOUNGSTOWN, OH, p. A508
SELF REGIONAL HEALTHCARE, GREENWOOD, SC, p. A567
SELMA COMMUNITY HOSPITAL, SELMA, CA, p. A95
SENECA HEALTHCARE DISTRICT, CHESTER, CA, p. A59
SENTARA ALBEMARLE MEDICAL CENTER, ELIZABETH CITY, NC, p. A468
SENTARA CAREPLEX HOSPITAL, HAMPTON, VA, p. A677
SENTARA HALIFAX REGIONAL HOSPITAL, SOUTH BOSTON, VA, p. A684
SENTARA LEIGH HOSPITAL, NORFOLK, VA, p. A680
SENTARA MARTHA JEFFERSON HOSPITAL, CHARLOTTESVILLE, VA, p. A674
SENTARA NORFOLK GENERAL HOSPITAL, NORFOLK, VA, p. A680
SENTARA NORTHERN VIRGINIA MEDICAL CENTER, WOODBRIDGE, VA, p. A685
SENTARA OBICI HOSPITAL, SUFFOLK, VA, p. A684
SENTARA PRINCESS ANNE HOSPITAL, VIRGINIA BEACH, VA, p. A684
SENTARA RMH MEDICAL CENTER, HARRISONBURG, VA, p. A677
SENTARA VIRGINIA BEACH GENERAL HOSPITAL, VIRGINIA BEACH, VA, p. A685
SENTARA WILLIAMSBURG REGIONAL MEDICAL CENTER, WILLIAMSBURG, VA, p. A685
SEQUOIA HOSPITAL, REDWOOD CITY, CA, p. A85
SERENITY SPRINGS SPECIALTY HOSPITAL, RUSTON, LA, p. A291
SETON HEALTH ST. MARY'S HOSPITAL, TROY, NY, p. A460
SETON HLTH SYST–ST MARY'S, TROY, NY, p. A460
SETON MEDICAL CENTER, DALY CITY, CA, p. A61
SETON MEDICAL CENTER COASTSIDE, MOSS BEACH, CA, p. A78
SETON MEDICAL CENTER HARKER HEIGHTS, HARKER HEIGHTS, TX, p. A623
SEVEN HILLS HOSPITAL, HENDERSON, NV, p. A409
SEVIER COUNTY MEDICAL CENTER, DE QUEEN, AR, p. A45

SEVIER VALLEY HOSPITAL, RICHFIELD, UT, p. A668
SEWICKLEY VALLEY HOSPITAL, (A DIVISION OF VALLEY MEDICAL FACILITIES), SEWICKLEY, PA, p. A555
SEYMOUR HOSPITAL, SEYMOUR, TX, p. A652
SHADYSIDE HOSPITAL, PITTSBURGH, PA, p. A551
SHAMROCK GENERAL HOSPITAL, SHAMROCK, TX, p. A652
SHANDS AT VISTA, GAINESVILLE, FL, p. A132
SHANDS CHILDRENS HOSPITAL, GAINESVILLE, FL, p. A132
SHANNON MEDICAL CENTER, SAN ANGELO, TX, p. A648
SHANNON REHABILITATION HOSPITAL, AN AFFILIATE OF ENCOMPASS HEALTH, SAN ANGELO, TX, p. A648
SHARE MEDICAL CENTER, ALVA, OK, p. A509
SHARKEY–ISSAQUENA COMMUNITY HOSPITAL, ROLLING FORK, MS, p. A368
SHARON HOSPITAL, SHARON, CT, p. A118
SHARON REGIONAL MEDICAL CENTER, SHARON, PA, p. A555
SHARP CHULA VISTA MEDICAL CENTER, CHULA VISTA, CA, p. A59
SHARP CORONADO HOSPITAL, CORONADO, CA, p. A60
SHARP CORONADO HOSPITAL AND HEALTHCARE CENTER, CORONADO, CA, p. A60
SHARP GROSSMONT HOSPITAL, LA MESA, CA, p. A68
SHARP HEALTHCARE MURRIETA, MURRIETA, CA, p. A79
SHARP MARY BIRCH HOSPITAL FOR WOMEN AND NEWBORNS, SAN DIEGO, CA, p. A89
SHARP MEMORIAL HOSPITAL, SAN DIEGO, CA, p. A89
SHARP MESA VISTA HOSPITAL, SAN DIEGO, CA, p. A90
SHASTA REGIONAL MEDICAL CENTER, REDDING, CA, p. A85
SHELBY BAPTIST MEDICAL CENTER, ALABASTER, AL, p. A15
SHELTERING ARMS INSTITUTE, MIDLOTHIAN, VA, p. A679
SHELTERING ARMS INSTITUTE, RICHMOND, VA, p. A682
SHENANDOAH MEDICAL CENTER, SHENANDOAH, IA, p. A243
SHENANGO VALLEY CAMPUS, FARRELL, PA, p. A540
SHENANGO VALLEY MEDICAL CENTER, FARRELL, PA, p. A540
SHEPHERD CENTER, ATLANTA, GA, p. A158
SHEPPARD PRATT, BALTIMORE, MD, p. A302
SHERIDAN COMMUNITY HOSPITAL, SHERIDAN, MI, p. A338
SHERIDAN COUNTY HEALTH COMPLEX, HOXIE, KS, p. A251
SHERIDAN MEMORIAL HOSPITAL, PLENTYWOOD, MT, p. A394
SHERIDAN MEMORIAL HOSPITAL, SHERIDAN, WY, p. A728
SHERIDAN VA MEDICAL CENTER, SHERIDAN, WY, p. A728
SHERMAN OAKS HOSPITAL, LOS ANGELES, CA, p. A75
SHIRLEY RYAN ABILITYLAB, CHICAGO, IL, p. A191
SHOALS HOSPITAL, MUSCLE SHOALS, AL, p. A23
SHODAIR CHILDREN'S HOSPITAL, HELENA, MT, p. A393
SHORE MEDICAL CENTER, SOMERS POINT, NJ, p. A428
SHOREPOINT HEALTH PORT CHARLOTTE, PORT CHARLOTTE, FL, p. A147
SHOREPOINT HEALTH PUNTA GORDA, PUNTA GORDA, FL, p. A148
SHOSHONE MEDICAL CENTER, KELLOGG, ID, p. A181
SHREVEPORT –OVERTON BROOKS VA MEDICAL CENTER, SHREVEPORT, LA, p. A293
SHREVEPORT REHABILITATION HOSPITAL, SHREVEPORT, LA, p. A293
SHRINERS CHILDREN'S – NORTHERN CALIFORNIA, SACRAMENTO, CA, p. A87
SHRINERS CHILDREN'S OHIO, DAYTON, OH, p. A494
SHRINERS CHILDREN'S PHILADELPHIA, PHILADELPHIA, PA, p. A550
SHRINERS HOSPITALS FOR CHILDREN, GALVESTON, TX, p. A621
SHRINERS HOSPITALS FOR CHILDREN–BOSTON, BOSTON, MA, p. A311
SHRINERS HOSPITALS FOR CHILDREN–CHICAGO, CHICAGO, IL, p. A191
SHRINERS HOSPITALS FOR CHILDREN–GREENVILLE, GREENVILLE, SC, p. A567
SHRINERS HOSPITALS FOR CHILDREN–HONOLULU, HONOLULU, HI, p. A176
SHRINERS HOSPITALS FOR CHILDREN–NORTHERN CALIFORNIA, SACRAMENTO, CA, p. A87
SHRINERS HOSPITALS FOR CHILDREN–PORTLAND, PORTLAND, OR, p. A531
SHRINERS HOSPITALS FOR CHILDREN–SALT LAKE CITY, SALT LAKE CITY, UT, p. A669
SHRINERS HOSPITALS FOR CHILDREN–SPOKANE, SPOKANE, WA, p. A696
SHRINERS HOSPITALS FOR CHILDREN–SPRINGFIELD, SPRINGFIELD, MA, p. A318
SHRINERS HOSPITALS FOR CHILDREN–ST. LOUIS, SAINT LOUIS, MO, p. A385
SIBLEY MEMORIAL HOSPITAL, WASHINGTON, DC, p. A124
SIDNEY HEALTH CENTER, SIDNEY, MT, p. A396
SIDNEY REGIONAL MEDICAL CENTER, SIDNEY, NE, p. A406

SIERRA NEVADA MEMORIAL HOSPITAL, GRASS VALLEY, CA, p. A66
SIERRA TUCSON, TUCSON, AZ, p. A41
SIERRA VIEW MEDICAL CENTER, PORTERVILLE, CA, p. A84
SIERRA VISTA HOSPITAL, SACRAMENTO, CA, p. A87
SIERRA VISTA HOSPITAL, TRUTH OR CONSEQUENCES, NM, p. A437
SIERRA VISTA REGIONAL MEDICAL CENTER, SAN LUIS OBISPO, CA, p. A93
SIGNATURE HEALTHCARE BROCKTON HOSPITAL, BROCKTON, MA, p. A311
SIGNATURE PSYCHIATRIC HOSPITAL, KANSAS CITY, MO, p. A377
SILOAM SPRINGS REGIONAL HOSPITAL, SILOAM SPRINGS, AR, p. A53
SILVER CROSS HOSPITAL, NEW LENOX, IL, p. A203
SILVER HILL HOSPITAL, NEW CANAAN, CT, p. A117
SILVER LAKE HOSPITAL LTACH, NEWARK, NJ, p. A425
SILVER LAKE MEDICAL CENTER–INGLESIDE HOSPITAL, ROSEMEAD, CA, p. A86
SILVER OAKS BEHAVIORAL HOSPITAL, NEW LENOX, IL, p. A203
SIMPSON GENERAL HOSPITAL, MENDENHALL, MS, p. A366
SINAI HOSPITAL OF BALTIMORE, BALTIMORE, MD, p. A301
SINGING RIVER GULFPORT, GULFPORT, MS, p. A363
SINGING RIVER HEALTH SYSTEM, PASCAGOULA, MS, p. A367
SINGING RIVER HOSPITAL, PASCAGOULA, MS, p. A367
SINGING RIVER OCEAN SPRINGS, OCEAN SPRINGS, MS, p. A367
SIOUX CENTER HEALTH, SIOUX CENTER, IA, p. A243
SIOUX FALLS SPECIALTY HOSPITAL, SIOUX FALLS, SD, p. A577
SIOUX FALLS VAMC, SIOUX FALLS, SD, p. A577
SISKIN HOSPITAL FOR PHYSICAL REHABILITATION, CHATTANOOGA, TN, p. A581
SISTER KENNY INSTITUTE, MINNEAPOLIS, MN, p. A351
SISTER KENNY REHABILITATION INSTITUTE, MINNEAPOLIS, MN, p. A351
SISTERS OF CHARITY HOSPITAL OF BUFFALO, BUFFALO, NY, p. A440
SISTERSVILLE GENERAL HOSPITAL, SISTERSVILLE, WV, p. A704
SKAGIT VALLEY HOSPITAL, MOUNT VERNON, WA, p. A692
SKY LAKES MEDICAL CENTER, KLAMATH FALLS, OR, p. A528
SKY RIDGE MEDICAL CENTER, LONE TREE, CO, p. A111
SKYLINE HEALTH, WHITE SALMON, WA, p. A698
SKYLINE HOSPITAL, WHITE SALMON, WA, p. A698
SKYLINE MADISON CAMPUS, MADISON, TN, p. A587
SLEEPY EYE MEDICAL CENTER, SLEEPY EYE, MN, p. A355
SLIDELL MEMORIAL HOSPITAL, SLIDELL, LA, p. A293
SLIDELL MEMORIAL HOSPITAL EAST, SLIDELL, LA, p. A293
SMC REGIONAL MEDICAL CENTER, OSCEOLA, AR, p. A52
SMITH COUNTY MEMORIAL HOSPITAL, SMITH CENTER, KS, p. A260
SMITH HOSPITAL, VALDOSTA, GA, p. A173
SMOKEY POINT BEHAVIORAL HOSPITAL, MARYSVILLE, WA, p. A691
SMP HEALTH – ST. ALOISIUS, HARVEY, ND, p. A481
SMP HEALTH – ST. ANDREW'S, BOTTINEAU, ND, p. A479
SMP HEALTH – ST. KATERI, ROLLA, ND, p. A483
SMYTH COUNTY COMMUNITY HOSPITAL, MARION, VA, p. A679
SNOQUALMIE VALLEY HEALTH, SNOQUALMIE, WA, p. A695
SNOQUALMIE VALLEY HOSPITAL DISTRICT, SNOQUALMIE, WA, p. A695
SOCORRO GENERAL HOSPITAL, SOCORRO, NM, p. A437
SOIN MEDICAL CENTER, BEAVERCREEK, OH, p. A486
SOJOURN AT SENECA SENIOR BEHAVIORAL HEALTH, TIFFIN, OH, p. A504
SOLARA HOSPITAL HARLINGEN–BROWNSVILLE CAMPUS, BROWNSVILLE, TX, p. A604
SOLARA SPECIALTY HOSPITALS HARLINGEN–BROWNSVILLE, BROWNSVILLE, TX, p. A604
SOLARA SPECIALTY HOSPITALS MCALLEN, MCALLEN, TX, p. A638
SOLDIERS AND SAILORS MEMORIAL HOSPITAL, PENN YAN, NY, p. A456
SOMERVILLE HOSPITAL, SOMERVILLE, MA, p. A318
SONOMA DEVELOPMENTAL CENTER, ELDRIDGE, CA, p. A62
SONOMA SPECIALTY HOSPITAL, SEBASTOPOL, CA, p. A95
SONOMA VALLEY HOSPITAL, SONOMA, CA, p. A96
SONOMA WEST MEDICAL CENTER, SEBASTOPOL, CA, p. A95
SONORA BEHAVIORAL HEALTH HOSPITAL, TUCSON, AZ, p. A41
SOUTH ARKANSAS REGIONAL HOSPITAL, EL DORADO, AR, p. A45

Index of Hospitals / SSM Health St. Mary's Hospital – Jefferson City

SOUTH BALDWIN REGIONAL MEDICAL CENTER, FOLEY, AL, p. A19
SOUTH BAY HOSPITAL, SUN CITY CENTER, FL, p. A151
SOUTH BEACH PSYCHIATRIC CENTER, NEW YORK, NY, p. A452
SOUTH BIG HORN COUNTY HOSPITAL, BASIN, WY, p. A726
SOUTH CAROLINA DEPARTMENT OF CORRECTIONS HOSPITAL, COLUMBIA, SC, p. A565
SOUTH CENTRAL HEALTH, WISHEK, ND, p. A483
SOUTH CENTRAL KANSAS MEDICAL CENTER, ARKANSAS CITY, KS, p. A246
SOUTH CENTRAL REGIONAL MEDICAL CENTER, LAUREL, MS, p. A365
SOUTH COAST GLOBAL MEDICAL CENTER, SANTA ANA, CA, p. A93
SOUTH COAST MEDICAL CENTER, LAGUNA BEACH, CA, p. A69
SOUTH COUNTY HOSPITAL, WAKEFIELD, RI, p. A561
SOUTH DAVIS COMMUNITY HOSPITAL, BOUNTIFUL, UT, p. A664
SOUTH FLORIDA BAPTIST HOSPITAL, PLANT CITY, FL, p. A147
SOUTH FLORIDA STATE HOSPITAL, HOLLYWOOD, FL, p. A133
SOUTH GEORGIA MEDICAL CENTER, VALDOSTA, GA, p. A173
SOUTH GEORGIA MEDICAL CENTER BERRIEN CAMPUS, NASHVILLE, GA, p. A169
SOUTH GEORGIA MEDICAL CENTER LANIER CAMPUS, LAKELAND, GA, p. A166
SOUTH LINCOLN MEDICAL CENTER, KEMMERER, WY, p. A727
SOUTH LYON MEDICAL CENTER, YERINGTON, NV, p. A413
SOUTH MISSISSIPPI COUNTY REGIONAL MEDICAL CENTER, OSCEOLA, AR, p. A52
SOUTH MISSISSIPPI STATE HOSPITAL, PURVIS, MS, p. A368
SOUTH OAKS HOSPITAL, AMITYVILLE, NY, p. A438
SOUTH PENINSULA HOSPITAL, HOMER, AK, p. A28
SOUTH PLAINS REHABILITATION HOSPITAL, AN AFFILIATE OF UMC AND ENCOMPASS HEALTH, LUBBOCK, TX, p. A636
SOUTH POINTE HOSPITAL, WARRENSVILLE HEIGHTS, OH, p. A506
SOUTH SHORE HOSPITAL, CHICAGO, IL, p. A191
SOUTH SHORE HOSPITAL, SOUTH WEYMOUTH, MA, p. A318
SOUTH SHORE UNIVERSITY HOSPITAL, BAY SHORE, NY, p. A439
SOUTH SUNFLOWER COUNTY HOSPITAL, INDIANOLA, MS, p. A363
SOUTH TEXAS HEALTH SYSTEM, EDINBURG, TX, p. A615
SOUTH TEXAS HOSPITAL, HARLINGEN, TX, p. A623
SOUTH TEXAS REHABILITATION HOSPITAL, BROWNSVILLE, TX, p. A605
SOUTH TEXAS SPINE AND SURGICAL HOSPITAL, SAN ANTONIO, TX, p. A651
SOUTH TEXAS SURGICAL HOSPITAL, CORPUS CHRISTI, TX, p. A609
SOUTH TEXAS VETERANS HCS, SAN ANTONIO, TX, p. A651
SOUTH TEXAS VETERANS HEALTHCARE SYSTEM AUDIE L MURPHY, SAN ANTONIO, TX, p. A651
SOUTHCOAST BEHAVIORAL HEALTH, DARTMOUTH, MA, p. A313
SOUTHCOAST HOSPITALS GROUP, FALL RIVER, MA, p. A313
SOUTHEAST ALABAMA MEDICAL CENTER, DOTHAN, AL, p. A18
SOUTHEAST BAPTIST HOSPITAL, SAN ANTONIO, TX, p. A651
SOUTHEAST COLORADO HOSPITAL DISTRICT, SPRINGFIELD, CO, p. A113
SOUTHEAST GEORGIA HEALTH SYSTEM BRUNSWICK CAMPUS, BRUNSWICK, GA, p. A159
SOUTHEAST GEORGIA HEALTH SYSTEM CAMDEN CAMPUS, SAINT MARYS, GA, p. A170
SOUTHEAST IOWA REGIONAL MEDICAL CENTER, WEST BURLINGTON CAMPUS, WEST BURLINGTON, IA, p. A245
SOUTHEAST MISSOURI MENTAL HEALTH CENTER, FARMINGTON, MO, p. A375
SOUTHEAST REGIONAL MEDICAL CENTER, KENTWOOD, LA, p. A284
SOUTHEAST REHABILITATION HOSPITAL, LAKE VILLAGE, AR, p. A49
SOUTHEASTERN REGIONAL MEDICAL CENTER, NEWNAN, GA, p. A169
SOUTHEASTERN REGIONAL REHABILITATION CENTER, FAYETTEVILLE, NC, p. A468
SOUTHERN ARIZONA VETERANS AFFAIRS HEALTH CARE SYSTEM, TUCSON, AZ, p. A41
SOUTHERN CALIFORNIA HOSPITAL AT CULVER CITY, CULVER CITY, CA, p. A61
SOUTHERN CALIFORNIA HOSPITAL AT HOLLYWOOD, LOS ANGELES, CA, p. A75
SOUTHERN CALIFORNIA HOSPITAL AT VAN NUYS, LOS ANGELES, CA, p. A75
SOUTHERN COOS HOSPITAL AND HEALTH CENTER, BANDON, OR, p. A525
SOUTHERN HILLS HOSPITAL AND MEDICAL CENTER, LAS VEGAS, NV, p. A410
SOUTHERN INDIANA REHABILITATION HOSPITAL, NEW ALBANY, IN, p. A225
SOUTHERN INYO HEALTHCARE DISTRICT, LONE PINE, CA, p. A70
SOUTHERN KENTUCKY REHABILITATION HOSPITAL, BOWLING GREEN, KY, p. A263
SOUTHERN MAINE HEALTH CARE – BIDDEFORD MEDICAL CENTER, BIDDEFORD, ME, p. A296
SOUTHERN NEVADA ADULT MENTAL HEALTH SERVICES, LAS VEGAS, NV, p. A410
SOUTHERN NEVADA HCS, NORTH LAS VEGAS, NV, p. A412
SOUTHERN NEW HAMPSHIRE MEDICAL CENTER, NASHUA, NH, p. A416
SOUTHERN OHIO MEDICAL CENTER, PORTSMOUTH, OH, p. A502
SOUTHERN OREGON–WHITE CITY VETERANS AFFAIRS REHABILITATION CENTER AND CLINICS, WHITE CITY, OR, p. A533
SOUTHERN REGIONAL MEDICAL CENTER, RIVERDALE, GA, p. A170
SOUTHERN SURGICAL HOSPITAL, SLIDELL, LA, p. A293
SOUTHERN TENNESSEE REGIONAL HEALTH SYSTEM–LAWRENCEBURG, LAWRENCEBURG, TN, p. A586
SOUTHERN TENNESSEE REGIONAL HEALTH SYSTEM–PULASKI, PULASKI, TN, p. A592
SOUTHERN TENNESSEE REGIONAL HEALTH SYSTEM–SEWANEE, SEWANEE, TN, p. A593
SOUTHERN TENNESSEE REGIONAL HEALTH SYSTEM–WINCHESTER, WINCHESTER, TN, p. A594
SOUTHERN VIRGINIA MENTAL HEALTH INSTITUTE, DANVILLE, VA, p. A675
SOUTHERN WINDS HOSPITAL, HIALEAH, FL, p. A133
SOUTHLAKE CAMPUS, MERRILLVILLE, IN, p. A223
SOUTHSIDE HOSPITAL, BAY SHORE, NY, p. A439
SOUTHVIEW HOSPITAL AND FAMILY HEALTH CENTER, DAYTON, OH, p. A494
SOUTHWELL MEDICAL, ADEL, GA, p. A156
SOUTHWEST CONNECTICUT MENTAL HEALTH SYSTEM, BRIDGEPORT, CT, p. A115
SOUTHWEST GENERAL HEALTH CENTER, MIDDLEBURG HEIGHTS, OH, p. A500
SOUTHWEST HEALTH, PLATTEVILLE, WI, p. A719
SOUTHWEST HEALTH CENTER NURSING HOME, CUBA CITY, WI, p. A709
SOUTHWEST HEALTH SYSTEM, CORTEZ, CO, p. A105
SOUTHWEST HEALTHCARE SERVICES, BOWMAN, ND, p. A479
SOUTHWEST HEALTHCARE SYSTEM, MURRIETA, CA, p. A79
SOUTHWEST MEDICAL CENTER, LIBERAL, KS, p. A253
SOUTHWEST MISSISSIPPI REGIONAL MEDICAL CENTER, MCCOMB, MS, p. A366
SOUTHWESTERN MEDICAL CENTER, LAWTON, OK, p. A514
SOUTHWESTERN VERMONT MEDICAL CENTER, BENNINGTON, VT, p. A671
SOUTHWESTERN VIRGINIA MENTAL HEALTH INSTITUTE, MARION, VA, p. A679
SOUTHWOOD PSYCHIATRIC HOSPITAL, PITTSBURGH, PA, p. A551
SOVAH HEALTH–DANVILLE, DANVILLE, VA, p. A675
SOVAH HEALTH–MARTINSVILLE, MARTINSVILLE, VA, p. A679
SPALDING REHABILITATION HOSPITAL, AURORA, CO, p. A103
SPANISH PEAKS REGIONAL HEALTH CENTER AND VETERANS COMMUNITY LIVING CENTER, WALSENBURG, CO, p. A114
SPARROW CLINTON HOSPITAL, SAINT JOHNS, MI, p. A337
SPARROW REGIONAL CHILDREN'S CENTER, LANSING, MI, p. A331
SPARROW SPECIALTY HOSPITAL, LANSING, MI, p. A331
SPARTA COMMUNITY HOSPITAL, SPARTA, IL, p. A208
SPARTANBURG HOSPITAL FOR RESTORATIVE CARE, SPARTANBURG, SC, p. A570
SPARTANBURG MEDICAL CENTER – CHURCH STREET CAMPUS, SPARTANBURG, SC, p. A570
SPARTANBURG REHABILITATION INSTITUTE, SPARTANBURG, SC, p. A570
SPAULDING HOSPITAL FOR CONTINUING MEDICAL CARE CAMBRIDGE, CAMBRIDGE, MA, p. A312
SPAULDING REHABILITATION HOSPITAL, CHARLESTOWN, MA, p. A312
SPAULDING REHABILITATION HOSPITAL CAPE COD, EAST SANDWICH, MA, p. A313
SPEARE MEMORIAL HOSPITAL, PLYMOUTH, NH, p. A417
SPEARFISH SURGERY CENTER, SPEARFISH, SD, p. A577
SPECIALISTS HOSPITAL SHREVEPORT, SHREVEPORT, LA, p. A293
SPECIALTY HOSP OF SANTA ANA, SANTA ANA, CA, p. A93
SPECIALTY HOSPITAL, MONROE, LA, p. A289
SPECIALTY HOSPITAL, WEST COVINA, CA, p. A101
SPECIALTY HOSPITAL OF CENTRAL JERSEY, LAKEWOOD, NJ, p. A422
SPECIALTY HOSPITAL OF HOUSTON, HOUSTON, TX, p. A627
SPECIALTY HOSPITAL OF LORAIN, AMHERST, OH, p. A484
SPECIALTY REHABILITATION HOSPITAL, LULING, TX, p. A287
SPECIALTY REHABILITATION HOSPITAL OF COUSHATTA, COUSHATTA, LA, p. A280
SPECTRUM HEALTH – BLODGETT CAMPUS, GRAND RAPIDS, MI, p. A328
SPECTRUM HEALTH – BUTTERWORTH, GRAND RAPIDS, MI, p. A328
SPECTRUM HEALTH BIG RAPIDS HOSPITAL, BIG RAPIDS, MI, p. A322
SPECTRUM HEALTH GERBER MEMORIAL, FREMONT, MI, p. A327
SPECTRUM HEALTH LAKELAND WATERVLIET HOSPITAL, WATERVLIET, MI, p. A340
SPECTRUM HEALTH LUDINGTON HOSPITAL, LUDINGTON, MI, p. A332
SPECTRUM HEALTH PENNOCK, HASTINGS, MI, p. A329
SPECTRUM HEALTH REED CITY HOSPITAL, REED CITY, MI, p. A336
SPECTRUM HEALTH UNITED HOSPITAL, GREENVILLE, MI, p. A329
SPECTRUM HEALTH ZEELAND COMMUNITY HOSPITAL, ZEELAND, MI, p. A341
SPENCER HOSPITAL, SPENCER, IA, p. A244
SPOKANE VAMC, SPOKANE, WA, p. A696
SPOONER HEALTH, SPOONER, WI, p. A721
SPOTSYLVANIA REGIONAL MEDICAL CENTER, FREDERICKSBURG, VA, p. A676
SPRING GROVE HOSPITAL CENTER, BALTIMORE, MD, p. A302
SPRING HOSPITAL, SPRING, TX, p. A654
SPRING MOUNTAIN SAHARA, LAS VEGAS, NV, p. A410
SPRING MOUNTAIN TREATMENT CENTER, LAS VEGAS, NV, p. A410
SPRING VALLEY HOSPITAL MEDICAL CENTER, LAS VEGAS, NV, p. A411
SPRING VIEW HOSPITAL, LEBANON, KY, p. A268
SPRINGBROOK BEHAVIORAL HEALTH, TRAVELERS REST, SC, p. A571
SPRINGBROOK HOSPITAL, BROOKSVILLE, FL, p. A127
SPRINGFIELD HOSPITAL, SPRINGFIELD, PA, p. A555
SPRINGFIELD HOSPITAL, SPRINGFIELD, VT, p. A672
SPRINGFIELD HOSPITAL CENTER, SYKESVILLE, MD, p. A307
SPRINGFIELD MEMORIAL HOSPITAL, SPRINGFIELD, IL, p. A209
SPRINGFIELD REGIONAL MEDICAL CENTER, SPRINGFIELD, OH, p. A504
SPRINGHILL MEDICAL CENTER, MOBILE, AL, p. A22
SPRINGHILL MEDICAL CENTER, SPRINGHILL, LA, p. A293
SPRINGHILL MEMORIAL HOSPITAL, MOBILE, AL, p. A22
SPRINGWOODS BEHAVIORAL HEALTH HOSPITAL, FAYETTEVILLE, AR, p. A46
SSM CARDINAL GLENNON CHILDREN'S HOSPITAL, SAINT LOUIS, MO, p. A384
SSM HEALTH CARDINAL GLENNON CHILDREN'S HOSPITAL, SAINT LOUIS, MO, p. A384
SSM HEALTH DEPAUL HOSPITAL – ST. LOUIS, BRIDGETON, MO, p. A372
SSM HEALTH GOOD SAMARITAN HOSPITAL, MOUNT VERNON, IL, p. A202
SSM HEALTH MONROE CLINIC, MONROE, WI, p. A718
SSM HEALTH RIPON COMMUNITY HOSPITAL, RIPON, WI, p. A721
SSM HEALTH SAINT LOUIS UNIVERSITY HOSPITAL – SOUTH CAMPUS, SAINT LOUIS, MO, p. A384
SSM HEALTH SAINT LOUIS UNIVERSITY HOSPITAL, SAINT LOUIS, MO, p. A384
SSM HEALTH ST. AGNES HOSPITAL – FOND DU LAC, FOND DU LAC, WI, p. A711
SSM HEALTH ST. ANTHONY HOSPITAL – MIDWEST, MIDWEST CITY, OK, p. A515
SSM HEALTH ST. ANTHONY HOSPITAL – OKLAHOMA CITY, OKLAHOMA CITY, OK, p. A518
SSM HEALTH ST. ANTHONY HOSPITAL – SHAWNEE, SHAWNEE, OK, p. A520
SSM HEALTH ST. CLARE HOSPITAL – FENTON, FENTON, MO, p. A375
SSM HEALTH ST. CLARE HOSPITAL–BARABOO, BARABOO, WI, p. A707
SSM HEALTH ST. JOSEPH – ST. CHARLES, SAINT CHARLES, MO, p. A383
SSM HEALTH ST. JOSEPH – WENTZVILLE, WENTZVILLE, MO, p. A388
SSM HEALTH ST. JOSEPH HOSPITAL – LAKE SAINT LOUIS, LAKE SAINT LOUIS, MO, p. A379
SSM HEALTH ST. MARY'S HOSPITAL – JEFFERSON CITY, JEFFERSON CITY, MO, p. A376

Index of Hospitals / SSM Health St. Mary's Hospital – St. Louis

SSM HEALTH ST. MARY'S HOSPITAL – ST. LOUIS, SAINT LOUIS, MO, p. A385
SSM HEALTH ST. MARY'S HOSPITAL, MADISON, WI, p. A714
SSM HEALTH ST. MARY'S HOSPITAL CENTRALIA, CENTRALIA, IL, p. A187
SSM HEALTH ST. MARY'S HOSPITAL JANESVILLE, JANESVILLE, WI, p. A713
SSM HEALTH WAUPUN MEMORIAL HOSPITAL, WAUPUN, WI, p. A724
SSM REHABILITATION HOSPITAL, BRIDGETON, MO, p. A372
SSM SELECT REHABILITATION HOSPITAL, RICHMOND HEIGHTS, MO, p. A382
SSM ST. JOSEPH – WENTZVILLE, WENTZVILLE, MO, p. A388
ST ANTHONY CONTINUING CARE CTR, ROCK ISLAND, IL, p. A207
ST CLARE'S HOSPITAL/BOONTON, BOONTON TOWNSHIP, NJ, p. A418
ST CLARE'S HOSPITAL/DENVILLE, DENVILLE, NJ, p. A420
ST David's REHAB HOSPITAL, AUSTIN, TX, p. A600
ST ELIZABETH MED CENTER, LAFAYETTE, IN, p. A222
ST FRANCIS HEALTH CENTER, COLORADO SPRINGS, CO, p. A105
ST FRANCIS HOME, WILLIAMSVILLE, NY, p. A462
ST FRANCIS HOSPITAL CRANBERRY, CRANBERRY TOWNSHIP, PA, p. A537
ST FRANCIS HOSPITAL OF BUFFALO, BUFFALO, NY, p. A440
ST JEROME HOSPITAL, BATAVIA, NY, p. A438
ST JOHN MEDICAL CENTER, STEUBENVILLE, OH, p. A504
ST JOHN'S EPISCOPAL HOME, NEW YORK, NY, p. A452
ST JOHN'S REGIONAL HEALTH CTR, SALINA, KS, p. A259
ST JOSEPH'S MERCY HOSP–EAST, MOUNT CLEMENS, MI, p. A334
ST JOSEPH'S MERCY HOSPITAL, CLINTON TOWNSHIP, MI, p. A324
ST JOSEPH'S–TRI COUNTY HOSP, ROMEO, MI, p. A336
ST LUKE'S HOSP OF NEW BEDFORD, NEW BEDFORD, MA, p. A316
ST LUKE'S HOSPITAL – ALLENTOWN CAMPUS, ALLENTOWN, PA, p. A534
ST LUKE'S HOSPITAL, DAVENPORT, IA, p. A234
ST LUKE'S HOSPITAL, SAGINAW, MI, p. A337
ST LUKE'S LUTHERAN HOSPITAL, SAN ANTONIO, TX, p. A651
ST LUKE'S MEM HOSPITAL CENTER, UTICA, NY, p. A460
ST LUKE'S SOUTH SHORE, CUDAHY, WI, p. A709
ST MARY HOSPITAL, QUINCY, IL, p. A206
ST MARY OF THE PLAINS HOSPITAL, LUBBOCK, TX, p. A636
ST MARY'S HOSPITAL AND HOME, WINSTED, MN, p. A357
ST VINCENT CHILDREN'S HOSPITAL, INDIANAPOLIS, IN, p. A220
ST. AGNES HOSPITAL, FOND DU LAC, WI, p. A711
ST. ALBANS PRIMARY AND EXTENDED CARE CENTER, NEW YORK, NY, p. A452
ST. ALOISIUS MEDICAL CENTER, HARVEY, ND, p. A481
ST. ANDREW'S HEALTH CENTER, BOTTINEAU, ND, p. A479
ST. ANNE HOSPITAL, BURIEN, WA, p. A688
ST. ANTHONY COMMUNITY HOSPITAL, WARWICK, NY, p. A461
ST. ANTHONY HOSPITAL, GIG HARBOR, WA, p. A690
ST. ANTHONY HOSPITAL, LAKEWOOD, CO, p. A110
ST. ANTHONY NORTH HEALTH CAMPUS, WESTMINSTER, CO, p. A114
ST. ANTHONY NORTH HOSPITAL, WESTMINSTER, CO, p. A114
ST. ANTHONY REGIONAL HOSPITAL, CARROLL, IA, p. A231
ST. ANTHONY SOUTH, OKLAHOMA CITY, OK, p. A518
ST. ANTHONY'S HOSPITAL, SAINT PETERSBURG, FL, p. A149
ST. ANTHONY'S REHABILITATION HOSPITAL, LAUDERDALE LAKES, FL, p. A137
ST. BARNABAS HOSPITAL, NEW YORK, NY, p. A452
ST. BERNARD HOSPITAL AND HEALTH CARE CENTER, CHICAGO, IL, p. A191
ST. BERNARD PARISH HOSPITAL, CHALMETTE, LA, p. A279
ST. BERNARDINE MEDICAL CENTER, SAN BERNARDINO, CA, p. A88
ST. BERNARDS FIVE RIVERS, POCAHONTAS, AR, p. A52
ST. BERNARDS MEDICAL CENTER, JONESBORO, AR, p. A48
ST. CATHERINE HOSPITAL – DODGE CITY, DODGE CITY, KS, p. A248
ST. CATHERINE HOSPITAL, EAST CHICAGO, IN, p. A215
ST. CATHERINE HOSPITAL, GARDEN CITY, KS, p. A249
ST. CATHERINE OF SIENA HOSPITAL, SMITHTOWN, NY, p. A459
ST. CATHERINE OF SIENA MEDICAL CENTER, SMITHTOWN, NY, p. A459
ST. CATHERINE'S REHABILITATION HOSPITAL, NORTH MIAMI, FL, p. A142
ST. CHARLES BEND, BEND, OR, p. A525
ST. CHARLES HOSPITAL, PORT JEFFERSON, NY, p. A456

ST. CHARLES MADRAS, MADRAS, OR, p. A529
ST. CHARLES PARISH HOSPITAL, LULING, LA, p. A287
ST. CHARLES PRINEVILLE, PRINEVILLE, OR, p. A531
ST. CHARLES REDMOND, REDMOND, OR, p. A531
ST. CHARLES SURGICAL HOSPITAL, NEW ORLEANS, LA, p. A290
ST. CHRISTOPHER'S HOSPITAL FOR CHILDREN, PHILADELPHIA, PA, p. A550
ST. CLAIR HEALTH, PITTSBURGH, PA, p. A551
ST. CLAIRE REGIONAL MEDICAL CENTER, MOREHEAD, KY, p. A272
ST. CLARE HOSPITAL, LAKEWOOD, WA, p. A691
ST. CLARE'S HOSPITAL/DOVER, DOVER, NJ, p. A420
ST. CLOUD VA HEALTH CARE SYSTEM, SAINT CLOUD, MN, p. A354
ST. CLOUD VAMC, SAINT CLOUD, MN, p. A354
ST. CROIX REGIONAL MEDICAL CENTER, ST CROIX FALLS, WI, p. A722
ST. David's MEDICAL CENTER, AUSTIN, TX, p. A600
ST. David's NORTH AUSTIN MEDICAL CENTER, AUSTIN, TX, p. A600
ST. David's ROUND ROCK MEDICAL CENTER, ROUND ROCK, TX, p. A648
ST. David's SOUTH AUSTIN MEDICAL CENTER, AUSTIN, TX, p. A600
ST. DOMINIC–JACKSON MEMORIAL HOSPITAL, JACKSON, MS, p. A364
ST. ELIAS SPECIALTY HOSPITAL, ANCHORAGE, AK, p. A27
ST. ELIZABETH COMMUNITY HOSPITAL, RED BLUFF, CA, p. A85
ST. ELIZABETH DEARBORN, LAWRENCEBURG, IN, p. A222
ST. ELIZABETH EDGEWOOD, EDGEWOOD, KY, p. A265
ST. ELIZABETH FLORENCE, FLORENCE, KY, p. A265
ST. ELIZABETH FORT THOMAS, FORT THOMAS, KY, p. A266
ST. ELIZABETH GRANT, WILLIAMSTOWN, KY, p. A275
ST. ELIZABETH HOSPITAL, ENUMCLAW, WA, p. A689
ST. ELIZABETH HOSPITAL, GONZALES, LA, p. A282
ST. ELIZABETH MEDICAL CENTER–NORTH, COVINGTON, KY, p. A264
ST. ELIZABETH TOLUCA LAKE CONVALESCENT HOSPITAL, LOS ANGELES, CA, p. A75
ST. ELIZABETH'S MEDICAL CENTER, BRIGHTON, MA, p. A311
ST. FRANCIS – EMORY HEALTHCARE, COLUMBUS, GA, p. A161
ST. FRANCIS HOSPITAL, COLUMBUS, GA, p. A161
ST. FRANCIS HOSPITAL, FEDERAL WAY, WA, p. A690
ST. FRANCIS HOSPITAL, WILMINGTON, DE, p. A122
ST. FRANCIS HOSPITAL AND HEART CENTER, ROSLYN, NY, p. A458
ST. FRANCIS MEDICAL CENTER, LYNWOOD, CA, p. A76
ST. FRANCIS MEDICAL CENTER, MONROE, LA, p. A289
ST. FRANCIS MEMORIAL HOSPITAL, WEST POINT, NE, p. A407
ST. FRANCIS REGIONAL MEDICAL CENTER, SHAKOPEE, MN, p. A355
ST. GEORGE REGIONAL HOSPITAL, SAINT GEORGE, UT, p. A668
ST. HELENA PARISH HOSPITAL, GREENSBURG, LA, p. A282
ST. JAMES BEHAVIORAL HEALTH HOSPITAL, GONZALES, LA, p. A282
ST. JAMES HOSPITAL, HORNELL, NY, p. A444
ST. JAMES HOSPITALS AND HEALTH CENTERS – OLYMPIA FIELDS CAMPUS, OLYMPIA FIELDS, IL, p. A204
ST. JAMES PARISH HOSPITAL, LUTCHER, LA, p. A287
ST. JOHN MACOMB–OAKLAND HOSPITAL, WARREN, MI, p. A340
ST. JOHN OWASSO, OWASSO, OK, p. A519
ST. JOHN PROVIDENCE MACOMB–OAKLAND HOSPITAL, OAKLAND CENTER, MADISON HEIGHTS, MI, p. A332
ST. JOHN REHABILITATION HOSPITAL, BROKEN ARROW, OK, p. A510
ST. JOHN SAPULPA, SAPULPA, OK, p. A520
ST. JOHN'S CHILDREN'S HOSPITAL, SPRINGFIELD, MO, p. A387
ST. JOHN'S EPISCOPAL HOSPITAL, NEW YORK, NY, p. A453
ST. JOHN'S HEALTH, JACKSON, WY, p. A727
ST. JOHN'S MERCY CHILDREN'S HOSPITAL, SAINT LOUIS, MO, p. A385
ST. JOHN'S REGIONAL MEDICAL CENTER, OXNARD, CA, p. A82
ST. JOHN'S RIVERSIDE HOSPITAL, YONKERS, NY, p. A462
ST. JOSEPH HEALTH SERVICES OF RHODE ISLAND, NORTH PROVIDENCE, RI, p. A560
ST. JOSEPH HOSPITAL, BANGOR, ME, p. A295
ST. JOSEPH HOSPITAL, BETHPAGE, NY, p. A439
ST. JOSEPH HOSPITAL, NASHUA, NH, p. A416
ST. JOSEPH HOSPITAL EUREKA, EUREKA, CA, p. A62
ST. JOSEPH HOSPITAL FOR SPECIALTY CARE, PROVIDENCE, RI, p. A561

ST. JOSEPH HOSPITAL ORANGE, ORANGE, CA, p. A82
ST. JOSEPH MEDICAL CENTER, HOUSTON, TX, p. A628
ST. JOSEPH MEDICAL CENTER, KANSAS CITY, MO, p. A378
ST. JOSEPH MEDICAL CENTER, TACOMA, WA, p. A697
ST. JOSEPH MEDICAL CENTER–DOWNTOWN READING, READING, PA, p. A553
ST. JOSEPH MEMORIAL HOSPITAL, MURPHYSBORO, IL, p. A203
ST. JOSEPH MERCY ANN ARBOR, YPSILANTI, MI, p. A341
ST. JOSEPH MERCY CHELSEA, CHELSEA, MI, p. A324
ST. JOSEPH MERCY LIVINGSTON HOSPITAL, HOWELL, MI, p. A330
ST. JOSEPH MERCY OAKLAND, PONTIAC, MI, p. A335
ST. JOSEPH REGIONAL MEDICAL CENTER, LEWISTON, ID, p. A182
ST. JOSEPH'S BEHAVIORAL HEALTH CENTER, STOCKTON, CA, p. A97
ST. JOSEPH'S CHILDREN'S HOSPITAL OF TAMPA, TAMPA, FL, p. A152
ST. JOSEPH'S HOSPITAL, ASHEVILLE, NC, p. A463
ST. JOSEPH'S HOSPITAL, BUCKHANNON, WV, p. A699
ST. JOSEPH'S HOSPITAL, SAVANNAH, GA, p. A171
ST. JOSEPH'S HOSPITAL, TAMPA, FL, p. A152
ST. JOSEPH'S HOSPITAL AND MEDICAL CENTER, PHOENIX, AZ, p. A36
ST. JOSEPH'S HOSPITAL HEALTH CENTER, SYRACUSE, NY, p. A460
ST. JOSEPH'S MEDICAL CENTER, STOCKTON, CA, p. A97
ST. JOSEPH'S MERCY–NORTH, ROMEO, MI, p. A336
ST. JOSEPH'S UNIVERSITY MEDICAL CENTER, PATERSON, NJ, p. A426
ST. JOSEPH'S WOMEN'S HOSPITAL – TAMPA, TAMPA, FL, p. A152
ST. JUDE CHILDREN'S RESEARCH HOSPITAL, MEMPHIS, TN, p. A589
ST. JUDE MEDICAL CENTER, FULLERTON, CA, p. A65
ST. LAWRENCE PSYCHIATRIC CENTER, OGDENSBURG, NY, p. A455
ST. LAWRENCE REHABILITATION HOSPITAL, LAWRENCEVILLE, NJ, p. A423
ST. LOUIS CHILDREN'S HOSPITAL, SAINT LOUIS, MO, p. A384
ST. LOUIS FORENSIC TREATMENT CENTER, SAINT LOUIS, MO, p. A384
ST. LOUIS PSYCHIATRIC REHABILITATION CENTER, SAINT LOUIS, MO, p. A384
ST. LOUIS REGIONAL PSYCHIATRIC STABILIZATION CENTER, SAINT LOUIS, MO, p. A384
ST. LOUISE REGIONAL HOSPITAL, GILROY, CA, p. A65
ST. LUKE COMMUNITY HEALTHCARE, RONAN, MT, p. A395
ST. LUKE HOSPITAL AND LIVING CENTER, MARION, KS, p. A254
ST. LUKE'S ANDERSON CAMPUS, EASTON, PA, p. A539
ST. LUKE'S BAPTIST HOSPITAL, SAN ANTONIO, TX, p. A651
ST. LUKE'S BEHAVIORAL HEALTH CENTER, PHOENIX, AZ, p. A36
ST. LUKE'S BOISE MEDICAL CENTER, BOISE, ID, p. A179
ST. LUKE'S CAMPUS, UTICA, NY, p. A460
ST. LUKE'S CARBON CAMPUS, LEHIGHTON, PA, p. A544
ST. LUKE'S CORNWALL HOSPITAL – CORNWALL CAMPUS, CORNWALL, NY, p. A441
ST. LUKE'S DES PERES HOSPITAL, SAINT LOUIS, MO, p. A386
ST. LUKE'S EASTON CAMPUS, EASTON, PA, p. A539
ST. LUKE'S ELMORE, MOUNTAIN HOME, ID, p. A182
ST. LUKE'S EPISCOPAL HOSPITAL, PONCE, PR, p. A734
ST. LUKE'S HEALTH – LAKESIDE HOSPITAL, THE WOODLANDS, TX, p. A657
ST. LUKE'S HEALTH – MEMORIAL LIVINGSTON, LIVINGSTON, TX, p. A635
ST. LUKE'S HEALTH – PATIENTS MEDICAL CENTER, PASADENA, TX, p. A643
ST. LUKE'S HEALTH – SUGAR LAND HOSPITAL, SUGAR LAND, TX, p. A655
ST. LUKE'S HEALTH – THE VINTAGE HOSPITAL, HOUSTON, TX, p. A628
ST. LUKE'S HEALTH – THE WOODLANDS HOSPITAL, THE WOODLANDS, TX, p. A658
ST. LUKE'S HOSPITAL – WARREN CAMPUS, PHILLIPSBURG, NJ, p. A427
ST. LUKE'S HOSPITAL, CHESTERFIELD, MO, p. A373
ST. LUKE'S HOSPITAL, COLUMBUS, NC, p. A466
ST. LUKE'S HOSPITAL, DULUTH, MN, p. A346
ST. LUKE'S HOSPITAL, NEW BEDFORD, MA, p. A316
ST. LUKE'S HOSPITAL, NEWBURGH, NY, p. A454
ST. LUKE'S HOSPITAL–MINERS CAMPUS, COALDALE, PA, p. A537
ST. LUKE'S JEROME, JEROME, ID, p. A181

ST. LUKE'S MAGIC VALLEY MEDICAL CENTER, TWIN FALLS, ID, p. A184
ST. LUKE'S MCCALL, MCCALL, ID, p. A182
ST. LUKE'S MEDICAL CENTER, CROSBY, ND, p. A480
ST. LUKE'S MERIDIAN MEDICAL CENTER, MERIDIAN, ID, p. A182
ST. LUKE'S MONROE CAMPUS, STROUDSBURG, PA, p. A555
ST. LUKE'S NAMPA, NAMPA, ID, p. A182
ST. LUKE'S QUAKERTOWN CAMPUS, QUAKERTOWN, PA, p. A553
ST. LUKE'S REGIONAL MEDICAL CENTER, BOISE, ID, p. A180
ST. LUKE'S REHABILITATION HOSPITAL, BOISE, ID, p. A180
ST. LUKE'S REHABILITATION HOSPITAL, CHESTERFIELD, MO, p. A373
ST. LUKE'S SUGAR LAND HOSPITAL, SUGAR LAND, TX, p. A655
ST. LUKE'S UNIVERSITY HOSPITAL – BETHLEHEM CAMPUS, BETHLEHEM, PA, p. A535
ST. LUKE'S WOOD RIVER MEDICAL CENTER, KETCHUM, ID, p. A182
ST. MARK'S HOSPITAL, SALT LAKE CITY, UT, p. A669
ST. MARY MEDICAL CENTER, APPLE VALLEY, CA, p. A56
ST. MARY MEDICAL CENTER, HOBART, IN, p. A218
ST. MARY MEDICAL CENTER, LANGHORNE, PA, p. A543
ST. MARY MEDICAL CENTER LONG BEACH, LONG BEACH, CA, p. A71
ST. MARY MERCY LIVONIA HOSPITAL, LIVONIA, MI, p. A332
ST. MARY REHABILITATION HOSPITAL, LANGHORNE, PA, p. A543
ST. MARY'S GENERAL HOSPITAL, PASSAIC, NJ, p. A426
ST. MARY'S GOOD SAMARITAN HOSPITAL, GREENSBORO, GA, p. A164
ST. MARY'S HEALTH, COTTONWOOD, ID, p. A181
ST. MARY'S HEALTH CARE SYSTEM, ATHENS, GA, p. A156
ST. MARY'S HEALTHCARE, AMSTERDAM, NY, p. A438
ST. MARY'S HOSPITAL, COTTONWOOD, ID, p. A181
ST. MARY'S HOSPITAL, RHINELANDER, WI, p. A720
ST. MARY'S HOSPITAL AMSTERDAM, AMSTERDAM, NY, p. A438
ST. MARY'S HOSPITAL AND REHABILITATION CENTER, MINNEAPOLIS, MN, p. A351
ST. MARY'S MEDICAL CENTER, BLUE SPRINGS, MO, p. A371
ST. MARY'S MEDICAL CENTER, HUNTINGTON, WV, p. A701
ST. MARY'S MEDICAL CENTER, WEST PALM BEACH, FL, p. A154
ST. MARY'S OF MICHIGAN, SAGINAW, MI, p. A337
ST. MARY'S REGIONAL MEDICAL CENTER, ENID, OK, p. A512
ST. MARY'S REGIONAL MEDICAL CENTER, LEWISTON, ME, p. A298
ST. MARY'S SACRED HEART HOSPITAL, LAVONIA, GA, p. A166
ST. MARY-CORWIN MEDICAL CENTER, PUEBLO, CO, p. A113
ST. MICHAEL MEDICAL CENTER, SILVERDALE, WA, p. A695
ST. MICHAEL'S ELITE HOSPITAL, SUGAR LAND, TX, p. A655
ST. MICHAEL'S HOSPITAL, STEVENS POINT, WI, p. A722
ST. MICHAEL'S HOSPITAL AVERA, TYNDALL, SD, p. A577
ST. PETER'S HEALTH, HELENA, MT, p. A393
ST. PETER'S HOSPITAL, ALBANY, NY, p. A457
ST. PETERSBURG GENERAL HOSPITAL, SAINT PETERSBURG, FL, p. A149
ST. ROSE DOMINICAN HOSPITALS – ROSE DE LIMA CAMPUS, HENDERSON, NV, p. A409
ST. ROSE DOMINICAN HOSPITALS – SAN MARTIN CAMPUS, LAS VEGAS, NV, p. A411
ST. ROSE DOMINICAN HOSPITALS – SIENA CAMPUS, HENDERSON, NV, p. A409
ST. ROSE HOSPITAL, HAYWARD, CA, p. A67
ST. TAMMANY HEALTH SYSTEM, COVINGTON, LA, p. A280
ST. THOMAS MORE HOSPITAL, CANON CITY, CO, p. A104
ST. VINCENT HEALTH, LEADVILLE, CO, p. A111
ST. VINCENT PEDIATRIC REHABILITATION CENTER, INDIANAPOLIS, IN, p. A220
ST. VINCENT'S BEHAVIORAL HEALTH, WESTPORT, CT, p. A120
ST. VINCENT'S BIRMINGHAM, BIRMINGHAM, AL, p. A17
ST. VINCENT'S BLOUNT, ONEONTA, AL, p. A23
ST. VINCENT'S EAST, BIRMINGHAM, AL, p. A17
ST. VINCENT'S MEDICAL CENTER, BRIDGEPORT, CT, p. A115
ST. VINCENT'S ST. CLAIR, PELL CITY, AL, p. A23
STAFFORD COUNTY HOSPITAL, STAFFORD, KS, p. A260
STAFFORD HOSPITAL, STAFFORD, VA, p. A684
STAMFORD HEALTH, STAMFORD, CT, p. A119
STAMFORD HOSPITAL, STAMFORD, CT, p. A119
STANDING ROCK SERVICE UNIT, FORT YATES HOSPITAL, INDIAN HEALTH SERVICE, DHHS, FORT YATES, ND, p. A481
STANFORD HEALTH CARE – VALLEYCARE, PLEASANTON, CA, p. A83
STANFORD HEALTH CARE, PALO ALTO, CA, p. A82

STANFORD HEALTH CARE TRI-VALLEY, PLEASANTON, CA, p. A83
STANTON COUNTY HOSPITAL, JOHNSON, KS, p. A251
STAR VALLEY HEALTH, AFTON, WY, p. A726
STARR COUNTY MEMORIAL HOSPITAL, RIO GRANDE CITY, TX, p. A647
STARR REGIONAL MEDICAL CENTER, ATHENS, TN, p. A579
STATE CORRECTIONAL INSTITUTION AT CAMP HILL, CAMP HILL, PA, p. A536
STATE HOSPITAL NORTH, OROFINO, ID, p. A183
STATE HOSPITAL SOUTH, BLACKFOOT, ID, p. A179
STATE PENITENTIARY HOSPITAL, WALLA WALLA, WA, p. A698
STATEN ISLAND UNIVERSITY HOSPITAL, NEW YORK, NY, p. A453
STE. GENEVIEVE COUNTY MEMORIAL HOSPITAL, STE GENEVIEVE, MO, p. A387
STEELE MEMORIAL MEDICAL CENTER, SALMON, ID, p. A183
STEPHENS COUNTY HOSPITAL, TOCCOA, GA, p. A173
STEPHENS MEMORIAL HOSPITAL, BRECKENRIDGE, TX, p. A604
STERLING REGIONAL MEDCENTER, STERLING, CO, p. A113
STERLING SURGICAL HOSPITAL, SLIDELL, LA, p. A293
STERLINGTON REHABILITATION HOSPITAL, BASTROP, LA, p. A277
STEVEN AND ALEXANDRA COHEN CHILDREN'S MEDICAL CENTER OF NEW YORK, NEW YORK, NY, p. A453
STEVENS COMMUNITY MEDICAL CENTER, MORRIS, MN, p. A351
STEVENS COUNTY HOSPITAL, HUGOTON, KS, p. A251
STEWART & LYNDA RESNICK NEUROPSYCHIATRIC HOSPITAL AT UCLA, LOS ANGELES, CA, p. A75
STEWART MEMORIAL COMMUNITY HOSPITAL, LAKE CITY, IA, p. A239
STILLWATER BILLINGS CLINIC, COLUMBUS, MT, p. A390
STILLWATER MEDICAL BLACKWELL, BLACKWELL, OK, p. A510
STILLWATER MEDICAL CENTER, STILLWATER, OK, p. A521
STILLWATER MEDICAL PERRY, PERRY, OK, p. A519
STOCKTON REGIONAL REHABILITATION HOSPITAL, STOCKTON, CA, p. A97
STONE COUNTY MEDICAL CENTER, MOUNTAIN VIEW, AR, p. A51
STONECREST CENTER, DETROIT, MI, p. A326
STONESPRINGS HOSPITAL CENTER, DULLES, VA, p. A675
STONEWALL MEMORIAL HOSPITAL, ASPERMONT, TX, p. A598
STONY BROOK UNIVERSITY HOSPITAL, STONY BROOK, NY, p. A459
STONY BROOK CHILDREN'S HOSPITAL, STONY BROOK, NY, p. A459
STORMONT VAIL HEALTH – FLINT HILLS CAMPUS, JUNCTION CITY, KS, p. A251
STORMONT VAIL HEALTH, TOPEKA, KS, p. A260
STORY COUNTY MEDICAL CENTER, NEVADA, IA, p. A240
STOUGHTON HEALTH, STOUGHTON, WI, p. A722
STRAITH HOSPITAL FOR SPECIAL SURGERY, SOUTHFIELD, MI, p. A339
STRATEGIC BEHAVIORAL HEALTH, LLC, GARNER, NC, p. A468
STRAUB MEDICAL CENTER, HONOLULU, HI, p. A176
STREAMWOOD BEHAVIORAL HEALTH CENTER, STREAMWOOD, IL, p. A209
STREAMWOOD BEHAVIORAL HEALTHCARE SYSTEM, STREAMWOOD, IL, p. A209
STRONG MEMORIAL HOSPITAL OF THE UNIVERSITY OF ROCHESTER, ROCHESTER, NY, p. A457
STURDY MEMORIAL HOSPITAL, ATTLEBORO, MA, p. A309
STURGIS HOSPITAL, STURGIS, MI, p. A338
SUBURBAN COMMUNITY HOSPITAL, EAST NORRITON, PA, p. A539
SUBURBAN HOSPITAL, BETHESDA, MD, p. A303
SULLIVAN COUNTY COMMUNITY HOSPITAL, SULLIVAN, IN, p. A227
SULLIVAN COUNTY MEMORIAL HOSPITAL, MILAN, MO, p. A380
SUMMA AKRON CITY HOSPITAL, AKRON, OH, p. A484
SUMMA BARBERTON CITIZENS HOSPITAL, BARBERTON, OH, p. A485
SUMMA HEALTH SYSTEM – AKRON CAMPUS, AKRON, OH, p. A484
SUMMA HEALTH SYSTEM, AKRON, OH, p. A484
SUMMA REHAB HOSPITAL, AKRON, OH, p. A484
SUMMA SAINT THOMAS HOSPITAL, AKRON, OH, p. A484
SUMMERLIN HOSPITAL MEDICAL CENTER, LAS VEGAS, NV, p. A411
SUMMERS COUNTY ARH HOSPITAL, HINTON, WV, p. A701
SUMMERSVILLE REGIONAL MEDICAL CENTER, SUMMERSVILLE, WV, p. A705

SUMMIT BEHAVIORAL HEALTHCARE, CINCINNATI, OH, p. A489
SUMMIT HEALTHCARE REGIONAL MEDICAL CENTER, SHOW LOW, AZ, p. A39
SUMMIT MEDICAL CENTER, CASPER, WY, p. A726
SUMMIT MEDICAL CENTER, EDMOND, OK, p. A512
SUMMIT MEDICAL CENTER, OAKLAND, CA, p. A81
SUMMIT OAKS HOSPITAL, SUMMIT, NJ, p. A428
SUMMIT PACIFIC MEDICAL CENTER, ELMA, WA, p. A689
SUMMIT SURGICAL, HUTCHINSON, KS, p. A251
SUMMITRIDGE HOSPITAL, LAWRENCEVILLE, GA, p. A166
SUMNER COUNTY HOSPITAL DISTRICT 1, CALDWELL, KS, p. A247
SUMNER REGIONAL MEDICAL CENTER, GALLATIN, TN, p. A583
SUN BEHAVIORAL COLUMBUS, COLUMBUS, OH, p. A492
SUN BEHAVIORAL DELAWARE, GEORGETOWN, DE, p. A121
SUN BEHAVIORAL HOUSTON, HOUSTON, TX, p. A628
SUN BEHAVIORAL KENTUCKY, ERLANGER, KY, p. A265
SUN COAST HOSPITAL, LARGO, FL, p. A137
SUNCOAST BEHAVIORAL HEALTH CENTER, BRADENTON, FL, p. A127
SUNNYVIEW REHABILITATION HOSPITAL, SCHENECTADY, NY, p. A459
SUNRISE CANYON HOSPITAL, LUBBOCK, TX, p. A636
SUNRISE HOSPITAL AND MEDICAL CENTER, LAS VEGAS, NV, p. A411
SUNVIEW MEDICAL CENTER, WEST PALM BEACH, FL, p. A154
SUNY DOWNSTATE HEALTH SCIENCES UNIVERSITY, NEW YORK, NY, p. A453
SURGEONS CHOICE MEDICAL CENTER, SOUTHFIELD, MI, p. A338
SURGERY SPECIALTY HOSPITALS OF AMERICA, PASADENA, TX, p. A643
SURGICAL HOSPITAL AT SOUTHWOODS, YOUNGSTOWN, OH, p. A508
SURGICAL HOSPITAL OF OKLAHOMA, OKLAHOMA CITY, OK, p. A519
SURGICAL INSTITUTE OF READING, WYOMISSING, PA, p. A558
SURGICAL SPECIALTY CENTER OF BATON ROUGE, BATON ROUGE, LA, p. A278
SURPRISE VALLEY HEALTH CARE DISTRICT, CEDARVILLE, CA, p. A59
SUSAN B. ALLEN MEMORIAL HOSPITAL, EL DORADO, KS, p. A248
SUTTER AMADOR HOSPITAL, JACKSON, CA, p. A68
SUTTER AUBURN FAITH HOSPITAL, AUBURN, CA, p. A56
SUTTER CENTER FOR PSYCHIATRY, SACRAMENTO, CA, p. A87
SUTTER COAST HOSPITAL, CRESCENT CITY, CA, p. A61
SUTTER DAVIS HOSPITAL, DAVIS, CA, p. A61
SUTTER DELTA MEDICAL CENTER, ANTIOCH, CA, p. A55
SUTTER HEALTH KAHI MOHALA, EWA BEACH, HI, p. A175
SUTTER LAKESIDE HOSPITAL, LAKEPORT, CA, p. A69
SUTTER MATERNITY AND SURGERY CENTER OF SANTA CRUZ, SANTA CRUZ, CA, p. A94
SUTTER MEDICAL CENTER, SACRAMENTO, SACRAMENTO, CA, p. A87
SUTTER ROSEVILLE MEDICAL CENTER, ROSEVILLE, CA, p. A86
SUTTER SANTA ROSA REGIONAL HOSPITAL, SANTA ROSA, CA, p. A95
SUTTER SOLANO MEDICAL CENTER, VALLEJO, CA, p. A100
SUTTER SURGICAL HOSPITAL – NORTH VALLEY, YUBA CITY, CA, p. A102
SUTTER TRACY COMMUNITY HOSPITAL, TRACY, CA, p. A98
SWAIN COMMUNITY HOSPITAL, A DUKE LIFEPOINT HOSPITAL, BRYSON CITY, NC, p. A464
SWEDISH EDMONDS, EDMONDS, WA, p. A689
SWEDISH HOSPITAL, CHICAGO, IL, p. A191
SWEDISH ISSAQUAH, ISSAQUAH, WA, p. A690
SWEDISH MEDICAL CENTER, ENGLEWOOD, CO, p. A107
SWEDISH MEDICAL CENTER–FIRST HILL, SEATTLE, WA, p. A694
SWEDISHAMERICAN – A DIVISION OF UW HEALTH, ROCKFORD, IL, p. A207
SWEENY COMMUNITY HOSPITAL, SWEENY, TX, p. A655
SWEETWATER HOSPITAL, SWEETWATER, TN, p. A594
SWISHER MEMORIAL HEALTHCARE SYSTEM, TULIA, TX, p. A658
SYCAMORE SHOALS HOSPITAL, ELIZABETHTON, TN, p. A582
SYCAMORE SPRINGS, LAFAYETTE, IN, p. A222
SYRACUSE AREA HEALTH, SYRACUSE, NE, p. A406
SYRACUSE VETERANS AFFAIRS MEDICAL CENTER, SYRACUSE, NY, p. A460
SYRINGA HOSPITAL AND CLINICS, GRANGEVILLE, ID, p. A181

Index of Hospitals / Tahoe Forest Hospital District

T

TAHOE FOREST HOSPITAL DISTRICT, TRUCKEE, CA, p. A98
TALLAHASSEE MEMORIAL HEALTHCARE, TALLAHASSEE, FL, p. A151
TALLAHATCHIE GENERAL HOSPITAL, CHARLESTON, MS, p. A360
TAMARACK HEALTH ASHLAND MEDICAL CENTER, ASHLAND, WI, p. A707
TAMARACK HEALTH HAYWARD MEDICAL CENTER, HAYWARD, WI, p. A713
TAMPA GENERAL HOSPITAL, TAMPA, FL, p. A152
TAMPA GENERAL HOSPITAL BROOKSVILLE, BROOKSVILLE, FL, p. A127
TAMPA GENERAL HOSPITAL CHILDREN'S MEDICAL CENTER, TAMPA, FL, p. A152
TAMPA GENERAL HOSPITAL CRYSTAL RIVER, CRYSTAL RIVER, FL, p. A129
TANNER MEDICAL CENTER-CARROLLTON, CARROLLTON, GA, p. A160
TANNER MEDICAL CENTER–VILLA RICA, VILLA RICA, GA, p. A173
TANNER MEDICAL CENTER/EAST ALABAMA, WEDOWEE, AL, p. A26
TAUNTON STATE HOSPITAL, TAUNTON, MA, p. A319
TAYLOR HARDIN SECURE MEDICAL FACILITY, TUSCALOOSA, AL, p. A25
TAYLOR HOSPITAL, RIDLEY PARK, PA, p. A553
TAYLOR REGIONAL HOSPITAL, CAMPBELLSVILLE, KY, p. A264
TAYLOR REGIONAL HOSPITAL, HAWKINSVILLE, GA, p. A165
TAYLORVILLE MEMORIAL HOSPITAL, TAYLORVILLE, IL, p. A210
T. C. THOMPSON CHILDREN'S HOSPITAL, CHATTANOOGA, TN, p. A581
TEAYS VALLEY HOSPITAL, HURRICANE, WV, p. A702
TELECARE HERITAGE PSYCHIATRIC HEALTH CENTER, OAKLAND, CA, p. A81
TEMECULA VALLEY HOSPITAL, TEMECULA, CA, p. A97
TEMPE ST. LUKE'S HOSPITAL, TEMPE, AZ, p. A39
TEMPLE HEALTH-CHESTNUT HILL HOSPITAL, PHILADELPHIA, PA, p. A550
TEMPLE REHABILITATION HOSPITAL, TEMPLE, TX, p. A656
TEMPLE UNIVERSITY HOSPITAL, PHILADELPHIA, PA, p. A550
TEMPLE UNIVERSITYHOSPITAL – JEANES CAMPUS, PHILADELPHIA, PA, p. A550
TEN BROECK HOSPITAL, HICKORY, NC, p. A470
TENNESSEE VALLEY HCS – NASHVILLE AND MURFREESBORO, NASHVILLE, TN, p. A590
TENNESSEE VALLEY HEALTHCARE SYSTEM, NASHVILLE, TN, p. A590
TENNOVA HEALTHCARE – CLEVELAND, CLEVELAND, TN, p. A581
TENNOVA HEALTHCARE REGIONAL HOSPITAL OF JACKSON, JACKSON, TN, p. A584
TENNOVA HEALTHCARE-CLARKSVILLE, CLARKSVILLE, TN, p. A581
TENNOVA HEALTHCARE–JEFFERSON MEMORIAL HOSPITAL, JEFFERSON CITY, TN, p. A584
TENNOVA HEALTHCARE–LAFOLLETTE MEDICAL CENTER, LA FOLLETTE, TN, p. A586
TENNOVA HEALTHCARE–LEBANON MCFARLAND CAMPUS, LEBANON, TN, p. A586
TENNOVA NEWPORT MEDICAL CENTER, NEWPORT, TN, p. A591
TENNOVA NORTH KNOXVILLE MEDICAL CENTER, POWELL, TN, p. A592
TERENCE CARDINAL COOKE HEALTH CARE CENTER, NEW YORK, NY, p. A453
TERRE HAUTE REGIONAL HOSPITAL, TERRE HAUTE, IN, p. A228
TERREBONNE GENERAL HEALTH SYSTEM, HOUMA, LA, p. A283
TERRELL STATE HOSPITAL, TERRELL, TX, p. A656
TETON VALLEY HEALTH CARE, DRIGGS, ID, p. A181
TEWKSBURY HOSPITAL, TEWKSBURY, MA, p. A319
TEXARKANA EMERGENCY CENTER & HOSPITAL, TEXARKANA, TX, p. A657
TEXAS CENTER FOR INFECTIOUS DISEASE, SAN ANTONIO, TX, p. A651
TEXAS CHILDREN'S HOSPITAL, HOUSTON, TX, p. A628
TEXAS CHILDREN'S HOSPITAL NORTH AUSTIN CAMPUS, AUSTIN, TX, p. A601
TEXAS COUNTY MEMORIAL HOSPITAL, HOUSTON, MO, p. A376
TEXAS HEALTH ARLINGTON MEMORIAL HOSPITAL, ARLINGTON, TX, p. A598
TEXAS HEALTH CENTER FOR DIAGNOSTIC & SURGERY, PLANO, TX, p. A645
TEXAS HEALTH FRISCO, FRISCO, TX, p. A621
TEXAS HEALTH HARRIS METHODIST HOSPITAL ALLIANCE, FORT WORTH, TX, p. A620
TEXAS HEALTH HARRIS METHODIST HOSPITAL AZLE, AZLE, TX, p. A601
TEXAS HEALTH HARRIS METHODIST HOSPITAL CLEBURNE, CLEBURNE, TX, p. A607
TEXAS HEALTH HARRIS METHODIST HOSPITAL FORT WORTH, FORT WORTH, TX, p. A620
TEXAS HEALTH HARRIS METHODIST HOSPITAL HURST-EULESS-BEDFORD, BEDFORD, TX, p. A602
TEXAS HEALTH HARRIS METHODIST HOSPITAL SOUTHLAKE, SOUTHLAKE, TX, p. A653
TEXAS HEALTH HARRIS METHODIST HOSPITAL SOUTHWEST FORT WORTH, FORT WORTH, TX, p. A620
TEXAS HEALTH HARRIS METHODIST HOSPITAL STEPHENVILLE, STEPHENVILLE, TX, p. A654
TEXAS HEALTH HEART & VASCULAR HOSPITAL ARLINGTON, ARLINGTON, TX, p. A598
TEXAS HEALTH HOSPITAL FRISCO, FRISCO, TX, p. A621
TEXAS HEALTH HOSPITAL MANSFIELD, MANSFIELD, TX, p. A637
TEXAS HEALTH HOSPITAL ROCKWALL, ROCKWALL, TX, p. A647
TEXAS HEALTH HUGULEY HOSPITAL FORT WORTH SOUTH, BURLESON, TX, p. A606
TEXAS HEALTH PRESBYTERIAN HOSPITAL ALLEN, ALLEN, TX, p. A595
TEXAS HEALTH PRESBYTERIAN HOSPITAL DALLAS, DALLAS, TX, p. A612
TEXAS HEALTH PRESBYTERIAN HOSPITAL DENTON, DENTON, TX, p. A614
TEXAS HEALTH PRESBYTERIAN HOSPITAL FLOWER MOUND, FLOWER MOUND, TX, p. A618
TEXAS HEALTH PRESBYTERIAN HOSPITAL KAUFMAN, KAUFMAN, TX, p. A631
TEXAS HEALTH PRESBYTERIAN HOSPITAL OF ROCKWALL, ROCKWALL, TX, p. A647
TEXAS HEALTH PRESBYTERIAN HOSPITAL PLANO, PLANO, TX, p. A645
TEXAS HEALTH SPECIALTY HOSPITAL, FORT WORTH, TX, p. A620
TEXAS HEALTH SPRINGWOOD, BEDFORD, TX, p. A602
TEXAS INSTITUTE FOR SURGERY AT TEXAS HEALTH PRESBYTERIAN DALLAS, DALLAS, TX, p. A612
TEXAS NEUROREHAB CENTER, AUSTIN, TX, p. A601
TEXAS ORTHOPEDIC HOSPITAL, HOUSTON, TX, p. A628
TEXAS REHABILITATION HOSPITAL OF ARLINGTON, ARLINGTON, TX, p. A598
TEXAS REHABILITATION HOSPITAL OF FORT WORTH, FORT WORTH, TX, p. A620
TEXAS REHABILITATION HOSPITAL OF KELLER, KELLER, TX, p. A632
TEXAS SCOTTISH RITE HOSPITAL FOR CHILDREN, DALLAS, TX, p. A612
TEXAS SURGICAL HOSPITAL, PLANO, TX, p. A645
TEXOMA MEDICAL CENTER, DENISON, TX, p. A613
TEXSAN HEART HOSPITAL, SAN ANTONIO, TX, p. A651
THAYER COUNTY HEALTH SERVICES, HEBRON, NE, p. A401
THE ACADIA HOSPITAL, BANGOR, ME, p. A295
THE ALLEN PAVILION, NEW YORK, NY, p. A453
THE AROOSTOOK MEDICAL CENTER, PRESQUE ISLE, ME, p. A299
THE BARBARA BUSH CHILDREN'S HOSPITAL, PORTLAND, ME, p. A298
THE BLACKBERRY CENTER, SAINT CLOUD, FL, p. A148
THE BRIDGEWAY, NORTH LITTLE ROCK, AR, p. A51
THE BRISTOL-MYERS SQUIBB CHILDREN'S HOSPITAL, NEW BRUNSWICK, NJ, p. A425
THE BROOK AT DUPONT, LOUISVILLE, KY, p. A270
THE BROOK HOSPITAL – KMI, LOUISVILLE, KY, p. A270
THE CHILDEN'S REGIONAL HOSPITAL AT COOPER, CAMDEN, NJ, p. A419
THE CHILDREN'S CENTER REHABILITATION HOSPITAL, BETHANY, OK, p. A510
THE CHILDREN'S HOME OF PITTSBURGH, PITTSBURGH, PA, p. A551
THE CHILDREN'S HOSPITAL, AMARILLO, TX, p. A596
THE CHILDREN'S HOSPITAL AT BRONSON, KALAMAZOO, MI, p. A331
THE CHILDREN'S HOSPITAL AT MONMOUTH MEDICAL CENTER, LONG BRANCH, NJ, p. A423
THE CHILDREN'S HOSPITAL AT PROVIDENCE, ANCHORAGE, AK, p. A27
THE CHILDREN'S HOSPITAL AT SAINT FRANCIS, TULSA, OK, p. A523
THE CHILDREN'S HOSPITAL OF MONTEFIORE, NEW YORK, NY, p. A453
THE CHILDREN'S INN AT NIH, BETHESDA, MD, p. A303
THE CHILDREN'S INSTITUTE OF PITTSBURGH, PITTSBURGH, PA, p. A551
THE CHRIST HOSPITAL HEALTH NETWORK, CINCINNATI, OH, p. A489
THE COLONY ER HOSPITAL, THE COLONY, TX, p. A657
THE CONNECTICUT HOSPICE, BRANFORD, CT, p. A115
THE CORE INSTITUTE SPECIALTY HOSPITAL, PHOENIX, AZ, p. A37
THE GENERAL, BATON ROUGE, LA, p. A278
THE HCMC DEPARTMENT OF PEDIATRICS, MINNEAPOLIS, MN, p. A351
THE HEART HOSPITAL AT DEACONESS GATEWAY, NEWBURGH, IN, p. A225
THE HORSHAM CLINIC, AMBLER, PA, p. A534
THE HOSPITAL AT HEBREW SENIOR CARE, WEST HARTFORD, CT, p. A120
THE HOSPITAL AT WESTLAKE MEDICAL CENTER, WEST LAKE HILLS, TX, p. A662
THE HOSPITAL OF CENTRAL CONNECTICUT, NEW BRITAIN, CT, p. A117
THE HOSPITALS OF PROVIDENCE EAST CAMPUS – TENET HEALTHCARE, EL PASO, TX, p. A617
THE HOSPITALS OF PROVIDENCE HORIZON CITY CAMPUS, HORIZON CITY, TX, p. A624
THE HOSPITALS OF PROVIDENCE MEMORIAL CAMPUS – TENET HEALTHCARE, EL PASO, TX, p. A617
THE HOSPITALS OF PROVIDENCE SIERRA CAMPUS – TENET HEALTHCARE, EL PASO, TX, p. A617
THE HOSPITALS OF PROVIDENCE TRANSMOUNTAIN CAMPUS – TENET HEALTHCARE, EL PASO, TX, p. A617
THE HSC PEDIATRIC CENTER, WASHINGTON, DC, p. A124
THE JEWISH HOSPITAL – MERCY HEALTH, CINCINNATI, OH, p. A489
THE MEADOWS PSYCHIATRIC CENTER, CENTRE HALL, PA, p. A536
THE MEDICAL CENTER AT ALBANY, ALBANY, KY, p. A263
THE MEDICAL CENTER AT BOWLING GREEN, BOWLING GREEN, KY, p. A264
THE MEDICAL CENTER AT CAVERNA, HORSE CAVE, KY, p. A267
THE MEDICAL CENTER AT RUSSELLVILLE, RUSSELLVILLE, KY, p. A274
THE MEDICAL CENTER OF SOUTHEAST TEXAS, PORT ARTHUR, TX, p. A645
THE MOUNT SINAI HOSPITAL, NEW YORK, NY, p. A453
THE NEUROMEDICAL CENTER REHABILITATION HOSPITAL, BATON ROUGE, LA, p. A278
THE OSUCCC – JAMES, COLUMBUS, OH, p. A493
THE OUTER BANKS HOSPITAL, NAGS HEAD, NC, p. A473
THE PAVILION, CHAMPAIGN, IL, p. A187
THE PAVILION AT WILLIAMSBURG PLACE, WILLIAMSBURG, VA, p. A685
THE PHYSICIANS CENTRE HOSPITAL, BRYAN, TX, p. A605
THE QUEEN'S MEDICAL CENTER, HONOLULU, HI, p. A176
THE REHABILITATION HOSPITAL OF MONTANA, BILLINGS, MT, p. A390
THE REHABILITATION INSTITUTE OF OHIO, DAYTON, OH, p. A494
THE REHABILITATION INSTITUTE OF ST. LOUIS, SAINT LOUIS, MO, p. A384
THE SPINE HOSPITAL OF LOUISIANA AT THE NEUROMEDICAL CENTER, BATON ROUGE, LA, p. A278
THE UNIVERSITY OF KANSAS HOSPITAL, KANSAS CITY, KS, p. A252
THE UNIVERSITY OF TOLEDO MEDICAL CENTER, TOLEDO, OH, p. A505
THE UNIVERSITY OF VERMONT HEALTH NETWORK – ALICE HYDE MEDICAL CENTER, MALONE, NY, p. A445
THE UNIVERSITY OF VERMONT HEALTH NETWORK CENTRAL VERMONT MEDICAL CENTER, BERLIN, VT, p. A671
THE UNIVERSITY OF VERMONT HEALTH NETWORK ELIZABETHTOWN COMMUNITY HOSPITAL, ELIZABETHTOWN, NY, p. A442
THE UNIVERSITY OF VERMONT HEALTH NETWORK PORTER MEDICAL CENTER, MIDDLEBURY, VT, p. A671
THE UNIVERSITY OF VERMONT HEALTH NETWORK–CHAMPLAIN VALLEY PHYSICIANS HOSPITAL, PLATTSBURGH, NY, p. A456
THE VINES, OCALA, FL, p. A143
THE WILLIAM W. BACKUS HOSPITAL, NORWICH, CT, p. A118
THE WILLOUGH AT NAPLES, NAPLES, FL, p. A142
THE WOMEN'S HOSPITAL, NEWBURGH, IN, p. A225
THE WOODS AT PARKSIDE, GAHANNA, OH, p. A496
THEDA CARE MEDICAL CENTER – WILD ROSE, WILD ROSE, WI, p. A725
THEDACARE MEDICAL CENTER–BERLIN, BERLIN, WI, p. A708

THEDACARE MEDICAL CENTER–NEW LONDON, NEW LONDON, WI, p. A718
THEDACARE MEDICAL CENTER–SHAWANO, SHAWANO, WI, p. A721
THEDACARE MEDICAL CENTER–WAUPACA, WAUPACA, WI, p. A724
THEDACARE REGIONAL MEDICAL CENTER–APPLETON, APPLETON, WI, p. A707
THEDACARE REGIONAL MEDICAL CENTER–NEENAH, NEENAH, WI, p. A718
THIBODAUX REGIONAL HEALTH SYSTEM, THIBODAUX, LA, p. A294
THOMAS B. FINAN CENTER, CUMBERLAND, MD, p. A303
THOMAS E. CREEK DEPARTMENT OF VETERANS AFFAIRS MEDICAL CENTER, AMARILLO, TX, p. A596
THOMAS H. BOYD MEMORIAL HOSPITAL, CARROLLTON, IL, p. A187
THOMAS HOSPITAL, FAIRHOPE, AL, p. A19
THOMAS JEFFERSON UNIVERSITY HOSPITAL, PHILADELPHIA, PA, p. A550
THOMAS MEMORIAL HOSPITAL, SOUTH CHARLESTON, WV, p. A705
THOMASVILLE REGIONAL MEDICAL CENTER, THOMASVILLE, AL, p. A25
THOREK MEMORIAL HOSPITAL, CHICAGO, IL, p. A191
THOREK MEMORIAL HOSPITAL ANDERSONVILLE, CHICAGO, IL, p. A191
THREE CROSSES REGIONAL HOSPITAL, LAS CRUCES, NM, p. A435
THREE GABLES SURGERY CENTER, PROCTORVILLE, OH, p. A503
THREE RIVERS BEHAVIORAL HEALTH, WEST COLUMBIA, SC, p. A571
THREE RIVERS HEALTH, BASIN, WY, p. A726
THREE RIVERS HEALTH SYSTEM, INC., THREE RIVERS, MI, p. A339
THREE RIVERS HOSPITAL, BREWSTER, WA, p. A687
THREE RIVERS HOSPITAL, WAVERLY, TN, p. A594
THREE RIVERS MEDICAL CENTER, LOUISA, KY, p. A269
THROCKMORTON COUNTY MEMORIAL HOSPITAL, THROCKMORTON, TX, p. A658
TIBOR RUBIN VA MEDICAL CENTER, LONG BEACH, CA, p. A71
TIDALHEALTH NANTICOKE, SEAFORD, DE, p. A122
TIDALHEALTH PENINSULA, SALISBURY, MD, p. A307
TIDALHEALTH PENINSULA REGIONAL, SALISBURY, MD, p. A307
TIDELANDS GEORGETOWN MEMORIAL HOSPITAL, GEORGETOWN, SC, p. A566
TIDELANDS HEALTH REHABILITATION HOSPITAL, AN AFFILIATE OF ENCOMPASS HEALTH, MURRELLS INLET, SC, p. A569
TIDELANDS WACCAMAW COMMUNITY HOSPITAL, MURRELLS INLET, SC, p. A569
TIFT REGIONAL MEDICAL CENTER, TIFTON, GA, p. A172
TIMPANOGOS REGIONAL HOSPITAL, OREM, UT, p. A667
TIOGA MEDICAL CENTER, TIOGA, ND, p. A483
TIPPAH COUNTY HOSPITAL, RIPLEY, MS, p. A368
TIRR MEMORIAL HERMANN, HOUSTON, TX, p. A628
TITUS REGIONAL MEDICAL CENTER, MOUNT PLEASANT, TX, p. A640
TITUSVILLE AREA HOSPITAL, TITUSVILLE, PA, p. A555
T.J. SAMSON COMMUNITY HOSPITAL, GLASGOW, KY, p. A266
T.J. HEALTH COLUMBIA, COLUMBIA, KY, p. A264
TMC BONHAM HOSPITAL, BONHAM, TX, p. A604
TMC FOR CHILDREN, TUCSON, AZ, p. A41
TMC HEALTH, TUCSON, AZ, p. A41
TOBEY HOSPITAL, WAREHAM, MA, p. A319
TOLEDO CHILDREN'S HOSPITAL, TOLEDO, OH, p. A505
TOMAH HEALTH, TOMAH, WI, p. A723
TOMAH VA MEDICAL CENTER, TOMAH, WI, p. A723
TOMAH VAMC, TOMAH, WI, p. A723
TOPS SURGICAL SPECIALTY HOSPITAL, HOUSTON, TX, p. A628
TORRANCE MEMORIAL MEDICAL CENTER, TORRANCE, CA, p. A98
TORRANCE STATE HOSPITAL, TORRANCE, PA, p. A555
TOTALLY KIDS REHABILITATION HOSPITAL, LOMA LINDA, CA, p. A70
TOUCHETTE REGIONAL HOSPITAL, CENTREVILLE, IL, p. A187
TOURO INFIRMARY, NEW ORLEANS, LA, p. A290
TOWN AND COUNTRY HOSPITAL, TAMPA, FL, p. A152
TOWNER COUNTY MEDICAL CENTER, CANDO, ND, p. A479
TOWNSEN MEMORIAL HOSPITAL, HUMBLE, TX, p. A629
TRACE REGIONAL HOSPITAL, HOUSTON, MS, p. A363
TRADITION MEDICAL CENTER, PORT ST LUCIE, FL, p. A147
TRANSYLVANIA REGIONAL HOSPITAL, BREVARD, NC, p. A464
TREASURE VALLEY HOSPITAL, BOISE, ID, p. A180

TREGO COUNTY–LEMKE MEMORIAL HOSPITAL, WAKEENEY, KS, p. A261
TRENTON PSYCHIATRIC HOSPITAL, TRENTON, NJ, p. A429
TRI-CITY MEDICAL CENTER, OCEANSIDE, CA, p. A81
TRI-COUNTY HOSPITAL, WADENA, MN, p. A356
TRI-STATE MEMORIAL HOSPITAL, CLARKSTON, WA, p. A688
TRI VALLEY HEALTH SYSTEM, CAMBRIDGE, NE, p. A398
TRIANGLE SPRINGS HOSPITAL, RALEIGH, NC, p. A474
TRICITIES HOSPITAL, HOPEWELL, VA, p. A678
TRIDENT MEDICAL CENTER, CHARLESTON, SC, p. A563
TRIGG COUNTY HOSPITAL, CADIZ, KY, p. A264
TRIHEALTH REHABILITATION HOSPITAL, CINCINNATI, OH, p. A490
TRINITAS HOSPITAL – JERSEY STREET CAMPUS, ELIZABETH, NJ, p. A420
TRINITAS HOSPITAL – NEW POINT CAMPUS, ELIZABETH, NJ, p. A420
TRINITAS REGIONAL MEDICAL CENTER, ELIZABETH, NJ, p. A421
TRINITY HEALTH, MINOT, ND, p. A482
TRINITY HEALTH ANN ARBOR HOSPITAL, YPSILANTI, MI, p. A341
TRINITY HEALTH GRAND HAVEN HOSPITAL, GRAND HAVEN, MI, p. A328
TRINITY HEALTH GRAND RAPIDS HOSPITAL, GRAND RAPIDS, MI, p. A328
TRINITY HEALTH LIVINGSTON HOSPITAL, HOWELL, MI, p. A330
TRINITY HEALTH LIVONIA HOSPITAL, LIVONIA, MI, p. A332
TRINITY HEALTH MUSKEGON HOSPITAL, MUSKEGON, MI, p. A334
TRINITY HEALTH OAKLAND HOSPITAL, PONTIAC, MI, p. A335
TRINITY HEALTH SAINT MARY'S – GRAND RAPIDS, GRAND RAPIDS, MI, p. A328
TRINITY HEALTH SHELBY HOSPITAL, SHELBY, MI, p. A338
TRINITY HEALTH SYSTEM, STEUBENVILLE, OH, p. A504
TRINITY HOSPITAL, WEAVERVILLE, CA, p. A101
TRINITY HOSPITAL, WOLF POINT, MT, p. A396
TRINITY HOSPITAL TWIN CITY, DENNISON, OH, p. A494
TRINITY KENMARE COMMUNITY HOSPITAL, KENMARE, ND, p. A482
TRINITY MEDICAL, FERRIDAY, LA, p. A282
TRINITY MOLINE, MOLINE, IL, p. A202
TRINITY SPRINGS PAVILION–EAST, FORT WORTH, TX, p. A620
TRIOS HEALTH, KENNEWICK, WA, p. A690
TRIPLER ARMY MEDICAL CENTER, HONOLULU, HI, p. A176
TRISTAR ASHLAND CITY MEDICAL CENTER, ASHLAND CITY, TN, p. A579
TRISTAR CENTENNIAL MEDICAL CENTER, NASHVILLE, TN, p. A591
TRISTAR GREENVIEW REGIONAL HOSPITAL, BOWLING GREEN, KY, p. A264
TRISTAR HENDERSONVILLE MEDICAL CENTER, HENDERSONVILLE, TN, p. A584
TRISTAR HORIZON MEDICAL CENTER, DICKSON, TN, p. A582
TRISTAR NORTHCREST MEDICAL CENTER, SPRINGFIELD, TN, p. A593
TRISTAR SKYLINE MEDICAL CENTER, NASHVILLE, TN, p. A591
TRISTAR SOUTHERN HILLS MEDICAL CENTER, NASHVILLE, TN, p. A591
TRISTAR STONECREST MEDICAL CENTER, SMYRNA, TN, p. A593
TRISTAR SUMMIT MEDICAL CENTER, HERMITAGE, TN, p. A584
TROUSDALE MEDICAL CENTER, HARTSVILLE, TN, p. A584
TROY REGIONAL MEDICAL CENTER, TROY, AL, p. A25
TRUMBULL MEMORIAL HOSPITAL, WARREN, OH, p. A506
TRUMBULL REGIONAL MEDICAL CENTER, WARREN, OH, p. A506
TRUSTPOINT HOSPITAL, MURFREESBORO, TN, p. A590
TRUSTPOINT REHABILITATION HOSPITAL OF LUBBOCK, LUBBOCK, TX, p. A636
TSEHOOTSOOI MEDICAL CENTER, FORT DEFIANCE, AZ, p. A31
TUALITY FOREST GROVE HOSPITAL, FOREST GROVE, OR, p. A527
TUBA CITY REGIONAL HEALTH CARE CORPORATION, TUBA CITY, AZ, p. A40
TUCSON VA MEDICAL CENTER, TUCSON, AZ, p. A41
TUFTS MEDICAL CENTER, BOSTON, MA, p. A311
TUG VALLEY ARH REGIONAL MEDICAL CENTER, SOUTH WILLIAMSON, KY, p. A274
TULANE–LAKESIDE HOSPITAL, METAIRIE, LA, p. A288
TULSA CENTER FOR BEHAVIORAL HEALTH, TULSA, OK, p. A523
TULSA ER & HOSPITAL, TULSA, OK, p. A523
TULSA REHABILITATION HOSPITAL, TULSA, OK, p. A523
TULSA SPINE AND SPECIALTY HOSPITAL, TULSA, OK, p. A523

TURKEY CREEK MEDICAL CENTER, KNOXVILLE, TN, p. A586
TURNING POINT HOSPITAL, MOULTRIE, GA, p. A169
TURQUOISE LODGE HOSPITAL, ALBUQUERQUE, NM, p. A433
TUSCALOOSA VA MEDICAL CENTER, TUSCALOOSA, AL, p. A25
TUSCALOOSA VAMC, TUSCALOOSA, AL, p. A25
TUSKEGEE DIVISION, TUSKEGEE, AL, p. A25
TWEETEN LUTHERAN HLTH CARE CTR, SPRING GROVE, MN, p. A355
TWELVE CLANS UNITY HOSPITAL, WINNEBAGO, NE, p. A407
TWIN CITIES COMMUNITY HOSPITAL, TEMPLETON, CA, p. A97
TWIN COUNTY REGIONAL HEALTHCARE, GALAX, VA, p. A677
TWIN LAKES REGIONAL MEDICAL CENTER, LEITCHFIELD, KY, p. A268
TWIN VALLEY BEHAVIORAL HEALTHCARE, COLUMBUS, OH, p. A493
TWINBROOK NURSING & CONV HOME, ERIE, PA, p. A540
TYLER CONTINUECARE HOSPITAL, TYLER, TX, p. A659
TYLER COUNTY HOSPITAL, WOODVILLE, TX, p. A663
TYLER HOLMES MEMORIAL HOSPITAL, WINONA, MS, p. A370

U

UAB HIGHLANDS, BIRMINGHAM, AL, p. A17
UAMS MEDICAL CENTER, LITTLE ROCK, AR, p. A50
UC DAVIS MEDICAL CENTER, SACRAMENTO, CA, p. A87
UC DAVIS REHABILITATION HOSPITAL, SACRAMENTO, CA, p. A88
UC SAN DIEGO HEALTH – EAST CAMPUS, SAN DIEGO, CA, p. A90
UC SAN DIEGO MEDICAL CENTER – HILLCREST, SAN DIEGO, CA, p. A90
UC SAN DIEGO SHILEY EYE CENTER, LA JOLLA, CA, p. A68
UCF LAKE NONA MEDICAL CENTER, ORLANDO, FL, p. A144
UCHEALTH BROOMFIELD HOSPITAL, BROOMFIELD, CO, p. A104
UCHEALTH GRANDVIEW HOSPITAL, COLORADO SPRINGS, CO, p. A105
UCHEALTH GREELEY HOSPITAL, GREELEY, CO, p. A109
UCHEALTH HIGHLANDS RANCH HOSPITAL, HIGHLANDS RANCH, CO, p. A109
UCHEALTH LONGS PEAK HOSPITAL, LONGMONT, CO, p. A111
UCHEALTH MEDICAL CENTER OF THE ROCKIES, LOVELAND, CO, p. A112
UCHEALTH MEMORIAL HOSPITAL, COLORADO SPRINGS, CO, p. A105
UCHEALTH PARKVIEW MEDICAL CENTER, PUEBLO, CO, p. A113
UCHEALTH PIKES PEAK REGIONAL HOSPITAL, WOODLAND PARK, CO, p. A114
UCHEALTH POUDRE VALLEY HOSPITAL, FORT COLLINS, CO, p. A108
UCHEALTH YAMPA VALLEY MEDICAL CENTER, STEAMBOAT SPRINGS, CO, p. A113
UCHICAGO MEDICINE ADVENTHEALTH BOLINGBROOK, BOLINGBROOK, IL, p. A186
UCHICAGO MEDICINE ADVENTHEALTH GLENOAKS, GLENDALE HEIGHTS, IL, p. A196
UCHICAGO MEDICINE ADVENTHEALTH HINSDALE, HINSDALE, IL, p. A198
UCHICAGO MEDICINE ADVENTHEALTH LA GRANGE, LA GRANGE, IL, p. A199
UCHICAGO MEDICINE INGALLS MEMORIAL, HARVEY, IL, p. A197
UCI HEALTH – LOS ALAMITOS, LOS ALAMITOS, CA, p. A71
UCI HEALTH – PLACENTIA LINDA, PLACENTIA, CA, p. A83
UCI HEALTH, ORANGE, CA, p. A82
UCI MEDICAL CENTER, ORANGE, CA, p. A82
UCLA MEDICAL CENTER–SANTA MONICA, SANTA MONICA, CA, p. A95
UCLA WEST VALLEY MEDICAL CENTER, LOS ANGELES, CA, p. A75
UCONN, JOHN DEMPSEY HOSPITAL, FARMINGTON, CT, p. A116
UCSF BENIOFF CHILDREN'S HOSPITAL OAKLAND, OAKLAND, CA, p. A81
UCSF CHILDREN'S HOSPITAL, SAN FRANCISCO, CA, p. A91
UCSF HEALTH SAINT FRANCIS HOSPITAL, SAN FRANCISCO, CA, p. A91
UCSF HEALTH ST. MARY'S HOSPITAL, SAN FRANCISCO, CA, p. A91
UCSF MEDICAL CENTER, SAN FRANCISCO, CA, p. A91
UF HEALTH JACKSONVILLE, JACKSONVILLE, FL, p. A135

UF HEALTH REHAB HOSPITAL, GAINESVILLE, FL, p. A132
UF HEALTH SHANDS HOSPITAL, GAINESVILLE, FL, p. A133
UF HEALTH ST. JOHN'S, SAINT AUGUSTINE, FL, p. A148
UF HEALTH THE VILLAGES HOSPITAL, THE VILLAGES, FL, p. A153
UH AVON REHABILITATION HOSPITAL, AVON, OH, p. A485
UH BEACHWOOD MEDICAL CENTER, BEACHWOOD, OH, p. A486
UH LAKE HEALTH MEDICAL CENTER, WILLOUGHBY, OH, p. A507
UH REGIONAL HOSPITALS, CHARDON, OH, p. A488
UH REHABILITATION HOSPITAL, BEACHWOOD, OH, p. A486
UH ST. JOHN MEDICAL CENTER, WESTLAKE, OH, p. A507
UHS CHENANGO MEMORIAL HOSPITAL, NORWICH, NY, p. A454
UHS DELAWARE VALLEY HOSPITAL, WALTON, NY, p. A461
UINTAH BASIN MEDICAL CENTER, ROOSEVELT, UT, p. A668
UK HEALTHCARE GOOD SAMARITAN, LEXINGTON, KY, p. A269
UK KING'S DAUGHTERS MEDICAL CENTER, ASHLAND, KY, p. A263
UMASS MEMORIAL HEALTH – HARRINGTON, SOUTHBRIDGE, MA, p. A318
UMASS MEMORIAL HEALTHALLIANCE–CLINTON HOSPITAL, LEOMINSTER, MA, p. A315
UMASS MEMORIAL MEDICAL CENTER, WORCESTER, MA, p. A320
UMASS MEMORIAL–MARLBOROUGH HOSPITAL, MARLBOROUGH, MA, p. A315
UMHC–SYLVESTER COMPREHENSIVE CANCER CENTER, MIAMI, FL, p. A141
UNC HEALTH BLUE RIDGE, MORGANTON, NC, p. A473
UNC HEALTH CALDWELL, LENOIR, NC, p. A471
UNC HEALTH CHATHAM, SILER CITY, NC, p. A476
UNC HEALTH JOHNSTON, SMITHFIELD, NC, p. A476
UNC HEALTH LENOIR, KINSTON, NC, p. A471
UNC HEALTH NASH, ROCKY MOUNT, NC, p. A475
UNC HEALTH PARDEE, HENDERSONVILLE, NC, p. A470
UNC HEALTH REX, RALEIGH, NC, p. A475
UNC HEALTH ROCKINGHAM, EDEN, NC, p. A467
UNC HEALTH SOUTHEASTERN, LUMBERTON, NC, p. A472
UNC HEALTH WAYNE, GOLDSBORO, NC, p. A469
UNICOI COUNTY HOSPITAL, ERWIN, TN, p. A583
UNIMED MEDICAL CENTER, MINOT, ND, p. A482
UNION CAMPUS, LYNN, MA, p. A315
UNION COUNTY GENERAL HOSPITAL, CLAYTON, NM, p. A434
UNION GENERAL HOSPITAL, BLAIRSVILLE, GA, p. A159
UNION GENERAL HOSPITAL, FARMERVILLE, LA, p. A281
UNION HOSPITAL, LYNN, MA, p. A315
UNION HOSPITAL, TERRE HAUTE, IN, p. A228
UNION HOSPITAL CLINTON, CLINTON, IN, p. A214
UNION MEDICAL CENTER, UNION, SC, p. A571
UNITED HEALTH SERVICES HOSPITALS–BINGHAMTON, BINGHAMTON, NY, p. A439
UNITED HOME, NEW ROCHELLE, NY, p. A447
UNITED HOSPITAL, GRAND FORKS, ND, p. A481
UNITED HOSPITAL, SAINT PAUL, MN, p. A355
UNITED HOSPITAL CENTER, BRIDGEPORT, WV, p. A699
UNITED HOSPITAL DISTRICT, BLUE EARTH, MN, p. A343
UNITED MEDICAL CENTER, WASHINGTON, DC, p. A124
UNITED MEDICAL HEALTHWEST NEW ORLEANS, LLC, GRETNA, LA, p. A282
UNITED MEDICAL REHABILITATION HOSPITAL–HAMMOND, HAMMOND, LA, p. A283
UNITED MEMORIAL MEDICAL CENTER, BATAVIA, NY, p. A439
UNITED REGIONAL HEALTH CARE SYSTEM, WICHITA FALLS, TX, p. A663
UNITY HEALTH – JACKSONVILLE, JACKSONVILLE, AR, p. A48
UNITY HEALTH – NEWPORT, NEWPORT, AR, p. A51
UNITY HEALTH, SEARCY, AR, p. A53
UNITY HEALTH MIDPOINT, NEWPORT, AR, p. A51
UNITY HOSPITAL, FRIDLEY, MN, p. A347
UNITY HOSPITAL, ROCHESTER, NY, p. A458
UNITY MEDICAL & SURGICAL HOSPITAL, MISHAWAKA, IN, p. A224
UNITY MEDICAL CENTER, GRAFTON, ND, p. A481
UNITY MEDICAL CENTER, MANCHESTER, TN, p. A587
UNITY PHYSICIANS HOSPITAL, MISHAWAKA, IN, p. A224
UNITY PSYCH CARE–MEMPHIS, MEMPHIS, TN, p. A589
UNITY PSYCHIATRIC CARE–CLARKSVILLE, CLARKSVILLE, TN, p. A581
UNITY PSYCHIATRIC CARE–COLUMBIA, COLUMBIA, TN, p. A581
UNITY PSYCHIATRIC CARE–HUNTSVILLE, HUNTSVILLE, AL, p. A21
UNITY PSYCHIATRIC CARE–MARTIN, MARTIN, TN, p. A587
UNITYPOINT HEALTH – ALLEN HOSPITAL, WATERLOO, IA, p. A244
UNITYPOINT HEALTH – DES MOINES, DES MOINES, IA, p. A235
UNITYPOINT HEALTH – FINLEY HOSPITAL, DUBUQUE, IA, p. A235
UNITYPOINT HEALTH – GRINNELL REGIONAL MEDICAL CENTER, GRINNELL, IA, p. A236
UNITYPOINT HEALTH – JONES REGIONAL MEDICAL CENTER, ANAMOSA, IA, p. A230
UNITYPOINT HEALTH – MARSHALLTOWN, MARSHALLTOWN, IA, p. A240
UNITYPOINT HEALTH – PEORIA, PEORIA, IL, p. A206
UNITYPOINT HEALTH – ST. LUKE'S HOSPITAL, CEDAR RAPIDS, IA, p. A232
UNITYPOINT HEALTH – ST. LUKES'S SIOUX CITY, SIOUX CITY, IA, p. A243
UNITYPOINT HEALTH – TRINITY BETTENDORF, BETTENDORF, IA, p. A231
UNITYPOINT HEALTH – TRINITY MOLINE, MOLINE, IL, p. A202
UNITYPOINT HEALTH – TRINITY MUSCATINE, MUSCATINE, IA, p. A240
UNITYPOINT HEALTH – TRINITY REGIONAL MEDICAL CENTER, FORT DODGE, IA, p. A236
UNITYPOINT HEALTH – TRINITY ROCK ISLAND, ROCK ISLAND, IL, p. A207
UNITYPOINT HEALTH MERITER, MADISON, WI, p. A714
UNITYPOINT HEALTH–DES MOINES, DES MOINES, IA, p. A235
UNIV OF NEW MEXICO HOSPITAL, ALBUQUERQUE, NM, p. A433
UNIVERSITY BEHAVIORAL HEALTH OF DENTON, DENTON, TX, p. A614
UNIVERSITY EVERETT TOWER, OKLAHOMA CITY, OK, p. A519
UNIVERSITY HEALTH, SAN ANTONIO, TX, p. A651
UNIVERSITY HEALTH–LAKEWOOD MEDICAL CENTER, KANSAS CITY, MO, p. A378
UNIVERSITY HEALTH–TRUMAN MEDICAL CENTER, KANSAS CITY, MO, p. A378
UNIVERSITY HOSPITAL, AUGUSTA, GA, p. A158
UNIVERSITY HOSPITAL, COLUMBIA, MO, p. A374
UNIVERSITY HOSPITAL, MADISON, WI, p. A714
UNIVERSITY HOSPITAL, NEWARK, NJ, p. A425
UNIVERSITY HOSPITAL, SAN JUAN, PR, p. A736
UNIVERSITY HOSPITAL AND MEDICAL CENTER, TAMARAC, FL, p. A151
UNIVERSITY HOSPITAL MCDUFFIE, THOMSON, GA, p. A172
UNIVERSITY HOSPITAL SCHOOL, IOWA CITY, IA, p. A238
UNIVERSITY HOSPITAL SUMMERVILLE, AUGUSTA, GA, p. A158
UNIVERSITY HOSPITALS AHUJA MEDICAL CENTER, BEACHWOOD, OH, p. A486
UNIVERSITY HOSPITALS BEACHWOOD MEDICAL CENTER, BEACHWOOD, OH, p. A486
UNIVERSITY HOSPITALS CLEVELAND MEDICAL CENTER, CLEVELAND, OH, p. A491
UNIVERSITY HOSPITALS CONNEAUT MEDICAL CENTER, CONNEAUT, OH, p. A493
UNIVERSITY HOSPITALS ELYRIA MEDICAL CENTER, ELYRIA, OH, p. A495
UNIVERSITY HOSPITALS EXTENDED CARE CAMPUS, CHARDON, OH, p. A488
UNIVERSITY HOSPITALS GEAUGA MEDICAL CENTER, CHARDON, OH, p. A488
UNIVERSITY HOSPITALS GENEVA MEDICAL CENTER, GENEVA, OH, p. A496
UNIVERSITY HOSPITALS LAKE HEALTH, WILLOUGHBY, OH, p. A507
UNIVERSITY HOSPITALS PARMA MEDICAL CENTER, PARMA, OH, p. A502
UNIVERSITY HOSPITALS PORTAGE MEDICAL CENTER, RAVENNA, OH, p. A503
UNIVERSITY HOSPITALS RAINBOW BABIES AND CHILDREN'S, CLEVELAND, OH, p. A491
UNIVERSITY HOSPITALS SAMARITAN MEDICAL CENTER, ASHLAND, OH, p. A485
UNIVERSITY HOSPITALS ST. JOHN MEDICAL CENTER, WESTLAKE, OH, p. A507
UNIVERSITY HOSPITALSTRIPOINT MEDICAL CENTER, CONCORD TOWNSHIP, OH, p. A493
UNIVERSITY MEDICAL CENTER, LAS VEGAS, NV, p. A411
UNIVERSITY MEDICAL CENTER, LUBBOCK, TX, p. A636
UNIVERSITY MEDICAL CENTER, NEW ORLEANS, LA, p. A290
UNIVERSITY MEDICAL CENTER OF EL PASO, EL PASO, TX, p. A617
UNIVERSITY MEDICAL CENTER–PSYCHIATRIC UNIT, LAFAYETTE, LA, p. A286
UNIVERSITY OF ALABAMA HOSPITAL, BIRMINGHAM, AL, p. A17
UNIVERSITY OF CALIFORNIA, DAVIS MEDICAL CENTER, SACRAMENTO, CA, p. A88
UNIVERSITY OF CHICAGO COMER CHILDREN'S HOSPITAL, CHICAGO, IL, p. A191
UNIVERSITY OF CHICAGO MEDICAL CENTER, CHICAGO, IL, p. A192
UNIVERSITY OF CINCINNATI MEDICAL CENTER, CINCINNATI, OH, p. A490
UNIVERSITY OF COLORADO HOSPITAL, AURORA, CO, p. A103
UNIVERSITY OF ILLINOIS HOSPITAL, CHICAGO, IL, p. A192
UNIVERSITY OF IOWA CHILDREN'S HOSPITAL, IOWA CITY, IA, p. A238
UNIVERSITY OF IOWA HEALTH CARE MEDICAL CENTER DOWNTOWN, IOWA CITY, IA, p. A238
UNIVERSITY OF IOWA HEALTH NETWORK REHABILITATION HOSPITAL, CORALVILLE, IA, p. A233
UNIVERSITY OF IOWA HOSPITALS & CLINICS, IOWA CITY, IA, p. A238
UNIVERSITY OF IOWA HOSPITALS AND CLINICS, IOWA CITY, IA, p. A238
UNIVERSITY OF IOWA REHABILITATION HOSPITAL, A VENTURE WITH ENCOMPASS HEALTH, CORALVILLE, IA, p. A233
UNIVERSITY OF KANSAS HEALTH SYSTEM GREAT BEND CAMPUS, GREAT BEND, KS, p. A250
UNIVERSITY OF KANSAS HEALTH SYSTEM ST. FRANCIS CAMPUS, TOPEKA, KS, p. A261
UNIVERSITY OF KENTUCKY ALBERT B. CHANDLER HOSPITAL, LEXINGTON, KY, p. A269
UNIVERSITY OF MARYLAND BALTIMORE WASHINGTON MEDICAL CENTER, GLEN BURNIE, MD, p. A304
UNIVERSITY OF MARYLAND CAPITAL REGION HEALTH AT LAUREL REGIONAL MEDICAL CENTER, LAUREL, MD, p. A305
UNIVERSITY OF MARYLAND CAPITAL REGION HEALTH PRINCE GEORGE'S HOSPITAL CENTER, LARGO, MD, p. A305
UNIVERSITY OF MARYLAND CAPITAL REGION MEDICAL CENTER, LARGO, MD, p. A305
UNIVERSITY OF MARYLAND CHARLES REGIONAL MEDICAL CENTER, LA PLATA, MD, p. A305
UNIVERSITY OF MARYLAND MEDICAL CENTER, BALTIMORE, MD, p. A301
UNIVERSITY OF MARYLAND MEDICAL CENTER MIDTOWN CAMPUS, BALTIMORE, MD, p. A301
UNIVERSITY OF MARYLAND REHABILITATION & ORTHOPAEDIC INSTITUTE, BALTIMORE, MD, p. A302
UNIVERSITY OF MARYLAND SHORE MEDICAL CENTER AT CHESTERTOWN, CHESTERTOWN, MD, p. A303
UNIVERSITY OF MARYLAND SHORE MEDICAL CENTER AT EASTON, EASTON, MD, p. A304
UNIVERSITY OF MARYLAND ST. JOSEPH MEDICAL CENTER, TOWSON, MD, p. A307
UNIVERSITY OF MARYLAND UPPER CHESAPEAKE MEDICAL CENTER, BEL AIR, MD, p. A302
UNIVERSITY OF MICHIGAN HEALTH – WEST, WYOMING, MI, p. A341
UNIVERSITY OF MICHIGAN HEALTH–SPARROW CARSON, CARSON CITY, MI, p. A323
UNIVERSITY OF MICHIGAN HEALTH–SPARROW EATON, CHARLOTTE, MI, p. A323
UNIVERSITY OF MICHIGAN HEALTH–SPARROW IONIA, IONIA, MI, p. A330
UNIVERSITY OF MICHIGAN HEALTH–SPARROW LANSING, LANSING, MI, p. A332
UNIVERSITY OF MICHIGAN MEDICAL CENTER, ANN ARBOR, MI, p. A321
UNIVERSITY OF MINNESOTA CHILDREN'S HOSPITAL, FAIRVIEW, MINNEAPOLIS, MN, p. A351
UNIVERSITY OF MINNESOTA HOSPITAL AND CLINIC, MINNEAPOLIS, MN, p. A351
UNIVERSITY OF MISSISSIPPI MEDICAL CENTER, JACKSON, MS, p. A364
UNIVERSITY OF MISSISSIPPI MEDICAL CENTER GRENADA, GRENADA, MS, p. A362
UNIVERSITY OF MISSISSIPPI MEDICAL CENTER HOLMES COUNTY, LEXINGTON, MS, p. A365
UNIVERSITY OF MISSOURI HEALTH CARE, COLUMBIA, MO, p. A374
UNIVERSITY OF MN HOSPITAL, MINNEAPOLIS, MN, p. A351
UNIVERSITY OF NEW MEXICO HOSPITALS, ALBUQUERQUE, NM, p. A433
UNIVERSITY OF NORTH CAROLINA HOSPITALS, CHAPEL HILL, NC, p. A465
UNIVERSITY OF TENNESSEE MEDICAL CENTER, KNOXVILLE, TN, p. A586
UNIVERSITY OF TEXAS M.D. ANDERSON CANCER CENTER, HOUSTON, TX, p. A628
UNIVERSITY OF TEXAS MEDICAL BRANCH, GALVESTON, TX, p. A621
UNIVERSITY OF TEXAS SOUTHWESTERN MEDICAL CENTER, DALLAS, TX, p. A612
UNIVERSITY OF UTAH HEALTH, SALT LAKE CITY, UT, p. A669

UNIVERSITY OF VERMONT MEDICAL CENTER, BURLINGTON, VT, p. A671
UNIVERSITY PEDIATRIC HOSPITAL, RIO PIEDRAS, PR, p. A734
UNIVERSITY POINTE SURGICAL HOSPITAL, WEST CHESTER, OH, p. A506
UNM CHILDREN'S PSYCH HOSPITAL, ALBUQUERQUE, NM, p. A433
UNM SANDOVAL REGIONAL MEDICAL CENTER, INC., RIO RANCHO, NM, p. A436
UOFL HEALTH – JEWISH HOSPITAL, LOUISVILLE, KY, p. A270
UOFL HEALTH – MARY AND ELIZABETH HOSPITAL, LOUISVILLE, KY, p. A270
UOFL HEALTH – PEACE HOSPITAL, LOUISVILLE, KY, p. A270
UOFL HEALTH – SHELBYVILLE HOSPITAL, SHELBYVILLE, KY, p. A274
UOFL HEALTH – UOFL HOSPITAL, LOUISVILLE, KY, p. A270
UP HEALTH SYSTEM – BELL, ISHPEMING, MI, p. A330
UP HEALTH SYSTEM – MARQUETTE, MARQUETTE, MI, p. A333
UP HEALTH SYSTEM – PORTAGE, HANCOCK, MI, p. A329
UP HEALTH SYSTEM–BELL, ISHPEMING, MI, p. A330
UPLAND HILLS HEALTH, DODGEVILLE, WI, p. A709
UPMC ALTOONA, ALTOONA, PA, p. A534
UPMC BEDFORD, EVERETT, PA, p. A540
UPMC CARLISLE, CARLISLE, PA, p. A536
UPMC CHAUTAUQUA, JAMESTOWN, NY, p. A444
UPMC CHILDREN'S HOSPITAL OF PITTSBURGH, PITTSBURGH, PA, p. A551
UPMC COLE, COUDERSPORT, PA, p. A537
UPMC COMMUNITY OSTEOPATHIC, HARRISBURG, PA, p. A541
UPMC EAST, MONROEVILLE, PA, p. A546
UPMC GREENE, WAYNESBURG, PA, p. A556
UPMC HAMOT, ERIE, PA, p. A540
UPMC HANOVER, HANOVER, PA, p. A541
UPMC HARRISBURG, HARRISBURG, PA, p. A541
UPMC HORIZON, FARRELL, PA, p. A540
UPMC JAMESON, NEW CASTLE, PA, p. A547
UPMC KANE, KANE, PA, p. A543
UPMC LITITZ, LITITZ, PA, p. A544
UPMC MAGEE–WOMENS HOSPITAL, PITTSBURGH, PA, p. A551
UPMC MCKEESPORT, MCKEESPORT, PA, p. A545
UPMC MEMORIAL, YORK, PA, p. A559
UPMC MERCY, PITTSBURGH, PA, p. A552
UPMC MONTEFIORE, PITTSBURGH, PA, p. A552
UPMC MUNCY, MUNCY, PA, p. A546
UPMC NORTHWEST, SENECA, PA, p. A554
UPMC PASSAVANT, PITTSBURGH, PA, p. A552
UPMC PASSAVANT CRANBERRY, CRANBERRY TOWNSHIP, PA, p. A537
UPMC PRESBYTERIAN, PITTSBURGH, PA, p. A552
UPMC SOMERSET, SOMERSET, PA, p. A555
UPMC ST. MARGARET, PITTSBURGH, PA, p. A552
UPMC SUSQUEHANNA DIVINE PROVIDENCE, WILLIAMSPORT, PA, p. A558
UPMC WASHINGTON, WASHINGTON, PA, p. A556
UPMC WELLSBORO, WELLSBORO, PA, p. A557
UPMC WESTERN MARYLAND, CUMBERLAND, MD, p. A304
UPMC WILLIAMSPORT, WILLIAMSPORT, PA, p. A558
UPMC–PRESBYTERIAN, PITTSBURGH, PA, p. A552
UPPER CONNECTICUT VALLEY HOSPITAL, COLEBROOK, NH, p. A414
UPPER VALLEY MEDICAL CENTER, TROY, OH, p. A505
UPSON REGIONAL MEDICAL CENTER, THOMASTON, GA, p. A172
UPSTATE UNIVERSITY HOSPITAL, SYRACUSE, NY, p. A460
USA HEALTH CHILDREN'S & WOMEN'S HOSPITAL, MOBILE, AL, p. A22
USA HEALTH PROVIDENCE HOSPITAL, MOBILE, AL, p. A22
USA HEALTH UNIVERSITY HOSPITAL, MOBILE, AL, p. A22
U. S. AIR FORCE HOSPITAL, HAMPTON, VA, p. A677
U. S. AIR FORCE MEDICAL CENTER KEESLER, KEESLER AFB, MS, p. A364
U. S. AIR FORCE REGIONAL HOSPITAL, EGLIN AFB, FL, p. A131
U. S. AIR FORCE REGIONAL HOSPITAL, ELMENDORF AFB, AK, p. A28
U. S. NAVAL HOSPITAL GUAM, AGANA, GU, p. A730
U. S. PENITENTIARY INFIRMARY, LEWISBURG, PA, p. A544
U. S. PUBLIC HEALTH SERVICE INDIAN HOSPITAL, CASS LAKE, MN, p. A344
U. S. PUBLIC HEALTH SERVICE INDIAN HOSPITAL, CROWNPOINT, NM, p. A434
U. S. PUBLIC HEALTH SERVICE INDIAN HOSPITAL, EAGLE BUTTE, SD, p. A573
U. S. PUBLIC HEALTH SERVICE INDIAN HOSPITAL, PARKER, AZ, p. A34
U. S. PUBLIC HEALTH SERVICE INDIAN HOSPITAL, PINE RIDGE, SD, p. A575
U. S. PUBLIC HEALTH SERVICE INDIAN HOSPITAL, ROSEBUD, SD, p. A576
U. S. PUBLIC HEALTH SERVICE INDIAN HOSPITAL, WAGNER, SD, p. A578
U. S. PUBLIC HEALTH SERVICE INDIAN HOSPITAL, ZUNI, NM, p. A437
U. S. PUBLIC HEALTH SERVICE INDIAN HOSPITAL–SELLS, SELLS, AZ, p. A38
U. S. PUBLIC HEALTH SERVICE INDIAN HOSPITAL–WHITERIVER, WHITERIVER, AZ, p. A41
U. S. PUBLIC HEALTH SERVICE PHOENIX INDIAN MEDICAL CENTER, PHOENIX, AZ, p. A37
USC ARCADIA HOSPITAL, ARCADIA, CA, p. A56
USC NORRIS COMPREHENSIVE CANCER CENTER AND HOSPITAL, LOS ANGELES, CA, p. A75
USC VERDUGO HILLS HOSPITAL, GLENDALE, CA, p. A66
USMD HOSPITAL AT ARLINGTON, ARLINGTON, TX, p. A598
UT HEALTH ATHENS, ATHENS, TX, p. A598
UT HEALTH CARTHAGE, CARTHAGE, TX, p. A607
UT HEALTH EAST TEXAS REHABILITATION HOSPITAL, TYLER, TX, p. A659
UT HEALTH HENDERSON, HENDERSON, TX, p. A624
UT HEALTH JACKSONVILLE, JACKSONVILLE, TX, p. A630
UT HEALTH NORTH CAMPUS TYLER, TYLER, TX, p. A659
UT HEALTH PITTSBURG, PITTSBURG, TX, p. A644
UT HEALTH QUITMAN, QUITMAN, TX, p. A646
UT HEALTH TYLER, TYLER, TX, p. A659
UTAH NEUROPSYCHIATRIC INST, SALT LAKE CITY, UT, p. A669
UTAH STATE HOSPITAL, PROVO, UT, p. A667
UTAH VALLEY HOSPITAL, PROVO, UT, p. A667
UTAH VALLEY SPECIALTY HOSPITAL, PROVO, UT, p. A668
UTHEALTH HARRIS COUNTY PSYCHIATRIC CENTER, HOUSTON, TX, p. A628
UVA ENCOMPASS HEALTH REHABILITATION HOSPITAL, CHARLOTTESVILLE, VA, p. A674
UVA HEALTH CULPEPER MEDICAL CENTER, CULPEPER, VA, p. A675
UVA HEALTH HAYMARKET MEDICAL CENTER, HAYMARKET, VA, p. A677
UVA HEALTH PRINCE WILLIAM MEDICAL CENTER, MANASSAS, VA, p. A679
UVA HEALTH UNIVERSITY MEDICAL CENTER, CHARLOTTESVILLE, VA, p. A674
UVA HEALTH UNIVERSITY MEDICAL CENTER IVY, CHARLOTTESVILLE, VA, p. A674
UVALDE MEMORIAL HOSPITAL, UVALDE, TX, p. A659
UW HEALTH REHABILITATION HOSPITAL, MADISON, WI, p. A715
UW HEALTH SWEDISHAMERICAN HOSPITAL, ROCKFORD, IL, p. A207
UW MEDICINE/HARBORVIEW MEDICAL CENTER, SEATTLE, WA, p. A695
UW MEDICINE/UNIVERSITY OF WASHINGTON MEDICAL CENTER, SEATTLE, WA, p. A695
UW MEDICINE/VALLEY MEDICAL CENTER, RENTON, WA, p. A693

V

VA CENTRAL CALIFORNIA HEALTH CARE SYSTEM, FRESNO, CA, p. A65
VA CENTRAL IOWA HEALTH CARE SYSTEM–DES MOINES, DES MOINES, IA, p. A235
VA PALO ALTO HEALTH CARE SYSTEM, PALO ALTO, CA, p. A82
VA PALO ALTO HEALTH CARE SYSTEM–LIVERMORE DIVISION, LIVERMORE, CA, p. A69
VA PALO ALTO HEATH CARE SYSTEM, PALO ALTO, CA, p. A82
VA PUGET SOUND HEALTHCARE SYSTEM – SEATTLE, SEATTLE, WA, p. A695
VA ST. LOUIS HEALTH CARE SYSTEM, SAINT LOUIS, MO, p. A384
VA TEXAS VALLEY COASTAL HCS, HARLINGEN, TX, p. A624
VAIL HEALTH, VAIL, CO, p. A114
VAL VERDE REGIONAL MEDICAL CENTER, DEL RIO, TX, p. A613
VALIR REHABILITATION HOSPITAL, OKLAHOMA CITY, OK, p. A519
VALLE VISTA HEALTH SYSTEM, GREENWOOD, IN, p. A218
VALLEY BAPTIST MEDICAL CENTER–BROWNSVILLE, BROWNSVILLE, TX, p. A605
VALLEY BAPTIST MEDICAL CENTER–HARLINGEN, HARLINGEN, TX, p. A624
VALLEY BEHAVIORAL HEALTH SYSTEM, BARLING, AR, p. A43
VALLEY CHILDREN'S HEALTHCARE, MADERA, CA, p. A76
VALLEY COMMUNITY HOSPITAL, PAULS VALLEY, OK, p. A519
VALLEY COUNTY HEALTH SYSTEM, ORD, NE, p. A404
VALLEY FORGE MEDICAL CENTER, NORRISTOWN, PA, p. A547
VALLEY HEALTH – HAMPSHIRE MEMORIAL HOSPITAL, ROMNEY, WV, p. A704
VALLEY HEALTH – PAGE MEMORIAL HOSPITAL, LURAY, VA, p. A678
VALLEY HEALTH – SHENANDOAH MEMORIAL HOSPITAL, WOODSTOCK, VA, p. A686
VALLEY HEALTH – WAR MEMORIAL HOSPITAL, BERKELEY SPRINGS, WV, p. A699
VALLEY HEALTH – WARREN MEMORIAL HOSPITAL, FRONT ROYAL, VA, p. A677
VALLEY HEALTH – WINCHESTER MEDICAL CENTER, WINCHESTER, VA, p. A685
VALLEY HOSPITAL, PARAMUS, NJ, p. A426
VALLEY HOSPITAL MEDICAL CENTER, LAS VEGAS, NV, p. A411
VALLEY HOSPITAL PHOENIX, PHOENIX, AZ, p. A37
VALLEY MEMORIAL, LIVERMORE, CA, p. A69
VALLEY PRESBYTERIAN HOSPITAL, LOS ANGELES, CA, p. A75
VALLEY REGIONAL HOSPITAL, CLAREMONT, NH, p. A414
VALLEY REGIONAL MEDICAL CENTER, BROWNSVILLE, TX, p. A605
VALLEY SPRINGS BEHAVIORAL HEALTH HOSPITAL, HOLYOKE, MA, p. A314
VALLEY VIEW HOSPITAL, GLENWOOD SPRINGS, CO, p. A108
VALLEY VIEW MEDICAL CENTER, FORT MOHAVE, AZ, p. A31
VALLEY WEST HEALTH CENTER, EUGENE, OR, p. A526
VALLEYCARE MEDICAL CENTER, LIVERMORE, CA, p. A70
VALLEYWISE HEALTH, PHOENIX, AZ, p. A37
VALOR HEALTH, EMMETT, ID, p. A181
VAN BUREN COUNTY HOSPITAL, KEOSAUQUA, IA, p. A238
VAN DIEST MEDICAL CENTER, WEBSTER CITY, IA, p. A245
VAN MATRE ENCOMPASS HEALTH REHABILITATION HOSPITAL, ROCKFORD, IL, p. A207
VANCOUVER MEMORIAL HOSPITAL, VANCOUVER, WA, p. A698
VANDERBILT BEDFORD HOSPITAL, SHELBYVILLE, TN, p. A593
VANDERBILT PSYCHIATRIC HOSPITAL, NASHVILLE, TN, p. A591
VANDERBILT STALLWORTH REHABILITATION HOSPITAL, NASHVILLE, TN, p. A591
VANDERBILT TULLAHOMA HARTON HOSPITAL, TULLAHOMA, TN, p. A594
VANDERBILT UNIVERSITY MEDICAL CENTER, NASHVILLE, TN, p. A591
VANDERBILT WILSON COUNTY HOSPITAL, LEBANON, TN, p. A586
VANTAGE POINT OF NORTHWEST ARKANSAS, FAYETTEVILLE, AR, p. A46
VASSAR BROTHERS MEDICAL CENTER, POUGHKEEPSIE, NY, p. A456
VAUGHAN REGIONAL MEDICAL CENTER, SELMA, AL, p. A24
VCU HEALTH COMMUNITY MEMORIAL HOSPITAL, SOUTH HILL, VA, p. A684
VCU HEALTH SYSTEM CHILDREN'S MEDICAL CENTER, RICHMOND, VA, p. A683
VCU HEALTH TAPPAHANNOCK HOSPITAL, TAPPAHANNOCK, VA, p. A684
VCU MEDICAL CENTER, RICHMOND, VA, p. A683
VEGAS VALLEY REHABILITATION HOSPITAL, LAS VEGAS, NV, p. A411
VENCOR HOSPITAL–CORAL GABLES, CORAL GABLES, FL, p. A128
VENTURA COUNTY MEDICAL CENTER, VENTURA, CA, p. A100
VERDE VALLEY MEDICAL CENTER, COTTONWOOD, AZ, p. A31
VERITAS COLLABORATIVE, DUNWOODY, GA, p. A163
VERITAS COLLABORATIVE, DURHAM, NC, p. A467
VERMILION BEHAVIORAL HEALTH SYSTEMS – NORTH CAMPUS, LAFAYETTE, LA, p. A286
VERMILION BEHAVIORAL HEALTH SYSTEMS SOUTH, LAFAYETTE, LA, p. A286
VERMONT PSYCHIATRIC CARE HOSPITAL, BERLIN, VT, p. A671
VERNON MEMORIAL HEALTHCARE, ELK MOUND, WI, p. A710
VETERAN AFFAIRS HUDSON VALLEY HEALTH CARE SYSTEM–CASTLE POINT CAMPUS, WAPPINGERS FALLS, NY, p. A461
VETERAN AFFAIRS HUDSON VALLEY HEALTH CARE SYSTEM–CASTLE POINT DIVISION, WAPPINGERS FALLS, NY, p. A461
VETERANS ADM MEDICAL CENTER, EAST ORANGE, NJ, p. A420

Index of Hospitals / Veterans Adm Medical Center

VETERANS ADM MEDICAL CENTER, NASHVILLE, TN, p. A591
VETERANS ADM MEDICAL CENTER, PITTSBURGH, PA, p. A552
VETERANS AFF MEDICAL CENTER, PITTSBURGH, PA, p. A552
VETERANS AFFAIRS ANN ARBOR HEALTHCARE SYSTEM, ANN ARBOR, MI, p. A321
VETERANS AFFAIRS BLACK HILLS HEALTH CARE SYSTEM, FORT MEADE, SD, p. A573
VETERANS AFFAIRS BOSTON HEALTHCARE SYSTEM, WEST ROXBURY, MA, p. A319
VETERANS AFFAIRS BOSTON HEALTHCARE SYSTEM BROCKTON DIVISION, BROCKTON, MA, p. A312
VETERANS AFFAIRS CARIBBEAN HEALTHCARE SYSTEM, SAN JUAN, PR, p. A736
VETERANS AFFAIRS CENTRAL WESTERN MASSACHUSETTS HEALTHCARE SYSTEM, LEEDS, MA, p. A315
VETERANS AFFAIRS CONNECTICUT HEALTHCARE SYSTEM, WEST HAVEN, CT, p. A120
VETERANS AFFAIRS EASTERN KANSAS HEALTH CARE SYSTEM–COLMERY-O'NEIL VETERANS AFFAIRS MEDICAL CENTER, TOPEKA, KS, p. A261
VETERANS AFFAIRS EASTERN KANSAS HEALTH CARE SYSTEM–DWIGHT D. EISENHOWER VETERANS AFFAIRS MEDICAL CENTER, LEAVENWORTH, KS, p. A253
VETERANS AFFAIRS HUDSON VALLEY HEALTH CARE SYSTEM, MONTROSE, NY, p. A446
VETERANS AFFAIRS HUDSON VALLEY HEALTH CARE SYSTEM–MONTROSE DIVISION, MONTROSE, NY, p. A446
VETERANS AFFAIRS ILLIANA HEALTH CARE SYSTEM, DANVILLE, IL, p. A192
VETERANS AFFAIRS MARYLAND HEALTH CARE SYSTEM–BALTIMORE DIVISION, BALTIMORE, MD, p. A302
VETERANS AFFAIRS MARYLAND HEALTH CARE SYSTEM–PERRY POINT DIVISION, PERRY POINT, MD, p. A306
VETERANS AFFAIRS MED CENTER, KERRVILLE, TX, p. A632
VETERANS AFFAIRS MED CENTER, LAS ANIMAS, CO, p. A111
VETERANS AFFAIRS MED CENTER, LINCOLN, NE, p. A402
VETERANS AFFAIRS MED CENTER, MARION, IN, p. A223
VETERANS AFFAIRS MED CENTER, PALO ALTO, CA, p. A82
VETERANS AFFAIRS MED CENTER, PERRY POINT, MD, p. A306
VETERANS AFFAIRS MED CENTER, TACOMA, WA, p. A697
VETERANS AFFAIRS MEDICAL CENTER, HOT SPRINGS, SD, p. A574
VETERANS AFFAIRS MEDICAL CENTER, LAKE CITY, FL, p. A136
VETERANS AFFAIRS MEDICAL CENTER, WEST HAVEN, CT, p. A120
VETERANS AFFAIRS MEDICAL CENTER, WEST ROXBURY, MA, p. A319
VETERANS AFFAIRS MEDICAL CENTER HOT SPRINGS CAMPUS, HOT SPRINGS, SD, p. A574
VETERANS AFFAIRS MEDICAL CENTER WEST ROXBURY DIVISION, WEST ROXBURY, MA, p. A319
VETERANS AFFAIRS NEBRASKA–WESTERN IOWA HEALTH CARE SYSTEM – LINCOLN, LINCOLN, NE, p. A402
VETERANS AFFAIRS NEW JERSEY HEALTH CARE SYSTEM, EAST ORANGE, NJ, p. A420
VETERANS AFFAIRS NEW JERSEY HEALTH CARE SYSTEM, LYONS, NJ, p. A423
VETERANS AFFAIRS NEW YORK HARBOR HEALTHCARE SYSTEM, NEW YORK, NY, p. A453
VETERANS AFFAIRS NORTH TEXAS HEALTH CARE SYSTEM, DALLAS, TX, p. A612
VETERANS AFFAIRS NORTHERN INDIANA HEALTH CARE SYSTEM, FORT WAYNE, IN, p. A217
VETERANS AFFAIRS NORTHERN INDIANA HEALTH CARE SYSTEM–MARION CAMPUS, MARION, IN, p. A223
VETERANS AFFAIRS NY HARBOR HEALTHCARE SYSTEM – MANHATTAN CAMPUS, NEW YORK, NY, p. A453
VETERANS AFFAIRS PALO ALTO HEALTH CARE SYSTEM, LIVERMORE DIVISION, LIVERMORE, CA, p. A70
VETERANS AFFAIRS PITTSBURGH HEALTHCARE SYSTEM, PITTSBURGH, PA, p. A552
VETERANS AFFAIRS PUGET SOUND HEALTH CARE SYSTEM–AMERICAN LAKE DIVISION, TACOMA, WA, p. A697
VETERANS AFFAIRS ROSEBURG HEALTHCARE SYSTEM, ROSEBURG, OR, p. A531
VETERANS AFFAIRS SIERRA NEVADA HEALTH CARE SYSTEM, RENO, NV, p. A412
VETERANS AFFAIRS ST. LOUIS HEALTH CARE SYSTEM, SAINT LOUIS, MO, p. A384
VETERANS AFFAIRS WESTERN NEW YORK HEALTHCARE SYSTEM–BATAVIA DIVISION, BATAVIA, NY, p. A439
VETERANS AFFAIRS WESTERN NEW YORK HEALTHCARE SYSTEM–BUFFALO DIVISION, BUFFALO, NY, p. A440
VETERANS HEALTH CARE SYSTEM OF THE OZARKS, FAYETTEVILLE, AR, p. A46
VETERANS MEMORIAL HOSPITAL, WAUKON, IA, p. A245
VHC HEALTH, ARLINGTON, VA, p. A673

VIA CHRISTI BEHAVIORAL HEALTH CENTER, WICHITA, KS, p. A262
VIA CHRISTI ST. JOSEPH, WICHITA, KS, p. A262
VIBRA HIGHLANDS REHABILITATION HOSPITAL OF EL PASO, EL PASO, TX, p. A617
VIBRA HOSPITAL – TAYLOR CAMPUS, LINCOLN PARK, MI, p. A332
VIBRA HOSPITAL OF BOISE, BOISE, ID, p. A180
VIBRA HOSPITAL OF CENTRAL DAKOTAS, MANDAN, ND, p. A482
VIBRA HOSPITAL OF CHARLESTON, MT. PLEASANT, SC, p. A569
VIBRA HOSPITAL OF CLEAR LAKE, WEBSTER, TX, p. A661
VIBRA HOSPITAL OF DENVER, THORNTON, CO, p. A114
VIBRA HOSPITAL OF FARGO, FARGO, ND, p. A481
VIBRA HOSPITAL OF HOUSTON, HOUSTON, TX, p. A628
VIBRA HOSPITAL OF NORTHERN CALIFORNIA, REDDING, CA, p. A85
VIBRA HOSPITAL OF RICHMOND, RICHMOND, VA, p. A682
VIBRA HOSPITAL OF SACRAMENTO, FOLSOM, CA, p. A63
VIBRA HOSPITAL OF SOUTHEASTERN MASSACHUSETTS, NEW BEDFORD, MA, p. A316
VIBRA HOSPITAL OF WESTERN MASSACHUSETTS–CENTRAL CAMPUS, ROCHDALE, MA, p. A317
VIBRA HOSPITALS OF SOUTHEASTERN MICHIGAN – TAYLOR CAMPUS, LINCOLN PARK, MI, p. A332
VIBRA REHABILITATION HOSPITAL OF AMARILLO, AMARILLO, TX, p. A596
VIBRA REHABILITATION HOSPITAL RANCHO MIRAGE, RANCHO MIRAGE, CA, p. A84
VIBRA SPECIALTY HOSPITAL OF PORTLAND, PORTLAND, OR, p. A531
VICKSBURG MEDICAL CENTER, VICKSBURG, MS, p. A369
VICTOR VALLEY GLOBAL MEDICAL CENTER, VICTORVILLE, CA, p. A100
VIDANT BEAUFORT HOSPITAL, WASHINGTON, NC, p. A477
VIDANT BERTIE HOSPITAL, WINDSOR, NC, p. A478
VIDANT CHOWAN HOSPITAL, EDENTON, NC, p. A467
VIDANT DUPLIN HOSPITAL, KENANSVILLE, NC, p. A471
VIDANT EDGECOMBE HOSPITAL, TARBORO, NC, p. A477
VIDANT MEDICAL CENTER, GREENVILLE, NC, p. A470
VIDANT NORTH HOSPITAL, ROANOKE RAPIDS, NC, p. A475
VIDANT ROANOKE–CHOWAN HOSPITAL, AHOSKIE, NC, p. A463
VILLA FELICIANA MEDICAL COMPLEX, JACKSON, LA, p. A283
VINCENT'S CHILTON HOSPITAL, CLANTON, AL, p. A18
VIRGINIA BAPTIST HOSPITAL, LYNCHBURG, VA, p. A679
VIRGINIA BEACH PSYCHIATRIC CENTER, VIRGINIA BEACH, VA, p. A685
VIRGINIA GAY HOSPITAL, VINTON, IA, p. A244
VIRGINIA MASON MEDICAL CENTER, SEATTLE, WA, p. A695
VIRTUA MARLTON, MARLTON, NJ, p. A423
VIRTUA MEMORIAL, MOUNT HOLLY, NJ, p. A424
VIRTUA MOUNT HOLLY HOSPITAL, MOUNT HOLLY, NJ, p. A424
VIRTUA OUR LADY OF LOURDES HOSPITAL, CAMDEN, NJ, p. A419
VIRTUA VOORHEES, VOORHEES, NJ, p. A430
VIRTUA WILLINGBORO HOSPITAL, WILLINGBORO, NJ, p. A431
VISALIA COMMUNITY HOSPITAL, VISALIA, CA, p. A100
VISTA DEL MAR HOSPITAL, VENTURA, CA, p. A100
VISTA HEALTH, WAUKEGAN, IL, p. A210
VISTA MEDICAL CENTER EAST, WAUKEGAN, IL, p. A210

W

WABASH GENERAL HOSPITAL, MOUNT CARMEL, IL, p. A202
WACO VETERANS AFFAIRS HOSPITAL, WACO, TX, p. A660
WADLEY REGIONAL MEDICAL CENTER, TEXARKANA, TX, p. A657
WADLEY REGIONAL MEDICAL CENTER AT HOPE, HOPE, AR, p. A47
WAGNER COMMUNITY MEMORIAL HOSPITAL AVERA, WAGNER, SD, p. A578
WAGONER COMMUNITY HOSPITAL, WAGONER, OK, p. A523
WAKE FOREST BAPTIST MEDICAL CENTER, WINSTON-SALEM, NC, p. A478
WAKEMED CARY HOSPITAL, CARY, NC, p. A464
WAKEMED NORTH FAMILY HEALTH AND WOMEN'S HOSPITAL, RALEIGH, NC, p. A475
WAKEMED RALEIGH CAMPUS, RALEIGH, NC, p. A475
WALDEN BEHAVIORAL CARE, WALTHAM, MA, p. A319
WALDO COUNTY GENERAL HOSPITAL, BELFAST, ME, p. A296
WALKER BAPTIST MEDICAL CENTER, JASPER, AL, p. A21
WALLOWA MEMORIAL HOSPITAL, ENTERPRISE, OR, p. A526

WALTER B. JONES ALCOHOL AND DRUG ABUSE TREATMENT CENTER, GREENVILLE, NC, p. A470
WALTER P. REUTHER PSYCHIATRIC HOSPITAL, WESTLAND, MI, p. A340
WALTER REED NATIONAL MILITARY MEDICAL CENTER, BETHESDA, MD, p. A303
WALTHALL COUNTY GENERAL HOSPITAL, TYLERTOWN, MS, p. A369
WALTHALL GENERAL HOSPITAL, TYLERTOWN, MS, p. A369
WALTON REHABILITATION HOSPITAL, AN AFFILIATE OF ENCOMPASS HEALTH, AUGUSTA, GA, p. A158
WAMEGO HEALTH CENTER, WAMEGO, KS, p. A261
WAR MEMORIAL HOSPITAL, SAULT SAINTE MARIE, MI, p. A338
WARD MEMORIAL HOSPITAL, MONAHANS, TX, p. A640
WARM SPRINGS MEDICAL CENTER, WARM SPRINGS, GA, p. A173
WARM SPRINGS REHABILITATION HOSPITAL OF KYLE, KYLE, TX, p. A633
WARM SPRINGS REHABILITATION HOSPITAL OF SAN ANTONIO, SAN ANTONIO, TX, p. A651
WARNER HOSPITAL AND HEALTH SERVICES, CLINTON, IL, p. A192
WARRACK HOSPITAL CAMPUS, SANTA ROSA, CA, p. A95
WARREN GENERAL HOSPITAL, WARREN, PA, p. A556
WARREN STATE HOSPITAL, WARREN, PA, p. A556
WASHAKIE MEDICAL CENTER, WORLAND, WY, p. A729
WASHINGTON ADVENTIST HOSPITAL, TAKOMA PARK, MD, p. A307
WASHINGTON COUNTY HOSPITAL, CHATOM, AL, p. A17
WASHINGTON COUNTY HOSPITAL, NASHVILLE, IL, p. A203
WASHINGTON COUNTY HOSPITAL, WASHINGTON, KS, p. A261
WASHINGTON COUNTY HOSPITAL AND CLINICS, WASHINGTON, IA, p. A244
WASHINGTON COUNTY MEMORIAL HOSPITAL, POTOSI, MO, p. A382
WASHINGTON COUNTY REGIONAL MEDICAL CENTER, SANDERSVILLE, GA, p. A170
WASHINGTON DC VETERANS AFFAIRS MEDICAL CENTER, WASHINGTON, DC, p. A124
WASHINGTON HOSPITAL HEALTHCARE SYSTEM, FREMONT, CA, p. A64
WASHINGTON REGIONAL MEDICAL CENTER, FAYETTEVILLE, AR, p. A46
WASHINGTON REGIONAL MEDICAL CENTER, PLYMOUTH, NC, p. A474
WASHINGTON REGIONAL MEDICAL SYSTEM, FAYETTEVILLE, AR, p. A46
WATAUGA MEDICAL CENTER, BOONE, NC, p. A464
WATERBURY HOSPITAL, WATERBURY, CT, p. A119
WATERTOWN REGIONAL MEDICAL CENTER, WATERTOWN, WI, p. A723
WATSONVILLE COMMUNITY HOSPITAL, WATSONVILLE, CA, p. A100
WAUKESHA COUNTY MENTAL HEALTH CENTER, WAUKESHA, WI, p. A723
WAUKESHA MEMORIAL HOSPITAL, WAUKESHA, WI, p. A724
WAUPUN MEMORIAL HOSPITAL, WAUPUN, WI, p. A724
WAVERLY HEALTH CENTER, WAVERLY, IA, p. A245
WAYNE COUNTY HOSPITAL, MONTICELLO, KY, p. A271
WAYNE COUNTY HOSPITAL AND CLINIC SYSTEM, CORYDON, IA, p. A233
WAYNE GENERAL HOSPITAL, WAYNE, NJ, p. A430
WAYNE GENERAL HOSPITAL, WAYNESBORO, MS, p. A369
WAYNE HEALTHCARE, GREENVILLE, OH, p. A497
WAYNE MEDICAL CENTER, WAYNESBORO, TN, p. A594
WAYNE MEMORIAL HOSPITAL, HONESDALE, PA, p. A542
WAYNE MEMORIAL HOSPITAL, JESUP, GA, p. A165
WEATHERFORD REGIONAL HOSPITAL, WEATHERFORD, OK, p. A524
WEBSTER COUNTY COMMUNITY HOSPITAL, RED CLOUD, NE, p. A405
WEBSTER COUNTY MEMORIAL HOSPITAL, WEBSTER SPRINGS, WV, p. A705
WEED ARMY COMMUNITY HOSPITAL, FORT IRWIN, CA, p. A63
WEEKS MEDICAL CENTER, LANCASTER, NH, p. A415
WEIRTON MEDICAL CENTER, WEIRTON, WV, p. A705
WEISBROD MEMORIAL COUNTY HOSPITAL, EADS, CO, p. A107
WEISER MEMORIAL HOSPITAL, WEISER, ID, p. A184
WEISMAN CHILDREN'S REHABILITATION HOSPITAL, MARLTON, NJ, p. A424
WEISS MEMORIAL HOSPITAL, CHICAGO, IL, p. A192
WEKIVA SPRINGS, JACKSONVILLE, FL, p. A135
WELCH COMMUNITY HOSPITAL, WELCH, WV, p. A705
WELIA HEALTH, MORA, MN, p. A351
WELKIND FACILITY, CHESTER, NJ, p. A419

Index of Hospitals / Women and Children's Hospital

WELLBRIDGE HEALTHCARE GREATER DALLAS, PLANO, TX, p. A645
WELLBRIDGE HEALTHCARE OF FORT WORTH, FORT WORTH, TX, p. A620
WELLFOUND BEHAVIORAL HEALTH HOSPITAL, TACOMA, WA, p. A697
WELLINGTON REGIONAL MEDICAL CENTER, WELLINGTON, FL, p. A154
WELLSPAN CHAMBERSBURG HOSPITAL, CHAMBERSBURG, PA, p. A536
WELLSPAN EPHRATA COMMUNITY HOSPITAL, EPHRATA, PA, p. A539
WELLSPAN GETTYSBURG HOSPITAL, GETTYSBURG, PA, p. A540
WELLSPAN GOOD SAMARITAN HOSPITAL, LEBANON, PA, p. A544
WELLSPAN PHILHAVEN, MOUNT GRETNA, PA, p. A546
WELLSPAN SURGERY AND REHABILITATION HOSPITAL, YORK, PA, p. A559
WELLSPAN WAYNESBORO HOSPITAL, WAYNESBORO, PA, p. A556
WELLSPAN YORK HOSPITAL, YORK, PA, p. A559
WELLSTAR COBB HOSPITAL, AUSTELL, GA, p. A159
WELLSTAR DOUGLAS HOSPITAL, DOUGLASVILLE, GA, p. A163
WELLSTAR KENNESTONE HOSPITAL, MARIETTA, GA, p. A167
WELLSTAR MCG HEALTH, AUGUSTA, GA, p. A158
WELLSTAR NORTH FULTON HOSPITAL, ROSWELL, GA, p. A170
WELLSTAR PAULDING HOSPITAL, HIRAM, GA, p. A165
WELLSTAR SPALDING REGIONAL HOSPITAL, GRIFFIN, GA, p. A164
WELLSTAR SYLVAN GROVE HOSPITAL, JACKSON, GA, p. A165
WELLSTAR WEST GEORGIA MEDICAL CENTER, LAGRANGE, GA, p. A166
WELLSTAR WINDY HILL HOSPITAL, MARIETTA, GA, p. A168
WELLSTONE REGIONAL HOSPITAL, JEFFERSONVILLE, IN, p. A221
WENTWORTH-DOUGLASS HOSPITAL, DOVER, NH, p. A414
WERNERSVILLE STATE HOSPITAL, WERNERSVILLE, PA, p. A557
WESLACO REGIONAL REHABILITATION HOSPITAL, WESLACO, TX, p. A662
WESLEY MEDICAL CENTER, WICHITA, KS, p. A262
WESLEY WOODS CENTER, ATLANTA, GA, p. A158
WESLEY WOODS GERIATRIC HOSPITAL OF EMORY UNIVERSITY, ATLANTA, GA, p. A158
WEST ANAHEIM MEDICAL CENTER, ANAHEIM, CA, p. A55
WEST BOCA MEDICAL CENTER, BOCA RATON, FL, p. A126
WEST CALCASIEU CAMERON HOSPITAL, SULPHUR, LA, p. A293
WEST CARROLL MEMORIAL HOSPITAL, OAK GROVE, LA, p. A290
WEST CENTRAL GEORGIA REGIONAL HOSPITAL, COLUMBUS, GA, p. A161
WEST CHASE HOUSTON HOSPITAL, HOUSTON, TX, p. A629
WEST CHESTER HOSPITAL, WEST CHESTER, OH, p. A506
WEST COVINA MEDICAL CENTER, WEST COVINA, CA, p. A101
WEST FELICIANA HOSPITAL, SAINT FRANCISVILLE, LA, p. A292
WEST FLORIDA HOSPITAL, PENSACOLA, FL, p. A147
WEST FLORIDA REHABILITATION INSTITUTE, PENSACOLA, FL, p. A147
WEST GABLES REHABILITATION HOSPITAL, MIAMI, FL, p. A141
WEST HILLS HOSPITAL AND MEDICAL CENTER, LOS ANGELES, CA, p. A76
WEST HOLT MEDICAL SERVICES, ATKINSON, NE, p. A397
WEST JEFFERSON MEDICAL CENTER, MARRERO, LA, p. A288
WEST MARION COMMUNITY HOSPITAL, OCALA, FL, p. A143
WEST OAKS HOSPITAL, HOUSTON, TX, p. A629
WEST PALM BEACH VETERANS AFFAIRS MEDICAL CENTER, WEST PALM BEACH, FL, p. A155
WEST PENN HOSPITAL, PITTSBURGH, PA, p. A552
WEST PINES AT LUTHERAN MED CTR, WHEAT RIDGE, CO, p. A114
WEST RIVER REGIONAL MEDICAL CENTER, HETTINGER, ND, p. A481
WEST SPRINGS HOSPITAL, GRAND JUNCTION, CO, p. A109
WEST SUBURBAN MEDICAL CENTER, OAK PARK, IL, p. A204
WEST TENNESSEE HEALTHCARE BOLIVAR HOSPITAL, BOLIVAR, TN, p. A579
WEST TENNESSEE HEALTHCARE CAMDEN HOSPITAL, CAMDEN, TN, p. A579
WEST TENNESSEE HEALTHCARE DYERSBURG HOSPITAL, DYERSBURG, TN, p. A582

WEST TENNESSEE HEALTHCARE MILAN HOSPITAL, MILAN, TN, p. A589
WEST TENNESSEE HEALTHCARE REHABILITATION HOSPITAL CANE CREEK, A PARTNERSHIP WITH ENCOMPASS HEALTH, MARTIN, TN, p. A587
WEST TENNESSEE HEALTHCARE REHABILITATION HOSPITAL JACKSON, A PARTNERSHIP WITH ENCOMPASS HEALTH, JACKSON, TN, p. A584
WEST TENNESSEE HEALTHCARE VOLUNTEER HOSPITAL, MARTIN, TN, p. A587
WEST TEXAS VA HEALTH CARE SYSTEM, BIG SPRING, TX, p. A604
WEST TEXAS VETERANS AFFAIRS HEALTH CARE SYSTEM, BIG SPRING, TX, p. A604
WEST VALLEY MEDICAL CENTER, CALDWELL, ID, p. A180
WEST VIRGINIA UNIVERSITY HOSPITALS, MORGANTOWN, WV, p. A703
WESTBOROUGH BEHAVIORAL HEALTHCARE HOSPITAL, WESTBOROUGH, MA, p. A319
WESTCHESTER MEDICAL CENTER, VALHALLA, NY, p. A461
WESTERLY HOSPITAL, WESTERLY, RI, p. A561
WESTERN ARIZONA REGIONAL MEDICAL CENTER, BULLHEAD CITY, AZ, p. A30
WESTERN MARYLAND HOSPITAL CENTER, HAGERSTOWN, MD, p. A305
WESTERN MASSACHUSETTS HOSPITAL, WESTFIELD, MA, p. A319
WESTERN MENTAL HEALTH INSTITUTE, BOLIVAR, TN, p. A579
WESTERN MISSOURI MEDICAL CENTER, WARRENSBURG, MO, p. A388
WESTERN NEW YORK CHILDREN'S PSYCHIATRIC CENTER, WEST SENECA, NY, p. A462
WESTERN PSYCHIATRIC INSTITUTE AND CLINIC, PITTSBURGH, PA, p. A552
WESTERN RESERVE HOSPITAL, CUYAHOGA FALLS, OH, p. A493
WESTERN STATE HOSPITAL, HOPKINSVILLE, KY, p. A267
WESTERN STATE HOSPITAL, STAUNTON, VA, p. A684
WESTERN STATE HOSPITAL, TACOMA, WA, p. A697
WESTERN WISCONSIN HEALTH, BALDWIN, WI, p. A707
WESTFIELD MEMORIAL HOSPITAL, WESTFIELD, NY, p. A462
WESTFIELDS HOSPITAL AND CLINIC, NEW RICHMOND, WI, p. A718
WESTON COUNTY HEALTH SERVICES, NEWCASTLE, WY, p. A727
WESTPARK SPRINGS, RICHMOND, TX, p. A646
WETZEL COUNTY HOSPITAL, NEW MARTINSVILLE, WV, p. A703
W. G. (BILL) HEFFNER VETERANS AFFAIRS MEDICAL CENTER, SALISBURY, NC, p. A476
WHEATLAND MEMORIAL HEALTHCARE, HARLOWTON, MT, p. A393
WHEELING HOSPITAL, WHEELING, WV, p. A706
WHIDBEYHEALTH, COUPEVILLE, WA, p. A688
WHIDDEN MEMORIAL HOSPITAL, EVERETT, MA, p. A313
WHITE COUNTY MEDICAL CENTER – SOUTH CAMPUS, SEARCY, AR, p. A53
WHITE MOUNTAIN REGIONAL MEDICAL CENTER, SPRINGERVILLE, AZ, p. A39
WHITE PLAINS HOSPITAL CENTER, WHITE PLAINS, NY, p. A462
WHITE RIVER HEALTH, BATESVILLE, AR, p. A43
WHITE RIVER JUNCTION VETERANS AFFAIRS MEDICAL CENTER, WHITE RIVER JUNCTION, VT, p. A672
WHITE RIVER MEDICAL CENTER, BATESVILLE, AR, p. A43
WHITE ROCK MEDICAL CENTER, DALLAS, TX, p. A613
WHITESBURG ARH HOSPITAL, WHITESBURG, KY, p. A275
WHITFIELD REGIONAL HOSPITAL, DEMOPOLIS, AL, p. A18
WHITING FORENSIC DIVISION OF CONNECTICUT VALLEY HOSPITAL, MIDDLETOWN, CT, p. A117
WHITING FORENSIC HOSPITAL, MIDDLETOWN, CT, p. A117
WHITINSVILLE HOSPITAL, WHITINSVILLE, MA, p. A319
WHITINSVILLE MEDICAL CENTER, WHITINSVILLE, MA, p. A319
WHITMAN HOSPITAL AND MEDICAL CENTER, COLFAX, WA, p. A688
WHITTIER HOSPITAL MEDICAL CENTER, WHITTIER, CA, p. A101
WHITTIER PAVILION, HAVERHILL, MA, p. A314
WHITTIER REHABILITATION HOSPITAL, BRADFORD, MA, p. A311
WHITTIER REHABILITATION HOSPITAL, WESTBOROUGH, MA, p. A319
WICHITA COUNTY HEALTH CENTER, LEOTI, KS, p. A253
WICHITA VAMC, WICHITA, KS, p. A262
WICKENBURG COMMUNITY HOSPITAL, WICKENBURG, AZ, p. A41
WILBARGER GENERAL HOSPITAL, VERNON, TX, p. A659
WILCOX MEDICAL CENTER, LIHUE, HI, p. A177

WILKES-BARRE GENERAL HOSPITAL, WILKES-BARRE, PA, p. A558
WILKES-BARRE VETERANS AFFAIRS MEDICAL CENTER, WILKES-BARRE, PA, p. A558
WILLAMETTE VALLEY MEDICAL CENTER, MCMINNVILLE, OR, p. A529
WILLAPA HARBOR HOSPITAL, SOUTH BEND, WA, p. A696
WILLIAM BEAUMONT ARMY MEDICAL CENTER, EL PASO, TX, p. A617
WILLIAM BEE RIRIE HOSPITAL, ELY, NV, p. A408
WILLIAM J. MCCORD ADOLESCENT TREATMENT FACILITY, ORANGEBURG, SC, p. A569
WILLIAM NEWTON HOSPITAL, WINFIELD, KS, p. A262
WILLIAM R. SHARPE, JR. HOSPITAL, WESTON, WV, p. A706
WILLIAM S. HALL PSYCHIATRIC INSTITUTE, COLUMBIA, SC, p. A565
WILLIAM S. MIDDLETON MEMORIAL VETERANS' HOSPITAL, MADISON, WI, p. A715
WILLIAMS COUNTY GEN HOSPITAL, MONTPELIER, OH, p. A500
WILLIAMSON MEDICAL CENTER, FRANKLIN, TN, p. A583
WILLINGWAY HOSPITAL, STATESBORO, GA, p. A172
WILLIS KNIGHTON NORTH, SHREVEPORT, LA, p. A293
WILLIS-KNIGHT BOSSIER, BOSSIER CITY, LA, p. A279
WILLIS-KNIGHTON NORTH, SHREVEPORT, LA, p. A293
WILLIS-KNIGHTON PIERREMONT, SHREVEPORT, LA, p. A293
WILLIS-KNIGHTON SOUTH, SHREVEPORT, LA, p. A293
WILLOW CREEK BEHAVIORAL HEALTH, GREEN BAY, WI, p. A712
WILLOW CREST HOSPITAL, MIAMI, OK, p. A515
WILLOW ROCK CENTER, SAN LEANDRO, CA, p. A92
WILLOW SPRINGS CENTER, RENO, NV, p. A412
WILLOW VIEW MENTAL HLTH SYSTEM, SPENCER, OK, p. A521
WILLS EYE HOSPITAL, PHILADELPHIA, PA, p. A550
WILLS MEMORIAL HOSPITAL, WASHINGTON, GA, p. A174
WILMA N. VAZQUEZ MEDICAL CENTER, VEGA BAJA, PR, p. A736
WILMED NURSING CARE CENTER, WILSON, NC, p. A478
WILMINGTON TREATMENT CENTER, WILMINGTON, NC, p. A478
WILMINGTON VETERANS AFFAIRS MEDICAL CENTER, WILMINGTON, DE, p. A122
WILSON MEDICAL CENTER, NEODESHA, KS, p. A255
WILSON MEDICAL CENTER, WILSON, NC, p. A478
WILSON MEMORIAL HOSPITAL, SIDNEY, OH, p. A503
WILSON MEMORIAL REG MED CTR, JOHNSON CITY, NY, p. A444
WILSON MEMORIAL REGIONAL MEDICAL CENTER, JOHNSON CITY, NY, p. A444
WINCHESTER HOSPITAL, WINCHESTER, MA, p. A320
WINDHAM HOSPITAL, WILLIMANTIC, CT, p. A120
WINDHAVEN PSYCHIATRIC HOSPITAL, PRESCOTT VALLEY, AZ, p. A37
WINDMOOR HEALTHCARE OF CLEARWATER, CLEARWATER, FL, p. A128
WINDOM AREA HEALTH, WINDOM, MN, p. A357
WINDSOR-LAURELWOOD CENTER FOR BEHAVIORAL MEDICINE, WILLOUGHBY, OH, p. A507
WINKLER COUNTY MEMORIAL HOSPITAL, KERMIT, TX, p. A632
WINN ARMY COMMUNITY HOSPITAL, HINESVILLE, GA, p. A165
WINN PARISH MEDICAL CENTER, WINNFIELD, LA, p. A294
WINNEBAGO MENTAL HEALTH INSTITUTE, WINNEBAGO, WI, p. A725
WINNER REGIONAL HEALTHCARE CENTER, WINNER, SD, p. A578
WINNESHIEK MEDICAL CENTER, DECORAH, IA, p. A234
WINNIE PALMER HOSPITAL FOR WOMEN AND BABIES, ORLANDO, FL, p. A145
WINNMED, DECORAH, IA, p. A234
WINONA HEALTH, WINONA, MN, p. A357
WINSTON MEDICAL CENTER, LOUISVILLE, MS, p. A365
WINTER HAVEN HOSPITAL, WINTER HAVEN, FL, p. A155
WINTER PARK MEMORIAL HOSPITAL, WINTER PARK, FL, p. A155
WIREGRASS MEDICAL CENTER, GENEVA, AL, p. A20
WITHAM HEALTH SERVICES, LEBANON, IN, p. A222
W. J. MANGOLD MEMORIAL HOSPITAL, LOCKNEY, TX, p. A635
WOMACK ARMY MEDICAL CENTER, FORT BRAGG, NC, p. A468
WOMAN'S HOSPITAL, BATON ROUGE, LA, p. A278
WOMAN'S HOSPITAL OF TEXAS, HOUSTON, TX, p. A629
WOMEN & INFANTS HOSPITAL OF RHODE ISLAND, PROVIDENCE, RI, p. A561
WOMEN AND CHILDREN'S HOSP, CHARLESTON, WV, p. A700
WOMEN AND CHILDREN'S HOSPITAL, BUFFALO, NY, p. A440

WOMEN'S AND CHILDREN'S HOSPITAL, LAFAYETTE, LA, p. A286
WOMEN'S HOSPITAL, LOS ANGELES, CA, p. A76
WOMEN'S HOSPITAL-INDIANAPOLIS, INDIANAPOLIS, IN, p. A220
WOOD COUNTY HOSPITAL, BOWLING GREEN, OH, p. A487
WOODLAND HEALTHCARE, WOODLAND, CA, p. A101
WOODLAND HEIGHTS MEDICAL CENTER, LUFKIN, TX, p. A637
WOODLAND MEMORIAL HOSPITAL, WOODLAND, CA, p. A101
WOODLAND SPRINGS HOSPITAL, CONROE, TX, p. A608
WOODLAWN HOSPITAL, ROCHESTER, IN, p. A226
WOODWINDS HEALTH CAMPUS, WOODBURY, MN, p. A357
WOOSTER COMMUNITY HOSPITAL, WOOSTER, OH, p. A507
WORCESTER HAHNEMANN HOSPITAL, WORCESTER, MA, p. A320
WORCESTER MEMORIAL HOSPITAL, WORCESTER, MA, p. A320
WORCESTER RECOVERY CENTER AND HOSPITAL, WORCESTER, MA, p. A320
WRANGELL MEDICAL CENTER, WRANGELL, AK, p. A29
WRAY COMMUNITY DISTRICT HOSPITAL, WRAY, CO, p. A114
WRIGHT MEMORIAL HOSPITAL, TRENTON, MO, p. A387
WRIGHT PATTERSON MEDICAL CENTER, WRIGHT-PATTERSON AFB, OH, p. A507
WVU MEDICINE – BARNESVILLE HOSPITAL, BARNESVILLE, OH, p. A485
WVU MEDICINE – HARRISON COMMUNITY HOSPITAL, CADIZ, OH, p. A487
WVU MEDICINE JACKSON GENERAL HOSPITAL, RIPLEY, WV, p. A704
WVU MEDICINE POTOMAC VALLEY HOSPITAL, KEYSER, WV, p. A702
WVU MEDICINE UNIONTOWN HOSPITAL, UNIONTOWN, PA, p. A556
WYANDOT MEMORIAL HOSPITAL, UPPER SANDUSKY, OH, p. A505
WYCKOFF HEIGHTS MEDICAL CENTER, NEW YORK, NY, p. A453
WYNN HOSPITAL, UTICA, NY, p. A460
WYOMING BEHAVIORAL INSTITUTE, CASPER, WY, p. A726
WYOMING COUNTY COMMUNITY HOSPITAL, WARSAW, NY, p. A461
WYOMING MEDICAL CENTER, CASPER, WY, p. A726
WYOMING STATE HOSPITAL, EVANSTON, WY, p. A727
WYTHE COUNTY COMMUNITY HOSPITAL, WYTHEVILLE, VA, p. A686

Y

YALE NEW HAVEN HOSPITAL, NEW HAVEN, CT, p. A118
YALE PSYCHIATRIC INSTITUTE, NEW HAVEN, CT, p. A118
YALOBUSHA GENERAL HOSPITAL, WATER VALLEY, MS, p. A369
YANCEY COMMUNITY MEDICAL CENTER, BURNSVILLE, NC, p. A464
YAVAPAI REGIONAL MEDICAL CENTER, PRESCOTT, AZ, p. A37
YOAKUM COMMUNITY HOSPITAL, YOAKUM, TX, p. A663
YOAKUM COUNTY HOSPITAL, DENVER CITY, TX, p. A614
YONKERS GENERAL HOSPITAL, YONKERS, NY, p. A462
YORK GENERAL, YORK, NE, p. A407
YORK HOSPITAL, YORK, ME, p. A299
YOUTH VILLAGES INNER HARBOUR CAMPUS, DOUGLASVILLE, GA, p. A163
YUKON–KUSKOKWIM DELTA REGIONAL HOSPITAL, BETHEL, AK, p. A27
YUMA DISTRICT HOSPITAL, YUMA, CO, p. A114
YUMA REGIONAL MEDICAL CENTER, YUMA, AZ, p. A42
YUMA REHABILITATION HOSPITAL, AN AFFILIATION OF ENCOMPASS HEALTH AND YUMA REGIONAL MEDICAL CENTER, YUMA, AZ, p. A42

Z

ZALE LIPSHY UNIV HOSPITAL, DALLAS, TX, p. A613
ZUCKER HILLSIDE HOSPITAL, NEW YORK, NY, p. A453
ZUCKERBERG SAN FRANCISCO GENERAL HOSPITAL AND TRAUMA CENTER, SAN FRANCISCO, CA, p. A91

Index of Health Care Professionals

This section is an index of the key health care professionals for the hospitals and/or health care systems listed in this publication. The index is in alphabetical order, by individual, followed by the title, institutional affiliation, city, state and page reference to the hospital and/or health care system listing in section A and/or B.

A

AAGARD, Kim, Chief Financial Officer, Astera Health, Wadena, MN, p. A356
AALBORG, Chase, Chief Operating Officer, Adventhealth Littleton, Littleton, CO, p. A111
AASVED, Craig E., Chief Executive Officer, Shodair Children's Hospital, Helena, MT, p. A393
ABAD, Ann, President, Missouri Baptist Medical Center, Saint Louis, MO, p. A385
ABAIR, Cynthia, Associate Director, Jennifer Moreno Department of Veterans Affairs Medical Center, San Diego, CA, p. A88
ABAN, Chona, Controller, Kindred Hospital Chicago–Northlake, Northlake, IL, p. A204
ABANG, Toni, M.D., Medical Director, Encompass Health Rehabilitation Hospital of Lakeview, Elizabethtown, KY, p. A265
ABBATE, Anthony, Director of Information Services, San Ramon Regional Medical Center, San Ramon, CA, p. A93
ABBOTT, Ed, Vice President Finance, Methodist Richardson Medical Center, Richardson, TX, p. A646
ABBOTT, Justin, M.D., Medical Director, Sevier Valley Hospital, Richfield, UT, p. A668
ABBOTT, Peggy L., President and Chief Executive Officer, Ouachita County Medical Center, Camden, AR, p. A44
ABBOTT, Rhonda
  Senior Vice President and Chief Executive Officer, Memorial Hermann Rehabilitation Hospital – Katy, Katy, TX, p. A631
  Senior Vice President and Chief Executive Officer, Tirr Memorial Hermann, Houston, TX, p. A628
ABBOUD, Josie, R.N., FACHE, President and Chief Executive Officer, Nebraska Methodist Hospital, Omaha, NE, p. A404
ABDA, William, Chief Human Resources Officer, Clarks Summit State Hospital, Clarks Summit, PA, p. A537
ABDELKARIM, Riad Z., M.D., Vice President and Chief Medical Officer, Providence St. Mary Medical Center, Apple Valley, CA, p. A56
ABDO, Abed, Chief Financial Officer, St. Jude Children's Research Hospital, Memphis, TN, p. A589
ABEL, Danielle, Vice President of Patient Care Services, Chi Lakewood Health, Baudette, MN, p. A343
ABEL, Jared
  Chief Executive Officer, Amberwell Health, Atchison, KS, p. A246
  Chief Executive Officer, Amberwell Hiawatha, Hiawatha, KS, p. A250
ABEL, Jeffrey, M.D., Chief Medical Officer, Ogden Regional Medical Center, Ogden, UT, p. A666
ABEL, Kevin
  Chief Executive Officer, Logan Health – Whitefish, Whitefish, MT, p. A396
  Chief Executive Officer, Logan Health, Kalispell, MT, p. A393
ABEL, Stacy L, Vice President People and Culture, Craig Hospital, Englewood, CO, p. A107
ABELLERA, Roland, Vice President and Chief Operating Officer, St. Bernard Hospital And Health Care Center, Chicago, IL, p. A191
ABELY, Susan Cerrone
  Chief Information Officer, St. Josep. Health Services of Rhode Island, North Providence, RI, p. A560
  Vice President and Chief Information Officer, Roger Williams Medical Center, Providence, RI, p. A561
ABERCROMBIE, Zach, Chief Financial Officer, Citizens Baptist Medical Center, Talladega, AL, p. A24
ABERLE, James, President, Legacy Mount Hood Medical Center, Gresham, OR, p. A527
ABERNATHY, Clint, President, Texas Health Harris Methodist Hospital Alliance, Fort Worth, TX, p. A620
ABERNATHY, Marietta Kaye, Chief Nursing Officer, Atrium Health Stanly, Albemarle, NC, p. A463
ABERNETHY, Allen, Chief Executive Officer, Musc Health Black River Medical Center, Cades, SC, p. A562

ABEY, Michelle, Chief Financial Officer, Stoughton Health, Stoughton, WI, p. A722
ABLA, Mike, Director of Nursing, Griffin Memorial Hospital, Norman, OK, p. A516
ABNEY, Stuart, Controller, Jasper Memorial Hospital, Monticello, GA, p. A168
ABRAHAM, Akram, M.D., Chief of Staff, Harmon Memorial Hospital, Hollis, OK, p. A513
ABRAHAM, Brian, Regional Chief Executive Officer, Clearsky Rehabilitation Hospital of Flower Mound, Flower Mound, TX, p. A618
ABRAHAM, JiJi
  Area Chief Financial Officer, Kaiser Permanente Moreno Valley Medical Center, Moreno Valley, CA, p. A78
  Chief Financial Officer, Kaiser Permanente Riverside Medical Center, Riverside, CA, p. A86
ABRAHAMSON-BATY, Sherri, Director Patient Care Services, Cambridge Medical Center, Cambridge, MN, p. A344
ABRAHAMY, Ran, M.D., Chief of Staff, HCA Florida Woodmont Hospital, Tamarac, FL, p. A151
ABRAMS, Jose, Chief Information Officer, St. Luke's Episcopal Hospital, Ponce, PR, p. A734
ABREU, Iris, Supervisor Human Resources, Hospital Hima De Humacao, Humacao, PR, p. A733
ABREU, John, Vice President and Chief Financial Officer, Portneuf Medical Center, Pocatello, ID, p. A183
ABRUTZ, Josep. F. Jr, Administrator, Cameron Regional Medical Center, Cameron, MO, p. A372
ABSALON, Jeffrey
  M.D., Chief Physician Officer, St. Charles Bend, Bend, OR, p. A525
  M.D., Chief Physician Officer, St. Charles Redmond, Redmond, OR, p. A531
ABSHIER, Trey, Chief Executive Officer, Ascension Sacred Heart Emerald Coast, Miramar Beach, FL, p. A141
ACEBO, Raymond, M.D., Administrator/Chief Medical Officer, Christus Spohn Hospital Corpus Christi Shoreline, Corpus Christi, TX, p. A608
ACETO, Anthony, Vice President Human Resources, Norwalk Hospital, Norwalk, CT, p. A118
ACEVEDO, Edwin Orama, Financial Supervisor, Hospital Buen Samaritano, Aguadilla, PR, p. A730
ACEVEDO, Elizabeth, Director Human Resources, Houston Methodist Willowbrook Hospital, Houston, TX, p. A626
ACEVEDO, Jose
  M.D., President and Chief Executive Officer, Geneva General Hospital, Geneva, NY, p. A443
  M.D., President and Chief Executive Officer, Soldiers And Sailors Memorial Hospital, Penn Yan, NY, p. A456
ACEVEDO, Ramon, Supervisor Information Systems, Hospital Menonita Ponce, Coto Laurel, PR, p. A732
ACHEBE, James Bob, M.D., President Medical Staff, South Shore Hospital, Chicago, IL, p. A191
ACHTER, Dick, Chief Financial Officer, Barrett Hospital & Healthcare, Dillon, MT, p. A391
ACHURY, Dario, Director of Information Management, St. Anthony's Rehabilitation Hospital, Lauderdale Lakes, FL, p. A137
ACKERMAN, Kenneth F.
  FACHE, Chair, Hospital Operation, Mayo Clinic Hospital – Rochester, Rochester, MN, p. A353
  FACHE, Hospital Administrator, Mayo Clinic Health System In Cannon Falls, Cannon Falls, MN, p. A344
ACKERSON, David, Chief Information Officer, Fred Hutchinson Cancer Center, Seattle, WA, p. A694
ACKERT, Sara, Executive Director and Chief Executive Officer, Royal C. Johnson Veterans' Memorial Hospital, Sioux Falls, SD, p. A576
ACKLEY, Michael
  Chief Financial Officer, Kentucky River Medical Center, Jackson, KY, p. A267
  Chief Financial Officer, Three Rivers Medical Center, Louisa, KY, p. A269
ACKLIN, Traci, M.D., Chief of Staff, Montgomery General Hospital, Montgomery, WV, p. A702
ACKMAN, Jeffrey D., M.D., Chief of Staff, Shriners Hospitals for Children–Chicago, Chicago, IL, p. A191
ACOSTA, Ivan, M.D., Medical Director, Hospital De La Concepcion, San German, PR, p. A734

ACOSTA, Louis, M.D., Chief of Staff, La Downtown Medical Center, Llc, Los Angeles, CA, p. A73
ACOSTA, Todd, R.N., Chief Nursing Officer, Hood Memorial Hospital, Amite, LA, p. A276
ACOSTA-CARLSON, Francisca, M.D., Chief of Staff, Lexington Regional Health Center, Lexington, NE, p. A401
ACREE, Charis L, Vice President and Chief Operating Officer, Wellstar West Georgia Medical Center, Lagrange, GA, p. A166
ACUS, Scott, Chief Executive Officer, Denver Springs, Englewood, CO, p. A107
ADAIR, Alonna, R.N., MSN, Chief Nurse Executive, Claremore Indian Hospital, Claremore, OK, p. A511
ADAIR, Dale K, M.D., Chief Medical Officer, Wernersville State Hospital, Wernersville, PA, p. A557
ADAIR, Julie, Interim Corporate Chief Human Resources Officer, Fresno Heart And Surgical Hospital, Fresno, CA, p. A64
ADAM, Nazir A., M.D., Chief Medical Officer, Musc Health – Orangeburg, Orangeburg, SC, p. A569
ADAM, Sheryl, Chief Financial Officer, Hanover Hospital, Hanover, KS, p. A250
ADAM, Suzanne, D.O., Medical Director, Encompass Health Rehabilitation Hospital of Reading, Reading, PA, p. A553
ADAMO, James D., M.D., Medical Director, Harbor Oaks Hospital, New Baltimore, MI, p. A334
ADAMO, Peter J.
  Regional Market President, SW Region/President, Penn Highlands Mon Valley, Penn Highlands Connellsville, Connellsville, PA, p. A537
  Regional Market President, SW Region/President, Penn Highlands Mon Valley, Penn Highlands Mon Valley, Monongahela, PA, p. A546
ADAMS, Amy Lynn., Chief Executive Officer, Encompass Health Rehabilitation Hospital of Nittany Valley, Pleasant Gap, PA, p. A552
ADAMS, Bob, Director Information Services, Bay Area Hospital, Coos Bay, OR, p. A526
ADAMS, Carla, Chief Nursing Officer, Northern Nevada Medical Center, Sparks, NV, p. A413
ADAMS, Carrie, Chief Operating Officer, Meritus Health, Hagerstown, MD, p. A305
ADAMS, Cathleen, Chief Nursing Officer, Carepartners Rehabilitation Hospital, Asheville, NC, p. A463
ADAMS, Charlotte, Director of Human Resources, Carolina Pines Regional Medical Center, Hartsville, SC, p. A568
ADAMS, Chris, Vice President Patient Care Services, SSM Health Good Samaritan Hospital, Mount Vernon, IL, p. A202
ADAMS, Cynthia, Vice President Human Resources, Tristar Stonecrest Medical Center, Smyrna, TN, p. A593
ADAMS, Cynthia D, Ph.D., R.N., Chief Nursing Officer, Ascension St. Vincent Indianapolis Hospital, Indianapolis, IN, p. A219
ADAMS, Denise, Human Resources Generalist, Hancock County Hospital, Sneedville, TN, p. A593
ADAMS, Emmy
  Chief Financial Officer, Aspen Grove Behavioral Hospital, Orem, UT, p. A666
  Chief Financial Officer, Mayhill Hospital, Denton, TX, p. A614
ADAMS, Essie, Director of Nursing, Kedren Community Health Center, Los Angeles, CA, p. A73
ADAMS, Felicia M, MS, Chief Nursing Officer, Adventist Health Columbia Gorge, The Dalles, OR, p. A532
ADAMS, Gini, Director Employee and Public Relations, Yuma District Hospital, Yuma, CO, p. A114
ADAMS, Heather, Chief Nursing Officer, JFK Memorial Hospital, Indio, CA, p. A67
ADAMS, J'Dee, Chief Executive Officer, North Canyon Medical Center, Gooding, ID, p. A181
ADAMS, Jan, Chief Financial Officer, Covington Behavioral Health, Covington, LA, p. A280
ADAMS, Jason, M.D.
  Medical Staff President, Forest Health Medical Center, Ypsilanti, MI, p. A341
  Chief Operating Officer, Chi Saint Josep. Health – Saint Josep. East, Lexington, KY, p. A268
  Chief Operating Officer, Chi Saint Josep. Health, Lexington, KY, p. A268

Index of Health Care Professionals

Index of Health Care Professionals / Adams

Preisdent, Christus St. Michael Health System, Texarkana, TX, p. A656
President, Christus St. Michael Health System, Texarkana, TX, p. A656
ADAMS, Jill B.
Chief Operating Officer and Chief Financial Officer, HCA Florida Lake City Hospital, Lake City, FL, p. A136
Interim Chief Executive Officer, HCA Florida Lake City Hospital, Lake City, FL, p. A136
ADAMS, Jo, Director Human Resources, Donalsonville Hospital, Donalsonville, GA, p. A163
ADAMS, John, Hospital Chief Executive officer, Presbyterian Santa Fe Medical Center, Santa Fe, NM, p. A437
ADAMS, Karen, Vice President Human Resources, Baxter Health, Mountain Home, AR, p. A51
ADAMS, Kelly, Chief Executive Officer, Mesa View Regional Hospital, Mesquite, NV, p. A411
ADAMS, Kimberly, Manager Human Resources, Carroll County Memorial Hospital, Carrollton, KY, p. A264
ADAMS, Lana, Chief Financial Officer, White Rock Medical Center, Dallas, TX, p. A613
ADAMS, Leslie, Chief Nursing Executive, Chi Saint Josep. Health – Saint Josep. Berea, Berea, KY, p. A263
ADAMS, Mark B., Chief Executive Officer, Ogden Regional Medical Center, Ogden, UT, p. A666
ADAMS, Mark C., M.D., Chief Medical Officer, El Camino Health, Mountain View, CA, p. A79
ADAMS, Marlene J, Director Human Resources, Schneider Regional Medical Center, Saint Thomas, VI, p. A736
ADAMS, Marsha, Interim Director Human Resources, Texas Health Harris Methodist Hospital Cleburne, Cleburne, TX, p. A607
ADAMS, Martin D., CPA, Vice President Finance and Chief Financial Officer, Paris Community Hospital, Paris, IL, p. A205
ADAMS, Mary Jane, R.N., MSN, Senior Vice President and Chief Nursing Officer, Uofl Health – Uofl Hospital, Louisville, KY, p. A270
ADAMS, Matthew, President, Ascension St. John Broken Arrow, Broken Arrow, OK, p. A510
ADAMS, Nancy D., R.N., Senior Vice President and Chief Operating Officer, UPMC Western Maryland, Cumberland, MD, p. A304
ADAMS, Norma, Director Human Resources, Southern Regional Medical Center, Riverdale, GA, p. A170
ADAMS, Patsy, Vice President Human Resources, Adventhealth Redmond, Rome, GA, p. A170
ADAMS, Renee, Director Information Technology, Chan Soon-Shiong Medical Center At Windber, Windber, PA, p. A558
ADAMS, Rob, Chief Executive Officer, Quillen Rehabilitation Hospital, A Joint Venture of Ballad Health And Encompass Health, Johnson City, TN, p. A585
ADAMS, Robert H, Vice President Operations, Hackensack Meridian Health Jersey Shore University Medical Center, Neptune, NJ, p. A424
ADAMS, Robert H.
President, Western Region, Hackettstown Medical Center, Hackettstown, NJ, p. A421
President, Western Region, Newton Medical Center, Newton, NJ, p. A426
ADAMS, Robin, Director Human Resources, Reeves Memorial Medical Center, Bernice, LA, p. A278
ADAMS, Russell, M.D., Chief Medical Officer, Unitypoint Health – Marshalltown, Marshalltown, IA, p. A240
ADAMS, Shannon, Chief Financial Officer, Avera Holy Family Hospital, Estherville, IA, p. A236
ADAMS, Sharon, President, Danbury Hospital, Danbury, CT, p. A115
ADAMS, Shaun, Chief Financial Officer, Southern Tennessee Regional Health System–Winchester, Winchester, TN, p. A594
ADAMS, Shawn, Chief Financial Officer, Christus Southeast Texas Hospital – St. Elizabeth, Beaumont, TX, p. A602
ADAMS, Susan, Chief Nursing Officer and Chief Operating Officer, Specialty Hospital of Lorain, Amherst, OH, p. A484
ADAMS, T Gard, M.D., Chief of Staff, Mclaren Caro Region, Caro, MI, p. A323
ADAMS, Winnie R, Chief Nursing Officer, Astria Sunnyside Hospital, Sunnyside, WA, p. A696
ADAMSKI, Joseph, Chief Nursing Officer, Encompass Health Rehabilitation Hospital of Concord, Concord, NH, p. A414
ADAMSON, James
Chief Executive Officer, Idaho Falls Community Hospital, Idaho Falls, ID, p. A181
Chief Executive Officer, Mountain View Hospital, Idaho Falls, ID, p. A181
ADAMSON, Nancy, Chief Nursing Officer, Banner Del E. Webb Medical Center, Sun City West, AZ, p. A39
ADCOCK, Brad, Chief Financial Officer, Union General Hospital, Farmerville, LA, p. A281
ADCOCK, Dana, Chief Executive Officer, Mason District Hospital, Havana, IL, p. A197
ADCOCK, Robert S., FACHE, President and Chief Executive Officer, Springfield Hospital, Springfield, VT, p. A672
ADDESSI, Shasta, Interim Senior Vice President and Area Manager, Kaiser Permanente South San Francisco Medical Center, South San Francisco, CA, p. A96
ADDINGTON, Tom, Chief Information Officer, Saint Michael's Medical Center, Newark, NJ, p. A425
ADDISON, John Bruce, D.O., Chief Medical Officer, Mccamey County Hospital District, Mccamey, TX, p. A638
ADDISON, Lenora, Vice President Patient Care and Nursing, Medstar Harbor Hospital, Baltimore, MD, p. A301
ADDISON, Lewis C, Senior Vice President and Chief Financial Officer, Centra Lynchburg General Hospital, Lynchburg, VA, p. A678
ADDLESPERGER, John, D.O., Chief Medical Officer, Sheridan Memorial Hospital, Sheridan, WY, p. A728
ADDO, Deborah, Executive Vice Preisdent and Chief Operating Officer, Penn State Health Hampden Medical Center, Enola, PA, p. A539
ADEEL, Mohammed, Medical Director, Encompass Health Deaconess Rehabilitation Hospital, Newburgh, IN, p. A225
ADELEKAN, Ade, Chief Nursing Officer, Continuecare Hospital At Medical Center (Odessa), Odessa, TX, p. A641
ADEMA, Carolyn, Senior Vice President, St. Tammany Health System, Covington, LA, p. A280
ADEN, Susie, Director, Inpatient Services, Pocahontas Community Hospital, Pocahontas, IA, p. A242
ADEOYE, Martins, M.D., Chief Medical Officer, Miracare Behavioral Health Care, Tinley Park, IL, p. A210
ADER, Michael H, M.D., Vice President Medical Affairs, UPMC Hanover, Hanover, PA, p. A541
ADERS, Deb, MS, R.N., Vice President Patient Care Services, Chief Nursing Officer, Yuma Regional Medical Center, Yuma, AZ, p. A42
ADESSO, Patrick
Director Information Technology and Systems, HCA Florida Memorial Hospital, Jacksonville, FL, p. A134
Director Information Technology and Systems, Pam Health Specialty Hospital of Jacksonville, Jacksonville, FL, p. A135
ADIGA, Raghu
M.D., Chief Medical Officer, Liberty Hospital, Liberty, MO, p. A379
M.D., President and Chief Executive Officer, Liberty Hospital, Liberty, MO, p. A379
ADKINS, Gary W, Chief Executive Officer, Parkview Noble Hospital, Kendallville, IN, p. A221
ADKINS, Kevin, Director Human Resources, Medical City Green Oaks Hospital, Dallas, TX, p. A611
ADKINS, Melisa, Chief Executive Officer, Uofl Health – Mary And Elizabeth Hospital, Louisville, KY, p. A270
ADKINS, Michael T., Chief Executive Officer, Cleveland Emergency Hospital, Humble, TX, p. A629
ADKINS, Paige, Chief Financial Officer, Camc Greenbrier Valley Medical Center, Ronceverte, WV, p. A704
ADKINS, Raymond, Chief Information Officer, Tidalhealth Peninsula Regional, Salisbury, MD, p. A307
ADKINS, Scott, Manager Information Technology, Vernon Memorial Healthcare, Elk Mound, WI, p. A710
ADKINS, Tyler, Chief Financial Officer, Vaughan Regional Medical Center, Selma, AL, p. A24
ADLER, Josh, M.D., Chief Medical Officer, UCSF Medical Center, San Francisco, CA, p. A91
ADLER, Kenneth, M.D., Medical Director, Arrowhead Behavioral Health Hospital, Maumee, OH, p. A499
ADLER, Marc, M.D., Senior Vice President and Chief of Hospital Operations, Long Island Community Hospital, Patchogue, NY, p. A455
ADLER, Maurita, Director Information Services, Gottlieb Memorial Hospital, Melrose Park, IL, p. A201
ADMA, Vishal, M.D., Medical Director, KVC Prairie Ridge Psychiatric Hospital, Kansas City, KS, p. A251
ADORNATO, Sara F., Chief Executive Officer, Barnes-Kasson County Hospital, Susquehanna, PA, p. A555
ADREAN, Christina, Chief Executive Officer, Pam Specialty Hospital of Victoria North, Victoria, TX, p. A660
ADRIAANSE, Steven W, Vice President and Chief Human Resources Officer, Tallahassee Memorial Healthcare, Tallahassee, FL, p. A151
ADRIANO, Elizabeth M., MC, USN, Director, Naval Medical Center San Diego, San Diego, CA, p. A89
ADVEY, Linda, Manager Information Systems, Glenbeigh Hospital And Outpatient Centers, Rock Creek, OH, p. A503
AERTKER, Robert J., M.D., III, Chief of Staff, Ochsner Acadia General Hospital, Crowley, LA, p. A280
AFENYA, Kenneth, M.D., Chief of Staff, Baptist Memorial Hospital–Tipton, Covington, TN, p. A582
AFLAK, Ziba, Chief Financial Officer, Kindred Hospital–San Francisco Bay Area, San Leandro, CA, p. A92
AFZAL, Muhammed, M.D., Chief of Staff, Sutter Medical Center, Sacramento, Sacramento, CA, p. A87
AGANA, Ben, M.D., Medical Director, Encompass Health Rehabilitation Hospital of The Woodlands, Conroe, TX, p. A608
AGENBROAD, Connie, Chief Executive Officer, Othello Community Hospital, Othello, WA, p. A692
AGLIECO, Fabio, D.O., Chief of Staff, Sweeny Community Hospital, Sweeny, TX, p. A655
AGLOINGA, Roy, Chief Administrative Officer, Norton Sound Regional Hospital, Nome, AK, p. A29
AGNEW, Claire, Chief Financial Officer, Valleywise Health, Phoenix, AZ, p. A37
AGOSTO, Paula M, R.N., MSN, Senior Vice President and Chief Nursing Officer, Children's Hospital of Philadelphia, Philadelphia, PA, p. A548
AGRAWAL, Abha, M.D., FACHE, President and Chief Executive Officer, Lawrence General Hospital, Lawrence, MA, p. A314
AGRELA, Ramona, Associate Chancellor & Chief Human Resources Executive, UCI Health, Orange, CA, p. A82
AGRESTI, Katie, R.N., Director Patient Care Services, Lecom Health Millcreek Community Hospital, Erie, PA, p. A540
AGUAS, Hugo, Vice President Human Resources, Inova Alexandria Hospital, Alexandria, VA, p. A673
AGUERO, Samuel, Chief Operating Officer, Adventhealth Deland, Deland, FL, p. A130
AGUILAR, Gretchen, Director Patient Care and Chief Nursing Officer, Three Rivers Hospital, Brewster, WA, p. A687
AGUILAR, Marisa
Chief Operating Officer, Valley Baptist Medical Center–Brownsville, Brownsville, TX, p. A605
Interim Chief Nursing Officer, Valley Baptist Medical Center–Brownsville, Brownsville, TX, p. A605
AGUILLARD, Clay
R.N., Chief Executive Officer, Seaside Health System – Baton Rouge, Baton Rouge, LA, p. A278
R.N., Director of Nursing, Apollo Behavioral Health Hospital, Baton Rouge, LA, p. A277
AGUILLARD, Shelly, Vice President Human Resources, Christus Ochsner St. Patrick, Lake Charles, LA, p. A286
AGUINAGA, Miguel, M.D., FACS, Medical Director, Advanced Care Hospital of White County, Searcy, AR, p. A53
AGWUNOBI, Andrew, M.D., Chief Executive Officer, Uconn, John Dempsey Hospital, Farmington, CT, p. A116
AHAINE, Israel, Chief Nursing Officer, West Oaks Hospital, Houston, TX, p. A629
AHEARN, Patrick, Chief Executive Officer, Community Medical Center, Toms River, NJ, p. A429
AHL, Dennis, Director Information Technology, Jefferson Community Health And Life, Fairbury, NE, p. A399
AHLERS, Tim, Chief Executive Officer, Guttenberg Municipal Hospital And Clinics, Guttenberg, IA, p. A237
AHMAD, Shariq, M.D., Chief of Staff, Baptist Hospitals of Southeast Texas, Beaumont, TX, p. A602
AHMED, Ashraf, M.D., Senior Vice President Physician and Hospital Services, Aultman Alliance Community Hospital, Alliance, OH, p. A484
AHMED, Imtiaz, Chief of Staff, Mercy Hospital Ada, Ada, OK, p. A509
AHMED, Mohammed Shafeeq., M.D., President, Johns Hopkins Howard County Medical Center, Columbia, MD, p. A303
AHMED, Omar, Acting Manager Human Resources, Veterans Affairs Caribbean Healthcare System, San Juan, PR, p. A736
AHMED, Sajid, Chief Information and Innovation Officer, Mlk Community Healthcare, Los Angeles, CA, p. A74
AHMED, Shabeer A, M.D., Clinical Director, Community Behavioral Health Hospital – Annandale, Annandale, MN, p. A342
AHRENS, C Todd., FACHE, President and Chief Executive Officer, Hannibal Regional Hospital, Hannibal, MO, p. A376
AIELLO, Louis, Senior Vice President and Chief Financial Officer, Wynn Hospital, Utica, NY, p. A460
AIKEN, Avery, Chief Financial Officer, Smith County Memorial Hospital, Smith Center, KS, p. A260
AIKEN, Patsy, Coordinator Human Resource, Monument Health Spearfish Hospital, Spearfish, SD, p. A577
AIKEN, Richard, M.D., Medical Director, Lakeland Behavioral Health System, Springfield, MO, p. A386
AIKIN, Brent
D.O., Chief Medical Officer, Banner Churchill Community Hospital, Fallon, NV, p. A408
D.O., Chief Medical Officer, Banner Lassen Medical Center, Susanville, CA, p. A97
AILOR, Lorie
Chief Executive Officer, Lutheran Hospital of Indiana, Fort Wayne, IN, p. A216
Chief Executive Officer, Chief Administrative Officer, Network Vice President Orthopedics and Sports,

A784 Index of Health Care Professionals

Orthopaedic Hospital of Lutheran Health Network, Fort Wayne, IN, p. A216
AINTABLIAN, Susan, Chief Information Officer, Olive View–Ucla Medical Center, Los Angeles, CA, p. A74
AIONA, Michael, M.D., Chief of Staff, Shriners Hospitals for Children–Portland, Portland, OR, p. A531
AIRHART, Steven
  Chief Executive Officer, Hartgrove Behavioral Health System, Chicago, IL, p. A189
  Group Chief Executive Officer, Garfield Park Behavioral Hospital, Chicago, IL, p. A189
AIROSUS, Diane
  Chief Financial Officer, Arbour H. R. I. Hospital, Brookline, MA, p. A312
  Chief Financial Officer, Pembroke Hospital, Pembroke, MA, p. A317
AISEN, Mindy, M.D., Chief Medical Officer, Rancho Los Amigos National Rehabilitation Center, Downey, CA, p. A62
AISENBREY, Lisa, Administrator Human Resources and Support Services, Sidney Health Center, Sidney, MT, p. A396
AIYELAWO, Pius, Chief Operating Officer, Nih Clinical Center, Bethesda, MD, p. A302
AJANAH, Muhammed, M.D., Clinical Director, Clifton T. Perkins Hospital Center, Jessup. MD, p. A305
AJMAL, Farooq, Vice President and Chief Information Officer, Nassau University Medical Center, East Meadow, NY, p. A442
AKBAR, Adnan
  Chief Medical Officer, Acute Care, Renown Regional Medical Center, Reno, NV, p. A412
  Chief Medical Officer, Acute Care, Renown South Meadows Medical Center, Reno, NV, p. A412
AKENBERGER, Gary, Chief Operating Officer, Promedica Toledo Hospital, Toledo, OH, p. A505
AKENS, Rick, Director Human Resources and Labor Relations, Methodist Medical Center of Oak Ridge, Oak Ridge, TN, p. A591
AKERS, Earl, Supervisor Information Technology, Salina Surgical Hospital, Salina, KS, p. A259
AKERS, Melanie, R.N., Vice President Women's and Children's Services, Cabell Huntington Hospital, Huntington, WV, p. A701
AKERSON, Jeffrey D., M.D., Chief Medical Officer, Nebraska Medicine – Bellevue, Bellevue, NE, p. A398
AKHRAS, Omar, M.D., Chief of Staff, Putnam General Hospital, Eatonton, GA, p. A163
AKHTAR, M. Osman, Chief Operating Officer, M Health Fairview St. John's Hospital, Maplewood, MN, p. A349
AKIF, Joe, Chief Clinical Officer and Chief Nursing Officer, Warren General Hospital, Warren, PA, p. A556
AKIN, Pam, R.N., MSN, Chief Nursing Officer, Whitman Hospital And Medical Center, Colfax, WA, p. A688
AKINS, Tina, Director Human Resources, Lost Rivers Medical Center, Arco, ID, p. A179
AKIYOSHI, Derek, Chief Executive Officer, Leahi Hospital, Honolulu, HI, p. A175
AKKUB, Laura, Director Human Resources, Magnolia Regional Medical Center, Magnolia, AR, p. A50
AKOPYAN, George, Director Human Resources, Centinela Hospital Medical Center, Inglewood, CA, p. A67
AL RAYES, Rachid, Chief Operating Officer, Atrium Medical Center, Stafford, TX, p. A654
AL-HASHMI, Samer, M.D., Chief Medical Staff, Stevens County Hospital, Hugoton, KS, p. A251
ALAGAR, Ravi, M.D., Medical Director, Pam Health Specialty Hospital of Pittsburgh, Oakdale, PA, p. A547
ALAM, Marie Rose., M.D., Chief Executive Officer, Spring Grove Hospital Center, Baltimore, MD, p. A302
ALAM, Md
  Chief Information Officer, NYC Health + Hospitals/Jacobi, New York, NY, p. A451
  Chief Information Officer, NYC Health + Hospitals/Metropolitan, New York, NY, p. A451
ALAM, Muhammad M, M.D., Medical Director, Turning Point Hospital, Moultrie, GA, p. A169
ALAMEDDINE, Hala
  Chief Executive Officer, Kindred Hospital Sugar Land, Sugar Land, TX, p. A654
  Chief Nursing Executive, Kindred Hospital Sugar Land, Sugar Land, TX, p. A654
ALASZEWSKI, Lydia, Chief Nursing Officer, Select Specialty Hospital – Macomb County, Mount Clemens, MI, p. A334
ALBA, Jose, President, Centracare – Long Prairie, Long Prairie, MN, p. A349
ALBA, Pamela, Chief Executive Officer, Willow Springs Center, Reno, NV, p. A412
ALBANY, Karen, Chief Information Officer, Naval Medical Center, Portsmouth, VA, p. A681
ALBAUM, Michael, M.D., Senior Vice President and Chief Medical Officer, Southern Maine Health Care – Biddeford Medical Center, Biddeford, ME, p. A296

ALBERS, Craig, President and Chief Operating Officer, Mercy Health – St. Vincent Medical Center, Toledo, OH, p. A504
ALBERT, Shannon, Director of Operations, Carson Valley Medical Center, Gardnerville, NV, p. A408
ALBERTS, Patrick J, Senior Vice President and Chief Operating Officer, Penn Highlands Mon Valley, Monongahela, PA, p. A546
ALBERTSON, Christopher
  Chief Executive Officer and President, SMP Health – St. Kateri, Rolla, ND, p. A483
  President and Chief Executive Officer, SMP Health – St. Andrew's, Bottineau, ND, p. A479
ALBIN, James
  Chief Information Officer, Chi St Luke's Health – Baylor St Luke's Medical Center, Houston, TX, p. A625
  Chief Information Officer, Theda Care Medical Center – Wild Rose, Wild Rose, WI, p. A725
ALBOSTA, Kevin, Vice President, Chief Financial Officer, Covenant Healthcare, Saginaw, MI, p. A336
ALBRECHT, John, Chief of Staff, Union Hospital Clinton, Clinton, IN, p. A214
ALBRECHT, Sandra, Interim Chief Financial Officer, Singing River Health System, Pascagoula, MS, p. A367
ALBRIGHT, Bill, Director Human Resources, Stewart Memorial Community Hospital, Lake City, IA, p. A239
ALBRIGHT, Kimberly, Chief Financial Officer, Lakeland Community Hospital, Haleyville, AL, p. A20
ALBRIGHT, Sara Z, Vice President Human Resources, Bassett Medical Center, Cooperstown, NY, p. A441
ALBRIGHT, Tina, Director Human Resources, National Park Medical Center, Hot Springs, AR, p. A48
ALCOCER, Deborah, Chief Information Officer, South Texas Rehabilitation Hospital, Brownsville, TX, p. A605
ALCUINO, Don, Chief Financial Officer, Carewell Health Medical Center, East Orange, NJ, p. A420
ALDANA, Eladio, Manager Information Systems, College Hospital Costa Mesa, Costa Mesa, CA, p. A60
ALDER, Cal, Director Information Technology, Rock County Hospital, Bassett, NE, p. A397
ALDERGATE, John, Director, Human Resources, Cleveland Clinic Union Hospital, Dover, OH, p. A495
ALDERMAN, Una, Chief Executive Officer, Northern Idaho Advanced Care Hospital, Post Falls, ID, p. A183
ALDERSON, Jane, R.N., Chief Nursing Officer, Manhattan Surgical, Manhattan, KS, p. A254
ALDRED, Linda W, Senior Vice President, Texas Children's Hospital, Houston, TX, p. A628
ALDRICH, Alan, Chief Financial Officer, Central Montana Medical Center, Lewistown, MT, p. A393
ALDRICH, Meghan, President, Sisters of Charity Hospital of Buffalo, Buffalo, NY, p. A440
ALDRIDGE, Brett, President, Gulf Breeze Hospital, Gulf Breeze, FL, p. A133
ALDRIDGE, Cassandra Haynes, Chief Human Resources Officer, Phoebe Sumter Medical Center, Americus, GA, p. A156
ALDRIDGE, Kenneth, M.D., Vice President Medical Affairs, Dch Regional Medical Center, Tuscaloosa, AL, p. A25
ALEEM, Asaf, M.D., Medical Director, Peachford Behavioral Health System, Atlanta, GA, p. A157
ALEXANDA, Lisa, M.D., Vice President Medical Affairs, Parrish Medical Center, Titusville, FL, p. A153
ALEXANDER, Alan B., FACHE, Vice President and Administrator, The Medical Center At Caverna, Horse Cave, KY, p. A267
ALEXANDER, Amy, Chief Executive Officer, Ridgeview Institute – Smyrna, Smyrna, GA, p. A171
ALEXANDER, April, Director Human Resources, NYC Health + Hospitals/Metropolitan, New York, NY, p. A451
ALEXANDER, Bobby, R.N., Chief Nursing Officer, Pinnacle Pointe Behavioral Healthcare System, Little Rock, AR, p. A50
ALEXANDER, Brenda, System Vice President, Human Resources, SSM Health St. Mary's Hospital Centralia, Centralia, IL, p. A187
ALEXANDER, Craig, Chief Operating Officer, Thomas B. Finan Center, Cumberland, MD, p. A303
ALEXANDER, David, Senior Vice President and Chief Financial Officer, St. Joseph's University Medical Center, Paterson, NJ, p. A426
ALEXANDER, Debra, Chief Information Officer, Lifeways Behavioral Hospital, Boise, ID, p. A179
ALEXANDER, Drew, Chief Nursing Officer, Cedar County Memorial Hospital, El Dorado Springs, MO, p. A374
ALEXANDER, Fred, M.D., Medical Director, Kaiser Permanente West Los Angeles Medical Center, Los Angeles, CA, p. A73
ALEXANDER, James L.
  R.N., Chief Nursing Officer, First Surgical Hospital, Bellaire, TX, p. A603

R.N., Chief Nursing Officer/Operating Chief Executive Officer, First Surgical Hospital, Bellaire, TX, p. A603
ALEXANDER, Jane, Director Facility Administrative Services, Sagamore Children's Psychiatric Center, Dix Hills, NY, p. A442
ALEXANDER, Jennifer, Director, Human Resources, Encompass Health Rehabilitation Hospital of North Tampa, Lutz, FL, p. A138
ALEXANDER, Jeremy, Chief Financial Officer, Southeast Iowa Regional Medical Center, West Burlington Campus, West Burlington, IA, p. A245
ALEXANDER, Josette, Director, Human Resources, Ohiohealth Rehabilitation Hospital, Columbus, OH, p. A492
ALEXANDER, Michael, FACHE, Chief Executive Officer, Hillsboro Area Hospital, Hillsboro, IL, p. A198
ALEXANDER, Thomas, Chief Executive Officer, East Houston Hospitals & Clinics, Houston, TX, p. A625
ALEXANDER–HINES, Joyce, R.N., MSN, Associate Director, Patient Care Services, Fayetteville Veterans Affairs Medical Center, Fayetteville, NC, p. A468
ALEXIADES, Nikolas, Chief Financial Officer, Monmouth Medical Center, Southern Campus, Lakewood, NJ, p. A422
ALFANO, Alan, M.D., Medical Director, UVA Encompass Health Rehabilitation Hospital, Charlottesville, VA, p. A674
ALFANO, Anthony, Vice President Executive Director, Montefiore New Rochelle, New Rochelle, NY, p. A447
ALFATLAWI, Lamia, Chief Operating Officer, Straith Hospital for Special Surgery, Southfield, MI, p. A338
ALFORD, Charles, Vice President Financial Services, ECU Health Edgecombe Hospital, Tarboro, NC, p. A477
ALFORD, Karla, Chief Information Officer, Greater Regional Health, Creston, IA, p. A234
ALFORD, Michelle, R.N., MSN, Director of Nursing, Washington County Hospital, Chatom, AL, p. A17
ALFRED, Lorrie, Director Human Resources, Southern Surgical Hospital, Slidell, LA, p. A293
ALFS, Abby, Chief Human Resources Officer, Fillmore County Hospital, Geneva, NE, p. A400
ALGER, Steve, Senior Vice President and Chief Financial Officer, Lakes Regional Healthcare, Spirit Lake, IA, p. A244
ALI, Irfan, Director Information Services, Saint Agnes Medical Center, Fresno, CA, p. A65
ALI, Mirza Z, M.D., Chief of Staff, Wilkes–Barre Veterans Affairs Medical Center, Wilkes–Barre, PA, p. A558
ALI, Muhammad, M.D., Chief Medical Officer, Sanford Tracy Medical Center, Tracy, MN, p. A356
ALI, Syed, M.D., Chief Medical Officer, Aurora Medical Center – Bay Area, Marinette, WI, p. A715
ALI, Syed Asif, M.D., Chief of Staff, Syracuse Veterans Affairs Medical Center, Syracuse, NY, p. A460
ALI–KHAN, Mir, M.D., Medical Director, Canyon Ridge Hospital, Chino, CA, p. A59
ALI–KHAN, Mujtaba, D.O., Chief Medical Officer, HCA Houston Healthcare Conroe, Conroe, TX, p. A608
ALICE, Patricia K., Chief Executive Officer, Arizona Orthopedic Surgical Hospital, Chandler, AZ, p. A30
ALICEA, Luis, Chief Information Officer, Doctors' Center Hospital San Juan, San Juan, PR, p. A734
ALICEA PEREZ, Eneida, Interim Nursing Director, Hospital Buen Samaritano, Aguadilla, PR, p. A730
ALIFF, Sarah, Ph.D., Chief Nursing Officer, Hot Springs County Hospital District, Thermopolis, WY, p. A728
ALKHOULI, Hassan, M.D.
  Chief Medical Officer, Garden Grove Hospital And Medical Center, Garden Grove, CA, p. A65
  Chief Medical Officer, West Anaheim Medical Center, Anaheim, CA, p. A55
  Medical Director, Huntington Beach Hospital, Huntington Beach, CA, p. A67
ALLA, Vamseedhar, M.D., Director Medical Staff, Connecticut Veterans Home And Hospital, Rocky Hill, CT, p. A118
ALLAMAN, Robin, Chief Nursing Officer, Kearny County Hospital, Lakin, KS, p. A252
ALLARD, Joan, Director Human Resources, Adventhealth Heart of Florida, Davenport, FL, p. A129
ALLARD, Marie, Finance Manager, Ascension Brighton Center for Recovery, Brighton, MI, p. A323
ALLARD, Piper, Chief Operating Officer, Weston County Health Services, Newcastle, WY, p. A727
ALLATT, Richard, M.D., Medical Director, Encompass Health Rehabilitation Hospital of Nittany Valley, Pleasant Gap. PA, p. A552
ALLDREDGE, Kim, Director Human Resources, Lawrence County Memorial Hospital, Lawrenceville, IL, p. A200
ALLEMAN, Scott, Senior Vice President Patient Care Services and Chief Nursing Officer, UW Medicine/Valley Medical Center, Renton, WA, p. A693
ALLEMAN, Tara, Chief Financial Officer, Ochsner Medical Center – Kenner, Kenner, LA, p. A284
ALLEN, Alice A, R.N., MS, Chief Nursing Officer, Northeastern Nevada Regional Hospital, Elko, NV, p. A408

Index of Health Care Professionals

Index of Health Care Professionals / Allen

ALLEN, Audrey, Coordinator Benefits, Dallas County Medical Center, Fordyce, AR, p. A46
ALLEN, Brian, M.D., President Medical Staff, Georgetown Community Hospital, Georgetown, KY, p. A266
ALLEN, Candice, Director of Nursing, Rio Grande Hospital, Del Norte, CO, p. A106
ALLEN, Carly, Hospital Administrator, Wrangell Medical Center, Wrangell, AK, p. A29
ALLEN, Carolyn
Chief Financial Officer, Saint Michael's Medical Center, Newark, NJ, p. A425
Vice President and Chief Financial Officer, Camden Clark Medical Center, Parkersburg, WV, p. A703
ALLEN, Dawn, R.N., Chief Clinical Officer, Centracare – Redwood, Redwood Falls, MN, p. A353
ALLEN, Devon, M.D., Chief of Medical Staff, Samuel Simmonds Memorial Hospital, Barrow, AK, p. A27
ALLEN, Donald, Chief Operating Officer, Unity Physicians Hospital, Mishawaka, IN, p. A224
ALLEN, Janel, Senior Vice President and Chief Human Resources Officer, Children's Nebraska, Omaha, NE, p. A404
ALLEN, Jason
Chief Operating Officer, Brook Lane, Hagerstown, MD, p. A304
Director Patient Care Services, Brook Lane, Hagerstown, MD, p. A304
ALLEN, Jean, Human Resources Director, Bleckley Memorial Hospital, Cochran, GA, p. A160
ALLEN, John
Chief Information Officer, Holzer Medical Center, Gallipolis, OH, p. A496
President and Chief Executive Officer, Prairie Lakes Healthcare System, Watertown, SD, p. A578
ALLEN, Judy, Human Resource Specialist, Carl Albert Community Mental Health Center, Mcalester, OK, p. A514
ALLEN, Kandice K., R.N., Chief Executive Officer, Share Medical Center, Alva, OK, p. A509
ALLEN, Karen A.
R.N., President, Clarion Hospital, Clarion, PA, p. A537
R.N., President, Butler & Clarion Hospitals, Butler Memorial Hospital, Butler, PA, p. A536
ALLEN, Keith
Senior Vice President and Chief Human Resources Officer, Froedtert And The Medical College of Wisconsin Froedtert Hospital, Milwaukee, WI, p. A717
Senior Vice President and Chief Human Resources Officer, Froedtert Menomonee Falls Hospital, Menomonee Falls, WI, p. A716
ALLEN, Keith M., Medical Center Director, Roseburg Va Medical Center, Roseburg, OR, p. A531
ALLEN, Kena C, Chief Financial Officer, Mccurtain Memorial Hospital, Idabel, OK, p. A514
ALLEN, Kent, Director Human Resources, Mymichigan Medical Center West Branch, West Branch, MI, p. A340
ALLEN, Linda M, Vice President Human Resources, The Children's Institute of Pittsburgh, Pittsburgh, PA, p. A551
ALLEN, Lori, Chief Operating Officer, Patterson Health Center, Anthony, KS, p. A246
ALLEN, Lucretia, Director Human Resources, Sweetwater Hospital, Sweetwater, TN, p. A594
ALLEN, Lyndon, Director Information Systems, Canton–Potsdam Hospital, Potsdam, NY, p. A456
ALLEN, Mark, Chief Operating Officer, Marian Regional Medical Center, Santa Maria, CA, p. A94
ALLEN, Maryjo, Chief Nursing Officer, Halifax Health/Uf Health Medical Center of Deltona, Deltona, FL, p. A130
ALLEN, Mike
Director Information Services, Adventhealth Shawnee Mission, Merriam, KS, p. A255
Director Information Services, Shriners Hospitals for Children–Spokane, Spokane, WA, p. A696
Director Information Technology, Shriners Hospitals for Children–Salt Lake City, Salt Lake City, UT, p. A669
ALLEN, Myrna, R.N., MS, Chief Operating and Nursing Officer, Mlk Community Healthcare, Los Angeles, CA, p. A74
ALLEN, Nancy, R.N., MS, Director, Patient Services and Chief Nursing Executive, Carle Eureka Hospital, Eureka, IL, p. A194
ALLEN, Nikki, Patient Care Executive, Sutter Amador Hospital, Jackson, CA, p. A68
ALLEN, Patty, St. John's Vice President Finance, HSHS St. John's Hospital, Springfield, IL, p. A209
ALLEN, R Keith, Senior Vice President Human Resources, University of Maryland Medical Center, Baltimore, MD, p. A301
ALLEN, Richard, Chief Executive Officer, Warren General Hospital, Warren, PA, p. A556
ALLEN, Robert, M.D., Chief Medical Officer, Mercy Hospital of Folsom, Folsom, CA, p. A63
ALLEN, Teresa M., Commanding Officer, Naval Hospital Jacksonville, Jacksonville, FL, p. A135
ALLEN, Timothy M, Vice President Human Resources, United Hospital Center, Bridgeport, WV, p. A699
ALLEN, Vicki, R.N., MS
Vice President Patient Care Services and Chief Nursing Officer, Harnett Health System, Dunn, NC, p. A467
Chief Financial Officer, Chicot Memorial Medical Center, Lake Village, AR, p. A49
ALLEN–DAVIS, Jandel, M.D., President and Chief Executive Officer, Craig Hospital, Englewood, CO, p. A107
ALLENDE–RUIZ, Luis R., Chief Executive Officer, Hialeah Hospital, Hialeah, FL, p. A133
ALLENSWORTH, Ed, M.D., Medical Director, Saint Francis Hospital Vinita, Vinita, OK, p. A523
ALLENSWORTH, Kenneth W., FACHE, Medical Center Director, Martinsburg Veterans Affairs Medical Center, Martinsburg, WV, p. A702
ALLERS, Ashley, Chief Financial Officer, Van Diest Medical Center, Webster City, IA, p. A245
ALLEX, Carnie, President, Centracare – Redwood, Redwood Falls, MN, p. A353
ALLEY, David, Chief Financial Officer, Starr Regional Medical Center, Athens, TN, p. A579
ALLEY, Delaine, Chief Executive Officer, Acoma–Canoncito–Laguna Hospital, Acoma, NM, p. A432
ALLEY, Jon, D.O., President Medical Staff, Cameron Memorial Community Hospital, Angola, IN, p. A212
ALLEY, Steve B, M.D., Chief of Staff, Crosbyton Clinic Hospital, Crosbyton, TX, p. A610
ALLEY, William, Chief Nursing Officer, Twin County Regional Healthcare, Galax, VA, p. A677
ALLGOOD, Libby, Chief Financial Officer, Kittitas Valley Healthcare, Ellensburg, WA, p. A689
ALLICON, Keary T, Vice President Finance and Chief Financial Officer, Baystate Wing Hospital, Palmer, MA, p. A317
ALLINSON, Randy, R.N., Chief Nursing Officer, Central Valley Medical Center, Nephi, UT, p. A666
ALLISON, Lorraine, Human Resource Partner, Peacehealth Peace Island Medical Center, Friday Harbor, WA, p. A690
ALLISON, Morgan, Chief Executive Officer, Kiowa County Memorial Hospital, Greensburg, KS, p. A250
ALLISON, Shannon, Finance Manager, Ascension St. Thomas Three Rivers, Waverly, TN, p. A594
ALLISON, Steve, Director Human Resources, Logan County Hospital, Oakley, KS, p. A256
ALLISON, William E., Senior Vice President and Chief Operating Officer, Administration, Mount Sinai South Nassau, Oceanside, NY, p. A454
ALLORE, Gary
President, Trinity Health Grand Haven Hospital, Grand Haven, MI, p. A328
President, Trinity Health Muskegon Hospital, Muskegon, MI, p. A334
President, Trinity Health Shelby Hospital, Shelby, MI, p. A338
ALLPORT, Jeff, Vice President, Chief Information Officer, Valley Presbyterian Hospital, Los Angeles, CA, p. A75
ALLRED, Al W, Chief Financial Officer, Adventhealth New Smyrna Beach, New Smyrna Beach, FL, p. A142
ALLRED, B Dee, M.D., President Medical Staff, Holy Cross Hospital – Jordan Valley, West Jordan, UT, p. A670
ALLRED, Brandi, Chief Nursing Officer, Eastern Idaho Regional Medical Center, Idaho Falls, ID, p. A181
ALLRED, Lowell C, M.D., Chief of Staff, Columbia Basin Hospital, Ephrata, WA, p. A689
ALLRED, William, M.D., Vice President Medical Affairs, Ascension St. John Medical Center, Tulsa, OK, p. A522
ALLSOP, Brian, Director Human Resources, Central Valley Medical Center, Nephi, UT, p. A666
ALLSTOTT, Patti, Administrative Coordinator Human Resources and Grant Writer, Pioneer Memorial Hospital, Heppner, OR, p. A527
ALLUSON, Valerie, M.D., Chief Medical Officer, Hackensack Meridian Mountainside Medical Center, Montclair, NJ, p. A424
ALMAUHY, Deborah, R.N., Chief Nursing Officer, Emory Rehabilitation Hospital, Atlanta, GA, p. A157
ALMEIDA, Sergio, Director Information Systems, HCA Houston Healthcare West, Houston, TX, p. A626
ALMEIDA, Sharon, Chief Executive Officer, Banner Rehabilitation Hospital Phoenix, Phoenix, AZ, p. A35
ALMEIDA–SUAREZ, Mario, M.D., Chief of Staff, Larkin Community Hospital–South Miami Campus, South Miami, FL, p. A150
ALMETER, Connie, Chief Nursing Officer, Wyoming County Community Hospital, Warsaw, NY, p. A461
ALMETER, Marilyn, Chief Nursing Officer, United Memorial Medical Center, Batavia, NY, p. A439
ALMODAVAR, William, M.D., Director Medical, First Hospital Panamericano, Cidra, PR, p. A732
ALMODOVAR, Gustavo, Executive Director, Hospital De La Concepcion, San German, PR, p. A734
ALMOHAMMED, Salah, Chief of Staff, UT Health Carthage, Carthage, TX, p. A607
ALO, Kathleen, Chief Nursing Officer, Mammoth Hospital, Mammoth Lakes, CA, p. A76
ALONSO, Gwen, Chief Nursing Officer, Adventhealth Zephyrhills, Zephyrhills, FL, p. A155
ALONSO, Jose', M.D., Medical Director, San Juan Capestrano Hospital, San Juan, PR, p. A735
ALONZO, Patti, Manager Human Resources, Pacifica Hospital of The Valley, Los Angeles, CA, p. A74
ALPERT, Jeffrey, M.D., Medical Director, Wichita County Health Center, Leoti, KS, p. A253
ALPERT, Len, Director Human Resources, Larkin Community Hospital Behavioral Health Services, Hollywood, FL, p. A133
ALRASHEDY, Farhad H, M.D., Chief Medical Officer, Ferry County Memorial Hospital, Republic, WA, p. A693
ALSADON, Danielle, Clinic/Hospital Manager, Trinity Kenmare Community Hospital, Kenmare, ND, p. A482
ALSIP, Bryan, M.D., Executive Vice President, Chief Medical Officer, University Health, San Antonio, TX, p. A651
ALSTAD, Nancy, Director Human Resources, Fort Healthcare, Fort Atkinson, WI, p. A711
ALT, Melinda, Chief Financial Officer, Audubon County Memorial Hospital And Clinics, Audubon, IA, p. A230
ALTAJAR, Sam, M.D., Chief of Staff, Desoto Memorial Hospital, Arcadia, FL, p. A125
ALTARAS, June, R.N.
President and Market Leader, Multicare Auburn Medical Center, Auburn, WA, p. A687
R.N., President and Market Leader, Multicare Covington Medical Center, Covington, WA, p. A688
ALTENBURGER, Andy, Chief Information Officer, Johnson Regional Medical Center, Clarksville, AR, p. A44
ALTHOEN, David, Director Financial Planning and Analysis, Forest Health Medical Center, Ypsilanti, MI, p. A341
ALTHOUSE, Douglas, Chief Medical Staff, Kearney County Health Services, Minden, NE, p. A402
ALTMAN, Alexander B III, Chief Financial Officer, Union County General Hospital, Clayton, NM, p. A434
ALTMAN, Brett, FACHE, Chief Executive Officer, Cass Health, Atlantic, IA, p. A230
ALTMAN, Deana, Interim Chief Nursing Officer, Harney District Hospital, Burns, OR, p. A526
ALTMAN, Harold, M.D., Chief Medical Officer, Acmh Hospital, Kittanning, PA, p. A543
ALTMAN, Rebecca A., R.N., Senior Vice President and Chief Administrative Officer, University of Maryland Medical Center Midtown Campus, Baltimore, MD, p. A301
ALTOM, Andy, President and Chief Executive Officer, Methodist Behavioral Hospital, Maumelle, AR, p. A50
ALTOSE, Murray, M.D., Chief of Staff, Northeast Ohio Va Healthcare System, Cleveland, OH, p. A491
ALTSHULER, Keith, President and Chief Administrative Officer, Fort Sanders Regional Medical Center, Knoxville, TN, p. A585
ALURI, Bapu, M.D., Chief Medical Officer, Yuma Rehabilitation Hospital, An Affiliation of Encompass Health And Yuma Regional Medical Center, Yuma, AZ, p. A42
ALVARADO, Felicita E., Administrator, Hospital Psiquiatrico Correccional, San Juan, PR, p. A735
ALVARADO, Rafael, Chief Executive Officer, Dr. Pila's Hospital, Ponce, PR, p. A733
ALVARADO, Ramona, Interim Manager Human Resources, Adventist Health Reedley, Reedley, CA, p. A85
ALVAREZ, Dena C, R.N., Chief Operating Officer and Chief Compliance Officer, Brodstone Memorial Hospital, Superior, NE, p. A406
ALVAREZ, Janie, Accounting Director, Cornerstone Regional Hospital, Edinburg, TX, p. A615
ALVAREZ, Jose, M.D., Chief Medical Staff, Circles of Care, Melbourne, FL, p. A138
ALVAREZ, Maria Charlotte, M.D., Chief of Staff, Sheridan Community Hospital, Sheridan, MI, p. A338
ALVAREZ, Marie, Chief Executive Officer, Rio Vista Behavioral Health, El Paso, TX, p. A617
ALVAREZ, Valerie, Executive Assistant, Adventist Health Reedley, Reedley, CA, p. A85
ALVEY, Raymond, Chief Financial Officer, SSM Health Saint Louis University Hospital, Saint Louis, MO, p. A384
ALVILLAR, Melissa, MSN, R.N., Chief Nursing Officer, Comanche County Memorial Hospital, Lawton, OK, p. A514
ALVIS, Kimberly, CPA, Chief Financial Officer, Kirby Medical Center, Monticello, IL, p. A202
ALWIN, Scott, Chief Executive Officer, Hot Springs County Hospital District, Thermopolis, WY, p. A728
ALWIN–POPP, Susan, R.N., Vice President of Clinical Services/Chief Clinical Officer, Edgerton Hospital And Health Services, Edgerton, WI, p. A710

A786 Index of Health Care Professionals

Index of Health Care Professionals

Index of Health Care Professionals / Anderson

ALZEIN, Bashar, M.D., President Medical Staff, Illini Community Hospital, Pittsfield, IL, p. A206
AMADO, Mitchell, Senior Vice President Finance and Chief Financial Officer, Glens Falls Hospital, Glens Falls, NY, p. A443
AMANTEA, Paul, Director Finance, University Hospitals Geauga Medical Center, Chardon, OH, p. A488
AMAR, Gino, Administrator, Kohala Hospital, Kohala, HI, p. A177
AMARANTOS, Stacie, Chief Operating Officer, Catalina Island Medical Center, Avalon, CA, p. A56
AMBROSIANI, Michael, Chief Financial Officer, Knox Community Hospital, Mount Vernon, OH, p. A501
AMBUEHL, Lisa, Chief Nursing Officer, Salem Township Hospital, Salem, IL, p. A208
AMERSON, Jeff, Director Information System, HCA Florida West Hospital, Pensacola, FL, p. A146
AMES, Lance
Chief Executive Officer, South Texas Health System, Edinburg, TX, p. A615
Interim Chief Executive Officer, South Texas Health System, Edinburg, TX, p. A615
AMICK, Kevin, Executive Director, W. G. (Bill) Heffner Veterans Affairs Medical Center, Salisbury, NC, p. A476
AMIN, Saad, Medical Director Hospital, Kindred Hospital–Greensboro, Greensboro, NC, p. A469
AMMONS, Angela, Administrator and Chief Executive Officer, Clinch Memorial Hospital, Homerville, GA, p. A165
AMODO, Mitch, Vice President and Chief Financial Officer, Garnet Health Medical Center, Middletown, NY, p. A446
AMOH, Eric, Chief Executive Officer, Psychiatric Institute of Washington, Washington, DC, p. A124
AMORE TALON, Mia, Chief Financial Officer, Prairie County Hospital District, Terry, MT, p. A396
AMOROSE, Carl, Vice President Finance, Norton Hospital, Louisville, KY, p. A270
AMOROSO, Mitze, Chief Information Officer, Terence Cardinal Cooke Health Care Center, New York, NY, p. A453
AMOS, Michael Paul, Chief Operating Officer, Lakewood Regional Medical Center, Lakewood, CA, p. A69
AMOS, Robert, Vice President and Chief Financial Officer, Valley Health – Winchester Medical Center, Winchester, VA, p. A685
AMOS, Stacey S., Hospital Commander/Ozark Market Director, General Leonard Wood Army Community Hospital, Fort Leonard Wood, MO, p. A375
AMRICH, Jason, Chief Executive Officer, Gunnison Valley Health, Gunnison, CO, p. A109
AMSBERRY, Shelly, Director of Nursing, Jennie M. Melham Memorial Medical Center, Broken Bow, NE, p. A398
AMSTUTZ, Charles, Director of Information Technology, Cascade Medical, Leavenworth, WA, p. A691
AMSTUTZ, Terry Lee., FACHE, Chief Executive Officer, Mcgehee Hospital, Mcgehee, AR, p. A50
AMYX, Maleigha, Chief Information Officer, Rockcastle Regional Hospital And Respiratory Care Center, Mount Vernon, KY, p. A272
ANANI, Anthony, Chief Medical Officer, Cook Children's Medical Center – Prosper, Prosper, TX, p. A646
ANASTASI, Frank, Chief Financial Officer, Pennsylvania Hospital, Philadelphia, PA, p. A549
ANAYA, Sandra J., R.N., Chief Executive Officer, Palo Verde Hospital, Blythe, CA, p. A58
ANCHONDO, Laura, Administrator Human Resources, Kindred Hospital El Paso, El Paso, TX, p. A616
ANDELL, Amy, Chief Financial Officer, Breckinridge Memorial Hospital, Hardinsburg, KY, p. A266
ANDERER, Tammy, Ph.D.
Chief Administrative Officer, Geisinger Lewistown Hospital, Lewistown, PA, p. A544
Vice President of Clinical Operations for the North Central Region, Geisinger Jersey Shore Hospital, Jersey Shore, PA, p. A542
Vice President of Clinical Operations for the North Central Region, Geisinger Medical Center Muncy, Muncy, PA, p. A546
ANDERS, Anna, R.N., MSN, Vice President and Chief Nursing Officer, Carson Tahoe Health, Carson City, NV, p. A408
ANDERS, James M Jr, Administrator and Chief Operating Officer, Kennedy Krieger Institute, Baltimore, MD, p. A300
ANDERS, Robert, Chief Financial Officer, Ouachita County Medical Center, Camden, AR, p. A44
ANDERSEN, Connie, R.N., MS, Chief Nursing Officer, Sarasota Memorial Hospital – Sarasota, Sarasota, FL, p. A150
ANDERSEN, Donia L, Director of Nursing, Centennial Peaks Hospital, Louisville, CO, p. A112
ANDERSEN, Janet, Chief Financial Officer, UT Health Quitman, Quitman, TX, p. A646
ANDERSEN, John, Manager Information Systems, Astria Sunnyside Hospital, Sunnyside, WA, p. A696
ANDERSEN, Kurt, M.D., President – Central Iowa Division, Mercyone Des Moines Medical Center, Des Moines, IA, p. A235
ANDERSEN, Michelle, R.N., Chief Nursing Officer, Manning Regional Healthcare Center, Manning, IA, p. A239
ANDERSEN, Sue
Chief Executive Officer, Marian Regional Medical Center, Santa Maria, CA, p. A94
Vice President and Service Area and Chief Financial Officer, Marian Regional Medical Center, Santa Maria, CA, p. A94
ANDERSEN, Tracy, Chief Information Officer, St. Mary's Regional Medical Center, Enid, OK, p. A512
ANDERSEN, Travis, President and Chief Executive Officer, UW Health Swedishamerican Hospital, Rockford, IL, p. A207
ANDERSEN, Wendy, Director Human Resources, Eastern Idaho Regional Medical Center, Idaho Falls, ID, p. A181
ANDERSON, Alison, Chief Nursing Officer, Select Specialty Hospital–Sioux Falls, Sioux Falls, SD, p. A577
ANDERSON, Allen K., President and Chief Executive Officer, St. Anthony Regional Hospital, Carroll, IA, p. A231
ANDERSON, Angela L., Manager Human Resource, Kansas Spine & Specialty Hospital, Wichita, KS, p. A262
ANDERSON, Angie, Director Information Technology, Crawford County Memorial Hospital, Denison, IA, p. A234
ANDERSON, Arthur
Chief Financial Officer, Crozer–Chester Medical Center, Upland, PA, p. A556
Chief Financial Officer, Grand View Health, Sellersville, PA, p. A554
ANDERSON, Benjamin, President and Chief Executive Officer, Hutchinson Regional Medical Center, Hutchinson, KS, p. A251
ANDERSON, Brad, Chief Financial Officer, Community Memorial Hospital, Cloquet, MN, p. A345
ANDERSON, Brady, Chief Human Resource Officer, Utah Valley Hospital, Provo, UT, p. A667
ANDERSON, Brian, Chief Financial Officer, Adventist Health Simi Valley, Simi Valley, CA, p. A96
ANDERSON, Calandra, Vice President Patient Care and Chief Nursing Officer, Mclaren Oakland, Pontiac, MI, p. A335
ANDERSON, Carter, Administrator, Montana State Hospital, Warm Springs, MT, p. A396
ANDERSON, Charles, M.D., Chief Medical Officer, Desert Regional Medical Center, Palm Springs, CA, p. A82
ANDERSON, Cherri, Chief Nursing Officer, Banner Behavioral Health Hospital – Scottsdale, Scottsdale, AZ, p. A38
ANDERSON, Christine, Chief Nursing Officer and Vice President of Patient Care Services, Lincolnhealth, Damariscotta, ME, p. A296
ANDERSON, Conde Nevin, M.D., Chief of Staff, Detar Healthcare System, Victoria, TX, p. A660
ANDERSON, Craig, Director Management Information Systems, River Bend Hospital, West Lafayette, IN, p. A229
ANDERSON, Dale, Chief Executive Officer, Sabine Medical Center, Many, LA, p. A288
ANDERSON, Dana, R.N., Administrator, Long–Term Acute Care Hospital, Mosaic Life Care At St. Joseph, Saint Joseph, MO, p. A383
ANDERSON, Dave, FACHE, Vice President Administration, Atrium Health Union, Monroe, NC, p. A472
ANDERSON, David, Chief Executive Officer, Jackson Purchase Medical Center, Mayfield, KY, p. A271
ANDERSON, Derek, Executive Director, Northern Westchester Hospital, Mount Kisco, NY, p. A446
ANDERSON, DeVry, Chief Medical Officer, St. David's South Austin Medical Center, Austin, TX, p. A600
ANDERSON, Donna, Chief Executive Officer, Southeast Missouri Mental Health Center, Farmington, MO, p. A375
ANDERSON, Edwin, M.D., Chief of Staff and Chief Medical Officer, Bigfork Valley Hospital, Bigfork, MN, p. A343
ANDERSON, Gina, Human Resources Officer, Riverview Regional Medical Center, Carthage, TN, p. A579
ANDERSON, Heather, Chief Nursing Officer, Spring Hospital, Spring, TX, p. A654
ANDERSON, Heidi
Chief Executive Officer, Forks Community Hospital, Forks, WA, p. A690
Chief Nursing Officer, Arbor Health, Morton Hospital, Morton, WA, p. A691
ANDERSON, Jay, Chief Operating Officer, Ohio State University Wexner Medical Center, Columbus, OH, p. A492
ANDERSON, Jeremy, M.D., Medical Staff President, Good Shepherd Health Care System, Hermiston, OR, p. A527
ANDERSON, John G.
FACHE, Chief Executive Officer and Administrator, Baptist Anderson Regional Medical Center – South, Meridian, MS, p. A366
FACHE, Chief Executive Officer and Administrator, Baptist Anderson Regional Medical Center, Meridian, MS, p. A366
ANDERSON, Jonathan, Medical Director, Western State Hospital, Staunton, VA, p. A684
ANDERSON, Joseph, Chief Medical Officer, Idaho Falls Community Hospital, Idaho Falls, ID, p. A181
ANDERSON, Justine, Chief Financial Officer, Perham Health, Perham, MN, p. A352
ANDERSON, Kathleen, Director, Acute Clinical Systems, Prisma Health Laurens County Hospital, Clinton, SC, p. A564
ANDERSON, Kenneth, M.D., Vice President and Chief Medical Officer, Baptist Health Louisville, Louisville, KY, p. A269
ANDERSON, Kristin, Director, Human Resources, California Hospital Medical Center, Los Angeles, CA, p. A72
ANDERSON, Libby, Chief Financial Officer, Satanta District Hospital And Long Term Care, Satanta, KS, p. A259
ANDERSON, Louis, Chief Financial Officer, Mcleod Health Cheraw, Cheraw, SC, p. A563
ANDERSON, Mark
Chief Financial Officer, North Oaks Medical Center, Hammond, LA, p. A282
Chief Financial Officer, North Oaks Rehabilitation Hospital, Hammond, LA, p. A282
ANDERSON, Mark T, Chief Financial Officer, Sovah Health–Danville, Danville, VA, p. A675
ANDERSON, Melissa, MSN, R.N., Acting Chief Executive Officer, Aspen Mountain Medical Center, Rock Springs, WY, p. A728
ANDERSON, Michael
M.D., Chief Medical Officer, St. Josep. Medical Center, Tacoma, WA, p. A697
President/Chief Executive Officer, Fort Healthcare, Fort Atkinson, WI, p. A711
ANDERSON, Michael Bruce, Ph.D., Chief Operating Officer, St. Louis Forensic Treatment Center, Saint Louis, MO, p. A384
ANDERSON, Mickey, M.D., Vice President Medical Affairs, Chi Saint Josep. Health – Flaget Memorial Hospital, Bardstown, KY, p. A263
ANDERSON, Paula, Administrative Director Human Resources, Endless Mountains Health Systems, Montrose, PA, p. A546
ANDERSON, Rhena
Chief Nursing Officer, Nexus Specialty Hospital, Shenandoah, TX, p. A652
Chief Nursing Officer, Nexus Specialty Hospital The Woodlands, The Woodlands, TX, p. A657
ANDERSON, Rhonda, Executive Vice President Finance and Chief Financial Officer, Ascension Columbia St. Mary's Hospital Milwaukee, Milwaukee, WI, p. A716
ANDERSON, Rick, M.D., Senior Vice President and Chief Medical Officer, TMC Health, Tucson, AZ, p. A41
ANDERSON, Rob J., Chief Executive Officer, The Hospitals of Providence Memorial Campus – Tenet Healthcare, El Paso, TX, p. A617
ANDERSON, Robert C, Interim Chief Financial Officer, Alameda Hospital, Alameda, CA, p. A55
ANDERSON, Rohan, Chief Information Officer, Doctors Memorial Hospital, Bonifay, FL, p. A126
ANDERSON, Rosemary, Administrator, Ccc At Pineview Hospital, Lakeside, AZ, p. A33
ANDERSON, Scott, Chief Medical Officer, Banner Del E. Webb Medical Center, Sun City West, AZ, p. A39
ANDERSON, Sharla, Chief Executive Officer, Christus Trinity Mother Frances Rehabilitation Hospital, A Partner of Encompass Health, Tyler, TX, p. A658
ANDERSON, Shelly, Hospital President, Memorial Sloan Kettering Cancer Center, New York, NY, p. A449
ANDERSON, Sims, Manager Facility Automation, Terrell State Hospital, Terrell, TX, p. A656
ANDERSON, Stephanie, Executive Vice President and Chief Operating Officer, Woman's Hospital, Baton Rouge, LA, p. A278
ANDERSON, Stephen, M.D., Chief Medical Officer, Plymouth Medical Center, Plymouth, IN, p. A226
ANDERSON, Sue, President and Chief Executive Officer, French Hospital Medical Center, San Luis Obispo, CA, p. A93
ANDERSON, Susan, Director Information Systems, Texas Health Presbyterian Hospital Plano, Plano, TX, p. A645
ANDERSON, Suzanne P., Nurse Administrator, Intermountain Medical Center, Murray, UT, p. A666
ANDERSON, Tara Beth., President, Baptist Medical Center Nassau, Fernandina Beach, FL, p. A131
ANDERSON, Terry, R.N., Director of Nursing Services, Ccm Health, Montevideo, MN, p. A351
ANDERSON, Thomas
M.D., Vice President Medical Affairs, Wellspan Chambersburg Hospital, Chambersburg, PA, p. A536
M.D., Vice President Medical Affairs, Wellspan Waynesboro Hospital, Waynesboro, PA, p. A556

 Index of Health Care Professionals A787

Index of Health Care Professionals

Index of Health Care Professionals / Anderson

Vice President Medical Affairs, Lakeview Hospital, Stillwater, MN, p. A355
ANDERSON, Todd, Chief Financial Officer, Mercyhealth Hospital And Physician Clinic–Crystal Lake, Crystal Lake, IL, p. A192
ANDERSON, Traci, Chief Financial Officer, Memorial Hospital, Seminole, TX, p. A652
ANDERSON, Valerie, Chief Nursing Officer, Select Specialty Hospital–Tri Cities, Bristol, TN, p. A579
ANDERSON, William, Medical Director, Rosebud Health Care Center, Forsyth, MT, p. A391
ANDERT, Nancy, Director Human Resources, Murray County Medical Center, Slayton, MN, p. A355
ANDERTON, Scott, Chief Financial Officer, Piedmont Macon, Macon, GA, p. A167
ANDRADA, Sally, Chief Information Officer, UCI Health – Los Alamitos, Los Alamitos, CA, p. A71
ANDRADE, Cristain, M.D., Vice President, Chief Medical Officer, Rome Health, Rome, NY, p. A458
ANDRADE, Marise, Controller, Southern Inyo Healthcare District, Lone Pine, CA, p. A70
ANDRE, Katelyn, Human Resource Coordinator, Select Specialty Hospital – Macomb County, Mount Clemens, MI, p. A334
ANDREAS, Ginger, Coordinator Personnel and Credentialing, El Camp. Memorial Hospital, El Campo, TX, p. A616
ANDREASEN, Raymond, M.D., Chief Medical Officer–Inpatient, California Medical Facility, Vacaville, CA, p. A99
ANDRES, Chad, Chief Information Officer, Desert View Hospital, Pahrump. NV, p. A412
ANDRES, Elizabeth, Director Human Resources, Atascadero State Hospital, Atascadero, CA, p. A56
ANDRES, Leonidas, M.D., Chief of Staff, Riceland Medical Center, Winnie, TX, p. A663
ANDRES, Macia
Assistant Vice President Finance (Controller), Baptist Health South Florida, Doctors Hospital, Coral Gables, FL, p. A128
Director of Finance, Baptist Health South Florida, Baptist Hospital of Miami, Miami, FL, p. A139
ANDRESEN, Daniel, Chief information Officer, Mercy Medical Center Merced, Merced, CA, p. A77
ANDREWS, Carolle, Vice President, Interim Human Resources Officer, Uconn, John Dempsey Hospital, Farmington, CT, p. A116
ANDREWS, Charles, Director Information Technology, West Springs Hospital, Grand Junction, CO, p. A109
ANDREWS, David, Manager Information Systems, Chicot Memorial Medical Center, Lake Village, AR, p. A49
ANDREWS, Fred, Director of Nursing, North Shore Health, Grand Marais, MN, p. A347
ANDREWS, Jade E., Regional Chief Financial Officer, Minden Medical Center, Minden, LA, p. A288
ANDREWS, Jim, President and Chief Executive Officer, Deborah Heart And Lung Center, Browns Mills, NJ, p. A419
ANDREWS, John, M.D., Chief of Staff, UT Health Tyler, Tyler, TX, p. A659
ANDREWS, Kathy, Chief Financial Officer, Kindred Hospital Philadelphia, Philadelphia, PA, p. A549
ANDREWS, Kevin, Chief Operating Officer, Emory Saint Joseph's Hospital, Atlanta, GA, p. A157
ANDREWS, Kiacie, Chief Executive Officer, Cornerstone Specialty Hospitals Little Rock, Little Rock, AR, p. A50
ANDREWS, Lisa, Director Human Resources, Lancaster Rehabilitation Hospital, Lancaster, PA, p. A543
ANDREWS, Michael, Coordinator Information Systems, Harlan County Health System, Alma, NE, p. A397
ANDREWS, Mike, Associate Administrator and Chief Operating Officer, Och Regional Medical Center, Starkville, MS, p. A369
ANDREWS, Rebecca
Chief Financial Officer, Vibra Hospital of Northern California, Redding, CA, p. A85
Senior Vice President and Administrator, Wakemed Raleigh Campus, Raleigh, NC, p. A475
ANDREWS, Ryan, M.D., Chief Medical Officer, Aspirus Wausau Hospital, Inc., Wausau, WI, p. A724
ANDREWS, Sue E., Chief Financial Officer, O'Connor Hospital, Delhi, NY, p. A442
ANDREWS, Susan E., Chief Executive Officer, Touro Infirmary, New Orleans, LA, p. A290
ANDREWS, Terri, Director Information Technology, Cone Health Alamance Regional Medical Center, Burlington, NC, p. A464
ANDRIC, Belma, Vice President and Chief Medical Officer, Lakeside Medical Center, Belle Glade, FL, p. A125
ANDRUS, Helen
Chief Financial Officer, Providence Mount Carmel Hospital, Colville, WA, p. A688
Chief Financial Officer, Providence St. Joseph's Hospital, Chewelah, WA, p. A688
Chief Financial Officer, Providence St. Luke's Rehabilitation Medical Center, Spokane, WA, p. A696
ANDRUS, Jonathon, President/Chief Executive Officer, Fairchild Medical Center, Yreka, CA, p. A102
ANELLI, Jill, Director, Human Resources, Musc Health Columbia Medical Center Downtown, Columbia, SC, p. A564
ANEWISHKI, Tesa, President and Chief Executive Officer, Loretto Hospital, Chicago, IL, p. A190
ANFINSON, Julie, Chief Human Resources Officer, Mercyone Siouxland Medical Center, Sioux City, IA, p. A243
ANGELL, Deborah, Chief Financial Officer, Syracuse Veterans Affairs Medical Center, Syracuse, NY, p. A460
ANGELL, Nancy, Associate Administrator Personnel, Sagamore Children's Psychiatric Center, Dix Hills, NY, p. A442
ANGELO, Elizabeth, President and Chief Nursing Officer, Carle Foundation Hospital, Urbana, IL, p. A210
ANGELO, Gregory, Chief Fiscal Program, James J. Peters Veterans Affairs Medical Center, New York, NY, p. A448
ANGELO, Thomas, Chief Executive Officer, Centra Southside Community Hospital, Farmville, VA, p. A676
ANGELUCCI, Patricia A, MS, R.N., Director Patient Care Services, Thedacare Medical Center–Shawano, Shawano, WI, p. A721
ANGERAMI, Deborah
Chief Executive Officer, Phoebe Putney Memorial Hospital, Albany, GA, p. A156
Chief Operating Officer, Health First Viera Hospital, Melbourne, FL, p. A139
Chief Operating Officer, Health First Community Hospitals, Health First Cap. Canaveral Hospital, Cocoa Beach, FL, p. A128
Chief Operating Officer, Health First Community Hospitals, Health First Palm Bay Hospital, Palm Bay, FL, p. A145
ANGERMEIER, Elizabeth, Director of Nursing, Evansville Psychiatric Children Center, Evansville, IN, p. A216
ANGLE, Mary Ann, R.N., FACHE, Chief Nursing Officer, Tristar Summit Medical Center, Hermitage, TN, p. A584
ANGLIM, John, Human Resources Client Manager, Providence Seaside Hospital, Seaside, OR, p. A532
ANGLIN, Jason, Chief Executive Officer, Nevada Regional Medical Center, Nevada, MO, p. A381
ANGLIN, Kristine, Human Resources Manager, Willow Springs Center, Reno, NV, p. A412
ANGOURAS, Yannis, Chief Executive Officer, Heritage Oaks Hospital, Sacramento, CA, p. A86
ANIL, Gokhan, Chief Medical Officer, Mayo Clinic Health System In Mankato, Mankato, MN, p. A349
ANISKO RYAN, Karen, Director Business Development and Communications, UC San Diego Medical Center – Hillcrest, San Diego, CA, p. A90
ANNECHARICO, Mary Alice
System Vice President and Chief Information Officer, Henry Ford Hospital, Detroit, MI, p. A325
System Vice President and Chief Information Officer, Henry Ford West Bloomfield Hospital, West Bloomfield, MI, p. A340
System Vice President and Chief Information Officer, Henry Ford Wyandotte Hospital, Wyandotte, MI, p. A341
ANNESSER, Sue, Director Information Systems, Freeman Neosho Hospital, Neosho, MO, p. A381
ANSHUTZ, Margie, Chief Development Officer, Hamilton Center, Terre Haute, IN, p. A228
ANSI, Azena, Manager Health Information Management, Horizon Specialty Hospital, Las Vegas, NV, p. A410
ANSLEY, Pamela, Director Finance, Sutter Center for Psychiatry, Sacramento, CA, p. A87
ANTCZAK, Brett, Chief Executive Officer, Odessa Memorial Healthcare Center, Odessa, WA, p. A692
ANTCZAK, Kenneth, Vice President Human Resources, Trinity Health Livonia Hospital, Livonia, MI, p. A332
ANTHONY, Harry C., M.D., Chief Medical Officer, Tidalhealth Nanticoke, Seaford, DE, p. A122
ANTHONY, Kim, Director Human Resources, Burke Medical Center, Waynesboro, GA, p. A174
ANTHONY, Mark, Executive Vice President and Chief Operating Officer, Ascension Borgess Hospital, Kalamazoo, MI, p. A331
ANTHONY, Michelle, Chief Nursing Officer, Encompass Health Rehabilitation Hospital of Richmond, Richmond, VA, p. A682
ANTHONY, Paula
Vice President Information Services, UT Health Pittsburg, Pittsburg, TX, p. A644
Vice President Information Services, UT Health Tyler, Tyler, TX, p. A659
ANTHONY, Shelton, Hospital Administrator, Prevost Memorial Hospital, Donaldsonville, LA, p. A281
ANTINELLI, Mark, Manager Human Resources, Syracuse Veterans Affairs Medical Center, Syracuse, NY, p. A460
ANTINORI, James, M.D., Chief of Staff, Mountain West Medical Center, Tooele, UT, p. A670
ANTLE, Sue, Director of Nursing, Casey County Hospital, Liberty, KY, p. A269
ANTOINE, Greg, M.D., Chief of Staff, Fayetteville Veterans Affairs Medical Center, Fayetteville, NC, p. A468
ANTON, Lourdes, Director Human Resources, Larkin Community Hospital–Palm Springs Campus, Hialeah, FL, p. A133
ANTONACCI, Amy, MSN, R.N., Vice President Nursing Services, Aultman Alliance Community Hospital, Alliance, OH, p. A484
ANTONECCHIA, Paul, M.D., Vice President Medical Affairs and Chief Medical Officer, St. John's Riverside Hospital, Yonkers, NY, p. A462
ANTONIADES, Michael A., President, UChicago Medicine Ingalls Memorial, Harvey, IL, p. A197
ANTONIADES, Stathis, President, University Hospitals Cleveland Medical Center, Cleveland, OH, p. A491
ANTONUCCI, Lawrence
M.D., President/Chief Executive Officer, Gulf Coast Medical Center, Fort Myers, FL, p. A131
M.D., President/Chief Executive Officer, Lee Memorial Hospital, Fort Myers, FL, p. A132
ANTRUM, Sheila, R.N., President, UCSF Medical Center, San Francisco, CA, p. A91
ANWAR, Muhammad, M.D., Chief Medical Officer, Encino Hospital Medical Center, Encino, CA, p. A62
ANYEBE, Abiola, Market Chief Executive Officer, Kindred Hospital Dallas Central, Dallas, TX, p. A611
ANZALDUA, Brandon, Chief Executive Officer, Gonzales Healthcare Systems, Gonzales, TX, p. A622
ANZURES, Rosey, Acting Chief Financial Officer, Central Texas Veterans Hcs/Temple Tx, Temple, TX, p. A656
APIKI, Zessica L, Accountant, Molokai General Hospital, Kaunakakai, HI, p. A177
APODACA, Mark
Chief Executive Officer, Kindred Hospital Paramount, Paramount, CA, p. A82
Chief Executive Officer, Kindred Hospital South Bay, Gardena, CA, p. A65
Chief Executive Officer, Kindred Hospital–Los Angeles, Los Angeles, CA, p. A73
APOLINAR, Adam, Chief Executive Officer, Uvalde Memorial Hospital, Uvalde, TX, p. A659
APOLIONA, Nicole, M.D., Medical Director, Kula Hospital, Kula, HI, p. A177
APONTE, Miguel, Supervisor Management Information Systems, Wilma N. Vazquez Medical Center, Vega Baja, PR, p. A736
APPERSON, Amy, R.N., Chief Executive Officer, Vermilion Behavioral Health Systems – North Campus, Lafayette, LA, p. A286
APPLE, Douglas, M.D., Chief Clinical Officer Ascension Michigan & Interim President and CEO Ascension Genesys, Ascension Genesys Hospital, Grand Blanc, MI, p. A327
APPLEBAUM, Jonathan D., President and Chief Operating Officer, Novant Health Thomasville Medical Center, Thomasville, NC, p. A477
APPLEBY, Jane, M.D., Chief Medical Officer, Trident Medical Center, Charleston, SC, p. A563
APPLEGEET, Carol, MSN, R.N., Vice President and Chief Nursing Officer, Kettering Health Hamilton, Hamilton, OH, p. A497
APPLETON, Joe, M.D., Chief of Surgery, West Tennessee Healthcare Milan Hospital, Milan, TN, p. A589
APPLEWOOD, David, Chief Financial Officer, Grant Memorial Hospital, Petersburg, WV, p. A703
APPLIN–JONES, Camille, Senior Vice President and Area Manager, Kaiser Permanente Panorama City Medical Center, Los Angeles, CA, p. A73
APRILE, Patricia, Chief Operating Officer, Southern Maine Health Care – Biddeford Medical Center, Biddeford, ME, p. A296
AQUILIA, Joanne, Vice President Operations, Bethesda Hospital East, Boynton Beach, FL, p. A126
ARA, Farideh, Interim Chief Nursing Officer, Cha Hollywood Presbyterian Medical Center, Los Angeles, CA, p. A72
ARAB, Samer, M.D., Chief Medical Officer, Frio Regional Hospital, Pearsall, TX, p. A643
ARAD, Lana, Chief Financial Officer, Good Samaritan Hospital – San Jose, San Jose, CA, p. A92
ARAGON, Juliette, Finance Director, Turquoise Lodge Hospital, Albuquerque, NM, p. A433
ARAGON, LeAnne, Chief Executive Officer, Medical Behavioral Hospital of Northern Arizona, Prescott, AZ, p. A37
ARAKELIAN, Armen
Chief Information Officer, Fulton County Medical Center, Mc Connellsburg, PA, p. A545
Chief Information Officer, Penn Highlands Huntingdon, Huntingdon, PA, p. A542

A788 Index of Health Care Professionals

Index of Health Care Professionals / Arthur

Index of Health Care Professionals

ARANDA, Heather R, R.N., MSN, Chief Nursing Officer, F. W. Huston Medical Center, Winchester, KS, p. A262
ARANIO, Lani, Regional Director Human Resources, Samuel Mahelona Memorial Hospital, Kapaa, HI, p. A177
ARATOW, Michael, M.D., Chief Information Officer, San Mateo Medical Center, San Mateo, CA, p. A93
ARAU, Molly, Chief Executive Officer, Encompass Health Rehabilitation Hospital of Largo, Largo, FL, p. A137
ARAUJO, Marianne D, R.N., Ph.D., FACHE, Vice President Nursing and Chief Nurse Executive, Advocate Good Shepherd Hospital, Barrington, IL, p. A186
ARAUJO, Markeeta, Chief Nursing Officer, Desert View Hospital, Pahrump, NV, p. A412
ARBAUGH, Ronnie, Director Human Resources, Grant Memorial Hospital, Petersburg, WV, p. A703
ARBON, Terron, R.N., Chief Nursing Officer, Holy Cross Hospital – Salt Lake, Salt Lake City, UT, p. A668
ARCANGELI, Barbara J., Vice President Human Resources, Newport Hospital, Newport, RI, p. A560
ARCE, Daisy, President Medical Staff, Weslaco Regional Rehabilitation Hospital, Weslaco, TX, p. A662
ARCENEAUX, Larrie, Chief Clinical Officer, KPC Promise Hospital of Baton Rouge, Baton Rouge, LA, p. A277
ARCENEAUX, Trina, Assistant Chief Financial Officer, KPC Promise Hospital of Baton Rouge, Baton Rouge, LA, p. A277
ARCH, Chrissy, Chief Financial Officer, Cherokee Indian Hospital, Cherokee, NC, p. A466
ARCHAMBEAULT, Shirley, Chief Information Officer, Medical City Lewisville, Lewisville, TX, p. A634
ARCHBOLD, Todd, Chief Executive Officer, Prairiecare Brooklyn Park, Brooklyn Park, MN, p. A344
ARCHER, Allie, Chief Executive Officer and Chief Nursing Officer, Morgan County Arh Hospital, West Liberty, KY, p. A275
ARCHER, Doug, President and Chief Executive Officer, Mark Twain Medical Center, San Andreas, CA, p. A88
ARCHER, Joe, Chief Information Officer, Victor Valley Global Medical Center, Victorville, CA, p. A100
ARCHER, Stuart
Chief Executive Officer, Oceans Behavioral Health of Waco, Waco, TX, p. A660
Chief Executive Officer, Oceans Behavioral Hospital of Tupelo, Tupelo, MS, p. A369
ARCHER–DUSTE, Helen, Chief Operating Officer, Kaiser Permanente San Francisco Medical Center, San Francisco, CA, p. A91
ARCHEY, Eugene, Chief Information Technology, Greater Los Angeles Hcs, Los Angeles, CA, p. A72
ARCHIBOLD, Robert, Director, Human Resources, St. Anthony North Hospital, Westminster, CO, p. A114
ARCHIBONG, Henry, Vice President, Information Services and Technology, University of Maryland Capital Region Medical Center, Largo, MD, p. A305
ARCHULETA, Michael, Chief Information Technology Officer, Mt. San Rafael Hospital, Trinidad, CO, p. A114
ARCIDI, Alfred J., M.D., Chief Executive Officer, Whittier Pavilion, Haverhill, MA, p. A314
ARDEMAGNI, Jeff, Chief Financial Officer, Medical City Arlington, Arlington, TX, p. A597
ARDESHNA, Harish, Pulmonologist & Chief Medical Officer, Bluffton Regional Medical Center, Bluffton, IN, p. A213
ARDION, Doug, M.D., Chief Medical Officer, Nch Baker Hospital, Naples, FL, p. A142
ARDOAN, Cody, Director Human Resources, Acadian Medical Center, Eunice, LA, p. A281
ARDOIN, Cody, Director Human Resources, Mercy Regional Medical Center, Ville Platte, LA, p. A294
ARDOIN, Kevin, Chief Executive Officer, Oakdale Community Hospital, Oakdale, LA, p. A290
ARDOLIC, Brahim, M.D., Chief Executive Officer, Staten Island University Hospital, New York, NY, p. A453
AREAUX, Rene, Vice President and Chief Operating Officer, Springhill Medical Center, Mobile, AL, p. A22
ARELLANO, Edgar Alejandro, Chief Information Technologist, Three Rivers Hospital, Brewster, WA, p. A687
ARENA, Gregg, M.D., Chief of Staff, Northern Louisiana Medical Center, Ruston, LA, p. A291
ARENDS, Candace, R.N., Chief Nursing Officer, United Hospital District, Blue Earth, MN, p. A343
ARGO, Brian, Chief Executive Officer, Conway Medical Center, Conway, SC, p. A565
ARGUELLO–VASQUEZ, Mabel, R.N., Executive Nurse Administrator, New Mexico Behavioral Health Institute At Las Vegas, Las Vegas, NM, p. A435
ARGUETA, Emma, Chief Nursing Officer, Central Desert Behavioral Health Hospital, Albuquerque, NM, p. A432
ARGYROS, Gregory J., M.D., President, Medstar Washington Hospital Center, Washington, DC, p. A124
ARIGAN, Helen, Director Human Resources, Encompass Health Rehabilitation Hospital of Huntington, Huntington, WV, p. A701
ARION, Elaine
Vice President, Chief Nursing Officer, Ridgeview Medical Center, Waconia, MN, p. A356
Vice President, Chief Nursing Officer, Ridgeview Sibley Medical Center, Arlington, MN, p. A342
ARISPE, Joe, Director Information Systems, Medical City Decatur, Decatur, TX, p. A613
ARIZMENDEZ, Maria Elena, M.D., Medical Director, Baylor Scott & White Institute for Rehabilitation – Lakeway, Lakeway, TX, p. A633
ARIZPE, Robert C., Superintendent, San Antonio State Hospital, San Antonio, TX, p. A650
ARKEMA, Ashley, Director of Human Resources, Pella Regional Health Center, Pella, IA, p. A242
ARKIN, Melissa, Chief Executive Officer, Parkridge Medical Center, Chattanooga, TN, p. A580
ARLEDGE, Denton, Vice President and Chief Information Officer, Wakemed Cary Hospital, Cary, NC, p. A464
ARLEDGE, Nicholas, Chief Executive Officer, Carlsbad Medical Center, Carlsbad, NM, p. A433
ARLEDGE, William, Administrator and Chief Financial Officer, Genesis Behavioral Hospital, Breaux Bridge, LA, p. A279
ARLIEN, Dana, M.D., Chief Medical Officer, Willow Springs Center, Reno, NV, p. A412
ARMAND, Sandra, Director, Ochsner Lafayette General Medical Center, Lafayette, LA, p. A285
ARMBRUSTER, Kent A W, M.D., Vice President Medical Affairs, OSF Healthcare Little Company of Mary Medical Center, Evergreen Park, IL, p. A195
ARMENTOR, Lance, Chief Executive Officer, Opelousas General Health System, Opelousas, LA, p. A291
ARMFIELD, Ben, Chief Financial Officer, Fresno Heart And Surgical Hospital, Fresno, CA, p. A64
ARMIJO, Mary, Chief Operating Officer, Memorial Medical Center, Las Cruces, NM, p. A435
ARMOUR, Dale, Chief Financial Officer, Melbourne Regional Medical Center, Melbourne, FL, p. A139
ARMOUR, John, Chief Financial Officer, HCA Houston Healthcare Southeast, Pasadena, TX, p. A643
ARMSTEAD, Russell, Executive Director, Lexington Vamc, Lexington, KY, p. A268
ARMSTRONG, Alan, M.D., Chief Medical Officer, Pine Rest Christian Mental Health Services, Grand Rapids, MI, p. A328
ARMSTRONG, Caroline, D.O., M.D., Chief of Staff, Grant Memorial Hospital, Petersburg, WV, p. A703
ARMSTRONG, Eleze
Chief Operating Officer, Sierra Vista Regional Medical Center, San Luis Obispo, CA, p. A93
President, Twin Cities Community Hospital, Templeton, CA, p. A97
ARMSTRONG, Gary, President and Chief Financial Officer, Methodist Rehabilitation Center, Jackson, MS, p. A364
ARMSTRONG, Kyle
Chief Operating Officer, Baylor University Medical Center, Dallas, TX, p. A610
President Central Region of BSW Health, Baylor Scott & White Medical Center–Uptown, Dallas, TX, p. A610
President Central Region of BSW Health, Baylor University Medical Center, Dallas, TX, p. A610
ARMSTRONG, Mark, M.D., Medical Director, Baylor Scott & White Medical Center–Uptown, Dallas, TX, p. A610
ARMSTRONG, Paula, Chief Financial Officer, Kaiser Permanente Fresno Medical Center, Fresno, CA, p. A65
ARMSTRONG, Robert, M.D., Chief Medical Officer, Sanpete Valley Hospital, Mount Pleasant, UT, p. A666
ARMSTRONG, Robert E., Senior Vice President and Chief Operating Officer, Lima Memorial Health System, Lima, OH, p. A498
ARMSTRONG, Roger, Vice President Finance and Chief Financial Officer, Carle Health Proctor Hospital, Peoria, IL, p. A206
ARMSTRONG, Stacey
Interim President, WVU Medicine – Barnesville Hospital, Barnesville, OH, p. A485
Interim President, WVU Medicine – Harrison Community Hospital, Cadiz, OH, p. A487
ARMSTRONG, William C
Senior Vice President and Chief Financial Officer, Mercy Medical Center, Rockville Centre, NY, p. A458
Vice President and Chief Financial Officer, St. Francis Hospital And Heart Center, Roslyn, NY, p. A458
ARMSTRONG–HUFF, Glenda, Assistant Superintendent, Texas Center for Infectious Disease, San Antonio, TX, p. A651
ARNDELL, Scott, Chief Financial Officer, Owensboro Health Twin Lakes Regional Medical Center, Leitchfield, KY, p. A268
ARNDT, Tiffani, Chief Nursing Officer, Grand Island Regional Medical Center, Grand Island, NE, p. A400
ARNER, Steven C.
President and Chief Operating Officer, Carilion Franklin Memorial Hospital, Rocky Mount, VA, p. A683
President and Chief Operating Officer, Hospital Administrator, Carilion Roanoke Memorial Hospital, Roanoke, VA, p. A683
ARNESON, Brenda, Administrative Assistant, SMP Health – St. Andrew's, Bottineau, ND, p. A479
ARNETT, Jacob, Chief Information Technology Officer, Lakeside Behavioral Health System, Memphis, TN, p. A588
ARNETT, James, Market President–Madison, Unitypoint Health Meriter, Madison, WI, p. A714
ARNETT, Sallie, Vice President Information Systems, Licking Memorial Hospital, Newark, OH, p. A501
ARNETT, Stuart
Regional Vice President Finance, Aurora Lakeland Medical Center, Elkhorn, WI, p. A710
Vice President Finance and Chief Financial Officer, Aurora Medical Center Burlington, Burlington, WI, p. A709
ARNHART, Carol, Vice President Finance and Chief Financial Officer, Siskin Hospital for Physical Rehabilitation, Chattanooga, TN, p. A581
ARNOLD, Ann, M.D., Medical Director, Medical City Plano, Plano, TX, p. A645
ARNOLD, Bill, Executive Vice President, RWJBarnabas Health, President Southern Region, Chief Executive Officer, Ro, Robert Wood Johnson University Hospital, New Brunswick, NJ, p. A425
ARNOLD, Dustin, D.O., Chief Medical Officer, Unitypoint Health – St. Luke's Hospital, Cedar Rapids, IA, p. A232
ARNOLD, Jane, Market President, UnityPoint Health – Sioux City, Unitypoint Health – St. Lukes's Sioux City, Sioux City, IA, p. A243
ARNOLD, Kimberly N, R.N., Chief Nursing Officer and Interim Chief Quality Officer, Integris Health Woodward Hospital, Woodward, OK, p. A524
ARNOLD, Michele, M.D., Vice President and Chief Medical Officer, Intermountain Health St. Mary's Regional Hospital, Grand Junction, CO, p. A109
ARNOLD, Scott, Senior Vice President Information Systems, Tamp. General Hospital, Tampa, FL, p. A152
ARNTZ, Mary, Manager Business Office and Executive Assistant, Physicians' Medical Center, New Albany, IN, p. A225
AROCHA, Joe, Chief of Staff, Alleghany Health, Sparta, NC, p. A476
ARORA, Pamela
Senior Vice President and Chief Information Officer, Children's Medical Center Plano, Plano, TX, p. A644
Senior Vice President Information Systems, Children's Medical Center Dallas, Dallas, TX, p. A611
ARORA, Sat, M.D., President Medical and Dental Staff, Crozer–Chester Medical Center, Upland, PA, p. A556
ARQUETTE, Darrin, President, Regional Acute Care, Michigan and President, ProMedica Monroe Regional Hospital, Promedica Monroe Regional Hospital, Monroe, MI, p. A333
ARRANTS, Diane, Chief Information Officer, Musc Health Kershaw Medical Center, Camden, SC, p. A562
ARROGANTE, Revelyn, M.D., Medical Director, Northern Colorado Rehabilitation Hospital, Johnstown, CO, p. A110
ARROWOOD, Melina, Chief Nursing Officer, Transylvania Regional Hospital, Brevard, NC, p. A464
ARROYO, Edgar, Hospital Commander, Irwin Army Community Hospital, Junction City, KS, p. A251
ARROYO, Luis A
Chief Financial Officer, Hima San Pablo Caguas, Caguas, PR, p. A731
Chief Financial Officer, Hospital Hima De Humacao, Humacao, PR, p. A733
Chief Financial Officer, Hospital San Pablo Del Este Hima Fajardo, Fajardo, PR, p. A732
ARSENAULT, Lisa, Vice President Human Resources and Compliance, Millinocket Regional Hospital, Millinocket, ME, p. A298
ARSURA, Edward, M.D., Chief Medical Officer, Richmond University Medical Center, New York, NY, p. A452
ARTENSTEIN, Andrew, M.D., Chief Physician Executive, Chief Academic Officer and President, Baystate Medical Practices, Baystate Medical Center, Springfield, MA, p. A318
ARTERBURN, Catherine T, R.N., Vice President Human Resources, Sidney Regional Medical Center, Sidney, NE, p. A406
ARTHUR, Cynthia, Fiscal Director, Piedmont Geriatric Hospital, Burkeville, VA, p. A674
ARTHUR, John
Chief Financial Officer, Ascension St. Vincent Mercy, Elwood, IN, p. A215
Chief Financial Officer, Ascension St. Vincent Randolph, Winchester, IN, p. A229
ARTHUR, Rita K, Director Human Resources, Adventhealth Littleton, Littleton, CO, p. A111

Index of Health Care Professionals

Index of Health Care Professionals / Artman

ARTMAN, David S, Chief Operating Officer, Weirton Medical Center, Weirton, WV, p. A705
ARTS–STRENKE, Cindy, R.N., Chief Operating Officer and Chief Nursing Officer, Marshfield Medical Center – Rice Lake, Rice Lake, WI, p. A720
ARUNAMATA, Peti, Interim Area Director Information Technology, Kaiser Permanente San Francisco Medical Center, San Francisco, CA, p. A91
ARVIDSON, Betty, Chief Financial Officer, Riverview Health, Crookston, MN, p. A345
ARVIN, Jon A, M.D., Chief Medical Officer, Rockcastle Regional Hospital And Respiratory Care Center, Mount Vernon, KY, p. A272
ARVON, Christina, Administrator and Chief Executive Officer, Charleston Surgical Hospital, Charleston, WV, p. A700
ASADA, Bonnie, Chief Nursing Officer, Alvarado Parkway Institute Behavioral Health System, La Mesa, CA, p. A68
ASAFTEI, Laura, Administrative Director, Adventhealth Zephyrhills, Zephyrhills, FL, p. A155
ASAOKA, Danny
Executive Director Information Systems, Long Beach Medical Center, Long Beach, CA, p. A71
Executive Director Information Systems, Miller Children's & Women's Hospital Long Beach, Long Beach, CA, p. A71
ASBURY, Wesley, M.D., President Medical Staff, Princeton Community Hospital, Princeton, WV, p. A704
ASCHOFF, Jodi, Chief Financial Officer, Osmond General Hospital, Osmond, NE, p. A405
ASH, Michael A, President, Chief Operating Officer, Nebraska Medicine – Nebraska Medical Center, Omaha, NE, p. A404
ASH, Richard M., Chief Executive Officer, United Hospital District, Blue Earth, MN, p. A343
ASH, Teresa, Chief Operating Officer, Mercy Health – Anderson Hospital, Cincinnati, OH, p. A489
ASHAI, Daud, M.D., Chief Medical Officer, Baylor Scott & White Surgical Hospital Fort Worth, Fort Worth, TX, p. A619
ASHBY, Anthony
President, Chi Health Immanuel, Omaha, NE, p. A403
Vice President and Chief Operating Officer, Chi Health Immanuel, Omaha, NE, p. A403
ASHBY, F Michael, M.D., Vice President and Medical Director, Sentara Martha Jefferson Hospital, Charlottesville, VA, p. A674
ASHBY, Kim, Vice President of Finance, Baptist Health Deaconess Madisonville, Inc., Madisonville, KY, p. A271
ASHBY, Natalie
Chief Nursing Officer, St. George Regional Hospital, Saint George, UT, p. A668
President, St. George Regional Hospital, Saint George, UT, p. A668
ASHBY, Pamela, Vice President Human Resources, Medstar National Rehabilitation Hospital, Washington, DC, p. A123
ASHBY, Rae A., Director Human Resources, Sullivan County Memorial Hospital, Milan, MO, p. A380
ASHCOM, Thomas L., M.D., Ph.D., Chief Executive Officer, Kansas Heart Hospital, Wichita, KS, p. A261
ASHENFELTER, Kathy, Chief Financial Officer, Swedish Medical Center, Englewood, CO, p. A107
ASHER, Barbara, Chief Executive Officer, U. S. Public Health Service Indian Hospital, Parker, AZ, p. A34
ASHLEY, Ada, HIM Director, Lifebrite Community Hospital of Stokes, Danbury, NC, p. A466
ASHLEY, Dennis H, Vice President Human Resources, Montefiore Mount Vernon, Mount Vernon, NY, p. A446
ASHLEY, Kent, Chief Financial Officer, Mesa Springs, Fort Worth, TX, p. A620
ASHLEY, Sharon, MSN, Chief Nursing Officer, Adams County Regional Medical Center, Seaman, OH, p. A503
ASHLOCK, Janet, Chief Nursing Officer, Morehouse General Hospital, Bastrop. LA, p. A277
ASHLOCK, Ryan
Interim President, Adventist Health Castle, Kailua, HI, p. A176
President, Sierra Vista Regional Medical Center, San Luis Obispo, CA, p. A93
ASHMENT, Kerry, Chief Executive Officer, Landmark Hospital of Columbia, Columbia, MO, p. A374
ASHTON, Michael, Administrator, Bayhealth, Dover, DE, p. A121
ASHWORTH, Fred, Chief Financial Officer, Regional Medical Center of San Jose, San Jose, CA, p. A92
ASHWORTH, Jerry
Senior Vice President and Chief Executive Officer, Memorial Hermann – Texas Medical Center, Houston, TX, p. A627
Senior Vice President and Chief Executive Officer, Memorial Hermann Katy Hospital, Katy, TX, p. A631
ASIC, Jason, President, Mercy Health – Kings Mills Hospital, Mason, OH, p. A499
ASKEW, Pam, R.N., Vice President Patient Care Services, Unitypoint Health – Trinity Muscatine, Muscatine, IA, p. A240
ASLIN, Paul, Chief Operating Officer, Chambers Health, Anahuac, TX, p. A597
ASMUS, Trevor, Chief Executive Officer, Las Encinas Hospital, Pasadena, CA, p. A83
ASP, Josh, Chief Financial Officer, Welia Health, Mora, MN, p. A351
ASPEL, Tracy, Chief Nursing Officer, Northern Inyo Hospital, Bishop. CA, p. A58
ASPLUND, David, Chief Operating Officer, MPTF/Motion Picture & Television Fund, Los Angeles, CA, p. A74
ASSAAD, Haney, Vice President Medical Affairs, Trinity Health Grand Haven Hospital, Grand Haven, MI, p. A328
ASTACIO, Benjamin, Director Human Resources, Bella Vista Hospital, Mayaguez, PR, p. A733
ASTLEFORD, Daniel, Vice President Operations, Lafayette Regional Health Center, Lexington, MO, p. A379
ATADERO, Robyn, R.N., Chief Nursing Officer, Pioneers Memorial Healthcare District, Brawley, CA, p. A58
ATCHISON, Garfield, President and Chief Executive Officer, Mclaren Northern Michigan, Petoskey, MI, p. A335
ATCHISON, Marcie
Vice President Human Resources, Long Beach Medical Center, Long Beach, CA, p. A71
Vice President Human Resources, Miller Children's & Women's Hospital Long Beach, Long Beach, CA, p. A71
ATCHLEY, Mark, Vice President and Chief Financial Officer, Medical City Dallas, Dallas, TX, p. A611
ATENCIO, Maria A, R.N., Acting Chief Executive Officer and Chief Nursing Officer, Cibola General Hospital, Grants, NM, p. A434
ATENCIO, Maria A., R.N., Acting Chief Executive Officer and Chief Nursing Officer, Cibola General Hospital, Grants, NM, p. A434
ATHERTON, Dorie, Manager Human Resources, University Behavioral Health of Denton, Denton, TX, p. A614
ATHEY, Alycia, Director of Nursing, Elbow Lake Medical Center, Elbow Lake, MN, p. A346
ATKINS, Christa, Administrator, Commonwealth Regional Specialty Hospital, Bowling Green, KY, p. A263
ATKINS, James, PharmD, Chief Operating Officer, Piedmont Henry Hospital, Stockbridge, GA, p. A172
ATKINS, Jim, Director Employee Services, St. Luke's Rehabilitation Hospital, Boise, ID, p. A180
ATKINS, Melissa, CPA, Chief Executive Officer, Graham County Hospital, Hill City, KS, p. A250
ATKINS, Tracy, Chief Operating and Nursing Officer, Orchard Hospital, Gridley, CA, p. A66
ATKINSON, Andrew, Chief Operating Officer, Fulton State Hospital, Fulton, MO, p. A375
ATKINSON, James, M.D., Medical Director, UCLA Medical Center–Santa Monica, Santa Monica, CA, p. A95
ATKINSON, Johnie M, Chief Human Resources Officer, Saint Vincent Hospital, Erie, PA, p. A540
ATTEBURY, Mary, Chief Operating Officer, Northwest Missouri Psychiatric Rehabilitation Center, Saint Joseph, MO, p. A383
ATTLESEY–PRIES, Jacqueline M
MS, R.N., Chief Nursing Officer & Chief Operating Officer, Boulder Community Health, Boulder, CO, p. A104
MS, R.N., Chief Nursing Officer/Chief Operating Officer, Boulder Community Health, Boulder, CO, p. A104
ATWAL, Money, Chief Information Officer, Hilo Medical Center, Hilo, HI, p. A175
ATWOOD, Brian, M.D., Associate Medical Director, Carle Richland Memorial Hospital, Olney, IL, p. A204
ATWOOD, Julie, Director Human Resources, San Bernardino Mountains Community Hospital, Lake Arrowhead, CA, p. A69
ATWOOD, Linda, Chief Nursing Officer, Merit Health Woman's Hospital, Flowood, MS, p. A362
AUBEL, Eugenia, President, Mercy Health – St. Elizabeth Boardman Hospital, Boardman, OH, p. A486
AUBRY, Michael, Director Information Systems, Adventist Health Hanford, Hanford, CA, p. A66
AUBUCHON, Christy, Director Personnel, Washington County Memorial Hospital, Potosi, MO, p. A382
AUCKER, Kendra A.
Senior Vice President, WellSpan North Region/President, WellSpan Evangelical Community Hosp., Evangelical Community Hospital, Lewisburg, PA, p. A544
Vice President Operations, Evangelical Community Hospital, Lewisburg, PA, p. A544
AUCKERMAN, Graydon Todd, Chief Nursing Officer, Ohiohealth Rehabilitation Hospital, Columbus, OH, p. A492
AUD, Pam, Chief Clinical Officer, Andalusia Health, Andalusia, AL, p. A15
AUDETT, John R, M.D., Medical Director Clinical Affairs, Overlook Medical Center, Summit, NJ, p. A428
AUGSBURGER, Marc, R.N., President and Chief Executive Officer, Edgerton Hospital And Health Services, Edgerton, WI, p. A710
AUGSBURGER, Tod, FACHE, President and Chief Executive Officer, Lexington Medical Center, West Columbia, SC, p. A571
AUGUST, Brad, Director Information Systems, Fairfield Memorial Hospital, Fairfield, IL, p. A195
AUGUST, Prudence, Chief Information Officer, Palomar Medical Center Escondido, Escondido, CA, p. A62
AUGUSTIN, Marcus, Chief Executive Officer, Annie Jeffrey Memorial County Health Center, Osceola, NE, p. A405
AUGUSTIN, Robert, Director Human Resources, Southern Tennessee Regional Health System–Lawrenceburg, Lawrenceburg, TN, p. A586
AUGUSTIN, W Walter, CPA, III, Vice President Financial Services and Chief Financial Officer, University of Maryland Rehabilitation & Orthopaedic Institute, Baltimore, MD, p. A302
AUGUSTUS, Charles A., M.D., Chief Medical Officer, Baptist Health South Florida, Homestead Hospital, Homestead, FL, p. A134
AUGUSTUS, Richard, M.D., Chief Medical Officer, West Valley Medical Center, Caldwell, ID, p. A180
AUGUSTYN, Carissa Dawn–Noelle, Chief Nursing Officer, Yuma Rehabilitation Hospital, An Affiliation of Encompass Health And Yuma Regional Medical Center, Yuma, AZ, p. A42
AUGUSTYN, Stacy, MSN, R.N., Chief Executive Officer, Coffey County Hospital, Burlington, KS, p. A247
AUGUSTYNIAK, Becky, Director Human Resources, Piedmont Columbus Regional Northside, Columbus, GA, p. A161
AUNE, Dixie Lee, Chief Nursing Officer, Dmc Sinai–Grace Hospital, Detroit, MI, p. A325
AURAND, Brendan, Director, Human Resources, Fairmount Behavioral Health System, Philadelphia, PA, p. A548
AURILIO, Lisa, R.N., MSN, Chief Operating Officer, Akron Children's Hospital, Akron, OH, p. A484
AUSTIN, Aaron
Division Vice President Human Resources Administration, Chi Health Creighton University Medical Center – Bergan Mercy, Omaha, NE, p. A403
Division Vice President, Human Resources, Chi Health Good Samaritan, Kearney, NE, p. A401
AUSTIN, Bill, Senior Vice President of Finance, Coastal Virginia Rehabilitation, Yorktown, VA, p. A686
AUSTIN, Dan
Director Information Technology, Arkansas Methodist Medical Center, Paragould, AR, p. A52
Manager Data Processing, Ashley County Medical Center, Crossett, AR, p. A45
AUSTIN, Donnica, Chief Executive Officer, John H. Stroger Jr. Hospital of Cook County, Chicago, IL, p. A190
AUSTIN, Gene, Chief Executive Officer, Kansas City Orthopaedic Institute, Leawood, KS, p. A253
AUSTIN, Geoff, Chief Operating Officer, UW Medicine/ University of Washington Medical Center, Seattle, WA, p. A695
AUSTIN, Logan, Chief Operating Officer, Our Lady of The Lake Regional Medical Center, Baton Rouge, LA, p. A278
AUSTIN, Melissa, Hospital Director, Walter Reed National Military Medical Center, Bethesda, MD, p. A303
AUSTIN, Pam, Senior Vice–President, Chief Information Officer, Bristol Regional Medical Center, Bristol, TN, p. A579
AUSTIN, Sherri, MSN, R.N., Chief Nursing Officer, Wrangell Medical Center, Wrangell, AK, p. A29
AUSTIN, Tommye, Ph.D., R.N., MSN, Chief Nursing Executive, University Health, San Antonio, TX, p. A651
AUSTIN, W William Jr, Senior Vice President Finance, Riverside Shore Memorial Hospital, Onancock, VA, p. A681
AUSTIN, Warren, M.D., Vice President Medical Affairs, Bon Secours Maryview Medical Center, Portsmouth, VA, p. A681
AUSTIN–MOORE, Gale, Director Area Technology, Kaiser Permanente Vallejo Medical Center, Vallejo, CA, p. A99
AUSTRIA, Ramon, R.N., Chief Nursing Officer, Baylor Scott & White Institute for Rehabilitation – Lakeway, Lakeway, TX, p. A633
AUTELLI, Oscar, Chief Information Officer, Los Angeles General Medical Center, Los Angeles, CA, p. A74
AUTHUR, Tanya, Chief Information Officer, Summa Health System – Akron Campus, Akron, OH, p. A484
AUTIN, Jeremy
Chief Executive Officer, Compass Behavioral Center of Alexandria, Alexandria, LA, p. A276
Chief Executive Officer, Compass Behavioral Center of Marksville, Marksville, LA, p. A288
AUTLER, Tracy Lynn, R.N., Chief Nursing and Quality Officer, Bonner General Health, Sandpoint, ID, p. A184
AUTREY, Pamela Spencer, R.N., Ph.D., MSN, Chief Nursing Officer, Medical West, Bessemer, AL, p. A16
AVANT, Andre, Facility Automation Manager, Texas Center for Infectious Disease, San Antonio, TX, p. A651

A790 Index of Health Care Professionals

AVELINO, Ardel, Vice President and Chief Operating Officer, St. Mary Medical Center Long Beach, Long Beach, CA, p. A71
AVELINO, Joseph, Chief Executive Officer, College Medical Center, Long Beach, CA, p. A70
AVERETTE, Beverly, Chief Financial Officer, Greene County Health System, Eutaw, AL, p. A19
AVERILL, Clark, Director Information Technology, Aspirus St. Luke's Hospital, Duluth, MN, p. A346
AVERNA, Russell
  Vice President Human Resources, Spaulding Rehabilitation Hospital, Charlestown, MA, p. A312
  Vice President of Human Resources, Spaulding Rehabilitation Hospital Cap. Cod, East Sandwich, MA, p. A313
AVERY, Donald R., FACHE, President and Chief Executive Officer, Fairview Park Hospital, Dublin, GA, p. A163
AVERY, Scott B., Chief Operating Officer, Paris Regional Medical Center, Paris, TX, p. A642
AVIADO, Gail
  MSN, R.N., Chief Executive Officer, Montclair Hospital Medical Center, Montclair, CA, p. A78
  MSN, R.N., Chief Executive Officer/Interim CEO of Chino Valley Medical Center, Chino Valley Medical Center, Chino, CA, p. A59
  MSN, R.N., Chief Nursing Officer, Montclair Hospital Medical Center, Montclair, CA, p. A78
AVIGDOR, Lauren, Director Human Resources, Advanced Specialty Hospital of Toledo, Toledo, OH, p. A504
AVILA, Brandi, Chief Nursing Officer, Martin County Hospital District, Stanton, TX, p. A654
AVILA, Patrick, Chief Executive Officer, Northeast Regional Medical Center, Kirksville, MO, p. A378
AVVISATO, Michael, Senior Vice President and Chief Financial Officer, Allied Services Scranton Rehabilitation Hospital, Scranton, PA, p. A554
AVVISATO, Mike, Vice President and Chief Financial Officer, John Heinz Institute of Rehabilitation Medicine, Wilkes-Barre, PA, p. A557
AWALT, Scott, Chief Financial Officer, Sanford Hillsboro Medical Center, Hillsboro, ND, p. A482
AWAN, Naveed, FACHE, Chief Executive Officer, St. Helena Parish Hospital, Greensburg, LA, p. A282
AWINO, Adebola, Chief Nursing Officer/Interim Chief Executive Offier, Continuecare Hospital At Medical Center (Odessa), Odessa, TX, p. A641
AWOLOWO, Yinusa, Business Officer, Kingsboro Psychiatric Center, New York, NY, p. A448
AWWAD, Emad, Director Care Delivery Sites Information Systems and Technology, Lakeview Hospital, Stillwater, MN, p. A355
AXTELL, Vicki, Director Human Resources, Livingston Healthcare, Livingston, MT, p. A394
AYALA, Jose L, M.D., Chief Medical Officer, Valley Baptist Medical Center-Brownsville, Brownsville, TX, p. A605
AYALA, Lisa, R.N., Director Human Resources, Pam Health Specialty Hospital of Jacksonville, Jacksonville, FL, p. A135
AYALA, Shirley, Director Human Resources, First Hospital Panamericano, Cidra, PR, p. A732
AYCOCK, Mark, Chief Operating Officer, Spartanburg Medical Center – Church Street Campus, Spartanburg, SC, p. A570
AYCOCK, Will, Chief Executive Officer, Select Specialty Hospital Hampton Roads, Newport News, VA, p. A680
AYERS, Jessi
  Chief Financial Officer, Central Carolina Hospital, Sanford, NC, p. A476
  Chief Financial Officer, Person Memorial Hospital, Roxboro, NC, p. A475
AYERS, Matthew, Chief Administrative Officer, Norton Hospital, Louisville, KY, p. A270
AYOUB, John J., FACHE, Chief Executive Officer, Mobridge Regional Hospital, Mobridge, SD, p. A575
AYRES, Robert, Director Information Systems, Firelands Regional Health System, Sandusky, OH, p. A503
AYRES, Sam, Chief Executive Officer, Select Specialty Hospital–Des Moines, Des Moines, IA, p. A235
AYRES, Shane, Chief Financial Officer, Sanford Wheaton Medical Center, Wheaton, MN, p. A357
AZAR, Richard
  Chief Operating Officer, Stewart & Lynda Resnick Neuropsychiatric Hospital At Ucla, Los Angeles, CA, p. A75
  Chief Operation Officer, Ronald Reagan Ucla Medical Center, Los Angeles, CA, p. A75
AZATIAN, Ashot, M.D., Medical Director, Oceans Behavioral Hospital of Lubbock, Lubbock, TX, p. A636
AZCONA, Alain
  Chief Executive Officer, Aurora Behavioral Healthcare San Diego, San Diego, CA, p. A88
  Director Business Development, Aurora Behavioral Healthcare San Diego, San Diego, CA, p. A88

AZCUY, Karla, Acting Chief Human Resources Officer, Portland Hcs, Portland, OR, p. A530
AZEVEDO, Michael, M.D., Medical Director, San Joaquin Valley Rehabilitation Hospital, Fresno, CA, p. A65
AZIZ, Samir, M.D., Medical Director, Fairfax Behavioral Health, Kirkland, WA, p. A691

B

BAAS, Dina, Director Financial Services, Orange City Area Health System, Orange City, IA, p. A241
BABAKANIAN, Ed; Chief Information Officer, UC San Diego Medical Center – Hillcrest, San Diego, CA, p. A90
BABB, Cindy, Executive Director Human Resources and Organizational Effectiveness, Ascension St. Vincent Kokomo, Kokomo, IN, p. A221
BABB, Dan, President and Chief Executive Officer, Dmc Rehabilitation Institute of Michigan, Detroit, MI, p. A325
BABB, Kathy, Manager Human Resources, Clifton Springs Hospital And Clinic, Clifton Springs, NY, p. A441
BABCOCK, Jordon, Chief Executive Officer, Springwoods Behavioral Health Hospital, Fayetteville, AR, p. A46
BABCOCK, Kimberly, Administrative Director of Operations, Kalkaska Memorial Health Center, Kalkaska, MI, p. A331
BABCOCK, Robert, M.D., Interim Chief of Staff, Bath Veterans Affairs Medical Center, Bath, NY, p. A439
BABE, Heather, M.D., Chief of Staff, Shenandoah Medical Center, Shenandoah, IA, p. A243
BABER, Jonathan, Director Information Technology, Central State Hospital, Petersburg, VA, p. A681
BABERS, Wesley, Chief Executive Officer, White Mountain Regional Medical Center, Springerville, AZ, p. A39
BABICH, Eli, Chief Nursing Officer, Select Specialty Hospital–Pittsburgh/Upmc, Pittsburgh, PA, p. A551
BABLY, Stacy, Chief Human Resources, Rogers Behavioral Health, Oconomowoc, WI, p. A718
BABUSCIO, Cathy, Director Human Resources, Mat-Su Regional Medical Center, Palmer, AK, p. A29
BACHA, Fadi, M.D., Chief Medical Officer, Select Specialty Hospital–Central Kentucky, Danville, KY, p. A265
BACHELDOR, H Lee, D.O., Chief Medical Officer, Ascension River District Hospital, East China, MI, p. A326
BACHELIER, Erin, Human Resource Administrator, Ranken Jordan Pediatric Bridge Hospital, Maryland Heights, MO, p. A380
BACHMAN, John Page, Corporate Vice President, Ascension St. John Medical Center, Tulsa, OK, p. A522
BACHMAN, Roberta, Director Human Resources, Riverview Behavioral Health, Texarkana, AR, p. A54
BACHMEIER, Susan T., MSN, R.N., Chief Nursing Officer, Atrium Health Wake Forest Baptist Davie Medical Center, Bermuda Run, NC, p. A463
BACK, Barbara, Manager Human Resources, Encino Hospital Medical Center, Encino, CA, p. A62
BACKUS, Coleen Elizabeth, Chief Nursing Officer, Ascension Seton Medical Center Austin, Austin, TX, p. A599
BACKUS, Michael, President and Chief Executive Officer, Oswego Hospital, Oswego, NY, p. A455
BACON, Jeff
  D.O., Chief Medical Officer, East Morgan County Hospital, Brush, CO, p. A104
  D.O., Chief Medical Officer, Ogallala Community Hospital, Ogallala, NE, p. A403
  D.O., Chief Medical Officer, Sterling Regional Medcenter, Sterling, CO, p. A113
BADEN, Robert M, Chief Financial Officer, Lompoc Valley Medical Center, Lompoc, CA, p. A70
BADEN, Thomas Jr, Chief Information Officer, Community Behavioral Health Hospital – Rochester, Rochester, MN, p. A353
BADER, Destiny, Director of Nursing, Saunders Medical Center, Wahoo, NE, p. A406
BADGER, Jeff
  Chief Financial Officer, Ascension Calumet Hospital, Chilton, WI, p. A709
  Chief Financial Officer, Ascension Northeast Wisconsin Mercy Hospital, Oshkosh, WI, p. A719
  Chief Financial Officer, Ascension Northeast Wisconsin St. Elizabeth Hospital, Appleton, WI, p. A707
BADINGER, Sandy
  Chief Executive Officer, Slidell Memorial Hospital, Slidell, LA, p. A293
  Chief Executive Officer, Slidell Memorial Hospital East, Slidell, LA, p. A293

BAEHL, Robyn
  Chief Nursing Officer, Select Specialty Hospital–Evansville, Evansville, IN, p. A216
  Interim Chief Executive Officer, Select Specialty Hospital–Evansville, Evansville, IN, p. A216
BAENEN, Sharla, MSN, R.N., President Mental Well Being, Vice President Emergency Medicine, Hospitalists & Medical Subspecialist, Bellin Psychiatric Center, Green Bay, WI, p. A712
BAER, Douglas M., Chief Executive Officer, Brooks Rehabilitation Hospital, Jacksonville, FL, p. A134
BAEZ, Janet, Director, University Hospital, San Juan, PR, p. A736
BAEZ, Juan, M.D., President Medical Staff, Robert Wood Johnson University Hospital Rahway, Rahway, NJ, p. A427
BAFFONE, Karen, R.N., Chief Nursing Officer, Tahoe Forest Hospital District, Truckee, CA, p. A98
BAGGERLY, Karen, Chief Nursing Officer and Vice President, Covenant Medical Center, Lubbock, TX, p. A636
BAGGETT, Al, M.D., Interim Chief of Staff, Taylor Regional Hospital, Hawkinsville, GA, p. A165
BAGGETT, Margarita
  MSN, R.N., Chief Nursing Officer, UC San Diego Medical Center – Hillcrest, San Diego, CA, p. A90
  MSN, R.N., Interim Chief Operating Officer, UC San Diego Medical Center – Hillcrest, San Diego, CA, p. A90
BAGGIO, Natalie, R.N., President and Chief Operating Officer, Corewell Health Lakeland Hospitals, Saint Joseph, MI, p. A337
BAGLEY, Brenda, Director Human Resources, TMC Bonham Hospital, Bonham, TX, p. A604
BAGNALL, Andrew
  FACHE, President and Chief Executive Officer, St. Luke's Des Peres Hospital, Saint Louis, MO, p. A386
  FACHE, President and Chief Executive Officer, St. Luke's Hospital, Chesterfield, MO, p. A373
BAGNELL, Kelly, M.D., Chief of Staff, Providence St. Josep. Medical Center, Polson, MT, p. A395
BAHLS, Fredrick, M.D., Chief of Staff, VA Central Iowa Health Care System–Des Moines, Des Moines, IA, p. A235
BAIG, Mirza N., M.D., Ph.D., Chief Executive Officer, White Rock Medical Center, Dallas, TX, p. A613
BAILES, Debbie, R.N., Director of Nursing, Caldwell Memorial Hospital, Columbia, LA, p. A280
BAILEY, Ann, Assistant Director Administration, Central State Hospital, Petersburg, VA, p. A681
BAILEY, Becky
  R.N., Director Nursing, Kansas Surgery And Recovery Center, Wichita, KS, p. A262
  Director Human Resources, Lincoln Hospital, Davenport, WA, p. A688
BAILEY, Brenda, Chief Executive Officer, Highland Springs Hospital, Highland Hills, OH, p. A497
BAILEY, Bruce P.
  President & Chief Executive Officer, Tidelands Georgetown Memorial Hospital, Georgetown, SC, p. A566
  President & Chief Executive Officer, Tidelands Waccamaw Community Hospital, Murrells Inlet, SC, p. A569
BAILEY, Cori
  Accountant, Tyler Holmes Memorial Hospital, Winona, MS, p. A370
  Chief Executive Officer, Tyler Holmes Memorial Hospital, Winona, MS, p. A370
BAILEY, Dan, Director Information Systems, Norton Sound Regional Hospital, Nome, AK, p. A29
BAILEY, David, FACHE, President, Community Hospital of Bremen, Bremen, IN, p. A213
BAILEY, Dianne, Chief Information Officer, Pana Community Hospital, Pana, IL, p. A205
BAILEY, Heather, Chief Human Resources Officer, Jefferson Healthcare, Port Townsend, WA, p. A693
BAILEY, Hope, Vice President Nursing, Three Rivers Health System, Inc., Three Rivers, MI, p. A339
BAILEY, Jodi J, Human Resources Director, Odessa Memorial Healthcare Center, Odessa, WA, p. A692
BAILEY, John E., Chief Financial Officer, Moore County Hospital District, Dumas, TX, p. A615
BAILEY, Jonathan D., Chief Executive Officer and Administrator, Hansford Hospital, Spearman, TX, p. A653
BAILEY, Jonathan T, Chief Operating Officer, Stamford Health, Stamford, CT, p. A119
BAILEY, Jordana Ane, Chief Operating Officer, NYC Health + Hospitals/Jacobi, New York, NY, p. A451
BAILEY, Joy, Director Information Technology, Sutter Amador Hospital, Jackson, CA, p. A68
BAILEY, Joyce, Vice President Patient Care, Chi St. Anthony Hospital, Pendleton, OR, p. A530
BAILEY, Larry, FACHE, Chief Operating Officer, Indiana University Health Bedford Hospital, Bedford, IN, p. A212
BAILEY, Leisa, M.D., Chief of Staff, Doctors Memorial Hospital, Bonifay, FL, p. A126

Index of Health Care Professionals

Index of Health Care Professionals / Bailey

BAILEY, Meagan, Chief Executive Officer, Encompass Health Rehabilitation Hospital of Richardson, Richardson, TX, p. A646
BAILEY, Patricia, Chief Nursing Officer, Minden Medical Center, Minden, LA, p. A288
BAILEY, Rachel
Chief Executive Officer, KPC Promise Hospital of Dallas, Dallas, TX, p. A611
Chief Executive Officer, KPC Promise Hospital of Wichita Falls, Wichita Falls, TX, p. A662
BAILEY, Robert W, Chief Information Officer, Hawthorn Center, Northville, MI, p. A334
BAILEY, Scott
Chief Executive Officer, National Park Medical Center, Hot Springs, AR, p. A48
Chief Financial Officer, Saint Francis Hospital Muskogee, Muskogee, OK, p. A515
Chief Operating Officer, Saint Mary's Regional Medical Center, Russellville, AR, p. A53
BAILEY, Terra, Chief Nursing Officer, Allen Parish Community Healthcare, Kinder, LA, p. A285
BAILEY, Thomas, Chief Operating Officer, Bothwell Regional Health Center, Sedalia, MO, p. A386
BAILEY–NEWELL, Susan, Vice President Human Resources, Chi St Luke's Health – Baylor St Luke's Medical Center, Houston, TX, p. A625
BAILEY–OETKER, Jessica, Director Quality and Medical Staff, Providence Willamette Falls Medical Center, Oregon City, OR, p. A530
BAILLARGEON, Stephanie Lakeman, R.N., Chief Nursing Officer, Down East Community Hospital, Machias, ME, p. A298
BAIN, Joel, Director Information Services, Tristar Summit Medical Center, Hermitage, TN, p. A584
BAIN, Mark, Chief Human Resources, Veterans Affairs Connecticut Healthcare System, West Haven, CT, p. A120
BAIN, Pat, Chief Nursing Officer, Lower Bucks Hospital, Bristol, PA, p. A535
BAIO, Katie, Human Resource Director, UChicago Medicine Adventhealth Bolingbrook, Bolingbrook, IL, p. A186
BAIR, Ada, Chief Executive Officer, Memorial Hospital Association, Carthage, IL, p. A187
BAIRD, David, Chief Information Officer, Lds Hospital, Salt Lake City, UT, p. A669
BAIRD, Donna, Vice President Corporate Services, Ascension Sacred Heart Bay, Panama City, FL, p. A145
BAIRD, Glen, M.D., Chief of Staff, Shriners Hospitals for Children–Spokane, Spokane, WA, p. A696
BAIRD, JOHN, Chief Executive Officer, Ascension Saint Josep. – Chicago, Chicago, IL, p. A188
BAISCH, Kim, R.N., Associate Vice President Patient Care Services, St. Anne Hospital, Burien, WA, p. A688
BAISDEN, Monica, Director Human Resources, Memorial Hermann Northeast, Humble, TX, p. A629
BAJ–WRIGHT, Irena, Director Human Resources, Southwest Connecticut Mental Health System, Bridgeport, CT, p. A115
BAJAK, Tony, Chief Operating Officer, Good Samaritan Medical Center, West Palm Beach, FL, p. A154
BAJARI, Pamela R, R.N., Nurse Executive MHSATS, Community Behavioral Health Hospital – Rochester, Rochester, MN, p. A353
BAK, Katharine, Chief Nursing Office and Vice President of Patient Care Services, Brattleboro Retreat, Brattleboro, VT, p. A671
BAKAR, Anne L.
President and Chief Executive Officer, Telecare Heritage Psychiatric Health Center, Oakland, CA, p. A81
President and Chief Executive Officer, Willow Rock Center, San Leandro, CA, p. A92
BAKER, Alison, M.D., Chief of Staff, Missouri Baptist Sullivan Hospital, Sullivan, MO, p. A387
BAKER, Bonnie
M.D., Chief Medical Services, Veterans Health Care System of The Ozarks, Fayetteville, AR, p. A46
Vice President Finance and Chief Financial Officer, Butler Hospital, Providence, RI, p. A560
BAKER, Christina, Chief Nursing Officer, Fairfield Memorial Hospital, Fairfield, IL, p. A195
BAKER, Cindi, Chief Operating Officer, Riverwood Healthcare Center, Aitkin, MN, p. A342
BAKER, Damon, D.O., Chief Medical Officer, Oklahoma State University Medical Center, Tulsa, OK, p. A522
BAKER, Daniel, Executive Director, Lenox Hill Hospital, New York, NY, p. A449
BAKER, Deborah
Vice President, Nursing, Johns Hopkins Hospital, Baltimore, MD, p. A300
Vice President, Patient Care Services, Mount Auburn Hospital, Cambridge, MA, p. A312
BAKER, Denis, Chief Information Officer, Sarasota Memorial Hospital – Sarasota, Sarasota, FL, p. A150
BAKER, Erin, Chief Nursing Officer, Eminent Medical Center, Richardson, TX, p. A646
BAKER, Frank, Chief Information Officer, Mary Breckinridge Arh Hospital, Hyden, KY, p. A267
BAKER, J Matthew, M.D., President Medical Staff, Bertrand Chaffee Hospital, Springville, NY, p. A459
BAKER, Jackie, Chief Operating Officer, Cedar Ridge, Oklahoma City, OK, p. A516
BAKER, Jason, Administrator, Christus Dubuis Hospital of Beaumont, Beaumont, TX, p. A602
BAKER, Jeff, Chief Executive Officer, Hickory Trail Hospital, Desoto, TX, p. A614
BAKER, Joel, D.O., Chief Medical Officer, Wayne County Hospital And Clinic System, Corydon, IA, p. A233
BAKER, John, R.N., Chief Nursing Officer, Cleveland Clinic Union Hospital, Dover, OH, p. A495
BAKER, Kim
Senior Vice President Hospital Operations, Samaritan Hospital – Main Campus, Troy, NY, p. A460
Senior Vice President, Hospital Operations, Sunnyview Rehabilitation Hospital, Schenectady, NY, p. A459
BAKER, Maia, MSN, Chief Nurse Executive, Rio Grande State Center/South Texas Health Care System, Harlingen, TX, p. A623
BAKER, Mark A., Chief Executive Officer, Jack Hughston Memorial Hospital, Phenix City, AL, p. A24
BAKER, Matt, Director of Information Technology, Memorial Community Hospital And Health System, Blair, NE, p. A398
BAKER, Melissa
Director, Human Resources, Providence Little Company of Mary Medical Center – Torrance, Torrance, CA, p. A98
Director, Human Resources, Providence Little Company of Mary Medical Center San Pedro, Los Angeles, CA, p. A75
BAKER, Michelle, Director Information Systems, Indiana University Health White Memorial Hospital, Monticello, IN, p. A224
BAKER, Nichelle A, Chair Human Resources, Mayo Clinic Hospital In Arizona, Phoenix, AZ, p. A36
BAKER, Paige, MSN, R.N., Chief Nursing Officer, Lee's Summit Medical Center, Lee's Summit, MO, p. A379
BAKER, Paula F, President and Chief Executive Officer, Freeman Health System, Joplin, MO, p. A377
BAKER, Paula F., President and Chief Executive Officer, Freeman Health System, Joplin, MO, p. A377
BAKER, R Hal, M.D., Vice President and Chief Information Officer, Wellspan York Hospital, York, PA, p. A559
BAKER, Ray, Director Information Technology Operations, Canyon Vista Medical Center, Sierra Vista, AZ, p. A39
BAKER, Reese, Director Information Systems, Crittenden Community Hospital, Marion, KY, p. A271
BAKER, Sharon, Director Support Services, Community Fairbanks Recovery Center, Indianapolis, IN, p. A219
BAKER, Steve, President and Chief Operating Officer, Columbus Regional Hospital, Columbus, IN, p. A214
BAKER, Vanya, Director, Atrium Health Wake Forest Baptist Wilkes Medical Center, North Wilkesboro, NC, p. A474
BAKERMAN, Michael, M.D., Chief Medical Officer, HCA Florida Lawnwood Hospital, Fort Pierce, FL, p. A132
BAKEWELL, Nancy
Administrator, Monroe Hospital, Bloomington, IN, p. A213
Chief Nursing Officer, Monroe Hospital, Bloomington, IN, p. A213
BAKHTIER, Hasan, M.D., Medical Director, Incompass Healthcare, Lawrenceburg, IN, p. A222
BAKICH, Sandy, Director Information Management, Adventist Health Delano, Delano, CA, p. A61
BALASIA, Tim, Chief Financial Officer, Johnson Memorial Hospital, Franklin, IN, p. A217
BALASUBRAMONY, Suresh, M.D., Chief Medical Officer, Minnie Hamilton Healthcare Center, Grantsville, WV, p. A701
BALASUNDARAM, Anusuya, M.D., Medical Director, Hampton Behavioral Health Center, Westampton, NJ, p. A430
BALAZY, Thomas E, M.D., Medical Director, Craig Hospital, Englewood, CO, p. A107
BALCAVAGE, Thomas, Vice President Chief Patient Safety and Quality Officer, Jefferson Stratford Hospital, Stratford, NJ, p. A428
BALCEZAK, Thomas, M.D., Senior Vice President Medical Affairs and Chief Medical Officer, Yale New Haven Hospital, New Haven, CT, p. A118
BALDAUF, Robb, Coordinator Information Systems, Cleveland Clinic Akron General Lodi Hospital, Lodi, OH, p. A498
BALDERRAMA, Eva, President, Ascension Saint Josep. – Elgin, Elgin, IL, p. A194
BALDERRAMA, Jose, Vice President Human Resources, Valley Hospital, Paramus, NJ, p. A426
BALDETTI, Nicholas, Chief Operating Officer and Chief Quality Officer, Hutchinson Regional Medical Center, Hutchinson, KS, p. A251
BALDOSARO, Thomas, Chief Financial Officer, Inspira Medical Center–Vineland, Vineland, NJ, p. A430
BALDRIDGE, Dava, R.N., Chief Nursing Officer, Hillcrest Hospital South, Tulsa, OK, p. A522
BALDWIN, Barbara, Chief Information Officer, Luminis Health Anne Arundel Medical Center, Annapolis, MD, p. A300
BALDWIN, Brooke, R.N., Vice President and Chief Nursing Executive, Ohsu Hospital, Portland, OR, p. A530
BALDWIN, Ellen, R.N., Chief Nursing Officer, Texas Health Center for Diagnostic & Surgery, Plano, TX, p. A645
BALDWIN, Erin, M.P.H., Chief Operating Officer, Mahaska Health, Oskaloosa, IA, p. A241
BALDWIN, Linda, Chief Nursing Officer, Ogallala Community Hospital, Ogallala, NE, p. A403
BALDWIN, Nathan, M.D., President Medical Staff, Baptist Memorial Hospital–Booneville, Booneville, MS, p. A360
BALDWIN, Stephen, Chief Operating Officer, Touro Infirmary, New Orleans, LA, p. A290
BALDWIN, Steve
Manager Information Technology, Wyoming State Hospital, Evanston, WY, p. A727
Vice President Finance, The Willough At Naples, Naples, FL, p. A142
BALES, Alicia, Senior Director, Chief Executive Officer and Chief Nursing Officer, Carilion Tazewell Community Hospital, Tazewell, VA, p. A684
BALES, Brian, Director Plant Operations, Encompass Health Rehabilitation Hospital of Princeton, Princeton, WV, p. A704
BALES, Glenn, Chief Financial Officer, Providence Saint Josep. Medical Center, Burbank, CA, p. A58
BALES–CHUBB, Denyse, Chief Executive Officer, Adventhealth Palm Coast, Palm Coast, FL, p. A145
BALK, Lavern, Chief Financial Officer, Quad Cities Rehabilitation Institute, The, Moline, IL, p. A202
BALKO, Tom, Manager Information Systems, Centracare – Redwood, Redwood Falls, MN, p. A353
BALL, Cassie, Chief Financial Officer, Colleton Medical Center, Walterboro, SC, p. A571
BALL, Charlie, Chief Operating Officer, Specialty Rehabilitation Hospital of Coushatta, Coushatta, LA, p. A280
BALL, Connie, Chief Financial Officer, Specialty Rehabilitation Hospital of Coushatta, Coushatta, LA, p. A280
BALL, Craig, Chief Executive Officer, Specialty Rehabilitation Hospital of Coushatta, Coushatta, LA, p. A280
BALL, James, Chief Operating Officer, Executive, St. Anthony's Rehabilitation Hospital, Lauderdale Lakes, FL, p. A137
BALL, Jim, Chief Operating Officer, St. Catherine's Rehabilitation Hospital, North Miami, FL, p. A142
BALL, Rodney, Vice President Finance, Atrium Health Cabarrus, Concord, NC, p. A466
BALLANCE, William, Chief of Medical Staff, ECU Health Bertie Hospital, Windsor, NC, p. A478
BALLARD, Jerry, Director Information Systems, HCA Florida Lake Monroe Hospital, Sanford, FL, p. A149
BALLARD, John, Chief Executive Officer, Frankfort Regional Medical Center, Frankfort, KY, p. A266
BALLARD, Lorraine L, Director Human Resources, St. Helena Parish Hospital, Greensburg, LA, p. A282
BALLARD, Perry W. MSN, RN, Chief Nursing Officer, Jackson Purchase Medical Center, Mayfield, KY, p. A271
BALLARD, Terri, Chief Nursing Officer, Encompass Health Rehabilitation Hospital of Northern Kentucky, Edgewood, KY, p. A265
BALLEW, Cheryl, Human Resources Director, Encompass Health Rehabilitation Hospital of Las Vegas, Las Vegas, NV, p. A410
BALLEW, Natalia, Chief Financial Officer, Physicians Surgical Hospital – Quail Creek, Amarillo, TX, p. A596
BALLIETT, Matt, Chief Information Officer, Coal County General Hospital, Coalgate, OK, p. A511
BALLIN, Daniel, Administrator, Coastal Virginia Rehabilitation, Yorktown, VA, p. A686
BALLINGHOFF, James R, MSN, R.N., DNP, RN, Chief Nursing Officer and Associate Executive Director, Penn Presbyterian Medical Center, Philadelphia, PA, p. A549
BALLMAN, Patricia, Director, Westfield Memorial Hospital, Westfield, NY, p. A462
BALLOU, Michele, M.D., Chief Medical Staff, Lewisgale Hospital Alleghany, Low Moor, VA, p. A678
BALSER, Jeffrey R., M.D., Ph.D., President and Chief Executive Officer Vanderbilt Medical Center and Dean, Vanderbilt University Scho, Vanderbilt University Medical Center, Nashville, TN, p. A591
BALT, David, D.O., Chief Medical Officer, Avera Queen of Peace Hospital, Mitchell, SD, p. A575
BALTZ, Phyllis, Hospital President, Methodist Hospital of Sacramento, Sacramento, CA, p. A87

A792 Index of Health Care Professionals

Index of Health Care Professionals / Barnes

BALU, Vasanth
- Senior Vice President and Chief Information Officer, Excela Frick Hospital, Mount Pleasant, PA, p. A546
- Senior Vice Prssident and Chief Information Officer, Excela Health Latrobe Hospital, Latrobe, PA, p. A544
- Senior Vice Prssident and Chief Information Officer, Excela Health Westmoreland Hospital, Greensburg, PA, p. A541

BALULGA, Josefina, M.D., Clinical Director, Florida State Hospital, Chattahoochee, FL, p. A127
BALZ, Pat, Vice President Operations Human Resources, Baylor Scott & White Medical Center – Temple, Temple, TX, p. A656
BAMAN, Raj, D.O., President Medical Staff, Samaritan North Lincoln Hospital, Lincoln City, OR, p. A528
BAMBERGER, Vanessa A, Human Resources Manager, Hodgeman County Health Center, Jetmore, KS, p. A251
BAMBRICK, Cathy, Administrator, Astria Toppenish Hospital, Toppenish, WA, p. A697
BAMBURG, Jeanna, FACHE, Chief Executive Officer, Woman's Hospital of Texas, Houston, TX, p. A629
BAME, Jeremiah, R.N., Chief Nursing Officer, Piedmont Athens Regional Medical Center, Athens, GA, p. A156
BAMIRO, Lana, Chief Executive Officer and Chief Operating Officer, Kindred Hospital–San Antonio, San Antonio, TX, p. A649
BAMMEL, Paul, Vice President, Mayo Clinic Health System – Northland In Barron, Barron, WI, p. A708
BANAS, Mark, M.D., Chief Medical Officer, Aspirus Rhinelander Hospital, Rhinelander, WI, p. A720
BANBURY, Brian, Director Site Information Systems, Advocate Christ Medical Center, Oak Lawn, IL, p. A204
BANCHY, Pamela, Chief Information Officer, Western Reserve Hospital, Cuyahoga Falls, OH, p. A493
BANDEH, Jamal, Chief Operating Officer, Prague Regional Memorial Hospital, Prague, OK, p. A520
BANDFIELD–KEOUGH, Kathryn, Vice President Patient Care Services, Munson Healthcare Cadillac Hospital, Cadillac, MI, p. A323
BANDLA, H., M.D., Chief Clinical Affairs, Walter P. Reuther Psychiatric Hospital, Westland, MI, p. A340
BANDY, Dawn, Chief Financial Officer, Grant Regional Health Center, Lancaster, WI, p. A714
BANDY, Jennifer, Human Resource Business Partner, Atrium Health Wake Forest Baptist Davie Medical Center, Bermuda Run, NC, p. A463
BANDY, P Ross, M.D., Chief Medical Officer and Chief of Staff, Levi Hospital, Hot Springs National Park, AR, p. A48
BANE, Brian R, Vice President Human Resources, Rush Memorial Hospital, Rushville, IN, p. A227
BANE, William, Chief Financial Officer, Inova Loudoun Hospital, Leesburg, VA, p. A678
BANGA, Alok, M.D., Medical Director, Sierra Vista Hospital, Sacramento, CA, p. A87
BANICH, Soula, President, Indiana University Health North Hospital, Carmel, IN, p. A214
BANIEWICZ, John, M.D., Chief Medical Officer, University Hospitals Lake Health, Willoughby, OH, p. A507
BANK, Carol J, Vice President Human Resources, Aspirus Divine Savior Hospital & Clinics, Portage, WI, p. A720
BANKER, Julie G, R.N., MSN, Chief Nursing Officer, Lehigh Regional Medical Center, Lehigh Acres, FL, p. A137
BANKERS, Diane, Chief Nursing Officer, Welia Health, Mora, MN, p. A351
BANKS, Elizabeth, Chief Executive Officer, Summit Behavioral Healthcare, Cincinnati, OH, p. A489
BANKS, Matthew, Chief Executive Officer, Crestwood Medical Center, Huntsville, AL, p. A20
BANKS, Maureen
- Chief Nursing Officer, Spaulding Rehabilitation Hospital, Charlestown, MA, p. A312
- Chief Operating Officer, Spaulding Rehabilitation Hospital, Charlestown, MA, p. A312

BANKS, Patricia, Chief Executive Officer, Ely–Bloomenson Community Hospital, Ely, MN, p. A346
BANKS, Penny, R.N., Administrator, St. Charles Surgical Hospital, New Orleans, LA, p. A290
BANKS, Robbi, Vice President, Human Resources, Medical Center Health System, Odessa, TX, p. A642
BANKS, Walter, Director Human Resources, Baptist Memorial Hospital–Desoto, Southaven, MS, p. A369
BANKSTON, Doug, Director Technical Services, North Oaks Medical Center, Hammond, LA, p. A282
BANKTSON, Julie, Manager Human Resources, Munson Healthcare Paul Oliver Memorial Hospital, Frankfort, MI, p. A327
BANNA, Shannon A.
- Chief Financial Officer, Northside Hospital, Atlanta, GA, p. A157
- Chief Financial Officer, Northside Hospital Gwinnett/Duluth, Lawrenceville, GA, p. A166

BANNER, Fred, Chief Information Officer, Shore Medical Center, Somers Point, NJ, p. A428
BANNER, Manuela, FACHE, R.N., President and Chief Executive Officer, Memorial Community Hospital And Health System, Blair, NE, p. A398
BANOS, Edward, President and Chief Executive Officer, University Health, San Antonio, TX, p. A651
BANSAL, Rina, M.D., President, Inova Alexandria Hospital, Alexandria, VA, p. A673
BANTZ, Steve, Manager Information Technology, Grundy County Memorial Hospital, Grundy Center, IA, p. A236
BANUEDOS, Jorge, Director Human Resources, Dsh Metropolitan, Norwalk, CA, p. A80
BAQUET, Shawn, Chief of Staff, Iberia Medical Center, New Iberia, LA, p. A289
BARAKAT, Tawfik, M.D., President, Medical Staff, Mercyhealth Hospital And Medical Center – Harvard, Harvard, IL, p. A197
BARANOFF, Peter R.
- Corporate Chief Executive Officer, Managing Director, Hemet Global Medical Center, Hemet, CA, p. A67
- Corporate Chief Executive Officer, Managing Director, Menifee Global Medical Center, Sun City, CA, p. A97

BARANSKI, Kenneth, Chief Financial Officer, Hills & Dales Healthcare, Cass City, MI, p. A323
BARANSKI, Monica, MS, R.N., President, Mclaren Bay Region, Bay City, MI, p. A322
BARBADIAN, John, Vice President Human Resources, Adventist Health – Tulare, Tulare, CA, p. A98
BARBAREE, Jerry, Director Human Resources, Baptist Memorial Hospital – Memphis, Memphis, TN, p. A588
BARBARIN, LaSharndra, Chief Executive Officer, Medical City Arlington, Arlington, TX, p. A597
BARBEE, Daniel, Interim President, Mercy Health – St. Vincent Medical Center, Toledo, OH, p. A504
BARBER, Eric A., President and Chief Executive Officer, Mary Lanning Healthcare, Hastings, NE, p. A400
BARBER, Keith, CPA, Chief Executive Officer, Houston Methodist Willowbrook Hospital, Houston, TX, p. A626
BARBER, Michael, Chief Operating Officer, Penn Medicine Chester County Hospital, West Chester, PA, p. A557
BARBER, Richard, M.D., Chief Medical Officer, Atrium Health Wake Forest Baptist Wilkes Medical Center, North Wilkesboro, NC, p. A474
BARBER, Roxann E.
- President and Chief Executive Officer, Ascension St. Alexius, Hoffman Estates, IL, p. A198
- Regional Ambulatory Care and Ancillary Services Officer, Ascension Mercy, Aurora, IL, p. A185

BARBER, Scott, Chief Executive Officer, West Tennessee Healthcare Dyersburg Hospital, Dyersburg, TN, p. A582
BARBERA, Charles, M.D., President and Chief Executive Officer, Reading Hospital, West Reading, PA, p. A557
BARBO, Steve, R.N., Chief Executive Officer, Citizens Medical Center, Columbia, LA, p. A280
BARBOUR, Alexis, Director Finance, Columbus Springs Dublin, Dublin, OH, p. A495
BARBOUR, Michael B, Chief Nursing Officer, Emerald Coast Behavioral Hospital, Panama City, FL, p. A145
BARCLAY, Duane, D.O., Chief Medical Officer, Emory Hillandale Hospital, Lithonia, GA, p. A166
BARCLAY, Jeremy, FACHE, Chief Executive Officer, St. David's North Austin Medical Center, Austin, TX, p. A600
BARCLAY, Rick, Vice President Support Services, Mercy Hospital Northwest Arkansas, Rogers, AR, p. A52
BARCUS, Krista, Human Resources Leader, Mosaic Medical Center – Maryville, Maryville, MO, p. A380
BARD, Jeffrey, President, Aurora Medical Center of Oshkosh, Oshkosh, WI, p. A719
BARDEN, Sean
- Executive Vice President and Chief Financial Officer, Mary Washington Hospital, Fredericksburg, VA, p. A676
- Executive Vice President and Chief Financial Officer, Stafford Hospital, Stafford, VA, p. A684

BARDIER, Catherine, Vice President, Human Resources, Elliot Hospital, Manchester, NH, p. A416
BARDWELL, Carol A, R.N., MSN, Chief Nurse Executive, Martha's Vineyard Hospital, Oak Bluffs, MA, p. A317
BARDWELL, Sheila, Director Information Systems, Baptist Memorial Hospital–Golden Triangle, Columbus, MS, p. A361
BAREFOOT, Denise, Director of Information Technology, Carolina Pines Regional Medical Center, Hartsville, SC, p. A568
BAREIS, Charles, M.D., Medical Director, Macneal Hospital, Berwyn, IL, p. A186
BARELA, Barbara, Director Human Resources, Gila Regional Medical Center, Silver City, NM, p. A437
BARELA, Chris, Chief Financial Officer, Laurel Ridge Treatment Center, San Antonio, TX, p. A650

BARFIELD, Donna, Chief Nursing Officer, West Tennessee Healthcare Volunteer Hospital, Martin, TN, p. A587
BARGEN, Jim, Chief Operating Officer, Box Butte General Hospital, Alliance, NE, p. A397
BARGFREDE, Rebecca Conroy, Chief Transformational Officer, Bitterroot Health – Daly Hospital, Hamilton, MT, p. A392
BARHAM, Ed, M.D., Chief of Staff, Merit Health Woman's Hospital, Flowood, MS, p. A362
BARIOLA, Christopher L., Chief Executive Officer, Baptist Memorial Rehabilitation Hospital, Germantown, TN, p. A583
BARKAAT, Syed, Chief Executive Officer, Spring Hospital, Spring, TX, p. A654
BARKER, Alanna, Director of Human Resources, Hartgrove Behavioral Health System, Chicago, IL, p. A189
BARKER, Karen, Vice President and Chief Information Officer, Sinai Hospital of Baltimore, Baltimore, MD, p. A301
BARKER, Kathryn L, Chief Human Resources Management, Veterans Health Care System of The Ozarks, Fayetteville, AR, p. A46
BARKER, Kristi, Administrator, Wyoming State Hospital, Evanston, WY, p. A727
BARKER, Russell, Information Officer, U. S. Public Health Service Indian Hospital–Whiteriver, Whiteriver, AZ, p. A41
BARKER JOHNSON, Cheri, MSN, Executive Vice President/Chief Nursing Officer, Woman's Hospital, Baton Rouge, LA, p. A278
BARKMAN, Joseph, Vice President Financial Services, Oaklawn Psychiatric Center, Goshen, IN, p. A218
BARKSDALE, Mary, Director Human Resources, Person Memorial Hospital, Roxboro, NC, p. A475
BARLAGE, Seth, Associate Medical Center Director, John J. Pershing Veterans' Administration Medical Center, Poplar Bluff, MO, p. A382
BARLEY, Tammy, Director, Human Resources, Encompass Health Rehabilitation Hospital of Jonesboro, Jonesboro, AR, p. A48
BARLIS, Ellen, Chief Financial Officer, NYC Health + Hospitals/Jacobi, New York, NY, p. A451
BARLOW, Carol, Chief Financial Officer, Bailey Medical Center, Owasso, OK, p. A519
BARLOW, Mark, M.D., Chief Medical Officer and President Medical Staff, Vibra Hospital of Clear Lake, Webster, TX, p. A661
BARLOW, Roddex, Chief Operating Officer, The Hospitals of Providence Memorial Campus – Tenet Healthcare, El Paso, TX, p. A617
BARLOW, Sereka, Chief Operating Officer, The Hospitals of Providence Sierra Campus – Tenet Healthcare, El Paso, TX, p. A617
BARLOW, Valerie, Senior Vice President and Administrator, Wakemed Raleigh Campus, Raleigh, NC, p. A475
BARMECHA, Jitendra, M.D., M.P.H., Senior Vice President and Chief Information Officer, St. Barnabas Hospital, New York, NY, p. A452
BARNARD, Kerri, Director Human Resources, Larned State Hospital, Larned, KS, p. A252
BARNCORD, Sharon, Human Resource Business Partner, Kaiser Permanente South San Francisco Medical Center, South San Francisco, CA, p. A96
BARND, Kristi
- Chief Executive Officer, Henry County Hospital, Napoleon, OH, p. A501
- Chief Operating Officer, Henry County Hospital, Napoleon, OH, p. A501

BARNELL, Phil, Chief Medical Officer, HSHS St. Mary's Hospital, Decatur, IL, p. A193
BARNES, Alan, Chief Financial Officer, North Star Behavioral Health System, Anchorage, AK, p. A27
BARNES, Becky, Chief Operating Officer, St. David's North Austin Medical Center, Austin, TX, p. A600
BARNES, Betty, Director Human Resources, Chicago Behavioral Hospital, Des Plaines, IL, p. A193
BARNES, Bridget, Vice President and Chief Information Officer, Ohsu Hospital, Portland, OR, p. A530
BARNES, Deborah, Vice President and Chief Information Officer, Children's Hospital of The King's Daughters, Norfolk, VA, p. A680
BARNES, Gary, Senior Vice President, Chief Information Officer, Medical Center Health System, Odessa, TX, p. A642
BARNES, Jacqueline, Manager Health Information, Select Specialty Hospital–Jackson, Jackson, MS, p. A364
BARNES, Jeff, Director Information Technology, Girard Medical Center, Girard, KS, p. A249
BARNES, Karen, Interim Chief Nursing Officer, Logan Regional Medical Center, Logan, WV, p. A702
BARNES, Kimber, Director of Human Resources, Family Health West, Fruita, CO, p. A108
BARNES, Larry, Vice President Information Technology, Salina Regional Health Center, Salina, KS, p. A259

Index of Health Care Professionals / Barnes

BARNES, LaTasha, Chief Financial Officer, Bayfront Health St. Petersburg, Saint Petersburg, FL, p. A148
BARNES, Marla, Director of Nursing, Pushmataha Hospital, Antlers, OK, p. A509
BARNES, Michael, Chief Information Officer, Logan Health – Whitefish, Whitefish, MT, p. A396
BARNES, Nancy, MSN, Vice President and Chief Nursing Officer, Mcleod Health Loris, Loris, SC, p. A568
BARNES, P. Marie, Director, Human Resources, North Mississipp. Medical Center–Pontotoc, Pontotoc, MS, p. A368
BARNES, Shannon, Chief Human Resource Officer, Bonner General Health, Sandpoint, ID, p. A184
BARNES, Sherry, Director Health Information and Quality Management, Rolling Hills Hospital, Ada, OK, p. A509
BARNETT, DeLynn K, Director Human Resources, Lake Chelan Health, Chelan, WA, p. A688
BARNETT, Julia, Chief Nursing Officer, Union General Hospital, Blairsville, GA, p. A159
BARNETT, Kelly, Human Resource Officer, Brownfield Regional Medical Center, Brownfield, TX, p. A604
BARNETT, Laura, Executive Director, Human Resources, Brigham And Women's Faulkner Hospital, Boston, MA, p. A310
BARNETT, Nicole, Chief Nursing Officer, Mercy Health – Anderson Hospital, Cincinnati, OH, p. A489
BARNETT, Pam, R.N., Director of Nursing, Highland District Hospital, Hillsboro, OH, p. A497
BARNETT, Shawn
  Senior Vice President and Chief Financial Officer, Chi St. Vincent Hot Springs, Hot Springs, AR, p. A48
  Senior Vice President and Chief Financial Officer, Chi St. Vincent Morrilton, Morrilton, AR, p. A51
  Senior Vice President and Chief Financial Officer, Chi St. Vincent North, Sherwood, AR, p. A53
BARNETT, Steve, FACHE, President and Chief Executive Officer, Mckenzie Health System, Sandusky, MI, p. A337
BARNETT, Timothy R., M.D., Vice President, Cleveland Clinic Lutheran Hospital, Cleveland, OH, p. A490
BARNETT, Tom, Chief Information Officer, Highland Hospital, Rochester, NY, p. A457
BARNETTE, Brian, Chief Information Officer, Shepherd Center, Atlanta, GA, p. A158
BARNEY, Sam
  Administrator, Essentia Health Moose Lake, Moose Lake, MN, p. A351
  Administrator, Essentia Health Sandstone, Sandstone, MN, p. A355
BARNHARDT, Bonnie, Executive Director Human Resources, Ridgeview Le Sueur Medical Center, Le Sueur, MN, p. A348
BARNHART, Cody, Chief Administrative Officer, Oro Valley Hospital, Oro Valley, AZ, p. A34
BARNHART, David, Director Information Systems, Rockledge Regional Medical Center, Rockledge, FL, p. A148
BARNHART, J. T.
  President, OSF Heart of Mary Medical Center, Urbana, IL, p. A210
  President, OSF Sacred Heart Medical Center, Danville, IL, p. A192
BARNO, Jill, M.D., Chief Medical Officer, Ohiohealth Berger Hospital, Circleville, OH, p. A490
BAROLETTI, Steven, Chief Executive Officer, Pembroke Hospital, Pembroke, MA, p. A317
BARONET, Rod, Chief Executive Officer, Red River Behavioral Center, Bossier City, LA, p. A279
BARR, Ann
  Chief Information Officer – Bay Area, California Pacific Medical Center–Mission Bernal Campus, San Francisco, CA, p. A90
  Chief Information Officer – Bay Area, California Pacific Medical Center–Van Ness Campus, San Francisco, CA, p. A90
  Chief Information Officer, Sutter Health Bay Area, Sutter Maternity And Surgery Center of Santa Cruz, Santa Cruz, CA, p. A94
  Interim Chief Financial Officer, Adventhealth Dade City, Dade City, FL, p. A129
BARR, Brent, Chief Information Officer, Minnie Hamilton Healthcare Center, Grantsville, WV, p. A701
BARR, Kristine, Vice President Communication Services, Ohiohealth O'Blenness Hospital, Athens, OH, p. A485
BARR, Kyle J
  Senior Vice President, Chief Team Resources Officer, Mease Countryside Hospital, Safety Harbor, FL, p. A148
  Senior Vice President, Chief Team Resources Officer, Mease Dunedin Hospital, Dunedin, FL, p. A130
  Senior Vice President, Chief Team Resources Officer, Morton Plant North Bay Hospital, New Port Richey, FL, p. A142

BARR, Sheldon, President, VCU Health Community Memorial Hospital, South Hill, VA, p. A684
BARRA, Jon, Director Human Resources, Wyoming Behavioral Institute, Casper, WY, p. A726
BARRALL, Audrey
  Director Human Resources, Adventist Health Clear Lake, Clearlake, CA, p. A59
  Director Human Resources, Adventist Health St. Helena, Saint Helena, CA, p. A88
BARRERA, Edward, Director Communications, Encino Hospital Medical Center, Encino, CA, p. A62
BARRERA-RICHARDS, Ursula, Human Resource Director, Northwest Ohio Psychiatric Hospital, Toledo, OH, p. A505
BARRERE, Davie Ann, Coordinator Information Technology, Dahl Memorial Healthcare Association, Ekalaka, MT, p. A391
BARRETT, Anne J, Associate Executive Director Human Resources, South Shore University Hospital, Bay Shore, NY, p. A439
BARRETT, Bill, Manager Human Resources, AHS Sherman Medical Center, Sherman, TX, p. A652
BARRETT, Cindy, Administrative Assistant, Dsh Patton, Patton, CA, p. A83
BARRETT, Damon, Chief Operating Officer, HCA Florida Jfk Hospital, Atlantis, FL, p. A125
BARRETT, Hannah, Director of Nursing, North Sunflower Medical Center, Ruleville, MS, p. A368
BARRETT, James W. Jr, Chief Executive Officer, Richardson Medical Center, Rayville, LA, p. A291
BARRETT, Jason, Chief Executive Officer, Northwest Texas Healthcare System, Amarillo, TX, p. A596
BARRETT, John, Regional Director Human Resources, Franciscan Health Michigan City, Michigan City, IN, p. A223
BARRETT, Pam, Human Resources Director, Colorado River Medical Center, Needles, CA, p. A80
BARRICK, Lisa, Chief Executive Officer, Encompass Health Rehabilitation Hospital of Scottsdale, Scottsdale, AZ, p. A38
BARRIENT, Mac Jr, Administrator, North Oaks Rehabilitation Hospital, Hammond, LA, p. A282
BARRILLEAUX, Scott G., FACHE, Chief Executive Officer, Baptist Health Medical Center – Drew County, Monticello, AR, p. A50
BARRIO, Gabe, M.D., Chief of Staff, Whidbeyhealth, Coupeville, WA, p. A688
BARRIONUEVO, Walter C., Director Information Services, Winter Haven Hospital, Winter Haven, FL, p. A155
BARRIOS, Luis, Chief Information Officer, Veterans Affairs New York Harbor Healthcare System, New York, NY, p. A453
BARRON, Kathleen, Executive Director, Temple University Hospital, Philadelphia, PA, p. A550
BARRON, Steven R. Esq, Chief Executive Officer, San Gorgonio Memorial Hospital, Banning, CA, p. A57
BARROW, Andy, Chief Financial Officer, Cone Health Moses Cone Hospital, Greensboro, NC, p. A469
BARROW, Robert, Chief Executive Officer, Pontiac General Hospital, Pontiac, MI, p. A335
BARROWS, Cheryl, Vice President Human Resources, Sturdy Memorial Hospital, Attleboro, MA, p. A309
BARRY, Rick, Director Information Systems, Baylor Scott & White Medical Center–Frisco, Frisco, TX, p. A621
BARSOM, Michael, M.D., Executive Director, Dsh Metropolitan, Norwalk, CA, p. A80
BARSTAD, Stacy
  Chief Executive Officer, Sanford Tracy Medical Center, Tracy, MN, p. A356
  Chief Executive Officer, Sanford Westbrook Medical Center, Westbrook, MN, p. A357
BARTA, Brian, Chief Executive Officer, William Newton Hospital, Winfield, KS, p. A262
BARTAL, Ely
  M.D., Chief Executive Officer, Kansas Surgery And Recovery Center, Wichita, KS, p. A262
  M.D., Chief Executive Officer and Medical Director, Kansas Surgery And Recovery Center, Wichita, KS, p. A262
BARTELL, Michael
  Chief Executive Officer, Encompass Health Lakeshore Rehabilitation Hospital, Birmingham, AL, p. A16
  Chief Executive Officer, Encompass Health Rehabilitation Hospital of Shelby County, Pelham, AL, p. A23
BARTELS, Dara, Chief Executive Officer, Mile Bluff Medical Center, Mauston, WI, p. A715
BARTELS, Jennifer, Director Human Resources, Pawnee County Memorial Hospital And Rural Health Clinic, Pawnee City, NE, p. A405
BARTH, Marci, Chief Nursing Officer, SBL Fayette County Hospital And Long Term Care, Vandalia, IL, p. A210
BARTHEL, Gayle, Coordinator Human Resources, Select Specialty Hospital – Flint, Flint, MI, p. A327

BARTHOLOMEW, Brenda
  Chief Executive Officer, Gunnison Valley Hospital, Gunnison, UT, p. A665
  Chief Nursing Officer, Gunnison Valley Hospital, Gunnison, UT, p. A665
BARTHOLOMEW, Christian, Chief Human Resources Officer, Saint Vincent Hospital, Worcester, MA, p. A320
BARTHOLOMEW, K A, M.D., Medical Director, Faulkton Area Medical Center, Faulkton, SD, p. A573
BARTILSON, Jim, Manager Information Systems, South Peninsula Hospital, Homer, AK, p. A28
BARTKOSKI, Tony, M.D., Chief of Medical Staff, Nemaha Valley Community Hospital, Seneca, KS, p. A260
BARTLETT, Beth, MSN, R.N., Vice President Nursing, Chi Health Saint Francis, Grand Island, NE, p. A400
BARTLETT, Freda, Director of Nursing, Crosbyton Clinic Hospital, Crosbyton, TX, p. A610
BARTLETT, Karolyn, Assistant Administrator, Mayo Clinic Health System – Northland In Barron, Barron, WI, p. A708
BARTLETT, Ronald E, Chief Financial Officer, Boston Medical Center, Boston, MA, p. A310
BARTLETT, Thomas G. III, Administrator, Ochsner Laird Hospital, Union, MS, p. A369
BARTLETT, Wayne, Director Information Systems, UC San Diego Health – East Campus, San Diego, CA, p. A90
BARTLEY, Scott C., M.D., Chief of Staff, St. Cloud Va Health Care System, Saint Cloud, MN, p. A354
BARTLEY, Tracy, Manager Information Technology, Bath Community Hospital, Hot Springs, VA, p. A678
BARTOLETTI, Freddy, M.D., Chief of Staff, Community Hospital of Anaconda, Anaconda, MT, p. A389
BARTOLOTTA, Carmen J., R.N., Vice President, Patient Care Services and Chief Nursing Officer, Missouri Baptist Sullivan Hospital, Sullivan, MO, p. A387
BARTON, Douglas
  M.D., Chief Medical Officer, SSM Health St. Josep. – St. Charles, Saint Charles, MO, p. A383
  M.D., Interim President, SSM Health St. Josep. – St. Charles, Saint Charles, MO, p. A383
BARTON, Kelly, President, Mainehealth Behavioral Health At Spring Harbor, Westbrook, ME, p. A299
BARTON, Michelle, Chief Operating Officer, Milford Valley Memorial Hospital, Milford, UT, p. A665
BARTON, Thomas, M.D., Medical Director, Top. Surgical Specialty Hospital, Houston, TX, p. A628
BARTON, Vikki, R.N., Chief Nursing Officer, Collingsworth General Hospital, Wellington, TX, p. A661
BARTOW, Byran, Director, Winnebago Mental Health Institute, Winnebago, WI, p. A725
BARWIS, Kurt A., FACHE, President and Chief Executive Officer, Bristol Health, Bristol, CT, p. A115
BARYLSKE, Ben, Chief Financial Officer, St. Bernards Medical Center, Jonesboro, AR, p. A48
BARYMON, Randall, Chief Executive Officer, St. Bernards Five Rivers, Pocahontas, AR, p. A52
BASA, Rhea, Director Human Resources, Morrill County Community Hospital, Bridgeport, NE, p. A398
BASALAY, Erin, PsyD, Chief Executive Officer, Rock Springs, Georgetown, TX, p. A622
BASEY, Marjorie, Chief Financial Officer, Rehabilitation Hospital of Indiana, Indianapolis, IN, p. A220
BASH, Camille, Chief Financial Officer, Luminis Health Doctors Community Medical Center, Lanham, MD, p. A305
BASHAM, Mark, M.D., Chief Medical Officer, Greenwood County Hospital, Eureka, KS, p. A249
BASQUE, Tonya, Chief Nursing Officer, Freestone Medical Center, Fairfield, TX, p. A618
BASRIA, Deborah, Human Resources Payroll Administrator, Kindred Hospital Bay Area–Tampa, Tampa, FL, p. A152
BASS, Darren, FACHE, Chief Executive Officer, North Region, Saint Luke's North Hospital – Barry Road, Kansas City, MO, p. A378
BASS, Keith, Medical Center Director, West Texas Va Health Care System, Big Spring, TX, p. A604
BASS, Kevin R., Commander, Evans U. S. Army Community Hospital, Fort Carson, CO, p. A107
BASS, Louis A., Chief Executive Officer, RMC Anniston, Anniston, AL, p. A15
BASSETT, Keri, Human Resources Business Partner, Florida State Hospital, Chattahoochee, FL, p. A127
BASSO, Marty
  Chief Financial Officer, Sibley Memorial Hospital, Washington, DC, p. A124
  Senior Vice President Finance, Suburban Hospital, Bethesda, MD, p. A303
BASTARACHE, Maurice, Chief Information Officer, Chesapeake Regional Medical Center, Chesapeake, VA, p. A674
BASTIANELLO, Carol, Director Human Resources, Aspirus Iron River Hospital, Iron River, MI, p. A330

Index of Health Care Professionals / Beattie

Index of Health Care Professionals

BASTING, Gregory
M.D., Vice President Medical Affairs, Allied Services Scranton Rehabilitation Hospital, Scranton, PA, p. A554
M.D., Vice President Medical Affairs, John Heinz Institute of Rehabilitation Medicine, Wilkes–Barre, PA, p. A557
BATA, Katie
Vice President Human Resources, Advocate Illinois Masonic Medical Center, Chicago, IL, p. A188
Vice President Human Resources, Advocate Lutheran General Hospital, Park Ridge, IL, p. A205
BATAL, Lucille M., Administrator, Baldpate Hospital, Georgetown, MA, p. A314
BATCHELOR, Dale, M.D., Chief Medical Officer, Ascension Saint Thomas Hospital, Nashville, TN, p. A590
BATCHELOR, Daniela, Director Human Resources, Springhill Medical Center, Mobile, AL, p. A22
BATCHLOR, Elaine, M.D., M.P.H., Chief Executive Officer, Mlk Community Healthcare, Los Angeles, CA, p. A74
BATDORF, Karyn
Director Human Resources, Mercy Health – West Hospital, Cincinnati, OH, p. A489
Director of Human Resources, Monroe Hospital, Bloomington, IN, p. A213
BATEMAN, Bryan S., Chief Executive Officer, Physicians Surgical Hospital – Quail Creek, Amarillo, TX, p. A596
BATEMAN, Devin, M.D., Chief Medical Officer, Adventhealth Parker, Parker, CO, p. A112
BATEMAN, Gary, Chief Information Technology, Adair County Health System, Greenfield, IA, p. A236
BATEMAN, Jana, R.N., Chief Nursing Officer, UT Health Jacksonville, Jacksonville, TX, p. A630
BATEMAN, Mark T, Interim Chief Operating Officer, Saint Agnes Medical Center, Fresno, CA, p. A65
BATES, Christine, Chief Nursing Officer, Shodair Children's Hospital, Helena, MT, p. A393
BATES, Don, Chief Executive Officer, Golden Plains Community Hospital, Borger, TX, p. A604
BATES, Earl, Director Information Technology, Western Mental Health Institute, Bolivar, TN, p. A579
BATES, Joe, M.D., Clinical Director, Rusk State Hospital, Rusk, TX, p. A648
BATES, Margaret, Chief of Staff, PIH Health Good Samaritan Hospital, Los Angeles, CA, p. A74
BATES, Ondrea, Senior Vice President, Operations and Continuum of Care, Henry Ford Jackson Hospital, Jackson, MI, p. A331
BATES, Robert A., Chief Financial Officer, Ascension St. Vincent Carmel Hospital, Carmel, IN, p. A213
BATH, Harneet, M.D., Vice President, Chief Medicine Officer, OSF Saint Anthony Medical Center, Rockford, IL, p. A207
BATISTA, David J., Chief Executive Officer, Doctors Hospital of Riverside/Executive Vice President, AHMC Healthcare, In, Parkview Community Hospital Medical Center, Riverside, CA, p. A86
BATISTE, Michele, Director Human Resources, Mon Health Preston Memorial Hospital, Kingwood, WV, p. A702
BATKE, Miriam, Interim Chief Human Resource Officer, Fisher–Titus Medical Center, Norwalk, OH, p. A501
BATRASH, Ahmad, Chief of Staff, Kansas City Va Medical Center, Kansas City, MO, p. A377
BATSCHELET, Wendy, MSN, R.N., Chief Nursing Officer, Geisinger Medical Center Muncy, Muncy, PA, p. A546
BATSHAW, Mark L, M.D., Physician–in–Chief, Executive Vice President and Chief Academic Officer, Children's National Hospital, Washington, DC, p. A123
BATTEY, Patrick M., FACS, M.D., Chief Executive Officer, Piedmont Atlanta Hospital, Atlanta, GA, p. A158
BATTISTA, Edward
Vice President Human Resources, California Pacific Medical Center–Mission Bernal Campus, San Francisco, CA, p. A90
Vice President Human Resources, California Pacific Medical Center–Van Ness Campus, San Francisco, CA, p. A90
Vice President Human Resources, Good Samaritan Hospital – San Jose, San Jose, CA, p. A92
BATTLES, Lindsay, Director Human Resources, Encompass Health Rehabilitation Hospital of Dallas, Dallas, TX, p. A611
BATTS, Kayla, Manager Human Resources, Baptist Health La Grange, La Grange, KY, p. A268
BATTY, Jill I, Chief Financial Officer, Cambridge Health Alliance, Cambridge, MA, p. A312
BATTY, Mark, Chief Operating Officer, Mason Health, Shelton, WA, p. A695
BATY, Krista
R.N., Chief Administrative & Nursing Officer, Hendrick Medical Center Brownwood, Brownwood, TX, p. A605
R.N., Chief Executive Officer, Hendrick Medical Center, Abilene, TX, p. A595
BATZ, Raymond R., Commanding Officer, Naval Hospital Beaufort, Beaufort, SC, p. A562
BATZEL, Linnane, M.D., Senior Vice President Quality and Medical Affairs and Chief Medical Officer, UPMC Altoona, Altoona, PA, p. A534
BAUER, Denise, Director of Human Resources, Rochelle Community Hospital, Rochelle, IL, p. A207
BAUER, Jeremy, Chief Executive Officer, West Holt Medical Services, Atkinson, NE, p. A397
BAUER, Jessica
President, Aurora Medical Center In Washington County, Hartford, WI, p. A712
President, Aurora Medical Center Summit, Summit, WI, p. A722
BAUER, John
Chief Operating Officer, Pam Specialty Hospital of Covington, Covington, LA, p. A280
Vice President, Chief Financial Officer, Dignity Health Arizona General Hospital Mesa, Llc, Mesa, AZ, p. A33
BAUER, Jonathan, Vice President Information Systems and Chief Information Officer, Atlantic General Hospital, Berlin, MD, p. A302
BAUER, Lindy, Chief Nursing Officer, Council Oak Comprehensive Healthcare, Tulsa, OK, p. A522
BAUER, Roberta, M.D., Acting Chair Medical Staff, Cleveland Clinic Children's Hospital for Rehabilitation, Cleveland, OH, p. A490
BAUER, Sandra A., Director Human Resources, Jefferson Community Health And Life, Fairbury, NE, p. A399
BAUER, Shar, Executive Secretary, South Central Health, Wishek, ND, p. A483
BAUER, Tracy, Chief Executive Officer, Midwest Medical Center, Galena, IL, p. A195
BAUER, William, Vice President Finance and Chief Financial Officer, Lehigh Valley Hospital – Hazleton, Hazleton, PA, p. A541
BAUGHMAN, Nathan, Chief Nursing Officer, Putnam County Memorial Hospital, Unionville, MO, p. A388
BAUM, Anne, President, Lehigh Valley Hospital–Cedar Crest, Allentown, PA, p. A534
BAUM, David, M.D., Senior Vice President Medical Services, F. F. Thompson Hospital, Canandaigua, NY, p. A440
BAUMAN, Chris, Director of Nursing, Ballard Rehabilitation Hospital, San Bernardino, CA, p. A88
BAUMAN, Jonathan, M.D., Chief Medical Officer, Four Winds Hospital, Katonah, NY, p. A444
BAUMGARTNER, Jennifer, Chief Information Officer, Perkins County Health Services, Grant, NE, p. A400
BAUNCHALK, James M, Deputy Chief Clinical Services, Dwight David Eisenhower Army Medical Center, Fort Gordon, GA, p. A164
BAUSCHKA, Martha F., R.N., Vice President and Chief Nursing Officer, Southwest General Health Center, Middleburg Heights, OH, p. A500
BAUTE, Corey
Vice President Human Resources, Franciscan Health Indianapolis, Indianapolis, IN, p. A219
Vice President of Human Resource, Franciscan Health Carmel, Carmel, IN, p. A213
BAUTISTA, Ricardo, Chief Executive Officer, Sonoma Specialty Hospital, Sebastopol, CA, p. A95
BAVA, Michele, Director Human Resources, Doctors Medical Center of Modesto, Modesto, CA, p. A77
BAVERSO, Lou, Chief Operating Officer President, Central Pennsylvania Region, UPMC Harrisburg, Harrisburg, PA, p. A541
BAW, Joseph, Chief Operating Officer, Riveredge Hospital, Forest Park, IL, p. A195
BAWAHAB, Atif
Chief Executive Officer, Insight Hospital And Medical Center, Chicago, IL, p. A189
Chief Executive Officer, Insight Surgical Hospital, Warren, MI, p. A340
BAXA, Erin, M.D., Chief Medical Officer, Osborne County Memorial Hospital, Osborne, KS, p. A256
BAXLEY, Edmond Russell. III, President and Chief Executive Officer, Beaufort Memorial Hospital, Beaufort, SC, p. A562
BAXTER, Joshua, Director, Information Systems, Powell Valley Health Care, Powell, WY, p. A728
BAXTER, Kyle, Chief Operating Officer, Musc Health Florence Medical Center, Florence, SC, p. A566
BAXTER, W. Gregory, M.D., Senior Vice President Medical Affairs and Chief Medical Officer, Elliot Hospital, Manchester, NH, p. A416
BAXTER, W. Gregory., M.D., President and Chief Executive Officer, Elliot Hospital, Manchester, NH, p. A416
BAYARDO, Fernando, M.D., Chief Medical Officer, Presbyterian Espanola Hospital, Espanola, NM, p. A434
BAYER, Brian, Information Technology Site Leader, Kalamazoo Psychiatric Hospital, Kalamazoo, MI, p. A331
BAYOUMY, Sam, Interim Chief Executive Officer, Kessler Institute for Rehabilitation, West Orange, NJ, p. A430
BAYTOS, David G., President, Methodist Healthcare Olive Branch Hospital, Olive Branch, MS, p. A367
BAYUS, Robin, Chief Financial Officer, Rancho Los Amigos National Rehabilitation Center, Downey, CA, p. A62
BAZEMORE, Daniel, Chief Financial Officer, Franklin Memorial Hospital, Farmington, ME, p. A297
BEA, Javon R.
President and Chief Executive Officer, Mercyhealth Hospital And Medical Center – Harvard, Harvard, IL, p. A197
President and Chief Executive Officer, Mercyhealth Hospital And Medical Center – Walworth, Lake Geneva, WI, p. A714
President and Chief Executive Officer, Mercyhealth Hospital And Physician Clinic–Crystal Lake, Crystal Lake, IL, p. A192
President and Chief Executive Officer, Mercyhealth Hospital And Trauma Center – Janesville, Janesville, WI, p. A713
President and Chief Executive Officer, Mercyhealth Javon Bea Hospital – Riverside Campus, Rockford, IL, p. A207
BEACH, Karrie, Vice President Finance, Syracuse Area Health, Syracuse, NE, p. A406
BEACH, Sarah, Director of Nursing, Jerold Phelp. Community Hospital, Garberville, CA, p. A65
BEAGLE, Ashley, Director of Nursing, Doctors' Memorial Hospital, Perry, FL, p. A147
BEAL, Christopher, M.D., Chief of Staff, Sparrow Clinton Hospital, Saint Johns, MI, p. A337
BEAL, Dwight, Chief Fiscal Services, Jack C. Montgomery Department of Veterans Affairs Medical Center, Muskogee, OK, p. A515
BEAL, Rachel, Chief Operating Officer, Poplar Springs Hospital, Petersburg, VA, p. A681
BEAL, Walter Edwin., Chief Executive Officer, Central Regional Hospital, Butner, NC, p. A464
BEALES, Julie, M.D., Chief of Staff, Hunter Holmes Mcguire Veterans Affairs Medical Center–Richmond, Richmond, VA, p. A683
BEALS, Kristin, Commander, David Grant Usaf Medical Center, Travis Air Force Base, CA, p. A98
BEAM, William, M.D., Chief of Staff, Cornerstone Specialty Hospitals Huntington, Huntington, WV, p. A701
BEAMAN, Frank, Chief Executive Officer, Faith Community Hospital, Jacksboro, TX, p. A630
BEAMES, Bo, Chief Executive Officer, Miners' Colfax Medical Center, Raton, NM, p. A436
BEAMON, Ron
Chief Financial Officer, St. Joseph's Hospital, Tampa, FL, p. A152
Vice President, Chief Financial Officer, Winter Haven Hospital, Winter Haven, FL, p. A155
BEAN, Todd, Chief Medical Officer, Cass Health, Atlantic, IA, p. A230
BEAR, John, Hospital Administrator Officer and Supervisor Human Resources, Lawton Indian Hospital, Lawton, OK, p. A514
BEARD, Bert
Chief Executive Officer, Maria Parham Health, Duke Lifepoint Healthcare, Henderson, NC, p. A470
Chief Executive Officer, Person Memorial Hospital, Roxboro, NC, p. A475
BEARD, Bradley, Chief Operating Officer, Essentia Health Duluth, Duluth, MN, p. A346
BEARD, Chris, Chief Nursing Officer, Brownfield Regional Medical Center, Brownfield, TX, p. A604
BEARD, Joan, Chief Nursing Officer, Northwest Florida Community Hospital, Chipley, FL, p. A128
BEARD, Rhonda, Director Human Resources, Palestine Regional Medical Center–East, Palestine, TX, p. A642
BEARD, Robert, Chief Clinical Officer, Amg Specialty Hospital Northwest Indiana, Crown Point, IN, p. A214
BEARDEN, Stephen, Chief Financial Officer, Tristar Hendersonville Medical Center, Hendersonville, TN, p. A584
BEARDSLEY, Katie, Chief Human Resources Officer, Sharp Mesa Vista Hospital, San Diego, CA, p. A90
BEASLEY, Carla
R.N., MSN, Administrator, Archbold Mitchell, Camilla, GA, p. A160
R.N., MSN, Director of Nursing, Archbold Mitchell, Camilla, GA, p. A160
BEASLEY, Craig, M.D., Chief Medical Officer, Throckmorton County Memorial Hospital, Throckmorton, TX, p. A658
BEASLEY, Jared, R.N., Vice President Patient Care, Parkview Lagrange Hospital, Lagrange, IN, p. A222
BEASLEY, Ruth, Director Human Resources, Vanderbilt Stallworth Rehabilitation Hospital, Nashville, TN, p. A591
BEASLEY, Tareka, Director Human Resources, Riverwoods Behavioral Health System, Riverdale, GA, p. A170
BEATTIE, Kathryn, M.D., Senior Vice President and Chief Medical Officer, UW Medicine/Valley Medical Center, Renton, WA, p. A693

Index of Health Care Professionals

Index of Health Care Professionals / Beattie

BEATTIE, Mac, Computer Network Specialist, Deer's Head Hospital Center, Salisbury, MD, p. A307
BEATTY, Alan L, Vice President Human Resources, Shore Medical Center, Somers Point, NJ, p. A428
BEATTY, Ann, Director Human Resources, Cleveland Clinic Fairview Hospital, Cleveland, OH, p. A490
BEATY, Susan R, R.N., Administrator, Firsthealth Moore Regional Hospital, Pinehurst, NC, p. A474
BEAUBIEN, Troy, Director Information Services, Manatee Memorial Hospital, Bradenton, FL, p. A126
BEAUCHAMP, Bill, Chief Financial Officer, St. Luke's Health – Sugar Land Hospital, Sugar Land, TX, p. A655
BEAUCHANE, Nichole, Director Information Technology, Riverview Health, Crookston, MN, p. A345
BEAUDOIN, Dale, Vice President Human Resources, Lewisgale Medical Center, Boones Mill, VA, p. A674
BEAUDOIN, Paul, Chief Financial Officer, Day Kimball Hospital, Putnam, CT, p. A118
BEAUDRY, Bo, Chief Executive Officer, Ascension St. John Medical Center, Tulsa, OK, p. A522
BEAULAC, Gary, Chief Operating Officer, Henry Ford Macomb Hospital, Clinton Township, MI, p. A324
BEAULIEU, Brent, Chief Financial Officer, Baptist Health Extended Care Hospital, Little Rock, AR, p. A49
BEAULIEU, Gregory, Commander, U. S. Air Force Hospital, Hampton, VA, p. A677
BEAULIEU, Lynn, Chief Nursing Officer, Walton Rehabilitation Hospital, An Affiliate of Encompass Health, Augusta, GA, p. A158
BEAULIEU, Michael Gregory, M.D., Chief Medical Officer, Helen Newberry Joy Hospital & Healthcare Center, Newberry, MI, p. A334
BEAUVAIS, Robert P., Chief Hospital Executive, Carepoint Health Hoboken University Medical Center, Hoboken, NJ, p. A422
BEAVER, Michael D., Chief Executive Officer, Methodist Stone Oak Hospital, San Antonio, TX, p. A650
BEAVER, Patrick, MSN, R.N., Chief Nursing Officer, East Cooper Medical Center, Mount Pleasant, SC, p. A568
BEAVER, Rhonda, Chief Administrative Officer, Creek Nation Community Hospital, Okemah, OK, p. A516
BECHAMPS, Gerald
M.D., Vice President Medical Affairs, Valley Health – Hampshire Memorial Hospital, Romney, WV, p. A704
M.D., Vice President Medical Affairs, Valley Health – War Memorial Hospital, Berkeley Springs, WV, p. A699
BECHTEL, Kathleen, MSN, R.N., Vice President Patient Care Services and Chief Nursing Officer, Froedtert And The Medical College of Wisconsin Froedtert Hospital, Milwaukee, WI, p. A717
BECK, Adam, Market Chief Executive Officer, Select Specialty Hospital–Camp Hill, Camp Hill, PA, p. A536
BECK, Allan, Chief Executive Officer, Baylor Orthopedic And Spine Hospital At Arlington, Arlington, TX, p. A597
BECK, Ann
Chief Financial Officer, Renown Rehabilitation Hospital, Reno, NV, p. A412
Chief Financial Officer, Renown South Meadows Medical Center, Reno, NV, p. A412
BECK, Brian, Vice President Human Resources, Oak Valley Hospital, Oakdale, CA, p. A80
BECK, Brody, Director Information Technology, Minidoka Memorial Hospital, Rupert, ID, p. A183
BECK, David S., Chief Operating Officer, Lane Regional Medical Center, Zachary, LA, p. A294
BECK, Debbie, Manager Human Resource and Payroll, Ochiltree General Hospital, Perryton, TX, p. A643
BECK, Howard, M.D., Chief of Staff, Grace Surgical Hospital, Lubbock, TX, p. A636
BECK, J Christopher, D.O., President Medical Staff, Aspen Valley Hospital, Aspen, CO, p. A103
BECK, Jason, President and Chief Executive Officer, Columbus Regional Healthcare System, Whiteville, NC, p. A477
BECK, Rebecca
Chief Executive Officer, Holston Valley Medical Center, Kingsport, TN, p. A585
Chief Executive Officer, Indian Path Community Hospital, Kingsport, TN, p. A585
BECK, Steve, MS, Chief Human Resource Officer, Kearney Regional Medical Center, Kearney, NE, p. A401
BECK STELLA, Caitlin, Chief Executive Officer, Memorial Regional Hospital, Hollywood, FL, p. A133
BECKER, Anita, R.N., Nurse Executive, Director of Patient Care Services, Shriners Hospitals for Children–Honolulu, Honolulu, HI, p. A176
BECKER, Brian, Vice President Medical Affairs and Chief Medical Officer, Ascension Providence, Waco, TX, p. A660
BECKER, Cindy, Vice President and Chief Operating Officer, Highland Hospital, Rochester, NY, p. A457
BECKER, Colleen, Chief Nursing Officer, OSF Healthcare Saint Anthony's Health Center, Alton, IL, p. A185
BECKER, Eric, Chief Executive Officer, Texas Orthopedic Hospital, Houston, TX, p. A628
BECKER, Kathleen R., M.P.H., JD, Chief Executive Officer, University of New Mexico Hospitals, Albuquerque, NM, p. A433
BECKER, Kathy, Ph.D., R.N., Vice President and Chief Nursing Officer, Aurora West Allis Medical Center, West Allis, WI, p. A724
BECKER, Preston, Chief Executive Officer, Steele Memorial Medical Center, Salmon, ID, p. A183
BECKER, Ralp. W, Vice President, Chief Financial Officer, Saint Mary's Hospital, Waterbury, CT, p. A119
BECKER, Sherri P., Chief Executive Officer, Regency North Central Ohio – Cleveland East, Warrensville Heights, OH, p. A506
BECKES, Hap. Director Information Systems, Sullivan County Community Hospital, Sullivan, IN, p. A227
BECKFORD, Crystal, Chief Nursing Officer, Luminis Health Doctors Community Medical Center, Lanham, MD, p. A305
BECKHAM, Blue, Interim Chief Information Officer, Wickenburg Community Hospital, Wickenburg, AZ, p. A41
BECKHAM, Steve, Director Human Resources, Magee General Hospital, Magee, MS, p. A365
BECKHAM, Steward, Director, Chief Operating Officer, Saint Elizabeths Hospital, Washington, DC, p. A124
BECKLUN, Megan, Director Human Resources, Antelop. Memorial Hospital, Neligh, NE, p. A403
BECKMAN, Dee, MSN, R.N., Chief Nursing Officer, Baptist Health Lexington, Lexington, KY, p. A268
BECKMANN, Lauren, Vice President Patient Services and Chief Nursing Officer, Barnes–Jewish St. Peters Hospital, Saint Peters, MO, p. A386
BECKNER, Jana, Director Human Resources, Lewisgale Hospital Pulaski, Pulaski, VA, p. A681
BECKNER, Michelle, Chief Financial Officer, Hays Medical Center, Hays, KS, p. A250
BECKSVOORT, Jennifer F, Senior Human Resource Business Partner, Corewell Health Zeeland Hospital, Zeeland, MI, p. A341
BECKWITH, Jami, Director Human Resources, Choctaw Nation Health Care Center, Talihina, OK, p. A521
BEDELL, Mikael, M.D., Medical Director, Cascade Medical Center, Cascade, ID, p. A180
BEDFORD, Tim, Chief Executive Officer, Emerald Coast Behavioral Hospital, Panama City, FL, p. A145
BEDI, Andrew, Chief Executive Officer, The Medical Center At Russellville, Russellville, KY, p. A274
BEDICK, Jennifer L., Deputy Commander Nursing, Tripler Army Medical Center, Honolulu, HI, p. A176
BEDNAR, Jan, R.N., MS, Chief Nursing Officer, Saint Clare's Denville Hospital, Denville, NJ, p. A420
BEDSOLE, Jessica, Director, Human Resources, Wellstar Paulding Hospital, Hiram, GA, p. A165
BEDZYK, J. Paul, Deputy Director Administration, Elmira Psychiatric Center, Elmira, NY, p. A443
BEEBE, Chris T, Director Human Resources, Raleigh General Hospital, Beckley, WV, p. A699
BEEBY, Lori, Vice President Support Services, Community Hospital, Mccook, NE, p. A402
BEECHY, Andrew, Manager Information Technology Systems, Lee's Summit Medical Center, Lee's Summit, MO, p. A379
BEED, Donna E, Chief Information Management Division, Tripler Army Medical Center, Honolulu, HI, p. A176
BEEDLE, Chester
Chief Financial Officer, Kern Valley Healthcare District, Lake Isabella, CA, p. A69
Interim Chief Financial Officer, Adventist Health Tehachap. Valley, Tehachapi, CA, p. A97
BEEDY, Scott, Chief Financial Officer, Hansford Hospital, Spearman, TX, p. A653
BEEG, Gregg M., FACHE, President and Chief Executive Officer, Oaklawn Hospital, Marshall, MI, p. A333
BEEHN, Holly, Director Human Resources, Southwest Health, Platteville, WI, p. A719
BEEL, Frank, Chief Executive Officer, Twin Valley Behavioral Healthcare, Columbus, OH, p. A493
BEELER, Janelle E, Human Resource Manager, Baraga County Memorial Hospital, L'Anse, MI, p. A331
BEER, Nicole K., Chief Nursing Officer, The Pavilion At Williamsburg Place, Williamsburg, VA, p. A685
BEER, Ronald R.
FACHE, Chief Administrative Officer, Geisinger Community Medical Center, Scranton, PA, p. A554
FACHE, Chief Administrative Officer, Geisinger Wyoming Valley Medical Center, Wilkes Barre, PA, p. A557
BEESON, Nicole, Senior Vice President, Patient Care Services and Chief Nursing Officer, University of Maryland St. Josep. Medical Center, Towson, MD, p. A307
BEGALSKE, Kathy, Chief Nursing Officer, Gundersen Palmer Lutheran Hospital And Clinics, West Union, IA, p. A245
BEGAN, Victoria D., R.N., MS, President and Chief Executive Officer, San Carlos Apache Healthcare Corporation, Peridot, AZ, p. A34
BEGAY, Trudy, Human Resources Specialist, Hop. Health Care Center, Keams Canyon, AZ, p. A32
BEGAYE, Lorraine, Supervisory Human Resource Specialist, Chinle Comprehensive Health Care Facility, Chinle, AZ, p. A31
BEGG, William V., M.D., III, Vice President Medical Affairs, Vassar Brothers Medical Center, Poughkeepsie, NY, p. A456
BEGGANE, Thomas, Manager Human Resources, Olive View–Ucla Medical Center, Los Angeles, CA, p. A74
BEGGS, Shawn, Administrator, Finance, Corewell Health Trenton Hospital, Trenton, MI, p. A339
BEGLIOMINI, Robert, President, LVH Cedar Crest and Lehigh Region, Lehigh Valley Hospital–Cedar Crest, Allentown, PA, p. A534
BEHAN, Lawrence, Vice President Administration and Finance, Chief Financial Officer, Walden Behavioral Care, Waltham, MA, p. A319
BEHL, Mark, President and Chief Executive Officer, Northbay Medical Center, Fairfield, CA, p. A63
BEHM, Anthony, D.O., Chief of Staff, Erie Veterans Affairs Medical Center, Erie, PA, p. A539
BEHNER, Bruce M, Chief Operating Officer, Knox Community Hospital, Mount Vernon, OH, p. A501
BEHNKEN, Nick, IT Director, Red Bud Regional Hospital, Red Bud, IL, p. A207
BEHR, Maria
President, Three Rivers Health System, Inc., Three Rivers, MI, p. A339
Vice President Operations, Three Rivers Health System, Inc., Three Rivers, MI, p. A339
BEHRENDT, Darcy, R.N., Vice President, Patient Care Services, Chi Health Missouri Valley, Missouri Valley, IA, p. A240
BEHRENDTSEN, Ole
M.D., Interim Director, Santa Barbara County Psychiatric Health Facility, Santa Barbara, CA, p. A94
M.D., Medical Director, Santa Barbara County Psychiatric Health Facility, Santa Barbara, CA, p. A94
BEHRENS, Karen, Director Technology Services, OSF Saint Clare Medical Center, Princeton, IL, p. A206
BEIDELSCHIES, Sandra, MSN, R.N., Vice President Patient Services, Wood County Hospital, Bowling Green, OH, p. A487
BEIERMAN, Jennifer, Director Human Resources, Boone County Health Center, Albion, NE, p. A397
BEIGHLE, John, Flight Chief Medical Information Systems, Wright Patterson Medical Center, Wright–Patterson Afb, OH, p. A507
BEIGI, Richard
M.D., President and Professor, UPMC Mercy, Pittsburgh, PA, p. A552
M.D., President and Professor UPSOM, UPMC Magee–Womens Hospital, Pittsburgh, PA, p. A551
BEIKMAN, Sara, Director of Nursing, Clay County Medical Center, Clay Center, KS, p. A247
BEILER, Jeffrey A. II, Director, Lebanon Veterans Affairs Medical Center, Lebanon, PA, p. A544
BEINDIT, Dawn, Labor Relations Partner, Ascension River District Hospital, East China, MI, p. A326
BEINHAUR, Karen Lewis, Chief Nursing Officer, New London Hospital, New London, NH, p. A416
BEIRL, Luke
PharmD, Chief Executive Officer, Tamarack Health Hayward Medical Center, Hayward, WI, p. A713
PharmD, Interim Chief Executive Officer, Tamarack Health Ashland Medical Center, Ashland, WI, p. A707
BEISSEL, Rachel, Chief Nursing Officer, Southern Coos Hospital And Health Center, Bandon, OR, p. A525
BEISWENGER, Joel, Chief Executive Officer, Astera Health, Wadena, MN, p. A356
BEITCHER, Robert, President/Chief Executive Officer, MPTF/Motion Picture & Television Fund, Los Angeles, CA, p. A74
BEITEL, Suzanne, Senior Vice President and Chief Financial Officer, Seattle Children's Hospital, Seattle, WA, p. A694
BEITING, Mark, Area Chief Executive Officer – Sutter East Bay Hospitals, Alta Bates Summit Medical Center – Summit Campus, Oakland, CA, p. A80
BEITZEL, Mark, Director Information Systems, Advocate Lutheran General Hospital, Park Ridge, IL, p. A205
BEJNAR, Darla, M.D., Chief Medical Officer, Socorro General Hospital, Socorro, NM, p. A437
BELAIR, Norman, Senior Vice President and Chief Financial Officer, Southern Maine Health Care – Biddeford Medical Center, Biddeford, ME, p. A296

A796 Index of Health Care Professionals

Index of Health Care Professionals / Benton

Index of Health Care Professionals

BELCASTRO, Marc, D.O., Chief Medical Officer, Miami Valley Hospital, Dayton, OH, p. A494
BELCHER, Debbie
Director Human Resource, Baylor Scott & White Institute for Rehabilitation – Lakeway, Lakeway, TX, p. A633
Director, Human Resources, Cross Creek Hospital, Austin, TX, p. A600
BELCHER, Laura, FACHE, Administrator, The Medical Center At Albany, Albany, KY, p. A263
BELDECOS, Athena, M.D., Medical Director, Vibra Hospital of Charleston, Mt. Pleasant, SC, p. A569
BELEC, Tim, Chief Information Officer, Jefferson County Health Center, Fairfield, IA, p. A236
BELFI, Brian
M.D., Executive Director, Kirby Forensic Psychiatric Center, New York, NY, p. A448
M.D., Executive Director, Manhattan Psychiatric Center–Ward's Island, New York, NY, p. A449
BELGARDE, Donna, Human Resources Specialist, Quentin N. Burdick Memorial Healthcare Facility, Belcourt, ND, p. A479
BELHASEN, F K, M.D., Medical Director, Paintsville Arh Hospital, Paintsville, KY, p. A273
BELKOSKI, Dave, Chief Financial Officer, Piedmont Mcduffie, Thomson, GA, p. A172
BELKOSKI, David, Senior Vice President and Chief Financial Officer, Piedmont Augusta, Augusta, GA, p. A158
BELL, Alex, Interim Chief Executive Officer, St. Luke's Hospital, Columbus, NC, p. A466
BELL, Beth, Chief Executive Officer, Weisbrod Memorial County Hospital, Eads, CO, p. A107
BELL, Billie, R.N., Chief Executive Officer, Medina Regional Hospital, Hondo, TX, p. A624
BELL, Brenda, Chief Nursing Officer, University of Iowa Health Network Rehabilitation Hospital, Coralville, IA, p. A233
BELL, Brian, Associate Administrator and Chief Operating Officer, National Park Medical Center, Hot Springs, AR, p. A48
BELL, Cindy, Director Finance, Willow Crest Hospital, Miami, OK, p. A515
BELL, Heath, Vice President, Information Services, Northwestern Medicine Valley West Hospital, Sandwich, IL, p. A208
BELL, Hollis, M.D., Esq, Medical Director, Mercy Rehabilition Hospital Springfield, Springfield, MO, p. A387
BELL, Kae, Chief Financial Officer, Brentwood Hospital, Shreveport, LA, p. A292
BELL, Karen
Chief Nursing Officer, Adventhealth Gordon, Calhoun, GA, p. A160
Chief Nursing Officer, Adventhealth Murray, Chatsworth, GA, p. A160
BELL, Kristine, Administrator, Christus St. Michael Rehabilitation Hospital, Texarkana, TX, p. A656
BELL, Madeline, President and Chief Executive Officer, Children's Hospital of Philadelphia, Philadelphia, PA, p. A548
BELL, Mary, Vice President People and Culture, Novant Health Ballantyne Medical Center, Charlotte, NC, p. A465
BELL, Michael, Chief Executive Officer, Hackensack Meridian Health Pascack Valley Medical Center, Westwood, NJ, p. A430
BELL, Michael J., President, North Shore Medical Center, Miami, FL, p. A140
BELL, Randall C, M.D., Medical Director, Pam Specialty Hospital of San Antonio Center, San Antonio, TX, p. A650
BELL, Roderick, Chief Financial Officer, College Hospital Cerritos, Cerritos, CA, p. A59
BELL, Roseanna, Chief Nursing Officer, Peacehealth St. Josep. Medical Center, Bellingham, WA, p. A687
BELL, Sammie Jr, Chief Financial Officer, Tallahatchie General Hospital, Charleston, MS, p. A360
BELL, Scot, Chief Medical Officer, Baptist Anderson Regional Medical Center, Meridian, MS, p. A366
BELL, Sonja, Coordinator Human Resources, Sedgwick County Health Center, Julesburg, CO, p. A110
BELL, Stuart, M.D., Vice President, Medical Affairs, Medstar Union Memorial Hospital, Baltimore, MD, p. A301
BELL, Tammie, Director Human Resources, West Tennessee Healthcare Volunteer Hospital, Martin, TN, p. A587
BELL, W Scot, M.D., Chief Medical Officer, Ochsner Rush Medical Center, Meridian, MS, p. A366
BELLAMY, David, Chief Financial Officer, Mclaren Northern Michigan, Petoskey, MI, p. A335
BELLATTY, Christine, Acting Director of Nursing, Dorothea Dix Psychiatric Center, Bangor, ME, p. A295
BELLEAU, Christopher, M.D., Medical Director, Sage Rehabilitation Hospital, Baton Rouge, LA, p. A278
BELLEAU, Donella, Director Human Resources, Graham County Hospital, Hill City, KS, p. A250
BELLEW, Johnny, Chief Executive Officer, Pam Rehabilitation Hospital of Clear Lake, Webster, TX, p. A661
BELMONT, Chris, Chief Information Officer, Memorial Hospital At Gulfport, Gulfport, MS, p. A362
BELONGEA, M. Anselma, Chief Operating Officer, OSF Healthcare Saint Anthony's Health Center, Alton, IL, p. A185
BELSKY, Joshua, Chief Executive Officer, Greystone Park Psychiatric Hospital, Morris Plains, NJ, p. A424
BELTZ, John, Chief Financial Officer, Hendry Regional Medical Center, Clewiston, FL, p. A128
BELZER, Leslie, Director Human Resources, Howard County Medical Center, Saint Paul, NE, p. A405
BEMENT, Douglas J, Chief Financial Officer, Lutheran Kosciusko Hospital, Warsaw, IN, p. A229
BEN, Sabrina, Director Human Resources, North Star Behavioral Health System, Anchorage, AK, p. A27
BENAVIDES, Christina, Director Employee Services, Otto Kaiser Memorial Hospital, Kenedy, TX, p. A632
BENCOMO, Dennis, JD, MSN, R.N., Chief Executive Officer, Select Specialty Hospital–The Villages, Oxford, FL, p. A145
BENDER, Bob, Vice–President Hospital Finance and Operations, Northeast Market, Bristol Regional Medical Center, Bristol, TN, p. A579
BENDER, Brad, M.D., Chief of Staff, North Florida/South Georgia Veteran's Health System, Gainesville, FL, p. A132
BENDER, David B, M.D., Chief Medical Staff, Grafton City Hospital, Grafton, WV, p. A701
BENDINELLI, Emily, Director of Nurses, Ashley County Medical Center, Crossett, AR, p. A45
BENDING, Tammy
Vice President, Theda Care Medical Center – Wild Rose, Wild Rose, WI, p. A725
Vice President, Critical Access Hospital, Thedacare Medical Center–Berlin, Berlin, WI, p. A708
BENEDICT, Brian, Director of Information Technology, Murray–Calloway County Hospital, Murray, KY, p. A272
BENEDICT, Joy M, Director Human Resources, Baptist Health Richmond, Richmond, KY, p. A273
BENEFIELD, Marlene, Director Human Resources, Atrium Health Floyd Cherokee Medical Center, Centre, AL, p. A17
BENEPAL, Jaspreet, Chief Nursing Officer, Contra Costa Regional Medical Center, Martinez, CA, p. A76
BENET, Miguel, M.D., Chief Medical Officer, Medical City Las Colinas, Irving, TX, p. A630
BENFIELD, Angie
Director Human Resources, Cherokee Medical Center, Gaffney, SC, p. A566
Human Resources Generalist, Union Medical Center, Union, SC, p. A571
BENFIELD, Justin
Chief Executive Officer, Prisma Health Laurens County Hospital, Clinton, SC, p. A564
Chief Operations Executive, Prisma Health Hillcrest Hospital, Simpsonville, SC, p. A570
Southern Region Chief Operating Officer, Prisma Health Laurens County Hospital, Clinton, SC, p. A564
BENGSTON, Jennifer, M.D., Chief Medical Officer, Valley County Health System, Ord, NE, p. A404
BENGYAK, Daniel, Vice President, Administrative Services, Montefiore St. Luke's Cornwall, Newburgh, NY, p. A454
BENHAM, D'Linda, Director of Nursing, Fisher County Hospital District, Rotan, TX, p. A647
BENINK, Eric, M.D., Chief Medical Officer, Medical City Arlington, Arlington, TX, p. A597
BENITEZ, Juan, Chief Executive Office and Executive Director, San Juan City Hospital, San Juan, PR, p. A736
BENITEZ, Pedro, M.D., Medical Director, Hospital De Damas, Ponce, PR, p. A734
BENJAMIN, Lucia, Chief Nursing Officer, West Gables Rehabilitation Hospital, Miami, FL, p. A141
BENNER, Brenda, Director Human Resources, Encompass Health Rehabilitation Hospital of Sarasota, Sarasota, FL, p. A149
BENNETT, Angela, Chief Nursing Officer, Dekalb Regional Medical Center, Fort Payne, AL, p. A19
BENNETT, Anthony, M.D., Chief Clinical Affairs, Baptist Health Medical Center–Little Rock, Little Rock, AR, p. A49
BENNETT, April
Chief Executive Officer, Boundary Community Hospital, Bonners Ferry, ID, p. A180
President, Baptist Health Medical Center – Conway, Conway, AR, p. A44
BENNETT, Bart
Chief Financial Officer, Springbrook Behavioral Health, Travelers Rest, SC, p. A571
Chief Information Technology Officer, Springbrook Behavioral Health, Travelers Rest, SC, p. A571
BENNETT, Courtney, Human Resource Manager, Alleghany Health, Sparta, NC, p. A476
BENNETT, Darnell, Director Finance, Horizon Specialty Hospital, Las Vegas, NV, p. A410
BENNETT, E Kyle., President and Chief Executive Officer, Memorial Hospital And Health Care Center, Jasper, IN, p. A220
BENNETT, Edwin, Controller, Turning Point Hospital, Moultrie, GA, p. A169
BENNETT, Fay, Vice President Employee Services, Guadalup. Regional Medical Center, Seguin, TX, p. A652
BENNETT, Gary, M.D., Chief of Medical Staff, Chapman Global Medical Center, Orange, CA, p. A81
BENNETT, Kay R
System Director Human Resources, Baptist Medical Center South, Montgomery, AL, p. A22
Vice President Human Resources, Baptist Medical Center East, Montgomery, AL, p. A22
BENNETT, Kimberly, R.N., Director of Nursing, Christus Dubuis Hospital of Alexandria, Alexandria, LA, p. A276
BENNETT, Laurie
Director Human Resources, Sarasota Memorial Hospital – Sarasota, Sarasota, FL, p. A150
Vice President, Human Resources, Sarasota Memorial Hospital – Venice, North Venice, FL, p. A142
BENNETT, Leo, M.D., Deputy Commander Clinical Services, Bassett Army Community Hospital, Fort Wainwright, AK, p. A28
BENNETT, Lisa, Chief Financial Officer, Waverly Health Center, Waverly, IA, p. A245
BENNETT, Mary Ann
Chief Nursing Officer, Glendora Hospital, Glendora, CA, p. A66
Chief Operating Officer and Chief Nursing Officer, Springbrook Behavioral Health, Travelers Rest, SC, p. A571
Director of Nursing, Springbrook Behavioral Health, Travelers Rest, SC, p. A571
BENNETT, Melissa, Chief Nursing Officer, Trumbull Regional Medical Center, Warren, OH, p. A506
BENNETT, Patti, Chief Nursing Officer, Nacogdoches Medical Center, Nacogdoches, TX, p. A640
BENNETT, Randall, Assistant Administrator, Uintah Basin Medical Center, Roosevelt, UT, p. A668
BENNETT, Richard, Administrator, The Willough At Naples, Naples, FL, p. A142
BENNETT, Rick, Director, The Blackberry Center, Saint Cloud, FL, p. A148
BENNETT, Robert, M.D., Medical Director, Millwood Hospital, Arlington, TX, p. A597
BENNETT, Samuel, Chief Executive Officer, Springbrook Hospital, Brooksville, FL, p. A127
BENNETT, Sharon, Manager Information Systems, Cobre Valley Regional Medical Center, Globe, AZ, p. A32
BENNETT, Sheila, R.N., Vice President & Chief Nursing Officer, Atrium Health Floyd Medical Center, Rome, GA, p. A170
BENNETT, Tony N., Chief Executive Officer, Encompass Health Rehabilitation Hospital of Panama City, Panama City, FL, p. A146
BENNETT, Will, Chief Financial Officer, Candler County Hospital, Metter, GA, p. A168
BENNETT III, Walter, FACHE, Chief Executive Officer, Musc Health – Orangeburg, Orangeburg, SC, p. A569
BENNION, Hailey, Chief Clinical Officer, Nexus Children's Hospital Houston, Houston, TX, p. A627
BENOIT, Linda, Human Resource Officer, Langdon Prairie Health, Langdon, ND, p. A482
BENOIT, Paul, Associate Administrator, Central Louisiana State Hospital, Pineville, LA, p. A291
BENOIT, William, President, University Hospitals Portage Medical Center, Ravenna, OH, p. A503
BENSEN, Carol, MSN, R.N., Chief Nursing Officer, Providence St. Patrick Hospital, Missoula, MT, p. A394
BENSON, Cheryl, Chief Operating Officer, Wernersville State Hospital, Wernersville, PA, p. A557
BENSON, Karla, Executive Assistant, Throckmorton County Memorial Hospital, Throckmorton, TX, p. A658
BENSON, Kathryn, Human Resources Partner, Avera St. Anthony's Hospital, O'Neill, NE, p. A403
BENSON, Michael, M.D., President Medical Staff, AHS Sherman Medical Center, Sherman, TX, p. A652
BENTLEY, Erica, Vice President Nursing, Ascension Saint Josep. – Elgin, Elgin, IL, p. A194
BENTLEY, Scott, Chief Financial Officer, Woman's Hospital of Texas, Houston, TX, p. A629
BENTLEY, Tom, MS, Interim Chief Information Officer, Ohio State University Wexner Medical Center, Columbus, OH, p. A492
BENTON, Edred, Chief Executive Officer, Cleveland Area Hospital, Cleveland, OK, p. A511
BENTON, Nancy, Assistant Director Patient Care Services, Mann–Grandstaff Department of Veterans Affairs Medical Center, Spokane, WA, p. A696

Index of Health Care Professionals

Index of Health Care Professionals / Bentz

BENTZ, Douglas E., Chief Executive Officer, Roane General Hospital, Spencer, WV, p. A705
BENVENUTTI, Cathy, Human Resource Director, Ochsner Medical Center – Hancock, Bay Saint Louis, MS, p. A359
BENWARE, Joel, Vice President Information Technology and Compliance, Northwestern Medical Center, Saint Albans, VT, p. A672
BENZ, Robert, M.D., Chief Medical Officer, Lankenau Medical Center, Wynnewood, PA, p. A558
BENZEL, Cindy, Manager Human Resources, Sanford Vermillion Medical Center, Vermillion, SD, p. A577
BENZING, Janet, Chief Administrative Officer, Delta Health – Northwest Regional, Clarksdale, MS, p. A360
BERARDI, Paula, Manager Human Resources, Bournewood Health Systems, Brookline, MA, p. A312
BERCHER, Richard, M.D., Chief Medical Officer, Paris Regional Medical Center, Paris, TX, p. A642
BERCI, Haya, Executive Director of Nursing, Joyce Eisenberg–Keefer Medical Center, Reseda, CA, p. A85
BERCIER, Paula, M.D., Chief Medical Officer, Quentin N. Burdick Memorial Healthcare Facility, Belcourt, ND, p. A479
BERDAL, Ritche, Chief Nursing Officer, Cornerstone Specialty Hospitals Tucson, Tucson, AZ, p. A40
BERENS, Jeff, MS, Chief Nursing Officer, Sanford Vermillion Medical Center, Vermillion, SD, p. A577
BERENTES, Amy, R.N., MSN, Chief Nursing Officer, Cgh Medical Center, Sterling, IL, p. A209
BERETTA, Dante, M.D., Chief of Staff, Centracare – Melrose, Melrose, MN, p. A350
BERG, Gary L, D.O., Chief Medical Officer, Ascension Macomb–Oakland Hospital, Warren Campus, Warren, MI, p. A340
BERG, Jon, M.D., Chief of Staff, Northwood Deaconess Health Center, Northwood, ND, p. A482
BERG, Katie, Chief Financial Officer, Cuyuna Regional Medical Center, Crosby, MN, p. A345
BERG, Tony L., M.D., Chief of Staff, Winner Regional Healthcare Center, Winner, SD, p. A578
BERG, William, Chief Information Officer, Naval Hospital Pensacola, Pensacola, FL, p. A146
BERGE, Ron, Executive Vice President and Chief Operating Officer, National Jewish Health, Denver, CO, p. A106
BERGEAUX, Scott, M.D., Chief Medical Staff, Ochsner Abrom Kaplan Memorial Hospital, Kaplan, LA, p. A284
BERGEMANN, John, Director Human Resources, Crouse Health, Syracuse, NY, p. A460
BERGER, David, M.D., Senior Vice President and Chief Operating Officer, Leesburg Regional Medical Center, Leesburg, FL, p. A137
BERGER, George, Controller, Encompass Health Rehabilitation Hospital of Altoona, Altoona, PA, p. A534
BERGER, Kathy, R.N., Chief Nursing Officer, Robley Rex Department of Veterans Affairs Medical Center, Louisville, KY, p. A270
BERGER, Robert, M.D., Medical Director, Southwest Connecticut Mental Health System, Bridgeport, CT, p. A115
BERGERON, Pierre, Information Services Director, Wellington Regional Medical Center, Wellington, FL, p. A154
BERGFORT, Joe, Chief Information Officer, UCSF Medical Center, San Francisco, CA, p. A91
BERGH, Christopher, Chief Operating Officer, Oklahoma City Rehabilitation Hospital, Oklahoma City, OK, p. A518
BERGHERM, Bruce, Chief Executive Officer, Adventhealth Tampa, Tampa, FL, p. A152
BERGHOLM, Brenda, MSN, R.N., Chief Nursing Officer, Caribou Medical Center, Soda Springs, ID, p. A184
BERGMAN, Chris, Chief Financial Officer, Dayton Children's Hospital, Dayton, OH, p. A493
BERGMAN, Jim, Director Human Resources, Northeast Regional Medical Center, Kirksville, MO, p. A378
BERGMAN–EVANS, Brenda, Chief Nursing Officer, Chi Health Midlands, Papillion, NE, p. A405
BERGMANN, Michael
President, Ascension Calumet Hospital, Chilton, WI, p. A709
President, Ascension Northeast Wisconsin St. Elizabeth Hospital, Appleton, WI, p. A707
BERGMEIER, Cindy, Chief Executive Officer, Tristar Horizon Medical Center, Dickson, TN, p. A582
BERGQUIST, Susan, Human Resources Generalist, Kindred Hospital–La Mirada, La Mirada, CA, p. A68
BERGSTEDT, Sharon, Director of Nursing, Alaska Psychiatric Institute, Anchorage, AK, p. A27
BERGSTROM, Jenny, Project Manager Information Technology, North Central Kansas Medical Center, Concordia, KS, p. A248
BERGSTROM, Michael, Chief Financial Officer, Harlingen Medical Center, Harlingen, TX, p. A623
BERINI, Deborah, President, SSM Health Depaul Hospital – St. Louis, Bridgeton, MO, p. A372
BERKOWITZ, David J, Vice President and Chief Operating Officer, Hackensack Meridian Health Palisades Medical Center, North Bergen, NJ, p. A426
BERKRAM, Treasure, Chief Financial Officer, Logan Health – Cut Bank, Cut Bank, MT, p. A391
BERLINGHOFF, Kathleen, Director Human Resources, Sharon Hospital, Sharon, CT, p. A118
BERLOT, Alvin, M.D., Medical Director, Bucktail Medical Center, Renovo, PA, p. A553
BERLOWITZ, Dan, M.D., M.P.H., Acting Chief of Staff, Bedford Veterans Affairs Medical Center, Edith Nourse Rogers Memorial Veterans Hospital, Bedford, MA, p. A309
BERLUCCHI, Scott A., FACHE, President, Auburn Community Hospital, Auburn, NY, p. A438
BERLYN, Maria, Assistant Vice President Nursing Services, John Heinz Institute of Rehabilitation Medicine, Wilkes–Barre, PA, p. A557
BERMAN, Alan S., M.D., Medical Director, Mountain Valley Regional Rehabilitation Hospital, Prescott Valley, AZ, p. A37
BERMAN, Manuel S, FACHE, President and Chief Executive Officer, Ohsu Health Hillsboro Medical Center, Hillsboro, OR, p. A528
BERMUDEZ, Ada, Director Human Resources, Hospital De La Concepcion, San German, PR, p. A734
BERMUDEZ, Armand, M.D., Medical Director, Select Specialty Hospital of Southeast Ohio, Newark, OH, p. A501
BERMUDEZ, Yuri, M.D., Chief of Staff, South Texas Health System, Edinburg, TX, p. A615
BERNAL, Enrique, Chief Financial Officer, Methodist Hospital, San Antonio, TX, p. A650
BERNAL, Hector
Chief Executive Officer, Pam Rehabilitation Hospital of Corpus Christi, Corpus Christi, TX, p. A609
Chief Executive Officer, Post Acute Medical Specialty Hospital of Corpus Christi – North, Corpus Christi, TX, p. A609
BERNAL, Maria Mercedes Torres., Administrator, Hospital De Damas, Ponce, PR, p. A734
BERNARD, David P., FACHE, Chief Executive Officer, Houston Methodist The Woodlands Hospital, The Woodlands, TX, p. A657
BERNARD, Donald P, Chief Financial Officer, St. John's Regional Medical Center, Oxnard, CA, p. A82
BERNARD, Doug, M.D., Chief Medical Officer, White River Health, Batesville, AR, p. A43
BERNARD, Eliese, President, Wellstar Cobb Hospital, Austell, GA, p. A159
BERNARD, Jose, Vice President Medical Affairs, United Hospital, Saint Paul, MN, p. A355
BERNARD, Mark L., Chief Executive Officer, Resolute Health, New Braunfels, TX, p. A641
BERNARD, Matthew
M.D., Chief Executive Officer, Covington Trace Er & Hospital, Mandeville, LA, p. A287
M.D., Chief Medical Officer, Covington Trace Er & Hospital, Mandeville, LA, p. A287
BERNARD, Robert, M.D., Chief of Staff, Alexandria Va Medical Center, Pineville, LA, p. A291
BERNARD, Traci, R.N., President, Chief Executive Officer and Chief Operating Officer, Texas Health Harris Methodist Hospital Southlake, Southlake, TX, p. A653
BERNARDO, Maria, M.D., Chief of Staff, Bullock County Hospital, Union Springs, AL, p. A25
BERNASEK, Robert, M.D., Chief Medical Officer, Southeast Georgia Health System Camden Campus, Saint Marys, GA, p. A170
BERNATIS, Terry D., Director Human Resources, Community Healthcare System, Onaga, KS, p. A256
BERND, Jason, President and Chief Operating Officer, Novant Health Matthews Medical Center, Matthews, NC, p. A472
BERNERT–YAP, Kellie, Director Human Resources, Vibra Specialty Hospital of Portland, Portland, OR, p. A531
BERNEY, Bernadette, Director Human Resources, Pullman Regional Hospital, Pullman, WA, p. A693
BERNHARDT, Alison
Chief Financial Officer, UPMC Carlisle, Carlisle, PA, p. A536
Chief Financial Officer, UPMC Harrisburg, Harrisburg, PA, p. A541
BERNHARDT–KADLEC, Peggy, Chief Human Resources Officer, Searhc Mt. Edgecumbe Hospital, Sitka, AK, p. A29
BERNICK, Michael, Executive Vice President and Chief Financial Officer, Clarity Child Guidance Center, San Antonio, TX, p. A649
BERNIER, Stephanie, Chief Executive Officer, Canyon Ridge Hospital, Chino, CA, p. A59
BERNIER, Tori Louise, Chief Nursing Officer, Summit Pacific Medical Center, Elma, WA, p. A689
BERNING, Cynthia, President and Chief Executive Officer, Grand Lake Health System, Saint Marys, OH, p. A503
BERNS, Erin, Director Human Resources, Veterans Memorial Hospital, Waukon, IA, p. A245
BERNSEN, Tina, Chief Nursing Officer, Othello Community Hospital, Othello, WA, p. A692
BERNSTEIN, Lee
Regional Executive Vice President and Chief Operating Officer, SSM Health St. Clare Hospital – Fenton, Fenton, MO, p. A375
Regional Executive Vice President of Hospital and Chief Operating Officer, SSM Health St. Josep. Hospital – Lake Saint Louis, Lake Saint Louis, MO, p. A379
BERNSTEIN, Les, Chief Information Officer, Cookeville Regional Medical Center, Cookeville, TN, p. A582
BERNSTEIN, Michael, Chief Financial Officer, Adventist Health – Tulare, Tulare, CA, p. A98
BERRIOS, Elenia, Chief Nursing Officer, Hima San Pablo Caguas, Caguas, PR, p. A731
BERRIOS, Zulma, M.D., Chief Medical Officer, Baptist Health South Florida, West Kendall Baptist Hospital, Miami, FL, p. A139
BERRY, Carlos E., M.D., Acting Chief of Staff, Tuscaloosa Va Medical Center, Tuscaloosa, AL, p. A25
BERRY, Greg, Chief Financial Officer, Doctors Medical Center of Modesto, Modesto, CA, p. A77
BERRY, James T., FACHE, Chief Executive Officer, Northeastern Health System, Tahlequah, OK, p. A521
BERRY, Julie, Chief Information Officer, Saint Anne's Hospital, Fall River, MA, p. A313
BERRY, Matthew, Chief Executive Officer, Miracare Behavioral Health Care, Tinley Park, IL, p. A210
BERRY, Rebecca
Senior Director Human Resources, St. Charles Prineville, Prineville, OR, p. A531
Vice President Human Resources, St. Charles Bend, Bend, OR, p. A525
Vice President Human Resources, St. Charles Redmond, Redmond, OR, p. A531
BERRYMAN, John David, M.D., Chief of Staff, Beckley Veterans Affairs Medical Center, Beckley, WV, p. A699
BERRYMAN, William R, M.D., Chief of Staff, Grand Junction Va Medical Center, Grand Junction, CO, p. A108
BERSANTE, Syd, R.N., Interim President, St. Josep. Medical Center, Tacoma, WA, p. A697
BERSINGER, David, M.D., Chief of Staff, Mcleod Health Cheraw, Cheraw, SC, p. A563
BERTAGNOLE, Matthew, Chief Executive Officer, University Behavioral Health of Denton, Denton, TX, p. A614
BERTANY, Kathryn, M.D., President and Chief Executive Officer, Bozeman Health Deaconess Regional Medical Center, Bozeman, MT, p. A390
BERTAPELLE, Andrew, MSN, R.N., Chief Executive Officer, Schoolcraft Memorial Hospital, Manistique, MI, p. A333
BERTHIL, Emmanuel, Chief Clinical Officer, Vibra Hospital of Southeastern Massachusetts, New Bedford, MA, p. A316
BERTKE, Bradley J.
Chief Operating Officer, Mercy Health – West Hospital, Cincinnati, OH, p. A489
President and Chief Operating Officer, Mercy Health – West Hospital, Cincinnati, OH, p. A489
BERTON, Theresa Catherine
Chief Operating Officer and Chief Nursing Supervisor, Chapman Global Medical Center, Orange, CA, p. A81
Interim Chief Executive Officer/Chief Nursing Officer, Chapman Global Medical Center, Orange, CA, p. A81
BERTON, Theresa Catherine., Interim Chief Executive Officer, Chapman Global Medical Center, Orange, CA, p. A81
BERTRAND, Joan L., Vice President Human Resources, Adcare Hospital of Worcester, Worcester, MA, p. A320
BERTRAND, Kristie, Director Health Information Management, Acadian Medical Center, Eunice, LA, p. A281
BERTRAND, Michael, Chief Executive Officer, Abbeville General Hospital, Abbeville, LA, p. A276
BERTRAND, Neil W, Interim Chief Financial Officer, Cheyenne Regional Medical Center, Cheyenne, WY, p. A726
BERTSCH, John, M.D., Chief of Staff, Cleveland Clinic Euclid Hospital, Euclid, OH, p. A495
BESA, Ivan, Chief Executive Officer, Pam Rehabilitation Hospital of Humble, Humble, TX, p. A629
BESCOE, Bradley, President and Chief Executive Officer, Straith Hospital for Special Surgery, Southfield, MI, p. A338
BESIO, Adam, Chief Information Officer, Memorial Medical Center, Port Lavaca, TX, p. A645
BESPALEC, Jason, M.D., Chief of Staff, Fillmore County Hospital, Geneva, NE, p. A400
BESS, Amy, Chief Financial Officer, Mizell Memorial Hospital, Opp, AL, p. A23
BESS, Charles, M.D., Medical Director, WVU Medicine Potomac Valley Hospital, Keyser, WV, p. A702

A798 Index of Health Care Professionals

BESSE, Kim
  Executive Vice President and Chief Human Resource Officer, Children's Medical Center Dallas, Dallas, TX, p. A611
  Executive Vice President and Chief Human Resource Officer, Children's Medical Center Plano, Plano, TX, p. A644
BESSEY, Kerry, Senior Vice President and Chief Human Resources Officer, Memorial Sloan Kettering Cancer Center, New York, NY, p. A449
BESSLER, Christine, Vice President Information Services, Prohealth Oconomowoc Memorial Hospital, Oconomowoc, WI, p. A718
BESSLER, September, Director, Human Resources, Brookings Health System, Brookings, SD, p. A572
BESSON, Kathleen, Executive Vice President and Chief Operating Officer, Caromont Regional Medical Center, Gastonia, NC, p. A469
BESST, Kara, President and Chief Executive Officer, Gritman Medical Center, Moscow, ID, p. A182
BEST, Nikole, Chief Executive Officer, Baylor Scott & White Surgical Hospital–Sherman, Sherman, TX, p. A652
BESTEN, Robert, Chief Financial Officer, Mary Breckinridge Arh Hospital, Hyden, KY, p. A267
BESTGEN, Pat, Manager Human Resources, Cameron Regional Medical Center, Cameron, MO, p. A372
BESWICK, Elizabeth, Vice President Human Resources and Public Relations, Carteret Health Care, Morehead City, NC, p. A473
BETANCOURT, Erika, Coordinator Human Resources, Cornerstone Regional Hospital, Edinburg, TX, p. A615
BETTCHER, Sue, R.N., Vice President of Nursing Services, Community Hospital of Bremen, Bremen, IN, p. A213
BETTINELLI, Stephanie M, Vice President of Human Resources, Winchester Hospital, Winchester, MA, p. A320
BETTISON, Lance, Hospital Director, Kalamazoo Psychiatric Hospital, Kalamazoo, MI, p. A331
BETTS, Brooks, Director Information Systems and Chief Information Officer, Mainehealth Pen Bay Medical Center, Rockport, ME, p. A299
BETTS, Crystal
  Chief Financial Officer, Incline Village Community Hospital, Incline Village, NV, p. A409
  Chief Financial Officer, Tahoe Forest Hospital District, Truckee, CA, p. A98
BETTS, Kristen A
  Director Team Resources, St. Anthony's Hospital, Saint Petersburg, FL, p. A149
  Director Team Resources, St. Joseph's Hospital, Tampa, FL, p. A152
  Director Team Resources, Winter Haven Hospital, Winter Haven, FL, p. A155
BETTS, Tracy, Chief Financial Officer, Hardeman County Memorial Hospital, Quanah, TX, p. A646
BEUCLER, MSN, RN, BS–NE, FACHE, Lori A, R.N., Vice President and Chief Nursing Officer, UPMC Williamsport, Williamsport, PA, p. A558
BEUS, Lance, Chief Executive Officer, Dmc Huron Valley–Sinai Hospital, Commerce Township. MI, p. A324
BEVARD, Julie, Vice President Human Resources, Perkins County Health Services, Grant, NE, p. A400
BEVEL, John, Manager Information Systems, Shriners Children's – Northern California, Sacramento, CA, p. A87
BEVERLY, Esther, Vice President Human Resources, Tri–City Medical Center, Oceanside, CA, p. A81
BEVERLY, Michelle L., Chief Operating Officer, Abrazo Central Campus, Phoenix, AZ, p. A35
BEVIER, Mary, Chief Financial Officer, Bayou Bend Health System, Franklin, LA, p. A282
BEVIS, Madora, R.N., Chief Nursing Officer, Wayne Medical Center, Waynesboro, TN, p. A594
BEYER, Laurie, Senior Vice President and Chief Financial Officer, Christianacare, Union Hospital, Elkton, MD, p. A304
BEYER, Teri, Chief Information Officer, Quality, Centracare – Rice Memorial Hospital, Willmar, MN, p. A357
BEYER, Tommy, Director of Operations, Pam Rehabilitation Hospital of Victoria, Victoria, TX, p. A660
BEYMER, Alicia, Chief Administrative Officer, Peacehealth Sacred Heart Medical Center At Riverbend, Springfield, OR, p. A532
BEZARD, David, Chief Financial Officer, South Lyon Medical Center, Yerington, NV, p. A413
BHAGAT, Sarah, Chief Operating Officer and Vice President of Organizational Effectiveness, Lakeland Regional Health Medical Center, Lakeland, FL, p. A137
BHAMBRA, Jody, Chief Nursing Officer, Hartgrove Behavioral Health System, Chicago, IL, p. A189
BHARUCHA, Bomi, Chief Financial Officer, Reeves Regional Health, Pecos, TX, p. A643

BHATEJA, Renu, M.D., President Medical Staff, Ridgeview Psychiatric Hospital And Center, Oak Ridge, TN, p. A591
BHATIA, Sanjay, Chief Medical Officer, Lower Bucks Hospital, Bristol, PA, p. A535
BHAYANI, Sam B, M.D., Chief Medical Officer, Barnes–Jewish West County Hospital, Saint Louis, MO, p. A384
BHIMANI, Meenesh, M.D., Chief Operating Officer, El Camino Health, Mountain View, CA, p. A79
BHOORASINGH, Merlene, Administrator, Kindred Hospital Ocala, Ocala, FL, p. A143
BHUCHAR, Subodh, M.D., Chief of Staff, Kindred Hospital Sugar Land, Sugar Land, TX, p. A654
BIAGIONI, Donna K, R.N., MSN, Director of Nursing, Maniilaq Health Center, Kotzebue, AK, p. A29
BIALORUCKI, Tom, Chief Information Officer, Adena Pike Medical Center, Waverly, OH, p. A506
BIANCHI, Hannah, Chief Operating Officer, Mt. Ascutney Hospital And Health Center, Windsor, VT, p. A672
BIAS, Richard R, Chief Operating Officer, Lahey Hospital & Medical Center, Burlington, MA, p. A312
BIBAL, Antoinette, Director Human Resources, Kindred Hospital–Baldwin Park, Baldwin Park, CA, p. A57
BIBB, Jeff, Chief Operating Officer, Oklahoma Center for Orthopaedic And Multi–Specialty Surgery, Oklahoma City, OK, p. A518
BIBER, Carl, Chief Financial Officer, Columbus Regional Healthcare System, Whiteville, NC, p. A477
BIBLO, Lee, M.D., Chief Medical Officer, Froedtert And The Medical College of Wisconsin Froedtert Hospital, Milwaukee, WI, p. A717
BICKEL, George, Director, Information Systems, Merit Health Biloxi, Biloxi, MS, p. A359
BICKEL, Jim, Chief Executive Officer, Columbus Regional Hospital, Columbus, IN, p. A214
BICKFORD, Carmel, Chief Financial Officer, Wyoming Behavioral Institute, Casper, WY, p. A726
BICKFORD, David, Chief Information Officer, Melissa Memorial Hospital, Holyoke, CO, p. A109
BIDDLE, Keith, Chief Operating Officer, Rivers Health, Point Pleasant, WV, p. A704
BIDDLE, Kenneth, Controller, Kensington Hospital, Philadelphia, PA, p. A549
BIDES, Adrienne, Assistant Chief Financial Officer and Budget Analyst, Big Spring State Hospital, Big Spring, TX, p. A603
BIDLEMAN, Angie, Chief Nursing Officer, Ascension St. John Jane Phillips, Bartlesville, OK, p. A510
BIE, Gary E, CPA, Chief Financial Officer, Stony Brook University Hospital, Stony Brook, NY, p. A459
BIEBER, Courtney, Director Information Systems, Mercy Regional Medical Center, Ville Platte, LA, p. A294
BIEBER, Judi, Senior Vice President Human Resources, Beth Israel Deaconess Medical Center, Boston, MA, p. A309
BIEBER, Julie, Vice President, Bellin Health Oconto Hospital, Oconto, WI, p. A719
BIEDIGER, Daniel F, Vice President Human Resources, Firsthealth Moore Regional Hospital, Pinehurst, NC, p. A474
BIEGERT, Dara, Vice President Human Resources, Medical City Lewisville, Lewisville, TX, p. A634
BIEGLER, Elizabeth Anne
  R.N., Chief Nursing Officer, Ohiohealth Dublin Methodist Hospital, Dublin, OH, p. A495
  R.N., Chief Nursing Officer, Ohiohealth Grady Memorial Hospital, Delaware, OH, p. A494
BIEHL, Benjamin, M.D., Chief Medical Officer, Johnson County Hospital, Tecumseh, NE, p. A406
BIEKER, Jeff, Director Human Resource, Trego County–Lemke Memorial Hospital, Wakeeney, KS, p. A261
BIELECKI, Thomas A, Chief Financial Officer, Geisinger Wyoming Valley Medical Center, Wilkes Barre, PA, p. A557
BIEN, John, Vice President Finance, United Hospital, Saint Paul, MN, p. A355
BIERI, Bryan, Manager Finance, Kansas City Va Medical Center, Kansas City, MO, p. A377
BIERLE, Dennis, President, Chi Health Creighton University Medical Center – Bergan Mercy, Omaha, NE, p. A403
BIERMAN, Debra, Associate Executive Director Human Resources, North Shore University Hospital, Manhasset, NY, p. A445
BIERMAN, Joan, Vice President Finance, Cherokee Regional Medical Center, Cherokee, IA, p. A232
BIERMAN, Ronald L., President, Sebastian River Medical Center, Sebastian, FL, p. A150
BIERSACK, Matt, M.D., President, Trinity Health Grand Rapids Hospital, Grand Rapids, MI, p. A328
BIERSCHENK, Cindy, Director of Financial Services, Jenkins County Medical Center, Millen, GA, p. A168
BIERSCHENK, Kevin, Chief Executive Officer, Union General Hospital, Blairsville, GA, p. A159

BIERUT, Barbara, Chief Financial Officer, Encompass Health Rehabilitation Hospital of Sarasota, Sarasota, FL, p. A149
BIGANDO, Kelli, Chief Nursing Officer, Mercy Hospital Joplin, Joplin, MO, p. A377
BIGELOW, Timothy, Director Human Resources, Butler Hospital, Providence, RI, p. A560
BIGGAR, Carrie, Chief Financial Officer, HCA Florida Osceola Hospital, Kissimmee, FL, p. A136
BIGGERSTAFF, David, Vice President, Chief Operating Officer, Intermountain Health Saint Josep. Hospital, Denver, CO, p. A106
BIGGS, Carol Cassandra, Chief Nursing Executive, Jackson Health System, Miami, FL, p. A140
BIGGS, Daniel, Chief Operating Officer, Valley View Hospital, Glenwood Springs, CO, p. A108
BIGGS, Jeremy, President and Chief Administrative Officer, Methodist Medical Center of Oak Ridge, Oak Ridge, TN, p. A591
BIGGS, Kelly, M.D., Chief Medical Officer, Penn Highlands Tyrone, Tyrone, PA, p. A556
BIGGS, R. Lee, D.O., Chief Medical Officer, HCA Florida Blake Hospital, Bradenton, FL, p. A126
BIGLER, Pamela, R.N., Senior Vice President of Clinical Partnership. and Programs, Carle Foundation Hospital, Urbana, IL, p. A210
BIGNAULT, Jon, M.D., Chief of Staff, Athens–Limestone Hospital, Athens, AL, p. A15
BIGONEY, Rebecca
  Executive Vice President and Chief Medical Officer, Mary Washington Hospital, Fredericksburg, VA, p. A676
  Executive Vice President and Chief Medical Officer, Stafford Hospital, Stafford, VA, p. A684
BIGOS, Ardelle, R.N., MSN, Vice President Nursing, Geneva General Hospital, Geneva, NY, p. A443
BIHUNIAK, Peter, Vice President Finance, Robert Wood Johnson University Hospital Rahway, Rahway, NJ, p. A427
BILBREY, Leanne, Chief Nursing Officer, Director of Quality, Macon Community Hospital, Lafayette, TN, p. A586
BILBRO, Debbie
  Chief Executive Officer, Northside Hospital Gwinnett/Duluth, Lawrenceville, GA, p. A166
  President and Chief Executive Officer, Northside Hospital Gwinnett/Duluth, Lawrenceville, GA, p. A166
BILELLO, Rene, Manager Information System, Ochsner St. Mary, Morgan City, LA, p. A289
BILLECI, Theresa, Executive Director, Porterville Developmental Center, Porterville, CA, p. A84
BILLINGS, Jonathan E, Chief Operating Officer, Northwestern Medical Center, Saint Albans, VT, p. A672
BILLINGS, Mark, Chief Operating Officer, Halifax Health Medical Center of Daytona Beach, Daytona Beach, FL, p. A130
BILLINGS, Mary Ann, Director of Nursing, WVU Medicine Potomac Valley Hospital, Keyser, WV, p. A702
BILLINGSLEA, Anidra, Health Insurance Management, Encompass Health Rehabilitation Hospital of Montgomery, Montgomery, AL, p. A22
BILLINGTON, Carole, R.N., MSN, Vice President Operations, Chief Nursing Officer, Saint Anne's Hospital, Fall River, MA, p. A313
BILLMEYER, Joe, Director, Information Services, Mercyone Dubuque Medical Center, Dubuque, IA, p. A235
BILLS, James, Chief Executive Officer, Select Specialty Hospital Nashville, Nashville, TN, p. A590
BILLY, Frank, Chief Financial Officer, Kindred Hospital Bay Area–Tampa, Tampa, FL, p. A152
BILSON, Josep. P., Chief Executive Officer, Wills Eye Hospital, Philadelphia, PA, p. A550
BILUNKA, Dianne C, Director Human Resources, Clarion Psychiatric Center, Clarion, PA, p. A537
BINDER, Dore, M.D., Chief Medical Officer, Woman's Hospital, Baton Rouge, LA, p. A278
BINDERMAN, Judi, Chief Information Technology Officer and Chief Medical Informatics Officer, St. Francis Medical Center, Lynwood, CA, p. A76
BINDL, Karen, CPA, Controller, UW Health Rehabilitation Hospital, Madison, WI, p. A715
BINGHAM, Julie, IT Supervisor, San Juan Health Service District, Monticello, UT, p. A666
BINGHAM, Leslie, Senior Vice President and Chief Executive Officer, Valley Baptist Medical Center–Brownsville, Brownsville, TX, p. A605
BINGHAM, Paulette, Director Nursing Services, Heritage Valley Kennedy, Mckees Rocks, PA, p. A545
BINGMAN, Ryan, Director Operations, Grundy County Memorial Hospital, Grundy Center, IA, p. A236
BINKLEY, Sharon, Director Human Resources, Rural Wellness Fairfax, Fairfax, OK, p. A512
BIRCH, Misty, Director Human Resources, Castleview Hospital, Price, UT, p. A667

Index of Health Care Professionals
Index of Health Care Professionals / Birchmeier

BIRCHMEIER, Kevin, Director Human Resources, Covenant Healthcare, Saginaw, MI, p. A336
BIRD, Alan, Chief Executive Officer, Adams County Regional Medical Center, Seaman, OH, p. A503
BIRD, Erin
M.D., Chief Medical Officer, Adventhealth Central Texas, Killeen, TX, p. A632
M.D., Chief Medical Officer, Adventhealth Rollins Brook, Lampasas, TX, p. A633
BIRD, Jace, M.D., Chief Medical Officer, Missouri River Medical Center, Fort Benton, MT, p. A392
BIRD, Jeffrey C., M.D., President, Indiana University Health Ball Memorial Hospital, Muncie, IN, p. A224
BIRD, Lindsay, Director Finance, Cleveland Clinic South Pointe Hospital, Warrensville Heights, OH, p. A506
BIRD, Michele
Chief Human Resources Officer, Hemet Global Medical Center, Hemet, CA, p. A67
Chief Human Resources Officer, Menifee Global Medical Center, Sun City, CA, p. A97
BIRENBERG, Allan, Vice President Medical Affairs, Medstar Harbor Hospital, Baltimore, MD, p. A301
BIRI, Abel, Chief Executive Officer, Adventhealth Waterman, Tavares, FL, p. A153
BIRKEL, Sue M, R.N., Director of Nursing, Butler County Health Care Center, David City, NE, p. A399
BIRKHOFER, Colleen, Chief Nursing Officer, Trenton Psychiatric Hospital, Trenton, NJ, p. A429
BIRMELE, Justin, Chief Executive Officer, Adventhealth Orlando, Orlando, FL, p. A144
BIRMINGHAM, Karen, Director Human Resources, West Springs Hospital, Grand Junction, CO, p. A109
BIRSCHBACH, Nancy
Vice President and Chief Information Officer, SSM Health Ripon Community Hospital, Ripon, WI, p. A721
Vice President and Chief Information Officer, SSM Health St. Agnes Hospital – Fond Du Lac, Fond Du Lac, WI, p. A711
Vice President and Chief Information Officer, SSM Health Waupun Memorial Hospital, Waupun, WI, p. A724
BISCHOFF, Joy
MSN, R.N., President, Ohiohealth Hardin Memorial Hospital, Kenton, OH, p. A497
MSN, R.N., President, Ohiohealth Van Wert Hospital, Van Wert, OH, p. A505
BISCO–FLORA, Nancy, Chief Nursing Officer, Saint Michael's Medical Center, Newark, NJ, p. A425
BISDORF, Jonathan, Director Information Technology, Ohio Valley Surgical Hospital, Springfield, OH, p. A504
BISH, Carol, Human Resources Coordinator, Prisma Health North Greenville Hospital, Travelers Rest, SC, p. A571
BISHARA, Reemon, M.D., Medical Director, Coastal Harbor Treatment Center, Savannah, GA, p. A171
BISHOP, Amy Leigh, Director Human Resources, Red Bay Hospital, Red Bay, AL, p. A24
BISHOP, Ann
Chief Executive Officer and Administrator, Baptist Memorial Hospital–Booneville, Booneville, MS, p. A360
Chief Executive Officer and Administrator, Baptist Memorial Hospital–Union County, New Albany, MS, p. A367
BISHOP, Bill, Chief Information Officer, Colquitt Regional Medical Center, Moultrie, GA, p. A169
BISHOP, Brent, Associate Chief Operating Officer, Massena Hospital, Inc., Massena, NY, p. A446
BISHOP, Elizabeth, Business Office Manager, Salina Surgical Hospital, Salina, KS, p. A259
BISHOP, Glenda, Interim Chief Executive Officer, Quincy Valley Medical Center, Quincy, WA, p. A693
BISHOP, Janice E, R.N., Chief Nursing Officer, Tewksbury Hospital, Tewksbury, MA, p. A319
BISHOP, Jim, Chief Financial Officer, Sullivan County Community Hospital, Sullivan, IN, p. A227
BISHOP, Jody A., Chief Nursing Officer, Bon Secours St. Mary's Hospital, Richmond, VA, p. A682
BISHOP, John, Chief Executive Officer, Bitterroot Health – Daly Hospital, Hamilton, MT, p. A392
BISHOP, Steve, Chief Financial Officer, Up Health System – Portage, Hancock, MI, p. A329
BISHOP–MCWAIN, Toni, Vice President Chief Nursing Officer, Saratoga Hospital, Saratoga Springs, NY, p. A458
BISIG, John, Chief Nursing Officer, The Brook Hospital – Kmi, Louisville, KY, p. A270
BISSENDEN, Chris, Director Human Resources, Ogden Regional Medical Center, Ogden, UT, p. A666
BISSONETTE, Christine, R.N., Service Line Director for Acute Services, Kalkaska Memorial Health Center, Kalkaska, MI, p. A331
BISSONNETTE, Andre, Chief Financial Officer, Northeastern Vermont Regional Hospital, Saint Johnsbury, VT, p. A672
BISTERFELDT, Joanne, Chief Information Officer, Ascension All Saints, Racine, WI, p. A720
BITAR, Adib, M.D., Medical Director, Aurora Charter Oak Hospital, Covina, CA, p. A60
BITAR, Ali, M.D., Vice President Medical Affairs, Dmc Rehabilitation Institute of Michigan, Detroit, MI, p. A325
BITNER, Janet, Chief Operating Officer, Texas Neurorehab Center, Austin, TX, p. A601
BITSILLY, Christina, Human Resource Specialist, U. S. Public Health Service Indian Hospital, Crownpoint, NM, p. A434
BITSOLI, Deborah, CPA, President, Mercy Medical Center, Springfield, MA, p. A318
BITTNER, Augustine, Chief Information Officer, Robley Rex Department of Veterans Affairs Medical Center, Louisville, KY, p. A270
BITTNER, David, Chief Financial Officer, Mount Sinai Rehabilitation Hospital, Hartford, CT, p. A116
BITZ, Joan, Chief Nursing Officer, Meeker Memorial Hospital And Clinics, Litchfield, MN, p. A348
BIUSO, Joseph, M.D., Vice President and Chief of Medical Affairs, Atrium Health Floyd Medical Center, Rome, GA, p. A170
BIVANS, Michelle, Director Human Resources, Duncan Regional Hospital, Duncan, OK, p. A512
BIVINS, Tera, Chief Human Resources Officer, Iroquois Memorial Hospital And Resident Home, Watseka, IL, p. A210
BJELLAND, Tim Esq, Physician, Mile Bluff Medical Center, Mauston, WI, p. A715
BJERGA, Lisa, President and Chief Executive Officer, Lakewood Health System, Staples, MN, p. A355
BJERKE, Carolyn R, Director Human Resources, Mercy Hospital Kingfisher, Kingfisher, OK, p. A514
BJERKE, Craig, Executive Vice President and Chief Financial Officer, Methodist Charlton Medical Center, Dallas, TX, p. A612
BJERKE, Erik, Chief Executive Officer, Madison Healthcare Services, Madison, MN, p. A349
BJERKNES, Dan, Chief Executive Officer, Regional President, Avera St. Luke's Hospital, Aberdeen, SD, p. A572
BJORDAHL, Kevin, M.D., Chief Medical Officer, Milbank Area Hospital Avera, Milbank, SD, p. A574
BJORNSTAD, Brad, M.D., Vice President and Chief Medical Officer, Adventhealth Tampa, Tampa, FL, p. A152
BLABON, Gary, President and Chief Operating Officer, Novant Health Rowan Medical Center, Salisbury, NC, p. A475
BLACK, Amy, R.N., MSN, Chief Operating Officer, Sentara Martha Jefferson Hospital, Charlottesville, VA, p. A674
BLACK, Ashley, Chief Executive Officer, Encompass Health Rehabilitation Hospital of Morgantown, Morgantown, WV, p. A703
BLACK, Charles Jr, Chief Financial Officer, Rockcastle Regional Hospital And Respiratory Care Center, Mount Vernon, KY, p. A272
BLACK, Douglas, Vice President of Operations, Christian Hospital, Saint Louis, MO, p. A385
BLACK, Jason Esq, Vice President and Chief Nursing Officer, Glendale Memorial Hospital And Health Center, Glendale, CA, p. A66
BLACK, Jessica, Market Chief Executive Officer, Copper Springs Hospital, Avondale, AZ, p. A30
BLACK, Marcey, Chief Financial Officer, Northwest Florida Community Hospital, Chipley, FL, p. A128
BLACK, Maria, Chief Nursing Officer, Utah Valley Hospital, Provo, UT, p. A667
BLACK, Marilynn
Chief Information Officer, Northern Arizona Healthcare, Flagstaff Medical Center, Flagstaff, AZ, p. A31
Chief Information Officer, Northern Arizona Healthcare, Verde Valley Medical Center, Cottonwood, AZ, p. A31
BLACK, Michael, Director Human Resources, East Georgia Regional Medical Center, Statesboro, GA, p. A171
BLACK, Ronald, M.D., Chief Medical Officer, Clark Fork Valley Hospital, Plains, MT, p. A394
BLACK, Shannon, Chief Executive Officer, Manning Regional Healthcare Center, Manning, IA, p. A239
BLACK, Terri, Network Manager, Lucas County Health Center, Chariton, IA, p. A232
BLACK, Tim, Director Human Resources, Timpanogos Regional Hospital, Orem, UT, p. A667
BLACKBEAR, Annabelle, Human Resources Specialist, U. S. Public Health Service Indian Hospital, Pine Ridge, SD, p. A575
BLACKBURN, Donovan, Chief Executive Officer and Vice President of Board of Directors, Pikeville Medical Center, Pikeville, KY, p. A273
BLACKBURN, Greg, Chief Executive Officer, Dignity Health East Valley Rehabilitation Hospital, Chandler, AZ, p. A30
BLACKBURN, Mary, Vice President Operations and Chief Practice Officer, Hugh Chatham Health, Elkin, NC, p. A468
BLACKBURN, Susan, Chief Operating Officer, Providence St. Mary Medical Center, Walla Walla, WA, p. A698
BLACKFORD, Nate, President, Mosaic Medical Center – Maryville, Maryville, MO, p. A380
BLACKHAM, Cami, R.N., Nurse Administrator, Sevier Valley Hospital, Richfield, UT, p. A668
BLACKWELL, David, Vice President Operations, Baylor Scott & White Medical Center – Hillcrest, Waco, TX, p. A660
BLACKWELL, Kelsie, Chief Financial Officer, UCI Health – Placentia Linda, Placentia, CA, p. A83
BLACKWELL, Keslie, Chief Financial Officer, Abrazo Central Campus, Phoenix, AZ, p. A35
BLACKWELL, Timothy, Manager Human Resources, Rolling Hills Hospital, Ada, OK, p. A509
BLACKWOOD, Jim, Chief Executive Officer, Tallahatchie General Hospital, Charleston, MS, p. A360
BLACKWOOD, Mark, M.D., Chief of Staff, Bolivar Medical Center, Cleveland, MS, p. A361
BLADEN, Anthony M., Executive Vice President, Chief Operating Officer, Calverthealth Medical Center, Prince Frederick, MD, p. A306
BLAHA, Bill, Manager Information Technology, Astera Health, Wadena, MN, p. A356
BLAHNIK, David, Chief Operating Officer, Twin Valley Behavioral Healthcare, Columbus, OH, p. A493
BLAIN, Brenda, MSN, Senior Vice President and Chief Nursing Executive, Bayhealth, Dover, DE, p. A121
BLAIR, Christopher
Chief Administrative Officer, Siloam Springs Regional Hospital, Siloam Springs, AR, p. A53
Chief Executive Officer, Northwest Medical Center – Springdale, Springdale, AR, p. A53
BLAIR, Diane, Human Resources and Admissions, Chi Health Plainview, Plainview, NE, p. A405
BLAIR, Heidi L, Vice President Administration, Centerstone Hospital, Bradenton, FL, p. A126
BLAIR, Jan, Director Human Resources, Cmh Regional Health System, Wilmington, OH, p. A507
BLAIR, Mark, M.D., Medical Director, Columbus Springs Dublin, Dublin, OH, p. A495
BLAIR, Melinda Lee, Vice President and Chief Nursing Officer, Baptist Health Richmond, Richmond, KY, p. A273
BLAKE, Alan, M.D., President Medical Staff, Samaritan Lebanon Community Hospital, Lebanon, OR, p. A528
BLAKE, Daphne, R.N., MSN, Chief Nursing Officer, Guadalup. Regional Medical Center, Seguin, TX, p. A652
BLAKE, Diane, Chief Executive Officer, Cascade Medical, Leavenworth, WA, p. A691
BLAKE, Jean, Chief Nursing Officer, University Hospitals Cleveland Medical Center, Cleveland, OH, p. A491
BLAKE, Kelly, Chief Executive Officer, Select Specialty Hospital–Johnstown, Johnstown, PA, p. A543
BLAKE, Robert, Chief Human Resources Officer Southwest Market, Memorial Hermann Sugar Land Hospital, Sugar Land, TX, p. A654
BLAKELY, Michelle
FACHE, Ph.D., Associate Director, Jesse Brown Va Medical Center, Chicago, IL, p. A189
FACHE, Ph.D., Chief Operating Officer, Humboldt Park Health, Chicago, IL, p. A189
BLAKELY, Michelle Y.
Ph.D., FACHE, President, Advocate South Suburban Hospital, Hazel Crest, IL, p. A197
Ph.D., FACHE, President, Advocate Trinity Hospital, Chicago, IL, p. A188
BLAKENEY, Dell, Vice President and Chief Information Officer, South Central Regional Medical Center, Laurel, MS, p. A365
BLAKEY GORMAN, Mary, Director Human Resources, Northwest Missouri Psychiatric Rehabilitation Center, Saint Joseph, MO, p. A383
BLALOCK, Tracey, MSN, R.N., Chief Nurse Executive, Atrium Health Navicent The Medical Center, Macon, GA, p. A167
BLANCHARD, Charmaine, Chief Nursing Officer, Encompass Health Rehabilitation Hospital, An Affiliate of Martin Health, Stuart, FL, p. A150
BLANCHARD, Jeremy, M.D., Chief Medical Officer, North Mississipp. Medical Center – Tupelo, Tupelo, MS, p. A369
BLANCHARD, Jordan, M.D., Chief of Medical Staff, Weiser Memorial Hospital, Weiser, ID, p. A184
BLANCHARD, Susan, R.N., Chief Nursing Officer, Encompass Health Rehabilitation Hospital of Albuquerque, Albuquerque, NM, p. A432
BLANCHARD, Timothy D, Chief Financial Officer, Kingman Regional Medical Center, Kingman, AZ, p. A32
BLANCHAT, Tim, Chief Information Officer, Catawba Valley Medical Center, Hickory, NC, p. A470
BLANCO, Andres, Director Management Information Systems, HCA Florida Westside Hospital, Plantation, FL, p. A147
BLAND, Andrew C., M.D., Vice President and Chief Medical Officer, Hamilton Medical Center, Dalton, GA, p. A162
BLAND, Casey, Director of Nursing, Ochsner Rush Medical Center, Meridian, MS, p. A366

A800 Index of Health Care Professionals

BLANEY, Gerard
    Vice President Finance and Interim Chief Financial Officer, Einstein Medical Center Philadelphia, Philadelphia, PA, p. A548
    Vice President, Finance, Jefferson Einstein Montgomery Hospital, East Norriton, PA, p. A538
BLANK, Kim
    Director Human Resources, Elbow Lake Medical Center, Elbow Lake, MN, p. A346
    Director Human Resources, Lake Region Healthcare Corporation, Fergus Falls, MN, p. A347
BLANKE, Kerry Lee
    Chief Financial Officer, Thedacare Medical Center–Shawano, Shawano, WI, p. A721
    Director Financial Services, Thedacare Medical Center–Waupaca, Waupaca, WI, p. A724
BLANKENHORN, Ann, Chief Nursing Officer, Pottstown Hospital, Pottstown, PA, p. A553
BLANKENSHIP, Diana, Director Human Resources, Welch Community Hospital, Welch, WV, p. A705
BLANKENSHIP, Jeff
    CPA, Chief Financial Officer, Pathways of Tennessee, Jackson, TN, p. A584
    CPA, Vice President and Chief Financial Officer, Jackson–Madison County General Hospital, Medina, TN, p. A588
BLANSKY, Richard, M.D., Chief Medical Officer, Guthrie Lourdes Hospital, Binghamton, NY, p. A439
BLANTON, Forest
    Chief Information Officer, Memorial Hospital Pembroke, Pembroke Pines, FL, p. A146
    Chief Information Officer, Memorial Hospital West, Pembroke Pines, FL, p. A146
    Senior VP and Chief Information Officer, Memorial Hospital Miramar, Miramar, FL, p. A141
BLANTON, James, Chief Financial Officer, UT Health East Texas Rehabilitation Hospital, Tyler, TX, p. A659
BLANTON, Kevin, D.O., Chief of Staff, Goodall–Witcher Hospital, Clifton, TX, p. A607
BLANTON, Ron, Chief Fiscal Services, Boise Va Medical Center, Boise, ID, p. A179
BLANTON, Sherry, Human Resource Director, Doctors' Memorial Hospital, Perry, FL, p. A147
BLASER, Joseph, Chief Medical Officer, SBL Fayette County Hospital And Long Term Care, Vandalia, IL, p. A210
BLASER, Karla, Director Human Resources, Unitypoint Health – Trinity Muscatine, Muscatine, IA, p. A240
BLASING, Amy
    R.N., MSN, Chief Executive Officer, Lovelace Westside Hospital, Albuquerque, NM, p. A432
    R.N., MSN, Chief Executive Officer, Lovelace Women's Hospital, Albuquerque, NM, p. A433
BLASKO, Edward, Chief of Staff, Atrium Health Anson, Wadesboro, NC, p. A477
BLASY, Christopher, D.O., Chief of Staff, Carl Vinson Veterans Affairs Medical Center, Dublin, GA, p. A163
BLAUER, Michael, Administrator, Cassia Regional Hospital, Burley, ID, p. A180
BLAUS, Deidre A., Interim Chief Administrative Officer, Robert Wood Johnson University Hospital Somerset, Somerville, NJ, p. A428
BLAUSTEIN, Ron, Chief Financial Officer, Ann & Robert H. Lurie Children's Hospital of Chicago, Chicago, IL, p. A188
BLAUWET, Cheri, Chief Medical Officer, Spaulding Rehabilitation Hospital, Charlestown, MA, p. A312
BLAUWET, Judy, M.P.H., R.N., Senior Vice President Operations, Avera Mckennan Hospital And University Health Center, Sioux Falls, SD, p. A576
BLAYLOCK, Arlen, Chief Operating Officer and Chief Nursing Officer, St. Luke's Magic Valley Medical Center, Twin Falls, ID, p. A184
BLAYLOCK, Darrell, Chief Executive Officer, Dekalb Regional Medical Center, Fort Payne, AL, p. A19
BLAYLOCK, Kevin, Chief Executive Officer, Oklahoma Spine Hospital, Oklahoma City, OK, p. A518
BLAZAKIS, Shelly, Director Human Resources Services, Scripp. Memorial Hospital–La Jolla, La Jolla, CA, p. A68
BLAZEK, Dennis, Chief Information Officer, Clarke County Hospital, Osceola, IA, p. A241
BLAZEK, Robert, System Director, Human Resources Business Partners, Endeavor Health Elmhurst Hospital, Elmhurst, IL, p. A194
BLAZIER, Patty, Chief Nursing Officer, Hamilton Memorial Hospital District, Mcleansboro, IL, p. A201
BLEAK, Jason, Chief Executive Officer, Battle Mountain General Hospital, Battle Mountain, NV, p. A408
BLECHA, Timothy, M.D., Medical Director, Brodstone Memorial Hospital, Superior, NE, p. A406
BLEECKER, Leigh, Chief Financial Officer, Duke Raleigh Hospital, Raleigh, NC, p. A474

BLENDERMAN, Robert, Senior Vice President and Chief Operating Officer, New York–Presbyterian Queens, New York, NY, p. A450
BLENK, David, President and Chief Executive Officer, Livengrin Foundation, Bensalem, PA, p. A535
BLESI, Michael, Director Information Technology, Rainy Lake Medical Center, International Falls, MN, p. A348
BLESSING, Brian, Chief Financial Officer, Texas Health Harris Methodist Hospital Azle, Azle, TX, p. A601
BLEVINS, Bonnie, R.N., Chief Financial Officer, Faith Community Hospital, Jacksboro, TX, p. A630
BLEVINS, Dean, Chief Executive Officer, Encompass Health Rehabilitation Hospital of Northern Kentucky, Edgewood, KY, p. A265
BLEVINS, Denzil, Director Information Systems, Montgomery General Hospital, Montgomery, WV, p. A702
BLEVINS, Emily, Chief Executive Officer, Select Specialty Hospital of Southeast Ohio, Newark, OH, p. A501
BLEVINS, Lindsey, Chief Executive Officer, Crestwyn Behavioral Health, Memphis, TN, p. A588
BLEVINS, Matthew H, Chief Operating Officer, Flowers Hospital, Dothan, AL, p. A18
BLEVINS, Pam
    R.N., Director Information Technology Member Hospitals Mission, Mission Hospital Mcdowell, Marion, NC, p. A472
    R.N., Director, Clinical Informatics, Blue Ridge Regional Hospital, Spruce Pine, NC, p. A476
BLIGHTON, Gordon, Director Resource Management, Naval Hospital Camp Pendleton, Camp Pendleton, CA, p. A58
BLINDE, Mark, Director, Information Technology, Grand Island Regional Medical Center, Grand Island, NE, p. A400
BLINKHORN, Richard, Executive Vice President and Chief Physician Executive, Metrohealth Medical Center, Cleveland, OH, p. A491
BLISS, Howard, Director of Information Systems, Helen Newberry Joy Hospital & Healthcare Center, Newberry, MI, p. A334
BLIVEN, Donna, Vice President Patient Care Services and Chief Nursing Officer, Jones Memorial Hospital, Wellsville, NY, p. A461
BLOCHLINGER, Pamela, Acting Vice President Finance, North Central Kansas Medical Center, Concordia, KS, p. A248
BLOCK, Annie, Director Human Resources, Poplar Community Hospital, Poplar, MT, p. A395
BLOCK, Deb, MSN, Director of Nursing, Stephens County Hospital, Toccoa, GA, p. A173
BLOCK, Linn, Chief Executive Officer, Stewart Memorial Community Hospital, Lake City, IA, p. A239
BLODGETT, Debbie, Director Fiscal Services, Ochiltree General Hospital, Perryton, TX, p. A643
BLOEMER, Brad
    Chief Financial Officer, Arkansas Methodist Medical Center, Paragould, AR, p. A52
    Chief Financial Officer, Henry County Medical Center, Paris, TN, p. A592
    President and Chief Executive Officer, Arkansas Methodist Medical Center, Paragould, AR, p. A52
BLOEMKER, Jeff, Chief Executive Officer, Ray County Hospital And Healthcare, Richmond, MO, p. A382
BLOMBERG, Emily, President, Regions Hospital, Saint Paul, MN, p. A354
BLOMQUIST, David, Director Information Technology, Mckenzie–Willamette Medical Center, Springfield, OR, p. A532
BLOMSTEDT, Jason, Chief of Staff, Community Hospital, Mccook, NE, p. A402
BLOOD, Barbara
    Director Human Resources, Lourdes Counseling Center, Richland, WA, p. A694
    Executive Director Human Resources, Lourdes Health, Pasco, WA, p. A692
BLOOM, Barry, Chief Executive Officer, Jeff Davis Hospital, Hazlehurst, GA, p. A165
BLOOM, Laura, Director Human Resources, Coffee Regional Medical Center, Douglas, GA, p. A163
BLOOM, Rob, Chief Financial Officer, Carthage Area Hospital, Carthage, NY, p. A441
BLOOMQUIST, Aaron
    Vice President, Chief Financial Officer, Ridgeview Medical Center, Waconia, MN, p. A356
    Vice President, Chief Financial Officer, Ridgeview Sibley Medical Center, Arlington, MN, p. A342
BLOSE, Brittany M., Director of Nursing, Reading Hospital Rehabilitation At Wyomissing, Wyomissing, PA, p. A558
BLOUNT, Robin, Chief Medical Officer, Boone Hospital Center, Columbia, MO, p. A374
BLUBAUGH, Mark, D.O., Medical Director, Tulsa Er & Hospital, Tulsa, OK, p. A523
BLUE, Jan L, Vice President Human Resources, Hoag Memorial Hospital Presbyterian, Newport Beach, CA, p. A80

BLUE, Lee Ann, MSN, R.N., Chief Nursing Officer and Executive Vice President Patient Care Services, Eskenazi Health, Indianapolis, IN, p. A219
BLUHM, Tom, Director Information Systems, Island Health, Anacortes, WA, p. A687
BLUM, Donald A., M.D., Chief of Staff, Wetzel County Hospital, New Martinsville, WV, p. A703
BLUM, Gavin, Chief Financial Officer, Kearney County Health Services, Minden, NE, p. A402
BLUMENTHAL, Rachel, Human Resources Generalist, North Platte Valley Medical Center, Saratoga, WY, p. A728
BLUNK, Jim, D.O., Chief Medical Officer, Caldwell Regional Medical Center, Caldwell, KS, p. A247
BLURTON, Cheri
    Director Human Resources, SMC Regional Medical Center, Osceola, AR, p. A52
    Director Human Resources, HIPAA Privacy Officer, Great River Medical Center, Blytheville, AR, p. A43
BLYE, Colleen M, Executive Vice President and Chief Financial Officer, Montefiore Medical Center, New York, NY, p. A449
BLYTHE, Thomas W, System Vice President Human Resources, SSM Health Good Samaritan Hospital, Mount Vernon, IL, p. A202
BOARD, Patricia, Vice President Human Resources, Community Hospital of Bremen, Bremen, IN, p. A213
BOATMAN, Robert, Director Information Technology, Richmond State Hospital, Richmond, IN, p. A226
BOBBITT, James, Vice President Human Resources, Group Ministry Market, Ascension Saint Agnes, Baltimore, MD, p. A300
BOBO, Matt, Chief Information Officer, Meade District Hospital, Meade, KS, p. A254
BOCCELLATO, Judy, R.N., MSN, Chief Nursing Officer, Specialty Hospital of Central Jersey, Lakewood, NJ, p. A422
BOCHATON, Philippe, President, Baylor Scott & White Medical Center – Round Rock, Round Rock, TX, p. A647
BOCKENEK, William, M.D., Chief Medical Officer, Carolinas Rehabilitation, Charlotte, NC, p. A465
BOCKER, Jennifer, M.D., Chief Medical Officer, HCA Florida Sarasota Doctors Hospital, Sarasota, FL, p. A149
BODE, Edwin J, Chief Financial Officer, Adventist Health Columbia Gorge, The Dalles, OR, p. A532
BODE, Heather, Chief Executive Officer, Faulkton Area Medical Center, Faulkton, SD, p. A573
BODENHAM, Steve, Senior Manager Clinical Engineering, Indiana University Health North Hospital, Carmel, IN, p. A214
BODENNER, Nancy, Director Human Resources, Mymichigan Medical Center Tawas, Tawas City, MI, p. A339
BODENSTEINER, Kim, Chief Financial Officer, Essentia Health–Fosston, Fosston, MN, p. A347
BODIN, Donna L, Vice President, Woman's Hospital, Baton Rouge, LA, p. A278
BODINE, Maureen, Chief Clinical Officer, Kindred Hospital–San Diego, San Diego, CA, p. A89
BODLOVIC, Kirk
    Vice President and Chief Financial Officer, Providence St. Josep. Medical Center, Polson, MT, p. A395
    WMSA Chief Financial Officer, Providence St. Patrick Hospital, Missoula, MT, p. A394
BODNAR, Darrell, Director Information, Weeks Medical Center, Lancaster, NH, p. A415
BOECKMANN, Patricia, R.N., Chief Operating Officer and Chief Nursing Officer, Straub Medical Center, Honolulu, HI, p. A176
BOEHM, Denise, Chief Nurse Executive, Washington Dc Veterans Affairs Medical Center, Washington, DC, p. A124
BOEHM, Donna, MSN, M.P.H., R.N., Chief Nursing Officer, North Arkansas Regional Medical Center, Harrison, AR, p. A47
BOEHMER, Bernard, M.D., Medical Director, Cassia Regional Hospital, Burley, ID, p. A180
BOEMER, Sally Mason
    Chief Financial Officer, Salem Hospital, Salem, MA, p. A318
    Senior Vice President Finance, Massachusetts General Hospital, Boston, MA, p. A310
BOEMMEL, Michael, Vice President and Chief Financial Officer, Medstar National Rehabilitation Hospital, Washington, DC, p. A123
BOEN, Stefanie, Chief Nursing Officer, Skyline Health, White Salmon, WA, p. A698
BOER, Jeff, Director Information Technology, Pulaski Memorial Hospital, Winamac, IN, p. A229
BOERGER, Kathy, Director Human Resources, Upper Valley Medical Center, Troy, OH, p. A505
BOERSCHEL, Viva, Director of Nursing, Floyd County Medical Center, Charles City, IA, p. A232
BOESE, Chris, Vice President and Chief Nursing Officer, Regions Hospital, Saint Paul, MN, p. A354

Index of Health Care Professionals / Bogard

BOGARD, Tim, Manager Information Technology, Highland District Hospital, Hillsboro, OH, p. A497
BOGARDUS, Tim, Chief Executive Officer, Oasis Hospital, Phoenix, AZ, p. A36
BOGERS, Christina, Chief Clinical Officer, Logan Health – Whitefish, Whitefish, MT, p. A396
BOGGESS, Carrie
  Human Resource Generalist, Carilion Giles Community Hospital, Pearisburg, VA, p. A681
  Human Resources Generalist, Carilion Tazewell Community Hospital, Tazewell, VA, p. A684
BOGGS, Cathy, Executive Director and Administrator, Community Fairbanks Recovery Center, Indianapolis, IN, p. A219
BOGLE, Bryan, Chief Executive Officer, Kit Carson County Memorial Hospital, Burlington, CO, p. A104
BOGLE, William J, Director Information Systems, North Arkansas Regional Medical Center, Harrison, AR, p. A47
BOGOLIN, Lore, MSN, R.N., Vice President Patient Care Services and Chief Nursing Officer, Vassar Brothers Medical Center, Poughkeepsie, NY, p. A456
BOHACH, Christopher, DPM, Chief of Staff, Mercy Health – Willard Hospital, Willard, OH, p. A507
BOHALL, Karen, Director Human Resources, UPMC Chautauqua, Jamestown, NY, p. A444
BOHATY, Richard, Director Information Technology, Chi Health St Elizabeth, Lincoln, NE, p. A402
BOHLIN, Sarah, Human Resources Director, North Carolina Specialty Hospital, Durham, NC, p. A467
BOHN, Terry, Director, Human Resources, Orange County Global Medical Center, Inc., Santa Ana, CA, p. A93
BOHNEN, Christa N, Director Human Resources, Ellsworth County Medical Center, Ellsworth, KS, p. A249
BOIK, Reyne, Director Human Resources, Cascade Medical, Leavenworth, WA, p. A691
BOIKE, Darlene, Chief Financial Officer, Ccm Health, Montevideo, MN, p. A351
BOILEAU, Michel, M.D., Chief Clinical Officer, St. Charles Prineville, Prineville, OR, p. A531
BOILY, Cindy
  MSN, R.N., Senior Vice President and Chief Nursing Officer, Wakemed Cary Hospital, Cary, NC, p. A464
  MSN, R.N., Senior Vice President and Chief Nursing Officer, Wakemed Raleigh Campus, Raleigh, NC, p. A475
BOIS, Alain, R.N., Director of Nursing, Northern Maine Medical Center, Fort Kent, ME, p. A297
BOJO, Rolland, R.N., President and Chief Executive Officer, UHS Delaware Valley Hospital, Walton, NY, p. A461
BOKON, Mark, Chief Information Officer, Northwest Medical Center – Springdale, Springdale, AR, p. A53
BOLAND, Albert, Vice President Operations, UPMC Jameson, New Castle, PA, p. A547
BOLAND, E. Kay, R.N., MS, Vice President and Chief Nursing Officer, United Health Services Hospitals–Binghamton, Binghamton, NY, p. A439
BOLAND, Giles W., M.D., President, Brigham And Women's Hospital, Boston, MA, p. A310
BOLANDER, Patrick, Chief Financial Officer, Slidell Memorial Hospital, Slidell, LA, p. A293
BOLANDER, Patrick C
  Chief Financial Officer, East Cooper Medical Center, Mount Pleasant, SC, p. A568
  Chief Financial Officer, Georgetown Community Hospital, Georgetown, KY, p. A266
BOLANOS, Jimmy, Chief Operating Officer, Adventhealth South Overland Park, Overland Park, KS, p. A257
BOLCAVAGE, Ted, Vice President Division Controller, Inpatient, Ohiohealth Rehabilitation Hospital, Columbus, OH, p. A492
BOLDA, Craig, Chief Operating Officer, St. Catherine Hospital, East Chicago, IN, p. A215
BOLDT, Stephanie, President and Chief Executive Officer, Crete Area Medical Center, Crete, NE, p. A399
BOLDUC, Tiana, Chief Information Officer, Mercy Hospital Ozark, Ozark, AR, p. A52
BOLEN, Shannon, Director Human Resources, Baptist Memorial Hospital–Booneville, Booneville, MS, p. A360
BOLES, Glen
  Chief Financial Officer, Christus Health Shreveport–Bossier, Shreveport, LA, p. A292
  Vice President and Chief Financial Officer, Christus St. Michael Health System, Texarkana, TX, p. A656
  Vice President and Chief Financial Officer, Christus St. Michael Rehabilitation Hospital, Texarkana, TX, p. A656
BOLES, Steven Lee., Chief Executive Officer, Hunt Regional Medical Center, Greenville, TX, p. A623
BOLEWARE, Mike, Administrator, Franklin County Memorial Hospital, Meadville, MS, p. A366
BOLEY, Sarah, Director Human Resources, Wetzel County Hospital, New Martinsville, WV, p. A703

BOLIN, Cris, Chief Financial Officer, Grand River Hospital District, Rifle, CO, p. A113
BOLIN, Kari, Chief Nursing Officer, HCA Florida Putnam Hospital, Palatka, FL, p. A145
BOLIN, Paul
  Chief Financial Officer, Williamson Medical Center, Franklin, TN, p. A583
  Vice President and Chief Human Resources Officer, The Acadia Hospital, Bangor, ME, p. A295
BOLINE, Steve, Chief Financial Officer, Seneca Healthcare District, Chester, CA, p. A59
BOLINGER, John, M.D., Vice President Medical Affairs, Union Hospital, Terre Haute, IN, p. A228
BOLLARD, Robert, Chief Financial Officer, Encompass Health Rehabilitation Hospital of Henderson, Henderson, NV, p. A409
BOLLICH, Mary, Director of Nurses, Amg Specialty Hospital–Lafayette, Lafayette, LA, p. A285
BOLLINGER, Bill, Chief Information Officer, Carroll County Memorial Hospital, Carrollton, MO, p. A373
BOLLMAN, Brooke, Chief Executive Officer, Salem Memorial District Hospital, Salem, MO, p. A386
BOLLMANN, Brett, Chief Executive Officer, Memorial Hospital, Chester, IL, p. A188
BOLLU, Prabhu, Director Information Technology, AHS Sherman Medical Center, Sherman, TX, p. A652
BOLOGNA, Donna, Manager, Human Resources, AHN Wexford Hospital, Wexford, PA, p. A557
BOLOGNA, Monica, R.N., Chief Nursing Officer, West Jefferson Medical Center, Marrero, LA, p. A288
BOLOGNANI, Laurie J, Human Resources Officer, Speare Memorial Hospital, Plymouth, NH, p. A417
BOLOR, Erlinda, R.N., Chief Nursing Officer, San Joaquin General Hospital, French Camp, CA, p. A64
BOLTER, Cindy, Chief Nursing and Operations Officer, John Muir Behavioral Health Center, Concord, CA, p. A60
BOLTON, Katlin, R.N., Chief Nursing Officer, Rapides Regional Medical Center, Alexandria, LA, p. A276
BOLTON, Stacy, Chief Technology Officer, Lakeland Regional Health Medical Center, Lakeland, FL, p. A137
BOMAN, Jeff, Chief Nursing Officer, Chadron Community Hospital And Health Services, Chadron, NE, p. A398
BOMAR, Jacob, Director Information Technology, Hardin Medical Center, Savannah, TN, p. A592
BOMGAARS, Scott, M.D., Vice President Medical Affairs, Methodist Jennie Edmundson Hospital, Council Bluffs, IA, p. A234
BOMSTAD, Heather
  MSN, R.N., Vice President Patient Care Services and Chief Nursing Officer, OSF Saint Paul Medical Center, Mendota, IL, p. A201
  MSN, R.N., Vice President, Chief Nursing Officer, OSF Saint Elizabeth Medical Center, Ottawa, IL, p. A204
BONACORSO, Donna, R.N., Chief Nursing Officer, Community Medical Center, Toms River, NJ, p. A429
BONACQUISTI, Gary, M.D., Chief Medical Officer, Texas Health Hospital Rockwall, Rockwall, TX, p. A647
BONAR, Carrie, Chief Information Officer, Southern California Hospital At Culver City, Culver City, CA, p. A61
BONAR, Robert Jr, Chief Executive Officer, Children's Minnesota, Minneapolis, MN, p. A350
BONAZZOLA, Michael, M.D., Interim Chief Medical Officer, Ohsu Hospital, Portland, OR, p. A530
BOND, Rodney, Director of Information Technology, Northern Regional Hospital, Mount Airy, NC, p. A473
BONDI, Blaise, Interim Chief Financial Officer, Rehoboth Mckinley Christian Health Care Services, Gallup, NM, p. A434
BONDS, Juanita Bates., M.D., President and Chief Executive Officer, Bliant Specialty Hospital, New Orleans, LA, p. A290
BONDURANT, Barry, Chief Executive Officer and Administrator, Baptist Memorial Hospital–Union City, Union City, TN, p. A594
BONDURANT, Charles, Chief Information Officer, Memorial Health Meadows Hospital, Vidalia, GA, p. A173
BONE, Janice, Human Resources, Marshall County Hospital, Benton, KY, p. A263
BONELLO, Joseph, R.N., Chief Nursing Officer, Holland Hospital, Holland, MI, p. A330
BONET, Carmen, Executive Director, Hospital De Psiquiatria, San Juan, PR, p. A735
BONEY, Rebecca, R.N., Chief Nursing Officer, Encompass Health Rehabilitation Hospital of Middletown, Middletown, DE, p. A121
BONI, Shirley M, Administrative Officer, San Carlos Apache Healthcare Corporation, Peridot, AZ, p. A34
BONILLA, Felicita, Administrator, Hospital De La Concepcion, San German, PR, p. A734
BONJOUR, Richard C, Chief Information Officer, Sauk Prairie Healthcare, Prairie Du Sac, WI, p. A720

BONKO, Margaret (Maggie), Chief Executive Officer, Orlando Health – Health Central Hospital, Ocoee, FL, p. A143
BONNECARRERE, Anthony, Controller, St. Bernard Parish Hospital, Chalmette, LA, p. A279
BONNER, Brad L., Executive Director, Human Resources and General Counsel, Crawford County Memorial Hospital, Denison, IA, p. A234
BONNER, Gwen, Chief Operating Officer, Saint Francis Hospital–Bartlett, Bartlett, TN, p. A579
BONNER, Jason, Interim Chief Financial, Accounting Analyst, Morehouse General Hospital, Bastrop, LA, p. A277
BONNER, Kimber, R.N., Vice President Patient Care Services, Chi Health Good Samaritan, Kearney, NE, p. A401
BONNER, Lenne
  Chief Executive Officer, Clearwater Valley Health, Orofino, ID, p. A183
  President, St. Mary's Health, Cottonwood, ID, p. A181
BONNER, Robert, Chief Financial Officer, Glendora Hospital, Glendora, CA, p. A66
BONNEY, Megan, President, Chi St. Vincent North, Sherwood, AR, p. A53
BONO, Anthony Jr, Chief Nursing Officer, AHN Grove City, Grove City, PA, p. A541
BONOMO, Carrie, M.D., Chief of Staff, Trinity Medical, Ferriday, LA, p. A282
BONTHRON, Rikki S, Chief Financial Officer, Franklin Hospital District, Benton, IL, p. A186
BONTRAGER, Mandy, Director Nursing, Holton Community Hospital, Holton, KS, p. A250
BONZO, Kelly, Director, Baptist Health Richmond, Richmond, KY, p. A273
BOOKER, Angela, Director of Nursing Services, Teton Valley Health Care, Driggs, ID, p. A181
BOOKER, Carolyn, R.N., Chief Nursing Officer, Northside Hospital Forsyth, Cumming, GA, p. A162
BOONE, Donna, MS, R.N., Chief Nursing Officer, Medical City Weatherford, Weatherford, TX, p. A661
BOONE, Elwood Bernard. III, FACHE, Division President, Sentara Virginia Beach General Hospital, Virginia Beach, VA, p. A685
BOONE, Richard, Chief Financial Officer, Johnson City Medical Center, Johnson City, TN, p. A585
BOORAS, Laura, Vice President Human Resources, Piedmont Macon, Macon, GA, p. A167
BOORE, Chad, Chief Operations Officer, Mercyone North Iowa Medical Center, Mason City, IA, p. A240
BOORNAZIAN, John, M.D., Chief Medical Officer, Huggins Hospital, Wolfeboro, NH, p. A417
BOOTH, Brad, Market Director, Information Services, Northwest Medical Center Sahuarita, Sahuarita, AZ, p. A38
BOOTH, Christy, Chief Human Resources Officer, Doctors Memorial Hospital, Bonifay, FL, p. A126
BOOTH, Cynthia, Chief Medical Officer, Banner Payson Medical Center, Payson, AZ, p. A34
BOOTH, Daniel
  Vice President Operations, Northern Light Inland Hospital, Waterville, ME, p. A299
  Vice President Operations and Chief Human Resources Officer, Northern Light Inland Hospital, Waterville, ME, p. A299
BOOTH, Donny, Chief Executive Officer, Permian Regional Medical Center, Andrews, TX, p. A597
BOOTH, Leslie, Human Resources Director, Houston County Community Hospital, Erin, TN, p. A582
BORCHERS, Jonathan, M.D., Chief Medical Officer, Washington County Memorial Hospital, Potosi, MO, p. A382
BORCHERT, Barry, Vice President Finance, Reedsburg Area Medical Center, Reedsburg, WI, p. A720
BORCHI, Daniel, Chief Information Officer, Carilion New River Valley Medical Center, Christiansburg, VA, p. A675
BORDELON, James L., M.D., Jr, Chief of Staff, Avoyelles Hospital, Marksville, LA, p. A288
BORDEN, Eric, Chief Operating Officer and Chief Financial Officer, Jewell County Hospital, Mankato, KS, p. A254
BORDERS, James, M.D., Chief Medical Officer, Baptist Health Lexington, Lexington, KY, p. A268
BORDO, David
  M.D., Chief Medical Officer, Ascension Holy Family, Des Plaines, IL, p. A193
  M.D., Interim Co–Chief Executive Officer and Chief Medical Officer, Ascension Resurrection, Chicago, IL, p. A188
  M.D., Vice President and Chief Medical Officer, Community First Medical Center, Chicago, IL, p. A189
BOREL, Patricia, Chief Financial Officer, Mercyone Elkader Medical Center, Elkader, IA, p. A236
BOREN, Kevin
  Chief Financial Officer, Essentia Health Duluth, Duluth, MN, p. A346
  Chief Financial Officer, Essentia Health Northern Pines, Aurora, MN, p. A343

Index of Health Care Professionals / Bowling

BORENS, Dwan, Chief Nursing Officer, Ascension St. John Broken Arrow, Broken Arrow, OK, p. A510
BORER, Tom, Vice President Operations, Promedica Fostoria Community Hospital, Fostoria, OH, p. A496
BORGERSON, Carol, Chief Financial Officer, Madison Healthcare Services, Madison, MN, p. A349
BORGSTROM, Christopher, Associate Administrator, Coastal Carolina Hospital, Hardeeville, SC, p. A568
BORIS, Diane, Chief Financial Officer, Lehigh Valley Hospital – Schuylkill, Pottsville, PA, p. A553
BORIS, Jamie, M.D., President Medical Staff, UPMC Greene, Waynesburg, PA, p. A556
BORLAND, Wray, Chief Executive Officer, Encompass Health Rehabilitation Hospital of Plano, Plano, TX, p. A644
BORNICK, Brian, Chief Information Officer, Minneapolis Va Health Care System, Minneapolis, MN, p. A351
BORNMANN, Debora, Chief Executive Officer, Cornerstone Specialty Hospitals Tucson, Tucson, AZ, p. A40
BOROWSKI, Thomas, FACHE, President, Hudson Hospital And Clinic, Hudson, WI, p. A713
BORREGO, Edward, Chief Exectuve Officer, Jackson Health System, Miami, FL, p. A140
BORRENPOHL, James, Market Site Director, Community Hospital of San Bernardino, San Bernardino, CA, p. A88
BORSOS, Dean B., Medical Center Director, James H. Quillen Department of Veterans Affairs Medical Center, Johnson City, TN, p. A585
BORTEL, Karol, Vice President Financial Services, Wood County Hospital, Bowling Green, OH, p. A487
BORTKE, Todd, Director Information Systems, Chi St. Alexius Health Bismarck, Bismarck, ND, p. A479
BORTZ, Tammy, Director of Finance, Peterson Healthcare And Rehabilitation Hospital, Wheeling, WV, p. A706
BORUS, Zachary A., M.D., Medical Chief of Staff, Lakes Regional Healthcare, Spirit Lake, IA, p. A244
BORYSZAK, Martin W., President, Mercy Hospital, Buffalo, NY, p. A440
BOS, Robbi E, Vice President Human Resources, Sauk Prairie Healthcare, Prairie Du Sac, WI, p. A720
BOSA, Jill, Chief Executive Officer, Southern Indiana Rehabilitation Hospital, New Albany, IN, p. A225
BOSCH, Randy T., Associate Vice President Human Resources, Unity Health – Jacksonville, Jacksonville, AR, p. A48
BOSCIA, Michael, Controller, Encompass Health Rehabilitation Hospital of Cumming, Cumming, GA, p. A162
BOSCO, John, Senior Vice President and Chief Information Officer, Long Island Jewish Medical Center, New Hyde Park, NY, p. A447
BOSHUT, Sami, Chief Information Officer, Jamaica Hospital Medical Center, New York, NY, p. A448
BOSLEY, Elizabeth, R.N., FACHE, Vice President Patient Services and Chief Nursing Officer, St. Mary's Medical Center, Huntington, WV, p. A701
BOSSARD, Neva, Chief Nursing Officer, Lewis County General Hospital, Lowville, NY, p. A445
BOSSE, Allison, Chief Executive Officer and Administrator, Baptist Memorial Hospital for Women, Memphis, TN, p. A588
BOSSE, Patrick, Chief Administrative Officer, Roper St. Francis Berkeley Hospital, Summerville, SC, p. A570
BOST, Cecelia, Chief Operating Officer, Alliance Healthcare System, Holly Springs, MS, p. A363
BOST, Marcus, Director Information Services and Chief Information Officer, Adena Greenfield Medical Center, Greenfield, OH, p. A497
BOSTER, Brian, M.D., Medical Director, Select Specialty Hospital–Cincinnati, Cincinnati, OH, p. A489
BOSTIC, Deborah, R.N., Chief Nursing Officer, Texas Health Presbyterian Hospital Denton, Denton, TX, p. A614
BOSTIC, William, Administrative Assistant Human Resources, Surprise Valley Health Care District, Cedarville, CA, p. A59
BOSTON–LEARY, Katie, Vice President and Chief Nursing Officer, UMPGHC, University of Maryland Capital Region Medical Center, Largo, MD, p. A305
BOSTROM, Stuart, M.D., Director Medical Affairs, Sutter Roseville Medical Center, Roseville, CA, p. A86
BOSTWICK, John, Chief Financial Officer, Rutherford Regional Health System, Rutherfordton, NC, p. A475
BOSTWICK, Monte J., Market Chief Executive Officer, Chi St. Luke's Health Memorial Lufkin, Lufkin, TX, p. A636
BOSTWICK, Shari, Director Human Resources, New London Hospital, New London, NH, p. A416
BOSWELL, Debbie, Chief Operating Officer and Chief Nursing Officer, Mercy Medical Center, Roseburg, OR, p. A531
BOSWELL, Diane, Director Human Resources and Marketing, Salem Township Hospital, Salem, IL, p. A208
BOSWELL, John, Chief Human Resources Officer, UVA Health University Medical Center, Charlottesville, VA, p. A674

BOSWELL, William D., M.D., Jr, Chief Medical Officer, City of Hope's Helford Clinical Research Hospital, Duarte, CA, p. A62
BOSWINKEL, Jan, M.D., Vice President Medical Operations and Chief Safety Officer, Children's Hospital of Philadelphia, Philadelphia, PA, p. A548
BOSWORTH, Dawn, Director Human Resources, Arrowhead Behavioral Health Hospital, Maumee, OH, p. A499
BOTAK, Geoff, Chief Executive Officer, Malvern Institute, Malvern, PA, p. A545
BOTHNER, Joan, M.D., Chief Medical Officer, Children's Hospital Colorado, Aurora, CO, p. A103
BOTHUN, Crystal, Chief Financial Officer, Johnson Memorial Health Services, Dawson, MN, p. A345
BOTINE, Gary, Vice President, Chief Financial Officer, Mary Greeley Medical Center, Ames, IA, p. A230
BOTLER, Joel, M.D., Chief Medical Officer, Mainehealth Maine Medical Center, Portland, ME, p. A298
BOTNEY, Mitchell, M.D., Vice President Medical Affairs and Chief Medical Officer, Missouri Baptist Medical Center, Saint Louis, MO, p. A385
BOTTENFIELD, Dana, Vice President Human Resources, St. Jude Children's Research Hospital, Memphis, TN, p. A589
BOTTGER, Barry, Chief Financial Officer, Republic County Hospital, Belleville, KS, p. A246
BOTTOM, Paige, Director Operations, Wilmington Treatment Center, Wilmington, NC, p. A478
BOUCHER, Christopher Paul, Director of Information Services, Grace Cottage Hospital, Townshend, VT, p. A672
BOUCHER, Travis, Chief Financial Officer, Speare Memorial Hospital, Plymouth, NH, p. A417
BOUCK, Nancy, Senior Director, Human Resources, Mclaren Thumb Region, Bad Axe, MI, p. A322
BOUCOT, Mark G.
  FACHE, President and Chief Executive Officer, Garrett Regional Medical Center, Oakland, MD, p. A306
  FACHE, President and Chief Executive Officer, WVU Medicine Potomac Valley Hospital, Keyser, WV, p. A702
BOUDREAU, Susan E., President, Mobile Infirmary Medical Center, Mobile, AL, p. A21
BOUDREAUX, Angela, Director Information Technology, St. Charles Parish Hospital, Luling, LA, p. A287
BOUDREAUX, Scott, Chief Operating Officer, Cypress Pointe Surgical Hospital, Hammond, LA, p. A287
BOUE, Lourdes, Chief Executive Officer, Baptist Health South Florida, West Kendall Baptist Hospital, Miami, FL, p. A139
BOUGHAL, Ginni, Director Health Information and Information Technology, Peacehealth Peace Harbor Medical Center, Florence, OR, p. A527
BOUHAROUN, Khalil, Chief Information Officer, The Hsc Pediatric Center, Washington, DC, p. A124
BOUIT, Michele, Vice President of Finance, Chief Financial Officer, Northbay Medical Center, Fairfield, CA, p. A63
BOULENGER, Albert Leon, R.N., Chief Executive Officer, Baptist Health South Florida, Baptist Hospital of Miami, Miami, FL, p. A139
BOUQUET RONSONET, Sheena
  Vice President, Ochsner Lafayette General Medical Center, Lafayette, LA, p. A285
  Vice President Human Resources, Ochsner University Hospital & Clinics, Lafayette, LA, p. A286
BOUQUIO, George, Director Human Resources, South Beach Psychiatric Center, New York, NY, p. A452
BOURGEOIS, Jeff
  FACHE, Chief Executive Officer, Saline Memorial Hospital, Benton, AR, p. A43
  FACHE, Interim Chief Executive Officer, Valley View Medical Center, Fort Mohave, AZ, p. A31
BOURLAND, Don, Vice President Human Resources, Peacehealth Peace Harbor Medical Center, Florence, OR, p. A527
BOURLAND, Renee, Human Resources Specialist, San Antonio State Hospital, San Antonio, TX, p. A650
BOURLAND, Trent, Chief Executive Officer, Coal County General Hospital, Coalgate, OK, p. A511
BOURN, Cris, Chief Executive Officer, Select Specialty Hospital – Belhaven, Jackson, MS, p. A364
BOURN, Jennifer, Director, Health Information Services and Medical Staff Services, Centerpointe Hospital, Saint Charles, MO, p. A383
BOURNE, Kara, R.N., MSN, Chief Nursing Officer and Chief Operating Officer, Foothill Regional Medical Center, Tustin, CA, p. A99
BOURNE, Kimberly L., President and Chief Executive Officer, Taylorville Memorial Hospital, Taylorville, IL, p. A210
BOURQUE, Teresa, Sr. Administrator for Nursing/Chief Nurse, Hurley Medical Center, Flint, MI, p. A326
BOUSEMAN, Cesiley, Chief Executive Officer, Cedar Ridge, Oklahoma City, OK, p. A516

BOUTAIN, Thomas, Information Services Executive, North Central Health Care, Wausau, WI, p. A724
BOUTWELL, Wayne B. Jr, Chief Executive Officer, Encompass Health Rehabilitation Hospital of Bluffton, Bluffton, SC, p. A562
BOUYEA, Lawanda Janine, Director Human Resources, Natividad, Salinas, CA, p. A88
BOVA, Sheila, Chief Financial Officer, Kindred Hospital–Albuquerque, Albuquerque, NM, p. A432
BOVIO, Ernest L. Jr, Senior Vice President & President Novant Health New Hanover Regional Medical Center & Coastal Market, Novant Health New Hanover Regional Medical Center, Wilmington, NC, p. A478
BOWDEN, Thomas, President, Rockledge Regional Medical Center, Rockledge, FL, p. A148
BOWE, Christopher
  M.D., Chief Medical Officer, Medical Affairs, St. Mary's Regional Medical Center, Lewiston, ME, p. A298
  M.D., President, Mid Coast Hospital, Brunswick, ME, p. A296
BOWEN, Aaron, Chief Executive Officer, Arizona State Hospital, Phoenix, AZ, p. A35
BOWEN, Bonnie, Director Human Resources, Huntsville Memorial Hospital, Huntsville, TX, p. A629
BOWEN, Christine, R.N., Chief Nursing Officer, Dmc Harper University Hospital, Detroit, MI, p. A325
BOWEN, John, President, Parkview Regional Medical Center, Fort Wayne, IN, p. A217
BOWEN, Rodger W, M.P.H., Chief Financial Officer, Scenic Mountain Medical Center, Big Spring, TX, p. A603
BOWEN, Stephen, Chief Executive Officer, Lavaca Medical Center, Hallettsville, TX, p. A623
BOWEN, Tim, FACHE, President, Baylor Scott & White Medical Center at – Mckinney, Mckinney, TX, p. A638
BOWER, David, M.D., Chief of Staff, Atlanta Veterans Affairs Medical Center, Decatur, GA, p. A162
BOWER, Kay, Associate Director for Patient Care Services, Battle Creek Veterans Affairs Medical Center, Battle Creek, MI, p. A322
BOWERMAN, Stephen, President and Chief Executive Officer, Midland Memorial Hospital, Midland, TX, p. A639
BOWERS, Daniel, Chief Operating Officer, Riverside Community Hospital, Riverside, CA, p. A86
BOWERS, David N, M.D., Medical Director, Siskin Hospital for Physical Rehabilitation, Chattanooga, TN, p. A581
BOWERS, Dusty A., Chief Executive Officer, Acuity Specialty Hospital–Ohio Valley At Weirton, Weirton, WV, p. A705
BOWERS, Jamelle, M.D., Vice President Medical, Mercy Health – Anderson Hospital, Cincinnati, OH, p. A489
BOWERS, Melodee, Director Human Resources, Carle Hoopeston Regional Health Center, Hoopeston, IL, p. A198
BOWERS, Michael E., Regional Executive Vice President and Chief Operating Officer, SSM Health St. Josep. – St. Charles, Saint Charles, MO, p. A383
BOWERS, Sharon, R.N., Manager of Community, Public and Employee Relations, Sheridan Community Hospital, Sheridan, MI, p. A338
BOWERS, Tracy
  Vice President Human Resources and Administrative Services, UVA Health Haymarket Medical Center, Haymarket, VA, p. A677
  Vice President Human Resources and Administrative Services, UVA Health Prince William Medical Center, Manassas, VA, p. A679
BOWERY, Leslie, Director of Standards and Compliance, Cumberland Hospital for Children And Adolescents, New Kent, VA, p. A679
BOWES, Arthur, Senior Vice President Human Resources, Salem Hospital, Salem, MA, p. A318
BOWES, William, Chief Financial Officer, UAMS Medical Center, Little Rock, AR, p. A50
BOWIE, John, Chief Operating Officer, Morehouse General Hospital, Bastrop. LA, p. A277
BOWLEG, Teresa, R.N., Chief Nursing Officer, Erlanger Western Carolina Hospital, Murphy, NC, p. A473
BOWLES, Patrica, R.N., Chief Nursing Officer, Franklin County Medical Center, Preston, ID, p. A183
BOWLES, Tara, Employee Relations Director, Rawlins County Health Center, Atwood, KS, p. A246
BOWLINE, Brandon, Chief Operating Officer, Claxton–Hepburn Medical Center, Ogdensburg, NY, p. A455
BOWLING, Donald, M.D., Chief Medical Staff, Bon Secours – Southampton Medical Center, Franklin, VA, p. A676
BOWLING, Karen, Chief Information Officer, St. Mary's Regional Medical Center, Lewiston, ME, p. A298
BOWLING, Karen L., MSN, R.N., President and Chief Executive Officer, Princeton Community Hospital, Princeton, WV, p. A704
BOWLING, Kay, Chief Executive Officer, Centra Specialty Hospital, Lynchburg, VA, p. A679

Index of Health Care Professionals

Index of Health Care Professionals / Bowling

BOWLING, Kelli, Chief Culture Officer, Door County Medical Center, Sturgeon Bay, WI, p. A722
BOWLING, Nancy, Director Human Resources, North Alabama Shoals Hospital, Muscle Shoals, AL, p. A23
BOWMAN, Bo, Chief Executive Officer, Kindred Hospital San Antonio Central, San Antonio, TX, p. A649
BOWMAN, Dyan, Director Human Resources, Newberry County Memorial Hospital, Newberry, SC, p. A569
BOWMAN, Erin, Director, Julian F. Keith Alcohol And Drug Abuse Treatment Center, Black Mountain, NC, p. A464
BOWMAN, Josep. E, Chief Financial Officer, Tristar Stonecrest Medical Center, Smyrna, TN, p. A593
BOWMAN, Julia C, Chief Financial Officer, Hancock County Health System, Britt, IA, p. A231
BOWMAN, Kenneth, Chief Executive Officer, UW Health Rehabilitation Hospital, Madison, WI, p. A715
BOWMAN, Kristin, Chief Executive Officer, Broward Health Coral Springs, Coral Springs, FL, p. A129
BOWMAN, Mark, M.D., President Medical Staff, Adventist Health Tillamook, Tillamook, OR, p. A533
BOWMAN, William, M.D., Vice President Medical Affairs, Cone Health Moses Cone Hospital, Greensboro, NC, p. A469
BOWSER, John, Vice President, Chief Financial Officer, OSF Saint Luke Medical Center, Kewanee, IL, p. A199
BOX, Darrel, Chief Executive Officer, Lafayette Regional Health Center, Lexington, MO, p. A379
BOX, Justin K.
Senior Vice President & Chief Information Officer, Mary Washington Hospital, Fredericksburg, VA, p. A676
Senior Vice President and Chief Information Officer, Stafford Hospital, Stafford, VA, p. A684
BOXELL, Shelley
R.N., Chief Nursing Officer, Rehabilitation Hospital of Fort Wayne, Fort Wayne, IN, p. A217
R.N., Interim Chief Operating Officer, Rehabilitation Hospital of Fort Wayne, Fort Wayne, IN, p. A217
BOYCE, Charlotte, Chief Nursing Officer, Encompass Health Rehabilitation Hospital of North Memphis, A Partner of Methodist Healthcare, Memphis, TN, p. A588
BOYD, Aaron, M.D., FACHE, Co–Chief Executive Officer, Norman Regional Health System, Norman, OK, p. A516
BOYD, Andre A., FACHE, Sr, Chief Operating Officer, The Christ Hospital Health Network, Cincinnati, OH, p. A489
BOYD, Donald
Chief Executive Officer, Kaleida Health, Buffalo, NY, p. A440
President and Chief Executive Officer, Kaleida Health, Buffalo, NY, p. A440
BOYD, Kenneth, President, Baptist Health Paducah, Paducah, KY, p. A272
BOYD, Kim, Chief Financial Officer, Buchanan General Hospital, Grundy, VA, p. A677
BOYD, Robert, Chief Human Resource Officer, Gateway Regional Medical Center, Granite City, IL, p. A196
BOYD, Roy, Chief Financial Officer, Wilkes–Barre General Hospital, Wilkes–Barre, PA, p. A558
BOYD, Steven, R.N., Nurse Executive, Levi Hospital, Hot Springs National Park, AR, p. A48
BOYD, Travis, Manager, Information Technology, Mercy Hospital Lincoln, Troy, MO, p. A387
BOYER, Charlene, Chief Nursing Officer, Kaiser Permanente Oakland Medical Center, Oakland, CA, p. A81
BOYER, Cheryl T.
Vice President Human Resources, Levindale Hebrew Geriatric Center And Hospital, Baltimore, MD, p. A300
Vice President Human Resources, Sinai Hospital of Baltimore, Baltimore, MD, p. A301
BOYER, Jim, Vice President Information Technology and Chief Information Officer, Rush Memorial Hospital, Rushville, IN, p. A227
BOYER, Roderick, M.D., Medical Director, Select Specialty Hospital – Downriver, Wyandotte, MI, p. A341
BOYER, Steve, M.D., Chief Medical Officer, Regional West Garden County, Oshkosh, NE, p. A405
BOYKIN, Doyle, R.N., MSN, Administrator, Presbyterian Hospital, Albuquerque, NM, p. A433
BOYLAN, Patti
Assistant Vice President Finance, Baptist Health South Florida, Homestead Hospital, Homestead, FL, p. A134
Assistant Vice President, Finance (Controller), Baptist Health South Florida, Mariners Hospital, Tavernier, FL, p. A153
Assistant Vice President, Finance (Controller), Baptist Health South Florida, West Kendall Baptist Hospital, Miami, FL, p. A139
Assistant Vice President, Finance (Controller), Fishermen's Hospital, Marathon, FL, p. A138
BOYLE, James W, M.D., Chief Medical Officer, UPMC Passavant, Pittsburgh, PA, p. A552
BOYLE, Kathy, R.N., Ph.D., Chief Nursing Officer, Denver Health, Denver, CO, p. A106
BOYLE, Lisa
M.D., President, Medstar Georgetown University Hospital, Washington, DC, p. A123
M.D., Vice President Medical Affairs and Medical Director, Medstar Georgetown University Hospital, Washington, DC, p. A123
BOYLE, Patrick R
Vice President Human Resources, Geneva General Hospital, Geneva, NY, p. A443
Vice President Human Resources, Soldiers And Sailors Memorial Hospital, Penn Yan, NY, p. A456
BOYLE, Thomas W., President and Chief Executive Officer, St. Lawrence Rehabilitation Hospital, Lawrenceville, NJ, p. A423
BOYLES, Clay
Director Human Resources, Peachford Behavioral Health System, Atlanta, GA, p. A157
Executive Director, Human Resources, Piedmont Newnan Hospital, Newnan, GA, p. A169
BOYLES, Lee, President, MT|WY Market and President, St. Vincent Regional Hospital, SCL Health Mt – St. Vincent Healthcare, Billings, MT, p. A390
BOYLES, Mary Gen, Chief Nursing Officer, Encompass Health Rehabilitation Hospital of Altoona, Altoona, PA, p. A534
BOYNTON, James P Jr, Chief Financial Officer, Carolina Center for Behavioral Health, Greer, SC, p. A567
BOYNTON, Stephanie
Administrator, Erlanger Bledsoe Hospital, Pikeville, TN, p. A592
Vice President and Chief Executive Officer, Erlanger Western Carolina Hospital, Murphy, NC, p. A473
BOYO, Tosan O., Chief Operating Officer, Zuckerberg San Francisco General Hospital And Trauma Center, San Francisco, CA, p. A91
BOYSEN, Doug, Chief Legal Counsel and Vice President Human Resources, Good Samaritan Regional Medical Center, Corvallis, OR, p. A526
BOYSEN, James, M.D., Executive Medical Director, Texas Neurorehab Center, Austin, TX, p. A601
BOZZUTO, Elizabeth, R.N., Chief Nursing Officer and Vice President, Saint Mary's Hospital, Waterbury, CT, p. A119
BRAAM, Richard, Vice President, Operations and Chief Financial Officer, Bristol Health, Bristol, CT, p. A115
BRAASCH, David A., FACHE, President, Alton Memorial Hospital, Alton, IL, p. A185
BRABANT, Christopher, President and Chief Executive Officer, HSHS St. Clare Memorial Hospital, Oconto Falls, WI, p. A719
BRABY, Heath, Director Fiscal Services, Shriners Hospitals for Children–Salt Lake City, Salt Lake City, UT, p. A669
BRACEY, Donny, Director Information Services, Marion General Hospital, Columbia, MS, p. A361
BRACK, Nancy R., Vice President Human Resources, Syracuse Area Health, Syracuse, NE, p. A406
BRACKEEN, Steven W., Chief Nursing Officer, Helena Regional Medical Center, Helena, AR, p. A47
BRACKEN, Thomas H, M.D., Vice President Medical Affairs, Mille Lacs Health System, Onamia, MN, p. A352
BRACKETT, Lori, Director Human Resources, Encompass Health Rehabilitation Hospital of Bakersfield, Bakersfield, CA, p. A57
BRACKLEY, Donna, R.N., MSN, Senior Vice President Patient Care Services, John Muir Health, Concord Medical Center, Concord, CA, p. A60
BRACKS, Adam, Chief Executive Officer, Southwestern Medical Center, Lawton, OK, p. A514
BRACY, Dale, Chief Financial Officer, College Hospital Costa Mesa, Costa Mesa, CA, p. A60
BRADBURY, Monica, Chief Executive Officer, Clarks Summit State Hospital, Clarks Summit, PA, p. A537
BRADDOCK, Mary B, Director Human Resources, Palo Pinto General Hospital, Mineral Wells, TX, p. A639
BRADFORD, Beth, Director Human Resources, Atrium Health Floyd Medical Center, Rome, GA, p. A170
BRADFORD, Jeremy, President and Chief Executive Officer, Calverthealth Medical Center, Prince Frederick, MD, p. A306
BRADFORD, John, Chief Financial Officer, Murray–Calloway County Hospital, Murray, KY, p. A272
BRADFORD, Scot, Chief Information Officer, Baylor Scott & White Medical Center – Trophy Club, Trophy Club, TX, p. A658
BRADFORD, Susan, Director Nursing, Kansas Heart Hospital, Wichita, KS, p. A261
BRADICK, Joe, Chief Financial Officer, Forks Community Hospital, Forks, WA, p. A690
BRADLEY, Betsy, Coordinator Performance Improvement, Central State Hospital, Milledgeville, GA, p. A168
BRADLEY, Connie
R.N., MSN, FACHE, Chief Nursing Officer, Health First Cap. Canaveral Hospital, Cocoa Beach, FL, p. A128
R.N., MSN, FACHE, Chief Nursing Officer, Health First Palm Bay Hospital, Palm Bay, FL, p. A145
R.N., MSN, FACHE, Senior Vice President and Chief Nursing Officer, Health First Viera Hospital, Melbourne, FL, p. A139
BRADLEY, Constance, FACHE, R.N., Vice President and Chief Operating Officer, Wellstar Kennestone Hospital, Marietta, GA, p. A167
BRADLEY, Eric, Director Computer Information Services, Summit Behavioral Healthcare, Cincinnati, OH, p. A489
BRADLEY, Sara, Chief Financial Officer, Oklahoma State University Medical Center, Tulsa, OK, p. A522
BRADLEY, Stacye, R.N., Chief Nursing Officer, Union County General Hospital, Clayton, NM, p. A434
BRADLEY, Warren, Chief Executive Officer, College Hospital Costa Mesa, Costa Mesa, CA, p. A60
BRADLY, Vivian, Chief Nursing Officer, Atrium Medical Center, Stafford, TX, p. A654
BRADSHAW, Benjamin, M.D., President Medical Staff, Texas Health Presbyterian Hospital Kaufman, Kaufman, TX, p. A631
BRADSHAW, David
Chief Information Officer, Memorial Hermann – Texas Medical Center, Houston, TX, p. A627
Chief Information Officer, Memorial Hermann Greater Heights Hospital, Houston, TX, p. A627
Chief Information, Planning and Marketing Officer, Memorial Hermann Memorial City Medical Center, Houston, TX, p. A627
BRADSHAW, Jeremy, Market President, Holy Cross Hospital – Salt Lake, Salt Lake City, UT, p. A668
BRADSHAW, Justin, Chief Executive Officer, Banner Desert Medical Center, Mesa, AZ, p. A33
BRADSHAW, Pamela, R.N., Vice President, Chief Operating Officer and Chief Nursing Officer, Shannon Medical Center, San Angelo, TX, p. A648
BRADSHAW, Rita, Director Human Resources, Chatuge Regional Hospital And Nursing Home, Hiawassee, GA, p. A165
BRADSTREET, Eric, M.D., Chief of Medical Staff, Olathe Medical Center, Olathe, KS, p. A256
BRADTMILLER DNP, RN, Theresa, MSN, R.N., Nursing Talent and Development Leader, Adams Memorial Hospital, Decatur, IN, p. A215
BRADY, Christopher, Interim Chief Executive Officer, Mercyone Elkader Medical Center, Elkader, IA, p. A236
BRADY, James, Area Information Officer, Kaiser Permanente Orange County Anaheim Medical Center, Anaheim, CA, p. A55
BRADY, Jeff
Chief Information Officer, Tug Valley Arh Regional Medical Center, South Williamson, KY, p. A274
Director Information Systems, Hazard Arh Regional Medical Center, Hazard, KY, p. A267
Director Information Systems, Mcdowell Arh Hospital, Mcdowell, KY, p. A271
Director Information Systems, Morgan County Arh Hospital, West Liberty, KY, p. A275
BRADY, John, Vice President Physician Services and Organizational Planning, Northwestern Medicine Marianjoy Rehabilitation Hospital, Wheaton, IL, p. A210
BRADY, Karen, R.N., MSN, Vice President, Chief Nursing Officer, Legacy Silverton Medical Center, Silverton, OR, p. A532
BRADY, Kit, Vice President of People Strategy, Gillette Children's Specialty Healthcare, Saint Paul, MN, p. A354
BRADY, Mike, Director Information Technology, Up Health System – Bell, Ishpeming, MI, p. A330
BRADY, Tim, Director Information Systems, Mt. Washington Pediatric Hospital, Baltimore, MD, p. A301
BRAGDON, Carol, Director Human Resources, Ascension Saint Thomas Rutherford, Murfreesboro, TN, p. A590
BRAGG, Craig, Chief Executive Officer, Trustpoint Rehabilitation Hospital of Lubbock, Lubbock, TX, p. A636
BRAGG, Deborah L., Senior Vice President, Finance, Decatur Memorial Hospital, Decatur, IL, p. A192
BRAGG, Krista A.
MSN, Chief Operating Officer, Allegheny Valley Hospital, Natrona Heights, PA, p. A547
MSN, Chief Operating Officer, Forbes Hospital, Monroeville, PA, p. A546
BRAGG, Lisa, Vice President Human Resources, Knox Community Hospital, Mount Vernon, OH, p. A501
BRAIN, David, Interim Vice President Finance, SCL Health Mt – St. James Healthcare, Butte, MT, p. A390
BRAITHWAITE, Robert, President and Chief Executive Officer, Hoag Memorial Hospital Presbyterian, Newport Beach, CA, p. A80
BRAKOVICH, Betsy, R.N., MSN, Vice President and Chief Nursing Officer, Wellstar Windy Hill Hospital, Marietta, GA, p. A168

A804 Index of Health Care Professionals

Index of Health Care Professionals / Brewer

Index of Health Care Professionals

BRALY, Cindy Ridge, MAAL, R.N., Chief Nursing Officer, Surgical Hospital of Oklahoma, Oklahoma City, OK, p. A519
BRANCH, Terrance, Chief Information Management, Fort Belvoir Community Hospital, Fort Belvoir, VA, p. A676
BRAND, Trevor, Chief Executive Officer, Sutter Delta Medical Center, Antioch, CA, p. A55
BRANDENBURG, Ronald, Vice President and Chief Financial Officer, Holy Cross Hospital, Fort Lauderdale, FL, p. A131
BRANDIS, Destin, Chief Information Officer, William Bee Ririe Hospital, Ely, NV, p. A408
BRANDON, Deborah, Director Total Quality Management, Eastern Louisiana Mental Health System, Jackson, LA, p. A283
BRANDON, Heather, Vice President of Finance, Grant, Ohiohealth Grant Medical Center, Columbus, OH, p. A492
BRANDON, Wendy H., Chief Executive Officer, UCF Lake Nona Medical Center, Orlando, FL, p. A144
BRANDOS, Orla, Vice President of Patient Care Services and Chief Nursing Officer, Newport Hospital, Newport, RI, p. A560
BRANDSTATER, Ronda, Vice President Patient Care, Kettering Health Dayton, Dayton, OH, p. A494
BRANDT, Debbie, Director Human Resources, Community Hospital, Munster, IN, p. A224
BRANDT, Lauren, Chief Clinical Officer, Central Texas Rehabilitation Hospital, Austin, TX, p. A599
BRANDT, Melanie Esq, Chief Nursing Officer, Harbor Regional Health, Aberdeen, WA, p. A687
BRANDT, Nolan, Chief Finance Officer, Madigan Army Medical Center, Tacoma, WA, p. A697
BRANDT, Rob, Chief Executive Officer, Mountainview Medical Center, White Sulphur Springs, MT, p. A396
BRANDT, Steve, M.D., Chief of Staff, Dale Medical Center, Ozark, AL, p. A23
BRANN, Terry, Chief Financial Officer, Mainegeneral Medical Center, Augusta, ME, p. A295
BRANNAN, Debbie
Chief Financial Officer, George Regional Hospital, Lucedale, MS, p. A365
Chief Financial Officer, Greene County Hospital, Leakesville, MS, p. A365
BRANNEN, Charles C, Senior Vice President and Chief Operating Officer, Southeast Alabama Medical Center, Dothan, AL, p. A18
BRANNIGAN, Timothy, Director Information Services, Intermountain Health Platte Valley Hospital, Brighton, CO, p. A104
BRANNON, Jeffrey M., Chief Executive Officer, Flowers Hospital, Dothan, AL, p. A18
BRANNON, Jim, Vice President Human Resources, Atlantic General Hospital, Berlin, MD, p. A302
BRANNON, Linda, Vice President Human Resources, Circles of Care, Melbourne, FL, p. A138
BRANNON, Rebecca, R.N., Chief Nursing Officer, Thomas Memorial Hospital, South Charleston, WV, p. A705
BRANSCUM, Suzette, Director of Nursing, Vantage Point of Northwest Arkansas, Fayetteville, AR, p. A46
BRANT, Johnny, Chief Financial Officer, Welch Community Hospital, Welch, WV, p. A705
BRANT, Mick, FACHE, Chief Executive Officer, Gothenburg Health, Gothenburg, NE, p. A400
BRANT–LUCICH, Kim, Director, Information Systems, Providence Little Company of Mary Medical Center San Pedro, Los Angeles, CA, p. A75
BRASEL, James, Chief Financial Officer, Ascension St. John Jane Phillips, Bartlesville, OK, p. A510
BRASH, David L., Chief Executive Officer, Logan Regional Medical Center, Logan, WV, p. A702
BRASS, Steven, Chief Medical Officer, Harris Health System, Bellaire, TX, p. A603
BRASSER, Brian, Chief Operating Officer, Corewell Health Butterworth Hospital, Grand Rapids, MI, p. A328
BRASSINGER, Cindy, Chief Operating Officer, Vibra Hospitals of Southeastern Michigan – Taylor Campus, Lincoln Park, MI, p. A332
BRATCHER, Tammy
Director Information Technology, SMC Regional Medical Center, Osceola, AR, p. A52
Director System Information Technology, Great River Medical Center, Blytheville, AR, p. A43
BRATKO, Eddie, President, Multicare Tacoma General Hospital, Tacoma, WA, p. A697
BRAUDT, Theresa Lynn, Chief Nursing Officer, Gundersen Boscobel Area Hospital And Clinics, Boscobel, WI, p. A708
BRAUDT, Theresa Lynn., Administrator, Gundersen Boscobel Area Hospital And Clinics, Boscobel, WI, p. A708
BRAUGHTON, David, Chief Operating Officer, Lifestream Behavioral Center, Leesburg, FL, p. A137
BRAUN, Peggy, R.N., Vice President Patient Care Services and Chief Nurse Executive, Sentara Virginia Beach General Hospital, Virginia Beach, VA, p. A685
BRAUN, Richard G, CPA, Jr, Executive Vice President and Chief Financial Officer, Niagara Falls Memorial Medical Center, Niagara Falls, NY, p. A454
BRAUN, Tim, Chief Operation Officer, Carroll County Memorial Hospital, Carrollton, MO, p. A373
BRAVERMAN, Kelly, FACHE, President and Chief Executive Officer, Witham Health Services, Lebanon, IN, p. A222
BRAVO, Gena, President/Chief Executive Officer, Woodland Memorial Hospital, Woodland, CA, p. A101
BRAVO, Stacey, Vice President Human Resources, Medical City Denton, Denton, TX, p. A614
BRAWLEY, Carrie, Administrator, Unity Psychiatric Care–Martin, Martin, TN, p. A587
BRAWNER, Patricia, Vice President–Nursing, Hannibal Regional Hospital, Hannibal, MO, p. A376
BRAXTON, Edwin R, Director Human Resources, Lompoc Valley Medical Center, Lompoc, CA, p. A70
BRAY, Jason, Chief Information Officer, Mcalester Regional Health Center, Mcalester, OK, p. A515
BRAY, John, M.D., Medical Director, Select Specialty Hospital–Pensacola, Pensacola, FL, p. A147
BRAY, Karen A, R.N., MSN, Vice President Patient Care Services, UPMC Washington, Washington, PA, p. A556
BRAY, Pam, Director of Nursing and Director Inpatient Services, UPMC Kane, Kane, PA, p. A543
BRAYFORD, Amy
Chief Human Resources Officer, Geisinger Medical Center, Danville, PA, p. A538
Chief Human Resources Officer, Geisinger Medical Center Muncy, Muncy, PA, p. A546
BRAYTON, Jackie, Vice President Human Resources, Portsmouth Regional Hospital, Portsmouth, NH, p. A417
BRAZ, Marcus, Chief Executive Officer, Encompass Health Rehabilitation Hospital of Sarasota, Sarasota, FL, p. A149
BRAZEL, Gary, M.D., Chief Medical Officer, Ascension St. Vincent Mercy, Elwood, IN, p. A215
BRAZIL, Wendy, Chief Operating Officer, Neosho Memorial Regional Medical Center, Chanute, KS, p. A247
BRCIC, Alen, Vice President, Mercyhealth Hospital And Physician Clinic–Crystal Lake, Crystal Lake, IL, p. A192
BREA, Christie, Manager Human Resources, KPC Promise Hospital of Phoenix, Mesa, AZ, p. A34
BREAKWELL, Michael, R.N., Nurse Executive, Twin Valley Behavioral Healthcare, Columbus, OH, p. A493
BREAL, Kenny, President, North Baldwin Infirmary, Bay Minette, AL, p. A16
BREAULT, Stephanie, Chief Financial Officer, Northwestern Medical Center, Saint Albans, VT, p. A672
BREAZEALE, Scott, Chief Nursing Officer, Neshoba General, Philadelphia, MS, p. A367
BREDESON, Christopher, Chief Operating Officer, Evergreenhealth, Kirkland, WA, p. A691
BREDTHAUER, Vicki, R.N., Director of Nursing, Valley County Health System, Ord, NE, p. A404
BREECE, Dan
D.O., Chief Medical Officer, Sistersville General Hospital, Sistersville, WV, p. A704
D.O., President, Sistersville General Hospital, Sistersville, WV, p. A704
D.O., Vice President Physician Services and Chief Medical Officer, Marietta Memorial Hospital, Marietta, OH, p. A499
BREEDEN, Patricia, M.D., Chief of Staff, Lexington Vamc, Lexington, KY, p. A268
BREEDEN, Susan M., Chief Executive Officer and Administrator, Baptist Memorial Hospital–Carroll County, Huntingdon, TN, p. A584
BREEDLOVE, Stacey, Chief Nursing Officer, Christus St. Michael Rehabilitation Hospital, Texarkana, TX, p. A656
BREEDVELD, Stacey, R.N., MSN, Associate Director for Patient Care, Veterans Affairs Ann Arbor Healthcare System, Ann Arbor, MI, p. A321
BREEN, Charles J, M.D., Medical Director, Sanford Hillsboro Medical Center, Hillsboro, ND, p. A482
BREEN, Sue, Chief Financial Officer, Western State Hospital, Tacoma, WA, p. A697
BREEN, Thomas, Vice President and Chief Financial Officer, South County Hospital, Wakefield, RI, p. A561
BREGIER, Heather, Administrator, Chief Executive Officer, Sanford Behavioral Health Center, Thief River Falls, MN, p. A356
BREHMER, Jennifer, Director Patient Care, New Ulm Medical Center, New Ulm, MN, p. A352
BREIDENBACH, Kim B, Medical Director, Gundersen Tri–County Hospital And Clinics, Whitehall, WI, p. A725
BREIDSTER, Cara, Chief Financial Officer, Indiana University Health Arnett Hospital, Lafayette, IN, p. A222
BREITBACH, Dave, Chief Financial Officer, Crossing Rivers Health, Prairie Du Chien, WI, p. A720
BREITENBACH, Ray, M.D., Chief of Staff, Pontiac General Hospital, Pontiac, MI, p. A335
BREITFELDER, Michelle, Chief Nursing Officer, Piedmont Mountainside Hospital, Jasper, GA, p. A165
BREITLING, Bryan
Chief Executive Officer, Avera Dells Area Hospital, Dell Rapids, SD, p. A573
Chief Executive Officer, Avera Flandreau Hospital, Flandreau, SD, p. A573
BREKKE, Erin, Director Human Resources, Burgess Health Center, Onawa, IA, p. A241
BRELAND, Kelly R, CPA, Director Support Services, Mississipp. State Hospital, Whitfield, MS, p. A370
BREMER, David, D.O., Chief of Staff, Mymichigan Medical Center Clare, Clare, MI, p. A324
BRENDEL, Michael J., R.N., President, Kettering Health Dayton, Dayton, OH, p. A494
BRENDEN, Stephanie D, Vice President Finance, Columbia Memorial Hospital, Astoria, OR, p. A525
BRENDLER, Stephen, Director Information Systems, Hilton Head Hospital, Hilton Head Island, SC, p. A568
BRENKLE, George, Chief Information Officer, Umass Memorial Medical Center, Worcester, MA, p. A320
BRENN, Andrea, R.N., Chief Nursing Officer, Texoma Medical Center, Denison, TX, p. A613
BRENNAN, Angela, M.D., Chief of Staff, Howard County Medical Center, Saint Paul, NE, p. A405
BRENNAN, Lina, Site Administrator, Soldiers And Sailors Memorial Hospital, Penn Yan, NY, p. A456
BRENNAN, Maria Lariccia, R.N., Chief Nursing Officer, Penn State Health St. Joseph, Reading, PA, p. A553
BRENNAN, Noreen Bridget, Chief Nursing Officer, NYC Health + Hospitals/Metropolitan, New York, NY, p. A451
BRENNAN, Patrick, Director Information System Technology, SSM Health Saint Louis University Hospital, Saint Louis, MO, p. A384
BRENNAN, Patrick J, M.D., Senior Vice President and Chief Medical Officer, Hospital of The University of Pennsylvania, Philadelphia, PA, p. A549
BRENNAN, Theresa, M.D., Chief Medical Officer, University of Iowa Hospitals & Clinics, Iowa City, IA, p. A238
BRENNER, Pattie, R.N., Chief Nursing Officer, Encompass Health Rehabilitation Hospital of Largo, Largo, FL, p. A137
BRENNER, Robert William., M.D., FACHE, President and Chief Executive Officer, President, Valley Health, Valley Hospital, Paramus, NJ, p. A426
BRENNER, William, Chief Financial Officer, Kindred Hospital–Indianapolis, Indianapolis, IN, p. A220
BRES, Thomas, Senior Vice President and Chief Administrative Officer, University of Michigan Health–Sparrow Lansing, Lansing, MI, p. A332
BRESCIA, Michael J, M.D., Executive Medical Director, Calvary Hospital, New York, NY, p. A447
BRESLIN, Susan, R.N., MSN, Vice President Patient Care Services and Chief Nursing Officer, Emory Decatur Hospital, Decatur, GA, p. A162
BRESNAHAN, Patti, Director Human Resources, Cleveland Clinic Mercy Hospital, Canton, OH, p. A487
BRETTNER, Eric, Chief Financial Officer, Marinhealth Medical Center, Greenbrae, CA, p. A66
BREUDER, Andrew, M.D., Chief of Staff, Manchester Veterans Affairs Medical Center, Manchester, NH, p. A416
BREUER, Rick, Chief Executive Officer and Administrator, Community Memorial Hospital, Cloquet, MN, p. A345
BREUM, Linda G, R.N., MSN, Chief Nursing Officer, Adventhealth New Smyrna Beach, New Smyrna Beach, FL, p. A142
BREVING, Joel, M.D., Medical Director, Central Louisiana State Hospital, Pineville, LA, p. A291
BREVING, Robert, M.D., Chief of Staff, National Park Medical Center, Hot Springs, AR, p. A48
BREWER, Becca, Chief Operations Officer, Falls Community Hospital And Clinic, Marlin, TX, p. A638
BREWER, Douglas, M.D., Chief Medical Officer, Erlanger Medical Center, Chattanooga, TN, p. A580
BREWER, Douglas L., Chief Executive Officer, Whitfield Regional Hospital, Demopolis, AL, p. A18
BREWER, Glenn, Chief Financial Officer, The Brook Hospital – Kmi, Louisville, KY, p. A270
BREWER, Jackie, Director, Human Resources, Lake Behavioral Hospital, Waukegan, IL, p. A210
BREWER, Justin
Chief Operating Officer, HCA Houston Healthcare West, Houston, TX, p. A626
Interim Chief Executive Officer, HCA Houston Healthcare Pearland, Pearland, TX, p. A643
BREWER, Kaye, Chief Human Resources Officer, Maury Regional Medical Center, Columbia, TN, p. A581
BREWER, Luke, Chief Executive Officer, Swisher Memorial Healthcare System, Tulia, TX, p. A658
BREWER, Peter G., Administrator, Shriners Hospitals for Children–Spokane, Spokane, WA, p. A696

 Index of Health Care Professionals A805

BREWER, Rebecca, FACHE, Chief Operating Officer, Adventhealth Lake Wales, Lake Wales, FL, p. A136
BREWER, Ruby RN, Senior Vice President, Chief Nursing and Quality Officer, East Jefferson General Hospital, Metairie, LA, p. A288
BREWER, Traci, R.N., Chief Clinical Officer, Kindred Hospital Dallas Central, Dallas, TX, p. A611
BREWER, MPH, Aimee, President and Chief Executive Officer, Sturdy Memorial Hospital, Attleboro, MA, p. A309
BREXLER, James L., FACHE, President and Chief Executive Officer, Doylestown Health, Doylestown, PA, p. A538
BREZA, Lisa
   R.N., Chief Administrative Officer, Robert Wood Johnson University Hospital At Hamilton, Hamilton, NJ, p. A422
   R.N., Vice President and Chief Nursing Officer, Robert Wood Johnson University Hospital At Hamilton, Hamilton, NJ, p. A422
BREZNY, Angie, Director Human Resources, Prague Regional Memorial Hospital, Prague, OK, p. A520
BRIA, Susan, Chief Nursing Officer, Shelby Baptist Medical Center, Alabaster, AL, p. A15
BRIAN, David, Chief Information Officer, Shriners Children's Ohio, Dayton, OH, p. A494
BRICE ROSHELL, Jade, M.D., Chief Medical Officer, Shelby Baptist Medical Center, Alabaster, AL, p. A15
BRICK-TURIN, Andrew, Chief Financial Officer, Desert Winds Hospital, Las Vegas, NV, p. A410
BRICKER, Jan, R.N., Chief Nursing Officer, Mount Carmel Rehabilitation Hospital, Westerville, OH, p. A507
BRICKHOUSE, Jerimiah
   Chief Information Officer, St. Charles Bend, Bend, OR, p. A525
   Chief Information Officer, St. Charles Redmond, Redmond, OR, p. A531
BRIDEN, David, Chief Information Officer, Exeter Hospital, Exeter, NH, p. A415
BRIDGELAND, Aaron
   Director Finance, Ascension Southeast Wisconsin Hospital – Franklin Campus, Franklin, WI, p. A711
   Director Finance, Ascension St. Francis Hospital, Milwaukee, WI, p. A716
   Director Finance, Midwest Orthopedic Specialty Hospital, Franklin, WI, p. A711
BRIDGES, Alan J, M.D., Chief of Staff, William S. Middleton Memorial Veterans' Hospital, Madison, WI, p. A715
BRIDGES, Angela, R.N., Chief Executive Officer, Mount Carmel Rehabilitation Hospital, Westerville, OH, p. A507
BRIDGES, Barbara, R.N., Chief Nursing Officer, Indiana Spine Hospital, Carmel, IN, p. A214
BRIDGES, Bill, Chief Executive Officer, Texas County Memorial Hospital, Houston, MO, p. A376
BRIDGES, Carol, M.D., Medical Director, Billings Clinic Broadwater, Townsend, MT, p. A396
BRIDGES, James M, Executive Vice President and Chief Operating Officer, Prisma Health Baptist Hospital, Columbia, SC, p. A565
BRIDGES, Jane Ann, Chief Financial Officer, Nacogdoches Memorial Hospital, Nacogdoches, TX, p. A640
BRIDGES, Kimberly, Chief Financial Officer, Byrd Regional Hospital, Leesville, LA, p. A287
BRIDGES, Mary, Director Human Resources, Ouachita County Medical Center, Camden, AR, p. A44
BRIDGES, Richard, M.D., Chief of Staff, Hood Memorial Hospital, Amite, LA, p. A276
BRIDGES, William, M.D., Chief Medical Officer, Texas Rehabilitation Hospital of Fort Worth, Fort Worth, TX, p. A620
BRIDGES-KEE, Lorinnsa, Vice President Human Resources, UNC Health Blue Ridge, Morganton, NC, p. A473
BRIDGEWATER, Melinda, Director, Information Services, Montana State Hospital, Warm Springs, MT, p. A396
BRIESEMEISTER, Eric, Chief Executive Officer, Unitypoint Health – Jones Regional Medical Center, Anamosa, IA, p. A230
BRIETE, Mark, M.D., Vice President Medical Affairs, Mercy Hospital Jefferson, Festus, MO, p. A375
BRIGGS, Deborah, Vice President Human Resources, Marketing, Volunteer Services and Community Relations, Ellenville Regional Hospital, Ellenville, NY, p. A442
BRIGGS, Gary, Vice President Human Resources, Tristar Southern Hills Medical Center, Nashville, TN, p. A591
BRIGGS, Michael, M.D., Chief Medical Officer, Essentia Health Fargo, Fargo, ND, p. A480
BRIGGS, Sharlet M., President, Kettering Health Main Campus, Kettering, OH, p. A497
BRIGGS, Stacey, Chief Financial Officer, Hodgeman County Health Center, Jetmore, KS, p. A251
BRIGGS, Thomas, Chief Financial Officer, Alliancehealth Madill, Madill, OK, p. A514
BRIGHAM, Randy, Chief Human Resource Officer, Estes Park Health, Estes Park, CO, p. A107
BRIGHT, Kim, M.D., Clinical Director, Springfield Hospital Center, Sykesville, MD, p. A307
BRIGHT, Shawn, Chief Executive Officer, Crittenden Community Hospital, Marion, KY, p. A271
BRIGNAC, Natalie, Chief Nursing Officer, Mercy Regional Medical Center, Ville Platte, LA, p. A294
BRILEY, Jay, FACHE, President, ECU Health Medical Center, Greenville, NC, p. A470
BRILL, Beth K., Senior Director Human Resources, WVU Medicine – Barnesville Hospital, Barnesville, OH, p. A485
BRILL, Karen, R.N., Chief Nursing Officer, Vice President Care, Gillette Children's Specialty Healthcare, Saint Paul, MN, p. A354
BRILLI, Richard, M.D., Chief Medical Officer, Nationwide Children's Hospital, Columbus, OH, p. A492
BRILLIANT, Steven, M.D., Chief of Staff, Ioannis A. Lougaris Veterans' Administration Medical Center, Reno, NV, p. A412
BRIM, Celena, Chief Financial Officer, Palestine Regional Medical Center–East, Palestine, TX, p. A642
BRINDLE, Charles B, M.D., Chief Medical Staff, Iowa Specialty Hospital–Belmond, Belmond, IA, p. A230
BRINER, Junior, Chief Operating Officer, Lawrence Memorial Hospital, Walnut Ridge, AR, p. A54
BRINKERHOFF, Douglas, M.D., Clinical Director, San Carlos Apache Healthcare Corporation, Peridot, AZ, p. A34
BRINKERHOFF, Kenley, Chief Information Officer, St. George Regional Hospital, Saint George, UT, p. A668
BRINKHAUS, Theresa, Chief Financial Officer, St. Helena Parish Hospital, Greensburg, LA, p. A282
BRINKLEY, Charles III, Chief Financial Officer, Maury Regional Medical Center, Columbia, TN, p. A581
BRINKMAN, Dan
   R.N., Chief Executive Officer, Hilo Medical Center, Hilo, HI, p. A175
   R.N., Chief Operating Officer, Hilo Medical Center, Hilo, HI, p. A175
BRINKMAN, Janet, Director Human Resources, Common Spirit St. Elizabeth Hospital, Fort Morgan, CO, p. A108
BRINSON, Pam, Nurse Executive, South Mississipp. State Hospital, Purvis, MS, p. A368
BRINTON, Kody, Chief Executive Officer, Daniels Memorial Healthcare Center, Scobey, MT, p. A395
BRIONES, Melba, M.D., Medical Director, Evansville State Hospital, Evansville, IN, p. A216
BRISBOE, Mark
   President, Sparrow Clinton Hospital, Saint Johns, MI, p. A337
   President, University of Michigan Health–Sparrow Carson, Carson City, MI, p. A323
BRISCOE, Betsy, Chief Executive Officer, Pecos County Memorial Hospital, Fort Stockton, TX, p. A619
BRISCOE, Charles G, FACHE, Chief Operating Officer, Houston Medical Center, Warner Robins, GA, p. A173
BRISCOE, Charles G., FACHE, President and Chief Executive Officer, Houston Medical Center, Warner Robins, GA, p. A173
BRISENDINE, Chad
   Chief Information Officer, St. Luke's Quakertown Campus, Quakertown, PA, p. A553
   Chief Information Officer, St. Luke's University Hospital – Bethlehem Campus, Bethlehem, PA, p. A535
   Vice President and Chief Information Officer, St. Luke's Hospital–Miners Campus, Coaldale, PA, p. A537
BRISTER, Marilyn, M.D., Chief of Staff, Texas Health Harris Methodist Hospital Stephenville, Stephenville, TX, p. A654
BRITNER, Joe, Chief Operating Officer, HCA Florida Kendall Hospital, Miami, FL, p. A139
BRITO, Manuela, Chief Financial Officer Post Acute Care, NYC Health + Hospitals/Henry J Carter Specialty Hospital And Medical Center, New York, NY, p. A451
BRITON, Emily M., President, Medstar Montgomery Medical Center, Olney, MD, p. A306
BRITT, Kevin, Chief Operating Officer, Reynolds Memorial Hospital, Glen Dale, WV, p. A700
BRITT, Key, Associate Director, Greenwood Leflore Hospital, Greenwood, MS, p. A362
BRITT, Linda, Director Information Systems, Baptist Memorial Hospital–North Mississippi, Oxford, MS, p. A367
BRITT, Suzanne, Director Human Resources, Samaritan Hospital, Macon, MO, p. A380
BRITT, Tommy, Vice President of Human Resources, Wellstar West Georgia Medical Center, Lagrange, GA, p. A166
BRITTON, Downapha, Chief Nursing Officer, Coast Plaza Hospital, Norwalk, CA, p. A80
BRITTON, Natalie, Manager Employee Relations, Legacy Silverton Medical Center, Silverton, OR, p. A532
BRITTON, William N, Associate Administrator Finance, Nemours Children's Hospital, Delaware, Wilmington, DE, p. A122
BRIX, Hsiu-chin, R.N., Director of Nursing, St. Lawrence Rehabilitation Hospital, Lawrenceville, NJ, p. A423
BRKA, Adnan, Chief Nursing Officer, Holston Valley Medical Center, Kingsport, TN, p. A585
BROADWATER, Veleaka, Director Human Resource, Encompass Health Rehabilitation Hospital, Shreveport, LA, p. A292
BROADWAY, Chris, Manager Information Technology, Mayers Memorial Hospital District, Fall River Mills, CA, p. A63
BROBST, Mary, R.N., MSN, Senior Vice President Patient Care Services and Chief Nursing Officer, Mercy Medical Center – Cedar Rapids, Cedar Rapids, IA, p. A231
BROCATO, Ray, Chief Financial Officer, Rolling Hills Hospital, Franklin, TN, p. A583
BROCCARD, Alain, M.D., Chief Medical Officer, Ascension St. Vincent Seton Specialty Hospital, Indianapolis, IN, p. A219
BROCK, B. J., Nursing Director, Higgins General Hospital, Bremen, GA, p. A159
BROCK, Jacqueline Dawn, Chief Nursing Officer, Harris Health System, Bellaire, TX, p. A603
BROCK, Jamie, Vice President Human Resources, Chan Soon–Shiong Medical Center At Windber, Windber, PA, p. A558
BROCK, Lisa M, Chief Human Resource Officer, Overlake Medical Center And Clinics, Bellevue, WA, p. A687
BROCK, Melinda, Director Human Resources, Integris Health Woodward Hospital, Woodward, OK, p. A524
BROCK, Nancy, Chief Financial Officer, Houston Methodist Continuing Care Hospital, Katy, TX, p. A631
BROCK, Robert
   Chief Financial Officer and Vice President, Adventhealth Rollins Brook, Lampasas, TX, p. A633
   Vice President Finance, Arh Our Lady of The Way, Martin, KY, p. A271
BROCK, Shea C., Chief Financial Officer, Navarro Regional Hospital, Corsicana, TX, p. A609
BROCK, Steve, Chief Financial Officer, Newman Memorial Hospital, Shattuck, OK, p. A520
BROCK, Tammy, MSN, R.N., Chief Nursing Officer, Rockcastle Regional Hospital And Respiratory Care Center, Mount Vernon, KY, p. A272
BROCK, Theresa, Vice President Nursing, Good Shepherd Health Care System, Hermiston, OR, p. A527
BROCK, Timothy, M.D., Chief Medical Officer, Willamette Valley Medical Center, Mcminnville, OR, p. A529
BROCK, William, Chief Information Officer, Atlanta Veterans Affairs Medical Center, Decatur, GA, p. A162
BROCKHAUS, Jennifer, Chief Information Officer, Sidney Regional Medical Center, Sidney, NE, p. A406
BROCKHOUSE, Dena M, Director Human Resources, University of Iowa Health Care Medical Center Downtown, Iowa City, IA, p. A238
BROCKMAN, Sheila, Chief Executive Officer, Trace Regional Hospital, Houston, MS, p. A363
BROCKMAN, Vicki, R.N., Chief Nursing Officer, Texas Health Harris Methodist Hospital Cleburne, Cleburne, TX, p. A607
BROCKMAN–WEBER, Steven
   President Seton Southwest & Northwest, Ascension Seton Northwest, Austin, TX, p. A599
   President Seton Southwest & Northwest, Ascension Seton Southwest, Austin, TX, p. A599
   System Chief Nursing Officer, Ascension Seton Bastrop. Bastrop. TX, p. A601
   System Chief Nursing Officer, Ascension Seton Edgar B. Davis Hospital, Luling, TX, p. A637
   System Chief Nursing Officer, Ascension Seton Highland Lakes, Burnet, TX, p. A606
BROCKMEYER, Heather, Human Resource Administrative Officer, Nevada Regional Medical Center, Nevada, MO, p. A381
BROCKMEYER, JoEllyn, Director Human Resources, Indiana University Health White Memorial Hospital, Monticello, IN, p. A224
BROCKUS, Harry, Chief Executive Officer, Deaconess Illinois Union County, Anna, IL, p. A185
BRODBECK, Kathleen MSN, RN–B, Chief Nursing Officer, St. James Hospital, Hornell, NY, p. A444
BRODBECK, Lisa, Chief Financial Officer, Medical City Lewisville, Lewisville, TX, p. A634
BRODERICK, Amy, Senior Division President, Pam Health Rehabilitation Hospital of Miamisburg, Miamisburg, OH, p. A500
BRODERSEN, Benjamin, President and Chief Operating Officer, Novant Health Ballantyne Medical Center, Charlotte, NC, p. A465
BRODHEAD, Roderick, Chief Medical Officer, Aspirus Eagle River Hospital, Eagle River, WI, p. A710
BRODHEAD, Ross
   Manager Human Resources, Ascension St. Vincent Mercy, Elwood, IN, p. A215
   Senior Director, Human Resource, Ascension St. Vincent Anderson, Anderson, IN, p. A212

Index of Health Care Professionals / Brown

Index of Health Care Professionals

Senior Director, Human Resources, Ascension St. Vincent Carmel Hospital, Carmel, IN, p. A213
BRODIAN, Craig R, Vice President Human Resources, Johns Hopkins Bayview Medical Center, Baltimore, MD, p. A300
BRODINE, Deborah, President, UPMC Presbyterian, Pittsburgh, PA, p. A552
BRODY, Anne Marie, Director Information Systems Customer Service, Providence Saint Josep. Medical Center, Burbank, CA, p. A58
BROEKHUIS, Arlyn
Chief Information Officer, Sanford Medical Center Fargo, Fargo, ND, p. A481
Vice President and Chief Information Officer, Sanford Usd Medical Center, Sioux Falls, SD, p. A577
BROERMANN, Robert
Senior Vice President and Chief Financial Officer, Sentara Leigh Hospital, Norfolk, VA, p. A680
Senior Vice President and Chief Financial Officer, Sentara Norfolk General Hospital, Norfolk, VA, p. A680
Senior Vice President and Chief Financial Officer, Sentara Princess Anne Hospital, Virginia Beach, VA, p. A684
BROFMAN, John, M.D., Chief Medical Officer, RML Specialty Hospital, Hinsdale, IL, p. A198
BROGAN, Michael, Controller, Encompass Health Rehabilitation Institute of Libertyville, Libertyville, IL, p. A200
BROHAWN, Bill, Chief of Staff, Trace Regional Hospital, Houston, MS, p. A363
BROKAW, Sara, President and Chief Nursing Officer, Bellevue Hospital, The, Bellevue, OH, p. A486
BROLLINI, Andrea, MSN, R.N., Chief Nursing Officer, Santa Clara Valley Medical Center, San Jose, CA, p. A92
BROMLEY, Trudy, Vice President Human Resources, HCA Florida Jfk Hospital, Atlantis, FL, p. A125
BRONHARD, John Edward, CPA, II, Corporate Vice President, Chief Financial Officer and Treasurer, Umass Memorial Healthalliance–Clinton Hospital, Leominster, MA, p. A315
BRONSON, Becki, Chief Information Officer, Cedar City Hospital, Cedar City, UT, p. A664
BROOCKS, Kelli C, Director Human Resources, Public Relations and Physician Recruitment, Beauregard Health System, De Ridder, LA, p. A281
BROOKER, Chris E., Chief Financial Officer, Willamette Valley Medical Center, Mcminnville, OR, p. A529
BROOKER, Doug A., Chief Financial Officer, Whitfield Regional Hospital, Demopolis, AL, p. A18
BROOKER, Paula, Director Information Services, Rivers Health, Point Pleasant, WV, p. A704
BROOKER, Susan E, R.N., Chief Clinical Officer, Vibra Specialty Hospital of Portland, Portland, OR, p. A531
BROOKES, Jeffrey
M.D., Chief Medical Officer, Parkview Lagrange Hospital, Lagrange, IN, p. A222
M.D., Medical Director, Parkview Whitley Hospital, Columbia City, IN, p. A214
BROOKMAN, Mark
Chief Information Officer, Medical Center At Scottsville, Scottsville, KY, p. A274
Chief Information Officer, The Medical Center At Albany, Albany, KY, p. A263
Chief Information Officer, The Medical Center At Bowling Green, Bowling Green, KY, p. A264
Vice President and Chief Information Officer, Medical Center At Franklin, Franklin, KY, p. A266
Vice President, Chief Information Officer, The Medical Center At Caverna, Horse Cave, KY, p. A267
BROOKS, Albert, M.D., Chief Medical Staff Services, Washington Hospital Healthcare System, Fremont, CA, p. A64
BROOKS, Anthony, Chief Information Officer, Miami Veterans Affairs Healthcare System, Miami, FL, p. A140
BROOKS, April, Chief Nursing Officer, Encompass Health Rehabilitation Hospital of Columbia, Columbia, SC, p. A564
BROOKS, Brian, Information Manager, Dewitt Hospital & Nursing Home, Dewitt, AR, p. A45
BROOKS, Cheri, R.N., Chief Nursing Officer, King's Daughters Medical Center, Brookhaven, MS, p. A360
BROOKS, Clint, Chief Operating Officer, Fairbanks Memorial Hospital, Fairbanks, AK, p. A28
BROOKS, Clyde, M.D., Chief Medical Officer, Carteret Health Care, Morehead City, NC, p. A473
BROOKS, David, M.D., Chief Medical Officer, Valley View Hospital, Glenwood Springs, CO, p. A108
BROOKS, Gary, Chief Operating Officer, Pam Specialty Hospital of Reno, Sparks, NV, p. A413
BROOKS, Gloria, Chief Operating Officer, Pali Momi Medical Center, Aiea, HI, p. A175
BROOKS, J Michael, M.D., Chief Medical Officer, Calverthealth Medical Center, Prince Frederick, MD, p. A306
BROOKS, Jacob, President, SSM Health St. Josep. – St. Charles, Saint Charles, MO, p. A383
BROOKS, Jeffrey, M.D., Chief Medical Officer, Parkview Huntington Hospital, Huntington, IN, p. A218
BROOKS, Lisa, Administrator, Comanche County Hospital, Coldwater, KS, p. A247
BROOKS, Lori, Director Human Resources, Red Bud Regional Hospital, Red Bud, IL, p. A207
BROOKS, Nick, Director of Information Systems, HCA Florida Citrus Hospital, Inverness, FL, p. A134
BROOKS, Robert M., FACHE, President and Chief Operating Officer, St. Christopher's Hospital for Children, Philadelphia, PA, p. A550
BROOKS, Scott, Chief Executive Officer, Jacobson Memorial Hospital Care Center, Elgin, ND, p. A480
BROOKS, Steven Michael, Vice President Human Resources, Ohiohealth Southeastern Medical Center, Cambridge, OH, p. A487
BROOKS, Troy, Chief Financial Officer, Conway Regional Health System, Conway, AR, p. A44
BROOKSHIRE, Tim
FACHE, Chief Operations Executive, Prisma Health Greenville Memorial Hospital, Greenville, SC, p. A567
FACHE, Chief Operations Executive, Prisma Health North Greenville Hospital, Travelers Rest, SC, p. A571
BROOKSHIRE–HEAVIN, Keri S., Senior Vice President, Chief Operating Officer and Chief Nursing Officer, Phelp. Health, Rolla, MO, p. A382
BROOM, Matthew, Vice President of Medical Affairs and Chief Medical Officer, SSM Health Saint Louis University Hospital, Saint Louis, MO, p. A384
BROOME, Josep. Scott.
M.P.H., FACHE, Chief Executive Officer, Musc Health Chester Medical Center, Chester, SC, p. A564
M.P.H., FACHE, Chief Executive Officer, Musc Health Lancaster Medical Center, Lancaster, SC, p. A568
BROPHY, Beth, Interim VP for Human Resources, Hurley Medical Center, Flint, MI, p. A326
BROPHY, Christopher, Chief Executive Officer, Crossing Rivers Health, Prairie Du Chien, WI, p. A720
BROSE, Tamara, Director Human Resources, Thayer County Health Services, Hebron, NE, p. A401
BROSIOUS, Megan M.
Chief Administrative Officer, Central Region, Geisinger Medical Center, Danville, PA, p. A538
Chief Administrative Officer, Central Region, Geisinger–Bloomsburg Hospital, Bloomsburg, PA, p. A535
BROSIUS, William, Chief Financial Officer, University of Maryland Capital Region Medical Center, Largo, MD, p. A305
BROSNAHAN, Jan, Chief Financial Officer, Winona Health, Winona, MN, p. A357
BROSTROM, Kyle J., Chief Executive Officer, Holy Cross Hospital – Davis, Layton, UT, p. A665
BROTEN, Kurt, Chief Financial Officer, Vista Del Mar Hospital, Ventura, CA, p. A100
BROTHMAN, Daniel J.
Chief Executive Officer, Garden Grove Hospital And Medical Center, Garden Grove, CA, p. A65
Chief Executive Officer, Huntington Beach Hospital, Huntington Beach, CA, p. A67
BROTHMAN, Joe, Assistant Vice President, Information Systems, Medstar Washington Hospital Center, Washington, DC, p. A124
BROUDER, Pamela, Associate Chief Nursing Officer, Missouri Baptist Medical Center, Saint Louis, MO, p. A385
BROUGHMAN, Robin, R.N., Ph.D., Chief Nursing Officer, Lewisgale Hospital Alleghany, Low Moor, VA, p. A678
BROUGHMAN, Wade
Chief Financial Officer, Southcoast Hospitals Group. Fall River, MA, p. A313
Executive Vice President and Chief Financial Officer, Riverside Regional Medical Center, Newport News, VA, p. A680
BROUILLETTE, Blaine, Director Information Technology, Avoyelles Hospital, Marksville, LA, p. A288
BROUK, Jonathan, President, Our Lady of The Lake Regional Medical Center, Baton Rouge, LA, p. A278
BROUSSARD, Heidi, Chief Nursing Officer, Abbeville General Hospital, Abbeville, LA, p. A276
BROUSSARD, Jessica, Chief Financial Officer, Mercy Regional Medical Center, Ville Platte, LA, p. A294
BROUWER, Heath, Administrator, Douglas County Memorial Hospital, Armour, SD, p. A572
BROVOLD, Nathan, Chief Nursing Officer, Lifecare Medical Center, Roseau, MN, p. A354
BROW, Benjamin, Vice President of Finance, Mclaren Lapeer Region, Lapeer, MI, p. A332
BROWN, Alisa, Administrative Assistant, Dewitt Hospital & Nursing Home, Dewitt, AR, p. A45
BROWN, Angel, Director Human Resources, Morton Plant Hospital, Clearwater, FL, p. A128
BROWN, B Blaine, Vice President and General Counsel, Prattville Baptist Hospital, Prattville, AL, p. A24
BROWN, Barbra, MS, R.N., Interim Chief Nursing Officer and Vice President of Nursing, Alice Peck Day Memorial Hospital, Lebanon, NH, p. A415
BROWN, Bartley, D.O., Chief of Staff, St. Joseph's Hospital, Buckhannon, WV, p. A699
BROWN, Benjamin, Chief Executive Officer, Dominion Hospital, Falls Church, VA, p. A675
BROWN, Bryan, Executive Director, Mercy Hospital Fort Smith, Fort Smith, AR, p. A47
BROWN, Chad J.
Dr.PH, FACHE, M.P.H., President, Atrium Health Wake Forest Baptist Wilkes Medical Center, North Wilkesboro, NC, p. A474
Dr.PH, FACHE, M.P.H., President, South and West Areas, Atrium Health Wake Forest Baptist Lexington Medical Center, Lexington, NC, p. A472
BROWN, Charna, Chief Nursing Officer, Cullman Regional Medical Center, Cullman, AL, p. A18
BROWN, Cheryl, Chief Executive Officer, Henderson Health Care Services, Henderson, NE, p. A401
BROWN, Chistiane, Assistant Vice President, Medstar Montgomery Medical Center, Olney, MD, p. A306
BROWN, Chris, Chief Executive Officer, Haywood Regional Medical Center, Clyde, NC, p. A466
BROWN, Christi, Director Human Resources, Our Lady of The Angels Hospital, Bogalusa, LA, p. A279
BROWN, Chrystal, Director Human Resources, Loretto Hospital, Chicago, IL, p. A190
BROWN, Chuck, Administrator, Bethesda North Hospital, Cincinnati, OH, p. A488
BROWN, Crystal, M.D., Medical Director, Atrium Health Navicent Peach, Macon, GA, p. A167
BROWN, Cullen, Chief Executive Officer, HCA Florida Poinciana Hospital, Kissimmee, FL, p. A136
BROWN, Cynthia, Director of Nursing, Hill Hospital of Sumter County, York, AL, p. A26
BROWN, Damon, President, Mountain Vista Medical Center, Mesa, AZ, p. A34
BROWN, Daniel, M.D., Ph.D., Medical Director, Hospital Operations, Mayo Clinic Hospital – Rochester, Rochester, MN, p. A353
BROWN, Darin, Chief Financial Officer, Henry Community Health, New Castle, IN, p. A225
BROWN, David A, Human Resources Director, Crestwood Medical Center, Huntsville, AL, p. A20
BROWN, Deana, Director Administrative Services, Franciscan Health Rensselear, Rensselaer, IN, p. A226
BROWN, DeAnn, Administrator, Garfield Memorial Hospital, Panguitch, UT, p. A667
BROWN, Deborah, Chief Nursing Officer, The Medical Center At Russellville, Russellville, KY, p. A274
BROWN, Debra L, Area Financial Officer, Kaiser Permanente Manteca Medical Center, Manteca, CA, p. A76
BROWN, Denise, Vice President Human Resources, Ascension Saint Josep. – Chicago, Chicago, IL, p. A188
BROWN, Doris, Chief Executive Officer, Osborne County Memorial Hospital, Osborne, KS, p. A256
BROWN, Douglas, Chief Financial Officer, Northridge Hospital Medical Center, Los Angeles, CA, p. A74
BROWN, Ed
Chief Financial Officer, Cibola General Hospital, Grants, NM, p. A434
Chief Information Officer, Atrium Health Navicent The Medical Center, Macon, GA, p. A167
BROWN, Eric, M.D., Physician Executive, Prisma Health Richland Hospital, Columbia, SC, p. A565
BROWN, Geoffrey
Chief Information Officer, Piedmont Fayette Hospital, Fayetteville, GA, p. A164
Chief Information Officer, Piedmont Mountainside Hospital, Jasper, GA, p. A165
Vice President Information Systems, Inova Fairfax Medical Campus, Falls Church, VA, p. A676
BROWN, Greg, President, Ascension St. Vincent's Blount, Oneonta, AL, p. A23
BROWN, Howard, Chief Financial Officer, Orlando Health – Health Central Hospital, Ocoee, FL, p. A143
BROWN, Hugh, Chief Executive Officer, St. David's Medical Center, Austin, TX, p. A600
BROWN, James, Chief Operating Officer, Townsen Memorial Hospital, Humble, TX, p. A629
BROWN, James H, Chief Financial Officer, Centerpoint Medical Center, Independence, MO, p. A376
BROWN, Janice, Chief Financial Officer, Coosa Valley Medical Center, Sylacauga, AL, p. A24
BROWN, Jason
M.D., Chief Medical Officer, Banner Goldfield Medical Center, Apache Junction, AZ, p. A30

Index of Health Care Professionals / Brown

Director, Kettering Health Miamisburg, Miamisburg, OH, p. A500
Director Information Systems, Sanford Sheldon Medical Center, Sheldon, IA, p. A243

BROWN, Jay
Senior Vice President, Chief Information Officer, West Chester Hospital, West Chester, OH, p. A506
Vice President and Chief Information Officer, University of Cincinnati Medical Center, Cincinnati, OH, p. A490

BROWN, Jeffrey P, M.D., Chief Medical Officer, Indiana University Health Arnett Hospital, Lafayette, IN, p. A222
BROWN, Jennifer L, Chief Financial Officer, Chadron Community Hospital And Health Services, Chadron, NE, p. A398
BROWN, Jill, Chief Financial Officer, Miller County Hospital, Colquitt, GA, p. A161

BROWN, Jim
Chief Executive Officer, HCA Houston Healthcare Kingwood, Kingwood, TX, p. A633
Director Information Technology, Lynn County Hospital District, Tahoka, TX, p. A655

BROWN, John, M.D., Chief Medical Officer, Gritman Medical Center, Moscow, ID, p. A182
BROWN, Jon, Chief Information Officer, Mission Hospital, Asheville, NC, p. A463
BROWN, Joni, Director Human Resources, Rehabilitation Hospital of Indiana, Indianapolis, IN, p. A220

BROWN, Josep. C.
Vice President Operations, Baylor Scott & White Medical Center – Plano, Plano, TX, p. A644
Vice President Operations, Baylor Scott & White Medical Center – Round Rock, Round Rock, TX, p. A647

BROWN, Judy, Chief Nursing Officer, Mitchell County Regional Health Center, Osage, IA, p. A241
BROWN, Karen C, Vice President Chief Operating Officer, OSF Saint Anthony Medical Center, Rockford, IL, p. A207
BROWN, Katie, Coordinator Human Resources, Pocahontas Memorial Hospital, Buckeye, WV, p. A699

BROWN, Kendra
MSN, R.N., Chief Nursing Officer, Kearney County Health Services, Minden, NE, p. A402
Job Requisition Coordinator, Rusk State Hospital, Rusk, TX, p. A648

BROWN, Kenneth A, Vice President and Chief Human Resource Officer, Pratt Regional Medical Center, Pratt, KS, p. A258
BROWN, Kris, Associate Director, Bay Pines Veterans Affairs Healthcare System, Bay Pines, FL, p. A125
BROWN, LaTonya, Interim Chief Operating Officer and Chief Financial Officer, UNC Health Rockingham, Eden, NC, p. A467
BROWN, Lewis, Director Information Technology, Bsa Hospital, Llc, Amarillo, TX, p. A596
BROWN, Lisa, Director of Nursing, Pearl River County Hospital, Poplarville, MS, p. A368
BROWN, Lorenzo, Chief Executive Officer West Volusia Market, Adventhealth Fish Memorial, Orange City, FL, p. A143
BROWN, Lori, Chief Nursing Officer, Baptist Memorial Hospital–Union City, Union City, TN, p. A594
BROWN, Lori J., R.N., FACHE, Chief Nursing Officer, Hennepin Healthcare, Minneapolis, MN, p. A350
BROWN, Luke, Chief Financial Officer, Nationwide Children's Hospital – Toledo, Toledo, OH, p. A504
BROWN, Marcy, Senior Vice President and Chief Operating Officer, Hoag Memorial Hospital Presbyterian, Newport Beach, CA, p. A80
BROWN, Margaret, Director Medical Records, Vantage Point of Northwest Arkansas, Fayetteville, AR, p. A46
BROWN, Mark R, Chief Nursing Officer, AHMC Seton Medical Center, Daly City, CA, p. A61
BROWN, Markham, M.D., Chief Medical Staff, Mike O'Callaghan Federal Hospital, Nellis Afb, NV, p. A411
BROWN, Marlon, Human Resources, Essex County Hospital Center, Cedar Grove, NJ, p. A419
BROWN, Martin, Vice President Information Services and Chief Information Officer, Nathan Littauer Hospital And Nursing Home, Gloversville, NY, p. A443
BROWN, Mary Beth, Director Human Resources, Bertrand Chaffee Hospital, Springville, NY, p. A459
BROWN, Michael, D.O., Chief of Staff, TMC Bonham Hospital, Bonham, TX, p. A604
BROWN, Mike, Chief Financial Officer, Carlinville Area Hospital, Carlinville, IL, p. A187
BROWN, Molly B., Chief Operating Officer, University of Mississippi. Medical Center Grenada, Grenada, MS, p. A362
BROWN, Natalie, Chief Human Resources Management Services, Lt. Col. Luke Weathers, Jr. Va Medical Center, Memphis, TN, p. A588
BROWN, Pam, Human Resources Manager, Unity Psychiatric Care–Columbia, Columbia, TN, p. A581

BROWN, Pat, R.N., Chief Nursing Officer, San Gorgonio Memorial Hospital, Banning, CA, p. A57
BROWN, Patsy, Site Coordinator Human Resources, Erlanger Bledsoe Hospital, Pikeville, TN, p. A592
BROWN, Penny D., Human Resource Representative, Broaddus Hospital, Philippi, WV, p. A704
BROWN, Philip. D.O., Vice President Medical Affairs, The University of Vermont Health Network Central Vermont Medical Center, Berlin, VT, p. A671

BROWN, Phyllis
Chief Executive Officer, Marshall Medical Center, Lewisburg, TN, p. A587
Chief Executive Officer, Wayne Medical Center, Waynesboro, TN, p. A594

BROWN, Randal, M.D., Chief of Medical Staff, Guadalup. County Hospital, Santa Rosa, NM, p. A437
BROWN, Regenia, Vice President Human Resources, Magnolia Regional Health Center, Corinth, MS, p. A361
BROWN, Rickie F, Chief Financial Officer, Monroe County Medical Center, Tompkinsville, KY, p. A274
BROWN, Rita, Director Human Resources, Richardson Medical Center, Rayville, LA, p. A291
BROWN, Robert, Chief Operating Officer, Parkview Community Hospital Medical Center, Riverside, CA, p. A86
BROWN, Roberta, Chief Nursing Officer, Community Hospital of Staunton, Staunton, IL, p. A209
BROWN, Royce, Chief Executive Officer, Adventhealth Lake Wales, Lake Wales, FL, p. A136
BROWN, Ryan, Vice President, Operations, Johns Hopkins Howard County Medical Center, Columbia, MD, p. A303
BROWN, Scott, Chief Financial Officer, Valir Rehabilitation Hospital, Oklahoma City, OK, p. A519
BROWN, Shannon, Hospital Administrator, Oceans Behavioral Hospital Katy, Katy, TX, p. A631

BROWN, Sharon
Deputy Commander Nursing, Winn Army Community Hospital, Hinesville, GA, p. A165
Vice President Human Resources, Sierra View Medical Center, Porterville, CA, p. A84
Vice President Patient Care and Chief Nursing Officer, St. Mary Medical Center, Langhorne, PA, p. A543

BROWN, Sherry, Director Human Resources, Cleveland Area Hospital, Cleveland, OK, p. A511

BROWN, Stacey L.
Chief Executive Officer, Odessa Regional Medical Center, Odessa, TX, p. A642
President, Scenic Mountain Medical Center, Big Spring, TX, p. A603

BROWN, Stephen A, Chief Financial Officer, Grace Cottage Hospital, Townshend, VT, p. A672

BROWN, Steve
M.D., Chief Quality Officer, Saint Alphonsus Regional Medical Center, Boise, ID, p. A179
Chief Information Officer, Wellstar Sylvan Grove Hospital, Jackson, GA, p. A165
Director Information Systems, Wellstar Spalding Regional Hospital, Griffin, GA, p. A164
Health Services Director, U. S. Penitentiary Infirmary, Lewisburg, PA, p. A544

BROWN, Steven
M.D., Medical Director, Wyoming Behavioral Institute, Casper, WY, p. A726
Vice President Finance, Baptist Anderson Regional Medical Center – South, Meridian, MS, p. A366
Vice President Finance, Baptist Anderson Regional Medical Center, Meridian, MS, p. A366
Vice President Fiscal Affairs, Mary Rutan Hospital, Bellefontaine, OH, p. A486

BROWN, Susan
Chief Human Resources Officer, Wellstar North Fulton Hospital, Roswell, GA, p. A170
Chief Nursing Officer, El Paso Behavioral Health System, El Paso, TX, p. A616

BROWN, Tammi, Regional Hospital Administrator, East Central Regional Hospital, Augusta, GA, p. A158
BROWN, Terry L, Chief Financial Officer, HCA Florida Raulerson Hospital, Okeechobee, FL, p. A143

BROWN, Theodore
Chief Operating Officer, Community Howard Regional Health, Kokomo, IN, p. A221
Vice President Financial Services, Community Howard Regional Health, Kokomo, IN, p. A221

BROWN, Thomas W., Chief Executive Officer, Brookhaven Hospital, Tulsa, OK, p. A522
BROWN, Todd A, M.D., Medical Director, Logan Regional Hospital, Logan, UT, p. A665
BROWN, Traci, Director Human Resources, Medical Arts Hospital, Lamesa, TX, p. A633
BROWN, Wendy W, M.D., M.P.H., Chief of Staff, Jesse Brown Va Medical Center, Chicago, IL, p. A189

BROWN, William A., Chief Medical Officer, Lake Charles Memorial Hospital, Lake Charles, LA, p. A286
BROWN–ROBERTS, Bonita, Director Information Systems, Advocate Trinity Hospital, Chicago, IL, p. A188
BROWNE, Colleen, Vice President and Chief People Officer, LMH Health, Lawrence, KS, p. A253

BROWNE, John
Assistant Administrator Finance, Kindred Hospital–Brea, Brea, CA, p. A58
Senior Chief Financial Officer, Kindred Hospital Riverside, Perris, CA, p. A83

BROWNE, Mark
M.D., Chief Medical Officer, Roane Medical Center, Harriman, TN, p. A583
M.D., Covenant Health, Senior Vice President and Chief Medical Officer, Methodist Medical Center of Oak Ridge, Oak Ridge, TN, p. A591

BROWNEWELL, Victoria, Chief Nursing Officer, Houston Methodist West Hospital, Houston, TX, p. A626
BROWNING, Deborah, MSN, R.N., Chief Executive Officer, USA Health Children's & Women's Hospital, Mobile, AL, p. A22
BROWNING, Douglas, Chief Financial Officer, Texas Health Center for Diagnostic & Surgery, Plano, TX, p. A645
BROWNING, Michael, Chief Financial Officer, Madison Health, London, OH, p. A498
BROWNING, Susan, President, Vassar Brothers Medical Center, Poughkeepsie, NY, p. A456
BROWNLEE, Tamarah, Vice President, Human Resources, Indiana University Health West Hospital, Avon, IN, p. A212
BROWNSTEIN, Richard, M.D., Chief of Staff, Delta Health – Northwest Regional, Clarksdale, MS, p. A360
BROYLES, Susan, Director Human Resources and Safety, Unicoi County Hospital, Erwin, TN, p. A583
BRUCE, Blackhart, M.D., Chief of Staff, Oak Valley Hospital, Oakdale, CA, p. A80
BRUCE, Caleigh, Director of Human Resources/Chief Compliance Officer, Ferrell Hospital, Eldorado, IL, p. A194
BRUCE, Jason, Executive Vice President of Healthcare and Director of Boys Town National Research Hospital and Clin, Boys Town National Research Hospital, Omaha, NE, p. A403
BRUCE, Jordan, Administrator, Norwood Health Center, Marshfield, WI, p. A715
BRUCE, Karen, Director of Nursing, Newport News Behavioral Health Center, Newport News, VA, p. A680
BRUCE, Marion, Chief Executive Officer, Muenster Memorial Hospital, Muenster, TX, p. A640

BRUCE, Michael
Chief Executive Officer, Elmore Community Hospital, Wetumpka, AL, p. A26
Chief Executive Officer, Lake Martin Community Hospital, Dadeville, AL, p. A18
Chief Financial Officer, Elmore Community Hospital, Wetumpka, AL, p. A26

BRUCHHAUS, John, M.D., Chief Medical Officer, St. Francis Medical Center, Monroe, LA, p. A289
BRUCKNER, Alison, Chief Operating Officer, Cass Health, Atlantic, IA, p. A230
BRUDNICKI, Gary F, Senior Executive Vice President, Chief Operating Officer and Chief Financial Officer, Westchester Medical Center, Valhalla, NY, p. A461
BRUEGGEMANN, Marty, Chief Medical Officer, Multicare Yakima Memorial Hospital, Yakima, WA, p. A698
BRUENING, Teri Tipton, MSN, Chief Nursing Officer and Vice President Patient Care Services, Nebraska Methodist Hospital, Omaha, NE, p. A404
BRUENS, Dennis, Vice President Operations, St. Thomas More Hospital, Canon City, CO, p. A104
BRUGGEMAN, Chris, Chief Operating Officer, Riverview Health, Crookston, MN, p. A345
BRUGGER, Diane, FACHE, Chief Executive Officer, Antelop. Memorial Hospital, Neligh, NE, p. A403
BRUHL, Lisa G., Hospital Administrator, Lallie Kemp Medical Center, Independence, LA, p. A283
BRUHL, Steven, Chief Medical Officer, Mercy Health – Tiffin Hospital, Tiffin, OH, p. A504
BRUHN, Julie, R.N., MS, Associate Director Patient Care and Nurse Executive, Fargo Va Medical Center, Fargo, ND, p. A480
BRUHN, Michelle, Executive Vice President, Chief Financial Officer, Phoenix Children's, Phoenix, AZ, p. A36
BRUINS, Melanie, Chief Talent Officer, Marshfield Medical Center – Beaver Dam, Beaver Dam, WI, p. A708
BRUMFIELD, Rita, R.N., MSN, Chief Nursing Officer, Ste. Genevieve County Memorial Hospital, Ste Genevieve, MO, p. A387
BRUMMER, Amy, MSN, Chief Nursing Officer, Saint Luke's North Hospital – Barry Road, Kansas City, MO, p. A378
BRUMMETT, Vincent, Chief Administrative Officer, Merit Health Central, Jackson, MS, p. A364

Index of Health Care Professionals / Bullock

BRUNDISE, Cynthia, Vice President Human Resources, SSM Health St. Anthony Hospital – Oklahoma City, Oklahoma City, OK, p. A518
BRUNELLE, Diane, MSN, R.N., Director Patient Care Services and Chief Nursing Officer, Shriners Hospitals for Children–Springfield, Springfield, MA, p. A318
BRUNER, Deborah, Chief Executive Officer and Administrator, Minneola District Hospital, Minneola, KS, p. A255
BRUNING, Troy, Director Information Technology, Meeker Memorial Hospital And Clinics, Litchfield, MN, p. A348
BRUNKE, Renea, Vice President Human Resources, Chandler Regional Medical Center, Chandler, AZ, p. A30
BRUNN, Mary E., R.N., Acting Associate Director Nursing, Clement J. Zablocki Veterans' Administration Medical Center, Milwaukee, WI, p. A717
BRUNO, Catherine, FACHE, Chief Information Officer, Northern Light Eastern Maine Medical Center, Bangor, ME, p. A295
BRUNO, John P, Senior Vice President Human Resources, St. Joseph's University Medical Center, Paterson, NJ, p. A426
BRUNS, Susan, Chief Nursing Officer, Phoebe Sumter Medical Center, Americus, GA, p. A156
BRUNSCHEON, Keagan, Manager, Human Resources, Grundy County Memorial Hospital, Grundy Center, IA, p. A236
BRUNSING, Alisa A., Chief Financial Officer, Franciscan Healthcare, West Point, NE, p. A407
BRUNSON, Joan, M.D., Medical Director, Mercy Behavioral Hospital Llc, Lecompte, LA, p. A287
BRUNSON, Pamela J, Director Human Resources, South Baldwin Regional Medical Center, Foley, AL, p. A19
BRUNT, C Hal, M.D., Medical Director, Lakeside Behavioral Health System, Memphis, TN, p. A588
BRUNTON, Hope, Chief Manpower Branch, Irwin Army Community Hospital, Junction City, KS, p. A251
BRUNTZ, Troy, CPA, President and Chief Executive Officer, Community Hospital, Mccook, NE, p. A402
BRUSCO, Louis, M.D., Chief Medical Officer, Hackensack Meridian Health Raritan Bay Medical Center, Perth Amboy, NJ, p. A427
BRUTON, Christine, Chief Financial Officer, Baptist Medical Center East, Montgomery, AL, p. A22
BRUTON, Jeff, Director Human Resources, Fairview Park Hospital, Dublin, GA, p. A163
BRYAN, Darlene, R.N., Chief Nursing Officer, Humboldt General Hospital, Winnemucca, NV, p. A413
BRYAN, Jason, Director Human Resources, Middle Park Health–Kremmling, Kremmling, CO, p. A110
BRYAN, Kenneth E, FACHE, President and Chief Executive Officer, Harnett Health System, Dunn, NC, p. A467
BRYAN, Linda, Vice President Human Resources, HCA Florida Fawcett Hospital, Port Charlotte, FL, p. A147
BRYAN, Lynda, Vice President Human Resources, HCA Florida Northwest Hospital, Margate, FL, p. A138
BRYANT, Amy, Chief Financial Officer, Cornerstone Specialty Hospitals Southwest Louisiana, Lake Charles, LA, p. A286
BRYANT, Dawn, Vice President Human Resources, North Kansas City Hospital, North Kansas City, MO, p. A381
BRYANT, Gary
Chief Financial Officer, Carepoint Health Bayonne Medical Center, Bayonne, NJ, p. A418
Executive Vice President and Chief Financial Officer, Carepoint Health Christ Hospital, Jersey City, NJ, p. A422
BRYANT, Gayla, R.N., Administrator, United Medical Healthwest New Orleans, Llc, Gretna, LA, p. A282
BRYANT, Holly, Chief Financial Officer, Tioga Medical Center, Tioga, ND, p. A483
BRYANT, Joe, Chief Executive Officer, Amg Specialty Hospital Northwest Indiana, Crown Point, IN, p. A214
BRYANT, Karen L., Chief Executive Officer, Prowers Medical Center, Lamar, CO, p. A111
BRYANT, Lidia, Director Human Resources, Ottumwa Regional Health Center, Ottumwa, IA, p. A241
BRYANT, Marcia, R.N., MSN, RN, Vice President, Clinical Operations, The Outer Banks Hospital, Nags Head, NC, p. A473
BRYANT, Pam, Director Human Resources, Helen Keller Hospital, Sheffield, AL, p. A24
BRYANT, Preston, Chief Executive Officer, Kindred Hospital–Greensboro, Greensboro, NC, p. A469
BRYANT, Rachel, Chief Operating Officer, Wyoming Medical Center, Casper, WY, p. A726
BRYANT, Ronald
President, Baystate Franklin Medical Center, Greenfield, MA, p. A314
President, Baystate Noble Hospital, Westfield, MA, p. A319
President, Baystate Wing Hospital, Palmer, MA, p. A317
BRYANT, Rusty, Director Information Technology, Baptist Health Medical Center – Drew County, Monticello, AR, p. A50
BRYANT, Samantha, Chief Nursing Officer, Rhea Medical Center, Dayton, TN, p. A582
BRYANT, Valerie, Chief Financial Officer, Tennova Healthcare–Clarksville, Clarksville, TN, p. A581
BRYANT–MOBLEY, Phyllis, M.D., Director Medical Services, William S. Hall Psychiatric Institute, Columbia, SC, p. A565
BRYCE, Keith, Vice President Finance and Chief Financial Officer, Mt. Graham Regional Medical Center, Safford, AZ, p. A38
BRYER, Alex, Director Information Management, Los Robles Health System, Thousand Oaks, CA, p. A97
BRYNER, Jennifer, Director Nursing, Petersburg Medical Center, Petersburg, AK, p. A29
BRYNES, Jeremy M., Chief Executive Officer, Elite Hospital Kingwood, Kingwood, TX, p. A632
BRYSON, Kellie, Director Human Resources, The Hospital At Westlake Medical Center, West Lake Hills, TX, p. A662
BRZEZINSKI, Christina, Chief Nursing Officer, Coastal Carolina Hospital, Hardeeville, SC, p. A568
BUCCELLATO, Vito, Chief Hospital Executive, Hackensack Meridian Health Jersey Shore University Medical Center, Neptune, NJ, p. A424
BUCCI, Andrea, Chief Executive Officer, Heartland Behavioral Healthcare, Massillon, OH, p. A499
BUCCI, Annette, Vice President Human Resources, Burke Rehabilitation Hospital, White Plains, NY, p. A462
BUCCIARELLI, Brant, Chief Information Officer, Riverview Health, Noblesville, IN, p. A225
BUCH, Naishadh, Chief Operating Officer, Lompoc Valley Medical Center, Lompoc, CA, p. A70
BUCHANAN, Donna, Director of Nursing, Rural Wellness Stroud, Stroud, OK, p. A521
BUCHANAN, Jean, Director Human Resources, Broughton Hospital, Morganton, NC, p. A473
BUCHANAN, Kyle, President, Helen Keller Hospital, Sheffield, AL, p. A24
BUCHANAN, Robert, Chief Information Officer, Anna Jaques Hospital, Newburyport, MA, p. A316
BUCHANAN, Rodney, MSN, R.N., Interim President, Westfield Memorial Hospital, Westfield, NY, p. A462
BUCHANAN, Sonja, Chief Executive Officer, Encompass Health Rehabilitation Hospital, A Partner of Washington Regional, Fayetteville, AR, p. A46
BUCHANAN, Toni, Chief Financial Officer, Unicoi County Hospital, Erwin, TN, p. A583
BUCHANAN, Tracy, Chief Executive Officer and President, Carepartners Rehabilitation Hospital, Asheville, NC, p. A463
BUCHE, Karen, Chief Human Resource Officer, Douglas County Community Mental Health Center, Omaha, NE, p. A404
BUCHELE, Paula, Chief Human Resources, Bay Pines Veterans Affairs Healthcare System, Bay Pines, FL, p. A125
BUCHER, Ben, Chief Executive Officer, Towner County Medical Center, Cando, ND, p. A479
BUCHHEIT, Anne, Coordinator Mental Health Local Information Systems, Buffalo Psychiatric Center, Buffalo, NY, p. A440
BUCHHOLZ, Kari, Director Health Information Management, South Central Health, Wishek, ND, p. A483
BUCK, Linda K, Vice President Human Resources, Carle Health Proctor Hospital, Peoria, IL, p. A206
BUCK, Nathan, R.N., Nursing Manager, Grove Creek Medical Center, Blackfoot, ID, p. A179
BUCK, Shelly, President, Riddle Hospital, Media, PA, p. A546
BUCKLEY, Brooke Mattern, M.D., FACS, Chief Medical Officer, Henry Ford Wyandotte Hospital, Wyandotte, MI, p. A341
BUCKLEY, David, Acting Chief Information Management Services, Oklahoma City Va Medical Center, Oklahoma City, OK, p. A518
BUCKLEY, James, Chief Executive Officer, Northlake Behavioral Health System, Mandeville, LA, p. A287
BUCKLEY, John, M.D., President Medical Staff, Vibra Hospital of Denver, Thornton, CO, p. A114
BUCKLEY, Kalvin, Director Information Systems, Woodland Heights Medical Center, Lufkin, TX, p. A637
BUCKLEY, Karen L, R.N., Regional Chief Nurse Executive, Community Behavioral Health Center, Fresno, CA, p. A64
BUCKLEY, Martha, Chief Medical Informatics Officer, Fairfield Medical Center, Lancaster, OH, p. A498
BUCKLEY, Robert G., M.D., Medical Center Director, Captain James A. Lovell Federal Health Care Center, North Chicago, IL, p. A203
BUCKMAN, Janet, Chief Financial Officer, Hedrick Medical Center, Chillicothe, MO, p. A373
BUCKMINSTER, Joe, Manager Information Technology, Community Medical Center, Inc., Falls City, NE, p. A399
BUCKNER, Twila, R.N., Chief Nursing Officer, Cass Regional Medical Center, Harrisonville, MO, p. A376
BUCKNOR, Jermaine, Chief Financial Officer, Northwest Health Physicians' Specialty Hospital, Fayetteville, AR, p. A46
BUCKWORTH, Ben, Human Resources Administrative Director, Primary Children's Hospital, Salt Lake City, UT, p. A669
BUCZKOWSKI, Laura, Senior Vice President and Chief Financial Officer, Wellspan York Hospital, York, PA, p. A559
BUDA, Jeff, Chief Information Officer, Atrium Health Floyd Medical Center, Rome, GA, p. A170
BUDD, Ned
President and Chief Executive Officer, Thorek Memorial Hospital, Chicago, IL, p. A191
President and Chief Executive Officer, Thorek Memorial Hospital Andersonville, Chicago, IL, p. A191
BUDZINSKI, Anthony James (Jim), R.N., II, Executive Vice President and Chief Financial Officer, Wellstar Kennestone Hospital, Marietta, GA, p. A167
BUDZINSKY, Chris
Vice President Nursing and Chief Nursing Officer Alexian Brothers Acute Care Ministries, Ascension St. Alexius, Hoffman Estates, IL, p. A198
Vice President, Nursing and Chief Nursing Officer, Ascension Alexian Brothers, Elk Grove Village, IL, p. A194
BUE, Cheryl, Health Information Transcriptionist, Faulkton Area Medical Center, Faulkton, SD, p. A573
BUEGLER, Carisa, Director of Operations, New Ulm Medical Center, New Ulm, MN, p. A352
BUEHLER, Bonnie J.
Chief Information Officer, St. Mary Medical Center, Langhorne, PA, p. A543
Chief Information Technology, Nazareth Hospital, Philadelphia, PA, p. A549
BUEHRLE, Jeff, Chief Financial Officer, Banner – University Medical Center South, Tucson, AZ, p. A40
BUELL, Jack, Director Information Services, Sutter Lakeside Hospital, Lakeport, CA, p. A69
BUENAVIDEZ, Nanette, Chief Nursing Officer, Arrowhead Regional Medical Center, Colton, CA, p. A60
BUER, Shane, Vice President, Human Resources, Mercyone Clinton Medical Center, Clinton, IA, p. A233
BUFFENBARGER, Andrew, FACHE, Chief Compliance Officer, Director of Human Resources & Risk Management, Kirby Medical Center, Monticello, IL, p. A202
BUFFINGTON, Mike, Manager Information Technology, Kansas Medical Center, Andover, KS, p. A246
BUFKIN, Ben, Human Resource Director, Bolivar Medical Center, Cleveland, MS, p. A361
BUFORD, Leslie, Chief Hospital Executive, Lakeside Women's Hospital, Oklahoma City, OK, p. A517
BUGALLO–MUROS, Mariana, Vice President, Human Resources, Anna Jaques Hospital, Newburyport, MA, p. A316
BUGAYONG, Carol, Human Resources Director, Encompass Health Rehabilitation Hospital of Tallahassee, Tallahassee, FL, p. A151
BUGNA, Eric, M.D., Chief of Staff, Eastern Plumas Health Care, Portola, CA, p. A84
BUGNAKI, Paul, Adminstrator, Humboldt County Mental Health, Eureka, CA, p. A62
BUHLKE, Brian, M.D., Medical Director, Genoa Medical Facilities, Genoa, NE, p. A400
BUI, Steven, M.D., Chief of Staff, Orange County Global Medical Center, Inc., Santa Ana, CA, p. A93
BUICE, Johnathan, Chief Information Officer, Upson Regional Medical Center, Thomaston, GA, p. A172
BUIT, Timothy A., President and Chief Executive Officer, Bellevue Hospital, The, Bellevue, OH, p. A486
BUKAC, Amy, M.D., Medical Director, Providence Seward Medical Center, Seward, AK, p. A29
BULEN, Susan R., M.D., Medical Director, Encompass Health Rehabilitation Hospital of Northwest Tucson, Tucson, AZ, p. A40
BULLARD, John, Director Information Technology, Intermountain Health St. Mary's Regional Hospital, Grand Junction, CO, p. A109
BULLARD, Patrick, Chief Financial Officer, Fayetteville Veterans Affairs Medical Center, Fayetteville, NC, p. A468
BULLARO, Guy, Chief Executive Officer, HCA Florida West Hospital, Pensacola, FL, p. A146
BULLER, Lisa, Regional Vice President and Chief Information Officer, Cascade Valley Hospital, Arlington, WA, p. A687
BULLINGTON, Benjamin P, M.D., Chief of Staff, Pioneer Medical Center, Big Timber, MT, p. A389
BULLINGTON, Gina, Chief Nursing Officer, Tristar Horizon Medical Center, Dickson, TN, p. A582
BULLMAN, Jody, President, Selby General Hospital, Marietta, OH, p. A499
BULLOCK, David, Director Information Services, Northwest Medical Center, Tucson, AZ, p. A40
BULLOCK, Deann, M.D., Chief Medical Officer, Nashville General Hospital, Nashville, TN, p. A590

Index of Health Care Professionals

Index of Health Care Professionals

Index of Health Care Professionals / Bullock

BULLOCK, Lance, M.D., Medical Director, St. James Behavioral Health Hospital, Gonzales, LA, p. A282
BULLOCK, Scott, Director Information Systems, Barstow Community Hospital, Barstow, CA, p. A57
BULMAN, Laurie, Director Human Resources, Winnmed, Decorah, IA, p. A234
BULMASH, Jack, M.D., Chief of Staff, Edward Hines, Jr. Veterans Affairs Hospital, Hines, IL, p. A198
BUMAN, Karen, MSN, Chief Nursing Officer, Myrtue Medical Center, Harlan, IA, p. A237
BUNCH, David V., Chief Executive Officer, Raleigh General Hospital, Beckley, WV, p. A699
BUNCH, Mark, Director Finance, Othello Community Hospital, Othello, WA, p. A692
BUNCH, Rita A.
M.P.H., FACHE, Division President, Sentara Martha Jefferson Hospital, Charlottesville, VA, p. A674
M.P.H., FACHE, Vice President of Operations, Sentara Careplex Hospital, Hampton, VA, p. A677
BUNCH, Terri
MSN, R.N., MSN, Chief Nursing Officer, Stone County Medical Center, Mountain View, AR, p. A51
MSN, R.N., MSN, Chief Nursing Officer, White River Health, Batesville, AR, p. A43
BUND, Linda, Chief Information Officer and Director Education, James J. Peters Veterans Affairs Medical Center, New York, NY, p. A448
BUNDT, Thomas S., Ph.D., FACHE, Executive Director, VA Puget Sound Healthcare System – Seattle, Seattle, WA, p. A695
BUNDY, Melissa, Chief Executive Officer, Coon Memorial Hospital, Dalhart, TX, p. A610
BUNDY, Michael N.
Chief Executive Officer, Prisma Health Baptist Hospital, Columbia, SC, p. A565
Chief Executive Officer, Prisma Health Baptist Parkridge Hospital, Columbia, SC, p. A564
Chief Executive Officer, Prisma Health Richland Hospital, Columbia, SC, p. A565
Chief Executive Officer, Prisma Health Tuomey Hospital, Sumter, SC, p. A570
BUNKER, Marla, Vice President Nursing and Chief Operating Officer, Mymichigan Medical Center Sault, Sault Sainte Marie, MI, p. A338
BUNN, Barry, M.D., Chief of Staff, ECU Health Edgecombe Hospital, Tarboro, NC, p. A477
BUNNELL, Craig A., Chief Medical Officer, Dana–Farber Cancer Institute, Boston, MA, p. A310
BUNNELL, Emily Ann, Chief Nurse Executive, Senior Director of Acute Care, UPMC Cole, Coudersport, PA, p. A537
BUNNER, Blake, Chief Executive Officer, Encompass Health Deaconess Rehabilitation Hospital, Newburgh, IN, p. A225
BUNSELMEYER, Becky, Director Information Services, Memorial Hospital, Chester, IL, p. A188
BUNTEN, Sherry
R.N., FACHE, Director Patient Care Services, Aspirus Langlade Hospital, Antigo, WI, p. A707
R.N., FACHE, President, Aspirus Langlade Hospital, Antigo, WI, p. A707
BUNTYN, Diane, MSN, R.N., Vice President Patient Care Services, Southeast Alabama Medical Center, Dothan, AL, p. A18
BUONGIORNO, Michael J
Executive Vice President Finance and Chief Financial Officer, Bryn Mawr Hospital, Bryn Mawr, PA, p. A536
Vice President Finance, Lankenau Medical Center, Wynnewood, PA, p. A558
BUPP, Steven, M.D., Medical Director, Sonora Behavioral Health Hospital, Tucson, AZ, p. A41
BURAS, Jay, Chief Operating Officer, Avala, Covington, LA, p. A280
BURBANK, Jimmy, Chief Information Officer, U. S. Public Health Service Indian Hospital, Crownpoint, NM, p. A434
BURCH, Andrea, MS, R.N., President, Lutheran Medical Center, Wheat Ridge, CO, p. A114
BURCH, Debra, Chief Nursing Officer, Burke Medical Center, Waynesboro, GA, p. A174
BURCH, Lee, Director Management Information Systems, Tamp. General Hospital Brooksville, Brooksville, FL, p. A127
BURCH, Tina, Chief Executive Officer and Chief Nursing Officer, Doctors Hospital of Manteca, Manteca, CA, p. A76
BURCHELL, Pam, Director Human Resources, HCA Florida Lawnwood Hospital, Fort Pierce, FL, p. A132
BURCHETT, Shelby, Chief Executive Officer, Southeast Iowa Regional Medical Center, West Burlington Campus, West Burlington, IA, p. A245
BURCHETT, Travis, Troop Commander Human Resources, Colonel Florence A. Blanchfield Army Community Hospital, Fort Campbell, KY, p. A265
BURCZEUSKI, Jason
Controller, Arms Acres, Carmel, NY, p. A441
Controller, Conifer Park, Glenville, NY, p. A443
BURD, David, President and Chief Executive Officer, Methodist Jennie Edmundson Hospital, Council Bluffs, IA, p. A234
BURDEN, Matthew J., President and Chief Executive Officer, Porter–Starke Services, Valparaiso, IN, p. A228
BURDETTE, Marie, Chief Nursing Officer, East Georgia Regional Medical Center, Statesboro, GA, p. A171
BURDICK, Ginny
Senior Vice President and Chief Human Resources Officer, Clovis Community Medical Center, Clovis, CA, p. A60
Vice President Human Resources, Community Behavioral Health Center, Fresno, CA, p. A64
Vice President Human Resources, Community Regional Medical Center, Fresno, CA, p. A64
BURDICK, Hoyt J., M.D., Vice President Medical Affairs, Cabell Huntington Hospital, Huntington, WV, p. A701
BURG, Sherry, Chief Nursing Officer, Fairview Range, Hibbing, MN, p. A348
BURGESS, Angela, Chief Information Officer, Randolp. Health, Asheboro, NC, p. A463
BURGESS, Daniel, Chief Information Officer, Mainegeneral Medical Center, Augusta, ME, p. A295
BURGESS, John, Director Information Services, Hocking Valley Community Hospital, Logan, OH, p. A498
BURGESS, Steven, Administrator Human Resources, Henrico Doctors' Hospital, Richmond, VA, p. A682
BURGESS, Ty, Chief Executive Officer, Reunion Rehabilitation Hospital Plano, Plano, TX, p. A645
BURGOS, Odette, Supervisor Human Resources, San Jorge Children's And Women Hospital, Santurce, PR, p. A736
BURGUS, Aurelis, Nursing Director, Ryder Memorial Hospital, Humacao, PR, p. A733
BURICK, Adam
M.D., Chief Medical Officer, Pam Specialty Hospital of Covington, Covington, LA, p. A280
M.D., Chief Medical Officer, Pam Specialty Hospital of Victoria North, Victoria, TX, p. A660
BURICK, Marsha, Chief Financial Officer, Central Florida Behavioral Hospital, Orlando, FL, p. A144
BURINGRUD, Duane, M.D., Chief Medical and Quality Officer, Palomar Medical Center Escondido, Escondido, CA, p. A62
BURISH, Brent
Chief Executive Officer, HCA Florida Pasadena Hospital, Saint Petersburg, FL, p. A149
Chief Executive Officer, HCA Florida St. Petersburg Hospital, Saint Petersburg, FL, p. A149
BURK, Thomas J, Chief Operating Officer, Danville State Hospital, Danville, PA, p. A538
BURKE, Brian, M.D., President Medical Staff, Fairview Hospital, Great Barrington, MA, p. A314
BURKE, Brigid, Chief Financial Officer, Logan Health – Conrad, Conrad, MT, p. A390
BURKE, Dorothy, Chief Financial Officer, Southeast Colorado Hospital District, Springfield, CO, p. A113
BURKE, Greg, M.D., Medical Director, Geisinger Encompass Health Rehabilitation Hospital, Danville, PA, p. A538
BURKE, Jack J, MS, R.N., Chief Operating Officer and Chief Nursing Officer, Antelop. Valley Medical Center, Lancaster, CA, p. A69
BURKE, James
M.D., Senior Vice President and Chief Medical Officer, Honorhealth Scottsdale Osborn Medical Center, Scottsdale, AZ, p. A38
M.D., Senior Vice President and Chief Medical Officer, Honorhealth Scottsdale Shea Medical Center, Scottsdale, AZ, p. A38
BURKE, James M., Vice President Finance, Chief Nursing Executive Medical Surgical Hospitals, Kent Hospital, Warwick, RI, p. A561
BURKE, Jeff, Chief Information Officer, Bon Secours Richmond Community Hospital, Richmond, VA, p. A682
BURKE, John, Chief Financial Officer, Montefiore Nyack Hospital, Nyack, NY, p. A454
BURKE, Marsha, Senior Vice President and Chief Financial Officer, Wellstar Windy Hill Hospital, Marietta, GA, p. A168
BURKE, Paul, Administrator, Shamrock General Hospital, Shamrock, TX, p. A652
BURKE, Rebecca, R.N., MS, Senior Vice President and Chief Nursing Officer, Kent Hospital, Warwick, RI, p. A561
BURKE, Richard Aron, M.D., Chief Medical Officer, Community Hospital–Fairfax, Fairfax, MO, p. A375
BURKE, Rose, Associate Director Patient Care Services, Marion Veterans Affairs Medical Center, Marion, IL, p. A200
BURKE, Ryan Esq, Vice President, Human Resources, Emanate Health Inter–Community Hospital, Covina, CA, p. A61
BURKE, Tim, Chief Executive Officer, Pam Specialty Hospital of Covington, Covington, LA, p. A280
BURKE, Timothy, M.D., Medical Director, The Brook Hospital – Kmi, Louisville, KY, p. A270
BURKEL, Greg, Chief Financial Officer, Regional Health Services of Howard County, Cresco, IA, p. A234
BURKEL, Gregory, Chief Financial Officer, Mitchell County Regional Health Center, Osage, IA, p. A241
BURKET, Mark, Chief Executive Officer, Platte Health Center Avera, Platte, SD, p. A575
BURKETT, Doug, Manager Information Technology, Regional Medical Center of Central Alabama, Greenville, AL, p. A20
BURKETT, Eric, M.D., Vice President Medical Affairs, Monmouth Medical Center, Long Branch Campus, Long Branch, NJ, p. A423
BURKETT, Evan, Chief Human Resource Officer, Sanford Usd Medical Center, Sioux Falls, SD, p. A577
BURKETT, Jenny S., USN, Director, Naval Hospital Camp Pendleton, Camp Pendleton, CA, p. A58
BURKEY, Brent, M.D., President and Chief Executive Officer, Fisher–Titus Medical Center, Norwalk, OH, p. A501
BURKHARDT, Jennifer, Chief Human Resources Officer, Olympic Medical Center, Port Angeles, WA, p. A693
BURKHARDT, Raye M., Chief Nurse Executive, Kaiser Permanente Fontana Medical Center, Fontana, CA, p. A63
BURKHART, Brad, Assistant Administrator, Harlan Arh Hospital, Harlan, KY, p. A266
BURKHART, Steven, M.D., Chief Medical Officer, Crittenden Community Hospital, Marion, KY, p. A271
BURKS, Felicia, Chief Financial Officer, U. S. Air Force Regional Hospital, Elmendorf Afb, AK, p. A28
BURKS, Matt, Director Information Technology, Unity Medical Center, Manchester, TN, p. A587
BURKS, Melvin, Chief Executive Officer, Hamilton Center, Terre Haute, IN, p. A228
BURKS, Tami, Comptroller, Rankin County Hospital District, Rankin, TX, p. A646
BURLESON, Stan, M.D., Chief Medical Staff, Dewitt Hospital & Nursing Home, Dewitt, AR, p. A45
BURLING, Chris, M.D., Chief of Staff, Titus Regional Medical Center, Mount Pleasant, TX, p. A640
BURLINGAME DEAL, Penney, FACHE, R.N., Chief Executive Officer, Onslow Memorial Hospital, Jacksonville, NC, p. A471
BURMEISTER, Keith, President, Promedica Defiance Regional Hospital, Defiance, OH, p. A494
BURMESTER, Mark A, Vice President Strategy and Communications, Kaiser Sunnyside Medical Center, Clackamas, OR, p. A526
BURNAM, Gregg
Chief Financial Officer and Chief Operating Officer, Mangum Regional Medical Center, Mangum, OK, p. A514
Chief Information Officer and Manager Business Office, Mangum Regional Medical Center, Mangum, OK, p. A514
BURNELL, Lori, R.N., Ph.D., Senior Vice President and Chief Nursing Officer, Valley Presbyterian Hospital, Los Angeles, CA, p. A75
BURNETT, Anthony, M.D., Medical Director, Julian F. Keith Alcohol And Drug Abuse Treatment Center, Black Mountain, NC, p. A464
BURNETT, Brad, Chief Financial Officer, Heart of Texas Healthcare System, Brady, TX, p. A604
BURNETT, Brenda, R.N., Vice President Patient Care Services and Chief Nursing Officer, Titusville Area Hospital, Titusville, PA, p. A555
BURNETT, Cindi, Chief Human Resources Officer, Madison County Memorial Hospital, Madison, FL, p. A138
BURNETT, David Mark., President and Chief Executive Officer, Scott County Hospital, Scott City, KS, p. A259
BURNETT, Michael, Chief Executive Officer, Piedmont Athens Regional Medical Center, Athens, GA, p. A156
BURNETT, Tasha, Director of Nursing, Falls Community Hospital And Clinic, Marlin, TX, p. A638
BURNETTE, Sheri, R.N., Chief Executive Officer, Cornerstone Specialty Hospitals Bossier City, Bossier City, LA, p. A279
BURNHAM, Natalie, Chief Operating Officer, Carthage Area Hospital, Carthage, NY, p. A441
BURNHAM, Sharon, Director of Nursing, Simpson General Hospital, Mendenhall, MS, p. A366
BURNLEY, Charles, Vice President, Chief Nursing Officer, Richland Hospital, Richland Center, WI, p. A720
BURNS, Aaron, President and Chief Executive Officer, Leconte Medical Center, Sevierville, TN, p. A593
BURNS, Becky L, Manager Health Information Management, Ellinwood District Hospital, Ellinwood, KS, p. A248
BURNS, Bruce R., Chief Financial Officer, Concord Hospital, Concord, NH, p. A414
BURNS, Gary, Chief Executive Officer, Perimeter Behavioral Hospital of New Orleans, Kenner, LA, p. A284
BURNS, Helen K
Ph.D., R.N., Senior Vice President and Chief Nursing Officer, Excela Frick Hospital, Mount Pleasant, PA, p. A546

A810 Index of Health Care Professionals

Index of Health Care Professionals / Byers

Index of Health Care Professionals

Ph.D., R.N., Senior Vice President and Chief Nursing Officer, Excela Health Latrobe Hospital, Latrobe, PA, p. A544
Ph.D., R.N., Senior Vice President and Chief Nursing Officer, Excela Health Westmoreland Hospital, Greensburg, PA, p. A541
BURNS, Helene M, R.N., Senior Vice President and Chief Nursing Officer, Jefferson Stratford Hospital, Stratford, NJ, p. A428
BURNS, Jeff, Manager of Information Technology, Mary Free Bed Rehabilitation Hospital, Grand Rapids, MI, p. A328
BURNS, Katherine, Vice President Human Resources, Atrium Health Wake Foret Baptist High Point Medical Center, High Point, NC, p. A470
BURNS, Kathryn I., R.N., Director of Nursing, Medicine Lodge Memorial Hospital, Medicine Lodge, KS, p. A254
BURNS, Larry P Jr, Chief Operating Officer, Dignity Health Yavapai Regional Medical Center, Prescott, AZ, p. A37
BURNS, Patrick, Vice President Finance, Acmh Hospital, Kittanning, PA, p. A543
BURNS, Rhonda, Director Human Resources, Caldwell Medical Center, Princeton, KY, p. A273
BURNS, Steve, Chief Operating Officer, Cumberland County Hospital, Burkesville, KY, p. A264
BURNS, Steven, Director Fiscal Services, Summit Behavioral Healthcare, Cincinnati, OH, p. A489
BURNS, Tom
M.D., Chief of Staff, The Hospital At Westlake Medical Center, West Lake Hills, TX, p. A662
Chief Operating Officer and Chief Nurse Executive, St. Rose Dominican Hospitals – Rose De Lima Campus, Henderson, NV, p. A409
President and Chief Executive Officer, St. Rose Dominican Hospitals – San Martin Campus, Las Vegas, NV, p. A411
BURNS–CHISTENSON, Katherine, Human Resource Director, Grand Itasca Clinic And Hospital, Grand Rapids, MN, p. A347
BURNS–TISDALE, Susan, Senior Vice President Clinical Operations, Interim CNO, Exeter Hospital, Exeter, NH, p. A415
BURNSIDE, Brian, FACHE, President and Chief Executive Officer, Carlinville Area Hospital, Carlinville, IL, p. A187
BURRELL, Carol H, Chief Executive Officer, Northeast Georgia Medical Center, Gainesville, GA, p. A164
BURRELL, Carol H., Chief Executive Officer, Northeast Georgia Medical Center Lumpkin, Dahlonega, GA, p. A162
BURRELL, Sonni, Director Human Resources, Canyon Vista Medical Center, Sierra Vista, AZ, p. A39
BURRESS, Lori, Vice President Patient Services and Chief Nursing Officer, Mt. Graham Regional Medical Center, Safford, AZ, p. A38
BURRIS, Bradley D., Chief Executive Officer, Pipestone County Medical Center, Pipestone, MN, p. A352
BURRIS, Caroline F., Chief Operating Officer, HCA Florida Fort Walton–Destin Hospital, Fort Walton Beach, FL, p. A132
BURRIS, Lisa, Director Human Resources, Southern Indiana Rehabilitation Hospital, New Albany, IN, p. A225
BURRISS, Jessica, Chief Financial Officer, Encompass Health Rehabilitation Hospital of Columbia, Columbia, SC, p. A564
BURROUGHS, Shawn, Director of Information Services, Northeastern Vermont Regional Hospital, Saint Johnsbury, VT, p. A672
BURROWS, Jennifer, R.N., Chief Executive, Providence St. Vincent Medical Center, Portland, OR, p. A531
BURROWS, Susan M, Vice President Human Resources, Mlk Community Healthcare, Los Angeles, CA, p. A74
BURRUS, Gary, Director Information Technology, Winner Regional Healthcare Center, Winner, SD, p. A578
BURT, Alan, Director Information Services, Sunrise Hospital And Medical Center, Las Vegas, NV, p. A411
BURT, Linda K, Corporate Vice President Finance, Nebraska Methodist Hospital, Omaha, NE, p. A404
BURT, Noel F, Ph.D., Chief Human Resources Officer, Cone Health Moses Cone Hospital, Greensboro, NC, p. A469
BURT, Suzanne M.
Chief Human Resources Officer, Mercyone Cedar Falls Medical Center, Cedar Falls, IA, p. A231
Chief Human Resources Officer, Mercyone Oelwein Medical Center, Oelwein, IA, p. A241
Chief Human Resources Officer, Mercyone Waterloo Medical Center, Waterloo, IA, p. A244
BURTCH, Gloria, Director Human Resources, Cornerstone of Medical Arts Center Hospital, Fresh Meadows, NY, p. A443
BURTCHELL, Scott, Director Information Systems, Northern Light Maine Coast Hospital, Ellsworth, ME, p. A297
BURTON, Angela, Privacy Officer, Wayne County Hospital, Monticello, KY, p. A271
BURTON, Charles, Chief Human Resources, Carl R. Darnall Army Medical Center, Fort Hood, TX, p. A618
BURTON, James, Vice President and Chief Information Officer, Valley Health, Valley Health – Shenandoah Memorial Hospital, Woodstock, VA, p. A686
BURTON, Kevin, Administrator, Unity Health – Jacksonville, Jacksonville, AR, p. A48
BURTON, Luanne, Director Human Resources, Encompass Health Rehabilitation Hospital of Columbia, Columbia, SC, p. A564
BURTON, Robert, Manager Finance, Utah State Hospital, Provo, UT, p. A667
BURTON, Stacey R., Director Human Resources, Muscogee Creek Nation Medical Center, Okmulgee, OK, p. A519
BURY, Peter, Vice President Finance, Ohiohealth Riverside Methodist Hospital, Columbus, OH, p. A492
BUSBY, Jay, M.D., President Medical Staff, Franklin Medical Center, Winnsboro, LA, p. A294
BUSCAGLIA, Jonathan, M.D., Chief Medical Officer, Stony Brook University Hospital, Stony Brook, NY, p. A459
BUSCH, Rebecca, Chief Financial Officer, Spooner Health, Spooner, WI, p. A721
BUSCH, Steve, Chief Operating Officer, Midwest Medical Center, Galena, IL, p. A195
BUSH, Amy
R.N., Chief Administrative Officer, West Virginia University Hospitals, Morgantown, WV, p. A703
R.N., Vice President Operations, UPMC Mckeesport, Mckeesport, PA, p. A545
BUSH, Bruce A., M.D., Interim Chief Medical Officer, Indiana Regional Medical Center, Indiana, PA, p. A542
BUSH, Chad, Managing Director, Elitecare Emergency Hospital, League City, TX, p. A634
BUSH, Stephen, Chief Financial Officer, TMC Health, Tucson, AZ, p. A41
BUSH, Steven, Chief Medical Officer, Crossing Rivers Health, Prairie Du Chien, WI, p. A720
BUSH, Wayne, M.D., Chief of Staff, Tristar Greenview Regional Hospital, Bowling Green, KY, p. A264
BUSHART, Phyllis, R.N., Chief Operating Officer, Providence Cedars–Sinai Tarzana Medical Center, Los Angeles, CA, p. A74
BUSHELL, Michael, President, Saint Anne's Hospital, Fall River, MA, p. A313
BUSHEY, Dale, Chief Financial Officer, Oss Health, York, PA, p. A558
BUSHMAN, Jerry, Chief Nursing Officer, Brigham City Community Hospital, Brigham City, UT, p. A664
BUSHNELL, Kim
R.N., Vice President, Patient Care Services, Mercy Medical Center, Baltimore, MD, p. A301
R.N., Vice President, Patient Care Services and Chief Nursing Officer, Northwest, Northwest Hospital, Randallstown, MD, p. A306
BUSKEY, Dawn M.
President, Acute Care, Promedica Toledo Hospital, Toledo, OH, p. A505
President, ProMedica Acute Care, Promedica Bay Park Hospital, Oregon, OH, p. A502
BUSKEY, Irene, Director Human Resources, Bon Secours – Southside Medical Center, Petersburg, VA, p. A681
BUSKILL, Lynn, Chief Operations Officer, John C. Fremont Healthcare District, Mariposa, CA, p. A76
BUSNELLO, Joao, M.D., Chief Medical Officer, Montrose Behavioral Health Hospital, Chicago, IL, p. A190
BUSS, Theresa L, Regional Vice President Human Resources, Windham Hospital, Willimantic, CT, p. A120
BUSSELL, Walter
Chief Financial Officer, Memorial Hospital West, Pembroke Pines, FL, p. A146
Chief Financial Officer, Memorial Regional Hospital, Hollywood, FL, p. A133
BUSSIERE, Mark, Administrator Human Resources, New Hampshire Hospital, Concord, NH, p. A414
BUSSINGER, Brandy, Director of Nursing, Brown County Hospital, Ainsworth, NE, p. A397
BUSSLER, David, Chief Information Officer, Sheridan Community Hospital, Sheridan, MI, p. A338
BUTCHER, Allen R
Chief Financial Officer, Candler Hospital–Savannah, Savannah, GA, p. A170
Chief Financial Officer, St. Joseph's Hospital, Savannah, GA, p. A171
BUTCHER, Gina, Chief Financial Officer, Garden City Hospital, Garden City, MI, p. A327
BUTCHER, Kay, Director Health Information Management, Mon Health Stonewall Jackson Memorial Hospital, Weston, WV, p. A705
BUTE, Phil, Manager Information Technology, Clay County Hospital, Flora, IL, p. A195
BUTERBAUGH, Roger W, Chief Human Resources Officer, Charlie Norwood Veterans Affairs Medical Center, Augusta, GA, p. A158
BUTKER, Jeff, Chief Information Officer, Sovah Health–Martinsville, Martinsville, VA, p. A679
BUTLER, Amanda, Chief Executive Officer, Seven Hills Hospital, Henderson, NV, p. A409
BUTLER, Brad, Network Administrator, Cox Barton County Memorial Hospital, Lamar, MO, p. A379
BUTLER, Carol A, R.N., MSN, VP Patient Care Services & Operations, St. Anthony North Hospital, Westminster, CO, p. A114
BUTLER, Catherine, M.D., Chief Medical Staff, Hancock County Health System, Britt, IA, p. A231
BUTLER, Chris, Chief Information Officer, Monmouth Medical Center, Long Branch Campus, Long Branch, NJ, p. A423
BUTLER, Dana, M.D., Medical Director, Sunrise Canyon Hospital, Lubbock, TX, p. A636
BUTLER, David
Chief Executive Officer, Mckenzie–Willamette Medical Center, Springfield, OR, p. A532
Chief Financial Officer, Ochsner Specialty Hospital, Meridian, MS, p. A366
BUTLER, Debby
Director Human Resources, Wadley Regional Medical Center, Texarkana, TX, p. A657
Director Human Resources, Wadley Regional Medical Center At Hope, Hope, AR, p. A47
BUTLER, LaDonna Esq, Chief Nursing Officer, Encompass Health Rehabilitation Hospital of Tustin, Tustin, CA, p. A99
BUTLER, Linda H., M.D., Chief Medical Officer, UNC Health Rex, Raleigh, NC, p. A475
BUTLER, Margaret, Vice President Human Resources, Abbott Northwestern Hospital, Minneapolis, MN, p. A350
BUTLER, Paulette, Chief Executive Officer, Patients Choice Medical Center of Smith County, Raleigh, MS, p. A368
BUTLER, Randy, Chief Financial Officer, HCA Florida West Hospital, Pensacola, FL, p. A146
BUTLER, Rosemary M, R.N., MSN, Chief Nurse Executive, Kaiser Permanente Riverside Medical Center, Riverside, CA, p. A86
BUTLER, Stuart, Director Information Technology, Sweeny Community Hospital, Sweeny, TX, p. A655
BUTT, Shiraz, M.D., Medical Director, Chicago Behavioral Hospital, Des Plaines, IL, p. A193
BUTT, Zaahra, Chief Executive Officer, Select Specialty Hospital – Macomb County, Mount Clemens, MI, p. A334
BUTTELL, Phil, Chief Executive Officer, Los Robles Health System, Thousand Oaks, CA, p. A97
BUTTER, Hazel, Manager Human Resources, Hammond–Henry Hospital, Geneseo, IL, p. A196
BUTTERFIELD, Chad, Chief Executive Officer, Greene County Medical Center, Jefferson, IA, p. A238
BUTTERFIELD, Cindy, Director, Fiscal and Administrative Services, Connecticut Valley Hospital, Middletown, CT, p. A117
BUTTERFIELD, Don, Interim Chief Executive Officer, Reno Behavioral Healthcare Hospital, Reno, NV, p. A412
BUTTERMORE, Bruce
Director Human Resources, Parkview Lagrange Hospital, Lagrange, IN, p. A222
Manager Human Resources, Parkview Noble Hospital, Kendallville, IN, p. A221
BUTTS, Cody, President, Cherokee Medical Center, Gaffney, SC, p. A566
BUTTS, Michele, Chief Executive Officer, Encompass Health Rehabilitation Hospital of Desert Canyon, Las Vegas, NV, p. A410
BUTTS, Paula Yvonne, Chief Nursing Officer, Piedmont Henry Hospital, Stockbridge, GA, p. A172
BUTTS, Ursula N, FACHE, Vice President of Patient Care Services, VCU Health Community Memorial Hospital, South Hill, VA, p. A684
BUTZINE, Bart, Director Information Technology, Community Hospital, Grand Junction, CO, p. A108
BUTZLER, Hilary, Director Human Resources, Cumberland Healthcare, Cumberland, WI, p. A709
BUUCK, Brian, Chief Executive Officer, Ridgeview Psychiatric Hospital And Center, Oak Ridge, TN, p. A591
BUYOK, Tammy K., President, Multicare Yakima Memorial Hospital, Yakima, WA, p. A698
BUZZAS, G. Rodney, M.D., Chief Medical Officer, St. Rose Dominican Hospitals – Siena Campus, Henderson, NV, p. A409
BYARS, Stephanie, Chief Nursing Officer, Unity Medical Center, Manchester, TN, p. A587
BYDA, Jeff, Vice President Information Technology, Mercy Fitzgerald Hospital, Darby, PA, p. A538
BYERS, Grant, Senior Vice President and Chief Financial Officer, South Georgia Medical Center, Valdosta, GA, p. A173
BYERS, John, M.D., Medical Director, Select Specialty Hospital–Tri Cities, Bristol, TN, p. A579
BYERS, Suzann, Director of Nursing, Southern Indiana Rehabilitation Hospital, New Albany, IN, p. A225

Index of Health Care Professionals / Byers

BYERS, Tracy P., FACHE, Chief Executive Officer, Lauderdale Community Hospital, Ripley, TN, p. A592
BYERS, William J., Chief Information Officer, UPMC Western Maryland, Cumberland, MD, p. A304
BYLER, Karen, Information Technology Generalist, Warren State Hospital, Warren, PA, p. A556
BYNUM, Justin, Chief Financial Officer, Saint Anthony Hospital, Chicago, IL, p. A191
BYORICK, Joseph, Senior Vice President and Chief Financial Officer, Penn Medicine Lancaster General Health, Lancaster, PA, p. A543
BYRAM, Ashley, Superintendent, Osawatomie State Hospital At Adair Acute Care, Osawatomie, KS, p. A256
BYRD, Catherine, Vice President Patient Services, Parkview Noble Hospital, Kendallville, IN, p. A221
BYRD, David T., Chief Executive Officer, The Hospitals of Providence Transmountain Campus – Tenet Healthcare, El Paso, TX, p. A617
BYRD, Greg, Vice President Medical Affairs, Valley Health – Shenandoah Memorial Hospital, Woodstock, VA, p. A686
BYRD, O Wayne, M.D., Chief of Staff, Ochsner Watkins Hospital, Quitman, MS, p. A368
BYRD–PELAEZ, Brenda, Chief Human Resources Management Office, Martinsburg Veterans Affairs Medical Center, Martinsburg, WV, p. A702
BYRNE, Bobbie, M.D., Chief Information Officer, Aurora Medical Center – Manitowoc County, Two Rivers, WI, p. A723
BYRNE, Frank J, Vice President Finance, Newport Hospital, Newport, RI, p. A560
BYRNE, John, M.D., Vice President and Chief Medical Officer, Chi St Luke's Health – Baylor St Luke's Medical Center, Houston, TX, p. A625
BYROM, David, Chief Executive Officer, Coryell Health, Gatesville, TX, p. A622

C

CAAMANO, Tero, Director Information Technology, Saint Clare's Denville Hospital, Denville, NJ, p. A420
CABALLERO, Rogelio, Chief Information Systems, San Jorge Children's And Women Hospital, Santurce, PR, p. A736
CABE, Jacque, Chief Financial Officer, UW Medicine/University of Washington Medical Center, Seattle, WA, p. A695
CABIBBO, Tiffany, Executive Vice President and Chief Nursing Officer, Mount Nittany Medical Center, State College, PA, p. A555
CABIGAO, Edwin, Chief Nursing Officer, San Francisco Campus for Jewish Living, San Francisco, CA, p. A91
CABIRO, Michael, Chief Executive Officer, Encompass Health Rehabilitation Hospital of Pearland, Pearland, TX, p. A643
CABLE, Cammie, Chief Human Resource Officer, Intermountain Medical Center, Murray, UT, p. A666
CABRERA, Ana, Vice President, Chief Nursing Officer, Baptist Health South Florida, Homestead Hospital, Homestead, FL, p. A134
CABRERA, Irma, Finance Director, Hospital San Carlos Borromeo, Moca, PR, p. A733
CABRERA, Sheelah, Chief Information Officer, La Rabida Children's Hospital, Chicago, IL, p. A190
CABUNOC, Brenda, Chief Human Resources, Greater Los Angeles Hcs, Los Angeles, CA, p. A72
CACCAMISE, Chad, Director Information Services, United Memorial Medical Center, Batavia, NY, p. A439
CACCAMO, Michael
  M.D., Chief Medical Officer, Kettering Health Greene Memorial, Xenia, OH, p. A508
  M.D., Chief Medical Officer, Soin Medical Center, Beavercreek, OH, p. A486
CACCHIONE, Joseph, M.D., Chief Executive Officer, Thomas Jefferson University Hospital, Philadelphia, PA, p. A550
CADAVID, Marly, Chief Nursing Officer, Ascension Sacred Heart Rehabilitation Hospital, Mequon, WI, p. A716
CADE, Paul, Chief Executive Officer and Administrator, Baptist Memorial Hospital – Memphis, Memphis, TN, p. A588
CADENA, Cyd, Vice President, Jay Hospital, Jay, FL, p. A135
CADIEUX, Marc
  Corporate Vice President and Chief Financial Officer, Children's Hospital of Wisconsin–Fox Valley, Neenah, WI, p. A718
  Corporate Vice President and Chief Financial Officer, Children's Wisconsin, Milwaukee, WI, p. A717
CADIGAN, Elizabeth, R.N., MSN, Senior Vice President Patient Care Services and Chief Nursing Officer, Cambridge Health Alliance, Cambridge, MA, p. A312

CADOGAN, David, Chief Medical Officer, Alaska Regional Hospital, Anchorage, AK, p. A27
CADORETTE, Brenda E, Chief Nursing Officer, Berkshire Medical Center, Pittsfield, MA, p. A317
CADWELL, Carrie, PsyD, Chief Executive Officer, 4C Health, Logansport, IN, p. A222
CADWELL, Jason, Chief Financial Officer, 4C Health, Logansport, IN, p. A222
CADY, Thomas, Vice President Human Resources, Heywood Hospital, Gardner, MA, p. A314
CADY, Tina, Controller, The Women's Hospital, Newburgh, IN, p. A225
CAFASSO, Michael
  Chief Executive Officer, Commonspirit – St. Mary-Corwin Hospital, Pueblo, CO, p. A112
  Chief Executive Officer, St. Thomas More Hospital, Canon City, CO, p. A104
CAGLE, Jennifer, Director of Nursing, North Mississipp. Medical Center–Hamilton, Hamilton, AL, p. A20
CAGLE, Karen, Chief Nursing Officer, Select Specialty Hospital Nashville, Nashville, TN, p. A590
CAGLE, LaDonna, HIM Appeals Coordinator III, Monroe Hospital, Bloomington, IN, p. A213
CAGLE, Lynn, Chief Nursing Officer, Parkwest Medical Center, Knoxville, TN, p. A586
CAGNA, Ralp. A
  Director Information Technology, Cleveland Clinic South Pointe Hospital, Warrensville Heights, OH, p. A506
  Director Information Technology Operations, Cleveland Clinic Health System South Market, Cleveland Clinic Marymount Hospital, Garfield Heights, OH, p. A496
CAHILL, Joseph, Executive Vice President and Chief Operating Officer, South Shore Hospital, South Weymouth, MA, p. A318
CAHILL, Patricia, Vice President, Patient Care Services and Chief Nursing Officer, Bronxcare Health System, New York, NY, p. A447
CAHO–MOONEY, Linda, Chief Financial Officer, Claiborne County Medical Center, Port Gibson, MS, p. A368
CAHOJ, Lindsey, Chief Nursing Officer, Select Specialty Hospital–Wichita, Wichita, KS, p. A262
CAHOJ, Nicholas, M.D., Chief of Staff, Community Healthcare System, Onaga, KS, p. A256
CAILLOUET, Danna, R.N., Chief Nursing Officer, Thibodaux Regional Health System, Thibodaux, LA, p. A294
CAIN, Brenda, Vice President and Chief Executive Officer, Jackson Health System, Miami, FL, p. A140
CAIN, Mark, Chief Executive Officer, Tennova Healthcare–Lafollette Medical Center, La Follette, TN, p. A586
CAIN, Roxie, Chief Financial Officer, Big Horn Hospital, Hardin, MT, p. A392
CAIN, Tom, Chief Executive Officer, Huntington Creek Recovery Center, Shickshinny, PA, p. A555
CAINE, Jamie, Director of Human Resources, Multicare Valley Hospital, Spokane Valley, WA, p. A696
CAINE, Natalie, Chief Administrative Officer, Mayo Clinic Hospital – Rochester, Rochester, MN, p. A353
CAIRNS, Craig, M.D., Vice President Medical Affairs, Licking Memorial Hospital, Newark, OH, p. A501
CALAIS, C Matthew, Senior Vice President and Chief Information Officer, Legacy Good Samaritan Medical Center, Portland, OR, p. A530
CALAMARI, Jacquelyn, MSN, MS, Chief Nursing Officer and Vice President, Patient Care Services, Middlesex Health, Middletown, CT, p. A117
CALANDRIELLO, John, Vice President and Chief Financial Officer, Hackensack Meridian Health Palisades Medical Center, North Bergen, NJ, p. A426
CALARCO, Marge, Chief Nursing Executive, University of Michigan Medical Center, Ann Arbor, MI, p. A321
CALAWAY, Shearmaine, Director Human Resources, East Mississipp. State Hospital, Meridian, MS, p. A366
CALBY, Elizabeth, Vice President Human Resources, Advocate Good Samaritan Hospital, Downers Grove, IL, p. A193
CALDARI, Patricia, Vice President, Richmond University Medical Center, New York, NY, p. A452
CALDEIRA, Amy, Director Information Technology and Systems, HCA Florida Fort Walton–Destin Hospital, Fort Walton Beach, FL, p. A132
CALDER, Gina
  M.P.H., FACHE, President, Midstate Medical Center, Meriden, CT, p. A116
  M.P.H., FACHE, President, The Hospital of Central Connecticut, New Britain, CT, p. A117
CALDERA, Ken, Director Human Resources, Kessler Institute for Rehabilitation, West Orange, NJ, p. A430
CALDERON, Lizmari, Director Finance, Hospital De La Concepcion, San German, PR, p. A734
CALDWELL, Andrew, Chief Financial Officer, City of Hop. Atlanta, Newnan, GA, p. A169

CALDWELL, Carolyn P., FACHE, President and Chief Executive Officer, St. Mary Medical Center Long Beach, Long Beach, CA, p. A71
CALDWELL, Dan, Chief Executive Officer, South Texas Health System, Edinburg, TX, p. A615
CALDWELL, Darren, Chief Executive Officer, Mercy Hospital Berryville, Berryville, AR, p. A43
CALDWELL, Eric, Director Finance, Northside Hospital Forsyth, Cumming, GA, p. A162
CALDWELL, Lisa, Chief Nursing Officer, Encompass Health Rehabilitation Hospital of Huntington, Huntington, WV, p. A701
CALDWELL, Matthew T., Market President, Bon Secours St. Francis Health System, Greenville, SC, p. A566
CALDWELL, Noah, Vice President and Chief Information Officer, Mount Sinai South Nassau, Oceanside, NY, p. A454
CALDWELL, Paul, Facility Coordinator Information Technology Customer Relations, Page Hospital, Page, AZ, p. A34
CALDWELL, Samantha, Chief Executive Officer, Dignity Health East Valley Rehabilitation Hospital – Gilbert, Gilbert, AZ, p. A32
CALDWELL, Steve, Vice President Finance and Chief Financial Officer, SSM Health St. Mary's Hospital, Madison, WI, p. A714
CALEY, Carl
  Chief Financial Officer, Forest View Psychiatric Hospital, Grand Rapids, MI, p. A328
  Chief Financial Officer, Spring Valley Hospital Medical Center, Las Vegas, NV, p. A411
CALHOUN, Cathy, Director Human Resources, River Point Behavioral Health, Jacksonville, FL, p. A135
CALHOUN, Joshua, M.D., Medical Director, Hawthorn Children Psychiatric Hospital, Saint Louis, MO, p. A385
CALHOUN, Michael, Chief Executive Officer, Citizens Memorial Hospital, Bolivar, MO, p. A371
CALHOUN, Rob, President and Chief Executive Offricer, West Jefferson Medical Center, Marrero, LA, p. A288
CALHOUN, Timothy
  Vice President Finance and Chief Financial Officer, Corewell Health Lakeland Hospitals, Saint Joseph, MI, p. A337
  Vice President Finance, Chief Financial Officer, Corewell Health Watervliet Hospital, Watervliet, MI, p. A340
CALHOUN, William, FACHE, Chief Executive, Providence St. Patrick Hospital, Missoula, MT, p. A394
CALIA, Christopher, Vice President Human Resources, Chi St. Luke's Health Brazosport, Lake Jackson, TX, p. A633
CALIFORNIA, Randy, Chief Operating Officer, Warren General Hospital, Warren, PA, p. A556
CALIME, Erica, Director Human Resources, Carrollton Regional Medical Center, Carrollton, TX, p. A606
CALIVA, Todd, FACHE, Chief Executive Officer, HCA Houston Healthcare Clear Lake, Webster, TX, p. A661
CALKIN, Steven, D.O., Vice President Medical Affairs, Mclaren Oakland, Pontiac, MI, p. A335
CALKINS, Megan, R.N., Chief Nursing Officer, T. J. Samson Community Hospital, Glasgow, KY, p. A266
CALKINS, Paul, M.D., Chief Medical Officer, Indiana University Health North Hospital, Carmel, IN, p. A214
CALL, Stacie
  R.N., Vice President Patient Care and Chief Nursing Officer, East Liverpool City Hospital, East Liverpool, OH, p. A495
  Chief Nursing Officer, Mercy Health – St. Elizabeth Boardman Hospital, Boardman, OH, p. A486
CALLAHAN, Ame, Acting Manager Resource Management Service, Bob Stump Department of Veterans Affairs Medical Center, Prescott, AZ, p. A37
CALLAHAN, Christopher M, Vice President Human Resources, Exeter Hospital, Exeter, NH, p. A415
CALLAHAN, Kelly, Public Information Officer, Elgin Mental Health Center, Elgin, IL, p. A194
CALLAHAN, Larry A., Senior Vice President Human Resources, Grady Health System, Atlanta, GA, p. A157
CALLAHAN, Mark, Chief Operating Officer, Mary Lanning Healthcare, Hastings, NE, p. A400
CALLAHAN, Neil, Chief Executive Officer, Brooke Glen Behavioral Hospital, Fort Washington, PA, p. A540
CALLAHAN, William, Chief Information Management Division, Bayne-Jones Army Community Hospital, Fort Polk, LA, p. A282
CALLAN, Michael, Executive Vice President and Chief Financial Officer, Kidspeace Children's Hospital, Orefield, PA, p. A547
CALLAS, Robin B
  Human Resource Director, Springbrook Behavioral Health, Travelers Rest, SC, p. A571
  Vice President Human Resources, Rutherford Regional Health System, Rutherfordton, NC, p. A475
CALLAWAY, Blair, Chief Financial Officer, Texas Orthopedic Hospital, Houston, TX, p. A628
CALLENDER, Wesley Scott, Administrator, Mercy Health Love County, Marietta, OK, p. A514

Index of Health Care Professionals / Capers

Index of Health Care Professionals

CALLENS, Don, M.D., Chief Medical Officer, Liberty Dayton Regional Medical Center, Liberty, TX, p. A634
CALLENS, Paul A., Ph.D., Director, North Mississipp. State Hospital, Tupelo, MS, p. A369
CALLERY, Sally, Director Human Resources, Great Falls Clinic Hospital, Great Falls, MT, p. A392
CALLICOAT, William, President, Multicare Capital Medical Center, Olympia, WA, p. A692
CALLISTE, Gregory, Ph.D., FACHE, Chief Executive Officer, NYC Health + Hospitals/Woodhull, New York, NY, p. A452
CALLMAN, Mark, M.D., Chief Medical Officer, HCA Florida Fawcett Hospital, Port Charlotte, FL, p. A147
CALLOWAY, Maria
R.N., MSN, Chief Nursing Officer, HCA Florida Lake Monroe Hospital, Sanford, FL, p. A149
Chief Nursing Officer, Musc Health Columbia Medical Center Downtown, Columbia, SC, p. A564
CALLUM, David, Chief Financial Officer, Sebastian River Medical Center, Sebastian, FL, p. A150
CALUBAQUIB, Evelyn, Chief Nursing Officer, Greater El Monte Community Hospital, South El Monte, CA, p. A96
CALVERT, Mandy, Director Information Systems, Southern Coos Hospital And Health Center, Bandon, OR, p. A525
CALVERT, Sarah, Chief Nursing Officer, Mcgehee Hospital, Mcgehee, AR, p. A50
CALVIN, Irene, Vice President Human Resources, South Oaks Hospital, Amityville, NY, p. A438
CALVIN, Jeff, Chief Financial Officer, Michiana Behavioral Health Center, Plymouth, IN, p. A226
CAMACHO, Leslie, R.N., Director of Nursing, Commonwealth Health Center, Saipan, MARIANA ISLANDS, p. A730
CAMARDELLO, Heidi, Vice President Patient Care Services and Chief Nursing Officer, Little Falls Hospital, Little Falls, NY, p. A445
CAMARENA, Elizabeth, Chief Human Resource Officer, Palmetto General Hospital, Hialeah, FL, p. A133
CAMERON, Carl, Director Information Systems, Holyoke Medical Center, Holyoke, MA, p. A314
CAMERON, Kim, Manager Health Information Services, Patients' Hospital of Redding, Redding, CA, p. A85
CAMERON, Shanna, Chief Financial Officer, Seton Medical Center Harker Heights, Harker Heights, TX, p. A623
CAMERON, Shauna, FACHE, Chief Executive Officer, Houlton Regional Hospital, Houlton, ME, p. A297
CAMILLUS, Joe, Chief Operating Officer, Boston Medical Center, Boston, MA, p. A310
CAMMACK, Geri, R.N., Director of Nursing, Lost Rivers Medical Center, Arco, ID, p. A179
CAMMENGA, Randall, M.D., Vice President Medical Affairs, Goshen Health, Goshen, IN, p. A217
CAMP, David, Director Human Resources, St. Mary's Regional Medical Center, Enid, OK, p. A512
CAMP, Kendra, R.N., Chief Executive Officer, Amg Specialty Hospital–Albuquerque, Albuquerque, NM, p. A432
CAMP–FRY, Zaynah, Chief Executive Officer, Encompass Health Rehabilitation Hospital of Miami, Cutler Bay, FL, p. A129
CAMPA, Melissa, Controller, Kindred Hospital El Paso, El Paso, TX, p. A616
CAMPANA, Thomas, M.D., Chief of Staff, Corewell Health Reed City Hospital, Reed City, MI, p. A336
CAMPANELLA, Alfred, Chief Information Officer, Virtua Voorhees, Voorhees, NJ, p. A430
CAMPANILE, Vicki, R.N., MS, Chief Nursing Officer, Monadnock Community Hospital, Peterborough, NH, p. A417
CAMPAS, Janice, Chief Financial Officer, Wichita County Health Center, Leoti, KS, p. A253
CAMPBELL, Al, FACHE, R.N., President, Winchester Hospital, Winchester, MA, p. A320
CAMPBELL, Alicia, Vice President, Facility Executive, Atrium Health Pineville, Charlotte, NC, p. A465
CAMPBELL, Amy, Chief Financial Officer, Community Hospital North, Indianapolis, IN, p. A219
CAMPBELL, Andrew, Associate Executive Director, NYC Health + Hospitals/South Brooklyn Health, New York, NY, p. A452
CAMPBELL, April, Director Human Resources, Billings Clinic Broadwater, Townsend, MT, p. A396
CAMPBELL, Bernard M, Administrator Human Resources, Lewisgale Hospital Alleghany, Low Moor, VA, p. A678
CAMPBELL, Brian, Director Professional Services, U. S. Public Health Service Indian Hospital–Whiteriver, Whiteriver, AZ, p. A41
CAMPBELL, C Scott, Market Chief Executive Officer, Physicians Regional – Pine Ridge, Naples, FL, p. A142
CAMPBELL, Christine, Controller, Vanderbilt Stallworth Rehabilitation Hospital, Nashville, TN, p. A591
CAMPBELL, Cinthia, Chief Nursing Officer, Encompass Health Rehabilitation Hospital of Chattanooga, Chattanooga, TN, p. A580
CAMPBELL, Dean, Vice President Information Services and Chief Information Officer, PIH Health Good Samaritan Hospital, Los Angeles, CA, p. A74
CAMPBELL, Debra, R.N., Administrator, Riverside Regional Medical Center, Newport News, VA, p. A680
CAMPBELL, Dennis
II, R.N., Interim President, ECU Health North Hospital, Roanoke Rapids, NC, p. A475
R.N., President, ECU Health Medical Center, Greenville, NC, p. A470
CAMPBELL, Emily, Assistant Vice President People and Patient Experience, The University of Vermont Health Network – Alice Hyde Medical Center, Malone, NY, p. A445
CAMPBELL, Eric, Chief Financial Officer, Oswego Hospital, Oswego, NY, p. A455
CAMPBELL, Ivy, Director of Nursing, Community Medical Center, Inc., Falls City, NE, p. A399
CAMPBELL, Jaime, President and Chief Executive Officer, Intermountain Health Platte Valley Hospital, Brighton, CO, p. A104
CAMPBELL, Jennie, Chief Financial Officer, Midcoast Central – Llano, Llano, TX, p. A635
CAMPBELL, Jessica, Chief Executive Officer, Wellstone Regional Hospital, Jeffersonville, IN, p. A221
CAMPBELL, John
Chief Information Officer, Spaulding Hospital for Continuing Medical Care Cambridge, Cambridge, MA, p. A312
Chief Information Officer, Spaulding Rehabilitation Hospital, Charlestown, MA, p. A312
Chief Information Officer, Spaulding Rehabilitation Hospital Cap. Cod, East Sandwich, MA, p. A313
CAMPBELL, Keith, Chief Medical Officer, Tristar Hendersonville Medical Center, Hendersonville, TN, p. A584
CAMPBELL, Kevin, Chief Executive Officer, Ascension Saint Thomas Hickman, Centerville, TN, p. A580
CAMPBELL, Levi, R.N., Interim Chief Nursing Officer, Prisma Health Tuomey Hospital, Sumter, SC, p. A570
CAMPBELL, Matthew J. Esq, Regional Chief Executive Officer, Select Specialty Hospital – Corewell Health Grand Rapids, Grand Rapids, MI, p. A328
CAMPBELL, Melissa, Chief Financial Officer and Controller, Mercy Rehabilition Hospital Springfield, Springfield, MO, p. A387
CAMPBELL, Melvin, M.D., Medical Staff Chairman, Brown County Hospital, Ainsworth, NE, p. A397
CAMPBELL, Pamela, M.D., Medical Director, Lincoln Prairie Behavioral Health Center, Springfield, IL, p. A209
CAMPBELL, Paul, Director Technology Support and Operations, UT Health East Texas Rehabilitation Hospital, Tyler, TX, p. A659
CAMPBELL, Rhonda, Chief Executive Officer, Liberty Dayton Regional Medical Center, Liberty, TX, p. A634
CAMPBELL, Sandra M., R.N., Chief Nursing Officer, Dodge County Hospital, Eastman, GA, p. A163
CAMPBELL, Scott, Chief Executive Officer, University of Kansas Health System St. Francis Campus, Topeka, KS, p. A261
CAMPBELL, Shari, Chief Operating Officer, Kearny County Hospital, Lakin, KS, p. A252
CAMPBELL, Sharon J, Director, Human Resources, Adventhealth Hendersonville, Hendersonville, NC, p. A470
CAMPBELL, Stephen J, Chief Operating Officer, Pioneers Memorial Healthcare District, Brawley, CA, p. A58
CAMPBELL, Suzannah, President, Ascension St. Vincent's East, Birmingham, AL, p. A16
CAMPBELL, Suzanne, R.N., Director Patient Services, Monument Health Spearfish Hospital, Spearfish, SD, p. A577
CAMPBELL, Teresa, R.N., Chief Nursing Executive, Sutter Lakeside Hospital, Lakeport, CA, p. A69
CAMPBELL, Vicky, Vice President Mental Health and Support Services, Ascension Providence, Waco, TX, p. A660
CAMPBELL, Whitney, Chief Financial Officer, Johnson Regional Medical Center, Clarksville, AR, p. A44
CAMPEAU, Arleen, R.N., Vice President Patient Care Services, Chief Nursing Officer, Powell Valley Health Care, Powell, WY, p. A728
CAMPION, Matthew, Administrator, Avera Hand County Memorial Hospital, Miller, SD, p. A574
CAMPOS, Adrian, Chief Executive Officer, Pam Specialty Hospital of Las Vegas, Las Vegas, NV, p. A410
CAMPOS, Emilio, Department Head Information Technology, Guadalup. County Hospital, Santa Rosa, NM, p. A437
CAMPOVERDE, Jacqueline, Business Manager, Essex County Hospital Center, Cedar Grove, NJ, p. A419
CAMPS, Lourdes, Chief Operating Officer, Hialeah Hospital, Hialeah, FL, p. A133
CANALE, Joseph, Business Manager, Trenton Psychiatric Hospital, Trenton, NJ, p. A429
CANALES, Antonio, Chief Financial Officer, Cleveland Emergency Hospital, Humble, TX, p. A629
CANALES, Joe
Director Human Resources, Ascension Seton Edgar B. Davis Hospital, Luling, TX, p. A637
Director Human Resources, Ascension Seton Shoal Creek, Austin, TX, p. A599
Vice President Human Resources, Ascension Seton Medical Center Austin, Austin, TX, p. A599
Vice President Human Resources, Ministry Market Texas, Dell Seton Medical Center At The University of Texas, Austin, TX, p. A600
Vice President, Ascension and Human Resources Officer, Texas Market, Ascension Seton Northwest, Austin, TX, p. A599
CANARD, Robert Shannon., Chief Executive Officer, Select Specialty Hospital–Jackson, Jackson, MS, p. A364
CANCEL, Diana, Director Human Resources, Glendora Hospital, Glendora, CA, p. A66
CANDELA, Chris, President and Chief Executive Officer, Mclaren Flint, Flint, MI, p. A327
CANDILIS, Phillip. M.D., Director, Medical Affairs, Saint Elizabeths Hospital, Washington, DC, p. A124
CANDILL, James W, M.D., President Medical Staff, Charleston Surgical Hospital, Charleston, WV, p. A700
CANDULLO, Carl, Chief Information Officer, Adventhealth Ocala, Ocala, FL, p. A143
CANEDO, Jim, Chief Financial Officer, College Medical Center, Long Beach, CA, p. A70
CANESTARO, Jasmine, Assistant Vice President, Operations, Schuyler Hospital, Montour Falls, NY, p. A446
CANFIELD, Brian, President and Chief Executive Officer, Blessing Hospital, Quincy, IL, p. A206
CANFIELD, Michael, Chief Information Officer, Augusta Health, Fishersville, VA, p. A676
CANFIELD, Tammy, Chief Information Officer, Wynn Hospital, Utica, NY, p. A460
CANIZARO, Tom, Vice President and Chief Financial Officer, South Central Regional Medical Center, Laurel, MS, p. A365
CANLAS, Emma, Chief Financial Officer, Valley View Medical Center, Fort Mohave, AZ, p. A31
CANNIFF, Christopher, Executive Director, Human Resources, Umass Memorial Health – Harrington, Southbridge, MA, p. A318
CANNING, John, Chief Financial Officer, Blythedale Children's Hospital, Valhalla, NY, p. A460
CANNON, Brenda, R.N., Director of Nursing, Greeneville Community Hospital East, Greeneville, TN, p. A583
CANNON, Colleen
Chief Financial Officer, South Central Health, Wishek, ND, p. A483
Chief Financial Officer and Chief Operational Officer, SMP Health – St. Aloisius, Harvey, ND, p. A481
Chief Operating Officer and Chief Financial Officer, SMP Health – St. Aloisius, Harvey, ND, p. A481
CANNON, Don, Chief Financial Officer, St. George Regional Hospital, Saint George, UT, p. A668
CANNON, Gayle, Director Human Resources, Childress Regional Medical Center, Childress, TX, p. A607
CANNON, Heather, M.D., Medical Director, Neshoba General, Philadelphia, MS, p. A367
CANNON, Linda, Chief Medical Records Services, San Diego County Psychiatric Hospital, San Diego, CA, p. A89
CANNON, Lorraine, Chief Financial Officer, Olympic Medical Center, Port Angeles, WA, p. A693
CANNON, William, M.D., Medical Director, Fort Healthcare, Fort Atkinson, WI, p. A711
CANO, Daniel, M.D., Chief Medical Officer, Citizens Medical Center, Victoria, TX, p. A660
CANSLER, Vicki A, Chief Human Resource Officer, Piedmont Atlanta Hospital, Atlanta, GA, p. A158
CANTLEY, J Scott., President and Chief Executive Officer, Marietta Memorial Hospital, Marietta, OH, p. A499
CANTRE, Pedro Laureano, Chief Nursing Officer, Cardiovascular Center of Puerto Rico And The Caribbean, San Juan, PR, p. A734
CANTRELL, David, CPA, Vice President and Chief Financial Officer, UCLA West Valley Medical Center, Los Angeles, CA, p. A75
CANTU, Andrew, Chief Financial Officer, Kern Medical, Bakersfield, CA, p. A57
CANTU, Janie, Director Human Resources, Crosbyton Clinic Hospital, Crosbyton, TX, p. A610
CANTWELL, Angela, R.N., MSN, Chief Executive Officer, Friends Hospital, Philadelphia, PA, p. A548
CAPECE, Vincent G. Jr, President and Chief Executive Officer, Middlesex Health, Middletown, CT, p. A117
CAPERS, Travis, FACHE, Chief Executive Officer, Regional Community Hospitals, Vanderbilt Bedford Hospital, Shelbyville, TN, p. A593

© 2025 AHA Guide Index of Health Care Professionals **A813**

Index of Health Care Professionals

Index of Health Care Professionals / Capili

CAPILI, Anthony, M.D., Chief of Staff, Chambers Health, Anahuac, TX, p. A597
CAPIOLA, Richard, M.D., Chief Medical Officer, Baton Rouge Behavioral Hospital, Baton Rouge, LA, p. A277
CAPITELLI, Robert, M.D., Senior Vice President and Chief Medical Officer, St. Tammany Health System, Covington, LA, p. A280
CAPITULO, Kathleen, Ph.D., R.N., Chief Nurse Executive, James J. Peters Veterans Affairs Medical Center, New York, NY, p. A448
CAPIZZI, Thomas, Vice President Human Resources, Choc Children's At Mission Hospital, Mission Viejo, CA, p. A77
CAPLE, Jocelyn, M.D., Interim President and Chief Executive Officer, Valley Regional Hospital, Claremont, NH, p. A414
CAPO, Ann Marie, R.N., Chief Nursing Officer, Vice President, Quality and Patient Services, Uconn, John Dempsey Hospital, Farmington, CT, p. A116
CAPOTE, Henry, Interim Chief Financial Officer, Coral Gables Hospital, Coral Gables, FL, p. A128
CAPOTE, Jerry
M.D., Chief Medical Officer, Broward Health Imperial Point, Fort Lauderdale, FL, p. A131
M.D., Chief Medical Officer, Broward Health North, Deerfield Beach, FL, p. A130
CAPPEL, Blaine, Director Information Systems, Memorial Health System, Abilene, KS, p. A246
CAPPLEMAN, Troy, M.D., Chief of Staff, Tippah County Hospital, Ripley, MS, p. A368
CAPPS, Anita
R.N., Chief Nursing Executive, Community Hospital South, Indianapolis, IN, p. A219
R.N., Hospital Administrator and Chief Nurse Executive, Community Hospital South, Indianapolis, IN, p. A219
CAPPS, Jeremy, Chief Executive Officer, Delta Health System, Dumas, AR, p. A45
CAPPS, Kim, Chief Financial Officer, University of Michigan Health–Sparrow Eaton, Charlotte, MI, p. A323
CAPPS, Melissa, Site Leader Information Technology, St. Luke's Magic Valley Medical Center, Twin Falls, ID, p. A184
CAPPS, Rick, Chief Financial Officer, Cumberland County Hospital, Burkesville, KY, p. A264
CAPRICO, Rick, Chief Financial Officer, Garnet Health Medical Center – Catskills, Harris Campus, Harris, NY, p. A444
CAPSHAW, Marcia
Administrator, West Central Georgia Regional Hospital, Columbus, GA, p. A161
Chief Operating Officer, West Central Georgia Regional Hospital, Columbus, GA, p. A161
CAPUANO, Tony, Chief Operating Officer, Saint Francis Hospital Muskogee, Muskogee, OK, p. A515
CAPUTO, Joseph, Vice President, Operations, Mercy Specialty Hospital Southeast Kansas, Galena, KS, p. A249
CAPUTO, Louis, Chief Executive Officer, Tristar Stonecrest Medical Center, Smyrna, TN, p. A593
CARABALLO, Amanda, Nursing Director, Hospital De La Concepcion, San German, PR, p. A734
CARACCIOLO, Kevin, Chief Human Resources Officer, Palm Beach Gardens Medical Center, Palm Beach Gardens, FL, p. A145
CARACCIOLO, Mary Jo, Human Resource Director, Wellington Regional Medical Center, Wellington, FL, p. A154
CARBALLO, Francisco R., M.D., Medical Director, Hospital Hima De Humacao, Humacao, PR, p. A733
CARBONE, Dominick, M.D., Chief of Staff, Hugh Chatham Health, Elkin, NC, p. A468
CARBONE, Karen
M.D., Chief Medical Officer, Dmc Detroit Receiving Hospital & University Health Center, Detroit, MI, p. A325
M.D., Chief Medical Officer, Dmc Harper University Hospital, Detroit, MI, p. A325
CARD, Dean
Chief Financial Officer, Kindred Hospital South Florida–Fort Lauderdale, Fort Lauderdale, FL, p. A131
Chief Financial Officer, Kindred Hospital The Palm Beaches, Riviera Beach, FL, p. A148
CARD, Jennifer, Chief Executive Officer, Canyon Creek Behavioral Health, Temple, TX, p. A656
CARDA, Greg, Vice President Finance, Missouri Delta Medical Center, Sikeston, MO, p. A386
CARDA, Vern, Chief Executive Officer, Estes Park Health, Estes Park, CO, p. A107
CARDENAS, Lydia, Director Human Resources, River Crest Hospital, San Angelo, TX, p. A648
CARDENAS, Mark, Director Plant Operations, Vibra Hospital of Northern California, Redding, CA, p. A85
CARDENAS, Mitzi
Executive Chief Administrative Officer, University Health–Lakewood Medical Center, Kansas City, MO, p. A378
Executive Chief Administrative Officer, University Health–Truman Medical Center, Kansas City, MO, p. A378
CARDENAS, Noel J., FACHE, Senior Vice President and Chief Executive Officer, Memorial Hermann Greater Heights Hospital, Houston, TX, p. A627
CARDIFF, Michael, Systems Supervisor, Ochsner Abrom Kaplan Memorial Hospital, Kaplan, LA, p. A284
CARDONA, Alysia, Chief Operating Officer, Hop. Health Care Center, Keams Canyon, AZ, p. A32
CARDOZA, Phuong, Chief Executive Officer, West Oaks Hospital, Houston, TX, p. A629
CARDWELL, Marian, Chief Financial Officer, WVU Medicine Potomac Valley Hospital, Keyser, WV, p. A702
CAREW LYONS, Aimee, Ph.D., R.N., Chief Nursing Officer, Nantucket Cottage Hospital, Nantucket, MA, p. A316
CAREY, Ann
Chief Information Officer, Ascension St. Vincent's Southside, Jacksonville, FL, p. A134
Vice President and Chief Information Officer, Ascension St. Vincent's Riverside, Jacksonville, FL, p. A134
CAREY, Calvin
Chief Financial Officer, Mt. San Rafael Hospital, Trinidad, CO, p. A114
Chief Financial Officer, Summit Medical Center, Casper, WY, p. A726
CAREY, Daniel, M.D., President, Corewell Health William Beaumont University Hospital, Royal Oak, MI, p. A336
CAREY, Eric R, Vice President Information Systems and Chief Information Officer, Valley Hospital, Paramus, NJ, p. A426
CAREY, Robin, Director of Nursing, Jasper Memorial Hospital, Monticello, GA, p. A168
CARIGSON, John, Chief Financial Officer, Covenant Specialty Hospital, Lubbock, TX, p. A636
CARIKER, Kelly, Chief Information Officer, North Valley Hospital, Tonasket, WA, p. A697
CARIUS, Glenda, R.N., MSN, Chief Executive Officer, Encompass Health Rehabilitation Hospital of Clermont, Clermont, FL, p. A128
CARLE, Chris, Senior Vice President and Chief Operating Officer, St. Elizabeth Florence, Florence, KY, p. A265
CARLETON, David
Chief Information Officer, Heritage Valley Beaver, Beaver, PA, p. A535
Chief Information Officer, Sewickley Valley Hospital, (A Division of Valley Medical Facilities), Sewickley, PA, p. A555
CARLISLE, Brenda H., R.N., Chief Executive Officer, University of Alabama Hospital, Birmingham, AL, p. A17
CARLISLE, Charles, Director, East Mississipp. State Hospital, Meridian, MS, p. A366
CARLISLE, Sandy, Manager Human Resources, Holzer Medical Center – Jackson, Jackson, OH, p. A497
CARLOS, Ilona, M.D., President Medical Staff, Thorek Memorial Hospital, Chicago, IL, p. A191
CARLSON, Andrew, Chief Executive Officer, Denton Rehab, Denton, TX, p. A613
CARLSON, Beth, R.N., Chief Nurse Executive, St. Rose Dominican Hospitals – Siena Campus, Henderson, NV, p. A409
CARLSON, Daniel, M.D., Chief Medical Officer, Holston Valley Medical Center, Kingsport, TN, p. A585
CARLSON, Kellie, Director Human Resources, Coastal Harbor Treatment Center, Savannah, GA, p. A171
CARLSON, Kim, Director Human Resources, Essentia Health Northern Pines, Aurora, MN, p. A343
CARLSON, Lisa, Chief Financial Officer, Adena Pike Medical Center, Waverly, OH, p. A506
CARLSON, Richard, Chief Financial Officer, Crawford Memorial Hospital, Robinson, IL, p. A207
CARLSON, Sandee, Director of Nursing, Essentia Health Duluth, Duluth, MN, p. A346
CARLSON, Sarah, Director Human Resources, Essentia Health–St. Joseph's Medical Center, Brainerd, MN, p. A344
CARLSON, Scott, Director, Mary Greeley Medical Center, Ames, IA, p. A230
CARLSON, Shannon, Chief Operating Officer, Lifecare Medical Center, Roseau, MN, p. A354
CARLSON, Wendie, Chief Human Resources Officer, Jackson–Madison County General Hospital, Medina, TN, p. A588
CARLSON, Wendy, Director Human Resources, Pathways of Tennessee, Jackson, TN, p. A584
CARLTON, Andrew, Chief Executive Officer, Mesa Springs, Fort Worth, TX, p. A620
CARLTON, Roy, Chief Financial Officer, Walter B. Jones Alcohol And Drug Abuse Treatment Center, Greenville, NC, p. A470
CARLUCCI, Ashley M.
R.N., Chief Nursing Officer, University Hospitals Conneaut Medical Center, Conneaut, OH, p. A493
R.N., Chief Nursing Officer, University Hospitals Geneva Medical Center, Geneva, OH, p. A496
CARLYLE, Dave, Director Human Resources, Wayne County Hospital And Clinic System, Corydon, IA, p. A233
CARMAN, Susan, Chief Information Officer, United Health Services Hospitals–Binghamton, Binghamton, NY, p. A439
CARMAN, Thomas H., President and Chief Executive Officer, Samaritan Medical Center, Watertown, NY, p. A461
CARMEN, Lee, Associate Vice President Health Care Information Systems, University of Iowa Hospitals & Clinics, Iowa City, IA, p. A238
CARMICHAEL, Craig, President and Chief Operating Officer, Senior Vice President, LifeBridge Health, Northwest Hospital, Randallstown, MD, p. A306
CARMICHAEL, Gavin H, FACHE, Chief Operating Officer, Alaska Psychiatric Institute, Anchorage, AK, p. A27
CARMODY, Erika, Interim Chief Nursing Officer, Regional West Medical Center, Scottsbluff, NE, p. A406
CARMODY, James, Vice President Human Resources, Wilkes–Barre General Hospital, Wilkes–Barre, PA, p. A558
CARNAHAN, Robert H. II, R.N., Chief Executive Officer, Banner Churchill Community Hospital, Fallon, NV, p. A408
CARNES, Ruth, Director Human Resources, Ochsner American Legion Hospital, Jennings, LA, p. A284
CARNEY, Adrienne, R.N., Director Nursing and Surgical Services, Kearney Regional Medical Center, Kearney, NE, p. A401
CARNEY, Courtney Bishop., Chief Executive Officer, Pinnacle Pointe Behavioral Healthcare System, Little Rock, AR, p. A50
CARNEY, Eric
President and Chief Executive Officer, Monmouth Medical Center, Long Branch Campus, Long Branch, NJ, p. A423
President and Chief Executive Officer, Monmouth Medical Center, Southern Campus, Lakewood, NJ, p. A422
CARNEY, Judi, M.D., President Medical Staff, Baptist Memorial Hospital for Women, Memphis, TN, p. A588
CARO, Vique, Chief Information Officer, Cincinnati Veterans Affairs Medical Center, Cincinnati, OH, p. A488
CAROLINA, Dorinda, Chief Human Resources Officer, Jefferson Health Northeast, Philadelphia, PA, p. A549
CARON, Jacqueline, Chief Human Resources, Birmingham Va Medical Center, Birmingham, AL, p. A16
CARON, Roger
Chief Executive Officer, Nexus Children's Hospital Houston, Houston, TX, p. A627
Chief Executive Officer, Nexus Speciality Hospital – The Woodlands Campus, The Woodlands, TX, p. A657
Chief Executive Officer, Nexus Specialty Hospital The Woodlands, The Woodlands, TX, p. A657
CARON, William J., Medical Center Director, North Las Vegas Va Medical Center, North Las Vegas, NV, p. A412
CAROSELLI, Cynthia A., R.N., Ph.D., Chief Nursing Officer, Veterans Affairs New York Harbor Healthcare System, New York, NY, p. A453
CAROZZA, Sally, Director Human Resources, West Penn Hospital, Pittsburgh, PA, p. A552
CARPENTER, Curt, Manager Information Technology, Coquille Valley Hospital, Coquille, OR, p. A526
CARPENTER, Deb, Director Information Technology, Lourdes Health, Pasco, WA, p. A692
CARPENTER, Eric, Chief Executive Officer, Eastern State Hospital, Medical Lake, WA, p. A691
CARPENTER, Garen, Chief Executive Officer, Van Buren County Hospital, Keosauqua, IA, p. A238
CARPENTER, Jackie, Office Manager, Rock County Hospital, Bassett, NE, p. A397
CARPENTER, Jennifer, Chief Nursing Officer, Northern Louisiana Medical Center, Ruston, LA, p. A291
CARPENTER, Shawn, Chief Executive Officer, Pearl River County Hospital, Poplarville, MS, p. A368
CARPENTER, Stephanie, Director of Nursing Services, Columbia County Health System, Dayton, WA, p. A689
CARPER, Joleen, Vice President Quality and Risk, Tri–State Memorial Hospital, Clarkston, WA, p. A688
CARR, Ann, R.N., Chief Nursing Officer, Saint Francis Hospital Vinita, Vinita, OK, p. A523
CARR, Celia, MSN, R.N., Director of Nursing, Christus Coushatta Health Care Center, Coushatta, LA, p. A280
CARR, David, M.D., Physician Medical Director, The Rehabilitation Institute of St. Louis, Saint Louis, MO, p. A384
CARR, Deborah, Vice President Human Resources, Garnet Health Medical Center, Middletown, NY, p. A446
CARR, Desiree, Director Human Resources, Minidoka Memorial Hospital, Rupert, ID, p. A183
CARR, James
Chief Information Officer, NYC Health + Hospitals/Bellevue, New York, NY, p. A450
Chief Information Officer, NYC Health + Hospitals/Lincoln, New York, NY, p. A451

A814 Index of Health Care Professionals

Index of Health Care Professionals / Case

Index of Health Care Professionals

CARR, Julie R., Chief Nursing Officer, Roane General Hospital, Spencer, WV, p. A705
CARR, Kay
Chief Information Officer, Bryn Mawr Hospital, Bryn Mawr, PA, p. A536
Chief Information Officer, Bryn Mawr Rehabilitation Hospital, Malvern, PA, p. A545
Chief Information Officer, Lankenau Medical Center, Wynnewood, PA, p. A558
Senior Vice President and Chief Information Officer, Paoli Hospital, Paoli, PA, p. A547
CARR, Randall, Director Human Resources, Roane Medical Center, Harriman, TN, p. A583
CARR, Sheila, Chief Executive Officer, Wekiva Springs, Jacksonville, FL, p. A135
CARRADINE, Damon, Director Information Technology, Highland Hospital, Charleston, WV, p. A700
CARRANZA, Diana, Associate Director, Veterans Affairs Illiana Health Care System, Danville, IL, p. A192
CARRASCO, Carlos, Chief Operating Officer, Orlando Health Orlando Regional Medical Center, Orlando, FL, p. A144
CARRASCO, Michelle, Director Human Resources, Palo Verde Behavioral Health, Tucson, AZ, p. A40
CARRASCO, Victor, Chief Executive Officer, Memorial Hospital of Gardena, Gardena, CA, p. A65
CARRASQUILLO, Carmen, M.D., Medical Director, Industrial Hospital, San Juan, PR, p. A735
CARREJO, Angela, Director Human Resources, Nor–Lea Hospital District, Lovington, NM, p. A435
CARRELLI, Bobbie, Director Human Resources, Summit Behavioral Healthcare, Cincinnati, OH, p. A489
CARREON, Aleana, Executive Director, Sonoma Developmental Center, Eldridge, CA, p. A62
CARRERO, Milton D, M.D., Medical Director, Mayaguez Medical Center, Mayaguez, PR, p. A733
CARRICO, Tom, Vice President of Operations, Baptist Health Hardin, Elizabethtown, KY, p. A265
CARRIER, Craig
Chief Financial Officer, American Fork Hospital, American Fork, UT, p. A664
Chief Financial Officer, Orem Community Hospital, Orem, UT, p. A667
CARRIER, Jeffrey
President, Baptist Health Western Region, Baptist Health – Van Buren, Van Buren, AR, p. A54
President, Baptist Health Western Region, Baptist Health– Fort Smith, Fort Smith, AR, p. A46
CARRIERE, Archie, Information Technology Technician, Northlake Behavioral Health System, Mandeville, LA, p. A287
CARRIGG, John M.
Executive Vice President and Chief Operating Officer, United Health Services Hospitals–Binghamton, Binghamton, NY, p. A439
President and Chief Executive Officer, United Health Services Hospitals–Binghamton, Binghamton, NY, p. A439
CARRIKER, Burton, Chief Executive Officer, Eagle View Behavioral Health, Bettendorf, IA, p. A230
CARRILLO, Irma, Director Human Resources, Ashford Presbyterian Community Hospital, San Juan, PR, p. A734
CARRILLO, Todd, Chief Information Officer, Yoakum County Hospital, Denver City, TX, p. A614
CARRILLO, Zulema, Superintendent, El Paso Psychiatric Center, El Paso, TX, p. A616
CARRINGER, Rick, Vice President and Chief Financial Officer, Methodist Medical Center of Oak Ridge, Oak Ridge, TN, p. A591
CARRINGTON, Kristy
R.N., Chief Executive Officer, Providence Regional Medical Center Everett, Everett, WA, p. A689
R.N., Chief Executive Officer, Providence Swedish Edmonds, Edmonds, WA, p. A689
CARRINGTON, Maxine Cenac, Senior Vice President and Chief Human Resources Officer, Long Island Jewish Medical Center, New Hyde Park, NY, p. A447
CARRION, Gloria, Chief Financial Offricer, Atrium Medical Center, Stafford, TX, p. A654
CARROCINO, Joanne, FACHE, President and Chief Executive Officer, Cooper University Hospital Cap. Regional, Cap. May Court House, NJ, p. A419
CARROLL, Candice R., Nurse Executive, Riverside Regional Medical Center, Newport News, VA, p. A680
CARROLL, Eric, Chief Executive Officer, Greeneville Community Hospital East, Greeneville, TN, p. A583
CARROLL, Jack, Director Human Resources, Spaulding Hospital for Continuing Medical Care Cambridge, Cambridge, MA, p. A312
CARROLL, Jacqueline, Director Human Resources, Los Alamos Medical Center, Los Alamos, NM, p. A435
CARROLL, JAIME
R.N., Vice President Nursing, Sentara Albemarle Medical Center, Elizabeth City, NC, p. A468
Department Head, Walter Reed National Military Medical Center, Bethesda, MD, p. A303
CARROLL, James H, Chief Information Officer, University Hospitals St. John Medical Center, Westlake, OH, p. A507
CARROLL, Jan, MSN, M.P.H., R.N., Chief Nursing Officer, Canton–Potsdam Hospital, Potsdam, NY, p. A456
CARROLL, John, M.D., Chief Medical Officer, St. James Hospital, Hornell, NY, p. A444
CARROLL, Jonathan, Chief Information Officer, Uconn, John Dempsey Hospital, Farmington, CT, p. A116
CARROLL, Karen Manuel, R.N., Vice President Patient Care Services, Beaufort Memorial Hospital, Beaufort, SC, p. A562
CARROLL, Keisha, Chief Nursing Officer, Behavioral Health of Rocky Top. Rocky Top. TN, p. A592
CARROLL, Kristen, M.D., Chief of Staff, Shriners Hospitals for Children–Salt Lake City, Salt Lake City, UT, p. A669
CARROLL, Leonard, M.D., Chief of Staff, Hendry Regional Medical Center, Clewiston, FL, p. A128
CARROLL, Linda, Chief Nursing Officer and Vice President, Patient Care Services, Saint Peter's Healthcare System, New Brunswick, NJ, p. A425
CARROLL, Patricia, President and Chief Hospital Executive, Hackensack Meridian Health Raritan Bay Medical Center, Perth Amboy, NJ, p. A427
CARROLL, Patrick, M.D., Chief Medical Officer, St. George Regional Hospital, Saint George, UT, p. A668
CARROLL, Peggy, Chief Information Officer, Northwestern Medicine Palos Hospital, Palos Heights, IL, p. A205
CARROLL, Richard
M.D., Chief Medical officer, UChicago Medicine Adventhealth Bolingbrook, Bolingbrook, IL, p. A186
M.D., Vice President and Chief Medical Officer, UChicago Medicine Adventhealth Glenoaks, Glendale Heights, IL, p. A196
CARROLL, Susan T., FACHE, President, Inova Loudoun Hospital, Leesburg, VA, p. A678
CARROLL, Terri L, Vice President Financial Services, Hillsboro Area Hospital, Hillsboro, IL, p. A198
CARROLL, Vanessa, Chief Medical Officer, Multicare Mary Bridge Children's Hospital And Health Center, Tacoma, WA, p. A697
CARROLL, William, M.D., Chief Medical Executive, Sutter Santa Rosa Regional Hospital, Santa Rosa, CA, p. A95
CARRUTHERS, Kadir, M.D., Medical Officer, Encompass Health Rehabilitation Hospital of North Tampa, Lutz, FL, p. A138
CARSON, Carole, Director of Nursing Operations, Rehabilitation Hospital of Southern New Mexico, Las Cruces, NM, p. A435
CARSON, Chad, Director of Nursing, Lake Behavioral Hospital, Waukegan, IL, p. A210
CARSON, Kara Jo, Chief Financial Officer, Pinckneyville Community Hospital, Pinckneyville, IL, p. A206
CARSON, Stacy, President, Select Specialty Hospital – Laurel Highlands, Latrobe, PA, p. A544
CARSON, Whisper, Manager Human Resource, Scott County Hospital, Scott City, KS, p. A259
CARSTENS, Craig, Chief Financial Officer, Floyd County Medical Center, Charles City, IA, p. A232
CARSTENSEN, Karla, Director Patient Care, Avera Dells Area Hospital, Dell Rapids, SD, p. A573
CARTAGENA, Maria, M.D., Chief Medical Officer, Brylin Hospitals, Buffalo, NY, p. A440
CARTER, Andrea, M.D., Chief Medical Officer, Samaritan Healthcare, Moses Lake, WA, p. A692
CARTER, Barbara, Chief Nursing Officer, Cimarron Memorial Hospital, Boise City, OK, p. A510
CARTER, Carolyn Lizann, Chief Nursing Officer, Broward Health Coral Springs, Coral Springs, FL, p. A129
CARTER, Christen, Director Public Relations, Roosevelt Warm Springs Rehabilitation And Specialty Hospitals, Warm Springs, GA, p. A173
CARTER, Dennis, M.D., Chief of Staff, Eastern Oklahoma Medical Center, Poteau, OK, p. A520
CARTER, Donna, Chief Information Officer and Security Officer, Russell Medical, Alexander City, AL, p. A15
CARTER, Douglas S, M.D., Vice President and Chief Medical Officer, Major Hospital, Shelbyville, IN, p. A227
CARTER, Gloria, Chief Nurse Executive Officer, St. Mary Medical Center Long Beach, Long Beach, CA, p. A71
CARTER, Gregory, M.D., Chief Medical Officer, Providence St. Luke's Rehabilitation Medical Center, Spokane, WA, p. A696
CARTER, James, Interim Chief Executive Officer, Mclaren Bay Region, Bay City, MI, p. A322
CARTER, Jason A., Chief Operating Officer, Duke Regional Hospital, Durham, NC, p. A467
CARTER, Jessica Y, Chief Financial Officer, Crisp Regional Hospital, Cordele, GA, p. A161
CARTER, Jim, Chief Operating Officer, Archbold Grady, Cairo, GA, p. A159
CARTER, Josh, Chief Executive Officer, Western Mental Health Institute, Bolivar, TN, p. A579
CARTER, Lacey, MSN, Chief Nursing Officer, Ozarks Healthcare, West Plains, MO, p. A388
CARTER, Leonard, Campus Administrator, South Georgia Medical Center, Valdosta, GA, p. A173
CARTER, Leonard M, Chief Human Resources Officer, FHN Memorial Hospital, Freeport, IL, p. A195
CARTER, Malinda Yvonne, Vice President Human Resources, Saint Anthony Hospital, Chicago, IL, p. A191
CARTER, Marcia, Director Human Resources, Bluegrass Community Hospital, Versailles, KY, p. A274
CARTER, Michael
M.D., Chief Medical Officer, Houston County Community Hospital, Erin, TN, p. A582
Administrator Information Technology, Northwest Ohio Psychiatric Hospital, Toledo, OH, p. A505
CARTER, Misty, Chief Human Resource Officer and Ancillary Services, Great Plains Regional Medical Center, Elk City, OK, p. A512
CARTER, Nate, Interim Chief Executive Officer and Chief Operating Officer, Portneuf Medical Center, Pocatello, ID, p. A183
CARTER, Priscilla, Chief Financial Officer, Premier Specialty Hospital of El Paso, El Paso, TX, p. A617
CARTER, Rebecca W., MSN, R.N., FACHE, President, Firsthealth Montgomery Memorial Hospital, Troy, NC, p. A477
CARTER, Richard
M.D., Chief Medical Director, Hamilton County Hospital, Syracuse, KS, p. A260
M.D., Chief of Staff, Tennova Healthcare–Jefferson Memorial Hospital, Jefferson City, TN, p. A584
CARTER, Shane, R.N., President, Ascension Northeast Wisconsin Mercy Hospital, Oshkosh, WI, p. A719
CARTER, Steve, Chief Information Officer, Mon Health Medical Center, Morgantown, WV, p. A703
CARTER, Teresa, Vice President Patient Care Services, Onecore Health, Oklahoma City, OK, p. A518
CARTER, Vickie, Information Systems Director, Sumner Regional Medical Center, Gallatin, TN, p. A583
CARTRIGHT, Rebecca, FACHE, Chief Executive Officer, Midlands Regional Rehabilitation Hospital, Elgin, SC, p. A565
CARTWRIGHT, Bryan, Chief Information Technology Officer, Missouri River Medical Center, Fort Benton, MT, p. A392
CARTWRIGHT, David, Director Management Information Systems, Sovah Health–Danville, Danville, VA, p. A675
CARTWRIGHT, Debra, Chief Financial Officer, St. Josep. Medical Center, Kansas City, MO, p. A378
CARTWRIGHT, Debra L, Senior Vice President, Chief Financial Officer, LMH Health, Lawrence, KS, p. A253
CARTWRIGHT, Kathleen, Director Human Resources, Mountain Vista Medical Center, Mesa, AZ, p. A34
CARUGATI, Diane, Chief Operating Officer, Friends Hospital, Philadelphia, PA, p. A548
CARUSO, Diane M, MSN, Chief Nursing Officer, Encompass Health Rehabilitation Hospital of Scottsdale, Scottsdale, AZ, p. A38
CARUSO, Maria, Chief Financial Officer, HCA Florida Pasadena Hospital, Saint Petersburg, FL, p. A149
CARVER, Carol, MSN, R.N., Vice President Patient Services, Clarity Child Guidance Center, San Antonio, TX, p. A649
CARVER, Deborah, Chief Nursing Officer, Providence Cedars–Sinai Tarzana Medical Center, Los Angeles, CA, p. A74
CARVER, Gary J., M.D., Chief Medical Officer, Coshocton Regional Medical Center, Coshocton, OH, p. A493
CARVETH, Barbara, Chief Financial Officer, University of Colorado Hospital, Aurora, CO, p. A103
CARYNSKI, Paula A., MS, R.N., President, OSF Saint Anthony Medical Center, Rockford, IL, p. A207
CASALI, Sherry, R.N., Market Chief Nursing Officer, Unitypoint Health Meriter, Madison, WI, p. A714
CASANOVA, Mark, Chief Executive Officer, Terre Haute Regional Hospital, Terre Haute, IN, p. A228
CASANOVA, Robert Bernier, Chief Financial Officer, Industrial Hospital, San Juan, PR, p. A735
CASAREZ, Margaret, Chief Financial Officer, San Joaquin Valley Rehabilitation Hospital, Fresno, CA, p. A65
CASDORPH, Michael, Ph.D., Chief Information Officer, Wellstar Mcg Health, Augusta, GA, p. A158
CASE, Cliff, Chief Financial Officer, Mineral Community Hospital, Superior, MT, p. A396
CASE, Ed, Executive Vice President and Chief Financial Officer, Shirley Ryan Abilitylab, Chicago, IL, p. A191

 Index of Health Care Professionals A815

Index of Health Care Professionals

Index of Health Care Professionals / Caserta

CASERTA, Kevin
M.D., Chief Medical Officer, Providence Centralia Hospital, Centralia, WA, p. A688
M.D., Chief Medical Officer, Providence St. Peter Hospital, Olympia, WA, p. A692
CASEY, Allison, Director, Gadsden Regional Medical Center, Gadsden, AL, p. A20
CASEY, Dina, Human Resources Officer, Lane County Hospital, Dighton, KS, p. A248
CASEY, Kevin, M.D., Chief Clinical Officer, Mercy Health – St. Rita's Medical Center, Lima, OH, p. A498
CASEY, Lindsey, MSN, R.N., Senior Vice President, Chief Nursing Officer, Children's Hospital New Orleans, New Orleans, LA, p. A290
CASH, Jeff, Senior Vice President and Chief Information Officer, Mercy Medical Center – Cedar Rapids, Cedar Rapids, IA, p. A231
CASHDOLLAR, Amy, Chief Operating Officer and Chief Innovation Officer, AHN Wexford Hospital, Wexford, PA, p. A557
CASHMAN, Tim, Chief Financial Officer, Estes Park Health, Estes Park, CO, p. A107
CASIANO, Manuel, M.D., Senior Vice President Medical Affairs, Frederick Health, Frederick, MD, p. A304
CASILLAS, Mary
Chief Executive Officer, Hazel Hawkins Memorial Hospital, Hollister, CA, p. A67
Chief Operating Officer, Hazel Hawkins Memorial Hospital, Hollister, CA, p. A67
CASILLAS, Rosalind C, Chief Nursing Officer, Lawrence Memorial Hospital, Walnut Ridge, AR, p. A54
CASNER, Trina, FACHE, President and Chief Executive Officer, Pana Community Hospital, Pana, IL, p. A205
CASOLA, Frances, Senior Vice President Operations, Saint Joseph's Medical Center, Yonkers, NY, p. A462
CASON, Amy, MSN, Chief Nursing Officer, Tristar Stonecrest Medical Center, Smyrna, TN, p. A593
CASON, Cathy, Chief Financial Officer, Jeff Davis Hospital, Hazlehurst, GA, p. A165
CASON, Diane, Chief Information Officer, Controller and Director Human Resources, Lake Butler Hospital, Lake Butler, FL, p. A136
CASON, Will, Vice President Human Resources, Mercy Health – St. Rita's Medical Center, Lima, OH, p. A498
CASS, Paul, D.O., Chief Medical & Clinical Integration Officer, Wentworth–Douglass Hospital, Dover, NH, p. A414
CASSADY, Perry, M.D., Medical Director, Physicians' Medical Center, New Albany, IN, p. A225
CASSADY, Richard L., CPA, Executive Vice–President and Chief Operating Officer, Acuity Specialty Hospital–Ohio Valley At Weirton, Weirton, WV, p. A705
CASSAI, Mary, Executive Vice President and Chief Operating Officer, Hospital for Special Surgery, New York, NY, p. A448
CASSEDY, Ryan, Chief Executive Officer, Options Behavioral Health System, Indianapolis, IN, p. A220
CASSEL, Kari, Senior Vice President and Chief Information Officer, UF Health Jacksonville, Jacksonville, FL, p. A135
CASSELL, Sally D, Manager Human Resources, Ozark Health Medical Center, Clinton, AR, p. A44
CASSETTA, Carmella, Chief Information Officer, Hoag Memorial Hospital Presbyterian, Newport Beach, CA, p. A80
CASSIDY, Donna
Administrator, Ascension Borgess Hospital, Kalamazoo, MI, p. A331
Chief Nursing Executive, Bronson South Haven Hospital, South Haven, MI, p. A338
Hospital Administrator, Ascension St. Vincent Salem, Salem, IN, p. A227
CASSIDY, Josep. J, Vice President, Holy Redeemer Hospital, Meadowbrook, PA, p. A545
CASSINGHAM, Brandi, R.N., Chief Nursing Officer, Saddleback Medical Center, Laguna Hills, CA, p. A69
CASTAñEDA, Edmundo, Executive Vice President and Chief Operating Officer, Parkland Health, Dallas, TX, p. A612
CASTALDO, Jennifer, R.N., Vice President, Patient Care and Chief Nursing Officer, Henry Mayo Newhall Hospital, Valencia, CA, p. A99
CASTANEDA, Jennifer, Interim Chief Executive Officer, El Paso Behavioral Health System, El Paso, TX, p. A616
CASTANEDA, Marissa, Chief Operating Officer and Director Marketing, Doctor's Hospital At Renaissance, Edinburg, TX, p. A615
CASTEEL, Brian, Information Technology Technician, Hardin County General Hospital, Rosiclare, IL, p. A208
CASTEEL, Rick, Vice President Management Information Systems and Chief Information Officer, University of Maryland Upper Chesapeake Medical Center, Bel Air, MD, p. A302
CASTELBERRY, Lindsey, Vice President Human Resources and General Counsel, White River Health, Batesville, AR, p. A43
CASTER, Patrick, President and Chief Executive Officer, St. John's Regional Medical Center, Oxnard, CA, p. A82
CASTER, Tiffany
Chief Operating Officer, UCSF Health Saint Francis Hospital, San Francisco, CA, p. A91
Chief Operating Officer, UCSF Health St. Mary's Hospital, San Francisco, CA, p. A91
CASTILLE, Meghan, R.N., Director of Nursing, Louisiana Extended Care Hospital of Natchitoches, Natchitoches, LA, p. A289
CASTILLO, Carlos, R.N., Chief Nursing Officer, The Hospitals of Providence Sierra Campus – Tenet Healthcare, El Paso, TX, p. A617
CASTILLO, Carol, Medical Director, Sonoma Developmental Center, Eldridge, CA, p. A62
CASTILLO, Edgar, Chief Financial Officer, Larkin Community Hospital–South Miami Campus, South Miami, FL, p. A150
CASTILLO, Paul, Chief Financial Officer, University of Michigan Medical Center, Ann Arbor, MI, p. A321
CASTILLO, Ralp. A., CPA, Chief Executive Officer, Morgan Medical Center, Madison, GA, p. A167
CASTILLO, Randall, Chief Executive Officer, Providence St. Mary Medical Center, Apple Valley, CA, p. A56
CASTILLO, Renee, Chief Nursing Officer, Plains Memorial Hospital, Dimmitt, TX, p. A614
CASTILLO, Rita S, R.N., Vice President, Quality, Risk and Safety, Methodist Hospital South, Jourdanton, TX, p. A631
CASTLE, Eric, Director Information Services, HCA Florida Lawnwood Hospital, Fort Pierce, FL, p. A132
CASTLE, sarah, Chief Executive Officer, Pam Specialty Hospital of Reno, Sparks, NV, p. A413
CASTLEMAN, Pam, MSN, Chief Nursing Officer, Regional One Health, Memphis, TN, p. A589
CASTON, David, Chief Executive Officer, Reeves Memorial Medical Center, Bernice, LA, p. A278
CASTOR, Susan, Chief Nursing Officer, Encompass Health Rehabilitation Hospital of Toms River, Toms River, NJ, p. A429
CASTRO, Ana, Director Information Technology, Gerald Champion Regional Medical Center, Alamogordo, NM, p. A432
CASTRO, Aristides, Director Finance, Hospital San Francisco, San Juan, PR, p. A735
CASTRO, Craig S.
Chief Information Officer, Community Regional Medical Center, Fresno, CA, p. A64
President and Chief Executive Officer, Community Health Systems, Clovis Community Medical Center, Clovis, CA, p. A60
President and Chief Executive Officer, Community Health Systems, Community Behavioral Health Center, Fresno, CA, p. A64
President and Chief Executive Officer, Community Health Systems, Community Regional Medical Center, Fresno, CA, p. A64
President and Chief Executive Officer, Community Health Systems, Fresno Heart And Surgical Hospital, Fresno, CA, p. A64
CASTRO, Darcy, Director Human Resources, Garfield Medical Center, Monterey Park, CA, p. A78
CASTRO, Jill, M.D., Medical Director, Encompass Health Rehabilitation Hospital of Littleton, Littleton, CO, p. A111
CASTRO, Marie, Chief Financial Officer, Midland Memorial Hospital, Midland, TX, p. A639
CASTRO, Pete, D.O., Chief of Staff, Heart of Texas Healthcare System, Brady, TX, p. A604
CASTRO, Richard, Chief Executive Officer, San Joaquin General Hospital, French Camp, CA, p. A64
CASTRO, Ruben, Chief Executive Officer, Abrazo Scottsdale Campus, Phoenix, AZ, p. A35
CASTROMAN, Marinella, Chief Execuitve Officer, Select Specialty Hospital–Orlando North, Orlando, FL, p. A144
CASTRONUEVO, Joseph, Director Information Management, St. Lawrence Rehabilitation Hospital, Lawrenceville, NJ, p. A423
CASWELL, Lori, Director Information Technology, Good Samaritan Medical Center, Brockton, MA, p. A311
CASWELL, Penny, Director of Nursing, Bloomington Meadows Hospital, Bloomington, IN, p. A212
CATALA, Lucy, Vice President Finance, Baylor Scott & White All Saints Medical Center – Fort Worth, Fort Worth, TX, p. A619
CATALDO, Linda, Human Resources Secretary, Prevost Memorial Hospital, Donaldsonville, LA, p. A281
CATANIA, Josep. M., Chief Executive Officer, St. Anthony's Rehabilitation Hospital, Lauderdale Lakes, FL, p. A137
CATAUDELLA, Mary, Corporate Director Human Resources, Jersey City Medical Center, Jersey City, NJ, p. A422
CATENA, Cornelio R., FACHE, President, Lehigh Valley Hospital – Pocono, East Stroudsburg, PA, p. A539
CATES, Brett, Director Information Services, Medical City Weatherford, Weatherford, TX, p. A661
CATES, Jessica
Fiscal Manager, Western State Hospital, Hopkinsville, KY, p. A267
Interim Facility Director, Western State Hospital, Hopkinsville, KY, p. A267
CATHEY, Laurin, Senior Vice President, Chief Human Resource Officer, Children's Minnesota, Minneapolis, MN, p. A350
CATHEY, Michele, Interim Chief Financial officer, Martin County Hospital District, Stanton, TX, p. A654
CATINO, Anne, MS, R.N., Vice President and Chief Nursing Officer, Holy Redeemer Hospital, Meadowbrook, PA, p. A545
CATTALANI, Mark, M.D., Clinical Director, Richard H. Hutchings Psychiatric Center, Syracuse, NY, p. A460
CATTELL, JoAnne, Chief Nursing Officer, HCA Florida St. Petersburg Hospital, Saint Petersburg, FL, p. A149
CATTELL, Nancy E, Vice President Human Resources, Liberty Hospital, Liberty, MO, p. A379
CATTON, Carolyn, Interim Chief Patient Care Officer, Marshfield Medical Center – Beaver Dam, Beaver Dam, WI, p. A708
CAUBLE, David
Executive Vice President and Chief Financial Officer, Children's Mercy Hospital Kansas, Overland Park, KS, p. A257
President and Chief Executive Officer, Sky Lakes Medical Center, Klamath Falls, OR, p. A528
CAUDILL, Allan, M.D., Chief of Staff, Bronson South Haven Hospital, South Haven, MI, p. A338
CAUDILL, David, Chief Executive Officer, Russell Regional Hospital, Russell, KS, p. A258
CAUGHELL, David, M.D., Chief of Staff, Ascension St. John Nowata, Nowata, OK, p. A516
CAUGHEY, Michelle, M.D., Physician In Chief, Kaiser Permanente South San Francisco Medical Center, South San Francisco, CA, p. A96
CAUGHMAN, Katie
Chief Financial Officer, Ascension St. John Broken Arrow, Broken Arrow, OK, p. A510
Chief Financial Officer, Ascension St. John Owasso, Owasso, OK, p. A519
CAULEY, Chris, FACHE, Interim Medical Center Director, John D. Dingell Department of Veterans Affairs Medical Center, Detroit, MI, p. A325
CAUSEY, Cynthia, Associate Administrator Human and Mission Services, Mcleod Health Dillon, Dillon, SC, p. A565
CAUSON, Jim, President and Chief Executive Officer, Memorial Hospital of Stilwell, Stilwell, OK, p. A521
CAUSSEAUX, Heather, Vice President of Operations, Sentara Northern Virginia Medical Center, Woodbridge, VA, p. A685
CAUWENBERG, Jude, M.D., Chief of Staff, Ashtabula County Medical Center, Ashtabula, OH, p. A485
CAVACOS, Mike P., MSN, Chief Nursing Officer, Methodist Medical Center of Oak Ridge, Oak Ridge, TN, p. A591
CAVAGNARO, Charles E
III, M.D., Interim President, Umass Memorial Healthalliance–Clinton Hospital, Leominster, MA, p. A315
M.D., III, Interim Chief Medical officer, Umass Memorial Medical Center, Worcester, MA, p. A320
CAVAGNARO, Charles E.
III, M.D., Interim President, Umass Memorial Healthalliance–Clinton Hospital, Leominster, MA, p. A315
III, M.D., Interim President, Umass Memorial–Marlborough Hospital, Marlborough, MA, p. A315
CAVANAUGH, Cheryl, Senior Director Human Resources, Valley Regional Hospital, Claremont, NH, p. A414
CAVANAUGH, Paul, Director Human Resources, Friends Hospital, Philadelphia, PA, p. A548
CAVANAUGH, Steven, Chief Financial Officer, Promedica Toledo Hospital, Toledo, OH, p. A505
CAVAZOS, David–Paul, Chief Executive Officer, Unitypoint Health – Grinnell Regional Medical Center, Grinnell, IA, p. A236
CAVE, Jason, JD, Executive Medical Center Director, Dallas Va North Texas Hcs, Dallas, TX, p. A611
CAVEN, Tom, M.D., Vice President, Medical Director, Dell Seton Medical Center At The University of Texas, Austin, TX, p. A600
CAVERNO, John
Chief Human Resources Officer, Excela Frick Hospital, Mount Pleasant, PA, p. A546
Chief Human Resources Officer, Excela Health Westmoreland Hospital, Greensburg, PA, p. A541
CAVES, Chandler, M.D., Chief Medical Officer, Theda Care Medical Center – Wild Rose, Wild Rose, WI, p. A725
CAVITT, Bryan, President, Ascension St. John Jane Phillips, Bartlesville, OK, p. A510

A816 Index of Health Care Professionals

Index of Health Care Professionals / Chapdelaine

Index of Health Care Professionals

CAWLEY, Karen, Chief Executive Officer, Select Specialty Hospital–Phoenix, Phoenix, AZ, p. A36
CAWLEY, Kevin J, Interim Chief Financial Officer, Mclaren Thumb Region, Bad Axe, MI, p. A322
CAWLEY, Patrick J., M.D., FACHE, Chief Executive Officer, MUSC Health and Vice President for Health Affairs, University, Musc Health University Medical Center, Charleston, SC, p. A563
CAYER, Gerald R., Chief Executive Officer, Lewis County General Hospital, Lowville, NY, p. A445
CAYO, Guybertho, Chief Executive Officer, UT Health Pittsburg, Pittsburg, TX, p. A644
CAYTON, Mical, Area Information Officer, Kaiser Permanente Antioch Medical Center, Antioch, CA, p. A55
CAZARES, Erik, Chief Executive Officer, The Hospitals of Providence Sierra Campus – Tenet Healthcare, El Paso, TX, p. A617
CAZAYOUX, John, Chief Financial Officer, Pointe Coupee General Hospital, New Roads, LA, p. A290
CAZES, Anna Leah, Senior Vice President, Chief Operating Officer and Chief Nursing Officer, Adventist Healthcare Fort Washington Medical Center, Fort Washington, MD, p. A304
CECAVA, Eric, President and Chief Executive Officer, Mclaren Port Huron, Port Huron, MI, p. A336
CECH, Bob, Regional Finance Officer, Ascension Saint Mary – Chicago, Chicago, IL, p. A188
CECIL, Bruce, Chief Financial Officer, Fresno Surgical Hospital, Fresno, CA, p. A64
CECIL, Janell, R.N., MSN, Senior Vice President and Chief Nursing Officer, University of Tennessee Medical Center, Knoxville, TN, p. A586
CECIL, Jason, Vice President, Information, Capital Region Medical Center, Jefferson City, MO, p. A376
CECIL, Jon C
Chief Human Resource Officer, Cap. Coral Hospital, Cap. Coral, FL, p. A127
Chief Human Resource Officer, Gulf Coast Medical Center, Fort Myers, FL, p. A131
Chief Human Resource Officer, Lee Memorial Hospital, Fort Myers, FL, p. A132
CEDENO LLORENS, Arturo, M.D., Medical Director, Hospital Buen Samaritano, Aguadilla, PR, p. A730
CEDILLO, Alaina
Administrator, Jefferson Davis Community Hospital, Prentiss, MS, p. A368
Administrator, Marion General Hospital, Columbia, MS, p. A361
CEJA, Daniel, Interim Chief Financial Officer, North Sunflower Medical Center, Ruleville, MS, p. A368
CELLA, Ann S, R.N., Senior Vice President, Patient Care Services, St. Francis Hospital And Heart Center, Roslyn, NY, p. A458
CELLA, Robert, M.D., Chief Medical Officer, St. Peter's Hospital, Albany, NY, p. A438
CELNIK, Pablo, Chief Executive Officer, Shirley Ryan Abilitylab, Chicago, IL, p. A191
CELSOR, Reba, Chief Executive Officer, Spring View Hospital, Lebanon, KY, p. A268
CEMENO, Michael J, Chief Information Officer, Waterbury Hospital, Waterbury, CT, p. A119
CENTENO, Robert, M.D., Chief Medical Officer, Governor Juan F. Luis Hospital, Christiansted, VI, p. A736
CENTENO, Yarisis, Executive Director, I. Gonzalez Martinez Oncologic Hospital, Hato Rey, PR, p. A732
CEPEDA, Aaron, Director Nursing Operations, South Texas Rehabilitation Hospital, Brownsville, TX, p. A605
CERALDI, Christopher, M.D., Chief of Staff, Abbeville Area Medical Center, Abbeville, SC, p. A562
CERCEK, Robert J., President, Ohiohealth Riverside Methodist Hospital, Columbus, OH, p. A492
CERCEO, Richard, Chief Executive Officer, Kindred Hospital Chicago–Northlake, Northlake, IL, p. A204
CERFOLIO, Robert J., M.D., Chief Operating Officer, Nyu Langone Hospitals, New York, NY, p. A452
CERIMELE, Joseph, D.O., Medical Director, Hillside Rehabilitation Hospital, Warren, OH, p. A506
CERISE, Fred, M.D., Chief Executive Officer, Parkland Health, Dallas, TX, p. A612
CERNAVA, Joanne, Director Human Resources, Kessler Marlton Rehabilitation, Marlton, NJ, p. A423
CERNAVA, Tia A, Chief Financial Officer, Pomerene Hospital, Millersburg, OH, p. A500
CERNEY, Ryan D., Administrator, Community Behavioral Health Hospital – Baxter, Baxter, MN, p. A343
CERNOCH, Desiree, Director of Nurses, El Camp. Memorial Hospital, El Campo, TX, p. A616
CERRA, Jane, Market Nurse Executive and Chief Nursing Officer, Select Specialty Hospital–Milwaukee, Milwaukee, WI, p. A717
CERVINO, Noel A., President and Chief Executive Officer, University of Maryland Charles Regional Medical Center, La Plata, MD, p. A305
CESAREZ, Margaret, Chief Financial Officer, Gateway Rehabilitation Hospital, Florence, KY, p. A265
CESCA, Kenneth W, Vice President Human Resources, Midstate Medical Center, Meriden, CT, p. A116
CESKO, David, M.D., Chief of Staff, Memorial Hospital of Carbon County, Rawlins, WY, p. A728
CHA, Wontae, Chief Operating Officer, Cha Hollywood Presbyterian Medical Center, Los Angeles, CA, p. A72
CHABALOWSKI, Edward, Vice President, Finance and Chief Financial Officer, East Region, Penn State Health Lancaster Medical Center, Lancaster, PA, p. A543
CHACKO, Benson
President, Methodist Southlake Hospital, Southlake, TX, p. A653
Vice President, Operations, Baylor Scott & White Medical Center – Lake Pointe, Rowlett, TX, p. A648
CHACON, Barbara, Chief Financial Officer, The Core Institute Specialty Hospital, Phoenix, AZ, p. A37
CHACON, Chanda, M.P.H., FACHE, President and Chief Executive Officer, Children's Nebraska, Omaha, NE, p. A404
CHADEK, Richard, M.D., Clinical Director, Lawton Indian Hospital, Lawton, OK, p. A514
CHADHA, Beenu
Chief Financial Officer, San Ramon Regional Medical Center, San Ramon, CA, p. A93
Interim Chief Executive Officer and Chief Financial Officer, San Ramon Regional Medical Center, San Ramon, CA, p. A93
CHADOCK, Brandon
Chief Administrative Officer, Sistersville General Hospital, Sistersville, WV, p. A704
Interim Chief Executive Officer, Pershing General Hospital, Lovelock, NV, p. A411
CHADWICK, LeeAnn, Chief Nursing Officer, Mymichigan Medical Center Alma, Alma, MI, p. A321
CHADWICK, Robyn, President, Ascension Via Christi St. Francis, Mulvane, KS, p. A255
CHAFFIN, Adam, Finance and Billing Coordinator, The Woods At Parkside, Gahanna, OH, p. A496
CHAFFIN, Jared, Chief Executive Officer and Chief Financial Officer, Friend Community Healthcare System, Friend, NE, p. A400
CHAFFIN, Linda, Director Medical Review, Baptist Memorial Hospital–Booneville, Booneville, MS, p. A360
CHAHANOVICH, Jen, President and Chief Executive Officer, Wilcox Medical Center, Lihue, HI, p. A177
CHAKAMBA, Carli, Chief Executive Officer, Pam Health Specialty Hospital of Pittsburgh, Oakdale, PA, p. A547
CHALFANT, Cathie, Director Human Resources, Harrison County Community Hospital, Bethany, MO, p. A371
CHALIAN, Christopher, M.D., Medical Director, Casa Colina Hospital And Centers for Healthcare, Pomona, CA, p. A84
CHALK, Jackie, Director Human Resources, Encompass Health Rehabilitation Hospital of Largo, Largo, FL, p. A137
CHALKE, Dennis, Senior Vice President, Chief Financial Officer and Treasurer, Baystate Medical Center, Springfield, MA, p. A318
CHALONER, Robert S.
President, Central Region, Marshfield Medical Center – Neilsville, Neillsville, WI, p. A718
President, Central Region, Marshfield Medical Center, Marshfield, WI, p. A715
CHALPHANT, Steve, Director Information Management Service Line, Columbia Va Health Care System, Columbia, SC, p. A564
CHALUPA, Rebecca, MSN, R.N., Chief Nursing Officer, Houston Methodist Baytown Hospital, Baytown, TX, p. A601
CHAMBERLAIN, Denise, Executive Vice President, Chief Financial Officer, Endeavor Health Edward Hospital, Naperville, IL, p. A203
CHAMBERLAIN, Diana, Director Human Resources, Carthage Area Hospital, Carthage, NY, p. A441
CHAMBERLAIN, Kayla, Chief Financial Officer, Salem Memorial District Hospital, Salem, MO, p. A386
CHAMBERLIN, Brad, Director of Finance, OSF Saint Elizabeth Medical Center, Ottawa, IL, p. A204
CHAMBERLIN, Kim, Vice President Patient Services and Chief Nursing Officer, Mercyone North Iowa Medical Center, Mason City, IA, p. A240
CHAMBERS, Gwen, Executive Director Human Resources, USC Arcadia Hospital, Arcadia, CA, p. A56
CHAMBERS, Matthew
Chief Information Officer, Baylor Scott & White Medical Center – Round Rock, Round Rock, TX, p. A647
Chief Information Officer, Baylor Scott & White Medical Center – Temple, Temple, TX, p. A656
CHAMBERS, Orie Jr, Vice President Patient Care Services and Chief Nursing Officer, Wellspan Ephrata Community Hospital, Ephrata, PA, p. A539
CHAMBERS, Tami, President and Chief Executive Officer, Grant Regional Health Center, Lancaster, WI, p. A714
CHAMBERS HASKINS, Laurel, Chief Executive Officer, Mineral Community Hospital, Superior, MT, p. A396
CHAMBERS LEWIS, Lorraine, Executive Director, Long Island Jewish Medical Center, New Hyde Park, NY, p. A447
CHAMBLEE, Jane, Manager Human Resources, North Mississipp. Medical Center–Iuka, Iuka, MS, p. A363
CHAMBLESS, Lesley
Assistant Vice President Human Resources, Atrium Health Lincoln, Lincolnton, NC, p. A472
Assistant Vice President Workforce Relations, Atrium Health Cabarrus, Concord, NC, p. A466
CHAMBLISS, James W, Chief of Staff, Magnolia Regional Medical Center, Magnolia, AR, p. A50
CHAMPAGNE, Charles D., Chief Executive Officer, Northeast Rehabilitation Hospital, Salem, NH, p. A417
CHAMPAVANNARATH, Vilakon, Director Information Systems, Bartow Regional Medical Center, Bartow, FL, p. A125
CHAMPION, Joshua I, Director, Adventhealth Palm Coast, Palm Coast, FL, p. A145
CHAMPLIN, Chris, President, Adventist Health And Rideout, Marysville, CA, p. A77
CHAN, Ed, FACHE, Market President, Hawaii, Kaiser Permanente Medical Center, Honolulu, HI, p. A175
CHAN, Eric, M.D., Chief Executive Officer, Surgery Specialty Hospitals of America, Pasadena, TX, p. A643
CHAN, Joyce, Chief Human Resources Officer, Centracare – Melrose, Melrose, MN, p. A350
CHAN, Thomas T., Chief Financial Officer, Meritus Health, Hagerstown, MD, p. A305
CHANAA, Ziad, M.D., Chief of Staff, Boone Memorial Hospital, Madison, WV, p. A702
CHANCE, Andre, Chief Financial Officer, Veterans Affairs New York Harbor Healthcare System, New York, NY, p. A453
CHANCE, Tammara, D.O., Chief Medical Officer, Broadlawns Medical Center, Des Moines, IA, p. A234
CHAND, Raj, M.D., President, Inova Fair Oaks Hospital, Fairfax, VA, p. A675
CHANDLER, Aileen, Chief Nursing Officer, Banner Lassen Medical Center, Susanville, CA, p. A97
CHANDLER, Carla, Vice President and Chief Financial Officer, Emory University Hospital, Atlanta, GA, p. A157
CHANDLER, Christopher, Chief Executive Officer, Monroe Regional Hospital, Aberdeen, MS, p. A359
CHANDLER, Ryan, Chief Executive Officer, Piedmont Columbus Regional Midtown, Columbus, GA, p. A161
CHANDLER, Sherri, Chief Executive Officer, Rolling Hills Hospital, Ada, OK, p. A509
CHANDLER, Stephen, Chief Executive Officer, Trident Medical Center, Charleston, SC, p. A563
CHANDLER, Vincent, Director Information Services, Porterville Developmental Center, Porterville, CA, p. A84
CHANDLER, Wendy
Regional Vice President Human Resources, Christus St. Frances Cabrini Hospital, Alexandria, LA, p. A276
Vice President Human Resources, Christus Health Shreveport–Bossier, Shreveport, LA, p. A292
Vice President Human Resources, Christus St. Michael Health System, Texarkana, TX, p. A656
CHANDRAN, Kutty, M.D., Regional Medical Officer, Broward Health Coral Springs, Coral Springs, FL, p. A129
CHANDRASENA, Anita, M.D., Vice President Medical Affairs, Sequoia Hospital, Redwood City, CA, p. A85
CHANEY, Dawne, Chief Executive Officer, Select Specialty Hospital–Akron, Akron, OH, p. A484
CHANEY, Martin, M.D., Chief Executive Officer, Maury Regional Medical Center, Columbia, TN, p. A581
CHANG, Alex
Chief Operating Officer, HCA Florida Englewood Hospital, Englewood, FL, p. A131
President and Chief Executive Officer, Ascension St. Vincent Evansville, Evansville, IN, p. A216
CHANG, Angel, M.D., Medical Director, Palomar Health Rehabilitation Institute, Escondido, CA, p. A62
CHANG, Jason, President & Chief Executive Officer, The Queen's Medical Center, Honolulu, HI, p. A176
CHANG, Jeen–Soo, M.D., MS, President and Chief Medical Officer, Holy Cross Hospital, Chicago, IL, p. A189
CHANG, Michael, M.D., Chief Medical Officer, USA Health Children's & Women's Hospital, Mobile, AL, p. A22
CHANG, Sang–ick, M.D., M.P.H., Chief Medical Officer, Highland Hospital, Oakland, CA, p. A80
CHANNELL, Lesley
Vice President Human Resources, Reston Hospital Center, Reston, VA, p. A682
Vice President Human Resources, Dominion Hospital, Falls Church, VA, p. A675
CHAPDELAINE, Debora R., Manager Information Technology, Aurora Medical Center Kenosha, Kenosha, WI, p. A713

Index of Health Care Professionals / Chapital

CHAPITAL, Alyssa B, M.D., Medical Director, Mayo Clinic Hospital, Mayo Clinic Hospital In Arizona, Phoenix, AZ, p. A36
CHAPLIN, Steven, M.D., Medical Director, Sutter Health Kahi Mohala, Ewa Beach, HI, p. A175
CHAPMAN, Bradley J., President, Memorial Hospital, North Conway, NH, p. A417
CHAPMAN, Cully, Chief Financial Officer, Lutheran Hospital of Indiana, Fort Wayne, IN, p. A216
CHAPMAN, Donna Lynn, R.N., Chief Nursing Officer, Mckay-Dee Hospital, Ogden, UT, p. A666
CHAPMAN, Emily, Chief Medical Officer, Children's Minnesota, Minneapolis, MN, p. A350
CHAPMAN, Jeffrey, M.D., Chief Medical Officer, Cheyenne Regional Medical Center, Cheyenne, WY, p. A726
CHAPMAN, John T.
   Chief Operative Officer, San Antonio Regional Hospital, Upland, CA, p. A99
   President and Chief Executive Officer, San Antonio Regional Hospital, Upland, CA, p. A99
CHAPMAN, Jon, Fiscal Officer, Western State Hospital, Staunton, VA, p. A684
CHAPMAN, Karen
   Director Human Resources, Musc Health Chester Medical Center, Chester, SC, p. A564
   Human Resources Director, Musc Health Lancaster Medical Center, Lancaster, SC, p. A568
CHAPMAN, Kathleen Esq, Deputy Director, Patient Care Services, Portland Hcs, Portland, OR, p. A530
CHAPMAN, Kathy, R.N., Chief Clinical Officer and Vice President of Patient Services, Ascension Borgess Allegan Hospital, Allegan, MI, p. A321
CHAPMAN, Patrick, Ed.D., Chief Executive Officer, Tippah County Hospital, Ripley, MS, p. A368
CHAPMAN, Rachel, Nurse Manager, Noland Hospital Birmingham, Birmingham, AL, p. A17
CHAPMAN, Rick, Chief Information Officer, Kindred Hospital North Florida, Green Cove Springs, FL, p. A133
CHAPMAN, Roland, Chief Information Officer, Northern Navajo Medical Center, Shiprock, NM, p. A437
CHAPMAN, Scott, Chief Executive Officer, Kansas Spine & Specialty Hospital, Wichita, KS, p. A262
CHAPMAN, Teresa, Vice President Human Resources, Northwestern Medicine Marianjoy Rehabilitation Hospital, Wheaton, IL, p. A210
CHAPMAN, Terina, Director of Nursing, Northern Utah Rehabilitation Hospital, South Ogden, UT, p. A670
CHAPPELL, Pamela, R.N., Assistant Administrator, Specialty Hospital, Monroe, LA, p. A289
CHAPPELL, Robert, M.D., Chief Medical Officer and Chief Quality Officer, Huntsville Hospital, Huntsville, AL, p. A21
CHAPPELL, Teresa, Chief Information Officer, UNC Health Johnston, Smithfield, NC, p. A476
CHAPPLE, Scott, Chief Operating Officer, Oroville Hospital, Oroville, CA, p. A82
CHARARA, Kassem, Chief Medical Officer, Corewell Health Taylor Hospital, Taylor, MI, p. A339
CHARBENEAU, Ryan, M.D., Chief Medical Officer, St. David's North Austin Medical Center, Austin, TX, p. A600
CHARBONNIER, Kathleen, MSN, R.N., Interim Chief Nursing Officer, Massachusetts Eye And Ear, Boston, MA, p. A310
CHARDAVOYNE, Alan, Chief Financial Officer, The University of Vermont Health Network Elizabethtown Community Hospital, Elizabethtown, NY, p. A442
CHARLAT, Richard A, Chief of Staff, Iowa City Va Health System, Iowa City, IA, p. A238
CHARLES, Charlotte, Director Acute Patient Services, Madison Regional Health System, Madison, SD, p. A574
CHARLES, Sally, Coordinator Human Resources, Grace Surgical Hospital, Lubbock, TX, p. A636
CHARLTON, Beth
   R.N., President and Chief Executive Officer, Covenant Healthcare, Saginaw, MI, p. A336
   R.N., President and Chief Executive Officer, Covenant Healthcare, Covenant Healthcare, Saginaw, MI, p. A336
CHARLTON, Francis, M.D., Jr, Chief Medical Staff, UCSF Health St. Mary's Hospital, San Francisco, CA, p. A91
CHARLTON, Judie, M.D., Chief Medical Officer, West Virginia University Hospitals, Morgantown, WV, p. A703
CHARLTON, Michael, President and Chief Executive Officer, Atlanticare Regional Medical Center, Atlantic City Campus, Atlantic City, NJ, p. A418
CHARMEL, Patrick, President and Chief Executive Officer, Griffin Health, Derby, CT, p. A115
CHARTIER, Bridgett, Director of Nursing, Beartooth Billings Clinic, Red Lodge, MT, p. A395
CHARTIER, Terry
   Director, Information Systems, Mercyone New Hampton Medical Center, New Hampton, IA, p. A240
   Director, Information Systems, Mercyone North Iowa Medical Center, Mason City, IA, p. A240

CHARVAT, Peter, M.D., Chief Medical Officer, St. Joseph's Hospital, Tampa, FL, p. A152
CHASE, Amy, Chief Financial Officer, Wyoming County Community Hospital, Warsaw, NY, p. A461
CHASE, Jean
   Regional Manager Information Services, Aurora Lakeland Medical Center, Elkhorn, WI, p. A710
   Regional Manager Information Services, Aurora Medical Center Burlington, Burlington, WI, p. A709
CHASE, Kena, Chief Nursing Officer, Lourdes Health, Pasco, WA, p. A692
CHASE, Kyle, Chief Financial Officer, Glacial Ridge Health System, Glenwood, MN, p. A347
CHASE, Layla, Interim Chief Financial Officer, Bunkie General Hospital, Bunkie, LA, p. A279
CHASE, Pansy, Director Human Resources, ECU Health Duplin Hospital, Kenansville, NC, p. A471
CHASE, Robert, M.D., Physician Advisor, West Suburban Medical Center, Oak Park, IL, p. A204
CHASE, Susan, Vice President, Carolinas Rehabilitation, Charlotte, NC, p. A465
CHASSE, Floyd, Vice President Human Resources, Erlanger Medical Center, Chattanooga, TN, p. A580
CHASTAIN, James G., FACHE, Director, Mississipp. State Hospital, Whitfield, MS, p. A370
CHASTAIN, Stephen L, M.D., Chief Medical Officer, Encompass Health Rehabilitation Hospital, An Affiliate of Martin Health, Stuart, FL, p. A150
CHASTANG, Mark J., M.P.H., Chief Executive Officer, Saint Elizabeths Hospital, Washington, DC, p. A124
CHASTANT, Lee J. III, Chief Executive Officer, West Feliciana Hospital, Saint Francisville, LA, p. A292
CHATANI, Kumar
   Chief Information Officer, Mount Sinai Health System, Mount Sinai Morningside, New York, NY, p. A449
   Chief Information Officer, Mount Sinai Health System, New York Eye And Ear Infirmary of Mount Sinai, New York, NY, p. A450
   Senior Vice President and Chief Information Officer Mount Sinai Health System, Mount Sinai Beth Israel, New York, NY, p. A449
   Senior Vice President and Chief Information Officer Mount Sinai Health System, The Mount Sinai Hospital, New York, NY, p. A453
CHATELAIN, Alicia, Director Human Resource, Hood Memorial Hospital, Amite, LA, p. A276
CHATELAIN, Vincent, Director Business Development, River Oaks Hospital, New Orleans, LA, p. A290
CHATHAM, Heather, Administrator, Mercy Hospital Healdton, Healdton, OK, p. A513
CHATLEY, Alice M, R.N., MSN, Vice President Acute Care Services, SSM Health St. Mary's Hospital – Jefferson City, Jefferson City, MO, p. A376
CHATMAN, Hubert, Chief Civilian Personnel, Wright Patterson Medical Center, Wright-Patterson Afb, OH, p. A507
CHATMAN, Jim, Chief Financial Officer, Maria Parham Health, Duke Lifepoint Healthcare, Henderson, NC, p. A470
CHATTERJEE, Kanan, M.D., Chief of Staff, Lebanon Veterans Affairs Medical Center, Lebanon, PA, p. A544
CHATULUKA, Victor, Chief Executive Officer, Doctors Neuropsychiatric Hospital, Bremen, IN, p. A213
CHAUDHARY, Shahid, M.D., Chief Medical Officer, Avera St. Luke's Hospital, Aberdeen, SD, p. A572
CHAUDHURI, Sumanta
   M.D., Chief Medical Officer, Hemet Global Medical Center, Hemet, CA, p. A67
   M.D., Chief Medical Officer, Menifee Global Medical Center, Sun City, CA, p. A97
CHAUDRY, Ramesh, M.D., Medical Director, Piedmont Geriatric Hospital, Burkeville, VA, p. A674
CHAUDRY, Zafar, M.D., Senior Vice President and Chief Information Officer, Seattle Children's Hospital, Seattle, WA, p. A694
CHAUHAN, Varsha, Chief Executive Officer, Encompass Health Rehabilitation Hospital of Henderson, Henderson, NV, p. A409
CHAUHAN, Varun, Chief Executive Officer, Vibra Hospital of Sacramento, Folsom, CA, p. A63
CHAVARRIA, Annmarie, Senior Vice President and Chief Nursing Officer, Tamp. General Hospital, Tampa, FL, p. A152
CHAVEZ, Kevin
   Central District Chief Executive Officer, Kindred Hospital-Baldwin Park, Baldwin Park, CA, p. A57
   Central District Chief Executive Officer, Kindred Hospital-Brea, Brea, CA, p. A58
CHAVEZ, Shari, Chief Nursing Officer, Swedish Medical Center, Englewood, CO, p. A107
CHAVEZ, Steven, Vice President Finance and Operations, Kettering Health Main Campus, Kettering, OH, p. A497

CHAVEZ, Virgil, Director Information Technology, Tsehootsooi Medical Center, Fort Defiance, AZ, p. A31
CHAVEZ STUMP, Tammie, R.N., Chief Executive Officer, Union County General Hospital, Clayton, NM, p. A434
CHAVIS, Anthony D, M.D., Vice President Enterprise Medical Officer, Community Hospital Foundation, Community Hospital of The Monterey Peninsula, Monterey, CA, p. A78
CHAYER, Olivia, Director, Human Resources, York Hospital, York, ME, p. A299
CHECK, Arthur, M.D., Chief Medical Officer, Story County Medical Center, Nevada, IA, p. A240
CHECKETTS, Lannie
   Chief Financial Officer, Saint Alphonsus Medical Center – Nampa, Nampa, ID, p. A182
   Chief Financial Officer, Saint Alphonsus Medical Center – Ontario, Ontario, OR, p. A529
CHEE, Darlene, Acting Chief Executive Officer, Chinle Comprehensive Health Care Facility, Chinle, AZ, p. A31
CHEEK, Michael, Chief Financial Officer, Christus Good Shepherd Medical Center–Marshall, Marshall, TX, p. A638
CHEEK, Ramona, MS, R.N., Chief Nursing Officer, Mercy Health – Fairfield Hospital, Fairfield, OH, p. A495
CHEEMA, Linde, Vice President Human Resources, Sequoia Hospital, Redwood City, CA, p. A85
CHEESEMAN, Karen, President and Chief Executive Officer, Mackinac Straits Health System, Inc., Saint Ignace, MI, p. A337
CHEKURU, Naidu, M.D., Chief Medical Officer, Covenant Specialty Hospital, Lubbock, TX, p. A636
CHELLAPPA, Sheila, M.D., Chief of Staff, Coatesville Veterans Affairs Medical Center, Coatesville, PA, p. A537
CHEN, Bonny, M.D., Vice President and Chief Medical Officer, UChicago Medicine Adventhealth Hinsdale, Hinsdale, IL, p. A198
CHEN, David
   M.D., Chief Medical Officer, Multicare Deaconess Hospital, Spokane, WA, p. A696
   M.D., Chief Medical Officer, Multicare Valley Hospital, Spokane Valley, WA, p. A696
CHEN, Linda, Chief Financial Officer, Hackensack Meridian Mountainside Medical Center, Montclair, NJ, p. A424
CHEN, Mako, M.D., Medical Director, Mercy Rehabilitation Hospital Fort Smith, Fort Smith, AR, p. A47
CHEN, Philip, M.D., Medical Director, University of Iowa Health Network Rehabilitation Hospital, Coralville, IA, p. A233
CHEN, Stephen, M.D., Chief Medicare, Alhambra Hospital Medical Center, Alhambra, CA, p. A55
CHEN, Van, M.D., Medical Director, Ballard Rehabilitation Hospital, San Bernardino, CA, p. A88
CHENEY, David, President and Chief Executive Officer, Flagstaff Medical Center, Flagstaff, AZ, p. A31
CHENG, Rebecca
   Chief Financial Officer, California Hospital Medical Center, Los Angeles, CA, p. A72
   Chief Financial Officer, Glendale Memorial Hospital And Health Center, Glendale, CA, p. A66
CHENG, Ringo, Director Information Technology, Surgery Specialty Hospitals of America, Pasadena, TX, p. A643
CHENIER, Lawrence, Chief Medical Officer, Madison Parish Hospital, Tallulah, LA, p. A293
CHENOWETH, Judy, Chief Nursing Officer, Russell County Hospital, Russell Springs, KY, p. A274
CHERAMIE, Bennett, Vice President Information Technology, Baton Rouge General Medical Center, Baton Rouge, LA, p. A277
CHERAY, James, M.D., Chief Medical Officer, Menorah Medical Center, Overland Park, KS, p. A257
CHERMSIDE, Paula L., Chief Administrative Officer, Aspirus Ironwood Hospital & Clinics, Inc., Ironwood, MI, p. A330
CHERRY, Brian, Chief Executive Officer, Chi St. Vincent Sherwood Rehabilitation Hospital, A Partner of Encompass Health, Sherwood, AR, p. A53
CHERRY, Deano, Chief Information Officer, UPMC Kane, Kane, PA, p. A543
CHERRY, Jean, Executive Vice President, Commonwealth Regional Specialty Hospital, Bowling Green, KY, p. A263
CHERRY, Jonathan M., President and Chief Executive Officer, Lifestream Behavioral Center, Leesburg, FL, p. A137
CHERRY, Michael, Chief Financial Officer, Tennova Healthcare–Lafollette Medical Center, La Follette, TN, p. A586
CHERRY, Robert, M.D., Chief Medical and Quality Officer, Ronald Reagan Ucla Medical Center, Los Angeles, CA, p. A75
CHERRY, Shay, Administrator, Hale County Hospital, Greensboro, AL, p. A20
CHESLEK, Ingrid, R.N., Chief Nursing Officer, Mary Free Bed Rehabilitation Hospital, Grand Rapids, MI, p. A328
CHESLEY, Judy S, M.D., Chief of Staff, Sanford Luverne Medical Center, Luverne, MN, p. A349
CHESLEY, Randy, Director Information Technology, Copley Hospital, Morrisville, VT, p. A672

A818   Index of Health Care Professionals   © 2025 AHA Guide

Index of Health Care Professionals / Christophel

Index of Health Care Professionals

CHESLEY, Walter, Senior Vice President Human Resources, Hennepin Healthcare, Minneapolis, MN, p. A350
CHESSARE, John B., M.D., M.P.H., FACHE, President and Chief Executive Officer, Gbmc Healthcare, Baltimore, MD, p. A302
CHESSON, Andrew, Chief Medical Officer, Catawba Valley Medical Center, Hickory, NC, p. A470
CHESSUM, George
Senior Vice President and Chief Information Officer, Community First Medical Center, Chicago, IL, p. A189
Senior Vice President Information Systems and Chief Information Officer, Ascension Saint Josep. – Chicago, Chicago, IL, p. A188
Vice President Information Systems, Ascension Saint Francis, Evanston, IL, p. A194
CHESTER, Julie, Vice President Human Resources, University Hospitals Cleveland Medical Center, Cleveland, OH, p. A491
CHESTER, Linnes L, USAF, MSC, Administrator, Mike O'Callaghan Federal Hospital, Nellis Afb, NV, p. A411
CHESTER, William, Manager Human Resources, Grand Junction Va Medical Center, Grand Junction, CO, p. A108
CHESTNUT–RAULS, Monica, Vice President Human Resources, Peconic Bay Medical Center, Riverhead, NY, p. A457
CHEUNG, Alan, M.D., Vice President Medical Affairs, Adventist Health Castle, Kailua, HI, p. A176
CHEUNG, Marilou, Assistant Administrator Finance, Kaiser Permanente Woodland Hills Medical Center, Los Angeles, CA, p. A73
CHEVERE, Carlos, M.D., Medical Director, I. Gonzalez Martinez Oncologic Hospital, Hato Rey, PR, p. A732
CHHABRA, Ankit, Director Finance, Cleveland Clinic Fairview Hospital, Cleveland, OH, p. A490
CHIANESE, Charles, Vice President, Chief Operating Officer, Children's Specialized Hospital, New Brunswick, NJ, p. A424
CHIANTELLA, Christopher, M.D., Chief Medical Officer, Inova Loudoun Hospital, Leesburg, VA, p. A678
CHIAVETTA, Robert, Vice President Finance, United Memorial Medical Center, Batavia, NY, p. A439
CHIBAYA, Daniel, Chief Information Officer, Adventist Health And Rideout, Marysville, CA, p. A77
CHICARELLI, Michael, R.N., Chief Operating Officer, University of New Mexico Hospitals, Albuquerque, NM, p. A433
CHICKEN, Kurt, Director Support Services, Gundersen Palmer Lutheran Hospital And Clinics, West Union, IA, p. A245
CHIDESTER, Annamarie, R.N., Vice President, Patient Care Services, St. Joseph's Hospital, Buckhannon, WV, p. A699
CHIEDA, Katie, Chief Nursing Officer, Fisher–Titus Medical Center, Norwalk, OH, p. A501
CHIEFFO, Ron, Chief Information Officer, Colorado River Medical Center, Needles, CA, p. A80
CHILCOTE, Lesalee, Chief Executive Officer, Chi St. Vincent Hot Springs Rehabilitation Hospital, A Partner of Encompass Health, Hot Springs, AR, p. A48
CHILCOTT, Stephen, Associate Director Human Resources, UC Davis Medical Center, Sacramento, CA, p. A87
CHILD, Clint, R.N., President, Saint Alphonsus Medical Center – Nampa, Nampa, ID, p. A182
CHILDERS, Bethany, Director Human Resources, Methodist Fremont Health, Fremont, NE, p. A400
CHILDERS, Linda, Director Human Resources, Wallowa Memorial Hospital, Enterprise, OR, p. A526
CHILDREE, Phillip. Chief Financial Officer, Flowers Hospital, Dothan, AL, p. A18
CHILDS, Michelle, Chief Human Resources Officer, Salinas Valley Health, Salinas, CA, p. A88
CHILES, Morton, M.D., Chief Medical Officer, UVA Health Culpeper Medical Center, Culpeper, VA, p. A675
CHILESE, Melody, Chief Nurse Executive, Hawthorn Children Psychiatric Hospital, Saint Louis, MO, p. A385
CHILESKI, Andy, Chief Information Officer and Vice President Facilities, Ohiohealth Berger Hospital, Circleville, OH, p. A490
CHILL, Martha O'Regan, Interim Chief Information Officer, Hancock County Hospital, Sneedville, TN, p. A593
CHILTON, Bryan, Director Information Systems, Navarro Regional Hospital, Corsicana, TX, p. A609
CHILTON, Hal, Senior Vice President and Chief Operating Officer, Adventist Health St. Helena, Saint Helena, CA, p. A88
CHIN, Ellyn, Vice President Finance, Gottlieb Memorial Hospital, Melrose Park, IL, p. A201
CHINBURG, Paul, M.D., Medical Director, Lane County Hospital, Dighton, KS, p. A248
CHING, Angelica
Director Information Systems, Garfield Medical Center, Monterey Park, CA, p. A78
Director Information Systems, Monterey Park Hospital, Monterey Park, CA, p. A78
CHINN, Tammie, Director Marketing and Public Relations, Camc Plateau Medical Center, Oak Hill, WV, p. A703
CHINN, Terri, Vice President Finance, Intermountain Health St. Mary's Regional Hospital, Grand Junction, CO, p. A109
CHINN, William A., President, Penn Highlands Dubois, Dubois, PA, p. A538
CHINNOCK, Richard, Chief Medical Officer, LLUCH, Loma Linda University Children's Hospital, Loma Linda, CA, p. A70
CHIOLO, Denise, Chief Human Resources Officer, Phoenixville Hospital, Phoenixville, PA, p. A550
CHIPMAN, Glen, Chief Financial Officer, Healthsource Saginaw Inc., Saginaw, MI, p. A337
CHISHOLM, Sharon, Entity Human Resource Officer, Texas Health Presbyterian Hospital Allen, Allen, TX, p. A595
CHISOLM, Sarah, Chief Executive Officer, Beacham Memorial Hospital, Magnolia, MS, p. A365
CHITCHYAN, Ara, M.D., Medical Director, Roosevelt Warm Springs Rehabilitation And Specialty Hospitals, Warm Springs, GA, p. A173
CHITTUM, Janae, Chief Nursing Officer, Clinton Regional Hospital, Clinton, OK, p. A511
CHITWOOD, Claire, Chief Operating Officer, Slidell Memorial Hospital, Slidell, LA, p. A293
CHIUSANO, Jennifer, R.N., Chief Nursing Officer, Saint Francis Hospital, Memphis, TN, p. A589
CHIVERS, John, Chief Executive Officer, Lower Umpqua Hospital District, Reedsport, OR, p. A531
CHMELICEK, Thomas, M.D., Chief Medical Officer, Oneida Healthcare, Oneida, NY, p. A455
CHMURA, David, Chief Information Officer, Copper Queen Community Hospital, Bisbee, AZ, p. A30
CHO, Eugene, Senior Vice President/Area Manager, Baldwin Park, Kaiser Permanente Baldwin Park Medical Center, Baldwin Park, CA, p. A57
CHOATE, Matthew, Chief Nursing Officer, The University of Vermont Health Network Central Vermont Medical Center, Berlin, VT, p. A671
CHOBANIAN, Nishan, M.D., Vice President of the Practices and Senior Physician Executive, Northern Light Inland Hospital, Waterville, ME, p. A299
CHOCKLETT, Wyatt, Chief Operating Officer, HCA Florida Largo Hospital, Largo, FL, p. A137
CHOINKA, Keith A, Vice President Information Systems and Chief Information Officer, St. Josep. Hospital, Nashua, NH, p. A416
CHOLEWA, Gerald M.
MSN, R.N., Chief Executive Officer, Chicago Behavioral Hospital, Des Plaines, IL, p. A193
MSN, R.N., Interim Chief Executive Officer, Smokey Point Behavioral Hospital, Marysville, WA, p. A691
CHON, Jun, M.D., Chief Medical Officer, The University of Vermont Health Network Elizabethtown Community Hospital, Elizabethtown, NY, p. A442
CHONG, Johnnette, Chief Financial Officer, Los Angeles Community Hospital At Los Angeles, Los Angeles, CA, p. A74
CHOPRA, Praveen, Chief Information Officer, Gundersen Lutheran Medical Center, La Crosse, WI, p. A713
CHORD, Ginger, Coordinator Human Resources, Monument Health Sturgis Hospital, Sturgis, SD, p. A577
CHOU, David, Vice President, Chief Information and Digital Officer, Children's Mercy Kansas City, Kansas City, MO, p. A377
CHOU, Rebecca, Director Information Systems, Palestine Regional Medical Center–East, Palestine, TX, p. A642
CHOWDHURY, Tarif TC, Chief Executive Officer, Encompass Health Rehabilitation Hospital of North Tampa, Lutz, FL, p. A138
CHOY, Ann N., Manager Human Resources and Payroll, Kuakini Medical Center, Honolulu, HI, p. A175
CHOZINSKI, Josep. P, M.D., Deputy Commander Clinical Services, Brooke Army Medical Center, Fort Sam Houston, TX, p. A618
CHRISTENSEN, Carl
Senior Vice President and Chief Information Officer, Northwestern Memorial HealthCare, Northwestern Memorial Hospital, Chicago, IL, p. A190
Senior Vice President, Chief Information Officer, Northwestern Medicine Kishwaukee Hospital, Dekalb, IL, p. A193
CHRISTENSEN, Claudia, Director, Human Resources, Mills–Peninsula Medical Center, Burlingame, CA, p. A58
CHRISTENSEN, Connie, Chief Financial Officer, Morrill County Community Hospital, Bridgeport, NE, p. A398
CHRISTENSEN, David, M.D., Senior Vice President and Chief Medical Officer, Valley Children's Healthcare, Madera, CA, p. A76
CHRISTENSEN, Elizabeth B, Director Human Resources, Northern Light Mercy Hospital, Portland, ME, p. A298
CHRISTENSEN, Eric, Chief Executive Officer, Select Specialty Hospital–Wichita, Wichita, KS, p. A262
CHRISTENSEN, G N, M.D., Chief Medical Officer, William Bee Ririe Hospital, Ely, NV, p. A408
CHRISTENSEN, Gwen, Vice President, Finance, Aurora Baycare Medical Center, Green Bay, WI, p. A712
CHRISTENSEN, Jay, FACHE, Chief Financial Officer, Lucas County Health Center, Chariton, IA, p. A232
CHRISTENSEN, Jeff
Chief Executive Officer, Encompass Health Rehabilitation Hospital of Northwest Tucson, Tucson, AZ, p. A40
Chief Executive Officer, Encompass Health Rehabilitation Institute of Tucson, Tucson, AZ, p. A40
CHRISTENSEN, Kim, Interim Chief Nursing Executive, Sheridan Community Hospital, Sheridan, MI, p. A338
CHRISTENSEN, Maria, Chief Executive Officer, Trenton Psychiatric Hospital, Trenton, NJ, p. A429
CHRISTENSEN, Marti, Director of Psychiatric Nursing, Douglas County Community Mental Health Center, Omaha, NE, p. A404
CHRISTENSEN, Michael, Chief Executive Officer, Bennett County Hospital And Nursing Home, Martin, SD, p. A574
CHRISTENSEN, Ryan, Chief Operatng Officer, St. Rose Dominican Hospitals – Siena Campus, Henderson, NV, p. A409
CHRISTENSEN, Scott
FACHE, Chief Executive Officer, Delta Health–The Medical Center, Greenville, MS, p. A362
FACHE, Chief Executive Officer, King's Daughters Medical Center, Brookhaven, MS, p. A360
CHRISTENSEN, Todd, Vice President, Finance, Grand Itasca Clinic And Hospital, Grand Rapids, MN, p. A347
CHRISTENSEN, Troy, Chief Executive Officer, Teton Valley Health Care, Driggs, ID, p. A181
CHRISTENSEN, W R, M.D., Chief of Staff, UT Health Pittsburg, Pittsburg, TX, p. A644
CHRISTENSON, Erik, Chief Executive Officer, Heart of America Medical Center, Rugby, ND, p. A483
CHRISTENSON, Ron, Chief Financial Officer, Morris County Hospital, Council Grove, KS, p. A248
CHRISTENSON, Shannon, Director Human Resources, Aurora West Allis Medical Center, West Allis, WI, p. A724
CHRISTIAN, Alan, Commanding Officer, Naval Hospital Pensacola, Pensacola, FL, p. A146
CHRISTIAN, Geoffrey, Chief Operating Officer, Baylor Scott & White Hospital Medical Center – College Station, College Station, TX, p. A607
CHRISTIAN, Karolyne, Director Human Resources, Byrd Regional Hospital, Leesville, LA, p. A287
CHRISTIAN, Lynn, MSN, R.N., Senior Director Acute Care Nursing, Centracare – Monticello, Monticello, MN, p. A351
CHRISTIAN, Michael, President, Ascension St. John Sapulpa, Sapulpa, OK, p. A520
CHRISTIANO, Barbara, Vice President, Patient Care Services and Chief Nursing Officer, Penn Medicine Princeton Medical Center, Plainsboro, NJ, p. A427
CHRISTIANSEN, Anne, Chief Financial Officer, Pioneer Memorial Hospital And Health Services, Viborg, SD, p. A578
CHRISTIANSEN, Hilary, Chief Financial Officer, George C. Grap. Community Hospital, Hamburg, IA, p. A237
CHRISTIANSEN, Keith, Chief Nursing Officer, Select Specialty Hospital–Erie, Erie, PA, p. A540
CHRISTIANSEN, Sadie, Director Human Resources, Perham Health, Perham, MN, p. A352
CHRISTIANSEN, Sara, Interim Director Human Resources, Ridgeview Sibley Medical Center, Arlington, MN, p. A342
CHRISTIANSON, Chase, Chief Executive Officer, HCA Florida Gulf Coast Hospital, Panama City, FL, p. A146
CHRISTIE, Janet L., Senior Vice President Human Resources, UF Health Shands Hospital, Gainesville, FL, p. A133
CHRISTINE, Gerald, Chief Financial Officer, Lakewood Ranch Medical Center, Bradenton, FL, p. A126
CHRISTION, Lydia, Director Human Resources, Encompass Health Rehabilitation Hospital of Dothan, Dothan, AL, p. A18
CHRISTISON, George, M.D., Medical Director, Dsh Patton, Patton, CA, p. A83
CHRISTMAN, Lawrence, Chief Financial Officer and Chief Operating Officer, Riverview Health, Noblesville, IN, p. A225
CHRISTMAN, Thomas C, Director Plant Operations, Kindred Hospital–St. Louis, Saint Louis, MO, p. A383
CHRISTNER, Jane, Chief Nursing Officer, Mclaren Thumb Region, Bad Axe, MI, p. A322
CHRISTOPH, Rebecca, Director Nursing and Patient Care Services, Mid–Valley Hospital And Clinics, Omak, WA, p. A692
CHRISTOPHEL, Randal, President and Chief Executive Officer, Goshen Health, Goshen, IN, p. A217

© 2025 AHA Guide Index of Health Care Professionals A819

Index of Health Care Professionals

Index of Health Care Professionals / Christy

CHRISTY, Richard, Information Technology Manager, Houston County Community Hospital, Erin, TN, p. A582
CHRISTY, Rose, Executive Director of Medical Services, Hamilton Center, Terre Haute, IN, p. A228
CHU, Betty, M.D., Chief Medical Officer and Vice President of Medical Affairs, Henry Ford West Bloomfield Hospital, West Bloomfield, MI, p. A340
CHUA, Jesus, M.D., Chief of Staff, Bayou Bend Health System, Franklin, LA, p. A282
CHUE, Bevins, M.D., Medical Director, Encompass Health Rehabilitation Hospital of Desert Canyon, Las Vegas, NV, p. A410
CHUGDEN, Robert, M.D., Chief Medical Officer, West Jefferson Medical Center, Marrero, LA, p. A288
CHUKWUMA, Lilian, Chief Financial Officer, United Medical Center, Washington, DC, p. A124
CHUN, Ryan, Information Resources Management, San Francisco Va Health Care System, San Francisco, CA, p. A91
CHUNG, Esther, Chief Operating Officer, St. David's Medical Center, Austin, TX, p. A600
CHUNG, Jason
M.D., Vice President, Medical Affairs and Chief Medical Officer, SSM Health St. Anthony Hospital – Midwest, Midwest City, OK, p. A515
M.D., Vice President, Medical Affairs and Chief Medical Officer, SSM Health St. Anthony Hospital – Shawnee, Shawnee, OK, p. A520
CHUNG, Maria, CPA, Director Fiscal Services, Shriners Hospitals for Children–Boston, Boston, MA, p. A311
CHUNG, Michael, Chief Financial Officer, Greater El Monte Community Hospital, South El Monte, CA, p. A96
CHUNG, William, M.D., Chief of Staff, Chinese Hospital, San Francisco, CA, p. A90
CHUQUIN, Nicolas, President, Riverside Shore Memorial Hospital, Onancock, VA, p. A681
CHURCH, Brian, Senior Vice President and Chief Financial Officer, Phoebe Putney Memorial Hospital, Albany, GA, p. A156
CHURCH, Kim
Manager Human Resources, G. Werber Bryan Psychiatric Hospital, Columbia, SC, p. A564
Manager Human Resources, William S. Hall Psychiatric Institute, Columbia, SC, p. A565
CHURCH, Rhonda, Director Human Resources, Riverbend Rehabilitation Hospital, Bastrop, LA, p. A277
CHURCHILL, Brigitte, Director of Human Resources, Memorial Satilla Health, Waycross, GA, p. A174
CHURCHILL, Larry, Director Information Services, Integris Health Woodward Hospital, Woodward, OK, p. A524
CHURCHILL, Sandi, Vice President Business Development and Operations, Professional Services, Advocate Good Samaritan Hospital, Downers Grove, IL, p. A193
CHURCHWELL, Kevin B. M.D., President and Chief Operating Officer, Boston Children's Hospital, Boston, MA, p. A310
CHURCHWELL, Kevin B., M.D., Chief Executive Officer, Boston Children's Hospital, Boston, MA, p. A310
CIANCIOTTO CROYLE, Allison, Vice President of Human Resources, Mercy Medical Center, Rockville Centre, NY, p. A458
CIANFLONE, Laura, Director Human Resources, Kenmore Mercy Hospital, Kenmore, NY, p. A444
CICCARELLI, John, Director Information Technology, Parkview Community Hospital Medical Center, Riverside, CA, p. A86
CICCHELLI, Duane, Director, Information Technology Services, San Gorgonio Memorial Hospital, Banning, CA, p. A57
CICCONE, Josie, Director, Human Resources, Garden City Hospital, Garden City, MI, p. A327
CICERI, David P, M.D., Chief Medical Officer, Baylor Scott & White Continuing Care Hospital–Temple, Temple, TX, p. A656
CICIRETTI, Mary Louise, Director Human Resources, Riddle Hospital, Media, PA, p. A546
CIHA, Clayton, President and Chief Executive Officer, Ascension Alexian Brothers Behavioral Health Hospital, Hoffman Estates, IL, p. A198
CIMINO, Michael A. Jr, Chief Financial Officer, Banner Behavioral Health Hospital – Scottsdale, Scottsdale, AZ, p. A38
CIMMINO, Denise, MSN, R.N., Assistant Vice President, Nursing and Patient Care Services, Carepoint Health Christ Hospital, Jersey City, NJ, p. A422
CINTRON, Jacob, FACHE, President and Chief Executive Officer, University Medical Center of El Paso, El Paso, TX, p. A617
CIOFFI, Cheryl, R.N., Senior Vice President, Chief Operating Officer and Chief Nursing Officer, Frederick Health, Frederick, MD, p. A304
CIOTA, Mark, M.D., Chief Executive Officer, Mayo Clinic Health System – Albert Lea And Austin, Albert Lea, MN, p. A342
CIRALDO, Lou, Information Services Representative, University Hospitals Geauga Medical Center, Chardon, OH, p. A488
CIRBA, Michael, Chief Information Officer, Good Shepherd Specialty Hospital, Bethlehem, PA, p. A535
CIRO, Maria, Director Human Resources, Select Specialty Hospital – Atlantic City, Atlantic City, NJ, p. A418
CIROCCO, Anthony, Chief Financial Officer, Dignity Health Arizona General Hospital, Laveen, AZ, p. A33
CITA, Bob, Chief Information Officer, Searhc Mt. Edgecumbe Hospital, Sitka, AK, p. A29
CITAK, Michael, M.D., Chief Medical Officer, Lake Cumberland Regional Hospital, Somerset, KY, p. A274
CITARA, Frank, Chief Hospital Executive, Hackensack Meridian Health Ocean University Medical Center, Brick Township, NJ, p. A419
CITRO, Tina, R.N., President and Vice President Operations, Wellspan Ephrata Community Hospital, Ephrata, PA, p. A539
CIUDAD, Charlotte, R.N., Associate Chief Nursing Officer, Banner – University Medical Center Phoenix, Phoenix, AZ, p. A35
CIUFO, Donna, R.N., Vice President and Chief Nurse Executive, Hackensack Meridian Health Southern Ocean Medical Center, Manahawkin, NJ, p. A423
CIVIC, Dave, M.D., Associate Director Clinical Services, U. S. Public Health Service Phoenix Indian Medical Center, Phoenix, AZ, p. A37
CIVITELLO, Dean
Vice President Human Resources, Saint Joseph's Medical Center, Yonkers, NY, p. A462
Vice President, Human Resources, Public Relations and Development, The University of Vermont Health Network–Champlain Valley Physicians Hospital, Plattsburgh, NY, p. A456
CLAASSENS, Nicolise, Nurse Executive, West Central Georgia Regional Hospital, Columbus, GA, p. A161
CLABAUGH, John, Director Human Resources, Saint Luke's East Hospital, Lee's Summit, MO, p. A379
CLACK, Deborah, Chief Nursing Officer, Hunt Regional Medical Center, Greenville, TX, p. A623
CLAIBORNE, Aimee M., Chief Human Resources Officer, Dartmouth–Hitchcock Medical Center, Lebanon, NH, p. A416
CLANCY, Kenneth, Chief Human Resources Officer, Chillicothe Veterans Affairs Medical Center, Chillicothe, OH, p. A488
CLAPP, Ann R, Director Human Resources, Encompass Health Rehabilitation Hospital of Texarkana, Texarkana, TX, p. A657
CLAPP, Nicole, R.N., MSN, FACHE, President, Mercyone Centerville Medical Center, Centerville, IA, p. A232
CLAPP, William, M.D., Chief of Medical Staff, Deaconess Union County Hospital, Morganfield, KY, p. A272
CLARK, Allan W, M.D., Medical Director, Southwood Psychiatric Hospital, Pittsburgh, PA, p. A551
CLARK, Ashley, Coordinator Human Resources, Noland Hospital Birmingham, Birmingham, AL, p. A17
CLARK, Ben, Vice President and Chief Information Officer, Centra Lynchburg General Hospital, Lynchburg, VA, p. A678
CLARK, Charity, Chief Operating Officer, Mcpherson Hospital, Inc., Mcpherson, KS, p. A254
CLARK, Christopher
D.O., President, AHN Grove City, Grove City, PA, p. A541
D.O., President, Saint Vincent Hospital, Erie, PA, p. A540
CLARK, Dale M., Vice President and Chief Executive Officer, Smyth County Community Hospital, Marion, VA, p. A679
CLARK, David D.
FACHE, Area Chief Executive Officer – Sutter East Bay Hospitals, Alta Bates Summit Medical Center – Summit Campus, Oakland, CA, p. A80
FACHE, Area Chief Executive Officer, Sutter East Bay Hospitals, Alta Bates Summit Medical Center–Alta Bates Campus, Berkeley, CA, p. A57
CLARK, Debra, Chief Nursing Officer, Shorepoint Health Port Charlotte, Port Charlotte, FL, p. A147
CLARK, Denise, Chief Nursing Officer, Holy Cross Hospital, Taos, NM, p. A437
CLARK, Heidi, Administrative Director of Nursing, Cox Monett Hospital, Inc, Monett, MO, p. A380
CLARK, Janice, Manager Human Resources, Garfield Park Behavioral Hospital, Chicago, IL, p. A189
CLARK, Jason, Director Information Systems, Greenwood County Hospital, Eureka, KS, p. A249
CLARK, Jeff, Director Information Systems, Graham Regional Medical Center, Graham, TX, p. A622
CLARK, Jeffrey, Chief Nursing Officer, Cornerstone Specialty Hospitals Southwest Louisiana, Lake Charles, LA, p. A286
CLARK, Jeremy L., Chief Executive Officer, Brookwood Baptist Medical Center, Birmingham, AL, p. A16
CLARK, Karen
MS, R.N., Vice President Operations, Advocate South Suburban Hospital, Hazel Crest, IL, p. A197
Director Administrative Services, Sonoma Developmental Center, Eldridge, CA, p. A62
Vice President Patient Care Services, St. Mary's Regional Medical Center, Lewiston, ME, p. A298
CLARK, Kent, M.D., Chief Medical Affairs and Quality, Waldo County General Hospital, Belfast, ME, p. A296
CLARK, Lisa, Director Human Resources, Willamette Valley Medical Center, Mcminnville, OR, p. A529
CLARK, Mark, Human Resources Liaison, U. S. Air Force Regional Hospital, Elmendorf Afb, AK, p. A28
CLARK, Mark A, Vice President Operations, SSM Health Good Samaritan Hospital, Mount Vernon, IL, p. A202
CLARK, Michael
Executive Vice President and Chief Financial Officer, FHN Memorial Hospital, Freeport, IL, p. A195
Fiscal Administrative Manager, Connecticut Veterans Home And Hospital, Rocky Hill, CT, p. A118
CLARK, N. Travis.
President, Valley Health – Page Memorial Hospital, Luray, VA, p. A678
President, Valley Health – Shenandoah Memorial Hospital, Woodstock, VA, p. A686
CLARK, Nancy, Vice President Human Resources, Regional Medical Center of San Jose, San Jose, CA, p. A92
CLARK, Patrick, Manager Information Technology, Sunnyview Rehabilitation Hospital, Schenectady, NY, p. A459
CLARK, Paula, Administrative Assistant and Director Human Resources, Nocona General Hospital, Nocona, TX, p. A641
CLARK, Paulette, Chief Human Resource Officer, Roseland Community Hospital, Chicago, IL, p. A190
CLARK, Peggy, Chief Nurse Executive, Sutter Santa Rosa Regional Hospital, Santa Rosa, CA, p. A95
CLARK, Randy, President, Northern Light Sebasticook Valley Hospital, Pittsfield, ME, p. A298
CLARK, Renee, M.D., Executive Vice President and Chief Operating Officer, Southcoast Hospitals Group. Fall River, MA, p. A313
CLARK, Rhonda, Interim Chief Nursing Officer, Alta Vista Regional Hospital, Las Vegas, NM, p. A435
CLARK, Robert J., President and Chief Executive Officer, Bristol Bay Area Health Corporation, Dillingham, AK, p. A28
CLARK, Robin, Chief Nursing Officer, Select Specialty Hospital–Greensboro, Greensboro, NC, p. A469
CLARK, Rodney, Chief Operating Officer, North Sunflower Medical Center, Ruleville, MS, p. A368
CLARK, Ron, M.D., Vice President Clinical Activities and Chief Medical Officer, VCU Medical Center, Richmond, VA, p. A683
CLARK, Sharon, Director Human Resources, Hillsboro Area Hospital, Hillsboro, IL, p. A198
CLARK, Shawn, Director Information Systems, The Physicians Centre Hospital, Bryan, TX, p. A605
CLARK, Teresa, Chief Executive Officer and Administrator, Wichita County Health Center, Leoti, KS, p. A253
CLARK, Theo, Director Financial Services, KPC Promise Hospital of Phoenix, Mesa, AZ, p. A34
CLARK, Thomas A.
President, MercyOne Western Division, Mercyone Primghar Medical Center, Primghar, IA, p. A242
President, MercyOne Western Division, Mercyone Siouxland Medical Center, Sioux City, IA, p. A243
CLARK, Tim, Chief Executive Officer, Acute Care Services, Adventhealth Heart of Florida, Davenport, FL, p. A129
CLARK, Troy, Chief Executive Officer, Encompass Health Rehabilitation Hospital of Kingsport, Kingsport, TN, p. A585
CLARK, William, M.D., Chief Clinical Affairs, Caro Center, Caro, MI, p. A323
CLARK, William H, Chief Financial Officer, Caldwell Memorial Hospital, Columbia, LA, p. A280
CLARKE, Clifton, Vice President Medical Management, Advocate Illinois Masonic Medical Center, Chicago, IL, p. A188
CLAROS, Elizabeth, Administrator Personnel Services, Guam Memorial Hospital Authority, Tamuning, GU, p. A730
CLARY, Elizabeth P, Vice President Behavioral Health, Parkwest Medical Center, Knoxville, TN, p. A586
CLARY, Robert, M.D., Medical Director, Logan Health – Cut Bank, Cut Bank, MT, p. A391
CLATANOFF, Kris, Director Human Resources, St. Josep. Medical Center, Houston, TX, p. A628
CLAUNCH, Jeremy, Chief Financial Officer, Power County Hospital District, American Falls, ID, p. A179
CLAUSSEN, Tammy, Chief Human Resource Officer, Tri Valley Health System, Cambridge, NE, p. A398
CLAVELL, Luis, M.D., Medical Director, San Jorge Children's And Women Hospital, Santurce, PR, p. A736

A820 Index of Health Care Professionals

© 2025 AHA Guide

Index of Health Care Professionals

Index of Health Care Professionals / Coffey

CLAVETTE, Patti, Interim Chief Financial Officer, Wickenburg Community Hospital, Wickenburg, AZ, p. A41
CLAWSON, Tonya, Manager Human Resources, Mercyone Centerville Medical Center, Centerville, IA, p. A232
CLAXTON, Tracey, Chief Financial Officer, Musc Health Chester Medical Center, Chester, SC, p. A564
CLAY, David, Chief Executive Officer, Lower Keys Medical Center, Key West, FL, p. A136
CLAY, Elysia, Chief Nursing Officer, Encompass Health Rehabilitation Hospital of Dallas, Dallas, TX, p. A611
CLAY, Jennie, Executive Director, Nap. State Hospital, Napa, CA, p. A79
CLAY, Mark, President, Ascension St. John Owasso, Owasso, OK, p. A519
CLAYBROOK, Paul, CEO/Administrator, Garfield County Health Center, Jordan, MT, p. A393
CLAYCOMB, Tony A., R.N., President, Mosaic Life Care At St. Josep. – Medical Center, Saint Joseph, MO, p. A383
CLAYTON, Julie B, Chief Nursing Officer, Barton Memorial Hospital, South Lake Tahoe, CA, p. A96
CLAYTON, Kent G., Chief Executive Officer, UCI Health – Los Alamitos, Los Alamitos, CA, p. A71
CLEARY, Gerard M., M.D., Senior Vice President, Chief of Staff and Chief Medical Officer, Jefferson Abington Health, Abington, PA, p. A534
CLEARY, Steven R, Chief Financial Officer, Overland Park Regional Medical Center, Overland Park, KS, p. A257
CLEAVER, Chuck, Vice President and Chief Financial Officer, Cleveland Clinic Martin North Hospital, Stuart, FL, p. A150
CLECKLER, Jason, Chief Executive Officer, Middle Park Health–Kremmling, Kremmling, CO, p. A110
CLEGG, Travis, Vice President, Operations, Adventist Health Castle, Kailua, HI, p. A176
CLELAND, Dub, Chief Financial Officer, Oklahoma Surgical Hospital, Tulsa, OK, p. A522
CLELAND, William H, M.D., Chief Medical Officer, University of Mississipp. Medical Center, Jackson, MS, p. A364
CLEMEN, Linda, Vice President and Chief Nursing Officer, Katherine Shaw Bethea Hospital, Dixon, IL, p. A193
CLEMENS, Gina Tess
PharmD, Market Chief Executive Officer, Mercy Rehabilitation Hospital Oklahoma City, Oklahoma City, OK, p. A517
PharmD, Market Chief Executive Officer, Mercy Rehabilitation Hospital Oklahoma City South, Oklahoma City, OK, p. A517
CLEMENT, Bernie, Chief Information Officer, Thibodaux Regional Health System, Thibodaux, LA, p. A294
CLEMENT, Charles, Chief Executive Officer, Searhc Mt. Edgecumbe Hospital, Sitka, AK, p. A29
CLEMENTS, Gabriel, Chief Executive Officer, Lee's Summit Medical Center, Lee's Summit, MO, p. A379
CLEMENTS, James, Chief Executive Officer, Cullman Regional Medical Center, Cullman, AL, p. A18
CLEMENTS, John R, Chief Financial Officer, Mccullough–Hyde Memorial Hospital/Trihealth, Oxford, OH, p. A502
CLEMENTS, Morgan, Director of Human Resources, Anmed Rehabilitation Hospital, Anderson, SC, p. A562
CLEMMENSEN, Scott
Vice President Human Resources and Leadership Enhancement, Capital Health Medical Center–Hopewell, Pennington, NJ, p. A427
Vice President Human Resources and Leadership Enhancement, Capital Health Regional Medical Center, Trenton, NJ, p. A429
CLEMMER, Deb, Vice President Human Resources, Bothwell Regional Health Center, Sedalia, MO, p. A386
CLER, Leslie, M.D., Chief Medical Officer, Methodist Dallas Medical Center, Dallas, TX, p. A612
CLEVELAND, Austin B., Chief Executive Officer, Vibra Hospital of Clear Lake, Webster, TX, p. A661
CLEVELAND, Cynthia, Ph.D., R.N., Associate Director for Patient Care Services and Nurse Executive, Birmingham Va Medical Center, Birmingham, AL, p. A16
CLEVENGER, Erin R.
Chief Nursing Officer, Memorial Medical Center, Port Lavaca, TX, p. A645
Interim Chief Executive Officer, Memorial Medical Center, Port Lavaca, TX, p. A645
CLIFFORD, Joan, R.N., FACHE, Medical Center Director and Chief Executive Officer, Bedford Veterans Affairs Medical Center, Edith Nourse Rogers Memorial Veterans Hospital, Bedford, MA, p. A309
CLIFFORD, Michael J, Director Finance, Wayne Memorial Hospital, Honesdale, PA, p. A542
CLIFT, Kym, FACHE, Chief Executive Officer, Tri–State Memorial Hospital, Clarkston, WA, p. A688
CLINE, Carl T., Vice President, Carilion Clinic and Hospital Administrator, Carilion Franklin Memorial Hospital, Rocky Mount, VA, p. A683
CLINE, Michael
Chief Executive Officer, Baptist Medical Center, San Antonio, TX, p. A648
Chief Executive Officer, Valley Baptist Medical Center–Harlingen, Harlingen, TX, p. A624
CLINE, Vickie, Director Human Resources, Mosaic Medical Center – Albany, Albany, MO, p. A371
CLINGENPEEL, Jeremy, Chief Executive Officer, Cheyenne County Hospital, Saint Francis, KS, p. A259
CLINGER, Dallas, Administrator, Power County Hospital District, American Falls, ID, p. A179
CLINITE, Ed, D.O., Chief of Staff, Adventist Health Sonora, Sonora, CA, p. A96
CLINTON, Laurie, Chief Human Resources Officer, Natchaug Hospital, Mansfield Center, CT, p. A116
CLINTON, Lee M., FACHE, President and Chief Executive Officer, Titusville Area Hospital, Titusville, PA, p. A555
CLINTON, Lori, Chief Nursing Officer, Sparta Community Hospital, Sparta, IL, p. A208
CLIPP, Jerry, Manager Human Resources, Washakie Medical Center, Worland, WY, p. A729
CLISTER, Martha L, Director Human Resources, Canonsburg Hospital, Canonsburg, PA, p. A536
CLOHSEY, Maria, Director of Nursing, Johnson Rehabilitation Institute At Hackensack Meridian Health Ocean Medical Center, Brick, NJ, p. A418
CLONCH, Les, Chief Information Officer, Scottish Rite for Children, Dallas, TX, p. A612
CLONTS, Jolene, Director Human Resources, Logan Regional Hospital, Logan, UT, p. A665
CLOPTON, Michelle, Director, Human Resources, Reunion Rehabilitation Hospital Denver, Denver, CO, p. A107
CLOSE, Debra, Chief Executive Officer, Dukes Memorial Hospital, Peru, IN, p. A226
CLOUATRE, Angela, MSN, R.N., Chief Nursing Officer, The General, Baton Rouge, LA, p. A278
CLOUD, Avery, Chief Information Officer, Our Lady of The Lake Regional Medical Center, Baton Rouge, LA, p. A278
CLOUD, Sylvia, Director Human Resources, La Downtown Medical Center, Llc, Los Angeles, CA, p. A73
CLOUGH–BERRY, Cherie, Vice President, Finance, Hampstead Hospital & Residential Treatment Facility, Hampstead, NH, p. A415
CLOUSE DAY, Sherry, Vice President Finance, Mercy Hospital Berryville, Berryville, AR, p. A43
CLOUTIER, Jonathan, Manager, Information Services, Buffalo Hospital, Buffalo, MN, p. A344
CLOUTIER, Michael, Director Information Services, Trios Health, Kennewick, WA, p. A690
CLOWERS, Jennifer, Regional Chief Financial Officer, Our Lady of The Lake Regional Medical Center, Baton Rouge, LA, p. A278
CLOWES, Jennifer, Chief Executive Officer, Billings Clinic Broadwater, Townsend, MT, p. A396
CLUBINE, Karla, Chief Executive Officer, Pershing Memorial Hospital, Brookfield, MO, p. A372
CLUCK, Robert N, M.D., Vice President and Medical Director, Texas Health Arlington Memorial Hospital, Arlington, TX, p. A598
CLUNIE, Lisa, Chief Executive Officer, Harrison County Hospital, Corydon, IN, p. A214
CLUNN, Amy, M.D., Medical Director, Encompass Health Rehabilitation Hospital of Ocala, Ocala, FL, p. A143
CLUTTS, Kathaleen, Chief Human Resources Officer, St. Luke's Des Peres Hospital, Saint Louis, MO, p. A386
CLYBURN, Mackenzie, Vice President, Operations, Baptist Health Medical Center–Little Rock, Little Rock, AR, p. A49
CLYNE, Mary Ellen, Ph.D., President and Chief Executive Officer, Clara Maass Medical Center, Belleville, NJ, p. A418
COAKLEY, Jeffrey, President and Chief Executive Officer, Community Memorial Hospital, Hamilton, NY, p. A444
COATES, Jennifer, Coordinator Information Technology, Purcell Municipal Hospital, Purcell, OK, p. A520
COATES, Robert, M.D., Vice President, Medical Affairs, Hunterdon Healthcare, Flemington, NJ, p. A421
COATS, John, M.D., Chief Medical Staff, Morehouse General Hospital, Bastrop. LA, p. A277
COATS, Kevin
Chief Financial Officer, Baylor Scott & White Medical Center–Frisco, Frisco, TX, p. A621
Chief Operating Officer and Chief Financial Officer, Baylor Scott & White Medical Center–Frisco, Frisco, TX, p. A621
COBARRUBIAS, Samuel, M.D., Chief of Staff, Clinch Memorial Hospital, Homerville, GA, p. A165
COBB, April, Chief Nursing Officer, Encompass Health Lakeshore Rehabilitation Hospital, Birmingham, AL, p. A16
COBB, Janice M, R.N., Chief Nursing Officer, Tennessee Valley Hcs – Nashville And Murfreesboro, Nashville, TN, p. A590
COBB, Jeff, Information Technologist, Guthrie County Hospital, Guthrie Center, IA, p. A237
COBB, Lindsay, Director Human Resources, Cypress Grove Behavioral Health, Bastrop. LA, p. A277
COBB, Tammy, Chief Financial Officer, Vanderbilt Bedford Hospital, Shelbyville, TN, p. A593
COBURN, Brad, Vice President, Human Resources, HCA Florida Orange Park Hospital, Orange Park, FL, p. A144
COBURN, Meridith
Vice President Information Services, Saint Francis Hospital, Tulsa, OK, p. A523
Vice President, Information Systems, Saint Francis Hospital South, Tulsa, OK, p. A523
COBURN, Paul, Chief Financial Officer, Cypress Grove Behavioral Health, Bastrop. LA, p. A277
COBURN, Thomas C., M.D., Chief Medical Officer, Middle Park Health–Kremmling, Kremmling, CO, p. A110
COCCHI, Dean, Chief Financial Officer, UF Health Jacksonville, Jacksonville, FL, p. A135
COCHRAN, Avril, R.N., Vice President Patient Care Services, North Country Hospital And Health Center, Newport, VT, p. A672
COCHRAN, Daniel
President, Adventist Healthcare Shady Grove Medical Center, Rockville, MD, p. A306
Vice President and Chief Financial Officer, Adventist Healthcare Shady Grove Medical Center, Rockville, MD, p. A306
COCHRAN, Jennifer, Director Human Relations, Northern Cochise Community Hospital, Willcox, AZ, p. A41
COCHRAN, Lena, Director of Finance, Highlands–Cashiers Hospital, Highlands, NC, p. A470
COCHRAN, Lisa, Chief Executive Officer, Kindred Hospital–Albuquerque, Albuquerque, NM, p. A432
COCHRAN, Liz, Operations Executive, Adventist Health Glendale, Glendale, CA, p. A66
COCHRAN, Tom, Chief Medical Officer, Upper Connecticut Valley Hospital, Colebrook, NH, p. A414
COCHRAN, Willie, M.D., Jr, Chief of Staff, Southern Regional Medical Center, Riverdale, GA, p. A170
COCHRANE, Donna R., Chief Nursing Officer, Liberty Regional Medical Center, Hinesville, GA, p. A165
COCHRANE, Robert K., Vice President Finance and Chief Financial Officer, Frisbie Memorial Hospital, Rochester, NH, p. A417
COCKAYNE, Heather, Chief Financial Officer, Clifton–Fine Hospital, Star Lake, NY, p. A459
COCKFIELD, Costa King
Chief Nursing Officer, Musc Health Black River Medical Center, Cades, SC, p. A562
Chief Nursing Officer, Musc Health Florence Medical Center, Florence, SC, p. A566
COCKRELL, Christopher, Executive Director Human Resources, USA Health Providence Hospital, Mobile, AL, p. A22
CODER, Charles
Vice President, UVA Health Haymarket Medical Center, Haymarket, VA, p. A677
Vice President, UVA Health Prince William Medical Center, Manassas, VA, p. A679
CODER, Denise, Chief Human Resource Officer, Cass Health, Atlantic, IA, p. A230
CODY, Karla, Chief Executive Officer, Pam Health Specialty Hospital of Tulsa, Tulsa, OK, p. A522
CODY, Kyllan, Chief Executive Officer, Encompass Health Rehabilitation Hospital of City View, Fort Worth, TX, p. A619
COE, Jason, M.D., Medical Director, Covington Behavioral Health, Covington, LA, p. A280
COE, Susan
Regional Vice President Human Resources, University of Maryland Shore Medical Center At Easton, Easton, MD, p. A304
Vice President Human Resources, University of Maryland Shore Medical Center At Chestertown, Chestertown, MD, p. A303
COELLO, Jennifer, Vice President, Operations and Administrator, Valley Health – Warren Memorial Hospital, Front Royal, VA, p. A677
COEN, Vickie, Chief Clinical Officer and Nurse Executive, Pana Community Hospital, Pana, IL, p. A205
COFFEE, Paula, Director Human Resources, Mymichigan Medical Center Saginaw, Saginaw, MI, p. A337
COFFEE, Robert, Chief Information Officer, Creek Nation Community Hospital, Okemah, OK, p. A516
COFFELL, Randy, Manager Human Resources, Mid–Valley Hospital And Clinics, Omak, WA, p. A692
COFFEY, Douglas W, R.N., MSN, Chief Nursing Officer, St. Mary's Regional Medical Center, Enid, OK, p. A512
COFFEY, Joseph, Director Facility Administration, Rochester Psychiatric Center, Rochester, NY, p. A457

Index of Health Care Professionals

Index of Health Care Professionals / Coffey

COFFEY, M. Justin, Vice President and Chief Information Officer, Medical Director Center for Brain Stimulation, Menninger Clinic, Houston, TX, p. A627
COFFING, Sylvia K, R.N., MSN, Chief Nursing and Compliance Officer, Unity Physicians Hospital, Mishawaka, IN, p. A224
COFFMAN, Brian, Director Information System, National Park Medical Center, Hot Springs, AR, p. A48
COFFMAN, Joan M., FACHE, President and Chief Executive Officer, St. Tammany Health System, Covington, LA, p. A280
COGGINS, David, MS, Chief Executive Officer, Encompass Health Rehabilitation Hospital of New England, Woburn, MA, p. A320
COGGINS, Lisa, Chief Nursing Officer, Morton Hospital And Medical Center, Taunton, MA, p. A319
COGLIANO, Michael Sr, President, Wellspan Gettysburg Hospital, Gettysburg, PA, p. A540
COHEE, Jonathan, Chief Executive Officer, Delta Health, Delta, CO, p. A106
COHEE, Thomas W., M.D., Chief of Staff, Franciscan Healthcare, West Point, NE, p. A407
COHEN, Jason, M.D., Chief Medical Officer, Logan Health – Whitefish, Whitefish, MT, p. A396
COHEN, Kathleena, MSN, R.N., Director of Nursing, Hampton Behavioral Health Center, Westampton, NJ, p. A430
COHEN, Kenneth L., M.D., Chief Medical Officer, Adventist Health White Memorial Montebello, Montebello, CA, p. A78
COHEN, Lisa, Chief Financial Officer, New London Hospital, New London, NH, p. A416
COHEN, Mark, M.D., Chief Medical Officer, Piedmont Atlanta Hospital, Atlanta, GA, p. A158
COHEN, Philip A., Chief Executive Officer, Monterey Park Hospital, Monterey Park, CA, p. A78
COHN, David, Interim Chief Executive Officer, The Osuccc – James, Columbus, OH, p. A493
COKER, Cindy, Vice President, Patient Care Services, ECU Health Chowan Hospital, Edenton, NC, p. A467
COKER, Robert, M.D., Medical Director, Deer's Head Hospital Center, Salisbury, MD, p. A307
COKER, Tina, MSN, Chief Nursing Officer, Henderson Hospital, Henderson, NV, p. A409
COLADONATO, Angela R., R.N., MSN, Chief Nursing Officer, Penn Medicine Chester County Hospital, West Chester, PA, p. A557
COLAMARIA, James, Director of Nursing, Four Winds Hospital, Saratoga Springs, NY, p. A458
COLAS, Chuck, M.D., Medical Director, Surprise Valley Health Care District, Cedarville, CA, p. A59
COLBERT, TameKia, Administrator, Louisiana Extended Care Hospital of Natchitoches, Natchitoches, LA, p. A289
COLBURN, Douglas, Chief Information Officer, Piedmont Columbus Regional Northside, Columbus, GA, p. A161
COLBY, Dennis, M.D., Chief of Staff, Iowa Specialty Hospital–Clarion, Clarion, IA, p. A232
COLBY, Karen M, MS, Chief Nursing Officer, Shirley Ryan Abilitylab, Chicago, IL, p. A191
COLCHER, Robert E, M.D., Medical Director, Valley Forge Medical Center, Norristown, PA, p. A547
COLE, Bernadette, R.N., Chief Nursing Officer, Munson Healthcare Charlevoix Hospital, Charlevoix, MI, p. A323
COLE, Beth, Director Information Services, Lewisgale Medical Center, Boones Mill, VA, p. A674
COLE, Carlene, Manager Human Resources, Kittson Healthcare, Hallock, MN, p. A348
COLE, Dale, Director, Human Resources, Corona Regional Medical Center, Corona, CA, p. A60
COLE, Donas, FACHE, President, Baylor Scott & White Medical Center – Lake Pointe, Rowlett, TX, p. A648
COLE, Dylan, Chief Medical Officer, Moab Regional Hospital, Moab, UT, p. A666
COLE, F Sessions, M.D., Chief Medical Officer, St. Louis Children's Hospital, Saint Louis, MO, p. A384
COLE, Jason
Regional Chief Financial Officer, Baylor Scott & White Medical Center – Round Rock, Round Rock, TX, p. A647
Senior Director, Management Information Systems, Suburban Hospital, Bethesda, MD, p. A303
COLE, Kristin B, R.N., Chief Nursing Officer, Springhill Medical Center, Springhill, LA, p. A293
COLE, Lori, Director Information Technology, UNC Health Wayne, Goldsboro, NC, p. A469
COLE, Robert, Chief Operating Officer, Connecticut Mental Health Center, New Haven, CT, p. A117
COLE, Sherry, Chief Nursing Officer, Grandview Medical Center, Birmingham, AL, p. A16
COLE, William Clifford, M.D., Chief of Staff, Leconte Medical Center, Sevierville, TN, p. A593
COLEMAN, Alisa, President, Baptist Health Deaconess Madisonville, Inc., Madisonville, KY, p. A271
COLEMAN, Anne, Administrator, Ascension St. Vincent Indianapolis Hospital, Indianapolis, IN, p. A219
COLEMAN, Connie, R.N., Chief Nursing Officer, Wyoming Medical Center, Casper, WY, p. A726
COLEMAN, Curt, FACHE, President, Chi Health Good Samaritan, Kearney, NE, p. A401
COLEMAN, D. Scott, M.D., Medical Director, Livingston Healthcare, Livingston, MT, p. A394
COLEMAN, Donna, Coordinator Human Resources, Jackson County Hospital District, Edna, TX, p. A616
COLEMAN, Edie, Chief Financial Officer, NYC Health + Hospitals/Metropolitan, New York, NY, p. A451
COLEMAN, Gregory, Commanding Officer, U. S. Air Force Regional Hospital, Eglin Afb, FL, p. A131
COLEMAN, Jim Jr, Chief Executive Officer, Erlanger Medical Center, Chattanooga, TN, p. A580
COLEMAN, Karen, Director of Nursing, Grove Hill Memorial Hospital, Grove Hill, AL, p. A20
COLEMAN, Kevin, M.D., Chief Medical Officer, Grand River Hospital District, Rifle, CO, p. A113
COLEMAN, Linda G., Chief Nursing Officer, Candler County Hospital, Metter, GA, p. A168
COLEMAN, Melissa, Director Human Resources, Encompass Health Rehabilitation Hospital of Sewickley, Sewickley, PA, p. A554
COLEMAN, Robert, Chief Executive Officer and Administrator, Baptist Memorial Hospital–Golden Triangle, Columbus, MS, p. A361
COLEMAN, Shane, Chief Operating Officer, Palo Pinto General Hospital, Mineral Wells, TX, p. A639
COLEMAN, Stacy, MS, President, SSM Health St. Anthony Hospital – Midwest, Midwest City, OK, p. A515
COLEMAN, Stanley, Director Human Resources, Texas Rehabilitation Hospital of Arlington, Arlington, TX, p. A598
COLERICK, Steven, Chief Executive Officer, Buena Vista Regional Medical Center, Storm Lake, IA, p. A244
COLETTA, Antonio
Vice President Human Resources, Carle Bromenn Medical Center, Normal, IL, p. A203
Vice President Human Resources, Carle Eureka Hospital, Eureka, IL, p. A194
COLETTA, Diane, Vice President Human Resources, Royal Oaks Hospital, Windsor, MO, p. A388
COLETTI, Edmund, Chief Executive Officer, Helen Hayes Hospital, West Haverstraw, NY, p. A461
COLEY, Aaron, Chief Financial Officer, Orange County, Saddleback Medical Center, Laguna Hills, CA, p. A69
COLEY, Brenda
Executive Director, Adventhealth Central Texas, Killeen, TX, p. A632
Executive Director, Adventhealth Rollins Brook, Lampasas, TX, p. A633
COLGAN, Teresa
Chief Executive Officer, Henry County Health Center, Mount Pleasant, IA, p. A240
Vice President Nursing, Southeast Iowa Regional Medical Center, West Burlington Campus, West Burlington, IA, p. A245
COLGLAZIER, Garrett, Director Health Information Management, Sabetha Community Hospital, Sabetha, KS, p. A259
COLL, Shawni, D.O., Chief Medical Officer, Tahoe Forest Hospital District, Truckee, CA, p. A98
COLLADO, Raquel, Vice President Human Resources, New York Community Hospital, New York, NY, p. A450
COLLAZO, Margaret, MSN, R.N., Chief Nursing Officer, Temple Health–Chestnut Hill Hospital, Philadelphia, PA, p. A550
COLLAZO, Marian, Director Finance, Hospital Menonita Ponce, Coto Laurel, PR, p. A732
COLLETT, John, Vice President and Chief Financial Officer, Cayuga Medical Center At Ithaca, Ithaca, NY, p. A444
COLLETT, Josh, Director Human Resources, Pineville Community Health Center, Pineville, KY, p. A273
COLLETTI, Teresa, Director Patient Services, South Florida Baptist Hospital, Plant City, FL, p. A147
COLLEY, Sarah
Senior Vice President and Chief Human Resource Officer, Methodist Healthcare Memphis Hospitals, Memphis, TN, p. A589
Senior Vice President Human Resources, Regional One Health, Memphis, TN, p. A589
COLLIER, Brad, Director, Piedmont Newton Hospital, Covington, GA, p. A162
COLLIER, Erin, Chief Executive Officer, Encompass Health Rehabilitation Hospital of Montgomery, Montgomery, AL, p. A22
COLLIER, Jack, M.D., Chief of Staff, Mountainview Hospital, Las Vegas, NV, p. A410
COLLINS, Alesha Danielle, MSN, R.N., Chief Nursing Officer, Howard Memorial Hospital, Nashville, AR, p. A51
COLLINS, Bobby, Director Human Resources, Lonesome Pine Hospital, Big Stone Gap. VA, p. A673
COLLINS, Chauncey, Chief Operating Officer and Chief Financial Officer, Austen Riggs Center, Stockbridge, MA, p. A318
COLLINS, Daniel, M.D., Clinical Director, New Mexico Behavioral Health Institute At Las Vegas, Las Vegas, NM, p. A435
COLLINS, Edmund, Chief Information Officer, Cleveland Clinic Martin North Hospital, Stuart, FL, p. A150
COLLINS, Ethan, R.N., Chief Nursing Officer, Smyth County Community Hospital, Marion, VA, p. A679
COLLINS, Frances, Director of Nursing, Elizabeth Parsons Ware Packard Mental Health Center, Springfield, IL, p. A209
COLLINS, Harold E, JD, Chief Financial Officer, Franciscan Healthcare Munster, Munster, IN, p. A224
COLLINS, Jeff, Chief Medical Officer, Providence St. Joseph's Hospital, Chewelah, WA, p. A688
COLLINS, John
Corporate Chief Financial Officer, Chapman Global Medical Center, Orange, CA, p. A81
Chief Financial Officer, Anaheim Global Medical Center, Anaheim, CA, p. A55
Chief Financial Officer, Orange County Global Medical Center, Inc., Santa Ana, CA, p. A93
Chief Financial Officer, South Coast Global Medical Center, Santa Ana, CA, p. A93
COLLINS, John F, President and Chief Executive Officer, Nyu Langone Hospitals, New York, NY, p. A452
COLLINS, John R, Chief Financial Officer, Hemet Global Medical Center, Hemet, CA, p. A67
COLLINS, Kevin J., M.D., Medical Director, Chi St. Vincent Sherwood Rehabilitation Hospital, A Partner of Encompass Health, Sherwood, AR, p. A53
COLLINS, Kimberly, M.D., Chief of Staff, Ascension Saint Thomas Dekalb, Smithville, TN, p. A593
COLLINS, Lainie, Human Resources Partner, Ascension St. Vincent Clay Hospital, Brazil, IN, p. A213
COLLINS, Leonora, Chief Nursing Officer, Nashville General Hospital, Nashville, TN, p. A590
COLLINS, Pam, Director Human Resources, Avala, Covington, LA, p. A280
COLLINS, Pamela, Vice President Chief Patient Services Officer, Mccullough–Hyde Memorial Hospital/Trihealth, Oxford, OH, p. A502
COLLINS, Richard F, M.D., Executive Vice President and Chief Medical Officer, Jefferson Hospital, Jefferson Hills, PA, p. A542
COLLINS, Ricky M, M.D., Chief of Staff, Whitesburg Arh Hospital, Whitesburg, KY, p. A275
COLLINS, Ronald, Chief Financial Officer, Pamp. Regional Medical Center, Pampa, TX, p. A642
COLLINS, Seamus, President, Northwestern Medicine Lake Forest Hospital, Lake Forest, IL, p. A200
COLLINS, Sharon, Chief Information Officer, Salem Veterans Affairs Medical Center, Salem, VA, p. A683
COLLINS, Stacey, R.N., Site Administrator, Chief Nursing Officer, Diley Ridge Medical Center, Canal Winchester, OH, p. A487
COLLINS, Timothy, Vice President, Chief Operations Executive, Scripp. Green Hospital, La Jolla, CA, p. A68
COLLINS, Traci
Chief Nursing Officer, Athens–Limestone Hospital, Athens, AL, p. A15
President, Athens–Limestone Hospital, Athens, AL, p. A15
COLLIPP, Dan, M.D., Chief of Staff, Wayne Memorial Hospital, Jesup. GA, p. A165
COLLISON, June M., President, Community Hospital of San Bernardino, San Bernardino, CA, p. A88
COLLOM, Bobbie, Nursing Director, North Runnels Hospital, Winters, TX, p. A663
COLMAN, Gerard, Chief Operating Officer, Aurora West Allis Medical Center, West Allis, WI, p. A724
COLMENARES, Derek
M.D., Chief Medical Officer, SSM Health Ripon Community Hospital, Ripon, WI, p. A721
M.D., Chief Medical Officer, SSM Health St. Agnes Hospital – Fond Du Lac, Fond Du Lac, WI, p. A711
M.D., Chief Medical Officer, SSM Health Waupun Memorial Hospital, Waupun, WI, p. A724
COLOMBO, Armando, Chief Executive Officer, Menninger Clinic, Houston, TX, p. A627
COLOMBO, Maria Carmen
R.N., Chief Nursing Officer, Sharp Mary Birch Hospital for Women And Newborns, San Diego, CA, p. A89
R.N., Chief Nursing Officer, Sharp Mesa Vista Hospital, San Diego, CA, p. A90
COLON, Anthony, Director, Veterans Affairs Northern Indiana Health Care System, Fort Wayne, IN, p. A217
COLON, Carmen, Chief Executive Officer, Ryder Memorial Hospital, Humacao, PR, p. A733

A822 Index of Health Care Professionals

Index of Health Care Professionals / Conroy

Index of Health Care Professionals

COLON, Julio, Financial Director, Hospital De Damas, Ponce, PR, p. A734
COLON, Omar, M.D., Medical Director, Encompass Health Rehabilitation Hospital of Plano, Plano, TX, p. A644
COLONNELLI, Kimberly Ann, Chief Operating Officer and Chief Nurse Executive, Kaiser Permanente San Rafael Medical Center, San Rafael, CA, p. A93
COLORADO, Judy, R.N., Chief Nursing Officer, Monmouth Medical Center, Southern Campus, Lakewood, NJ, p. A422
COLSDEN, Kristen, Director of Nursing, Osmond General Hospital, Osmond, NE, p. A405
COLSON, Wayne, Chief Financial Officer, Southwestern Medical Center, Lawton, OK, p. A514
COLTHARP, Missy, Director, Baptist Memorial Hospital–Union County, New Albany, MS, p. A367
COLTON, Jan, M.D., Acting Clinical Director, U. S. Public Health Service Indian Hospital, Pine Ridge, SD, p. A575
COLVARD, Dusty, Manager Information Technology, Adventist Health Tehachap. Valley, Tehachapi, CA, p. A97
COLVERT, Richard, Chief Information Officer, Royal Oaks Hospital, Windsor, MO, p. A388
COLVIN, Garren
Chief Executive Officer, St. Elizabeth Dearborn, Lawrenceburg, IN, p. A222
Chief Executive Officer, St. Elizabeth Edgewood, Edgewood, KY, p. A265
Chief Executive Officer, St. Elizabeth Florence, Florence, KY, p. A265
Chief Executive Officer, St. Elizabeth Fort Thomas, Fort Thomas, KY, p. A266
Chief Executive Officer, St. Elizabeth Grant, Williamstown, KY, p. A275
COLVIN, William, Human Resources Officer, Claiborne Memorial Medical Center, Homer, LA, p. A283
COLWELL, Dean, D.O., Vice President Medical Affairs, Ohiohealth Doctors Hospital, Columbus, OH, p. A492
COLWELL, Jordan, R.N., Chief Nursing Officer, Box Butte General Hospital, Alliance, NE, p. A397
COLWELL, Melodie, Chief Financial Officer, Baptist Health Medical Center – Drew County, Monticello, AR, p. A50
COLYER, Valeri J
Director Human Resources, Dickenson Community Hospital, Clintwood, VA, p. A675
Director Human Resources, Norton Community Hospital, Norton, VA, p. A680
COMAIANNI, Sheri, Vice President Human Resources, Bakersfield Memorial Hospital, Bakersfield, CA, p. A56
COMBETTA, Jeffery, M.D., Medical Director, Riverbend Rehabilitation Hospital, Bastrop, LA, p. A277
COMBS, Jennifer, Chief Financial Officer, Jackson County Memorial Hospital, Altus, OK, p. A509
COMBS, Mike, Manager Information Technology, Holdenville General Hospital, Holdenville, OK, p. A513
COMBS, Scott, NWSA Chief Financial Officer, Providence Regional Medical Center Everett, Everett, WA, p. A689
COMBS, Will, Director Information Technology, WVU Medicine – Harrison Community Hospital, Cadiz, OH, p. A487
COMER, Jeff, PsyD, Chief Executive Officer, Summit Healthcare Regional Medical Center, Show Low, AZ, p. A39
COMER, Jeff W., Chief Executive Officer, Fresno Surgical Hospital, Fresno, CA, p. A64
COMER, Jennifer, M.D., Medical Director, Valle Vista Health System, Greenwood, IN, p. A218
COMER, Randy
Chief Financial Officer, Athens–Limestone Hospital, Athens, AL, p. A15
Chief Operating Officer, Athens–Limestone Hospital, Athens, AL, p. A15
COMER, Scott M, Vice President Human Resources, Marshall Medical Center, Placerville, CA, p. A83
COMER, William J., President, Mountain Vista Medical Center, Mesa, AZ, p. A34
COMERFORD, Jennifer, Manager Information Services, Midstate Medical Center, Meriden, CT, p. A116
COMISSIONG, Tina A. Esq, Chief Executive Officer, Schneider Regional Medical Center, Saint Thomas, VI, p. A736
COMITO, Arthur, Chief Financial Officer, St. Luke's Easton Campus, Easton, PA, p. A539
COMP, Susan, Senior Vice President and Chief Nursing Officer, UPMC Harrisburg, Harrisburg, PA, p. A541
COMPTON, Brenda, Manager Information Technology, Plumas District Hospital, Quincy, CA, p. A84
COMPTON, Carri, Administrative Officer, Heartland Behavioral Health Services, Nevada, MO, p. A381
COMPTON, Mark, Chief Financial Officer, Greeneville Community Hospital East, Greeneville, TN, p. A583
COMPTON, Meghan, Executive Vice President, Chief Clinic Operations Officer, Altru Health System, Grand Forks, ND, p. A481
COMPTON, Randy, Information Technology and System Director, The Medical Center At Russellville, Russellville, KY, p. A274
CONABOY, William P., Chief Executive Officer, Allied Services Scranton Rehabilitation Hospital, Scranton, PA, p. A554
CONANT, Cathy, Chief Human Resources and Personnel, Eastern Plumas Health Care, Portola, CA, p. A84
CONANT, Merrill, M.D., Chief of Staff, St. Catherine Hospital – Dodge City, Dodge City, KS, p. A248
CONANT, Sonya, Senior Director Human Resources, Alaska Native Medical Center, Anchorage, AK, p. A27
CONAWAY, E Edwin, M.D., Vice President Medical Affairs and Chief Medical Officer, Ohiohealth Southeastern Medical Center, Cambridge, OH, p. A487
CONCANNON, Laura, M.D., Regional Chief Medical Officer, Ascension Saint Mary – Chicago, Chicago, IL, p. A188
CONCEPCION, Walter, Chief Executive Officer, West Gables Rehabilitation Hospital, Miami, FL, p. A141
CONDE STERLING, Tania, President, Multy Medical Rehabilitation Hospital San Juan, San Juan, PR, p. A735
CONDIT, Brian
M.D., Chief Medical Officer, Johnston Memorial Hospital, Abingdon, VA, p. A673
M.D., Vice President Chief Medical Officer, Virginia Operations Medical Staff Services, Russell County Medical Center, Lebanon, VA, p. A678
CONDIT, Edward, President and Chief Executive Officer, St. Mary's General Hospital, Passaic, NJ, p. A426
CONDOLUCI, David, M.D., Senior Vice President and Chief Medical Officer, Jefferson Stratford Hospital, Stratford, NJ, p. A428
CONDON, William, President, Ascension Sacred Heart Pensacola, Pensacola, FL, p. A146
CONDRIN, Michael, Chief Administrator/System Chief Operating Officer, UC Davis Medical Center, Sacramento, CA, p. A87
CONDRY, Donna, Director Human Resources, Unitypoint Health – Jones Regional Medical Center, Anamosa, IA, p. A230
CONE, Maryann, Chief Operating Officer, Sharp Grossmont Hospital, La Mesa, CA, p. A68
CONFALONE, Daniel, Chief Financial Officer and Vice President Finance, St. Mary Medical Center, Langhorne, PA, p. A543
CONFER, James, Manager Information Systems, Clarion Hospital, Clarion, PA, p. A537
CONGDON, James B, M.D., Medical Director, The Horsham Clinic, Ambler, PA, p. A534
CONGER, Sue, Chief Operating Officer, Eastside Psychiatric Hospital, Tallahassee, FL, p. A151
CONKLIN, Maggie C
M.P.H., Interim Chief Nurse Officer, UVA Health Prince William Medical Center, Manassas, VA, p. A679
M.P.H., Interim Chief Nursing Officer, UVA Health Haymarket Medical Center, Haymarket, VA, p. A677
CONKLIN, Michael E Jr, Chief Financial Officer, St. Josep. Health Services of Rhode Island, North Providence, RI, p. A560
CONKLIN, Stacey A, Chief Nursing Officer, Mount Sinai South Nassau, Oceanside, NY, p. A454
CONKLING, Victoria, Vice President, Patient Services and Chief Nursing Officer, UHS Delaware Valley Hospital, Walton, NY, p. A461
CONLEY, Christopher, M.D., President of the Medical Staff, Tristar Skyline Medical Center, Nashville, TN, p. A591
CONLEY, Eric, President, Froedtert And The Medical College of Wisconsin Froedtert Hospital, Milwaukee, WI, p. A717
CONLEY, Joanna J., FACHE, Chief Executive Officer, Doctors Hospital, Augusta, GA, p. A158
CONLEY, Kenneth, Chief Financial Officer, Baptist Memorial Hospital – Calhoun, Calhoun City, MS, p. A360
CONLEY, Kirkpatrick, Senior Vice President, Regional President, Central, Sentara Careplex Hospital, Hampton, VA, p. A677
CONLEY, Melissa, Director Human Resources, Midwest Medical Center, Galena, IL, p. A195
CONLEY, Michelle E, R.N., Chief Nursing Officer, Jefferson Health Northeast, Philadelphia, PA, p. A549
CONLEY, Teressa, Vice President and Chief Operating Officer, St. Rose Dominican Hospitals – Rose De Lima Campus, Henderson, NV, p. A409
CONLEY, Theresa, Manager Human Resources, Cherokee Regional Medical Center, Cherokee, IA, p. A232
CONLON, John, M.D., Chief Medical Officer, Saint Anne's Hospital, Fall River, MA, p. A313
CONN, Chris, Chief Financial Officer, HCA Florida Poinciana Hospital, Kissimmee, FL, p. A136
CONN, Stephanie
Chief Executive Officer, Coshocton Regional Medical Center, Coshocton, OH, p. A493
Chief Executive Officer, East Liverpool City Hospital, East Liverpool, OH, p. A495
CONNAWAY, Jessica, Director Human Resources, Deaconess Illinois Crossroads, Mount Vernon, IL, p. A202
CONNEL, Lorene, Chief Human Resources Management Service, Rocky Mountain Regional Va Medical Center, Aurora, CO, p. A103
CONNELL, Eric, Chief Executive Officer, North Big Horn Hospital District, Lovell, WY, p. A727
CONNELL, Lawrence B., Medical Center Director, Providence Veterans Affairs Medical Center, Providence, RI, p. A560
CONNELL, Pam, Manager Human Resources, Windsor–Laurelwood Center for Behavioral Medicine, Willoughby, OH, p. A507
CONNELLEY, Bertha Mary, Director Human Resources, Austen Riggs Center, Stockbridge, MA, p. A318
CONNELLY, Jac, Chief Financial Officer, Rose Medical Center, Denver, CO, p. A107
CONNELLY, Kathryn, Manager Information Technology, Connecticut Valley Hospital, Middletown, CT, p. A117
CONNELLY, Michael P., CPA, FACHE, Executive Vice President and Chief Financial Officer, Melrosewakefield Healthcare, Melrose, MA, p. A315
CONNELLY, Steven, M.D., President and Chief Medical Officer, Park Nicollet Methodist Hospital, Saint Louis Park, MN, p. A354
CONNER, Chad, Administrator, Northern Louisiana Medical Center, Ruston, LA, p. A291
CONNER, Jeff, M.D., Chief Medical Staff, Loma Linda University Medical Center–Murrieta, Murrieta, CA, p. A79
CONNER, June, R.N., Chief Operating Officer, Emory University Hospital, Atlanta, GA, p. A157
CONNER, Leslie, M.P.H., Chief Executive Officer, Santa Cruz County Psychiatric Health Facility, Santa Cruz, CA, p. A94
CONNER, Stacey, Human Resources Director, Ed Fraser Memorial Hospital, Macclenny, FL, p. A138
CONNERTON, Kathryn, President and Chief Executive Officer, Guthrie Lourdes Hospital, Binghamton, NY, p. A439
CONNICK, Mary, Chief Financial Officer, San Francisco Campus for Jewish Living, San Francisco, CA, p. A91
CONNOLLY, Christine, M.D., Chief of Staff, Keefe Memorial Hospital, Cheyenne Wells, CO, p. A104
CONNOLLY, Teresa, R.N., Chief Nursing Officer, Mayo Clinic Hospital In Arizona, Phoenix, AZ, p. A36
CONNOR, Paul J. III, Chief Administrative Officer, Stony Brook University Hospital, Stony Brook, NY, p. A459
CONNOR, William, Assistant Administrator and Director Human Resources, River Hospital, Alexandria Bay, NY, p. A438
CONNOR KENT, Stephanie, Chief Executive Officer and Interim Chief Nursing Officer, Sutter Maternity And Surgery Center of Santa Cruz, Santa Cruz, CA, p. A94
CONNORS, Lawrence J, Chief Operating Officer, HSHS St. Mary's Hospital Medical Center, Green Bay, WI, p. A712
CONNORS, Michael
Senior Vice President and Chief Financial Officer, Cap. Cod Hospital, Hyannis, MA, p. A314
Senior Vice President and Chief Financial Officer, Falmouth Hospital, Falmouth, MA, p. A313
CONNORS, Robert, M.D., President, Helen DeVos Children's Hospital, Corewell Health Butterworth Hospital, Grand Rapids, MI, p. A328
CONNY, Sophia, Deputy Administrative Officer, U. S. Public Health Service Indian Hospital, Pine Ridge, SD, p. A575
CONRAD, Daniel S, M.D., President, Abbott Northwestern Hospital, Minneapolis, MN, p. A350
CONRAD, Elizabeth P., Senior Vice President and Chief Human Resource Officer, Lahey Hospital & Medical Center, Burlington, MA, p. A312
CONRAD, Heidi, Vice President and Chief Financial Officer, Regions Hospital, Saint Paul, MN, p. A354
CONRAD, Matthew
Chief Operating Officer, Mountainview Regional Medical Center, Las Cruces, NM, p. A435
Interim Chief Executive Officer and Chief Operating Officer, Mountainview Regional Medical Center, Las Cruces, NM, p. A435
CONRATH, Mark, Chief Financial Officer, Drumright Regional Hospital, Drumright, OK, p. A511
CONROW–VERVERIS, Stacy, Director Human Resources, Mineral Community Hospital, Superior, MT, p. A396
CONROY, Joanne M., M.D., Chief Executive Officer and President, Dartmouth–Hitchcock Medical Center, Lebanon, NH, p. A416
CONROY, Mike, Chief Financial Officer, Methodist Mckinney Hospital, Mckinney, TX, p. A638
CONROY, Tim, Chief Information Officer, Cary Medical Center, Caribou, ME, p. A296
CONROY, Tracy, Chief Executive Officer, Daviess Community Hospital, Washington, IN, p. A229

Index of Health Care Professionals

Index of Health Care Professionals / Consbruck

CONSBRUCK, Todd, Administrator, Sleep. Eye Medical Center, Sleep. Eye, MN, p. A355
CONSIGLIO, Gayle, Chief Information Officer, Mclaren Lapeer Region, Lapeer, MI, p. A332
CONSIGNEY, Ginger, Vice President Human Resources, Lake Charles Memorial Hospital, Lake Charles, LA, p. A286
CONSOLVER, Roberta
Chief Executive Officer/Chief Clinical Officer, Healthbridge Children's Hospital, Orange, CA, p. A81
Chief Information Officer, Healthbridge Children's Hospital, Orange, CA, p. A81
CONSTANT, Jean–Charles, Administrator, Dover Behavioral Health System, Dover, DE, p. A121
CONSTANTINE–CASTILLO, DHA, DNP, Candi, MSN, R.N., Chief Executive Officer, Harlingen Medical Center, Harlingen, TX, p. A623
CONTE, John, Director Facility Services and Real Estate, Wayne Memorial Hospital, Honesdale, PA, p. A542
CONTE, Thomas, M.D., President, Medical Staff, Ohiohealth Van Wert Hospital, Van Wert, OH, p. A505
CONTI, John, Director Finance, Shriners Hospitals for Children–Greenville, Greenville, SC, p. A567
CONTI, Stephen, Controller, Gifford Medical Center, Randolph, VT, p. A672
CONTRERAS, Amy Esq, Chief Nursing Officer, Milford Valley Memorial Hospital, Milford, UT, p. A665
CONTRERAS, Cristina, Chief Executive Officer, NYC Health + Hospitals/Metropolitan, New York, NY, p. A451
CONTRERAS–SOTO, Alex, President, Palmetto General Hospital, Hialeah, FL, p. A133
CONVERY, Luanne, Vice President Patient Care Services, Putnam Hospital, Carmel, NY, p. A441
CONWAY, Jimmy, M.D., President Medical Staff, Northwest Surgical Hospital, Oklahoma City, OK, p. A517
CONWAY, Kevin, Chief Information Officer, UPMC Mercy, Pittsburgh, PA, p. A552
CONWILL, Michael, Director Human Resources, Corpus Christi Medical Center – Doctors Regional, Corpus Christi, TX, p. A609
CONYERS, Robin, Administrator, Chi Health Creighton University Medical Center – Bergan Mercy, Omaha, NE, p. A403
COOGAN, Ben, Chief Executive Officer, Medical City Plano, Plano, TX, p. A645
COOK, Aaron, Director Information Services, Christus Ochsner Lake Area Hospital, Lake Charles, LA, p. A286
COOK, Alan, Chief Medical Officer, Central Regional Hospital, Butner, NC, p. A464
COOK, Anthony, M.D., Chief of Staff, Avera Holy Family Hospital, Estherville, IA, p. A236
COOK, Brooke, Director of Nursing, Carolina Dunes Behavioral Health, Leland, NC, p. A471
COOK, Carla, Director of Nursing, Scotland County Hospital, Memphis, MO, p. A380
COOK, Courtney L., Vice President of Nursing and Patient Care Services, Northern Light Inland Hospital, Waterville, ME, p. A299
COOK, Daniel, Director of Finance, Aurora Medical Center – Bay Area, Marinette, WI, p. A715
COOK, Darrin
Chief Executive Officer and Administrator, Horizon Specialty Hospital, Las Vegas, NV, p. A410
Chief Operating Officer, Saint Vincent Hospital, Worcester, MA, p. A320
COOK, David, Manager Information Systems, Christus Dubuis Hospital of Hot Springs, Hot Springs National Park, AR, p. A48
COOK, David A, Vice President and Chief Financial Officer, University Hospitals Elyria Medical Center, Elyria, OH, p. A495
COOK, Elizabeth, Chief Information Officer, Mizell Memorial Hospital, Opp. AL, p. A23
COOK, G. Anthony, M.D., Medical Director, Hemphill County Hospital District, Canadian, TX, p. A606
COOK, Greg
Chief Executive Officer, Castleview Hospital, Price, UT, p. A667
President and Chief Executive Officer, Upper Connecticut Valley Hospital, Colebrook, NH, p. A414
COOK, Heidi, Chief Nursing Officer, Warner Hospital And Health Services, Clinton, IL, p. A192
COOK, James, PRMCE Chief Medical Officer, Providence Regional Medical Center Everett, Everett, WA, p. A689
COOK, Jana, Vice President and Chief Financial Officer, Phelp. Health, Rolla, MO, p. A382
COOK, John
Interim Chief Information Officer, UC Davis Medical Center, Sacramento, CA, p. A87
Vice President and Chief Financial Officer, Mercyhealth Hospital And Trauma Center – Janesville, Janesville, WI, p. A713
COOK, Jon, Chief Executive Officer, Rehabilitation Hospital of Northern Arizona, Flagstaff, AZ, p. A31
COOK, Kim, Interim Clinical Applications Services Manager, Tri–City Medical Center, Oceanside, CA, p. A81
COOK, LaMont, Chief Executive Officer, Webster County Community Hospital, Red Cloud, NE, p. A405
COOK, Linda, Vice President Human Resources, Providence St. Josep. Hospital Eureka, Eureka, CA, p. A62
COOK, Marcia, Director Information Technology, Bates County Memorial Hospital, Butler, MO, p. A372
COOK, Mary Ann, Director of Nursing, Red Lake Indian Health Service Hospital, Red Lake, MN, p. A353
COOK, Mary Ann., Chief Executive Officer, Red Lake Service Unit, Red Lake Indian Health Service Hospital, Red Lake, MN, p. A353
COOK, Natalie
Administrative Director of Human Resources, Manchester Memorial Hospital, Manchester, CT, p. A116
Administrative Director, Human Resources, Rockville General Hospital, Vernon, CT, p. A119
COOK, Nichole, Chief Financial Officer, Ozarks Healthcare, West Plains, MO, p. A388
COOK, Pamela W, Chief Financial Officer, Trace Regional Hospital, Houston, MS, p. A363
COOK, Patrick, Vice President Support Services, Morgan Medical Center, Madison, GA, p. A167
COOK, Paul, M.D., Chief Medical Officer, Midcoast Central – Llano, Llano, TX, p. A635
COOK, Robert, Chief Nursing Officer, Twin Cities Community Hospital, Templeton, CA, p. A97
COOK, Sheliah, Director Human Resources, Boone Memorial Hospital, Madison, WV, p. A702
COOK, Stacey M, MS, Vice President, Human Resources, University of Maryland Charles Regional Medical Center, La Plata, MD, p. A305
COOK, Thomas M, Chief Financial Officer, Good Samaritan Hospital, Vincennes, IN, p. A228
COOK, Wendy J., Chief Financial Officer, Piedmont Athens Regional Medical Center, Athens, GA, p. A156
COOK, William
Associate Warden Business Service, California Mens Colony Correctional Treatment Center, San Luis Obispo, CA, p. A92
Director, Southern Virginia Mental Health Institute, Danville, VA, p. A675
President and Chief Executive Officer, Vail Health, Vail, CO, p. A114
COOKE, Barbara, Director Health Information Systems, Montefiore Mount Vernon, Mount Vernon, NY, p. A446
COOKE, David
R.N., Chief Nursing Officer, Sutter Surgical Hospital – North Valley, Yuba City, CA, p. A102
R.N., Chief Operating Officer, Hi–Desert Medical Center, Joshua Tree, CA, p. A68
COOKE, Nancy, Chief Executive Officer, Martin County Hospital District, Stanton, TX, p. A654
COOKE, Rebecca L, Director Human Resources, Kearney County Health Services, Minden, NE, p. A402
COOKE, Timothy J., Medical Center Director and Chief Executive Officer, Orlando Va Medical Center, Orlando, FL, p. A144
COOKE, William, M.D., Chief of Staff, Gundersen St. Joseph's Hospital And Clinics, Hillsboro, WI, p. A713
COOLEY, Andrew, M.D., Chief Medical Officer, Eastern State Hospital, Lexington, KY, p. A268
COOLEY, Jennifer, Director of Nursing, Rock Springs, Georgetown, TX, p. A622
COOLEY, Richard
M.D., Chief Physician Executive, HSHS St. Clare Memorial Hospital, Oconto Falls, WI, p. A719
M.D., Chief Physician Executive, HSHS St. Nicholas Hospital, Sheboygan, WI, p. A721
COOMBS, James, Chief Executive Officer, Grand River Hospital District, Rifle, CO, p. A113
COOMBS, Jodi, R.N., Executive Vice President, Chief Operating Officer, Children's Mercy Hospital Kansas, Overland Park, KS, p. A257
COOMBS, Teri, R.N., Director Nursing Services, Cascade Medical Center, Cascade, ID, p. A180
COOMLER, Mimi, R.N., Senior Vice President and Chief Operating Officer, TMC Health, Tucson, AZ, p. A41
COONER, Suzanne, MSN, R.N., Chief Executive Officer, Audubon County Memorial Hospital And Clinics, Audubon, IA, p. A230
COONEY, Lauri Ann, Director Nursing, Wheatland Memorial Healthcare, Harlowton, MT, p. A393
COONEY, Marina, Medical Director, Montgomery County Emergency Service, Norristown, PA, p. A547
COONS, Jeff, Chief Executive Officer, Memphis Mental Health Institute, Memphis, TN, p. A588
COOPER, Alisa, Manager Financial Resources, Michael E. Debakey Department of Veterans Affairs Medical Center, Houston, TX, p. A627
COOPER, Alison, Chief Financial Officer, Ward Memorial Hospital, Monahans, TX, p. A640
COOPER, Brenda, Director Quality and Human Resources, Lecom Health Corry Memorial Hospital, Corry, PA, p. A537
COOPER, Casey, Chief Executive Officer, Cherokee Indian Hospital, Cherokee, NC, p. A466
COOPER, Corey, Chief Executive Officer, Select Specialty Hospital–Fort Myers, Fort Myers, FL, p. A132
COOPER, Curtis, Manager Information Systems, Pioneers Medical Center, Meeker, CO, p. A112
COOPER, Douglas, M.D., Chief Medical Officer, Grundy County Memorial Hospital, Grundy Center, IA, p. A236
COOPER, Ian, Chief Executive Officer, Tulsa Rehabilitation Hospital, Tulsa, OK, p. A523
COOPER, Jack, M.D., Chief Medical Officer, Baptist Health South Florida, Doctors Hospital, Coral Gables, FL, p. A128
COOPER, Jerry, Director, Information Technology, Richland Hospital, Richland Center, WI, p. A720
COOPER, Jessica, Executive Director, Good Shepherd Penn Partners, Philadelphia, PA, p. A548
COOPER, Mike, Chief Executive Officer, Fairfield Memorial Hospital, Fairfield, IL, p. A195
COOPER, Pamela, Director Finance, Providence Seaside Hospital, Seaside, OR, p. A532
COOPER, Robert, M.D., Chief Medical Officer, Faith Community Hospital, Jacksboro, TX, p. A630
COOPER, Tim, Chief Financial Officer, Prosser Memorial Health, Prosser, WA, p. A693
COOPER–LEHKI, Christi, Chief Clinical Officer, Highland–Clarksburg Hospital, Clarksburg, WV, p. A700
COOPER–LOHR, Willie, Chief Financial Officer, WVU Medicine – Barnesville Hospital, Barnesville, OH, p. A485
COOPERMAN, Todd, M.D., Medical Director, Encompass Health Rehabilitation Hospital of Tinton Falls, A Joint Venture With Monmouth Medical Center, Tinton Falls, NJ, p. A429
COOPWOOD, Reginald W., M.D., President and Chief Executive Officer, Regional One Health, Memphis, TN, p. A589
COOTS, Aaron, Information Technology Director, Mason District Hospital, Havana, IL, p. A197
COPE, Brent A., President, The Medical Center of Southeast Texas, Port Arthur, TX, p. A645
COPE, Dave, Director Information Systems, Marshall County Hospital, Benton, KY, p. A263
COPE, Kathryn, Chief Operating Officer, Mainehealth Maine Medical Center, Portland, ME, p. A298
COPE, Mary, R.N., Chief Clinical Officer, Spanish Peaks Regional Health Center And Veterans Community Living Center, Walsenburg, CO, p. A114
COPE, Yvette Renee, Chief Nurse Executive, Lompoc Valley Medical Center, Lompoc, CA, p. A70
COPELAND, Carolyn, Business Administrator, Madison State Hospital, Madison, IN, p. A223
COPELAND, Darlinda, Chief Operating Officer, Adventhealth Daytona Beach, Daytona Beach, FL, p. A129
COPELAND, Gail, Director Management Information Systems, Crossridge Community Hospital, Wynne, AR, p. A54
COPELAND, Gearline, R.N., Chief Nursing Officer, Ascension Saint Thomas Highlands, Sparta, TN, p. A593
COPELAND, Stephen, Chief Financial Officer, Cypress Creek Hospital, Houston, TX, p. A625
COPELAND, Willie Mae, Chief Financial Officer, Harmon Memorial Hospital, Hollis, OK, p. A513
COPELAND, Yolanda, R.N., Senior Vice President Patient Care Services and Chief Nursing Officer, Ascension Saint Agnes, Baltimore, MD, p. A300
COPEN, Greg, Chief Information Officer, Haywood Regional Medical Center, Clyde, NC, p. A466
COPENHAVER, Kathy, Director Human Resources, Haven Behavioral Hospital of Eastern Pennsylvania, Reading, PA, p. A553
COPES, Tammy, Director Information Systems, Mymichigan Medical Center Standish, Standish, MI, p. A338
COPLIN, Rebecca, Chief Executive Officer, Providence Seaside Hospital, Seaside, OR, p. A532
COPPEDGE, Mitch, M.D., Chief Medical Officer, Grady Memorial Hospital, Chickasha, OK, p. A511
COPPLE, Brad
Vice President Operations, Northwestern Medicine Valley West Hospital, Sandwich, IL, p. A208
Vice President, Operations, Northwestern Medicine Kishwaukee Hospital, Dekalb, IL, p. A193
COPPLE, Robert C., FACHE, President, Ascension Via Christi Hospital, Manhattan, Manhattan, KS, p. A254

A824 Index of Health Care Professionals

Index of Health Care Professionals / Cottrell

Index of Health Care Professionals

CORAZON, Jesus M
Controller, Encompass Health Rehabilitation Hospital of Manati, Manati, PR, p. A733
Controller, Encompass Health Rehabilitation Hospital of San Juan, San Juan, PR, p. A735
CORBEIL, John, Chief Executive Officer, HCA Houston Healthcare Kingwood, Kingwood, TX, p. A633
CORBET, Mark, Interim Chief Financial Officer, Los Angeles General Medical Center, Los Angeles, CA, p. A74
CORBETT, David, M.D., Chief of Staff, Northwest Medical Center, Winfield, AL, p. A26
CORBETT, Shaun, M.D., Chief Medical Officer, Miami Jewish Health, Miami, FL, p. A140
CORBI, Kelly, President and Chief Executive Officer, Melrosewakefield Healthcare, Melrose, MA, p. A315
CORBIN, Loren, Chief Nursing Officer, Hillsdale Hospital, Hillsdale, MI, p. A329
CORBIN, Michelle, M.D., Chief of Staff, Deer Lodge Medical Center, Deer Lodge, MT, p. A391
CORBIN, William, Vice President and Chief Human Resources Officer, Mcdonough District Hospital, Macomb, IL, p. A200
CORCIMIGLIA, Michael, Chief Operating Officer, Wyoming County Community Hospital, Warsaw, NY, p. A461
CORCORAN, Frank, R.N., Chief Executive Officer, Sierra Vista Hospital, Truth Or Consequences, NM, p. A437
CORCORAN, John Russell, Vice President Medical Affairs, South County Hospital, Wakefield, RI, p. A561
CORCORAN, Josep. C., D.O., Division Chief Medical Officer, Southern Hills Hospital And Medical Center, Las Vegas, NV, p. A410
CORCORAN, Kevin, Chief Financial Officer, HCA Florida Westside Hospital, Plantation, FL, p. A147
CORCORAN, Nancy R, Senior Vice President Human Resources and Quality Service, Hackensack Meridian Health Hackensack University Medical Center, Hackensack, NJ, p. A421
CORCORAN, Rose, R.N., Chief Nursing Executive, Sutter Coast Hospital, Crescent City, CA, p. A61
CORD, Jennifer, R.N., Chief Nursing Officer, Providence Mission Hospital Mission Viejo, Mission Viejo, CA, p. A77
CORDEAU, Peter, President, Norwalk Hospital, Norwalk, CT, p. A118
CORDER, Earline, Chief Fiscal, Charlie Norwood Veterans Affairs Medical Center, Augusta, GA, p. A158
CORDER, Scott, Controller, Encompass Health Rehabilitation Hospital At Cincinnati, Cincinnati, OH, p. A489
CORDERO, Edwin, Chief Financial Officer, Valley Baptist Medical Center–Brownsville, Brownsville, TX, p. A605
CORDES, Debra, Chief Nursing Officer, Rehabilitation Hospital of Indiana, Indianapolis, IN, p. A220
CORDIA, Jennifer, Vice President and Chief Nursing Executive, Christian Hospital, Saint Louis, MO, p. A385
CORDOVA, Mandelyn, R.N., Director of Nurses, Guadalup. County Hospital, Santa Rosa, NM, p. A437
CORDOVA, Martin, Director Information Services, Centinela Hospital Medical Center, Inglewood, CA, p. A67
CORDOVA, Sheila
Chief Operating Officer and Chief Nursing Officer, Aurora Charter Oak Hospital, Covina, CA, p. A60
Director Clinical Services and Chief Operating Officer, Aurora Charter Oak Hospital, Covina, CA, p. A60
CORDOVES, America, Controller, Sunview Medical Center, West Palm Beach, FL, p. A154
CORDUM, Shelly L., MSN, R.N., Chief Nursing Officer, Merit Health River Oaks, Flowood, MS, p. A362
CORDY, Roy, M.D., President Medical Staff, SMP Health – St. Kateri, Rolla, ND, p. A483
COREA, Rohan, Director Healthcare Information Technology, College Medical Center, Long Beach, CA, p. A70
COREY, Mark, Chief Financial Officer, Behavioral Center of Michigan, Warren, MI, p. A340
CORKERY, Thomas B, D.O., Chief Medical Officer, Canonsburg Hospital, Canonsburg, PA, p. A536
CORLEY, Becky, Director Human Resources, Tyler Holmes Memorial Hospital, Winona, MS, p. A370
CORLEY, Craig, Chief Financial Officer, Bhc Alhambra Hospital, Rosemead, CA, p. A86
CORLEY, Janet, Accountant, Malvern Institute, Malvern, PA, p. A545
CORLEY, Juli, Chief Information Officer, Edgefield County Healthcare, Edgefield, SC, p. A565
CORLEY, Lesa, Director of Nursing, Broaddus Hospital, Philippi, WV, p. A704
CORN, Rick, Chief Information Officer, Huntsville Hospital, Huntsville, AL, p. A21
CORNEJO, C Susan
Chief Financial Officer, Ascension Sacred Heart Pensacola, Pensacola, FL, p. A146
Chief Operating Officer, USA Health Providence Hospital, Mobile, AL, p. A22
CORNELIUS, David, Director Information Systems, Parkridge Medical Center, Chattanooga, TN, p. A580
CORNELIUS, Margaret E, Vice President Human Resources, Wyckoff Heights Medical Center, New York, NY, p. A453
CORNELIUS, Michelle
Director Human Resources, Aspirus Tomahawk Hospital, Tomahawk, WI, p. A723
Director Human Resources, Howard Young Medical Center, Inc., Woodruff, WI, p. A725
Director Human Resources for Northern Region, Aspirus Eagle River Hospital, Eagle River, WI, p. A710
Director Human Resources for the Northern Region, Aspirus Rhinelander Hospital, Rhinelander, WI, p. A720
CORNELIUS, Senta, Director Human Resources, West Valley Medical Center, Caldwell, ID, p. A180
CORNELIUS, Teresa, R.N., Chief Operating Officer and Chief Nursing Officer, HSHS St. Joseph's Hospital Highland, Highland, IL, p. A197
CORNET, Trina, JD, Vice President Human Resources, Jamaica Hospital Medical Center, New York, NY, p. A448
CORNETT, Sheila, Manager Human Resources, Hazard Arh Regional Medical Center, Hazard, KY, p. A267
CORNETT, Suzanne, Director Human Resources, Southern Kentucky Rehabilitation Hospital, Bowling Green, KY, p. A263
CORNISH, James W., M.D., Medical Director, Livengrin Foundation, Bensalem, PA, p. A535
CORNWALL, Rick, HIT Site Coordinator, Advocate Condell Medical Center, Libertyville, IL, p. A200
CORNWALL, Thomas, M.D., Medical Director, Holly Hill Hospital, Raleigh, NC, p. A474
CORNWELL, Cheryl J, Chief Financial Officer, Lake District Hospital, Lakeview, OR, p. A528
CORNWELL, Daniel, Command Officer, U. S. Naval Hospital Guam, Agana, GU, p. A730
CORONA JR., Robert J., Chief Executive Officer, Upstate University Hospital, Syracuse, NY, p. A460
CORONEL, Jorge, Chief Information Officer, Regional Hospital of Scranton, Scranton, PA, p. A554
CORPORA, Don, Executive Vice President and Chief Human Resources Officer, Cleveland Clinic Akron General, Akron, OH, p. A484
CORRA, Michelle, Administrator, Human Resources, Corewell Health Trenton Hospital, Trenton, MI, p. A339
CORRADO, Theresa, Director Finance, St. Luke's Quakertown Campus, Quakertown, PA, p. A553
CORREA, Elizabeth, Director Information Management, Big Spring State Hospital, Big Spring, TX, p. A603
CORREA, Leo, Chief Executive Officer and Administrator, St. Catherine Hospital, East Chicago, IN, p. A215
CORREA, Maria de los Angeles, M.D., Medical Director, Hospital Metropolitano, San Juan, PR, p. A735
CORREA, Omar, Chief Financial Officer, Texas Neurorehab Center, Austin, TX, p. A601
CORREA, Sharon, Chief Information Officer, Adventist Health Glendale, Glendale, CA, p. A66
CORRELL, Anne, Chief Clinical Officer, Kindred Hospital–Greensboro, Greensboro, NC, p. A469
CORRIGAN, Jeffrey T.
Vice President Human Resources, Brattleboro Retreat, Brattleboro, VT, p. A671
Vice President Human Resources, Day Kimball Hospital, Putnam, CT, p. A118
CORRIGAN, Paula, Vice President and Chief Financial Officer, OSF Saint James – John W. Albrecht Medical Center, Pontiac, IL, p. A206
CORRY, Craig
Chief Financial Officer, Cedar City Hospital, Cedar City, UT, p. A664
Chief Financial Officer, Garfield Memorial Hospital, Panguitch, UT, p. A667
CORS, William K., M.D., Senior Medical Director, Lehigh Valley Hospital – Pocono, East Stroudsburg, PA, p. A539
CORSO, Michael
President & Chief Executive Officer, UPMC Bedford, Everett, PA, p. A540
President and Chief Executive Officer, UPMC Altoona/Bedford, UPMC Altoona, Altoona, PA, p. A534
CORTES, Anais, Chief of Staff, Palmetto General Hospital, Hialeah, FL, p. A133
CORTI, Ronald J., President and Chief Executive Officer, St. John's Riverside Hospital, Yonkers, NY, p. A462
CORUM, Sharon, Chief Financial Officer, Kingwood Pines Hospital, Kingwood, TX, p. A632
CORUNA, Chris, Chief Nursing Officer, Carewell Health Medical Center, East Orange, NJ, p. A420
CORWIN, Nancy
Chief Nursing Officer, Summit Surgical, Hutchinson, KS, p. A251
Chief Operating Officer, Summit Surgical, Hutchinson, KS, p. A251
CORWIN, Steven J., M.D., President and Chief Executive Officer, New York–Presbyterian Hospital, New York, NY, p. A450
CORZINE, Judy, Vice President of IT & Chief Information Officer, Stormont Vail Health, Topeka, KS, p. A260
COSBY, Christopher, President and Chief Executive Officer, Parkridge Medical Center, Chattanooga, TN, p. A580
COSBY, Dwan, Manager Human Resources, Mclaren Oakland, Pontiac, MI, p. A335
COSBY, Ernestine Y., Vice President Clinical Services and Chief Nursing Officer, Sheppard Pratt, Baltimore, MD, p. A302
COSTA, Christopher P., M.D., Chief of Staff, Gordon Memorial Health Services, Gordon, NE, p. A400
COSTA, Joe
Acting Chief Fiscal Officer, Veterans Affairs Boston Healthcare System Brockton Division, Brockton, MA, p. A312
Chief Financial Officer, Veterans Affairs Boston Healthcare System, West Roxbury, MA, p. A319
COSTA, Mark E, Executive Director, Kaiser Permanente Orange County Anaheim Medical Center, Anaheim, CA, p. A55
COSTA, Michael, President and Chief Executive Officer, Gifford Medical Center, Randolph, VT, p. A672
COSTA, Michael G, Vice President Human Resources, Chi St. Josep. Regional Health Center, Bryan, TX, p. A605
COSTAKIS, Angie, Chief Information Officer, Claiborne Memorial Medical Center, Homer, LA, p. A283
COSTANTINO, Vincent, Vice President Operations and Human Resources, Hackensack Meridian Health Raritan Bay Medical Center, Perth Amboy, NJ, p. A427
COSTANZO, Kristin L., Direct–In–Market Lead Human Relations Partner, Ascension St. Vincent's Blount, Oneonta, AL, p. A23
COSTANZO, Rosemary, Chief Nursing Officer, New Hampshire Hospital, Concord, NH, p. A414
COSTELLA, Jeane L, Vice President, New York–Presbyterian/Hudson Valley Hospital, Cortlandt Manor, NY, p. A442
COSTELLO, Jeff
Chief Financial Officer, Elkhart General Hospital, Elkhart, IN, p. A215
Chief Financial Officer, Beacon Health System, Memorial Hospital of South Bend, South Bend, IN, p. A227
COSTELLO, Jodi, Chief Executive Officer, Select Specialty Hospital–Youngstown, Youngstown, OH, p. A508
COSTELLO, Karen
Chief Executive Officer, SCL Health Mt – St. James Healthcare, Butte, MT, p. A390
President, Holy Rosary Healthcare, Miles City, MT, p. A394
COSTIC, Andrew, Vice President of Regional Finance, Aspirus Keweenaw Hospital, Laurium, MI, p. A332
COSTIGAN, Tricia, FACHE, President, Northern Light Inland Hospital, Waterville, ME, p. A299
COTE, Gerri, Chief Operating Officer, Brattleboro Retreat, Brattleboro, VT, p. A671
COTE, Mary, Director Human Resources, New England Rehabilitation Hospital of Portland, Portland, ME, p. A298
COTHERN, Val, Chief Human Resources Officer, Valley Community Hospital, Pauls Valley, OK, p. A519
COTT, Gary, M.D., Executive Vice President Medical and Clinical Services, National Jewish Health, Denver, CO, p. A106
COTTEN, Brandon, Chief Financial Officer, Dewitt Hospital & Nursing Home, Dewitt, AR, p. A45
COTTER, Bonny, Chief Nursing Officer, Baraga County Memorial Hospital, L'Anse, MI, p. A331
COTTER, Carole
Senior Vice President and Chief Information Officer, Emma Pendleton Bradley Hospital, East Providence, RI, p. A560
Senior Vice President and Chief Information Officer, Rhode Island Hospital, Providence, RI, p. A561
Vice President and Chief Information Officer, Miriam Hospital, Providence, RI, p. A560
COTTERILL, allison MSN, RN, Chief Nursing Officer, Mercy General Hospital, Sacramento, CA, p. A87
COTTINGHAM, Jerod, Director Information Systems, Carlinville Area Hospital, Carlinville, IL, p. A187
COTTLE, Jeremy, Ph.D., Chief Executive Officer, Aspen Grove Behavioral Hospital, Orem, UT, p. A666
COTTLE, Mike, Information Technology Director, Nmc Health, Newton, KS, p. A255
COTTO, Hector L, M.D., Medical Director, Hospital San Francisco, San Juan, PR, p. A735
COTTON, C Gerald, Interim Chief Operating Officer, Baptist Medical Center – Leake, Carthage, MS, p. A360
COTTON, Michael, Chief Financial Officer, Grandview Medical Center, Birmingham, AL, p. A16
COTTRELL, Cheryl
R.N., Vice President and Chief Nursing Officer, Baptist Health South Florida, Mariners Hospital, Tavernier, FL, p. A153

R.N., Vice President and Chief Nursing Officer, Fishermen's Hospital, Marathon, FL, p. A138
COTTRILL, Brian, Chief Information Officer, United Hospital Center, Bridgeport, WV, p. A699
COUBAL, Steve, Manager Information Technology and Systems, Johnson Memorial Health Services, Dawson, MN, p. A345
COUCH, Beulah, Director Human Resources, Mary Breckinridge Arh Hospital, Hyden, KY, p. A267
COUCH, Bill, Chief Financial Officer, Ashley County Medical Center, Crossett, AR, p. A45
COUCH, Jamie, Interim Chief Executive Officer, Adventhealth Manchester, Manchester, KY, p. A271
COUCHMAN, Diane, Interim Vice President, Human Resources, Calverthealth Medical Center, Prince Frederick, MD, p. A306
COUGHENOUR, DPT, CLD, Derek, Medical Center Director, James E. Van Zandt Veterans Affairs Medical Center, Altoona, PA, p. A534
COUGHLIN, Ann, Director Human Resources, Boundary Community Hospital, Bonners Ferry, ID, p. A180
COUGHLIN, Kevin B., President and Chief Executive Officer, Beth Israel Deaconess Hospital–Plymouth, Plymouth, MA, p. A317
COULE, Phillip. M.D., Chief Medical Officer, Wellstar Mcg Health, Augusta, GA, p. A158
COULSTON, Joy, Chief Executive Officer, Powell Valley Health Care, Powell, WY, p. A728
COULTER, Barbara
　Director Information Systems, Franciscan Health Indianapolis, Indianapolis, IN, p. A219
　Director Information Systems, Franciscan Health Mooresville, Mooresville, IN, p. A224
COUNTS, Virginia, Manager Human Resources, Baylor Scott & White Medical Center – Brenham, Brenham, TX, p. A604
COUNTY-TEEMER, Vickie, Coordinator Human Resources, Archbold Mitchell, Camilla, GA, p. A160
COURIS, John D., Chief Executive Officer, Tamp. General Hospital, Tampa, FL, p. A152
COURTOIS, Harold, Chief Executive Officer, Memorial Health System, Abilene, KS, p. A246
COURTOIS, Robert, Vice President Finance, Munson Healthcare Otsego Memorial Hospital, Gaylord, MI, p. A327
COURY, Justin, Chief Executive Officer, Tristar Hendersonville Medical Center, Hendersonville, TN, p. A584
COUSAR, Myra, Director Human Resources, Baptist Memorial Hospital–Tipton, Covington, TN, p. A582
COUSINEAU, Cathy, Director Human Resources, Kaiser Permanente Woodland Hills Medical Center, Los Angeles, CA, p. A73
COUTURE, Maureen, Chief Nursing Officer and Vice President Nursing, Encompass Health Cardinal Hill Rehabilitation Hospital, Lexington, KY, p. A268
COVA, Matthew, Chief Executive Officer, Regional Medical Center of San Jose, San Jose, CA, p. A92
COVAULT, Julie, Vice President Finance, Wilson Memorial Hospital, Sidney, OH, p. A503
COVAULT, Myra, Associate Vice President of Human Resources, Baptist Health Hardin, Elizabethtown, KY, p. A265
COVELL, Nancy, Director Human Resources, Cameron Memorial Community Hospital, Angola, IN, p. A212
COVELLI, Margaret, R.N., Chief Nursing Officer, Spring Valley Hospital Medical Center, Las Vegas, NV, p. A411
COVERT, Kathy, MSN, Vice President Workforce Development and Organizational Development, Schneck Medical Center, Seymour, IN, p. A227
COVERT, Michael H., FACHE, President and Chief Operating Officer, Northeast Georgia Medical Center, Gainesville, GA, p. A164
COVERT, Terri, Vice President Human Resources, Providence Mission Hospital Mission Viejo, Mission Viejo, CA, p. A77
COVINGTON, Casey, M.D., President Elect, Medical Staff, Jennie Stuart Medical Center, Hopkinsville, KY, p. A267
COVINGTON, Jerome, M.D., Chief Medical Officer, Lower Keys Medical Center, Key West, FL, p. A136
COVONE, Ann Marie, Senior Vice President and Chief Financial Officer, Terence Cardinal Cooke Health Care Center, New York, NY, p. A453
COWAN, Christopher, Senior Vice President and Chief Human Resources Officer, Christianacare, Newark, DE, p. A122
COWAN, Ronald M, Vice President Information Systems, Geisinger Lewistown Hospital, Lewistown, PA, p. A544
COWART, Mark, Facility Chief Information Officer, Carl Vinson Veterans Affairs Medical Center, Dublin, GA, p. A163
COWLES, John, Chief Financial Officer, La Downtown Medical Center, Llc, Los Angeles, CA, p. A73
COWLING, Phyllis A., CPA, President and Chief Executive Officer, United Regional Health Care System, Wichita Falls, TX, p. A663

COX, Amber, Director Human Resources, UT Health Carthage, Carthage, TX, p. A607
COX, Brian, Director Information Systems, Baptist Health Floyd, New Albany, IN, p. A225
COX, Carla C., Chief Nursing Officer, Indiana University Health Ball Memorial Hospital, Muncie, IN, p. A224
COX, Chandler, Director Human Resources, Mena Regional Health System, Mena, AR, p. A50
COX, Christopher, Chief Nursing Officer, Baptist Health Extended Care Hospital, Little Rock, AR, p. A49
COX, David, Chief Executive Officer, Rehabilitation Hospital of The Northwest, Post Falls, ID, p. A183
COX, Debbie D., Administrative Director Human Resources, Christus Santa Rosa Hospital – San Marcos, San Marcos, TX, p. A651
COX, Dianne E, Vice President of Human Resources, Kaweah Health Medical Center, Visalia, CA, p. A100
COX, Dina, Director Human Resources, Kansas Rehabilitation Hospital, Topeka, KS, p. A260
COX, Dorothy, Manager Information Systems, Hackettstown Medical Center, Hackettstown, NJ, p. A421
COX, Gwen, Director Nursing Services, Klickitat Valley Health, Goldendale, WA, p. A690
COX, James, Chief Executive Officer, Arkansas Continued Care Hospital of Jonesboro, Jonesboro, AR, p. A48
COX, Jason, Chief Operating Officer, Musc Health Black River Medical Center, Cades, SC, p. A562
COX, Jeffrey
　Chief Information Officer, Glendora Hospital, Glendora, CA, p. A66
　Director Information Technology, San Dimas Community Hospital, San Dimas, CA, p. A90
COX, Keith, Chief Executive Officer, Minden Medical Center, Minden, LA, p. A288
COX, Kenneth, Interim Chief Financial Officer, Mckenzie County Healthcare System, Watford City, ND, p. A483
COX, Leigh, Chief Information Officer, Wellstar Windy Hill Hospital, Marietta, GA, p. A168
COX, Lynna B, Director Health Information Services, Anson General Hospital, Anson, TX, p. A597
COX, Randy, Chief Information Officer, Ascension St. Vincent Indianapolis Hospital, Indianapolis, IN, p. A219
COX, Sandra, Controller, Permian Regional Medical Center, Andrews, TX, p. A597
COX, Sheila, Director Human Resources, Cibola General Hospital, Grants, NM, p. A434
COX, Steven, M.D., Chief Medical Officer, UT Health North Campus Tyler, Tyler, TX, p. A659
COYE, Ed
　Director Information Technology, Transylvania Regional Hospital, Brevard, NC, p. A464
　Director Information Technology Mission Health System Hospitals, Angel Medical Center, Franklin, NC, p. A468
COYLE, Michael F., Chief Executive Officer, Veterans Memorial Hospital, Waukon, IA, p. A245
COYNE, Rose, Interim CFO, Haywood Regional Medical Center, Clyde, NC, p. A466
COZART, Adrienne, Senior Vice President Human Resources, University Medical Center, Lubbock, TX, p. A636
CRABB, David W, M.D., Chief Medical Officer, Eskenazi Health, Indianapolis, IN, p. A219
CRABB, Ian, M.D., Chief Medical Officer, Orthonebraska Hospital, Omaha, NE, p. A404
CRABBE, Amy J.
　Senior Vice President Human Resources, Watauga Medical Center, Boone, NC, p. A464
　Vice President People Services, Charles A. Cannon Jr. Memorial Hospital, Newland, NC, p. A473
CRABTREE, Robert, M.D., Chief of Staff and Medical Director, Physicians Surgical Hospital – Quail Creek, Amarillo, TX, p. A596
CRABTREE, Susan, Director Human Resources, Adventist Health Simi Valley, Simi Valley, CA, p. A96
CRACROFT, Davis, M.D., Senior Director Medical Affairs, Scripp. Mercy Hospital, San Diego, CA, p. A89
CRAFT, Brian, Group Finance Officer, Texas Health Presbyterian Hospital Dallas, Dallas, TX, p. A612
CRAFT, Christina, Director Information Systems, Washington Regional Medical Center, Plymouth, NC, p. A474
CRAFT, Kirby, Chief Information Officer, Magee General Hospital, Magee, MS, p. A365
CRAGGS, Chris, Deputy Director, Winnebago Mental Health Institute, Winnebago, WI, p. A725
CRAIG, Alan, M.D., Chief Medical Officer, Princeton Baptist Medical Center, Birmingham, AL, p. A17
CRAIG, Celine H, Chief Human Resource and Regulatory Officer, King's Daughters Medical Center, Brookhaven, MS, p. A360
CRAIG, Donnette, Director Human Resources, Christus Coushatta Health Care Center, Coushatta, LA, p. A280

CRAIG, Emmett
　Chief Human Resources Officer, Knap. Medical Center, Weslaco, TX, p. A662
　Director Human Resources, Harlingen Medical Center, Harlingen, TX, p. A623
CRAIG, Jeff, Chief Human Resource Management, Veterans Affairs Maryland Health Care System–Baltimore Division, Baltimore, MD, p. A302
CRAIG, Mike
　Chief Financial Officer, Indiana University Health Bloomington Hospital, Bloomington, IN, p. A213
　Vice President, Chief Financial Officer, Indiana University Health Bedford Hospital, Bedford, IN, p. A212
CRAIG, Pamela, R.N., Chief Nursing Officer, Seton Medical Center Harker Heights, Harker Heights, TX, p. A623
CRAIG, Patrice, Manager Human Resources, Tucson Va Medical Center, Tucson, AZ, p. A41
CRAIG, Rebecca W, Vice President and Chief Financial Officer, UNC Health Wayne, Goldsboro, NC, p. A469
CRAIG, Scott, M.D., Medical Director, Encompass Health Rehabilitation Hospital of Franklin, Franklin, TN, p. A583
CRAIG, Sherry, Director Human Resources, Trace Regional Hospital, Houston, MS, p. A363
CRAIG, Stacey, Chief Executive Officer, Select Specialty Hospital–Savannah, Savannah, GA, p. A171
CRAIG, Steven, Ph.D., Chief Executive Officer, Surgeons Choice Medical Center, Southfield, MI, p. A338
CRAIG, William J., CPA, Chief Financial Officer, Howard Memorial Hospital, Nashville, AR, p. A51
CRAIGIN, Melanie Jane., Chief Executive Officer and Administrator, Ascension St. Vincent Williamsport, Williamsport, IN, p. A229
CRAIN, Michelle B., R.N., MSN, Vice President, Our Lady of Lourdes Regional Medical Center, Lafayette, LA, p. A286
CRAMBES, Terry, Manager Finance, Warren State Hospital, Warren, PA, p. A556
CRAMER, James R
　Vice President and Chief Information Officer, Honorhealth Scottsdale Osborn Medical Center, Scottsdale, AZ, p. A38
　Vice President and Chief Information Officer, Honorhealth Scottsdale Shea Medical Center, Scottsdale, AZ, p. A38
CRAMER, Lonnie, President and Chief Executive Officer, UCHealth Memorial Hospital, Colorado Springs, CO, p. A105
CRANDELL, Kristy, M.D., Medical Staff President, Red Bay Hospital, Red Bay, AL, p. A24
CRANFORD, Melvin, Chief Fiscal Services, Cheyenne Va Medical Center, Cheyenne, WY, p. A726
CRANK, Christina, Administrator, Chief Nursing Officer, Ascension St. Vincent Jennings, North Vernon, IN, p. A225
CRANKER, John, Chief Information Officer, Carthage Area Hospital, Carthage, NY, p. A441
CRATE, Kyle, President, SSM Health St. Clare Hospital – Fenton, Fenton, MO, p. A375
CRATTY, Michael
　M.D., Chief Medical Officer, Heritage Valley Beaver, Beaver, PA, p. A535
　M.D., Chief Medical Officer, Sewickley Valley Hospital, (A Division of Valley Medical Facilities), Sewickley, PA, p. A555
CRAVEN, Bruce, Chief Financial Officer, Providence Medical Center, Wayne, NE, p. A406
CRAVEN, Darcy, President and Chief Executive Officer, John D. Archbold Memorial Hospital, Thomasville, GA, p. A172
CRAVEY, Lavonda, Chief Financial Officer, Coffee Regional Medical Center, Douglas, GA, p. A163
CRAW, David, Coordinator Information Technology, Dundy County Hospital, Benkelman, NE, p. A398
CRAWFORD, Allen, Chief Nursing Officer, Jeff Davis Hospital, Hazlehurst, GA, p. A165
CRAWFORD, Arnita, Director Human Resources, Woman's Hospital of Texas, Houston, TX, p. A629
CRAWFORD, Brenda, Chief Financial Officer, Council Oak Comprehensive Healthcare, Tulsa, OK, p. A522
CRAWFORD, Jim, Chief Financial Officer, Lawrence Medical Center, Moulton, AL, p. A23
CRAWFORD, John W
　Chief Financial Officer, Ascension St. John Sapulpa, Sapulpa, OK, p. A520
　Chief Financial Officer, Muscogee Creek Nation Medical Center, Okmulgee, OK, p. A519
CRAWFORD, Linda, R.N., MSN, Chief Nursing Officer, Cookeville Regional Medical Center, Cookeville, TN, p. A582
CRAWFORD, Lucinda, Vice President Financial Services, ECU Health Duplin Hospital, Kenansville, NC, p. A471
CRAWFORD, Marc, Chief Operating Officer, Regions Behavioral Hospital, Baton Rouge, LA, p. A278

Index of Health Care Professionals / Cruson

CRAWFORD, Pam, R.N., Ph.D., Vice President of Nursing and Chief Nursing Officer, Ohiohealth Mansfield Hospital, Mansfield, OH, p. A499
CRAWFORD, Susan, Manager Human Resources, SBL Fayette County Hospital And Long Term Care, Vandalia, IL, p. A210
CRAWFORD, Thomas, Chicago Market Chief Information Officer, Weiss Memorial Hospital, Chicago, IL, p. A192
CRAWFORD, Tom
  Vice President Human Resources, Emory Hillandale Hospital, Lithonia, GA, p. A166
  Vice President Human Resources, Emory Long–Term Acute Care, Decatur, GA, p. A162
CRAWFORD, Wendy, Chief Human Resource Officer, Honorhealth Scottsdale Thompson Peak Medical Center, Scottsdale, AZ, p. A38
CRAYTON, Cory
  Director Information Systems, Northeast Georgia Medical Center Barrow, Winder, GA, p. A174
  Director of Information Systems, Piedmont Walton Hospital, Monroe, GA, p. A168
CRAYTON, Karen, Chief Executive Officer, United Medical Rehabilitation Hospital–Hammond, Hammond, LA, p. A283
CREAMER, Ken, Chief Human Resource, Thomas E. Creek Department of Veterans Affairs Medical Center, Amarillo, TX, p. A596
CREASMAN, Ginny L.
  Associate Director, Richard L. Roudebush Veterans Affairs Medical Center, Indianapolis, IN, p. A220
  Director, Veterans Affairs Ann Arbor Healthcare System, Ann Arbor, MI, p. A321
CREEL, Keith, Vice President Operations, Christus Good Shepherd Medical Center–Marshall, Marshall, TX, p. A638
CREEL, Mary Ann, Chief Information Resource Management, Martinsburg Veterans Affairs Medical Center, Martinsburg, WV, p. A702
CREIGHTON, Peggy F, R.N., Director of Nursing, Deaconess Union County Hospital, Morganfield, KY, p. A272
CRELIA, Denise Benningfield., Market Chief Executive Office & Chief Nursing Executive, Cornerstone Specialty Hospitals Muskogee, Muskogee, OK, p. A515
CRENSHAW, Rachel H., Chief Operating Officer, Jack Hughston Memorial Hospital, Phenix City, AL, p. A24
CRENSHAW, William, M.D., Chief of Staff, Lady of The Sea General Hospital, Cut Off, LA, p. A281
CREPEAU, Diana, Director Human Resources, Encompass Health Rehabilitation Hospital of Colorado Springs, Colorado Springs, CO, p. A105
CREPS, Barbara, Director Human Resources and Accounting, Okeene Municipal Hospital, Okeene, OK, p. A516
CREQUE, J C, Director Management Information Systems, Schneider Regional Medical Center, Saint Thomas, VI, p. A736
CRESTA, Debra, President, Exeter Hospital, Exeter, NH, p. A415
CREVLING, Charles, Chief Financial Officer, Valley View Hospital, Glenwood Springs, CO, p. A108
CREWS, Carol
  Chief Financial Officer, Higgins General Hospital, Bremen, GA, p. A159
  Chief Financial Officer, Tanner Medical Center–Carrollton, Carrollton, GA, p. A160
  Senior Vice President and Chief Financial Officer, Tanner Medical Center–Villa Rica, Villa Rica, GA, p. A173
CREWSE, Britt
  CPA, Chief Executive Officer, University of Mississipp. Medical Center, Jackson, MS, p. A364
  CPA, Southern Region President, Mainehealth Maine Medical Center, Portland, ME, p. A298
  CPA, Southern Region President, Southern Maine Health Care – Biddeford Medical Center, Biddeford, ME, p. A296
CRIBBS, Susan, D.O., Chief of Staff, Adventist Health Tehachap. Valley, Tehachapi, CA, p. A97
CRIDER, Leonard Greg., Administrator, Sage Rehabilitation Hospital, Baton Rouge, LA, p. A278
CRIDER, Terry, Information Technology Site Manager, Nea Baptist Memorial Hospital, Jonesboro, AR, p. A48
CRILLY, Tom
  Executive Vice President and Chief Financial Officer, Unity Hospital, Rochester, NY, p. A458
  Executive Vice President, Chief Financial Officer, Rochester Regional Health, Newark–Wayne Community Hospital, Newark, NY, p. A454
CRIM, Marcia, MSN, R.N., Chief Executive Officer & Chief Nursing Officer, USMD Hospital At Arlington, Arlington, TX, p. A598
CRINER, Mark, Director Information Technology, Memorial Health Care Systems, Seward, NE, p. A406
CRINION, Shannon, Chief Executive Officer, Baptist Neighborhood Hospital At Thousand Oaks, San Antonio, TX, p. A649
CRIPE, Kimberly C.
  President and Chief Executive Officer, Children's Hospital of Orange County, Orange, CA, p. A81
  President/CEO, Choc Children's At Mission Hospital, Mission Viejo, CA, p. A77
CRIPPS, Eric, Chief Financial Officer, Specialists Hospital Shreveport, Shreveport, LA, p. A293
CRISTY, Kirk, Vice President Finance, Sanford Medical Center Bismarck, Bismarck, ND, p. A479
CRISWELL, Jodie, Vice President of Fiscal Services, Hammond–Henry Hospital, Geneseo, IL, p. A196
CRITCHLEY, Dan, Chief Information Officer, Banner – University Medical Center Tucson, Tucson, AZ, p. A40
CRNKOVIC, Elaine, Chief Executive Officer, Appalachian Behavioral Healthcare, Athens, OH, p. A485
CROCE, Martin, M.D., Senior Vice President and Chief Medical Officer, Regional One Health, Memphis, TN, p. A589
CROCKER, Daniel, M.D., Chief Medical Officer, Pam Specialty Hospital of Rocky Mount, Rocky Mount, NC, p. A475
CROCKETT, James Scott, M.D., Chief of Staff, Falls Community Hospital And Clinic, Marlin, TX, p. A638
CROCKETT, John, Chief Information Officer, Guidance Center, Flagstaff, AZ, p. A31
CROCKETT, Mandy Lee
  Director Human Resources, San Luis Valley Health, Alamosa, CO, p. A103
  Director Human Resources, San Luis Valley Health Conejos County Hospital, La Jara, CO, p. A110
CROCKETT, Richard, Director, Overton Brooks Veterans' Administration Medical Center, Shreveport, LA, p. A292
CROFFUT, Tom, Chief Financial Officer, Centerpointe Hospital, Saint Charles, MO, p. A383
CROFT, Bryan
  Executive Vice President and Chief Operating Officer, Cedars–Sinai Medical Center, Los Angeles, CA, p. A72
  Executive Vice President, Hospital Operations & Chief Operating Officer, Cedars–Sinai Marina Del Rey Hospital, Marina Del Rey, CA, p. A76
CROFT, Kim, R.N., Executive Director Human Resources, Pomerene Hospital, Millersburg, OH, p. A500
CROFTON, Michael
  Chief Financial Officer, Good Samaritan Hospital, Cincinnati, OH, p. A489
  Senior Vice President and Chief Financial Officer, Bethesda North Hospital, Cincinnati, OH, p. A488
CROKER, James, Director Information Systems, St. Bernardine Medical Center, San Bernardino, CA, p. A88
CROLAND, Jennifer, Chief Nursing Officer, Vice President Patient Care, OSF Saint Francis Medical Center, Peoria, IL, p. A206
CROLEY, John S., Chief Executive Officer and Chief Financial Officer, Texas Institute for Surgery At Texas Health Presbyterian Dallas, Dallas, TX, p. A612
CROME, Christopher, M.D., Chief Medical Officer, Genesis Health System, Genesis Medical Center – Davenport, Davenport, IA, p. A234
CROMMWELL, Andre, Chief Executive Officer, Strategic Behavioral Health, Llc, Garner, NC, p. A468
CRONE, Timothy, M.D., Vice President, Cleveland Clinic Mercy Hospital, Canton, OH, p. A487
CRONER, Robert, Senior Vice President and Chief Human Resources Officer, Children's Hospital of Philadelphia, Philadelphia, PA, p. A548
CRONIN, David J, Regional Vice President Human Resources, Good Samaritan Medical Center, Brockton, MA, p. A311
CRONIN–WAELDE, Deborah L, MSN, R.N., Senior Vice President Clinical Operations and Chief Nursing Officer, Melrosewakefield Healthcare, Melrose, MA, p. A315
CROOKS, John, Chair Information Services, Mayo Clinic Hospital In Florida, Jacksonville, FL, p. A135
CROOM, Jon–Paul, President, Wellstar North Fulton Hospital, Roswell, GA, p. A170
CROPPER, Ronnie, Chief Operating Officer, Warren State Hospital, Warren, PA, p. A556
CROSBY, Paul R., Chief Executive Officer, Lindner Center of Hope, Mason, OH, p. A499
CROSBY, Robert, Chief Financial Officer, Athol Hospital, Athol, MA, p. A309
CROSS, Carol, CPA, Chief Financial Officer, Northeast Regional Medical Center, Kirksville, MO, p. A378
CROSS, Kyle, Director of Support Services, Greene County General Hospital, Linton, IN, p. A222
CROSS, Lynda, R.N., Director of Nurses, Nemaha Valley Community Hospital, Seneca, KS, p. A260
CROSS, Patricia, Chief Executive Officer, Life Line Hospital, Steubenville, OH, p. A504
CROSS, Renee, Chief Financial Officer, HCA Florida Lawnwood Hospital, Fort Pierce, FL, p. A132
CROSSAN, Eric, Chief Executive Officer, Walton Rehabilitation Hospital, An Affiliate of Encompass Health, Augusta, GA, p. A158
CROSSLAND, Jeanne, Director of Nursing, Shamrock General Hospital, Shamrock, TX, p. A652
CROSSLEY, Kent, M.D., Chief of Staff, Minneapolis Va Health Care System, Minneapolis, MN, p. A351
CROSSMAN, Margaret
  M.D., Chief Medical Officer, Halifax Health Medical Center of Daytona Beach, Daytona Beach, FL, p. A130
  M.D., Chief Medical Officer, Halifax Health/Uf Health Medical Center of Deltona, Deltona, FL, p. A130
CROTEAU, Gary, Assistant Vice President and Chief Information Officer, South County Hospital, Wakefield, RI, p. A561
CROTTY, Glenn Jr, M.D., President and Chief Executive Officer, Charleston Area Medical Center, Charleston, WV, p. A700
CROTTY, Renee, Coordinator Marketing and Public Relations, Multicare Capital Medical Center, Olympia, WA, p. A692
CROUCH, Amy, Chief Financial Officer, Promedica Coldwater Regional Hospital, Coldwater, MI, p. A324
CROUCH, Chester, Nobis Rehabilitation Partners President and Chief Executive Officer, Oklahoma City Rehabilitation Hospital, Oklahoma City, OK, p. A518
CROUCH, James, Vice President Technical Services, Mosaic Medical Center – Albany, Albany, MO, p. A371
CROUCH, Jodie, Assistant Vice President, Information Services, Ochsner Lsu Health Shreveport – St. Mary Medical Center, Llc, Shreveport, LA, p. A292
CROUCH, Matthew, Chief Executive Officer and Managing Director, Peachford Behavioral Health System, Atlanta, GA, p. A157
CROUCH, Ryan, M.D., Chief Medical Officer, Grand Island Regional Medical Center, Grand Island, NE, p. A400
CROUSE, Autumn, Chief Financial Officer, Behavioral Hospital of Bellaire, Houston, TX, p. A625
CROUT, Tom, MS, Director Human Resources, Central Louisiana State Hospital, Pineville, LA, p. A291
CROW, Angie, Director Finance, Ascension Saint Thomas Hospital for Specialty Surgery, Nashville, TN, p. A590
CROW, Ronda, Chief Nursing Officer, Moore County Hospital District, Dumas, TX, p. A615
CROWDER, Lonna, Director of Nursing, Phillip. County Hospital, Malta, MT, p. A394
CROWE, Arthur, Director Information Systems, Peconic Bay Medical Center, Riverhead, NY, p. A457
CROWE, Charmaine, Team Manager, Nursing and Infection Prevention, Johnson County Community Hospital, Mountain City, TN, p. A590
CROWE, Danny, Chief Financial Officer, Decatur Morgan Hospital, Decatur, AL, p. A18
CROWE, Darren, Chief Executive Officer, Crow/Northern Cheyenne Hospital, Crow Agency, MT, p. A391
CROWELL, Pamela, Director, Sheridan Va Medical Center, Sheridan, WY, p. A728
CROWELL, Robin, Chief Nursing Officer and Chief Operating Officer, Ascension Saint Thomas Hickman, Centerville, TN, p. A580
CROWL, Steve, Director of Information Services, Davis Medical Center, Elkins, WV, p. A700
CRUIKSHANK, Jennifer, R.N., Chief Executive Officer, Riverside University Health System–Medical Center, Moreno Valley, CA, p. A78
CRUM, Aaron, M.D., Chief Medical Officer, Assistant Chief Executive Officer and Senior Vice President, Pikeville Medical Center, Pikeville, KY, p. A273
CRUM, Dennis L, Senior Vice President and Chief Financial Officer, Tift Regional Medical Center, Tifton, GA, p. A172
CRUM, Jarett
  Chief Hospital Officer, Eastpointe Hospital, Daphne, AL, p. A18
  Hospital Director, Baypointe Behavioral Health, Mobile, AL, p. A21
CRUMLEY, Vickie L, Chief Human Resources Officer, Mary Rutan Hospital, Bellefontaine, OH, p. A486
CRUMP, John, M.D., Medical Staff President, Howard Young Medical Center, Inc., Woodruff, WI, p. A725
CRUMP, Rick, Chief Financial Officer, Lakeland Behavioral Health System, Springfield, MO, p. A386
CRUMPLER, John, R.N., Director of Nursing, Red River Behavioral Center, Bossier City, LA, p. A279
CRUMPTON, Lindsay Barker
  Market Chief Nursing Officer, Sovah Health–Danville, Danville, VA, p. A675
  Market Chief Nursing Officer, Sovah Health–Martinsville, Martinsville, VA, p. A679
CRUMPTON, Patsy Sue, R.N., Chief Nursing Officer, National Park Medical Center, Hot Springs, AR, p. A48
CRUNK, Frances H, Chief Financial Officer, Adventhealth Ocala, Ocala, FL, p. A143
CRUSON, Jim, Chief Information Officer, Riverview Behavioral Health, Texarkana, AR, p. A54

Index of Health Care Professionals

CRUTCHFIELD, David, Vice President, Information Services & Chief Information Officer, Conway Medical Center, Conway, SC, p. A565
CRUZ, Arlene, Director, Rush Oak Park Hospital, Oak Park, IL, p. A204
CRUZ, Carlos, Interim Chief Executive Officer, Keralty Hospital Miami, Miami, FL, p. A140
CRUZ, Janice, Executive Director, Metropolitano De La Montana, Utuado, PR, p. A736
CRUZ, Josep. V, Chief Information Officer, Ryder Memorial Hospital, Humacao, PR, p. A733
CRUZ, Julia, Chief Financial Officer, San Juan Capestrano Hospital, San Juan, PR, p. A735
CRUZ, Marie, Administrator, Centro De Salud Conductual Menonita–Cima, Aibonito, PR, p. A731
CRUZ, Michael, Chief Executive Officer, Bsa Hospital, Llc, Amarillo, TX, p. A596
CRUZ, Miguel
 M.D., Medical Director, Bella Vista Hospital, Mayaguez, PR, p. A733
 Medical Staff Credentialing Coordinator, Encompass Health Rehabilitation Hospital of Miami, Cutler Bay, FL, p. A129
CRUZ, Obed, Vice President and Chief Nursing Officer, UChicago Medicine Adventhealth Bolingbrook, Bolingbrook, IL, p. A186
CRUZ, Randi, Chief Nursing Officer, Encompass Health Rehabilitation Hospital of Round Rock, Round Rock, TX, p. A647
CRUZ CORREA, Jesus, Chief Medical Officer, St. Luke's Episcopal Hospital, Ponce, PR, p. A734
CRUZ CORREA, Marcia, Administrator, Hospital Centro Comprensivo De Cancer, Universidad De Puerto Rico, San Juan, PR, p. A735
CRUZ VIVALDI, Dominao, Executive Director, Hospital San Francisco, San Juan, PR, p. A735
CRUZ–VIVALDI, Domingo, Executive Director, Hospital Pavia–Santurce, San Juan, PR, p. A735
CRYER, Selena, Director Human Resources, Ennis Regional Medical Center, Ennis, TX, p. A618
CUBELLIS, Guido J., Chief Executive Officer, Vibra Hospital of Houston, Houston, TX, p. A628
CUELLAR, Eddie, Vice President Information Systems, Methodist Hospital, San Antonio, TX, p. A650
CUEVAS, Gilberto, Director Human Resources, Hospital De Damas, Ponce, PR, p. A734
CUEVAS, Jacki, Director Health Information Services, Regional Rehabilitation Hospital, Phenix City, AL, p. A24
CUFF, Randy, Chief Operating Officer, Central Valley Medical Center, Nephi, UT, p. A666
CULBERT, Devon, Controller, The Hospital At Westlake Medical Center, West Lake Hills, TX, p. A662
CULBERTSON, Tabitha, President, Centra Lynchburg General Hospital, Lynchburg, VA, p. A678
CULBRETH, David
 Administrator, Kula Hospital, Kula, HI, p. A177
 Administrator, Lanai Community Hospital, Lanai City, HI, p. A177
CULLEN, John, M.D., Chief of Staff and Medical Director Long Term Care, Providence Valdez Medical Center, Valdez, AK, p. A29
CULLEN, Kelly, R.N., Executive Vice President and Chief Operating Officer, Tamp. General Hospital, Tampa, FL, p. A152
CULLEN, Neil, Director Human Resources, Encompass Health Rehabilitation Hospital of Northwest Tucson, Tucson, AZ, p. A40
CULLEY, Robert, D.O., Chief Medical Officer, VCU Health Tappahannock Hospital, Tappahannock, VA, p. A684
CULLINAN, Kevin, Chief Executive Officer, St. Anthony Hospital, Lakewood, CO, p. A110
CULLISON, Rebecca, President, Methodist Healthcare Memphis Hospitals, Memphis, TN, p. A589
CULLOM, Christopher, FACHE, Chief Operating Officer, Thomas Jefferson University Hospitals, Thomas Jefferson University Hospital, Philadelphia, PA, p. A550
CULP, Melinda, Executive Director, Administrator, Saint Francis Hospital Vinita, Vinita, OK, p. A523
CULPEPPER, Yvonne, MSN, R.N., Senior Vice President of Nursing and Professional Services, Chief Operating Officer and Chief Nursing Officer, Hendricks Regional Health, Danville, IN, p. A215
CULVER, Douglas, Chief Financial Officer, Mercy Hospital Carthage, Carthage, MO, p. A373
CULVER, Shawna, Director Information Systems, St. Catherine Hospital – Dodge City, Dodge City, KS, p. A248
CUMBIE, Dan L, Chief Nursing Officer, Flowers Hospital, Dothan, AL, p. A18
CUMBIE, Robert, Administrator, Jasper Memorial Hospital, Monticello, GA, p. A168
CUMBO, Adam, Chief Financial Officer, Dukes Memorial Hospital, Peru, IN, p. A226

CUMMINGS, Allana, Chief Information Officer, Children's Healthcare of Atlanta, Atlanta, GA, p. A157
CUMMINGS, Brooke, Chief Financial Officer, Our Lady of The Angels Hospital, Bogalusa, LA, p. A279
CUMMINGS, Gabrielle, President, Endeavor Health Evanston Hospital, Evanston, IL, p. A195
CUMMINGS, Jerry, Chief Operating Officer, Putnam County Memorial Hospital, Unionville, MO, p. A388
CUMMINGS, Kelly, Chief Nursing Officer, Jefferson Lansdale Hospital, Lansdale, PA, p. A544
CUMMINGS, Rae, Chief Operating Officer, Boulder City Hospital, Boulder City, NV, p. A408
CUMMINGS, Spencer, President and Chief Executive Officer, Cap. Fear Valley Bladen County Hospital, Elizabethtown, NC, p. A468
CUMMINGS, Steve
 M.D., Chief of Medical Staff, Stillwater Medical Center, Stillwater, OK, p. A521
 Interim President & Chief Executive Officer, Brattleboro Retreat, Brattleboro, VT, p. A671
CUMMINGS, Steven, Chief Operating Officer and Chief Information Officer, Baystate Noble Hospital, Westfield, MA, p. A319
CUMMINGS, Vickie, Vice President of Human Resources, Trident Medical Center, Charleston, SC, p. A563
CUMMINGS SMITH, Hatch Jr, Administrator, Midcoast Central – Llano, Llano, TX, p. A635
CUMMINS, Frank L, Vice President Human Resources, Honorhealth Deer Valley Medical Center, Phoenix, AZ, p. A35
CUMMINS, Ron V., Senior Vice President and Chief Operating Officer, University of Maryland Medical Center, Baltimore, MD, p. A301
CUNNINGHAM, Dennis J., M.D., Chief Medical Officer, Mclaren Macomb, Mount Clemens, MI, p. A333
CUNNINGHAM, Gail, Chief Medical Officer, University of Maryland St. Josep. Medical Center, Towson, MD, p. A307
CUNNINGHAM, James C, M.D., Chief Medical Officer, Cook Children's Medical Center, Fort Worth, TX, p. A619
CUNNINGHAM, Jason, Chief Operating Officer, HCA Florida Osceola Hospital, Kissimmee, FL, p. A136
CUNNINGHAM, Joseph, Chief Medical Officer, Council Oak Comprehensive Healthcare, Tulsa, OK, p. A522
CUNNINGHAM, Julie, Associate Administrator and Chief Human Resources Officer, Pioneers Memorial Healthcare District, Brawley, CA, p. A58
CUNNINGHAM, Keith W, M.D., Medical Director, Encompass Health Rehabilitation Hospital of Scottsdale, Scottsdale, AZ, p. A38
CUNNINGHAM, Michael, Vice President for Advancement, Anmed Cannon, Pickens, SC, p. A569
CUNNINGHAM, Michelle P., Chief Executive Officer, Encompass Health Rehabilitation Hospital of Harmarville, Pittsburgh, PA, p. A551
CUNNINGHAM, Regina, Ph.D., R.N., Chief Executive Officer, Hospital of The University of Pennsylvania, Philadelphia, PA, p. A549
CUNNINGHAM, Robert, Chief Operations Officer, Olmsted Medical Center, Rochester, MN, p. A354
CUNNINGHAM, Sam, Director Ascension Seton Shoal Creek, Ascension Seton Shoal Creek, Austin, TX, p. A599
CUPPS, Cheryl, Director Finance, Griffin Memorial Hospital, Norman, OK, p. A516
CURD, R Blake., M.D., Chief Executive Officer, Sioux Falls Specialty Hospital, Sioux Falls, SD, p. A577
CURETON, Michael
 FACHE, Chief Executive Officer, Sutter Amador Hospital and Sutter Davis Hospital, Sutter Amador Hospital, Jackson, CA, p. A68
 FACHE, Chief Executive Officer, Sutter Amador Hospital and Sutter Davis Hospital, Sutter Davis Hospital, Davis, CA, p. A61
CURNEL, Robin, MSN, Chief Operating Officer and Chief Nursing Officer, Crittenden Community Hospital, Marion, KY, p. A271
CURNES, Lisa, R.N., Medical Center Director/Chief Executive Officer, VA Central Iowa Health Care System–Des Moines, Des Moines, IA, p. A235
CURNUTT, Melody, CPA, Chief Financial Officer, Greenwood County Hospital, Eureka, KS, p. A249
CURRAN, Denise, Chief Financial Officer, Canyon Creek Behavioral Health, Temple, TX, p. A656
CURRAN, Dezerae, Director Human Resources, Osawatomie State Hospital At Adair Acute Care, Osawatomie, KS, p. A256
CURRAN, Maria, Vice President Human Resources, VCU Medical Center, Richmond, VA, p. A683
CURRAN, Michael, Chief Executive Officer, Regional Hospital of Scranton, Scranton, PA, p. A554
CURRAN, Todd A., M.D., President Medical Staff, Oss Health, York, PA, p. A558

CURRAN–MEULI, Jane
 President, SSM Health Monroe Clinic, Monroe, WI, p. A718
 President, SSM Health St. Mary's Hospital Janesville, Janesville, WI, p. A713
CURREN, Robert
 Director Information Technology, Center for Behavioral Medicine, Kansas City, MO, p. A377
 Western Region Chief Information Technology Officer, Northwest Missouri Psychiatric Rehabilitation Center, Saint Joseph, MO, p. A383
CURRIE, Scott D, Vice President and Chief Financial Officer, Mymichigan Medical Center Midland, Midland, MI, p. A333
CURRY, Christopher, President, OSF Transitional Care Hospital, Peoria, IL, p. A206
CURRY, Darryl B.
 Senior Vice President, Area Manager, Napa–Solano Area, Kaiser Permanente Vacaville Medical Center, Vacaville, CA, p. A99
 Senior Vice President, Area Manager, Napa–Solano Area, Kaiser Permanente Vallejo Medical Center, Vallejo, CA, p. A99
CURRY, Jeffrey T
 Executive Vice President and Chief Financial Officer, Excela Frick Hospital, Mount Pleasant, PA, p. A546
 Executive Vice President and Chief Financial Officer, Excela Health Westmoreland Hospital, Greensburg, PA, p. A541
CURRY, Stephen A, Director Information Services, Princeton Community Hospital, Princeton, WV, p. A704
CURRY, Steve, Regional Director Human Resources, 4C Health, Logansport, IN, p. A222
CURRY, Timothy, Chief Executive Officer, Avoyelles Hospital, Marksville, LA, p. A288
CURRY–PELYAK, Mary Jane, R.N., Vice President and Chief Clinical Officer, UF Health The Villages Hospital, The Villages, FL, p. A153
CURTI, Tate, Senior Vice President and Chief Operating Officer, Southern New Hampshire Medical Center, Nashua, NH, p. A416
CURTIS, Bryan, Chief Information Officer, Memorial Regional Health, Craig, CO, p. A105
CURTIS, George, Chief Information Officer, Houston Medical Center, Warner Robins, GA, p. A173
CURTIS, Joy U, Senior Vice President Human Resources, Cambridge Health Alliance, Cambridge, MA, p. A312
CURTIS, Michael, Chief Administrative Officer, Mckenzie County Healthcare System, Watford City, ND, p. A483
CURTIS, Shawn
 Chief Financial Officer, Barstow Community Hospital, Barstow, CA, p. A57
 Chief Financial Officer, Northern Nevada Medical Center, Sparks, NV, p. A413
CURTIS, Tracie, Business Partner Human Resources, Cleveland Clinic Medina Hospital, Medina, OH, p. A500
CURTRIGHT, Jonathan W., Chief Operating Officer, Ou Health – University of Oklahoma Medical Center, Oklahoma City, OK, p. A518
CURVIN, Thomas J, M.D., Chief of Staff, Rankin County Hospital District, Rankin, TX, p. A646
CUSACK, Michele, Senior Vice President and Chief Financial Officer, South Shore University Hospital, Bay Shore, NY, p. A439
CUSANO, Susan, Director Human Resources, Four Winds Hospital, Katonah, NY, p. A444
CUSHING, Heidi, Chief Financial Officer, Harlan County Health System, Alma, NE, p. A397
CUSHMAN, Bonnie, Chief Financial Officer, Northern Colorado Rehabilitation Hospital, Johnstown, CO, p. A110
CUSTER, Joshua, Chief Financial Officer, Northwest Medical Center Sahuarita, Sahuarita, AZ, p. A38
CUSTER, Lindsey, Director Human Resources, VCU Health Tappahannock Hospital, Tappahannock, VA, p. A684
CUSTIN, Melinda, Chief Information Officer, JPS Health Network, Fort Worth, TX, p. A619
CUSUMANO, Margaret M, R.N., MSN, Vice President Patient Care Services and Chief Nursing Officer, Saint Joseph's Medical Center, Yonkers, NY, p. A462
CUTHRELL, Rob, Director of Human Resources, Coastal Virginia Rehabilitation, Yorktown, VA, p. A686
CUTOLO, Edward, M.D., Jr, Chief of Staff, James A. Haley Veterans' Hospital–Tampa, Tampa, FL, p. A152
CUTRELL, Carrie, Chief Nursing Officer, Arkansas Valley Regional Medical Center, La Junta, CO, p. A110
CUTSFORTH, Shawn, Information Systems Officer, Pioneer Memorial Hospital, Heppner, OR, p. A527
CUTTER, Elise, FACHE, Chief Executive Officer, Superintendent, Island Health, Anacortes, WA, p. A687
CUTTS, Jennifer, M.D., Chief Medical Officer, York Hospital, York, ME, p. A299
CUZZOLA, Anthony, Vice President, Administrator, JFK Johnson Rehabilitation Institute At Hackensack Meridian Health, Edison, NJ, p. A420

Index of Health Care Professionals / Darcy

Index of Health Care Professionals

CYBORON, Abigail, Chief Executive Officer, Chase County Community Hospital, Imperial, NE, p. A401
CYE, Mark, Chief Financial Officer, Warren General Hospital, Warren, PA, p. A556
CYR, Kristin, R.N., MSN, Senior Nursing Executive and Vice President of Patient Care Services, Northern Light Maine Coast Hospital, Ellsworth, ME, p. A297
CYTLAK, David
Chief Financial Officer, Blanchard Valley Hospital, Findlay, OH, p. A496
Vice President Finance, Bluffton Hospital, Bluffton, OH, p. A486
CZAJKOWSKI, Cheryl, Associate Director Patient and Nursing Services, Syracuse Veterans Affairs Medical Center, Syracuse, NY, p. A460
CZAPLINSKI, Cindy, MSN, R.N., Vice President Operations, Vassar Brothers Medical Center, Poughkeepsie, NY, p. A456
CZYMBOR, Mary, Chief Medical Officer, Milford Regional Medical Center, Milford, MA, p. A316
CZYZ, AnneMarie, R.N., Ed.D., President and Chief Executive Officer, Rome Health, Rome, NY, p. A458

D

DAANE, John, Information Systems Officer, Crossing Rivers Health, Prairie Du Chien, WI, p. A720
DACE–MURKEY, Deidra, Chief Nursing Officer, Rehabilitation Institute of Southern Illinois, Llc, The, Shiloh, IL, p. A208
DACUS, Keith, MSC, Chief Executive Officer, St. Charles Parish Hospital, Luling, LA, p. A287
DADD, Steven, Flight Commander Resource Management, U. S. Air Force Hospital, Hampton, VA, p. A677
DADO, Joe
Chief Information Officer, Conemaugh Memorial Medical Center, Johnstown, PA, p. A542
Chief Information Officer, Conemaugh Miners Medical Center, Hastings, PA, p. A541
DAEGER, Brian, Chief Financial Officer and Vice President Financial Services, Margaret Mary Health, Batesville, IN, p. A212
DAFFRON, Eric Allen, Division Director, Information Systems, Southeast Alabama Medical Center, Dothan, AL, p. A18
DAGENBACH, Pete, Chief Financial Officer, Adams County Regional Medical Center, Seaman, OH, p. A503
DAGGETT, Jake
Market Chief Executive Officer, Texas Rehabilitation Hospital of Fort Worth, Fort Worth, TX, p. A620
Market Chief Executive Officer, Texas Rehabilitation Hospital of Keller, Keller, TX, p. A632
D'AGOSTINO, Christopher, Chief Medical Officer, Ascension Alexian Brothers Behavioral Health Hospital, Hoffman Estates, IL, p. A198
DAHDUL, Adnan, M.D., Medical Director, Encompass Health Rehabilitation Hospital of Western Massachusetts, Ludlow, MA, p. A315
DAHER, Amyra, MSN, R.N., Chief Nursing Officer, University Medical Center of El Paso, El Paso, TX, p. A617
DAHLHAUSEN, Daniel J., M.D., Chief, Medical Staff, Anmed Cannon, Pickens, SC, p. A569
DAHLQUIST, Clay, M.D., Chief Medical Officer, Waverly Health Center, Waverly, IA, p. A245
DAHLSTRAND, David, Chief, OI&T, Hunter Holmes Mcguire Veterans Affairs Medical Center–Richmond, Richmond, VA, p. A683
DAHMAN, Sheri, Chief Nursing Officer, Hoke Hospital, Raeford, NC, p. A474
DAIGLE, Charles D., Chief Executive Officer, Ochsner Medical Center – Baton Rouge, Baton Rouge, LA, p. A278
DAIGLE, Cindy, Chief Financial Officer, Northern Maine Medical Center, Fort Kent, ME, p. A297
DAIGLE, Jennifer, R.N., Director of Nursing and Utilization Review, Carolina Center for Behavioral Health, Greer, SC, p. A567
DAIGLE, Richard
Chief Information Officer, Manchester Memorial Hospital, Manchester, CT, p. A116
Chief Information Officer, Rockville General Hospital, Vernon, CT, p. A119
DAIGLE, Suggie, Administrator, Riceland Medical Center, Winnie, TX, p. A663
DAIKER, David, Chief Information Resource Management, Veterans Affairs Nebraska–Western Iowa Health Care System – Lincoln, Lincoln, NE, p. A402
DAILEY, Gina, Chief Financial Officer, Pinnacle Pointe Behavioral Healthcare System, Little Rock, AR, p. A50
DAILEY, Glenn, Chief Executive Officer, Ochsner University Hospital & Clinics, Lafayette, LA, p. A286
DAILEY, Jacqueline, Chief Information Officer, West Penn Hospital, Pittsburgh, PA, p. A552
DAILEY, James, Director Information Services, Good Samaritan Medical Center, West Palm Beach, FL, p. A154
DAILEY, Richard R, D.O., President Medical Staff, Ellett Memorial Hospital, Appleton City, MO, p. A371
DAISE, Travis, M.D., Chief Medical Officer, Goodland Regional Medical Center, Goodland, KS, p. A250
DAISLEY, Samuel, D.O., Vice President Medical Affairs, UPMC Horizon, Farrell, PA, p. A540
DAJCZAK, Stanislaw, M.D., Chief of Staff, Promedica Defiance Regional Hospital, Defiance, OH, p. A494
DALBY, William, Director Fiscal Services, Shriners Children's – Northern California, Sacramento, CA, p. A87
DALE, Jackson, Director Management Information Services, Johnston Memorial Hospital, Abingdon, VA, p. A673
DALEY, Robert
CPA, Chief Financial Officer, Black River Memorial Hospital, Black River Falls, WI, p. A708
CPA, Vice President Fiscal and Information Technology Services, Black River Memorial Hospital, Black River Falls, WI, p. A708
DALGAI, Netrisha, Director of Operations, Navajo Health Foundation – Sage Memorial Hospital, Ganado, AZ, p. A31
DALLER, Sue, R.N., Assistant Administrator Nursing, Hermann Area District Hospital, Hermann, MO, p. A376
DALLIS, Donna, R.N., Vice President Patient Care, Northeastern Health System, Tahlequah, OK, p. A521
DALPOAS, Dolan, FACHE, President and Chief Executive Officer, Lincoln Memorial Hospital, Lincoln, IL, p. A200
DALTON, Dana L., Chief Nursing Officer, Palmdale Regional Medical Center, Palmdale, CA, p. A82
DALTON, Deana, Human Resources, San Juan Health Service District, Monticello, UT, p. A666
DALTON, Leigh, Director of Nursing and Patient Care Services, Highland Hospital, Charleston, WV, p. A700
DALTON, Nissi, Manager Human Resources, Baylor Scott & White Institute for Rehabilitation–Fort Worth, Fort Worth, TX, p. A619
DALTON, Valerie, R.N., Administrator, Oceans Behavioral Hospital of Baton Rouge – South, Baton Rouge, LA, p. A277
DALTON, Wayne, Chief Financial Officer, Lakeview Hospital, Bountiful, UT, p. A664
DALY, Cindy, R.N., Director of Nursing, Syringa Hospital And Clinics, Grangeville, ID, p. A181
DALY, Derek, Chief Executive Officer, Tomah Health, Tomah, WI, p. A723
DALY, Linda, Vice President Human Resources, Auburn Community Hospital, Auburn, NY, p. A438
DALY, Thomas M, CPA, Chief Financial Officer, University Hospital, Newark, NJ, p. A425
DAMBOISE, Robin, Director Human Resources, Northern Maine Medical Center, Fort Kent, ME, p. A297
DAMIANO, Louis
M.D., Chief Executive Officer, Holy Cross Germantown Hospital, Germantown, MD, p. A304
M.D., Chief Executive Officer, Holy Cross Hospital, Silver Spring, MD, p. A307
D'AMICO, David St. Anthony's Rehabilitation Hospital, Lauderdale Lakes, FL, p. A137
D'AMICO, Paul, M.D., Chief of Staff, Atrium Health Stanly, Albemarle, NC, p. A463
DAMMEYER, Matt, Ph.D., Chief Executive Officer, Memorial Hospital of Converse County, Douglas, WY, p. A727
DAMODARAN, A N, M.D., President Medical Staff, Northwest Health – Starke, Knox, IN, p. A221
DAMON, Kerry, Director Human Resources, Baystate Franklin Medical Center, Greenfield, MA, p. A314
D'AMORE, Seanna, Director Human Resources, Penn Highlands Elk, Saint Marys, PA, p. A554
DAMRON, Don, Chief Executive Officer, Ascension St. Vincent Kokomo, Kokomo, IN, p. A221
DAMRON, Paul, Chief Financial Officer, HCA Florida Highlands Hospital, Sebring, FL, p. A150
DAMRON, Tony, Senior Vice President and Chief Information Officer, Pikeville Medical Center, Pikeville, KY, p. A273
D'AMBROSIO, Matthew, MSN, R.N., Chief Nursing Officer, Encompass Health Rehabilitation Hospital of San Antonio, San Antonio, TX, p. A649
DANCY, Peter C. Jr, FACHE, Medical Center Director, Alexandria Va Medical Center, Pineville, LA, p. A291
DANDORPH, Michael J., Chief Executive Officer, Tufts Medical Center, Boston, MA, p. A311
DANE, Brenda, Director, Human Resources, HCA Florida Highlands Hospital, Sebring, FL, p. A150
DANE, Jeff, Executive Vice President and Chief Financial Officer, University Medical Center, Lubbock, TX, p. A636
DANEFF, Jeffrey, Chief Financial Officer, Northwest Health – Porter, Valparaiso, IN, p. A228
DANELLO, Sherry
MSN, R.N., Vice President and Chief Nursing Officer, Candler Hospital–Savannah, Savannah, GA, p. A170
MSN, R.N., Vice President and Chief Nursing Officer, St. Joseph's Hospital, Savannah, GA, p. A171
D'ANGELO, John, D.O., Vice President, Chief Medical Officer, Trinitas Regional Medical Center, Elizabeth, NJ, p. A421
D'ANGINA, Joseph, Chief Financial Officer, Mercy Medical Center Redding, Redding, CA, p. A85
DANIEL, Karen
Chief Executive Officer, Warm Springs Medical Center, Warm Springs, GA, p. A173
Director Human Resources, Bibb Medical Center, Centreville, AL, p. A17
DANIEL, Ron, Manager Information Systems, Matheny Medical And Educational Center, Peapack, NJ, p. A426
DANIEL, S., M.D., Chief Medical Officer, Spring Valley Hospital Medical Center, Las Vegas, NV, p. A411
DANIEL, Steven, Chief Executive Officer, Christus Surgical Hospital, Corpus Christi, TX, p. A608
DANIELS, Alex, Chief Nurse Executive, U. S. Public Health Service Indian Hospital, Crownpoint, NM, p. A434
DANIELS, Amy, R.N., Director of Nursing, Oceans Behavioral Hospital of Deridder, Deridder, LA, p. A281
DANIELS, Andy Esq, FACHE, Co–CEO, Aspire Rural Health System, Hills & Dales Healthcare, Cass City, MI, p. A323
DANIELS, Betty, M.D., Chief of Staff, St. Bernardine Medical Center, San Bernardino, CA, p. A88
DANIELS, Buddy, Chief Executive Officer, UT Health Athens, Athens, TX, p. A598
DANIELS, Craig M, Chief Financial Officer, Moab Regional Hospital, Moab, UT, p. A666
DANIELS, Don, Executive Vice President and Chief Operating Officer, UW Health Swedishamerican Hospital, Rockford, IL, p. A207
DANIELS, Forrest, Chief Executive Officer, Eastern Shore Hospital Center, Cambridge, MD, p. A303
DANIELS, Janette, Chief Executive Officer, Select Specialty Hospital–Tulsa Midtown, Tulsa, OK, p. A523
DANIELS, Kristin, Manager Human Resources, Sutter Center for Psychiatry, Sacramento, CA, p. A87
DANIELS, Mark, M.D., Vice President/Chief Medical Officer, Northwestern Medicine Delnor Hospital, Geneva, IL, p. A196
DANIELS, Robbie, Chief Information Officer, Fulton County Health Center, Wauseon, OH, p. A506
DANIELS, S Janette, Director Human Resources, Encompasss Health Rehabilitation Hospital of Fort Smith, Fort Smith, AR, p. A47
DANIELS, Sarah, Vice President, Information Technology, Mayo Clinic Health System In Mankato, Mankato, MN, p. A349
DANIELS, Todd, M.D., Medical Director, Encompass Health Rehabilitation Hospital of Arlington, Arlington, TX, p. A597
DANIELS, Troy P, Chief Human Resources Officer, Forrest General Hospital, Hattiesburg, MS, p. A363
DANIELYAN, Arman, M.D., Chief of Staff, John Muir Behavioral Health Center, Concord, CA, p. A60
DANILKO, Ashli, Chief Executive Officer, St. Michael's Hospital Avera, Tyndall, SD, p. A577
DANN, Doreen, R.N., Chief Operating Officer, Victor Valley Global Medical Center, Victorville, CA, p. A100
DANNEL, Elizabeth, Administrator, Operations Manager, Dallas Va North Texas Hcs, Dallas, TX, p. A611
DANNENBERG, Walt C., FACHE, Medical Center Director, Tibor Rubin Va Medical Center, Long Beach, CA, p. A71
DANOWSKI, Dale, R.N., Vice President, Patient Care Services, St. Vincent's Medical Center, Bridgeport, CT, p. A115
DANSBY, Tommy, Chief Medical Officer, Cypress Grove Behavioral Health, Bastrop, LA, p. A277
DANSIE, Kimberly, Chief Human Resource Officer, Riverton Hospital, Riverton, UT, p. A668
DANUSER, James, Chief Information Officer, VA Central Iowa Health Care System–Des Moines, Des Moines, IA, p. A235
DAOUD, Joudat, M.D., Chief of Staff, Promedica Coldwater Regional Hospital, Coldwater, MI, p. A324
D'APOLLO, Julie, R.N., Director of Nursing, Hampstead Hospital & Residential Treatment Facility, Hampstead, NH, p. A415
D'AQUILA, Richard, President, Yale New Haven Hospital, New Haven, CT, p. A118
DARBONNE, Tina, Chief Financial Officer, Central Louisiana State Hospital, Pineville, LA, p. A291
DARBY, Sharon, R.N., FACHE, Vice President, Clinical Operations, Children's Hospital of Richmond At Vcu, Richmond, VA, p. A682
DARCY, Deborah, Human Resources, Cornerstone Specialty Hospitals Tucson, Tucson, AZ, p. A40

 Index of Health Care Professionals **A829**

Index of Health Care Professionals
Index of Health Care Professionals / Dardano

DARDANO, Anthony, M.D., Chief Medical Officer, Delray Medical Center, Delray Beach, FL, p. A130
DARDEAU, Sean T., FACHE, Chief Executive Officer, Texoma Medical Center, Denison, TX, p. A613
DAREY, Kimberley, Chief Executive Officer, Endeavor Health Elmhurst Hospital, Elmhurst, IL, p. A194
DAREY, Roland, M.D., Medical Director, Wamego Health Center, Wamego, KS, p. A261
DARLING, Cory, Chief Executive Officer, Ascension St. Vincent's St. Johns County, Saint Johns, FL, p. A148
DARMELIO, Matthew P, Chief of Staff, Mon Health Medical Center, Morgantown, WV, p. A703
DARNAUER, Kristina, M.D., Chief of Staff, Hospital District No 1 of Rice County, Lyons, KS, p. A254
DARNAUER, Patricia, Administrator, Harris Health System, Bellaire, TX, p. A603
DARNELL, Chris, Administrator, Bozeman Health Big Sky Medical Center, Big Sky, MT, p. A389
DARNELL, Linda, Director Management Information Systems, Norton King's Daughters' Health, Madison, IN, p. A223
DARNER, Tonya, Chief Executive Officer, Up Health System – Marquette, Marquette, MI, p. A333
DARRIGO, Melinda, Interim Chief Operating Officer, Metrowest Medical Center, Framingham, MA, p. A313
DARRINGTON, Gilbert, Director Human Resources, Jackson Hospital And Clinic, Montgomery, AL, p. A22
DARVIN, Ken, M.D., Chief of Staff, Rural Wellness Stroud, Stroud, OK, p. A521
DASARO, Lynda, Director Human Resources, Sutter Roseville Medical Center, Roseville, CA, p. A86
DASCENZO, Douglas R, R.N., Chief Nursing Officer, Trinity Health Oakland Hospital, Pontiac, MI, p. A335
DASCOULIAS, Kristine, Chief Nursing Officer, Memorial Hospital, North Conway, NH, p. A417
DASHIELD, Luanne, Chief Operating Officer, Deer's Head Hospital Center, Salisbury, MD, p. A307
DASKALAKIS, Tom G., Chief Executive Officer, Cmh Regional Health System, Wilmington, OH, p. A507
DASKEVICH, Cris
FACHE, Chief Executive Officer Children's Hosp SA & SVP Maternal Svces CHRISTUS Health, Christus Santa Rosa Health System, San Antonio, TX, p. A649
FACHE, Senior Vice President, Maternal Services and Chief Executive Officer, Christus Children's, San Antonio, TX, p. A649
DASSENKO, Dennis, Chief Information Officer, Essentia Health Duluth, Duluth, MN, p. A346
DAUBERT, Stephanie
Chief Financial Officer, Nebraska Medicine – Bellevue, Bellevue, NE, p. A398
Chief Financial Officer, Nebraska Medicine – Nebraska Medical Center, Omaha, NE, p. A404
DAUBY, Randall W., Chief Executive Officer, Pinckneyville Community Hospital, Pinckneyville, IL, p. A206
DAUERMAN, Rebecca, R.N., Vice President, Administrator Mental Health Services and Chief Nursing Officer, Christian Health, Wyckoff, NJ, p. A431
DAUGHDRILL, Diane, Director Human Resources, Jefferson Davis Community Hospital, Prentiss, MS, p. A368
DAUGHDRILL, Richard P., R.N., Administrator, Greene County Hospital, Leakesville, MS, p. A365
DAUGHERTY, Don, Director Information Systems, Fleming County Hospital, Flemingsburg, KY, p. A265
DAUGHERTY, Jessica, Chief Executive Officer, Cleveland Clinic Rehabilitation Hospital, Avon, OH, p. A485
DAUGHERTY, Marney, Worklife Services Consultant, Ascension Brighton Center for Recovery, Brighton, MI, p. A323
DAUGHERTY, Stephen J.
Chief Executive Officer, Piedmont Macon, Macon, GA, p. A167
Chief Executive Officer, Piedmont Macon North, Macon, GA, p. A167
Interim Chief Executive Officer, Piedmont Macon, Macon, GA, p. A167
D'AURIA, Joseph, Director Finance, Morristown Medical Center, Morristown, NJ, p. A424
DAUTERIVE, F Ralph, M.D., Vice President Medical Affairs, Ochsner Medical Center – Baton Rouge, Baton Rouge, LA, p. A278
DAVACHI, Khosrow, Chief Medical Officer, Bridgepoint Continuing Care Hospital – National Harborside, Washington, DC, p. A123
DAVE, Bhasker J, M.D., Superintendent, Independence Mental Health Institute, Independence, IA, p. A238
DAVE, Bhasker J., M.D., Superintendent, Independence Mental Health Institute, Independence, IA, p. A238
DAVE', Rajesh J, M.D., Executive Vice President and Chief Medical Officer, United Health Services Hospitals–Binghamton, Binghamton, NY, p. A439
DAVENPORT, Allison, Chief Executive Officer, Riveredge Hospital, Forest Park, IL, p. A195
DAVENPORT, Douglas, Interim Chief Financial Officer, University of Iowa Health Care Medical Center Downtown, Iowa City, IA, p. A238
DAVENPORT, Ginger, Director Human Resources, KPC Promise Hospital of Dallas, Dallas, TX, p. A611
DAVENPORT, Michael, D.O., President, Medical Staff, Saint Luke's South Hospital, Overland Park, KS, p. A257
DAVID, Daphne, Chief Executive Officer, Tristar Summit Medical Center, Hermitage, TN, p. A584
DAVID, Robert G., President and Chief Executive Officer, Mclaren Central Michigan, Mount Pleasant, MI, p. A334
DAVIDOW, Daniel N, M.D., Medical Director, Cumberland Hospital for Children And Adolescents, New Kent, VA, p. A679
DAVIDSON, Camille, Administrator and Chief Executive Officer, Stanton County Hospital, Johnson, KS, p. A251
DAVIDSON, Diane, Senior Vice President Human Resources, Essentia Health Duluth, Duluth, MN, p. A346
DAVIDSON, Dianne, Chief Executive Officer, Union General Hospital, Farmerville, LA, p. A281
DAVIDSON, Elizabeth, R.N., Vice President, Patient Care Services, OSF Saint James – John W. Albrecht Medical Center, Pontiac, IL, p. A206
DAVIDSON, Gary
M.D., Medical Director, Select Specialty Hospital–Johnstown, Johnstown, PA, p. A543
Senior Vice President and Chief Information Officer, Penn Medicine Lancaster General Health, Lancaster, PA, p. A543
DAVIDSON, James, Director of Information Services, Ferry County Memorial Hospital, Republic, WA, p. A693
DAVIDSON, James N., Troop Commander, Tripler Army Medical Center, Honolulu, HI, p. A176
DAVIDSON, Judy, R.N., I, Chief Nursing Officer, Northwest Health – Porter, Valparaiso, IN, p. A228
DAVIDSON, Rocky, Chief Financial Officer, Larkin Community Hospital Behavioral Health Services, Hollywood, FL, p. A133
DAVIDSON, Stephen, Director Human Resources, Lafayette Regional Health Center, Lexington, MO, p. A379
DAVIDSON, Stuart, M.D., Chief Medical Officer, Mount Desert Island Hospital, Bar Harbor, ME, p. A295
DAVIDSON, Tori, R.N., Chief Nursing Officer, Tsehootsooi Medical Center, Fort Defiance, AZ, p. A31
DAVIDSON, Verno
R.N., Interim Chief Nursing Officer, Multicare Capital Medical Center, Olympia, WA, p. A692
R.N., Interim Chief Nursing Officer, Southern Tennessee Regional Health System–Pulaski, Pulaski, TN, p. A592
DAVIDYOCK, John M., M.D., Vice President and Chief Medical Officer, Winter Haven Hospital, Winter Haven, FL, p. A155
DAVILA, Susan, Chief Executive Officer, Desert View Hospital, Pahrump. NV, p. A412
DAVIN, Joni, Director Information and Business Management Service Line, Eastern Kansas Hcs, Topeka, KS, p. A260
DAVINI, John, Vice President, St. Rose Hospital, Hayward, CA, p. A67
DAVIS, Amelia, Director of Nursing, Crossridge Community Hospital, Wynne, AR, p. A54
DAVIS, Andrew L Jr, Chief Operating Officer, Erie County Medical Center, Buffalo, NY, p. A440
DAVIS, Andy, Chief Operating Officer, Ascension St. Vincent's Birmingham, Birmingham, AL, p. A16
DAVIS, Anne, Director Human Resources, Mason District Hospital, Havana, IL, p. A197
DAVIS, Astrid, R.N., Chief Nursing Officer, Wellspan York Hospital, York, PA, p. A559
DAVIS, Autherine, Director Human Resources, D. W. Mcmillan Memorial Hospital, Brewton, AL, p. A17
DAVIS, Ben, President and Chief Executive Officer, Glencoe Regional Health, Glencoe, MN, p. A347
DAVIS, Betty, Director Administrative Services, Porterville Developmental Center, Porterville, CA, p. A84
DAVIS, Boyd
III, Chief Executive Officer, Encompass Health Rehabilitation Hospital of Abilene, Abilene, TX, p. A595
III, Interim Chief Executive Officer, Encompass Health Rehabilitation Hospital of Midland Odessa, Midland, TX, p. A639
DAVIS, Brenda, Chief Executive Officer, Caprock Hospital, Bryan, TX, p. A605
DAVIS, Brent, Chief Financial Officer, Central Valley Medical Center, Nephi, UT, p. A666
DAVIS, Charissa, Chief Nursing Officer and Director of Nursing, Oasis Behavioral Health – Chandler, Chandler, AZ, p. A31
DAVIS, Charlotte C, Director Human Resources, Lincoln Trail Behavioral Health System, Radcliff, KY, p. A273
DAVIS, Cheryl, M.D., Chief Medical Officer, Scotland Health Care System, Laurinburg, NC, p. A471
DAVIS, Christopher, Chief Operating Officer, De Soto Regional Health System, Mansfield, LA, p. A288
DAVIS, Cynthia, Chief Information Officer, Loyola University Medical Center, Maywood, IL, p. A201
DAVIS, Dan
MSN, R.N., Nurse Administrator, Park City Hospital, Park City, UT, p. A667
Managing Director and Chief Financial Officer, Integris Southwest Medical Center, Oklahoma City, OK, p. A517
DAVIS, Daniel E, Chief Financial Officer, HCA Houston Healthcare Kingwood, Kingwood, TX, p. A633
DAVIS, Darcy, Chief Financial Officer, Lakeside Medical Center, Belle Glade, FL, p. A125
DAVIS, David, Chief Operating Officer, Western Maryland Hospital Center, Hagerstown, MD, p. A305
DAVIS, Debra K., Director of Operations, Winner Regional Healthcare Center, Winner, SD, p. A578
DAVIS, Deland, Chief Financial Officer, Quentin N. Burdick Memorial Healthcare Facility, Belcourt, ND, p. A479
DAVIS, Dustin, Chief Executive Officer, Woodland Springs Hospital, Conroe, TX, p. A608
DAVIS, Elaine, Chief Nursing Officer and Vice President Patient Services, RMC Anniston, Anniston, AL, p. A15
DAVIS, Evan, Director Technology and Environmental Services, Barbourville Arh Hospital, Barbourville, KY, p. A263
DAVIS, Gannon, Director Human Resources, Medical West, Bessemer, AL, p. A16
DAVIS, Gary, Vice President Information Systems, Baptist Medical Center, San Antonio, TX, p. A648
DAVIS, Gary S., Chief Financial Officer, North Okaloosa Medical Center, Crestview, FL, p. A129
DAVIS, Heather
M.D., Chief of Staff, Novant Health Pender Medical Center, Burgaw, NC, p. A464
Administrator, Ochsner Scott Regional, Morton, MS, p. A367
DAVIS, Howard Z, M.D., Chief Medical Officer, Providence Cedars–Sinai Tarzana Medical Center, Los Angeles, CA, p. A74
DAVIS, Janice, Interim Director Human Resources, Gifford Medical Center, Randolph, VT, p. A672
DAVIS, Jeff, Chief Financial Officer, Harrison County Hospital, Corydon, IN, p. A214
DAVIS, Jeremy P., President and Chief Executive Officer, Grande Ronde Hospital, La Grande, OR, p. A528
DAVIS, John, Chief Human Resources Officer, Bristol Bay Area Health Corporation, Dillingham, AK, p. A28
DAVIS, Johnnie, Director Human Resources, Medicine Lodge Memorial Hospital, Medicine Lodge, KS, p. A254
DAVIS, Jon, Chief Financial Officer, Community Hospital–Fairfax, Fairfax, MO, p. A375
DAVIS, Josh, R.N., Chief Executive Officer, Mountain Valley Regional Rehabilitation Hospital, Prescott Valley, AZ, p. A37
DAVIS, Kassi, Director Patient Care Services, Willow Crest Hospital, Miami, OK, p. A515
DAVIS, Kelly, Chief Nursing Officer, Anmed Rehabilitation Hospital, Anderson, SC, p. A562
DAVIS, Kenneth
M.D., Chief Medical Officer, Christus Santa Rosa Health System, San Antonio, TX, p. A649
Assistant Vice President Information Systems, Kennedy Krieger Institute, Baltimore, MD, p. A300
DAVIS, LaKeitha, Director Human Resources, South Arkansas Regional Hospital, El Dorado, AR, p. A45
DAVIS, Lance, PharmD, Associate Director, Miami Veterans Affairs Healthcare System, Miami, FL, p. A140
DAVIS, Lora, FACHE, Chief Executive Officer, Regional Rehabilitation Hospital, Phenix City, AL, p. A24
DAVIS, Lorraine, Vice President Human Resources, Horn Memorial Hospital, Ida Grove, IA, p. A237
DAVIS, Margaret, Chief Operating Officer, Pecos County Memorial Hospital, Fort Stockton, TX, p. A619
DAVIS, Mark
M.D., Chief of Staff, Newberry County Memorial Hospital, Newberry, SC, p. A569
Director Information Systems, Lake Taylor Transitional Care Hospital, Norfolk, VA, p. A680
DAVIS, Marla, Interim Chief Nursing Officer, Prosser Memorial Health, Prosser, WA, p. A693
DAVIS, Matt, FACHE, Chief Executive Officer, HCA Houston Healthcare Conroe, Conroe, TX, p. A608
DAVIS, Myra, Senior Vice President and Chief Information Officer, Texas Children's Hospital, Houston, TX, p. A628
DAVIS, Myrna, Manager Human Resources, Palo Verde Hospital, Blythe, CA, p. A58
DAVIS, Orlando, M.D., Medical Director, The Meadows Psychiatric Center, Centre Hall, PA, p. A536

A830 Index of Health Care Professionals

DAVIS, Patricia, Chief Nursing Officer, South Central Kansas Medical Center, Arkansas City, KS, p. A246
DAVIS, Paul, Chief Nursing Officer, Lincoln County Health System, Fayetteville, TN, p. A583
DAVIS, Paula M, Chief Human Resources Officer, Sonoma Valley Hospital, Sonoma, CA, p. A96
DAVIS, Rachel, Director, Sharp Coronado Hospital, Coronado, CA, p. A60
DAVIS, Randy
  Chief Executive Officer, Cumberland Medical Center, Crossville, TN, p. A582
  Vice President and Chief Information Officer, Cgh Medical Center, Sterling, IL, p. A209
DAVIS, Regana, Vice President Human Resources, Tri-State Memorial Hospital, Clarkston, WA, p. A688
DAVIS, Richard
  Chief Financial Officer, George Washington University Hospital, Washington, DC, p. A123
  President and Chief Executive Officer, Cooperman Barnabas Medical Center, Livingston, NJ, p. A423
DAVIS, Rick, Chief Operating Officer and Support Services, Coshocton Regional Medical Center, Coshocton, OH, p. A493
DAVIS, Robert, Chief Nursing Officer, Adventhealth Palm Coast, Palm Coast, FL, p. A145
DAVIS, Roger K, Director Human Resources, Bourbon Community Hospital, Paris, KY, p. A273
DAVIS, Ronald Anthony, Chief Financial Officer – UCLA Hospital System, Stewart & Lynda Resnick Neuropsychiatric Hospital At Ucla, Los Angeles, CA, p. A75
DAVIS, Roy, M.D., Chief Medical Officer, Providence Alaska Medical Center, Anchorage, AK, p. A27
DAVIS, Scott
  Manager Information Technology, Arkansas Surgical Hospital, North Little Rock, AR, p. A51
  President/Chief Executive Officer, Swedish Medical Center, Englewood, CO, p. A107
DAVIS, Shawn, Chief Information Officer, Tuba City Regional Health Care Corporation, Tuba City, AZ, p. A40
DAVIS, Sondra, Vice President Human Resources & System Development, Harnett Health System, Dunn, NC, p. A467
DAVIS, Stan, FACHE, Senior Vice President and Chief Operating Officer, Cook Children's Medical Center – Prosper, Prosper, TX, p. A646
DAVIS, Stephanie, Controller, Encompass Health Rehabilitation Hospital of Colorado Springs, Colorado Springs, CO, p. A105
DAVIS, Steve, President and Chief Executive Officer, Cincinnati Children's Hospital Medical Center, Cincinnati, OH, p. A488
DAVIS, Takeisha C., M.D., M.P.H., President and Chief Executive Officer, New Orleans East Hospital, New Orleans, LA, p. A290
DAVIS, Talbert, Human Resources Manager, Spring Hospital, Spring, TX, p. A654
DAVIS, Tamara, R.N., Chief Nurse Executive Officer, Sutter Davis Hospital, Davis, CA, p. A61
DAVIS, Tammy, Director Human Resources, Deaconess Illinois Union County, Anna, IL, p. A185
DAVIS, Terry, Manager Information Systems, Amberwell Health, Atchison, KS, p. A246
DAVIS, Teshia, Chief Clinical Officer, Carolinas Continuecare Hospital At Pineville, Charlotte, NC, p. A465
DAVIS, Toby, Chief Nursing Officer, Good Samaritan Hospital, Bakersfield, CA, p. A57
DAVIS, Todd
  M.D., Executive Vice President, Chief Medical Officer, Caromont Regional Medical Center, Gastonia, NC, p. A469
  Executive Director of Information Systems, Hendricks Regional Health, Danville, IN, p. A215
DAVIS, Tommy, M.D., Chief of Staff, Oakdale Community Hospital, Oakdale, LA, p. A290
DAVIS, Tracye B., FACHE, Medical Center Director, Maine Veterans Affairs Medical Center, Augusta, ME, p. A295
DAVIS, Tyler, Chief Executive Officer, Erlanger Behavioral Hospital, Chattanooga, TN, p. A580
DAVIS, Tyson, Chief Financial Officer, Adventhealth Tampa, Tampa, FL, p. A152
DAVIS, Valerie
  Administrator, Mercy Hospital Aurora, Aurora, MO, p. A371
  Administrator, Mercy Hospital Cassville, Cassville, MO, p. A373
  Administrator, Mercy Hospital Aurora, Mercy St. Francis Hospital, Mountain View, MO, p. A381
DAVIS, Verlene, Director Human Resources, Blue Mountain Hospital District, John Day, OR, p. A528
DAVIS, Vicki, Chief Executive Officer, Amg Specialty Hospital – Las Vegas, Las Vegas, NV, p. A409

DAVIS, Wayne, Manager Human Resources, Jesse Brown Va Medical Center, Chicago, IL, p. A189
DAVIS, Wendy, Associate Vice President and Chief Human Resource Officer, The University of Toledo Medical Center, Toledo, OH, p. A505
DAVIS, William
  Chief Administrative Officer, Deaconess Illinois Crossroads, Mount Vernon, IL, p. A202
  Chief Administrative Officer, Deaconess Illinois Medical Center, Marion, IL, p. A200
  Chief Financial Officer, Rapides Regional Medical Center, Alexandria, LA, p. A276
DAVISON, Justin, President and Chief Executive Officer, Saint Francis Medical Center, Cap. Girardeau, MO, p. A372
DAVISON, Katie, Vice President, Human Resources, UNC Health Nash, Rocky Mount, NC, p. A475
DAVISON, Trish, R.N., Chief Nursing Officer, Regional West Garden County, Oshkosh, NE, p. A405
DAVISSON, Deborah, MSN, Chief Nursing Officer and Vice President, Patient Care Services, Holy Cross Hospital, Chicago, IL, p. A189
DAWSEY, Stephanie, R.N., Chief Executive Officer, Amg Physical Rehabilitation Hospital, Covington, LA, p. A280
DAWSON, Kane A., Chief Executive Officer, Mission Regional Medical Center, Mission, TX, p. A640
DAWSON, Kevin, Chief Information Officer, Howard University Hospital, Washington, DC, p. A123
DAWSON, Theresa, MSN, R.N., Chief Nursing Officer, Oaklawn Hospital, Marshall, MI, p. A333
DAWSON, Trang, Chief Information Officer, Baylor Scott & White Emergency Hospitals–Aubrey, Aubrey, TX, p. A598
DAX, Jennifer, Director Human Resources, Gundersen Boscobel Area Hospital And Clinics, Boscobel, WI, p. A708
DAY, Gordy, M.D., Medical Director, Schleicher County Medical Center, Eldorado, TX, p. A618
DAY, John M., Chief Executive Officer, Unity Physicians Hospital, Mishawaka, IN, p. A224
DAY, Mark, Chief Financial Officer, HCA Florida Twin Cities Hospital, Niceville, FL, p. A142
DAY, Regina
  Director of Finance, Hancock County Hospital, Sneedville, TN, p. A593
  Executive Vice President of Finance, Lonesome Pine Hospital, Big Stone Gap. VA, p. A673
DAY, Scott, Vice President Human Resources, Lutheran Medical Center, Wheat Ridge, CO, p. A114
DAY, Sherry Clouse
  CPA, Chief Financial Officer, Mercy Hospital Cassville, Cassville, MO, p. A373
  CPA, Chief Financial Officer, Mercy St. Francis Hospital, Mountain View, MO, p. A381
DAY, Therese, Chief Financial Officer, Umass Memorial Medical Center, Worcester, MA, p. A320
DAY, Victoria, Chief Financial Officer and Vice President of Ancillary Services, Sharp Coronado Hospital, Coronado, CA, p. A60
DAYOTAS, Andrea, Interim Chief Executive Officer, Adcare Hospital of Worcester, Worcester, MA, p. A320
DE AQUINO, Walmir Wally, Chief Executive Officer, Adventhealth Palm Coast Parkway, Palm Coast, FL, p. A145
DE BOND, Virginia, Chief Financial Officer, Nexus Speciality Hospital – The Woodlands Campus, The Woodlands, TX, p. A657
DE FARIA, Ludmila, M.D., Chief Medical Officer, Eastside Psychiatric Hospital, Tallahassee, FL, p. A151
DE JESUS, Alexander, M.D., Medical Director, Encompass Health Rehabilitation Hospital of Sarasota, Sarasota, FL, p. A149
DE LA CRUZ, Rosemary, Chief Financial Officer, Hospital Menonita Guayama, Guayama, PR, p. A732
DE LA GARZA, Josiah, Chief Executive Officer, Baylor Surgical Hospital At Las Colinas, Irving, TX, p. A630
DE LA PAZ, Christine, Director Human Resources, Aurora Charter Oak Hospital, Covina, CA, p. A60
DE LEON, Aurea, Chief Human Resources Officer, Hospital Universitario Dr. Ramon Ruiz Arnau, Bayamon, PR, p. A731
DE LEON, Darcy, Executive Director, Human Resources, Adventist Health Howard Memorial, Willits, CA, p. A101
DE LEON, Dennis, M.D., Associate Chief Medical Officer and Vice President Medical Affairs, St. Anne Hospital, Burien, WA, p. A688
DE LEON, Sherilene, Chief Financial Officer, Park Royal Hospital, Fort Myers, FL, p. A132
DE LOS SANTOS, Conrad, President Medical Staff, Medical West, Bessemer, AL, p. A16
DE LOS SANTOS, Ruben, M.D., Chief Medical Officer, Fort Duncan Regional Medical Center, Eagle Pass, TX, p. A615
DE MELO, Dennis, Chief Information Officer, Heber Valley Hospital, Heber City, UT, p. A665

DE ONIS, Luis, Interim Chief Human Resources Officer, Stony Brook University Hospital, Stony Brook, NY, p. A459
DE PIANO, Linda, Ph.D., Chief Executive Officer, Sunview Medical Center, West Palm Beach, FL, p. A154
DE SHAZO, Sheri, R.N., FACHE, President, Advocate Sherman Hospital, Elgin, IL, p. A194
DE SIMON JOHNSON, Lauren, Senior Vice President, Chief Human Resources Officer, Southcoast Hospitals Group. Fall River, MA, p. A313
DEAK, Terry, Chief Financial Officer, Adventist Health Lodi Memorial, Lodi, CA, p. A70
DEAKYNE, John R, Chief Financial Officer, Saint Mary's Regional Medical Center, Reno, NV, p. A412
DEAL, Lisa, Budget Analyst, U. S. Public Health Service Indian Hospital, Eagle Butte, SD, p. A573
DEAL, Roy, Chief Medical Officer, Emerald Coast Behavioral Hospital, Panama City, FL, p. A145
DEAN, Aimee, Executive Director, St. Lawrence Psychiatric Center, Ogdensburg, NY, p. A455
DEAN, Douglas B, Chief Human Resources Officer, Children's of Alabama, Birmingham, AL, p. A16
DEAN, Holly, Chief Executive Officer, Shelby Baptist Medical Center, Alabaster, AL, p. A15
DEAN, Jason, Administrator, Ephraim Mcdowell Fort Logan Hospital, Stanford, KY, p. A274
DEAN, Joel, Director Information Services, Piedmont Medical Center, Rock Hill, SC, p. A570
DEAN, Laura L, Director Human Resources, Wilson Medical Center, Neodesha, KS, p. A255
DEAN, Ronald, President and Chief Executive Officer, South Georgia Medical Center, Valdosta, GA, p. A173
DEAN, Sam, Chief Executive Officer, Merit Health River Oaks, Flowood, MS, p. A362
DEAN, Thomas, M.D., Chief of Staff, Avera Weskota Memorial Hospital, Wessington Springs, SD, p. A578
DEANGELIS, Lisa, M.D., Acting Physician–in–Chief, Memorial Sloan Kettering Cancer Center, New York, NY, p. A449
DEARDORFF, Chad, Chief Financial Officer, Pam Health Specialty Hospital of Heritage Valley, Beaver, PA, p. A535
DEARDORFF, John A., President and Chief Executive, Northern Virginia Market, Reston Hospital Center, Reston, VA, p. A682
DEARY, Shirley, Director Human Resources, Glenbeigh Hospital And Outpatient Centers, Rock Creek, OH, p. A503
DEATER, Gary A, Vice President Administration, Human Resources and Risk Management, Witham Health Services, Lebanon, IN, p. A222
DEATON, David, FACHE, Chief Executive Officer, Ozark Health Medical Center, Clinton, AR, p. A44
DEATON, Eric, Executive Vice President, Chief Operating Officer and Corporate Operating, Hancock County Hospital, Sneedville, TN, p. A593
DEATON, Mike, Chief Financial Officer, Ozark Health Medical Center, Clinton, AR, p. A44
DEATON, Susan Renodin, Human Resources Director, The Medical Center At Russellville, Russellville, KY, p. A274
DEBEVEC, Teresa, Chief Executive Officer and Administrator, Cook Hospital & Care Center, Cook, MN, p. A345
DEBILT, Alisha, Human Resources Director, Mountrail County Medical Center, Stanley, ND, p. A483
DEBLANC, Hunt, M.D., Chief of Staff, Opelousas General Health System, Opelousas, LA, p. A291
DEBLIEUX, Dawna, Vice President Patient Care Services and Chief Nurse Executive, Natchitoches Regional Medical Center, Natchitoches, LA, p. A289
DEBLOIS, Georgean, M.D., Chairman Medical Staff, Cjw Medical Center, Richmond, VA, p. A683
DEBLOUW, Christina, R.N., Chief Executive Officer, Select Specialty Hospital – Flint, Flint, MI, p. A327
DEBOER, Cynthia D, Chief Financial Officer, Cedar Springs Hospital, Colorado Springs, CO, p. A104
DEBOER, Kenneth C., Regional President for Mid–Missouri, SSM Health St. Mary's Hospital – Jefferson City, Jefferson City, MO, p. A376
DEBOLT, Kelly Ann., R.N., Chief Executive Officer, Select Specialty Hospital – Saginaw, Saginaw, MI, p. A337
DEBOLT, Larry W, Chief Financial Officer, Bluffton Regional Medical Center, Bluffton, IN, p. A213
DEBONO, Julie, Director, Human Resources, Umass Memorial Healthalliance–Clinton Hospital, Leominster, MA, p. A315
DEBORD, Thomas, Chief Operating Officer, Overlake Medical Center And Clinics, Bellevue, WA, p. A687
DECARLO, Donald, M.D., President, University Hospitals Geauga Medical Center, Chardon, OH, p. A488
DECASPERIS, Ilyssa, Director of Human Resources, Parkview Community Hospital Medical Center, Riverside, CA, p. A86
DECELIS, Lori, Director Human Resources, Hampton Behavioral Health Center, Westampton, NJ, p. A430
DECHABERT, Rebecca, Acting Director Personnel, New York State Psychiatric Institute, New York, NY, p. A450

Index of Health Care Professionals

Index of Health Care Professionals / Dechant

DECHANT, David, Chief Human Resources Officer, Tomah Va Medical Center, Tomah, WI, p. A723
DECHANT, Laura, Chief Nursing Officer, Reunion Rehabilitation Hospital Denver, Denver, CO, p. A107
DECKARD, Rick, Chief Fiscal Service, Chillicothe Veterans Affairs Medical Center, Chillicothe, OH, p. A488
DECKARD, Steven D, Vice President Human Resources, Indiana University Health Bloomington Hospital, Bloomington, IN, p. A213
DECKER, Ashlie, Chief Executive Officer, Honorhealth Rehabilitation Hospital, Scottsdale, AZ, p. A38
DECKER, Chad, Director Human Resources, Winona Health, Winona, MN, p. A357
DECKER, Diann, Chief Human Resource Officer, Aspen Grove Behavioral Hospital, Orem, UT, p. A666
DECKER, Janet, Assistant Vice President, Information Systems, Medstar Union Memorial Hospital, Baltimore, MD, p. A301
DECKER, Jeanine, Manager Human Resources, Arizona State Hospital, Phoenix, AZ, p. A35
DECKER, Stacey L., MS, R.N., Chief Hospital Executive and Chief Nursing Officer, Lakeside Women's Hospital, Oklahoma City, OK, p. A517
DECKER, William (Kevir), Chief Executive Officer, West Tennessee Healthcare Volunteer Hospital, Martin, TN, p. A587
DECREMER, Dean, Information Systems Manager, Marshfield Medical Center – Dickinson, Iron Mountain, MI, p. A330
DECUBELLIS, Jennifer, Chief Executive Officer, Hennepin Healthcare, Minneapolis, MN, p. A350
DEDOMINICO, Tony, Chief Operating Officer, Ascension Seton Northwest, Austin, TX, p. A599
DEE, Thomas A., President and Chief Executive Officer, Southwestern Vermont Medical Center, Bennington, VT, p. A671
DEEB, Nana, Chief Executive Officer, Palmdale Regional Medical Center, Palmdale, CA, p. A82
DEEDS, Michelle, Chief Executive Officer, Pocahontas Memorial Hospital, Buckeye, WV, p. A699
DEEKEN, Debra Jean, R.N., Interim Chief Nursing Officer, Capital Region Medical Center, Jefferson City, MO, p. A376
DEEN, Cecelia Esq, Chief Nursing Officer, Southeast Colorado Hospital District, Springfield, CO, p. A113
DEETER, Joe, MS, Director Information Systems, Clifton–Fine Hospital, Star Lake, NY, p. A459
DEFAZIO, Vanessa, Chief Human Resources Officer, Highland–Clarksburg Hospital, Clarksburg, WV, p. A700
DEFIGUIEREDO, Kathy, Director, Information Technology, St. Luke's Health – Memorial Livingston, Livingston, TX, p. A635
DEFILIPPI, Bianca, Chief Executive Officer, Vista Medical Center East, Waukegan, IL, p. A210
DEFILLIPO, Emily, Chief Executive Officer, Vibra Hospital of Northern California, Redding, CA, p. A85
DEFOE, Michael, Chief Financial Officer, Thayer County Health Services, Hebron, NE, p. A401
DEFOE, Mike, Chief Financial Officer, OSF Saint Clare Medical Center, Princeton, IL, p. A206
DEFRANCESCO, Anthony, Associate Director, Tibor Rubin Va Medical Center, Long Beach, CA, p. A71
DEFRANCESCO, Jennifer A., Medical Center Director, Dayton Veterans Affairs Medical Center, Dayton, OH, p. A493
DEFREECE, Daniel, M.D., President, Chi Health St. Mary's, Nebraska City, NE, p. A402
DEFREECE, Todd, Senior Vice President of Operations, Essentia Health–St. Joseph's Medical Center, Brainerd, MN, p. A344
DEGEAR, David O, M.D., Vice President Medical Affairs, Westfields Hospital And Clinic, New Richmond, WI, p. A718
DEGENAARS, Joel, Chief Financial Officer, Wentworth–Douglass Hospital, Dover, NH, p. A414
DEGENNARO, Melanie, Vice President of Human Resources, Emory University Hospital, Atlanta, GA, p. A157
DEGENNARO, Vincent, M.D., Chief of Staff, Miami Veterans Affairs Healthcare System, Miami, FL, p. A140
DEGNAN, William, Vice President Finance, Jefferson Health Northeast, Philadelphia, PA, p. A549
DEGNER, Keith, Chief Financial Officer, Granite Hills Hospital, West Allis, WI, p. A724
DEGRAVELLE, Eric, Vice President Professional Services, Thibodaux Regional Health System, Thibodaux, LA, p. A294
DEGROOD, Robert, M.D., Chief Medical Staff, Musc Health Marion Medical Center, Mullins, SC, p. A569
DEGROOT, Daniel, President and Chief Executive Officer, Stoughton Health, Stoughton, WI, p. A722
DEHAAI, Sarah, R.N., Director of Nursing, Avera Hand County Memorial Hospital, Miller, SD, p. A574
DEHART, Kristen, Chief Executive Officer, Excelsior Springs Hospital, Excelsior Springs, MO, p. A374
DEHAVEN, Bryce, Chief Financial Officer, Medical Center of Aurora, Aurora, CO, p. A103
DEHERRERA, Barbara, Chief Nursing Officer, Garfield County Public Hospital District, Pomeroy, WA, p. A692
DEHNING, Cielo, M.D., Medical Director, Mid–America Rehabilitation Hospital, Shawnee Mission, KS, p. A260
DEIBEL, Justin, Senior Vice President and Chief Financial Officer, Mercy Medical Center, Baltimore, MD, p. A301
DEININGER, Robert Craig., President and Chief Executive Officer, Adventhealth Orlando, Orlando, FL, p. A144
DEITRICK, Diana, Director Information Services, Devereux Hospital And Children's Center of Florida, Melbourne, FL, p. A138
DEJONG, Tyler
President, Chi Health St Elizabeth, Lincoln, NE, p. A402
Vice President, Operational Finance, Chi Health Midlands, Papillion, NE, p. A405
Vice President, Operational Finance, Chi Health St Elizabeth, Lincoln, NE, p. A402
DEKEYZER, Ron, Regional Director Information Systems, Christus St. Vincent Regional Medical Center, Santa Fe, NM, p. A436
DEKEZEL, Lisa
R.N., President, OSF Holy Family Medical Center, Monmouth, IL, p. A202
R.N., President, OSF St. Mary Medical Center, Galesburg, IL, p. A196
DEKOK, Joni, Chief Nursing Officer, Sanford Sheldon Medical Center, Sheldon, IA, p. A243
DEKONING, Bernard L., M.D., Chief of Staff, Columbia Va Health Care System, Columbia, SC, p. A564
DEKREY, Dale, MS, Associate Director Operations and Resources, Fargo Va Medical Center, Fargo, ND, p. A480
DEKREY, Daniel, M.D., Chief of Staff, Sanford Bemidji Medical Center, Bemidji, MN, p. A343
DEL CARMEN, Marcela G., President, Massachusetts General Hospital, Boston, MA, p. A310
DEL CASTILLO, Daniel, Chief Executive Officer, Encompass Health Rehabilitation Hospital of San Juan, San Juan, PR, p. A735
DEL FARNO, George, Chief Executive Officer, Pam Health Rehabilitation Hospital of Georgetown, Georgetown, DE, p. A121
DEL GAUDIO, Frank J., Department and Hospital Center Director, Essex County Hospital Center, Cedar Grove, NJ, p. A419
DEL MAR TORRES HERNANDEZ, Maria, Administrator, Hospital Menonita De Cayey, Cayey, PR, p. A732
DEL PIZZO, Michelle, President, UPMC Memorial, York, PA, p. A559
DEL RIO, R Maxilimien, M.D., Medical Director, Northern Virginia Mental Health Institute, Falls Church, VA, p. A676
DEL TORO, Gustavo, M.D., Chief Medical Officer, Wyckoff Heights Medical Center, New York, NY, p. A453
DEL TORO, Ivan E, M.D., Medical Director, Hima San Pablo Caguas, Caguas, PR, p. A731
DELA MERCED, Maria Gloria, Hospital Executive, St. Louise Regional Hospital, Gilroy, CA, p. A65
DELAHANTY, Paula
Regional Chief Nursing Officer, Mainehealth Pen Bay Medical Center, Rockport, ME, p. A299
Regional Chief Nursing Officer, Waldo County General Hospital, Belfast, ME, p. A296
DELAHOUSSAYE, Renee D., R.N., Vice President, Chief Nursing Officer, Ochsner Lafayette General Medical Center, Lafayette, LA, p. A285
DELANCEY, Darlene, Director, Albany Stratton Veterans Affairs Medical Center, Albany, NY, p. A438
DELANEY, Bryan, Director Information Technology, Deaconess Illinois Crossroads, Mount Vernon, IL, p. A202
DELANEY, Conor P., M.D., Ph.D., Chief Executive Officer and President, Cleveland Clinic Florida, Weston, FL, p. A155
DELANEY, Kristi, Director, Human Resources, Siskin Hospital for Physical Rehabilitation, Chattanooga, TN, p. A581
DELANO, John, Chief Information Officer, Southwest Region, Texas Health Huguley Hospital Fort Worth South, Burleson, TX, p. A606
DELAROSA, Michael, Chief Executive Officer, Rush Specialty Hospital, Chicago, IL, p. A190
DELATTE, Sandra, Director Human Resources, Villa Feliciana Medical Complex, Jackson, LA, p. A283
DELAVAN, Karen, Interim Director Human Resources, Comanche County Medical Center, Comanche, TX, p. A608
DELBOCCIO, Suzanne, Chief Nursing Officer, Havasu Regional Medical Center, Lake Havasu City, AZ, p. A32
DELDUCA, Michael, Associate Medical Center Director, Syracuse Veterans Affairs Medical Center, Syracuse, NY, p. A460
DELEON, Arsenio V, M.D., Chief Medical Officer, Select Specialty Hospital – Macomb County, Mount Clemens, MI, p. A334
DELEON, Dennis, M.D., Chief Medical Officer, King Region, St. Francis Hospital, Federal Way, WA, p. A690
DELEON, J. Michael, FACHE, Chief Executive Officer, Baylor Scott & White Institute for Rehabilitation–Fort Worth, Fort Worth, TX, p. A619
DELEON, John, Chief Executive Officer, Methodist Stone Oak Hospital, San Antonio, TX, p. A650
DELEON, Sherilene, Chief Financial Officer, Spring Mountain Treatment Center, Las Vegas, NV, p. A410
DELFS, Michael, President and Chief Executive Officer, Jamestown Regional Medical Center, Jamestown, ND, p. A482
DELGADO, Eric, Chief Financial Officer, Lakewood Regional Medical Center, Lakewood, CA, p. A69
DELGADO, Lupe, Coordinator Human Resources, Kindred Hospital Sugar Land, Sugar Land, TX, p. A654
DELGRECO, Trish, Director of Nursing, Ohiohealth Shelby Hospital, Shelby, OH, p. A503
DELIEN, Rudie, Director of Human Resources, Devereux Advanced Behavioral Health Georgia, Kennesaw, GA, p. A166
DELLA FLORA, Thomas, Vice President and Chief Information Officer, Catholic Medical Center, Manchester, NH, p. A416
DELLEA, Eugene A., President, Fairview Hospital, Great Barrington, MA, p. A314
DELLICKER, Sandra, Director of Human Resources, Saint Anne's Hospital, Fall River, MA, p. A313
DELLOCONO, John, Senior Vice President and Chief Financial Officer, Centrastate Healthcare System, Freehold, NJ, p. A421
DELOACH, Stephen, Regional Information Management Executive, Christus St. Michael Health System, Texarkana, TX, p. A656
DELONE, J. Bret, M.D., Vice President, Medical Affairs, Penn State Health Holy Spirit Medical Center, Camp Hill, PA, p. A536
DELONG, Patricia, Chief Nursing Officer, Essentia Health–St. Joseph's Medical Center, Brainerd, MN, p. A344
DELORENZO, David, Senior Director Human Resources, Sisters of Charity Hospital of Buffalo, Buffalo, NY, p. A440
DELORME, Robert, Vice President Medical Affairs, Community Memorial Hospital, Hamilton, NY, p. A444
DELROSSI, Stephen
Chief Executive Officer, Northern Inyo Hospital, Bishop, CA, p. A58
Chief Financial Officer, The Meadows Psychiatric Center, Centre Hall, PA, p. A536
DELVEAUX, Joe, Manager Information Services, St. Francis Regional Medical Center, Shakopee, MN, p. A355
DEMARCO, Cindy, Chief Executive Officer, Lake Behavioral Hospital, Waukegan, IL, p. A210
DEMARCO, Tom, Interim Chief Executive Officer, Lincoln Prairie Behavioral Health Center, Springfield, IL, p. A209
DEMARCO, Victor, Chief Financial Officer, Bronxcare Health System, New York, NY, p. A447
DEMASIE, Dennis, Vice President Information Systems and Chief Information Officer, Rush–Copley Medical Center, Aurora, IL, p. A186
DEMATTEO, Kathleen, Chief Information Officer, Danbury Hospital, Danbury, CT, p. A115
DEMBLA, Preeti, Chief Medical Officer and Medical Director, Rehabilitation Hospital of Fort Wayne, Fort Wayne, IN, p. A217
DEMERICH, Lois B, Director Human Resources, Sentara Williamsburg Regional Medical Center, Williamsburg, VA, p. A685
DEMERS, Stephen, Chief Executive Officer, Memorial Hospital Miramar, Miramar, FL, p. A141
DEMERS, Vickie, Chief Executive Officer, Andalusia Health, Andalusia, AL, p. A15
DEMETRIADES, James
Chief Executive Officer, Penn Medicine Princeton Medical Center, Plainsboro, NJ, p. A427
Vice President, Operations, Penn Medicine Princeton Medical Center, Plainsboro, NJ, p. A427
DEMING, Mark, Administrator, Finance and Support, Corewell Health Taylor Hospital, Taylor, MI, p. A339
DEMING, Peggy, Executive Vice President and Chief Financial Officer, University Health, San Antonio, TX, p. A651
DEMING, Terra, Director Human Resources, Munson Healthcare Otsego Memorial Hospital, Gaylord, MI, p. A327
DEMKE, Jason, Chief Operator Officer, Mercy Hospital Fort Smith, Fort Smith, AR, p. A47
DEMLAKIAN, Vahan, Director of Human Resources, Gateways Hospital And Mental Health Center, Los Angeles, CA, p. A72
DEMMEL, Ruth, M.D., Chief Medical Officer, Perkins County Health Services, Grant, NE, p. A400
DEMORLIS, John, M.D., Chief Medical Staff, Salem Memorial District Hospital, Salem, MO, p. A386

A832 Index of Health Care Professionals

Index of Health Care Professionals / Dew

Index of Health Care Professionals

DEMORROW, Dawn P, Chief Human Resources Service, Wilkes–Barre Veterans Affairs Medical Center, Wilkes–Barre, PA, p. A558
DEMOSS, Jill, Finance Manager, Guttenberg Municipal Hospital And Clinics, Guttenberg, IA, p. A237
DEMOTTE, Mike, Chief Financial Officer, Lds Hospital, Salt Lake City, UT, p. A669
DEMPSEY, Jeff, Chief Operating Officer, Nationwide Children's Hospital – Toledo, Toledo, OH, p. A504
DEMPSEY, Jeffrey, President, Mercy Health – St. Vincent Medical Center, Toledo, OH, p. A504
DEMPSEY, John J., Chief Executive Officer, Little Colorado Medical Center, Winslow, AZ, p. A41
DEMPSEY, Melanie, Vice President and Chief Financial Officer, Davis Medical Center, Elkins, WV, p. A700
DEMPSEY, William J., Chief Executive Officer, Webster County Memorial Hospital, Webster Springs, WV, p. A705
DENEFF, Randall, Vice President Finance, Mary Free Bed Rehabilitation Hospital, Grand Rapids, MI, p. A328
DENEGRI, David, Chief Financial Officer, Parkwood Behavioral Health System, Olive Branch, MS, p. A367
DENG, Mei, Chief Financial Officer, T. J. Samson Community Hospital, Glasgow, KY, p. A266
DENHAM, Stephanie, Chief Financial Officer and Human Resources Officer, Phillip. County Hospital, Malta, MT, p. A394
DENIGRIS, Deborah, Chief Nursing Officer, Kingsboro Psychiatric Center, New York, NY, p. A448
DENIKE, Michael, D.O., Vice President, Medical Affairs, Blanchard Valley Hospital, Findlay, OH, p. A496
DENIL, Alison, Chief Executive Officer, Willow Creek Behavioral Health, Green Bay, WI, p. A712
DENIRO, Lori, Regional Chief Nursing Officer, Mercy Health – St. Elizabeth Youngstown Hospital, Youngstown, OH, p. A508
DENISIENKO, Mary, Vice President Human Resources, Northwestern Medicine Palos Hospital, Palos Heights, IL, p. A205
DENISON, Rita, Director of Information Systems, Sturgis Hospital, Sturgis, MI, p. A338
DENKER, Jill, Executive Director Human Resources, Lexington Regional Health Center, Lexington, NE, p. A401
DENMARK, Donald, M.D., Chief Medical Officer, Carondelet St. Joseph's Hospital, Tucson, AZ, p. A40
DENNETT, Bryan, M.D., Chief of Staff, William Newton Hospital, Winfield, KS, p. A262
DENNING, Kimberly, R.N., Medical Director, Jack C. Montgomery Department of Veterans Affairs Medical Center, Muskogee, OK, p. A515
DENNIS, Kera, Assistant Administrator, Finance, UW Medicine/Harborview Medical Center, Seattle, WA, p. A695
DENNIS, Michael, Executive Director, William J. Mccord Adolescent Treatment Facility, Orangeburg, SC, p. A569
DENNISON, Cynthia, Chief Financial Officer, Mercy Health – Allen Hospital, Oberlin, OH, p. A501
DENNY, Donald, M.D., Senior Vice President, Medical Affairs, Penn Medicine Princeton Medical Center, Plainsboro, NJ, p. A427
DENO, Mark S.
FACHE, Chief Executive Officer, Medical City Mckinney, Mckinney, TX, p. A638
FACHE, Chief Executive Officer, Medical City North Hills, North Richland Hills, TX, p. A641
DENSON, Anna, Human Resources Specialist, Choctaw Health Center, Philadelphia, MS, p. A367
DENSON, Paula Lajean, M.D., President, Tyler County Hospital, Woodville, TX, p. A663
DENT, Bruce, Human Resources Director, Heber Valley Hospital, Heber City, UT, p. A665
DENTE, Deborah, Site Finance Officer, Newark Beth Israel Medical Center, Newark, NJ, p. A425
DENTEN, Jane, MSN, R.N., Chief Nurse Executive, Advocate Lutheran General Hospital, Park Ridge, IL, p. A205
DENTON, Christopher, Chief Financial Officer, Henrico Doctors' Hospital, Richmond, VA, p. A682
DENTON, Genise, Manager Human Resources, John J. Pershing Veterans' Administration Medical Center, Poplar Bluff, MO, p. A382
DENTON, Joe, Executive Vice President and Chief Financial Officer, Mobile Infirmary Medical Center, Mobile, AL, p. A21
DENTON, Renee, Chief Operating Officer, Freeman Neosho Hospital, Neosho, MO, p. A381
DENTON, Roy, M.D., Chief Medical Officer, Conway Regional Rehabilitation Hospital, Conway, AR, p. A44
DENTON, T. Anthony, JD, Senior Vice President and Chief Environmental Social and Governance Officer, University of Michigan Medical Center, Ann Arbor, MI, p. A321
DENTONI, Terry, Chief Nursing Officer, Zuckerberg San Francisco General Hospital And Trauma Center, San Francisco, CA, p. A91
DENUCCI, Alex, Chief Financial Officer, Franciscan Children's, Brighton, MA, p. A311
DEPKO, Mike, Director Information Technology, Brown County Hospital, Ainsworth, NE, p. A397
DEPLONTY, Sandy, Chief Information Officer and Senior Director, Ancillary Services, Mymichigan Medical Center Sault, Sault Sainte Marie, MI, p. A338
DEPOMPEI, Patricia
President, University Hospitals Cleveland Medical Center, Cleveland, OH, p. A491
President, University Hospitals Rainbow Babies And Children's, Cleveland, OH, p. A491
DEPOOTER, Stephen, Chief Information Officer, Humboldt Park Health, Chicago, IL, p. A189
DEPOY, Amber, Interim Chief Nursing Officer, Mcdonough District Hospital, Macomb, IL, p. A200
DEPPERMAN, Kristi, Chief Financial Officer, Lt. Col. Luke Weathers, Jr. Va Medical Center, Memphis, TN, p. A588
DEPPERT, Eric, M.D., Chief Medical Officer, Sebastian River Medical Center, Sebastian, FL, p. A150
DEPRATO, Jeremy, Director Information Technology, The Spine Hospital of Louisiana At The Neuromedical Center, Baton Rouge, LA, p. A278
D'ERAMO, John, Chief Operating Officer, Connecticut Valley Hospital, Middletown, CT, p. A117
DERAMUS, Brenda, Manager Human Resources, Sutter Lakeside Hospital, Lakeport, CA, p. A69
DEROCHE, Richard, Manager Information Technology, Multicare Deaconess Hospital, Spokane, WA, p. A696
DERONCEREY, Josiane, Director Human Resources, Carepoint Health Christ Hospital, Jersey City, NJ, p. A422
DERONDE, Kevin, Chief Executive Officer, Mahaska Health, Oskaloosa, IA, p. A241
DEROSSETTE, Stephanie, Human Resources Business Partner, Eastern State Hospital, Lexington, KY, p. A268
DEROSSITT, James, M.D., Chief of Staff, Forrest City Medical Center, Forrest City, AR, p. A46
DEROUEN, George Patrick., Administrator, Christus Dubuis Hospital of Alexandria, Alexandria, LA, p. A276
DEROUEN, Jason, Director Management Information Systems, Grace Surgical Hospital, Lubbock, TX, p. A636
DERRICK, Tony, MSN, R.N., Vice President and Chief Nursing Officer, Mcleod Regional Medical Center, Florence, SC, p. A566
DERRICO, Patricia, FACHE, R.N., Chief Nursing Officer, Piedmont Macon North, Macon, GA, p. A167
DERSCH, Stephen, M.D., President Medical Staff, Regency Hospital of Florence, Florence, SC, p. A566
DERUS, Charles, M.D., Vice President Medical Management, Advocate Good Samaritan Hospital, Downers Grove, IL, p. A193
DERUYTER, David N., M.D., President Medical Staff, Select Specialty Hospital Midtown Atlanta, Atlanta, GA, p. A158
DERYNCK, Dodie, Chief Nursing Officer, Avera Marshall Regional Medical Center, Marshall, MN, p. A350
DESAI, Colleen, Chief Nursing Officer, Holyoke Medical Center, Holyoke, MA, p. A314
DESAI, Nimesh, M.D., Medical Director, Massena Hospital, Inc., Massena, NY, p. A446
DESAI, Shailesh, M.D., Chief of Staff, Mercyone Primghar Medical Center, Primghar, IA, p. A242
DESALVO, Susan, Manager Human Resources, Bath Veterans Affairs Medical Center, Bath, NY, p. A439
DESANTIS, John, Interim Chief Financial Officer, Glenwood Regional Medical Center, West Monroe, LA, p. A294
DESANTIS, Vincent, Vice President Finance, Phelp. Memorial Hospital Center, Sleep. Hollow, NY, p. A459
DESART, Amy, Vice President, Chief Financial Officer, Missouri Baptist Medical Center, Saint Louis, MO, p. A385
DESCHENE, Normand E., FACHE, Chief Executive Officer, Lowell General Hospital, Lowell, MA, p. A315
DESEI, Nitin, M.D., Medical Director, Regional Rehabilitation Hospital, Phenix City, AL, p. A24
DESIMONE, Maureen, Chief Operating Officer, Blythedale Children's Hospital, Valhalla, NY, p. A460
DESIMONE, Shane, M.D., Chief of Staff, Jane Todd Crawford Hospital, Greensburg, KY, p. A266
DESJARDINS, Isabelle, M.D., Chief Medical Officer, University of Vermont Medical Center, Burlington, VT, p. A671
DESJEUNES, Carol, Vice President and Chief Operating Officer, Psychiatric Institute of Washington, Washington, DC, p. A124
DESMOND, Debbie, Director Human Resources, Sentara Martha Jefferson Hospital, Charlottesville, VA, p. A674
DESMOND, Heather, Chief Financial Officer, Bibb Medical Center, Centreville, AL, p. A17
DESMOND, Jeffrey, M.D., Chief Medical Officer, University of Michigan Medical Center, Ann Arbor, MI, p. A321
DESMOND, Matthew, Regional President, Bon Secours St. Francis and Mount Pleasant Hospitals & Vice President of Operati, Bon Secours St. Francis Hospital, Charleston, SC, p. A563
DESOTELLE, Robert C., President and Chief Executive Officer, Continuing Care Hospital, Lexington, KY, p. A268
DESOTO, James
M.D., Vice President Medical Affairs, Mercy Medical Center Redding, Redding, CA, p. A85
M.D., Vice President Medical Affairs, St. Elizabeth Community Hospital, Red Bluff, CA, p. A85
DESROCHES, Jeff, Director Information Systems, AHMC Anaheim Regional Medical Center, Anaheim, CA, p. A55
DESROSIERS, Chelsea Lee
CPA, Chief Financial Officer, Cary Medical Center, Caribou, ME, p. A296
CPA, Chief Operating Officer, Cary Medical Center, Caribou, ME, p. A296
DESTEFANO, Stephen, Chief Financial Officer, Magee Rehabilitation, Philadelphia, PA, p. A549
DETREMPE, Russell, Chief Executive Officer, Fulton State Hospital, Fulton, MO, p. A375
DETTERMAN, Lynn, Senior Vice President, President, ThedaCare South Region, Thedacare Regional Medical Center–Neenah, Neenah, WI, p. A718
DETTMER, Brantley, Chief Operating Officer, Kaiser Westside Medical Center, Hillsboro, OR, p. A527
DETWILER, Eric, Director Information Technology, Barnes–Kasson County Hospital, Susquehanna, PA, p. A555
DEUTCHMAN, Adam, M.D., FACS, Chief Medical Officer, Steele Memorial Medical Center, Salmon, ID, p. A183
DEUTSCH, Stephen, Vice President Operations and Support, Spencer Hospital, Spencer, IA, p. A244
DEVALL, Michael, Chief Financial Officer, Lane Regional Medical Center, Zachary, LA, p. A294
DEVANATHAN, Raja, M.D., Chief Medical Officer, Amg Specialty Hospital Northwest Indiana, Crown Point, IN, p. A214
DEVARAJ, Kiran S., Chief Medical Officer and Chief Clinical Officer, Highland Hospital, Charleston, WV, p. A700
DEVARAJAN, Vadakkipalayam N., Chief Medical Staff, St. Charles Parish Hospital, Luling, LA, p. A287
DEVASTHALI, Deepak
Chief Operating Officer, St. Anne Hospital, Burien, WA, p. A688
Chief Operating Officer, Vice President, St. Elizabeth Hospital, Enumclaw, WA, p. A689
DEVAULT, Jennifer, Vice President Associate Services, F. F. Thompson Hospital, Canandaigua, NY, p. A440
DEVAULT, Rosanne, Chief Financial Officer, Mckenzie–Willamette Medical Center, Springfield, OR, p. A532
DEVAULT, Roseann M, Chief Financial Officer, Tennova Healthcare–Jefferson Memorial Hospital, Jefferson City, TN, p. A584
DEVAUX, Sheri, Information Technology Manager, Connecticut Veterans Home And Hospital, Rocky Hill, CT, p. A118
DEVENNY, Jay, FACHE, Chief Executive Officer, Medical City Dallas, Dallas, TX, p. A611
DEVENY, T. Clifford, M.D., Chief Executive Officer, Summa Health System – Akron Campus, Akron, OH, p. A484
DEVERA, Rozelle, Director of Information Systems, Gateways Hospital And Mental Health Center, Los Angeles, CA, p. A72
DEVEREUX, Chris, Human Resources Director, Business Partner, Endeavor Health Edward Hospital, Naperville, IL, p. A203
DEVILLE, Linda F., Chief Executive Officer, Bunkie General Hospital, Bunkie, LA, p. A279
DEVIN, Brian V., Chief Executive Officer, Pappas Rehabilitation Hospital for Children, Canton, MA, p. A312
DEVINE, Kathleen, R.N., Senior Vice President and Chief Nursing Executive, Cooper University Health Care, Camden, NJ, p. A419
DEVINE, Kathryn, Vice President Human Resources, UPMC Presbyterian, Pittsburgh, PA, p. A552
DEVINE, Nancy, Chief Nursing Officer, Daviess Community Hospital, Washington, IN, p. A229
DEVINE, Sarah M., M.D., Chief of Staff, Myrtue Medical Center, Harlan, IA, p. A237
DEVITA, James, M.D., Chief Medical Officer, Tewksbury Hospital, Tewksbury, MA, p. A319
DEVITO, Josep. M, Vice President Finance and Chief Operating Officer, Geisinger–Bloomsburg Hospital, Bloomsburg, PA, p. A535
DEVLIN, James, Director Information Systems, Orlando Health St. Cloud Hospital, Saint Cloud, FL, p. A148
DEVORE, Druery, Chief of Medical Staff, Northern Regional Hospital, Mount Airy, NC, p. A473
DEVORE, Kathy, R.N., Administrator, Christus Dubuis Hospital of Hot Springs, Hot Springs National Park, AR, p. A48
DEW, Douglas, M.D., President Medical Staff, UF Health St. John's, Saint Augustine, FL, p. A148

 Index of Health Care Professionals A833

Index of Health Care Professionals

Index of Health Care Professionals / Dewan

DEWAN, Vijay, M.D., Clinical Director, Lincoln Regional Center, Lincoln, NE, p. A402
DEWANE, Patti, Chief Financial Officer and Treasurer, UW Health Swedishamerican Hospital, Rockford, IL, p. A207
DEWEESE, Ryan, Chief Executive Officer, Spotsylvania Regional Medical Center, Fredericksburg, VA, p. A676
DEWITT, Aaron, Chief Medical Officer, The General, Baton Rouge, LA, p. A278
DEWITT, Jocelyn, Ph.D., Vice President and Chief Information Officer, University Hospital, Madison, WI, p. A714
DEWORTH, Gerald M, Associate Director, Carl Vinson Veterans Affairs Medical Center, Dublin, GA, p. A163
DEWS, Teresa, M.D., Vice President, Cleveland Clinic Euclid Hospital, Euclid, OH, p. A495
DEXTER, Nadine, R.N., MSN, Chief Executive Officer, Highland Hospital, Charleston, WV, p. A700
DEYARMIN, James A, Controller, Children's Hospital of Richmond At Vcu, Richmond, VA, p. A682
DEYNOODT, Mary, Interim Chief Executive Officer and Chief Operating Officer, Ochsner Medical Center, New Orleans, LA, p. A289
DEYO–ALLERS, Margaret, Vice President, Chief Nursing Officer, Montefiore St. Luke's Cornwall, Newburgh, NY, p. A454
DEYOUNG, Keith, M.D., Chief Medical Staff, Wallowa Memorial Hospital, Enterprise, OR, p. A526
DEYOUNG, Peter, M.D., Chief Medical Officer, Methodist Stone Oak Hospital, San Antonio, TX, p. A650
DHAMI, Sukhraj
Chief Financial Officer, Encompass Health Rehabilitation Hospital of Modesto, Modesto, CA, p. A77
Interim Chief Executive Officer, Encompass Health Rehabilitation Hospital of Modesto, Modesto, CA, p. A77
DHANJY, Muhtar, Comptroller, Texas Surgical Hospital, Plano, TX, p. A645
DHAWAN, Ajay, M.D., Chief of Staff, Veterans Affairs Northern Indiana Health Care System, Fort Wayne, IN, p. A217
DHAWAN, Rahul, M.D., Chief Medical Officer, St. Francis Medical Center, Lynwood, CA, p. A76
DHILLON, Amrit, Chief Operating Officer, HCA Florida St. Petersburg Hospital, Saint Petersburg, FL, p. A149
DHILLON, Avtar
M.D., Medical Director, Newport News Behavioral Health Center, Newport News, VA, p. A680
M.D., Medical Director, The Pavilion At Williamsburg Place, Williamsburg, VA, p. A685
DHULIPALA, Vasudeva, M.D., Medical Director, Encompass Health Rehabilitation Hospital of Alexandria, Alexandria, LA, p. A276
DI BERNARDO, Deborah, Chief Information Officer, Saint Joseph's Medical Center, Yonkers, NY, p. A462
DIAL, Jeffery, Chief Executive Officer, ECU Health Duplin Hospital, Kenansville, NC, p. A471
DIAL, Jody S, Chief Financial Officer, Timpanogos Regional Hospital, Orem, UT, p. A667
DIAL, Ray D., Director of Nursing, Nebraska Medicine – Bellevue, Bellevue, NE, p. A398
DIALTO, Margaret, Regional Chief Human Resource Officer, Staten Island University Hospital, New York, NY, p. A453
DIAMOND, Erin Dianne., R.N., Chief Executive Officer, Sterling Surgical Hospital, Slidell, LA, p. A293
DIAMOND, Kevin M., M.D., Chief Medical Officer, Lawrence Memorial Hospital, Walnut Ridge, AR, p. A54
DIAMOND, Robert, Senior Vice President and Chief Operating Officer, Kaleida Health, Buffalo, NY, p. A440
DIAMOND, Timothy, Chief Information Officer, Methodist Hospitals, Gary, IN, p. A217
DIAMOND, JD, Anne, President, Bridgeport Hospital, Bridgeport, CT, p. A115
DIAS, Katie, D.O., President, Mosaic Medical Center – Albany, Albany, MO, p. A371
DIAZ, Evelyn, R.N., Chief Nursing Officer, Encompass Health Rehabilitation Hospital of Manati, Manati, PR, p. A733
DIAZ, Janine, Human Resources Manager, Emory Rehabilitation Hospital, Atlanta, GA, p. A157
DIAZ, Jesse, Chief Information Officer, Phoebe Putney Memorial Hospital, Albany, GA, p. A156
DIAZ, Jimmy, Director Information Technology, Odessa Regional Medical Center, Odessa, TX, p. A642
DIAZ, Jose, Director Information Systems, Ascension St. Vincent Evansville, Evansville, IN, p. A216
DIAZ, Ron, Manager Operations, Albany Stratton Veterans Affairs Medical Center, Albany, NY, p. A438
DIAZ, Steve, M.D., Chief Medical Officer, Mainegeneral Medical Center, Augusta, ME, p. A295
DIAZ GARCIA, Rogelio, Executive Director, Hospital Menonita Guayama, Guayama, PR, p. A732
DIAZ GUZMAN, Victor, Executive Director, University Pediatric Hospital, Rio Piedras, PR, p. A734
DIAZ VAZQUEZ, Pedro, Administrator, Hospital Menonita Humacao, Humacao, PR, p. A733
DIBACCO, David J, Interim Chief Operating Officer, Olean General Hospital, Olean, NY, p. A455
DIBNER, David A, FACHE, Senior Vice President Hospital Operations and Musculoskeletal Strategic Areas, Nyu Langone Hospitals, New York, NY, p. A452
DICESARE, Jan, Vice President Financial Operations, Ascension St. Vincent's East, Birmingham, AL, p. A16
DICICCO, Marilyn, Director Human Resources, Temple Health–Chestnut Hill Hospital, Philadelphia, PA, p. A550
DICK, Andy, Director Information Services, Saline Memorial Hospital, Benton, AR, p. A43
DICK, Darinda, MSN, R.N., President and Chief Executive Officer, Western Missouri Medical Center, Warrensburg, MO, p. A388
DICK, Lynette, Director of Support Services, Ellsworth County Medical Center, Ellsworth, KS, p. A249
DICK, Mandy MSN, RN, Chief Nursing Officer, AHS Sherman Medical Center, Sherman, TX, p. A652
DICK, Mollie, Coordinator Human Resources, Wayne County Hospital, Monticello, KY, p. A271
DICKENS, Betty, Director Human Resources, Sierra Tucson, Tucson, AZ, p. A41
DICKERSON, Gene, M.D., Vice President Medical Affairs, Prisma Health Tuomey Hospital, Sumter, SC, p. A570
DICKERSON, Kathy
Chief Financial Officer, Encompass Health Rehabilitation Hospital of Arlington, Arlington, TX, p. A597
Interim Controller, Encompass Health Rehabilitation Hospital of Texarkana, Texarkana, TX, p. A657
DICKERSON, Melody, R.N., MSN, Senior Vice President, Chief Nursing Officer, VHC Health, Arlington, VA, p. A673
DICKERSON, Michelle
Chief Nursing Officer, Frye Regional Medical Center, Hickory, NC, p. A470
Chief Nursing Officer, Tennova Healthcare–Clarksville, Clarksville, TN, p. A581
DICKERSON, Sandra, Chief Executive Officer, Greenwood County Hospital, Eureka, KS, p. A249
DICKERSON, Taylor, Chief Information Officer, HCA Florida Lake City Hospital, Lake City, FL, p. A136
DICKERSON, Toby, Chief Information Resources Management Services, Durham Va Health Care System, Durham, NC, p. A467
DICKEY, Ashley, Director Human Resources, Benson Hospital, Benson, AZ, p. A30
DICKEY, John M, Chief Administrative Officer, Mayo Clinic Health System In Eau Claire, Eau Claire, WI, p. A710
DICKEY, Mark, Director Business Development, Valir Rehabilitation Hospital, Oklahoma City, OK, p. A519
DICKEY, Sarah J., Human Resource Director, Marshall Browning Hospital, Du Quoin, IL, p. A193
DICKEY, Sarah S., Executive Director, Human Resource People and Culture, Mahaska Health, Oskaloosa, IA, p. A241
DICKINSON, Cathy C.
Chief Human Resources, Baptist Health Extended Care Hospital, Little Rock, AR, p. A49
Vice President Human Resources, Baptist Health Medical Center – North Little Rock, North Little Rock, AR, p. A51
DICKLICH–COBB, Cristy, Chief Nursing Officer, Memorial Hospital of Converse County, Douglas, WY, p. A727
DICKMAN, Kathy, Director of Information Systems, St. Elizabeth Dearborn, Lawrenceburg, IN, p. A222
DICKS, Mandy, Director of Nursing, Lake Butler Hospital, Lake Butler, FL, p. A136
DICKSON, Anita, Director Human Resources, St. Bernards Five Rivers, Pocahontas, AR, p. A52
DICKSON, Scott, Director Information Technology, Reeves Memorial Medical Center, Bernice, LA, p. A278
DIDDLE, Derrick, Director of Information Technology, Family Health West, Fruita, CO, p. A108
DIDRIKSON, Lynne, M.D., Chief Medical Officer, Langdon Prairie Health, Langdon, ND, p. A482
DIEDERICH, John A., FACHE, President and Chief Executive Officer, Rush–Copley Medical Center, Aurora, IL, p. A186
DIEDRICH, Michele, R.N., Chief Nursing Officer, Vice President Patient Care, Baptist Health Medical Center–Little Rock, Little Rock, AR, p. A49
DIEDRICK, Kellie
Interim Vice President, Thedacare Medical Center–Shawano, Shawano, WI, p. A721
Vice President, Thedacare Medical Center–New London, New London, WI, p. A718
Vice President, Thedacare Medical Center–Waupaca, Waupaca, WI, p. A724
DIEHL, Lesa, Chief Executive Officer, Thomas B. Finan Center, Cumberland, MD, p. A303
DIEHL, Ryan, Chief Nursing Officer, Montrose Behavioral Health Hospital, Chicago, IL, p. A190
DIERKENS, Janelle, Chief Administration Officer, New York State Psychiatric Institute, New York, NY, p. A450
DIERKER, Anne, Vice President Hospital Services, Carle Health Pekin Hospital, Pekin, IL, p. A205
DIERS, Suzanne, R.N., Director Patient Care Services, Shriners Hospitals for Children–Portland, Portland, OR, p. A531
DIESTEL, Peter, Senior Vice President and Chief Operating Officer, Valley Hospital, Paramus, NJ, p. A426
DIETER, Brian, President and Chief Executive Officer, Mary Greeley Medical Center, Ames, IA, p. A230
DIETERICH, Kevin, Director Information Services, Northern Light Inland Hospital, Waterville, ME, p. A299
DIETRICH, Brenda, Chief Human Resources Officer, Banner Boswell Medical Center, Sun City, AZ, p. A39
DIETRICH, Ken, Chief Medical Officer, Summit Pacific Medical Center, Elma, WA, p. A689
DIETRICH MELLON, Jill K., JD, FACHE, Executive Director, Chief Executive Officer, Northeast Ohio Va Healthcare System, Cleveland, OH, p. A491
DIETRICK, Brian, Director Information Systems, Wilson Medical Center, Wilson, NC, p. A478
DIETSCH, Barry
Chief Financial Officer, Virginia Gay Hospital, Vinton, IA, p. A244
Interim executive leader (Currently CFO), Virginia Gay Hospital, Vinton, IA, p. A244
DIETSCH, Lindsay, R.N., Director of Nursing, United Medical Rehabilitation Hospital–Hammond, Hammond, LA, p. A283
DIETZ, Michael, Administrator, U. S. Air Force Hospital, Hampton, VA, p. A677
DIETZE, Zachary K.
Chief Executive Officer, UT Health North Campus Tyler, Tyler, TX, p. A659
Chief Executive Officer, UT Health Tyler, Tyler, TX, p. A659
DIEUDONNE, Nicole, R.N., MSN, Director of Nursing, DGH, Miami Jewish Health, Miami, FL, p. A140
DIEUVEUIL, Harry, Vice President and Chief Human Resources Officer, Saint Peter's Healthcare System, New Brunswick, NJ, p. A425
DIFRANCO, Vincent, Chief Executive Officer, W. J. Mangold Memorial Hospital, Lockney, TX, p. A635
DIGEROLAMO, Anthony, R.N., MSN, Chief Executive Officer, Bridgepoint Continuing Care Hospital, Marrero, LA, p. A288
DIGIAMARINO, Edward, M.D., President of Medical Staff, San Antonio Regional Hospital, Upland, CA, p. A99
DIGUILIO, Jason, Controller, UH Avon Rehabilitation Hospital, Avon, OH, p. A485
DIIESO, Nicholas T, R.N., Chief Operating Officer, Mount Auburn Hospital, Cambridge, MA, p. A312
DIKE, Charles, M.D., Chief of Staff, Sanford Worthington Medical Center, Worthington, MN, p. A358
DIKOS, Julie A., President and Chief Executive Officer, Asheville Specialty Hospital, Asheville, NC, p. A463
DILIEGRO, Nancy, Ph.D., FACHE, President and Chief Executive Officer, Trinitas Regional Medical Center, Elizabeth, NJ, p. A421
DILL, Danielle, Executive Director, Central New York Psychiatric Center, Marcy, NY, p. A446
DILLARD, Sharon, Chief Nursing Officer, HCA Florida Poinciana Hospital, Kissimmee, FL, p. A136
DILLEHUNT, David B
Chief Information Officer, Firsthealth Montgomery Memorial Hospital, Troy, NC, p. A477
Chief Information Officer, Firsthealth Moore Regional Hospital, Pinehurst, NC, p. A474
DILLEY, Chad, President, Ascension St. Vincent Carmel Hospital, Carmel, IN, p. A213
DILLEY, Emily, Chief Executive Officer, Cumberland Healthcare, Cumberland, WI, p. A709
DILLIE, Codie, Chief Executive Officer, Select Specialty Hospital–Quad Cities, Davenport, IA, p. A234
DILLION, Tim, Vice President of Human Resources, Devereux Hospital And Children's Center of Florida, Melbourne, FL, p. A138
DILLMAN, Theresa Anne, MSN, R.N., Chief Nursing Officer, Associate Executive Director, Patient Services, Glen Cove Hospital, Glen Cove, NY, p. A443
DILLON, Jim, Chief Financial Officer, Rangely District Hospital, Rangely, CO, p. A113
DILLON, Lorie, Chief Executive Officer, Geisinger Encompass Health Rehabilitation Hospital, Danville, PA, p. A538
DILLON, Minty, Chief Executive Officer, Good Samaritan Hospital, Bakersfield, CA, p. A57
DILLON, Nacole, Administrator, Walthall General Hospital, Tylertown, MS, p. A369
DILMORE, Shawn
Chief Executive Officer, Select Specialty Hospital–Tallahassee, Tallahassee, FL, p. A151
Market Chief Executive Officer, Select Specialty Hospital – Willingboro, Willingboro, NJ, p. A430
DILORETO, David, M.D., Executive Vice President and Chief Medical Officer, Ascension Saint Francis, Evanston, IL, p. A194

A834 Index of Health Care Professionals

Index of Health Care Professionals / Dolbee

Index of Health Care Professionals

DIMARE, John, M.D., Medical Director, Emanate Health Foothill Presbyterian Hospital, Glendora, CA, p. A66
DIMEK, Carolyn, Superintendent, Dorothea Dix Psychiatric Center, Bangor, ME, p. A295
DIMITROVA, Gergana, M.D., Medical Director, Carolina Center for Behavioral Health, Greer, SC, p. A567
DIMM, Adam, Chief Executive Officer, Penn Highlands Huntingdon, Huntingdon, PA, p. A542
DIMMICK, Scott, Senior Vice President and Chief Human Resources Officer, Lakeland Regional Health Medical Center, Lakeland, FL, p. A137
DINARDO, Mark, Chief Nursing Officer, Encompass Health Rehabilitation Hospital of Modesto, Modesto, CA, p. A77
DINEEN, C. Renae, Chief Nursing Officer, Northern Cochise Community Hospital, Willcox, AZ, p. A41
DINGER, Bradley
Chief Financial Officer, UPMC Chautauqua, Jamestown, NY, p. A444
Chief Financial Officer, UPMC Hamot, Erie, PA, p. A540
Chief Financial Officer, UPMC Kane, Kane, PA, p. A543
Chief Financial Officer, UPMC Northwest, Seneca, PA, p. A554
DINGILIAN, John, M.D., Chief Medical Officer, Adventist Health Simi Valley, Simi Valley, CA, p. A96
DINGLEDINE, Jon, Chief Financial Officer and Chief Operating Officer, Mercer Health, Coldwater, OH, p. A491
DINGLER, Chance, M.D., Chief Medical Officer, Nocona General Hospital, Nocona, TX, p. A641
DINHAM, Vilma L, R.N., Chief Nursing Officer, Encino Hospital Medical Center, Encino, CA, p. A62
DINKHA, Duncan, M.D., Chief of Staff, Morrison Community Hospital, Morrison, IL, p. A202
DINKINS, Vicki, Director Human Resources, South Georgia Medical Center Lanier Campus, Lakeland, GA, p. A166
DION, Jeffrey P., Vice President and Chief Financial Officer, Holy Family Hospital, Methuen, MA, p. A316
DIPALMA, Maureen, Chief Financial Officer, Tewksbury Hospital, Tewksbury, MA, p. A319
DIPAOLA, Robert, Executive Vice President for Health Affairs, University of Kentucky Albert B. Chandler Hospital, Lexington, KY, p. A269
DIPIETRO, Sandra P, Chief Financial Officer, St. Tammany Health System, Covington, LA, p. A280
DIPPEL, Doug, R.N., MSN, Chief Executive Officer, Rolling Plains Memorial Hospital, Sweetwater, TX, p. A655
DIRKES, Nick, Chief Executive Officer, Frances Mahon Deaconess Hospital, Glasgow, MT, p. A392
DISANTE, Ginger, Chief Nursing Executive, Christus Health Shreveport–Bossier, Shreveport, LA, p. A292
DISBROW, Wendy, President and Chief Executive Officer, St. James Hospital, Hornell, NY, p. A444
DISHMAN, Kevin, M.D., Chief Medical Officer, Stormont Vail Health, Topeka, KS, p. A260
DISLER, Jordi K.
Market President, Parkview Noble Hospital, Kendallville, IN, p. A221
President, Parkview Lagrange Hospital, Lagrange, IN, p. A222
DISPOTO, Martha, R.N., I, Chief Nurse Executive, Anaheim Medical Center, Kaiser Permanente Orange County Anaheim Medical Center, Anaheim, CA, p. A55
DISQUE, Laura, MSN, R.N., Chief Executive Officer, Rio Grande Regional Hospital, Mcallen, TX, p. A638
DISTEFANO, Mike, Chief Medical Officer, Children's Hospital Colorado – Colorado Springs, Colorado Springs, CO, p. A105
DISWOOD, Lavenia, R.N., Chief Nurse Executive, Northern Navajo Medical Center, Shiprock, NM, p. A437
DITMANSON, Paul, M.D., Clinical Director, Red Lake Indian Health Service Hospital, Red Lake, MN, p. A353
DITTBENNER, Beth, Regional Director, Human Resources, Mayo Clinic Health System In Mankato, Mankato, MN, p. A349
DITTO, Debbie, CPA, Controller, Lincoln Trail Behavioral Health System, Radcliff, KY, p. A273
DITURO, Beth, Divisional Chief Information Officer, Lenox Hill Hospital, New York, NY, p. A449
DITZLER, Andru, Chief Information Officer, Lebanon Veterans Affairs Medical Center, Lebanon, PA, p. A544
DIVINS, Brooke N., Director Human Resources, Clarion Hospital, Clarion, PA, p. A537
DIX, Theresa, MSN, R.N., Chief Nursing Officer, Wythe County Community Hospital, Wytheville, VA, p. A686
DIXON, Christy, Chief Human Resources Officer, Encompass Health Rehabilitation Hospital of Humble, Humble, TX, p. A629
DIXON, Debbie, Director Human Resources, Pamp. Regional Medical Center, Pampa, TX, p. A642
DIXON, Deidre, Chief Executive Officer, Northside Hospital, Atlanta, GA, p. A157
DIXON, Del, Chief Information Officer, South Shore Hospital, South Weymouth, MA, p. A318
DIXON, Florine, Chief Operating Officer, Memorial Hospital Association, Carthage, IL, p. A187
DIXON, Gregg
Chief Financial Officer, Asheville Specialty Hospital, Asheville, NC, p. A463
Chief Financial Officer, Carepartners Rehabilitation Hospital, Asheville, NC, p. A463
DIXON, John, Chief Medical Officer, Mobile Infirmary Medical Center, Mobile, AL, p. A21
DIXON, Lisa, Business Partner and Human Resource Director, Endeavor Health Linden Oaks Hospital, Naperville, IL, p. A203
DIXON, Mary E., MSN, R.N., Interim Chief Nursing Officer, UVA Health University Medical Center, Charlottesville, VA, p. A674
DIXON, Michael L, Vice President, Human Resources, Corewell Health William Beaumont University Hospital, Royal Oak, MI, p. A336
DIXON, Shannon, Chief Financial Officer, Weisbrod Memorial County Hospital, Eads, CO, p. A107
DOAK, Mark, Interim President, Davis Medical Center, Elkins, WV, p. A700
DOAK, Scott
System Vice President, Human Resources, University of North Carolina Hospitals, Chapel Hill, NC, p. A465
Vice President, Human Resources, UNC Health Rex, Raleigh, NC, p. A475
DOAN, Angela, Chief Financial Officer, Norton Scott Hospital, Scottsburg, IN, p. A227
DOANE, Peter
M.D., Chief Medical Officer, Concord Hospital – Franklin, Franklin, NH, p. A415
M.D., Chief Medical Officer, Concord Hospital – Laconia, Laconia, NH, p. A415
DOBBINS, Callie F., R.N., MSN, Vice President and Facility Executive, Atrium Health's Carolinas Medical Center, Charlotte, NC, p. A465
DOBBINS, Jim, Vice President and Chief Human Resources Officer, UNC Health Lenoir, Kinston, NC, p. A471
DOBBINS, Thomas Tom, M.D., Chief of Staff, Byrd Regional Hospital, Leesville, LA, p. A287
DOBBS, Jacee, Chief Information Officer, Citizens Medical Center, Colby, KS, p. A247
DOBBS, Stephanie, Chief Nursing Officer, Sanford Clear Lake Medical Center, Clear Lake, SD, p. A572
DOBIE, Linda, R.N., JD, Vice President, Legal Affairs, Torrance Memorial Medical Center, Torrance, CA, p. A98
DOBIN, Jennifer
Chief Human Resources Officer, Carewell Health Medical Center, East Orange, NJ, p. A420
Executive Vice President Human Resources, Carepoint Health Bayonne Medical Center, Bayonne, NJ, p. A418
DOBIZL, Howard
Director Information Services for the Northern Region, Aspirus Rhinelander Hospital, Rhinelander, WI, p. A720
Director Information Technology Services, Aspirus Eagle River Hospital, Eagle River, WI, p. A710
Director Information Technology Services, Aspirus Tomahawk Hospital, Tomahawk, WI, p. A723
Director Information Technology Services, Howard Young Medical Center, Inc., Woodruff, WI, p. A725
DOBKIN, Eric D, M.D., Vice President Medical Affairs, Suburban Hospital, Bethesda, MD, p. A303
DOBOSH, Josep. J Jr, Vice President and Chief Financial Officer, Children's Specialized Hospital, New Brunswick, NJ, p. A424
DOBRAWA, Stanley
Area Information Officer, Kaiser Permanente San Rafael Medical Center, San Rafael, CA, p. A93
Area Information Officer, Kaiser Permanente Santa Rosa Medical Center, Santa Rosa, CA, p. A95
DOBRINSKI, Sandra, Director of Nursing, Comanche County Hospital, Coldwater, KS, p. A247
DOBROVICH, Michael, M.D., Chief Medical Officer, University Hospitals St. John Medical Center, Westlake, OH, p. A507
DOBSON, Glenn E, Vice President, Finance and Chief Financial Officer, Aspirus Iron River Hospital, Iron River, MI, p. A330
DOBSON, Trey, M.D., Chief Medical Officer, Southwestern Vermont Medical Center, Bennington, VT, p. A671
DOBY, Kathryn, Chief Administrative Officer, Alleghany Health, Sparta, NC, p. A476
DOCTOR, LaFreda, Director, Human Resources, Encompass Health Rehabilitation Hospital of Bluffton, Bluffton, SC, p. A562
DODD, John, Vice President Human Resources, Central Peninsula Hospital, Soldotna, AK, p. A29
DODD, Kathy M, Director of Nursing, Southern Virginia Mental Health Institute, Danville, VA, p. A675
DODD, Pam, Chief Operating Officer, Harper County Community Hospital, Buffalo, OK, p. A510
DODDS, George, M.D., Medical Director, Gouverneur Hospital, Gouverneur, NY, p. A443
DODDS, Rick, Chief Executive Officer, Adventhealth Littleton, Littleton, CO, p. A111
DODDS, Sheryl, Chief Clinical Officer, Adventhealth Orlando, Orlando, FL, p. A144
DODERER, Marcella
FACHE, Chief Executive Officer, Arkansas Children's Northwest, Springdale, AR, p. A53
FACHE, President and Chief Executive Officer, Arkansas Children's Hospital, Little Rock, AR, p. A49
DODGE, Terry, M.D., Chief of Staff, Musc Health Chester Medical Center, Chester, SC, p. A564
DODSON, Carrie, Director of Nursing, Wellstone Regional Hospital, Jeffersonville, IN, p. A221
DODSON, Louise
R.N., Chief Nursing Officer, Wagoner Community Hospital, Wagoner, OK, p. A523
R.N., Chief Operating Officer and Chief Nursing Officer, Wagoner Community Hospital, Wagoner, OK, p. A523
DODSON, Paige, M.D., M.P.H., Chief Medical Officer, Susan B. Allen Memorial Hospital, El Dorado, KS, p. A248
DOEHRING, Christopher
M.D., Vice President Medical Affairs, Franciscan Health Indianapolis, Indianapolis, IN, p. A219
M.D., Vice President of Medical Affairs, Franciscan Health Carmel, Carmel, IN, p. A213
DOEHRMANN, Melissa, Director Patient Care Services, Mercyone Newton Medical Center, Newton, IA, p. A241
DOELING, Mariann, R.N., President, Chi St. Alexius Health Devils Lake, Devils Lake, ND, p. A480
DOELLING, James, Hospital Director, Edward Hines, Jr. Veterans Affairs Hospital, Hines, IL, p. A198
DOERFLER, Mary P., Chief Human Resources Officer, Central Texas Veterans Hcs/Temple Tx, Temple, TX, p. A656
DOERGE, Jean, R.N., MSN, Nurse Executive, Providence Swedish Edmonds, Edmonds, WA, p. A689
DOERGE, Jean B, MS, R.N., Chief Nursing Executive, Unitypoint Health – Trinity Bettendorf, Bettendorf, IA, p. A231
DOERR, Brian, Chief Information Officer, Continuecare Hospital At Baptist Health Corbin, Corbin, KY, p. A264
DOGGETT, Geri, Director Business, East Mississipp. State Hospital, Meridian, MS, p. A366
DOGGETT, Sherri L, Vice President Patient Services, Mercyone Centerville Medical Center, Centerville, IA, p. A232
DOHERTY, Allison, Chief Financial Officer, The Spine Hospital of Louisiana At The Neuromedical Center, Baton Rouge, LA, p. A278
DOHERTY, Brooke, Director, People Services, Mercy Rehabilitation Hospital South, Saint Louis, MO, p. A385
DOHERTY, Bryan, Management Information Technology Services I, Sagamore Children's Psychiatric Center, Dix Hills, NY, p. A442
DOHERTY, Dan, Chief Executive Officer, Ascension Alexian Brothers, Elk Grove Village, IL, p. A194
DOHERTY, Donna, R.N., Vice President of Nursing and Chief Nursing Officer, Beth Israel Deaconess Hospital–Plymouth, Plymouth, MA, p. A317
DOHERTY, Holly, Chief Executive Officer, Mayhill Hospital, Denton, TX, p. A614
DOHERTY, Ray, Director Information Technology, Cmh Regional Health System, Wilmington, OH, p. A507
DOHERTY, Shaun, Chief Executive Officer, The Pavilion, Champaign, IL, p. A187
DOHM, Thomas J., President and Chief Executive Officer, Morris Hospital & Healthcare Centers, Morris, IL, p. A202
DOHMANN, Eileen L
R.N., Senior Vice President and Chief Nursing Officer, Mary Washington Hospital, Fredericksburg, VA, p. A676
R.N., Senior Vice President and Chief Nursing Officer, Stafford Hospital, Stafford, VA, p. A684
DOIDGE, John C, Vice President Finance, Glencoe Regional Health, Glencoe, MN, p. A347
DOKSUM, Kathryn, Director Finance, Samaritan North Lincoln Hospital, Lincoln City, OR, p. A528
DOLAN, Mary, Regional Director Information Services and HIPAA Security Official, Shriners Hospitals for Children–Boston, Boston, MA, p. A311
DOLAN, Mike, Executive Vice President and Medical Chief Operating Officer, Gundersen Lutheran Medical Center, La Crosse, WI, p. A713
DOLAN, Steve, Chief Information Officer, Eastpointe Hospital, Daphne, AL, p. A18
DOLBEE, Hilary, Chief Financial Officer, Monroe Hospital, Bloomington, IN, p. A213

Index of Health Care Professionals

Index of Health Care Professionals / Dolbin

DOLBIN, Kathy, Director of Human Resources, Mercy Health – Allen Hospital, Oberlin, OH, p. A501
DOLL, Jennifer, Interim Chief Financial Officer, Ohsu Hospital, Portland, OR, p. A530
DOLL, Jessica, Chief Nursing Officer, Baylor Surgical Hospital At Las Colinas, Irving, TX, p. A630
DOLORESCO, Laureen, R.N., Associate Director for Patient Care and Nursing Services, James A. Haley Veterans' Hospital–Tampa, Tampa, FL, p. A152
DOMALESKI, Vareen O'Keefe, MS, R.N., Vice Patient Care Services and Chief Nursing Officer, Emma Pendleton Bradley Hospital, East Providence, RI, p. A560
DOMANN, Debbie, Director of Operations, Fillmore County Hospital, Geneva, NE, p. A400
DOMANSKY, John, Vice President Operations, Rutherford Regional Health System, Rutherfordton, NC, p. A475
DOMAYER, Cory, Chief Financial Officer, Adventhealth Palm Coast, Palm Coast, FL, p. A145
DOMINGO, Connie, M.D., Medical Director, Weisman Children's Rehabilitation Hospital, Marlton, NJ, p. A424
DOMINGUE, Buffy H., Chief Executive Officer, Ochsner Lafayette General Medical Center, Lafayette, LA, p. A285
DOMINGUEZ, Brenda, Director Human Resources, Cypress Creek Hospital, Houston, TX, p. A625
DOMINICCI, Sandra, Nursing Director, Hospital De Damas, Ponce, PR, p. A734
DOMINIQUE, Ravon, Chief Nursing Officer, Brentwood Hospital, Shreveport, LA, p. A292
DOMINISSE, Lisa, President and Chief Executive Officer, Radiant Health, Marion, IN, p. A223
DOMINSKI, Paul, Vice President Human Resources, Park Nicollet Methodist Hospital, Saint Louis Park, MN, p. A354
DOMMER, Matthew N., M.D., Vice President Medical Affairs and Chief Operating Officer, Bronson Lakeview Hospital, Paw Paw, MI, p. A335
DOMON, Steven, M.D., Medical Director, Arkansas State Hospital, Little Rock, AR, p. A49
DONAHEY, Kenneth C., Chief Executive Officer, Oviedo Medical Center, Oviedo, FL, p. A145
DONAHOE, Ashley
Chief Executive Officer, Encompass Health Rehabilitation Hospital of Arlington, Arlington, TX, p. A597
Chief Executive Officer, Encompass Health Rehabilitation Hospital of The Mid–Cities, Bedford, TX, p. A602
DONAHUE, Edward, M.D., Chief Medical Officer, St. Joseph's Hospital And Medical Center, Phoenix, AZ, p. A36
DONAHUE, Kristine
R.N., President, Corewell Health Taylor Hospital, Taylor, MI, p. A339
R.N., President, Corewell Health Trenton Hospital, Trenton, MI, p. A339
R.N., President, Corewell Health Wayne Hospital, Wayne, MI, p. A340
DONAHUE, Michael, M.D., Medical Director, Select Specialty Hospital–Pittsburgh/Upmc, Pittsburgh, PA, p. A551
DONAHUE, Ruth, R.N., Chief Nursing Officer, Harrison County Hospital, Corydon, IN, p. A214
DONAHUE, Samantha, Director Human Resources, Crossing Rivers Health, Prairie Du Chien, WI, p. A720
DONAHUE, Theresa, Chief Executive Officer, Bertrand Chaffee Hospital, Springville, NY, p. A459
DONALD, Steve, M.D., Chief of Staff, Washington County Hospital, Chatom, AL, p. A17
DONALDSON, Brooke G., Chief Executive Officer, Jackson Hospital, Marianna, FL, p. A138
DONALDSON, David
Chief Executive Officer, HCA Florida Mercy Hospital, Miami, FL, p. A140
President and Chief Executive Assistant, Presbyterian/St. Luke's Medical Center, Denver, CO, p. A106
DONALDSON, Jill, President, Medstar Harbor Hospital, Baltimore, MD, p. A301
DONALDSON, Les, M.D., Chief of Staff, Roosevelt General Hospital, Portales, NM, p. A436
DONALDSON, Lori, Chief Financial Officer, UC San Diego Medical Center – Hillcrest, San Diego, CA, p. A90
DONALDSON, Nesha, Chief Operating Officer, Cullman Regional Medical Center, Cullman, AL, p. A18
DONATELLE, Lawrence, M.D., Vice President Medical Affairs, Ascension Northeast Wisconsin St. Elizabeth Hospital, Appleton, WI, p. A707
DONATO, Cyndy, Vice President, Human Resources, Missouri Baptist Medical Center, Saint Louis, MO, p. A385
DONELAN, Matthias B, M.D., Chief of Staff, Shriners Hospitals for Children–Boston, Boston, MA, p. A311
DONENWIRTH, Karl, Vice President Information Services, Northcoast Behavioral Healthcare, Northfield, OH, p. A501
DONET, Andrew P.
Chief Executive Officer, Kindred Hospital–New Jersey Morris County, Dover, NJ, p. A420
Market Chief Executive Officer, Kindred Hospital Philadelphia, Philadelphia, PA, p. A549
DONGILLI, Paul
Jr, Ph.D., FACHE, President and Chief Executive Officer, Madonna Rehabilitation Hospital, Lincoln, NE, p. A402
Jr, Ph.D., FACHE, President and Chief Executive Officer, Madonna Rehabilitation Specialty Hospital Lincoln, Lincoln, NE, p. A402
Jr, Ph.D., FACHE, President and Chief Executive Officer, Madonna Rehabilitation Specialty Hospital Omaha, Omaha, NE, p. A404
DONHAM, Guyle, M.D., Chief of Staff, Comanche County Medical Center, Comanche, TX, p. A608
DONICA, Joanna, Director Human Resource, Pam Rehabilitation Hospital of Beaumont, Beaumont, TX, p. A602
DONLEY, Linda, Vice President Operations, Ira Davenport Memorial Hospital, Bath, NY, p. A439
DONLEY, Patricia F., R.N., MSN, President, Wellspan Good Samaritan Hospital, Lebanon, PA, p. A544
DONLIN, John
Director Human Resources, Shriners Hospitals for Children–Springfield, Springfield, MA, p. A318
Regional Director Human Resources – Boston, Erie, and Springfield, Shriners Hospitals for Children–Boston, Boston, MA, p. A311
DONNELLY, James E, Chief Nursing Officer and Vice President Patient Care Services, UPMC Hamot, Erie, PA, p. A540
DONNELLY, Sheryl, Human Resources Specialist, State Hospital South, Blackfoot, ID, p. A179
DONNELY, Lisa, Controller II, Central Texas Rehabilitation Hospital, Austin, TX, p. A599
DONNENWERTH, Mike, DPM, Chief Medical Officer, Winona Health, Winona, MN, p. A357
DONOFRIO, Kathryn, Chief Nursing Officer, Endeavor Health Swedish Hospital, Chicago, IL, p. A189
DONOGHUE, Alicia, Director Human Resources, Eastpointe Hospital, Daphne, AL, p. A18
DONOHUE, Mary Ann T, Ph.D., R.N., Chief Patient Care Services Officer, Stony Brook University Hospital, Stony Brook, NY, p. A459
DONOHUE, Vince
Chief Financial Officer, Delta Community Medical Center, Delta, UT, p. A664
Chief Financial Officer, Fillmore Community Hospital, Fillmore, UT, p. A665
Chief Financial Officer, Sanpete Valley Hospital, Mount Pleasant, UT, p. A666
DONOVAN, Andrew
Director Information Technology, Ascension Southeast Wisconsin Hospital – Elmbrook Campus, Brookfield, WI, p. A708
Regional Director Information Services, Ascension Southeast Wisconsin Hospital – St. Joseph's Campus, Milwaukee, WI, p. A716
DONOVAN, Jenny, Director Human Resources, Wright Memorial Hospital, Trenton, MO, p. A387
DONOVAN, Mary, Controller, Encompass Health Rehabilitation Institute of Tucson, Tucson, AZ, p. A40
DONOVAN, Mike, Chief Financial Officer, Lemuel Shattuck Hospital, Jamaica Plain, MA, p. A314
DONOVAN, Terri, Vice President of Finance, Mercyone Des Moines Medical Center, Des Moines, IA, p. A235
DONSON, Elliott, Chief Information Specialist, Lincoln Hospital, Davenport, WA, p. A688
DONZE, Richard D, D.O., Senior Vice President Medical Affairs, Penn Medicine Chester County Hospital, West Chester, PA, p. A557
DOODY, Kris A., Chief Executive Officer, Cary Medical Center, Caribou, ME, p. A296
DOOKEERAM, David, Chief Operating Officer, Adventhealth Porter, Denver, CO, p. A106
DOOLEY, Mark, Chief Executive Officer, Gadsden Regional Medical Center, Gadsden, AL, p. A20
DOOLEY, Paige, R.N., MSN, Hospital Administrator, Vice President and Chief Nurse Executive, Community Hospital East, Indianapolis, IN, p. A219
DOOLING, Edward, Vice President, Human Resources, Masonicare Health Center, Wallingford, CT, p. A119
DOOLITTLE, Doak, M.D., Chief of Staff, Phillip. County Health Systems, Phillipsburg, KS, p. A258
DOOM, Stephanie, Chief Financial Officer, Baptist Health Lexington, Lexington, KY, p. A268
DOORENBOS, Pamela, M.D., Vice President, Medical Affairs, Maple Grove Hospital, Maple Grove, MN, p. A349
DOORN, Douglas, Chief Executive Officer, Avera Sacred Heart Hospital, Yankton, SD, p. A578
DORAK, John, Director, Information Systems, Nicholas H. Noyes Memorial Hospital, Dansville, NY, p. A442
DORAN, Ken, Interim Chief Executive Officer, Carson Tahoe Health, Carson City, NV, p. A408
DORAN, T, M.D., Chief of Staff, OSF Saint Clare Medical Center, Princeton, IL, p. A206
DORIA, Thomas
Vice President and Patient Services – West, Morton Plant North Bay Hospital, New Port Richey, FL, p. A142
Vice President and Patient Services West, St. Anthony's Hospital, Saint Petersburg, FL, p. A149
Vice President Patient Services – West, Morton Plant Hospital, Clearwater, FL, p. A128
Vice President, Patient Services and Chief Nursing Officer, Mease Countryside Hospital, Safety Harbor, FL, p. A148
Vice President, Patient Services and Chief Nursing Officer, Mease Dunedin Hospital, Dunedin, FL, p. A130
DORIAN, Armand, M.D., FACHE, Chief Executive Officer, USC Verdugo Hills Hospital, Glendale, CA, p. A66
DORION, Heath, Physician Administrator, Mercy Health – St. Elizabeth Boardman Hospital, Boardman, OH, p. A486
DORITY, Paula, Director Human Resources, Martin County Hospital District, Stanton, TX, p. A654
DORMAN, Christopher
Chief Executive Officer, Southwell Medical, Adel, GA, p. A156
President and Chief Executive Officer, Tift Regional Medical Center, Tifton, GA, p. A172
DORMAN, Doug, Vice President Human Resources, Prisma Health Greenville Memorial Hospital, Greenville, SC, p. A567
DORMAN, Julie, Human Resources Director, Parkwood Behavioral Health System, Olive Branch, MS, p. A367
DORNOFF, Edward G., Associate Director, Battle Creek Veterans Affairs Medical Center, Battle Creek, MI, p. A322
DOROGY, Sharon, Chief Information Officer, The Children's Institute of Pittsburgh, Pittsburgh, PA, p. A551
DOROTHY, Jonnie, Senior Director Human Resources, Massena Hospital, Inc., Massena, NY, p. A446
DORR, Amy
Vice President Human Resources, Mclaren Greater Lansing, Lansing, MI, p. A331
Vice President Human Resources, Mclaren Lapeer Region, Lapeer, MI, p. A332
DORSCH, Anthony, Chief Financial Officer, Providence Alaska Medical Center, Anchorage, AK, p. A27
DORSEY, Kyle, FACHE, President, Baptist Medical Center Jacksonville, Jacksonville, FL, p. A134
DORSEY, William, M.D., Board Chairman and Chief Executive Officer, Jackson Park Hospital And Medical Center, Chicago, IL, p. A189
DORST, Jake, Chief Information Officer, Tahoe Forest Hospital District, Truckee, CA, p. A98
D'ORTENZIO, Gabe, Director of Human Resources, Weirton Medical Center, Weirton, WV, p. A705
DORTON, Patty, Director of Nursing, Buchanan General Hospital, Grundy, VA, p. A677
D'ORTONA, Cary, President, Orlando Health Orlando Regional Medical Center, Orlando, FL, p. A144
DORUNDO, Cynthia M.
Chief Executive Officer, AHN Hempfield Neighborhood Hospital, Greensburg, PA, p. A540
Market Chief Executive Officer, AHN Hempfield Neighborhood Hospital, Greensburg, PA, p. A540
DOS SANTOS, Frank, D.O., Chief Medical Officer, Clara Maass Medical Center, Belleville, NJ, p. A418
DOSI, Abhishek, Senior Vice President and Area Manager, Santa Rose Service Area, Kaiser Permanente Santa Rosa Medical Center, Santa Rosa, CA, p. A95
D'SOUZA, Carol, Chief Human Resources Officer, Banner Casa Grande Medical Center, Casa Grande, AZ, p. A30
D'SOUZA, Gladys, Chief Nursing Officer, Barlow Respiratory Hospital, Los Angeles, CA, p. A71
DOSS, Delilah, Director, Human Resources, Mountainview Regional Medical Center, Las Cruces, NM, p. A435
DOSS, Justin, Chief Executive Officer, Baptist Hospitals of Southeast Texas, Beaumont, TX, p. A602
DOSS, Mounir F
Executive Vice President and Chief Financial Officer, Flushing Hospital Medical Center, New York, NY, p. A448
Executive Vice President and Chief Financial Officer, Jamaica Hospital Medical Center, New York, NY, p. A448
DOSSETT, Jeffrey, Southwest Kansas City Market Chief Operating Officer, Olathe Medical Center, Olathe, KS, p. A256
DOSSETT, Phyllis, Director of Clinical Services, Hancock County Hospital, Sneedville, TN, p. A593
DOSTAL, Drew H.
FACHE, Regional Market Leader, Corewell Health Big Rapids Hospital, Big Rapids, MI, p. A322
FACHE, Regional Market Leader, Corewell Health Greenville Hospital, Greenville, MI, p. A329

A836 Index of Health Care Professionals

FACHE, Regional Market Leader, North Region, Corewell Health Ludington Hospital, Ludington, MI, p. A332
FACHE, Regional Market Leader, North Region, Corewell Health Reed City Hospital, Reed City, MI, p. A336
DOSTALIK, Kathleen, Chief Executive Officer, Haven Behavioral Senior Care of Albuquerque, Albuquerque, NM, p. A432
DOTTOR, Wende, Medical Center Director, North Florida/South Georgia Veteran's Health System, Gainesville, FL, p. A132
DOTY, Dean, Chief Executive Officer, Gulfport Behavioral Health System, Gulfport, MS, p. A362
DOTY, Jennifer, Chief Executive Officer, Sidney Health Center, Sidney, MT, p. A396
DOTY, Lisa, Manager Human Resources, Desert View Hospital, Pahrump. NV, p. A412
DOUBLE, Ron
  Chief Information Officer, Parkview Huntington Hospital, Huntington, IN, p. A218
  Chief Information Officer, Parkview Noble Hospital, Kendallville, IN, p. A221
  Chief Information Technology Officer, Parkview Lagrange Hospital, Lagrange, IN, p. A222
DOUCETTE, Diane
  R.N., President and Chief Operating Officer, Mount Carmel New Albany Surgical Hospital, New Albany, OH, p. A501
  R.N., President and Chief Operating Officer, Mount Carmel St. Ann's, Westerville, OH, p. A507
DOUCETTE, Elmer H, Chief Financial Officer, Redington–Fairview General Hospital, Skowhegan, ME, p. A299
DOUD, Tony
  Controller, Mymichigan Medical Center Standish, Standish, MI, p. A338
  Controller, Mymichigan Medical Center Tawas, Tawas City, MI, p. A339
DOUGHERTY, Christopher J., President and Chief Executive Officer, Brattleboro Memorial Hospital, Brattleboro, VT, p. A671
DOUGHERTY, Chuck, Chief Information Officer, Shenandoah Medical Center, Shenandoah, IA, p. A243
DOUGHERTY, David, Chief Information Management Officer, Irwin Army Community Hospital, Junction City, KS, p. A251
DOUGHERTY, James, Commander, U. S. Air Force Medical Center Keesler, Keesler Afb, MS, p. A364
DOUGHERTY, Terry, Director Human Resources, Bryn Mawr Hospital, Bryn Mawr, PA, p. A536
DOUGHTY, Cathy, Vice President Human Resources, Sheppard Pratt, Baltimore, MD, p. A302
DOUGHTY, Linda, Chief Nursing Officer, Alaska Regional Hospital, Anchorage, AK, p. A27
DOUGHTY, Stephanie
  Chief Financial Officer, UCHealth Medical Center of The Rockies, Loveland, CO, p. A112
  Chief Financial Officer, UCHealth Poudre Valley Hospital, Fort Collins, CO, p. A108
DOUGLAS, Andy, Manager Information Technology, Burnett Medical Center, Grantsburg, WI, p. A711
DOUGLAS, Debbie, Director Human Resources, Putnam County Memorial Hospital, Unionville, MO, p. A388
DOUGLAS, Errol A., MS, Vice President, Human Resources, Roswell Park Comprehensive Cancer Center, Buffalo, NY, p. A440
DOUGLAS, Johnna, Manager, Human Resources, Massac Memorial Hospital, Metropolis, IL, p. A202
DOUGLAS, Justin, R.N., MSN, Chief Executive Officer, Lemuel Shattuck Hospital, Jamaica Plain, MA, p. A314
DOUGLAS, Kay
  Executive Director, Musc Health Black River Medical Center, Cades, SC, p. A562
  Human Resources Director, Musc Health Florence Medical Center, Florence, SC, p. A566
DOUGLAS, Pam, Chief Nursing Officer, Putnam General Hospital, Eatonton, GA, p. A163
DOUGLAS, Paul, Vice President Human Resources, Baton Rouge General Medical Center, Baton Rouge, LA, p. A277
DOVER, Chris, CPA, Chief Financial Officer, Wilbarger General Hospital, Vernon, TX, p. A659
DOVER, Deborah L, Senior Vice–President of Human Resources, Bristol Regional Medical Center, Bristol, TN, p. A579
DOW, Alan, Chief Financial Officer, Southern Coos Hospital And Health Center, Bandon, OR, p. A525
DOW, Laura, Chief Financial Officer, Memorial Health University Medical Center, Savannah, GA, p. A171
DOWD, Philip. IT Director, Clinch Memorial Hospital, Homerville, GA, p. A165
DOWDLE, Paula, Chief Operating Officer, Jefferson Healthcare, Port Townsend, WA, p. A693

DOWDY, Stacy
  R.N., Administrator, Chief Nursing Officer, Sevier County Medical Center, De Queen, AR, p. A45
  R.N., Chief Nursing Officer, Sevier County Medical Center, De Queen, AR, p. A45
DOWELL, James, Chief Executive Officer, Little River Medical Center, Inc., Ashdown, AR, p. A43
DOWERS, Cindy, Chief Nursing Officer, Harsha Behavioral Center, Terre Haute, IN, p. A228
DOWLING, Deanna, R.N., Chief Nursing Officer, KPC Promise Hospital of Wichita Falls, Wichita Falls, TX, p. A662
DOWLING, Lisa, Manager Finance, Mercy Hospital Tishomingo, Tishomingo, OK, p. A521
DOWLING, Sally, M.D., Vice President Medical Affairs, Atlantic General Hospital, Berlin, MD, p. A302
DOWN, Melanie Falls, Site Manager, Crow/Northern Cheyenne Hospital, Crow Agency, MT, p. A391
DOWNARD, Diane, Chief Financial Officer, Coal County General Hospital, Coalgate, OK, p. A511
DOWNES, Patrick, President, St. Joseph's Hospital, Tampa, FL, p. A152
DOWNIE, Beth, Chief Information Officer, Newton–Wellesley Hospital, Newton Lower Falls, MA, p. A316
DOWNING, James R., M.D., Chief Executive Officer, St. Jude Children's Research Hospital, Memphis, TN, p. A589
DOWNING, Jeff, R.N., MS, Chief Nursing Officer, National Jewish Health, Denver, CO, p. A106
DOWNS, Bryan, Director Information Systems, Central Peninsula Hospital, Soldotna, AK, p. A29
DOWNS, Lisa M, R.N., Chief Nursing Officer, Sarah D. Culbertson Memorial Hospital, Rushville, IL, p. A208
DOWNS, Patricia, Director Human Resources, Northern Nevada Medical Center, Sparks, NV, p. A413
DOWNS, Steven
  Chief Financial Officer, Musc Health Black River Medical Center, Cades, SC, p. A562
  Chief Financial Officer, St. Luke's Des Peres Hospital, Saint Louis, MO, p. A386
DOXY, Eric, Administrator, Middle Tennessee Mental Health Institute, Nashville, TN, p. A590
DOYLE, Craig, Director and Chief Information Officer, St. Tammany Health System, Covington, LA, p. A280
DOYLE, Declan, President, St. Catherine of Siena Hospital, Smithtown, NY, p. A459
DOYLE, John
  Chief Financial Officer, Confluence Health Hospital – Central Campus, Wenatchee, WA, p. A698
  Chief Financial Officer, Confluence Health Hospital – Mares Campus, Wenatchee, WA, p. A698
  Vice President Finance, Paoli Hospital, Paoli, PA, p. A547
DOYLE, Kelly, Chief Executive Officer, Rothman Orthopaedic Specialty Hospital, Bensalem, PA, p. A535
DOYLE, Mark, President and Chief Executive Officer, Holy Cross Hospital, Fort Lauderdale, FL, p. A131
DOYLE, Matthew, CPA, President and Chief Executive Officer, Methodist Hospitals, Gary, IN, p. A217
DOYLE, Michael
  M.D., Executive Director and Chief Medical Officer, Health Alliance Hospital – Broadway Campus, Kingston, NY, p. A445
  M.D., Executive Director and Chief Medical Officer, Health Alliance Hospital – Mary's Avenue Campus, Kingston, NY, p. A445
DOZIER, Carol
  Chief Financial Officer, Lifestream Behavioral Center, Leesburg, FL, p. A137
  President and Chief Executive Officer, Norton King's Daughters' Health, Madison, IN, p. A223
DOZIER, Michael
  Senior Vice President, Chief Information Officer, Ochsner University Hospital & Clinics, Lafayette, LA, p. A286
  Vice President, Chief Information Officer, Ochsner Lafayette General Medical Center, Lafayette, LA, p. A285
DRAEGER, Anne, Chief Nursing Officer, Owatonna Hospital, Owatonna, MN, p. A352
DRAEGER, Trish, Chief Nursing Officer, Encompass Health Deaconess Rehabilitation Hospital, Newburgh, IN, p. A225
DRAIME, D. Eric
  Vice President and Chief Financial Officer, Avita Ontario Hospital, Ontario, OH, p. A502
  Vice President and Chief Financial Officer, Galion Community Hospital, Galion, OH, p. A496
DRAKE, Archie
  Chief Executive Officer, Dmc Children's Hospital of Michigan, Detroit, MI, p. A325
  Chief Operating Officer, Valley Baptist Medical Center–Harlingen, Harlingen, TX, p. A624
DRAKE, Carolyn, Director of Nursing, West Tennessee Healthcare Milan Hospital, Milan, TN, p. A589

DRAKE, Derek Scott., Chief Executive Officer, Orange County Global Medical Center, Inc., Santa Ana, CA, p. A93
DRAKE, Megan, Chief Operating Officer, Shelby Baptist Medical Center, Alabaster, AL, p. A15
DRANSFIELD, Darin, Chief Executive Officer, Franklin County Medical Center, Preston, ID, p. A183
DRAPER, Jason
  Chief Financial Officer, West Tennessee Healthcare Volunteer Hospital, Martin, TN, p. A587
  Vice President and Chief Support Officer, Parkwest Medical Center, Knoxville, TN, p. A586
DRAPER, Vivian, Chief Financial Officer, U. S. Public Health Service Indian Hospital–Sells, Sells, AZ, p. A38
DREESEN, Andy, Chief Executive Officer, St. Vincent Health, Leadville, CO, p. A111
DREGNEY, James, Vice President Finance and Operations, Chief Financial Officer, Sauk Prairie Healthcare, Prairie Du Sac, WI, p. A720
DREHER, Craig, Chief Information Officer, Northern Light Mercy Hospital, Portland, ME, p. A298
DREHER, Ronald, Finance Officer, Robert J. Dole Department of Veterans Affairs Medical And Regional Office Center, Wichita, KS, p. A262
DREHR, Sammie, Chief Nursing Officer, Detar Healthcare System, Victoria, TX, p. A660
DREICER, Jarret, FACHE, President, Baptist Medical Center Beaches, Jacksonville Beach, FL, p. A135
DRENTH, Nancy E, R.N., Director Ancillary Services, Sanford Luverne Medical Center, Luverne, MN, p. A349
DRESSER, Paula, Chief Nursing Officer, Orleans Community Health, Medina, NY, p. A446
DRESSLER, Kaeli, R.N., MSN, Chief Nursing Officer, Peterson Health, Kerrville, TX, p. A632
DREW, Jeff, Fiscal Officer, Aleda E. Lutz Department of Veterans Affairs Medical Center, Saginaw, MI, p. A336
DREW, Laura, Chief Operating Officer, Piedmont Columbus Regional Northside, Columbus, GA, p. A161
DREWS, Manty, Chief Information Officer, Adventist Health Sonora, Sonora, CA, p. A96
DREXLER, Diane, R.N., Chief Nursing Officer, Dignity Health Yavapai Regional Medical Center, Prescott, AZ, p. A37
DREY, Mistie, Chief Executive Officer, Community Memorial Hospital, Burke, SD, p. A572
DRIEMEYER, Jed, Director of Human Resources, HSHS St. Joseph's Hospital Breese, Breese, IL, p. A187
DRIESSNACK, Hans, Chief Executive Officer, Abrazo West Campus, Goodyear, AZ, p. A32
DRIGGERS, Steve, M.D., Chief Medical Officer, Holy Family Memorial, Manitowoc, WI, p. A715
DRINKWATER, Jinia, R.N., Director Patient Care Services, Encompass Health Rehabilitation Hospital of Braintree, Braintree, MA, p. A311
DRINKWATER, Linda, Chief Financial Officer, Waldo County General Hospital, Belfast, ME, p. A296
DRINKWITZ, Jeremy
  President, Mercy Joplin Communities, Mercy Hospital Carthage, Carthage, MO, p. A373
  President, Mercy Joplin Communities, Mercy Hospital Joplin, Joplin, MO, p. A377
DRISCOLL, Kelly, R.N., FACHE, President and Chief Executive Officer, Faith Regional Health Services, Norfolk, NE, p. A403
DRISCOLL, Mark, Chief Information Officer, Jackson County Memorial Hospital, Altus, OK, p. A509
DRISCOLL, Philip J., Chief Executive Officer, Kessler Institute for Rehabilitation, West Orange, NJ, p. A430
DRISKILL, Chris, M.D., Chief of Staff, Covenant Health Hobbs Hospital, Hobbs, NM, p. A435
DRONE, Marilyn
  R.N., MSN, Chief Executive Officer, Victor Valley Global Medical Center, Victorville, CA, p. A100
  R.N., MSN, Vice President, CNO, Providence St. Mary Medical Center, Apple Valley, CA, p. A56
DRUMMOND, Danielle, MS, FACHE, President and Chief Executive Officer, Lakeland Regional Health Medical Center, Lakeland, FL, p. A137
DRVARIC, David M, M.D., Chief of Staff, Shriners Hospitals for Children–Springfield, Springfield, MA, p. A318
DRY, Cynthia
  MSN, Chief Nursing Officer, Ennis Regional Medical Center, Ennis, TX, p. A618
  MSN, Chief Nursing Officer, Parkview Regional Hospital, Mexia, TX, p. A639
DRY, Laurence
  Chief Operating Officer, Acute Care Hospitals Northern Region, Ascension Alexian Brothers, Elk Grove Village, IL, p. A194
  Chief Operating Officer, Acute Care Hospitals Northern Region, Ascension St. Alexius, Hoffman Estates, IL, p. A198

Index of Health Care Professionals

Index of Health Care Professionals / Dryden

DRYDEN, Shawn, FACHE, President and Chief Executive Officer, Ranken Jordan Pediatric Bridge Hospital, Maryland Heights, MO, p. A380

DRYMON, Lisa, Manager, Rural Wellness Fairfax, Fairfax, OK, p. A512

DRZEWIECKI–BURGER, Mary Jo, Administrative Manager, Caro Center, Caro, MI, p. A323

DU LAC, Joseph, Senior Vice President, Chief Operating Officer, Bronson Battle Creek Hospital, Battle Creek, MI, p. A322

DU PONT, Karen, Chief Human Resource Officer, Casa Colina Hospital And Centers for Healthcare, Pomona, CA, p. A84

DUANE, Paul K
- Chief Financial Officer and Office of Health Reform, Prisma Health Baptist Hospital, Columbia, SC, p. A565
- Chief Financial Officer and Office of Health Reform, Prisma Health Richland Hospital, Columbia, SC, p. A565

DUARTE, Ray, Director, Information Technology and Services, Monmouth Medical Center, Southern Campus, Lakewood, NJ, p. A422

DUBOIS, Brady, Chief Executive Officer, Boone Hospital Center, Columbia, MO, p. A374

DUBROW, Melissa, Vice President Wellspan Health and President WellSpan Waynesboro Hospital, Wellspan Waynesboro Hospital, Waynesboro, PA, p. A556

DUBRUYNE, Sharon, Director Human Resources, College Hospital Costa Mesa, Costa Mesa, CA, p. A60

DUBY, Heather, Administrator, Oceans Behavioral Hospital of Amarillo, Amarillo, TX, p. A596

DUCHARME, Jacqueline
- Worcester Recovery Center And Hospital, Worcester, MA, p. A320
- Chief Operating Officer and Interim Chief Executive Officer, Worcester Recovery Center And Hospital, Worcester, MA, p. A320

DUCHARME, Maria
- R.N., President, Miriam Hospital, Providence, RI, p. A560
- R.N., Senior Vice President Patient Care Services and Chief Nursing Officer, Miriam Hospital, Providence, RI, p. A560

DUCHEMIN, MaDena, Assistant Administrator Human Resources, Tricities Hospital, Hopewell, VA, p. A678

DUCHENE, Pamela, R.N., Vice President Patient Care Services, Chief Nursing Officer, Southwestern Vermont Medical Center, Bennington, VT, p. A671

DUCHESNEAU, Angy, Senior Director Human Resources, Lakeview Hospital, Stillwater, MN, p. A355

DUCK, Sigsbee, M.D., President, Medical Staff, Memorial Hospital of Sweetwater County, Rock Springs, WY, p. A728

DUCKERT, Jon, FACHE, Chief Executive Officer, Baylor Scott & White Medical Center – Sunnyvale, Sunnyvale, TX, p. A655

DUCKETT, Jonathan, Chief Executive Officer, Haven Behavioral Hospital of Dayton, Dayton, OH, p. A493

DUCKWORTH, Bob, Director Information Systems, Medical West, Bessemer, AL, p. A16

DUDLEY, Edward L III, Executive Vice President and Chief Financial Officer, Catholic Medical Center, Manchester, NH, p. A416

DUDLEY, Heather, Director Administrative Services, Brookhaven Hospital, Tulsa, OK, p. A522

DUDLEY, Lauren, Chief Executive Officer, Lewisgale Hospital Montgomery, Blacksburg, VA, p. A673

DUDLEY, Susanna, Director of Operations, Pam Specialty Hospital of Dayton, Miamisburg, OH, p. A500

DUDLEY, W. Steve, CPA, Chief Financial Officer, Ed Fraser Memorial Hospital, Macclenny, FL, p. A138

DUEMMEL, John, Chief Executive Officer, Select Specialty Hospital–Pittsburgh/Upmc, Pittsburgh, PA, p. A551

DUET, Kendrick, Chief Operating Officer, Leonard J. Chabert Medical Center, Houma, LA, p. A283

DUFF, James, M.D., Chief Medical Officer, Cox Medical Center Branson, Branson, MO, p. A372

DUFF, Jim, Chief Financial Officer, Colorado Mental Health Institute At Pueblo, Pueblo, CO, p. A112

DUFF, Mary Claire, CPA, Chief Financial Officer, Ridgeview Psychiatric Hospital And Center, Oak Ridge, TN, p. A591

DUFFEE, Patrick, Director Medical Information Systems, Delta Specialty Hospital, Memphis, TN, p. A588

DUFFEY, Pamela
- R.N., Chief Nursing Officer, Texas Health Specialty Hospital, Fort Worth, TX, p. A620
- R.N., Chief Operating Officer and Chief Nursing Officer, Texas Health Specialty Hospital, Fort Worth, TX, p. A620
- R.N., Vice President/Chief Operating Office/Chief Nursing Officer, Texas Health Specialty Hospital, Fort Worth, TX, p. A620

DUFFIN, Kelly L, Operations Officer, Intermountain Medical Center, Murray, UT, p. A666

DUFFIN, Kelly L., President, Layton Hospital, Layton, UT, p. A665

DUFFORD, Shawn, M.D., Vice President Medical Affairs and Chief Medical Officer, Intermountain Health Saint Josep. Hospital, Denver, CO, p. A106

DUFFY, Beth, President and Chief Operating Officer, Jefferson Einstein Montgomery Hospital, East Norriton, PA, p. A538

DUFFY, Daniel, D.O., Chief Medical Director, Healthsource Saginaw Inc., Saginaw, MI, p. A337

DUFFY, Kenneth, M.D., Medical Director, Seiling Municipal Hospital, Seiling, OK, p. A520

DUFFY, Marie Theresa, Chief Hospital Executive, Executive Vice President System Clinical Integration and Standards, Carepoint Health Christ Hospital, Jersey City, NJ, p. A422

DUFFY, Pamela
- MSN, R.N., Vice President Operations and Chief Nursing Executive, Northwestern Medicine Valley West Hospital, Sandwich, IL, p. A208
- MSN, R.N., Vice President Operations and Chief Nursing Officer, Northwestern Medicine Kishwaukee Hospital, Dekalb, IL, p. A193

DUFFY, Timothy W, General Director, Albany Medical Center, Albany, NY, p. A438

DUFFY, William, Interim Chief Nursing Officer, Humboldt Park Health, Chicago, IL, p. A189

DUFRAYNE, Francis, M.D., Chief Medical Officer, Owensboro Health Regional Hospital, Owensboro, KY, p. A272

DUFT, Ryan, R.N., Chief Nursing Officer, Fredonia Regional Hospital, Fredonia, KS, p. A249

DUGAN, Elizabeth, Ph.D., R.N., MSN, Chief Nursing Officer, Inova Loudoun Hospital, Leesburg, VA, p. A678

DUGAN, Gary, M.D., Vice President Medical Affairs, Penn Highlands Dubois, Dubois, PA, p. A538

DUGGAL, Harpreet, M.D., Medical Director, Department of Health and Human Services, Humboldt County Mental Health, Eureka, CA, p. A62

DUGGAN, James E, Director Human Resources, Western Massachusetts Hospital, Westfield, MA, p. A319

DUGGAN, Peggy M., M.D., Executive Vice President and Chief Medical Officer, Tamp. General Hospital, Tampa, FL, p. A152

DUGGAN, Tonya, Director Human Resources, Northern Louisiana Medical Center, Ruston, LA, p. A291

DUGGER, Curtis R., Chief Financial Officer, Memorial Hospital of Converse County, Douglas, WY, p. A727

DUGGER, Sandy
- Chief Executive Officer, Banner Lassen Medical Center, Susanville, CA, p. A97
- Chief Executive Officer, Platte County Memorial Hospital, Wheatland, WY, p. A729

DUHAIME, Robert A, R.N., Senior Vice President Clinical Operations and Chief Nursing Officer, Catholic Medical Center, Manchester, NH, p. A416

DUHANEY–WEST, Aphriekah, Senior Vice President, Area Manager, Central Valley, Kaiser Permanente Manteca Medical Center, Manteca, CA, p. A76

DUHE, Louis, Senior Director Information Technology, George Washington University Hospital, Washington, DC, p. A123

DUHE, Louis H., Executor Director, Information Services, Piedmont Athens Regional Medical Center, Athens, GA, p. A156

DUKE, Ezekiel, M.D., Chief of Staff, Knox County Hospital, Knox City, TX, p. A633

DUKE, Kelly, Chief Executive Officer, Select Specialty Hospital–Oklahoma City, Oklahoma City, OK, p. A518

DUKE, Lee M, M.D., II, Senior Vice President and Chief Physician Executive, Penn Medicine Lancaster General Health, Lancaster, PA, p. A543

DUKES, Brenda, Director Human Resources, Sonoma Developmental Center, Eldridge, CA, p. A62

DUKOFF, Ruth, M.D., Medical Director, North Star Behavioral Health System, Anchorage, AK, p. A27

DULANEY, Kim Wiley., Vice President of Revenue Cycle, Holzer Medical Center – Jackson, Jackson, OH, p. A497

DULANEY, Paul, M.D., Chief of Staff, Troy Regional Medical Center, Troy, AL, p. A25

DULING, Ruth, Chief Executive Officer, Girard Medical Center, Girard, KS, p. A249

DULL, David, M.D., Chief Medical Officer, Penrose–St. Francis Health Services, Colorado Springs, CO, p. A105

DULL, Kevin B
- Senior Vice President Human Potential, Multicare Auburn Medical Center, Auburn, WA, p. A687
- Senior Vice President Human Potential, Multicare Good Samaritan Hospital, Puyallup. WA, p. A693
- Senior Vice President Human Potential, Multicare Mary Bridge Children's Hospital And Health Center, Tacoma, WA, p. A697
- Senior Vice President Human Potential, Multicare Tacoma General Hospital, Tacoma, WA, p. A697

DULNY, David
- Chief Financial Officer, Providence Medical Center, Kansas City, KS, p. A252
- Chief Financial Officer, Saint John Hospital, Leavenworth, KS, p. A253

DUMAIS, Mark, M.D., Chief Medical Officer, Northridge Hospital Medical Center, Los Angeles, CA, p. A74

DUMAL, Jennifer, R.N., Senior Vice President, Patient Care Services and Chief Nursing Officer, Memorial Hospital At Gulfport, Gulfport, MS, p. A362

DUMKE, Steve, FACHE, Executive Vice President and Chief Operating Officer, Christian Health, Wyckoff, NJ, p. A431

DUMONSEAU, Kent
- Vice President Finance and Information Services, Tamarack Health Ashland Medical Center, Ashland, WI, p. A707
- Vice President Finance and Information Services, Tamarack Health Hayward Medical Center, Hayward, WI, p. A713

DUNAVAN, Chad, R.N., Vice President, Chief Nursing Officer, Medical Center Health System, Odessa, TX, p. A642

DUNCAN, Allison, Chief Financial Officer, Arrowhead Behavioral Health Hospital, Maumee, OH, p. A499

DUNCAN, Barbara, Chief Financial Officer, Northeast Georgia Medical Center Habersham, Demorest, GA, p. A162

DUNCAN, Charles, M.D., Medical Director, Kindred Hospital–San Antonio, San Antonio, TX, p. A649

DUNCAN, Cindy
- Director Human Resources, Roosevelt General Hospital, Portales, NM, p. A436
- Manager Human Resources, Plains Regional Medical Center, Clovis, NM, p. A434

DUNCAN, Cynthia, Chief Executive Officer, Roger Mills Memorial Hospital, Cheyenne, OK, p. A511

DUNCAN, Erika, Vice President Human Resources, St. Joseph's Hospital Health Center, Syracuse, NY, p. A460

DUNCAN, Greg, President and Chief Executive Officer, Incompass Healthcare, Lawrenceburg, IN, p. A222

DUNCAN, Jeremy, Director Information Systems, Lawrence Medical Center, Moulton, AL, p. A23

DUNCAN, Jimmy, Senior Vice President and Chief People Officer, Arkansas Children's Hospital, Little Rock, AR, p. A49

DUNCAN, Joani, Chief Human Resource Officer, Ann & Robert H. Lurie Children's Hospital of Chicago, Chicago, IL, p. A188

DUNCAN, Karen, President and Chief Executive Officer, JPS Health Network, Fort Worth, TX, p. A619

DUNCAN, Larry, Vice President and Administrator Children's Hospital, Renown Regional Medical Center, Reno, NV, p. A412

DUNCAN, Leeann, Director Patient Care Services, Harbor Oaks Hospital, New Baltimore, MI, p. A334

DUNCAN, Linda, Director Human Resources, Lee's Summit Medical Center, Lee's Summit, MO, p. A379

DUNCAN, Lora, Chief Nursing Officer, Optim Medical Center – Tattnall, Reidsville, GA, p. A169

DUNCAN, Lyman, Chief Financial Officer, San Juan Health Service District, Monticello, UT, p. A666

DUNCAN, Michael J., President and Chief Executive Officer, Penn Medicine Chester County Hospital, West Chester, PA, p. A557

DUNCAN, Nathan, Chief Executive Officer, Lakeland Behavioral Health System, Springfield, MO, p. A386

DUNCAN, Thomas M, Executive Vice President and Chief Financial Officer, Miami Valley Hospital, Dayton, OH, p. A494

DUNCAN, Traci A, R.N., Vice President, Chief Nursing Officer, Northbay Medical Center, Fairfield, CA, p. A63

DUNCKHORST, Robyn, R.N., Chief Executive Officer, Humboldt General Hospital, Winnemucca, NV, p. A413

DUNFEE, Marcia, Chief Nursing Officer, Riverview Health Institute, Dayton, OH, p. A494

DUNFORD, Bill, Manager, Northside Hospital Cherokee, Canton, GA, p. A160

DUNHAM, Cathy, Chief Human Resources Officer, Mcpherson Hospital, Inc., Mcpherson, KS, p. A254

DUNIO, Gina, Chief Human Resources, James E. Van Zandt Veterans Affairs Medical Center, Altoona, PA, p. A534

DUNKEL, Jason
- Chief Executive Officer, Adventhealth Sebring, Sebring, FL, p. A150
- Chief Executive Officer, Adventhealth Wauchula, Wauchula, FL, p. A154

DUNKER, Karla, Chief Financial Officer, Sedgwick County Health Center, Julesburg, CO, p. A110

DUNKIEL, Barbara, Director Human Resources, Encompass Health Rehabilitation Hospital of Sunrise, Sunrise, FL, p. A151

DUNKIN, Jackie J., Director Human Resources, Intermountain Health Platte Valley Hospital, Brighton, CO, p. A104

DUNKIN, John, Executive Director, Ascension Alexian Brothers, Elk Grove Village, IL, p. A194

A838 Index of Health Care Professionals

DUNKLE, David, President and Chief Executive Officer and Vice President Medical Affairs, Johnson Memorial Hospital, Franklin, IN, p. A217
DUNLAP, Cyndy, R.N., FACHE, Chief Nursing Officer, Ascension Providence, Waco, TX, p. A660
DUNLAVEY, Jerry
 Chief Executive Officer, Garnet Health Medical Center – Catskills, Callicoon Campus, Callicoon, NY, p. A440
 Chief Executive Officer, Garnet Health Medical Center – Catskills, Harris Campus, Harris, NY, p. A444
DUNLOP, James H
 CPA, Jr, Chief Financial Officer, Sisters of Charity Hospital of Buffalo, Buffalo, NY, p. A440
 CPA, Jr, Executive Vice President and Chief Financial Officer, Kenmore Mercy Hospital, Kenmore, NY, p. A444
 CPA, Jr, Senior Vice President Finance and Chief Financial Officer, Mercy Hospital, Buffalo, NY, p. A440
DUNMYER, Daniel C.
 Chief Executive Officer, Landmark Hospital of Southwest Florida, Naples, FL, p. A141
 Chief Executive Officer, Select Specialty Hospital – Morgantown, Morgantown, WV, p. A703
DUNN, Ajani N., M.D., Chief Administrative Officer, Mayo Clinic Hospital In Florida, Jacksonville, FL, p. A135
DUNN, Denise, R.N., Chief Nursing Officer, Baptist Health Deaconess Madisonville, Inc., Madisonville, KY, p. A271
DUNN, E D, Vice President Human Resources, Virtua Mount Holly Hospital, Mount Holly, NJ, p. A424
DUNN, Hope, Chief Nursing Officer, Encompass Health Rehabilitation Hospital of East Valley, Mesa, AZ, p. A33
DUNN, Jack, M.D., Chief of Staff, La Paz Regional Hospital, Parker, AZ, p. A34
DUNN, Janice, Chief Financial Officer, Plymouth Medical Center, Plymouth, IN, p. A226
DUNN, Jim, Ph.D., FACHE, Chief Human Resource Officer, Atrium Health's Carolinas Medical Center, Charlotte, NC, p. A465
DUNN, Leonard, M.D., Chief Medical Officer, Baycare Alliant Hospital, Dunedin, FL, p. A130
DUNN, Margie, Director Human Resources, Middle Tennessee Mental Health Institute, Nashville, TN, p. A590
DUNN, Nicholas, Director Information Systems, Mena Regional Health System, Mena, AR, p. A50
DUNN, Rosemary, R.N., Chief Nursing Officer, Cooper University Hospital Cap. Regional, Cap. May Court House, NJ, p. A419
DUNN, Sheila, Assistant Administrator Human Resources, Dale Medical Center, Ozark, AL, p. A23
DUNN, Tandra, Director of Nursing, San Luis Valley Health Conejos County Hospital, La Jara, CO, p. A110
DUNN, Terry, Director Information Technology, Battle Mountain General Hospital, Battle Mountain, NV, p. A408
DUNNING, David K., Medical Center Director, James A. Haley Veterans' Hospital–Tampa, Tampa, FL, p. A152
DUNNING, Nan, Human Resources Manager, Paris Community Hospital, Paris, IL, p. A205
DUNNING, Thomas, President, North Shore Medical Center, Miami, FL, p. A140
DUNNING, Thomas M., Chief Executive Officer, Texas Surgical Hospital, Plano, TX, p. A645
DUNNIWAY, Heidi, M.D., Chief Medical Officer, Ascension St. Vincent Evansville, Evansville, IN, p. A216
DUNPHEY, Paul, President, New York–Presbyterian/Hudson Valley Hospital, Cortlandt Manor, NY, p. A442
DUNPHY–ALEXANDER, Shannon, Director, Mercyhealth Hospital And Medical Center – Harvard, Harvard, IL, p. A197
DUPONT, Laurel
 Chief Executive Officer, Northshore Rehabilitation Hospital, Lacombe, LA, p. A285
 Chief Executive Officer, Ochsner Rehabilitaton Hospital West Campus, Jefferson, LA, p. A284
DUPPER, Harold, Chief Financial Officer, Cobre Valley Regional Medical Center, Globe, AZ, p. A32
DUPREE, Eric, M.D., Chief of Staff, Winn Parish Medical Center, Winnfield, LA, p. A294
DUPREE, Lucy G, Director Human Resources, Columbia Memorial Hospital, Astoria, OR, p. A525
DUPREY, Irma, Administrator Medical Records, Hospital Universitario Dr. Ramon Ruiz Arnau, Bayamon, PR, p. A731
DUQUETTE, Connie
 Director Human Resources, Sharp Mary Birch Hospital for Women And Newborns, San Diego, CA, p. A89
 Director Human Resources, Sharp Memorial Hospital, San Diego, CA, p. A89
DUQUETTE, William M., Chief Executive Officer, Baptist Health South Florida, South Miami Miami, FL, p. A139
DURAN, Andres, Chief Executive Officer, Dimmit Regional Hospital, Carrizo Springs, TX, p. A606

DURAN, Jody, Manager Information Systems, Livingston Healthcare, Livingston, MT, p. A394
DURAN, Tracy, Administrator, Stormont Vail Health – Flint Hills Campus, Junction City, KS, p. A251
DURAND, Crista F., President, Newport Hospital, Newport, RI, p. A560
DURAND, Mark, Assistant Administrator Operations, Christus Southeast Texas Jasper Memorial, Jasper, TX, p. A630
DURBAK, Ivan, Chief Information Officer, Bronxcare Health System, New York, NY, p. A447
DURBIN, Melissa Ann, R.N., MSN, Chief Nursing Officer, Boca Raton Regional Hospital, Boca Raton, FL, p. A126
DURFLINGER, Kathy
 Vice President and Chief Nursing Officer, Avita Ontario Hospital, Ontario, OH, p. A502
 Vice President and Chief Nursing Officer, Galion Community Hospital, Galion, OH, p. A496
DURGIN, Manal, Network Medical Director, Devereux Hospital And Children's Center of Florida, Melbourne, FL, p. A138
DURHAM, Karla, Director of Information Systems, Baptist Health Deaconess Madisonville, Inc., Madisonville, KY, p. A271
DURHAM, Linda, Director Human Resources, Henderson County Community Hospital, Lexington, TN, p. A587
DURHAM, Thomas, Chief Nursing Officer, Ferry County Memorial Hospital, Republic, WA, p. A693
DURIS, Deb, Director of Nursing, Northwest Ohio Psychiatric Hospital, Toledo, OH, p. A505
DURNIAT–SUSHRSTEDT, Karen, Nurse Executive, Appalachian Behavioral Healthcare, Athens, OH, p. A485
DURNIOK, Brian
 President, UPMC Chautauqua, Jamestown, NY, p. A444
 President, UPMC Hamot, Erie, PA, p. A540
 President, UPMC Northwest, Seneca, PA, p. A554
 Vice President Operations, UPMC Northwest, Seneca, PA, p. A554
DUROCHER, Steven, M.D., Chief Medical Officer, Piedmont Walton Hospital, Monroe, GA, p. A168
DURON, Christine, Interim Chief Executive Officer, Denver Regional Rehabilitation Hospital, Thornton, CO, p. A113
DURON, Kety, Vice President Human Resources, Stanford Health Care, Palo Alto, CA, p. A82
DUROVICH, Christopher J., President and Chief Executive Officer, Children's Medical Center Dallas, Dallas, TX, p. A611
DURR, Michael, CPA, Chief Financial Officer, Miami Jewish Health, Miami, FL, p. A140
DURRETT, Johnathan, Chief Executive Officer, Fredonia Regional Hospital, Fredonia, KS, p. A249
DURST, Geoff, Vice President Finance, Avera St. Luke's Hospital, Aberdeen, SD, p. A572
DURST, Sue, R.N., MS, Vice President Plant Operations, Mclaren Macomb, Mount Clemens, MI, p. A333
DURSTELER, Courtney, Chief Human Resources Officer, Franklin County Medical Center, Preston, ID, p. A183
DUSANG, Nina, Chief Financial Officer, Woman's Hospital, Baton Rouge, LA, p. A278
DUTHE, Robert J, Director Information Systems and Chief Information Officer, Guthrie Cortland Regional Medical Center, Cortland, NY, p. A441
DUTLA, M.D., Chief Medical Staff, Holzer Medical Center – Jackson, Jackson, OH, p. A497
DUTMERS, David, Manager, Information Services, Corewell Health Greenville Hospital, Greenville, MI, p. A329
DUTTON, Angela, Chief Human Resources Management Service, Robley Rex Department of Veterans Affairs Medical Center, Louisville, KY, p. A270
DUTTON, Teresa, R.N., Chief Nursing Officer, Baylor Scott & White Surgical Hospital–Sherman, Sherman, TX, p. A652
DUVAL, Megan Picou, Chief Nursing Officer, Physicians Medical Center, Houma, LA, p. A283
DUVAL, Rob, Chief Human Resources Officer, Emma Pendleton Bradley Hospital, East Providence, RI, p. A560
DUVALL, Richard
 Chief Executive Officer, Carthage Area Hospital, Carthage, NY, p. A441
 President and Chief Executive Officer, Claxton–Hepburn Medical Center, Ogdensburg, NY, p. A455
DUVALL, Wendy, Chief Financial Officer, Heartland Behavioral Health Services, Nevada, MO, p. A381
DUVVURI, Vikas, M.D., Medical Director, Fremont Hospital, Fremont, CA, p. A64
DWIGHT, John, Regional Vice President and Chief Information Officer, Skagit Valley Hospital, Mount Vernon, WA, p. A692
DWORAK, Paige, FACHE, President and Chief Executive Officer, Carewell Health Medical Center, East Orange, NJ, p. A420
DWORKIN, Jack H, M.D., Vice President Medical Affairs and Chief Medical Officer, Centrastate Healthcare System, Freehold, NJ, p. A421

DWORKIN, Paul, M.D., Physician–in–Chief, Connecticut Children's, Hartford, CT, p. A116
DWYER, Cathy, Senior Administrator Information Systems, Burke Rehabilitation Hospital, White Plains, NY, p. A462
DWYER, James P
 D.O., Executive Vice President and Chief Medical Officer, Virtua Mount Holly Hospital, Mount Holly, NJ, p. A424
 D.O., Executive Vice President and Chief Medical Officer, Virtua Voorhees, Voorhees, NJ, p. A430
DWYER, Susan, Vice President Finance, Aurora Psychiatric Hospital, Wauwatosa, WI, p. A724
DYBDAL, Landon, Chief Executive Officer, Ruby Valley Medical Center, Sheridan, MT, p. A396
DYCHE, Ginny, Director Community Relations, Aspen Valley Hospital, Aspen, CO, p. A103
DYE, Chris, Director Information Systems, Arh Our Lady of The Way, Martin, KY, p. A271
DYE, Dana, R.N., Vice President, Baptist Memorial Hospital – Memphis, Memphis, TN, p. A588
DYE, David Bryan, M.D., Chief Medical Officer, Purcell Municipal Hospital, Purcell, OK, p. A520
DYE, Emily, Vice President Human Resources, Tristar Summit Medical Center, Hermitage, TN, p. A584
DYE, Leslie, Chief Executive Officer, PHS Santa Fe Indian Hospital, Santa Fe, NM, p. A436
DYE, Purcell
 Ph.D., Chief Executive Officer, Spring Mountain Sahara, Las Vegas, NV, p. A410
 Ph.D., Chief Executive Officer, Spring Mountain Treatment Center, Las Vegas, NV, p. A410
DYER, Edward L, Chief Executive Officer, Cornerstone Specialty Hospitals Austin Round Rock, Austin, TX, p. A599
DYER, Karen, Chief Executive Officer, SBL Fayette County Hospital And Long Term Care, Vandalia, IL, p. A210
DYER, Robert, Chief Executive Officer, Cozad Community Health System, Cozad, NE, p. A399
DYKEHOUSE, Rodney, Senior Vice President Information Services, Prohealth Waukesha Memorial Hospital, Waukesha, WI, p. A723
DYKSTERHOUSE, Trevor J., President, Forest Health Medical Center, Ypsilanti, MI, p. A341
DYKSTRA, Lisa, Senior Vice President and Chief Information Officer, Ann & Robert H. Lurie Children's Hospital of Chicago, Chicago, IL, p. A188
DYLE, Amanda
 Chief Financial Officer, Princeton Baptist Medical Center, Birmingham, AL, p. A17
 Chief Financial Officer, Walker Baptist Medical Center, Jasper, AL, p. A21
DYSART–CREDEUR, Amy, Administrator, Oceans Behavioral Hospital of Broussard, Broussard, LA, p. A279
DZIEDZICKI, Ron, R.N., Chief Operating Officer, University Hospitals Cleveland Medical Center, Cleveland, OH, p. A491

E

EADS, Barry
 R.N., Chief Nursing Officer, Encompass Health Rehabilitation Hospital of Gadsden, Gadsden, AL, p. A19
 R.N., Chief Nursing Officer, Medical Center Enterprise, Enterprise, AL, p. A19
EADS, Ted, Interim Chief Nursing Officer, Ascension St. Vincent Carmel Hospital, Carmel, IN, p. A213
EADY, Bruce, R.N., MSN, Chief Executive Officer, St. Luke's Rehabilitation Hospital, Chesterfield, MO, p. A373
EAGAR, Troy, Director Human Resources, Mountain Valley Regional Rehabilitation Hospital, Prescott Valley, AZ, p. A37
EAKER, Blake, Interim Director Information Services, Uvalde Memorial Hospital, Uvalde, TX, p. A659
EAMRANOND, Pracha, M.D., Senior Vice President Population Health and Medical Affairs, Lawrence General Hospital, Lawrence, MA, p. A314
EANES, Janine, Senior Human Resources Business Partner, UNC Health Rockingham, Eden, NC, p. A467
EARLE, Cletis, Senior Vice President and Chief Information Officer, Penn State Health Hampden Medical Center, Enola, PA, p. A539
EARLY, Drew, President and Chief Executive Officer, Decatur Memorial Hospital, Decatur, IL, p. A192
EARLY, Elfie, Manager Data Services, Georgia Regional Hospital At Atlanta, Decatur, GA, p. A162
EARLY, Elizabeth, FACHE, President, Gottlieb Memorial Hospital, Melrose Park, IL, p. A201

Index of Health Care Professionals / Early

EARLY, Gerald L, M.D., Chief Medical Officer, Pullman Regional Hospital, Pullman, WA, p. A693
EARNSHAW, Dallas, Superintendent, Utah State Hospital, Provo, UT, p. A667
EASLEY, Evan, M.D., Chief Medical Officer, Carson Valley Medical Center, Gardnerville, NV, p. A408
EASLEY, Mike, Vice President and Chief Operating Officer, Sabine County Hospital, Hemphill, TX, p. A624
EAST, Becky, CPA, Senior Vice President, Chief Financial Officer, Bronson Lakeview Hospital, Paw Paw, MI, p. A335
EAST, Stephen H, Chief Financial Officer, Thibodaux Regional Health System, Thibodaux, LA, p. A294
EASTBURG, Mark C., Ph.D., President and Chief Executive Officer, Pine Rest Christian Mental Health Services, Grand Rapids, MI, p. A328
EASTER, Susan, Chief Nursing Officer, Palacios Community Medical Center, Palacios, TX, p. A642
EASTERWOOD, Diane J, Human Resources Business Partner, Kaiser Permanente San Francisco Medical Center, San Francisco, CA, p. A91
EASTHOPE, Kerry, Area Finance Officer, Kaiser Permanente Antioch Medical Center, Antioch, CA, p. A55
EATON, Eric, Chief Executive Officer, Hillcrest Hospital Henryetta, Henryetta, OK, p. A513
EATON, Lisa J., R.N., Chief Nursing Officer, Grace Cottage Hospital, Townshend, VT, p. A672
EATON, Philip. Chief Executive Officer, Mountain West Medical Center, Tooele, UT, p. A670
EAVENSON, Steve, Vice President Finance, Trinity Health Grand Rapids Hospital, Grand Rapids, MI, p. A328
EAVES, Dan, Chief Executive Officer, Marshall Browning Hospital, Du Quoin, IL, p. A193
EBBETT, Patricia, Chief Human Resources Officer, Catawba Hospital, Catawba, VA, p. A674
EBELING, April, Chief Executive Officer, Amg Specialty Hospital–Lafayette, Lafayette, LA, p. A285
EBELTOFT, Perry, Chief Executive Officer, Encompass Health Rehabilitation Hospital of Murrieta, Murrieta, CA, p. A79
EBENAL, Shelley, Chief Executive Officer, Fairbanks Memorial Hospital, Fairbanks, AK, p. A28
EBERHARDT, Lisa, Chief Nursing Officer, Clark Fork Valley Hospital, Plains, MT, p. A394
EBERHARDT, Scott, MSN, R.N., Chief Nursing Officer, Pam Rehabilitation Hospital of Jupiter, Jupiter, FL, p. A136
EBERS, Layne, Director Human Resources and Marketing, Pike County Memorial Hospital, Louisiana, MO, p. A379
EBERSOLE, Nathan, Controller, Calhoun Liberty Hospital, Blountstown, FL, p. A126
EBERT, Larry W. Jr, Chief Executive Officer, Piedmont Eastside Medical Center, Snellville, GA, p. A171
EBERT, Meg, Administrator, Noxubee General Hospital, Macon, MS, p. A365
EBKE, Russell, M.D., Chief of Staff, Crete Area Medical Center, Crete, NE, p. A399
EBLIN, Steven E., Chief Executive Officer, UNC Health Rockingham, Eden, NC, p. A467
EBNER, Joseph, M.D., Chief Medical Officer, Speare Memorial Hospital, Plymouth, NH, p. A417
EBRIGHT, Brian, Chief Financial Officer, Holy Cross Hospital – Salt Lake, Salt Lake City, UT, p. A668
ECHAVARRIA, Jose A., Chief Executive Officer, Woodland Heights Medical Center, Lufkin, TX, p. A637
ECKELS, Dan, Chief Financial Officer, Washington Regional Medical System, Fayetteville, AR, p. A46
ECKENFELS, Dan, President, Mercy Jefferson Communities, Mercy Hospital Jefferson, Festus, MO, p. A375
ECKENFELS, Susan, Chief Financial Officer, Ste. Genevieve County Memorial Hospital, Ste Genevieve, MO, p. A387
ECKERT, Mary L., President and Chief Executive Officer, Lecom Health Millcreek Community Hospital, Erie, PA, p. A540
ECKLER, Patrick, Administrator, Villa Feliciana Medical Complex, Jackson, LA, p. A283
ECKMAN, Jonathan R., Medical Center Director, Veterans Affairs Maryland Health Care System–Baltimore Division, Baltimore, MD, p. A302
ECKSTEIN, Becca, Executive Director, Veritas Collaborative, Durham, NC, p. A467
ECKSTEIN, William, Chief Executive Officer and Chief Financial Officer, Columbus Specialty Hospital, Columbus, GA, p. A161
ECONOMIDES, Rachelle, R.N., Chief Executive Officer, Amg Specialty Hospital–Houma, Houma, LA, p. A283
EDALATI, David, M.D., Medical Director, Meadowbrook Rehabilitation Hospital, Gardner, KS, p. A249
EDDEY, Gary E, M.D., Medical Director, Matheny Medical And Educational Center, Peapack, NJ, p. A426
EDDINGTON, Paul, CPA, Affiliate Vice President and Chief Financial Officer, Jacksonville Memorial Hospital, Jacksonville, IL, p. A199
EDDINGTON, Tonya, Coordinator Human Resources, Select Specialty Hospital–Springfield, Springfield, MO, p. A387
EDDLEMAN, Patricia, Fiscal Officer, Heartland Behavioral Healthcare, Massillon, OH, p. A499
EDELMAN, Scott, Executive Director and Chief Executive Officer, Burke Rehabilitation Hospital, White Plains, NY, p. A462
EDELSTEIN, Tracy, MSN, R.N., Chief Nursing Officer, Wellington Regional Medical Center, Wellington, FL, p. A154
EDEN, Tina M, Director of Nursing, Virginia Gay Hospital, Vinton, IA, p. A244
EDENFIELD, Janet, Director Financial Services, Georgia Regional Hospital At Savannah, Savannah, GA, p. A171
EDENFIELD, Todd, R.N., Administrator, Houston Medical Center, Warner Robins, GA, p. A173
EDENS, Melanie, Chief Operating Officer, Nea Baptist Memorial Hospital, Jonesboro, AR, p. A48
EDGAR, Josep. H, Senior Vice President Operations, Wellspan Gettysburg Hospital, Gettysburg, PA, p. A540
EDGAR, JP, President, Jefferson County Hospital, Waurika, OK, p. A524
EDGAR, Nancy, Vice President Human Resources, Methodist Hospital, San Antonio, TX, p. A650
EDGAR, Steven, FACHE, President and Chief Executive Officer, Medical City Denton, Denton, TX, p. A614
EDGE, Jeffery, Chief Executive Officer, Ochsner Medical Center – Hancock, Bay Saint Louis, MS, p. A359
EDGE, Lee, Administrator, Louisiana Behavioral Health, Shreveport, LA, p. A292
EDGEWORTH, Mitchell C., President, Tristar Centennial Medical Center, Nashville, TN, p. A591
EDIN, Scott D, Vice President, Finance and Chief Financial Officer, Northfield Hospital And Clinics, Northfield, MN, p. A352
EDINGTON, Brent, Director Information Services, Pomerene Hospital, Millersburg, OH, p. A500
EDIS, Peter D., Chief Executive Officer, Mckenzie County Healthcare System, Watford City, ND, p. A483
EDLER, Susie, R.N., Chief Nursing Officer, Dallas Behavioral Healthcare Hospital, Desoto, TX, p. A614
EDMINSTER, Sue
 Vice President Human Resources, SSM Health Ripon Community Hospital, Ripon, WI, p. A721
 Vice President Human Resources, SSM Health St. Agnes Hospital – Fond Du Lac, Fond Du Lac, WI, p. A711
 Vice President Human Resources, SSM Health Waupun Memorial Hospital, Waupun, WI, p. A724
EDMISTEN, Cathy, R.N., FACHE, Chief Executive Officer, HCA Florida South Shore Hospital, Sun City Center, FL, p. A151
EDMONDS, Kelly, Chief Financial Officer, Western Maryland Hospital Center, Hagerstown, MD, p. A305
EDMONDSON, Bobby, Controller, Regional Rehabilitation Hospital, Phenix City, AL, p. A24
EDMONDSON, Cory, President and Chief Executive Officer, Peterson Health, Kerrville, TX, p. A632
EDMONDSON, James H., Chief Executive Officer, Hardin Medical Center, Savannah, TN, p. A592
EDMUNDS, Liza, Director Human Resources, Tennova Healthcare–Clarksville, Clarksville, TN, p. A581
EDNIE, Brent, M.D., Chief Medical Officer, Torrance State Hospital, Torrance, PA, p. A555
EDWARDS, Aaron, Chief Executive Officer, Lake Chelan Health, Chelan, WA, p. A688
EDWARDS, Angela Imelda, R.N., Chief Nurse Executive, NYC Health + Hospitals/Woodhull, New York, NY, p. A452
EDWARDS, Annette, Chief Financial Officer, Odessa Memorial Healthcare Center, Odessa, WA, p. A692
EDWARDS, Ashley, Chief Nursing Officer, Rome Health, Rome, NY, p. A458
EDWARDS, Becky, Manager Human Resources, Irwin County Hospital, Ocilla, GA, p. A169
EDWARDS, Bruce
 Vice President Human Resources, Heritage Valley Beaver, Beaver, PA, p. A535
 Vice President Human Resources, Sewickley Valley Hospital, (A Division of Valley Medical Facilities), Sewickley, PA, p. A555
EDWARDS, Chris
 M.D., Chief Medical Officer, Piedmont Columbus Regional Midtown, Columbus, GA, p. A161
 M.D., Chief Medical Officer, Piedmont Columbus Regional Northside, Columbus, GA, p. A161
EDWARDS, Dana, Controller, Encompass Health Rehabilitation Hospital of Savannah, Savannah, GA, p. A171
EDWARDS, David, Chief Executive Officer, Twelve Clans Unity Hospital, Winnebago, NE, p. A407
EDWARDS, Dennis, M.D., Vice President Medical Affairs, Chi Health Good Samaritan, Kearney, NE, p. A401
EDWARDS, Gordon, Chief Financial Officer, Akron Children's Hospital, Akron, OH, p. A484
EDWARDS, Gregg
 Chief People Officer, Asante Rogue Regional Medical Center, Medford, OR, p. A529
 Chief People Officer, Asante Three Rivers Medical Center, Grants Pass, OR, p. A527
 Vice President Human Resources, Asante Ashland Community Hospital, Ashland, OR, p. A525
EDWARDS, Heidi, Chief Nursing Officer, Charleston Area Medical Center, Charleston, WV, p. A700
EDWARDS, Jeff, Manager Information Services, Adventist Health Mendocino Coast, Fort Bragg, CA, p. A63
EDWARDS, Jonita, Director Human Resources, Dmc Children's Hospital of Michigan, Detroit, MI, p. A325
EDWARDS, Kathleen, Manager Information Systems Operation, Encompass Health Rehabilitation Hospital of Altoona, Altoona, PA, p. A534
EDWARDS, Lyndon C.
 Chief Operating Officer, Loma Linda University Children's Hospital, Loma Linda, CA, p. A70
 Chief Operating Officer, Loma Linda University Medical Center, Loma Linda, CA, p. A70
 Chief Operating Officer, Loma Linda University Medical Center–Murrieta, Murrieta, CA, p. A79
EDWARDS, Marti, MSN, R.N., Chief Nursing Officer, RML Specialty Hospital, Hinsdale, IL, p. A198
EDWARDS, Matt, Vice President Nursing Services and Chief Nursing Officer, Baptist Anderson Regional Medical Center, Meridian, MS, p. A366
EDWARDS, Michelle, Executive Vice President Information Technology, Prisma Health Baptist Hospital, Columbia, SC, p. A565
EDWARDS, Michelle E., Interim DCIO of Operations, Musc Health – Orangeburg, Orangeburg, SC, p. A569
EDWARDS, Nicki E, Ph.D., R.N., Interim Chief Nursing Officer, Sierra Vista Regional Medical Center, San Luis Obispo, CA, p. A93
EDWARDS, Rebecca, Chief Human Resources Officer, Penn Highlands Brookville, Brookville, PA, p. A535
EDWARDS, Rick, Vice President and Chief Financial Officer, Hancock Regional Hospital, Greenfield, IN, p. A218
EDWARDS, Robert
 Administrator, Unity Psych Care–Memphis, Memphis, TN, p. A589
 Chief Nursing Officer, Lakeside Behavioral Health System, Memphis, TN, p. A588
EDWARDS, Samuel, M.D., Chief of Staff, Adventhealth Deland, Deland, FL, p. A130
EDWARDS, Scott, Chief Operating Officer, Norton Scott Hospital, Scottsburg, IN, p. A227
EDWARDS, Susan, Vice President Human Resources, UVA Health Culpeper Medical Center, Culpeper, VA, p. A675
EDWARDS, Susan A.
 President and Chief Executive Officer, Prohealth Oconomowoc Memorial Hospital, Oconomowoc, WI, p. A718
 President and Chief Executive Officer, Prohealth Waukesha Memorial Hospital, Waukesha, WI, p. A723
EDWARDS, Theresa, R.N., Chief Nursing Officer, Kansas Spine & Specialty Hospital, Wichita, KS, p. A262
EDWARDS, Todd, Director Information Management Systems, Chi St. Luke's Health Brazosport, Lake Jackson, TX, p. A633
EDWARDS, William, Information Technology Generalist, Wernersville State Hospital, Wernersville, PA, p. A557
EGAN, Joseph, Vice President and Chief Informational Officer, Valley Children's Healthcare, Madera, CA, p. A76
EGAN, Timothy, President and Chief Executive Officer, Roseland Community Hospital, Chicago, IL, p. A190
EGBERT, Jeff, Interim Chief Executive Officer, Southeast Colorado Hospital District, Springfield, CO, p. A113
EGERTON, W Eugene, M.D., Chief Medical Officer, University of Maryland Medical Center Midtown Campus, Baltimore, MD, p. A301
EGGEN, Caity, Chief Human Resource Officer, Cuyuna Regional Medical Center, Crosby, MN, p. A345
EGGERS, Judy, Manager Human Resources, Alliance Healthcare System, Holly Springs, MS, p. A363
EGGLESTON, Brett, Chief Executive Officer, Callaway District Hospital, Callaway, NE, p. A398
EGGLESTON, Lara
 Finance Manager, University Hospitals Conneaut Medical Center, Conneaut, OH, p. A493
 Finance Manager, University Hospitals Geneva Medical Center, Geneva, OH, p. A496
EGGLESTON, Ryan, Chief Financial Officer, Desert View Hospital, Pahrump. NV, p. A412
EGYUD, Amber, R.N., Chief Nursing Officer and Chief Operating Officer, Chesapeake Regional Medical Center, Chesapeake, VA, p. A674

Index of Health Care Professionals / Elmblad

EHASZ, James, Chief Financial Officer, Copper Queen Community Hospital, Bisbee, AZ, p. A30
EHLER, Phyllis, Director Human Resources, Avera St. Benedict Health Center, Parkston, SD, p. A575
EHLERS, Jeffrey, Chief Financial Officer, Memorial Health, Marysville, OH, p. A499
EHLINGER, Forrest, System Chief Financial Officer, Benefis Health System, Great Falls, MT, p. A392
EHLKE, Ranae, Administrative Secretary and Coordinator Risk Management and Human Resources, Trinity Kenmare Community Hospital, Kenmare, ND, p. A482
EHLY, Ronda S, R.N., Chief Nursing Officer, Mary Lanning Healthcare, Hastings, NE, p. A400
EHN, Jerry, Chief Operating Officer, Northfield Hospital And Clinics, Northfield, MN, p. A352
EHN, Nicole, M.D., Chief of Staff, Van Diest Medical Center, Webster City, IA, p. A245
EHRAT, Michael, Chief Executive Officer, HCA Florida Fawcett Hospital, Port Charlotte, FL, p. A147
EHRICH, Laurie, Chief Communications Officer, Wayne County Hospital And Clinic System, Corydon, IA, p. A233
EHRLICH, Frank
M.D., Chief Medical Officer, Health Alliance Hospital – Broadway Campus, Kingston, NY, p. A445
M.D., Chief Medical Officer, Health Alliance Hospital – Mary's Avenue Campus, Kingston, NY, p. A445
EHRLICH, Susan P., M.D., Chief Executive Officer, Zuckerberg San Francisco General Hospital And Trauma Center, San Francisco, CA, p. A91
EHTISHAM, Saad, FACHE, Senior Vice President and President Novant Health Presbyterian Medical Center & Greater Charlotte Ma, Novant Health Presbyterian Medical Center, Charlotte, NC, p. A466
EICHER, Natasha, President and Chief Executive Officer, Parkview Dekalb Hospital, Auburn, IN, p. A212
EIDE, Tom, Chief Financial Officer, Prairie St. John's, Fargo, ND, p. A480
EIDE, Trevor, M.D., Chief Medical Officer, Frisbie Memorial Hospital, Rochester, NH, p. A417
EIG, Blair
M.D., Senior Vice President Medical Affairs, Holy Cross Hospital, Silver Spring, MD, p. A307
M.D., Vice President and Chief Medical Officer, Medical Affairs, Holy Cross Germantown Hospital, Germantown, MD, p. A304
EIKE, Gail, Chief Financial Officer, Sanford Jackson Medical Center, Jackson, MN, p. A348
EILBRACHT, Hans, Chief Information Officer, Hamilton Center, Terre Haute, IN, p. A228
EIMERS, Katy, Human Resources Officer, Syringa Hospital And Clinics, Grangeville, ID, p. A181
EIPE, Joseph, M.D., Chief Medical Officer, Pacifica Hospital of The Valley, Los Angeles, CA, p. A74
EISCHENS, Karla, Chief Executive Officer, Sanford Bemidji Medical Center, Bemidji, MN, p. A343
EISCHENS, Shelby, Chief Medical Officer, Brookings Health System, Brookings, SD, p. A572
EISELE, Karla, M.D., Clinical Director, State Hospital North, Orofino, ID, p. A183
EISEN, Robert A, Vice President Human Resources, Northern California Region, Providence Queen of The Valley Medical Center, Napa, CA, p. A79
EISENMANN, Claudia A., FACHE, President, Texas Health Harris Methodist Hospital Stephenville, Stephenville, TX, p. A654
EISMAN, Michael, M.D., Medical Director, Schuyler Hospital, Montour Falls, NY, p. A446
EITZEN, Tamara, Chief Nursing Officer, Fairview Regional Medical Center, Fairview, OK, p. A512
EKENGREN, Francie H, M.D., Chief Medical Officer, Wesley Medical Center, Wichita, KS, p. A262
EKEREN, Douglas R.
FACHE, Regional President and Chief Executive Officer, Avera Queen of Peace Hospital, Mitchell, SD, p. A575
FACHE, Regional President and Chief Executive Officer, Administration, Avera Sacred Heart Hospital, Yankton, SD, p. A578
EKUNDAYO, Adedayo, Ph.D., Director of Nursing, Bridgepoint Continuing Care Hospital – Capitol Hill, Washington, DC, p. A123
EL KHALILI, Nizar, M.D., Medical Director, Sycamore Springs, Lafayette, IN, p. A222
EL MUSSELMANI, Wafa, R.N., Chief Nursing Officer, East Los Angeles Doctors Hospital, Los Angeles, CA, p. A72
EL–DALATI, Sam, M.D., Chief Medical Officer, Mercy Health – Lorain Hospital, Lorain, OH, p. A498
EL–SOLH, Ali, M.D., Interim Chief of Staff, Veterans Affairs Western New York Healthcare System–Buffalo Division, Buffalo, NY, p. A440
ELAM, Lora, R.N., Chief Nursing Officer, Wayne County Hospital, Monticello, KY, p. A271
ELAM, Moses D, M.D., Physician–in–Chief, Kaiser Permanente Manteca Medical Center, Manteca, CA, p. A76
ELARBEE, Vernon, Director of Human Resources, Adventhealth North Pinellas, Tarpon Springs, FL, p. A153
ELBEN, Jordan, Director of Human Resources, St. Josep. Regional Medical Center, Lewiston, ID, p. A182
ELBERT, Darlene M., R.N., MS, Chief Executive Officer, Kossuth Regional Health Center, Algona, IA, p. A230
ELBERT, Lee, Chief Financial Officer, Franklin General Hospital, Hampton, IA, p. A237
ELDER, Beth, Chief Executive Officer, South Plains Rehabilitation Hospital, An Affiliate of Umc And Encompass Health, Lubbock, TX, p. A636
ELDER, Bruce, Information Technology, Breckinridge Memorial Hospital, Hardinsburg, KY, p. A266
ELDER, Deborah, Director Human Resources, Scenic Mountain Medical Center, Big Spring, TX, p. A603
ELDIDY, Rene, M.D., Chief of Staff, Centracare – Long Prairie, Long Prairie, MN, p. A349
ELDRED, Jamie, Controller, Klickitat Valley Health, Goldendale, WA, p. A690
ELDRIDGE, Donna, Chief Financial Officer, Richardson Medical Center, Rayville, LA, p. A291
ELDRIDGE, Janet, Director Human Resources and Personnel, Archbold Brooks, Quitman, GA, p. A169
ELDRIDGE, Jim, Area Financial Officer, Kaiser Permanente Sacramento Medical Center, Sacramento, CA, p. A86
ELDRIDGE, Laurie, Chief Financial Officer, Marshall Medical Center, Placerville, CA, p. A83
ELDRIDGE, Lisa, Human Resources Officer, Thomas H. Boyd Memorial Hospital, Carrollton, IL, p. A187
ELFERT, Mike, Director Information Services, Virtua Willingboro Hospital, Willingboro, NJ, p. A431
ELGARICO, David, Chief Executive Officer, Trios Health, Kennewick, WA, p. A690
ELIAS, Jose, Director Information Technology, Fort Duncan Regional Medical Center, Eagle Pass, TX, p. A615
ELICH, Elizabeth, Chief Human Resources Officer, Piedmont Medical Center, Rock Hill, SC, p. A570
ELIOT, Jason L, Vice President Human Resources, Integris Baptist Medical Center, Oklahoma City, OK, p. A517
ELKINGTON, Bruce, Regional Chief Information Officer, St. Clare Hospital, Lakewood, WA, p. A691
ELKINGTON, Mark, M.D., Chief Medical Officer, Willow Crest Hospital, Miami, OK, p. A515
ELKINS, Carl, Director Information Technology, Adventhealth Rollins Brook, Lampasas, TX, p. A633
ELKINS, Cindy, Chief Executive Officer, Lonesome Pine Hospital, Big Stone Gap. VA, p. A673
ELKINS, James N., FACHE, Director, Texas Center for Infectious Disease, San Antonio, TX, p. A651
ELKINS, Wendy, Director Operations, Dundy County Hospital, Benkelman, NE, p. A398
ELLEDGE, David, Controller, Select Specialty Hospital–North Knoxville, Powell, TN, p. A592
ELLEN, Jonathan D, M.D., Medical Director, Encompass Health Rehabilitation Hospital of Memphis, A Partner of Methodist Healthcare, Memphis, TN, p. A588
ELLENBURG, Cynthia, Director Health Information Services, Prisma Health Baptist Easley Hospital, Easley, SC, p. A565
ELLER, Bill, Director Information Technology, El Camp. Memorial Hospital, El Campo, TX, p. A616
ELLER, Melinda, Chief Executive Officer, Memorial Hermann Surgical Hospital Kingwood, Kingwood, TX, p. A633
ELLER, Steven M
Chief Human Resources Officer, Memorial Hospital of South Bend, South Bend, IN, p. A227
Vice President Human Resources, Elkhart General Hospital, Elkhart, IN, p. A215
ELLER, Troy, Chief Financial Officer, Guthrie County Hospital, Guthrie Center, IA, p. A237
ELLERSON, Thomas, Chief Information Officer, Guthrie Lourdes Hospital, Binghamton, NY, p. A439
ELLERT, William, M.D., Medical Director, Carondelet St. Mary's Hospital, Tucson, AZ, p. A40
ELLINGTON, Christopher, President and Chief Executive Officer, UNC Health Southeastern, Lumberton, NC, p. A472
ELLIOTT, Amy, M.D., Director Medical Affairs, Allina Health Faribault Medical Center, Faribault, MN, p. A346
ELLIOTT, Barb, Chief Financial Officer, Community Fairbanks Recovery Center, Indianapolis, IN, p. A219
ELLIOTT, Eric
Chief Financial Officer, Behavioral Health Center of Porter Village, Norman, OK, p. A515
Chief Financial Officer, Louisiana Behavioral Health, Shreveport, LA, p. A292
Chief Financial Officer, Oceans Behavioral Hospital of Amarillo, Amarillo, TX, p. A596
Chief Financial Officer, Oceans Behavioral Hospital of Lubbock, Lubbock, TX, p. A636
Chief Financial Officer, Oceans Behavioral Hospital of Tupelo, Tupelo, MS, p. A369
ELLIOTT, Jim
Director Human Resources, Bryce Hospital, Tuscaloosa, AL, p. A25
Director Human Resources, Mary's Harper Geriatric Psychiatry Center, Tuscaloosa, AL, p. A25
ELLIOTT, Kimberly, Chief Nursing Officer, Holy Cross Germantown Hospital, Germantown, MD, p. A304
ELLIOTT, Laura, Director Human Resources, Northeastern Nevada Regional Hospital, Elko, NV, p. A408
ELLIOTT, Lee Ann, R.N., Director of Nursing, Denton Rehab, Denton, TX, p. A613
ELLIOTT, Marlene L, MSN, R.N., Chief Nursing Officer, Coulee Medical Center, Grand Coulee, WA, p. A690
ELLIOTT, Michael
M.D., Chief Medical Officer and Senior Vice President of Medical Affairs, Avera Mckennan Hospital And University Health Center, Sioux Falls, SD, p. A576
Controller, Indianhead Medical Center, Shell Lake, WI, p. A721
ELLIOTT, R James, Vice President Human Resources, Charlotte Hungerford Hospital, Torrington, CT, p. A119
ELLIOTT, Randi, MSN, Chief Nursing Officer, Baylor Scott & White Medical Center–Frisco, Frisco, TX, p. A621
ELLIOTT, Rhonda M., Director Information Technology and Meaningful Use, Person Memorial Hospital, Roxboro, NC, p. A475
ELLIOTT, Robin, Personnel Officer, Community Memorial Hospital, Sumner, IA, p. A244
ELLIOTT, Shane, Associate Director Administration, Jerry L. Pettis Memorial Veterans' Hospital, Loma Linda, CA, p. A70
ELLIOTT, Wendy C., President, Ohiohealth Southeastern Medical Center, Cambridge, OH, p. A487
ELLIS, Amanda, Chief Financial Officer, Barbourville Arh Hospital, Barbourville, KY, p. A263
ELLIS, Angela, R.N., Chief Nursing Officer, Terre Haute Regional Hospital, Terre Haute, IN, p. A228
ELLIS, Cynthia, Chief Nursing Officer, Merit Health Rankin, Brandon, MS, p. A360
ELLIS, Deb
Director Human Resource, Stillwater Medical Blackwell, Blackwell, OK, p. A510
Director Human Resources, Stillwater Medical Perry, Perry, OK, p. A519
ELLIS, Kristin, Controller, Munson Healthcare Cadillac Hospital, Cadillac, MI, p. A323
ELLIS, Lisa, Chief Operating Officer, SSM Health St. Anthony Hospital – Midwest, Midwest City, OK, p. A515
ELLIS, Mark, Director Information Technology, Lakeview Hospital, Bountiful, UT, p. A664
ELLIS, Michael, M.D., Chief Medical Officer, The University of Toledo Medical Center, Toledo, OH, p. A505
ELLIS, Michael J., FACHE, Chief Executive Officer, SSM Health St. Anthony Hospital – Shawnee, Shawnee, OK, p. A520
ELLIS, Michelle, Director Human Resources, Whitman Hospital And Medical Center, Colfax, WA, p. A688
ELLIS, Mike, Chief Financial Officer, Lake Chelan Health, Chelan, WA, p. A688
ELLIS, Nichole, Chief Medical Officer, Hillsdale Hospital, Hillsdale, MI, p. A329
ELLIS, Richard, President, Vanderbilt Tullahoma Harton Hospital, Tullahoma, TN, p. A594
ELLIS, Scott, D.O., Chief Medical Officer, Memorial Regional Health, Craig, CO, p. A105
ELLIS, Tammy, FACHE, R.N., Vice President Patient Services, Texas Health Huguley Hospital Fort Worth South, Burleson, TX, p. A606
ELLIS, Thomas J, Vice President Human Resources, Mt. Washington Pediatric Hospital, Baltimore, MD, p. A301
ELLIS, Wendel, D.O., Chief Medical Staff, Greeley County Health Services, Tribune, KS, p. A261
ELLISON, Darcy, R.N., MSN, Senior Vice President, Chief Nursing Officer and Inpatient Flow, Ascension St. Vincent Evansville, Evansville, IN, p. A216
ELLISON, Keith, Chief Nursing Officer, Big Bend Regional Medical Center, Alpine, TX, p. A596
ELLISON, Mike, Information Systems Lead, Summersville Regional Medical Center, Summersville, WV, p. A705
ELLISON, Patricia, Chief Financial Officer, Wellstone Regional Hospital, Jeffersonville, IN, p. A221
ELLSWORTH, Anthon, Director Information Technology, Mt. Graham Regional Medical Center, Safford, AZ, p. A38
ELLWANGER, Dina
R.N., President and Chief Nursing Officer, Saint Alphonsus Medical Center – Ontario, Ontario, OR, p. A529
R.N., President, Eastern Oregon, Saint Alphonsus Medical Center – Baker City, Baker City, OR, p. A525
ELMBLAD, Tracey, Director of IT, Up Health System – Marquette, Marquette, MI, p. A333

Index of Health Care Professionals

Index of Health Care Professionals / Elmore

ELMORE, Kevin, Chief Information Officer, Covenant Hospital–Levelland, Levelland, TX, p. A634
ELROD, Emily
 R.N., Chief Nursing Officer, Ascension Saint Thomas Dekalb, Smithville, TN, p. A593
 R.N., Director of Nursing, Ascension Saint Thomas Stones River, Woodbury, TN, p. A594
ELROD, Keri, Administrator, Willis Knighton North, Shreveport, LA, p. A293
ELSESSER, William, Administrator, Noland Hospital Montgomery, Montgomery, AL, p. A23
ELSWICK, Beth, Administrative Assistant, Summers County Arh Hospital, Hinton, WV, p. A701
ELWELL, Richard, Senior Vice President and Chief Financial Officer, Elliot Hospital, Manchester, NH, p. A416
ELWELL, Russell, M.D., Medical Director, Westfield Memorial Hospital, Westfield, NY, p. A462
EMAMGHORAISHI, Anna, Human Resources, Inspire Specialty Hospital, Midwest City, OK, p. A515
EMANUEL, Kate, Director Human Resources, Clarke County Hospital, Osceola, IA, p. A241
EMANUEL, Sandra, Chief Executive Officer, Peak Behavioral Health Services, Santa Teresa, NM, p. A437
EMBREY, Jeffrey, M.D., Chief Medical Officer, Baylor Scott & White Medical Center–Irving, Irving, TX, p. A630
EMBREY, Richard, M.D., Chief Medical Officer, Augusta Health, Fishersville, VA, p. A676
EMBURY, Stuart, M.D., Chief Medical Officer, Phelp. Memorial Health Center, Holdrege, NE, p. A401
EMDUR, Larry, D.O., Chief Medical Officer, UC San Diego Health – East Campus, San Diego, CA, p. A90
EMERSON, Leah, Director of Nursing, St. Luke Community Healthcare, Ronan, MT, p. A395
EMERSON, Sherri Leigh, Chief Operating Officer, Texas Health Heart & Vascular Hospital Arlington, Arlington, TX, p. A598
EMERY, Andrew, Chief Executive Officer, Tennova Healthcare–Clarksville, Clarksville, TN, p. A581
EMERY, John
 President, Bon Secours Memorial Regional Medical Center, Mechanicsville, VA, p. A679
 President, Bon Secours Rappahannock General Hospital, Kilmarnock, VA, p. A678
EMGE, Joann, Chief Executive Officer, Sparta Community Hospital, Sparta, IL, p. A208
EMIG, Laura, Director Marketing Operations, Encompass Health Rehabilitation Hospital of York, York, PA, p. A558
EMMETT, Brett, Chief Operating Officer, Hendrick Medical Center Brownwood, Brownwood, TX, p. A605
EMMINGER, Dianne, Vice President Information Services, Acmh Hospital, Kittanning, PA, p. A543
EMPEY, Dennis, Chief Financial Officer, Trinity Kenmare Community Hospital, Kenmare, ND, p. A482
EMPEY, Nathan, Chief Finanial Officer, Utah Valley Hospital, Provo, UT, p. A667
ENCAPERA, Kimberly, M.D., Medical Director, Rehabilitation Hospital of Southern New Mexico, Las Cruces, NM, p. A435
ENCE, Michael, Computer Specialist, Sanpete Valley Hospital, Mount Pleasant, UT, p. A666
ENCKE, Faye, Director Information Management, Encompass Health Rehabilitation Hospital of Richmond, Richmond, VA, p. A682
ENDEN, Jay, M.D., Medical Director, South Shore University Hospital, Bay Shore, NY, p. A439
ENDERLE, Carol, R.N., MSN, President, Chi St. Alexius Health Dickinson, Dickinson, ND, p. A480
ENDOM, Beth W, R.N., MSN, Vice President and Chief Nursing Officer, South Central Regional Medical Center, Laurel, MS, p. A365
ENDSLEY, Scott, Chief Financial Officer, Fisher–Titus Medical Center, Norwalk, OH, p. A501
ENG, Jeffrey, M.D., Medical Director, Encompass Health Rehabilitation Hospital of Montgomery, Montgomery, AL, p. A22
ENGBERS, Jon, M.D., President, Hegg Health Center Avera, Rock Valley, IA, p. A242
ENGBRECHT, Chad, Chief Financial Officer, Alvarado Parkway Institute Behavioral Health System, La Mesa, CA, p. A68
ENGELKE, Brian, Chief Financial Officer, Community Hospital of Staunton, Staunton, IL, p. A209
ENGESSER, Edward, Chief Financial Officer and Chief Information Officer, Barlow Respiratory Hospital, Los Angeles, CA, p. A71
ENGFEHR, Tricia A, Chief Human Resources, Selby General Hospital, Marietta, OH, p. A499
ENGLAND, Dave, Director Human Resources, Lakeland Behavioral Health System, Springfield, MO, p. A386
ENGLAND, Leslie, Chief of Staff, Merit Health Natchez, Natchez, MS, p. A367
ENGLAND, Mary Ann, Chief Nurse Executive, Wilcox Medical Center, Lihue, HI, p. A177
ENGLAND, Richard N, Chief Financial Officer, Palo Verde Behavioral Health, Tucson, AZ, p. A40
ENGLAND, Teresa, R.N., Ph.D., Nurse Executive, Salem Veterans Affairs Medical Center, Salem, VA, p. A683
ENGLE, Dana E., Chief Executive Officer, Madison Health, London, OH, p. A498
ENGLE, Harold, R.N., Chief Executive Officer, The Physicians Centre Hospital, Bryan, TX, p. A605
ENGLE, Lisa, Director Information Technology, Texoma Medical Center, Denison, TX, p. A613
ENGLE, Sharon, Director Clinical Services, Noland Hospital Birmingham, Birmingham, AL, p. A17
ENGLEHART, Jay, M.D., Medical Director, Southeast Missouri Mental Health Center, Farmington, MO, p. A375
ENGLERTH, LaDonna, Administrator and Chief Executive Officer, East Carroll Parish Hospital, Lake Providence, LA, p. A287
ENGLISH, Anne L, Vice President Human Resources, Oneida Healthcare, Oneida, NY, p. A455
ENGLISH, Dennis, M.D., Vice President Medical Affairs, UPMC Magee–Womens Hospital, Pittsburgh, PA, p. A551
ENGLISH, Jeff, Vice President Human Resources, St. Mary's Health Care System, Athens, GA, p. A156
ENGLISH, Julene, Director Human Resources, Kentfield Hospital, Kentfield, CA, p. A68
ENGLISH, Kathy L, R.N., MSN, Executive Vice President and Chief Operating Officer, Children's Nebraska, Omaha, NE, p. A404
ENGLISH, Laurie, Senior Vice President and Chief Human Resource Officer, Excela Health Latrobe Hospital, Latrobe, PA, p. A544
ENGSTROM, Chad P, Director Human Resources, Westfields Hospital And Clinic, New Richmond, WI, p. A718
ENGSTROM, Frederick, M.D., Chief Medical Officer, Brattleboro Retreat, Brattleboro, VT, p. A671
ENJADY, Rainey, Administrative Officer, Mescalero Public Health Service Indian Hospital, Mescalero, NM, p. A436
ENNEN, Mark S, Director of Finance, HSHS Holy Family Hospital In Greenville, Greenville, IL, p. A196
ENNIS, Debra, Vice President and Chief Nursing Officer, Texas Health Harris Methodist Hospital Southlake, Southlake, TX, p. A653
ENNIS, Virgil, Chief Information Officer, Helen Hayes Hospital, West Haverstraw, NY, p. A461
ENOCHS, Darren, Director Human Resources, KPC Promise Hospital of Overland Park, Overland Park, KS, p. A257
ENOKA, Christina, Director Human Resources and Risk Management, Sutter Health Kahi Mohala, Ewa Beach, HI, p. A175
ENRICO–SIMON, Agnes, M.D., President Medical Staff, Rivers Health, Point Pleasant, WV, p. A704
ENRIQUEZ, Kelly
 President, Mease Hospitals, Mease Countryside Hospital, Safety Harbor, FL, p. A148
 President, Mease Hospitals, Mease Dunedin Hospital, Dunedin, FL, p. A130
ENSLEY, Terrasina, Director Human Resources, Fannin Regional Hospital, Blue Ridge, GA, p. A159
ENSMINGER, Jennifer, Chief Operating Officer, College Medical Center, Long Beach, CA, p. A70
ENSRUDE, Layne, Chief Financial Officer, First Care Health Center, Park River, ND, p. A483
ENTIN, Ari, Chief Information Officer, Natividad, Salinas, CA, p. A88
ENTLER, Paul, D.O., Medical Director, Sparrow Specialty Hospital, Lansing, MI, p. A331
ENTWISTLE, David, President and Chief Executive Officer, Stanford Health Care, Palo Alto, CA, p. A82
ENTZMINGER, Julie, Manager Human Resources, Chi Oakes Hospital, Oakes, ND, p. A483
EOLOFF, Eric, President, Mercy Washington, Mercy Hospital Washington, Washington, MO, p. A388
EPPERSON, Elysia, Director Human Resources, UT Health Jacksonville, Jacksonville, TX, p. A630
EPPERSON, Jeff, Chief Financial Officer, Millwood Hospital, Arlington, TX, p. A597
EPPERSON, Joel, M.D., Chief of Staff, Arkansas Methodist Medical Center, Paragould, AR, p. A52
EPPLER, Todd, FACHE, Chief Executive Officer, De Soto Regional Health System, Mansfield, LA, p. A288
EPPLEY, Colette, Chief Human Resource Officer, St. George Regional Hospital, Saint George, UT, p. A668
EPPS, Donna
 Vice President and Chief Human Resources Officer, Lawrence + Memorial Hospital, New London, CT, p. A118
 Vice President, Chief Human Resource Officer, Westerly Hospital, Westerly, RI, p. A561
EPPS, Michelle L., MSN, R.N., Chief Nursing Officer, Stonesprings Hospital Center, Dulles, VA, p. A675
EPSTEIN, Michael, M.D., Senior Vice President Medical Affairs, Johns Hopkins All Children's Hospital, Saint Petersburg, FL, p. A149
ERAAS, Jamie, President and Chief Executive Officer, Tioga Medical Center, Tioga, ND, p. A483
ERDMAN, Beth, Chief Financial Officer, Unitypoint Health Meriter, Madison, WI, p. A714
ERDMAN, Donja, Chief Financial Officer, Shoshone Medical Center, Kellogg, ID, p. A181
ERDMAN, John, M.D., Chief of Staff, Chi Memorial Hospital – Georgia, Fort Oglethorpe, GA, p. A164
ERDMANN, Chrissie, Executive Vice President Finance, Chief Financial Officer, Nch Baker Hospital, Naples, FL, p. A142
ERDMANN, Michael, M.D., Chief of Staff, Clement J. Zablocki Veterans' Administration Medical Center, Milwaukee, WI, p. A717
ERDOS, Joseph, M.D., Chief Information Officer, Veterans Affairs Connecticut Healthcare System, West Haven, CT, p. A120
EREMAN, Melissa, R.N., Chief Nursing Officer, Coleman County Medical Center, Coleman, TX, p. A607
ERGLE, Jeanine, Chief Financial Officer, Bay Pines Veterans Affairs Healthcare System, Bay Pines, FL, p. A125
ERICKSON, Brent J, Administrator, Wright Patterson Medical Center, Wright–Patterson Afb, OH, p. A507
ERICKSON, Doug, Chief Financial Officer, Prague Regional Memorial Hospital, Prague, OK, p. A520
ERICKSON, Jake
 Chief Executive Officer, Bingham Memorial Hospital, Blackfoot, ID, p. A179
 Chief Executive Officer, Grove Creek Medical Center, Blackfoot, ID, p. A179
ERICKSON, Karyn, Director Human Resources, Delta Specialty Hospital, Memphis, TN, p. A588
ERICKSON, Laura, R.N., Chief Nursing Officer, Logan Health – Conrad, Conrad, MT, p. A390
ERICKSON, Melissa, R.N., Chief Nursing Officer, Black River Memorial Hospital, Black River Falls, WI, p. A708
ERICKSON, Michael
 Northern Region President, Mymichigan Medical Center Saginaw, Saginaw, MI, p. A337
 Northern Region President, Mymichigan Medical Center Standish, Standish, MI, p. A338
 Northern Region President, Mymichigan Medical Center Tawas, Tawas City, MI, p. A339
ERICKSON, Nancy
 Administrator Information Systems, Kossuth Regional Health Center, Algona, IA, p. A230
 Human Resource Director, Southern Inyo Healthcare District, Lone Pine, CA, p. A70
ERICKSON, Robert J.
 Market President and Chief Executive Officer and President and Chief Executive Officer, HSHS St. Mary's Hospital Medical Center, Green Bay, WI, p. A712
 Market President and Chief Executive Officer and President and Chief Executive Officer, HSHS St. Vincent Hospital, Green Bay, WI, p. A712
ERICKSON, Ty
 Chief Administrative Officer, Marshfield Medical Center – Minocqua, Minocqua, WI, p. A717
 Chief Administrative Officer, Marshfield Medical Center – Park Falls, Park Falls, WI, p. A719
ERICKSON, Vonnie, Human Resource Manager, Ccm Health, Montevideo, MN, p. A351
ERICSON, Allen
 Chief Executive Officer, Froedtert Community Hospital – New Berlin, New Berlin, WI, p. A718
 Chief Operating Officer, Community Hospital Division and President, St. Joseph's Hospital, Froedtert Menomonee Falls Hospital, Menomonee Falls, WI, p. A716
 President, Froedtert Community Hospital – New Berlin, New Berlin, WI, p. A718
 President, Froedtert West Bend Hospital, West Bend, WI, p. A724
ERICSON, Bob, Chief Financial Officer, Hemphill County Hospital District, Canadian, TX, p. A606
ERIXON, Stephen M, Chief Executive Officer, Sagewest Health Care, Riverton, WY, p. A728
ERKEN, Carole L, Human Resources Leader, Kaiser Permanente Panorama City Medical Center, Los Angeles, CA, p. A73
ERLANDSON, Lesley, Human Resources Manager, Jamestown Regional Medical Center, Jamestown, ND, p. A482
ERMANN, William, Chief Executive Officer, Madison Parish Hospital, Tallulah, LA, p. A293
ERNST, William E. Jr, Chief Executive Officer, Allegiance Behavioral Health Center of Plainview, Plainview, TX, p. A644

Index of Health Care Professionals / Ewing

Index of Health Care Professionals

ERTEL, Matthew, Chief Financial Officer, Gibson Area Hospital And Health Services, Gibson City, IL, p. A196
ERUKHIMOU, Jeffrey, M.D., Medical Director, Pam Health Specialty Hospital of Heritage Valley, Beaver, PA, p. A535
ERVIN, Paul D., Interim Chief Financial Officer, Mena Regional Health System, Mena, AR, p. A50
ERVIN, Richard, Chief Financial Officer, HCA Houston Healthcare Tomball, Tomball, TX, p. A658
ERVING–MENGEL, Tammi, R.N., MSN, Vice President, Chief Nursing Officer, Atrium Health Wake Foret Baptist High Point Medical Center, High Point, NC, p. A470
ERWAY, Robert, Director for Administration, Bronx Psychiatric Center, New York, NY, p. A447
ERWIN, Connie, Manager, Samaritan Lebanon Community Hospital, Lebanon, OR, p. A528
ERWIN, Dennise, Chief Executive Officer, Horizon Medical Center, Llc, Denton, TX, p. A613
ERWIN, Patricia, R.N., Chief Nursing Officer, Oakdale Community Hospital, Oakdale, LA, p. A290
ESCANDON, Christy, R.N., Chief Nursing Officer, Lovelace Regional Hospital – Roswell, Roswell, NM, p. A436
ESCHENBRENNER, Wade
Chief Financial Officer, Lexington Regional Health Center, Lexington, NE, p. A401
Interim Chief Executive Officer, Lexington Regional Health Center, Lexington, NE, p. A401
ESCOBAR, Carlos R., FACHE, Director, Veterans Affairs Caribbean Healthcare System, San Juan, PR, p. A736
ESFAHANI, Reza, M.D., Medical Director, Reunion Rehabilitation Hospital Denver, Denver, CO, p. A107
ESHLEMAN, James, D.O., President Medical Staff, Mainehealth Stephens Hospital, Norway, ME, p. A298
ESLAVA, Lee, Chief Medical Officer, South Baldwin Regional Medical Center, Foley, AL, p. A19
ESPARZA, Becky, Human Resources, Crane Memorial Hospital, Crane, TX, p. A609
ESPARZA, Caroline
R.N., Senior Vice President, Chief Operating Officer and Chief Nurse Officer, Adventist Health Simi Valley, Simi Valley, CA, p. A96
R.N., Sr. VP, COO & CNO, Adventist Health Simi Valley, Simi Valley, CA, p. A96
ESPARZA, Ernesto, MSN, Director of Nursing, Cottonwood Creek Behavioral Hospital, Meridian, ID, p. A182
ESPARZA, Nathan, Chief Financial Officer, Abrazo Scottsdale Campus, Phoenix, AZ, p. A35
ESPARZA, Rachael, Human Resource Coordinator, Hill Regional Hospital, Hillsboro, TX, p. A624
ESPELAND, Darryl
D.O., Chief Medical Staff, Fallon Medical Complex, Baker, MT, p. A389
D.O., Medical Director, Dahl Memorial Healthcare Association, Ekalaka, MT, p. A391
ESPELAND, David, Chief Executive Officer, Fallon Medical Complex, Baker, MT, p. A389
ESPINA, Francisco, Director Finance, Hospital Pavia–Santurce, San Juan, PR, p. A735
ESPINOLA, Trina, M.D., Chief Medical Officer, Bayfront Health St. Petersburg, Saint Petersburg, FL, p. A148
ESPINOZA, Judy, Chief Human Resources Officer, Ascension Via Christi St. Francis, Mulvane, KS, p. A255
ESPINOZA, Richard, Chief Administrative Officer, Highland Hospital, Oakland, CA, p. A80
ESPOSITO, Anthony, President, Crozer–Chester Medical Center, Upland, PA, p. A556
ESPOSITO, Mary H, Assistant Executive Director, Devereux Advanced Behavioral Health Georgia, Kennesaw, GA, p. A166
ESPOSITO, Pamela, Director Administration, Buffalo Psychiatric Center, Buffalo, NY, p. A440
ESPY, Christine, Division Director, Adventist Health Columbia Gorge, The Dalles, OR, p. A532
ESQUIVEL, Carmen P, R.N., Chief Nursing Officer, Dimmit Regional Hospital, Carrizo Springs, TX, p. A606
ESROCK, Brett A.
Chief Executive Officer, Health First Holmes Regional Medical Center, Melbourne, FL, p. A139
President, Health First Cap. Canaveral Hospital, Cocoa Beach, FL, p. A128
President, Health First Palm Bay Hospital, Palm Bay, FL, p. A145
President, Health First Viera Hospital, Melbourne, FL, p. A139
ESSELMAN, Charlotte, Director Finance, Marshfield Medical Center – Weston, Weston, WI, p. A725
ESSMYER, Dale, M.D., Chief of Staff, Sullivan County Memorial Hospital, Milan, MO, p. A380
ESTAY, Mike, Chief Financial Officer, Hood Memorial Hospital, Amite, LA, p. A276
ESTES, Benton D, Materials Management, Baptist Medical Center – Yazoo, Yazoo City, MS, p. A370
ESTES, Jessica, Chief Executive Officer, Cumberland Hall Hospital, Hopkinsville, KY, p. A267
ESTES, Mary, Director Information Systems, St. Luke's Des Peres Hospital, Saint Louis, MO, p. A386
ESTES, Stephen A., Chief Executive Officer, Rockcastle Regional Hospital And Respiratory Care Center, Mount Vernon, KY, p. A272
ESTEVEZ, Aurora, M.D., Chief Medical Officer, Texas Health Presbyterian Hospital Dallas, Dallas, TX, p. A612
ESTRADA, Jack, Chief Administrative Officer, Peacehealth Peace Island Medical Center, Friday Harbor, WA, p. A690
ESTRIDGE, Christopher J., Commander, U. S. Air Force Medical Center Keesler, Keesler Afb, MS, p. A364
ETCHASON, Barbara, HR Manager, West Gables Rehabilitation Hospital, Miami, FL, p. A141
ETCITTY, Ronnye, Director Human Resources, Rehoboth Mckinley Christian Health Care Services, Gallup, NM, p. A434
ETHERIDGE, Darold, Vice President and Chief Financial Officer, Wellstar Cobb Hospital, Austell, GA, p. A159
ETHRIDGE, Sandy, Interim Chief Operating Officer, Baptist Medical Center, San Antonio, TX, p. A648
ETTER, Carl J., Chief Executive Officer, Scripp. Memorial Hospital–La Jolla, La Jolla, CA, p. A68
ETTESTAD, Donita, R.N., MS, Chief Nursing Officer, Rainy Lake Medical Center, International Falls, MN, p. A348
ETZEL, Glen T., M.D., Chief of Staff, Castleview Hospital, Price, UT, p. A667
ETZLER, Randal M., Chief Human Resources Officer, Yuma Regional Medical Center, Yuma, AZ, p. A42
EUBANKS, Bill, Senior Vice President and Chief Information Officer, University Medical Center, Lubbock, TX, p. A636
EUBANKS, Trey, M.D., President, Methodist Healthcare Memphis Hospitals, Memphis, TN, p. A589
EULIARTE, Mary Ann
R.N., Chief Nursing Officer, Memorial Hermann Rehabilitation Hospital – Katy, Katy, TX, p. A631
R.N., Chief Operating Officer, Memorial Hermann Rehabilitation Hospital – Katy, Katy, TX, p. A631
EUSTACE, Scott, Director Health Information Technology, Trenton Psychiatric Hospital, Trenton, NJ, p. A429
EVANCHO, Timothy R., Chief Financial Officer, Ohiohealth Southeastern Medical Center, Cambridge, OH, p. A487
EVANDER, Justin N., Chief Financial Officer, Kaiser Sunnyside Medical Center, Clackamas, OR, p. A526
EVANS, Brian G., FACHE, Chief Executive Officer, Clarke County Hospital, Osceola, IA, p. A241
EVANS, Cindy, R.N., MS, Chief Nursing Officer, Legacy Good Samaritan Medical Center, Portland, OR, p. A530
EVANS, Dave, Chief Financial Officer, Community Hospital of San Bernardino, San Bernardino, CA, p. A88
EVANS, Dwight, M.D., Chief of Staff, Jerry L. Pettis Memorial Veterans' Hospital, Loma Linda, CA, p. A70
EVANS, Eric
Chief Executive Officer, Corpus Christi Medical Center – Doctors Regional, Corpus Christi, TX, p. A609
Chief Executive Officer, Sky Ridge Medical Center, Lone Tree, CO, p. A111
EVANS, George, Vice President and Chief Information Officer, Candler Hospital–Savannah, Savannah, GA, p. A170
EVANS, Heath, President and Chief Executive Officer, Kingman Regional Medical Center, Kingman, AZ, p. A32
EVANS, Janice, Chief Financial Officer, John J. Madden Mental Health Center, Hines, IL, p. A198
EVANS, Jeff W., Vice President Information and Technology, Hannibal Regional Hospital, Hannibal, MO, p. A376
EVANS, Jeremy, Vice President Operations, Kootenai Health, Coeur D'Alene, ID, p. A180
EVANS, Kari, Chief Operating Officer, Grant Memorial Hospital, Petersburg, WV, p. A703
EVANS, Lagina Sheffield., R.N., Chief Executive Officer, Optim Medical Center – Screven, Sylvania, GA, p. A172
EVANS, Lola, Director of Nursing, Surgeons Choice Medical Center, Southfield, MI, p. A338
EVANS, Lorrie, Director Human Resources, Laurel Oaks Behavioral Health Center, Dothan, AL, p. A18
EVANS, Melinda S
Vice President Finance, Chi Saint Josep. Health – Saint Josep. East, Lexington, KY, p. A268
Vice President Finance, Chi Saint Josep. Health, Lexington, KY, p. A268
EVANS, Michael C., Chief Executive Officer and Deputy Director of Finance and Administration, Santa Barbara County Psychiatric Health Facility, Santa Barbara, CA, p. A94
EVANS, Michelle, Administrator, Elgin Mental Health Center, Elgin, IL, p. A194
EVANS, Ronald A., M.D., Chief Medical Officer, Citizens Memorial Hospital, Bolivar, MO, p. A371
EVANS, Sam, Chief Human Resources Management, G.V. (Sonny) Montgomery Department of Veterans Affairs Medical Center, Jackson, MS, p. A364
EVANS, Scott
PharmD, Senior Vice President and Market Chief Executive Officer, Sharp HealthCare Regional Hospitals, Sharp Grossmont Hospital, La Mesa, CA, p. A68
PharmD, Senior Vice President/Market Chief Executive Officer, Sharp HealthCare Regional Hospitals, Sharp Chula Vista Medical Center, Chula Vista, CA, p. A59
PharmD, Senior Vice President/Market Chief Executive Officer, Sharp HealthCare Regional Hospitals, Sharp Coronado Hospital, Coronado, CA, p. A60
EVANS, Susan, Chief Nursing Officer, Old Vineyard Behavioral Health Services, Winston–Salem, NC, p. A478
EVANS, Tim, Assistant Financial Director, Devereux Children's Behavioral Health Center, Malvern, PA, p. A545
EVANS, Timothy, Vice President and Chief Financial Officer, Self Regional Healthcare, Greenwood, SC, p. A567
EVANS–HARRISON, Martina, R.N., MSN, Chief Nurse Executive, Methodist Hospital of Sacramento, Sacramento, CA, p. A87
EVE, John, Vice President Human Resources and Education, Wilson Memorial Hospital, Sidney, OH, p. A503
EVELIUS, Karen, Director Human Resources, Medstar Harbor Hospital, Baltimore, MD, p. A301
EVELY, James C., President, Methodist Mckinney Hospital, Mckinney, TX, p. A638
EVELYN, David M, M.D., Vice President Medical Affairs, Cayuga Medical Center At Ithaca, Ithaca, NY, p. A444
EVENS, James, Executive Director, Human Resources and General Services, UPMC Cole, Coudersport, PA, p. A537
EVENSON, Margie, Manager Human Resources, Osceola Medical Center, Osceola, WI, p. A719
EVERDING, Dawn
Chief Hospital Administrator and Chief Financial Officer, Community Memorial Hospital, Sumner, IA, p. A244
Chief Hospital Administrator/Chief Financial Officer, Community Memorial Hospital, Sumner, IA, p. A244
EVERETT, Happy, Chief Nursing Officer, Roper St. Francis Mount Pleasant Hospital, Mount Pleasant, SC, p. A568
EVERETT, John, Chief Financial Officer, Cogdell Memorial Hospital, Snyder, TX, p. A653
EVERETT, Michael, Chief Executive Officer, Taylor Regional Hospital, Campbellsville, KY, p. A264
EVERETT, Neil, Vice President Human Resources, University Hospitals Portage Medical Center, Ravenna, OH, p. A503
EVERETT, Stephanie, Chief Executive Officer, Mountrail County Medical Center, Stanley, ND, p. A483
EVERHART, Martin S, Senior Vice President Human Resources, Robert Wood Johnson University Hospital, New Brunswick, NJ, p. A425
EVERLY, Nanette, Manager Human Resources and Administrative Assistant, Jefferson County Health Center, Fairfield, IA, p. A236
EVERS, Andrea, Director Information Technology, Haxtun Hospital District, Haxtun, CO, p. A109
EVERT, Barbara
M.D., Vice President Medical Affairs, Ohiohealth Dublin Methodist Hospital, Dublin, OH, p. A495
M.D., Vice President Medical Affairs, Ohiohealth Grady Memorial Hospital, Delaware, OH, p. A494
EVINS, Starling C, M.D., Chief of Staff, Williamson Medical Center, Franklin, TN, p. A583
EVISCHI, Deland, Regional Chief Financial Officer, Southern Illinois, SSM Health Good Samaritan Hospital, Mount Vernon, IL, p. A202
EVOLGA, Nancy K, Director Human Resources, Adventhealth New Smyrna Beach, New Smyrna Beach, FL, p. A142
EWALD, Ronald, Chief Financial Officer, Inova Fairfax Medical Campus, Falls Church, VA, p. A676
EWELL, Dorene L, Director of Human Resources and Development, Harrisburg Medical Center, Harrisburg, IL, p. A197
EWELL, Sandy, Chief Nursing Officer, Timpanogos Regional Hospital, Orem, UT, p. A667
EWING, Brenda, Chief Information Officer, Cleveland Emergency Hospital, Humble, TX, p. A629
EWING, Catherine, M.D., Chief Nursing Officer, Baylor Scott & White Institute for Rehabilitation–Fort Worth, Fort Worth, TX, p. A619
EWING, Hella, R.N., Vice President Patient Care Services and Chief Nursing Officer, East Tennessee Children's Hospital, Knoxville, TN, p. A585
EWING, Reginald S. III, Commanding Officer, Naval Hospital Camp Lejeune, Camp Lejeune, NC, p. A464
EWING, Steven, Chief Financial Officer, Medical Center Health System, Odessa, TX, p. A642
EWING, Thomas
Director Information Technology, Sentara Careplex Hospital, Hampton, VA, p. A677
Director Information Technology, Sentara Northern Virginia Medical Center, Woodbridge, VA, p. A685

Index of Health Care Professionals

Index of Health Care Professionals / Exline

EXLINE, Kathleen, R.N., Chief Administrative Officer, Norton Clark Hospital, Jeffersonville, IN, p. A221
EXLINE, Michael
Chief Financial Officer, Carrus Rehabilitation Hospital, Sherman, TX, p. A653
Chief Financial Officer, Carrus Specialty Hospital, Sherman, TX, p. A653
EYE, Jeffrey L, R.N., MSN, Vice President Patient Care Services, Murray–Calloway County Hospital, Murray, KY, p. A272
EYLER, Sandra, MS, Chief Nursing Officer, Sheltering Arms Institute, Midlothian, VA, p. A679
EZZIE, Michael, Director of Medical Education and Interim Vice President of Medical Affairs, Ohiohealth Grant Medical Center, Columbus, OH, p. A492

F

FABER, Chris, Human Resources Analyst, Stanford Health Care Tri–Valley, Pleasanton, CA, p. A83
FABER, Tammy, Director Human Resources, Hegg Health Center Avera, Rock Valley, IA, p. A242
FABIAN, Alan J., Chief Executive Officer, Lewisgale Medical Center, Boones Mill, VA, p. A674
FABIANO, Tom, Director Human Resources, Mount Auburn Hospital, Cambridge, MA, p. A312
FABIN, Peggy, Director Human Resources, Phillip. County Health Systems, Phillipsburg, KS, p. A258
FABRICK, Peter, Vice President Clinical Operations, Mountain View Hospital, Idaho Falls, ID, p. A181
FABRY, Joseph, D.O., Chief of Staff, Sutter Maternity And Surgery Center of Santa Cruz, Santa Cruz, CA, p. A94
FACKRELL, Sherlyn, Finance Controller, Grover C. Dils Medical Center, Caliente, NV, p. A408
FADALE, Sean, FACHE, President and Chief Executive Officer, Nathan Littauer Hospital And Nursing Home, Gloversville, NY, p. A443
FADLER, Jeannie, R.N., Vice President Patient Care Services, Saint Francis Medical Center, Cap. Girardeau, MO, p. A372
FAERBER, Craig, Interim Chief Financial Officer, Memorial Hospital At Gulfport, Gulfport, MS, p. A362
FAGAN, Erin, Manager Human Resources, George Washington University Hospital, Washington, DC, p. A123
FAGAN, Mary, MSN, R.N., Chief Nursing Officer, Rady Children's Hospital – San Diego, San Diego, CA, p. A89
FAGBONGBE, Eniola, M.D., Chief Medical Staff, Grove Hill Memorial Hospital, Grove Hill, AL, p. A20
FAGERBERG, Lesley, Vice President Fiscal Services, Heart of The Rockies Regional Medical Center, Salida, CO, p. A113
FAGERSTROM, Joel, Executive Vice President and Chief Operating Officer, St. Luke's Hospital–Miners Campus, Coaldale, PA, p. A537
FAGG, Cindy, Fiscal Officer, Battle Mountain General Hospital, Battle Mountain, NV, p. A408
FAHEY, Dana, Manager Management Information Systems, Santa Barbara County Psychiatric Health Facility, Santa Barbara, CA, p. A94
FAHEY, Stephen P, Executive Director, Sierra Tucson, Tucson, AZ, p. A41
FAHEY, Stephen P., Chief Executive Officer, Arbour Hospital, Boston, MA, p. A309
FAHEY, Walter, Chief Information Officer, Maimonides Medical Center, New York, NY, p. A449
FAHN, J'Patrick, D.O., Chief Medical Officer, Chi St. Alexius Health Bismarck, Bismarck, ND, p. A479
FAIN, Nona, Ph.D., R.N., Director of Nursing, Belmont Behavioral Health System, Philadelphia, PA, p. A548
FAIRBANKS, Bruce, Vice President and Chief Financial Officer, Mercy Hospital Southeast, Cap. Girardeau, MO, p. A372
FAIRBANKS, Patricia J
R.N., Vice President, Chief Nursing Officer, Endeavor Health Edward Hospital, Naperville, IL, p. A203
R.N., Vice President, Chief Nursing Officer, Endeavor Health Linden Oaks Hospital, Naperville, IL, p. A203
FAIRCHILD, David, M.D., Chief Medical Officer, Tufts Medical Center, Boston, MA, p. A311
FAIRFAX, Tom, Director Information Systems, Bothwell Regional Health Center, Sedalia, MO, p. A386
FAIRFAX, Walter, M.D., Chief Medical Officer, Kootenai Health, Coeur D'Alene, ID, p. A180
FAIRLEY, Dawn Ann, M.D., Chief of Staff, Putnam County Memorial Hospital, Unionville, MO, p. A388
FAIRLEY, Michelle, R.N., Chief Nursing Officer, Iroquois Memorial Hospital And Resident Home, Watseka, IL, p. A210
FAISON–CLARK, Lauren, Chief Executive Officer, Doctors' Memorial Hospital, Perry, FL, p. A147
FALCONE, Lynn, Chief Executive Officer, Cuero Regional Hospital, Cuero, TX, p. A610
FALGOUT, Charlene, Chief Nursing Officer, Sagewest Health Care, Riverton, WY, p. A728
FALIVENA, Richard, D.O., M.P.H., Vice President and Chief Medical Officer, Saratoga Hospital, Saratoga Springs, NY, p. A458
FALK, Chelsie, Chief Executive Officer, Sanford Wheaton Medical Center, Wheaton, MN, p. A357
FALKENBERRY, Jody, Director Information Systems, Monroe County Hospital, Monroeville, AL, p. A22
FALLIS, Susan, Chief Nursing Officer, Buffalo Psychiatric Center, Buffalo, NY, p. A440
FALLON, Laurence, JD, JD, Executive Vice President, Chief Legal and Human Resources Officer, Carle Foundation Hospital, Urbana, IL, p. A210
FALTERMAN, James B, M.D., Jr, Medical Director, Ochsner University Hospital & Clinics, Lafayette, LA, p. A286
FANALE, Linda, Chief Financial Officer, Conemaugh Miners Medical Center, Hastings, PA, p. A541
FANKHAUSER, John, M.D., Chief Executive Officer, Ventura County Medical Center, Ventura, CA, p. A100
FANNIN, Allyson, Human Resources Officer, Lasalle General Hospital, Jena, LA, p. A284
FANTANO, Gene, Chief Financial Officer, Aurora Behavioral Healthcare San Diego, San Diego, CA, p. A88
FARAH, Katie, M.D., Chief Medical Officer, AHN Wexford Hospital, Wexford, PA, p. A557
FARAH, Tony, M.D., President Medical Staff, Allegheny General Hospital, Pittsburgh, PA, p. A551
FARANO, Cynthia, Director Human Resources and Compliance Officer, Wills Eye Hospital, Philadelphia, PA, p. A550
FARBER, Benjamin, R.N., Vice President, Patient Care and Chief Nursing Officer, Eisenhower Health, Rancho Mirage, CA, p. A84
FARBER, Bobbi, M.D., Chief Medical Officer, St. Francis – Emory Healthcare, Columbus, GA, p. A161
FARBER, Stephen D., Chief Financial Officer, Kindred Hospital–New Jersey Morris County, Dover, NJ, p. A420
FARBERMAN, Daniel, Director Human Resource, Wyoming County Community Hospital, Warsaw, NY, p. A461
FARELL, Clay, Chief Executive Officer, St. Francis Medical Center, Lynwood, CA, p. A76
FARGASON, Crayton A, M.D., Medical Director, Children's of Alabama, Birmingham, AL, p. A16
FARGUSON, Jack, Director Information Technology, TMC Bonham Hospital, Bonham, TX, p. A604
FARINA, Albert M, Chief Financial Officer, Montefiore Mount Vernon, Mount Vernon, NY, p. A446
FARINA, Jonathan, Chief Information Officer, Brattleboro Memorial Hospital, Brattleboro, VT, p. A671
FARKAS, Laura, Director Human Resources, Fairview Hospital, Great Barrington, MA, p. A314
FARMER, Crystal, MSN, R.N., FACHE, Chief Operating Officer and Chief Nursing Officer, Augusta Health, Fishersville, VA, p. A676
FARMER, Pat, Coordinator Human Resources and Safety Officer, Institute for Orthopaedic Surgery, Lima, OH, p. A498
FARMER, Troye, Hospital Administrator, Cimarron Memorial Hospital, Boise City, OK, p. A510
FARMER, William, M.D., Chief of Staff, Evergreen Medical Center, Evergreen, AL, p. A19
FARNHAM, Diane, Acting Director Human Resources, Lallie Kemp Medical Center, Independence, LA, p. A283
FARNHAM, Krista, Chief Executive, Providence Portland Medical Center, Portland, OR, p. A530
FARO, Joan, M.D., Chief Medical Officer, Mather Hospital, Port Jefferson, NY, p. A456
FAROOQUI, Sana, Chief Operating Officer, Spring Hospital, Spring, TX, p. A654
FARR, Lorraine, Manager Human Resources, Georgia Regional Hospital At Atlanta, Decatur, GA, p. A162
FARR, Ronald, Chief Financial Officer, Uofl Health – Jewish Hospital, Louisville, KY, p. A270
FARR, William L, M.D., Chief Medical Officer, Piedmont Augusta, Augusta, GA, p. A158
FARRAGE, Jim, M.D., Medical Director, Southern Kentucky Rehabilitation Hospital, Bowling Green, KY, p. A263
FARRAND, Cynthia B, President, Cone Health Moses Cone Hospital, Greensboro, NC, p. A469
FARRELL, Brenda, Vice President Finance, Long Island Community Hospital, Patchogue, NY, p. A455
FARRELL, Coleen M, Vice President Human Resources, Mid Coast Hospital, Brunswick, ME, p. A296
FARRELL, Darin, Chief Executive Officer, Weatherford Regional Hospital, Weatherford, OK, p. A524
FARRELL, George, M.D., Chief Medical Officer, Clinch Valley Medical Center, Richlands, VA, p. A682
FARRELL, Mike, Interim President, Advocate Christ Medical Center, Oak Lawn, IL, p. A204
FARRELL, Roy, M.D., Chief Medical Officer, Carondelet Holy Cross Hospital, Nogales, AZ, p. A34
FARRELL, Steven E, M.D., Chief Medical Officer, Forrest General Hospital, Hattiesburg, MS, p. A363
FARRELL, Terence, President, Mercy Hospital Ada, Ada, OK, p. A509
FARRELL, Teresa, Chief Human Resources Officer, Nacogdoches Medical Center, Nacogdoches, TX, p. A640
FARRELLY, Irene, Vice President and Chief Information Officer, Brooklyn Hospital Center, New York, NY, p. A447
FARRER, Brandy H, R.N., Chief Nursing Officer, Medical City Denton, Denton, TX, p. A614
FARRINGTON, Robyn, Chief Nursing Officer, Broward Health Medical Center, Fort Lauderdale, FL, p. A131
FARRIS, Jason, Chief Nursing Officer, Inspire Specialty Hospital, Midwest City, OK, p. A515
FARRIS, Michelle, Chief Nursing Officer, HCA Florida Osceola Hospital, Kissimmee, FL, p. A136
FARRISH, John, Health Information Director, University of Mississipp. Medical Center Grenada, Grenada, MS, p. A362
FARROW, Rachel, Administrator, Seiling Municipal Hospital, Seiling, OK, p. A520
FARWELL, Brenda
Director Human Resources, Providence Medical Center, Kansas City, KS, p. A252
Director Human Resources, Saint John Hospital, Leavenworth, KS, p. A253
FASANO, Philip. Chief Information Officer, Kaiser Permanente Sacramento Medical Center, Sacramento, CA, p. A86
FASHINA, Olawale, M.D., Chief of Staff, Central Texas Veterans Hcs/Temple Tx, Temple, TX, p. A656
FAST, Alanna, Chief Executive Officer, St. Bernard Parish Hospital, Chalmette, LA, p. A279
FAST, Gary, M.D., Medical Director, Prairie View, Newton, KS, p. A256
FASTHORSE, Lena, Supervisor Human Resource, U. S. Public Health Service Indian Hospital–Whiteriver, Whiteriver, AZ, p. A41
FATCH, Casey, Chief Executive Officer, Shasta Regional Medical Center, Redding, CA, p. A85
FATTIG, Marty, Chief Executive Officer, Nemaha County Hospital, Auburn, NE, p. A397
FAUBION, Matthew, M.D., Clinical Director, Kerrville State Hospital, Kerrville, TX, p. A632
FAUCHER, Kimberly, M.D., Chief Medical Officer, Adventist Health Howard Memorial, Willits, CA, p. A101
FAUCHEUX, Lisa, Director Human Resources, St. James Parish Hospital, Lutcher, LA, p. A287
FAUGHNDER, Kevin, Chief Executive Officer, Norton County Hospital, Norton, KS, p. A256
FAUL, Jennifer, Chief Operating Officer, Prairie St. John's, Fargo, ND, p. A480
FAUL, Phyllis, R.N., Chief Nursing Officer, Acadia–St. Landry Hospital, Church Point, LA, p. A280
FAULIS, Karen
Chief Executive Officer, Hi–Desert Medical Center, Joshua Tree, CA, p. A68
Chief Executive Officer, JFK Memorial Hospital, Indio, CA, p. A67
FAULK, Robin, Senior Vice President, Chief Human Resources Officer, Children's Mercy Hospital Kansas, Overland Park, KS, p. A257
FAULKNER, Cheryl, Director of Nursing, Mckenzie County Healthcare System, Watford City, ND, p. A483
FAULKNER, Cynthia, R.N., Chief Nursing Executive, Novant Health Pender Medical Center, Burgaw, NC, p. A464
FAULKNER, Kristi, Vice President Organizational Growth, United Regional Health Care System, Wichita Falls, TX, p. A663
FAULKNER, Laura, Chief Human Resource Management Service, Lexington Vamc, Lexington, KY, p. A268
FAULKNER, Sharon
R.N., Administrator, Sage Specialty Hospital (Ltac), Denham Springs, LA, p. A281
R.N., Chief Nursing Officer, Sage Specialty Hospital (Ltac), Denham Springs, LA, p. A281
FAUS, Doug, FACHE, Chief Executive Officer, Ivinson Memorial Hospital, Laramie, WY, p. A727
FAUST, Cheryl, Chief Nursing Officer, Edgefield County Healthcare, Edgefield, SC, p. A565
FAUTHEREE, Greg, M.D., Medical Director, The Spine Hospital of Louisiana At The Neuromedical Center, Baton Rouge, LA, p. A278
FAVATA, Valerie, R.N., MS, Chief Nursing Officer, Oswego Hospital, Oswego, NY, p. A455
FAY, Brian, Director Information Systems, Sidney Health Center, Sidney, MT, p. A396
FAYEN, Edward J, Associate Administrator Operations and Support, Washington Hospital Healthcare System, Fremont, CA, p. A64

A844 Index of Health Care Professionals

Index of Health Care Professionals / Ferrell

Index of Health Care Professionals

FAZIO, Charles, Chief Health Officer and Medical Director Health Plan, Regions Hospital, Saint Paul, MN, p. A354
FAZIO, Corey, M.D., Chief Medical Officer, Bellevue Hospital, The, Bellevue, OH, p. A486
FEAGIN, Bridgett, Senior Vice President and Chief Financial Officer, Connecticut Children's, Hartford, CT, p. A116
FEASEL, Jeff
Chief Executive Officer, Halifax Health/Uf Health Medical Center of Deltona, Deltona, FL, p. A130
President and Chief Executive Officer, Halifax Health Medical Center of Daytona Beach, Daytona Beach, FL, p. A130
FEASTER, Amy, Senior Vice President, Chief Digital Information Officer, Children's Hospital Colorado – Colorado Springs, Colorado Springs, CO, p. A105
FEATHER, Leroy P, Vice President Finance, Community Hospitals And Wellness Centers, Bryan, OH, p. A487
FEATHERSTON, Jennifer, Chief Executive Officer, Stevens County Hospital, Hugoton, KS, p. A251
FEAZELL, Kayla, Chief Executive Officer, Encompass Health Rehabilitation Hospital of Pensacola, Pensacola, FL, p. A146
FEBRY, Ricardo, M.D., Medical Director, Bliant Specialty Hospital, New Orleans, LA, p. A290
FEBUS, Steven, Chief Financial Officer, Pullman Regional Hospital, Pullman, WA, p. A693
FEDDERS, Neil, Chief Executive Officer, Trihealth Rehabilitation Hospital, Cincinnati, OH, p. A490
FEDIE, Corey J., Chief Executive Officer, East Adams Rural Healthcare, Ritzville, WA, p. A694
FEDORA, Deborah, Director Human Resources, Paoli Hospital, Paoli, PA, p. A547
FEELEY, Daniel, Interim Chief Financial Officer, Medstar Southern Maryland Hospital Center, Clinton, MD, p. A303
FEEMAN, Kimberly
President, Pennsylvania Psychiatric Institute, Harrisburg, PA, p. A541
Senior Vice President and Chief Operating Officer, Wellspan Good Samaritan Hospital, Lebanon, PA, p. A544
FEEN, Jim, Senior Vice President and Chief Information Officer, Southcoast Hospitals Group. Fall River, MA, p. A313
FEENEY, Daniel, M.D., Medical Director, Brentwood Hospital, Shreveport, LA, p. A292
FEGAN, Claudia, M.D., Chief Medical Officer, John H. Stroger Jr. Hospital of Cook County, Chicago, IL, p. A190
FEGHALI, Georges
M.D., Senior Vice President Quality and Chief Medical Officer, Bethesda North Hospital, Cincinnati, OH, p. A488
M.D., Senior Vice President Quality and Chief Medical Officer, Good Samaritan Hospital, Cincinnati, OH, p. A489
FEHR, Daniel, Chief Financial Officer, Community Memorial Healthcare, Marysville, KS, p. A254
FEHRING, Marcia, Chief Financial Officer, Horn Memorial Hospital, Ida Grove, IA, p. A237
FEICKERT, Brent, Chief Financial Officer, Jefferson County Health Center, Fairfield, IA, p. A236
FEIDT, Leslie, Chief Information Officer, Erie County Medical Center, Buffalo, NY, p. A440
FEIGENBAUM, Avi, Chief Executive Officer, Northbrook Behavioral Health Hospital, Blackwood, NJ, p. A418
FEILNER, Margaret, Director Information Services, SSM Health St. Josep. – St. Charles, Saint Charles, MO, p. A383
FEINBERG, Daniel, M.D., Chief Medical Officer, Pennsylvania Hospital, Philadelphia, PA, p. A549
FEINBERG, Jason
M.D., Vice President Medical Affairs and Chief Medical Officer, Geneva General Hospital, Geneva, NY, p. A443
M.D., Vice President Medical Affairs and Chief Medical Officer, Soldiers And Sailors Memorial Hospital, Penn Yan, NY, p. A456
FEINOUR, Jamie, President and Chief Operating Officer, Novant Health Charlotte Orthopaedic Hospital, Charlotte, NC, p. A466
FEISAL, J Philip. Preident, Spartanburg Medical Center – Church Street Campus, Spartanburg, SC, p. A570
FEISAL, J Philip., President and Chief Executive Officer, Spartanburg Medical Center – Church Street Campus, Spartanburg, SC, p. A570
FEIST, Patricia, Manager Human Resources, Crook County Medical Services District, Sundance, WY, p. A728
FEISTHAMEL, Chris, Chief Operating Officer, Eleanor Slater Hospital, Cranston, RI, p. A560
FEISTRITZER, Nancye R., Chief Nursing Officer, Emory University Hospital, Atlanta, GA, p. A157
FELDMAN, Brian, Commanding Officer, Naval Medical Center, Portsmouth, VA, p. A681
FELDMAN, David L.
Executive Vice President and Treasurer, Circles of Care, Melbourne, FL, p. A138
President and Chief Executive Officer, Circles of Care, Melbourne, FL, p. A138
FELDMAN, Deborah A., President and Chief Executive Officer, Dayton Children's Hospital, Dayton, OH, p. A493
FELDSTEIN, Charles S, M.D., Vice President Medical Affairs, St. Rose Hospital, Hayward, CA, p. A67
FELICE, Michael, Chief Financial Officer, Poplar Springs Hospital, Petersburg, VA, p. A681
FELICETTI, Jacqueline, Chief Human Resource Officer, Penn Medicine Chester County Hospital, West Chester, PA, p. A557
FELICIANO, Myrna Quinones, M.D., Medical Director, University Pediatric Hospital, Rio Piedras, PR, p. A734
FELICIANO, Pablo, Manager Human Resources, Veterans Affairs Central Western Massachusetts Healthcare System, Leeds, MA, p. A315
FELIZ, Miriam, M.D., Medical Director, St. Catherine's Rehabilitation Hospital, North Miami, FL, p. A142
FELKNER, Josep. G
Chief Financial Officer, Health First Viera Hospital, Melbourne, FL, p. A139
Executive Vice President and Chief Financial Officer, Health First Palm Bay Hospital, Palm Bay, FL, p. A145
Senior Vice President Finance and Chief Financial Officer, Health First Cap. Canaveral Hospital, Cocoa Beach, FL, p. A128
FELL, David, M.D., Chief Medical Officer, Tulsa Spine And Specialty Hospital, Tulsa, OK, p. A523
FELLER, Julie, Executive Director Human Resources, Harbor Regional Health, Aberdeen, WA, p. A687
FELLOWS, Rhonda, R.N., Chief Nursing Officer, Van Buren County Hospital, Keosauqua, IA, p. A238
FELLOWS, Steven A
Executive Vice President and Chief Operating Officer, Goleta Valley Cottage Hospital, Santa Barbara, CA, p. A94
Executive Vice President and Chief Operating Officer, Santa Barbara Cottage Hospital, Santa Barbara, CA, p. A94
Executive Vice President and Chief Operating Officer, Santa Ynez Valley Cottage Hospital, Solvang, CA, p. A96
FELTMAN, Steven, CPA, Chief Financial Officer, Essentia Health–Virginia, Virginia, MN, p. A356
FELTON, David
Manager Information Systems, Waldo County General Hospital, Belfast, ME, p. A296
Regional Chief Information Officer, Lincolnhealth, Damariscotta, ME, p. A296
FELTON, Jon, Chief Operations Officer, Summit Healthcare Regional Medical Center, Show Low, AZ, p. A39
FELTS, Dave, Chief Information Systems, Logan Regional Hospital, Logan, UT, p. A665
FELTZ, Stacy, Manager Human Resource, Hillsdale Hospital, Hillsdale, MI, p. A329
FENDT, Phil, Chief Financial Officer, Memorial Community Health, Aurora, NE, p. A397
FENN, Mark, Director Human Resources, Pulaski Memorial Hospital, Winamac, IN, p. A229
FENNELL, Charles, Vice President Information Management, St. Joseph's Hospital Health Center, Syracuse, NY, p. A460
FENNELL, Colin, M.D., Chief Medical Officer, Riverview Health, Crookston, MN, p. A345
FENNELL, David, M.D., Acting Medical Director, Atascadero State Hospital, Atascadero, CA, p. A56
FENOUGHTY, Michelle, M.D., President and Chief Executive Officer, Hendricks Regional Health, Danville, IN, p. A215
FENSKE, Bill, Chief Financial Officer, Centracare – Rice Memorial Hospital, Willmar, MN, p. A357
FENTON, David, Administrator, Lifeways Behavioral Hospital, Boise, ID, p. A179
FENTON, Shaun, Chief Executive Officer, Westpark Springs, Richmond, TX, p. A646
FEOLA, Ferd, Chief Information Officer, Lehigh Valley Hospital – Pocono, East Stroudsburg, PA, p. A539
FERCH, Wayne, President and Chief Executive Officer, Adventist Health Hanford, Hanford, CA, p. A66
FERDOUS, Riza, Health Services Director, Ossining Correctional Facilities Hospital, Ossining, NY, p. A455
FERGUS, Janie
Director and Chief Information Officer, Chi Saint Josep. Health – Saint Josep. East, Lexington, KY, p. A268
Director and Chief Information Officer, Chi Saint Josep. Health, Lexington, KY, p. A268
FERGUS, Linda, Manager Information Technology, Allegheny Valley Hospital, Natrona Heights, PA, p. A547
FERGUSON, Allison, Director Human Resources, Avoyelles Hospital, Marksville, LA, p. A288
FERGUSON, Cheryl L, Associate Administrator, Sanford Canby Medical Center, Canby, MN, p. A344
FERGUSON, Clifford, Director Information Technology and Systems, HCA Houston Healthcare Southeast, Pasadena, TX, p. A643
FERGUSON, Daniel, Chief of Staff, AHN Grove City, Grove City, PA, p. A541
FERGUSON, Deborah
Director, Human Resources, Sentara Albemarle Medical Center, Elizabeth City, NC, p. A468
Human Resources Consultant, Sentara Obici Hospital, Suffolk, VA, p. A684
FERGUSON, Denise, Chief Nursing Officer, Baptist Memorial Hospital–Collierville, Collierville, TN, p. A581
FERGUSON, Denise L., Administrator, Mount Grant General Hospital, Hawthorne, NV, p. A409
FERGUSON, G Thomas, Senior Vice President and Chief Human Resources Officer, New York–Presbyterian Hospital, New York, NY, p. A450
FERGUSON, Gordon B., President and Chief Executive Officer, Ascension Saint Thomas Rutherford, Murfreesboro, TN, p. A590
FERGUSON, Jared, Chief Executive Officer, Longleaf Hospital, Alexandria, LA, p. A276
FERGUSON, Karen, Director Human Resources, Johnson County Healthcare Center, Buffalo, WY, p. A726
FERGUSON, Michael, Chief Financial Officer, Harbor Oaks Hospital, New Baltimore, MI, p. A334
FERGUSON, Nina L, Director Human Resources, Little Colorado Medical Center, Winslow, AZ, p. A41
FERGUSON, Randy, Information Systems Manager, Fairchild Medical Center, Yreka, CA, p. A102
FERGUSON, Rick, Chief Executive Officer, Oklahoma Surgical Hospital, Tulsa, OK, p. A522
FERGUSON, Tonya, Director Human Resources, Encompass Health Rehabilitation Hospital of Richmond, Richmond, VA, p. A682
FERGUSON, Zeta, Chief Human Resources, Atlanta Veterans Affairs Medical Center, Decatur, GA, p. A162
FERIA, Jorge, M.D., President Medical Staff, Wilma N. Vazquez Medical Center, Vega Baja, PR, p. A736
FERNANDEZ, Arthur, Chief Financial Officer, First Hospital Panamericano, Cidra, PR, p. A732
FERNANDEZ, Benigno J, M.D., Executive Medical Director, Laurel Ridge Treatment Center, San Antonio, TX, p. A650
FERNANDEZ, Jaime, Chief Executive Officer, Kempsville Center for Behavioral Health, Norfolk, VA, p. A680
FERNANDEZ, Jean, Chief Information Officer, Beth Israel Deaconess Hospital–Milton, Milton, MA, p. A316
FERNANDEZ, John, Chief Operating Officer, United Hospital Center, Bridgeport, WV, p. A699
FERNANDEZ, Lilly, Director Human Resources, Palmdale Regional Medical Center, Palmdale, CA, p. A82
FERNANDEZ, Nicole, R.N., MS, President, Endeavor Health Evanston Hospital, Evanston, IL, p. A195
FERNANDEZ, Ricardo, Administrator, Chicago–Read Mental Health Center, Chicago, IL, p. A189
FERNANDEZ, Richard W., President and Chief Executive Officer, Beth Israel Deaconess Hospital–Milton, Milton, MA, p. A316
FERNANDEZ, Ruben D, R.N., Vice President and Chief Nursing Officer, Hackensack Meridian Health Palisades Medical Center, North Bergen, NJ, p. A426
FERNANDEZ, Tracey, Chief Financial Officer, Peacehealth Southwest Medical Center, Vancouver, WA, p. A698
FERNANDEZ DEL VALLE, Arthur J, Chief Financial Officer, Cardiovascular Center of Puerto Rico And The Caribbean, San Juan, PR, p. A734
FERNYAK, Susan, M.D., Interim Chief Medical Officer & Chief Quality Officer, San Mateo Medical Center, San Mateo, CA, p. A93
FERRACANE, Tony, Vice President Human Resources, St. Mary Medical Center, Hobart, IN, p. A218
FERRANTI, Jeffrey, M.D., Chief Information Officer, Duke University Hospital, Durham, NC, p. A467
FERRANTI, Sue, M.D., Interim Chief Medical Officer, Eleanor Slater Hospital, Cranston, RI, p. A560
FERRARA, Carol, Director Human Resources, Saint Luke's South Hospital, Overland Park, KS, p. A257
FERRARO, Claudio J, President, Ascension Via Christi St. Francis, Mulvane, KS, p. A255
FERRAROTTI, Gianna, Director Human Resources North Region, Ohiohealth Marion General Hospital, Marion, OH, p. A499
FERREIRA, Daniel, Director Management Information Systems, Hospital De La Concepcion, San German, PR, p. A734
FERRELL, Eileen Brennan, MS, R.N., Vice President and Chief Nursing Officer, Medstar Georgetown University Hospital, Washington, DC, p. A123

Index of Health Care Professionals

Index of Health Care Professionals / Ferrell

FERRELL, Jennifer, Chief Nursing Officer, Encompass Health Rehabilitation Hospital of Memphis, A Partner of Methodist Healthcare, Memphis, TN, p. A588
FERRELL, Ronald, Chief Information Officer, Raymond G. Murphy Department of Veterans Affairs Medical Center, Albuquerque, NM, p. A433
FERREN, Alison, President and Chief Operating Officer, Jefferson Abington Health, Abington, PA, p. A534
FERRIS, David, Chief Nursing Officer and Vice President Patient Care Services, Claxton–Hepburn Medical Center, Ogdensburg, NY, p. A455
FERRIS, Joseph, Chief Financial Officer, Black Hills Hcs, Fort Meade, SD, p. A573
FERRIS, Norma, R.N., MS, Chief Nursing Officer, Spring Mountain Treatment Center, Las Vegas, NV, p. A410
FERRONI, Karen, M.D., Medical Director, Holyoke Medical Center, Holyoke, MA, p. A314
FERRY, Jennilyn
Chief Financial Officer, Heber Valley Hospital, Heber City, UT, p. A665
Chief Financial Officer, Park City Hospital, Park City, UT, p. A667
FESS, Jennifer, Chief Executive Officer, Select Specialty Hospital – Cleveland Fairhill, Cleveland, OH, p. A491
FETTO, Julie, R.N., Chief Nursing Officer, Cleveland Clinic Medina Hospital, Medina, OH, p. A500
FEUNNING, Charles, M.D., Chief Medical Officer, Western Reserve Hospital, Cuyahoga Falls, OH, p. A493
FEUQUAY, Derek, M.D., Chief Medical Officer, Flagstaff Medical Center, Flagstaff, AZ, p. A31
FIBIYI, Abayomi, Chief Human Resources Officer, North Vista Hospital, North Las Vegas, NV, p. A412
FICARA, Cheryl A., R.N., MS, President, Hartford Hospital, Hartford, CT, p. A116
FICCHI, Adrienne, Vice President Information Management, Philadelphia Veterans Affairs Medical Center, Philadelphia, PA, p. A550
FICICCHY, Teri, R.N., MSN, Chief Nursing Officer, Bon Secours St. Francis Health System, Greenville, SC, p. A566
FICK, Beverly, Chief Nursing Officer, Desert Regional Medical Center, Palm Springs, CA, p. A82
FIDLER, Soniya, MS, President, UCHealth Yamp. Valley Medical Center, Steamboat Springs, CO, p. A113
FIELD, Clifford, M.D., Medical Director, Ka'U Hospital, Pahala, HI, p. A177
FIELD, Laurie, Director Human Resources, Eaton Rapids Medical Center, Eaton Rapids, MI, p. A326
FIELDER, Barb, Vice President Finance, Chelsea Hospital, Chelsea, MI, p. A324
FIELDER, Jaf, President and Chief Executive Officer, Willis Knighton North, Shreveport, LA, p. A293
FIELDHOUSE, Cheryl, Chief Nursing Officer, Encompass Health Rehabilitation Hospital of Greenville, Greenville, SC, p. A567
FIELDING, Colene, Manager Business Office, Baylor Scott & White Medical Center–Uptown, Dallas, TX, p. A610
FIELDING, Laura M, Administrative Director Organizational Development, Holy Family Memorial, Manitowoc, WI, p. A715
FIELDS, Greg, Director Information Technology, Elbert Memorial Hospital, Elberton, GA, p. A163
FIERER, Jonathan, M.D., Chief of Staff, Martinsburg Veterans Affairs Medical Center, Martinsburg, WV, p. A702
FIERRO, Barbara, Director, Human Resources, St. Francis Hospital And Heart Center, Roslyn, NY, p. A458
FIETEK, Denise, Information Technology, Rio Grande Hospital, Del Norte, CO, p. A106
FIFE, Stephen, President and Chief Financial Officer, Cap. Fear Valley Bladen County Hospital, Elizabethtown, NC, p. A468
FIFERLICK, Beverly, Chief Financial Officer, Jamestown Regional Medical Center, Jamestown, ND, p. A482
FIGGINS, Tara, Director Human Resources, Holy Cross Hospital – Davis, Layton, UT, p. A665
FIGUEROA, George, M.D., Chief Medical Officer, Banner Gateway Medical Center, Gilbert, AZ, p. A31
FIGUEROA, Maria, Director Human Resources, Ryder Memorial Hospital, Humacao, PR, p. A733
FIGUEROA, Roseann, Director Human Resources, Doctors Hospital of Laredo, Laredo, TX, p. A634
FIGUEROA PERALTA, Wanda, President and Chief Executive Officer, Rivervalley Behavioral Health Hospital, Owensboro, KY, p. A272
FILER, Christine, Director Human Resources, Encompass Health Rehabilitation Hospital of Altoona, Altoona, PA, p. A534
FILES, Ashley S., Director Human Resources, Public Relations and Marketing, Winn Parish Medical Center, Winnfield, LA, p. A294
FILES, Carol, Chief Financial Officer, East Houston Hospitals & Clinics, Houston, TX, p. A625
FILIPINI, Alfred, Manager Human Resources, Ancora Psychiatric Hospital, Hammonton, NJ, p. A422
FILIPOWICZ, Thomas, M.D., Medical Director, St. Luke's Quakertown Campus, Quakertown, PA, p. A553
FILLER, Richard, Chief Financial Officer, Ohiohealth Berger Hospital, Circleville, OH, p. A490
FILLER, Scott, Chief Executive Officer, Encompass Health Rehabilitation Hospital of Altoona, Altoona, PA, p. A534
FILLINGIM, Jed, Acting Chief Operating Officer and Associate Director, G.V. (Sonny) Montgomery Department of Veterans Affairs Medical Center, Jackson, MS, p. A364
FILLIPO, Brian, M.D., Chief Medical Officer, Guthrie Robert Packer Hospital, Sayre, PA, p. A554
FILLMAN, Donald, M.D., Chief Medical Officer, Guthrie County Hospital, Guthrie Center, IA, p. A237
FILLMAN, T Orvin, Dr.PH, Vice President, Operations, Rogers Behavioral Health, Oconomowoc, WI, p. A718
FILOSA, Frank, Fiscal Manager, Washington Dc Veterans Affairs Medical Center, Washington, DC, p. A124
FILOSA, Shannon M., Executive Director Women's and Children, Saint Francis Hospital, Tulsa, OK, p. A523
FILPI, Jeanette, Chief Executive Officer, Early Medical Center, Blakely, GA, p. A159
FILSON, Debbie, Chief Financial Officer, Ashland Health Center, Ashland, KS, p. A246
FINCH, John
Chief Information and Community Officer, Health Alliance Hospital – Mary's Avenue Campus, Kingston, NY, p. A445
Vice President Information Services, Health Alliance Hospital – Broadway Campus, Kingston, NY, p. A445
FINCH, Kim, Chief Nursing Officer, Lutheran Kosciusko Hospital, Warsaw, IN, p. A229
FINCH, Robert D., Director, Human Resources, Piedmont Athens Regional Medical Center, Athens, GA, p. A156
FINCH, Roy, Chief Operating Officer, Longview Regional Medical Center, Longview, TX, p. A635
FINCH, Sally, Chief Nursing Officer, Atoka County Medical Center, Atoka, OK, p. A510
FINCH, Steve, Chief Financial Officer, Guidance Center, Flagstaff, AZ, p. A31
FINCHER, Jodi
R.N., Chief Executive Officer, St. Josep. Medical Center, Kansas City, MO, p. A378
R.N., Vice President Patient Care Services, Saint John Hospital, Leavenworth, KS, p. A253
FINDLAY, Andrew L., Deputy Commander Clinical Services, Tripler Army Medical Center, Honolulu, HI, p. A176
FINDLAY, Kelly, Director of Nurses, Pawnee County Memorial Hospital And Rural Health Clinic, Pawnee City, NE, p. A405
FINDLEY, Amber, Senior Director Nursing Services and NRC Administrator, Rivers Health, Point Pleasant, WV, p. A704
FINE, Mathew N., M.D., Chief Medical Officer, Oroville Hospital, Oroville, CA, p. A82
FINELLI, Frederick, M.D., Vice President Medical Affairs, Medstar Montgomery Medical Center, Olney, MD, p. A306
FINESTEIN, Brian, Chief Executive Officer, Saint Clare's Denville Hospital, Denville, NJ, p. A420
FINETTI, Yoany, R.N., Vice President Patient Care Services Chief Nurse Officer, Barnes–Jewish West County Hospital, Saint Louis, MO, p. A384
FINK, Renee, CPA, Chief Financial Officer, Dundy County Hospital, Benkelman, NE, p. A398
FINK, Tom, Vice President Regional Finance Officer, Fairview Range, Hibbing, MN, p. A348
FINK, Walter, Chief Medical Officer, Multicare Good Samaritan Hospital, Puyallup. WA, p. A693
FINKE, Jill, FACHE, Interim Chief Executive Officer, Foundation Surgical Hospital of San Antonio, San Antonio, TX, p. A649
FINKEL, Naomi, Nurse Executive, Montgomery County Emergency Service, Norristown, PA, p. A547
FINLAYSON, Susan D, MSN, R.N., Senior Vice President of MMC Operations, Mercy Medical Center, Baltimore, MD, p. A301
FINLEY, Alan
Chief Operating Officer, Conway Regional Health System, Conway, AR, p. A44
President, Dardanelle Regional Medical Center, Dardanelle, AR, p. A45
FINLEY, Delvecchio
FACHE, Interim Chief Executive Officer, Atrium Health Navicent Baldwin, Milledgeville, GA, p. A168
FACHE, President and Chief Executive Officer, Atrium Health Navicent The Medical Center, Macon, GA, p. A167
FINLEY, Elizabeth Jane, Senior Vice President and Area Manager, Kaiser Permanente Zion Medical Center, San Diego, CA, p. A89
FINLEY, Elizabeth Jane.
Senior Vice President and Area Manager, Kaiser Foundation Hospital – San Marcos, San Marcos, CA, p. A93
Senior Vice President and Area Manager, Kaiser Permanente Zion Medical Center, San Diego, CA, p. A89
FINLEY, Kelly, Customer Site Executive, Mclaren Oakland, Pontiac, MI, p. A335
FINLEY, Kevan, MS, Chief Executive Officer, Cottonwood Creek Behavioral Hospital, Meridian, ID, p. A182
FINLEY, Tommy, Chief Information Officer, Rutherford Regional Health System, Rutherfordton, NC, p. A475
FINN, Patricia, Chief Executive Officer, Fulton County Health Center, Wauseon, OH, p. A506
FINNEGAN, Mary Jane, Chief Nursing Officer, St. Catherine of Siena Hospital, Smithtown, NY, p. A459
FINNERTY, Kimberley, MSN, R.N., Chief Nursing Officer, Jefferson Hospital, Jefferson Hills, PA, p. A542
FINNEY, David, R.N., Vice President Nursing, UHS Chenango Memorial Hospital, Norwich, NY, p. A454
FINNEY, Michele, Chief Executive Officer, Desert Regional Medical Center, Desert Regional Medical Center, Palm Springs, CA, p. A82
FINSTAD, Gary A, M.D., Chief of Staff, Kern Valley Healthcare District, Lake Isabella, CA, p. A69
FIORE–LOPEZ, Nicolette, Ph.D., R.N., Chief Nursing Officer, St. Charles Hospital, Port Jefferson, NY, p. A456
FIORET, Phil, M.D., Vice President Medical Affairs, UK King's Daughters Medical Center, Ashland, KY, p. A263
FIORICA, James
M.D., Chief Medical Officer, Sarasota Memorial Hospital – Sarasota, Sarasota, FL, p. A150
M.D., Chief Medical Officer, Sarasota Memorial Hospital – Venice, North Venice, FL, p. A142
FIRMAN, Russell, M.D., Chief Medical Officer, Guthrie Cortland Regional Medical Center, Cortland, NY, p. A441
FIRTCH, William, M.D., Physician In Chief, Kaiser Permanente Redwood City Medical Center, Redwood City, CA, p. A85
FISCARELLI, Conner Mikhail., Chief Executive Officer, Gove County Medical Center, Quinter, KS, p. A258
FISCHELS, Diane, Senior Vice President and Chief Operating Officer, Mercyone North Iowa Medical Center, Mason City, IA, p. A240
FISCHER, Cheyana Deane, Chief Nursing Officer, Health First Holmes Regional Medical Center, Melbourne, FL, p. A139
FISCHER, Jason
Chief Information Officer, PIH Health Downey Hospital, Downey, CA, p. A61
Chief Information Officer, PIH Health Whittier Hospital, Whittier, CA, p. A101
FISCHER, JC, Director Human Resources, Mercy Health – Lorain Hospital, Lorain, OH, p. A498
FISCHER, Lisa, Director Human Resources, Brown County Hospital, Ainsworth, NE, p. A397
FISCHER, Lukas
R.N., Chief Executive Officer, Linton Regional Medical Center, Linton, ND, p. A482
R.N., Chief Executive Officer, South Central Health, Wishek, ND, p. A483
FISCHER, Rebecca J, Chief Financial Officer, NYC Health + Hospitals/Bellevue, New York, NY, p. A450
FISCHER, Robert
M.D., Medical Center Director, Mann–Grandstaff Department of Veterans Affairs Medical Center, Spokane, WA, p. A696
M.D., Medical Director, Methodist Hospital for Surgery, Addison, TX, p. A595
FISCHER, Sandra, Director Human Resources, W. G. (Bill) Heffner Veterans Affairs Medical Center, Salisbury, NC, p. A476
FISCHER, Steven P, Chief Financial Officer, Beth Israel Deaconess Medical Center, Boston, MA, p. A309
FISCHER, Tamara, Chief Nursing Officer, Okeene Municipal Hospital, Okeene, OK, p. A516
FISER, David, Vice President and Chief Information Officer, Cleveland Clinic Akron General, Akron, OH, p. A484
FISH, Carolyn, Director Human Resources, Mission Community Hospital, Los Angeles, CA, p. A74
FISH, Elizabeth
Chief Information Officer, University of Maryland Shore Medical Center At Easton, Easton, MD, p. A304
Information Technology Site Executive, University of Maryland Charles Regional Medical Center, La Plata, MD, p. A305
Senior Director Site Executive and Information Technology, University of Maryland Shore Medical Center At Chestertown, Chestertown, MD, p. A303
FISH, Eric, M.D., President and Chief Executive Officer, Schneck Medical Center, Seymour, IN, p. A227
FISH, Francis James, Vice President and Chief Financial Officer, Mile Bluff Medical Center, Mauston, WI, p. A715

A846 Index of Health Care Professionals

Index of Health Care Professionals
Index of Health Care Professionals / Fletcher

FISHEL, Stephanie, Vice President Patient Care Services and Chief Nursing Officer, Nathan Littauer Hospital And Nursing Home, Gloversville, NY, p. A443
FISHER, Alan, Chief Executive Officer, Woodlawn Hospital, Rochester, IN, p. A226
FISHER, Charles, Chief Executive Officer, U. S. Public Health Service Indian Hospital, Eagle Butte, SD, p. A573
FISHER, David
Director Information Systems, UPMC Lititz, Lititz, PA, p. A544
Vice President Human Resources, Signature Healthcare Brockton Hospital, Brockton, MA, p. A311
FISHER, Diane, R.N., VP, Patient Care Services, Munson Healthcare Otsego Memorial Hospital, Gaylord, MI, p. A327
FISHER, J. Matthew, Chief Financial Officer, Russell Medical, Alexander City, AL, p. A15
FISHER, Jeannie, Coordinator Information Technology, Webster County Memorial Hospital, Webster Springs, WV, p. A705
FISHER, Jennifer A, Manager Human Resources, Henry County Hospital, Napoleon, OH, p. A501
FISHER, John
M.D., Chief Medical Officer, Mlk Community Healthcare, Los Angeles, CA, p. A74
Interim Chief Executive Officer, Carrollton Springs, Carrollton, TX, p. A606
FISHER, Jonathan, Chief Financial Officer, Adventhealth Parker, Parker, CO, p. A112
FISHER, Kenneth, M.D., President, Medical Staff, Adventist Healthcare Fort Washington Medical Center, Fort Washington, MD, p. A304
FISHER, Kerry, M.D., Medical Director, Lds Hospital, Salt Lake City, UT, p. A669
FISHER, Lynn, M.D., Chief of Staff, Rooks County Health Center, Plainville, KS, p. A258
FISHER, Mahana, M.D., Medical Director, Blue Mountain Hospital, Blanding, UT, p. A664
FISHER, Mark, Chief Human Resources Officer, UCI Health – Los Alamitos, Los Alamitos, CA, p. A71
FISHER, Mathew, M.D., Medical Director, Springbrook Behavioral Health, Travelers Rest, SC, p. A571
FISHER, Patricia, M.D., Chief Medical Officer, Hackensack Meridian Health Ocean University Medical Center, Brick Township. NJ, p. A419
FISHER, Robert E, Chief Financial Officer, Coquille Valley Hospital, Coquille, OR, p. A526
FISHER, Ryan
Director Human Resources, Bluffton Hospital, Bluffton, OH, p. A486
Director of Human Resources, Blanchard Valley Hospital, Findlay, OH, p. A496
FISHER, Sharon
M.D., Chief of Staff, Bartlett Regional Hospital, Juneau, AK, p. A28
R.N., Chief Nursing Officer, Penn Highlands Tyrone, Tyrone, PA, p. A556
FISHER, Teresa
R.N., Chief Nursing Officer, Fort Loudoun Medical Center, Lenoir City, TN, p. A586
Chief Nursing Officer, Lakewood Health System, Staples, MN, p. A355
FISHER, Thomas, Senior Vice President and Chief Financial Officer, University of Tennessee Medical Center, Knoxville, TN, p. A586
FISHER, Vicky, Ph.D., R.N., Chief Nurse Executive, Catawba Hospital, Catawba, VA, p. A674
FISHER–FORD, Karen, Director of Health Information Management, West Central Georgia Regional Hospital, Columbus, GA, p. A161
FISHKIN, Edward, M.D., Medical Director, NYC Health + Hospitals/Woodhull, New York, NY, p. A452
FISHMAN, Aaron, Vice President, Finance, Nantucket Cottage Hospital, Nantucket, MA, p. A316
FISK, Amber, Director Human Resources, Memorial Hospital of Sweetwater County, Rock Springs, WY, p. A728
FISK, Anita, Director Human Resources, Three Rivers Hospital, Brewster, WA, p. A687
FISK, Kathryn M, Chief Human Resources Officer, El Camino Health, Mountain View, CA, p. A79
FISK, Kellee J., Chief People and Strategy Officer, Altru Health System, Grand Forks, ND, p. A481
FISLER, Eileen, Chief Financial Officer, Pacifica Hospital of The Valley, Los Angeles, CA, p. A74
FISLER, Elyse
Chief Nursing Officer, Wellspan Chambersburg Hospital, Chambersburg, PA, p. A536
Chief Nursing Officer, Wellspan Waynesboro Hospital, Waynesboro, PA, p. A556
FITCH, Andrew, Chief Financial Officer, Providence St. Elias Specialty Hospital, Anchorage, AK, p. A27
FITCH, James A, Director Human Resources, Houston Methodist Continuing Care Hospital, Katy, TX, p. A631
FITCH, John A, Vice President Human Resources, Campbell County Health, Gillette, WY, p. A727
FITCH, Ron
President/UCHealth Pikes Peak Regional Hospital/ Grandview Hospital/Operations and Military Affairs/U, UCHealth Grandview Hospital, Colorado Springs, CO, p. A105
President/UCHealth Pikes Peak Regional Hospital/ Grandview Hospital/Operations and Military Affairs/U, UCHealth Pikes Peak Regional Hospital, Woodland Park, CO, p. A114
FITE, David, Director Information Technology, Towner County Medical Center, Cando, ND, p. A479
FITE, Theresa, R.N., Chief Financial Officer, Fleming County Hospital, Flemingsburg, KY, p. A265
FITTERMAN, Nick, M.D., Executive Director, Huntington Hospital, Huntington, NY, p. A444
FITTS, Barry
Chief Information Officer, Hillside Rehabilitation Hospital, Warren, OH, p. A506
Chief Information Officer, Trumbull Regional Medical Center, Warren, OH, p. A506
FITZGERALD, Amy, Human Resources Manager, Copley Hospital, Morrisville, VT, p. A672
FITZGERALD, Kerri, Executive Director, Johnson Rehabilitation Institute At Hackensack Meridian Health Ocean Medical Center, Brick, NJ, p. A418
FITZGERALD, Michelle, R.N., Chief Executive Officer, Encompass Health Rehabilitation Hospital of Cap. Coral, Cap. Coral, FL, p. A127
FITZGERALD, Mike
Chief Financial Officer, St. Clare Hospital, Lakewood, WA, p. A691
Chief Financial Officer, St. Francis Hospital, Federal Way, WA, p. A690
Chief Financial Officer, St. Josep. Medical Center, Tacoma, WA, p. A697
Chief Financial Officer, St. Michael Medical Center, Silverdale, WA, p. A695
FITZGERALD, Patty, Staff Services, Munson Healthcare Charlevoix Hospital, Charlevoix, MI, p. A323
FITZGERALD, Philip, Chief Executive Officer, Havasu Regional Medical Center, Lake Havasu City, AZ, p. A32
FITZGERALD, Shane, Chief Operating Officer, Uofl Health – Mary And Elizabeth Hospital, Louisville, KY, p. A270
FITZGERALD, Trisha, Chief Nursing Officer, North Central Surgical Center, Dallas, TX, p. A612
FITZMAURICE, Dennis, Vice President, Professional Services, Community First Medical Center, Chicago, IL, p. A189
FITZPATRICK, Anna, Director Human Resources, St. Anthony Regional Hospital, Carroll, IA, p. A231
FITZPATRICK, Bridget, Chief Operating Officer, Bon Secours St. Francis Medical Center, Midlothian, VA, p. A679
FITZPATRICK, Daniel, Director Human Resources, Whitesburg Arh Hospital, Whitesburg, KY, p. A275
FITZPATRICK, James, M.D., Vice President Medical Affairs, Kenmore Mercy Hospital, Kenmore, NY, p. A444
FITZPATRICK, Leigh Ann, Superintendent, Kerrville State Hospital, Kerrville, TX, p. A632
FITZPATRICK, Patrick J., Commanding Officer, Naval Hospital Bremerton, Bremerton, WA, p. A687
FITZSIMMONS, Brendan, Medical Director, North Platte Valley Medical Center, Saratoga, WY, p. A728
FITZSIMMONS, Shaun, Director Information Technology Services, Community Medical Center, Toms River, NJ, p. A429
FITZSIMONS, Patricia Sue, R.N., Ph.D., Senior Vice President Patient Services, Yale New Haven Hospital, New Haven, CT, p. A118
FITZTHUM, John, Chief Operating Officer and Admiistrator, St. Catherine Hospital – Dodge City, Dodge City, KS, p. A248
FLACK, Charles, Interim Chief Information Officer, Orange County Global Medical Center, Inc., Santa Ana, CA, p. A93
FLAHERTY, John
Chief Financial Officer, Encompass Health Rehabilitation Hospital of Western Massachusetts, Ludlow, MA, p. A315
Controller, Fairlawn Rehabilitation Hospital, Worcester, MA, p. A320
FLAHERTY, Linda, R.N., Senior Vice President, Patient Care Services, Mclean Hospital, Belmont, MA, p. A309
FLAHERTY, Patrick, Director Management Information, Naval Hospital Bremerton, Bremerton, WA, p. A687
FLAHERTY, Tom, Assistant Administrator, Los Angeles County Central Jail Hospital, Los Angeles, CA, p. A74
FLAHERTY–OXLER, Karen Ann., MSN, R.N., Medical Center Director, Philadelphia Veterans Affairs Medical Center, Philadelphia, PA, p. A550
FLAKE, Leslie, Senior Vice President, Finance, Corewell Health Butterworth Hospital, Grand Rapids, MI, p. A328
FLAMING, Patrick, R.N., Director Inpatient Operations, Prairie View, Newton, KS, p. A256
FLAMM, Cindy, Manager Quality, Choate Mental Health Center, Anna, IL, p. A185
FLANAGAN, Craig, Chief Financial Officer, Unitypoint Health – Allen Hospital, Waterloo, IA, p. A244
FLANAGAN, Michael J., President and Chief Executive Officer, St. Clair Health, Pittsburgh, PA, p. A551
FLANAGAN, Thomas, M.D., Medical Director, Aurora Behavioral Healthcare San Diego, San Diego, CA, p. A88
FLANARY, Tresha, R.N., Chief Clinical Services Officer, Wamego Health Center, Wamego, KS, p. A261
FLANDERS, David, Chief Executive Officer, Optim Medical Center – Tattnall, Reidsville, GA, p. A169
FLANIGAN, Erin J, Vice President Human Resources, Wentworth–Douglass Hospital, Dover, NH, p. A414
FLANNERY, Maureen, Vice President Clinic Operations, Straub Medical Center, Honolulu, HI, p. A176
FLANNERY, Patrick, Chief Executive Officer and Administrator, Kate Dishman Rehabilitation Hospital, Beaumont, TX, p. A602
FLANNERY, Robert, Chief Financial Officer, University Hospital, Madison, WI, p. A714
FLANZ, Bruce J.
President and Chief Executive Officer, Flushing Hospital Medical Center, New York, NY, p. A448
President and Chief Executive Officer, Jamaica Hospital Medical Center, New York, NY, p. A448
FLASCHENRIEM, Julie, Chief Information Officer, Park Nicollet Methodist Hospital, Saint Louis Park, MN, p. A354
FLASHER, Sara, Chief Nurse Executive, Warren State Hospital, Warren, PA, p. A556
FLATOW, Evan, M.D., President, Mount Sinai Morningside, New York, NY, p. A449
FLATT, G Wayne, D.O., Chief Medical Director, Pushmataha Hospital, Antlers, OK, p. A509
FLATTERY, William, Vice President and Administrator Western Division, Carilion New River Valley Medical Center, Christiansburg, VA, p. A675
FLECHLER, Leslie, Chief Executive Officer, Lincoln Trail Behavioral Health System, Radcliff, KY, p. A273
FLECKENSTEIN, Casey, Nurse Manager, Monroe County Hospital, Forsyth, GA, p. A164
FLEEGEL, Monica, Director Human Resources, Mayo Clinic Health System – Albert Lea And Austin, Albert Lea, MN, p. A342
FLEENOR, Dennis, R.N., Administrator, Muleshoe Area Medical Center, Muleshoe, TX, p. A640
FLEET, Aaron, R.N., Chief Nursing Officer, Baylor Scott & White Texas Spine & Joint Hospital–Tyler, Tyler, TX, p. A658
FLEISCHMANN, Craig, Vice President Finance, University of Maryland Medical Center Midtown Campus, Baltimore, MD, p. A301
FLEISCHMANN, Tim, Chief Financial Officer, Ohsu Health Hillsboro Medical Center, Hillsboro, OR, p. A528
FLEISHMAN, Samuel A, M.D., Chief Medical Officer, Cap. Fear Valley Medical Center, Fayetteville, NC, p. A468
FLEITES, Fernando, Senior Vice President Human Resources, Bon Secours St. Francis Health System, Greenville, SC, p. A566
FLEMER, David Andrew. Jr, Chief Executive Officer, Arkansas Valley Regional Medical Center, La Junta, CO, p. A110
FLEMING, Jared, Director, Information Services, Lourdes Counseling Center, Richland, WA, p. A694
FLEMING, Joshua, Vice President Chief Clinical Officer, Leesburg Regional Medical Center, Leesburg, FL, p. A137
FLEMING, Michael, Chief People Officer, Banner – University Medical Center Phoenix, Phoenix, AZ, p. A35
FLEMING, Michele, Chief Executive Officer, Western Maryland Hospital Center, Hagerstown, MD, p. A305
FLEMING, Shane
Chief Financial Officer, Capital Health Medical Center– Hopewell, Pennington, NJ, p. A427
Chief Financial Officer, Capital Health Regional Medical Center, Trenton, NJ, p. A429
FLEMMING, Libby, Controller and Chief Information Officer, South Georgia Medical Center Lanier Campus, Lakeland, GA, p. A166
FLESNER, Lynn, Director of Nursing, Glacial Ridge Health System, Glenwood, MN, p. A347
FLETCHER, Gemma, Interim Chief Executive Officer, Encompass Health Rehabilitation Institute of Libertyville, Libertyville, IL, p. A200
FLETCHER, James, M.D., Medical Staff President, Cascade Valley Hospital, Arlington, WA, p. A687
FLETCHER, Jennifer, Chief of Staff, Decatur County Memorial Hospital, Greensburg, IN, p. A218

© 2025 AHA Guide Index of Health Care Professionals A847

Index of Health Care Professionals / Fletcher

FLETCHER, Kathy, R.N., MSN, Interim Chief Nursing Officer, Val Verde Regional Medical Center, Del Rio, TX, p. A613
FLETCHER, Kevin, Director Information Systems, Medical City Mckinney, Mckinney, TX, p. A638
FLETCHER, Michael, M.D., Vice President and Chief Medical Officer, Hancock Regional Hospital, Greenfield, IN, p. A218
FLETCHER, Stephanie L, CPA, Chief Financial Officer, Union General Hospital, Blairsville, GA, p. A159
FLETT, Will, Vice President Finance and Chief Financial Officer, Avera Queen of Peace Hospital, Mitchell, SD, p. A575
FLICKEMA, James, Vice President Market Development, Munson Healthcare Otsego Memorial Hospital, Gaylord, MI, p. A327
FLICKINGER, Kenneth E, Chief Financial Officer, Penn Medicine Chester County Hospital, West Chester, PA, p. A557
FLINN, Charles, Vice President, Chief Operating Officer, Saint Mary's Hospital, Waterbury, CT, p. A119
FLINT, Dan, Director Healthcare Information Systems, Wyoming County Community Hospital, Warsaw, NY, p. A461
FLINT, Jennifer, Chief Financial Officer, Ochsner Laird Hospital, Union, MS, p. A369
FLINT, Ruth, Chief Nursing Officer, St. Josep. Medical Center, Tacoma, WA, p. A697
FLIPPO, Mary Elizabeth, R.N., MSN, Vice President and Chief Nursing Officer, Cleveland Clinic Martin North Hospital, Stuart, FL, p. A150
FLITTON, Emileh, Administrator, Oceans Behavioral Health Center Permian Basin, Midland, TX, p. A639
FLOOD, James, Director Information Systems, Claxton-Hepburn Medical Center, Ogdensburg, NY, p. A455
FLOOD, Sherri, Chief Executive Officer, The Brook Hospital - Kmi, Louisville, KY, p. A270
FLORENTINE, Stephen J., Administrator, Riverbend Rehabilitation Hospital, Bastrop. LA, p. A277
FLORES, Adrian, Chief Executive Officer, Houston Behavioral Healthcare Hospital, Houston, TX, p. A626
FLORES, Andrea, Director, Information Systems, Providence Little Company of Mary Medical Center - Torrance, Torrance, CA, p. A98
FLORES, Debbie
  Chief Executive Officer, Banner Behavioral Health Hospital - Scottsdale, Scottsdale, AZ, p. A38
  Chief Executive Officer, Banner Thunderbird Medical Center, Glendale, AZ, p. A32
FLORES, Debra A.
  R.N., FACHE, Senior Vice President and Area Manager, Kaiser Permanente Fremont Medical Center, Fremont, CA, p. A64
  R.N., FACHE, Senior Vice President and Area Manager, Kaiser Permanente San Leandro Medical Center, San Leandro, CA, p. A92
FLORES, Jerome
  Chief Financial Officer, Sunrise Canyon Hospital, Lubbock, TX, p. A636
  Chief Financial Officer and Chief Operating Officer, Kahuku Medical Center, Kahuku, HI, p. A176
FLORES, Linda, R.N., MSN, Vice President Nursing Services, UCHealth Parkview Medical Center, Pueblo, CO, p. A113
FLORES, Rick, Chief Executive Officer, Big Bend Regional Medical Center, Alpine, TX, p. A596
FLORKOWSKI, Douglas, Chief Executive Officer, Crawford Memorial Hospital, Robinson, IL, p. A207
FLOURA, Kamal, M.D., Medical Director, Eastern State Hospital, Medical Lake, WA, p. A691
FLOWE, Kenneth, M.D., Chief Medical Officer, Centracare - Rice Memorial Hospital, Willmar, MN, p. A357
FLOWERS, Amy, Controller, Encompass Health Rehabilitation Hospital of Princetcn, Princeton, WV, p. A704
FLOWERS, Deborah, Director Human Resources, Monroe County Hospital, Forsyth, GA, p. A164
FLOWERS, Frank M.
  M.D., Area Medical Director, Kaiser Permanente Moreno Valley Medical Center, Moreno Valley, CA, p. A78
  M.D., Area Medical Director, Kaiser Permanente Riverside Medical Center, Riverside, CA, p. A86
FLOWERS, Michael, Director Information Management, Calhoun Liberty Hospital, Blountstown, FL, p. A126
FLOWERS, Scott, Interim President and Chief Operating Officer, St. Josep. Medical Center, Houston, TX, p. A628
FLOWERS, Susan S, MSN, R.N., Chief Nursing Officer, Cumberland County Hospital, Burkesville, KY, p. A264
FLOWERS, Taylor, Senior Vice President Human Resources, Onslow Memorial Hospital, Jacksonville, NC, p. A471
FLOYD, Duane, Vice President Human Resources and Professional Services, Watertown Regional Medical Center, Watertown, WI, p. A723
FLOYD, Kiley, Chief Executive Officer, Nemaha Valley Community Hospital, Seneca, KS, p. A260

FLOYD, Leroy, M.D., Chief Medical Officer, Garnet Health Medical Center, Middletown, NY, p. A446
FLOYD, Miranda, R.N., Chief Nursing Officer, Mosaic Medical Center - Albany, Albany, MO, p. A371
FLOYD, Robert, D.O., Chief Medical Staff, Davis County Hospital And Clinics, Bloomfield, IA, p. A231
FLOYD, Terri, Chief Financial Officer, Bates County Memorial Hospital, Butler, MO, p. A372
FLUCKEY, Kari, Director of Human Resources, Grand Island Regional Medical Center, Grand Island, NE, p. A400
FLUGUM, Aaron, Chief Executive Officer, Mercyone New Hampton Medical Center, New Hampton, IA, p. A240
FLUKE, Cinda, R.N., Chief Nursing Officer, Chi Saint Josep. Health – Saint Josep. Mount Sterling, Mount Sterling, KY, p. A272
FLUTY, Lisa, Director Information Services, Baptist Health Lexington, Lexington, KY, p. A268
FLYGARE, Matthew, Director Human Resources, Mountain West Medical Center, Tooele, UT, p. A670
FLYNN, Brian, Chief Human Resources Officer, Veterans Affairs Northern Indiana Health Care System, Fort Wayne, IN, p. A217
FLYNN, Dan, Chief Nursing Officer, Covington Trace Er & Hospital, Mandeville, LA, p. A287
FLYNN, Julianne, M.D., Executive Director, South Texas Veterans Healthcare System Audie L Murphy, San Antonio, TX, p. A651
FLYNN, Kristin, Chief Human Resources Officer, Sierra Vista Regional Medical Center, San Luis Obispo, CA, p. A93
FLYNN, Matt, Vice President/Chief Financial Officer, Northwestern Medicine Delnor Hospital, Geneva, IL, p. A196
FLYNN, Matthew J, Chief Financial Officer West Region, Northwestern Medicine Valley West Hospital, Sandwich, IL, p. A208
FLYNN, Patrick, Chief Financial Officer, Warm Springs Medical Center, Warm Springs, GA, p. A173
FLYNT, Mac
  Chief Executive Officer and Administrator, Baptist Medical Center - Attala, Kosciusko, MS, p. A365
  Chief Executive Officer and Administrator, Baptist Medical Center - Yazoo, Yazoo City, MS, p. A370
FOARD, Mesa, Director Information technology, William S. Hall Psychiatric Institute, Columbia, SC, p. A565
FOCHT, Glenn, M.D., President, Anna Jaques Hospital, Newburyport, MA, p. A316
FOGARTY, John M., President and Chief Executive Officer, Beth Israel Deaconess Hospital-Needham, Needham, MA, p. A316
FOGELSON, Julia, R.N., Chief Operating Officer and Chief Nursing Executive, French Hospital Medical Center, San Luis Obispo, CA, p. A93
FOGG, Robert W, Director Finance, Lake Taylor Transitional Care Hospital, Norfolk, VA, p. A680
FOISTER, Greer, Chief Executive Officer, Sonora Behavioral Health Hospital, Tucson, AZ, p. A41
FOLDS, Jesse, Director of Information Technologies, Merit Health Wesley, Hattiesburg, MS, p. A363
FOLEY, Chris, Chief of Medicine, Children's Hospital of The King's Daughters, Norfolk, VA, p. A680
FOLEY, James T, CPA, Vice President and Chief Financial Officer, Shore Medical Center, Somers Point, NJ, p. A428
FOLEY, John, Chief Information Officer, Allegheny General Hospital, Pittsburgh, PA, p. A551
FOLEY, Michael, M.D., Chief Medical Officer, North Okaloosa Medical Center, Crestview, FL, p. A129
FOLEY, Regina, R.N., FACHE, Vice President Nursing and Operations, Hackensack Meridian Health Ocean University Medical Center, Brick Township. NJ, p. A419
FOLK, Jeffrey R, M.D., Vice President Medical Affairs and Chief Medical Officer, Piedmont Newnan Hospital, Newnan, GA, p. A169
FOLKENBERG, Todd, Chief Executive Officer, Adventhealth Porter, Denver, CO, p. A106
FOLL, Gary R, Chief Financial Officer, Amberwell Health, Atchison, KS, p. A246
FOLLETT, Traci, Director Clinical Informatics, Sierra View Medical Center, Porterville, CA, p. A84
FOLSOM, Lori S, Assistant Vice President Human Resources, Tift Regional Medical Center, Tifton, GA, p. A172
FOLTZ, Merri, Director of Human Resources, Mount Carmel Rehabilitation Hospital, Westerville, OH, p. A507
FONDESSY, Terrence, M.D., Vice President Medical Affairs, Promedica Fostoria Community Hospital, Fostoria, OH, p. A496
FONKEN, Paul, M.D., Chief of Staff, Estes Park Health, Estes Park, CO, p. A107
FONTAINE, Barbara, Vice President, Nursing, Ascension Sacred Heart Emerald Coast, Miramar Beach, FL, p. A141

FONTENAULT, Richard, Director Information Systems, Medical City Green Oaks Hospital, Dallas, TX, p. A611
FONTENELLE, Mary, Executive Nurse Director, Eastern Louisiana Mental Health System, Jackson, LA, p. A283
FONTENOT, Ashley, Chief Executive Officer, Mercy Regional Medical Center, Ville Platte, LA, p. A294
FONTENOT, Jude
  Administrator, Ochsner Lafayette General Medical Center, Lafayette, LA, p. A285
  Chief Operating Officer, Ochsner Lafayette General Medical Center, Lafayette, LA, p. A285
FONTENOT, Michael, Chief Financial Officer, Claiborne Memorial Medical Center, Homer, LA, p. A283
FONTENOT, Robert, Director Human Resources, Kingwood Pines Hospital, Kingwood, TX, p. A632
FONTENOT, Tanya, Director of Nursing, Mercy Behavioral Hospital Llc, Lecompte, LA, p. A287
FONZIE, Juril, Director Human Resources, Helena Regional Medical Center, Helena, AR, p. A47
FOOTE, Donald E, Fiscal Officer, Wilkes-Barre Veterans Affairs Medical Center, Wilkes-Barre, PA, p. A558
FOOTE, John, Chief Information Officer, Manchester Veterans Affairs Medical Center, Manchester, NH, p. A416
FORBES, Brenda
  Controller, Encompasss Health Rehabilitation Hospital of Fort Smith, Fort Smith, AR, p. A47
  Interim Controller, Encompass Health Rehabilitation Hospital of Alexandria, Alexandria, LA, p. A276
FORBES, Dan, Vice President Human Resources, Ohsu Hospital, Portland, OR, p. A530
FORBES, Jonathan, Director Human Resources, Ashtabula County Medical Center, Ashtabula, OH, p. A485
FORBES, Ronald O, M.D., Medical Director, Central State Hospital, Petersburg, VA, p. A681
FORBORT, Gordy, Interim Chief Financial Officer, Burnett Medical Center, Grantsburg, WI, p. A711
FORD, Alisa, Vice President Human Resources, The University of Kansas Hospital, Kansas City, KS, p. A252
FORD, Angelique, Administrator Human Resources, Spring Valley Hospital Medical Center, Las Vegas, NV, p. A411
FORD, Audra, Chief Financial Officer, Madison County Health Care System, Winterset, IA, p. A245
FORD, Frank, President, St. Luke's University Hospital - Bethlehem Campus, Bethlehem, PA, p. A535
FORD, James, Director Human Resources, Baptist Health - Van Buren, Van Buren, AR, p. A54
FORD, Jessica, Interim Chief Executive Officer, Falls Community Hospital And Clinic, Marlin, TX, p. A638
FORD, John, Information Technology Director, The Brook Hospital – Kmi, Louisville, KY, p. A270
FORD, Karen, Chief Nursing Officer, Sabine Medical Center, Many, LA, p. A288
FORD, LeeAnn, Director Human Resources and Imaging, The Physicians Centre Hospital, Bryan, TX, p. A605
FORD, Mary Carroll, Chief Information Officer, Jefferson Einstein Montgomery Hospital, East Norriton, PA, p. A538
FORD, Michael, Vice President Patient Services, Wood County Hospital, Bowling Green, OH, p. A487
FORD, Nathan, Chief Executive Officer, Encompass Health Rehabilitation Hospital of Parkersburg, Parkersburg, WV, p. A703
FORD, Tim, President and Chief Executive Officer, Randolp. Health, Asheboro, NC, p. A463
FORD, Veronica, Vice President Human Resources, University of Maryland Capital Region Medical Center, Largo, MD, p. A305
FORDE, Kerry, Chief Operating Officer, Kaiser Permanente Zion Medical Center, San Diego, CA, p. A89
FORDYCE, Brian, Director Information Technology, Roosevelt Medical Center, Culbertson, MT, p. A391
FOREMAN, Christopher, Director Human Resources, Santa Rosa Medical Center, Milton, FL, p. A141
FOREMAN, Kim, M.D., Chief of Staff, Baylor Scott & White Texas Spine & Joint Hospital-Tyler, Tyler, TX, p. A658
FOREMAN, Lee Ann
  Vice President Human Resources, Mississipp. Baptist Medical Center, Jackson, MS, p. A364
  Vice President Human Resources, Select Specialty Hospital - Belhaven, Jackson, MS, p. A364
FOREMAN, Nena, Chief Nursing Officer, Palo Verde Hospital, Blythe, CA, p. A58
FORESTER, John C.
  Interim President, Braxton County Memorial Hospital, Gassaway, WV, p. A700
  Interim President, Summersville Regional Medical Center, Summersville, WV, p. A705
FORET, Chris, M.D., Chief of Staff, Riverside Medical Center, Franklinton, LA, p. A282
FORET, Robert, Chief Financial Officer, Yoakum Community Hospital, Yoakum, TX, p. A663

FORGE, Brenda J, Vice President, Human Resources, Regional West Medical Center, Scottsbluff, NE, p. A406
FORGE, Matthew, Chief Executive Officer, Pullman Regional Hospital, Pullman, WA, p. A693
FORGET, Theresa, Executive Director, Human Resources, Johns Hopkins Howard County Medical Center, Columbia, MD, p. A303
FORKEL, Todd, Chief Executive Officer, Altru Health System, Grand Forks, ND, p. A481
FORKNER, Christine, Executive Vice President and Chief Financial Officer, National Jewish Health, Denver, CO, p. A106
FORNIER–JOHNSON, Michelle, Group Vice President Human Resources, St. Anthony Hospital, Lakewood, CO, p. A110
FORREST, Brian, Vice President Human Resources, Cayuga Medical Center At Ithaca, Ithaca, NY, p. A444
FORREST, Devon, Chief Executive Officer, Guidance Center, Flagstaff, AZ, p. A31
FORREST, Kevin, FACHE, Medical Center Director, Manchester Veterans Affairs Medical Center, Manchester, NH, p. A416
FORREST, LaDessa, Chief Executive Officer, Encompass Health Rehabilitation Hospital of Albuquerque, Albuquerque, NM, p. A432
FORREST, Qualenta, Executive Vice President, Chief People and Talent Officer, Tamp. General Hospital, Tampa, FL, p. A152
FORREST, Shannon C., R.N., Chief Nursing Officer, Christus St. Frances Cabrini Hospital, Alexandria, LA, p. A276
FORRESTER, John M, Director Information Services, Hamilton Medical Center, Dalton, GA, p. A162
FORSCH, Randall T, M.D., M.P.H., Chief Medical Officer, Chelsea Hospital, Chelsea, MI, p. A324
FORSHA, Barbara, Interim Medical Center Director, Louis A. Johnson Veterans Affairs Medical Center, Clarksburg, WV, p. A700
FORSTER, Tracy B, R.N., Senior Director of Nursing, Novant Health Matthews Medical Center, Matthews, NC, p. A472
FORSYTH, Kurt
 President, Delta Community Medical Center, Delta, UT, p. A664
 President, Fillmore Community Hospital, Fillmore, UT, p. A665
FORSYTH, Larry, Director Information Services, Ou Health – University of Oklahoma Medical Center, Oklahoma City, OK, p. A518
FORT, Glenn, Chief Medical Officer, Landmark Medical Center, Woonsocket, RI, p. A561
FORTENBERRY, Denise, Chief Nursing Officer and Chief Compliance Officer, Cypress Pointe Surgical Hospital, Hammond, LA, p. A282
FORTENBERRY, Doris, Coordinator Human Resources, Delta Health System, Dumas, AR, p. A45
FORTENBERRY, Rob, Chief Information Officer, Mann–Grandstaff Department of Veterans Affairs Medical Center, Spokane, WA, p. A696
FORTIN, Amanda, Manager Finance, Decatur Health Systems, Oberlin, KS, p. A256
FORTIN, Laura, R.N., Chief Operating Officer, St. Josep. Medical Center, Houston, TX, p. A628
FORTMANN, Tony, Chief Financial Officer, Buchanan County Health Center, Independence, IA, p. A238
FORTNEY, John
 Chief Medical Officer, Adena Pike Medical Center, Waverly, OH, p. A506
 Senior System Medical Advisor, Adena Regional Medical Center, Chillicothe, OH, p. A488
FORTUNE, Julia C., Acting Administrator/Risk Manager, Port St. Lucie Hospital, Port St Lucie, FL, p. A147
FOSBERG, Renee, Chief Information Officer, Emerson Hospital, Concord, MA, p. A313
FOSINA, Michael, M.P.H., FACHE, President, New York–Presbyterian Hospital, New York, NY, p. A450
FOSNESS, Nick, Chief Executive Officer, Marshall County Healthcare Center Avera, Britton, SD, p. A572
FOSNOCHT, Kevin, M.D., Chief Medical Officer and Associate Executive Director, Penn Presbyterian Medical Center, Philadelphia, PA, p. A549
FOSS, Coleman, Senior Vice President and Hospital President, Wellstar West Georgia Medical Center, Lagrange, GA, p. A166
FOSS, David, Chief Information Officer, New London Hospital, New London, NH, p. A416
FOSS, R Coleman, Chief Executive Officer, Tennova Healthcare – Cleveland, Cleveland, TN, p. A581
FOSTER, Angelia, Chief Administrative Officer, Marshfield Medical Center – Beaver Dam, Beaver Dam, WI, p. A708
FOSTER, Angie, Chief Nursing Officer, Evanston Regional Hospital, Evanston, WY, p. A727
FOSTER, Barbara A, Regional Human Resources Director, Select Specialty Hospital–Wilmington, Wilmington, DE, p. A122

FOSTER, Becky
 Employee Relations Specialist, Sanford Tracy Medical Center, Tracy, MN, p. A356
 Employee Relations Specialist, Sanford Westbrook Medical Center, Westbrook, MN, p. A357
FOSTER, Bob, Chief Information Officer, South Georgia Medical Center, Valdosta, GA, p. A173
FOSTER, Carolyn, Chief Financial Officer, Peacehealth Peace Island Medical Center, Friday Harbor, WA, p. A690
FOSTER, Charles, Regional Director Human Resources, Christus Southeast Texas Hospital – St. Elizabeth, Beaumont, TX, p. A602
FOSTER, Chris, Director Health Information Management, Deer Lodge Medical Center, Deer Lodge, MT, p. A391
FOSTER, Daniel J, Chief Financial Officer, Northern Utah Rehabilitation Hospital, South Ogden, UT, p. A670
FOSTER, Gary
 R.N., Associate Administrator, Banner Estrella Medical Center, Phoenix, AZ, p. A35
 R.N., Chief Operating Officer, Peacehealth Southwest Medical Center, Vancouver, WA, p. A698
 Vice President and Chief Financial Officer, Saratoga Hospital, Saratoga Springs, NY, p. A458
FOSTER, Kennetha, Chief Nursing Officer, Mission Regional Medical Center, Mission, TX, p. A640
FOSTER, Larry, R.N., MSN, Chief Executive Officer, Kindred Hospital–San Francisco Bay Area, San Leandro, CA, p. A92
FOSTER, Matthew, Chief Executive Officer and Superintendent, Neurodiagnostic Institute And Advanced Treatment Center, Indianapolis, IN, p. A220
FOSTER, Michael, Director Information Systems, East Cooper Medical Center, Mount Pleasant, SC, p. A568
FOSTER, Mickey W., Chief Executive Officer, Firsthealth Moore Regional Hospital, Pinehurst, NC, p. A474
FOSTER, Mike, Manager Information Systems, Moab Regional Hospital, Moab, UT, p. A666
FOSTER, Mitzi, Director Information Services, Southern Tennessee Regional Health System–Pulaski, Pulaski, TN, p. A592
FOSTER, Nancy, Vice President, Human Resources, Hendricks Regional Health, Danville, IN, p. A215
FOSTER, Patti, Chief Operations Officer, Cleveland Emergency Hospital, Humble, TX, p. A629
FOSTER, Rebecca, MSN, R.N., Chief Nursing Officer, Cumberland Medical Center, Crossville, TN, p. A582
FOSTER, Robert, Director Human Resources, Regional Medical Center of Central Alabama, Greenville, AL, p. A20
FOSTER, Stephanie, MSN, R.N., Chief Nursing Officer, Longview Regional Medical Center, Longview, TX, p. A635
FOSTER, Steven
 President and Chief Executive Officer, St. Luke's Health – Patients Medical Center, Pasadena, TX, p. A643
 President and Chief Executive Officer, St. Luke's Health – Sugar Land Hospital, Sugar Land, TX, p. A655
FOSTER, Terri, Hospital Finance Officer, Baylor Scott & White Medical Center – Grapevine, Grapevine, TX, p. A622
FOSTER, Timothy, Acting Chief Medical Officer, Newton–Wellesley Hospital, Newton Lower Falls, MA, p. A316
FOTIADIS, George, M.D., Chief of Staff, Clarke County Hospital, Osceola, IA, p. A241
FOTTER, Robert, Chief Financial Officer, Pennsylvania Psychiatric Institute, Harrisburg, PA, p. A541
FOUCH, Loren, Chief Executive Officer, Millwood Hospital, Arlington, TX, p. A597
FOUGERE, John, Chief Financial Officer, Acadian Medical Center, Eunice, LA, p. A281
FOUGHT, Scott, Vice President Finance, Promedica Bay Park Hospital, Oregon, OH, p. A502
FOULKE, Elvia, Executive Vice President and Chief Operating Officer, Emanate Health Foothill Presbyterian Hospital, Glendora, CA, p. A66
FOUNTAIN, Wesley D, Chief Financial Officer, St. David's South Austin Medical Center, Austin, TX, p. A600
FOURNIER JOHNSON, Michelle, Chief Human Resource Officer, Denver Health, Denver, CO, p. A106
FOUSE, Carla, Chief Nursing Officer, Ascension St. Vincent Randolph, Winchester, IN, p. A229
FOUSE, Sarah, Associate Director of Patient Services, Captain James A. Lovell Federal Health Care Center, North Chicago, IL, p. A203
FOUST, Lisa
 Senior Vice President Human Resources, John Muir Behavioral Health Center, Concord, CA, p. A60
 Senior Vice President Human Resources, John Muir Health, Concord Medical Center, Concord, CA, p. A60
 Senior Vice President, Human Resources, John Muir Medical Center, Walnut Creek, Walnut Creek, CA, p. A100
FOUST–COFIELD, Misti, R.N., Vice President and Chief Nursing Officer, Reid Health, Richmond, IN, p. A226

FOUTS, Phillip
 Chief Financial Officer, Dekalb Regional Medical Center, Fort Payne, AL, p. A19
 Chief Financial Officer, Fannin Regional Hospital, Blue Ridge, GA, p. A159
FOUTZ, Patricia, Director Human Resources, Bath Community Hospital, Hot Springs, VA, p. A678
FOWLER, Barry, Director Human and System Resources, Clark Fork Valley Hospital, Plains, MT, p. A394
FOWLER, Brian
 Chief Executive Officer, Arkansas Surgical Hospital, North Little Rock, AR, p. A51
 Information Technology Director, Jeff Davis Hospital, Hazlehurst, GA, p. A165
FOWLER, D. Ryan., President, Chi Mercy Health, Valley City, ND, p. A483
FOWLER, Jennifer Central State Hospital, Louisville, KY, p. A269
FOWLER, Kate, Chief Financial Officer, West Valley Medical Center, Caldwell, ID, p. A180
FOWLER, Kevin
 Chief Financial Officer, Ferrell Hospital, Eldorado, IL, p. A194
 Director Finance, Putnam County Hospital, Greencastle, IN, p. A218
FOWLER, Marcia, Chief Executive Officer, Bournewood Health Systems, Brookline, MA, p. A312
FOWLER, Maureen, Director Human Resources, Conifer Park, Glenville, NY, p. A443
FOWLER, Rita, Vice President of Nursing and Chief Nursing Officer, SSM Health Saint Louis University Hospital, Saint Louis, MO, p. A384
FOWLER, Ruth, Senior Vice President and Chief Financial Officer, Children's Healthcare of Atlanta, Atlanta, GA, p. A157
FOWLER, Steven, M.D., President Medical Staff, Genesis Medical Center, Dewitt, De Witt, IA, p. A234
FOX, Alan, Chief Financial Officer, UCSF Health Saint Francis Hospital, San Francisco, CA, p. A91
FOX, Carol J., M.D., Senior Vice President and Chief Medical Officer, Excela Health Latrobe Hospital, Latrobe, PA, p. A544
FOX, Chris, Division President, Louisiana Extended Care Hospital of Lafayette, Lafayette, LA, p. A285
FOX, Christine, MSN, R.N., Interim Chief Nursing Officer, Corewell Health Watervliet Hospital, Watervliet, MI, p. A340
FOX, David R., FACHE, Chief Executive Officer, Merit Health River Region, Vicksburg, MS, p. A369
FOX, Debra, Chief Nursing Officer, University Medical Center, Las Vegas, NV, p. A411
FOX, Devin, M.D., Vice President Medical Operations, Chi Health Creighton University Medical Center – Bergan Mercy, Omaha, NE, p. A403
FOX, Jay
 FACHE, President, Baylor Scott & White Medical Center – Austin, Austin, TX, p. A599
 FACHE, President, Baylor Scott & White Medical Center – Buda, Buda, TX, p. A605
 FACHE, President, Baylor Scott & White Medical Center – Pflugerville, Pflugerville, TX, p. A644
 FACHE, President, Baylor Scott & White Medical Center – Round Rock, Round Rock, TX, p. A647
 FACHE, President, Baylor Scott & White Medical Center – Taylor, Taylor, TX, p. A655
 FACHE, President BSWH Austin Area, Baylor Scott & White Emergency Medical Center– Cedar Park, Cedar Park, TX, p. A607
FOX, Jerome
 Chief Information Officer, Alton Memorial Hospital, Alton, IL, p. A185
 Senior Vice President and Chief Information Officer, Memorial Hospital Belleville, Belleville, IL, p. A186
FOX, Jessica, Director of Human Resources, Aspirus Riverview Hospital And Clinics, Inc., Wisconsin Rapids, WI, p. A725
FOX, John, M.D., Medical Director, Select Specialty Hospital – San Diego, San Diego, CA, p. A89
FOX, Judi Kennedy., President and Chief Executive Officer, Rutland Regional Medical Center, Rutland, VT, p. A672
FOX, Julie, M.D., Chief Medical Officer, Lone Peak Hospital, Draper, UT, p. A665
FOX, Randy, Director Performance Improvement and Risk Management, Lakeland Behavioral Health System, Springfield, MO, p. A386
FOX, Starla, Director of Nursing, Bristol Bay Area Health Corporation, Dillingham, AK, p. A28
FOX, Susan, President and Chief Executive Officer, White Plains Hospital Center, White Plains, NY, p. A462
FOY, Gregory S., Risk Manager, Scheurer Health, Pigeon, MI, p. A335

Index of Health Care Professionals

Index of Health Care Professionals / Frachiseur

FRACHISEUR, Kenny, Chief Information Officer, Ouachita County Medical Center, Camden, AR, p. A44
FRACHISEUR, Trey, Chief Human Resources Officer, Sevier County Medical Center, De Queen, AR, p. A45
FRACICA, Philip. M.D., Chief Medical Officer, Bothwell Regional Health Center, Sedalia, MO, p. A386
FRACK, Darla, MSN, Vice President, Patient Services, St. Luke's Anderson Campus, Easton, PA, p. A539
FRAGEN, Andrew, M.D., Chief Medical Officer, Community Hospital of San Bernardino, San Bernardino, CA, p. A88
FRAGOSO, Lucio, President and Chief Executive Officer, Children's Hospital New Orleans, New Orleans, LA, p. A290
FRAHER, Francis D, Vice President, Finance, Northwestern Memorial Hospital, Northwestern Memorial Hospital, Chicago, IL, p. A190
FRAIOLA, Anthony, Associate Administrator Administrative and Support Services, Hawaii State Hospital, Kaneohe, HI, p. A177
FRAKER, Steve
Chief Financial Officer, Banner Churchill Community Hospital, Fallon, NV, p. A408
Chief Financial Officer, Banner Lassen Medical Center, Susanville, CA, p. A97
FRALICKER, Tammy, MS, R.N., Chief Nursing Officer, Crawford Memorial Hospital, Robinson, IL, p. A207
FRAME, Angela, Chief Financial Officer, Jackson General Hospital, Ripley, WV, p. A704
FRAME, Daphne, R.N., Director of Nursing, Oceans Behavioral Hospital of Opelousas, Opelousas, LA, p. A291
FRAME, Ken, Chief Nursing Officer, Ashtabula County Medical Center, Ashtabula, OH, p. A485
FRANCE, Cheryl, M.D., Chief Medical Officer, William R. Sharpe, Jr. Hospital, Weston, WV, p. A706
FRANCE, James, M.D., Chief of Staff, Conway Regional Health System, Conway, AR, p. A44
FRANCIS, Carolyn, R.N., MSN, Director of Nursing, Lasalle General Hospital, Jena, LA, p. A284
FRANCIS, Jeff
Vice President Finance and Chief Financial Officer, Methodist Jennie Edmundson Hospital, Council Bluffs, IA, p. A234
Vice President, Chief Financial Officer, Methodist Fremont Health, Fremont, NE, p. A400
FRANCIS, Keaton, Chief Hospital Executive, Integris Health Enid Hospital, Enid, OK, p. A512
FRANCIS, Lana B., Chief Executive Officer, Lasalle General Hospital, Jena, LA, p. A284
FRANCIS, Perry, Supervisory Information Technology Specialist, Chinle Comprehensive Health Care Facility, Chinle, AZ, p. A31
FRANCIS, Rebekah
JD, Chief Financial Officer, Aurora Behavioral Health System East, Tempe, AZ, p. A39
JD, Chief Financial Officer, Aurora Behavioral Health System West, Glendale, AZ, p. A32
FRANCISCO, Gerard E, M.D., Chief Medical Officer, Tirr Memorial Hermann, Houston, TX, p. A628
FRANCKOWIAK, Debra, Executive Director, Children's Hospital of Wisconsin–Fox Valley, Neenah, WI, p. A718
FRANCO, Glenda, Director, Human Resources, Vibra Hospital of Sacramento, Folsom, CA, p. A63
FRANCO, Luis, M.D., Medical Director, United Medical Rehabilitation Hospital–Hammond, Hammond, LA, p. A283
FRANCO, Richard, Chief Financial Officer, Community First Medical Center, Chicago, IL, p. A189
FRANCO, Richard A., Vice President and Chief Financial Officer, Northwestern Medicine Lake Forest Hospital, Lake Forest, IL, p. A200
FRANCO, Roger, Director Human Resources, St. John's Episcopal Hospital, New York, NY, p. A453
FRANCO, Rosemary, Chief Nursing Officer, Cochran Memorial Hospital, Morton, TX, p. A640
FRANCOIS, Brennan, Chief Executive Officer, Sun Behavioral Houston, Houston, TX, p. A628
FRANCOIS, Fritz, M.D., Chief Medical Officer, Nyu Langone Hospitals, New York, NY, p. A452
FRANK, Anthony, M.D., Senior Vice President and Chief Medical Officer, UNC Health Blue Ridge, Morganton, NC, p. A473
FRANK, Barbara, Human Resource Specialist, Caro Center, Caro, MI, p. A323
FRANK, Cathrine, M.D., Chairperson, Henry Ford Kingswood Hospital, Ferndale, MI, p. A326
FRANK, Daniel, Chief Financial Officer, Craig Hospital, Englewood, CO, p. A107
FRANK, Debra, Chief Financial Officer, Ness County Hospital District No 2, Ness City, KS, p. A255
FRANK, Jessie, Assistant Vice President, Information Services, Ochsner Lsu Health Shreveport – Monroe Medical Center, Monroe, LA, p. A288
FRANK, Joseph
Interim President, Penn State Health St. Joseph, Reading, PA, p. A553
Regional Hospital President, East Region, Penn State Health Lancaster Medical Center, Lancaster, PA, p. A543
Regional Hospital President, East Region, Penn State Health St. Joseph, Reading, PA, p. A553
FRANK, Kim, Chief Human Resources Officer, Virginia Gay Hospital, Vinton, IA, p. A244
FRANK, Mitchell, Chief Financial Officer, Vanderbilt Tullahoma Harton Hospital, Tullahoma, TN, p. A594
FRANK, Patricia, Chief Nursing Officer, Henry County Hospital, Napoleon, OH, p. A501
FRANK, Robert A
Senior Vice President of Operations, University of Maryland Shore Medical Center At Chestertown, Chestertown, MD, p. A303
Senior Vice President of Operations, University of Maryland Shore Medical Center At Easton, Easton, MD, p. A304
FRANK, Thomas, President & Chief Executive Officer, North Country Hospital And Health Center, Newport, VT, p. A672
FRANK–LIGHTFOOT, Loraine, Vice President and Market Chief Nursing Officer, Novant Health Forsyth Medical Center, Winston–Salem, NC, p. A478
FRANKE, Jessica, Chief Executive Officer, Pam Rehabilitation Hospital of Fargo, Fargo, ND, p. A480
FRANKE, Paul, M.D., Chief Medical Officer, Alaska Native Medical Center, Anchorage, AK, p. A27
FRANKEL, Harris, M.D., Chief Medical Officer, Chief Compliance Officer, Nebraska Medicine – Nebraska Medical Center, Omaha, NE, p. A404
FRANKEL, Michele, Associate Executive Director Finance, Glen Cove Hospital, Glen Cove, NY, p. A443
FRANKEN, Stephanie, Vice President Operational Finance, Chi St. Alexius Health Dickinson, Dickinson, ND, p. A480
FRANKL, Angie, Director Human Resources, Adair County Health System, Greenfield, IA, p. A236
FRANKLIN, Chuck, M.D., Chief Medical Staff, Weston County Health Services, Newcastle, WY, p. A727
FRANKLIN, Ed, Chief Human Resources Officer, Page Hospital, Page, AZ, p. A34
FRANKLIN, Jennifer, R.N., Chief Clinical Officer, Yoakum Community Hospital, Yoakum, TX, p. A663
FRANKLIN, Kimberly, Director, Human Resource, Encompass Health Rehabilitation Hospital of Pensacola, Pensacola, FL, p. A146
FRANKLIN, Matthew, Director Human Resources, Warren General Hospital, Warren, PA, p. A556
FRANKLIN, Michael A., FACHE, Chief Executive Officer, Encompass Health Rehabilitation Hospital of Ocala, Ocala, FL, p. A143
FRANKLIN, Michelle, Chief Executive Officer, Sullivan County Community Hospital, Sullivan, IN, p. A227
FRANKLIN, Tammy, Manager Personnel and Marketing, Covenant Hospital–Levelland, Levelland, TX, p. A634
FRANKO, Stephen, Vice President Finance and Chief Financial Officer, Regional Hospital of Scranton, Scranton, PA, p. A554
FRANKOVITCH, John C., President and Chief Executive Officer, Weirton Medical Center, Weirton, WV, p. A705
FRANKS, Cathy RN, Chief Operating Officer, Izard County Medical Center, Calico Rock, AR, p. A44
FRANKS, Charles, Chief Human Resources, Northeast Ohio Va Healthcare System, Cleveland, OH, p. A491
FRANKS, Dennis
FACHE, Chief Executive Officer, Neosho Memorial Regional Medical Center, Chanute, KS, p. A247
Interim Chief Financial Officer, Pontiac General Hospital, Pontiac, MI, p. A335
Vice President Operations, Pontiac General Hospital, Pontiac, MI, p. A335
FRANOVICH, Tracey, R.N., President and Chief Executive Officer, Mclaren Macomb, Mount Clemens, MI, p. A333
FRANSEN, Mitchell, Chief Financial Officer, Mesa View Regional Hospital, Mesquite, NV, p. A411
FRANSON, John K, M.D., Chief Medical Staff, Caribou Medical Center, Soda Springs, ID, p. A184
FRANTZ, Vincent, M.D., Chief of Staff, Plumas District Hospital, Quincy, CA, p. A84
FRANZ, Eric, Vice President, Finance and Chief Financial Officer, Graham Hospital, Canton, IL, p. A187
FRANZ, Staci, Director Human Resources, Providence St. Luke's Rehabilitation Medical Center, Spokane, WA, p. A696
FRANZEN, Danelle, Chief Operating Officer, Great Plains Health, North Platte, NE, p. A403
FRARDO, Virgil, M.D., Medical Director, Encompass Health Rehabilitation Hospital of Wichita Falls, Wichita Falls, TX, p. A662
FRASCA, Edith, Controller and Chief Financial Officer, The Pavilion, Champaign, IL, p. A187
FRASCH, Sara, Chief Human Resource Officer, University of New Mexico Hospitals, Albuquerque, NM, p. A433
FRASER, Cathryn H., Chief Human Resources Officer, Mayo Clinic Health System In Sparta, Sparta, WI, p. A721
FRASER, James, Administrator Finance, Ascension Via Christi Hospital, Manhattan, Manhattan, KS, p. A254
FRASER, Sherry, Administrator, Christus Santa Rosa Health System, San Antonio, TX, p. A649
FRASIER, Nora, R.N., FACHE, Chief Nursing Officer, Methodist Mansfield Medical Center, Mansfield, TX, p. A637
FRASURE, Jane, Human Resources, Midcoast Central – Llano, Llano, TX, p. A635
FRAUENHOFER, Chris
Chief Financial Officer, Northern Light Maine Coast Hospital, Ellsworth, ME, p. A297
Vice President of Finance, Northern Light Inland Hospital, Waterville, ME, p. A299
FRAYSER, Jay, MSN, R.N., Administrator, Texas Health Harris Methodist Hospital Hurst–Euless–Bedford, Bedford, TX, p. A602
FRAZIER, Amy, Supervisor Management Information Systems, Wetzel County Hospital, New Martinsville, WV, p. A703
FRAZIER, Brandon, Chief Financial Officer, HCA Houston Healthcare Conroe, Conroe, TX, p. A608
FRAZIER, Derrick A., FACHE, President, OSF Saint James – John W. Albrecht Medical Center, Pontiac, IL, p. A206
FRAZIER, James P. III, Chief Executive Officer, Beaumont Emergency Hospital, Beaumont, TX, p. A602
FRAZIER, Joel L, M.D., Medical Director, Onecore Health, Oklahoma City, OK, p. A518
FREAS, Mary Ann, Senior Vice President and Chief Financial Officer, Southwest General Health Center, Middleburg Heights, OH, p. A500
FRED, Mark
R.N., Chief Operating Officer, Kirby Medical Center, Monticello, IL, p. A202
R.N., Chief Operating Offier, Chief Information Officer, Kirby Medical Center, Monticello, IL, p. A202
FREDEBOELLING, Elizabeth, Chief Nursing Officer, Dell Children's Medical Center of Central Texas, Austin, TX, p. A600
FREDERICK, Brenda, Director Human Resources, Laurel Ridge Treatment Center, San Antonio, TX, p. A650
FREDERICK, Dessa, Manager Human Resources, St. James Behavioral Health Hospital, Gonzales, LA, p. A282
FREDERICK, Gretchen A, R.N., Director Patient Care Services, Buffalo Hospital, Buffalo, MN, p. A344
FREDERICK, John, Chief Financial Officer, West Central Georgia Regional Hospital, Columbus, GA, p. A161
FREDERICK, Ryannon, Chief Nursing Officer, Mayo Clinic Hospital In Florida, Jacksonville, FL, p. A135
FREDERICKS, David, Chief Executive Officer, Encompass Health Rehabilitation Hospital of Lakeview, Elizabethtown, KY, p. A265
FREDERICKSON, Kathy, Information Systems Site Lead, Sutter Delta Medical Center, Antioch, CA, p. A55
FREDETTE, Beth, Chief Information Officer, Dayton Children's Hospital, Dayton, OH, p. A493
FREDRICK, Joyce, Associate Director, Veterans Affairs Central Western Massachusetts Healthcare System, Leeds, MA, p. A315
FREDRICK, Rick, Director Information Technology, Cottage Hospital, Woodsville, NH, p. A417
FREDRICKSON, Kelley, Director Information Services, Medical City Fort Worth, Fort Worth, TX, p. A620
FREDRICKSON, Mark A, M.D., Medical Director, Encompass Health Rehabilitation Hospital of Midland Odessa, Midland, TX, p. A639
FREE, Johnathan, Information Security Officer, Fairbanks Memorial Hospital, Fairbanks, AK, p. A28
FREEBORN, Fawn, Human Resources Generalist, Schoolcraft Memorial Hospital, Manistique, MI, p. A333
FREEBURN, Mark, Chief Executive Officer, Penn State Health Rehabilitation Hospital, Hummelstown, PA, p. A542
FREED, Nancy, Chief Financial Officer, Seiling Municipal Hospital, Seiling, OK, p. A520
FREED, Stuart
M.D., Chief Medical Officer, Confluence Health Hospital – Central Campus, Wenatchee, WA, p. A698
M.D., Medical Director, Confluence Health Hospital – Mares Campus, Wenatchee, WA, p. A698
FREED–SIGURDSSON, Anna, M.D., Medical Director, Encompass Health Rehabilitation Hospital of Dallas, Dallas, TX, p. A611
FREEDMAN, Kenneth, M.D., Chief Medical Officer, Lemuel Shattuck Hospital, Jamaica Plain, MA, p. A314
FREEHILL, Sarah, Chief Nursing Officer, Arbuckle Memorial Hospital, Sulphur, OK, p. A521
FREELAND, R Alan, M.D., Chief Clinical Officer, Twin Valley Behavioral Healthcare, Columbus, OH, p. A493

A850 Index of Health Care Professionals

Index of Health Care Professionals
Index of Health Care Professionals / Fry

FREEMAN, Brian, FACHE, Senior Vice President, President West Area, Atrium Health Stanly, Albemarle, NC, p. A463
FREEMAN, Diane, R.N., Assistant Vice President and Chief Nursing Officer, St. Luke's Health – Lakeside Hospital, The Woodlands, TX, p. A657
FREEMAN, Dominic, Chief Information Officer, Community Healthcare System, Onaga, KS, p. A256
FREEMAN, Gail, Chief Nursing Officer, San Gabriel Valley Medical Center, San Gabriel, CA, p. A91
FREEMAN, Jerry, Chief, Human Resources Management Services, Durham Va Health Care System, Durham, NC, p. A467
FREEMAN, Julie, Commander, Winn Army Community Hospital, Hinesville, GA, p. A165
FREEMAN, Kimberlee
Vice President of Patient Care Services/Chief Nursing Officer, Wayne Healthcare, Greenville, OH, p. A497
Vice President Patient Care Services and Chief Nursing Officer, Wayne Healthcare, Greenville, OH, p. A497
FREEMAN, Marianne, Vice President Human Resources, Piedmont Rockdale Hospital, Conyers, GA, p. A161
FREEMAN, Michael
Director Human Resources, Alta Vista Regional Hospital, Las Vegas, NM, p. A435
Director Human Resources, Huhukam Memorial Hospital, Sacaton, AZ, p. A37
FREEMAN, Mike, Director Information Technology, Sentara Williamsburg Regional Medical Center, Williamsburg, VA, p. A685
FREEMAN, Peggy, Chief Physicians Services Officer, Marshfield Medical Center – Dickinson, Iron Mountain, MI, p. A330
FREEMAN, Randolph, M.D., Vice President Medical Affairs, Memorial Hospital Belleville, Belleville, IL, p. A186
FREEMAN, Richard, FACS, M.D., Chief Clinical Officer, Loyola University Medical Center, Maywood, IL, p. A201
FREEMAN, Robert, Director Human Resources, Baptist Health–Fort Smith, Fort Smith, AR, p. A46
FREEMAN–BROWN, Samantha, Assistant Administrator, Respiratory Director, Lifebrite Community Hospital of Stokes, Danbury, NC, p. A466
FREGOLI, Fabian, M.D., Chief Medical Officer, Trinity Health Oakland Hospital, Pontiac, MI, p. A335
FREID–SCHEPPKE, Denise, Chief Accounting Officer, Oakleaf Surgical Hospital, Altoona, WI, p. A707
FREIER, Toby, President, New Ulm Medical Center, New Ulm, MN, p. A352
FREIJ, Walid, M.D., Chief of Staff, Vaughan Regional Medical Center, Selma, AL, p. A24
FREILICH, Josh, Vice President and Chief Nurse Executive, Mercy Hospital of Folsom, Folsom, CA, p. A63
FREIMARK, Jeffrey P., Chief Executive Officer, Miami Jewish Health, Miami, FL, p. A140
FREISCHLAG, Julie Ann., M.D., FACS, Chief Executive Officer, Atrium Health Wake Forest Baptist, Winston–Salem, NC, p. A478
FREITAG, Donald, M.D., Chief Medical Officer, Lynn County Hospital District, Tahoka, TX, p. A655
FREITAG, Vanessa, Chief Operating Officer, Mercyone Des Moines Medical Center, Des Moines, IA, p. A235
FRELING, Eric, M.D., Director Medical Staff Affairs, Memorial Hospital West, Pembroke Pines, FL, p. A146
FRENCH, Dean O, M.D., Chief of Staff, Faith Regional Health Services, Norfolk, NE, p. A403
FRENCH, Holly, Chief Financial Officer, Newman Regional Health, Emporia, KS, p. A249
FRENCH, Lori, Manager Human Resources, Fulton State Hospital, Fulton, MO, p. A375
FRENCH, Toni, Manager Human Resources, Callaway District Hospital, Callaway, NE, p. A398
FRENCH, Tracy
Chief Financial Officer, Banner Goldfield Medical Center, Apache Junction, AZ, p. A30
Chief Financial Officer, Banner Ironwood Medical Center, San Tan Valley, AZ, p. A38
FRENGLE, Kelley
Director, Human Resources, Peacehealth St. John Medical Center, Longview, WA, p. A691
Senior Director, Human Resources, Peacehealth Southwest Medical Center, Vancouver, WA, p. A698
FRENIER, Karen, Chief Human Resources Officer, Orlando Health – Health Central Hospital, Ocoee, FL, p. A143
FRERER, Mary
Chief Human Resources Officer, Freeman Health System, Joplin, MO, p. A377
Chief Human Resources Officer, Freeman Neosho Hospital, Neosho, MO, p. A381
FRERICHS, Craig, Chief Information Technology Service, Grand Junction Va Medical Center, Grand Junction, CO, p. A108
FRESQUEZ, Juan, President, Methodist Mansfield Medical Center, Mansfield, TX, p. A637
FREUDENBERGER, Joe, Chief Executive Officer, Oakbend Medical Center, Richmond, TX, p. A646
FREUND, Jenn, MSN, R.N., Chief Nursing Officer, Trident Medical Center, Charleston, SC, p. A563
FREY, Jack, Acting Business Manager, Greystone Park Psychiatric Hospital, Morris Plains, NJ, p. A424
FREY, James Jr, Acting Manager Human Resources, Greystone Park Psychiatric Hospital, Morris Plains, NJ, p. A424
FREY, Jeff, Business Administrator, Elizabeth Parsons Ware Packard Mental Health Center, Springfield, IL, p. A209
FREY, Michael, Chief Executive Officer, Pineville Community Health Center, Pineville, KY, p. A273
FREY, Paul, Director Information Technology Applications, Orthoindy Hospital, Indianapolis, IN, p. A220
FREY, Rachel, Director Human Resources, Athens–Limestone Hospital, Athens, AL, p. A15
FREYER, Mary, Chief Operating Officer, OSF Healthcare Little Company of Mary Medical Center, Evergreen Park, IL, p. A195
FREYER, Sharon, R.N., Chief Nursing Officer, Baptist Health Paducah, Paducah, KY, p. A272
FREYMULLER, Robert S., Chief Executive Officer, Summerlin Hospital Medical Center, Las Vegas, NV, p. A411
FREYSINGER, Edward E., Chief Executive Officer, St. Josep. Regional Medical Center, Lewiston, ID, p. A182
FRIARTE, Pedro, Director of Physician Services, Coral Gables Hospital, Coral Gables, FL, p. A128
FRIAS, Patricio A., M.D., President and Chief Executive Officer, Rady Children's Hospital – San Diego, San Diego, CA, p. A89
FRICK, Mary Jo, Director Finance, St. Catherine's Rehabilitation Hospital, North Miami, FL, p. A142
FRICKE, Rhett D., Chief Executive Officer/Administrator, Ballinger Memorial Hospital, Ballinger, TX, p. A601
FRIDAY, Lisa, Director Human Resources, Christus Ochsner Lake Area Hospital, Lake Charles, LA, p. A286
FRIDKIN, Marjorie, M.D., Chief Medical Officer, Garrett Regional Medical Center, Oakland, MD, p. A306
FRIED, Guy, M.D., Chief Medical Officer, Magee Rehabilitation, Philadelphia, PA, p. A549
FRIED, Tera, Manager Human Resources, West River Regional Medical Center, Hettinger, ND, p. A481
FRIEDEN, Robert
Vice President Information Systems, Genesis Medical Center – Davenport, Davenport, IA, p. A234
Vice President Information Systems, Genesis Medical Center, Silvis, Silvis, IL, p. A208
Vice President, Information Services and Chief Information Officer, Genesis Medical Center–Aledo, Aledo, IL, p. A185
FRIEDENBACH, Daryl, Director Fiscal Services, Floyd Valley Healthcare, Le Mars, IA, p. A239
FRIEDLY, Jenni
Market President, UnityPoint Health – Waterloo, Unitypoint Health – Allen Hospital, Waterloo, IA, p. A244
Market President, UnityPoint Health – Waterloo, Unitypoint Health – Marshalltown, Marshalltown, IA, p. A240
FRIEDMAN, Jonathan, Public Affairs Officer, Captain James A. Lovell Federal Health Care Center, North Chicago, IL, p. A203
FRIEDMAN, Lloyd, M.D., Interim President and Chief Operating Officer, Bridgeport Hospital, Bridgeport, CT, p. A115
FRIEL, Donald F., Executive Vice President, Holy Redeemer Hospital, Meadowbrook, PA, p. A545
FRIELING, Jeff
Chief Information Officer, Pathways of Tennessee, Jackson, TN, p. A584
Vice President and Chief Information Officer, Jackson–Madison County General Hospital, Medina, TN, p. A588
Vice President Information Systems, West Tennessee Healthcare Camden Hospital, Camden, TN, p. A579
FRIEND, Chad, Director, T. J. Samson Community Hospital, Glasgow, KY, p. A266
FRIERSON, Cathy, Chief Human Resource Officer, Danbury Hospital, Danbury, CT, p. A115
FRIES, Richard W
Vice President Finance, AHN Grove City, Grove City, PA, p. A541
Vice President Finance, Allegheny General Hospital, Pittsburgh, PA, p. A551
FRIESEN, Lorie, Director of Nursing, Mercy Hospital Inc., Moundridge, KS, p. A255
FRIESEN, Lynette, Manager Human Resources, Henderson Health Care Services, Henderson, NE, p. A401
FRIGO, Dave
Vice President Financial Planning and Treasury, Cleveland Clinic Akron General, Akron, OH, p. A484
Director Finance and Controller, Cleveland Clinic Akron General Lodi Hospital, Lodi, OH, p. A498
Senior Director Financial Operations, Cleveland Clinic Union Hospital, Dover, OH, p. A495
FRIGY, Alan, M.D., President Medical Staff, Pana Community Hospital, Pana, IL, p. A205
FRILEY, Ryan, CPA, Area Controller, Mercy Rehabilitation Hospital South, Saint Louis, MO, p. A385
FRIMODIG, Mindy, D.O., President Medical Staff ThedaCare Physicians Shawano, Thedacare Medical Center–Shawano, Shawano, WI, p. A721
FRISBEE, Kent, Director Human Resources, Ascension Saint Thomas Highlands, Sparta, TN, p. A593
FRISINA, Marcy, Chief Nursing Officer, HCA Florida South Shore Hospital, Sun City Center, FL, p. A151
FRITSCH, William, M.D., Medical Director, Landmark Hospital of Cap. Girardeau, Cap. Girardeau, MO, p. A372
FRITTON, Amy, Controller, Sierra Tucson, Tucson, AZ, p. A41
FRITTS, Doris, R.N., Executive Director, Same Day Surgery Center, Rapid City, SD, p. A576
FRITTS, Robert G., Chief Financial Officer and Senior Vice President, UNC Health Blue Ridge, Morganton, NC, p. A473
FRITZ, Brian
Chief Financial Officer, UPMC Horizon, Farrell, PA, p. A540
Chief Financial Officer, UPMC Jameson, New Castle, PA, p. A547
Chief Financial Officer, UPMC Passavant, Pittsburgh, PA, p. A552
Chief Financial Officer, UPMC St. Margaret, Pittsburgh, PA, p. A552
President, Excela Frick Hospital, Mount Pleasant, PA, p. A546
President, Excela Health Latrobe Hospital, Latrobe, PA, p. A544
President, Westmoreland, Latrobe, Frick Hospitals, Excela Health Westmoreland Hospital, Greensburg, PA, p. A541
FRITZ, Howard P, M.D., Vice President, Medical Affairs and Chief Medical Officer, Glens Falls Hospital, Glens Falls, NY, p. A443
FRITZ, Melissa, R.N., Chief Nursing Officer, Park Nicollet Methodist Hospital, Saint Louis Park, MN, p. A354
FRITZ, Robert, Chief Information Officer, Brook Lane, Hagerstown, MD, p. A304
FRIX, Candice, Vice President and Chief Nursing Officer, St. Mary's Health Care System, Athens, GA, p. A156
FROCHTZWAJG, Stanley, M.D., Chief Medical Officer, Community Memorial Hospital – Ventura, Ventura, CA, p. A100
FROEMKE, Janet, Human Resources Officer, Chi Lisbon Health, Lisbon, ND, p. A482
FROESE, Kristi
R.N., Chief Nursing Officer, St. Luke's Health – Memorial Livingston, Livingston, TX, p. A635
R.N., Vice President Clinical Operations, St. Luke's Health – Memorial Livingston, Livingston, TX, p. A635
FROH, Chris, Senior Coordinator Human Resources, Select Specialty Hospital–Milwaukee, Milwaukee, WI, p. A717
FROHNHOFER, Erin J
Director Human Resources, Southwood Psychiatric Hospital, Pittsburgh, PA, p. A551
Vice President Human Resources, Heritage Valley Kennedy, Mckees Rocks, PA, p. A545
FROISLAND, Jeffrey R, Chief Financial Officer, Mayo Clinic Hospital In Arizona, Phoenix, AZ, p. A36
FROMM, Daniel, Chief Financial Officer, North Memorial Health Hospital, Robbinsdale, MN, p. A353
FROMME, Richard, Chief Financial Officer, Langdon Prairie Health, Langdon, ND, p. A482
FROMMELT, William, Director Operations and Finance, River Falls Area Hospital, River Falls, WI, p. A721
FROSCH, Kevin, Chief Financial Officer, Medina Regional Hospital, Hondo, TX, p. A624
FROSCHAUER, Beth, Director, Human Resources, Palomar Health Rehabilitation Institute, Escondido, CA, p. A62
FROST, Christine, Chief Nursing Officer, Luminis Health Anne Arundel Medical Center, Annapolis, MD, p. A300
FROST, Eric, Associate Vice President Human Resources, Upstate University Hospital, Syracuse, NY, p. A460
FROST, Sarah
Chief Executive Officer, Banner – University Medical Center South, Tucson, AZ, p. A40
Chief Executive Officer, Banner – University Medical Center Tucson, Tucson, AZ, p. A40
Chief, Lifespan Hospital Operations, and President, Rhode Island Hospital and Hasbro Children's Hosp. Rhode Island Hospital, Providence, RI, p. A561
FROWNFELTER, Penny, Chief Nursing Officer, Encompass Health Rehabilitation Hospital of Nittany Valley, Pleasant Gap. PA, p. A552
FRUGE, Janie D., FACHE, Chief Executive Officer, West Calcasieu Cameron Hospital, Sulphur, LA, p. A293
FRY, Kenneth, Chief Financial Officer, Saint Alphonsus Regional Medical Center, Boise, ID, p. A179
FRY, Mackenzi Texas Rehabilitation Hospital of Fort Worth, Fort Worth, TX, p. A620

Index of Health Care Professionals **A851**

Index of Health Care Professionals

Index of Health Care Professionals / Fry

FRY, Matthew
FACHE, President and Chief Executive Officer, Central Illinois Market, HSHS Good Shepherd Hospital, Shelbyville, IL, p. A208
FACHE, President and Chief Executive Officer, Central Illinois Market, HSHS St. Anthony's Memorial Hospital, Effingham, IL, p. A194
FACHE, President and Chief Executive Officer, Central Illinois Market, HSHS St. Francis Hospital, Litchfield, IL, p. A200
FACHE, President and Chief Executive Officer, Central Illinois Market, HSHS St. Mary's Hospital, Decatur, IL, p. A193
FACHE, President and Chief Executive Officer, Central Illinois Market and President and Chief Executive Off, HSHS St. John's Hospital, Springfield, IL, p. A209
FRY, Robin, CPA, Market Controller, Kindred Hospital Dallas Central, Dallas, TX, p. A611
FRY, Terry, R.N., Chief Nursing Officer, Upper Valley Medical Center, Troy, OH, p. A505
FRYAR, Marri, Executive Director, Fayetteville Veterans Affairs Medical Center, Fayetteville, NC, p. A468
FRYE, Kelly D, Director Human Resources, Montgomery General Hospital, Montgomery, WV, p. A702
FRYE, Matthew, Acting Chies Executive Officer, Fort Belknap Service Unit, Harlem, MT, p. A393
FRYE, Terri, Information Technology Officer, Weston County Health Services, Newcastle, WY, p. A727
FRYFOGLE, Anthoney, Chief Information Officer, George Regional Hospital, Lucedale, MS, p. A365
FRYSZTAK, Christopher, CPA, Chief Financial Officer, Western Arizona Regional Medical Center, Bullhead City, AZ, p. A30
FUCHSEL, Stephanie, Human Resources Director, Pam Rehabilitation Hospital of Tavares, Tavares, FL, p. A153
FUENTES, Frances, Human Resources Director, Encompass Health Rehabilitation Hospital of The Mid–Cities, Bedford, TX, p. A602
FUENTES, Leticia, Nursing Director, San Jorge Children's And Women Hospital, Santurce, PR, p. A736
FUENTES, Michelle, Chief Executive Officer and President, Adventhealth Castle Rock, Castle Rock, CO, p. A104
FUENTES, Miguel A Jr, President and Chief Executive Officer, Bronxcare Health System, New York, NY, p. A447
FUENTES, Miguel A. Jr, President and Chief Executive Officer, Bronxcare Health System, New York, NY, p. A447
FUENTES, Rodemil, Chief Operating Officer, Carewell Health Medical Center, East Orange, NJ, p. A420
FUERSTENBERG, Donna, Fiscal Chief, Sheridan Va Medical Center, Sheridan, WY, p. A728
FUGATTE, Cheryl, MSN, Vice President and Chief Nursing Officer, Uofl Health – Jewish Hospital, Louisville, KY, p. A270
FUGITT, Jacki L., Director Employee Relations, OSF Saint Francis Medical Center, Peoria, IL, p. A206
FUGLEBERG, Jason Russell., R.N., Chief Executive Officer, Southern Tennessee Regional Health System–Pulaski, Pulaski, TN, p. A592
FUGLER, Shawna, R.N., Chief Nursing Officer, Memorial Hermann Surgical Hospital Kingwood, Kingwood, TX, p. A633
FUHRMAN, Bradley, M.D., Physician in Chief, El Paso Children's Hospital, El Paso, TX, p. A616
FUHRMAN, Dennis, Vice President Finance, Essentia Health Fargo, Fargo, ND, p. A480
FUHRO, Mary, Chief Nursing Officer, Newark Beth Israel Medical Center, Newark, NJ, p. A425
FUHS, Veronica
Chief Executive Officer, Davis County Hospital And Clinics, Bloomfield, IA, p. A231
Chief Executive Officer, Monroe County Hospital And Clinics, Albia, IA, p. A230
FULCHER, Kimberly
Chief Human Resources Officer, Halifax Health Medical Center of Daytona Beach, Daytona Beach, FL, p. A130
Senior Vice President and Chief Human Resources Officer, Halifax Health/Uf Health Medical Center of Deltona, Deltona, FL, p. A130
FULKERSON, Judy, Director Human Resources, Tristar Greenview Regional Hospital, Bowling Green, KY, p. A264
FULKERSON, Kimberly, Chief Nursing Officer, Dupont Hospital, Fort Wayne, IN, p. A216
FULKERSON, Richard, Director Fiscal Services, Shriners Hospitals for Children–Springfield, Springfield, MA, p. A318
FULKS, Chris, Vice President Finance, Lake Huron Medical Center, Port Huron, MI, p. A336
FULLER, Cara
Vice President Human Resources, Unitypoint Health – Trinity Bettendorf, Bettendorf, IA, p. A231
Vice President Human Resources, Unitypoint Health – Trinity Rock Island, Rock Island, IL, p. A207
FULLER, Cheryl, Director Information Resources, Kansas Neurological Institute, Topeka, KS, p. A260
FULLER, Christopher, Chief Executive Officer, Novant Health Rehabilitation Hospital, An Affiliate of Encompass Health, Winston Salem, NC, p. A478
FULLER, Dale
Vice President and Chief Information Officer, UPMC Altoona, Altoona, PA, p. A534
Vice President, Chief Information Officer, UPMC Somerset, Somerset, PA, p. A555
FULLER, David, Vice President of Human Resources, The University of Vermont Health Network Porter Medical Center, Middlebury, VT, p. A671
FULLER, Harrington, Information Technology Director, Hendry Regional Medical Center, Clewiston, FL, p. A128
FULLER, Jane, Vice President Human Resources, HCA Florida North Florida Hospital, Gainesville, FL, p. A132
FULLER, Jeremy, Director Information Systems, HCA Houston Healthcare Conroe, Conroe, TX, p. A608
FULLER, Marion, Chief of Staff, Munson Healthcare Manistee Hospital, Manistee, MI, p. A332
FULLER SPENCER, Carrie, Chief Financial Officer, Highland Hospital, Rochester, NY, p. A457
FULLER–WILLIAMS, Vonetta, Director Human Resources Strategic and Business Services, Baylor Scott & White Medical Center–Irving, Irving, TX, p. A630
FULLUM, Jane, Vice President Patient Care Services, East Alabama Medical Center, Opelika, AL, p. A23
FULTON, Lynn, Chief Executive Officer, Maui Memorial Medical Center, Wailuku, HI, p. A177
FUNDERBURG, Michelle, Director Human Resources, Stephens Memorial Hospital, Breckenridge, TX, p. A604
FUNDERBURK, Mark, President and Chief Executive Officer, University Medical Center, Lubbock, TX, p. A636
FUNG, Adrian, Director Information Systems, Vanderbilt Wilson County Hospital, Lebanon, TN, p. A586
FUNK, Luann A, Administrative Assistant and Manager Human Resources, Pana Community Hospital, Pana, IL, p. A205
FUNKHOUSER, Krisy L, Manager Human Resources, Willap. Harbor Hospital, South Bend, WA, p. A696
FUNTANILLA, Alan V., Executive Vice President, Chief Operating Officer, Guam Regional Medical City, Dededo, GU, p. A730
FUQUA, David, Director Human Resources Management, Ochsner Lsu Health Shreveport – Academic Medical Center, Shreveport, LA, p. A292
FUQUA, David G., Chief Executive Officer, Marshall County Hospital, Benton, KY, p. A263
FUQUA, Leon, Chief Operating Officer, Medical City Decatur, Decatur, TX, p. A613
FURER, Darnell F, MS, R.N., Vice President Patient Care Services and Chief Nursing Officer, Lehigh Valley Hospital – Schuylkill, Pottsville, PA, p. A553
FURLANI, Thomas, M.D., Chief Information Officer, Roswell Park Comprehensive Cancer Center, Buffalo, NY, p. A440
FURLOW, Pete, Chief Information Officer, RMC Anniston, Anniston, AL, p. A15
FURNAS, David, Chief Information Officer, Gila Regional Medical Center, Silver City, NM, p. A437
FURNISS, Scott, Vice President and Chief Financial Officer, Ascension Saint Agnes, Baltimore, MD, p. A300
FUSCHILLO, Ronald, Chief Information Officer, Harris Health System, Bellaire, TX, p. A603
FUSELIER, Gerald, Chief Operating Officer, Savoy Medical Center, Mamou, LA, p. A287
FUSELIER, Jarrett, Assistant Vice President Nursing, St. Charles Parish Hospital, Luling, LA, p. A287
FUSILERO, Jane, Vice President Chief Nursing Officer, H. Lee Moffitt Cancer Center And Research Institute, Tampa, FL, p. A152
FUSTON, Kathie, Director Human Resources, Moore County Hospital District, Dumas, TX, p. A615
FUTCH, Margaret A., Chief Executive Officer, Encompass Health Rehabilitation Hospital of Dothan, Dothan, AL, p. A18
FUTRAL, Cindy, Director Human Resources, Elmore Community Hospital, Wetumpka, AL, p. A26
FUTRELL, Bradley, Chief Operating Officer, Pinckneyville Community Hospital, Pinckneyville, IL, p. A206
FUTRELL, Cynthia, MSN, R.N., Chief Nursing Officer, Marion Health, Marion, IN, p. A223

G

GAAL, James G, M.D., Chief of Medical Staff, Jackson General Hospital, Ripley, WV, p. A704
GABALDON, Karen, Chief Management Information Systems, West Palm Beach Veterans Affairs Medical Center, West Palm Beach, FL, p. A155
GABEL, Christopher, Chief Operating Officer, Larkin Community Hospital Behavioral Health Services, Hollywood, FL, p. A133
GABEL, Kelly, Chief of Staff, Citizens Medical Center, Colby, KS, p. A247
GABEL, Marcia
Chief Financial Officer, Lane County Hospital, Dighton, KS, p. A248
Chief Financial Officer and Co–Chief Executive Officer, Lane County Hospital, Dighton, KS, p. A248
GABELE, Danielle, R.N., Chief Nursing Executive, Ventura County Medical Center, Ventura, CA, p. A100
GABLE, Beth, Administrative Assistant, Jasper General Hospital, Bay Springs, MS, p. A359
GABORIAULT, Randall, Chief Information Officer, Christianacare, Newark, DE, p. A122
GABRICK, Sara S, R.N., Chief Nursing Officer, Winona Health, Winona, MN, p. A357
GABRIEL, Scott F, President, Parkview Whitley Hospital, Columbia City, IN, p. A214
GABRIEL, Scott F., President, Parkview Whitley Hospital, Columbia City, IN, p. A214
GABRIEL, Shannon, Chief Nursing Officer, River Place Behavioral Health, La Place, LA, p. A285
GABRIEL, Shirley, Vice President and Chief Information Officer, Piedmont Augusta, Augusta, GA, p. A158
GABRIEL, Stacey, R.N., President and Chief Executive Officer, Hocking Valley Community Hospital, Logan, OH, p. A498
GABRIELE, Joan, Deputy Executive Director, NYC Health + Hospitals/Queens, New York, NY, p. A451
GABRYEL, Timothy, M.D., Vice President Medical Affairs and Medical Director, Mercy Hospital, Buffalo, NY, p. A440
GABUAT, Jesse, Chief Nursing Officer, HCA Florida Aventura Hospital, Aventura, FL, p. A125
GAC, Deborah, Vice President Human Resources, Valley Presbyterian Hospital, Los Angeles, CA, p. A75
GADALLAH, Yousri, M.D., Chief Medical Officer, Pershing General Hospital, Lovelock, NV, p. A411
GADDAM, Sumalatha, Senior Vice President and Chief Information Officer, Kent Hospital, Warwick, RI, p. A561
GADDAM, Summa, Chief Information Officer, Butler Hospital, Providence, RI, p. A560
GADDIS, Cathryn H, Director Human Resources, Rivervalley Behavioral Health Hospital, Owensboro, KY, p. A272
GADDY, Kortney, CPA, Chief Financial Officer, Copiah County Medical Center, Hazlehurst, MS, p. A363
GADDY, Pam, Director, Patient Care Services and Chief Nursing Officer, Firsthealth Montgomery Memorial Hospital, Troy, NC, p. A477
GADE, Swami P, M.D., Medical Director, Tioga Medical Center, Tioga, ND, p. A483
GAEDE, John, Chief Information Officer, Sky Lakes Medical Center, Klamath Falls, OR, p. A528
GAFFOLI, Jill, Director Human Resources, Physicians Regional – Pine Ridge, Naples, FL, p. A142
GAFFORD, Deborah, Chief Financial Officer, Menorah Medical Center, Overland Park, KS, p. A257
GAFFORD, Grady Paul, Chief Financial Officer, Brownfield Regional Medical Center, Brownfield, TX, p. A604
GAFFORD, Michelle, Chief Executive Officer, Mitchell County Hospital, Colorado City, TX, p. A608
GAGE, Bobby, Director Information Technology, Wabash General Hospital, Mount Carmel, IL, p. A202
GAGE, Kevin, Chief Financial Officer, Stamford Health, Stamford, CT, p. A119
GAGE, Mark, D.O., Medical Director, Brookhaven Hospital, Tulsa, OK, p. A522
GAGE, Susan, Financial Manager, Veterans Affairs Western New York Healthcare System–Buffalo Division, Buffalo, NY, p. A440
GAGE, Weldon, Executive Vice President, Chief Financial Officer, Texas Children's Hospital North Austin Campus, Austin, TX, p. A601
GAGLIO, Anthony, CPA, Senior Vice President and Chief Financial Officer, Menninger Clinic, Houston, TX, p. A627
GAGNE, Cheryl I, Vice President Patient Care Services and Chief Nursing Officer, Southern New Hampshire Medical Center, Nashua, NH, p. A416
GAGNE, Margaret, R.N., MS, Chief Nursing Officer, University of Vermont Medical Center, Burlington, VT, p. A671
GAGNON, Andy, Manager Information Technology, Ascension Via Christi Hospital, Manhattan, Manhattan, KS, p. A254
GAILLARD, Timothy, Chief Operating Officer, Wellstar Mcg Health, Augusta, GA, p. A158
GAINES, April R., Chief Nursing Officer, Crete Area Medical Center, Crete, NE, p. A399
GAINES, Jared, M.D., Chief Medical Officer, Fort Lauderdale Behavioral Health Center, Oakland Park, FL, p. A143
GAINES, Jeffrey, M.D., Vice President and Chief Medical Officer, Newport Hospital, Newport, RI, p. A560

A852 Index of Health Care Professionals

GAINES, Susan, Chief Nursing Officer, Madison Parish Hospital, Tallulah, LA, p. A293
GAINEY, Rachel, Chief Executive Officer, Vice President McLeod Health, Mcleod Health Clarendon, Manning, SC, p. A568
GAINEY, Shari W
  Chief Human Resource Officer, Tanner Medical Center–Villa Rica, Villa Rica, GA, p. A173
  Human Resource Director, Higgins General Hospital, Bremen, GA, p. A159
GAITHER, Cecil W., Interim Chief Executive Officer, Parkview Hospital, Wheeler, TX, p. A662
GAJ, Steve, Facility Chief Information Officer, Northeast Ohio Va Healthcare System, Cleveland, OH, p. A491
GAJARAJ, Krishnaswamy, M.D., Medical Director, Arbour H. R. I. Hospital, Brookline, MA, p. A312
GAJEWSKI, Christie, Director Human Resources, Pinckneyville Community Hospital, Pinckneyville, IL, p. A206
GALANG, Michael
  M.D., Chief Information Officer, Mercy Hospital, Buffalo, NY, p. A440
  M.D., Chief Information Officer, Sisters of Charity Hospital of Buffalo, Buffalo, NY, p. A440
GALARNEAU, Ciprian, Director Information Systems, Tri Valley Health System, Cambridge, NE, p. A398
GALARNEAU, Gerard, M.D., Regional Chief Medical Officer, Garnet Health Medical Center – Catskills, Harris Campus, Harris, NY, p. A444
GALBRAITH, Kathleen B., FACHE, President, Lankenau Medical Center, Wynnewood, PA, p. A558
GALE, Gabrielle, Chief Financial Officer, Lighthouse Behavioral Health Hospital, Conway, SC, p. A565
GALE, Melissa, Chief Executive Officer, Landmann–Jungman Memorial Hospital Avera, Scotland, SD, p. A576
GALE, Michael, Chief Financial Officer, Bournewood Health Systems, Brookline, MA, p. A312
GALER, Lana, Chief Nursing Officer, Texas Rehabilitation Hospital of Fort Worth, Fort Worth, TX, p. A620
GALEY, John P, M.D., Chief Medical Officer, Schoolcraft Memorial Hospital, Manistique, MI, p. A333
GALIANA, Amy S., Chief Human Resource Officer, Highland Hospital, Rochester, NY, p. A457
GALIPEAU, Michelle, Director Human Resources, Ascension St. Vincent's Birmingham, Birmingham, AL, p. A16
GALKOWSKI, James, Associate Director for Operations, Fayetteville Veterans Affairs Medical Center, Fayetteville, NC, p. A468
GALLAGHER, Chris, M.D., Chief Medical Officer, Christus Mother Frances Hospital – Sulphur Springs, Sulphur Springs, TX, p. A655
GALLAGHER, Deborah, Manager Human Resources, Ojai Valley Community Hospital, Ojai, CA, p. A81
GALLAGHER, Doug, Director Human Resources, Carolinas Continuecare Hospital At Pineville, Charlotte, NC, p. A465
GALLAGHER, Jeannie
  Banner Mckee Medical Center, Loveland, CO, p. A112
  Chief Human Resource Officer, Banner North Colorado Medical Centernorth Colorado Medical Center, Greeley, CO, p. A109
GALLAGHER, Karen, Vice President Human Resources and Learning, Brooks Rehabilitation Hospital, Jacksonville, FL, p. A134
GALLAGHER, Karen M, MSN, Chief Nursing Office, Vice President Operations, Ascension St. Mary – Kankakee, Kankakee, IL, p. A199
GALLAGHER, Michael, Administrator, Child And Adolescent Behavioral Health Services, Willmar, MN, p. A357
GALLAGHER, Pamela J, Chief Financial Officer, Catawba Valley Medical Center, Hickory, NC, p. A470
GALLAGHER, Regen, D.O., Chief Medical Officer, Cary Medical Center, Caribou, ME, p. A296
GALLAGHER, Sherry, Director Nursing, Department of Health and Human Services, Humboldt County Mental Health, Eureka, CA, p. A62
GALLAHER, Sarah, Chief Operating Officer, Covington Trace Er & Hospital, Mandeville, LA, p. A287
GALLAHOM, Gerty, Director Human Resources, Maniilaq Health Center, Kotzebue, AK, p. A29
GALLARDO, Kathleen, Chief Nursing Officer, Select Specialty Hospital – Flint, Flint, MI, p. A327
GALLARDO, Laura, Chief Operating Officer, Kaiser Permanente Panorama City Medical Center, Los Angeles, CA, p. A73
GALLARDO, Ysidro, Associate Administrator Human Resources, Hazel Hawkins Memorial Hospital, Hollister, CA, p. A67
GALLAY, Emily, Vice President and Chief Information Officer, Corewell Health Lakeland Hospitals, Saint Joseph, MI, p. A337

GALLEGOS, Colleen, Director Human Resources, Guadalup. County Hospital, Santa Rosa, NM, p. A437
GALLEGOS, Kelly, Chief Nursing Officer, UCHealth Yamp. Valley Medical Center, Steamboat Springs, CO, p. A113
GALLEGOS, Ken, Director Support Services and Information Technology, Medina Regional Hospital, Hondo, TX, p. A624
GALLEY, Pamela
  Senior Vice President and Area Manager, Diablo Service Area, Kaiser Permanente Walnut Creek Medical Center, Walnut Creek, CA, p. A100
  Senior Vice President/Area Manager, Diablo Service Area, Kaiser Permanente Antioch Medical Center, Antioch, CA, p. A55
GALLIART, Mark, Chief Executive Officer, Mcbride Orthopedic Hospital, Oklahoma City, OK, p. A517
GALLO, Carrie, Chief Nursing Officer, Western Reserve Hospital, Cuyahoga Falls, OH, p. A493
GALLO, Ronald, Director Human Resources, Blythedale Children's Hospital, Valhalla, NY, p. A460
GALLOGLY-SIMON, Catherine A, R.N., MS, Chief Nursing Officer, Wyckoff Heights Medical Center, New York, NY, p. A453
GALLUCCI, Vince
  Senior Vice President Human Resources, Ascension Northeast Wisconsin Mercy Hospital, Oshkosh, WI, p. A719
  Senior Vice President Human Resources, Ascension Northeast Wisconsin St. Elizabeth Hospital, Appleton, WI, p. A707
GALLUP, Jared, Chief Information Officer, Cassia Regional Hospital, Burley, ID, p. A180
GALOFARO, Brian J., M.D., Chief Medical Officer, Our Lady of The Angels Hospital, Bogalusa, LA, p. A279
GALT, Nick
  Chief Financial Officer, Medical City Las Colinas, Irving, TX, p. A630
  Chief Financial Officer, Medical City North Hills, North Richland Hills, TX, p. A641
GALUP, Richard
  Chief Operating Officer, Jefferson Health Northeast, Philadelphia, PA, p. A549
  Chief Operating Officer, Jefferson Stratford Hospital, Stratford, NJ, p. A428
  President, Jefferson Health Northeast, Philadelphia, PA, p. A549
GALUSHA, Fred, Chief Information Officer, Providence St. Luke's Rehabilitation Medical Center, Spokane, WA, p. A696
GALYON, Darlene, Director Human Resources, Choctaw Memorial Hospital, Hugo, OK, p. A513
GAMACHE, Cynthia, R.N., Vice President and Chief Nursing Officer, Baptist Hospital, Pensacola, FL, p. A146
GAMB, Pamela, Manager Human Resources, Aurora Psychiatric Hospital, Wauwatosa, WI, p. A724
GAMBLA, Kurt, D.O., Chief Medical Officer, Beaufort Memorial Hospital, Beaufort, SC, p. A562
GAMBLE, Brian, President, Karmanos Cancer Center, Detroit, MI, p. A326
GAMBLE, Kathleen, Fiscal Officer, Dsh Patton, Patton, CA, p. A83
GAMBLE, Laura, Chief Executive Officer, Pender Community Hospital, Pender, NE, p. A405
GAMBLE, Mike, M.D., Chief Medical Officer, Greene County General Hospital, Linton, IN, p. A222
GAMBOA, Eileen, Vice President Human Resources, HCA Houston Healthcare Southeast, Oakbend Medical Center, Richmond, TX, p. A646
GAMEZ, Kriss, Director Human Resources, Baylor Scott & White Medical Center – Plano, Plano, TX, p. A644
GAMINO, Randall, Director Perot Site, St. Joseph's Medical Center, Stockton, CA, p. A97
GAMMIERE, Thomas A, Chief Executive Officer, Scripp. Mercy Hospital, San Diego, CA, p. A89
GAMMON, Lisa
  Chief Executive Officer, Novato Community Hospital, Novato, CA, p. A80
  Chief Nursing Executive, Novato Community Hospital, Novato, CA, p. A80
GANDHI, Tejas, Ph.D., Chief Operating Officer, Baystate Medical Center, Springfield, MA, p. A318
GANDY, Galina, Vice President Information Technology, Columbia Memorial Hospital, Astoria, OR, p. A525
GANGADHAR, Shiva, M.D., Medical Director, Community Rehabilitation Hospital South, Greenwood, IN, p. A218
GANGER, Craig, Chief Financial Officer, Upper Valley Medical Center, Troy, OH, p. A505
GANGULY, Indranil, Vice President and Chief Information Officer, Hackensack Meridian Health Jfk Medical Center, Edison, NJ, p. A420

GANGULY, Neal, Chief Information Officer, JFK Johnson Rehabilitation Institute At Hackensack Meridian Health, Edison, NJ, p. A420
GANN, Glenn, Vice President and Administrator, Southeast Georgia Health System Camden Campus, Saint Marys, GA, p. A170
GANNON, Ronnie, Director Information Services, Tristar Southern Hills Medical Center, Nashville, TN, p. A591
GANS, Bruce M., M.D., Executive Vice President and Chief Medical Officer, Kessler Institute for Rehabilitation, West Orange, NJ, p. A430
GANSEMER, Sheila, R.N., Vice President Patient Care Services and Chief Nursing Officer, Ascension Southeast Wisconsin Hospital – Franklin Campus, Franklin, WI, p. A711
GANSKE, Jary M.
  Chief Executive Officer and VP of Finance, Methodist Midlothian Medical Center, Midlothian, TX, p. A639
  Chief Financial Officer, Methodist Mansfield Medical Center, Mansfield, TX, p. A637
GANSZ, Phil, Director Information Technology, Colleton Medical Center, Walterboro, SC, p. A571
GANT, Curtis, Chief Financial Officer, New Mexico Rehabilitation Center, Roswell, NM, p. A436
GANTHIER, Sem, FACHE, Executive Director, Operations, Musc Health – Orangeburg, Orangeburg, SC, p. A569
GANTT, Cynthia J, Chief of Staff, Naval Medical Center, Portsmouth, VA, p. A681
GANTZER, Ann M.
  Ph.D., R.N., Chief Nursing Officer, Good Samaritan Medical Center, Lafayette, CO, p. A110
  Ph.D., R.N., Interim Chief Nursing Officer, Lutheran Medical Center, Wheat Ridge, CO, p. A114
GARAY, Kenneth, M.D., Chief Medical Officer, Jersey City Medical Center, Jersey City, NJ, p. A422
GARBANZOS, Del, Director Human Resources, Adventist Health Delano, Delano, CA, p. A61
GARBARINO, James, Chief Financial Officer, Clay County Medical Center, Clay Center, KS, p. A247
GARBER, Mary, Vice President Finance, Mercy Hospital Ada, Ada, OK, p. A509
GARCIA, Antonio M
  Chief Nursing Officer, Long Beach Medical Center, Long Beach, CA, p. A71
  Chief Nursing Officer, Miller Children's & Women's Hospital Long Beach, Long Beach, CA, p. A71
GARCIA, Aymette, Manager Human Resources, Wilma N. Vazquez Medical Center, Vega Baja, PR, p. A736
GARCIA, Charla, Human Resource Officer, Uvalde Memorial Hospital, Uvalde, TX, p. A659
GARCIA, Danette, Director Human Resources, Encompass Health Valley of The Sun Rehabilitation Hospital, Glendale, AZ, p. A32
GARCIA, EM Vitug.
  Ph.D., Chief Executive Officer, Encino Hospital Medical Center, Encino, CA, p. A62
  Ph.D., Chief Executive Officer, Sherman Oaks Hospital, Los Angeles, CA, p. A75
GARCIA, Estevan, M.D., Chief Medical Officer, Cooley Dickinson Hospital, Northampton, MA, p. A316
GARCIA, Evangeline, M.D., Clinical Director, Eastern Shore Hospital Center, Cambridge, MD, p. A303
GARCIA, Georgina R.
  R.N., Chief Executive Officer, Kaiser Permanente Fontana Medical Center, Fontana, CA, p. A63
  R.N., Senior Vice President, Area Manager for San Bernardino County, Kaiser Permanente Fontana Medical Center, Fontana, CA, p. A63
GARCIA, Gerard, Chief Human Resource Officer, University Hospital, Newark, NJ, p. A425
GARCIA, Idalia, Chief Human Resources Officer, Hospital De Psiquiatria, San Juan, PR, p. A735
GARCIA, Iris, Director, Information Services, Sunview Medical Center, West Palm Beach, FL, p. A154
GARCIA, Irma, Job Coordinator, Rio Grande State Center/South Texas Health Care System, Harlingen, TX, p. A623
GARCIA, Jacob, Chief Information Officer, Little Colorado Medical Center, Winslow, AZ, p. A41
GARCIA, Jannina, Director of Human Resources, Adventhealth Fish Memorial, Orange City, FL, p. A143
GARCIA, Joannie, CPA, Director Finance, Hospital Perea, Mayaguez, PR, p. A733
GARCIA, Jose
  M.D., Chief Medical Staff, Dundy County Hospital, Benkelman, NE, p. A398
  Chief Human Resources Officer, San Juan City Hospital, San Juan, PR, p. A736
GARCIA, Karen, MSN, R.N., Chief Nursing Officer, Baptist Hospitals of Southeast Texas, Beaumont, TX, p. A602

Index of Health Care Professionals

Index of Health Care Professionals / Garcia

GARCIA, Kathleen, Controller, St. John's Episcopal Hospital, New York, NY, p. A453
GARCIA, Luis Mario Jr, Director Human Resources, Houston Methodist Sugar Land Hospital, Sugar Land, TX, p. A654
GARCIA, Margaret, Manager Human Resources, Baylor Scott & White Medical Center–Frisco, Frisco, TX, p. A621
GARCIA, Michael, Chief Executive Officer, Houston Methodist Sugar Land Hospital, Sugar Land, TX, p. A654
GARCIA, Michael A., Vice President and Chief Information Officer, Jackson Health System, Miami, FL, p. A140
GARCIA, Orlando, M.D., Chief Medical Officer, Hialeah Hospital, Hialeah, FL, p. A133
GARCIA, Robert W, M.D., Chief Medical Officer, Iraan General Hospital, Iraan, TX, p. A630
GARCIA, Roland
Senior Vice President and Chief Information Officer, Baptist Medical Center Beaches, Jacksonville Beach, FL, p. A135
Senior Vice President and Chief Information Officer, Baptist Medical Center Jacksonville, Jacksonville, FL, p. A134
GARCIA, Sharon, Human Resources Representative, Medina Regional Hospital, Hondo, TX, p. A624
GARCIA, Shawn, Manager Human Resources, Memorial Hospital Los Banos, Los Banos, CA, p. A76
GARCIA, Sylvia, Chief Accounting Officer, South Texas Spine And Surgical Hospital, San Antonio, TX, p. A651
GARCIA, Tracy, MS, Chief Nursing Officer, Cheyenne Regional Medical Center, Cheyenne, WY, p. A726
GARCIN, Hector Troche, Human Resources Director, St. Luke's Episcopal Hospital, Ponce, PR, p. A734
GARD, Emily, Chief Clinical Officer, Kindred Hospital–San Francisco Bay Area, San Leandro, CA, p. A92
GARDEPE, Cynthia, Director, Human Resources, UHS Delaware Valley Hospital, Walton, NY, p. A461
GARDINER, Karen, Human Resources Director, Shorepoint Health Port Charlotte, Port Charlotte, FL, p. A147
GARDNER, Carla, Director of Nursing, Munson Healthcare Grayling Hospital, Grayling, MI, p. A329
GARDNER, Geoffrey, Senior Vice President Operational Finance and Revenue Cycle, Novant Health Ballantyne Medical Center, Charlotte, NC, p. A465
GARDNER, Greg, Senior Vice President and Chief Financial Officer, Cleveland Clinic Indian River Hospital, Vero Beach, FL, p. A154
GARDNER, Jacque, Chief Executive Officer, Mccone County Health Center, Circle, MT, p. A390
GARDNER, James D, M.D., Vice President and Chief Medical Officer, Prohealth Waukesha Memorial Hospital, Waukesha, WI, p. A723
GARDNER, Kristin Day, Chief Nursing Officer, Ohiohealth Berger Hospital, Circleville, OH, p. A490
GARDNER, Michelle, M.D., Clinical Director, Dorothea Dix Psychiatric Center, Bangor, ME, p. A295
GARDNER, Patrick, M.D., Associate Vice President, Medical Affairs, St. Joseph's Hospital, Froedtert West Bend Hospital, West Bend, WI, p. A724
GARDNER, Sharon, Manager Information Systems, SSM Health St. Josep. Hospital – Lake Saint Louis, Lake Saint Louis, MO, p. A379
GARDNER, William, MSN, Chief Clinical Officer, Summit Healthcare Regional Medical Center, Show Low, AZ, p. A39
GARDNER, Zoe, Manager Human Resources, Sharp Chula Vista Medical Center, Chula Vista, CA, p. A59
GARISON, Jerri, R.N., President, Baylor Scott & White Medical Center – Plano, Plano, TX, p. A644
GARLAND, Pamela, R.N., Chief Nursing Officer, Northside Hospital Gwinnett/Duluth, Lawrenceville, GA, p. A166
GARMAN, Denise M, Director Human Resources, Wellspan Good Samaritan Hospital, Lebanon, PA, p. A544
GARMAN, Michael, Chief Financial Officer, Avera St. Anthony's Hospital, O'Neill, NE, p. A403
GARMANY, Kandi, Interim Chief Financial Officer, Gadsden Regional Medical Center, Gadsden, AL, p. A20
GARNAS, David, Administrator, North Central Kansas Medical Center, Concordia, KS, p. A248
GARNER, Douglas, Vice President, Thomas Hospital, Fairhope, AL, p. A19
GARNER, John, D.O., Medical Director, Culberson Hospital, Van Horn, TX, p. A659
GARNER, Mario J., Ed.D., FACHE, Chief Executive Officer, St. Luke's Health – The Vintage Hospital, Houston, TX, p. A628
GARNER, Matthew, Chief Executive Officer, Broward Health North, Deerfield Beach, FL, p. A130
GARNER, Stephen, Chief Executive Officer, Abrazo Arrowhead Campus, Glendale, AZ, p. A32
GARNER, Tiffinie, Chief Financial Officer, Baylor Scott & White Texas Spine & Joint Hospital–Tyler, Tyler, TX, p. A658
GARNETT, Mark, M.D., Chief of Staff, Hansford Hospital, Spearman, TX, p. A653
GAROFOLA, Aaron, Chief Executive Officer, Uofl Health – Shelbyville Hospital, Shelbyville, KY, p. A274
GARONE, Marlene, M.D., Vice President Medical Affairs and Medical Director, UPMC Chautauqua, Jamestown, NY, p. A444
GARRED, John, M.D., Sr, Chief Medical Officer, Burgess Health Center, Onawa, IA, p. A241
GARREN–OSTER, Cynthia
Human Resource Manager, South Coast Global Medical Center, Santa Ana, CA, p. A93
Human Resources Manager, Chapman Global Medical Center, Orange, CA, p. A81
GARRETT, Dana M., R.N., Nursing Services Administrator, Taylor Regional Hospital, Campbellsville, KY, p. A264
GARRETT, David B
Senior Vice President and Chief Information Officer, Novant Health Brunswick Medical Center, Bolivia, NC, p. A464
Senior Vice President and Chief Information Officer, Novant Health Charlotte Orthopaedic Hospital, Charlotte, NC, p. A466
Senior Vice President and Chief Information Officer, Novant Health Forsyth Medical Center, Winston–Salem, NC, p. A478
Senior Vice President and Chief Information Officer, Novant Health Huntersville Medical Center, Huntersville, NC, p. A470
Senior Vice President and Chief Information Officer, Novant Health Matthews Medical Center, Matthews, NC, p. A472
Senior Vice President and Chief Information Officer, Novant Health Medical Park Hospital, Winston–Salem, NC, p. A478
Senior Vice President and Chief Information Officer, Novant Health Rowan Medical Center, Salisbury, NC, p. A475
Senior Vice President and Chief Information Officer, Novant Health Thomasville Medical Center, Thomasville, NC, p. A477
Senior Vice President and Chief Information Officer, UVA Health Haymarket Medical Center, Haymarket, VA, p. A677
Senior Vice President and Chief Information Officer, UVA Health Prince William Medical Center, Manassas, VA, p. A679
Senior Vice President Information Technology, Novant Health Presbyterian Medical Center, Charlotte, NC, p. A466
GARRETT, Josh, Chief of Staff, Northeast Georgia Medical Center Habersham, Demorest, GA, p. A162
GARRETT, Kevin C., M.D., Medical Executive, East Region, M Health Fairview Woodwinds Hospital, Woodbury, MN, p. A357
GARRETT, Matthew, Director Information Systems, Flowers Hospital, Dothan, AL, p. A18
GARRETT, Scott, Director of IS, Ottumwa Regional Health Center, Ottumwa, IA, p. A241
GARRETT, Sharon, Chief Executive Officer, Encompass Health Rehabilitation Hospital of Dallas, Dallas, TX, p. A611
GARRICK, Renee, M.D., Executive Medical Director, Westchester Medical Center, Valhalla, NY, p. A461
GARRIGAN, Ami, M.D., Chief of Staff, Fall River Health Services, Hot Springs, SD, p. A574
GARRIOTT, Edie, Director Human Resources, Community Hospital South, Indianapolis, IN, p. A219
GARRISON, Christopher, M.D., Medical Director, Central Texas Rehabilitation Hospital, Austin, TX, p. A599
GARRISON, Eric L, Chief Information Officer, Greeneville Community Hospital East, Greeneville, TN, p. A583
GARRISON, Wes St. Luke's Health – Sugar Land Hospital, Sugar Land, TX, p. A655
GARRITY, Elizabeth, Director Human Resources, Hudson Regional Hospital, Secaucus, NJ, p. A428
GARRITY, Nerissa, Chief Financial Officer, Kula Hospital, Kula, HI, p. A177
GARROW, Dina, Chief Nursing Officer and Chief Operating Officer, Kindred Hospital–Baldwin Park, Baldwin Park, CA, p. A57
GARTHWAITE, Tom, President, Winter Haven Hospital, Winter Haven, FL, p. A155
GARTMAN, Kathy Degenstein, Chief Nursing Officer, South Arkansas Regional Hospital, El Dorado, AR, p. A45
GARTNER, Katie, Director Health Information Management, Chi Health Good Samaritan, Kearney, NE, p. A401
GARTON, Debra, R.N., Chief Nursing Officer, Oss Health, York, PA, p. A558
GARVEY, Rita, Chief Nursing Officer, Lawrence County Memorial Hospital, Lawrenceville, IL, p. A200
GARVEY, Thomas J, Senior Vice President Operations and Chief Financial Officer, Endeavor Health Swedish Hospital, Chicago, IL, p. A189
GARVIN, Maria, Chief Financial Officer, UCF Lake Nona Medical Center, Orlando, FL, p. A144
GARY, Al, COO, Simpson General Hospital, Mendenhall, MS, p. A366
GARZA, Art, FACHE, Chief Executive Officer, Las Palmas Medical Center, El Paso, TX, p. A616
GARZA, Ismelda
Chief Information Officer, Cuero Regional Hospital, Cuero, TX, p. A610
Director Information Systems, Comanche County Medical Center, Comanche, TX, p. A608
GARZA, Laura, Manager Information Technology, Hereford Regional Medical Center, Hereford, TX, p. A624
GARZA, Leo, Chief Executive Officer, South Texas Rehabilitation Hospital, Brownsville, TX, p. A605
GARZA, Ruben, Chief Executive Officer, Dallas Medical Center, Dallas, TX, p. A611
GARZA, Teri, Director Health Information Services, Knap. Medical Center, Weslaco, TX, p. A662
GARZA, Tom, Director Fiscal and Support, Rio Grande State Center/South Texas Health Care System, Harlingen, TX, p. A623
GASAWAY, Rob, Vice President Finance, Hannibal Regional Hospital, Hannibal, MO, p. A376
GASBARRE, Christopher, D.O., Community Medical Director, Monument Health Spearfish Hospital, Spearfish, SD, p. A577
GASH, Deborah
Chief Information Officer, Saint Luke's Hospital of Kansas City, Kansas City, MO, p. A378
Chief Information Officer, Saint Luke's South Hospital, Overland Park, KS, p. A257
GASKILL, Paulette Sue, Executive Director of Nursing, Ascension St. Vincent Clay Hospital, Brazil, IN, p. A213
GASKINS, Michael, Director Information Technology, Lincoln Health, Hugo, CO, p. A110
GASKINS, Michael W., President, UPMC Hanover, Hanover, PA, p. A541
GASPAR, Gabrielle, M.D., Chief Medical Officer, Doctors Medical Center of Modesto, Modesto, CA, p. A77
GASQUE, James, M.D., Chief Hospital Services, U. S. Air Force Medical Center Keesler, Keesler Afb, MS, p. A364
GASSELING, Cassie
Chief Executive Officer, Kimball Health Services, Kimball, NE, p. A401
Chief Financial Officer, Kimball Health Services, Kimball, NE, p. A401
GASTINEAU, Trent, Chief Executive Officer, Tulsa Spine And Specialty Hospital, Tulsa, OK, p. A523
GASTON, Tammy, Chief Information Officer, Smith County Memorial Hospital, Smith Center, KS, p. A260
GATES, Lisa, Chief Nursing Officer, Southwest Health System, Cortez, CO, p. A105
GATES, Misty, Chief Financial Officer, Forrest City Medical Center, Forrest City, AR, p. A46
GATES, Rose, Director Human Resources, Tamarack Health Hayward Medical Center, Hayward, WI, p. A713
GATES, Tracy, Vice President Operations and Chief Operating Officer, Guthrie Cortland Regional Medical Center, Cortland, NY, p. A441
GATHERS, Mary
Director Information Systems, Mckay–Dee Hospital, Ogden, UT, p. A666
Director Information Systems, Utah Valley Hospital, Provo, UT, p. A667
Manager Information Systems, American Fork Hospital, American Fork, UT, p. A664
GATLIFF, Peggy, Chief Financial Officer, HCA Florida Northside Hospital, Saint Petersburg, FL, p. A149
GATLIFF, Rob, Chief of Medical Staff, Washington County Regional Medical Center, Sandersville, GA, p. A170
GATO, Carlos A, Director of Human Resources, Fort Lauderdale Behavioral Health Center, Oakland Park, FL, p. A143
GATRELL, Kristi, Chief Executive Officer, Big Horn Hospital, Hardin, MT, p. A392
GATTO, Tony, Director Management Information Systems, Flushing Hospital Medical Center, New York, NY, p. A448
GAUER, Natalie, Administrator, Milbank Area Hospital Avera, Milbank, SD, p. A574
GAUG, Mathew P.
Executive Director of Information Technology, Lima Memorial Health System, Lima, OH, p. A498
Vice President Information Systems and Chief Information Officer, Memorial Hospital And Health Care Center, Jasper, IN, p. A220
GAUGHAN, Thomas, M.D., Chief Medical Officer, Kingman Regional Medical Center, Kingman, AZ, p. A32
GAUL, Mike, Director Information Technology, Golden Valley Memorial Healthcare, Clinton, MO, p. A373
GAULT, Cindy L., Chief Financial Officer, Union Medical Center, Union, SC, p. A571

A854 Index of Health Care Professionals

Index of Health Care Professionals / George

GAURON, Patricia, Director Human Resources, Holy Family Hospital, Methuen, MA, p. A316
GAUSE, Levi Nathan, M.D., Chief Information Officer and Vice President Health System Informatics, Southeast Iowa Regional Medical Center, West Burlington Campus, West Burlington, IA, p. A245
GAUTHIER, Celeste, Mental Hospital Administrator 2, Central Louisiana State Hospital, Pineville, LA, p. A291
GAUTHIER, Paul, Chief Information Resources Management, Fort Harrison Va Medical Center, Fort Harrison, MT, p. A392
GAUTNEY, Steven, FACHE, President and Chief Executive Officer, Crisp Regional Hospital, Cordele, GA, p. A161
GAVIN, Donald, Chief Financial Officer, Southern Tennessee Regional Health System–Pulaski, Pulaski, TN, p. A592
GAVIN, Eliza, Chief Executive Officer, Regency Hospital of Meridian, Meridian, MS, p. A366
GAVIN, Patrick J., M.P.H., President and Chief Executive Officer, Hunterdon Healthcare, Flemington, NJ, p. A421
GAVIN, Todd, Chief Medical Officer, Madelia Health, Madelia, MN, p. A349
GAVORA, George, Director Program Evaluation, Kingsboro Psychiatric Center, New York, NY, p. A448
GAVULIC, Melany
  R.N., President & Chief Executive Officer, Hurley Medical Center, Flint, MI, p. A326
  R.N., Senior Vice President Operations & COO, Hurley Medical Center, Flint, MI, p. A326
GAW, Kris, Chief Operating Officer, Denver Health, Denver, CO, p. A106
GAWITH, Marlene, Director of Nursing, Ottawa County Health Center, Minneapolis, KS, p. A255
GAWLER, William, Chief Information Officer, Chillicothe Veterans Affairs Medical Center, Chillicothe, OH, p. A488
GAWNE, Bernard B, M.D., Vice President and Chief Medical Officer, The Christ Hospital Health Network, Cincinnati, OH, p. A489
GAY, Christophe, M.D., Chief of Staff, Midcoast Medical Center – Bellville, Bellville, TX, p. A603
GAY, Heywood Kyle, M.D., Physician, Optim Medical Center – Screven, Sylvania, GA, p. A172
GAY, Kent E., M.D., Chief of Medical Staff, Arkansas Valley Regional Medical Center, La Junta, CO, p. A110
GAY, Kristi
  Chief Financial Officer, Chi St. Luke's Health Memorial Lufkin, Lufkin, TX, p. A636
  Chief Financial Officer, Chi St. Luke's Health Memorial San Augustine, San Augustine, TX, p. A651
GAY, Michael, Chief Operating Officer, Northeast Georgia Medical Center Habersham, Demorest, GA, p. A162
GAY, Perry, Chief Executive Officer, Lutheran Downtown Hospital, Fort Wayne, IN, p. A216
GAYNE, William, Chief Financial Officer, Medstar Washington Hospital Center, Washington, DC, p. A124
GAYTKO, Caren, Chief Nursing Officer, Regency Hospital of Minneapolis, Golden Valley, MN, p. A347
GAZAWAY, William, Information Technology Security Officer, Integris Health Ponca City Hospital, Ponca City, OK, p. A519
GAZECKI, Cindy, Senior Vice President, Hospital Operations, Seattle Children's Hospital, Seattle, WA, p. A694
GEAGHAN, Jeff
  Chief Information Officer, Franciscan Healthcare, West Point, NE, p. A407
  Chief Information Officer, Valley County Health System, Ord, NE, p. A404
GEARHART, Heidi, Director Information Systems, Arkansas Valley Regional Medical Center, La Junta, CO, p. A110
GEARY, David S, Chief Financial Officer, Cache Valley Hospital, North Logan, UT, p. A666
GEARY, Herb J
  Chief Nursing Officer, Santa Ynez Valley Cottage Hospital, Solvang, CA, p. A96
  Vice President Patient Care Services and Chief Nursing Officer, Santa Barbara Cottage Hospital, Santa Barbara, CA, p. A94
GEBAUER, Laurie, Director Patient Care, Orange City Area Health System, Orange City, IA, p. A241
GEBHARD, Scott
  Chief Operating Officer, JFK Johnson Rehabilitation Institute At Hackensack Meridian Health, Edison, NJ, p. A420
  Executive VP and Chief Operating Officer, Hackensack Meridian Health Jfk Medical Center, Edison, NJ, p. A420
GEBHART, Cheryl
  Chief Human Resources Officer, Ohsu Health Hillsboro Medical Center, Hillsboro, OR, p. A528
  Director Human Resources Providence Health Plan and Providence Medical Group, Providence Newberg Medical Center, Newberg, OR, p. A529

GEBHART, Ronald J, M.D., Chief of Staff, George E. Wahlen Department of Veterans Affairs Medical Center, Salt Lake City, UT, p. A668
GEBHART, Ryan, FACHE, President, Baylor Scott & White Medical Center – Centennial, Frisco, TX, p. A621
GEBHART, Steve, Vice President, Patient Services, Mercy Hospital Waldron, Waldron, AR, p. A54
GECKLE, Rachel, Chief Human Resource Officer, Fulton County Health Center, Wauseon, OH, p. A506
GEDDES WIRTH, Lauren
  Chief Medical Officer, New London Hospital, New London, NH, p. A416
  Interim President and Chief Executive Officer, New London Hospital, New London, NH, p. A416
GEDDINGS, Toni, Director Human Resources, Cullman Regional Medical Center, Cullman, AL, p. A18
GEDIES, Lucille, Chief Financial Officer, Mildred Mitchell–Bateman Hospital, Huntington, WV, p. A701
GEE, Kyle
  Chief Financial Officer, Beartooth Billings Clinic, Red Lodge, MT, p. A395
  Chief Financial Officer, Pioneer Medical Center, Big Timber, MT, p. A389
  Regional Vice President Financial Operations, Roundup Memorial Healthcare, Roundup. MT, p. A395
GEERTS, Jodi, Chief Executive Officer, Waverly Health Center, Waverly, IA, p. A245
GEESEY, Wanda, Director Human Resources, Pennsylvania Psychiatric Institute, Harrisburg, PA, p. A541
GEHA, Andrew, D.O., President Medical Staff, Floyd Valley Healthcare, Le Mars, IA, p. A239
GEHLAUF, Dee Ann, Vice President Business and Organization Development, Marietta Memorial Hospital, Marietta, OH, p. A499
GEHLHAUSEN, Sherri, Chief Financial Officer, Logansport Memorial Hospital, Logansport, IN, p. A223
GEHRIG, Ryan T.
  FACHE, President, Mercy Hospital Fort Smith, Fort Smith, AR, p. A47
  FACHE, President, Mercy Hospital Northwest Arkansas, Rogers, AR, p. A52
GEHRING, Betty, Finance Director, Operations, Thedacare Medical Center–New London, New London, WI, p. A718
GEHRING, Jay, Director Information Systems, Kingman Community Hospital, Kingman, KS, p. A252
GEHRING, Mikaela, Chief Operating Officer, Compass Memorial Healthcare, Marengo, IA, p. A239
GEHRING, Samuel, M.D., Chief of Staff, Fleming County Hospital, Flemingsburg, KY, p. A265
GEIB, Ryan, President,Mercy Southeast Communities, Mercy Hospital Southeast, Cap. Girardeau, MO, p. A372
GEIER, Joyce, Director Nursing, Girard Medical Center, Girard, KS, p. A249
GEIER, Kathy, Director of Nursing, Chase County Community Hospital, Imperial, NE, p. A401
GEIGER, Deb, Executive Director of Acute Care, Harbor Beach Community Hospital Inc., Harbor Beach, MI, p. A329
GEIGLE, Joseph, Director Human Resources, Kettering Health Hamilton, Hamilton, OH, p. A497
GEIL, Kristie A, Vice President and Chief Nursing Officer, Aurora Medical Center Kenosha, Kenosha, WI, p. A713
GEISLER, Linda W, R.N., FACHE, Vice President Patient Services, Centrastate Healthcare System, Freehold, NJ, p. A421
GEISSLER, Bonnie, R.N., Chief Nursing Officer, Vice President Patient Care Services, Clara Maass Medical Center, Belleville, NJ, p. A418
GEIST, Jim, Executive Vice President and Chief Operating Officer, Skagit Valley Hospital, Mount Vernon, WA, p. A692
GEISTER, Bennett, President, Oklahoma City Communities, Mercy Hospital Oklahoma City, Oklahoma City, OK, p. A517
GEITZ, Cheri, Director Human Resources, Hansen Family Hospital, Iowa Falls, IA, p. A238
GEIVER, Betsy, Chief Human Resources Officer, Royal C. Johnson Veterans' Memorial Hospital, Sioux Falls, SD, p. A576
GELDENHUYS, Albert
  Chief Executive Officer, Cypress Pointe Surgical Hospital, Hammond, LA, p. A282
  Chief Financial Officer, Cypress Pointe Surgical Hospital, Hammond, LA, p. A282
GELDHOF, Jay
  Director Information Systems, Greater El Monte Community Hospital, South El Monte, CA, p. A96
  Director Information Systems, Whittier Hospital Medical Center, Whittier, CA, p. A101
GELL, Daniel
  MSN, Market Chief Executive Officer, Ascension Wisconsin Hospital – Menomonee Falls Campus, Menomonee Falls, WI, p. A715

  MSN, Regional Chief Nursing Officer, Ascension Wisconsin Hospital – Menomonee Falls Campus, Menomonee Falls, WI, p. A715
GELLASCH, Tara L, Chief Medical Officer, United Memorial Medical Center, Batavia, NY, p. A439
GELLER, Harold S., Chief Executive Officer, Chi St. Anthony Hospital, Pendleton, OR, p. A530
GELLER, Mark, M.D., President and Chief Executive Officer, Montefiore Nyack Hospital, Nyack, NY, p. A454
GELLER, Warren, President and Chief Executive Officer, Englewood Health, Englewood, NJ, p. A421
GEMBOL, Leslie, MSN, R.N., Chief Nursing Officer, Baylor Scott & White Medical Center – Round Rock, Round Rock, TX, p. A647
GEMENY, Anna
  Regional Director Human Resources, Baylor Scott & White The Heart Hospital Denton, Denton, TX, p. A613
  Regional Director Human Resources, Baylor Scott & White The Heart Hospital Plano, Plano, TX, p. A644
GENC, Zafer L., Chief Executive Officer, La Paz Regional Hospital, Parker, AZ, p. A34
GENESIO, Sabina, Finance Officer for Institutes, Colorado Mental Health Institute At Fort Logan, Denver, CO, p. A106
GENEVRO, Thomas A, Vice President Human Resources, Butler Memorial Hospital, Butler, PA, p. A536
GENGLE, Tim F, Director Human Resources, Trinity Health Grand Haven Hospital, Grand Haven, MI, p. A328
GENGLER, Laraine, Chief Financial Officer, Lindsborg Community Hospital, Lindsborg, KS, p. A253
GENNA, Nick, Administrator, Treasure Valley Hospital, Boise, ID, p. A180
GENNARO, John, FACHE, Director, Erie Veterans Affairs Medical Center, Erie, PA, p. A539
GENOVESE, Vincent P, M.D., President Medical Staff, Owensboro Health Muhlenberg Community Hospital, Greenville, KY, p. A266
GENSERT, Kurt G, FACHE, R.N., Vice President Operations, Intermountain Health Platte Valley Hospital, Brighton, CO, p. A104
GENTILE, John
  M.D., Vice President Medical Affairs, Alta Bates Summit Medical Center – Summit Campus, Oakland, CA, p. A80
  M.D., Vice President Medical Affairs, Alta Bates Summit Medical Center–Alta Bates Campus, Berkeley, CA, p. A57
GENTNER, Kim, Chief Financial Officer, Deckerville Community Hospital, Deckerville, MI, p. A324
GENTRY, Julia
  Chief Nursing Officer, Northern Colorado, Banner Fort Collins Medical Center, Fort Collins, CO, p. A108
  Chief Nursing Officer, Northern Colorado, Banner Mckee Medical Center, Loveland, CO, p. A112
  Chief Nursing Officer, Northern Colorado, Banner North Colorado Medical Centernorth Colorado Medical Center, Greeley, CO, p. A109
GENTRY, Laura, Chief Executive Officer, Atrium Health Navicent Peach, Macon, GA, p. A167
GENTRY, Lee, FACHE, Chief Executive Officer, Continuecare Hospital At Baptist Health Paducah, Paducah, KY, p. A273
GENTRY, Margie, Controller, T. J. Samson Community Hospital, Glasgow, KY, p. A266
GEOGHEGAN, Jeffrey, Chief Financial Officer, Uconn, John Dempsey Hospital, Farmington, CT, p. A116
GEORGE, Alan E, Chief Operating Officer, St. Francis – Emory Healthcare, Columbus, GA, p. A161
GEORGE, Alan E., President, Bon Secours Mary Immaculate Hospital, Newport News, VA, p. A679
GEORGE, Brad, Director Information Systems, Parkland Medical Center, Derry, NH, p. A414
GEORGE, Daniel M, Executive Vice President, Operations, Covenant Healthcare, Saginaw, MI, p. A336
GEORGE, Denise, R.N., President, Northern Dutchess Hospital, Rhinebeck, NY, p. A457
GEORGE, Gary, Senior Vice President Human Resources, Mercy Health – St. Vincent Medical Center, Toledo, OH, p. A504
GEORGE, Jerrica, FACHE, Chief Executive Officer, Methodist Hospital, San Antonio, TX, p. A650
GEORGE, P A, M.D., Chief of Staff, Madison Medical Center, Fredericktown, MO, p. A375
GEORGE, Saju, Regional Chief Executive Officer – Prime Healthcare Michigan Market, Garden City Hospital, Garden City, MI, p. A327
GEORGE, Susan, R.N., M.P.H., Associate Director Patient Care Services, Martinsburg Veterans Affairs Medical Center, Martinsburg, WV, p. A702
GEORGE, Trace, Chief Financial Officer, North Runnels Hospital, Winters, TX, p. A663
GEORGE, Tracy L, Chief Financial Officer, St. James Parish Hospital, Lutcher, LA, p. A287

© 2025 AHA Guide

Index of Health Care Professionals / George

GEORGE, William, M.D., Chief of Staff, Beartooth Billings Clinic, Red Lodge, MT, p. A395
GEORGE-RAY, Stephanie, Superintendent, Riverview Psychiatric Center, Augusta, ME, p. A295
GEORGES, Angelo, M.D., President Medical and Dental Staff, Wheeling Hospital, Wheeling, WV, p. A706
GEORGESON, Keith, M.D., Chief Executive, Providence Sacred Heart Medical Center & Children's Hospital, Spokane, WA, p. A696
GEORGOFF, Julie, Vice President of Finance and Chief Financial Officer, Magruder Memorial Hospital, Port Clinton, OH, p. A502
GEPFORD, John, Director Information Systems, Evergreenhealth Monroe, Monroe, WA, p. A691
GEPHART, Anandita, M.D., Chief Medical Officer, Ascension Saint Josep. – Elgin, Elgin, IL, p. A194
GERACI, Nichole
  Chief Operating Officer, Acmh Hospital, Kittanning, PA, p. A543
  President and Chief Executive Officer, Acmh Hospital, Kittanning, PA, p. A543
GERARD, Greg Donavan., President, Baptist Health Richmond, Richmond, KY, p. A273
GERARD, Jennifer
  R.N., Assistant Vice President, Nursing and Hospital Administration, Ochsner Abrom Kaplan Memorial Hospital, Kaplan, LA, p. A284
  R.N., Chief Nursing Officer, Ochsner Abrom Kaplan Memorial Hospital, Kaplan, LA, p. A284
GERARDI, Joe, R.N., Chief Operating Officer, Chief Nursing Officer, Community Hospital, Grand Junction, CO, p. A108
GERBER, Allen, M.D., Chief of Staff, Baptist Health Medical Center–Hot Spring County, Malvern, AR, p. A50
GERBER, Andrew J.
  M.D., Ph.D., President and Chief Executive Officer, Silver Hill Hospital, New Canaan, CT, p. A117
  M.D., Ph.D., President and Medical Director, Silver Hill Hospital, New Canaan, CT, p. A117
GERBER, Greg, M.D., Chief Medical Officer, Aurora Lakeland Medical Center, Elkhorn, WI, p. A710
GERDES, Isaac
  Chief Executive Officer, Pioneer Memorial Hospital And Health Services, Viborg, SD, p. A578
  Chief Executive Officer, Sanford Webster Medical Center, Webster, SD, p. A578
GERDTS, Nicole, Director, Quality and Risk, University of Iowa Health Network Rehabilitation Hospital, Coralville, IA, p. A233
GERE, Zsaber, Chief Human Resource Officer, Banner Behavioral Health Hospital – Scottsdale, Scottsdale, AZ, p. A38
GERETY, Meghan, M.D., Chief of Staff, Raymond G. Murphy Department of Veterans Affairs Medical Center, Albuquerque, NM, p. A433
GHERHART, Paul, Chief Financial Officer, Sanford Canton–Inwood Medical Center, Canton, SD, p. A572
GERHOLD, John, Chief Executive Officer, HCA Florida Lake Monroe Hospital, Sanford, FL, p. A149
GERING, Paul, M.D., Vice President Medical Affairs, Saint Alphonsus Medical Center – Ontario, Ontario, OR, p. A529
GERKE, Daniel, Chief Nursing Officer, Wright Patterson Medical Center, Wright-Patterson Afb, OH, p. A507
GERKE, Sarah, Manager Human Resources, Warner Hospital And Health Services, Clinton, IL, p. A192
GERKEN, Jennifer, R.N., Chief Financial Officer, Kansas Spine & Specialty Hospital, Wichita, KS, p. A262
GERLACH, Carl, Chief Financial Officer, Curry General Hospital, Gold Beach, OR, p. A527
GERLACH, Matthew S
  Chief Operating Officer, Children's Hospital of Orange County, Orange, CA, p. A81
  Chief Operating Officer, Choc Children's At Mission Hospital, Mission Viejo, CA, p. A77
GERMANY, Alan, Chief Operating Officer, Adventist Health – Tulare, Tulare, CA, p. A98
GERNDT, Angie, Human Resources Manager, Mercyone Elkader Medical Center, Elkader, IA, p. A236
GERONIMO, Veronica, Administrator and Chief Executive Officer, U. S. Public Health Service Indian Hospital–Sells, Sells, AZ, p. A38
GERRITS, Brad, Director Information Systems, Marshfield Medical Center – Rice Lake, Rice Lake, WI, p. A720
GERSON, Elaine, Chief Clinical Officer and General Counsel, Aspen Valley Hospital, Aspen, CO, p. A103
GERSTENBERGER, Linda
  Vice President Human Resources, St. Rose Dominican Hospitals – San Martin Campus, Las Vegas, NV, p. A411
  Vice President Human Resources, St. Rose Dominican Hospitals – Siena Campus, Henderson, NV, p. A409

GERSTNER, Nancy, Manager Human Resources, Robert J. Dole Department of Veterans Affairs Medical And Regional Office Center, Wichita, KS, p. A262
GERTEN, Michael, Chief Executive Officer, Haskell Regional Hospital, Stigler, OK, p. A521
GERVELER, Patrick M, Vice President Finance and Chief Financial Officer, Blessing Hospital, Quincy, IL, p. A206
GESSLER, Kevin M.
  Chief Financial Officer, Mon Health Preston Memorial Hospital, Kingwood, WV, p. A702
  Interim Chief Financial Officer, Grafton City Hospital, Grafton, WV, p. A701
GESSLING, Heather, M.D., Chief Medical Officer, Moberly Regional Medical Center, Moberly, MO, p. A380
GESSNER, Christopher A., President and Chief Executive Officer, Akron Children's Hospital, Akron, OH, p. A484
GETCHIUS, Joseph, Director Information Technology, Benewah Community Hospital, Saint Maries, ID, p. A183
GETSAY, Timothy, Chief of Performance and Integration, Gillette Children's Specialty Healthcare, Saint Paul, MN, p. A354
GETTINGER, Thomas
  Executive Vice President and Chief Operating Officer, Mary Washington Hospital, Fredericksburg, VA, p. A676
  Executive Vice President and Chief Operating Officer, Stafford Hospital, Stafford, VA, p. A684
GETTINGS, Scott, M.D., Senior Vice President and Chief Medical Officer, Health First Viera Hospital, Melbourne, FL, p. A139
GETTS, Alissa, Chief Nursing Officer, Atlantic Rehabilitation Institute, Madison, NJ, p. A423
GETTYS, Sky, Chief Financial Officer, Fairfield Medical Center, Lancaster, OH, p. A498
GETZ, Liz, Chief Information Officer, Aultman Hospital, Canton, OH, p. A487
GEURTS, Chuck, Manager Information Technology Client Services, Aurora Baycare Medical Center, Green Bay, WI, p. A712
GEWECKE, Tyler, Information Technology Technician, Fillmore County Hospital, Geneva, NE, p. A400
GFELLER, Michael, Director Information Systems, Medical City Plano, Plano, TX, p. A645
GHAEMMAGHAMI, Chris A., M.D., Executive Vice President, Chief Physician Executive and Chief Clinical Officer, Jackson Health System, Miami, FL, p. A140
GHAFFARI, Bahram, President, Adventist Health Delano, Delano, CA, p. A61
GHAFOOR, Tariq, Medical Director, Aurora Behavioral Health System East, Tempe, AZ, p. A39
GHERINGHELLI, Thomas, Senior Vice President, Chief Financial Officer, New England Baptist Hospital, Boston, MA, p. A311
GHERKE, Sheila, Director Human Resources, Minnie Hamilton Healthcare Center, Grantsville, WV, p. A701
GHIDOTTI, Craig J, Vice President Human Resources, University Hospitals Lake Health, Willoughby, OH, p. A507
GHINASSI, Frank A., Ph.D., President and Chief Executive Officer, Rutgers University Behavioral Healthcare, Piscataway, NJ, p. A427
GHION, christopher, Vice President and Chief Information Officer, Adventist Healthcare Shady Grove Medical Center, Rockville, MD, p. A306
GIAGUINTO, Shelly, Chief Financial Officer, Highland–Clarksburg Hospital, Clarksburg, WV, p. A700
GIAMPA, Patricia L, Chief Nursing Officer, Searhc Mt. Edgecumbe Hospital, Sitka, AK, p. A29
GIANG, Vernon
  M.D., Chief Medical Executive, California Pacific Medical Center–Mission Bernal Campus, San Francisco, CA, p. A90
  M.D., Chief Medical Executive, California Pacific Medical Center–Van Ness Campus, San Francisco, CA, p. A90
GIANGARDELLA, Mike, Vice President Finance and Administration, Salem Regional Medical Center, Salem, OH, p. A503
GIANNINI, Francis
  Associate Director, Southwest Connecticut Mental Health System, Bridgeport, CT, p. A115
  Interim Chief Executive Officer, Southwest Connecticut Mental Health System, Bridgeport, CT, p. A115
GIANNONE, John, M.D., Delaware Valley Hospital Medical Director, UHS Delaware Valley Hospital, Walton, NY, p. A461
GIANNOSA, Amy, Director Human Resources, Havenwyck Hospital, Inc., Auburn Hills, MI, p. A322
GIANSANTE, Joseph, Vice President Human Resources, Ellis Medicine, Schenectady, NY, p. A458
GIARDINA, Deborah, Director Human Resources and Medical Staff Services, Rehabilitation Hospital of Fort Wayne, Fort Wayne, IN, p. A217

GIARDINO, Angelo, M.D., Chief Medical Officer, Primary Children's Hospital, Salt Lake City, UT, p. A669
GIBB, Matthew, M.D., Executive Vice President and System Chief Medical Officer, Carle Foundation Hospital, Urbana, IL, p. A210
GIBBENS, Lori, Controller, Encompass Health Rehabilitation Hospital of Erie, Erie, PA, p. A539
GIBBERMAN, Val, M.D., Acting Chief of Staff, Hampton Veterans Affairs Medical Center, Hampton, VA, p. A677
GIBBES, Gregg
  Chief Executive Officer, Covington County Hospital, Collins, MS, p. A361
  Chief Executive Officer, Magee General Hospital, Magee, MS, p. A365
  Chief Executive Officer, Simpson General Hospital, Mendenhall, MS, p. A366
  President and Chief Executive Officer, South Central Regional Medical Center, Laurel, MS, p. A365
GIBBONS, Barbara, Vice President Patient Care Services, St. Josep. Hospital, Bethpage, NY, p. A439
GIBBONS, Brian P., Chief Executive Officer, Astria Sunnyside Hospital, Sunnyside, WA, p. A696
GIBBONS, Jason, Chief Financial Officer, Minidoka Memorial Hospital, Rupert, ID, p. A183
GIBBS, Christopher Michael, Director Information Management Systems, Taylor Regional Hospital, Campbellsville, KY, p. A264
GIBBS, Diane, Director, Operations, Winter Haven Hospital, Winter Haven, FL, p. A155
GIBBS, Jeffrey S., M.D., Regional Vice President Medical Affairs, Skagit Valley Hospital, Mount Vernon, WA, p. A692
GIBBS, Kenneth, President and Chief Executive Officer, Maimonides Medical Center, New York, NY, p. A449
GIBBS, Michael, President, Avera Heart Hospital of South Dakota, Sioux Falls, SD, p. A576
GIBBS, Parker, M.D., Chief Medical Officer, UF Health Shands Hospital, Gainesville, FL, p. A133
GIBBS, Tim, Director of Information Technology, Information Security Officer, Children's Hospital of Richmond At Vcu, Richmond, VA, p. A682
GIBBS, Vickie, Director Nursing, Phillip. County Health Systems, Phillipsburg, KS, p. A258
GIBBS–MCELVY, Shelana, M.D., Medical Director, Encompass Health Rehabilitation Hospital of Sewickley, Sewickley, PA, p. A554
GIBNEY, Thomas, Senior Vice President and Chief Financial Officer, Montefiore St. Luke's Cornwall, Newburgh, NY, p. A454
GIBSON, Armetria, Human Resources Generalist, Select Specialty Hospital Midtown Atlanta, Atlanta, GA, p. A158
GIBSON, Belinda D, R.N., Senior Vice President Patient Services, Bsa Hospital, Llc, Amarillo, TX, p. A596
GIBSON, Jack, Administrator, Noland Hospital Tuscaloosa, Tuscaloosa, AL, p. A25
GIBSON, Joel, Vice President Human Resources, Henry Ford Macomb Hospital, Clinton Township, MI, p. A324
GIBSON, Mary Helen, Director Human Resources, Floyd Valley Healthcare, Le Mars, IA, p. A239
GIBSON, Matthew, Ph.D., FACHE, Chief Executive Officer, Siskin Hospital for Physical Rehabilitation, Chattanooga, TN, p. A581
GIBSON, Megan, Nurse Manager, River Bend Hospital, West Lafayette, IN, p. A229
GIBSON, Todd, Chief Financial Officer, Medical City Denton, Denton, TX, p. A614
GICCA, Ron, Chief Executive Officer, Melbourne Regional Medical Center, Melbourne, FL, p. A139
GICZI, Mary Beth, Director Human Resources, Encompass Health Rehabilitation Hospital of Scottsdale, Scottsdale, AZ, p. A38
GIEGER, Julie
  Chief Financial Officer, Lackey Memorial Hospital, Forest, MS, p. A362
  Chief Financial Officer, Monroe Regional Hospital, Aberdeen, MS, p. A359
GIER, Jennifer, Director Human Resources, Brynn Marr Hospital, Jacksonville, NC, p. A471
GIERTUGA, Garry, Site Manager Human Resources, UChicago Medicine Adventhealth La Grange, La Grange, IL, p. A199
GIESE, Kristine A, Chief Operating Officer, Providence Medical Center, Wayne, NE, p. A406
GIESECKE, Guy, Chief Executive Officer, University of Mississipp. Medical Center, Jackson, MS, p. A364
GIGLIOTTI, Vicki, Chief Clinical Officer, Moab Regional Hospital, Moab, UT, p. A666
GIL, Julio, Manager Information Services, Hazel Hawkins Memorial Hospital, Hollister, CA, p. A67
GILBERT, Alicia, Vice President, Regions Hospital, Saint Paul, MN, p. A354

GILBERT, Carla, Director Finance, Cedar County Memorial Hospital, El Dorado Springs, MO, p. A374
GILBERT, Christy
  President and Chief Operating Officer, Doctors Neuropsychiatric Hospital, Bremen, IN, p. A213
  President and Chief Operating Officer, Medical Behavioral Hospital of Clear Lake, Houston, TX, p. A629
  President and Chief Operating Officer, Medical Behavioral Hospital of Mishawaka, Mishawaka, IN, p. A223
  President and Chief Operating Officer, Medical Behavioral Hospital of Northern Arizona, Prescott, AZ, p. A37
  President and Chief Operating Officer, Neurobehavioral Hospital of Nw Indiana/Greater Chicago, Crown Point, IN, p. A215
  President and Chief Operating Officer, Neuropsychiatric Hospital of Indianapolis, Indianapolis, IN, p. A220
  President and Chief Operating Officer, Phoenix Medical Psychiatric Hospital, Phoenix, AZ, p. A36
GILBERT, Jack, Vice President Finance and Facilities, Advocate Illinois Masonic Medical Center, Chicago, IL, p. A188
GILBERT, Kevin, R.N., Vice President, Confluence Health Hospital – Mares Campus, Wenatchee, WA, p. A698
GILBERT, Kim, R.N., Chief Nursing Officer, Electra Memorial Hospital, Electra, TX, p. A618
GILBERT, Peter N., Senior Vice President and Chief Operations Officer, University of Kentucky Albert B. Chandler Hospital, Lexington, KY, p. A269
GILBERT, Sarah, Chief Operating Officer and Assistant Vice President, Bayfront Health St. Petersburg, Saint Petersburg, FL, p. A148
GILBERT, Thomas, Director Information Technology Services, Lake Cumberland Regional Hospital, Somerset, KY, p. A274
GILBERT, Thomas D.
  FACHE, Chief Executive Officer, Wadley Regional Medical Center, Texarkana, TX, p. A657
  FACHE, Chief Executive Officer, Wadley Regional Medical Center At Hope, Hope, AR, p. A47
GILBERT, Tim J., President and Administrator, Maniilaq Health Center, Kotzebue, AK, p. A29
GILBERTSON, Gerry, FACHE, Chief Operating Officer, Centracare – Melrose, Melrose, MN, p. A350
GILBERTSON, Nicholle, Chief Executive Officer, Ringgold County Hospital, Mount Ayr, IA, p. A240
GILDON, Lisa
  Group Financial Officer, Texas Health Presbyterian Hospital Allen, Allen, TX, p. A595
  Vice President and Chief Financial Officer, Texas Health Presbyterian Hospital Plano, Plano, TX, p. A645
GILES, Charles, M.D., President Medical Staff, T.J. Health Columbia, Columbia, KY, p. A264
GILES, Dolly, Chief Nursing Officer, Pike County Memorial Hospital, Louisiana, MO, p. A379
GILES, Jared, FACHE, Chief Executive Officer, Southwest Healthcare System, Murrieta, CA, p. A79
GILES, Steve, Chief Information Officer, Cha Hollywood Presbyterian Medical Center, Los Angeles, CA, p. A72
GILGEN, Steve, Chief Financial Officer, Prowers Medical Center, Lamar, CO, p. A111
GILJUM, Anthony, Chief Information Officer, Sheridan Va Medical Center, Sheridan, WY, p. A728
GILKEY, Edward, M.D., Vice President Medical Affairs, St. Luke's Hospital – Warren Campus, Phillipsburg, NJ, p. A427
GILL, Ben, President and Chief Executive Officer, Southern Ohio Medical Center, Portsmouth, OH, p. A502
GILL, Duane B., Acting Director, Fort Harrison Va Medical Center, Fort Harrison, MT, p. A392
GILL, Jagdip Kaur, Chief Operating Officer, Kaiser Permanente Baldwin Park Medical Center, Baldwin Park, CA, p. A57
GILL, Jon, Chief Operating Officer, Great Plains Regional Medical Center, Elk City, OK, p. A512
GILL, Jonathan, Chief Executive Officer, Pamp. Regional Medical Center, Pampa, TX, p. A642
GILL, Mandeep, Chief Operating Officer, Memorial Hospital of Sweetwater County, Rock Springs, WY, p. A728
GILL, Mark, Vice President Finance and Chief Financial Officer, Cooper University Hospital Cap. Regional, Cap. May Court House, NJ, p. A419
GILL, Sandip. R.N., Chief Nursing Officer, Texas Health Presbyterian Hospital Flower Mound, Flower Mound, TX, p. A618
GILLAM, Sally A, R.N., Chief Nursing Officer, St. David's South Austin Medical Center, Austin, TX, p. A600
GILLARD, Austin M., FACHE, Chief Executive Officer, Clay County Medical Center, Clay Center, KS, p. A247
GILLELAND, Dana
  Chief Executive Officer, Chief Financial Officer, Niobrara Community Hospital, Lusk, WY, p. A727
  Chief Financial Officer, Iroquois Memorial Hospital And Resident Home, Watseka, IL, p. A210
GILLEN, Mark T
  Director Finance and Operations, Owatonna Hospital, Owatonna, MN, p. A352
  Director of Operations, Owatonna Hospital, Owatonna, MN, p. A352
GILLENWATER, Laura, Chief Financial Officer, Sevier County Medical Center, De Queen, AR, p. A45
GILLES, Ken
  Associate Chief Information Officer, Essentia Health St. Mary's – Detroit Lakes, Detroit Lakes, MN, p. A345
  Chief Information Officer, Essentia Health Fargo, Fargo, ND, p. A480
GILLESPIE, Anne, R.N., Associate Director Patient Care and Nursing Services, Jerry L. Pettis Memorial Veterans' Hospital, Loma Linda, CA, p. A70
GILLESPIE, Bob
  Chief Executive Officer, Connally Memorial Medical Center, Floresville, TX, p. A618
  Chief Operating Officer, Connally Memorial Medical Center, Floresville, TX, p. A618
GILLESPIE, Christina L., Chief Executive Officer, Harrison County Community Hospital, Bethany, MO, p. A371
GILLESPIE, Karen, Director Human Resources, Anderson County Hospital, Garnett, KS, p. A249
GILLESPIE, Lisa, M.D., Chief Medical Officer, Piedmont Rockdale Hospital, Conyers, GA, p. A161
GILLESPIE, Megan, R.N., FACHE, Chief Executive Officer, Sutter Santa Rosa Regional Hospital, Santa Rosa, CA, p. A95
GILLESPIE, Tim, Manager Information Systems, Carle Richland Memorial Hospital, Olney, IL, p. A204
GILLETTE, Karen, Associate Director Patient Care Services, Lt. Col. Luke Weathers, Jr. Va Medical Center, Memphis, TN, p. A588
GILLETTE, Nicole, R.N., Chief Nursing Officer, Mymichigan Medical Center West Branch, West Branch, MI, p. A340
GILLETTE, Tom, Senior Vice President and Chief Information Officer, Mount Sinai Medical Center, Miami Beach, FL, p. A141
GILLIAM, David, M.D., Medical Director, Bloomington Meadows Hospital, Bloomington, IN, p. A212
GILLIAM, Leslie, Director Health Information Management, Dominion Hospital, Falls Church, VA, p. A675
GILLIAN, Tom, Chief Operating Officer, River Bend Hospital, West Lafayette, IN, p. A229
GILLILAND, Michael, M.D., Chief of Staff, Chi St. Luke's Health Brazosport, Lake Jackson, TX, p. A633
GILLILAND, Michelle, Director of Nursing, River Park Hospital, Huntington, WV, p. A701
GILLILAND, Sharon, Chief of Staff, Baraga County Memorial Hospital, L'Anse, MI, p. A331
GILLILAND, Terry
  M.D., Chief Medical Officer, Sentara Leigh Hospital, Norfolk, VA, p. A680
  M.D., Senior Vice President and Chief Medical Officer, Sentara Princess Anne Hospital, Virginia Beach, VA, p. A684
GILLIS, Anne, Chief Financial Officer, Holy Cross Hospital, Silver Spring, MD, p. A307
GILLIS, Wayne, Chief Executive Officer, Great Falls Clinic Hospital, Great Falls, MT, p. A392
GILLMAN, Kreg, Chief Executive Officer, Salt Lake Behavioral Health, Salt Lake City, UT, p. A669
GILLY, Mike, Chief Information Officer, Our Lady of The Angels Hospital, Bogalusa, LA, p. A279
GILMAN, James K., M.D., Chief Executive Officer, Nih Clinical Center, Bethesda, MD, p. A302
GILMAN, Kim
  Chief Executive Officer, Phoebe Worth Medical Center, Sylvester, GA, p. A172
  Chief Nursing Officer, Phoebe Worth Medical Center, Sylvester, GA, p. A172
GILMORE, BJ, Chief Nursing Officer, SCL Health Mt – St. Vincent Healthcare, Billings, MT, p. A390
GILMORE, Hugh V, M.D., Vice President Medical Affairs, Ascension Seton Williamson, Round Rock, TX, p. A647
GILMORE, Phillip K., FACHE, Chief Executive Officer, Ashley County Medical Center, Crossett, AR, p. A45
GILMORE, Stephen, Chief Financial Officer, Piedmont Medical Center, Rock Hill, SC, p. A570
GILPIN, Michael W., Vice President Human Resources, Sampson Regional Medical Center, Clinton, NC, p. A466
GILPIN, Nicholas, D.O., Chief Medical Director, Infection Control and Section Head of Infectious Disease, Corewell Health Beaumont Grosse Pointe Hospital, Grosse Pointe, MI, p. A329
GILSON, Sheila, R.N., Chief Operating Officer, Kaiser Permanente Redwood City Medical Center, Redwood City, CA, p. A85
GIN, Nancy, M.D., Area Associate Medical Director, Kaiser Permanente Orange County Anaheim Medical Center, Anaheim, CA, p. A55
GINGRAS, Sean, CPA, Chief Financial Officer, Centerstone Hospital, Bradenton, FL, p. A126
GINGRICH, Curtis
  M.D., President, Ohiohealth Mansfield Hospital, Mansfield, OH, p. A499
  M.D., President, Ohiohealth Shelby Hospital, Shelby, OH, p. A503
GINGRICH, Joye, Director Patient Care Services and Chief Nursing Officer, Penn Highlands Huntingdon, Huntingdon, PA, p. A542
GINGRICH, Mary, Director Health Care Services, Kansas Neurological Institute, Topeka, KS, p. A260
GINN, Bobby, Chief Executive Officer, Tamp. General Hospital Brooksville, Brooksville, FL, p. A127
GINN, Doug, Executive Vice President Operations, Peak Behavioral Health Services, Santa Teresa, NM, p. A437
GINN, Mallory, Chief Financial Officer, Southwest Mississipp. Regional Medical Center, Mccomb, MS, p. A366
GINNATY, Rayn, Vice President Nursing, Benefis Health System, Great Falls, MT, p. A392
GINSBERG, Jo-Ann M., R.N., MSN, Medical Center Executive Director, Robley Rex Department of Veterans Affairs Medical Center, Louisville, KY, p. A270
GIOIA, Anthony, Chief Financial Officer, Orthoindy Hospital, Indianapolis, IN, p. A220
GIORDANO, Kevin T.
  Chief Operating Officer, Brigham And Women's Hospital, Boston, MA, p. A310
  President, Brigham And Women's Faulkner Hospital, Boston, MA, p. A310
GIORDANO, Paul D., Senior Vice President, Human Resources, Mount Sinai South Nassau, Oceanside, NY, p. A454
GIORDANO, Peter, Senior Director Human Resources, WVU Medicine – Harrison Community Hospital, Cadiz, OH, p. A487
GIORDANO, Roger, M.D., Medical Director, Encompass Health Rehabilitation Hospital of Richmond, Richmond, VA, p. A682
GIORDANO, Susan, Chief Nursing Officer, Hackensack Meridian Health Pascack Valley Medical Center, Westwood, NJ, p. A430
GIPP, Jana, Chief Executive Officer, Standing Rock Service Unit, Fort Yates Hospital, Indian Health Service, Dhhs, Fort Yates, ND, p. A481
GIPSON, Hilary, Director of Nursing, Rolling Hills Hospital, Franklin, TN, p. A583
GIPSON, Linda Stephens, MSN, Ph.D., Chief Nursing Officer, Whidbeyhealth, Coupeville, WA, p. A688
GIRADO, Harold, Vice President, Chief Nursing Officer, Baptist Health South Florida, Baptist Hospital of Miami, Miami, FL, p. A139
GIRARD, Thomas R
  Vice President Human Resources, Lincolnhealth, Damariscotta, ME, p. A296
  Vice President Human Resources, Mainehealth Pen Bay Medical Center, Rockport, ME, p. A299
GIRARDEAU, Brian, Director Information System, East Georgia Regional Medical Center, Statesboro, GA, p. A171
GIRARDIER, Cheryl, Director Information Technology, Lecom Health Millcreek Community Hospital, Erie, PA, p. A540
GIRARDY, James, M.D., Vice President, Chief Surgical Officer, OSF Saint Anthony Medical Center, Rockford, IL, p. A207
GIRTY, Tara, Director Human Resources, Kiowa District Healthcare, Kiowa, KS, p. A252
GISI, Dale, President, Thedacare Regional Medical Center– Appleton, Appleton, WI, p. A707
GISLER, Greg, Chief Financial Officer, Mcbride Orthopedic Hospital, Oklahoma City, OK, p. A517
GISLESON, Joni, Director Finance, Gundersen Palmer Lutheran Hospital And Clinics, West Union, IA, p. A245
GITHINJI, Sam, Chief Information Security Officer, Children's Minnesota, Minneapolis, MN, p. A350
GITMAN, Michael
  M.D., Executive Director, Long Island Jewish Medical Center, New Hyde Park, NY, p. A447
  M.D., Medical Director, North Shore University Hospital, Manhasset, NY, p. A445
GITTELMAN, Michael B
  Administrator, UMHC–Sylvester Comprehensive Cancer Center, Miami, FL, p. A141
  Chief Executive Officer, UMHC–Sylvester Comprehensive Cancer Center, Miami, FL, p. A141
GITTLER, Michelle, M.D., Medical Director, Schwab Rehabilitation Hospital, Chicago, IL, p. A191
GITZINGER, Matthew, Director of Operations, ECU Health Duplin Hospital, Kenansville, NC, p. A471

Index of Health Care Professionals

Index of Health Care Professionals / Giudice

GIUDICE, William A, Vice President and Chief Financial Officer, Tallahassee Memorial Healthcare, Tallahassee, FL, p. A151
GIVEN, Christopher, Regional Vice President, Finance, St. Vincent's Medical Center, Bridgeport, CT, p. A115
GIVENS, Michael K., FACHE, Administrator, St. Bernards Medical Center, Jonesboro, AR, p. A48
GIVENS, Patricia, R.N., Chief Nursing Officer, Children's Hospital Colorado, Aurora, CO, p. A103
GIVENS, Seth, Chief Human Resource Officer, Baptist Health Medical Center – Drew County, Monticello, AR, p. A50
GIZZI, Jason, Controller, Encompass Health Rehabilitation Hospital of Morgantown, Morgantown, WV, p. A703
GJOLBERG, Skip Jr, FACHE, President and Chief Executive Officer, St. Joseph's Hospital, Buckhannon, WV, p. A699
GLADEN, Tracy, Chief Financial Officer, Twin Valley Behavioral Healthcare, Columbus, OH, p. A493
GLANVILLE, Tristan, Chief Financial Officer, Adirondack Health, Saranac Lake, NY, p. A458
GLANZER, Elgin, Chief Financial Officer, Memorial Health System, Abilene, KS, p. A246
GLASBERG, Michael, Senior Vice President, Chief Operating Officer, Dameron Hospital, Stockton, CA, p. A96
GLASER, Ruth, President and Chief Operating Officer, Novant Health Pender Medical Center, Burgaw, NC, p. A464
GLASGO, Leah, R.N., Market President, UnityPoint Health – Fort Dodge, Unitypoint Health – Trinity Regional Medical Center, Fort Dodge, IA, p. A236
GLASNAPP, Sherry L., Director, Douglas County Community Mental Health Center, Omaha, NE, p. A404
GLASS, Kyle, Chief Financial Officer, Adventhealth Deland, Deland, FL, p. A130
GLASSCOCK, Sheryl, Chief Nursing Officer, Lake Cumberland Regional Hospital, Somerset, KY, p. A274
GLAUBKE, Nancy, Chief Executive Officer, Valley County Health System, Ord, NE, p. A404
GLAVIN, Jolene, R.N., MSN, Director Nursing, Salina Surgical Hospital, Salina, KS, p. A259
GLAZIER, Stephen, Chief Operating Officer, Uthealth Harris County Psychiatric Center, Houston, TX, p. A628
GLEASON, Jeffrey J, M.D., Chief Medical Officer, Cookeville Regional Medical Center, Cookeville, TN, p. A582
GLEASON, Joe, Chief Executive Officer, HCA Florida Highlands Hospital, Sebring, FL, p. A150
GLEASON, Vallerie L., President and Chief Executive Officer, Nmc Health, Newton, KS, p. A255
GLEN, Diane M, Assistant Administrator, Barnes–Jewish West County Hospital, Saint Louis, MO, p. A384
GLENDENING, Mary, FACHE, Administrator, Shriners Hospitals for Children, Galveston, TX, p. A621
GLENN, Chris, Chief Financial Officer, HCA Florida Orange Park Hospital, Orange Park, FL, p. A144
GLENN, Gary
Director Information Technology, Carrus Rehabilitation Hospital, Sherman, TX, p. A653
Director Information Technology, Carrus Specialty Hospital, Sherman, TX, p. A653
GLENN, Michael, M.D., Chief Medical Officer, Virginia Mason Medical Center, Seattle, WA, p. A695
GLENN, Mike, Chief Executive Officer, Jefferson Healthcare, Port Townsend, WA, p. A693
GLENN, Wil A, Director Communications, Larry B. Zieverink, Sr. Alcoholism Treatment Center, Raleigh, NC, p. A474
GLENNING, Robert, Executive Vice President Finance and Chief Financial Officer, Hackensack Meridian Health Hackensack University Medical Center, Hackensack, NJ, p. A421
GLESSNER, Theresa, Chief Nursing Officer, Eastern Region, Newark–Wayne Community Hospital, Newark, NY, p. A454
GLICK, Jennifer, Manager Clinical Informatics, Oaklawn Psychiatric Center, Goshen, IN, p. A218
GLIDDEN, Nancy, Chief Financial Officer and Vice President Finance, Northern Light Mayo Hospital, Dover–Foxcroft, ME, p. A297
GLIDEWELL, Calvin E Jr, Chief Executive Officer, Broward Health Medical Center, Fort Lauderdale, FL, p. A131
GLIDEWELL, Calvin E. Jr, Interim Chief Executive Officer, Broward Health Imperial Point, Fort Lauderdale, FL, p. A131
GLIHA, Jennie, Chief Human Resource Officer, Aurelia Osborn Fox Memorial Hospital, Oneonta, NY, p. A455
GLIMCHER, Laurie H., President and Chief Executive Officer, Dana–Farber Cancer Institute, Boston, MA, p. A310
GLIMP, Richard
M.D., Chief Medical Officer, Providence Little Company of Mary Medical Center – Torrance, Torrance, CA, p. A98
M.D., Chief Medical Officer, Providence Little Company of Mary Medical Center San Pedro, Los Angeles, CA, p. A75
GLINES, Grant L, Vice President Operation Finance, Mercy Medical Center, Roseburg, OR, p. A531
GLODT, Brian B., Chief of Medical Staff, U. S. Air Force Hospital, Hampton, VA, p. A677
GLONER, James, Senior Vice President, Behavioral Wellness Center At Girard, The, Philadelphia, PA, p. A548
GLORIA–BARRAZA, Patricia, Coordinator Human Resources, Mayhill Hospital, Denton, TX, p. A614
GLOSEMEYER–SAMSEL, Talitha, M.P.H., FACHE, Chief Executive Officer, Pam Health Specialty Hospital of Oklahoma City, Oklahoma City, OK, p. A518
GLOVER, Cynthia, R.N., Vice President and Chief Nursing Officer, Reston Hospital Center, Reston, VA, p. A682
GLOVER, Doug, Controller, William S. Hall Psychiatric Institute, Columbia, SC, p. A565
GLOVER, Jason, Chief Executive Officer, Memorial Hermann – Texas Medical Center, Houston, TX, p. A627
GLOWA, Meghan, Director Human Resources, Sunnyview Rehabilitation Hospital, Schenectady, NY, p. A459
GLOWCZEWSKI, Jason
Chief Operating Officer, University Hospitals Conneaut Medical Center, Conneaut, OH, p. A493
Chief Operating Officer, University Hospitals Geneva Medical Center, Geneva, OH, p. A496
GLUCHOWSKI, Jeanne, Executive Director, Conifer Park, Glenville, NY, p. A443
GLUECK, Dane, M.D., Chief of Staff, Progress West Hospital, O Fallon, MO, p. A381
GLUM, Derrick, Chief Executive Officer, Saint Mary's Regional Medical Center, Reno, NV, p. A412
GLUNK, Daniel, M.D., Chief Quality Officer, UPMC Wellsboro, Wellsboro, PA, p. A557
GLYER, David
Vice President Finance, Community Memorial Hospital – Ventura, Ventura, CA, p. A100
Vice President Finance, Ojai Valley Community Hospital, Ojai, CA, p. A81
GLYNN, Cindy, Director Human Resources, Regional Rehabilitation Hospital, Phenix City, AL, p. A24
GLYNN, John
Chief Information Officer, Rochester General Hospital, Rochester, NY, p. A457
Executive Vice President, Chief Information Officer, Rochester Regional Health, Newark–Wayne Community Hospital, Newark, NY, p. A454
Senior Vice President and Chief Information Officer, Unity Hospital, Rochester, NY, p. A458
GLYNN, Margaret, M.D., Chief Medical Officer, North Mississipp. Medical Center–Iuka, Iuka, MS, p. A363
GLYNN, Shari, Vice President Finance and Chief Financial Officer, Eaton Rapids Medical Center, Eaton Rapids, MI, p. A326
GNAM, Gwen, R.N., MSN, Chief Nursing Officer, Henry Ford Hospital, Detroit, MI, p. A325
GNANN, Andrew, President, Ascension Seton Williamson, Round Rock, TX, p. A647
GOACHER, Brad, Vice President Administration, Alton Memorial Hospital, Alton, IL, p. A185
GOAD, Jeff, Chief Information Officer, Williamson Medical Center, Franklin, TN, p. A583
GOAD, Pat, Director Human Resources, Hillcrest Hospital Claremore, Claremore, OK, p. A511
GOBEL, Bret, Chief Financial Officer, Sierra Vista Hospital, Truth Or Consequences, NM, p. A437
GOBELL, James, Chief Financial Officer, Unitypoint Health – St. Lukes's Sioux City, Sioux City, IA, p. A243
GOBER, Kirby, Chief Executive Officer, Throckmorton County Memorial Hospital, Throckmorton, TX, p. A658
GOCHENOUR, Julia, Manager Information Systems, West River Regional Medical Center, Hettinger, ND, p. A481
GOCHNOUR, Eric, Chief Human Resource Officer, Cassia Regional Hospital, Burley, ID, p. A180
GODAMUNNE, Karim, M.D., Chief Medical Officer, Wellstar North Fulton Hospital, Roswell, GA, p. A170
GODBEE, Mitchell, Chief of Staff, Capital Region Medical Center, Jefferson City, MO, p. A376
GODBOLD, Steven, Vice President Operations and Chief Operating Officer, East Tennessee Children's Hospital, Knoxville, TN, p. A585
GODDARD, Mark, M.D., Medical Director, Encompass Health Rehabilitation Hospital At Cincinnati, Cincinnati, OH, p. A489
GODDARD, Nichole, Chief Operating Officer, South Region, Community Hospital South, Indianapolis, IN, p. A219
GODFREY, John, M.D., Vice President and Chief Executive Officer, Baptist Health Hardin, Elizabethtown, KY, p. A265
GODFREY, Katrina, Director Human Resources, Mercy Hospital Ada, Ada, OK, p. A509
GODFREY, Kristine, Director Human Resources, Tennova Healthcare – Cleveland, Cleveland, TN, p. A581
GODFREY, Larry, Chief Executive Officer, Baton Rouge Behavioral Hospital, Baton Rouge, LA, p. A277
GODFRIN, Sheri, Chief Executive Officer, Rehabilitation Hospital of Rhode Island, North Smithfield, RI, p. A560
GODINEZ, Andrea, Chief Nursing Officer, Palomar Health Rehabilitation Institute, Escondido, CA, p. A62
GODLEY, James R, Vice President of Human Resources, Northern Light Mayo Hospital, Dover–Foxcroft, ME, p. A297
GODLEY, Patrick, Chief Financial Officer, Contra Costa Regional Medical Center, Martinez, CA, p. A76
GODOY, Charette, Chief Financial Officer, Willow Springs Center, Reno, NV, p. A412
GODWIN, Herman A, M.D., Jr, Senior Vice President and Medical Director, Watauga Medical Center, Boone, NC, p. A464
GODWIN, Robin M.
MSN, Administrator, Ascension Sacred Heart Bay, Panama City, FL, p. A145
MSN, Vice President of Nursing, Ascension Sacred Heart Gulf, Port St Joe, FL, p. A147
GOEB–BURKETT, Michele, R.N., MSN, Chief Nursing Officer, Adventhealth Daytona Beach, Daytona Beach, FL, p. A129
GOEBEL, Bret, Chief Financial Officer, Guadalup. County Hospital, Santa Rosa, NM, p. A437
GOEBEL, Cecilia B, R.N., Chief Nursing Officer, Susan B. Allen Memorial Hospital, El Dorado, KS, p. A248
GOEBEL, Dennis, Chief Executive Officer, Southwest Healthcare Services, Bowman, ND, p. A479
GOEBEL, Donna, M.D., Chief Nursing Officer, Mitchell County Hospital, Colorado City, TX, p. A608
GOEBEL, Michael, Chief Executive Officer, Adventhealth Parker, Parker, CO, p. A112
GOEDDE, Ronald, Chief Executive Officer, Paulding County Hospital, Paulding, OH, p. A502
GOEHRING, Jennifer, R.N., Assistant Chief Nursing Officer, Ascension Via Christi Hospital, Manhattan, Manhattan, KS, p. A254
GOEL, Amitabh, M.D., Chief Medical Officer, University Hospitals Geneva Medical Center, Geneva, OH, p. A496
GOEL, Ash, Senior Vice President Information Technology and Chief Information/Medical Informatics Officer, Bronson Lakeview Hospital, Paw Paw, MI, p. A335
GOEL, Vineet, Chief Medical Officer, Atrium Health Lincoln, Lincolnton, NC, p. A472
GOELZER, Mark L., M.D., Director Medical Affairs, Mercyhealth Hospital And Trauma Center – Janesville, Janesville, WI, p. A713
GOERKE, John, Chief Nursing Officer, Presbyterian/St. Luke's Medical Center, Denver, CO, p. A106
GOETTSCH, Barry, FACHE, Chief Executive Officer, Compass Memorial Healthcare, Marengo, IA, p. A239
GOFF, Gary E., M.D., Medical Director, KPC Promise Hospital of Dallas, Dallas, TX, p. A611
GOGGIN, Daniel, Chief Financial Officer, UT Health Tyler, Tyler, TX, p. A659
GOGGIN, Kathy
Director of Finance, Devereux Advanced Behavioral Health Georgia, Kennesaw, GA, p. A166
Director, Finance & Support Services, Devereux Advanced Behavioral Health Georgia, Kennesaw, GA, p. A166
GOINES, Lynn, Chief Financial Officer, Massac Memorial Hospital, Metropolis, IL, p. A202
GOLAN, Marc
Chief Financial Officer, Franciscan Health Crown Point, Crown Point, IN, p. A214
Chief Financial Officer, Franciscan Health Hammond, Hammond, IN, p. A218
Regional Chief Financial Officer, Franciscan Health Michigan City, Michigan City, IN, p. A223
GOLD, Barbara, M.D., Chief Medical Officer, M Health Fairview University of Minnesota Medical Center, Minneapolis, MN, p. A350
GOLD, Joseph, M.D., Chief Medical Officer, Mclean Hospital, Belmont, MA, p. A309
GOLD, Larry, Vice President, Information Services, Bon Secours – Southern Virginia Medical Center, Emporia, VA, p. A675
GOLDA, David
Vice President Hospital and Administrator, St. Charles Redmond, Redmond, OR, p. A531
Vice President, Hospital Administrator, St. Charles Bend, Bend, OR, p. A525
GOLDAMMER, Kyle, Chief Financial Officer, Sioux Falls Specialty Hospital, Sioux Falls, SD, p. A577
GOLDBECK, Brandon, Chief Executive Officer, Orthopaedic Hospital of Wisconsin, Glendale, WI, p. A711
GOLDBERG, David
M.D., Board Vice Chair and Chief Clinical Officer, Froedtert Community Hospital – New Berlin, New Berlin, WI, p. A718
M.D., Vice President Medical Affairs and Chief Medical Officer, Froedtert Menomonee Falls Hospital, Menomonee Falls, WI, p. A716

Index of Health Care Professionals / Goodwin

President and Chief Executive Officer, Mon Health System, Executive Vice President, Vandalia Health, Mon Health Medical Center, Morgantown, WV, p. A703
GOLDBERG, Frederick, M.D., Vice President Medical Affairs and Chief Medical Officer, Nathan Littauer Hospital And Nursing Home, Gloversville, NY, p. A443
GOLDBERG, Gary, M.D., Chief Medical Officer, Queen's North Hawaii Community Hospital, Kamuela, HI, p. A176
GOLDBERG, Paul R, Chief Financial Officer, Jersey City Medical Center, Jersey City, NJ, p. A422
GOLDBERG, Stephanie J, MSN, R.N., Senior Vice President and Chief Nursing Officer, Hospital for Special Surgery, New York, NY, p. A448
GOLDEN, Christopher, Director Information Systems, Natchitoches Regional Medical Center, Natchitoches, LA, p. A289
GOLDEN, Joy, Chief Executive Officer, Lakeside Behavioral Health System, Memphis, TN, p. A588
GOLDEN, William, M.D., Chief Medical Officer, East Alabama Medical Center, Opelika, AL, p. A23
GOLDENSTEIN, Rachel, R.N., Chief Nursing Officer, Buchanan County Health Center, Independence, IA, p. A238
GOLDESBERRY–CURRY, Christine, Director of Strategic Finance–CAH, Taylorville Memorial Hospital, Taylorville, IL, p. A210
GOLDFARB, I William, Chief Medical Officer, West Penn Hospital, Pittsburgh, PA, p. A552
GOLDFARB, Timothy, Interim Chief Executive Officer, Ohsu Hospital, Portland, OR, p. A530
GOLDFRACH, Andrew, Chief Executive Officer, Arrowhead Regional Medical Center, Colton, CA, p. A60
GOLDHAGEN, Michele, M.D., Chief Medical Officer, Russell Medical, Alexander City, AL, p. A15
GOLDIS, Glenn, Chief Medical Officer, Kern Medical, Bakersfield, CA, p. A57
GOLDMAN, Daniel, M.D., Chief Medical Officer, Bethesda Hospital East, Boynton Beach, FL, p. A126
GOLDMAN, Eric, Chief Executive Officer, HCA Florida Lawnwood Hospital, Fort Pierce, FL, p. A132
GOLDMAN, Kris, Director Human Resources, Shriners Hospitals for Children–Salt Lake City, Salt Lake City, UT, p. A669
GOLDSMITH, Cheri L.
Director Financial Services, Parkland Health Center – Farmington Community, Farmington, MO, p. A375
Director Financial Services, Parkland Health Center–Bonne Terre, Bonne Terre, MO, p. A371
GOLDSMITH, Dana L, M.D., Vice President Medical Affairs, Mainehealth Pen Bay Medical Center, Rockport, ME, p. A299
GOLDSTEIN, Allan, M.D., Medical Director and Chief of Staff, Select Specialty Hospital–Birmingham, Birmingham, AL, p. A17
GOLDSTEIN, David, M.D., Chief Medical Officer, Contra Costa Regional Medical Center, Martinez, CA, p. A76
GOLDSTEIN, Gerald, M.D., Senior Vice President and Chief Medical Officer, UPMC Western Maryland, Cumberland, MD, p. A304
GOLDSTEIN, Jennifer Price, Chief Medical Officer, Wilkes–Barre General Hospital, Wilkes–Barre, PA, p. A558
GOLDSTEIN, Steven I.
President and Chief Executive Officer, Highland Hospital, Rochester, NY, p. A457
President and Chief Executive Officer, Strong Memorial Hospital of The University of Rochester, Rochester, NY, p. A457
GOLDSZER, Robert, M.D., Senior Vice President and Chief Medical Officer, Mount Sinai Medical Center, Miami Beach, FL, p. A141
GOLDWIRE, Seth Chandler., Interim Chief Executive Officer, Atrium Health Anson, Wadesboro, NC, p. A477
GOLICH, Jake, Interim Chief Executive Officer, Pinewood Springs, Columbia, TN, p. A581
GOLIGHTLY, Beverly, Director Information Technology, Ascension St. Vincent's East, Birmingham, AL, p. A16
GOLKE, Rynae, Director Human Resources, Jacobson Memorial Hospital Care Center, Elgin, ND, p. A480
GOLLAHER, Jeffrey, Chief Executive Officer, Hendricks Community Hospital Association, Hendricks, MN, p. A348
GOLOLOBOV, Alexey, Chief Financial Officer, Silver Lake Hospital Ltach, Newark, NJ, p. A425
GOLOVAN, Ronald, M.D., Vice President Medical Operations, Cleveland Clinic Lutheran Hospital, Cleveland, OH, p. A490
GOMBAR, Greg A, Chief Financial Officer, Atrium Health University City, Charlotte, NC, p. A465
GOMES, Bob, Chief Executive Officer, Harney District Hospital, Burns, OR, p. A526
GOMES, Carol, MS, FACHE, Chief Executive Officer and Chief Operating Officer, Stony Brook University Hospital, Stony Brook, NY, p. A459
GOMES, Robert, FACHE, Chief Executive Officer, Community Medical Center, Missoula, MT, p. A394
GOMEZ, Denise, Assistant Vice President Information Systems, Unitypoint Health Meriter, Madison, WI, p. A714
GOMEZ, Dianna, Controller, UVA Encompass Health Rehabilitation Hospital, Charlottesville, VA, p. A674
GOMEZ, Dolores, M.D., Chief Medical Officer, Memorial Medical Center, Las Cruces, NM, p. A435
GOMEZ, Dolores S., R.N., Chief Operating Officer, Mills–Peninsula Medical Center, Burlingame, CA, p. A58
GOMEZ, Gloria, M.D., Medical Director, East Mississipp. State Hospital, Meridian, MS, p. A366
GOMEZ, Jay Michael, Chief Financial Officer, Memorial Hermann Surgical Hospital Kingwood, Kingwood, TX, p. A633
GOMEZ, Jesse, Vice President Human Resources, UT Health North Campus Tyler, Tyler, TX, p. A659
GOMEZ, Nico, Chief Executive Officer, Bethany Children's Health Center, Bethany, OK, p. A510
GOMEZ, Omar, M.D., Chief of Staff, Cornerstone Regional Hospital, Edinburg, TX, p. A615
GOMEZ, Richard, Assistant Vice President Information Technology Division, Hillcrest Medical Center, Tulsa, OK, p. A522
GOMEZ, Robin, R.N., MSN, Chief Executive Officer, Kindred Hospital–San Diego, San Diego, CA, p. A89
GOMEZ, Tad, MS, President, Loyola University Medical Center, Maywood, IL, p. A201
GOMPF, Shelly, Director Human Resources, Alomere Health, Alexandria, MN, p. A342
GONCZ, Gray, Vice President of Medical Affairs, Trinity Health System, Steubenville, OH, p. A504
GONGAWARE, Robert, Chief Financial Officer, Indiana Regional Medical Center, Indiana, PA, p. A542
GONSENHAUSER, Iahn
Chief Medical Officer, Cap. Coral Hospital, Cap. Coral, FL, p. A127
Chief Medical Officer, Lee Memorial Hospital, Fort Myers, FL, p. A132
GONYO, Katelyn, Director of Human Resources, Prohealth Rehabilitation Hospital of Wisconsin, Waukesha, WI, p. A723
GONZALES, Amy, Director of Human Resources, Mckenzie County Healthcare System, Watford City, ND, p. A483
GONZALES, Angela, Manager Human Resources, San Mateo Medical Center, San Mateo, CA, p. A93
GONZALES, David, Chief Medical Officer, Christus St. Vincent Regional Medical Center, Santa Fe, NM, p. A436
GONZALES, Ed
Vice President Human Resources, Marian Regional Medical Center, Santa Maria, CA, p. A94
Vice President Human Resources, St. John's Regional Medical Center, Oxnard, CA, p. A82
GONZALES, Jan, Director Human Resources, North Valley Hospital, Tonasket, WA, p. A697
GONZALES, Mike, Chief Financial Officer, Select Specialty Hospital – San Diego, San Diego, CA, p. A89
GONZALES, Mindy, Chief Human Resources Officer, Othello Community Hospital, Othello, WA, p. A692
GONZALES, Rachel Ann., Chief Executive Officer, Madisonhealth, Rexburg, ID, p. A183
GONZALEZ, Agustin, Director Finance, Hospital Pavia Arecibo, Arecibo, PR, p. A731
GONZALEZ, Alan, Chief Operating Officer, Fort Duncan Regional Medical Center, Eagle Pass, TX, p. A615
GONZALEZ, Anthony, Executive Director, Mohawk Valley Psychiatric Center, Utica, NY, p. A460
GONZALEZ, Aurelio, Chief Financial Officer, HCA Florida Woodmont Hospital, Tamarac, FL, p. A151
GONZALEZ, David
M.D., Medical Director, Brook Lane, Hagerstown, MD, p. A304
Chief Clinical Officer, East Houston Hospitals & Clinics, Houston, TX, p. A625
GONZALEZ, Dinah L., Chief Financial Officer, Knap. Medical Center, Weslaco, TX, p. A662
GONZALEZ, Elizabeth, CPA, Financial Director, Hospital Pavia Yauco, Yauco, PR, p. A736
GONZALEZ, Enid Y., Chief Executive Officer, Rehabilitation Hospital of Naples, Naples, FL, p. A142
GONZALEZ, Erin, Chief Human Resources Officer, Abrazo Scottsdale Campus, Phoenix, AZ, p. A35
GONZALEZ, Jacqueline Lytle, Senior Vice President and Chief Nursing Officer, Nicklaus Children's Hospital, Miami, FL, p. A140
GONZALEZ, Jaime, Administrator, St. Catherine's Rehabilitation Hospital, North Miami, FL, p. A142
GONZALEZ, Jorge F., M.D., Vice President and Chief Nursing Officer, Adventhealth Wauchula, Wauchula, FL, p. A154
GONZALEZ, Jorge Matta., Executive Director, University Hospital, San Juan, PR, p. A736
GONZALEZ, Laura, Interim Chief Nurse Executive, South Shore Hospital, Chicago, IL, p. A191
GONZALEZ, Luis, FACHE, Chief Executive Officer, Haven Behavioral Hospital of Phoenix, Phoenix, AZ, p. A35
GONZALEZ, Omar, Corporate Director Information Technology Clinical Engineering, Bayfront Health St. Petersburg, Saint Petersburg, FL, p. A148
GONZALEZ, Rafael, M.D., Medical Director, Ashford Presbyterian Community Hospital, San Juan, PR, p. A734
GONZALEZ, Roberto, Executive Director Human Resources, Carepoint Health Hoboken University Medical Center, Hoboken, NJ, p. A422
GONZALEZ, Rodney, M.D., Medical Center Director, Thomas E. Creek Department of Veterans Affairs Medical Center, Amarillo, TX, p. A596
GONZLEZ FIGUEROA, Adrin, Executive Director, Hospital Pavia Arecibo, Arecibo, PR, p. A731
GOOCH, Monica, Chief Executive Officer, Rusk Rehabilitation Hospital, Columbia, MO, p. A374
GOOD, Jeff, President, Northwestern Medicine Palos Hospital, Palos Heights, IL, p. A205
GOOD, Jo, Director of Nursing, Palmetto Lowcountry Behavioral Health, Charleston, SC, p. A563
GOOD, Vance A, M.D., Chief Medical Staff, Guthrie Troy Community Hospital, Troy, PA, p. A556
GOODALL, David, M.D., Chief Medical Staff, Essentia Health–Deer River, Deer River, MN, p. A345
GOODBALIAN, Terry
Regional Chief Financial Officer, Henry Ford West Bloomfield Hospital, West Bloomfield, MI, p. A340
Vice President Finance and Chief Financial Officer, Henry Ford Macomb Hospital, Clinton Township. MI, p. A324
Vice President, Finance and Chief Financial Officer, Henry Ford Wyandotte Hospital, Wyandotte, MI, p. A341
GOODE, Crystal, President/Chief Nursing Officer, Christus Southeast Texas Jasper Memorial, Jasper, TX, p. A630
GOODE, Jennifer, Director Human Resources, Russell County Hospital, Russell Springs, KY, p. A274
GOODE, Lori, Director Human Resources, Baptist Memorial Hospital–Union County, New Albany, MS, p. A367
GOODE, Richard P., Executive Vice President and Chief Financial Officer, Children's Medical Center Dallas, Dallas, TX, p. A611
GOODE, Vicky, Director Human Resources, Pam Specialty Hospital of Rocky Mount, Rocky Mount, NC, p. A475
GOODIN, Scott, Interim Chief Financial Officer, Delta Health–The Medical Center, Greenville, MS, p. A362
GOODING, Lari, Chief Executive Officer, Allendale County Hospital, Fairfax, SC, p. A566
GOODLETT, Lisa, Administrator Finance and Support Services, Musc Health University Medical Center, Charleston, SC, p. A563
GOODMAN, Brenda, Chief Nursing Officer, Atrium Health Navicent Peach, Macon, GA, p. A167
GOODMAN, Darrell, Chief Information Officer, Hi–Desert Medical Center, Joshua Tree, CA, p. A68
GOODMAN, David M, Ph.D., Chief Information Officer, Veterans Affairs Boston Healthcare System, West Roxbury, MA, p. A319
GOODMAN, Mary Jo, Chief Operating Officer, HCA Houston Healthcare Medical Center, Houston, TX, p. A625
GOODMAN, Steven, Chief Operating Officer, Willow Crest Hospital, Miami, OK, p. A515
GOODMAN, William H., Vice President Medical Affairs, Chief Medical Officer, Catholic Medical Center, Manchester, NH, p. A416
GOODNO, Janell, Chief Executive Officer, Kiowa District Healthcare, Kiowa, KS, p. A252
GOODNOW, John H., Chief Executive Officer, Benefis Health System, Great Falls, MT, p. A392
GOODRICH, C Harlan, Vice President and Chief Information Officer, Mymichigan Medical Center Midland, Midland, MI, p. A333
GOODRICH, Craig, Chief Financial Officer, Virginia Mason Medical Center, Seattle, WA, p. A695
GOODRICH, Tanner, Senior Vice President, Operations – West Market, Essentia Health St. Mary's – Detroit Lakes, Detroit Lakes, MN, p. A345
GOODROW, Darrin, Chief Information Officer, The University of Vermont Health Network Elizabethtown Community Hospital, Elizabethtown, NY, p. A442
GOODSTEIN, Ruth, Controller, Encompass Health Rehabilitation Hospital of Sunrise, Sunrise, FL, p. A151
GOODWIN, Jeremy, M.D., President, Medical Staff, Monroe County Hospital, Forsyth, GA, p. A164
GOODWIN, Matthew, Chief Nursing Officer, Windsor–Laurelwood Center for Behavioral Medicine, Willoughby, OH, p. A507
GOODWIN, Tom, Administrator, Daniel Drake Center for Post Acute Care, Cincinnati, OH, p. A489

© 2025 AHA Guide Index of Health Care Professionals **A859**

Index of Health Care Professionals / Goodwin

GOODWIN, W Jarrad, M.D., Director, UMHC–Sylvester Comprehensive Cancer Center, Miami, FL, p. A141
GOPALAKRISHNAN, Paari
  M.D., Chief Medical Officer, Kent Hospital, Warwick, RI, p. A561
  M.D., President and Chief Operating Officer, Kent Hospital, Warwick, RI, p. A561
GOPALAM, Gopinath, Administrator and Chief Executive Officer, Apollo Behavioral Health Hospital, Baton Rouge, LA, p. A277
GOPINATH, Anil, FACHE, M.D., Regional Chief Medical Officer, Ascension Mercy, Aurora, IL, p. A185
GORAB, Robert, M.D., Chief Medical Officer, Hoag Orthopedic Institute, Irvine, CA, p. A67
GORANSON, Ken, Chief Financial Officer, Benson Hospital, Benson, AZ, p. A30
GORBY, Cherie, Chief Operations Officer, UCHealth Memorial Hospital, Colorado Springs, CO, p. A105
GORCZYCA, Julie A, R.N., Chief Nursing Officer, Ascension Genesys Hospital, Grand Blanc, MI, p. A327
GORDIN, Peggy, Vice President, Patient Care Services and Chief Nursing Officer, St. Louis Children's Hospital, Saint Louis, MO, p. A384
GORDON, Alyson, Chief Human Resources Officer, Duke Raleigh Hospital, Raleigh, NC, p. A474
GORDON, Cyndy, Chief Operating Officer, Adventist Health And Rideout, Marysville, CA, p. A77
GORDON, Kevin, M.D., Chief of Staff, Alliancehealth Durant, Durant, OK, p. A512
GORDON, LaCrystal
  Chief Nursing Officer, Harris Regional Hospital, Sylva, NC, p. A477
  Chief Nursing Officer, Swain Community Hospital, A Duke Lifepoint Hospital, Bryson City, NC, p. A464
GORDON, Mandy, Human Resource Coordinator, Phoebe Worth Medical Center, Sylvester, GA, p. A172
GORDON, Mark
  Chief Nursing Officer, Kern Valley Healthcare District, Lake Isabella, CA, p. A69
  President, Cone Health Alamance Regional Medical Center, Burlington, NC, p. A464
GORDON, Michael, M.D., Chief Medical Officer, Carthage Area Hospital, Carthage, NY, p. A441
GORDON, Robert, Manager, Information Services, ECU Health North Hospital, Roanoke Rapids, NC, p. A475
GORDON, Steve
  Chief Executive Officer, Longview Regional Medical Center, Longview, TX, p. A635
  Director Human Resources, HCA Florida Lake City Hospital, Lake City, FL, p. A136
GORDON, Thomas, Chief Information Officer, Virtua Marlton, Marlton, NJ, p. A423
GORDON, Wayne
  Chief Financial Officer, Memorial Hermann Rehabilitation Hospital – Katy, Katy, TX, p. A631
  Chief Financial Officer, Tirr Memorial Hermann, Houston, TX, p. A628
GORDON, Will
  Vice President and Chief Administrative Officer, Abbeville Area Medical Center, Abbeville, SC, p. A562
  Vice President and Chief Administrative Officer, Edgefield County Healthcare, Edgefield, SC, p. A565
GORE, Carol, MSN, R.N., Chief Nursing Officer, Saint Mary's Regional Medical Center, Russellville, AR, p. A53
GORE, Lesley, Human Resources Director, North Mississipp. Medical Center–Eupora, Eupora, MS, p. A361
GORE, Tim, Chief Financial Officer, Rivendell Behavioral Health Hospital, Bowling Green, KY, p. A263
GOREAU, Judy, R.N., Director of Nursing, Eastside Psychiatric Hospital, Tallahassee, FL, p. A151
GORELICK, Marc, M.D., President and Chief Executive Officer, Children's Minnesota, Minneapolis, MN, p. A350
GOREY, Peter, Administrative Coordinator, Rockland Children's Psychiatric Center, Orangeburg, NY, p. A455
GORLEWSKI, Todd, Senior Vice President and Chief Financial Officer, St. Barnabas Hospital, New York, NY, p. A452
GORMAN, Deitrick, M.D., Chief of Staff, Reeves Regional Health, Pecos, TX, p. A643
GORMAN, Jodie, Director Human Resources, Salem Memorial District Hospital, Salem, MO, p. A386
GORMLEY, Ann H, Senior Vice President Human Resources, UPMC Harrisburg, Harrisburg, PA, p. A541
GORMSEN, David, D.O., Senior Vice President and Chief Medical Officer, Cleveland Clinic Mercy Hospital, Canton, OH, p. A487
GORN, Angela, Vice President, Norton Sound Regional Hospital, Nome, AK, p. A29
GORS, Ann, Division President and Chief Executive Officer Kentfield Hospital, Kentfield Hospital San Francisco, Kentfield Hospital, Kentfield, CA, p. A68

GOSE, Jelinda Doris, MSN, R.N., Chief Nursing Officer, HCA Florida Trinity Hospital, Trinity, FL, p. A153
GOSEY, J, M.D., Medical Director, Southern Surgical Hospital, Slidell, LA, p. A293
GOSHIA, Rob, Chief Financial Officer, Paulding County Hospital, Paulding, OH, p. A502
GOSLEE, Belle, Chief Nursing Officer, Encompass Health Rehabilitation Hospital of Salisbury, Salisbury, MD, p. A307
GOSS, Darin
  FACHE, Chief Executive Officer, Providence Centralia Hospital, Centralia, WA, p. A688
  FACHE, Chief Executive Officer, Providence St. Peter Hospital, Olympia, WA, p. A692
GOSS, Ella M., MSN, R.N., Chief Executive Officer, Providence Alaska Medical Center, Anchorage, AK, p. A27
GOSS, Hannah, Chief Nursing Officer, Pam Health Rehabilitation Hospital of Georgetown, Georgetown, DE, p. A121
GOSS, J. Richard, M.D., M.P.H., Medical Director, UW Medicine/Harborview Medical Center, Seattle, WA, p. A695
GOSS, Norma, R.N., Chief Nursing Officer, Chi Saint Josep. Health – Flaget Memorial Hospital, Bardstown, KY, p. A263
GOSS, Roger, Chief Information Officer, North Sunflower Medical Center, Ruleville, MS, p. A368
GOSSELIN, Gail
  Director Human Resources, Landmark Medical Center, Woonsocket, RI, p. A561
  Director Human Resources, Rehabilitation Hospital of Rhode Island, North Smithfield, RI, p. A560
GOSSENS, Kevin J, Director Human Resources, Thedacare Medical Center–Waupaca, Waupaca, WI, p. A724
GOSSETT, Lisa, MSN, R.N., Chief Nursing Officer, Ohiohealth Riverside Methodist Hospital, Columbus, OH, p. A492
GOTTI, Sreekant, Director Information Systems, Desert Valley Hospital, Victorville, CA, p. A100
GOTTLE, L. Gill, Senior Vice President and Chief Financial Officer, Robert Wood Johnson University Hospital At Hamilton, Hamilton, NJ, p. A422
GOTTLIEB, Harold, M.D., Chief Medical Officer, Memorial Hermann Memorial City Medical Center, Houston, TX, p. A627
GOTTLIEB, Jonathan, M.D., Senior Vice President and Chief Medical Officer, University of Maryland Medical Center, Baltimore, MD, p. A301
GOTTSCHALL, Dan, Vice President, Medical Officer, St. Vincent's Medical Center, Bridgeport, CT, p. A115
GOTTSHALL, Steve
  Chief Financial Officer, Adventhealth Gordon, Calhoun, GA, p. A160
  Chief Financial Officer, Adventhealth Murray, Chatsworth, GA, p. A160
GOUGEON, Michele L, Executive Vice President and Chief Operating Officer, Mclean Hospital, Belmont, MA, p. A309
GOUGH, Michelle MSN, RN–B, Chief Nursing Officer, Southwest Mississipp. Regional Medical Center, Mccomb, MS, p. A366
GOUGH, Thomas J., Executive Vice President & Chief Operating Officer, Wakemed Cary Hospital, Cary, NC, p. A464
GOULD, Christine, Director Human Resources, Martha's Vineyard Hospital, Oak Bluffs, MA, p. A317
GOULD, Dana L., Chief Executive Officer, Broaddus Hospital, Philippi, WV, p. A704
GOULD, Jacquelyn M, MS, R.N., Vice President Patient Care Services and Chief Nursing Officer, Wellspan Good Samaritan Hospital, Lebanon, PA, p. A544
GOULD, Tamara, R.N., Vice President Clinical Services and Chief Nursing Officer, Wabash General Hospital, Mount Carmel, IL, p. A202
GOULD, William R, Vice President Human Resources, Intermountain Health Saint Josep. Hospital, Denver, CO, p. A106
GOULET, James P, Vice President Operations, Columbus Community Hospital, Columbus, NE, p. A399
GOURLEY, Candice, President, Baylor Scott & White Continuing Care Hospital–Temple, Temple, TX, p. A656
GOUTHRO, Robert, M.D., Chief Medical Officer, North Central Health Care, Wausau, WI, p. A724
GOVE, Cynthia A, Chief Operating Officer, Hampstead Hospital & Residential Treatment Facility, Hampstead, NH, p. A415
GOVINDAIAH, Rajesh G., M.D., Chief Medical Officer, Springfield Memorial Hospital, Springfield, IL, p. A209
GOVORCHIN, Pete
  President and Chief Executive Officer, City of Hop. Chicago, Zion, IL, p. A211
  Senior Vice President Operations, City of Hop. Chicago, Zion, IL, p. A211
GOWEN, Tina, System Controller, Westfield Memorial Hospital, Westfield, NY, p. A462

GOWER, Gary, Chief Information Officer, Appling Healthcare System, Baxley, GA, p. A159
GOWLER, Barbara, Human Resources Manager, Washington County Hospital, Nashville, IL, p. A203
GOYAL, Deepak, M.D., Chief of Staff, Jacobson Memorial Hospital Care Center, Elgin, ND, p. A480
GOYKOVICH, Stephen, D.O., Chief Medical Officer, Geisinger Jersey Shore Hospital, Jersey Shore, PA, p. A542
GOYNE, Stacie, Chief Executive Officer, Oklahoma City Rehabilitation Hospital, Oklahoma City, OK, p. A518
GOZA, Brian, Chief Information Officer, Hemphill County Hospital District, Canadian, TX, p. A606
GRABER, Donald, M.D., Medical Director, Richmond State Hospital, Richmond, IN, p. A226
GRABOSO, Rebecca, Vice President and Chief Nurse Executive, Hackensack Meridian Health Riverview Medical Center, Red Bank, NJ, p. A428
GRABOWSKI, Alec
  Chief Executive Officer, Davis Regional Medical Center, Statesville, NC, p. A477
  Chief Executive Officer, Lake Norman Regional Medical Center, Mooresville, NC, p. A472
GRACE, Jeffery, M.D., Clinical Director, Buffalo Psychiatric Center, Buffalo, NY, p. A440
GRACE, Michael
  Ed.D., FACHE, President, West Virginia University Hospitals, Morgantown, WV, p. A703
  Chief Executive Officer, Select Specialty Hospital – Ann Arbor, Ypsilanti, MI, p. A341
GRACE, Richard, Chief Administrative Officer, Mayo Clinic Health System In Saint James, Saint James, MN, p. A354
GRADDY, Steve W
  Chief Financial Officer, Freeman Health System, Joplin, MO, p. A377
  Chief Financial Officer, Freeman Neosho Hospital, Neosho, MO, p. A381
GRADNEY, Angel, Chief Executive Officer, Kindred Hospital Clear Lake, Webster, TX, p. A661
GRADY, John M, Associate Director, Veterans Affairs Hudson Valley Health Care System, Montrose, NY, p. A446
GRADY, Kevin
  M.D., East Region President, Ascension Macomb–Oakland Hospital, Warren Campus, Warren, MI, p. A340
  M.D., East Region President, Ascension River District Hospital, East China, MI, p. A326
  M.D., East Region President, Ascension St. John Hospital, Detroit, MI, p. A325
GRADY, Raymond, FACHE, Chief Executive Officer, Franciscan Health Olympia Fields, Olympia Fields, IL, p. A204
GRAF, John, Senior Vice President, Watertown Regional Medical Center, Watertown, WI, p. A723
GRAGG, Connie, Director Human Resources, Saint Mary's Regional Medical Center, Russellville, AR, p. A53
GRAGG, Jodi, Interim Chief Nursing Executive, Multicare Mary Bridge Children's Hospital And Health Center, Tacoma, WA, p. A697
GRAGG, Martha, R.N., MSN, Chief Executive Officer, Sullivan County Memorial Hospital, Milan, MO, p. A380
GRAHAM, Bill, President, Sequoia Hospital, Redwood City, CA, p. A85
GRAHAM, Brenda, Chief Nursing Officer, Barbourville Arh Hospital, Barbourville, KY, p. A263
GRAHAM, Brooke, Human Resources Manager, Franklin Woods Community Hospital, Johnson City, TN, p. A584
GRAHAM, Christopher, Chief Executive Officer, Caldwell Regional Medical Center, Caldwell, KS, p. A247
GRAHAM, Christopher W, Chief Financial Officer, Community Memorial Hospital, Hamilton, NY, p. A444
GRAHAM, Connie, Public Information Officer, Mercy Health Love County, Marietta, OK, p. A514
GRAHAM, Jeff, President and Chief Executive Officer, Adena Regional Medical Center, Chillicothe, OH, p. A488
GRAHAM, John
  M.D., Vice President Medical Affairs, Day Kimball Hospital, Putnam, CT, p. A118
  Chief Financial Officer, Jefferson Hospital, Louisville, GA, p. A166
GRAHAM, John W, FACHE, Chief Administrative Officer, Jefferson Stratford Hospital, Stratford, NJ, p. A428
GRAHAM, Jon, Chief Finance Officer, ECU Health Roanoke–Chowan Hospital, Ahoskie, NC, p. A463
GRAHAM, Kathryn, Director Communications and Community Relations, Novato Community Hospital, Novato, CA, p. A80
GRAHAM, Michelle
  M.D., Vice President Medical Affairs, Ascension Southeast Wisconsin Hospital – Franklin Campus, Franklin, WI, p. A711
  M.D., Vice President Medical Affairs, Ascension St. Francis Hospital, Milwaukee, WI, p. A716

GRAHAM, Scott, Chief Executive Officer, Three Rivers Hospital, Brewster, WA, p. A687
GRAHAM, Shauna, Director of Professional Services Human Resources, Marketing Foundation, Merrick Medical Center, Central City, NE, p. A398
GRAHAM, Susan, R.N., Nurse Executive, Healthsource Saginaw Inc., Saginaw, MI, p. A337
GRAHAM, Timothy, JD, Medical Center Director, Veterans Affairs New York Harbor Healthcare System, New York, NY, p. A453
GRAHAM, Yolanda, M.D., Medical Director, Devereux Advanced Behavioral Health Georgia, Kennesaw, GA, p. A166
GRAMER, Johanna, Director Human Resources, Mimbres Memorial Hospital, Deming, NM, p. A434
GRAMLEY, Kevin, Chief Executive Officer, Edgewood Surgical Hospital, Transfer, PA, p. A555
GRAMS, Shannon, Chief Executive Officer, Select Specialty Hospital–Fort Smith, Fort Smith, AR, p. A47
GRAMZA, Jeanne, Director Finance, Ascension All Saints, Racine, WI, p. A720
GRANADO-VILLAR, Deise, M.D., Chief Medical Officer and Senior Vice President Medical Affairs, Nicklaus Children's Hospital, Miami, FL, p. A140
GRANATH, Brad, M.D., Chief of Staff, Humboldt General Hospital, Winnemucca, NV, p. A413
GRANATO, Jerome
  M.D., Senior Vice President and Chief Medical Officer, Excela Frick Hospital, Mount Pleasant, PA, p. A546
  M.D., Senior Vice President and Chief Medical Officer, Excela Health Westmoreland Hospital, Greensburg, PA, p. A541
GRANCHALEK, Gustav E., President, Endeavor Health Evanston Hospital, Evanston, IL, p. A195
GRAND, Lawrence N, MS, R.N., Chief Operating Officer, Hunterdon Healthcare, Flemington, NJ, p. A421
GRAND, Michael, Director of Finance, New Ulm Medical Center, New Ulm, MN, p. A352
GRANNELL, James, Chief Medical Officer, Sturgis Hospital, Sturgis, MI, p. A338
GRANT, Cheryl, Director Information Systems, Coastal Carolina Hospital, Hardeeville, SC, p. A568
GRANT, Gail, Director Human Resources, Chi St. Francis Health, Breckenridge, MN, p. A344
GRANT, Mikki, Chief Information Officer, Fort Belknap Service Unit, Harlem, MT, p. A393
GRANT, Timothy M., M.D., Chief Medical Officer, Parkridge Medical Center, Chattanooga, TN, p. A580
GRANT, Tonya, Director Human Resources, T.J. Health Columbia, Columbia, KY, p. A264
GRANT, Will, Interim Chief Financial Officer, Clarion Hospital, Clarion, PA, p. A537
GRANTHAM, Charlie, Manager Information Systems, Musc Health Marion Medical Center, Mullins, SC, p. A569
GRAPER, Lisa, R.N., MSN, Chief Nursing Officer, AHN Wexford Hospital, Wexford, PA, p. A557
GRASER, David, Vice President and Chief Information Officer, Hillcrest Hospital South, Tulsa, OK, p. A522
GRASS, Linda J., President, St. Luke's Easton Campus, Easton, PA, p. A539
GRATE, Anthony, Controller, Kindred Hospital–Greensboro, Greensboro, NC, p. A469
GRATRIX, Katie E., Administrative Assistant III, Alaska Psychiatric Institute, Anchorage, AK, p. A27
GRATZ, Silvia, D.O., Chief Medical Officer, Fairmount Behavioral Health System, Philadelphia, PA, p. A548
GRAU, Teri, R.N., Vice President Operations and Chief Nursing Officer, University of Cincinnati Medical Center, Cincinnati, OH, p. A490
GRAUL, Andrew, Administrator, Shriners Hospitals for Children–Honolulu, Honolulu, HI, p. A176
GRAVES, Amanda, Chief Information Systems, Washington Dc Veterans Affairs Medical Center, Washington, DC, p. A124
GRAVES, Bruce, M.D., Chief of Staff, Hale Ho'Ola Hamakua, Honokaa, HI, p. A175
GRAVES, Buddy, Chief Information Officer, Southern Surgical Hospital, Slidell, LA, p. A293
GRAVES, Deborah, R.N., President, Memorial Hospital Belleville, Belleville, IL, p. A186
GRAY, Amy, Chief Executive Officer, Chi St. Josep. Health Rehabilitation Hospital, An Affiliate of Encompass Health, Bryan, TX, p. A605
GRAY, Anthony, Chief Financial Officer, Olive View–Ucla Medical Center, Los Angeles, CA, p. A74
GRAY, Bob, Chief Financial Officer, Aspire Hospital, Conroe, TX, p. A608
GRAY, Brian, Chief Executive Officer, Michiana Behavioral Health Center, Plymouth, IN, p. A226
GRAY, Carrie, Director of Nursing, Riverview Behavioral Health, Texarkana, AR, p. A54

GRAY, Christine, Chief Human Resource Officer, Lifeways Behavioral Hospital, Boise, ID, p. A179
GRAY, Cynthia, Interim Chief Financial Officer, SSM Health St. Anthony Hospital – Midwest, Midwest City, OK, p. A515
GRAY, Eric, Chief Financial Officer, Encompass Health Rehabilitation Hospital of Memphis, A Partner of Methodist Healthcare, Memphis, TN, p. A588
GRAY, Jane, Interim Chief Operating Officer, Phoebe Putney Memorial Hospital, Albany, GA, p. A156
GRAY, Janis
  Chief Information Officer, Dupont Hospital, Fort Wayne, IN, p. A216
  Chief Information Officer, Rehabilitation Hospital of Fort Wayne, Fort Wayne, IN, p. A217
GRAY, Jason, M.D., Chief Medical Officer, Mercy Medical Center, Roseburg, OR, p. A531
GRAY, Judy, Vice President Human Resources, St. Peter's Hospital, Albany, NY, p. A438
GRAY, Karen D, Director Human Resources, Vibra Hospitals of Southeastern Michigan – Taylor Campus, Lincoln Park, MI, p. A332
GRAY, Keith, M.D., FACS, President and Chief Executive Officer, University of Tennessee Medical Center, Knoxville, TN, p. A586
GRAY, Kris David, Chief Medical Officer, Adventhealth Daytona Beach, Daytona Beach, FL, p. A129
GRAY, Lori, Chief Executive Officer, Choate Mental Health Center, Anna, IL, p. A185
GRAY, Marty, R.N., Director of Nursing, Wyandot Memorial Hospital, Upper Sandusky, OH, p. A505
GRAY, Mary, Director Human Resources, Lehigh Regional Medical Center, Lehigh Acres, FL, p. A137
GRAY, Megan, Interim Chief Executive Officer and Chief Nursing Officer, Frisbie Memorial Hospital, Rochester, NH, p. A417
GRAY, Mike, Corporate Vice President Human Resources, UT Health Tyler, Tyler, TX, p. A659
GRAY, Patricia, Director Health Information Management, Cumberland Hall Hospital, Hopkinsville, KY, p. A267
GRAY, Richard, M.D., Vice President Operations, Mayo Clinic Hospital In Arizona, Phoenix, AZ, p. A36
GRAY, Roshanda, Assistant Administrator, Memorial Medical Center, Port Lavaca, TX, p. A645
GRAY, Sarah, Vice President Information Services, East Alabama Medical Center, Opelika, AL, p. A23
GRAY, Shannon
  Chief Financial Officer, South Central Kansas Medical Center, Arkansas City, KS, p. A246
  Interim Administrator, South Central Kansas Medical Center, Arkansas City, KS, p. A246
GRAY, Stephen
  Chief Administration Officer, Sutter Maternity And Surgery Center of Santa Cruz, Santa Cruz, CA, p. A94
  Chief Executive Officer, Watsonville Community Hospital, Watsonville, CA, p. A100
GRAY, Tami, Chief Financial Officer, Irwin County Hospital, Ocilla, GA, p. A169
GRAY, Teresa, Chief Hospital Executive, Integris Canadian Valley Hospital, Yukon, OK, p. A524
GRAY, Thomas, M.D., Medical Director, Montana State Hospital, Warm Springs, MT, p. A396
GRAY, Tracy
  Chief Information Officer, Archbold Grady, Cairo, GA, p. A159
  Chief Information Officer, Archbold Mitchell, Camilla, GA, p. A160
  Senior Vice President Information Services, John D. Archbold Memorial Hospital, Thomasville, GA, p. A172
GRAYBEAL, Phillip
  CPA, Chief Financial Officer, Valley Health – Page Memorial Hospital, Luray, VA, p. A678
  CPA, Chief Financial Officer, Valley Health – Warren Memorial Hospital, Front Royal, VA, p. A677
  CPA, Vice President, Finance, Valley Health – Shenandoah Memorial Hospital, Woodstock, VA, p. A686
GRAYBILL, Matthew P, Vice President, Human Resources and Chief Administrative Officer, Dayton Children's Hospital, Dayton, OH, p. A493
GRAYSON, Barbara, Vice President Human Resources, Mercy Hospital Washington, Washington, MO, p. A388
GRAZIANO, Jill, R.N., Senior Vice President, President and Chief Operating Officer, Unity Hospital, Rochester, NY, p. A458
GREAKER, Mark, Chief Information Officer, New York–Presbyterian Queens, New York, NY, p. A450
GREAR, Esther, Director Hospital Social Work and Assistant Hospital Administrator, Polara Health, Prescott Valley, AZ, p. A37
GREASON, Linda, Vice President Human Resources, Milford Regional Medical Center, Milford, MA, p. A316

GRECCO, Jamie
  Chief Human Resource Executive, NYC Health + Hospitals/Jacobi, New York, NY, p. A451
  Director Human Resources Post Acute, NYC Health + Hospitals/Henry J Carter Specialty Hospital And Medical Center, New York, NY, p. A451
GRECO, Andrew, Chief Financial Officer, Calvary Hospital, New York, NY, p. A447
GRECO, Margaret, Chief Human Resources, Keller Army Community Hospital, West Point, NY, p. A462
GREEAR, Joy
  President and Chief Operating Officer, Novant Health Ballantyne Medical Center, Charlotte, NC, p. A465
  President and Chief Operating Officer, Novant Health Mint Hill Medical Center, Charlotte, NC, p. A466
GREELEY, Donna, Director Human Resources, Spalding Rehabilitation Hospital, Aurora, CO, p. A103
GREELEY, Gerald, Chief Information Officer, Signature Healthcare Brockton Hospital, Brockton, MA, p. A311
GREELY, John H., Senior Vice President and Chief Operating Officer, University of Maryland Baltimore Washington Medical Center, Glen Burnie, MD, p. A304
GREEMAN, Josh, Chief Executive Officer, Select Specialty Hospital–Central Kentucky, Danville, KY, p. A265
GREEN, Adrienne, M.D., President and Chief Executive Officer, San Francisco Campus for Jewish Living, San Francisco, CA, p. A91
GREEN, Amber, R.N., Chief Operating Officer and Chief Nursing Officer, St. Luke's Mccall, Mccall, ID, p. A182
GREEN, Barbara, Director Human Resources, O'Connor Hospital, Delhi, NY, p. A442
GREEN, Brenda, Director of Nursing, Ruby Valley Medical Center, Sheridan, MT, p. A396
GREEN, Bridget, Chief Human Resources Officer, Northside Hospital Gwinnett/Duluth, Lawrenceville, GA, p. A166
GREEN, Christopher, Chief Financial Officer, HCA Florida Citrus Hospital, Inverness, FL, p. A134
GREEN, Dante'
  FACHE, Chief Operating Officer, Kaiser Permanente Oakland Medical Center, Oakland, CA, p. A81
  FACHE, Interim Senior Vice President & Area Manager, East Bay Area, Kaiser Permanente Oakland Medical Center, Oakland, CA, p. A81
GREEN, David
  Chief Human Resources, West Palm Beach Veterans Affairs Medical Center, West Palm Beach, FL, p. A155
  Manager Information Technology, W. J. Mangold Memorial Hospital, Lockney, TX, p. A635
GREEN, David F., M.D., Chief Medical Officer, Concord Hospital, Concord, NH, p. A414
GREEN, Debra Jane, R.N., Director of Nursing, Turquoise Lodge Hospital, Albuquerque, NM, p. A433
GREEN, Elizabeth, Chief Human Resources Officer, Cooper University Health Care, Camden, NJ, p. A419
GREEN, Gayle, Director of Nursing, Hale Ho'Ola Hamakua, Honokaa, HI, p. A175
GREEN, John
  President and Chief Executive Officer, Iredell Health System, Statesville, NC, p. A477
  Vice President Finance, St. Peter's Health, Helena, MT, p. A393
GREEN, Jon
  R.N., Chief Executive Officer, Bleckley Memorial Hospital, Cochran, GA, p. A160
  R.N., Chief Executive Officer, Taylor Regional Hospital, Hawkinsville, GA, p. A165
GREEN, Julie, Vice President Human Resources, Cheshire Medical Center, Keene, NH, p. A415
GREEN, Justin, M.D., Ph.D., FACS, Chief Medical Officer, Los Alamos Medical Center, Los Alamos, NM, p. A435
GREEN, Karen, Chief Information Officer, Brooks Rehabilitation Hospital, Jacksonville, FL, p. A134
GREEN, Kaye, FACHE, Chief Executive Officer, Roosevelt General Hospital, Portales, NM, p. A436
GREEN, Ladonna, Director Human Resources, Glen Rose Medical Center, Glen Rose, TX, p. A622
GREEN, Lance, Chief Financial Officer, Lakeland Regional Health Medical Center, Lakeland, FL, p. A137
GREEN, Lori, Chief Executive, California Medical Facility, Vacaville, CA, p. A99
GREEN, Meredith, Senior Vice President and Chief Nursing Officer, Washington Regional Medical System, Fayetteville, AR, p. A46
GREEN, Patrick, FACHE, Chief Executive Officer, UF Health Jacksonville, Jacksonville, FL, p. A135
GREEN, Paul, Chief Clinical Officer, Kindred Hospital–Aurora, Aurora, CO, p. A103
GREEN, Rose Marie, Director Human Resources, Humboldt General Hospital, Winnemucca, NV, p. A413

Index of Health Care Professionals

Index of Health Care Professionals / Green

GREEN, Steve, Comptroller, Jasper General Hospital, Bay Springs, MS, p. A359
GREEN, Susan, Senior Vice President Finance, Chief Financial Officer, Lowell General Hospital, Lowell, MA, p. A315
GREEN, Vince, Chief Operating Officer, Lutheran Downtown Hospital, Fort Wayne, IN, p. A216
GREEN, Vincent, Medical Director, Prisma Health Laurens County Hospital, Clinton, SC, p. A564
GREEN–CHEATWOOD, Toni, M.D., Vice President and Chief Medical Officer, Good Samaritan Medical Center, Lafayette, CO, p. A110
GREENAWALT, Janelle, Director Human Resources, Wellspan Philhaven, Mount Gretna, PA, p. A546
GREENBERG, Mark, M.D., Medical Director, Gulf Coast Medical Center, Fort Myers, FL, p. A131
GREENBLATT, James, M.D., Chief Medical Officer, Vice President Medical Clinical Services, Walden Behavioral Care, Waltham, MA, p. A319
GREENE, Arthur, M.D., Vice President Medical Affairs, Sentara Careplex Hospital, Hampton, VA, p. A677
GREENE, Beth, Chief Operating Officer, Cherokee Indian Hospital, Cherokee, NC, p. A466
GREENE, Bradley, Chief Financial Officer, Wellstar Douglas Hospital, Douglasville, GA, p. A163
GREENE, Casey, Market President–UnityPoint Health Cedar Rapids, Unitypoint Health – St. Luke's Hospital, Cedar Rapids, IA, p. A232
GREENE, Charles, Chief Information Technology Officer, Och Regional Medical Center, Starkville, MS, p. A369
GREENE, Chelsea, Manager Human Resources, Guttenberg Municipal Hospital And Clinics, Guttenberg, IA, p. A237
GREENE, Cora, Senior Director, Chief Nursing Officer, Novant Health Rowan Medical Center, Salisbury, NC, p. A475
GREENE, Cynthia, Chief Executive Officer, Select Specialty Hospital–Augusta, Augusta, GA, p. A158
GREENE, Erin, Coordinator Human Resources, Kindred Hospital–San Francisco Bay Area, San Leandro, CA, p. A92
GREENE, Melodi, R.N., MS, Chief Nursing Officer, Community Howard Regional Health, Kokomo, IN, p. A221
GREENE, Neely, Chief Operating Officer, Trinity Medical, Ferriday, LA, p. A282
GREENE, Palmer, R.N., Chief Nursing Officer, Sierra Vista Hospital, Truth Or Consequences, NM, p. A437
GREENE, Philip. M.D., Chief Executive Officer, Frye Regional Medical Center, Hickory, NC, p. A470
GREENE, Robert, Director Information Technology, Riverbridge Specialty Hospital, Vidalia, LA, p. A294
GREENE, Scott, Chief Information Officer, Tennova Healthcare–Clarksville, Clarksville, TN, p. A581
GREENE, Todd, Chief Executive Officer, Physicians Surgical Hospital – Quail Creek, Amarillo, TX, p. A596
GREENE, Tracie, Director Human Resources, Brigham City Community Hospital, Brigham City, UT, p. A664
GREENFIELD, Tadd S., Chief Executive Officer, Cabinet Peaks Medical Center, Libby, MT, p. A394
GREENMAN, Heidi, Interim Chief Executive Officer, Western Arizona Regional Medical Center, Bullhead City, AZ, p. A30
GREENMAN, Sharon, Director Human Resources, Melissa Memorial Hospital, Holyoke, CO, p. A109
GREENSLIT, Mark, M.D., Chief Medical Staff, Colleton Medical Center, Walterboro, SC, p. A571
GREENWALD, Derek
  Chief Nursing Officer, Star Valley Health, Afton, WY, p. A726
  Chief Nursing Officer, Syracuse Area Health, Syracuse, NE, p. A406
GREENWOOD, Annette June, Chief Nursing Officer, Riverside Community Hospital, Riverside, CA, p. A86
GREENWOOD, Les, M.D., President, Medical Staff, Holy Cross Hospital – Davis, Layton, UT, p. A665
GREENWOOD, Susan, R.N., Chief Nursing Officer, Hendrick Medical Center, Abilene, TX, p. A595
GREER, Jinger
  CPA, Chief Financial Officer, Delhi Hospital, Delhi, LA, p. A281
  CPA, Interim Administrator, Delhi Hospital, Delhi, LA, p. A281
GREER, Stephanie
  President, Avery Healthcare Market, Appalachian Regional Behavioral Health, Linville, NC, p. A472
  President, Avery Healthcare Market, Charles A. Cannon Jr. Memorial Hospital, Newland, NC, p. A473
GREER, Troy, Interim Chief Executive Officer, Lovelace Unm Rehabilitation Hospital, Albuquerque, NM, p. A432
GREGG, Richard, M.D., Medical Director, Pam Specialty Hospital of Dayton, Miamisburg, OH, p. A500
GREGG, Shawna, Director Human Resources, Porterville Developmental Center, Porterville, CA, p. A84
GREGG, Sherry, Chief Information Technology Officer, Beckley Veterans Affairs Medical Center, Beckley, WV, p. A699
GREGG, Travis, FACHE, Chief Operating Officer, Bryan Medical Center, Lincoln, NE, p. A401
GREGGAIN, Don, M.D., Physician Network Director, Tri–State Memorial Hospital, Clarkston, WA, p. A688
GREGONIS, Michael, Comptroller, Naval Hospital Jacksonville, Jacksonville, FL, p. A135
GREGOR, Brian, Manager Information Technology Operations, Glendale Memorial Hospital And Health Center, Glendale, CA, p. A66
GREGORIAN, Myra, Vice President and Chief Human Resources Officer, Children's Hospital Los Angeles, Los Angeles, CA, p. A72
GREGORICH, Miki, Director Human Resources, Pioneer Medical Center, Big Timber, MT, p. A389
GREGORY, Ben, Chief Executive Officer, Walter B. Jones Alcohol And Drug Abuse Treatment Center, Greenville, NC, p. A470
GREGORY, Cody, Comptroller, Beaver County Memorial Hospital, Beaver, OK, p. A510
GREGORY, Jan, Chief of Human Resources, Crittenden Community Hospital, Marion, KY, p. A271
GREGORY, Jay, M.D., Chief Medical Officer, Saint Francis Hospital Muskogee, Muskogee, OK, p. A515
GREGORY, Jim, Controller, Thorek Memorial Hospital Andersonville, Chicago, IL, p. A191
GREGORY, Jody, Chief Executive Officer, Encompass Health Rehabilitation Hospital of Wichita Falls, Wichita Falls, TX, p. A662
GREGORY, Jody S, R.N., Chief Nursing Officer, Encompass Health Rehabilitation Hospital of Wichita Falls, Wichita Falls, TX, p. A662
GREGORY, Phyllis, Registered Health Information Administrator, Southern Inyo Healthcare District, Lone Pine, CA, p. A70
GREGORY, Sean, Chief Executive, Columbia Network, Peacehealth Southwest Medical Center, Vancouver, WA, p. A698
GREGORY, Shawn, Chief Financial Officer, HCA Florida St. Petersburg Hospital, Saint Petersburg, FL, p. A149
GREGORY, Trip. Senior Vice President Human Resources, Prisma Health Baptist Hospital, Columbia, SC, p. A565
GREGSON, Jennifer, Chief Administrative Officer, Red Bud Regional Hospital, Red Bud, IL, p. A207
GREIMAN, Alan W., Chief Executive Officer and President, Royal Oaks Hospital, Windsor, MO, p. A388
GREINER, Walter, Chief Financial Officer, Atlanticare Regional Medical Center, Atlantic City Campus, Atlantic City, NJ, p. A418
GREINER, William, M.D., Chief of Staff, F. W. Huston Medical Center, Winchester, KS, p. A262
GRENDON, M Todd, M.D., President Medical Staff, Ascension Saint Josep. – Chicago, Chicago, IL, p. A188
GRESHAM, Alicia, Chief Executive Officer, Pennsylvania Hospital, Philadelphia, PA, p. A549
GRESHAM, Paula, Vice President, Hospital Administrator, Tanner Medical Center–Villa Rica, Villa Rica, GA, p. A173
GREW, Terry, Chief Business Office, Hampton Veterans Affairs Medical Center, Hampton, VA, p. A677
GREY, Drew, Chief Operating Officer, Tennova North Knoxville Medical Center, Powell, TN, p. A592
GREY, Michael, M.D., Interim Chief Medical Officer, Saint Francis Hospital, Hartford, CT, p. A116
GREY, Mitzi, Chief Operating Officer, Bath Community Hospital, Hot Springs, VA, p. A678
GRICUS, Peggy, R.N., Vice President, Patient Care Services and Chief Nursing Officer, Silver Cross Hospital, New Lenox, IL, p. A203
GRIDLEY, Mark, FACHE, President and Chief Executive Officer, FHN Memorial Hospital, Freeport, IL, p. A195
GRIEP, John, M.D., Chief Medical Director, St. Catherine Hospital, East Chicago, IN, p. A215
GRIEST, Mary, Vice President Finance and Chief Financial Officer, University Hospitals Samaritan Medical Center, Ashland, OH, p. A485
GRIFFES, Carol, Administrator, Duane L. Waters Hospital, Jackson, MI, p. A330
GRIFFEY, Jennifer
  Chief Financial Officer, Brattleboro Memorial Hospital, Brattleboro, VT, p. A671
  Chief Financial Officer, Encompass Health Rehabilitation Hospital of Bluffton, Bluffton, SC, p. A562
GRIFFIN, Amy, Vice President Patient Care Services, John D. Archbold Memorial Hospital, Thomasville, GA, p. A172
GRIFFIN, Anthony, M.D., Chief Medical Officer, Jacksonville Memorial Hospital, Jacksonville, IL, p. A199
GRIFFIN, Betty, Interim Chief Nursing Officer, Musc Health Chester Medical Center, Chester, SC, p. A564
GRIFFIN, Brian
  Chief Financial Officer, Springhill Medical Center, Springhill, LA, p. A293
  Director of Medical Affairs, Houlton Regional Hospital, Houlton, ME, p. A297
GRIFFIN, Charles, Director of Nursing, Clay County Hospital, Ashland, AL, p. A15
GRIFFIN, Cindy
  Chief Nursing Officer, Liberty Dayton Regional Medical Center, Liberty, TX, p. A634
  Director Human Resources, Medical Center Barbour, Eufaula, AL, p. A19
GRIFFIN, Douglas, M.D., Vice President Medical Officer, Sanford Medical Center Fargo, Fargo, ND, p. A481
GRIFFIN, Eugeniya, Chief Financial Officer, Mountrail County Medical Center, Stanley, ND, p. A483
GRIFFIN, Holly, R.N., Chief Nursing Officer, Lady of The Sea General Hospital, Cut Off, LA, p. A281
GRIFFIN, Jarvis T.
  Assistant Director Administration and Chief Operating Officer, Piedmont Geriatric Hospital, Burkeville, VA, p. A674
  Chief Executive Officer, Facility Director, Hiram W. Davis Medical Center, Petersburg, VA, p. A681
GRIFFIN, Jeannine, M.D., Chief of Staff, Memorial Medical Center, Port Lavaca, TX, p. A645
GRIFFIN, Jeff, Assistant Vice President Finance, Atrium Health Anson, Wadesboro, NC, p. A477
GRIFFIN, Joe, Chief Executive Officer, Saint Alphonsus Regional Rehabilitation Hospital, An Affiliate of Encompass Health, Boise, ID, p. A179
GRIFFIN, Kathryn, Chief Nurse Executive, Terrell State Hospital, Terrell, TX, p. A656
GRIFFIN, Matthew, M.D., Chief Medical Officer, Trinity Health Livonia Hospital, Livonia, MI, p. A332
GRIFFIN, Philip. Director of Operations, Rochester Psychiatric Center, Rochester, NY, p. A457
GRIFFIN, Wes, Division Human Resources Manager, UT Health East Texas Rehabilitation Hospital, Tyler, TX, p. A659
GRIFFIN–JONES, Christie, R.N., Chief Nursing Officer, Encompass Health Rehabilitation Hospital of Humble, Humble, TX, p. A629
GRIFFIN–MAHON, Selena, Assistant Vice President Human Resources, Bronxcare Health System, New York, NY, p. A447
GRIFFIS, Daniel, M.D., Chief Medical Officer, Syringa Hospital And Clinics, Grangeville, ID, p. A181
GRIFFIS, Tiffany, Chief Executive Officer, Eastern Oklahoma Medical Center, Poteau, OK, p. A520
GRIFFITH, Barbara
  M.D., President, Duke Raleigh Hospital, Raleigh, NC, p. A474
  Vice President Human Resources, St. Anthony's Rehabilitation Hospital, Lauderdale Lakes, FL, p. A137
GRIFFITH, David, M.D., Medical Director, Texas Center for Infectious Disease, San Antonio, TX, p. A651
GRIFFITH, Jeanne, Chief Nursing Officer, Coryell Health, Gatesville, TX, p. A622
GRIFFITH, Joshua, Manager Human Resources, Presbyterian Espanola Hospital, Espanola, NM, p. A434
GRIFFITH, Kyndel, Chief Nursing Officer, Texarkana Emergency Center & Hospital, Texarkana, TX, p. A657
GRIFFITH, Maria, Director Human Resources, Signature Psychiatric Hospital, Kansas City, MO, p. A377
GRIFFITH, Patti, R.N., MS, Chief Nursing Officer, Methodist Hospital for Surgery, Addison, TX, p. A595
GRIFFITH, Susan M, Finance Business Partner Specialist, Eastern State Hospital, Lexington, KY, p. A268
GRIFFITHS, Mark, Director Management Information Systems, Incline Village Community Hospital, Incline Village, NV, p. A409
GRIFKA, Ronald, M.D., FACC, President, University of Michigan Health – West, Wyoming, MI, p. A341
GRIGG, Dan, Chief Executive Officer, Wallowa Memorial Hospital, Enterprise, OR, p. A526
GRIGG, William E., Senior Vice President and Chief Financial Officer, USC Arcadia Hospital, Arcadia, CA, p. A56
GRIGGS, Erika, Chief Operating Officer, Iron County Medical Center, Pilot Knob, MO, p. A382
GRIGGS, Shannon, Interim Chief Executive Officer, Research Medical Center, Kansas City, MO, p. A378
GRIGGS, Stacie, MIS Analyst, North Mississipp. Medical Center–West Point, West Point, MS, p. A370
GRIGSBY, Jan, Vice President and Chief Financial Officer, Springhill Medical Center, Mobile, AL, p. A22
GRIGSON, John A, Vice President and Chief Financial Officer, Covenant Medical Center, Lubbock, TX, p. A636
GRILL, Laura D., R.N., Chief Executive Officer, East Alabama Medical Center, Opelika, AL, p. A23
GRILLS, Kathy, Director Human Resources, Encompass Health Rehabilitation Hospital of Harmarville, Pittsburgh, PA, p. A551
GRIM, Andrew, Chief Financial Officer, San Gabriel Valley Medical Center, San Gabriel, CA, p. A91

A862 Index of Health Care Professionals

Index of Health Care Professionals / Guillory

Index of Health Care Professionals

GRIM, Charles, D.D.S., Secretary of Health, Chickasaw Nation Medical Center, Ada, OK, p. A509
GRIMES, Paula, R.N., MSN, Chief Nursing Officer, Nea Baptist Memorial Hospital, Jonesboro, AR, p. A48
GRIMES, Teresa G., Chief Executive Officer, Washington County Hospital, Chatom, AL, p. A17
GRIMES, Walter, Director Information Technology, Christus Good Shepherd Medical Center–Marshall, Marshall, TX, p. A638
GRIMLEY, Karen A, Chief Nursing Executive, Ronald Reagan Ucla Medical Center, Los Angeles, CA, p. A75
GRIMM, Debra, MS, R.N., Vice President and Chief Nursing Officer, Long Island Community Hospital, Patchogue, NY, p. A455
GRIMM, Tamara, R.N., Chief Clinical Officer and Chief Nursing Officer, Cornerstone Specialty Hospitals Bossier City, Bossier City, LA, p. A279
GRIMM, William, Chief Information Officer, Henry County Hospital, Napoleon, OH, p. A501
GRIMMER, Michael, Chief Operating Officer, Athol Hospital, Athol, MA, p. A309
GRIMSHAW, Matthew, Market Chief Executive Officer, Trinity Health System, Steubenville, OH, p. A504
GRINER, Alisa R, Director, Human Resources, Memorial Health University Medical Center, Savannah, GA, p. A171
GRINER, Ginny, Director Human Resources, George E. Weems Memorial Hospital, Apalachicola, FL, p. A125
GRINNELL, Jeannine M., Interim Chief Executive Officer, UW Medicine/Valley Medical Center, Renton, WA, p. A693
GRIPPI, Michael, M.D., Chief Medical Officer, Good Shepherd Penn Partners, Philadelphia, PA, p. A548
GRISH, John, Chief Financial Officer, Johnson Memorial Hospital, Stafford Springs, CT, p. A119
GRISHOW, Cathy, Director Human Resources, Ellett Memorial Hospital, Appleton City, MO, p. A371
GRISIER, Douglas, D.O., Medical Director, Encompass Health Rehabilitation Hospital of Erie, Erie, PA, p. A539
GRISNAK, Karen, R.N., Chief Operating Officer and Assistant Administrator Quality Services, Kaiser Permanente Vallejo Medical Center, Vallejo, CA, p. A99
GRISPINO, Frank, Vice President Operations, Mosaic Medical Center – Maryville, Maryville, MO, p. A380
GRISSOM, Robyn, Director of Human Resources, OSF Healthcare Saint Anthony's Health Center, Alton, IL, p. A185
GRISSOM, Tina, Chief Information Technology Officer, Arkansas State Hospital, Little Rock, AR, p. A49
GROCHALA, Eugene
Vice President Information Systems, Capital Health Medical Center–Hopewell, Pennington, NJ, p. A427
Vice President Information Systems, Capital Health Regional Medical Center, Trenton, NJ, p. A429
GROEN, Kathleen, Chief Human Resources Officer, Providence Regional Medical Center Everett, Everett, WA, p. A689
GROENIG, Matt, Vice President Finance, St. Luke's Mccall, Mccall, ID, p. A182
GROEPER, William E, Vice President Finance, Beloit Health System, Beloit, WI, p. A708
GROLEMUND, Dan, Chief Executive Officer, Lecom Health Corry Memorial Hospital, Corry, PA, p. A537
GRONERT, Thomas, Chief Information Officer, University of Maryland St. Josep. Medical Center, Towson, MD, p. A307
GRONOW, Thomas, President and Chief Executive Officer, University of Colorado Hospital, Aurora, CO, p. A103
GROS, Mark, Director Human Resources, United Medical Rehabilitation Hospital–Hammond, Hammond, LA, p. A283
GROSECLOSE, Cathy, Vice President Patient Care Services, Grady Memorial Hospital, Chickasha, OK, p. A511
GROSETH, Bradley D.
Chief Administrative Officer, Marshfield Medical Center – Rice Lake, Rice Lake, WI, p. A720
President – West Market, Marshfield Medical Center – Eau Claire Hospital, Eau Claire, WI, p. A710
President, Marshfield Medical Center – Ladysmith, Ladysmith, WI, p. A714
GROSHANS, Adam, Market President, Mercy Health – Springfield Regional Medical Center, Springfield, OH, p. A504
GROSS, Anne H, Senior Vice President, Patient Care Services and Chief Nursing Officer, Dana–Farber Cancer Institute, Boston, MA, p. A310
GROSS, Barry L, M.D., Executive Vice President and Chief Medical Officer, Riverside Regional Medical Center, Newport News, VA, p. A680
GROSS, Cathy, Director Health Information Management Systems, Wrangell Medical Center, Wrangell, AK, p. A29
GROSS, Christian
Chief Operating Officer, Baptist Health – Van Buren, Van Buren, AR, p. A54
Vice President, Operations, Baptist Health–Fort Smith, Fort Smith, AR, p. A46
GROSS, Cindy, Director of Finance, Barnes–Jewish St. Peters Hospital, Saint Peters, MO, p. A386
GROSS, Kevin J., FACHE, Interim Chief Executive Officer, Hillcrest Hospital South, Tulsa, OK, p. A522
GROSS, Kristin, Director Information Technology Center, Avera Mckennan Hospital And University Health Center, Sioux Falls, SD, p. A576
GROSS, Len, Chief Human Resources Officer, Sheridan Memorial Hospital, Sheridan, WY, p. A728
GROSS, Mark
Chief Finance Officer, Hillsdale Hospital, Hillsdale, MI, p. A329
Executive Vice President and Chief Financial Officer, Bronson South Haven Hospital, South Haven, MI, p. A338
Vice President Finance and Chief Financial Officer, Trinity Health Grand Haven Hospital, Grand Haven, MI, p. A328
GROSS, Paul, Human Services and Finance Officer, Larry B. Zieverink, Sr. Alcoholism Treatment Center, Raleigh, NC, p. A474
GROSS, Peter A, M.D., Senior Vice President and Chief Medical Officer, Hackensack Meridian Health Hackensack University Medical Center, Hackensack, NJ, p. A421
GROSS, Randy, Chief Executive Officer, Encompass Health Rehabilitation Hospital of Sunrise, Sunrise, FL, p. A151
GROSS, Tina, MSN, R.N., President and Chief Nursing Officer, Sparrow Specialty Hospital, Lansing, MI, p. A331
GROSSER, Joy
Chief Information Officer, UW Medicine/Harborview Medical Center, Seattle, WA, p. A695
Chief Information Officer, UW Medicine/University of Washington Medical Center, Seattle, WA, p. A695
GROSSMAN, Drew
Chief Executive Officer, Baptist Health South Florida, Mariners Hospital, Tavernier, FL, p. A153
Chief Executive Officer, Fishermen's Hospital, Marathon, FL, p. A138
GROSSMAN, Hannah, M.D., Chief Medical Officer, Los Robles Health System, Thousand Oaks, CA, p. A97
GROSSMAN, Robert I., M.D., Chief Executive Officer, Nyu Langone Hospitals, New York, NY, p. A452
GROSTEFON, Gregory, Superintendent, Logansport State Hospital, Logansport, IN, p. A223
GROTE, Brad, Chief Operating Officer, Glendale Memorial Hospital And Health Center, Glendale, CA, p. A66
GROTELUSCHEN, Ronald J., Chief Financial Officer, Coastal Carolina Hospital, Hardeeville, SC, p. A568
GROTH, McGarrett, Chief of Staff, Amberwell Health, Atchison, KS, p. A246
GROVE, Gene, M.D., Chief of Staff, Elkhart General Hospital, Elkhart, IN, p. A215
GROVE, Jeri, Chief Nursing Officer, Scott County Hospital, Scott City, KS, p. A259
GROVE, Lucy, Human Resources Director, Up Health System – Marquette, Marquette, MI, p. A333
GROVE, Sarah, M.D., Medical Director, Mount Carmel Rehabilitation Hospital, Westerville, OH, p. A507
GROVER, James, Manager Data Processing, Atascadero State Hospital, Atascadero, CA, p. A56
GROVES, Tandy, Director Human Resources, Bailey Medical Center, Owasso, OK, p. A519
GROW, Julie E., Chief Financial Officer, Hocking Valley Community Hospital, Logan, OH, p. A498
GROWSE, Michael, M.D., Clinical Director, Federal Medical Center, Lexington, KY, p. A268
GRUBB, Michael
Chief Financial Officer, Bridgepoint Continuing Care Hospital – National Harborside, Washington, DC, p. A123
Senior Chief Financial Officer, Bridgepoint Continuing Care Hospital – Capitol Hill, Washington, DC, p. A123
GRUBB, Nora, Chief Financial Officer, Big Sandy Medical Center, Big Sandy, MT, p. A389
GRUBBS, John, Chief Executive Officer, SSM Select Rehabilitation Hospital, Richmond Heights, MO, p. A382
GRUBER, Scott, M.D., Chief of Staff, John D. Dingell Department of Veterans Affairs Medical Center, Detroit, MI, p. A325
GRUEN, Jeremy, Director Information Systems, Pike County Memorial Hospital, Louisiana, MO, p. A379
GRUHONJIC, Osman, Chief Financial Officer, Lehigh Regional Medical Center, Lehigh Acres, FL, p. A137
GRUN, Joseph, Chief Information Officer, New York State Psychiatric Institute, New York, NY, p. A450
GRUNDIG, Kevin, Chief Human Resource Officer, Veterans Affairs New York Harbor Healthcare System, New York, NY, p. A453
GRUNHOVD, April, Vice President of Patient Care Services and Chief Nursing Officer, Riverview Health, Crookston, MN, p. A345
GRUTA, Fernando, President, Ascension Mercy, Aurora, IL, p. A185
GRUVER, Laquita, Fiscal Officer, Grand Junction Va Medical Center, Grand Junction, CO, p. A108
GRZYBOWSKI, John, M.D., Medical Director, Mayo Clinic Health System – Albert Lea And Austin, Albert Lea, MN, p. A342
GUADAGNOLI, Donald, M.D., Chief Medical Officer, Cap. Cod Hospital, Hyannis, MA, p. A314
GUAJARDO, Carlos, Chief Financial Officer, South Texas Health System, Edinburg, TX, p. A615
GUAJARDO, Michael, Director Finance, Christus Spohn Hospital Alice, Alice, TX, p. A595
GUARINO, Celia, R.N., MSN, Vice President and Chief Nursing Officer, Holy Cross Hospital, Silver Spring, MD, p. A307
GUARINO, Rick, M.D., Vice President Medical Affairs, Wilson Medical Center, Wilson, NC, p. A478
GUARNI, Andrew, Chief Financial Officer, Hoag Memorial Hospital Presbyterian, Newport Beach, CA, p. A80
GUARNIERI, Candace, Chief Financial Officer, Phoebe Worth Medical Center, Sylvester, GA, p. A172
GUARRACINO, Joseph, Senior Vice President and Chief Financial Officer, White Plains Hospital Center, White Plains, NY, p. A462
GUARRERA, Frank, Executive Vice President and Chief Financial Officer, MPTF/Motion Picture & Television Fund, Los Angeles, CA, p. A74
GUAY, Amy, Chief Financial Officer, Spaulding Rehabilitation Hospital, Charlestown, MA, p. A312
GUBER, Casey, President and Chief Executive Officer, Rose Medical Center, Denver, CO, p. A107
GUBERMAN, Wayne, Director Finance, Matheny Medical And Educational Center, Peapack, NJ, p. A426
GUDAHL, Shanna, Manager Human Resources, United Hospital District, Blue Earth, MN, p. A343
GUEDE, Carmen, Chief Operating Officer, San Juan City Hospital, San Juan, PR, p. A736
GUEHLSTORF, Daniel, M.D., Chief of Staff, Midwest Orthopedic Specialty Hospital, Franklin, WI, p. A711
GUELKER, Rhonda, Senior Director Finance, Rolling Plains Memorial Hospital, Sweetwater, TX, p. A655
GUENTHER, Theresa L., Chief Executive Officer, Avera Creighton Hospital, Creighton, NE, p. A399
GUERRA, Tony, Chief Financial Officer, Sharp Mesa Vista Hospital, San Diego, CA, p. A90
GUERRERO, Bonnie, Director Human Resources, Valley View Medical Center, Fort Mohave, AZ, p. A31
GUERRERO, Kerrie, R.N., MSN, Vice President and Chief Nursing Officer, Houston Methodist The Woodlands Hospital, The Woodlands, TX, p. A657
GUERRERO, Marisa, Director Human Resources, Laredo Specialty Hospital, Laredo, TX, p. A634
GUERRIERO, John A., D.O., III, Chief of Staff, Berwick Hospital Center, Berwick, PA, p. A535
GUESMAN, Kim, R.N., Chief Nursing Officer, Corewell Health Farmington Hills Hospital, Farmington Hills, MI, p. A326
GUEST, William, M.D., Senior Vice President and Chief Medical Officer, Tift Regional Medical Center, Tifton, GA, p. A172
GUGEL, Paul, Manager Information Technology, Marlette Regional Hospital, Marlette, MI, p. A333
GUGLIELMI, Diane, Vice President, Human Resources, Ohiohealth Berger Hospital, Circleville, OH, p. A490
GUGLIELMO, Elaine, Vice President Human Resources and Organizational Development, Stamford Health, Stamford, CT, p. A119
GUIDO, Kathleen, Chief Nursing Officer, Palmetto General Hospital, Hialeah, FL, p. A133
GUIDO–ALLEN, Debra, R.N., FACHE, President, Corewell Health Dearborn Hospital, Dearborn, MI, p. A324
GUIDRY, Charles W, Chief Information Officer, Abbeville General Hospital, Abbeville, LA, p. A276
GUIDRY, Linda, Human Resources Generalist, Ochsner Abrom Kaplan Memorial Hospital, Kaplan, LA, p. A284
GUIDRY, Lloyd, Chief Executive Officer, Lady of The Sea General Hospital, Cut Off, LA, p. A281
GUIDRY, Stephanie A., Chief Executive Officer, Bayou Bend Health System, Franklin, LA, p. A282
GUIDRY, Trisha, Administrator, Baton Rouge Rehabilitation Hospital, Baton Rouge, LA, p. A277
GUILD, Anthony, Chief Executive Officer, Columbus Springs Dublin, Dublin, OH, p. A495
GUILFOIL, Thomas, Director Human Resources, Baystate Wing Hospital, Palmer, MA, p. A317
GUILLAUME, Kristen, Vice President and Chief Information Officer, North Kansas City Hospital, North Kansas City, MO, p. A381
GUILLORY, Cayle P., Administrator, Oceans Behavioral Hospital of Opelousas, Opelousas, LA, p. A291
GUILLORY, Larry, Chief Human Resources Officer, Baylor Scott & White Emergency Hospitals–Aubrey, Aubrey, TX, p. A598

Index of Health Care Professionals

Index of Health Care Professionals / Guillory

GUILLORY, Nicholas D, MSN, Chief Operating Officer, Oceans Behavioral Hospital of Lake Charles, Lake Charles, LA, p. A286
GUILLORY, Nicholas D., MSN, Interim Administrator, Executive Vice President, Regional Operations, Oceans Behavioral Hospital of Deridder, Deridder, LA, p. A281
GUILLORY, Pamela, Chief Operating Officer and Chief Nursing Officer, Methodist Hospital South, Jourdanton, TX, p. A631
GUIMARAES, Antonio, M.D., Clinical Director, U. S. Public Health Service Indian Hospital, Cass Lake, MN, p. A344
GUIMENTO, Robert, President, New York–Presbyterian Hospital, New York, NY, p. A450
GUINA, Michelle, Manager Human Resources, Sutter Surgical Hospital – North Valley, Yuba City, CA, p. A102
GUINANE, Gerard, Vice President Human Resources, UW Health Swedishamerican Hospital, Rockford, IL, p. A207
GUIRL, Nadine T, Senior Vice President Human Resources, Prohealth Waukesha Memorial Hospital, Waukesha, WI, p. A723
GUISE, Linda, Senior Human Resource Consultant, Indiana University Health Jay Hospital, Portland, IN, p. A226
GUITTAP, Taylor, Chief Financial Officer, Good Samaritan Medical Center, West Palm Beach, FL, p. A154
GULCZEWSKI, Vicki, Chief Executive Officer, Baptist Medical Center, San Antonio, TX, p. A648
GULL, Joann Bernadette, Chief Nursing Officer, NYC Health + Hospitals/Elmhurst, New York, NY, p. A451
GULLATT, Thomas, M.D., President, St. Francis Medical Center, Monroe, LA, p. A289
GULLINGSRUD, Timothy, Chief Executive Officer, Ogallala Community Hospital, Ogallala, NE, p. A403
GUM, Jessica, Controller, Encompass Health Rehabilitation Hospital of Parkersburg, Parkersburg, WV, p. A703
GUMATO, Sixta, M.D., Chief Medical Officer, Crane Memorial Hospital, Crane, TX, p. A609
GUMBEL, Wendy, Director of Human Resources, Encompass Health Deaconess Rehabilitation Hospital, Newburgh, IN, p. A225
GUMBS, Milton A, M.D., Vice President and Medical Director, Bronxcare Health System, New York, NY, p. A447
GUMMADI, Subhaker, M.D., Chief Medical Staff, KPC Promise Hospital of Baton Rouge, Baton Rouge, LA, p. A277
GUMP, Jeremy, Interim Chief Executive Officer, Sturgis Hospital, Sturgis, MI, p. A338
GUMP, Linda A., Chief Clinical Services Officer, Aurora Medical Center Kenosha, Kenosha, WI, p. A713
GUNABALAN, Ryan, Chief Executive Officer, Behavioral Center of Michigan, Warren, MI, p. A340
GUNASEKARAN, Suresh, President and Chief Executive Officer, UCSF Medical Center, San Francisco, CA, p. A91
GUNDLAPALLI, Madhu, M.D., Clinical Director, Utah State Hospital, Provo, UT, p. A667
GUNKEL, Jeff, Chief Information Officer, Jamestown Regional Medical Center, Jamestown, ND, p. A482
GUNN, Deborah, Chief Information Officer, W. G. (Bill) Heffner Veterans Affairs Medical Center, Salisbury, NC, p. A476
GUNNELL, Nancy, Chief Human Resource Officer, West Suburban Medical Center, Oak Park, IL, p. A204
GUNTHER, Anne, R.N., MSN, President, Aultman Hospital, Canton, OH, p. A487
GUNTHER, Kurt, Chief Executive Officer, Arbour H. R. I. Hospital, Brookline, MA, p. A312
GUNTLOW, Ann Marie, Chief Nursing Officer, Ellenville Regional Hospital, Ellenville, NY, p. A442
GUNUKULA, Srinivas, M.D., Chief of Staff, Dallas Regional Medical Center, Mesquite, TX, p. A639
GUOYAVATIN, Kora
Chief Financial Officer, Garden Grove Hospital And Medical Center, Garden Grove, CA, p. A65
Chief Financial Officer, West Anaheim Medical Center, Anaheim, CA, p. A55
GUPTA, Anil, M.D., Chief of Staff, Kindred Hospital–Baldwin Park, Baldwin Park, CA, p. A57
GUPTA, Arun, M.D., Vice President Medical Affairs, Cleveland Clinic South Pointe Hospital, Warrensville Heights, OH, p. A506
GUPTA, Ashok K, M.D., Chief of Staff, Eaton Rapids Medical Center, Eaton Rapids, MI, p. A326
GUPTA, John, Executive Vice President and Chief Operating Officer, Brooklyn Hospital Center, New York, NY, p. A447
GUPTA, Saurabh, Chief Medical Officer, Rockford Center, Newark, DE, p. A122
GUPTA, Vijay D, M.D., President and Chief Executive Officer, Franciscan Healthcare Munster, Munster, IN, p. A224
GURGA, Jean J., Executive Medical Center Director, VA Palo Alto Health Care System, VA Palo Alto Heath Care System, Palo Alto, CA, p. A82
GURR, Lory, Chief Human Resources Division, Evans U. S. Army Community Hospital, Fort Carson, CO, p. A107
GURRAD, Trece, Vice President Patient Care Services, Columbia Memorial Hospital, Astoria, OR, p. A525
GURROLA, Jose Luis, Chief Operating Officer, Artesia General Hospital, Artesia, NM, p. A433
GURULE, Eric, Chief Information Officer, Turquoise Lodge Hospital, Albuquerque, NM, p. A433
GURUNG, Anju, M.D., Chief Medical Officer, Mahnomen Health, Mahnomen, MN, p. A349
GUSHEE, Dean, M.D., Medical Director, Mason Health, Shelton, WA, p. A695
GUSHO, Michael, Chief Financial Officer, Trinity Health Oakland Hospital, Pontiac, MI, p. A335
GUSMANO, Jane, Vice President Finance, Memorial Hospital Belleville, Belleville, IL, p. A186
GUSTAFSON, Brian, Chief Financial Officer, Fort Harrison Va Medical Center, Fort Harrison, MT, p. A392
GUSTAFSON, Connie, Director of Nursing, Jacobson Memorial Hospital Care Center, Elgin, ND, p. A480
GUSTE, Allison, Chief Nursing Officer, University Medical Center, New Orleans, LA, p. A290
GUSTIN, Michael, Information Technology, John J. Pershing Veterans' Administration Medical Center, Poplar Bluff, MO, p. A382
GUTHMILLER, Martin W., Chief Executive Officer, Orange City Area Health System, Orange City, IA, p. A241
GUTHRIE, Pamela A, Chief Human Resources Officer, Hillcrest Hospital Pryor, Pryor, OK, p. A520
GUTHRIE, Shauna, M.D., Chief Medical Officer, Maria Parham Health, Duke Lifepoint Healthcare, Henderson, NC, p. A470
GUTIERREZ, Lori, Chief Financial Officer, Rochelle Community Hospital, Rochelle, IL, p. A207
GUTIERREZ, Michelle
Executive Director Human Resources, Orange Coast Medical Center, Fountain Valley, CA, p. A64
Executive Director Human Resources, Orange County, Saddleback Medical Center, Laguna Hills, CA, p. A69
GUTIERREZ, Noe, Chief Financial Officer, Lake Granbury Medical Center, Granbury, TX, p. A622
GUTIERREZ, Santiago, M.D., Chief Medical Officer, Doctors Hospital of Laredo, Laredo, TX, p. A634
GUTIERREZ, Vickie, Hospital Administrator and Chief Nursing Officer, Dr. Dan C. Trigg Memorial Hospital, Tucumcari, NM, p. A437
GUTIERREZ, Victor A, M.D., Medical Director, Allegiance Behavioral Health Center of Plainview, Plainview, TX, p. A644
GUTJAHR, Susan, Reimbursement Specialist, Sparta Community Hospital, Sparta, IL, p. A208
GUTNICK, Michael, Executive Vice President and Chief Financial Officer, Memorial Sloan Kettering Cancer Center, New York, NY, p. A449
GUTOWSKI, Jennifer S., FACHE, Director, Tucson Va Medical Center, Tucson, AZ, p. A41
GUTSCHENRITTER, John, Chief Financial Officer, Wilson Medical Center, Neodesha, KS, p. A255
GUTTENBERG, Ellen, Chief Operating Officer, Frances Mahon Deaconess Hospital, Glasgow, MT, p. A392
GUTTIN, Enrique, M.D., FACS, Chief of Staff, Wilmington Veterans Affairs Medical Center, Wilmington, DE, p. A122
GUTTMACHER, Laurence, M.D., Clinical Director, Rochester Psychiatric Center, Rochester, NY, p. A457
GUTZEIT, Michael, M.D., Chief Medical Officer, Children's Wisconsin, Milwaukee, WI, p. A717
GUY, Kimberly, President, St. Joseph's Hospital, Tampa, FL, p. A152
GUYETTE, William, M.D., President Medical Staff, Livingston Hospital And Healthcare Services, Salem, KY, p. A274
GUYTON, Nat'e, R.N., MSN, Chief Operating Officer, California Hospital Medical Center, Los Angeles, CA, p. A72
GUZ, Andrew, Chief Executive Officer, Lakewood Ranch Medical Center, Bradenton, FL, p. A126
GUZMAN, David, Chief Financial Officer, NYC Health + Hospitals/Elmhurst, New York, NY, p. A451
GUZMAN, Lisa, Human Resource Vice President, Redlands Community Hospital, Redlands, CA, p. A85
GWATKIN, Elizabeth, Vice President Human Resources, Northeastern Vermont Regional Hospital, Saint Johnsbury, VT, p. A672
GWYN, Andrea, Chief Operating Officer, Terre Haute Regional Hospital, Terre Haute, IN, p. A228
GYNTHER, Tracy, R.N., Vice President and Chief Nursing Officer, Wellstar West Georgia Medical Center, Lagrange, GA, p. A166

H

HAACK, Sally, Vice President and Director of Human Resources, St. Francis Regional Medical Center, Shakopee, MN, p. A355
HAACK, Wanda, MSN, R.N., Chief Nursing Officer, Genesis Medical Center, Dewitt, De Witt, IA, p. A234
HAAG, Adam, Manager Information Technology, Coffey County Hospital, Burlington, KS, p. A247
HAAGENSON, Deb, R.N., Vice President of Patient Care, Chi St. Joseph's Health, Park Rapids, MN, p. A352
HAAK, Karen S., R.N., MSN, Chief Nursing Officer, Good Samaritan Hospital, Vincennes, IN, p. A228
HAAS, Christine, Chief Information Officer, Geisinger Jersey Shore Hospital, Jersey Shore, PA, p. A542
HAAS, Steven J
Chief Financial Officer, Health Alliance Hospital – Broadway Campus, Kingston, NY, p. A445
Chief Financial Officer, Health Alliance Hospital – Mary's Avenue Campus, Kingston, NY, p. A445
HAAS, Susan, Director Human Resources, Aurora Behavioral Healthcare San Diego, San Diego, CA, p. A88
HAASE, Patricia, Director Information Technology and Communications, Marian Regional Medical Center, Santa Maria, CA, p. A94
HAASE, Ronald, Chief Administrative Officer, Verde Valley Medical Center, Cottonwood, AZ, p. A31
HAASE, Russ, Director Human Resources, Aurora Medical Center of Oshkosh, Oshkosh, WI, p. A719
HAASKEN, Timothy W, Chief Financial Officer, Lewisgale Hospital Montgomery, Blacksburg, VA, p. A673
HABIB, Noel, M.D., Chief Medical Officer, Huhukam Memorial Hospital, Sacaton, AZ, p. A37
HACHEY, Michael
Senior Vice President and Chief Financial Officer, Emerson Hospital, Concord, MA, p. A313
Senior Vice President and Chief Financial Officer, Northern Light Mercy Hospital, Portland, ME, p. A298
HACKBARTH, John, CPA, Senior Vice President Finance and Chief Financial Officer, Owensboro Health Regional Hospital, Owensboro, KY, p. A272
HACKER, Phillip. Chief Financial Officer, Stone County Medical Center, Mountain View, AR, p. A51
HACKETT, Leslie, Chief Nursing Officer, Covenant Hospital Plainview, Plainview, TX, p. A644
HACKSTEDDE, Anita
M.D., President and Chief Executive Officer, Salem Regional Medical Center, Salem, OH, p. A503
M.D., Vice President Medical Affairs, Salem Regional Medical Center, Salem, OH, p. A503
HACKWORTH, Lisa B, Vice President Human Resources, Holzer Medical Center, Gallipolis, OH, p. A496
HADAR, Janet, President, University of North Carolina Hospitals, Chapel Hill, NC, p. A465
HADAWAY, Krystal, Director Human Resources, Healthsource Saginaw Inc., Saginaw, MI, p. A337
HADDAD, Housam, M.D., Chief of Staff, Casey County Hospital, Liberty, KY, p. A269
HADDADIN, Maen, M.D., President Medical Staff, Chi Health Mercy Corning, Corning, IA, p. A233
HADDEN, Scott, M.D., Medical Staff President, Santiam Hospital, Stayton, OR, p. A532
HADDOX, Melissa, Controller, Encompass Health Rehabilitation Hospital of Cypress, Houston, TX, p. A625
HADEN, Meg, Chief Operating Officer, Austin Oaks Hospital, Austin, TX, p. A599
HADLEY, Gerard, Vice President Finance for Brigham & Women's Faulkner Hospital and Vice President Finance and Controller, Brigham And Women's Faulkner Hospital, Boston, MA, p. A310
HADLEY, H Roger, M.D., Vice President, Medical Affairs, Loma Linda University Medical Center, Loma Linda, CA, p. A70
HADLEY, Steven N, Chief Financial Officer, Kansas Medical Center, Andover, KS, p. A246
HADLEY, Susan, MS, Chief Nursing Officer, Marshfield Medical Center – Dickinson, Iron Mountain, MI, p. A330
HAEHN, Debra, Chief Financial Officer, Clay County Memorial Hospital, Henrietta, TX, p. A624
HAENELT, Michael, Chief Information Management, Weed Army Community Hospital, Fort Irwin, CA, p. A63
HAESEMEYER, Allan, M.D., Chief of Staff, Indianhead Medical Center, Shell Lake, WI, p. A721
HAESEMEYER, Christa, Chief Nursing Officer, Lincoln County Hospital, Lincoln, KS, p. A253
HAFEMAN, Paula
Chief Nursing Officer, HSHS St. Clare Memorial Hospital, Oconto Falls, WI, p. A719
Chief Nursing Officer, HSHS St. Mary's Hospital Medical Center, Green Bay, WI, p. A712
HAFFEY, Robert, R.N., Chief Executive Officer and President, Signature Healthcare Brockton Hospital, Brockton, MA, p. A311
HAFFNER, John, M.D., Chief Medical Officer, St. Anthony's Hospital, Saint Petersburg, FL, p. A149
HAFIZ, Irfan, Vice President Medical Affairs, Northwestern Medicine Mchenry, Mchenry, IL, p. A201

A864 Index of Health Care Professionals

Index of Health Care Professionals
Index of Health Care Professionals / Halstenson

HAGAN, Donald E, Chief Financial Officer, Detar Healthcare System, Victoria, TX, p. A660
HAGAN, Eric, R.N., Executive Vice President and Administrator, Medical Center At Scottsville, Scottsville, KY, p. A274
HAGAN, Frank, Senior Vice President Finance, Saint Joseph's Medical Center, Yonkers, NY, p. A462
HAGEDORN, Tammy, Chief Human Resource Officer, Genesis Medical Center–Aledo, Aledo, IL, p. A185
HAGEL, Bonnie, Chief Financial Officer, Logan County Hospital, Oakley, KS, p. A256
HAGELBERG, Robbi, Vice President Nursing Services and Chief Nursing Officer, Lakeview Hospital, Stillwater, MN, p. A355
HAGELTHORN, Diane, Human Resources Generalist, Modoc Medical Center, Alturas, CA, p. A55
HAGEN, Mary, R.N., MSN, VP and Chief Nursing Officer, Unitypoint Health – Allen Hospital, Waterloo, IA, p. A244
HAGEN, Paulette, Human Resources and Administrative Services Director, Centracare – Paynesville, Paynesville, MN, p. A352
HAGEN, SHRM–CP, Lynne D, Human Resources Officer, Avera Mckennan Hospital And University Health Center, Sioux Falls, SD, p. A576
HAGENS, Paul, Vice President Human Resources, Luminis Health Doctors Community Medical Center, Lanham, MD, p. A305
HAGER, Robin, Chief Executive Officer, Kindred Hospital Las Vegas–Sahara, Henderson, NV, p. A409
HAGERSTROM, Paige A, System Director of Talent Management, St. Josep. Hospital, Bangor, ME, p. A295
HAGERTY, Cindy, Assistant Chief Nurse Officer and Administrator of Operations, Ascension Via Christi Rehabilitation Hospital, Wichita, KS, p. A261
HAGGARD, Tommy, Chief Executive Officer, Bourbon Community Hospital, Paris, KY, p. A273
HAGGERTY, Cheryl Kay, Chief Nursing Officer, Assistant Chief Executive Officer, Mercyone New Hampton Medical Center, New Hampton, IA, p. A240
HAGLUND, Nicole
Interim Chief Executive Officer and Chief Nursing Officer, Providence Medical Center, Wayne, NE, p. A406
Vice President of Nursing Services, Providence Medical Center, Wayne, NE, p. A406
HAGOOD, Teena, Chief Nursing Officer, Kimble Hospital, Junction, TX, p. A631
HAGWELL, Mick, Chief Financial Officer, Aspirus Ironwood Hospital & Clinics, Inc., Ironwood, MI, p. A330
HAGY, Kelly, Director Human Resources, Cumberland Hall Hospital, Hopkinsville, KY, p. A267
HAGY, Michelle, Senior Vice President and Chief Financial Officer, Pikeville Medical Center, Pikeville, KY, p. A273
HAHEY, Joanne A
Senior Vice President and Chief Financial Officer, University of Maryland Shore Medical Center At Easton, Easton, MD, p. A304
Vice President Finance and Chief Financial Officer, University of Maryland Shore Medical Center At Chestertown, Chestertown, MD, p. A303
HAHN, Jen, Finance Manager, University Hospitals Portage Medical Center, Ravenna, OH, p. A503
HAHN, Kurt, M.D., Acting Clinical Director, Elmira Psychiatric Center, Elmira, NY, p. A443
HAHN, Lisa, R.N., Chief Executive Officer, AHMC Anaheim Regional Medical Center, Anaheim, CA, p. A55
HAHN, Lori, Vice President Nursing Services, Chi St. Alexius Health Williston, Williston, ND, p. A483
HAHN, Stephen, Deputy to the President and Chief Operating Officer, University of Texas M.D. Anderson Cancer Center, Houston, TX, p. A628
HAIGH, Sara, Associate Director, Durham Va Health Care System, Durham, NC, p. A467
HAIN, Jim, Chief Operating Officer, Lexington Regional Health Center, Lexington, NE, p. A401
HAINES, Alex, Chief Executive Officer, St. Luke Hospital And Living Center, Marion, KS, p. A254
HAIR, Denise J., Vice President of Nursing Services and Chief Nursing Officer, Dameron Hospital, Stockton, CA, p. A96
HAIR, William T., Chief Financial Officer, Abbeville General Hospital, Abbeville, LA, p. A276
HAISLIP, Heidi, M.D., Chief of Staff, Alliancehealth Madill, Madill, OK, p. A514
HAISLIP, Wendy, Chief Nursing Officer, Indiana Regional Medical Center, Indiana, PA, p. A542
HAIZLIP, Thomas M, M.D., Jr, Chief of Staff, Charles A. Cannon Jr. Memorial Hospital, Newland, NC, p. A473
HAJEK, Julie, Director Human Resources, St. David's Medical Center, Austin, TX, p. A600
HALBERT, Jeff, Chief Executive Officer, Select Specialty Hospital–St. Louis, Saint Charles, MO, p. A383
HALBROOK, Gerrie, Chief Financial Officer, Good Samaritan Hospital, Bakersfield, CA, p. A57
HALDEMAN, Larry, M.D., Executive Vice President and Chief Medical Officer, Wellstar Windy Hill Hospital, Marietta, GA, p. A168
HALDER, Ranjay, M.D., Chief Medical Director, Centerstone Hospital, Bradenton, FL, p. A126
HALE, Danny, Director Human Resources, Southwestern Medical Center, Lawton, OK, p. A514
HALE, Donna, Director of Nursing, Baptist Memorial Rehabilitation Hospital, Germantown, TN, p. A583
HALE, Ken, Executive Director of Operations, Mercy Health – Allen Hospital, Oberlin, OH, p. A501
HALE, Kim, R.N., Chief Nursing and Operating Officer, Legent North Houston Surgical Hospital, Tomball, TX, p. A658
HALE, Kirsten
Coordinator Health Information Services, University Hospitals Conneaut Medical Center, Conneaut, OH, p. A493
Coordinator Health Information Systems and Coding, University Hospitals Geneva Medical Center, Geneva, OH, p. A496
HALE, Renae, Chief Nursing Officer, Lincoln Prairie Behavioral Health Center, Springfield, IL, p. A209
HALE, Steven D., FACHE, Chief Executive Officer, Weiser Memorial Hospital, Weiser, ID, p. A184
HALE, Tonia, R.N., Chief Executive Officer and Chief Nursing Officer, Blue Ridge Regional Hospital, Spruce Pine, NC, p. A476
HALEN, Catherine, Vice President Human Resources, Beebe Healthcare, Lewes, DE, p. A121
HALES, Brent, Chief Financial Officer, Uintah Basin Medical Center, Roosevelt, UT, p. A668
HALES, Joe, Chief Information Officer, Primary Children's Hospital, Salt Lake City, UT, p. A669
HALEY, DeLeigh, Chief Executive Officer, UT Health Jacksonville, Jacksonville, TX, p. A630
HALEY, James, M.D., Senior Vice President and Chief Medical Officer, Unity Hospital, Rochester, NY, p. A458
HALEY, Kelsey, Chief Executive Officer, Hemphill County Hospital District, Canadian, TX, p. A606
HALEY, Thomas
Information Technology Services Site Director, Chi Health Mercy Council Bluffs, Council Bluffs, IA, p. A233
Information Technology Systems Site Director, Chi Health Lakeside, Omaha, NE, p. A403
Information Technology Systems Site Director, Chi Health Midlands, Papillion, NE, p. A405
HALFEN, John, M.D., Medical Director, Lakewood Health System, Staples, MN, p. A355
HALIMI, Hamid, M.D., Medical Director, Select Specialty Hospital – Ann Arbor, Ypsilanti, MI, p. A341
HALL, Becky, R.N., Director Nursing, Rumford Hospital, Rumford, ME, p. A299
HALL, Catherine, Manager Human Resources, Jefferson Hospital, Louisville, GA, p. A166
HALL, Dan, R.N., Chief Operating Officer, Ascension St. John Owasso, Owasso, OK, p. A519
HALL, David
Chief Financial Officer, Sierra Nevada Memorial Hospital, Grass Valley, CA, p. A66
Chief Information Officer, Pineville Community Health Center, Pineville, KY, p. A273
Senior Vice President and Chief Operating Officer, University of Tennessee Medical Center, Knoxville, TN, p. A586
HALL, Elizabeth, Chief Human Resources Officer, New Braunfels Er & Hospital, New Braunfels, TX, p. A641
HALL, Geoffrey, Chief Executive Officer, California Rehabilitation Institute, Los Angeles, CA, p. A72
HALL, George
M.D., Vice President Medical Affairs, St. Elizabeth Florence, Florence, KY, p. A265
M.D., Vice President Medical Affairs, St. Elizabeth Fort Thomas, Fort Thomas, KY, p. A266
HALL, Ginger, Chief Nursing Officer, Emanuel Medical Center, Swainsboro, GA, p. A172
HALL, James, M.D., Chief Medical Officer, Pamp. Regional Medical Center, Pampa, TX, p. A642
HALL, Jeanne, Director Information Systems, Shriners Hospitals for Children–St. Louis, Saint Louis, MO, p. A385
HALL, Jim, Acting Chief Information Officer, John L. Mcclellan Memorial Veterans' Hospital, Little Rock, AR, p. A50
HALL, John, Chief Medical Officer, Knox Community Hospital, Mount Vernon, OH, p. A501
HALL, Kathy, R.N., Chief Executive Officer, Northern Louisiana Medical Center, Ruston, LA, p. A291
HALL, Kenneth C, R.N., Chief Nursing Officer, Saint Josep. Health System, Mishawaka, IN, p. A224
HALL, Kent
M.D., Chief Medical Officer, The University of Vermont Health Network – Alice Hyde Medical Center, Malone, NY, p. A445
M.D., Vice President and Chief Medical Officer, The University of Vermont Health Network–Champlain Valley Physicians Hospital, Plattsburgh, NY, p. A456
HALL, Kristy, Chief Executive Officer, Mountain Lakes Medical Center, Clayton, GA, p. A160
HALL, Margaret, M.D., Chief Medical Officer, Lakeside Women's Hospital, Oklahoma City, OK, p. A517
HALL, Mary A, Chief Medical Staff, Mcdowell Arh Hospital, Mcdowell, KY, p. A271
HALL, Megan, Chief Executive Officer, Rehabilitation Hospital of Overland Park, Overland Park, KS, p. A257
HALL, Melissa, MSN, R.N., Vice President of Clinical Affairs and Chief Nursing Officer, Calverthealth Medical Center, Prince Frederick, MD, p. A306
HALL, Melissa K., Chief Executive Officer, Susan B. Allen Memorial Hospital, El Dorado, KS, p. A248
HALL, Michael D., Chief Executive Officer, Moberly Regional Medical Center, Moberly, MO, p. A380
HALL, Morrison, Chief Financial Officer, Novant Health Pender Medical Center, Burgaw, NC, p. A464
HALL, Rana, Chief Nursing Officer, HCA Florida Northwest Hospital, Margate, FL, p. A138
HALL, Richard, Chief Executive Officer, Samuel Simmonds Memorial Hospital, Barrow, AK, p. A27
HALL, Sally, Manager Human Resources, South Texas Spine And Surgical Hospital, San Antonio, TX, p. A651
HALL, Stephanie
M.D., Chief Medical Officer, Keck Hospital of Usc, Los Angeles, CA, p. A73
M.D., Chief Medical Officer, USC Verdugo Hills Hospital, Glendale, CA, p. A66
M.D., Medical Director, USC Norris Comprehensive Cancer Center And Hospital, Los Angeles, CA, p. A75
HALL, Steve, Chief Financial Officer, Carle Health Pekin Hospital, Pekin, IL, p. A205
HALL, Tara, Commander, Moncrief Army Community Hospital, Fort Jackson, SC, p. A566
HALL, Terry E., Chief of Staff, Harrison County Community Hospital, Bethany, MO, p. A371
HALL, Trudy
M.D., Vice President Medical Affairs and Interim Chief Executive Officer, University of Maryland Capital Region Medical Center, Largo, MD, p. A305
M.D., Vice President, Medical Affairs, University of Maryland Capital Region Medical Center, Largo, MD, p. A305
HALLAL, Joseph, M.D., Chief Medical Officer, Inova Fairfax Medical Campus, Falls Church, VA, p. A676
HALLAM, Elizabeth, R.N., Chief Executive Officer, Select Specialty Hospital–Springfield, Springfield, MO, p. A387
HALLATT, Jennifer
Chief Operating Officer, Mercyhealth Hospital And Medical Center – Harvard, Harvard, IL, p. A197
Vice President, Mercyhealth Hospital And Medical Center – Walworth, Lake Geneva, WI, p. A714
Vice President, Mercyhealth Hospital And Physician Clinic–Crystal Lake, Crystal Lake, IL, p. A192
HALLEY, Andrea, Vice President of Non–Clinical Operations/ Director Human Resources, Hopedale Medical Complex, Hopedale, IL, p. A198
HALLIDAY, Lisa, Director Accounting Services, Taylor Regional Hospital, Hawkinsville, GA, p. A165
HALLIWILL, Donald B
Chief Financial Officer, Carilion Franklin Memorial Hospital, Rocky Mount, VA, p. A683
Executive Vice President and Chief Financial Officer, Carilion Roanoke Memorial Hospital, Roanoke, VA, p. A683
HALLMARK, Todd, Executive Officer of Health Operations, Choctaw Nation Health Care Center, Talihina, OK, p. A521
HALLOCK, Mirya, Chief Executive Officer, Brown County Hospital, Ainsworth, NE, p. A397
HALLORAN, Teresa, Ph.D., R.N., Vice President Nursing Services, Memorial Hospital Belleville, Belleville, IL, p. A186
HALPIN, Kim, Director Human Resources, Arms Acres, Carmel, NY, p. A441
HALSTEAD, Lisa, Chief Nursing Officer, Integris Miami Hospital, Miami, OK, p. A515
HALSTEAD, Rhonda
President, Penn Highlands Dubois, Dubois, PA, p. A538
Region President for Huntington and Tyrone, Penn Highlands Tyrone, Tyrone, PA, p. A556
Region President, Huntingdon & Tyrone, Penn Highlands Huntingdon, Huntingdon, PA, p. A542
HALSTENSON, Jake, Chief Financial Officer, River's Edge Hospital And Clinic, Saint Peter, MN, p. A355

Index of Health Care Professionals / Halter

HALTER, Bev, Director Human Resources and Payroll, Logan Health Chester, Chester, MT, p. A390
HALTOM, Shannon, Vice President, Patient Care Services, Chi St. Luke's Health Brazosport, Lake Jackson, TX, p. A633
HALVORSEN, Lisa, Chief Nurse Executive, Providence Milwaukie Hospital, Milwaukie, OR, p. A529
HALVORSON, Marla, Vice President, Chief Human Resources Officer, Aspirus St. Luke's Hospital, Duluth, MN, p. A346
HAMAN, Timothy, M.D., Vice President Medical Affairs, Christus Ochsner St. Patrick, Lake Charles, LA, p. A286
HAMATY, Edward G., D.O., Chief Medical Officer, Select Specialty Hospital – Willingboro, Willingboro, NJ, p. A430
HAMB, Aaron, M.D., Chief Medical Officer, Provident Hospital of Cook County, Chicago, IL, p. A190
HAMBLIN, Garth, Chief Financial Officer, Bear Valley Community Hospital, Big Bear Lake, CA, p. A58
HAMBLIN, Scott, M.D., President Medical Staff, White Mountain Regional Medical Center, Springerville, AZ, p. A39
HAMBRIDGE, Mark, Director Information Systems, Livingston Regional Hospital, Livingston, TN, p. A587
HAMBY, Kelley, Vice President Patient Care, Baptist Health Medical Center – North Little Rock, North Little Rock, AR, p. A51
HAMEL, Ryan, Chief People Officer, Northwestern Medical Center, Saint Albans, VT, p. A672
HAMILL, Dave H., President and Chief Executive Officer, Hampton Regional Medical Center, Varnville, SC, p. A571
HAMILTON, Adriana H, Chief Human Resources Officer, Hunter Holmes Mcguire Veterans Affairs Medical Center–Richmond, Richmond, VA, p. A683
HAMILTON, Aggie, Chief Human Resources, Fort Harrison Va Medical Center, Fort Harrison, MT, p. A392
HAMILTON, Brandy, Chief Executive Officer, Suncoast Behavioral Health Center, Bradenton, FL, p. A127
HAMILTON, Catherine
   MSN, R.N., Administrator, Hedrick Medical Center, Chillicothe, MO, p. A373
   MSN, R.N., Administrator, Wright Memorial Hospital, Trenton, MO, p. A387
   MSN, R.N., Chief Nursing Officer, Hedrick Medical Center, Chillicothe, MO, p. A373
HAMILTON, Chanda, Chief Information Officer, Clifton T. Perkins Hospital Center, Jessup. MD, p. A305
HAMILTON, Dan, Chief Operating Officer, Nor–Lea Hospital District, Lovington, NM, p. A435
HAMILTON, David, Chief Information Officer, Southwest Mississipp. Regional Medical Center, Mccomb, MS, p. A366
HAMILTON, Garrett, Chief Executive Officer, Cumberland Hospital for Children And Adolescents, New Kent, VA, p. A679
HAMILTON, Geoff, Interim Chief Financial Officer, Arbor Health, Morton Hospital, Morton, WA, p. A691
HAMILTON, Hunter
   Chief Executive Officer, Hawkins County Memorial Hospital, Rogersville, TN, p. A592
   Chief Executive Officer/Administrator, Hancock County Hospital, Sneedville, TN, p. A593
HAMILTON, Jennifer, Chief Financial Officer, Sagewest Health Care, Riverton, WY, p. A728
HAMILTON, John Dennis., Interim Chief Operating Officer, Capital Region Medical Center, Jefferson City, MO, p. A376
HAMILTON, Kevin M., M.D., Chief Medical Officer, Tristar Summit Medical Center, Hermitage, TN, p. A584
HAMILTON, Marci, Chief Nursing Officer, Orthopaedic Hospital of Lutheran Health Network, Fort Wayne, IN, p. A216
HAMILTON, Marilyn, Director Human Resources, KPC Promise Hospital of Baton Rouge, Baton Rouge, LA, p. A277
HAMILTON, Michelle, Human Resource Manager, Turning Point Hospital, Moultrie, GA, p. A169
HAMILTON, Nancy, Chief Human and Learning Resources, Veterans Affairs New Jersey Health Care System, East Orange, NJ, p. A420
HAMILTON, Patricia, R.N., Director of Nursing, Mildred Mitchell–Bateman Hospital, Huntington, WV, p. A701
HAMILTON, Randal S., Chief Executive Officer, Encompass Health Rehabilitation Hospital of Savannah, Savannah, GA, p. A171
HAMILTON, Randy, Chief Administrative Officer, Norton Hospital, Louisville, KY, p. A270
HAMILTON, Scott, Vice President and Chief Financial Officer, Parkwest Medical Center, Knoxville, TN, p. A586
HAMILTON, Shanon, Administrator, Ascension St. Vincent's Chilton, Clanton, AL, p. A18
HAMILTON, Sharon, Chief Nursing Officer, Encompass Health Rehabilitation Hospital of Panama City, Panama City, FL, p. A146
HAMILTON, Terry, President, Ascension Macomb–Oakland Hospital, Warren Campus, Warren, MI, p. A340

HAMILTON–BEYER, Maggie, Chief Financial Officer, Knoxville Hospital & Clinics, Knoxville, IA, p. A239
HAMLIN, Faye, Manager Human Resources, Julian F. Keith Alcohol And Drug Abuse Treatment Center, Black Mountain, NC, p. A464
HAMM, Sonja, Vice President Human and Foundation Resources, Lakes Regional Healthcare, Spirit Lake, IA, p. A244
HAMMAKER, Barry, M.D., Chief Medical Officer and Chief Clinical Officer, Vail Health, Vail, CO, p. A114
HAMMAN, Baron L, M.D., Chief Medical Officer, Texas Health Heart & Vascular Hospital Arlington, Arlington, TX, p. A598
HAMMER, Rebecca J, Chief Financial Officer, Pocahontas Memorial Hospital, Buckeye, WV, p. A699
HAMMES, Paul, Chief Executive Officer, Hugh Chatham Health, Elkin, NC, p. A468
HAMMETT, Doran, Chief Financial Officer, Petersburg Medical Center, Petersburg, AK, p. A29
HAMMOCK, Preston W., President, Cone Health Moses Cone Hospital, Greensboro, NC, p. A469
HAMMOND, Flora, M.D., Chief Medical Affairs, Rehabilitation Hospital of Indiana, Indianapolis, IN, p. A220
HAMMOND, Michael
   Chief Financial Officer, Virtua Our Lady of Lourdes Hospital, Camden, NJ, p. A419
   Chief Financial Officer, Virtua Willingboro Hospital, Willingboro, NJ, p. A431
HAMMOND, Nancy, M.D., Vice President, Chief Medical Officer, Ascension Saint Agnes, Baltimore, MD, p. A300
HAMMOND, Patti, Chief Operating Officer, Adirondack Health, Saranac Lake, NY, p. A458
HAMMOND, Reed, Chief Executive Officer, HCA Florida Memorial Hospital, Jacksonville, FL, p. A134
HAMMONDS, Janie, Human Resources Officer, Columbus Community Hospital, Columbus, TX, p. A608
HAMMONS, Joshua, Chief Executive Officer, Highland Hills Medical Center, Senatobia, MS, p. A369
HAMNER, Candy, Vice President and Chief Nursing Officer, Levindale Hebrew Geriatric Center And Hospital, Baltimore, MD, p. A300
HAMNER, Carla, Hospital Administrator, Mon Health Marion Neighborhood Hospital, White Hall, WV, p. A706
HAMNER, James, Regional Information Technology Director, SSM Health Depaul Hospital – St. Louis, Bridgeton, MO, p. A372
HAMON, Eric
   Executive Vice President and Chief Financial Officer, Driscoll Children's Hospital, Corpus Christi, TX, p. A609
   President and Chief Executive Officer, Driscoll Children's Hospital, Corpus Christi, TX, p. A609
HAMPF, Carl, M.D., Chief Medical Officer, Ascension Saint Thomas Hospital for Specialty Surgery, Nashville, TN, p. A590
HAMPTON, Angie, Director Human Resources, Northwest Health – Porter, Valparaiso, IN, p. A228
HAMPTON, Danita, Chief Executive Officer, Mcdowell Arh Hospital, Mcdowell, KY, p. A271
HAMPTON, Elizabeth, MS, R.N., Chief Nursing Officer, Kit Carson County Memorial Hospital, Burlington, CO, p. A104
HAMPTON, Jeff, Director Information Systems, Lehigh Regional Medical Center, Lehigh Acres, FL, p. A137
HAMPTON, Mary Ann, MSN, R.N., Chief Nursing Officer, St. Luke's Des Peres Hospital, Saint Louis, MO, p. A386
HAMRICK, Jan, Chief Financial Officer, Dodge County Hospital, Eastman, GA, p. A163
HAMSCHER, Janice L., MSN, Executive Vice President, Chief Nursing Officer, Altru Health System, Grand Forks, ND, p. A481
HAMSTRA, Nancy, Chief Operating Officer, University Hospital, Newark, NJ, p. A425
HAMULA, Michelle, Director of Nursing and Quality, Chan Soon–Shiong Medical Center At Windber, Windber, PA, p. A558
HANCOCK, J Brian, M.D., Chief of Staff, Fargo Va Medical Center, Fargo, ND, p. A480
HANCOCK, K. Kelly, R.N., Chief Caregiver Officer and Rich Family Chief Caregiver Chair, Cleveland Clinic, Cleveland, OH, p. A490
HANCOCK, Kerry, Director Human Resources, Bacon County Hospital And Health System, Alma, GA, p. A156
HANCOCK, Lori, Chief Business Officer, West Palm Beach Veterans Affairs Medical Center, West Palm Beach, FL, p. A155
HANCOCK, Myrna, Director Financial Services, Choctaw Health Center, Philadelphia, MS, p. A367
HANCOCK, Sharon, Chief Human Resources Officer, Mccullough–Hyde Memorial Hospital/Trihealth, Oxford, OH, p. A502

HANCOCK, Todd
   Market President and Chief Executive Officer, Christus Good Shepherd Medical Center–Marshall, Marshall, TX, p. A638
   President, Christus Good Shepherd Medical Center–Marshall, Marshall, TX, p. A638
HANDLER, Michael, M.D., Vice President Medical Affairs and Chief Medical Officer, SSM Health St. Josep. Hospital – Lake Saint Louis, Lake Saint Louis, MO, p. A379
HANDLEY, Charles
   Chief Financial Officer, The Hospitals of Providence Memorial Campus – Tenet Healthcare, El Paso, TX, p. A617
   Chief Financial Officer, The Hospitals of Providence Sierra Campus – Tenet Healthcare, El Paso, TX, p. A617
   Chief Financial Officer, Vibra Hospital of Houston, Houston, TX, p. A628
HANDLEY, Donna
   President, The William W. Backus Hospital, Norwich, CT, p. A118
   President, Windham Hospital, Willimantic, CT, p. A120
HANDLEY, Jack, M.D., Chief Medical Officer, Evergreenhealth Monroe, Monroe, WA, p. A691
HANDLEY, Rhonda, Chief Financial Officer, Columbia Basin Hospital, Ephrata, WA, p. A689
HANDOL, Nelson, M.D., Medical Director, Laurel Oaks Behavioral Health Center, Dothan, AL, p. A18
HANDWERK, Ashley, Director, Human Resources, Medstar Union Memorial Hospital, Baltimore, MD, p. A301
HANEFELD, Darlene, Chief Human Resources Officer, Banner Churchill Community Hospital, Fallon, NV, p. A408
HANER, Todd, R.N., Chief Nursing Officer, HCA Florida Blake Hospital, Bradenton, FL, p. A126
HANEY, Kathryn, Controller, Encompass Health Valley of The Sun Rehabilitation Hospital, Glendale, AZ, p. A32
HANEY, Lisa, Chief Executive Officer, St. Mary Rehabilitation Hospital, Langhorne, PA, p. A543
HANGER, Kelvin, President and Chief Operating Officer, Good Samaritan Hospital, Cincinnati, OH, p. A489
HANIGAN, Hank
   FACHE, Chief Executive Officer, Whitman Hospital And Medical Center, Colfax, WA, p. A688
   FACHE, Interim Chief Financial Officer, Whitman Hospital And Medical Center, Colfax, WA, p. A688
HANISCH, Denise, M.D., Chief of Staff, Avera St. Mary's Hospital, Pierre, SD, p. A575
HANKEY, Babette, President and Chief Executive Officer, Aspire Health Partners, Orlando, FL, p. A144
HANKINS, Brad, Chief Operating Quality Officer, Lake Chelan Health, Chelan, WA, p. A688
HANKINS, J. William., Chief Executive Officer, Avala, Covington, LA, p. A280
HANKINS, Steven D., Chief Operating Officer, Good Samaritan Medical Center, Lafayette, CO, p. A110
HANKS, John, Director Information Systems, East Tennessee Children's Hospital, Knoxville, TN, p. A585
HANKS, Steven
   M.D., President and Chief Executive Officer, St. Peter's Hospital, Albany, NY, p. A438
   M.D., President and Chief Executive Officer, St. Joseph's Health and St. Peter's Health Partners, Samaritan Hospital – Main Campus, Troy, NY, p. A460
HANKS, Susan, Chief Information Officer, Riverton Hospital, Riverton, UT, p. A668
HANLEY, Bob, Senior Vice President and Chief Human Resources Officer, University of Chicago Medical Center, Chicago, IL, p. A192
HANLEY, Mathew, Chief Financial Officer, OSF Healthcare Saint Anthony's Health Center, Alton, IL, p. A185
HANLON, Jerad, Chief Executive Officer, West Boca Medical Center, Boca Raton, FL, p. A126
HANNA, Casey, M.D., Chief of Staff, Wagoner Community Hospital, Wagoner, OK, p. A523
HANNA, Robb, Executive Director Information Technology, Lexington Regional Health Center, Lexington, NE, p. A401
HANNAGAN, Jason, Chief Executive Officer, Southwest Kansas City Market, and Senior Vice President, Kansas City Divisi, Olathe Medical Center, Olathe, KS, p. A256
HANNAH, Frances, Administrator/Financial Manager/CPT/AMB Operator, Surprise Valley Health Care District, Cedarville, CA, p. A59
HANNAH, Jill, Director Human Resources, The Osuccc – James, Columbus, OH, p. A493
HANNAPEL, Andrew, Chief Medical Officer, UNC Health Chatham, Siler City, NC, p. A476
HANNERS, Brandy, Chief Financial Officer, Sovah Health–Martinsville, Martinsville, VA, p. A679
HANNON, Patricia, Chief Nursing Officer, Vaughan Regional Medical Center, Selma, AL, p. A24

Index of Health Care Professionals / Harkins

Index of Health Care Professionals

HANNU, Theresa, Vice President, Chief Nursing Officer, Aspirus St. Luke's Hospital, Duluth, MN, p. A346
HANSCOM, Kristine, Chief Financial Officer, Tufts Medical Center, Boston, MA, p. A311
HANSCOME, Joyce, Chief Information Officer, Luminis Health Doctors Community Medical Center, Lanham, MD, p. A305
HANSEL, Jimmie W., Ph.D., Chief Executive Officer, Edwards County Medical Center, Kinsley, KS, p. A252
HANSELMAN, Matthew, Chief Financial Officer, Ascension Sacred Heart Rehabilitation Hospital, Mequon, WI, p. A716
HANSEN, Carolyn, Chief Nursing Officer, Bingham Memorial Hospital, Blackfoot, ID, p. A179
HANSEN, Chris, Senior Vice President and Chief Information Officer, The University of Kansas Hospital, Kansas City, KS, p. A252
HANSEN, Diane
President and Chief Executive Officer, Palomar Medical Center Escondido, Escondido, CA, p. A62
President and Chief Executive Officer, Palomar Medical Center Poway, Poway, CA, p. A84
HANSEN, Ellen Dempsey, Chief Nursing Officer, University of Mississipp. Medical Center, Jackson, MS, p. A364
HANSEN, Gayle B
R.N., Chief Integration Officer, Mayo Clinic Health System In Saint James, Saint James, MN, p. A354
R.N., Chief Operating Officer, Mayo Clinic Health System In Fairmont, Fairmont, MN, p. A346
HANSEN, James, Chief Financial Officer, Summit Pacific Medical Center, Elma, WA, p. A689
HANSEN, Jay, Director Information Services, Prisma Health Oconee Memorial Hospital, Seneca, SC, p. A570
HANSEN, Julie S, Chief Financial Officer, Mayo Clinic Health System In Sparta, Sparta, WI, p. A721
HANSEN, Karen, Vice President and Chief Operating Officer, Tamarack Health Ashland Medical Center, Ashland, WI, p. A707
HANSEN, Kristy, CPA, Chief Financial Officer, Myrtue Medical Center, Harlan, IA, p. A237
HANSEN, Kyle, Corporate Director Information Systems, Riverside Medical Center, Kankakee, IL, p. A199
HANSEN, Kyle A., President, Utah Valley Hospital, Provo, UT, p. A667
HANSEN, Laurie
Director of Administration, Johnson County Healthcare Center, Buffalo, WY, p. A726
Vice President of Operations, Emory Johns Creek Hospital, Johns Creek, GA, p. A166
HANSEN, Michael T., FACHE, President and Chief Executive Officer, Columbus Community Hospital, Columbus, NE, p. A399
HANSEN, Steven, Director Information Technology, Healdsburg Hospital, Healdsburg, CA, p. A67
HANSFORD, Jessica, Chief Executive Officer, Clarion Psychiatric Center, Clarion, PA, p. A537
HANSON, Brent, Chief Executive Officer, Select Specialty Hospital–Kansas City, Kansas City, KS, p. A252
HANSON, Denise, Information Technology Specialist, St. Cloud Va Health Care System, Saint Cloud, MN, p. A354
HANSON, Emily, M.D., President, Medical Staff, St. Josep. Memorial Hospital, Murphysboro, IL, p. A203
HANSON, Gregory S., M.D., President and Chief Executive Officer, Clark Fork Valley Hospital, Plains, MT, p. A394
HANSON, Jane E.
R.N., Chief Executive Officer, Dignity Health Arizona General Hospital, Laveen, AZ, p. A33
R.N., President and Chief Executive Officer, Dignity Health Arizona General Hospital Mesa, Llc, Mesa, AZ, p. A33
HANSON, Jesica, Vice President Finance and Chief Financial Officer, Mercyone Siouxland Medical Center, Sioux City, IA, p. A243
HANSON, Jim, Director Information Systems, Avera Queen of Peace Hospital, Mitchell, SD, p. A575
HANSON, June, Chief Nursing Officer, Up Health System – Bell, Ishpeming, MI, p. A330
HANSON, Lesley, Director Human Resources, Lake District Hospital, Lakeview, OR, p. A528
HANSON, Mary Ann, Director Personnel, Cherokee Mental Health Institute, Cherokee, IA, p. A232
HANSON, Paul, Chief Financial Officer, Great Falls Clinic Hospital, Great Falls, MT, p. A392
HANSON, Paul A., FACHE, President, Sanford Usd Medical Center, Sioux Falls, SD, p. A577
HANSON, Rhonda, Director Human Resources, Huron Regional Medical Center, Huron, SD, p. A574
HANSON, Rita
M.D., Vice President Medical Affairs, Ascension Southeast Wisconsin Hospital – Elmbrook Campus, Brookfield, WI, p. A708
M.D., Vice President Medical Affairs, Ascension Southeast Wisconsin Hospital – St. Joseph's Campus, Milwaukee, WI, p. A716
HANSON, Tamra, Human Resource Manager, Dorothea Dix Psychiatric Center, Bangor, ME, p. A295
HANSON, Troy, Chief Operating Officer, Bitterroot Health – Daly Hospital, Hamilton, MT, p. A392
HANZLIK, Debra Dawn, R.N., Director of Nursing, Niobrara Valley Hospital, Lynch, NE, p. A402
HAPPEL, Terry J, M.D., Vice President and Chief Medical Officer, Chandler Regional Medical Center, Chandler, AZ, p. A30
HAQQANI, Rahim, M.D., Medical Director, Dallas Behavioral Healthcare Hospital, Desoto, TX, p. A614
HAQUE, Syed, Vice President and Chief Information Officer, Loretto Hospital, Chicago, IL, p. A190
HARA, Karen, Personnel Management Specialist, Hawaii State Hospital, Kaneohe, HI, p. A177
HARALDSON, Richard, CPA, FACHE, Chief Executive Officer, Beatrice Community Hospital And Health Center, Beatrice, NE, p. A398
HARALSON, Gregory
FACHE, President, Baylor Scott & White Medical Center – Temple, Temple, TX, p. A656
FACHE, Senior Vice President and Chief Executive Officer, Memorial Hermann – Texas Medical Center, Houston, TX, p. A627
HARARI, Jack L, M.D., Chief Medical Officer, West Boca Medical Center, Boca Raton, FL, p. A126
HARBAUGH, Charles, Director Human Resources, Mountain Lakes Medical Center, Clayton, GA, p. A160
HARBAUGH, Ken, Vice President and Chief Financial Officer, OSF Saint Francis Medical Center, Peoria, IL, p. A206
HARBERSON, Stacy, Chief Operating Officer, Howard Memorial Hospital, Nashville, AR, p. A51
HARBERTS, Jerry, Information Technologist, Madison Healthcare Services, Madison, MN, p. A349
HARBIN, Cathy
Chief Nursing Officer, Roosevelt Warm Springs Long Term Acute Care Hospital, Warm Springs, GA, p. A173
Chief Nursing Officer, Roosevelt Warm Springs Rehabilitation And Specialty Hospitals, Warm Springs, GA, p. A173
HARBIN, Jason, Director of Nursing, Ward Memorial Hospital, Monahans, TX, p. A640
HARBISON, Damon R.
President, SSM Health Good Samaritan Hospital, Mount Vernon, IL, p. A202
President, SSM Health St. Mary's Hospital Centralia, Centralia, IL, p. A187
HARCHENKO, Vern, M.D., Chief of Staff, Chi St. Alexius Health Garrison, Garrison, ND, p. A481
HARCLERODE, Timothy
R.N., FACHE, Chief Executive Officer, Conemaugh Meyersdale Medical Center, Meyersdale, PA, p. A546
R.N., FACHE, Chief Executive Officer, Conemaugh Miners Medical Center, Hastings, PA, p. A541
R.N., FACHE, Chief Executive Officer, Conemaugh Nason Medical Center, Roaring Spring, PA, p. A553
R.N., FACHE, Chief Operating Officer, Conemaugh Memorial Medical Center, Johnstown, PA, p. A542
HARCOURT, Jenifer, Chief Operating Officer, Riverwoods Behavioral Health System, Riverdale, GA, p. A170
HARCOURT, Roxane, Interim Administrator, UF Health Shands Hospital, Gainesville, FL, p. A133
HARDACRE, Jerry, M.D., Chief of Staff, Ascension All Saints, Racine, WI, p. A720
HARDAN, Terry, Director Human Resources, Longview Regional Medical Center, Longview, TX, p. A635
HARDCASTLE, Brad, Chief Financial Officer, South Baldwin Regional Medical Center, Foley, AL, p. A19
HARDCASTLE, Kathy, Director Human Resources, Texas Health Presbyterian Hospital Denton, Denton, TX, p. A614
HARDEE, Gary R, M.D., Medical Director, Plains Memorial Hospital, Dimmitt, TX, p. A614
HARDEE, Jenny, MSN, Chief Executive Officer, Mcleod Health Dillon, Dillon, SC, p. A565
HARDEN, Diane P
Chief Financial Officer, Leesburg Regional Medical Center, Leesburg, FL, p. A137
Senior Vice President and Chief Financial Officer, UF Health The Villages Hospital, The Villages, FL, p. A153
HARDEN, Jeffrey M, Chief Nursing Officer, Memorial Health Meadows Hospital, Vidalia, GA, p. A173
HARDESTY, Keith, Chief Financial Officer, Springfield Hospital Center, Sykesville, MD, p. A307
HARDICK, Cindy, Human Resources Coordinator, Select Specialty Hospital – Ann Arbor, Ypsilanti, MI, p. A341
HARDIE, Rebecca Kay, Chief Nursing Officer, Baylor Scott & White Medical Center – Hillcrest, Waco, TX, p. A660
HARDIN, Cecil, CPA, Chief Financial Officer, Catawba Hospital, Catawba, VA, p. A674
HARDIN, James, Human Resources Officer, Sheridan Va Medical Center, Sheridan, WY, p. A728
HARDIN, Leslie, Chief Executive Officer and Chief Financial Officer, Seymour Hospital, Seymour, TX, p. A652
HARDIN, Marci, Manager Information Technology, Nevada Regional Medical Center, Nevada, MO, p. A381
HARDIN, Mark, M.D., Medical Director, Ed Fraser Memorial Hospital, Macclenny, FL, p. A138
HARDIN, Nicholas, FACHE, Chief Executive Officer, Encompass Health Rehabilitation Hospital of Katy, Katy, TX, p. A631
HARDING, Denise, Director Human Resources, Plumas District Hospital, Quincy, CA, p. A84
HARDING, Edward A., FACHE, President, Aurora Medical Center – Bay Area, Marinette, WI, p. A715
HARDING, Geoff, Chief Clinical Officer, KPC Promise Hospital of Salt Lake, Salt Lake City, UT, p. A668
HARDING, Gwen, Site Manager Information Systems, Bon Secours Memorial Regional Medical Center, Mechanicsville, VA, p. A679
HARDING, Helen, Chief Nursing Officer, Fairfield Medical Center, Lancaster, OH, p. A498
HARDING, Samantha, Chief Executive Officer, Nelson County Health System, Mcville, ND, p. A482
HARDISON, Randall, M.D., Chief Medical Officer, Arizona Orthopedic Surgical Hospital, Chandler, AZ, p. A30
HARDMAN, Joe, M.D., Chief Medical Officer, Ohsu Health Hillsboro Medical Center, Hillsboro, OR, p. A528
HARDY, Bob, Chief Operating Officer, Opelousas General Health System, Opelousas, LA, p. A291
HARDY, Geoff, Administrator, South Georgia Medical Center Lanier Campus, Lakeland, GA, p. A166
HARDY, James, D.O., Chief of Staff, Dayton Veterans Affairs Medical Center, Dayton, OH, p. A493
HARDY, Janice, Chief Human Resource Management Service, Central Alabama Va Medical Center–Montgomery, Montgomery, AL, p. A22
HARDY, Kevin, Chief Financial Officer, Encompass Health Rehabilitation Hospital of Treasure Coast, Vero Beach, FL, p. A154
HARDY, LaBon, Chief Information Officer, Ralp. H. Johnson Veterans Affairs Medical Center, Charleston, SC, p. A563
HARDY, Raymond, Controller, Encompass Health Rehabilitation Hospital of Las Vegas, Las Vegas, NV, p. A410
HARDY, Valonia, Chief Healthy Living Officer, Tsehootsooi Medical Center, Fort Defiance, AZ, p. A31
HARESNAPE, Julie, Coordinator Human Resources, Smith County Memorial Hospital, Smith Center, KS, p. A260
HARFORD, Todd, Chief Operating Officer, University Hospitals Elyria Medical Center, Elyria, OH, p. A495
HARGENS, Scott James., Chief Executive Officer, Select Specialty Hospital–Sioux Falls, Sioux Falls, SD, p. A577
HARGER, Anita
Chief Human Resource Officer, Kingman Regional Medical Center, Kingman, AZ, p. A32
Director Human Resources, Mercy Gilbert Medical Center, Gilbert, AZ, p. A32
HARGETT, Stephen A, Senior Vice President and Chief Financial Officer, Cedars–Sinai Marina Del Rey Hospital, Marina Del Rey, CA, p. A76
HARGIS, Bryan
CPA, FACHE, Chief Executive Officer, Great River Medical Center, Blytheville, AR, p. A43
CPA, FACHE, Chief Executive Officer, SMC Regional Medical Center, Osceola, AR, p. A52
HARGRAVE, Dallas, Human Resources Director, Bartlett Regional Hospital, Juneau, AK, p. A28
HARGRAVE, David, Chief Information Officer, Ward Memorial Hospital, Monahans, TX, p. A640
HARGRODER, Ty, M.D., Chief of Staff, Acadia–St. Landry Hospital, Church Point, LA, p. A280
HARGROVE, Ben, Human Resources Director, Lifestream Behavioral Center, Leesburg, FL, p. A137
HARGROVE, Jeno, R.N., Director of Nursing, Columbus Community Hospital, Columbus, TX, p. A608
HARGROVE, Tressa B, Director Human Resources, Jackson Purchase Medical Center, Mayfield, KY, p. A271
HARKER, Jodie, Director Human Resources, Van Diest Medical Center, Webster City, IA, p. A245
HARKEY, Shirley S., M.D., R.N., FACHE, Interim Vice President and Chief Nursing Officer, UNC Health Lenoir, Kinston, NC, p. A471
HARKINS, Jennifer, Executive Director, Coatesville Veterans Affairs Medical Center, Coatesville, PA, p. A537
HARKINS, Shelly
M.D., Chief Medical Officer, HSHS St. Elizabeth's Hospital, O Fallon, IL, p. A204
M.D., Chief Medical Officer, St. Peter's Health, Helena, MT, p. A393

Index of Health Care Professionals

Index of Health Care Professionals / Harkleroad

HARKLEROAD, Rod
R.N., Chief Executive Officer, Riverview Regional Medical Center, Carthage, TN, p. A579
R.N., Chief Executive Officer, Sumner Regional Medical Center, Gallatin, TN, p. A583
HARKNESS, Bryan, R.N., Chief Nursing Officer, Ottumwa Regional Health Center, Ottumwa, IA, p. A241
HARKNESS, Charles, D.O., Vice President Medical Affairs, Southeast Alabama Medical Center, Dothan, AL, p. A18
HARLAN, Kevin W.
President, Atrium Medical Center, Middletown, OH, p. A500
President, Upper Valley Medical Center, Troy, OH, p. A505
HARLESS, Andrea, Director Information Services, Wythe County Community Hospital, Wytheville, VA, p. A686
HARLESS, Cheryl, Chief Nursing Officer, Doctors Medical Center of Modesto, Modesto, CA, p. A77
HARLESS, Rebecca, Chief Executive Officer, Camc Greenbrier Valley Medical Center, Ronceverte, WV, p. A704
HARLING, Roxanne, Chief Nursing Officer, Lincoln Memorial Hospital, Lincoln, IL, p. A200
HARLOW, Dayle, Chief Financial Officer, Fillmore County Hospital, Geneva, NE, p. A400
HARLOW, Donald, Director of Information Services, Mountainview Regional Medical Center, Las Cruces, NM, p. A435
HARLOW, Tammy, Chief Operating Officer, Elbert Memorial Hospital, Elberton, GA, p. A163
HARMATZ, Alan, M.D., Chief Medical Officer, HCA Florida Brandon Hospital, Brandon, FL, p. A127
HARMON, Andre, Chief Human Resource Officer, Deer's Head Hospital Center, Salisbury, MD, p. A307
HARMON, Connie, Director of Nursing, Corewell Health Watervliet Hospital, Watervliet, MI, p. A340
HARMON, David, D.O., Vice President Medical Services, Rivervalley Behavioral Health Hospital, Owensboro, KY, p. A272
HARMON, James
Information Technology, Cypress Creek Hospital, Houston, TX, p. A625
Network Administrator, West Oaks Hospital, Houston, TX, p. A629
HARMON, Jennifer, Director of Human Resources, Orlando Health St. Cloud Hospital, Saint Cloud, FL, p. A148
HARMON, Thomas, M.D., Vice President Medical Affairs, Ohiohealth Riverside Methodist Hospital, Columbus, OH, p. A492
HARMS, Arlene, Chief Executive Officer, Rio Grande Hospital, Del Norte, CO, p. A106
HARMS, George, Chief Financial Officer, Pawnee Valley Community Hospital, Larned, KS, p. A253
HARNED, Barbara, R.N., MSN, Chief Nursing Officer, Monroe County Hospital, Monroeville, AL, p. A22
HARNESS, Phil, Chief Executive Officer, Doctor's Hospital, Leawood, KS, p. A253
HARNEY, Geraldine, Chief Financial Officer, U. S. Public Health Service Phoenix Indian Medical Center, Phoenix, AZ, p. A37
HARNEY, Sean Patrick, Chief Medical Officer, Employed Provider Clinics, Lewis County General Hospital, Lowville, NY, p. A445
HARPER, Cindy, Manager Patient Data, Westfield Memorial Hospital, Westfield, NY, p. A462
HARPER, David
Chief Information Officer, Wills Memorial Hospital, Washington, GA, p. A174
Director, Site Information Systems, Carle Eureka Hospital, Eureka, IL, p. A194
HARPER, James F, Senior Vice President and Chief Human Resources Officer, Tidelands Georgetown Memorial Hospital, Georgetown, SC, p. A566
HARPER, Kirk, R.N., Chief Nursing Officer, Kadlec Regional Medical Center, Richland, WA, p. A694
HARPER, R Andrew, M.D., Medical Director, Uthealth Harris County Psychiatric Center, Houston, TX, p. A628
HARPER, Ryan, Chief Operating Officer, Carondelet St. Mary's Hospital, Tucson, AZ, p. A40
HARPER, Shirley, Chief Financial Officer, Mercy Health – Clermont Hospital, Batavia, OH, p. A486
HARPER, Wally G, Vice President Human Resources, Gaylord Specialty Healthcare, Wallingford, CT, p. A119
HARPER, William F, M.D., Chief of Staff, Birmingham Va Medical Center, Birmingham, AL, p. A16
HARREL, Mark, Chief Executive Officer, Phelp. Memorial Health Center, Holdrege, NE, p. A401
HARRELL, Aaron, Director, Grove Hill Memorial Hospital, Grove Hill, AL, p. A20
HARRELL, Dale E., Commander, 88th Medical Group. Wright–Patterson AFB, Wright Patterson Medical Center, Wright–Patterson Afb, OH, p. A507
HARRELL, Joy, R.N., Chief Nursing Officer, Mimbres Memorial Hospital, Deming, NM, p. A434
HARRELL, Michael, R.N., Chief Executive Officer, Riverbridge Specialty Hospital, Vidalia, LA, p. A294
HARRELL, Paula, Chief Nursing Officer, Regional One Health Extended Care Hospital, Memphis, TN, p. A589
HARRELL, Steven W, FACHE, Chief Operating Officer, Adventhealth New Smyrna Beach, New Smyrna Beach, FL, p. A142
HARRER, Seth, M.D., Chief of Staff, Buena Vista Regional Medical Center, Storm Lake, IA, p. A244
HARRIER, Margie
MSN, R.N., Medical Center Chief Operations Officer, Kaiser Permanente Orange County Anaheim Medical Center, Anaheim, CA, p. A55
MSN, R.N., Senior Vice President/Area Manager, South Bay, Kaiser Permanente South Bay Medical Center, Los Angeles, CA, p. A73
HARRILSON, Annette, Chief Clinical Officer, Select Specialty Hospital Midtown Atlanta, Atlanta, GA, p. A158
HARRINGTON, Dawn, Chief Information Officer, University of New Mexico Hospitals, Albuquerque, NM, p. A433
HARRINGTON, Georgia, Senior Vice President and Chief Operations Officer, Centra Lynchburg General Hospital, Lynchburg, VA, p. A678
HARRINGTON, Hal, Vice President Human Resources, Merit Health River Region, Vicksburg, MS, p. A369
HARRINGTON, Jason, FACHE, President and Chief Executive Officer, Lakes Regional Healthcare, Spirit Lake, IA, p. A244
HARRINGTON, Jeff
Senior Vice President, Chief Financial Officer, Children's Hospital Colorado – Colorado Springs, Colorado Springs, CO, p. A105
Senior Vice President, Chief Financial Officer, Children's Hospital Colorado, Aurora, CO, p. A103
HARRINGTON, Jennifer, Chief Operating Officer, Luminis Health Anne Arundel Medical Center, Annapolis, MD, p. A300
HARRINGTON, Kathleen, Vice President Human Resources, Beth Israel Deaconess Hospital–Milton, Milton, MA, p. A316
HARRINGTON, Lane, Chief Nursing Officer, Upson Regional Medical Center, Thomaston, GA, p. A172
HARRIS, Alicia, Director Fiscal Services, Mississipp. State Hospital, Whitfield, MS, p. A370
HARRIS, Allen, M.D., Clinical Director, South Mississipp. State Hospital, Purvis, MS, p. A368
HARRIS, Angela, Chief Executive Officer, Riverwoods Behavioral Health System, Riverdale, GA, p. A170
HARRIS, Ben, Chief Executive Officer, HCA Florida Kendall Hospital, Miami, FL, p. A139
HARRIS, Betty J, Director Human Resources, Southern California Hospital At Culver City, Culver City, CA, p. A61
HARRIS, Burt
Chief Financial Officer, Canyon Ridge Hospital, Chino, CA, p. A59
Chief Financial Officer, Fort Lauderdale Behavioral Health Center, Oakland Park, FL, p. A143
HARRIS, C Martin
M.D., Chief Information Officer, Cleveland Clinic Children's Hospital for Rehabilitation, Cleveland, OH, p. A490
M.D., Chief Information Officer, Cleveland Clinic Fairview Hospital, Cleveland, OH, p. A490
M.D., Chief Information Officer, Cleveland Clinic Lutheran Hospital, Cleveland, OH, p. A490
HARRIS, Charles, Chief Executive Officer, Natividad, Salinas, CA, p. A88
HARRIS, Darian, Chief Executive Officer, Mills–Peninsula Medical Center, Burlingame, CA, p. A58
HARRIS, Donna, Chief Executive Officer, Encompass Health Rehabilitation Hospital of Waco, Robinson, TX, p. A647
HARRIS, Dory, Director Human Resource, Teton Valley Health Care, Driggs, ID, p. A181
HARRIS, Ethan, Manager Information Systems, Mid–Valley Hospital And Clinics, Omak, WA, p. A692
HARRIS, Jan, R.N., Director of Nursing, Stonewall Memorial Hospital, Aspermont, TX, p. A598
HARRIS, Janice M, Director Human Resources, University Medical Center of El Paso, El Paso, TX, p. A617
HARRIS, Jen, Director Health Information Management, Chase County Community Hospital, Imperial, NE, p. A401
HARRIS, Jerald, Chief Information Officer, Vibra Hospital of Clear Lake, Webster, TX, p. A661
HARRIS, Jim, Director Information Technology, Grafton City Hospital, Grafton, WV, p. A701
HARRIS, Jo ell, R.N., Chief Nursing Officer, Forest View Psychiatric Hospital, Grand Rapids, MI, p. A328
HARRIS, John, Chief Executive Officer, Memorial Medical Center, Las Cruces, NM, p. A435
HARRIS, John B., Vice President Finance and Chief Financial Officer, Community Hospital Anderson, Anderson, IN, p. A212
HARRIS, Julie
Chief Financial Officer, Riceland Medical Center, Winnie, TX, p. A663
Controller, Anmed Rehabilitation Hospital, Anderson, SC, p. A562
HARRIS, Karen, R.N., Chief Nursing and Operations Officer, Henry Ford West Bloomfield Hospital, West Bloomfield, MI, p. A340
HARRIS, Kathy, Vice President, Mercyhealth Hospital And Trauma Center – Janesville, Janesville, WI, p. A713
HARRIS, Kevin, Director Information Systems, Titus Regional Medical Center, Mount Pleasant, TX, p. A640
HARRIS, Laci, MSN, R.N., Chief Executive Officer, Crane Memorial Hospital, Crane, TX, p. A609
HARRIS, Laurie, Chief Accountant, Kerrville State Hospital, Kerrville, TX, p. A632
HARRIS, Lee, Assistant Administrator Support Services, Memorial Hospital And Manor, Bainbridge, GA, p. A159
HARRIS, Leslie, MSN, R.N., Chief Nursing Officer, Forrest City Medical Center, Forrest City, AR, p. A46
HARRIS, Lisa E., M.D., Chief Executive Officer, Eskenazi Health, Indianapolis, IN, p. A219
HARRIS, Mark D, Deputy Commander Clinical Services, Fort Belvoir Community Hospital, Fort Belvoir, VA, p. A676
HARRIS, Miriam, Director Finance, Oklahoma Forensic Center, Vinita, OK, p. A523
HARRIS, Parker, Chief Executive Officer and Administrator, Baptist Memorial Hospital–Tipton, Covington, TN, p. A582
HARRIS, R Brian, M.D., Chief of Staff, Reeves Memorial Medical Center, Bernice, LA, p. A278
HARRIS, Robert M, M.D., President Medical and Dental Staff, Bergen New Bridge Medical Center, Paramus, NJ, p. A426
HARRIS, Ryan, Chief Executive Officer, Mayers Memorial Hospital District, Fall River Mills, CA, p. A63
HARRIS, Shelly, Chief Executive Officer, Quentin N. Burdick Memorial Healthcare Facility, Belcourt, ND, p. A479
HARRIS, Shirley, M.D., President Medical Staff, Mosaic Medical Center – Maryville, Maryville, MO, p. A380
HARRIS, Spencer, Chief Financial Officer, Kadlec Regional Medical Center, Richland, WA, p. A694
HARRIS, Stuart, M.D., Chief of Staff, Trigg County Hospital, Cadiz, KY, p. A264
HARRIS, Susan
R.N., Chief Operating Officer, Atrium Health Navicent The Medical Center, Macon, GA, p. A167
Director Fiscal Services, Shriners Children's Ohio, Dayton, OH, p. A494
HARRIS, Sylvia, Fiscal Director, Moccasin Bend Mental Health Institute, Chattanooga, TN, p. A580
HARRIS, Thomas, Chief Operating POfficer, Gillette Children's Specialty Healthcare, Saint Paul, MN, p. A354
HARRIS, Timothy, M.D., Chief Quality Officer, Texas Health Presbyterian Hospital Denton, Denton, TX, p. A614
HARRIS, Vena, Director Human Resources, Minneola District Hospital, Minneola, KS, p. A255
HARRIS, William R, Chief Information Officer, Lawton Indian Hospital, Lawton, OK, p. A514
HARRIS, Z. Leah, M.D., Chief Physician, Dell Children's Medical Center of Central Texas, Austin, TX, p. A600
HARRISON, Bruce, Chief Executive Officer, Iron County Medical Center, Pilot Knob, MO, p. A382
HARRISON, Chris, Manager Information Systems, Campbell County Health, Gillette, WY, p. A727
HARRISON, Denise, Associate Director, Omaha Va Medical Center, Omaha, NE, p. A404
HARRISON, Douglass, Chief Executive Officer, Wheeling Hospital, Wheeling, WV, p. A706
HARRISON, Dyan, Manager Health Information, Ochiltree General Hospital, Perryton, TX, p. A643
HARRISON, George E., M.D., Chief Medical Officer, Fairview Park Hospital, Dublin, GA, p. A163
HARRISON, Jeffrey, Market Chief Executive Officer, Kindred Hospital Bay Area–Tampa, Tampa, FL, p. A152
HARRISON, Jo L, Vice President of Patient Care Services, Southwest Medical Center, Liberal, KS, p. A253
HARRISON, Kathleen, Chief Executive Officer, Tidalhealth Peninsula Regional, Salisbury, MD, p. A307
HARRISON, Mary, Interim Health Director, Choctaw Health Center, Philadelphia, MS, p. A367
HARRISON, Nicole, R.N., CNO, Tirr Memorial Hermann, Houston, TX, p. A628
HARRISON, Pam
MSN, Chief Executive Officer, Continuecare Hospital At Baptist Health Corbin, Corbin, KY, p. A264
MSN, Chief Nursing Officer, Continuecare Hospital At Baptist Health Corbin, Corbin, KY, p. A264
HARRISON, Randy, Chief Financial Officer, Raleigh General Hospital, Beckley, WV, p. A699
HARRISON, Theresa M., Site Director, Dr. Solomon Carter Fuller Mental Health Center, Boston, MA, p. A310

A868 Index of Health Care Professionals

Index of Health Care Professionals / Haushalter

Index of Health Care Professionals

HARRON, Rick, Chief Financial Officer, Dominican Hospital, Santa Cruz, CA, p. A94
HARROP, Elizabeth, Director, Human Resources, Marshfield Medical Center – Park Falls, Park Falls, WI, p. A719
HARROP, Phil, Chief Executive Officer, Integris Southwest Medical Center, Oklahoma City, OK, p. A517
HARSHAWAT, Paras, M.D., Medical Director, Harsha Behavioral Center, Terre Haute, IN, p. A228
HARSHAWAT, Roopam, President and Chief Executive Officer, Harsha Behavioral Center, Terre Haute, IN, p. A228
HARSY, Brice, Chief Financial Officer, Marshall Browning Hospital, Du Quoin, IL, p. A193
HART, Amy, Chief Executive Officer, Cuyuna Regional Medical Center, Crosby, MN, p. A345
HART, Betsy, Chief Executive Officer, Glendale Memorial Hospital And Health Center, Glendale, CA, p. A66
HART, Denise, Director Human Resources, Sullivan County Community Hospital, Sullivan, IN, p. A227
HART, Donna, Chief Information Officer, Provident Hospital of Cook County, Chicago, IL, p. A190
HART, Elizabeth, R.N., MSN, Chief Nursing Officer, Providence Saint Josep. Medical Center, Burbank, CA, p. A58
HART, Gary, M.D., Chief Medical Officer, Cody Regional Health, Cody, WY, p. A726
HART, James, M.D., Medical Director, Rolling Hills Hospital, Franklin, TN, p. A583
HART, John, Chief Executive Officer, Wray Community District Hospital, Wray, CO, p. A114
HART, Joline, Vice President Human Resources, Franklin Memorial Hospital, Farmington, ME, p. A297
HART, Joseph, Director Finance and Support Services, Putnam Hospital, Carmel, NY, p. A441
HART, Lisa, Chief Executive Officer, Elkview General Hospital, Hobart, OK, p. A513
HART, Mike, System Assistant Vice President, Information Systems, Hendrick Medical Center, Abilene, TX, p. A595
HART, Monique, Chief Financial Officer, Baptist Memorial Hospital–Tipton, Covington, TN, p. A582
HART, Pat, Director Human Resources, Three Rivers Medical Center, Louisa, KY, p. A269
HART, Randy F., Manager, Information Technology Regional Operations, Indian Path Community Hospital, Kingsport, TN, p. A585
HART, Scott, Controller, Encompass Health Rehabilitation Hospital of Lakeview, Elizabethtown, KY, p. A265
HART, Susan, Chief Executive Officer, Encompass Health Cardinal Hill Rehabilitation Hospital, Lexington, KY, p. A268
HART–FLYNN, Wilma, Ph.D., R.N., Chief Nursing Officer, Morristown–Hamblen Healthcare System, Morristown, TN, p. A589
HARTBERG, David, Chief Executive Officer, Vernon Memorial Healthcare, Elk Mound, WI, p. A710
HARTE, Brian J.
M.D., President, Cleveland Clinic Akron General, Akron, OH, p. A484
M.D., President, Cleveland Clinic Akron General Lodi Hospital, Lodi, OH, p. A498
HARTGRAVES, Steve L.
Chief Executive Officer, Harmon Memorial Hospital, Hollis, OK, p. A513
President and Chief Executive Officer, Jackson County Memorial Hospital, Altus, OK, p. A509
HARTKE, Michael, President, Endeavor Health Northwest Community Hospital, Arlington Heights, IL, p. A185
HARTL, Sharon, Chief Executive Officer, Encompass Health Rehabilitation Hospital of Concord, Concord, NH, p. A414
HARTLEY, Barbara, Chief Medical Officer, Benson Hospital, Benson, AZ, p. A30
HARTLEY, Diane L, Director of Patient Care Services, Corewell Health Wayne Hospital, Wayne, MI, p. A340
HARTLEY, Michael, MS, Chief Nursing Officer, Holly Hill Hospital, Raleigh, NC, p. A474
HARTLEY, Randall W, Chief Operating Officer, Nemours Children's Hospital, Orlando, FL, p. A144
HARTLEY, Shauna, Administrator, Turquoise Lodge Hospital, Albuquerque, NM, p. A433
HARTLEY, Shawn, Chief Financial Officer, UNC Health Nash, Rocky Mount, NC, p. A475
HARTLEY, Wannah, Controller, Winkler County Memorial Hospital, Kermit, TX, p. A632
HARTMAN, Don, Director Human Resources, Sutter Davis Hospital, Davis, CA, p. A61
HARTMAN, Mark, Interim Chief Financial Officer, St. Josep. Medical Center, Houston, TX, p. A628
HARTMAN, Sally, Senior Vice President, Riverside Regional Medical Center, Newport News, VA, p. A680
HARTMANN, Doreen, Chief Financial Officer, St. Joseph's Behavioral Health Center, Stockton, CA, p. A97
HARTMANN, Peter M, M.D., Vice President Medical Affairs, Wellspan York Hospital, York, PA, p. A559
HARTMANN, Rob, Assistant Director Human Resources Management, Ochsner Lsu Health Shreveport – Monroe Medical Center, Monroe, LA, p. A288
HARTNETT, Tammy, Employee Relations Manager, Unitypoint Health – St. Lukes's Sioux City, Sioux City, IA, p. A243
HARTSELL, Henry, Ph.D., Executive Director, Griffin Memorial Hospital, Norman, OK, p. A516
HARTSELL, Scott, Chief Operating Officer, Tamp. General Hospital Brooksville, Brooksville, FL, p. A127
HARTSOCK, Aaron, Associate Vice President, Clinical Operations, Western Region, Geisinger Lewistown Hospital, Lewistown, PA, p. A544
HARTUNG, Andy, Assistant Vice President of Information Systems and Chief Information Officer, Self Regional Healthcare, Greenwood, SC, p. A567
HARTWELL, Tim, Chief Human Resources, Marion Veterans Affairs Medical Center, Marion, IL, p. A200
HARTWICK, Bryan
Vice President Human Resources, Alton Memorial Hospital, Alton, IL, p. A185
Vice President Human Resources, Christian Hospital, Saint Louis, MO, p. A385
HARTWIG, Michael, M.D., Esq, Chief of Staff, Stillwater Medical Perry, Perry, OK, p. A519
HARTZ, Kimberly, Chief Executive Officer, Washington Hospital Healthcare System, Fremont, CA, p. A64
HARTZOG, Rick, Chief Information Officer, Merit Health Madison, Canton, MS, p. A360
HARVEY, Alisha, Director of Finance, Houston County Community Hospital, Erin, TN, p. A582
HARVEY, Jennifer, Director Human Resources, Golden Plains Community Hospital, Borger, TX, p. A604
HARVEY, John
M.D., Chief Executive Officer, Oklahoma Heart Hospital, Oklahoma City, OK, p. A518
M.D., Chief Executive Officer, Oklahoma Heart Hospital South Campus, Oklahoma City, OK, p. A518
HARVEY, Kathy, D.O., Chief Medical Officer, Logan Regional Medical Center, Logan, WV, p. A702
HARVEY, Linda, Chief Financial Officer, West Feliciana Hospital, Saint Francisville, LA, p. A292
HARVEY, Michael, FACHE, President and Chief Executive Officer, Syracuse Area Health, Syracuse, NE, p. A406
HARVEY, Paul
President and Chief Executive Officer, Christus Mother Frances Hospital – Winnsboro, Winnsboro, TX, p. A663
President/Chief Executive Officer, Christus Mother Frances Hospital – Sulphur Springs, Sulphur Springs, TX, p. A655
HARVILL, Brian
President, ECU Health Bertie Hospital, Windsor, NC, p. A478
President, ECU Health Chowan Hospital, Edenton, NC, p. A467
President, ECU Health Roanoke–Chowan Hospital, Ahoskie, NC, p. A463
HARVIN, Schley, Information Technology Technician, Hood Memorial Hospital, Amite, LA, p. A276
HARWOOD, Daniel, M.D., Chief of Staff, Trinity Hospital, Weaverville, CA, p. A101
HASBROUCK, Matthew Steven., Chief Executive Officer, St. Mark's Hospital, Salt Lake City, UT, p. A669
HASHMI, Mubashir, Chief Information Officer, Pacifica Hospital of The Valley, Los Angeles, CA, p. A74
HASKELL, Jeffrey, M.D., Chief Medical Staff, Lost Rivers Medical Center, Arco, ID, p. A179
HASKETT, Russ, Vice President Information Technology, Eagle View Behavioral Health, Bettendorf, IA, p. A230
HASKINS, Don, Administrative Director Human Resources, Southwest Mississipp. Regional Medical Center, Mccomb, MS, p. A366
HASLETT, Tom, Interim Chief Information Officer, Macneal Hospital, Berwyn, IL, p. A186
HASNI, Kamran, M.D., Chief of Medical Staff, Barbourville Arh Hospital, Barbourville, KY, p. A263
HASS, Roxanne, Director of Nursing, Chi St. Josep. Health Madison Hospital, Madisonville, TX, p. A637
HASSAN, Tariq, M.D., Associate Director of Patient Care, Captain James A. Lovell Federal Health Care Center, North Chicago, IL, p. A203
HASSANI, Dahlia, Vice President of Medical Affairs, Baylor Scott & White All Saints Medical Center – Fort Worth, Fort Worth, TX, p. A619
HASSELBRACK, Jeni, Director Human Resources, Adventhealth Gordon, Calhoun, GA, p. A160
HASSELL, Michael, Chief Executive Officer, Melissa Memorial Hospital, Holyoke, CO, p. A109
HAST, Anne S., R.N., Chief Executive Officer, Advanced Surgical Hospital, Washington, PA, p. A556
HASTIN–HULSEY, Kathy, Administrative Assistant Human Resources, Dardanelle Regional Medical Center, Dardanelle, AR, p. A45
HASTINGS, Clare, R.N., Ph.D., Chief Nurse Officer, Nih Clinical Center, Bethesda, MD, p. A302
HASTINGS, Elaine, MSN, R.N., Chief Nursing Officer, Piedmont Medical Center, Rock Hill, SC, p. A570
HASTINGS, Sarah, Chief Human Resources Officer, Abrazo Arrowhead Campus, Glendale, AZ, p. A32
HASTINGS, Sarah M, Executive Director, Ridgeview Medical Center, Waconia, MN, p. A356
HATCH, Brooke, Director Human Resource, Bradley County Medical Center, Warren, AR, p. A54
HATCH, Tammy, Manager, Northern Light Sebasticook Valley Hospital, Pittsfield, ME, p. A298
HATCHEL, Kimberly Kay, Senior Vice President, Chief Operating Officer, Bronson Methodist Hospital, Kalamazoo, MI, p. A331
HATCHER, Amy, Executive Vice President and Chief Financial Officer, Children's Nebraska, Omaha, NE, p. A404
HATCHER, Julie, Vice President Human Resources, O'Connor Hospital, San Jose, CA, p. A92
HATCHES, Ann
Director, Human Resources, Holy Cross Hospital, Chicago, IL, p. A189
Interim Director Human Resources, Mount Sinai Hospital, Chicago, IL, p. A190
HATFIELD, Jesse, M.D., Chief Medical Officer, Mercy Hospital Joplin, Joplin, MO, p. A377
HATFIELD, Jonathan
Chief Executive Officer, Klickitat Valley Health, Goldendale, WA, p. A690
Supervisor Information Technology, Klickitat Valley Health, Goldendale, WA, p. A690
HATFIELD, Rhonda, Chief Nursing Officer and Vice President of Clinical Operations, Chi Memorial, Chattanooga, TN, p. A580
HATHCOCK, Claudette
Administrative Director Human Resources, University of Mississipp. Medical Center Grenada, Grenada, MS, p. A362
Human Resources Director, University of Mississipp. Medical Center Holmes County, Lexington, MS, p. A365
HATIC, Safet, M.D., President Medical Staff, Wayne Healthcare, Greenville, OH, p. A497
HATIRAS, Spiros, FACHE, President and Chief Executive Officer, Holyoke Medical Center, Holyoke, MA, p. A314
HATLESTAD, Jill, Vice President Human Resources and Marketing, Glencoe Regional Health, Glencoe, MN, p. A347
HATMAKER, Michael, Vice President Support Services and Admin Nursing Home, Leconte Medical Center, Sevierville, TN, p. A593
HATTEM–SCHIFFMAN, Marita
FACHE, Regional President, Mymichigan Medical Center Alma, Alma, MI, p. A321
FACHE, Regional President, Mymichigan Medical Center Clare, Clare, MI, p. A324
HATTER, Jason, Chief Human Resource Officer, Princeton Baptist Medical Center, Birmingham, AL, p. A17
HATTERER–HOAG, Dawn, Director Human Resources, Psychiatric Institute of Washington, Washington, DC, p. A124
HATTON, Cathy, Interim Chief Hospital Executive, Valley Community Hospital, Pauls Valley, OK, p. A519
HATTON, Tad, Vice President Chief Operating Officer, Ascension Seton Medical Center Austin, Austin, TX, p. A599
HAUBL, Eileen, Senior Vice President and Chief Financial Officer, Providence Mission Hospital Mission Viejo, Mission Viejo, CA, p. A77
HAUG, Darin L., D.O., Chief Medical Officer, Fitzgibbon Hospital, Marshall, MO, p. A380
HAUGE, Meri, R.N., MSN, Associate Director of Patient Care Services and Nurse Executive, St. Cloud Va Health Care System, Saint Cloud, MN, p. A354
HAUGER, Clint, Chief Executive Officer, North Tamp. Behavioral Health, Wesley Chapel, FL, p. A154
HAUGHEY, Tracie, Chief Executive Officer and Chief Financial Officer, Wills Memorial Hospital, Washington, GA, p. A174
HAUPERT, John M., FACHE, President and Chief Executive Officer, Grady Health System, Atlanta, GA, p. A157
HAUPT, Carolyn, Chief Financial Officer, Peacehealth United General Medical Center, Sedro–Woolley, WA, p. A695
HAUSAUER, Patricia K, Director Finance, Baptist Medical Center Nassau, Fernandina Beach, FL, p. A131
HAUSER, Claudia, Chief Executive Officer, Pam Rehabilitation Hospital of Clear Lake, Webster, TX, p. A661
HAUSER, Megan, Director Human Resources, Shriners Children's Philadelphia, Philadelphia, PA, p. A550
HAUSHALTER, Richard L, Senior Vice President Operations and Chief Operating Officer, Sentara Rmh Medical Center, Harrisonburg, VA, p. A677

© 2025 AHA Guide Index of Health Care Professionals **A869**

Index of Health Care Professionals

Index of Health Care Professionals / Hausmann

HAUSMANN, Jena, President and Chief Executive Officer, Children's Hospital Colorado, Aurora, CO, p. A103
HAUSMANN, Lisa, President and Chief Executive Officer, Mercy Hospital of Folsom, Folsom, CA, p. A63
HAVARD, Greg, Chief Executive Officer, George Regional Hospital, Lucedale, MS, p. A365
HAVEN, Adrian C, Site Manager, Gallup Indian Medical Center, Gallup. NM, p. A434
HAVENHILL–JACOBS, Tamara, Chief Information Officer, Bozeman Health Deaconess Regional Medical Center, Bozeman, MT, p. A390
HAVENS, Derek, Interim President, Chi Health Mercy Council Bluffs, Council Bluffs, IA, p. A233
HAVENS, Jennifer, R.N., FACHE, Market President, UnityPoint Health – Dubuque, Unitypoint Health – Finley Hospital, Dubuque, IA, p. A235
HAVERICAK, Heather, Chief Executive Officer, Delray Medical Center, Delray Beach, FL, p. A130
HAVERLY, Kim, Chief Executive Officer, Carroll County Memorial Hospital, Carrollton, KY, p. A264
HAVERSTOCK, Loren, Manager Human Resources, Harrison County Hospital, Corydon, IN, p. A214
HAVRILLA, David A, Chief Financial Officer, Medstar Montgomery Medical Center, Olney, MD, p. A306
HAWIG, Scott
Senior Vice President Finance, Chief Financial Officer and Treasurer, Froedtert And The Medical College of Wisconsin Froedtert Hospital, Milwaukee, WI, p. A717
Senior Vice President Finance, Chief Financial Officer and Treasurer, Froedtert Community Hospital – New Berlin, New Berlin, WI, p. A718
Senior Vice President of Finance, Chief Financial Officer and Treasurer, Froedtert Menomonee Falls Hospital, Menomonee Falls, WI, p. A716
Senior Vice President of Finance, Chief Financial Officer and Treasurer, Froedtert West Bend Hospital, West Bend, WI, p. A724
HAWKEY, Tammy, Manager Information Technology Client Services, Marshfield Medical Center – Weston, Weston, WI, p. A725
HAWKINS, Bryan, Controller, Firsthealth Montgomery Memorial Hospital, Troy, NC, p. A477
HAWKINS, Cynthia, Chief Human Resources Officer, Saint Elizabeths Hospital, Washington, DC, p. A124
HAWKINS, Ellis, FACHE, President, Ascension Saint Mary – Chicago, Chicago, IL, p. A188
HAWKINS, Jason F.
Chief Administrative Officer, Peacehealth Cottage Grove Community Medical Center, Cottage Grove, OR, p. A526
Chief Administrative Officer, Peacehealth Peace Harbor Medical Center, Florence, OR, p. A527
HAWKINS, Julie, MSN, R.N., Chief Nursing Officer, Witham Health Services, Lebanon, IN, p. A222
HAWKINS, Sheri, Chief Nursing Officer, Adventhealth Shawnee Mission, Merriam, KS, p. A255
HAWKINS, Tami, R.N., MSN, Vice President Patient Care and Chief Nursing Officer, Texas Health Hospital Rockwall, Rockwall, TX, p. A647
HAWKINSON, Curtis R., Chief Executive Officer, Community Memorial Healthcare, Marysville, KS, p. A254
HAWLEY, Gina, Dr.PH, Chief Operating Officer, University of Utah Health, Salt Lake City, UT, p. A669
HAWLEY, Jason, Director of Information Services and Security, Yuma District Hospital, Yuma, CO, p. A114
HAWS, Bradley, Chief Executive Officer, University of Iowa Hospitals & Clinics, Iowa City, IA, p. A238
HAWTHORNE, Caryn, Vice President Finance and Chief Finance Officer, East Tennessee Children's Hospital, Knoxville, TN, p. A585
HAWTOF, Jeffrey, M.D., Vice President Medical Operations and Informatics, Beebe Healthcare, Lewes, DE, p. A121
HAY, Fraser, FACHE, President, Texas Health Presbyterian Hospital Plano, Plano, TX, p. A645
HAYDEN, Crystal, FACHE, R.N., President and Chief Executive Officer, UNC Health Lenoir, Kinston, NC, p. A471
HAYDEN, James, M.D., Chief Medical Officer, Penn Highlands Huntingdon, Huntingdon, PA, p. A542
HAYDEN, Jamie, Chief Financial Officer, Eastland Memorial Hospital, Eastland, TX, p. A615
HAYDEN, John
Senior Vice President and Chief Human Resources Officer, Bronson Lakeview Hospital, Paw Paw, MI, p. A335
Senior Vice President and Human Resources Officer, Bronson Battle Creek Hospital, Battle Creek, MI, p. A322
Vice President and Chief Human Resources Officer, Bronson Methodist Hospital, Kalamazoo, MI, p. A331
HAYDEN, Karen, Director Health Information Services, Performance Improvement and Risk Management, Valle Vista Health System, Greenwood, IN, p. A218
HAYDEN–PUGH, Beverly P., R.N., Senior Vice President and Chief Nursing Officer, Valley Children's Healthcare, Madera, CA, p. A76
HAYES, Amy Christine, Chief Nursing Officer, Encompass Health Rehabilitation Hospital of North Tampa, Lutz, FL, p. A138
HAYES, David R, Chief Financial Officer, T.J. Health Columbia, Columbia, KY, p. A264
HAYES, Deborah, R.N., MS, MSN, President and Chief Executive Officer, The Christ Hospital Health Network, Cincinnati, OH, p. A489
HAYES, Donald, Chief Financial Officer, Wythe County Community Hospital, Wytheville, VA, p. A686
HAYES, Elaine, Controller, Uofl Health – Mary And Elizabeth Hospital, Louisville, KY, p. A270
HAYES, Farrell, Chief Financial Officer, Chi Memorial Hospital – Georgia, Fort Oglethorpe, GA, p. A164
HAYES, James L, Director Human Resources, Western State Hospital, Hopkinsville, KY, p. A267
HAYES, Jo, Chief Nursing Officer, Horn Memorial Hospital, Ida Grove, IA, p. A237
HAYES, Kevin, M.D., Chief of Staff, Monroe Regional Hospital, Aberdeen, MS, p. A359
HAYES, Lisa G., Chief Clinical Officer, Central Indiana Amg Specialty Hospital, Muncie, IN, p. A224
HAYES, Lynnette, Chief Nursing Officer, Golden Valley Memorial Healthcare, Clinton, MO, p. A373
HAYES, Sharon, Chief Executive Officer, Encompass Health Rehabilitation Hospital of Lakeland, Lakeland, FL, p. A136
HAYES, Stacy, R.N., Chief Nursing Officer, Arizona Spine And Joint Hospital, Mesa, AZ, p. A33
HAYES, Susan, Director Human Resources, UNC Health Southeastern, Lumberton, NC, p. A472
HAYES, Tammy A., R.N., MS, Chief Nurse Executive, Hospital and Long Term Care Center Administrator, Northfield Hospital And Clinics, Northfield, MN, p. A352
HAYES, Warren, Chief of Staff, Montgomery County Memorial Hospital, Red Oak, IA, p. A242
HAYES, William M., Chief Executive Officer, Northside Hospital Cherokee, Canton, GA, p. A160
HAYGOOD, Rachel Joy, Director Information Technology, Tyler County Hospital, Woodville, TX, p. A663
HAYHURST, Leslie, Director Information Systems, UPMC Greene, Waynesburg, PA, p. A556
HAYN, Jed, Chief Information Officer, Walter B. Jones Alcohol And Drug Abuse Treatment Center, Greenville, NC, p. A470
HAYNES, Deatosha D., Interim Associates Director for Patient, Biloxi Va Medical Center, Biloxi, MS, p. A359
HAYNES, Elaine S, R.N., MSN, Vice President Patient Services and Chief Nursing Executive, Atrium Health Lincoln, Lincolnton, NC, p. A472
HAYNES, Jamil, Regional Director Human Resources, Integris Miami Hospital, Miami, OK, p. A515
HAYNES, Jill, Financial Coach, Bath Veterans Affairs Medical Center, Bath, NY, p. A439
HAYNES, John H, M.D., Jr, Chief of Medical Staff, North Caddo Medical Center, Vivian, LA, p. A294
HAYNES, Laurie, Chief Financial Officer, HCA Florida Gulf Coast Hospital, Panama City, FL, p. A146
HAYNES, Mark, M.D., Chief of Staff, Claiborne Memorial Medical Center, Homer, LA, p. A283
HAYNES, Robert Gerard., FACHE, Chief Executive Officer, Guadalup. Regional Medical Center, Seguin, TX, p. A652
HAYNES, Tina, Chief Executive Officer, Claiborne Memorial Medical Center, Homer, LA, p. A283
HAYNES, William, Director Information Technology, Central Louisiana State Hospital, Pineville, LA, p. A291
HAYREH, Davinder, M.D., Medical Director, St. Louis Forensic Treatment Center, Saint Louis, MO, p. A384
HAYS, Chuck, President and Chief Executive Officer, Mainegeneral Medical Center, Augusta, ME, p. A295
HAYS, Kathie, MSN, R.N., Chief Nursing Officer, West Chester Hospital, West Chester, OH, p. A506
HAYS, Larry, Director Information Technology, Southern Virginia Mental Health Institute, Danville, VA, p. A675
HAYS, Richard, M.D., Chief Medical Officer, Wellington Regional Medical Center, Wellington, FL, p. A154
HAYS, Richard O, Chief Fiscal Service, North Las Vegas Va Medical Center, North Las Vegas, NV, p. A412
HAYS, Timothy A, Vice President Human Resources, UNC Health Johnston, Smithfield, NC, p. A476
HAYTAIAN, Mike, Head Director Information Resources Management, Naval Hospital Jacksonville, Jacksonville, FL, p. A135
HAYWOOD, Nancy
Chief Financial Officer, Ascension Genesys Hospital, Grand Blanc, MI, p. A327
Chief Financial Officer, Mymichigan Medical Center Saginaw, Saginaw, MI, p. A337
HAYWOOD, Stephanie, Director Human Resources, Southern Virginia Mental Health Institute, Danville, VA, p. A675
HAZELBAKER, Matthew, M.D., President Medical Staff, Memorial Health, Marysville, OH, p. A499
HEAD, David, M.D., Chief Medical Staff, Norton Sound Regional Hospital, Nome, AK, p. A29
HEAD, Susan, Director Nursing Services, Blackfeet Community Hospital, Saint Mary, MT, p. A395
HEALEY, Lauren, Human Resources Director, Encompass Health Rehabilitation Hospital of New England, Woburn, MA, p. A320
HEALY, John, Manager Information Technology, Friends Hospital, Philadelphia, PA, p. A548
HEALY, Peter J., Divisional President, Metro Boston and President of Beth Israel Deaconess Medical Center, Beth Israel Deaconess Medical Center, Boston, MA, p. A309
HEALY–COLLIER, Kathy, President, Mercy Health – Anderson Hospital, Cincinnati, OH, p. A489
HEARD, Alex, M.D., Chief Medical Officer, Falmouth Hospital, Falmouth, MA, p. A313
HEARD, Charles, M.D., Chief of Staff, Orlando Health Orlando Regional Medical Center, Orlando, FL, p. A144
HEARD, Heather, Director Human Resources, Holdenville General Hospital, Holdenville, OK, p. A513
HEARD, John E., Chief Executive Officer, Chicot Memorial Medical Center, Lake Village, AR, p. A49
HEARD, M Denise, Director Business Services, North Mississipp. Medical Center–Pontotoc, Pontotoc, MS, p. A368
HEARING, Tim, Associate Information Technology Director, HCA Florida Raulerson Hospital, Okeechobee, FL, p. A143
HEARNE, Diane, Director Human Resources, Arizona Spine And Joint Hospital, Mesa, AZ, p. A33
HEARNSBERGER, John
M.D., Chief of Staff, Howard Memorial Hospital, Nashville, AR, p. A51
M.D., Interim Chief Executive Officer, Howard Memorial Hospital, Nashville, AR, p. A51
HEATH, Benjamin, Chief Financial Officer, Cedar Ridge, Oklahoma City, OK, p. A516
HEATH, Ed, FACHE, Chief Executive Officer, Owensboro Health Muhlenberg Community Hospital, Greenville, KY, p. A266
HEATH, Marsha, Human Resources Manager, Carle Richland Memorial Hospital, Olney, IL, p. A204
HEATH, Megan
Chief Executive Officer and Chief Nursing Officer, Gordon Memorial Health Services, Gordon, NE, p. A400
Chief Nursing Officer, Gordon Memorial Health Services, Gordon, NE, p. A400
HEATH, Merry, Chief Nursing Officer, Piedmont Fayette Hospital, Fayetteville, GA, p. A164
HEATH, Susan, R.N., Senior Vice President and Chief Nursing Officer, Seattle Children's Hospital, Seattle, WA, p. A694
HEATH, William D., Chief Executive Officer, Encompass Health Rehabilitation Hospital of Tallahassee, Tallahassee, FL, p. A151
HEATHERLY, Steve
Chief Executive Officer, Sovah Health–Danville, Danville, VA, p. A675
Chief Executive Officer, Sovah Health–Martinsville, Martinsville, VA, p. A679
HEATHERLY–LLOYD, Sara, Chief Operating Officer, Tennova Healthcare–Lafollette Medical Center, La Follette, TN, p. A586
HEATON, Crystal, Director of Finance, Ascension St. Vincent Warrick, Boonville, IN, p. A213
HEAVNER, Jason, M.D., Senior Vice President and Chief Medical Officer, University of Maryland Baltimore Washington Medical Center, Glen Burnie, MD, p. A304
HEBBERD, Hilda, R.N., MSN, Senior Director Clinical Services, Marlette Regional Hospital, Marlette, MI, p. A333
HEBEL, Barbara, Vice President Human Resources, Doylestown Health, Doylestown, PA, p. A538
HEBERT, Bryan, Director Information Systems, The Medical Center of Southeast Texas, Port Arthur, TX, p. A645
HEBERT, Carol, Director Human Resources, The Medical Center of Southeast Texas, Port Arthur, TX, p. A645
HEBERT, Jeffrey C., Vice President Finance, Chief Financial Officer, Littleton Regional Healthcare, Littleton, NH, p. A416
HEBERT, Kim, Chief Financial Officer, Ochsner Lafayette General Medical Center, Lafayette, LA, p. A285
HEBERT, Raquel, Business Manager, Memorial Hermann Surgical Hospital–First Colony, Sugar Land, TX, p. A654
HEBERT, Timothy, Director Human Resources, Ochsner St. Mary, Morgan City, LA, p. A289
HEBGEN, Lynn, MSN, R.N., Vice President of Nursing, Upland Hills Health, Dodgeville, WI, p. A709

A870 Index of Health Care Professionals

Index of Health Care Professionals / Henderson

Index of Health Care Professionals

HEBL, James
M.D., Regional Vice President, Mayo Clinic Health System In Mankato, Mankato, MN, p. A349
M.D., Regional Vice President, Mayo Clinic Health System In New Prague, New Prague, MN, p. A351
M.D., Regional Vice President, Mayo Clinic Health System In Saint James, Saint James, MN, p. A354
HEBRA, Andre, M.D., Chief Medical Officer, Nemours Children's Hospital, Orlando, FL, p. A144
HECHLER, Tracy, Healthcare Director Information Services, Cjw Medical Center, Richmond, VA, p. A683
HECHT, David, M.D., Chief of Staff, James H. Quillen Department of Veterans Affairs Medical Center, Johnson City, TN, p. A585
HECKER, Cynthia
R.N., Chief Executive Officer, UW Medicine/University of Washington Medical Center, Seattle, WA, p. A695
R.N., Chief Executive Officer, UW Medical Center, UW Medicine/University of Washington Medical Center, Seattle, WA, p. A695
HECKER, Julie, Vice President, Operations, UPMC Mercy, Pittsburgh, PA, p. A552
HECKER, Lisa A, Director Human Resources, Hedrick Medical Center, Chillicothe, MO, p. A373
HECKERMAN, Ray, Chief Executive Officer and Managing Director, Coastal Harbor Treatment Center, Savannah, GA, p. A171
HECKERT, Robert J. Jr, Chief Executive Officer, Gerald Champion Regional Medical Center, Alamogordo, NM, p. A432
HEDBERG, Beth, R.N., Director Nursing, Lindsborg Community Hospital, Lindsborg, KS, p. A253
HEDDE, Charles C, M.D., Chief Medical Officer, Good Samaritan Hospital, Vincennes, IN, p. A228
HEDDEN, Tyler, Senior Vice President/Area Manager, Kaiser Permanente Fresno Medical Center, Fresno, CA, p. A65
HEDGE, William, Chief Executive Officer, Central Indiana Amg Specialty Hospital, Muncie, IN, p. A224
HEDLEY, Kenneth, President, Northwestern Medicine Central Dupage Hospital, Winfield, IL, p. A211
HEDLUND, Chris, Director Information Systems, Community Hospital–Fairfax, Fairfax, MO, p. A375
HEEMANN, John, Vice President and Chief Information Officer, Aspire Hospital, Conroe, TX, p. A608
HEFFERNAN, Paul F, Vice President Human Resources, Women & Infants Hospital of Rhode Island, Providence, RI, p. A561
HEFFERS, Margaret, Assistant Vice President Human Resources, Geisinger Wyoming Valley Medical Center, Wilkes Barre, PA, p. A557
HEFLIN, Erick, R.N., Chief Executive Officer, Amg Specialty Hospital – Oklahoma City, Oklahoma City, OK, p. A516
HEFNER, Donna J., R.N., President and Chief Executive Officer, Sierra View Medical Center, Porterville, CA, p. A84
HEFNER, Katherine, MSN, Chief Nursing Officer, St. Luke's Hospital, Columbus, NC, p. A466
HEFNER, Kathy, Chief Nursing Officer, Mission Hospital Mcdowell, Marion, NC, p. A472
HEGGEM, Mark, M.D., Chief Medical Officer, Riverwood Healthcare Center, Aitkin, MN, p. A342
HEGGEN, Steve, Administrative Director Human Resources, Lutheran Downtown Hospital, Fort Wayne, IN, p. A216
HEGGER, John, Director Information Systems, Deaconess Illinois Union County, Anna, IL, p. A185
HEGLAND, Larry T, M.D., Chief Medical Officer, Decatur Memorial Hospital, Decatur, IL, p. A192
HEGLAND, Ty, Chief Executive Officer, Prairie St. John's, Fargo, ND, p. A480
HEGSTROM, Michael T, M.D., Chief Medical Officer, Geisinger Lewistown Hospital, Lewistown, PA, p. A544
HEIDT, Robert, Director Information Systems, Pembina County Memorial Hospital And Wedgewood Manor, Cavalier, ND, p. A480
HEIFNER, Bruce, Chief Financial Officer, Pella Regional Health Center, Pella, IA, p. A242
HEIKKINEN, Todd, Manager Sports Medicine and Rehabilitation Services, Orthopaedic Hospital of Wisconsin, Glendale, WI, p. A711
HEILMAN, Brooke, Chief Financial Officer, Bowdle Hospital, Bowdle, SD, p. A572
HEILMAN, Christopher, Chief Executive Officer, Acuity Specialty Hospital–Ohio Valley At Weirton, Weirton, WV, p. A705
HEILPERN, Katherine, M.D., President, Yale New Haven Hospital, New Haven, CT, p. A118
HEIM, Chad, Management Information System Director, Lifestream Behavioral Center, Leesburg, FL, p. A137
HEIM, Nicole, Chief Information Officer, Milford Regional Medical Center, Milford, MA, p. A316
HEIMALL, Michael S., Medical Center Director, Washington Dc Veterans Affairs Medical Center, Washington, DC, p. A124
HEIMAN, Thomas, Vice President Information Services and Chief Information Officer, Mather Hospital, Port Jefferson, NY, p. A456
HEIN, Janet
Chief Executive Officer, Encompass Health Rehabilitation Hospital of Erie, Erie, PA, p. A539
Chief Executive Officer, Summa Rehab Hospital, Akron, OH, p. A484
HEIN, Jodi, Chief Nursing Officer, Providence Holy Cross Medical Center, Los Angeles, CA, p. A75
HEINE, Ann, Chief Executive Officer, Surgical Specialty Center of Baton Rouge, Baton Rouge, LA, p. A278
HEINEMEIER, Robert, Interim Chief Financial Officer, Sonoma Specialty Hospital, Sebastopol, CA, p. A95
HEINISCH, Sheri, Compliance Officer, Chi Lisbon Health, Lisbon, ND, p. A482
HEINONEN, Ryan, MSN, R.N., Chief Executive Officer, Up Health System – Portage, Hancock, MI, p. A329
HEINRICH, Bill, Chief Financial Officer, Adventhealth Zephyrhills, Zephyrhills, FL, p. A155
HEINRICH, Caleb, Chief Financial Officer, Adventhealth North Pinellas, Tarpon Springs, FL, p. A153
HEINRICH, Michael G., Senior Vice President and Chief Financial Officer, Unitypoint Health – St. Luke's Hospital, Cedar Rapids, IA, p. A232
HEINRICHS, Leann, M.D., Chief of Staff, Thayer County Health Services, Hebron, NE, p. A401
HEINS, Patrick, President, ECU Health Edgecombe Hospital, Tarboro, NC, p. A477
HEINSOHN, Carmel, M.D., Medical Director, Bournewood Health Systems, Brookline, MA, p. A312
HEINZMAN, Jerry, Senior Vice President and Chief Financial Officer, Sampson Regional Medical Center, Clinton, NC, p. A466
HEINZMANN, Bill, Director Human Resources, Texoma Medical Center, Denison, TX, p. A613
HEISE, James, Chief Medical Officer, Door County Medical Center, Sturgeon Bay, WI, p. A722
HEISE, Teresa, Coordinator Management Information Systems, Pender Community Hospital, Pender, NE, p. A405
HEISEL, Diane, Acting Director, Center for Forensic Psychiatry, Saline, MI, p. A337
HEISER, Eric, Chief Information Resource Management, Royal C. Johnson Veterans' Memorial Hospital, Sioux Falls, SD, p. A576
HEISMEYER, Joyce, Chief Operating Officer, Kansas Heart Hospital, Wichita, KS, p. A261
HEISSER, Randy, M.D., Medical Director, Kindred Hospital–Chattanooga, Chattanooga, TN, p. A580
HEITHAUS, Carolyn, Chief Financial Officer, Calverthealth Medical Center, Prince Frederick, MD, p. A306
HEITRITTER, Joe, Chief Executive Officer, Osceola Regional Health Center, Sibley, IA, p. A243
HEITZMAN, Cynthia, R.N., Chief Nursing Officer, Tamp. General Hospital Crystal River, Crystal River, FL, p. A129
HEITZMAN, David, Chief Administrative Officer and Chief Nursing Officer, New Braunfels Er & Hospital, New Braunfels, TX, p. A641
HELBER, LeeAnn, President, Ohiohealth O'Bleness Hospital, Athens, OH, p. A485
HELD, Jeffrey, M.D., Vice President, Medical Affairs, Penn State Health St. Joseph, Reading, PA, p. A553
HELFER, Cassandra, Chief Financial Officer, Ralp. H. Johnson Veterans Affairs Medical Center, Charleston, SC, p. A563
HELGESON, Heidi E, M.D., Chief Medical Officer, Rio Grande Hospital, Del Norte, CO, p. A106
HELLA, Timothy, Chief Information Officer, Munson Healthcare Otsego Memorial Hospital, Gaylord, MI, p. A327
HELLAND, Don, M.D., Chief Medical Officer, Roosevelt Medical Center, Culbertson, MT, p. A391
HELLE, Dan, Human Resources Officer, Iowa City Va Health System, Iowa City, IA, p. A238
HELLE, Tara, Human Resources Lead, Palo Alto County Health System, Emmetsburg, IA, p. A236
HELLEBUSCH, William, Administrator, Hermann Area District Hospital, Hermann, MO, p. A376
HELLELAND, Brian, Chief Executive, Orange County High Desert Service Area, Providence St. Josep. Hospital Orange, Orange, CA, p. A81
HELLENTHAL, Nicholas, M.D., Chief Medical Officer, Bassett Medical Center, Cooperstown, NY, p. A441
HELLER, Michael, Chief Financial Officer, Lecom Health Corry Memorial Hospital, Corry, PA, p. A537
HELLER, Tom, Vice President Operations and Human Resources, Camden Clark Medical Center, Parkersburg, WV, p. A703
HELLINGER, Jeffrey, Chief Financial Officer, Lewis County General Hospital, Lowville, NY, p. A445
HELM, Benny, Chief Financial Officer, North Runnels Hospital, Winters, TX, p. A663
HELMERS, Richard
M.D., Chief Executive Officer, Mayo Clinic Health System In La Crosse, La Crosse, WI, p. A714
M.D., Chief Executive Officer, Mayo Clinic Health System In Sparta, Sparta, WI, p. A721
M.D., Regional Vice President, Mayo Clinic Health System – Chippewa Valley In Bloomer, Bloomer, WI, p. A708
M.D., Regional Vice President, Mayo Clinic Health System – Northland In Barron, Barron, WI, p. A708
M.D., Regional Vice President, Mayo Clinic Health System – Oakridge In Osseo, Osseo, WI, p. A719
M.D., Regional Vice President, Mayo Clinic Health System – Red Cedar In Menomonie, Menomonie, WI, p. A716
M.D., Regional Vice President, Mayo Clinic Health System In Eau Claire, Eau Claire, WI, p. A710
HELMICKI, Soni, Chief Executive Officer, Wellbridge Healthcare of Fort Worth, Fort Worth, TX, p. A620
HELMKE, Joel, Chief Operating Officer, Fox Chase Cancer Center, Philadelphia, PA, p. A548
HELMS, Ella Raye., Chief Executive Officer, Cogdell Memorial Hospital, Snyder, TX, p. A653
HELMS, James, President and Chief Executive Officer, Jones Memorial Hospital, Wellsville, NY, p. A461
HELMS, Joseph, Director Information Systems, Dekalb Regional Medical Center, Fort Payne, AL, p. A19
HELPER, Mark A, Corporate Vice President and Chief Financial Officer, Munson Medical Center, Traverse City, MI, p. A339
HELSPER, Richard S, Chief Operating Officer, Genesis Healthcare System, Zanesville, OH, p. A508
HELSTROM, James
M.D., Chief Medical Officer, Fox Chase Cancer Center, Philadelphia, PA, p. A548
M.D., Interim Chief Medical Officer, Temple Health–Chestnut Hill Hospital, Philadelphia, PA, p. A550
HELTON, Fay, Director Medical Records, Red River Hospital, Llc, Wichita Falls, TX, p. A662
HELTON, R.J, D.O., Chief of Staff, Coal County General Hospital, Coalgate, OK, p. A511
HELTON, Stephanie, Chief Financial Officer, Weatherford Regional Hospital, Weatherford, OK, p. A524
HELVEY, John, Chief Information Officer, Orchard Hospital, Gridley, CA, p. A66
HEMANN, Randy, M.D., Chief Medical Officer, Olmsted Medical Center, Rochester, MN, p. A354
HEMATILLAKE, M. Ganga, M.D., Chief of Staff, White River Junction Veterans Affairs Medical Center, White River Junction, VT, p. A672
HEMBREE, Greg, Senior Vice President and Chief Financial Officer, St. Francis – Emory Healthcare, Columbus, GA, p. A161
HEMEON, Frank, Interim Chief Financial Officer, Evergreenhealth, Kirkland, WA, p. A691
HEMMER, Chris, Director Finance, Aurora West Allis Medical Center, West Allis, WI, p. A724
HEMMERT, Ryan, Chief Executive Officer, Regency Hospital of Columbus, Columbus, OH, p. A492
HEMPEL, Stephen, M.D., President Medical Staff, Corewell Health Lakeland Hospitals, Saint Joseph, MI, p. A337
HEMPHILL, Dana, Manager Human Resources, Shoshone Medical Center, Kellogg, ID, p. A181
HEMPHILL, Robyn, Chief Executive Officer and Chief Nursing Officer, Monroe Surgical Hospital, Monroe, LA, p. A288
HEMPLER, Shannan, Director Human Resources, Norton County Hospital, Norton, KS, p. A256
HEMSATH, Randolph, M.D., Medical Director, Suncoast Behavioral Health Center, Bradenton, FL, p. A127
HEMSTEAD, Peter, Chief Executive Officer, Riverside Community Hospital, Riverside, CA, p. A86
HENDEL, Dawna, R.N., Chief Nursing Officer and Vice President Patient Care Services, Providence Saint John's Health Center, Santa Monica, CA, p. A95
HENDERSHOT, Richard
Chief Financial Officer, Casey County Hospital, Liberty, KY, p. A269
Chief Financial Officer, Jane Todd Crawford Hospital, Greensburg, KY, p. A266
HENDERSON, Claudia, Chief Human Resources, St. Elizabeth's Medical Center, Brighton, MA, p. A311
HENDERSON, David K, M.D., Deputy Director Clinical Care, Nih Clinical Center, Bethesda, MD, p. A302
HENDERSON, David M, Director Human Resources, Summersville Regional Medical Center, Summersville, WV, p. A705
HENDERSON, Deborah, Acting Chief Financial Officer, Harry S. Truman Memorial Veterans' Hospital, Columbia, MO, p. A374

© 2025 AHA Guide
Index of Health Care Professionals **A871**

Index of Health Care Professionals / Henderson

HENDERSON, Gary, Chief Information Resources Management Services, Huntington Veterans Affairs Medical Center, Huntington, WV, p. A702
HENDERSON, Jace, Chief Financial Officer, Parkview Hospital, Wheeler, TX, p. A662
HENDERSON, Jessica, Manager Human Resources, Fitzgibbon Hospital, Marshall, MO, p. A380
HENDERSON, John
   Chief Human Resources Management, James H. Quillen Department of Veterans Affairs Medical Center, Johnson City, TN, p. A585
   Chief Information Officer, Choc Children's At Mission Hospital, Mission Viejo, CA, p. A77
   Vice President and Chief Information Officer, Children's Hospital of Orange County, Orange, CA, p. A81
HENDERSON, Kathy, Director Human Resources, Willow Crest Hospital, Miami, OK, p. A515
HENDERSON, Lisa
   Chief Operating Officer, Palacios Community Medical Center, Palacios, TX, p. A642
   Chief Operations Officer, Palacios Community Medical Center, Palacios, TX, p. A642
HENDERSON, Melody Lynn, Ph.D., R.N., Chief Operating Officer and Chief Nursing Officer, Golden Plains Community Hospital, Borger, TX, p. A604
HENDERSON, Michelle, Chief Nursing Officer, Abrazo Central Campus, Phoenix, AZ, p. A35
HENDERSON, Mike, Human Resources Director, Forest View Psychiatric Hospital, Grand Rapids, MI, p. A328
HENDERSON, Pamela S, Vice President Human Resources, Memorial Hospital of Carbondale, Carbondale, IL, p. A187
HENDERSON, Paula
   Chief Human Resources Officer, University of Mississipp. Medical Center, Jackson, MS, p. A364
   Vice President Human Resources, University of Maryland Medical Center Midtown Campus, Baltimore, MD, p. A301
   Vice President Human Resources, University of Maryland Rehabilitation & Orthopaedic Institute, Baltimore, MD, p. A302
HENDERSON, Rex, M.D., Chief of Staff, Mission Hospital Mcdowell, Marion, NC, p. A472
HENDERSON, Sue, Human Resource Manager, Smyth County Community Hospital, Marion, VA, p. A679
HENDERSON, Travis, M.D., Chief of Staff, Mobridge Regional Hospital, Mobridge, SD, p. A575
HENDERSON, Vickie, M.D., Chief Medical Officer, Saint Mary's Regional Medical Center, Russellville, AR, p. A53
HENDERSON, Volante, Director Human Resources, Walton Rehabilitation Hospital, An Affiliate of Encompass Health, Augusta, GA, p. A158
HENDRICK, Kirk, Director Information Systems, HCA Florida Northside Hospital, Saint Petersburg, FL, p. A149
HENDRICKS, Marcia, FACHE, R.N., Chief Executive Officer, Madison County Health Care System, Winterset, IA, p. A245
HENDRICKS, Sharon, Chief Administrative Officer, Levindale Hebrew Geriatric Center And Hospital, Baltimore, MD, p. A300
HENDRICKS WOODS, Nicole Smith., FACHE, Chief Executive Officer, Encompass Health Rehabilitation Hospital of Columbia, Columbia, SC, p. A564
HENDRICKSEN, Sherry, R.N., MSN, Chief Nursing Officer, Continuecare Hospital At Hendrick Medical Center, Abilene, TX, p. A595
HENDRICKSON, Cristin, Chief Executive Officer, George C. Grap. Community Hospital, Hamburg, IA, p. A237
HENDRICKSON, Leslie, Director Human Resources, Coteau Des Prairies Hospital, Sisseton, SD, p. A577
HENDRICKSON, Michelle, Human Resources Director, Pam Health Rehabilitation Hospital of Greater Indiana, Clarksville, IN, p. A214
HENDRICKSON, Roman, M.D., Medical Director, Ruby Valley Medical Center, Sheridan, MT, p. A396
HENDRIX, Angie, Director of Nursing, Evergreen Medical Center, Evergreen, AL, p. A19
HENDRIX, Billie, R.N., Director of Nursing, W. J. Mangold Memorial Hospital, Lockney, TX, p. A635
HENDRIX, Jamie, Vice President Patient Care Services, Prairie Ridge Health, Inc., Columbus, WI, p. A709
HENDRIX, Michael
   Chief Financial Officer, St. Josep. Hospital, Bangor, ME, p. A295
   Chief Financial Officer, St. Mary's Regional Medical Center, Lewiston, ME, p. A298
HENDRY, Christopher, M.D., Chief Medical Officer, Atrium Health Navicent The Medical Center, Macon, GA, p. A167
HENDRYX, Joel, M.D., Chief Medical Officer, University Medical Center of El Paso, El Paso, TX, p. A617

HENES, Jean M., MSN, R.N., Director of Nursing, Avera Creighton Hospital, Creighton, NE, p. A399
HENESSEE, Nolan, Vice President and Chief Information Officer, St. Joseph's Hospital, Savannah, GA, p. A171
HENINGER, Bev, Director of Nursing, Trinity Kenmare Community Hospital, Kenmare, ND, p. A482
HENKE, Georgia, Operational Account Manager, OSF Healthcare Saint Anthony's Health Center, Alton, IL, p. A185
HENKENIUS, Jim, Chief Financial Officer, Stewart Memorial Community Hospital, Lake City, IA, p. A239
HENLEY, Martha, Chief Executive Officer, Unity Medical Center, Manchester, TN, p. A587
HENNEBOLD, Julie, R.N., Interim Chief Nursing Officer, Winner Regional Healthcare Center, Winner, SD, p. A578
HENNELLY, John, President and Chief Executive Officer, Sonoma Valley Hospital, Sonoma, CA, p. A96
HENNEMAN, Craig, President, Centracare – Paynesville, Paynesville, MN, p. A352
HENNENBERG, Shayla, Director Human Resources, Essentia Health-Ada, Ada, MN, p. A342
HENNESSY, John, Chief Executive Officer, Bonner General Health, Sandpoint, ID, p. A184
HENNIGAN, Michael, M.D., Medical Director, Encompass Health Rehabilitation Hospital of Panama City, Panama City, FL, p. A146
HENNIKA, Billi Jo, Vice President Operations, Mckenzie Health System, Sandusky, MI, p. A337
HENNING, Cindy, R.N., Chief Nursing Officer, HCA Houston Healthcare Northwest, Houston, TX, p. A626
HENNIS, Michelle
   Administrative Director Financial Services, Grace Hospital, Cleveland, OH, p. A490
   Interim President and Chief Executive Officer, Grace Hospital, Cleveland, OH, p. A490
HENNIS, Tamra, Chief Executive Officer, Vibra Hospital of Charleston, Mt. Pleasant, SC, p. A569
HENRICHS, Mark, Chief Financial Officer, University of Iowa Hospitals & Clinics, Iowa City, IA, p. A238
HENRICI, Michael, Associate Administrator, Roxborough Memorial Hospital, Philadelphia, PA, p. A550
HENRICKS, William, Ph.D., Vice President and Chief Operating Officer, Ascension Seton Shoal Creek, Austin, TX, p. A599
HENRY, Andrea
   Chief Executive Officer, Sweetwater Hospital, Sweetwater, TN, p. A594
   Director of Nursing, Sweetwater Hospital, Sweetwater, TN, p. A594
HENRY, Anna, Chief Information Officer, Kimble Hospital, Junction, TX, p. A631
HENRY, Brad
   Chief Executive Officer, Providence Willamette Falls Medical Center, Oregon City, OR, p. A530
   Interim Chief Executive Officer, Providence Milwaukie Hospital, Milwaukie, OR, p. A529
HENRY, Chris, Associate Administrator and Chief Financial Officer, Washington Hospital Healthcare System, Fremont, CA, p. A64
HENRY, David
   FACHE, Chief Executive Officer, Merit Health Madison, Canton, MS, p. A360
   President and Chief Executive Officer, Northern Montana Hospital, Havre, MT, p. A393
HENRY, Debbie, Vice President and Chief Financial Officer, Baxter Health, Mountain Home, AR, p. A51
HENRY, Donna, Vice President of Nursing Services, 4C Health, Logansport, IN, p. A222
HENRY, Eric, Senior Vice President/Area Manager, Greater San Jose Service Area, Kaiser Permanente San Jose Medical Center, San Jose, CA, p. A92
HENRY, Hannah, Interim Vice President of Human Resources, Emory Johns Creek Hospital, Johns Creek, GA, p. A166
HENRY, Heather, Information Technology Manager, Hammond–Henry Hospital, Geneseo, IL, p. A196
HENRY, James L, Director Human Resources, Sea Pines Rehabilitation Hospital, An Affiliate of Encompass Health, Melbourne, FL, p. A139
HENRY, Joy, R.N., Chief of Nursing, Faith Community Hospital, Jacksboro, TX, p. A630
HENRY, Joyce, Controller, Encompass Health Rehabilitation Hospital of York, York, PA, p. A558
HENRY, Kelsea, Chief Financial Officer, Memorial Regional Health, Craig, CO, p. A105
HENRY, Peter, M.D., Chief Medical Officer, Essentia Health–St. Joseph's Medical Center, Brainerd, MN, p. A344
HENRY, Roshonda, Chief Nursing Officer, Encompass Health Rehabilitation Hospital of Cypress, Houston, TX, p. A625
HENRY, Tim, Accountant, Chatuge Regional Hospital And Nursing Home, Hiawassee, GA, p. A165

HENRY, William
   Chief Executive Officer, Fannin Regional Hospital, Blue Ridge, GA, p. A159
   Director Human Resources, UT Health Henderson, Henderson, TX, p. A624
   Director Human Resources, UT Health Quitman, Quitman, TX, p. A646
HENSEL, David, Director Financial Operations, Ohiohealth Grady Memorial Hospital, Delaware, OH, p. A494
HENSEL, Derek MHL, BNS, Controller, Encompass Health Rehabilitation Hospital of Pensacola, Pensacola, FL, p. A146
HENSEL, Edward, Chief Information Officer, Tomah Va Medical Center, Tomah, WI, p. A723
HENSH, Emily, Chief Executive Officer, Pam Health Specialty Hospital of Heritage Valley, Beaver, PA, p. A535
HENSLEE, Maureen, Chief Financial Officer, Lower Keys Medical Center, Key West, FL, p. A136
HENSLEIGH, David, Director Medical Staff, Clay County Hospital, Ashland, AL, p. A15
HENSLEY, Angela, Director of Nursing, Pathways of Tennessee, Jackson, TN, p. A584
HENSLEY, Anna
   Chief Operating Officer, Ohiohealth Dublin Methodist Hospital, Dublin, OH, p. A495
   Chief Operating Officer, Ohiohealth Grady Memorial Hospital, Delaware, OH, p. A494
HENSLEY, Barry, Director Information Systems, Logan Regional Medical Center, Logan, WV, p. A702
HENSLEY, Kristy, Director Human Resources, Orthoindy Hospital, Indianapolis, IN, p. A220
HENSON, Judith
   Vice President Patient Care Services, Southeast Georgia Health System Brunswick Campus, Brunswick, GA, p. A159
   Vice President, Patient Care Services, Southeast Georgia Health System Camden Campus, Saint Marys, GA, p. A170
HENSON, Lily, M.D., President and Chief Executive Officer, Piedmont Augusta, Augusta, GA, p. A158
HENSON, Maureen, Vice President Human Resources, Monument Health Rapid City Hospital, Rapid City, SD, p. A576
HENSON, Pam, Executive Director, Pathways of Tennessee, Jackson, TN, p. A584
HENTZ, Amber, Chief Executive Officer, Park Royal Hospital, Fort Myers, FL, p. A132
HENWOOD, Kellie J., Interim Chief Financial Officer, Desoto Memorial Hospital, Arcadia, FL, p. A125
HENZE, Rick, Chief Financial Officer, St. Mary's Healthcare, Amsterdam, NY, p. A438
HEPNER, Tim, M.D., Chief Medical Officer, Ascension St. John Owasso, Owasso, OK, p. A519
HERALD, Kathleen R, Vice President and Chief Information Officer, Lexington Medical Center, West Columbia, SC, p. A571
HERB, Beth, Administrator, State Correctional Institution At Camp Hill, Camp Hill, PA, p. A536
HERBECK, Marilyn, Coordinator Human Resources, Community Hospital of Staunton, Staunton, IL, p. A209
HERBEL, Aaron, Administrator, Mercy Hospital Inc., Moundridge, KS, p. A255
HERBER, Steven C.
   M.D., FACS, President, Adventist Health St. Helena, Saint Helena, CA, p. A88
   M.D., FACS, President, Adventist Health Vallejo, Vallejo, CA, p. A99
HERBERGER, Eva, Administrator Human Resources, USC Verdugo Hills Hospital, Glendale, CA, p. A66
HERBERT, Daniel, M.D., Medical Administrative Officer, Millinocket Regional Hospital, Millinocket, ME, p. A298
HERBERT, Teresa, M.D., Chief Medical Officer, Adventhealth Hendersonville, Hendersonville, NC, p. A470
HERBOLD, Charlotte, Manager Business Officer, Garfield County Health Center, Jordan, MT, p. A393
HERBST, Gary K., Chief Executive Officer, Kaweah Health Medical Center, Visalia, CA, p. A100
HERDELIN, Jeffrey, Vice President Human Resources, Kindred Hospital Indianapolis North, Indianapolis, IN, p. A220
HERDER, Debbie, Controller, KPC Promise Hospital of Wichita Falls, Wichita Falls, TX, p. A662
HEREFORD, James, Executive Vice President, Chief Operating Officer, M Health Fairview Bethesda Hospital, Saint Paul, MN, p. A354
HERFORT, Oliver, M.D., Chief Medical Officer, Valley Regional Hospital, Claremont, NH, p. A414
HERING, John
   M.D., Chief Medical Officer, Centracare – Monticello, Monticello, MN, p. A351
   M.D., President and Chief Medical Officer, Centracare – Monticello, Monticello, MN, p. A351

HERING, Kristine, R.N., Chief Nursing Officer, Speare Memorial Hospital, Plymouth, NH, p. A417
HERKIMER, Eileen, Director Human Resources, United Memorial Medical Center, Batavia, NY, p. A439
HERMAN, David C., M.D., Chief Executive Officer, Essentia Health Duluth, Duluth, MN, p. A346
HERMAN, John J., FACHE, Chief Executive Officer, Penn Medicine Lancaster General Health, Lancaster, PA, p. A543
HERMAN, Kelsey B., Director Human Resources, Arkansas Valley Regional Medical Center, La Junta, CO, p. A110
HERMANN, Terri, R.N., Chief Nursing Officer, Franklin Hospital District, Benton, IL, p. A186
HERMES, Cliff, Administrator, Oceans Behavioral Hospital Biloxi, Biloxi, MS, p. A359
HERMES, Dina, Chief Financial Officer, Golden Plains Community Hospital, Borger, TX, p. A604
HERMOSA, Mercy, Director of Information System, Coral Gables Hospital, Coral Gables, FL, p. A128
HERNANDEZ, Ashley, Chief Information Technology Officer, Novant Health Pender Medical Center, Burgaw, NC, p. A464
HERNANDEZ, Carmelo, M.D., Chief Medical Officer, San Luis Valley Health, Alamosa, CO, p. A103
HERNANDEZ, Dennis, M.D., Chief Medical Officer, Adventhealth New Smyrna Beach, New Smyrna Beach, FL, p. A142
HERNANDEZ, Diane
  Area Finance Officer, Kaiser Permanente San Rafael Medical Center, San Rafael, CA, p. A93
  Area Finance Officer, Kaiser Permanente Santa Rosa Medical Center, Santa Rosa, CA, p. A95
HERNANDEZ, Dinorah Esq, Executive Director, Hospital Pavia Yauco, Yauco, PR, p. A736
HERNANDEZ, Elisa, Chief Human Resource Officer, Miami Jewish Health, Miami, FL, p. A140
HERNANDEZ, Hector, Chief Executive Officer, Los Angeles Community Hospital At Los Angeles, Los Angeles, CA, p. A74
HERNANDEZ, Holly, Chief Financial Officer, Newport News Behavioral Health Center, Newport News, VA, p. A680
HERNANDEZ, Janira, Coordinator Human Resources, Hospital Metropolitano Dr. Susoni, Arecibo, PR, p. A731
HERNANDEZ, Joseph, M.D., Medical Director, San Antonio Behavioral Healthcare Hospital, San Antonio, TX, p. A650
HERNANDEZ, Kim, Chief Human Resources Officer, Sage Specialty Hospital (Ltac), Denham Springs, LA, p. A281
HERNANDEZ, Kristen, Director Human Resources, Encompass Health Rehabilitation Hospital of Albuquerque, Albuquerque, NM, p. A432
HERNANDEZ, Lilly, Human Resources Director, Catalina Island Medical Center, Avalon, CA, p. A56
HERNANDEZ, Luz Maria, Director Human Resources, I. Gonzalez Martinez Oncologic Hospital, Hato Rey, PR, p. A732
HERNANDEZ, Matt, Director of Information Technology and System, HCA Florida Kendall Hospital, Miami, FL, p. A139
HERNANDEZ, Nelia, Chief Financial Officer, Iraan General Hospital, Iraan, TX, p. A630
HERNANDEZ, Reyna, Assistant Vice President, Finance (Controller), Baptist Health South Florida, South Miami Hospital, Miami, FL, p. A139
HERNANDEZ, Ricky, Director Human Resources, Mercy Rehabilitation Hospital Fort Smith, Fort Smith, AR, p. A47
HERNANDEZ, Roberto, Administrator and Executive Director, Multy Medical Rehabilitation Hospital San Juan, San Juan, PR, p. A735
HERNANDEZ, Susan
  R.N., Chief Nurse Executive, University of Texas Southwestern Medical Center, Dallas, TX, p. A612
  R.N., Chief Nursing Officer, Rice Medical Center, Eagle Lake, TX, p. A615
HERNANDEZ, Yoely, Chief Executive Officer, Larkin Community Hospital Behavioral Health Services, Hollywood, FL, p. A133
HERNANDEZ-KEEBLE, Sonia, Superintendent, Rio Grande State Center/South Texas Health Care System, Harlingen, TX, p. A623
HERNANDEZ-LICHTL, Javier, Chief Executive Officer, Baptist Health South Florida, Doctors Hospital, Coral Gables, FL, p. A128
HERNDON, Amy, Chief Finance Officer, Morristown-Hamblen Healthcare System, Morristown, TN, p. A589
HERNDON, Robert Scott
  Chief Financial Officer, Ascension Seton Shoal Creek, Austin, TX, p. A599
  Vice President Chief Financial Officer, Ascension Seton Medical Center Austin, Austin, TX, p. A599
HERNDON, Sandra, CPA, Chief Financial Officer, Bleckley Memorial Hospital, Cochran, GA, p. A160

HERNDON, Scott
  FACHE, Chief Financial Officer, Ministry Market Texas, Dell Seton Medical Center At The University of Texas, Austin, TX, p. A600
  FACHE, Chief Financial Officer, Texas Market, Ascension Seton Northwest, Austin, TX, p. A599
HEROLD, Amy, M.D., Chief Medical Officer, Providence Queen of The Valley Medical Center, Napa, CA, p. A79
HEROLD, Mary, Director Human Resources, Share Medical Center, Alva, OK, p. A509
HEROLD, Matthew
  Vice President, Chief Medical Officer, Ridgeview Le Sueur Medical Center, Le Sueur, MN, p. A348
  Vice President, Chief Medical Officer, Ridgeview Medical Center, Waconia, MN, p. A356
  Vice President, Chief Medical Officer, Ridgeview Sibley Medical Center, Arlington, MN, p. A342
HERPFER, Caroline, Chief Nursing Officer, Arizona Orthopedic Surgical Hospital, Chandler, AZ, p. A30
HERR, Brenda, Chief Nursing Officer, East Adams Rural Healthcare, Ritzville, WA, p. A694
HERR, Michael, Chief Operating Officer, Starr Regional Medical Center, Athens, TN, p. A579
HERRARA, Espie, Chief Financial Officer, Peak Behavioral Health Services, Santa Teresa, NM, p. A437
HERRERA, Jocelyn A.
  Director Human Resources, Kaiser Permanente Orange County Anaheim Medical Center, Anaheim, CA, p. A55
  Human Resources Director, Kaiser Permanente Zion Medical Center, San Diego, CA, p. A89
HERRERA, Veronica, Director Human Resources, Las Encinas Hospital, Pasadena, CA, p. A83
HERRERA, Yamila, Director Human Resources, Hialeah Hospital, Hialeah, FL, p. A133
HERRERO, Carmelo, M.D., Medical Director, Hospital Menonita Humacao, Humacao, PR, p. A733
HERRICK, Brian, M.D., Chief Information Officer, Cambridge Health Alliance, Cambridge, MA, p. A312
HERRING, Davey, M.D., Chief Medical Officer, Dorminy Medical Center, Fitzgerald, GA, p. A164
HERRING, Michael, R.N., Chief Executive Officer, Banner Gateway Medical Center, Gilbert, AZ, p. A31
HERRING, Randy, M.D., Chief of Staff, Coon Memorial Hospital, Dalhart, TX, p. A610
HERRING, Sherry, Chief Nursing Officer, UVA Encompass Health Rehabilitation Hospital, Charlottesville, VA, p. A674
HERRINGTON, Ashley, Chief Executive Officer, Owensboro Health Twin Lakes Regional Medical Center, Leitchfield, KY, p. A268
HERRINGTON, Bruce, M.D., Chief Medical Officer, South Georgia Medical Center Lanier Campus, Lakeland, GA, p. A166
HERRINGTON, Kristal, Senior Director, Human Resources, Twin County Regional Healthcare, Galax, VA, p. A677
HERRMAN, Edward, R.N., FACHE, President and Chief Executive Officer, Hays Medical Center, Hays, KS, p. A250
HERRON, Katherine, Director Human Resources, Richard H. Hutchings Psychiatric Center, Syracuse, NY, p. A460
HERRON, Mary, Chief Financial Officer, St. Mark's Hospital, Salt Lake City, UT, p. A669
HERRON, Shon, Director, Finance, Anmed Cannon, Pickens, SC, p. A569
HERSEN, Jon, President, Legacy Salmon Creek Medical Center, Vancouver, WA, p. A698
HERSHBERGER, Brandy
  Chief Nursing Officer, HCA Florida Fawcett Hospital, Port Charlotte, FL, p. A147
  CNO, VP Patient Care Services, UPMC Presbyterian, Pittsburgh, PA, p. A552
HERSHBERGER, Scott, Acting Chief Information Management Services, Battle Creek Veterans Affairs Medical Center, Battle Creek, MI, p. A322
HERSHMAN, Michael E., Director, Richard L. Roudebush Veterans Affairs Medical Center, Indianapolis, IN, p. A220
HERSHMAN, Sharon, R.N., Chief Nursing Officer, Providence Holy Family Hospital, Spokane, WA, p. A696
HERSKOVITZ, Paul, Administrator, Cornerstone Behavioral Health Hospital of Union County, Berkeley Heights, NJ, p. A418
HERTEL, Holly, Director Nursing, Larned State Hospital, Larned, KS, p. A252
HERTZ, Karl Edward., Administrator, Providence Kodiak Island Medical Center, Kodiak, AK, p. A28
HERZBERG, Deborah L., R.N., MS, FACHE, Chief Executive Officer, Avera Holy Family Hospital, Estherville, IA, p. A236
HERZL-BETZ, Kenneth, M.D., Chief Medical Officer, Arnot Ogden Medical Center, Elmira, NY, p. A442
HERZOG, Dean, Chief Financial Officer, Kona Community Hospital, Kealakekua, HI, p. A177
HERZOG, Vearnail, Chief Executive Officer, Allegiance Specialty Hospital of Greenville, Greenville, MS, p. A362

HESCH, Dennis, Executive Vice President Finance, System Chief Financial Officer, Carle Foundation Hospital, Urbana, IL, p. A210
HESKETH, Matthew, President, Good Samaritan Medical Center, Brockton, MA, p. A311
HESKIN, Paul, Chief Nursing Officer, Adventhealth Avista, Louisville, CO, p. A111
HESLEP, Marchelle, Human Resources Director, Perry County Memorial Hospital, Tell City, IN, p. A227
HESMAN, Tasha N., R.N., Senior Executive, Patient Care Services, Beatrice Community Hospital And Health Center, Beatrice, NE, p. A398
HESPEN, Barbara K., R.N., President, Monument Health Custer Hospital, Custer, SD, p. A573
HESS, Cory, President and Chief Executive Officer, Harnett Health System, Dunn, NC, p. A467
HESS, David F., M.D., President and Chief Executive Officer, United Hospital Center, Bridgeport, WV, p. A699
HESS, Heidi, Chief Nursing Officer, Genesis Medical Center-Aledo, Aledo, IL, p. A185
HESS, Kent, Chief Executive Officer, Sun Behavioral Columbus, Columbus, OH, p. A492
HESS, Michael, M.D., Chief Medical Officer, Lakeview Hospital, Bountiful, UT, p. A664
HESS, Pamela, Chief Financial Officer, Ascension Saint Thomas Hospital, Nashville, TN, p. A590
HESS, Philip D., President, Wellspan Philhaven, Mount Gretna, PA, p. A546
HESS, Steve
  Vice President Information Services and Chief Information Officer, UCHealth Medical Center of The Rockies, Loveland, CO, p. A112
  Vice President Information Services and Chief Information Officer, University of Colorado Hospital, Aurora, CO, p. A103
HESS, Steven, Chief Operating Officer, Miami Jewish Health, Miami, FL, p. A140
HESS, Susan, Director Human Resources, Penn Highlands Huntingdon, Huntingdon, PA, p. A542
HESSAMI, Sam, M.D., Chief Medical Officer, Arrowhead Regional Medical Center, Colton, CA, p. A60
HESSE, Fred, M.D., Medical Director, Arms Acres, Carmel, NY, p. A441
HESSELRODE, Renee, Director Health Information Management, Landmark Hospital of Cap. Girardeau, Cap. Girardeau, MO, p. A372
HESSHEIMER, Susan, Director Human Resources, Johnson County Hospital, Tecumseh, NE, p. A406
HESSING, Jeffrey, M.D., Medical Director, Treasure Valley Hospital, Boise, ID, p. A180
HESSMAN, Mary Pat, Chief Fiscal, Northport Veterans Affairs Medical Center, Northport, NY, p. A454
HESTER, Amber, Area Chief Executive Officer, Rehabilitation Hospital of Henry, Mcdonough, GA, p. A168
HESTER, Charles H., CPA, Jr, Chief Financial Officer, Delta Health – Northwest Regional, Clarksdale, MS, p. A360
HESTER, Joey, Chief Executive Officer, Medical Center Enterprise, Enterprise, AL, p. A19
HESTER, Josh, Chief Operating Officer, Gadsden Regional Medical Center, Gadsden, AL, p. A20
HESTER, Joshua
  Chief Executive Officer, Dmc Detroit Receiving Hospital & University Health Center, Detroit, MI, p. A325
  Chief Executive Officer, Dmc Harper University Hospital, Detroit, MI, p. A325
HESTER, Joyce, CPA, Senior Vice President and Chief Financial Officer, Christus Mother Frances Hospital – Tyler, Tyler, TX, p. A658
HESTER, Kathy
  Chief Nursing Officer, Ascension St. Vincent's Southside, Jacksonville, FL, p. A134
  Chief Nursing Officer, HCA Florida Orange Park Hospital, Orange Park, FL, p. A144
HESTER, Michael, Chief Executive Officer and Chief Financial Officer, Burke Medical Center, Waynesboro, GA, p. A174
HESTON, Catherine, Chief Nursing Officer, Three Rivers Medical Center, Louisa, KY, p. A269
HETHERINGTON, Ray, Network Administrator, Wheatland Memorial Healthcare, Harlowton, MT, p. A393
HETLETVED, Beth, Director of Nurses, Chi St. Alexius Health Garrison, Garrison, ND, p. A481
HETT, Samantha, Manager Human Resources, Satanta District Hospital And Long Term Care, Satanta, KS, p. A259
HETTICH, E Paul, Chief Financial Officer, Brylin Hospitals, Buffalo, NY, p. A440
HETTINGER, JoAnn, R.N., Director of Patient Care Services, Avera Weskota Memorial Hospital, Wessington Springs, SD, p. A578

HETTINGER, MaryLou, Director Quality Management, Devereux Children's Behavioral Health Center, Malvern, PA, p. A545
HETTLER, Aidan, Chief Executive Officer, Sedgwick County Health Center, Julesburg, CO, p. A110
HETU, Maureen, Chief Information Officer, Virtua Our Lady of Lourdes Hospital, Camden, NJ, p. A419
HETZ, Mark
　Chief Information Officer, Asante Ashland Community Hospital, Ashland, OR, p. A525
　Chief Information Officer, Asante Rogue Regional Medical Center, Medford, OR, p. A529
　Chief Information Officer, Asante Three Rivers Medical Center, Grants Pass, OR, p. A527
HEUPEL, Eric, Chief Executive Officer, Ashley Medical Center, Ashley, ND, p. A479
HEURTIN, John, Chief Financial Officer, Lee's Summit Medical Center, Lee's Summit, MO, p. A379
HEWSTON, MaryAnn, R.N., Chief Nurse Executive, Meadville Medical Center, Meadville, PA, p. A545
HEXEM, Greg, Chief Financial Officer, Northeastern Nevada Regional Hospital, Elko, NV, p. A408
HEYN, Matthew M., Chief Executive Officer, Oak Valley Hospital, Oakdale, CA, p. A80
HEYWOOD, Matthew, President and Chief Executive Officer, Aspirus Wausau Hospital, Inc., Wausau, WI, p. A724
HIATT, Tim, Chief Information Officer, Brodstone Memorial Hospital, Superior, NE, p. A406
HIBBARD, Carrie, Human Resource Business Partner, Adventist Healthcare Rehabilitation, Rockville, MD, p. A306
HIBSCHMAN, Kimberly
　Chief Financial Officer, Conway Behavioral Health, Conway, AR, p. A44
　Chief Financial Officer, Riverview Behavioral Health, Texarkana, AR, p. A54
HICKEL, Ashley, Chief Operating Officer, Frankfort Regional Medical Center, Frankfort, KY, p. A266
HICKEY, Beth, Vice President, Finance, Advocate Lutheran General Hospital, Park Ridge, IL, p. A205
HICKEY, Christopher, Chief Financial Officer and Senior Vice President, The University of Vermont Health Network – Alice Hyde Medical Center, Malone, NY, p. A445
HICKEY, Conner, Chief Operating Officer, Woodland Heights Medical Center, Lufkin, TX, p. A637
HICKEY, Marcia H, Senior Vice President Operations, The Hospital At Hebrew Senior Care, West Hartford, CT, p. A120
HICKEY–BOYNTON, Meg
　Chief Financial Officer, Community Hospital of Anaconda, Anaconda, MT, p. A389
　Director Human Resources and Marketing, Community Hospital of Anaconda, Anaconda, MT, p. A389
HICKEY–TOEDTMANN, Cristina, Senior Director, Human Resources, Nantucket Cottage Hospital, Nantucket, MA, p. A316
HICKLING, Andrea, Vice President of Finance and Chief Financial Officer, Northern Regional Hospital, Mount Airy, NC, p. A473
HICKMAN, Art, Chief Executive Officer, Perimeter Behavioral Hospital of West Memphis, West Memphis, AR, p. A54
HICKMAN, Monica, Director Fiscal Services, Shriners Hospitals for Children–Spokane, Spokane, WA, p. A696
HICKS, Amanda Lea., R.N., Chief Executive Officer, Hop. Health Care Center, Keams Canyon, AZ, p. A32
HICKS, Christia, Vice President Human Resources, Eskenazi Health, Indianapolis, IN, p. A219
HICKS, Crystal, R.N., Chief Nursing Officer, Harrison County Community Hospital, Bethany, MO, p. A371
HICKS, Dana, Director of Nursing, Izard County Medical Center, Calico Rock, AR, p. A44
HICKS, Deborah, Senior Vice President, Chief People and Culture Officer, Dana–Farber Cancer Institute, Boston, MA, p. A310
HICKS, Janelle, R.N., Vice President Patient Services, Hocking Valley Community Hospital, Logan, OH, p. A498
HICKS, Joan, Chief Information Officer, University of Alabama Hospital, Birmingham, AL, p. A17
HICKS, Mary Jane, Hospital Director, William S. Hall Psychiatric Institute, Columbia, SC, p. A565
HICKS, Michael L, Senior Vice President and Chief Operating Officer, UChicago Medicine Ingalls Memorial, Harvey, IL, p. A197
HICKS, Scott, Vice President, Norton Clark Hospital, Jeffersonville, IN, p. A221
HICKS, Teresa, Chief Financial Officer, Allendale County Hospital, Fairfax, SC, p. A566
HICKS, Terri, Chief Executive Officer, The Spine Hospital of Louisiana At The Neuromedical Center, Baton Rouge, LA, p. A278
HICKS, Tim
　Administrator, Muscogee Creek Nation Medical Center, Okmulgee, OK, p. A519
　Administrator, Muscogee Creek Nation Physical Rehabilitation Center, Okmulgee, OK, p. A519
　Chief Operating Officer, Hospital Services, Council Oak Comprehensive Healthcare, Tulsa, OK, p. A522
HICKS, William, Chief Executive Officer, NYC Health + Hospitals/Bellevue, New York, NY, p. A450
HICKS–ARSENAULT, Nancy J., R.N., Interim Chief Executive Officer, Cherry County Hospital, Valentine, NE, p. A406
HICKSON, Stan, Chief Executive Officer, Encompass Health Rehabilitation Hospital of Newnan, Newnan, GA, p. A169
HIDAY, Holly, Director Human Resources, Kalamazoo Psychiatric Hospital, Kalamazoo, MI, p. A331
HIEB, Dorothy, Director Human Resources, Sanford Chamberlain Medical Center, Chamberlain, SD, p. A572
HIEB, Laura, R.N., Chief Nursing Officer, Bellin Hospital, Green Bay, WI, p. A712
HIESTAND, John J., M.D., Vice President Medical Affairs, Promedica Memorial Hospital, Fremont, OH, p. A496
HIGA, Russel, JD, Regional Director Human Resources, Leahi Hospital, Honolulu, HI, p. A175
HIGDON, Kevin J, Chief Financial Officer, Saint Josep. Health System, Mishawaka, IN, p. A224
HIGGINBOTHAM, Beau
　Chief Operating Officer, Ascension Saint Agnes, Baltimore, MD, p. A300
　Interim Chief Executive Officer, Chief Strategy Officer and Chief Operating Officer, Ascension Saint Agnes, Baltimore, MD, p. A300
HIGGINBOTHAM, Lee
　Chief Executive Officer, Lewisgale Hospital Alleghany, Low Moor, VA, p. A678
　Chief Executive Officer, Mission Hospital Mcdowell, Marion, NC, p. A472
HIGGINS, Alana, Regional Information Management Executive, Christus St. Michael Rehabilitation Hospital, Texarkana, TX, p. A656
HIGGINS, Henry, M.D., Chief Executive Officer, Brushy Creek Family Hospital, Round Rock, TX, p. A647
HIGGINS, Jennifer Sue, R.N., Vice President, Operations and Chief Nurse Executive, Gulf Coast Medical Center, Fort Myers, FL, p. A131
HIGGINS, Kevin A, Chief Financial Officer, Olmsted Medical Center, Rochester, MN, p. A354
HIGGINS, Rodney, Chief Financial Officer, Multicare Deaconess Hospital, Spokane, WA, p. A696
HIGGINS, Thomas, M.D., Chief Medical Officer, Baystate Franklin Medical Center, Greenfield, MA, p. A314
HIGGINS, William, M.D., Vice President Medical Affairs, New York–Presbyterian/Hudson Valley Hospital, Cortlandt Manor, NY, p. A442
HIGGINS BOWERS, Shirley, Senior Vice President Human Resources, Hackensack Meridian Health Jfk Medical Center, Edison, NJ, p. A420
HIGH, Kim, Chief Financial Officer, Baptist Memorial Hospital–Union County, New Albany, MS, p. A367
HIGHFILL, Andrea, Chief Nursing Officer, Carson Valley Medical Center, Gardnerville, NV, p. A408
HIGHTOWER, Bernita, Chief Human Resources, Benning Martin Army Community Hospital, Fort Benning, GA, p. A164
HIGHTOWER, Heather, Director of Nursing, Turning Point Hospital, Moultrie, GA, p. A169
HIGHTOWER, Skip
　Chief Financial Officer, Archbold Brooks, Quitman, GA, p. A169
　Chief Financial Officer, Archbold Grady, Cairo, GA, p. A159
　Senior Vice President and Chief Financial Officer, Archbold Mitchell, Camilla, GA, p. A160
　Senior Vice President and Chief Financial Officer, John D. Archbold Memorial Hospital, Thomasville, GA, p. A172
HIJECK, Thomas W., R.N., MS, Vice President Nursing Services and Chief Nursing Officer, Umass Memorial Health – Harrington, Southbridge, MA, p. A318
HILAMAN, Brad L, M.D., JD, Chief Medical Officer, Dosher Memorial Hospital, Southport, NC, p. A476
HILDEBRAND, Dan, Chief Information Officer, Logansport Memorial Hospital, Logansport, IN, p. A223
HILDEBRAND, Randall, M.D., Chief Medical Officer, University of Kansas Health System Great Bend Campus, Great Bend, KS, p. A250
HILDEBRANDT, James, D.O., Vice President Medical Affairs, Sarah Bush Lincoln Health Center, Mattoon, IL, p. A201
HILDRETH, Beth, Vice President Human Resources, Ohiohealth Mansfield Hospital, Mansfield, OH, p. A499
HILDRETH, Joe, Technician, Desktop Support, Ascension St. Thomas Three Rivers, Waverly, TN, p. A594
HILDWEIN, Robin, Chief Information Officer, Boca Raton Regional Hospital, Boca Raton, FL, p. A126
HILFIGER, Janie Marie., R.N., President, UPMC Cole, Coudersport, PA, p. A537
HILL, Beth, Director Human Resources, Russell County Medical Center, Lebanon, VA, p. A678
HILL, Candice, Chief Executive Officer, Mid–Jefferson Extended Care Hospital of Beaumont, Beaumont, TX, p. A602
HILL, Cheryl, Vice President Human Resources, Ascension Columbia St. Mary's Hospital Milwaukee, Milwaukee, WI, p. A716
HILL, Chris, Information Technology, Anchor Hospital, Atlanta, GA, p. A156
HILL, Deborah Ann., Chief Executive Officer, Montgomery General Hospital, Montgomery, WV, p. A702
HILL, Herbert, Director Human Resources, Klickitat Valley Health, Goldendale, WA, p. A690
HILL, Jack
　Chief Operating Officer and Administrator, The Jewish Hospital – Mercy Health, Cincinnati, OH, p. A489
　Vice President and Chief Operating Officer, Union Hospital Clinton, Clinton, IN, p. A214
HILL, James Lee. Sr, M.D., Chief Operating Officer, University Hospitals Parma Medical Center, Parma, OH, p. A502
HILL, James P, Senior Vice President Administrative Services, Medstar Washington Hospital Center, Washington, DC, p. A124
HILL, Jason, M.D., Chief Medical Officer, Choctaw Nation Health Care Center, Talihina, OK, p. A521
HILL, Jill, Director Information Technology, Utah State Hospital, Provo, UT, p. A667
HILL, Kalisha, M.D., Chief Medical Officer, Ascension St. Mary – Kankakee, Kankakee, IL, p. A199
HILL, Karen
　Departmental Personnel Officer, Zuckerberg San Francisco General Hospital And Trauma Center, San Francisco, CA, p. A91
　Director Human Resources, Baylor Scott & White Institute for Rehabilitation – Dallas, Dallas, TX, p. A610
HILL, Kerry, Chief Financial Officer, Vista Medical Center East, Waukegan, IL, p. A210
HILL, Leo, Chief Information Officer, Massachusetts Eye And Ear, Boston, MA, p. A310
HILL, M. Scott.
　President and Chief Executive Officer, Piedmont Columbus Regional Midtown, Columbus, GA, p. A161
　President and Chief Executive Officer, Piedmont Columbus Regional Northside, Columbus, GA, p. A161
HILL, Nancy, R.N., Chief Nursing Officer, Johnson Regional Medical Center, Clarksville, AR, p. A44
HILL, Nancy L, R.N., MSN, Chief Operating Officer, Medical City North Hills, North Richland Hills, TX, p. A641
HILL, Ryan, Senior Financial Advisor, Essentia Health St. Mary's – Detroit Lakes, Detroit Lakes, MN, p. A345
HILL, Stephen, Vice President and Chief Nursing Officer, Valley Baptist Medical Center–Harlingen, Harlingen, TX, p. A624
HILL, Stuart
　Vice President and Treasurer, Unity Health – Jacksonville, Jacksonville, AR, p. A48
　Vice President and Treasurer, Unity Health, Searcy, AR, p. A53
HILL, Timothy, Chief Operating Officer, UAMS Medical Center, Little Rock, AR, p. A50
HILL, Tracy
　M.D., Chief Medical Officer, Orem Community Hospital, Orem, UT, p. A667
　M.D., Chief Medical Officer, Utah Valley Hospital, Provo, UT, p. A667
HILL, Tyler, D.O., Chief Medical Officer, Sierra Nevada Memorial Hospital, Grass Valley, CA, p. A66
HILL–DAVIS, Nancy L, Senior Vice President and Chief Talent Officer, Mercy Medical Center – Cedar Rapids, Cedar Rapids, IA, p. A231
HILLARD, Mary, MSN, R.N., Chief Nursing Officer, Longmont United Hospital, Longmont, CO, p. A111
HILLARY, Maureen, Chief Nursing Officer, University of Michigan Health-Sparrow Eaton, Charlotte, MI, p. A323
HILLESTAD, Catherine, Chief Executive Officer, Adair County Health System, Greenfield, IA, p. A236
HILLESTAD, Tammy, Chief Nursing Officer, Brookings Health System, Brookings, SD, p. A572
HILLIARD, David J, D.O., Chief of Staff, WVU Medicine – Barnesville Hospital, Barnesville, OH, p. A485
HILLIARD, Jamie, Director of Information Technology, University of Kansas Health System St. Francis Campus, Topeka, KS, p. A261
HILLIS–CLARK, Patricia, Executive Director, Devereux Children's Behavioral Health Center, Malvern, PA, p. A545
HILLMAN, Brandon, R.N., Administrator, Christus Coushatta Health Care Center, Coushatta, LA, p. A280

HILLS, Cindi, Director Human Resources, Riverwood Healthcare Center, Aitkin, MN, p. A342
HILLYER, Lisa L, Human Resources Manager, Box Butte General Hospital, Alliance, NE, p. A397
HILSENBECK, Kelly, MSN, R.N., Chief Nursing Officer, Waverly Health Center, Waverly, IA, p. A245
HILT, Monica, President, Virginia Mason Medical Center, Seattle, WA, p. A695
HILTON, Aaron, President, Lawrence Memorial Hospital, Walnut Ridge, AR, p. A54
HILTON, Christopher, Chief Financial Officer, East Georgia Regional Medical Center, Statesboro, GA, p. A171
HILTON, Craig, Chief Executive Officer and Managing Director, Hampton Behavioral Health Center, Westampton, NJ, p. A430
HILTON, Daniel, M.D., Chief of Staff, Fountain Valley Regional Hospital And Medical Center, Fountain Valley, CA, p. A64
HILTON, Lois, Director Human Resources, Desoto Memorial Hospital, Arcadia, FL, p. A125
HILTON, Neil A., FACHE, Chief Executive Officer, Perkins County Health Services, Grant, NE, p. A400
HILTON–SIEBERT, Stephanie
  FACHE, MSN, Chief Executive Officer, Marion Health, Marion, IN, p. A223
  FACHE, MSN, President and Chief Executive Officer, Marion Health, Marion, IN, p. A223
HILTUNEN, Theresa, Entity Information Officer, Penn Presbyterian Medical Center, Philadelphia, PA, p. A549
HILTZ, Paul C, FACHE, Chief Executive Officer, Nch Baker Hospital, Naples, FL, p. A142
HILTZ, Paul C., FACHE, Chief Executive Officer, Nch Baker Hospital, Naples, FL, p. A142
HIMES, Geoffrey, Interim Chief Financial Officer, Metrohealth Medical Center, Cleveland, OH, p. A491
HINCHEY, Paul P.
  President and Chief Executive Officer, Candler Hospital–Savannah, Savannah, GA, p. A170
  President and Chief Executive Officer, St. Joseph's Hospital, Savannah, GA, p. A171
HINCKLEY, Fran X., Chief Information Officer, Salem Hospital, Salem, MA, p. A318
HINDMAN, Ashley
  Chief Executive Officer, Harris Regional Hospital, Sylva, NC, p. A477
  Chief Executive Officer, Swain Community Hospital, A Duke Lifepoint Hospital, Bryson City, NC, p. A464
HINDMAN, Jennifer, Vice President, Hospital Administrator, Community Hospital North, Indianapolis, IN, p. A219
HINDS, Bob, Executive Director, Bradford Health Services At Huntsville, Madison, AL, p. A21
HINE, Kristy
  Associate Vice President Finance, Geisinger Lewistown Hospital, Lewistown, PA, p. A544
  Chief Financial Officer, Geisinger Medical Center Muncy, Muncy, PA, p. A546
HINE, Rhonda, R.N., Interim Chief Nursing Executive, Mason District Hospital, Havana, IL, p. A197
HINER, Jill, Vice President and Chief Financial Officer, Western Reserve Hospital, Cuyahoga Falls, OH, p. A493
HINER, Peggy, Director Human Resources, Wheatland Memorial Healthcare, Harlowton, MT, p. A393
HINES, Andrew, Administrator, St. James Behavioral Health Hospital, Gonzales, LA, p. A282
HINES, JeDonne, Chief Financial Officer, Intermountain Hospital, Boise, ID, p. A179
HINES, Linda, Vice President Information Technology and Information Systems, University of Maryland Rehabilitation & Orthopaedic Institute, Baltimore, MD, p. A302
HINES, Lisa, Director of Performance Improvement, Eastern Shore Hospital Center, Cambridge, MD, p. A303
HINES, Mary Beth, D.O., Chief Medical Officer, Up Health System – Portage, Hancock, MI, p. A329
HINES, Stacy, Administrator, D. W. Mcmillan Memorial Hospital, Brewton, AL, p. A17
HINESLEY, Jay
  FACHE, Chief Executive Officer, Musc Health Florence Medical Center, Florence, SC, p. A566
  FACHE, Chief Executive Officer, Musc Health Marion Medical Center, Mullins, SC, p. A569
HINKLE, Matthew, R.N., Chief Operating Officer, Piedmont Medical Center, Rock Hill, SC, p. A570
HINKLE, Stacey, Director Information Technology, Banner Desert Medical Center, Mesa, AZ, p. A33
HINNER, William J
  Vice President Financial Analysis and Planning, Aspirus Steven's Point Hospital & Clinics, Inc., Stevens Point, WI, p. A722
  Vice President Financial Analysis and Planning Ministry Health Care, Marshfield Medical Center, Marshfield, WI, p. A715

HINO, Raymond T., FACHE, Chief Executive Officer, Southern Coos Hospital And Health Center, Bandon, OR, p. A525
HINOJOSA, Anna, MSN, R.N., Interim Chief Nursing Officer, Knap. Medical Center, Weslaco, TX, p. A662
HINRICHS, Becky Kay, Vice President Human Resources, Riverside Medical Center, Kankakee, IL, p. A199
HINRICHS, Sandy, Director Human Resources, Burnett Medical Center, Grantsburg, WI, p. A711
HINSHAW, Bruce, Director Human Resources, Artesia General Hospital, Artesia, NM, p. A433
HINSON, Lee, Chief Nursing Officer, Merit Health Natchez, Natchez, MS, p. A367
HINSON, Renee, Chief Executive Officer, Emory Rehabilitation Hospital, Atlanta, GA, p. A157
HINTZ, Lori, Coordinator Information Systems, Rochester Psychiatric Center, Rochester, NY, p. A457
HINTZE, Paul, M.D., Vice President Medical Affairs, Mercy Hospital St. Louis, Saint Louis, MO, p. A385
HIOTT, Jimmy O. III, Chief Executive Officer, Colleton Medical Center, Walterboro, SC, p. A571
HIPKISS, Tom, Vice President Finance, Forbes Hospital, Monroeville, PA, p. A546
HIPP, Bradley, Chief Financial Officer, Banner – University Medical Center Tucson, Tucson, AZ, p. A40
HIPP, Sarah, Director of Marketing, Desoto Memorial Hospital, Arcadia, FL, p. A125
HIRKALER, Kim, Director Human Resources, Bon Secours Community Hospital, Port Jervis, NY, p. A456
HIRKO, Mark, M.D., FACS, President, Putnam Hospital, Carmel, NY, p. A441
HIROMOTO, Brenda, Director of Nursing, Rehabilitation Hospital of The Pacific, Honolulu, HI, p. A176
HIRSCH, Leslie D., FACHE, President and Chief Executive Officer, Saint Peter's Healthcare System, New Brunswick, NJ, p. A425
HIRSCH, Noomi, Chief Executive Officer, Encompass Health Rehabilitation Hospital of Littleton, Littleton, CO, p. A111
HIRSCH, Ted W, Senior Executive Director, Logan Health, Kalispell, MT, p. A393
HIRSCH, Vicki, R.N., Director of Nursing, Lallie Kemp Medical Center, Independence, LA, p. A283
HIRSCH–LANUTE, Hirsch–Lanute, Interim Vice President and Chief Nursing Officer, Penn State Health Hampden Medical Center, Enola, PA, p. A539
HIRST, Barb, R.N., Vice President Human Resources and Chief Nursing Officer, Salem Regional Medical Center, Salem, OH, p. A503
HISE, Landon, Chief Executive Officer, Oklahoma Center for Orthopaedic And Multi–Specialty Surgery, Oklahoma City, OK, p. A518
HISEY, Commie, D.O., Chief of Staff, Gonzales Healthcare Systems, Gonzales, TX, p. A622
HISLOP, Donald Ayers, R.N., Jr, Chief Nursing Officer, Los Alamos Medical Center, Los Alamos, NM, p. A435
HITCHCOCK, Sherri, Chief Financial Officer, Mcdonough District Hospital, Macomb, IL, p. A200
HITE DAVIS, Anissa J, Vice President Human Resources, St. Joseph's Hospital, Buckhannon, WV, p. A699
HITT, Melissa, Director of Nursing, Highland–Clarksburg Hospital, Clarksburg, WV, p. A700
HITT, Patricia A, Associate Director, Grand Junction Va Medical Center, Grand Junction, CO, p. A108
HITTMEIER, Robert, Chief Executive Officer, Adolescent Hospital, Montrose Behavioral Health Hospital, Chicago, IL, p. A190
HIXSON, Kim, Chief Financial Officer, Pender Community Hospital, Pender, NE, p. A405
HJEMBO, Philip. Chief Financial Officer, St. Elizabeth Hospital, Enumclaw, WA, p. A689
HLAHOL, Jan, Manager Human Resources, Cleveland Clinic Children's Hospital for Rehabilitation, Cleveland, OH, p. A490
HLUCHY, Nicholas, Business Analyst, Support Services Manager, Baton Rouge Rehabilitation Hospital, Baton Rouge, LA, p. A277
HO, Kingman, M.D., Senior Vice President, Chief Medical and Care Innovation Officer, Henry Mayo Newhall Hospital, Valencia, CA, p. A99
HO–SHING, Viodelda, Deputy Director Administration, Creedmoor Psychiatric Center, New York, NY, p. A448
HOAG, Abby, Director, Human Resources, UH Avon Rehabilitation Hospital, Avon, OH, p. A485
HOAGBIN, Joseph
  M.D., Chief Medical Officer, Chi Health Immanuel, Omaha, NE, p. A403
  M.D., Chief Quality Officer, Chi Health Mercy Council Bluffs, Council Bluffs, IA, p. A233
HOAR, Brad, Director Information and Technology, Cedar Park Regional Medical Center, Cedar Park, TX, p. A607

HOARD, Kaylee S., Chief Financial Officer, Cook Hospital & Care Center, Cook, MN, p. A345
HOARD, Shelly RN, Director of Nursing, Cypress Grove Behavioral Health, Bastrop, LA, p. A277
HOBACK, Kim, Supervisor Information Systems, Athens–Limestone Hospital, Athens, AL, p. A15
HOBART, Robert, Director Management Information Systems, Heartland Behavioral Healthcare, Massillon, OH, p. A499
HOBBS, Donna, Nurse Executive, U. S. Public Health Service Indian Hospital–Sells, Sells, AZ, p. A38
HOBBS, Ed, Director Information Services, Parkview Dekalb Hospital, Auburn, IN, p. A212
HOBBS, Emilie, Director Human Resources, Woodland Heights Medical Center, Lufkin, TX, p. A637
HOBBS, Keith, FACHE, President and Chief Executive Officer, Torrance Memorial Medical Center, Torrance, CA, p. A98
HOBBS, Mike, Chief Financial Officer, Clay County Hospital, Flora, IL, p. A195
HOBBS, Steve E.
  Chief Financial Officer, North Alabama Medical Center, Florence, AL, p. A19
  Chief Financial Officer, North Alabama Shoals Hospital, Muscle Shoals, AL, p. A23
HOBBS, Tommy, Chief Executive Officer, Johnson Regional Medical Center, Clarksville, AR, p. A44
HOBDY, Amy L, Vice President of Human Resources, Tristar Hendersonville Medical Center, Hendersonville, TN, p. A584
HOBGOOD, Marcus, Director Information Services, Ochsner Lsu Health Shreveport – Academic Medical Center, Shreveport, LA, p. A292
HOBSON, Christopher Brian, Chief Operating Officer, Bristol Regional Medical Center, Bristol, TN, p. A579
HOBSON, James M., Chief Executive Officer, Magnolia Regional Health Center, Corinth, MS, p. A361
HOBSON, Loveland, Chief Executive Office, Unicoi County Hospital, Erwin, TN, p. A583
HOBSON, Tamara, Director of Nursing, North Platte Valley Medical Center, Saratoga, WY, p. A728
HOCATE, Crispin P, Professional and Support Services Officer, Texas Health Presbyterian Hospital Allen, Allen, TX, p. A595
HOCHENBERG, Paul S, Executive Director, Westchester Medical Center, Valhalla, NY, p. A461
HOCHSTETLER, Amy, Chief Financial Officer, Orthopaedic Hospital of Lutheran Health Network, Fort Wayne, IN, p. A216
HOCHSTETLER, Lisa, R.N., Chief Nursing Officer, Tristar Hendersonville Medical Center, Hendersonville, TN, p. A584
HOCK, Douglas G, Executive Vice President and Chief Operating Officer, Children's Hospital of Philadelphia, Philadelphia, PA, p. A548
HOCKENBERRY, Michael A., Senior Vice President and Chief Operating Officer, UPMC Hanover, Hanover, PA, p. A541
HOCKERSMITH, Lisa K., Vice President Human Resources, Kern Medical, Bakersfield, CA, p. A57
HOCKERT, Steve, Interim Chief Executive Officer, Onecore Health, Oklahoma City, OK, p. A518
HOCKING, Barbara, Chief Nursing Officer, St. Luke's Regional Medical Center, Boise, ID, p. A180
HOCKING, Dale E, Chief Financial Officer, Jupiter Medical Center, Jupiter, FL, p. A136
HOCKING, Patrick
  Chief Financial Officer, Asante Ashland Community Hospital, Ashland, OR, p. A525
  Chief Financial Officer, Asante Rogue Regional Medical Center, Medford, OR, p. A529
  Chief Financial Officer, Asante Three Rivers Medical Center, Grants Pass, OR, p. A527
HOCUM, Timothy, Chief Financial Officer, Providence Kodiak Island Medical Center, Kodiak, AK, p. A28
HODGE, David Jr, Chief Operating Officer, Valley Children's Healthcare, Madera, CA, p. A76
HODGE, Ian, Chief Executive Officer, Select Specialty Hospital–Durham, Durham, NC, p. A467
HODGE, Lisa, Director, Human Resources, Rolling Hills Hospital, Franklin, TN, p. A583
HODGE, Montie, Vice President Information Technology and Chief Information Officer, Regional West Medical Center, Scottsbluff, NE, p. A406
HODGE, Stacie, Director of Nursing, Washington County Hospital, Nashville, IL, p. A203
HODGES, Calvin, Director Human Resources, Integris Health Ponca City Hospital, Ponca City, OK, p. A519
HODGES, Craig, Director Information Services, Ochsner Medical Center – Hancock, Bay Saint Louis, MS, p. A359
HODGES, Dawn, Director Human Resources, Grand River Hospital District, Rifle, CO, p. A113

Index of Health Care Professionals
Index of Health Care Professionals / Hodges

HODGES, Jay, Chief Financial Officer, Chambers Health, Anahuac, TX, p. A597
HODGES, Leisha, Human Resources Officer, Eastland Memorial Hospital, Eastland, TX, p. A615
HODGES, Randall H, FACHE, Vice President and Administrator, Charleston Area Medical Center, Charleston, WV, p. A700
HODGIN, Robin, R.N., Vice President of Patient Services and Chief Nursing Officer, Northern Regional Hospital, Mount Airy, NC, p. A473
HODGSON, Judith Ann, Chief Nursing Officer, Cheyenne County Hospital, Saint Francis, KS, p. A259
HODSHIRE, Jeremiah J., President and Chief Executive Officer, Hillsdale Hospital, Hillsdale, MI, p. A329
HODSON, Don, M.D., Chief Medical Officer, St. Luke Hospital And Living Center, Marion, KS, p. A254
HOEFER, Bill
FACHE, President and Regional Market Leader, Corewell Health Zeeland Hospital, Zeeland, MI, p. A341
FACHE, Regional Market Leader, Corewell Health Pennock Hospital, Hastings, MI, p. A329
HOEFS, Dennis, Manager Information Technology, New Mexico Rehabilitation Center, Roswell, NM, p. A436
HOEG, Robin, Chief Operating Officer, Winona Health, Winona, MN, p. A357
HOEHNS, Brent, M.D., Chief of Medical Staff, Knoxville Hospital & Clinics, Knoxville, IA, p. A239
HOEKSTRA, James, M.D., President, Atrium Health Wake Foret Baptist High Point Medical Center, High Point, NC, p. A470
HOELL, Paul, M.D., President Medical Staff, Thedacare Medical Center–New London, New London, WI, p. A718
HOELSCHER, Cassidy, Chief Executive Officer, Rehabilitation Institute of Southern Illinois, Llc, The, Shiloh, IL, p. A208
HOELSCHER, Steven C, Chief Operating Officer, Valley Regional Medical Center, Brownsville, TX, p. A605
HOERTZ, Joanne, Vice President of Nursing, Brooks Rehabilitation Hospital, Jacksonville, FL, p. A134
HOESCH, Marty, Director Information Systems, North Suburban Medical Center, Thornton, CO, p. A113
HOEY, Amy J., R.N., MS, President, Lowell General Hospital, Lowell, MA, p. A315
HOFER, Maggie, Human Resources Representative, Hawarden Regional Healthcare, Hawarden, IA, p. A237
HOFF, Deanna, R.N., Director of Nursing, Bacon County Hospital And Health System, Alma, GA, p. A156
HOFF, Linda, Senior Vice President and Chief Financial Officer, Legacy Mount Hood Medical Center, Gresham, OR, p. A527
HOFF, Margaret, Account Manager, Brown County Community Treatment Center, Green Bay, WI, p. A712
HOFFER, Nolan, Administrator Rehabilitation Services, St. Luke's Rehabilitation Hospital, Boise, ID, p. A180
HOFFMAN, Brad, Administrative Director Human Resources, Adventhealth Shawnee Mission, Merriam, KS, p. A255
HOFFMAN, Brian
M.D., Chief Medical Services, Veterans Affairs Boston Healthcare System, West Roxbury, MA, p. A319
Chief Human, Beaufort Memorial Hospital, Beaufort, SC, p. A562
HOFFMAN, Carole, Vice President Human Resources, HCA Florida Brandon Hospital, Brandon, FL, p. A127
HOFFMAN, Daniel, M.D., Administrative Medical Director, SSM Health Good Samaritan Hospital, Mount Vernon, IL, p. A202
HOFFMAN, Debbie, Vice President Patient Services, Mosaic Medical Center – Maryville, Maryville, MO, p. A380
HOFFMAN, Debra, Human Resources Manager, Kern Valley Healthcare District, Lake Isabella, CA, p. A69
HOFFMAN, Donna R, Chief Human Resource Officer, Mercyone Des Moines Medical Center, Des Moines, IA, p. A235
HOFFMAN, Howard, M.D., Medical Director, Psychiatric Institute of Washington, Washington, DC, p. A124
HOFFMAN, Jerry, Chief Financial Officer, Platte Health Center Avera, Platte, SD, p. A575
HOFFMAN, Marcus, Area Chief Financial Officer, Kaiser Permanente Orange County Anaheim Medical Center, Anaheim, CA, p. A55
HOFFMAN, Rex, M.D., Chief Medical Officer, Providence Holy Cross Medical Center, Los Angeles, CA, p. A75
HOFFMAN, Robert P, R.N., Chief Nursing Officer, Wilkes–Barre General Hospital, Wilkes–Barre, PA, p. A558
HOFFMAN, Tom, Manager Information Systems, Wayne Memorial Hospital, Honesdale, PA, p. A542
HOFFMAN, Val, Chief Financial Officer, Avera Granite Falls, Granite Falls, MN, p. A348
HOFFMANN, Wanda, Director Human Resources, River Oaks Hospital, New Orleans, LA, p. A290
HOFFPAUIR, Chad, Chief Executive Officer, Jennings Senior Care Hospital, Jennings, LA, p. A284
HOFIUS, Chuck, FACHE, Chief Executive Officer, Perham Health, Perham, MN, p. A352
HOFMAN, William, Manager Information Technology, Atrium Health Wake Forest Baptist Wilkes Medical Center, North Wilkesboro, NC, p. A474
HOFSTETTER, Phil A., Chief Executive Officer, Petersburg Medical Center, Petersburg, AK, p. A29
HOGAN, Brian, Chief Executive Officer and Administrator, Baptist Memorial Hospital–Desoto, Southaven, MS, p. A369
HOGAN, Judith, Comptroller and Director Resources and Logistics, Naval Hospital Bremerton, Bremerton, WA, p. A687
HOGAN, Michael, Chief Resource Management, General Leonard Wood Army Community Hospital, Fort Leonard Wood, MO, p. A375
HOGAN, Richard H, CPA, Chief Financial Officer, Landmark Hospital of Cap. Girardeau, Cap. Girardeau, MO, p. A372
HOGAN, Sean, FACHE, President, Mercy South St. Louis Communities, Mercy Hospital South, Saint Louis, MO, p. A385
HOGAN, Timothy J., FACHE, President, Chief Hospital Executive, Hackensack Meridian Health Riverview Medical Center, Red Bank, NJ, p. A428
HOGDSON, Judy, R.N., Chief Nursing Officer, Hospital District No 1 of Rice County, Lyons, KS, p. A254
HOGUE, Vicky, R.N., Vice President Patient Services and Chief Nursing Officer, Wellstar Paulding Hospital, Hiram, GA, p. A165
HOHN, Craig, Chief Executive Officer, Avera Merrill Pioneer Hospital, Rock Rapids, IA, p. A242
HOLBERT, Brandon, Director, Information Services, HCA Florida Ocala Hospital, Ocala, FL, p. A143
HOLBROOK, Chip, M.D., Chief of Staff, Simpson General Hospital, Mendenhall, MS, p. A366
HOLBROOK, Curtis, M.D., Chief Medical Officer, Baylor Scott & White Surgical Hospital–Sherman, Sherman, TX, p. A652
HOLBROOK, Donald, Chief Executive Officer, State Penitentiary Hospital, Walla Walla, WA, p. A698
HOLCOMB, Holly, R.N., Chief Executive Officer, Childress Regional Medical Center, Childress, TX, p. A607
HOLCOMB, Michelle, Human Resources, Webster County Memorial Hospital, Webster Springs, WV, p. A705
HOLDEN, Carol, Chief Financial Officer, Northern Cochise Community Hospital, Willcox, AZ, p. A41
HOLDER, Hal
Regional Chief Financial Officer, SSM Health St. Josep. Hospital – Lake Saint Louis, Lake Saint Louis, MO, p. A379
Regional Chief Financial Officer–Hospital Operations, SSM Health St. Clare Hospital – Fenton, Fenton, MO, p. A375
HOLDER, Kasey, M.D., Vice President Medical Affairs, St. Bernards Medical Center, Jonesboro, AR, p. A48
HOLDER, Kelly, Administrator, Hamilton County Hospital, Syracuse, KS, p. A260
HOLDER, Michelle, Nurse Executive, Straith Hospital for Special Surgery, Southfield, MI, p. A338
HOLDER, Sophia G., Executive Vice President and Chief Financial Officer, Children's Hospital of Philadelphia, Philadelphia, PA, p. A548
HOLDER, Spencer, Chief Financial Officer, Trinity Medical, Ferriday, LA, p. A282
HOLDER–HOOPER, Donna, Chief Human Resource Officer, Encompass Health Rehabilitation Hospital, An Affiliate of Martin Health, Stuart, FL, p. A150
HOLEKAMP, Nicholas, M.D., Chief Medical Officer, Ranken Jordan Pediatric Bridge Hospital, Maryland Heights, MO, p. A380
HOLGUIN, Brenda, Manager Human Resources, El Paso Behavioral Health System, El Paso, TX, p. A616
HOLGUIN, Mindee, Manager Human Resources, Sierra Vista Hospital, Truth Or Consequences, NM, p. A437
HOLIFIELD, Tracy, Director Information Systems, Merit Health Central, Jackson, MS, p. A364
HOLINER, Joel, M.D., Executive Medical Director, Medical City Green Oaks Hospital, Dallas, TX, p. A611
HOLLAND, Brad D., President and Chief Executive Officer, Hendrick Medical Center, Abilene, TX, p. A595
HOLLAND, Charles, President and Chief Executive Officer, St. Bernard Hospital And Health Care Center, Chicago, IL, p. A191
HOLLAND, David
Chief Information Officer, Herrin Hospital, Herrin, IL, p. A197
Vice President Chief Innovation Officer, Memorial Hospital of Carbondale, Carbondale, IL, p. A187
Vice President Information Services, St. Josep. Memorial Hospital, Murphysboro, IL, p. A203
HOLLAND, Gabrielle, Chief Financial Officer, Baylor Surgical Hospital At Las Colinas, Irving, TX, p. A630
HOLLAND, Kevin, Administrator, Memorial Hospital At Stone County, Wiggins, MS, p. A370
HOLLAND, Kwi, Vice President Information Services, Knox Community Hospital, Mount Vernon, OH, p. A501
HOLLAND, Megan, Chief Medical Officer and Family Practitioner, Southern Coos Hospital And Health Center, Bandon, OR, p. A525
HOLLAND, Michael, M.D., Chief Executive Officer, Rehabilitation Hospital of Jennings, Jennings, LA, p. A284
HOLLAND, Penny, Associate Director for Patient Care Services, Aleda E. Lutz Department of Veterans Affairs Medical Center, Saginaw, MI, p. A336
HOLLAND, Shannon S.
R.N., MSN, Chief Nursing Officer, Billings Clinic, Billings, MT, p. A389
R.N., MSN, Chief Nursing Officer, Multicare Valley Hospital, Spokane Valley, WA, p. A696
HOLLAND, Sharron, Chief Financial Officer, Baptist Memorial Hospital–Carroll County, Huntingdon, TN, p. A584
HOLLAND, Stace, Chief Executive Officer, Thomas H. Boyd Memorial Hospital, Carrollton, IL, p. A187
HOLLAND, Stephen, M.D., Vice President Chief Medical Officer and Medical Director, Gaylord Specialty Healthcare, Wallingford, CT, p. A119
HOLLEMAN, James, M.D., Chief of Staff, St. Luke's Hospital, Columbus, NC, p. A466
HOLLEMAN, Stephen B, Chief Financial Officer, Shepherd Center, Atlanta, GA, p. A158
HOLLENBERG, Anthony, M.D., President, Boston Medical Center, Boston, MA, p. A310
HOLLEY, Brenda
R.N., Chief Nursing Officer, Lovelace Westside Hospital, Albuquerque, NM, p. A432
R.N., Chief Nursing Officer, Lovelace Women's Hospital, Albuquerque, NM, p. A433
HOLLIDAY, Jonathan, Manager Information Technology, Mercyone Elkader Medical Center, Elkader, IA, p. A236
HOLLIN, Sheara, Chief Operating Officer, Hospital of The University of Pennsylvania, Philadelphia, PA, p. A549
HOLLINGER, Theresa, Chief Nursing Officer, Newport Hospital And Health Services, Newport, WA, p. A692
HOLLINGS, Derrick O., Chief Financial Officer, Hennepin Healthcare, Minneapolis, MN, p. A350
HOLLINGSWORTH, Carl, Chief Financial Officer, Artesia General Hospital, Artesia, NM, p. A433
HOLLINGSWORTH, Christine, Chief Financial Officer, Carl T. Hayden Veterans' Administration Medical Center, Phoenix, AZ, p. A35
HOLLINGSWORTH, Sherri, Chief Human Resources Officer, PIH Health Downey Hospital, Downey, CA, p. A61
HOLLIS, Gary W, Comptroller, Arkansas State Hospital, Little Rock, AR, p. A49
HOLLIS, Lauren, Chief Human Resources Officer, North Mississipp. Medical Center–West Point, West Point, MS, p. A370
HOLLISTER, Jerry, Chief Executive Officer, Northeastern Center, Auburn, IN, p. A212
HOLLISTER, Richard, President of Medical Staff, Exeter Hospital, Exeter, NH, p. A415
HOLLOMON, Brian, Chief Financial Officer, Blount Memorial Hospital, Maryville, TN, p. A587
HOLLOWAY, Becky
Vice President, Human Resources, Doctors Neuropsychiatric Hospital, Bremen, IN, p. A213
Vice President, Human Resources, Medical Behavioral Hospital of Clear Lake, Houston, TX, p. A629
Vice President, Human Resources, Medical Behavioral Hospital of Mishawaka, Mishawaka, IN, p. A223
Vice President, Human Resources, Medical Behavioral Hospital of Northern Arizona, Prescott, AZ, p. A37
Vice President, Human Resources, Neurobehavioral Hospital of Nw Indiana/Greater Chicago, Crown Point, IN, p. A215
Vice President, Human Resources, Neuropsychiatric Hospital of Indianapolis, Indianapolis, IN, p. A220
Vice President, Human Resources, Phoenix Medical Psychiatric Hospital, Phoenix, AZ, p. A36
HOLLOWAY, Kristina, Chief Human Resources Officer, Healdsburg Hospital, Healdsburg, CA, p. A67
HOLLOWAY, Myra, Director Human Resources Management, Central State Hospital, Milledgeville, GA, p. A168
HOLLOWAY, Whitney, Chief Financial Officer, Berwick Hospital Center, Berwick, PA, p. A535
HOLM, Mary Ann, Office Clerk, Tioga Medical Center, Tioga, ND, p. A483
HOLM, Stan
FACHE, Chief Executive Officer, Banner Boswell Medical Center, Sun City, AZ, p. A39
FACHE, Chief Executive Officer, Banner Del E. Webb Medical Center, Sun City West, AZ, p. A39

A876 Index of Health Care Professionals

Index of Health Care Professionals
Index of Health Care Professionals / Horn

HOLMAN, Resha T, Chief Nurse Executive Officer, Northridge Hospital Medical Center, Los Angeles, CA, p. A74
HOLMAN, Steve M.
FACHE, Chief Executive Officer, Union Hospital Clinton, Clinton, IN, p. A214
FACHE, President and Chief Executive Officer, Union Hospital, Terre Haute, IN, p. A228
HOLMES, Dawne, Chief Financial Officer, Greenwood Leflore Hospital, Greenwood, MS, p. A362
HOLMES, Diana, Chief Nursing Officer, Central Regional Hospital, Butner, NC, p. A464
HOLMES, Ginnie, Chief Financial Officer, Electra Memorial Hospital, Electra, TX, p. A618
HOLMES, Heather, Director Health Information Systems, Merit Health Rankin, Brandon, MS, p. A360
HOLMES, Heidi, Chief Information Officer, Oklahoma State University Medical Center, Tulsa, OK, p. A522
HOLMES, Jim R., President/Chief Executive Officer, Redlands Community Hospital, Redlands, CA, p. A85
HOLMES, John, Business Manager, Ancora Psychiatric Hospital, Hammonton, NJ, p. A422
HOLMES, Kamara, Director of Nursing, Beacon Behavioral Hospital, Lutcher, LA, p. A287
HOLMES, Katrina, Chief Nursing Officer, Sutter Auburn Faith Hospital, Auburn, CA, p. A56
HOLMES, Nicholas M.
M.D., President, UCSF Benioff Children's Hospitals, SVP Children's Services UCSF Health, UCSF Benioff Children's Hospital Oakland, Oakland, CA, p. A81
M.D., President, UCSF Benioff Children's Hospitals, SVP Children's Services UCSF Health, UCSF Medical Center, San Francisco, CA, p. A91
HOLMES, Phillip Walter, M.D., Chief of Staff, Elbow Lake Medical Center, Elbow Lake, MN, p. A346
HOLMES, Ray, Chief Nursing Officer, Slidell Memorial Hospital, Slidell, LA, p. A293
HOLMES, Terry R, M.D., Clinical Director, Moccasin Bend Mental Health Institute, Chattanooga, TN, p. A580
HOLMES, Tim
Chief Executive Officer, Navos, Seattle, WA, p. A694
Interim President, Multicare Good Samaritan Hospital, Puyallup. WA, p. A693
HOLMES, Troy, Chief Financial Officer, Advanced Specialty Hospital of Toledo, Toledo, OH, p. A504
HOLMSTROM, Ashley, Chief Nursing Officer, Abrazo West Campus, Goodyear, AZ, p. A32
HOLMSTROM, Rebecca, Chief Nursing Officer, Ely–Bloomenson Community Hospital, Ely, MN, p. A346
HOLMSTROM, Tallulah
M.D., Chief Medical Officer, Carolina Pines Regional Medical Center, Hartsville, SC, p. A568
M.D., Chief Medical Officer, Musc Health Kershaw Medical Center, Camden, SC, p. A562
HOLSAPPLE, Kim, Human Resource Specialist, Chester Mental Health Center, Chester, IL, p. A188
HOLSCHBACH, Dennis, Chief Financial Officer, Ruby Valley Medical Center, Sheridan, MT, p. A396
HOLSON, Debbie C, R.N., MSN, Chief Operating Officer, The Hsc Pediatric Center, Washington, DC, p. A124
HOLSON, Debbie C., R.N., MSN, Chief Operating Officer, The Hsc Pediatric Center, Washington, DC, p. A124
HOLST, David, M.D., Chief of Staff, Mercy Medical Center Mount Shasta, Mount Shasta, CA, p. A79
HOLSTEN, Robyn, Human Resources Director, Salt Lake Behavioral Health, Salt Lake City, UT, p. A669
HOLT, Albert E., M.D., IV, Chief Medical Officer, HCA Florida Memorial Hospital, Jacksonville, FL, p. A134
HOLT, Bebe, Chief Nursing Officer, Scotland Health Care System, Laurinburg, NC, p. A471
HOLT, Clayton, Chief Executive Officer, San Juan Health Service District, Monticello, UT, p. A666
HOLT, David, Director, Portland Hcs, Portland, OR, p. A530
HOLT, Jeffrey J., Chief Operating Officer, Clara Maass Medical Center, Belleville, NJ, p. A418
HOLT, Julie, R.N., MSN, Chief Nursing Officer, The Christ Hospital Health Network, Cincinnati, OH, p. A489
HOLT, Kory
Assistant Vice President for Financial Integration, Avera Flandreau Hospital, Flandreau, SD, p. A573
Division Controller Network Operations, Avera Dells Area Hospital, Dell Rapids, SD, p. A573
HOLT, Peter, M.D., Director Medical Affairs, Saint Luke's Hospital of Kansas City, Kansas City, MO, p. A378
HOLT, Richard, R.N., Associate Director Patient Care Services, VA St. Louis Health Care System, Saint Louis, MO, p. A384
HOLT, Sherry, Director Human Resources, Unity Medical Center, Manchester, TN, p. A587
HOLT, Tabetha, Director of Human Resources, Riverside Walter Reed Hospital, Gloucester, VA, p. A677
HOLT, Will, Director Information Technology, Harrison County Community Hospital, Bethany, MO, p. A371
HOLTHAUS, Julie K, Director Human Resources, Sabetha Community Hospital, Sabetha, KS, p. A259
HOLTHAUS, Monica, Chief Financial Officer, Community Healthcare System, Onaga, KS, p. A256
HOLTMAN, Jean, Vice President, Human Resources, Providence St. Mary Medical Center, Apple Valley, CA, p. A56
HOLTZ, George, Adminstrative Director Human Resources, Adventist Health White Memorial Montebello, Montebello, CA, p. A78
HOLTZ, Jennifer, Director Finance, Centracare – Paynesville, Paynesville, MN, p. A352
HOLTZ, Keith M, Chief Administrative Office, Cook Children's Medical Center – Prosper, Prosper, TX, p. A646
HOLTZ, Noel, M.D., Chief Medical Officer, Wellstar Douglas Hospital, Douglasville, GA, p. A163
HOLTZMAN, Michael, M.D., Medical Director, Kindred Hospital–St. Louis, Saint Louis, MO, p. A383
HOLUBEK, William, M.D., Chief Medical Officer, University Hospital, Newark, NJ, p. A425
HOLYOAK, Mark C.
FACHE, Chief Executive Officer, Lourdes Counseling Center, Richland, WA, p. A694
FACHE, Chief Executive Officer, Lourdes Health, Pasco, WA, p. A692
HOLZBOG, Doug
Market Chief Executive Officer, Ennis Regional Medical Center, Ennis, TX, p. A618
Market Chief Executive Officer, Palestine Regional Medical Center–East, Palestine, TX, p. A642
Market Chief Executive Officer, Parkview Regional Hospital, Mexia, TX, p. A639
HOLZER, Traci, Chief Human Resources Officer, Doctors Hospital of Manteca, Manteca, CA, p. A76
HOMYK, Linda
Chief Nursing Officer, Heritage Valley Beaver, Beaver, PA, p. A535
Chief Nursing Officer, Sewickley Valley Hospital, (A Division of Valley Medical Facilities), Sewickley, PA, p. A555
HONAKER, Jennifer, Chief Financial Officer, Tricities Hospital, Hopewell, VA, p. A678
HONEA, Bruce, Director Information Services, Christus Coushatta Health Care Center, Coushatta, LA, p. A280
HONEA, Michael, Chief Executive Officer, Glen Rose Medical Center, Glen Rose, TX, p. A622
HONERLAW, Elayne
Chief Clinical Officer, Kindred Hospital The Palm Beaches, Riviera Beach, FL, p. A148
Chief Executive Officer, Kindred Hospital The Palm Beaches, Riviera Beach, FL, p. A148
HONEYCUTT, Cynthia, Director Human Resources, Moccasin Bend Mental Health Institute, Chattanooga, TN, p. A580
HONEYCUTT, Robert, President, Christus Santa Rosa Hospital – San Marcos, San Marcos, TX, p. A651
HONOMICHL, Robin, Chief Executive Officer, Eastern Iowa Rehabilitation Hospital, Coralville, IA, p. A233
HONSINGER, Melissa, Chief Operating Officer, St. Luke's Rehabilitation Hospital, Boise, ID, p. A180
HOOD, Cliff, Chief Operating Officer, Central Regional Hospital, Butner, NC, p. A464
HOOD, Gary, Chief Information Officer, SBL Fayette County Hospital And Long Term Care, Vandalia, IL, p. A210
HOOD, Kathy, Administrative Assistant Human Resources, Union General Hospital, Blairsville, GA, p. A159
HOOD, Ron, M.D., Chief of Staff, Sutter Amador Hospital, Jackson, CA, p. A68
HOOD, Sam, Director Human Resources, Deaconess Illinois Medical Center, Marion, IL, p. A200
HOOD, Thomas, Chief Operating Officer, King's Daughters Medical Center, Brookhaven, MS, p. A360
HOOD, Tom, Chief Executive Officer, Wilson Medical Center, Neodesha, KS, p. A255
HOOD, Tyler, Chief Administrative Officer, Medical Center of Aurora, Aurora, CO, p. A103
HOODY, Dan, M.D., MSC, Interim Chief Medical Officer, Hennepin Healthcare, Minneapolis, MN, p. A350
HOOK, Diane, Chief Financial Officer, Wayne County Hospital And Clinic System, Corydon, IA, p. A233
HOOKER, Justin, M.D., Chief of Staff, Logan Health Shelby, Shelby, MT, p. A395
HOOKER, Melvin, Chief Human Resources, Raymond G. Murphy Department of Veterans Affairs Medical Center, Albuquerque, NM, p. A433
HOOKER, Rita, Administrative Director Information Services, Bon Secours St. Francis Health System, Greenville, SC, p. A566
HOOKS, Kurtis, Chief Executive Officer, Virginia Beach Psychiatric Center, Virginia Beach, VA, p. A685
HOOLAHAN, Susan E, R.N., MSN, Vice President Patient Care Services and Chief Nursing Officer, UPMC Passavant, Pittsburgh, PA, p. A552
HOOP, Heather, Human Resources Generalist, Adams County Regional Medical Center, Seaman, OH, p. A503
HOOPER, Grady A., Chief Executive Officer, Hamilton General Hospital, Hamilton, TX, p. A623
HOOPER, Jason R., President and Chief Executive Officer, KVC Prairie Ridge Psychiatric Hospital, Kansas City, KS, p. A251
HOOPER, Robert A, Director Human Resources, Tristar Skyline Medical Center, Nashville, TN, p. A591
HOOPINGARNER, Darrick, Chief Operating Officer, Dupont Hospital, Fort Wayne, IN, p. A216
HOOPINGARNER, Traci, R.N., Chief Nursing Officer, LMH Health, Lawrence, KS, p. A253
HOOVER, Garrett W, FACHE, President and Chief Operating Officer, Senior Vice President LifeBridge Health, Carroll Hospital, Westminster, MD, p. A308
HOOVER, Garrett W., FACHE, President and Chief Operating Officer, Senior Vice President LifeBridge Health, Carroll Hospital, Westminster, MD, p. A308
HOOVER, Jeremy Steven, Chief Information Officer, Kiowa County Memorial Hospital, Greensburg, KS, p. A250
HOOVER, John, Chief Executive Officer, Medical City Fort Worth, Fort Worth, TX, p. A620
HOOVER, Paul, President, Kettering Health Hamilton, Hamilton, OH, p. A497
HOPE, Lisa R, Director Human Resources, Owensboro Health Muhlenberg Community Hospital, Greenville, KY, p. A266
HOPE, Steve, Vice President Corporate Services, Methodist Rehabilitation Center, Jackson, MS, p. A364
HOPE, William IV, Chief of Medical Staff, ECU Health Chowan Hospital, Edenton, NC, p. A467
HOPKINS, Bill, Director of Operations, Northern Cochise Community Hospital, Willcox, AZ, p. A41
HOPKINS, Frances F, Chief Financial Officer, Sabine Medical Center, Many, LA, p. A288
HOPKINS, Jason, Director, Human Resources, Hamilton Medical Center, Dalton, GA, p. A162
HOPKINS, John, M.D., Chief of Staff, Avera Hand County Memorial Hospital, Miller, SD, p. A574
HOPKINS, Joy, Vice President Patient Care Services, OSF St. Francis Hospital And Medical Group. Escanaba, MI, p. A326
HOPKINS, Kelli, Director Human Resources, Baptist Health Medical Center–Hot Spring County, Malvern, AR, p. A50
HOPKINS, Ken
Vice President and Chief Executive Officer, Madonna Rehabilitation Specialty Hospital Lincoln, Lincoln, NE, p. A402
Vice President Finance and Chief Financial Officer, Norman Regional Health System, Norman, OK, p. A516
HOPKINS, Kevin, Vice President of Operations, Chi Memorial Hospital – Georgia, Fort Oglethorpe, GA, p. A164
HOPKINS, Larry, Chief Medical Officer, Indiana University Health Tipton Hospital, Tipton, IN, p. A228
HOPKINS, Michelle, Vice President of Human Resources, Mary Lanning Healthcare, Hastings, NE, p. A400
HOPKINS, Paul, Director, Kansas City Va Medical Center, Kansas City, MO, p. A377
HOPKINS, Ronald, D.O., Chief of Staff, Nor–Lea Hospital District, Lovington, NM, p. A435
HOPKINS, William, Director Finance, Carolinas Rehabilitation, Charlotte, NC, p. A465
HOPP, Eva, Chief Nurse Executive, Pinckneyville Community Hospital, Pinckneyville, IL, p. A206
HOPPER, Tasha
MSN, R.N., FACHE, Chief Executive Officer, The Hospitals of Providence East Campus – Tenet Healthcare, El Paso, TX, p. A617
MSN, R.N., FACHE, Chief Executive Officer, The Hospitals of Providence Sierra Campus – Tenet Healthcare, El Paso, TX, p. A617
HOPSON, W Briggs, M.D., Clinical Medical Director, Merit Health River Region, Vicksburg, MS, p. A369
HOPWOOD, James, Chief Financial Officer, Riverbridge Specialty Hospital, Vidalia, LA, p. A294
HORAN, Gary S, FACHE, President and Chief Executive Officer, Trinitas Regional Medical Center, Elizabeth, NJ, p. A421
HORATH, Kevin, Vice President Human Resources, Decatur Memorial Hospital, Decatur, IL, p. A192
HORECKA, Richard, Chief Medical Officer, Centracare – Benson, Benson, MN, p. A343
HORINECK, Kim, Chief Human Resource Officer, Goodland Regional Medical Center, Goodland, KS, p. A250
HORINEK, ReChelle, Chief Financial Officer, Trego County–Lemke Memorial Hospital, Wakeeney, KS, p. A261
HORN, Debbie, Controller, Texas Rehabilitation Hospital of Arlington, Arlington, TX, p. A598

Index of Health Care Professionals

Index of Health Care Professionals / Horn

HORN, Jon, M.D., Chief of Staff, Northeast Georgia Medical Center Barrow, Winder, GA, p. A174
HORN, LeeAnn, Chief Nurse Executive, Providence Kodiak Island Medical Center, Kodiak, AK, p. A28
HORN, Sarah
Chief Nursing Officer, Salem Health West Valley, Dallas, OR, p. A526
Chief Nursing Officer, Salem Hospital, Salem, OR, p. A532
HORN, Syndi, Director Information Systems, Memorial Hospital Association, Carthage, IL, p. A187
HORNBOGEN, Abigail Lynn, MS, R.N., Vice President, Patient Care and Chief Nursing Officer, Rush–Copley Medical Center, Aurora, IL, p. A186
HORNBURG, Tom, Director Information Systems, Mason Health, Shelton, WA, p. A695
HORNE, Beth, System Administrator Information Technology, Mon Health Preston Memorial Hospital, Kingwood, WV, p. A702
HORNE, Eilene, Manager Human Resources, Mountain View Hospital, Idaho Falls, ID, p. A181
HORNE, J Mark, Senior Vice President, Ambulatory Services and Chief Operating Officer, Grand View Health, Sellersville, PA, p. A554
HORNE, Perry, Chief Nursing Officer, Orlando Health St. Cloud Hospital, Saint Cloud, FL, p. A148
HORNE, Willus Mark, M.D., Chief Medical Officer, South Central Regional Medical Center, Laurel, MS, p. A365
HORNED EAGLE, Michael, Chief Executive Officer, U. S. Public Health Service Indian Hospital, Wagner, SD, p. A578
HORNER, Bryan, President and Chief Executive Officer, Shannon Medical Center, San Angelo, TX, p. A648
HORNER, Cheryl, Supervisor Data Processing, Community Hospital of Staunton, Staunton, IL, p. A209
HORNER, Eva, Assistant Executive Director Operations, Devereux Hospital And Children's Center of Florida, Melbourne, FL, p. A138
HORNER, John M., President and Chief Executive Officer, Major Hospital, Shelbyville, IN, p. A227
HORNSBY, Brooke Broussard, Chief Nursing Officer, Ochsner American Legion Hospital, Jennings, LA, p. A284
HORNSBY, Donny, Director Fiscal Services, Memphis Mental Health Institute, Memphis, TN, p. A588
HORNUNG, Dona, Director Information and Technology Services, Doctors Hospital, Augusta, GA, p. A158
HORNUNG, Kurt, Director, HCA Florida Trinity Hospital, Trinity, FL, p. A153
HORRIGAN, Timothy, M.D., Chief Quality Officer, Unitypoint Health – Allen Hospital, Waterloo, IA, p. A244
HORSLEY, Steve, Vice President and Chief Information Officer, Cone Health Moses Cone Hospital, Greensboro, NC, p. A469
HORST, Adam, Chief Financial Officer, Mayo Clinic Hospital – Rochester, Rochester, MN, p. A353
HORST, Brad, Director Human Resources, HCA Houston Healthcare Clear Lake, Webster, TX, p. A661
HORST, Joanna, MSN, R.N., Chief Nursing Officer, St. Christopher's Hospital for Children, Philadelphia, PA, p. A550
HORSTMAN, Jennifer M, R.N., Chief Nursing Officer and Chief Information Officer, Community Fairbanks Recovery Center, Indianapolis, IN, p. A219
HORSTMANN, Steve, Vice President Operations, North Memorial Health Hospital, Robbinsdale, MN, p. A353
HORTON, Alan, Chief Executive Officer, Putnam General Hospital, Eatonton, GA, p. A163
HORTON, Greg, Director Support Services, State Hospital South, Blackfoot, ID, p. A179
HORTON, Jerrilyn, R.N., Chief Nursing Officer, Dewitt Hospital & Nursing Home, Dewitt, AR, p. A45
HORTON, Jim, Chief Executive Officer, Rankin County Hospital District, Rankin, TX, p. A646
HORTON, Joseph
Assistant Administrator, Middlesboro Arh Hospital, Middlesboro, KY, p. A271
Community Chief Executive Officer, Harlan Arh Hospital, Harlan, KY, p. A266
HORTON, Kenny, Director Information Systems, Walker Baptist Medical Center, Jasper, AL, p. A21
HORTON, Landon, Director of Nursing, Valley Behavioral Health System, Barling, AR, p. A43
HORTON, Marie, Director Associate Relations, Bartow Regional Medical Center, Bartow, FL, p. A125
HORTON, Warren, Information Technologist, Baptist Health Medical Center–Stuttgart, Stuttgart, AR, p. A54
HORTON, Wendy Michelle.
PharmD, FACHE, Chief Executive Officer, UVA Health University Medical Center, Charlottesville, VA, p. A674
PharmD, FACHE, Chief Executive Officer, UVA Health University Medical Center Ivy, Charlottesville, VA, p. A674
HORVAT, Kami, Chief Financial Officer, West Covina Medical Center, West Covina, CA, p. A101
HORVATH, Alex
Vice President and Chief Human Resources Officer, TMC Health, Tucson, AZ, p. A41
Vice President Human Resources, Methodist Hospitals, Gary, IN, p. A217
HORVATH, Holly, Director of Nursing, Sunview Medical Center, West Palm Beach, FL, p. A154
HORVATH, Joanne, Vice President Finance, Theda Care Medical Center – Wild Rose, Wild Rose, WI, p. A725
HOSS, Laurna, Human Resource Coordinator, Select Specialty Hospital–Omaha, Omaha, NE, p. A404
HOSTEENEZ, Vivie, Chief Financial Officer, San Carlos Apache Healthcare Corporation, Peridot, AZ, p. A34
HOSTETTER, Lynne, Vice President Human Resources, The Hsc Pediatric Center, Washington, DC, p. A124
HOTA, Bala, Interim Chief Information Officer, John H. Stroger Jr. Hospital of Cook County, Chicago, IL, p. A190
HOTCHKISS, Jason, CPA, Chief Financial Officer, Trinity Health, Minot, ND, p. A482
HOTCHKISS, Kaleigh, Controller, Encompass Health Rehabilitation Hospital of Northwest Tucson, Tucson, AZ, p. A40
HOTOVY, Patrick, M.D., Chief of Staff, York General, York, NE, p. A407
HOUCHIN, Kim, Chief Nursing Officer, Minnie Hamilton Healthcare Center, Grantsville, WV, p. A701
HOUGH, Nathan, Chief Executive Officer, Bigfork Valley Hospital, Bigfork, MN, p. A343
HOUGHTON, Roxan, Director Human Resources, Riverbridge Specialty Hospital, Vidalia, LA, p. A294
HOULE, David, Executive Vice President and Chief Financial Officer, The Hospital At Hebrew Senior Care, West Hartford, CT, p. A120
HOULIHAN, David, M.D., Chief of Staff, Tomah Va Medical Center, Tomah, WI, p. A723
HOULTON, Andrew, M.D., Chief Medical Officer, North Memorial Health Hospital, Robbinsdale, MN, p. A353
HOUMANN, Lars D, President, Adventhealth Orlando, Orlando, FL, p. A144
HOUNSHELL, Jacqueline, Chief Financial Officer, Leconte Medical Center, Sevierville, TN, p. A593
HOURANY, Joseph, Chief Medical Officer, Montclair Hospital Medical Center, Montclair, CA, p. A78
HOUSAND, Jill, Director Human Resources, USMD Hospital At Arlington, Arlington, TX, p. A598
HOUSE, Alan, Interim Chief Financial Officer, Copley Hospital, Morrisville, VT, p. A672
HOUSE, David
Vice President, Baptist Health Extended Care Hospital, Little Rock, AR, p. A49
Vice President and Chief Information Officer, Baptist Health Medical Center – North Little Rock, North Little Rock, AR, p. A51
Vice President and Chief Information Officer, Baptist Health Medical Center–Arkadelphia, Arkadelphia, AR, p. A43
Vice President and Chief Information Officer, Baptist Health Medical Center–Little Rock, Little Rock, AR, p. A49
Vice President and Chief Information Officer, Baptist Health Rehabilitation Institute, Little Rock, AR, p. A49
HOUSE, John, M.D., Chief of Staff, Eureka Springs Hospital, Eureka Springs, AR, p. A45
HOUSEMAN, Jamie, President, Mercy Health – Urbana Hospital, Urbana, OH, p. A505
HOUSER, Clark, Chief Executive Officer, Okeene Municipal Hospital, Okeene, OK, p. A516
HOUSER, David, M.D., Vice President Medical Affairs, Monument Health Rapid City Hospital, Rapid City, SD, p. A576
HOUSER, Kurt, Chief Human Resources Officer, University Medical Center, Las Vegas, NV, p. A411
HOUSER, Sara, Chief Nursing Officer, Ashe Memorial Hospital, Jefferson, NC, p. A471
HOUSH, Joe, District Director Human Resources, Kindred Hospital–Indianapolis, Indianapolis, IN, p. A220
HOUSMAN, Bradley W., M.D., Chief Medical Officer, Baptist Health Paducah, Paducah, KY, p. A272
HOUSTON, Jerry, Director Information Systems, Jennie Stuart Medical Center, Hopkinsville, KY, p. A267
HOUSTON–RAASIKH, Ceonne, Chief Nursing Officer, Keck Hospital of Usc, Los Angeles, CA, p. A73
HOVDENES, Jodi Lynn., R.N., President, Chi St Alexius Health Carrington, Carrington, ND, p. A479
HOVENS, Michael R., M.D., Chief Medical Officer, Panola Medical Center, Batesville, MS, p. A359
HOWALD, Nick
Chief Executive Officer, Tristar Southern Hills Medical Center, Nashville, TN, p. A591
Chief Operating Officer, Tristar Skyline Medical Center, Nashville, TN, p. A591
HOWARD, Andrew, Chief Executive Officer, Select Specialty Hospital–Birmingham, Birmingham, AL, p. A17
HOWARD, Cameron, Chief Operating Officer, Medical City Plano, Plano, TX, p. A645
HOWARD, Catherine, Director Human Resources, Sentara Halifax Regional Hospital, South Boston, VA, p. A684
HOWARD, Cindy, Director Financial Services, Nell J. Redfield Memorial Hospital, Malad City, ID, p. A182
HOWARD, Dan, Chief Information Officer, USA Health Children's & Women's Hospital, Mobile, AL, p. A22
HOWARD, Daniel, Chief Financial Officer, Maine Veterans Affairs Medical Center, Augusta, ME, p. A295
HOWARD, Darcy, Interim Chief Financial Officer, Lincoln Health, Hugo, CO, p. A110
HOWARD, Gary L, Senior Vice President and Chief Financial Officer, Hamilton Medical Center, Dalton, GA, p. A162
HOWARD, Greg M
Director Human Resource, Health Alliance Hospital – Broadway Campus, Kingston, NY, p. A445
Vice President Human Resources, Health Alliance Hospital – Mary's Avenue Campus, Kingston, NY, p. A445
HOWARD, Gwenyth, Vice President Finance, St. Thomas More Hospital, Canon City, CO, p. A104
HOWARD, Krystal, System Chief Financial Officer, United Medical Rehabilitation Hospital–Hammond, Hammond, LA, p. A283
HOWARD, Loy M., Chief Operating Officer, Tanner Medical Center–Carrollton, Carrollton, GA, p. A160
HOWARD, Mary, Director Human Resources, Winnebago Mental Health Institute, Winnebago, WI, p. A725
HOWARD, Melissa, Chief Nurse Executive, ICH & FPH, Emanate Health Inter–Community Hospital, Covina, CA, p. A61
HOWARD, Michael, Chief Executive Officer, Southern Tennessee Regional Health System–Lawrenceburg, Lawrenceburg, TN, p. A586
HOWARD, Mike, Chief Operating Officer, North Alabama Medical Center, Florence, AL, p. A19
HOWARD, Opal R, Executive Director Human Resources, Adventhealth Daytona Beach, Daytona Beach, FL, p. A129
HOWARD, Ron, Chief Financial Officer, Holly Hill Hospital, Raleigh, NC, p. A474
HOWARD, Sabra, Manager Human Resources, Harlan Arh Hospital, Harlan, KY, p. A266
HOWARD, Teresa, Manager Human Resources, Yoakum County Hospital, Denver City, TX, p. A614
HOWARD, Tim, Chief Human Resources Officer, Abrazo Central Campus, Phoenix, AZ, p. A35
HOWARD, Tom, Chief Financial Officer, Texas Health Presbyterian Hospital Flower Mound, Flower Mound, TX, p. A618
HOWARD–CROW, Dallis
Chief Human Resources Officer, Emory University Hospital Midtown, Atlanta, GA, p. A157
Chief Human Resources Officer, UCHealth Yamp. Valley Medical Center, Steamboat Springs, CO, p. A113
HOWAT, Greg, Vice President Human Resources, Northern Light Eastern Maine Medical Center, Bangor, ME, p. A295
HOWDEN, William, Vice President Nursing, Good Samaritan Regional Medical Center, Corvallis, OR, p. A526
HOWE, Christopher L., R.N., Interim Chief Executive Officer, Wilkes–Barre General Hospital, Wilkes–Barre, PA, p. A558
HOWE, James L, Director Human Resources, Pinnacle Pointe Behavioral Healthcare System, Little Rock, AR, p. A50
HOWE, Vicki, Health Information Management, Ness County Hospital District No 2, Ness City, KS, p. A255
HOWELL, Amy M, Director Human Resources, St. Luke's Behavioral Health Center, Phoenix, AZ, p. A36
HOWELL, Bradley C., Chief Executive Officer, Regional West Garden County, Oshkosh, NE, p. A405
HOWELL, Diana, Director Human Resources, HCA Houston Healthcare Conroe, Conroe, TX, p. A608
HOWELL, Kristie, System Information Technology Director, Bon Secours – Southampton Medical Center, Franklin, VA, p. A676
HOWELL, Nathan, President and Chief Executive Officer, Mainegeneral Medical Center, Augusta, ME, p. A295
HOWELL, Patty, M.D., Chief Medical Officer, Eastern Idaho Regional Medical Center, Idaho Falls, ID, p. A181
HOWELL, Ronene, Director Health Information Management, Bryce Hospital, Tuscaloosa, AL, p. A25
HOWELL, Sheri, Deputy Commander Nursing, Brooke Army Medical Center, Fort Sam Houston, TX, p. A618
HOWELL, Timothy W., R.N., Senior Vice President, Patient Care Services, University Medical Center, Lubbock, TX, p. A636
HOWELL, Todd, Chief Executive Officer, Beckley Arh Hospital, Beckley, WV, p. A699
HOWELLS, Brian, Administrator, Wamego Health Center, Wamego, KS, p. A261

A878 Index of Health Care Professionals

Index of Health Care Professionals / Hulett

Index of Health Care Professionals

HOWELLS, Stephen, Chief Financial Officer, Kane County Hospital, Kanab, UT, p. A665
HOWERTER, Mark, M.D., Chief Medical Officer, Columbus Community Hospital, Columbus, NE, p. A399
HOWERTON, Russell M, M.D., Chief Medical Officer, Atrium Health Wake Forest Baptist, Winston–Salem, NC, p. A478
HOWERTON, Shawn, M.D., Chief Executive Officer and President, Medical Staff, Sampson Regional Medical Center, Clinton, NC, p. A466
HOY, Jonathan B, Chief Financial Officer, Duke Regional Hospital, Durham, NC, p. A467
HOY, Sarah M, Chief Nursing Officer, Coffeyville Regional Medical Center, Coffeyville, KS, p. A247
HOYER, Sara, Director Administrative Services, Kansas Neurological Institute, Topeka, KS, p. A260
HOYLE, Lisa, R.N., Chief Nursing Officer, John C. Fremont Healthcare District, Mariposa, CA, p. A76
HOYOS, Kent, Chief Information Officer, Pomona Valley Hospital Medical Center, Pomona, CA, p. A84
HOYT, Nancy Gerilyn, R.N., Vice President Operations, Clinical and Chief Nursing Officer, Commonspirit – Mercy Hospital, Durango, CO, p. A107
HRIT, Barbara, Controller, Corewell Health Farmington Hills Hospital, Farmington Hills, MI, p. A326
HRUBIAK, Dan, Associate Computer Program Analyst, Western New York Children's Psychiatric Center, West Seneca, NY, p. A462
HRUBY, Deidre, Director of Patient Care, Madelia Health, Madelia, MN, p. A349
HSIEH, Sam, M.D., FACS, Chief of Staff and Chief Medical Officer, Coulee Medical Center, Grand Coulee, WA, p. A690
HSU, Wah Chung, Senior Vice President Finance, San Antonio Regional Hospital, Upland, CA, p. A99
HUANG, Edwin, M.D., Interim President, Mount Auburn Hospital, Cambridge, MA, p. A312
HUANG, Hanna
Administrator and Chief Operating Officer, Laredo Rehabilitation Hospital, Laredo, TX, p. A634
Administrator and Chief Operating Officer, Laredo Specialty Hospital, Laredo, TX, p. A634
HUANG, Joseph, M.D., Chief Medical and Quality Officer, Legacy Silverton Medical Center, Silverton, OR, p. A532
HUBBARD, Bill, Vice President, Operations, Atrium Health Cabarrus, Concord, NC, p. A466
HUBBARD, Brenda E., Corporate Director, Human Resources, Cap. Fear Valley Bladen County Hospital, Elizabethtown, NC, p. A468
HUBBARD, Brent, FACHE, Interim Chief Executive Officer, Integris Baptist Medical Center, Oklahoma City, OK, p. A517
HUBBARD, Daniel, Chief Financial Officer, Royal C. Johnson Veterans' Memorial Hospital, Sioux Falls, SD, p. A576
HUBBARD, Gwen, Chief Nursing Officer, Sierra Vista Hospital, Sacramento, CA, p. A87
HUBBARD, Kathy
Controller, Ocean Beach Hospital And Medical Clinics, Ilwaco, WA, p. A690
Manager Human Resources, Nell J. Redfield Memorial Hospital, Malad City, ID, p. A182
HUBBARD, Lisa, Vice President and Chief Nursing Executive, Mercy Medical Center Mount Shasta, Mount Shasta, CA, p. A79
HUBBARD, Rosie, R.N., Administrative Director of Nursing, Cox Barton County Memorial Hospital, Lamar, MO, p. A379
HUBBELL, Heather, Director of Patient Care, Avera Flandreau Hospital, Flandreau, SD, p. A573
HUBBS, Olas A. III, FACHE, President and Chief Executive Officer, Memorial Health, Marysville, OH, p. A499
HUBEL, Edward T, FACHE, President, Baptist Medical Center Jacksonville, Jacksonville, FL, p. A134
HUBER, Dalton, Chief Financial Officer, Campbell County Health, Gillette, WY, p. A727
HUBER, Josep. M, Chief Financial Officer, Hospital of The University of Pennsylvania, Philadelphia, PA, p. A549
HUBER, Patricia
Chief Executive Officer, Sojourn At Seneca Senior Behavioral Health, Tiffin, OH, p. A504
Chief Nursing Officer, Sojourn At Seneca Senior Behavioral Health, Tiffin, OH, p. A504
HUBER, Timothy
Vice President Finance, Mercyone Cedar Falls Medical Center, Cedar Falls, IA, p. A231
Vice President Finance, Mercyone Oelwein Medical Center, Oelwein, IA, p. A241
Vice President Finance, Mercyone Waterloo Medical Center, Waterloo, IA, p. A244
HUBLEY, Grover, M.D., President Medical Staff, Chi St. Josep. Health Madison Hospital, Madisonville, TX, p. A637
HUBLING, Anne, R.N., President and Chief Nurse Executive, Northwestern Medicine Marianjoy Rehabilitation Hospital, Wheaton, IL, p. A210
HUBSCHMAN, Gary
Administrative Director Finance, Sutter Auburn Faith Hospital, Auburn, CA, p. A56
Administrative Director Finance, Sutter Roseville Medical Center, Roseville, CA, p. A86
HUCKABEE, Mike, Network Administrator, Coryell Health, Gatesville, TX, p. A622
HUCKABY, Don, Chief Information Management Service, Rocky Mountain Regional Va Medical Center, Aurora, CO, p. A103
HUDA, Edith, Director Human Resources, Daniels Memorial Healthcare Center, Scobey, MT, p. A395
HUDAK, Corey, Director, Human Resources, UPMC Memorial, York, PA, p. A559
HUDGENS, Roselyn, Director Human Resources, Ballinger Memorial Hospital, Ballinger, TX, p. A601
HUDGINS, Laura E, Assistant Administrator, Jasper Memorial Hospital, Monticello, GA, p. A168
HUDGINS, Paul C., Senior Vice President, Carilion Franklin Memorial Hospital, Rocky Mount, VA, p. A683
HUDSON, Beth, Chief Nursing Officer, Baylor Scott & White Institute for Rehabilitation – Dallas, Dallas, TX, p. A610
HUDSON, Delilah, Controller, Covington County Hospital, Collins, MS, p. A361
HUDSON, Janell, Director, Nursing and Clinical Services, Sanford Thief River Falls Medical Center, Thief River Falls, MN, p. A356
HUDSON, Jason Dan., R.N., Chief Executive Officer, Pam Specialty Hospital of Victoria North, Victoria, TX, p. A660
HUDSON, Jeralene, Director, Ascension St. Vincent Fishers, Fishers, IN, p. A216
HUDSON, Kenneth J, Chief Financial Officer, VA Puget Sound Healthcare System – Seattle, Seattle, WA, p. A695
HUDSON, Kent, Chief Financial Officer, Kingman Community Hospital, Kingman, KS, p. A252
HUDSON, Maggie, President and Chief Executive Officer, Santiam Hospital, Stayton, OR, p. A532
HUDSON, Mike, Administrator, Federal Correctional Institute Hospital, Littleton, CO, p. A111
HUDSON, Norma, Chief Financial Officer, Del Amo Behavioral Health System, Torrance, CA, p. A98
HUDSON, Patricia, Administrator, John J. Madden Mental Health Center, Hines, IL, p. A198
HUDSON, Robbi, Chief Executive Officer, Kindred Hospital North Florida, Green Cove Springs, FL, p. A133
HUDSON, Shannon, Chief Executive Officer, Beacon Behavioral Hospital, Luverne, AL, p. A21
HUDSON–JINKS, Therese M., R.N., MSN, Chief Nursing Officer, Tufts Medical Center, Boston, MA, p. A311
HUELSKAMP, Donald, Interim Chief Financial Officer, WVU Medicine – Harrison Community Hospital, Cadiz, OH, p. A487
HUERTA, Brad, Chief Executive Officer and Administrator, Lost Rivers Medical Center, Arco, ID, p. A179
HUERTA, Guillermo, M.D., Chief Medical Officer, Select Specialty Hospital–Omaha, Omaha, NE, p. A404
HUERTA, Jose, Chief Executive Officer, Everest Rehabilitation Hospital of El Paso, El Paso, TX, p. A616
HUERTER, Holly
Vice President Human Resources, Methodist Jennie Edmundson Hospital, Council Bluffs, IA, p. A234
Vice President Human Resources, Nebraska Methodist Hospital, Omaha, NE, p. A404
HUESMAN, Carol, Chief Information Officer, Major Hospital, Shelbyville, IN, p. A227
HUETTL, Patricia, Vice President Finance and Chief Financial Officer, Holy Family Memorial, Manitowoc, WI, p. A715
HUFF, Jeff, Assistant Administrator Finance, Fayette Medical Center, Fayette, AL, p. A19
HUFF, Michael H., Chief Executive Officer, Olney Hamilton Hospital, Olney, TX, p. A642
HUFF, Shelley E, Regional Program Manager, Indiana University Health Tipton Hospital, Tipton, IN, p. A228
HUFFINE, Daniel, Chief Financial Officer, St. David's Medical Center, Austin, TX, p. A600
HUFFMAN, David, Vice President and Controller, Select Specialty Hospital–Wilmington, Wilmington, DE, p. A122
HUFFMAN, Joshua, M.D., Chief Medical Staff, Chi Saint Josep. Health – Saint Josep. Berea, Berea, KY, p. A263
HUFFMAN, Michael Trevor., Chief Executive Officer, Jacksonville Memorial Hospital, Jacksonville, IL, p. A199
HUFFMAN, Patricia, Controller, Encompass Health Rehabilitation Hospital of Franklin, Franklin, TN, p. A583
HUFFMAN, Sherry, Administrator Human Resources, Corewell Health Dearborn Hospital, Dearborn, MI, p. A324
HUFFMAN, Teresa, Chief Executive Officer, Texas Rehabilitation Hospital of Arlington, Arlington, TX, p. A598
HUFFMAN, Tim, Western Region Director, Information Systems Business Relationships, Baylor Scott & White Medical Center–Irving, Irving, TX, p. A630
HUFFNER, William
M.D., Chief Medical Officer, University of Maryland Shore Medical Center At Chestertown, Chestertown, MD, p. A303
M.D., Chief Medical Officer, University of Maryland Shore Medical Center At Easton, Easton, MD, p. A304
HUFFSTUTLER, Brandon, Chief Information Officer, Electra Memorial Hospital, Electra, TX, p. A618
HUFNAGEL, Keith, Director Human Resources, Stillwater Medical Center, Stillwater, OK, p. A521
HUGAR, Josep. G., Chief Executive Officer, Sacramento Rehabilitation Hospital, Llc, Sacramento, CA, p. A87
HUGGINS, Lois, Chief Human Resources Officer and Senior Vice President Human Resources, Shirley Ryan Abilitylab, Chicago, IL, p. A191
HUGGINS, Michael C, Administrator Network System, Eastern Oklahoma Medical Center, Poteau, OK, p. A520
HUGGLER, Jerry, Chief, Finance, Reunion Rehabilitation Hospital Denver, Denver, CO, p. A107
HUGHES, April, Chief Financial Officer, Peachford Behavioral Health System, Atlanta, GA, p. A157
HUGHES, Bill, Chief Nursing Officer, Granville Health System, Oxford, NC, p. A474
HUGHES, Chad
Chief Information Officer, North Texas State Hospital, Wichita Falls Campus, Wichita Falls, TX, p. A662
Information Officer, North Texas State Hospital, Vernon, TX, p. A659
HUGHES, Chantel, Chief Financial Officer, Seven Hills Hospital, Henderson, NV, p. A409
HUGHES, Charlie, Chief Executive Officer, Northwest Ohio Psychiatric Hospital, Toledo, OH, p. A505
HUGHES, David L., Administrator, Crenshaw Community Hospital, Luverne, AL, p. A21
HUGHES, Douglas, R.N., President and Chief Executive Officer, Grand View Health, Sellersville, PA, p. A554
HUGHES, Dustan, M.D., Vice President Medical Affairs, Saint Alphonsus Medical Center – Nampa, Nampa, ID, p. A182
HUGHES, Elisabeth, Director Human Resources and Community Relations, Fairview Regional Medical Center, Fairview, OK, p. A512
HUGHES, James, Director Human Resources, Lake Cumberland Regional Hospital, Somerset, KY, p. A274
HUGHES, Jessica, Director Finance, Hawarden Regional Healthcare, Hawarden, IA, p. A237
HUGHES, Kelly
Chief Executive Officer, Coulee Medical Center, Grand Coulee, WA, p. A690
Chief Financial Officer, Coulee Medical Center, Grand Coulee, WA, p. A690
HUGHES, Lee, R.N., Chief Nursing Officer, Flint River Hospital, Montezuma, GA, p. A168
HUGHES, Leigh Ann, Chief Financial Officer, Hardin Medical Center, Savannah, TN, p. A592
HUGHES, Lori, R.N., MSN, Chief Nursing Officer, Vice President Operations and Patient Care Services, Cottage Hospital, Woodsville, NH, p. A417
HUGHES, Mark A., M.D., Medical Director, River Park Hospital, Huntington, WV, p. A701
HUGHES, Matt, Chief Financial Officer, HCA Florida University Hospital, Davie, FL, p. A129
HUGHES, Robert K., Chief Executive Officer, NYC Health + Hospitals/Henry J Carter Specialty Hospital And Medical Center, New York, NY, p. A451
HUGHES, Sascha, Chief Executive Officer, Fairfax Behavioral Health, Kirkland, WA, p. A691
HUGHES, Susan, Interim Director Human Resources, Winner Regional Healthcare Center, Winner, SD, p. A578
HUGHES, Terry, Director Information Systems, Nantucket Cottage Hospital, Nantucket, MA, p. A316
HUGHES, Thomas, President, St. Josep. Health Services of Rhode Island, North Providence, RI, p. A560
HUGHES, Veronica, Chief Nursing Officer, Mesilla Valley Hospital, Las Cruces, NM, p. A435
HUGHES–MICKEL, Leann, Chief Information Officer, Touro Infirmary, New Orleans, LA, p. A290
HUGHS, Mary, Chief Human Resources Officer, Guthrie Lourdes Hospital, Binghamton, NY, p. A439
HUGHSON, John R., Chief Executive Officer, Frio Regional Hospital, Pearsall, TX, p. A643
HUGO, Chris, M.D., Chief of Staff, Guttenberg Municipal Hospital And Clinics, Guttenberg, IA, p. A237
HUGUELEY, Sandra, Vice President Nursing, Mercy Health – Clermont Hospital, Batavia, OH, p. A486
HUITT, Leslie, Chief Executive Officer, Bradley County Medical Center, Warren, AR, p. A54
HULBERT, Kim, R.N., R.N., Chief Clinical Officer, Madison County Health Care System, Winterset, IA, p. A245
HULETT, Rachelle, Vice President Human Resources, Mclaren Flint, Flint, MI, p. A327

Index of Health Care Professionals / Hulett

HULETT, Wendi, Chief Nursing Officer, Artesia General Hospital, Artesia, NM, p. A433
HULL, Brad, Chief Financial Officer, Dale Medical Center, Ozark, AL, p. A23
HULL, Debbie, Chief Financial Officer, Fisher County Hospital District, Rotan, TX, p. A647
HULL, Ken, Director Human Resources, Inova Fairfax Medical Campus, Falls Church, VA, p. A676
HULSE, Mark, MSN, Chief Digital Officer, City of Hope's Helford Clinical Research Hospital, Duarte, CA, p. A62
HULSEY, Cathy, Manager of Human Resources, Chi Memorial Hospital – Georgia, Fort Oglethorpe, GA, p. A164
HULSEY, Grant, Director Information Technology, Baylor Scott & White Surgical Hospital–Sherman, Sherman, TX, p. A652
HULSEY, Kelly, MSN, R N., Chief Nursing Officer, Piedmont Atlanta Hospital, Atlanta, GA, p. A158
HUM, Monica A., Chief Executive Officer, Piedmont Rockdale Hospital, Conyers, GA, p. A161
HUMBERT, Gilbert Glenn, R.N., Jr, Market Chief Nursing Officer, Our Lady of Lourdes Regional Medical Center, Lafayette, LA, p. A286
HUMBLE, Kathryn G., Senior Executive, Human Resource Services, Beatrice Community Hospital And Health Center, Beatrice, NE, p. A398
HUMBLE, Linnea, Director of Finance, Sutter Lakeside Hospital, Lakeport, CA, p. A69
HUME, Diana, Manager Human Resources, Methodist Mckinney Hospital, Mckinney, TX, p. A638
HUMES, Karen, Chief Information Officer, Titusville Area Hospital, Titusville, FA, p. A555
HUMMEL, Angela, Vice President Human Resources, Evangelical Community Hospital, Lewisburg, PA, p. A544
HUMMELKE, Arlita, Manager Human Resources, Mercy Hospital Tishomingo, Tishomingo, OK, p. A521
HUMMER, Denise, R.N., Vice President Administrative Services, Community Memorial Hospital, Hamilton, NY, p. A444
HUMPAL, Jenny, Chief Nursing Officer, White Rock Medical Center, Dallas, TX, p. A613
HUMPHREY, Eric
 Senior Vice President Human Resources, Froedtert Community Hospital – New Berlin, New Berlin, WI, p. A718
 Senior Vice President, Chief Human Resources Officer, Froedtert West Bend Hospital, West Bend, WI, p. A724
HUMPHREY, James, Vice President Talent Resources and Human Resources for South Side Operating Group. Penrose–St. Francis Health Services, Colorado Springs, CO, p. A105
HUMPHREY, Randy, Chief Financial Officer, Merit Health Wesley, Hattiesburg, MS, p. A363
HUMPHREY, Richard, Executive Vice President and Chief Financial Officer, Parkland Health, Dallas, TX, p. A612
HUMPHREY, Robert Dale, Chief Executive Officer, Ascension Saint Thomas River Park, Mc Minnville, TN, p. A587
HUMPHREYS, Lynn, Director Human Resources, Henry County Health Center, Mount Pleasant, IA, p. A240
HUMPHRIES, Vickie Witcher
 Director Human Resources, Bon Secours Maryview Medical Center, Portsmouth, VA, p. A681
 Vice President Human Resources, Bon Secours Mary Immaculate Hospital, Newport News, VA, p. A679
HUNDAL, Ranjit, M.D., Senior Vice President and Chief Medical Officer, Providence Redwood Memorial Hospital, Fortuna, CA, p. A63
HUNDORFEAN, Richard C., Chief Executive Officer, Musc Health Rehabilitation Hospital, An Affiliate of Encompass Health, Charleston, SC, p. A563
HUNGER, Bryan, Chief Executive Officer, Jefferson County Health Center, Fairfield, IA, p. A236
HUNGER, Dennis, Chief Operating Officer, Ottumwa Regional Health Center, Ottumwa, IA, p. A241
HUNSAKER, Mike, Chief Operating Officer, Star Valley Health, Afton, WY, p. A726
HUNSBERGER, Tom, Director Human Resources, Olmsted Medical Center, Rochester, MN, p. A354
HUNSICKER, Elizabeth, Chief Executive Officer, Eastern Idaho Regional Medical Center, Idaho Falls, ID, p. A181
HUNT, Amy, Director Human Resources, Menorah Medical Center, Overland Park, KS, p. A257
HUNT, Arel, Chief Executive Officer, Bear Lake Memorial Hospital, Montpelier, ID, p. A182
HUNT, Carter, Chief Executive Officer, Falmouth Hospital, Falmouth, MA, p. A313
HUNT, Cheryl Esq, Chief Nursing Officer, St. Peter's Health, Helena, MT, p. A393
HUNT, Christopher, Director, Information Technologies, FISO, Helena Regional Medical Center, Helena, AR, p. A47
HUNT, Deloris, Chief Human Resources Officer, University of Michigan Medical Center, Ann Arbor, MI, p. A321

HUNT, Don, M.D., Vice President Patient Centered Care and Chief Nursing Officer, UT Health North Campus Tyler, Tyler, TX, p. A659
HUNT, Jeffery B, Vice President, Business Development and Support Services, Roane General Hospital, Spencer, WV, p. A705
HUNT, John R., Chief Executive Officer, Encompass Health Rehabilitation Hospital of Western Massachusetts, Ludlow, MA, p. A315
HUNT, Julie, R.N., MS, Chief Nursing Officer, Oro Valley Hospital, Oro Valley, AZ, p. A34
HUNT, Karen, Executive Director, Harsha Behavioral Center, Terre Haute, IN, p. A228
HUNT, Lynelle, Director of Nursing, Quentin N. Burdick Memorial Healthcare Facility, Belcourt, ND, p. A479
HUNT, Nick, Interim Director of Nursing, Mercy Hospital Waldron, Waldron, AR, p. A54
HUNT, Richard, M.D., Chief Operating Officer, Kaiser Sunnyside Medical Center, Clackamas, OR, p. A526
HUNT, Sharon
 Chief Financial Officer, Hereford Regional Medical Center, Hereford, TX, p. A624
 Interim Chief Financial Officer, Pecos County Memorial Hospital, Fort Stockton, TX, p. A619
HUNT, Vanessa, Director Human Resources, HCA Houston Healthcare Tomball, Tomball, TX, p. A658
HUNT, William Robert, Chief Financial Officer, Reynolds Memorial Hospital, Glen Dale, WV, p. A700
HUNTER, Byron, Vice President Human Resources, Cooper University Hospital Cap. Regional, Cap. May Court House, NJ, p. A419
HUNTER, Diana, Director of Nursing, Fort Belknap Service Unit, Harlem, MT, p. A393
HUNTER, George, Interim Chief Human Resources Officer, Tuba City Regional Health Care Corporation, Tuba City, AZ, p. A40
HUNTER, John G., M.D., FACS, Executive Vice President and Chief Executive Officer, Ohsu Hospital, Portland, OR, p. A530
HUNTER, Kimberly D., MSN, R.N., Chief Nurse Executive, University of Iowa Hospitals & Clinics, Iowa City, IA, p. A238
HUNTER, Mary Ann, Director Nursing Services, Prisma Health Baptist Easley Hospital, Easley, SC, p. A565
HUNTER, Melissa, Chief Nursing Officer, Lake Regional Health System, Osage Beach, MO, p. A381
HUNTER, Melvin, Hospital Administrator, Atascadero State Hospital, Atascadero, CA, p. A56
HUNTER, Sarah, Interim Chief Operating Officer, Northwest Health – Porter, Valparaiso, IN, p. A228
HUNTER, Stephanie, Chief Human Resources Officer, Veterans Affairs Ann Arbor Healthcare System, Ann Arbor, MI, p. A321
HUNTER, Terri Lynn, R.N., Vice President and Chief Nursing Officer, Washington Hospital Healthcare System, Fremont, CA, p. A64
HUNTER, Tracy, Chief Human Resources Officer, East Cooper Medical Center, Mount Pleasant, SC, p. A568
HUNTINGTON, Jonathan, M.D., Ph.D., M.P.H., Chief Medical Officer, Dartmouth–Hitchcock Medical Center, Lebanon, NH, p. A416
HUNTLEY, Adrienne
 Chief Human Resources Officer, Saint Francis Hospital–Bartlett, Bartlett, TN, p. A579
 Director Human Resources, Encompass Health Rehabilitation Hospital of North Memphis, A Partner of Methodist Healthcare, Memphis, TN, p. A588
HUNTLEY, Devin, Chief Operating Officer, Providence St. Josep. Medical Center, Polson, MT, p. A395
HUNTON, David, M.D., Chief Medical Officer, Mercy Hospital Fort Smith, Fort Smith, AR, p. A47
HUNTSINGER, Kelli, Chief Operating Officer, Northern Inyo Hospital, Bishop. CA, p. A58
HUPP, Diane, R.N., President, UPMC Children's Hospital of Pittsburgh, Pittsburgh, PA, p. A551
HURD, Debra J., MS, R.N., Vice President and Chief Nursing Officer, M Health Fairview Woodwinds Hospital, Woodbury, MN, p. A357
HURD, Ross, Chief Information Officer, Lake Chelan Health, Chelan, WA, p. A688
HURFORD, Bill, Chief Medical Officer, University of Cincinnati Medical Center, Cincinnati, OH, p. A490
HURLEY, Al, West Region Chief Operating Officer, Essentia Health Fargo, Fargo, ND, p. A480
HURLEY, Jeff, Vice President Human Resources, UF Health St. John's, Saint Augustine, FL, p. A148
HUROWITZ, Marc P., D.O., Chief Executive Officer, Temple University Hospital, Philadelphia, PA, p. A550
HURSH, John, Vice President Human Resources, Cox North Hospital, Springfield, MO, p. A386

HURSHE, Joseph, MMc President & Chief Executive Officer, Munson Medical Center, Traverse City, MI, p. A339
HURST, David, Chief Nursing Officer, Alta View Hospital, Sandy, UT, p. A669
HURST, Kyle, Chief Operations Officer, Northwest Ohio Psychiatric Hospital, Toledo, OH, p. A505
HURST, Paul, M.D., Chief Medical Officer, Banner Heart Hospital, Mesa, AZ, p. A33
HURST, Steve, Information Technology Specialist, Haskell Regional Hospital, Stigler, OK, p. A521
HURT, Carol Anne, Chief Nursing Officer, Tippah County Hospital, Ripley, MS, p. A368
HURT, Christie, M.D., Chief of Staff and Medical Director, Mercy Hospital Aurora, Aurora, MO, p. A371
HURT, Kelly, Chief Human Resources Officer Northern Colorado and Western Region, Banner Fort Collins Medical Center, Fort Collins, CO, p. A108
HURT, Todd, Chief Executive Officer, Intermountain Hospital, Boise, ID, p. A179
HURWITZ, Steven, Senior Vice President Shared Services, Seattle Children's Hospital, Seattle, WA, p. A694
HUSAIN, Syed Arshad, M.D., Executive Vice President and Chief Medical Officer, Royal Oaks Hospital, Windsor, MO, p. A388
HUSEBY, Custer, Chief Executive Officer, Vibra Hospital of Fargo, Fargo, ND, p. A481
HUSHER, Phillip
 Chief Financial Officer, Freeman Regional Health Services, Freeman, SD, p. A573
 Interim Co–Chief Executive Officer, Freeman Regional Health Services, Freeman, SD, p. A573
HUSO, Brian, Chief Executive Officer, Granite County Medical Center, Philipsburg, MT, p. A394
HUSS, Cathy, Chief Financial Officer, Lifecare Medical Center, Roseau, MN, p. A354
HUSS, Eric, Chief Financial Officer, Butler Memorial Hospital, Butler, PA, p. A536
HUSSAIN, Iftikhar, Chief Financial Officer, El Camino Health, Mountain View, CA, p. A79
HUSSEY, Jamie, Chief Information Officer, Jackson Hospital, Marianna, FL, p. A138
HUSSEY, Stephen, M.D., Chief of Staff, Lake District Hospital, Lakeview, OR, p. A528
HUSSON, Charles, Regional Chief Medical Officer, Ascension Genesys Hospital, Grand Blanc, MI, p. A327
HUSTEDT, Dale, President, Aspirus Stanley Hospital & Clinics, Inc., Stanley, WI, p. A722
HUSTON, Jennifer, Chief Nursing Officer, Adventhealth Lake Wales, Lake Wales, FL, p. A136
HUSTON, William R, Senior Vice President and Chief Financial Officer, Scottish Rite for Children, Dallas, TX, p. A612
HUTCHENRIDER, E. Kenneth. Jr, FACHE, President, Methodist Richardson Medical Center, Richardson, TX, p. A646
HUTCHENS, Alisha C., President and Chief Operating Officer, Novant Health Medical Park Hospital, Winston–Salem, NC, p. A478
HUTCHENS, Zachary, M.D., Chief Medical Officer, Ascension Saint Thomas Hickman, Centerville, TN, p. A580
HUTCHESON, Lorie, Vice President of Human Resources, Shepherd Center, Atlanta, GA, p. A158
HUTCHESON, Lou Ellen, M.D., Chief of Staff, Bacon County Hospital And Health System, Alma, GA, p. A156
HUTCHINGS, Diane, R.N., MS, Interim Chief Executive Officer, St. Michael's Elite Hospital, Sugar Land, TX, p. A655
HUTCHINGS, Lisa, Chief Financial Officer, Dmc Children's Hospital of Michigan, Detroit, MI, p. A325
HUTCHINS, Anne, M.D., Chief of Staff, Salem Veterans Affairs Medical Center, Salem, VA, p. A683
HUTCHISON, Barbra, Director Medical Records, Delhi Hospital, Delhi, LA, p. A281
HUTCHION, Florence N., M.D., Chief of Staff, Ralp. H. Johnson Veterans Affairs Medical Center, Charleston, SC, p. A563
HUTCHISON, Lewis, Vice President Operations and Quality, Ashtabula County Medical Center, Ashtabula, OH, p. A485
HUTCHSIN, Joel, M.D., Chief Medical Staff, Holton Community Hospital, Holton, KS, p. A250
HUTH, Michael, Chief Financial Officer, Sycamore Springs, Lafayette, IN, p. A222
HUTH, Thomas, M.D., Vice President Medical Affairs, Reid Health, Richmond, IN, p. A226
HUTKA, Michael, Chief Executive Officer, Temple Rehabilitation Hospital, Temple, TX, p. A656
HUTSON, Clint, President and Chief Operating Officer, Bethesda North Hospital, Cincinnati, OH, p. A488
HUTSON, Joy M, Director Human Resources, Merit Health Rankin, Brandon, MS, p. A360
HUTSON, Marty, Chief Financial Officer, St. Mary's Health Care System, Athens, GA, p. A156

Index of Health Care Professionals / Isom

HUTSON, Wayne
  Chief Financial Officer, Union Hospital Clinton, Clinton, IN, p. A214
  Executive Vice President and Chief Financial Officer, Union Hospital, Terre Haute, IN, p. A228
HUTT, Si William., President, Heber Valley Hospital, Heber City, UT, p. A665
HUVAL, Shadelle, Director Finance, Ochsner St. Martin Hospital, Breaux Bridge, LA, p. A279
HUYNH, Thai, M.D., Chief of Medical Staff, El Camp. Memorial Hospital, El Campo, TX, p. A616
HVIDING, Brittany, Senior Human Resources Director, Banner Gateway Medical Center, Gilbert, AZ, p. A31
HWU, Patrick, M.D., President and Chief Executive Officer, H. Lee Moffitt Cancer Center And Research Institute, Tampa, FL, p. A152
HYATT, David W, FACHE, Chief Executive Officer, Riverview Health, Noblesville, IN, p. A225
HYATT, David W., FACHE, Chief Executive Officer, Riverview Health, Noblesville, IN, p. A225
HYATT, Lakisha, Chief Executive Officer, Connecticut Valley Hospital, Middletown, CT, p. A117
HYATT, Ronnie, Senior Vice President Finance and Chief Financial Officer, Bon Secours St. Francis Health System, Greenville, SC, p. A566
HYBERGER, Trey, Director Information Technology, Baptist Health Hardin, Elizabethtown, KY, p. A265
HYDE, Devon, President and Chief Executive Officer, Lake Charles Memorial Hospital, Lake Charles, LA, p. A286
HYDE, Garrick, President, Chi St. Alexius Health Williston, Williston, ND, p. A483
HYDE, Robert, Human Resources Business Partner, Kaiser Permanente Santa Clara Medical Center, Santa Clara, CA, p. A94
HYDE, Shannon, Director Human Resources, Encompass Health Rehabilitation Hospital of Morgantown, Morgantown, WV, p. A703
HYDE, Stephanie, R.N., MSN, Chief Executive Officer, Tyler Continuecare Hospital, Tyler, TX, p. A659
HYDE, Steve, Chief Executive Officer, Paris Regional Medical Center, Paris, TX, p. A642
HYDER, LouAnn, Director Information Integrity Management, Encompass Health Cardinal Hill Rehabilitation Hospital, Lexington, KY, p. A268
HYEK, Michael, President, Morrow County Hospital, Mount Gilead, OH, p. A501
HYLAND, Donna W., President and Chief Executive Officer, Children's Healthcare of Atlanta, Atlanta, GA, p. A157
HYLAND, Jaquelyn, M.D., Chief Medical Officer, University of Kansas Health System St. Francis Campus, Topeka, KS, p. A261
HYLAND–HILL, Barbara M, R.N., Chief Nursing Officer, Providence Regional Medical Center Everett, Everett, WA, p. A689
HYLTON, Heather, Vice President, Finance, Camc Plateau Medical Center, Oak Hill, WV, p. A703
HYMAN, Bruce, M.D., Vice President Clinical Performance, Advocate Sherman Hospital, Elgin, IL, p. A194
HYMBAUGH, Mitzi, Chief Personnel, Ringgold County Hospital, Mount Ayr, IA, p. A240
HYNDS, Robin, MSN, R.N., Executive Vice President and Chief Operating Officer, Lawrence General Hospital, Lawrence, MA, p. A314
HYNES, Kristi, Director Human Resources, Georgetown Behavioral Health Institute, Georgetown, TX, p. A622
HYNES, Mary, Manager Information Services, United Hospital District, Blue Earth, MN, p. A343
HYNOSKI, Michael, Chief Information Resource Management, James E. Van Zandt Veterans Affairs Medical Center, Altoona, PA, p. A534
HYTRY, Steven M., PsyD, Chief Executive Officer, Pacific Grove Hospital, Riverside, CA, p. A86

I

IACHETTI, Lisa, President and Chief Hospital Executive, Hackensack Meridian Health Palisades Medical Center, North Bergen, NJ, p. A426
IACUONE, Karen
  Chief Nursing Officer, Pioneers Medical Center, Meeker, CO, p. A112
  Chief Nursing Officer and Chief Operating Officer, Pioneers Medical Center, Meeker, CO, p. A112
IANDOLO, Joseph, Vice President, Operations, UPMC Memorial, York, PA, p. A559
IANNACO, Robert, Administrator, Whittier Rehabilitation Hospital, Bradford, MA, p. A311

IBARRA, Daniel, Chief Financial Officer, Crane Memorial Hospital, Crane, TX, p. A609
IBARRA, Kyle, Director Information Systems, Stormont Vail Health – Flint Hills Campus, Junction City, KS, p. A251
IBRAHIM, Tajudeen, Interim Business Administrator, Elgin Mental Health Center, Elgin, IL, p. A194
IBUSHI–THOMPSON, Leila, MSN, R.N., Chief Nurse Executive, Kaiser Permanente Baldwin Park Medical Center, Baldwin Park, CA, p. A57
IDBEIS, Badr, M.D., Chief Executive Officer, Kansas Medical Center, Andover, KS, p. A246
IDOINE–FRIES, Julie
  FACHE, Chief Executive Officer, Cleveland Clinic Rehabilitation Hospital, Avon, OH, p. A485
  FACHE, Chief Executive Officer, Regency North Central Ohio – Cleveland East, Warrensville Heights, OH, p. A506
IDSTEIN, Mary, Chief Financial Officer, Porter–Starke Services, Valparaiso, IN, p. A228
IERARDI, Josep. P., Chief Executive Officer, Wayne Memorial Hospital, Jesup. GA, p. A165
IERO, Tony, Director Management Information Systems, Behavioral Wellness Center At Girard, The, Philadelphia, PA, p. A548
IFABIYI, Candace, FACHE, Medical Center Director, VA St. Louis Health Care System, Saint Louis, MO, p. A384
IGO, Angela, MSN, R.N., Chief Nursing Officer, Fitzgibbon Hospital, Marshall, MO, p. A380
IMHOFF, Sarah, Business Administrator, Chester Mental Health Center, Chester, IL, p. A188
IMLER, Jim
  Director Human Resources, Gothenburg Health, Gothenburg, NE, p. A400
  Director Human Resources, Kimball Health Services, Kimball, NE, p. A401
IMMORDINO, Jonathan R, Chief Financial Officer, Rockledge Regional Medical Center, Rockledge, FL, p. A148
IMSEIS, Mikhail, M.D., Chief of Staff, Ness County Hospital District No 2, Ness City, KS, p. A255
IN, Henry, Director Human Resources, Dallas Behavioral Healthcare Hospital, Desoto, TX, p. A614
INGE, Laura, MSN, R.N., Chief Executive Officer, Kindred Hospital Northland, Kansas City, MO, p. A377
INGE, Ray, Vice President Human Resources, Pomona Valley Hospital Medical Center, Pomona, CA, p. A84
INGLE, Alyssa, Chief Executive Officer, Perimeter Behavioral Hospital of Springfield, Springfield, MO, p. A387
INGRAHAM, Christopher, Chief Nursing Officer, Lakes Regional Healthcare, Spirit Lake, IA, p. A244
INGRAM, David, Chief Executive Officer, Acadian Medical Center, Eunice, LA, p. A281
INGRAM, Karen, Director Human Resources, Baptist Memorial Hospital for Women, Memphis, TN, p. A588
INGRAM, Nathan Daniel., Chief Executive Officer and Owner, Lone Star Behavioral Health, Cypress, TX, p. A610
INHOFE, Kyle, Chief Human Resources Officer, Oklahoma City Va Medical Center, Oklahoma City, OK, p. A518
INMAN, Debbie, Chief Nursing Officer, Physicians Surgical Hospital – Quail Creek, Amarillo, TX, p. A596
INMAN, Joanne, Division President, Sentara Leigh Hospital, Norfolk, VA, p. A680
INO, Alan, Chief Financial Officer, PIH Health Good Samaritan Hospital, Los Angeles, CA, p. A74
INOUYE, Valerie, Chief Financial Officer, Zuckerberg San Francisco General Hospital And Trauma Center, San Francisco, CA, p. A91
INSERRA, Toni A., Administrator, South Lyon Medical Center, Yerington, NV, p. A413
INSKEEP, Johnathan, Chief Information Officer, Caribou Medical Center, Soda Springs, ID, p. A184
INZANA, Lou, Chief Financial Officer and MaineHealth Associate Chief Financial Officer, Mainehealth Maine Medical Center, Portland, ME, p. A298
IQBAL, Nayyar, M.D., Director Medical Staff, Western State Hospital, Hopkinsville, KY, p. A267
IRELAND, Amy, Chief Financial Officer, Carroll County Memorial Hospital, Carrollton, MO, p. A373
IRELAND, Daniel P.
  FACHE, President and Chief Operating Officer, Finger Lakes Rural Hospitals, Clifton Springs Hospital And Clinic, Clifton Springs, NY, p. A441
  FACHE, President and Chief Operating Officer, Finger Lakes Rural Hospitals, Newark–Wayne Community Hospital, Newark, NY, p. A454
  FACHE, President and Chief Operating Officer, Finger Lakes Rural Hospitals, United Memorial Medical Center, Batavia, NY, p. A439
IRION, Val, M.D., Medical Director, Specialists Hospital Shreveport, Shreveport, LA, p. A293

IRISH, Kevin
  Chief Information Officer, Concord Hospital – Franklin, Franklin, NH, p. A415
  Chief Information Officer, Concord Hospital – Laconia, Laconia, NH, p. A415
IRIZARRI, David, Director Information Technology, HCA Florida Northwest Hospital, Margate, FL, p. A138
IRIZARRY, David
  Chief Executive Officer, Corpus Christi Medical Center – Doctors Regional, Corpus Christi, TX, p. A609
  Chief Executive Officer, Valley Regional Medical Center, Brownsville, TX, p. A605
IRIZARRY, Lourdes, M.D., Chief of Staff, Albany Stratton Veterans Affairs Medical Center, Albany, NY, p. A438
IRIZARRY, Sigfredo, Information Technology Director, Ashford Presbyterian Community Hospital, San Juan, PR, p. A734
IRIZARRY MORALES, Annabelle, Administrator, Hospital San Pablo, Bayamon, PR, p. A731
IROEGBU, Nkem, M.D., M.P.H., President, Aurora St. Luke's Medical Center, Milwaukee, WI, p. A717
IRVIN, Debbie, Director Health Information Management, Bhc Alhambra Hospital, Rosemead, CA, p. A86
IRVIN, Donna, Director Human Resources, Baylor Scott & White Medical Center – Trophy Club, Trophy Club, TX, p. A658
IRVIN, Mary, R.N., MSN, Senior Vice President and Chief Nursing Officer, Bethesda North Hospital, Cincinnati, OH, p. A488
IRVIN, Michael, Chief Executive Officer, HCA Florida Trinity Hospital, Trinity, FL, p. A153
IRVIN, Miriam, CNO, Encompass Health Rehabilitation Hospital, A Partner of Washington Regional, Fayetteville, AR, p. A46
IRVING, Edith E, R.N., MS, FACHE, Chief Nursing Officer, West Valley Medical Center, Caldwell, ID, p. A180
IRVING, Kelly Ann MSN, RN–B, Associate Director for Patient Care Services, Michael E. Debakey Department of Veterans Affairs Medical Center, Houston, TX, p. A627
IRVING, Mark, Manager Management Information Systems, OSF St. Francis Hospital And Medical Group. Escanaba, MI, p. A326
IRWIN, Robert G, Vice President Information Systems, Robert Wood Johnson University Hospital, New Brunswick, NJ, p. A425
IRWIN, Vivian, Chief Financial Officer and Controller, Encompass Health Rehabilitation Hospital of Midland Odessa, Midland, TX, p. A639
ISAAC, Lisa, Chief Nursing Officer, Choctaw Nation Health Care Center, Talihina, OK, p. A521
ISAAC, Regina, Director of Nursing, Choctaw Health Center, Philadelphia, MS, p. A367
ISAACKS, Scott R., FACHE, Director and Chief Executive Officer, Ralp. H. Johnson Veterans Affairs Medical Center, Charleston, SC, p. A563
ISAACS, Alicia, Superintendent and Medical Director, Madison State Hospital, Madison, IN, p. A223
ISAACS, Diane, Director of Nursing, Ouachita County Medical Center, Camden, AR, p. A44
ISAACS, Michael R, Vice President Human Resources, Vista Medical Center East, Waukegan, IL, p. A210
ISAACSON, Sara, Chief Nursing Officer, Mad River Community Hospital, Arcata, CA, p. A56
ISADO, Jose, M.D., Medical Director, Auxilio Mutuo Hospital, San Juan, PR, p. A734
ISBELL, Samantha, R.N., Chief Nursing Officer, Olney Hamilton Hospital, Olney, TX, p. A642
ISBELL, Sherri, Chief Information Officer, Virginia Gay Hospital, Vinton, IA, p. A244
ISBELL, Todd, R.N., MSN, Chief Nursing Officer, Memorial Health University Medical Center, Savannah, GA, p. A171
ISENMANN, Debra, Human Resources Generalist, Cox Monett Hospital, Inc, Monett, MO, p. A380
ISHIZUKA, Paul
  Chief Financial Officer, Skagit Valley Hospital, Mount Vernon, WA, p. A692
  Regional Vice President and Chief Financial Officer, Cascade Valley Hospital, Arlington, WA, p. A687
ISHKANIAN, Gary, M.D., Vice President Medical Affairs, Montefiore Mount Vernon, Mount Vernon, NY, p. A446
ISKANDAR, Said, M.D., Chief Medical Officer, Sentara Halifax Regional Hospital, South Boston, VA, p. A684
ISLAM, Asad, M.D., Chief Medical Officer, Mayhill Hospital, Denton, TX, p. A614
ISLEY, L. Lee., FACHE, Ph.D., President and Chief Executive Officer, UNC Health Nash, Rocky Mount, NC, p. A475
ISMAIL, Asad, M.D., Medical Director, Wellstone Regional Hospital, Jeffersonville, IN, p. A221
ISMAIL, Hummayun, M.D., Medical Director, Select Specialty Hospital–Wilmington, Wilmington, DE, p. A122
ISOM, Julie, Director Human Resources, Lakeview Hospital, Bountiful, UT, p. A664

Index of Health Care Professionals / Ison

ISON, Tamara
  Chief Financial Officer, Wellstar Sylvan Grove Hospital, Jackson, GA, p. A165
  Chief Operating Officer, Wellstar Spalding Regional Hospital, Griffin, GA, p. A164
  Senior Vice President and President, Wellstar Spalding Regional Hospital, Griffin, GA, p. A164
  Senior Vice President and President, Wellstar Sylvan Grove Hospital, Jackson, GA, p. A165
ISON, William G, Human Resources Manager, Select Specialty Hospital–Tri Cities, Bristol, TN, p. A579
ISRAEL, Corry, Director Human Resources, St. Catherine Hospital – Dodge City, Dodge City, KS, p. A248
ISRAEL, Michael D., President and Chief Executive Officer, Westchester Medical Center, Valhalla, NY, p. A461
ISSACS, Cynthia, Chief Executive Officer, Solara Specialty Hospitals Harlingen–Brownsville, Brownsville, TX, p. A604
ISSAI, Alice H.
  President, Adventist Health Glendale, Glendale, CA, p. A66
  President, Adventist Health Simi Valley, Simi Valley, CA, p. A96
ITANI, Sam, Chief Executive Officer, Corona Regional Medical Center, Corona, CA, p. A60
ITO, Derek, Director Human Resources, Shriners Hospitals for Children–Honolulu, Honolulu, HI, p. A176
IVERSON, Amber, Chief Nursing Officer, Orem Community Hospital, Orem, UT, p. A667
IVERSON, Caryn, MSN, Chief Nursing Officer, Memorial Medical Center, Las Cruces, NM, p. A435
IVES, Matthew
  Chief Executive Officer and Chief Financial Officer, Keokuk County Hospital & Clinics, Sigourney, IA, p. A243
  Interim Chief Executive Officer and Chief Financial Officer, Keokuk County Hospital & Clinics, Sigourney, IA, p. A243
IVES, Shawna, CPA, Chief Financial Officer, White River Health, Batesville, AR, p. A43
IVES ERICKSON, Jeanette R, MS, R.N., Senior Vice President Patient Care and Chief Nurse, Massachusetts General Hospital, Boston, MA, p. A310
IVEY, Kim, Director of Human Resources, Cumberland Hospital for Children And Adolescents, New Kent, VA, p. A679
IVEY, Misty, Human Resources Manager, Washington County Regional Medical Center, Sandersville, GA, p. A170
IVIE, Brian K.
  President and Chief Executive Officer, Cascade Valley Hospital, Arlington, WA, p. A687
  President and Chief Executive Officer, Skagit Valley Hospital, Mount Vernon, WA, p. A692
IVY, Michael, M.D., Senior Vice President for Medical Affairs and Chief Medical Officer, Bridgeport Hospital, Bridgeport, CT, p. A115
IVY, Tristan, Chief Executive Officer, Santa Rosa Behavioral Healthcare Hospital, Santa Rosa, CA, p. A95
IYER, Raju, Senior Vice President and Chief Financial Officer, UCSF Medical Center, San Francisco, CA, p. A91
IZAKOVIC, Martin, M.D., Vice President Medical Staff Affairs and Chief Medical Officer, University of Iowa Health Care Medical Center Downtown, Iowa City, IA, p. A238
IZZI, Denine, Senior Director Information Technology, Robert Wood Johnson University Hospital Rahway, Rahway, NJ, p. A427

J

JABBARPOUR, Yad, M.D., Chief of Staff, Catawba Hospital, Catawba, VA, p. A674
JABLONSKI, Kevin, Chief Nursing Officer, Christus Mother Frances Hospital – Winnsboro, Winnsboro, TX, p. A663
JABLONSKI, Kevin M, Chief Nursing Officer, UT Health Athens, Athens, TX, p. A598
JABLONSKI, Mark, Vice President Mission Integration, Providence St. Jude Medical Center, Fullerton, CA, p. A65
JABOUR, Leon John
  Regional Chief Information Officer, Wellspan Ephrata Community Hospital, Ephrata, PA, p. A539
  Regional Chief Information Officer, Wellspan Good Samaritan Hospital, Lebanon, PA, p. A544
JACK, Claudia L, Director Associate Relations, Tamp. General Hospital Brooksville, Brooksville, FL, p. A127
JACK, Shannon, Administrator, Indianhead Medical Center, Shell Lake, WI, p. A721
JACKES, Frederick D, Assistant Administrator and Director Human Resources, Valley Forge Medical Center, Norristown, PA, p. A547
JACKIEWICZ, Thomas E., President, University of Chicago Medical Center, Chicago, IL, p. A192
JACKMAN, Casey, Chief Operating Officer, Idaho Falls Community Hospital, Idaho Falls, ID, p. A181
JACKMAN–HAVEY, Stephanie, Chief Financial Officer, Metrowest Medical Center, Framingham, MA, p. A313
JACKSON, Alan, M.D., Medical Director, Roseland Community Hospital, Chicago, IL, p. A190
JACKSON, Amy L., Commander, Keller Army Community Hospital, West Point, NY, p. A462
JACKSON, Angelica, Director of Nursing, Anchor Hospital, Atlanta, GA, p. A156
JACKSON, Carolyn, Chief Executive Officer, Saint Vincent Hospital, Worcester, MA, p. A320
JACKSON, Cindy
  Director Human Resources, Phelp. Memorial Health Center, Holdrege, NE, p. A401
  Market Chief Executive Officer, Kindred Hospital South Florida–Fort Lauderdale, Fort Lauderdale, FL, p. A131
JACKSON, Corey D., Executive Vice President and Chief Talent Officer, Parkland Health, Dallas, TX, p. A612
JACKSON, Courtney, Coordinator Human Resources, Atoka County Medical Center, Atoka, OK, p. A510
JACKSON, Cynthia, Vice President Human Resources, HCA Florida Raulerson Hospital, Okeechobee, FL, p. A143
JACKSON, Darryl, D.O., Chief of Staff, Prague Regional Memorial Hospital, Prague, OK, p. A520
JACKSON, David, Chief Financial Officer, Baptist Medical Center – Leake, Carthage, MS, p. A360
JACKSON, Donna, Chief Nursing Officer, Houston County Community Hospital, Erin, TN, p. A582
JACKSON, Erin, Human Resources Specialist, Baptist Medical Center Nassau, Fernandina Beach, FL, p. A131
JACKSON, Evan, Chief Information Officer and Vice President, Planning and Business Development, Middlesex Health, Middletown, CT, p. A117
JACKSON, F Cameron., Hospital Commander, Weed Army Community Hospital, Fort Irwin, CA, p. A63
JACKSON, Frank D. III, Facility Chief Information Officer, Veterans Affairs Illiana Health Care System, Danville, IL, p. A192
JACKSON, Gary, D.O., Medical Director, Lincoln County Medical Center, Ruidoso, NM, p. A436
JACKSON, Holly, Chief Operating Officer, HCA Florida Gulf Coast Hospital, Panama City, FL, p. A146
JACKSON, James, M.D., Chief of Staff, Cornerstone Specialty Hospitals Bossier City, Bossier City, LA, p. A279
JACKSON, James E.T.
  M.P.H., Chief Executive Officer, Alameda Hospital, Alameda, CA, p. A55
  M.P.H., Chief Executive Officer, Highland Hospital, Oakland, CA, p. A80
  M.P.H., Interim Chief Executive Officer, Highland Hospital, Oakland, CA, p. A80
JACKSON, James H. Jr, Chief Executive Officer, Och Regional Medical Center, Starkville, MS, p. A369
JACKSON, Jeanette, Chief Executive Officer, Laurel Oaks Behavioral Health Center, Dothan, AL, p. A18
JACKSON, Jeffrey, M.D., Medical Director, Houston Methodist Sugar Land Hospital, Sugar Land, TX, p. A654
JACKSON, Jennifer
  R.N., MSN, Vice President of Operations and Chief Nursing Officer, West Chester Hospital, West Chester, OH, p. A506
  Director Human Resources, Madison County Health Care System, Winterset, IA, p. A245
JACKSON, Joanne, Administrator Human Resources, Community Relations and Quality Improvement, Amery Hospital And Clinic, Amery, WI, p. A707
JACKSON, Joel, Chief Executive Officer, Three Rivers Health, Basin, WY, p. A726
JACKSON, John J, President, Firsthealth Moore Regional Hospital, Pinehurst, NC, p. A474
JACKSON, Judy, Director Health Information Management and Privacy Officer, Shodair Children's Hospital, Helena, MT, p. A393
JACKSON, Kiland, Chief Information Officer, Bunkie General Hospital, Bunkie, LA, p. A279
JACKSON, Krista, Chief Executive Officer, Johnson County Rehabilitation Hospital, Overland Park, KS, p. A257
JACKSON, Lynn, Chief Executive Officer, Northside Hospital Forsyth, Cumming, GA, p. A162
JACKSON, Marcus, Chief Operating Officer, Medical City Las Colinas, Irving, TX, p. A630
JACKSON, Margaret G., R.N., Vice President Patient Care Services and Chief Nursing Officer, Suny Downstate Health Sciences University, New York, NY, p. A453
JACKSON, Meg, Director Information Technology, Beauregard Health System, De Ridder, LA, p. A281
JACKSON, Melinda R, Director Human Resources, Bates County Memorial Hospital, Butler, MO, p. A372
JACKSON, Melonie, Human Resource Business Partner, Corewell Health Big Rapids Hospital, Big Rapids, MI, p. A322
JACKSON, Michael, M.D., Assistant Chief Medical Officer, Integris Health Enid Hospital, Enid, OK, p. A512
JACKSON, Patsy, Director of Nursing, Jay Hospital, Jay, FL, p. A135
JACKSON, Reese, President and Chief Executive Officer, Chesapeake Regional Medical Center, Chesapeake, VA, p. A674
JACKSON, Robert
  Chief Financial Officer, Alliance Health Center, Meridian, MS, p. A366
  Chief Financial Officer, Signature Psychiatric Hospital, Kansas City, MO, p. A377
JACKSON, Robin E., Ph.D., Chief Executive Officer, Charlie Norwood Veterans Affairs Medical Center, Augusta, GA, p. A158
JACKSON, Stephanie L, M.D., Vice President and Chief Medical Officer, Honorhealth Scottsdale Thompson Peak Medical Center, Scottsdale, AZ, p. A38
JACKSON, Todd, Chief Executive Officer, HCA Florida Twin Cities Hospital, Niceville, FL, p. A142
JACKSON, Tom, Chief Financial Officer, Tristar Centennial Medical Center, Nashville, TN, p. A591
JACKSON, William L, Chief Medical Officer, Inova Alexandria Hospital, Alexandria, VA, p. A673
JACKSON–GEHRIS, Patti, President, UPMC Williamsport, Williamsport, PA, p. A558
JACOB, Hiram, Chief Operating Officer, HCA Florida Citrus Hospital, Inverness, FL, p. A134
JACOB, Sony, Senior Vice President, Chief Information Officer, Froedtert Community Hospital – New Berlin, New Berlin, WI, p. A718
JACOBI, Elizabeth
  Associate Director Human Resources, Rancho Los Amigos National Rehabilitation Center, Downey, CA, p. A62
  Human Resources Director, Los Angeles General Medical Center, Los Angeles, CA, p. A74
JACOBO, Maria E., Executive Director, Hospital Hima De Humacao, Humacao, PR, p. A733
JACOBS, Anastasia, Chief Human Resources Officer, Robert Wood Johnson University Hospital Somerset, Somerville, NJ, p. A428
JACOBS, Andrea, Chief Operating Officer, Cleveland Clinic South Pointe Hospital, Warrensville Heights, OH, p. A506
JACOBS, Brian, M.D., Vice President Chief Information Officer and Chief Medical Information Officer, Children's National Hospital, Washington, DC, p. A123
JACOBS, Greg, Manager, Mclaren Bay Special Care, Bay City, MI, p. A322
JACOBS, Hannah, Senior Vice President and Chief Financial Officer, Frederick Health, Frederick, MD, p. A304
JACOBS, Ian, Chief, Human Resource Management Service, Louis A. Johnson Veterans Affairs Medical Center, Clarksburg, WV, p. A700
JACOBS, Jenny
  Director Human Resources, OSF Holy Family Medical Center, Monmouth, IL, p. A202
  Director Human Resources, OSF St. Mary Medical Center, Galesburg, IL, p. A196
JACOBS, Julie, Director Human Resources, Oklahoma Forensic Center, Vinita, OK, p. A523
JACOBS, Lori, Chief Financial Officer, Edgefield County Healthcare, Edgefield, SC, p. A565
JACOBS, Robert
  Regional Director Information Management, Christus Southeast Texas Hospital – St. Elizabeth, Beaumont, TX, p. A602
  Regional Information Management Executive, Christus Southeast Texas Jasper Memorial, Jasper, TX, p. A630
JACOBS, Ronnie, M.D., Chief Medical Officer, Asheville Specialty Hospital, Asheville, NC, p. A463
JACOBS, Stacy, Chief Nursing Officer, Millwood Hospital, Arlington, TX, p. A597
JACOBS, Trace, Director Information Technology, Santiam Hospital, Stayton, OR, p. A532
JACOBS, Yolanda, Coordinator Human Resources, Vibra Hospital of Clear Lake, Webster, TX, p. A661
JACOBSEN, Barry, CPA, Chief Executive Officer, Myrtue Medical Center, Harlan, IA, p. A237
JACOBSON, Becky, Vice President Finance, Ascension St. Vincent Heart Center, Indianapolis, IN, p. A218
JACOBSON, Carlton, Vice President of Finance, Adventist Health Clear Lake, Clearlake, CA, p. A59
JACOBSON, Carolyn
  Chief Human Resource Officer, M Health Fairview Woodwinds Hospital, Woodbury, MN, p. A357
  Chief Human Resources Officer, M Health Fairview St. John's Hospital, Maplewood, MN, p. A349

Index of Health Care Professionals / Jean–Louis

Index of Health Care Professionals

JACOBSON, Ches, Chief Nursing Officer, Delta Community Medical Center, Delta, UT, p. A664
JACOBSON, Gary, M.D., Chief Medical Officer, Pembroke Hospital, Pembroke, MA, p. A317
JACOBSON, Janet, Director Human Resources, Lakewood Health System, Staples, MN, p. A355
JACOBSON, Jenny, Manager Human Resources, Sanford Hillsboro Medical Center, Hillsboro, ND, p. A482
JACOBSON, Mark, D.O., Vice President Medical Affairs, Wellspan Ephrata Community Hospital, Ephrata, PA, p. A539
JACOBSON, Randolph, Chief Financial Officer, Hackensack Meridian Health Carrier Clinic, Belle Mead, NJ, p. A418
JACOBSON, Renae A., Human Resources Officer, Ralp. H. Johnson Veterans Affairs Medical Center, Charleston, SC, p. A563
JACOBSON, Sam, Director Management Information Systems, Community Memorial Hospital, Cloquet, MN, p. A345
JACOBSON, Shirley
Chief Financial Officer, Community Behavioral Health Hospital – Alexandria, Alexandria, MN, p. A342
Chief Financial Officer, Community Behavioral Health Hospital – Rochester, Rochester, MN, p. A353
JACQUAY, Dena M, Chief Human Resource Officer, Parkview Huntington Hospital, Huntington, IN, p. A218
JACQUES, Alistair, Chief Information Officer, Senior Vice President, M Health Fairview St. John's Hospital, Maplewood, MN, p. A349
JACQUES, Stephany
R.N., President, Bridgton Hospital, Bridgton, ME, p. A296
R.N., President, Rumford Hospital, Rumford, ME, p. A299
JACQUES, Teresa, Interim Chief Financial Officer, Adventist Health Reedley, Reedley, CA, p. A85
JADCZAK, Audrey
R.N., FACHE, Vice President Chief Nursing Officer, Virtua Our Lady of Lourdes Hospital, Camden, NJ, p. A419
R.N., FACHE, Vice President/Chief Nursing Officer, Virtua Willingboro Hospital, Willingboro, NJ, p. A431
JADEJA, Neerav
Administrator, Paradise Valley Hospital, National City, CA, p. A79
Chief Executive Officer, Paradise Valley Hospital, National City, CA, p. A79
JAEGER, Shiuvaun, M.D., Chief of Staff, Tri Valley Health System, Cambridge, NE, p. A398
JAEGER–JACKSON, Kelley, Chief Executive Officer, Sutter Solano Medical Center, Vallejo, CA, p. A100
JAFFE, Richard, M.D., Medical Director, Belmont Behavioral Health System, Philadelphia, PA, p. A548
JAFFER, Amir, M.D., Senior Vice President Medical Affairs, New York–Presbyterian Queens, New York, NY, p. A450
JAGASIA, Shubhada, President and Chief Executive Officer, Ascension Saint Thomas Hospital, Nashville, TN, p. A590
JAGER, Jonathon R, Chief Information Officer, St. Francis – Emory Healthcare, Columbus, GA, p. A161
JAGER, Linda, Director Finance, Avera Weskota Memorial Hospital, Wessington Springs, SD, p. A578
JAGGI, Michael, D.O., Vice President and Chief Medical Officer, Hurley Medical Center, Flint, MI, p. A326
JAGIELSKI, Helena Maria., Administrator, Providence Seward Medical Center, Seward, AK, p. A29
JAGOE, Patricia, Assistant Vice President Patient Care, Johnson Memorial Hospital, Stafford Springs, CT, p. A119
JAHAN, Mohammad S, M.D., Clinical Director, Middle Tennessee Mental Health Institute, Nashville, TN, p. A590
JAHN, Gregory L., R.N., Chief Executive Officer, St. Luke's Behavioral Health Center, Phoenix, AZ, p. A36
JAHN, Kim C, Chief Plant Operations and Chief Information Officer, Manning Regional Healthcare Center, Manning, IA, p. A239
JAHNIG, Jay A, Chief Executive Officer, Faulkton Area Medical Center, Faulkton, SD, p. A573
JAHRE, Jeffrey, M.D., Vice President Medical and Academic Affairs, St. Luke's University Hospital – Bethlehem Campus, Bethlehem, PA, p. A535
JAIN, Anil
Chief Financial Officer, St. Francis Medical Center, Lynwood, CA, p. A76
Interim Chief Financial Officer, Emanuel Medical Center, Turlock, CA, p. A98
JAIN, Ashok, M.D., Senior Vice President and Chief Medical Officer, Corewell Health Wayne Hospital, Wayne, MI, p. A340
JAKACKI, Emily Cochran., President, Northwestern Medicine Delnor Hospital, Geneva, IL, p. A196
JAKOUBECK, Denise, Director Human Resources, Hancock County Health System, Britt, IA, p. A231
JAKUBOWSKI, Michael, M.D., Chief Medical Officer, Mary Free Bed Rehabilitation Hospital, Grand Rapids, MI, p. A328
JALOMO, Angie, Chief Nursing Officer, Lynn County Hospital District, Tahoka, TX, p. A655
JAMES, Annette, R.N., MSN, Chief Nursing Officer, Creek Nation Community Hospital, Okemah, OK, p. A516
JAMES, Carl H., Chief Financial Officer, Mountainview Hospital, Las Vegas, NV, p. A410
JAMES, Carla, Chief Nursing Officer, Encompass Health Rehabilitation Hospital of Savannah, Savannah, GA, p. A171
JAMES, Curtis, FACHE, Chief Executive Officer, Thomasville Regional Medical Center, Thomasville, AL, p. A25
JAMES, Dixieanne
President and Chief Operating Officer, Magee Rehabilitation, Philadelphia, PA, p. A549
President and Chief Operating Officer, Thomas Jefferson University Hospital, Philadelphia, PA, p. A550
President and Chief Operating Officer, Central Region, Einstein Medical Center Philadelphia, Philadelphia, PA, p. A548
JAMES, Donald, D.O., Senior Vice President and Chief Medical Officer, Phelp. Health, Rolla, MO, p. A382
JAMES, Douglas, Chief Nursing Officer, Caldwell Medical Center, Princeton, KY, p. A273
JAMES, Jaime, Entity Finance Officer, Texas Health Harris Methodist Hospital Hurst–Euless–Bedford, Bedford, TX, p. A602
JAMES, Janet, Director Human Resources, Trigg County Hospital, Cadiz, KY, p. A264
JAMES, Joan, M.D., Medical Director, Eagle View Behavioral Health, Bettendorf, IA, p. A230
JAMES, Jobie, Chief Financial Officer, West Calcasieu Cameron Hospital, Sulphur, LA, p. A293
JAMES, Karen, Regional Director, Human Resources, The William W. Backus Hospital, Norwich, CT, p. A118
JAMES, Michael
Chief Operating Officer, Turning Point Hospital, Moultrie, GA, p. A169
Chief Operations Officer, Jackson Hospital And Clinic, Montgomery, AL, p. A22
Information Technology Technical Support Specialist 1, Villa Feliciana Medical Complex, Jackson, LA, p. A283
JAMES, Robert L, Director Human Resources, Corewell Health Wayne Hospital, Wayne, MI, p. A340
JAMES, Taya, Director, Mercy Hospital Berryville, Berryville, AR, p. A43
JAMES, Teri, Chief Financial Officer, Lafayette Regional Health Center, Lexington, MO, p. A379
JAMES, Thomas L, M.D., Chief Medical Officer, Trumbull Regional Medical Center, Warren, OH, p. A506
JAMES, Wesley, Chief Financial Officer, Piedmont Henry Hospital, Stockbridge, GA, p. A172
JAMES–NIELSEN, Lori, President, Ohsu Health Hillsboro Medical Center, Hillsboro, OR, p. A528
JAMESON, David, M.D., Chief of Staff, Annie Jeffrey Memorial County Health Center, Osceola, NE, p. A405
JAMIESON, Donna F., Ph.D., R.N., President, Aurora Medical Center Kenosha, Kenosha, WI, p. A713
JAMIN, David, Chief Financial Officer, St. Mary's Regional Medical Center, Enid, OK, p. A512
JAMISON, Marsha, Chief Nursing Officer, St. Catherine Hospital – Dodge City, Dodge City, KS, p. A248
JAMROSE, Todd I, Chief Clinical Officer, Appalachian Behavioral Healthcare, Athens, OH, p. A485
JANDIAL, Rajnish, M.D., Chief Medical Officer, San Dimas Community Hospital, San Dimas, CA, p. A90
JANERELLA, Wendy, Controller, Bucktail Medical Center, Renovo, PA, p. A553
JANGDHARI, Kalautie, Medical Center Director, Miami Veterans Affairs Healthcare System, Miami, FL, p. A140
JANICAK, Dan, Chief Financial Officer, University of Mississipp. Medical Center, Jackson, MS, p. A364
JANIS, Terry, Assistant Vice President, HCA Houston Healthcare Medical Center, Houston, TX, p. A625
JANKOWSKI, Carrie, President, Mercy Health – Allen Hospital, Oberlin, OH, p. A501
JANKOWSKI, Stan, Vice President and Chief Information Officer, Hospital for Special Care, New Britain, CT, p. A117
JANLOO, Arman, M.D., Chief Medical Staff, Rural Wellness Fairfax, Fairfax, OK, p. A512
JANOSO, John R., Chief Executive Officer, Fairfield Medical Center, Lancaster, OH, p. A498
JANSEN, David, Vice President Human Resources, Karmanos Cancer Center, Detroit, MI, p. A326
JANSEN, John, Management Information Specialist, Hawaii State Hospital, Kaneohe, HI, p. A177
JANSEN, Robert, M.D., Chief Medical Officer, Grady Health System, Atlanta, GA, p. A157
JANSEZIAN, Krikor, Ph.D., Chief Operating Officer, SCL Health Mt – St. Vincent Healthcare, Billings, MT, p. A390
JANSSEN, Kathy, Director Medical Records, Mountrail County Medical Center, Stanley, ND, p. A483
JANSSEN, Svetlana, Chief Nursing Officer, Encompass Health Rehabilitation Institute of Libertyville, Libertyville, IL, p. A200
JANTZEN, Daniel, Chief Financial Officer, Dartmouth–Hitchcock Medical Center, Lebanon, NH, p. A416
JANTZEN, Tammi, Chief Operating Officer, Okeene Municipal Hospital, Okeene, OK, p. A516
JANUS, Tammy, Senior Vice President Human Resources, Mercy Medical Center, Baltimore, MD, p. A301
JANZEN, Wes, Chief Information Officer, Wamego Health Center, Wamego, KS, p. A261
JAO, Bernadette Yap. Chief Nursing Executive, Associate Director Patient and Nursing Services, Veterans Affairs Connecticut Healthcare System, West Haven, CT, p. A120
JAQUA, Terry, Human Resources Director, Whittier Hospital Medical Center, Whittier, CA, p. A101
JAQUEZ, Jason
Director Human Resources, Greater El Monte Community Hospital, South El Monte, CA, p. A96
Human Resource Director, AHMC Anaheim Regional Medical Center, Anaheim, CA, p. A55
JARAMILLO, Ashley, Chief Financial Officer, White Mountain Regional Medical Center, Springerville, AZ, p. A39
JARAMILLO, Charles, Chief Operating Officer, New Mexico Behavioral Health Institute At Las Vegas, Las Vegas, NM, p. A435
JARBOE, Joe, Director Human Resources, Lutheran Kosciusko Hospital, Warsaw, IN, p. A229
JARMER, Ryan, Chief Information Officer, Naval Medical Center San Diego, San Diego, CA, p. A89
JAROPILLO, Erwin, Director Information Systems, Adventhealth Lake Wales, Lake Wales, FL, p. A136
JAROS, Allegra, President, Baptist Medical Center Jacksonville, Jacksonville, FL, p. A134
JAROSINSKI, Steve, Chief Executive Officer, Pulaski Memorial Hospital, Winamac, IN, p. A229
JARREAU, Jeff
Chief Human Resources Officer, North Oaks Medical Center, Hammond, LA, p. A282
Senior Vice President, Human Resources, North Oaks Health System, North Oaks Rehabilitation Hospital, Hammond, LA, p. A282
JARREAU, Valerie Sparks, R.N., Chief Nursing Officer, Pointe Coupee General Hospital, New Roads, LA, p. A290
JARRETT, Adam D, M.D., Executive Vice President and Chief Medical Officer, Holy Name Medical Center, Teaneck, NJ, p. A429
JARRY, Patricia, Manager Human Resources, Crenshaw Community Hospital, Luverne, AL, p. A21
JARVIS, Dinah, Director of Nursing, Pineville Community Health Center, Pineville, KY, p. A273
JARVIS, Keith, Director Information Systems, Longview Regional Medical Center, Longview, TX, p. A635
JARVIS, Tammy, Vice President Clinical Services and Chief Nursing Officer, Texas Institute for Surgery At Texas Health Presbyterian Dallas, Dallas, TX, p. A612
JASINSKI, Lindsey, Chief Administrative Officer, Eastern State Hospital, Lexington, KY, p. A268
JASPER, Harry, Chief Financial Officer, Jerold Phelp. Community Hospital, Garberville, CA, p. A65
JASPER, Jerry
Interim Chief Executive Officer, Arise Austin Medical Center, Austin, TX, p. A598
Interim Chief Executive Officer, The Hospital At Westlake Medical Center, West Lake Hills, TX, p. A662
JAURON, Jason, Director Human Resources, Orange City Area Health System, Orange City, IA, p. A241
JAVERSACK, Dawn, Vice President and Chief Financial Officer, Boca Raton Regional Hospital, Boca Raton, FL, p. A126
JAVOIS, Laurent D., Regional Executive Officer, St. Louis Forensic Treatment Center, Saint Louis, MO, p. A384
JAVOIS, Rosalie, Chief Financial Officer, Governor Juan F. Luis Hospital, Christiansted, VI, p. A736
JAWORSKI, James, Chief Information Officer, Adventist Health White Memorial Montebello, Montebello, CA, p. A78
JAY, Richard, D.O., Chief of Staff, North Big Horn Hospital District, Lovell, WY, p. A727
JAYACHANDRAN, Vijay, M.D., President, Texas Health Heart & Vascular Hospital Arlington, Arlington, TX, p. A598
JEAKLE, James, Chief Medical Officer, Munson Healthcare Charlevoix Hospital, Charlevoix, MI, p. A323
JEAN–BAPTISTE, Joan, Vice President Human Resources, Governor Juan F. Luis Hospital, Christiansted, VI, p. A736
JEAN–FRANCOIS, Michale, Chief Medical Officer, Adventhealth South Overland Park, Overland Park, KS, p. A257
JEAN–LOUIS, Marie S, R.N., Chief Nursing Officer, Creedmoor Psychiatric Center, New York, NY, p. A448

Index of Health Care Professionals

Index of Health Care Professionals / Jean–Mary

JEAN–MARY, Ralph, Chief Executive Officer, Intermountain Medical Center, Murray, UT, p. A666
JEANSONNE, Corey, Chief Nursing Officer, Bunkie General Hospital, Bunkie, LA, p. A279
JEDLICKA, Colleen, R.N., JD, Chief Nursing Officer, Comanche County Medical Center, Comanche, TX, p. A608
JEFFERIES, Kanika, Executive Director, New York City Children's Center, New York, NY, p. A450
JEFFERS, Lynn, Chief Medical Officer St. John's Regional Medical Center and St. John's Hospital Camarillo, St. John's Regional Medical Center, Oxnard, CA, p. A82
JEFFERS, Zane, President and Chief Executive Officer, Levi Hospital, Hot Springs National Park, AR, p. A48
JEFFERSON, Glenn, Chief Medical Officer, Garfield County Public Hospital District, Pomeroy, WA, p. A692
JEFFERSON, Kelly
MSN, President, OSF St. Francis Hospital And Medical Group. Escanaba, MI, p. A326
MSN, Vice President, Operations, OSF St. Francis Hospital And Medical Group. Escanaba, MI, p. A326
JEFFERY, Jeremy, Regional Chief Financial Officer, Jefferson Regional, Pine Bluff, AR, p. A52
JEFFRESS, Chuck, Vice President Fiscal Services, Chi St. Luke's Health Brazosport, Lake Jackson, TX, p. A633
JEFFREY, Paul A, President, Cone Health Moses Cone Hospital, Greensboro, NC, p. A469
JEFFRIES, John, Director Finance, HSHS St. Joseph's Hospital Breese, Breese, IL, p. A187
JEFFS, Carla, Chief Financial Officer, Cornerstone Specialty Hospitals Huntington, Huntington, WV, p. A701
JEHAN, Sayed, M.D., Interim Medical Director, Larned State Hospital, Larned, KS, p. A252
JELALIAN, Christine, M.D., Medical Director, Montefiore St. Luke's Cornwall, Newburgh, NY, p. A454
JELDEN, Dennis, M.D., Chief of Staff, Melissa Memorial Hospital, Holyoke, CO, p. A109
JELESKY, Beth, MSN, Chief Nursing Officer, Ascension Alexian Brothers Behavioral Health Hospital, Hoffman Estates, IL, p. A198
JELKS, Kim, Fiscal Officer, Villa Feliciana Medical Complex, Jackson, LA, p. A283
JENE, Suzanne L., Chief Operating Officer, Tennessee Valley Hcs – Nashville And Murfreesboro, Nashville, TN, p. A590
JENKINS, Bonnie
Chief Financial Officer, Mercy General Hospital, Sacramento, CA, p. A87
Chief Financial Officer, Methodist Hospital of Sacramento, Sacramento, CA, p. A87
JENKINS, Brian, Director Human Resources, Arbour–Fuller Hospital, Attleboro, MA, p. A309
JENKINS, Debbie, Chief Human Resources Management Service, Ioannis A. Lougaris Veterans' Administration Medical Center, Reno, NV, p. A412
JENKINS, Denise, Chief Clinical Officer, Kindred Hospital–Brea, Brea, CA, p. A58
JENKINS, Devin
MSN, Chief Executive Officer and Chief Operating Officer, Specialists Hospital Shreveport, Shreveport, LA, p. A293
MSN, Chief Operating Officer, Specialists Hospital Shreveport, Shreveport, LA, p. A293
JENKINS, Jim, Chief Financial Officer, Huntsville Memorial Hospital, Huntsville, TX, p. A629
JENKINS, Jimmy, M.D., Chief Medical Officer, Stormont Vail Health – Flint Hills Campus, Junction City, KS, p. A251
JENKINS, Jonna, Vice President of Patient Care Services, Chief Nursing Officer. Hutchinson Regional Medical Center, Hutchinson, KS, p. A251
JENKINS, Keith, Director, Human Resources, Kettering Health Dayton, Dayton, OH, p. A494
JENKINS, Kerri, Senior Vice President and Chief Operating Officer, North Kansas City Hospital, North Kansas City, MO, p. A381
JENKINS, Linda, R.N., Vice President Patient Care Services, Providence St. Jude Medical Center, Fullerton, CA, p. A65
JENKINS, Maynard, Regional Vice President Human Resources, Sutter Maternity And Surgery Center of Santa Cruz, Santa Cruz, CA, p. A94
JENKINS, Michelle, M.D., President Medical Staff, Herrin Hospital, Herrin, IL, p. A197
JENKINS, Ruth, Chief Financial Officer, Ridgeview Institute – Smyrna, Smyrna, GA, p. A171
JENKINS, Timothy, M.D., Area Medical Director and Chief of Staff, Kaiser Permanente Fontana Medical Center, Fontana, CA, p. A63
JENNETTE, Brian, Chief Financial Officer, Northside Hospital Cherokee, Canton, GA, p. A160
JENNEY, Stephen, Vice President of Finance, South Shore Hospital, South Weymouth, MA, p. A318
JENNINGS, Jason
FACHE, President, Baylor Scott & White Hospital Medical Center – College Station, College Station, TX, p. A607
FACHE, President, Baylor Scott & White Medical Center – Brenham, Brenham, TX, p. A604
JENNINGS, Keith, Chief Information Officer, Massachusetts General Hospital, Boston, MA, p. A310
JENNINGS, Marilyn, Director Human Resources, Arise Austin Medical Center, Austin, TX, p. A598
JENNINGS, Mark, Chief Information Officer, Saint Anthony Hospital, Chicago, IL, p. A191
JENNINGS, Peter, M.D., Chief Medical Officer, Ascension Sacred Heart Pensacola, Pensacola, FL, p. A146
JENNINGS, Shane, Chief Medical Officer, Baptist Health–Fort Smith, Fort Smith, AR, p. A46
JENNINGS, Shayla, Human Resources Director, Montgomery County Memorial Hospital, Red Oak, IA, p. A242
JENNINGS, William, President, Fairfield Region, St. Vincent's Medical Center, Bridgeport, CT, p. A115
JENNY, Paul, Chief Financial Officer, Cincinnati Children's Hospital Medical Center, Cincinnati, OH, p. A488
JENSEMA, Christine
Chief Human Resources Officer, HSHS St. Clare Memorial Hospital, Oconto Falls, WI, p. A719
Chief Human Resources Officer, HSHS St. Vincent Hospital, Green Bay, WI, p. A712
Chief People Officer, HSHS St. Mary's Hospital Medical Center, Green Bay, WI, p. A712
Chief People Officer, HSHS St. Nicholas Hospital, Sheboygan, WI, p. A721
JENSEN, Amy, Director Human Resources, Promedica Coldwater Regional Hospital, Coldwater, MI, p. A324
JENSEN, Annelise, Vice President and Chief Nursing Officer, Methodist Healthcare Olive Branch Hospital, Olive Branch, MS, p. A367
JENSEN, Beth, Director Clinic Operations, Mobridge Regional Hospital, Mobridge, SD, p. A575
JENSEN, Christopher, Chief Financial Officer, Three Rivers Behavioral Health, West Columbia, SC, p. A571
JENSEN, Dave, Director Human Resources, Performance Improvement and Risk Management, Mountain View Hospital, Gadsden, AL, p. A20
JENSEN, Janette, Manager Human Resources, Avera Holy Family Hospital, Estherville, IA, p. A236
JENSEN, Jeff
D.O., Vice President, Medical Affairs, Morton Plant Hospital, Clearwater, FL, p. A128
D.O., Vice President, Medical Affairs, Morton Plant North Bay Hospital, New Port Richey, FL, p. A142
JENSEN, Jennifer L., Chief Human Resource Officer, Layton Hospital, Layton, UT, p. A665
JENSEN, Mary, Controller, Mountain View Hospital, Gadsden, AL, p. A20
JENSEN, Melissa A, Director, Nursing and Clinical Operations, University of Kansas Health System Great Bend Campus, Great Bend, KS, p. A250
JENSEN, Neal, Chief Executive Officer, Cobre Valley Regional Medical Center, Globe, AZ, p. A32
JENSEN, Paul, M.D., Chief of Staff, Regional Health Services of Howard County, Cresco, IA, p. A234
JENSEN, Renee K., Chief Executive Officer, Snoqualmie Valley Health, Snoqualmie, WA, p. A695
JENSEN, Ron, D.O., Chief Medical Officer and Vice President, Baylor Scott & White Medical Center – Grapevine, Grapevine, TX, p. A622
JENSEN, Ryan, Chief Executive Officer, Henrico Doctors' Hospital, Richmond, VA, p. A682
JENSEN, Sherry, Vice President, Financial Services, ECU Health North Hospital, Roanoke Rapids, NC, p. A475
JENSEN, Steve, Chief Financial Officer, Lifeways Behavioral Hospital, Boise, ID, p. A179
JENSEN, Tom, Chief Executive Officer, Harbor Regional Health, Aberdeen, WA, p. A687
JENSEN, Troy, Director Human Resources, Encompass Health Rehabilitation Hospital of Utah, Sandy, UT, p. A669
JENSEN, Twyla, Director Human Resources, Pioneers Medical Center, Meeker, CO, p. A112
JENTZ, Amy, M.D., Chief of Staff, University of Michigan Health–Sparrow Ionia, Ionia, MI, p. A330
JEPPESEN, Kelly, Chief Medical Officer, San Juan Health Service District, Monticello, UT, p. A666
JEPSEN, Christinia, R.N., Chief Executive Officer, Calhoun Liberty Hospital, Blountstown, FL, p. A126
JERDEE, Amy L., R.N., President, St. Francis Regional Medical Center, Shakopee, MN, p. A355
JERGER, Greg, Chief Financial Officer, Memorial Health Care Systems, Seward, NE, p. A406
JERNIGAN, Pam, Chief Financial Officer, Unity Medical Center, Manchester, TN, p. A587
JEROME, Jerome, M.D., Clinic Medical Director, Cascade Medical, Leavenworth, WA, p. A691
JESCH, Doug, Director Human Resources, Northwest Health – Starke, Knox, IN, p. A221
JESIOLOWSKI, Craig A.
FACHE, President and Chief Executive Officer, Memorial Hospital of Carbondale, Carbondale, IL, p. A187
FACHE, Vice President and Administrator, St. Josep. Memorial Hospital, Murphysboro, IL, p. A203
JESSIE, Scott, Chief Nursing Officer, Upstate University Hospital, Syracuse, NY, p. A460
JESSOP, Reuben
Chief Executive Officer, Northern Utah Rehabilitation Hospital, South Ogden, UT, p. A670
Chief Executive Officer, Utah Valley Specialty Hospital, Provo, UT, p. A668
JESSUP, Daniel
Chief Financial Officer, Legacy Silverton Medical Center, Silverton, OR, p. A532
Chief Financial Officer, Wallowa Memorial Hospital, Enterprise, OR, p. A526
JESTER, Denise, Chief Financial Officer, Tidalhealth Nanticoke, Seaford, DE, p. A122
JESTILA–PELTOLA, Gail, Chief Financial Officer, Baraga County Memorial Hospital, L'Anse, MI, p. A331
JESURASA, Jebashini, Vice President, Chief Information Technology Officer, Wyckoff Heights Medical Center, New York, NY, p. A453
JETER, John
Chief Executive Officer, Bristol Regional Medical Center, Bristol, TN, p. A579
Chief Executive Officer, Johnston Memorial Hospital, Abingdon, VA, p. A673
JETT, Christopher, Chief Executive Officer, Johnson City Medical Center, Johnson City, TN, p. A585
JETTERGREN, Tess, Director Clinical Informatics, Essentia Health St. Mary's Medical Center, Duluth, MN, p. A346
JEUNEHOMME, Patti, Director Human Resources, Hot Springs County Hospital District, Thermopolis, WY, p. A728
JEWETT, Jess, Chief Medical Officer, Cache Valley Hospital, North Logan, UT, p. A666
JEX, Kerri, R.N., Chief Nursing Officer, Bear Valley Community Hospital, Big Bear Lake, CA, p. A58
JEZSU, Peggy, Chief Nursing Officer, UC San Diego Health – East Campus, San Diego, CA, p. A90
JHA, Gautam, M.D., Chief of Staff, Salem Township Hospital, Salem, IL, p. A208
JIMENEZ, Betzaida, Director Human Resources, Hospital De La Universidad De Puerto Rico/Dr. Federico Trilla, Carolina, PR, p. A732
JIMENEZ, Edward, President and Chief Executive Officer, University Hospital, Newark, NJ, p. A425
JIMENEZ, Eric, Chief Information Officer, Artesia General Hospital, Artesia, NM, p. A433
JIMENEZ, Gerson, M.D., Medical Director, Hospital Menonita Guayama, Guayama, PR, p. A732
JIMENEZ, Guillermo, Director Finance, Castaner General Hospital, Castaner, PR, p. A732
JIMENEZ, Ramonita, R.N., Chief Nursing Officer, Hackensack Meridian Health Hackensack University Medical Center, Hackensack, NJ, p. A421
JIMMERSON, Kevin, Business Manager, Independence Mental Health Institute, Independence, IA, p. A238
JIN, Marvin, M.D., Medical Director, Parkside Psychiatric Hospital And Clinic, Tulsa, OK, p. A522
JIROVEC, David, Director Finance, Aspirus Merrill Hospital & Clinics, Inc., Merrill, WI, p. A716
JOBE, Kenneth Lynn, Director Human Resources, Tyler County Hospital, Woodville, TX, p. A663
JOBIN, Michael, Chief Information Officer, Mercy Hospital Perry, Perryville, MO, p. A382
JODWAY, Timothy, Chief Financial Administrator, Corewell Health Dearborn Hospital, Dearborn, MI, p. A324
JOHANNSEN, Lee, M.D., Vice President and Chief Medical Officer, Christus Santa Rosa Hospital – San Marcos, San Marcos, TX, p. A651
JOHANSON, Amanda, Chief Executive Officer, Triangle Springs Hospital, Raleigh, NC, p. A474
JOHE, David, M.D., President Medical Staff, Penn Highlands Elk, Saint Marys, PA, p. A554
JOHN, Aleyamma, R.N., Director of Nursing, Kensington Hospital, Philadelphia, PA, p. A549
JOHNS, Dale, FACHE, Chief Executive Officer, Mercy Medical Center Merced, Merced, CA, p. A77
JOHNS, Dawn, Director Human Resources, Colquitt Regional Medical Center, Moultrie, GA, p. A169
JOHNS, Jeffery, M.D., Medical Director, Vanderbilt Stallworth Rehabilitation Hospital, Nashville, TN, p. A591
JOHNS, Paul, Chief Operating Officer, Orlando Health South Lake Hospital, Clermont, FL, p. A128
JOHNS, Thomas Bradford, M.D., Medical Director, Ridgeview Institute – Smyrna, Smyrna, GA, p. A171
JOHNSEN, Liz, Chief Operations Officer, Lifeways Behavioral Hospital, Boise, ID, p. A179

A884 Index of Health Care Professionals

JOHNSON, Aaron, Vice President Patient Care Services and Chief Nursing Officer, Chi St. Alexius Health Devils Lake, Devils Lake, ND, p. A480
JOHNSON, Adam, Chief Operating Officer, Adventhealth Ocala, Ocala, FL, p. A143
JOHNSON, Alan, Interim Chief Information Officer, United Medical Center, Washington, DC, p. A124
JOHNSON, Allen
  Chief Financial Officer, University Health–Lakewood Medical Center, Kansas City, MO, p. A378
  Chief Financial Officer, University Health–Truman Medical Center, Kansas City, MO, p. A378
JOHNSON, Amy R, R.N., Quality Improvement Safety Officer, Star Valley Health, Afton, WY, p. A726
JOHNSON, Arlan D., Chief Executive Officer, Howard County Medical Center, Saint Paul, NE, p. A405
JOHNSON, Ashley, Director Human Resource, Mccamey County Hospital District, Mccamey, TX, p. A638
JOHNSON, Becky, Director Human Resources, Oakdale Community Hospital, Oakdale, LA, p. A290
JOHNSON, Belinda, R.N., Chief Nursing Officer/Chief Clinical Officer, Russellville Hospital, Russellville, AL, p. A24
JOHNSON, Blake, M.D., Chief of Staff, Holy Cross Hospital – Salt Lake, Salt Lake City, UT, p. A668
JOHNSON, Brandi, Site Manager Technology Information Systems, Corewell Health Reed City Hospital, Reed City, MI, p. A336
JOHNSON, Brenda, Director Human Resources, Baptist Memorial Hospital–Collierville, Collierville, TN, p. A581
JOHNSON, Brent, Commander, Mike O'Callaghan Federal Hospital, Nellis Afb, NV, p. A411
JOHNSON, Brett, Chief Executive Officer, Eleanor Slater Hospital, Cranston, RI, p. A560
JOHNSON, Brian
  M.D., Chief Medical Officer, Aurora Baycare Medical Center, Green Bay, WI, p. A712
  President and Chief Executive Officer, West Penn Hospital, Pittsburgh, PA, p. A552
JOHNSON, Bryan L., President, Intermountain Health St. Mary's Regional Hospital, Grand Junction, CO, p. A109
JOHNSON, Bryan N, M.D., Chief Medical Officer, Whitman Hospital And Medical Center, Colfax, WA, p. A688
JOHNSON, C Thomas III, Vice President Finance and Chief Financial Officer, UNC Health Southeastern, Lumberton, NC, p. A472
JOHNSON, Caleb, Chief Financial Officer, Plumas District Hospital, Quincy, CA, p. A84
JOHNSON, Candace, Ph.D., President and Chief Executive Officer, Roswell Park Comprehensive Cancer Center, Buffalo, NY, p. A440
JOHNSON, Casey R, Chief Financial Officer, Riverwood Healthcare Center, Aitkin, MN, p. A342
JOHNSON, Cheryl, Regional Chief Information Officer, St. Josep. Medical Center, Kansas City, MO, p. A378
JOHNSON, Chris, M.D., Chief of Staff, Mercy Hospital Northwest Arkansas, Rogers, AR, p. A52
JOHNSON, Christina, M.D., Sacramento Market President, Mercy General Hospital, Sacramento, CA, p. A87
JOHNSON, Collette, Chief Financial Officer, Palo Alto County Health System, Emmetsburg, IA, p. A236
JOHNSON, Cynthia J, R.N., Chief Nurse Officer, Sunrise Hospital And Medical Center, Las Vegas, NV, p. A411
JOHNSON, Danielle, Chief Operating Officer, Adventhealth Fish Memorial, Orange City, FL, p. A143
JOHNSON, Darren, M.D., Chief of Staff, West Tennessee Healthcare Dyersburg Hospital, Dyersburg, TN, p. A582
JOHNSON, David, Manager Information Services, Providence Kodiak Island Medical Center, Kodiak, AK, p. A28
JOHNSON, Debra, R.N., Chief Administrator, Corewell Health Lakeland Hospitals, Saint Joseph, MI, p. A337
JOHNSON, Deeann, Director Human Resources, Ascension Saint Thomas River Park, Mc Minnville, TN, p. A587
JOHNSON, Denise, M.D., Medical Director, Meadville Medical Center, Meadville, PA, p. A545
JOHNSON, Dennis B., Chief Executive Officer, Catawba Valley Medical Center, Hickory, NC, p. A470
JOHNSON, Derek Sr, Chief Operating Officer, Franklin Hospital District, Benton, IL, p. A186
JOHNSON, Diana G, Acting Chief Human Resources Officer, Novato Community Hospital, Novato, CA, p. A80
JOHNSON, Dino
  R.N., Chief Operating Officer, St. Anthony Hospital, Gig Harbor, WA, p. A690
  R.N., Interim Chief Operating Officer, St. Francis Hospital, Federal Way, WA, p. A690
JOHNSON, Douglas E
  Chief Financial Officer, Lakeview Hospital, Stillwater, MN, p. A355
  Vice President, Chief Financial Officer, Hudson Hospital And Clinic, Hudson, WI, p. A713

JOHNSON, Drew, Chief Financial Officer, Holdenville General Hospital, Holdenville, OK, p. A513
JOHNSON, Earle
  Area Information Officer, Kaiser Permanente Panorama City Medical Center, Los Angeles, CA, p. 73
  Area Information Officer, Kaiser Permanente Woodland Hills Medical Center, Los Angeles, CA, p. 73
JOHNSON, Eddie, Chief Information Technology Officer, Kansas City Va Medical Center, Kansas City, MO, p. A377
JOHNSON, Eric M., Director, United Medical Center, Washington, DC, p. A124
JOHNSON, Eunice, M.D., Chief Medical Staff, Kentucky River Medical Center, Jackson, KY, p. A267
JOHNSON, Gigi, Chief Nursing Officer, Kindred Hospital–Chattanooga, Chattanooga, TN, p. A580
JOHNSON, Greg, IT Coordinator, North Shore Health, Grand Marais, MN, p. A347
JOHNSON, Greg K, Chief Operating Officer, Colquitt Regional Medical Center, Moultrie, GA, p. A169
JOHNSON, Heather, Director of Finance, Operations and Business Development, Buffalo Hospital, Buffalo, MN, p. A344
JOHNSON, Helen, Chief Executive Officer, Helen Newberry Joy Hospital & Healthcare Center, Newberry, MI, p. A334
JOHNSON, J Christopher, Chief Nursing Officer, Holy Cross Hospital – Davis, Layton, UT, p. A665
JOHNSON, J. Ronald., Medical Center Director, Hunter Holmes Mcguire Veterans Affairs Medical Center–Richmond, Richmond, VA, p. A683
JOHNSON, James, Chief Executive Officer, Franklin Hospital District, Benton, IL, p. A186
JOHNSON, Jamie
  R.N., Vice President Nursing, Community Hospital of Anaconda, Anaconda, MT, p. A389
  Director Human Resources, Miners' Colfax Medical Center, Raton, NM, p. A436
JOHNSON, Jane, MSN, R.N., Executive Medical Center Director, Cincinnati Veterans Affairs Medical Center, Cincinnati, OH, p. A488
JOHNSON, Jani L., R.N., MSN, Chief Executive Officer, Saint Luke's Hospital of Kansas City, Kansas City, MO, p. A378
JOHNSON, Jarrod G., FACHE, President, UPMC Carlisle, Carlisle, PA, p. A536
JOHNSON, Jason, Controller, F. W. Huston Medical Center, Winchester, KS, p. A262
JOHNSON, Jay R., FACHE, President and Chief Executive Officer, Duncan Regional Hospital, Duncan, OK, p. A512
JOHNSON, Jayne, Director Human Resources, Great Plains Health, North Platte, NE, p. A403
JOHNSON, Jeff, Director Information Systems, Ascension Saint Thomas River Park, Mc Minnville, TN, p. A587
JOHNSON, Jessica, Chief Financial Officer, Emanuel Medical Center, Swainsboro, GA, p. A172
JOHNSON, Jimmy, Chief Financial Officer, Blue Mountain Hospital, Blanding, UT, p. A664
JOHNSON, Joe
  FACHE, President and Chief Executive Officer, Adventhealth Carrollwood, Tampa, FL, p. A151
  Chief Nursing Officer, Helen Newberry Joy Hospital & Healthcare Center, Newberry, MI, p. A334
JOHNSON, Joel, M.D., Chief Medical Staff, First Care Health Center, Park River, ND, p. A483
JOHNSON, John
  M.D., Chief of Staff, Camc Greenbrier Valley Medical Center, Ronceverte, WV, p. A704
  M.D., Clinical Director, U. S. Public Health Service Indian Hospital, Crownpoint, NM, p. A434
JOHNSON, Juantina, Chief of Staff, Choctaw Health Center, Philadelphia, MS, p. A367
JOHNSON, Judith, Controller, Encompass Health Rehabilitation Hospital of Largo, Largo, FL, p. A137
JOHNSON, Kathryn
  Chief Nursing Officer, Casa Colina Hospital And Centers for Healthcare, Pomona, CA, p. A84
  Manager Human Resources, Marketing and Public Relations, Ascension St. Vincent Jennings, North Vernon, IN, p. A225
JOHNSON, Kathy, Interim Chief Executive Officer, Johnson Memorial Health Services, Dawson, MN, p. A345
JOHNSON, Kawanda
  Ph.D., MSN, Administrator, Ochsner Choctaw General, Butler, AL, p. A17
  Ph.D., MSN, Administrator, Ochsner Watkins Hospital, Quitman, MS, p. A368
  Ph.D., MSN, Administrator and Executive Vice President, Ochsner Specialty Hospital, Meridian, MS, p. A366
JOHNSON, Kayla, R.N., Vice President Patient Care Services and Chief Nursing Officer, St. Francis Medical Center, Monroe, LA, p. A289

JOHNSON, Kelly
  R.N., Chief Nursing Officer, Ascension St. John Sapulpa, Sapulpa, OK, p. A520
  Director Human Resources, Madison Healthcare Services, Madison, MN, p. A349
  Senior Vice President, Chief Nursing Officer, Children's Hospital Los Angeles, Los Angeles, CA, p. A72
JOHNSON, Kelly M, Chief Nursing Officer, The Queen's Medical Center, Honolulu, HI, p. A176
JOHNSON, Ken
  Chief Physician Executive, HSHS St. Mary's Hospital Medical Center, Green Bay, WI, p. A712
  Chief Physician Executive, HSHS St. Vincent Hospital, Green Bay, WI, p. A712
JOHNSON, Kendall
  Chief Financial Officer, Baton Rouge General Medical Center, Baton Rouge, LA, p. A277
  Interim Chief Executive Officer, Ascension Saint Francis, Evanston, IL, p. A194
JOHNSON, Kevin, Chief Executive Officer, Mountain View Hospital, Payson, UT, p. A667
JOHNSON, Kimberly A, R.N., MSN, Vice President Patient Care and Chief Nursing Officer, Aspirus Riverview Hospital And Clinics, Inc., Wisconsin Rapids, WI, p. A725
JOHNSON, Kristen, Chief Nursing Officer, Southwest Healthcare System, Murrieta, CA, p. A79
JOHNSON, Kyle
  Chief Information Officer, The Aroostook Medical Center, Presque Isle, ME, p. A299
  Corporate Director, Information Technology, Reunion Rehabilitation Hospital Denver, Denver, CO, p. A107
  Vice President Finance, East Liverpool City Hospital, East Liverpool, OH, p. A495
JOHNSON, LaTeka Tanette., Chief Executive Officer, KPC Promise Hospital of Baton Rouge, Baton Rouge, LA, p. A277
JOHNSON, Laurie, Director – Human Resources, Mercy Hospital Pittsburg, Pittsburg, KS, p. A258
JOHNSON, Linda, R.N., Vice President, Patient Services Risk Management and Chief Nursing Officer, Heart of The Rockies Regional Medical Center, Salida, CO, p. A113
JOHNSON, Lori, Chief Operating Officer, Lucas County Health Center, Chariton, IA, p. A232
JOHNSON, Marianne, Chief Nursing Officer, Trace Regional Hospital, Houston, MS, p. A363
JOHNSON, Marie
  Chief Nursing Officer, Carrus Rehabilitation Hospital, Sherman, TX, p. A653
  Chief Nursing Officer, Carrus Specialty Hospital, Sherman, TX, p. A653
JOHNSON, Marissa, Chief Human Resource Officer, Alta View Hospital, Sandy, UT, p. A669
JOHNSON, Mark, Chief Information Officer, West Holt Medical Services, Atkinson, NE, p. A397
JOHNSON, Mary, Chief Nursing Officer, Falmouth Hospital, Falmouth, MA, p. A313
JOHNSON, Matt, Chief Executive Officer, Loring Hospital, Sac City, IA, p. A242
JOHNSON, Megan Elizabeth., President, Intermountain Spanish Fork Hospital, Spanish Fork, UT, p. A670
JOHNSON, Melissa, Chief Financial Officer, Baptist Medical Center South, Montgomery, AL, p. A22
JOHNSON, Michael, M.D., Medical Director, Salina Surgical Hospital, Salina, KS, p. A259
JOHNSON, Michael B, Vice President, Operations, Northwestern Medicine Delnor Hospital, Geneva, IL, p. A196
JOHNSON, Michael G., CPA, Chief Financial Officer, Ochsner Abrom Kaplan Memorial Hospital, Kaplan, LA, p. A284
JOHNSON, Monte, Vice President, Medical Affairs, St. Francis Regional Medical Center, Shakopee, MN, p. A355
JOHNSON, Nancy, Chief Nursing Officer, Select Specialty Hospital–North Knoxville, Powell, TN, p. A592
JOHNSON, Nanette, Chief Nursing Officer, Orthopaedic Hospital of Wisconsin, Glendale, WI, p. A711
JOHNSON, Nate, Chief Information Officer, HCA Florida Highlands Hospital, Sebring, FL, p. A150
JOHNSON, Neil, Chief Operating Officer, Eskenazi Health, Indianapolis, IN, p. A219
JOHNSON, Pamela
  R.N., Chief Nursing Officer, Mccurtain Memorial Hospital, Idabel, OK, p. A514
  Treasurer and Chief Financial Officer, Geneva General Hospital, Geneva, NY, p. A443
  Treasurer and Chief Financial Officer, Soldiers And Sailors Memorial Hospital, Penn Yan, NY, p. A456
JOHNSON, Patrick, Director Human Resources, Logan Health – Conrad, Conrad, MT, p. A390
JOHNSON, Penny, Chief Executive Officer, Texas Health Huguley Hospital Fort Worth South, Burleson, TX, p. A606

Index of Health Care Professionals / Johnson

JOHNSON, Peri, Human Resources Director, West Central Georgia Regional Hospital, Columbus, GA, p. A161

JOHNSON, Peter A, Interim Chief Information Officer, Monadnock Community Hospital, Peterborough, NH, p. A417

JOHNSON, Peter B., Chief Executive Officer, Springhill Medical Center, Springhill, LA, p. A293

JOHNSON, Phillip. Vice President, Chief Human Resources Officer, St. Luke's Regional Medical Center, Boise, ID, p. A180

JOHNSON, Ralph
  Chief Information Officer, Franklin Memorial Hospital, Farmington, ME, p. A297
  Chief Information Officer, Southern Maine Health Care – Biddeford Medical Center, Biddeford, ME, p. A296

JOHNSON, Raymond
  Chief Administrative Officer, Ascension Saint Thomas Dekalb, Smithville, TN, p. A593
  Chief Administrative Officer, Ascension Saint Thomas Stones River, Woodbury, TN, p. A594

JOHNSON, Regina E., Chief Nurse Executive, Piedmont Geriatric Hospital, Burkeville, VA, p. A674

JOHNSON, Ric, Associate Administrator, Mountain View Hospital, Payson, UT, p. A667

JOHNSON, Richard, M.D., Chief of Medical Staff, Chi St. Alexius Health Devils Lake, Devils Lake, ND, p. A480

JOHNSON, Robb, Director Operations, Hamilton Center, Terre Haute, IN, p. A228

JOHNSON, Roger, M.D., Chief of Staff, Cheyenne Va Medical Center, Cheyenne, WY, p. A726

JOHNSON, Ronald W., FACHE, President and Chief Executive Officer, Shore Medical Center, Somers Point, NJ, p. A428

JOHNSON, Russell W., President and Chief Executive Officer, LMH Health, Lawrence, KS, p. A253

JOHNSON, Ryan K, Controller, Corewell Health Greenville Hospital, Greenville, MI, p. A329

JOHNSON, Sam, M.D., Chief Medical Officer, Northeast Georgia Medical Center, Gainesville, GA, p. A148

JOHNSON, Scott H., Executive Vice President and Chief Financial Officer, St. Luke's Hospital, Chesterfield, MO, p. A373

JOHNSON, Sean, Chief Executive Officer, Walker Baptist Medical Center, Jasper, AL, p. A21

JOHNSON, Shanna
  FACHE, Interim President, Henry Ford Macomb Hospital, Clinton Township. MI, p. A324
  FACHE, President, Henry Ford West Bloomfield Hospital, West Bloomfield, MI, p. A340

JOHNSON, Sharon, Director Health Information Management, Western State Hospital, Staunton, VA, p. A684

JOHNSON, Sheila, Chief Nursing Officer, Ascension Columbia St. Mary's Hospital Milwaukee, Milwaukee, WI, p. A716

JOHNSON, Shelly
  Administrator and President, Riverside Walter Reed Hospital, Gloucester, VA, p. A677
  Chief Operating Officer, Corewell Health Gerber Hospital, Fremont, MI, p. A327

JOHNSON, Sheryl, Chief Information Officer, UW Health Swedishamerican Hospital, Rockford, IL, p. A207

JOHNSON, Shirley, Chief Clinical Operations Officer, Roswell Park Comprehensive Cancer Center, Buffalo, NY, p. A440

JOHNSON, Shrea, Director Human Resources, Alliance Health Center, Meridian, MS, p. A366

JOHNSON, Stephanie, Controller, Encompass Health Rehabilitation Hospital of Greenville, Greenville, SC, p. A567

JOHNSON, Talicia, Director Human Resources, Brentwood Hospital, Shreveport, LA, p. A292

JOHNSON, Thomas, Director Information Systems, Penn Highlands Brookville, Brookville, PA, p. A535

JOHNSON, Timothy, President and Chief Executive Officer, Eaton Rapids Medical Center, Eaton Rapids, MI, p. A326

JOHNSON, Todd, Chief Financial Officer, Longview Regional Medical Center, Longview, TX, p. A635

JOHNSON, Tom, Chief Human Resource Officer, Minneapolis Va Health Care System, Minneapolis, MN, p. A351

JOHNSON, Tonya
  Director of Finance, Mercyone Clinton Medical Center, Clinton, IA, p. A233
  Director of Finance, Mercyone Dubuque Medical Center, Dubuque, IA, p. A235

JOHNSON, Tracy
  Chief Executive Officer, Memorial Hospital of Texas County Authority, Guymon, OK, p. A513
  Vice President Patient Care Services/Chief Nursing Officer, Pratt Regional Medical Center, Pratt, KS, p. A258

JOHNSON, Tripp, Assistant Vice President Operations, RMC Anniston, Anniston, AL, p. A15

JOHNSON, Vern, Director Information Technology, Sullivan County Memorial Hospital, Milan, MO, p. A380

JOHNSON, Vernon, Chief Executive Officer, Dale Medical Center, Ozark, AL, p. A23

JOHNSON, Wade C., MS, FACHE, Chief Executive Officer, St. Peter's Health, Helena, MT, p. A393

JOHNSON, Whitney
  President, Allina Health Faribault Medical Center, Faribault, MN, p. A346
  President, Owatonna Hospital, Owatonna, MN, p. A352

JOHNSON, William, Director Information Systems, North Alabama Shoals Hospital, Muscle Shoals, AL, p. A23

JOHNSON, William F, Chief Medical Officer, Tennova Healthcare – Cleveland, Cleveland, TN, p. A581

JOHNSON, William Micah, MSN, R.N., Chief Nursing Officer, Christus Santa Rosa Hospital – San Marcos, San Marcos, TX, p. A651

JOHNSON, Yvonne, M.D., Chief Medical Offficer, Baptist Health South Florida, South Miami Hospital, Miami, FL, p. A139

JOHNSON CARLSON, Pam, R.N., Chief Nursing Officer, Children's Nebraska, Omaha, NE, p. A404

JOHNSON VANKUREN, Jill, President and Chief Executive Officer, Saratoga Hospital, Saratoga Springs, NY, p. A458

JOHNSON–HATCHER, Dawn, Interim Chief Financial Officer, Vice President Finance, Lake Charles Memorial Hospital, Lake Charles, LA, p. A286

JOHNSON–MEKOTA, Judith, FACHE, Director, Iowa City Va Health System, Iowa City, IA, p. A238

JOHNSON–MILLER, Kimberly, Chief Financial Officer, Carl Vinson Veterans Affairs Medical Center, Dublin, GA, p. A163

JOHNSON–THREAT, Yvette, Vice President Medical Affairs, Medstar Southern Maryland Hospital Center, Clinton, MD, p. A303

JOHNSRUD, Carolyn, Manager Human Resources, Missouri River Medical Center, Fort Benton, MT, p. A392

JOHNSRUD, Jill, Director of Nursing, Essentia Health–Graceville, Graceville, MN, p. A347

JOHNSTON, Christopher, Chief Administrative Officer, Peacehealth United General Medical Center, Sedro–Woolley, WA, p. A695

JOHNSTON, Diann, R.N., MSN, Vice President of Patient Care Services, Monmouth Medical Center, Long Branch Campus, Long Branch, NJ, p. A423

JOHNSTON, Don, Chief Information Officer, San Joaquin General Hospital, French Camp. CA, p. A64

JOHNSTON, John, Chief Medical Officer, Ochsner Specialty Hospital, Meridian, MS, p. A366

JOHNSTON, Kelly, Interim Chief Financial Officer, Delta Health, Delta, CO, p. A106

JOHNSTON, LaDonna
  Administrator, Unity Health – Newport, Newport, AR, p. A51
  Interim President and Chief Executive Officer, Unity Health, Searcy, AR, p. A53

JOHNSTON, Matthew, Chief Operating Officer, HCA Florida Trinity Hospital, Trinity, FL, p. A153

JOHNSTON, Michael Eric, FACHE, President, Mercy Hospital, Coon Rapids, MN, p. A345

JOHNSTON, Michael Eric., FACHE, President Southern Market, Mercy Hospital, Mercy Hospital, Coon Rapids, MN, p. A345

JOHNSTON, Michael V, M.D., Chief Medical Officer and Senior Vice President Medical Programs, Kennedy Krieger Institute, Baltimore, MD, p. A300

JOHNSTON, Mike
  Chief Executive Officer, Decatur County Hospital, Leon, IA, p. A239
  Director Facilities Operations, Union General Hospital, Blairsville, GA, p. A159

JOHNSTON, Monte, Manager Human Resources, Coquille Valley Hospital, Coquille, OR, p. A526

JOHNSTON, Patricia, Vice President Information Services, Texas Health Harris Methodist Hospital Azle, Azle, TX, p. A601

JOHNSTON, Phyllis M., Vice President, Catawba Valley Medical Center, Hickory, NC, p. A470

JOHNSTON, Susan, Vice President Human Resources, East Alabama Medical Center, Opelika, AL, p. A23

JOHNSTON, Susanne, Manager Human Resources, Lincoln County Medical Center, Ruidoso, NM, p. A436

JOHNSTON, Word, Medical Director, Covington County Hospital, Collins, MS, p. A361

JOHRENDT, JT, Information Technology Network Specialist, Edgerton Hospital And Health Services, Edgerton, WI, p. A710

JOICE, Jason, M.D., Chief Medical Staff, Hillcrest Hospital Pryor, Pryor, OK, p. A520

JOLITZ, Julie, Administrator, Ascension Sacred Heart Rehabilitation Hospital, Mequon, WI, p. A716

JOLLEY, Colby, D.O., Acting Chief of Staff, Haxtun Hospital District, Haxtun, CO, p. A109

JOLLEY, Sherry, Administrator, Red Bay Hospital, Red Bay, AL, p. A24

JOLLEY GREENE, Jill, MSN, R.N., President, Spartanburg Hospital for Restorative Care, Spartanburg, SC, p. A570

JOLLY, Kimberly, Vice President and Chief Nursing Officer, Mcleod Health Clarendon, Manning, SC, p. A568

JONES, Adrienne, Director Human Resources, Creedmoor Psychiatric Center, New York, NY, p. A448

JONES, Alesia, Chief Human Resources Officer, University of Alabama Hospital, Birmingham, AL, p. A17

JONES, Allan, Controller, Encompass Health Rehabilitation Hospital of Jonesboro, Jonesboro, AR, p. A48

JONES, America, R.N., Chief Executive Officer, Kindred Hospital El Paso, El Paso, TX, p. A616

JONES, Andrew
  M.D., Chief Executive Officer, Confluence Health Hospital – Central Campus, Wenatchee, WA, p. A698
  M.D., Chief Executive Officer, Confluence Health Hospital – Mares Campus, Wenatchee, WA, p. A698

JONES, Anitra, Director Human Resources, Encompass Health Rehabilitation Hospital of Middletown, Middletown, DE, p. A121

JONES, Anthony, Chief Operating Officer, Intensive Specialty Hospital – Shreveport Campus, Shreveport, LA, p. A292

JONES, Austin
  CPA, Chief Financial Officer, Chi St. Josep. Health Burleson Hospital, Caldwell, TX, p. A606
  CPA, Chief Financial Officer, Chi St. Josep. Health Grimes Hospital, Navasota, TX, p. A641

JONES, Beth
  Chief Operating Officer, Reeves Memorial Medical Center, Bernice, LA, p. A278
  Director of Nursing, Reeves Memorial Medical Center, Bernice, LA, p. A278
  Regional Administrator, Georgia Regional Hospital At Savannah, Savannah, GA, p. A171

JONES, Bill, Chief Financial Officer, Florida State Hospital, Chattahoochee, FL, p. A127

JONES, Brain, Director of Information Technology, Multicare Valley Hospital, Spokane Valley, WA, p. A696

JONES, Brian, Chief Information Officer, Billings Clinic, Billings, MT, p. A389

JONES, Carol, Controller and Manager Business Office, Coryell Health, Gatesville, TX, p. A622

JONES, Carol S., MSN, R.N., Interim Chief Nursing Officer, Morristown Medical Center, Morristown, NJ, p. A424

JONES, Charlene, Chief Nursing Officer, Peterson Healthcare And Rehabilitation Hospital, Wheeling, WV, p. A706

JONES, Christian, Chief Operating Officer, Boone Hospital Center, Columbia, MO, p. A374

JONES, Connie, Director Human Resources, Community Behavioral Health Hospital – Rochester, Rochester, MN, p. A353

JONES, Dana R., R.N., MSN, Chief Operating Officer, Springhill Medical Center, Springhill, LA, p. A293

JONES, David
  M.D., Chief Medical Officer, Beauregard Health System, De Ridder, LA, p. A281
  Chief Financial Officer, Ascension Alexian Brothers Behavioral Health Hospital, Hoffman Estates, IL, p. A198
  Service Chief, Riverside Shore Memorial Hospital, Onancock, VA, p. A681

JONES, David A, JD, Executive Vice President of Human Resources and Organizational Learning, Wellstar Kennestone Hospital, Marietta, GA, p. A167

JONES, David C., Administrator, North Caddo Medical Center, Vivian, LA, p. A294

JONES, David J., Market President, Critical Access Hospitals (NE, IA, MN), Chi Health Missouri Valley, Missouri Valley, IA, p. A240

JONES, Debbie, Director of Nursing, Brookhaven Hospital, Tulsa, OK, p. A522

JONES, Denise, R.N., Chief Nursing Officer, Willis Knighton North, Shreveport, LA, p. A293

JONES, Donald J., FACHE, Administrator, Fayette Medical Center, Fayette, AL, p. A19

JONES, Douglas A, Chief Operating Officer, Forrest General Hospital, Hattiesburg, MS, p. A363

JONES, Elaine, M.D., President Medical Staff, Roger Williams Medical Center, Providence, RI, p. A561

JONES, Elizabeth, Chief Operating Officer, Lake Cumberland Regional Hospital, Somerset, KY, p. A274

JONES, Evelyn, R.N., Vice President Nursing Services, St. Bernard Hospital And Health Care Center, Chicago, IL, p. A191

JONES, Florence, President, Methodist Healthcare Memphis Hospitals, Memphis, TN, p. A589

JONES, Greg, Chief Financial Officer, Wayne Memorial Hospital, Jesup. GA, p. A165

Index of Health Care Professionals / Joy
Index of Health Care Professionals

JONES, Holly A, Administrative Director Nursing Services, Illini Community Hospital, Pittsfield, IL, p. A206
JONES, Holly A., Administrator, Illini Community Hospital, Pittsfield, IL, p. A206
JONES, Jace
Chief Administrative Officer, Ascension Seton Bastrop, Bastrop, TX, p. A601
Chief Administrative Officer, Ascension Seton Edgar B. Davis Hospital, Luling, TX, p. A637
Chief Executive Officer and Administrator, Ascension Seton Smithville, Smithville, TX, p. A653
JONES, Janice, M.D., Chief of Staff, Mercy Health – Clermont Hospital, Batavia, OH, p. A486
JONES, Jason L.
R.N., Chief Executive Officer, Hillcrest Hospital Claremore, Claremore, OK, p. A511
R.N., Chief Executive Officer, Hillcrest Hospital Pryor, Pryor, OK, p. A520
JONES, Jeff, Director Human Resources, Kettering Health Greene Memorial, Xenia, OH, p. A508
JONES, Jennifer, Chief Executive Officer, Gateway Rehabilitation Hospital, Florence, KY, p. A265
JONES, Jeremy A., Administrator, Arbuckle Memorial Hospital, Sulphur, OK, p. A521
JONES, John
M.D., Chief Medical Officer, Unitypoint Health – St. Lukes's Sioux City, Sioux City, IA, p. A243
Chief Executive Officer, Encompass Health Rehabilitation Hospital of Florence, Florence, SC, p. A566
JONES, Joshua, Director Human Resources, Evanston Regional Hospital, Evanston, WY, p. A727
JONES, Joyce, Director Human Resources, Encompass Health Rehabilitation Hospital of Kingsport, Kingsport, TN, p. A585
JONES, Judy, Chief Clinical Officer, Arkansas Surgical Hospital, North Little Rock, AR, p. A51
JONES, Julie L., R.N., Chief Executive Officer, Community Hospital–Fairfax, Fairfax, MO, p. A375
JONES, Karen, Administrative Director of Human Resources, Marion Health, Marion, IN, p. A223
JONES, Karol, Chief Nursing Officer, Huntsville Hospital, Huntsville, AL, p. A21
JONES, Kathy, Director Human Resources, Jackson Medical Center, Jackson, AL, p. A21
JONES, Keith, Chief Information Officer, Fulton State Hospital, Fulton, MO, p. A375
JONES, Ken M, Chief Operating Officer, UCSF Medical Center, San Francisco, CA, p. A91
JONES, Kenneth, Chief Executive Officer, HCA Florida Northwest Hospital, Margate, FL, p. A138
JONES, Kimberly, Director Human Resources, The Spine Hospital of Louisiana At The Neuromedical Center, Baton Rouge, LA, p. A278
JONES, Kyle, Chief Financial Officer, Marshall Medical Center, Lewisburg, TN, p. A587
JONES, Lance, Chief Executive Officer, Cjw Medical Center, Richmond, VA, p. A683
JONES, Lee, R.N., Chief Nursing Officer, Claiborne Memorial Medical Center, Homer, LA, p. A283
JONES, Liston, M.D., Medical Director, Springhill Medical Center, Mobile, AL, p. A22
JONES, Louis, Director Management Information Systems, Adventhealth Heart of Florida, Davenport, FL, p. A129
JONES, M Steven.
Regional President, University Hospitals Conneaut Medical Center, Conneaut, OH, p. A493
Regional President, University Hospitals Geneva Medical Center, Geneva, OH, p. A496
JONES, Mark, Chief Financial Officer, Methodist Hospital Hill Country, Fredericksburg, TX, p. A620
JONES, Marsha
R.N., Director Nursing, Baptist Medical Center – Yazoo, Yazoo City, MS, p. A370
R.N., Director of Nursing, Baptist Medical Center – Yazoo, Yazoo City, MS, p. A370
JONES, Matthew, Chief Operating Officer and Senior Vice President, The University of Vermont Health Network – Alice Hyde Medical Center, Malone, NY, p. A445
JONES, Maud, Manager Medical Records, Top. Surgical Specialty Hospital, Houston, TX, p. A628
JONES, Mike, Executive Director, Marshall Medical Center, Placerville, CA, p. A83
JONES, Mitchell, Director Information Technology, Little River Medical Center, Inc., Ashdown, AR, p. A43
JONES, Pamela K., Executive Director of Finance, Baptist Health Corbin, Corbin, KY, p. A264
JONES, Pat, Director Information Systems, Merit Health River Oaks, Flowood, MS, p. A362
JONES, Patrice, R.N., MSN, DNP, RN, Vice President and Chief Nursing Officer, UF Health Jacksonville, Jacksonville, FL, p. A135
JONES, Phyllis, Chief Human Resources, Columbia Va Health Care System, Columbia, SC, p. A564
JONES, Rachel, Chief Financial Officer, Watsonville Community Hospital, Watsonville, CA, p. A100
JONES, Reginald, Business Manager, Georgia Regional Hospital At Atlanta, Decatur, GA, p. A162
JONES, Richard, M.D., Medical Director, Encompass Health Rehabilitation Hospital of Richardson, Richardson, TX, p. A646
JONES, Rob, Director of Nursing and Operations, Physicians' Medical Center, New Albany, IN, p. A225
JONES, Robert, Director Management Information Systems, Trinity Health Oakland Hospital, Pontiac, MI, p. A335
JONES, Roger, M.D., Interim Chief of Staff, Tennessee Valley Hcs – Nashville And Murfreesboro, Nashville, TN, p. A590
JONES, Ruth, Chief Clinical Officer, Regency Hospital of Northwest Arkansas – Springdale, Springdale, AR, p. A53
JONES, Ruth Ann
Ed.D., MSN, R.N., Senior Vice President, Chief Nursing Officer, University of Maryland Shore Medical Center At Chestertown, Chestertown, MD, p. A303
Ed.D., MSN, R.N., Senior Vice President, Chief Nursing Officer, University of Maryland Shore Medical Center At Easton, Easton, MD, p. A304
JONES, Ryan
Chief Executive Officer, Aultman Alliance Community Hospital, Alliance, OH, p. A484
President, Aultman Orrville Hospital, Orrville, OH, p. A502
JONES, Sarah, Chief Nurse Executive, St. Louis Forensic Treatment Center, Saint Louis, MO, p. A384
JONES, Scott, Vice President and Facility Executive, Atrium Health's Carolinas Medical Center, Charlotte, NC, p. A465
JONES, Sean, Director Human Resources, Merit Health Central, Jackson, MS, p. A364
JONES, Shannon, M.D., Medical Director and Attending Psychiatrist, Evansville Psychiatric Children Center, Evansville, IN, p. A216
JONES, Sharon, Chief Financial Officer, Evergreen Medical Center, Evergreen, AL, p. A19
JONES, Sherry J, Chief Financial Officer, Crestwood Medical Center, Huntsville, AL, p. A20
JONES, Stacy, Chief Nursing Officer, Encompass Health Rehabilitation Hospital of Morgantown, Morgantown, WV, p. A703
JONES, Stephanie, R.N., Chief Nursing Officer, Santa Rosa Medical Center, Milton, FL, p. A141
JONES, Stephen K, M.D., Vice President Medical Staff Affairs, St. Rose Dominican Hospitals – Rose De Lima Campus, Henderson, NV, p. A409
JONES, Steven K, M.D., Medical Director, Carle Eureka Hospital, Eureka, IL, p. A194
JONES, Theresa L., Manager Human Resources, St. Luke Community Healthcare, Ronan, MT, p. A395
JONES, Tim, Chief Executive Officer, Heart of Texas Healthcare System, Brady, TX, p. A604
JONES, Timothy P., Chief Operating Officer, Concord Hospital, Concord, NH, p. A414
JONES, Tom, Chief Information Officer, Fitzgibbon Hospital, Marshall, MO, p. A380
JONES, Tracey, Director Human Resources, Jackson Park Hospital And Medical Center, Chicago, IL, p. A189
JONES, Traci
Chief Financial Officer, USA Health Children's & Women's Hospital, Mobile, AL, p. A22
Chief Financial Officer, USA Health University Hospital, Mobile, AL, p. A22
JONES, Tracie, Director Information Services, Missouri Baptist Medical Center, Saint Louis, MO, p. A385
JONES, Vera A., Chief Operating Officer, Copley Hospital, Morrisville, VT, p. A672
JONES, Vernita, Site Manager, PHS Santa Fe Indian Hospital, Santa Fe, NM, p. A436
JONES, Vernon II, Chief Executive Officer, Rapides Regional Medical Center, Alexandria, LA, p. A276
JONES, Victoria, Chief Executive Officer, Highland–Clarksburg Hospital, Clarksburg, WV, p. A700
JONES, Wendy, Interim Chief Financial Officer, Northern Light Blue Hill Hospital, Blue Hill, ME, p. A296
JONES, William G.
M.D., Chief Medical Officer, Baylor Scott & White Medical Center – Sunnyvale, Sunnyvale, TX, p. A655
M.D., President and Chief Medical Officer, Chi St. Vincent Infirmary, Little Rock, AR, p. A49
JONES, Yvette A, Health Information Management Director, HCA Florida Putnam Hospital, Palatka, FL, p. A145
JONGSMA, Michael, R.N., Chief Nursing Officer, Providence Little Company of Mary Medical Center – Torrance, Torrance, CA, p. A98
JOOS, David, President, Abbott Northwestern Hospital, Minneapolis, MN, p. A350
JORDAN, Allen, Interim Chief Executive Officer, Grove Hill Memorial Hospital, Grove Hill, AL, p. A20
JORDAN, Amy
Chief Financial Officer, Rock Springs, Georgetown, TX, p. A622
Chief Human Resources Officer, Community Hospital, Grand Junction, CO, p. A108
JORDAN, Andrew, M.D., Chief of Staff, Vanderbilt Wilson County Hospital, Lebanon, TN, p. A586
JORDAN, Bradley, Chief Executive Officer, Select Specialty Hospital–Greensboro, Greensboro, NC, p. A469
JORDAN, Christy D, R.N., JD, Chief Operating Officer/Legal Counsel, Southeast Georgia Health System Brunswick Campus, Brunswick, GA, p. A159
JORDAN, Clay, R.N., Chief Executive Officer, Tri Valley Health System, Cambridge, NE, p. A398
JORDAN, Eric, Chief Executive Officer, Jasper General Hospital, Bay Springs, MS, p. A359
JORDAN, Gary W., FACHE, Chief Executive Officer, Cherokee Regional Medical Center, Cherokee, IA, p. A232
JORDAN, Heather, Director Human Resources, St. Luke's Health – Memorial Livingston, Livingston, TX, p. A635
JORDAN, Kim, Chief Operating officer, Lehigh Valley Hospital – Pocono, East Stroudsburg, PA, p. A539
JORDAN, Marie Kim, R.N., Senior Vice President and Chief Nursing Officer, Lehigh Valley Hospital–Cedar Crest, Allentown, PA, p. A534
JORDAN, Patrick III, Chief Operating Officer, Dartmouth–Hitchcock Medical Center, Lebanon, NH, p. A416
JORDAN, Quincy, M.D., Chief of Staff, Flint River Hospital, Montezuma, GA, p. A168
JORDAN, Regginald, Executive Director, Montefiore Mount Vernon, Mount Vernon, NY, p. A446
JORDAN, Rhonda R, Chief Human Resources Officer, Virtua Marlton, Marlton, NJ, p. A423
JORDAN, Terry, M.D., Chief of Staff, Alliance Health Center, Meridian, MS, p. A366
JORDAN, Traci S., MS, R.N., Chief Nursing Officer, Ochsner Lsu Health Shreveport – Monroe Medical Center, Monroe, LA, p. A288
JORDEN BEST, Rosemary, Director Human Resources, Penn Highlands Tyrone, Tyrone, PA, p. A556
JORE, Bernie, Chief Nursing Officer, Mymichigan Medical Center Saginaw, Saginaw, MI, p. A337
JORGENSEN, Jacob, Chief Information Officer, Floyd Valley Healthcare, Le Mars, IA, p. A239
JORGENSON, Craig, M.D., Chief of Staff, Boulder City Hospital, Boulder City, NV, p. A408
JOSEPH, Adrienne, Ph.D., Chief Executive Officer, Houston Methodist Baytown Hospital, Baytown, TX, p. A601
JOSEPH, James, M.D., President Medical Staff, Geisinger–Bloomsburg Hospital, Bloomsburg, PA, p. A535
JOSEPH, Jason, Vice President, Information Services, Corewell Health Butterworth Hospital, Grand Rapids, MI, p. A328
JOSEPH–TAYLOR, Terri, Chief Human Resource Manager, Slidell Memorial Hospital East, Slidell, LA, p. A293
JOSHI, Maulik, President and Chief Executive Officer, Meritus Health, Hagerstown, MD, p. A305
JOSHI, Nirmal
M.D., Senior Vice President Medical Affairs and Chief Medical Officer, UPMC Harrisburg, Harrisburg, PA, p. A541
M.D., System Chief Medical Officer, Mount Nittany Medical Center, State College, PA, p. A555
JOSLIN, Charlie, M.D., Chief of Staff, Ellinwood District Hospital, Ellinwood, KS, p. A248
JOSLYN, E Allen, M.D., Chief Medical Officer, Centra Bedford Memorial Hospital, Bedford, VA, p. A673
JOSLYN, J Scott, Senior Vice President and Chief Information Officer, Saddleback Medical Center, Laguna Hills, CA, p. A69
JOUD, Mohammad A, M.D., Chief of Staff, Tamp. General Hospital Brooksville, Brooksville, FL, p. A127
JOUDEH, Jalal
M.D., Chief Medical Officer, Specialty Rehabilitation Hospital of Coushatta, Coushatta, LA, p. A280
M.D., Chief of Staff, Dequincy Memorial Hospital, Dequincy, LA, p. A281
JOURDEN, Marti, FACHE, Chief Quality Officer, SSM Health St. Anthony Hospital – Oklahoma City, Oklahoma City, OK, p. A518
JOY, Michelle L., FACHE, President and Chief Executive Officer, Carson Tahoe Health, Carson City, NV, p. A408
JOY, Mike, Administrator, Finance, Mercy Hospital Pittsburg, Pittsburg, KS, p. A258
JOY, Roland Eugene Jr, Vice President and Chief Nursing Officer, Adventhealth Hendersonville, Hendersonville, NC, p. A470
JOY, Saju, M.D., Chief Executive Officer, Musc Health University Medical Center, Charleston, SC, p. A563

© 2025 AHA Guide
Index of Health Care Professionals A887

JOY, Susan, Chief Nursing Officer, Hillside Rehabilitation Hospital, Warren, OH, p. A506
JOYAL, Shirley, Director Information Systems, Regional Medical Center of San Jose, San Jose, CA, p. A92
JOYCE, Allyson, Vice President Human Resources, Mclaren Caro Region, Caro, MI, p. A323
JOYCE, John, President, Ascension Columbia St. Mary's Hospital Milwaukee, Milwaukee, WI, p. A716
JOYCE, Maria, Chief Financial Officer, Nih Clinical Center, Bethesda, MD, p. A302
JOYNER, Jeff, FACHE, Division President, Sentara Northern Virginia Medical Center, Woodbridge, VA, p. A685
JOZEFIAK, Jennifer, Information Officer, Fairlawn Rehabilitation Hospital, Worcester, MA, p. A320
JUAREZ, Edward, M.D., Chief Medical Officer, Kindred Hospital El Paso, El Paso, TX, p. A616
JUAREZ, Elizabeth, M.D., Chief Medical Officer, Harlingen Medical Center, Harlingen, TX, p. A623
JUAREZ, Rose, Chief Civilian Personnel Branch, Brooke Army Medical Center, Fort Sam Houston, TX, p. A618
JUBAS, John, Vice President Finance, The Children's Institute of Pittsburgh, Pittsburgh, PA, p. A551
JUCHNOWICZ, Jean E, Director Human Resources, Merit Health Natchez, Natchez, MS, p. A367
JUDD, Martin H., Regional President and Chief Executive Officer, Ascension Saint Mary – Chicago, Chicago, IL, p. A188
JUDICE, Kelly Paige., Interim Chief Executive Officer, Ochiltree General Hospital, Perryton, TX, p. A643
JUDLIN, Karen Ann, Director Human Resources, St. Charles Parish Hospital, Luling, LA, p. A287
JUDYCKI-CREPEAULT, Christine, Chief Financial Officer, Adcare Hospital of Worcester, Worcester, MA, p. A320
JUHL, Valerie, Director of Health, Madelia Health, Madelia, MN, p. A349
JULE, Janet, Chief Nurse Executive, Kaiser Permanente Antioch Medical Center, Antioch, CA, p. A55
JULIAN, Bell, Associate Executive Director and Chief Financial Officer, The Osuccc – James, Columbus, OH, p. A493
JULIAN, Steve, M.D., Vice President Medical Affairs, Sentara Obici Hospital, Suffolk, VA, p. A684
JULIANA, Rich, Director Human Resources, Silver Hill Hospital, New Canaan, CT, p. A117
JUMPING EAGLE, Sara, Clinical Director, Standing Rock Service Unit, Fort Yates Hospital, Indian Health Service, Dhhs, Fort Yates, ND, p. A481
JUNEAU, Cindy K., Chief Nursing Officer, Avoyelles Hospital, Marksville, LA, p. A288
JUNEAU, James B, Interim Chief Executive Officer, Opelousas General Health System, Opelousas, LA, p. A291
JUNEAU, Tina Louise, Director Human Resources, Bunkie General Hospital, Bunkie, LA, p. A279
JUNG, Darra, Director of Nursing, Union General Hospital, Farmerville, LA, p. A281
JUNGELS, Trisha, R.N., Chief Nursing Officer and Vice President Clinical Services, Jamestown Regional Medical Center, Jamestown, ND, p. A482
JUNGWIRTH, Scott, Chief Human Resources Officer, Providence Alaska Medical Center, Anchorage, AK, p. A27
JUNKINS, Curt M., Chief Executive Officer, Lake Granbury Medical Center, Granbury, TX, p. A622
JURADO, Jorge I., Interim Chief Executive Officer, Val Verde Regional Medical Center, Del Rio, TX, p. A613
JURCZYK, John Albert., FACHE, President, St. Josep. Hospital, Nashua, NH, p. A416
JURGENS, Chad, Senior Executive, Financial Services, Beatrice Community Hospital And Health Center, Beatrice, NE, p. A398
JURY, Tina M., R.N., Chief Hospital Operations, Anmed Medical Center, Anderson, SC, p. A562
JUST, Lisa, Patient Service Area President South Wisconsin, President, Aurora Medical Center Mount Pleasant, Aurora Medical Center Kenosha, Kenosha, WI, p. A713
JUST, Paula
  Chief Human Resources Officer, Health First Cap. Canaveral Hospital, Cocoa Beach, FL, p. A128
  Chief Human Resources Officer, Health First Holmes Regional Medical Center, Melbourne, FL, p. A139
  Chief Human Resources Officer, Health First Palm Bay Hospital, Palm Bay, FL, p. A145
  Chief Human Resources Officer, Health First Viera Hospital, Melbourne, FL, p. A139
JUSTICE, Brandi, Interim Director, Central State Hospital, Petersburg, VA, p. A681
JUSTICE, Jay D.
  Chief Human Resource Officer, Adena Regional Medical Center, Chillicothe, OH, p. A488
  Chief Human Resources Officer, Adena Pike Medical Center, Waverly, OH, p. A506
JUSTICE, Kansas, Senior Vice President and Chief Operating Officer, Pikeville Medical Center, Pikeville, KY, p. A273
JUSTICE, Kim, Vice President Planning and Operations, Atlantic General Hospital, Berlin, MD, p. A302
JUSTIN, Patrick, Chief Financial Officer, United Hospital District, Blue Earth, MN, p. A343
JUSTIN-TANNER, Karen, R.N., Chief Nursing Officer, Fairbanks Memorial Hospital, Fairbanks, AK, p. A28
JUSTUS, Jason, Chief Executive Officer, Pomerene Hospital, Millersburg, OH, p. A500
JUTILA, Kathy, M.D., Chief of Staff, Wheatland Memorial Healthcare, Harlowton, MT, p. A393
JUTZ, Kimberly, Administrator, Community Behavioral Health Hospital – Alexandria, Alexandria, MN, p. A342
JYRKAS, Wade A, Director Computer Information Systems, Lake Region Healthcare Corporation, Fergus Falls, MN, p. A347

K

KA'AKIMAKA, Holly, Director Human Resources, Hilo Medical Center, Hilo, HI, p. A175
KAARE, Rae, Chief Administrative Officer, Aspirus Iron River Hospital, Iron River, MI, p. A330
KABERLINE, Gene, Chief Financial Officer, Susan B. Allen Memorial Hospital, El Dorado, KS, p. A248
KABITZKE-GROTH, Terry, R.N., Chief Nursing Officer, Aurora Medical Center In Washington County, Hartford, WI, p. A712
KACHIGION, Claudia, M.D., Medical Director, Alton Mental Health Center, Alton, IL, p. A185
KADDOURI, Sami, M.D., Medical Director, Cornerstone of Medical Arts Center Hospital, Fresh Meadows, NY, p. A443
KADIVAR, Aryan, M.D., Chief Medical Officer, Southwestern Medical Center, Lawton, OK, p. A514
KAFKA, Rich, M.D., Chief Medical Officer, Avera Gregory Hospital, Gregory, SD, p. A574
KAHL, Larry, Chief Operating Officer, Adventist Health Columbia Gorge, The Dalles, OR, p. A532
KAHL, Vicky, Director Human Resources, Valley Regional Medical Center, Brownsville, TX, p. A605
KAHLE, Russ, Chief Information Officer, Logan County Hospital, Oakley, KS, p. A256
KAHLE, Ty
  Assistant Vice President Human Resources, Deaconess Union County Hospital, Morganfield, KY, p. A272
  Vice President Human Resources, Deaconess Henderson Hospital, Henderson, KY, p. A267
KAHLER, John G., M.D., Radiologist, Whitfield Regional Hospital, Demopolis, AL, p. A18
KAHLY-MCMAHON, Heidi
  Vice President Human Resources, Genesis Medical Center, Silvis, Silvis, IL, p. A208
  Vice President Human Resources Genesis Health System, Genesis Medical Center – Davenport, Davenport, IA, p. A234
KAHN, Russell, Administrator, Mercy Behavioral Hospital Llc, Lecompte, LA, p. A287
KAHO, Clint
  President, Baptist Health La Grange, La Grange, KY, p. A268
  Vice President, Baptist Health Louisville, Louisville, KY, p. A269
KAHRS, Amy, Director of Finance, Franklin County Memorial Hospital, Franklin, NE, p. A399
KAINO, Linda, Chief Nursing Officer, Ocean Beach Hospital And Medical Clinics, Ilwaco, WA, p. A690
KAISER, James, Site Director Information Technology, Upper Valley Medical Center, Troy, OH, p. A505
KAISER, Janet, R.N., Chief Nursing Officer, Kansas Medical Center, Andover, KS, p. A246
KAISER, Ken, Coordinator Information Systems, Grant Regional Health Center, Lancaster, WI, p. A714
KAISER, Russell, Interim Chief Executive Officer and Chief Nursing Officer, The Colony Er Hospital, The Colony, TX, p. A657
KAKUDA, James, M.D., Chief of Staff, Pali Momi Medical Center, Aiea, HI, p. A175
KALAFUS, Lisa, MSN, R.N., Chief Nursing Officer, Gaylord Specialty Healthcare, Wallingford, CT, p. A119
KALAJAINEN, Kimberly, FACHE, Chief Administrative Officer, Saint Mary's Hospital, Waterbury, CT, p. A119
KALANIHUIA, Janice, President, Molokai General Hospital, Kaunakakai, HI, p. A177
KALAVAR, Jagadeesh S, M.D., Chief of Staff, Michael E. Debakey Department of Veterans Affairs Medical Center, Houston, TX, p. A627
KALCHIK, Kevin, CPA, President, Mymichigan Medical Center Sault, Sault Sainte Marie, MI, p. A338
KALE, Debra, Vice President Human Resources, Atrium Health Cleveland, Shelby, NC, p. A476
KALEEL, Reza
  Chief Executive, Kadlec Regional Medical Center, Richland, WA, p. A694
  Chief Executive, Providence St. Mary Medical Center, Walla Walla, WA, p. A698
  Executive Vice President and Chief Operating Officer, Intermountain Health St. Mary's Regional Hospital, Grand Junction, CO, p. A109
KALINA, Andrea, Vice President External Affairs and Chief Human Resources Officer, St. Clair Health, Pittsburgh, PA, p. A551
KALINA, Margaret L, R.N., KalinaDirector of Patient Services and Chief Nursing Officer, Alomere Health, Alexandria, MN, p. A342
KALINSKI, Cami, Chief Financial Officer, Frances Mahon Deaconess Hospital, Glasgow, MT, p. A392
KALKA, Gina, R.N., Chief Nursing Officer, Pecos County Memorial Hospital, Fort Stockton, TX, p. A619
KALKANIS, Steven, M.D., Chief Executive Officer, Henry Ford Hospital, Detroit, MI, p. A325
KALKMAN, Joe, Chief Administrative Officer, Chief Human Resources Officer, Executive Vice President, Centracare – St. Cloud Hospital, Saint Cloud, MN, p. A354
KALKOWSKI, Kelly, Chief Executive Officer, Niobrara Valley Hospital, Lynch, NE, p. A402
KALKUT, Gary, M.D., Senior Vice President and Chief Medical Officer, Montefiore Medical Center, New York, NY, p. A449
KALLAS, Kathryn, Interim Administrator, Anoka Metro Regional Treatment Center, Anoka, MN, p. A342
KALLBERG, Diana, Administrator, Essentia Health Northern Pines, Aurora, MN, p. A343
KALLEVIG, Daryl, Chief Information Officer, Riverwood Healthcare Center, Aitkin, MN, p. A342
KALMAN, Arthur, M.D., Medical Director, Encompass Health Rehabilitation Hospital of Pensacola, Pensacola, FL, p. A146
KALSMAN, Stephen L, Area Finance Officer, Kaiser Permanente San Jose Medical Center, San Jose, CA, p. A92
KALTENBACH, Gretchen, R.N., Chief Operating Officer, Genesis Behavioral Hospital, Breaux Bridge, LA, p. A279
KALUA, Patricia, Chief Nurse Executive, Kona Community Hospital, Kealakekua, HI, p. A177
KAMAL, Mohsin, Chief Information Officer, Spring Hospital, Spring, TX, p. A654
KAMAROUSKY, Gabriel, President, Geisinger St. Luke's Hospital, Orwigsburg, PA, p. A547
KAMBER, Sean, Chief Executive Officer, Medical City Weatherford, Weatherford, TX, p. A661
KAMBEROS, Peter N, Chief Operating Officer, Thorek Memorial Hospital, Chicago, IL, p. A191
KAMBIC, Phillip M., President and Chief Executive Officer, Riverside Medical Center, Kankakee, IL, p. A199
KAMBOJ, Pradeep. M.D., Chief Medical Staff, Adventist Health – Tulare, Tulare, CA, p. A98
KAMENS, Eric, Regional Director Information Systems, Shriners Hospitals for Children–Springfield, Springfield, MA, p. A318
KAMERMAYER, Angela K, MS, Chief Nursing Officer, Integris Health Edmond Hospital, Edmond, OK, p. A512
KAMGUIA, Rebecca, Administrative Director Human Resources, Bon Secours Memorial Regional Medical Center, Mechanicsville, VA, p. A679
KAMINSKI, Gene, Vice President Human Resources and Hospitality Services, Mclaren Northern Michigan, Petoskey, MI, p. A335
KAMINSKI, Tammy, Vice President, Human Resources, Tristar Centennial Medical Center, Nashville, TN, p. A591
KAMINSKI, Toni, Director Human Resources, Medical Center Enterprise, Enterprise, AL, p. A19
KAMINSKY, Kathleen A., MS, R.N., Senior Vice President Patient Care Services, Englewood Health, Englewood, NJ, p. A421
KAMLOT-WRIGHT, Deborah, Vice President, Human Resources, HCA Florida Citrus Hospital, Inverness, FL, p. A134
KAMMERER, James M., Vice President Support Services, Southeast Iowa Regional Medical Center, West Burlington Campus, West Burlington, IA, p. A245
KAMMERUD, Shawn, Manager Information Services, Osceola Medical Center, Osceola, WI, p. A719
KAMPWERTH, Dennis, Director Management Information Systems, Gateway Regional Medical Center, Granite City, IL, p. A196
KANAPARTI, V.R., M.D., Director Medical Services, Kalamazoo Psychiatric Hospital, Kalamazoo, MI, p. A331

Index of Health Care Professionals / Kedzierski

Index of Health Care Professionals

KANDOW, Casey
Chief Operating Officer, Mclaren Greater Lansing, Lansing, MI, p. A331
Interim President and Chief Executive Officer, Mclaren Greater Lansing, Lansing, MI, p. A331
KANE, Addy, Chief Financial Officer, Roger Williams Medical Center, Providence, RI, p. A561
KANE, Kelli R, Director of Finance, Barnes–Kasson County Hospital, Susquehanna, PA, p. A555
KANE, Robert E., President, UPMC Williamsport, Williamsport, PA, p. A558
KANE, Steve, Director Information Technology, Lower Bucks Hospital, Bristol, PA, p. A535
KANE, Thomas, R.N., Vice President Patient Services and Chief Nursing Officer, Munson Healthcare Manistee Hospital, Manistee, MI, p. A332
KANE, Trisha, Director Human Resources, Continuecare Hospital At Hendrick Medical Center, Abilene, TX, p. A595
KANESHIRO, Shela, Chief Nursing Officer, Orange Coast Medical Center, Fountain Valley, CA, p. A64
KANIA, Kathy, Associate Executive Director and Chief Information Officer, Staten Island University Hospital, New York, NY, p. A453
KANNA, Balavenkatesh, M.D., M.P.H., FACHE, Medical Center Director, James J. Peters Veterans Affairs Medical Center, New York, NY, p. A448
KANNADAY, Colleen, FACHE, President, Carle Bromenn Medical Center, Normal, IL, p. A203
KANNAN, Vidhya
Chief Executive Officer, Encompass Health Rehabilitation Hospital of East Valley, Mesa, AZ, p. A33
Chief Executive Officer, Encompass Health Rehabilitation Hospital of Northern Virginia, Aldie, VA, p. A673
KANTELAS, Sandra Jean, Chief Nursing Officer, University Hospitals Elyria Medical Center, Elyria, OH, p. A495
KANTOS, Craig A., Chief Executive Officer, Coteau Des Prairies Hospital, Sisseton, SD, p. A577
KANUCH, James A
Vice President Finance, Allegheny Valley Hospital, Natrona Heights, PA, p. A547
Vice President Finance, West Penn Hospital, Pittsburgh, PA, p. A552
KANWAL, Neeraj, M.D., Vice President, Medical Affairs, Promedica Toledo Hospital, Toledo, OH, p. A505
KAPER, Jonathan, Chief Medical Officer, Corewell Health Trenton Hospital, Trenton, MI, p. A339
KAPLAN, Alan, M.D., Chief Executive Officer, University Hospital, Madison, WI, p. A714
KAPLAN, Eric, Chief Operating Officer, Shorepoint Health Port Charlotte, Port Charlotte, FL, p. A147
KAPLAN, Ronald, Chief Financial Officer, Behavioral Wellness Center At Girard, The, Philadelphia, PA, p. A548
KAPLAN, Tamra, PharmD, Senior Vice President, Operations, Phoenix Children's, Phoenix, AZ, p. A36
KAPLANIS, Gene, Director Information Technology, Alaska Regional Hospital, Anchorage, AK, p. A27
KAPRE, Sheela, M.D., Chief Medical Officer, San Joaquin General Hospital, French Camp, CA, p. A64
KARA, Amynah, M.D., Chief Medical Officer, Baylor Scott & White Emergency Hospitals–Aubrey, Aubrey, TX, p. A598
KARAM, Annah, Chief Human Resources Officer, San Gorgonio Memorial Hospital, Banning, CA, p. A57
KARAM, Christopher J, Chief Operating Officer, Saint Josep. Health System, Mishawaka, IN, p. A224
KARAM, Christopher J., President, Plymouth Medical Center, Plymouth, IN, p. A226
KARANJA, Diana, R.N., Director of Nursing, Saint John Vianney Hospital, Downingtown, PA, p. A538
KARANJAI, Rajohn, M.D., Chief Medical Officer, Sidney Health Center, Sidney, MT, p. A396
KARCZ, Chrisi, Chief Nursing Officer, Van Matre Encompass Health Rehabilitation Hospital, Rockford, IL, p. A207
KAREL, Thomas L, Vice President Organization and Talent Effectiveness, Trinity Health Grand Rapids Hospital, Grand Rapids, MI, p. A328
KARIM, Parvez, M.D., Chief Medical Officer, Allegiance Specialty Hospital of Greenville, Greenville, MS, p. A362
KARL, Don
Chief Executive Officer, Las Palmas Medical Center, El Paso, TX, p. A616
Chief Operating Officer, Las Palmas Medical Center, El Paso, TX, p. A616
Interim Chief Executive Officer, Las Palmas Medical Center, El Paso, TX, p. A616
KARLAPUDI, Sudhakar, Chief Medical Officer and Patient Safety Officer, Northwest, Peacehealth St. Josep. Medical Center, Bellingham, WA, p. A687
KARLIX, Krysla, Chief Executive Officer, Medical City Green Oaks Hospital, Dallas, TX, p. A611
KARLSEN, Brooke, MSN, R.N., Regional Vice President, Operations, St. Vincent's Medical Center, Bridgeport, CT, p. A115
KARN, Cielette, M.D., Chief of Staff, Sagewest Health Care, Riverton, WY, p. A728
KARNER, Diana M.
R.N., MSN, Chief Nursing Executive, California Pacific Medical Center–Mission Bernal Campus, San Francisco, CA, p. A90
R.N., MSN, Chief Nursing Officer, California Pacific Medical Center–Van Ness Campus, San Francisco, CA, p. A90
KARNITZ, Susan, Chief Nursing Director, Hutchinson Health, Hutchinson, MN, p. A348
KARP, Bob, M.D., Chief Medical Officer, United Hospital District, Blue Earth, MN, p. A343
KARSOS, Felicia, R.N., Chief Nursing Officer, Hudson Regional Hospital, Secaucus, NJ, p. A428
KARSTEN, Paul H, Vice President Finance and Chief Financial Officer, Pine Rest Christian Mental Health Services, Grand Rapids, MI, p. A328
KARSTETTER, James M., R.N., II, Vice President and Chief Nursing Officer, UPMC Western Maryland, Cumberland, MD, p. A304
KARTCHNER, Gary, R.N., MSN, Chief Executive Officer, Benson Hospital, Benson, AZ, p. A30
KASHMAN, Scott, President, Ascension St. Vincent's Riverside, Jacksonville, FL, p. A134
KASIRYE, Yusuf, M.D., Chief of Staff, Marshfield Medical Center – Park Falls, Park Falls, WI, p. A719
KASITZ, Todd, Vice President Finance, Nmc Health, Newton, KS, p. A255
KASPER, Katie, Chief Clinical Officer, UH Avon Rehabilitation Hospital, Avon, OH, p. A485
KASPER, Yobi, Chief Information Officer, East Houston Hospitals & Clinics, Houston, TX, p. A625
KASS, Andrew J A, M.D., Assistant Superintendent, Albert J. Solnit Children's Center, Middletown, CT, p. A116
KASSAB, Kelly
Chief Operating Officer, Canonsburg Hospital, Canonsburg, PA, p. A536
Chief Operating Officer, Jefferson Hospital, Jefferson Hills, PA, p. A542
KASSER, Michael
Chief Financial Officer, Herrin Hospital, Herrin, IL, p. A197
Vice President Chief Financial Officer and Treasurer, Memorial Hospital of Carbondale, Carbondale, IL, p. A187
KASSIS, Maher, M.D., Chief Medical Staff, Mercy Health – Marcum And Wallace, Irvine, KY, p. A267
KASTEN, Karen, Chief Executive Officer, Centerpointe Hospital, Saint Charles, MO, p. A383
KATES, Josh, Information Technology Analyst, Elizabeth Parsons Ware Packard Mental Health Center, Springfield, IL, p. A209
KATNENI, Jitendra P., M.D., Medical Director, Select Specialty Hospital – Flint, Flint, MI, p. A327
KATO, Laura, Vice President Human Resources, St. Francis Medical Center, Lynwood, CA, p. A76
KATSCHKE, R William, M.D., Jr, Medical Director, Grover C. Dils Medical Center, Caliente, NV, p. A408
KATZ, Jeffrey, M.D., Chief Medical Officer, Memorial Hermann – Texas Medical Center, Houston, TX, p. A627
KATZ, Michael, Vice President Human Resources, Canton–Potsdam Hospital, Potsdam, NY, p. A456
KATZ, Michelle, Director Human Resources, Encompass Health Rehabilitation Hospital of Nittany Valley, Pleasant Gap, PA, p. A552
KATZ, Richard, M.D., Vice President Medical Affairs, Mt. Washington Pediatric Hospital, Baltimore, MD, p. A301
KATZ, Robert, M.D., Chief of Staff, Columbus Community Hospital, Columbus, TX, p. A608
KATZ, Yair
Chief Financial Officer, Long Beach Medical Center, Long Beach, CA, p. A71
Chief Financial Officer, Miller Children's & Women's Hospital Long Beach, Long Beach, CA, p. A71
KATZDORN, Rhonda L, Executive Director, Human Resources, Delta Health, Delta, CO, p. A106
KAUFFMAN, Angie, Chief Executive Officer, South Texas Spine And Surgical Hospital, San Antonio, TX, p. A651
KAUFFMAN, Gail, Director Human Resources, Berwick Hospital Center, Berwick, PA, p. A535
KAUFMAN, Cheryl
Director Health Information Management, Adventhealth Dade City, Dade City, FL, p. A129
Information Technology Technician, Coteau Des Prairies Hospital, Sisseton, SD, p. A577
KAUFMAN, Dan, Director Information Services, Paulding County Hospital, Paulding, OH, p. A502
KAUFMAN, Irvin A, M.D., Chief Medical Officer, Rady Children's Hospital – San Diego, San Diego, CA, p. A89
KAUFMAN, Robert
Director Financial Services, Central State Hospital, Petersburg, VA, p. A681
Fiscal Officer, Hiram W. Davis Medical Center, Petersburg, VA, p. A681
KAUFMAN, Samuel, Chief Executive Officer, Henderson Hospital, Henderson, NV, p. A409
KAUFMAN, Seth, M.D., Chief Medical Officer, Northbay Medical Center, Fairfield, CA, p. A63
KAUL, Kamlesh, M.D., Chief of Staff, Logansport Memorial Hospital, Logansport, IN, p. A223
KAUL, Stephanie, Interim Chief Financial Officer, Chi St. Alexius Health Bismarck, Bismarck, ND, p. A479
KAUP, Jack, Chief Executive Officer, Black Hills Surgical Hospital, Rapid City, SD, p. A575
KAUPA, Michael, Executive Vice President and Chief Operating Officer, Park Nicollet Methodist Hospital, Saint Louis Park, MN, p. A354
KAUR, Gurvinder, President and Market Leader, Saint Agnes Medical Center, Fresno, CA, p. A65
KAUZLARICH, Sidney A., M.D., Medical Director, Douglas County Community Mental Health Center, Omaha, NE, p. A404
KAVANAGH, Darina, R.N., MSN, Chief Nursing Officer, Good Samaritan Hospital – San Jose, San Jose, CA, p. A92
KAVANAGH, Sean, Director Information Technology, Logan Health – Conrad, Conrad, MT, p. A390
KAVANAUGH, Cassie, Chief Nursing Officer, Cleveland Emergency Hospital, Humble, TX, p. A629
KAVANAUGH, Paul B., President and Chief Executive Officer, Community Care Hospital, New Orleans, LA, p. A290
KAVANAUGH, Samantha, Chief Financial Officer, Riverview Psychiatric Center, Augusta, ME, p. A295
KAVTARADZE, David, M.D., Chief of Staff, Crisp Regional Hospital, Cordele, GA, p. A161
KAY, Kirk, Chief Financial Officer, Omaha Va Medical Center, Omaha, NE, p. A404
KAY, Robert W, Senior Vice President and Chief Financial Officer, Springfield Memorial Hospital, Springfield, IL, p. A209
KAYE, Erika, Chief Executive Officer, Reunion Rehabilitation Hospital Denver, Denver, CO, p. A107
KAYE, Jessie, Chief Executive Officer, Prairie View, Newton, KS, p. A256
KAYROUZ, Thomas, M.D., Chief Medical Officer, Anmed Medical Center, Anderson, SC, p. A562
KAYSER, Sonya J, Human Resources Officer, Avera Marshall Regional Medical Center, Marshall, MN, p. A350
KAZMIERCZAK, Sara Marie, R.N., Director of Nursing, North Valley Health Center, Warren, MN, p. A357
KAZMIERCZAK, Stanley, Controller, Ascension Saint Josep. – Chicago, Chicago, IL, p. A188
KEANE, Dennis M., Vice President Finance and Chief Financial Officer, St. John's Riverside Hospital, Yonkers, NY, p. A462
KEANE, Fran, Vice President Human Resources, Centrastate Healthcare System, Freehold, NJ, p. A421
KEANE, Merry–Ann, MSN, FACHE, Chief Executive Officer, Ocean Beach Hospital And Medical Clinics, Ilwaco, WA, p. A690
KEANE, Valerie E, FACHE, Chief Nursing Executive, Sentara Northern Virginia Medical Center, Woodbridge, VA, p. A685
KEARNEY, Elizabeth, R.N., Chief Executive Officer, Arizona Spine And Joint Hospital, Mesa, AZ, p. A33
KEARNEY, Karen, Vice President Inpatient Rehabilitation Services, John Heinz Institute of Rehabilitation Medicine, Wilkes–Barre, PA, p. A557
KEARNEY, Lynn, Vice President Nursing, Robert Wood Johnson University Hospital Somerset, Somerville, NJ, p. A428
KEARNEY, M Clark, Vice President Human Resources, Saint Mary's Hospital, Waterbury, CT, p. A119
KEARNS, Debbie
Chief Executive Officer, Community Hospital, Oklahoma City, OK, p. A516
Chief Executive Officer, Northwest Surgical Hospital, Oklahoma City, OK, p. A517
KEASTER, Lorna, Interim Chief Nursing Officer, HSHS Holy Family Hospital In Greenville, Greenville, IL, p. A196
KEATING, Todd, Chief Financial Officer, University of Vermont Medical Center, Burlington, VT, p. A671
KEATON, Tony, Director Information Systems, Roane General Hospital, Spencer, WV, p. A705
KECK, Catherine, Chief Financial Officer, Decatur County Memorial Hospital, Greensburg, IN, p. A218
KEDDINGTON, Richard, Chief Executive Officer, Watertown Regional Medical Center, Watertown, WI, p. A723
KEDZIERSKI, Kelly, R.N., BSN, RN, Director of Quality, Cordova Community Medical Center, Cordova, AK, p. A28

Index of Health Care Professionals A889

Index of Health Care Professionals / Kee

KEE, Agnes, Financial Manager, Gallup Indian Medical Center, Gallup, NM, p. A434
KEE, Robert, Chief Information Officer, NYC Health + Hospitals/South Brooklyn Health, New York, NY, p. A452
KEEF, Shaun, Chief Financial Officer, Eastern Oklahoma Medical Center, Poteau, OK, p. A520
KEEF, Shaun Patrick., Chief Executive Officer, Central Peninsula Hospital, Soldotna, AK, p. A29
KEEFE, Eileen, Chief Nursing Officer, Parkland Medical Center, Derry, NH, p. A414
KEEFE, Erin, Ed.D., R.N., Chief Nursing Executive Officer, St. Bernardine Medical Center, San Bernardino, CA, p. A88
KEEFE, John, Chief Financial Officer, Carrollton Regional Medical Center, Carrollton, TX, p. A606
KEEFER, Russ, Chief Human Resources Officer, Trios Health, Kennewick, WA, p. A590
KEEGAN, Justin, Director Support Services, Avera Gregory Hospital, Gregory, SD, p. A574
KEEL, Barry L.
  Administrator, North Mississipp. Medical Center–Iuka, Iuka, MS, p. A363
  Administrator, North Mississipp. Medical Center–West Point, West Point, MS, p. A370
KEEL, Brooks, M.D., President, Augusta University, Wellstar Mcg Health, Augusta, GA, p. A158
KEELE, Paula
  Manager Information Systems, OSF Heart of Mary Medical Center, Urbana, IL, p. A210
  Manager Information Systems, OSF Sacred Heart Medical Center, Danville, IL, p. A192
KEELER, Jason, Executive Vice President and Chief Operating Officer, University of Chicago Medical Center, Chicago, IL, p. A192
KEELER, Karl, Chief Executive, Los Angeles Valley Service Area, Providence Saint Josep. Medical Center, Burbank, CA, p. A58
KEELEY, Katherine, M.D., Chief of Staff, Sunrise Hospital And Medical Center, Las Vegas, NV, p. A411
KEELINE, Leah, Clinical Informatics Specialist, Catalina Island Medical Center, Avalon, CA, p. A56
KEELING, Kathy, Director of Nursing, Rehabilitation Hospital of Rhode Island, North Smithfield, RI, p. A560
KEELING, Michele A., President, Saint Francis Hospital Muskogee, Muskogee, OK, p. A515
KEELING, Terri, Vice President Information Systems, UPMC Mckeesport, Mckeesport, PA, p. A545
KEEN, Kris, Chief Information Officer, Cameron Memorial Community Hospital, Angola, IN, p. A212
KEENAN, Bob, Chief Medical Officer, H. Lee Moffitt Cancer Center And Research Institute, Tampa, FL, p. A152
KEENAN, Kevin, M.D., Physician Advisor, East Cooper Medical Center, Mount Pleasant, SC, p. A568
KEENAN, Nancy C, R.N., Senior Vice President and Chief Nursing Officer, Houston Methodist Willowbrook Hospital, Houston, TX, p. A626
KEENAN, Richard, Senior Vice President Finance and Chief Financial Officer, Valley Hospital, Paramus, NJ, p. A426
KEENE, Amy, R.N., Chief Nursing Officer, Byrd Regional Hospital, Leesville, LA, p. A287
KEENE, Emilie, FACHE, Interim Chief Operating Officer, Prisma Health Baptist Parkridge Hospital, Columbia, SC, p. A564
KEENE, Tony, Chief Executive Officer, Ferrell Hospital, Eldorado, IL, p. A194
KEENER, Jayd, Co–Chief Executive Officer, Garfield County Public Hospital District, Pomeroy, WA, p. A692
KEENER, Vicki, Administrative Assistant and Director Human Resources, Little River Medical Center, Inc., Ashdown, AR, p. A43
KEEPSEAGLE, Joelle, Director of Nursing, Standing Rock Service Unit, Fort Yates Hospital, Indian Health Service, Dhhs, Fort Yates, ND, p. A481
KEESBURY, Drew
  Chief Financial Officer, Northwest Health – La Porte, La Porte, IN, p. A221
  Chief Financial Officer, Northwest Health – Starke, Knox, IN, p. A221
KEESEE, Alan, Chief Executive Officer, HCA Florida Ocala Hospital, Ocala, FL, p. A143
KEEVER, Jerry, Administrator, Sharkey–Issaquena Community Hospital, Rolling Fork, MS, p. A368
KEGLEY, Shawn, Director Information Services, Research Medical Center, Kansas City, MO, p. A378
KEHIAYAN, Nancy, Director of Nursing, Colorado Mental Health Institute at Fort Logan, Denver, CO, p. A106
KEHRBERG, Mark W
  M.D., Chief Medical Officer, Ascension Calumet Hospital, Chilton, WI, p. A709
  M.D., Senior Vice President and Chief Medical Officer, Ascension Northeast Wisconsin Mercy Hospital, Oshkosh, WI, p. A719

KEHUS, Frank, Associate Director for Operations, Marion Veterans Affairs Medical Center, Marion, IL, p. A200
KEIDAN, Ben, CMO/Senior Physician Executive, Boulder Community Health, Boulder, CO, p. A104
KEIL, James, M.D., Chief Medical Officer, Niobrara Valley Hospital, Lynch, NE, p. A402
KEILMAN, Stacey, Chief Executive Officer, Torrance State Hospital, Torrance, PA, p. A555
KEIRNS, Melody, Manager Human Resources, F. W. Huston Medical Center, Winchester, KS, p. A262
KEISER, Trish, Comptroller, Avera Gregory Hospital, Gregory, SD, p. A574
KEITH, Bridgette, Director Human Resources, Encompass Health Rehabilitation Hospital of Northern Kentucky, Edgewood, KY, p. A265
KEITH, Darlene, Chief Information Systems, Alleghany Health, Sparta, NC, p. A476
KEITH, Jeannie, R.N., Nurse Executive, Shriners Hospitals for Children, Galveston, TX, p. A621
KEITH, Jessica, Chief Executive Officer, Norristown State Hospital, Norristown, PA, p. A547
KEITH, Marty, Chief Human Resources Officer, Saint Francis Hospital, Memphis, TN, p. A589
KELBAUGH, Brian, Chief Financial Officer, Summersville Regional Medical Center, Summersville, WV, p. A705
KELBLY, Kevin, Senior Vice President Finance and Corporate Fiscal Affairs, Carroll Hospital, Westminster, MD, p. A308
KELEMAN, Michael
  Chief Executive Officer, Providence Redwood Memorial Hospital, Fortuna, CA, p. A63
  Chief Executive Officer, Providence St. Josep. Hospital Eureka, Eureka, CA, p. A62
KELLAR, Brian
  Chief Executive Officer, Banner Baywood Medical Center, Mesa, AZ, p. A33
  Chief Executive Officer, Banner Goldfield Medical Center, Apache Junction, AZ, p. A30
  Chief Executive Officer, Banner Heart Hospital, Mesa, AZ, p. A33
  Chief Executive Officer, Banner Ironwood Medical Center, San Tan Valley, AZ, p. A38
KELLAR, Mark, R.N., Interim Chief Nursing Officer, Our Lady of The Angels Hospital, Bogalusa, LA, p. A279
KELLEHER, Mary, Vice President Human Resources, Holyoke Medical Center, Holyoke, MA, p. A314
KELLEHER, Mary Lou, R.N., MSN, Vice President, Nursing, Franciscan Children's, Brighton, MA, p. A311
KELLEHER, Michael, Chief Medical Officer, Ann & Robert H. Lurie Children's Hospital of Chicago, Chicago, IL, p. A188
KELLEHER, William H, Director, Veterans Affairs Boston Healthcare System Brockton Division, Brockton, MA, p. A312
KELLENBARGER, Lance, Site Director Information Systems, St. Catherine Hospital, Garden City, KS, p. A249
KELLER, Anita M., R.N., MSN, Chief Nursing Officer, Johnson Memorial Hospital, Franklin, IN, p. A217
KELLER, Ann, Supervisor Health Information Management, Walton Rehabilitation Hospital, An Affiliate of Encompass Health, Augusta, GA, p. A158
KELLER, Gretchen, Director Health Information, Neosho Memorial Regional Medical Center, Chanute, KS, p. A247
KELLER, James
  M.D., Vice President, Medical Management, Advocate Trinity Hospital, Chicago, IL, p. A188
  Chief Information Officer, Ascension Borgess–Lee Hospital, Dowagiac, MI, p. A326
  Director Human Resources, Nea Baptist Memorial Hospital, Jonesboro, AR, p. A48
KELLER, Jim, Site Director Information Services, Trinity Health Grand Rapids Hospital, Grand Rapids, MI, p. A328
KELLER, Justin, Chief Information Officer, Murray County Medical Center, Slayton, MN, p. A355
KELLER, Ken, President/Chief Executive Officer, Bakersfield Memorial Hospital, Bakersfield, CA, p. A56
KELLER, Marsha, Director Human Resources, UPMC Kane, Kane, PA, p. A543
KELLER, Maryalice, Vice President Brand and Talent Management, Unity Hospital, Rochester, NY, p. A458
KELLER, Patricia, MSN, R.N., Nurse Administrator, Mayo Clinic Health System – Northland In Barron, Barron, WI, p. A708
KELLER, Ruey, Acting Chief Information Officer, Jennifer Moreno Department of Veterans Affairs Medical Center, San Diego, CA, p. A88
KELLER, Scott, Director Information Technology, Community Memorial Healthcare, Marysville, KS, p. A254
KELLER, Stewart, M.D., Medical Director, Mesa Springs, Fort Worth, TX, p. A620
KELLER, Thomas W., President and Chief Executive Officer, Ozarks Healthcare, West Plains, MO, p. A388

KELLERMAN, Laurie, MSN, Chief Clinical Officer, Marshall Browning Hospital, Du Quoin, IL, p. A193
KELLEY, Brent, Director Information Technology, Nor–Lea Hospital District, Lovington, NM, p. A435
KELLEY, Chad, Chief Operating Officer, Mercyone Newton Medical Center, Newton, IA, p. A241
KELLEY, Danny, Administrative Director, Health Information Technology, Norman Regional Health System, Norman, OK, p. A516
KELLEY, Jalinda, Secretary of Interior Services, Chickasaw Nation Medical Center, Ada, OK, p. A509
KELLEY, James, Chief Human Resources Officer, Desert Regional Medical Center, Palm Springs, CA, p. A82
KELLEY, Janice, Chief Financial Officer, Marshall County Hospital, Benton, KY, p. A263
KELLEY, Julie, M.D., Chief of Staff, Red Bud Regional Hospital, Red Bud, IL, p. A207
KELLEY, Kinzie, Chief Operating Officer, Valley Community Hospital, Pauls Valley, OK, p. A519
KELLEY, Lewis, Chief Operating Officer, Union General Hospital, Blairsville, GA, p. A159
KELLEY, Mary, Director Human Resources, The Outer Banks Hospital, Nags Head, NC, p. A473
KELLEY, Sarah Hi, Executive Director of Human Resources and Support Services, Ste. Genevieve County Memorial Hospital, Ste Genevieve, MO, p. A387
KELLEY, Sharon, Chief Financial Officer, Clifton Springs Hospital And Clinic, Clifton Springs, NY, p. A441
KELLEY, Steven L., President and Chief Executive Officer, Ellenville Regional Hospital, Ellenville, NY, p. A442
KELLEY, Sue, Chief Financial Officer, Cordell Memorial Hospital, Cordell, OK, p. A511
KELLEY, Thomas J., Executive Vice President and Chief Financial Officer, Froedtert South – Kenosha Medical Center, Kenosha, WI, p. A713
KELLEY, Warren, Chief Information Officer, Reynolds Memorial Hospital, Glen Dale, WV, p. A700
KELLIHER, Brandon, Chief Information Officer, Great Plains Health, North Platte, NE, p. A403
KELLOGG, Ben, Administrator, Oceans Behavioral Hospital Longview, Longview, TX, p. A635
KELLOGG, Benjamin, M.D., Chief of Staff, Rhea Medical Center, Dayton, TN, p. A582
KELLS, Anne, Interim Chief Financial Officer, Appleton Area Health, Appleton, MN, p. A342
KELLUM, Craig, Director Management Information Systems, Cap. Fear Valley Bladen County Hospital, Elizabethtown, NC, p. A468
KELLUM, Kyle, President and Chief Executive Officer, Jennie M. Melham Memorial Medical Center, Broken Bow, NE, p. A398
KELLY, Adelane, Chief Financial Officer, Eastern New Mexico Medical Center, Roswell, NM, p. A436
KELLY, Brian
  M.D., Vice President Medical Affairs and Medical Director, Sturdy Memorial Hospital, Attleboro, MA, p. A309
  Acting Chief Fiscal Service, San Francisco Va Health Care System, San Francisco, CA, p. A91
  Vice President Finance, Advocate South Suburban Hospital, Hazel Crest, IL, p. A197
KELLY, Brian E., M.D., President Medical Staff, Gundersen Saint Elizabeth's Hospital & Clinics, Wabasha, MN, p. A356
KELLY, Bryan T., M.D., President and Chief Executive Officer, Hospital for Special Surgery, New York, NY, p. A448
KELLY, Charles, D.O., Vice President Medical Affairs and Chief Medical Officer, Henry Ford Macomb Hospital, Clinton Township, MI, p. A324
KELLY, Colan, Chief Financial Officer, Pineville Community Health Center, Pineville, KY, p. A273
KELLY, Dan, R.N., Chief Nursing Officer, Memorial Hermann Memorial City Medical Center, Houston, TX, p. A627
KELLY, Daniel J., Chief Executive Officer, Republic County Hospital, Belleville, KS, p. A246
KELLY, Diane P., R.N., President, Greenwich Hospital, Greenwich, CT, p. A116
KELLY, Edward, Chief Executive Officer and President, Milford Regional Medical Center, Milford, MA, p. A316
KELLY, James J.
  Jr, Interim Chief Executive Officer, UF Health Shands Hospital, Gainesville, FL, p. A133
  Jr, Senior Vice President and Chief Financial Officer, UF Health Shands Hospital, Gainesville, FL, p. A133
KELLY, John, R.N., Chief Nursing Officer and Chief Operating Officer, Umass Memorial–Marlborough Hospital, Marlborough, MA, p. A315
KELLY, Kathy
  Chief Executive Officer, Kindred Hospital–Sycamore, Sycamore, IL, p. A209
  Market Chief Executive Officer, Kindred Chicago Lakeshore, Chicago, IL, p. A190

Market Chief Executive Officer, Kindred Hospital Chicago–Northlake, Northlake, IL, p. A204
KELLY, Kevin M., Commander, Benning Martin Army Community Hospital, Fort Benning, GA, p. A164
KELLY, Leo, Vice President Medical Management, Advocate Lutheran General Hospital, Park Ridge, IL, p. A205
KELLY, Mark, Chief Executive Officer, Baptist Memorial Restorative Care Hospital, Memphis, TN, p. A588
KELLY, Maura, Vice President Fiscal Services, Mainehealth Pen Bay Medical Center, Rockport, ME, p. A299
KELLY, Michael
　Vice President, Christian Hospital, Saint Louis, MO, p. A385
　Vice President Operations, Missouri Baptist Medical Center, Saint Louis, MO, p. A385
KELLY, Misty, Chief Executive Officer and Administrator, Oceans Behavioral Hospital of Lake Charles, Lake Charles, LA, p. A286
KELLY, Patrick J., FACHE, Director, Minneapolis Va Health Care System, Minneapolis, MN, p. A351
KELLY, Ray, R.N., MSN, Vice President Chief Nursing Officer, Texas Health Harris Methodist Hospital Hurst–Euless–Bedford, Bedford, TX, p. A602
KELLY, Robert E, M.D., President, New York–Presbyterian Hospital, New York, NY, p. A450
KELLY, Sara, D.O., Chief Medical Officer, Rapides Regional Medical Center, Alexandria, LA, p. A276
KELLY, Shannon, Director Human Resources, Arbor Health, Morton Hospital, Morton, WA, p. A691
KELLY, Stephen, M.D., Chief Medical Officer, SSM Health St. Mary's Hospital – St. Louis, Saint Louis, MO, p. A385
KELLY, Steve, Chief Executive Officer, Austin Oaks Hospital, Austin, TX, p. A599
KELLY, Virginia, Chief Financial Officer, Eastside Psychiatric Hospital, Tallahassee, FL, p. A151
KELMAN, Gregory, M.D., Area Medical Director, Kaiser Permanente Woodland Hills Medical Center, Los Angeles, CA, p. A73
KELSCH, Leah, Executive Director, Sanford Medical Center Bismarck, Bismarck, ND, p. A479
KELTNER, Burt, Administrator, Prairie County Hospital District, Terry, MT, p. A396
KEM, Mark, Vice President Finance and Chief Financial Officer, Chandler Regional Medical Center, Chandler, AZ, p. A30
KEMKER, S E, M.D., President Medical Staff, Ascension St. Vincent Salem, Salem, IN, p. A227
KEMMERER, Jan, Director of Nursing, Mitchell County Hospital Health Systems, Beloit, KS, p. A247
KEMP, Marlo, Vice President and Chief Financial Officer, Roseland Community Hospital, Chicago, IL, p. A190
KEMP, Susie, Chief Financial Officer, Fulton State Hospital, Fulton, MO, p. A375
KEMPF, Gary L., R.N., Chief Executive Officer, Houston Methodist Continuing Care Hospital, Katy, TX, p. A631
KEMPF, Josh, Chief Operating Officer, Medical City Dallas, Dallas, TX, p. A611
KEMPH, Joshua, Chief Executive Officer, Integris Baptist Medical Center, Oklahoma City, OK, p. A517
KEMPIAK, Matthew, Director Human Resources and Administrative Services, Memorial Hospital of Gardena, Gardena, CA, p. A65
KEMPINSKI, Paul D.
　MS, FACHE, Chief Executive Officer, Children's Mercy Hospital Kansas, Overland Park, KS, p. A257
　MS, FACHE, President and Chief Executive Officer, Children's Mercy Kansas City, Kansas City, MO, p. A377
KEMPTON, Matthew, Chief Executive Officer, Willap. Harbor Hospital, South Bend, WA, p. A696
KENAGY, John Jay
　Ph.D., Senior Vice President and Chief Information Officer, Legacy Meridian Park Medical Center, Tualatin, OR, p. A533
　Ph.D., Senior Vice President and Chief Information Officer, Legacy Mount Hood Medical Center, Gresham, OR, p. A527
KENAGY, Rob, M.D., President and Chief Executive Officer, Stormont Vail Health, Topeka, KS, p. A260
KENDALL, Abigail, Chief Nursing Officer, Lake Granbury Medical Center, Granbury, TX, p. A622
KENDALL, Amy, Chief Executive Officer, Kindred Hospital Central Tampa, Tampa, FL, p. A152
KENDALL, Anthony
　Vice President Human Resources, Baptist Health Medical Center–Arkadelphia, Arkadelphia, AR, p. A43
　Vice President Human Resources, Baptist Health Medical Center–Little Rock, Little Rock, AR, p. A49
　Vice President Human Resources, Baptist Health Rehabilitation Institute, Little Rock, AR, p. A49

KENDALL, Clint, R.N., Chief Executive Officer and Chief Nursing Officer, Angel Medical Center, Franklin, NC, p. A468
KENDALL, Dorothy, Medical Director, William J. Mccord Adolescent Treatment Facility, Orangeburg, SC, p. A569
KENDALL, Nancy L, Chief Nursing Officer, Encompass Health Rehabilitation Hospital of Bluffton, Bluffton, SC, p. A562
KENDLE, Melinda
　Director Fiscal Management, Evansville State Hospital, Evansville, IN, p. A216
　Manager Business Office, Evansville Psychiatric Children Center, Evansville, IN, p. A216
KENDLER, Lisa
　Chief Financial Officer, Memorial Hermann Memorial City Medical Center, Houston, TX, p. A627
　Chief Financial Officer, Memorial Hermann Sugar Land Hospital, Sugar Land, TX, p. A654
KENDRICK, Donovan, M.D., Chief Medical Officer, Baptist Medical Center South, Montgomery, AL, p. A22
KENDRICK, Justin
　Senior Vice President and Chief Executive Officer, Memorial Hermann Greater Heights Hospital, Houston, TX, p. A627
　Senior Vice President and Chief Executive Officer, Memorial Hermann Northeast, Humble, TX, p. A629
KENDRICK, Ray, Chief Human Resources Officer, Memorial Hospital Miramar, Miramar, FL, p. A141
KENINGER, Luke, Information Technology Client Leader, Winona Health, Winona, MN, p. A357
KENLEY, William A, FACHE, Chief Executive Officer, Anmed Medical Center, Anderson, SC, p. A562
KENLEY, William A., FACHE, Chief Executive Officer, Anmed Medical Center, Anderson, SC, p. A562
KENNEDY, Anita J, Vice President Operations, Methodist Hospital of Sacramento, Sacramento, CA, p. A87
KENNEDY, Carol, Chief Clinical Officer, Barrett Hospital & Healthcare, Dillon, MT, p. A391
KENNEDY, Connie, Director Human Resources, Marlette Regional Hospital, Marlette, MI, p. A333
KENNEDY, Danielle, Director of Nursing, Montefiore New Rochelle, New Rochelle, NY, p. A447
KENNEDY, Darla, Chief Information Officer, Foothill Regional Medical Center, Tustin, CA, p. A99
KENNEDY, Diana, Director Human Resources, Meadowview Regional Medical Center, Maysville, KY, p. A271
KENNEDY, Eric, Chief Executive Officer, Belmont Pines Hospital, Youngstown, OH, p. A508
KENNEDY, Jessica, D.O., Chief Medical Officer, Adair County Health System, Greenfield, IA, p. A236
KENNEDY, Jill M, R.N., Chief Nursing Executive, Providence Group. Bon Secours Memorial Regional Medical Center, Mechanicsville, VA, p. A679
KENNEDY, John, M.D., Vice President of Medical Affairs, Mercy Health – Fairfield Hospital, Fairfield, OH, p. A495
KENNEDY, Kay V, Chief Nurse Executive, Wellstar Cobb Hospital, Austell, GA, p. A159
KENNEDY, Kimberly, Manager Human Resources, OSF Saint Paul Medical Center, Mendota, IL, p. A201
KENNEDY, Larkin, Chief Executive Officer, Ochsner Rush Medical Center, Meridian, MS, p. A366
KENNEDY, Nancy A., M.D., Chief Medical Officer, St. Elizabeth Dearborn, Lawrenceburg, IN, p. A222
KENNEDY, Peter, Chief Operating Officer, HCA Florida Northside Hospital, Saint Petersburg, FL, p. A149
KENNEDY, R. Scott, M.D., Chief Medical Officer and Safety Officer, Olympic Medical Center, Port Angeles, WA, p. A693
KENNEDY, Robert, Chief Operating Officer, Holston Valley Medical Center, Kingsport, TN, p. A585
KENNEDY, Ryan
　Chief Financial Officer, Holy Name Medical Center, Teaneck, NJ, p. A429
　Chief Operating Officer, Kingman Regional Medical Center, Kingman, AZ, p. A32
KENNEDY, Stephen, Superintendent, Bridgewater State Hospital, Bridgewater, MA, p. A311
KENNEMER, Darline, Controller, Methodist Rehabilitation Hospital, Dallas, TX, p. A612
KENNEY, Mary Ellen, Chief Human Services, Manchester Veterans Affairs Medical Center, Manchester, NH, p. A416
KENNEY, Ronda, Chief Operating Officer, Eastern State Hospital, Medical Lake, WA, p. A691
KENNINGTON, Lynn
　Chief Financial Officer, Canyon Vista Medical Center, Sierra Vista, AZ, p. A39
　Chief Financial Officer, Conemaugh Memorial Medical Center, Johnstown, PA, p. A542
KENNISON, Barbara, Director Clinical Services, Aurora Behavioral Healthcare San Diego, San Diego, CA, p. A88

KENNY, Carolyn, Executive Vice President Clinical Care, Children's Healthcare of Atlanta, Atlanta, GA, p. A157
KENT, Blair M.
　Executive Vice President/Chief Executive Officer, Long Beach Medical Center, Long Beach Medical Center, Long Beach, CA, p. A71
　Executive Vice President/Chief Executive Officer, Long Beach Medical Center, Miller Children's & Women's Hospital Long Beach, Long Beach, CA, p. A71
KENT, David
　M.D., Chief Medical Officer, Lifeways Behavioral Hospital, Boise, ID, p. A179
　Chief Executive Officer, Piedmont Henry Hospital, Stockbridge, GA, p. A172
KENT, Mary, Administrator, Johnson County Hospital, Tecumseh, NE, p. A406
KENT, Robert, D.O., President and Chief Executive Officer, Western Reserve Hospital, Cuyahoga Falls, OH, p. A493
KENT, William, President and Chief Executive Officer, Matheny Medical And Educational Center, Peapack, NJ, p. A426
KENTERA, Amy, Chief Information Officer, Conifer Park, Glenville, NY, p. A443
KENTFIELD, Melinda Johanna, R.N., Chief Nursing Officer, Methodist Fremont Health, Fremont, NE, p. A400
KENTON, Bart, Chief Financial Officer, Holton Community Hospital, Holton, KS, p. A250
KENWOOD, Linda S, R.N., MSN, Chief Nursing Officer and Chief Operating Officer, Shore Medical Center, Somers Point, NJ, p. A428
KEPLINGER, Ron, Chief Information Officer, Western Maryland Hospital Center, Hagerstown, MD, p. A305
KEPNER, Donald L, Chief Financial Officer, Ashtabula County Medical Center, Ashtabula, OH, p. A485
KERBS, Curtis, Regional Chief Information Officer, Memorial Hospital, North Conway, NH, p. A417
KERCHENSKI, Marlene, Chief Nurse, U. S. Air Force Hospital, Hampton, VA, p. A677
KERI, Alison, Director Human Resources, Amberwell Hiawatha, Hiawatha, KS, p. A250
KERIAN–MASTERS, Carol, R.N., Chief Nursing Officer, Regional Health Services of Howard County, Cresco, IA, p. A234
KERLING, Norma, Interim Chief Executive Officer and Chief Clinical Officer, Cuba Memorial Hospital, Cuba, NY, p. A442
KERMEN, John, D.O., Chief Medical Staff, Adventist Health Mendocino Coast, Fort Bragg, CA, p. A63
KERN, Douglas W.
　Chief Executive Officer, Northcoast Behavioral Healthcare, Northfield, OH, p. A501
　Chief Executive Officer, Windsor–Laurelwood Center for Behavioral Medicine, Willoughby, OH, p. A507
KERNAN, Jackie
　R.N., MSN, President, OSF Saint Clare Medical Center, Princeton, IL, p. A206
　R.N., MSN, President, OSF Saint Luke Medical Center, Kewanee, IL, p. A199
KERNELL, Shane, Chief Executive Officer, Graham Regional Medical Center, Graham, TX, p. A622
KERNIVAN, Lorna, Chief Operating Officer, HCA Florida Palms West Hospital, Loxahatchee, FL, p. A138
KERNS, Kellie, Director, Human Resources, Eagle View Behavioral Health, Bettendorf, IA, p. A230
KERNS, Zach
　Vice President, Finance, Berkeley Medical Center, Martinsburg, WV, p. A702
　Vice President, Finance, Jefferson Medical Center, Ranson, WV, p. A704
KERR, Jonathan, Acting Director, Veterans Affairs Central Western Massachusetts Healthcare System, Leeds, MA, p. A315
KERR, Karen
　R.N., President, Bartow Regional Medical Center, Bartow, FL, p. A125
　R.N., President, South Florida Baptist Hospital, Plant City, FL, p. A147
KERR, Michael, Chief Executive Officer, Vibra Specialty Hospital of Portland, Portland, OR, p. A531
KERRIGAN, Chris
　Interim Chief Operating Officer, Banner Fort Collins Medical Center, Fort Collins, CO, p. A108
　Interim Chief Operating Officer, Banner Mckee Medical Center, Loveland, CO, p. A112
　Interim Chief Operating Officer, Banner North Colorado Medical Centernorth Colorado Medical Center, Greeley, CO, p. A109
KERRINS, David, Vice President Information Services and Chief Information Officer, Dameron Hospital, Stockton, CA, p. A96
KERSCHL, Walter, Chief Medical Officer, Camden Clark Medical Center, Parkersburg, WV, p. A703

Index of Health Care Professionals / Kerswill

KERSWILL, Randy, M.D., Medical Director, Winnebago Mental Health Institute, Winnebago, WI, p. A725
KERWOOD, Lori A, Director Human Resources, Cooley Dickinson Hospital, Northampton, MA, p. A316
KESSLER, Alexander, M.D., Chief of Staff, Northside Hospital Cherokee, Canton, GA, p. A160
KESSLER, Charlene, R.N., Director of Nursing, Beacon Behavioral Hospital, Bunkie, LA, p. A279
KESSLER, David, M.D., Clinical Director, U. S. Public Health Service Indian Hospital, Zuni, NM, p. A437
KESSNER, Jennifer, Financial Director, Roosevelt Medical Center, Culbertson, MT, p. A391
KESTER, Andy
  Vice President, Chief Information Officer, Ridgeview Medical Center, Waconia, MN, p. A356
  Vice President, Chief Information Officer, Ridgeview Sibley Medical Center, Arlington, MN, p. A342
KESTER, Kris, Chief Financial Officer, Livingston Healthcare, Livingston, MT, p. A394
KESTERSON, Matt
  Director Information Services, Wadley Regional Medical Center, Texarkana, TX, p. A657
  Director Information Services, Wadley Regional Medical Center At Hope, Hope, AR, p. A47
KETCH, Lynn
  Human Resources Recruiter Generalist, Integris Canadian Valley Hospital, Yukon, OK, p. A524
  Regional Director Integris Southwest Medical Center, Integris Southwest Medical Center, Oklahoma City, OK, p. A517
KETCHAM, Krista, Chief Financial Officer, Buena Vista Regional Medical Center, Storm Lake, IA, p. A244
KETCHAM, Michael, President, Medical Staff, Lonesome Pine Hospital, Big Stone Gap, VA, p. A673
KETCHEM, Tami, Human Resource Director, Up Health System – Bell, Ishpeming, MI, p. A330
KETCHUM, David, PharmD, Chief Executive Officer, Pemiscot Memorial Health System, Hayti, MO, p. A376
KETERI, Dan, R.N., Chief Executive Officer, Samaritan Albany General Hospital, Albany, OR, p. A525
KETTERHAGEN, James P, M.D., Senior Vice President and Chief Medical Officer, UofL Health – Jewish Hospital, Louisville, KY, p. A270
KETTERLING, Kimberly A., R.N., Vice President Patient Care Services, Chi Oakes Hospital, Oakes, ND, p. A483
KETTERMAN, Patricia P., R.N., President and Chief Administrative Officer, Claiborne Medical Center, Tazewell, TN, p. A594
KETTLER, Paul, M.D., Vice President Medical Affairs, M Health Fairview Ridges Hospital, Burnsville, MN, p. A344
KEY, Buffy
  Chief Executive Officer, Cookeville Regional Medical Center, Cookeville, TN, p. A582
  Chief Operating Officer, Cookeville Regional Medical Center, Cookeville, TN, p. A582
KEY, Jennifer, Chief Nursing Officer, Piedmont Newnan Hospital, Newnan, GA, p. A169
KEYONNIE, Christine, CPA, Chief Financial Officer, Tuba City Regional Health Care Corporation, Tuba City, AZ, p. A40
KHADE, Kashmira, Coordinator Non-Clinical Services, Behavioral Center of Michigan, Warren, MI, p. A340
KHADEMI, Allen M., M.D., Vice President Medical Affairs, Christian Health, Wyckoff, NJ, p. A431
KHALEGHI, Trisha
  MSN, R.N., Senior Vice President and Market Chief Executive Officer, Sharp HealthCare Metropolitan Hospitals, Sharp Mary Birch Hospital for Women And Newborns, San Diego, CA, p. A89
  MSN, R.N., Senior Vice President and Market Chief Executive Officer, Sharp HealthCare Metropolitan Hospitals, Sharp Memorial Hospital, San Diego, CA, p. A89
  MSN, R.N., Senior Vice President and Market Chief Executive Officer, Sharp HealthCare Metropolitan Hospitals, Sharp Mesa Vista Hospital, San Diego, CA, p. A90
KHALIQUE, Tania, Director Human Resources, Select Specialty Hospital – San Diego, San Diego, CA, p. A89
KHAN, Amir, Chief Executive Officer, Oakwood Springs, Oklahoma City, OK, p. A517
KHAN, Atique, M.D., Medical Director, University Behavioral Health of Denton, Denton, TX, p. A614
KHAN, Dan, M.D., Chief Medical Officer, Yoakum County Hospital, Denver City, TX, p. A614
KHAN, Faraz, Chief Financial Officer, Denver Health, Denver, CO, p. A106
KHAN, Sarfraz, Medical Director, Meridian Health Services, Muncie, IN, p. A224
KHAN, Talha, Vice President Medical Affairs, St. Croix Regional Medical Center, St Croix Falls, WI, p. A722

KHAN, Waheed, M.D., President Medical Staff, Summers County Arh Hospital, Hinton, WV, p. A701
KHANCHANDANI, Ashok, Chief Financial Officer, Oroville Hospital, Oroville, CA, p. A82
KHANDELWAL, Ashish, M.D., Medical Director, Encompass Health Rehabilitation Hospital of Middletown, Middletown, DE, p. A121
KHARONOV, Arthur, Vice President Nursing, Silver Lake Hospital Ltach, Newark, NJ, p. A425
KHATAMI, Manoochehr, M.D., Medical Director, Hickory Trail Hospital, Desoto, TX, p. A614
KHAVKIN, Lisa, Vice President Human Resources, Huntington Hospital, Huntington, NY, p. A444
KHDOUR, Adel, M.D., Chief Medical Officer, Indiana University Health White Memorial Hospital, Monticello, IN, p. A224
KHEMKA, Hemant
  Chief Financial Officer, Surgery Specialty Hospitals of America, Pasadena, TX, p. A643
  Chief Operating Officer, Surgery Specialty Hospitals of America, Pasadena, TX, p. A643
KHIAMI, Ahmad, Chief of Staff, Beckley Arh Hospital, Beckley, WV, p. A699
KHIM FUGATE, Guay, Chief Operations Officer, Kindred Hospital Riverside, Perris, CA, p. A83
KHOERL, Thomas, Vice President Finance, Corewell Health Big Rapids Hospital, Big Rapids, MI, p. A322
KHOO, Alex, Interim Area Finance Officer, Kaiser Permanente San Francisco Medical Center, San Francisco, CA, p. A91
KHOSRAVI, Sasha, D.O., Chief Medical Officer, Clive Behavioral Health, Clive, IA, p. A233
KHOURI, Lara, Executive Vice President and Chief Operating Officer, Children's Hospital Los Angeles, Los Angeles, CA, p. A72
KHULMANN, Sabrina, R.N., Chief Nursing Officer, Winn Parish Medical Center, Winnfield, LA, p. A294
KIBAR, Nizar, M.D., Chief Medical Staff, Kiowa County Memorial Hospital, Greensburg, KS, p. A250
KIBBY, Rosalinda, Superintendent and Administrator, Columbia Basin Hospital, Ephrata, WA, p. A689
KIDD, Amanda Lusk, Chief Nursing Officer, Encompass Health Rehabilitation Hospital of Florence, Florence, SC, p. A566
KIDD, David, Manager Human Resources, Sentara Careplex Hospital, Hampton, VA, p. A677
KIDDER, David M., D.O., Chief Medical Officer, Garfield County Health Center, Jordan, MT, p. A393
KIDDER, Suzanne F, Human Resources Officer, Opelousas General Health System, Opelousas, LA, p. A291
KIEBZAK, Stanley F, R.N., Chief Nursing Officer, Encompass Health Rehabilitation Hospital The Vintage, Houston, TX, p. A625
KIEF, Brian, President, Aspirus Riverview Hospital And Clinics, Inc., Wisconsin Rapids, WI, p. A725
KIEFER, Michael L, FACHE, Director, Central Texas Veterans Hcs/Temple Tx, Temple, TX, p. A656
KIEFER, Michael L., FACHE, Medical Center Director, Central Texas Veterans Hcs/Temple Tx, Temple, TX, p. A656
KIEFER, William
  Chief Executive Officer, Ottumwa Regional Health Center, Ottumwa, IA, p. A241
  Chief Nursing Officer, TMC Bonham Hospital, Bonham, TX, p. A604
  Chief Operations Officer, Canyon Vista Medical Center, Sierra Vista, AZ, p. A39
KIEFFER, Kelley
  Chief Nursing Officer, Banner Baywood Medical Center, Mesa, AZ, p. A33
  Chief Nursing Officer, Banner Gateway Medical Center, Gilbert, AZ, p. A31
  Chief Nursing Officer, Banner Heart Hospital, Mesa, AZ, p. A33
KIEHL, Tiffany, Chief Executive Officer, Mid-America Rehabilitation Hospital, Shawnee Mission, KS, p. A260
KIELY, Sharon, M.D., Senior Vice President Medical Affairs and Chief Medical Officer, Stamford Health, Stamford, CT, p. A119
KIENITZ, Mikaela, Chief Executive Officer, Boone County Hospital, Boone, IA, p. A231
KIERNAN, Richard
  Regional Chief Human Resources Officer, Monmouth Medical Center, Southern Campus, Lakewood, NJ, p. A422
  Vice President Human Resources, Monmouth Medical Center, Long Branch Campus, Long Branch, NJ, p. A423
KIFAIEH, Nizar, M.D., President and Chief Executive Officer, Hudson Regional Hospital, Secaucus, NJ, p. A428
KIGER, Tom, Director Information Systems, Trinity Health System, Steubenville, OH, p. A504
KIGHT, Sheila, Director Human Resources, Tristar Horizon Medical Center, Dickson, TN, p. A582

KILBORN, Mark, Director Information Systems, Springhill Medical Center, Mobile, AL, p. A22
KILE, Steven E, Vice President Human Resources, Indiana University Health North Hospital, Carmel, IN, p. A214
KILGORE, Julie, Vice President, Human Resources, Broadlawns Medical Center, Des Moines, IA, p. A234
KILLINGER, William, M.D., Chief Medical Officer, HCA Houston Healthcare Clear Lake, Webster, TX, p. A661
KILPACK, Lee, Chief Executive Officer, Marian Center, Salt Lake City, UT, p. A669
KILPATRICK, Von, Chief Nursing Officer, St. Vincent Health, Leadville, CO, p. A111
KIM, Anne, Chief Financial Officer, Riveredge Hospital, Forest Park, IL, p. A195
KIM, Donald, M.D., Chief Medical Officer, Memorial Regional Hospital, Hollywood, FL, p. A133
KIM, Eric, Chief Information Officer, Las Encinas Hospital, Pasadena, CA, p. A83
KIM, Eugene P., M.D., Chief Medical Officer, Providence St. Jude Medical Center, Fullerton, CA, p. A65
KIM, Hyon Su, M.D., Medical Director, Northlake Behavioral Health System, Mandeville, LA, p. A287
KIM, John, Chief Financial Officer, Anchor Hospital, Atlanta, GA, p. A156
KIM, Wendy, Vice President, Nursing and Chief Nursing Officer, Henry Ford Jackson Hospital, Jackson, MI, p. A331
KIMBALL, Joe, D.O., Chief of Staff, Madison County Health Care System, Winterset, IA, p. A245
KIMBALL, Tim, Chief Nursing Officer, Northwest Health Physicians' Specialty Hospital, Fayetteville, AR, p. A46
KIMBERLING-CASAD, Ashley, President of Springfield Hospitals, Cox North Hospital, Springfield, MO, p. A386
KIMBLE, Becky, R.N., Chief Nursing Officer, Encompass Health Rehabilitation Hospital of Jonesboro, Jonesboro, AR, p. A48
KIMBLE, D. Gay, Chief Human Resource Officer, Susan B. Allen Memorial Hospital, El Dorado, KS, p. A248
KIMBLE, Robert J., Chief Financial Officer, William R. Sharpe, Jr. Hospital, Weston, WV, p. A706
KIMBRELL, Jason L., Chief Executive Officer, HCA Florida Palms West Hospital, Loxahatchee, FL, p. A138
KIMBREW, Missey, Director Human Resources, Grafton City Hospital, Grafton, WV, p. A701
KIMBROUGH, Pam, M.D., Vice President Medical Affairs, Mercy Hospital Ardmore, Ardmore, OK, p. A510
KIMMEL, Kyle, Chief Financial Officer, Bacon County Hospital And Health System, Alma, GA, p. A156
KIMMEL, Stephen, Chief Financial Officer, Cook Children's Medical Center, Fort Worth, TX, p. A619
KIMMET, Ashley, Human Resources, Logan Health – Cut Bank, Cut Bank, MT, p. A391
KIMMET, Jackie, Chief Human Resource Officer, River's Edge Hospital And Clinic, Saint Peter, MN, p. A355
KIMPLE, Robin, Director Information Services, Wellspan Gettysburg Hospital, Gettysburg, PA, p. A540
KIMZEY, Mike, Chief Executive Officer, Surgical Hospital of Oklahoma, Oklahoma City, OK, p. A519
KINARD, Tifani
  Chief Executive Officer, Atrium Health Floyd Cherokee Medical Center, Centre, AL, p. A17
  Chief Nursing Officer, Atrium Health Floyd Cherokee Medical Center, Centre, AL, p. A17
  Vice President of Rural Health in SAM, Atrium Health Floyd Polk Medical Center, Cedartown, GA, p. A160
KINCAID, Kevin, Chief Executive Officer, Knoxville Hospital & Clinics, Knoxville, IA, p. A239
KINCAID, Rachael, Chief Nursing Officer, South Peninsula Hospital, Homer, AK, p. A28
KINCAID, Steve, Information Technology Manager, Eastern State Hospital, Lexington, KY, p. A268
KINDER, Barbara, R.N., Chief Clinical Officer, Clark Regional Medical Center, Winchester, KY, p. A275
KINDLER, Dean
  M.D., Regional President and Chief Executive Officer, Ascension Borgess Allegan Hospital, Allegan, MI, p. A321
  M.D., Regional President and Chief Executive Officer, Ascension Borgess Hospital, Kalamazoo, MI, p. A331
  M.D., Regional President and Chief Executive Officer, Ascension Borgess-Lee Hospital, Dowagiac, MI, p. A326
KINDRED, Deanne, Vice President Finance, Baylor Scott & White Medical Center – Plano, Plano, TX, p. A644
KINDSCHI, Mark, Director Human Resources, Edgerton Hospital And Health Services, Edgerton, WI, p. A710
KING, Abner, Chief Executive Officer, Syringa Hospital And Clinics, Grangeville, ID, p. A181
KING, Beth, Chief Executive Officer, Jersey Community Hospital, Jerseyville, IL, p. A199
KING, Brent R, Chief Medical Officer and Chief Physician, Nemours Children's Hospital, Delaware, Wilmington, DE, p. A122

KING, Carole, Chief Human Resources Officer, Ascension Wisconsin Hospital – Menomonee Falls Campus, Menomonee Falls, WI, p. A715
KING, Chris, Director Information Services, Ohiohealth Marion General Hospital, Marion, OH, p. A499
KING, Christopher, Director Operations and Administrative Services, Matheny Medical And Educational Center, Peapack, NJ, p. A426
KING, Daniel, Director, Information Systems, Musc Health Columbia Medical Center Downtown, Columbia, SC, p. A564
KING, Doug
  M.D., Director Clinical Services, Western Mental Health Institute, Bolivar, TN, p. A579
  Senior Vice President and Chief Information Officer, Northwestern Medicine Delnor Hospital, Geneva, IL, p. A196
KING, Glenn
  R.N., MSN, Vice President and Chief Nursing Officer, Mymichigan Medical Center Gladwin, Gladwin, MI, p. A327
  R.N., MSN, Vice President, Chief Nursing Officer, Mymichigan Medical Center Clare, Clare, MI, p. A324
KING, Heath, President, Wellstar Douglas Hospital, Douglasville, GA, p. A163
KING, Heather, President and Chief Operating Officer, Novant Health Brunswick Medical Center, Bolivia, NC, p. A464
KING, Jay, Vice President Human Resources, Mercy Hospital Downtown, Bakersfield, CA, p. A57
KING, Jo Nell, Director of Nursing, Northlake Behavioral Health System, Mandeville, LA, p. A287
KING, Joanie, Chief Financial Officer, Carteret Health Care, Morehead City, NC, p. A473
KING, JoAnne, Chief Operating Officer, Adventhealth Palm Coast, Palm Coast, FL, p. A145
KING, Katie, R.N., Chief Nursing Officer, Mountain View Hospital, Payson, UT, p. A667
KING, Katrina, R.N., Senior Director, Nursing, Novant Health Huntersville Medical Center, Huntersville, NC, p. A470
KING, Kim, Director Human Resources and Public Relations, Baptist Memorial Hospital–Carroll County, Huntingdon, TN, p. A584
KING, Kyle
  President, Adventist Health Columbia Gorge, The Dalles, OR, p. A532
  President, Adventist Health Portland, Portland, OR, p. A530
KING, Levi J., Director Human Resources, Conway Behavioral Health, Conway, AR, p. A44
KING, Louie
  Chief Executive Officer, Benefis Teton Medical Center, Choteau, MT, p. A390
  President, Harry Bold Nursing Home Administrator, Missouri River Medical Center, Fort Benton, MT, p. A392
KING, Matt
  Chief Financial Officer, HCA Florida Fort Walton–Destin Hospital, Fort Walton Beach, FL, p. A132
  Senior Director of Finance, Banner Payson Medical Center, Payson, AZ, p. A34
  Senior Finance Director, Page Hospital, Page, AZ, p. A34
KING, Micheal, Controller, Corewell Health Pennock Hospital, Hastings, MI, p. A329
KING, Mike, Chief Financial Officer and Chief Operating Officer, JFK Memorial Hospital, Indio, CA, p. A67
KING, Monica, Chief Information Officer, Oakdale Community Hospital, Oakdale, LA, p. A290
KING, Paul
  M.D., Medical Director, Parkwood Behavioral Health System, Olive Branch, MS, p. A367
  President/Chief Executive Officer, Lucile Packard Children's Hospital Stanford, Palo Alto, CA, p. A82
KING, Ray, M.D., Senior Vice President, Medical Affairs and Chief Medical Officer, Henry Ford Jackson Hospital, Jackson, MI, p. A331
KING, Rick, Chief Financial Officer, Kaiser Foundation Hospital – San Marcos, San Marcos, CA, p. A93
KING, Ronnie B., Chief Nursing Officer, Ochsner Rehabilitaton Hospital West Campus, Jefferson, LA, p. A284
KING, Ryan, Chief Financial Officer, Legent North Houston Surgical Hospital, Tomball, TX, p. A658
KING, Sammy, Controller, Encompass Health Rehabilitation Hospital of Ocala, Ocala, FL, p. A143
KING, Sandra, Chief Nursing Officer, Sagamore Children's Psychiatric Center, Dix Hills, NY, p. A442
KING, Tamara, R.N., MSN, Chief Nurse Executive, Shepherd Center, Atlanta, GA, p. A158
KING, Thomas, Vice President, Operations, Natchaug Hospital, Mansfield Center, CT, p. A116
KING, Val, Chief Information Officer, Val Verde Regional Medical Center, Del Rio, TX, p. A613

KINGRY, Jennifer, Chief Financial Officer, Ascension St. Vincent's Blount, Oneonta, AL, p. A23
KINGSLEY, Christi, Vice President Human Resources, West Calcasieu Cameron Hospital, Sulphur, LA, p. A293
KINGSTON, Eileen M, R.N., Nurse Executive, Associate Director Patient Care, Omaha Va Medical Center, Omaha, NE, p. A404
KINGSTON, Eileen M.
  R.N., Acting Director, Chief Executive Officer, Omaha Va Medical Center, Omaha, NE, p. A404
  R.N., Acting Director, Chief Executive Officer, Veterans Affairs Nebraska–Western Iowa Health Care System – Lincoln, Lincoln, NE, p. A402
KINGSTON, Mary Beth, Ph.D., R.N., MSN, Executive Vice President and Chief Nursing Officer, Aurora Medical Center of Oshkosh, Oshkosh, WI, p. A719
KINLEN, Thomas, Superintendent, Larned State Hospital, Larned, KS, p. A252
KINMAN, Amanda, Director of Finance, Chi Saint Josep. Health – Saint Josep. Mount Sterling, Mount Sterling, KY, p. A272
KINMAN, Brett, Chief Executive Officer, Magnolia Regional Medical Center, Magnolia, AR, p. A50
KINNEER, James W., Chief Human Resource Officer, Indiana Regional Medical Center, Indiana, PA, p. A542
KINNEY, Aric, President, Aurora Medical Center – Sheboygan County, Sheboygan, WI, p. A721
KINNEY, Janet, Interim Chief Executive Officer, Medical Center Barbour, Eufaula, AL, p. A19
KINNEY, Thomas, Chief Human Resource Officer, St. John's Health, Jackson, WY, p. A727
KINSEL, Mike, Controller, Federal Medical Center, Lexington, KY, p. A268
KINSELLA, Daniel F, Vice President and Chief Information Officer, Northwestern Medicine Central Dupage Hospital, Winfield, IL, p. A211
KINSELLA, Kathleen, President, OSF Healthcare Little Company of Mary Medical Center, Evergreen Park, IL, p. A195
KINSELLA, Matthew, Chief Financial Officer, SSM Health St. Mary's Hospital Centralia, Centralia, IL, p. A187
KINSEY, Daniel, M.D., Medical Director, Oaklawn Psychiatric Center, Goshen, IN, p. A218
KINTZ, Ronald J
  Chief Financial Officer, Ira Davenport Memorial Hospital, Bath, NY, p. A439
  Vice President and Treasurer, Arnot Ogden Medical Center, Elmira, NY, p. A442
KINYON, Craig C., President and Chief Executive Officer, Reid Health, Richmond, IN, p. A226
KINZIC, Elizabeth, M.D., Chief of Staff, Share Medical Center, Alva, OK, p. A509
KIO, Kenneth, Manager Human Resources, Albany Stratton Veterans Affairs Medical Center, Albany, NY, p. A438
KIPP, Christine, R.N., MSN, Interim Chief Nursing Officer and Chief Operating Officer, Anna Jaques Hospital, Newburyport, MA, p. A316
KIPP, Kris M, Executive Director, Patient Services and Chief Nursing Officer, The Osuccc – James, Columbus, OH, p. A493
KIRACOFE, Darin, Director Information Resource Management, Broughton Hospital, Morganton, NC, p. A473
KIRALY, Denise G, Director, Human Resources and Organization Development, Lima Memorial Health System, Lima, OH, p. A498
KIRBY, Brendan, M.D., Medical Director, Riverview Psychiatric Center, Augusta, ME, p. A295
KIRBY, Elizabeth, Chief Executive Officer, Monroe County Hospital, Monroeville, AL, p. A22
KIRBY, Elizabeth A, Senior Director Human Resources, Aurora Medical Center – Manitowoc County, Two Rivers, WI, p. A723
KIRBY, James M. II, President and Chief Executive Officer, UNC Health Pardee, Hendersonville, NC, p. A470
KIRBY, Jared
  Chief Financial Officer, Memorial Health Meadows Hospital, Vidalia, GA, p. A173
  Interim Chief Executive Officer, Memorial Health Meadows Hospital, Vidalia, GA, p. A173
KIRBY, John, Senior Vice President, Virtua Health and President of Virtua Mount Holly and Virtua Willingboro hosp. Virtua Willingboro Hospital, Willingboro, NJ, p. A431
KIRBY, Juliana Kay, R.N., MSN, Chief Nursing Officer, Adventist Health Tehachap. Valley, Tehachapi, CA, p. A97
KIRBY, Penny V, MSN, Chief Nursing Officer, Livingston Regional Hospital, Livingston, TN, p. A587
KIRBY, Ruby
  Chief Executive Officer, West Tennessee Healthcare Bolivar Hospital, Bolivar, TN, p. A579

  Chief Executive Officer, West Tennessee Healthcare Camden Hospital, Camden, TN, p. A579
KIRBY, Tracy
  Assistant Vice President Business Relationship Management, Chi St. Vincent Hot Springs, Hot Springs, AR, p. A48
  Assistant Vice President Business Relationship Management, Chi St. Vincent Infirmary, Little Rock, AR, p. A49
  Assistant Vice President Business Relationship Management, Chi St. Vincent Morrilton, Morrilton, AR, p. A51
KIRBY, Tracy L, MS, R.N., Vice President Patient Care Services and Chief Nursing Officer, United Hospital, Saint Paul, MN, p. A355
KIRCH, Cyndi
  Vice President Human Resources, Mercy General Hospital, Sacramento, CA, p. A87
  Vice President Human Resources, Methodist Hospital of Sacramento, Sacramento, CA, p. A87
KIRCHER, Janelle, MSN, R.N., Chief Executive Officer, Mitchell County Hospital Health Systems, Beloit, KS, p. A247
KIRCHNER, Kent, M.D., Chief of Staff, G.V. (Sonny) Montgomery Department of Veterans Affairs Medical Center, Jackson, MS, p. A364
KIRCHNER, Susan M, Director Human Resources, Four Winds Hospital, Saratoga Springs, NY, p. A458
KIRISITS, Christopher, Chief Nursing Officer, Rochester Psychiatric Center, Rochester, NY, p. A457
KIRITANI, Tracy, Vice President and Chief Financial Officer, Clovis Community Medical Center, Clovis, CA, p. A60
KIRK, Darlene, Manager Finance, U. S. Public Health Service Indian Hospital, Crownpoint, NM, p. A434
KIRK, Donald, M.D., Chief of Staff, Star Valley Health, Afton, WY, p. A726
KIRK, J. Douglas, M.D., Chief Medical Officer, UC Davis Medical Center, Sacramento, CA, p. A87
KIRK, Jean, Chief Financial Officer, Bennett County Hospital And Nursing Home, Martin, SD, p. A574
KIRK, Paul, Vice President, Woman's Hospital, Baton Rouge, LA, p. A278
KIRK, Vanessa, Director of Nursing, Kiowa County Memorial Hospital, Greensburg, KS, p. A250
KIRKBRIDE, James B., Chief Executive Officer, Ellsworth County Medical Center, Ellsworth, KS, p. A249
KIRKER, Donna, R.N., MS, Vice President Patient Services and Chief Nursing Officer, Glens Falls Hospital, Glens Falls, NY, p. A443
KIRKER, Lynda I, Chief Financial Officer, UF Health St. John's, Saint Augustine, FL, p. A148
KIRKHAM, Brett, Chief Executive Officer, El Camp. Memorial Hospital, El Campo, TX, p. A616
KIRKLAND, Jeremiah
  President and Chief Operating Officer, Good Samaritan Hospital, Cincinnati, OH, p. A489
  President and Chief Operating Officer, Mccullough–Hyde Memorial Hospital/Trihealth, Oxford, OH, p. A502
KIRKLAND–ROSE, Tina, Coordinator Human Resources, Select Specialty Hospital–Central Kentucky, Danville, KY, p. A265
KIRKLEY, Scott, M.D., BJC Chief Medical Officer Group Liaison, Parkland Health Center – Farmington Community, Farmington, MO, p. A375
KIRKS, Linda, Vice President and Chief Financial Officer, Christus Santa Rosa Health System, San Antonio, TX, p. A649
KIRSHNER, Arthur N, Chief Information Management, Winn Army Community Hospital, Hinesville, GA, p. A165
KIRSHNER, David L., Chief Financial Officer, Strong Memorial Hospital of The University of Rochester, Rochester, NY, p. A457
KIRTON, Carl, Ph.D., Chief Nursing Officer, University Hospital, Newark, NJ, p. A425
KISACKY, Christina A, Vice President, Operations, UHS Chenango Memorial Hospital, Norwich, NY, p. A454
KISER, Danita, Chief Nursing Officer, Piedmont Mcduffie, Thomson, GA, p. A172
KISER, Greg, Chief Executive Officer, Three Rivers Medical Center, Louisa, KY, p. A269
KISER, Harrison, Chief Operating Officer, Ascension Saint Thomas Hospital, Nashville, TN, p. A590
KISER, James, Chief Executive Officer, Holy Cross Hospital, Taos, NM, p. A437
KISER, Pamela, R.N., MS, Chief Nursing Executive and Vice President of Nursing, Ascension St. John Medical Center, Tulsa, OK, p. A522
KISHNER, Janice, R.N., FACHE, Chief Clinical Officer, St. Bernard Parish Hospital, Chalmette, LA, p. A279
KISKADDON, Robert, M.D., Chief Medical Officer, UNC Health Pardee, Hendersonville, NC, p. A470

Index of Health Care Professionals

Index of Health Care Professionals / Kisner

KISNER, Angela, Director Human Resources and Coordinator Medical Staff, Landmark Hospital of Cap. Girardeau, Cap. Girardeau, MO, p. A372
KISTLER, Beckie, Director of Finance, Uofl Health – Peace Hospital, Louisville, KY, p. A270
KITCH, Barrett, M.D., Senior Vice President, Clinical Affairs and Chief Medical Officer, Emerson Hospital, Concord, MA, p. A313
KITCHENS, Kody, Chief Executive Officer, Cochran Memorial Hospital, Morton, TX, p. A640
KITTNER, Bonnie, R.N.. Chief Nursing Officer, Adventist Health Mendocino Coast, Fort Bragg, CA, p. A63
KITTOE, Michael, Chief Financial Officer, Katherine Shaw Bethea Hospital, Dixon, IL, p. A193
KLAMFOTH, William, Administrator, Christus Southeast Texas Orthopedic Specialty Center, Beaumont, TX, p. A602
KLANG, Adam, M.D., Chief Medical Officer, Bakersfield Rehabilitation Hospital, Bakersfield, CA, p. A57
KLANN, Andrew, D.O., Chief of Staff, Southwest Health, Platteville, WI, p. A719
KLAPPER, Allan, M.D., President, AHN Wexford Hospital, Wexford, PA, p. A557
KLASEK, Chance, CPA, Chief Financial Officer, Jefferson Community Health And Life, Fairbury, NE, p. A399
KLASS, Cheryl, President, Kaleida Health, Buffalo, NY, p. A440
KLASSEN, Brad, Information Technology Coordinator, Sanford Worthington Medical Center, Worthington, MN, p. A358
KLASSEN, Karen, Controller, Encompass Health Rehabilitation Hospital of Chattanooga, Chattanooga, TN, p. A580
KLATT, Monica
Chief Financial Officer, UPMC Altoona, Altoona, PA, p. A534
Chief Financial Officer, UPMC Bedford, Everett, PA, p. A540
Chief Financial Officer, UPMC Somerset, Somerset, PA, p. A555
KLAUER, Kevin, D.O., Chief Medical Officer, HCA Florida Ocala Hospital, Ocala, FL, p. A143
KLAWITER, Trey, President, Methodist Hospital for Surgery, Addison, TX, p. A595
KLAWITTER, Kyle, Vice President Human Resources, Summa Health System – Akron Campus, Akron, OH, p. A484
KLAY, Chris
FACHE, President and Chief Executive Officer, Southern Illinois Market, HSHS Holy Family Hospital In Greenville, Greenville, IL, p. A196
FACHE, President and Chief Executive Officer, Southern Illinois Market, HSHS St. Joseph's Hospital Breese, Breese, IL, p. A187
FACHE, President and Chief Executive Officer, Southern Illinois Market, HSHS St. Joseph's Hospital Highland, Highland, IL, p. A197
FACHE, President and Chief Executive Officer, Southern Illinois Market and President and Chief Executive Of, HSHS St. Elizabeth's Hospital, O Fallon, IL, p. A204
KLEAM, Douglas V., President, St. Bernardine Medical Center, San Bernardino, CA, p. A88
KLECKNER, Christine, Medical Center Director, William S. Middleton Memorial Veterans' Hospital, Madison, WI, p. A715
KLEEMAN, Debbie, Director Information Systems, Perry County Memorial Hospital, Tell City, IN, p. A227
KLEEN, Kathy, Chief Nursing Officer, Astera Health, Wadena, MN, p. A356
KLEFFMAN, Angela, Director of Ancillary Services, Bigfork Valley Hospital, Bigfork, MN, p. A343
KLEFFMAN, Kirby, Chief Executive Officer, Bowdle Hospital, Bowdle, SD, p. A572
KLEHN, Paul, Chief Information Technology Officer, Liberty Hospital, Liberty, MO, p. A379
KLEIN, Aron
Vice President Finance, Carle Bromenn Medical Center, Normal, IL, p. A203
Vice President of Finance, Carle Eureka Hospital, Eureka, IL, p. A194
KLEIN, Barbara, R.N., Director of Nursing, Arms Acres, Carmel, NY, p. A441
KLEIN, Bernard, M.D., Chief Executive, Providence Holy Cross Medical Center, Los Angeles, CA, p. A75
KLEIN, Cindy C, Vice President Human Resources, Peacehealth St. Josep. Medical Center, Bellingham, WA, p. A687
KLEIN, David G., M.D., Chief Executive Officer, Marinhealth Medical Center, Greenbrae, CA, p. A66
KLEIN, Diany, Vice President Human Resources, Community Memorial Hospital – Ventura, Ventura, CA, p. A100
KLEIN, Edward A, Chief Financial Officer, UNC Health Johnston, Smithfield, NC, p. A476
KLEIN, Jacqueline, Chief Financial Officer, Marshfield Medical Center – Rice Lake, Rice Lake, WI, p. A720
KLEIN, Jillyn, Chief Operating Officer, Howard County Medical Center, Saint Paul, NE, p. A405
KLEIN, Kenneth, M.D., Vice President Medical Affairs, Beloit Health System, Beloit, WI, p. A708
KLEIN, Korrey, M.D., President and Chief Executive Offricer, Family Health West, Fruita, CO, p. A108
KLEIN, Kyle, Assistant Chief Financial Officer, Mercy Health – West Hospital, Cincinnati, OH, p. A489
KLEIN, Perry, Chief Engineering, Mann–Grandstaff Department of Veterans Affairs Medical Center, Spokane, WA, p. A696
KLEIN, Scott M., M.D., Chief Executive Officer, Mt. Washington Pediatric Hospital, Baltimore, MD, p. A301
KLEIN, Terrence, Ph.D., Vice President and Chief Operating Officer, Franciscan Health Crawfordsville, Crawfordsville, IN, p. A214
KLEINE, Doug, IT Director, Providence St. Mary Medical Center, Apple Valley, CA, p. A56
KLEINHANZL, Thomas A., President and Chief Executive Officer, Frederick Health, Frederick, MD, p. A304
KLEINSASSER, Dustin, Manager, Information Technology, Fall River Health Services, Hot Springs, SD, p. A574
KLEINSMITH, Carmen, MSN, R.N., Chief Nurse Executive, Unitypoint Health – St. Luke's Hospital, Cedar Rapids, IA, p. A232
KLENKE, Lisa R., R.N., Chief Executive Officer, Mercer Health, Coldwater, OH, p. A491
KLENKE, Michael, Chief Information Security Officer, West Calcasieu Cameron Hospital, Sulphur, LA, p. A293
KLEPPEN, Roxy, Director Human Resource, Sheridan Memorial Hospital, Plentywood, MT, p. A394
KLESS, Adam
Chief Nursing Officer, HCA Florida Highlands Hospital, Sebring, FL, p. A150
Chief Nursing Officer, HCA Florida Raulerson Hospital, Okeechobee, FL, p. A143
KLESS, Kurt, Chief Nursing Officer, The University of Toledo Medical Center, Toledo, OH, p. A505
KLESSENS, Thomas
Chief Financial Officer, Landmark Medical Center, Woonsocket, RI, p. A561
Chief Financial Officer, Rehabilitation Hospital of Rhode Island, North Smithfield, RI, p. A560
KLEVEN, Brian, Chief Financial Officer, St. Rose Dominican Hospitals – Siena Campus, Henderson, NV, p. A409
KLEWENO–WALLEY, Sommer, Chief Executive Officer, UW Medicine/Harborview Medical Center, Seattle, WA, p. A695
KLIEWER, Chad, Information Technology Specialist, Mercy Hospital Kingfisher, Kingfisher, OK, p. A514
KLINDWORTH, Jacinta, Chief Medical Officer, Sakakawea Medical Center, Hazen, ND, p. A481
KLINE, Brian S, Vice President and Chief Financial Officer, Penn Highlands Dubois, Dubois, PA, p. A538
KLINE, Daniel B, Vice President, Site Administrator, St. Joseph's University Medical Center, Paterson, NJ, p. A426
KLINE, Julie
R.N., Senior Vice President Patient Services, Adventist Health Sonora, Sonora, CA, p. A96
Chief Human Resource Officer, Mercyone North Iowa Medical Center, Mason City, IA, p. A240
KLINE, Melissa, Chief Nursing Officer, Metrohealth Medical Center, Cleveland, OH, p. A491
KLINGA, Maria, Director Management Information Systems, Silver Hill Hospital, New Canaan, CT, p. A117
KLINGEMAN, Jennifer, Director of Nursing, Chester Mental Health Center, Chester, IL, p. A188
KLINGENBERG, Pat, Director Human Resources, Towner County Medical Center, Cando, ND, p. A479
KLINGLER, Stacie, R.N., Vice President of Patient Services, Franciscan Health Rensselear, Rensselaer, IN, p. A226
KLINGSEIS, Robert, Director Information Systems, Desert Regional Medical Center, Palm Springs, CA, p. A82
KLINISKE, Nathan, Chief Executive Officer, Encompass Health Rehabilitation Hospital of Colorado Springs, Colorado Springs, CO, p. A105
KLINK, Sheryl, Chief Financial Officer, Piedmont Atlanta Hospital, Atlanta, GA, p. A158
KLINKNER, Donna M, Chief Financial Officer, Madelia Health, Madelia, MN, p. A349
KLITSCH, John J., President, Texas Health Presbyterian Hospital Flower Mound, Flower Mound, TX, p. A618
KLOCKENGA, Kevin A., President/Chief Executive Officer, Henry Mayo Newhall Hospital, Valencia, CA, p. A99
KLOCKMAN, Dena
Chief Financial Officer, East Morgan County Hospital, Brush, CO, p. A104
Chief Financial Officer, Ogallala Community Hospital, Ogallala, NE, p. A403
KLOCKO, Daniel, Vice President Human Resources, Kootenai Health, Coeur D'Alene, ID, p. A180
KLOECKNER, Vicki, Director Human Resources, HSHS Holy Family Hospital In Greenville, Greenville, IL, p. A196
KLOEWER, Ron, Chief Executive Officer, Montgomery County Memorial Hospital, Red Oak, IA, p. A242
KLOPFER, Anthony Rudy., FACHE, Director, Eastern Kansas Hcs, Topeka, KS, p. A260
KLOPP, Amanda, Director, Innovation and Clinical Integration, Penn State Health St. Joseph, Reading, PA, p. A553
KLOSTERMAN, Mark, FACHE, President and Chief Executive Officer, Wilson Memorial Hospital, Sidney, OH, p. A503
KLOSTERMEIER, Janice, Senior Vice President and Chief Financial Officer, Valley Presbyterian Hospital, Los Angeles, CA, p. A75
KLUGE, David, M.D., Chief of Staff, Great Falls Clinic Hospital, Great Falls, MT, p. A392
KNACKSTEDT, Cameron, D.O., Chief Medical Staff, Harlan County Health System, Alma, NE, p. A397
KNACKSTEDT, Nathan, D.O., Chief of Staff, Clara Barton Medical Center, Hoisington, KS, p. A250
KNAK, Roger, Administrator and Chief Executive Officer, Fairview Regional Medical Center, Fairview, OK, p. A512
KNAPIK, Steven, M.D., Chief of Staff, Bear Valley Community Hospital, Big Bear Lake, CA, p. A58
KNAPP, Beverly Ann, Chief Operating Officer, Adventhealth Hendersonville, Hendersonville, NC, p. A470
KNAPP, Brian A, Vice President Operations, M Health Fairview Ridges Hospital, Burnsville, MN, p. A344
KNE, Tanya, M.D., Chief Medical Officer, Banner Desert Medical Center, Mesa, AZ, p. A33
KNECHT, Brian J, Chief Operating Officer, Regional Medical Center of San Jose, San Jose, CA, p. A92
KNECHT, John, Chief Medical Staff, Linton Regional Medical Center, Linton, ND, p. A482
KNECHT, Maria, R.N., MSN, President, Endeavor Health Evanston Hospital, Evanston, IL, p. A195
KNEELAND, Misty, Chief Medical Staff, South Arkansas Regional Hospital, El Dorado, AR, p. A45
KNEISEL, Kristin, Interim Director, Information Services, Alice Peck Day Memorial Hospital, Lebanon, NH, p. A415
KNEPP, Gary, D.O., Regional Chief Medical Officer and Chief Quality Officer, Carle Health Methodist Hospital, Peoria, IL, p. A205
KNEPP, Keith
M.D., Regional President, Carle Health Methodist Hospital, Peoria, IL, p. A205
M.D., Regional President, Carle Health Pekin Hospital, Pekin, IL, p. A205
M.D., Regional President, Carle Health Proctor Hospital, Peoria, IL, p. A206
KNEPPER, Scott, M.D., Chief Medical Officer, New Braunfels Er & Hospital, New Braunfels, TX, p. A641
KNIEVEL, Lon, Chief Executive Officer, Osmond General Hospital, Osmond, NE, p. A405
KNIFFIN, Fred, M.D., Chief Medical Officer, The University of Vermont Health Network Porter Medical Center, Middlebury, VT, p. A671
KNIGHT, Beth, Chief Nursing Officer, Nacogdoches Memorial Hospital, Nacogdoches, TX, p. A640
KNIGHT, Bethany, M.D., Chief of Staff, Izard County Medical Center, Calico Rock, AR, p. A44
KNIGHT, Christopher D., Vice President Finance and Chief Financial Officer, Reid Health, Richmond, IN, p. A226
KNIGHT, Don, Assistant Administrator and Risk Manager, Ochsner St. Mary, Morgan City, LA, p. A289
KNIGHT, Jennifer, Manager Human Resources, Wellspan Waynesboro Hospital, Waynesboro, PA, p. A556
KNIGHT, Kimber, Chief Financial Officer, Braxton County Memorial Hospital, Gassaway, WV, p. A700
KNIGHT, Laura, Chief Nursing Officer, Merit Health Central, Jackson, MS, p. A364
KNIGHT, Mark T, Executive Vice President and Chief Financial Officer, Jackson Health System, Miami, FL, p. A140
KNIGHT, Michael, M.D., Medical Director, Hampstead Hospital & Residential Treatment Facility, Hampstead, NH, p. A415
KNIGHT, Reginald Q., Chief Medical Officer, Aurelia Osborn Fox Memorial Hospital, Oneonta, NY, p. A455
KNIGHT, Scott, Chief Executive Officer, Sutter Tracy Community Hospital, Tracy, CA, p. A98
KNIGHT, Terry, Public Information Officer and Administrative Assistant, California Mens Colony Correctional Treatment Center, San Luis Obispo, CA, p. A92
KNIGHT, Warren, Chief Financial Officer, Baton Rouge Behavioral Hospital, Baton Rouge, LA, p. A277
KNIGHT, Wayne
Chief Financial Officer, Indiana University Health Frankfort, Frankfort, IN, p. A217
Director Finance, Ascension St. Vincent Clay Hospital, Brazil, IN, p. A213

A894 Index of Health Care Professionals

Index of Health Care Professionals / Koppenhaver

Index of Health Care Professionals

KNIGHT, Wesley
Chief Financial Officer, UT Health Athens, Athens, TX, p. A598
Chief Financial Officer, UT Health Henderson, Henderson, TX, p. A624
KNIPP, Cindi, Director Human Resources, Rooks County Health Center, Plainville, KS, p. A258
KNIPPERS, Ashley, Chief Financial Officer, Longleaf Hospital, Alexandria, LA, p. A276
KNISLEY, Shane, President, Bon Secours Maryview Medical Center, Portsmouth, VA, p. A681
KNITT, Lori, Chief Nursing Officer, Aurora Medical Center – Sheboygan County, Sheboygan, WI, p. A721
KNOBLOCH, Stanley, Director of Finance, Sanford Sheldon Medical Center, Sheldon, IA, p. A243
KNOCKE, Michael, Chief Information Officer, Kansas Spine & Specialty Hospital, Wichita, KS, p. A262
KNODE, Scott, Chief Financial Officer, Veterans Memorial Hospital, Waukon, IA, p. A245
KNOEPFFLER, Susan, R.N., Vice President Nursing, Huntington Hospital, Huntington, NY, p. A444
KNOEPFLEIN, Susan, Chief Nurse Executive, Fulton State Hospital, Fulton, MO, p. A375
KNOEPFLER, David, M.D., Chief Medical Officer, Overlake Medical Center And Clinics, Bellevue, WA, p. A687
KNOERL, Thomas, Vice President Finance, Corewell Health Reed City Hospital, Reed City, MI, p. A336
KNOTHE, Lisa, Vice President, Chief Human Resources Officer, Children's Specialized Hospital, New Brunswick, NJ, p. A424
KNOWLES, B K, D.O., Chief of Staff, Pershing Memorial Hospital, Brookfield, MO, p. A372
KNOWLES, Christy, Chief Human Resources Officer, Coosa Valley Medical Center, Sylacauga, AL, p. A24
KNOWLES, John, Director Human Resources, Clinch Valley Medical Center, Richlands, VA, p. A682
KNOWLES, Robert, M.D., Chief of Staff, Ascension Saint Thomas Highlands, Sparta, TN, p. A593
KNOWLES-SMITH, Peter, M.D., Medical Director, Bennett County Hospital And Nursing Home, Martin, SD, p. A574
KNOX, Fred, Chief Executive Officer, Rivendell Behavioral Health Services, Benton, AR, p. A43
KNOX, Jody, Chief Operating Officer, Kindred Hospital Rancho, Rancho Cucamonga, CA, p. A84
KNOX, John, Senior Vice President and Chief Information Officer, Atrium Health University City, Charlotte, NC, p. A465
KNOX, Roland, Chief Executive Officer, Mt. Graham Regional Medical Center, Safford, AZ, p. A38
KNOX, Stacey A., Administrator, Rock County Hospital, Bassett, NE, p. A397
KNUDSEN, Jessica
Chief Executive Officer, Clarity Child Guidance Center, San Antonio, TX, p. A649
Chief Operating Officer and Director Performance Improvement and Risk Management, Holly Hill Hospital, Raleigh, NC, p. A474
KNUDSEN, Mark, Director Fiscal Services, Shriners Hospitals for Children–Portland, Portland, OR, p. A531
KNUDSEN, Matthew, Director, Information Systems, Sheppard Pratt, Baltimore, MD, p. A302
KNUDSON, Aaron, Chief Medical Officer, Page Hospital, Page, AZ, p. A34
KNUDSON, Jenny, Controller, Amberwell Hiawatha, Hiawatha, KS, p. A250
KNUDTEN, Kristine, M.D., Vice President Medical Affairs, Glencoe Regional Health, Glencoe, MN, p. A347
KNUTH, Kerry, Chief Operating Officer, Mercy Health – Defiance Hospital, Defiance, OH, p. A494
KNUTSON, Andy, Chief Financial Officer, Mille Lacs Health System, Onamia, MN, p. A352
KNUTSON, Holly, Manager Information Technology, Kittson Healthcare, Hallock, MN, p. A348
KNUTSON, John P, M.D., Chief Medical Staff, Delta Health, Delta, CO, p. A106
KNUTSON, Larry, Director Finance, Centracare – Long Prairie, Long Prairie, MN, p. A349
KNYCH, Stephen, M.D., Chief Medical Officer, Adventhealth Fish Memorial, Orange City, FL, p. A143
KO, Dicken S.C., M.D., Vice President of Medical Affairs and Chief Medical Officer, St. Elizabeth's Medical Center, Brighton, MA, p. A311
KO, Tommy, M.D., Chief Medical Officer, St. Josep. Medical Center, Kansas City, MO, p. A378
KOAST, Eric, Vice President Information Technology and Chief Information Officer, Marietta Memorial Hospital, Marietta, OH, p. A499
KOBIS, David A., Chief Executive Officer, Wyoming County Community Hospital, Warsaw, NY, p. A461
KOBOLD, Luke, Chief Executive Officer, Stillwater Billings Clinic, Columbus, MT, p. A390
KOCH, Colleen, M.D., MS, Group Senior Vice President and Chief Operating Officer, New York–Presbyterian Hospital, New York, NY, p. A450
KOCH, Douglas Edward.
Chief Executive Officer, Governor Juan F. Luis Hospital, Christiansted, VI, p. A736
Chief Executive Officer, Kearney Regional Medical Center, Kearney, NE, p. A401
KOCH, Eric, Chief Nursing Officer, Northern Montana Hospital, Havre, MT, p. A393
KOCH, Holly, Chief Financial Officer, Girard Medical Center, Girard, KS, p. A249
KOCH, Jamie, R.N., Chief Nursing Officer, Thayer County Health Services, Hebron, NE, p. A401
KOCH, Josep. G.
Chief Executive Officer, Fleming County Hospital, Flemingsburg, KY, p. A265
Chief Executive Officer, Meadowview Regional Medical Center, Maysville, KY, p. A271
KOCH, Shane, Chief Executive Officer, The Brook At Dupont, Louisville, KY, p. A270
KOCHIE, Daniel A, CPA, Chief Financial Officer, Samaritan Hospital – Main Campus, Troy, NY, p. A460
KOCHIS, Mary Ellen, MSN, R.N., Administrator Nursing Operations, Corewell Health Dearborn Hospital, Dearborn, MI, p. A324
KOCOUREK, Cathie A., President, Aurora Medical Center – Manitowoc County, Two Rivers, WI, p. A723
KOCSIS, Dana
Vice President Nursing and Operations, Cleveland Clinic Akron General Lodi Hospital, Lodi, OH, p. A498
Vice President, Nursing and Operations, Cleveland Clinic Akron General Lodi Hospital, Lodi, OH, p. A498
KOCSIS, Violet, Chief Human Resources Officer, Hunterdon Healthcare, Flemington, NJ, p. A421
KOCZENT, Kurt, Executive Vice President and Chief Operating Officer, F. F. Thompson Hospital, Canandaigua, NY, p. A440
KOEBKE, Troy L
Director Human Resources, Bellin Psychiatric Center, Green Bay, WI, p. A712
Director Human Resources Management, Bellin Hospital, Green Bay, WI, p. A712
Human Resource Director, Bellin Health Oconto Hospital, Oconto, WI, p. A719
KOEHLER, Amy, Director Human Resources, HSHS Good Shepherd Hospital, Shelbyville, IL, p. A208
KOEHLER, Joseph, Market Chief Executive Officer, Mercy Rehabilitation Hospital St. Louis, Chesterfield, MO, p. A373
KOELE, Craig, Chief Executive Officer, Cornerstone Specialty Hospitals Muskogee, Muskogee, OK, p. A515
KOENIG, Donald E.
Jr, Chief Operating Officer, Mercy Health – St. Josep. Warren Hospital, Warren, OH, p. A506
Jr, Executive Vice President and Regional Chief Operating Officer, President, St. Elizabeth Youngstown Hospital, Mercy Health – St. Elizabeth Youngstown Hospital, Youngstown, OH, p. A508
Director, Veterans Affairs Pittsburgh Healthcare System, Pittsburgh, PA, p. A552
KOENIG, Lori, Assistant Finance Director, Cleveland Clinic Avon Hospital, Avon, OH, p. A485
KOENIG, Mary, Chief Financial Officer, Vernon Memorial Healthcare, Elk Mound, WI, p. A710
KOEPKE, Eldon, Chief Financial Officer, Mitchell County Hospital Health Systems, Beloit, KS, p. A247
KOERNER, Jill, Manager Employee Relations, Weisman Children's Rehabilitation Hospital, Marlton, NJ, p. A424
KOERNIG, Felissa
President and Chief Executive Officer, Oneida Healthcare, Oneida, NY, p. A455
President and Chief Operating Officer, Guthrie Robert Packer Hospital, Sayre, PA, p. A554
KOESSL, Brenda, R.N., Director of Nursing Services, Frances Mahon Deaconess Hospital, Glasgow, MT, p. A392
KOESTER, Jean, Manager Human Resources, Limestone Medical Center, Groesbeck, TX, p. A623
KOESTERER, Susan, Vice President, Finance, Alton Memorial Hospital, Alton, IL, p. A185
KOETTING, Edward, Chief Financial Officer, Bedford Veterans Affairs Medical Center, Edith Nourse Rogers Memorial Veterans Hospital, Bedford, MA, p. A309
KOGANTI, Ravikanth, Vice President Information Technology, Englewood Health, Englewood, NJ, p. A421
KOHANKE, Crystal H, Group Vice President, Human Resources, Christus Santa Rosa Health System, San Antonio, TX, p. A649
KOHL, Randy T., M.D., Deputy Director, Health Services, Nebraska Penal And Correctional Hospital, Lincoln, NE, p. A402
KOHLER, Douglas, M.D., Vice President Medical Operations, Cleveland Clinic Marymount Hospital, Garfield Heights, OH, p. A496
KOHLER, Tracy, Chief Executive Officer, Kindred Hospital–Houston Northwest, Houston, TX, p. A626
KOHR, Kathy, Chief Financial Officer, Mymichigan Medical Center West Branch, West Branch, MI, p. A340
KOHUT, Karli, President and Chief Executive Officer, Silver Lake Hospital Ltach, Newark, NJ, p. A425
KOLACZ, Nicole Marie, R.N., Chief Nursing Officer, Aultman Hospital, Canton, OH, p. A487
KOLACZEK, Rick, Chief Operating Officer, Merit Health Wesley, Hattiesburg, MS, p. A363
KOLB, Edward M., M.D., Medical Director, Boys Town National Research Hospital, Omaha, NE, p. A403
KOLDA, Tena, Director of Nursing, Community Memorial Hospital, Redfield, SD, p. A576
KOLLMAN, Matt, Chief Executive Officer, Skyline Health, White Salmon, WA, p. A698
KOLLMEYER, Sherry, Vice President Human Resources, Youth Villages Inner Harbour Campus, Douglasville, GA, p. A163
KOLODZIEJCYK, Wanda S, Director Human Resources, Cuero Regional Hospital, Cuero, TX, p. A610
KOLODZIEJCZYK, Clayton, Chief Financial Officer, Meadowview Regional Medical Center, Maysville, KY, p. A271
KOLSETH, Shelley V, Chief Financial Officer, HCA Florida West Tamp. Hospital, Tampa, FL, p. A152
KOMAN, Stuart, Ph.D., President and Chief Executive Officer, Walden Behavioral Care, Waltham, MA, p. A319
KOMANDURI, Ramanujam, M.D., Chief of Staff, North Las Vegas Va Medical Center, North Las Vegas, NV, p. A412
KOMAR, Ellen M, R.N., Senior Vice President Patient Care Services and Chief Nursing Officer, Stamford Health, Stamford, CT, p. A119
KOME, Hunter
Chief Operations Executive, Prisma Health Baptist Easley Hospital, Easley, SC, p. A565
Chief Operations Executive, Prisma Health Oconee Memorial Hospital, Seneca, SC, p. A570
KOMER, Claudia, M.D., Chief Medical Officer, Saint Michael's Medical Center, Newark, NJ, p. A425
KOMINS, Jeff, M.D., Chief Medical Officer, Mercy Fitzgerald Hospital, Darby, PA, p. A538
KONARSKI, Debbie, Chief Financial Officer, Pottstown Hospital, Pottstown, PA, p. A553
KONECNE, Robin, Manager Human Resources, Kit Carson County Memorial Hospital, Burlington, CO, p. A104
KONG, Mei, Chief Operating Officer, NYC Health + Hospitals/ South Brooklyn Health, New York, NY, p. A452
KONGARA, Rama, Chief Financial Officer, St. James Behavioral Health Hospital, Gonzales, LA, p. A282
KONIECZEK, Raymond, Chief Human Resources Officer, JFK Memorial Hospital, Indio, CA, p. A67
KONIG, Angie, Senior Director Human Resources, Mitchell County Regional Health Center, Osage, IA, p. A241
KONKEL, Robert, Manager Finance, James A. Haley Veterans' Hospital–Tampa, Tampa, FL, p. A152
KONSAVAGE, Christian, M.D., Chief of Staff, Cumberland County Hospital, Burkesville, KY, p. A264
KOOIMAN, Thomas
Administrator, Avera Tyler, Tyler, MN, p. A356
Chief Executive Officer, Avera Granite Falls, Granite Falls, MN, p. A348
KOOISTRA, Josh, M.D., Senior Vice President, Chief Medical Officer, Corewell Health Butterworth Hospital, Grand Rapids, MI, p. A328
KOOKEN, Kyron J., MS, Chief Executive Officer, Pam Rehabilitation Hospital of Allen, Allen, TX, p. A595
KOON, Rion, Chief Information Management Division, William Beaumont Army Medical Center, El Paso, TX, p. A617
KOONCE, Jonathan, Chief Executive Officer, Highlands Arh Regional Medical Center, Prestonsburg, KY, p. A273
KOONS, Marley Lyn., Chief Executive Officer, Kearny County Hospital, Lakin, KS, p. A252
KOONTZ, Jeffrey, Chief Administrator Officer, Hillside Rehabilitation Hospital, Warren, OH, p. A506
KOOVAKADA, Philip. President, Orlando Health – Health Central Hospital, Ocoee, FL, p. A143
KOOYMAN, James, Human Resources Manager, Seneca Healthcare District, Chester, CA, p. A59
KOPEL, Samuel, M.D., Medical Director, Maimonides Medical Center, New York, NY, p. A449
KOPIN, Jeffrey D., Senior Vice President and Chief Medical Officer, Northwestern Medicine Lake Forest Hospital, Lake Forest, IL, p. A200
KOPPELMAN, Benjamin, President, Chi St. Joseph's Health, Park Rapids, MN, p. A352
KOPPENHAVER, Colleen, Interim Chief Financial Officer, Ascension Resurrection, Chicago, IL, p. A188

KOPPERUD, Gordon, Director Operations, Sanford Westbrook Medical Center, Westbrook, MN, p. A357
KOPSER, Mark
  Interim Chief Financial Officer, Ascension Wisconsin Hospital – Menomonee Falls Campus, Menomonee Falls, WI, p. A715
  Interim Chief Financial Officer, Dignity St. Rose – Craig Ranch, North Las Vegas, NV, p. A411
KORDAHL, Rebecca, R.N., Associate Director, Patient Care Services, William S. Middleton Memorial Veterans' Hospital, Madison, WI, p. A715
KORDUCKI, Stanley R., President, Wood County Hospital, Bowling Green, OH, p. A487
KORDUPEL, Maureen
  Director Information Technology Relationship Manager, Mercy Health – St. Elizabeth Boardman Hospital, Boardman, OH, p. A486
  Director Relationship Manager, Mercy Health – St. Elizabeth Youngstown Hospital, Youngstown, OH, p. A508
KORF, Rick, Chief Financial Officer, Yuma District Hospital, Yuma, CO, p. A114
KORKMAS, Ross, Chief Executive Officer, Palo Pinto General Hospital, Mineral Wells, TX, p. A639
KORN, Roy, M.D., Medical Director, Cobleskill Regional Hospital, Cobleskill, NY, p. A441
KORNBLATT, Lynne R, Chief Human Resources Officer, Einstein Medical Center Philadelphia, Philadelphia, PA, p. A548
KORNELE, Alyson, Chief Executive Officer, West River Regional Medical Center, Hettinger, ND, p. A481
KORNFIELD, Lee, M.D., Medical Director, St. Luke's Rehabilitation Hospital, Boise, ID, p. A180
KORNRUMPF, Rodney, Chief Executive Officer, The Meadows Psychiatric Center, Centre Hall, PA, p. A536
KOROM, Nancy K
  Chief Nursing Officer and Vice President, Children's Hospital of Wisconsin–Fox Valley, Neenah, WI, p. A718
  Chief Nursing Officer and Vice President, Children's Wisconsin, Milwaukee, WI, p. A717
KORPELA, Donita, R.N., Director of Patient Care Services, Essentia Health Moose Lake, Moose Lake, MN, p. A351
KORPIEL, Michael, President, Mercy San Juan Medical Center, Carmichael, CA, p. A58
KORTE, Fred, Chief Financial Officer, Mclaren Flint, Flint, MI, p. A327
KORTH–WHITE, Kirsten, Munson Healthcare Grayling Hospital President and Chief Executive Officer and MHC East Region Presid, Munson Healthcare Grayling Hospital, Grayling, MI, p. A329
KOSANOVICH, John, M.D., Executive Vice President Physician Enterprise and Chief Executive Officer, Covenant Medical Group, Covenant Healthcare, Saginaw, MI, p. A336
KOSANOVICH, John P, President, Watertown Regional Medical Center, Watertown, WI, p. A723
KOSE, William H., M.D., Vice President Quality and Medical Affairs, Bluffton Hospital, Bluffton, OH, p. A486
KOSEK, Kevin, Associate Director Operations, Iowa City Va Health System, Iowa City, IA, p. A238
KOSLOW, Howard B, President and Chief Executive Officer, Riverbridge Specialty Hospital, Vidalia, LA, p. A294
KOSMAN, Beth, Director Health Information Management, Ringgold County Hospital, Mount Ayr, IA, p. A240
KOSNIK, Linda, R.N., MSN, Chief Nursing Officer and Vice President, Patient Care Services, Sinai Hospital of Baltimore, Baltimore, MD, p. A301
KOSNOSKY, David, M.D., Chief Medical Officer, University Hospitals Geauga Medical Center, Chardon, OH, p. A488
KOSTER, Chad, Chief Executive Officer, Sheridan County Health Complex, Hoxie, KS, p. A251
KOSTER, Tracy, Director Human Resources, Carlinville Area Hospital, Carlinville, IL, p. A187
KOSTERS, Gregory J, D.O., Chief Medical Officer, Osceola Regional Health Center, Sibley, IA, p. A243
KOSTOK, Barbara, Manager Human Resources, Punxsutawney Area Hospital, Punxsutawney, PA, p. A553
KOTAL, Clint, Chief Executive Officer, Methodist Hospital Hill Country, Fredericksburg, TX, p. A620
KOTIL, Drew, Director Information Technology, Crete Area Medical Center, Crete, NE, p. A399
KOTIN, Kathy, Chief Financial Officer, Banner – University Medical Center Phoenix, Phoenix, AZ, p. A35
KOTRBA, Mitchell, Chief Financial Officer, North Valley Health Center, Warren, MN, p. A357
KOTSALOS, Mantah, VP & President, WellSpan Philhaven, Wellspan Philhaven, Mount Gretna, PA, p. A546
KOTTOOR, Jose, Chief Executive Officer, Lake Huron Medical Center, Port Huron, MI, p. A328
KOULOVATOS, James E., Chief Executive Officer, Clay County Memorial Hospital, Henrietta, TX, p. A624

KOUNTZ, David, M.D., Senior Vice President Medical Affairs, Hackensack Meridian Health Jersey Shore University Medical Center, Neptune, NJ, p. A424
KOUSKOLEKAS, Anthony, FACHE, President, Pelham Medical Center, Greer, SC, p. A567
KOUTOUZOS, Connie L.
  R.N., MSN, President and Chief Executive Officer, Mclaren Caro Region, Caro, MI, p. A323
  R.N., MSN, President and Chief Executive Officer, Mclaren Thumb Region, Bad Axe, MI, p. A322
KOUTSOUMPAS, Tom, President and Chief Executive Officer, Capital Caring, Arlington, VA, p. A673
KOVAC, John, Facility Chief Information Officer, Veterans Affairs Pittsburgh Healthcare System, Pittsburgh, PA, p. A552
KOVACEVICH, Kyle, Chief Financial Officer, North Country Hospital And Health Center, Newport, VT, p. A672
KOVACH, Andrew L, Vice President Human Resources and Chief Administrative Officer, Newton Medical Center, Newton, NJ, p. A426
KOVACS, Tina
  Chief Financial Officer, Saint Francis Hospital, Memphis, TN, p. A589
  Chief Financial Officer, Saint Francis Hospital–Bartlett, Bartlett, TN, p. A579
  Interim Chief Financial Officer, Saint Vincent Hospital, Worcester, MA, p. A320
KOVAL, Matthew, M.D., Vice President Medical Affairs, Kidspeace Children's Hospital, Orefield, PA, p. A547
KOVAR, Kelley, R.N., Chief Nursing Officer, Adventhealth Littleton, Littleton, CO, p. A111
KOVOLYAN, Amanda, M.D., Chief Medical Officer, Bucyrus Community Hospital, Bucyrus, OH, p. A487
KOVSKI, Christopher, Senior Vice President Human Resources, Penn Highlands Mon Valley, Monongahela, PA, p. A546
KOWALCZYK, David, Vice President Human Resources, Eisenhower Health, Rancho Mirage, CA, p. A84
KOWALSKI, David, Chief Executive Officer, Kindred Hospital–La Mirada, La Mirada, CA, p. A68
KOWNACKI, Dawn, Director Human Resources, Brooke Glen Behavioral Hospital, Fort Washington, PA, p. A540
KOWNACKI, Hamila
  R.N., Chief Executive Officer, California Pacific Medical Center–Davies Campus, San Francisco, CA, p. A90
  R.N., Chief Executive Officer, California Pacific Medical Center–Mission Bernal Campus, San Francisco, CA, p. A90
  R.N., Chief Executive Officer, California Pacific Medical Center–Van Ness Campus, San Francisco, CA, p. A90
KOZAR, Michael A., Chief Executive Officer, Northwest Florida Community Hospital, Chipley, FL, p. A128
KOZEL, Kenneth D., FACHE, President and Chief Executive Officer, University of Maryland Shore Medical Center At Easton, Easton, MD, p. A304
KOZEL, Mary Ann, Chief Fiscal, Wilmington Veterans Affairs Medical Center, Wilmington, DE, p. A122
KOZIK, Kelly, Director Human Resources, Encompass Health Rehabilitation Hospital of Reading, Reading, PA, p. A553
KOZIKUSKI, Courtney
  Chief Financial Officer, Stillwater Medical Blackwell, Blackwell, OK, p. A510
  Chief Financial Officer, Stillwater Medical Perry, Perry, OK, p. A519
  President & Chief Financial Officer, Stillwater Medical Perry, Perry, OK, p. A519
  President and Chief Financial Officer, Stillwater Medical Blackwell, Blackwell, OK, p. A510
KOZIN, Scott, M.D., Chief of Staff, Shriners Children's Philadelphia, Philadelphia, PA, p. A550
KOZIOL, Michael J, Chief Financial Officer, Holyoke Medical Center, Holyoke, MA, p. A314
KOZYRA, John, Chief Executive Officer, Avera St. Anthony's Hospital, O'Neill, NE, p. A403
KRABLIN, Brett, M.D., Chief of Staff, Mercy Hospital Kingfisher, Kingfisher, OK, p. A514
KRAFT, Carly, Human Resources Director, Pam Health Rehabilitation Hospital of Westminster, Westminster, CO, p. A114
KRAFT, Chris, Director Information Systems, York General, York, NE, p. A407
KRAFT, John, Chief Financial Officer, Woodlawn Hospital, Rochester, IN, p. A226
KRAFVE, Jake Matthew, Chief Financial Officer, Royal Oaks Hospital, Windsor, MO, p. A388
KRAHNERT, John F, M.D., Chief Medical Officer, Firsthealth Moore Regional Hospital, Pinehurst, NC, p. A474
KRAJEWSKI, David, Senior Vice President and Chief Financial Officer, Sinai Hospital of Baltimore, Baltimore, MD, p. A301

KRAJICEK, John, Chief Financial Officer, Research Medical Center, Kansas City, MO, p. A378
KRAJNA–MATHERLY, Anna, Human Resources Leader, Kaiser Permanente Santa Rosa Medical Center, Santa Rosa, CA, p. A95
KRAMER, Aaron, Chief Executive Officer, Adirondack Health, Saranac Lake, NY, p. A458
KRAMER, Andrea, Chief Medical Officer, Essentia Health Moose Lake, Moose Lake, MN, p. A351
KRAMER, Blake, Administrator, Franklin Medical Center, Winnsboro, LA, p. A294
KRAMER, Danette
  Chief Executive Officer, Regional Medical Center, Manchester, IA, p. A239
  Chief Financial Officer, Regional Medical Center, Manchester, IA, p. A239
KRAMER, Janie, Chief Operating Officer, Sharp Memorial Hospital, San Diego, CA, p. A89
KRAMER, Kathryn, M.D., President Medical Staff, Carle Health Pekin Hospital, Pekin, IL, p. A205
KRAMER, Kevin, Chief Executive Officer, Modoc Medical Center, Alturas, CA, p. A55
KRAMER, Kyle, Chief Executive Officer, Day Kimball Hospital, Putnam, CT, p. A118
KRAMER, Michael, President, The Jewish Hospital – Mercy Health, Cincinnati, OH, p. A489
KRAMER, Susan, Director of Human Resources, Levi Hospital, Hot Springs National Park, AR, p. A48
KRAMPITS, Carrie, Director Human Resources, Mckenzie Health System, Sandusky, MI, p. A337
KRASS, Todd, Chief Executive Officer, Belton Regional Medical Center, Belton, MO, p. A371
KRAUKLIS, Gene
  Regional Vice President Human Resources, Aurora Lakeland Medical Center, Elkhorn, WI, p. A710
  Regional Vice President Human Resources, Aurora Medical Center Burlington, Burlington, WI, p. A709
KRAUS, Jason, Director Human Resources, Magruder Memorial Hospital, Port Clinton, OH, p. A502
KRAUS, John, M.D., Chief Medical Officer, Bryn Mawr Rehabilitation Hospital, Malvern, PA, p. A545
KRAUSE, Christa, Chief Nursing Officer, Door County Medical Center, Sturgeon Bay, WI, p. A722
KRAUSE, Donna, Chief Information Officer, Harry S. Truman Memorial Veterans' Hospital, Columbia, MO, p. A374
KRAUSE, Kim, Director Human Resources, Baylor Scott & White Heart & Vascular Hospital–Dallas, Dallas, TX, p. A610
KRAUSE, Matt, Chief Administrative Officer, Aspirus Keweenaw Hospital, Laurium, MI, p. A332
KRAUSE, Michelle, M.D., Senior Vice Chancellor, UAMS Health and Chief Executive Officer, UAMS Medical Center, Little Rock, AR, p. A50
KRAUSE, Steven, Manager Information Technology, Franciscan Healthcare Munster, Munster, IN, p. A224
KRAUSE, Wade, M.D., Chief Medical Officer, Connally Memorial Medical Center, Floresville, TX, p. A618
KRAUTSCHEID, Steven P, Ancillary Services Administrator, Ohsu Health Hillsboro Medical Center, Hillsboro, OR, p. A528
KRAVETZ, Michael, M.D., Medical Director, Encompass Health Valley of The Sun Rehabilitation Hospital, Glendale, AZ, p. A32
KRAVETZ, Todd, Chief of Staff, Wickenburg Community Hospital, Wickenburg, AZ, p. A41
KRC, Juie, Chief Financial Officer, UT Health North Campus Tyler, Tyler, TX, p. A659
KREATSOULAS, Nicholas, Vice President Medical Affairs, Mercy Health – St. Josep. Warren Hospital, Warren, OH, p. A506
KREBS, Christine
  Director of Nursing, Aspirus Tomahawk Hospital, Tomahawk, WI, p. A723
  Director or Nursing, Aspirus Rhinelander Hospital, Rhinelander, WI, p. A720
KREBS, Cindy, District Director Human Resources, Matagorda Regional Medical Center, Bay City, TX, p. A601
KREBS, George, M.D., Chief Medical Officer, Broughton Hospital, Morganton, NC, p. A473
KREBS, Shantel, Chief Executive Officer, Avera St. Mary's Hospital, Pierre, SD, p. A575
KREELEY, Chris, Director Nursing, Kessler Marlton Rehabilitation, Marlton, NJ, p. A423
KREHBIEL, Rod, M.D., Chief of Staff, Klickitat Valley Health, Goldendale, WA, p. A690
KREIDER, David, Controller, Wellspan Ephrata Community Hospital, Ephrata, PA, p. A539
KREIDLER, Marlene, Executive Director Human Resources, Adventist Health Bakersfield, Bakersfield, CA, p. A56

Index of Health Care Professionals / Kunkel

KREIL, Stacy
Chief Nursing Officer, Adventhealth Sebring, Sebring, FL, p. A150
Chief Nursing Officer, Adventhealth Wauchula, Wauchula, FL, p. A154
KREITNER, Jason, FACHE, Senior Vice President and Chief Operarting Officer, Hackensack Meridian Health Hackensack University Medical Center, Hackensack, NJ, p. A421
KREITZER, Teri, Director Human Resources, Saint Francis Medical Center, Cap. Girardeau, MO, p. A372
KREJCI, Kathy Blair, Chief Nursing Officer, Marshall Medical Center, Placerville, CA, p. A83
KRELL, G Christopher, M.D., Chief of Staff, South Lincoln Medical Center, Kemmerer, WY, p. A727
KRELSTEIN, Michael, M.D., Medical Director, San Diego County Psychiatric Hospital, San Diego, CA, p. A89
KRESHON, James, M.D., Medical Director, Encompass Health Rehabilitation Hospital of Harmarville, Pittsburgh, PA, p. A551
KRETSCHMAN, Robin, MSN, R.N., Vice President Patient Care Services, Marshfield Medical Center, Marshfield, WI, p. A715
KRETSCHMER, Suzanne, Chief Executive Officer, Cornerstone Specialty Hospitals Conroe, Conroe, TX, p. A608
KRETZ, Blake, FACHE, President, Texas Health Arlington Memorial Hospital, Arlington, TX, p. A598
KRETZINGER, Curt, Chief Operating Officer, Mosaic Life Care At St. Josep. – Medical Center, Saint Joseph, MO, p. A383
KRETZSCHMER, Kendra, Patient Care System Leader, Scheurer Health, Pigeon, MI, p. A335
KREUTNER, Ron, Chief Financial Officer, San Joaquin General Hospital, French Camp. CA, p. A64
KREUTZER, Anne, Chief Executive Officer, Yuma District Hospital, Yuma, CO, p. A114
KREUTZER, Kevin, Chief Financial Officer, Russell Regional Hospital, Russell, KS, p. A258
KRIDEL, Jeff, Senior Director, Information Technology Operations, Carewell Health Medical Center, East Orange, NJ, p. A420
KRIEGER, Cathy, Human Resources Director, Greene County Medical Center, Jefferson, IA, p. A238
KRIEGER, Mark, Vice President and Chief Financial Officer, Barnes–Jewish Hospital, Saint Louis, MO, p. A383
KRIEGER, Tim, Director Information Systems, Harnett Health System, Dunn, NC, p. A467
KRIER, Jennifer, Vice President Human Resources, Wesley Medical Center, Wichita, KS, p. A262
KRILICH, Chad
M.D., Chief Med Officer–AMC/CMC, Multicare Auburn Medical Center, Auburn, WA, p. A687
M.D., Chief Medical Officer, Providence Santa Rosa Memorial Hospital, Santa Rosa, CA, p. A95
KRINKE, Susan, Chief Executive Officer, Kindred Hospital Lima, Lima, OH, p. A498
KRIPAKARAN, Kasturi, M.D., Medical Director, Elizabeth Parsons Ware Packard Mental Health Center, Springfield, IL, p. A209
KRIPINSKI, Laura, Chief Nursing Officer, Forks Community Hospital, Forks, WA, p. A690
KRISHNA, M. S., M.D., Chief of Medical Staff, Deaconess Gibson Hospital, Princeton, IN, p. A226
KRISHNAN, Radha, M.D., Chief Medical Officer, Antelop. Valley Medical Center, Lancaster, CA, p. A69
KRISHNASWAMY, Jaikumar, Chief Executive Officer, Doctors Medical Center of Modesto, Modesto, CA, p. A77
KRODEL, Scott, Vice President Information Systems, Johnson Memorial Hospital, Franklin, IN, p. A217
KROESE, Brandi, Director Operations, West Springs Hospital, Grand Junction, CO, p. A109
KROESE, Robert D, FACHE, Chief Executive Officer, Pella Regional Health Center, Pella, IA, p. A242
KROESE, Robert D., FACHE, Chief Executive Officer, Pella Regional Health Center, Pella, IA, p. A242
KROLICKI, Karen, Director, Human Resources, Corewell Health Taylor Hospital, Taylor, MI, p. A339
KROLIK, Phillip. Vice President, Finance, Mercy Hospital, Coon Rapids, MN, p. A345
KRONENBERG, Seth, M.D., President and Chief Executive Officer, Crouse Health, Syracuse, NY, p. A460
KROSOFF, Mary June, Chief Human Resources Officer, Penn Highlands Connellsville, Connellsville, PA, p. A537
KROUSE, Michael
Chief Information Officer, Ohiohealth Doctors Hospital, Columbus, OH, p. A492
Chief Information Officer, Ohiohealth Grant Medical Center, Columbus, OH, p. A492
Chief Information Officer, Ohiohealth Riverside Methodist Hospital, Columbus, OH, p. A492
Chief Information Officer Information Services, Ohiohealth Grady Memorial Hospital, Delaware, OH, p. A494
Senior Vice President Chief Information Officer, Ohiohealth Dublin Methodist Hospital, Dublin, OH, p. A495
KRUEGER, Christine, M.D., Chief of Staff, Munising Memorial Hospital, Munising, MI, p. A334
KRUEGER, Ellen, Director Human Resources, Chadron Community Hospital And Health Services, Chadron, NE, p. A398
KRUEGER, Eric
Chief Financial Officer, Insight Hospital And Medical Center, Chicago, IL, p. A189
Finance Officer, Adventist Health Glendale, Glendale, CA, p. A66
KRUEGER, James G., M.D., Ph.D., Chief Executive Officer, Rockefeller University Hospital, New York, NY, p. A452
KRUEGER, Justin, FACHE, President, Mercy Health – Fairfield Hospital, Fairfield, OH, p. A495
KRUG, James, Affiliate Vice President, Information Systems and Support Services, Jacksonville Memorial Hospital, Jacksonville, IL, p. A199
KRUG, Robert J., M.D., President and Executive Medical Director, Mount Sinai Rehabilitation Hospital, Hartford, CT, p. A116
KRUGEL, Gary M, Chief Financial Officer, Humboldt Park Health, Chicago, IL, p. A189
KRUGER, Dale K., Chief Executive Officer, Mahnomen Health, Mahnomen, MN, p. A349
KRUGER, George, CPA, Chief Financial Officer, Comanche County Memorial Hospital, Lawton, OK, p. A514
KRUGER, Jason, Chief Medical Officer and Vice President, Chi Health St Elizabeth, Lincoln, NE, p. A402
KRUMMEL, Dere, Director Information Systems, Ochsner Medical Center – Kenner, Kenner, LA, p. A284
KRUMP, Carrie, Senior Director, Sanford Bagley Medical Center, Bagley, MN, p. A343
KRUPA, Charles, Chief Information Officer and Public Information Officer, Southwest Health System, Cortez, CO, p. A105
KRUPA, Michael P., Ed.D., Chief Executive Officer, Miravista Behavioral Health Center, Holyoke, MA, p. A314
KRUPALA, Judith, R.N., Chief Nursing Officer, Cuero Regional Hospital, Cuero, TX, p. A610
KRUSE, Marcia, R.N., Director Nursing, Logan County Hospital, Oakley, KS, p. A256
KRUSE, Victoria, Manager Human Resources, Franklin General Hospital, Hampton, IA, p. A237
KRUSIE, Kathleen R, FACHE, President, Community Hospital East, Indianapolis, IN, p. A219
KRUYER–COLLINS, Emyle, Chief Human Resources Officer, Unity Physicians Hospital, Mishawaka, IN, p. A224
KRUZEL, Janet, Business Office Manager, Centracare – Melrose, Melrose, MN, p. A350
KRUZICK, Michael, Acting Chief Financial Officer, Norwalk Hospital, Norwalk, CT, p. A118
KRUZNER, Melinda, Chief Financial Officer, Lexington Medical Center, West Columbia, SC, p. A571
KRYDER, Dan, M.D., Chief Medical Officer, Alomere Health, Alexandria, MN, p. A342
KRYSTOWIAK, Thomas P, Chief Financial Officer, Thedacare Medical Center–Berlin, Berlin, WI, p. A708
KRZASTEK, Sue, Vice President Human Resources, Augusta Health, Fishersville, VA, p. A676
KU, Evelyn, R.N., MSN, Chief Executive Officer, Alhambra Hospital Medical Center, Alhambra, CA, p. A55
KUBALA, Joseph
Chief Financial Officer, Ascension St. Vincent Jennings, North Vernon, IN, p. A225
Director Financial and Support Services, Ascension St. Vincent Salem, Salem, IN, p. A227
KUBALL, Lana, Director Administrative Services, Lucas County Health Center, Chariton, IA, p. A232
KUBE, Don, M.D., Chief Medical Officer, Marshfield Medical Center – Dickinson, Iron Mountain, MI, p. A330
KUBICEK, Jim, Vice President, Operations, Rogers Behavioral Health, Oconomowoc, WI, p. A718
KUBOUSHEK, David, Chief, Fiscal Service, Durham Va Health Care System, Durham, NC, p. A467
KUCERA, Katie
Chief Financial Officer, Carson Tahoe Health, Carson City, NV, p. A408
interim Chief Financial Officer Acute Services, Renown Regional Medical Center, Reno, NV, p. A412
KUCERA, Kim, Chief Operating Officer, Mille Lacs Health System, Onamia, MN, p. A352
KUCICH, Vincent
FACHE, FACS, M.D., Chief Medical Officer, OSF Heart of Mary Medical Center, Urbana, IL, p. A210
FACHE, FACS, M.D., Chief Medical Officer, OSF Sacred Heart Medical Center, Danville, IL, p. A192
KUCKEWICH, Mike, Director Information Systems, Terre Haute Regional Hospital, Terre Haute, IN, p. A228
KUDLA, Angela, MSN, R.N., Chief Nursing Officer, Select Specialty Hospital – Downriver, Wyandotte, MI, p. A341
KUDRNA, Raumi, Chief Nursing Officer, Chi St. Alexius Health Bismarck, Bismarck, ND, p. A479
KUEHLER, Sheila, R.N., Director of Nursing, Knox County Hospital, Knox City, TX, p. A633
KUEHLER, Stephen A., Administrator and Chief Executive Officer, Knox County Hospital, Knox City, TX, p. A633
KUEHN, Aaron, Administrator, Ness County Hospital District No 2, Ness City, KS, p. A255
KUEHN, David, Chief Financial Officer, Marshfield Medical Center – Ladysmith, Ladysmith, WI, p. A714
KUENNEN, Patrice, Chief Executive Officer, Gundersen Palmer Lutheran Hospital And Clinics, West Union, IA, p. A245
KUEPERS, Kathleen, Chief Executive Officer, Memorial Hospital of Lafayette County, Darlington, WI, p. A709
KUEVEN, John, President, Northeast Georgia Medical Center, Gainesville, GA, p. A164
KUHAR, Peggy A R.N., MSN, Chief Nursing Officer, University Hospitals Geauga Medical Center, Chardon, OH, p. A488
KUHLMAN, Ian, Manager Information Technology, HSHS Good Shepherd Hospital, Shelbyville, IL, p. A208
KUHN, Anita, Controller, Texas County Memorial Hospital, Houston, MO, p. A376
KUHN, Margueritte, M.D., Vice President Medical Affairs, Mymichigan Medical Center Midland, Midland, MI, p. A333
KUHN, Steve, Chief Executive Officer, River Park Hospital, Huntington, WV, p. A701
KUHNS, Jay, Vice President Human Resources, Johns Hopkins All Children's Hospital, Saint Petersburg, FL, p. A149
KUHRT, Sharon, Chief Nursing Officer, New England Rehabilitation Hospital of Portland, Portland, ME, p. A298
KUJAWA, Kallie, Chief Operating Officer, Bozeman Health Deaconess Regional Medical Center, Bozeman, MT, p. A390
KUKELHAN, Alison, Manager Human Resources, Adams Memorial Hospital, Decatur, IN, p. A215
KUKOYI, Oladip. A., M.D., Executive Director, Chief Executive Officer, Birmingham Va Medical Center, Birmingham, AL, p. A16
KULHANEK, Linda, Chief Financial Officer, Memorial Hermann Katy Hospital, Katy, TX, p. A631
KULICK, Daniel, M.D., Chief of Staff, Marlette Regional Hospital, Marlette, MI, p. A333
KULIK, Alec G, Administrator, Cleveland Clinic Children's Hospital for Rehabilitation, Cleveland, OH, p. A490
KULISZ, Michael
D.O., Chief Medical Officer, Northwestern Medicine Kishwaukee Hospital, Dekalb, IL, p. A193
D.O., Vice President, Chief Medical Officer, Northwestern Medicine Valley West Hospital, Sandwich, IL, p. A208
KULMA, Mariarose, R.N., Vice President Patient Services, UT Health Tyler, Tyler, TX, p. A659
KUMAR, Daryn J.
President, UCSF Health Saint Francis Hospital, San Francisco, CA, p. A91
President, UCSF Health St. Mary's Hospital, San Francisco, CA, p. A91
KUMAR, Deborah W, MSN, Chief Nursing Officer, Adventhealth Carrollwood, Tampa, FL, p. A151
KUMAR, Jaya, M.D., Chief Medical Officer, Medical City Mckinney, Mckinney, TX, p. A638
KUMAR, Nanda, M.D., Chief of Staff, Vibra Hospital of Northern California, Redding, CA, p. A85
KUMAR, Naveen, M.D., Physician–in–Chief, Kaiser Permanente San Rafael Medical Center, San Rafael, CA, p. A93
KUMAR, Priya, Chief Medical Officer and Vice President of Medical Affairs, Self Regional Healthcare, Greenwood, SC, p. A567
KUMAR, Raji
Managing Partner and Chief Executive Officer, Crescent Medical Center Lancaster, Lancaster, TX, p. A634
Managing Partner and Chief Executive Officer, Hill Regional Hospital, Hillsboro, TX, p. A624
KUMMER, Margaret, Chief Human Resource Officer, Citizens Medical Center, Colby, KS, p. A247
KUNDE, Dan, Chief Executive Officer, Pam Rehabilitation Hospital of Centennial Hills, Las Vegas, NV, p. A410
KUNDU, Nabarun, Chief Executive Officer, New England Rehabilitation Hospital of Portland, Portland, ME, p. A298
KUNERT, Alicia, MS, R.N., Executive Director, Conway Regional Rehabilitation Hospital, Conway, AR, p. A44
KUNKEL, Elisabeth J., M.D., Professor, Pennsylvania State College of Medicine, Pennsylvania Psychiatric Institute, Harrisburg, PA, p. A541

© 2025 AHA Guide Index of Health Care Professionals A897

Index of Health Care Professionals

KUNKEL, Tara, R.N., MSN, Chief Nursing Officer, The Meadows Psychiatric Center, Centre Hall, PA, p. A536
KUNNAPPILLY, Chester, M.D., Chief Executive Officer, San Mateo Medical Center, San Mateo, CA, p. A93
KUNZ, Alicia, Director of Acute Care, Fall River Health Services, Hot Springs, SD, p. A574
KUNZ, Donna, System Director Human Resources, Saint Luke's North Hospital – Barry Road, Kansas City, MO, p. A378
KUNZA, Mary Kay, Manager Human Resources, Mercy Hospital Lincoln, Troy, MO, p. A387
KUOPUS, Lisa, Chief Nursing Officer, Legent Orthopedic + Spine Hospital, San Antonio, TX, p. A438
KUPLEN, Carol, R.N., MSN, President, St. Luke's University Hospital – Bethlehem Campus, Bethlehem, PA, p. A535
KUPPLER, Sylvia, Chief Financial Officer, Belmont Pines Hospital, Youngstown, OH, p. A508
KURAITIS, Kestutis V, M.D., Chief of Staff, Pioneers Memorial Healthcare District, Brawley, CA, p. A58
KURCAB, Jeff
　Chief Financial Officer, Lewisgale Hospital Pulaski, Pulaski, VA, p. A681
　Chief Financial Officer, Poplar Bluff Regional Medical Center, Poplar Bluff, MO, p. A382
KURTZ, Kris, Chief Financial Officer, University of Michigan Health – West, Wyoming, MI, p. A341
KURTZ, Maria
　Director Human Resources, Lutheran Hospital of Indiana, Fort Wayne, IN, p. A216
　Director Human Resources, Orthopaedic Hospital of Lutheran Health Network, Fort Wayne, IN, p. A216
KURTZ, Thomas F Jr, Chief Operating Officer, Georgia Regional Hospital At Savannah, Savannah, GA, p. A171
KURTZ, Thomas M., President and Chief Executive Officer, Chan Soon-Shiong Medical Center At Windber, Windber, PA, p. A558
KURTZ, Tom, Vice President Information Services and Chief Information Officer, Memorial Healthcare, Owosso, MI, p. A334
KURTZIG, Joshua, Interim President, Valir Rehabilitation Hospital, Oklahoma City, OK, p. A519
KURZ, Kenneth R, M.D., Chief of Staff, Midstate Medical Center, Meriden, CT, p. A116
KUSCHE, Kristopher, Vice President and Chief Information Officer, Albany Medical Center, Albany, NY, p. A438
KUSHNER, Michael S., Senior Vice President and Chief Talent Officer, Nicklaus Children's Hospital, Miami, FL, p. A140
KUSLER, Julie, Manager Information Services, Avera St. Luke's Hospital, Aberdeen, SD, p. A572
KUSNIERZ, William J., Vice President and Chief Financial Officer, Mercy Health – Springfield Regional Medical Center, Springfield, OH, p. A504
KUTASINSKI-MARTIN, Donna, Controller, Atlantic Rehabilitation Institute, Madison, NJ, p. A423
KUTCH, John M., President and Chief Executive Officer, Trinity Health, Minot, ND, p. A482
KUTNER, Jean, M.D., Chief Medical Officer, University of Colorado Hospital, Aurora, CO, p. A103
KUVLIEV, Enio, M.D., Chief of Staff, Clark Regional Medical Center, Winchester, KY, p. A275
KUVSHINOFF, Boris, M.D., II, Chief Medical Officer, Roswell Park Comprehensive Cancer Center, Buffalo, NY, p. A440
KUYKENDALL, Jana, Chief Executive Officer, Pam Specialty Hospital of Luling, Luling, TX, p. A637
KUZEE, Ann, Executive Director Human Resources, Riverview Health, Noblesville, IN, p. A225
KVAPIL, Denise, Chief Nursing Officer, Saint Vincent Hospital, Worcester, MA, p. A320
KWIESIELEWICZ, Nancy
　Human Resources Manager, Aspirus Merrill Hospital & Clinics, Inc., Merrill, WI, p. A716
　Human Resources Manager, Marshfield Medical Center – Weston, Weston, WI, p. A725
KYHNELL, Koreen H, Vice President Human Resources, Indiana University Health Arnett Hospital, Lafayette, IN, p. A222
KYLER, Yvonne
　Director Human Resources, Texas Health Arlington Memorial Hospital, Arlington, TX, p. A598
　Director Human Resources, Texas Health Heart & Vascular Hospital Arlington, Arlington, TX, p. A598
KYRIACOU, Jonathan, Chief Operating Officer, The Mount Sinai Hospital, New York, NY, p. A453
KYWI, Alberto
　Chief Information Officer, Goleta Valley Cottage Hospital, Santa Barbara, CA, p. A94
　Chief Information Officer, Santa Barbara Cottage Hospital, Santa Barbara, CA, p. A94
KYZAR, Debbie, Interim Chief Financial Officer, Ochsner St. Mary, Morgan City, LA, p. A289

L

LA CROIX, Kent, Chief Information Officer, Schoolcraft Memorial Hospital, Manistique, MI, p. A333
LAAS, Michele, R.N., Chief Nursing Officer, Bothwell Regional Health Center, Sedalia, MO, p. A386
LABADIE, Wendy, Chief Human Resource Officer, Banner Estrella Medical Center, Phoenix, AZ, p. A35
LABAGNARA, James, M.D., Vice President Medical Affairs, St. Joseph's University Medical Center, Paterson, NJ, p. A426
LABARBERA, Sonja, President and Chief Executive Officer, Gaylord Specialty Healthcare, Wallingford, CT, p. A119
LABARCA, Laurie
　President, Ascension Via Christi Hospital On St. Teresa, Wichita, KS, p. A261
　President, Ascension Via Christi Rehabilitation Hospital, Wichita, KS, p. A261
LABELLE, Douglas, M.D., Chief Medical Officer, Up Health System – Bell, Ishpeming, MI, p. A330
LABELLE, James
　M.D., Chief Medical Officer, Scripp. Green Hospital, La Jolla, CA, p. A68
　M.D., Chief Medical Officer, Scripp. Memorial Hospital–La Jolla, La Jolla, CA, p. A68
LABER, Susan, R.N., Chief Nursing Officer, HCA Florida Pasadena Hospital, Saint Petersburg, FL, p. A149
LABONTE, Karen Y., Chief Nursing Officer, Unity Health – Jacksonville, Jacksonville, AR, p. A48
LABONTE, Robin, Leader Financial Care, York Hospital, York, ME, p. A299
LABRIOLA, Suzanne M., D.O., Chief Medical Officer, Allegheny Valley Hospital, Natrona Heights, PA, p. A547
LABRIOLA, Terri, Human Resources Officer, Sierra Nevada Memorial Hospital, Grass Valley, CA, p. A66
LACAZE, Todd, Chief Financial Officer, Riverside Community Hospital, Riverside, CA, p. A86
LACEFIELD, Gayla, Director Human Resources, Howard Memorial Hospital, Nashville, AR, p. A51
LACEFIELD, Leonard, Chief Executive Officer, Clinton Regional Hospital, Clinton, OK, p. A511
LACEY, Paul M., Chief Medical Staff, North Valley Hospital, Tonasket, WA, p. A697
LACHER, Paula A, MSN, R.N., Chief Nursing Officer, West Penn Hospital, Pittsburgh, PA, p. A552
LACHINA, Ignazio, M.D., Medical Director, Encompass Health Rehabilitation Hospital of Cypress, Houston, TX, p. A625
LACHNEY, Cheryl, Director of Nursing, Compass Behavioral Center of Alexandria, Alexandria, LA, p. A276
LACHOWSKY, John, M.D., Chief Medical Officer, Mercy Hospital Ozark, Ozark, AR, p. A52
LACKEY, Lori, Chief Financial Officer, Sabetha Community Hospital, Sabetha, KS, p. A259
LACKMAN, Vickie, Human Resource Director, Peninsula Region, St. Michael Medical Center, Silverdale, WA, p. A695
LACOT, Ivette, Director Human Resources, Hospital Menonita Guayama, Guayama, PR, p. A732
LACY, Dwight, Chief Operating Officer, Eagle View Behavioral Health, Bettendorf, IA, p. A230
LACY, Julie, Chief Financial Officer, Crete Area Medical Center, Crete, NE, p. A399
LACY, Rodney, Leader Human Resources, SSM Health Depaul Hospital – St. Louis, Bridgeton, MO, p. A372
LACY, Tyson, Chief Executive Officer and Superintendent, Lincoln Hospital, Davenport, WA, p. A688
LADAROLA, Sandra, Chief Nursing Officer, Waterbury Hospital, Waterbury, CT, p. A119
LADD, Bill, Director Information Services, Western Missouri Medical Center, Warrensburg, MO, p. A388
LADD, Robert
　M.D., Interim Chief Executive Officer, Rush County Memorial Hospital, La Crosse, KS, p. A252
　M.D., Medical Director, Rush County Memorial Hospital, La Crosse, KS, p. A252
LADLEY, Herbert D., M.D., Chief Medical Officer, Indian Path Community Hospital, Kingsport, TN, p. A585
LADNER, Warren, Senior Vice President, Chief Financial Officer, Harrisburg Medical Center, Harrisburg, IL, p. A197
LADWIG, Michael, M.D., Chief of Staff, Marion Veterans Affairs Medical Center, Marion, IL, p. A200
LAFERNEY, Jimmy, M.D., Vice President Medical Staff Affairs, Baylor Scott & White Medical Center–Frisco, Frisco, TX, p. A621
LAFEVER, Carla, President, Aurora Medical Center Grafton, Grafton, WI, p. A711

LAFFEY, Leah, R.N., Chief Executive Officer, Encompass Health Rehabilitation Hospital of Sewickley, Sewickley, PA, p. A554
LAFLAMME, Christine, R.N., MSN, Chief Nursing Officer, Ascension Seton Smithville, Smithville, TX, p. A653
LAFLEUR, Robert, Chief Executive Officer, Clearsky Rehabilitation Hospital of Rosepine, Leesville, LA, p. A287
LAFRANCOIS, Gregory, President, Northern Light Eastern Maine Medical Center, Bangor, ME, p. A295
LAGASSE, David A, Senior Vice President Fiscal Affairs, Mclean Hospital, Belmont, MA, p. A309
LAGNESE, John, M.D., Vice President Medical Affairs, UPMC St. Margaret, Pittsburgh, PA, p. A552
LAGROU, Robert, D.O., Medical Director, Henry Ford Kingswood Hospital, Ferndale, MI, p. A326
LAGUNA–KENNEDY, Joanne, Vice President and Chief Operating Officer, Cedars–Sinai Marina Del Rey Hospital, Marina Del Rey, CA, p. A76
LAHAYE, Daniel, Director of Operations, Savoy Medical Center, Mamou, LA, p. A287
LAHIRI, Anupam, Chief Executive Officer, Select Specialty Hospital – West Tennessee, Jackson, TN, p. A584
LAHOUT, Brenda, Chief Nurse Executive, Danville State Hospital, Danville, PA, p. A538
LAHTI, Mary G, Director Human Resources, Parkland Medical Center, Derry, NH, p. A414
LAIBINIS, Walter, M.D., Chief Medical Officer, UPMC Wellsboro, Wellsboro, PA, p. A557
LAIBLE, Anna, Administrator, Carle Eureka Hospital, Eureka, IL, p. A194
LAIL, Steve
　Chief Executive Officer, Calais Community Hospital, Calais, ME, p. A296
　Chief Executive Officer, Down East Community Hospital, Machias, ME, p. A298
LAIOSA, Sarah, M.D., Chief Medical Staff, Harney District Hospital, Burns, OR, p. A526
LAIRD, Alan, M.D., Chief Medical Officer, Orange City Area Health System, Orange City, IA, p. A241
LAIRD, Charles, Chief Executive Officer, St. David's South Austin Medical Center, Austin, TX, p. A600
LAIRD, Laci, Administrator, Oceans Behavioral Hospital Lufkin, Lufkin, TX, p. A637
LAIRD, Melinda, MS, R.N., Administrator and Director of Nursing, Cordell Memorial Hospital, Cordell, OK, p. A511
LAIRD, Shaw, Chief Information Officer, Musc Health Chester Medical Center, Chester, SC, p. A564
LAKE, Chandra, Associate Director, Sheridan Va Medical Center, Sheridan, WY, p. A728
LAKE, Nathan, Vice President Human Resources, Prairie Lakes Healthcare System, Watertown, SD, p. A578
LAKE, Peter M, M.D., Chief Medical Officer, Rogers Behavioral Health, Oconomowoc, WI, p. A718
LAKE, Ryan, Director Information Technology, Glencoe Regional Health, Glencoe, MN, p. A347
LAKEY, Travis, Chief Financial Officer, Mayers Memorial Hospital District, Fall River Mills, CA, p. A63
LALAS, Angela
　CPA, Chief Financial Officer, Loma Linda University Children's Hospital, Loma Linda, CA, p. A70
　CPA, Chief Financial Officer, Loma Linda University Medical Center, Loma Linda, CA, p. A70
　CPA, Chief Financial Officer, Loma Linda University Medical Center–Murrieta, Murrieta, CA, p. A79
LALIBERTE, John, Chief Information Officer, Ascension St. Vincent's Blount, Oneonta, AL, p. A23
LALICH, Michael, M.D., Area Medical Director, Kaiser Foundation Hospital – San Marcos, San Marcos, CA, p. A93
LALIOTIS, Anna, Chief Executive Officer, Mesilla Valley Hospital, Las Cruces, NM, p. A435
LALLI, Benjamin, Director of Nursing, Eagle View Behavioral Health, Bettendorf, IA, p. A230
LALLI, Kathleen, Chief Executive Officer, Kensington Hospital, Philadelphia, PA, p. A549
LALLY, Robert P Jr, Vice President Finance, Medstar Franklin Square Medical Center, Baltimore, MD, p. A302
LALUZERNE, Andrew, Chief Financial Officer, Door County Medical Center, Sturgeon Bay, WI, p. A722
LAM, Thomas, Chief Medical Officer, Garfield Medical Center, Monterey Park, CA, p. A78
LAMADELEINE, Joseph, Chief Financial Officer, Veterans Affairs Connecticut Healthcare System, West Haven, CT, p. A120
LAMANTEER, Mike, M.D., Senior Vice President Medical Affairs, Bsa Hospital, Llc, Amarillo, TX, p. A596
LAMARCHE, Maximo, M.D., Chief Medical Officer, Amg Specialty Hospital–Lafayette, Lafayette, LA, p. A285
LAMB, Andrew, M.D., Chief of Staff, Cone Health Alamance Regional Medical Center, Burlington, NC, p. A464

Index of Health Care Professionals / Lapointe

Index of Health Care Professionals

LAMB, Cindy, Director Human Resources, Logan Health Shelby, Shelby, MT, p. A395
LAMB, Deanna, Director Human Resources, Central Carolina Hospital, Sanford, NC, p. A476
LAMB, Hope, Manager Human Resources, Kimble Hospital, Junction, TX, p. A631
LAMB, Joshua, Vice President Operations, Christus Health Shreveport–Bossier, Shreveport, LA, p. A292
LAMBERT, Amand, Director Human Resources, Allen Parish Community Healthcare, Kinder, LA, p. A285
LAMBERT, Barbara, Director Healthcare Compliance, Eastern State Hospital, Williamsburg, VA, p. A685
LAMBERT, Cheryl, Chief Financial Officer, Select Specialty Hospital – Atlantic City, Atlantic City, NJ, p. A418
LAMBERT, James M., FACHE, Chief Executive Officer, Memorial Hospital And Manor, Bainbridge, GA, p. A159
LAMBERT, Karen A., FACHE, President, Advocate Good Shepherd Hospital, Barrington, IL, p. A186
LAMBERT, Lynn, Chief Financial Officer, Harnett Health System, Dunn, NC, p. A467
LAMBERT, Paul, M.D., Chief of Staff, Boise Va Medical Center, Boise, ID, p. A179
LAMBERT, Randall C., Chief Executive Officer, Select Specialty Hospital–Pensacola, Pensacola, FL, p. A147
LAMBERT, Suzanne, R.N., Regional Chief Nursing Officer and Support Services, Ascension Saint Mary – Chicago, Chicago, IL, p. A188
LAMBERT, Tony, Administrator, Cypress Grove Behavioral Health, Bastrop. LA, p. A277
LAMBRECHT, Katrina, JD, Chief Operating Officer, University Hospital, Columbia, MO, p. A374
LAMEBULL, Charlotte, Administrative Officer, Fort Belknap Service Unit, Harlem, MT, p. A393
LAMEN, Drake M., M.D., President and Chief Executive Officer, UHS Chenango Memorial Hospital, Norwich, NY, p. A454
LAMERS, Jamon
Director Finance, Aspirus Eagle River Hospital, Eagle River, WI, p. A710
Director Finance, Aspirus Rhinelander Hospital, Rhinelander, WI, p. A720
Director Finance, Aspirus Tomahawk Hospital, Tomahawk, WI, p. A723
Director Finance, Howard Young Medical Center, Inc., Woodruff, WI, p. A725
LAMEY, Mark, Commander, U. S. Air Force Regional Hospital, Elmendorf Afb, AK, p. A28
LAMEY, Rebecca, Vice President Human Resources, Mainegeneral Medical Center, Augusta, ME, p. A295
LAMLE, Sandra, Chief Financial Officer, Okeene Municipal Hospital, Okeene, OK, p. A516
LAMM, Eileen, Regional Chief Financial Officer, SSM Health Depaul Hospital – St. Louis, Bridgeton, MO, p. A372
LAMMERS, Sandra, Coordinator Human Resources and Finance, Chi Health Mercy Corning, Corning, IA, p. A233
LAMONT, Jennifer, Chief Financial Officer, West Suburban Medical Center, Oak Park, IL, p. A204
LAMOTHE, Henri, Chief Medical Officer, Olean General Hospital, Olean, NY, p. A455
LAMOUREUX, Laurie, Director of Finance, Cooley Dickinson Hospital, Northampton, MA, p. A316
LAMPE, Michael, M.D., Chief of Staff, Kossuth Regional Health Center, Algona, IA, p. A230
LAMPE, Tammy K, Director Human Resources, Edwards County Medical Center, Kinsley, KS, p. A252
LAMPLEY, Joseph, D.O., Chief of Staff, Fisher County Hospital District, Rotan, TX, p. A647
LAMPTON, Lucius, M.D., Medical Director, Beacham Memorial Hospital, Magnolia, MS, p. A365
LANCASTER, Brian, Executive Director Information Management, Nebraska Medicine – Bellevue, Bellevue, NE, p. A398
LANCASTER, Chris, President, Baylor Scott & White Medical Center – Hillcrest, Waco, TX, p. A660
LANCASTER, Penny, Controller, Cascade Medical Center, Cascade, ID, p. A180
LANCETTE, Peter, Chief Executive Officer, Fairlawn Rehabilitation Hospital, Worcester, MA, p. A320
LANCIOTTI, Kevin, Chief Financial Officer, Vice President Finance, Geisinger Medical Center, Danville, PA, p. A538
LAND, Alison G., Chief Executive Officer, Brentwood Behavioral Healthcare of Mississippi, Flowood, MS, p. A361
LAND, Susann, M.D., Chief Medical Officer, Texas Health Harris Methodist Hospital Hurst–Euless–Bedford, Bedford, TX, p. A602
LAND, Teresa Kay, R.N., Chief Nursing Officer, Vice President Nursing, Methodist Charlton Medical Center, Dallas, TX, p. A612
LANDAU, Kenneth G, CPA, Chief Financial Officer, Helen Newberry Joy Hospital & Healthcare Center, Newberry, MI, p. A334
LANDAVERDE, Helen Arteaga., Chief Executive Officer, NYC Health + Hospitals/Elmhurst, New York, NY, p. A451
LANDERS, Alice, Administrative Director Operations, Texas Health Harris Methodist Hospital Hurst–Euless–Bedford, Bedford, TX, p. A602
LANDERS, MS, RN, Kimberly Ann, FACHE, Vice President Patient Care Services, Morris Hospital & Healthcare Centers, Morris, IL, p. A202
LANDINI, Kristin
Vice President Human Resources, Advocate South Suburban Hospital, Hazel Crest, IL, p. A197
Vice President, Human Resources, Advocate Trinity Hospital, Chicago, IL, p. A188
LANDIS, Janie, Chief Financial Officer, Russell County Hospital, Russell Springs, KY, p. A274
LANDMAN, Adam, M.D., Chief Information Officer, Brigham And Women's Hospital, Boston, MA, p. A310
LANDON, Anna, Chief Nursing Officer, Mercy Hospital Washington, Washington, MO, p. A388
LANDRAU, Erika, Director Human Resources, Encompass Health Rehabilitation Hospital of Manati, Manati, PR, p. A733
LANDRENEAU, John Derrick., R.N., Chief Executive Officer, Amg Specialty Hospital–Zachary, Zachary, LA, p. A294
LANDRETH, Sandy, Director Human Resources, Seiling Municipal Hospital, Seiling, OK, p. A520
LANDRETH, Shannan, Information Systems, Livingston Hospital And Healthcare Services, Salem, KY, p. A274
LANDRUM, David, Chief Police Services, Atascadero State Hospital, Atascadero, CA, p. A56
LANDRY, Adam, Director of Information Systems, Northern Maine Medical Center, Fort Kent, ME, p. A297
LANDRY, Candy, Chief Human Resource Officer, Eastside Psychiatric Hospital, Tallahassee, FL, p. A151
LANDRY, Donna F.
Chief Operating Officer, Our Lady of Lourdes Regional Medical Center, Lafayette, LA, p. A286
Interim President, Acadiana Market, Our Lady of Lourdes Regional Medical Center, Lafayette, LA, p. A286
LANDRY, Jeanne, Vice President Human Resources, Emory Saint Joseph's Hospital, Atlanta, GA, p. A157
LANDRY, Kyle, Chief Operating Officer, St. David's South Austin Medical Center, Austin, TX, p. A600
LANDRY, Lisa G., Human Resources Director, Redington–Fairview General Hospital, Skowhegan, ME, p. A299
LANE, Andrea, Chief Financial Officer, AHS Sherman Medical Center, Sherman, TX, p. A652
LANE, Andrew, Chief Financial Officer, Medical City Fort Worth, Fort Worth, TX, p. A620
LANE, Charles A., Chief Medical Officer, Anderson Hospital, Maryville, IL, p. A201
LANE, Christopher, President and Chief Executive Officer, VHC Health, Arlington, VA, p. A673
LANE, Diron
Director Information Systems, Lewisgale Hospital Montgomery, Blacksburg, VA, p. A673
Director Information Systems, Lewisgale Hospital Pulaski, Pulaski, VA, p. A681
LANE, Kevin
D.O., Chief of Staff, Hardeman County Memorial Hospital, Quanah, TX, p. A646
Vice President Information Systems, Silver Cross Hospital, New Lenox, IL, p. A203
LANE, Kim, Chief Fiscal Service, Overton Brooks Veterans' Administration Medical Center, Shreveport, LA, p. A292
LANE, Michael, Chief Executive Officer, Sutter Coast Hospital, Crescent City, CA, p. A61
LANE, Mike, Chief Operating Officer, Twin Cities Community Hospital, Templeton, CA, p. A97
LANE, Richard, Chief Financial Officer, Mid–America Rehabilitation Hospital, Shawnee Mission, KS, p. A260
LANE, Sara, Chief Financial Officer, Acuity Specialty Hospital–Ohio Valley At Weirton, Weirton, WV, p. A705
LANE, Sonia, Interim Chief Nursing Officer, UCI Health, Orange, CA, p. A82
LANEAUX, Eleanor, Director Information Systems, UCI Health – Placentia Linda, Placentia, CA, p. A83
LANER, Richard Jr, Manager Information Systems, Miners' Colfax Medical Center, Raton, NM, p. A436
LANG, Cyndi, Director Information Services, French Hospital Medical Center, San Luis Obispo, CA, p. A93
LANG, Gary, M.D., Clinical Director, Claremore Indian Hospital, Claremore, OK, p. A511
LANG, Gordon, M.D., Chief of Staff, Trego County–Lemke Memorial Hospital, Wakeeney, KS, p. A261
LANG, Jeff, Chief Executive Officer, Coquille Valley Hospital, Coquille, OR, p. A526
LANG, John Christopher., FACHE, Chief Executive Officer, Cass Regional Medical Center, Harrisonville, MO, p. A376
LANG, Joseph, M.D., Chief of Staff, Carolinas Continuecare Hospital At Pineville, Charlotte, NC, p. A465
LANG, Nicholas P, M.D., Chief Medical Officer, UAMS Medical Center, Little Rock, AR, p. A50
LANG, Richard, Ed.D., Vice President and Chief Information Officer, Doylestown Health, Doylestown, PA, p. A538
LANG, Richard T, Chief Financial Officer, Gouverneur Hospital, Gouverneur, NY, p. A443
LANG, Robin Lynn, Vice President, Chief Information Officer, Caromont Regional Medical Center, Gastonia, NC, p. A469
LANGAN, Lynn, Chief Nursing Officer, Quillen Rehabilitation Hospital, A Joint Venture of Ballad Health And Encompass Health, Johnson City, TN, p. A585
LANGBEHN, Cody, Chief Executive Officer, Central Montana Medical Center, Lewistown, MT, p. A393
LANGBEHN, Jennifer, Medical Director, Mayo Clinic Health System In Saint James, Saint James, MN, p. A354
LANGDON, Ashlee, Controller, Yalobusha General Hospital, Water Valley, MS, p. A369
LANGE–AHMED, Suzanne, Chief Nursing Officer, Garnet Health Medical Center – Catskills, Callicoon Campus, Callicoon, NY, p. A440
LANGENBERG, Shannon, Director Human Resources, Jackson County Regional Health Center, Maquoketa, IA, p. A239
LANGENFELD, John, Medical Records Coordinator, Arizona Orthopedic Surgical Hospital, Chandler, AZ, p. A30
LANGEVIN, Seth M., Vice President and Administrator, Renown Rehabilitation Hospital, Reno, NV, p. A412
LANGFORD, Scott
Administrator, Beaver Valley Hospital, Beaver, UT, p. A664
Administrator, Milford Valley Memorial Hospital, Milford, UT, p. A665
LANGFORD, Terrie, Director Human Resources, Baylor Scott & White Surgical Hospital–Sherman, Sherman, TX, p. A652
LANGLAND, Robert, Senior Vice President and Chief Financial Officer, Stormont Vail Health, Topeka, KS, p. A260
LANGLINIAS, Amy, Chief Financial Officer, Iberia Medical Center, New Iberia, LA, p. A289
LANGLITZ, Sara, Controller, Kindred Hospital Houston Medical Center, Houston, TX, p. A626
LANGLOIS, John, Chief Executive Officer, Riverview Regional Medical Center, Gadsden, AL, p. A20
LANGLOTZ, Ronald, Vice President, Nursing and Chief Nursing Officer, Johns Hopkins Howard County Medical Center, Columbia, MD, p. A303
LANGMEAD, Paula A.
Acting Chief, Hospital Administration, Clifton T. Perkins Hospital Center, Jessup. MD, p. A305
Chief Executive Officer, Springfield Hospital Center, Sykesville, MD, p. A307
LANGSTON, Phillip W., Administrator, Lawrence County Hospital, Monticello, MS, p. A366
LANIER, Donna, R.N., Chief Nursing Officer, Delta Specialty Hospital, Memphis, TN, p. A588
LANKOWICZ, Andrew Joseph., Chief Executive Officer, Cass Lake Service Unit, U. S. Public Health Service Indian Hospital, Cass Lake, MN, p. A344
LANKOWICZ, Genevieve, M.D., Chief Medical Officer, Saint Josep. Health System, Mishawaka, IN, p. A224
LANNING, John, Chief Executive Officer, Three Crosses Regional Hospital, Las Cruces, NM, p. A435
LANNOM, Tera, Chief Nurse Executive, Harrisburg Medical Center, Harrisburg, IL, p. A197
LANNOYE, Craig, Vice President Operations, Wilson Memorial Hospital, Sidney, OH, p. A503
LANOUE, Cheryl, Chief Financial Officer, Ottawa County Health Center, Minneapolis, KS, p. A255
LANSDOWNE, Lynn
Vice President Labor Relations and Human Resources, Lehigh Valley Hospital – Hazleton, Hazleton, PA, p. A541
Vice President Labor Relations and Human Resources, Lehigh Valley Hospital – Pocono, East Stroudsburg, PA, p. A539
Vice President Labor Relations and Human Resources, Lehigh Valley Hospital – Schuylkill, Pottsville, PA, p. A553
LANTZY, William, Chief Financial Officer, Dmc Huron Valley–Sinai Hospital, Commerce Township. MI, p. A324
LANZA, Nicholas, Controller, St. Mary's General Hospital, Passaic, NJ, p. A426
LAPERLE, Linda M, Vice President Administrative Services, Androscoggin Valley Hospital, Berlin, NH, p. A414
LAPLANT, Dawn, Manager Health Information Management, Brown County Community Treatment Center, Green Bay, WI, p. A712
LAPLANTE, Lisa, Chief Administrative Officer, Evergreenhealth Monroe, Monroe, WA, p. A691
LAPOINTE, Ellen M., Chief Executive Officer, New Hampshire Hospital, Concord, NH, p. A414

© 2025 AHA Guide Index of Health Care Professionals **A899**

Index of Health Care Professionals / Lapp

LAPP, Philip. Vice President of Medical Affairs, Medical Director, Endocrinology, Rutland Regional Medical Center, Rutland, VT, p. A672
LAPRISE, Christine, Vice President of Human Resources, Bristol Health, Bristol, CT, p. A115
LAQUINTZ, Diane, President, St. Luke's Hospital–Miners Campus, Coaldale, PA, p. A537
LARA, Anne, Chief Information Officer, Christianacare, Union Hospital, Elkton, MD, p. A304
LARA, Sergio, M.D., Chief Medical Officer, Covenant Hospital Plainview, Plainview, TX, p. A644
LARABIE, Shawn, Chief Nursing Officer, San Antonio Behavioral Healthcare Hospital, San Antonio, TX, p. A650
LARAMIE, Robert, Chief Information Officer, Beverly Hospital, Beverly, MA, p. A309
LARAMIE, Wayne, Vice President Nursing, SSM Health St. Clare Hospital – Fenton, Fenton, MO, p. A375
LARCAS, John, M.D., Acting Medical Director, Choate Mental Health Center, Anna, IL, p. A185
LAREAU, Daniel, Executive Director, Operations and Information, Ascension St. Vincent Carmel Hospital, Carmel, IN, p. A213
LARIMER, Cynthia, M.D., Chief of Staff, Lake Butler Hospital, Lake Butler, FL, p. A136
LARIMORE, Rhonda
   Vice President Human Resources, UPMC Magee–Womens Hospital, Pittsburgh, PA, p. A551
   Vice President, Human Resources, UPMC Children's Hospital of Pittsburgh, Pittsburgh, PA, p. A551
LARISCY, Christopher, M.D., Chief of Staff, Davis Regional Medical Center, Statesville, NC, p. A477
LARISCY, Robin Barton, M.D., Medical Director, Mary's Harper Geriatric Psychiatry Center, Tuscaloosa, AL, p. A25
LARKIN, Kevin
   Chief Financial Officer, Ascension Saint Josep. – Elgin, Elgin, IL, p. A194
   Regional Chief Financial Officer, Ascension Mercy, Aurora, IL, p. A185
LARKIN, Kim, Chief Information Officer, Washington County Hospital, Nashville, IL, p. A203
LARKIN, Matthew, Chief Operating Officer, Portsmouth Regional Hospital, Portsmouth, NH, p. A417
LARKIN, Sarah, Chief Executive Officer, SSM Select Rehabilitation Hospital, Richmond Heights, MO, p. A382
LARKIN–SKINNER, Melissa, Chief Executive Officer, Centerstone Hospital, Bradenton, FL, p. A126
LARKINS, Mark, Interim Chief Information Officer, Saint Elizabeths Hospital, Washington, DC, p. A124
LARMER, Jennifer, R.N., Chief Clinical Officer, Lincoln Hospital, Davenport, WA, p. A688
LARNER, Cheryl, Chief Financial Officer, Sentara Careplex Hospital, Hampton, VA, p. A677
LAROSA, Vincent
   Director of Information Systems, Landmark Medical Center, Woonsocket, RI, p. A561
   Director of Information Technology Services, Rehabilitation Hospital of Rhode Island, North Smithfield, RI, p. A560
LARRALDE, Bernardo II, Chief Information Officer, Miami Jewish Health, Miami, FL, p. A140
LARRISON, Robert G., President, Carolinas Rehabilitation, Charlotte, NC, p. A465
LARSEN, Bill, Vice President Human Resources, Driscoll Children's Hospital, Corpus Christi, TX, p. A609
LARSEN, Brenda, R.N., Vice President Operations, Unitypoint Health – St. Lukes's Sioux City, Sioux City, IA, p. A243
LARSEN, Catherine M, Director Marketing, Sutter Tracy Community Hospital, Tracy, CA, p. A98
LARSEN, Donald, M.D., Chief Medical Officer, Providence Saint John's Health Center, Santa Monica, CA, p. A95
LARSEN, Kevin, Associate Vice President, Business and Ancillary Services, Uconn, John Dempsey Hospital, Farmington, CT, p. A116
LARSEN, Ryan C., FACHE, Chief Executive Officer, Community Medical Center, Inc., Falls City, NE, p. A399
LARSEN–ENGELKES, Tamera J, Chief Nursing Officer, Avera Mckennan Hospital And University Health Center, Sioux Falls, SD, p. A576
LARSON, Bill, Vice President Finance and Chief Financial Officer, Torrance Memorial Medical Center, Torrance, CA, p. A98
LARSON, Derek, Information Technology Network, Lakes Regional Healthcare. Spirit Lake, IA, p. A244
LARSON, Erick, Vice President and Chief Information Officer, Adventist Health Columbia Gorge, The Dalles, OR, p. A532
LARSON, Erick J., President and Chief Executive Officer, Huron Regional Medical Center, Huron, SD, p. A574
LARSON, Jay, Chief Information Officer, Summit Healthcare Regional Medical Center, Show Low, AZ, p. A39
LARSON, Jennifer, M.D., Chief of Staff, Blue Ridge Regional Hospital, Spruce Pine, NC, p. A476

LARSON, Jon, M.D., Medical Director, Encompass Health Rehabilitation Institute of Tucson, Tucson, AZ, p. A40
LARSON, Karla, Director Human Resources, Stevens Community Medical Center, Morris, MN, p. A351
LARSON, Kay, R.N., Chief Nursing Officer, Essentia Health St. Mary's – Detroit Lakes, Detroit Lakes, MN, p. A345
LARSON, Michael, Vice President Chief Information Officer, Mymichigan Medical Center Clare, Clare, MI, p. A324
LARSON, Mike, Chief Operating Officer, Essentia Health–St. Joseph's Medical Center, Brainerd, MN, p. A344
LARSON, Pamela, Division Director Financial Services, Hutchinson Health, Hutchinson, MN, p. A348
LARSON, Ronald, Chief Financial Officer, Jennifer Moreno Department of Veterans Affairs Medical Center, San Diego, CA, p. A88
LARSON, Ryan, CPA, Chief Financial Officer, Steele Memorial Medical Center, Salmon, ID, p. A183
LARSON, Scott C., Chief Executive Officer, Sanford Canton–Inwood Medical Center, Canton, SD, p. A572
LARSON, Shelly, Chief Financial Officer, Hot Springs County Hospital District, Thermopolis, WY, p. A728
LARSON, Steve, M.D., Director Information Systems, Mercyone Siouxland Medical Center, Sioux City, IA, p. A243
LARSON, Tammy, Chief Financial Officer, Towner County Medical Center, Cando, ND, p. A479
LARSON, Theresa, MSN, R.N., Vice President, Nursing and Clinical Services, Sanford Medical Center Fargo, Fargo, ND, p. A481
LARSON, Tracy, MS, Vice President Patient Care Services and Chief Nursing Officer, Mercyone Siouxland Medical Center, Sioux City, IA, p. A243
LARSON, Valerie, M.D., Chief Medical Officer, Avera Dells Area Hospital, Dell Rapids, SD, p. A573
LARSON, Walt, Vice President Finance, Adventist Health Tillamook, Tillamook, OR, p. A533
LARSON, Wendy, Chief Clinical Officer, KPC Promise Hospital of Phoenix, Mesa, AZ, p. A34
LASATER, Laci, R.N., Chief Nursing Officer, Christus Spohn Hospital Kleberg, Kingsville, TX, p. A632
LASCANO, Terrance, Administrative Officer, U. S. Public Health Service Indian Hospital, Cass Lake, MN, p. A344
LASECKI, Cynthia, M.D., Chief Medical Officer, Bellin Hospital, Green Bay, WI, p. A712
LASELL, Jon, Chief Executive Officer, Medical City Mental Health & Wellness Center – Frisco, Frisco, TX, p. A621
LASHBROOK, Amy, Chief Financial Officer, Community Hospital of Bremen, Bremen, IN, p. A213
LASHER, Karen, Chief Nursing Officer, Vanderbilt Stallworth Rehabilitation Hospital, Nashville, TN, p. A591
LASHLEY, Eulanie, President and Chief Executive Officer, Texas Health Hospital Mansfield, Mansfield, TX, p. A637
LASKOWSKI, Rose, R.N., Director, Caro Center, Caro, MI, p. A323
LASKY, John Jr, Vice President, Chief Human Resources Officer, Temple University Hospital, Philadelphia, PA, p. A550
LASOTA, John, Assistant Finance Officer, Clement J. Zablocki Veterans' Administration Medical Center, Milwaukee, WI, p. A717
LASSON, Scott, Chief Executive Officer, Bailey Medical Center, Owasso, OK, p. A519
LATEEF, Omar, D.O., President and Chief Executive Officer, Rush University Medical Center, Chicago, IL, p. A191
LATER, Elizabeth B., R.N., Chief Nursing Officer, St. Francis – Emory Healthcare, Columbus, GA, p. A161
LATIBEAUDIERE, Jorge, Chief Financial Officer, Covenant Health Hobbs Hospital, Hobbs, NM, p. A435
LATIMER, Timothy, Chief Financial Officer, University of Kansas Health System Great Bend Campus, Great Bend, KS, p. A250
LATIOLAIS, Ryan J, Director Information Systems, Our Lady of Lourdes Regional Medical Center, Lafayette, LA, p. A286
LATNEY, Cynthia, Chief Nursing Officer, Penrose–St. Francis Health Services, Colorado Springs, CO, p. A105
LATO, Barb, Chief Nursing Officer, Aspirus Medford Hospital & Clinics, Medford, WI, p. A715
LATTANZI, Katie, Chief Operating Officer, St. David's Round Rock Medical Center, Round Rock, TX, p. A648
LATTERNER, Renee, Director Human Resources, Adventhealth Lake Wales, Lake Wales, FL, p. A136
LATTO, Janet B., Chief Nursing Officer and Disaster Officer, Pacifica Hospital of The Valley, Los Angeles, CA, p. A74
LATULIPPE, Steve, President Medical Staff, East Liverpool City Hospital, East Liverpool, OH, p. A495
LAU, James, M.D., Area Medical Director, Kaiser Permanente Panorama City Medical Center, Los Angeles, CA, p. A73
LAUBENTHAL, Sherrie L, R.N., Chief Nursing Officer, Clarinda Regional Health Center, Clarinda, IA, p. A232
LAUDON, Heather, Director Information Technology Services, Tomah Health, Tomah, WI, p. A723

LAUDON, Larry A., Administrator, Community Behavioral Health Hospital – Bemidji, Bemidji, MN, p. A343
LAUE, Edward Arthur, M.D., Chief Medical Officer, Texas Health Hospital Mansfield, Mansfield, TX, p. A637
LAUE, Jerry, Administrator, Ascension St. Vincent Clay Hospital, Brazil, IN, p. A213
LAUER, Bill, Chief Information Officer, Morris County Hospital, Council Grove, KS, p. A248
LAUF, Michael K., President and Chief Executive Officer, Cap. Cod Hospital, Hyannis, MA, p. A314
LAUFLE, Chuck, Director of Information Services, San Luis Valley Health, Alamosa, CO, p. A103
LAUGHLIN, Jennifer, Chief Information Officer, Watertown Regional Medical Center, Watertown, WI, p. A723
LAUGHLIN, Paige, Chief Operating Officer, HCA Florida Blake Hospital, Bradenton, FL, p. A126
LAUGHLIN, Thomas, Chief Executive Officer, Encompass Health Rehabilitation Hospital of St. Augustine, St Augustine, FL, p. A150
LAUGHLIN, Warren, Vice President Human Resources, Longmont United Hospital, Longmont, CO, p. A111
LAUNIUS, Billie, Director Business Finance, Dallas County Medical Center, Fordyce, AR, p. A46
LAURENTS, W Robert, CPA, Chief Financial Officer, Madison Parish Hospital, Tallulah, LA, p. A293
LAURENZANA, John, Chief Executive Officer, Encompass Health Rehabilitation Hospital of Petersburg, Petersburg, VA, p. A681
LAURETANO, Arthur, M.D., Chief Medical Officer, Lowell General Hospital, Lowell, MA, p. A315
LAURETO, Rose Ann
   Chief Information Officer, Promedica Fostoria Community Hospital, Fostoria, OH, p. A496
   Corporate Vice President Information Resources, Promedica Bay Park Hospital, Oregon, OH, p. A502
LAURIDSEN, Amy, Director Human Resources, Northern Colorado Rehabilitation Hospital, Johnstown, CO, p. A110
LAURIHA, Fran, Chief Nursing Officer, Pomerene Hospital, Millersburg, OH, p. A500
LAURIN, George M, Interim Director Human Resources, Crisp Regional Hospital, Cordele, GA, p. A161
LAUTER, Keith A.
   Chief Financial Officer, Franciscan Health Carmel, Carmel, IN, p. A213
   Regional Chief Financial Officer, Franciscan Health Indianapolis, Indianapolis, IN, p. A219
   Vice President Finance, Franciscan Health Crawfordsville, Crawfordsville, IN, p. A214
LAUTEREN, Mark, Chief Information Officer, USA Health University Hospital, Mobile, AL, p. A22
LAUTNER, Marty, Vice President Finance and Chief Financial Officer, Encompass Health Cardinal Hill Rehabilitation Hospital, Lexington, KY, p. A268
LAUTT, Julie, CPA, Vice President, Operational Finance, Avera Mckennan Hospital And University Health Center, Sioux Falls, SD, p. A576
LAUVE, Lisa R., R.N., Regional Chief Nursing Executive and Chief Operating Officer, Christus St. Frances Cabrini Hospital, Alexandria, LA, p. A276
LAUVER, David, M.D., Chief Division Hospital Based Care, Central Maine Medical Center, Lewiston, ME, p. A297
LAVELLE, John P., M.D., Chief Medical Officer, Parkview Hospital, Wheeler, TX, p. A662
LAVENDER, Darrell Lee., Chief Executive Officer, Riverside Medical Center, Franklinton, LA, p. A282
LAVENDER, John Kenneth, Chief Information Officer, Lincoln County Health System, Fayetteville, TN, p. A583
LAVIGNETTE, Brooke, Director of Nursing, Sycamore Springs, Lafayette, IN, p. A222
LAVIOLETTE, Judy
   M.D., Chief Medical Officer, Texas Health Harris Methodist Hospital Azle, Azle, TX, p. A601
   M.D., Chief Medical Officer, Texas Health Harris Methodist Hospital Cleburne, Cleburne, TX, p. A607
LAVIOLETTE, Steph, Chief Executive Officer, Pam Health Specialty Hospital of Denver, Denver, CO, p. A106
LAVIS, Brittany, Chief Executive Officer, Dmc Harper University Hospital, Detroit, MI, p. A325
LAVOIE, Brad, Chief Financial Officer, Coastal Harbor Treatment Center, Savannah, GA, p. A171
LAW, Charles, Ph.D., Facility Director, Catawba Hospital, Catawba, VA, p. A674
LAW, Johnny, Area Information Officer, Kaiser Permanente Oakland Medical Center, Oakland, CA, p. A81
LAWHORN, David, M.D., Chief Medical Officer, Shoshone Medical Center, Kellogg, ID, p. A181
LAWHORN, Renee, Director Medical Records, UT Health Carthage, Carthage, TX, p. A607
LAWHORNE, Thomas, Chief Financial Officer, HCA Florida Bayonet Point Hospital, Hudson, FL, p. A134

Index of Health Care Professionals / Lee

Index of Health Care Professionals

LAWLER, Anne, Director Human Resources, North Mississipp. Medical Center–Hamilton, Hamilton, AL, p. A20
LAWLER, Kay, Business Office Manager, North Mississipp. Medical Center–West Point, West Point, MS, p. A370
LAWLER, Patrick, Chief Executive Officer, Youth Villages Inner Harbour Campus, Douglasville, GA, p. A163
LAWLESS, JoBeth, Chief Nursing Officer, Nursing Services and Director Emergency Management Services, Lucas County Health Center, Chariton, IA, p. A232
LAWLESS, John, Chief Financial Officer, Oakdale Community Hospital, Oakdale, LA, p. A290
LAWLESS, Rosalie, Director Human Resources, Fairlawn Rehabilitation Hospital, Worcester, MA, p. A320
LAWONN, Kenneth
Senior Vice President and Chief Information Officer, Chi Health Mercy Corning, Corning, IA, p. A233
Senior Vice President and Chief Information Officer, Chi Health Schuyler, Schuyler, NE, p. A405
Senior Vice President and Chief Information Officer, Sharp Grossmont Hospital, La Mesa, CA, p. A68
Senior Vice President and Chief Information Officer, Sharp Memorial Hospital, San Diego, CA, p. A89
Senior Vice President Information Systems, Sharp Mesa Vista Hospital, San Diego, CA, p. A90
LAWRENCE, Brian, Chief Executive Officer, Coffeyville Regional Medical Center, Coffeyville, KS, p. A247
LAWRENCE, Dana, Controller, West Tennessee Healthcare Bolivar Hospital, Bolivar, TN, p. A579
LAWRENCE, Earline, Chief Operating Officer, Garfield County Health Center, Jordan, MT, p. A393
LAWRENCE, Glenda, R.N., Chief Nursing Officer, Red River Hospital, Llc, Wichita Falls, TX, p. A662
LAWRENCE, Jonathan I, President and Chief Executive Officer, Arnot Ogden Medical Center, Elmira, NY, p. A442
LAWRENCE, Jonathan I., President and Chief Executive Officer, Arnot Ogden Medical Center, Elmira, NY, p. A442
LAWRENCE, Kelsey, Manager Information Technology, Union County General Hospital, Clayton, NM, p. A434
LAWRENCE, Mark, Director Information Systems, Saint Francis Hospital–Bartlett, Bartlett, TN, p. A579
LAWRENCE, Michael, Chief Financial Officer, UChicago Medicine Ingalls Memorial, Harvey, IL, p. A197
LAWRENCE, Paige, Assistant Administrator, University of Mississipp. Medical Center Holmes County, Lexington, MS, p. A365
LAWRENCE, Richard H., Administrator, Behavioral Health of Rocky Top. Rocky Top. TN, p. A592
LAWRENCE, Stephanie
Chief Financial Officer, Kentfield Hospital, Kentfield, CA, p. A68
Chief Financial Officer, Vibra Specialty Hospital of Portland, Portland, OR, p. A531
LAWRENCE, Tiffany, President and Chief Executive Officer, Sanford Medical Center Fargo, Fargo, ND, p. A481
LAWRENSON, Victoria
Chief Operating Officer, Bullock County Hospital, Union Springs, AL, p. A25
Chief Operating Officer, Crenshaw Community Hospital, Luverne, AL, p. A21
LAWRIMORE, Luke, Chief Executive Officer, Altru Rehabilitation Hospital, Grand Forks, ND, p. A481
LAWSON, Andy, Chief Human Resource Officer, Lds Hospital, Salt Lake City, UT, p. A669
LAWSON, Beth
Chief Executive Officer, Sunrise Canyon Hospital, Lubbock, TX, p. A636
Chief Nursing Officer, Union Medical Center, Union, SC, p. A571
LAWSON, Chad, Chief Information Officer, St. Anthony Regional Hospital, Carroll, IA, p. A231
LAWSON, Crystal, Director Human Resource, Specialists Hospital Shreveport, Shreveport, LA, p. A293
LAWSON, David C., Senior Vice President Human Resources, St. Clare Hospital, Lakewood, WA, p. A691
LAWSON, Eric, Chief Executive Officer, HCA Florida North Florida Hospital, Gainesville, FL, p. A132
LAWSON, Jessica, Director of Nursing, Greenwood Regional Rehabilitation Hospital, Greenwood, SC, p. A567
LAWSON, Judy, Director Information Services, Norton Community Hospital, Norton, VA, p. A680
LAWSON, Linda B., Chief Nursing Officer, The Hospitals of Providence Transmountain Campus – Tenet Healthcare, El Paso, TX, p. A617
LAWSON, Linda Kathryn, Chief Nursing Officer, Huntsville Memorial Hospital, Huntsville, TX, p. A629
LAWSON, Michael, President, Ohiohealth Grant Medical Center, Columbus, OH, p. A492
LAWSON, Penny, Human Resource Director, Quillen Rehabilitation Hospital, A Joint Venture of Ballad Health And Encompass Health, Johnson City, TN, p. A585
LAWSON, Sandra K., Interim Director Fiscal Services, Shriners Hospitals for Children–St. Louis, Saint Louis, MO, p. A385
LAWSON, T. Douglas, Ph.D., FACHE, Chief Executive Officer, Chi St Luke's Health – Baylor St Luke's Medical Center, Houston, TX, p. A625
LAY, A K, M.D., Jr, Chief Medical Officer, Jasper General Hospital, Bay Springs, MS, p. A359
LAYUGAN, Melvin, Director Human Resources, Horizon Specialty Hospital, Las Vegas, NV, p. A410
LAZROFF, Gary, Vice President Human Resources, University Hospitals St. John Medical Center, Westlake, OH, p. A507
LAZURE, Julie L., R.N., MSN, Vice President, Nurse Executive, Nebraska Medicine – Bellevue, Bellevue, NE, p. A398
LAZZARO, Frank A. III, Chief Human Resources Officer, Phelp. Health, Rolla, MO, p. A382
LE, Emily, Director Information Technology and Services, Woman's Hospital of Texas, Houston, TX, p. A629
LE, Jennifer, Chief Financial Officer, Southern Hills Hospital And Medical Center, Las Vegas, NV, p. A410
LE, Tuan, Chief Executive Officer, Select Specialty Hospital – San Diego, San Diego, CA, p. A89
LE GLOAHEC, Victor, Chief Operating Officer, Doctors Hospital of Laredo, Laredo, TX, p. A634
LEA, Lindsay, Chief Nursing Officer, Upper Connecticut Valley Hospital, Colebrook, NH, p. A414
LEA, Rich, Vice President Operations, Cleveland Clinic Euclid Hospital, Euclid, OH, p. A495
LEACH, Dana, Director Human Resources, SSM Health St. Anthony Hospital – Midwest, Midwest City, OK, p. A515
LEACH, Deonca, Director, Human Resources, Carolinas Rehabilitation, Charlotte, NC, p. A465
LEACH, Ryan, Chief Information Officer, HSHS St. John's Hospital, Springfield, IL, p. A209
LEACH, Todd, Vice President and Chief Information Officer, University of Texas Medical Branch, Galveston, TX, p. A621
LEACH, Travis, FACHE, Chief Executive Officer, West Valley Medical Center, Caldwell, ID, p. A180
LEADBETTER, Dan, Information Technology Systems Site Lead, Chi Lakewood Health, Baudette, MN, p. A343
LEADBETTER, Raymond J. Jr, Revenue Cycle Consultant, Appling Healthcare System, Baxley, GA, p. A159
LEAHY, Mary
M.D., Chief Executive Officer, Bon Secours Community Hospital, Port Jervis, NY, p. A456
M.D., Chief Executive Officer, Good Samaritan Regional Medical Center, Suffern, NY, p. A459
M.D., Chief Executive Officer, St. Anthony Community Hospital, Warwick, NY, p. A461
LEAHY, Mary P, Regional Vice President, Chief Human Resources Officer, Providence St. Josep. Hospital Orange, Orange, CA, p. A81
LEAHY, Rosanne, Vice President Nursing Services, Carolinaeast Health System, New Bern, NC, p. A473
LEAKE, Neta F, Administrative Assistant Human Resources, West Feliciana Hospital, Saint Francisville, LA, p. A292
LEAKEY, Kim, R.N., Chief Nursing Officer, Lafayette Regional Health Center, Lexington, MO, p. A379
LEAL, Carlos, Director Information Technology, Valley Regional Medical Center, Brownsville, TX, p. A605
LEAL, Jorge E., FACHE, Chief Executive Officer, Laredo Medical Center, Laredo, TX, p. A634
LEAL, Josep. M, M.D., Jr, Chief of Staff, Glendive Medical Center, Glendive, MT, p. A392
LEAMING, James, M.D., Interim Vice President Medical Affairs and Staff Development, Penn State Health Hampden Medical Center, Enola, PA, p. A539
LEAMON, Jim, Chief Financial Officer, HCA Florida Jfk Hospital, Atlantis, FL, p. A125
LEAR, Jarad, Interim Director of Information Services, Deaconess Gibson Hospital, Princeton, IN, p. A226
LEAR, Richard
Director Information Systems, St. David's Medical Center, Austin, TX, p. A600
Director Information Systems, St. David's South Austin Medical Center, Austin, TX, p. A600
LEARSON, Jerome, Manager Information Technology and Chief Security Officer, Palo Verde Hospital, Blythe, CA, p. A58
LEARY, Edward B.
Chief Executive Officer, Vibra Hospital of Southeastern Massachusetts, New Bedford, MA, p. A316
Chief Executive Officer, Vibra Hospital of Western Massachusetts–Central Campus, Rochdale, MA, p. A317
LEASE, Faye, Chief Nursing Officer, Reeves Regional Health, Pecos, TX, p. A643
LEASE–HOMEYER, Cheryl, Lead Information Technology Business Partner, Mercy Hospital Carthage, Carthage, MO, p. A373
LEASURE, Sandie, Senior Vice President Human Resources, Ohiohealth O'Bleness Hospital, Athens, OH, p. A485
LEAVITT, Jared, Chief Operating Officer, Kern Medical, Bakersfield, CA, p. A57
LEBARON, Kenneth M., R.N., Administrator, Ochsner Lafayette General Medical Center, Lafayette, LA, p. A285
LEBEAU, Michelle
President, The University of Vermont Health Network – Alice Hyde Medical Center, Malone, NY, p. A445
President and Chief Operating Officer, The University of Vermont Health Network–Champlain Valley Physicians Hospital, Plattsburgh, NY, p. A456
LEBER, Corey
R.N., Associate Vice President of Nursing, Promedica Toledo Hospital, Toledo, OH, p. A505
R.N., Associate Vice President Operations, Promedica Memorial Hospital, Fremont, OH, p. A496
LEBER, Ian, M.D., Chief Medical Officer, Hackensack Meridian Health Bayshore Community Hospital, Holmdel, NJ, p. A422
LEBLANC, Fernis
Chief Executive Officer, Leonard J. Chabert Medical Center, Houma, LA, p. A283
Chief Executive Officer, Bayou Region, Ochsner St. Anne General Hospital, Raceland, LA, p. A291
LEBLANC, Karen, Director, Applications, Samaritan Hospital – Main Campus, Troy, NY, p. A460
LEBLANC, Terri
Chief Executive and Nursing Officer, Legent Orthopedic + Spine Hospital, San Antonio, TX, p. A650
Chief Executive and Nursing Officer, Legent Orthopedic Hospital Carrollton, Carrollton, TX, p. A606
LEBOWITZ, Howard, M.D., Chief Medical Officer, Specialty Hospital of Central Jersey, Lakewood, NJ, p. A422
LEBRON, Juan, M.D., Medical Director, Sea Pines Rehabilitation Hospital, An Affiliate of Encompass Health, Melbourne, FL, p. A139
LEBRON, Sonia M, Human Resources Specialist, Industrial Hospital, San Juan, PR, p. A735
LECHICH, Anthony, M.D., Chief Medical Officer, Terence Cardinal Cooke Health Care Center, New York, NY, p. A453
LECHUGA, Mario, Director Human Resources, Turquoise Lodge Hospital, Albuquerque, NM, p. A433
LECKELT, Mitchell D., FACHE, Chief Executive Officer, Up Health System – Bell, Ishpeming, MI, p. A330
LECKER, Marijo, Vice President, Sentara Martha Jefferson Hospital, Charlottesville, VA, p. A674
LECKEY, Scott, Chief Financial Officer, Banner Desert Medical Center, Mesa, AZ, p. A33
LECONTE, Georges, Chief Executive Officer, NYC Health + Hospitals/Harlem, New York, NY, p. A451
LEDBETTER, Joy, Regional Chief Human Resources Officer, Carle Health Methodist Hospital, Peoria, IL, p. A205
LEDBETTER, Thomas Glenn, M.D., Chief Medical Officer, Baylor Scott & White Medical Center–Waxahachie, Waxahachie, TX, p. A660
LEDDEN, Edwin L, Assistant Administrator and Director Human Resources, Henry County Medical Center, Paris, TN, p. A592
LEDELL, Michelle
Director Human Resource, M Health Fairview Ridges Hospital, Burnsville, MN, p. A344
Director Human Resources, M Health Fairview Southdale Hospital, Edina, MN, p. A346
LEDERMAN, Joel, Director Information Systems, Promedica Coldwater Regional Hospital, Coldwater, MI, p. A324
LEDFORD, Keith, M.D., Chief of Staff, Scenic Mountain Medical Center, Big Spring, TX, p. A603
LEDUA, Akapusi, Chief Executive Officer, Lyndon B. Johnson Tropical Medical Center, Pago Pago, AMERICAN SAMOA, p. A730
LEE, Amy
Chief Operating Officer, Nantucket Cottage Hospital, Nantucket, MA, p. A316
President, Nantucket Cottage Hospital, Nantucket, MA, p. A316
LEE, Brett
Chief Administrative Officer, Northwest Medical Center Sahuarita, Sahuarita, AZ, p. A38
Chief Executive Officer, Northwest Medical Center Sahuarita, Sahuarita, AZ, p. A38
LEE, Brett D., President, Texas Health Hospital Frisco, Frisco, TX, p. A621
LEE, Byong, Chief Information Officer, Limestone Medical Center, Groesbeck, TX, p. A623
LEE, Cheryl, Human Resources Director, North Alabama Medical Center, Florence, AL, p. A19
LEE, Cheryl D, R.N., MSN, Vice President of Patient Care Services and Chief Nursing Officer, University of Maryland

Index of Health Care Professionals

Index of Health Care Professionals / Lee

Rehabilitation & Orthopaedic Institute, Baltimore, MD, p. A302
LEE, Clare, Chief Operating Officer, Mercy General Hospital, Sacramento, CA, p. A87
LEE, David, Chief Executive Officer, Otto Kaiser Memorial Hospital, Kenedy, TX, p. A632
LEE, Debra, Chief Medical Officer, Sentara Northern Virginia Medical Center, Woodbridge, VA, p. A685
LEE, Dennis, Vice President and Chief Information Officer, Cabell Huntington Hospital, Huntington, WV, p. A701
LEE, Eric A., President and Chief Executive Officer, Jennie Stuart Medical Center, Hopkinsville, KY, p. A267
LEE, James A. Jr, Administrator, Midcoast Medical Center – Bellville, Bellville, TX, p. A603
LEE, James R, M.D., Chief of Staff, Hamilton General Hospital, Hamilton, TX, p. A623
LEE, Janelle
Vice President Human Resources, Miami County Medical Center, Paola, KS, p. A257
Vice President Human Resources, Olathe Medical Center, Olathe, KS, p. A256
LEE, Jenny, Human Resources Generalist, Essentia Health–Graceville, Graceville, MN, p. A347
LEE, John, M.D., Chief Information Officer, AHN Wexford Hospital, Wexford, PA, p. A557
LEE, John Paul, M.D., Chief of Staff, Lackey Memorial Hospital, Forest, MS, p. A362
LEE, Karen, Director Human Resources, Gallup Indian Medical Center, Gallup. NM, p. A434
LEE, Kendra, JD, Chief Operating Officer, Bedford Veterans Affairs Medical Center, Edith Nourse Rogers Memorial Veterans Hospital, Bedford, MA, p. A309
LEE, Kenneth, Division Chair, Human Resource Advisory, Mayo Clinic Health System In Eau Claire, Eau Claire, WI, p. A710
LEE, Kim, Chief Operating Officer, Faith Community Hospital, Jacksboro, TX, p. A630
LEE, Kristina, Director Human Resources, Chi St. Josep. Health Grimes Hospital, Navasota, TX, p. A641
LEE, Kwon, Chief Information Officer, Pennsylvania Hospital, Philadelphia, PA, p. A549
LEE, Loretta, Acting Chief Nursing Officer, Chi St Luke's Health – Baylor St Luke's Medical Center, Houston, TX, p. A625
LEE, Michael D, Chief Human Resources Officer, Adirondack Health, Saranac Lake, NY, p. A458
LEE, Mihi, Chief Financial Officer, Mission Community Hospital, Los Angeles, CA, p. A74
LEE, Mike, R.N., Chief Nursing Officer, Matagorda Regional Medical Center, Bay City, TX, p. A601
LEE, Min Y., PharmD, Chief Operating Officer, UVA Health University Medical Center, Charlottesville, VA, p. A674
LEE, Nancy, R.N., MSN, Vice President Patient Care Services and Chief Nursing Officer, Stanford Health Care, Palo Alto, CA, p. A82
LEE, Nathan W, Chief Executive Officer, Mary Breckinridge Arh Hospital, Hyden, KY, p. A267
LEE, Randy, M.D., Senior Vice President Medical Affairs, Community Hospital South, Indianapolis, IN, p. A219
LEE, Reginald, Chief Executive Officer, Bridgepoint Continuing Care Hospital – National Harborside, Washington, DC, p. A123
LEE, Ryan D., FACHE, Chief Executive Officer, Coastal Carolina Hospital, Hardeeville, SC, p. A568
LEE, S. Kwon, M.D., Chief of Staff, Vibra Hospital of Sacramento, Folsom. CA, p. A63
LEE, Stacey
CPA, JD, Vice President and Administrator, Ridgeview Le Sueur Medical Center, Le Sueur, MN, p. A348
CPA, JD, Vice President/Administrator, Ridgeview Sibley Medical Center, Arlington, MN, p. A342
LEE, Terri
Chief Information Officer, Higgins General Hospital, Bremen, GA, p. A159
Chief Information Officer, Tanner Medical Center–Villa Rica, Villa Rica, GA, p. A173
Executive Director, Jim Taliaferro Community Mental Health Center, Lawton, OK, p. A514
LEE, Thomas G, Chief Financial Officer, Medicine Lodge Memorial Hospital, Medicine Lodge, KS, p. A254
LEE, Twilla
Chief Executive Officer, Bob Wilson Memorial Grant County Hospital, Ulysses, KS, p. A261
Chief Executive Officer, St. Catherine Hospital – Dodge City, Dodge City, KS, p. A248
Chief Executive Officer, St. Catherine Hospital, Garden City, KS, p. A249
LEE, Ulondia D., R.N., MSN, Chief Nursing OFficer, Medical City Fort Worth, Fort Worth, TX, p. A620
LEE, W. Bryan, President, Bon Secours Richmond Community Hospital, Richmond, VA, p. A682
LEE, W. Bryan., President, Bon Secours St. Mary's Hospital, Richmond, VA, p. A682
LEE, Wendy, Chief Nursing Officer, Regional Rehabilitation Hospital, Phenix City, AL, p. A24
LEE, William H., Chief Executive Officer, Evans Memorial Hospital, Claxton, GA, p. A160
LEEGSTRA, Ruurd, Chief Financial Officer, Silver Hill Hospital, New Canaan, CT, p. A117
LEEK, Lynn, Executive Vice President of Finance and Chief Financial Officer, Wabash General Hospital, Mount Carmel, IL, p. A202
LEEPER, Doug, Chief Information Officer, Kaweah Health Medical Center, Visalia, CA, p. A100
LEEPER, Kevin Alan., Chief Executive Officer, Morris County Hospital, Council Grove, KS, p. A248
LEESMAN, Keenan, Director Information Systems, Lincoln Memorial Hospital, Lincoln, IL, p. A200
LEFEVRE, Denise, Chief Information Officer, Oroville Hospital, Oroville, CA, p. A82
LEFF, Marc, Vice President Human Resources, St. John's Riverside Hospital, Yonkers, NY, p. A462
LEFFLER, Stephen, M.D., President and Chief Operating Officer, University of Vermont Medical Center, Burlington, VT, p. A671
LEFKOW, Frances, Director Human Resources, La Rabida Children's Hospital, Chicago, IL, p. A190
LEFTERIS, Chad T.
Chief Executive Officer, UCI Health, Orange, CA, p. A82
Chief Operating Officer, UCI Health, Orange, CA, p. A82
LEFTON, Ruth, Chief Operating Officer, Einstein Medical Center Philadelphia, Philadelphia, PA, p. A548
LEFTWICH, Hal W., FACHE, Chief Executive Officer, Big South Fork Medical Center, Oneida, TN, p. A592
LEGASPI, Johnson, Director Information Systems, Alhambra Hospital Medical Center, Alhambra, CA, p. A55
LEGAY, Jeff, Chief Financial Officer, UNC Health Chatham, Siler City, NC, p. A476
LEGE, Christopher, Chief Executive Officer, Touro Infirmary, New Orleans, LA, p. A290
LEGEND, Rachel, Chief Executive Officer, Arbour–Fuller Hospital, Attleboro, MA, p. A309
LEGER, Bernard, Chief Executive Officer, Detar Healthcare System, Victoria, TX, p. A660
LEGER, Lynn, Director Information Systems, Ridgeview Institute – Smyrna, Smyrna, GA, p. A171
LEGG, Alyce, Vice President Human Resources, University Hospitals Samaritan Medical Center, Ashland, OH, p. A485
LEGG, Debra Lynn, Associate Director Patient Care Services and Nurse Executive, Beckley Veterans Affairs Medical Center, Beckley, WV, p. A699
LEGGETT, Sandra, Chief Operating Officer, Amberwell Health, Atchison, KS, p. A246
LEGGETT, Sandy, R.N., MSN, Chief Operations Officer, Community Medical Center, Missoula, MT, p. A394
LEGGIO, Benjamin, M.D., Chief Medical Officer, De Soto Regional Health System, Mansfield, LA, p. A288
LEGLEITER, Brenda, Director Quality and Human Resources, Rush County Memorial Hospital, La Crosse, KS, p. A252
LEGRAND, Kila, Executive Director, Sanford Aberdeen Medical Center, Aberdeen, SD, p. A572
LEHMAN, Lindsey, Associate Administrator, Hospital Operations, Mayo Clinic Hospital – Rochester, Rochester, MN, p. A353
LEHMAN, Ronda
PharmD, Chief Operating Officer, SRPS, Mercy Health – St. Rita's Medical Center, Lima, OH, p. A498
PharmD, President, Mercy Health – St. Rita's Medical Center, Lima, OH, p. A498
LEHMAN, Sandi, Chief Financial Officer, Humboldt General Hospital, Winnemucca, NV, p. A413
LEHMAN, Travis, M.D., Medical Director, Wilbarger General Hospital, Vernon, TX, p. A659
LEHN, Matthew, Chief Executive Officer, Ohiohealth Rehabilitation Hospital, Columbus, OH, p. A492
LEHN, Toby, Director of Nurses, Concho County Hospital, Eden, TX, p. A615
LEHNHOF–WATTS, Laurie, Administrator and Chief Nursing Officer, UT Health East Texas Rehabilitation Hospital, Tyler, TX, p. A659
LEIBMAN, Maurice, M.D., Chief Medical Officer, Memorial Hermann Greater Heights Hospital, Houston, TX, p. A627
LEIF, Sue, R.N., Director Human Resources, Annie Jeffrey Memorial County Health Center, Osceola, NE, p. A405
LEIGHTON, Martha, Senior Vice President and Chief Nursing Officer, Elliot Hospital, Manchester, NH, p. A416
LEIGHTON, Richard, Financial Application Analyst, Unity Physicians Hospital, Mishawaka, IN, p. A224
LEINEN, Rick J, Chief Financial Officer, Montgomery County Memorial Hospital, Red Oak, IA, p. A242
LEININGER, Bethany, Manager Human Resource, Hillcrest Hospital Cushing, Cushing, OK, p. A511
LEISHER, George
Jr, Chief Human Resources Officer, Antelop. Valley Medical Center, Lancaster, CA, p. A69
Jr, Vice President Human Resources, Cha Hollywood Presbyterian Medical Center, Los Angeles, CA, p. A72
LEISHER, Karla, Business Office Manager, Beaver County Memorial Hospital, Beaver, OK, p. A510
LEISING, Elizabeth
Chief Nursing Officer and Vice President Patient Services, Margaret Mary Health, Batesville, IN, p. A212
Interim Chief Executive Officer and President, Margaret Mary Health, Batesville, IN, p. A212
LEIST, Frank, Human Resources Manager, Piedmont Mountainside Hospital, Jasper, GA, p. A165
LEITERMAN, Gretchen, Chief Operating Officer, SSM Health Saint Louis University Hospital, Saint Louis, MO, p. A384
LEITNER, Jeff, Director, Facilities Management, Encompass Health Rehabilitation Hospital of Cumming, Cumming, GA, p. A162
LEITNER, Mark
FACHE, Administrator, UT Health Henderson, Henderson, TX, p. A624
FACHE, Chief Executive Officer, UT Health Carthage, Carthage, TX, p. A607
LEJA, Loretta, M.D., Chief of Staff, Mackinac Straits Health System, Inc., Saint Ignace, MI, p. A337
LEJEUNE, Michael, Chief Executive Officer, Acadia–St. Landry Hospital, Church Point, LA, p. A280
LEJSEK, Shari, Administrator, Patients' Hospital of Redding, Redding, CA, p. A85
LELAND, Joni, Director Human Resources, Gonzales Healthcare Systems, Gonzales, TX, p. A622
LELAND, Rebecca, Executive Director, Rockland Children's Psychiatric Center, Orangeburg, NY, p. A455
LEM, Alan
Vice President Finance, M Health Fairview Ridges Hospital, Burnsville, MN, p. A344
Vice President Finance, M Health Fairview Southdale Hospital, Edina, MN, p. A346
LEMAIRE, Josep. M
Executive Vice President, Hackensack Meridian Health Southern Ocean Medical Center, Manahawkin, NJ, p. A423
Executive Vice President Finance, Hackensack Meridian Health Riverview Medical Center, Red Bank, NJ, p. A428
LEMASTERS, Ryan, Chief Operating Officer, Timpanogos Regional Hospital, Orem, UT, p. A667
LEMAY, Catherine, Vice President Finance, Millinocket Regional Hospital, Millinocket, ME, p. A298
LEMAY, Robert Raymond, R.N., Chief Nursing Officer, The Physicians Centre Hospital, Bryan, TX, p. A605
LEMBCKE, Brad, M.D., Vice President Medical Staff Affairs, Baylor University Medical Center, Dallas, TX, p. A610
LEMBCKE, Bradley T., M.D., President, Chi St Luke's Health – Baylor St Luke's Medical Center, Houston, TX, p. A625
LEMEL, Mark, Chief of Staff, Transylvania Regional Hospital, Brevard, NC, p. A464
LEMELLE, Natalie, Chief Financial Officer, Vermilion Behavioral Health Systems – North Campus, Lafayette, LA, p. A286
LEMIEUX, Harry, Chief Information Officer, Umass Memorial Health – Harrington, Southbridge, MA, p. A318
LEMKE, Michelle, Administrator Human Resources and Support Services, Ridgecrest Regional Hospital, Ridgecrest, CA, p. A86
LEMLE, Trent, Chief Financial Officer, Adena Fayette Medical Center, Washington Court House, OH, p. A506
LEMMER, Donn J, Chief Financial Officer and Chief Operating Officer, Munson Healthcare Manistee Hospital, Manistee, MI, p. A332
LEMMERMAN, Deborah, Chief People Officer, Hebrew Rehabilitation Center, Roslindale, MA, p. A317
LEMMING, Harry
Chief Executive Officer, Glen Oaks Hospital, Greenville, TX, p. A623
Interim Chief Executive Officer, Texoma Medical Center, Denison, TX, p. A613
LEMMONS, Joe, D.O., Chief of Staff, Lehigh Regional Medical Center, Lehigh Acres, FL, p. A137
LEMOINE, Kirk, Chief Executive Officer, Bienville Medical Center, Arcadia, LA, p. A277
LEMON, Rita, Director Human Resources, Avera Queen of Peace Hospital, Mitchell, SD, p. A575
LEMONTE, David
Chief Executive Officer, HCA Florida Aventura Hospital, Aventura, FL, p. A125
Vice President and Chief Operating Officer, Christus Spohn Hospital Kleberg, Kingsville, TX, p. A632

A902 Index of Health Care Professionals

Index of Health Care Professionals

Index of Health Care Professionals / Lewis

LENA, Ela C., President and Chief Executive Officer, Southern Regional Medical Center, Riverdale, GA, p. A170
LENAHAN, Kevin
Director Corporate Accounting, Budgets, Grants and Reimbursements, Newton Medical Center, Newton, NJ, p. A426
Vice President Finance and Chief Financial Officer, Overlook Medical Center, Summit, NJ, p. A428
LENAMOND, Kevin, Information Management Service Line Executive, Michael E. Debakey Department of Veterans Affairs Medical Center, Houston, TX, p. A627
LENANE, Naomi, Chief Information Officer, Dana–Farber Cancer Institute, Boston, MA, p. A310
LENARZ, Sandy, Chief Nursing Officer, Grand Itasca Clinic And Hospital, Grand Rapids, MN, p. A347
LENDARIS, Antonia, Chief Nursing Operations Officer, Chinese Hospital, San Francisco, CA, p. A90
LENDARIS, Nia, MS, R.N., Regional Vice President Patient Care, Adventist Health St. Helena, Saint Helena, CA, p. A88
LENFANT, Rodney, Chief Financial Officer, Oakbend Medical Center, Richmond, TX, p. A646
LENGFELDER, Valerie, M.D., Chief of Staff, Powell Valley Health Care, Powell, WY, p. A728
LENIOR, Frank, Vice President Human Resources, St. Dominic–Jackson Memorial Hospital, Jackson, MS, p. A364
LENKO, Paul, Section Head Information Technology, Mayo Clinic Hospital In Arizona, Phoenix, AZ, p. A36
LENNON, Colin, Chief Financial Officer, Richard L. Roudebush Veterans Affairs Medical Center, Indianapolis, IN, p. A220
LENNON, Roslyn J, R.N., MS, Chief Nursing Officer, West Suburban Medical Center, Oak Park, IL, p. A204
LENTENBRINK, Laura, Vice President, Human Resources, Ascension Borgess Hospital, Kalamazoo, MI, p. A331
LENZA, Robert, Chief Executive Officer, Methodist Hospital, San Antonio, TX, p. A650
LEON, Daniel, Chief Financial Officer, Sherman Oaks Hospital, Los Angeles, CA, p. A75
LEON, Luis, Chief Operating Officer, Desert Valley Hospital, Victorville, CA, p. A100
LEONARD, Barry I, Vice President of Finance, Encompass Health Rehabilitation Hospital of Braintree, Braintree, MA, p. A311
LEONARD, Beckie, R.N., Chief Nursing Officer, Foundation Surgical Hospital of San Antonio, San Antonio, TX, p. A649
LEONARD, Billie, Chief Executive Officer, Saint John Hospital, Leavenworth, KS, p. A253
LEONARD, Bruce, M.D., Medical Director and Chief of Psychiatry, Colorado Mental Health Institute At Fort Logan, Denver, CO, p. A106
LEONARD, Donavan, Chief Financial Officer, Baptist Memorial Hospital–Booneville, Booneville, MS, p. A360
LEONARD, Edward F, Executive Vice President and Chief Operating Officer, White Plains Hospital Center, White Plains, NY, p. A462
LEONARD, George, M.D., Chief Medical Officer, Madigan Army Medical Center, Tacoma, WA, p. A697
LEONARD, James, M.D., Chief Executive Officer, Northwest Health – Porter, Valparaiso, IN, p. A228
LEONARD, Jayne, M.D., Family Medicine, Ashe Memorial Hospital, Jefferson, NC, p. A471
LEONARD, Julie, Chief Financial Officer, Boundary Community Hospital, Bonners Ferry, ID, p. A180
LEONARD, Kevin, Vice President, Finance, Henry Ford Jackson Hospital, Jackson, MI, p. A331
LEONARD, Mark, Vice President Finance, Corewell Health Beaumont Troy Hospital, Troy, MI, p. A339
LEONARD, Robert, Director Information Services, Sierra Vista Regional Medical Center, San Luis Obispo, CA, p. A93
LEONARD, Steven E., President and Chief Executive Officer, Tidalhealth Peninsula Regional, Salisbury, MD, p. A307
LEONARD, William H., President, Atrium Health University City, Charlotte, NC, p. A465
LEONDAR, Kimberly, Director Human Resources, Texas Health Harris Methodist Hospital Stephenville, Stephenville, TX, p. A654
LEONELIS, Lisa, Chief Information Officer, George E. Wahlen Department of Veterans Affairs Medical Center, Salt Lake City, UT, p. A668
LEOPARD, Erik, Manager Human Resource, Methodist Hospital for Surgery, Addison, TX, p. A595
LEOPARD, Jimmy, FACHE, Chief Executive Officer, Wagoner Community Hospital, Wagoner, OK, p. A523
LEOPOLD, Michael, Chief Operating Officer, Broward Health Coral Springs, Coral Springs, FL, p. A129
LEPAGE, Kenneth C., FACHE, Chief Executive Officer, Select Specialty Hospital – Battle Creek, Battle Creek, MI, p. A322
LEPAK, Jason
M.D., Medical Director, Ascension St. John Broken Arrow, Broken Arrow, OK, p. A510
M.D., Medical Director, Ascension St. John Sapulpa, Sapulpa, OK, p. A520
LEPPER, Dale, Chief Information Officer, Antelop. Valley Medical Center, Lancaster, CA, p. A69
LEPPKE, Ben, Chief Information Officer, Satanta District Hospital And Long Term Care, Satanta, KS, p. A259
LEQUEUX, Veronica, Vice President Human Resources, HCA Florida Blake Hospital, Bradenton, FL, p. A126
LERCH, Gail
R.N., Executive Vice President Human Resources, Straub Medical Center, Honolulu, HI, p. A176
R.N., Vice President, Kapiolani Medical Center for Women & Children, Honolulu, HI, p. A175
R.N., Vice President Human Resources, Pali Momi Medical Center, Aiea, HI, p. A175
LERCH, Shawn, Chief Executive Officer, Sauk Prairie Healthcare, Prairie Du Sac, WI, p. A720
LERNER, Jerome, M.D., Medical Director, Sierra Tucson, Tucson, AZ, p. A41
LEROY, Michael
Senior Vice President and Chief Information Officer, Dmc Detroit Receiving Hospital & University Health Center, Detroit, MI, p. A325
Senior Vice President and Chief Information Officer, Dmc Harper University Hospital, Detroit, MI, p. A325
LESCH, Jason, Chief Financial Officer, Auburn Community Hospital, Auburn, NY, p. A438
LESEMANN, Julie, Chief Operating Officer and Assistant Administrator, Cook Hospital & Care Center, Cook, MN, p. A345
LESIAK, Cindy, Vice President Patient Care Services and Director of Nursing, Boone County Health Center, Albion, NE, p. A397
LESINS, Ross, Chief Information Officer, Casa Colina Hospital And Centers for Healthcare, Pomona, CA, p. A84
LESKO, Joan, Director Technical Support and Services, Kidspeace Children's Hospital, Orefield, PA, p. A547
LESLIE, Andrea M., MSN, R.N., Senior Vice President, Hospital Operations, Corewell Health Butterworth Hospital, Grand Rapids, MI, p. A328
LESLIE, Desdemona, Finance Officer, U. S. Public Health Service Indian Hospital–Whiteriver, Whiteriver, AZ, p. A41
LESLIE, Donald P, M.D., Medical Director, Shepherd Center, Atlanta, GA, p. A158
LESLIE, Kelly, Chief Financial Officer, Ferry County Memorial Hospital, Republic, WA, p. A693
LESLIE, Steve, Chief Financial Officer, Fairbanks Memorial Hospital, Fairbanks, AK, p. A28
LESLIE–PUHUYAOMA, Katrina
D.D.S., Chief Executive Officer, Gallup Indian Medical Center, Gallup. NM, p. A434
D.D.S., Chief Executive Officer, Northern Navajo Medical Center, Shiprock, NM, p. A437
LESNICK, Kelly, Resource Manager Flight Commander, Wright Patterson Medical Center, Wright–Patterson Afb, OH, p. A507
LESNIEWSKI, Amy, Associate Director Patient Care Services, Alexandria Va Medical Center, Pineville, LA, p. A291
LESSARD, Greg
Chief Executive Officer, Pam Specialty Hospital of San Antonio Center, San Antonio, TX, p. A650
Chief Executive Officer, Post Acute Medical Specialty Hospital of Texarkana – North, Texarkana, TX, p. A657
LESSMANN, Eric, Chief of Staff, South Sunflower County Hospital, Indianola, MS, p. A363
LESTE, Jim, Chief Administrative Officer, University of Iowa Hospitals & Clinics, Iowa City, IA, p. A238
LESTER, Lisa, Chief Nursing Officer, Encompass Health Rehabilitation Hospital of Princeton, Princeton, WV, p. A704
LESTER, Ron, Chief Human Resources, Cheyenne Va Medical Center, Cheyenne, WY, p. A726
LESTER, William, M.D., Vice President Medical Affairs, Encompass Health Cardinal Hill Rehabilitation Hospital, Lexington, KY, p. A268
LETCHWORTH, Mike, Manager Information Systems, Cherry Hospital, Goldsboro, NC, p. A469
LETEXIER, Lisa, Chief Executive Officer, Pembina County Memorial Hospital And Wedgewood Manor, Cavalier, ND, p. A480
LETHI, Scott, R.N., FACHE, Chief Nursing Officer, Fort Duncan Regional Medical Center, Eagle Pass, TX, p. A615
LETT, Patrick, M.D., Medical Doctor, Medical Center Enterprise, Enterprise, AL, p. A19
LEU, Christopher, President, Texas Health Harris Methodist Hospital Cleburne, Cleburne, TX, p. A607
LEUBNER, Kristel, D.O., Chief of Staff, Chi St. Josep. Health Burleson Hospital, Caldwell, TX, p. A606
LEUDECKE, Amelia, Director Human Resources, Encompass Health Rehabilitation Hospital of Round Rock, Round Rock, TX, p. A647
LEUNG, Lawrence, M.D., Chief of Staff, VA Palo Alto Heath Care System, Palo Alto, CA, p. A82
LEURCK, Mary P, Human Resources Director, UChicago Medicine Adventhealth Hinsdale, Hinsdale, IL, p. A198
LEVANGER, Nathan, M.D., Chief of Staff, Teton Valley Health Care, Driggs, ID, p. A181
LEVECK, Dianna, Chief Administrative Officer, Genesis Healthcare System, Zanesville, OH, p. A508
LEVEILLEE, Mary, Senior Vice President Patient Care Services and Chief Nursing Officer, Butler Hospital, Providence, RI, p. A560
LEVELING, Jim, Director Information Technology, Kansas City Orthopaedic Institute, Leawood, KS, p. A253
LEVER, Roger, M.D., President Medical Staff, The Outer Banks Hospital, Nags Head, NC, p. A473
LEVERING, Pamela, Chief Nursing Officer, Niagara Falls Memorial Medical Center, Niagara Falls, NY, p. A454
LEVERING, Theresa, Director Human Resources, HCA Florida Sarasota Doctors Hospital, Sarasota, FL, p. A149
LEVI, Daniela, Chief Medical Officer, Montefiore New Rochelle, New Rochelle, NY, p. A447
LEVI, John, Director Human Resources, St. Lawrence Rehabilitation Hospital, Lawrenceville, NJ, p. A423
LEVIN, Alan M., MSN, R.N., Chief Nursing Officer, New York–Presbyterian Queens, New York, NY, p. A450
LEVINE, David, Chief Medical Officer, Fisher–Titus Medical Center, Norwalk, OH, p. A501
LEVINE, Larry L., President and Chief Executive Officer, Blythedale Children's Hospital, Valhalla, NY, p. A460
LEVINE, Robert V, Executive Vice President and Chief Operating Officer, Flushing Hospital Medical Center, New York, NY, p. A448
LEVINE, Stuart M., M.D., President, Medstar Franklin Square Medical Center, Baltimore, MD, p. A302
LEVINSON, Adam, Associate Director, Information Services, Rutgers University Behavioral Healthcare, Piscataway, NJ, p. A427
LEVIS, Randolph, Chief Financial Officer, Saint Vincent Hospital, Erie, PA, p. A540
LEVISON, Julie, Director Human Resources, Providence Medford Medical Center, Medford, OR, p. A529
LEVITAN, Kenneth, President and Chief Executive Officer, Einstein Medical Center Philadelphia, Philadelphia, PA, p. A548
LEVITOW, John L Jr, Vice President Patient Care Services and Chief Nursing Officer, Frisbie Memorial Hospital, Rochester, NH, p. A417
LEVITZ, Michele, Director Finance, St. Luke's Hospital–Miners Campus, Coaldale, PA, p. A537
LEVY, Becky
Chief Financial Officer, Paradise Valley Hospital, National City, CA, p. A79
Chief Financial Officer, Shasta Regional Medical Center, Redding, CA, p. A85
Chief Operating Officer, Shasta Regional Medical Center, Redding, CA, p. A85
LEVY, Dana, Chief Nursing Officer, University of Maryland Charles Regional Medical Center, La Plata, MD, p. A305
LEVY, Jennifer C., Director Human Resources, Texas Institute for Surgery At Texas Health Presbyterian Dallas, Dallas, TX, p. A612
LEVY, Marlow
President, Mercy Fitzgerald Hospital, Darby, PA, p. A538
President, St. Francis Hospital, Wilmington, DE, p. A122
LEVY, Scott S, M.D., Vice President and Chief Medical Officer, Doylestown Health, Doylestown, PA, p. A538
LEVY, Susan M, M.D., Vice President Medical Affairs, Levindale Hebrew Geriatric Center And Hospital, Baltimore, MD, p. A300
LEWALLEN, Stephen B., Hospital Administrator, Florida State Hospital, Chattahoochee, FL, p. A127
LEWANDOWSKI, James, Vice President Human Resources, OSF Saint Clare Medical Center, Princeton, IL, p. A206
LEWANDOWSKI, Jim, Interim Director of Human Resources, Carson Tahoe Health, Carson City, NV, p. A408
LEWANDOWSKI, Terri, Director Financial Services, Aspirus Stanley Hospital & Clinics, Inc., Stanley, WI, p. A722
LEWELLEN, Patsy, Interim Chief Nursing Officer, Moberly Regional Medical Center, Moberly, MO, p. A380
LEWELLEN, Thomas, D.O., Chief of Staff, Delta Health System, Dumas, AR, p. A45
LEWERKE, Jane, Manager Human Resources, Bob Stump Department of Veterans Affairs Medical Center, Prescott, AZ, p. A37
LEWIS, Alene, R.N., Chief Nursing Officer, Raleigh General Hospital, Beckley, WV, p. A699
LEWIS, Alonzo, President, Trinity Health Ann Arbor Hospital, Ypsilanti, MI, p. A341

© 2025 AHA Guide Index of Health Care Professionals A903

LEWIS, Angela, Senior Vice President Administration, Cookeville Regional Medical Center, Cookeville, TN, p. A582
LEWIS, Aundrea, Interim Chief Executive Officer, UofL Health – Peace Hospital, Louisville, KY, p. A270
LEWIS, Brandon, Director of Information Technology, Ivinson Memorial Hospital, Laramie, WY, p. A727
LEWIS, Cameron, Chief Executive Officer, Lubbock Heart & Surgical Hospital, Lubbock, TX, p. A636
LEWIS, Christine, Assistant Administrator, Finance, Hermann Area District Hospital, Hermann, MO, p. A376
LEWIS, Colleen, Director Human Resources, Texas Neurorehab Center, Austin, TX, p. A601
LEWIS, Courtney, Director Human Resources, Houston Methodist Baytown Hospital, Baytown, TX, p. A601
LEWIS, Craig, Chief Financial Officer, Sentara Albemarle Medical Center, Elizabeth City, NC, p. A468
LEWIS, Dana, Director Clinical Services, Southern Kentucky Rehabilitation Hospital, Bowling Green, KY, p. A263
LEWIS, Daniel
  Chief Medical Officer, Hancock County Hospital, Sneedville, TN, p. A593
  Chief Medical Officer, Hawkins County Memorial Hospital, Rogersville, TN, p. A592
  Executive Vice President and Chief Operating Officer, Metrohealth Medical Center, Cleveland, OH, p. A491
LEWIS, Dave, Director Information Services, Mosaic Medical Center – Maryville, Maryville, MO, p. A380
LEWIS, Dennis, M.D., Chief of Staff, Ashley Regional Medical Center, Vernal, UT, p. A670
LEWIS, Doug
  Chief Financial Officer, St. Luke's Rehabilitation Hospital, Boise, ID, p. A180
  Chief Financial Officer, Wheatland Memorial Healthcare, Harlowton, MT, p. A393
LEWIS, Douglas, Chief Financial Officer, Boulder City Hospital, Boulder City, NV, p. A408
LEWIS, Eugene, Chief Human Resources Officer, Marinhealth Medical Center, Greenbrae, CA, p. A66
LEWIS, Gordon, Chief Executive Officer, Burnett Medical Center, Grantsburg, WI, p. A711
LEWIS, Irvan Wick, Vice President Human Resources, Mt. Graham Regional Medical Center, Safford, AZ, p. A38
LEWIS, J Steve, Director Finance, Youth Villages Inner Harbour Campus, Douglasville, GA, p. A163
LEWIS, Jacob, Chief Financial Officer, Mark Twain Medical Center, San Andreas, CA, p. A88
LEWIS, Jeff, Administrator, Waukesha County Mental Health Center, Waukesha, WI, p. A723
LEWIS, Kent, Director Information Services, Southwestern Medical Center, Lawton, OK, p. A514
LEWIS, Marcus, Chief Executive Officer, First Care Health Center, Park River, ND, p. A483
LEWIS, Marie, Human Resources Liaison, VA St. Louis Health Care System, Saint Louis, MO, p. A384
LEWIS, Monica, Chief Executive Officer, Winn Parish Medical Center, Winnfield, LA, p. A294
LEWIS, Myron D.
  Chief Executive Officer, Blanchard Valley Hospital, Findlay, OH, p. A496
  Chief Executive Officer, Bluffton Hospital, Bluffton, OH, p. A486
LEWIS, Pam, Chief Compliance Officer, William R. Sharpe, Jr. Hospital, Weston, WV, p. A706
LEWIS, Paul, Chief Executive Officer, Shoshone Medical Center, Kellogg, ID, p. A181
LEWIS, Paula, Interim Chief Nursing Officer, St. Bernards Five Rivers, Pocahontas, AR, p. A52
LEWIS, Robin, Chief Financial Officer, Kiowa District Healthcare, Kiowa, KS, p. A252
LEWIS, Sharon, Director Information Systems, Forbes Hospital, Monroeville, PA, p. A546
LEWIS, Thomas D, Chief Operating Officer, Clifton T. Perkins Hospital Center, Jessup, MD, p. A305
LEWIS, Trevor, Chief Financial Officer, Bitterroot Health – Daly Hospital, Hamilton, MT, p. A392
LEWIS, Vicki, FACHE, President and Chief Executive Officer, Coffee Regional Medical Center, Douglas, GA, p. A163
LEWIS, Vickie, Chief Executive Officer, Central Florida Behavioral Hospital, Orlando, FL, p. A144
LEWIS–TAYLOR, Tracey, Chief Operating Officer, Stanford Health Care Tri–Valley, Pleasanton, CA, p. A83
LEWISTON, Jamie, R.N., MSN, Chief Nursing Officer, Aurora Psychiatric Hospital, Wauwatosa, WI, p. A724
LEYDEN, Andrea RN, Chief Nursing Officer, Washington County Hospital And Clinics, Washington, IA, p. A244
LI, Charles, M.D., Administrator, Georgia Regional Hospital At Atlanta, Decatur, GA, p. A162
LI, Eric, M.D., Chief Medical Officer, United Medical Center, Washington, DC, p. A124
LI, Jia F., FACHE, Health Care System Director, San Francisco Va Health Care System, San Francisco, CA, p. A91
LI, Ronald, Vice President Management Information Systems, Bergen New Bridge Medical Center, Paramus, NJ, p. A426
LI, Stephen, Vice President Management Information Systems, Jersey City Medical Center, Jersey City, NJ, p. A422
LI, Xiao H., M.D., Chief of Staff, Surgery Specialty Hospitals of America, Pasadena, TX, p. A643
LIANG, Bonnie, Divisional Finance Officer, Sutter Maternity And Surgery Center of Santa Cruz, Santa Cruz, CA, p. A94
LIANG, Lorrie
  Senior Vice President and President of WellStar Kennestone and WellStar Windy Hill, Wellstar Kennestone Hospital, Marietta, GA, p. A167
  Senior Vice President and President of WellStar Kennestone and WellStar Windy Hill, Wellstar Windy Hill Hospital, Marietta, GA, p. A168
LIBBY, Kenneth, Vice President Finance, VCU Health Community Memorial Hospital, South Hill, VA, p. A684
LIBCKE, Julia, R.N., President, Schwab Rehabilitation Hospital, Chicago, IL, p. A191
LIBERATORE, Kristi, Vice President and Chief Financial Officer, Providence St. Josep. Hospital Orange, Orange, CA, p. A81
LICHIUS, Sylvia Marie, R.N., Chief Nursing Officer, Morrill County Community Hospital, Bridgeport, NE, p. A398
LICHNEROWICZ, Darcy, Chief Executive Officer, Southcoast Behavioral Health, Dartmouth, MA, p. A313
LICHTENWALNER, Tom, Vice President Finance, St. Luke's University Hospital – Bethlehem Campus, Bethlehem, PA, p. A535
LICHTY, Scott, M.D., Physician, Sanford Sheldon Medical Center, Sheldon, IA, p. A243
LIDDELL, Sean, Manager Regional Service Information Technology, Unitypoint Health – Trinity Muscatine, Muscatine, IA, p. A240
LIDDY, Casey, President, Ohiohealth Berger Hospital, Circleville, OH, p. A490
LIDHOLM, Helen, Chief Executive Officer, Northern Nevada Medical Center, Sparks, NV, p. A413
LIDIAK, Brian, Chief Executive Officer, Warm Springs Rehabilitation Hospital of San Antonio, San Antonio, TX, p. A651
LIEBERMAN, Steven L, M.D., Chief of Staff, Veterans Affairs New Jersey Health Care System, East Orange, NJ, p. A420
LIEBERS, David, M.D., Chief Medical Officer and Vice President Medical Affairs, Ellis Medicine, Schenectady, NY, p. A458
LIEBMAN, Jeffrey H.
  Chief Executive Officer, Roger Williams Medical Center, Providence, RI, p. A561
  Chief Executive Officer, St. Josep. Health Services of Rhode Island, North Providence, RI, p. A560
LIEBSCHER, Julia, Vice President Operations and Chief Nurse Executive, Lee Memorial Hospital, Fort Myers, FL, p. A132
LIECHTY, Dillon, Interim Chief Executive Officer, Caribou Medical Center, Soda Springs, ID, p. A184
LIEFER, Alan, M.D., President Medical Staff, Memorial Hospital, Chester, IL, p. A188
LIESCHING, Timothy, M.D., Chief Medical Officer, Lahey Hospital & Medical Center, Burlington, MA, p. A312
LIESEN, Daniel, M.D., Chief Medical Officer, Vista Medical Center East, Waukegan, IL, p. A210
LIESMANN, George, M.D., Chief Medical Officer, Blessing Hospital, Quincy, IL, p. A206
LIETTE, Cindy, Vice President Patient Care Services, Mercer Health, Coldwater, OH, p. A491
LIFFERTH, Geoffrey, M.D., Chief Medical Officer, Sumner Regional Medical Center, Gallatin, TN, p. A583
LIGHT, Asher, M.D., Medical Director, Baylor Scott & White Institute for Rehabilitation–Fort Worth, Fort Worth, TX, p. A619
LIGHT, Laura, Director Human Resources, St. David's North Austin Medical Center, Austin, TX, p. A600
LIGHTBOURNE, Olieth, Chief Nursing Officer, Streamwood Behavioral Healthcare System, Streamwood, IL, p. A209
LIGHTCAP, Debora, Director Human Resources, Mercy Medical Center, Roseburg, OR, p. A531
LIGHTFOOT, William M, M.D., Vice President Medical Services, USA Health Providence Hospital, Mobile, AL, p. A22
LIGHTNER, Matthew, M.D., Chief Medical Staff, Scott County Hospital, Scott City, KS, p. A259
LIGON, Kim, Director Information Services, Dch Regional Medical Center, Tuscaloosa, AL, p. A25
LIGON, Lynda, Chief Nursing Officer, Warm Springs Medical Center, Warm Springs, GA, p. A173
LIKES, Randle L, M.D., Chief Medical Officer, Timpanogos Regional Hospital, Orem, UT, p. A667
LILES, Jerry, D.O., Chief Medical Officer, Christus Spohn Hospital Alice, Alice, TX, p. A595
LILES, Richard A, M.D., Medical Director, Encompass Health Rehabilitation Hospital of Largo, Largo, FL, p. A137
LILLIS, Marc, Chief Operating Officer, Orlando Health St. Cloud Hospital, Saint Cloud, FL, p. A148
LIM, David, Chief Financial Officer, Lower Bucks Hospital, Bristol, PA, p. A535
LIM, Rosemarie, M.D., Chief Medical Officer, Paradise Valley Hospital, National City, CA, p. A79
LIMA, Robert, Director Information Systems, Pappas Rehabilitation Hospital for Children, Canton, MA, p. A312
LIMBAGA, Aries J., R.N., Chief Executive Officer, Rancho Los Amigos National Rehabilitation Center/System Chief Nursing Offic, Rancho Los Amigos National Rehabilitation Center, Downey, CA, p. A62
LIMM, Whitney, M.D., Executive Vice President and Chief Physician Executive, The Queen's Medical Center, Honolulu, HI, p. A176
LIN, George, M.D., Physician Advisor, Hackensack Meridian Health Pascack Valley Medical Center, Westwood, NJ, p. A430
LIN, James Y, D.O., Chief of Staff, Lecom Health Millcreek Community Hospital, Erie, PA, p. A540
LINAFELTER, Robb, Chief Executive Officer, Lincoln Surgical Hospital, Lincoln, NE, p. A402
LINARES, Manuel, Chief Executive Officer, Broward Health Medical Center, Fort Lauderdale, FL, p. A131
LIND, Jonathan, President, Endeavor Health Swedish Hospital, Chicago, IL, p. A189
LIND, Mark, Chief Information Officer, Mammoth Hospital, Mammoth Lakes, CA, p. A76
LINDAUER, Randy L., Ph.D., FACHE, Chief Executive Officer, Weston County Health Services, Newcastle, WY, p. A727
LINDBERG, Bob, Chief Operating Officer, Cumberland Healthcare, Cumberland, WI, p. A709
LINDBERG, Michael, M.D., Chief Medical Officer, Monadnock Community Hospital, Peterborough, NH, p. A417
LINDEMAN, Barry K, Director Human Resources, Encompass Health Cardinal Hill Rehabilitation Hospital, Lexington, KY, p. A268
LINDEMAN, Gretchen, Director of Human Resources, Monterey Park Hospital, Monterey Park, CA, p. A78
LINDEMANN, Fran, Director Finance, Kell West Regional Hospital, Wichita Falls, TX, p. A662
LINDEN, Elizabeth, MSN, R.N., Chief Operating Officer and Vice President, Indiana University Health University Hospital, Indianapolis, IN, p. A220
LINDEN, Kelly, President and Chief Executive Officer, Casa Colina Hospital And Centers for Healthcare, Pomona, CA, p. A84
LINDER, James, M.D., Chief Executive Officer, Nebraska Medicine – Nebraska Medical Center, Omaha, NE, p. A404
LINDFORS, Teresa, Vice President Growth and Development, Stoughton Health, Stoughton, WI, p. A722
LINDQUIST, James
  Chief Nursing Officer, Hackensack Meridian Health Jfk Medical Center, Edison, NJ, p. A420
  Chief Nursing Officer, JFK Johnson Rehabilitation Institute At Hackensack Meridian Health, Edison, NJ, p. A420
LINDQUIST, Peter, Vice President and Chief Nursing Officer, USA Health Providence Hospital, Mobile, AL, p. A22
LINDQUIST, Steve, Assistant Vice President, Behavioral Health, Avera Mckennan Hospital And University Health Center, Sioux Falls, SD, p. A576
LINDSAY, Kelly, Chief Operating Officer, HCA Florida Brandon Hospital, Brandon, FL, p. A127
LINDSAY–BELL, Davida, Area Human Resources Leader, Kaiser Permanente Antioch Medical Center, Antioch, CA, p. A55
LINDSAY–WOOD, Elizabeth, Interim Chief Information Officer, Overlook Medical Center, Summit, NJ, p. A428
LINDSEY, Don, Vice President and Chief Information Officer, Tallahassee Memorial Healthcare, Tallahassee, FL, p. A151
LINDSEY, Hugh, M.D., Chief Medical Officer, University of Michigan Health–Sparrow Eaton, Charlotte, MI, p. A323
LINDSEY, Kim, Chief Human Resources Officer, Mercy Health – Lourdes Hospital, Paducah, KY, p. A273
LINDSEY, Nikki, Administrator and Chief Executive Officer, Dakota Regional Medical Center, Cooperstown, ND, p. A480
LINDSEY, Rob, Vice President Strategic, Business Partner, Ochsner Lsu Health Shreveport – St. Mary Medical Center, Llc, Shreveport, LA, p. A292
LINDSEY, Robbie, Chief Information Officer, Owensboro Health Twin Lakes Regional Medical Center, Leitchfield, KY, p. A268
LINDSEY, Tony, M.D., Chief of Staff, University of North Carolina Hospitals, Chapel Hill, NC, p. A465
LINDSTROM, David, M.D., Vice President Medical Affairs, Promedica Bay Park Hospital, Oregon, OH, p. A502

Index of Health Care Professionals / Loesche

Index of Health Care Professionals

LINE, Michael, Chief Medical Officer, Greene County Medical Center, Jefferson, IA, p. A238
LINES, Brian
Chief Executive Officer, Lone Peak Hospital, Draper, UT, p. A665
Chief Operating Officer, Ogden Regional Medical Center, Ogden, UT, p. A666
LING, Lori, Information Technician, Windom Area Health, Windom, MN, p. A357
LINGEN, Tom, M.D., Chief of Staff, Cumberland Healthcare, Cumberland, WI, p. A709
LINGERFELT, Jeffrey, Chief Executive Officer, Bath Community Hospital, Hot Springs, VA, p. A678
LINGLE, David, Directors Council Chairman and Chief of Staff, ECU Health Roanoke–Chowan Hospital, Ahoskie, NC, p. A463
LINGO, Jessica, Human Resource Generalist, Story County Medical Center, Nevada, IA, p. A240
LINK, Nathan, M.D., Medical Director, NYC Health + Hospitals/Bellevue, New York, NY, p. A450
LINKENHOKER, Ellen Y, Chief Nursing Officer, Lewisgale Hospital Montgomery, Blacksburg, VA, p. A673
LINN, Steven C, M.D., Chief Medical Officer, Inspira Medical Center–Vineland, Vineland, NJ, p. A430
LINNELL, Jon E., Chief Executive Officer, North Valley Health Center, Warren, MN, p. A357
LINNINGTON, Darryl, Chief Financial Officer, Mcalester Regional Health Center, Mcalester, OK, p. A515
LINSCHEID, Carol, Vice President Human Resources, Enloe Health, Chico, CA, p. A59
LINSCOTT, Jason, CPA, President, Texas Health Hospital Rockwall, Rockwall, TX, p. A647
LINSCOTT, Mark, Interim Administrator, Sutter Health Kahi Mohala, Ewa Beach, HI, p. A175
LINSE, Margaret, Administrative Secretary and Director Human Resources, West Holt Medical Services, Atkinson, NE, p. A397
LINSKEY, Chris, M.D., Acting Chief Medical Officer, Guidance Center, Flagstaff, AZ, p. A31
LINSTROM, Joseph, Vice President Operations, Suburban Hospital, Bethesda, MD, p. A303
LINTON, Dwight, Director Human Resources, Detar Healthcare System, Victoria, TX, p. A660
LINTON, Tina, Chief Nursing Officer, Palo Pinto General Hospital, Mineral Wells, TX, p. A639
LINTZ, Gordon, President and Chief Administrative Officer, Morristown–Hamblen Healthcare System, Morristown, TN, p. A589
LINZMAN, Rob, D.O., Chief of Staff, Jefferson County Hospital, Waurika, OK, p. A524
LIONARONS, JoAnn, Director, Burdett Birth Center, Troy, NY, p. A460
LIPE, Curt, Vice President, Chief Financial Officer, OSF St. Mary Medical Center, Galesburg, IL, p. A196
LIPINSKI, Gary, M.D., Chief Medical Officer, Ascension Saint Josep. – Joliet, Joliet, IL, p. A199
LIPMAN, Brian, M.D., Medical Director and Medical Staff Services, Prohealth Oconomowoc Memorial Hospital, Oconomowoc, WI, p. A718
LIPMAN, Henry D, Senior Vice President, Financial Strategy and External Relations, Concord Hospital – Franklin, Franklin, NH, p. A415
LIPNER, Zach, Vice President Human Resources, Newark Beth Israel Medical Center, Newark, NJ, p. A425
LIPPERT, Brandt, Vice President Human Resources, Adena Greenfield Medical Center, Greenfield, OH, p. A497
LIPPINCOTT, Ken, M.D., Chief of Staff, North Mississipp. State Hospital, Tupelo, MS, p. A369
LIPPMANN, Frederick, Chief of Staff, University Medical Center, Las Vegas, NV, p. A411
LIPSCOMB, Tracy, CPA, Vice President Financial Services and Chief Financial Officer, Garrett Regional Medical Center, Oakland, MD, p. A306
LIPSON, Wayne, M.D., Chief Physician Executive, Baptist Health Deaconess Madisonville, Inc., Madisonville, KY, p. A271
LIPTAK, Valenda M., Chief Executive Officer, Western Massachusetts Hospital, Westfield, MA, p. A319
LIPTON, Pat, Director Team Resources, South Florida Baptist Hospital, Plant City, FL, p. A147
LIPYANSKAYA, Svetlana, Chief Executive Officer, NYC Health + Hospitals/South Brooklyn Health, New York, NY, p. A452
LIRA, Kim, Chief Executive Officer, Southwood Psychiatric Hospital, Pittsburgh, PA, p. A551
LIRAKIS, Kathy, R.N., Chief Nursing Officer, Northern Light Blue Hill Hospital, Blue Hill, ME, p. A296
LIRIO, Ruel R., M.D., Clinical Physician Advisor, Corewell Health Zeeland Hospital, Zeeland, MI, p. A341
LISITANO, Richard
President, Lawrence + Memorial Hospital, New London, CT, p. A118
President, Westerly Hospital, Westerly, RI, p. A561
LISOVICZ, Jason, President/Chief Executive Officer, Altus Lumberton Hospital, Lumberton, TX, p. A637
LISS, Rita, Vice President Fiscal Services and Chief Financial Officer, Boone County Health Center, Albion, NE, p. A397
LISTI, Daniel, Chief Executive Officer, Princeton Baptist Medical Center, Birmingham, AL, p. A17
LISTON, Allison, Director, Human Resources, Cedar Crest Hospital And Residential Treatment Center, Belton, TX, p. A603
LISTON, John, Chief Operating Officer, Mclaren Port Huron, Port Huron, MI, p. A336
L'ITALIEN, Mark, Director Information Services, Salem Regional Medical Center, Salem, OH, p. A503
LITER, Jennifer Lynn, Vice President of Inpatient Services, Norton King's Daughters' Health, Madison, IN, p. A223
LITKA, Calvin, R.N., Director of Nursing, The Horsham Clinic, Ambler, PA, p. A534
LITOVITZ, Gary, M.D., Medical Director, Dominion Hospital, Falls Church, VA, p. A675
LITSINGER, James, CPA, Chief Operating Officer, Sheltering Arms Institute, Midlothian, VA, p. A679
LITTERER, Karen Christine, R.N., MSN, Administrator and Chief Operating Officer, Ascension Seton Highland Lakes, Burnet, TX, p. A606
LITTERER, Karen Christine., R.N., MSN, Chief Administrator and Chief Nursing Officer, Ascension Seton Highland Lakes, Burnet, TX, p. A606
LITTLE, Amy A, Vice President Patient Services, Indiana University Health Bedford Hospital, Bedford, IN, p. A212
LITTLE, Carl, Chief Executive Officer, Houston Methodist Clear Lake Hospital, Houston, TX, p. A626
LITTLE, Denise, Director Human Resources, St. Elizabeth Community Hospital, Red Bluff, CA, p. A85
LITTLE, James P, M.D., Medical Director, Encompass Health Rehabilitation Hospital of Kingsport, Kingsport, TN, p. A585
LITTLE, Joi, Chief Human Resources Officer, Dmc Sinai–Grace Hospital, Detroit, MI, p. A325
LITTLE, Suzanne, Human Resources Specialist, Columbia Basin Hospital, Ephrata, WA, p. A689
LITTLE, William, Chief Executive Officer, Carolina Pines Regional Medical Center, Hartsville, SC, p. A568
LITTLEFIELD, Karen, Director Human Resources, Waldo County General Hospital, Belfast, ME, p. A296
LITTLEJOHN, Matthew
FACHE, Chief Executive Officer, Musc Health Columbia Medical Center Downtown, Columbia, SC, p. A564
FACHE, Chief Executive Officer, Musc Health Kershaw Medical Center, Camden, SC, p. A562
LITTLESON, Steven G, FACHE, Chief Operating and Integration Officer, Penn Medicine Lancaster General Health, Lancaster, PA, p. A543
LITTLESON, Steven G., FACHE, President and Chief Executive Officer, Central Maine Medical Center, Lewiston, ME, p. A297
LITTLETON, Paula, Chief Financial Officer, Lake Regional Health System, Osage Beach, MO, p. A381
LITTRELL, Angela P., CPA, President and Chief Executive Officer, Fitzgibbon Hospital, Marshall, MO, p. A380
LIUZZA, Jed M.
Chief Human Resources Officer, Hutchinson Regional Medical Center, Hutchinson, KS, p. A251
Chief Human Resources Officer, Ou Health – University of Oklahoma Medical Center, Oklahoma City, OK, p. A518
LIVELY, Corey, Chief Executive Officer, Great Plains Regional Medical Center, Elk City, OK, p. A512
LIVERMAN, Brett, Chief Financial Officer, Alleghany Health, Sparta, NC, p. A476
LIVIN, Lee, Chief Financial Officer, Dignity Health Yavapai Regional Medical Center, Prescott, AZ, p. A37
LIVINGSTON, Carolyn, Director Human Resources, Holy Cross Hospital – Salt Lake, Salt Lake City, UT, p. A668
LIVINGSTON, Charles, Chief Executive Officer, Midwest Surgical Hospital, Omaha, NE, p. A404
LIVINGSTON, Denise, Director Human Resources, St. Mary Medical Center Long Beach, Long Beach, CA, p. A71
LIVINGSTON, Keith
Senior Vice President and Chief Information Officer, Thedacare Regional Medical Center–Appleton, Appleton, WI, p. A707
Senior Vice President and Chief Information Officer, Thedacare Regional Medical Center–Neenah, Neenah, WI, p. A718
LIVINGSTON, Richard, M.D., Medical Director, Valley Behavioral Health System, Barling, AR, p. A43
LIVINGSTON, Sam, Information Resource Consultant, G. Werber Bryan Psychiatric Hospital, Columbia, SC, p. A564
LIVSEY, Don, Vice President and Chief Information Officer, UCSF Benioff Children's Hospital Oakland, Oakland, CA, p. A81
LIZZA, Beth, Chief Nursing Officer, Ohio Valley Surgical Hospital, Springfield, OH, p. A504
LLANO, Manuel R., Chief Executive Officer, Fort Lauderdale Behavioral Health Center, Oakland Park, FL, p. A143
LLECHU, Armando, Chief Administrative Officer, Lee Memorial Hospital, Fort Myers, FL, p. A132
LLEWELLYN, Michael R, Chief Operating Officer, Laguna Honda Hospital And Rehabilitation Center, San Francisco, CA, p. A91
LLORENS, Michelle, Executive Director, Devereux Hospital And Children's Center of Florida, Melbourne, FL, p. A138
LLOYD, Chuck, Chief Executive Officer, Benewah Community Hospital, Saint Maries, ID, p. A183
LLOYD, Donald H. II, President and Chief Executive Officer, St. Claire Regional Medical Center, Morehead, KY, p. A272
LLOYD, Richard, D.O., Chief of Staff, Harbor Beach Community Hospital Inc., Harbor Beach, MI, p. A329
LLOYD, Russell E., Medical Center Director, Wilkes–Barre Veterans Affairs Medical Center, Wilkes–Barre, PA, p. A558
LOBERG, Rachel, R.N., Chief Nursing Officer, Advocate Condell Medical Center, Libertyville, IL, p. A200
LOCATELLI, Eduardo, M.D., Interim Chief Medical Officer, Holy Cross Hospital, Fort Lauderdale, FL, p. A131
LOCEY, Vicky, R.N., MSN, Chief Operating Officer and Chief Nursing Executive, Kaiser Permanente Santa Rosa Medical Center, Santa Rosa, CA, p. A95
LOCHALA, Richard, Chief of Staff, Mena Regional Health System, Mena, AR, p. A50
LOCHNER, Lisa, President, Missouri Baptist Sullivan Hospital, Sullivan, MO, p. A387
LOCKARD, Dennis, FACHE, Chief Financial Officer, Coshocton Regional Medical Center, Coshocton, OH, p. A493
LOCKCUFF, Todd, Chief Financial Officer, Inova Alexandria Hospital, Alexandria, VA, p. A673
LOCKE, Cheryl, Vice President and Chief Human Resource Officer, Atrium Health Wake Forest Baptist, Winston–Salem, NC, p. A478
LOCKE, Marianne, R.N., MSN, Associate Director Patient Care Services, Edward Hines, Jr. Veterans Affairs Hospital, Hines, IL, p. A198
LOCKE, Stuart, Chief Executive Officer, Southern Kentucky Rehabilitation Hospital, Bowling Green, KY, p. A263
LOCKERD, Marie Paul, M.D., Chief Medical Officer, Sanford Jackson Medical Center, Jackson, MN, p. A348
LOCKETT, Kevin, Interim Chief Financial Officer, Mayo Clinic Hospital In Florida, Jacksonville, FL, p. A135
LOCKHART, Jimmy Wayne, M.D., Medical Director, Encompass Health Rehabilitation Hospital of Treasure Coast, Vero Beach, FL, p. A154
LOCKLEAR, Ann, Vice President, Human Resources, Scotland Health Care System, Laurinburg, NC, p. A471
LOCKLIER, Olivia, Vice President Organizational Effectiveness, Ascension Sacred Heart Rehabilitation Hospital, Mequon, WI, p. A716
LOCKRIDGE, Michael, Chief Financial Officer, Northern Louisiana Medical Center, Ruston, LA, p. A291
LOCKWOOD, Melissa
Chief Administration Officer, Grafton City Hospital, Grafton, WV, p. A701
Chief Executive Officer, Mon Health Preston Memorial Hospital, Kingwood, WV, p. A702
LODOLCE, Jodi, Chief Nursing Officer, HCA Florida St. Lucie Hospital, Port St Lucie, FL, p. A147
LOE, Cindy, R.N., Director of Nursing, Essentia Health Northern Pines, Aurora, MN, p. A343
LOEB, Amy E., Ed.D., R.N., Executive Director, Peconic Bay Medical Center, Riverhead, NY, p. A457
LOECKE, Steven
M.D., Chief Medical Officer, Banner Fort Collins Medical Center, Fort Collins, CO, p. A108
M.D., Chief Medical Officer, Banner Mckee Medical Center, Loveland, CO, p. A112
LOEFFELHOLZ, Tim, Account Executive Information Technology, Unitypoint Health – Finley Hospital, Dubuque, IA, p. A235
LOEHR, Andrew, Senior Vice President and Chief Operating Officer, Children's of Alabama, Birmingham, AL, p. A16
LOELIGER, Eric, Vice President of Medical Affairs, Asante Three Rivers Medical Center, Grants Pass, OR, p. A527
LOERA, Arnold, M.D., Clinical Director, Bristol Bay Area Health Corporation, Dillingham, AK, p. A28
LOERINC, Albert, M.D., Medical Director, Vibra Hospital of Southeastern Massachusetts, New Bedford, MA, p. A316
LOESCHE, Nora, Southwest Kansas City Market Finance Director, Olathe Medical Center, Olathe, KS, p. A256

Index of Health Care Professionals / Loescher

LOESCHER, Cori, R.N., Chief Nursing Officer and Vice President of Patient Care Services, Brigham And Women's Faulkner Hospital, Boston, MA, p. A310
LOEWENSTEIN, Howard, Chief Information Resource Management Services, Jesse Brown Va Medical Center, Chicago, IL, p. A189
LOFFING, David, Chief Operating Officer, University of Illinois Hospital, Chicago, IL, p. A192
LOFGREN, Richard P., M.D., M.P.H., Chief Executive Officer, Ou Health – University of Oklahoma Medical Center, Oklahoma City, OK, p. A518
LOFQUIST, Barry D., Chief Executive Officer, Christus Mother Frances Hospital – Jacksonville, Jacksonville, TX, p. A630
LOFTIS, Dennis
Senior Vice President and Chief Information Officer, Riverside Regional Medical Center, Newport News, VA, p. A680
Senior Vice President of Information Systems, Coastal Virginia Rehabilitation, Yorktown, VA, p. A686
LOFTIS, Michelle, Human Resources Officer, Ferry County Memorial Hospital, Republic, WA, p. A693
LOFTUS, John, M.D., Chief of Staff, Kaiser Permanente Oakland Medical Center, Oakland, CA, p. A81
LOFTUS, Philip
Ph.D., Chief Information Officer, Aurora West Allis Medical Center, West Allis, WI, p. A724
Ph.D., Vice President and Chief Information Officer, Aurora Medical Center of Oshkosh, Oshkosh, WI, p. A719
Ph.D., Vice President and Chief Information Officer, Aurora Psychiatric Hospital, Wauwatosa, WI, p. A724
Ph.D., Vice President and Chief Information Officer, Aurora St. Luke's Medical Center, Milwaukee, WI, p. A717
LOFTUS, Terry, M.D., Chief Medical Officer, Medical City Fort Worth, Fort Worth, TX, p. A620
LOGAN, Angela
Chief Executive Officer, Cameron Memorial Community Hospital, Angola, IN, p. A212
Chief Nursing Officer, Lutheran Hospital of Indiana, Fort Wayne, IN, p. A216
LOGAN, Ann P., R.N., Ph.D., Chief Hospital Executive, Carepoint Health Hoboken University Medical Center, Hoboken, NJ, p. A422
LOGAN, Denise, Director Human Resources, Specialty Rehabilitation Hospital of Coushatta, Coushatta, LA, p. A280
LOGAN, John, M.D., Chief Medical Officer, Deaconess Henderson Hospital, Henderson, KY, p. A267
LOGAN, Matthew T., M.D., President and Chief Executive Officer, Self Regional Healthcare, Greenwood, SC, p. A567
LOGAN, Renee, Chief Financial Officer, Murray County Medical Center, Slayton, MN, p. A355
LOGAN–OWENS, Michelle, Ph.D., R.N., Chief Operating Officer, Mcleod Regional Medical Center, Florence, SC, p. A566
LOGOZZO, Vince, Director Information Technology, Aultman Orrville Hospital, Orrville, OH, p. A502
LOGSDON, Amy, Chief Nursing Officer, Encompass Health Rehabilitation Hospital of Lakeview, Elizabethtown, KY, p. A265
LOGSDON, Terri, Chief Financial Officer, Hickory Trail Hospital, Desoto, TX, p. A614
LOHMAN, Eric, M.D., Chief of Staff, Meadowview Regional Medical Center, Maysville, KY, p. A271
LOHR, Christa M., R.N., Chief Clinical Officer, Oklahoma City Rehabilitation Hospital, Oklahoma City, OK, p. A518
LOHR, Daniel E, Regional Vice President Finance, Windham Hospital, Willimantic, CT, p. A120
LOHRMAN, Josep. W, Chief Executive Officer, Annie Jeffrey Memorial County Health Center, Osceola, NE, p. A405
LOHSTRETER, Thomas, M.D., Chief of Staff, Kittson Healthcare, Hallock, MN, p. A348
LOKKE, Kimberly, Chief Human Resources Officer, Central Desert Behavioral Health Hospital, Albuquerque, NM, p. A432
LOKKEN, Christine, Chief Financial Officer, Bigfork Valley Hospital, Bigfork, MN, p. A343
LOLLEY, Tim, MSN, Chief Nursing Officer, Merit Health Madison, Canton, MS, p. A360
LOLLIS, Sylvia, Director Human Resources, HCA Florida Osceola Hospital, Kissimmee, FL, p. A136
LOLLO, Trisha, President, St. Louis Children's Hospital, Saint Louis, MO, p. A384
LOMAN, Sarah, Director Human Resources, Penobscot Valley Hospital, Lincoln, ME, p. A298
LOMAX, William, Chief Executive Officer, Houston County Community Hospital, Erin, TN, p. A582
LOMBA, Maria R, Medical Director, New Braunfels Regional Rehabilitation Hospital, New Braunfels, TX, p. A641
LOMBARD, Lisa, Chief Medical Officer, Ohiohealth Rehabilitation Hospital, Columbus, OH, p. A492
LOMBARDI, David, Site Chief Information Officer, Huntington Hospital, Huntington, NY, p. A444
LOMBARDO, Alan
Chief Executive Officer, Sheltering Arms Institute, Midlothian, VA, p. A679
Chief Executive Officer, Sheltering Arms Institute, Richmond, VA, p. A682
LOMMER, Dan, Vice President, Operations, Riverview Health Institute, Dayton, OH, p. A494
LONDON, Ashley, R.N., Administrator, Chi St. Luke's Health Memorial San Augustine, San Augustine, TX, p. A651
LONERGAN, Araceli, Chief Executive Officer, Foothill Regional Medical Center, Tustin, CA, p. A99
LONES, Malachi, Chief Nursing Officer, Hamilton County Hospital, Syracuse, KS, p. A260
LONEY, Chris, Director Personnel, Thomas B. Finan Center, Cumberland, MD, p. A303
LONG, Amy, Administrator, Mayo Clinic Health System In Fairmont, Fairmont, MN, p. A346
LONG, Anne, Chief Executive Officer, Harbor Oaks Hospital, New Baltimore, MI, p. A334
LONG, Brian, FACHE, President and Chief Executive Officer, Memorial Healthcare, Owosso, MI, p. A334
LONG, David, Chief Executive Officer, Pam Health Specialty Hospital of Wilkes–Barre, Wilkes Barre, PA, p. A557
LONG, Dennis, Director Human Resources, Western Missouri Medical Center, Warrensburg, MO, p. A388
LONG, Douglas, President, Dameron Hospital, Stockton, CA, p. A96
LONG, Floyd R, Chief Executive Officer, NYC Health + Hospitals/Henry J Carter Specialty Hospital And Medical Center, New York, NY, p. A451
LONG, Floyd R., Executive Director, NYC Health + Hospitals/ Henry J Carter Specialty Hospital And Medical Center, New York, NY, p. A451
LONG, Gregory L
M.D., Chief Medical Officer, Thedacare Regional Medical Center–Appleton, Appleton, WI, p. A707
M.D., Chief Medical Officer, Thedacare Regional Medical Center–Neenah, Neenah, WI, p. A718
LONG, Gretchen, Manager Human Resources, Shriners Children's Ohio, Dayton, OH, p. A494
LONG, Heather
R.N., Chief Executive Officer, Leesburg Regional Medical Center, Leesburg, FL, p. A137
R.N., Senior Vice President and Chief Operating Officer, UF Health The Villages Hospital, The Villages, FL, p. A153
LONG, Ingrid
Chief Executive Officer and Chief Nursing Officer, Community Hospital, Torrington, WY, p. A729
Chief Nursing Officer, Platte County Memorial Hospital, Wheatland, WY, p. A729
LONG, Jeremy
Chief Information Officer, Ascension St. Vincent Heart Center, Indianapolis, IN, p. A218
Manager Information Systems, Ascension St. Vincent Salem, Salem, IN, p. A227
LONG, Jonathan Ray, M.D., Chief of Staff, Weatherford Regional Hospital, Weatherford, OK, p. A524
LONG, Josep. Michael, M.D., Medical Director, Encompass Health Rehabilitation Hospital of Albuquerque, Albuquerque, NM, p. A432
LONG, Judy M, R.N., MS, Chief Nursing Officer and Chief Operating Officer, Appling Healthcare System, Baxley, GA, p. A159
LONG, Karen K., Medical Center Director, Tomah Va Medical Center, Tomah, WI, p. A723
LONG, Lisa, M.D., Physician, Vice Chief of Staff, Up Health System – Marquette, Marquette, MI, p. A333
LONG, Michelle
Regional Human Resource Manager, Lincoln Memorial Hospital, Lincoln, IL, p. A200
Regional Human Resource Manager, Taylorville Memorial Hospital, Taylorville, IL, p. A210
LONG, Mike, Chief Financial Officer, National Park Medical Center, Hot Springs, AR, p. A48
LONG, Richard, M.D., Chief Medical Officer, UPMC Hamot, Erie, PA, p. A540
LONG, Stephanie, President and Chief Executive Officer, River Bend Hospital, West Lafayette, IN, p. A229
LONG, Steven V., FACHE, President and Chief Executive Officer, Hancock Regional Hospital, Greenfield, IN, p. A218
LONG, Theresa, Chief Executive Officer, Danville State Hospital, Danville, PA, p. A538
LONGABAUGH, James, M.D., Chief Executive Officer, Sabetha Community Hospital, Sabetha, KS, p. A259
LONGACRE, Mark E.
FACHE, President, Chi Health Lakeside, Omaha, NE, p. A403
FACHE, President, Chi Health Midlands, Papillion, NE, p. A405
LONGBRAKE, Jeffery, Interim Vice President, Chief Financial Officer, Richland Hospital, Richland Center, WI, p. A720
LONGDO, Derrick, Director Information Systems, Marshfield Medical Center – Neilsville, Neillsville, WI, p. A718
LONGEST, Bruce, M.D., President Medical Staff, Baptist Memorial Hospital – Calhoun, Calhoun City, MS, p. A360
LONGEST, Sonya, M.D., Chief Medical Officer, Walter B. Jones Alcohol And Drug Abuse Treatment Center, Greenville, NC, p. A470
LONGLEY, Frank, Business Partner Information Technology, Cleveland Clinic Medina Hospital, Medina, OH, p. A500
LONGLEY, Michael, M.D., Chief Medical Officer, Adventhealth North Pinellas, Tarpon Springs, FL, p. A153
LONGMORE, David, Chief Information Officer, Wilkes–Barre Veterans Affairs Medical Center, Wilkes–Barre, PA, p. A558
LONGMUIR, Marla, M.D., Chief Medical Officer, Mountrail County Medical Center, Stanley, ND, p. A483
LONGNECKER, Stacy, Chief of Staff, Ortonville Area Health Services, Ortonville, MN, p. A352
LONGO, Joseph, Chief Information Officer, Parkland Health, Dallas, TX, p. A612
LONGO, Marybeth, Manager Human Resources, Trenton Psychiatric Hospital, Trenton, NJ, p. A429
LONGSTREET, Laura, Chief Executive Officer, Belmont Behavioral Health System, Philadelphia, PA, p. A548
LONGTIN, Brett
Chief Financial Officer, Elbow Lake Medical Center, Elbow Lake, MN, p. A346
Chief Financial Officer, Lake Region Healthcare Corporation, Fergus Falls, MN, p. A347
LONGWELL, Connie, Chief Executive Officer, Elkhorn Valley Rehabilitation Hospital, Casper, WY, p. A726
LOOMIS, Randy, Chief Financial Officer, Dallas County Hospital, Perry, IA, p. A242
LOONEY, Zane, Chief Information Officer, St. Bernard Parish Hospital, Chalmette, LA, p. A279
LOOS, Greg, Chief Operating Officer, Black Hills Surgical Hospital, Rapid City, SD, p. A575
LOOSBROCK, Tammy, Chief Executive Officer and Administrator, Sanford Luverne Medical Center, Luverne, MN, p. A349
LOOSEMORE, Tim
Director, Franciscan Health Crown Point, Crown Point, IN, p. A214
Regional Director Information Systems, Franciscan Health Michigan City, Michigan City, IN, p. A223
LOOSER, Justin, Chief Executive Officer, Hampstead Hospital & Residential Treatment Facility, Hampstead, NH, p. A415
LOOSLI, Angela, Assistant Administrator, Operations, State Hospital South, Blackfoot, ID, p. A179
LOPACHIN, Vicki L., M.D., Chief Medical Officer, The Mount Sinai Hospital, New York, NY, p. A453
LOPAS, Mary, Chief Information Officer, Door County Medical Center, Sturgeon Bay, WI, p. A722
LOPER, Carly
Acting Chief Executive Officer, Pioneers Memorial Healthcare District, Brawley, CA, p. A58
Chief Financial Officer, Pioneers Memorial Healthcare District, Brawley, CA, p. A58
LOPEZ, Aaron Lee., Chief Executive Officer, Clearsky Rehabilitation Hospital of Weatherford, Weatherford, TX, p. A661
LOPEZ, Augustine, Chief Financial Officer, Salinas Valley Health, Salinas, CA, p. A88
LOPEZ, Cesar, R.N., Director of Nurses, Chi St. Josep. Health Grimes Hospital, Navasota, TX, p. A641
LOPEZ, Enrique, M.D., Medical Director, Larry B. Zieverink, Sr. Alcoholism Treatment Center, Raleigh, NC, p. A474
LOPEZ, Ericca, Director Human Resources, Canyon Ridge Hospital, Chino, CA, p. A59
LOPEZ, Ivonne, Director Human Resources, Hospital Menonita Humacao, Humacao, PR, p. A733
LOPEZ, Jose, M.D., Medical Staff President, Indiana University Health Paoli Hospital, Paoli, IN, p. A226
LOPEZ, Leonardo, President Medical Staff, OSF Saint Paul Medical Center, Mendota, IL, p. A201
LOPEZ, Leroy, Chief Financial Officer, The Jewish Hospital – Mercy Health, Cincinnati, OH, p. A489
LOPEZ, Lesbia, Chief Nursing Officer, Doctors' Center Hospital San Juan, San Juan, PR, p. A734
LOPEZ, Lisa M, Director Human Resources, San Joaquin General Hospital, French Camp. CA, p. A64
LOPEZ, Maritza, M.D., Chief of Staff, Sanford Canby Medical Center, Canby, MN, p. A344
LOPEZ, Rene, Chief Executive Officer, Knap. Medical Center, Weslaco, TX, p. A662
LOPEZ, Robert, Chief Medical Officer, Highland Community Hospital, Picayune, MS, p. A368

Index of Health Care Professionals / Luebcke

Index of Health Care Professionals

LOPEZ, Rosalio J, M.D., Senior Vice President and Chief Medical Officer, PIH Health Whittier Hospital, Whittier, CA, p. A101
LOPEZ, Steven, M.D., Chief Medical Officer, Palmetto Lowcountry Behavioral Health, Charleston, SC, p. A563
LOPEZ, Susan Nordstrom., President, Advocate Illinois Masonic Medical Center, Chicago, IL, p. A188
LOPEZ, Trish, Area Chief Financial Officer, Kaiser Permanente Fontana Medical Center, Fontana, CA, p. A63
LOPEZ, Valerie, CPA, Chief Financial Officer, Uvalde Memorial Hospital, Uvalde, TX, p. A659
LOPEZ–CEPERO, Joe, Chief Nursing Officer, Good Samaritan Medical Center, West Palm Beach, FL, p. A154
LOPP, Rhonda, Chief Executive Officer, Eminent Medical Center, Richardson, TX, p. A646
LORD, Gregory D, M.D., Chief Medical Officer, Clearsky Rehabilitation Hospital of Leesville, Leesville, LA, p. A287
LORD, Jeff, Director of Nursing, Connecticut Veterans Home And Hospital, Rocky Hill, CT, p. A118
LOREN, Alan, M.D., Chief Medical Officer, Endeavor Health Northwest Community Hospital, Arlington Heights, IL, p. A185
LORENTZ, Derick, Chief Financial Officer, Grand Island Regional Medical Center, Grand Island, NE, p. A400
LORENZ, Paul E.
Chief Executive Officer, Santa Clara Valley Healthcare, O'Connor Hospital, San Jose, CA, p. A92
Chief Executive Officer, Santa Clara Valley Healthcare, Santa Clara Valley Medical Center, San Jose, CA, p. A92
LORENZEN, Shelli, Chief Human Resources Officer, Manning Regional Healthcare Center, Manning, IA, p. A239
LORIS, Adam, Chief Executive Officer, Barstow Community Hospital, Barstow, CA, p. A57
LORMAND, Jared, Vice President Information Technology, Opelousas General Health System, Opelousas, LA, p. A291
LORTON, Donald E, Executive Vice President, Centra Bedford Memorial Hospital, Bedford, VA, p. A673
LOSING, Crystal, Chief Nursing Officer, Logan Health – Cut Bank, Cut Bank, MT, p. A391
LOSKOSKI, Van, Chief Executive Officer, Stephens County Hospital, Toccoa, GA, p. A173
LOTHE, Eric L, FACHE, Executive Vice President and Chief Operating Officer, Unitypoint Health–Des Moines, Des Moines, IA, p. A235
LOTT, Benjamin, Chief Executive Officer, Copiah County Medical Center, Hazlehurst, MS, p. A363
LOTT, Cynthia, Director Human Resources, Northern Virginia Mental Health Institute, Falls Church, VA, p. A676
LOTT, Laura, Chief Executive Officer, Eastern Louisiana Mental Health System, Jackson, LA, p. A283
LOTT, Rodney, Director Management Information Systems and Facility Operations, Midcoast Central – Llano, Llano, TX, p. A635
LOTZ, Abby, MSN, R.N., Chief Executive Officer, Beartooth Billings Clinic, Red Lodge, MT, p. A395
LOTZE, Eberhard, M.D., Chief Medical Officer, Woman's Hospital of Texas, Houston, TX, p. A629
LOUBERT, Cheryl, M.D., Chief Medical Staff, Mymichigan Medical Center Gladwin, Gladwin, MI, p. A327
LOUDEN CORBETT, Jeanette L, Chief Human Resources Officer, Highland Hospital, Oakland, CA, p. A80
LOUGHRAN, Michael, Vice President Human Resources, Kennedy Krieger Institute, Baltimore, MD, p. A300
LOUK, Rodney, Chief Operating Officer, UPMC Washington, Washington, PA, p. A556
LOUME, Ibrahima, Controller, Mount Carmel Rehabilitation Hospital, Westerville, OH, p. A507
LOVATO, Anthony, Director Information Technology, Coon Memorial Hospital, Dalhart, TX, p. A610
LOVDAHL, Brian A., Chief Executive Officer, Ccm Health, Montevideo, MN, p. A351
LOVE, Alex, Acting Manager Human Resources, Alexandria Va Medical Center, Pineville, LA, p. A291
LOVE, Bianca, Assistant Administrator Human Resources, Trinity Hospital Twin City, Dennison, OH, p. A494
LOVE, E Clifford, Director Fiscal Services, Eastern State Hospital, Williamsburg, VA, p. A685
LOVE, Glenn Neil, M.D., Medical Director, Hilton Head Hospital, Hilton Head Island, SC, p. A568
LOVE, Matthew, Chief Executive Officer, Nicklaus Children's Hospital, Miami, FL, p. A140
LOVE, Tami, Chief Financial Officer, Memorial Hospital of Sweetwater County, Rock Springs, WY, p. A728
LOVE, Tim, Director Information Services, Reid Health, Richmond, IN, p. A226
LOVEJOY, David, Chief Operations Officer, Riverview Psychiatric Center, Augusta, ME, p. A295
LOVEJOY, Rob
Chief Operating Officer, Sanford Behavioral Health Center, Thief River Falls, MN, p. A356
Director, Operations, Sanford Thief River Falls Medical Center, Thief River Falls, MN, p. A356
LOVELACE, Alan, Vice President and Chief Financial Officer, Stillwater Medical Center, Stillwater, OK, p. A521
LOVELACE, Christina, Director Human Resources, Gunnison Valley Health, Gunnison, CO, p. A109
LOVELACE, Corey, Chief Executive Officer, HCA Florida St. Lucie Hospital, Port St Lucie, FL, p. A147
LOVELACE, Lisa, Chief Executive Officer, Tennova Healthcare – Cleveland, Cleveland, TN, p. A581
LOVELADY, Shawn M., Chief Executive Officer, Oss Health, York, PA, p. A558
LOVELESS, Craig
Chief Executive Officer, Goodland Regional Medical Center, Goodland, KS, p. A250
Chief Executive Officer, Rawlins County Health Center, Atwood, KS, p. A246
LOVELESS, Jane Doll, Vice President, Chief Information Officer, Grand View Health, Sellersville, PA, p. A554
LOVELESS, Kurt, Chief Executive Officer, Kane County Hospital, Kanab, UT, p. A665
LOVELL, Mark, Vice President and Chief Financial Officer, Prisma Health Tuomey Hospital, Sumter, SC, p. A570
LOVELL, Stephanie, Vice President and General Counsel, Boston Medical Center, Boston, MA, p. A310
LOVELL, Terrence, Vice President Human Resources, Christianacare, Union Hospital, Elkton, MD, p. A304
LOVELLETTE, Teresa A, Manager Human Resources, Herrin Hospital, Herrin, IL, p. A197
LOVERA, Carlos, Director Information Systems, Montrose Regional Health, Montrose, CO, p. A112
LOVERING, Keith, Information Technician, Miller County Hospital, Colquitt, GA, p. A161
LOVERING, Richard, Corporate Vice President Human Resources and Organizational Development, Atlanticare Regional Medical Center, Atlantic City Campus, Atlantic City, NJ, p. A418
LOVETT, Chad Lovett, Chief Executive Officer, Central Prison Hospital, Raleigh, NC, p. A474
LOVING, Tonya, Director of Human Resources, UVA Encompass Health Rehabilitation Hospital, Charlottesville, VA, p. A674
LOVINGER, Warren, M.D., Chief Medical Officer, Nevada Regional Medical Center, Nevada, MO, p. A381
LOVINGOOD, Toni, Chief Operating Officer, Erlanger Western Carolina Hospital, Murphy, NC, p. A473
LOVRICH, John
Chief Financial Officer, Catalina Island Medical Center, Avalon, CA, p. A56
Chief Financial Officer, Glenn Medical Center, Willows, CA, p. A101
LOW, Kern
M.D., Chief Medical Officer, Commonspirit – St. Mary–Corwin Hospital, Pueblo, CO, p. A112
M.D., Chief Medical Officer, St. Thomas More Hospital, Canon City, CO, p. A104
LOW, Lewis
M.D., Chief Medical Officer, Legacy Mount Hood Medical Center, Gresham, OR, p. A527
M.D., Senior Vice President and Chief Medical Officer, Legacy Meridian Park Medical Center, Tualatin, OR, p. A533
M.D., Senior Vice President and Chief Medical Officer, Legacy Salmon Creek Medical Center, Vancouver, WA, p. A698
LOWE, Bren T., Chief Executive Officer, Vice President, McLeod Health, Mcleod Health Cheraw, Cheraw, SC, p. A563
LOWE, E. Rick., Chief Executive Officer, Encompass Health Rehabilitation Hospital of Cumming, Cumming, GA, p. A162
LOWE, Joe, Director Management Information Systems, Cumberland Medical Center, Crossville, TN, p. A582
LOWE, Kristen, Chief Executive Officer, Post Acute/Warm Springs Specialty Hospital of San Antonio, San Antonio, TX, p. A650
LOWE, Rob, Director, Healthcare Information Management, Onslow Memorial Hospital, Jacksonville, NC, p. A471
LOWE, Scott
Director Human Resource, Mcalester Regional Health Center, Mcalester, OK, p. A515
Market Chief Executive Officer, Physicians Regional – Pine Ridge, Naples, FL, p. A142
LOWELL, David, M.D., Chief Medical Officer, Spaulding Rehabilitation Hospital Cap. Cod, East Sandwich, MA, p. A313
LOWENTHAL, David, M.D., Clinical Director, New York State Psychiatric Institute, New York, NY, p. A450
LOWENTHAL, Steve B, M.D., M.P.H., FACS, Senior Vice President Medical Affairs and Chief Medical Officer, Rush–Copley Medical Center, Aurora, IL, p. A186
LOWERY, Brad
Chief Executive Officer, Atmore Community Hospital, Atmore, AL, p. A15
Director of Operations, Atmore Community Hospital, Atmore, AL, p. A15
LOWERY, John, M.D., Deputy Commander Clinical Services, General Leonard Wood Army Community Hospital, Fort Leonard Wood, MO, p. A375
LOWERY, Josh, Director of Human Resources, Baptist Memorial Hospital–North Mississippi, Oxford, MS, p. A367
LOWMAN, LeeAnn, Director Human Resources, Lake Taylor Transitional Care Hospital, Norfolk, VA, p. A680
LOWREY, Linda, Human Resources Officer, Atmore Community Hospital, Atmore, AL, p. A15
LOWRY, David, M.D., Chief Executive Officer, UNC Health Caldwell, Lenoir, NC, p. A471
LOWRY, Emma L., M.D., Acting Facility Director, Chief Executive Officer, Piedmont Geriatric Hospital, Burkeville, VA, p. A674
LOYA, Velma, Administrative Human Resource Coordinator, Rice Medical Center, Eagle Lake, TX, p. A615
LOYD, Chris, Director Human Resources, Methodist Richardson Medical Center, Richardson, TX, p. A646
LOYD BROWN, Bernita, Vice President and Administrator, Lake Charles Memorial Hospital, Lake Charles, LA, p. A286
LOYKE, Christopher, Chief Medical Officer, University Hospitals Parma Medical Center, Parma, OH, p. A502
LOYO–RODRIGUEZ, Raul J, Administrative Analyst III, San Diego County Psychiatric Hospital, San Diego, CA, p. A89
LOZADA, Leonardo J, M.D., Chief Physician Executive, Saint Luke's North Hospital – Barry Road, Kansas City, MO, p. A378
LOZANO, Catherine, Chief Executive Officer, The Hospitals of Providence Horizon City Campus, Horizon City, TX, p. A624
LOZANO, Eli, Commander, Bassett Army Community Hospital, Fort Wainwright, AK, p. A28
LOZANO, Elias B., Executive Officer, Tripler Army Medical Center, Honolulu, HI, p. A176
LOZANO, Michelle C., Chief Executive Officer and Hospital Administrator, Oceans Behavioral Hospital of Corpus Christi, Corpus Christi, TX, p. A609
LUBARSKY, Neil, Senior Vice President, Finance and Chief Financial Officer, Thomas Jefferson University Hospital, Philadelphia, PA, p. A550
LUBECK, Monica, Senior Vice President and Chief Financial Officer, Miami County Medical Center, Paola, KS, p. A257
LUBINSKY, Jeanie, Chief Financial Officer, Mayo Clinic Health System – Red Cedar In Menomonie, Menomonie, WI, p. A716
LUCAS, Benny Lee Jr, Chief Nursing Executive, St. Joseph's Behavioral Health Center, Stockton, CA, p. A97
LUCAS, Christine, Chief of Staff, Deaconess Illinois Union County, Anna, IL, p. A185
LUCAS, Kelly, Chief Information Officer, Sampson Regional Medical Center, Clinton, NC, p. A466
LUCAS, Marshall, M.D., Medical Director, Cypress Creek Hospital, Houston, TX, p. A625
LUCCHESI, Michael, M.D., Chief Medical Officer; Chair, Emergency Medicine, Suny Downstate Health Sciences University, New York, NY, p. A453
LUCE, Paul W., R.N., MSN, Administrator, Miami County Medical Center, Paola, KS, p. A257
LUCENA QUILES, Yelitza, Chief Executive Officer, Hospital Episcopal San Lucas Metro, San Juan, PR, p. A735
LUCERO, Brenda, Chief Clinical Officer, Vibra Hospital of Clear Lake, Webster, TX, p. A661
LUCERO, Kim, Interim Chief Executive Officer, Mt. San Rafael Hospital, Trinidad, CO, p. A114
LUCERO, Lupe, Manager Business Office, Presbyterian Espanola Hospital, Espanola, NM, p. A434
LUCEY, Jeffery, M.D., Clinical Director, Kingsboro Psychiatric Center, New York, NY, p. A448
LUCIA, Sandra J, Director Health Information and Corporate Compliance Officer, Hampstead Hospital & Residential Treatment Facility, Hampstead, NH, p. A415
LUCIANO, Lisa, D.O., Medical Director, Johnson Rehabilitation Institute At Hackensack Meridian Health Ocean Medical Center, Brick, NJ, p. A418
LUCIER, Robbyn, Director Human Resources, Up Health System – Portage, Hancock, MI, p. A329
LUCKE, Kim, Vice President Finance, Northern Montana Hospital, Havre, MT, p. A393
LUCORE, Charles, M.D., President, St. Francis Hospital And Heart Center, Roslyn, NY, p. A458
LUDFORD, Brad, Chief Financial Officer, Bozeman Health Deaconess Regional Medical Center, Bozeman, MT, p. A390
LUDWIG, Walter, President, Kenmore Mercy Hospital, Kenmore, NY, p. A444
LUEBCKE, Diane, R.N., Director Nursing, Community Memorial Healthcare, Marysville, KS, p. A254

Index of Health Care Professionals

Index of Health Care Professionals / Lueders

LUEDERS, Kathy, R.N., Director of Nursing–Acute Care, Gundersen Saint Elizabeth's Hospital & Clinics, Wabasha, MN, p. A356
LUEHRS, Bill, Chief Human Resources Officer, Endeavor Health Evanston Hospital, Evanston, IL, p. A195
LUEHRS, Paul R, Chief Operating Officer, Mercy San Juan Medical Center, Carmichael, CA, p. A58
LUELLEN, John
M.D., Chief Operating Officer, Heritage Valley Beaver, Beaver, PA, p. A535
M.D., Chief Operating Officer, Sewickley Valley Hospital, (A Division of Valley Medical Facilities), Sewickley, PA, p. A555
M.D., Market President, Mercy Health – Lorain Hospital, Lorain, OH, p. A498
M.D., Market President, Mercy Health – St. Elizabeth Youngstown Hospital, Youngstown, OH, p. A508
LUFKIN, Kirk, M.D., VPMA, Mclaren Northern Michigan, Petoskey, MI, p. A335
LUGER, Gerald, M.D., President Medical Staff, Gottlieb Memorial Hospital, Melrose Park, IL, p. A201
LUGO, Cesar, Director Human Resources, Victor Valley Global Medical Center, Victorville, CA, p. A100
LUGO, Maria, Director of Nurses, Multy Medical Rehabilitation Hospital San Juan, San Juan, PR, p. A735
LUHRS, Jason J., Vice President Fiscal Services, Westfields Hospital And Clinic, New Richmond, WI, p. A718
LUKASICK, Melissa, Chief Financial Officer, Loyola University Medical Center, Maywood, IL, p. A201
LUKENS, Mark, President, The Acadia Hospital, Bangor, ME, p. A295
LUKENS, Tammy, Director Information, Lutheran Kosciusko Hospital, Warsaw, IN, p. A229
LUKISH, Kris, Human Resources Officer, Cjw Medical Center, Richmond, VA, p. A683
LUKSAN, Abel, M.D., Chief Medical Officer, Mary Lanning Healthcare, Hastings, NE, p. A400
LULICH, Diane, Director Human Resources, Tamarack Health Ashland Medical Center, Ashland, WI, p. A707
LULL, Todd, Director Information Technology, Southwest Health, Platteville, WI, p. A719
LUM, Bing, PharmD, Executive Vice President, Colorado River Medical Center, Needles, CA, p. A80
LUMPKINS, Deborah, MSN, Chief Operating Officer, Maury Regional Medical Center, Columbia, TN, p. A581
LUMPP, Karen, Senior Vice President and Chief Financial Officer, Trinitas Regional Medical Center, Elizabeth, NJ, p. A421
LUMSDEN, Chris A., President and Chief Executive Officer, Northern Regional Hospital, Mount Airy, NC, p. A473
LUNA, Raul D., Chief Nurse Executive, El Paso Psychiatric Center, El Paso, TX, p. A616
LUNA, Tony, M.D., Chief of Staff, Minneola District Hospital, Minneola, KS, p. A255
LUND, Dennis, M.D., Chief Medical Officer, Lucile Packard Children's Hospital Stanford, Palo Alto, CA, p. A82
LUND, Elizabeth, M.D., Chief of Staff, West Tennessee Healthcare Volunteer Hospital, Martin, TN, p. A587
LUND, Maggie A., Chief Human Resources Officer, Theda Care Medical Center – Wild Rose, Wild Rose, WI, p. A725
LUNDAL, David, Senior Vice President Information Systems and Chief Information Officer, Ascension Holy Family, Des Plaines, IL, p. A193
LUNDBERG, Lanetta, Vice President Culture and People, Peacehealth Ketchikan Medical Center, Ketchikan, AK, p. A28
LUNDBERG, Maggie, R.N., Chief Nursing Officer, Cooperman Barnabas Medical Center, Livingston, NJ, p. A423
LUNDBLAD, Jackie, President and Chief Executive Officer, Wickenburg Community Hospital, Wickenburg, AZ, p. A41
LUNDBYE, Justin, President, Good Samaritan Hospital Medical Center, West Islip. NY, p. A461
LUNDE, Eric E., President and Chief Executive Officer, Adventhealth Deland, Deland, FL, p. A130
LUNDE, Susan, R.N., Director of Nursing, Fallon Medical Complex, Baker, MT, p. A389
LUNDERGAN, Dan, Chief Executive Officer, University of Utah Health, Salt Lake City, UT, p. A669
LUNDY, Kelly, Chief Information Officer, Peacehealth St. Josep. Medical Center, Bellingham, WA, p. A687
LUNDY, Marcel, Chief Information Officer, Putnam General Hospital, Eatonton, GA, p. A163
LUNDY, Noah, Director of Human Resources, Northern Light Maine Coast Hospital, Ellsworth, ME, p. A297
LUNDY–PAINE, Robert, Director Information Systems, Alameda Hospital, Alameda, CA, p. A55
LUNNEBORG, Brandi, Chief Executive Officer, Lakeview Hospital, Stillwater, MN, p. A355
LUNNEY, Kathleen, MS, R.N., Vice President Patient Care Services and Chief Nursing Officer, Montefiore Nyack Hospital, Nyack, NY, p. A454
LUNSFORD, Cindy, Executive Vice President and Chief Operating Officer, Tidalhealth Peninsula Regional, Salisbury, MD, p. A307
LUNSFORD, Kaye W, System Director Human Resources, Ascension St. Vincent's Southside, Jacksonville, FL, p. A134
LUNT, Kimberly, Controller, Encompass Health Rehabilitation Hospital of North Tampa, Lutz, FL, p. A138
LUNTZ, Adam, Chief Financial Officer, Aultman Orrville Hospital, Orrville, OH, p. A502
LUOMA, Michael, M.D., Chief of Staff, Aspirus Keweenaw Hospital, Laurium, MI, p. A332
LUPINACCI, Michael, M.D., Medical Director, Encompass Health Rehabilitation Hospital of Mechanicsburg, Mechanicsburg, PA, p. A545
LUREMAN, Proctor, President and Chief Executive Officer, Broadlawns Medical Center, Des Moines, IA, p. A234
LUSINS, John, M.D., Medical Director, Oceans Behavioral Hospital of Corpus Christi, Corpus Christi, TX, p. A609
LUSK, Clifford Dale, M.D., Senior Vice President of Corporate Quality and Safety and Executive Medical Officer, Mcleod Regional Medical Center, Florence, SC, p. A566
LUSSIER, Shirley G, Vice President Human Resources, Northeast Rehabilitation Hospital, Salem, NH, p. A417
LUSTERIO, Efren, Director of Nursing, Behavioral Center of Michigan, Warren, MI, p. A340
LUTERBACH, Robert M, Chief Operating Officer, Kaiser Permanente Los Angeles Medical Center, Los Angeles, CA, p. A73
LUTERBACH, Robert M., Interim Senior Vice President/Area Manager, Los Angeles/Chief Operating Officer, Kaiser Permanente Los Angeles Medical Center, Los Angeles, CA, p. A73
LUTHER, Lori, CPA, Chief Operating Officer, Indiana University Health Ball Memorial Hospital, Muncie, IN, p. A224
LUTHER, Tracie, Director Employee and Labor Relations, Brooks–Tlc Hospital System, Inc., Dunkirk, NY, p. A442
LUTHER, Vera, M.D., Chief of Staff, Sabine County Hospital, Hemphill, TX, p. A624
LUTKENHAUS, Tiffany, Chief Nursing Officer, Muenster Memorial Hospital, Muenster, TX, p. A640
LUTTRINGER, Eric, Vice President, Finance and Chief Financial Officer, St. Clair Health, Pittsburgh, PA, p. A551
LUTZ, Andrea, Director of Ancillary Services, Community Healthcare System, Onaga, KS, p. A256
LUTZ, Barb, Director of Human Resources, Compliance and Informatics, Fall River Health Services, Hot Springs, SD, p. A574
LUTZ, Barbara, Vice President Human Resources, Heart of The Rockies Regional Medical Center, Salida, CO, p. A113
LUTZ, Carrie L., Chief Executive Officer, Holton Community Hospital, Holton, KS, p. A250
LUTZ, Denise, Chief Human Resources Officer, Chi St. Alexius Health Dickinson, Dickinson, ND, p. A480
LUTZ, Don, Director Information Technology, St. Luke's Easton Campus, Easton, PA, p. A539
LUTZ, Kevin, DPM, Chief Operating Officer, Grant, Ohiohealth Grant Medical Center, Columbus, OH, p. A492
LUTZ, Roger, Chief Information Officer, Butler Memorial Hospital, Butler, PA, p. A536
LUTZ, Terry, Chief Financial Officer, Scheurer Health, Pigeon, MI, p. A335
LUX, Teresa M, President and Chief Operating Officer, Froedtert West Bend Hospital, West Bend, WI, p. A724
LUX, Teresa M., President and Chief Operating Officer, Froedtert Menomonee Falls Hospital, Menomonee Falls, WI, p. A716
LYDON, Jean, MS, R.N., System Vice President Operations, Chief Nursing Officer, Endeavor Health Elmhurst Hospital, Elmhurst, IL, p. A194
LYLE, Janet, Chief Human Resources and Allied Health Services, Springfield Hospital, Springfield, VT, p. A672
LYMAN, Jeremy, Chief Executive Officer, Blue Mountain Hospital, Blanding, UT, p. A664
LYMBEROPOULOS, Nick, Chief Executive Officer, Providence Cedars–Sinai Tarzana Medical Center, Los Angeles, CA, p. A74
LYNAM, Sheila, M.D., Chief Medical Officer, Peacehealth St. John Medical Center, Longview, WA, p. A691
LYNCE, Danialle
Business Partner Human Resources, University Hospitals Conneaut Medical Center, Conneaut, OH, p. A493
Business Partner Human Resources, University Hospitals Geneva Medical Center, Geneva, OH, p. A496
Manager Human Resources, University Hospitals Geauga Medical Center, Chardon, OH, p. A488
LYNCH, Becky, Manager Business Entity Management and Information Systems, OSF St. Mary Medical Center, Galesburg, IL, p. A196
LYNCH, Cecelia, R.N., MS, Vice President Patient Care Services and Chief Nursing Officer, Lowell General Hospital, Lowell, MA, p. A315
LYNCH, Danile, Chief Operating Officer, Saint Luke Institute, Silver Spring, MD, p. A307
LYNCH, Elizabeth A, Vice President Human Resources, The Hospital of Central Connecticut, New Britain, CT, p. A117
LYNCH, G Michael, M.D., Chief Medical Officer, Inova Fair Oaks Hospital, Fairfax, VA, p. A675
LYNCH, James, M.D., Senior Vice President and Chief Medical Officer, Corewell Health Beaumont Troy Hospital, Troy, MI, p. A339
LYNCH, John, M.D., President, Barnes–Jewish Hospital, Saint Louis, MO, p. A383
LYNCH, Marc, D.O., Chief of Staff, Kindred Hospital–Ontario, Ontario, CA, p. A81
LYNCH, Margaret, Chief of Support Operations, Holy Cross Hospital, Taos, NM, p. A437
LYNCH, Megan, Manager Human Resources, Johnson Memorial Health Services, Dawson, MN, p. A345
LYNCH, Michael T., M.D., Chief Medical Officer, Alice Peck Day Memorial Hospital, Lebanon, NH, p. A415
LYNCH, Thomas, President and Director, Fred Hutchinson Cancer Center, Seattle, WA, p. A694
LYNCH, Tim
Director of Finance, M Health Fairview Lakes Medical Center, Wyoming, MN, p. A358
Director of Finance, M Health Fairview Northland Medical Center, Princeton, MN, p. A353
LYNCH, Torie A, Manager Human Resources, Central Montana Medical Center, Lewistown, MT, p. A393
LYNCH, William, Executive Vice President and Chief Operating Officer, Jamaica Hospital Medical Center, New York, NY, p. A448
LYNCH–KILIC, Cathy, Vice President Human Resources, St. Mary's General Hospital, Passaic, NJ, p. A426
LYND, Samuel, Chief Executive Officer and Administrator, Nea Baptist Memorial Hospital, Jonesboro, AR, p. A48
LYNE, Marjorie, Associate Director for Patient Care Services, Hunter Holmes Mcguire Veterans Affairs Medical Center–Richmond, Richmond, VA, p. A683
LYNN, Christina, M.D., Medical Director, Three Rivers Behavioral Health, West Columbia, SC, p. A571
LYNN, Michelle
Chief Executive Officer, Hospital for Behavioral Medicine, Worcester, MA, p. A320
Chief Executive Officer, Westborough Behavioral Healthcare Hospital, Westborough, MA, p. A319
LYNN, Samuel, Director Human Resources, Northwest Texas Healthcare System, Amarillo, TX, p. A596
LYNNE, Donna, Chief Executive Officer, Denver Health, Denver, CO, p. A106
LYNSKEY, Jeanne, Vice President and Chief Financial Officer, Milford Regional Medical Center, Milford, MA, p. A316
LYON, Julie
M.D., Chief Medical Officer, Madonna Rehabilitation Hospital, Lincoln, NE, p. A402
M.D., Chief Medical Officer, Madonna Rehabilitation Specialty Hospital Lincoln, Lincoln, NE, p. A402
M.D., Chief Medical Officer, Madonna Rehabilitation Specialty Hospital Omaha, Omaha, NE, p. A404
LYON, Steve, Senior Director Human Resources, Grande Ronde Hospital, La Grande, OR, p. A528
LYON, Tami, Director Human Resources, Community Memorial Hospital, Burke, SD, p. A572
LYONS, Althea C, Vice President Human Resources and Development, Beverly Hospital, Beverly, MA, p. A309
LYONS, Denise, Chief Nursing Officer, Cumberland Hall Hospital, Hopkinsville, KY, p. A267
LYONS, Jim, President, Hutchinson Health, Hutchinson, MN, p. A348
LYONS, Lenny, President, Orem Community Hospital, Orem, UT, p. A667
LYONS, Michael, Regional Director Information Services, Shriners Hospitals for Children, Galveston, TX, p. A621
LYONS, Micki, Chief Executive Officer, Crook County Medical Services District, Sundance, WY, p. A728
LYONS, Rowena L., Human Resource Manager, Indian Path Community Hospital, Kingsport, TN, p. A585
LYREN, Joseph, Chief Financial Officer, Ohiohealth Mansfield Hospital, Mansfield, OH, p. A499
LYSAGHT, William, Chief Financial Officer, Kindred Hospital Las Vegas–Sahara, Henderson, NV, p. A409
LYTHGOE, Derek
Chief Financial Officer, Banner Baywood Medical Center, Mesa, AZ, p. A33
Chief Financial Officer, Banner Heart Hospital, Mesa, AZ, p. A33

A908 Index of Health Care Professionals

M

MA, Gene, M.D., President and Chief Executive Officer, Tri-City Medical Center, Oceanside, CA, p. A81
MAAMARI, Marcela, Chief Operating Officer, United Medical Center, Washington, DC, p. A124
MABRY, Brad, Administrator, Physicians Behavioral Hospital, Shreveport, LA, p. A292
MACAFEE, Francis M, Vice President Finance and Chief Financial Officer, Guthrie Corning Hospital, Corning, NY, p. A441
MACDONALD, Joan, R.N., MSN, Chief Nursing Officer, Vice President Nursing Services, Aurelia Osborn Fox Memorial Hospital, Oneonta, NY, p. A455
MACDONALD, Laurie, Vice President Finance, Penn Highlands Elk, Saint Marys, PA, p. A554
MACDONALD, Neil, Vice President, Operations, Medstar Union Memorial Hospital, Baltimore, MD, p. A301
MACDONELL, Jean
President and Chief Executive Officer, Fairview Range, Hibbing, MN, p. A348
President and Chief Executive Officer, Grand Itasca Clinic And Hospital, Grand Rapids, MN, p. A347
MACDOUGALL, David, Chief Financial Officer, United Health Services Hospitals–Binghamton, Binghamton, NY, p. A439
MACE, T. Paul, Chief Medical Officer, Singing River Gulfport, Gulfport, MS, p. A363
MACEVOY, Bonnie, Chief of Staff, Mad River Community Hospital, Arcata, CA, p. A56
MACFADYEN, James, M.D., Medical Director, Saint John Vianney Hospital, Downingtown, PA, p. A538
MACFIE, Helen
Chief Operating Officer, Long Beach Medical Center, Long Beach, CA, p. A71
Chief Operating Officer, Miller Children's & Women's Hospital Long Beach, Long Beach, CA, p. A71
MACGREGOR, Jay, Vice President Medical Affairs, Mercy Hospital, Coon Rapids, MN, p. A345
MACH, Robert, FACHE, Chief Executive Officer, Arbor Health, Morton Hospital, Morton, WA, p. A691
MACHOKA, Alistair M., Chief Executive Officer, Corona Regional Medical Center, Corona, CA, p. A60
MACHORRO, Vicky, R.N., Chief Nursing Officer, Kittitas Valley Healthcare, Ellensburg, WA, p. A689
MACIAG, Jeanne, Director of Nursing, Rosebud Health Care Center, Forsyth, MT, p. A391
MACIAS, Teresa, Administrator, California Mens Colony Correctional Treatment Center, San Luis Obispo, CA, p. A92
MACK, Charles, Vice President Finance and Chief Financial Officer, Merit Health Natchez, Natchez, MS, p. A367
MACK, Kristina, Manager, Human Resources, San Dimas Community Hospital, San Dimas, CA, p. A90
MACKAY, Cristal, Chief Operating Officer, Banner Desert Medical Center, Mesa, AZ, p. A33
MACKEN–MARBLE, Kelly, Chief Executive Officer, Osceola Medical Center, Osceola, WI, p. A719
MACKENROTH, Robin D., Chief Operating Officer, Kaiser Permanente Riverside Medical Center, Riverside, CA, p. A86
MACKEY, Denise
Administrator, Hale Ho'Ola Hamakua, Honokaa, HI, p. A175
Administrator, Ka'U Hospital, Pahala, HI, p. A177
MACKINNON, Paul, MS, R.N., Chief Operating Officer, Umass Memorial Healthalliance–Clinton Hospital, Leominster, MA, p. A315
MACKSOOD, Dan, Regional Senior Vice President and Chief Financial Officer, Good Samaritan Hospital Medical Center, West Islip. NY, p. A461
MACLAUGHLIN, Jeremy, Director Human Resources, Citizens Memorial Hospital, Bolivar, MO, p. A371
MACLENNAN, Alex, Chief Human Resources Officer, Tahoe Forest Hospital District, Truckee, CA, p. A98
MACLEOD, Deborah, MS, R.N., Vice President Nursing and Patient Care Services, Mid Coast Hospital, Brunswick, ME, p. A296
MACMILLAN, Don, MS, Senior Director of Information Services, Regional Chief Information Officer, Mainehealth Maine Medical Center, Portland, ME, p. A298
MACOGAY, Melissa, Vice President and Chief Nursing Officer, Johns Hopkins All Children's Hospital, Saint Petersburg, FL, p. A149
MACRI, Fredrick, Executive Vice President, Rhode Island Hospital, Providence, RI, p. A561

MACYK, Irene
R.N., MS, Ph.D., Chief Nursing Officer, North Shore University Hospital, Manhasset, NY, p. A445
R.N., MS, Ph.D., Executive Director, South Shore University Hospital, Bay Shore, NY, p. A439
MADAN, Sunil I., M.D., Chief Medical Officer and Chief Population Health Officer, Luminis Health Doctors Community Medical Center, Lanham, MD, p. A305
MADDEN, R. Craig, Director Employee Relations, Reynolds Memorial Hospital, Glen Dale, WV, p. A700
MADDOX, Dale, Chief Financial Officer, South Arkansas Regional Hospital, El Dorado, AR, p. A45
MADDOX, Jamie, Chief Nursing Officer, Christus Mother Frances Hospital – Jacksonville, Jacksonville, TX, p. A630
MADER, Elaine, M.D., Chief of Staff, Integris Miami Hospital, Miami, OK, p. A515
MADER, Frank, Director Information Services, East Liverpool City Hospital, East Liverpool, OH, p. A495
MADER, Vikki, Director Health Information Services, Pratt Regional Medical Center, Pratt, KS, p. A258
MADIGAN, Catherine, Chief Nursing Executive, University of North Carolina Hospitals, Chapel Hill, NC, p. A465
MADKINS, Catrina, Controller and Chief Financial Officer, Encompass Health Rehabilitation Hospital of Plano, Plano, TX, p. A644
MADRID, Melissa, R.N., Chief Nursing Officer, Harper County Community Hospital, Buffalo, OK, p. A510
MADRIGAL, Monica
Chief Executive Officer, Select Specialty Hospital–Miami Lakes, Miami Lakes, FL, p. A141
Interim Chief Executive Officer, Select Specialty Hospital–Miami, Miami, FL, p. A140
MADSEN, Greg T., Vice President, Hospital Administrator Carilion Rockbridge Community Hospital, Carilion Rockbridge Community Hospital, Lexington, VA, p. A678
MAEKAWA, Steve, Chief Financial Officer, Garfield Medical Center, Monterey Park, CA, p. A78
MAES, Jillian, Director Marketing and Public Relations, St. Thomas More Hospital, Canon City, CO, p. A104
MAES, Stephen, Director Information Systems, Franciscan Health Olympia Fields, Olympia Fields, IL, p. A204
MAESTAS, Sadie, Interim Chief Nursing Officer, Copper Queen Community Hospital, Bisbee, AZ, p. A30
MAESTRE, Jaime, Executive Director, Mayaguez Medical Center, Mayaguez, PR, p. A733
MAEWAL, Param, M.D., Chief Medical Officer, Cleveland Emergency Hospital, Humble, TX, p. A629
MAGALON, Stefanie, Interim Chief Executive Officer, Conway Behavioral Health, Conway, AR, p. A44
MAGDANGAL, Connie, Executive Vice President and Chief Financial Officer, Bergen New Bridge Medical Center, Paramus, NJ, p. A426
MAGEE, Becky, Chief Information Officer, Washington Regional Medical System, Fayetteville, AR, p. A46
MAGEE, James L., Executive Director, Piggott Health System, Piggott, AR, p. A52
MAGEE, Robert A, Director Human Resources, Shriners Hospitals for Children, Galveston, TX, p. A621
MAGEE, William F, Chief Financial Officer, Alliance Healthcare System, Holly Springs, MS, p. A363
MAGER, Angela N, Director, Human Resources, Kadlec Regional Medical Center, Richland, WA, p. A694
MAGES, Jill, Chief Human Resource Officer, Myrtue Medical Center, Harlan, IA, p. A237
MAGGARD, Amanda, President and Chief Executive Officer, Adventhealth Orlando, Orlando, FL, p. A144
MAGHAZEHE, Al
Ph.D., FACHE, President and Chief Executive Officer, Capital Health Medical Center–Hopewell, Pennington, NJ, p. A427
Ph.D., FACHE, President and Chief Executive Officer, Capital Health Regional Medical Center, Trenton, NJ, p. A429
MAGID, Philip. Director Fiscal Services, Shriners Hospitals for Children–Chicago, Chicago, IL, p. A191
MAGNER, Kile, Administrator, Ellinwood District Hospital, Ellinwood, KS, p. A248
MAGNESS, Grant, Chief Executive Officer, Top. Surgical Specialty Hospital, Houston, TX, p. A628
MAGNUSON, Johna, Director Nursing, Hillsboro Community Hospital, Hillsboro, KS, p. A250
MAGRANE, Brian
M.D., Chief Medical Officer, Baptist Health South Florida, Mariners Hospital, Tavernier, FL, p. A153
M.D., Chief Medical Officer, Fishermen's Hospital, Marathon, FL, p. A138
MAGRO, Michael
Jr, D.O., President, Nazareth Hospital, Philadelphia, PA, p. A549
Jr, D.O., President, St. Mary Medical Center, Langhorne, PA, p. A543

MAGU, Bharat, M.D., Chief Medical Officer, Yuma Regional Medical Center, Yuma, AZ, p. A42
MAGUIRE, Christina
President and Chief Executive Officer, Mount Desert Island Hospital, Bar Harbor, ME, p. A295
Senior Vice President, Chief Operating Officer and Chief Financial Officer, Mount Desert Island Hospital, Bar Harbor, ME, p. A295
MAGUIRE, David L, M.D., Vice President Medical Affairs, Baystate Wing Hospital, Palmer, MA, p. A317
MAGUREAN, Vickie
Chief Financial Officer, HCA Florida Englewood Hospital, Englewood, FL, p. A131
Chief Financial Officer, HCA Florida Fawcett Hospital, Port Charlotte, FL, p. A147
Chief Financial Officer, Tamp. General Hospital Crystal River, Crystal River, FL, p. A129
MAGUTA, Sam, Coordinator Information Systems, Devereux Advanced Behavioral Health Georgia, Kennesaw, GA, p. A166
MAHAJAN, Naman, Chief Executive Officer, Baylor Scott & White Medical Center – Grapevine, Grapevine, TX, p. A622
MAHAN, Vic
Chief Information Officer, Chino Valley Medical Center, Chino, CA, p. A59
Director Information Systems, Garden Grove Hospital And Medical Center, Garden Grove, CA, p. A65
Director Information Technology, La Palma Intercommunity Hospital, La Palma, CA, p. A69
Director Information Technology, West Anaheim Medical Center, Anaheim, CA, p. A55
MAHAR, Priscilla, Chief Operating Officer, Corewell Health Greenville Hospital, Greenville, MI, p. A329
MAHER, Donna, R.N., Chief Operating Officer, Morton Hospital And Medical Center, Taunton, MA, p. A319
MAHER, Sean, Director Human Resources, Devereux Children's Behavioral Health Center, Malvern, PA, p. A545
MAHER, Thomas, Chief Executive Officer and Administrator, Boulder City Hospital, Boulder City, NV, p. A408
MAHERA, Tina, M.D., Chief Medical Officer, Garfield Park Behavioral Hospital, Chicago, IL, p. A189
MAHL, Morgan G, Director Human Resources, St. Luke's Hospital – Warren Campus, Phillipsburg, NJ, p. A427
MAHLE, Thomas J., Chief Executive Officer, Palm Point Behavioral Health, Titusville, FL, p. A153
MAHMOOD, AHSan, M.D., Chief Medical Officer, Hamilton Center, Terre Haute, IN, p. A228
MAHNEKE, Suzette, Associate Vice President of Nursing, UChicago Medicine Adventhealth Glenoaks, Glendale Heights, IL, p. A196
MAHONEY, Bryan, Chief Financial Officer, Columbia Memorial Hospital, Hudson, NY, p. A444
MAHONEY, Nicole, Chief Financial Officer, Pioneer Memorial Hospital, Heppner, OR, p. A527
MAHONEY, Sandee, Chief Financial Officer, Community Medical Center, Missoula, MT, p. A394
MAHONEY, William K., FACHE, President and Senior Vice President, Community Hospital Group. Cox Medical Center Branson, Branson, MO, p. A372
MAHR–CHAN, Lydia, Director of Human Resources, Chinese Hospital, San Francisco, CA, p. A90
MAIDEN, Phillip G, M.D., Medical Director, Belmont Pines Hospital, Youngstown, OH, p. A508
MAIER, Cindy, R.N., Director of Nursing, Ness County Hospital Hospital District No 2, Ness City, KS, p. A255
MAIER, Walter M., Chief of Staff, San Bernardino Mountains Community Hospital, Lake Arrowhead, CA, p. A69
MAIETTA, Carol, Vice President Human Resources and Chief Learning Officer, Ascension St. Vincent's East, Birmingham, AL, p. A16
MAIJALA, Jake, Chief Human Resource Officer, Penn Highlands Dubois, Dubois, PA, p. A538
MAIN, Cleo, Finance Officer, Blackfeet Community Hospital, Saint Mary, MT, p. A395
MAIN, Theresa, R.N., President, Genesis Medical Center, Silvis, Silvis, IL, p. A208
MAINE, David N., M.D., President and Chief Executive Officer, Mercy Medical Center, Baltimore, MD, p. A301
MAINES, Stephanie, Chief Nursing Officer, Deaconess Illinois Crossroads, Mount Vernon, IL, p. A202
MAIRE, Jeffrey, M.D., Chief of Staff, Audubon County Memorial Hospital And Clinics, Audubon, IA, p. A230
MAIZE, Makyla, Director Information Services, Washington County Hospital And Clinics, Washington, IA, p. A244
MAJAUSKAS, Joel, Chief Information Officer, Clifton Springs Hospital And Clinic, Clifton Springs, NY, p. A441
MAJCHRZAK, John, Chief Financial Officer, Touchette Regional Hospital, Centreville, IL, p. A187
MAJDALANI, Elias, Director Management Information Systems, Mildred Mitchell–Bateman Hospital, Huntington, WV, p. A701

Index of Health Care Professionals

Index of Health Care Professionals / Majeski

MAJESKI, Denise, MSN, R.N., Vice President Operations and Chief Nurse Executive, Northwestern Medicine Lake Forest Hospital, Lake Forest, IL, p. A200
MAJETICH, Stephen D, CPA, Chief Financial Officer, Southwestern Vermont Medical Center, Bennington, VT, p. A671
MAJHAIL, Ruby, Chief Financial Officer, St. Luke's Behavioral Health Center, Phoenix, AZ, p. A36
MAJOR, Aprille, Director Human Resources, Foothill Regional Medical Center, Tustin, CA, p. A99
MAJOR, Kerry, R.N., MSN, Chief Nursing Officer, Cleveland Clinic Florida, Weston, FL, p. A155
MAJOR, Pattie, Chief Financial Officer, Paintsville Arh Hospital, Paintsville, KY, p. A273
MAJORS, Valerie, Director Information Services, Western State Hospital, Hopkinsville, KY, p. A267
MAJZUN, Rick, FACHE, Chief Operating Officer, Lucile Packard Children's Hospital Stanford, Palo Alto, CA, p. A82
MAK, David, Chief Financial Officer, El Camp. Memorial Hospital, El Campo, TX, p. A616
MAKAROFF, Jason, Chief Operating Officer and Associate Vice President, Adventist Healthcare Rehabilitation, Rockville, MD, p. A306
MAKELA, Taylor, Director Information Technology, Baraga County Memorial Hospital, L'Anse, MI, p. A331
MAKI, Jacquelyn, Chief Nursing Officer, Oakleaf Surgical Hospital, Altoona, WI, p. A707
MAKORO, Leslie, Director Information management Systems, Merit Health Natchez, Natchez, MS, p. A367
MAKOSKY, Michael D., Chief Executive Officer, Fulton County Medical Center, Mc Connellsburg, PA, p. A545
MAKSOUD, Jane
R.N., Senior Vice President Human Resources and Labor Relations, The Mount Sinai Hospital, New York, NY, p. A453
R.N., Senior Vice President Human Resources and Labor Relations, Mount Sinai Health System, Mount Sinai Beth Israel, New York, NY, p. A449
R.N., Senior Vice President Human Resources and Labor Relations, Mount Sinai Health System, Mount Sinai Morningside, New York, NY, p. A449
R.N., Senior Vice President Human Resources and Labor Relations, Mount Sinai Health System, New York Eye And Ear Infirmary of Mount Sinai, New York, NY, p. A450
MAKSYMOW, Michael, Vice President Information Systems, Beebe Healthcare, Lewes, DE, p. A121
MALAKAR, Crystal, Team Leader Inpatient Nursing, Bellin Psychiatric Center, Green Bay, WI, p. A712
MALAKOFF, Stacey, Executive Vice President and Chief Financial Officer, Hospital for Special Surgery, New York, NY, p. A448
MALAMED, Michael, M.D., Chief of Staff, Sherman Oaks Hospital, Los Angeles, CA, p. A75
MALAN, Glen, Vice President Information Technology and Chief Information Officer, Endeavor Health Northwest Community Hospital, Arlington Heights, IL, p. A185
MALAS, Joe, CPA, Eastern Division Vice President, Chief Financial Officer, Genesis Medical Center – Davenport, Davenport, IA, p. A234
MALAY, Jo, M.P.H., R.N., Hospital Administrator, Southern Nevada Adult Mental Health Services, Las Vegas, NV, p. A410
MALCOLM, Cole, Chief Financial Officer, Boone Memorial Hospital, Madison, WV, p. A702
MALCOLM, Dru Michele, MSN, R.N., Vice President and Chief Nursing Officer, Johnson City Medical Center, Johnson City, TN, p. A585
MALCOLMSON, James F, M.D., Chief of Staff, Sierra Vista Hospital, Truth Or Consequences, NM, p. A437
MALDONADO, April, Vice President Human Resources, Oklahoma City Rehabilitation Hospital, Oklahoma City, OK, p. A518
MALENSEK, Frank, M.D., Chief Medical Officer, Ascension St. Vincent's East, Birmingham, AL, p. A16
MALEY, Shelley, Director Human Resources, St. Luke's Quakertown Campus, Quakertown, PA, p. A553
MALIK, Azfar
M.D., Chief Medical Officer, Centerpointe Hospital, Saint Charles, MO, p. A383
M.D., Chief Medical Officer, Signature Psychiatric Hospital, Kansas City, MO, p. A377
MALIK, Chuck
Director Information Systems, Advocate Good Shepherd Hospital, Barrington, IL, p. A186
Director Information Systems, Advocate Illinois Masonic Medical Center, Chicago, IL, p. A188
MALINA, Joanne J, M.D., Chief of Staff, Veterans Affairs Hudson Valley Health Care System, Montrose, NY, p. A446
MALINDZAK, Edward, Chief Human Resources Officer, Prohealth Oconomowoc Memorial Hospital, Oconomowoc, WI, p. A718
MALJOVEC, John, M.D., Medical Director, Warren General Hospital, Warren, PA, p. A556
MALLETT, Belinda, R.N., MS, Vice President, Patient Care and Clinical Services, Soin Medical Center, Beavercreek, OH, p. A486
MALLETT, Teresa, Chief Financial Officer, Madison Regional Health System, Madison, SD, p. A574
MALLICOAT, Robert E., Chief Executive Officer, Select Specialty Hospital Daytona Beach, Daytona Beach, FL, p. A130
MALLIK, Subodh, M.D., Chief of Staff, Pecos County Memorial Hospital, Fort Stockton, TX, p. A619
MALLING, Timothy, M.D., Chief of Staff, Centracare – Paynesville, Paynesville, MN, p. A352
MALLON, Ben, Chief Executive Officer, Prohealth Rehabilitation Hospital of Wisconsin, Waukesha, WI, p. A723
MALLONEE, Teresa, Director Human Resources, Angel Medical Center, Franklin, NC, p. A468
MALLORY, Brenda, M.D., Medical Director, Penn State Health Rehabilitation Hospital, Hummelstown, PA, p. A542
MALLOY, Patrick C., M.D., Chief of Staff, Veterans Affairs New York Harbor Healthcare System, New York, NY, p. A453
MALLOY, Peter, Chief Information Officer, Cheshire Medical Center, Keene, NH, p. A415
MALM, Brad, Director Human Resources and Education, Lindsborg Community Hospital, Lindsborg, KS, p. A253
MALMSTROM, Ron, Information Research Specialist, Parsons State Hospital And Training Center, Parsons, KS, p. A258
MALONE, Barbara, M.D., Chief Medical Officer, Nantucket Cottage Hospital, Nantucket, MA, p. A316
MALONE, Brenna, Manager Human Resources, Weiser Memorial Hospital, Weiser, ID, p. A184
MALONE, Ginger MSN, RN–B, Chief Nursing Officer, SSM Health St. Mary's Hospital, Madison, WI, p. A714
MALONE, Meredith, Chief Financial Officer, West Tennessee Healthcare Dyersburg Hospital, Dyersburg, TN, p. A582
MALONE, Michael, Vice President and Chief Human Resources Officer, VHC Health, Arlington, VA, p. A673
MALONE, Patty, M.D., Chief Medical Officer, Ocean Beach Hospital And Medical Clinics, Ilwaco, WA, p. A690
MALONEY, Catherine, Chief Operating Officer, Emory University Hospital, Atlanta, GA, p. A157
MALONEY, Christopher, M.D., Senior Vice President, Medical Affairs and Chief Medical Officer, Children's Nebraska, Omaha, NE, p. A404
MALONEY, Jay, M.D., Chief of Staff, Cabinet Peaks Medical Center, Libby, MT, p. A394
MALONEY, Patrick J.
Chief Executive Officer, Franciscan Health Dyer, Dyer, IN, p. A215
Chief Executive Officer, Franciscan Health Hammond, Hammond, IN, p. A218
Chief Executive Officer, Franciscan Healthcare Munster, Munster, IN, p. A224
MALONEY, Paul V, Vice President Finance, Behavioral Health Network, Natchaug Hospital, Mansfield Center, CT, p. A116
MALOTT, Deanna, Director Human Resources, Henry Community Health, New Castle, IN, p. A225
MALOTT, Gregg, Chief Financial Officer, Pulaski Memorial Hospital, Winamac, IN, p. A229
MALOTTE, Rebecca, Executive Director and Chief Nursing Officer, Deaconess Midtown Hospital, Evansville, IN, p. A216
MALSED, Brad, Area Chief Financial Officer, Kaiser Permanente Los Angeles Medical Center, Los Angeles, CA, p. A73
MALSEED, Timothy James, Chief Information Officer, Keck Hospital of Usc, Los Angeles, CA, p. A73
MALSEED, TJ, Vice President and Chief Information Officer, Children's Hospital Los Angeles, Los Angeles, CA, p. A72
MALYSZEK, Richard, M.D., Chief of Staff, UCHealth Pikes Peak Regional Hospital, Woodland Park, CO, p. A114
MAMMONE, Tina, Ph.D., R.N., Chief Nursing Officer, VCU Medical Center, Richmond, VA, p. A683
MANDAL, Alan, Vice President Financial Operations, Scripp. Memorial Hospital–La Jolla, La Jolla, CA, p. A68
MANDAL, Konoy, M.D., Medical Director, Centennial Peaks Hospital, Louisville, CO, p. A112
MANDANAS, Renato, M.D., Chief Medical Officer, Oswego Hospital, Oswego, NY, p. A455
MANDEL, Ernest I.
M.D., Executive Vice President Health Care and Hebrew Senior Living Chief Medical Officer and Chief Qualit, Hebrew Rehabilitation Center, Roslindale, MA, p. A317
M.D., Executive Vice President Health Care and Hebrew Senior Living Chief Medical Officer and Chief Quality Officer, Hebrew Rehabilitation Center, Roslindale, MA, p. A317
MANDELL, Barry, Vice President, Special Projects, Jackson Park Hospital And Medical Center, Chicago, IL, p. A189
MANDERINO, Michelle, Chief Human Resources, North Florida/South Georgia Veteran's Health System, Gainesville, FL, p. A132
MANDHAN, Narain, M.D., Chief Medical Officer, Kirby Medical Center, Monticello, IL, p. A202
MANDI, Deepak, M.D., Chief of Staff, West Palm Beach Veterans Affairs Medical Center, West Palm Beach, FL, p. A155
MANETH, Laura, Human Resources Businss Partner, University of Kansas Health System Great Bend Campus, Great Bend, KS, p. A250
MANFREDO, John, Chief Operating Officer, Norman Regional Health System, Norman, OK, p. A516
MANGAN, Melissa, Vice President of Finance and Chief Financial Officer, Prairie Ridge Health, Inc., Columbus, WI, p. A709
MANGIN, Chris, Chief Executive Officer, Ochsner Lsu Health Shreveport – Academic Medical Center, Shreveport, LA, p. A292
MANGIONE, Ellen, M.D., Chief of Staff, Rocky Mountain Regional Va Medical Center, Aurora, CO, p. A103
MANGONA, John, Vice President, Chief Information Officer and Compliance Officer, Saratoga Hospital, Saratoga Springs, NY, p. A458
MANGUM, Lisa, Chief Nursing Officer, North Canyon Medical Center, Gooding, ID, p. A181
MANGUM, Rozanne, Administrative Assistant and Director Human Resources, Grover C. Dils Medical Center, Caliente, NV, p. A408
MANIATIS, Theodore, M.D., Medical Director, Staten Island University Hospital, New York, NY, p. A453
MANKER, Marcia
Chief Executive Officer, Executive Vice President, Memorial Care Orange County Region, Orange Coast Medical Center, Fountain Valley, CA, p. A64
Chief Executive Officer/Executive Vice President, MemorialCare Orange County Region, Saddleback Medical Center, Laguna Hills, CA, p. A69
MANKINS, Mark L, M.D., Chief of Staff, Olney Hamilton Hospital, Olney, TX, p. A642
MANKOSKI, Susan, Vice President Human Resources, SSM Health St. Mary's Hospital – Jefferson City, Jefferson City, MO, p. A376
MANLAGNIT, Maybelle, Senior Accounting Officer, Dsh Metropolitan, Norwalk, CA, p. A80
MANLEY, John, Director Information Systems, Jackson General Hospital, Ripley, WV, p. A704
MANN, Corey, Director Human Resources, Memorial Health Care Systems, Seward, NE, p. A406
MANN, Deborah, CPA, Vice President Finance and Chief Financial Officer, Schneck Medical Center, Seymour, IN, p. A227
MANN, Erin, R.N., Chief Nursing Officer, Mccamey County Hospital District, Mccamey, TX, p. A638
MANN, Karen, R.N., Chief Nursing Officer, Shoshone Medical Center, Kellogg, ID, p. A181
MANN, Lori, R.N., MSN, Chief Nursing Officer, Rusk Rehabilitation Hospital, Columbia, MO, p. A374
MANN, Rex, M.D., Chief Medical Officer, Ochiltree General Hospital, Perryton, TX, p. A643
MANN, Rhonda
Chief Nursing Officer, Franklin Woods Community Hospital, Johnson City, TN, p. A584
Chief Operating Officer, Raleigh General Hospital, Beckley, WV, p. A699
MANNER, Jennifer, Director of Nursing, Oceans Behavioral Hospital of Lubbock, Lubbock, TX, p. A636
MANNI, Joseph, Executive Vice President and Chief Operating Officer, Deborah Heart And Lung Center, Browns Mills, NJ, p. A419
MANNI, Kymberlee Jean, Chief Operating Officer, UMHC–Sylvester Comprehensive Cancer Center, Miami, FL, p. A141
MANNI, Kymberlee Jean., Chief Executive Officer, UMHC–Sylvester Comprehensive Cancer Center, Miami, FL, p. A141
MANNING, Angela, Director Health Information Services, Encompass Health Rehabilitation Hospital of Sunrise, Sunrise, FL, p. A151
MANNING, Austin
Chief Executive Officer, Timpanogos Regional Hospital, Orem, UT, p. A667
Chief Operating Officer, Los Robles Health System, Thousand Oaks, CA, p. A97
MANNING, Claude, Chief Financial Officer, Palacios Community Medical Center, Palacios, TX, p. A642
MANNING, Donald, M.D., Clinical Director, Georgia Regional Hospital At Savannah, Savannah, GA, p. A171

A910 Index of Health Care Professionals

Index of Health Care Professionals

Index of Health Care Professionals / Marks

MANNING, James, Administrator, Pathway Rehabilitation Hospital of Bossier, Bossier City, LA, p. A279
MANNING, JoAnn
Chief Financial Officer, Emory Johns Creek Hospital, Johns Creek, GA, p. A166
Chief Financial Officer, Emory Saint Joseph's Hospital, Atlanta, GA, p. A157
MANNING, Kimberly, Chief Nursing Officer, Washington Regional Medical Center, Plymouth, NC, p. A474
MANNING, Laura, Administrative Director, Guthrie Corning Hospital, Corning, NY, p. A441
MANNING, Lori, Administrator Human Resources, Western State Hospital, Tacoma, WA, p. A697
MANNING, Nicholas, Chief Operating Officer, Eastern Idaho Regional Medical Center, Idaho Falls, ID, p. A181
MANNION, Stephen, Assistant Vice President Information Systems Customer Service, Medstar Franklin Square Medical Center, Baltimore, MD, p. A302
MANNISTE, Eileen, MSN, Chief Nursing Officer, Broward Health North, Deerfield Beach, FL, p. A130
MANNIX, Mary N., FACHE, President and Chief Executive Officer, Augusta Health, Fishersville, VA, p. A676
MANNON, Jane, Vice President Human Resources, Penn State Milton S. Hershey Medical Center, Hershey, PA, p. A542
MANNS, Bill
President and Chief Executive Officer, Bronson Battle Creek Hospital, Battle Creek, MI, p. A322
President and Chief Executive Officer, Bronson Methodist Hospital, Kalamazoo, MI, p. A331
President and Chief Executive Officer, Bronson South Haven Hospital, South Haven, MI, p. A338
President and Chief Executive Officer, Bronson Healthcare Group. Bronson Lakeview Hospital, Paw Paw, MI, p. A335
MANNY, Martin, Director, I.S., Providence St. Mary Medical Center, Walla Walla, WA, p. A698
MANOLAKIS, John, Chief Executive Officer, Navarro Regional Hospital, Corsicana, TX, p. A609
MANOPELLA, Joseph, President, Mercy Medical Center, Rockville Centre, NY, p. A458
MANRING, Shannon, Director Human Resources, Lifebrite Community Hospital of Stokes, Danbury, NC, p. A466
MANSFIELD, Deena, Director Human Resources, Ashley Regional Medical Center, Vernal, UT, p. A670
MANSKE, Kristin, Chief Executive Officer, Greenwood Regional Rehabilitation Hospital, Greenwood, SC, p. A567
MANSKE, Lou Ann, Vice President Human Resources, Madonna Rehabilitation Hospital, Lincoln, NE, p. A402
MANSON, David, Manager Human Resources, Santa Clara Valley Medical Center, San Jose, CA, p. A92
MANSON, Kelly, Chief Financial Officer, Ioannis A. Lougaris Veterans' Administration Medical Center, Reno, NV, p. A412
MANSON, Lisa, Director Ambulatory Services, Guttenberg Municipal Hospital And Clinics, Guttenberg, IA, p. A237
MANSON, Stephanie, FACHE, President, Acadiana Market, Our Lady of Lourdes Regional Medical Center, Lafayette, LA, p. A286
MANSTEDT, Chase, Chief Financial Officer, Saunders Medical Center, Wahoo, NE, p. A406
MANSUE, Amy B.
President and Chief Executive Officer, Inspira Medical Center Mullica Hill, Mullica Hill, NJ, p. A424
President and Chief Executive Officer, Inspira Medical Center–Vineland, Vineland, NJ, p. A430
MANSUKHANI, Martin, Chief Financial Officer, Desert Valley Hospital, Victorville, CA, p. A100
MANTERNACH, Paul, M.D., Senior Vice President Physician Integration and Chief Medical Officer, Mercyone North Iowa Medical Center, Mason City, IA, p. A240
MANTOOTH, Charles, President and Chief Executive Officer, Watauga Medical Center, Boone, NC, p. A464
MANTZ, David, President and Chief Executive Officer, Dallas County Medical Center, Fordyce, AR, p. A46
MANUBENS, Claudio, M.D., Chief of Staff, Adventhealth Heart of Florida, Davenport, FL, p. A129
MANUEL, Shasta, Executive Director Finance, SSM Health St. Anthony Hospital – Oklahoma City, Oklahoma City, OK, p. A518
MANUEL, Wendy, Vice President and Chief Financial Officer, Rehabilitation Hospital of The Pacific, Honolulu, HI, p. A176
MANUS, Kim
Chief Financial Officer, Newport Hospital And Health Services, Newport, WA, p. A692
Interim CEO/CFO, Newport Hospital And Health Services, Newport, WA, p. A692
MANYBANSENG, Belen, R.N., Chief Nursing Officer, Trinity Hospital, Weaverville, CA, p. A101
MANZO, Arnold D, Vice President Human Resources, Cooperman Barnabas Medical Center, Livingston, NJ, p. A423
MANZO–LUNA, Hilda, Chief Nursing Officer, La Palma Intercommunity Hospital, La Palma, CA, p. A69
MANZOOR, Amir, M.D., Medical Director, Select Specialty Hospital–Panama City, Panama City, FL, p. A146
MAPARA, Anupam, M.D., Chief of Staff, Sutter Delta Medical Center, Antioch, CA, p. A55
MAPLES, Michael, M.D., Vice President and Chief Medical Officer, Mississipp. Baptist Medical Center, Jackson, MS, p. A364
MARAAN, Sheila, Director of Nursing, Brynn Marr Hospital, Jacksonville, NC, p. A471
MARANDI, Hossain, M.D., FACHE, President, SSM Health Cardinal Glennon Children's Hospital, Saint Louis, MO, p. A384
MARANO, Deena, Human Resources Director, Community Hospital of San Bernardino, San Bernardino, CA, p. A88
MARAS, Greg, Vice President Human Resources, Meadville Medical Center, Meadville, PA, p. A545
MARASA, Richard, M.D., President Medical Staff, Springfield Hospital, Springfield, VT, p. A672
MARBLE, Kevin, Director Information Technology, Oklahoma Forensic Center, Vinita, OK, p. A523
MARBLEY, Courtney J., Chief Operating Officer, New Orleans East Hospital, New Orleans, LA, p. A290
MARCANTANO, Mark R., Enterprise Vice President, President, Chief Executive, Delaware Valley Operations, Nemours Children's Hospital, Delaware, Wilmington, DE, p. A122
MARCANTEL, Bill, Chief Information Systems, Allen Parish Community Healthcare, Kinder, LA, p. A285
MARCEAUX, Caroline, MSN, R.N., Assistant Vice President, Nursing and Hospital Administration, Ochsner Acadia General Hospital, Crowley, LA, p. A280
MARCELIN, Fitzgerald, M.D., Chief of Staff, Bon Secours – Southern Virginia Medical Center, Emporia, VA, p. A675
MARCHAND, Gary, Interim Chief Executive Officer, Greenwood Leflore Hospital, Greenwood, MS, p. A362
MARCHANT, Joseph, Administrator, Bibb Medical Center, Centreville, AL, p. A17
MARCHESINI, Philip. Chief Executive Officer, HCA Florida Northside Hospital, Saint Petersburg, FL, p. A149
MARCHIK, Katie A
Chief Financial Officer, Unitypoint Health – Trinity Rock Island, Rock Island, IL, p. A207
Vice President, Consolidated Services, UnityPoint Health and Chief Financial Officer, Trinity Regional Health System, Unitypoint Health – Trinity Muscatine, Muscatine, IA, p. A240
MARCIANO, Paolo G, M.D., Chief Medical Officer, Corewell Health Dearborn Hospital, Dearborn, MI, p. A324
MARCO, James E Jr, Interim Vice President, Human Resources, Oswego Hospital, Oswego, NY, p. A455
MARCO, Wendy, R.N., Chief Nursing Officer, Osceola Regional Health Center, Sibley, IA, p. A243
MARCOTTE, Eric, M.D., Chief Medical Officer, Riverview Health, Noblesville, IN, p. A225
MARCOTTE, Lynn, Chief Financial Officer, Mclaren Oakland, Pontiac, MI, p. A335
MARCOTTE, Melissa, Chief Financial Officer, Rainy Lake Medical Center, International Falls, MN, p. A348
MARCOUX, Kelly Keefe, MSN, Vice President, Patient Care Services and Chief Nursing Officer, Children's Specialized Hospital, New Brunswick, NJ, p. A424
MARCOVICI, Mia, M.D., Chief Medical Officer, Norristown State Hospital, Norristown, PA, p. A547
MARCOWITZ, David, M.D., Chief of Staff, Lucas County Health Center, Chariton, IA, p. A232
MARCUCCI, John, M.D., Vice President Medical Affairs, Baylor Scott & White Medical Center – Plano, Plano, TX, p. A644
MARCUM, Amie, Human Resources Coordinator, Continuecare Hospital At Baptist Health Corbin, Corbin, KY, p. A264
MARCUS, Shannon, Chief Executive Officer, Three Rivers Behavioral Health, West Columbia, SC, p. A571
MARCZEWSKI, Les, M.D., Chief Medical Officer, Loring Hospital, Sac City, IA, p. A242
MARDY, Paul, Chief Information Technology Officer, Tennessee Valley Hcs – Nashville And Murfreesboro, Nashville, TN, p. A590
MAREK, Kyle
President, Carteret Health Care, Morehead City, NC, p. A473
Vice President General Services and Chief Information Officer, Carteret Health Care, Morehead City, NC, p. A473
MAREK, Rick, Vice President Medical Information Systems, Warm Springs Rehabilitation Hospital of San Antonio, San Antonio, TX, p. A651
MARGENAU, Randall, Chief Information Officer, William S. Middleton Memorial Veterans' Hospital, Madison, WI, p. A715
MARGOSCHIS, Shanthi
MSN, R.N., Chief Executive Officer, Sutter Auburn Faith Hospital, Auburn, CA, p. A56
MSN, R.N., Chief Operating Officer, Kaiser Permanente San Jose Medical Center, San Jose, CA, p. A92
MARIANI, Marilyn, R.N., Chief Nursing Officer, Lakeview Hospital, Bountiful, UT, p. A664
MARIANI, Meleah, Chief Nursing Officer, Corewell Health Ludington Hospital, Ludington, MI, p. A332
MARICN, Tanya, Interim Vice President Human Resources, Mercy Hospital Springfield, Springfield, MO, p. A387
MARIETTA, John, M.D., Chief Medical Officer, St. David's Medical Center, Austin, TX, p. A600
MARIETTA, Megan, Chief Executive Officer, HCA Houston Healthcare West, Houston, TX, p. A626
MARIN, Jessica, Chief Operating Officer, Research Medical Center, Kansas City, MO, p. A378
MARIN, Loyman, Chief Human Resources, Miami Veterans Affairs Healthcare System, Miami, FL, p. A140
MARIN, Octavio, Vice President Long Term Care and Ambulatory Care Services, Bronxcare Health System, New York, NY, p. A447
MARIN, Veronica, Chief Financial Officer, Red Bud Regional Hospital, Red Bud, IL, p. A207
MARINARI, Debra, Associate Vice President Hospital Operations, Stafford Hospital, Stafford, VA, p. A684
MARINARO, Jon, M.D., Chief Medical Officer, Kindred Hospital–Albuquerque, Albuquerque, NM, p. A432
MARINELLI, Steve, Chief Executive Officer, Choctaw Regional Medical Center, Ackerman, MS, p. A359
MARINELLO, Anthony, Chief Operating Officer, University Medical Center, Las Vegas, NV, p. A411
MARINI, Frank, Senior Vice President and Chief Information Officer, TMC Health, Tucson, AZ, p. A41
MARINO, A Michael, M.D., Senior Vice President Medical Administration, Greenwich Hospital, Greenwich, CT, p. A116
MARINO, Christopher, M.D., Chief of Staff, Lt. Col. Luke Weathers, Jr. Va Medical Center, Memphis, TN, p. A588
MARINO, Joseph, Chief Financial Officer, Suburban Community Hospital, East Norriton, PA, p. A539
MARINO, Marchita H, Vice President Human Resources, Rockledge Regional Medical Center, Rockledge, FL, p. A148
MARINO, Matt, Chief Financial Officer, Saint Luke's South Hospital, Overland Park, KS, p. A257
MARINOFF, Peter Jr, Munson Healthcare Cadillac Hospital Community President and Munson Healthcare South Region President, Munson Healthcare Cadillac Hospital, Cadillac, MI, p. A323
MARION, Alli, Chief Executive Officer, Rebound Behavioral Health, Lancaster, SC, p. A568
MARION, Amy, Chief Human Resource Officer, Walter B. Jones Alcohol And Drug Abuse Treatment Center, Greenville, NC, p. A470
MARION, Kristie Lorraine, Chief Executive Officer and Chief Nurse Executive, Memorial Hospital Los Banos, Los Banos, CA, p. A76
MARION, Kristie Lorraine., Chief Executive Officer and Chief Nurse Executive, Memorial Hospital Los Banos, Los Banos, CA, p. A76
MARIOTTI, Denise J., Chief Human Resource Officer, Hospital of The University of Pennsylvania, Philadelphia, PA, p. A549
MARIS, Peter, Director Human Resources, NYC Health + Hospitals/Elmhurst, New York, NY, p. A451
MARKENSON, David, M.D., Chief Medical Officer, Sky Ridge Medical Center, Lone Tree, CO, p. A111
MARKER, John, MSN, R.N., Chief Nursing Officer, Medical City North Hills, North Richland Hills, TX, p. A641
MARKESINO, Patricia A, FACHE, Chief Nurse Executive and Chief Operating Officer, Providence Willamette Falls Medical Center, Oregon City, OR, p. A530
MARKGRAF, SHRM–SCP, SPHR, Janelle K., Director Human Resources and Off Campus Services, Aspirus Langlade Hospital, Antigo, WI, p. A707
MARKHAM, Barbara, Chief Financial Officer, Glendive Medical Center, Glendive, MT, p. A392
MARKHAM, Kevin, Chief Financial Officer, Eastpointe Hospital, Daphne, AL, p. A18
MARKOS, Valerie, Chief Nursing Officer, Ed Fraser Memorial Hospital, Macclenny, FL, p. A138
MARKOWITZ, Stuart, M.D., Chief Medical Officer, Hartford Hospital, Hartford, CT, p. A116
MARKOWSKI, Stan, Chief Financial Officer, Palmetto Lowcountry Behavioral Health, Charleston, SC, p. A563
MARKS, Craig J., FACHE, Chief Executive Officer, Prosser Memorial Health, Prosser, WA, p. A693

© 2025 AHA Guide Index of Health Care Professionals **A911**

Index of Health Care Professionals

Index of Health Care Professionals / Marks

MARKS, Kimberly W., President, Bon Secours – Southampton Medical Center, Franklin, VA, p. A676
MARKS, Michael, M.D., Chief of Staff, Norwalk Hospital, Norwalk, CT, p. A118
MARKS, Peter, Vice President & Chief Information Officer, Wakemed Raleigh Campus, Raleigh, NC, p. A475
MARKS, Rhonda, Chief Nursing Officer, Rochelle Community Hospital, Rochelle, IL, p. A207
MARKS, Sara
President and Chief Executive Officer, King's Daughters Medical Center Ohio, Portsmouth, OH, p. A502
President and Chief Executive Officer, UK King's Daughters Medical Center, Ashland, KY, p. A263
Senior Vice President and Chief Operating Officer, UK King's Daughters Medical Center, Ashland, KY, p. A263
MARLATT, Pam, Business Systems Director, Essentia Health–St. Joseph's Medical Center, Brainerd, MN, p. A344
MARLER, Ruth, Chief Nursing Officer and Chief Operating Officer, UNC Health Johnston, Smithfield, NC, p. A476
MARLER, Steven R, Assistant Administrator, Parkland Health Center – Farmington Community, Farmington, MO, p. A375
MARLETTE, Andy, Chief Operating Officer, Valir Rehabilitation Hospital, Oklahoma City, OK, p. A519
MARLEY, Amelia, Chief Information Officer, Bassett Medical Center, Cooperstown, NY, p. A441
MARLEY, Charles, D.O., Vice President Medical Affairs, Wellspan Gettysburg Hospital, Gettysburg, PA, p. A540
MARLEY, Lee, Vice President, Information Services Chief Application Officer, Presbyterian Hospital, Albuquerque, NM, p. A433
MARLEY, Michael, Chief Information Officer, Veterans Affairs Central Western Massachusetts Healthcare System, Leeds, MA, p. A315
MARLOW, Billy, Executive Director and Administrator, North Sunflower Medical Center, Ruleville, MS, p. A368
MARLOWE, Cameron M., Chief Executive Officer, Blue Mountain Hospital District, John Day, OR, p. A528
MARMANDE, Susanne, Administrator, Infirmary Long Term Acute Care Hospital, Mobile, AL, p. A21
MARMERSTEIN, Robert, Chief Executive Officer, HCA Houston Healthcare Tomball, Tomball, TX, p. A658
MARNEY, Terri A, R.N., Director of Nursing, Plains Regional Medical Center, Clovis, NM, p. A434
MARON, Michael, President and Chief Executive Officer, Holy Name Medical Center, Teaneck, NJ, p. A429
MARONEY, Gerry, Chief Information Officer and Security Officer, Gaylord Specialty Healthcare, Wallingford, CT, p. A119
MAROSTICA, Tony, Chief Compliance and Human Resource Officer, Spanish Peaks Regional Health Center And Veterans Community Living Center, Walsenburg, CO, p. A114
MAROTTA, Diane, Vice President Human Resources, Mather Hospital, Port Jefferson, NY, p. A456
MAROUN, Christiane, M.D., Chief of Staff, Lifescape, Sioux Falls, SD, p. A576
MARQUARDT, Thomas, M.D., Interim Chief Medical Officer, Winnmed, Decorah, IA, p. A234
MARQUES, Michael, Vice President and Chief Information Officer Information Technology, Halifax Health/Uf Health Medical Center of Deltona, Deltona, FL, p. A130
MARR, Debbie, Administrative Assistant and Director Human Resources, Fredonia Regional Hospital, Fredonia, KS, p. A249
MARRAN, Mary, MS, President and Chief Operating Officer; Interim President, The Providence Center, Butler Hospital, Providence, RI, p. A560
MARRERO, Jamie L, M.D., Medical Director, Encompass Health Rehabilitation Hospital of Manati, Manati, PR, p. A733
MARRERO, Javier Marrero., Executive Director, Cardiovascular Center of Puerto Rico And The Caribbean, San Juan, PR, p. A734
MARRERO, Jose, Director Finance, San Jorge Children's And Women Hospital, Santurce, PR, p. A736
MARRERO, Marisela, M.D., President, St. Elizabeth's Medical Center, Brighton, MA, p. A311
MARRERO GONZALEZ, Mara, Executive Director, Bella Vista Hospital, Mayaguez, PR, p. A733
MARRONI, Denise
Chief Financial Officer, Providence Centralia Hospital, Centralia, WA, p. A688
Chief Financial Officer, Providence St. Peter Hospital, Olympia, WA, p. A692
MARRS, Deborah, Chief Nursing Officer, William Newton Hospital, Winfield, KS, p. A262
MARRUFO, Gabriel, Chief Financial Officer, Methodist Stone Oak Hospital, San Antonio, TX, p. A650
MARSEE, DeWayne, Director Information Systems, Mercer Health, Coldwater, OH, p. A491
MARSH, Allen, Chief Operating Officer, Medical City Lewisville, Lewisville, TX, p. A634
MARSH, Amy, Chief Financial Officer, Fairfield Memorial Hospital, Fairfield, IL, p. A195
MARSH, J. Michael., President and Chief Executive Officer, Overlake Medical Center And Clinics, Bellevue, WA, p. A687
MARSH, Linda, Vice President Financial Services and Chief Financial Officer, Alhambra Hospital Medical Center, Alhambra, CA, p. A55
MARSH, Mark A., President and Chief Executive Officer, Owensboro Health Regional Hospital, Owensboro, KY, p. A272
MARSH, Mitch, Interim Executive Director, Terence Cardinal Cooke Health Care Center, New York, NY, p. A453
MARSH, Robert, Chief Executive Officer, Centerpointe Hospital of Columbia, Columbia, MO, p. A374
MARSH, Toby, MSN, R.N., Interim Chief Patient Care Services Officer, UC Davis Medical Center, Sacramento, CA, p. A87
MARSH, Wallace, Director of Information Technology, Willow Springs Center, Reno, NV, p. A412
MARSHAK, Glenn, M.D., Chief of Staff, Mission Community Hospital, Los Angeles, CA, p. A74
MARSHALL, David R, R.N., Ph.D., Senior Vice President, Chief Nursing Executive, Cedars-Sinai Medical Center, Los Angeles, CA, p. A72
MARSHALL, Deborah K, Vice President Public Relations, Good Samaritan Regional Medical Center, Suffern, NY, p. A459
MARSHALL, James I., President and Chief Executive Officer, Uintah Basin Medical Center, Roosevelt, UT, p. A668
MARSHALL, Joe
Chief Executive Officer, Colorado Mental Health Institute At Pueblo, Pueblo, CO, p. A112
Chief Executive Officer, Lillian M. Hudspeth Memorial Hospital, Sonora, TX, p. A653
Chief Operating Officer, Lillian M. Hudspeth Memorial Hospital, Sonora, TX, p. A653
MARSHALL, John, Chief Nursing Officer, Calais Community Hospital, Calais, ME, p. A296
MARSHALL, Judy, Director Human Resources, Holy Cross Hospital, Taos, NM, p. A437
MARSHALL, Kenneth P., Chief Executive Officer, Uofl Health – Uofl Hospital, Louisville, KY, p. A270
MARSHALL, Michael
Chief Operating Officer, Anderson Hospital, Maryville, IL, p. A201
Vice President Finance and Chief Financial Officer, Anderson Hospital, Maryville, IL, p. A201
MARSHALL, Patricia, Assistant Administrator Human Resources, UPMC Greene, Waynesburg, PA, p. A556
MARSHALL, Ryan, Chief Financial Officer, Doctors Hospital of Manteca, Manteca, CA, p. A76
MARSHBURN, Deborah, Chief Nursing Executive, Cap. Fear Valley Medical Center, Fayetteville, NC, p. A468
MARSICO, Nick, President and Chief Executive Officer, Magruder Memorial Hospital, Port Clinton, OH, p. A502
MARSO, Paul, Vice President Human Resources, Avera St. Mary's Hospital, Pierre, SD, p. A575
MARTANIUK, Jean, Director Human Resources, Mt. Ascutney Hospital And Health Center, Windsor, VT, p. A672
MARTE, Maria, Administrator, Doctor's Center of Bayamon, Bayamon, PR, p. A731
MARTELL, Gustavo, M.D., Chief Medical Officer, The Hospitals of Providence Transmountain Campus – Tenet Healthcare, El Paso, TX, p. A617
MARTELL, Shirley, Chief Executive Officer, Select Specialty Hospital – Richmond, Richmond, VA, p. A682
MARTENS, Angela, Chief Financial Officer, Cumberland Healthcare, Cumberland, WI, p. A709
MARTENS, Troy, Chief Operating Officer, Unitypoint Health – Trinity Regional Medical Center, Fort Dodge, IA, p. A236
MARTHONE, Frances
Ph.D., MSN, R.N., Administrator, Shriners Hospitals for Children–Boston, Boston, MA, p. A311
Ph.D., MSN, R.N., Administrator, Shriners Hospitals for Children–Springfield, Springfield, MA, p. A318
MARTI, Maria L, Director Fiscal Services, Auxilio Mutuo Hospital, San Juan, PR, p. A734
MARTIN, Aaron, Chief Financial Officer, Eastern Idaho Regional Medical Center, Idaho Falls, ID, p. A181
MARTIN, Adam, Chief Executive Officer, Southern Tennessee Regional Health System–Winchester, Winchester, TN, p. A594
MARTIN, Amanda, Manager Human Resources, Ohio Valley Surgical Hospital, Springfield, OH, p. A504
MARTIN, Amy, Chief Human Resource Officer, Cedar City Hospital, Cedar City, UT, p. A664
MARTIN, Angelia, M.D., Chief of Staff, Mosaic Medical Center – Albany, Albany, MO, p. A371
MARTIN, Barbara
Chief Executive Officer, Community First Medical Center, Chicago, IL, p. A189
Chief Nursing Officer, Mercy Health – St. Vincent Medical Center, Toledo, OH, p. A504
President, Ascension Saint Josep. – Joliet, Joliet, IL, p. A199
MARTIN, Brent, Chief Executive Officer, Shreveport Rehabilitation Hospital, Shreveport, LA, p. A293
MARTIN, Brian, Vice President Medical Affairs, UPMC Children's Hospital of Pittsburgh, Pittsburgh, PA, p. A551
MARTIN, Bruce A, Vice President Human Resources, Carolinaeast Health System, New Bern, NC, p. A473
MARTIN, Carmen, Associate Administrator, Auxilio Mutuo Hospital, San Juan, PR, p. A734
MARTIN, Charity, Controller and Regional Business Officer Manager, Greenwood Regional Rehabilitation Hospital, Greenwood, SC, p. A567
MARTIN, Cheryl, Chief Information Officer, Prisma Health Tuomey Hospital, Sumter, SC, p. A570
MARTIN, Chris, Chief Operating Officer, Atoka County Medical Center, Atoka, OK, p. A510
MARTIN, Christine M, Vice President and Chief Financial Officer, Atrium Health Cleveland, Shelby, NC, p. A476
MARTIN, Cindy Jo., Senior Hospital Administrator, Cherokee Nation W.W. Hastings Hospital, Tahlequah, OK, p. A521
MARTIN, Clifford G
M.D., Regional Vice President and Chief Medical Officer, OSF Holy Family Medical Center, Monmouth, IL, p. A202
M.D., Regional Vice President and Chief Medical Officer, OSF Saint Luke Medical Center, Kewanee, IL, p. A199
M.D., Regional Vice President and Chief Medical Officer, OSF St. Mary Medical Center, Galesburg, IL, p. A196
MARTIN, Connie
President and Chief Administrative Officer, Fort Loudoun Medical Center, Lenoir City, TN, p. A586
Vice President and Chief Support Officer, Methodist Medical Center of Oak Ridge, Oak Ridge, TN, p. A591
MARTIN, Corey, M.D., Director Medical Affairs, Buffalo Hospital, Buffalo, MN, p. A344
MARTIN, Cyndie, Director, Coal County General Hospital, Coalgate, OK, p. A511
MARTIN, David, Assistant Administrator, Multicare Valley Hospital, Spokane Valley, WA, p. A696
MARTIN, David W, M.D., Vice President Chief Medical Officer, Ascension Seton Medical Center Austin, Austin, TX, p. A599
MARTIN, Deborah
Regional Vice President Human Resources, Cascade Valley Hospital, Arlington, WA, p. A687
Regional Vice President Human Resources, Skagit Valley Hospital, Mount Vernon, WA, p. A692
MARTIN, Debra, Chief Nursing Officer, Hamilton General Hospital, Hamilton, TX, p. A623
MARTIN, Denny, D.O., President, University of Michigan Health–Sparrow Lansing, University of Michigan Health–Sparrow Lansing, Lansing, MI, p. A332
MARTIN, Elizabeth J., Hospital President, VCU Health Tappahannock Hospital, Tappahannock, VA, p. A684
MARTIN, Erik, R.N., Vice President Patient Care Services and Chief Nursing Officer, Norton Children's Hospital, Louisville, KY, p. A269
MARTIN, Garland, M.D., Chief of Staff, Appling Healthcare System, Baxley, GA, p. A159
MARTIN, Gregg
Chief Information Officer, Arnot Ogden Medical Center, Elmira, NY, p. A442
Chief Information Officer, Ira Davenport Memorial Hospital, Bath, NY, p. A439
MARTIN, Harvey C, M.D., Medical Director, Red River Hospital, Llc, Wichita Falls, TX, p. A662
MARTIN, Holly
Director Human Resource, Iowa Specialty Hospital–Belmond, Belmond, IA, p. A230
Human Resources Leader, Iowa Specialty Hospital–Clarion, Clarion, IA, p. A232
MARTIN, James, Chief Information Officer, River Park Hospital, Huntington, WV, p. A701
MARTIN, James D
Chief Financial Officer, Hawthorn Children Psychiatric Hospital, Saint Louis, MO, p. A385
Chief Financial Officer, St. Louis Forensic Treatment Center, Saint Louis, MO, p. A384
MARTIN, Jason, M.D., Medical Director, Ascension Seton Northwest, Austin, TX, p. A599
MARTIN, Jeffrey H, M.D., Chief of Staff, Erlanger Western Carolina Hospital, Murphy, NC, p. A473
MARTIN, Jeremy, Chief Operating Officer, St. James Parish Hospital, Lutcher, LA, p. A287
MARTIN, Jessica, Director Human Resources, Logan Regional Medical Center, Logan, WV, p. A702

A912 Index of Health Care Professionals

Index of Health Care Professionals / Massey

Index of Health Care Professionals

MARTIN, Jessie, R.N., Chief Nursing Executive, Chi St. Alexius Health Turtle Lake Hospital, Turtle Lake, ND, p. A483
MARTIN, Josh, Chief Executive Officer, Summit Pacific Medical Center, Elma, WA, p. A689
MARTIN, Karen
R.N., MSN, Chief Nursing Officer, Marshall Medical Center, Lewisburg, TN, p. A587
Chief Nursing Officer, Musc Health Lancaster Medical Center, Lancaster, SC, p. A568
MARTIN, Keith, M.D., Chief Medical Officer, FHN Memorial Hospital, Freeport, IL, p. A195
MARTIN, Kelly, Chief Financial Officer, Fairchild Medical Center, Yreka, CA, p. A102
MARTIN, Kelly K., Vice President, Human Resources, Texas Health Presbyterian Hospital Plano, Plano, TX, p. A645
MARTIN, Kenneth A, M.D., Chief of Staff, Arkansas Surgical Hospital, North Little Rock, AR, p. A51
MARTIN, Kevin, M.P.H., R.N., FACHE, Administrator, Shriners Hospitals for Children–Salt Lake City, Salt Lake City, UT, p. A669
MARTIN, Kevin P., M.D., Chief Medical Officer, Four Winds Hospital, Saratoga Springs, NY, p. A458
MARTIN, Konnie
Chief Executive Officer, San Luis Valley Health, Alamosa, CO, p. A103
President and Chief Executive Officer, San Luis Valley Health Conejos County Hospital, La Jara, CO, p. A110
MARTIN, Kory Lann, M.D., Chief of Staff, Seymour Hospital, Seymour, TX, p. A652
MARTIN, Kristina, Chief Information Officer, Curry General Hospital, Gold Beach, OR, p. A527
MARTIN, Leslee, Manager Information Technology, HSHS St. Elizabeth's Hospital, O Fallon, IL, p. A204
MARTIN, Marlana, Director Human Resources, Benewah Community Hospital, Saint Maries, ID, p. A183
MARTIN, Mary, FACHE, Chief Operating Officer, Duke University Hospital, Durham, NC, p. A467
MARTIN, Michelle, Executive Medical Center Director, Battle Creek Veterans Affairs Medical Center, Battle Creek, MI, p. A322
MARTIN, Nikki
Chief Financial Officer, Christus Ochsner Lake Area Hospital, Lake Charles, LA, p. A286
Chief Financial Officer, Christus Ochsner St. Patrick, Lake Charles, LA, p. A286
Chief Financial Officer, Christus Southeast Texas Jasper Memorial, Jasper, TX, p. A630
MARTIN, Patrick
M.D., Medical Director, Wilmington Treatment Center, Wilmington, NC, p. A478
Director Information Systems, Calvary Hospital, New York, NY, p. A447
MARTIN, Patsy, Manager Human Resources, Denton Rehab, Denton, TX, p. A613
MARTIN, Paul, Chief Medical Officer, Kettering Health Dayton, Dayton, OH, p. A494
MARTIN, Paul J, Director Human Resources, Kaiser Permanente Los Angeles Medical Center, Los Angeles, CA, p. A73
MARTIN, Ric, Information Specialist, Madison State Hospital, Madison, IN, p. A223
MARTIN, Richard, MSN, R.N., Senior Vice President and Chief Nursing Officer, Hoag Memorial Hospital Presbyterian, Newport Beach, CA, p. A80
MARTIN, Sabrina
Chief Executive Officer, Advanced Care Hospital of Southern New Mexico, Las Cruces, NM, p. A435
Chief Executive Officer, Rehabilitation Hospital of Southern New Mexico, Las Cruces, NM, p. A435
MARTIN, Sharon E, M.D., Ph.D., President Medical Staff, Fulton County Medical Center, Mc Connellsburg, PA, p. A545
MARTIN, Sheila, Chief Nursing Officer, Cmh Regional Health System, Wilmington, OH, p. A507
MARTIN, Sherri, M.D., President Medical Staff, Adventhealth Shawnee Mission, Merriam, KS, p. A255
MARTIN, Stacy L, Director Human Resources, Grant Regional Health Center, Lancaster, WI, p. A714
MARTIN, Susan, Chief Financial Officer and Vice President, Finance, Middlesex Health, Middletown, CT, p. A117
MARTIN, Tim, Chief Operating Officer, Cabell Huntington Hospital, Huntington, WV, p. A701
MARTIN, Tom, Senior Vice President, Strategy and Information Technology Officer, Evergreenhealth, Kirkland, WA, p. A691
MARTIN, Val, Director Financial Management Services Center, George E. Wahlen Department of Veterans Affairs Medical Center, Salt Lake City, UT, p. A668
MARTIN, Wendy, Chief Executive Officer, Jefferson Hospital, Louisville, GA, p. A166
MARTIN–LINNARD, Tamara, R.N., Chief Clinical Officer, Great Plains Health, North Platte, NE, p. A403
MARTIN–PRATT, Diane, Director Information Systems, Niagara Falls Memorial Medical Center, Niagara Falls, NY, p. A454
MARTINEK, Jacquelyn, R.N., Group Chief Nursing Officer, Brookwood Baptist Medical Center, Birmingham, AL, p. A16
MARTINELLI, Tony
PharmD, President and Chief Executive Officer, Reynolds Memorial Hospital, Glen Dale, WV, p. A700
PharmD, President and Chief Executive Officer, Wetzel County Hospital, New Martinsville, WV, p. A703
MARTINEZ, Albino, Director Budget and Finance, Miners' Colfax Medical Center, Raton, NM, p. A436
MARTINEZ, Darlene, Director Finance, New Mexico Behavioral Health Institute At Las Vegas, Las Vegas, NM, p. A435
MARTINEZ, Eddie, Chief Financial Officer, El Paso Ltac Hospital, El Paso, TX, p. A616
MARTINEZ, Edward, Chief Information Officer, Nicklaus Children's Hospital, Miami, FL, p. A140
MARTINEZ, Eleanor, Chief Nursing Officer, Alhambra Hospital Medical Center, Alhambra, CA, p. A55
MARTINEZ, Francisco, Executive Director, Hospital San Antonio, Mayaguez, PR, p. A733
MARTINEZ, Frank, Senior Vice President Human Resources, East Jefferson General Hospital, Metairie, LA, p. A288
MARTINEZ, Homero S. III, Director, VA Texas Valley Coastal Hcs, Harlingen, TX, p. A624
MARTINEZ, Jason, Director Information Technology, West Valley Medical Center, Caldwell, ID, p. A180
MARTINEZ, Jeanine, Director Human Resources, Putnam General Hospital, Eatonton, GA, p. A163
MARTINEZ, Jose, M.D., Chief Medical Officer, HCA Florida Northwest Hospital, Margate, FL, p. A138
MARTINEZ, Josue, Coordinator Information Systems, University Hospital, San Juan, PR, p. A736
MARTINEZ, Kathryn J, Chief Operating Officer and Chief Nursing Officer, FHN Memorial Hospital, Freeport, IL, p. A195
MARTINEZ, Kelley, Hospital Administrator, Mangum Regional Medical Center, Mangum, OK, p. A514
MARTINEZ, Leanne, Chief Executive Officer and Administrator, Fisher County Hospital District, Rotan, TX, p. A647
MARTINEZ, Lee, Chief Information Officer, Cooley Dickinson Hospital, Northampton, MA, p. A316
MARTINEZ, Lonnie, Chief Executive Officer, Reunion Rehabilitation Hospital Inverness, Englewood, CO, p. A107
MARTINEZ, Louisa, Director of Nursing, Frio Regional Hospital, Pearsall, TX, p. A643
MARTINEZ, Maria, Chief Nursing Officer, La Paz Regional Hospital, Parker, AZ, p. A34
MARTINEZ, Michelle
Chief Executive Officer, U. S. Public Health Service Indian Hospital–Whiteriver, Whiteriver, AZ, p. A41
Controller, Encompass Health Rehabilitation Hospital of Albuquerque, Albuquerque, NM, p. A432
MARTINEZ, Ozalina, R.N., Director of Nursing, Northeastern Health System Sequoyah, Sallisaw, OK, p. A520
MARTINEZ, Regina M, Director Human Resources, La Paz Regional Hospital, Parker, AZ, p. A34
MARTINEZ, Scott, Executive Director Finance, Mercy Hospital Jefferson, Festus, MO, p. A375
MARTINEZ, Suzanne, Director Human Resources, Centennial Peaks Hospital, Louisville, CO, p. A112
MARTINEZ, Terri, Chief Financial Officer, Plains Memorial Hospital, Dimmitt, TX, p. A614
MARTINEZ, Tina, Director Human Resources, J. D. Mccarty Center for Children With Developmental Disabilities, Norman, OK, p. A516
MARTINEZ, Virginia, Director Human Resources, Copper Queen Community Hospital, Bisbee, AZ, p. A30
MARTINEZ, Yolanda, Chief Fiscal Services, Edward Hines, Jr. Veterans Affairs Hospital, Hines, IL, p. A198
MARTINEZ, Yvette, Director Human Resources, Sutter Auburn Faith Hospital, Auburn, CA, p. A56
MARTINEZ–TORRES, Daniel, Chief Executive Officer, Wellbridge Healthcare Greater Dallas, Plano, TX, p. A645
MARTINSON, Erling, M.D., Medical Director, Nelson County Health System, Mcville, ND, p. A482
MARTINSON, Tiffany, Director Human Resources, Norton Sound Regional Hospital, Nome, AK, p. A29
MARTN, Heather, Chief Financial Officer, Windsor–Laurelwood Center for Behavioral Medicine, Willoughby, OH, p. A507
MARTOCCIO, Debora, R.N., Chief Operating Officer, Adventhealth Connerton, Land O'Lakes, FL, p. A137
MARTONE, Nancy M, Vice President and Chief Human Resources Officer, Hospital for Special Care, New Britain, CT, p. A117
MARTUCCI, Kathleen, Chief Operating Officer, Helen Hayes Hospital, West Haverstraw, NY, p. A461
MARTZ, Dean
Chief Medical Officer, Providence Holy Family Hospital, Spokane, WA, p. A696
Chief Medical Officer, Providence Sacred Heart Medical Center & Children's Hospital, Spokane, WA, p. A696
MARTZ, Michael, Senior Vice President and Chief Information Officer, Mount Nittany Medical Center, State College, PA, p. A555
MARTZ, Michele R., CPA, President, UPMC Western Maryland, Cumberland, MD, p. A304
MARVIN, Ryan, Support Services Director, Rawlins County Health Center, Atwood, KS, p. A246
MARX, Edward, Chief Information Officer, Cleveland Clinic, Cleveland, OH, p. A490
MARX, Geoffrey, M.D., Chief Medical Officer, Piedmont Athens Regional Medical Center, Athens, GA, p. A156
MARX, Kenneth, Chief Financial Officer, Ranken Jordan Pediatric Bridge Hospital, Maryland Heights, MO, p. A380
MARX, Tomasine, Chief Financial Officer and Chief Operating Officer, Ascension Providence Rochester Hospital, Rochester, MI, p. A336
MARX, Troy, Human Resources Director, Upland Hills Health, Dodgeville, WI, p. A709
MARZOLF, Steve, R.N., Chief Nursing Officer, Corewell Health Pennock Hospital, Hastings, MI, p. A329
MASHAK–EKERN, Jane, Fiscal Officer, Tomah Va Medical Center, Tomah, WI, p. A723
MASHBURN, Jerry, Senior Vice President and Chief Financial Officer, HCA Florida Mercy Hospital, Miami, FL, p. A140
MASIELLO, Matthew, M.D., Chief Medical Officer, The Children's Institute of Pittsburgh, Pittsburgh, PA, p. A551
MASINGALE, Jason, Chief Operating Officer, Arkansas Methodist Medical Center, Paragould, AR, p. A52
MASKELL, Denise, Chief Information Officer, Springfield Hospital Center, Sykesville, MD, p. A307
MASMELA, Alex, Chief Operating Officer, HCA Florida Lawnwood Hospital, Fort Pierce, FL, p. A132
MASON, AJ, Chief Financial Officer, Humboldt County Memorial Hospital, Humboldt, IA, p. A237
MASON, Bret, Chief Financial Officer, New Hampshire Hospital, Concord, NH, p. A414
MASON, Delicia Y, Vice President of Nursing Operations, Children's of Alabama, Birmingham, AL, p. A16
MASON, H F, M.D., Chief Medical Officer, Baptist Memorial Hospital–Union County, New Albany, MS, p. A367
MASON, Jill K, MS, R.N., Chief Nursing Officer, Blessing Hospital, Quincy, IL, p. A206
MASON, John, Chief Information Officer, Methodist Hospital Hill Country, Fredericksburg, TX, p. A620
MASON, Kay, Chief Financial Officer, Texas Health Heart & Vascular Hospital Arlington, Arlington, TX, p. A598
MASON, Phyllis, M.D., Chief Medical Officer, Natchitoches Regional Medical Center, Natchitoches, LA, p. A289
MASON, Rhonda, Vice President of Patient Care Services, Tri–State Memorial Hospital, Clarkston, WA, p. A688
MASON, Robin, Chief Human Resources Officer, Cleveland Emergency Hospital, Humble, TX, p. A629
MASON, Sandra, MSN, R.N., Director Nursing Services and Senior Nurse Executive, Robert E. Bush Naval Hospital, Twentynine Palms, CA, p. A99
MASON, Stacie
Vice President and Chief Financial Officer, Integris Grove Hospital, Grove, OK, p. A513
Vice President, Regional Chief Financial Officer, Integris Health Enid Hospital, Enid, OK, p. A512
MASON, William, Chief Executive Officer and Managing Director, Rockford Center, Newark, DE, p. A122
MASON, William R, Chief Operating Officer, Brooke Glen Behavioral Hospital, Fort Washington, PA, p. A540
MASON–JONES, Taryn, Chief Nurse Executive, Norristown State Hospital, Norristown, PA, p. A547
MASOOD, Shahid, M.D., Clinical Director, Mildred Mitchell–Bateman Hospital, Huntington, WV, p. A701
MASSA, Rhonda, Director of Nursing, Clarion Psychiatric Center, Clarion, PA, p. A537
MASSAAD, Aziz, M.D., Medical Staff President, Down East Community Hospital, Machias, ME, p. A298
MASSARO, Thomas, M.D., Chief Medical Officer, New Mexico Rehabilitation Center, Roswell, NM, p. A436
MASSELLA, Joan, Administrative Vice President and Chief Nursing Officer, St. Clair Health, Pittsburgh, PA, p. A551
MASSENGALE, David
Chief Financial Officer, Deaconess Union County Hospital, Morganfield, KY, p. A272
Vice President and Chief Financial Officer, Deaconess Henderson Hospital, Henderson, KY, p. A267
MASSEY, Gina, Vice President Human Resources, Clarity Child Guidance Center, San Antonio, TX, p. A649
MASSEY, Mark, Chief Financial Officer, St. Catherine Hospital – Dodge City, Dodge City, KS, p. A248

Index of Health Care Professionals

Index of Health Care Professionals / Massey

MASSEY, Rocco K., Interim Chief Executive Officer, Arh Our Lady of The Way, Martin, KY, p. A271
MASSEY, Steven, President and Chief Executive Officer, Westfields Hospital And Clinic, New Richmond, WI, p. A718
MASSEY, Tami, M.D., Chief of Medical Staff, Edgefield County Healthcare, Edgefield, SC, p. A565
MASSEY, Terry, Chief Fiscal Services, Beckley Veterans Affairs Medical Center, Beckley, WV, p. A699
MASSIELLO, Martin J.
Executive Vice President and Chief Operating Officer, Eisenhower Health, Rancho Mirage, CA, p. A84
President/Chief Executive Officer, Eisenhower Health, Rancho Mirage, CA, p. A84
MASSIMILLA, John P., FACHE, WSH Vice President and President of Wellspan Chambersburg, Wellspan Chambersburg Hospital, Chambersburg, PA, p. A536
MASSINI, Stephen M., Chief Executive Officer, Penn State Health, Penn State Milton S. Hershey Medical Center, Hershey, PA, p. A542
MASSMAN, Patty, Director of Nursing, Avera Granite Falls, Granite Falls, MN, p. A348
MASSOUH, Rafik, M.D., Chief of Staff, Mercy Health – Allen Hospital, Oberlin, OH, p. A501
MAST, Delvin, R.N., Director of Nursing, Weatherford Regional Hospital, Weatherford, OK, p. A524
MAST, Duane, M.D., Medical Director, Hocking Valley Community Hospital, Logan, OH, p. A498
MAST, Joelle, Ph.D., M.D., Chief Medical Officer, Blythedale Children's Hospital, Valhalla, NY, p. A460
MASTALERZ, Beata, Executive Director, Phelp. Memorial Hospital Center, Sleep. Hollow, NY, p. A459
MASTER, Moiz, M.D., Medical Director of Quality, Piedmont Mountainside Hospital, Jasper, GA, p. A165
MASTERS, Emily, Chief Human Relations Officer, Windom Area Health, Windom, MN, p. A357
MASTERS, Ken, Director Information Technology, Chambers Memorial Hospital, Danville, AR, p. A45
MASTERS, Kim, M.D., Medical Director, Saint Simons By–The–Sea Hospital, Saint Simons Island, GA, p. A170
MASTERS, Regina, R.N., MSN, Director of Nursing, Continuing Care Hospital, Lexington, KY, p. A268
MASTERSON, Beau, Chief Executive Officer, Barbourville Arh Hospital, Barbourville, KY, p. A263
MASTERSON, David J., Division President, Sentara Obici Hospital, Suffolk, VA, p. A684
MASTERSON, Paul, Chief Financial Officer, Genesis Healthcare System, Zanesville, OH, p. A508
MASTERSON, Sammie, Director Human Resources, Harney District Hospital, Burns, OR, p. A526
MASTROIANNI, Anthony, Regional Vice President Finance, The William W. Backus Hospital, Norwich, CT, p. A118
MASTROIANNI, Thomas, Director, Human Resources, ECU Health North Hospital, Roanoke Rapids, NC, p. A475
MASTROMANO, Christopher, Chief Executive Officer, NYC Health + Hospitals/Jacobi, New York, NY, p. A451
MASZAK, Edward, Chief Financial Officer, Gateway Regional Medical Center, Granite City, IL, p. A196
MATA, Maribel, Director Information Services, Doctors Hospital of Laredo, Laredo, TX, p. A634
MATA–GUERRERO, Rita, Director of Nursing, Weslaco Regional Rehabilitation Hospital, Weslaco, TX, p. A662
MATAI, Divya, Chief Financial Officer, Northwest Texas Healthcare System, Amarillo, TX, p. A596
MATCHETT, Glenda, Chief Executive Officer, Dallas Regional Medical Center, Mesquite, TX, p. A639
MATCHETT, Jarred, Chief Financial Officer, Fox Chase Cancer Center, Philadelphia, PA, p. A548
MATEJICKA, Anthony, D.O., M.P.H., Vice President, Chief Medical Officer, Montefiore Nyack Hospital, Nyack, NY, p. A454
MATEJKA, Cheryl
Chief Financial Officer, Mercy Hospital St. Louis, Saint Louis, MO, p. A385
Chief Financial Officer, Mercy Hospital Washington, Washington, MO, p. A388
MATENS, Brett, FACHE, Chief Executive Officer, St. David's Medical Center, Austin, TX, p. A600
MATHAI, George, M.D., Chief of Staff, Ascension St. Thomas Three Rivers, Waverly, TN, p. A594
MATHAI, Matt, M.D., Medical Director, Select Specialty Hospital–Milwaukee, Milwaukee, WI, p. A717
MATHEIS, Tracey
Chief Financial Officer, Moberly Regional Medical Center, Moberly, MO, p. A380
Chief Operating Officer, Moberly Regional Medical Center, Moberly, MO, p. A380
MATHERS, Larry, M.D., Chief of Staff, Tennova Newport Medical Center, Newport, TN, p. A591
MATHES, Lisa L., Human Resources Director, Southwest Medical Center, Liberal, KS, p. A253
MATHEW, Finny, President, Oklahoma State University Medical Center, Tulsa, OK, p. A522
MATHEWS, Gary, M.D., Medical Doctor, Beaver County Memorial Hospital, Beaver, OK, p. A510
MATHEWS, Kristopher, Chief Executive Officer, Dundy County Hospital, Benkelman, NE, p. A398
MATHEWS, Nimmy, Acting Director Quality Management, San Carlos Apache Healthcare Corporation, Peridot, AZ, p. A34
MATHEWS, Paul G., CPA, Chief Executive Officer, Hardtner Medical Center, Olla, LA, p. A291
MATHEWS, Thomas, Chief Financial Officer, Unitypoint Health–Des Moines, Des Moines, IA, p. A235
MATHEWSON, Patricia, Chief Nursing Officer, Adventist Health – Tulare, Tulare, CA, p. A98
MATHIEU, Angie, System Director Information Technology and Regional Chief Information Officer, The William W. Backus Hospital, Norwich, CT, p. A118
MATHIEU, Lori, MSN, Chief Nursing Officer and Chief Operating Officer, Glenwood Regional Medical Center, West Monroe, LA, p. A294
MATHIS, Alison, Chief Nursing Officer, Copiah County Medical Center, Hazlehurst, MS, p. A363
MATHIS, Ashley, Privacy Officer, Columbus Community Hospital, Columbus, TX, p. A608
MATHIS, Christina, Chief Executive Officer, Medical City Plano, Plano, TX, p. A645
MATHIS, Patricia, Associate Director Patient Care Service, Richard L. Roudebush Veterans Affairs Medical Center, Indianapolis, IN, p. A220
MATHIS, Rebecca
Chief Financial Officer, UChicago Medicine Adventhealth La Grange, La Grange, IL, p. A199
Vice President and Chief Financial Officer, UChicago Medicine Adventhealth Hinsdale, Hinsdale, IL, p. A198
MATHIS, Richard, Chief Executive Officer, Valley Community Hospital, Pauls Valley, OK, p. A519
MATHIS, Robin, Director Human Resources, Methodist Healthcare Olive Branch Hospital, Olive Branch, MS, p. A367
MATHISEN, Arthur, FACHE, Chief Executive Officer, Good Shepherd Health Care System, Hermiston, OR, p. A527
MATHUR, Ashish, M.D., Chief of Staff, Siloam Springs Regional Hospital, Siloam Springs, AR, p. A53
MATHURIN, Emile, M.D., Jr, Medical Director, Encompass Health Rehabilitation Hospital of Humble, Humble, TX, p. A629
MATHURIN, Venra, Vice President Human Resources, Interfaith Medical Center, New York, NY, p. A448
MATINCHEV, Borian, M.D., Medical Director, Encompass Health Rehabilitation Hospital, A Partner of Washington Regional, Fayetteville, AR, p. A46
MATISH, Elizabeth, Chief Executive Officer, Henrico Doctors' Hospital, Richmond, VA, p. A682
MATLOCK, Kourtney, President, Baptist Health Rehabilitation Institute, Little Rock, AR, p. A49
MATNEY, James L., President and Chief Executive Officer, Colquitt Regional Medical Center, Moultrie, GA, p. A169
MATNEY, Patty, Human Resources Consultant, Ascension Saint Thomas Hickman, Centerville, TN, p. A580
MATNEY, Tim, Chief Financial Officer, Logan Regional Medical Center, Logan, WV, p. A702
MATOS, Patricia, Chief Nursing Officer, Stewart & Lynda Resnick Neuropsychiatric Hospital At Ucla, Los Angeles, CA, p. A75
MATSINGER, John, D.O., Chief Medical Officer, Virtua Marlton, Marlton, NJ, p. A423
MATSON, Kevin, Interim Chief Executive Officer, Northeast Georgia Medical Center Habersham, Demorest, GA, p. A162
MATTERN, Bonnie, Director Human Resources, Chi St. Alexius Health Devils Lake, Devils Lake, ND, p. A480
MATTERN, Joe, M.D., Chief Medical Officer, Jefferson Healthcare, Port Townsend, WA, p. A693
MATTERN, Karen, Director of Human Resources, Shriners Hospitals for Children–Spokane, Spokane, WA, p. A696
MATTES, Bryan, Associate Administrator, Crossridge Community Hospital, Wynne, AR, p. A54
MATTEUCCI, Dolly, Executive Director, Nap. State Hospital, Napa, CA, p. A79
MATTHEWS, Adora, M.D., Medical Director, Encompass Health Rehabilitation Hospital of Florence, Florence, SC, p. A566
MATTHEWS, Bryan C., Medical Center Director, Carl T. Hayden Veterans' Administration Medical Center, Phoenix, AZ, p. A35
MATTHEWS, Carol, Director Human Resources, Saline Memorial Hospital, Benton, AR, p. A43
MATTHEWS, Deborah
Chief Nursing Officer, Tanner Medical Center–Carrollton, Carrollton, GA, p. A160
Senior Vice President, Tanner Medical Center–Villa Rica, Villa Rica, GA, p. A173
MATTHEWS, Edward, Chief Financial Officer, San Dimas Community Hospital, San Dimas, CA, p. A90
MATTHEWS, Judith, Nurse Executive, VCU Health Tappahannock Hospital, Tappahannock, VA, p. A684
MATTHEWS, Kristopher, Chief Operating Officer, Decatur Health Systems, Oberlin, KS, p. A256
MATTHEWS, Lori, Vice President Information Technology System, Banner Baywood Medical Center, Mesa, AZ, p. A33
MATTHEWS, Melissa, Director Human Resources, Dahl Memorial Healthcare Association, Ekalaka, MT, p. A391
MATTHEWS, Oliver, M.D., Chief Medical Officer, North Alabama Medical Center, Florence, AL, p. A19
MATTHEWS, Ted D., Chief Executive Officer, Anson General Hospital, Anson, TX, p. A597
MATTHEY, Michael, Facility Chief Information Officer, Louis A. Johnson Veterans Affairs Medical Center, Clarksburg, WV, p. A700
MATTHIAS, Mark, M.D., Vice President, Medical Affairs, and Physician Vice President, Acute Care Division, Centracare – St. Cloud Hospital, Saint Cloud, MN, p. A354
MATTHIESSEN, Matthew, Chief Financial Officer, North Valley Hospital, Tonasket, WA, p. A697
MATTICE, Gloria, R.N., Director Patient Care, George C. Grap. Community Hospital, Hamburg, IA, p. A237
MATTINGLY, Marty, Administrator, Ascension St. Vincent Warrick, Boonville, IN, p. A213
MATTISON, Denise, Director Finance and Accounting Services, Mayo Clinic Health System In Eau Claire, Eau Claire, WI, p. A710
MATTLY, Sheila, Chief Nursing Officer, Wayne County Hospital And Clinic System, Corydon, IA, p. A233
MATTNER, Matthew
Chief Operating Officer, Cleveland Clinic Lutheran Hospital, Cleveland, OH, p. A490
Chief Operations Officer, Fisher–Titus Medical Center, Norwalk, OH, p. A501
MATTSON, Jodi, Director of Nursing, Cedar Springs Hospital, Colorado Springs, CO, p. A104
MATTSON, Kent D.
Chief Executive Officer, Elbow Lake Medical Center, Elbow Lake, MN, p. A346
Chief Executive Officer, Lake Region Healthcare Corporation, Fergus Falls, MN, p. A347
MATTSON, Wayne, Management Information Systems Specialist, Rogers Behavioral Health, Oconomowoc, WI, p. A718
MATUS, Jose, M.D., Director Medical, Carrus Rehabilitation Hospital, Sherman, TX, p. A653
MATUSIAK, Matthew, Chief Executive Officer, Dallas Behavioral Healthcare Hospital, Desoto, TX, p. A614
MATUSZEWSKI, Jonathon
Hospital Administrator, Ascension Southeast Wisconsin Hospital – Franklin Campus, Franklin, WI, p. A711
Hospital Administrator, Ascension St. Francis Hospital, Milwaukee, WI, p. A716
MATUSZKIEWICZ, Marcin, M.D., Chief of Staff and Medical Director, Jerold Phelp. Community Hospital, Garberville, CA, p. A65
MATZIGKEIT, Linda, Senior Vice President Human Resources, Children's Healthcare of Atlanta, Atlanta, GA, p. A157
MAUGHAN, Daniel J. MSN,RN, C, President and Chief Executive Officer, Montefiore St. Luke's Cornwall, Newburgh, NY, p. A454
MAURER, Jackie, Fiscal Officer, Julian F. Keith Alcohol And Drug Abuse Treatment Center, Black Mountain, NC, p. A464
MAURER, Linda, Vice President Patient Care Services, Wilson Memorial Hospital, Sidney, OH, p. A503
MAURER, Marsha L., R.N., MS, Chief Nursing Officer Patient Care Services, Beth Israel Deaconess Medical Center, Boston, MA, p. A309
MAURICE, Timothy, Chief Financial Officer, UC Davis Medical Center, Sacramento, CA, p. A87
MAURIN, Michael J, Chief Financial Officer, Southern Surgical Hospital, Slidell, LA, p. A293
MAUS, Adam
Administrator, Chi St. Alexius Health Garrison, Garrison, ND, p. A481
Administrator, Chi St. Alexius Health Turtle Lake Hospital, Turtle Lake, ND, p. A483
MAVROMATIS, Lou, Vice President Information Technology, Medstar Southern Maryland Hospital Center, Clinton, MD, p. A303
MAXIE, Bryan K., Administrator, Highland Community Hospital, Picayune, MS, p. A368
MAXWELL, Dale, Executive Vice President and Chief Financial Officer, Presbyterian Hospital, Albuquerque, NM, p. A433

A914 Index of Health Care Professionals

Index of Health Care Professionals / McCarthy

Index of Health Care Professionals

MAXWELL, Ronnie, Director Information Systems, Glenwood Regional Medical Center, West Monroe, LA, p. A294
MAY, Brandon, President, Morton Plant North Bay Hospital, New Port Richey, FL, p. A142
MAY, Kevin B
Chief Financial Officer, Watauga Medical Center, Boone, NC, p. A464
System Director Finance, Charles A. Cannon Jr. Memorial Hospital, Newland, NC, p. A473
MAY, Robin, Director Information Systems, Platte County Memorial Hospital, Wheatland, WY, p. A729
MAY, Ronald B, M.D., Vice President Medical Affairs, Carolinaeast Health System, New Bern, NC, p. A473
MAY, Scott, Area Director Technology, Kaiser Permanente Santa Clara Medical Center, Santa Clara, CA, p. A94
MAY, Sonja, Director Human Resources, Morton County Health System, Elkhart, KS, p. A248
MAY, Todd, M.D., Chief Medical Officer, Zuckerberg San Francisco General Hospital And Trauma Center, San Francisco, CA, p. A91
MAY, Troy, Chief Information Officer, Uofl Health – Uofl Hospital, Louisville, KY, p. A270
MAYBEN, Casey, Chief Nursing Officer, UT Health Pittsburg, Pittsburg, TX, p. A644
MAYCOCK, Adam
President and Chief Executive Officer, UChicago Medicine Adventhealth Hinsdale, Hinsdale, IL, p. A198
President and Chief Executive Officer, UChicago Medicine Adventhealth La Grange, La Grange, IL, p. A199
MAYEAUX, Scott, Director of Human Resources, Tristar Northcrest Medical Center, Springfield, TN, p. A593
MAYER, David, Chief of Staff, Wayne County Hospital, Monticello, KY, p. A271
MAYER, Dean, M.D., Chief Medical Officer, Riverton Hospital, Riverton, UT, p. A668
MAYER, Denise, MSN, R.N., Chief Nursing Officer, Pam Rehabilitation Hospital of Tavares, Tavares, FL, p. A153
MAYER, Joanne St. Joseph's Hospital, Tampa, FL, p. A152
MAYER, John W., Chief Financial Officer, San Juan Regional Medical Center, Farmington, NM, p. A434
MAYER, William, M.D., Vice President Medical Staff Services, St. Mary's Healthcare, Amsterdam, NY, p. A438
MAYES, Libby, Human Resource Director, Ephraim Mcdowell Regional Medical Center, Danville, KY, p. A264
MAYES, Precious Velvet., President and Chief Executive Officer, Pacifica Hospital of The Valley, Los Angeles, CA, p. A74
MAYES, Terri A, Vice President and Chief Nursing Officer, Valley Health – Warren Memorial Hospital, Front Royal, VA, p. A677
MAYEWSKI, Raymond
M.D., Chief Medical Officer, Highland Hospital, Rochester, NY, p. A457
M.D., Chief Medical Officer, Strong Memorial Hospital of The University of Rochester, Rochester, NY, p. A457
MAYFIELD, Michael Bradley, M.D., Chief of Staff, Chicot Memorial Medical Center, Lake Village, AR, p. A49
MAYFIELD, William, M.D., Chief of Staff, Tristar Stonecrest Medical Center, Smyrna, TN, p. A593
MAYHLE, Douglas, M.D., Medical Director, Nicholas H. Noyes Memorial Hospital, Dansville, NY, p. A442
MAYLE, Connie, Vice President Administrative Services, UPMC Horizon, Farrell, PA, p. A540
MAYNARD, BJ, Chief Information Officer, Ashe Memorial Hospital, Jefferson, NC, p. A471
MAYNARD, Bob, Chief Information Officer, Fairview Regional Medical Center, Fairview, OK, p. A512
MAYNARD, Waylon, Chief Executive Officer, Pam Health Rehabilitation Hospital of Greater Indiana, Clarksville, IN, p. A214
MAYO, Hal, Chief Financial Officer, Liberty Dayton Regional Medical Center, Liberty, TX, p. A634
MAYO, Jim, M.D., Clinical Director, Cherry Hospital, Goldsboro, NC, p. A469
MAYO, Randy, Director Information Technology, William Newton Hospital, Winfield, KS, p. A262
MAYO, Robert
M.D., Chief Medical Officer, Rochester General Hospital, Rochester, NY, p. A457
M.D., Executive Vice President, Chief Medical Officer, Rochester Regional Health, Newark–Wayne Community Hospital, Newark, NY, p. A454
MAYORGA, Oliver
M.D., Chief Medical Officer, Lawrence + Memorial Hospital, New London, CT, p. A118
M.D., Chief Medical Officer, Westerly Hospital, Westerly, RI, p. A561
MAYS, Dawn, Chief Nursing Officer, Norton Scott Hospital, Scottsburg, IN, p. A227
MAYS, Raymond, M.D., Medical Director, River Crest Hospital, San Angelo, TX, p. A648
MAYS, Sherrie, MSN, R.N., Vice President and Chief Nursing Officer, Baptist Health Corbin, Corbin, KY, p. A264
MAYSENT, Patty, M.P.H., Chief Executive Officer, UC San Diego Medical Center – Hillcrest, San Diego, CA, p. A90
MAYSON, Mark J, M.D., Medical Director, Prisma Health Baptist Hospital, Columbia, SC, p. A565
MAZANEC, Lori, Chief Executive Officer, Box Butte General Hospital, Alliance, NE, p. A397
MAZEK, Mariusz, Vice President Information Technology and Chief Information Officer, Roseland Community Hospital, Chicago, IL, p. A190
MAZOUR, Linda, M.D., President, Franklin County Memorial Hospital, Franklin, NE, p. A399
MAZUREK, Michele A, Chief Nursing Officer, Mount Sinai Hospital, Chicago, IL, p. A190
MAZZA, Mary, Director Human Resources, Encompass Health Rehabilitation Hospital of Western Massachusetts, Ludlow, MA, p. A315
MAZZARELLI, Anthony J., JD, M.D., Co–President and Chief Executive Officer, Cooper University Health Care, Camden, NJ, p. A419
MAZZO, Joseph, Chief Executive Officer, Tricities Hospital, Hopewell, VA, p. A678
MAZZOLA, Joseph, D.O., Vice President of Medical Affairs, Iredell Health System, Statesville, NC, p. A477
MAZZONI, Dean, President and Chief Executive Officer, Franciscan Health Michigan City, Michigan City, IN, p. A223
MAZZUCA, Darryl, Director Management Information Systems, OSF Healthcare Little Company of Mary Medical Center, Evergreen Park, IL, p. A195
MAZZUCA, Phillip J., Chief Executive Officer, Williamson Medical Center, Franklin, TN, p. A583
MBENGA, Saul, Manager Information Technology, Alliance Healthcare System, Holly Springs, MS, p. A363
MCADAMS, David, Chief Financial Officer, Lindner Center of Hope, Mason, OH, p. A499
MCADOO, Jackie, Chief Financial Officer, Grady Memorial Hospital, Chickasha, OK, p. A511
MCAFEE, Sean, Chief Operating Officer, Ascension St. Vincent's St. Johns County, Saint Johns, FL, p. A148
MCAFEE, Thomas J.
President, Northwestern Memorial Hospital, Chicago, IL, p. A190
Region President, Northwestern Medicine Mchenry, Mchenry, IL, p. A201
MCALISTER, Julene, Administrator, Accord Rehabilitation Hospital, Plaquemine, LA, p. A291
MCALISTER, Stephanie, Controller, Tippah County Hospital, Ripley, MS, p. A368
MCALLISTER, Guy, Vice President and Chief Information Officer, Tift Regional Medical Center, Tifton, GA, p. A172
MCALLISTER, Ric, Chief Executive Officer, Creekside Behavioral Health, Kingsport, TN, p. A585
MCALLISTER, Yvonne, Senior Director Human Resources, Southern Maine Health Care – Biddeford Medical Center, Biddeford, ME, p. A296
MCALOON, Richard, Vice President Human Resources, Hartford Hospital, Hartford, CT, p. A116
MCALPINE, Kimberly, Facility Director, Taylor Hardin Secure Medical Facility, Tuscaloosa, AL, p. A25
MCANDREWS, Kevin
Vice President Human Resources, Nexus Specialty Hospital, Shenandoah, TX, p. A652
Vice President, Human Resources, Nexus Specialty Hospital The Woodlands, The Woodlands, TX, p. A657
MCANULTY, Jonathan, Chief Executive Officer, West Tennessee Healthcare Rehabilitation Hospital Cane Creek, A Partnership With Encompass Health, Martin, TN, p. A587
MCARTOR, Dana, R.N., Director of Nursing, Perkins County Health Services, Grant, NE, p. A400
MCASKILL, L. Craig, M.D., Chief Medical Officer, HCA Florida Englewood Hospital, Englewood, FL, p. A131
MCAULIFFE, Christopher, R.N., Market Chief Executive Officer, Integris Health Community Hospital At Council Crossing, Oklahoma City, OK, p. A517
MCAVOY, Tim, M.D., Medical Director, Prohealth Rehabilitation Hospital of Wisconsin, Waukesha, WI, p. A723
MCBEE, Jeff, Administrator, Presbyterian Hospital, Albuquerque, NM, p. A433
MCBEE, John, Chief of Staff, Chi St. Anthony Hospital, Pendleton, OR, p. A530
MCBREARTY, Michael, M.D., Vice President Medical Affairs, Thomas Hospital, Fairhope, AL, p. A19
MCBRIDE, Brandon
Operations Officer, Logan Regional Hospital, Logan, UT, p. A665
President, Logan Regional Hospital, Logan, UT, p. A665
MCBRIDE, Dina, Chief Operating Officer and Director Human Resources, East Adams Rural Healthcare, Ritzville, WA, p. A694
MCBRIDE, Grace, Regional Chief Nursing Officer, Ascension Mercy, Aurora, IL, p. A185
MCBRIDE, Jason, Chief Executive Officer, Pawhuska Hospital, Pawhuska, OK, p. A519
MCBRIDE, Lamar, Chief Executive Officer, Vibra Hospital of Denver, Thornton, CO, p. A114
MCBROOM, Robert, M.D., Medical Director, KPC Promise Hospital of Wichita Falls, Wichita Falls, TX, p. A662
MCBRYDE, Robin, Chief Information Officer, Alexandria Va Medical Center, Pineville, LA, p. A291
MCCAA, Karen, R.N., Vice President Patient Care Services and Chief Nursing Officer, Baptist Medical Center South, Montgomery, AL, p. A22
MCCABE, Patrick, Senior Vice President Finance and Chief Financial Officer, Bridgeport Hospital, Bridgeport, CT, p. A115
MCCABE, Rhonda, Chief Executive Officer, Nacogdoches Memorial Hospital, Nacogdoches, TX, p. A640
MCCABE, Steve, Chief Executive Officer, Carolina Dunes Behavioral Health, Leland, NC, p. A471
MCCAFFERTY, Michael, Chief Executive Officer, Sheridan Memorial Hospital, Sheridan, WY, p. A728
MCCAHILL, Mary, Chief Nursing Officer, Thorek Memorial Hospital, Chicago, IL, p. A191
MCCAIN, Rebecca J., Chief Executive Officer, Electra Memorial Hospital, Electra, TX, p. A618
MCCALL, Brad D.
Vice President Operations, Baylor Scott & White The Heart Hospital Denton, Denton, TX, p. A613
Vice President Operations, Baylor Scott & White The Heart Hospital Plano, Plano, TX, p. A644
MCCALL, Harlo, Chief Executive Officer, Ascension St. John Rehabilitation Hospital, An Affiliate of Encompass Health – Owasso, Owasso, OK, p. A519
MCCALL, Lee, Chief Executive Officer, Neshoba General, Philadelphia, MS, p. A367
MCCALLISTER, Bob, Director Human Resources, Baptist Memorial Hospital–Golden Triangle, Columbus, MS, p. A361
MCCALLISTER, Darla, Chief Financial Officer, Lakeside Women's Hospital, Oklahoma City, OK, p. A517
MCCALLISTER, Dianne, M.D., Chief Medical Officer, Medical Center of Aurora, Aurora, CO, p. A103
MCCALLUM, Shawn, Chief Executive Officer, Reunion Rehabilitation Hospital Peoria, Peoria, AZ, p. A34
MCCAMPBELL, Kellie, Coordinator Human Resources, Kindred Hospital–Chattanooga, Chattanooga, TN, p. A580
MCCAMPBELL, Marcia, M.D., Chief Medical Officer, Shasta Regional Medical Center, Redding, CA, p. A85
MCCANDLESS, David, Vice President Medical Affairs, UPMC Northwest, Seneca, PA, p. A554
MCCANN, Barbara, Director Human Resources, Sunrise Canyon Hospital, Lubbock, TX, p. A636
MCCANN, Kyle, Chief Operating Officer, St. Joseph's Hospital, Savannah, GA, p. A171
MCCANN, Lew, Director Management Information Systems, OSF Holy Family Medical Center, Monmouth, IL, p. A202
MCCARTAN, Mary E, Manager Human Resources, Tibor Rubin Va Medical Center, Long Beach, CA, p. A71
MCCARTER, Alyssa, Chief Financial Officer, W. J. Mangold Memorial Hospital, Lockney, TX, p. A635
MCCARTER, Deborah
R.N., MSN, Vice President and Chief Nursing Officer, OSF Heart of Mary Medical Center, Urbana, IL, p. A210
R.N., MSN, Vice President and Chief Nursing Officer, OSF Sacred Heart Medical Center, Danville, IL, p. A192
MCCARTER, Scott, Chief Information Officer, Karmanos Cancer Center, Detroit, MI, p. A326
MCCARTHY, Cynthia L, Chief Nursing Officer, Texas Health Harris Methodist Hospital Stephenville, Stephenville, TX, p. A654
MCCARTHY, Katherine, Director Human Resources, Arbour H. R. I. Hospital, Brookline, MA, p. A312
MCCARTHY, Kevin L.
Chief Administrative Officer, Concord Hospital – Franklin, Franklin, NH, p. A415
Chief Administrative Officer and Vice President, Support Services, Concord Hospital – Laconia, Laconia, NH, p. A415
MCCARTHY, Maureen, M.D., Chief of Staff, Carl T. Hayden Veterans' Administration Medical Center, Phoenix, AZ, p. A35
MCCARTHY, Rick, Chief Information Officer, White Plains Hospital Center, White Plains, NY, p. A462
MCCARTHY, Sandra Mac, Chief Nursing Officer, Arnot Ogden Medical Center, Elmira, NY, p. A442

© 2025 AHA Guide Index of Health Care Professionals **A915**

Index of Health Care Professionals
Index of Health Care Professionals / McCarthy

MCCARTHY, Tim, President Puerto Rico Division, First Hospital Panamericano, Cidra, PR, p. A732
MCCARTHY, Tonia, Chief Nursing Officer, Spring View Hospital, Lebanon, KY, p. A268
MCCARTIN, Nikki, Chief Executive Officer, Pam Rehabilitation Hospital of Jupiter, Jupiter, FL, p. A136
MCCARTNEY, Adam, Chief Information Officer, Arrowhead Regional Medical Center, Colton, CA, p. A60
MCCARTNEY, Daryl, M.D., President Medical Staff, Emanuel Medical Center, Swainsboro, GA, p. A172
MCCARTNEY, Mary Ellen, Chief Human Resource Officer, Gundersen Lutheran Medical Center, La Crosse, WI, p. A713
MCCARTY, Daniel P, Chief Operating Officer, Orange City Area Health System, Orange City, IA, p. A241
MCCARTY, Kirk
R.N., MSN, Chief Executive Officer, Menorah Medical Center, Overland Park, KS, p. A257
R.N., MSN, Chief Executive Officer, Research Medical Center, Kansas City, MO, p. A378
MCCARTY, Melany
R.N., Chief Clinical Officer, KPC Promise Hospital of Amarillo, Amarillo, TX, p. A596
R.N., Chief Executive Officer, KPC Promise Hospital of Amarillo, Amarillo, TX, p. A596
MCCARTY, Tim, Chief Information Officer, Oakbend Medical Center, Richmond, TX, p. A646
MCCARTY, Wendy, Director Human Resources, Hillsboro Community Hospital, Hillsboro, KS, p. A250
MCCARVER, Scott
Chief Operating Officer, Vanderbilt Wilson County Hospital, Lebanon, TN, p. A586
President, Vanderbilt Wilson County Hospital, Lebanon, TN, p. A586
MCCASKILL, Rodney, M.D., Interim Chief Medical Officer, UNC Health Johnston, Smithfield, NC, p. A476
MCCASLIN, Anna, Director Finance, Boys Town National Research Hospital, Omaha, NE, p. A403
MCCASLIN, Jami, Director Human Resources, Providence Hood River Memorial Hospital, Hood River, OR, p. A528
MCCAULEY, Cynthia, Chief Executive Officer, St. Mary's Medical Center, West Palm Beach, FL, p. A154
MCCAULEY, Dudley, Controller, Lincoln County Medical Center, Ruidoso, NM, p. A436
MCCAULEY, Jason, Administrator, Ascension St. John Nowata, Nowata, OK, p. A516
MCCAULEY, Sue E, Director Finance, Mercyone Primghar Medical Center, Primghar, IA, p. A242
MCCAWLEY, Thomas J, Vice President, Beloit Health System, Beloit, WI, p. A708
MCCHESNEY, Brett D., Chief Executive Officer, Helen M. Simpson Rehabilitation Hospital, Harrisburg, PA, p. A541
MCCHESNEY, Lisa D, R.N., Senior Director Information Systems, UPMC Hamot, Erie, PA, p. A540
MCCLAIN, James, Deputy Director, Clement J. Zablocki Veterans' Administration Medical Center, Milwaukee, WI, p. A717
MCCLAIN, Richard, M.D., Chief Medical Officer, Chickasaw Nation Medical Center, Ada, OK, p. A509
MCCLAIN–CLOWER, April, Director of Patient Care, Valley Health – Shenandoah Memorial Hospital, Woodstock, VA, p. A686
MCCLANAHAN, Gary, Chief Information Officer, Northeastern Health System Sequoyah, Sallisaw, OK, p. A520
MCCLANAHAN, Tammy L., Chief Administrative Officer, Norton Hospital, Louisville, KY, p. A270
MCCLARIGAN, Linda, R.N., Chief Nursing Officer, Adirondack Health, Saranac Lake, NY, p. A458
MCCLASKEY, Cynthia, Ph.D., Director, Southwestern Virginia Mental Health Institute, Marion, VA, p. A679
MCCLAY, Robert, Chief Executive Officer, Harmon Medical And Rehabilitation Hospital, Las Vegas, NV, p. A410
MCCLEARY, Heather, Director Human Resources, Coulee Medical Center, Grand Coulee, WA, p. A690
MCCLEESE, Randy
Chief Information Officer, Deaconess Henderson Hospital, Henderson, KY, p. A267
Chief Information Officer, Deaconess Union County Hospital, Morganfield, KY, p. A272
MCCLELLAN, Kathryn
Chief Information Officer, Memorial Health University Medical Center, Savannah, GA, p. A171
Senior Vice President and Chief Information Officer, Froedtert West Bend Hospital, West Bend, WI, p. A724
MCCLELLAND, Patricia, Director Human Resources, South Texas Health System, Edinburg, TX, p. A615
MCCLINTICK, Cliff, Chief Information Officer, Lindner Center of Hope, Mason, OH, p. A499
MCCLOSKEY, Louis, Chief Human Resources, Wilmington Veterans Affairs Medical Center, Wilmington, DE, p. A122
MCCLUNG, James W., Chief Executive Officer, Select Specialty Hospital–St. Louis, Saint Charles, MO, p. A383
MCCLUNG, Lyle, M.D., Chief of Staff, Carilion Rockbridge Community Hospital, Lexington, VA, p. A678
MCCLURE, Jordan
Chief Executive Officer, Select Specialty Hospital Nashville, Nashville, TN, p. A590
Chief Executive Officer, Select Specialty Hospital– Wilmington, Wilmington, DE, p. A122
MCCLURE, Kenneth, M.D., Chief of Staff, Longview Regional Medical Center, Longview, TX, p. A635
MCCLURE–CHESSIER, Patricia, Chief Administrative Officer, Montrose Behavioral Health Hospital, Chicago, IL, p. A190
MCCLURG, Cathy, Director Human Resources, William Newton Hospital, Winfield, KS, p. A262
MCCLURG, Chris, Vice President Finance and Chief Financial Officer, St. Claire Regional Medical Center, Morehead, KY, p. A272
MCCLUSKEY, Diane M, Chief Human Resources Officer, Twin Cities Community Hospital, Templeton, CA, p. A97
MCCLUSKEY, Scott Elton, Chief Financial Officer, Tyler County Hospital, Woodville, TX, p. A663
MCCLUSKEY, Tabb, M.D., Chief Medical Officer, Hendricks Community Hospital Association, Hendricks, MN, p. A348
MCCLUSKEY, Zachary, Chief Executive Officer, HCA Florida Fort Walton–Destin Hospital, Fort Walton Beach, FL, p. A132
MCCOBB, David, Chief Information Officer, Emanate Health Foothill Presbyterian Hospital, Glendora, CA, p. A66
MCCOIC, Kristie
Administrator, Gundersen St. Joseph's Hospital And Clinics, Hillsboro, WI, p. A713
Clinic Operations Officer and Director Human Resources, Gundersen St. Joseph's Hospital And Clinics, Hillsboro, WI, p. A713
MCCOLL, Karen, M.D., Chief Medical Officer, Memorial Health Meadows Hospital, Vidalia, GA, p. A173
MCCOLLEM, Darren, Chief Operating Officer, Banner Gateway Medical Center, Gilbert, AZ, p. A31
MCCOLLOUGH, Brooke, President, Adventist Health Lodi Memorial, Lodi, CA, p. A70
MCCOLLUM, Joann, Chief Nursing Officer, Bolivar Medical Center, Cleveland, MS, p. A361
MCCOLLUM, Kathleen, President and Chief Executive Officer, University of Maryland Baltimore Washington Medical Center, Glen Burnie, MD, p. A304
MCCOLM, Denni, Chief Information Officer, Citizens Memorial Hospital, Bolivar, MO, p. A371
MCCOMB, Canise A, Director Human Resources, Graham Hospital, Canton, IL, p. A187
MCCOMBS, Amy S., MSN, R.N., Chief Operating Officer, Renown Regional Medical Center, Reno, NV, p. A412
MCCONKEY, Teresa L, MSN, R.N., Vice President of Nursing and Chief Nursing Officer, Graham Hospital, Canton, IL, p. A187
MCCONNACHIE, Angela
MSN, R.N., Co–CEO, Aspire Rural Health System, Marlette Regional Hospital, Marlette, MI, p. A333
MSN, R.N., Co–Chief Executive Officer, Aspire Rural Health System, Deckerville Community Hospital, Deckerville, MI, p. A324
MCCONNELL, Adam
Chief Financial Officer, Granville Health System, Oxford, NC, p. A474
Interim Chief Executive Officer, Granville Health System, Oxford, NC, p. A474
MCCONNELL, Collete, Chief Financial Officer, Kossuth Regional Health Center, Algona, IA, p. A230
MCCONNELL, George, Director, Morris Village Alcohol And Drug Addiction Treatment Center, Columbia, SC, p. A564
MCCONNELL, Linda M, R.N., MSN, FACHE, Associate Medical Center Director Patient Care Services, James H. Quillen Department of Veterans Affairs Medical Center, Johnson City, TN, p. A585
MCCONNELL, Lisa, Chief Nursing Officer, Mayo Clinic Health System In Mankato, Mankato, MN, p. A349
MCCONNELL, Nicole, Senior Vice President, Human Resources, SHDS, Corewell Health Butterworth Hospital, Grand Rapids, MI, p. A328
MCCONNELL, Patrick G, Chief Financial Officer, Cody Regional Health, Cody, WY, p. A726
MCCONNELL, Ron, Chief Operating Officer, UPMC Altoona, Altoona, PA, p. A534
MCCOO, Myron, Vice President, Human Resources, Memorial Hospital At Gulfport, Gulfport, MS, p. A362
MCCORKLE, David, Chief Executive Officer, Citizens Medical Center, Colby, KS, p. A247
MCCORMACK, Holly, R.N., Chief Executive Officer, Cottage Hospital, Woodsville, NH, p. A417
MCCORMACK, J. David., Chief Executive Officer, Vaughan Regional Medical Center, Selma, AL, p. A24
MCCORMACK, Jane, R.N., MSN, Vice President, Chief Nursing Officer and Nursing and Patient Care Services, Unity Hospital, Rochester, NY, p. A458
MCCORMICK, Brad, Chief Financial Officer, Natchitoches Regional Medical Center, Natchitoches, LA, p. A289
MCCORMICK, Brenda, Chief Financial Officer, Senior Vice President, Children's Minnesota, Minneapolis, MN, p. A350
MCCORMICK, Daniel, M.D., President and Chief Executive Officer, Franciscan Health Crown Point, Crown Point, IN, p. A214
MCCORMICK, David, Chief Financial Officer, Northwest Hospital, Assistant Vice President, Finance, LifeBridge Health, Northwest Hospital, Randallstown, MD, p. A306
MCCORMICK, Dee Dawn, Director Personnel and Human Resources, Coon Memorial Hospital, Dalhart, TX, p. A610
MCCORMICK, Jason, Interim Chief Financial Officer, Melissa Memorial Hospital, Holyoke, CO, p. A109
MCCORMICK, Jayne, M.D., Chief Medical Officer CDS, Presbyterian Hospital, Albuquerque, NM, p. A433
MCCORMICK, Kevin, M.D., Associate Medical Director, Jones Memorial Hospital, Wellsville, NY, p. A461
MCCORMICK, Pam, Director Human Resources, Permian Regional Medical Center, Andrews, TX, p. A597
MCCORMICK, Taylor, Chief Financial Officer, West Holt Medical Services, Atkinson, NE, p. A397
MCCOY, Andrea C.S., M.D., Chief Medical Officer, Cooper University Hospital Cap. Regional, Cap. May Court House, NJ, p. A419
MCCOY, Craig, Chief Executive Officer and Managing Director, Centennial Hills Hospital Medical Center, Las Vegas, NV, p. A409
MCCOY, Doug, Chief Executive Officer, Eastern Plumas Health Care, Portola, CA, p. A84
MCCOY, Janice M, MS, R.N., Chief Clinical Officer, Select Specialty Hospital–The Villages, Oxford, FL, p. A145
MCCOY, Jessica, Director Human Resources, Cedar Springs Hospital, Colorado Springs, CO, p. A104
MCCOY, Josh
Senior Operations Executive Officer, Adena Fayette Medical Center, Washington Court House, OH, p. A506
Senior Operations Executive Officer, Regional Vice President, Adena Greenfield Medical Center, Greenfield, OH, p. A497
MCCOY, Melissa, Vice President and Chief Financial Officer, West Virginia University Hospitals, Morgantown, WV, p. A703
MCCOY, Michael Jerry, M.D., Chief Medical Officer, Southeast Iowa Regional Medical Center, West Burlington Campus, West Burlington, IA, p. A245
MCCOY, Michael Jerry., M.D., President and Chief Executive Officer, Southeast Iowa Regional Medical Center, West Burlington Campus, West Burlington, IA, p. A245
MCCOY, Shawn W., Chief Executive Officer, Deaconess Midtown Hospital, Evansville, IN, p. A216
MCCRAW, Nicki, Assistant Vice President Human Resources, UW Medicine/Harborview Medical Center, Seattle, WA, p. A695
MCCREA, Kim, Chief Human Resources Officer, Ortonville Area Health Services, Ortonville, MN, p. A352
MCCREA, Yvette, Chief Human Resources, Winn Army Community Hospital, Hinesville, GA, p. A165
MCCREADY, David, President and Chief Executive Officer, Southcoast Hospitals Group. Fall River, MA, p. A313
MCCREARY, Michael, Chief of Services, Mercy Hospital Washington, Washington, MO, p. A388
MCCREARY, William, Vice President and Chief Information Officer, The University of Toledo Medical Center, Toledo, OH, p. A505
MCCRIMMON, Scott, Manager Information Technology, Bob Stump Department of Veterans Affairs Medical Center, Prescott, AZ, p. A37
MCCROSKEY, Mark, Vice President Operations, Northeastern Health System, Tahlequah, OK, p. A521
MCCUE, Jennifer, Director Patient Care, Summersville Regional Medical Center, Summersville, WV, p. A705
MCCUE, Raymond, M.D., Vice President, Medical Affairs and Chief Medical Officer, Chesapeake Regional Medical Center, Chesapeake, VA, p. A674
MCCUE, Robert N, Vice President Finance, Mid Coast Hospital, Brunswick, ME, p. A296
MCCUE, Steven, Chief Financial Officer, Umass Memorial–Marlborough Hospital, Marlborough, MA, p. A315
MCCULLEY, Becky, Chief Operations Officer, University of Texas Southwestern Medical Center, Dallas, TX, p. A612
MCCULLEY, Larry W., Chief Executive Officer, Touchette Regional Hospital, Centreville, IL, p. A187
MCCULLOCH, Christina, President, Sharon Hospital, Sharon, CT, p. A118

A916 Index of Health Care Professionals

Index of Health Care Professionals / McGill

Index of Health Care Professionals

MCCULLOCH, Greg, CPA, President, Adventist Health Sonora, Sonora, CA, p. A96
MCCULLOCH, Liz, Chief Information Resource Management Systems, Cheyenne Va Medical Center, Cheyenne, WY, p. A726
MCCULLOUGH, Barbara A, Vice President Human Resources, UPMC Washington, Washington, PA, p. A556
MCCULLOUGH, Erin, Chief Clinical Officer, Kindred Hospital Philadelphia, Philadelphia, PA, p. A549
MCCULLOUGH, Mary Kelly, Associate Director Patient Care Services, Lexington Vamc, Lexington, KY, p. A268
MCCULLOUGH, Patrick, M.D., Chief Medical Services, Summit Behavioral Healthcare, Cincinnati, OH, p. A489
MCCULLOUGH, Wadra, Chief Nursing Officer, Wellstar Spalding Regional Hospital, Griffin, GA, p. A164
MCCULLY, Michael, Chief Operating Officer, Northport Veterans Affairs Medical Center, Northport, NY, p. A454
MCCUNE, Becky A, Director Human Resources, Community Relations and Education, Coffeyville Regional Medical Center, Coffeyville, KS, p. A247
MCCURDY, Brent, Director Management Information, St. Croix Regional Medical Center, St Croix Falls, WI, p. A722
MCCUTCHAN, Matt, Chief Financial Officer, Greater Regional Health, Creston, IA, p. A234
MCDADE, Len, Chief Executive Officer, Ochsner Extended Care Hospital, New Orleans, LA, p. A289
MCDANALD, Matt, M.D., Chief Medical Officer, Baptist Health La Grange, La Grange, KY, p. A268
MCDANEL, Joyce, Vice President Human Resources and Education, Unitypoint Health–Des Moines, Des Moines, IA, p. A235
MCDANIEL, Amy, Chief Executive Officer, Iowa Specialty Hospital–Belmond, Belmond, IA, p. A230
MCDANIEL, Donald E III, Chief Financial Officer, Paris Regional Medical Center, Paris, TX, p. A642
MCDANIEL, Justin, R.N., Administrator, Oceans Behavioral Hospital of Alexandria, Alexandria, LA, p. A276
MCDANIEL, Kaylee, Administrator, Sabine County Hospital, Hemphill, TX, p. A624
MCDANIEL, Kim, Director Human Resources, Encompass Health Rehabilitation Hospital of Montgomery, Montgomery, AL, p. A22
MCDANIEL, LaDonna, Financial Manager, Prattville Baptist Hospital, Prattville, AL, p. A24
MCDANIEL, Levi, M.D., Chief of Staff, Wabash General Hospital, Mount Carmel, IL, p. A202
MCDANIEL, Patrick, Chief Executive Officer, Palmetto Lowcountry Behavioral Health, Charleston, SC, p. A563
MCDANIEL, Randy, Information Systems Director, Jackson Purchase Medical Center, Mayfield, KY, p. A271
MCDANIEL, Suzie Q, Chief Human Resource Officer, Bay Area Hospital, Coos Bay, OR, p. A526
MCDANIEL, Yasmene, Chief Executive Officer, HCA Houston Healthcare Southeast, Pasadena, TX, p. A643
MCDAVID, Clarence, Vice President Human Resources, Rose Medical Center, Denver, CO, p. A107
MCDERMOTT, James, M.D., Chief of Staff, Sedan City Hospital, Sedan, KS, p. A259
MCDERMOTT, Mary, MSN, MS, R.N., Senior Vice President Patient Care Services and Chief Nursing Officer, Phelp. Memorial Hospital Center, Sleep. Hollow, NY, p. A459
MCDERMOTT, Michael P., M.D., President and Chief Executive Officer, Mary Washington Hospital, Fredericksburg, VA, p. A676
MCDEVITT, Robert J, M.D., Chief of Staff, Wilson Memorial Hospital, Sidney, OH, p. A503
MCDONAGH, Andrew, M.D., Chief Medical Officer, Aurora West Allis Medical Center, West Allis, WI, p. A724
MCDONALD, Amanda, MSN, Chief Nurse Executive, Kerrville State Hospital, Kerrville, TX, p. A632
MCDONALD, Andrew, Chief Finance Officer, Mountainview Regional Medical Center, Las Cruces, NM, p. A435
MCDONALD, Carl, Chief Human Resources Officer, Broward Health North, Deerfield Beach, FL, p. A130
MCDONALD, Connie, Chief Financial Officer, Marion Veterans Affairs Medical Center, Marion, IL, p. A200
MCDONALD, Edward A, Chief Financial Officer, Adventist Health Vallejo, Vallejo, CA, p. A99
MCDONALD, Elizabeth, Director Human Resources, Wayne Memorial Hospital, Honesdale, PA, p. A542
MCDONALD, Gary, Associate Administrator Human Resources, Stone County Medical Center, Mountain View, AR, p. A51
MCDONALD, Gregory, Vice President Finance and Chief Financial Officer, Roswell Park Comprehensive Cancer Center, Buffalo, NY, p. A440
MCDONALD, Jeff, Information Technology Manager, Adventhealth Wauchula, Wauchula, FL, p. A154
MCDONALD, John
FACHE, Chief Executive Officer, Centerpoint Medical Center, Independence, MO, p. A376
FACHE, Chief Operating Officer, Northwest Texas Healthcare System, Amarillo, TX, p. A596
M.D., Chief Medical Officer, Medical City North Hills, North Richland Hills, TX, p. A641
MCDONALD, Mark, M.D., President and Chief Executive Officer, Institute for Orthopaedic Surgery, Lima, OH, p. A498
MCDONALD, Matthew B. III, President and Chief Executive Officer, Children's Specialized Hospital, New Brunswick, NJ, p. A424
MCDONALD, Ruth A., M.D., Chief Medical Officer, Seattle Children's Hospital, Seattle, WA, p. A694
MCDONALD, Shari, Chief Nursing Officer, Rochester General Hospital, Rochester, NY, p. A457
MCDONALD, Shelly, Chief Human Resources Officer, Ness County Hospital District No 2, Ness City, KS, p. A255
MCDONALD, Stanton B, M.D., Medical Director, Heber Valley Hospital, Heber City, UT, p. A665
MCDONALD, Susan, Vice President, Medical Affairs, Sentara Rmh Medical Center, Harrisonburg, VA, p. A677
MCDONALD–PINKETT, Shelly, Chief Medical Officer, Howard University Hospital, Washington, DC, p. A123
MCDONELL, Stephanie, Vice President and Chief Information Officer, United Regional Health Care System, Wichita Falls, TX, p. A663
MCDONNELL, Jennifer, Director, Human Resources, Southern Hills Hospital And Medical Center, Las Vegas, NV, p. A410
MCDONNELL, Kevin, Chief Hospital Executive, Atlanticare Regional Medical Center, Atlantic City Campus, Atlantic City, NJ, p. A418
MCDONNELL, Michael, M.D., Chief Medical Officer, Insight Hospital And Medical Center, Chicago, IL, p. A189
MCDONNELL, Stephen C, Chief Financial Officer, Chesapeake Regional Medical Center, Chesapeake, VA, p. A674
MCDONOUGH, Amy K, Chief Nursing Officer, Van Diest Medical Center, Webster City, IA, p. A245
MCDOUGAL, Tom R. Jr, FACHE, Chief Executive Officer, Manatee Memorial Hospital, Bradenton, FL, p. A126
MCDOUGLE, Mark, Executive Vice President and Chief Operating Officer, Maimonides Medical Center, New York, NY, p. A449
MCDOWELL, Kim, Chief Nursing Officer and Chief Operating Officer, Bartlett Regional Hospital, Juneau, AK, p. A28
MCDOWELL, Paul L
Deputy Chief Financial Officer, Mission Hospital, Asheville, NC, p. A463
Vice President Finance and Chief Financial Officer, UK King's Daughters Medical Center, Ashland, KY, p. A263
MCDOWELL, Richard
M.D., Medical Director, Kona Community Hospital, Kealakekua, HI, p. A177
Chief Financial Officer, Ridge Behavioral Health System, Lexington, KY, p. A269
MCDOWELL, Wendy, R.N., Director of Nursing, Weisbrod Memorial County Hospital, Eads, CO, p. A107
MCDOWN, Missy, Director Information Systems, Mercy Hospital Pittsburg, Pittsburg, KS, p. A258
MCDRURY, Martha M, R.N., Chief Operating Officer and Chief Nursing Officer, Holy Family Hospital, Methuen, MA, p. A316
MCEACHIN, Brenda, Human Resources Director, Jeff Davis Hospital, Hazlehurst, GA, p. A165
MCELDOWNEY, Erin, Manager Human Resources, Haven Behavioral Hospital of Phoenix, Phoenix, AZ, p. A35
MCELMURRAY, Dodie
FACHE, Chief Executive Officer, University of Mississipp. Medical Center Grenada, Grenada, MS, p. A362
FACHE, Chief Executive Officer, University of Mississipp. Medical Center Holmes County, Lexington, MS, p. A365
MCELRATH, Matthew
Chief Human Resources Officer, Keck Hospital of Usc, Los Angeles, CA, p. A73
Chief Human Resources Officer, USC Norris Comprehensive Cancer Center And Hospital, Los Angeles, CA, p. A75
MCELROY, Kevin, Chief Human Resources Officer, Mackinac Straits Health System, Inc., Saint Ignace, MI, p. A337
MCENIRY, Allen
Executive Director, Patrick B. Harris Psychiatric Hospital, Anderson, SC, p. A562
Interim Director, G. Werber Bryan Psychiatric Hospital, Columbia, SC, p. A564
MCENTEE, Chris, Network Specialist, Van Buren County Hospital, Keosauqua, IA, p. A238
MCENTEE, Kara, Chief Financial Officer, Van Buren County Hospital, Keosauqua, IA, p. A238
MCENTIRE, Ann, MSN, R.N., Chief Nursing Officer, Citizens Baptist Medical Center, Talladega, AL, p. A24
MCEUEN, Jacqueline, Coordinator Human Resources, Midcoast Medical Center – Bellville, Bellville, TX, p. A603
MCEVILLY, Kerrie, President and Chief Executive Officer, Stevens Community Medical Center, Morris, MN, p. A351
MCEWAN, Kevin K, R.N., Chief Nursing Officer, Madisonhealth, Rexburg, ID, p. A183
MCEWEN, Michelle, President and Chief Executive Officer, Speare Memorial Hospital, Plymouth, NH, p. A417
MCFADYEN, David M., FACHE, President, Saint Alphonsus Regional Medical Center, Boise, ID, p. A179
MCFALL, Cathy, Human Resources Manager, Kiowa County Memorial Hospital, Greensburg, KS, p. A250
MCFALL–ROBERTS, Ebuni, Director Human Resources, Holly Hill Hospital, Raleigh, NC, p. A474
MCFARLAND, Dustin, Interim Chief Executive Officer, Encompass Health Rehabilitation Hospital of Middletown, Middletown, DE, p. A121
MCFARLAND, Kenneth D., Chief Executive Officer, UC San Diego Health – East Campus, San Diego, CA, p. A90
MCFARLAND, Nita, Director of Nursing, Kingman Community Hospital, Kingman, KS, p. A252
MCFARLAND, Rhonda
Director Human Resources, Atrium Health Anson, Wadesboro, NC, p. A477
Director Human Resources, Atrium Health Union, Monroe, NC, p. A472
MCFARLAND, Rodney, M.D., Medical Director, Freeman Neosho Hospital, Neosho, MO, p. A381
MCFARLAND, Tracee, Chief Financial Officer, Claiborne Medical Center, Tazewell, TN, p. A594
MCFARLANE, Michael
Chief Executive Officer, Hawthorn Children Psychiatric Hospital, Saint Louis, MO, p. A385
Chief Human Resource Officer, St. Louis Forensic Treatment Center, Saint Louis, MO, p. A384
Chief Operating Officer, Hawthorn Children Psychiatric Hospital, Saint Louis, MO, p. A385
Director Human Resources, St. Louis Forensic Treatment Center, Saint Louis, MO, p. A384
MCFERRAN, Virginia, Chief Information Officer, UCLA Medical Center–Santa Monica, Santa Monica, CA, p. A95
MCGAHAN, Thomas P., M.D., Chief Medical Officer, Emory Saint Joseph's Hospital, Atlanta, GA, p. A157
MCGAHEY, Nikki, Information Officer, Jefferson County Hospital, Waurika, OK, p. A524
MCGARIGLE, Kristine, R.N., Vice President Patient Care, Aspirus Merrill Hospital & Clinics, Inc., Merrill, WI, p. A716
MCGARVEY, Missy, Chief Information Officer, Twin Valley Behavioral Healthcare, Columbus, OH, p. A493
MCGEACHY, Kevin M., Executive Director, Mather Hospital, Port Jefferson, NY, p. A456
MCGEE, Angela, Vice President Nursing Services, Aultman Orrville Hospital, Orrville, OH, p. A502
MCGEE, Genemarie, R.N., MS, Chief Nursing Officer, Sentara Leigh Hospital, Norfolk, VA, p. A680
MCGEE, Jarrod, Chief Executive Officer, Pam Health Rehabilitation Hospital of El Paso, El Paso, TX, p. A617
MCGEE, Jessica
Chief Financial Officer, Amg Specialty Hospital–Lafayette, Lafayette, LA, p. A285
Chief Financial Officer, Sage Specialty Hospital (Ltac), Denham Springs, LA, p. A281
MCGEE, Terry, Chief Operations Officer, Central State Hospital, Milledgeville, GA, p. A168
MCGEEHAN, Paul, M.D., Chief Medical Staff, Lecom Health Corry Memorial Hospital, Corry, PA, p. A537
MCGETTIGAN, Ryan, Chief Information Officer, Coatesville Veterans Affairs Medical Center, Coatesville, PA, p. A537
MCGHAN, Clayton, Interim West Hawaii Regional Chief Executive Officer, Kona Community Hospital, Kealakekua, HI, p. A177
MCGHEE, Craig, FACHE, Midwest Market Administrator, Shriners Hospitals for Children–Chicago, Chicago, IL, p. A191
MCGHEE, Kenneth, Vice President of Finance, Jackson Park Hospital And Medical Center, Chicago, IL, p. A189
MCGHEE, Michael, M.D., Medical Director, Unity Psychiatric Care–Clarksville, Clarksville, TN, p. A581
MCGIBBON, Monica, Chief Nursing Officer, Terence Cardinal Cooke Health Care Center, New York, NY, p. A453
MCGILL, Brittini, MSN, R.N., Chief Nursing Officer, Norman Regional Health System, Norman, OK, p. A516
MCGILL, Martha
Executive Vice President and Chief Operating Officer, Nicklaus Children's Hospital, Miami, FL, p. A140
President, Central Florida, Nemours Children's Hospital, Orlando, FL, p. A144

Index of Health Care Professionals

Index of Health Care Professionals / McGill

MCGILL, Rusty, System Director Information Technology, Indiana University Health Arnett Hospital, Lafayette, IN, p. A222
MCGILL, Suzanne, Director of Nursing, Atmore Community Hospital, Atmore, AL, p. A15
MCGILL, Timothy W., Chief Executive Officer, Livingston Regional Hospital, Livingston, TN, p. A587
MCGILVRAY, Greg, Chief Financial Officer, Medical Center Enterprise, Enterprise, AL, p. A19
MCGIMSEY, Erika, Controller, Uofl Health – Shelbyville Hospital, Shelbyville, KY, p. A274
MCGINLEY, Mary Ann, Ph.D., Senior Vice President, Patient Services and Chief Nursing Officer, Thomas Jefferson University Hospital, Philadelphia, PA, p. A550
MCGINNIS, Brian, Director Finance, Aurora Medical Center of Oshkosh, Oshkosh, WI, p. A719
MCGINNIS, Christina, Director Information Technology, Menorah Medical Center, Overland Park, KS, p. A257
MCGINNIS, Jeff, M.D., President Medical Staff, Chi Saint Josep. Health – Saint Josep. Mount Sterling, Mount Sterling, KY, p. A272
MCGINNIS, Paula, Chief Executive Officer, St. Joseph's Hospital, Tampa, FL, p. A152
MCGINTY–THOMPSON, Melissa
Administrator, Chief Nursing Officer and Clinical Officer, Centracare – Benson, Benson, MN, p. A343
Chief Nursing Officer, Centracare – Benson, Benson, MN, p. A343
MCGIRL, John, Chief Human Resources Officer, Nch Baker Hospital, Naples, FL p. A142
MCGLADE, Jim
Director Human Resources, United Hospital, Saint Paul, MN, p. A355
Vice President, Human Resources, Mercy Hospital, Coon Rapids, MN, p. A345
MCGLEW, Timothy, Chief Executive Officer, Kern Valley Healthcare District, Lake Isabella, CA, p. A69
MCGLON, Tracy, Director Human Resources, HCA Florida Gulf Coast Hospital, Panama City, FL, p. A146
MCGONNELL, James, Chief Financial Officer, Los Alamos Medical Center, Los Alamos, NM, p. A435
MCGOVERN, Charles, Chief of Staff, Margaret Mary Health, Batesville, IN, p. A212
MCGOVERN, Joanne, MSN, R.N., Chief Executive Officer, Select Specialty Hospital – Atlantic City, Atlantic City, NJ, p. A418
MCGOVERN, Julia, Vice President Human Resources, Chilton Medical Center, Pompton Plains, NJ, p. A427
MCGOVERN, Julie, Vice President Human Resources, Luminis Health Anne Arundel Medical Center, Annapolis, MD, p. A300
MCGOVERN, Kimberly, Manager Human Resources, Hackettstown Medical Center, Hackettstown, NJ, p. A421
MCGOVERN, Pam, Director Technology, Huggins Hospital, Wolfeboro, NH, p. A417
MCGOWAN, Marion A., Senior Vice President and Chief Operating Officer, St. Clair Health, Pittsburgh, PA, p. A551
MCGOWEN, Bernard A, M.D., Medical Director, Kindred Hospital Tarrant County–Arlington, Arlington, TX, p. A597
MCGOWIN, Norman F, M.D., III, Chief of Staff, Regional Medical Center of Central Alabama, Greenville, AL, p. A20
MCGRATH, John, Chief Information Officer, Mclaren Port Huron, Port Huron, MI, p. A336
MCGRATH, Kelly, Chief Medical Officer, Clearwater Valley Health, Orofino, ID, p. A183
MCGRATH, Lynn, M.D., Vice President Medical Affairs, Deborah Heart And Lung Center, Browns Mills, NJ, p. A419
MCGRAW, Belinda, Director Human Resources, Boulder City Hospital, Boulder City, NV, p. A408
MCGRAW, Kathleen, M.D., Chief Medical Officer, Brattleboro Memorial Hospital, Brattleboro, VT, p. A671
MCGRAW, Scott, M.D., Medical Director, Baylor Surgical Hospital At Las Colinas, Irving, TX, p. A630
MCGREEVY, John, FACHE, Chief Executive Officer, Christus Mother Frances Hospital – Tyler, Tyler, TX, p. A658
MCGREGOR, Catherine, Deputy Director Facility and Administrative Services, Capital District Psychiatric Center, Albany, NY, p. A438
MCGREGOR, Donna, FACHE, President, Canton–Potsdam Hospital, Potsdam, NY, p. A456
MCGREGOR, Julie
Director Human Resources, Uofl Health – Mary And Elizabeth Hospital, Louisville, KY, p. A270
Vice President and Chief People Officer, Uofl Health – Jewish Hospital, Louisville, KY, p. A270
Vice President, Human Resources and Organization Development, Columbus Regional Hospital, Columbus, IN, p. A214
MCGREGOR, Robert, M.D., Chief Medical Officer, Akron Children's Hospital, Akron, OH, p. A484
MCGREW, David S, Chief Financial Officer, San Mateo Medical Center, San Mateo, CA, p. A93
MCGREW, Deborah A, Vice President and Chief Operating Officer, University of Texas Medical Branch, Galveston, TX, p. A621
MCGREW, Diane, Chief Nurse Executive, Montgomery County Memorial Hospital, Red Oak, IA, p. A242
MCGRIFF, Marchelle M, Chief Nursing Executive, Sutter Medical Center, Sacramento, Sacramento, CA, p. A87
MCGRUE, Van, R.N., MSN, Chief Nursing Officer, Princeton Baptist Medical Center, Birmingham, AL, p. A17
MCGUE, Lisa, Controller, Encompass Health Rehabilitation Hospital of Northern Kentucky, Edgewood, KY, p. A265
MCGUIGAN, Kevin, M.D., Medical Director, St. Lawrence Rehabilitation Hospital, Lawrenceville, NJ, p. A423
MCGUILL, Gail, R.N., MSN, Chief Nursing Officer and Administrative Director of Patient Care Services, Shriners Hospitals for Children–Salt Lake City, Salt Lake City, UT, p. A669
MCGUINNESS, Patrick, Chief Information Management, Keller Army Community Hospital, West Point, NY, p. A462
MCGUIRE, Ann M., Regional Vice President Human Resources, Indiana University Health Ball Memorial Hospital, Muncie, IN, p. A224
MCGUIRE, Christie, R.N., Chief Nursing Officer, Salinas Valley Health, Salinas, CA, p. A88
MCGUIRE, Cynthia K., FACHE, President and Chief Executive Officer, Monadnock Community Hospital, Peterborough, NH, p. A417
MCGUIRE, Patrick, Chief Financial Officer, Michigan Market, Ascension Macomb–Oakland Hospital, Warren Campus, Warren, MI, p. A340
MCGUIRE, Shane A., Chief Executive Officer, Columbia County Health System, Dayton, WA, p. A689
MCGUIRK, Christina Marie, R.N., Chief Nursing Officer, Orlando Health – Health Central Hospital, Ocoee, FL, p. A143
MCGUIRT, Jacob
Chief Executive Officer, Pam Rehabilitation Hospital of Tavares, Tavares, FL, p. A153
Chief Executive Officer, Pam Specialty Hospital of Sarasota, Sarasota, FL, p. A150
MCGURK, Kevin, Controller, Bellin Psychiatric Center, Green Bay, WI, p. A712
MCGUSTY, Tricia, Interim Chief Executive Officer, HCA Houston Healthcare Northwest, Houston, TX, p. A626
MCHUGH, Colin T., President and Chief Executive Officer, Southern New Hampshire Medical Center, Nashua, NH, p. A416
MCHUGH, Frank, Vice President Finance Chief Financial Officer, Franciscan Health Olympia Fields, Olympia Fields, IL, p. A204
MCHUGH, Matthew, Director Information Services, Vaughan Regional Medical Center, Selma, AL, p. A24
MCHUGH, Ryan, M.D., Chief of Staff, The Medical Center of Southeast Texas, Port Arthur, TX, p. A645
MCILROY, Gail, Director Medical Records, KPC Promise Hospital of Wichita Falls, Wichita Falls, TX, p. A662
MCILVAIN, Spencer, Director of Human Resources, Peterson Healthcare And Rehabilitation Hospital, Wheeling, WV, p. A706
MCILWAIN, T Pinckney, M.D., Vice President and Chief Medical Officer, Charleston Area Medical Center, Charleston, WV, p. A700
MCINTIRE, Cheryl, Chief Executive Officer and Chief Financial Officer, Lehigh Regional Medical Center, Lehigh Acres, FL, p. A137
MCINTOSH, Craig, Chief Information Officer, Northwest Specialty Hospital, Post Falls, ID, p. A183
MCINTOSH, Eric D., Vice President Human Resources, UPMC Jameson, New Castle, PA, p. A547
MCINTOSH, Ernasha, Interim Director of Nursing, Navajo Health Foundation – Sage Memorial Hospital, Ganado, AZ, p. A31
MCINTOSH, Joe, Director Management Information Systems, Logansport State Hospital, Logansport, IN, p. A223
MCINTOSH, Tyler, Chief Financial Officer, Creek Nation Community Hospital, Okemah, OK, p. A516
MCINTYRE, Cindy, R.N., Administrative Director Clinical Services, Magee General Hospital, Magee, MS, p. A365
MCIWAIN, John, Director Human Resources, Wayne Memorial Hospital, Jesup, GA, p. A165
MCKALE, Brigitte, MSN, FACHE, Vice President and Chief Nurse Executive, Pali Momi Medical Center, Aiea, HI, p. A175
MCKAY, Amy, Chief Nursing Officer, Mid–America Rehabilitation Hospital, Shawnee Mission, KS, p. A260
MCKAY, Andrea
President, Cox Barton County Memorial Hospital, Lamar, MO, p. A379
President, Cox Monett Hospital, Inc, Monett, MO, p. A380
MCKAY, Daniel E., Chief Executive Officer, Ephraim Mcdowell Regional Medical Center, Danville, KY, p. A264
MCKAY, Ronda, R.N., Vice President Patient Care Services, Chief Nursing Officer, Community Hospital, Munster, IN, p. A224
MCKEAN, Heather, Director of Patient Care Services, Providence Seward Medical Center, Seward, AK, p. A29
MCKEE, Debra, R.N., Chief Clinical Officer and Chief Nursing Officer, Grand Lake Health System, Saint Marys, OH, p. A503
MCKEE, Michele, Vice President and Chief Financial Officer, St. Louis Children's Hospital, Saint Louis, MO, p. A384
MCKEE, Willis P, M.D., Jr, Chief Medical Officer, Frankfort Regional Medical Center, Frankfort, KY, p. A266
MCKEEBY, Ben, Senior Vice President and Chief Information Officer, Grady Health System, Atlanta, GA, p. A157
MCKEEBY, Jon W, Chief Information Officer, Nih Clinical Center, Bethesda, MD, p. A302
MCKEEN, Marcia, Director Human Resources, Twin Valley Behavioral Healthcare, Columbus, OH, p. A493
MCKELDIN, Pat, Human Resource Business Partner, Kaiser Permanente Manteca Medical Center, Manteca, CA, p. A76
MCKELLEB, Jalyn, MSN, R.N., Chief Nursing Executive Officer, St. Rose Dominican Hospitals – San Martin Campus, Las Vegas, NV, p. A411
MCKENDALL, Michael, Vice President, Operations, East Jefferson General Hospital, Metairie, LA, p. A288
MCKENDREE, Rodney, Senior Vice President and Chief Financial Officer, Nemours Children's Hospital, Orlando, FL, p. A144
MCKENNA, Dennis
M.D., Interim Vice President Medical Affairs, Albany Medical Center, Albany, NY, p. A438
M.D., President and Chief Executive Officer, Albany Medical Center, Albany, NY, p. A438
MCKENNA, Donald, President, Penn State Milton S. Hershey Medical Center, Hershey, PA, p. A542
MCKENNA, Quinn, Chief Operating Officer, Stanford Health Care, Palo Alto, CA, p. A82
MCKENNERY, Kay, Chief Executive Officer, Cross Creek Hospital, Austin, TX, p. A600
MCKENNEY, Jennifer, M.D., Chief Medical Officer, Fredonia Regional Hospital, Fredonia, KS, p. A249
MCKENRICK, Robert W., Medical Center Director, Raymond G. Murphy Department of Veterans Affairs Medical Center, Albuquerque, NM, p. A433
MCKENZIE, Jackie, Director Administrative Services, Beacham Memorial Hospital, Magnolia, MS, p. A365
MCKENZIE, Margaret
M.D., Vice President, Cleveland Clinic Marymount Hospital, Garfield Heights, OH, p. A496
M.D., Vice President, Cleveland Clinic South Pointe Hospital, Warrensville Heights, OH, p. A506
MCKENZIE, Sandra D., President and Chief Executive Officer, Hamilton Medical Center, Dalton, GA, p. A162
MCKENZIE, Shawn, Chief Executive Officer, Seneca Healthcare District, Chester, CA, p. A59
MCKENZIE, Troy, Chief information Officer, Faith Community Hospital, Jacksboro, TX, p. A630
MCKEON, Sean, Director, Information Technology, Franciscan Children's, Brighton, MA, p. A311
MCKEOWN, Kevin, Chief Financial Officer, HCA Florida Memorial Hospital, Jacksonville, FL, p. A134
MCKERNAN, Kathleen S., Director Information Systems, Pioneers Memorial Healthcare District, Brawley, CA, p. A58
MCKERRIGAN, Jeanne, Chief Financial Officer, Regional West Medical Center, Scottsbluff, NE, p. A406
MCKEVETT, Timothy M., President and Chief Executive Officer, Beloit Health System, Beloit, WI, p. A708
MCKIBBEN, Sean, President and Chief Operating Officer, Mount Carmel East Hospital, Columbus, OH, p. A491
MCKIDDY, Paul, Director Information Technology, Monroe County Medical Center, Tompkinsville, KY, p. A274
MCKIE, Kathy, Director Human Resources, Montrose Regional Health, Montrose, CO, p. A112
MCKILLIP, Ed, Vice President Finance, Riddle Hospital, Media, PA, p. A546
MCKIMMY, Doyle L., FACHE, Chief Executive Officer, Jewell County Hospital, Mankato, KS, p. A254
MCKINLEY, Alton, Chief Financial Officer, Dallas Va North Texas Hcs, Dallas, TX, p. A611
MCKINLEY, Ivy
Director Human Resources, Ascension Holy Family, Des Plaines, IL, p. A193
Regional Human Resources Officer, Community First Medical Center, Chicago, IL, p. A189
MCKINLEY, John, Director, Information Technology, Incompass Healthcare, Lawrenceburg, IN, p. A222

A918 Index of Health Care Professionals

Index of Health Care Professionals / McNeel

Index of Health Care Professionals

MCKINLEY, Mike, Information Security Officer, West Texas Va Health Care System, Big Spring, TX, p. A604
MCKINLEY, Ronald, Ph.D., Vice President Human Resources and Employee Services, University of Texas Medical Branch, Galveston, TX, p. A621
MCKINNEY, Brenda, Chief Executive Officer, Reeves Regional Health, Pecos, TX, p. A643
MCKINNEY, Bruce, Business Officer, Administrative Services, Central Prison Hospital, Raleigh, NC, p. A474
MCKINNEY, Camillia, Chief Executive Officer, San Antonio Behavioral Healthcare Hospital, San Antonio, TX, p. A650
MCKINNEY, Dana, Chief Nursing Officer, Select Specialty Hospital–Madison, Madison, WI, p. A714
MCKINNEY, Daniel, Chief Executive Officer, Grandview Medical Center, Birmingham, AL, p. A16
MCKINNEY, James, Warden, Iowa Medical And Classification Center, Coralville, IA, p. A233
MCKINNEY, Rex, President and Chief Executive Officer, Decatur County Memorial Hospital, Greensburg, IN, p. A218
MCKINNEY, Thomas, FACHE, Chief Executive Officer, Baptist Medical Center, San Antonio, TX, p. A648
MCKINNON, Mark, M.D., Chief of Staff, North Runnels Hospital, Winters, TX, p. A663
MCKINNON, Ron, Chief Information Officer, Ellis Medicine, Schenectady, NY, p. A458
MCKINSTRY, Merissa, Chief Operating Officer, Columbus Springs Dublin, Dublin, OH, p. A495
MCKNIGHT, Stephanie, Hospital Nursing Manager, Sanford Bagley Medical Center, Bagley, MN, p. A343
MCKNIGHT, Tim, M.D., Chief of Staff, Trinity Hospital Twin City, Dennison, OH, p. A494
MCKOY, Lori, Business Partner, Novant Health Pender Medical Center, Burgaw, NC, p. A464
MCKULA, Tim, Vice President Information Systems and Chief Information Officer, Shirley Ryan Abilitylab, Chicago, IL, p. A191
MCKUNE, Jeff, Chief Health Informatics Officer, Phelp. Health, Rolla, MO, p. A382
MCLAIN, Allen, M.D., Chief of Staff, Grisell Memorial Hospital District One, Ransom, KS, p. A258
MCLAIN, James D., Executive Director, Clement J. Zablocki Veterans' Administration Medical Center, Milwaukee, WI, p. A717
MCLAIN, John R., Chief Executive Officer, Starr Regional Medical Center, Athens, TN, p. A579
MCLARTY, Collin, Chief Executive Officer, Yoakum County Hospital, Denver City, TX, p. A614
MCLARTY, Walter L
Chief Human Resources Officer, Bethesda North Hospital, Cincinnati, OH, p. A488
Chief Human Resources Officer, Good Samaritan Hospital, Cincinnati, OH, p. A489
MCLAUGHLIN, Amy, CPA, Chief Financial Officer, Manning Regional Healthcare Center, Manning, IA, p. A239
MCLAUGHLIN, Collin, Chief Executive Officer, Valley Hospital Medical Center, Las Vegas, NV, p. A411
MCLAUGHLIN, Diana J., Chief Financial Officer, Memorial Hospital, North Conway, NH, p. A417
MCLAUGHLIN, Kathryn
Chief Nursing Officer, Hemet Global Medical Center, Hemet, CA, p. A67
Chief Nursing Officer, Memorial Hospital of Gardena, Gardena, CA, p. A65
MCLAUGHLIN, Leslie, Director of Business Development, Michiana Behavioral Health Center, Plymouth, IN, p. A226
MCLAUGHLIN, Michael, M.D., Chief Medical Officer, Health First Holmes Regional Medical Center, Melbourne, FL, p. A139
MCLAUGHLIN, Pamela, Chief Financial Officer, Encompass Health Rehabilitation Hospital of Austin, Austin, TX, p. A600
MCLAUGHLIN, Rebecca, Chief Human Resource Officer, Banner Goldfield Medical Center, Apache Junction, AZ, p. A30
MCLAUGHLIN, Richard
M.D., President and Chief Executive Officer, Phoenixville Hospital, Phoenixville, PA, p. A550
M.D., President and Chief Executive Officer, Pottstown Hospital, Pottstown, PA, p. A553
MCLAUGHLIN, Sherry, Director Human Resources, Forrest City Medical Center, Forrest City, AR, p. A46
MCLAUGHLIN, Steve, M.D., Chief Medical Officer, University of New Mexico Hospitals, Albuquerque, NM, p. A433
MCLAWS, Douglas, D.O., Chief Medical Officer, Manning Regional Healthcare Center, Manning, IA, p. A239
MCLEAN, Chris, Chief Administrative Officer, Methodist Healthcare Memphis Hospitals, Memphis, TN, p. A589
MCLEAN, Cindy J, R.N., MSN, Director of Nursing, Central Prison Hospital, Raleigh, NC, p. A474
MCLEAN, Georgia, Director Human Resources, Mount Sinai Medical Center, Miami Beach, FL, p. A141
MCLEAN, Sandra MSN, RN, Vice President and Chief Nursing Officer, Baptist Health South Florida, West Kendall Baptist Hospital, Miami, FL, p. A139
MCLENDON, Carla
Director Human Resources, Appling Healthcare System, Baxley, GA, p. A159
Director Information Resource Management Services, Charles George Veterans Affairs Medical Center, Asheville, NC, p. A463
MCLENDON, John
Senior Vice President and Chief Information Officer, UChicago Medicine Adventhealth Bolingbrook, Bolingbrook, IL, p. A186
Vice President and Chief Information Officer, Johns Hopkins All Children's Hospital, Saint Petersburg, FL, p. A149
MCLENDON, Tom, President and Chief Executive Officer, Evergreen Medical Center, Evergreen, AL, p. A19
MCLEOD, John Will, Chief Executive Officer, Mcleod Regional Medical Center, Florence, SC, p. A566
MCLEOD, John Will., Chief Executive Officer, Mcleod Regional Medical Center, Florence, SC, p. A566
MCLEOD, Les, Director of Nursing Services, Blue Mountain Hospital District, John Day, OR, p. A528
MCLEOD, Margie, Director Information Technology, North Canyon Medical Center, Gooding, ID, p. A181
MCLEOD, Michael, M.D., Chief Medical Officer, Cuero Regional Hospital, Cuero, TX, p. A610
MCLEOD, Sheldon, Chief Executive Officer, NYC Health + Hospitals/Kings County, New York, NY, p. A451
MCLERRAN, Andrea, Chief Executive Officer, Monroe County Medical Center, Tompkinsville, KY, p. A274
MCLIN, Robert D., President and Chief Executive Officer, Good Samaritan Hospital, Vincennes, IN, p. A228
MCLOONE, Paul
M.D., Chief Medical Officer, Unitypoint Health – Trinity Bettendorf, Bettendorf, IA, p. A231
M.D., Chief Medical Officer, Unitypoint Health – Trinity Rock Island, Rock Island, IL, p. A207
MCMAHAN, Steve, M.D., Chief Medical Officer, Glenwood Regional Medical Center, West Monroe, LA, p. A294
MCMAHON, Andrew, Chief Fiscal Officer, Veterans Affairs Central Western Massachusetts Healthcare System, Leeds, MA, p. A315
MCMAHON, Chris, Chief Operating Officer, The Medical Center of Southeast Texas, Port Arthur, TX, p. A645
MCMAHON, Elaine, Administrator, Kwajalein Hospital, Kwajalein Atoll, MARSHALL ISLANDS, p. A730
MCMAHON, Eugene
Senior Vice President and Chief Medical Officer, Capital Health Medical Center–Hopewell, Pennington, NJ, p. A427
Senior Vice President and Chief Medical Officer, Capital Health Regional Medical Center, Trenton, NJ, p. A429
MCMAHON, Leigh, MS, R.N., Executive Vice President Patient Care Services and Chief Nursing Officer, White Plains Hospital Center, White Plains, NY, p. A462
MCMAHON, Nancy, Vice President Human Resources, Miriam Hospital, Providence, RI, p. A560
MCMANAMAN, Craig, M.D., Chief of Staff, Mclaren Thumb Region, Bad Axe, MI, p. A322
MCMANMON, Kristin, President, Ascension All Saints, Racine, WI, p. A720
MCMANUS, Doug, Chief Medical Officer, Aurora Medical Center Grafton, Grafton, WI, p. A711
MCMANUS, Marybeth, Chief Nursing Officer, Long Island Jewish Medical Center, New Hyde Park, NY, p. A447
MCMANUS, Ronald, Senior Vice President Clinical Services and Business Entities, Peconic Bay Medical Center, Riverhead, NY, p. A457
MCMASTER, Dawn, Human Resources Director, Encompass Health Rehabilitation Hospital of Franklin, Franklin, TN, p. A583
MCMASTER, Sandra
Regional Chief Information Officer, Kauai Veterans Memorial Hospital, Waimea, HI, p. A178
Regional Chief Information Officer, Samuel Mahelona Memorial Hospital, Kapaa, HI, p. A177
MCMATH, Mark W, Chief Information Officer, Musc Health University Medical Center, Charleston, SC, p. A563
MCMENAMIN, Anneliese, Chief Human Resource Officer, Inspira Medical Center–Vineland, Vineland, NJ, p. A430
MCMICHAEL, Derek, Administrator, Community Howard Regional Health, Kokomo, IN, p. A221
MCMILLAN, Deborah, Director Human Resources, Glenn Medical Center, Willows, CA, p. A101
MCMILLAN, Donn, Senior Director, IST Client Liaison, Peacehealth Southwest Medical Center, Vancouver, WA, p. A698
MCMILLAN, Douglas A., Administrator and Chief Executive Officer, Cody Regional Health, Cody, WY, p. A726
MCMILLAN, Jennifer
Chief Financial Officer, Community Hospital, Torrington, WY, p. A729
Chief Financial Officer, Platte County Memorial Hospital, Wheatland, WY, p. A729
Chief Financial Officer, Washakie Medical Center, Worland, WY, p. A729
MCMILLAN, Sheila, Chief Financial Officer, Park Nicollet Methodist Hospital, Saint Louis Park, MN, p. A354
MCMILLIN, David, President and Chief Executive Officer, Methodist Rehabilitation Center, Jackson, MS, p. A364
MCMILLIN, Lori, Administrator, Mercy Hospital Tishomingo, Tishomingo, OK, p. A521
MCMILLION, Kelley, Chief Nursing Officer, Clay County Memorial Hospital, Henrietta, TX, p. A624
MCMINN, Ken, Director Information Technology, Scotland County Hospital, Memphis, MO, p. A380
MCMINN, Melvin, Director Human Resources, Wernersville State Hospital, Wernersville, PA, p. A557
MCMINOWAY, Kelly, R.N., Vice President, Nursing, Baptist Health Floyd, New Albany, IN, p. A225
MCMULLAN, Cheryl, Chief Financial Officer, Baylor Scott & White Medical Center–Waxahachie, Waxahachie, TX, p. A660
MCMULLAN, Heidi, R.N., Chief Nursing Officer, Wellspan Philhaven, Mount Gretna, PA, p. A546
MCMULLAN, Rosemary, Chief Human Resources, Mayo Clinic Hospital In Florida, Jacksonville, FL, p. A135
MCMURRAY, Rob, Chief Financial Officer, Christianacare, Newark, DE, p. A122
MCMURRAY, Sharon, Director, Human Resources, Rock Springs, Georgetown, TX, p. A622
MCNABB, Dana, Human Resources Manager, Field Memorial Community Hospital, Centreville, MS, p. A360
MCNABB, Kie, Chief Nursing Officer, Beauregard Health System, De Ridder, LA, p. A281
MCNABB, Teresita, FACHE, R.N., Vice President Nursing Services, Terrebonne General Health System, Houma, LA, p. A283
MCNAIR, Lisa, CPA, Senior Vice President and Chief Financial Officer, Chi St. Josep. Regional Health Center, Bryan, TX, p. A605
MCNAIR, Rebekah, Director Human Resources, Encompass Health Rehabilitation Hospital of Chattanooga, Chattanooga, TN, p. A580
MCNAIR, Scott, Chief Financial Officer, Neshoba General, Philadelphia, MS, p. A367
MCNALLY, Colleen, M.D., Chief Medical Officer, Sharp Mary Birch Hospital for Women And Newborns, San Diego, CA, p. A89
MCNALLY, Joseph, M.D., Medical Director, Streamwood Behavioral Healthcare System, Streamwood, IL, p. A209
MCNALLY, Kathy, Chief Nursing Officer, Encompass Health Rehabilitation Hospital At Cincinnati, Cincinnati, OH, p. A489
MCNALLY, Lou–Ann, Executive Director Human Resources and Staff Development, Claxton–Hepburn Medical Center, Ogdensburg, NY, p. A455
MCNAMARA, Edward, Executive Director, Margaretville Hospital, Margaretville, NY, p. A446
MCNAMARA, John, M.D., Senior Vice President, Chief Medical Officer, Torrance Memorial Medical Center, Torrance, CA, p. A98
MCNAMARA, Marilyn, M.D., Chief Medical Officer, Southwest General Health Center, Middleburg Heights, OH, p. A500
MCNAMARA, Mike, Chief Information Officer, George L. Mee Memorial Hospital, King City, CA, p. A68
MCNAMARA, Steve, Chief Financial Officer, Orange Coast Medical Center, Fountain Valley, CA, p. A64
MCNAMARA, Thomas, D.O., Vice President Medical Affairs, Wellstar Cobb Hospital, Austell, GA, p. A159
MCNAMARA, Timothy M, Senior Vice President Human Resources, Olean General Hospital, Olean, NY, p. A455
MCNAMEE, Hugar, D.O., Chief Medical Officer, Adventhealth Zephyrhills, Zephyrhills, FL, p. A155
MCNAUGHTON, Kathy, Chief Information Officer, Nemaha County Hospital, Auburn, NE, p. A397
MCNAUGHTON, Richard, Chief Information Management Service, Maine Veterans Affairs Medical Center, Augusta, ME, p. A295
MCNEA, Melvin, President and Chief Executive Officer, Regional West Medical Center, Scottsbluff, NE, p. A406
MCNEAR, Michael, M.D., Chief Medical Officer, Jersey Community Hospital, Jerseyville, IL, p. A199
MCNEEL, Jacob, D.O., Chief of Staff, Camc Plateau Medical Center, Oak Hill, WV, p. A703
MCNEEL, Wakelin, M.D., Medical Director, Bhc Alhambra Hospital, Rosemead, CA, p. A86

Index of Health Care Professionals

Index of Health Care Professionals / McNeely

MCNEELY, Sheri, Chief Financial Officer, Winn Parish Medical Center, Winnfield, LA, p. A294
MCNEIL, Ane, Vice President Human Resources, Trinity Health Oakland Hospital, Pontiac, MI, p. A335
MCNEILL, Michael, Chief Financial Management, Raymond G. Murphy Department of Veterans Affairs Medical Center, Albuquerque, NM, p. A433
MCNICHOLS, Janiece, Chief Financial Officer, Commonspirit – St. Mary–Corwin Hospital, Pueblo, CO, p. A112
MCNITT, Kelly, R.N., Chief Nursing Officer, Steele Memorial Medical Center, Salmon, ID, p. A183
MCNULTY, Bruce, Chief Medical Officer, Endeavor Health Swedish Hospital, Chicago, IL, p. A189
MCNULTY, Timothy, Director Human Resources, Mainehealth Behavioral Health At Spring Harbor, Westbrook, ME, p. A299
MCNUTT, Mike
  Assistant Administrator, Covenant Hospital Plainview, Plainview, TX, p. A644
  Chief Executive Officer, Lamb Healthcare Center, Littlefield, TX, p. A634
MCNUTT, Pamela
  Senior Vice President and Chief Information Officer, Methodist Dallas Medical Center, Dallas, TX, p. A612
  Senior Vice President and Chief Information Officer, Methodist Mansfield Medical Center, Mansfield, TX, p. A637
  Senior Vice President and Chief Information Officer, Methodist Richardson Medical Center, Richardson, TX, p. A646
  Vice President Information Systems, Methodist Charlton Medical Center, Dallas, TX, p. A612
MCPHERSON, Timothy, Emergency Room Director, Tristar Ashland City Medical Center, Ashland City, TN, p. A579
MCPHERSON, Valarie, MSN, R.N., Chief Operating Officer and Chief Nursing Officer, Hackensack Meridian Mountainside Medical Center, Montclair, NJ, p. A424
MCPHIE, Cindie, Chief Executive Officer, Rehabilitation Hospital of Northern Indiana, Mishawaka, IN, p. A224
MCQUILLEN, Daniel Paul, M.D., Chief of Medical Staff, Mercyone New Hampton Medical Center, New Hampton, IA, p. A240
MCQUILLEN, Debra, Vice President, Chief Operations Executive, Scripp. Mercy Hospital, San Diego, CA, p. A89
MCQUILLEN, Paul, M.D., Chief Medical Officer, Ascension St. John Jane Phillips, Bartlesville, OK, p. A510
MCQUISTAN, Bob, Vice President Finance, York General, York, NE, p. A407
MCQUISTON, Mike, Administrative Director Human Resources, Medical City Decatur, Decatur, TX, p. A613
MCRAE, Ashley, Chief Clinical Officer, Kindred Hospital North Florida, Green Cove Springs, FL, p. A133
MCREYNOLDS, John, Chief Executive Officer, North Valley Hospital, Tonasket, WA, p. A697
MCRIMMON, Dana, Chief Financial Officer, Mesilla Valley Hospital, Las Cruces, NM, p. A435
MCROBERTS, Kevin G., FACHE, Chief Executive Officer, Lake Regional Health System, Osage Beach, MO, p. A381
MCSHAN, Audrey, Facility Director, Bryce Hospital, Tuscaloosa, AL, p. A25
MCSWEENEY, Christine, FACHE, Chief Executive Officer, Holy Cross Hospital – Jordan Valley, West Jordan, UT, p. A670
MCTAGGART, Jac
  Chief Executive Officer, Sanford Hillsboro Medical Center, Hillsboro, ND, p. A482
  Chief Executive Officer, Sanford Mayville Medical Center, Mayville, ND, p. A482
MCTIGRIT, Chris, Manager Information Technology, Delta Health System, Dumas, AR, p. A45
MCTIGUE, Michael
  Chief Information Officer, Clara Maass Medical Center, Belleville, NJ, p. A418
  Chief Information Officer, Cooperman Barnabas Medical Center, Livingston, NJ, p. A423
MCTIGUE, DNP, RNC, CENP, Mary, Vice President Patient Care Services and Chief Nursing Officer, Trinitas Regional Medical Center, Elizabeth, NJ, p. A421
MCVAY, Tara
  Chief Executive Officer, Logansport Memorial Hospital, Logansport, IN, p. A223
  Chief Nursing Officer, Logansport Memorial Hospital, Logansport, IN, p. A223
MCVEIGH, Bruce W.
  Chief Operating Officer, Exceptional Community Hospital Maricopa, Maricopa, AZ, p. A33
  Chief Operating Officer, Exceptional Community Hospital Yuma, Yuma, AZ, p. A41
MCVEIGH, Kevin, Chief Human Resources Officer, Banner Desert Medical Center, Mesa, AZ, p. A33
MCVEIGH, Sean, M.D., Chief of Medical Staff, Wayne Memorial Hospital, Honesdale, PA, p. A542
MCVEY, Cecilia, Chief, Nursing Service, Veterans Affairs Boston Healthcare System, West Roxbury, MA, p. A319
MCVEY, Eric A, M.D., III, Executive Vice President Medical Affairs and Quality, St. Dominic–Jackson Memorial Hospital, Jackson, MS, p. A364
MCVEY, Lynn, Chief Operating Officer, Hudson Regional Hospital, Secaucus, NJ, p. A428
MCVEY, Marian Lorraine, Chief Nursing Officer, Prisma Health North Greenville Hospital, Travelers Rest, SC, p. A571
MCWAY, Jacob, Senior Vice President and Chief Financial Officer, Cox North Hospital, Springfield, MO, p. A386
MCWHERTER, Joe, Chief Financial Officer, Baptist Memorial Hospital–Desoto, Southaven, MS, p. A369
MCWHORTER, Juli, R.N., MSN, Chief Executive Officer, Northwest Health Physicians' Specialty Hospital, Fayetteville, AR, p. A46
MEACHAM, Byanka, Director Human Resources, Montgomery County Emergency Service, Norristown, PA, p. A547
MEACHEM, Michelle, Director Human Resources, The University of Vermont Health Network Elizabethtown Community Hospital, Elizabethtown, NY, p. A442
MEAD, Linda, Director Human Resources, Margaretville Hospital, Margaretville, NY, p. A446
MEAD, Richard, Senior Director Human Resources, UCSF Health Saint Francis Hospital, San Francisco, CA, p. A91
MEAD, Rick, Human Resources Leader, Kaiser Permanente Oakland Medical Center, Oakland, CA, p. A81
MEADE, Andrew, Chief Executive Officer, Encompass Health Rehabilitation Hospital of San Antonio, San Antonio, TX, p. A649
MEADE, Robert C., Chief Executive Officer, HCA Florida Sarasota Doctors Hospital, Sarasota, FL, p. A149
MEADE, Teresa, R.N., Chief Nursing Officer, Boone Memorial Hospital, Madison, WV, p. A702
MEADOR, Joe, Chief financial Officer, Augusta Health, Fishersville, VA, p. A676
MEADOWS, Barbara, Chief Financial Manager, Captain James A. Lovell Federal Health Care Center, North Chicago, IL, p. A203
MEADOWS, Danny, M.D., Medical Director, Logansport State Hospital, Logansport, IN, p. A223
MEADOWS, Sheila M, Chief Human Resources Officer, Mission Hospital, Asheville, NC, p. A463
MEADOWS, Theresa, Chief Information Officer, Cook Children's Medical Center, Fort Worth, TX, p. A619
MEANEY, Chris Ann, Senior Vice President, Chief Operating Officer and Chief Nursing Officer, Bristol Health, Bristol, CT, p. A115
MEANS, Dennis, M.D., Vice President Medical Affairs, Carilion New River Valley Medical Center, Christiansburg, VA, p. A675
MEANS, Paul, M.D., President Medical Staff, Penn Highlands Connellsville, Connellsville, PA, p. A537
MEARNS, Stephanie, Vice President Patient Care Services and Chief Nurse Executive, AHMC Seton Medical Center, Daly City, CA, p. A61
MEARS, Terry, Director Information Systems, Duke Regional Hospital, Durham, NC, p. A467
MECHAM, Cindy, Health Information Director, Mountain View Hospital, Payson, UT, p. A667
MECKEL, Marsha S, R.N., Vice President Clinical Services and Chief Nursing Executive, Community Hospital Anderson, Anderson, IN, p. A212
MECKEL, Marsha S., R.N., Hospital Administrator, Community Hospital Anderson, Anderson, IN, p. A212
MEDAGLIA, Guy A., President and Chief Executive Officer, Saint Anthony Hospital, Chicago, IL, p. A191
MEDCIROS, Ron, Director Applied Information Technology, Worcester Recovery Center And Hospital, Worcester, MA, p. A320
MEDINA, Alberto, Information Technology Senior Consultant, Hospital Manati Medical Center, Manati, PR, p. A733
MEDINA, Betsmari, Director Human Resources, Mayaguez Medical Center, Mayaguez, PR, p. A733
MEDINA, Ed, M.D., Medical Director, Phillip. County Hospital, Malta, MT, p. A394
MEDINA, Eleanor, M.D., Chief Medical Officer, Behavioral Center of Michigan, Warren, MI, p. A340
MEDINA, Glorimar, M.D., Executive Vice President and Administrator, Harris Health System, Bellaire, TX, p. A603
MEDINA, Letemia, Administrator, Baylor Scott & White Emergency Hospitals–Aubrey, Aubrey, TX, p. A598
MEDINA, Luz D, Controller, Bayamon Medical Center, Bayamon, PR, p. A731
MEDINA, Marco, Chief Information Officer, Stanton County Hospital, Johnson, KS, p. A251
MEDINA, Obdulia, MSN, MSN, Associate Director for Administrative Support, Clinical Management and Ambulatory Care, Ashford Presbyterian Community Hospital, San Juan, PR, p. A734
MEDINA, Shelby, Chief Executive Officer, Windom Area Health, Windom, MN, p. A357
MEDINA CRUZ, Victor L.
  M.D., Executive Director, Hospital Cuidado Agudo Especializado En Pacientes Politraumatizados, San Juan, PR, p. A736
  M.D., Executive Director, Hospital Universitario Dr. Ramon Ruiz Arnau, Bayamon, PR, p. A731
MEDINA RIVERA, Obdulia, Executive Director, Doctors Center Manati, Manati, PR, p. A733
MEDLEY, Barry, Director Information Systems, Southwell Medical, Adel, GA, p. A156
MEDLEY, Dennis
  Chief Executive Officer, Physicians' Medical Center, New Albany, IN, p. A225
  Chief Executive Officer and Administrator, Physicians' Medical Center, New Albany, IN, p. A225
MEDLEY, India, Chief Nursing Officer, Howard University Hospital, Washington, DC, p. A123
MEDLIN, John, Chief Nursing Officer, North Carolina Specialty Hospital, Durham, NC, p. A467
MEDOVICH, Lisa, Chief Financial Officer, Peterson Health, Kerrville, TX, p. A632
MEEKER, Brian, D.O., President Medical Staff, Virginia Gay Hospital, Vinton, IA, p. A244
MEEKER, Chris, M.D., Chief Medical Officer, Sanford Medical Center Bismarck, Bismarck, ND, p. A479
MEEKER, Christina, Director Human Resources, Strategic Behavioral Health, Llc, Garner, NC, p. A468
MEEKINS, Lance, Chief Executive Officer, Nocona General Hospital, Nocona, TX, p. A641
MEEKINS, Michelle, Manager Human Resources, Sentara Virginia Beach General Hospital, Virginia Beach, VA, p. A685
MEEKS, Deborah, Chief Nursing Officer, Harlingen Medical Center, Harlingen, TX, p. A623
MEENK, Susan, Vice President Human Resources, Providence St. Peter Hospital, Olympia, WA, p. A692
MEESE, Larry R. Jr, FACHE, Chief Executive Officer, Lane Regional Medical Center, Zachary, LA, p. A294
MEESIG, Deborah, M.D., Chief of Staff, Chillicothe Veterans Affairs Medical Center, Chillicothe, OH, p. A488
MEGEHEE, Mark, Vice President and Chief Information Officer, Decatur Morgan Hospital, Decatur, AL, p. A18
MEGGS, Christi, Director, Musc Health Marion Medical Center, Mullins, SC, p. A569
MEGLI, Cami, Controller, Morrison Community Hospital, Morrison, IL, p. A202
MEGLIOLA, Donna M, Assistant Vice President, Johnson Memorial Hospital, Stafford Springs, CT, p. A119
MEGUIAR, Ramon V, M.D., Chief Medical Officer, Memorial Health University Medical Center, Savannah, GA, p. A171
MEHAFFEY, M. Beth, Senior Vice President Human Resources, Baptist Medical Center Jacksonville, Jacksonville, FL, p. A134
MEHINDRU, Vinay
  M.D., Medical Director, Rockledge Regional Medical Center, Rockledge, FL, p. A148
  M.D., Vice President/Chief Medical Officer, Adventhealth Waterman, Tavares, FL, p. A153
MEHJIAN, George, M.D., Chief Medical Officer, Gateway Regional Medical Center, Granite City, IL, p. A196
MEHR, Nicholle, Vice President Operations, Mclaren Oakland, Pontiac, MI, p. A335
MEHTA, Anuj, M.D., Chief Medical Officer, Carewell Health Medical Center, East Orange, NJ, p. A420
MEHTA, Kalpana, Chief Fiscal Services, Jesse Brown Va Medical Center, Chicago, IL, p. A189
MEHTA, Umesh, M.D., Chief Medical Officer, Hackensack Meridian Health Carrier Clinic, Belle Mead, NJ, p. A418
MEIDINGER, Sue, Manager Business Office, Linton Regional Medical Center, Linton, ND, p. A482
MEIER, Adam, MSN, R.N., Chief Nursing Officer, University of Kansas Health System St. Francis Campus, Topeka, KS, p. A261
MEIER, John, Chief Executive Officer, Aurora Charter Oak Hospital, Covina, CA, p. A60
MEIER, Suzanne S, System Director, Compensation and Human Resources Technology, Memorial Hermann Memorial City Medical Center, Houston, TX, p. A627
MEIERS, Dawn, Coordinator Medical Staff and Personnel Services, Insight Surgical Hospital, Warren, MI, p. A340
MEIGS, Jeffrey L, Chief Financial Officer, Weiss Memorial Hospital, Chicago, IL, p. A192
MEIGS, John, M.D., Jr, Chief of Staff, Bibb Medical Center, Centreville, AL, p. A17
MEINDEL, Nympha, R.N., Chief Information Officer, North Shore University Hospital, Manhasset, NY, p. A445

A920 Index of Health Care Professionals

Index of Health Care Professionals / Meskan

Index of Health Care Professionals

MEINERS, David, President, Mercy Hospital St. Louis, Saint Louis, MO, p. A385
MEKHAEL, Hani, M.D., Chief Staff, Havenwyck Hospital, Inc., Auburn Hills, MI, p. A322
MELAHN, William L, M.D., Vice President Medical Affairs and Chief Medical Officer, St. Claire Regional Medical Center, Morehead, KY, p. A272
MELAHOURES, Holly, D.O., Chief Medical Officer, Mercyone Newton Medical Center, Newton, IA, p. A241
MELAN, Kristen, Director Human Resources Administration, Good Shepherd Specialty Hospital, Bethlehem, PA, p. A535
MELANCON, Eric, Chief of Staff, Ochsner St. Mary, Morgan City, LA, p. A289
MELAND, Jeff, M.D., Vice President, Chief Medical Officer, Northfield Hospital And Clinics, Northfield, MN, p. A352
MELARAGNO, Robert, Vice President Finance, Ohiohealth O'Bleness Hospital, Athens, OH, p. A485
MELBOURNE, John, M.D., Medical Director, Conifer Park, Glenville, NY, p. A443
MELBY, Larry, Chief Executive Officer, Select Specialty Hospital–Palm Beach, Lake Worth, FL, p. A136
MELBY, Rachel, Vice President, Chief Financial Officer, Crawford County Memorial Hospital, Denison, IA, p. A234
MELCHER, Nancy, Chief Nursing Officer, Wellstar North Fulton Hospital, Roswell, GA, p. A170
MELCHIOR, Eric L, Executive Vice President and Chief Financial Officer, Gbmc Healthcare, Baltimore, MD, p. A302
MELCHIORRE, Lisa, R.N., MS, Chief Operating Officer and Chief Nursing Officer, St. Luke's Elmore, Mountain Home, ID, p. A182
MELEAR, Brian, Chief Executive Officer, HCA Florida Raulerson Hospital, Okeechobee, FL, p. A143
MELEAR, David, Chief Executive Officer, Cedar Hills Hospital, Portland, OR, p. A531
MELENDEZ, Alma, Controller, Dimmit Regional Hospital, Carrizo Springs, TX, p. A606
MELENDEZ, Jose, M.D., Chief Medical Officer, UCHealth Memorial Hospital, Colorado Springs, CO, p. A105
MELGAR, Joy, MSN, R.N., Chief Nursing Officer, Avala, Covington, LA, p. A280
MELINE, Brenda, Manager Human Resources, Patients' Hospital of Redding, Redding, CA, p. A85
MELL, Kevin, Vice President Operations, Medstar Montgomery Medical Center, Olney, MD, p. A306
MELLETT, David, Chief Financial Officer, Harrison Memorial Hospital, Cynthiana, KY, p. A264
MELLGREN, Gustave, M.D., Chief of Staff, Glacial Ridge Health System, Glenwood, MN, p. A347
MELLO, Brett, Chief Information Officer, Cayuga Medical Center At Ithaca, Ithaca, NY, p. A444
MELLO, Paul, Manager Data Processing, Dsh Metropolitan, Norwalk, CA, p. A80
MELLOWS, George, Facility Director, Hawthorn Center, Northville, MI, p. A334
MELNIKOFF, Jean, Vice President Human Resources, Kaiser Permanente Medical Center, Honolulu, HI, p. A175
MELTON, Anne, Interim Chief Nursing Officer, Rutherford Regional Health System, Rutherfordton, NC, p. A475
MELTON, Chad, President, St. Michael Medical Center, Silverdale, WA, p. A695
MELTON, Josh, Chief Information Officer, St. Bernards Medical Center, Jonesboro, AR, p. A48
MELTVEDT, Robert, M.D., Jr, Vice President Medical Affairs, Valley Health – Warren Memorial Hospital, Front Royal, VA, p. A677
MELTZER, David B, Chief Financial Officer, Texas Health Presbyterian Hospital Denton, Denton, TX, p. A614
MELVILLE, Carol, Director Human Resources, HCA Houston Healthcare West, Houston, TX, p. A626
MENCINI, Brandon
Chief Executive Officer, Asante Ashland Community Hospital, Ashland, OR, p. A525
Chief Executive Officer, Asante Rogue Regional Medical Center, Medford, OR, p. A529
MENDELOWITZ, Susan, R.N., FACHE, Executive Vice President and Chief Operating Officer, Bergen New Bridge Medical Center, Paramus, NJ, p. A426
MENDENHALL, Matthew, M.D., Chief Medical Officer, Adventhealth Littleton, Littleton, CO, p. A111
MENDEZ, Alex A, Executive Vice President and Chief Financial Officer, Mount Sinai Medical Center, Miami Beach, FL, p. A141
MENDEZ, Kim K, Ed.D., R.N., Chief Nurse Officer, NYC Health + Hospitals/Bellevue, New York, NY, p. A450
MENDEZ, Lincoln S., Chief Executive Officer, Boca Raton Regional Hospital, Boca Raton, FL, p. A126
MENDEZ, Nicholas Paul., Chief Executive Officer and Director of Nursing, Pam Specialty Hospital of Hammond, Hammond, LA, p. A283
MENDIOLA–BALDERAS, Rosie L, Director Information Systems, South Texas Health System, Edinburg, TX, p. A615
MENDOZA, Carlos, Controller, Baptist Memorial Rehabilitation Hospital, Germantown, TN, p. A583
MENDOZA, Christopher, Chief Executive Officer, Integris Health Ponca City Hospital, Ponca City, OK, p. A519
MENDOZA, Dana, Chief Information Officer, Maui Memorial Medical Center, Wailuku, HI, p. A177
MENDOZA, Joseph
M.D., Medical Director, Porterville Developmental Center, Porterville, CA, p. A84
Chief Financial Officer, Hillcrest Hospital Cushing, Cushing, OK, p. A511
Chief Financial Officer, Hillcrest Hospital Henryetta, Henryetta, OK, p. A513
Chief Financial Officer, Hillcrest Medical Center, Tulsa, OK, p. A522
MENDOZA, Melissa, Chief Financial Officer, HCA Houston Healthcare Medical Center, Houston, TX, p. A625
MENDOZA, Yolanda, Director Human Resources, Rehabilitation Hospital of Southern New Mexico, Las Cruces, NM, p. A435
MENDOZA DAYAO, Jerome, MS, R.N., Chief Nursing Officer, Wynn Hospital, Utica, NY, p. A460
MENDRZYCKI, Jennifer, Chief Executive Officer, TMC Health, Tucson, AZ, p. A41
MENDYKA, Nick, Chief Financial Officer, UVA Health University Medical Center, Charlottesville, VA, p. A674
MENEFEE, Jason J, Chief Financial Officer, Mccamey County Hospital District, Mccamey, TX, p. A638
MENEFEE, Jason J., Chief Executive Officer, Mccamey County Hospital District, Mccamey, TX, p. A638
MENEN, Michael, M.D., Chief Medical Officer, Bon Secours St. Francis Medical Center, Midlothian, VA, p. A679
MENGENHAUSEN, Jeff, Chief Executive Officer, Montrose Regional Health, Montrose, CO, p. A112
MENGLE, Scott
Vice President Human Resources, Penn State Health St. Joseph, Reading, PA, p. A553
Vice President, Human Resources, East Region, Penn State Health Lancaster Medical Center, Lancaster, PA, p. A543
MENKES, Jeffrey, President and Chief Executive Officer, Calvary Hospital, New York, NY, p. A447
MENKOSKY, Paula, Chief Human Resources Officer, Mayo Clinic Hospital – Rochester, Rochester, MN, p. A353
MENNONNA, Guy, Senior Vice President Human Resources, Bergen New Bridge Medical Center, Paramus, NJ, p. A426
MENON, Rema, M.D., Clinical Director, Parsons State Hospital And Training Center, Parsons, KS, p. A258
MENSCH, Alan, M.D., Senior Vice President Medical Affairs, Plainview Hospital, Plainview, NY, p. A456
MENSEN, Amy, Chief Operating Officer, Regional Medical Center, Manchester, IA, p. A239
MENTHCOAST, Lynn, Chief Fiscal Service, Tennessee Valley Hcs – Nashville And Murfreesboro, Nashville, TN, p. A590
MENTZEL, Bridget, System Director Human Resources, Mercy Health – Clermont Hospital, Batavia, OH, p. A486
MENTZER, Kai, Interim Director, G.V. (Sonny) Montgomery Department of Veterans Affairs Medical Center, Jackson, MS, p. A364
MENTZER, Larry, Chief Human Resources Officer, Roseburg Va Medical Center, Roseburg, OR, p. A531
MENZEL, Colette, Ph.D., Chief Operating Officer and Chief Financial Officer, Antelop. Valley Medical Center, Lancaster, CA, p. A69
MENZEL, Kimberly, Senior Vice President and Area Manager, Kaiser Permanente Roseville Medical Center, Roseville, CA, p. A86
MENZIE, Sue, R.N., Director Patient Care, Sierra Tucson, Tucson, AZ, p. A41
MERCADO, Felix V., Chief Financial Officer, Lawrence General Hospital, Lawrence, MA, p. A314
MERCADO, Gloria, Director of Nursing, Mennonite General Hospital, Aibonito, PR, p. A731
MERCADO, Leda Marta R, Chief Operating Officer, Hospital Menonita De Cayey, Cayey, PR, p. A732
MERCER, David, Coordinator Information Systems, Baptist Memorial Hospital–Union City, Union City, TN, p. A594
MERCER, Jonathan, FACHE, Senior Vice President, Chief Operating Officer, UNC Health Blue Ridge, Morganton, NC, p. A473
MERCER, Shawna, Director Human Resources, Kansas Neurological Institute, Topeka, KS, p. A260
MERCER, William, M.D., Director, Peterson Healthcare And Rehabilitation Hospital, Wheeling, WV, p. A706
MERCHANT, Deven, M.D., Chief Medical Executive, Sutter Davis Hospital, Davis, CA, p. A61
MERCHANT, Robert, Interim Medical Center Director & Executive Director, Ambulatory Care Services, Greater Los Angeles Hcs, Los Angeles, CA, p. A72
MERCIER, Murry, Chief Information Officer, Promedica Toledo Hospital, Toledo, OH, p. A505
MERCKENS, Natalie, Chief Executive Officer, Ballard Rehabilitation Hospital, San Bernardino, CA, p. A88
MERCURI, Ralph, Vice President and Chief Financial Officer, Major Hospital, Shelbyville, IN, p. A227
MERE, Mohammed J., Chief Information Officer, Oneida Healthcare, Oneida, NY, p. A455
MEREDITH, Katie, Chief Nursing Officer, Select Specialty Hospital–Central Kentucky, Danville, KY, p. A265
MEREDITH, Keith, Chief Operating Officer, Salem Regional Medical Center, Salem, OH, p. A503
MEREDITH, Ty, Chief Executive Officer, Peak View Behavioral Health, Colorado Springs, CO, p. A105
MEREK, Gloria, Director of Nursing, Springfield Hospital Center, Sykesville, MD, p. A307
MERGEN, Lynn M., Chief Executive Officer, Lutheran Kosciusko Hospital, Warsaw, IN, p. A229
MERILLO, Myra, Supervisor Health Information Management, Encompass Health Rehabilitation Hospital of Spring Hill, Brooksville, FL, p. A127
MERINGOLO, Francis, Vice President Human Resources, Umass Memorial–Marlborough Hospital, Marlborough, MA, p. A315
MERKEL, Rebecca, Privacy Officer, Franciscan Health Carmel, Carmel, IN, p. A213
MERKLE, John F., Medical Center Director, Tuscaloosa Va Medical Center, Tuscaloosa, AL, p. A25
MERKLEY, Jason R., Chief Executive Officer, Brookings Health System, Brookings, SD, p. A572
MERKLIN, Paul, Assistant Administrator, Chief Financial Officer, Macon Community Hospital, Lafayette, TN, p. A586
MERRIFIELD, Matthew, Chief Executive Officer, Aiken Regional Medical Centers, Aiken, SC, p. A562
MERRIGAN, Mary C, Manager Public Relations, Sanford Vermillion Medical Center, Vermillion, SD, p. A577
MERRILL, Cheryl Bhima, MSN, R.N., Senior Vice President Patient Care Services and Chief Nursing Officer, Salem Hospital, Salem, MA, p. A318
MERRILL, Chuck, M.D., Vice President Medical Affairs, Marian Regional Medical Center, Santa Maria, CA, p. A94
MERRILL, Rick W.
Chief Executive Officer, Cook Children's Medical Center – Prosper, Prosper, TX, p. A646
System President and Chief Executive Officer, Cook Children's Medical Center, Fort Worth, TX, p. A619
MERRITT, Anneke, R.N., Chief Nursing Officer, Northwestern Medical Center, Saint Albans, VT, p. A672
MERRITT, Becky A, Director Human Resources, Houston Methodist Clear Lake Hospital, Houston, TX, p. A626
MERRITT, Belinda, M.D., Medical Director, West Tennessee Healthcare Rehabilitation Hospital Cane Creek, A Partnership With Encompass Health, Martin, TN, p. A587
MERRITT, Bradley, M.D., Medical Director, Christus Trinity Mother Frances Rehabilitation Hospital, A Partner of Encompass Health, Tyler, TX, p. A658
MERRITT, Janet, Chief Financial Officer, Ascension St. Vincent Williamsport, Williamsport, IN, p. A229
MERRITT, Trevor, Director Human Resources, Star Valley Health, Afton, WY, p. A726
MERRY, Duane, Chief Information Officer, Little Falls Hospital, Little Falls, NY, p. A445
MERRYMAN, Mary, Regional Director Information Management, Christus Health Shreveport–Bossier, Shreveport, LA, p. A292
MERRYWELL, Paul, Chief Information Officer, Sycamore Shoals Hospital, Elizabethton, TN, p. A582
MERSON, John, M.D., Chief of Staff, John Muir Health, Concord Medical Center, Concord, CA, p. A60
MERZ, Stephen, Chief Operating Officer, Sheppard Pratt, Baltimore, MD, p. A302
MESA, Gustavo, Chief Information Officer, San Juan City Hospital, San Juan, PR, p. A736
MESAROS, Dennis
Administrator, St. Luke's Regional Medical Center, Boise, ID, p. A180
Vice President, Population Health/Regional Acute Care Operations, St. Luke's Regional Medical Center, Boise, ID, p. A180
MESIC, John, M.D., Chief Medical Officer, Sutter Auburn Faith Hospital, Auburn, CA, p. A56
MESICK, Marc, Vice President and Chief Financial Officer, Ellis Medicine, Schenectady, NY, p. A458
MESKAN, Paula
R.N., Chief Executive Officer, River's Edge Hospital And Clinic, Saint Peter, MN, p. A355

Index of Health Care Professionals

Index of Health Care Professionals / Mesoras

R.N., Chief Nursing Officer, River's Edge Hospital And Clinic, Saint Peter, MN, p. A355
MESORAS, Amber, Chief Human Resources Officer, Veterans Affairs Pittsburgh Healthcare System, Pittsburgh, PA, p. A552
MESSA–GILL, Nicole, Manager Human Resources, Northlake Behavioral Health System, Mandeville, LA, p. A287
MESSELT, Mary Jo
Manager Human Resources, Mercy Hospital Watonga, Watonga, OK, p. A524
Senior Human Resources Manager, Mercy Hospital Logan County, Guthrie, OK, p. A513
MESSER, Adam, President, Dell Seton Medical Center At The University of Texas, Austin, TX, p. A600
MESSER, Kelly, Director of Finance, Devereux Hospital And Children's Center of Florida, Melbourne, FL, p. A138
MESSER, Mark
D.O., Clinical Director, Terrell State Hospital, Terrell, TX, p. A656
D.O., Interim Superintendent, Terrell State Hospital, Terrell, TX, p. A656
MESSERSMITH, Scott E, Director Human Resources, Columbus Community Hospital, Columbus, NE, p. A399
MESSINA, Arlene, R.N., MSN, Director of Nursing, Riverside Doctors' Hospital Williamsburg, Williamsburg, VA, p. A685
MESSINA, Daniel J., Ph.D., FACHE, President and Chief Executive Officer, Richmond University Medical Center, New York, NY, p. A452
MESSMAN, Catherine, Chief Financial Officer, Mills–Peninsula Medical Center, Burlingame, CA, p. A58
MESTAS, Lisa, Associate Administrator and System Chief Nursing Officer, USA Health University Hospital, Mobile, AL, p. A22
MESTER, Sulynn, R.N., Chief Nursing Officer, Childress Regional Medical Center, Childress, TX, p. A607
MESZLER, Lori A., Chief Financial Officer, Helen Hayes Hospital, West Haverstraw, NY, p. A461
METCALF, Angie L, Vice President and Chief Human Resource Officer, Cleveland Clinic Martin North Hospital, Stuart, FL, p. A150
METCALF, Chris, Director of Nursing, Utah State Hospital, Provo, UT, p. A667
METCALF, Kathleen, Chief Information Officer, University Hospitals Samaritan Medical Center, Ashland, OH, p. A485
METCALF, Peter, M.D., President Medical Staff, Genesis Medical Center, Silvis, Silvis, IL, p. A208
METCALFE, Kevan
FACHE, Chief Executive Officer, Anaheim Global Medical Center, Anaheim, CA, p. A55
FACHE, Chief Executive Officer, South Coast Global Medical Center, Santa Ana, CA, p. A93
METELKO, Lindsey, Chief Nursing Officer, Castleview Hospital, Price, UT, p. A667
METHVEN, Jeffrey M., President and Chief Executive Officer, St. Mary's Healthcare, Amsterdam, NY, p. A438
METHVIN, Jeff, Manager Information Technology, St. Luke Hospital And Living Center, Marion, KS, p. A254
METIKO, Olushola, M.D., Medical Director, Central Prison Hospital, Raleigh, NC, p. A474
METINKO, Andrew, M.D., Chief Medical Officer, The Hsc Pediatric Center, Washington, DC, p. A124
METIVIER, Roberta, Vice President Human Resources and Administrator, Western Main Nursing Home, Mainehealth Stephens Hospital, Norway, ME, p. A298
METRO, Michelle, Vice President Nursing, North Central Kansas Medical Center, Concordia, KS, p. A248
METSKER, Matthew, President, St. Clare Hospital, Lakewood, WA, p. A691
METTEAUER, Kenneth, Chief Financial Officer, Adventhealth Redmond, Rome, GA, p. A170
METZ, Amy, MSN, R.N., Chief Executive Officer, Regency Hospital of Florence, Florence, SC, p. A566
METZ, Bruce, Ph.D., Senior Vice President and Chief Information Officer, Lahey Hospital & Medical Center, Burlington, MA, p. A312
METZ, Carl, Vice President, Ephraim Mcdowell Fort Logan Hospital, Stanford, KY, p. A274
METZGER, Alysha, Director Human Resources, Methodist Hospital Hill Country, Fredericksburg, TX, p. A620
METZGER, Cynthia, Chief Nursing and Operations Officer, Little River Medical Center, Inc., Ashdown, AR, p. A43
METZGER, Richard, Interim Chief Executive Officer, USA Health Providence Hospital, Mobile, AL, p. A22
MEUER, Lynn, Interim Chief Nursing Officer, Sibley Memorial Hospital, Washington, DC, p. A124
MEURER, Bryan, Director Information Systems, Mat–Su Regional Medical Center, Palmer, AK, p. A29
MEYER, Anthony, M.D., Medical Director, Aurora Psychiatric Hospital, Wauwatosa, WI, p. A724
MEYER, Barb, Executive Director of Nursing, Gibson Area Hospital And Health Services, Gibson City, IL, p. A196
MEYER, Brian, Senior Vice President and Chief Administrative Officer, Phoenix Children's, Phoenix, AZ, p. A36
MEYER, Cameron, CPA, Chief Financial Officer, Hutchinson Regional Medical Center, Hutchinson, KS, p. A251
MEYER, Cheryl, MSN, Director of Nursing, Haven Behavioral Hospital of Dayton, Dayton, OH, p. A493
MEYER, Cindy, Chief Executive Officer, Rogers Behavioral Health, Oconomowoc, WI, p. A718
MEYER, Daniel T, President, Aurora Baycare Medical Center, Green Bay, WI, p. A712
MEYER, Gordon, Director Human Resources, Surgeons Choice Medical Center, Southfield, MI, p. A338
MEYER, Jennifer, M.D., Chief Medical Officer, East Jefferson General Hospital, Metairie, LA, p. A288
MEYER, Karen, Vice President Finance and Chief Financial Officer, Rush Memorial Hospital, Rushville, IN, p. A227
MEYER, Kurt A
Chief Human Resource Officer, Saint Josep. Health System, Mishawaka, IN, p. A224
Chief Human Resources Officer, Plymouth Medical Center, Plymouth, IN, p. A226
MEYER, Lorraine R, Chief Operating Officer, Community Healthcare System, Onaga, KS, p. A256
MEYER, Lorraine R., Interim Chief Executive Officer, Community Healthcare System, Onaga, KS, p. A256
MEYER, Michele C.
R.N., Chief Executive Officer, Washington County Memorial Hospital, Potosi, MO, p. A382
R.N., Vice President of Operations, Mercy Hospital Jefferson, Festus, MO, p. A375
MEYER, Morgan, Chief Financial Officer, Howard County Medical Center, Saint Paul, NE, p. A405
MEYER, Nate, Chief Financial Officer, Alomere Health, Alexandria, MN, p. A342
MEYER, Robert L., President and Chief Executive Officer, Phoenix Children's, Phoenix, AZ, p. A36
MEYER, Roger, M.D., Chief of Staff, Friend Community Healthcare System, Friend, NE, p. A400
MEYER, Ryan
Chief Operating Officer, Mercyone Cedar Falls Medical Center, Cedar Falls, IA, p. A231
Chief Operating Officer, Mercyone Oelwein Medical Center, Oelwein, IA, p. A241
Chief Operating Officer, Mercyone Waterloo Medical Center, Waterloo, IA, p. A244
Vice President Operations, Mercyone Waterloo Medical Center, Waterloo, IA, p. A244
MEYER, Timothy, M.D., Chief of Staff, Marshfield Medical Center – Neillsville, Neillsville, WI, p. A718
MEYER, Wessel H., M.D., Chief of Staff, VA Central California Health Care System, Fresno, CA, p. A65
MEYERS, Betty, Chief Financial Officer, Crook County Medical Services District, Sundance, WY, p. A728
MEYERS, Jeff, HR Generalist, Pershing General Hospital, Lovelock, NV, p. A411
MEYERS, John, M.D., Chief Medical Officer, White Rock Medical Center, Dallas, TX, p. A613
MEYERS, Josette
Area Chief Executive Officer, Encompass Health Rehabilitation Hospital of Toms River, Toms River, NJ, p. A429
Chief Executive Officer, Encompass Health Rehabilitation Hospital of York, York, PA, p. A558
MEYERS, Larry, Chief Information Officer, Wilson Memorial Hospital, Sidney, OH, p. A503
MEYERS, Mark S., M.D., Chief of Staff, Battle Mountain General Hospital, Battle Mountain, NV, p. A408
MEYERS, William, Chief Information Officer, St. Luke's Hospital, Chesterfield, MO, p. A373
MEZA, Eduardo, M.D., Medical Director, Prairie St. John's, Fargo, ND, p. A480
MEZA, Lourdes, Coordinator Human Resources, West Covina Medical Center, West Covina, CA, p. A101
MEZOFF, Adam, M.D., Vice President and Chief Medical Officer, Dayton Children's Hospital, Dayton, OH, p. A493
MHERABI, Nader, Senior Vice President and Vice Dean, Chief Information Officer, Nyu Langone Hospitals, New York, NY, p. A452
MIANO, Christena, Vice President, Human Resources, HCA Florida Trinity Hospital, Trinity, FL, p. A153
MICAN, Deborah, R.N., Chief Nursing Officer, Capital Health Medical Center–Hopewell, Pennington, NJ, p. A427
MICHAEL, Amy J, Chief Operating Officer, Sullivan County Memorial Hospital, Milan, MO, p. A380
MICHAEL, Elizabeth, R.N., MS, Vice President Patient Care Services and Chief Nursing Officer, Stillwater Medical Center, Stillwater, OK, p. A521
MICHAEL, Linda, Vice President, Chief Compliance Officer, Children's Hospital Colorado – Colorado Springs, Colorado Springs, CO, p. A105
MICHAEL, Richard, M.D., Vice President Medical Affairs, Christus Health Shreveport–Bossier, Shreveport, LA, p. A292
MICHAELS, Stephen T., M.D., FACHE, President, Medstar Southern Maryland Hospital Center, Clinton, MD, p. A303
MICHAJYSZYN, Christina, FACHE, Chief Executive Officer, Dmc Rehabilitation Institute of Michigan, Detroit, MI, p. A325
MICHALSKI, Carrie, President and Chief Executive Officer, Riverview Health, Crookston, MN, p. A345
MICHEL, George J, Chief Operating Officer, Larkin Community Hospital–South Miami Campus, South Miami, FL, p. A150
MICHEL, Randall, M.D., Chief of Staff, Lompoc Valley Medical Center, Lompoc, CA, p. A70
MICHEL–OGBORN, Deborah, Chief Information Resource Management, North Florida/South Georgia Veteran's Health System, Gainesville, FL, p. A132
MICHELE, Margorie, Chief Human Resources Officer, Penn Presbyterian Medical Center, Philadelphia, PA, p. A549
MICHELEN, Jeannith
Chief Implementation Officer, NYC Health + Hospitals/ Elmhurst, New York, NY, p. A451
Senior Associate Executive Director, NYC Health + Hospitals/Lincoln, New York, NY, p. A451
Senior Associate Executive Director, NYC Health + Hospitals/Queens, New York, NY, p. A451
MICHELSON, Soad, M.D., Senior Medical Director, Clarity Child Guidance Center, San Antonio, TX, p. A649
MICHENER, Scott, M.D., Chief Medical Officer, Comanche County Memorial Hospital, Lawton, OK, p. A514
MICHL, Michelle, Director Human Resources, Mercy Medical Center Mount Shasta, Mount Shasta, CA, p. A79
MICKELSEN, Ryan, President and Chief Executive Officer, SMP Health – St. Aloisius, Harvey, ND, p. A481
MICKELSON, Aaron
M.D., Chief Medical Officer, Dignity Health Arizona General Hospital, Laveen, AZ, p. A33
M.D., Chief Medical Officer, Dignity Health Arizona General Hospital Mesa, Llc, Mesa, AZ, p. A33
MICKIEWICZ, Nanette, M.D., President, Dominican Hospital, Santa Cruz, CA, p. A94
MICKLOS, Trevor, President, St. Luke's Hospital – Warren Campus, Phillipsburg, NJ, p. A427
MIDDENDORF, Bruce, M.D., Chief Medical Officer, St. Mary's Health Care System, Athens, GA, p. A156
MIDDLEBROOK, Dan, Chief Medical Officer, Ascension Wisconsin Hospital – Menomonee Falls Campus, Menomonee Falls, WI, p. A715
MIDDLEBROOKS, Mark, M.D., Medical Director, Noland Hospital Birmingham, Birmingham, AL, p. A17
MIDDLETON, Jackie, Vice President Human Resources, Methodist Dallas Medical Center, Dallas, TX, p. A612
MIDDLETON, James, MSN, R.N., Chief Nursing Officer, Knox Community Hospital, Mount Vernon, OH, p. A501
MIDDLETON, Robert Eldon, MSN, R.N., III, Vice President Ancillary Services, Chief Administrative Officer, Chief Construction Executive, Gerald Champion Regional Medical Center, Alamogordo, NM, p. A432
MIDGETT, Jenifer, President and Chief Executive Officer, Temp. St. Luke's Hospital, Tempe, AZ, p. A39
MIDGETT, Steve, R.N., Chief Nursing Officer, Encompass Health Rehabilitation Hospital of Sugar Land, Sugar Land, TX, p. A654
MIDKIFF, Rodney, Chief Executive Officer, Cornerstone Specialty Hospitals Huntington, Huntington, WV, p. A701
MIDTLIEN, Tonia, Information Systems Support Specialist, Gundersen Boscobel Area Hospital And Clinics, Boscobel, WI, p. A708
MIEDLER, Michael, M.D., Chief Medical Officer, Continuing Care Hospital, Lexington, KY, p. A268
MIESNER, Gail, Chief Financial Officer, Memorial Hospital, Chester, IL, p. A188
MIGLIETTA, Steven, Chief Financial Officer, Sarasota Memorial Hospital – Venice, North Venice, FL, p. A142
MIGOYA, Carlos A., President and Chief Executive Officer, Jackson Health System, Miami, FL, p. A140
MIKELL, Evarista, Assistant Finance Officer, William S. Middleton Memorial Veterans' Hospital, Madison, WI, p. A715
MIKES, Kim, Chief Executive Officer, Hoag Orthopedic Institute, Irvine, CA, p. A67
MIKHAIL, Ashraf, M.D., Medical Director, Brynn Marr Hospital, Jacksonville, NC, p. A471
MIKI, Nobuyuki, M.D., Vice President Medical Services and Chief Medical Officer, Kuakini Medical Center, Honolulu, HI, p. A175

A922 Index of Health Care Professionals

Index of Health Care Professionals / Miller

MIKITARIAN, George Jr, FACHE, President and Chief Executive Officer, Parrish Medical Center, Titusville, FL, p. A153
MIKKELSEN, Kallie, Vice President Nursing, Memorial Hospital of Sweetwater County, Rock Springs, WY, p. A728
MIKKELSON, Tom
  M.D., Interim Chief Operating Officer, Touchette Regional Hospital, Centreville, IL, p. A187
  M.D., Vice President Medical Affairs, Touchette Regional Hospital, Centreville, IL, p. A187
MIKLAVIC, Kirk
  Director Human Resources, Bridgton Hospital, Bridgton, ME, p. A296
  Director, Human Resources, Central Maine Medical Center, Lewiston, ME, p. A297
MIKLOS, Maggie, Director Human Resources, HCA Florida Northside Hospital, Saint Petersburg, FL, p. A149
MIKULIC, Jeannie, Director Human Resources, Providence Portland Medical Center, Portland, OR, p. A530
MILAM, Wendy, Chief Nursing Officer, Encompass Health Rehabilitation Hospital of Ocala, Ocala, FL, p. A143
MILAN, Isabel, R.N., Chief Nursing Officer, Los Angeles General Medical Center, Los Angeles, CA, p. A74
MILAND, Shelly
  Chief Financial Officer, Texas Health Specialty Hospital, Fort Worth, TX, p. A620
  Group Finance Officer, Texas Health Harris Methodist Hospital Cleburne, Cleburne, TX, p. A607
  Group Financial Officer, Texas Health Harris Methodist Hospital Fort Worth, Fort Worth, TX, p. A620
MILANO, Arthur D, Vice President Human Resources, Berkshire Medical Center, Pittsfield, MA, p. A317
MILATOVICH, Natasha, Association Vice President Human Resources, Adventist Health White Memorial, Los Angeles, CA, p. A71
MILAZZO, John
  Chief Financial Officer, Merit Health River Region, Vicksburg, MS, p. A369
  Chief Financial Officer, Southeast Georgia Health System Camden Campus, Saint Marys, GA, p. A170
MILBURN, Sandra, Director Human Resources, Encompass Health Rehabilitation Hospital of Memphis, A Partner of Methodist Healthcare, Memphis, TN, p. A588
MILBURN, Sharon, Chief Nursing Officer, Summers County Arh Hospital, Hinton, WV, p. A701
MILES, Ben, President, Chelsea Hospital, Chelsea, MI, p. A324
MILES, Dana, Chief Nursing Officer and Chief Clinical Officer, Delta Health System, Dumas, AR, p. A45
MILES, Erika, Chief Medical Officer, Essentia Health Sandstone, Sandstone, MN, p. A355
MILES, John, Chief Financial Officer, Piedmont Newnan Hospital, Newnan, GA, p. A169
MILES, Karen, M.D., Medical Director, Strategic Behavioral Health, Llc, Garner, NC, p. A468
MILES, Kerry
  Chief Information Officer, Providence St. Peter Hospital, Olympia, WA, p. A692
  Site Director, Providence Centralia Hospital, Centralia, WA, p. A688
MILES, Lee Ann, Chief Financial Officer, Harrison County Community Hospital, Bethany, MO, p. A371
MILES, Paul V
  Chief Operating Officer, Morgan County Arh Hospital, West Liberty, KY, p. A275
  Vice President Administration, Whitesburg Arh Hospital, Whitesburg, KY, p. A275
MILES, Scott, Chief Operating Officer, Forest View Psychiatric Hospital, Grand Rapids, MI, p. A328
MILES, Sybil J., R.N., Administrator, Sage Specialty Hospital (Ltac), Denham Springs, LA, p. A281
MILETO, Dottie, Chief Nursing Officer, Adventhealth Heart of Florida, Davenport, FL, p. A129
MILHALTSES, Dean, Chief Operating Officer, NYC Health + Hospitals/Queens, New York, NY, p. A451
MILHORN, Britta, Chief Executive Officer, Rehabilitation Hospital of Bristol, Bristol, VA, p. A674
MILIAN, Tony, Chief Financial Officer, Larkin Community Hospital–Palm Springs Campus, Hialeah, FL, p. A133
MILIAZZO, John A, Vice President and Chief Financial Officer, Southeast Georgia Health System Brunswick Campus, Brunswick, GA, p. A159
MILICEVIC, Heather, Vice President and Chief Human Resource Officer, Western Reserve Hospital, Cuyahoga Falls, OH, p. A493
MILLAN, Wilfredo Rabelo, Chief Operating Officer, Cardiovascular Center of Puerto Rico And The Caribbean, San Juan, PR, p. A734
MILLARD, Kathleen, Acting Director Nursing, Kalamazoo Psychiatric Hospital, Kalamazoo, MI, p. A331

MILLEN, Peter S, Chief Medical Officer MHSATS, Community Behavioral Health Hospital – Rochester, Rochester, MN, p. A353
MILLER, Aaron, Chief Executive Officer/Chief Operating Officer, First Baptist Medical Center, Dallas, TX, p. A611
MILLER, Alicia, Director Human Resources, Aspen Valley Hospital, Aspen, CO, p. A103
MILLER, Andy, Chief Financial Officer, Trident Medical Center, Charleston, SC, p. A563
MILLER, Barbie, Chief Financial Officer, Cimarron Memorial Hospital, Boise City, OK, p. A510
MILLER, Brent R, Manager Human Resources, Brown County Community Treatment Center, Green Bay, WI, p. A712
MILLER, Brian, Chief Executive Officer, Lovelace Medical Center, Albuquerque, NM, p. A432
MILLER, Brian F., Chief Executive Officer, Dewitt Hospital & Nursing Home, Dewitt, AR, p. A45
MILLER, Caitlin, MS, Chief Hospital Executive, Hackensack Meridian Health Bayshore Community Hospital, Holmdel, NJ, p. A422
MILLER, Candace N., President and Chief Executive Officer, Jackson General Hospital, Ripley, WV, p. A704
MILLER, Carol R, R.N., Chief Nursing Officer, Reynolds Memorial Hospital, Glen Dale, WV, p. A700
MILLER, Carrie, Director Human Resources, Promedica Defiance Regional Hospital, Defiance, OH, p. A494
MILLER, Chad
  Chief Financial Officer, Merit Health Biloxi, Biloxi, MS, p. A359
  Chief Financial Officer, West Jefferson Medical Center, Marrero, LA, p. A288
MILLER, Chandra, Director of Nursing, John J. Pershing Veterans' Administration Medical Center, Poplar Bluff, MO, p. A382
MILLER, Chris K., Chief Financial Officer, Highland Hospital, Charleston, WV, p. A700
MILLER, Christine
  Chief Human Resources Management Services, Maine Veterans Affairs Medical Center, Augusta, ME, p. A295
  General Counsel and Vice President Human Resources, UPMC Hanover, Hanover, PA, p. A541
MILLER, Clint, Chief Nursing Officer, Spooner Health, Spooner, WI, p. A721
MILLER, Connie, Vice President Human Resources, Overland Park Regional Medical Center, Overland Park, KS, p. A257
MILLER, Daniel
  Human Resources Business Partner, University Hospitals Parma Medical Center, Parma, OH, p. A502
  Vice President Human Resources, University Hospitals Elyria Medical Center, Elyria, OH, p. A495
MILLER, David C., M.D., M.P.H., Executive Vice Dean for Clinical Affairs and President, UM Health System, University of Michigan Medical Center, Ann Arbor, MI, p. A321
MILLER, Debra, Administrator, Crosbyton Clinic Hospital, Crosbyton, TX, p. A610
MILLER, Derek, Senior Vice President and Chief Financial Officer, Southeast Alabama Medical Center, Dothan, AL, p. A18
MILLER, Dillon D, M.D., Chief Medical Officer, Fannin Regional Hospital, Blue Ridge, GA, p. A159
MILLER, Dionne, Chief Operating Officer, Sutter Roseville Medical Center, Roseville, CA, p. A86
MILLER, Dyrek, M.D., Chief Medical Staff, ECU Health Duplin Hospital, Kenansville, NC, p. A471
MILLER, Elaine G, Director of Nursing, Oaklawn Psychiatric Center, Goshen, IN, p. A218
MILLER, Esteban, Chief Medical Officer, Black River Memorial Hospital, Black River Falls, WI, p. A708
MILLER, Gary L
  Regional Director Information Systems, Plymouth Medical Center, Plymouth, IN, p. A226
  Senior Director Information Systems, Saint Josep. Health System, Mishawaka, IN, p. A224
MILLER, Hope, Director of Medical Records, Peterson Healthcare And Rehabilitation Hospital, Wheeling, WV, p. A706
MILLER, J D
  M.D., Chief Medical Officer, Hazard Arh Regional Medical Center, Hazard, KY, p. A267
  M.D., Vice President Medical Affairs, Morgan County Arh Hospital, West Liberty, KY, p. A275
  M.D., Vice President Medical Affairs, Tug Valley Arh Regional Medical Center, South Williamson, KY, p. A274
MILLER, James
  Chief Executive Officer, Encompass Health Rehabilitation Hospital of Richmond, Richmond, VA, p. A682
  Chief Executive Officer, Rolling Hills Hospital, Franklin, TN, p. A583
  President of Lehigh Valley Health Muhlenberg and North Hampton Region, Lehigh Valley Health Network At Coordinated Health, Allentown, PA, p. A534

MILLER, James L, Chief Financial Officer, Baptist Medical Center – Yazoo, Yazoo City, MS, p. A370
MILLER, Jane E.
  Director Human Resources, Avera Creighton Hospital, Creighton, NE, p. A399
  Human Resources Officer, Avera Sacred Heart Hospital, Yankton, SD, p. A578
MILLER, Jason R.
  Chief Financial Officer, Christus St. Frances Cabrini Hospital, Alexandria, LA, p. A276
  Chief Financial Officer, The Medical Center of Southeast Texas, Port Arthur, TX, p. A645
MILLER, Jeff, Safety Officer, Citizens Memorial Hospital, Bolivar, MO, p. A371
MILLER, Jennifer, Chief Administrative Officer, University of Iowa Health Care Medical Center Downtown, Iowa City, IA, p. A238
MILLER, Jerry, Vice President, Information Services, Springfield Memorial Hospital, Springfield, IL, p. A209
MILLER, Joanne, R.N., MSN, Chief Nursing Officer, Baystate Medical Center, Springfield, MA, p. A318
MILLER, John E., Vice President, Finance, Orlando Health Orlando Regional Medical Center, Orlando, FL, p. A144
MILLER, Jon, Director Accounting and Information Services, Hancock Regional Hospital, Greenfield, IN, p. A218
MILLER, Joshua, Director Information Systems, Grand Lake Health System, Saint Marys, OH, p. A503
MILLER, Julie
  Chief Executive Officer, Valley Hospital Phoenix, Phoenix, AZ, p. A37
  Chief Operating Officer, Williamson Medical Center, Franklin, TN, p. A583
MILLER, Justin, Chief Information Officer and Associate Vice President, The University of Vermont Health Network – Alice Hyde Medical Center, Malone, NY, p. A445
MILLER, Kay J
  R.N., MSN, Chief Nursing Officer, UCHealth Greeley Hospital, Greeley, CO, p. A109
  R.N., MSN, Chief Nursing Officer, UCHealth Memorial Hospital, Colorado Springs, CO, p. A105
MILLER, Keith
  Chief Executive Officer, Lawrence County Memorial Hospital, Lawrenceville, IL, p. A200
  Chief Operating Officer, Daviess Community Hospital, Washington, IN, p. A229
MILLER, Ken, Chief Financial Officer, Beaufort Memorial Hospital, Beaufort, SC, p. A562
MILLER, Kris, Senior Human Resources Business Partner, Corewell Health Reed City Hospital, Reed City, MI, p. A336
MILLER, Krista, R.N., Chief Nursing Officer, Shriners Children's Philadelphia, Philadelphia, PA, p. A550
MILLER, Lana, Administrator, Elizabeth Parsons Ware Packard Mental Health Center, Springfield, IL, p. A209
MILLER, Laurie, Executive Assistant, Sakakawea Medical Center, Hazen, ND, p. A481
MILLER, Leanne R, Director Human Resources, Community Hospital, Mccook, NE, p. A402
MILLER, Lisa, Director Human Resources, Hendry Regional Medical Center, Clewiston, FL, p. A128
MILLER, Loren J., Administrator, Advanced Care Hospital of White County, Searcy, AR, p. A53
MILLER, Maria, Controller, Corewell Health Beaumont Grosse Pointe Hospital, Grosse Pointe, MI, p. A329
MILLER, Mark, FACHE, Chief Executive Officer, Tristar Skyline Medical Center, Nashville, TN, p. A591
MILLER, Mary, Vice President Finance and Business Development, Mt. Washington Pediatric Hospital, Baltimore, MD, p. A301
MILLER, Mary Beth, M.D., Chief of Staff, Cheyenne County Hospital, Saint Francis, KS, p. A259
MILLER, Mathew, M.D., Vice President and Chief Medical Officer, Providence St. Josep. Hospital Eureka, Eureka, CA, p. A62
MILLER, Megan, Chief Executive Officer, The Bridgeway, North Little Rock, AR, p. A51
MILLER, Michael J
  Director Human Resources, Barnes–Jewish St. Peters Hospital, Saint Peters, MO, p. A386
  Director Human Resources, Progress West Hospital, O Fallon, MO, p. A381
MILLER, Michele A, R.N., MSN, Vice President, Acute and Nursing Services, Rutgers University Behavioral Healthcare, Piscataway, NJ, p. A427
MILLER, Michelle, Chief Human Resources, UCI Health – Placentia Linda, Placentia, CA, p. A83
MILLER, Mitchell, M.D., Chief Medical Officer, Garfield Memorial Hospital, Panguitch, UT, p. A667
MILLER, Nicole, Director Human Resources, Riverside Shore Memorial Hospital, Onancock, VA, p. A681

Index of Health Care Professionals / Miller

MILLER, Patrick, Technology Coordinator, San Bernardino Mountains Community Hospital, Lake Arrowhead, CA, p. A69
MILLER, Paul, Director of Operations, Sanford Chamberlain Medical Center, Chamberlain, SD, p. A572
MILLER, Peter S, Chief Financial Officer, North Vista Hospital, North Las Vegas, NV, p. A412
MILLER, Phil, Chief Information Officer, Unity Health, Searcy, AR, p. A53
MILLER, Randy, M.D., Chief, Medical Staff, Acadian Medical Center, Eunice, LA, p. A281
MILLER, Redonda G., M.D., President, Johns Hopkins Hospital, Baltimore, MD, p. A300
MILLER, Richard B., Ph.D., Vice President Hospital Affairs and Chief Financial Officer, Suny Downstate Health Sciences University, New York, NY, p. A453
MILLER, Rick
   Chief Financial Officer, Allina Health Faribault Medical Center, Faribault, MN, p. A346
   Director, Operations and Finance, Allina Health Faribault Medical Center, Faribault, MN, p. A346
   President and Chief Operating Officer, Nationwide Children's Hospital – Toledo, Toledo, OH, p. A504
   President and Chief Operating Officer, Nationwide Children's Hospital, Columbus, OH, p. A492
MILLER, Robyn, Chief Nursing Officer, Belton Regional Medical Center, Belton, MO, p. A371
MILLER, Rod, Chief Information Technology, Community Hospital, Torrington, WY, p. A729
MILLER, Sandra, MSN, R.N., Interim Vice President, Patient Care Continuum and Chief Nursing Officer, Sarah Bush Lincoln Health Center, Mattoon, IL, p. A201
MILLER, Shane
   Chief Information Officer, HSHS St. Clare Memorial Hospital, Oconto Falls, WI, p. A719
   Chief Information Officer, HSHS St. Mary's Hospital Medical Center, Green Bay, WI, p. A712
   Chief Information Officer, HSHS St. Nicholas Hospital, Sheboygan, WI, p. A721
   Chief Information Officer, HSHS St. Vincent Hospital, Green Bay, WI, p. A712
MILLER, Stacy, Entity Human Resources Officer, Texas Health Presbyterian Hospital Dallas, Dallas, TX, p. A612
MILLER, Steve
   Director Information Systems, Baptist Medical Center South, Montgomery, AL, p. A22
   Vice President, Chief Operations Executive, Scripp. Memorial Hospital–Encinitas, Encinitas, CA, p. A62
MILLER, Susan, Financial Administrator, Faulkton Area Medical Center, Faulkton, SD, p. A573
MILLER, Susie, Deputy Administrator, Desert Willow Treatment Center, Las Vegas, NV, p. A410
MILLER, Tamara, FACHE, Chief Executive Officer and Administrator, Madison Regional Health System, Madison, SD, p. A574
MILLER, Ted, Vice President and Chief Financial Officer, Memorial Hospital And Health Care Center, Jasper, IN, p. A220
MILLER, Thomas
   M.D., Medical Director, University of Utah Health, Salt Lake City, UT, p. A669
   President, Aurora Baycare Medical Center, Green Bay, WI, p. A712
MILLER, Tiffany, Chief Executive Officer, Yoakum Community Hospital, Yoakum, TX, p. A663
MILLER, Tim, Chief Executive Officer, Cherry Hospital, Goldsboro, NC, p. A469
MILLER, Tracy, Chief Nursing Officer, Vice President, Patient Care Services, UPMC Memorial, York, PA, p. A559
MILLER, Valerie L, MSN, R.N., Director of Nursing, Major Hospital, Shelbyville, IN, p. A227
MILLER, Weston, M.D., Chief Medical Officer, Abbeville General Hospital, Abbeville, LA, p. A276
MILLER, William, Coordinator Management Information Systems, Livengrin Foundation, Bensalem, PA, p. A535
MILLER–BALFOUR, Pam, Director Human Resources, Socorro General Hospital, Socorro, NM, p. A437
MILLER–COLLETTE, Melody M, Director Human Resources, North Okaloosa Medical Center, Crestview, FL, p. A129
MILLICAN, Sharon, Associate Director, Patient Care Services, South Texas Veterans Healthcare System Audie L Murphy, San Antonio, TX, p. A651
MILLIGAN, Corbi, M.D., Chief Medical Officer, HCA Florida Trinity Hospital, Trinity, FL, p. A153
MILLIRON, Melissa, Regional Director of Human Resources, Acuity Specialty Hospital–Ohio Valley At Weirton, Weirton, WV, p. A705
MILLIS, David, M.D., Clinical Director, Thomas B. Finan Center, Cumberland, MD, p. A303
MILLS, Angela, Chief Medical Officer, Banner North Colorado Medical Centernorth Colorado Medical Center, Greeley, CO, p. A109
MILLS, Brent, Chief Executive Officer, Encompass Health Rehabilitation Hospital of North Alabama, Huntsville, AL, p. A20
MILLS, Chad, Senior Vice President, Chief Information Officer, Children's Mercy Hospital Kansas, Overland Park, KS, p. A257
MILLS, Dennis, Chief Human Resources Officer, San Ramon Regional Medical Center, San Ramon, CA, p. A93
MILLS, Gene, Director Information Technology, Scenic Mountain Medical Center, Big Spring, TX, p. A603
MILLS, Jerry, Chief Human Resources Management Services, San Francisco Va Health Care System, San Francisco, CA, p. A91
MILLS, Jim, Regional Director Information Technology, Sutter Medical Center, Sacramento, Sacramento, CA, p. A87
MILLS, John, Chief Operating Officer, Cleveland Clinic Avon Hospital, Avon, OH, p. A485
MILLS, John C, Senior Vice President Operations, Cleveland Clinic Fairview Hospital, Cleveland, OH, p. A490
MILLS, Kalen M, Director Human Resources, Southern Coos Hospital And Health Center, Bandon, OR, p. A525
MILLS, Marianne, R.N., Chairperson, Stanton County Hospital, Johnson, KS, p. A251
MILLS, Scott, M.D., Vice President Medical Staff Administration and Chief Medical Officer, Mid Coast Hospital, Brunswick, ME, p. A296
MILLS, Sean
   Chief Financial Officer, Guthrie Lourdes Hospital, Binghamton, NY, p. A439
   Chief Financial Officer, Samaritan Medical Center, Watertown, NY, p. A461
MILLS, Tylie, R.N., Chief Executive Officer, Pike County Memorial Hospital, Louisiana, MO, p. A379
MILLS, Vicki L, Chief Financial Officer, Anderson County Hospital, Garnett, KS, p. A249
MILLS–MATHEWS, Marcy, Director Human Resources, HCA Florida Palms West Hospital, Loxahatchee, FL, p. A138
MILLSAP, Claressa, Chief Executive Officer, Keefe Memorial Hospital, Cheyenne Wells, CO, p. A104
MILLSAP, Debra, Director of Nursing, River Crest Hospital, San Angelo, TX, p. A648
MILLSAPS, Janet
   Chief Human Resources Officer, Harris Regional Hospital, Sylva, NC, p. A477
   Vice President Human Resources, Haywood Regional Medical Center, Clyde, NC, p. A466
MILNE, C Dean, D.O., Medical Director, Pam Specialty Hospital of Las Vegas, Las Vegas, NV, p. A410
MILNER, Rene, Chief Medical Officer, Osceola Medical Center, Osceola, WI, p. A719
MILOVICH, David, Vice President Human Resources, Saint Mary's Regional Medical Center, Reno, NV, p. A412
MILSTEIN, Marc E., Vice President Information Resources, University of Texas Southwestern Medical Center, Dallas, TX, p. A612
MILTON, Kerry K., R.N., Chief Nursing Officer, St. Tammany Health System, Covington, LA, p. A280
MILTON, Paul A, Executive Vice President and Chief Operating Officer, Ellis Medicine, Schenectady, NY, p. A458
MILTON, Paul A., President and Chief Executive Officer, Ellis Medicine, Schenectady, NY, p. A458
MILTON, S. Byron, M.D., Medical Director, Emory Rehabilitation Hospital, Atlanta, GA, p. A157
MILUS, Lori, R.N., MSN, Director of Nursing, Aurora Behavioral Health System West, Glendale, AZ, p. A32
MIMS, Tammy, Chief Executive Officer, Liberty Regional Medical Center, Hinesville, GA, p. A165
MINADEO, John, M.D., Chief Medical Quality Officer, Northwestern Medical Center, Saint Albans, VT, p. A672
MINARD, Keith, Chief Information Officer, Chinese Hospital, San Francisco, CA, p. A90
MINCEY, Wallace D, Chief Executive Officer, Clinch Memorial Hospital, Homerville, GA, p. A165
MINCY, Jeffrey, Chief Executive Officer, North Platte Valley Medical Center, Saratoga, WY, p. A728
MINDEN, Philip. President, St. Joseph's Hospital, Tampa, FL, p. A152
MINEAR, Michael N., Senior Vice President and Chief Information Officer, Lehigh Valley Hospital–Cedar Crest, Allentown, PA, p. A534
MINEAU, Francine, Chief Nursing Officer, Baton Rouge Behavioral Hospital, Baton Rouge, LA, p. A277
MINEO, Michael, M.D., Interim Chief Medical Officer, Kaleida Health, Buffalo, NY, p. A440
MINER, Bill, M.D., Chief of Staff, Huron Regional Medical Center, Huron, SD, p. A574
MINER, Greg, Chief Executive Officer, Appleton Area Health, Appleton, MN, p. A342
MINER, John, Chief Financial Officer, Kindred Hospital Central Tampa, Tampa, FL, p. A152
MINGLE, Regina, Senior Vice President and Chief Leadership Officer, Penn Medicine Lancaster General Health, Lancaster, PA, p. A543
MINGS, William, M.D., Medical Director, Carl Albert Community Mental Health Center, Mcalester, OK, p. A514
MINIER, Lori, Chief Financial Officer, Benewah Community Hospital, Saint Maries, ID, p. A183
MINIER, Mary
   Chief Operating Officer, Indiana University Health Frankfort, Frankfort, IN, p. A217
   Chief Operating Officer, Indiana University Health White Memorial Hospital, Monticello, IN, p. A224
MINIOR, Devin, M.D., Chief Medical Officer, Banner Casa Grande Medical Center, Casa Grande, AZ, p. A30
MINKS, Michael H.
   Chief Information Officer, Ascension Seton Edgar B. Davis Hospital, Luling, TX, p. A637
   Chief Information Officer, Ascension Seton Northwest, Austin, TX, p. A599
   Chief Information Officer, Ascension Seton Shoal Creek, Austin, TX, p. A599
   Chief Information Officer VI, Ascension Seton Medical Center Austin, Austin, TX, p. A599
   Chief Information Officer VI, Dell Seton Medical Center At The University of Texas, Austin, TX, p. A600
MINNICK, Paul E, R.N., MSN, Senior Vice President and Chief Operating Officer, Virtua Voorhees, Voorhees, NJ, p. A430
MINNICK, Peggy, R.N., Chief Executive Officer, Bhc Alhambra Hospital, Rosemead, CA, p. A86
MINNIS, Rosanne, Business Officer, Rochester Psychiatric Center, Rochester, NY, p. A457
MINON, Maria
   M.D., Vice President Medical Affairs and Chief Medical Officer, Children's Hospital of Orange County, Orange, CA, p. A81
   M.D., Vice President Medical Affairs and Chief Medical Officer, Choc Children's At Mission Hospital, Mission Viejo, CA, p. A77
MINOR, Amy, Chief Nursing Officer, Troy Regional Medical Center, Troy, AL, p. A25
MINOR, Athena, Chief Nursing Officer, Ohio County Hospital, Hartford, KY, p. A267
MINOR, Beverly, Chief Human Resources, Schleicher County Medical Center, Eldorado, TX, p. A618
MINOR, Blaine, M.D., Chief of Staff, Adventhealth Murray, Chatsworth, GA, p. A160
MINSHEW, Tony L., Vice President, Patient Care Services, Conway Medical Center, Conway, SC, p. A565
MINSINGER, Linda, Vice President Hospital Division, Gifford Medical Center, Randolph, VT, p. A672
MINSKY, Bart R, Interim Vice President Human Resources, Adventist Health And Rideout, Marysville, CA, p. A77
MINTEER, Laura, Chief Human Resource Officer, Meritus Health, Hagerstown, MD, p. A305
MINTON, Tamra, R.N., MSN, Vice President Patient Care Services and Chief Nursing Officer, UPMC East, Monroeville, PA, p. A546
MINTONYE, Traci, Chief Financial Officer, River Hospital, Alexandria Bay, NY, p. A438
MINTZ, Michael, M.D., Chief Medical Officer, Christus Surgical Hospital, Corpus Christi, TX, p. A608
MINZEY, Darrick
   Vice President Finance, Advocate Condell Medical Center, Libertyville, IL, p. A200
   Vice President Finance, Aurora Lakeland Medical Center, Elkhorn, WI, p. A710
   Vice President Finance, Aurora Medical Center Burlington, Burlington, WI, p. A709
MIRABELLA, Ilene, Director Human Resources, Vibra Hospital of Southeastern Massachusetts, New Bedford, MA, p. A316
MIRANDA, Ada S, M.D., Medical Director, Hospital Metropolitano Dr. Susoni, Arecibo, PR, p. A731
MIRANDA, Casey D., Executive Vice President and Chief Operating Officer, Jackson County Memorial Hospital, Altus, OK, p. A509
MIRANDA, Ivette, Chief Executive Officer, Encompass Health Rehabilitation Hospital, An Affiliate of Martin Health, Stuart, FL, p. A150
MIRANDA, Kim, Chief Financial Officer, St. Elizabeth Community Hospital, Red Bluff, CA, p. A85
MIRANDA, Michael, Chief of Staff, Mercy Hospital Booneville, Booneville, AR, p. A44
MIRANDA, Samuel Jr, Chief Nursing Officer, Good Shepherd Specialty Hospital, Bethlehem, PA, p. A535

Index of Health Care Professionals / Molyneux

Index of Health Care Professionals

MIRANDA, Vicki, Vice President Human Resources, Dominican Hospital, Santa Cruz, CA, p. A94
MIRANDA, Victor Hernandez, M.D., Chief of Staff, Mennonite General Hospital, Aibonito, PR, p. A731
MIRATO, Shelly, Chief Executive Officer, Desert Winds Hospital, Las Vegas, NV, p. A410
MIRZABEGIAN, Edward, Chief Executive Officer, Antelop. Valley Medical Center, Lancaster, CA, p. A69
MISAJET, Jennifer, Interim Chief Nursing Officer, Mercyone Des Moines Medical Center, Des Moines, IA, p. A235
MISHLER, Sheila, Chief Executive Officer, Ascension St. Vincent Indianapolis Hospital, Indianapolis, IN, p. A219
MISKIMEN, Theresa, M.D., Vice President Medical Services, Rutgers University Behavioral Healthcare, Piscataway, NJ, p. A427
MISRA, Sahana, Acting Chief of Staff, Portland Hcs, Portland, OR, p. A530
MISSAGIA, Carlos
Chief Financial Officer, Medical Behavioral Hospital of Clear Lake, Houston, TX, p. A629
Chief Financial Officer, Medical Behavioral Hospital of Mishawaka, Mishawaka, IN, p. A223
Chief Financial Officer, Medical Behavioral Hospital of Northern Arizona, Prescott, AZ, p. A37
Chief Financial Officer, Neurobehavioral Hospital of Nw Indiana/Greater Chicago, Crown Point, IN, p. A215
Chief Financial Officer, Neuropsychiatric Hospital of Indianapolis, Indianapolis, IN, p. A220
Chief Financial Officer, Phoenix Medical Psychiatric Hospital, Phoenix, AZ, p. A36
MISSERITTI, Colomba, Director Human Resources, Rochester Psychiatric Center, Rochester, NY, p. A457
MISTRETTA, Michael, Vice President and Chief Information Officer, VHC Health, Arlington, VA, p. A673
MITCHELL, Adonna, Director Fiscal Services, North Mississipp. Medical Center–Eupora, Eupora, MS, p. A361
MITCHELL, Barbara
Director Human Resources, Oasis Behavioral Health – Chandler, Chandler, AZ, p. A31
Senior Vice President Marketing and Human Resources, UW Medicine/Valley Medical Center, Renton, WA, p. A693
MITCHELL, Bridgett, Chief Clinical Officer, Advanced Specialty Hospital of Toledo, Toledo, OH, p. A504
MITCHELL, Camelia, M.D., Medical Director, Texas Rehabilitation Hospital of Arlington, Arlington, TX, p. A598
MITCHELL, Cathy, Chief Eecutive Officer, Northwest Medical Center, Winfield, AL, p. A26
MITCHELL, David, Vice President Nursing, Baptist Neighborhood Hospital At Thousand Oaks, San Antonio, TX, p. A649
MITCHELL, Douglas W, Vice President and Chief Nursing Officer, West Virginia University Hospitals, Morgantown, WV, p. A703
MITCHELL, Errol, Chief Financial Officer, Integris Canadian Valley Hospital, Yukon, OK, p. A524
MITCHELL, Heath, Chief Operating Officer, Memorial Hospital, Seminole, TX, p. A652
MITCHELL, Ivan, Chief Executive Officer, Great Plains Health, North Platte, NE, p. A403
MITCHELL, Jenifer, R.N., Director of Nursing Services, Mineral Community Hospital, Superior, MT, p. A396
MITCHELL, Jodie, Facility Financial Director, Monument Health Sturgis Hospital, Sturgis, SD, p. A577
MITCHELL, Joseph, M.D., President and Chief Executive Officer, Franciscan Children's, Brighton, MA, p. A311
MITCHELL, Karen, Vice President Patient Care Services, Children's Hospital of The King's Daughters, Norfolk, VA, p. A680
MITCHELL, Kathy
R.N., Chief Nursing Officer, HCA Florida Sarasota Doctors Hospital, Sarasota, FL, p. A149
Chief Nursing Officer, Owensboro Health Muhlenberg Community Hospital, Greenville, KY, p. A266
Director Human Resources, Marshfield Medical Center – Rice Lake, Rice Lake, WI, p. A720
MITCHELL, Kent, Chief Financial Officer, Hamilton Memorial Hospital District, Mcleansboro, IL, p. A201
MITCHELL, Leah, R.N., Interim Chief Information Officer, Salem Hospital, Salem, OR, p. A532
MITCHELL, Marsha, Director Human Resources, Fleming County Hospital, Flemingsburg, KY, p. A265
MITCHELL, Mary S, Chief Resource Management Services, Birmingham Va Medical Center, Birmingham, AL, p. A16
MITCHELL, Morris, Director Human Resources, Poplar Springs Hospital, Petersburg, VA, p. A681
MITCHELL, Naomi, Director Human Resources, Kentucky River Medical Center, Jackson, KY, p. A267
MITCHELL, Perry, M.D., Chief of Staff, Little Colorado Medical Center, Winslow, AZ, p. A41
MITCHELL, Rhonda K., Director Human Resources, Mon Health Stonewall Jackson Memorial Hospital, Weston, WV, p. A705
MITCHELL, Richard R, Director Information Technology, Eagleville Hospital, Eagleville, PA, p. A538
MITCHELL, Roger A. Jr, M.D., President, Howard University Hospital, Washington, DC, p. A123
MITCHELL, Sarah, Director Finance, Mary's Harper Geriatric Psychiatry Center, Tuscaloosa, AL, p. A25
MITCHELL, Steve, Chief Operating Officer, Memorial Medical Center, Modesto, CA, p. A78
MITCHELL SANCHEZ, Lexi, D.O., Chief of Staff, Clay County Memorial Hospital, Henrietta, TX, p. A624
MITCHNECK, Barry, Chief Nursing Officer, Director of Patient Care Services, UPMC Lititz, Lititz, PA, p. A544
MITCHUM, Linda, Director of Nursing, William J. Mccord Adolescent Treatment Facility, Orangeburg, SC, p. A569
MITRY, Norman F.
President and Chief Executive Officer, Heritage Valley Beaver, Beaver, PA, p. A535
President and Chief Executive Officer, Heritage Valley Kennedy, Mckees Rocks, PA, p. A545
President and Chief Executive Officer, Sewickley Valley Hospital, (A Division of Valley Medical Facilities), Sewickley, PA, p. A555
MITTAL, Vikrant, M.D., Chief Medical Officer, Danville State Hospital, Danville, PA, p. A538
MIXON, Pam, Chief Operating Officer, Jenkins County Medical Center, Millen, GA, p. A168
MIXON, Robin
Administrator, North Mississipp. Medical Center–Eupora, Eupora, MS, p. A361
Administrator, North Mississipp. Medical Center–Hamilton, Hamilton, AL, p. A20
MIYASAWA, Patricia, CPA, Director Fiscal Service, Shriners Hospitals for Children–Honolulu, Honolulu, HI, p. A176
MIZE, David, Director of Information Technology, Marshall Medical Center North, Guntersville, AL, p. A20
MIZELL, Patty, Chief Financial Officer, Riverside Medical Center, Franklinton, LA, p. A282
MIZELL, Philip L, M.D., Medical Director, The Bridgeway, North Little Rock, AR, p. A51
MMEJE, Ikenna, President and Chief Executive Officer, USC Arcadia Hospital, Arcadia, CA, p. A56
MO, Lin H, M.P.H., President, Mount Sinai Beth Israel, New York, NY, p. A449
MOAD, Sharon, Human Resources Director Health Information Management, Elkview General Hospital, Hobart, OK, p. A513
MOAK, Jennifer, Business Office Manager, Lawrence County Hospital, Monticello, MS, p. A366
MOATS, Susan K.
R.N., Chief Nursing Officer, Baylor Scott & White The Heart Hospital Denton, Denton, TX, p. A613
R.N., Vice President Patient Care Services and Chief Nursing Officer, Baylor Scott & White The Heart Hospital Plano, Plano, TX, p. A644
MOCK, Presley, M.D., Chief of Staff, Texas Institute for Surgery At Texas Health Presbyterian Dallas, Dallas, TX, p. A612
MOCKUS, Tom, Director Information Services, Mount Desert Island Hospital, Bar Harbor, ME, p. A295
MOE, Jonathan, Chief Executive Officer, Palo Alto County Health System, Emmetsburg, IA, p. A236
MOEHRINGER, Candace, Chief Executive Officer, Select Specialty Hospital–Northern Kentucky, Fort Thomas, KY, p. A265
MOELLER, Deborah A, R.N., MS, Interim Chief Nursing Officer, Baylor Scott & White Medical Center – Sunnyvale, Sunnyvale, TX, p. A655
MOEN, Belinda, R.N., MSN, Interim Director of Nursing, Mountrail County Medical Center, Stanley, ND, p. A483
MOEN, Larry, Chief Financial Officer, Coteau Des Prairies Hospital, Sisseton, SD, p. A577
MOFFA, Salvatore, M.D., Vice President, Medical Affairs and Chief Medical Officer, Robert Wood Johnson University Hospital Somerset, Somerville, NJ, p. A428
MOFFAT, Jeanne, Manager Information Technology, Keefe Memorial Hospital, Cheyenne Wells, CO, p. A104
MOFFAT, Jennifer, Staff Accountant, Regional West Garden County, Oshkosh, NE, p. A405
MOFFATT, Dan, Chief Information Officer, Sanford Bemidji Medical Center, Bemidji, MN, p. A343
MOFFATT–BRUCE, Susan, President, Lahey Hospital & Medical Center, Burlington, MA, p. A312
MOFFET, Chris, Director Information Services, Bob Wilson Memorial Grant County Hospital, Ulysses, KS, p. A261
MOFFITT, Brenda L., Chief Nursing Officer, Memorial Health System, Abilene, KS, p. A246
MOGERMAN, Shauna, Chief Executive Officer, Roxbury Treatment Center, Shippensburg, PA, p. A555
MOGG, Cassie, Chief Executive Officer, Covenant Hospital Plainview, Plainview, TX, p. A644
MOGLE, Jeri, Assistant Executive Director Finance, Wills Eye Hospital, Philadelphia, PA, p. A550
MOHAMED, Antonia, Acting Chief Information Officer, Birmingham Va Medical Center, Birmingham, AL, p. A16
MOHAN, Amit, Ph.D., FACHE, President and Chief Executive Officer, Barlow Respiratory Hospital, Los Angeles, CA, p. A71
MOHAN, Rajesh, M.D., Chief Medical Officer, Monmouth Medical Center, Southern Campus, Lakewood, NJ, p. A422
MOHANDAS, Arjun, M.D., Chief of Staff, Ascension Seton Edgar B. Davis Hospital, Luling, TX, p. A637
MOHESKY, Deb, Chief Executive Officer, Longmont United Hospital, Longmont, CO, p. A111
MOHLER, Brittany, Director Human Resources, Essentia Health–Deer River, Deer River, MN, p. A345
MOHNK, Richard, Vice President Corporate Services, Bayhealth, Dover, DE, p. A121
MOHNKERN, Pearl, Vice President and Director Human Resources, Christus St. Vincent Regional Medical Center, Santa Fe, NM, p. A436
MOHR, Amanda, Chief Nursing Officer, Greater Regional Health, Creston, IA, p. A234
MOHR, Amy, Coordinator Human Resources, Forest Health Medical Center, Ypsilanti, MI, p. A341
MOHR, Angela, R.N., MS, President, SSM Health St. Anthony Hospital – Shawnee, Shawnee, OK, p. A520
MOHR, Jodi, Chief Executive Officer, Merrick Medical Center, Central City, NE, p. A398
MOHR, Liz, Assistant Chief Financial Officer, Mercy Health – Fairfield Hospital, Fairfield, OH, p. A495
MOHR, Steven, Senior Vice President and Chief Financial Officer, Huntington Health, Pasadena, CA, p. A83
MOHREN, Trevor, Chief Nursing Officer, Kimball Health Services, Kimball, NE, p. A401
MOK, Michelle, Chief Financial Officer, Redlands Community Hospital, Redlands, CA, p. A85
MOK, Timothy, Chief Medical Officer, Avera Marshall Regional Medical Center, Marshall, MN, p. A350
MOKRY, Deborah, Chief Nurse Executive, St. Louis Forensic Treatment Center, Saint Louis, MO, p. A384
MOL, Stacy E, CPA, Director Finance, Spencer Hospital, Spencer, IA, p. A244
MOLELUS, Elena, Manager Human Resources, Santa Barbara County Psychiatric Health Facility, Santa Barbara, CA, p. A94
MOLINA, Al, Chief Executive Officer, Kindred Hospital South Florida–Fort Lauderdale, Fort Lauderdale, FL, p. A131
MOLINA, Isabel, M.D., Chief Medical Officer, Lamb Healthcare Center, Littlefield, TX, p. A634
MOLL, Eric, Chief Executive Officer, Mason Health, Shelton, WA, p. A695
MOLL, Gudrun, R.N., MSN, Chief Nursing Officer, San Antonio Regional Hospital, Upland, CA, p. A99
MOLL, Jeffrey, M.D., Medical Director, Clarion Psychiatric Center, Clarion, PA, p. A537
MOLL, Michael A., M.D., Chief Medical Officer and Chief of Staff, Spanish Peaks Regional Health Center And Veterans Community Living Center, Walsenburg, CO, p. A114
MOLLER, Dan, M.D., Chief Medical Officer, Willis Knighton North, Shreveport, LA, p. A293
MOLLER, Lynn, Chief Financial Officer, Weston County Health Services, Newcastle, WY, p. A727
MOLLINER, Jose
Chief Operating Officer, Coral Gables Hospital, Coral Gables, FL, p. A128
Interim Chief Executive Officer, Coral Gables Hospital, Coral Gables, FL, p. A128
MOLLOHAN, Joan, Vice President Human Resources, Ochsner Medical Center, New Orleans, LA, p. A289
MOLLOY, Kevin, Senior Vice President and Chief Operating Officer, Mount Sinai Morningside, New York, NY, p. A449
MOLLOY, Reuben D, Chief Information Officer, Governor Juan F. Luis Hospital, Christiansted, VI, p. A736
MOLNAR, Becky, Director of Finance, Cleveland Clinic Medina Hospital, Medina, OH, p. A500
MOLONEY, Ellen, President and Chief Operating Officer, Newton–Wellesley Hospital, Newton Lower Falls, MA, p. A316
MOLONY, Kristin, Chief Executive Officer, Ochsner Stennis Hospital, De Kalb, MS, p. A361
MOLSBERGER, Shawn, President, Orlando Health Orlando Regional Medical Center, Orlando, FL, p. A144
MOLT, Brianna, Human Resources Director, Genoa Medical Facilities, Genoa, NE, p. A400
MOLYNEUX, Phyllis, Associate Administrator Human Resources and Education, Williamson Medical Center, Franklin, TN, p. A583

Index of Health Care Professionals

Index of Health Care Professionals / Momeyer

MOMEYER, Polly, Manager Human Resources, Lecom Health Millcreek Community Hospital, Erie, PA, p. A540
MOMTAZBAKHSH, Sassan, M.D., Medical Director, Cornerstone Specialty Hospitals Tucson, Tucson, AZ, p. A40
MONAHAN, Jane, Vice President Ministry, Spiritual Care and Human Resources, SSM Health Monroe Clinic, Monroe, WI, p. A718
MONASTERIO, Eugene A, M.D., Medical Director, Children's Hospital of Richmond At Vcu, Richmond, VA, p. A682
MONCHER, Daniel J, Vice President and Chief Financial Officer, Firelands Regional Health System, Sandusky, OH, p. A503
MONCRIEF, William, ORH IT Client Executive, Surgeons Choice Medical Center, Southfield, MI, p. A338
MONDA, Cam, D.O., Medical Director, Greenwood Regional Rehabilitation Hospital, Greenwood, SC, p. A567
MONDAY, Eric, Co–Chief Executive Officer, Executive Vice President for Health Affairs, University of Kentucky Albert B. Chandler Hospital, Lexington, KY, p. A269
MONETTE, Gregory C., Chief Operating Officer, Memorial Hospital of Gardena, Gardena, CA, p. A65
MONETTE, Steven, Chief Financial Officer, Brattleboro Retreat, Brattleboro, VT, p. A671
MONFILS, Michael, M.D., Chief of Medical Staff, Rochelle Community Hospital, Rochelle, IL, p. A207
MONGE, Candice, R.N., Chief Nurse Executive Officer, Marian Regional Medical Center, Santa Maria, CA, p. A94
MONGE, Jacqualyn
Director of Nursing, Aspirus Eagle River Hospital, Eagle River, WI, p. A710
Director of Nursing, Howard Young Medical Center, Inc., Woodruff, WI, p. A725
MONGEAU, Anne, Chief Nursing Officer, Eleanor Slater Hospital, Cranston, RI, p. A560
MONGER, Shelton, Director Information Technology, Wayne Healthcare, Greenville, OH, p. A497
MONICAL, Robert, Chief Executive Officer, Dunes Surgical Hospital, Dakota Dunes, SD, p. A573
MONICE, Pierre, President, Macneal Hospital, Berwyn, IL, p. A186
MONJE, Mary Anne
Chief Executive Officer, Chief Financial Officer, Whittier Hospital Medical Center, Whittier, CA, p. A101
Chief Financial Officer, AHMC Anaheim Regional Medical Center, Anaheim, CA, p. A55
Chief Operations Officer, AHMC Anaheim Regional Medical Center, Anaheim, CA, p. A55
MONJE, Mary Anne., Chief Executive Officer/Chief Financial Officer, Whittier Hospital Medical Center, Whittier, CA, p. A101
MONROE, Ame, Director Human Resources, Rolling Plains Memorial Hospital, Sweetwater, TX, p. A655
MONROE, Janet J., R.N., Executive Director, Rockland Psychiatric Center, Orangeburg, NY, p. A455
MONROE, Lori, Director of Nursing, Winnebago Mental Health Institute, Winnebago, WI, p. A725
MONROE, Temple, Director Nursing Operations, Wilson Medical Center, Neodesha, KS, p. A255
MONROY–MILLER, Cherry, M.D., Acting Medical Director, Greystone Park Psychiatric Hospital, Morris Plains, NJ, p. A424
MONSANTO, Monte, Chief Information Systems, Russell County Hospital, Russell Springs, KY, p. A274
MONSMA, Brian, President, Washington County Hospital, Nashville, IL, p. A203
MONSOUR, Joe, Chief Information Officer, Allegiance Behavioral Health Center of Plainview, Plainview, TX, p. A644
MONSRUD, Michele, Director Human Resources, Piedmont Walton Hospital, Monroe, GA, p. A168
MONTAGNESE, Robert A., President and Chief Executive Officer, Licking Memorial Hospital, Newark, OH, p. A501
MONTALBO, Tripp. Chief Executive Officer, HCA Houston Healthcare Clear Lake, Webster, TX, p. A661
MONTALVO, Eladio, Chief Executive Officer, Fort Duncan Regional Medical Center, Eagle Pass, TX, p. A615
MONTALVO, Jose, M.D., Medical Director, Hospital Del Maestro, San Juan, PR, p. A735
MONTANA, Jennifer, Manager Human Resources, Community Memorial Hospital, Hamilton, NY, p. A444
MONTANIO, John, Chief Financial Officer, Prevost Memorial Hospital, Donaldsonville, LA, p. A281
MONTANO, Maxine, R.N., Chief Nursing Officer, Rolling Plains Memorial Hospital, Sweetwater, TX, p. A655
MONTANO, Mayra, Director Information Systems, Hospital Metropolitano Dr. Susoni, Arecibo, PR, p. A731
MONTANTE, Carl, Director Information Systems and Information Technology, Shriners Hospitals for Children–Portland, Portland, OR, p. A531
MONTANYE, Richard, Director Information Systems, Hunt Regional Medical Center, Greenville, TX, p. A623
MONTANYE–IRELAND, Cherelle, Chief Hospital Executive, Peacehealth Southwest Medical Center, Vancouver, WA, p. A698
MONTGOMERY, James, Chief Nursing Officer, Bear River Valley Hospital, Tremonton, UT, p. A670
MONTGOMERY, Mark, M.D., Chief Medical Officer, Texas Health Harris Methodist Hospital Southwest Fort Worth, Fort Worth, TX, p. A620
MONTGOMERY, Mary Jim, R.N., MSN, FACHE, Chief Operating Officer, Crisp Regional Hospital, Cordele, GA, p. A161
MONTGOMERY, Michael Scott., Chief Executive Officer, Vice President, McLeod Health, Mcleod Health Loris, Loris, SC, p. A568
MONTGOMERY, Peggy, Director Medical Records, Arrowhead Behavioral Health Hospital, Maumee, OH, p. A499
MONTGOMERY, Roxie, Director of Nursing, Jane Todd Crawford Hospital, Greensburg, KY, p. A266
MONTGOMERY, Sheri, Acting Chief Executive Officer, Good Samaritan Medical Center, West Palm Beach, FL, p. A154
MONTGOMERY, Susan, Chief Nursing Officer, Asante Ashland Community Hospital, Ashland, OR, p. A525
MONTGOMERY, Tina, Chief Financial Officer, Sidney Health Center, Sidney, MT, p. A396
MONTOUR, Vina, Director Information Technology, U. S. Public Health Service Phoenix Indian Medical Center, Phoenix, AZ, p. A37
MONTOYA, Brooke, Director Human Resources, Lake Granbury Medical Center, Granbury, TX, p. A622
MONTOYA, Lillian, President and Chief Executive Officer, Christus St. Vincent Regional Medical Center, Santa Fe, NM, p. A436
MONZINGO, Ashley, Human Resources, Accounts Payable and Payroll, Top. Surgical Specialty Hospital, Houston, TX, p. A628
MOODY, Christy, R.N., Chief Nursing Officer, Carolina Pines Regional Medical Center, Hartsville, SC, p. A568
MOODY, Crystal R, Director Human Resources, Izard County Medical Center, Calico Rock, AR, p. A44
MOODY, David, Vice President Human Resources, Salina Regional Health Center, Salina, KS, p. A259
MOODY, James
Administrator, Donalsonville Hospital, Donalsonville, GA, p. A163
Chief Financial Officer, Donalsonville Hospital, Donalsonville, GA, p. A163
MOON, Diane, Chief Financial Officer, Adventist Health And Rideout, Marysville, CA, p. A77
MOON, James, Chief Financial Officer, Pana Community Hospital, Pana, IL, p. A205
MOON, John, Associate Director, Eastern Kansas Hcs, Topeka, KS, p. A260
MOON, Ryan, Chief Operating Officer, Palmdale Regional Medical Center, Palmdale, CA, p. A82
MOONEY, Claire Bradley, R.N., Senior Vice President an Chief Executive Officer, Penn State Health Lancaster Medical Center, Lancaster, PA, p. A543
MOONEY, Melissa, Director Human Resources, Mercy Rehabilition Hospital Springfield, Springfield, MO, p. A387
MOONEY, Robert W, M.D., Medical Director, Willingway Hospital, Statesboro, GA, p. A172
MOONEY, Susan E., M.D., MS, President and Chief Executive Officer, Alice Peck Day Memorial Hospital, Lebanon, NH, p. A415
MOORE, Amy, Human Resources, Olney Hamilton Hospital, Olney, TX, p. A642
MOORE, Betty, Business Manager, North Mississipp. Medical Center–Iuka, Iuka, MS, p. A363
MOORE, Bill, Chief Human Resources, El Centro Regional Medical Center, El Centro, CA, p. A62
MOORE, Brett, CPA, Assistant Administrator Finance, Sutter Amador Hospital, Jackson, CA, p. A68
MOORE, Brian, President and Chief Executive Officer, Bay Area Hospital, Coos Bay, OR, p. A526
MOORE, Carrie, Director Human Resources, Meadowbrook Rehabilitation Hospital, Gardner, KS, p. A249
MOORE, Cecelia B, CPA, Associate Vice Chancellor Finance, Vanderbilt University Medical Center, Nashville, TN, p. A591
MOORE, Dana, Chief Information Officer, Children's Hospital Colorado, Aurora, CO, p. A103
MOORE, Daniel J., CRDAMC Commander, Carl R. Darnall Army Medical Center, Fort Hood, TX, p. A618
MOORE, Deborah, Director Human Resources, Walter P. Reuther Psychiatric Hospital, Westland, MI, p. A340
MOORE, Diane C., Chief Financial Officer, Memorial Medical Center, Port Lavaca, TX, p. A645
MOORE, Donna, PsyD, Director, Eastern State Hospital, Williamsburg, VA, p. A685
MOORE, Edward H., President, Umass Memorial Health – Harrington, Southbridge, MA, p. A318
MOORE, Elizabeth, Chief Operating Officer, Silver Hill Hospital, New Canaan, CT, p. A117
MOORE, Emily, Director Human Resources and Information Technology, Haskell Memorial Hospital, Haskell, TX, p. A624
MOORE, Ethel L, M.D., Director of Medical Affairs, Fort Belknap Service Unit, Harlem, MT, p. A393
MOORE, Harold, Chief Information Technology Officer, Spartanburg Medical Center – Church Street Campus, Spartanburg, SC, p. A570
MOORE, J. Brandon., FACHE, Chief Executive Officer, Park Place Surgical Hospital, Lafayette, LA, p. A286
MOORE, Jason H, Vice President and Chief Operating Officer, Tallahassee Memorial Healthcare, Tallahassee, FL, p. A151
MOORE, Jody Dewen, District Director Human Resources, Kindred Hospital–San Diego, San Diego, CA, p. A89
MOORE, John, M.D., Medical Director, Granite County Medical Center, Philipsburg, MT, p. A394
MOORE, John A., FACHE, President, Bayfront Health St. Petersburg, Saint Petersburg, FL, p. A148
MOORE, John G, Vice President and Chief Financial Officer, Atrium Health Union, Monroe, NC, p. A472
MOORE, Karen, Vice President Information Technology and Chief Information Officer, Southern Regional Medical Center, Riverdale, GA, p. A170
MOORE, Karen O., FACHE, Senior Vice President Operations and Chief Nursing Officer, Lawrence General Hospital, Lawrence, MA, p. A314
MOORE, Kenneth, President, Laureate Psychiatric Clinic And Hospital, Tulsa, OK, p. A522
MOORE, Keri, Vice President Human Resources and Support Services, Presbyterian/St. Luke's Medical Center, Denver, CO, p. A106
MOORE, Kermit, R.N., Chief Operating Officer and Chief Nursing Officer, Nemaha County Hospital, Auburn, NE, p. A397
MOORE, Kevin, R.N., Hospital Administrator, South Georgia Medical Center Berrien Campus, Nashville, GA, p. A169
MOORE, Kyna
R.N., Chief Nursing Officer, Pocahontas Memorial Hospital, Buckeye, WV, p. A699
R.N., Director of Nursing, Bath Community Hospital, Hot Springs, VA, p. A678
MOORE, Leigh, Administrative Assistant Human Resources, Ochsner Watkins Hospital, Quitman, MS, p. A368
MOORE, Linda, Manager Human Resources, Seymour Hospital, Seymour, TX, p. A652
MOORE, Maisha, R.N., Interim Medical Center Director, VA Central California Health Care System, Fresno, CA, p. A65
MOORE, Margaret, Director Business Office, Sabine County Hospital, Hemphill, TX, p. A624
MOORE, Marie, Chief Nursing Officer, Mercy Hospital Springfield, Springfield, MO, p. A387
MOORE, Matthew, Director of Financial Reporting, Effingham Health System, Springfield, GA, p. A171
MOORE, Melinda, Director Human Resources, Multicare Deaconess Hospital, Spokane, WA, p. A696
MOORE, Michael
Director Information Systems, Troy Regional Medical Center, Troy, AL, p. A25
Interim Director, Rocky Mountain Regional Va Medical Center, Aurora, CO, p. A103
MOORE, Neil J., Chief Executive Officer, NYC Health + Hospitals/Queens, New York, NY, p. A451
MOORE, Nelda, Director Data Processing, Memorial Hospital And Manor, Bainbridge, GA, p. A159
MOORE, Patricia J, Director Human Resource, Valley Behavioral Health System, Barling, AR, p. A43
MOORE, Paul
R.N., Chief Clinical Officer, Mercy Rehabilition Hospital Springfield, Springfield, MO, p. A387
Chief Information Officer, Connecticut Mental Health Center, New Haven, CT, p. A117
MOORE, Paula, R.N., Chief Clinical Officer, Hugh Chatham Health, Elkin, NC, p. A468
MOORE, Randy, Chief Information Officer, Banner Lassen Medical Center, Susanville, CA, p. A97
MOORE, Rick
Chief Information Officer, Bethesda North Hospital, Cincinnati, OH, p. A488
Chief Information Officer, Good Samaritan Hospital, Cincinnati, OH, p. A489
MOORE, Robin A., Chief Human Resources Officer, Concord Hospital, Concord, NH, p. A414
MOORE, Samuel, Chief Financial Officer, University of Kansas Health System St. Francis Campus, Topeka, KS, p. A261
MOORE, Saunya, Chief Financial Officer, Parkside Psychiatric Hospital And Clinic, Tulsa, OK, p. A522

A926 Index of Health Care Professionals

MOORE, Shari, Chief Executive Officer, Methodist Rehabilitation Hospital, Dallas, TX, p. A612
MOORE, Susan, MS, R.N., Chief Nursing Officer, Gothenburg Health, Gothenburg, NE, p. A400
MOORE, Tammy Marie
  Chief Nursing Officer, Davis Regional Medical Center, Statesville, NC, p. A477
  Chief Nursing Officer, Lake Norman Regional Medical Center, Mooresville, NC, p. A472
MOORE, Tim, Vice President Finance, Illini Community Hospital, Pittsfield, IL, p. A206
MOORE, Travis W., R.N., Director of Nursing and Compliance Officer, Iron County Medical Center, Pilot Knob, MO, p. A382
MOORE, VonDa, Director of Nursing, Mercy Hospital Berryville, Berryville, AR, p. A43
MOORE, William, Chief Information Officer, Parrish Medical Center, Titusville, FL, p. A153
MOORE–CONNELLY, Marci
  M.D., Senior Vice President, Chief Medical Officer, Harrisburg Medical Center, Harrisburg, IL, p. A197
  M.D., Vice President Chief Medical Officer, Memorial Hospital of Carbondale, Carbondale, IL, p. A187
MOORER, Thad, Chief Information Officer, Eastside Psychiatric Hospital, Tallahassee, FL, p. A151
MOORHEAD, David, M.D., Chief Medical Officer, Adventhealth Orlando, Orlando, FL, p. A144
MOORHEAD, Emily, FACHE, President, Henry Ford Hospital and Central Market Operations, Henry Ford Jackson Hospital, Jackson, MI, p. A331
MOORHEAD, Michael, Chief Executive Officer, Stonewall Memorial Hospital, Aspermont, TX, p. A598
MOORING, Matt, Hospital Director, Central State Hospital, Louisville, KY, p. A269
MOOSS, Eric
  Chief Executive Officer, Bryan Medical Center, Lincoln, NE, p. A401
  President and Chief Executive Officer, Bryan Medical Center, Lincoln, NE, p. A401
MORACA, Lynn, Director Human Resources, Cleveland Clinic Akron General Lodi Hospital, Lodi, OH, p. A498
MORAHAN, John, Vice President Finance, St. Josep. Hospital, Bethpage, NY, p. A439
MORALES, Autumn, Chief Medical Staff Officer, Clarinda Regional Health Center, Clarinda, IA, p. A232
MORALES, Daniza
  Chief Information Officer, Hospital Menonita De Cayey, Cayey, PR, p. A732
  Manager Information System, Mennonite General Hospital, Aibonito, PR, p. A731
MORALES, Elsie, Chief Financial Officer, Hospital Universitario Dr. Ramon Ruiz Arnau, Bayamon, PR, p. A731
MORALES, Joel, Chief Financial Officer, Fort Duncan Regional Medical Center, Eagle Pass, TX, p. A615
MORALES, John R., Interim Chief Financial Officer, Loretto Hospital, Chicago, IL, p. A190
MORALES, Kathryn
  Director of Finance, Valley Health – Hampshire Memorial Hospital, Romney, WV, p. A704
  Director of Finance, Valley Health – War Memorial Hospital, Berkeley Springs, WV, p. A699
MORALES, Kristin, Chief Operating Officer, Umass Memorial Health – Harrington, Southbridge, MA, p. A318
MORALES, Trish, Director Human Resources, Lakewood Ranch Medical Center, Bradenton, FL, p. A126
MORAN, Alina, FACHE, FABC, President, California Hospital Medical Center, Los Angeles, CA, p. A72
MORAN, Debbie
  Executive Director, Carl Albert Community Mental Health Center, Mcalester, OK, p. A514
  Executive Director, Oklahoma Forensic Center, Vinita, OK, p. A523
MORAN, Mary, M.D., Pediatrician In Chief, St. Christopher's Hospital for Children, Philadelphia, PA, p. A550
MORAN MURPHY, Marybeth, Hospital Chief Executive Officer, Oceans Behavioral Hospital of Lubbock, Lubbock, TX, p. A636
MORANDEIRA, Ana, Director Marketing, San Juan Capestrano Hospital, San Juan, PR, p. A735
MORASKO, Jerome
  President and Chief Executive Officer, Avita Ontario Hospital, Ontario, OH, p. A502
  President and Chief Executive Officer, Bucyrus Community Hospital, Bucyrus, OH, p. A487
  President and Chief Executive Officer, Galion Community Hospital, Galion, OH, p. A496
MORASKO, Robert A., Chief Executive Officer, Heart of The Rockies Regional Medical Center, Salida, CO, p. A113
MORDECAI, Steve, Director Human Resources, Griffin Health, Derby, CT, p. A115

MOREFIELD, Terri, Deputy Chief Human Resources Division, Bassett Army Community Hospital, Fort Wainwright, AK, p. A28
MOREH, Swenda, Vice President and Chief Operating Officer, Bridgepoint Continuing Care Hospital – National Harborside, Washington, DC, p. A123
MOREIN, Sandy, Chief Nursing Officer, Iberia Medical Center, New Iberia, LA, p. A289
MORELAND, Janet D., Hospital Administrator, Lakeside Medical Center, Belle Glade, FL, p. A125
MORELL, Ixel, Chief Operating Officer, Sierra Vista Hospital, Sacramento, CA, p. A87
MORELLI, Gerald, Director Human Resources, Philadelphia Veterans Affairs Medical Center, Philadelphia, PA, p. A550
MORENO, Adrian, Chief Operating Officer, HCA Houston Healthcare Tomball, Tomball, TX, p. A658
MORENO, Debbie, R.N., Patient Care Executive, Adventist Health Lodi Memorial, Lodi, CA, p. A70
MORENO, Robin
  Chief Financial Officer, North Texas State Hospital, Wichita Falls Campus, Wichita Falls, TX, p. A662
  Financial Officer, North Texas State Hospital, Vernon, TX, p. A659
MORENO, Sandra, Chief Nursing Officer, Orange County Global Medical Center, Inc., Santa Ana, CA, p. A93
MORETTE, Josep. M, Executive Vice President, Methodist Rehabilitation Center, Jackson, MS, p. A364
MORGAN, Andrew
  President, Mercy Health – Tiffin Hospital, Tiffin, OH, p. A504
  President, Mercy Health – Willard Hospital, Willard, OH, p. A507
MORGAN, Charlene, Chief Nursing Officer, Henderson County Community Hospital, Lexington, TN, p. A587
MORGAN, David, Vice President and Chief Financial Officer, Bristol Bay Area Health Corporation, Dillingham, AK, p. A28
MORGAN, Dennis P, Chief of Staff, Baptist Memorial Hospital–North Mississippi, Oxford, MS, p. A367
MORGAN, Derek
  Vice President Human Resources, Kettering Health Main Campus, Kettering, OH, p. A497
  Vice President Human Resources, Kettering Health Miamisburg, Miamisburg, OH, p. A500
MORGAN, Eric, Chief Executive Officer, Prattville Baptist Hospital, Prattville, AL, p. A24
MORGAN, James, M.D., Chief Medical Officer, Memorial Hospital of Converse County, Douglas, WY, p. A727
MORGAN, Janelle, Interim Director of Nursing, Howard County Medical Center, Saint Paul, NE, p. A405
MORGAN, Jeff, Director Information Systems, Northeastern Nevada Regional Hospital, Elko, NV, p. A408
MORGAN, John, R.N., Chief Executive Officer, Jackson Parish Hospital, Jonesboro, LA, p. A284
MORGAN, Julie, Director of Nursing, St. Helena Parish Hospital, Greensburg, LA, p. A282
MORGAN, Lewus, Director, Information Technology, Mobridge Regional Hospital, Mobridge, SD, p. A575
MORGAN, Lois, R.N., MSN, Chief Administrative Officer, Chief Nursing Officer, Deaconess Gibson Hospital, Princeton, IN, p. A226
MORGAN, Loretta Y, Director Human Resources, Connally Memorial Medical Center, Floresville, TX, p. A618
MORGAN, Lori J., M.D., President/Chief Executive Officer, Huntington Health, Huntington Health, Pasadena, CA, p. A83
MORGAN, Mace, Director Information Systems, Minden Medical Center, Minden, LA, p. A288
MORGAN, Matthew, Associate Administrator, Hillcrest Hospital South, Tulsa, OK, p. A522
MORGAN, Nyle, Chief Information Officer, Sheridan Memorial Hospital, Sheridan, WY, p. A728
MORGAN, Rose
  MS, R.N., Vice President Patient Care Services, Princeton Community Hospital, Princeton, WV, p. A704
  MS, Interim Chief Nursing Officer, Onslow Memorial Hospital, Jacksonville, NC, p. A471
MORGAN, Shawn, Finance Officer, Northern Navajo Medical Center, Shiprock, NM, p. A437
MORGAN, Susan, Director of Nursing Services, Prairie County Hospital District, Terry, MT, p. A396
MORGAN, Teresa, Chief Financial Officer, Mcgehee Hospital, Mcgehee, AR, p. A50
MORGAN–FINE, Richard, IT Director, Clarinda Regional Health Center, Clarinda, IA, p. A232
MORICE, Tura, Chief Information Officer, Riverside University Health System–Medical Center, Moreno Valley, CA, p. A78
MORIN, Richard
  R.N., President CHRISTUS Spohn Hospital – Alice/Kleberg, Christus Spohn Hospital Alice, Alice, TX, p. A595

R.N., President CHRISTUS Spohn Hospital – Alice/Kleberg, Christus Spohn Hospital Beeville, Beeville, TX, p. A603
  R.N., President CHRISTUS Spohn Hospital – Alice/Kleberg, Christus Spohn Hospital Kleberg, Kingsville, TX, p. A632
MORIN, Robert J., Chief Financial Officer and Chief Operating Officer, Sturgis Hospital, Sturgis, MI, p. A338
MORIN–SCRIBNER, Nicole, Director Human Resources, St. Mary's Regional Medical Center, Lewiston, ME, p. A298
MORISCO, Antonietta, M.D., Medical Director, Chairman Anesthesiology, Jamaica Hospital Medical Center, New York, NY, p. A448
MORITZ, Kathy, Chief Nursing Officer, Winnmed, Decorah, IA, p. A234
MORITZ, Mary, Administrator Human Resources, Humboldt County Memorial Hospital, Humboldt, IA, p. A237
MORKRID, Shirley, Chief Nursing Officer, Logan Health Chester, Chester, MT, p. A390
MORLEY, Justin, Vice President of Operations, SSM Health St. Mary's Hospital – Jefferson City, Jefferson City, MO, p. A376
MORLOCK, Paul J, FACHE, Vice President Human Resources and Occupational Health, Children's Hospital of The King's Daughters, Norfolk, VA, p. A680
MORON, David, M.D., Clinical Director, Rio Grande State Center/South Texas Health Care System, Harlingen, TX, p. A623
MORONY, David, Chief Financial Officer, Casa Colina Hospital And Centers for Healthcare, Pomona, CA, p. A84
MORQUECHO, Adam, Director Information Technology, Huntington Beach Hospital, Huntington Beach, CA, p. A67
MORRELL, Dan, Manager Information Systems, Sierra Vista Hospital, Truth Or Consequences, NM, p. A437
MORRELL, Glen, M.D., Chief Medical Officer, Layton Hospital, Layton, UT, p. A665
MORRICAL, Michael, Chief Executive Officer, Encompass Health Rehabilitation Hospital of Treasure Coast, Vero Beach, FL, p. A154
MORRIONE, Thomas, Medical Director, New England Rehabilitation Hospital of Portland, Portland, ME, p. A298
MORRIS, Barbara, R.N., Chief Nursing Officer, Pam Rehabilitation Hospital of Beaumont, Beaumont, TX, p. A602
MORRIS, Christi, Director of Nursing, Chambers Health, Anahuac, TX, p. A597
MORRIS, Christopher
  Director Human Resources, Ascension Southeast Wisconsin Hospital – Elmbrook Campus, Brookfield, WI, p. A708
  Senior Director, Human Resources, Ascension Southeast Wisconsin Hospital – St. Joseph's Campus, Milwaukee, WI, p. A716
MORRIS, Clayton, Medical Director, Griffin Memorial Hospital, Norman, OK, p. A516
MORRIS, Dennis, Area Finance Officer, Kaiser Permanente Oakland Medical Center, Oakland, CA, p. A81
MORRIS, Donald, Vice President Human Resources, Hillcrest Medical Center, Tulsa, OK, p. A522
MORRIS, Douglas
  Chief Financial Officer, Amg Specialty Hospital Northwest Indiana, Crown Point, IN, p. A214
  Chief Financial Officer, Vibra Hospitals of Southeastern Michigan – Taylor Campus, Lincoln Park, MI, p. A332
MORRIS, Dylan, Director of Information Technology, Greene County General Hospital, Linton, IN, p. A222
MORRIS, Esther, Chief Human Resource Officer, North Shore Medical Center, Miami, FL, p. A140
MORRIS, Janet, Director Human Resources, Encompass Health Rehabilitation Hospital of Lakeview, Elizabethtown, KY, p. A265
MORRIS, Janice, Accountant, Crossridge Community Hospital, Wynne, AR, p. A54
MORRIS, Jarrett L
  Controller, Atrium Health Lincoln, Lincolnton, NC, p. A472
  Controller and Chief Information Officer, Atrium Health Lincoln, Lincolnton, NC, p. A472
MORRIS, Jerry
  Administrator, Higgins General Hospital, Bremen, GA, p. A159
  Vice President and Administrator, Tanner Medical Center–Villa Rica, Villa Rica, GA, p. A173
MORRIS, Jim
  Vice President Finance, Baptist Health La Grange, La Grange, KY, p. A268
  Vice President Finance, Baptist Health Louisville, Louisville, KY, p. A269
MORRIS, Jonelle, R.N., Chief Operating Officer, Medical Center & Clinics, Riverside University Health System–Medical Center, Moreno Valley, CA, p. A78
MORRIS, Kelly, Director of Human Resources, Macon Community Hospital, Lafayette, TN, p. A586

Index of Health Care Professionals / Morris

MORRIS, Kenneth R., President and Chief Executive Officer, Brooks-Tlc Hospital System, Inc., Dunkirk, NY, p. A442
MORRIS, Lisa, Vice President Human Resources, Swedish Medical Center, Englewood, CO, p. A107
MORRIS, Marsha, Manager Information Services, Fairview Park Hospital, Dublin, GA, p. A163
MORRIS, Mary, Chief Financial Officer, Purcell Municipal Hospital, Purcell, OK, p. A520
MORRIS, Nerissa E., Senior Vice President and Chief Human Resource Officer, Cincinnati Children's Hospital Medical Center, Cincinnati, OH, p. A488
MORRIS, R. Randall., Administrator, West Carroll Memorial Hospital, Oak Grove, LA, p. A290
MORRIS, Scott, Vice President Information Systems, Eskenazi Health, Indianapolis, IN, p. A219
MORRIS, Tara M., Interim Director, Human Resources, Musc Health – Orangeburg, Orangeburg, SC, p. A569
MORRIS, Tony, Business Manager, Cherokee Mental Health Institute, Cherokee, IA, p. A232
MORRIS, Will, Director Information Technology, Panola Medical Center, Batesville, MS, p. A359
MORRISON, Christopher, Chief Executive Officer, Ancora Psychiatric Hospital, Hammonton, NJ, p. A422
MORRISON, Deane, Chief Information Officer, Concord Hospital, Concord, NH, p. A414
MORRISON, Dereck, Assistant Administrator, Whitfield Regional Hospital, Demopolis, AL, p. A18
MORRISON, Dianne, Director Human Resources, Mizell Memorial Hospital, Opp. AL, p. A23
MORRISON, Greta M., Administrator, Assistant Vice President and Chief Nursing Officer, Russell County Medical Center, Lebanon, VA, p. A678
MORRISON, J. E., M.D., M.P.H., Chief Medical Officer, Baylor Scott & White Medical Center – Hillcrest, Waco, TX, p. A660
MORRISON, James A, Chief Information Officer, Madigan Army Medical Center, Tacoma, WA, p. A697
MORRISON, Kathy E., Executive Director Human Resources, St. Catherine Hospital, Garden City, KS, p. A249
MORRISON, Kevin, Chief Financial Officer, Dickenson Community Hospital, Clintwood, VA, p. A675
MORRISON, Maureen, Vice President, Finance, Advocate Trinity Hospital, Chicago, IL, p. A188
MORRISON, Michael, Chief Financial Officer, Tristar Skyline Medical Center, Nashville, TN, p. A591
MORRISON, Michele, R.N., M.P.H., President and Chief Hospital Executive, Hackensack Meridian Health Southern Ocean Medical Center, Manahawkin, NJ, p. A423
MORRISON, Olivia, Human Resource Manager, Encompass Health Rehabilitation Hospital of Parkersburg, Parkersburg, WV, p. A703
MORRISSETT, Barbara, Vice President Human Resources, UCSF Health St. Mary's Hospital, San Francisco, CA, p. A91
MORRISSETTE, Daniel, Chief Financial Officer, Stanford Health Care, Palo Alto, CA, p. A82
MORRISSEY, Moira
  Esq, Chief Executive Officer, Four Winds Hospital, Katonah, NY, p. A444
  Esq, Chief Executive Officer, Four Winds Hospital, Saratoga Springs, NY, p. A458
  Esq, Chief Operating Officer and General Counsel, Four Winds Hospital, Katonah, NY, p. A444
MORRISSEY, Una E, R.N., MSN, Senior Vice President Operations, Chief Operating Officer and Chief Nursing Officer, New York Community Hospital, New York, NY, p. A450
MORROW, Charles, M.D., Chief Medical Officer, Spartanburg Medical Center – Church Street Campus, Spartanburg, SC, p. A570
MORROW, Ginger, Entity Human Resources Officer, Texas Health Harris Methodist Hospital Fort Worth, Fort Worth, TX, p. A620
MORROW, Jennifer, Director Human Resources, San Joaquin Valley Rehabilitation Hospital, Fresno, CA, p. A65
MORROW, Laurie, Executive Director Human Resources, Washington Regional Medical System, Fayetteville, AR, p. A46
MORROW, Pat, Director Human Resources, Walker Baptist Medical Center, Jasper, AL, p. A21
MORROW, Randy, Vice President and Chief Operating Officer, Boone Hospital Center, Columbia, MO, p. A374
MORROW, Sarah, Vice President Human Resources, Capital Region Medical Center, Jefferson City, MO, p. A376
MORROW, Shawn
  FACHE, Market President, Unitypoint Health – Trinity Rock Island, Rock Island, IL, p. A207
  FACHE, Market President–UnityPoint Health Quad Cities, Unitypoint Health – Trinity Bettendorf, Bettendorf, IA, p. A231
  FACHE, Market President, UnityPoint Health – Quad Cities, Unitypoint Health – Trinity Muscatine, Muscatine, IA, p. A240
MORROW, W. Robert, M.D., Executive Vice President and Chief Medical Officer, Children's Medical Center Dallas, Dallas, TX, p. A611
MORROW NEELY, Laurie, Chief Nursing Officer, Merit Health River Region, Vicksburg, MS, p. A369
MORSCHAUSER, Roberta, Administrator, Brown County Community Treatment Center, Green Bay, WI, p. A712
MORSE, Courtney, Chief Nursing Officer, Select Specialty Hospital–Camp Hill, Camp Hill, PA, p. A536
MORSE, Craig, Chief Financial Officer, Carlsbad Medical Center, Carlsbad, NM, p. A433
MORSE, Jason, Director Information Technology, Cumberland Healthcare, Cumberland, WI, p. A709
MORSE, Rhonda, Chief Nursing Officer, Mercy Rehabilitation Hospital South, Saint Louis, MO, p. A385
MORSE, Robert, Chief Medical Officer, Providence Seaside Hospital, Seaside, OR, p. A532
MORSE, Rustin, M.D., Chief Medical Officer, Nationwide Children's Hospital – Toledo, Toledo, OH, p. A504
MORSTAD, Joan, Director Information Systems, Piedmont Macon, Macon, GA, p. A167
MORTENSEN, Lorrie, MSN, R.N., Director, Patient Care, Floyd Valley Healthcare, Le Mars, IA, p. A239
MORTENSEN, Shane
  Chief Financial Officer, San Luis Valley Health, Alamosa, CO, p. A103
  Chief Financial Officer, San Luis Valley Health Conejos County Hospital, La Jara, CO, p. A110
MORTENSON, June, R.N., Director of Nursing, Power County Hospital District, American Falls, ID, p. A179
MORTIMER, Kenneth, Medical Center Director, Chillicothe Veterans Affairs Medical Center, Chillicothe, OH, p. A488
MORTINSEN, Roy, M.D., Chief of Staff, Sanford Vermillion Medical Center, Vermillion, SD, p. A577
MORTON, David, M.D., Clinical Director, West Central Georgia Regional Hospital, Columbus, GA, p. A161
MORTON, Julie, Chief Nursing Officer and Chief Clinical Officer, Brooks-Tlc Hospital System, Inc., Dunkirk, NY, p. A442
MORTON, Leslie, Manager Human Resources, Riverview Regional Medical Center, Gadsden, AL, p. A20
MORTON, Lucas
  Regional Chief Financial Officer, OSF Heart of Mary Medical Center, Urbana, IL, p. A210
  Regional Chief Financial Officer, OSF Sacred Heart Medical Center, Danville, IL, p. A192
MORTON, Robert, M.D., Medical Director, Rolling Hills Hospital, Ada, OK, p. A509
MORTON, Stephanie, Chief Information Officer, Providence Alaska Medical Center, Anchorage, AK, p. A27
MORTON, Steve, M.D., Chief Medical Officer, Continuecare Hospital At Baptist Health Corbin, Corbin, KY, p. A264
MORTON ROWE, Laura, Director of Human Resources, Providence Saint John's Health Center, Santa Monica, CA, p. A95
MORTOZA, Angela, Chief Executive Officer, Dallas County Hospital, Perry, IA, p. A242
MOSBY, Charmaine T, Area Director Health Information Management, KPC Promise Hospital of Baton Rouge, Baton Rouge, LA, p. A277
MOSCA, Philip. M.D., President, Medical Staff, Integris Southwest Medical Center, Oklahoma City, OK, p. A517
MOSCHKAU, Don, Senior Director Human Resources, M Health Fairview University of Minnesota Medical Center, Minneapolis, MN, p. A350
MOSCOSO, Ricardo, M.D., Medical Director, University Hospital, San Juan, PR, p. A736
MOSEL, Lindy, Director of Nursing, Memorial Community Health, Aurora, NE, p. A397
MOSELY, Chisty, Director Information Management, Saint Simons By–The–Sea Hospital, Saint Simons Island, GA, p. A170
MOSER, Cindy, Director Human Resources, Allegheny Valley Hospital, Natrona Heights, PA, p. A547
MOSER, Joseph, M.D., Chief Medical Officer, University of Maryland Charles Regional Medical Center, La Plata, MD, p. A305
MOSER, Kevin, Vice President of Operations, Baptist Health Deaconess Madisonville, Inc., Madisonville, KY, p. A271
MOSER, Nathan, Information Technology Engineer, Audubon County Memorial Hospital And Clinics, Audubon, IA, p. A230
MOSER, Neal, M.D., Medical Director, Encompass Health Rehabilitation Hospital of Northern Kentucky, Edgewood, KY, p. A265
MOSER, Sharese, Director, Finance, Amberwell Hiawatha, Hiawatha, KS, p. A250
MOSESIAN, Robert, Controller, Encompass Health Rehabilitation Hospital of Bakersfield, Bakersfield, CA, p. A57
MOSHER, Guy W
  III, Manager Information Systems, Geneva General Hospital, Geneva, NY, p. A443
  III, Manager Information Systems, Soldiers And Sailors Memorial Hospital, Penn Yan, NY, p. A456
MOSHIER, John, Director Human Resources, Clara Barton Medical Center, Hoisington, KS, p. A250
MOSHIRPUR, Jasmin
  M.D., Chief Medical Officer, NYC Health + Hospitals/Queens, New York, NY, p. A451
  M.D., Dean and Medical Director, NYC Health + Hospitals/Elmhurst, New York, NY, p. A451
MOSIER, Dawn, Director Human Resources, Encompass Health Rehabilitation Institute of Tucson, Tucson, AZ, p. A40
MOSLEY, J. Christopher., Chief Executive Officer, HCA Florida Capital Hospital, Tallahassee, FL, p. A151
MOSLEY, Tonja, Chief Financial Officer, Wellington Regional Medical Center, Wellington, FL, p. A154
MOSMEYER, Kathleen C, Director Human Resources, Citizens Medical Center, Victoria, TX, p. A660
MOSS, Austin, Vice President Human Resources, Jennie Stuart Medical Center, Hopkinsville, KY, p. A267
MOSS, C Renee, M.D., Chief Medical Officer, Coastal Virginia Rehabilitation, Yorktown, VA, p. A686
MOSS, Jennifer, MS, R.N., Chief Clinical Officer, Kirby Medical Center, Monticello, IL, p. A202
MOSS, Keith A, Vice President & Chief Medical Informatics Officers, Riverside Medical Center, Kankakee, IL, p. A199
MOSS, Misty, Director Business Administration, Logansport State Hospital, Logansport, IN, p. A223
MOSS, Ray, Vice President and Chief Information Officer, Henry Mayo Newhall Hospital, Valencia, CA, p. A99
MOSS, Roberta, Chief Executive Officer, Kindred Hospital South Florida–Fort Lauderdale, Fort Lauderdale, FL, p. A131
MOSS, Shelby, Human Resource Officer, Sheridan County Health Complex, Hoxie, KS, p. A251
MOSS, Stuart, Chief Financial Officer, Kessler Marlton Rehabilitation, Marlton, NJ, p. A423
MOSS, Terry, Chief Operating Officer, Ivinson Memorial Hospital, Laramie, WY, p. A727
MOSS, Tyler, Chief Financial Officer, Milford Valley Memorial Hospital, Milford, UT, p. A665
MOTAKEF, Shahin
  FACHE, Chief Executive Officer, Baylor Scott & White Medical Center – Temple, Temple, TX, p. A656
  FACHE, President, Baylor Scott & White Medical Center – Temple, Temple, TX, p. A656
MOTEJZIK, Thomas, Director Information Systems, Carlsbad Medical Center, Carlsbad, NM, p. A433
MOTLEY, Yolanda, Chief Executive Officer, Encompass Health Rehabilitation Hospital of North Memphis, A Partner of Methodist Healthcare, Memphis, TN, p. A588
MOTONAGA, Gregg, M.D., Chief of Staff, Central Peninsula Hospital, Soldotna, AK, p. A29
MOTT, Daman, MSN, Chief Nursing Officer, Doctors Hospital of Laredo, Laredo, TX, p. A634
MOTT, William, Chief Operating Officer, Ascension Macomb–Oakland Hospital, Warren Campus, Warren, MI, p. A340
MOTTE, Michael J.
  Chief Executive Officer, Lower Bucks Hospital, Bristol, PA, p. A535
  Chief Executive Officer, Suburban Community Hospital, East Norriton, PA, p. A539
MOUGHAN, Jennifer L, Chief Human Resources Officer, Virtua Our Lady of Lourdes Hospital, Camden, NJ, p. A419
MOUISSET, Rena B, Director Human Resources and Contract Compliance, Ochsner St. Martin Hospital, Breaux Bridge, LA, p. A279
MOULTON, Susan, Director Health Information Management, Mainehealth Behavioral Health At Spring Harbor, Westbrook, ME, p. A299
MOUNIE, Mike, Director Finance, Sentara Obici Hospital, Suffolk, VA, p. A684
MOUNSEY, Victoria, Director Human Resources, Rehabilitation Hospital of Henry, Mcdonough, GA, p. A168
MOUNTAIN, J Michael, Chief Financial Officer, Rivervalley Behavioral Health Hospital, Owensboro, KY, p. A272
MOUSA, Ayman
  R.N., Chief Executive Officer, La Palma Intercommunity Hospital, La Palma, CA, p. A69
  R.N., Chief Executive Officer, West Anaheim Medical Center, Anaheim, CA, p. A55
MOUSA, Cindy, Director Human Resources, Touro Infirmary, New Orleans, LA, p. A290

Index of Health Care Professionals / Murphy

Index of Health Care Professionals

MOUSTAKAKIS, John, Senior Vice President Information Systems and Chief Information Officer, Westchester Medical Center, Valhalla, NY, p. A461
MOVSESIAN, Gregory, M.D., Acting Chief of Staff, Aleda E. Lutz Department of Veterans Affairs Medical Center, Saginaw, MI, p. A336
MOYA, Linda, Director Human Resources, Mesilla Valley Hospital, Las Cruces, NM, p. A435
MOYANO, Mathias
Chief Human Resource Officer, Delta Community Medical Center, Delta, UT, p. A664
Chief Human Resource Officer, Fillmore Community Hospital, Fillmore, UT, p. A665
MOYER, Alyssa, President, Wellspan York Hospital, York, PA, p. A559
MOYER, Dale, Vice President Information Systems, Evangelical Community Hospital, Lewisburg, PA, p. A544
MOYER, Douglas J., Division President, Sentara Rmh Medical Center, Harrisonburg, VA, p. A677
MOYER, Karen W, R.N., Senior Vice President and Chief Nursing Officer, Mount Sinai Medical Center, Miami Beach, FL, p. A141
MOYER, William, President, St. Luke's University Hospital – Bethlehem Campus, Bethlehem, PA, p. A535
MRAMOR, Joann, Director Human Resources, Tamp. General Hospital Crystal River, Crystal River, FL, p. A129
MUCHNICK, Ashley, Chief Operating Officer, Rogers Behavioral Health, Oconomowoc, WI, p. A718
MUCK, Erin, Chief Executive Officer, Crawford County Memorial Hospital, Denison, IA, p. A234
MUDD, Mike, Chief Operating Officer, Mercy Hospital Northwest Arkansas, Rogers, AR, p. A52
MUDEN, Todd, Section Head Information Management, Mayo Clinic Health System – Northland In Barron, Barron, WI, p. A708
MUDRY, Janel, Chief Operating Officer, UPMC Greene, Waynesburg, PA, p. A556
MUELLER, Charles, M.D., Chief of Staff, Texas County Memorial Hospital, Houston, MO, p. A376
MUELLER, Eric, Market Chief Executive Officer Phoenix Metro, Reunion Rehabilitation Hospital Phoenix, Phoenix, AZ, p. A36
MUELLER, Karen, R.N., Chief Nursing Officer, Mount Desert Island Hospital, Bar Harbor, ME, p. A295
MUELLER, Michael E., Chief Financial Officer, Orlando Health St. Cloud Hospital, Saint Cloud, FL, p. A148
MUENZER, Jared, M.D., Chief Physician Executive, Phoenix Children's, Phoenix, AZ, p. A36
MUGGLI, David D, FACHE, Chief Executive Officer, Select Specialty Hospital–Cincinnati, Cincinnati, OH, p. A489
MUHAMMAD, Mark, Manager Human Resources, Michael E. Debakey Department of Veterans Affairs Medical Center, Houston, TX, p. A627
MUHS, David, Chief Financial Officer, Henry County Health Center, Mount Pleasant, IA, p. A240
MUILENBURG, Jeff, Chief of Staff, Memorial Community Health, Aurora, NE, p. A397
MULDER, Doris, Vice President Nursing, Beloit Health System, Beloit, WI, p. A708
MULDERIG, Marsha L., R.N., MSN, Chief Nursing Officer, Crisp Regional Hospital, Cordele, GA, p. A161
MULDOON, Sean R
M.D., Chief Medical Officer, Kindred Hospital–New Jersey Morris County, Dover, NJ, p. A420
M.D., Senior Vice President and Chief Medical Officer–Kindred Healthcare, Hospital Division, Kindred Hospital Northland, Kansas City, MO, p. A377
MULIKIN, Rob, Director Information Systems, Los Alamos Medical Center, Los Alamos, NM, p. A435
MULIS, Becky, Director of Health Information Management Systems, 4C Health, Logansport, IN, p. A222
MULKERN, Nicole, Assistant Chief Financial Officer, Anna Jaques Hospital, Newburyport, MA, p. A316
MULKEY, Michael J., Chief Executive Officer, Willamette Valley Medical Center, Mcminnville, OR, p. A529
MULKEY, Peter, Chief Executive Officer, Clinch Valley Medical Center, Richlands, VA, p. A682
MULLEN, Michelle
Chief Clinical Officer, Bridgepoint Continuing Care Hospital – Capitol Hill, Washington, DC, p. A123
Chief Executive Officer, Continuecare Hospital At Madisonville, Madisonville, KY, p. A271
Chief Nursing Officer, Continuecare Hospital At Madisonville, Madisonville, KY, p. A271
MULLENDER, Monica, Director of Nursing, Osborne County Memorial Hospital, Osborne, KS, p. A256
MULLENS, Allen, M.D., Chief Medical Staff, Norton Community Hospital, Norton, VA, p. A680
MULLER, Donna L.
Vice President Finance, Southern Region, UPMC Hanover, Hanover, PA, p. A541
Vice President Finance, Southern Region, UPMC Memorial, York, PA, p. A559
MULLER, Oz, Director Human Resources, Adventhealth Porter, Denver, CO, p. A106
MULLERY, Barbara M, Vice President Administration, Robert Wood Johnson University Hospital Rahway, Rahway, NJ, p. A427
MULLIGAN, Marie, R.N., MSN, Chief Nursing Officer, Vice President Nursing, Mather Hospital, Port Jefferson, NY, p. A456
MULLINGS, Donna, Director of Nursing, Our Lady of The Lake Assumption Community Hospital, Napoleonville, LA, p. A289
MULLINS, Bandy, M.D., Chief of Staff, Summersville Regional Medical Center, Summersville, WV, p. A705
MULLINS, Brad, Director Information Technology, Gove County Medical Center, Quinter, KS, p. A258
MULLINS, Bryan, Chief Operating Officer, Johnston Memorial Hospital, Abingdon, VA, p. A673
MULLINS, Cindy, Director Information Technology, Saint Mary's Regional Medical Center, Reno, NV, p. A412
MULLINS, Dustin
Chief Human Resources, Bayne–Jones Army Community Hospital, Fort Polk, LA, p. A282
Chief Resource Management, Bayne–Jones Army Community Hospital, Fort Polk, LA, p. A282
MULLINS, Erin, D.O., Chief Medical Staff, Dickenson Community Hospital, Clintwood, VA, p. A675
MULLINS, Michelle, Chief Information Officer, Oklahoma Heart Hospital, Oklahoma City, OK, p. A518
MULLIS, Jeffrey
Interim Chief Financial Officer, Newberry County Memorial Hospital, Newberry, SC, p. A569
Interim Chief Financial Officer, Piedmont Walton Hospital, Monroe, GA, p. A168
Interim Chief Financial Officer, Shorepoint Health Port Charlotte, Port Charlotte, FL, p. A147
MULROONEY, JoAnn M, R.N., Chief Operating Officer, Trinity Health System, Steubenville, OH, p. A504
MULTACH, Mark, M.D., Chief Medical Officer, Mount Sinai Hospital, Chicago, IL, p. A190
MULTACK, Richard, D.O., Vice President Medical Management, Advocate South Suburban Hospital, Hazel Crest, IL, p. A197
MULVEHILL, Mitchell
Group Financial Officer, Texas Health Harris Methodist Hospital Southlake, Southlake, TX, p. A653
President, Texas Health Center for Diagnostic & Surgery, Plano, TX, p. A645
MULVEY, Lee, Human Resource Officer, Texas Health Harris Methodist Hospital Hurst–Euless–Bedford, Bedford, TX, p. A602
MUMFORD, Stephen, Chief Operating Officer, Baton Rouge General Medical Center, Baton Rouge, LA, p. A277
MUMOLIE, Gina, Senior Vice President Hospital Administration, Capital Health Regional Medical Center, Trenton, NJ, p. A429
MUMPOWER, Rebecca, Director Marketing, Mesilla Valley Hospital, Las Cruces, NM, p. A435
MUNA, Esther L., FACHE, Chief Executive Officer, Commonwealth Health Center, Saipan, MARIANA ISLANDS, p. A730
MUNCHEL, Bryan, Senior Vice President and Chief Information Officer, Pam Specialty Hospital of Covington, Covington, LA, p. A280
MUNGO, Paul, Vice President, Chief Nursing Officer, Baptist Health South Florida, South Miami Hospital, Miami, FL, p. A139
MUNGOVAN, Sandy, Chief Information Officer, Harbor–Ucla Medical Center, Torrance, CA, p. A98
MUNHOLLAND, Cleta, Administrator, Specialty Hospital, Monroe, LA, p. A289
MUNINGER, Barry, Chief Executive Officer, Kansas Rehabilitation Hospital, Topeka, KS, p. A260
MUNIR, Amjad, M.D., Medical Director, Encompass Health Rehabilitation Hospital of Chattanooga, Chattanooga, TN, p. A580
MUNLEY, William, Administrator, Shriners Hospitals for Children–Greenville, Greenville, SC, p. A567
MUNOZ, Alejandro, M.D., Chief Medical Officer, Cedar Crest Hospital And Residential Treatment Center, Belton, TX, p. A603
MUNOZ, Anthony, Chief, Civilian Human Resources Branch, Madigan Army Medical Center, Tacoma, WA, p. A697
MUNOZ, Astro, Executive Director, First Hospital Panamericano, Cidra, PR, p. A732
MUNOZ, Thalia H., R.N., MS, Chief Executive Officer, Starr County Memorial Hospital, Rio Grande City, TX, p. A647
MUNSHI, Imtiaz A, M.D., Chief of Staff, Richard L. Roudebush Veterans Affairs Medical Center, Indianapolis, IN, p. A220
MUNSON, James, R.N., Chief Executive Officer, Cobalt Rehabilitation Hospital of New Orleans, New Orleans, LA, p. A290
MUNSON, Jennifer, Chief Financial Officer, Three Rivers Hospital, Brewster, WA, p. A687
MUNTEFERING, Denise, Vice President Patient Care Services, Avera St. Benedict Health Center, Parkston, SD, p. A575
MUNTON, Christopher, Chief Executive Officer, Wilson Medical Center, Wilson, NC, p. A478
MUNTON, David, Chief Financial Officer, Twin County Regional Healthcare, Galax, VA, p. A677
MUNYAN, Lori, Director, Human Resources, Encompass Health Rehabilitation Hospital of Toms River, Toms River, NJ, p. A429
MURANSKY, Ed, Owner, Surgical Hospital At Southwoods, Youngstown, OH, p. A508
MURCHISON, Sandra, Director Medical Records, Coosa Valley Medical Center, Sylacauga, AL, p. A24
MURDAUGH, Laura, Finance Director, William J. Mccord Adolescent Treatment Facility, Orangeburg, SC, p. A569
MURDOCK, Guy, Vice President Human Resources, Nexus Children's Hospital Houston, Houston, TX, p. A627
MURDOCK, William R., President and Chief Executive Officer, Mcdonough District Hospital, Macomb, IL, p. A200
MURDOCK–LANGAN, Patricia
M.D., Chief Medical Officer, Chi Health Lakeside, Omaha, NE, p. A403
M.D., Chief Medical Officer, Chi Health Midlands, Papillion, NE, p. A405
MURDY, James B., Chief Financial Officer, Wheeling Hospital, Wheeling, WV, p. A706
MURILLO, Jeremias, M.D., Chief Medical Officer, Newark Beth Israel Medical Center, Newark, NJ, p. A425
MURIN, William J, Chief Human Resources Officer, UC San Diego Medical Center – Hillcrest, San Diego, CA, p. A90
MURNYACK, Laura, Interim Chief Executive Officer, Bucktail Medical Center, Renovo, PA, p. A553
MURO, Deborah, Chief Information Officer, El Camino Health, Mountain View, CA, p. A79
MURPHREE, Shari, Chief Executive Officer, Willow Crest Hospital, Miami, OK, p. A515
MURPHY, Bobbie, R.N., Chief Nursing Officer, Bristol Regional Medical Center, Bristol, TN, p. A579
MURPHY, Brian
M.D., Chief Executive Officer, Valley View Hospital, Glenwood Springs, CO, p. A108
Senior Director Admissions and Referral Services, Hebrew Rehabilitation Center, Roslindale, MA, p. A317
Vice President Information Systems, Sarah Bush Lincoln Health Center, Mattoon, IL, p. A201
MURPHY, Bruce, M.D., President and Chief Executive Officer, Arkansas Heart Hospital, Little Rock, AR, p. A49
MURPHY, Charles J, Associate Vice President Human Resources, Strong Memorial Hospital of The University of Rochester, Rochester, NY, p. A457
MURPHY, Christine, MS, Chief Operating Officer, Cypress Grove Behavioral Health, Bastrop. LA, p. A277
MURPHY, Colleen, M.D., Chief of Staff, Clay County Hospital, Flora, IL, p. A195
MURPHY, Elizabeth A, R.N., FACHE, Chief Nursing Officer, Trinity Health Grand Rapids Hospital, Grand Rapids, MI, p. A328
MURPHY, Evelyn, Chief Nursing Officer, St. Mary's Sacred Heart Hospital, Lavonia, GA, p. A166
MURPHY, J Patrick, Chief Financial Officer, North Baldwin Infirmary, Bay Minette, AL, p. A16
MURPHY, John B, M.D., Vice President Medical Affairs and Chief Medical Officer, Rhode Island Hospital, Providence, RI, p. A561
MURPHY, John M., M.D., President and Chief Executive Officer, Western Connecticut Health Network, Danbury Hospital, Danbury, CT, p. A115
MURPHY, Julie, Chief Financial Officer, Saint Luke's North Hospital – Barry Road, Kansas City, MO, p. A378
MURPHY, Kathy, Site Manager, Mescalero Public Health Service Indian Hospital, Mescalero, NM, p. A436
MURPHY, Kevin G, Chief Financial Officer, Signature Healthcare Brockton Hospital, Brockton, MA, p. A311
MURPHY, Kyle, Director Information Technology, Mayhill Hospital, Denton, TX, p. A614
MURPHY, Linda, Chief Financial Officer, Osborne County Memorial Hospital, Osborne, KS, p. A256
MURPHY, Lionel, Chief Executive Officer, Bethesda Rehabilitation Hospital, Baton Rouge, LA, p. A277
MURPHY, Margaret M, Chief Executive Officer, Kindred Hospital Philadelphia, Philadelphia, PA, p. A549
MURPHY, Marie, Director Human Resources, Effingham Health System, Springfield, GA, p. A171

© 2025 AHA Guide Index of Health Care Professionals **A929**

MURPHY, Mark, Administrator, Southeast Regional Medical Center, Kentwood, LA, p. A284
MURPHY, Mary S
  MSN, Regional Chief Nursing Officer, UChicago Medicine Adventhealth La Grange, La Grange, IL, p. A199
  MSN, Vice President and Chief Nursing Officer, UChicago Medicine Adventhealth Hinsdale, Hinsdale, IL, p. A198
MURPHY, Matthew, Chief Financial Officer, Compass Memorial Healthcare, Marengo, IA, p. A239
MURPHY, Maureen, M.D., Director of Medical Affairs, SSM Health St. Clare Hospital–Baraboo, Baraboo, WI, p. A707
MURPHY, Michael, M.D., JD, Chief Medical Officer, Sharp Grossmont Hospital, La Mesa, CA, p. A68
MURPHY, Michael D., FACHE, Chief Operaitng Officer, Hendrick Medical Center, Abilene, TX, p. A595
MURPHY, Nancy, Vice President, Human Resources, Franciscan Children's, Brighton, MA, p. A311
MURPHY, Rita, Director Human Resources, Cobre Valley Regional Medical Center, Globe, AZ, p. A32
MURPHY, Sheryl, Chief Nursing Officer and Director of Clinical Services, Peacehealth Peace Island Medical Center, Friday Harbor, WA, p. A690
MURPHY, Steve
  Director Information Systems, SSM Health St. Mary's Hospital Centralia, Centralia, IL, p. A187
  FM–East Region IS, SSM Health Good Samaritan Hospital, Mount Vernon, IL, p. A202
MURPHY, Terry
  FACHE, President and Chief Executive Officer, Bayhealth, Dover, DE, p. A121
  Director Information Services, Phoenixville Hospital, Phoenixville, PA, p. A550
MURPHY, Theresa, Chief Nursing Officer, USC Verdugo Hills Hospital, Glendale, CA, p. A66
MURPHY, Timothy
  R.N., Chief Nursing Officer, Encompass Health Rehabilitation Hospital of Desert Canyon, Las Vegas, NV, p. A410
  Vice President Human Resources, Mercy Hospital Joplin, Joplin, MO, p. A377
MURPHY, Tom, Chief Executive Officer, Minidoka Memorial Hospital, Rupert, ID, p. A183
MURPHY–FROBISH, Erin, Vice President Human Resources, Morris Hospital & Healthcare Centers, Morris, IL, p. A202
MURPHY–MIJARES, Mcnique, Chief Information Officer, Valley View Medical Center, Fort Mohave, AZ, p. A31
MURRAY, Alexander, Interim Associate Director, Biloxi Va Medical Center, Biloxi, MS, p. A359
MURRAY, Beverly, Director of Human Resources, Providence Cedars–Sinai Tarzana Medical Center, Los Angeles, CA, p. A74
MURRAY, Brian
  M.D., Medical Director, Erie County Medical Center, Buffalo, NY, p. A440
  Chief Financial Officer, Gunnison Valley Hospital, Gunnison, UT, p. A665
MURRAY, Cindy, R.N., Chief Nursing Officer and Chief Operating Officer, Baylor Scott & White Medical Center–Waxahachie, Waxahachie, TX, p. A660
MURRAY, Deborah, Executive Director, Capital District Psychiatric Center, Albany, NY, p. A438
MURRAY, Denise R., Chief Executive Officer, Anmed Rehabilitation Hospital, Anderson, SC, p. A562
MURRAY, Diana, Director Information Systems, Grand River Hospital District, Rifle, CO, p. A113
MURRAY, Karen, M.D., President, Cleveland Clinic Children's Hospital for Rehabilitation, Cleveland, OH, p. A490
MURRAY, Kent, M.D., Chief of Staff, Robert J. Dole Department of Veterans Affairs Medical And Regional Office Center, Wichita, KS, p. A262
MURRAY, Kevin, M.D., Director Medical Services, Lake Taylor Transitional Care Hospital, Norfolk, VA, p. A680
MURRAY, Kevin J, Senior Vice President, Mather Hospital, Port Jefferson, NY, p. A456
MURRAY, Marisa, CPA, Director Finance, HSHS St. Francis Hospital, Litchfield, IL, p. A200
MURRAY, Meggan, Assistant Vice President Finance, Terrebonne General Health System, Houma, LA, p. A283
MURRAY, Sherri, Chief Financial Officer, Montgomery General Hospital, Montgomery, WV, p. A702
MURRAY, Susan, FACHE, Chief Operating Officer, The Queen's Medical Center, Honolulu, HI, p. A176
MURRAY, Vanessa, Director of Finance, Adventist Healthcare Fort Washington Medical Center, Fort Washington, MD, p. A304
MURRELL, Joseph, Chief Executive Officer, Wayne County Hospital, Monticello, KY, p. A271
MURRILL, Michael
  Chief Executive Officer, Adventhealth Zephyrhills, Zephyrhills, FL, p. A155
  President and Chief Executive Officer, Adventhealth Connerton, Land O'Lakes, FL, p. A137
  President and Chief Executive Officer, Adventhealth Dade City, Dade City, FL, p. A129
MURROW, Carol, Vice President Business Development, Cox Medical Center Branson, Branson, MO, p. A372
MURRY, Jim, Chief Information Officer, Stony Brook University Hospital, Stony Brook, NY, p. A459
MURTAUGH, Karen B., Executive Director, Human Resources, RML Specialty Hospital, Hinsdale, IL, p. A198
MURTHY, Anand, FACHE, Interim Chief Executive Officer, Encompass Health Rehabilitation Hospital of Fredericksburg, Fredericksburg, VA, p. A676
MURTHY, Anandhi, Chief Medical Officer, WVU Medicine – Harrison Community Hospital, Cadiz, OH, p. A487
MURTHY, Bangalore, M.D., Director Medical Staff, Jackson Park Hospital And Medical Center, Chicago, IL, p. A189
MURZYN, Derek, Market Chief Executive Officer, Carolinas Continuecare Hospital At Pineville, Charlotte, NC, p. A465
MUSACK, Scott, Chief Information Officer, La Downtown Medical Center, Llc, Los Angeles, CA, p. A73
MUSANTE, David, M.D., Medical Director, North Carolina Specialty Hospital, Durham, NC, p. A467
MUSGRAVE, Chelsea, Director of Human Resources, Clay County Hospital, Flora, IL, p. A195
MUSKRAT, Lisa, Chief Executive Officer, Regency Hospital of Northwest Arkansas – Springdale, Springdale, AR, p. A53
MUSSI, Alexis, Chief Executive Officer, Southern Hills Hospital And Medical Center, Las Vegas, NV, p. A410
MUSSI, Natalie, President and Chief Executive Officer, Los Robles Health System, Thousand Oaks, CA, p. A97
MUSSO, Lewis C, Vice President Human Resources, Trinity Health System, Steubenville, OH, p. A504
MUSTARD, Ruth, R.N., MSN, Suffix, Associate Director Nursing and Patient Services, Columbia Va Health Care System, Columbia, SC, p. A564
MUSUNURU, J.R., M.D., Executive Director, Fond Du Lac County Mental Health Center, Fond Du Lac, WI, p. A710
MUTTERER, Michael, R.N., President and Chief Executive Officer, Silver Cross Hospital, New Lenox, IL, p. A203
MUTZ, Jeffrey S., Human Resources Director, Northfield Hospital And Clinics, Northfield, MN, p. A352
MUTZIGER, John, M.D., Chief Medical Officer, Ochsner Laird Hospital, Union, MS, p. A369
MWANIKI, Mary, Chief Financial Officer, Encompass Health Rehabilitation Hospital of The Mid–Cities, Bedford, TX, p. A602
MWEBE, David, M.D., Chief of Staff, Osmond General Hospital, Osmond, NE, p. A405
MYCROFT, Tina, Chief Financial Officer, Valley Children's Healthcare, Madera, CA, p. A76
MYERS, Becky, Human Resources Specialist, Illini Community Hospital, Pittsfield, IL, p. A206
MYERS, Chrissy, R.N., Director of Nursing, Unity Psychiatric Care–Clarksville, Clarksville, TN, p. A581
MYERS, Gabby, Human Resources Director, East Houston Hospitals & Clinics, Houston, TX, p. A625
MYERS, Grace, MSN, Vice President, Nurse Executive, Sentara Princess Anne Hospital, Virginia Beach, VA, p. A684
MYERS, Jan M, Chief Nursing Officer, Knoxville Hospital & Clinics, Knoxville, IA, p. A239
MYERS, Jerry, M.D., Chief Executive Officer and Medical Director, Kell West Regional Hospital, Wichita Falls, TX, p. A662
MYERS, John, President, Mercy Springfield Communities, Mercy Hospital Springfield, Springfield, MO, p. A387
MYERS, Julie
  Market Chief Executive Officer, Kindred Hospital Rancho, Rancho Cucamonga, CA, p. A84
  Market Chief Executive Officer, Kindred Hospital Riverside, Perris, CA, p. A83
  Market Chief Executive Officer, Kindred Hospital–Ontario, Ontario, CA, p. A81
MYERS, Kathy R, MS, R.N., Chief Nursing Officer, Tennova Healthcare–Lafollette Medical Center, La Follette, TN, p. A586
MYERS, Keith G., Chairman and Chief Executive Officer, Lhc Group – Home Healthcare, Lafayette, LA, p. A285
MYERS, Kevin
  Director Information Systems, Lake Granbury Medical Center, Granbury, TX, p. A622
  Director Information Technology, Wilson Medical Center, Neodesha, KS, p. A255
MYERS, Kimberly, Director Human Resources, Guthrie County Hospital, Guthrie Center, IA, p. A237
MYERS, Lisa, Director Human Resources, Heritage Oaks Hospital, Sacramento, CA, p. A86
MYERS, Michelle F., Director Human Resources, Adventhealth Wauchula, Wauchula, FL, p. A154
MYERS, Paul, M.D., Neonatologist and Chief Medical Officer, Children's Hospital of Wisconsin–Fox Valley, Neenah, WI, p. A718
MYERS, Philip. M.D., Vice President Medical Affairs, University Hospitals Samaritan Medical Center, Ashland, OH, p. A485
MYERS, Randy, Chief Information Officer, Rehoboth Mckinley Christian Health Care Services, Gallup. NM, p. A434
MYERS, Robert T, Chief Operating Officer, Goshen Health, Goshen, IN, p. A217
MYERS, Shane P, Chief Operating Officer, Iberia Medical Center, New Iberia, LA, p. A289
MYERS, Sheri, Vice President Patient Care Services, Mclaren Central Michigan, Mount Pleasant, MI, p. A334
MYERS, Tara, Director, Human Resources, Encompass Health Rehabilitation Hospital of Greenville, Greenville, SC, p. A567
MYERS, Theresa, Personnel Director, Fallon Medical Complex, Baker, MT, p. A389
MYERS, William, Chief Executive Officer, Montgomery County Emergency Service, Norristown, PA, p. A547
MYHAVER, Christopher, FACHE, Medical Center Director, Harry S. Truman Memorial Veterans' Hospital, Columbia, MO, p. A374
MYHRE, Tracy, R.N., MSN, Chief Nursing Officer, Tomah Health, Tomah, WI, p. A723
MYLAVARAPU, Sarada, M.D., Chief Medical Officer, Woodland Memorial Hospital, Woodland, CA, p. A101
MYLES, Tremayne, Chief Executive Officer, Select Specialty Hospital – Dallas Downtown, Desoto, TX, p. A614
MYSTER, Jennifer, President, Park Nicollet Methodist Hospital, Saint Louis Park, MN, p. A354
MYSZKOWSKI, Joseph, Vice President, Human Resources, UCF Lake Nona Medical Center, Orlando, FL, p. A144

N

NABULSHI, Sari A., M.D., Chief Medical Officer, Medical Center Health System, Odessa, TX, p. A642
NACEY, Marley, Director Finance, Sentara Virginia Beach General Hospital, Virginia Beach, VA, p. A685
NACHIMUTHU, Anbu
  Chief Executive Officer and Chairman, Carrus Behavioral Hospital, Sherman, TX, p. A652
  Chief Executive Officer and Chairman, Carrus Rehabilitation Hospital, Sherman, TX, p. A653
NACHTIGAL, Amy, Chief Financial Officer, Saint Luke's Hospital of Kansas City, Kansas City, MO, p. A378
NACHTRIEB, Han, Vice President Human Resources, Fred Hutchinson Cancer Center, Seattle, WA, p. A694
NACION, Glenn, Vice President Human Resources, Trinitas Regional Medical Center, Elizabeth, NJ, p. A421
NADEAU, Barbara, Chief Human Resources Management Service, White River Junction Veterans Affairs Medical Center, White River Junction, VT, p. A672
NADER, Keoni, Director Human Resources, Weiss Memorial Hospital, Chicago, IL, p. A192
NADER, Rick Lee, Chief Financial Officer, Haxtun Hospital District, Haxtun, CO, p. A109
NADKARNI, Manasi, M.D., Vice President Medical Affairs, Unitypoint Health – Trinity Muscatine, Muscatine, IA, p. A240
NADLE, Patricia A, R.N., Chief Nursing Officer, St. Josep. Health Services of Rhode Island, North Providence, RI, p. A560
NADLER, Tammy R, Chief Financial Officer, Golden Valley Memorial Healthcare, Clinton, MO, p. A373
NADOLNY, Stephanie
  President and Chief Executive Officer, Rehabilitation Hospital of The Pacific, Honolulu, HI, p. A176
  Vice President of Hospital Operations, Spaulding Rehabilitation Hospital Cap. Cod, East Sandwich, MA, p. A313
NAEGLER, Rick R., Market Chief Executive Officer, Northwest Medical Center – Springdale, Springdale, AR, p. A53
NAFZIGER, Laurie N., President and Chief Executive Officer, Oaklawn Psychiatric Center, Goshen, IN, p. A218
NAFZIGER, Steve, M.D., Vice President Medical Affairs, UCHealth Parkview Medical Center, Pueblo, CO, p. A113
NAG, Pratip. Vice President, Chief Medical Officer, Katherine Shaw Bethea Hospital, Dixon, IL, p. A193
NAGARAJ, Alaka, M.D., Medical Director, Regency Hospital of Minneapolis, Golden Valley, MN, p. A347
NAGARAJ, Raghava, M.D., Medical Director, Atrium Health Wake Forest Baptist Lexington Medical Center, Lexington, NC, p. A472

NAGATOSHI, Holly, R.N., Chief Nursing Officer, San Dimas Community Hospital, San Dimas, CA, p. A90
NAGEL, Hollie, MSN, Chief Nursing Officer, Community Medical Center, Missoula, MT, p. A394
NAGLER, Richard, M.D., Chief of Staff, Mayo Clinic Health System – Northland In Barron, Barron, WI, p. A708
NAGOWSKI, Michael, Chief Executive Officer, Cap. Fear Valley Medical Center, Fayetteville, NC, p. A468
NAGY, Jeff, Chief Financial Officer, River Bend Hospital, West Lafayette, IN, p. A229
NAGY, Ryan, M.D., President, Indiana University Health University Hospital, Indianapolis, IN, p. A220
NAHM, Christopher, M.D., Chief Medical Officer, Livingston Regional Hospital, Livingston, TN, p. A587
NAIBERK, Donald T., Administrator and Chief Executive Officer, Butler County Health Care Center, David City, NE, p. A399
NAIDU, Murali, M.D., FACS, Chief Executive Officer, Emanuel Medical Center, Turlock, CA, p. A98
NAIL, Cheryl, Chief Nursing Officer, HCA Florida Lawnwood Hospital, Fort Pierce, FL, p. A132
NAIR, Chand, M.D., Medical Director, Brooke Glen Behavioral Hospital, Fort Washington, PA, p. A540
NAIR, Vijayachandran, M.D., Chief of Staff, John J. Pershing Veterans' Administration Medical Center, Poplar Bluff, MO, p. A382
NAJIEB, La Donna, Vice President, Human Resources, San Antonio Regional Hospital, Upland, CA, p. A99
NAJIEB, LaDonna, Service Area Director Human Resources, Providence Saint Josep. Medical Center, Burbank, CA, p. A58
NAJJAR, Maher, M.D., Medical Director, Kindred Hospital Chicago–Northlake, Northlake, IL, p. A204
NAKAGAWA, Marc, Chief Financial Officer, Palmdale Regional Medical Center, Palmdale, CA, p. A82
NAKAMOTO, Kenneth, M.D., Vice President Medical Affairs, Pomona Valley Hospital Medical Center, Pomona, CA, p. A84
NAKAMURA, Bridget, Director Information Systems, Adventist Health Simi Valley, Simi Valley, CA, p. A96
NAKASUJI, Jody, Chief Financial Officer, Harbor–Ucla Medical Center, Torrance, CA, p. A98
NALDI, Robert, Chief Financial Officer, Maimonides Medical Center, New York, NY, p. A449
NALL, Brian, Chief Executive Officer, Kindred Hospital Seattle–First Hill, Seattle, WA, p. A694
NALL, Wes, Chief Financial Officer, Monroe County Hospital, Monroeville, AL, p. A22
NALL, William
  Chief Nursing Officer, Iraan General Hospital, Iraan, TX, p. A630
  Interim Chief Executive Officer, Iraan General Hospital, Iraan, TX, p. A630
NALLEY, Leanna W, Director Human Resources, Texas Health Harris Methodist Hospital Southwest Fort Worth, Fort Worth, TX, p. A620
NANCE, Brett, M.D., Chief Medical Officer, Bear River Valley Hospital, Tremonton, UT, p. A670
NANCE, Christi, R.N., MSN, Chief Nursing Officer, Northwest Specialty Hospital, Post Falls, ID, p. A183
NANZER, Michael, FACHE, Chief Executive Officer, Forest View Psychiatric Hospital, Grand Rapids, MI, p. A328
NAPOLITANO, Mary Pat, Director Human Resources, Specialty Hospital of Central Jersey, Lakewood, NJ, p. A422
NARANG, Steve, M.D., President and President, Pediatric Service Line, Inova Fairfax Medical Campus, Falls Church, VA, p. A676
NARANJO, Maria, Director Human Resources, Memorial Hospital West, Pembroke Pines, FL, p. A146
NARBUTAS, Virgis, Chief Executive Officer, Lakewood Regional Medical Center, Lakewood, CA, p. A69
NARROW, Ann, Director of Nursing, River Hospital, Alexandria Bay, NY, p. A438
NARVAEZ, Andrea, R.N., Chief Nursing Officer, Adventhealth Parker, Parker, CO, p. A112
NASEATH, LeGay Marie, Chief Nursing Officer, Banner Churchill Community Hospital, Fallon, NV, p. A408
NASER, Bashar, Chief Financial Officer, Gerald Champion Regional Medical Center, Alamogordo, NM, p. A432
NASER, Mohammad, R.N., MSN, Chief Executive Officer, Centinela Hospital Medical Center, Inglewood, CA, p. A67
NASER, Tarek, Chief Financial Officer, St. Mary's Medical Center, West Palm Beach, FL, p. A154
NASH, Daniel J, Chief Information Officer, Emanate Health Inter–Community Hospital, Covina, CA, p. A61
NASH, Ernest
  Chief Financial Officer, South Texas Rehabilitation Hospital, Brownsville, TX, p. A605
  Chief Financial Officer, Weslaco Regional Rehabilitation Hospital, Weslaco, TX, p. A662

NASH, Gayle, R.N., M.P.H., Chief Nursing Officer, Mountainview Regional Medical Center, Las Cruces, NM, p. A435
NASH, Jacqueline, Controller, Corewell Health Wayne Hospital, Wayne, MI, p. A340
NASH, Sandra, Chief Fiscal Service, James H. Quillen Department of Veterans Affairs Medical Center, Johnson City, TN, p. A585
NASH, Tanika, Chief Financial Officer, De Soto Regional Health System, Mansfield, LA, p. A288
NASH, Tim, M.D., Chief of Staff, Board Vice Chairman, Marshall Medical Center, Lewisburg, TN, p. A587
NASHID, Nadia, M.D., Chief of Staff, Windham Hospital, Willimantic, CT, p. A120
NASLUND, Kevin, Manager Information Technology, Cherokee Regional Medical Center, Cherokee, IA, p. A232
NASO, Leanne, Chief Operating Officer, Adventhealth Parker, Parker, CO, p. A112
NASRALLAH, Fadi, M.D., Vice President Medical Affairs, Christus Mother Frances Hospital – Tyler, Tyler, TX, p. A658
NASSIEF, Raymond, Senior Vice President, Hospital Operations and Support Services, John Muir Medical Center, Walnut Creek, Walnut Creek, CA, p. A100
NASSTROM, Jeff, D.O., Chief of Staff, Mitchell County Regional Health Center, Osage, IA, p. A241
NAST, Ed, M.D., Chief Medical Officer, HCA Florida Oak Hill Hospital, Brooksville, FL, p. A127
NATAL, Yesenia, Coordinator Human Resources, Hospital Pavia Arecibo, Arecibo, PR, p. A731
NATCHER, Charles, Chief Financial Officer, Kindred Hospital–Los Angeles, Los Angeles, CA, p. A73
NATH, Pravene, Chief Information Officer, Stanford Health Care, Palo Alto, CA, p. A82
NATHANSON, Andrea, Director Finance, Baystate Franklin Medical Center, Greenfield, MA, p. A314
NAU, James, Manager Computer and Applications Support, Delaware Psychiatric Center, New Castle, DE, p. A121
NAUGHTON, Stacey, Chief Executive Officer, Select Specialty Hospital–North Knoxville, Powell, TN, p. A592
NAUMAN, Michael B
  Chief Information Officer, Children's Wisconsin, Milwaukee, WI, p. A717
  Chief Information Officer and Corporate Vice President, Children's Hospital of Wisconsin–Fox Valley, Neenah, WI, p. A718
NAUMOWICH, Sarah, President, St. Joseph's Hospital, Tampa, FL, p. A152
NAVA, Madeline, Chief Executive Officer, HCA Florida University Hospital, Davie, FL, p. A129
NAVARRO, Beth Ann, Chief Clinical Officer, Kindred Hospital–Sycamore, Sycamore, IL, p. A209
NAVARRO, Ramomita, Director Human Resources, University Hospital, San Juan, PR, p. A736
NAVARRO, Tess, Chief Financial Officer, Laguna Honda Hospital And Rehabilitation Center, San Francisco, CA, p. A91
NAVAS, Manuel, M.D., Medical Director, Hospital San Pablo Del Este Hima Fajardo, Fajardo, PR, p. A732
NAWAHINE, Steve, Chief Executive Officer, Kahuku Medical Center, Kahuku, HI, p. A176
NAWROCKI, Edward, President, St. Luke's Anderson Campus, Easton, PA, p. A539
NAYLOR, Angela
  Inpatient Chief Operating Executive and Chief Nursing Executive of Behavioral Health Network, Navos, Seattle, WA, p. A694
  Interim Chief Executive Officer, Wellfound Behavioral Health Hospital, Tacoma, WA, p. A697
NAZ, Haroon, Chief Executive Officer, Pinnacle Hospital, Crown Point, IN, p. A215
NAZARIAN, Jeanette, M.D., Vice President, Medical Affairs and Chief Medical Officer, Johns Hopkins Howard County Medical Center, Columbia, MD, p. A303
NAZARIO, Uriel, M.D., Chief of Medical Staff, Kindred Hospital North Florida, Green Cove Springs, FL, p. A133
NAZE, Jesse, Chief Financial Officer, Fall River Health Services, Hot Springs, SD, p. A574
NAZEER, Imran, M.D., Chief of Staff, Woodland Heights Medical Center, Lufkin, TX, p. A637
NAZIR, Tariq, Interim Director Information Technology, Signature Psychiatric Hospital, Kansas City, MO, p. A377
NCHEGE, Onyeka, Executive Vice President and Chief Digital and Information Officer, Novant Health Ballantyne Medical Center, Charlotte, NC, p. A465
NDIFORCHU, Fombe, Chief Medical Officer, Long Beach Medical Center, Long Beach, CA, p. A71
NDOMEA, Feisal, Director Case Management, Kindred Hospital Sugar Land, Sugar Land, TX, p. A654

NDOW, Emmanuel, Chief Information Officer, Marion Health, Marion, IN, p. A223
NEAL, Alisha, Chief Financial Officer, Slidell Memorial Hospital East, Slidell, LA, p. A293
NEAL, Bob, Information Technology, University of Michigan Health–Sparrow Ionia, Ionia, MI, p. A330
NEAL, Kaley, Chief Financial Officer, Shenandoah Medical Center, Shenandoah, IA, p. A243
NEAL, Robert, Manager Information Technology Services, Newman Memorial Hospital, Shattuck, OK, p. A520
NEAL, Roger, Chief Operating Officer, Duncan Regional Hospital, Duncan, OK, p. A512
NEAL, Tom, Chief Executive Officer and Chief Nursing Officer, Highlands–Cashiers Hospital, Highlands, NC, p. A470
NEALE, Debra, R.N., Chief Nursing Officer, O'Connor Hospital, Delhi, NY, p. A442
NEALON, Matthew, Vice President, Chief Financial Officer, University of Cincinnati Medical Center, Cincinnati, OH, p. A490
NEAR, Holly, Chief Administrative Officer, Harsha Behavioral Center, Terre Haute, IN, p. A228
NEAT, Gary
  Chief Information Officer, Ephraim Mcdowell Regional Medical Center, Danville, KY, p. A264
  Director Information Systems, Ephraim Mcdowell Fort Logan Hospital, Stanford, KY, p. A274
NEBLETT, Meika, M.D., Chief Medical Officer, Community Medical Center, Toms River, NJ, p. A429
NECAS, Kevin, Chief Financial Officer, University Hospital, Columbia, MO, p. A374
NEEB, Verette, R.N., MSN, Chief Nursing Officer, Baylor Scott & White Medical Center–Uptown, Dallas, TX, p. A610
NEECE, Patrick, Chief Information Officer, Lake Regional Health System, Osage Beach, MO, p. A381
NEEDHAM, Denise
  PharmD, President, Mainehealth Pen Bay Medical Center, Rockport, ME, p. A299
  PharmD, President, Waldo County General Hospital, Belfast, ME, p. A296
NEEDHAM, Kim, Assistant Chief Executive Officer, Vista Medical Center East, Waukegan, IL, p. A210
NEEDHAM, Priscilla, CPA, Chief Financial Officer, Billings Clinic, Billings, MT, p. A389
NEEDHAM, Tammy, Chief Nursing Officer, UNC Health Chatham, Siler City, NC, p. A476
NEEDLES, Kim, Manager Business Office, Patients' Hospital of Redding, Redding, CA, p. A85
NEELEY, Scott, M.D., President and Chief Executive Officer, Sierra Nevada Memorial Hospital, Grass Valley, CA, p. A66
NEELY, Denise, Vice President and Chief Nursing Officer, Bronson Methodist Hospital, Kalamazoo, MI, p. A331
NEELY, Jill, Chief Financial Officer, Titusville Area Hospital, Titusville, PA, p. A555
NEELY, K. Dale., FACHE, Chief Executive Officer, Memorial Satilla Health, Waycross, GA, p. A174
NEELY, Kathy E.
  R.N., Interim Vice President Patient Care Services, Chi St. Vincent Infirmary, Little Rock, AR, p. A49
  R.N., Interim Vice President Patient Care Services, Chi St. Vincent Morrilton, Morrilton, AR, p. A51
NEELY, Randall, CEO, Simpson General Hospital, Mendenhall, MS, p. A366
NEENAN, Sharon, Interim Chief Nursing Officer, Grant, Ohiohealth Grant Medical Center, Columbus, OH, p. A492
NEERGHEEN, Chabilal, M.D., Medical Director, Western Massachusetts Hospital, Westfield, MA, p. A319
NEESEN, Cindy, Director of Information Technology, Butler County Health Care Center, David City, NE, p. A399
NEFF, Josh, Chief Executive Officer, Commonspirit – Mercy Hospital, Durango, CO, p. A107
NEFF, Kris, Chief Operating Officer, Samaritan Healthcare, Moses Lake, WA, p. A692
NEFF, William, M.D., Chief Medical Officer, UCHealth Medical Center of The Rockies, Loveland, CO, p. A112
NEGRON, Manuel, Chief Information Technology Service, Veterans Affairs Caribbean Healthcare System, San Juan, PR, p. A736
NEGULESCU, Catalina R., M.D., Medical Officer, Baton Rouge Rehabilitation Hospital, Baton Rouge, LA, p. A277
NEIDENBACH, John, Administrator, Northeast Georgia Medical Center Barrow, Winder, GA, p. A174
NEIGER, Kelly, Chief Financial Officer, Barton Memorial Hospital, South Lake Tahoe, CA, p. A96
NEIKIRK, Richard, Chief Executive Officer, Cumberland County Hospital, Burkesville, KY, p. A264
NEIL, William, Vice President and Chief Information Officer, Cleveland Clinic Indian River Hospital, Vero Beach, FL, p. A154
NEILSON, Carol, CPA, Area Controller, Encompass Health Rehabilitation Hospital of Pearland, Pearland, TX, p. A643

NEILSON, Erinn, Chief Nursing Officer, Minidoka Memorial Hospital, Rupert, ID, p. A183
NEILSON, Richard, Director of Information Services, Timpanogos Regional Hospital, Orem, UT, p. A667
NEIMAN, Carla A., Chief Financial Officer, Clark Fork Valley Hospital, Plains, MT, p. A394
NEISWONGER, Randy, Chief Operating Officer, Community Hospital, Munster, IN, p. A224
NEITZEL, Monte, Chief Executive Officer, Greater Regional Health, Creston, IA, p. A234
NELL, Sergio, Director Information Systems, Watsonville Community Hospital, Watsonville, CA, p. A100
NELLSCH, Verner, M.D., Chief of Staff, St. Luke's Health – Memorial Livingston, Livingston, TX, p. A635
NELSON, Allison
   Chief Financial Officer, Sanford Canby Medical Center, Canby, MN, p. A344
   Chief Financial Officer, Sanford Clear Lake Medical Center, Clear Lake, SD, p. A572
NELSON, Barbara J, Ph.D., R.N., Chief Nursing Executive, Sutter Roseville Medical Center, Roseville, CA, p. A86
NELSON, Barry, MSN, Vice President Nursing, Chief Nurse Executive, UNC Health Blue Ridge, Morganton, NC, p. A473
NELSON, Bill
   Chief Executive Officer, Mille Lacs Health System, Onamia, MN, p. A352
   Chief Executive Officer and Chair, Governing Board, West Covina Medical Center, West Covina, CA, p. A101
NELSON, Christopher, President, St. Josep. Hospital, Bethpage, NY, p. A439
NELSON, Clifford, Chief Financial Officer, Suncoast Behavioral Health Center, Bradenton, FL, p. A127
NELSON, Cory D., Administrator, Sioux Center Health, Sioux Center, IA, p. A243
NELSON, David, M.D., Medical Director, Barlow Respiratory Hospital, Los Angeles, CA, p. A71
NELSON, David A., President and Chief Executive Officer, Chi St. Francis Health, Breckenridge, MN, p. A344
NELSON, Dawn, Director Human Resources, Sagewest Health Care, Riverton, WY, p. A728
NELSON, Diane, R.N., Chief Nursing Officer, Kindred Hospital–Albuquerque, Albuquerque, NM, p. A432
NELSON, Elaine, R.N., MSN, Chief Nursing Officer, Texas Health Harris Methodist Hospital Fort Worth, Fort Worth, TX, p. A620
NELSON, Heather, Senior Vice President and Chief Information Officer, Boston Children's Hospital, Boston, MA, p. A310
NELSON, Jack, Vice President Finance and Chief Financial Officer, Heritage Valley Kennedy, Mckees Rocks, PA, p. A545
NELSON, Jackie, Director Human Resources, Hansford Hospital, Spearman, TX, p. A653
NELSON, James J, Senior Vice President Finance and Strategic Planning, Fort Healthcare, Fort Atkinson, WI, p. A711
NELSON, Jamie, Vice President and Chief Information Officer, Hospital for Special Surgery, New York, NY, p. A448
NELSON, Jennifer, Senior Human Resource Business Partner, Corewell Health Greenville Hospital, Greenville, MI, p. A329
NELSON, Jody, Chief Executive Officer, St. Luke's Medical Center, Crosby, ND, p. A480
NELSON, John, Chief of Staff, Merit Health Biloxi, Biloxi, MS, p. A359
NELSON, Joseph, M.D., President Medical Staff, Lewisgale Medical Center, Boones Mill, VA, p. A674
NELSON, Julia, Vice President of Human Resources, Northern Regional Hospital, Mount Airy, NC, p. A473
NELSON, Katey
   Chief Human Resource Officer, Sanpete Valley Hospital, Mount Pleasant, UT, p. A666
   Director Human Resources, Sevier Valley Hospital, Richfield, UT, p. A668
NELSON, Kellie, Director Human Resources, Aurora Medical Center Kenosha, Kenosha, WI, p. A713
NELSON, Kenneth E, R.N., III, Chief Nursing Officer, HSHS St. Vincent Hospital, Green Bay, WI, p. A712
NELSON, Kerri, Chief Financial Officer, Corewell Health Ludington Hospital, Ludington, MI, p. A332
NELSON, Kody, Chief Executive Officer, Sheridan Memorial Hospital, Plentywood, MT, p. A394
NELSON, Lucy, Director Finance, Vice President, Maniilaq Health Center, Kotzebue, AK, p. A29
NELSON, Lynn M., R.N., R.N., Chief Nursing Officer and Chief Operating Officer, St. John's Riverside Hospital, Yonkers, NY, p. A462
NELSON, Marlin Pete, Vice President Fiscal Services, Aspirus Divine Savior Hospital & Clinics, Portage, WI, p. A720
NELSON, Martha
   Chief Financial Officer, Antelop. Memorial Hospital, Neligh, NE, p. A403
   Chief Financial Officer, Niobrara Valley Hospital, Lynch, NE, p. A402
NELSON, Melissa, Assistant Administrator, Baptist Memorial Hospital for Women, Memphis, TN, p. A588
NELSON, Michael
   Chief Financial Officer, Select Specialty Hospital Midtown Atlanta, Atlanta, GA, p. A158
   Executive Vice President and Chief Financial Officer, Pomona Valley Hospital Medical Center, Pomona, CA, p. A84
NELSON, Nan, Senior Vice President Finance, Aurora St. Luke's Medical Center, Milwaukee, WI, p. A717
NELSON, Nancy, Director Human Resources, Intermountain Hospital, Boise, ID, p. A179
NELSON, Nick, Director Support Services, Adams Memorial Hospital, Decatur, IN, p. A215
NELSON, Raymond, Acting Chief Information Resource Management, Fargo Va Medical Center, Fargo, ND, p. A480
NELSON, Richard, Chief of Human Resources Management Services, John L. Mcclellan Memorial Veterans' Hospital, Little Rock, AR, p. A50
NELSON, Robert, Chief Executive Officer, Alta Vista Regional Hospital, Las Vegas, NM, p. A435
NELSON, Robin, Chief Financial Officer, Gundersen St. Joseph's Hospital And Clinics, Hillsboro, WI, p. A713
NELSON, Selena, Chief Financial Officer, Fallon Medical Complex, Baker, MT, p. A389
NELSON, Siri, Chief Executive Officer, Marshall Medical Center, Placerville, CA, p. A83
NELSON, Stewart R
   Vice President and Chief Financial Officer, Sentara Halifax Regional Hospital, South Boston, VA, p. A684
   Vice President and Chief Financial Officer, Sentara Martha Jefferson Hospital, Charlottesville, VA, p. A674
   Vice President and Chief Financial Officer, Sentara Rmh Medical Center, Harrisonburg, VA, p. A677
NELSON, Suzanne, R.N., Director of Nursing, Salt Lake Behavioral Health, Salt Lake City, UT, p. A669
NELSON, Tara, Chief Clinic Officer, Hutchinson Health, Hutchinson, MN, p. A348
NELSON, Tricia, Chief Financial Officer, Musc Health Rehabilitation Hospital, An Affiliate of Encompass Health, Charleston, SC, p. A563
NELSON, Trudy, Chief Human Resource Officer, Niobrara Valley Hospital, Lynch, NE, p. A402
NELSON–JONES, Susan, Director Human Resources, Adventist Health Tehachap. Valley, Tehachapi, CA, p. A97
NEMECHEK, Victor, M.D., Chief of Staff and Chief Medical Officer, Sheridan County Health Complex, Hoxie, KS, p. A251
NEMENS, Julie, Chief Administrative Officer, University of Maryland Rehabilitation & Orthopaedic Institute, Baltimore, MD, p. A302
NEMETH, Jim, FACHE, Chief Executive Officer, Oakleaf Surgical Hospital, Altoona, WI, p. A707
NEMI, Neil, Administrator Facility Information Center, Richard H. Hutchings Psychiatric Center, Syracuse, NY, p. A460
NESMITH, Nikki, Chief Nursing Officer, Evans Memorial Hospital, Claxton, GA, p. A160
NESPOLI, John L, President, St. Luke's University Hospital – Bethlehem Campus, Bethlehem, PA, p. A535
NESPOLI, John L., President, St. Luke's Carbon Campus, Lehighton, PA, p. A544
NESS, David L, Vice President Operations, Unitypoint Health – Grinnell Regional Medical Center, Grinnell, IA, p. A236
NESS, Joe, Chief Operating Officer, Ohsu Hospital, Portland, OR, p. A530
NESSEL, Mark, Executive Vice President and Chief Operating Officer, Virtua Our Lady of Lourdes Hospital, Camden, NJ, p. A419
NESSELRODT, Derek, Director Information Systems, Grant Memorial Hospital, Petersburg, WV, p. A703
NESTE, Donna, Chief Executive Officer, Wheatland Memorial Healthcare, Harlowton, MT, p. A393
NESTER, Brian A., D.O., President and Chief Executive Officer, Lehigh Valley Hospital–Cedar Crest, Allentown, PA, p. A534
NESTER, Darlene E.
   Chief Human Resources Officer, Hilton Head Hospital, Hilton Head Island, SC, p. A568
   Market Chief Human Resources Officer, Coastal Carolina Hospital, Hardeeville, SC, p. A568
NESTER, Michael, Chief Executive Officer, Winston Medical Center, Louisville, MS, p. A365
NESTER WOLFE, Cheryl R.
   R.N., President and Chief Executive Officer, Salem Health West Valley, Dallas, OR, p. A526
   R.N., President and Chief Executive Officer, Salem Hospital, Salem, OR, p. A532
NESTLER, Nicole, Division Director Human Resources, Chi Mercy Health, Valley City, ND, p. A483
NETTLES, Angela F, Vice President, Human Resources and Support Services, Musc Health Kershaw Medical Center, Camden, SC, p. A562
NETTLES, Robert, Director Human Resources, Mountainview Hospital, Las Vegas, NV, p. A410
NETZER, Craig, M.D., President Medical Staff, Wilcox Medical Center, Lihue, HI, p. A177
NEUBAUER, Stacy, R.N., Chief Executive Officer, Harlan County Health System, Alma, NE, p. A397
NEUBERT, Todd, President, Riverton Hospital, Riverton, UT, p. A668
NEUENDORF, Deborah, Vice President Administration, New York–Presbyterian/Hudson Valley Hospital, Cortlandt Manor, NY, p. A442
NEUENDORF, James, M.D., Medical Director, Saint Joseph's Medical Center, Yonkers, NY, p. A462
NEUFELD, Ellis, M.D., Chief Medical Officer, St. Jude Children's Research Hospital, Memphis, TN, p. A589
NEUGENT, Kevin, Chief Information Officer, University of Michigan Health–Sparrow Eaton, Charlotte, MI, p. A323
NEUJAHR, Elias
   Chief Executive Officer, VCU Medical Center, Richmond, VA, p. A683
   President, Children's Hospital of Richmond At Vcu, Richmond, VA, p. A682
NEUMAN, Keith A.
   Chief Information Officer, Lutheran Hospital of Indiana, Fort Wayne, IN, p. A216
   Chief Information Officer, Orthopaedic Hospital of Lutheran Health Network, Fort Wayne, IN, p. A216
NEUMAN, Michael J, Vice President Finance, Kennedy Krieger Institute, Baltimore, MD, p. A300
NEUMEISTER, Daniel P, Senior Vice President and Chief Operating Officer, Searhc Mt. Edgecumbe Hospital, Sitka, AK, p. A29
NEUNER, Kathy, R.N., Chief Nursing Officer, Norton Clark Hospital, Jeffersonville, IN, p. A221
NEUSCHWANGER, Elizabeth, Chief Nursing Officer, Ohiohealth Van Wert Hospital, Van Wert, OH, p. A505
NEUVIRTH, Stephanie, Chief Human Resource and Diversity Officer, City of Hope's Helford Clinical Research Hospital, Duarte, CA, p. A62
NEVILLE, Bette, R.N., MSN, Vice President and Chief Nursing Officer, Northern Light Mercy Hospital, Portland, ME, p. A298
NEVILLE, Lawrence, Chief Medical Officer, Peacehealth Southwest Medical Center, Vancouver, WA, p. A698
NEVILLE, Michelle, Chief Executive Officer, Greenleaf Behavioral Health Hospital, Valdosta, GA, p. A173
NEVILLE, Ryan T., FACHE, President Northeast Market, Holy Family Memorial, Manitowoc, WI, p. A715
NEVIN, James, M.D., Vice President and Chief Medical Officer, Carle Bromenn Medical Center, Normal, IL, p. A203
NEVIN, Janice E.
   M.D., M.P.H., President and Chief Executive Officer, Christianacare, Newark, DE, p. A122
   M.D., M.P.H., President and Chief Executive Officer, Christianacare, Union Hospital, Elkton, MD, p. A304
NEVINS, Norm, Manager Human Resources, Kansas Medical Center, Andover, KS, p. A246
NEWBOLD WELGE, Melissa, Chief Executive Officer, Anderson Rehabilitation Institute, Edwardsville, IL, p. A193
NEWBY, Doug, Chief Information Officer, Highlands Medical Center, Scottsboro, AL, p. A24
NEWBY, Jennifer, Vice President of Operational Finance and Chief Financial Officer, Memorial Community Hospital And Health System, Blair, NE, p. A398
NEWCOMB, James
   M.D., Vice President Medical, Slidell Memorial Hospital East, Slidell, LA, p. A293
   M.D., Vice President Medical Affairs, Slidell Memorial Hospital, Slidell, LA, p. A293
NEWCOMB, Michael
   D.O., Senior Vice President and Chief Operating Officer, Legacy Meridian Park Medical Center, Tualatin, OR, p. A533
   D.O., Senior Vice President and Chief Operating Officer, Legacy Mount Hood Medical Center, Gresham, OR, p. A527
   D.O., Senior Vice President and Chief Operating Officer, Legacy Salmon Creek Medical Center, Vancouver, WA, p. A698
NEWCOMBE, William, Chief Executive Officer and Managing Director, North Star Behavioral Health System, Anchorage, AK, p. A27

Index of Health Care Professionals / Nighman

NEWCOMER, Jeremy, Director Information Services, Elmira Psychiatric Center, Elmira, NY, p. A443
NEWCOMER, Peter, M.D., Chief Medical Officer, University Hospital, Madison, WI, p. A714
NEWELL, Dan, Chief Financial Officer, Highlands Medical Center, Scottsboro, AL, p. A24
NEWELL, Janice
Chief Information Officer, Providence Swedish Cherry Hill, Seattle, WA, p. A694
Chief Information Officer, Providence Swedish First Hill, Seattle, WA, p. A694
NEWELL, Richard, President and Chief Executive Officer, Temple Health–Chestnut Hill Hospital, Philadelphia, PA, p. A550
NEWEY, Mark, D.O., Chief of Staff, Mercy Hospital Healdton, Healdton, OK, p. A513
NEWHOUSE, Chuck, M.D., Chief of Staff, Boundary Community Hospital, Bonners Ferry, ID, p. A180
NEWHOUSE, Paul R., President, Union Medical Center, Union, SC, p. A571
NEWMAN, Carlotta Hannah, Human Resources Manager, Northeast Georgia Medical Center Barrow, Winder, GA, p. A174
NEWMAN, Cynthia, Manager Human Resources, Petersburg Medical Center, Petersburg, AK, p. A29
NEWMAN, Jennifer, Director of Human Resources, Grace Cottage Hospital, Townshend, VT, p. A672
NEWMAN, Jinny, Director Human Resources, Emanuel Medical Center, Swainsboro, GA, p. A172
NEWMAN, Karen, Ed.D., MSN, R.N., Vice President and Chief Nursing Officer, Baptist Health Louisville, Louisville, KY, p. A269
NEWMILLER, Vicki
President, Logan Health – Conrad, Conrad, MT, p. A390
President, Logan Health Shelby, Shelby, MT, p. A395
NEWSOM, Jeremiah, M.D., Medical Director, Ochsner Extended Care Hospital, New Orleans, LA, p. A289
NEWSOM, Terri T., Vice President of Finance and Chief Financial Officer, Prisma Health Greenville Memorial Hospital, Greenville, SC, p. A567
NEWSOME, George, Director, Commonwealth Center for Children And Adolescents, Staunton, VA, p. A684
NEWSOME, Joe, Chief Nursing Officer, Blount Memorial Hospital, Maryville, TN, p. A587
NEWSWANGER, Jeff, M.D., Chief Medical Officer, Adventhealth Manchester, Manchester, KY, p. A271
NEWTON, Ann, Chief Executive Officer, Chambers Health, Anahuac, TX, p. A597
NEWTON, Bradford, Chief Information Officer, North Memorial Health Hospital, Robbinsdale, MN, p. A353
NEWTON, Gail, R.N., MSN, Vice President Patient Care Services, St. Luke's Hospital – Warren Campus, Phillipsburg, NJ, p. A427
NEWTON, Jennifer, R.N., Chief Nursing Officer, Neosho Memorial Regional Medical Center, Chanute, KS, p. A247
NEWTON, Susan, Chief Operating Officer, Broward Health North, Deerfield Beach, FL, p. A130
NEWTON, Terri, Chief Nursing Officer, Lakewood Regional Medical Center, Lakewood, CA, p. A69
NEWTON, Wilma, Executive Vice President and Chief Financial Officer, Ascension St. Vincent's Birmingham, Birmingham, AL, p. A16
NEYENHOUSE, Rich, Director Information Technology, Thayer County Health Services, Hebron, NE, p. A401
NEZBETH, Jacqueline, Human Resources Officer, Select Specialty Hospital of Southeast Ohio, Newark, OH, p. A501
NG, Anthony, M.D., Vice President and Chief Medical Officer, The Acadia Hospital, Bangor, ME, p. A295
NG, Hong–Kin, M.D., Chief Medical Officer, Roane General Hospital, Spencer, WV, p. A705
NG, Thomas T., Chief Information Officer, Collingsworth General Hospital, Wellington, TX, p. A661
NG, Vincent
Director, Veterans Affairs Boston Healthcare System Brockton Division, Brockton, MA, p. A312
Medical Center Director, Veterans Affairs Boston Healthcare System, West Roxbury, MA, p. A319
NGIRAISUI, Clarinda, Director, Human Resources, Commonwealth Health Center, Saipan, MARIANA ISLANDS, p. A730
NGUYEN, Abby, R.N., Chief Nursing Officer, Genesis Healthcare System, Zanesville, OH, p. A508
NGUYEN, Anthony, Chief Executive Officer, San Gabriel Valley Medical Center, San Gabriel, CA, p. A91
NGUYEN, Bach, Director Information Systems, Northwest Texas Healthcare System, Amarillo, TX, p. A596
NGUYEN, Hai H., CPA, Vice President Finance, Livengrin Foundation, Bensalem, PA, p. A535
NGUYEN, Huy, M.D., Chief Executive Officer, Doctors Memorial Hospital, Bonifay, FL, p. A126
NGUYEN, Jinhee, Patient Care Executive, Adventist Health Glendale, Glendale, CA, p. A66
NGUYEN, Nga, Manager Human Resources and Organizational Development, Glendale Memorial Hospital And Health Center, Glendale, CA, p. A66
NGUYEN, Phuong Hoang, M.D., Chief Medical Officer, Santa Clara Valley Medical Center, San Jose, CA, p. A92
NGUYEN, Vu Thuy, M.D., Medical Director, Kaiser Permanente Baldwin Park Medical Center, Baldwin Park, CA, p. A57
NIBLOCK, Jenny, Chief Clinical Officer, Citizens Medical Center, Colby, KS, p. A247
NICAUD, Kent, President and Chief Executive Officer, Memorial Hospital At Gulfport, Gulfport, MS, p. A362
NICHELSON, Kathleen, Director Human Resources, The Horsham Clinic, Ambler, PA, p. A534
NICHOLAS, Angela, Vice President, Medical Affairs, Jefferson Einstein Montgomery Hospital, East Norriton, PA, p. A538
NICHOLAS, Chris, Chief Executive Officer, Renown Regional Medical Center, Reno, NV, p. A412
NICHOLAS, David, Chief Executive Officer, St. John Rehabilitation Hospital, Broken Arrow, OK, p. A510
NICHOLS, Bryan
Chief Financial Officer, Baylor Scott & White The Heart Hospital Denton, Denton, TX, p. A613
Chief Financial Officer, Baylor Scott & White The Heart Hospital Plano, Plano, TX, p. A644
NICHOLS, Carl W.
III, Chief Executive Officer, Select Specialty Hospital – Boardman, Boardman, OH, p. A486
III, Market Chief Executive Officer, Select Specialty Hospital – Boardman, Boardman, OH, p. A486
NICHOLS, Christopher, Chief Executive Officer, Fillmore County Hospital, Geneva, NE, p. A400
NICHOLS, Donna, R.N., Chief Nursing Officer, Goodall–Witcher Hospital, Clifton, TX, p. A607
NICHOLS, Greg, Chief Executive Officer, East Alabama Medical Center, Opelika, AL, p. A23
NICHOLS, Laura L, Director Human Resources, Hancock Regional Hospital, Greenfield, IN, p. A218
NICHOLS, Lisa, President, Ascension St. Vincent's St. Clair, Pell City, AL, p. A23
NICHOLS, Matt, Chief Financial Officer, St. Bernards Five Rivers, Pocahontas, AR, p. A52
NICHOLS, Nathan, Director of Finance, Sterling Regional Medcenter, Sterling, CO, p. A113
NICHOLS, Randy
Chief Financial Officer, Great River Medical Center, Blytheville, AR, p. A43
Chief Financial Officer, SMC Regional Medical Center, Osceola, AR, p. A52
NICHOLS, Robin, Interim Chief Financial Officer, Emory Decatur Hospital, Decatur, GA, p. A162
NICHOLS, Suzanne, Director Human Resources, Muleshoe Area Medical Center, Muleshoe, TX, p. A640
NICHOLS, Terry, Chief Executive Officer, Cedar County Memorial Hospital, El Dorado Springs, MO, p. A374
NICHOLSON, Britain, M.D., Chief Medical Officer, Massachusetts General Hospital, Boston, MA, p. A310
NICHOLSON, Charles, Vice President, Medical Affairs, Sentara Albemarle Medical Center, Elizabeth City, NC, p. A468
NICHOLSON, Chrissy, Vice President of Human Resources, Delta Health–The Medical Center, Greenville, MS, p. A362
NICHOLSON, Cindy, Director Human Resources, Shelby Baptist Medical Center, Alabaster, AL, p. A15
NICHOLSON, Debra, Manager Finance, Central Alabama Va Medical Center–Montgomery, Montgomery, AL, p. A22
NICHOLSON, Kristin, Coordinator Human Resources, Genesis Medical Center, Dewitt, De Witt, IA, p. A234
NICHOSON, Julia, M.D., Chief Medical Officer, Baptist Health Medical Center – Drew County, Monticello, AR, p. A50
NICKEL, Jarret, Operations Executive, North Central Health Care, Wausau, WI, p. A724
NICKEL, Kathleen, Director Communications, Mercy Medical Center, Roseburg, OR, p. A531
NICKELL, Jerry, Vice President Human Resource and Mission, Saint Alphonsus Medical Center – Baker City, Baker City, OR, p. A525
NICKELS, John, M.D., President Medical Staff, Grace Hospital, Cleveland, OH, p. A490
NICKELSON, Autumn Jesse.
Executive Director, Northwest Center for Behavioral Health, Woodward, OK, p. A524
Executive Director, Tulsa Center for Behavioral Health, Tulsa, OK, p. A523
NICKENS, John R.
IV, Chief Executive Officer, Children's Hospital New Orleans, New Orleans, LA, p. A290
IV, President and Chief Executive Officer, University Medical Center, New Orleans, LA, p. A290
NICKENS, Wesley, M.D., Chief of Staff, Collingsworth General Hospital, Wellington, TX, p. A661
NICKLES, Ashton, DPM, Chief Medical Officer, Mercyone Clinton Medical Center, Clinton, IA, p. A233
NICKOLES, Jennifer, President, Johns Hopkins Bayview Medical Center, Baltimore, MD, p. A300
NICKRAND, Tami, Director Information Technology, Harbor Beach Community Hospital Inc., Harbor Beach, MI, p. A329
NICKS, Bret, M.D., Chief Medical Officer and Chief of Staff, Atrium Health Wake Forest Baptist Davie Medical Center, Bermuda Run, NC, p. A463
NICOLAS, Fadi, M.D., Chief Medical Officer, Sharp Mesa Vista Hospital, San Diego, CA, p. A90
NICOLL, C. Diana, M.D., Ph.D., Chief of Staff, San Francisco Va Health Care System, San Francisco, CA, p. A91
NICOLSON, Lynne T, M.D., Medical Director, Sunnyview Rehabilitation Hospital, Schenectady, NY, p. A459
NICOSIA, Chris, Chief Financial Officer, Corpus Christi Medical Center – Doctors Regional, Corpus Christi, TX, p. A609
NIEDEREE, Laurie, M.D., Chief Medical Officer, Alta View Hospital, Sandy, UT, p. A669
NIELSEN, Ben
Vice President, Chief Operating Officer, Ridgeview Medical Center, Waconia, MN, p. A356
Vice President, Chief Operating Officer, Ridgeview Sibley Medical Center, Arlington, MN, p. A342
NIELSEN, Gregory, Chief Executive Officer, East Jefferson General Hospital, Metairie, LA, p. A288
NIELSEN, Gwen, Manager Human Resources, Indianhead Medical Center, Shell Lake, WI, p. A721
NIELSEN, Helen V
Director Human Resources, Lovelace Medical Center, Albuquerque, NM, p. A432
Director Human Resources, Lovelace Unm Rehabilitation Hospital, Albuquerque, NM, p. A432
NIELSEN, Kristine, Manager Human Resources, Memorial Community Hospital And Health System, Blair, NE, p. A398
NIELSEN, Randy, Director Information Technology, Arbor Health, Morton Hospital, Morton, WA, p. A691
NIELSEN, Wayne, Director Human Resources, HCA Florida Ocala Hospital, Ocala, FL, p. A143
NIELSON, Curtis, Chief Financial Officer, South Lincoln Medical Center, Kemmerer, WY, p. A727
NIELSON, Lars, M.D., Chief Medical Officer, Weeks Medical Center, Lancaster, NH, p. A415
NIELSON, P Douglas, M.D., Chief of Staff, Kahuku Medical Center, Kahuku, HI, p. A176
NIELSON, Yvonne, Chief Nursing Officer, Director Quality Management and Regulatory Compliance, Mountain West Medical Center, Tooele, UT, p. A670
NIEMALA, Amanda, Director of Information Services, Bigfork Valley Hospital, Bigfork, MN, p. A343
NIEMANN, Larry, Chief Executive Officer, KPC Promise Hospital of Phoenix, Mesa, AZ, p. A34
NIEMANN, Lynne, Director Nurses and Patient Care, Community Memorial Hospital, Sumner, IA, p. A244
NIENHUIS, Jamie, Chief Nursing Officer, Langdon Prairie Health, Langdon, ND, p. A482
NIERMANN, Micah, Chief Medical Officer, Gillette Children's Specialty Healthcare, Saint Paul, MN, p. A354
NIERSTEDT, Kelly
President, Orlando Health Orlando Regional Medical Center, Orlando, FL, p. A144
President, OSF Saint Francis Medical Center, Peoria, IL, p. A206
NIES, Lynn, Human Resources Officer, Erie Veterans Affairs Medical Center, Erie, PA, p. A539
NIESE, Mel, Chief Fiscal Service, VA Palo Alto Heath Care System, Palo Alto, CA, p. A82
NIESEN, Matthew, M.D., Chief of the Medical Staff, Prairie Ridge Health, Inc., Columbus, WI, p. A709
NIESSINK, Henry
Regional Director Information Technology Services, Mercy Medical Center Redding, Redding, CA, p. A85
Senior Manager Information Technology Systems, St. Elizabeth Community Hospital, Red Bluff, CA, p. A85
NIEVES, Deborah, Director Management Information Systems, Hospital San Francisco, San Juan, PR, p. A735
NIEVES, Erick, M.D., Medical Director, Hospital San Carlos Borromeo, Moca, PR, p. A733
NIEVES MARTINEZ, Ruthmaris, Chief Executive Officer, Encompass Health Rehabilitation Hospital of Manati, Manati, PR, p. A733
NIGG, Nicole, Chief Executive Officer, Mercyone Clive Rehabilitation Hospital, Clive, IA, p. A233
NIGH, Andrew, M.D., Chief of Staff, Indiana University Health West Hospital, Avon, IN, p. A212
NIGHMAN, Mike, Facility Coordinator Information Systems, Shelby Baptist Medical Center, Alabaster, AL, p. A15

Index of Health Care Professionals

© 2025 AHA Guide Index of Health Care Professionals A933

Index of Health Care Professionals

Index of Health Care Professionals / Nightengale

NIGHTENGALE, Randy, Chief Financial Officer, Bingham Memorial Hospital, Blackfoot, ID, p. A179
NIGON, Scott, Finance Senior Manager, Essentia Health St. Mary's Hospital of Superior, Superior, WI, p. A722
NIHALANI, Sunil, M.D., Chief Medical Staff, Adventhealth Lake Wales, Lake Wales, FL, p. A136
NIJOKA, Monica, Chief Nursing Officer, Baton Rouge General Medical Center, Baton Rouge, LA, p. A277
NIKAIDO, Mavis Hiroko, Vice President of Patient Services and Chief Nurse Executive, Kapiolani Medical Center for Women & Children, Honolulu, HI, p. A175
NIKITIN, Victoria, Chief Financial Officer, Harris Health System, Bellaire, TX, p. A603
NILES, EZ, Executive Director of Information Technology, Ozarks Healthcare, West Plains, MO, p. A388
NILES, Heather, Director Human Resources Operations, Mercyhealth Hospital And Medical Center – Harvard, Harvard, IL, p. A197
NILEST, Nicholas, Chief Executive Officer, New Braunfels Regional Rehabilitation Hospital, New Braunfels, TX, p. A641
NIMMO, Ben, M.D., Medical Director, Pinnacle Pointe Behavioral Healthcare System, Little Rock, AR, p. A50
NIMMO, Brian, Medical Center Director, Huntington Veterans Affairs Medical Center, Huntington, WV, p. A702
NIMS, Carrie, Director of Nursing, Post Acute/Warm Springs Specialty Hospital of San Antonio, San Antonio, TX, p. A650
NINNEMAN, David, Associate Director, Cincinnati Veterans Affairs Medical Center, Cincinnati, OH, p. A488
NIPPER, Nathan
Chief Operating Officer, Piedmont Fayette Hospital, Fayetteville, GA, p. A164
Vice President and Chief Operating Officer, Piedmont Newnan Hospital, Newnan, GA, p. A169
NIPPERT, Kathi, Acting Chief Human Resources Officer, Kansas City Va Medical Center, Kansas City, MO, p. A377
NISH, Paulette, Chief Nursing Officer, Geisinger Jersey Shore Hospital, Jersey Shore, PA, p. A542
NISKANEN, Brian, Chief Medical Officer, Welia Health, Mora, MN, p. A351
NISKANEN, Grant, M.D., Vice President Medical Affairs, Sky Lakes Medical Center, Klamath Falls, OR, p. A528
NISSEN, Beth
Director Human Resources, Troy Regional Medical Center, Troy, AL, p. A25
Human Resources Director, University of Iowa Health Network Rehabilitation Hospital, Coralville, IA, p. A233
NIU, Paul, Chief Medical Officer, Corona Regional Medical Center, Corona, CA, p. A60
NIX, Alisha, Director Human Resources, Wilbarger General Hospital, Vernon, TX, p. A659
NIX, Bo, Chief Information Officer, Madison Valley Medical Center, Ennis, MT, p. A391
NIXDORF, David L, Director Support Services, Frances Mahon Deaconess Hospital, Glasgow, MT, p. A392
NIXON, James, Chief Operating Officer, Memorial Health Meadows Hospital, Vidalia, GA, p. A173
NIXON, Myra, Director Human Resources, Encompass Health Rehabilitation Hospital of Concord, Concord, NH, p. A414
NIZAMI, Nassar, Chief Information Officer, Thomas Jefferson University Hospital, Philadelphia, PA, p. A550
NJAU, Caronline, Chief Nursing Officer & Senior Vice President, Patient Care, Children's Minnesota, Minneapolis, MN, p. A350
NNAJI, Felix, Chief Medical Staff, West Tennessee Healthcare Bolivar Hospital, Bolivar, TN, p. A579
NOAK, Amy, Director Human Resources, St. David's Round Rock Medical Center, Round Rock, TX, p. A648
NOBLE, Angel, Chief Nursing Officer, West Feliciana Hospital, Saint Francisville, LA, p. A292
NOBLE, Dave, Director of Nursing, Livingston Healthcare, Livingston, MT, p. A394
NOBLE, Mallie S., Chief Executive Officer, Mary Breckinridge Arh Hospital, Hyden, KY, p. A267
NOBLES, Diane, Nurse Executive, East Mississipp. State Hospital, Meridian, MS, p. A366
NOBLES, Sharon
Chief Financial Officer, North Mississipp. Medical Center – Tupelo, Tupelo, MS, p. A369
Interim Chief Financial Officer, Baptist Hospital, Pensacola, FL, p. A146
NOBLIN, Jeff, FACHE, President, Mainehealth Stephens Hospital, Norway, ME, p. A298
NOCKOWITZ, Richard, M.D., Medical Director, Ohio Hospital for Psychiatry, Columbus, OH, p. A492
NOE, Sharon, Chief Executive Officer, Pam Health Rehabilitation Hospital of Surprise, Surprise, AZ, p. A39
NOEL, Bill, Chief Operating Officer, Grand River Hospital District, Rifle, CO, p. A113
NOEL, Vicki, Vice President Human Resources, Southern Ohio Medical Center, Portsmouth, OH, p. A502
NOESS, Bobbi, Director of Nursing, Bowdle Hospital, Bowdle, SD, p. A572
NOFFSINGER, Sandy, Executive Assistant, Risk Manager and Director Marketing, Dundy County Hospital, Benkelman, NE, p. A398
NOGLER, Wendy, Director Human Resources, Lincoln County Health System, Fayetteville, TN, p. A583
NOLAN, Douglas, M.D., Medical Director, Cherokee Nation W.W. Hastings Hospital, Tahlequah, OK, p. A521
NOLAN, Heather, Director Information Services, Northern Louisiana Medical Center, Ruston, LA, p. A291
NOLAN, Jennifer
President, Chi Saint Josep. Health – Saint Josep. East, Lexington, KY, p. A268
President and Chief Executive Officer, Chi Saint Josep. Health – Flaget Memorial Hospital, Bardstown, KY, p. A263
NOLAN, Matthew, Chief Operating Officer, The University of Vermont Health Network Elizabethtown Community Hospital, Elizabethtown, NY, p. A442
NOLAN, Patrick, Vice President Finance and Chief Financial Officer, Gillette Children's Specialty Healthcare, Saint Paul, MN, p. A354
NOLAN, Roz, Chief Nursing Executive Officer, Community Hospital of San Bernardino, San Bernardino, CA, p. A88
NOLASCO, Wanda, Chief Nursing Officer, Fairmount Behavioral Health System, Philadelphia, PA, p. A548
NOLD, Pam, Chief Nurse Executive, Northwest Missouri Psychiatric Rehabilitation Center, Saint Joseph, MO, p. A383
NOLE, Penny, Director of Patient Care Services, The Medical Center At Caverna, Horse Cave, KY, p. A267
NOLES, Coy, Chief Financial Officer Consultant, Olney Hamilton Hospital, Olney, TX, p. A642
NOLFE, Sherry, MS, Chief Nursing Officer, Loma Linda University Children's Hospital, Loma Linda, CA, p. A70
NOLL, David, Director, Adventist Health St. Helena, Saint Helena, CA, p. A88
NOLL, Gerald A, Chief Financial Officer, Rogers Behavioral Health, Oconomowoc, WI, p. A718
NOLLEY, Dexter, Chief Human Resources Officer, Duke Regional Hospital, Durham, NC, p. A467
NOLTE, Darlene R, Chief Human Resource Officer, Saint Francis Hospital Vinita, Vinita, OK, p. A523
NONNEMAN, Lisa, Director Information Technology Services, Mary Lanning Healthcare, Hastings, NE, p. A400
NOONAN, Anna T., President and Chief Operating Officer, The University of Vermont Health Network Central Vermont Medical Center, Berlin, VT, p. A671
NOONAN, Kathryn, Director Information Management, Lemuel Shattuck Hospital, Jamaica Plain, MA, p. A314
NOONE, Thomas, M.D., Chief Medical Officer, Shorepoint Health Port Charlotte, Port Charlotte, FL, p. A147
NOPWASKEY, Cristen, Chief Information Officer, Weirton Medical Center, Weirton, WV, p. A705
NORD, Stanley K, Chief Financial Officer, HCA Houston Healthcare West, Houston, TX, p. A626
NORDAHL, Richard E., Senior Director, Sanford Sheldon Medical Center, Sheldon, IA, p. A243
NORDBERG, Traci, Chief Human Resources Officer, Vanderbilt University Medical Center, Nashville, TN, p. A591
NORDBY, Betsy, Director of Human Resources, St. Croix Regional Medical Center, St Croix Falls, WI, p. A722
NORDBY, Shawn A, Chief Financial Officer, Mary Lanning Healthcare, Hastings, NE, p. A400
NORDELL, Cindy, Chief Nursing Officer, Encompass Health Rehabilitation Hospital of Colorado Springs, Colorado Springs, CO, p. A105
NORDIN, Danna, Director Human Resources, Anchor Hospital, Atlanta, GA, p. A156
NORDLUND, Sarah, Director of Nursing, Garfield County Health Center, Jordan, MT, p. A393
NORDNESS, Michael, Chief Executive Officer, North Okaloosa Medical Center, Crestview, FL, p. A129
NORDSTROM, Janice, Director Human Resources, Landmark Hospital of Joplin, Joplin, MO, p. A377
NORDSTROM, Katie, Director Human Resources, Beartooth Billings Clinic, Red Lodge, MT, p. A395
NORDSVEN, Mellissa, Director, Human Resources, Chi St. Alexius Health Bismarck, Bismarck, ND, p. A479
NORDYKE, Charles, Chief Executive Officer, Clarinda Regional Health Center, Clarinda, IA, p. A232
NORDYKE, Melissa, Chief Financial Officer, Ascension Seton Smithville, Smithville, TX, p. A653
NORELDIN, Mohsen, M.D., President Medical Staff, Athol Hospital, Athol, MA, p. A309
NOREM, Ashley, Chief Information Systems, Northwest Health – Starke, Knox, IN, p. A221
NORICK, Laurence, M.D., Clinical Director, U. S. Public Health Service Indian Hospital, Parker, AZ, p. A34
NORKO, Michael A, M.D., Acting Chief Executive Officer, Connecticut Valley Hospital, Middletown, CT, p. A117
NORMAN, Daniel, Regional Service Manager, Unitypoint Health – Allen Hospital, Waterloo, IA, p. A244
NORMAN, Debbie
MSN, R.N., Chief Nursing Officer, Elkview General Hospital, Hobart, OK, p. A513
Director Human Resources, Central Louisiana Surgical Hospital, Alexandria, LA, p. A276
NORMAN, Jimmy, Chief Financial Officer, Mountain Lakes Medical Center, Clayton, GA, p. A160
NORMAN, Laura, Chief Development and Information Officer, Polara Health, Prescott Valley, AZ, p. A37
NORMAN, Lori, Chief Financial Officer, Encompass Health Rehabilitation Hospital of Gadsden, Gadsden, AL, p. A19
NORMAN, Michael L, Executive Vice President and Chief Operating Officer, Landmark Hospital of Cap. Girardeau, Cap. Girardeau, MO, p. A372
NORMINGTON–SLAY, Jeremy, FACHE, Chief Executive Officer, Firelands Regional Health System, Sandusky, OH, p. A503
NORQUEST, Cathy, Director Human Resources, York General, York, NE, p. A407
NORRICK, Michael, Director of Campus Operations, Prisma Health Laurens County Hospital, Clinton, SC, p. A564
NORRIS, Charles, Interim Chief Executive Officer, Brownfield Regional Medical Center, Brownfield, TX, p. A604
NORRIS, David, Chief Medical Staff, Sweetwater Hospital, Sweetwater, TN, p. A594
NORRIS, Lucy, Administrator Interim Chief Nursing Officer, Multicare Good Samaritan Hospital, Puyallup. WA, p. A693
NORSWORTHY, Autumn, Director of Nursing, St. Michael's Elite Hospital, Sugar Land, TX, p. A655
NORTH, Mark D., Chief Financial Officer, RMC Anniston, Anniston, AL, p. A15
NORTH, Ralene, Chief Nurse Executive, Massena Hospital, Inc., Massena, NY, p. A446
NORTH, Sarah, Chief Executive Officer, Baylor Scott & White Institute for Rehabilitation – Lakeway, Lakeway, TX, p. A633
NORTHCUTT, Lynn, Chief Information Officer, Musc Health Florence Medical Center, Florence, SC, p. A566
NORTHERN, Gail M., Director Human Resources, Blue Mountain Hospital, Blanding, UT, p. A664
NORTHUP, Carol, R.N., Chief Nursing Officer, Island Health, Anacortes, WA, p. A687
NORTON, Andrew J
M.D., Chief Medical Officer, Bryn Mawr Hospital, Bryn Mawr, PA, p. A536
M.D., Chief Medical Officer, Paoli Hospital, Paoli, PA, p. A547
NORTON, Bill, Chief Nursing Officer, Rehoboth Mckinley Christian Health Care Services, Gallup. NM, p. A434
NORTON, Carole, Chief Nursing Officer, Mon Health Stonewall Jackson Memorial Hospital, Weston, WV, p. A705
NORTON, Lizette O, Vice President, Human Resources, Loma Linda University Children's Hospital, Loma Linda, CA, p. A70
NORTON, Meg, Executive Vice President and Chief Administrative Officer, Rady Children's Hospital – San Diego, San Diego, CA, p. A89
NORTON, Robert G, President, Salem Hospital, Salem, MA, p. A318
NORTON, Sidney P., Chief Financial Officer, Primary Children's Hospital, Salt Lake City, UT, p. A669
NORTON, Susan, Vice President Human Resources, Wellstar Mcg Health, Augusta, GA, p. A158
NORTON–ROSKO, Peggy, R.N., MSN, Regional Chief Nursing Officer, Loyola University Medical Center, Maywood, IL, p. A201
NORVILLE, Amy, Vice President Support Services, St. Luke's Hospital, Columbus, NC, p. A466
NORWOOD, William, Vice President, Human Resources, Brattleboro Memorial Hospital, Brattleboro, VT, p. A671
NOSACKA, David
Chief Financial Officer, HSHS St. Elizabeth's Hospital, O Fallon, IL, p. A204
Southern Illinois Division Chief Financial Officer, HSHS St. Joseph's Hospital Highland, Highland, IL, p. A197
NOSBISCH, Don, Director Human Resources, Floyd County Medical Center, Charles City, IA, p. A232
NOSKIN, Gary, Senior Vice President and Chief Medical Officer, Northwestern Memorial Hospital, Northwestern Memorial Hospital, Chicago, IL, p. A190
NOSKO, Jeannine, Vice President Patient Care, Aspirus Wausau Hospital, Inc., Wausau, WI, p. A724
NOSTRANT, Hunter, FACHE, President, Mymichigan Medical Center Alpena, Alpena, MI, p. A321
NOTEMAN, Laurali, Director Human Resources, Kane County Hospital, Kanab, UT, p. A665

A934 Index of Health Care Professionals

Index of Health Care Professionals / Oduwole
Index of Health Care Professionals

NOTTER, Pat, R.N., Chief Nursing Officer and Director Quality, Melissa Memorial Hospital, Holyoke, CO, p. A109
NOTTINGHAM, Cheryl, Chief Financial Officer, Atlantic General Hospital, Berlin, MD, p. A302
NOTTMEIER, Travis, Administrator, Chester Mental Health Center, Chester, IL, p. A188
NOUNA, Nabil, M.D., Chief of Staff, Ascension Borgess Allegan Hospital, Allegan, MI, p. A321
NOVAK, Charles, M.D., Medical Director, Cottonwood Creek Behavioral Hospital, Meridian, ID, p. A182
NOVAK, Christopher, Chief Operating Officer, Ascension Alexian Brothers Behavioral Health Hospital, Hoffman Estates, IL, p. A198
NOVAK, Georgene, Director Human Resources, Littleton Regional Healthcare, Littleton, NH, p. A416
NOVAK, Jerald, Chief People Officer, University of Vermont Medical Center, Burlington, VT, p. A671
NOVAK, Kristen
Director, Human Resources, Hudson Hospital And Clinic, Hudson, WI, p. A713
Manager Human Resources, River Falls Area Hospital, River Falls, WI, p. A721
NOVAK, Matthew, President, Morton Plant Hospital, Clearwater, FL, p. A128
NOVAK, Michael
Vice President and Chief Operating Officer, Montefiore Nyack Hospital, Nyack, NY, p. A454
Vice President, Operations and Chief Information Officer, Saint Mary's Hospital, Waterbury, CT, p. A119
NOVELLO, Mimi, President and Chief Medical Officer, Medstar St. Mary's Hospital, Leonardtown, MD, p. A305
NOVELLO, Regina, R.N., Chief Operating Officer, Healdsburg Hospital, Healdsburg, CA, p. A67
NOVICK, Peggy, Vice President, Clinical Support and Outpatient Services, Milford Regional Medical Center, Milford, MA, p. A316
NOVOA LOYOLA, Jose E, M.D., Medical Director, Cardiovascular Center of Puerto Rico And The Caribbean, San Juan, PR, p. A734
NOVOSEL, Stacie, Vice President, Human Resources, HCA Florida South Shore Hospital, Sun City Center, FL, p. A151
NOVOTNY, April, MSN, R.N., Chief Nurse Executive, Lakeland Regional Health Medical Center, Lakeland, FL, p. A137
NOWACHEK, Debra S., Director Human Resources, Unitypoint Health – Grinnell Regional Medical Center, Grinnell, IA, p. A236
NOWICKI, Becky, Director Human Resources, Michiana Behavioral Health Center, Plymouth, IN, p. A226
NOWLIN, Jeff, Interim Chief Executive Officer, Integris Health Woodward Hospital, Woodward, OK, p. A524
NOWLING, Tara, Director Human Resources, Monroe County Hospital, Monroeville, AL, p. A22
NOYES, Vikki, Executive Vice President and Chief Operating Officer, Confluence Health Hospital – Central Campus, Wenatchee, WA, p. A698
NUAKO, Kofi, M.D., President Medical Staff, Baptist Memorial Hospital–Union City, Union City, TN, p. A594
NUDD, Brandon M., President and Chief Executive Officer, Adventhealth Hendersonville, Hendersonville, NC, p. A470
NUMMI, Lisa, MSN, R.N., Chief Executive Officer, HCA Florida Citrus Hospital, Inverness, FL, p. A134
NUNEZ, Humberto F., M.D., Chief Medical Officer, Mission Regional Medical Center, Mission, TX, p. A640
NUNEZ, Jennifer, Chief Executive Officer, Oasis Behavioral Health – Chandler, Chandler, AZ, p. A31
NUNEZ, Michael, Chief Financial Officer, University Medical Center of El Paso, El Paso, TX, p. A617
NUNEZ, Sheila, Director Human Resources, Eastern New Mexico Medical Center, Roswell, NM, p. A436
NUNN, Brian, R.N., Chief Executive Officer, HCA Florida Putnam Hospital, Palatka, FL, p. A145
NUNN, Chalmers, M.D., Chief Medical Officer and Senior Vice President, Centra Lynchburg General Hospital, Lynchburg, VA, p. A678
NUNN, Vernell, Chief Executive Officer, Summitridge Hospital, Lawrenceville, GA, p. A166
NUNNELEE, Almita, R.N., Chief Operating Officer and Chief Nursing Officer, St. Luke's Wood River Medical Center, Ketchum, ID, p. A182
NUNNELLY, Sarah, Executive Vice President and Chief Operating Officer, East Alabama Medical Center, Opelika, AL, p. A23
NURY, Alex, Chief Information Officer, Providence Cedars–Sinai Tarzana Medical Center, Los Angeles, CA, p. A74
NUSBAUM, Neil, M.D., Chief of Staff, Veterans Affairs Central Western Massachusetts Healthcare System, Leeds, MA, p. A315
NUSSBAUM, Mark, Vice President Operations, Cleveland Clinic Marymount Hospital, Garfield Heights, OH, p. A496
NUTTER, Robert F., President and Chief Executive Officer, Littleton Regional Healthcare, Littleton, NH, p. A416
NUTTING, Ron, M.D., Chief Medical Officer, Reading Hospital, West Reading, PA, p. A557
NWATUOBI, Joyce, Vice President Finance, Aurora Medical Center – Manitowoc County, Two Rivers, WI, p. A723
NWOKIKE, Jerome, M.D., Medical Director, Spring Mountain Treatment Center, Las Vegas, NV, p. A410
NYAMU, Samuel, M.D., Chief Medical Officer, Sanford Aberdeen Medical Center, Aberdeen, SD, p. A572
NYBERG, Becky T., Chief Financial Officer, Bloomington Meadows Hospital, Bloomington, IN, p. A212
NYIKES, Debra, Director Finance and Chief Financial Officer, Cleveland Clinic Children's Hospital for Rehabilitation, Cleveland, OH, p. A490
NYKAMP, Robert, Vice President and Chief Operating Officer, Pine Rest Christian Mental Health Services, Grand Rapids, MI, p. A328
NYLUND, Barbara, M.D., Chief of Staff, Novato Community Hospital, Novato, CA, p. A80
NYSTROM, Dale, M.D., Chief Medical Officer, Physician, Hawarden Regional Healthcare, Hawarden, IA, p. A237

O

OAKES, Julie P, R.N., Manager Risk and Quality, Ocean Beach Hospital And Medical Clinics, Ilwaco, WA, p. A690
OAKES FERRUCCI, Susan
MS, Chief Hospital Executive, Cobleskill Regional Hospital, Cobleskill, NY, p. A441
MS, Chief Hospital Executive, Little Falls Hospital, Little Falls, NY, p. A445
MS, Chief Hospital Executive, O'Connor Hospital, Delhi, NY, p. A442
OAKLEY, Lisa, Chief Financial Officer, Harper County Community Hospital, Buffalo, OK, p. A510
OAKLEY, Sarah G, R.N., MSN, Vice President Nursing, North Kansas City Hospital, North Kansas City, MO, p. A381
OAXACA, Norma, Director Human Resources, Peak Behavioral Health Services, Santa Teresa, NM, p. A437
OBERHEU, Todd, Hospital Chief Executive, Lincoln County Medical Center, Ruidoso, NM, p. A436
OBERMIER, Jenny, Senior Vice President, Chief Operating Officer and Chief Nursing Officer, York General, York, NE, p. A407
OBEY, Bianca A., Chief Financial Officer, Alexandria Va Medical Center, Pineville, LA, p. A291
O'BOYLE, Kevin, President, Legacy Good Samaritan Medical Center, Portland, OR, p. A530
O'BRIEN, Daniel R., Vice President and Chief Financial Officer, Community Hospital, Munster, IN, p. A224
O'BRIEN, Elizabeth, Chief Financial Officer, Northern Nevada Adult Mental Health Services, Sparks, NV, p. A413
O'BRIEN, Gina, M.D., Interim Chief Medical Officer, Cheshire Medical Center, Keene, NH, p. A415
O'BRIEN, Jane E, M.D., Medical Director, Franciscan Children's, Brighton, MA, p. A311
O'BRIEN, Karen, Director Human Resources, Gerald Champion Regional Medical Center, Alamogordo, NM, p. A432
O'BRIEN, Kevin, Chief Executive Officer, Harper County Community Hospital, Buffalo, OK, p. A510
O'BRIEN, Laureen, Chief Information Officer, Providence Newberg Medical Center, Newberg, OR, p. A529
O'BRIEN, Renee, Director Human Resources, Greater Binghamton Health Center, Binghamton, NY, p. A439
O'BRIEN, Tim, Chief Executive Officer, Hackensack Meridian Mountainside Medical Center, Montclair, NJ, p. A424
O'BRIEN–PARADIS, Katie, M.D., Chief Medical Officer, Chi Oakes Hospital, Oakes, ND, p. A483
O'BRYANT, G. Mark., President and Chief Executive Officer, Tallahassee Memorial Healthcare, Tallahassee, FL, p. A151
OCASIO, J Manuel, Vice President Human Resources, Holy Cross Hospital, Silver Spring, MD, p. A307
OCEGUERA, Louis, M.D., Medical Director, Little Falls Hospital, Little Falls, NY, p. A445
OCHOA, Mark S, M.D., Deputy Commander, Clinical Services, Irwin Army Community Hospital, Junction City, KS, p. A251
OCHOA, Nikki, Interim Chief Financial Officer, St. Joseph's Medical Center, Stockton, CA, p. A97
O'CONNELL, Brian, Director Information Services, North Star Behavioral Health System, Anchorage, AK, p. A27
O'CONNELL, Melody M, Director Human Resources, St. Bernard Parish Hospital, Chalmette, LA, p. A279
O'CONNELL, Sara, Director Human Resources, Mount Desert Island Hospital, Bar Harbor, ME, p. A295
O'CONNELL, Tim, Chief Financial Officer, Lincoln Hospital, Davenport, WA, p. A688
O'CONNOR, Alice M., Chief Executive Officer, Kindred Hospital–New Jersey Morris County, Dover, NJ, p. A420
O'CONNOR, Betty, Chief Nursing Officer, Crouse Health, Syracuse, NY, p. A460
O'CONNOR, Colleen, Director Human Resources, Centerstone Hospital, Bradenton, FL, p. A126
O'CONNOR, David, Executive Vice President and Chief Financial Officer, Caromont Regional Medical Center, Gastonia, NC, p. A469
O'CONNOR, Dennis, M.D., Medical Director, Ira Davenport Memorial Hospital, Bath, NY, p. A439
O'CONNOR, James, President, St. Charles Hospital, Port Jefferson, NY, p. A456
O'CONNOR, Joyce, Chief Operating Officer, Taunton State Hospital, Taunton, MA, p. A319
O'CONNOR, Kathy
Vice President Finance, Trinity Health Ann Arbor Hospital, Ypsilanti, MI, p. A341
Vice President Finance and Controller, Trinity Health Livingston Hospital, Howell, MI, p. A330
O'CONNOR, Kevin, D.O., President, Medical Staff, Corewell Health Greenville Hospital, Greenville, MI, p. A329
O'CONNOR, Michael P, M.D., Chief Medical Officer, Banner Baywood Medical Center, Mesa, AZ, p. A33
O'CONNOR, Patrick J, Chief Executive Officer, Kindred Hospital–New Jersey Morris County, Dover, NJ, p. A420
O'CONNOR, Tim, Area Finance Officer, Kaiser Permanente Santa Clara Medical Center, Santa Clara, CA, p. A94
O'CONNOR, Timothy P., Executive Vice President and Chief Financial Officer, Lahey Hospital & Medical Center, Burlington, MA, p. A312
O'CONNOR–SNYDER, Judy, R.N., Chief Nursing Officer, Mercy Hospital Lebanon, Lebanon, MO, p. A379
ODATO, David, Chief Administrative and Chief Human Resources Officer, UCSF Medical Center, San Francisco, CA, p. A91
O'DEA, Edward, Executive Vice President and Chief Financial Officer, Lehigh Valley Hospital–Cedar Crest, Allentown, PA, p. A534
O'DEA, James, Chief Executive Officer, Natchaug Hospital, Mansfield Center, CT, p. A116
ODEGAARD, Daniel, FACHE, Chief Executive Officer, Caldwell Medical Center, Princeton, KY, p. A273
O'DELL, Darrell, Director Information Services, Good Samaritan Hospital – San Jose, San Jose, CA, p. A92
O'DELL, Edward
D.O., Chief Medical Officer, Nazareth Hospital, Philadelphia, PA, p. A549
D.O., Chief Medical Officer, St. Mary Medical Center, Langhorne, PA, p. A543
ODELL, Michelle, Director of Public Affairs, Kaiser Permanente South Sacramento Medical Center, Sacramento, CA, p. A87
O'DELL, Michael
Chief Financial Officer, Box Butte General Hospital, Alliance, NE, p. A397
Chief Financial Officer, Sheridan County Health Complex, Hoxie, KS, p. A251
ODEN, Greg, Chief Medical Officer, Merit Health Central, Jackson, MS, p. A364
ODEN, Ryan, D.O., Chief of Staff, Arbuckle Memorial Hospital, Sulphur, OK, p. A521
ODEN, Tracie, Vice President, Human Resources, Northwest Hospital, Randallstown, MD, p. A306
ODETOYINBO, Adedapo, M.D., Chief Medical Office, Emory Johns Creek Hospital, Johns Creek, GA, p. A166
ODOM, David, Director, Information Technology, Chambers Health, Anahuac, TX, p. A597
ODOM, Jake, Chief Information Officer, Trinity Hospital, Weaverville, CA, p. A101
ODOM, Jennifer, Interim Director Human Resources, Flowers Hospital, Dothan, AL, p. A18
ODOM, Robbin, R.N., MSN, Chief Nursing Officer, West Calcasieu Cameron Hospital, Sulphur, LA, p. A293
O'DONNELL, Jan, Chief Nursing Officer, Christus Surgical Hospital, Corpus Christi, TX, p. A608
ODONELL, John, Director Information Systems, Cherokee Medical Center, Gaffney, SC, p. A566
O'DONNELL, John, Chief Operating Officer, Torrance State Hospital, Torrance, PA, p. A555
O'DONNELL, Michael F., CPA, Chief Financial Officer, Peconic Bay Medical Center, Riverhead, NY, p. A457
O'DONOGHUE, Brian, M.D., Chief Medical Officer, Breckinridge Memorial Hospital, Hardinsburg, KY, p. A266
ODUWOLE, Adedapo, M.D., Medical Director, Lighthouse Behavioral Health Hospital, Conway, SC, p. A565

Index of Health Care Professionals

Index of Health Care Professionals / Oehmke

OEHMKE, Brittni, Administrator, Hanover Hospital, Hanover, KS, p. A250
OERTEL, Robert, Chief Financial Officer, Abrazo Arrowhead Campus, Glendale, AZ, p. A32
OETTING, Phyllis, Director Human Resources, Mitchell County Hospital Health Systems, Beloit, KS, p. A247
OETZEL, Gerald P, Chief Financial Officer, Temple Health–Chestnut Hill Hospital, Philadelphia, PA, p. A550
OFFUTT, Dan, Manager Finance, Knox County Hospital, Knox City, TX, p. A633
O'FLANAGAN, Jayne, Director Human Resources, Incline Village Community Hospital, Incline Village, NV, p. A409
OFSTEDAL, Jeff, Manager Information Technology, Glacial Ridge Health System, Glenwood, MN, p. A347
OGANESYAN, Alen, Chief Information Officer, USC Arcadia Hospital, Arcadia, CA, p. A56
OGASAWARA, Keith, M.D., Associate Medical Director and Professional Chief of Staff, Kaiser Permanente Medical Center, Honolulu, HI, p. A175
OGAWA, Quin
Chief Financial Officer, Sutter Health Kahi Mohala, Ewa Beach, HI, p. A175
Vice President Finance and Chief Financial Officer, Kuakini Medical Center, Honolulu, HI, p. A175
OGDEN, Judy, Director Information Technology, Franklin Medical Center, Winnsboro, LA, p. A294
OGDEN, Lesley
M.D., Chief Executive Officer, Samaritan North Lincoln Hospital, Lincoln City, OR, p. A528
M.D., Chief Executive Officer, Samaritan Pacific Communities Hospital, Newport, OR, p. A529
OGG, Tom, Chief Information Officer, Olmsted Medical Center, Rochester, MN, p. A354
OGIER, Katie, Director of Nursing, Rock County Hospital, Bassett, NE, p. A397
OGILVIE, Richard, Chief Information Officer, Southwestern Vermont Medical Center, Bennington, VT, p. A671
OGLESBY, Lorie A., Director of Human Resources, Baptist Health Deaconess Madisonville, Inc., Madisonville, KY, p. A271
OGLESBY, Lorri, Chief Nursing Officer, Encompass Health Rehabilitation Hospital of Texarkana, Texarkana, TX, p. A657
OGLESBY–ODOM, Gwendolyn Marie, Chief Nursing Officer, Advocate Trinity Hospital, Chicago, IL, p. A188
OGROD, Eugene, M.D., Chief Medical Officer, HCA Houston Healthcare Kingwood, Kingwood, TX, p. A633
OHASHI, Curtis, Ph.D., Chief Operating Officer, Santa Clara Valley Medical Center, San Jose, CA, p. A92
O'HAODHA, Levon, Chief of Staff, Hudson Hospital And Clinic, Hudson, WI, p. A713
O'HARA, Denise, Vice President Human Resources, Wilson Medical Center, Wilson, NC, p. A478
O'HARA, Kathleen, Vice President Human Resources, Erie County Medical Center, Buffalo, NY, p. A440
O'HARA, Michael, Senior Executive Director Human Resources, Houston Medical Center, Warner Robins, GA, p. A173
O'HEARN, John, Interim Chief Executive Officer, Culberson Hospital, Van Horn, TX, p. A659
O'HERN, Mark
President, UPMC East, Monroeville, PA, p. A546
President, UPMC Mckeesport, Mckeesport, PA, p. A545
OHL, Connie, Acting Chief Human Resources, Veterans Affairs Illiana Health Care System, Danville, IL, p. A192
OHMART, Dean, Vice President Financial Services and Chief Financial Officer, Western Missouri Medical Center, Warrensburg, MO, p. A388
OHRT, James M, M.D., Director Medical Staff, Henderson Health Care Services, Henderson, NE, p. A401
OISHI, Gregg, President and Chief Executive Officer, Kuakini Medical Center, Honolulu, HI, p. A175
OJEDA, Guadalupe, R.N., Chief Nursing Officer, Community Hospital of Huntington Park, Huntington Park, CA, p. A67
OJILE, Ene, M.D., Medical Director, Rehabilitation Hospital of Henry, Mcdonough, GA, p. A168
OJOMO, Karanita, M.D., Chief of Staff, Lewisgale Hospital Pulaski, Pulaski, VA, p. A681
OKABE, David
Executive Vice President, Chief Financial Officer and Treasurer, Pali Momi Medical Center, Aiea, HI, p. A175
Executive Vice President, Chief Financial Officer and Treasurer, Straub Medical Center, Honolulu, HI, p. A176
Executive Vice President, Chief Financial Officer and Treasurer, Wilcox Medical Center, Lihue, HI, p. A177
Senior Vice President, Chief Financial Officer and Treasurer, Kapiolani Medical Center for Women & Children, Honolulu, HI, p. A175
O'KANE, Patricia, Associate Director, Veterans Affairs New Jersey Health Care System, East Orange, NJ, p. A420
O'KEEFE, John
Chief Executive Officer, Select Specialty Hospital–Gulfport, Gulfport, MS, p. A363
Chief Nursing Officer, Day Kimball Hospital, Putnam, CT, p. A118
O'KEEFE, Kathy
Executive Director, Pilgrim Psychiatric Center, Brentwood, NY, p. A439
Interim Executive Director, Sagamore Children's Psychiatric Center, Dix Hills, NY, p. A442
O'KEEFE, Michelle, Chief Executive Officer, Kessler Institute for Rehabilitation, West Orange, NJ, p. A430
O'KEEFE, Sharon L, President, University of Chicago Medical Center, University of Chicago Medical Center, Chicago, IL, p. A192
O'KEEFE, Trish, Ph.D., R.N., President, Morristown Medical Center, Morristown, NJ, p. A424
OKEN, Jeffrey, Vice President of Medical Affairs, Northwestern Medicine Marianjoy Rehabilitation Hospital, Wheaton, IL, p. A210
OKESON, Keith, President and Chief Executive Officer, Lifecare Medical Center, Roseau, MN, p. A354
OKEY, Suzi, Director of Nursing, Southwest Health, Platteville, WI, p. A719
OKONIEWSKI, Susan, M.D., Chief of Staff, Chi St. Gabriel's Health, Little Falls, MN, p. A349
OKOTH, Stacey–Ann, R.N., Senior Vice President and Chief Nursing Officer, Jefferson Abington Health, Abington, PA, p. A534
OKUHARA, Mary, Chief Human Resource Officer, Lakewood Regional Medical Center, Lakewood, CA, p. A69
OLANDER, Scott, Chief Financial Officer, Evergreenhealth Monroe, Monroe, WA, p. A691
OLASON, Roxanne, R.N., FACHE, Vice President and Chief Nursing Officer, Skagit Valley Hospital, Mount Vernon, WA, p. A692
OLDHAM, Jennie, Director Human Resources, Goodall–Witcher Hospital, Clifton, TX, p. A607
OLDHAM, Lawrence, Chief Financial Officer, Arise Austin Medical Center, Austin, TX, p. A598
OLDHAM, Marriner, M.D., Chief Medical Officer, U. S. Air Force Regional Hospital, Elmendorf Afb, AK, p. A28
OLDHAM, Nate, M.D., Chief Medical Officer, Ferrell Hospital, Eldorado, IL, p. A194
O'LEARY, Daniel H, M.D., Chief Medical Officer, Umass Memorial Healthalliance–Clinton Hospital, Leominster, MA, p. A315
O'LEARY, Kevin J, Senior Vice President and Chief Financial Officer, Exeter Hospital, Exeter, NH, p. A415
O'LEARY, Megan A, Vice President Human Resources and Rehabilitation Services, Mckenzie–Willamette Medical Center, Springfield, OR, p. A532
O'LEARY, Rand, FACHE, President, Henry Ford Wyandotte Hospital, Wyandotte, MI, p. A341
OLEKSYK, Mike, M.D., Vice President and Chief Medical Officer, Baptist Hospital, Pensacola, FL, p. A146
OLESTON, Caryn Lynn
FACHE, MSN, R.N., Chief Nursing Officer, Mercyhealth Hospital And Medical Center – Harvard, Harvard, IL, p. A197
FACHE, MSN, R.N., Chief Nursing Officer, Mercyhealth Hospital And Medical Center – Walworth, Lake Geneva, WI, p. A714
OLIA, Ali, Vice President, Mercyhealth Hospital And Physician Clinic–Crystal Lake, Crystal Lake, IL, p. A192
OLIGSCHLAEGER, David, Medical Staff President, HSHS Good Shepherd Hospital, Shelbyville, IL, p. A208
OLINDE, Chad E., CPA, Chief Executive Officer, Pointe Coupee General Hospital, New Roads, LA, p. A290
OLINGER, Richard P, Chief Financial Officer, Lecom Health Millcreek Community Hospital, Erie, PA, p. A540
OLINGER, Terry, Interim Chief Operating Officer, Trios Health, Kennewick, WA, p. A690
OLINSKI, Janis, R.N., Vice President Clinical Services, WVU Medicine – Harrison Community Hospital, Cadiz, OH, p. A487
OLIPHANT, Gerald P, Executive Vice President and Chief Operating Officer, Good Samaritan Hospital, Cincinnati, OH, p. A489
OLIPHANT, Jenny, Executive Vice President and Chief Operating Officer, Bethesda North Hospital, Cincinnati, OH, p. A488
OLIPHANT, Phillip. Chief Information Officer, U. S. Air Force Regional Hospital, Elmendorf Afb, AK, p. A28
OLIVARES, Andy, Chief Executive Officer, Lakeview Specialty Hospital And Rehab, Waterford, WI, p. A723
OLIVARES, Rafael, Controller, Starr County Memorial Hospital, Rio Grande City, TX, p. A647
OLIVAREZ, Freddy, Chief Executive Officer, Medical Arts Hospital, Lamesa, TX, p. A633
OLIVAREZ, Lorenzo, Senior Vice President and Chief Financial Officer, Bsa Hospital, Llc, Amarillo, TX, p. A596
OLIVAS, Ray, Chief Fiscal Service, West Texas Va Health Care System, Big Spring, TX, p. A604
OLIVE, Alan C., Chief Executive Officer, Ashley Regional Medical Center, Vernal, UT, p. A670
OLIVENCIA, Humberto, M.D., Medical Director, Hospital Perea, Mayaguez, PR, p. A733
OLIVER, Carlene, Superintendent, Evansville Psychiatric Children Center, Evansville, IN, p. A216
OLIVER, David, Director Information Systems, UK King's Daughters Medical Center, Ashland, KY, p. A263
OLIVER, Doug, Chief Financial Officer, Polara Health, Prescott Valley, AZ, p. A37
OLIVER, Michelle, Chief Nursing Executive, HSHS Good Shepherd Hospital, Shelbyville, IL, p. A208
OLIVER, Pamela A., M.D., Executive Vice President and Chief Medical Officer, Novant Health Ballantyne Medical Center, Charlotte, NC, p. A465
OLIVER, Patricia, Administrator, Weisman Children's Rehabilitation Hospital, Marlton, NJ, p. A424
OLIVER, Rick, Information Technology, Olney Hamilton Hospital, Olney, TX, p. A642
OLIVER, Rosalie, Senior Vice President and Chief Financial Officer, Adventhealth Wauchula, Wauchula, FL, p. A154
OLIVERA, Sue, Vice President, Aultman Hospital, Canton, OH, p. A487
OLIVERAS, Freddy, Chief Information Officer, Martin County Hospital District, Stanton, TX, p. A654
OLIVERAS LAGUNA, Ana, Administrator, Caribbean Medical Center, Fajardo, PR, p. A732
OLIVERIO, Robert, M.D., Vice President and Chief Medical Officer, Ambulatory Care and Population Health, Roper St. Francis Berkeley Hospital, Summerville, SC, p. A570
OLIVIER, Edward
Chief Financial Officer, Martha's Vineyard Hospital, Oak Bluffs, MA, p. A317
Chief Financial Officer, Northern Light Ca Dean Hospital, Greenville, ME, p. A297
OLLI, Cindy, R.N., Chief Nursing Officer, Schoolcraft Memorial Hospital, Manistique, MI, p. A333
OLLIE, Edwin J, Executive Vice President and Chief Financial Officer, Novant Health New Hanover Regional Medical Center, Wilmington, NC, p. A478
OLLSON, Joanne, Vice President Human Resources, Baystate Noble Hospital, Westfield, MA, p. A319
OLM–SHIPMAN, Bobby
Chief Executive Officer, Saint Luke's South Hospital, Overland Park, KS, p. A257
President and Chief Executive Officer, Saint Luke's East Hospital, Lee's Summit, MO, p. A379
OLNEY, Garry M., Chief Executive, Northern California, Providence Queen of The Valley Medical Center, Napa, CA, p. A79
OLS, Timothy A., FACHE, President, Baylor Scott & White Medical Center – Marble Falls, Marble Falls, TX, p. A637
OLSEN, Debbie, Human Resource Partner, University of Michigan Health–Sparrow Ionia, Ionia, MI, p. A330
OLSEN, Jennifer, M.D., Chief of Staff, North Canyon Medical Center, Gooding, ID, p. A181
OLSEN, Justin, JD, FACHE, Vice President and Chief Operating Officer, Johns Hopkins All Children's Hospital, Saint Petersburg, FL, p. A149
OLSEN, Ryan, Chief Operating Officer, Saddleback Medical Center, Laguna Hills, CA, p. A69
OLSEN, Sabrina, Chief Financial Officer, Duke University Hospital, Durham, NC, p. A467
OLSON, Aaron, Chief Executive Officer, North Dakota State Hospital, Jamestown, ND, p. A482
OLSON, Adrienne, R.N., FACHE, Chief Nursing Officer and Vice President, Patient Care Services, Bryan Medical Center, Lincoln, NE, p. A401
OLSON, Andrea, Vice President Patient Care, St. Croix Regional Medical Center, St Croix Falls, WI, p. A722
OLSON, Dave, Director of Nursing, Montana State Hospital, Warm Springs, MT, p. A396
OLSON, Diana
Chief Human Resources Officer, Mercy Health – Willard Hospital, Willard, OH, p. A507
Director Human Resources, Mercy Health – Tiffin Hospital, Tiffin, OH, p. A504
OLSON, Eric, Chief Financial Officer, Providence Portland Medical Center, Portland, OR, p. A530
OLSON, Forrest, M.D., Chief Medical Officer, Enloe Health, Chico, CA, p. A59
OLSON, Gary, Executive Director, North Central Health Care, Wausau, WI, p. A724
OLSON, John L., M.D., Medical Director, Marshfield Medical Center – Rice Lake, Rice Lake, WI, p. A720

A936 Index of Health Care Professionals

OLSON, Joni, Chief Executive Officer, Gundersen Tri-County Hospital And Clinics, Whitehall, WI, p. A725
OLSON, Kevin, Director Information Systems, SSM Health St. Anthony Hospital - Oklahoma City, Oklahoma City, OK, p. A518
OLSON, Kristi, Chief Executive Officer, Penrose-St. Francis Health Services, Colorado Springs, CO, p. A105
OLSON, Lacey, M.D., Chief Medical Staff, Sanford Chamberlain Medical Center, Chamberlain, SD, p. A572
OLSON, Lynn R, Director Human Resources, Hendricks Community Hospital Association, Hendricks, MN, p. A348
OLSON, Marcia
  Business Office Manager, Webster County Community Hospital, Red Cloud, NE, p. A405
  Director Finance and Controller, Monument Health Spearfish Hospital, Spearfish, SD, p. A577
OLSON, Mark
  M.D., Chief of Staff, Lincoln Health, Hugo, CO, p. A110
  Interim Chief Information Officer, Behavioral Health Network, Natchaug Hospital, Mansfield Center, CT, p. A116
OLSON, Michael R., Chief Executive Officer, Citizens Medical Center, Victoria, TX, p. A660
OLSON, Steven, Administrator Patient Care Services, Carthage Area Hospital, Carthage, NY, p. A441
OLSON, Tim
  Senior Vice President Finance, Thedacare Regional Medical Center-Appleton, Appleton, WI, p. A707
  Senior Vice President Finance, Thedacare Regional Medical Center-Neenah, Neenah, WI, p. A718
OLSON, Tracy L, Human Resource Officer, Avera St. Luke's Hospital, Aberdeen, SD, p. A572
OLSZYK, Mark, M.D., Vice President Medical Affairs and Chief Medical Officer, Carroll Hospital, Westminster, MD, p. A308
OLTMANN, Michael, M.D., Chief Medical Officer, Baptist Health Medical Center-Stuttgart, Stuttgart, AR, p. A54
O'MALLEY, Bert W. Jr, President and Chief Executive Officer, University of Maryland Medical Center, Baltimore, MD, p. A301
O'MALLEY, John F., FACHE, President, Trinity Health Livingston Hospital, Howell, MI, p. A330
O'MALLEY, Jon P., Chief Executive Officer, Select Specialty Hospital - Macomb County, Mount Clemens, MI, p. A334
O'MALLEY, Mary Jo, R.N., MS, Vice President Diagnostics and Support Services, Prohealth Oconomowoc Memorial Hospital, Oconomowoc, WI, p. A718
OMAN, Michelle
  D.O., Chief Medical Officer, Essentia Health Northern Pines, Aurora, MN, p. A343
  D.O., Chief Medical Officer, Essentia Health-Virginia, Virginia, MN, p. A356
OMILUSIK, Kevin, M.D., Chief Medical Officer, Munson Medical Center, Traverse City, MI, p. A339
OMOLARA, Khar, M.D., Chief Medical Staff, Jefferson County Hospital, Fayette, MS, p. A361
OMRAN, Yasser, M.D., President Medical Staff, Pomerene Hospital, Millersburg, OH, p. A500
ONCALE, Gerard, Director of Nursing, Perimeter Behavioral Hospital of New Orleans, Kenner, LA, p. A284
ONDERS, Robert, M.D., JD, Medical Director, Maniilaq Health Center, Kotzebue, AK, p. A29
O'NEAL, Catherine, M.D., Chief Medical Officer, Our Lady of The Lake Regional Medical Center, Baton Rouge, LA, p. A278
O'NEAL, Charlotte, Vice President Human Resources, Research Medical Center, Kansas City, MO, p. A378
O'NEAL, Jeffery D., FACHE, Chief Executive Officer, Brook Lane, Hagerstown, MD, p. A304
O'NEAL, Jessica, Chief Executive Officer, Medical City Las Colinas, Irving, TX, p. A630
O'NEAL, Lewis Stephen, R.N., MSN, Chief Nursing Officer, Chi Saint Josep. Health - Saint Josep. London, London, KY, p. A269
O'NEAL, Michael, M.D., Chief Medical Officer, Ochsner Lsu Health Shreveport - Monroe Medical Center, Monroe, LA, p. A288
O'NEAL, Timothy, Chief Nursing Officer, Poplar Bluff Regional Medical Center, Poplar Bluff, MO, p. A382
ONEAL, Karen, Chief Financial Officer, Burke Medical Center, Waynesboro, GA, p. A174
O'NEIL, Alan, Chief Executive Officer, Unity Medical Center, Grafton, ND, p. A481
O'NEIL, Sean K, Chief Operations Officer, Exeter Hospital, Exeter, NH, p. A415
O'NEILL, Beth, Chief Nursing Officer, Morgan Medical Center, Madison, GA, p. A167
O'NEILL, Bri, Chief Nursing Officer, Tristar Northcrest Medical Center, Springfield, TN, p. A593
O'NEILL, Jennifer A, R.N., Chief Operating Officer, Cooperman Barnabas Medical Center, Livingston, NJ, p. A423
O'NEILL, Lynn, R.N., Chief Nursing Officer, Medical City Lewisville, Lewisville, TX, p. A634
O'NEILL, Melissa, Vice President Human Resources, Advocate Sherman Hospital, Elgin, IL, p. A194
O'NEILL, Michael, M.D., Chief Medical Officer, Piedmont Eastside Medical Center, Snellville, GA, p. A171
O'NEILL, Stephan, Vice President Information Services, Hartford Hospital, Hartford, CT, p. A116
ONEILL, Steve, Chief Information Officer, NYC Health + Hospitals/Henry J Carter Specialty Hospital And Medical Center, New York, NY, p. A451
ONG, Richard B, Chief Information Officer, Saint Vincent Hospital, Erie, PA, p. A540
ONI, Buki, M.D., Chief Medical Officer, Trinity Kenmare Community Hospital, Kenmare, ND, p. A482
ONIFATHER, Jeff, Chief Financial Officer, Cornerstone of Medical Arts Center Hospital, Fresh Meadows, NY, p. A443
ONO, Craig, M.D., Chief of Staff, Shriners Hospitals for Children–Honolulu, Honolulu, HI, p. A176
ONOFRE, Bonnie, Chief Nursing Officer, Orlando Health South Lake Hospital, Clermont, FL, p. A128
OPBROEK, Steve, Manager Information Technology, Skyline Health, White Salmon, WA, p. A698
OPHAUG, Courtney, FACHE, Chief Executive Officer, Banner Estrella Medical Center, Phoenix, AZ, p. A35
OPHEIKENS, Robyn, Assistant Administrator Human Resources, St. Mark's Hospital, Salt Lake City, UT, p. A669
OPP, Andrew, M.D., Medical Chief of Staff, Saunders Medical Center, Wahoo, NE, p. A406
OPPONG, Bernard, D.O., Chief of Staff, Madison Health, London, OH, p. A498
OPRANDI, Allison, M.D., Chief Medical Officer, Aultman Hospital, Canton, OH, p. A487
OPRISKO, Judy P, Vice President, Allied Services Scranton Rehabilitation Hospital, Scranton, PA, p. A554
OPSTEDAHL, DeeAnna, R.N., Vice President Patient Care Services, Chi St. Alexius Health Dickinson, Dickinson, ND, p. A480
OPSUT, Jennifer
  Chief Executive Officer, Alaska Regional Hospital, Anchorage, AK, p. A27
  Interim Chief Operating Officer, West Valley Medical Center, Caldwell, ID, p. A180
OQUENDO, Tanja, Chief Human Resources Officer, Chi Saint Josep. Health - Flaget Memorial Hospital, Bardstown, KY, p. A263
ORAZINE, Jay, Director Information Services, Baptist Health Paducah, Paducah, KY, p. A272
ORDYNA, Daniel, Chief Executive Officer, Star Valley Health, Afton, WY, p. A726
O'REAR, Caleb F., Chief Executive Officer, Carrollton Regional Medical Center, Carrollton, TX, p. A606
OREGEL, Omar, Controller, Kindred Hospital–Ontario, Ontario, CA, p. A81
O'REILLY, Colin, D.O., Vice President and Chief Medical Officer, Children's Specialized Hospital, New Brunswick, NJ, p. A424
O'REILLY, Frank, Director, Dr. J. Corrigan Mental Health Center, Fall River, MA, p. A313
ORELLANA, Feliipe, Chief Medical Officer, Barnes-Jewish St. Peters Hospital, Saint Peters, MO, p. A386
OREN, Cole, R.N., Chief Nursing Officer, Select Specialty Hospital–Durham, Durham, NC, p. A467
OREOL, Harry, Acting Chief Executive Officer, Dsh Patton, Patton, CA, p. A83
ORIOL, Albert, Vice President Information Management and Chief Information Officer, Rady Children's Hospital - San Diego, San Diego, CA, p. A89
ORLANDO, Anthony T, Senior Vice President Finance, Englewood Health, Englewood, NJ, p. A421
ORLANDO, Kristin, Chief Executive Officer, Mid-Hudson Forensic Psychiatric Center, New Hampton, NY, p. A446
ORLANDO, Lorraine S, Vice President Human Resources, New York–Presbyterian Queens, New York, NY, p. A450
ORMOND, Jack, Chief Financial Officer, Cuba Memorial Hospital, Cuba, NY, p. A442
ORNELAS, Henry
  Chief Operating Officer, Los Angeles General Medical Center, Los Angeles, CA, p. A74
  Chief Operating Officer, Salinas Valley Health, Salinas, CA, p. A88
ORONA, Jennifer, Chief Financial Officer, Abrazo West Campus, Goodyear, AZ, p. A32
O'ROURKE, Jane, R.N., Chief Nursing Officer, Vice President Operations, St. Peter's Hospital, Albany, NY, p. A438
O'ROURKE, Michael
  Regional Human Resource Officer, Ascension Mercy, Aurora, IL, p. A185
  Regional Human Resources Director, Ascension Saint Josep. - Elgin, Elgin, IL, p. A194
OROZCO, Jorge, Chief Executive Officer, Los Angeles General Medical Center, Los Angeles, CA, p. A74
ORR, Karen
  Administrator and Chief Nursing Officer, Providence Medical Center, Kansas City, KS, p. A252
  Chief Nursing Officer, Providence Medical Center, Kansas City, KS, p. A252
ORR, Natassia, Chief Operating Officer, Broward Health Medical Center, Fort Lauderdale, FL, p. A131
ORRILL, Neil, Director of Finance, Optim Medical Center – Screven, Sylvania, GA, p. A172
ORSAK, Brian, Chief Financial Officer, St. Michael's Elite Hospital, Sugar Land, TX, p. A655
ORSAK, Shannon, Chief Medical Officer, St. Michael's Elite Hospital, Sugar Land, TX, p. A655
ORSINI, Alexander, M.D., Medical Director, Baptist Health Extended Care Hospital, Little Rock, AR, p. A49
ORSINI, John
  Executive Vice President and Chief Financial Officer, Northwestern Medicine Central Dupage Hospital, Winfield, IL, p. A211
  Senior Vice President, Chief Financial Officer, Northwestern Medicine Kishwaukee Hospital, Dekalb, IL, p. A193
ORSINI, Thomas J., President and Chief Executive Officer, Lake Taylor Transitional Care Hospital, Norfolk, VA, p. A680
ORT, Linda, Chief Financial Officer, Piggott Health System, Piggott, AR, p. A52
ORTEGA, Alisha, Director, Human Resource, Cottonwood Creek Behavioral Hospital, Meridian, ID, p. A182
ORTEGA, Becky, Manager Human Resources, Adventhealth Avista, Louisville, CO, p. A111
ORTEGA, Charlie, Administrative Director Information Systems, The Hospitals of Providence Sierra Campus – Tenet Healthcare, El Paso, TX, p. A617
ORTEGA, Debbie, Chief Human Resource Officer and Vice President Administrative Services, Huntington Health, Pasadena, CA, p. A83
ORTEGA, Jose, Chief Operating Officer, Greater El Monte Community Hospital, South El Monte, CA, p. A96
ORTEGO, Ashley, Director Human Resources and Marketing, Springhill Medical Center, Springhill, LA, p. A293
ORTEGON, Liisa, R.N., Division President, Sentara Norfolk General Hospital, Norfolk, VA, p. A680
ORTIZ, Andrew, Senior Vice President, Human Resources and Organization Development, Cedars-Sinai Medical Center, Los Angeles, CA, p. A72
ORTIZ, Bienvenido, Coordinator Information Systems, Hospital De Damas, Ponce, PR, p. A734
ORTIZ, Blas Jr, Assistant Superintendent and Public Information Officer, Rio Grande State Center/South Texas Health Care System, Harlingen, TX, p. A623
ORTIZ, Edson, Chief Information Officer, Hospital Pavia Yauco, Yauco, PR, p. A736
ORTIZ, Evelyn Padilla
  Director Human Resources, Hospital Menonita De Cayey, Cayey, PR, p. A732
  Director Human Resources, Mennonite General Hospital, Aibonito, PR, p. A731
ORTIZ, Francisco, M.D., Chief of Staff, Jackson County Hospital District, Edna, TX, p. A616
ORTIZ, Giovanni, Executive Director, Hospital Psiquiatrico Metropolitano, Cabo Rojo, PR, p. A731
ORTIZ, Jose O, Chief Financial Officer, Ryder Memorial Hospital, Humacao, PR, p. A733
ORTIZ, Migdalia, Director Human Resources, Hospital San Carlos Borromeo, Moca, PR, p. A733
ORTIZ, Nancy, Director Human Resource and Marketing, Frio Regional Hospital, Pearsall, TX, p. A643
ORTIZ, Nate, Vice President and Chief Operating Officer, Baptist Health South Florida, Baptist Hospital of Miami, Miami, FL, p. A139
ORTIZ, Norma, M.D., Medical Director, Bayamon Medical Center, Bayamon, PR, p. A731
ORTIZ BAEZ, Felix, Administrator, I. Gonzalez Martinez Oncologic Hospital, Hato Rey, PR, p. A732
ORTMEIER, Chelsea, Chief Financial Officer, Valley County Health System, Ord, NE, p. A404
ORTMYER, Robert
  President & Chief Operating Officer, The University of Vermont Health Network Porter Medical Center, Middlebury, VT, p. A671
  President, The University of Vermont Health Network Elizabethtown Community Hospital, Elizabethtown, NY, p. A442
ORTO, Victoria K, R.N., Chief Nursing and Patient Care Services Officer, Duke Regional Hospital, Durham, NC, p. A467
ORTOLANI, Philip A, Vice President Operations, Mid Coast Hospital, Brunswick, ME, p. A296

Index of Health Care Professionals

Index of Health Care Professionals / Orton

ORTON, Wendy, Chief Nursing Officer, Alleghany Health, Sparta, NC, p. A476
OSANTOSKI, Tina, Director Human Resources, Harbor Beach Community Hospital Inc., Harbor Beach, MI, p. A329
OSARIO, Cesar, Specialist Information Technology, Cedar Crest Hospital And Residential Treatment Center, Belton, TX, p. A603
OSBORN, Kim, Chief Financial Officer, Sequoia Hospital, Redwood City, CA, p. A85
OSBORN, Tom, D.O., Chief Medical Staff, Holdenville General Hospital, Holdenville, OK, p. A513
OSBORNE, Anna, Chief Human Resources Management Service, West Texas Va Health Care System, Big Spring, TX, p. A604
OSBORNE, Phil, Director Information Technology, Bourbon Community Hospital, Paris, KY, p. A273
OSBORNE, Stacey M., Chief Nursing Officer, Geisinger Lewistown Hospital, Lewistown, PA, p. A544
OSBURN, Muriel, Chief Financial Officer, River Place Behavioral Health, La Place, LA, p. A285
OSCADAL, Martin
Senior Vice President Human Resources, St. Elizabeth Florence, Florence, KY, p. A265
Senior Vice President Human Resources, St. Elizabeth Fort Thomas, Fort Thomas, KY, p. A266
Vice President Human Resources, St. Elizabeth Edgewood, Edgewood, KY, p. A265
OSEGARD, Jeff, Chief Information Officer, Cass Health, Atlantic, IA, p. A230
OSEHOBO, Philip, M.D., Chief Medical Officer, Wellstar Spalding Regional Hospital, Griffin, GA, p. A164
OSENTOWSKI, Chris, Chief Executive Officer, HCA Houston Healthcare Medical Center, Houston, TX, p. A625
OSER, William F.
M.D., Chief Medical Officer, JFK Johnson Rehabilitation Institute At Hackensack Meridian Health, Edison, NJ, p. A420
M.D., Senior Vice President and Chief Medical Officer, Hackensack Meridian Health Jfk Medical Center, Edison, NJ, p. A420
O'SHEA, James, Chief Operating Officer, Baton Rouge Behavioral Hospital, Baton Rouge, LA, p. A277
OSHIKI, Michael, M.D., MS, FACHE, President, Riverside Regional Medical Center, Newport News, VA, p. A680
OSHIRO, Shari Ann, Chief Medical Director, Rehabilitation Hospital of The Pacific, Honolulu, HI, p. A176
OSINSKI, Kathleen, Chief Human Resources Service, John D. Dingell Department of Veterans Affairs Medical Center, Detroit, MI, p. A325
OSKIN, Jeffrey L.
Senior Vice President and Chief Operating Officer, Charleston Area Medical Center, Charleston, WV, p. A700
Vice President and Administrator, Charleston Area Medical Center, Charleston, WV, p. A700
OSLIN, Dave, M.D., Chief of Staff, Philadelphia Veterans Affairs Medical Center, Philadelphia, PA, p. A550
OSSELLO, Susan, Chief Financial Officer, Granite County Medical Center, Philipsburg, MT, p. A394
OSTASZEWSKI, Patricia, MS, Chief Executive Officer, Encompass Health Rehabilitation Hospital of Toms River, Toms River, NJ, p. A429
OSTBLOOM, Jan, Human Resources Consultant, Uofl Health – Peace Hospital, Louisville, KY, p. A270
O'STEEN, Neil, Director Information Technology, Bacon County Hospital And Health System, Alma, GA, p. A156
OSTEEN, Tom J, Director Area Technology, Kaiser Permanente Manteca Medical Center, Manteca, CA, p. A76
OSTENSON, Scott, Chief Financial Officer, Jacobson Memorial Hospital Care Center, Elgin, ND, p. A480
OSTER, Kurt, Human Resources Officer, Carl Vinson Veterans Affairs Medical Center, Dublin, GA, p. A163
OSTERBERG, Valerie, Chief Financial Officer, Sanford Vermillion Medical Center, Vermillion, SD, p. A577
OSTERHOUT, David, Assistant Superintendent and Chief Financial Officer, El Paso Psychiatric Center, El Paso, TX, p. A616
OSTERLY, Eric, Chief Financial Officer, Adventhealth Fish Memorial, Orange City, FL, p. A143
OSTING, Lindsey, President, Ohiohealth Doctors Hospital, Columbus, OH, p. A492
OSTLIG, Jane, Chief Medical Officer, Sanford Mayville Medical Center, Mayville, ND, p. A482
OSTRANDER, Maria DC, R.N., MSN, Chief Nurse Executive, San Antonio State Hospital, San Antonio, TX, p. A650
OSTREM, Jill
President, River Falls Area Hospital, River Falls, WI, p. A721
President, United Hospital, Saint Paul, MN, p. A355
OSTROM, Julie, Chief Nursing Officer, Sierra Nevada Memorial Hospital, Grass Valley, CA, p. A66
OSTROW, Peter, M.D., President Medical Staff, Beth Israel Deaconess Hospital–Needham, Needham, MA, p. A316
O'SULLIVAN, Barbara, M.D., M.P.H., Medical Director, Rockefeller University Hospital, New York, NY, p. A452
O'SULLIVAN, Paul
FACHE, Chief Executive Officer, Memorial Hermann Greater Heights Hospital, Houston, TX, p. A627
FACHE, Chief Executive Officer, Memorial Hermann Memorial City Medical Center, Houston, TX, p. A627
OSWAL, Arvind, Chief Financial Officer, Arrowhead Regional Medical Center, Colton, CA, p. A60
OSWALD, Jessica, Chief Executive Officer, Providence St. Elias Specialty Hospital, Anchorage, AK, p. A27
OSWALD, Traci, Vice President Human Resources, Bucyrus Community Hospital, Bucyrus, OH, p. A487
OSWALD, Traci L
Vice President of Human Resources, Galion Community Hospital, Galion, OH, p. A496
Vice President, Chief Human Resources, Avita Ontario Hospital, Ontario, OH, p. A502
OTHOLE, Jean, Chief Executive Officer, U. S. Public Health Service Indian Hospital, Zuni, NM, p. A437
O'TOOL, Nick, Vice President Operational Finance, Chi Health Lakeside, Omaha, NE, p. A403
O'TOOLE, Maura
President, Northwestern Medicine Kishwaukee Hospital, Dekalb, IL, p. A193
President, Northwestern Medicine Valley West Hospital, Sandwich, IL, p. A208
OTOTT, Kelly, R.N., Chief Nursing Officer, Washington County Hospital, Washington, KS, p. A261
OTT, Darin, D.O., Chief of Staff, Kane County Hospital, Kanab, UT, p. A665
OTT, Eugene J. Jr, Chief Executive Officer, Eagleville Hospital, Eagleville, PA, p. A538
OTT, Laurie, Vice President Human Resources and President University Health Care Foundation, Piedmont Augusta, Augusta, GA, p. A158
OTT, Mark, M.D., Regional Chief Medical Director, Intermountain Medical Center, Murray, UT, p. A666
OTT, Pamela, Vice President Finance, Aurora Medical Center – Sheboygan County, Sheboygan, WI, p. A721
OTTE, Elaine, Chief Operating Officer, Clarinda Regional Health Center, Clarinda, IA, p. A232
OTTEN, Sharon A., Vice President Nursing, Advocate South Suburban Hospital, Hazel Crest, IL, p. A197
OTTENBACHER, John, Chief of Staff, Bowdle Hospital, Bowdle, SD, p. A572
OTTENS, Mark, Chief Nursing Officer, Baptist Memorial Hospital–North Mississippi, Oxford, MS, p. A367
OTTLEY, Shawn, R.N., Chief Clinical Officer, Cascade Medical, Leavenworth, WA, p. A691
OTTMAR, Kellie, Manager Information Services, East Adams Rural Healthcare, Ritzville, WA, p. A694
OTTO, Sara, Chief Compliance Officer, North Canyon Medical Center, Gooding, ID, p. A181
OUBRE, Chris, Information Technology Director, Singing River Gulfport, Gulfport, MS, p. A363
OUELETTE, Lisa, Director Human Resources, Corewell Health Beaumont Troy Hospital, Troy, MI, p. A339
OUELLETTE, Demetra, Chief Operating Officer, Rehabilitation Hospital of Rhode Island, North Smithfield, RI, p. A560
OUNGST, Laurie
Chief Administrative Officer, Aspirus Tomahawk Hospital, Tomahawk, WI, p. A723
Vice President, Operations, Aspirus Eagle River Hospital, Eagle River, WI, p. A710
OUSEY, Tracy, Director Human Resources, Washington County Hospital And Clinics, Washington, IA, p. A244
OUTHIER, Amy, Director Health Information Management, Weatherford Regional Hospital, Weatherford, OK, p. A524
OUTLAW, Debbie, R.N., Director Patient Care Services, Coastal Virginia Rehabilitation, Yorktown, VA, p. A686
OUTLAW, Laura, Chief Executive Officer, Center for Behavioral Health Maryland Heights, Maryland Heights, MO, p. A380
OVANDO, Benjamin, Chief Operations Officer, Rancho Los Amigos National Rehabilitation Center, Downey, CA, p. A62
OVERBY, Roger, Executive Director Information Systems, Greene County Medical Center, Jefferson, IA, p. A238
OVERMILLER, Tara
Chief Executive Officer, Phillip. County Health Systems, Phillipsburg, KS, p. A258
Chief Operating Officer, Phillip. County Health Systems, Phillipsburg, KS, p. A258
OVERSTREET, Alyson, Chief Financial Officer, Grove Hill Memorial Hospital, Grove Hill, AL, p. A20
OVERSTREET, Amy, Director Human Resources, Trousdale Medical Center, Hartsville, TN, p. A584
OVERTON, Deana, Director Human Resources, Mitchell County Hospital, Colorado City, TX, p. A608
OVERTON, Saundra, R.N., Chief Nursing Officer, Royal Oaks Hospital, Windsor, MO, p. A388
OVESON, Mark, M.D., Chief Medical Staff, Central Valley Medical Center, Nephi, UT, p. A666
OWEN, Amber, Regional Vice President, Human Resources, Texas Health Huguley Hospital Fort Worth South, Burleson, TX, p. A606
OWEN, Sabrina, Human Resources Officer, VA Central Iowa Health Care System–Des Moines, Des Moines, IA, p. A235
OWEN, Summer, Chief Financial Officer, Great Plains Health, North Platte, NE, p. A403
OWENS, Beverly, Controller, Atrium Health Navicent Rehabilitation Hospital, Macon, GA, p. A167
OWENS, Brian, Chief Operating Officer, Lindner Center of Hope, Mason, OH, p. A499
OWENS, Courtney, R.N., Chief Nursing Officer, Texas County Memorial Hospital, Houston, MO, p. A376
OWENS, Diane, Assistant Administrator, St. David's Medical Center, Austin, TX, p. A600
OWENS, Dwight, Chief Operating Officer, Indian Path Community Hospital, Kingsport, TN, p. A585
OWENS, Jill, M.D., President, Olean General Hospital, Olean, NY, p. A455
OWENS, Kevin, M.D., Chief Medical Officer, Minidoka Memorial Hospital, Rupert, ID, p. A183
OWENS, Mark, M.D., Vice President Medical Affairs, Mercy San Juan Medical Center, Carmichael, CA, p. A58
OWENS, Nancy, Administrator, Christus Dubuis Hospital of Fort Smith, Fort Smith, AR, p. A46
OWENS, Royce Bramer, Chief Operating Officer, Midcoast Central – Llano, Llano, TX, p. A635
OWENS, Stephanie, Manager Human Resources, Mcdowell Arh Hospital, Mcdowell, KY, p. A271
OWENSBY, Terri, R.N., Chief Nursing Executive, Kaiser Permanente South Sacramento Medical Center, Sacramento, CA, p. A87
OWINGS, Karen, MSN, Vice President, Patient Care Services, Medstar Union Memorial Hospital, Baltimore, MD, p. A301
OWINGS, Tripp, Chief Executive Officer, HCA Florida Brandon Hospital, Brandon, FL, p. A127
OWNES, Loyal, Chief Executive Officer, Beckett Springs, West Chester, OH, p. A506
OWREY, Donald R., President and Chief Executive Officer, Atlantic General Hospital, Berlin, MD, p. A302
OXFORD, Michelle
Chief Administrative Officer, Healdsburg Hospital, Healdsburg, CA, p. A67
Chief Administrative Officer, Petaluma Valley Hospital, Petaluma, CA, p. A83
OXFORD, Tammy, Director Human Resources, Bob Wilson Memorial Grant County Hospital, Ulysses, KS, p. A261
OXLEY, Dawn, R.N., Associate Director Patient Care Services and Nurse Executive, Iowa City Va Health System, Iowa City, IA, p. A238
OXTON, Alice, Director Information Technology, Sentara Obici Hospital, Suffolk, VA, p. A684
OZBORN, Charles A., M.D., Chief of Staff, North Mississippi Medical Center–Eupora, Eupora, MS, p. A361
OZBURN, Thomas H., FACHE, President and Chief Executive Officer, Tristar Centennial Medical Center, Nashville, TN, p. A591
OZEL, A Deniz, M.D., Chief Medical Officer, Northeast Rehabilitation Hospital, Salem, NH, p. A417
OZMENT, Mary, Chief Nursing Officer, Hillcrest Hospital Pryor, Pryor, OK, p. A520
OZMUN, Andrew
Chief Financial Officer, Alta View Hospital, Sandy, UT, p. A669
Chief Financial Officer, Riverton Hospital, Riverton, UT, p. A668
OZUAH, Philip O., M.D., Ph.D., Chief Executive Officer, Montefiore Medical Center, New York, NY, p. A449

P

PAARLBERG, Ted, Chief Executive Officer, Medical Behavioral Hospital of Mishawaka, Mishawaka, IN, p. A223
PAASCH, Michael
Regional Chief Information Officer, SSM Health St. Mary's Hospital – St. Louis, Saint Louis, MO, p. A385
Regional Vice President and Chief Information Officer, SSM Health Cardinal Glennon Children's Hospital, Saint Louis, MO, p. A384
Vice President, Regional Chief Information Officer, SSM Health St. Clare Hospital – Fenton, Fenton, MO, p. A375

A938 Index of Health Care Professionals

Index of Health Care Professionals / Parigi

Index of Health Care Professionals

PABLO, Gary M.
M.D., Chief Medical Officer, Ascension Sacred Heart Emerald Coast, Miramar Beach, FL, p. A141
M.D., Chief Medical Officer, Ascension Sacred Heart Gulf, Port St Joe, FL, p. A147
PABON, Jose O, Director Operations, Wilma N. Vazquez Medical Center, Vega Baja, PR, p. A736
PABON–RAMIREZ, Felix, Chief Information Officer, St. Charles Hospital, Port Jefferson, NY, p. A456
PACCA, Richard, M.D., Chief of Staff, Granville Health System, Oxford, NC, p. A474
PACCAPANICCIA, Dominic, Chief Operating Officer, Indiana Regional Medical Center, Indiana, PA, p. A542
PACE, Dewane, Chief Executive Officer, Haxtun Hospital District, Haxtun, CO, p. A109
PACE, Kathleen, MSN, R.N., Chief Nursing Officer, HCA Florida Englewood Hospital, Englewood, FL, p. A131
PACE, Kelly, Director Human Resource, Carolina Dunes Behavioral Health, Leland, NC, p. A471
PACEK, Thomas, Vice President Information Systems and Chief Information Officer, Inspira Medical Center–Vineland, Vineland, NJ, p. A430
PACHECO, Robert W, Vice President Finance, Women & Infants Hospital of Rhode Island, Providence, RI, p. A561
PACINI, Jenna, Human Resources Specialist, Belmont Behavioral Health System, Philadelphia, PA, p. A548
PACK, Natalie, Chief Financial Officer, St. David's North Austin Medical Center, Austin, TX, p. A600
PACK, William, Chief Financial Officer, Memorial Hermann – Texas Medical Center, Houston, TX, p. A627
PACKER, Eric, President, Cedar City Hospital, Cedar City, UT, p. A664
PACKER, Lee, Administrator, South Florida State Hospital, Hollywood, FL, p. A133
PACKER, Melanie, Administrative Assistant, Director of Human Resources, Clearsky Rehabilitation Hospital of Leesville, Leesville, LA, p. A287
PACKER, Steven J., M.D., President and Chief Executive Officer, Montage Health, Community Hospital of The Monterey Peninsula, Monterey, CA, p. A78
PACYNA, Andrew, Deputy Director, Northeast Ohio Va Healthcare System, Cleveland, OH, p. A491
PADDEN, Ernest C, Chief Financial Officer, Bon Secours Maryview Medical Center, Portsmouth, VA, p. A681
PADEN, Tawnya, Director Human Resources, Weatherford Regional Hospital, Weatherford, OK, p. A524
PADGETT, Doug, President/Chief Executive Officer/Chairman of the Board, Totally Kids Rehabilitation Hospital, Loma Linda, CA, p. A70
PADGETT, Shirley, Director Human Resources, Southwell Medical, Adel, GA, p. A156
PADILLA, Kathy, Chief Nursing Officer, Bitterroot Health – Daly Hospital, Hamilton, MT, p. A392
PADULA, Judy, MSN, R.N., Vice President Patient Care Services and Chief Nursing Officer, St. Joseph's University Medical Center, Paterson, NJ, p. A426
PAFFORD, Roger, M.D., Medical Director, Mineral Community Hospital, Superior, MT, p. A396
PAGE, Bob, Chief Executive Officer, The University of Kansas Hospital, Kansas City, KS, p. A252
PAGE, Cynthia, FACHE, Chief Executive Officer, Encompass Health Rehabilitation Hospital of Braintree, Braintree, MA, p. A311
PAGE, Deborah, Chief Human Resources Officer, Duke University Hospital, Durham, NC, p. A467
PAGE, Heather, MSN, Director of Nursing, Chi St. Josep. Health Burleson Hospital, Caldwell, TX, p. A606
PAGE, Jennifer, M.D., Medical Director, Mercy Rehabilitation Hospital South, Saint Louis, MO, p. A385
PAGE, Pattie, Director Marketing and Public Relations, Piedmont Eastside Medical Center, Snellville, GA, p. A171
PAGE, Robert III, Chief Information and Technology Officer, Lt. Col. Luke Weathers, Jr. Va Medical Center, Memphis, TN, p. A588
PAGE, Rodger
Market President, North State, St. Elizabeth Community Hospital, Red Bluff, CA, p. A85
President, Mercy Medical Center Mount Shasta, Mount Shasta, CA, p. A79
PAGE, Sue, Director Human Resources, Monroe County Medical Center, Tompkinsville, KY, p. A274
PAGE, William E, CPA, Chief Financial Officer, Franklin Medical Center, Winnsboro, LA, p. A294
PAGELER, Robert
Chief Information Officer, Confluence Health Hospital – Central Campus, Wenatchee, WA, p. A698
Chief Information Officer, Confluence Health Hospital – Mares Campus, Wenatchee, WA, p. A698
PAGET, Cindy, Chief Human Resources Officer, Forks Community Hospital, Forks, WA, p. A690
PAGLIUZZA, Greg, Chief Financial Officer, Unitypoint Health – Trinity Bettendorf, Bettendorf, IA, p. A231
PAGNINI, Janie, Administrator Accounting, Atascadero State Hospital, Atascadero, CA, p. A56
PAGUAGA, Ana, Director of Human Resources, Coral Gables Hospital, Coral Gables, FL, p. A128
PAHE, Gary, Manager Human Resources, Navajo Health Foundation – Sage Memorial Hospital, Ganado, AZ, p. A31
PAHL, Jodi, Chief Nurse Executive, Mercy Health – St. Rita's Medical Center, Lima, OH, p. A498
PAHUT, Rachel, Chief Nursing Officer, Great Falls Clinic Hospital, Great Falls, MT, p. A392
PAI, Ajith
PharmD, FACHE, Chief Executive Officer, Texas Health Harris Methodist Hospital Southwest Fort Worth, Fort Worth, TX, p. A620
PharmD, FACHE, President, Texas Health Harris Methodist Hospital Southwest Fort Worth, Fort Worth, TX, p. A620
PAINE, Chad, Director Client Services, Pottstown Hospital, Pottstown, PA, p. A553
PAINE, Lincoln, M.D., Medical Director, River Oaks Hospital, New Orleans, LA, p. A290
PAINE, Russ, Human Resources Officer, Erlanger Western Carolina Hospital, Murphy, NC, p. A473
PAINTER, Jeff, Network Administrator, Information Technology, Summit Pacific Medical Center, Elma, WA, p. A689
PAIRISH, Katherine, Chief Financial Officer, Eastern Plumas Health Care, Portola, CA, p. A84
PAIRMORE, James G., Commander, Dwight David Eisenhower Army Medical Center, Fort Gordon, GA, p. A164
PALADINO, James, Controller, New England Rehabilitation Hospital of Portland, Portland, ME, p. A298
PALAGI, Pam, Regional Vice President, Finance, SCL Health Mt – St. Vincent Healthcare, Billings, MT, p. A390
PALAZZO, Ettore, Chief Executive Officer, Evergreenhealth, Kirkland, WA, p. A691
PALERMO, Robert, Vice President Finance, Hackensack Meridian Health Ocean University Medical Center, Brick Township. NJ, p. A419
PALEY, Jonathon, Chief Medical Officer, Riverview Health Institute, Dayton, OH, p. A494
PALICKA, Martha, Director Information Systems, Bartlett Regional Hospital, Juneau, AK, p. A28
PALIGO, Terry, Chief Financial Officer, Deaconess Illinois Union County, Anna, IL, p. A185
PALKOWSKI, Chris, M.D., Physician in Chief, Kaiser Permanente Sacramento Medical Center, Sacramento, CA, p. A86
PALLIN, Angel, Senior Vice President of Operations, Mount Sinai Medical Center, Miami Beach, FL, p. A141
PALMER, Cathy, Chief Financial Officer, Torrance State Hospital, Torrance, PA, p. A555
PALMER, Charles, Director Information Technology, Tidalhealth Nanticoke, Seaford, DE, p. A122
PALMER, Debra L, MS, R.N., Chief Human Resources Officer and Corporate Compliance Officer, Fairfield Medical Center, Lancaster, OH, p. A498
PALMER, Janel M, Director Human Resources, Greenwood County Hospital, Eureka, KS, p. A249
PALMER, Katie, Manager Human Resources, Sanford Aberdeen Medical Center, Aberdeen, SD, p. A572
PALMER, Keith, Assistant Administrator, Winkler County Memorial Hospital, Kermit, TX, p. A632
PALMER, Kelly, D.O., Medical Director, State Hospital South, Blackfoot, ID, p. A179
PALMER, Melissa, Executive Director of Nursing, Delta Health, Delta, CO, p. A106
PALMER, Stephanie, Chief Nursing Officer, Encompass Health Valley of The Sun Rehabilitation Hospital, Glendale, AZ, p. A32
PALMIER, Michael L, Chief Human Resources Management, Overton Brooks Veterans' Administration Medical Center, Shreveport, LA, p. A292
PALMUCCI, Jeffrey, Chief Executive Officer, Vanderbilt Stallworth Rehabilitation Hospital, Nashville, TN, p. A591
PALO, Alan, Chief Financial Officer, Sarah D. Culbertson Memorial Hospital, Rushville, IL, p. A208
PALUMBO, Christopher M., Chief Executive Officer, Nebraska Spine Hospital, Omaha, NE, p. A404
PALUMBO, Michael, M.D., Executive Vice President and Medical Director, White Plains Hospital Center, White Plains, NY, p. A462
PAMPERIEN, Linda, Chief Financial Officer, Texas County Memorial Hospital, Houston, MO, p. A376
PANDO, Terry, R.N., Associate Executive Director and Chief Nursing Officer, Staten Island University Hospital, New York, NY, p. A453
PANDOLPH, Philip E., FACHE, President and Chief Executive Officer, Meadville Medical Center, Meadville, PA, p. A545
PANDYA, Kamel, Director Information Services, San Antonio Regional Hospital, Upland, CA, p. A99
PANESAR, Mandip. M.D., Medical Director, Wyoming County Community Hospital, Warsaw, NY, p. A461
PANESSO, Katherine, Chief Executive Officer, Larkin Community Hospital–Palm Springs Campus, Hialeah, FL, p. A133
PANI, Arabinda, Chief Medical Officer, HCA Houston Healthcare Northwest, Houston, TX, p. A626
PANIRY, David, Chief Financial Officer, HCA Florida Northwest Hospital, Margate, FL, p. A138
PANKEY, De'Niro, Director Information Systems, Corona Regional Medical Center, Corona, CA, p. A60
PANKEY, Susan Kay, Chief Nursing Officer, Davis County Hospital And Clinics, Bloomfield, IA, p. A231
PANKOWSKI, Charles, Manager Human Resources, Select Specialty Hospital–Columbus, Columbus, OH, p. A492
PANNAGL, Bryan, Chief Financial Officer, Christus Coushatta Health Care Center, Coushatta, LA, p. A280
PANNIKODE, Shalima, Senior Vice President and Chief Information and Digital Officer, Wellstar Kennestone Hospital, Marietta, GA, p. A167
PANNULLO, Ava, M.D., Vice President Medical Services and Physician in Chief, The Hospital At Hebrew Senior Care, West Hartford, CT, p. A120
PANSA, Leonard F, Senior Vice President Human Resources and Administrative Services, Mercy Medical Center, Springfield, MA, p. A318
PAOLUCCI, Benjamin, D.O., Chief of Staff, Insight Surgical Hospital, Warren, MI, p. A340
PAPA, Alan, President, University Hospitals Ahuja Medical Center, Beachwood, OH, p. A486
PAPA, AnnMarie, R.N., Vice President and Chief Nursing Officer, Jefferson Einstein Montgomery Hospital, East Norriton, PA, p. A538
PAPALIA, Fern, Director of Nursing, Essex County Hospital Center, Cedar Grove, NJ, p. A419
PAPALIA, Mark, President, UPMC Kane, Kane, PA, p. A543
PAPE, David, Vice President, Information Technology, Palomar Medical Center Poway, Poway, CA, p. A84
PAPKA, Lauren, Chief Administrative Officer, St. Mary's Sacred Heart Hospital, Lavonia, GA, p. A166
PAPPAN, Clayton, Director Human Resources and Marketing, South Central Kansas Medical Center, Arkansas City, KS, p. A246
PAPPAS, Michael, Chief Fiscal Service Officer, Northeast Ohio Va Healthcare System, Cleveland, OH, p. A491
PAPPAS, Sheryl L, Chief Financial Officer, Sanford Webster Medical Center, Webster, SD, p. A578
PAPPAS, Theron, Director Management Information Systems, Holy Family Memorial, Manitowoc, WI, p. A715
PARADIS, Brian, Chief Operating Officer, Adventhealth Orlando, Orlando, FL, p. A144
PARADIS, James, President, Paoli Hospital, Paoli, PA, p. A547
PARADIS, Jeanne, Director Information Services, The Acadia Hospital, Bangor, ME, p. A295
PARAS, Chris, Interim Executive Director, Brookdale Hospital Medical Center, New York, NY, p. A447
PARAUDA, Martina A, Director, Veterans Affairs New York Harbor Healthcare System, New York, NY, p. A453
PARAVATE, Chris, Chief Information Officer, Northeast Georgia Medical Center, Gainesville, GA, p. A164
PARAVISINI, Nilda, Director Human Resources, Hospital Manati Medical Center, Manati, PR, p. A733
PARCHMENT, Deborah, Executive Director, Kingsboro Psychiatric Center, New York, NY, p. A448
PARDEE, Wendy Ann., President and Chief Executive Officer, The Children's Institute of Pittsburgh, Pittsburgh, PA, p. A551
PAREEK, Yogesh, M.D., Clinical Director, Brown County Community Treatment Center, Green Bay, WI, p. A712
PAREKH, Darshan Shawn., PharmD, FACHE, Chief Executive Officer, Roxborough Memorial Hospital, Philadelphia, PA, p. A550
PARENT, Paula A., Chief Nursing Officer and Director of Human Resources, Cary Medical Center, Caribou, ME, p. A296
PARET, Jason, Chief Executive Officer, Catalina Island Medical Center, Avalon, CA, p. A56
PARHAM, Eva, R.N., Chief Nurse Executive, Central State Hospital, Petersburg, VA, p. A681
PARHAM, Michael, R.N., Chief Nursing Officer, Riverside Hospital, Alexandria, LA, p. A276
PARHAM, Tracy
University of North Carolina Hospitals, Chapel Hill, NC, p. A465
Health Care System Chief Information Officer, UNC Health Rex, Raleigh, NC, p. A475
PARIGI, John S II, Interim Chief Financial Officer, Healdsburg Hospital, Healdsburg, CA, p. A67

Index of Health Care Professionals

Index of Health Care Professionals / Parikh

PARIKH, Pranav, M.D., Vice President & Chief Medical Officer, Hannibal Regional Hospital, Hannibal, MO, p. A376
PARIS, Claire, M.D., Vice President and Chief Medical Officer, UNC Health Lenoir, Kinston, NC, p. A471
PARIS, David, Chief Executive Officer, Perry County General Hospital, Richton, MS, p. A368
PARIS, Heather, Chief Administrator Officer and Chief Financial Officer, Greene County Medical Center, Jefferson, IA, p. A238
PARIS, Karen, Controller, Crittenden Community Hospital, Marion, KY, p. A271
PARIS, Sherri, Chief Operating Officer, Providence Milwaukie Hospital, Milwaukie, OR, p. A529
PARIS, Trevor, M.D., Medical Director, Brooks Rehabilitation Hospital, Jacksonville, FL, p. A134
PARISI, James
Chief Executive Officer, St. Luke's Health – Lakeside Hospital, The Woodlands, TX, p. A657
Chief Executive Officer, St. Luke's Health – The Woodlands Hospital, The Woodlands, TX, p. A658
PARISKY, Yuri, M.D., Chief of Staff, Mammoth Hospital, Mammoth Lakes, CA, p. A76
PARK, Albert, M.D., Chief Medical Officer, Quad Cities Rehabilitation Institute, The, Moline, IL, p. A202
PARK, Charlton Gordon, Chief Financial Officer and Chief Analytics Officer, University of Utah Health, Salt Lake City, UT, p. A669
PARK, Chong S.
M.D., Chief Executive Officer, Canonsburg Hospital, Canonsburg, PA, p. A536
M.D., Chief Executive Officer, Jefferson Hospital, Jefferson Hills, PA, p. A542
PARK, Jessica, Director Accounting, Penn Highlands Brookville, Brookville, PA, p. A535
PARK, Jung, Interim Chief Information Officer, Connecticut Children's, Hartford, CT, p. A116
PARK, Kelly
R.N., Chief Executive Officer, Sweeny Community Hospital, Sweeny, TX, p. A655
R.N., Chief Nursing Officer, Sweeny Community Hospital, Sweeny, TX, p. A655
PARK, Rustin, Director of Nursing, Seven Hills Hospital, Henderson, NV, p. A409
PARKE, Carol, Chief Operating Officer, SUN Kentucky, Sun Behavioral Kentucky, Erlanger, KY, p. A265
PARKER, Charisse
Director Human Resources, Vanderbilt Bedford Hospital, Shelbyville, TN, p. A593
Director Human Resources, Vanderbilt Tullahoma Harton Hospital, Tullahoma, TN, p. A594
PARKER, Christopher, R.N., Executive Vice President and Chief Operating Officer, St. John's Episcopal Hospital, New York, NY, p. A453
PARKER, David, VP Information Technology, Magnolia Regional Health Center, Corinth, MS, p. A361
PARKER, Deanna, Director Human Resources, Dosher Memorial Hospital, Southport, NC, p. A476
PARKER, Erin, Senior Vice President and Chief Information Officer, Arkansas Children's Hospital, Little Rock, AR, p. A49
PARKER, Janie, Chief Financial Officer, Hardin County General Hospital, Rosiclare, IL, p. A208
PARKER, Jim, FACHE, Chief Executive Officer, Munising Memorial Hospital, Munising, MI, p. A334
PARKER, Judy, Chief Executive Officer, Encompass Health Rehabilitation Hospital of Reading, Reading, PA, p. A553
PARKER, Julie, Chief Executive Officer, Lighthouse Behavioral Health Hospital, Conway, SC, p. A565
PARKER, Lori, Chief Nursing Officer, Gonzales Healthcare Systems, Gonzales, TX, p. A622
PARKER, Lorraine, MSN, R.N., Chief Nursing Officer and Assistant Vice President, Bayfront Health St. Petersburg, Saint Petersburg, FL, p. A148
PARKER, Michael, M.D., Chief of Staff, Sharon Hospital, Sharon, CT, p. A118
PARKER, Ralph, Chief Executive Officer and Chief Nursing Officer, Page Hospital, Page, AZ, p. A34
PARKER, Richard, M.D., President, Cleveland Clinic Hillcrest Hospital, Cleveland, OH, p. A490
PARKER, Sandra K, M.D., Chief Medical Officer, Eastpointe Hospital, Daphne, AL, p. A18
PARKER, Susan, Chief Executive Officer, Kimble Hospital, Junction, TX, p. A631
PARKER, Theresa M, Regional Finance Director, Transylvania Regional Hospital, Brevard, NC, p. A464
PARKER, Tina, Director Human Resources, Encompass Health Rehabilitation Hospital of Midland Odessa, Midland, TX, p. A639
PARKER, Tom, Chief Executive Officer, Mammoth Hospital, Mammoth Lakes, CA, p. A76
PARKER, Travis, Director Human Resources, Southwest Health System, Cortez, CO, p. A105
PARKER, Valerie, M.D., Clinical Director, U. S. Public Health Service Indian Hospital, Rosebud, SD, p. A576
PARKER–BRADSHAW, Carmen, Vice President and Administrator, Saint Luke's Hospital of Kansas City, Kansas City, MO, p. A378
PARKHILL, Cherie, Chief Financial Officer, Crosbyton Clinic Hospital, Crosbyton, TX, p. A610
PARKHURST, Jennifer, Chief Financial Officer, City of Hope's Helford Clinical Research Hospital, Duarte, CA, p. A62
PARKINS, David, M.D., Chief of Staff, Watertown Regional Medical Center, Watertown, WI, p. A723
PARKINSON, Michelle A, Director Human Resources, Prairie St. John's, Fargo, ND, p. A480
PARKS, Audrey, Chief Information Officer, Salinas Valley Health, Salinas, CA, p. A88
PARKS, Cary, Chief Information Resource Management, Hampton Veterans Affairs Medical Center, Hampton, VA, p. A677
PARKS, Dave, Chief Information Officer, Three Rivers Health System, Inc., Three Rivers, MI, p. A339
PARKS, Jody, Administrator, Ottawa County Health Center, Minneapolis, KS, p. A255
PARKS, Kathi, Director of Nursing, South Lincoln Medical Center, Kemmerer, WY, p. A727
PARKS, Kelvin L., Chief Executive Officer, Select Specialty Hospital–Orlando North, Orlando, FL, p. A144
PARKS, Kyle, M.D., Chief of Staff, Evans Memorial Hospital, Claxton, GA, p. A160
PARKS, Michaela, Director of Finance, Pawnee County Memorial Hospital And Rural Health Clinic, Pawnee City, NE, p. A405
PARKS, Michelle, Administrator, Rivervalley Behavioral Health Hospital, Owensboro, KY, p. A272
PARKS, Peggy, R.N., Chief Nursing Officer, Northeast Regional Medical Center, Kirksville, MO, p. A378
PARKS, Sherry, R.N., MS, Chief Nursing Officer, Saint Alphonsus Regional Medical Center, Boise, ID, p. A179
PARKS, Vicki, Chief Executive Officer, Wythe County Community Hospital, Wytheville, VA, p. A686
PARMER, Michael, Chief Medical Officer, Carepartners Rehabilitation Hospital, Asheville, NC, p. A463
PARNEL, George, Chief Financial Officer, Clifton T. Perkins Hospital Center, Jessup, MD, p. A305
PARNELL, Linda, Chief Nursing Officer, Musc Health Marion Medical Center, Mullins, SC, p. A569
PAROBEK, Jim, President, Ohiohealth Marion General Hospital, Marion, OH, p. A499
PAROD, Daniel A.
President Central Region, Ascension St. Vincent Indianapolis Hospital, Indianapolis, IN, p. A219
President Central Region, Ascension St. Vincent Seton Specialty Hospital, Indianapolis, IN, p. A219
PARR, James
Chief Financial Officer, Salem Health West Valley, Dallas, OR, p. A526
Chief Financial Officer, Salem Hospital, Salem, OR, p. A532
PARR, Lynnette
Chief Operating Officer, Calais Community Hospital, Calais, ME, p. A296
Vice President Financial Services, Chief Financial Officer, Calais Community Hospital, Calais, ME, p. A296
PARRA, Joseph, M.D., Division Chief Medical Officer, Medical City Dallas, Dallas, TX, p. A611
PARRA, Kristin, Chief Executive Officer, Yuma Rehabilitation Hospital, An Affiliation of Encompass Health And Yuma Regional Medical Center, Yuma, AZ, p. A42
PARRA, Michelle, Director Human Resources, Kindred Hospital South Bay, Gardena, CA, p. A65
PARRADO, Carlos, M.D., Sr, Chief Medical Officer, Roosevelt Warm Springs Long Term Acute Care Hospital, Warm Springs, GA, p. A173
PARRINELLO, Kathleen M, Ph.D., Chief Operating Officer, Strong Memorial Hospital of The University of Rochester, Rochester, NY, p. A457
PARRIS, Brent, Vice President of Human Resources, Self Regional Healthcare, Greenwood, SC, p. A567
PARRIS, Misty, Vice President Operations, PHMG Northwest, Peacehealth St. Josep. Medical Center, Bellingham, WA, p. A687
PARRISH, Becky, Director Human Resources, Bon Secours – Southern Virginia Medical Center, Emporia, VA, p. A675
PARRISH, Carl, Chief Fiscal Service, James E. Van Zandt Veterans Affairs Medical Center, Altoona, PA, p. A534
PARRISH, Suann, Chief Financial Officer, Yoakum County Hospital, Denver City, TX, p. A614
PARRISH, Todd, M.D., Chief of Staff, UT Health Jacksonville, Jacksonville, TX, p. A630
PARRY, Kayla, Manager Human Resources, Ivinson Memorial Hospital, Laramie, WY, p. A727
PARRY, Mary, Vice President Operations and Chief Operating Officer, Oneida Healthcare, Oneida, NY, p. A455
PARRY, Timothy
R.N., Chief Operating Officer, Highland District Hospital, Hillsboro, OH, p. A497
R.N., President and Chief Executive Officer, Highland District Hospital, Hillsboro, OH, p. A497
PARSI, Kia
M.D., Chief Medical Officer, Chi St. Josep. Regional Health Center, Bryan, TX, p. A605
M.D., Chief Medical Officer, Chi St. Joseph's Health, Park Rapids, MN, p. A352
PARSLEY, George N, Chief Operating Officer, Detar Healthcare System, Victoria, TX, p. A660
PARSLEY, Patricia, Program Director, Access Hospital Dayton, Dayton, OH, p. A493
PARSON, Charlynne, Nurse Executive, Moccasin Bend Mental Health Institute, Chattanooga, TN, p. A580
PARSONS, Brent
Chief Executive Officer, Dupont Hospital, Fort Wayne, IN, p. A216
Chief Executive Officer, Western Arizona Regional Medical Center, Bullhead City, AZ, p. A30
PARSONS, John, R.N., Chief Nursing Officer, Trustpoint Rehabilitation Hospital of Lubbock, Lubbock, TX, p. A636
PARTEE, Paris I, Associate Administrator and Director Human Resources, John H. Stroger Jr. Hospital of Cook County, Chicago, IL, p. A190
PARTENZA, John, Vice President and Treasurer, Northern Westchester Hospital, Mount Kisco, NY, p. A446
PARTHEMORE, Warrenette, Director Human Resources, Promedica Memorial Hospital, Fremont, OH, p. A496
PARTIN, James R, M.D., Chief Medical Director, Methodist Hospital Hill Country, Fredericksburg, TX, p. A620
PARUCH, Randy J, Director, Information Systems, Holland Hospital, Holland, MI, p. A330
PASCASCIO, Dellone, Chief Nursing Officer, Olive View–Ucla Medical Center, Los Angeles, CA, p. A74
PASCO, Teri, Director Human Resources, East Liverpool City Hospital, East Liverpool, OH, p. A495
PASCUAL, Bolivar, M.D., Medical Director, Essex County Hospital Center, Cedar Grove, NJ, p. A419
PASCUZZI, Robert, Chief Financial Officer, Mercy San Juan Medical Center, Carmichael, CA, p. A58
PASLEY–RICH, Angela, Chief Executive Officer, The Pavilion At Williamsburg Place, Williamsburg, VA, p. A685
PASQUALE, Mark
Chief Information Officer, Integris Baptist Medical Center, Oklahoma City, OK, p. A517
Chief Information Officer, Integris Southwest Medical Center, Oklahoma City, OK, p. A517
PASS, Christian
Interim Chief Financial Officer, John Muir Health, Concord Medical Center, Concord, CA, p. A60
Senior Vice President & Chief Financial Officer, John Muir Medical Center, Walnut Creek, Walnut Creek, CA, p. A100
Senior Vice President and Chief Financial Officer, John Muir Behavioral Health Center, Concord, CA, p. A60
PASSAFARO, David, President, New England Baptist Hospital, Boston, MA, p. A311
PASSANANTE, Gregory, Hospital Administrator, Shriners Children's Philadelphia, Philadelphia, PA, p. A550
PASSARELLI, Theresa, Human Resources Generalist, Warm Springs Medical Center, Warm Springs, GA, p. A173
PASSMANN, Frederic K, M.D., Chief of Staff, Stonewall Memorial Hospital, Aspermont, TX, p. A598
PASSMORE, Gary, Chief Information Officer, Endless Mountains Health Systems, Montrose, PA, p. A546
PASTIAN, Andre, R.N., MSN, Chief Nursing Officer, Boulder City Hospital, Boulder City, NV, p. A408
PASTOR, Robert II, R.N., Chief Executive Officer, Rainy Lake Medical Center, International Falls, MN, p. A348
PASTORE, Raymond, M.D., Chief Medical Officer, St. John's Episcopal Hospital, New York, NY, p. A453
PASTRANA, Jose Guillermo., Executive Director, Hospital Menonita De Caguas, Caguas, PR, p. A731
PASZTOR, Barbara J.
R.N., Chief Nursing Executive, Blanchard Valley Hospital, Findlay, OH, p. A496
R.N., Chief Nursing Executive, Bluffton Hospital, Bluffton, OH, p. A486
PATCHELL, Lee, Lead Human Resources Business Partner, Presbyterian Hospital, Albuquerque, NM, p. A433
PATE, John, M.D., Chief Medical Officer, Astera Health, Wadena, MN, p. A356
PATE, Warren, Chief Financial Officer, HCA Florida South Shore Hospital, Sun City Center, FL, p. A151

A940 Index of Health Care Professionals

Index of Health Care Professionals / Paulus

Index of Health Care Professionals

PATEL, Amita, M.D., Medical Director, Haven Behavioral Hospital of Dayton, Dayton, OH, p. A493
PATEL, Bimal, President, Hartford and Northwest Regions, Charlotte Hungerford Hospital, Torrington, CT, p. A119
PATEL, Binesh, M.D., Chief Medical Officer, Mclaren Flint, Flint, MI, p. A327
PATEL, Deepak, M.D., Medical Director, Cumberland Hall Hospital, Hopkinsville, KY, p. A267
PATEL, Dilip. M.D., Chief of Staff, Greater El Monte Community Hospital, South El Monte, CA, p. A96
PATEL, Fatma, M.D., Vice President Medical Affairs, Niagara Falls Memorial Medical Center, Niagara Falls, NY, p. A454
PATEL, Govind, M.D., Medical Director, Encompass Health Rehabilitation Hospital of Morgantown, Morgantown, WV, p. A703
PATEL, Hema, Director Medical Records, Riverwoods Behavioral Health System, Riverdale, GA, p. A170
PATEL, Hiral, M.D., Chief Executive Officer, Mountainview Hospital, Las Vegas, NV, p. A410
PATEL, Karan
Chief Executive Officer, Inova Specialty Hospital, Alexandria, VA, p. A673
Interim Chief Executive Officer, Select Specialty Hospital Midtown Atlanta, Atlanta, GA, p. A158
PATEL, Maheshkumar, M.D., Medical Director, Center for Behavioral Medicine, Kansas City, MO, p. A377
PATEL, Malini, M.D., Medical Director, Elgin Mental Health Center, Elgin, IL, p. A194
PATEL, Malisha
Senior Vice President and Chief Executive Officer, Memorial Hermann Greater Heights Hospital, Houston, TX, p. A627
Senior Vice President and Chief Executive Officer, Memorial Hermann Sugar Land Hospital, Sugar Land, TX, p. A654
PATEL, Natu M, M.D., Chief of Staff, Phoebe Worth Medical Center, Sylvester, GA, p. A172
PATEL, Neel, Chief Executive Officer, Kessler Institute for Rehabilitation, West Orange, NJ, p. A430
PATEL, Nirav, M.D., Chief of Staff, UCI Health – Los Alamitos, Los Alamitos, CA, p. A71
PATEL, Paryus, M.D., Chief Medical Officer, Centinela Hospital Medical Center, Inglewood, CA, p. A67
PATEL, Prakash Chandra, M.D., Chief of Staff, Kindred Hospital–La Mirada, La Mirada, CA, p. A68
PATEL, Pravin, M.D., Acting President and Chief Executive Officer, Southern Virginia Mental Health Institute, Danville, VA, p. A675
PATEL, Pravinchandra, M.D., Chief Medical Officer, Barnes–Kasson County Hospital, Susquehanna, PA, p. A555
PATEL, Rakesh, D.O., Medical Director, Encompass Health Rehabilitation Hospital of Altoona, Altoona, PA, p. A534
PATEL, Shailesh, M.D., Medical Director, Anchor Hospital, Atlanta, GA, p. A156
PATEL, Shalin, M.D., Chief Medical Officer, Memorial Hermann Rehabilitation Hospital – Katy, Katy, TX, p. A631
PATEL, Sharad, M.D., Medical Director, Adventhealth Connerton, Land O'Lakes, FL, p. A137
PATEL, Shatish, M.D., Chief Medical Officer, Atrium Medical Center, Stafford, TX, p. A654
PATEL, Sneha, Chief Executive Officer, Coastal Harbor Treatment Center, Savannah, GA, p. A171
PATEL, Tanay M., M.D., Chief of Staff, Golden Plains Community Hospital, Borger, TX, p. A604
PATEL, Viraj, M.D., Chief Medical Officer, Unity Physicians Hospital, Mishawaka, IN, p. A224
PATER, Tom, Chief Financial Officer, RML Specialty Hospital, Hinsdale, IL, p. A198
PATHAK, Rajiv, Chief of Staff, Marshall Medical Center, Placerville, CA, p. A83
PATIL, Steve, Chief Financial Officer, W. G. (Bill) Heffner Veterans Affairs Medical Center, Salisbury, NC, p. A476
PATILLO, Laura, Manager Human Resources, Fresno Surgical Hospital, Fresno, CA, p. A64
PATIN, Al J., R.N., Chief Executive Officer, Ochsner Lafayette General Medical Center, Lafayette, LA, p. A285
PATINO, Beth, Chief Information Officer, Emory Decatur Hospital, Decatur, GA, p. A162
PATINO, Billy, Chief Information Officer, North Shore Medical Center, Miami, FL, p. A140
PATMAS, Michael, M.D., Interim Chief Medical Officer, Anna Jaques Hospital, Newburyport, MA, p. A316
PATRIAS, Thomas
FACHE, Chief Executive Officer, East Jefferson General Hospital, Metairie, LA, p. A288
FACHE, Chief Operating Officer, University Medical Center, New Orleans, LA, p. A290
PATRICK, Calvin II, Director Information Services, Adventhealth New Smyrna Beach, New Smyrna Beach, FL, p. A142
PATRICK, Chad, Chief Executive Officer, Mission Hospital, Asheville, NC, p. A463
PATRICK, Christian C, M.D., Chief Medical Officer, Baptist Memorial Hospital – Memphis, Memphis, TN, p. A588
PATRICK, Devin, Manager Human Resources, Utah State Hospital, Provo, UT, p. A667
PATRICK, Lisa, Chief Operating Officer, Caldwell Memorial Hospital, Columbia, LA, p. A280
PATRICK, Ronald, Chief Financial Officer, Northwest Medical Center, Tucson, AZ, p. A40
PATRICK, Samantha, Chief Financial Officer, Clark Regional Medical Center, Winchester, KY, p. A275
PATRICK, Sean, Director Information Systems, Gifford Medical Center, Randolph, VT, p. A672
PATTEN, William D. Jr, Interim Chief Executive Officer, Rehoboth Mckinley Christian Health Care Services, Gallup. NM, p. A434
PATTERSON, Barbara, Chief Financial Officer, Provident Hospital of Cook County, Chicago, IL, p. A190
PATTERSON, Camie, Chief Operating Officer, Manatee Memorial Hospital, Bradenton, FL, p. A126
PATTERSON, Christina, Chief Financial Officer, Ascension Saint Thomas River Park, Mc Minnville, TN, p. A587
PATTERSON, Dave, Chief Information Officer, Memorial Hospital of Converse County, Douglas, WY, p. A727
PATTERSON, David, Director Human Resources, Parkside Psychiatric Hospital And Clinic, Tulsa, OK, p. A522
PATTERSON, Devasha, Director of Human Resources, Delta Health – Northwest Regional, Clarksdale, MS, p. A360
PATTERSON, Diane, Senior Vice President, Chief Operating Officer and Chief Nursing Officer, Multicare Yakima Memorial Hospital, Yakima, WA, p. A698
PATTERSON, Elmore, Chief Executive Officer, Morehouse General Hospital, Bastrop. LA, p. A277
PATTERSON, Gregory
President, Barnes–Jewish St. Peters Hospital, Saint Peters, MO, p. A386
President, Progress West Hospital, O Fallon, MO, p. A381
Vice President and Chief Operating Officer, Progress West Hospital, O Fallon, MO, p. A381
PATTERSON, James, M.D., Chief of Medical Staff, Bates County Memorial Hospital, Butler, MO, p. A372
PATTERSON, Jan, Chief Nursing Officer, Avera St. Luke's Hospital, Aberdeen, SD, p. A572
PATTERSON, Jeff, Chief Executive Officer, Nacogdoches Medical Center, Nacogdoches, TX, p. A640
PATTERSON, Karen, Deputy Director Operations, Elmira Psychiatric Center, Elmira, NY, p. A443
PATTERSON, Larry R., Deputy Commander Administration, Bayne–Jones Army Community Hospital, Fort Polk, LA, p. A282
PATTERSON, Leah Ann, R.N., Chief Nursing Officer, Riverside University Health System–Medical Center, Moreno Valley, CA, p. A78
PATTERSON, Leigh
Chief Executive Officer, North Central Surgical Center, Dallas, TX, p. A612
Chief Financial Officer, North Central Surgical Center, Dallas, TX, p. A612
Chief Operating Officer, North Central Surgical Center, Dallas, TX, p. A612
PATTERSON, Lisa, Director Human Resources, Pointe Coupee General Hospital, New Roads, LA, p. A290
PATTERSON, Marcia, MSN, R.N., Chief Nursing Officer, Southern Tennessee Regional Health System–Lawrenceburg, Lawrenceburg, TN, p. A586
PATTERSON, Maria, Manager Health Information Management, Canyon Ridge Hospital, Chino, CA, p. A59
PATTERSON, Mark, M.D., Chief Medical Officer, Greeneville Community Hospital East, Greeneville, TN, p. A583
PATTERSON, Melanie, R.N., Vice President Patient Care Services and Chief Nursing Officer, Children's Hospital of Orange County, Orange, CA, p. A81
PATTERSON, Melinda, MSN, R.N., Chief Nursing Officer, Lone Peak Hospital, Draper, UT, p. A665
PATTERSON, Michael C.
Chief Executive Officer, Flint River Hospital, Montezuma, GA, p. A168
Chief Financial Officer, Flint River Hospital, Montezuma, GA, p. A168
PATTERSON, Mike, Director of Operations, Northside Hospital Cherokee, Canton, GA, p. A160
PATTERSON, Philip A., President Providence Health Center/Network, Ascension Providence, Waco, TX, p. A660
PATTERSON, Robert, Vice President Human Resources and Rehabilitation Services, The University of Vermont Health Network Central Vermont Medical Center, Berlin, VT, p. A671
PATTERSON, Russ
Director Information Technology, St. Rose Dominican Hospitals – Siena Campus, Henderson, NV, p. A409
Site Manager Information Technology, St. Rose Dominican Hospitals – San Martin Campus, Las Vegas, NV, p. A411
PATTERSON, Sam, Chief Financial Officer, Bay Area Hospital, Coos Bay, OR, p. A526
PATTERSON, Sean, Chief Executive Officer, Tristar Northcrest Medical Center, Springfield, TN, p. A593
PATTERSON, Stuart, M.D., Chief of Staff, Bartow Regional Medical Center, Bartow, FL, p. A125
PATTERSON, Todd, Chief Executive Officer, Washington County Hospital And Clinics, Washington, IA, p. A244
PATTERSON, Tony, Chief Financial Officer, Ephraim Mcdowell James B. Haggin Memorial Hospital, Harrodsburg, KY, p. A266
PATTI, Rosa, Chief Financial Officer, Cameron Regional Medical Center, Cameron, MO, p. A372
PATTISON, Kiera, R.N., Interim Chief Nursing Officer, Bozeman Health Deaconess Regional Medical Center, Bozeman, MT, p. A390
PATTON, Daniel, Director Information Systems, Henrico Doctors' Hospital, Richmond, VA, p. A682
PATTON, David J.
President, UPMC Horizon, Farrell, PA, p. A540
President, UPMC Jameson, New Castle, PA, p. A547
PATTON, Joy, Director Information Technology, Pamp. Regional Medical Center, Pampa, TX, p. A642
PATTON, Meghan
Vice President Human Resources, Jefferson Abington Health, Abington, PA, p. A534
Vice President Human Resources, Jefferson Lansdale Hospital, Lansdale, PA, p. A544
PATTON, William
Administrator, Allen County Regional Hospital, Iola, KS, p. A251
Administrator, Anderson County Hospital, Garnett, KS, p. A249
PATWA, Huned, Chief of Staff, Veterans Affairs Connecticut Healthcare System, West Haven, CT, p. A120
PAUGH, David, Chief Financial Officer, Memorial Hospital And Manor, Bainbridge, GA, p. A159
PAUL, Allison Kay, R.N., Chief Nursing Officer, HSHS St. John's Hospital, Springfield, IL, p. A209
PAUL, Darrick, Chief People Officer, Musc Health University Medical Center, Charleston, SC, p. A563
PAUL, Donn, Chief Human Resources, Lackey Memorial Hospital, Forest, MS, p. A362
PAUL, Jenny, CPA, Area Controller, Rehabilitation Hospital of Henry, Mcdonough, GA, p. A168
PAUL, Joseph, Chief Financial Officer, Broward Health Imperial Point, Fort Lauderdale, FL, p. A131
PAUL, Julie, R.N., Chief Nursing Officer, Acadian Medical Center, Eunice, LA, p. A281
PAUL, Lise, Vice President Reimbursement and Network Planning, Hebrew Rehabilitation Center, Roslindale, MA, p. A317
PAUL, Mary, Chief Information Officer, Ascension Columbia St. Mary's Hospital Milwaukee, Milwaukee, WI, p. A716
PAUL, West
M.D., Ph.D., Senior Vice President and Chief Quality and Medical Staff Officer, Wakemed Raleigh Campus, Raleigh, NC, p. A475
M.D., Ph.D., Senior Vice President, Chief Quality and Medical Staff Officer, Wakemed Cary Hospital, Cary, NC, p. A464
PAULEON, Merlinda, Chief Nursing Officer, Rehabilitation Hospital of Henry, Mcdonough, GA, p. A168
PAULEY, Clarence, Senior Vice President and Chief Human Resources Officer, University of Cincinnati Medical Center, Cincinnati, OH, p. A490
PAULMEYER, Steven, M.D., Senior Executive, Medical Services, Beatrice Community Hospital And Health Center, Beatrice, NE, p. A398
PAULS, Scott R, Director Information Technology– HealthNet Connect, Guttenberg Municipal Hospital And Clinics, Guttenberg, IA, p. A237
PAULSEN, Lisa, R.N., Chief Nursing Officer, Audubon County Memorial Hospital And Clinics, Audubon, IA, p. A230
PAULSEN, Susan, Director Human Resources, Northridge Hospital Medical Center, Los Angeles, CA, p. A74
PAULSON, Adam, President, Centracare – Sauk Centre, Sauk Centre, MN, p. A355
PAULSON, Erik, Director of Finance, J. D. Mccarty Center for Children With Developmental Disabilities, Norman, OK, p. A516
PAULSON, Gordon, Manager Human Resources, Glacial Ridge Health System, Glenwood, MN, p. A347
PAULUS, Terresa Ann
Chief Nursing Officer, Banner Goldfield Medical Center, Apache Junction, AZ, p. A30
Chief Nursing Officer, Banner Ironwood Medical Center, San Tan Valley, AZ, p. A38

Index of Health Care Professionals

Index of Health Care Professionals / Pauly

PAULY, Greg, President, Duke University Hospital, Durham, NC, p. A467
PAUTLER, John Steve, FACHE, Chief Executive Officer, Ste. Genevieve County Memorial Hospital, Ste Genevieve, MO, p. A387
PAVALONIS, Diane, Chief Nurse Executive, Western State Hospital, Staunton, VA, p. A684
PAVIA, Antoine, M.D., Medical Director, Hospital Pavia Arecibo, Arecibo, PR, p. A731
PAVIK, Sarah, Director Human Resources and Guest Services, Inova Loudoun Hospital, Leesburg, VA, p. A678
PAVILANIS, Charlotte J, R.N., Vice President of Clinical Services and Chief Nursing Officer, Sturgis Hospital, Sturgis, MI, p. A338
PAVLATOS, Thales, Medical Director, Ohio Valley Surgical Hospital, Springfield, OH, p. A504
PAWAR, Ganesh, M.D., Chief of Staff, Marshfield Medical Center – Ladysmith, Ladysmith, WI, p. A714
PAWLEK, Kenny, Administrator/Chief Executive Officer, Shriners Children's – Northern California, Sacramento, CA, p. A87
PAWLOWICZ, James E, Director Human Resources, Shriners Hospitals for Children–Chicago, Chicago, IL, p. A191
PAWLOWSKI, Phil, Chief Financial Officer, Glenbeigh Hospital And Outpatient Centers, Rock Creek, OH, p. A503
PAWOLA, Ken, Chief Operating Officer, RML Specialty Hospital, Hinsdale, IL, p. A198
PAXSON, Gary, FACHE, President and Chief Executive Officer, UNC Health Blue Ridge, Morganton, NC, p. A473
PAYA, Alejandro, D.O., Chief Medical Officer, HCA Florida Jfk Hospital, Atlantis, FL, p. A125
PAYNE, Angel, Clinical Director, Director of Nursing, Sonora Behavioral Health Hospital, Tucson, AZ, p. A41
PAYNE, Ellen, Chief Operating Officer, Georgetown Behavioral Health Institute, Georgetown, TX, p. A622
PAYNE, James, Director Information Systems, Southern Tennessee Regional Health System–Winchester, Winchester, TN, p. A594
PAYNE, Jason, Executive Vice President and Chief Operating Officer, Ochsner Rush Medical Center, Meridian, MS, p. A366
PAYNE, Judy H., Chief Executive Officer, Turning Point Hospital, Moultrie, GA, p. A169
PAYNE, Keela, Director Human Resources, Hamilton General Hospital, Hamilton, TX, p. A623
PAYNE, Kenneth G, Chief Financial Officer, Holzer Medical Center, Gallipolis, OH, p. A496
PAYNE, Michael, M.D., Chief of Staff, Dallas County Medical Center, Fordyce, AR, p. A46
PAYNE, Michael D., Medical Center Director, Robert J. Dole Department of Veterans Affairs Medical And Regional Office Center, Wichita, KS, p. A262
PAYNE, Rick, Director Information Systems, Santa Rosa Medical Center, Milton, FL, p. A141
PAYNE–BORDEN, Jacqueline, Chief Executive Officer, United Medical Center, Washington, DC, p. A124
PAYTON, Becky J, Vice President Human Resources, Mercy Hospital Oklahoma City, Oklahoma City, OK, p. A517
PAYTON, Robert, Chief Medical Officer, Endeavor Health Edward Hospital, Naperville, IL, p. A203
PAYTON, Willie Jr, Chief Operating Officer, Abrazo West Campus, Goodyear, AZ, p. A32
PAZDERNIK, Mary, Chief Financial Officer, Mahnomen Health, Mahnomen, MN, p. A349
PEA, Richard, Director Human Resources, Memorial Hospital And Health Care Center, Jasper, IN, p. A220
PEABODY, Kim, Chief Operating Officer, The Brook Hospital – Kmi, Louisville, KY, p. A270
PEACE, Lother E. III, President and Chief Executive Officer, Russell Medical, Alexander City, AL, p. A15
PEARCE, Barbara, Interim Chief Executive Officer, The Connecticut Hospice, Branford, CT, p. A115
PEARCE, Darren, Executive Director, Atrium Health Navicent Rehabilitation Hospital, Macon, GA, p. A167
PEARCE, Kelly, R.N., FACHE, Chief Executive Officer, St. Mary's Medical Center, Blue Springs, MO, p. A371
PEARCE, Marc B., Chief Executive Officer, Pam Specialty Hospital of Shreveport, Shreveport, LA, p. A292
PEARCH, William, Chief Information Officer, Yukon–Kuskokwim Delta Regional Hospital, Bethel, AK, p. A27
PEARCY, Joetta J, Director, Human Resources, Glendive Medical Center, Glendive, MT, p. A392
PEARCY, Steve, Director Human Resources, Community Hospital North, Indianapolis, IN, p. A219
PEARLMAN, Helen, Nurse Executive, Minneapolis Va Health Care System, Minneapolis, MN, p. A351
PEARSON, Christine, Chief Financial Officer, Anmed Medical Center, Anderson, SC, p. A562
PEARSON, Dawn, Director Human Resources, Encompass Health Rehabilitation Hospital of Vineland, Vineland, NJ, p. A429
PEARSON, Frank P., Director, Jennifer Moreno Department of Veterans Affairs Medical Center, San Diego, CA, p. A88
PEARSON, Gregory, Chief Executive Officer, Abrazo Central Campus, Phoenix, AZ, p. A35
PEARSON, Jeff, Vice President and Chief Information Officer, Christus Mother Frances Hospital – Tyler, Tyler, TX, p. A658
PEARSON, Kellie T., Chief Human Resource Officer, St. Christopher's Hospital for Children, Philadelphia, PA, p. A550
PEARSON, Kim Renee, Nursing Director, Essentia Health St. Mary's Hospital of Superior, Superior, WI, p. A722
PEARSON, Kim Renee., Administrator, Essentia Health St. Mary's Hospital of Superior, Superior, WI, p. A722
PEARSON, Madelyn, R.N., Senior Vice President Patient Care Services and Chief Nursing Officer, Brigham And Women's Hospital, Boston, MA, p. A310
PEARSON, Marshall, Director Management Information Systems, St. David's North Austin Medical Center, Austin, TX, p. A600
PEARSON, Matthew, Chief Executive Officer, Encompass Health Rehabilitation Hospital of Chattanooga, Chattanooga, TN, p. A580
PEARSON, Nancy, MSN, R.N., Director, Nursing, Novant Health Thomasville Medical Center, Thomasville, NC, p. A477
PEAVY, Mike
Chief Information Officer, Ochsner Rush Medical Center, Meridian, MS, p. A366
Chief Information Officer, Ochsner Specialty Hospital, Meridian, MS, p. A366
PEBURN, Eric
Chief Financial Officer, Halifax Health Medical Center of Daytona Beach, Daytona Beach, FL, p. A130
Chief Financial Officer, Halifax Health/Uf Health Medical Center of Deltona, Deltona, FL, p. A130
PECHOUS, Bryan, M.D., Vice President Medical Affairs, Unitypoint Health – Finley Hospital, Dubuque, IA, p. A235
PECK, Amy, R.N., Chief Nursing Officer, Memorial Regional Health, Craig, CO, p. A105
PECK, Darin, M.D., Chief of Staff, Northern Light Ca Dean Hospital, Greenville, ME, p. A297
PECK, Michael D, Assistant Administrator, Caribou Medical Center, Soda Springs, ID, p. A184
PECK, Robert C, M.D., Chief Medical Officer, Mayo Clinic Health System In Eau Claire, Eau Claire, WI, p. A710
PECKENPAUGH, Russell, Vice President Information Systems Administration, Marinhealth Medical Center, Greenbrae, CA, p. A66
PEDANO, Andrea D, D.O., Chief Medical Officer, Suburban Community Hospital, East Norriton, PA, p. A539
PEDDIE, Matthew Brian, Vice President and Chief Operating Officer, Long Island Community Hospital, Patchogue, NY, p. A455
PEDERSEN, Darren, Coordinator Information Technology, Weisman Children's Rehabilitation Hospital, Marlton, NJ, p. A424
PEDERSEN, Paul E, M.D., Vice President and Chief Medical Officer, OSF St. Josep. Medical Center, Bloomington, IL, p. A186
PEDERSEN, Rebecca, Chief Nursing Officer, Rush Specialty Hospital, Chicago, IL, p. A190
PEDERSON, Bryan, Human Resources Manager, Astera Health, Wadena, MN, p. A356
PEDERSON, Eilidh, Chief Executive Officer, Western Wisconsin Health, Baldwin, WI, p. A707
PEDERSON, Karn, Manager Health Information Management, Mckenzie County Healthcare System, Watford City, ND, p. A483
PEDLOW, Bernadette R, Senior Vice President Business and Chief Operating Officer, Albany Medical Center, Albany, NY, p. A438
PEDRETTI, Jennalee, Vice President Operations, Regional Health Services of Howard County, Cresco, IA, p. A234
PEDROZA, Fernando, Vice President Information Technology, UCHealth Poudre Valley Hospital, Fort Collins, CO, p. A108
PEEBLES, Wanda V., Chief Nursing Officer, JPS Health Network, Fort Worth, TX, p. A619
PEEK, Chris, Chief Executive Officer, Caromont Regional Medical Center, Gastonia, NC, p. A469
PEEK, Scott
FACHE, Chief Executive Officer, Chambers Memorial Hospital, Danville, AR, p. A45
Front Range Market President, Intermountain Health Saint Joseph. Hospital, Denver, CO, p. A106
PEELER, Cindy K, R.N., Chief Nursing Officer, Adair County Health System, Greenfield, IA, p. A236
PEELGREN, Jim, Chief Information Officer, Adventist Health – Tulare, Tulare, CA, p. A98
PEEPLES, Jonnitra, Chief Human Resource Officer, Select Specialty Hospital – Richmond, Richmond, VA, p. A682
PEER, Julianne
President, Penn Highlands Brookville, Brookville, PA, p. A535
President, Penn Highlands Elk, Saint Marys, PA, p. A554
PEERY, Lori, Chief Human Resource Management Services, VA Palo Alto Heath Care System, Palo Alto, CA, p. A82
PEET, Fred, Chief Information Officer, Yuma Regional Medical Center, Yuma, AZ, p. A42
PEFFER, Margo, Vice President, Human Resources, Mainehealth Maine Medical Center, Portland, ME, p. A298
PEGE, Diane, M.D., Vice President Medical Affairs, Sutter Lakeside Hospital, Lakeport, CA, p. A69
PEGLOW, Robert, Chief Administrative Officer, Ascension Saint Thomas Highlands, Sparta, TN, p. A593
PEIFFER, Paul, Chief Financial Officer and Vice President, Jackson Hospital And Clinic, Montgomery, AL, p. A22
PEIL, Michael, M.D., Chief Medical Director, OSF Transitional Care Hospital, Peoria, IL, p. A206
PEIRICK, Brent, Chief Operating Officer, Scotland County Hospital, Memphis, MO, p. A380
PEKOFSKE, Robert, Vice President Finance, Advocate Christ Medical Center, Oak Lawn, IL, p. A204
PELFREY, Joy S, R.N., MSN, Vice President and Chief Nursing Officer, Cabell Huntington Hospital, Huntington, WV, p. A701
PELHAM, Wesley Florida State Hospital, Chattahoochee, FL, p. A127
PELKEY, Melissa, Chief Executive Officer, Penobscot Valley Hospital, Lincoln, ME, p. A298
PELKOWSKI, Margaret, R.N., Vice President Patient Care Services, Calvary Hospital, New York, NY, p. A447
PELLEGRIN, Kimberley, Director, Human Resources, Red River Hospital, Llc, Wichita Falls, TX, p. A662
PELLEGRINO, Ron, Chief Operating Officer, West Virginia University Hospitals, Morgantown, WV, p. A703
PELLETIER, Lindsay, Chief Executive Officer, Silver Oaks Behavioral Hospital, New Lenox, IL, p. A203
PELLICONE, John T, M.D., Chief Medical Officer, NYC Health + Hospitals/Metropolitan, New York, NY, p. A451
PELTIER, Casey, Director Human Resources, Thibodaux Regional Health System, Thibodaux, LA, p. A294
PELTIER, Glenn, Chief Financial Officer, Christus Mother Frances Hospital – Winnsboro, Winnsboro, TX, p. A663
PELTIER, Robert
M.D., Chief Medical Officer, North Oaks Medical Center, Hammond, LA, p. A282
M.D., Senior Vice President, Chief Medical Officer, North Oaks Health System, North Oaks Rehabilitation Hospital, Hammond, LA, p. A282
PELTON, Ed, Chief of Staff, Chadron Community Hospital And Health Services, Chadron, NE, p. A398
PELTON, Gerele Dawn, Interim Chief Human Resources Officer, Billings Clinic, Billings, MT, p. A389
PEMBERTON, Stacy, Chief Nursing Officer, Grand River Hospital District, Rifle, CO, p. A113
PEMELTON, Debbie, Director Human Resources, Weslaco Regional Rehabilitation Hospital, Weslaco, TX, p. A662
PENA, Carolina, Assistant Director Administrator, Larkin Community Hospital–South Miami Campus, South Miami, FL, p. A150
PENA, Jessica, Manager Finance, Christus Spohn Hospital Kleberg, Kingsville, TX, p. A632
PENA, Terry, Chief Operating Officer and Chief Nursing Officer, San Bernardino Mountains Community Hospital, Lake Arrowhead, CA, p. A69
PENCO, Kris, Director Information Systems, Coffeyville Regional Medical Center, Coffeyville, KS, p. A247
PENDER, Carol, Assistant Vice President Human Resources, Walden Behavioral Care, Waltham, MA, p. A319
PENDER, Debra, MS, R.N., Vice President Nursing, Mercy Hospital Ardmore, Ardmore, OK, p. A510
PENDERGRAFT, Tina, Chief Executive Officer, Satanta District Hospital And Long Term Care, Satanta, KS, p. A259
PENDLEBURY, Sharon, Chief Executive Officer, South Texas Health System, Edinburg, TX, p. A615
PENDLETON, Brian, Chief Nursing Officer, Riverton Hospital, Riverton, UT, p. A668
PENDLETON, Gretchen, Director Human Resources, Suburban Community Hospital, East Norriton, PA, p. A539
PENDLETON, Timothy, M.D., President Medical Staff, Penn Highlands Brookville, Brookville, PA, p. A535
PENICK, Lisa, R.N., Chief Nursing Officer, Carroll County Memorial Hospital, Carrollton, KY, p. A264
PENLAND, Jennifer, Controller, Kindred Hospital Tarrant County–Arlington, Arlington, TX, p. A597
PENN, Cassie, Chief Operating Officer, Callaway District Hospital, Callaway, NE, p. A398

A942 Index of Health Care Professionals

Index of Health Care Professionals
Index of Health Care Professionals / Peterman

PENN, Nicholas A., Chief Financial Officer, Hopedale Medical Complex, Hopedale, IL, p. A198
PENNACCHIO, Suzanne, MSN, R.N., Chief Nursing Officer, NYC Health + Hospitals/Jacobi, New York, NY, p. A451
PENNER, Jerome, FACHE, Chief Executive Officer, Murray–Calloway County Hospital, Murray, KY, p. A272
PENNEY, Cindy L, R.N., Vice President Nursing, University of Iowa Health Care Medical Center Downtown, Iowa City, IA, p. A238
PENNEY, Jan, R.N., Vice President and Chief Nursing Officer, Mymichigan Medical Center Midland, Midland, MI, p. A333
PENNEY, Rozanna
Co–Chief Executive Officer, Athol Hospital, Athol, MA, p. A309
Co–Chief Executive Officer, Heywood Hospital, Gardner, MA, p. A314
PENNICK, Jeanette, Chief Nursing Officer, HCA Houston Healthcare Pearland, Pearland, TX, p. A643
PENNINGTON, Brian Keith., President and Chief Executive Officer, Medical West, Bessemer, AL, p. A16
PENNINGTON, Stephen G., Chief Executive Officer, East Georgia Regional Medical Center, Statesboro, GA, p. A171
PENNINO, Jackie, Director Human Resources, Old Vineyard Behavioral Health Services, Winston–Salem, NC, p. A478
PENNISSON, Jay M, Chief Financial Officer, Touro Infirmary, New Orleans, LA, p. A290
PENNY, Tracy, Interim Chief Executive Officer, Pam Rehabilitation Hospital of Allen, Allen, TX, p. A595
PENUEL, Jennifer, Director Human Resources, Madison Medical Center, Fredericktown, MO, p. A375
PEOPLES, Kathleen K, R.N., MS, Vice President of Nursing, Ascension St. Vincent Kokomo, Kokomo, IN, p. A221
PEOPLES, Kyle, Director Technology Management Services, Springfield Hospital, Springfield, VT, p. A672
PEOPLES, Lynn, Interim Chief Nursing Officer, Person Memorial Hospital, Roxboro, NC, p. A475
PEOPLES, Phyllis, Chief Executive Officer, Physicians Medical Center, Houma, LA, p. A283
PEOPLES, Phyllis L., President and Chief Executive Officer, Terrebonne General Health System, Houma, LA, p. A283
PEPITONE, Stephen, Interim Chief Financial Officer, Ochsner Medical Center – Baton Rouge, Baton Rouge, LA, p. A278
PEPPEL, David
Executive Director, Elmira Psychiatric Center, Elmira, NY, p. A443
Executive Director, Greater Binghamton Health Center, Binghamton, NY, p. A439
PEPPER, L. Douglas, M.D., President, Medical Staff, Penn Highlands Mon Valley, Monongahela, PA, p. A546
PEPPLER, Lisa, Financial Manager, Parkview Whitley Hospital, Columbia City, IN, p. A214
PERAL, Sherry, Director Information Systems, Oak Valley Hospital, Oakdale, CA, p. A80
PERALES, Lisa, Chief Nursing Officer, Fairlawn Rehabilitation Hospital, Worcester, MA, p. A320
PERALTA, Pennie, R.N., VP, Nursing & Chief Nursing Officer, Bon Secours St. Francis Hospital, Charleston, SC, p. A563
PERARD, Anie, M.D., President, Medical Staff, Clarion Hospital, Clarion, PA, p. A537
PERCELLO, Thomas, Executive Vice President, Finance and Chief Financial Officer, Deborah Heart And Lung Center, Browns Mills, NJ, p. A419
PEREA, Ely, Director & Chief Executive Officer, Covenant Specialty Hospital, Lubbock, TX, p. A636
PEREACE, Vicki, Manager Human Resources, William Bee Ririe Hospital, Ely, NV, p. A408
PEREIRA, Raul Ramos, M.D., Medical Director, Ryder Memorial Hospital, Humacao, PR, p. A733
PEREL, Michael
Regional Chief Financial Officer, Kauai Veterans Memorial Hospital, Waimea, HI, p. A178
Regional Chief Financial Officer, Samuel Mahelona Memorial Hospital, Kapaa, HI, p. A177
PEREZ, Berenice, Chief Nursing Officer, Ashford Presbyterian Community Hospital, San Juan, PR, p. A734
PEREZ, Carmen, Director Human Resources, Doctors' Center Hospital San Juan, San Juan, PR, p. A734
PEREZ, David, Vice President, Chief Information Officer, Eisenhower Health, Rancho Mirage, CA, p. A84
PEREZ, Eddie, R.N., Chief Clinical Officer and Chief Nurse Executive, Select Specialty Hospital – Willingboro, Willingboro, NJ, p. A430
PEREZ, Edwin, M.D., Chief of Medical Staff, Marshall County Hospital, Benton, KY, p. A263
PEREZ, Francisco, Manager Management Information Systems, Hospital De La Universidad De Puerto Rico/Dr. Federico Trilla, Carolina, PR, p. A732
PEREZ, Joe, Associate Director, South Texas Veterans Healthcare System Audie L Murphy, San Antonio, TX, p. A651
PEREZ, Lisa, R.N., Director Nursing, Meadowbrook Rehabilitation Hospital, Gardner, KS, p. A249
PEREZ, Mary E., MSN, Chief Nursing Officer, University of New Mexico Hospitals, Albuquerque, NM, p. A433
PEREZ, Maya, President, Baycare Alliant Hospital, Dunedin, FL, p. A130
PEREZ, Mercedes, Vice President Nursing, Larkin Community Hospital–South Miami Campus, South Miami, FL, p. A150
PEREZ, Nina, R.N., MSN, Chief Nursing Officer, North Okaloosa Medical Center, Crestview, FL, p. A129
PEREZ, Tony, M.D., President Medical Staff, Uofl Health – Shelbyville Hospital, Shelbyville, KY, p. A274
PEREZ–GUERRA, Francisco, Administrator, Gundersen Moundview Hospital & Clinics, Friendship. WI, p. A711
PEREZ–MIR, Ernesto, Chief Nursing Executive, Kaiser Foundation Hospital – San Marcos, San Marcos, CA, p. A93
PEREZ–POLA, Humberto, Executive Director, Hospital Metropolitano Dr. Susoni, Arecibo, PR, p. A731
PEREZ, III, Miguel, Chief Information Officer, Driscoll Children's Hospital, Corpus Christi, TX, p. A609
PERI, Gil, President, Indiana University Health University Hospital, Indianapolis, IN, p. A220
PERKERSON, Robyn, R.N., Administrator, Pam Specialty Hospital of Rocky Mount, Rocky Mount, NC, p. A475
PERKES, Neil C, Operations Officer, Logan Regional Hospital, Logan, UT, p. A665
PERKET, William, Vice President Human Resources, North Country Hospital And Health Center, Newport, VT, p. A672
PERKINS, Bill, Chief Executive Officer, Shannon Rehabilitation Hospital, An Affiliate of Encompass Health, San Angelo, TX, p. A648
PERKINS, Brett, M.D., Chief Medical Staff, Madison County Memorial Hospital, Madison, FL, p. A138
PERKINS, Chris, Director Information Services, Clinch Valley Medical Center, Richlands, VA, p. A682
PERKINS, Dan, Corporate Director Human Resources, Cornerstone Specialty Hospitals West Monroe, West Monroe, LA, p. A294
PERKINS, Kathryn
M.D., Chief Medical Officer, Banner Boswell Medical Center, Sun City, AZ, p. A39
M.D., Chief Medical Officer, Banner Thunderbird Medical Center, Glendale, AZ, p. A32
PERKINS, Lewis L., R.N., MSN, Jr, Chief Nursing Officer, Integris Baptist Medical Center, Oklahoma City, OK, p. A517
PERKINS, Mike, President, Baptist Health Medical Center–Little Rock, Little Rock, AR, p. A49
PERKINS, Richard, Chief Financial Officer, Baylor Scott & White Medical Center – Hillcrest, Waco, TX, p. A660
PERKINS, Sherry B., Ph.D., R.N., President, Luminis Health Anne Arundel Medical Center, Annapolis, MD, p. A300
PERKINS, Tom, Chief Information Officer, Shannon Medical Center, San Angelo, TX, p. A648
PERKINS–PEPPERS, Andrea, Chief Information Officer, Forks Community Hospital, Forks, WA, p. A690
PERKOVICH, Shayne, Chief Executive Officer, Bakersfield Rehabilitation Hospital, Bakersfield, CA, p. A57
PERL, Lawrence, M.D., Chief Medical Officer, Columbia Memorial Hospital, Hudson, NY, p. A444
PERLICH, Gwynn, Chief Operating Officer, Ascension St. Vincent Evansville, Evansville, IN, p. A216
PERLSTEIN, David A., M.D., President and Chief Executive Officer, St. Barnabas Hospital, New York, NY, p. A452
PERMANN, Darcy, Manager Business Office, Landmann–Jungman Memorial Hospital Avera, Scotland, SD, p. A576
PERNICE, Dominick, Chief Operating Officer, St. Catherine of Siena Hospital, Smithtown, NY, p. A459
PERNICE, Paul, Vice President Finance, Beebe Healthcare, Lewes, DE, p. A121
PERNO, William P., FACHE, Chief Executive Officer, Ohio Valley Surgical Hospital, Springfield, OH, p. A504
PERRAS, Josep. L.
M.D., Chief Medical Officer, Mt. Ascutney Hospital And Health Center, Windsor, VT, p. A672
M.D., President and Chief Executive Officer, Cheshire Medical Center, Keene, NH, p. A415
PERRON, Kirk, Controller, Jennings Senior Care Hospital, Jennings, LA, p. A284
PERROTTE, Kenneth, Director Operations, Rockland Children's Psychiatric Center, Orangeburg, NY, p. A455
PERROTTI, Paul R, CPA, Chief Financial Officer, Wellstar West Georgia Medical Center, Lagrange, GA, p. A166
PERRY, Carol, R.N., Vice President and Chief Nursing Officer, Stormont Vail Health, Topeka, KS, p. A260
PERRY, Cheryl
Chief Financial Officer, Integris Baptist Medical Center, Oklahoma City, OK, p. A517
Chief Financial Officer, Vibra Hospital of Southeastern Massachusetts, New Bedford, MA, p. A316
Executive Director Human Resources, Paris Regional Medical Center, Paris, TX, p. A642
PERRY, Cynthia, M.D., Chief of Staff, Stephens Memorial Hospital, Breckenridge, TX, p. A604
PERRY, Darrin Keith, Chief Information Officer and Senior Vice President, St. Jude Children's Research Hospital, Memphis, TN, p. A589
PERRY, Doug, M.D., Chief of Staff, Baptist Medical Center – Leake, Carthage, MS, p. A360
PERRY, Jeff, Director Information Technology, St. John's Regional Medical Center, Oxnard, CA, p. A82
PERRY, Joe, Chief Financial Officer, Howard University Hospital, Washington, DC, p. A123
PERRY, Julia, Director Human Resources, Regions Behavioral Hospital, Baton Rouge, LA, p. A278
PERRY, Karen, Chief Information Resource Management Services, James H. Quillen Department of Veterans Affairs Medical Center, Johnson City, TN, p. A585
PERRY, Kathleen, Senior Vice President and Chief Information Officer, Mercy Medical Center, Baltimore, MD, p. A301
PERRY, Matthew, Director Information Systems, Andalusia Health, Andalusia, AL, p. A15
PERRY, Matthew J, President and Chief Executive Officer, Genesis Healthcare System, Zanesville, OH, p. A508
PERRY, Matthew J., President and Chief Executive Officer, Genesis Healthcare System, Zanesville, OH, p. A508
PERRY, Nini, Chief Nursing Officer, Georgetown Behavioral Health Institute, Georgetown, TX, p. A622
PERRY, Rhonda S., Chief Financial Officer, Atrium Health Navicent The Medical Center, Macon, GA, p. A167
PERRY, Robert Keith, Senior Vice President, Chief Information Officer, Carilion Franklin Memorial Hospital, Rocky Mount, VA, p. A683
PERRY, Sharon, Chief Nursing Officer, Emanuel Medical Center, Turlock, CA, p. A98
PERRY, Shaun, Chief Information Officer, Mcgehee Hospital, Mcgehee, AR, p. A50
PERRY, Shawn, Chief Financial Officer, Adventhealth Ottawa, Ottawa, KS, p. A256
PERRY, Solette, Regional Director Human Resources, Kauai Veterans Memorial Hospital, Waimea, HI, p. A178
PERRY, Teresa J, Chief Financial Officer, Up Health System – Bell, Ishpeming, MI, p. A330
PERRY, Tim, Executive Director of Human Resources, Baptist Health Corbin, Corbin, KY, p. A264
PERRY, V Mark, Chief Financial Officer, Adventist Health Portland, Portland, OR, p. A530
PERRY GRIMES, Amy
Chief Executive Officer, Riverside Hospital, Alexandria, LA, p. A276
Chief Operating Officer, Riverside Hospital, Alexandria, LA, p. A276
PERRYMAN, Mike, Chief Financial Officer, Baptist Memorial Hospital–Union City, Union City, TN, p. A594
PERSING, Tamara Fetchina, Chief Nursing Officer, Evangelical Community Hospital, Lewisburg, PA, p. A544
PERT, Robert M, Vice President Finance and Chief Financial Officer, United Regional Health Care System, Wichita Falls, TX, p. A663
PERUGINO, Antonio, Vice President Finance, Hospitals, Vassar Brothers Medical Center, Poughkeepsie, NY, p. A456
PESCHEL, Colleen, Director Human Resources, Sutter Medical Center, Sacramento, Sacramento, CA, p. A87
PESKIN, Ted, M.D., Acute Care Medical Director, Hilo Medical Center, Hilo, HI, p. A175
PESONEN–JOHNSON, Alice, Chief Nursing Officer, Chi St. Francis Health, Breckenridge, MN, p. A344
PETE, Andrew, Chief Operating Officer, Fountain Valley Regional Hospital And Medical Center, Fountain Valley, CA, p. A64
PETER, David J.
M.D., Interim President and Chief Medical Officer, Cleveland Clinic Indian River Hospital, Vero Beach, FL, p. A154
M.D., Vice President and Chief Medical Officer, Cleveland Clinic Indian River Hospital, Vero Beach, FL, p. A154
PETER, Douglas G, M.D., Chief Medical Officer, Gallup Indian Medical Center, Gallup. NM, p. A434
PETER, Jan D, Vice President Fiscal Services and Chief Financial Officer, Good Shepherd Health Care System, Hermiston, OR, p. A527
PETER, John, M.D., Vice President Medical Affairs, SSM Health Cardinal Glennon Children's Hospital, Saint Louis, MO, p. A384
PETERMAN, John, Vice President and Chief Operating Officer, Riverside Regional Medical Center, Newport News, VA, p. A680

Index of Health Care Professionals

Index of Health Care Professionals / Peterman

PETERMAN, Tammy, R.N., MS, Executive Vice President, Chief Operating Officer and Chief Nursing Officer, The University of Kansas Hospital, Kansas City, KS, p. A252
PETERMEIER, Jill, Senior Executive Human Resources, Unitypoint Health – Marshalltown, Marshalltown, IA, p. A240
PETERS, Alana, Nurse Manager, Ascension St. Thomas Three Rivers, Waverly, TN, p. A594
PETERS, Candace, R.N., Director of Nursing, Webster County Community Hospital, Red Cloud, NE, p. A405
PETERS, Connie
R.N., President, Chi Health Plainview, Plainview, NE, p. A405
R.N., President, Chi Health Schuyler, Schuyler, NE, p. A405
PETERS, Dave, Chief Human Resources Officer, Veterans Affairs Nebraska–Western Iowa Health Care System – Lincoln, Lincoln, NE, p. A402
PETERS, Gerald, Vice President Information Technologies and Chief Information Officer, University Hospitals Lake Health, Willoughby, OH, p. A507
PETERS, Holli, Director Health Information Management, Holton Community Hospital, Holton, KS, p. A250
PETERS, John, Interim Chief Financial Officer, Providence Santa Rosa Memorial Hospital, Santa Rosa, CA, p. A95
PETERS, Mary
Chief Information Officer, Womack Army Medical Center, Fort Bragg, NC, p. A468
Chief Nursing Executive, Unitypoint Health – Finley Hospital, Dubuque, IA, p. A235
PETERS, Patrick, Administrator/Chief Executive Officer, Jackson County Regional Health Center, Maquoketa, IA, p. A239
PETERS, Wayne, Administrator, Southern Virginia Mental Health Institute, Danville, VA, p. A675
PETERS–LEWIS, Angelleen
Ph.D., R.N., President, Barnes–Jewish West County Hospital, Saint Louis, MO, p. A384
Ph.D., R.N., Vice President and Chief Operating Officer, Barnes–Jewish Hospital, Saint Louis, MO, p. A383
PETERSCHICK, Aubrey, Chief Executive Officer, Advanced Care Hospital of Montana, Billings, MT, p. A389
PETERSEN, Brenda, Human Resources, Sanford Wheaton Medical Center, Wheaton, MN, p. A357
PETERSEN, Cheryl
Chief Nursing Officer, Cook Children's Medical Center – Prosper, Prosper, TX, p. A646
Vice President and Chief Nursing Officer, Cook Children's Medical Center, Fort Worth, TX, p. A619
PETERSEN, Debbie, R.N., Chief Operating Officer and Chief Nursing Officer, Spalding Rehabilitation Hospital, Aurora, CO, p. A103
PETERSEN, Julie, CPA, Chief Executive Officer, Kittitas Valley Healthcare, Ellensburg, WA, p. A689
PETERSEN, Richard W, President and Chief Executive Officer, Mainehealth Maine Medical Center, Portland, ME, p. A298
PETERSEN, Susan, Human Resources, Lincoln Health, Hugo, CO, p. A110
PETERSEN, Tina, Chief Nursing Officer, Hillcrest Hospital Cushing, Cushing, OK, p. A511
PETERSON, Bill, Director Human Resources, Saint Francis Hospital Muskogee, Muskogee, OK, p. A515
PETERSON, Brett, Director of Information Services, Adventhealth North Pinellas, Tarpon Springs, FL, p. A153
PETERSON, Carrie, Director of Nursing, Henderson Health Care Services, Henderson, NE, p. A401
PETERSON, Chad, Chief Information Officer, Northwood Deaconess Health Center, Northwood, ND, p. A482
PETERSON, Cheryl, Business Office Manager, Surgical Institute of Reading, Wyomissing, PA, p. A558
PETERSON, Dan, Chief Executive Officer, Sutter Center for Psychiatry, Sacramento, CA, p. A87
PETERSON, David, Senior Vice President, Chief Technology Officer, Erlanger Medical Center, Chattanooga, TN, p. A580
PETERSON, Denise, R.N., FACHE, President and Chief Executive Officer, The Hospital At Hebrew Senior Care, West Hartford, CT, p. A120
PETERSON, Douglas R., President and Chief Executive Officer, Adventhealth Durand, Durand, WI, p. A709
PETERSON, Eric, Director, Ogden Regional Medical Center, Ogden, UT, p. A666
PETERSON, Erica
Chief Executive Officer, Sanford Chamberlain Medical Center, Chamberlain, SD, p. A572
Chief Executive Officer and Chief Financial Officer, Sanford Chamberlain Medical Center, Chamberlain, SD, p. A572
PETERSON, Ian, Chief Executive Officer, Pioneer Medical Center, Big Timber, MT, p. A389
PETERSON, James Kevin, Human Resources Leader, Kaiser Permanente South Sacramento Medical Center, Sacramento, CA, p. A87
PETERSON, Jeff, M.D., Chief of Staff, Essentia Health–Ada, Ada, MN, p. A342
PETERSON, Jeffrey, M.D., Medical Director, Dakota Regional Medical Center, Cooperstown, ND, p. A480
PETERSON, Jordan, Chief Executive Officer, Desert Parkway Behavioral Healthcare Hospital, Las Vegas, NV, p. A409
PETERSON, Josilyn, Chief Financial Officer, Ballinger Memorial Hospital, Ballinger, TX, p. A601
PETERSON, Judy, R.N., Chief Nursing Officer, UT Health Carthage, Carthage, TX, p. A607
PETERSON, Julie, Chief Financial Officer, Sutter Delta Medical Center, Antioch, CA, p. A55
PETERSON, Kathy, Director Information Services, OSF Saint Anthony Medical Center, Rockford, IL, p. A207
PETERSON, Katie, R.N., Chief Nursing Officer, Pender Community Hospital, Pender, NE, p. A405
PETERSON, Kenny, Chief Executive Officer, KPC Promise Hospital of Salt Lake, Salt Lake City, UT, p. A668
PETERSON, Larry, Chief Financial Officer, Allen County Regional Hospital, Iola, KS, p. A251
PETERSON, Linda, M.D., Vice President Medical Affairs, Mclaren Greater Lansing, Lansing, MI, p. A331
PETERSON, Mackenzie, M.D., Chief of Staff, Anderson County Hospital, Garnett, KS, p. A249
PETERSON, Mary, M.D., Executive Vice President and Chief Operating Officer, Driscoll Children's Hospital, Corpus Christi, TX, p. A609
PETERSON, Michael, M.D., Chief of Staff, Pineville Community Health Center, Pineville, KY, p. A273
PETERSON, Michael D.
FACHE, Chief Operating Officer, Northern Light Sebasticook Valley Hospital, Pittsfield, ME, p. A298
FACHE, President and Chief Executive Officer, Androscoggin Valley Hospital, Berlin, NH, p. A414
PETERSON, Robert
CPA, Chief Financial Officer, Hackettstown Medical Center, Hackettstown, NJ, p. A421
FACHE, Chief Executive Officer, Millinocket Regional Hospital, Millinocket, ME, p. A298
PETERSON, Ron, FACHE, President and Chief Executive Officer, Baxter Health, Mountain Home, AR, p. A51
PETERSON, Scott, Vice President of People and Organizational Development, Tidalhealth Peninsula Regional, Salisbury, MD, p. A307
PETERSON, Scott J.
Chief Executive Officer, Encompass Health Rehabilitation Hospital of Franklin, Franklin, TN, p. A583
Interim Chief Executive Officer, Van Matre Encompass Health Rehabilitation Hospital, Rockford, IL, p. A207
PETERSON, Seth, Director Information Services, Coshocton Regional Medical Center, Coshocton, OH, p. A493
PETERSON, Shelley, R.N., Vice President Patient Services and Chief Nursing Officer, Intermountain Health St. Mary's Regional Hospital, Grand Junction, CO, p. A109
PETERSON, Steve, M.D., Chief of Staff, Chi Health Plainview, Plainview, NE, p. A405
PETERSON, Steven, Chief Information Officer, Vice President of Operations, Garrett Regional Medical Center, Oakland, MD, p. A306
PETERSON, Tim, M.D., Chief of Staff, Meeker Memorial Hospital And Clinics, Litchfield, MN, p. A348
PETIK, Jason, Chief Executive Officer, Sidney Regional Medical Center, Sidney, NE, p. A406
PETINAUX, Bruno, M.D., Chief Medical Officer, George Washington University Hospital, Washington, DC, p. A123
PETIT, Ashley, Chief Information Officer, Northside Hospital Gwinnett/Duluth, Lawrenceville, GA, p. A166
PETITT, Michael
Director of Finance, Ascension Southeast Wisconsin Hospital – Elmbrook Campus, Brookfield, WI, p. A708
Director of Finance, Ascension Southeast Wisconsin Hospital – St. Joseph's Campus, Milwaukee, WI, p. A716
PETRICEVIC, Lili, Chief Executive Officer, Sheridan Community Hospital, Sheridan, MI, p. A338
PETRICK, Teresa G, President, UPMC Passavant, Pittsburgh, PA, p. A552
PETRIK, Jennifer, Interim Chief Nursing Officer, Multicare Deaconess Hospital, Spokane, WA, p. A696
PETRILLO, Mary Ann, R.N., MSN, Acting Associate Director Nursing and Patient Clinical Services, Bedford Veterans Affairs Medical Center, Edith Nourse Rogers Memorial Veterans Hospital, Bedford, MA, p. A309
PETRILLO, Nancy, Director Human Resources, Matheny Medical And Educational Center, Peapack, NJ, p. A426
PETRINA, Robert, Chief Financial Officer, Alta Bates Summit Medical Center–Alta Bates Campus, Berkeley, CA, p. A57
PETRINI, Lindsey
Chief Executive Officer, Piedmont Newton Hospital, Covington, GA, p. A162
Chief Operating Officer, Wellstar North Fulton Hospital, Roswell, GA, p. A170
PETRITZ, Jennifer J, Director Human Resources, UW Medicine/University of Washington Medical Center, Seattle, WA, p. A695
PETROV, John R.
Senior Vice President, Chief Human Resource Officer, Guthrie Robert Packer Hospital, Sayre, PA, p. A554
Senior Vice President, Chief Human Resource Officer, Guthrie Troy Community Hospital, Troy, PA, p. A556
PETROWER, Stacey, President, New York–Presbyterian Queens, New York, NY, p. A450
PETRY, Gary, M.D., Chief of Staff, St. Vincent Health, Leadville, CO, p. A111
PETTERSON–CARTER, Billie, Administrator, Schleicher County Medical Center, Eldorado, TX, p. A618
PETTIGREW, Dennis, Chief Operating Officer, Saint Michael's Medical Center, Newark, NJ, p. A425
PETTIJOHN, Kim, R.N., MSN, Chief Nursing Officer, The Spine Hospital of Louisiana At The Neuromedical Center, Baton Rouge, LA, p. A278
PETTIJOHN, Trent
M.D., Esq, Chief Medical Officer, Baylor Scott & White The Heart Hospital Denton, Denton, TX, p. A613
M.D., Esq, Chief Medical Officer, Baylor Scott & White The Heart Hospital Plano, Plano, TX, p. A644
PETTINATO, James, R.N., Chief Executive Officer, Wayne Memorial Hospital, Honesdale, PA, p. A542
PETTINGILL, Tammy, Interim Chief Executive Officer, Vibra Hospital of Boise, Boise, ID, p. A180
PETTIT, Amy, R.N., Vice President of Patient Care Services and Chief Nursing Officer, Schneck Medical Center, Seymour, IN, p. A227
PETTIT, Donny, Chief Financial Officer, Coon Memorial Hospital, Dalhart, TX, p. A610
PETTIT, Kevin, Chief Executive Officer, Clive Behavioral Health, Clive, IA, p. A233
PETTITE, Shirley F, Chief Human Resources Officer, Tennessee Valley Hcs – Nashville And Murfreesboro, Nashville, TN, p. A590
PETTORINI–D'AMICO, Susan, R.N., Chief Nursing Officer, Mercy Medical Center, Springfield, MA, p. A318
PETTREY, Lisa J., MSN, R.N., Chief Executive Officer, Select Specialty Hospital–Columbus, Columbus, OH, p. A492
PETTUS, Jay, Chief Financial Officer, Oviedo Medical Center, Oviedo, FL, p. A145
PETTY, Jane, Director Human Resources, Southern Tennessee Regional Health System–Pulaski, Pulaski, TN, p. A592
PETTY, Russ, M.D., Chief of Staff, Towner County Medical Center, Cando, ND, p. A479
PETULA, Ronald J.
Chief Financial Officer, Good Shepherd Rehabilitation Network, Allentown, PA, p. A534
Chief Financial Officer, Good Shepherd Specialty Hospital, Bethlehem, PA, p. A535
Vice President Finance, Good Shepherd Penn Partners, Philadelphia, PA, p. A548
PEVEY, Bradley, Chief Executive Officer, The Neuromedical Center Rehabilitation Hospital, Baton Rouge, LA, p. A278
PFAFF, Joni, Chief Nursing Officer, Grisell Memorial Hospital District One, Ransom, KS, p. A258
PFAFF, Tony, Chief Executive Officer, Deer Lodge Medical Center, Deer Lodge, MT, p. A391
PFALTZGRAFF, George, Chief Medical Officer, Hansen Family Hospital, Iowa Falls, IA, p. A238
PFAU, Ben, Chief Facility and Information Officer, Bay Area Hospital, Coos Bay, OR, p. A526
PFEFFER, Amy, Chief Financial Officer, Sturdy Memorial Hospital, Attleboro, MA, p. A309
PFEFFER, Daniel William, Chief Nurse Executive, Weisman Children's Rehabilitation Hospital, Marlton, NJ, p. A424
PFEIFER, Mark P, M.D., Senior Vice President and Chief Medical Officer, Uofl Health – Uofl Hospital, Louisville, KY, p. A270
PFEIFFER, Margaret, R.N., MSN, Vice President Patient Care Services, PIH Health Good Samaritan Hospital, Los Angeles, CA, p. A74
PFISTER, Joann M, Director Human Resources, Providence Willamette Falls Medical Center, Oregon City, OR, p. A530
PFISTER, Pam, Chief Executive Officer, Morrison Community Hospital, Morrison, IL, p. A202
PFISTER, Scott, Director Finance, Providence St. Vincent Medical Center, Portland, OR, p. A531
PFLEIGER, Dennis, President, St. Luke's Quakertown Campus, Quakertown, PA, p. A553
PFRANK, Kym, Senior Vice President and Chief Operating Officer, Union Hospital, Terre Haute, IN, p. A228
PHAM, Bong, Chief Medical Officer, Kit Carson County Memorial Hospital, Burlington, CO, p. A104

A944 Index of Health Care Professionals

Index of Health Care Professionals / Pilon

PHAM, K, M.D., Chief of Staff, Winkler County Memorial Hospital, Kermit, TX, p. A632
PHELAN, Cynthia, Vice President Human Resources, Lawrence General Hospital, Lawrence, MA, p. A314
PHELPS, Alan, Market Chief Financial Officer, Havasu Regional Medical Center, Lake Havasu City, AZ, p. A32
PHELPS, Craig, M.D., Chief of Staff, Great Plains Regional Medical Center, Elk City, OK, p. A512
PHELPS, Gail, R.N., Chief Nursing Officer, Haxtun Hospital District, Haxtun, CO, p. A109
PHELPS, Joel, President and Chief Executive Officer, Salina Regional Health Center, Salina, KS, p. A259
PHELPS, Kathleen, Director Human Resources, Treasure Valley Hospital, Boise, ID, p. A180
PHELPS, Michael, President and Chief Executive Officer, Ridgeview Medical Center, Waconia, MN, p. A356
PHETTEPLACE, Danial, Director Information Technology, Gundersen St. Joseph's Hospital And Clinics, Hillsboro, WI, p. A713
PHILIP, Merry, M.D., Chief Nursing Officer, University of Texas Medical Branch, Galveston, TX, p. A621
PHILLIPS, Alan M, Controller, Encompass Health Rehabilitation Hospital of Nittany Valley, Pleasant Gap. PA, p. A552
PHILLIPS, Barry, Executive Director Human Resources, West Tennessee Healthcare Camden Hospital, Camden, TN, p. A579
PHILLIPS, Bill, Vice President Information Services, University Health, San Antonio, TX, p. A651
PHILLIPS, Christopher, Chief Executive Officer, Encompass Health Rehabilitation Hospital, Shreveport, LA, p. A292
PHILLIPS, Courtney, Chief Executive Officer, South Sunflower County Hospital, Indianola, MS, p. A363
PHILLIPS, David D., Chief Operating Officer, Wheeling Hospital, Wheeling, WV, p. A706
PHILLIPS, Donna, President, Bryn Mawr Rehabilitation Hospital, Malvern, PA, p. A545
PHILLIPS, Frank, M.D., Chief of Staff, Cherokee Medical Center, Gaffney, SC, p. A566
PHILLIPS, Glenn, Director Information Systems, Gadsden Regional Medical Center, Gadsden, AL, p. A20
PHILLIPS, Jamie, Chief Operating Officer, UCSF Benioff Children's Hospital Oakland, Oakland, CA, p. A81
PHILLIPS, Jerome, Chief Executive Officer, Neurobehavioral Hospital of Nw Indiana/Greater Chicago, Crown Point, IN, p. A215
PHILLIPS, John, Vice President Information Services, Chi St. Josep. Regional Health Center, Bryan, TX, p. A605
PHILLIPS, John E., FACHE, President, Methodist Dallas Medical Center, Dallas, TX, p. A612
PHILLIPS, Jonathan, Chief Operating Officer, Ochsner Lsu Health Shreveport – Monroe Medical Center, Monroe, LA, p. A288
PHILLIPS, Kelly, M.D., M.P.H., Clinical Director and Chief Staff, Spring Grove Hospital Center, Baltimore, MD, p. A302
PHILLIPS, Kimberly A, Chief Financial Officer, The Children's Home of Pittsburgh, Pittsburgh, PA, p. A551
PHILLIPS, Lionel J, Vice President Financial Services, Fauquier Hospital, Warrenton, VA, p. A685
PHILLIPS, Mark, Chief Nursing Officer, The Hospitals of Providence Memorial Campus – Tenet Healthcare, El Paso, TX, p. A617
PHILLIPS, Mike, Chief Executive Officer, Wyoming Behavioral Institute, Casper, WY, p. A726
PHILLIPS, Monie III, Director Clinical Informatics, Jackson Parish Hospital, Jonesboro, LA, p. A284
PHILLIPS, Paul, Chief Financial Officer, Taylor Regional Hospital, Campbellsville, KY, p. A264
PHILLIPS, Richard, Chief Medical Officer, Baptist Health Floyd, New Albany, IN, p. A225
PHILLIPS, Robert, M.D., Ph.D., FACC, Executive Vice President and Chief Medical Officer, Houston Methodist Hospital, Houston, TX, p. A626
PHILLIPS, Sarah, Manager Human Resources, Morgan Medical Center, Madison, GA, p. A167
PHILLIPS, Shaun, PharmD, Chief Executive Officer, Canyon Vista Medical Center, Sierra Vista, AZ, p. A39
PHILLIPS, Tammy, Director, Information Systems, Texas Health Presbyterian Hospital Dallas, Dallas, TX, p. A612
PHINNEY, Cody, Administrator, Northern Nevada Adult Mental Health Services, Sparks, NV, p. A413
PHIPPS, Emily, Director Human Resources, Oklahoma Center for Orthopaedic And Multi-Specialty Surgery, Oklahoma City, OK, p. A518
PHIPPS, Jackie G, Director Human Resources, Johnston Memorial Hospital, Abingdon, VA, p. A673
PHIPPS ADAMS, Holly, Vice President of Human Resources, Carroll Hospital, Westminster, MD, p. A308
PHOENIX, Tim, Chief Executive Officer, Kindred Hospital–Louisville, Louisville, KY, p. A269

PIATKOWSKI, Shannon, Director Information Technology, HCA Florida Blake Hospital, Bradenton, FL, p. A126
PIAZZA, Doreen, MS, Executive Director, South Beach Psychiatric Center, New York, NY, p. A452
PIAZZA, Tony, Director Human Resources, Titus Regional Medical Center, Mount Pleasant, TX, p. A640
PICAZA, Jose, M.D., Chief of Staff, Unicoi County Hospital, Erwin, TN, p. A583
PICCIONE, Elizabeth A., M.D., President, UPMC Passavant, Pittsburgh, PA, p. A552
PICCIONE, Jennifer, Chief Nursing and Clinical Services Officer, Madison Health, London, OH, p. A498
PICKARD, Bert, Chief Financial Officer, North Mississipp. Medical Center Gilmore–Amory, Amory, MS, p. A359
PICKARTS, Lisa, Vice President Patient Services, Sauk Prairie Healthcare, Prairie Du Sac, WI, p. A720
PICKEL, Joseph, Director Resource Management, Walter Reed National Military Medical Center, Bethesda, MD, p. A303
PICKENS, Arlene G., Chief Executive Officer, Putnam County Memorial Hospital, Unionville, MO, p. A388
PICKER, Josephine, MSN, R.N., Director of Nursing, Asheville Specialty Hospital, Asheville, NC, p. A463
PICKERELL, Heidi, Chief Executive Officer, F. W. Huston Medical Center, Winchester, KS, p. A262
PICKERING, David, System Director, Applications, Endeavor Health Linden Oaks Hospital, Naperville, IL, p. A203
PICKETT, Jerry Lynn
  Chief Financial Officer, Goodall–Witcher Hospital, Clifton, TX, p. A607
  Interim Chief Financial Officer, Concho County Hospital, Eden, TX, p. A615
PICKETT, Lisa C, M.D., Chief Medical Officer, Duke University Hospital, Durham, NC, p. A467
PICKLER, Nancy, Director of Human Resources, Encompass Health Rehabilitation Hospital of East Valley, Mesa, AZ, p. A33
PICKREL, Kevan, M.D., Chief Medical Officer, Honorhealth Sonoran Crossing Medical Center, Phoenix, AZ, p. A36
PICOU, Timothy, Manager Information Technology, Lower Umpqua Hospital District, Reedsport, OR, p. A531
PIEFFER, Paul
  Chief Operating Officer, Great River Medical Center, Blytheville, AR, p. A43
  Chief Operating Officer, SMC Regional Medical Center, Osceola, AR, p. A52
PIEH, Samuel, Chief Executive Officer and Administrator, Baptist Memorial Hospital–Crittenden, West Memphis, AR, p. A54
PIEPER, Kevin, Chief Medical Officer, Kadlec Regional Medical Center, Richland, WA, p. A694
PIEPHOFF, Tonya, Hospital Administrator, Alton Mental Health Center, Alton, IL, p. A185
PIERCE, Christy, Director of Human Resources, Katherine Shaw Bethea Hospital, Dixon, IL, p. A193
PIERCE, Earl, Chief Financial Officer, Winner Regional Healthcare Center, Winner, SD, p. A578
PIERCE, Felicia
  R.N., Chief Nursing Officer, Great River Medical Center, Blytheville, AR, p. A43
  R.N., Chief Nursing Officer, SMC Regional Medical Center, Osceola, AR, p. A52
PIERCE, Ivan, MSN, R.N., Chief Nursing Officer, Riverside Walter Reed Hospital, Gloucester, VA, p. A677
PIERCE, James, Chief Executive Officer, Community Behavioral Health Hospital – Rochester, Rochester, MN, p. A353
PIERCE, Jeff M
  Chief Human Resource Officer, Marshall Medical Center, Lewisburg, TN, p. A587
  Manager Human Resources, Wayne Medical Center, Waynesboro, TN, p. A594
PIERCE, Jennifer, Administrative Director of Finance, SSM Health St. Anthony Hospital – Shawnee, Shawnee, OK, p. A520
PIERCE, John, President, Monument Health Rapid City Hospital, Rapid City, SD, p. A576
PIERCE, Kenneth, Chief Financial Officer, Brookhaven Hospital, Tulsa, OK, p. A522
PIERCE, Kristine, Director Human Resources, Newport News Behavioral Health Center, Newport News, VA, p. A680
PIERCE, Laura, Director Human Resources, Memorial Medical Center, Las Cruces, NM, p. A435
PIERCE, Michael L., Chief Executive Officer, Corpus Christi Rehabilitation Hospital, Corpus Christi, TX, p. A609
PIERCE, Pamela, Deputy Chief Executive Officer, Polara Health, Prescott Valley, AZ, p. A37
PIERCE, Pat, Director Information Systems, Lakewood Regional Medical Center, Lakewood, CA, p. A69

PIERCE, Reid, M.D., Chief Medical Officer, Jefferson Regional, Pine Bluff, AR, p. A52
PIERCE, Stonish
  FACHE, President and Chief Executive Officer, St. Mary's Good Samaritan Hospital, Greensboro, GA, p. A164
  FACHE, President and Chief Executive Officer, St. Mary's Health Care System, Athens, GA, p. A156
  FACHE, President and Chief Executive Officer, St. Mary's Sacred Heart Hospital, Lavonia, GA, p. A166
PIERCE, Tiffany, Director Human Resources, Wellstone Regional Hospital, Jeffersonville, IN, p. A221
PIERCE, Trent, R.N., Regional Vice President, HCA Rehabilitation Division, Central Texas Rehabilitation Hospital, Austin, TX, p. A599
PIERCE GRAHAM, Andrea, Chief Executive Officer, Appling Healthcare System, Baxley, GA, p. A159
PIERDON, Steven, M.D., Executive Vice President and Chief Medical Officer, Geisinger Wyoming Valley Medical Center, Wilkes Barre, PA, p. A557
PIERESCHI, Giovanni
  Vice President Enterprise Information and Chief Information Officer, Hima San Pablo Caguas, Caguas, PR, p. A731
  Vice President Management Information Systems, Hospital Hima De Humacao, Humacao, PR, p. A733
PIERLUISI, Guillermo, Vice President of Medical Affairs, Wellstar Paulding Hospital, Hiram, GA, p. A165
PIERRE, Tonia, Coordinator Human Resources, Our Lady of The Lake Assumption Community Hospital, Napoleonville, LA, p. A289
PIERRO, John, Executve Vice President and Chief Operating Officer, Lehigh Valley Hospital–Cedar Crest, Allentown, PA, p. A534
PIERSON, Cindy, Interim Chief Nursing Officer, Highlands–Cashiers Hospital, Highlands, NC, p. A470
PIERSON, Kyle A., Chief Financial Officer, Roane General Hospital, Spencer, WV, p. A705
PIERSON, Lois K., Chief Financial Officer, Uthealth Harris County Psychiatric Center, Houston, TX, p. A628
PIERSON, Michelle, M.D., Chief Medical Officer, Billings Clinic, Billings, MT, p. A389
PIETSCH, Al, CPA, Senior Vice President and Chief Financial Officer, University of Maryland Baltimore Washington Medical Center, Glen Burnie, MD, p. A304
PIFKO, Duane, Interim Director Financial Services, Daniel Drake Center for Post Acute Care, Cincinnati, OH, p. A489
PIGG, Russell
  Chief Executive Officer, North Alabama Medical Center, Florence, AL, p. A19
  Chief Executive Officer, North Alabama Shoals Hospital, Muscle Shoals, AL, p. A23
PIGOTT, Tom, Chief Operating Officer, Abbeville General Hospital, Abbeville, LA, p. A276
PIKE, Irving, M.D., Senior Vice President and Chief Medical Officer, John Muir Medical Center, Walnut Creek, Walnut Creek, CA, p. A100
PIKE, Jeff, R.N., Chief Operating Officer, Cleveland Clinic Union Hospital, Dover, OH, p. A495
PIKE, Pauline, Chief Operating Officer, Beverly Hospital, Beverly, MA, p. A309
PIKE, Randi, Director of Nursing, Pioneer Medical Center, Big Timber, MT, p. A389
PIKE, Ronald F, M.D., Medical Director, Adcare Hospital of Worcester, Worcester, MA, p. A320
PIKER, John F, M.D., Medical Director, Villa Feliciana Medical Complex, Jackson, LA, p. A283
PIKULA, Shirley, MSN, Associate Director Patient Center Care, San Francisco Va Health Care System, San Francisco, CA, p. A91
PIL, Pieter, M.D., Chief Medical Staff, Martha's Vineyard Hospital, Oak Bluffs, MA, p. A317
PILANT, Jason B., President and Chief Administrative Officer, Roane Medical Center, Harriman, TN, p. A583
PILCHER, Shane, Administrative Director Information Systems, Siskin Hospital for Physical Rehabilitation, Chattanooga, TN, p. A581
PILE, Larry, Director Human Resources, Deaconess Midtown Hospital, Evansville, IN, p. A216
PILE, Mindi L., Chief Operations Officer, Summit Medical Center, Casper, WY, p. A726
PILGRIM, Patti, Chief Financial Officer, Sutter Davis Hospital, Davis, CA, p. A61
PILKINGTON, Albert, Chief Executive Officer, Memorial Hospital, Seminole, TX, p. A652
PILLOT, Juan, M.D., Esq, Medical Director, Hospital Pavia Yauco, Yauco, PR, p. A736
PILNEY, Jeffrey, Chief Medical Officer, Pocahontas Memorial Hospital, Buckeye, WV, p. A699
PILON, Michele, President and Chief Nursing Officer, Transylvania Regional Hospital, Brevard, NC, p. A464

Index of Health Care Professionals / Pilot

PILOT, Dave, Chief Financial Officer, Essentia Health–St. Joseph's Medical Center, Brainerd, MN, p. A344
PIMPLE, Cathy, MS, Chief Executive Officer, Newman Regional Health, Emporia, KS, p. A249
PINA, Julie A., Assistant Vice President Patient Care Services and Chief Nursing Officer, Driscoll Children's Hospital, Corpus Christi, TX, p. A609
PINEIRO, Carlos M, President, Hospital Hima De Humacao, Humacao, PR, p. A733
PINELLE, Brian, R.N., Chief Nursing Officer, HCA Florida Gulf Coast Hospital, Panama City, FL, p. A146
PINER, Thomas J., Director for Resources Management, Naval Medical Center San Diego, San Diego, CA, p. A89
PINKELMAN, Janet M, Director Human Resources, Faith Regional Health Services, Norfolk, NE, p. A403
PINKERTON, Jay
   M.D., Chief Medical Officer, George Regional Hospital, Lucedale, MS, p. A365
   M.D., Chief of Staff, Greene County Hospital, Leakesville, MS, p. A365
PINO, Elena, Chief Operating Officer and Chief Nursing Officer, Premier Specialty Hospital of El Paso, El Paso, TX, p. A617
PINON, Richard, Chief Medical Officer, Eastern New Mexico Medical Center, Roswell, NM, p. A436
PINSKY, Karen, M.D., Chief Medical Information Officer, Penn Medicine Chester County Hospital, West Chester, PA, p. A557
PINTER, Tabatha
   Director of Nursing, George Regional Hospital, Lucedale, MS, p. A365
   Director of Nursing, Greene County Hospital, Leakesville, MS, p. A365
PINTO, Frank, Chief Information Officer, The Hospital of Central Connecticut, New Britain, CT, p. A117
PINTO, Mauricio, M.D., Chief Medical Officer, HCA Houston Healthcare Tomball, Tomball, TX, p. A658
PINTOZZI, Kerri, Chief Financial Officer, HCA Florida Lake City Hospital, Lake City, FL, p. A136
PIO RODA, Claro M, Dr.PH, Vice President, Finance and Chief Financial Officer, Johns Hopkins Howard County Medical Center, Columbia, MD, p. A303
PIPER, Kevin, Director Information Systems, Adventhealth Deland, Deland, FL, p. A130
PIPER, Vicky, Regional Vice President Human Resources, Loyola University Medical Center, Maywood, IL, p. A201
PIPGRASS, Michele, Chief Fiscal Service, Oklahoma City Va Medical Center, Oklahoma City, OK, p. A518
PIPP, Darren, M.D., Chief Medical Officer, SSM Health Monroe Clinic, Monroe, WI, p. A718
PIPPIN, Katie, R.N., Director of Nursing, East Carroll Parish Hospital, Lake Providence, LA, p. A287
PIPPIN, Kim, Chief Nursing Officer, Select Specialty Hospital–Augusta, Augusta, GA, p. A158
PIRANI, John, M.D., Chief Medical Officer, Gadsden Regional Medical Center, Gadsden, AL, p. A20
PIRO, Michael J, Chief Information Officer, St. John's Episcopal Hospital, New York, NY, p. A453
PIRRI, Christine, Vice President Human Resources, Little Falls Hospital, Little Falls, NY, p. A445
PIRTLE, Kathleen, Director Human Resources, Encompass Health Rehabilitation Hospital of Wichita Falls, Wichita Falls, TX, p. A662
PISANO, Thomas, M.D., Chief Professional Services, Connecticut Valley Hospital, Middletown, CT, p. A117
PISCIOTTA, Michael J., Chief Executive Officer, Southern Surgical Hospital, Slidell, LA, p. A293
PISICOTTA, Robert, Chief Nursing Officer, Baylor Scott & White Continuing Care Hospital–Temple, Temple, TX, p. A656
PISTERS, Peter, M.D., President and Chief Executive Officer, University of Texas M.D. Anderson Cancer Center, Houston, TX, p. A628
PITCHER, Ellen, Senior Vice President Patient Care Services and Chief Nursing Officer, St. Luke's Health – The Woodlands Hospital, The Woodlands, TX, p. A658
PITMAN, David R, Vice President Finance, Medstar Harbor Hospital, Baltimore, MD, p. A301
PITTMAN, Cyndi, Chief Financial Officer, Baptist Memorial Hospital – Memphis, Memphis, TN, p. A588
PITTMAN, Jennifer, Chief Financial Officer, Shelby Baptist Medical Center, Alabaster, AL, p. A15
PITTS, Celeste, Chief Financial Officer, Upper Connecticut Valley Hospital, Colebrook, NH, p. A414
PITTS, Lynn, Director Human Resources, Calhoun Liberty Hospital, Blountstown, FL, p. A126
PITTS, Robert, Executive Director, Wilmington Treatment Center, Wilmington, NC, p. A478
PITTS, Ryan, Chief Nursing Officer, Logan Health, Kalispell, MT, p. A393

PIVONKA, Mary, Director Quality Management, Rockland Children's Psychiatric Center, Orangeburg, NY, p. A455
PIZ, Tom, Director Human Resources, Fremont Hospital, Fremont, CA, p. A64
PIZARRO, Hugo A, Vice President Human Resources, Terence Cardinal Cooke Health Care Center, New York, NY, p. A453
PIZZI, Chris, Chief Executive Officer, Providence Medford Medical Center, Medford, OR, p. A529
PIZZINO, Mary, Chief Information Officer, Effingham Health System, Springfield, GA, p. A171
PLACE, Ronald J., M.D., President and Chief Executive Officer, Avera Mckennan Hospital And University Health Center, Sioux Falls, SD, p. A576
PLAGGEMEYER, Rikki, Director Acute Care Nursing, Monument Health Sturgis Hospital, Sturgis, SD, p. A577
PLAISANCE, Erika, Chief Nursing Officer, Ochsner Extended Care Hospital, New Orleans, LA, p. A289
PLAISANCE, Stephen, Chief Financial Officer, Meeker Memorial Hospital And Clinics, Litchfield, MN, p. A348
PLAKUN, Eric M., M.D., Medical Center Director and Chief Executive Officer, Austen Riggs Center, Stockbridge, MA, p. A318
PLAMANN, Joy, R.N., Senior Vice President Central Operations, President CentraCare – St. Cloud Hospital, Centracare – St. Cloud Hospital, Saint Cloud, MN, p. A354
PLAMONDON, Jason
   Chief Nursing Officer, Providence Seaside Hospital, Seaside, OR, p. A532
   Chief Operating Officer, Providence Seaside Hospital, Seaside, OR, p. A532
PLAMONDON, Richard, Vice President Finance and Chief Financial Officer, St. Josep. Hospital, Nashua, NH, p. A416
PLANT, Steven L, Chief Financial Officer, Cottage Hospital, Woodsville, NH, p. A417
PLANTE, Vanessa, Chief Clinical Officer, Prohealth Rehabilitation Hospital of Wisconsin, Waukesha, WI, p. A723
PLASEK, James, M.D., Chief of Staff, Memorial Health Care Systems, Seward, NE, p. A406
PLASS, Mary Ellen, MS, R.N., Senior Vice President and Chief Nursing Officer, Columbia Memorial Hospital, Hudson, NY, p. A444
PLATE, James, M.D., Chief of Staff, Kimball Health Services, Kimball, NE, p. A401
PLATEL, Raylene, M.D., Chief Medical Officer, HCA Florida Citrus Hospital, Inverness, FL, p. A134
PLATER, Queenie C.
   Vice President, Human Resources National Capital Region Johns Hopkins Medicine, Sibley Memorial Hospital, Washington, DC, p. A124
   Vice President, Human Resources National Capital Region Johns Hopkins Medicine, Suburban Hospital, Bethesda, MD, p. A303
PLATT, Dwayne, M.D., Chief Medical Officer, Conemaugh Meyersdale Medical Center, Meyersdale, PA, p. A546
PLATT, Shantel, Chief Executive Officer, Select Specialty Hospital–Pittsburgh/Upmc, Pittsburgh, PA, p. A551
PLAUTH, William, M.D., Vice President Operations and Chief Medical Officer, Commonspirit – Mercy Hospital, Durango, CO, p. A107
PLAVIAK, David J, Interim Chief Financial Officer, UVA Health Culpeper Medical Center, Culpeper, VA, p. A675
PLAVIN, Joshua, M.D., Medical Director Medicine Division, Gifford Medical Center, Randolph, VT, p. A672
PLAYER, Tamara, Chief Executive Officer, Polara Health, Prescott Valley, AZ, p. A37
PLAZA, Marta Rivera., Chief Executive Officer and Managing Director, San Juan Capestrano Hospital, San Juan, PR, p. A735
PLEDGER, Michelle, Coordinator Human Resources, Archbold Grady, Cairo, GA, p. A159
PLEMEL, Jeff, Director Health Information, Ccm Health, Montevideo, MN, p. A351
PLEMMONS, Debra, Chief Nursing Officer, Middle Park Health–Kremmling, Kremmling, CO, p. A110
PLESKOW, Eric D., President and Chief Executive Officer, Brylin Hospitals, Buffalo, NY, p. A440
PLESS, Katy, Director of Human Resources, Carepartners Rehabilitation Hospital, Asheville, NC, p. A463
PLUARD, Dennis, Vice President Finance and Support Services, Sarah Bush Lincoln Health Center, Mattoon, IL, p. A201
PLUMLEE, Steve, Chief Executive Officer, Select Specialty Hospital–North Knoxville, Powell, TN, p. A592
PLUMMER, Doug, Chief Operating Officer, Sabine Medical Center, Many, LA, p. A288
PLUNKETT, Alicia
   Chief Executive Officer, Parkwood Behavioral Health System, Olive Branch, MS, p. A367
   Chief Nurse Executive, Parkwood Behavioral Health System, Olive Branch, MS, p. A367

PLUNKETT, Isaac, Chief Financial Officer, Ascension St. Vincent's St. Clair, Pell City, AL, p. A23
PLYMELL, Shane, Chief Executive Officer, Shannon Medical Center, San Angelo, TX, p. A648
PLYWACZYNSKI, Russell J., CPA, Director of Finance, St. Joseph's Hospital, Buckhannon, WV, p. A699
POBLETE, Ronald, M.D., President Medical and Dental Staff, St. Mary's General Hospital, Passaic, NJ, p. A426
POCCHIARI, Michael, Director Human Resources, Singing River Gulfport, Gulfport, MS, p. A363
PODESTA, Charles H, Chief Information Officer, UCI Health, Orange, CA, p. A82
PODESWICK, Michelle, Director Human Resources, Rome Health, Rome, NY, p. A458
PODGES, Christopher J, Vice President and Chief Information Officer, Munson Medical Center, Traverse City, MI, p. A339
PODNOS, Yale D., M.D., Chief Medical Officer, UCLA West Valley Medical Center, Los Angeles, CA, p. A75
PODOLSKY, Daniel
   M.D., President, University of Texas Southwestern Medical Center, Dallas, TX, p. A612
   M.D., President and Professor, Department of Internal Medicine, University of Texas Southwestern Medical Center, Dallas, TX, p. A612
PODZIMEK, Marcia, Chief Human Resources Officer, Wagner Community Memorial Hospital Avera, Wagner, SD, p. A578
POE, Dale
   Vice President and Chief Financial Officer, Hawkins County Memorial Hospital, Rogersville, TN, p. A592
   Vice President Finance and Operations, Holston Valley Medical Center, Kingsport, TN, p. A585
POE, Terri Lyn, Chief Nursing Officer, University of Alabama Hospital, Birmingham, AL, p. A17
POEHLER, Kathy, Vice President, Human Resources, University of Maryland Baltimore Washington Medical Center, Glen Burnie, MD, p. A304
POFAHL, Barnetta, Director Human Resources, Wagoner Community Hospital, Wagoner, OK, p. A523
POFF, Heather, Director Human Resources, Princeton Community Hospital, Princeton, WV, p. A704
POFFENBARGER, John, Director Fiscal Services, Northern Virginia Mental Health Institute, Falls Church, VA, p. A676
POGAS, George, CPA, Senior Vice President and Chief Financial Officer, Witham Health Services, Lebanon, IN, p. A222
POGLIANO, Chris, M.D., Chief Medical Staff, Aspirus Ironwood Hospital & Clinics, Inc., Ironwood, MI, p. A330
POHJALA, Eric D., Vice President, Finance and Chief Financial Officer, Lima Memorial Health System, Lima, OH, p. A498
POHL, Ann-Marie J, Vice President and Chief Nursing Officer, Lima Memorial Health System, Lima, OH, p. A498
POHL, David F., M.D., Chief of Staff, Cornerstone Specialty Hospitals Austin Round Rock, Austin, TX, p. A599
POHL, David L., M.D., Chief of Staff, Hillcrest Hospital South, Tulsa, OK, p. A522
POHLMAN, John, Senior Vice President and Chief Financial Officer, Mount Sinai South Nassau, Oceanside, NY, p. A454
POISKER, Karen C, MSN, Vice President Patient Care Services and Chief Nursing Officer, Tidalhealth Peninsula Regional, Salisbury, MD, p. A307
POISSON, Keith R, Executive Vice President and Chief Operating Officer, Gbmc Healthcare, Baltimore, MD, p. A302
POITINGER, Kevin, Chief Executive Officer and Managing Director, Holly Hill Hospital, Raleigh, NC, p. A474
POKLADNIK, Rebekah, Human Resources Director, Oceans Behavioral Hospital of Corpus Christi, Corpus Christi, TX, p. A609
POKORZYNSKI, Debra, Vice President of Nursing, Mymichigan Medical Center Alpena, Alpena, MI, p. A321
POLAND, David, Interim Chief Human Resource Officer, AHN Grove City, Grove City, PA, p. A541
POLASHEK, Maurene, Chief Financial Officer, Oro Valley Hospital, Oro Valley, AZ, p. A34
POLASZEK, Julie, R.N., MSNSarasota Memorial Hospital – Venice, North Venice, FL, p. A142
POLEGA, Steve, Chief Nursing Officer, University of Michigan Health – West, Wyoming, MI, p. A341
POLHILL, James, M.D., Chief Medical Officer, Jefferson Hospital, Louisville, GA, p. A166
POLIKAITIS, Audrius, Chief Information Officer, University of Illinois Hospital, Chicago, IL, p. A192
POLING, Rodney, M.D., Medical Director, Unity Psychiatric Care–Columbia, Columbia, TN, p. A581
POLING, Susan Kay, Director Human Resources, Norton King's Daughters' Health, Madison, IN, p. A223
POLIS, Nikki S, Ph.D., Chief Nurse Executive, Methodist Healthcare Memphis Hospitals, Memphis, TN, p. A589
POLISKNOWSKI, John, Chief Nursing Officer, HCA Florida Northside Hospital, Saint Petersburg, FL, p. A149

POLITIS, Christos, M.D., Chief Medical Officer, HCA Florida West Tamp. Hospital, Tampa, FL, p. A152
POLITO, Janine, Chief Human Resources Officer, Banner Ironwood Medical Center, San Tan Valley, AZ, p. A38
POLIVKA, Maureen, Chief Nursing Officer, Methodist Hospital Hill Country, Fredericksburg, TX, p. A620
POLIZZOTTI, Barbara, Controller, Encompass Health Rehabilitation Hospital of New England, Woburn, MA, p. A320
POLIZZOTTO, Mike, Chief Medical Officer, UW Health Swedishamerican Hospital, Rockford, IL, p. A207
POLK, Brent, M.D., Chair Department of Pediatrics and Vice President Academic Affairs, Children's Hospital Los Angeles, Los Angeles, CA, p. A72
POLK, Claire, Chief Financial Officer, Lake Norman Regional Medical Center, Mooresville, NC, p. A472
POLK, Gregory, Chief Executive Officer, Kedren Community Health Center, Los Angeles, CA, p. A73
POLK, Monica, M.D., Chief Medical Officer, Salt Lake Behavioral Health, Salt Lake City, UT, p. A669
POLKOW, Craig, Vice President, Finance, Ascension St. Vincent Evansville, Evansville, IN, p. A216
POLLACK, Neil, Senior Administrator, Terence Cardinal Cooke Health Care Center, New York, NY, p. A453
POLLAK, Erich, M.D., Chief of Staff, West Covina Medical Center, West Covina, CA, p. A101
POLLARD, Anthony, D.O., Chief Medical Officer, Amg Specialty Hospital - Las Vegas, Las Vegas, NV, p. A409
POLLARD, Beau, Vice President and Baptist Hospital Administrator, Baptist Hospital, Pensacola, FL, p. A146
POLLARD-LEIGHTON, Heather, Director of Administrative Services, Upper Connecticut Valley Hospital, Colebrook, NH, p. A414
POLLART, Leslie, R.N., Chief Nursing Officer, Memorial Regional Hospital, Hollywood, FL, p. A133
POLLMAN, Brian, Chief Medical Officer, Hutchinson Health, Hutchinson, MN, p. A348
POLLOCK, Jeffrey, Chief Information Officer, Wentworth-Douglass Hospital, Dover, NH, p. A414
POLLOCK, Preston, Chief Operating Officer, Cobre Valley Regional Medical Center, Globe, AZ, p. A32
POLO, Fabian, Ph.D., Chief Executive Officer, Rehabilitation Hospital of Fort Wayne, Fort Wayne, IN, p. A217
POLO, Therese, Medical Staff President, Carlinville Area Hospital, Carlinville, IL, p. A187
POLSELLI, Donna, Chief Operating Officer, Franciscan Children's, Brighton, MA, p. A311
POLSTER, Peggy, Manager Personnel and Administrative Assistant, Falls Community Hospital And Clinic, Marlin, TX, p. A638
POLTAWSKY, Jeffrey S, Senior Vice President, University Hospital, Madison, WI, p. A714
POLTAWSKY, Jeffrey S., President and Market Leader, Multicare Mary Bridge Children's Hospital And Health Center, Tacoma, WA, p. A697
POLUNAS, David M., Director, Colorado Mental Health Institute At Fort Logan, Denver, CO, p. A106
POLZIN, Greg
 Chief Financial Officer, Iowa Specialty Hospital-Belmond, Belmond, IA, p. A230
 Chief Financial Officer, Iowa Specialty Hospital-Clarion, Clarion, IA, p. A232
PONCE, Agustin, Supervisor Maintenance, Castaner General Hospital, Castaner, PR, p. A732
PONCE, Josep. A, Chief Information Management, Dwight David Eisenhower Army Medical Center, Fort Gordon, GA, p. A164
PONCE, Martha, Director Information Technologies and Telecommunications, Providence Saint John's Health Center, Santa Monica, CA, p. A95
PONCZOCHA, John, Chief Executive Officer, Select Specialty Hospital - Downriver, Wyandotte, MI, p. A341
POND, Dwight, TIS Boise, Saint Alphonsus Regional Medical Center, Boise, ID, p. A179
POND-BELL, Michele, R.N., Nurse Administrator, Cassia Regional Hospital, Burley, ID, p. A180
PONDER, Beverly K, Executive Assistant and Human Resources Coordinator, Covington County Hospital, Collins, MS, p. A361
PONDER, David, Information Technology Officer, Claremore Indian Hospital, Claremore, OK, p. A511-
PONDER, Kathryn, Chief Financial Officer, Surgical Specialty Center of Baton Rouge, Baton Rouge, LA, p. A278
PONETA, Jan, Director Information Services, Mercy Hospital Jefferson, Festus, MO, p. A375
PONIERS, Keith David, Vice President and Chief Financial Officer, Hurley Medical Center, Flint, MI, p. A326
PONOZZO, Nancy Lynn, MSN, R.N., Chief Nursing Officer, Aspirus Iron River Hospital, Iron River, MI, p. A330
PONTICELLO, Nat, Vice President Human Resources, Valley Children's Healthcare, Madera, CA, p. A76

PONTIKES, Leon, M.D., Chief Medical Officer, Verde Valley Medical Center, Cottonwood, AZ, p. A31
PONTIOUS, Becky, Human Resources/Accounting, Loring Hospital, Sac City, IA, p. A242
PONTIOUS, Michael, M.D., Chief of Staff, St. Mary's Regional Medical Center, Enid, OK, p. A512
PONTON-CRUZ, Elyonel, Executive Director, St. Luke's Episcopal Hospital, Ponce, PR, p. A734
POOK, Lots, Chief Information Officer, National Jewish Health, Denver, CO, p. A106
POOL, Ashley, President, Highlands Medical Center, Scottsboro, AL, p. A24
POOLE, Aaron, Chief Financial Officer, St. Josep. Regional Medical Center, Lewiston, ID, p. A182
POOLE, Andrew J. III, Interim Chief Financial Officer, Oaklawn Hospital, Marshall, MI, p. A333
POOLE-ADAMS, Veronica
 R.N., Interim West Market President, Atrium Health Cleveland, Shelby, NC, p. A476
 R.N., Vice President, Facility Executive and Chief Nursing Executive, Atrium Health Cleveland, Shelby, NC, p. A476
POORE, Caleb, President and Chief Executive Officer, Boone County Health Center, Albion, NE, p. A397
POORE, Caleb Kelly, Chief Financial Officer, Callaway District Hospital, Callaway, NE, p. A398
POORE, Justin, D.O., Chief Medical Staff, North Central Kansas Medical Center, Concordia, KS, p. A248
POORE, Luke David., Chief Executive Officer, Kearney County Health Services, Minden, NE, p. A402
POOS, Joshua, M.D., President Medical Staff, Community Hospital of Staunton, Staunton, IL, p. A209
POPE, Alan R
 M.D., Chief Medical Officer, Virtua Our Lady of Lourdes Hospital, Camden, NJ, p. A419
 M.D., Vice President, Medical Affairs, Virtua Willingboro Hospital, Willingboro, NJ, p. A431
POPE, Alice H, Chief Financial Officer, Honorhealth Scottsdale Thompson Peak Medical Center, Scottsdale, AZ, p. A38
POPE, Brad W, Vice President Human Resources, Chi Memorial, Chattanooga, TN, p. A580
POPE, David L., President and Chief Executive Officer, Scotland Health Care System, Laurinburg, NC, p. A471
POPE, Diana, Director, Human Resources, Community Rehabilitation Hospital South, Greenwood, IN, p. A218
POPE, Eddie, Chief Information Officer, Lackey Memorial Hospital, Forest, MS, p. A362
POPE, Richard, Vice President Human Resources, Jackson County Memorial Hospital, Altus, OK, p. A509
POPE, Robert A., Director I, Ascension St. Vincent Anderson, Anderson, IN, p. A212
POPE, Susan, Director Human Resources, Wills Memorial Hospital, Washington, GA, p. A174
POPEJOY, Waite, Interim Chief Financial Officer, Wellstar Mcg Health, Augusta, GA, p. A158
POPELKA, EvaMarie, Chief Operating Officer, North Platte Valley Medical Center, Saratoga, WY, p. A728
POPHAN, Cameron, Chief Financial Officer, HCA Houston Healthcare Northwest, Houston, TX, p. A626
POPKIN, Stephen, Chief Executive Officer, Lompoc Valley Medical Center, Lompoc, CA, p. A70
POPLAWSKI, Christine, Chief Financial Officer, Cherokee Medical Center, Gaffney, SC, p. A566
POPLI, Anand, Medical Director, Porter-Starke Services, Valparaiso, IN, p. A228
POPOWYCZ, Alex
 Chief Information Officer, Health First Viera Hospital, Melbourne, FL, p. A139
 Senior Vice President and Chief Information Officer, Health First Cap. Canaveral Hospital, Cocoa Beach, FL, p. A128
 Senior Vice President and Chief Information Officer, Health First Palm Bay Hospital, Palm Bay, FL, p. A145
POPP, Adam, Director Information Systems, Avera St. Benedict Health Center, Parkston, SD, p. A575
POPP, Susan, Chief Financial Officer, Hill Regional Hospital, Hillsboro, TX, p. A624
POPPEN, Jeffrey, Chief Financial Officer, Sanford Aberdeen Medical Center, Aberdeen, SD, p. A572
POPPERT, Dale, M.D., Chief of Staff, Kaiser Permanente Antioch Medical Center, Antioch, CA, p. A55
POPPY, Bill, Chief Information Officer, Virginia Mason Medical Center, Seattle, WA, p. A695
POPRAWSKI, Teresa, Chief Medical Officer, Hartgrove Behavioral Health System, Chicago, IL, p. A189
PORADA, John, Chief Financial Officer, Tristar Southern Hills Medical Center, Nashville, TN, p. A591
PORCELLI, Cheri, MSN, R.N., Chief Nursing Officer, Deer's Head Hospital Center, Salisbury, MD, p. A307
PORCO, Albert, Director Management Information Systems, Hackensack Meridian Health Palisades Medical Center, North Bergen, NJ, p. A426

PORSA, Esmaeil, M.D., President and Chief Executive Officer, Harris Health System, Bellaire, TX, p. A603
PORTCHY, Mindy, Manager Human Resources, Summit Pacific Medical Center, Elma, WA, p. A689
PORTER, Bruce, Chief Financial Officer, Red River Hospital, Llc, Wichita Falls, TX, p. A662
PORTER, Daniel J., Senior Vice President and Chief Financial Officer, Dosher Memorial Hospital, Southport, NC, p. A476
PORTER, Glen, Vice President Human Resources, Essentia Health St. Mary's Medical Center, Duluth, MN, p. A346
PORTER, Greg, Chief Financial Officer, Rio Grande Hospital, Del Norte, CO, p. A106
PORTER, Heather, Chief Clinical Officer, Nmc Health, Newton, KS, p. A255
PORTER, James, Chief Financial Officer, Brookdale Hospital Medical Center, New York, NY, p. A447
PORTER, James P, Chief Financial Officer, St. Bernard Hospital And Health Care Center, Chicago, IL, p. A191
PORTER, Jim, Chief Financial Officer, Bon Secours - Southern Virginia Medical Center, Emporia, VA, p. A675
PORTER, Jody, R.N., Senior Vice President Patient Care Services and Chief Nursing Officer, Gbmc Healthcare, Baltimore, MD, p. A302
PORTER, Lance, President and Chief Executive Officer, Wyoming Medical Center, Casper, WY, p. A726
PORTER, Lisa, Director Human Resources, Leadership and Education, George E. Wahlen Department of Veterans Affairs Medical Center, Salt Lake City, UT, p. A668
PORTER, Lydia, Administrator, Osage Beach Center for Behavioral Health, Llc, Osage Beach, MO, p. A381
PORTER, Sharon, Chief Financial Officer, Pappas Rehabilitation Hospital for Children, Canton, MA, p. A312
PORTER, Stephen D., Chief Executive Officer, Piedmont Fayette Hospital, Fayetteville, GA, p. A164
PORTER, T J, Director Human Resources, Bennett County Hospital And Nursing Home, Martin, SD, p. A574
PORTER, Trever
 Chief Financial Officer, Layton Hospital, Layton, UT, p. A665
 Chief Financial Officer, Mckay-Dee Hospital, Ogden, UT, p. A666
PORTMAN, Angela, Chief Executive Officer, Breckinridge Memorial Hospital, Hardinsburg, KY, p. A266
PORTNER, Barry, M.D., Chief of Staff, Prowers Medical Center, Lamar, CO, p. A111
PORWOLL, Amy, Vice President of Information Systems, Centracare - St. Cloud Hospital, Saint Cloud, MN, p. A354
POSADAS, Lillian, Hospital Administrator, Chief Executive Officer, Guam Memorial Hospital Authority, Tamuning, GU, p. A730
POSCH, Tim B, Business Manager and Director Personnel, Parsons State Hospital And Training Center, Parsons, KS, p. A258
POSEY, Richard B, Director Human Resources, Prisma Health Baptist Easley Hospital, Easley, SC, p. A565
POST, Daniel, Chief Executive Officer, Banner - University Medical Center Phoenix, Phoenix, AZ, p. A35
POST, Eleanor, R.N., Chief Nursing Officer, Piedmont Rockdale Hospital, Conyers, GA, p. A161
POST, Gwen, R.N., Chief Nursing Officer, Sanford Worthington Medical Center, Worthington, MN, p. A358
POST, John, M.D., Medical Director, Morrill County Community Hospital, Bridgeport, NE, p. A398
POST, Kimberly
 R.N., Chief Operating Officer, Honorhealth Deer Valley Medical Center, Phoenix, AZ, p. A35
 R.N., Chief Operating Officer, Honorhealth John C. Lincoln Medical Center, Phoenix, AZ, p. A36
 R.N., Chief Operating Officer, Honorhealth Scottsdale Osborn Medical Center, Scottsdale, AZ, p. A38
 R.N., Chief Operating Officer, Honorhealth Scottsdale Shea Medical Center, Scottsdale, AZ, p. A38
 R.N., Chief Operating Officer, Honorhealth Scottsdale Thompson Peak Medical Center, Scottsdale, AZ, p. A38
 R.N., Chief Operating Officer, Honorhealth Sonoran Crossing Medical Center, Phoenix, AZ, p. A36
POST, Michael
 Chief Executive Officer, Poplar Community Hospital, Poplar, MT, p. A395
 Chief Executive Officer, Trinity Hospital, Wolf Point, MT, p. A396
POST, Michael A., Chief Executive Officer, Select Specialty Hospital-Erie, Erie, PA, p. A540
POSTULKA, Carol, Administrative Coordinator, Avera Gregory Hospital, Gregory, SD, p. A574
POTEATE, Kathy, Human Resources Manager, Hugh Chatham Health, Elkin, NC, p. A468
POTEETE, Robin, Manager Human Resources, Hawkins County Memorial Hospital, Rogersville, TN, p. A592

Index of Health Care Professionals

Index of Health Care Professionals / Potempa

POTEMPA, Debra, MSN, R.N., President, Parkview Wabash Hospital, Wabash, IN, p. A228
POTITADKUL, Wendy, Chief Information Officer, Sunrise Canyon Hospital, Lubbock, TX, p. A636
POTLURI, Vamsee, Director, Wilmington Veterans Affairs Medical Center, Wilmington, DE, p. A122
POTTER, Carolyn
Chief Human Resources Officer, Mclaren Bay Region, Bay City, MI, p. A322
Vice President Human Resources, Mclaren Bay Special Care, Bay City, MI, p. A322
Vice President Human Resources, Mclaren Central Michigan, Mount Pleasant, MI, p. A334
POTTER, Leah Voigt., Hospital Administrator, Community Behavioral Health Hospital – Fergus Falls, Fergus Falls, MN, p. A346
POTTER, Val, Director Human Resources, Ascension St. Vincent Salem, Salem, IN, p. A227
POTTS, Mary Ann, Director Personnel, Community Hospitals And Wellness Centers, Bryan, OH, p. A487
POUND, Steve, Vice President Human Resources, St. Joseph's Hospital, Savannah, GA, p. A171
POUND, Terry, Chief Financial Officer, Hospital District No 1 of Rice County, Lyons, KS, p. A254
POUND, Veronica, R.N., Hospital Chief Executive Officer, Chief Nursing Officer and Director, Home Health Care and Hospice, Socorro General Hospital, Socorro, NM, p. A437
POVEY, Jason, Chief Information Officer, Power County Hospital District, American Falls, ID, p. A179
POVICH, Mark, D.O., Medical Director, OSF St. Francis Hospital And Medical Group, Escanaba, MI, p. A326
POWE, Lee, Director Management Information Systems, Hugh Chatham Health, Elkin, NC, p. A468
POWEL, Linda J, M.D., Medical Director, Odessa Memorial Healthcare Center, Odessa, WA, p. A692
POWELL, Adam, Program Manager, Marion Veterans Affairs Medical Center, Marion, IL, p. A200
POWELL, Amber, Chief Administrative Officer, Deaconess Union County Hospital, Morganfield, KY, p. A272
POWELL, Amy, Director Human Resources, Johnson Regional Medical Center, Clarksville, AR, p. A44
POWELL, Audra, Chief Executive Officer, Pam Health Rehabilitation Hospital of Tulsa, Tulsa, OK, p. A522
POWELL, Candy, Administrator, Collingsworth General Hospital, Wellington, TX, p. A661
POWELL, Charles, Chief Financial Officer, Arkansas Surgical Hospital, North Little Rock, AR, p. A51
POWELL, D Jerome, M.D., Chief Information Officer, Strong Memorial Hospital of The University of Rochester, Rochester, NY, p. A457
POWELL, Hannah, Chief Nursing Officer, Mercy Hospital Kingfisher, Kingfisher, OK, p. A514
POWELL, Holly, Interim Chief Executive Officer, Continuecare Hospital At Palmetto Health Baptist, Columbia, SC, p. A564
POWELL, Jackie, Director Human Resources, Pemiscot Memorial Health System, Hayti, MO, p. A376
POWELL, Jimmy, Manager Human Resources, Harry S. Truman Memorial Veterans' Hospital, Columbia, MO, p. A374
POWELL, Josh, Facility Controller, Cox Monett Hospital, Inc, Monett, MO, p. A380
POWELL, Julie, Interim Chief Executive Officer, Mcalester Regional Health Center, Mcalester, OK, p. A515
POWELL, Karen S., Vice President, Human Resources, Mary Free Bed Rehabilitation Hospital, Grand Rapids, MI, p. A328
POWELL, Karrie S., MSN, R.N., Chief Nursing Officer, Musc Health – Orangeburg, Orangeburg, SC, p. A569
POWELL, Kay, Director Human Resources, Christus Southeast Texas Jasper Memorial, Jasper, TX, p. A630
POWELL, Mark, Chief Executive Officer, Select Specialty Hospital – Tucson, Tucson, AZ, p. A41
POWELL, Michelle, Chief Nursing Officer, Jefferson Regional, Pine Bluff, AR, p. A52
POWELL, Parker, Chief Executive Officer, Glendive Medical Center, Glendive, MT, p. A392
POWELL, Tammy, FACHE, M.P.H., President, SSM Health St. Anthony Hospital – Oklahoma City, Oklahoma City, OK, p. A518
POWELL, Traci, Director Human Resources, Encompass Health Rehabilitation Hospital of Panama City, Panama City, FL, p. A146
POWELL, Troy, Regional President, Roper Hospital and Berkeley Hospital, Roper Hospital, Charleston, SC, p. A563
POWELL, Virginia, Director Finance, Wilmington Treatment Center, Wilmington, NC, p. A478
POWELL–STAFFORD, Valerie L., President, Saint Francis Hospital, Hartford, CT, p. A116
POWER, Bob, Vice President Information Services, Good Samaritan Regional Medical Center, Corvallis, OR, p. A526
POWER, Robert
Chief Information Officer, Samaritan Pacific Communities Hospital, Newport, OR, p. A529
Vice President Information Services, Samaritan Lebanon Community Hospital, Lebanon, OR, p. A528
POWERS, Anthony, Interim President and Vice President of Patient Services, Baptist Health Corbin, Corbin, KY, p. A264
POWERS, Brent, M.D., Vice President/Chief Medical Officer, Lexington Medical Center, West Columbia, SC, p. A571
POWERS, Cynthia Ann, VP, ACNO, City of Hope's Helford Clinical Research Hospital, Duarte, CA, p. A62
POWERS, Felicia, Chief Executive Officer, Mercy Behavioral Hospital Llc, Lecompte, LA, p. A287
POWERS, Jamekia, Assistant Director Human Resources, Georgia Regional Hospital At Savannah, Savannah, GA, p. A171
POWERS, Katharine, MS, Chief Executive Officer, Baylor Scott & White Institute for Rehabilitation–Frisco, Frisco, TX, p. A621
POWERS, Kelli
Chief Financial Officer, Huntsville Hospital, Huntsville, AL, p. A21
President, Decatur Morgan Hospital, Decatur, AL, p. A18
POWERS, Mary
R.N., MSN, Senior Vice President and Chief Nursing Officer, Manchester Memorial Hospital, Manchester, CT, p. A116
R.N., MSN, Senior Vice President and Chief Nursing Officer, Rockville General Hospital, Vernon, CT, p. A119
POWERS, Michael, Director and Chief Executive Officer, J. D. Mccarty Center for Children With Developmental Disabilities, Norman, OK, p. A516
POWERS, Ryan J., Vice President Finance, Corewell Health Zeeland Hospital, Zeeland, MI, p. A341
POWERS, Tamara, R.N., Chief Executive Officer, Sutter Roseville Medical Center, Roseville, CA, p. A86
POWRIE, Raymond, M.D., Senior Vice President Quality and Clinical Effectiveness, Women & Infants Hospital of Rhode Island, Providence, RI, p. A561
POYNTER, Carmen, Director Human Resources, Rockcastle Regional Hospital And Respiratory Care Center, Mount Vernon, KY, p. A272
POYTHRESS, Antoine, Chief Executive Officer, Jenkins County Medical Center, Millen, GA, p. A168
PRABHAKARAN, Madhan, M.D., Chief Medical Officer, Palo Alto County Health System, Emmetsburg, IA, p. A236
PRACHEIL, Michael, Chief Financial Officer, Gothenburg Health, Gothenburg, NE, p. A400
PRACHT, Matthew, Vice President Finance, Scotland Health Care System, Laurinburg, NC, p. A471
PRADA, Janina
Director Information Services, University Medical Center of El Paso, El Paso, TX, p. A617
Director Information Technology, El Paso Children's Hospital, El Paso, TX, p. A616
PRAFKA, David, Ed.D., Director of Human Resources, ECU Health Edgecombe Hospital, Tarboro, NC, p. A477
PRAKASH, Amitabh, M.D., Chief Medical Officer, AHMC Anaheim Regional Medical Center, Anaheim, CA, p. A55
PRAKASH, Vijay, Information Technology Officer, Essex County Hospital Center, Cedar Grove, NJ, p. A419
PRASAD, Manoj
M.D., Group Chief Executive Officer, Weiss Memorial Hospital, Chicago, IL, p. A192
M.D., Group Chief Executive Officer, West Suburban Medical Center, Oak Park, IL, p. A204
PRASTO, Michael, M.D., Vice President and Chief Medical Officer, Grand View Health, Sellersville, PA, p. A554
PRATER, Jeffrey, Chief Executive Officer, Carson Valley Medical Center, Gardnerville, NV, p. A408
PRATER, Marsha A, Ph.D., R.N., Chief Nursing Officer Emeritus, Springfield Memorial Hospital, Springfield, IL, p. A209
PRATER, Robin, Director Human Resources, Rusk Rehabilitation Hospital, Columbia, MO, p. A374
PRATHER, Rachael, Chief Nursing Officer, Ferrell Hospital, Eldorado, IL, p. A194
PRATT, Audra, Chief Human Resource Officer, Ascension St. Vincent Indianapolis Hospital, Indianapolis, IN, p. A219
PRATT, Bailey, Chief Financial Officer, Ascension Saint Thomas Rutherford, Murfreesboro, TN, p. A590
PRATT, Debra, Chief Financial Officer, Washington County Memorial Hospital, Potosi, MO, p. A382
PRATT, Donna, Controller, North Platte Valley Medical Center, Saratoga, WY, p. A728
PRATT, Dustin, M.D., Chief of Staff, Childress Regional Medical Center, Childress, TX, p. A607
PRATT, Lisa D., Vice President, Human Resources, Mclean Hospital, Belmont, MA, p. A309
PRATT, MaryEllen, FACHE, Chief Executive Officer, St. James Parish Hospital, Lutcher, LA, p. A287
PRATT, Ramona, Chief Nursing Officer, PIH Health Whittier Hospital, Whittier, CA, p. A101
PRATT, Timothy J, M.D., Vice President Medical Affairs and Chief Medical Officer, SSM Health St. Clare Hospital – Fenton, Fenton, MO, p. A375
PRATT, Troy, Information Technology Site Director, Covenant Medical Center, Lubbock, TX, p. A636
PREAST, Joseph, Chief Executive Officer, Summers County Arh Hospital, Hinton, WV, p. A701
PRECOURT, Justin
Chief Nursing Officer, Umass Memorial Medical Center, Worcester, MA, p. A320
Interim President and Chief Nursing Officer, Umass Memorial Medical Center, Worcester, MA, p. A320
PREDUM, BJ, FACHE, President/Chief Executive Officer, Mercy Hospital Downtown, Bakersfield, CA, p. A57
PREIB, Barbara, Director of Nursing, Chicago Behavioral Hospital, Des Plaines, IL, p. A193
PREISINGER, Andrea, Director Human Resources, Menninger Clinic, Houston, TX, p. A627
PRELLBERG, Todd, Chief Information Officer, RML Specialty Hospital, Hinsdale, IL, p. A198
PREMO, Mark, Senior Director HC Intelligence, Providence Portland Medical Center, Portland, OR, p. A530
PRENTISS, Kristin, Chief Financial Officer, Specialty Hospital of Central Jersey, Lakewood, NJ, p. A422
PRESCOTT, Tina, Executive Vice President and Chief Operating Officer, Jackson–Madison County General Hospital, Medina, TN, p. A588
PRESLEY, Matthew, Chief Executive Officer, Select Specialty Hospital–Panama City, Panama City, FL, p. A146
PRESNELL, Elizabeth, Assistant Vice President of Finance, St. Luke's Hospital, Columbus, NC, p. A466
PRESSMAN, Sean, Chief Executive Officer, Lewisgale Hospital Pulaski, Pulaski, VA, p. A681
PRESTEGAARD, Benjamin, Chief Medical Officer, University Hospitals Portage Medical Center, Ravenna, OH, p. A503
PRESTON, Samuel L., Commander, Colonel Florence A. Blanchfield Army Community Hospital, Fort Campbell, KY, p. A265
PRESTON, Tara
Director Human Resources, Bingham Memorial Hospital, Blackfoot, ID, p. A179
Director Human Resources, Grove Creek Medical Center, Blackfoot, ID, p. A179
PRESTON, Traci R., Director of Nursing, Cap. Fear Valley Bladen County Hospital, Elizabethtown, NC, p. A468
PRESTRIDGE, Tim, President, Mercy Health – Clermont Hospital, Batavia, OH, p. A486
PRETE, Mark, M.D., Vice President Medical Affairs, Charlotte Hungerford Hospital, Torrington, CT, p. A119
PRETTYMAN, Edgar E., PsyD, Chief Executive Officer, Texas Neurorehab Center, Austin, TX, p. A601
PRETZLAFF, Robert, M.D., Chief Medical Officer, St. Rose Dominican Hospitals – San Martin Campus, Las Vegas, NV, p. A411
PREWITT, Margaret Elizabeth, Vice President Patient Services and Chief Nursing Officer, St. Catherine Hospital, Garden City, KS, p. A249
PRIBITKIN, Edmund A., M.D., Chief Medical Officer, Thomas Jefferson University Hospital, Philadelphia, PA, p. A550
PRICE, Amber, Division President, Sentara Williamsburg Regional Medical Center, Williamsburg, VA, p. A685
PRICE, Andy, Chief Information Officer, St. Claire Regional Medical Center, Morehead, KY, p. A272
PRICE, Bernard J, Chief Human Resources Officer, Atrium Health Navicent The Medical Center, Macon, GA, p. A167
PRICE, Connie, M.D., Chief Medical Officer, Denver Health, Denver, CO, p. A106
PRICE, Cory P., FACHE, Medical Center Director and Chief Executive Officer, West Palm Beach Veterans Affairs Medical Center, West Palm Beach, FL, p. A155
PRICE, David, M.D., Chief Medical Advisor, Tennova Healthcare–Clarksville, Clarksville, TN, p. A581
PRICE, Derek, Chief Executive Officer, Sierra Tucson, Tucson, AZ, p. A41
PRICE, Eric, Chief Financial Officer, Cordova Community Medical Center, Cordova, AK, p. A28
PRICE, John, Chief Financial Officer, Norton King's Daughters' Health, Madison, IN, p. A223
PRICE, John Stephen, M.D., Chief of Staff, Fairview Regional Medical Center, Fairview, OK, p. A512
PRICE, Kelley, R.N., Chief Nursing Officer, Battle Mountain General Hospital, Battle Mountain, NV, p. A408
PRICE, Kevin A
Vice President and Chief Operating Officer, Sparrow Clinton Hospital, Saint Johns, MI, p. A337
Vice President and Chief Operating Officer, University of Michigan Health–Sparrow Ionia, Ionia, MI, p. A330

A948 Index of Health Care Professionals

PRICE, Kim, Chief Executive Officer, Franklin General Hospital, Hampton, IA, p. A237
PRICE, Larry, Chief Executive Officer, Limestone Medical Center, Groesbeck, TX, p. A623
PRICE, Lori
  R.N., President and Chief Executive Officer, Central Indiana Region, Franciscan Health Carmel, Carmel, IN, p. A213
  R.N., President and Chief Executive Officer, Central Indiana Region, Franciscan Health Indianapolis, Indianapolis, IN, p. A219
  R.N., President and Chief Executive Officer, Central Indiana Region, Franciscan Health Mooresville, Mooresville, IN, p. A224
PRICE, Lorraine B, Associate Director, Hampton Veterans Affairs Medical Center, Hampton, VA, p. A677
PRICE, Manuel, Director Information Systems, Brookwood Baptist Medical Center, Birmingham, AL, p. A16
PRICE, Meredith
  Senior Vice President, Acute Operations, St. Joseph's Hospital Health Center, Syracuse, NY, p. A460
  Vice President Fiscal Services and Chief Financial Officer, St. Joseph's Hospital Health Center, Syracuse, NY, p. A460
PRICE, Mindy, R.N., Chief Executive Officer, Rosebud Health Care Center, Forsyth, MT, p. A391
PRICE, Patricia, MSN, R.N., Chief Nursing Officer, Adventhealth Ocala, Ocala, FL, p. A143
PRICE, Sam, Executive Vice President Finance/Chief Financial Officer, East Alabama Medical Center, Opelika, AL, p. A23
PRICE, Shari, Director Information Services, Baptist Health Louisville, Louisville, KY, p. A269
PRICE, Terry, Director Information Technology, Great Plains Regional Medical Center, Elk City, OK, p. A512
PRICE, Tonya, Chief Nursing Officer, Wilbarger General Hospital, Vernon, TX, p. A659
PRICE-GHARZEDDINE, Karen, R.N., MS, Chief Nursing Officer and Administrator, Centinela Hospital Medical Center, Inglewood, CA, p. A67
PRICE-YONTS, Melody, Chief Executive Officer, U. S. Public Health Service Indian Hospital, Rosebud, SD, p. A576
PRICKEL, Trisha, Information Systems Director, Margaret Mary Health, Batesville, IN, p. A212
PRIDDY, Ernest C III, Chief Financial Officer, Old Vineyard Behavioral Health Services, Winston-Salem, NC, p. A478
PRIDDY, Steven, M.D., VP of Physician Affairs/Chief Medical Officer, Ascension St. Vincent Carmel Hospital, Carmel, IN, p. A213
PRIDEAUX, Heather, Chief Financial Officer, Rawlins County Health Center, Atwood, KS, p. A246
PRIDGEN, Parker, Chief Executive Officer, Adventhealth Orlando, Orlando, FL, p. A144
PRIES, Kathleen M., Director Human Resources, Nazareth Hospital, Philadelphia, PA, p. A549
PRIEST, Bill, Chief Executive Officer, Plains Regional Medical Center, Clovis, NM, p. A434
PRIEST, David, Director Information Systems, Munson Healthcare Charlevoix Hospital, Charlevoix, MI, p. A323
PRIEST, Mike, M.D., Chief of Staff, Pawhuska Hospital, Pawhuska, OK, p. A519
PRIHODA, Matt, M.D., Chief of Staff, Washington County Hospital And Clinics, Washington, IA, p. A244
PRILUTSKY, Michael, President and Chief Executive Officer, Jersey City Medical Center, Jersey City, NJ, p. A422
PRIMACK, Matthew Lee., President, Advocate Condell Medical Center, Libertyville, IL, p. A200
PRIMEAU, Kristen
  Chief Executive Officer, Bloomington Meadows Hospital, Bloomington, IN, p. A212
  Chief Executive Officer, Valle Vista Health System, Greenwood, IN, p. A218
PRINCE, Clay, M.D., Chief Medical Officer, Madisonhealth, Rexburg, ID, p. A183
PRINCE, Kem, Manager of Finance, Parkview Noble Hospital, Kendallville, IN, p. A221
PRINCE, Sue, Director Information Systems, Northern Westchester Hospital, Mount Kisco, NY, p. A446
PRINCIPE, Hector Cintron, M.D., Director, Hospital Universitario Dr. Ramon Ruiz Arnau, Bayamon, PR, p. A731
PRINGLE-MILLER, Letitia, Administrative Director, Prisma Health Tuomey Hospital, Sumter, SC, p. A570
PRINTY, Wayne, Chief Financial Officer, Lincolnhealth, Damariscotta, ME, p. A296
PRIORE, Jacqueline, Chief Nursing Officer, Samaritan Hospital - Main Campus, Troy, NY, p. A460
PRISELAC, Thomas M., President and Chief Executive Officer, Cedars-Sinai Medical Center, Los Angeles, CA, p. A72
PRISTELSKI, Bradley, Division Vice President, Chief Information Officer, Dignity Health Arizona General Hospital Mesa, Llc, Mesa, AZ, p. A33

PRISTER, James R., President and Chief Executive Officer, RML Specialty Hospital, Hinsdale, IL, p. A198
PRITCHARD, Jason, Chief Financial Officer, Hackensack Meridian Health Pascack Valley Medical Center, Westwood, NJ, p. A430
PRITCHARD, Joann, Chief Financial Officer, Erie Veterans Affairs Medical Center, Erie, PA, p. A539
PRITCHETT, Greg, Chief Financial Officer, Cuero Regional Hospital, Cuero, TX, p. A610
PRIVETT, David Thomas., Executive Director, Western New York Children's Psychiatric Center, West Seneca, NY, p. A462
PROBASCO, Brent, Chief Financial Officer, Cass Regional Medical Center, Harrisonville, MO, p. A376
PROBST, Nancy, R.N., Chief Nursing Officer, Bigfork Valley Hospital, Bigfork, MN, p. A343
PROBUS, Kimberly, Chief Nursing Officer, Opelousas General Health System, Opelousas, LA, p. A291
PROCHASKA, Jodi, Chief Financial Officer, Butler County Health Care Center, David City, NE, p. A399
PROCHNOW, Bryan, Chief Financial Officer, Matagorda Regional Medical Center, Bay City, TX, p. A601
PROCTOR, Brandy, Director of Nursing, North Star Behavioral Health System, Anchorage, AK, p. A27
PROCTOR, David, Administrator, Three Gables Surgery Center, Proctorville, OH, p. A503
PROCTOR, Jason J, President, Christus Mother Frances Hospital - Tyler, Tyler, TX, p. A658
PROCTOR, Jason J., President, Christus Mother Frances Hospital - Tyler, Tyler, TX, p. A658
PROCTOR, Mark, Chief Financial Officer, South Plains Rehabilitation Hospital, An Affiliate of Umc And Encompass Health, Lubbock, TX, p. A636
PROCTOR, Quinn, Director Human Resources, Claremore Indian Hospital, Claremore, OK, p. A511
PROCTOR, Sandra, R.N., MS, Chief Nurse Executive, Memorial Medical Center, Modesto, CA, p. A78
PROCTOR, Stephen, Director of Human Resources/Risk, Russellville Hospital, Russellville, AL, p. A24
PROFOTA, Lori, Chief Operating Officer/Chief Nursing Officer, Springfield Hospital, Springfield, VT, p. A672
PRONGER, Derk F.
  President, Corewell Health Beaumont Grosse Pointe Hospital, Grosse Pointe, MI, p. A329
  President, Corewell Health Farmington Hills Hospital, Farmington Hills, MI, p. A326
PRONI, John, CPA, Manager Finance and Operations, Baycare Alliant Hospital, Dunedin, FL, p. A130
PROPP, Elizabeth R, Vice President Finance and Chief Financial Officer, Dameron Hospital, Stockton, CA, p. A96
PROSKOCIL, Danielle, Director Human Resources, Valley County Health System, Ord, NE, p. A404
PROSPER, Charles, Chief Executive, PeaceHealth Northwest, Peacehealth St. Josep. Medical Center, Bellingham, WA, p. A687
PROSSER, Alita, Chief Financial Officer, Baylor Scott & White Medical Center - Temple, Temple, TX, p. A656
PROSSER, Edna, Chief Nursing Officer, Ozark Health Medical Center, Clinton, AR, p. A44
PROSSER, Joseph, M.D., Chief Medical Officer, Texas Health Harris Methodist Hospital Fort Worth, Fort Worth, TX, p. A620
PROUD, James, Vice President Human Resources and Marketing, WVU Medicine Uniontown Hospital, Uniontown, PA, p. A556
PROVENZANO, Jeff
  Vice President and Chief Financial Officer, Mymichigan Medical Center Alma, Alma, MI, p. A321
  Vice President and Chief Financial Officer, Mymichigan Medical Center Clare, Clare, MI, p. A324
  Vice President and Chief Financial Officer, Mymichigan Medical Center Gladwin, Gladwin, MI, p. A327
PROVENZANO, Stacey, Chief Operating Officer, Greystone Park Psychiatric Hospital, Morris Plains, NJ, p. A424
PROVINCE, Wing, M.D., Chief Medical Officer, Park City Hospital, Park City, UT, p. A667
PRUESS, Mark, M.D., Chief Medical Staff, Sparta Community Hospital, Sparta, IL, p. A208
PRUETT, Angela
  Chief Nursing Officer, Riverview Regional Medical Center, Carthage, TN, p. A579
  Chief Nursing Officer, Trousdale Medical Center, Hartsville, TN, p. A584
PRUITT, Amanda
  Chief Financial Officer, Riverview Regional Medical Center, Carthage, TN, p. A579
  Chief Financial Officer, Trousdale Medical Center, Hartsville, TN, p. A584
PRUITT, Jeffrey, M.D., Chief of Staff, Mercy Health - Defiance Hospital, Defiance, OH, p. A494
PRUKOP, Jeff, Director Professional Services, Jackson County Hospital District, Edna, TX, p. A616

PRUNCHUNAS, Edward M, Executive Vice President and Chief Financial Officer, Cedars-Sinai Medical Center, Los Angeles, CA, p. A72
PRUNOSKE, Mark
  Chief Financial Officer, Nicholas H. Noyes Memorial Hospital, Dansville, NY, p. A442
  Chief Financial Officer and Senior Vice President Finance, F. F. Thompson Hospital, Canandaigua, NY, p. A440
PRUSIA, Jeff, Chief Financial Officer, Adventhealth South Overland Park, Overland Park, KS, p. A257
PRYBYLO, Mary, R.N., MSN, FACHE, President, St. Josep. Hospital, Bangor, ME, p. A295
PRYOR, Vincent, Senior Vice President and Chief Financial Officer, Silver Cross Hospital, New Lenox, IL, p. A203
PRZESTRZELSKI, David, Associate Director, Patient Care Services and Chief Nursing Executive, Charles George Veterans Affairs Medical Center, Asheville, NC, p. A463
PRZYBYLSKI, David, Controller, Sparrow Specialty Hospital, Lansing, MI, p. A331
PSAILA, Justin P, M.D., Vice President Medical Affairs, St. Luke's Anderson Campus, Easton, PA, p. A539
PSARRAS, James, M.D., Chief Medical Officer, Windsor-Laurelwood Center for Behavioral Medicine, Willoughby, OH, p. A507
PSCODNA, Susan, Director Human Resources, Mercy Health - Defiance Hospital, Defiance, OH, p. A494
PUCKETT, Doug
  President, Indiana University Health Tipton Hospital, Tipton, IN, p. A228
  President, Indiana University Health University Hospital, Indianapolis, IN, p. A220
  President, Indiana University Health West Hospital, Avon, IN, p. A212
PUCLIK, Becky, Division Chief People Officer, HSHS St. John's Hospital, Springfield, IL, p. A209
PUENTES, Francisco, Human Resource Officer, San Diego County Psychiatric Hospital, San Diego, CA, p. A89
PUFFENBERGER, James, Vice President and Chief Financial Officer, Mercy Health - Defiance Hospital, Defiance, OH, p. A494
PUFFENBERGER, Sheila, Manager Information Technology, Hillsdale Hospital, Hillsdale, MI, p. A329
PUGH, Larry, Vice President and Chief Financial Officer, Adventist Health White Memorial Montebello, Montebello, CA, p. A78
PUGH, Marcia, Chief Executive Officer, Greene County Health System, Eutaw, AL, p. A19
PUGH, Melodee, Director Human Resources, Navarro Regional Hospital, Corsicana, TX, p. A609
PUGH, Ryan
  Chief Financial Officer, Ashley Regional Medical Center, Vernal, UT, p. A670
  Chief Financial Officer, Castleview Hospital, Price, UT, p. A667
PUGLIESE, Heidi, Chief Executive Officer and Superintendent, Albert J. Solnit Children's Center, Middletown, CT, p. A116
PUGSLEY, Tim, Chief Information Officer, Orthonebraska Hospital, Omaha, NE, p. A404
PUKALA, Shirley, R.N., Assistant Administrator Operations, St. Lawrence Rehabilitation Hospital, Lawrenceville, NJ, p. A423
PULASKI, Jason, Controller, Encompass Health Rehabilitation Hospital of Reading, Reading, PA, p. A553
PULEO, Mark, Vice President and Chief Human Resources Officer, Henry Mayo Newhall Hospital, Valencia, CA, p. A99
PULIDO, Michael, Chief Administrative Officer, Mosaic Life Care At St. Josep. - Medical Center, Saint Joseph, MO, p. A383
PULIS, Autumn, Chief Nursing Officer, Select Specialty Hospital-Oklahoma City, Oklahoma City, OK, p. A518
PULLIAM, Elizabeth, Chief Financial Officer, Christus Mother Frances Hospital - Jacksonville, Jacksonville, TX, p. A630
PULLIN, Dennis W.
  FACHE, President and Chief Executive Officer, Virtua Marlton, Marlton, NJ, p. A423
  FACHE, President and Chief Executive Officer, Virtua Mount Holly Hospital, Mount Holly, NJ, p. A424
  FACHE, President and Chief Executive Officer, Virtua Voorhees, Voorhees, NJ, p. A430
PULLINS, Ruth
  Chief Human Resources Officer, University Health-Lakewood Medical Center, Kansas City, MO, p. A378
  Chief Human Resources Officer, University Health-Truman Medical Center, Kansas City, MO, p. A378
PULLMAN, Debbie, Director Finance, Avera Hand County Memorial Hospital, Miller, SD, p. A574
PULLMAN, Jayson, Chief Executive Officer, Hawarden Regional Healthcare, Hawarden, IA, p. A237
PULSCHER, Nathan, President, Healthpartners Olivia Hospital & Clinic, Olivia, MN, p. A352
PULVER, Dayna, Director of Nursing, Friend Community Healthcare System, Friend, NE, p. A400

PUMMEL, Keely, Director, Financial Operations, Ohiohealth Dublin Methodist Hospital, Dublin, OH, p. A495
PUMPHREY, Robbin, Chief Nursing Officer, Bullock County Hospital, Union Springs, AL, p. A25
PUNG, Margaret, R.N., Chief Nursing Officer, Uthealth Harris County Psychiatric Center, Houston, TX, p. A628
PUNJABI, Rishab, Chief Financial Officer, Kindred Hospital–La Mirada, La Mirada, CA, p. A68
PUORTO, Charlene, Chief Nursing Officer, Capital District Psychiatric Center, Albany, NY, p. A438
PURCELL, Deborah, Director of Information Technology, UNC Health Caldwell, Lenoir, NC, p. A471
PURCELL, Terrence J., President, Lehigh Valley Hospital – Schuylkill, Pottsville, PA, p. A553
PURCELL, Tom, Chief Medical Officer, UCHealth Highlands Ranch Hospital, Highlands Ranch, CO, p. A109
PURDY, Bruce, M.D., Chief of Staff, Muleshoe Area Medical Center, Muleshoe, TX, p. A640
PURINGTON, Denise, Vice President and Chief Information Officer, Elliot Hospital, Manchester, NH, p. A416
PURINTON, Sandy, Chief Nursing Officer, Trego County–Lemke Memorial Hospital, Wakeeney, KS, p. A261
PURKEYPILE, Dallas, Chief Executive Officer, Adventhealth South Overland Park, Overland Park, KS, p. A257
PURMONT, Tiffany, Supervisor Medical Records, Monroe County Hospital, Forsyth, GA, p. A164
PUROHIT, Divyesh, M.D., Chief of Staff, Sullivan County Community Hospital, Sullivan, IN, p. A227
PUROHIT, Kumar, Chief Financial Officer, Rockford Center, Newark, DE, p. A122
PUROHIT, Shamb, Chief Financial Officer, Colquitt Regional Medical Center, Moultrie, GA, p. A169
PURRINGTON, Janice, Coordinator Medical Records, Avera Hand County Memorial Hospital, Miller, SD, p. A574
PURTLE, Mark, M.D., Vice President Medical Affairs, Unitypoint Health–Des Moines, Des Moines, IA, p. A235
PURUSHOTHAM, Gary, Chief Executive Officer, Dmc Sinai–Grace Hospital, Detroit, MI, p. A325
PURVANCE, Clint, M.D., President and Chief Executive Officer, Barton Memorial Hospital, South Lake Tahoe, CA, p. A96
PURVES, Stephen A., FACHE, President and Chief Executive Officer, Valleywise Health, Phoenix, AZ, p. A37
PURVIS, Kevin, Chief Information Officer, Community Howard Regional Health, Kokomo, IN, p. A221
PURVIS, Michael, Chief Executive Officer, Candler County Hospital, Metter, GA, p. A168
PUSHARD, Roland, Director of Nursing, Riverview Psychiatric Center, Augusta, ME, p. A295
PUSTINA, Karl, Vice President Finance, Upland Hills Health, Dodgeville, WI, p. A709
PUTHOFF, Tim, President, Ascension St. Vincent's Birmingham, Birmingham, AL, p. A16
PUTNAM, Mark, M.D., Medical Director, Haven Behavioral Hospital of Eastern Pennsylvania, Reading, PA, p. A553
PUTNAM, Maureen M, Director Human Resources, Oss Health, York, PA, p. A558
PUTNAM-GILCHRIST, Dena, Chief Nursing Officer, Trios Health, Kennewick, WA, p. A690
PUVOGEL, LuAnn, R.N., Chief Executive Officer, Salina Surgical Hospital, Salina, KS, p. A259
PUZO, Thomas C., President and Chief Executive Officer, Cornerstone of Medical Arts Center Hospital, Fresh Meadows, NY, p. A443
PUZZUTO, David, M.D., Vice President Medical Affairs and Chief Medical Officer, Waterbury Hospital, Waterbury, CT, p. A119
PYGON, Bernard, M.D., Chief Medical Officer, University of Illinois Hospital, Chicago, IL, p. A192
PYLE, Diana, Director Human Resources and Executive Assistant to Chief Executive Officer, Cedar County Memorial Hospital, El Dorado Springs, MO, p. A374
PYLE, Julia, R.N., Chief Nursing Officer, Newman Regional Health, Emporia, KS, p. A249
PYLE FARRELL, Martha, Vice President Human Resources and General Counsel, Massachusetts Eye And Ear, Boston, MA, p. A310
PYRAH, Scott, Director Information Systems, St. Luke's Rehabilitation Hospital, Boise, ID, p. A180

Q

QADEER, Imran, President, Allegheny General Hospital, Pittsburgh, PA, p. A551
QUACKENBUSH, Kirk, M.D., Chief of Staff, Intermountain Health Platte Valley Hospital, Brighton, CO, p. A104
QUALLS, Alan Chief Executive Officer, Banner Fort Collins Medical Center, Fort Collins, CO, p. A108
Chief Executive Officer, Banner Mckee Medical Center, Loveland, CO, p. A112
Chief Executive Officer, Banner North Colorado Medical Centernorth Colorado Medical Center, Greeley, CO, p. A109
QUALLS, Brenda, Chief Financial Officer, Atrium Health Navicent Baldwin, Milledgeville, GA, p. A168
QUARANTE, Dino, CPA, Chief Financial Officer, Oasis Behavioral Health – Chandler, Chandler, AZ, p. A31
QUARLES, Christopher, M.D., Director Medical Services, Naval Hospital Jacksonville, Jacksonville, FL, p. A135
QUATROCHE, Thomas J. Jr, President and Chief Executive Officer, Erie County Medical Center, Buffalo, NY, p. A440
QUATTLEBAUM, Ryan, President and Chief Executive Officer, Adventhealth North Pinellas, Tarpon Springs, FL, p. A153
QUEBEDEAUX, Jay
FACHE, President, Baptist Health Medical Center–Arkadelphia, Arkadelphia, AR, p. A43
FACHE, President, Baptist Health Medical Center–Hot Spring County, Malvern, AR, p. A50
QUENAN, James, M.D., Chief Medical Officer, Amery Hospital And Clinic, Amery, WI, p. A707
QUICHOCHO, Vince, Manager Information Systems, Guam Memorial Hospital Authority, Tamuning, GU, p. A730
QUILLIN, Gayla, Administrator, Parmer Medical Center, Friona, TX, p. A620
QUIN, Robert, Regional Vice President Finance, and Chief Financial Officer, Carle Health Methodist Hospital, Peoria, IL, p. A205
QUINLAN, Patrick J, M.D., Chief Executive Officer, Ochsner Clinic Foundation & International Services, Exec. Director Ochsner Center for Community, Ochsner Medical Center, New Orleans, LA, p. A289
QUINLIVAN, Kathy, Director Management Information Systems, Avera Sacred Heart Hospital, Yankton, SD, p. A578
QUINN, Jennifer, Quality and Safety Coordinator, Thedacare Medical Center–Shawano, Shawano, WI, p. A721
QUINN, Judith, Vice President Patient Care Services, Cap. Cod Hospital, Hyannis, MA, p. A314
QUINN, Kevin J., Chief Executive Officer, Byrd Regional Hospital, Leesville, LA, p. A287
QUINN, Mary Ann
Administrative Assistant, Casey County Hospital, Liberty, KY, p. A269
Administrative Assistant, Jane Todd Crawford Hospital, Greensburg, KY, p. A266
QUINN, Mary Anna, Executive Vice President, Chief Administrative Officer, St. Jude Children's Research Hospital, Memphis, TN, p. A589
QUINN, Paul, Information Systems Manager, Kern Valley Healthcare District, Lake Isabella, CA, p. A69
QUINN, Tim, M.D., President and Chief Executive Officer, Mercy Medical Center – Cedar Rapids, Cedar Rapids, IA, p. A231
QUINONES, Yolanda, Director Finance, I. Gonzalez Martinez Oncologic Hospital, Hato Rey, PR, p. A732
QUINONEZ, Yolanda, Chief Financial Officer, Hospital De La Universidad De Puerto Rico/Dr. Federico Trilla, Carolina, PR, p. A732
QUINTANA, Francisco, Warden, Federal Medical Center, Lexington, KY, p. A268
QUINTANILLA, Dana, Director Human Resources, Sweeny Community Hospital, Sweeny, TX, p. A655
QUINTERO, Anthony, Interim Administrator, Glendora Hospital, Glendora, CA, p. A66
QUINTO, Mike, Chief Information Officer, Watauga Medical Center, Boone, NC, p. A464
QUINTON, Ben, Chief Executive Officer, Rock Regional Hospital, Derby, KS, p. A248
QUIRKE, David, Vice President Information Services, Frederick Health, Frederick, MD, p. A304
QUIROGA, Alejandro, M.D., President of Corewell Health West, Corewell Health Butterworth Hospital, Grand Rapids, MI, p. A328
QUITO, Arturo L, M.D., Chief of Staff, Erlanger Bledsoe Hospital, Pikeville, TN, p. A592
QUO, Justin, Chief of Staff, Chi Lakewood Health, Baudette, MN, p. A343
QVISTGAARD, Guy C, Chief Executive Officer, Highland Hospital, Oakland, CA, p. A80

R

RAAUM, Elizabeth, Manger Business Office, Roosevelt Medical Center, Culbertson, MT, p. A391
RABAGO, Janie, Chief Accountant, San Antonio State Hospital, San Antonio, TX, p. A650
RABE, Jeremy, Chief Executive Officer, Trego County–Lemke Memorial Hospital, Wakeeney, KS, p. A261
RABEL, Jonas
Chief Hospital Executive, Integris Grove Hospital, Grove, OK, p. A513
Chief Hospital Executive, Integris Miami Hospital, Miami, OK, p. A515
RABIDEAU, Ray, M.D., Senior Vice President and Chief Medical Officer, Memorial Hospital, North Conway, NH, p. A417
RABIN, Barry, M.D., Regional Medical Director, Endeavor Health Linden Oaks Hospital, Naperville, IL, p. A203
RABINE, Traci, Vice President Clinic Operations, Prairie Lakes Healthcare System, Watertown, SD, p. A578
RABINOWITZ, Jordy, Senior Vice President Human Resources Operations, Westchester Medical Center, Valhalla, NY, p. A461
RABON, Catherine
M.D., Regional Chief Medical Officer, Mcleod Health Clarendon, Manning, SC, p. A568
M.D., Regional Chief Medical Officer, Mcleod Health Dillon, Dillon, SC, p. A565
RABORN, Janelle, Chief Operating Officer, Lovelace Women's Hospital, Albuquerque, NM, p. A433
RACHAL, Paul, M.D., Chief Medical Officer, Pointe Coupee General Hospital, New Roads, LA, p. A290
RACICOT, Mark, Chief Executive Officer, Sea Pines Rehabilitation Hospital, An Affiliate of Encompass Health, Melbourne, FL, p. A139
RACINE–WELLS, Lisa, Interim Chief Executive Officer, Blackfeet Community Hospital, Saint Mary, MT, p. A395
RACKHAM, Dan, Chief Executive Officer, Samaritan Lebanon Community Hospital, Lebanon, OR, p. A528
RACZEK, James, M.D., Sr. Vice President of Operations and Chief Medical Officer, Northern Light Eastern Maine Medical Center, Bangor, ME, p. A295
RADANDT, Jeremiah, Executive Vice President Northern Market/Administrator, Children's Medical Center Plano, Plano, TX, p. A644
RADCLIFFE, Eric, M.D., Medical Director, United Hospital Center, Bridgeport, WV, p. A699
RADDEN, April, Vice President of Human Resources, HCA Florida Aventura Hospital, Aventura, FL, p. A125
RADER, Herbert, M.D., Advisor for Medical Affairs, New York Community Hospital, New York, NY, p. A450
RADER, Sandra
R.N., President, UPMC Presbyterian, Pittsburgh, PA, p. A552
R.N., President, UPMC Presbyterian, UPMC Presbyterian, Pittsburgh, PA, p. A552
RADER, W. Mark, Chief Executive Officer, Encompass Health Rehabilitation Hospital of Salisbury, Salisbury, MD, p. A307
RADFORD, Angie, R.N., Director of Nursing, Wills Memorial Hospital, Washington, GA, p. A174
RADIVOJEVIC, Vladimir, President and Chief Executive Officer, UChicago Medicine Adventhealth Glenoaks, Glendale Heights, IL, p. A196
RADKE, Erma, Director of Operations, Oakleaf Surgical Hospital, Altoona, WI, p. A707
RADNER, Allen, M.D., President and Chief Executive Officer, Salinas Valley Health, Salinas, CA, p. A88
RADOTICH, Maureen, Director Human Resources, Providence Valdez Medical Center, Valdez, AK, p. A29
RADUNSKY, Daniel, M.D., Medical Staff President, Union County General Hospital, Clayton, NM, p. A434
RADZEVICH, Jason, Vice President Finance, Beth Israel Deaconess Hospital–Plymouth, Plymouth, MA, p. A317
RADZISZEWSKI, Sylvia, Chief Operating Officer, University Hospitals Samaritan Medical Center, Ashland, OH, p. A485
RAEL, Matthew, Administrator, New Mexico Rehabilitation Center, Roswell, NM, p. A436
RAETZ, Elizabeth A, R.N., MSN, Vice President Nursing and Chief Nursing Officer, Chi Health St Elizabeth, Lincoln, NE, p. A402
RAFALA, Paula, Director, Human Resources, Memorial Medical Center, Modesto, CA, p. A78
RAFFERTY, Joyce, Vice President Finance, The University of Vermont Health Network–Champlain Valley Physicians Hospital, Plattsburgh, NY, p. A456
RAFFERTY, Patrick, Chief Operating Officer, Overland Park Regional Medical Center, Overland Park, KS, p. A257
RAFFERTY, Patrick W., Chief Operating Officer, Pipeline Los Angeles/Chief Executive Officer, Coast Plaza Hospital, Coast Plaza Hospital, Norwalk, CA, p. A80
RAFFETY, Leannette, Administrative Generalist, Rural Wellness Stroud, Stroud, OK, p. A521

Index of Health Care Professionals / Rath

RAFFOUL, John
FACHE, President, Adventist Health White Memorial, Los Angeles, CA, p. A71
FACHE, President, Adventist Health White Memorial Montebello, Montebello, CA, p. A78
RAFUS, Matthew, Chief Information Officer, White River Junction Veterans Affairs Medical Center, White River Junction, VT, p. A672
RAGAIN, Michael, M.D., Chief Medical Officer and Senior Vice President, University Medical Center, Lubbock, TX, p. A636
RAGAS, Rene J., FACHE, President and Chief Executive Officer, Woman's Hospital, Baton Rouge, LA, p. A278
RAGER, Claudia, R.N., Vice President Patient Care Services, Conemaugh Memorial Medical Center, Johnstown, PA, p. A542
RAGLAND, Albert
Superintendent, North Texas State Hospital, Vernon, TX, p. A659
Superintendent, North Texas State Hospital, Wichita Falls Campus, Wichita Falls, TX, p. A662
RAGLE, Bertha, Director Personnel, Crossridge Community Hospital, Wynne, AR, p. A54
RAGONESE–GREEN, Virginia, Chief Nursing Officer, Encompass Health Rehabilitation Hospital of Northwest Tucson, Tucson, AZ, p. A40
RAGSDALE, Mary
Chief Operating Officer, St. Joseph's Hospital And Medical Center, Phoenix, AZ, p. A36
Interim President and Chief Executive Officer, St. Joseph's Hospital And Medical Center, Phoenix, AZ, p. A36
RAGSDALE, Sarah Jane., R.N., Chief Executive Officer, Smith County Memorial Hospital, Smith Center, KS, p. A260
RAHDERT, Richard, M.D., Medical Director, River Bend Hospital, West Lafayette, IN, p. A229
RAHEEM, Robert, R.N., Chief Nursing Officer, Bayou Bend Health System, Franklin, LA, p. A282
RAHMAN, Syed, M.D., Chief of Staff, Horizon Specialty Hospital, Las Vegas, NV, p. A410
RAHN, Kevin, President Medical Staff, Orthopaedic Hospital of Lutheran Health Network, Fort Wayne, IN, p. A216
RAINA, Suresh, M.D., Vice President Medical Staff and Chief Medical Officer, Hackensack Meridian Health Palisades Medical Center, North Bergen, NJ, p. A426
RAINBOLT, Mike, Chief Financial Officer, Rivendell Behavioral Health Services, Benton, AR, p. A43
RAINES, Jill, R.N., Chief of Clinical Quality, Greene County General Hospital, Linton, IN, p. A222
RAINEY, Jackie, Chief Financial Officer, Little River Medical Center, Inc., Ashdown, AR, p. A43
RAINEY, Mark J, Director Human Resources, Texas Health Presbyterian Hospital Kaufman, Kaufman, TX, p. A631
RAINEY, Michelle L., Senior Vice President and Chief Nursing Officer, Pikeville Medical Center, Pikeville, KY, p. A273
RAINS, Celeste, D.O., Chief of Staff, Logan County Hospital, Oakley, KS, p. A256
RAINS, Debbie, Coordinator Health Information Management, Erlanger Bledsoe Hospital, Pikeville, TN, p. A592
RAINS, Jeff G., Chief Executive Officer, Baptist Medical Center East, Montgomery, AL, p. A22
RAINS, Jon Michael., President and Chief Operating Officer, Carrus Specialty Hospital, Sherman, TX, p. A653
RAINS, Paul, R.N., MSN, President, St. Joseph's Behavioral Health Center, Stockton, CA, p. A97
RAINS, Steve, Director Information Services, Banner Mckee Medical Center, Loveland, CO, p. A112
RAISNER, Gary, Chief Operating Officer, Norristown State Hospital, Norristown, PA, p. A547
RAJ, Bharath, M.D., Medical Director, Kingwood Pines Hospital, Kingwood, TX, p. A632
RAJEWSKI, Frank A, Chief Financial Officer, Rooks County Health Center, Plainville, KS, p. A258
RAJPARA, Suresh, M.D., Chief Medical Officer, Sunview Medical Center, West Palm Beach, FL, p. A154
RAJU, Vasudeva, M.D., Suffix, Chief, Long Term Acute Care Medicine, NYC Health + Hospitals/Henry J Carter Specialty Hospital And Medical Center, New York, NY, p. A451
RAK, Roger, Director Human Resources, South Shore Hospital, Chicago, IL, p. A191
RAKES, Lori, R.N., Chief Executive Officer, Piedmont Cartersville, Cartersville, GA, p. A160
RAKOV, Robert, M.D., Chief Medical Officer, Cogdell Memorial Hospital, Snyder, TX, p. A653
RAMA–BANAAG, Gemma, R.N., MSN, Chief Nursing Officer, Paradise Valley Hospital, National City, CA, p. A79
RAMAGE, Gary, M.D., Chief Medical Officer, Mckenzie County Healthcare System, Watford City, ND, p. A483
RAMAN, Jayashree, Vice President and Chief Information Officer, Reading Hospital, West Reading, PA, p. A557
RAMEY, Rita, Director Information Systems, Buchanan General Hospital, Grundy, VA, p. A677
RAMEY, Robert L., President, Baptist Health Hardin, Elizabethtown, KY, p. A265
RAMEY, Steve, Chief Financial Officer, Bon Secours – Southampton Medical Center, Franklin, VA, p. A676
RAMHOFER, Pam, Chief Information Officer, Sarasota Memorial Hospital – Venice, North Venice, FL, p. A142
RAMIREZ, Ana, Director of Nursing, Mesa Springs, Fort Worth, TX, p. A620
RAMIREZ, Arthur L.
M.D., Medical Director, El Paso Behavioral Health System, El Paso, TX, p. A616
M.D., Medical Director, Mesilla Valley Hospital, Las Cruces, NM, p. A435
RAMIREZ, Clara, Manager, French Hospital Medical Center, San Luis Obispo, CA, p. A93
RAMIREZ, Harvey, Chief Information Officer, Coleman County Medical Center, Coleman, TX, p. A607
RAMIREZ, Omar
Chief Operating Officer, California Hospitals, Southern California Hospital At Culver City, Culver City, CA, p. A61
Chief Operating Officer, California Hospitals, Southern California Hospital At Hollywood, Los Angeles, CA, p. A75
RAMIREZ, Ruben, M.D., Chief of Staff, Monterey Park Hospital, Monterey Park, CA, p. A78
RAMIREZ, Susan, Chief Nursing Officer, Encompass Health Rehabilitation Hospital of Las Vegas, Las Vegas, NV, p. A410
RAMIREZ, Willie, Manager Labor Relations, Laguna Honda Hospital And Rehabilitation Center, San Francisco, CA, p. A91
RAMIREZ DELGADO, Winston, Executive Director, Hospital Metropolitano San German, San German, PR, p. A734
RAMON, Maggie, Chief Financial Officer, Cochran Memorial Hospital, Morton, TX, p. A640
RAMOS, Eduardo, M.D., Medical Director, Encompass Health Rehabilitation Hospital of San Juan, San Juan, PR, p. A735
RAMOS, Gracie, Chief Human Resources Officer, Ogallala Community Hospital, Ogallala, NE, p. A403
RAMOS, Holly, R.N., Chief Clinical Officer, Kindred Hospital–Ontario, Ontario, CA, p. A81
RAMOS, Jessie, Manager Human Resources, Skyline Health, White Salmon, WA, p. A698
RAMOS, Jet, Head Staff Administration, Naval Hospital Camp Pendleton, Camp Pendleton, CA, p. A58
RAMOS, Laura, R.N., MSN, Chief Executive Officer, Providence St. Jude Medical Center, Fullerton, CA, p. A65
RAMOS, Raymond, FACHE, Chief Executive Officer, Select Specialty Hospital–Phoenix Downtown, Phoenix, AZ, p. A36
RAMPP, Randal D, M.D., Chief Medical Officer, Ascension Saint Thomas River Park, Mc Minnville, TN, p. A587
RAMSAMY, Dev, Chief Financial Officer, St. Rose Dominican Hospitals – San Martin Campus, Las Vegas, NV, p. A411
RAMSAY, Carla, Chief Human Resource Officer, Garfield Memorial Hospital, Panguitch, UT, p. A667
RAMSEY, Antonina, Senior Vice President and Chief Human Resource Officer, Henry Ford Hospital, Detroit, MI, p. A325
RAMSEY, Kristin, R.N., Senior Vice President and Chief Nursing Executive, Northwestern Memorial Hospital, Northwestern Memorial Hospital, Chicago, IL, p. A190
RAMSEY, Lisa, Chief Financial Officer, Prairie View, Newton, KS, p. A256
RAMSEY, Rance, Chief Executive Officer, Cornerstone Regional Hospital, Edinburg, TX, p. A615
RAMSEY, Rhonda, Controller, Encompass Health Deaconess Rehabilitation Hospital, Newburgh, IN, p. A225
RAMSEY, Ross
M.D., Chief of Staff, Scheurer Health, Pigeon, MI, p. A335
M.D., President and Chief Executive Officer, Scheurer Health, Pigeon, MI, p. A335
RAMSEY, Roy M., Executive Director, Bradford Health Services At Warrior Lodge, Warrior, AL, p. A26
RAMSEY, Thomas, Chief Financial Officer, Ochsner Medical Center – Hancock, Bay Saint Louis, MS, p. A359
RAMTHUN, Jane, Chief Financial Officer, Story County Medical Center, Nevada, IA, p. A240
RANA, Chaula, M.D., Medical Director, Encompass Health Rehabilitation Hospital of San Antonio, San Antonio, TX, p. A649
RANDALL, Cherry, Business Officer, Greater Binghamton Health Center, Binghamton, NY, p. A439
RANDALL, Kevin, Chief Financial Officer, Crouse Health, Syracuse, NY, p. A460
RANDALL, Lori, R.N., Executive Vice President, Chief Nursing Officer, Chief Operating Officer and Hospital Administrator, Family Health West, Fruita, CO, p. A108
RANDALL, Rebecca, Chief Nursing Officer, Greenwood County Hospital, Eureka, KS, p. A249
RANDALL, Stephen, Chief Operating Officer, Ochsner Lsu Health Shreveport – Academic Medical Center, Shreveport, LA, p. A292
RANDAZZO, Vince
Interim Chief Information Officer, The Hospitals of Providence Transmountain Campus – Tenet Healthcare, El Paso, TX, p. A617
Texas Regional Director Information Systems, Tenet Account, The Hospitals of Providence Memorial Campus – Tenet Healthcare, El Paso, TX, p. A617
RANDLE, Emily, Vice President Operations, Orange Coast Medical Center, Fountain Valley, CA, p. A64
RANDOLPH, Arianne, Director Human Resources, UCHealth Pikes Peak Regional Hospital, Woodland Park, CO, p. A114
RANDOLPH, Joseph, M.D., Chairman Medical Executive Committee, Orthoindy Hospital, Indianapolis, IN, p. A220
RANDOLPH, Karsten, Executive Vice President and Chief Financial Officer, Adventhealth Shawnee Mission, Merriam, KS, p. A255
RANDOLPH, Linda, Director Personnel Services, Washington County Hospital, Chatom, AL, p. A17
RANDOLPH, Mark A., Chief Executive Officer, Ochsner Lsu Health Shreveport – Monroe Medical Center, Monroe, LA, p. A288
RANEY, Hollie, Director of Nursing, Dallas County Medical Center, Fordyce, AR, p. A46
RANGE, Bonny, MSN, Chief Nursing Officer, Holy Family Memorial, Manitowoc, WI, p. A715
RANKIN, Cynthia, Chief Nursing Officer, Lovelace Unm Rehabilitation Hospital, Albuquerque, NM, p. A432
RANKIN, Keith, Chief Executive Officer and Managing Director, Ridge Behavioral Health System, Lexington, KY, p. A269
RANKIN, Linda, Chief Nursing Officer, Wickenburg Community Hospital, Wickenburg, AZ, p. A41
RANKIN, Sheila, Chief Executive Officer, Adventhealth Orlando, Orlando, FL, p. A144
RANNEY, Timothy, M.D., Chief Medical Officer, AHMC Seton Medical Center, Daly City, CA, p. A61
RANSOM, Ric A., Chief Executive Officer, University Hospital, Columbia, MO, p. A374
RAO, Kalapala, M.D., Medical Director, Encompass Health Rehabilitation Hospital of Parkersburg, Parkersburg, WV, p. A703
RAPENSKE, Jennifer, Manager Financial Services, Mercyone New Hampton Medical Center, New Hampton, IA, p. A240
RAPP, David, Chief Information Officer, Wheeling Hospital, Wheeling, WV, p. A706
RAPP, Ronald, Vice President Finance, UPMC Cole, Coudersport, PA, p. A537
RAPPACH, Shannon, Chief Fiscal Services, Dayton Veterans Affairs Medical Center, Dayton, OH, p. A493
RASCHKE, Judy, Director Human Resources, Pipestone County Medical Center, Pipestone, MN, p. A352
RASHID, Harun, Vice President and Chief Information Officer, Akron Children's Hospital, Akron, OH, p. A484
RASHID, Syed, Chief Executive Officer, Spring Hospital, Spring, TX, p. A654
RASHILLA, Matt, Chief Information and Application Officer, Penn Highlands Mon Valley, Monongahela, PA, p. A546
RASK, Brenda, Vice President Operations, Chi St Alexius Health Carrington, Carrington, ND, p. A479
RASKE, Jamie, Information Technology Lead, Avera St. Mary's Hospital, Pierre, SD, p. A575
RASMUSSEN, Diane, Director Human Resources, Cambridge Medical Center, Cambridge, MN, p. A344
RASMUSSEN, John, Vice President for Information Technology, Medstar Georgetown University Hospital, Washington, DC, p. A123
RASMUSSEN, Rick, Chief Executive Officer, Northwest Specialty Hospital, Post Falls, ID, p. A183
RASMUSSEN, Ron, M.D., Chief Medical Officer, HCA Florida Pasadena Hospital, Saint Petersburg, FL, p. A149
RASMUSSEN, Scott, Director Human Resources, Lincoln Regional Center, Lincoln, NE, p. A402
RASOOL, Chaudri, D.O., Chief of Staff, Gundersen Palmer Lutheran Hospital And Clinics, West Union, IA, p. A245
RASTER, Robert, M.D., Medical Director, Michiana Behavioral Health Center, Plymouth, IN, p. A226
RASTOGI, Abhinav, President and Chief Executive Officer, Temple University Hospital, Philadelphia, PA, p. A550
RASTOGI, Amit, M.D., Chief Executive, Jupiter Medical Center, Jupiter, FL, p. A136
RATAJ, Marianne, Chief Nursing Officer, Mercy Hospital Fort Smith, Fort Smith, AR, p. A47
RATCLIFF, David, M.D., Chief Medical Affairs, Washington Regional Medical System, Fayetteville, AR, p. A46
RATCLIFF, Paul, Director Information Services, Carrollton Regional Medical Center, Carrollton, TX, p. A606
RATH, Kevin, Vice President and Executive Director, Ascension St. Alexius, Hoffman Estates, IL, p. A198
RATH, Travis, Director Information Systems, Mcdonough District Hospital, Macomb, IL, p. A200

Index of Health Care Professionals

Index of Health Care Professionals

Index of Health Care Professionals / Rathgaber

RATHGABER, Scott W., M.D., Chief Executive Officer, Gundersen Lutheran Medical Center, La Crosse, WI, p. A713
RATLIFF, Ada
Chief Executive Officer, Claiborne County Medical Center, Port Gibson, MS, p. A368
Chief Information Officer, Claiborne County Medical Center, Port Gibson, MS, p. A368
RATLIFF, Bonnie, Chief Information Officer, Columbia Memorial Hospital, Hudson, NY, p. A444
RATLIFF, Kim, Director Health Information Management, Southwestern Virginia Mental Health Institute, Marion, VA, p. A679
RATLIFF, Simon
Chief Executive Officer, Northwest Health – La Porte, La Porte, IN, p. A221
Chief Executive Officer, Northwest Health – Starke, Knox, IN, p. A221
RATLIFF, Steve, Director Information Technology, Guadalup. Regional Medical Center, Seguin, TX, p. A652
RATLIFF, Tammy, Chief Executive Officer, Regency Hospital of Greenville, Greenville, SC, p. A567
RATNASAMY,FACHE, Sudandra, R.N., FACHE, Chief Executive Officer, Twin County Regional Healthcare, Galax, VA, p. A677
RATTLE, John, Chief Financial Officer, West Springs Hospital, Grand Junction, CO, p. A109
RATTLER, Crystal, Director of Nursing, Logan Health Shelby, Shelby, MT, p. A395
RATTRAY, Cindy Stewart, Director Human Resources, Uofl Health – Shelbyville Hospital, Shelbyville, KY, p. A274
RAU, Robin, Chief Executive Officer, Miller County Hospital, Colquitt, GA, p. A161
RAUB, Jessica, Director Health Information Management, Seven Hills Hospital, Henderson, NV, p. A409
RAUCH, Scott C, Vice President Human Resources, Reid Health, Richmond, IN, p. A226
RAUCH, Scott L., M.D., President and Psychiatrist in Chief, Mclean Hospital, Belmont, MA, p. A309
RAUH, Bradley W., Vice President, Chief Operating Officer, Southwest General Health Center, Middleburg Heights, OH, p. A500
RAUNER, Mary Ellen, R.N., Chief Nursing Officer, Suburban Community Hospital, East Norriton, PA, p. A539
RAUPERS, Debra, MSN, R.N., Chief Nursing Officer, Guthrie Corning Hospital, Corning, NY, p. A441
RAUSCH, Scott
Chief Executive Officer, Methodist Hospital, San Antonio, TX, p. A650
Chief Executive Officer, Spalding Rehabilitation Hospital, Aurora, CO, p. A103
President and Chief Executive Officer, Medical Center of Aurora, Aurora, CO, p. A103
RAUTIO, Wendy, Chief Financial Officer, Munising Memorial Hospital, Munising, MI, p. A334
RAVA, Linda Esq, Director Human Resources, Saint John Vianney Hospital, Downingtown, PA, p. A538
RAVE, Nick, President, Northwestern Medicine Mchenry, Mchenry, IL, p. A201
RAVELING, Lynn, Chief Financial Officer, Pocahontas Community Hospital, Pocahontas, IA, p. A242
RAWLINGS, Linda, Director Human Resources and Personnel, Ascension St. Thomas Three Rivers, Waverly, TN, p. A594
RAWLINGS, Michael, Interim Chief Operating Officer, NYC Health + Hospitals/Bellevue, New York, NY, p. A450
RAWLINGS, Patrick, Human Resources Director, Thomas Memorial Hospital, South Charleston, WV, p. A705
RAWLINGS, Sheri, Chief Information Officer, San Juan Regional Medical Center, Farmington, NM, p. A434
RAWLS, Jane
R.N., Interim Chie Nursing Officer, Christus Ochsner St. Patrick, Lake Charles, LA, p. A286
R.N., Interim Chief Nursing Officer, Christus Ochsner Lake Area Hospital, Lake Charles, LA, p. A286
RAWSON, Richard L, President and Chief Executive Officer, Adventist Health Hanford, Hanford, CA, p. A66
RAY, Beverly, Director Human Resources, West Tennessee Healthcare Dyersburg Hospital, Dyersburg, TN, p. A582
RAY, Denise, Chief Executive Officer, Piedmont Mountainside Hospital, Jasper, GA, p. A165
RAY, Diane, R.N., FACHE, Senior Vice President and Chief Operating Officer; Network Chief Nursing Officer, St. Luke's Hospital, Chesterfield, MO, p. A373
RAY, Donald, Vice President Operations, University of Maryland Medical Center Midtown Campus, Baltimore, MD, p. A301
RAY, Jerilyn, Manager Human Resources, St. Elizabeth Hospital, Enumclaw, WA, p. A689
RAY, Kirk M., President and Chief Executive Officer, Mclaren Greater Lansing, Lansing, MI, p. A331
RAY, Marge
Director Information Systems, Mercyone Cedar Falls Medical Center, Cedar Falls, IA, p. A231
Director Information Systems, Mercyone Waterloo Medical Center, Waterloo, IA, p. A244
RAY, Rachel, Chief Financial Officer, Unity Medical Center, Grafton, ND, p. A481
RAY, Trenda, Ph.D., Chief Nursing Officer, Baptist Health Medical Center – Conway, Conway, AR, p. A44
RAYBOURN, Gina, Director Health Information, Ellett Memorial Hospital, Appleton City, MO, p. A371
RAYBURN, Al, Chief Executive Officer, Encompass Health Rehabilitation Hospital of Gadsden, Gadsden, AL, p. A19
RAYMOND, Dee, Director Human Resources, Rosebud Health Care Center, Forsyth, MT, p. A391
RAYMOND, Greg
President, Southern Colorado Care System, Children's Hospital Colorado – Colorado Springs, Colorado Springs, CO, p. A105
Southern Region President, Children's Hospital Colorado, Aurora, CO, p. A103
RAYMOND, Heather, Area Public Relations Director, Kaiser Permanente Fontana Medical Center, Fontana, CA, p. A63
RAYMOND, Jane, Vice President and Chief Operating Officer, Reston Hospital Center, Reston, VA, p. A682
RAYMOND, Mindy, Vice President Human Resources, Boca Raton Regional Hospital, Boca Raton, FL, p. A126
RAYMOND, Scott, Director Information Systems, Orange Coast Medical Center, Fountain Valley, CA, p. A64
RAYNER, Evan J., Chief Executive Officer, Bear Valley Community Hospital, Big Bear Lake, CA, p. A58
RAYNER, Thomas J, Senior Vice President and Chief Operating Officer, Kaweah Health Medical Center, Visalia, CA, p. A100
RAYNES, Scott, President and Chief Executive Officer, Southeast Georgia Health System Brunswick Campus, Brunswick, GA, p. A159
RAYNOR, Robert, Human Resources Director, Park Royal Hospital, Fort Myers, FL, p. A132
RAYUDU, Subbu, M.D., Chief of Staff, Alliance Healthcare System, Holly Springs, MS, p. A363
RAZMIC, Tammy, Chief Executive Officer, Stonesprings Hospital Center, Dulles, VA, p. A675
REA, Jerry A., Ph.D., Superintendent, Parsons State Hospital And Training Center, Parsons, KS, p. A258
READ, Eddie, Interim Chief Financial Officer, Val Verde Regional Medical Center, Del Rio, TX, p. A613
READ, JoDee, Chief Executive Officer, Plumas District Hospital, Quincy, CA, p. A84
READ, John, Chief Nursing Officer, Allegiance Specialty Hospital of Greenville, Greenville, MS, p. A362
READ, Paul, R.N., MSN, Vice President and Chief Nursing Officer, Springhill Medical Center, Mobile, AL, p. A22
READ, Richard, Chief Financial Officer, HCA Florida Lake Monroe Hospital, Sanford, FL, p. A149
READER, G. Whitney, M.D., Chief Medical Officer, Kansas Medical Center, Andover, KS, p. A246
READER, Rhonda L, R.N., Chief Nursing Officer, Oneida Healthcare, Oneida, NY, p. A455
READING, Jared, M.D., Chief of Staff, Uvalde Memorial Hospital, Uvalde, TX, p. A659
READY, Janet L., Chief Operating Officer, St. Joseph's Hospital Health Center, Syracuse, NY, p. A460
REALE, Kelli, Vice President Human Resources, UPMC Mckeesport, Mckeesport, PA, p. A545
REALE, Kelli Ann, Vice President Human Resources, Southeast Georgia Health System Brunswick Campus, Brunswick, GA, p. A159
REAM, Tom, Regional Chief Information Officer, Sutter Auburn Faith Hospital, Auburn, CA, p. A56
REAMER, Roger J., Chief Executive Officer, Memorial Health Care Systems, Seward, NE, p. A406
REAMES, Jim, Director Human Resources, Bayfront Health St. Petersburg, Saint Petersburg, FL, p. A148
REANDEAU, Michael, Chief Information Officer, Mills–Peninsula Medical Center, Burlingame, CA, p. A58
REASONER, Vanessa, Chief Executive Officer, Grace Surgical Hospital, Lubbock, TX, p. A636
REASY, Stephanie
Administrator and Chief Executive Officer, Avera De Smet Memorial Hospital, De Smet, SD, p. A573
Administrator and Chief Executive Officer, Avera Weskota Memorial Hospital, Wessington Springs, SD, p. A578
REBER, Philip. Chief Operations Officer, Northern Nevada Medical Center, Sparks, NV, p. A413
REBOCK, Michael, Chief Medical Officer, Corewell Health Farmington Hills Hospital, Farmington Hills, MI, p. A326
RECA, Thomas Sr, Deputy Executive Director and Chief Financial Officer, Staten Island University Hospital, New York, NY, p. A453
RECHNER, Paula, M.D., Chief Medical Officer, Mymichigan Medical Center Sault, Sault Sainte Marie, MI, p. A338
RECHSTEINER, Hans, M.D., Chief of Staff, Burnett Medical Center, Grantsburg, WI, p. A711
RECKERT, Sandy, Director Communications and Public Affairs, Johns Hopkins Bayview Medical Center, Baltimore, MD, p. A300
RECTOR, Jeanne, Chief Nursing Officer, Carroll County Memorial Hospital, Carrollton, MO, p. A373
RECUPERO, David, Chief Financial Officer, San Gorgonio Memorial Hospital, Banning, CA, p. A57
REDD, Brook, M.D., Chief of Staff, Sanford Thief River Falls Medical Center, Thief River Falls, MN, p. A356
REDD, Dakota, R.N., Chief Clinical Officer, Kindred Hospital–St. Louis, Saint Louis, MO, p. A383
REDDEN, Chase, Chief Financial Officer, HCA Houston Healthcare Clear Lake, Webster, TX, p. A661
REDDING, Georgia, Director Human Resources, Forbes Hospital, Monroeville, PA, p. A546
REDDING, Lisa, Manager Human Resources, Morgan County Arh Hospital, West Liberty, KY, p. A275
REDDIX, Morgan, Administrator, Unity Psychiatric Care–Columbia, Columbia, TN, p. A581
REDDY, Challa, M.D., President Medical Staff, Northern Light Mayo Hospital, Dover–Foxcroft, ME, p. A297
REDDY, Lex, President and Chief Executive Officer, St. Rose Hospital, Hayward, CA, p. A67
REDDY, Sridhar, M.D., Chief Medical Officer, Lake Huron Medical Center, Port Huron, MI, p. A336
REDDY, Vikrum, M.D., Vice President and Chief Medical Officer, Wellstar Kennestone Hospital, Marietta, GA, p. A167
REDHORSE–CHARLEY, Gloria, Director Human Resources, Northern Navajo Medical Center, Shiprock, NM, p. A437
REDINGTON, James, M.D., Chief of Staff, Bath Community Hospital, Hot Springs, VA, p. A678
REDLER, Kathleen A., Chief Nursing Officer, Christus Good Shepherd Medical Center–Marshall, Marshall, TX, p. A638
REDMOND, Paula, Chief Executive Officer, Encompass Health Rehabilitation Hospital of Tustin, Tustin, CA, p. A99
REDRICK, Heather
Chief Nursing Officer, Emory Johns Creek Hospital, Johns Creek, GA, p. A166
Chief Operating Officer, Emory Johns Creek Hospital, Johns Creek, GA, p. A166
REECE, Morris A, EVP/COO, Ochsner Laird Hospital, Union, MS, p. A369
REECER, Jeff, FACHE, President, Texas Health Presbyterian Hospital Denton, Denton, TX, p. A614
REED, Alex
Chief Information Officer, Avita Ontario Hospital, Ontario, OH, p. A502
Chief Information Officer, Bucyrus Community Hospital, Bucyrus, OH, p. A487
Chief Information Officer, Galion Community Hospital, Galion, OH, p. A496
REED, Alicia, President, Chi Health Mercy Corning, Corning, IA, p. A233
REED, Amanda, Administrator, Essentia Health–Deer River, Deer River, MN, p. A345
REED, Anthony, MSN, R.N., Interim Administrator, Fulton County Hospital, Salem, AR, p. A53
REED, Cindy, Director Community Relations, Austin State Hospital, Austin, TX, p. A599
REED, Claudia
Interim Chief Financial Officer, Spaulding Hospital for Continuing Medical Care Cambridge, Cambridge, MA, p. A312
Interim Chief Financial Officer, Spaulding Rehabilitation Hospital Cap. Cod, East Sandwich, MA, p. A313
REED, Colton, Chief Executive Officer, Vista Del Mar Hospital, Ventura, CA, p. A100
REED, David Ashton, M.D., Chief Medical Officer, Louisiana Extended Care Hospital of Lafayette, Lafayette, LA, p. A285
REED, Fred, M.D., Chief of Staff, Lincoln Hospital, Davenport, WA, p. A688
REED, Helen, Director Health Information, North Mississipp. Medical Center–Eupora, Eupora, MS, p. A361
REED, Jennifer, Chief Executive Officer, Ferry County Memorial Hospital, Republic, WA, p. A693
REED, John E, M.D., Medical Director, Baptist Memorial Hospital–Golden Triangle, Columbus, MS, p. A361
REED, Karen
R.N., MSN, Chief Nursing Officer, Canyon Vista Medical Center, Sierra Vista, AZ, p. A39
Interim Chief Nursing Officer, Willamette Valley Medical Center, Mcminnville, OR, p. A529
REED, Kathleen, Manager Human Resources, Missouri Baptist Sullivan Hospital, Sullivan, MO, p. A387

A952 Index of Health Care Professionals

Index of Health Care Professionals / Remaley

Index of Health Care Professionals

REED, Katy, Chief Executive Officer, Encompass Health Rehabilitation Hospital of Cypress, Houston, TX, p. A625
REED, Kim, Director Human Resources, Dekalb Regional Medical Center, Fort Payne, AL, p. A19
REED, Kirby, Director Information Systems, Franciscan Health Rensselear, Rensselaer, IN, p. A226
REED, Leslie, Chief Financial Officer, Wright Memorial Hospital, Trenton, MO, p. A387
REED, Linda
Vice President and Chief Information Officer, St. Joseph's University Medical Center, Paterson, NJ, p. A426
Vice President Information Systems and Chief Information Officer, Newton Medical Center, Newton, NJ, p. A426
REED, Pamela R., Chief Executive Officer, Kindred Hospital Melbourne, Melbourne, FL, p. A139
REED, Renee
Director Human Resources, Ascension Via Christi Hospital, Manhattan, Manhattan, KS, p. A254
Director Human Resources, Wamego Health Center, Wamego, KS, p. A261
REED, Tim, Vice President and Chief Financial Officer, Multicare Yakima Memorial Hospital, Yakima, WA, p. A698
REED, Tina, Director of Human Resources, Encompass Health Rehabilitation Hospital of Modesto, Modesto, CA, p. A77
REED, Tracy Collings, Vice President Patient Care Services, Chief Nursing Officer, Siskin Hospital for Physical Rehabilitation, Chattanooga, TN, p. A581
REED, Zachary, Chief Operating Officer, Henrico Doctors' Hospital, Richmond, VA, p. A682
REEDER, Carol, R.N., Chief Nursing Officer, Providence St. Josep. Hospital Eureka, Eureka, CA, p. A62
REEDER, Elizabeth, Director Human Resources, Trinity Hospital, Weaverville, CA, p. A101
REEDER, Janet Lee, MSN, R.N., Chief Nurse Executive, Kaiser Westside Medical Center, Hillsboro, OR, p. A527
REEDER, Wendy, R.N., Chief Nursing Officer, Harrison Memorial Hospital, Cynthiana, KY, p. A264
REEDY, Janet, Manager Human Resources, St. Thomas More Hospital, Canon City, CO, p. A104
REEKS, Kimberly, Director, University Hospital, Columbia, MO, p. A374
REEL, Micah, Director of Bio–Med, WVU Medicine Potomac Valley Hospital, Keyser, WV, p. A702
REEL, Stephanie L, Senior Vice President Information Services, Johns Hopkins Hospital, Baltimore, MD, p. A300
REES, Matthew, Chief Executive Officer, Administrator, Jerold Phelp. Community Hospital, Garberville, CA, p. A65
REES, Stephen G., M.D., Vice President Medical Affairs, Ochsner Lafayette General Medical Center, Lafayette, LA, p. A285
REESE, Bert
Chief Information Officer, Sentara Leigh Hospital, Norfolk, VA, p. A680
Chief Information Officer, Sentara Norfolk General Hospital, Norfolk, VA, p. A680
Chief Information Officer, Sentara Princess Anne Hospital, Virginia Beach, VA, p. A684
REESE, Jeff, Chief Financial Officer, Rusk Rehabilitation Hospital, Columbia, MO, p. A374
REESE, Jeffrey, Chief Executive Officer, The Rehabilitation Institute of St. Louis, Saint Louis, MO, p. A384
REESE, Karin, R.N., MS, Chief Nursing Officer and Chief Administrative Officer, Marinhealth Medical Center, Greenbrae, CA, p. A66
REESE, Mike, Chief Financial Officer, Ou Health – University of Oklahoma Medical Center, Oklahoma City, OK, p. A518
REESE, Stephanie, Chief Executive Officer, Delta Specialty Hospital, Memphis, TN, p. A588
REESE, Todd, Director Human Performance, Adventist Health Castle, Kailua, HI, p. A176
REESMAN, David, Acting Director, Carl Vinson Veterans Affairs Medical Center, Dublin, GA, p. A163
REETZ, Brenda, FACHE, Chief Executive Officer, Greene County General Hospital, Linton, IN, p. A222
REETZ, Linda
R.N., President, University of Michigan Health–Sparrow Eaton, Charlotte, MI, p. A323
R.N., President, University of Michigan Health–Sparrow Ionia, Ionia, MI, p. A330
REETZ, Renee, Director Human Resources, Mymichigan Medical Center Standish, Standish, MI, p. A338
REEVE, Jay A., Ph.D., President and Chief Executive Officer, Eastside Psychiatric Hospital, Tallahassee, FL, p. A151
REEVES, Andrew, M.D., Director Medical Affairs, New Ulm Medical Center, New Ulm, MN, p. A352
REEVES, Danny, Chief Financial Officer, Penrose–St. Francis Health Services, Colorado Springs, CO, p. A105
REEVES, Katy, Vice President Human Resources, Fauquier Hospital, Warrenton, VA, p. A685
REEVES, Matthew, D.O., Esq, Chief Medical Officer, Atrium Medical Center, Middletown, OH, p. A500
REEVES, Michelle, R.N., Director of Nursing, Specialists Hospital Shreveport, Shreveport, LA, p. A293
REEVES, Mike
Chief Information Officer, Ascension St. John Owasso, Owasso, OK, p. A519
Vice President, Ascension St. John Medical Center, Tulsa, OK, p. A522
REEVES, Steve, M.D., Chief Medical Staff, Greater Regional Health, Creston, IA, p. A234
REEVES, Susan A., Ed.D., R.N., Chief Nursing Executive, Dartmouth–Hitchcock Medical Center, Lebanon, NH, p. A416
REEVES, Valerie, Chief Financial Officer, Integris Miami Hospital, Miami, OK, p. A515
REFFNER, Gina, Chief Financial Officer, Little Colorado Medical Center, Winslow, AZ, p. A41
REFNESS, Kristen, Director, Financial Operations, Endeavor Health Linden Oaks Hospital, Naperville, IL, p. A203
REGAN, Timothy, M.D., President and Chief Medical Officer, Lakeland Regional Health Medical Center, Lakeland, FL, p. A137
REGIER, Donald, M.D., Chief Medical Officer, Sedgwick County Health Center, Julesburg, CO, p. A110
REGIER, Steve, Chief Financial Officer, Kearney Regional Medical Center, Kearney, NE, p. A401
REGISTER, Kellie, Director of Nursing, Clinch Memorial Hospital, Homerville, GA, p. A165
REGO, Ashwin, Chief Information Officer, Ascension Wisconsin Hospital – Menomonee Falls Campus, Menomonee Falls, WI, p. A715
REGULA, John
Chief Information Officer, Allied Services Scranton Rehabilitation Hospital, Scranton, PA, p. A554
Chief Information Officer, John Heinz Institute of Rehabilitation Medicine, Wilkes–Barre, PA, p. A557
REHBEIN, Beth, Chief Nursing and Quality Officer, Story County Medical Center, Nevada, IA, p. A240
REHM, Janice, Manager Human Resources, USA Health Children's & Women's Hospital, Mobile, AL, p. A22
REHM, Micah, Chief Nursing Officer, Forrest General Hospital, Hattiesburg, MS, p. A363
REHN, Lindsay, Executive Director of Financial Operations, Wellstar Paulding Hospital, Hiram, GA, p. A165
REHN, Ronald G.
Chief Administrative Officer, Providence Mount Carmel Hospital, Colville, WA, p. A688
Chief Executive Officer, Providence St. Joseph's Hospital, Chewelah, WA, p. A688
REICH, David L., M.D., President and Chief Operating Officer, The Mount Sinai Hospital, New York, NY, p. A453
REICH, Joanne, R.N., Chief Nursing Officer, Jersey City Medical Center, Jersey City, NJ, p. A422
REICH, Joel R
M.D., Senior Vice President Medical Affairs, Manchester Memorial Hospital, Manchester, CT, p. A116
M.D., Senior Vice President Medical Affairs, Rockville General Hospital, Vernon, CT, p. A119
REICHARD, Steve, Manager Information Systems, Brigham City Community Hospital, Brigham City, UT, p. A664
REICHENBACH, Geri, Nurse Executive, Pam Health Specialty Hospital of Heritage Valley, Beaver, PA, p. A535
REICHLE, Paula, Senior Vice President and Chief Operating Officer, University of Michigan Health–Sparrow Lansing, Lansing, MI, p. A332
REICHMAN, Joseph, M.D., Vice President Medical Affairs and Clinical Effectiveness, Hackensack Meridian Health Riverview Medical Center, Red Bank, NJ, p. A428
REID, Bernadette, Vice President, Information Technology and Chief Information Officer, Torrance Memorial Medical Center, Torrance, CA, p. A98
REID, Bev, Chief Financial Officer, St. Luke Hospital And Living Center, Marion, KS, p. A254
REID, Colleen, Chief Financial Officer, Carson Valley Medical Center, Gardnerville, NV, p. A408
REID, Dereesa, Administrator, Shriners Hospitals for Children–Portland, Portland, OR, p. A531
REID, Jim, Vice President and Chief Information Officer, Covenant Children's Hospital, Lubbock, TX, p. A635
REID, Kelly, Human Resources Director, South Mississipp. State Hospital, Purvis, MS, p. A368
REID, Patricia, Director of Nursing, Marion General Hospital, Columbia, MS, p. A361
REID, Richard, Vice President Chief Finance Officer, University of Michigan Health–Sparrow Carson, Carson City, MI, p. A323
REID, Stephanie, R.N., Vice President of Patient Care Services and Chief Nursing Officer, Carroll Hospital, Westminster, MD, p. A308
REID, Wayne, Chief Executive Officer, Langdon Prairie Health, Langdon, ND, p. A482
REID TINIO, Gina, M.P.H., MS, Ph.D., Vice President, Chief Nurse Executive, Northwestern Medicine Delnor Hospital, Geneva, IL, p. A196
REIDER, Rochelle, Vice President Patient Care, Avera Queen of Peace Hospital, Mitchell, SD, p. A575
REIDER, Rodney, Chief Executive Officer, Conemaugh Memorial Medical Center, Johnstown, PA, p. A542
REIDY, Christopher, Site Financial Officer, Community Medical Center, Toms River, NJ, p. A429
REIDY, Margaret, M.D., Vice President Medical Affairs, UPMC Presbyterian, Pittsburgh, PA, p. A552
REIFSTECK, Jeff, Assistant Vice President Chief Information Officer, White River Health, Batesville, AR, p. A43
REILLY, Brian M, Chief Financial Officer, Robert Wood Johnson University Hospital, New Brunswick, NJ, p. A425
REILLY, Janelle, Market Chief Executive Officer, Chi Memorial, Chattanooga, TN, p. A580
REILLY, John, M.D., Vice President Medical Affairs and Chief Medical Officer, Mercy Medical Center, Rockville Centre, NY, p. A458
REILLY, Robert, Vice President and Chief Financial Officer, Luminis Health Anne Arundel Medical Center, Annapolis, MD, p. A300
REILLY, Tiffany, Director Human Resources, Lifescape, Sioux Falls, SD, p. A576
REIMER, Ronda, Chief Nursing Officer and Assistant Administrator, Franklin General Hospital, Hampton, IA, p. A237
REIMSCHISSEL, Elizabeth Meagan, Administrator and Associate Chief Nursing Officer, University of Texas Medical Branch, Galveston, TX, p. A621
REIN, Mitchell S, M.D., Chief Medical Officer, Salem Hospital, Salem, MA, p. A318
REINBOTH, Thomas, Chief Financial Officer, Roxborough Memorial Hospital, Philadelphia, PA, p. A550
REINEKE, James, Chief Nurse Executive, Providence Alaska Medical Center, Anchorage, AK, p. A27
REINER, Mark, Chief Medical Office, Executive, St. Anthony's Rehabilitation Hospital, Lauderdale Lakes, FL, p. A137
REINERT, Brenda, Director Human Resources, Tomah Health, Tomah, WI, p. A723
REINERT, Chad, Chief Information Officer, Hamilton General Hospital, Hamilton, TX, p. A623
REINHARD, Diane, R.N., Vice President of Patient Care Services, Craig Hospital, Englewood, CO, p. A107
REINHARDT, Tom, Chief Executive Officer, Cascade Medical Center, Cascade, ID, p. A180
REINKE, Aaron, M.D., Chief of Medical Staff, Newport Hospital And Health Services, Newport, WA, p. A692
REINKE, Bradley, M.D., Vice President Medical Affairs and Chief Medical Officer, Dameron Hospital, Stockton, CA, p. A96
REINKING, DN, Cheryl, R.N., MS, Chief Nursing Officer, El Camino Health, Mountain View, CA, p. A79
REINTJES, Stephen Sr, M.D., President and Chief Executive Officer, North Kansas City Hospital, North Kansas City, MO, p. A381
REIS, David, Ph.D., Interim Chief Information Officer, UMHC–Sylvester Comprehensive Cancer Center, Miami, FL, p. A141
REISELT, Doug
Vice President and Chief Information Officer, Baptist Memorial Hospital – Memphis, Memphis, TN, p. A588
Vice President and Chief Information Officer, Baptist Memorial Hospital–Collierville, Collierville, TN, p. A581
REISER, Jochen, President and Chief Executive Officer, University of Texas Medical Branch, Galveston, TX, p. A621
REISING, Robyn, R.N., Chief Nursing Officer, HSHS St. Mary's Hospital, Decatur, IL, p. A193
REISMAN, Ernestine O, Vice President Human Resources, Down East Community Hospital, Machias, ME, p. A298
REISS, Deanna, Hospital Director of Nursing, Devereux Children's Behavioral Health Center, Malvern, PA, p. A545
REITZ, Brent, President, Post Acute Care Services, Adventist Healthcare Rehabilitation, Rockville, MD, p. A306
REITZEL, David, Chief Information Officer, Brookdale Hospital Medical Center, New York, NY, p. A447
REKLIS, Chip. Director Information Systems, Scotland Health Care System, Laurinburg, NC, p. A471
REKOWSKI, Christian
Information Technology Director, Jenkins County Medical Center, Millen, GA, p. A168
Information Technology Manager, Optim Medical Center – Screven, Sylvania, GA, p. A172
RELPH, Daren, Chief Executive Officer, Wayne County Hospital And Clinic System, Corydon, IA, p. A233
REMALEY, Anne, Vice President Human Resources, Acmh Hospital, Kittanning, PA, p. A543

Index of Health Care Professionals

Index of Health Care Professionals / Rembert

REMBERT, Christine, MSN, R.N., Facility Director, Mary's Harper Geriatric Psychiatry Center, Tuscaloosa, AL, p. A25
REMBOLD, Abbey
Human Resources Senior Generalist, Valley Health – Hampshire Memorial Hospital, Romney, WV, p. A704
Human Resources Senior Generalist, Valley Health – War Memorial Hospital, Berkeley Springs, WV, p. A699
Manager, Human Resource Business Partnerships, Valley Health – Shenandoah Memorial Hospital, Woodstock, VA, p. A686
REMER, Joseph, Chief Financial Officer, Hartgrove Behavioral Health System, Chicago, IL, p. A189
REMINGTON, Amanda
Director Human Resources, Wellstar Spalding Regional Hospital, Griffin, GA, p. A164
Director Human Resources, Wellstar Sylvan Grove Hospital, Jackson, GA, p. A165
REMLEY, Richard, Chief Executive Officer, Medical Behavioral Hospital of Clear Lake, Houston, TX, p. A629
REMPSON, Joseph, Medical Director, Atlantic Rehabilitation Institute, Madison, NJ, p. A423
REMSPECHER, Mark, Director Human Resources, Southeast Missouri Mental Health Center, Farmington, MO, p. A375
RENDA, Nick, Chief Financial Officer, Merit Health Woman's Hospital, Flowood, MS, p. A362
RENDER-LEACH, Cynthia, Director Human Resources, Highland Community Hospital, Picayune, MS, p. A368
RENEAU, John D., Medical Director, Encompass Health Rehabilitation Hospital of Las Vegas, Las Vegas, NV, p. A410
RENEY, Michael L., Senior Vice President for Finance and Chief Financial Officer, Dana–Farber Cancer Institute, Boston, MA, p. A310
RENFREE, Mark, Chief Financial Officer, La Rabida Children's Hospital, Chicago, IL, p. A190
RENFROW, Michael B., Medical Center Director, Tennessee Valley Hcs – Nashville And Murfreesboro, Nashville, TN, p. A590
RENIER, Hugh
M.D., Vice President Medical Affairs, Essentia Health Duluth, Duluth, MN, p. A346
M.D., Vice President Medical Affairs, Essentia Health St. Mary's Medical Center, Duluth, MN, p. A346
RENKIEWICZ, Ginger L, Chief Clinical Officer, Chief Nursing Executive, and Chief Quality Officer, Unitypoint Health – Trinity Rock Island, Rock Island, IL, p. A207
RENN, Amy Katherine, Vice President, Nursing, Ascension Via Christi St. Francis, Mulvane, KS, p. A255
RENNEKER, James M, FACHE, MSN, R.N., Vice President and Chief Nursing Officer, Methodist Hospitals, Gary, IN, p. A217
RENNER, Dianne, Director Human Resources, Logansport State Hospital, Logansport, IN, p. A223
RENNER, Marie, Chief Executive Officer, Saint Simons By–The–Sea Hospital, Saint Simons Island, GA, p. A170
RENO, Kelly, R.N., Chief Nursing Officer, Menorah Medical Center, Overland Park, KS, p. A257
RENO, Mike, Chief Operating Officer, Methodist Hospital Hill Country, Fredericksburg, TX, p. A620
RENO, William, M.D., III, President Medical Staff, Merit Health Wesley, Hattiesburg, MS, p. A363
RENTAS, Margarita, R.N., Nursing Director, Castaner General Hospital, Castaner, PR, p. A732
RENTSCH, Richard E, President, Rural Wellness Stroud, Stroud, OK, p. A521
REOHR, Sara, Regional Controller, West Gables Rehabilitation Hospital, Miami, FL, p. A141
REPAC, Kimberly S., Senior Vice President and Chief Financial Officer, UPMC Western Maryland, Cumberland, MD, p. A304
REPASKY, Stephanie, PsyD, Interim Medical Center Director, Biloxi Va Medical Center, Biloxi, MS, p. A359
REPASS, Lois, Quality Assurance Specialist and Coordinator Performance Improvement, Northern Nevada Adult Mental Health Services, Sparks, NV, p. A413
REPETTI, Gregory George.
III, FACHE, President, Multicare Deaconess Hospital, Spokane, WA, p. A696
III, FACHE, President, Multicare Valley Hospital, Spokane Valley, WA, p. A696
RESCH, Ned, Chief Executive Officer, Sterling Regional Medcenter, Sterling, CO, p. A113
RESENDEZ, James R., FACHE, Chief Executive Officer, Nexus Specialty Hospital, Shenandoah, TX, p. A652
RESETAR, Gayle L, Executive Vice President and Chief Operating Officer, Tidelands Georgetown Memorial Hospital, Georgetown, SC, p. A566
RESLER, Lori, R.N., Chief Nurse, Sullivan County Community Hospital, Sullivan, IN, p. A227
RESSLER, David, Chief Executive Officer, Aspen Valley Hospital, Aspen, CO, p. A103
RESSLER, Dennis, Vice President, Finance and Chief Financial Officer, Hendricks Regional Health, Danville, IN, p. A215
RESTREPO, Nicolas, M.D., Vice President Medical Affairs, Valley Health – Winchester Medical Center, Winchester, VA, p. A685
RESTUCCIA, Michael, Chief Information Officer, Hospital of The University of Pennsylvania, Philadelphia, PA, p. A549
RETALIC, Tammy B., R.N., MS, Chief Nursing Officer, Hebrew Rehabilitation Center, Roslindale, MA, p. A317
RETHAMEL, Terry, Director of Support Services, Newport News Behavioral Health Center, Newport News, VA, p. A680
RETHORST, Richard, Chief of Medical Staff, Franklin Hospital District, Benton, IL, p. A186
RETTGER, Linda, M.D., President Medical Staff, UPMC Kane, Kane, PA, p. A543
RETTIG, Esther, M.D., Chief Medical Officer, Mcpherson Hospital, Inc., Mcpherson, KS, p. A254
RETTIG, Jeffrey, D.O., Chief of Staff, Limestone Medical Center, Groesbeck, TX, p. A623
RETZNER, Kim, Chief Executive Officer, Brentwood Springs, Newburgh, IN, p. A225
REULAND, Charles B., Sc.D., Executive Vice President and Chief Operatng Officer, Johns Hopkins Hospital, Baltimore, MD, p. A300
REUST, Michele, Controller, Memorial Hospital of Texas County Authority, Guymon, OK, p. A513
REUTTINGER, H. Rex, D.O., Chief Medical Officer, Administration, Garden City Hospital, Garden City, MI, p. A327
REVELS, Beverly, Director Human Resources, Sutter Amador Hospital, Jackson, CA, p. A68
REVELS, Tonya, Senior Strategic Business Partner, Mission Hospital Mcdowell, Marion, NC, p. A472
REVERMAN, Larry, Director Information Systems, Norton Clark Hospital, Jeffersonville, IN, p. A221
REVIEL, Jackie Costley., R.N., Chief Executive Officer, Allen Parish Community Healthcare, Kinder, LA, p. A285
REWERTS, Karen
System Vice President Finance, SSM Health St. Josep. – St. Charles, Saint Charles, MO, p. A383
System Vice President of Finance, SSM Health Cardinal Glennon Children's Hospital, Saint Louis, MO, p. A384
System Vice President of Finance, SSM Health St. Mary's Hospital – St. Louis, Saint Louis, MO, p. A385
REXFORD, Linda, Director Human Resources, Weeks Medical Center, Lancaster, NH, p. A415
REYES, Anthony, Information Technology Director, Commonwealth Health Center, Saipan, MARIANA ISLANDS, p. A730
REYES, Glenda, Chief Financial Officer, Northwest Medical Center, Winfield, AL, p. A26
REYES, Jody, R.N., Chief Operating Officer, Clinical Enterprise, University of Iowa Hospitals & Clinics, Iowa City, IA, p. A238
REYES, Netonua, MSN, Chief Operating Officer and Chief Nursing Officer, Broward Health Imperial Point, Fort Lauderdale, FL, p. A131
REYES, Raul, M.D., Medical Director, San Juan City Hospital, San Juan, PR, p. A736
REYES, Roxanne, Director of Nursing, Cornerstone Regional Hospital, Edinburg, TX, p. A615
REYES CONCEPCION, Marco A., Executive Director, Hospital Perea, Mayaguez, PR, p. A733
REYES MELéNDEZ, Alexander, Executive Director, Hospital Menonita Ponce, Coto Laurel, PR, p. A732
REYMAN, Reed, President, Chi St. Alexius Health Bismarck, Bismarck, ND, p. A479
REYNA, Krista, Chief Nursing Officer, Mcbride Orthopedic Hospital, Oklahoma City, OK, p. A517
REYNGOUDT, Mark, Chief Financial Officer, Reading Hospital, West Reading, PA, p. A557
REYNOLDS, Angela D, Chief Financial Officer, Lewisgale Medical Center, Boones Mill, VA, p. A674
REYNOLDS, Ashley, Chief Nursing Officer, San Juan Health Service District, Monticello, UT, p. A666
REYNOLDS, Christina, M.D., Medical Director, Encompass Health Rehabilitation Hospital, Shreveport, LA, p. A292
REYNOLDS, Denise, Chief Nursing Officer, Memorial Hospital Miramar, Miramar, FL, p. A141
REYNOLDS, Doug, Area Finance Officer, Kaiser Permanente Redwood City Medical Center, Redwood City, CA, p. A85
REYNOLDS, Ian, Chief Medical Officer, East Houston Hospitals & Clinics, Houston, TX, p. A625
REYNOLDS, James B M.D., Medical Director, Northwest Missouri Psychiatric Rehabilitation Center, Saint Joseph, MO, p. A383
REYNOLDS, Jay
M.D., Chief Medical Officer and Chief Clinical Officer, The Aroostook Medical Center, Presque Isle, ME, p. A299
M.D., President, The Aroostook Medical Center, Presque Isle, ME, p. A299
REYNOLDS, Katelyn, Manager Human Resources, Greeley County Health Services, Tribune, KS, p. A261
REYNOLDS, Lauren, Associate Director of Nursing, Baptist Health Medical Center–Stuttgart, Stuttgart, AR, p. A54
REYNOLDS, Lennetta M, Administrative Supervisor, Community Behavioral Health Hospital – Annandale, Annandale, MN, p. A342
REYNOLDS, Mike, Chief Financial Officer, Delta Specialty Hospital, Memphis, TN, p. A588
REYNOLDS, Paul, M.D., Medical Director, Coleman County Medical Center, Coleman, TX, p. A607
REYNOLDS, Robert, Director Information Systems, Mary Rutan Hospital, Bellefontaine, OH, p. A486
REYNOLDS, Ronald J., President, UPMC Muncy, Muncy, PA, p. A546
REYNOLDS, Scott, Vice President Finance, Mercy Hospital Springfield, Springfield, MO, p. A387
REYNOLDS, Stevanie, Chief Nursing Officer, Piedmont Walton Hospital, Monroe, GA, p. A168
REYNOLDS, Teresa, Chief Nursing Officer, Valley View Medical Center, Fort Mohave, AZ, p. A31
REYNOLDS, Todd, Chief Information Officer, Tamarack Health Ashland Medical Center, Ashland, WI, p. A707
REYNOLDS ROBERTS, Emily, Chief Executive Officer, Pioneer Memorial Hospital, Heppner, OR, p. A527
REYNOLDS–GOSSETTE, Youdie, Controller, Wilma N. Vazquez Medical Center, Vega Baja, PR, p. A736
REZAC, Julie A., R.N., Chief Executive Officer, Saunders Medical Center, Wahoo, NE, p. A406
RHEINHEIMER, Rick, Chief Clinical Officer, Kindred Hospital–Chattanooga, Chattanooga, TN, p. A580
RHINE, Kathleen, President and Chief Executive Officer, Mount Nittany Medical Center, State College, PA, p. A555
RHINEHART, Jennie R., Administrator and Chief Executive Officer, Community Hospital, Tallassee, AL, p. A25
RHOADES, Cory, Chief Financial Officer, Cook Children's Medical Center – Prosper, Prosper, TX, p. A646
RHOADES, Shelly, Chief Financial Officer, Clarion Psychiatric Center, Clarion, PA, p. A537
RHOADS, Becky, Executive Director, Veterans Affairs Connecticut Healthcare System, West Haven, CT, p. A120
RHOADS, Jack, M.D., Medical Director, Landmark Hospital of Joplin, Joplin, MO, p. A377
RHOADS, Pam, Chief Financial Officer, Fairfax Behavioral Health, Kirkland, WA, p. A691
RHODES, Eric, President, Advocate Good Samaritan Hospital, Downers Grove, IL, p. A193
RHODES, Helen, R.N., Associate Director Operations, Veterans Affairs Northern Indiana Health Care System, Fort Wayne, IN, p. A217
RHODES, Thomas, Chief Operating Officer (River Region), Ochsner Medical Center – Kenner, Kenner, LA, p. A284
RHODES, Tracey, Coordinator Human Resources, Evergreen Medical Center, Evergreen, AL, p. A19
RHODES–STARK, Kelly, Chief Medical Officer, Miami County Medical Center, Paola, KS, p. A257
RHOTON, Stephanie L., Director, Patient Care Services, Indian Path Community Hospital, Kingsport, TN, p. A585
RHYNE, Craig
M.D., FACS, Chief Medical Officer, Covenant Children's Hospital, Lubbock, TX, p. A635
M.D., FACS, Chief Medical Officer, Covenant Medical Center, Lubbock, TX, p. A636
RHYNE, Dennis, M.D., Acting Medical Director, Community Fairbanks Recovery Center, Indianapolis, IN, p. A219
RHYNE, Tim, Personnel Officer, Ventura County Medical Center, Ventura, CA, p. A100
RIAL, Joanne, Chief Financial Officer, Cumberland Hospital for Children And Adolescents, New Kent, VA, p. A679
RIALS, Joe, Director Fiscal Services, North Mississipp. State Hospital, Tupelo, MS, p. A369
RIALS, Loren
Chief Financial Officer, Musc Health Florence Medical Center, Florence, SC, p. A566
Chief Financial Officer, Musc Health Marion Medical Center, Mullins, SC, p. A569
RIANO, Omaira D., Chief Nursing Officer, Encompass Health Rehabilitation Hospital of Sunrise, Sunrise, FL, p. A151
RIBA, Chris, Director Human Resources, Western Wisconsin Health, Baldwin, WI, p. A707
RICARDO, Jennifer, Director of Human Resources, Keralty Hospital Miami, Miami, FL, p. A140
RICCI, Lynn, President and Chief Executive Officer, Hospital for Special Care, New Britain, CT, p. A117
RICCIARDI, Patrice, Director Human Resources, Silver Lake Hospital Ltach, Newark, NJ, p. A425

A954 Index of Health Care Professionals

Index of Health Care Professionals / Rieber

Index of Health Care Professionals

RICCIO, Dustin, M.D., President and Chief Executive Officer, St. Joseph's University Medical Center, Paterson, NJ, p. A426
RICCIONI, Michel
Chief Financial Officer, Petaluma Valley Hospital, Petaluma, CA, p. A83
Chief Financial Officer, Providence St. Josep. Hospital Eureka, Eureka, CA, p. A62
Chief Financial Officer, Queen's North Hawaii Community Hospital, Kamuela, HI, p. A176
Chief Financial Officer, The Queen's Medical Center, Honolulu, HI, p. A176
Vice President and Chief Financial Officer, Northern California Region, Providence Queen of The Valley Medical Center, Napa, CA, p. A79
RICE, Aimee, Human Resources Manager, Riverview Psychiatric Center, Augusta, ME, p. A295
RICE, Bernard
Chief Compliance Officer, Rangely District Hospital, Rangely, CO, p. A113
Chief Information Officer, Nemours Children's Hospital, Orlando, FL, p. A144
RICE, Carolyn, M.D., Director Medical Services, Naval Hospital Pensacola, Pensacola, FL, p. A146
RICE, Cathy, Director Support Services, Clifton–Fine Hospital, Star Lake, NY, p. A459
RICE, Craig, Chief Information Officer, Schneck Medical Center, Seymour, IN, p. A227
RICE, Mark, CPA, Chief Financial Officer, Geisinger Jersey Shore Hospital, Jersey Shore, PA, p. A542
RICE, Mark J.
Administrator, Ruston Regional Specialty Hospital, Ruston, LA, p. A291
Chief Executive Officer, Mid–Jefferson Extended Care Hospital of Beaumont, Beaumont, TX, p. A602
RICE, Peter, M.D., Medical Director, Peacehealth Ketchikan Medical Center, Ketchikan, AK, p. A28
RICH, Anna, Chief Financial Officer, Pam Specialty Hospital of Las Vegas, Las Vegas, NV, p. A410
RICH, Bill, Chief Executive Officer, Tennova North Knoxville Medical Center, Powell, TN, p. A592
RICH, Deborah, R.N., Chief Nursing Officer, Encompass Health Rehabilitation Hospital of New England, Woburn, MA, p. A320
RICH, Judy F., MSN, R.N., President and Chief Executive Officer, TMC Health, Tucson, AZ, p. A41
RICHARD, Andrea J., M.D., Chief Medical Officer, Warren State Hospital, Warren, PA, p. A556
RICHARD, Angelique, R.N., Ph.D., Vice President Clinical Nursing, Chief Nursing Officer and Associate Dean for Practice, College of Nursing, Rush University Medical Center, Chicago, IL, p. A191
RICHARD, Brandi, Chief Nursing Officer, Michiana Behavioral Health Center, Plymouth, IN, p. A226
RICHARD, Brent, Administrative Director Information Systems, Southern Ohio Medical Center, Portsmouth, OH, p. A502
RICHARD, Christina, Chief Executive Officer, Kindred Hospital Tarrant County–Arlington, Arlington, TX, p. A597
RICHARD, Thomas, Director Budget and Revenue Cycle, Centracare – Redwood, Redwood Falls, MN, p. A353
RICHARD, Tim, IT Coordinator, Crawford Memorial Hospital, Robinson, IL, p. A207
RICHARDS, Alaina, Chief Executive Officer, Compass Behavioral Center of Houma, Houma, LA, p. A283
RICHARDS, Christine, Chief of Staff, Richland Hospital, Richland Center, WI, p. A720
RICHARDS, Craig A., Chief Executive Officer, Mildred Mitchell–Bateman Hospital, Huntington, WV, p. A701
RICHARDS, Frank
Chief Information Officer, Geisinger Medical Center, Danville, PA, p. A538
Chief Information Officer, Geisinger Medical Center Muncy, Muncy, PA, p. A546
Chief Information Officer, Geisinger Wyoming Valley Medical Center, Wilkes Barre, PA, p. A557
RICHARDS, Jaena, Chief Financial Officer, Deer Lodge Medical Center, Deer Lodge, MT, p. A391
RICHARDS, Jennifer
Ph.D., R.N., Chief Nursing Officer, Renown Rehabilitation Hospital, Reno, NV, p. A412
Ph.D., R.N., Chief Nursing Officer, Renown South Meadows Medical Center, Reno, NV, p. A412
Ph.D., R.N., Chief Nursing Officer Acute Services, Renown Regional Medical Center, Reno, NV, p. A412
RICHARDS, Jon, Chief Financial Officer, Tennova Newport Medical Center, Newport, TN, p. A591
RICHARDS, Jonathan, Chief Financial Officer, David Grant Usaf Medical Center, Travis Air Force Base, CA, p. A98
RICHARDS, Judith, Director of Nursing, Adcare Hospital of Worcester, Worcester, MA, p. A320
RICHARDS, Kelly
Vice President and Chief Nursing Officer, Mercyone Cedar Falls Medical Center, Cedar Falls, IA, p. A231
Vice President and Chief Nursing Officer, Mercyone Oelwein Medical Center, Oelwein, IA, p. A241
Vice President and Chief Nursing Officer, Mercyone Waterloo Medical Center, Waterloo, IA, p. A244
RICHARDS, Nate, Director Information Technology, Mitchell County Hospital Health Systems, Beloit, KS, p. A247
RICHARDS, Samantha M
MSN, Vice President Patient Care Services and Chief Nursing Officer, Berkeley Medical Center, Martinsburg, WV, p. A702
MSN, Vice President Patient Care Services and Chief Nursing Officer, Jefferson Medical Center, Ranson, WV, p. A704
RICHARDS, Sheila K, Human Resources Director, Dallas Medical Center, Dallas, TX, p. A611
RICHARDS, Stanlee, R.N., MS, Chief Nurse Executive, NYC Health + Hospitals/Henry J Carter Specialty Hospital And Medical Center, New York, NY, p. A451
RICHARDS, Thom, Director Information Technology, Knoxville Hospital & Clinics, Knoxville, IA, p. A239
RICHARDSON, Angelique, Chief Executive Officer, Acadiana Rehabilitation, Lafayette, LA, p. A285
RICHARDSON, Crystal, Chief Nursing Officer, Select Specialty Hospital – Richmond, Richmond, VA, p. A682
RICHARDSON, David, M.D., Chief of Staff, Delta Specialty Hospital, Memphis, TN, p. A588
RICHARDSON, Denise, R.N., MSN, Senior Vice President and Chief Nursing Officer, St. Barnabas Hospital, New York, NY, p. A452
RICHARDSON, Dwayne, President, Trinity Hospital Twin City, Dennison, OH, p. A494
RICHARDSON, Greg H, Assistant Administrator Human Resources, Piedmont Newton Hospital, Covington, GA, p. A162
RICHARDSON, Heidi, Chief Nursing Officer, De Soto Regional Health System, Mansfield, LA, p. A288
RICHARDSON, Irene, Chief Executive Officer, Memorial Hospital of Sweetwater County, Rock Springs, WY, p. A728
RICHARDSON, Judy, M.D., President Medical Staff, Adventist Health Columbia Gorge, The Dalles, OR, p. A532
RICHARDSON, Karen K., Senior Vice President and Chief Financial Officer, Ascension Providence, Waco, TX, p. A660
RICHARDSON, Kevin, M.D., Chief of Staff, Southwest Mississipp. Regional Medical Center, Mccomb, MS, p. A366
RICHARDSON, Kirk, R.N., Senior Vice President, Chief Operating Officer, and Chief Nursing Officer, Bronson Lakeview Hospital, Paw Paw, MI, p. A335
RICHARDSON, Lonnie, Chief Information Officer, University Medical Center, Las Vegas, NV, p. A411
RICHARDSON, Nathaniel Jr, President and Chief Executive Officer, University of Maryland Capital Region Medical Center, Largo, MD, p. A305
RICHARDSON, Pamela, Business Manager, Central Regional Hospital, Butner, NC, p. A464
RICHARDSON, Paul McKinley Jr, Chief Medical Officer, Conway Medical Center, Conway, SC, p. A565
RICHARDSON, Robert
Information Technology Administrator, Northwest Health – Porter, Valparaiso, IN, p. A228
Interim President and Chief Executive Officer, Munson Healthcare Otsego Memorial Hospital, Gaylord, MI, p. A327
RICHARDSON, Robert Stephen. Jr, Administrator, Regions Behavioral Hospital, Baton Rouge, LA, p. A278
RICHARDSON, Rodney, Director of Information Technology, Baptist Health Corbin, Corbin, KY, p. A264
RICHARDSON, Sarah, Director Information Systems, Belton Regional Medical Center, Belton, MO, p. A371
RICHARDSON, Stanley, Coordinator Human Resources and Payroll Benefits, Kindred Hospital–San Antonio, San Antonio, TX, p. A649
RICHARDSON, Teresa, Chief Clinical Officer, Kindred Hospital Indianapolis North, Indianapolis, IN, p. A220
RICHARDSON, Terrie, Coordinator Human Resources, Select Specialty Hospital–Augusta, Augusta, GA, p. A158
RICHARDSON, Timothy J, M.D., Chief of Staff, Maine Veterans Affairs Medical Center, Augusta, ME, p. A295
RICHARDSON, Todd, Chief Information Officer, Aspirus Medford Hospital & Clinics, Medford, WI, p. A715
RICHASON, Amie A.
Vice President Human Resources, Leesburg Regional Medical Center, Leesburg, FL, p. A137
Vice President Human Resources, UF Health The Villages Hospital, The Villages, FL, p. A153
RICHAUD, Benjamin, Chief Executive Officer, East Jefferson General Hospital, Metairie, LA, p. A288
RICHBURG, Melanie, Chief Executive Officer, Lynn County Hospital District, Tahoka, TX, p. A655
RICHCREEK, Keith, Manager Technical Services, Lafayette Regional Health Center, Lexington, MO, p. A379
RICHENS, Ken, Chief Information Officer, Central Valley Medical Center, Nephi, UT, p. A666
RICHERT, Ed, M.D., Chief of Staff, Modoc Medical Center, Alturas, CA, p. A55
RICHERT, Tadd M, Chief Executive Officer, Penrose–St. Francis Health Services, Colorado Springs, CO, p. A105
RICHESON, Robert, Chief Operating Officer, Connecticut Department of Correction's Hospital, Somers, CT, p. A118
RICHETTI, Michael, Chief Financial Officer, Chilton Medical Center, Pompton Plains, NJ, p. A427
RICHHART, David, Chief Financial Officer, Logan Health – Whitefish, Whitefish, MT, p. A396
RICHMAN, Jonathan, M.D., Chief of Staff, Chase County Community Hospital, Imperial, NE, p. A401
RICHMOND, Andy, Director Information Technology, Choctaw Memorial Hospital, Hugo, OK, p. A513
RICHMOND, Christine, Director of Nursing, Community Care Hospital, New Orleans, LA, p. A290
RICHMOND, Deneen, R.N., President, Luminis Health Doctors Community Medical Center, Lanham, MD, p. A305
RICHMOND, Ira, Associate Director Patient Care Services, Veterans Affairs Pittsburgh Healthcare System, Pittsburgh, PA, p. A552
RICHMOND, Nathan Adam., Administrator, Carnegie Tri–County Municipal Hospital, Carnegie, OK, p. A510
RICHOUX, Jacquelyn, Chief Financial Officer, Lady of The Sea General Hospital, Cut Off, LA, p. A281
RICHTER, Daniel, M.D., Chief of Staff, Chi Health Missouri Valley, Missouri Valley, IA, p. A240
RICK, Bob, Vice President Information Technology, USMD Hospital At Arlington, Arlington, TX, p. A598
RICKENS, Chris, R.N., MS, Senior Vice President and Chief Nursing Officer, UPMC Altoona, Altoona, PA, p. A534
RICKS, Edward, Vice President and Chief Information Officer, Beaufort Memorial Hospital, Beaufort, SC, p. A562
RICKS, Loretha, Human Resources Supervisor, Bon Secours – Southampton Medical Center, Franklin, VA, p. A676
RICKS, Michael
Chief Executive, Los Angeles Coastal Service Area, Providence Little Company of Mary Medical Center – Torrance, Torrance, CA, p. A98
Chief Executive, Los Angeles Coastal Service Area, Providence Little Company of Mary Medical Center San Pedro, Los Angeles, CA, p. A75
Chief Executive, Los Angeles Coastal Service Area, Providence Saint John's Health Center, Santa Monica, CA, p. A95
RICO, Carrie, Chief Human Resource Officer, Keefe Memorial Hospital, Cheyenne Wells, CO, p. A104
RICO, Richard, Vice President and Chief Financial Officer, Sky Lakes Medical Center, Klamath Falls, OR, p. A528
RIDDER, Benjamin, Chief Executive Officer, Tennova Healthcare–Jefferson Memorial Hospital, Jefferson City, TN, p. A584
RIDDER, Terri, Director Human Resources, Franciscan Healthcare, West Point, NE, p. A407
RIDDLE, Joel, Senior Director Human Resources, Caromont Regional Medical Center, Gastonia, NC, p. A469
RIDDLE, Kent, Chief Executive Officer, Mary Free Bed Rehabilitation Hospital, Grand Rapids, MI, p. A328
RIDDLE, Ross, D.O., Medical Director, Elkview General Hospital, Hobart, OK, p. A513
RIDER, Lucinda, CFO, UHS Delaware Valley Hospital, Walton, NY, p. A461
RIDGE, Lisa Carolyn., Chief Executive Officer, Van Diest Medical Center, Webster City, IA, p. A245
RIDGE, Michele A R.N., Chief Operating Officer and Chief Nursing Officer, Indiana University Health Paoli Hospital, Paoli, IN, p. A226
RIDGEWAY–WASHINGTON, Ashley M., Senior Vice President, Chief Human Resources Officer, JPS Health Network, Fort Worth, TX, p. A619
RIDING, Cathan, Interim Chief Operating Officer, Wesley Medical Center, Wichita, KS, p. A262
RIDLEY, John, Executive Vice President & Chief Operating Officer, Decatur Memorial Hospital, Decatur, IL, p. A192
RIDLEY, Pam, Director Information Systems, Henry County Medical Center, Paris, TN, p. A592
RIDLEY, Zena, Director Human Resources, Harbor Oaks Hospital, New Baltimore, MI, p. A334
RIDNER, Sheila, R.N., Director of Nursing, Unity Psychiatric Care–Columbia, Columbia, TN, p. A581
RIEBER, Dan, Chief Financial Officer, UCHealth Memorial Hospital, Colorado Springs, CO, p. A105
RIEBER, Jim, Director Information Systems, Perham Health, Perham, MN, p. A352

Index of Health Care Professionals

Index of Health Care Professionals / Riechers

RIECHERS, Thomas, M.D., Chief Medical Staff, Mercy Hospital Washington, Washington, MO, p. A388
RIECK, Amy, Human Resources Officer, Greater Regional Health, Creston, IA, p. A234
RIEDLINGER, Floyd, Director Human Resources, West Jefferson Medical Center, Marrero, LA, p. A288
RIEG, Kevin, M.D., President Medical Staff, Ascension Via Christi Rehabilitation Hospital, Wichita, KS, p. A261
RIEGER, Bill, Chief Information Officer, UF Health St. John's, Saint Augustine, FL, p. A148
RIEGER, Tim, Chief Financial Officer, Mercy Health – St. Rita's Medical Center, Lima, OH, p. A498
RIEGERT, Patricia, Director Fiscal Services, Danville State Hospital, Danville, PA, p. A538
RIEKE, Diane, Director Patient Care Services, Patients' Hospital of Redding, Redding, CA, p. A85
RIEKS, Katie, Chief Nursing Officer, Hansen Family Hospital, Iowa Falls, IA, p. A238
RIER, Kirk, Chief Operating Officer, Iowa Specialty Hospital–Clarion, Clarion, IA, p. A232
RIES, Heather, Chief Nursing Officer, Regional Medical Center, Manchester, IA, p. A239
RIESER, Michael, M.D., Medical Director, Ridge Behavioral Health System, Lexington, KY, p. A269
RIETMAN, Cheryl, Chief Administrative Officer, Deaconess Midtown Hospital, Evansville, IN, p. A216
RIETSEMA, Wouter, M.D., Chief Quality and Information Officer, The University of Vermont Health Network–Champlain Valley Physicians Hospital, Plattsburgh, NY, p. A456
RIEVES, Cheryl, Chief Nurse Executive Lorain Region, Mercy Health – Allen Hospital, Oberlin, OH, p. A501
RIFFLE, Virginia, Vice President Patient Care Services, Samaritan North Lincoln Hospital, Lincoln City, OR, p. A528
RIGAS, Warren Alston, Executive Vice President and Chief Operating Officer, Atrium Health Floyd Medical Center, Rome, GA, p. A170
RIGDON, Alice W., Vice President Finance, Intermountain Health Saint Josep. Hospital, Denver, CO, p. A106
RIGDON, Edward, M.D., Chief Medical Officer, Merit Health Rankin, Brandon, MS, p. A360
RIGDON, Pam, Director Nursing, Ochsner Laird Hospital, Union, MS, p. A369
RIGGER, Kelly, Chief Executive Officer, Mental Health Services for Clark And Madison Counties, Springfield, OH, p. A503
RIGGLE, Vikki, Director Human Resources, Eastern Louisiana Mental Health System, Jackson, LA, p. A283
RIGGS, Amber, Controller, Community Rehabilitation Hospital South, Greenwood, IN, p. A218
RIGGS, Jennifer, R.N., Chief Nurse Officer, Mainegeneral Medical Center, Augusta, ME, p. A295
RIGGS, Kirsten
Chief Operating Officer, UNC Health Rex, Raleigh, NC, p. A475
Interim President and Chief Operating Officer, UNC Health Rex, Raleigh, NC, p. A475
RIGGS, Richard V., M.D., Senior Vice President Medical Affairs and Chief Medical Officer, Cedars–Sinai Medical Center, Los Angeles, CA, p. A72
RIGNEY, Alice, Chief Human Resources Officer, Abbeville Area Medical Center, Abbeville, SC, p. A562
RIGSBEE CARROLL, Cristina, Chief Operating Officer, Granville Health System, Oxford, NC, p. A474
RIGSBY, Diane, Chief Information Officer, Capital Caring, Arlington, VA, p. A673
RIKER, Yvette, Chief Operating Officer, Reeves Regional Health, Pecos, TX, p. A643
RILEY, Colleen, M.D., Medical Director, Laguna Honda Hospital And Rehabilitation Center, San Francisco, CA, p. A91
RILEY, Jennifer
Chief Executive Officer, Memorial Regional Health, Craig, CO, p. A105
Vice President Operations, Memorial Regional Health, Craig, CO, p. A105
RILEY, Jim, Director Information Technology, Wagoner Community Hospital, Wagoner, OK, p. A523
RILEY, Joe B., FACHE, President and Chief Executive Officer, Jackson Hospital And Clinic, Montgomery, AL, p. A22
RILEY, Kenneth, Director Information Systems, Baystate Wing Hospital, Palmer, MA, p. A317
RILEY, Mike, President and Chief Operating Officer, Novant Health Huntersville Medical Center, Huntersville, NC, p. A470
RILEY, Randy, Fiscal and Administrative Manager, Northwest Missouri Psychiatric Rehabilitation Center, Saint Joseph, MO, p. A383
RILEY, Susan, Director Human Resources, Encompass Health Rehabilitation Hospital of Miami, Cutler Bay, FL, p. A129
RILEY, Wayne J., M.D., M.P.H., President, Suny Downstate Health Sciences University, New York, NY, p. A453
RILEY, William, M.D., Jr, Chief of Staff, Memorial Hermann Sugar Land Hospital, Sugar Land, TX, p. A654
RILEY–BROWN, Michelle, President and Chief Executive Officer, Children's National Hospital, Washington, DC, p. A123
RINALDI, Anthony, Executive Vice President, Fairview Hospital, Great Barrington, MA, p. A314
RINALDI, Blythe, Vice President, Mayo Clinic Health System – Northland In Barron, Barron, WI, p. A708
RINDELS, Doris, Vice President Operations, Unitypoint Health – Grinnell Regional Medical Center, Grinnell, IA, p. A236
RINDFLEISCH, Jody, Manager Human Resources, Centracare – Redwood, Redwood Falls, MN, p. A353
RINEHART, Linda, Director Human Resources, Encompass Health Rehabilitation Hospital of Treasure Coast, Vero Beach, FL, p. A154
RINEHART, Rick, Vice President, Chief Information Officer, Carle Foundation Hospital, Urbana, IL, p. A210
RINEHART, Tyler, Chief Financial Officer, Center for Behavioral Medicine, Kansas City, MO, p. A377
RINEY, Kirsten S, MSN, R.N., Chief Nursing Officer, North Oaks Medical Center, Hammond, LA, p. A282
RING, Brian K., Chief Executive Officer, Henry Community Health, New Castle, IN, p. A225
RING, Caroline A, Chief Nursing Officer, Corewell Health Big Rapids Hospital, Big Rapids, MI, p. A322
RINGE, Kathy, Director Human Resources, Sage Rehabilitation Hospital, Baton Rouge, LA, p. A278
RINGER, Dave, M.D., Chief of Staff, St. Mary's Good Samaritan Hospital, Greensboro, GA, p. A164
RINKE, Joseph
Director Human Resources, Streamwood Behavioral Healthcare System, Streamwood, IL, p. A209
Director of Human Resources, Riveredge Hospital, Forest Park, IL, p. A195
RINKENBERGER, Sean, Chief Financial Officer, SMP Health – St. Andrew's, Bottineau, ND, p. A479
RINKER, John M., Chief Medical Officer, OSF Saint James – John W. Albrecht Medical Center, Pontiac, IL, p. A206
RINKS, Kevin, Chief Executive Officer, Ascension St. Vincent's Southside, Jacksonville, FL, p. A134
RIORDAN, Lena, R.N., Chief Nursing Officer, Northshore Rehabilitation Hospital, Lacombe, LA, p. A285
RIOS, Cindy, Chief Financial Officer, Alliancehealth Durant, Durant, OK, p. A512
RIOS, Damaris, Executive Nursing Director, Hospital Metropolitano Dr. Susoni, Arecibo, PR, p. A731
RIOS, Jose C, Director Information Services, Adventhealth Murray, Chatsworth, GA, p. A160
RIOS, Margot, R.N., Chief Nursing Officer, Christus Spohn Hospital Alice, Alice, TX, p. A595
RIOS, Riva, Chief Nursing Officer, Willow Springs Center, Reno, NV, p. A412
RIPPERGER, Ted, Administrative Director Human Resources, Atrium Medical Center, Middletown, OH, p. A500
RIPPEY, Wesley E, M.D., Chief Medical Officer, Adventist Health Portland, Portland, OR, p. A530
RISBY, Emile, M.D., Clinical Director, Georgia Regional Hospital At Atlanta, Decatur, GA, p. A162
RISHA, Holly, Administrative Director Human Resources, College Hospital Cerritos, Cerritos, CA, p. A59
RISINGER, Jeff, Director Human Resources, UAMS Medical Center, Little Rock, AR, p. A50
RISK, Carl W. II, President, Elkhart General Hospital, Elkhart, IN, p. A215
RISKA, Marilouise, Chief Executive Officer, Select Specialty Hospital – Downriver, Wyandotte, MI, p. A341
RISOVI, Carol, Human Resources, Chi St Alexius Health Carrington, Carrington, ND, p. A479
RISSE, Thomas, Chief Financial Officer and Vice President Business Services, Kaiser Permanente Medical Center, Honolulu, HI, p. A175
RITCHEY, James, Montana Region, Vice President Human Resources, SCL Health Mt – St. Vincent Healthcare, Billings, MT, p. A390
RITCHEY, Jim, Director Human Resources, Sky Ridge Medical Center, Lone Tree, CO, p. A111
RITCHIE, Andrew, President, UPMC St. Margaret, Pittsburgh, PA, p. A552
RITCHIE, Bruce, Vice President of Finance and Chief Financial Officer, Tidalhealth Peninsula Regional, Salisbury, MD, p. A307
RITCHIE, Eric, M.D., Clinical Director, Chinle Comprehensive Health Care Facility, Chinle, AZ, p. A31
RITCHIE, Jill, Director of Nursing, Ellinwood District Hospital, Ellinwood, KS, p. A248
RITCHIE, Jim, Director Management Information Systems, South Shore Hospital, Chicago, IL, p. A191
RITENOUR, Chad W.M., M.D., Chief Medical Officer, Emory University Hospital, Atlanta, GA, p. A157
RITON, John, Director Information Services, HCA Florida West Tamp. Hospital, Tampa, FL, p. A152
RITTENOUR, Melanie, Director Human Resources, Paulding County Hospital, Paulding, OH, p. A502
RITTER, Elizabeth, President, UPMC Harrisburg, Harrisburg, PA, p. A541
RITTER, Jane Taylor, R.N., Chief Nursing Officer, Wesley Medical Center, Wichita, KS, p. A262
RITTER, Robert G, FACHE, Associate Director, Harry S. Truman Memorial Veterans' Hospital, Columbia, MO, p. A374
RITZ, Andrew, Chief Operatiang Officer, Longmont United Hospital, Longmont, CO, p. A111
RIVAS, Ramon Rodriguez, M.D., Medical Director, Hospital Menonita Ponce, Coto Laurel, PR, p. A732
RIVERA, Angela, Chief Nursing Officer, Beckley Arh Hospital, Beckley, WV, p. A699
RIVERA, Camille, Interim Chief Information Officer, HCA Florida Mercy Hospital, Miami, FL, p. A140
RIVERA, Edgar, Chief Information Officer, Brownfield Regional Medical Center, Brownfield, TX, p. A604
RIVERA, Enrique, Chief Financial Officer, Bella Vista Hospital, Mayaguez, PR, p. A733
RIVERA, Frank, Chief Executive Officer, Premier Specialty Hospital of El Paso, El Paso, TX, p. A617
RIVERA, Jamie, Chief Financial Officer, Hospital Pavia Arecibo, Arecibo, PR, p. A731
RIVERA, Joe, Chief Information Technology Officer, Laredo Medical Center, Laredo, TX, p. A634
RIVERA, Jose Garcia, Director Human Resources, Hospital Buen Samaritano, Aguadilla, PR, p. A730
RIVERA, Julia, M.D., Chief of Staff, Jackson County Memorial Hospital, Altus, OK, p. A509
RIVERA, Luis, Director Human Resources, San Juan Capestrano Hospital, San Juan, PR, p. A735
RIVERA, Maria, Director Human Resources, HCA Florida Westside Hospital, Plantation, FL, p. A147
RIVERA, Moises, Interim Human Resource Director, Multy Medical Rehabilitation Hospital San Juan, San Juan, PR, p. A735
RIVERA, Orlando, Executive Director, Hospital San Pablo Del Este Hima Fajardo, Fajardo, PR, p. A732
RIVERA, Tiffany, Market Director, Human Resources, Northwest Medical Center Sahuarita, Sahuarita, AZ, p. A38
RIVERA, Zamarys, R.N., Chief Nursing Officer, Encompass Health Rehabilitation Hospital of San Juan, San Juan, PR, p. A735
RIVERA–SANTOS, Ivonne
Chief Financial Officer, Hospital Episcopal San Lucas Metro, San Juan, PR, p. A735
Director Finance, Hospital Menonita Humacao, Humacao, PR, p. A733
RIVERS, Eric, Chief Information Officer, Mission Community Hospital, Los Angeles, CA, p. A74
RIVERS, Ken, Chief Operating Officer, Fontana Medical Center, Kaiser Permanente Fontana Medical Center, Fontana, CA, p. A63
RIVERS, Nikki, R.N., Chief Nursing Officer and Interim Chief Executive Officer, Christus Santa Rosa Health System, San Antonio, TX, p. A649
RIVET, Brady, MSN, R.N., Chief Nursing Officer, River Oaks Hospital, New Orleans, LA, p. A290
RIVKIN, Oleg, Chief Executive Officer, Select Specialty Hospital–Northeast New Jersey, Rochelle Park, NJ, p. A428
RIZGALLAH, Ed, Vice President Information Services and Chief Information Officer, Christian Health, Wyckoff, NJ, p. A431
RIZK, Magdy, M.D., Chief of Staff, HCA Houston Healthcare West, Houston, TX, p. A626
RIZK, Norman, M.D., Chief Medical Officer, Stanford Health Care, Palo Alto, CA, p. A82
RIZK, Rob, Director Information Technology, Good Shepherd Health Care System, Hermiston, OR, p. A527
RIZKALLA, Nasseem, M.D., Chief Medical Officer, Aspirus Iron River Hospital, Iron River, MI, p. A330
RIZZO, Theresa, Administrator, Franklin County Memorial Hospital, Franklin, NE, p. A399
ROACH, Abbey, Chief Operating Officer, Vice President, Uofl Health – Peace Hospital, Louisville, KY, p. A270
ROACH, Bryan, Executive Vice President and Chief Financial Officer, Mount Nittany Medical Center, State College, PA, p. A555
ROACH, Crystal, Chief Financial Officer, Trustpoint Rehabilitation Hospital of Lubbock, Lubbock, TX, p. A636
ROACH, Dee A, M.D., Chief of Staff, Mitchell County Hospital, Colorado City, TX, p. A608
ROACH, Donna, MS, Chief Information Officer, University of Utah Health, Salt Lake City, UT, p. A669

A956 Index of Health Care Professionals

ROACH, Geoff, Director Human Resources, Barrett Hospital & Healthcare, Dillon, MT, p. A391
ROACH, James, D.O., Chief Medical Officer, Broward Health Medical Center, Fort Lauderdale, FL, p. A131
ROACH, Maureen, Senior Chief Financial Officer, Kindred Hospital–St. Louis, Saint Louis, MO, p. A383
ROACH, Renee
　System Vice President, SSM Health St. Josep. Hospital – Lake Saint Louis, Lake Saint Louis, MO, p. A379
　System Vice President, Human Resources, SSM Health St. Clare Hospital – Fenton, Fenton, MO, p. A375
ROADER, Charles, Vice President Finance, Edgerton Hospital And Health Services, Edgerton, WI, p. A710
ROAN, Linda Lyn, Chief Nursing Officer, East Morgan County Hospital, Brush, CO, p. A104
ROANHORSE, Anslem, Chief Executive Officer, U. S. Public Health Service Indian Hospital, Crownpoint, NM, p. A434
ROARK, Chris, Chief Information Officer, Stillwater Medical Center, Stillwater, OK, p. A521
ROARK, Darin, President and Chief Executive Officer, Wentworth–Douglass Hospital, Dover, NH, p. A414
ROARTY, Maureen, Executive Vice President Human Resources, Nassau University Medical Center, East Meadow, NY, p. A442
ROATCH, Randy, Chief Executive Officer, Summit Surgical, Hutchinson, KS, p. A251
ROB, Lee, Director Human Resources, Monroe Regional Hospital, Aberdeen, MS, p. A359
ROBB, Joy, Vice President Human Resources, Prairie View, Newton, KS, p. A256
ROBBENNOLT, Rena, Interim Administrator, Avera Missouri River Health Center, Gettysburg, SD, p. A574
ROBBINS, Donald
　M.D., Jr, Chief Staff, Hills & Dales Healthcare, Cass City, MI, p. A323
　Chief Executive Officer, Massac Memorial Hospital, Metropolis, IL, p. A202
ROBBINS, Joe, M.D., Vice President Medical Affairs, Sentara Williamsburg Regional Medical Center, Williamsburg, VA, p. A685
ROBBINS, Shannon, Chief Operating Officer, Ohio Hospital for Psychiatry, Columbus, OH, p. A492
ROBERGE, Jeremy, CPA, President and Chief Executive Officer, Huggins Hospital, Wolfeboro, NH, p. A417
ROBERSON, Ed, Director Information Systems, HCA Houston Healthcare Northwest, Houston, TX, p. A626
ROBERSON, Kim, Interim Chief Executive Officer, Lawrence Medical Center, Moulton, AL, p. A23
ROBERSON, Lynda, Senior Program Director, Rusk State Hospital, Rusk, TX, p. A648
ROBERSON, Meika, M.D., Chief Medical Officer, Carepoint Health Hoboken University Medical Center, Hoboken, NJ, p. A422
ROBERSON, Sammie, MSN, President and Chief Executive Officer, North Arkansas Regional Medical Center, Harrison, AR, p. A47
ROBERSON, Scott, President, Alta View Hospital, Sandy, UT, p. A669
ROBERT, Thomas W., Senior Vice President of Finance and Chief Financial Officer, Mercy Medical Center, Springfield, MA, p. A318
ROBERTS, Allyson, CPA, Chief Financial Officer, Nor–Lea Hospital District, Lovington, NM, p. A435
ROBERTS, Andrew, Interim Chief Human Resources Officer, Biloxi Va Medical Center, Biloxi, MS, p. A359
ROBERTS, Barbara, Chief Financial Officer, Robley Rex Department of Veterans Affairs Medical Center, Louisville, KY, p. A270
ROBERTS, Brad, Network Administrator, Swisher Memorial Healthcare System, Tulia, TX, p. A658
ROBERTS, Cathy, Vice President Mission Integration and Human Resources, Commonspirit – Mercy Hospital, Durango, CO, p. A107
ROBERTS, Celene, Chief Human Resource Officer, Park City Hospital, Park City, UT, p. A667
ROBERTS, Charles, M.D., Executive Vice President and Executive Medical Director, Children's Mercy Kansas City, Kansas City, MO, p. A377
ROBERTS, Curt L., Market Chief Executive Officer, Cornerstone Specialty Hospitals Austin Round Rock, Austin, TX, p. A599
ROBERTS, Cyndi, Director Human Resources, Medical City Fort Worth, Fort Worth, TX, p. A620
ROBERTS, David, M.D., Chief Medical Officer, Jackson–Madison County General Hospital, Medina, TN, p. A588
ROBERTS, Deborah, R.N., Chief Nursing Officer, The Core Institute Specialty Hospital, Phoenix, AZ, p. A37
ROBERTS, Debra, Director of Human Resources, St. Luke's Health – Lakeside Hospital, The Woodlands, TX, p. A657

ROBERTS, Heath M, Chief Operating Officer, Dmc Children's Hospital of Michigan, Detroit, MI, p. A325
ROBERTS, Jason
　Director Information System, Carson Valley Medical Center, Gardnerville, NV, p. A408
　Director of Information Services, Barton Memorial Hospital, South Lake Tahoe, CA, p. A96
ROBERTS, Jeff, Director Information Technology, Pinckneyville Community Hospital, Pinckneyville, IL, p. A206
ROBERTS, Jesse, Acting Chief Nursing Officer, Jackson Hospital, Marianna, FL, p. A138
ROBERTS, Justin, Chief Financial Officer, Piedmont Newton Hospital, Covington, GA, p. A162
ROBERTS, Kathryn, Director Human Resources, Mercyone Dubuque Medical Center, Dubuque, IA, p. A235
ROBERTS, Kevin A.
　FACHE, President and Chief Executive Officer, Adventhealth Central Texas, Killeen, TX, p. A632
　FACHE, President and Chief Executive Officer, Adventhealth Rollins Brook, Lampasas, TX, p. A633
ROBERTS, Kim, Chief Strategy Officer, Lucile Packard Children's Hospital Stanford, Palo Alto, CA, p. A82
ROBERTS, Laurel, R.N., MSN, Chief Operating Officer, Rolling Hills Hospital, Franklin, TN, p. A583
ROBERTS, Mark, Chief Operating Officer, Memorial Satilla Health, Waycross, GA, p. A174
ROBERTS, Meggin, Chief Executive Officer, Animas Surgical Hospital, Durango, CO, p. A107
ROBERTS, Michele, Vice President, Patient Care Services, Lehigh Valley Hospital – Pocono, East Stroudsburg, PA, p. A539
ROBERTS, Mike, Chief Technology Officer, Highlands Arh Regional Medical Center, Prestonsburg, KY, p. A273
ROBERTS, Nancy, Chief Operating Officer, Providence St. Vincent Medical Center, Portland, OR, p. A531
ROBERTS, Paul L., Director, Cheyenne Va Medical Center, Cheyenne, WY, p. A726
ROBERTS, Paula, Chief Nursing Officer, Cumberland Hospital for Children And Adolescents, New Kent, VA, p. A679
ROBERTS, Priscilla, Chief Executive Officer, Reception And Medical Center, Lake Butler, FL, p. A136
ROBERTS, Rob, Director Information Technology, Benson Hospital, Benson, AZ, p. A30
ROBERTS, Robert C
　Senior Vice President, Baptist Health Rehabilitation Institute, Little Rock, AR, p. A49
　Senior Vice President Financial Services, Baptist Health Medical Center – North Little Rock, North Little Rock, AR, p. A51
　Senior Vice President Financial Services, Baptist Health Medical Center–Little Rock, Little Rock, AR, p. A49
　Vice President and Chief Financial Officer, Baptist Health Medical Center–Arkadelphia, Arkadelphia, AR, p. A43
ROBERTS, Ronald Brent, M.D., Chief of Medical Staff, North Sunflower Medical Center, Ruleville, MS, p. A368
ROBERTS, Roslyn, Manager, Northside Hospital Cherokee, Canton, GA, p. A160
ROBERTS, Shayna Brooke, Director Human Resources, Northeastern Health System Sequoyah, Sallisaw, OK, p. A520
ROBERTS, Teresa, Chief Financial Officer, Ringgold County Hospital, Mount Ayr, IA, p. A240
ROBERTS, Todd P, Vice President Finance, Alice Peck Day Memorial Hospital, Lebanon, NH, p. A415
ROBERTS, Tony, CPA, Chief Financial Officer, Marion Health, Marion, IN, p. A223
ROBERTSHAW, Hazel, R.N., Ph.D., Chief Nursing Officer, Vice President Patient Services, F. F. Thompson Hospital, Canandaigua, NY, p. A440
ROBERTSON, Carla, Chief Operating Officer and Chief Financial Officer, Saline Memorial Hospital, Benton, AR, p. A43
ROBERTSON, Casey, President and Chief Executive Officer, Christus Health Shreveport–Bossier, Shreveport, LA, p. A292
ROBERTSON, Elizabeth, Area Controller, Encompass Health Rehabilitation Hospital of Dallas, Dallas, TX, p. A611
ROBERTSON, Laura
　R.N., Chief Executive Officer, Banner Desert Medical Center, Mesa, AZ, p. A33
　R.N., Chief Executive Officer, Banner Ocotillo Medical Center, Chandler, AZ, p. A30
ROBERTSON, Michael, Chief Executive Officer, Piedmont Newnan Hospital, Newnan, GA, p. A169
ROBERTSON, Misty, R.N., FACHE, Chief Operating Officer and Chief Nursing Officer, St. Luke's Nampa, Nampa, ID, p. A182
ROBERTSON, Steve
　Executive Vice President and Chief Information Officer, Straub Medical Center, Honolulu, HI, p. A176

　Executive Vice President Revenue Cycle Management and Chief Information Officer, Wilcox Medical Center, Lihue, HI, p. A177
　Senior Vice President, Pali Momi Medical Center, Aiea, HI, p. A175
　Vice President, Kapiolani Medical Center for Women & Children, Honolulu, HI, p. A175
ROBESON, Gail, Vice President Patient Services, Huron Regional Medical Center, Huron, SD, p. A574
ROBICHAUX, Andre', Chief Executive Officer, Compass Behavioral Center of Lafayette, Lafayette, LA, p. A285
ROBICHAUX, Martha, Chief Human Resources Officer, John C. Fremont Healthcare District, Mariposa, CA, p. A76
ROBICHEAUX, Brian, Chief Information Officer, Peterson Health, Kerrville, TX, p. A632
ROBICHEAUX, James Warren., FACHE, Chief Executive Officer, Matagorda Regional Medical Center, Bay City, TX, p. A601
ROBINETTE, Susie
　MSN, Chief Executive Officer, Kentucky River Medical Center, Jackson, KY, p. A267
　MSN, Chief Nursing Officer, Kentucky River Medical Center, Jackson, KY, p. A267
ROBINSON, Aaron, President and Chief Executive Officer, South County Hospital, Wakefield, RI, p. A561
ROBINSON, Adam M., M.D., Director, Veterans Affairs Maryland Health Care System–Baltimore Division, Baltimore, MD, p. A302
ROBINSON, Anthony, Manager, Human Resources, Mercy Hospital of Folsom, Folsom, CA, p. A63
ROBINSON, Bradley, Chief Financial Officer, Evans U. S. Army Community Hospital, Fort Carson, CO, p. A107
ROBINSON, Candace, Chief Medical Officer, New Orleans East Hospital, New Orleans, LA, p. A290
ROBINSON, Dakota, Interim Chief Financial Officer and Controller, North Caddo Medical Center, Vivian, LA, p. A294
ROBINSON, David
　D.O., Medical Director, St. Joseph's Behavioral Health Center, Stockton, CA, p. A97
　President Medical and Dental Staff, Community Hospital, Munster, IN, p. A224
ROBINSON, Denise M., M.P.H., R.N., Chief Nursing Officer, Loma Linda University Medical Center–Murrieta, Murrieta, CA, p. A79
ROBINSON, Elena, Chief Human Resources Officer, Hima San Pablo Caguas, Caguas, PR, p. A731
ROBINSON, Girard, M.D., Senior Vice President Medical and Clinical Affairs, Mainehealth Behavioral Health At Spring Harbor, Westbrook, ME, p. A299
ROBINSON, Herbert, M.D., Vice President, Chief Medical Information Officer, North Oaks Health System, North Oaks Rehabilitation Hospital, Hammond, LA, p. A282
ROBINSON, James L.
　III, PsyD, Senior Vice President/Area Manager, Sacramento and South Sacramento, Kaiser Permanente Sacramento Medical Center, Sacramento, CA, p. A86
　III, PsyD, Senior Vice President/Area Manager, Sacramento and South Sacramento, Kaiser Permanente South Sacramento Medical Center, Sacramento, CA, p. A87
ROBINSON, Jeanne, Director Human Resources, Inova Fair Oaks Hospital, Fairfax, VA, p. A675
ROBINSON, Jeffrey, President and Chief Executive Officer, Mclaren Bay Special Care, Bay City, MI, p. A322
ROBINSON, Jennifer B, Vice President Human Resources, HCA Florida St. Petersburg Hospital, Saint Petersburg, FL, p. A149
ROBINSON, Loren, M.D., Chief Medical Officer, Christus St. Michael Health System, Texarkana, TX, p. A656
ROBINSON, Mark, Associate Administrator and Chief Financial Officer, Hazel Hawkins Memorial Hospital, Hollister, CA, p. A67
ROBINSON, Mary, Chief Nursing Officer and Vice President Patient Care Services, Texas Health Harris Methodist Hospital Southwest Fort Worth, Fort Worth, TX, p. A620
ROBINSON, Phil, Chief Financial Officer, Saint Agnes Medical Center, Fresno, CA, p. A65
ROBINSON, Stephen Jr, FACHE, Chief Executive Officer, Ochsner Medical Center – Kenner, Kenner, LA, p. A284
ROBINSON, Susan Beth, Vice President Human Resources, St. Mary's Medical Center, Huntington, WV, p. A701
ROBINSON, Tim, Chief Executive Officer, Nationwide Children's Hospital, Columbus, OH, p. A492
ROBINSON, Trena, Director, Human Resources, Central Texas Rehabilitation Hospital, Austin, TX, p. A599
ROBINSON, Vance, Chief Information Officer, Iberia Medical Center, New Iberia, LA, p. A289
ROBINSON, William, Director Human Resources, Encompass Health Rehabilitation Hospital of Erie, Erie, PA, p. A539

Index of Health Care Professionals / Robison

ROBISON, Cheri, Human Resources Director, Riverview Health Institute, Dayton, OH, p. A494
ROBISON, Keith, Chief Information Officer, UPMC Chautauqua, Jamestown, NY, p. A444
ROBISON, Neely, Director Human Resources, The Bridgeway, North Little Rock, AR, p. A51
ROBISON, Rob, Director Information Technology, South Arkansas Regional Hospital, El Dorado, AR, p. A45
ROBISON, Ryan, Chief Nursing Officer, Sanpete Valley Hospital, Mount Pleasant, UT, p. A666
ROBISON, Wendell, M.D., Chief of Staff, Sheridan Va Medical Center, Sheridan, WY, p. A728
ROBITAILLE, Mark E, FACHE, President and Chief Executive Officer, Cleveland Clinic Martin North Hospital, Stuart, FL, p. A150
ROBL, Chris, Human Resources, Ellinwood District Hospital, Ellinwood, KS, p. A248
ROBLES, Burt, Vice President Information Services, Guthrie Robert Packer Hospital, Sayre, PA, p. A554
ROCHA, Julie, Vice President Human Resources, Mercy Medical Center Merced, Merced, CA, p. A77
ROCHE, Maurice, Chief Human Resources Officer, Howard University Hospital, Washington, DC, p. A123
ROCHELEAU, John, Vice President Business Support and Information Technology, Bellin Hospital, Green Bay, WI, p. A712
ROCHER, Leslie, Senior Vice President and Chief Medical Officer, Corewell Health William Beaumont University Hospital, Royal Oak, MI, p. A336
ROCK, Betty Ann, Vice President Nursing and Chief Nursing Officer, WVU Medicine Uniontown Hospital, Uniontown, PA, p. A556
ROCK, Brian, Director of Information Systems, VCU Health Community Memorial Hospital, South Hill, VA, p. A684
ROCK, David, Executive Vice President and Chief Operating Officer, Wyckoff Heights Medical Center, New York, NY, p. A453
ROCKWELL, Karla, Director of Nursing, Doctors Memorial Hospital, Bonifay, FL, p. A126
ROCKWOOD, John D., President, Medstar National Rehabilitation Hospital, Washington, DC, p. A123
ROCKWOOD, Sylvia, Director Human Resources, UPMC Carlisle, Carlisle, PA, p. A536
RODDEN, Celeste, Chief Information Officer, Hillcrest Hospital Claremore, Claremore, OK, p. A511
RODDY, Thomas, Chief Operating Officer, Ascension Saint Thomas Rutherford, Murfreesboro, TN, p. A590
RODEN, George
  Vice President Human Resources, Mercy Hospital Aurora, Aurora, MO, p. A371
  Vice President Human Resources, Mercy Hospital Cassville, Cassville, MO, p. A373
RODENBAUGH, Cathy, Director Human Resources, Holy Rosary Healthcare, Miles City, MT, p. A394
RODENBERGER, Wendy, Chief Nursing Officer and Vice President, Patient Services, Mary Rutan Hospital, Bellefontaine, OH, p. A486
RODENFELS, Cheryl, System Vice President, IT Operations, Ascension Saint Mary – Chicago, Chicago, IL, p. A188
RODER, Darla, Chief Operating Officer, Langdon Prairie Health, Langdon, ND, p. A482
RODERMAN, Nicki, Chief Nursing Officer, St. Mark's Hospital, Salt Lake City, UT, p. A669
RODEWALD, Amanda, Interim Chief Financial Officer, Daviess Community Hospital, Washington, IN, p. A229
RODGE, Mark, Director Information Systems, Eaton Rapids Medical Center, Eaton Rapids, MI, p. A326
RODGERS, April, Vice President, Human Resources, Holy Name Medical Center, Teaneck, NJ, p. A429
RODGERS, Dondie, Interim Chief Nursing Officer, Memorial Hospital of Texas County Authority, Guymon, OK, p. A513
RODGERS, Jamie
  Administrator, North Mississipp. Medical Center Gilmore–Amory, Amory, MS, p. A359
  Administrator, North Mississipp. Medical Center–Pontotoc, Pontotoc, MS, p. A368
RODGERS, Larry, Market Chief Executive Officer, Kindred Hospital–St. Louis, Saint Louis, MO, p. A383
RODOWICZ, Darlene, President and Chief Executive Officer, Berkshire Medical Center, Pittsfield, MA, p. A317
RODRIGUES, Pablo, M.D., Medical Director, KPC Promise Hospital of Amarillo, Amarillo, TX, p. A596
RODRIGUEZ, Alex
  Vice President and Chief Information Officer, St. Elizabeth Edgewood, Edgewood, KY, p. A265
  Vice President and Chief Information Officer, St. Elizabeth Florence, Florence, KY, p. A265
  Vice President and Chief Information Officer, St. Elizabeth Fort Thomas, Fort Thomas, KY, p. A266

RODRIGUEZ, Amy, Chief Executive Officer, Vibra Hospital of Clear Lake, Webster, TX, p. A661
RODRIGUEZ, Andre, Administrator, Hima San Pablo Caguas, Caguas, PR, p. A731
RODRIGUEZ, Anna Liza, Chief Nursing Officer, Fox Chase Cancer Center, Philadelphia, PA, p. A548
RODRIGUEZ, Asha, Vice President and Facility Executive, Atrium Health Cabarrus, Concord, NC, p. A466
RODRIGUEZ, Betsy, Vice President Human Resources, Barnes-Jewish Hospital, Saint Louis, MO, p. A383
RODRIGUEZ, Candie, Director Human Resources, Hospital Menonita Ponce, Coto Laurel, PR, p. A732
RODRIGUEZ, Edgardo, Director Management Information Systems, Auxilio Mutuo Hospital, San Juan, PR, p. A734
RODRIGUEZ, Heather, Chief Nursing Officer, Fresno Heart And Surgical Hospital, Fresno, CA, p. A64
RODRIGUEZ, Jaime, Chief Financial Officer, San Juan City Hospital, San Juan, PR, p. A736
RODRIGUEZ, Jose Luis., Executive Director, San Jorge Children's And Women Hospital, Santurce, PR, p. A736
RODRIGUEZ, Jose O, M.D., Medical Director, Castaner General Hospital, Castaner, PR, p. A732
RODRIGUEZ, Joshua, Chief Executive Officer, Windmoor Healthcare of Clearwater, Clearwater, FL, p. A128
RODRIGUEZ, Laura
  Chief Executive Officer, Kindred Hospital Houston Medical Center, Houston, TX, p. A626
  Director Medical Records, Hospital Del Maestro, San Juan, PR, p. A735
RODRIGUEZ, Leticia, Chief Executive Officer, Ward Memorial Hospital, Monahans, TX, p. A640
RODRIGUEZ, Maritza, Chief Financial Officer, Hospital Metropolitano, San Juan, PR, p. A735
RODRIGUEZ, Miguel, Medical Director, Caribbean Medical Center, Fajardo, PR, p. A732
RODRIGUEZ, Onel
  Chief Financial Officer, Broward Health Coral Springs, Coral Springs, FL, p. A129
  Chief Financial Officer, HCA Florida Aventura Hospital, Aventura, FL, p. A125
RODRIGUEZ, Oscar, Chief Fiscal Officer, Veterans Affairs Caribbean Healthcare System, San Juan, PR, p. A736
RODRIGUEZ, Ramon J., President and Chief Executive Officer, Wyckoff Heights Medical Center, New York, NY, p. A453
RODRIGUEZ, Randy, Hospital Administrator, State Hospital South, Blackfoot, ID, p. A179
RODRIGUEZ, Rudy, Human Resources Director, Arrowhead Regional Medical Center, Colton, CA, p. A60
RODRIGUEZ, Rufus, M.D., Medical Director, Mayo Clinic Health System In Fairmont, Fairmont, MN, p. A346
RODRIGUEZ, Sara
  Chief Financial Officer, Kindred Hospital Sugar Land, Sugar Land, TX, p. A654
  Human Resources, Ascension Seton Smithville, Smithville, TX, p. A653
RODRIGUEZ, Tammy, Vice President Patient Care Services, Adventhealth Central Texas, Killeen, TX, p. A632
RODRIGUEZ, Tomas, Chief Information Technology Officer, First Hospital Panamericano, Cidra, PR, p. A732
RODRIGUEZ, Tony, Director Human Resources, South Texas Rehabilitation Hospital, Brownsville, TX, p. A605
RODRIGUEZ, Vilma, Director Human Resources, Hospital San Pablo Del Este Hima Fajardo, Fajardo, PR, p. A732
RODRIGUEZ, Wilfredo, M.D., Chief of Staff, Battle Creek Veterans Affairs Medical Center, Battle Creek, MI, p. A322
RODRIGUEZ, Yolanda, Chief Nursing Officer, Bakersfield Rehabilitation Hospital, Bakersfield, CA, p. A57
RODRIGUEZ DIAZ, Yarimir, Executive Director, Hospital Del Maestro, San Juan, PR, p. A735
RODRIGUEZ SCHMIDT, Myriam T, Director Human Resources, Cardiovascular Center of Puerto Rico And The Caribbean, San Juan, PR, p. A734
RODRIQUEZ, Daisy, Director Human Resources, Fort Duncan Regional Medical Center, Eagle Pass, TX, p. A615
ROE, Jared, Chief Executive Officer, Ascension Saint Thomas Behavioral Health Hospital, Nashville, TN, p. A590
ROEBACK, Jason, Chief Operating Officer, AHN Grove City, Grove City, PA, p. A541
ROEBKEN, Curtis, M.D., Chief Medical Staff, Kentfield Hospital, Kentfield, CA, p. A68
ROEBUCK, Amanda, Chief Executive Officer, Genoa Medical Facilities, Genoa, NE, p. A400
ROEDEL, Megan, Chief Operating Officer, Center for Behavioral Medicine, Kansas City, MO, p. A377
ROEDER, Donna, Chief Financial Officer, Jackson County Regional Health Center, Maquoketa, IA, p. A239
ROEHLING, Alex, Chief Financial Officer, Holland Hospital, Holland, MI, p. A330
ROEHRLE, Andreas, Director Finance, Sentara Williamsburg Regional Medical Center, Williamsburg, VA, p. A685

ROES, Erin
  R.N., MSN, Chief Executive Officer, Central Louisiana Surgical Hospital, Alexandria, LA, p. A276
  R.N., MSN, Chief Operating Officer, Central Louisiana Surgical Hospital, Alexandria, LA, p. A276
ROESLER, Bruce E., FACHE, Chief Executive Officer, Richland Hospital, Richland Center, WI, p. A720
ROESLER, Dana, R.N., Chief Executive Officer, Desert Valley Hospital, Victorville, CA, p. A100
ROETMAN, James D., President and Chief Executive Officer, Pocahontas Community Hospital, Pocahontas, IA, p. A242
ROEVER, Judy, MSN, R.N., Chief Nursing Officer, Scenic Mountain Medical Center, Big Spring, TX, p. A603
ROGALSKI, Robert, President, Sharon Regional Medical Center, Sharon, PA, p. A555
ROGALSKI, Ted
  Administrator, Genesis Medical Center–Aledo, Aledo, IL, p. A185
  Administrator, Genesis Medical Center, Dewitt, De Witt, IA, p. A234
ROGAN, Edie, Manager Human Resources, Eastern State Hospital, Williamsburg, VA, p. A685
ROGAN, James, M.D., Chief Medical Officer, Perry County Memorial Hospital, Tell City, IN, p. A227
ROGERS, Aaron, Chief Executive Officer, Trinity Hospital, Weaverville, CA, p. A101
ROGERS, B. Carter, Chief of Staff, Piedmont Newton Hospital, Covington, GA, p. A162
ROGERS, Cathy M, Manager Human Resources, Prisma Health Laurens County Hospital, Clinton, SC, p. A564
ROGERS, Doris, Vice President Human Resources, Saint Luke's Hospital of Kansas City, Kansas City, MO, p. A378
ROGERS, Eric, Chief Information Officer, Hebrew Rehabilitation Center, Roslindale, MA, p. A317
ROGERS, Jeremy
  FACHE, Chief Financial Officer, Our Lady of Lourdes Regional Medical Center, Lafayette, LA, p. A286
  FACHE, Chief Operating Officer and Chief Financial Officer, St. Francis Medical Center, Monroe, LA, p. A289
  FACHE, Vice President and Chief Operating Officer, St. Francis Medical Center, Monroe, LA, p. A289
ROGERS, Jeremy H, Chief Human Resource Officer, Orem Community Hospital, Orem, UT, p. A667
ROGERS, Jerry, R.N., Director Nurses and Infection Control, Specialty Hospital, Monroe, LA, p. A289
ROGERS, Josep. J, Vice President and Chief Operating Officer, Providence Redwood Memorial Hospital, Fortuna, CA, p. A63
ROGERS, Kathy, Vice President Marketing, San Luis Valley Health Conejos County Hospital, La Jara, CO, p. A110
ROGERS, LaDonna, Executive Vice President Human Resources, T. J. Samson Community Hospital, Glasgow, KY, p. A266
ROGERS, Leslie M., President and Chief Executive Officer, South Shore Hospital, Chicago, IL, p. A191
ROGERS, Lucy, Chief Information Resource Management Systems, Dallas Va North Texas Hcs, Dallas, TX, p. A611
ROGERS, Marceline, Senior Vice President, Chief Operating Officer, Service Line Leader, Parkview Ortho Hospital, Fort Wayne, IN, p. A217
ROGERS, Mark G
  Interim Vice President Finance and Chief Financial Officer, Genesis Medical Center, Silvis, Silvis, IL, p. A208
  Vice President, Finance and Chief Financial Officer, Genesis Medical Center–Aledo, Aledo, IL, p. A185
ROGERS, Matt, Chief Financial Officer, Wellspan Philhaven, Mount Gretna, PA, p. A546
ROGERS, Maureen, Executive Director, Specialty Hospital of Central Jersey, Lakewood, NJ, p. A422
ROGERS, Patricia, Director of Nursing, Dahl Memorial Healthcare Association, Ekalaka, MT, p. A391
ROGERS, Paul, Interim Chief Financial Officer, Gila Regional Medical Center, Silver City, NM, p. A437
ROGERS, Randy, FACHE, Chief Executive Officer, Fountain Valley Regional Hospital And Medical Center, Fountain Valley, CA, p. A64
ROGERS, Rich, Vice President Information Services, Prisma Health Greenville Memorial Hospital, Greenville, SC, p. A567
ROGERS, Richard, M.D., Chief Medical Officer, Ascension Saint Thomas Rutherford, Murfreesboro, TN, p. A590
ROGERS, Robert T, M.D., II, Medical Director, Canton–Potsdam Hospital, Potsdam, NY, p. A456
ROGERS, Sherron, Chief Financial Officer, Johns Hopkins All Children's Hospital, Saint Petersburg, FL, p. A149
ROGERS, Tammy, Director Human Resources, Mt. San Rafael Hospital, Trinidad, CO, p. A114
ROGERS, Thomas J., M.D., Vice President, Cleveland Clinic Union Hospital, Dover, OH, p. A495

Index of Health Care Professionals / Rosenberg

Index of Health Care Professionals

ROGERS, Valerie J, Director of Nursing, Cherokee Nation W.W. Hastings Hospital, Tahlequah, OK, p. A521
ROGERS, William, Chief Medical Officer, North Mississipp. Medical Center Gilmore–Amory, Amory, MS, p. A359
ROGOLS, Kevin L., FACHE, Administrator/CEO, Kalkaska Memorial Health Center, Kalkaska, MI, p. A331
ROGOZ, Brian, Vice President Finance and Treasurer, The Hospital of Central Connecticut, New Britain, CT, p. A117
ROHAN, Colleen M., Director Human Resources, OSF Healthcare Little Company of Mary Medical Center, Evergreen Park, IL, p. A195
ROHAN, Patrick, FACHE, Chief Executive Officer, Good Samaritan Hospital – San Jose, San Jose, CA, p. A92
ROHLEDER, Scott, Chief Information Officer, Hays Medical Center, Hays, KS, p. A250
ROHMAN, Ryan
MSN, R.N., Chief Operating Officer, UCHealth Medical Center of The Rockies, Loveland, CO, p. A112
MSN, R.N., Chief Operating Officer, UCHealth Poudre Valley Hospital, Fort Collins, CO, p. A108
MSN, R.N., President, UCHealth Broomfield Hospital, Broomfield, CO, p. A104
MSN, R.N., President, UCHealth Longs Peak Hospital, Longmont, CO, p. A111
ROHRBACH, Dan D., President, Southwest Health, Platteville, WI, p. A719
ROHRBACK, Allen, Chief Executive Officer, Madison Valley Medical Center, Ennis, MT, p. A391
ROHRBACK, Jenny, Director Human Resource, Ruby Valley Medical Center, Sheridan, MT, p. A396
ROHRER, Harry, Chief Financial Officer, UMHC–Sylvester Comprehensive Cancer Center, Miami, FL, p. A141
ROIZ, JoAnn, Director Human Resources, Encompass Health Rehabilitation Hospital of Tustin, Tustin, CA, p. A99
ROJAS, Anna, Chief Executive Officer, Continuecare Hospital At Hendrick Medical Center, Abilene, TX, p. A595
ROJAS, Curtis, Interim Chief Financial Officer, Connally Memorial Medical Center, Floresville, TX, p. A618
ROJAS–SANCHEZ, Dina, Chief Executive Officer, Carondelet Holy Cross Hospital, Nogales, AZ, p. A34
ROKER, Christopher, Chief Executive Officer, NYC Health + Hospitals/Lincoln, New York, NY, p. A451
ROKOSZ, Gregory, D.O., Senior Vice President Medical and Academic Affairs, Cooperman Barnabas Medical Center, Livingston, NJ, p. A423
ROKUSEK, Brian, President and Chief Executive Officer, Thayer County Health Services, Hebron, NE, p. A401
ROLAND, Brian, Chief Executive Officer, Stephens Memorial Hospital, Breckenridge, TX, p. A604
ROLAND, John, R.N., Chief Operating Officer and Chief Nursing Officer, Bleckley Memorial Hospital, Cochran, GA, p. A160
ROLDAN, Lanyce, Chief Nursing Officer, Penn Medicine Lancaster General Health, Lancaster, PA, p. A543
ROLEK, Jim, Chief Human Resources Officer, Vice President, Clara Maass Medical Center, Belleville, NJ, p. A418
ROLEY, Margaret
Chief Executive Officer, South Baldwin Regional Medical Center, Foley, AL, p. A19
Chief Nursing Officer, South Baldwin Regional Medical Center, Foley, AL, p. A19
ROLFE, David, Chief Information Officer, Madonna Rehabilitation Hospital, Lincoln, NE, p. A402
ROLFF, Christi, Director Business Development, San Joaquin Valley Rehabilitation Hospital, Fresno, CA, p. A65
ROLING, Robin, FACHE, MS, R.N., Chief Operating Officer, Cheyenne Regional Medical Center, Cheyenne, WY, p. A726
ROLLI, Molli Martha, M.D., Medical Director, Mendota Mental Health Institute, Madison, WI, p. A714
ROLLINS, James, Chief Financial Officer, Arbour–Fuller Hospital, Attleboro, MA, p. A309
ROLLINS, Larry, Supervisor Information Technology, Mccamey County Hospital District, Mccamey, TX, p. A638
ROLLINS, Skip. Chief Information Officer, Freeman Health System, Joplin, MO, p. A377
ROLLINS, Vicki, President, La Downtown Medical Center, Llc, Los Angeles, CA, p. A73
ROMAN, Jody, Chief Human Resource Officer, Hillside Rehabilitation Hospital, Warren, OH, p. A506
ROMAN, Marina, M.D., Medical Director, Hospital De La Universidad De Puerto Rico/Dr. Federico Trilla, Carolina, PR, p. A732
ROMAN, Rebecca, Administrator, Whittier Rehabilitation Hospital, Westborough, MA, p. A319
ROMAN, Tracy, Chief Executive Officer, Memorial Medical Center, Modesto, CA, p. A78
ROMANELLO, Marcus, Chief Medical Officer, Kettering Health Hamilton, Hamilton, OH, p. A497
ROMANIA, Matt, Director of Nursing, UPMC Wellsboro, Wellsboro, PA, p. A557
ROMANICK, Odile, Chief information Officer, Day Kimball Hospital, Putnam, CT, p. A118
ROMANIELLO, Guy, Director Fiscal Services, Belmont Behavioral Health System, Philadelphia, PA, p. A548
ROMANO, Jean, Chief Nursing Officer, Good Shepherd Penn Partners, Philadelphia, PA, p. A548
ROMANO, William, Director Information Systems and Privacy, Wills Eye Hospital, Philadelphia, PA, p. A550
ROMANOWSKI, Ellen, Chief Nursing Officer, Encompass Health Rehabilitation Hospital of Miami, Cutler Bay, FL, p. A129
ROMANS, Alan, Director Information Technology, Ashland Health Center, Ashland, KS, p. A246
ROMEO, John, Chief Information Officer, Insight Hospital And Medical Center, Chicago, IL, p. A189
ROMERO, Brenda, Hospital Chief, Presbyterian Espanola Hospital, Espanola, NM, p. A434
ROMERO, Edward, Chief Financial Officer, Rehabilitation Hospital of Fort Wayne, Fort Wayne, IN, p. A217
ROMERO, Frank
M.D., Chief Medical Officer, Cox North Hospital, Springfield, MO, p. A386
M.D., Vice President Medical Affairs and Chief Medical Officer, Cox Monett Hospital, Inc, Monett, MO, p. A380
ROMERO, Kevin M., Chief Executive Officer, Lafayette Physical Rehabilitation Hospital, Lafayette, LA, p. A285
ROMERO, Matt, Chief Financial Officer, HCA Florida Oak Hill Hospital, Brooksville, FL, p. A127
ROMIG, Barbara DNP, RN, Chief Nursing Officer, Reading Hospital, West Reading, PA, p. A557
ROMIG, Glenn, Chief Financial Officer, HCA Florida Largo Hospital, Largo, FL, p. A137
ROMINE, Andrew
R.N., Chief Executive Officer, Shorepoint Health Port Charlotte, Port Charlotte, FL, p. A147
R.N., Chief Executive Officer, Shorepoint Health Punta Gorda, Punta Gorda, FL, p. A148
ROMITO, Edmund J, Chief Information Officer, Genesis Healthcare System, Zanesville, OH, p. A508
ROMO, Dianna, Director, Human Resources, Emanuel Medical Center, Turlock, CA, p. A98
ROMO, Justin, Director of Information Technology, Pocahontas Community Hospital, Pocahontas, IA, p. A242
ROMUALDO, Heather, Chief Information Officer, Intermountain Medical Center, Murray, UT, p. A666
RONAN, John
President, Northern Light Blue Hill Hospital, Blue Hill, ME, p. A296
President, Northern Light Maine Coast Hospital, Ellsworth, ME, p. A297
RONCA, Cyndi, Director Human Resources, HCA Florida Twin Cities Hospital, Niceville, FL, p. A142
RONDE, Christa, Assistant Chief Financial Officer, Palo Verde Hospital, Blythe, CA, p. A58
RONKE, Lisa, Director Finance, St. Michael's Hospital Avera, Tyndall, SD, p. A577
RONN, Michael, Hospital Commander, Tripler Army Medical Center, Honolulu, HI, p. A176
RONNISCH, Kim, Vice President Nursing and Chief Nursing Officer, Ascension Macomb–Oakland Hospital, Warren Campus, Warren, MI, p. A340
ROOD, Mandy, Vice President Human Resources, University of Michigan Health–Sparrow Eaton, Charlotte, MI, p. A323
ROOKER, Mark, Chief Executive Officer, Hillsboro Community Hospital, Hillsboro, KS, p. A250
ROONERY, Nicole, Chief Nursing Officer, Ivinson Memorial Hospital, Laramie, WY, p. A727
ROONEY, Al, Director Information Systems, SCL Health Mt – St. Vincent Healthcare, Billings, MT, p. A390
ROONEY, David, Administrator Operations, Winnmed, Decorah, IA, p. A234
ROONEY, Thomas, Chief Information Resource Management, Veterans Affairs Hudson Valley Health Care System, Montrose, NY, p. A446
ROOP, Terri
Assistant Vice President and Administrator, Dickenson Community Hospital, Clintwood, VA, p. A675
Director Patient Care Services, Dickenson Community Hospital, Clintwood, VA, p. A675
ROOSA, Carol, Vice President Information Services and Chief Information Officer, Athol Hospital, Athol, MA, p. A309
ROOSE, Robert
M.D., Chief Executive Officer, Johnson Memorial Hospital, Stafford Springs, CT, p. A119
M.D., Chief Medical Officer, Mercy Medical Center, Springfield, MA, p. A318
ROOT, Jim, Administrator, Gundersen Saint Elizabeth's Hospital & Clinics, Wabasha, MN, p. A356
ROOT, Rodney Mark, D.O., Vice President Medical Affairs, Bakersfield Memorial Hospital, Bakersfield, CA, p. A56
ROPER, Anne, Chief Executive Officer, UF Health Rehab Hospital, Gainesville, FL, p. A132
ROPER, Sandra, Chief Human Resources, General Leonard Wood Army Community Hospital, Fort Leonard Wood, MO, p. A375
ROQUE, John
MSN, R.N., Chief Nursing Officer, Medical Center of Aurora, Aurora, CO, p. A103
MSN, R.N., Chief Nursing Officer, Spalding Rehabilitation Hospital, Aurora, CO, p. A103
RORRER, Michael, M.D., Chief of Medical Staff, Carilion Tazewell Community Hospital, Tazewell, VA, p. A684
ROSA–TOLEDO, Luis R, M.D., Medical Director, Hospital Manati Medical Center, Manati, PR, p. A733
ROSADO, Jose Samuel, Chief Executive Officer, Bayamon Medical Center, Bayamon, PR, p. A731
ROSADO, Jose Samuel., Chief Executive Officer, Bayamon Medical Center, Bayamon, PR, p. A731
ROSALES, Alvina, R.N., Chief Nursing Officer, Tuba City Regional Health Care Corporation, Tuba City, AZ, p. A40
ROSAS, Efren, M.D., Physician in Chief, Kaiser Permanente San Jose Medical Center, San Jose, CA, p. A92
ROSATI, Rosemarie, Chief Operating Officer, Rutgers University Behavioral Healthcare, Piscataway, NJ, p. A427
ROSBOROUGH, Brian S, M.D., Chief Medical Officer, OSF Saint Elizabeth Medical Center, Ottawa, IL, p. A204
ROSCHMANN, Al, M.D., Chief of Staff, Peterson Health, Kerrville, TX, p. A632
ROSE, Blake, Chief Executive Officer, Cache Valley Hospital, North Logan, UT, p. A666
ROSE, Cheryl, Human Resources Director, Fulton County Medical Center, Mc Connellsburg, PA, p. A545
ROSE, Hugh, Vice President Fiscal Management, Northwestern Medicine Palos Hospital, Palos Heights, IL, p. A205
ROSE, Julia, R.N., Director of Nursing, Braxton County Memorial Hospital, Gassaway, WV, p. A700
ROSE, Kenneth, President and Chief Executive Officer, UChicago Medicine Adventhealth Bolingbrook, Bolingbrook, IL, p. A186
ROSE, Kim, Chief Information Technology, Crouse Health, Syracuse, NY, p. A460
ROSE, Laura L, Chief Financial Officer, Ascension St. Vincent Anderson, Anderson, IN, p. A212
ROSE, Mary, Chief Nursing Officer, Promedica Coldwater Regional Hospital, Coldwater, MI, p. A324
ROSE, Mary R, R.N., Chief Clinical Officer, Promedica Coldwater Regional Hospital, Coldwater, MI, p. A324
ROSE, May, Director Human Resources, Memorial Hospital, Chester, IL, p. A188
ROSE, Michaell, Chief Operating Officer, St. Joseph's Medical Center, Stockton, CA, p. A97
ROSE, Richard T, Associate Director, Manchester Veterans Affairs Medical Center, Manchester, NH, p. A416
ROSE, Robin, R.N., Chief Operating and Clinical Officer, Gibson Area Hospital And Health Services, Gibson City, IL, p. A196
ROSE, Robin M., Director of Human Resources, Greene County General Hospital, Linton, IN, p. A222
ROSE, Taylor, Chief Executive Officer, Barrett Hospital & Healthcare, Dillon, MT, p. A391
ROSEMORE, Michael, M.D., Medical Director, Encompass Health Lakeshore Rehabilitation Hospital, Birmingham, AL, p. A16
ROSEN, Barry, M.D., Vice President Medical Management, Advocate Good Shepherd Hospital, Barrington, IL, p. A186
ROSEN, Jules, M.D., Chief Medical Officer, West Springs Hospital, Grand Junction, CO, p. A109
ROSEN, Michael, M.D., Chief Medical Officer, Havasu Regional Medical Center, Lake Havasu City, AZ, p. A32
ROSEN, Raymond, FACHE, Vice President Operations, Wellspan York Hospital, York, PA, p. A559
ROSENA, Robens, Director Information Systems, Delray Medical Center, Delray Beach, FL, p. A130
ROSENBALM, Jennifer, Manager Business Office, Omaha Va Medical Center, Omaha, NE, p. A404
ROSENBAUM, Victor, Chief Operating Officer, Alaska Regional Hospital, Anchorage, AK, p. A27
ROSENBERG, Andrew, M.D., Chief Information Officer, University of Michigan Medical Center, Ann Arbor, MI, p. A321
ROSENBERG, Cynthia
Vice President, Chief Nursing Officer, Dignity Health Arizona General Hospital, Laveen, AZ, p. A33
Vice President, Chief Nursing Officer, Dignity Health Arizona General Hospital Mesa, Llc, Mesa, AZ, p. A33
ROSENBERG, Patricia A
R.N., MSN, Chief Nursing Officer, Palm Beach Gardens Medical Center, Palm Beach Gardens, FL, p. A145

Index of Health Care Professionals / Rosenberg

R.N., MSN, Chief Nursing Officer, Touro Infirmary, New Orleans, LA, p. A290
ROSENBERG, Steven, Chief Financial Officer, Danbury Hospital, Danbury, CT, p. A115
ROSENBERGER, Robert
  Chief Financial Officer, Heritage Valley Beaver, Beaver, PA, p. A535
  Chief Financial Officer, Sewickley Valley Hospital, (A Division of Valley Medical Facilities), Sewickley, PA, p. A555
ROSENBLATT, Mark, M.D., Ph.D., Chief Executive Officer, University of Illinois Hospital, Chicago, IL, p. A192
ROSENBURG, Deborah L, Vice President Human Resources, Chesapeake Regional Medical Center, Chesapeake, VA, p. A674
ROSENCRANCE, Daris, Chief Financial Officer, Mon Health Stonewall Jackson Memorial Hospital, Weston, WV, p. A705
ROSENCRANCE, J. Gregory, M.D., President and Chief Executive Officer, Thomas Memorial Hospital, South Charleston, WV, p. A705
ROSENCRANCE, J. Gregory., M.D., President and Chief Executive Officer, Thomas Memorial Hospital, South Charleston, WV, p. A705
ROSENDAHL, Lisa, Director Human Resources, St. Cloud Va Health Care System, Saint Cloud, MN, p. A354
ROSENFELD, Merryll, Vice President, Human Resources, Catholic Medical Center, Manchester, NH, p. A416
ROSENTHAL, Benjamin, Information Systems Director, South Sunflower County Hospital, Indianola, MS, p. A363
ROSENTHAL, Philip P., Executive Director, Lenox Hill Hospital, New York, NY, p. A449
ROSENTHAL, Raul, M.D., Interim Chief of Staff, Cleveland Clinic Florida, Weston, FL, p. A155
ROSEQUIST, Helen, Manager Information Systems, Warren General Hospital, Warren, PA, p. A556
ROSETTA, Kathy, Chief Nursing Officer, Laurel Ridge Treatment Center, San Antonio, TX, p. A650
ROSHAN, Payman, Senior Vice President and Area Manager, Orange County, Kaiser Permanente Orange County Anaheim Medical Center, Anaheim, CA, p. A55
ROSHETKO, Chet, Chief Nursing Officer, Eastern State Hospital, Medical Lake, WA, p. A691
ROSIER, Elisha, Chief Executive Officer, Plains Memorial Hospital, Dimmitt, TX, p. A614
ROSILES, Nancy, Director Human Resources, Encompass Health Rehabilitation Hospital of Arlington, Arlington, TX, p. A597
ROSKE, Jeff, D.O., Chief Medical Staff, Community Memorial Hospital, Sumner, IA, p. A244
ROSLER, Andrea P, Vice President Human Resources, Huntsville Hospital, Huntsville, AL, p. A21
ROSS, Adia, M.D., M.F.H., Chief Medical Officer, Duke Regional Hospital, Durham, NC, p. A467
ROSS, Allan, Chief Excecutive Officer, Ortonville Area Health Services, Ortonville, MN, p. A352
ROSS, Chad A., President and Chief Executive Officer, Mary Rutan Hospital, Bellefontaine, OH, p. A486
ROSS, Charles, M.D., Vice President Medical Affairs, Chilton Medical Center, Pompton Plains, NJ, p. A427
ROSS, Christopher J., Chief Information Technology Officer, Mayo Clinic Hospital – Rochester, Rochester, MN, p. A353
ROSS, Darrell, Chief Nursing Officer, Dequincy Memorial Hospital, Dequincy, LA, p. A281
ROSS, Denzil
  FACHE, Chief Operating Officer, Indiana University Health Paoli Hospital, Paoli, IN, p. A226
  FACHE, Chief Operating Officer, Lovelace Medical Center, Albuquerque, NM, p. A432
  FACHE, President, Indiana University Health Bedford Hospital, Bedford, IN, p. A212
  FACHE, President, Indiana University Health Bloomington Hospital, Bloomington, IN, p. A213
ROSS, Douglas B., M.D., President and Chief Medical Officer, Chi St. Vincent Hot Springs, Hot Springs, AR, p. A48
ROSS, Jacqueline, Chief Human Resources Officer, Mann–Grandstaff Department of Veterans Affairs Medical Center, Spokane, WA, p. A696
ROSS, James E., President and Chief Executive Officer, Jackson–Madison County General Hospital, Medina, TN, p. A588
ROSS, Jay
  Chief Financial Officer, Chi St. Joseph's Health, Park Rapids, MN, p. A352
  Vice President of Finance, Chi Lakewood Health, Baudette, MN, p. A343
ROSS, Jeffrey
  M.D., Chief Medical Officer, King's Daughters Medical Center, Brookhaven, MS, p. A360
  M.D., Medical Director, Amg Specialty Hospital–Albuquerque, Albuquerque, NM, p. A432
ROSS, Joan, President, Ascension Seton Hays, Kyle, TX, p. A633
ROSS, John, Vice President, Franciscan Health Mooresville, Mooresville, IN, p. A224
ROSS, Johnny Shane, Executive Medical Director, Encompass Health Rehabilitation Hospital of Austin, Austin, TX, p. A600
ROSS, Kevin, M.D., Chief of Medical Staff, Frances Mahon Deaconess Hospital, Glasgow, MT, p. A392
ROSS, Laurie, Chief Nursing Officer, Bon Secours – Southampton Medical Center, Franklin, VA, p. A676
ROSS, Mychelle, R.N., Chief Nursing Officer, Cherokee Medical Center, Gaffney, SC, p. A566
ROSS, Robert, Chief Operating Officer, Medstar Washington Hospital Center, Washington, DC, p. A124
ROSS, Shana, Vice President Human Resources, Bayhealth, Dover, DE, p. A121
ROSS, Yolanda, Director Human Resources, Millwood Hospital, Arlington, TX, p. A597
ROSS–COLE, Melissa, Director Human Resources, Regency Hospital of Northwest Arkansas – Springdale, Springdale, AR, p. A53
ROSSI, Coleen, Director Quality Services, Encompass Health Rehabilitation Hospital of Toms River, Toms River, NJ, p. A429
ROSSI, Lawrence, M.D., Clinical Director, Trenton Psychiatric Hospital, Trenton, NJ, p. A429
ROSSI, Mark F, Chief Operating Officer and General Counsel, Hopedale Medical Complex, Hopedale, IL, p. A198
ROSSI, Matthew, M.D., Chief Executive Officer, Hopedale Medical Complex, Hopedale, IL, p. A198
ROSVOLD, Robert, Director Finance, Virtua Voorhees, Voorhees, NJ, p. A430
ROSZHART, Jay M., President and Chief Executive Officer, Springfield Memorial Hospital, Springfield, IL, p. A209
ROTENBERRY–BAGGETT, Katie, Administrative Assistant and Human Resources, Yalobusha General Hospital, Water Valley, MS, p. A369
ROTERT, Angela Lynne, Chief Clinical Officer, Kindred Hospital–Indianapolis, Indianapolis, IN, p. A220
ROTGER, Lindsey, Chief Nursing Officer, West Tennessee Healthcare Rehabilitation Hospital Cane Creek, A Partnership With Encompass Health, Martin, TN, p. A587
ROTH, Chad, Director Information Services, Prairie View, Newton, KS, p. A256
ROTH, Diane, Chief Financial Officer, Piedmont Rockdale Hospital, Conyers, GA, p. A161
ROTH, Eugene, Vice President Information Services, Mercy Hospital St. Louis, Saint Louis, MO, p. A385
ROTH, Mark A.
  Chief Executive Officer, Encompass Health Valley of The Sun Rehabilitation Hospital, Glendale, AZ, p. A32
  Chief Financial Officer, Mountain Valley Regional Rehabilitation Hospital, Prescott Valley, AZ, p. A37
ROTH, Randy, Chief Medical Officer, Singing River Health System, Pascagoula, MS, p. A367
ROTH–MALLEK, Nancy, Vice President of Finance, Aspirus Riverview Hospital And Clinics, Inc., Wisconsin Rapids, WI, p. A725
ROTHBERG, Kathryn, Director Human Resources, Evergreenhealth Monroe, Monroe, WA, p. A691
ROTHBERGER, Richard, Corporate Executive Vice President and Chief Financial Officer, Scripp. Green Hospital, La Jolla, CA, p. A68
ROTHENBERGER, David, Chief Financial Officer, Summit Healthcare Regional Medical Center, Show Low, AZ, p. A39
ROTHERMICH, Michael, M.D., Chief of Staff, Hermann Area District Hospital, Hermann, MO, p. A376
ROTHMAN, Marc, M.D., Medical Director, Friends Hospital, Philadelphia, PA, p. A548
ROTHSCHILD, Marylee, M.D., Chief of Staff, Robley Rex Department of Veterans Affairs Medical Center, Louisville, KY, p. A270
ROTTINGHAUS, David, M.D., Director, Butler Memorial Hospital, Butler, PA, p. A536
ROTY, Christopher, President, Baptist Health Lexington, Lexington, KY, p. A268
ROUGH, Vicki, Chief Nursing Officer, Penn Highlands Connellsville, Connellsville, PA, p. A537
ROUILLARD, Smita, M.D., Physician in Chief, Kaiser Permanente Fresno Medical Center, Fresno, CA, p. A65
ROULEAU, Greg, Vice President Nursing, Mercy Medical Center Merced, Merced, CA, p. A77
ROUND, Laurie, MS, R.N., Vice President and Chief Nursing Officer, Carle Bromenn Medical Center, Normal, IL, p. A203
ROUNDS, Jason, FACHE, President and Chief Executive Officer, San Juan Regional Medical Center, Farmington, NM, p. A434
ROUNDY, Ann, Vice President of Employee and Support Services, Prairie Ridge Health, Inc., Columbus, WI, p. A709
ROUNSLEY, Joan, Director Human Resources, Geisinger Jersey Shore Hospital, Jersey Shore, PA, p. A542
ROUNSLEY, Karen, Controller, Encompass Health Rehabilitation Hospital of Salisbury, Salisbury, MD, p. A307
ROUSH, D. Channing., Facility Executive, Atrium Health's Carolinas Medical Center, Charlotte, NC, p. A465
ROUSSE, Michael, M.D., Chief Medical Officer, Northeastern Vermont Regional Hospital, Saint Johnsbury, VT, p. A672
ROUSSEAU, Mickie, Director Human Resources, Terrebonne General Health System, Houma, LA, p. A283
ROUSSEL, Steve
  Chief Financial Officer, Baylor Scott & White Medical Center at – Mckinney, Mckinney, TX, p. A638
  Vice President Finance, Baylor Scott & White Medical Center–Irving, Irving, TX, p. A630
ROUSSOS, Michael
  Administrator, University Health, San Antonio, TX, p. A651
  President, VCU Medical Center, Richmond, VA, p. A683
ROUTH, Lori, R.N., Nurse Administrator, Mayo Clinic Health System – Albert Lea And Austin, Albert Lea, MN, p. A342
ROUX, Roger, Chief Financial Officer, Rady Children's Hospital – San Diego, San Diego, CA, p. A89
ROUZER, Cindy, Director Human Resources, Spooner Health, Spooner, WI, p. A721
ROVITO, Kevin, Chief Financial Officer, Jackson Hospital, Marianna, FL, p. A138
ROW, Tracy, Manager Business Office, Fredonia Regional Hospital, Fredonia, KS, p. A249
ROW, Tyler, Director Information Technology, Fredonia Regional Hospital, Fredonia, KS, p. A249
ROWAN, Cary, Chief Financial Officer, Astria Sunnyside Hospital, Sunnyside, WA, p. A696
ROWAN, Mark, Vice President, Chief Information Officer, Rome Health, Rome, NY, p. A458
ROWAN, R C, Director Human Resources, Neosho Memorial Regional Medical Center, Chanute, KS, p. A247
ROWE, Chad, Human Resource Director, Aspirus Keweenaw Hospital, Laurium, MI, p. A332
ROWE, Jeanne M, M.D., Chief Medical Officer, Shore Medical Center, Somers Point, NJ, p. A428
ROWE, Melissa S., Chief Executive Officer, Grover C. Dils Medical Center, Caliente, NV, p. A408
ROWE, Paul W, Director Information Technology, St. Francis Hospital, Wilmington, DE, p. A122
ROWE, Scott, Chief Executive Officer, Encompass Health Rehabilitation Hospital of Chattanooga, Chattanooga, TN, p. A580
ROWE, Wilma, M.D., Senior Vice President Medical Affairs, Mercy Medical Center, Baltimore, MD, p. A301
ROWELL, Becky, R.N., Director, Allendale County Hospital, Fairfax, SC, p. A566
ROWELL, Julie, R.N., Chief Nursing Officer, Thomas Hospital, Fairhope, AL, p. A19
ROWELL, LeAnne, Director of Nursing, D. W. Mcmillan Memorial Hospital, Brewton, AL, p. A17
ROWLAND, Claire, Director Human Resources, Vermilion Behavioral Health Systems – North Campus, Lafayette, LA, p. A286
ROWLAND, Gerald, M.D., Chief Medical Officer, Cedar City Hospital, Cedar City, UT, p. A664
ROWLAND, Michael, M.D., Vice President Medical Affairs, Franklin Memorial Hospital, Farmington, ME, p. A297
ROWLAND, Nick
  Chief Executive Officer, Choctaw Memorial Hospital, Hugo, OK, p. A513
  Chief Executive Officer, Pushmataha Hospital, Antlers, OK, p. A509
  Chief Operating Officer, Pushmataha Hospital, Antlers, OK, p. A509
ROWLAND, Robert, M.D., Medical Director, Encompass Health Rehabilitation Hospital of Tallahassee, Tallahassee, FL, p. A151
ROWLAND, Ruby, Strategic Partner, Highlands–Cashiers Hospital, Highlands, NC, p. A470
ROWLAND, Ted, Chief of Medical Staff, Atoka County Medical Center, Atoka, OK, p. A510
ROWLANDS, Dewey R, Vice President and Chief Financial Officer, Rome Health, Rome, NY, p. A458
ROWLEY, Charla, Chief Executive Officer, Southwest Mississipp. Regional Medical Center, Mccomb, MS, p. A366
ROWLEY, Heather, R.N., Administrator, Singing River Gulfport, Gulfport, MS, p. A363
ROWLEY, Mike, Chief Executive Officer, Springbrook Behavioral Health, Travelers Rest, SC, p. A571
ROY, Ashley, Vice President of Nursing Services, Ochsner Specialty Hospital, Meridian, MS, p. A366
ROY, Jennifer, R.N., Chief Nursing Officer, Carondelet St. Mary's Hospital, Tucson, AZ, p. A40

Index of Health Care Professionals / Russell

Index of Health Care Professionals

ROY, Linda, R.N., Chief Nursing Officer, Walter B. Jones Alcohol And Drug Abuse Treatment Center, Greenville, NC, p. A470
ROY, Rock, Professional Services Director, Power County Hospital District, American Falls, ID, p. A179
ROY, Schindelheim, M.D., Chief of Staff, George L. Mee Memorial Hospital, King City, CA, p. A68
ROYAL, Keli, Chief Human Resources Officer, Shenandoah Medical Center, Shenandoah, IA, p. A243
ROYAL, Shawanna, R.N., Director Nursing, Strategic Behavioral Health, Llc, Garner, NC, p. A468
ROYAL, Ty, Executive Director of Human Resources and Support Services, Gibson Area Hospital And Health Services, Gibson City, IL, p. A196
ROYE, G. Dean, M.D., Senior Vice President of Medical Affairs and Chief Medical Officer, Miriam Hospital, Providence, RI, p. A560
ROYSTON, Aaron, Vice President, Rural Health Transformation and Executive Director, University of Maryland Shore Medical Center At Chestertown, Chestertown, MD, p. A303
ROZELL, Becky, Vice President, Human Resources, Madison Health, London, OH, p. A498
ROZENBOOM, Steve, Chief Financial Officer, Holy Cross Hospital, Taos, NM, p. A437
ROZENFELD, Jon, Market President, UnityPoint Health – Des Moines, Unitypoint Health–Des Moines, Des Moines, IA, p. A235
ROZIER, Derek, Chief Financial Officer, Liberty Regional Medical Center, Hinesville, GA, p. A165
ROZNOVSKY, Karen, Director Human Resources, Yoakum Community Hospital, Yoakum, TX, p. A663
RUBANO, Kathleen A, MSN, R.N., Chief Nursing Officer, Corpus Christi Medical Center – Doctors Regional, Corpus Christi, TX, p. A609
RUBE, David M, M.D., Clinical Director, New York City Children's Center, New York, NY, p. A450
RUBEN, Wanda, R.N., Chief Nursing Officer, Garden Grove Hospital And Medical Center, Garden Grove, CA, p. A65
RUBENS, Deborah, Director Human Resources, Shriners Children's – Northern California, Sacramento, CA, p. A87
RUBERG, Greg, FACHE, President and Chief Executive Officer, Aspirus Lake View Hospital, Two Harbors, MN, p. A356
RUBERTI, Charlene, Director Information Technology Development, Ancora Psychiatric Hospital, Hammonton, NJ, p. A422
RUBIN, Nancy, Vice President Human Resources, MPTF/ Motion Picture & Television Fund, Los Angeles, CA, p. A74
RUBIN, Vincent, Chief Financial Officer, Southern California Hospital At Culver City, Culver City, CA, p. A61
RUBINATE, Donna, R.N., Chief Operating Officer, Good Samaritan Medical Center, Brockton, MA, p. A311
RUBINO, Lucy, Hospital Administrator and Chief Executive Officer, Hudson County Meadowview Psychiatric Hospital, Secaucus, NJ, p. A428
RUBINO, Mark
M.D., President, Allegheny Valley Hospital, Natrona Heights, PA, p. A547
M.D., President, Forbes Hospital, Monroeville, PA, p. A546
RUBINSTEIN, Mitchell, M.D., Chief Medical Officer, HCA Florida St. Petersburg Hospital, Saint Petersburg, FL, p. A149
RUBIO, Felipe, M.D., Medical Director, Kindred Hospital–Dayton, Dayton, OH, p. A494
RUBLE, Chris, Chief Executive Officer, Quail Run Behavioral Health, Phoenix, AZ, p. A36
RUBLE, Justin
Director Human Resources, Jefferson Medical Center, Ranson, WV, p. A704
Director, Human Resources, Berkeley Medical Center, Martinsburg, WV, p. A702
RUBY, Blaine, M.D., Chief of Staff, Johnson County Healthcare Center, Buffalo, WY, p. A726
RUCH, Jordan, Vice President and Chief Information Officer, Robert Wood Johnson University Hospital Somerset, Somerville, NJ, p. A428
RUCHTI, Robert D., Chief Executive Officer, Buchanan General Hospital, Grundy, VA, p. A677
RUCKER, Alisa, Vice President Finance and Chief Financial Officer, UPMC Washington, Washington, PA, p. A556
RUCKER, Jodi
MSN, R.N., President and Chief Nursing Officer, Vice President of Patient Care Services, Promedica Fostoria Community Hospital, Fostoria, OH, p. A496
MSN, R.N., President and Chief Nursing Officer, Vice President of Patient Care Services, Promedica Memorial Hospital, Fremont, OH, p. A496
RUCKER, Rick, Chief Operating Officer, Highland Hospital, Charleston, WV, p. A700
RUDBERG, Susan, M.D., Chief Medical Officer, Fairview Range, Hibbing, MN, p. A348
RUDD, Barry, Chief Information Officer, Memorial Satilla Health, Waycross, GA, p. A174
RUDD, Jedd, Director of Ancillary Services and Safety, Mad River Community Hospital, Arcata, CA, p. A56
RUDD, Taylor, Chief Operating Officer, St. Josep. Regional Medical Center, Lewiston, ID, p. A182
RUDDEN, Elizabeth, Vice President Human Resources, Connecticut Children's, Hartford, CT, p. A116
RUDEK, Charles M.
Chief Information Officer, UPMC Jameson, New Castle, PA, p. A547
Chief Information Officer, UPMC St. Margaret, Pittsburgh, PA, p. A552
RUDISILL, Joe, Chief Executive Officer, HCA Florida Englewood Hospital, Englewood, FL, p. A131
RUDLOFF, Roger, M.D., President Medical Staff, Antelop. Memorial Hospital, Neligh, NE, p. A403
RUDQUIST, Debra, FACHE, President and Chief Executive Officer, Amery Hospital And Clinic, Amery, WI, p. A707
RUDY, Bret, M.D., Executive Director and Senior Vice President, Nyu Langone Hospitals, New York, NY, p. A452
RUDZIK, Donna, Director Human Resources, Christus Mother Frances Hospital – Sulphur Springs, Sulphur Springs, TX, p. A655
RUE, Loring, M.D., Senior Vice President, Quality Patient Safety and Clinical Effectiveness, University of Alabama Hospital, Birmingham, AL, p. A17
RUE, Robert, Chief Financial Officer, Ellenville Regional Hospital, Ellenville, NY, p. A442
RUECKERT, Sebastian
M.D., Chief Medical Officer, Christian Hospital, Saint Louis, MO, p. A385
M.D., Vice President and Chief Medical Officer, Alton Memorial Hospital, Alton, IL, p. A185
RUEDISUELI, Amy, Vice President of Finance, Mckenzie Health System, Sandusky, MI, p. A337
RUEDISUELI, Donna, MSN, R.N., Chief Nursing Officer, Nationwide Children's Hospital – Toledo, Toledo, OH, p. A504
RUELLO, Rocky, Vice President Human Resources, Mercy Hospital St. Louis, Saint Louis, MO, p. A385
RUFF, Robin, Chief Financial Officer, UCHealth Pikes Peak Regional Hospital, Woodland Park, CO, p. A114
RUFF, Victoria, M.D., Medical Director, Select Specialty Hospital–Columbus, Columbus, OH, p. A492
RUFFIN, Janet L, R.N., Chief Nursing Officer, Temecula Valley Hospital, Temecula, CA, p. A97
RUFFIN, Marshall, Chief Information Officer, Inova Fair Oaks Hospital, Fairfax, VA, p. A675
RUFFING, Cindy, Director Human Resources, Siloam Springs Regional Hospital, Siloam Springs, AR, p. A53
RUFFOLO, Josep. A., President and Chief Executive Officer, Niagara Falls Memorial Medical Center, Niagara Falls, NY, p. A454
RUFINO, Rick
Chief Executive Officer, East Los Angeles Doctors Hospital, Los Angeles, CA, p. A72
Chief Executive Officer, Kindred Hospital–La Mirada, La Mirada, CA, p. A68
RUFRANO, Thomas, Chief Executive Officer, Banner Rehabilitation Hospital Phoenix, Phoenix, AZ, p. A35
RUGGIERO, Joanne, Chief Exectuve Officer, Jackson Health System, Miami, FL, p. A140
RUGGIERO, Taren, R.N., MSN, Vice President and Chief Nursing Officer, Holy Cross Hospital, Fort Lauderdale, FL, p. A131
RUIZ, Irene, Area Human Resources Director, Kaiser Permanente Fontana Medical Center, Fontana, CA, p. A63
RUIZ, Kathleen, M.D., Associate Director Patient Care Services, Veterans Affairs Caribbean Healthcare System, San Juan, PR, p. A736
RUIZ, Patricia, R.N., Chief Nursing Officer, NYC Health + Hospitals/South Brooklyn Health, New York, NY, p. A452
RUIZ, Tony, Senior Vice President, Chief Operating Officer, Medical Center Health System, Odessa, TX, p. A642
RULAND, Jyl
Chief Financial Officer, Clearwater Valley Health, Orofino, ID, p. A183
Chief Financial Officer, St. Mary's Health, Cottonwood, ID, p. A181
RULE, Jonathan, Chief Hospital Executive, Integris Health Edmond Hospital, Edmond, OK, p. A512
RULLI, Sheila, Director Human Resources, Kidspeace Children's Hospital, Orefield, PA, p. A547
RUMMEL, Jennifer
Director Human Resources, Freestone Medical Center, Fairfield, TX, p. A618
Director Human Resources, UT Health Athens, Athens, TX, p. A598
RUMORO, Dino, D.O., M.P.H., Chief Executive Officer, Rush Oak Park Hospital, Oak Park, IL, p. A204
RUMPH, Jerald W.
FACHE, President, OSF Healthcare Saint Anthony's Health Center, Alton, IL, p. A185
FACHE, President, SSM Health St. Josep. Hospital – Lake Saint Louis, Lake Saint Louis, MO, p. A379
RUNDLE, Eduard, Vice President Human Resources, HCA Florida Mercy Hospital, Miami, FL, p. A140
RUNDLE, Mike, Interim Site Leader for Finance, Capital Region Medical Center, Jefferson City, MO, p. A376
RUNNELS, Clay, Vice President Chief Medical Officer Washington County, Johnson City Medical Center, Johnson City, TN, p. A585
RUNYAN, Mark, Director Information Services, Holy Cross Hospital – Salt Lake, Salt Lake City, UT, p. A668
RUNYON, Annette, Vice President and Administrator, Medical Center At Franklin, Franklin, KY, p. A266
RUNYON, Mark A, Chief Financial Officer, Tamp. General Hospital, Tampa, FL, p. A152
RUPA, Maitra, M.D., Acting Medical Director, Chester Mental Health Center, Chester, IL, p. A188
RUPERT, Duke, Chief Operating Officer, Allegheny General Hospital, Pittsburgh, PA, p. A551
RUPERT, James M., Chief Fiscal Services, Battle Creek Veterans Affairs Medical Center, Battle Creek, MI, p. A322
RUPERT, Michael J, Chief Financial Officer, Tibor Rubin Va Medical Center, Long Beach, CA, p. A71
RUPP, Robert, Chief Executive Officer, Forrest City Medical Center, Forrest City, AR, p. A46
RUPPEL, Roxanne C., President and Chief Operating Officer, Salem Hospital, Salem, MA, p. A318
RUPPERT, Jennifer, Chief Financial Officer, Iowa City Va Health System, Iowa City, IA, p. A238
RUPPERT SCHILLER, Kerri
Senior Vice President and Chief Financial Officer, Children's Hospital of Orange County, Orange, CA, p. A81
Senior Vice President and Chief Financial Officer, Choc Children's At Mission Hospital, Mission Viejo, CA, p. A77
RUSCH, Brett, M.D., Executive Director, White River Junction Veterans Affairs Medical Center, White River Junction, VT, p. A672
RUSH, Andrew G., President, UPMC Somerset, Somerset, PA, p. A555
RUSH, Ann Marie, Chief Financial Officer, Penobscot Valley Hospital, Lincoln, ME, p. A298
RUSH, Christopher
President, Marshall Medical Center North, Guntersville, AL, p. A20
President, Marshall Medical Center South, Boaz, AL, p. A17
RUSH, Cindy, Director Human Resources, Clay County Medical Center, Clay Center, KS, p. A247
RUSH, Meg, M.D., Interim President, Vanderbilt University Medical Center, Nashville, TN, p. A591
RUSHIN, Denise, Director Human Resources, Poplar Bluff Regional Medical Center, Poplar Bluff, MO, p. A382
RUSHLOW, David, Vice President Medical Affairs, Mayo Clinic Health System In La Crosse, La Crosse, WI, p. A714
RUSK, Scott, M.D., Chief Medical Officer, Providence St. Josep. Hospital Orange, Orange, CA, p. A81
RUSNAK, Greg, Executive Vice President and Chief Operating Officer, Prisma Health Greenville Memorial Hospital, Greenville, SC, p. A567
RUSS, Nicole L, Director Colleague Relations, Aultman Alliance Community Hospital, Alliance, OH, p. A484
RUSSELL, Bill, Senior Chief Information Officer, Providence Mission Hospital Mission Viejo, Mission Viejo, CA, p. A77
RUSSELL, Brandy, Technology and Analytics Officer, Council Oak Comprehensive Healthcare, Tulsa, OK, p. A522
RUSSELL, Brant, R.N., President and Chief Executive Officer, Ascension Providence Hospital, Southfield Campus, Southfield, MI, p. A338
RUSSELL, Dardanella, Chief Human Resources Management Service, Veterans Affairs Hudson Valley Health Care System, Montrose, NY, p. A446
RUSSELL, Donald
AMITA Health Senior Vice President and Chief Human Resources Officer, UChicago Medicine Adventhealth Glenoaks, Glendale Heights, IL, p. A196
Senior Vice President and Chief Human Resources Officer, Ascension Alexian Brothers, Elk Grove Village, IL, p. A194
Senior Vice President and Chief Human Resources Officer, Ascension St. Alexius, Hoffman Estates, IL, p. A198
RUSSELL, Erin, Controller, Kindred Hospital–San Antonio, San Antonio, TX, p. A649
RUSSELL, Freda, R.N., Administrator, Ascension St. Thomas Three Rivers, Waverly, TN, p. A594
RUSSELL, Georgette, Vice President of Talent & Organizational Effectiveness, University of Michigan Health–Sparrow Carson, Carson City, MI, p. A323

© 2025 AHA Guide Index of Health Care Professionals **A961**

Index of Health Care Professionals / Russell

RUSSELL, Holly, Chief Executive Officer, Trustpoint Hospital, Murfreesboro, TN, p. A590

RUSSELL, John D., President and Chief Executive Officer, Prairie Ridge Health, Inc., Columbus, WI, p. A709

RUSSELL, Jon
 Senior Vice President & Chief Information Officer, John Muir Medical Center, Walnut Creek, Walnut Creek, CA, p. A100
 Senior Vice President and Chief Information Officer, John Muir Health, Concord Medical Center, Concord, CA, p. A60

RUSSELL, Karen M, Director of Employee Relations, OSF Saint Elizabeth Medical Center, Ottawa, IL, p. A204

RUSSELL, Kathy, R.N., Chief Nursing Officer, Bluegrass Community Hospital, Versailles, KY, p. A274

RUSSELL, Kimberly, Chief Nursing Officer, Mercy Hospital Booneville, Booneville, AR, p. A44

RUSSELL, Laurie, Director Human Resources, Covenant Health Hobbs Hospital, Hobbs, NM, p. A435

RUSSELL, Melvin Bruce Jr, Chief Nursing Officer, Palomar Medical Center Escondido, Escondido, CA, p. A62

RUSSELL, Michael, Chief Operations Officer, Cross Creek Hospital, Austin, TX, p. A600

RUSSELL, Michelle, Chief Executive Officer, Community Rehabilitation Hospital South, Greenwood, IN, p. A218

RUSSELL, Patti, Vice President Nursing, Masonicare Health Center, Wallingford, CT, p. A119

RUSSELL, Ricky, Chief Human Resource Officer, Carondelet St. Mary's Hospital, Tucson, AZ, p. A40

RUSSELL, Robert J., MS, FACHE, Chief Executive Officer, Penn Presbyterian Medical Center, Philadelphia, PA, p. A549

RUSSELL, Robin, Executive Director, Castaner General Hospital, Castaner, PR, p. A732

RUSSELL, Shelly, Chief Executive Officer, Mitchell County Regional Health Center, Osage, IA, p. A241

RUSSELL, Sherrie
 AMITA Health Senior Vice President and Chief Information Officer, UChicago Medicine Adventhealth Glenoaks, Glendale Heights, IL, p. A196
 Senior Vice President & Chief Information Officer, Ascension Alexian Brothers, Elk Grove Village, IL, p. A194
 Senior Vice President and Chief Information Officer, Ascension St. Alexius, Hoffman Estates, IL, p. A198
 Vice President and Chief Information Officer, Ascension Alexian Brothers Behavioral Health Hospital, Hoffman Estates, IL, p. A198

RUSSELL, Susan
 Chief Financial Officer, Och Regional Medical Center, Starkville, MS, p. A369
 Chief Nursing Officer, Singing River Health System, Pascagoula, MS, p. A367

RUSSELL, Valerie, Interim Medical Center Director, Central Alabama Va Medical Center-Montgomery, Montgomery, AL, p. A22

RUSSELL-BERRING, Jess, Hospital Administrator, Lincoln Regional Center, Lincoln, NE, p. A402

RUSSELL-JENKINS, Shane, M.D., Medical Director, Polara Health, Prescott Valley, AZ, p. A37

RUSSO, Arthur, M.D., Director Medical Affairs, Umass Memorial Health – Harrington, Southbridge, MA, p. A318

RUSSO, Cindy, FACHE, MS, R.N., President, Trumbull Regional Medical Center, Warren, OH, p. A506

RUSSO, Kimberly, MS, Chief Executive Officer and Managing Director, George Washington University Hospital, Washington, DC, p. A123

RUSSO, Mike, Vice President Information Systems, Chi St. Josep. Health Grimes Hospital, Navasota, TX, p. A641

RUSSO, Paul M., FACHE, Director, Bay Pines Veterans Affairs Healthcare System, Bay Pines, FL, p. A125

RUST, Jeff, Information Technology Systems Site Manager, Chi St. Alexius Health Williston, Williston, ND, p. A483

RUST, Steve, Director, Human Resources, Scripp. Memorial Hospital-Encinitas, Encinitas, CA, p. A62

RUTH, Joseph, Executive Vice President and Chief Operating Officer, University of Michigan Health-Sparrow Lansing, Lansing, MI, p. A332

RUTHERFORD, Eddie, Director of Pharmacy, Tyler Holmes Memorial Hospital, Winona, MS, p. A370

RUTHERFORD, Jeremiah, Chief Medical Officer, Cornerstone Specialty Hospitals Muskogee, Muskogee, OK, p. A515

RUTHS, Steve, M.D., Chief Medical Officer, Vista Del Mar Hospital, Ventura, CA, p. A100

RUTKOWSKI, Jennifer, R.N., MSN, Vice President Professional Services, Grant Regional Health Center, Lancaster, WI, p. A714

RUTKOWSKI, Jim, Chief Financial Officer, United Hospital Center, Bridgeport, WV, p. A699

RUTLEDGE, Debra K, R.N., Vice President Nursing Services, Chi Health Plainview, Plainview, NE, p. A405

RUTLEDGE, Rebel, Director Human Resources, Grady Memorial Hospital, Chickasha, OK, p. A511

RUTTINO, Denao, Vice President. Chief Information Officer, Harrisburg Medical Center, Harrisburg, IL, p. A197

RYAN, Christie, Chief Nursing Officer, Encompass Health Rehabilitation Hospital of Sewickley, Sewickley, PA, p. A554

RYAN, Christina M, R.N., Chief Executive Officer and Chief Nursing Officer, The Women's Hospital, Newburgh, IN, p. A225

RYAN, Christina M., R.N., Chief Executive Officer, The Women's Hospital, Newburgh, IN, p. A225

RYAN, Christopher, Chief Information Officer, Auburn Community Hospital, Auburn, NY, p. A438

RYAN, Connie, Chief Nursing Officer, Select Specialty Hospital–Tulsa Midtown, Tulsa, OK, p. A523

RYAN, David P., Vice President Human Resources, Melrosewakefield Healthcare, Melrose, MA, p. A315

RYAN, Debora, R.N., Vice President Patient Care, St. Francis Regional Medical Center, Shakopee, MN, p. A355

RYAN, Dennis, Senior Vice President and Chief Financial Officer, Children's Hospital of The King's Daughters, Norfolk, VA, p. A680

RYAN, Frank, Chief Financial Officer, Manchester Veterans Affairs Medical Center, Manchester, NH, p. A416

RYAN, John, JD, Chief Executive Officer, Orthoindy Hospital, Indianapolis, IN, p. A220

RYAN, John Jack, M.D., Chief Medical Officer, Surgeons Choice Medical Center, Southfield, MI, p. A338

RYAN, Lisa M, Coordinator Human Resources, Hampstead Hospital & Residential Treatment Facility, Hampstead, NH, p. A415

RYAN, Megan C., Interim Chief Executive Officer and Chief Legal Officer, Nassau University Medical Center, East Meadow, NY, p. A442

RYAN, Mike, Director of Information Services, Gunnison Valley Hospital, Gunnison, UT, p. A665

RYAN, Patrice
 Vice President Human Resources, Goleta Valley Cottage Hospital, Santa Barbara, CA, p. A94
 Vice President Human Resources, Santa Barbara Cottage Hospital, Santa Barbara, CA, p. A94
 Vice President Human Resources, Santa Ynez Valley Cottage Hospital, Solvang, CA, p. A96

RYAN, Patricia, Interim Chief Executive Officer, John C. Fremont Healthcare District, Mariposa, CA, p. A76

RYAN, Patrick, Chief Executive Officer, William R. Sharpe, Jr. Hospital, Weston, WV, p. A706

RYAN, Patrick J., Chief Human Resources Officer, Helen Hayes Hospital, West Haverstraw, NY, p. A461

RYAN, Rebecca, Interim Director Human Resources and Employee Health, Adventist Health Ukiah Valley, Ukiah, CA, p. A99

RYAN, Robert
 M.D., Chief Medical Officer, Guadalup. Regional Medical Center, Seguin, TX, p. A652
 President and Chief Executive Officer, Otis R. Bowen Center for Human Services, Warsaw, IN, p. A229

RYAN, Sharon, Regional Controller, Select Specialty Hospital – Macomb County, Mount Clemens, MI, p. A334

RYAN, Tim, Chief Financial Officer, Centennial Peaks Hospital, Louisville, CO, p. A112

RYBA, Janice L., JD, Chief Executive Officer, St. Mary Medical Center, Hobart, IN, p. A218

RYBICKI, Cathy, Chief Operating Officer, Corewell Health Reed City Hospital, Reed City, MI, p. A336

RYCKMAN, George, D.O., Chief of Staff, Munson Healthcare Paul Oliver Memorial Hospital, Frankfort, MI, p. A327

RYDEN, Lura, Chief Nursing Officer, Banner Payson Medical Center, Payson, AZ, p. A34

RYDER, Jeff, Director Information Systems, Chi Saint Josep. Health – Saint Josep. Mount Sterling, Mount Sterling, KY, p. A272

RYDER, Ronald, D.O., President of the Medical Staff, Robert Wood Johnson University Hospital At Hamilton, Hamilton, NJ, p. A422

RYERSE, Dave, Chief Executive Officer, South Lincoln Medical Center, Kemmerer, WY, p. A727

RYLAND, Jennifer M, R.N., Chief Administrative Officer, Jackson Medical Center, Jackson, AL, p. A21

RYLAND, Jennifer M., R.N., Chief Executive Officer, Jackson Medical Center, Jackson, AL, p. A21

RYLE, Barry W., Chief Information Officer, Oswego Hospital, Oswego, NY, p. A455

RYMER, Brandy, Coordinator Human Resources, Adventhealth Murray, Chatsworth, GA, p. A160

RYON, Joel, M.D., Chief of Staff, Henry County Health Center, Mount Pleasant, IA, p. A240

RYSTROM, Jennifer, R.N., Chief Nursing Officer, West Holt Medical Services, Atkinson, NE, p. A397

RZOMP, Kimberly
 Vice President and Chief Financial Officer, Wellspan Chambersburg Hospital, Chambersburg, PA, p. A536
 Vice President Finance, Wellspan Waynesboro Hospital, Waynesboro, PA, p. A556

S

SAAD, Michael, Vice President and Chief Information Officer, University of Tennessee Medical Center, Knoxville, TN, p. A586

SAADAT, Annette, Human Resources Business Partner, Chi Saint Josep. Health – Saint Josep. Mount Sterling, Mount Sterling, KY, p. A272

SAADI, Thomas J., Commissioner, Connecticut Veterans Home And Hospital, Rocky Hill, CT, p. A118

SAALFELD, Thomas, Senior Vice President and Chief Operating Officer, St. Elizabeth Fort Thomas, Fort Thomas, KY, p. A266

SAARI, Heidi L, Director, Human Resources, Upper Connecticut Valley Hospital, Colebrook, NH, p. A414

SAAVEDRA, JayLynn, Chief Information Officer, U. S. Public Health Service Indian Hospital, Parker, AZ, p. A34

SABA, Yvette, R.N., President, Edward Hospital & South Institutes, Endeavor Health Edward Hospital, Naperville, IL, p. A203

SABANDIT, Elizabeth, Director Human Resources, Alhambra Hospital Medical Center, Alhambra, CA, p. A55

SABATINO, Marc, Medical Diretor, Rehabilitation Institute of Southern Illinois, Llc, The, Shiloh, IL, p. A208

SABELLA, Deborah, R.N., Chief Executive Officer, Landmark Hospital of Cap. Girardeau, Cap. Girardeau, MO, p. A372

SABHARRWAL, Parajeet, Chief Executive Officer, Minimally Invasive Surgery Hospital, Lenexa, KS, p. A253

SABHARWAL, Vicky, Vice President and Chief Executive Officer, Jackson Behavioral Health Hospital, Jackson Health System, Miami, FL, p. A140

SABIA, John, M.D., Vice President Medical Affairs, Northern Dutchess Hospital, Rhinebeck, NY, p. A457

SACHARSKI, Steve, Chief Financial Officer, Havenwyck Hospital, Inc., Auburn Hills, MI, p. A322

SACHDEV, Aruna, M.D., Medical Director, Pappas Rehabilitation Hospital for Children, Canton, MA, p. A312

SACHDEV, Vish, M.D., Chief Medical Officer, Brookwood Baptist Medical Center, Birmingham, AL, p. A16

SACHDEVA, Brittany, Vice President of Operations, Sanford Medical Center Fargo, Fargo, ND, p. A481

SACHDEVA, Sandeep. M.D., Vice President Medical Affairs, Providence Swedish Edmonds, Edmonds, WA, p. A689

SACHS, Henry T. III, M.D., President, Emma Pendleton Bradley Hospital, East Providence, RI, p. A560

SACK, Michael V, FACHE, Chief Executive Officer, Melrosewakefield Healthcare, Melrose, MA, p. A315

SACKETT, John, President SGMC and Executive Vice President and Chief Operating Officer, Adventist Healthcare Shady Grove Medical Center, Rockville, MD, p. A306

SACKMANN, Charles, M.D., Chief of Staff, East Adams Rural Healthcare, Ritzville, WA, p. A694

SACRISTE, Ashley, Chief Executive Officer, Laurel Ridge Treatment Center, San Antonio, TX, p. A650

SADA, Judy, Chief Financial Officer, Memorial Hospital Miramar, Miramar, FL, p. A141

SADDORIS, Debbie, Vice President Human Resources, Sarah Bush Lincoln Health Center, Mattoon, IL, p. A201

SADLER, Donna, Director Human Resources, Arkansas State Hospital, Little Rock, AR, p. A49

SADLER, Joy, Director Human Resources, Bear River Valley Hospital, Tremonton, UT, p. A670

SADLER, Lynn, Regional Director, Finance, Select Specialty Hospital – Tucson, Tucson, AZ, p. A41

SADOFF, Jennifer, Chief Executive Officer, Moab Regional Hospital, Moab, UT, p. A666

SADOWSKA, Anne, Chief Executive Officer, Rehabilitation Hospital of Western Wisconsin, Eau Claire, WI, p. A710

SADRO, Cheryl A, Executive Vice President Chief Business and Finance Officer, University of Texas Medical Branch, Galveston, TX, p. A621

SAELEE, Sheba, Chief Clinical Office and Chief Operating Officer, Vibra Hospital of Northern California, Redding, CA, p. A85

SAENZ, Luis J Rodriquez, M.D., Medical Director, Hospital Menonita De Cayey, Cayey, PR, p. A732

Index of Health Care Professionals

Index of Health Care Professionals / Sanchez

SAENZ, Melanie, Regional Human Resources Officer, Ascension Saint Mary – Chicago, Chicago, IL, p. A188
SAFAEE SEMIROMI, Masood, M.D., Chief Medical Officer, Mckay–Dee Hospital, Ogden, UT, p. A666
SAFDAR, Aamir, M.D., Chief Medical Officer, Riveredge Hospital, Forest Park, IL, p. A195
SAFFA, Steve, Director Human Resources, University of Kansas Health System St. Francis Campus, Topeka, KS, p. A261
SAFRIT, Frank, Ph.D., MSN, Chief Executive Officer, Grisell Memorial Hospital District One, Ransom, KS, p. A258
SAGE, Kelly, Chief Nursing Officer, HSHS St. Anthony's Memorial Hospital, Effingham, IL, p. A194
SAGE, Zachary, Director, Marion Veterans Affairs Medical Center, Marion, IL, p. A200
SAGMIT, Rodney, Chief Information Management, Tibor Rubin Va Medical Center, Long Beach, CA, p. A71
SAGUE, Jonathan, Chief Operating Officer, University Hospitals St. John Medical Center, Westlake, OH, p. A507
SAHA, Sanjay K, Chief Operating Officer, Sibley Memorial Hospital, Washington, DC, p. A124
SAHLI, Anna, Vice President of Operations, Saint Luke's South Hospital, Overland Park, KS, p. A257
SAHLOLBEI, Hossain, M.D., Chief of Staff, Palo Verde Hospital, Blythe, CA, p. A58
SAHLSTROM, Christopher, M.D., Chief of Staff, Mat–Su Regional Medical Center, Palmer, AK, p. A29
SAHMAUNT, Sarabeth, Supervisory Accountant, Lawton Indian Hospital, Lawton, OK, p. A514
SAINBERT, Wilmino, Chief Human Resources Management Service, Northport Veterans Affairs Medical Center, Northport, NY, p. A454
SAINI, Gurvir K MSN, RN, Chief Nursing Officer, HCA Houston Healthcare Southeast, Pasadena, TX, p. A643
SAINTZ, Jeffrey, Vice President Human Resources, Titusville Area Hospital, Titusville, PA, p. A555
SAIYED, Ashfaq, M.D., Medical Director, Irwin County Hospital, Ocilla, GA, p. A169
SAJID, Muhammad W., M.D., Medical Director, Lincoln Trail Behavioral Health System, Radcliff, KY, p. A273
SAKOVITS, Steven, Vice President Information Systems and Chief Information Officer, Stamford Health, Stamford, CT, p. A119
SALAKI, Jana, Regional Director Human Resources, Wellspan Ephrata Community Hospital, Ephrata, PA, p. A539
SALAMACHA, Rena, Chief Executive Officer, George L. Mee Memorial Hospital, King City, CA, p. A68
SALAMANCA, Mary, Director Human Resources, Encompass Health Rehabilitation Hospital of Spring Hill, Brooksville, FL, p. A127
SALAMONE, Joanna, Senior Vice President Clinical Services and Chief Nursing Officer, Southern Maine Health Care – Biddeford Medical Center, Biddeford, ME, p. A296
SALAS, Christina Lea.
Chief Executive Officer, Northern Colorado Long Term Acute Hospital, Johnstown, CO, p. A110
Chief Executive Officer, Northern Colorado Rehabilitation Hospital, Johnstown, CO, p. A110
SALAS, Dawn, Controller, Encompass Health Rehabilitation Hospital, An Affiliate of Martin Health, Stuart, FL, p. A150
SALAS, Victor, M.D., President Medical Staff, Unitypoint Health – Jones Regional Medical Center, Anamosa, IA, p. A230
SALAWAY, Tarek
Senior Vice President and Area Manager, Golden Gate Service Area, Kaiser Permanente San Francisco Medical Center, San Francisco, CA, p. A91
Senior Vice President/Area Manager, Golden Gate Service Area, Kaiser Permanente San Rafael Medical Center, San Rafael, CA, p. A93
SALAZAR, Christina, Chief Operating Officer, Advanced Care Hospital of Southern New Mexico, Las Cruces, NM, p. A435
SALAZAR, Eloisa, Chief Financial Officer, South Texas Veterans Healthcare System Audie L Murphy, San Antonio, TX, p. A651
SALAZAR, Leanne, Chief Operating Officer, HCA Florida Oak Hill Hospital, Brooksville, FL, p. A127
SALAZAR, Pamela, M.D., Chief of Staff, Walton Rehabilitation Hospital, An Affiliate of Encompass Health, Augusta, GA, p. A158
SALAZAR, Serafin, M.D., Chief of Staff, Parkview Community Hospital Medical Center, Riverside, CA, p. A86
SALCEDO, Nydimar, Chief Human Resources Officer, Castaner General Hospital, Castaner, PR, p. A732
SALCIDO, Tony, Director of Information Technology, Kearny County Hospital, Lakin, KS, p. A252
SALDIVAR, Antoninette, Vice President, Human Resources, Bridgepoint Continuing Care Hospital – National Harborside, Washington, DC, p. A123
SALDIVAR, Duke, FACHE, Interim Chief Executive Officer, Pam Rehabilitation Hospital of Round Rock, Round Rock, TX, p. A647
SALEEBY, Manhal, M.D., Chief of Staff, VCU Health Community Memorial Hospital, South Hill, VA, p. A684
SALEEM, David, Director Information Technology, Greystone Park Psychiatric Hospital, Morris Plains, NJ, p. A424
SALEM, Gary, M.D., Vice President Medical Affairs, Mclaren Lapeer Region, Lapeer, MI, p. A332
SALEM, Michael, M.D., President and Chief Executive Officer, National Jewish Health, Denver, CO, p. A106
SALGADO, Joe
M.D., Chief of Staff, Artesia General Hospital, Artesia, NM, p. A433
M.D., Interim Chief Executive Officer, Artesia General Hospital, Artesia, NM, p. A433
SALGUEIRO, Richard W., Medical Center Director, Grand Junction Va Medical Center, Grand Junction, CO, p. A108
SALIM, Saif, Chief Executive Officer, Atlantic Rehabilitation Institute, Madison, NJ, p. A423
SALINAS, Amaro, Assistant Administrator and Human Resource Officer, Starr County Memorial Hospital, Rio Grande City, TX, p. A647
SALINAS, Daniel, M.D., Senior Vice President and Chief Medical Officer, Children's Healthcare of Atlanta, Atlanta, GA, p. A157
SALINAS, Noe
Vice President Information Technology, Nexus Specialty Hospital, Shenandoah, TX, p. A652
Vice President Information Technology, Nexus Specialty Hospital The Woodlands, The Woodlands, TX, p. A657
SALING, Christopher, Chief Human Resource Officer, Mckay–Dee Hospital, Ogden, UT, p. A666
SALISBURY, Dennis, M.D., Vice President for Medical Affairs, SCL Health Mt – St. James Healthcare, Butte, MT, p. A390
SALISBURY, Renee A, Director Human Resources, OSF Saint Luke Medical Center, Kewanee, IL, p. A199
SALISBURY, Tracy
Director Human Resources, Hiram W. Davis Medical Center, Petersburg, VA, p. A681
Regional Manager Human Resources, Central State Hospital, Petersburg, VA, p. A681
SALL, Jordan, Chief of Staff, Corewell Health Gerber Hospital, Fremont, MI, p. A327
SALLER, William, Chief Financial Officer, Rio Grande Regional Hospital, Mcallen, TX, p. A638
SALLEY, Wanda, Vice President Human Resources, HCA Florida West Hospital, Pensacola, FL, p. A146
SALLIS, Tom, Director Information Systems, Baptist Health–Fort Smith, Fort Smith, AR, p. A46
SALMAN, Wael, M.D., Vice President Medical Affairs, Memorial Healthcare, Owosso, MI, p. A334
SALMANULLAH, Muhammad, Chief Medical Director, Encompass Health Rehabilitation Hospital of Concord, Concord, NH, p. A414
SALMONSON, Eric, Vice President and Chief Financial Officer, St. Anthony Regional Hospital, Carroll, IA, p. A231
SALNAS, Todd, Chief Operating Officer, Peacehealth Sacred Heart Medical Center At Riverbend, Springfield, OR, p. A532
SALOM, Ira, M.D., Clinical Director, Northern Navajo Medical Center, Shiprock, NM, p. A437
SALOME, Jenny, Chief Financial Officer and Assistant Administrator, Northwest Hills Surgical Hospital, Austin, TX, p. A600
SALOMON, Kathryn, Director Human Resources, Kona Community Hospital, Kealakekua, HI, p. A177
SALTER, Cherry B, Director of Nursing, Hardtner Medical Center, Olla, LA, p. A291
SALTONSTALL, Christine, Chief Financial Officer, Kindred Hospital–Baldwin Park, Baldwin Park, CA, p. A57
SALTZGABER, Lee, Chief Medical Officer, Gerald Champion Regional Medical Center, Alamogordo, NM, p. A432
SALUDES, Melvin, M.D., Medical Officer, Acuity Specialty Hospital–Ohio Valley At Weirton, Weirton, WV, p. A705
SALVADOR, Ed, Chief Financial Officer, Providence St. Jude Medical Center, Fullerton, CA, p. A65
SALVATI, Mario, Director Fiscal Services, Shriners Children's Philadelphia, Philadelphia, PA, p. A550
SALVI, Donna, Chief Nursing Officer, Watsonville Community Hospital, Watsonville, CA, p. A100
SALVINO, Sonia, Vice President Finance, University Hospitals Cleveland Medical Center, Cleveland, OH, p. A491
SALVITTI, Alfred P, Chief Financial Officer, Eagleville Hospital, Eagleville, PA, p. A538
SALWAN, Manav, Medical Director, Kindred Hospital–Sycamore, Sycamore, IL, p. A209
SALY, David, Director, Information Services, HCA Florida Largo Hospital, Largo, FL, p. A137
SALZMAN, Shona, Chief Operating Officer, William Newton Hospital, Winfield, KS, p. A262
SAMANI, Daniel, M.D.Community Medical Center, Inc., Falls City, NE, p. A399
SAMBASIVAN, Venkataraman, M.D., Chief Medical Officer, Lourdes Health, Pasco, WA, p. A692
SAMILO, Nick, Vice President Fiscal Services and Chief Financial Officer, Atrium Health Stanly, Albemarle, NC, p. A463
SAMMARCO, Michael, M.D., Chief Financial Officer, Erie County Medical Center, Buffalo, NY, p. A440
SAMMONS, Craig, Chief Financial Officer, Sky Ridge Medical Center, Lone Tree, CO, p. A111
SAMMS, Caswell, Network Chief Financial Officer, NYC Health + Hospitals/Lincoln, New York, NY, p. A451
SAMORA, Martha Esq, R.N., FACHE, Chief Executive Officer, Encompass Health Rehabilitation Hospital of Bakersfield, Bakersfield, CA, p. A57
SAMPAGA, Arthur, Chief Nursing Officer, Hilo Medical Center, Hilo, HI, p. A175
SAMPLE, Steven, Medical Center Director, Bob Stump Department of Veterans Affairs Medical Center, Prescott, AZ, p. A37
SAMPLES, Robert, Chief Executive Officer, Landmark Hospital of Joplin, Joplin, MO, p. A377
SAMPSON, Amy, President and Chief Executive Officer, Children's Hospital of The King's Daughters, Norfolk, VA, p. A680
SAMPSON, Bob
Senior Vice President, Human Resources, Evergreenhealth, Kirkland, WA, p. A691
Vice President Human Resources, Providence Redwood Memorial Hospital, Fortuna, CA, p. A63
SAMPSON, Jill, Director Human Resources, Lemuel Shattuck Hospital, Jamaica Plain, MA, p. A314
SAMROW, Kevin, Chief Executive Officer, Merit Health Natchez, Natchez, MS, p. A367
SAMS, James C., Chief of Staff, Mckenzie Health System, Sandusky, MI, p. A337
SAMSEL, Roy, Medical Center Director, Aleda E. Lutz Department of Veterans Affairs Medical Center, Saginaw, MI, p. A336
SAMSON, Ley
Chief Information Officer, Presbyterian/St. Luke's Medical Center, Denver, CO, p. A106
Director Management Information Systems, HCA Houston Healthcare Clear Lake, Webster, TX, p. A661
SAMSTEIN, Ivan, Executive Vice President and Chief Financial Officer, University of Chicago Medical Center, Chicago, IL, p. A192
SAMUDRALA, Siresha, M.D., Medical Director, Mercy Rehabilitation Hospital St. Louis, Chesterfield, MO, p. A373
SAMUEL, Nicole, Chief Financial Officer, Sierra Vista Hospital, Sacramento, CA, p. A87
SAMUELS, Christopher, Chief of Staff, Skyline Health, White Salmon, WA, p. A698
SAMUELSON, Kimberly, Director of Information Management, Highland–Clarksburg Hospital, Clarksburg, WV, p. A700
SAMYN, Mike, Vice President, Finance and Chief Financial Officer, Trinity Health Livonia Hospital, Livonia, MI, p. A332
SAMZ, Jeff, Chief Executive Officer, Huntsville Hospital, Huntsville, AL, p. A21
SANBORN, Randall, Director Information Systems, Garden City Hospital, Garden City, MI, p. A327
SANCHEZ, Alberto
Chief Executive Officer, Solara Specialty Hospitals Harlingen–Brownsville, Brownsville, TX, p. A604
Chief Executive Officer, Solara Specialty Hospitals Mcallen, Mcallen, TX, p. A638
SANCHEZ, Antonio, M.D., Executive Director, Northport Veterans Affairs Medical Center, Northport, NY, p. A454
SANCHEZ, Arnaldo Rodriguez, M.D., Chief Operating Officer, Hospital Menonita Guayama, Guayama, PR, p. A732
SANCHEZ, Emalie, Director Human Resources, Baylor Scott & White Medical Center–Uptown, Dallas, TX, p. A610
SANCHEZ, Esperanza, Chief Clinical Officer, Kindred Hospital–La Mirada, La Mirada, CA, p. A68
SANCHEZ, Freddie, Director Information Systems, Fountain Valley Regional Hospital And Medical Center, Fountain Valley, CA, p. A64
SANCHEZ, Holly, Chief Information Officer, Slidell Memorial Hospital, Slidell, LA, p. A293
SANCHEZ, Jose R., President and Chief Executive Officer, Humboldt Park Health, Chicago, IL, p. A189
SANCHEZ, Nancy, Senior Vice President and Vice Dean Human Resources, Nyu Langone Hospitals, New York, NY, p. A452
SANCHEZ, Oscar
Chief Financial Officer, Texas Rehabilitation Hospital of Fort Worth, Fort Worth, TX, p. A620

Index of Health Care Professionals

Index of Health Care Professionals / Sanchez

Chief Financial Officer, Texas Rehabilitation Hospital of Keller, Keller, TX, p. A632
SANCHEZ, Rebecca, R.N., M.P.H., Director of Nursing, Texas Center for Infectious Disease, San Antonio, TX, p. A651
SANCHEZ RODRIGUEZ, Yelitza, Chief Executive Officer, Hospital De La Universidad De Puerto Rico/Dr. Federico Trilla, Carolina, PR, p. A732
SANCHEZ–RICO, Gloria, Chief Nursing Officer and Vice President, Huntington Health, Pasadena, CA, p. A83
SANDAGER, Brian, Chief Information Officer, Lowell General Hospital, Lowell, MA, p. A315
SANDBULTE, Nyla H, R.N., Director of Nursing, Sanford Luverne Medical Center, Luverne, MN, p. A349
SANDEL, Lacey, Chief Executive Officer, Clearsky Rehabilitation Hospital of Leesville, Leesville, LA, p. A287
SANDEL, Sherri, D.O., Chief Medical Director, Northern Westchester Hospital, Mount Kisco, NY, p. A446
SANDENE, Jeff D, Executive Vice President and Chief Financial Officer, Charleston Area Medical Center, Charleston, WV, p. A700
SANDER, Cindy, Coordinator Human Resources, Kindred Hospital–St. Louis, Saint Louis, MO, p. A383
SANDERS, Amy, Chief Human Resources, Captain James A. Lovell Federal Health Care Center, North Chicago, IL, p. A203
SANDERS, Angela, Chief Executive Officer, Granite Hills Hospital, West Allis, WI, p. A724
SANDERS, Brian, M.D., Chief Medical Officer, Portsmouth Regional Hospital, Portsmouth, NH, p. A417
SANDERS, Hannah
M.D., Chief Executive Officer, Cordova Community Medical Center, Cordova, AK, p. A28
M.D., Medical Director, Cordova Community Medical Center, Cordova, AK, p. A28
SANDERS, Harv, Chief Financial Officer, Rhea Medical Center, Dayton, TN, p. A582
SANDERS, Jeffrey, M.D., Chief of Staff, Carson Tahoe Health, Carson City, NV, p. A408
SANDERS, Kelly B., Vice President Human Resources, Good Shepherd Health Care System, Hermiston, OR, p. A527
SANDERS, Kimberly, Chief Nursing Officer, Baptist Memorial Hospital–Carroll County, Huntingdon, TN, p. A584
SANDERS, Kirk S., M.D., Chief of Staff, Lifebrite Community Hospital of Stokes, Danbury, NC, p. A466
SANDERS, Kris, Chief Financial Officer, Methodist Healthcare Olive Branch Hospital, Olive Branch, MS, p. A367
SANDERS, Kyle, Chief Financial Officer, Nea Baptist Memorial Hospital, Jonesboro, AR, p. A48
SANDERS, Michael R, MS, Chief Operating Officer, KPC Promise Hospital of Baton Rouge, Baton Rouge, LA, p. A277
SANDERS, Patrick, Chief Operating Officer, Hartgrove Behavioral Health System, Chicago, IL, p. A189
SANDERS, R. Bradley, D.O., Executive Medical Director, Alvarado Parkway Institute Behavioral Health System, La Mesa, CA, p. A68
SANDERS, Robert, M.D., Chief Medical Officer, Texoma Medical Center, Denison, TX, p. A613
SANDERS, Sheila, Chief Nursing Officer, HCA Florida Oak Hill Hospital, Brooksville, FL, p. A127
SANDERS, Sheila M, Chief Information Officer, Emory University Hospital, Atlanta, GA, p. A157
SANDERS, Steve, Chief Financial Officer, Washington County Hospital And Clinics, Washington, IA, p. A244
SANDERS, Susie Sherrod, Chief Financial Officer, Cherry Hospital, Goldsboro, NC, p. A469
SANDHU, Harminder, M.D., Chief of Staff, Bridgepoint Continuing Care Hospital – Capitol Hill, Washington, DC, p. A123
SANDIFER, Ron, Chief Information Officer, Community Memorial Hospital – Ventura, Ventura, CA, p. A100
SANDIFER, Tawny, R.N., MSN, Chief Nursing Officer, Vice President of Patient Care Services, Columbus Community Hospital, Columbus, NE, p. A399
SANDIN, James H, M.D., Assistant Administrator Medical Affairs, Hunt Regional Medical Center, Greenville, TX, p. A623
SANDLIN, Michael, M.D., Chief of Staff, Muscogee Creek Nation Medical Center, Okmulgee, OK, p. A519
SANDMANN, Patty, Senior Director of Nursing, Burgess Health Center, Onawa, IA, p. A241
SANDS, Anthony B., Associate Chief Financial Officer, Musc Health – Orangeburg, Orangeburg, SC, p. A569
SANDS, Dennis, Chief Medical Officer, OSF Healthcare Saint Anthony's Health Center, Alton, IL, p. A185
SANDS, Tiffany, Manager Health Information, Arbuckle Memorial Hospital, Sulphur, OK, p. A521
SANDS, Tom, FACHE, President, Beverly Hospital, Beverly, MA, p. A309
SANDSTROM, C Bruce, Vice President and Chief Financial Officer, The Aroostook Medical Center, Presque Isle, ME, p. A299
SANFORD, Debbie F, R.N., MS, Administrator, Forrest General Hospital, Hattiesburg, MS, p. A363
SANFORD, Lisa, VP Patient Care/CNO, Holy Rosary Healthcare, Miles City, MT, p. A394
SANFORD, Ricca, Director Human Resources, Regional West Garden County, Oshkosh, NE, p. A405
SANFORD, Sharon K, Director Human Resources, Jersey Community Hospital, Jerseyville, IL, p. A199
SANFORD, Stacy, Administrator, Oceans Behavioral Hospital Abilene, Abilene, TX, p. A595
SANGER, David, M.D., Chief Medical Officer, Pawnee Valley Community Hospital, Larned, KS, p. A253
SANGER, Ken, R.N., Chief Nursing Officer and Chief Operations Officer, Lake Huron Medical Center, Port Huron, MI, p. A336
SANGER, Neal, Vice President Information Services, Mayo Clinic Health System In La Crosse, La Crosse, WI, p. A714
SANGHA, Harbaksh, M.D., Chief Medical Officer, Lake Regional Health System, Osage Beach, MO, p. A381
SANGHI, Harishankar, M.D., Clinical Director, St. Lawrence Psychiatric Center, Ogdensburg, NY, p. A455
SANGVAI, Devdutta, M.D., President, Duke Regional Hospital, Durham, NC, p. A467
SANKARAN, Jaya, M.D., Chief of Staff, Mymichigan Medical Center Standish, Standish, MI, p. A338
SANKE, Kristina, Chief Financial Officer, Orchard Hospital, Gridley, CA, p. A66
SANKEY, Kara, Chief Nursing Officer, Mercyhealth Hospital And Physician Clinic–Crystal Lake, Crystal Lake, IL, p. A192
SANKOORIKAL, Joseph, M.D., Chief Medical Staff, Kansas Rehabilitation Hospital, Topeka, KS, p. A260
SANKS, Claude, Chief Medical Staff, Effingham Health System, Springfield, GA, p. A171
SANSOM, Christine R, Chief Nursing Officer, Mclaren Port Huron, Port Huron, MI, p. A336
SANSONE, John, Vice President, Human Resources, Monadnock Community Hospital, Peterborough, NH, p. A417
SANTANA, Leticia, Administrator Medical Records, Bayamon Medical Center, Bayamon, PR, p. A731
SANTANGELO, Craig, Director Information Services, Medical City Arlington, Arlington, TX, p. A597
SANTANGELO, Joe, M.D., Vice President of Medical Affairs, Munson Healthcare Cadillac Hospital, Cadillac, MI, p. A323
SANTANGELO, John, Director Information Technology, Cleveland Clinic Florida, Weston, FL, p. A155
SANTARELLI, James, M.D., President Medical Staff, Aurora Medical Center Kenosha, Kenosha, WI, p. A713
SANTIAGO, Alejandro, Director Finance, Doctors' Center Hospital San Juan, San Juan, PR, p. A734
SANTIAGO, Anthony J., M.D., Chief Executive Officers, Huhukam Memorial Hospital, Sacaton, AZ, p. A37
SANTIAGO, Ernesto, Executive Director, Industrial Hospital, San Juan, PR, p. A735
SANTIAGO, Julio, M.D., Chief of Staff, Genesis Medical Center–Aledo, Aledo, IL, p. A185
SANTIAGO, Manuel, Chief Information Officer, Hospital Metropolitano, San Juan, PR, p. A735
SANTIAGO, Orlando, Human Resources Officer, Hospital Del Maestro, San Juan, PR, p. A735
SANTIAGO, Sugehi, Director, Hospital San Francisco, San Juan, PR, p. A735
SANTIAGO, Ubaldo, M.D., Chairman, Doctors' Center Hospital San Juan, San Juan, PR, p. A734
SANTIAGO ROSARIO, Carlos, Executive Director, Hospital Pavia–Hato Rey, San Juan, PR, p. A735
SANTIESTEBAN, Nancy, Director Patient Care Services, Presbyterian Espanola Hospital, Espanola, NM, p. A434
SANTINA, Ray, Director Information Systems, Psychiatric Institute of Washington, Washington, DC, p. A124
SANTISTEVAN, Vivian, Chief Human Resources, Tsehootsooi Medical Center, Fort Defiance, AZ, p. A31
SANTOEMMA, Dave, Chief Executive Officer, Central Carolina Hospital, Sanford, NC, p. A476
SANTORA, Judith
Chief Human Resource Officer, Cleveland Clinic Lutheran Hospital, Cleveland, OH, p. A490
Human Resources Business Partner, Cleveland Clinic Marymount Hospital, Garfield Heights, OH, p. A496
SANTORIO, Gino R., President and Chief Executive Officer, Mount Sinai Medical Center, Miami Beach, FL, p. A141
SANTOS, Daniel, Director Ancillary Services, Pacifica Hospital of The Valley, Los Angeles, CA, p. A74
SANTOS, Deborah, R.N., Chief Nursing Officer, Encompass Health Rehabilitation Hospital of Western Massachusetts, Ludlow, MA, p. A315
SANTOS, Gloria, Vice President, Nursing, Penn State Health Holy Spirit Medical Center, Camp Hill, PA, p. A536
SANTOS, Ismael, Director Human Resources, Valle Vista Health System, Greenwood, IN, p. A218
SANTOS, Lori, Chief Financial Officer, St. Peter's Hospital, Albany, NY, p. A438
SANTOS, Perlita, Chief Financial Officer, Commonwealth Health Center, Saipan, MARIANA ISLANDS, p. A730
SANTUCCI, James, Chief Operating Officer, Desert Regional Medical Center, Palm Springs, CA, p. A82
SANTULLI, Patricia, Director Human Resources, Elmira Psychiatric Center, Elmira, NY, p. A443
SANVILLE, David, Chief Financial Officer, Mt. Ascutney Hospital And Health Center, Windsor, VT, p. A672
SANWARI, Murtaza, Senior Vice President/Area Manager, Woodland Hills, Kaiser Permanente Woodland Hills Medical Center, Los Angeles, CA, p. A73
SANZONE, Frank, Manager Information Technology, Ascension Brighton Center for Recovery, Brighton, MI, p. A323
SAPMAZ, Cagri, Information Technology Director, Bolivar Medical Center, Cleveland, MS, p. A361
SAPORITO, Angie, Administrator, Mercy Hospital Columbus, Columbus, KS, p. A248
SAPORITO, Joann L., R.N., Vice President Nursing Services, Oak Valley Hospital, Oakdale, CA, p. A80
SAPP, Tracy, Director Human Resources, Encompass Health Rehabilitation Hospital of Ocala, Ocala, FL, p. A143
SAPPENFIELD, Debra, R.N., Chief Nursing Officer, Hemphill County Hospital District, Canadian, TX, p. A606
SAPPINGTON–CRITTENDEN, Shana, Chief Operating Officer, HCA Florida Westside Hospital, Plantation, FL, p. A147
SARBACHER, James, Chief Information Officer, State Hospital North, Orofino, ID, p. A183
SARDANA, Sadhana, M.D., Clinical Director, Rockland Children's Psychiatric Center, Orangeburg, NY, p. A455
SARDELLA, Jeff, Director Information Technology, Terrebonne General Health System, Houma, LA, p. A283
SARFATY, Beth, Chief Executive Officer, Encompass Health Rehabilitation Hospital of Tinton Falls, A Joint Venture With Monmouth Medical Center, Tinton Falls, NJ, p. A429
SARGEANT, William Martin.
Chief Executive Officer/Interim Chief, Office of Performance & Transformation, Keck Hospital of Usc, Los Angeles, CA, p. A73
Chief Executive Officer/Interim Chief, Office of Performance & Transformation, USC Norris Comprehensive Cancer Center And Hospital, Los Angeles, CA, p. A75
SARGENT, Kimberly, Vice President Patient Services, St. Luke's Hospital–Miners Campus, Coaldale, PA, p. A537
SARGENT, Kurt
CPA, Vice President Operational Finance, Chi St. Alexius Health Devils Lake, Devils Lake, ND, p. A480
CPA, Vice President, Operational Finance, Chi St Alexius Health Carrington, Carrington, ND, p. A479
SARGENT, Teresa, Vice President Human Resources, Saint Alphonsus Regional Medical Center, Boise, ID, p. A179
SARMENTO, Joann, Manager Human Resources, Fairchild Medical Center, Yreka, CA, p. A102
SARNECKI, Robert, Interim Chief Information Officer, Children's of Alabama, Birmingham, AL, p. A16
SARROS, Steven, Vice President and Chief Information Officer, Baptist Hospital, Pensacola, FL, p. A146
SARROUI, B, M.D., Chief of Staff, Advanced Specialty Hospital of Toledo, Toledo, OH, p. A504
SARTAIN, Jarred, M.D., President Medical Staff, North Mississipp. Medical Center–Hamilton, Hamilton, AL, p. A20
SARTAIN, Lisa M., Vice President, Human Resources, Bellevue Hospital, The, Bellevue, OH, p. A486
SARTORIUS, Matt, Chief Operating Officer, Abrazo Arrowhead Campus, Glendale, AZ, p. A32
SARVEPALLI, Raghu, M.D., Vice President of Medical Affairs, Mymichigan Medical Center Saginaw, Saginaw, MI, p. A337
SARVER, Troy, R.N., Chief Nursing Officer, Texas Orthopedic Hospital, Houston, TX, p. A628
SAS, Mary, Vice President, Valley Health – Hampshire Memorial Hospital, Romney, WV, p. A704
SASENARAINE, Roy, Chief Executive Officer, Valley Springs Behavioral Health Hospital, Holyoke, MA, p. A314
SASSER, Kelley, Director Information Systems, Adventhealth Zephyrhills, Zephyrhills, FL, p. A155
SATHER, Sonia, M.D., President Medical Staff, Spencer Hospital, Spencer, IA, p. A244
SATTAR, Parhez, Senior Director Information Technology, Grande Ronde Hospital, La Grande, OR, p. A528
SATTERWHITE, Glenda, Director of Nursing, Oklahoma Forensic Center, Vinita, OK, p. A523
SAUCERMAN–HOWARD, Kelli J. Cleveland Clinic Akron General, Akron, OH, p. A484
SAUDER, Chris, Vice President and Chief Financial Officer, Adventhealth Carrollwood, Tampa, FL, p. A151

A964 Index of Health Care Professionals

SAUER, Bernie, Director Information Technology, San Gabriel Valley Medical Center, San Gabriel, CA, p. A91
SAUER, Mary R, R.N., Chief Nursing Officer, Cleveland Clinic Avon Hospital, Avon, OH, p. A485
SAUERBREI, Teresa, Chief Nursing Officer, Compass Memorial Healthcare, Marengo, IA, p. A239
SAUERS, Preston
   Chief Executive Officer, Kingman Community Hospital, Kingman, KS, p. A252
   Chief Financial Officer, Ellsworth County Medical Center, Ellsworth, KS, p. A249
SAUL, Anthony J, Executive Vice President, Chief Financial Officer, Grady Health System, Atlanta, GA, p. A157
SAUM, Anita, Director Human Resources, Encompass Health Rehabilitation Hospital of Tinton Falls, A Joint Venture With Monmouth Medical Center, Tinton Falls, NJ, p. A429
SAUNDERS, Brooke, Vice President of Southeastern Market, Vibra Hospitals of Southeastern Michigan – Taylor Campus, Lincoln Park, MI, p. A332
SAUNDERS, John R, M.D., Senior Vice President Medical Affairs and Chief Medical Officer, Gbmc Healthcare, Baltimore, MD, p. A302
SAUNDERS, Jonathan, Chief Executive Officer, Baylor Scott & White Medical Center – Trophy Club, Trophy Club, TX, p. A658
SAUNDERS, M Patricia, R.N., MS, Vice President Nursing, UPMC Hanover, Hanover, PA, p. A541
SAURO, Anthony, Chief Information Officer, Pointe Coupee General Hospital, New Roads, LA, p. A290
SAUSEDO, Rhonda, Chief Nursing Officer, UCI Health – Placentia Linda, Placentia, CA, p. A83
SAUTER, Michael, M.D., Chief Medical Officer, St. Charles Hospital, Port Jefferson, NY, p. A456
SAVAGE, Elizabeth, Senior Vice President and Chief Human Resource Officer and Vice President Community Health and Wellness, Valley Health – Winchester Medical Center, Winchester, VA, p. A685
SAVAGE, Ginny, Director of Human Resources, Carolina Center for Behavioral Health, Greer, SC, p. A567
SAVAGE, Heather, Director Human Resources, The Rehabilitation Institute of St. Louis, Saint Louis, MO, p. A384
SAVAGE, Logan, Chief Executive Officer, Lafayette Regional Rehabilitation Hospital, Lafayette, IN, p. A222
SAVAGE, Steve, Chief Executive Officer, Bca Stonecrest Center, Detroit, MI, p. A325
SAVOCA, Kelly, Chief Financial Officer, Sheppard Pratt, Baltimore, MD, p. A302
SAVOY, F. Peter. III, Chief Executive Officer, Dequincy Memorial Hospital, Dequincy, LA, p. A281
SAVOY, Greg, M.D., Chief Medical Officer, Savoy Medical Center, Mamou, LA, p. A287
SAWA, Kendall, R.N., Chief Hospital Executive, Peacehealth St. John Medical Center, Longview, WA, p. A691
SAWALLISH, Trevor
   Chief Executive Officer, Maple Grove Hospital, Maple Grove, MN, p. A349
   Chief Executive Officer, North Memorial Health Hospital, Robbinsdale, MN, p. A353
   Senior Vice President Clinical Operations and Chief Operating Officer, Children's Minnesota, Minneapolis, MN, p. A350
SAWDEY, Don, M.D., Medical Director, Daniels Memorial Healthcare Center, Scobey, MT, p. A395
SAWICKI, Mitzi, Director of Nursing, Havenwyck Hospital, Inc., Auburn Hills, MI, p. A322
SAWTELL, William, Information Technology Leader, Kaiser Permanente Baldwin Park Medical Center, Baldwin Park, CA, p. A57
SAWYER, Anne, Chief Financial Officer, Wayne County Hospital, Monticello, KY, p. A271
SAWYER, Holly, Director and Human Resources Business Partner, Piedmont Fayette Hospital, Fayetteville, GA, p. A164
SAWYER, Josep. T. Jr, President and Chief Operating Officer, Guthrie Robert Packer Hospital, Sayre, PA, p. A554
SAWYER, Regina, Vice President Chief Nursing Officer, Kaweah Health Medical Center, Visalia, CA, p. A100
SAWYER, Stephen, Chief Financial Officer, Norton Community Hospital, Norton, VA, p. A680
SAWYER, Sydney, R.N., Chief Executive Officer, Lackey Memorial Hospital, Forest, MS, p. A362
SAXON, Kathy, R.N., Vice President Patient Care Services, Adventist Health Tillamook, Tillamook, OR, p. A533
SAYAH, Assaad
   M.D., Chief Executive Officer, Cambridge Health Alliance, Cambridge, MA, p. A312
   M.D., Chief Medical Officer, Cambridge Health Alliance, Cambridge, MA, p. A312
SAYLER, Elizabeth, M.D., Chief of Staff, Monument Health Lead–Deadwood Hospital, Deadwood, SD, p. A573

SAYLER, Roger, Finance Officer, Fargo Va Medical Center, Fargo, ND, p. A480
SAYLES, Debbie A, R.N., Vice President and Chief Nursing Officer, Scottish Rite for Children, Dallas, TX, p. A612
SAYLOR, Marie, Chief Executive Officer, Landmark Hospital of Athens, Athens, GA, p. A156
SAYRE, Amy, Director Human Resources, Pershing Memorial Hospital, Brookfield, MO, p. A372
SAYRE, Cindy, Ph.D., R.N., Chief Nursing Officer, UW Medicine/University of Washington Medical Center, Seattle, WA, p. A695
SBARDELLA, Steven P., M.D., FABC, President Clinical Operations and Chief Medical Officer, Melrosewakefield Healthcare, Melrose, MA, p. A315
SCAFIDDI, Darlene, R.N., MSN, Vice President Nursing and Patient Care Services, Pomona Valley Hospital Medical Center, Pomona, CA, p. A84
SCAGLIONE, Kim, Vice President Human Resources, Baptist Health Louisville, Louisville, KY, p. A269
SCALES, Melisa, Director of Nursing, Parkview Hospital, Wheeler, TX, p. A662
SCALES, Yolanda, R.N., Director of Nursing, Bethesda Rehabilitation Hospital, Baton Rouge, LA, p. A277
SCAMARDO, Luke P, M.D., II, Chief of Staff, Chi St. Josep. Health Grimes Hospital, Navasota, TX, p. A641
SCANLON, Donald
   Chief Corporate Services, Mount Sinai Health System, Mount Sinai Beth Israel, New York, NY, p. A449
   Chief Corporate Services, Mount Sinai Health System, Mount Sinai Morningside, New York, NY, p. A449
   Chief Corporate Services, Mount Sinai Health System, New York Eye And Ear Infirmary of Mount Sinai, New York, NY, p. A450
   Chief Financial Officer, The Mount Sinai Hospital, New York, NY, p. A453
SCANLON, Kerri
   R.N., Executive Director, Glen Cove Hospital, Glen Cove, NY, p. A443
   R.N., Executive Director, North Shore University Hospital, Manhasset, NY, p. A445
   R.N., Executive Director, Plainview Hospital, Plainview, NY, p. A456
SCANNELL, Donna, Vice President Information Technology, Kaiser Permanente Medical Center, Honolulu, HI, p. A175
SCANZERA, Christopher A, Vice President and Chief Information Officer, Atlanticare Regional Medical Center, Atlantic City Campus, Atlantic City, NJ, p. A418
SCARBORO, Parrish, Chief Executive Officer, San Dimas Community Hospital, San Dimas, CA, p. A90
SCARBROUGH, Keith, Director, Information Systems, Saint Francis Hospital, Memphis, TN, p. A589
SCARDINO, Diane M., Chief Administrative Officer, Norton Children's Hospital, Louisville, KY, p. A269
SCARLATTI, Shirley K, Associate Chief Nursing Officer, Parkridge Medical Center, Chattanooga, TN, p. A580
SCARLETT, Kamesha, Chief Information Resource Management, Veterans Affairs New Jersey Health Care System, East Orange, NJ, p. A420
SCARPELLI, Michael, Executive Director, South Oaks Hospital, Amityville, NY, p. A438
SCARTEZINA, Angie, Chief Nursing Officer, Primary Children's Hospital, Salt Lake City, UT, p. A669
SCEPANSKI, Theresa, Vice President People and Organizational Development, University Health, San Antonio, TX, p. A651
SCERCY, Charles, Corporate Director, Mary Washington Hospital, Fredericksburg, VA, p. A676
SCHAAB, Ben, Vice President, Chief Financial Officer, Cgh Medical Center, Sterling, IL, p. A209
SCHAAL, Dawn M., Medical Center Director, Veterans Affairs Hudson Valley Health Care System, Montrose, NY, p. A446
SCHACHTNER, Laurie, Director Operations, Ascension Saint Josep. – Elgin, Elgin, IL, p. A194
SCHAD, Todd, M.D., Medical Director, Sauk Prairie Healthcare, Prairie Du Sac, WI, p. A720
SCHADE, Sue, Interim Chief Information Officer, University Hospitals Cleveland Medical Center, Cleveland, OH, p. A491
SCHADLER, Gene, Superintendent, Evansville State Hospital, Evansville, IN, p. A216
SCHAEF, Toby, Director Information Technology, Memorial Hospital of Carbon County, Rawlins, WY, p. A728
SCHAEFER, Jamie, Vice President Finance, Avera Sacred Heart Hospital, Yankton, SD, p. A578
SCHAEFER, Kevin, Manager Information Services, River's Edge Hospital And Clinic, Saint Peter, MN, p. A355
SCHAEFER, Matthew, President and Chief Executive Officer, East Tennessee Children's Hospital, Knoxville, TN, p. A585
SCHAEFER, Michelle, Chief Financial Officer, Lillian M. Hudspeth Memorial Hospital, Sonora, TX, p. A653

SCHAEFFER, Andre, M.D., Chief of Staff, Union General Hospital, Blairsville, GA, p. A159
SCHAEFFER, Richard, Vice President Information Systems and Chief Information Officer, St. Clair Health, Pittsburgh, PA, p. A551
SCHAEFFER, Steven, Director of Finance, Central Louisiana Surgical Hospital, Alexandria, LA, p. A276
SCHAETTI, Susan, Chief Executive Officer, Kindred Hospital Tarrant County–Arlington, Arlington, TX, p. A597
SCHAFER, Michael, Chief Executive Officer and Administrator, Spooner Health, Spooner, WI, p. A721
SCHAFER, Mona, Regional Manager Human Resources, Milbank Area Hospital Avera, Milbank, SD, p. A574
SCHAFER, Natasha, Chief Executive Officer, Ohio Hospital for Psychiatry, Columbus, OH, p. A492
SCHAFFER, John, R.N., Director of Nursing, Clifton–Fine Hospital, Star Lake, NY, p. A459
SCHAFFER, Megan, Administrative Assistant, Surgical Institute of Reading, Wyomissing, PA, p. A558
SCHAFFER, Renee, Coordinator Human Resources, Select Specialty Hospital–Wichita, Wichita, KS, p. A262
SCHAFFER, Todd, M.D., President and Chief Executive Officer, Sanford Medical Center Bismarck, Bismarck, ND, p. A479
SCHAFSNITZ, Patricia, Director of Nursing Services, Mckenzie Health System, Sandusky, MI, p. A337
SCHALES, Marion, Chief Financial Officer, Highland Hospital, Oakland, CA, p. A80
SCHALL, Dee, R.N., Chief Nursing Officer, Baptist Health Medical Center–Hot Spring County, Malvern, AR, p. A50
SCHALSKI, Paula, Director Human Resources, Pushmataha Hospital, Antlers, OK, p. A509
SCHALTZ, Linda, MSN, R.N., Chief Nursing Officer, Corewell Health Zeeland Hospital, Zeeland, MI, p. A341
SCHAMP, Cindy K., FACHE, President, Baylor Scott & White Medical Center–Irving, Irving, TX, p. A630
SCHANDL, Brian, Chief Information Officer, Marshall Browning Hospital, Du Quoin, IL, p. A193
SCHANE, Kathryn, Chief Executive Officer, Haven Behavioral Hospital of Eastern Pennsylvania, Reading, PA, p. A553
SCHANEL, Judith A, R.N., MSN, FACHE, Chief Operating Officer, Cone Health Moses Cone Hospital, Greensboro, NC, p. A469
SCHAPP, Susan, Vice President Finance and Treasurer, Charlotte Hungerford Hospital, Torrington, CT, p. A119
SCHARENBROCK, Chris, M.D., Chief Medical Staff, David Grant Usaf Medical Center, Travis Air Force Base, CA, p. A98
SCHARFF, Tom, Director Information Services, HCA Florida Woodmont Hospital, Tamarac, FL, p. A151
SCHARNBERG, Cathi Rae, R.N., M.P.H., Vice President Patient Services, Avera Holy Family Hospital, Estherville, IA, p. A236
SCHARNHORST, Alicia, Human Resources and Administrative Assistant, Garfield County Public Hospital District, Pomeroy, WA, p. A692
SCHATTSCHNEIDER, Tami, Chief Nursing Officer, SSM Health St. Agnes Hospital – Fond Du Lac, Fond Du Lac, WI, p. A711
SCHAUER, Jason, M.D., Chief Medical Officer, Geisinger Medical Center Muncy, Muncy, PA, p. A546
SCHAUF, Jeffrey, Director Information Systems, Wesley Medical Center, Wichita, KS, p. A262
SCHAUF, Kyle, M.D., President Medical Staff, Integris Grove Hospital, Grove, OK, p. A513
SCHEERER, Dan, M.D., Chief Medical Officer, Genesis Healthcare System, Zanesville, OH, p. A508
SCHEETZ, Allison, M.D., Medical Director, Atrium Health Navicent Rehabilitation Hospital, Macon, GA, p. A167
SCHEFFLER, Tom, Chief Fiscal Officer, Veterans Affairs Maryland Health Care System–Baltimore Division, Baltimore, MD, p. A302
SCHEINBART, Lee
   M.D., Vice President Medical Affairs, Health First Community Hospitals, Health First Cap. Canaveral Hospital, Cocoa Beach, FL, p. A128
   M.D., Vice President Medical Affairs, Health First Community Hospitals, Health First Palm Bay Hospital, Palm Bay, FL, p. A145
SCHEINBLUM, Richard, Chief Financial Officer, Monadnock Community Hospital, Peterborough, NH, p. A417
SCHELBAR, E Joe, M.D., Medical Director, Select Specialty Hospital–Tulsa Midtown, Tulsa, OK, p. A523
SCHELL, James, M.D., Vice President Medical Affairs, Saint Francis Medical Center, Cap. Girardeau, MO, p. A372
SCHELL, Jonathan
   R.N., Chief Executive Officer, Hillcrest Hospital Cushing, Cushing, OK, p. A511
   Chief Nursing Officer, Baptist Health Medical Center – Drew County, Monticello, AR, p. A50

Index of Health Care Professionals

Index of Health Care Professionals / Schemenaur

SCHEMENAUR, Christina Marie., Vice President, Chief Operating Officer and Chief Nursing Officer, Indiana University Health Jay Hospital, Portland, IN, p. A226
SCHEMER, Tonia, Interim Chief Human Resources, Trinity Health Livingston Hospital, Howell, MI, p. A330
SCHEPICI, Denise, M.P.H., Chief Executive Officer and President, Martha's Vineyard Hospital, Oak Bluffs, MA, p. A317
SCHEPMANN, Jane, Vice President and Chief Nursing Officer, Clara Barton Medical Center, Hoisington, KS, p. A250
SCHEPPERS, Levi, Chief Executive Officer, Orthonebraska Hospital, Omaha, NE, p. A404
SCHEPPERS, Lisa, Chief Medical Officer, Regional West Medical Center, Scottsbluff, NE, p. A406
SCHER, Kathleen, Ed.D., R.N., Chief Nursing Officer, Jamaica Hospital Medical Center, New York, NY, p. A448
SCHERER, Timothy, M.D., Chief Medical Officer, Southern New Hampshire Medical Center, Nashua, NH, p. A416
SCHERLER, Jay, Vice President Finance and Chief Information Officer, Ascension Providence, Waco, TX, p. A660
SCHERLING, Adam, President, Grundy County Memorial Hospital, Grundy Center, IA, p. A236
SCHERPF, John, Chief Executive Officer, Banner Casa Grande Medical Center, Casa Grande, AZ, p. A30
SCHESLER, Stacy, Chief Operating Officer, The Children's Home of Pittsburgh, Pittsburgh, PA, p. A551
SCHEVING, Travis, Chief Financial Officer, Holy Rosary Healthcare, Miles City, MT, p. A394
SCHEXNAYDER, Glenn, M.D., Chief of Staff, Prevost Memorial Hospital, Donaldsonville, LA, p. A281
SCHEXNAYDRE, Renata, Chief Nursing Officer, Ochsner St. Anne General Hospital, Raceland, LA, p. A291
SCHEY, David, Chief Financial Officer, Brook Lane, Hagerstown, MD, p. A304
SCHICK, Eric
Chief Financial Officer, Saint Francis Hospital South, Tulsa, OK, p. A523
Senior Vice President and Chief Financial Officer, Saint Francis Health System, Saint Francis Hospital, Tulsa, OK, p. A523
Senior Vice President, Chief Administrative Officer and Chief Financial Officer, Laureate Psychiatric Clinic And Hospital, Tulsa, OK, p. A522
SCHIEBER, Steven M., FACHE, President, Chi Health Saint Francis, Grand Island, NE, p. A400
SCHIEFELBEIN, Shelia, Coordinator Human Resources, Northwest Florida Community Hospital, Chipley, FL, p. A128
SCHIERECK, Stacie, Director Management Services, Mendota Mental Health Institute, Madison, WI, p. A714
SCHIESL, Troy, Director Information Services, Bellin Psychiatric Center, Green Bay, WI, p. A712
SCHIESLER, Hannah, Interim Assistant Director Human Resources, Baptist Hospitals of Southeast Texas, Beaumont, TX, p. A602
SCHILLER, Ann Mattia, Vice President Human Resources, College Medical Center, Long Beach, CA, p. A70
SCHILLER, Jonathan, President and Chief Executive Officer, Garnet Health Medical Center, Middletown, NY, p. A446
SCHIMEROWSKI, Deb
Regional Chief Financial Officer, Ascension St. Mary – Kankakee, Kankakee, IL, p. A199
Regional Finance Officer, Ascension Saint Josep. – Joliet, Joliet, IL, p. A199
SCHIMMERS, Heather, Chief Operating Officer and Chief Nursing Officer, Gundersen Lutheran Medical Center, La Crosse, WI, p. A713
SCHIMMING, Christopher, M.D., Medical Director, Mayo Clinic Health System In Waseca, Waseca, MN, p. A357
SCHIMMING, Michael B, Director Financial Services, Shriners Hospitals for Children, Galveston, TX, p. A621
SCHIPPER, Brad J., Chief Operating Officer, Sanford Usd Medical Center, Sioux Falls, SD, p. A577
SCHIPPER, Jody, Director of Nursing, Grundy County Memorial Hospital, Grundy Center, IA, p. A236
SCHLABACH, Michael, M.D., Chief Medical Officer, Baylor Scott & White Medical Center – Brenham, Brenham, TX, p. A604
SCHLAGER, Robert, M.D., Chief Medical Officer, Northern Light Sebasticook Valley Hospital, Pittsfield, ME, p. A298
SCHLAGGAR, Bradley, M.D., President and Chief Executive Officer, Kennedy Krieger Institute, Baltimore, MD, p. A300
SCHLAUDERAFF, Cole, Director, Finance, Ridgeview Le Sueur Medical Center, Le Sueur, MN, p. A348
SCHLECHT, Dara, Chief Nursing Officer, Franciscan Healthcare, West Point, NE, p. A407
SCHLECHTER, Sandy, Chief Financial Officer, Pipestone County Medical Center, Pipestone, MN, p. A352
SCHLEETER, Larry C, Chief Human Resources Officer, Memorial Health, Marysville, OH, p. A499
SCHLEICHER, Larry, Manager Information Services, Warner Hospital And Health Services, Clinton, IL, p. A192
SCHLEIDER, Katherine
Interim President, Gouverneur Hospital, Senior Vice President of Operations, St. Lawrence Health, Gouverneur Hospital, Gouverneur, NY, p. A443
St. Lawrence Health Senior Vice President, Operations, Canton–Potsdam Hospital, Potsdam, NY, p. A456
SCHLEIF, John V, Senior Vice President and Chief Operating Officer, Henry Mayo Newhall Hospital, Valencia, CA, p. A99
SCHLENKER, Jim, Interim Chief Executive Officer, Lake District Hospital, Lakeview, OR, p. A528
SCHLESSMAN, Alissa, Administrator, Beaver County Memorial Hospital, Beaver, OK, p. A510
SCHLEY, Kurt, President, Ascension Southeast Wisconsin Hospital – Elmbrook Campus, Brookfield, WI, p. A708
SCHLICHTMAN, Beth A, Chief Human Resources Officer, Brodstone Memorial Hospital, Superior, NE, p. A406
SCHLIECH, Roxane K, Chief Financial Officer, Gundersen Tri–County Hospital And Clinics, Whitehall, WI, p. A725
SCHLUETER, Ann, Chief Operating Officer, Community Hospital–Fairfax, Fairfax, MO, p. A375
SCHLUNTZ, Ana, Director of Human Resources, Harlan County Health System, Alma, NE, p. A397
SCHLUTER, Robin M., Chief Executive Officer, Regional Health Services of Howard County, Cresco, IA, p. A234
SCHMAEDECKE, Dena, Vice President Human Resources, North Suburban Medical Center, Thornton, CO, p. A113
SCHMALLEN, Dede, Chief Human Resources Officer, Wickenburg Community Hospital, Wickenburg, AZ, p. A41
SCHMERBECK, Victor
Chief Executive Officer, Baylor Scott & White Emergency Hospital – Burleson, Burleson, TX, p. A606
Chief Executive Officer, Baylor Scott & White Emergency Hospitals–Aubrey, Aubrey, TX, p. A598
SCHMID, Nancy A, R.N., MS, Associate Director Patient Care Services, Coatesville Veterans Affairs Medical Center, Coatesville, PA, p. A537
SCHMIDT, Allen J, M.D., President, Medical Staff, Decatur Morgan Hospital, Decatur, AL, p. A18
SCHMIDT, Bobbi, Chief Nursing Officer, Select Specialty Hospital–Cincinnati, Cincinnati, OH, p. A489
SCHMIDT, Brent, President, Sevier Valley Hospital, Richfield, UT, p. A668
SCHMIDT, Constance, FACHE, R.N., Chief Executive Officer, St. Anthony North Hospital, Westminster, CO, p. A114
SCHMIDT, Janie, Director of Nursing, Greeley County Health Services, Tribune, KS, p. A261
SCHMIDT, Mark C.
President, Monument Health Lead–Deadwood Hospital, Deadwood, SD, p. A573
President, Monument Health Sturgis Hospital, Sturgis, SD, p. A577
SCHMIDT, Milan, Medical Director, North Shore Health, Grand Marais, MN, p. A347
SCHMIDT, Richard O Jr, President and Chief Executive Officer, Froedtert South – Kenosha Medical Center, Kenosha, WI, p. A713
SCHMIDT, Richard O. Jr, President and Chief Executive Officer, Froedtert South – Kenosha Medical Center, Kenosha, WI, p. A713
SCHMIDT, Robert F, Director Human Resources, Hocking Valley Community Hospital, Logan, OH, p. A498
SCHMIDT, Steve, Director Information Systems, Evans Memorial Hospital, Claxton, GA, p. A160
SCHMIDTBERGER, Sheryl, Chief Financial Officer, Integris Health Ponca City Hospital, Ponca City, OK, p. A519
SCHMIDTKE, Holly, FACHE, R.N., President, Aurora West Allis Medical Center, West Allis, WI, p. A724
SCHMIEDT, Jason, Chief Financial Officer, Clinch Valley Medical Center, Richlands, VA, p. A682
SCHMIER, Joseph, Interim Director Human Resources, Logan Health – Whitefish, Whitefish, MT, p. A396
SCHMIESING, Karee, Director of Nursing, Sleep. Eye Medical Center, Sleep. Eye, MN, p. A355
SCHMIT, Catie, President, Northwestern Medicine Mchenry, Mchenry, IL, p. A201
SCHMITS, Peggy, Director, Nursing Operations, New Braunfels Regional Rehabilitation Hospital, New Braunfels, TX, p. A641
SCHMITT, Amy
M.D., Chief Medical Officer, Providence Newberg Medical Center, Newberg, OR, p. A529
M.D., Interim Chief Executive Officer and Chief Medical Officer, Providence Newberg Medical Center, Newberg, OR, p. A529
SCHMITT, Joseph
III, Senior Vice President Finance and Chief Financial Officer, Henry Ford Hospital, Detroit, MI, p. A325
Chief Financial Officer, Greater Los Angeles Hcs, Los Angeles, CA, p. A72
Chief Information Officer, St. Elizabeth's Medical Center, Brighton, MA, p. A311
SCHMITT, Karl, M.D., Chief of Staff, St. Elizabeth Edgewood, Edgewood, KY, p. A265
SCHMITT, Lance, R.N., Chief Nursing Officer and Vice President, Nursing, Broadlawns Medical Center, Des Moines, IA, p. A234
SCHMITT, Robert C. II, CPA, FACHE, Chief Executive Officer, Gibson Area Hospital And Health Services, Gibson City, IL, p. A196
SCHMITTOU, Stephanie, MSN, R.N., Chief Nursing Officer, Magnolia Regional Medical Center, Magnolia, AR, p. A50
SCHMITZ, Bonnie
Chief Financial Officer, SSM Health Ripon Community Hospital, Ripon, WI, p. A721
Chief Financial Officer, SSM Health Waupun Memorial Hospital, Waupun, WI, p. A724
Vice President and Chief Financial Officer, SSM Health St. Agnes Hospital – Fond Du Lac, Fond Du Lac, WI, p. A711
SCHMITZ, Christopher, Associate Vice President, Director Human Resources, Stoughton Health, Stoughton, WI, p. A722
SCHMITZ, Cole
Chief Executive Officer, Legent Hospital for Special Surgery, Plano, TX, p. A644
Chief Executive Officer, Legent North Houston Surgical Hospital, Tomball, TX, p. A658
SCHMITZ, Douglas, Director of Nursing, Long–Term Acute Care Hospital, Mosaic Life Care At St. Joseph, Saint Joseph, MO, p. A383
SCHMITZ, Jessica, Director of Nursing, Roosevelt Medical Center, Culbertson, MT, p. A391
SCHMITZ, Joseph, Chief Financial Officer, St. Cloud Va Health Care System, Saint Cloud, MN, p. A354
SCHMOTZER, Dave, Chief Financial Officer, Bryn Mawr Rehabilitation Hospital, Malvern, PA, p. A545
SCHMUS, Angie, Chief Information Technology, Aleda E. Lutz Department of Veterans Affairs Medical Center, Saginaw, MI, p. A336
SCHNABEL, Annette D.
FACHE, President, Parkland Health Center–Bonne Terre, Bonne Terre, MO, p. A371
FACHE, President, Parkland Health Center Corporation, Parkland Health Center – Farmington Community, Farmington, MO, p. A375
SCHNACK, Tim H.
Chief Financial Officer, Chi Health Immanuel, Omaha, NE, p. A403
Chief Financial Officer, Chi Health Plainview, Plainview, NE, p. A405
Chief Financial Officer, Chi Health Schuyler, Schuyler, NE, p. A405
Vice President Financial Services, Chi Health Creighton University Medical Center – Bergan Mercy, Omaha, NE, p. A403
Vice President Operations Finance, Chi Health St. Mary's, Nebraska City, NE, p. A402
SCHNEDLER, Lisa W., FACHE, President and Chief Executive Officer, Upland Hills Health, Dodgeville, WI, p. A709
SCHNEIDER, Brenda, Chief Financial Officer, Skyline Health, White Salmon, WA, p. A698
SCHNEIDER, Brian, Chief Financial Officer, Dupont Hospital, Fort Wayne, IN, p. A216
SCHNEIDER, Erica
Chief Operating Officer, Kettering Health Miamisburg, Miamisburg, OH, p. A500
President, Kettering Health Dayton, Dayton, OH, p. A494
President KH Miamisburg & KH Washington Township. Kettering Health Miamisburg, Miamisburg, OH, p. A500
SCHNEIDER, Gina, Director Human Resources, Northwest Specialty Hospital, Post Falls, ID, p. A183
SCHNEIDER, Jennifer S., Vice President of Finance, Saint Francis Hospital, Hartford, CT, p. A116
SCHNEIDER, Jessie, Director Human Resources, Community Memorial Healthcare, Marysville, KS, p. A254
SCHNEIDER, John, Human Resources Director, HCA Florida Putnam Hospital, Palatka, FL, p. A145
SCHNEIDER, Kimberly, Director Human Resources, Pottstown Hospital, Pottstown, PA, p. A553
SCHNEIDER, Maureen, Ph.D., R.N., FACHE, President, Chilton Medical Center, Pompton Plains, NJ, p. A427
SCHNEIDER, Scott, Chief Executive Officer, Vibra Hospital of Central Dakotas, Mandan, ND, p. A482
SCHNEIDER, Shanon, Chief Information Officer, Greeley County Health Services, Tribune, KS, p. A261
SCHNEIDER, Stacie A, Director Human Resources, Aurora Medical Center – Sheboygan County, Sheboygan, WI, p. A721

A966 Index of Health Care Professionals

SCHNEIDER, Stephen, Manager Information Services, Alaska Psychiatric Institute, Anchorage, AK, p. A27
SCHNEIDER, Thomas D, D.O., Chief of Staff, Jack C. Montgomery Department of Veterans Affairs Medical Center, Muskogee, OK, p. A515
SCHNEIDER, Valerie, Director Human Resources, Gove County Medical Center, Quinter, KS, p. A258
SCHNELL, Dawn
  Administrator and Chief Executive Officer, Sanford Jackson Medical Center, Jackson, MN, p. A348
  Chief Nursing Officer, Sanford Jackson Medical Center, Jackson, MN, p. A348
SCHNELLER, Sharon L, Chief Nursing Officer, Olmsted Medical Center, Rochester, MN, p. A354
SCHNIER, Martin, D.O., Chief of Staff, West Texas Va Health Care System, Big Spring, TX, p. A604
SCHNITTKER, Kira, Director of Nursing, Ascension St. Vincent's Blount, Oneonta, AL, p. A23
SCHNITZLEIN, Carla, D.O., Medical Director, Natchaug Hospital, Mansfield Center, CT, p. A116
SCHNOOR, Jeff, Director Information Systems, Swedish Medical Center, Englewood, CO, p. A107
SCHOCK, Marilyn, President, UCHealth Greeley Hospital, Greeley, CO, p. A109
SCHOELLER, Betsy V, Director Human Resources and Education, Mary Greeley Medical Center, Ames, IA, p. A230
SCHOEN, Greg
  M.D., Regional Medical Director, M Health Fairview Northland Medical Center, Princeton, MN, p. A353
  M.D., Vice President Medical Affairs, M Health Fairview Lakes Medical Center, Wyoming, MN, p. A358
SCHOENDALER, Hannah, Chief Nursing Officer, Sheridan County Health Complex, Hoxie, KS, p. A251
SCHOENECKER, Perry L, M.D., Chief of Staff, Shriners Hospitals for Children-St. Louis, Saint Louis, MO, p. A385
SCHOENER, Timothy E
  Chief Information Officer, UPMC Memorial, York, PA, p. A559
  Chief Information Officer, UPMC Muncy, Muncy, PA, p. A546
  Senior Vice President and Chief Information Officer, UPMC Wellsboro, Wellsboro, PA, p. A557
  Vice President and Chief Information Officer, UPMC Williamsport, Williamsport, PA, p. A558
SCHOENIG, Thomas
  Chief Information Officer, Jupiter Medical Center, Jupiter, FL, p. A136
  Chief Information Officer, UChicago Medicine Adventhealth La Grange, La Grange, IL, p. A199
SCHOENIG, Tom, Regional Director Information Services, Valley Hospital Medical Center, Las Vegas, NV, p. A411
SCHOETTLE, Steve, M.D., Chief Medical Staff, Ozark Health Medical Center, Clinton, AR, p. A44
SCHOFIELD, Joseph, Chief Operating Officer, Suburban Community Hospital, East Norriton, PA, p. A539
SCHOFIELD, Sherry, Director Human Resources, Sovah Health-Martinsville, Martinsville, VA, p. A679
SCHOLEFIELD, Robert, MS, R.N., Executive Vice President and Chief Operating Officer, Wynn Hospital, Utica, NY, p. A460
SCHOLL, Shyanne, Interim Human Resources Director, Friend Community Healthcare System, Friend, NE, p. A400
SCHOLZ, Suzanne, Director Medical Records, The Horsham Clinic, Ambler, PA, p. A534
SCHOMBURG, Jennifer, President, Aurora St. Luke's Medical Center, Milwaukee, WI, p. A717
SCHONEBERY, Jeremy, Director Information Technology, Heart of America Medical Center, Rugby, ND, p. A483
SCHONS, Jeri, R.N., Chief Nursing Officer, Sanford Tracy Medical Center, Tracy, MN, p. A356
SCHOOL, Peggy, Director of Nursing, Thedacare Medical Center-New London, New London, WI, p. A718
SCHOPP, Mary Ellen, Senior Vice President Human Resources, Rush University Medical Center, Chicago, IL, p. A191
SCHORER, Emily
  Senior Vice President Human Resources, Cap. Cod Hospital, Hyannis, MA, p. A314
  Vice President, Human Resources, Falmouth Hospital, Falmouth, MA, p. A313
SCHOTT, Connie, Vice President, Human Resources, Ozarks Healthcare, West Plains, MO, p. A388
SCHOTTEL, Roxanne, Chief Executive Officer, Washington County Hospital, Washington, KS, p. A261
SCHOWENGERDT, Daniel, M.D., Chief of Staff, Comanche County Hospital, Coldwater, KS, p. A247
SCHRADER, Guillermo, M.D., Acting Medical Director, Eastern State Hospital, Williamsburg, VA, p. A685
SCHRADER, Rick, Chief Financial Officer, Southwest Health System, Cortez, CO, p. A105

SCHRAEDER, David, Director Information Systems, Russell Regional Hospital, Russell, KS, p. A258
SCHRAMM, Michael, Chief Executive Officer, Centracare - Rice Memorial Hospital, Willmar, MN, p. A357
SCHRAMM, Steven R, Chief Financial Officer, Mountain View Hospital, Payson, UT, p. A667
SCHRANK, Paul, Chief Executive Officer, Kindred Hospital Bay Area-Tampa, Tampa, FL, p. A152
SCHRANT, Benjamin, M.D., Chief of Staff, Northeast Regional Medical Center, Kirksville, MO, p. A378
SCHREFFLER, Mary Jane, Director Human Resources, The Meadows Psychiatric Center, Centre Hall, PA, p. A536
SCHREIBER, Anne, Manager Human Resources, Fairfax Behavioral Health, Kirkland, WA, p. A691
SCHREIBER, Elizabeth, R.N., Director Patient Care Services, Marshfield Medical Center - Park Falls, Park Falls, WI, p. A719
SCHREIER, Garett E., R.N., Associate Director, Nursing and Patient Care Services, Ralp. H. Johnson Veterans Affairs Medical Center, Charleston, SC, p. A563
SCHREINER, David, Ph.D., President and Chief Executive Officer, Katherine Shaw Bethea Hospital, Dixon, IL, p. A193
SCHREINER, Kimberly D, MSN, R.N., Vice President of Nursing & Chief Nursing Officer, Magruder Memorial Hospital, Port Clinton, OH, p. A502
SCHROCK, Bonnie W, FACHE, Chief Operating Officer, Baptist Health Paducah, Paducah, KY, p. A272
SCHRODER, Kristina, Chief Executive Officer, Encompass Health Rehabilitation Hospital of Sioux Falls, Sioux Falls, SD, p. A576
SCHRODER, Loren D, Chief Financial Officer, Phelp. Memorial Health Center, Holdrege, NE, p. A401
SCHROEDER, Brian D., M.D., Senior Vice President and Chief Medical Officer, University of Michigan Health-Sparrow Lansing, Lansing, MI, p. A332
SCHROEDER, Catherine, Deputy Chief Information Officer, Brigham And Women's Faulkner Hospital, Boston, MA, p. A310
SCHROEDER, Cygnet, D.O., Medical Director, Encompasss Health Rehabilitation Hospital of Fort Smith, Fort Smith, AR, p. A47
SCHROEDER, Destiny, Information Systems Director, Rawlins County Health Center, Atwood, KS, p. A246
SCHROEDER, Heather, R.N., Vice President Nursing, Aurora Baycare Medical Center, Green Bay, WI, p. A712
SCHROEDER, Joanne, FACHE, Munson Healthcare Charlevoix Hospital President and Chief Executive Officer, Munson Healthcare Charlevoix Hospital, Charlevoix, MI, p. A323
SCHROEDER, Rick, Interim Chief Executive Officer, Roundup Memorial Healthcare, Roundup. MT, p. A395
SCHROEDER, Russell, Chief Nursing Officer, Shorepoint Health Punta Gorda, Punta Gorda, FL, p. A148
SCHROEPPEL, Stacie, Director of Human Resources, Baptist Memorial Rehabilitation Hospital, Germantown, TN, p. A583
SCHROYER, Mike K., FACHE, MSN, R.N., President, Baptist Health Floyd, New Albany, IN, p. A225
SCHRUMPF, Jason, FACHE, Chief Executive Officer, Missouri Delta Medical Center, Sikeston, MO, p. A386
SCHRYVERS, Luke, Chief Executive Officer, Murray County Medical Center, Slayton, MN, p. A355
SCHUBACH, Michael, Chief People Officer, Carroll County Memorial Hospital, Carrollton, MO, p. A373
SCHUCK, Eric
  M.D., Chief Medical Officer, HCA Florida Fort Walton-Destin Hospital, Fort Walton Beach, FL, p. A132
  M.D., Chief Medical Officer, HCA Florida Twin Cities Hospital, Niceville, FL, p. A142
  M.D., Chief Medical Officer, Tristar Southern Hills Medical Center, Nashville, TN, p. A591
SCHUCK, Jennifer
  Chief Executive Officer, Emory Decatur Hospital, Decatur, GA, p. A162
  Chief Executive Officer, Emory Hillandale Hospital, Lithonia, GA, p. A166
  Chief Executive Officer, Emory Long-Term Acute Care, Decatur, GA, p. A162
SCHUCKMAN, Tim, Chief Financial Officer, Jennie M. Melham Memorial Medical Center, Broken Bow, NE, p. A398
SCHUE, Janine
  Executive Vice President, Chief Human Resources Officer, Rochester Regional Health, Newark-Wayne Community Hospital, Newark, NY, p. A454
  Senior Vice President Human Resources, Rochester General Hospital, Rochester, NY, p. A457
SCHUELER, Joe, Chief Financial Officer, Morrow County Hospital, Mount Gilead, OH, p. A501
SCHUERCH, Timothy, President and Chief Executive Officer, Maniilaq Health Center, Kotzebue, AK, p. A29
SCHUESSLER, Dwight, Chief Information Officer, Iowa City Va Health System, Iowa City, IA, p. A238

SCHUETZ, Gail, Associate Chief Nursing Officer, Olathe Medical Center, Olathe, KS, p. A256
SCHULER, Allison, R.N., Chief Nursing Officer, Baptist Medical Center – Attala, Kosciusko, MS, p. A365
SCHULHOF, K. Alicia., President, Johns Hopkins All Children's Hospital, Saint Petersburg, FL, p. A149
SCHULKOWSKI, Becky, President, Baycare Hospital Wesley Chapel, Wesley Chapel, FL, p. A154
SCHULTE, Mark, FACHE, Vice President of Operations, Monument Health Rapid City Hospital, Rapid City, SD, p. A576
SCHULTES, Jeremy, Chief Executive Officer, Fall River Health Services, Hot Springs, SD, p. A574
SCHULTES, Jeremy S., Administrator and Chief Executive Officer, Philip Health Services, Philip. SD, p. A575
SCHULTHEIS, Hal, Director Information Systems, Tristar Hendersonville Medical Center, Hendersonville, TN, p. A584
SCHULTZ, Bradley, Chief Financial Officer, Wesley Medical Center, Wichita, KS, p. A262
SCHULTZ, Diana
  Chief Executive Officer, Las Palmas Medical Center, El Paso, TX, p. A616
  Chief Executive Officer, Mesquite Rehabilitation Institute, Mesquite, TX, p. A639
  Chief Executive Officer, Mesquite Specialty Hospital, Mesquite, TX, p. A639
  Chief Executive Officer, Weslaco Regional Rehabilitation Hospital, Weslaco, TX, p. A662
SCHULTZ, Kurt
  Chief Financial Officer, Cornerstone Specialty Hospitals West Monroe, West Monroe, LA, p. A294
  Group Chief Financial Officer, Cornerstone Specialty Hospitals Tucson, Tucson, AZ, p. A40
SCHULTZ, Mary Kay, Director Human Resources, Sturgis Hospital, Sturgis, MI, p. A338
SCHULTZ, Merrilee, Chief Finance, Sanford Usd Medical Center, Sioux Falls, SD, p. A577
SCHULTZ, Patrick, Vice President Nursing, Sanford Medical Center Bismarck, Bismarck, ND, p. A479
SCHULTZ, Rachelle H., Ed.D., President and Chief Executive Officer, Winona Health, Winona, MN, p. A357
SCHULTZ, Sharon A, Chief Nurse Executive and Vice President, Tri-City Medical Center, Oceanside, CA, p. A81
SCHULTZ, Teresa L, R.N., Vice President, Patient Care, Rogers Behavioral Health, Oconomowoc, WI, p. A718
SCHULTZ, Vince, M.D., Chief Medical Officer, Munson Healthcare Grayling Hospital, Grayling, MI, p. A329
SCHULZ, Ken, Chief Operating Officer, North Dakota State Hospital, Jamestown, ND, p. A482
SCHULZ, Leah, Director of Nursing, North Dakota State Hospital, Jamestown, ND, p. A482
SCHULZ, Richard, Chief Executive Officer, Spartanburg Rehabilitation Institute, Spartanburg, SC, p. A570
SCHULZ, Susan G, Chief Nursing Officer, Corewell Health Trenton Hospital, Trenton, MI, p. A339
SCHUMACHER, Debbie
  Chief Human Resource Officer, Clearwater Valley Health, Orofino, ID, p. A183
  Chief Human Resource Officer, St. Mary's Health, Cottonwood, ID, p. A181
SCHUMACHER, Kevin, Director of Information Systems, Lifecare Medical Center, Roseau, MN, p. A354
SCHUMACHER, Rodney, Administrative Director, Shannon Medical Center, San Angelo, TX, p. A648
SCHUMANN, Vera, Director of Finance and Controller, North Shore Health, Grand Marais, MN, p. A347
SCHUSTER, Carol E, R.N., Chief Nursing Officer and Vice President Patient Care Services, Franciscan Health Crown Point, Crown Point, IN, p. A214
SCHUSTER, Christine C., R.N., President and Chief Executive Officer, Emerson Hospital, Concord, MA, p. A313
SCHUSTER, Janet, Chief Nursing Officer, Cleveland Clinic Lutheran Hospital, Cleveland, OH, p. A490
SCHUSTER, Lexie, Vice President Human Resources, PIH Health Good Samaritan Hospital, Los Angeles, CA, p. A74
SCHUSTER, Shane, Chief Operating Officer, Pender Community Hospital, Pender, NE, p. A405
SCHUSTER, Steve, Interim Senior Vice President, Human Resources, Phoenix Children's, Phoenix, AZ, p. A36
SCHUSTER, Todd, President, Saint Francis Hospital South, Tulsa, OK, p. A523
SCHUSTER, Tony
  M.D., Vice President, Chief Medical Officer, Mease Countryside Hospital, Safety Harbor, FL, p. A148
  M.D., Vice President, Chief Medical Officer, Mease Dunedin Hospital, Dunedin, FL, p. A130
SCHWAB, Bob, M.D., Chief Medical Officer, Texas Health Presbyterian Hospital Allen, Allen, TX, p. A595

Index of Health Care Professionals

Index of Health Care Professionals / Schwab

SCHWAB, Caryn A, Executive Director, The Mount Sinai Hospital, New York, NY, p. A453
SCHWABENBAUER, Mary Ann, Director Information Technology, Penn Highlands Elk, Saint Marys, PA, p. A554
SCHWAEGEL, Glen
Chief Financial Officer, Progress West Hospital, O Fallon, MO, p. A381
Vice President and Chief Financial Officer, Barnes–Jewish St. Peters Hospital, Saint Peters, MO, p. A386
SCHWAN, Karin, Chief Nursing Officer, Vice President Patient Care Services, University Hospitals Samaritan Medical Center, Ashland, OH, p. A485
SCHWANER, Charles III, Chief Financial Officer, HCA Florida Sarasota Doctors Hospital, Sarasota, FL, p. A149
SCHWANKE, Dan, FACHE, Interim President, Promedica Coldwater Regional Hospital, Coldwater, MI, p. A324
SCHWARTZ, Ave, Chief Information Officer, Austen Riggs Center, Stockbridge, MA, p. A318
SCHWARTZ, David
M.D., Chief Medical Officer, Saint Francis Hospital, Memphis, TN, p. A589
M.D., Chief Medical Officer, Saint Francis Hospital–Bartlett, Bartlett, TN, p. A579
SCHWARTZ, Jack, Director Information Technology, Kittitas Valley Healthcare, Ellensburg, WA, p. A689
SCHWARTZ, Jonathon, M.D., Chief Medical Officer, Spaulding Hospital for Continuing Medical Care Cambridge, Cambridge, MA, p. A312
SCHWARTZ, Kenneth V, M.D., Medical Director, Griffin Health, Derby, CT, p. A115
SCHWARTZ, Kim, Assistant Administrator Human Resources and Operations, Boone County Hospital, Boone, IA, p. A231
SCHWARTZ, Michael, M.D., Chief of Staff, College Hospital Costa Mesa, Costa Mesa, CA, p. A60
SCHWARTZ, Peggy, Vice President Human Resources, Wayne Healthcare, Greenville, OH, p. A497
SCHWARTZ, Peter, Director Information Systems, Hackensack Meridian Health Carrier Clinic, Belle Mead, NJ, p. A418
SCHWARTZ, Roberta, Ph.D., Executive Vice President, Houston Methodist Hospital, Houston, TX, p. A626
SCHWARTZ, Ronald, M.D., Medical Director, Masonicare Health Center, Wallingford, CT, p. A119
SCHWARTZ, Sharon, Director Medical Records, Baylor Scott & White Medical Center – Brenham, Brenham, TX, p. A604
SCHWARTZ, Stephanie L., FACHE, President, Overlook Medical Center, Summit, NJ, p. A428
SCHWARZ, John T., President, Bryn Mawr Hospital, Bryn Mawr, PA, p. A536
SCHWARZKOPF, Ruth, Chief Nursing Officer, St. Mary's Medical Center, West Palm Beach, FL, p. A154
SCHWECHHEIMER, Betsy L., Chief Executive Officer, Tewksbury Hospital, Tewksbury, MA, p. A319
SCHWEICKHARDT, Mary Jo, Vice President Human Resources, Medstar Georgetown University Hospital, Washington, DC, p. A123
SCHWEIGERT, Nicole, Director Human Resources, Texas Health Presbyterian Hospital Flower Mound, Flower Mound, TX, p. A618
SCHWEIKART, Jay, Chief Financial Officer, Kindred Hospital–Sycamore, Sycamore, IL, p. A209
SCHWEIZER, Kim, Director Human Resources, Excelsior Springs Hospital, Excelsior Springs, MO, p. A374
SCHWENN, Krystal, Chief Financial Officer, Phillip. County Health Systems, Phillipsburg, KS, p. A258
SCHWIEGER, Kay, Chief Human Resources Officer, Clement J. Zablocki Veterans' Administration Medical Center, Milwaukee, WI, p. A717
SCHWIND, David, Chief Financial Officer, Capital Caring, Arlington, VA, p. A673
SCHWINGLER, Joyce, Chief Financial Officer, Eureka Community Health Services Avera, Eureka, SD, p. A573
SCIARRA, Michael, M.D., Chief Medical Officer, Hudson Regional Hospital, Secaucus, NJ, p. A428
SCIARRO, Jason R., Chief Operating Officer, Butler Memorial Hospital, Butler, PA, p. A536
SCIMECA, Paul, President and Chief Executive Officer, Glens Falls Hospital, Glens Falls, NY, p. A443
SCIONTI, Jeff, Interim Chief Executive Officer, Parkland Medical Center, Derry, NH, p. A414
SCLAMA, Tony, M.D., Vice President Medical Affairs, Medstar Franklin Square Medical Center, Baltimore, MD, p. A302
SCOGGIN, Kevin, Chief Executive Officer, Methodist Hospital, San Antonio, TX, p. A650
SCOGGIN, Terry, Chief Executive Officer, Titus Regional Medical Center, Mount Pleasant, TX, p. A640
SCOGGINS, James
Chief Executive Officer, Arkansas State Hospital, Little Rock, AR, p. A49
Director of Nursing, Arkansas State Hospital, Little Rock, AR, p. A49
SCORZELLI, Gerard, Chief Financial Officer, Albany Stratton Veterans Affairs Medical Center, Albany, NY, p. A438
SCOTFORD, Lucrecia, Executive Vice President and Chief Operations Officer, Bristol Bay Area Health Corporation, Dillingham, AK, p. A28
SCOTT, Alan, M.D., Chief of Staff, East Georgia Regional Medical Center, Statesboro, GA, p. A171
SCOTT, Angie, Chief Executive Officer, Ridgeview Institute – Monroe, Monroe, GA, p. A168
SCOTT, Colleen M, Vice President Finance, Waterbury Hospital, Waterbury, CT, p. A119
SCOTT, Cullen, Acting Chief Executive Officer and Director of Operations for Surgical Care Affiliates, Northwest Hills Surgical Hospital, Austin, TX, p. A600
SCOTT, Damien, Chief Executive Officer, Emanuel Medical Center, Swainsboro, GA, p. A172
SCOTT, Daniel, Director of Information Systems, Good Samaritan Hospital, Vincennes, IN, p. A228
SCOTT, Doug, Vice President Human Resources, RMC Anniston, Anniston, AL, p. A15
SCOTT, Ernie, Director Human Resources, Natchitoches Regional Medical Center, Natchitoches, LA, p. A289
SCOTT, Henry, Executive Director, Technical Services, Piedmont Newnan Hospital, Newnan, GA, p. A169
SCOTT, James
M.D., Vice President Medical Affairs, Candler Hospital–Savannah, Savannah, GA, p. A170
M.D., Vice President Medical Affairs, St. Joseph's Hospital, Savannah, GA, p. A171
SCOTT, Jeffrey, Chief Information Officer, Ascension St. Vincent Kokomo, Kokomo, IN, p. A221
SCOTT, Jennifer, Director of Informatics, Carepartners Rehabilitation Hospital, Asheville, NC, p. A463
SCOTT, Jo Ellen, R.N., MS, Senior Vice President of Patient Care Services and Chief Nursing Officer, Indiana University Health Tipton Hospital, Tipton, IN, p. A228
SCOTT, Joy, Market Administrator, Ascension Via Christi St. Francis, Mulvane, KS, p. A255
SCOTT, Julie, Chief Nursing Officer, Encompass Health Rehabilitation Hospital of York, York, PA, p. A558
SCOTT, Karen M, Vice President Patient Care, Adventist Health Howard Memorial, Willits, CA, p. A101
SCOTT, Kelley M., Interim Chief Nursing Officer, Grant Memorial Hospital, Petersburg, WV, p. A703
SCOTT, LaNell, President, Christus Spohn Hospital Corpus Christi Shoreline, Corpus Christi, TX, p. A608
SCOTT, Lincoln, Vice President Human Resources, Mercy Hospital Southeast, Cap. Girardeau, MO, p. A372
SCOTT, Margie A., M.D., Medical Center Director, John L. Mcclellan Memorial Veterans' Hospital, Little Rock, AR, p. A50
SCOTT, Martha Lynn, Chief Patient Care Officer, Covington County Hospital, Collins, MS, p. A361
SCOTT, Monica, Chief Financial Officer, Great Plains Regional Medical Center, Elk City, OK, p. A512
SCOTT, Rhonda Adams, Ph.D., R.N., Market Chief Operating Officer and President, Chi Memorial, Chattanooga, TN, p. A580
SCOTT, Robert F, Vice President and Chief Human Resources Officer, Springfield Memorial Hospital, Springfield, IL, p. A209
SCOTT, Sam, Vice President Financial Services, St. Dominic–Jackson Memorial Hospital, Jackson, MS, p. A364
SCOTT, Sandra, M.D., Interim Chief Executive Officer, Interfaith Medical Center, New York, NY, p. A448
SCOTT, Sharon, Health Information Director, Allegiance Specialty Hospital of Greenville, Greenville, MS, p. A362
SCOTT, Steve, Chief Operating Officer, Sheridan Community Hospital, Sheridan, MI, p. A338
SCOTT, Steven, Chief Executive Officer, Phoenix Medical Psychiatric Hospital, Phoenix, AZ, p. A36
SCOTT, Steven M.
M.P.H., FACHE, President, SSM Health Saint Louis University Hospital, Saint Louis, MO, p. A384
M.P.H., FACHE, President, SSM Health St. Mary's Hospital – St. Louis, Saint Louis, MO, p. A385
SCOTT, Susan, Chief Operating Officer, Providence Holy Family Hospital, Spokane, WA, p. A696
SCOTT, Thomas G., CPA, Chief Financial Officer, Saint Clare's Denville Hospital, Denville, NJ, p. A420
SCOTT, Thomas W., FACHE, FABC, President and Chief Executive Officer, Centrastate Healthcare System, Freehold, NJ, p. A421
SCOTT, Todd, Chief Financial Officer, Vibra Hospital of Sacramento, Folsom, CA, p. A63
SCOTT, Travis, Service Unit Director, U. S. Public Health Service Indian Hospital, Pine Ridge, SD, p. A575
SCOTT, Veronica, Business Office Manager, Inspire Specialty Hospital, Midwest City, OK, p. A515
SCOTT, William
M.D., Vice President Medical Affairs, Regional Medical Center of San Jose, San Jose, CA, p. A92
Chief Financial Officer, KPC Promise Hospital of Overland Park, Overland Park, KS, p. A257
SCOTT, William P, M.D., Chief of Staff, Dardanelle Regional Medical Center, Dardanelle, AR, p. A45
SCOUFOS, Jennifer, M.D., Chief of Staff, Northeastern Health System Sequoyah, Sallisaw, OK, p. A520
SCOWN, Kent, Director Operations and Information Services, Jerold Phelp. Community Hospital, Garberville, CA, p. A65
SCREMIN, Karen, Vice President Finance, Lutheran Medical Center, Wheat Ridge, CO, p. A114
SCRIVO, Josep. A Jr, Director Human Resources, Mercy Hospital, Buffalo, NY, p. A440
SCROGGIN, Christy, Director Operations and Human Resources, Conway Regional Rehabilitation Hospital, Conway, AR, p. A44
SCROGGINS, Todd, Chief Financial Officer, Medical City Decatur, Decatur, TX, p. A613
SCROGGS, Amy, Chief Nursing Officer, Adventist Health Delano, Delano, CA, p. A61
SCRUGGS, Sherry, Chief Executive Officer, West Tennessee Healthcare Milan Hospital, Milan, TN, p. A589
SCRUGGS–MORRIS, Kisha, Chief Financial Officer, Montrose Behavioral Health Hospital, Chicago, IL, p. A190
SCUDDER, Angela K., MSN, R.N., Vice President Patient Care Services, St. Elizabeth Dearborn, Lawrenceburg, IN, p. A222
SCUDERI, Denise, Vice President Patient Care Services, Northern Light Mayo Hospital, Dover–Foxcroft, ME, p. A297
SCULCO, Dawn, Chief Nursing Officer, Valley View Hospital, Glenwood Springs, CO, p. A108
SCULL, Stephen W, Vice President Ethics and Compliance officer, Rapides Regional Medical Center, Alexandria, LA, p. A276
SCULLY, Charles, Chief Information Officer, Denver Health, Denver, CO, p. A106
SCULLY, Trish
Director Human Resources, Taunton State Hospital, Taunton, MA, p. A319
Manager Employment Services, Pappas Rehabilitation Hospital for Children, Canton, MA, p. A312
SCZYGELSKI, Sidney C, Senior Vice President Finance and Chief Financial Officer, Aspirus Wausau Hospital, Inc., Wausau, WI, p. A724
SEAGER, Jerry, Assistant Vice President and Chief Financial Officer, Inova Fair Oaks Hospital, Fairfax, VA, p. A675
SEAGO, Terri, Chief Financial Officer, Baptist Memorial Hospital–Collierville, Collierville, TN, p. A581
SEAGRAM, Patricia, Vice President Human Resources, Henry Ford Jackson Hospital, Jackson, MI, p. A331
SEAGROVES, Matthew, Chief Financial Officer, Tamp. General Hospital Brooksville, Brooksville, FL, p. A127
SEAHORN, Martha, Chief Nursing Officer, Gadsden Regional Medical Center, Gadsden, AL, p. A20
SEALE, Jonathan, Chief Information Officer, Erie Veterans Affairs Medical Center, Erie, PA, p. A539
SEALS, Amanda, Assistant Vice President, Human Resource Business Partner, Ochsner Medical Center – Baton Rouge, Baton Rouge, LA, p. A278
SEALS, Mary Beth, President, Lincoln County Health System, Fayetteville, TN, p. A583
SEALS, Robert, D.O., Medical Director, University of Michigan Health–Sparrow Carson, Carson City, MI, p. A323
SEAMON, Robert L., Chief Executive Officer, Copper Queen Community Hospital, Bisbee, AZ, p. A30
SEARLE, Anne, Chief Information Officer, Penn Medicine Princeton Medical Center, Plainsboro, NJ, p. A427
SEARLS, Barbara, Chief Financial Officer, Searhc Mt. Edgecumbe Hospital, Sitka, AK, p. A29
SEARLS, Gary, Chief Financial Officer, HCA Florida Brandon Hospital, Brandon, FL, p. A127
SEARS, Erin Clare, Associate Director of Operations, Providence Veterans Affairs Medical Center, Providence, RI, p. A560
SEARS, Marilyn, Chief Financial Officer, HSHS Good Shepherd Hospital, Shelbyville, IL, p. A208
SEARS, Tina, Director Patient Care Services, Sullivan County Memorial Hospital, Milan, MO, p. A380
SEARS, Wendi, Chief Nursing Officer, Banner Estrella Medical Center, Phoenix, AZ, p. A35
SEASE, Peggy, Vice President Human Resources, Dch Regional Medical Center, Tuscaloosa, AL, p. A25
SEBEK, Brenda Jean, R.N., Administrator, Chi Health St. Mary's, Nebraska City, NE, p. A402

A968 Index of Health Care Professionals

Index of Health Care Professionals / Sevilla

Index of Health Care Professionals

SEBENALER, Ginette, Associate Chief Financial Officer, Aspen Valley Hospital, Aspen, CO, p. A103
SECOR, April, R.N., Chief Nursing Officer, Hillcrest Hospital Henryetta, Henryetta, OK, p. A513
SECOR, Diane K, Director Human Resources, Lawrence Medical Center, Moulton, AL, p. A23
SECURRO, Matthew J., Vice President, Human Resources, Conway Medical Center, Conway, SC, p. A565
SEDMINIK, Vincent, Vice President and Administrator, Willis Knighton North, Shreveport, LA, p. A293
SEEDER, Rachael, Controller, Santiam Hospital, Stayton, OR, p. A532
SEELEY, Hollie, President and Chief Executive Officer, Sutter Medical Center, Sacramento, Sacramento, CA, p. A87
SEELEY, Kevin, Chief Information Officer, Mike O'Callaghan Federal Hospital, Nellis Afb, NV, p. A411
SEELEY, Pam, Chief Nursing Officer, Elmira Psychiatric Center, Elmira, NY, p. A443
SEELEY, Steven, Vice President, Chief Operating Officer, Chief Nursing Officer, Jupiter Medical Center, Jupiter, FL, p. A136
SEELY, Paula, Manager Human Resources, Kossuth Regional Health Center, Algona, IA, p. A230
SEEMS, Steven, Director of Information Technology, Phillip. County Health Systems, Phillipsburg, KS, p. A258
SEERUP, Kathleen, R.N., Senior Vice President, Chief Nursing and Operations Officer, Children's Hospital Colorado – Colorado Springs, Colorado Springs, CO, p. A105
SEESE, Rebecca, Chief Operating Officer, U. S. Air Force Regional Hospital, Elmendorf Afb, AK, p. A28
SEEVER, Jennifer, Regional Chief Financial Officer, Sedan City Hospital, Sedan, KS, p. A259
SEGAL, Jonathan, Chief Financial Officer, New York State Psychiatric Institute, New York, NY, p. A450
SEGAL, Rebecca, FACHE, President and Chief Executive Officer, Fauquier Hospital, Warrenton, VA, p. A685
SEGAL, Stanton, M.D., Chief Medical Officer, Jefferson Health Northeast, Philadelphia, PA, p. A549
SEGAL, Tanya, Director, St. Luke's Easton Campus, Easton, PA, p. A539
SEGAR–MILLER, Cindy, FACHE, R.N., President, St. Mary's Regional Medical Center, Lewiston, ME, p. A298
SEGARRA, Sergio, M.D., Chief Medical Officer, Baptist Health South Florida, Baptist Hospital of Miami, Miami, FL, p. A139
SEGAWA, Lance
Chief Executive Officer, Kauai Veterans Memorial Hospital, Waimea, HI, p. A178
Chief Executive Officer, Samuel Mahelona Memorial Hospital, Kapaa, HI, p. A177
SEGER, Clint, M.D., Chief Executive Officer, Billings Clinic, Billings, MT, p. A389
SEGIN, Robert
Chief Financial Officer, Virtua Mount Holly Hospital, Mount Holly, NJ, p. A424
Executive Vice President & Chief Financial Officer, Virtua Marlton, Marlton, NJ, p. A423
SEGUR, DNP, Jennifer, Chief Nursing Officer and Chief Clinical Officer, Adventhealth North Pinellas, Tarpon Springs, FL, p. A153
SEGURA, Mario, Director of Nursing, Starr County Memorial Hospital, Rio Grande City, TX, p. A647
SEHNERT, Laura, M.D., Chief Medical Officer, UCHealth Yamp. Valley Medical Center, Steamboat Springs, CO, p. A113
SEIBERT, Jenee, Chief Finance Officer, Fulton County Health Center, Wauseon, OH, p. A506
SEIBOLD, Spencer Garrett, M.D., Chief of Medical Staff, Power County Hospital District, American Falls, ID, p. A179
SEID, Lynette, Area Chief Financial Officer, Kaiser Permanente Zion Medical Center, San Diego, CA, p. A89
SEIDL, Doris A, Vice President Human Resources, Mclaren Port Huron, Port Huron, MI, p. A336
SEIDMAN, Robert
Chief Operating Officer, Health Alliance Hospital – Broadway Campus, Kingston, NY, p. A445
Chief Operating Officer, Health Alliance Hospital – Mary's Avenue Campus, Kingston, NY, p. A445
SEIFER, Jill, Vice President Human Resources, Oaklawn Psychiatric Center, Goshen, IN, p. A218
SEIFERT, Debra A, Director Human Resources, Lake Huron Medical Center, Port Huron, MI, p. A336
SEILER, Gregory A, Chief Executive Officer, Methodist Hospital, San Antonio, TX, p. A650
SEILER, Gregory A., Chief Executive Officer, Methodist Hospital South, Jourdanton, TX, p. A631
SEIM, Lori, R.N., Director Nursing Services, First Care Health Center, Park River, ND, p. A483
SEIN, Rafael, M.D., Medical Director, Multy Medical Rehabilitation Hospital San Juan, San Juan, PR, p. A735
SEIP, Jeffrey, M.D., Chief Medical Staff, Hi–Desert Medical Center, Joshua Tree, CA, p. A68
SEIPLE, Donald, President, St. Luke's Monroe Campus, Stroudsburg, PA, p. A555
SEIRER, Jeff, Interim Chief Financial Officer, Ascension Via Christi St. Francis, Mulvane, KS, p. A255
SEITZ, Kimberly A, Area Human Resources Leader, Kaiser Permanente Redwood City Medical Center, Redwood City, CA, p. A85
SEITZ, Tawnya, Chief Executive Officer and Chief Financial Officer, Lincoln County Hospital, Lincoln, KS, p. A253
SELBY, Eric, R.N., Chief Nursing Officer, Chicot Memorial Medical Center, Lake Village, AR, p. A49
SELBY, Victoria MHA, BSN, Vice President, Ancillary and Support Services, Community Hospital of San Bernardino, San Bernardino, CA, p. A88
SELF, Chris
Chief Executive Officer, Adventhealth Gordon, Calhoun, GA, p. A160
Chief Executive Officer, Adventhealth Murray, Chatsworth, GA, p. A160
SELFRIDGE, Tara, Manager Human Resources, Purcell Municipal Hospital, Purcell, OK, p. A520
SELHORST, Sonya, R.N., President and Chief Nursing Officer, Mercy Health – Defiance Hospital, Defiance, OH, p. A494
SELIG, Doug R, MSN, R.N., Vice President of Patient Services, Parkview Huntington Hospital, Huntington, IN, p. A218
SELIG, Doug R., MSN, R.N., President, Parkview Huntington Hospital, Huntington, IN, p. A218
SELIGMAN, David, Executive Director, Long Island Jewish Medical Center, New Hyde Park, NY, p. A447
SELIGMAN, Morris H, M.D., Chief Medical Officer and Chief Medical Information Officer, Sycamore Shoals Hospital, Elizabethton, TN, p. A582
SELINGER, Stephen, M.D., Chief Medical Officer, Luminis Health Anne Arundel Medical Center, Annapolis, MD, p. A300
SELL, Paula, Director Human Resources, Allen County Regional Hospital, Iola, KS, p. A251
SELL, Teri, Payroll and Personnel Coordinator, Jennie M. Melham Memorial Medical Center, Broken Bow, NE, p. A398
SELLA, John, Controller, Corewell Health Gerber Hospital, Fremont, MI, p. A327
SELLE, Ginger, Vice President Patient Care Services, SSM Health St. Clare Hospital–Baraboo, Baraboo, WI, p. A707
SELLE, Justin, Chief Executive Officer, HSHS St. Nicholas Hospital, Sheboygan, WI, p. A721
SELLERS, Laura, Director Information Systems, Youth Villages Inner Harbour Campus, Douglasville, GA, p. A163
SELLERS, Liz, R.N., MSN, Chief Executive Officer, Pioneers Medical Center, Meeker, CO, p. A112
SELLERS, Mary, Chief Information Officer, Navos, Seattle, WA, p. A694
SELLERS, Robert R., President, Clay County Hospital, Flora, IL, p. A195
SELLMAN, Elizabeth, President and Chief Operating Officer, Mount Sinai Beth Israel, New York, NY, p. A449
SELLS, Matt, Chief Executive Officer, Shenandoah Medical Center, Shenandoah, IA, p. A243
SELMAN, J Peter., FACHE, Chief Executive Officer, Baptist Medical Center South, Montgomery, AL, p. A22
SELMON, Patricia, Director Public Relations and Chief Human Resources, Jefferson County Hospital, Fayette, MS, p. A361
SELPH, Wendy, Director Human Resources, Dodge County Hospital, Eastman, GA, p. A163
SELSOR, Doug, Director Finance, Denton Rehab, Denton, TX, p. A613
SELVAM, A Panneer, M.D., Chief of Staff, Bob Stump Department of Veterans Affairs Medical Center, Prescott, AZ, p. A37
SELVICK, Carl, President and Chief Executive Officer, Black River Memorial Hospital, Black River Falls, WI, p. A708
SELVIDGE, Sandra, Chief Fiscal Service, Cincinnati Veterans Affairs Medical Center, Cincinnati, OH, p. A488
SELZ, Timothy P, Vice President, Garnet Health Medical Center, Middletown, NY, p. A446
SEMELSBERGER, Kimberly, CPA, Chief Financial Officer, Conemaugh Nason Medical Center, Roaring Spring, PA, p. A553
SEMERDJIAN, Nancy, R.N., Chief Nursing Officer, Endeavor Health Evanston Hospital, Evanston, IL, p. A195
SEMERE, Jana, Chief Nursing Officer, Leonard J. Chabert Medical Center, Houma, LA, p. A283
SEMINARO, Anthony J.
Chief Financial Officer, Mercy Health – St. Elizabeth Youngstown Hospital, Youngstown, OH, p. A508
Chief Financial Youngstown, Mercy Health – St. Elizabeth Boardman Hospital, Boardman, OH, p. A486
SEMRAU, Clint, President Medical Staff, Aspirus Medford Hospital & Clinics, Medford, WI, p. A715
SENDACH, Jon, Executive Director, North Shore University Hospital, Manhasset, NY, p. A445
SENDAYDIEGO, Fe, Director Information Systems, Sonoma Valley Hospital, Sonoma, CA, p. A96
SENDEN, Luke, Chief Executive Officer, Johnson County Healthcare Center, Buffalo, WY, p. A726
SENDROS, Isaac, President and Chief Executive Officer, Adventhealth Redmond, Rome, GA, p. A170
SENGER, Joshua, Chief Financial Officer, Chi St. Francis Health, Breckenridge, MN, p. A344
SENGER, Richard, Chief Financial Officer, Portsmouth Regional Hospital, Portsmouth, NH, p. A417
SENGER, Tricia, Chief Financial Officer, St. Luke's Elmore, Mountain Home, ID, p. A182
SENKER, Margaret, Chief Information Officer, Veterans Affairs Western New York Healthcare System–Buffalo Division, Buffalo, NY, p. A440
SENKER, Thomas J.
FACHE, President, Medstar Good Samaritan Hospital, Baltimore, MD, p. A300
FACHE, President, Medstar Union Memorial Hospital, Baltimore, MD, p. A301
SENNEFF, Robert G., FACHE, President and Chief Executive Officer, Graham Hospital, Canton, IL, p. A187
SENNETT, Paul, Chief Financial Officer, Centinela Hospital Medical Center, Inglewood, CA, p. A67
SENNISH, James, Vice President Human Resources, Firelands Regional Health System, Sandusky, OH, p. A503
SENSING, Phillip, Chief Financial Officer, Presbyterian/St. Luke's Medical Center, Denver, CO, p. A106
SEQUIN, Shannon, MSN, Chief Nursing Officer, Select Specialty Hospital – Saginaw, Saginaw, MI, p. A337
SERAFIN, Brady, Chief Executive Officer, Cedar Crest Hospital And Residential Treatment Center, Belton, TX, p. A603
SERENO, Joseph, Chief Financial Officer, Lovelace Women's Hospital, Albuquerque, NM, p. A433
SERGEANT, Lindy, Medical Staff President, Community Hospital of Bremen, Bremen, IN, p. A213
SERGIO, Barbara, President, Franklin Memorial Hospital, Farmington, ME, p. A297
SERKETICH, Steve, Manager Information Services, Aurora Medical Center – Sheboygan County, Sheboygan, WI, p. A721
SERNYAK, Michael, M.D., Director, Connecticut Mental Health Center, New Haven, CT, p. A117
SERRANO, Jorge L Matta., Administrator, Auxilio Mutuo Hospital, San Juan, PR, p. A734
SERRANO, Justin, Chief Executive Officer, Santa Rosa Medical Center, Milton, FL, p. A141
SERRANO, Lorenzo, Chief Executive Officer, Winkler County Memorial Hospital, Kermit, TX, p. A632
SERRATT, Jim, Chief Executive Officer, Parkside Psychiatric Hospital And Clinic, Tulsa, OK, p. A522
SERZAN, Megan, Director of Quality, Compliance, Risk & Safety, Asheville Specialty Hospital, Asheville, NC, p. A463
SESSIONS, Ben, Human Resources Director, Steele Memorial Medical Center, Salmon, ID, p. A183
SESSIONS, Jerry W., M.D., Chief Medical Staff, Springhill Medical Center, Springhill, LA, p. A293
SESTERHENN, Steven, Vice President, Unitypoint Health – Allen Hospital, Waterloo, IA, p. A244
SETHI, Sanjiv, M.D., Medical Director, Fulton State Hospital, Fulton, MO, p. A375
SETLIFF, Chad, Senior Vice President, President Novant Health Forsyth Medical Center and Greater Winston–Salem Mark, Novant Health Forsyth Medical Center, Winston–Salem, NC, p. A478
SETTLE, Andrea, Director Human Resources, Taylor Regional Hospital, Campbellsville, KY, p. A264
SETTLES, Allicia, Chief Nursing Officer, UT Health Quitman, Quitman, TX, p. A646
SETZER, Jeffery, Administrator Information Systems, J. D. Mccarty Center for Children With Developmental Disabilities, Norman, OK, p. A516
SETZER, Randy R, Financial Services Manager, Waukesha County Mental Health Center, Waukesha, WI, p. A723
SETZKORN–MEYER, Marsha, Director Public Relations and Marketing, Hillsboro Community Hospital, Hillsboro, KS, p. A250
SEVERE, Sandra, Senior Vice President, Chief Executive Officer, Jackson Health System, Miami, FL, p. A140
SEVERSON, Lynn, Chief Financial Officer, Prairie Lakes Healthcare System, Watertown, SD, p. A578
SEVILLA, Mark, R.N., Executive Director, Yale New Haven Hospital, New Haven, CT, p. A118

© 2025 AHA Guide Index of Health Care Professionals **A969**

Index of Health Care Professionals / Sewell

SEWELL, Lance
  Chief Financial Officer, Orlando Health South Lake Hospital, Clermont, FL, p. A128
  President and Chief Executive Officer, Orlando Health South Lake Hospital, Clermont, FL, p. A128
SEWICK, Alayne, Vice President Human Resources, Medical City Mckinney, Mckinney, TX, p. A638
SEXTON, Charles, Manager Human Resources, Cumberland Medical Center, Crossville, TN, p. A582
SEXTON, Cindy, Chief Financial Officer, St. David's Round Rock Medical Center, Round Rock, TX, p. A648
SEXTON, Kevin, Director Information Systems, Raleigh General Hospital, Beckley, WV, p. A699
SEYBOLD, Henry, Senior Vice President and Chief Financial Officer, North Kansas City Hospital, North Kansas City, MO, p. A381
SEYMOUR, Alex, Chief Executive Officer, Chi Franciscan Rehabilitation, Tacoma, WA, p. A697
SEYMOUR, Claudette, Director Personnel, Memphis Mental Health Institute, Memphis, TN, p. A588
SEYMOUR, Donna, Assistant Vice President, Finance (Controller), Bethesda Hospital East, Boynton Beach, FL, p. A126
SEYMOUR, Jose, Chief Information Resource Management, James A. Haley Veterans' Hospital–Tampa, Tampa, FL, p. A152
SEYMOUR, Robert, Chief Financial Officer/Senior Director Finance, Grande Ronde Hospital, La Grande, OR, p. A528
SEYMOUR, Sally, Chief Executive Officer, HCA Florida Bayonet Point Hospital, Hudson, FL, p. A134
SGARLATA, Lisa, MSN, Chief Patient Care Officer, Cap. Coral Hospital, Cap. Coral, FL, p. A127
SHACKELFORD, Gerald, Staff Support Specialist, Texas Center for Infectious Disease, San Antonio, TX, p. A651
SHACKELFORD, J. Larry., CPA, President and Chief Executive Officer, Washington Regional Medical System, Fayetteville, AR, p. A46
SHACKELFORD, Paul, M.D., Chief Medical Officer, ECU Health Medical Center, Greenville, NC, p. A470
SHACKELFORD, Teresa, Administrator, State Hospital North, Orofino, ID, p. A183
SHACKLETON, Carol, M.D., Medical Director, Gothenburg Health, Gothenburg, NE, p. A400
SHACKLETT, Shawna, Chief Financial Officer, UT Health Pittsburg, Pittsburg, TX, p. A644
SHADENSACK, Don, Vice President Clinical Services, OSF St. Mary Medical Center, Galesburg, IL, p. A196
SHADOWENS, Karen
  CPA, Chief Financial Officer, Ohiohealth Van Wert Hospital, Van Wert, OH, p. A505
  Chief Financial Officer, UNC Health Caldwell, Lenoir, NC, p. A471
SHAFER, Kenny
  Chief Executive Officer, Johnson City Medical Center, Johnson City, TN, p. A585
  Chief Operating Officer, Johnson City Medical Center, Johnson City, TN, p. A585
SHAFER, Robert, Vice President Finance, Mercyone Dyersville Medical Center, Dyersville, IA, p. A236
SHAFFER, Jeraldene, MSN, Chief Nursing Officer, Roseland Community Hospital, Chicago, IL, p. A190
SHAFICI, Khaled, M.D., President Medical Staff, Cornerstone Specialty Hospitals West Monroe, West Monroe, LA, p. A294
SHAFIU, Mohamed, M.D., Chief of Staff, Val Verde Regional Medical Center, Del Rio, TX, p. A613
SHAH, Beena, M.D., Chief of Staff and Chief Medical Officer, Anaheim Global Medical Center, Anaheim, CA, p. A55
SHAH, Jayendra H, M.D., Chief Medical Officer, Tucson Va Medical Center, Tucson, AZ, p. A41
SHAH, Paresh, Director Information Systems, Reston Hospital Center, Reston, VA, p. A682
SHAH, Rubin, Chief Executive Officer, East Houston Hospitals & Clinics, Houston, TX, p. A625
SHAH, Sameer, PharmD, President, Mount Sinai Hospital, Chicago, IL, p. A190
SHAH, Samir, M.D., Chief Executive Officer and Chief Medical Officer, Contra Costa Regional Medical Center, Martinez, CA, p. A76
SHAH, Syed, M.D., Chief of Staff, Pioneer Memorial Hospital And Health Services, Viborg, SD, p. A578
SHAH, Vital, M.D., Associate Director and Chief Medical Officer, Central State Hospital, Louisville, KY, p. A269
SHAHAN, Matthew, Chief Executive Officer, Campbell County Health, Gillette, WY, p. A727
SHAHI, Niloo, Chief Operating Officer, Olive View–Ucla Medical Center, Los Angeles, CA, p. A74
SHAHNAM, Melissa Shreves, Director Human Resources, Mon Health Medical Center, Morgantown, WV, p. A703

SHAHRYAR, Syed, M.D., Medical Director, KPC Promise Hospital of Phoenix, Mesa, AZ, p. A34
SHAHZADA, Kamran, M.D., Chief Medical Staff, South Central Kansas Medical Center, Arkansas City, KS, p. A246
SHAIFFER, Mandy, Chief Nursing Officer, Mt. San Rafael Hospital, Trinidad, CO, p. A114
SHAIKH, Azim, Chief Executive Officer, Riverview Health Institute, Dayton, OH, p. A494
SHAKOOR, Arif, Chief of Staff, HCA Florida Raulerson Hospital, Okeechobee, FL, p. A143
SHALK, Jennifer, Chief Executive Officer, Meadow Wood Behavioral Health System, New Castle, DE, p. A122
SHALLOCK, James R, Chief Financial Officer, Memorial Hermann Greater Heights Hospital, Houston, TX, p. A627
SHAMBURG, Steffen, M.D., Chief of Staff, Amberwell Hiawatha, Hiawatha, KS, p. A250
SHAMIEH, Samer, M.D., Chief Medical Officer, Avala, Covington, LA, p. A280
SHANAHAN, Thomas
  CPA, Chief Financial Officer and Senior Vice President, Hackensack Meridian Health Raritan Bay Medical Center, Perth Amboy, NJ, p. A427
  CPA, Chief Operating Officer, Hackensack Meridian Health Raritan Bay Medical Center, Perth Amboy, NJ, p. A427
  Vice President, Human Resources, Children's Hospital of Wisconsin–Fox Valley, Neenah, WI, p. A718
  Vice President, Human Resources, Children's Wisconsin, Milwaukee, WI, p. A717
SHANER, Danna, President, St. Elizabeth Hospital, Enumclaw, WA, p. A689
SHANKS–CONNORS, Tanya, R.N., MSN, Chief Nursing Officer, Peacehealth Southwest Medical Center, Vancouver, WA, p. A698
SHANLEY, Diane, Deputy Service Unit Director, U. S. Public Health Service Indian Hospital–Sells, Sells, AZ, p. A38
SHANLEY, Linda L., Vice President, Chief Information Officer, Saint Francis Hospital, Hartford, CT, p. A116
SHANLEY, Thomas, M.D., President and Chief Executive Officer, Ann & Robert H. Lurie Children's Hospital of Chicago, Chicago, IL, p. A188
SHANNON, Christine, Chief Nursing Officer, Miracare Behavioral Health Care, Tinley Park, IL, p. A210
SHANNON, Erik
  Chief Executive Officer, UVA Health Culpeper Medical Center, Culpeper, VA, p. A675
  Chief Executive Officer, UVA Health Haymarket Medical Center, Haymarket, VA, p. A677
  Chief Executive Officer, UVA Health Prince William Medical Center, Manassas, VA, p. A679
SHANNON, Greg, Chief Human Resources Officer, Golden Valley Memorial Healthcare, Clinton, MO, p. A373
SHANNON, Lori, President, Ascension St. Vincent Heart Center, Indianapolis, IN, p. A218
SHANNON, Patrick, Chief Executive Officer, Huntsville Memorial Hospital, Huntsville, TX, p. A629
SHANNON, Richard, M.D., Chief of Staff, Montrose Regional Health, Montrose, CO, p. A112
SHANNON, Scott, Director Finance, Socorro General Hospital, Socorro, NM, p. A437
SHAPE, Amy, Information Technology, North Dakota State Hospital, Jamestown, ND, p. A482
SHAPIRO, David, M.D., Vice President Medical Affairs and Chief Medical Officer, Ascension Columbia St. Mary's Hospital Milwaukee, Milwaukee, WI, p. A716
SHAPIRO, Marc, M.D., Chief Medical Officer, Adventist Health Clear Lake, Clearlake, CA, p. A59
SHARANGPANI, Rojesh, M.D., Chief of Staff, Multicare Capital Medical Center, Olympia, WA, p. A692
SHARKEY, Linda, R.N., MSN, Vice President Patient Care Services and Chief Nurse Executive, Fauquier Hospital, Warrenton, VA, p. A685
SHARLOW, Joseph, M.D., Chief of Staff, Ste. Genevieve County Memorial Hospital, Ste Genevieve, MO, p. A387
SHARMA, Adhi
  M.D., President, Mount Sinai South Nassau, Oceanside, NY, p. A454
  M.D., Senior Vice President, Medical Affairs and Chief Medical Officer, Mount Sinai South Nassau, Oceanside, NY, p. A454
SHARMA, Aika, M.D., President Medical Staff, Alameda Hospital, Alameda, CA, p. A55
SHARMA, Chandra, M.D., Chief of Staff, Welch Community Hospital, Welch, WV, p. A705
SHARMA, Priyam, Chief Executive Officer, Berwick Hospital Center, Berwick, PA, p. A535
SHARMA, Roger
  President and Chief Executive Officer, Emanate Health Foothill Presbyterian Hospital, Glendora, CA, p. A66
  President/Chief Executive Officer, Emanate Health Inter-Community Hospital, Covina, CA, p. A61

SHARMA, Satish C, M.D., Chief of Staff, Providence Veterans Affairs Medical Center, Providence, RI, p. A560
SHARON, Joesp. P., Associate Director, Wilkes–Barre Veterans Affairs Medical Center, Wilkes–Barre, PA, p. A558
SHARP, Alan
  Chief Financial Officer, Ascension Saint Thomas Dekalb, Smithville, TN, p. A593
  Chief Financial Officer, Ascension Saint Thomas Stones River, Woodbury, TN, p. A594
SHARP, ArvaDell, Director of Nursing, Pembina County Memorial Hospital And Wedgewood Manor, Cavalier, ND, p. A480
SHARP, Cindy, M.D., Chief Medical Officer, Madison Valley Medical Center, Ennis, MT, p. A391
SHARP, Gary, Director Information Technology, Southern Hills Hospital And Medical Center, Las Vegas, NV, p. A410
SHARP, Gina, FACHE, President, Endeavor Health Linden Oaks Hospital, Naperville, IL, p. A203
SHARP, Greg, M.D., Senior Vice President and Chief Medical Officer, Arkansas Children's Hospital, Little Rock, AR, p. A49
SHARP, Julie, Supervisor Human Resources, Chase County Community Hospital, Imperial, NE, p. A401
SHARP, Patrick, Chief Executive Officer, Asante Three Rivers Medical Center, Grants Pass, OR, p. A527
SHARP, Ray, Chief Information Officer, Katherine Shaw Bethea Hospital, Dixon, IL, p. A193
SHARP, Rebecca, Chief Financial Officer, Wagoner Community Hospital, Wagoner, OK, p. A523
SHARP, Richard, M.D., Medical Director, Christus St. Michael Rehabilitation Hospital, Texarkana, TX, p. A656
SHARP, Tony, Supervisor Information System, Sweetwater Hospital, Sweetwater, TN, p. A594
SHARPE, Deborah, R.N., Director of Nursing, West Springs Hospital, Grand Junction, CO, p. A109
SHARPTON, Debra, Director of Nursing, Devereux Advanced Behavioral Health Georgia, Kennesaw, GA, p. A166
SHARUM, Melinda
  Director Human Resources, Mercy Hospital Ardmore, Ardmore, OK, p. A510
  Director Human Resources, Mercy Hospital Healdton, Healdton, OK, p. A513
SHATRAW, Thomas, Director Human Resources, Samaritan Medical Center, Watertown, NY, p. A461
SHAUINGER, Beckie, Interim Chief Executive Officer, Rainier Springs Hospital, Vancouver, WA, p. A698
SHAULL, Heather, Chief Financial Officer, Adair County Health System, Greenfield, IA, p. A236
SHAULL, Ty, President and Chief Executive Officer, Wyandot Memorial Hospital, Upper Sandusky, OH, p. A505
SHAUNESSY, Celia, Vice President Human Resources, Aspirus Steven's Point Hospital & Clinics, Inc., Stevens Point, WI, p. A722
SHAVELSON, Karin, M.D., Chief Medical Officer, Marinhealth Medical Center, Greenbrae, CA, p. A66
SHAVER, Chris
  Vice President Human Resources, Covenant Children's Hospital, Lubbock, TX, p. A635
  Vice President Human Resources, Covenant Medical Center, Lubbock, TX, p. A636
  Vice President Human Resources, Covenant Specialty Hospital, Lubbock, TX, p. A636
SHAVER, Jennifer, Director of Nursing, Gouverneur Hospital, Gouverneur, NY, p. A443
SHAVER, John, Chief Financial Officer, Baystate Noble Hospital, Westfield, MA, p. A319
SHAVER, Robert D, M.D., Vice President Medical Affairs, Wellspan Good Samaritan Hospital, Lebanon, PA, p. A544
SHAW, Angie, Chief Executive Officer, Eureka Springs Hospital, Eureka Springs, AR, p. A45
SHAW, David, Director Information Technology, Forrest City Medical Center, Forrest City, AR, p. A46
SHAW, David B., Chief Executive Officer and Administrator, Nor–Lea Hospital District, Lovington, NM, p. A435
SHAW, Douglas A., Chief Executive Officer, Mad River Community Hospital, Arcata, CA, p. A56
SHAW, Greg, Vice President, Finance, Aspirus Medford Hospital & Clinics, Medford, WI, p. A715
SHAW, Howard, M.D., Chief Medical Officer, Medical City Denton, Denton, TX, p. A614
SHAW, Jan, Director Personnel, River Bend Hospital, West Lafayette, IN, p. A229
SHAW, Jean, Chief Financial Officer, Valley Regional Hospital, Claremont, NH, p. A414
SHAW, John C, M.D., Medical Director, Southern Indiana Rehabilitation Hospital, New Albany, IN, p. A225
SHAW, Kendra, Chief Information Officer, Western Wisconsin Health, Baldwin, WI, p. A707

Index of Health Care Professionals / Shirilla

Index of Health Care Professionals

SHAW, Kimberly
FACHE, President and Chief Executive Officer, Chi St. Josep. Regional Health Center, Bryan, TX, p. A605
FACHE, St. Josep. Market President, Chi St. Josep. Regional Health Center, Bryan, TX, p. A605
SHAW, Mandy, M.D., Chief of Staff, Sidney Regional Medical Center, Sidney, NE, p. A406
SHAW, Tristan, Chief Financial Officer, UChicago Medicine Adventhealth Bolingbrook, Bolingbrook, IL, p. A186
SHAW, Violet, R.N., Director of Nursing, Grafton City Hospital, Grafton, WV, p. A701
SHAWGO, Darla, Director Human Resources, Sparta Community Hospital, Sparta, IL, p. A208
SHAWN, D.J., Director Human Resources, Alliancehealth Madill, Madill, OK, p. A514
SHEA, Natalie, Chief Nursing Officer, Mercyone Elkader Medical Center, Elkader, IA, p. A236
SHEALEY, John P., Medical Center Director, Oscar G. Johnson Department of Veterans Affairs Medical Facility, Iron Mountain, MI, p. A330
SHEAR, Larry, Administrative Assistant, Norwood Health Center, Marshfield, WI, p. A715
SHEARER, Christopher, M.D., Chief Medical Officer, Honorhealth John C. Lincoln Medical Center, Phoenix, AZ, p. A36
SHEARER, Ron, M.D., Regional Medical Director, Peacehealth Peace Harbor Medical Center, Florence, OR, p. A527
SHEARN, Dan, R.N., MSN, Chief Nursing Officer, Carondelet St. Joseph's Hospital, Tucson, AZ, p. A40
SHEARS, Ann Marie, Vice President Patient Care Services, Robert Wood Johnson University Hospital Rahway, Rahway, NJ, p. A427
SHEEHAN, John, Chief Executive Officer, West Springs Hospital, Grand Junction, CO, p. A109
SHEEHAN, Karen, Vice President and Chief Information Officer, Endeavor Health Swedish Hospital, Chicago, IL, p. A189
SHEEHAN, T J, Chief Financial Officer, Lauderdale Community Hospital, Ripley, TN, p. A592
SHEEHAN, Terrence P, M.D., Medical Director, Adventist Healthcare Rehabilitation, Rockville, MD, p. A306
SHEEHY, Andrea, Chief Executive Officer, Rehabilitation Hospital of Northwest Ohio, Toledo, OH, p. A505
SHEETS, Cindy, Vice President Information Systems and Chief Information Officer, Ohiohealth Mansfield Hospital, Mansfield, OH, p. A499
SHEFFIELD, Aubrey, Administrative Assistant Human Resources and Public Relations, Grove Hill Memorial Hospital, Grove Hill, AL, p. A20
SHEFIELD, Jennifer, M.D., Chief of Staff, West River Regional Medical Center, Hettinger, ND, p. A481
SHEGOLEV, Igor, Vice President Human Resources, Carondelet St. Joseph's Hospital, Tucson, AZ, p. A40
SHEHATA, Nady, M.D., Vice President Medical Affairs, Sisters of Charity Hospital of Buffalo, Buffalo, NY, p. A440
SHEHI, G Michael, M.D., Medical Director, Mountain View Hospital, Gadsden, AL, p. A20
SHEHI, Jay, Chief Executive Officer, Alliance Health Center, Meridian, MS, p. A366
SHEIKH, Azad, Chief Medical Officer, Adventist Health And Rideout, Marysville, CA, p. A77
SHEINBEIN, David, Chief Medical Officer, Banner – University Medical Center South, Tucson, AZ, p. A40
SHELAST, Amanda, FACHE, President, Marshfield Medical Center – Dickinson, Iron Mountain, MI, p. A330
SHELBURNE, Dorie, Chief Executive Officer, Uofl Health – Jewish Hospital, Louisville, KY, p. A270
SHELBURNE, John D, M.D., Chief of Staff, Durham Va Health Care System, Durham, NC, p. A467
SHELDON, Monica, Chief Executive Officer, Northern Cochise Community Hospital, Willcox, AZ, p. A41
SHELFORD, Dave, Assistant Superintendent, Richmond State Hospital, Richmond, IN, p. A226
SHELL, John, M.D., Chief Medical Officer, Coffey County Hospital, Burlington, KS, p. A247
SHELLENBERGER, David, President, Saint John Vianney Hospital, Downingtown, PA, p. A538
SHELLS, Tammy, Chief Nursing Officer, Belmont Pines Hospital, Youngstown, OH, p. A508
SHELSTAD, Erik, M.D., Chief of Staff, Johnson Memorial Health Services, Dawson, MN, p. A345
SHELT, Elizabeth, Civilian Personnel Officer, Dwight David Eisenhower Army Medical Center, Fort Gordon, GA, p. A164
SHELTON, Amy, Chief Nursing Officer, Ascension St. Vincent's East, Birmingham, AL, p. A16
SHELTON, Angela, Chief Financial Officer, Jack Hughston Memorial Hospital, Phenix City, AL, p. A24
SHELTON, Carol, Director Human Resources, Lovelace Women's Hospital, Albuquerque, NM, p. A433
SHELTON, Darlene, Coordinator Team Resources, Baycare Alliant Hospital, Dunedin, FL, p. A130
SHELTON, Jared
FACHE, President, Texas Health Harris Methodist Hospital Fort Worth, Fort Worth, TX, p. A620
FACHE, President, Texas Health Harris Methodist Hospital Hurst–Euless–Bedford, Bedford, TX, p. A602
SHELTON, Kathy, Director Human Resources, UT Health Pittsburg, Pittsburg, TX, p. A644
SHELTON, Richard, M.D., Chief Medical Officer, Baptist Health Richmond, Richmond, KY, p. A273
SHELTON, Tom, Coordinator of Nursing Services, Porterville Developmental Center, Porterville, CA, p. A84
SHENEFIELD, Jason, FACHE, President, Chief Executive Officer, Phelp. Health, Rolla, MO, p. A382
SHENGLE, Lori, Director Information Technology, Morrill County Community Hospital, Bridgeport, NE, p. A398
SHENNAR, Arek, Chief Information Officer, Kingman Regional Medical Center, Kingman, AZ, p. A32
SHEPARD, Bridget, Vice President Human Resources, Wabash General Hospital, Mount Carmel, IL, p. A202
SHEPARD, Karen, Senior Vice President and Chief Financial Officer, St. Charles Prineville, Prineville, OR, p. A531
SHEPARD, Megan, Director Clinical Services, Odessa Memorial Healthcare Center, Odessa, WA, p. A692
SHEPARD, Melissa, Chief Financial Officer, Heart of America Medical Center, Rugby, ND, p. A483
SHEPARD, Sheila, Controller, Encompass Health Rehabilitation Hospital of Humble, Humble, TX, p. A629
SHEPARDSON, Dean, Chief Financial Officer, Banner Estrella Medical Center, Phoenix, AZ, p. A35
SHEPARDSON, Heather S, Vice President Human Resources, Carilion Roanoke Memorial Hospital, Roanoke, VA, p. A683
SHEPHARD, Bryan, Chief Financial Officer, Tristar Summit Medical Center, Hermitage, TN, p. A584
SHEPHARD, Russ, Senior Systems Analyst, West Tennessee Healthcare Dyersburg Hospital, Dyersburg, TN, p. A582
SHEPHERD, Jamie, Chief Executive Officer, Shepherd Center, Atlanta, GA, p. A158
SHEPHERD, Joshua
President, Buffalo Hospital, Buffalo, MN, p. A344
President, Cambridge Medical Center, Cambridge, MN, p. A344
SHEPHERD, Mary, Chief Operating Officer, Northside Hospital Gwinnett/Duluth, Lawrenceville, GA, p. A166
SHEPHERD, Tory
Market Chief Operating Officer, Sovah Health–Danville, Danville, VA, p. A675
Market Chief Operating Officer, Sovah Health–Martinsville, Martinsville, VA, p. A679
SHEPLER, Mary, R.N., Senior Vice President, Chief Nursing Officer, Evergreenhealth, Kirkland, WA, p. A691
SHEPPARD, Ballard, Ph.D., Chief Executive Officer, Hill Crest Behavioral Health Services, Birmingham, AL, p. A17
SHEPPARD, Sandy, Vice President Patient Services, Atrium Health Wake Forest Baptist Wilkes Medical Center, North Wilkesboro, NC, p. A474
SHEPPARD, Sharon, Manager Human Resources, Sycamore Shoals Hospital, Elizabethton, TN, p. A582
SHERBONDY, Lori, Director Human Resources, Battle Mountain General Hospital, Battle Mountain, NV, p. A408
SHERER, Susan, Chief Information Resource Management, Dayton Veterans Affairs Medical Center, Dayton, OH, p. A493
SHERMAN, Angelina, R.N., MSN, Chief Nursing Officer, The Rehabilitation Institute of St. Louis, Saint Louis, MO, p. A384
SHERMAN, Frederick C, M.D., Chief Medical Officer, The Children's Home of Pittsburgh, Pittsburgh, PA, p. A551
SHERMAN, Sheila, Vice President Patient Care Services, Vail Health, Vail, CO, p. A114
SHERMAN, Stephanie, Chief Human Resources Officer, West Boca Medical Center, Boca Raton, FL, p. A126
SHERON, William E., Chief Executive Officer, Wooster Community Hospital, Wooster, OH, p. A507
SHERRILL, Angela, Chief Information Officer, Ochsner Laird Hospital, Union, MS, p. A369
SHERRILL, Diane, R.N., Director of Nursing, Medical Arts Hospital, Lamesa, TX, p. A633
SHERRILL, Tyler, Chief Executive Officer, East Cooper Medical Center, Mount Pleasant, SC, p. A568
SHERROD, Michael, Chief Executive Officer, Tristar Greenview Regional Hospital, Bowling Green, KY, p. A264
SHERROD, Rhonda, Chief Executive Officer, Select Specialty Hospital–Gainesville, Gainesville, FL, p. A132
SHERRON, Tammy M., Vice President Finance, Carolinaeast Health System, New Bern, NC, p. A473
SHERRY, Mark A., Regional Director Human Resource Strategic Services, Austin/Round Rock Region, Baylor Scott & White Medical Center – Round Rock, Round Rock, TX, p. A647
SHERVA, Brock, Chief Executive Officer, Northwood Deaconess Health Center, Northwood, ND, p. A482
SHERWIN, Chuck H., FACHE, President, Mymichigan Medical Center Midland, Midland, MI, p. A333
SHERWOOD, Edward J M.D., Chief Executive Officer, Cornerstone Specialty Hospitals Austin Round Rock, Austin, TX, p. A599
SHERWOOD, Jennifer L, Division, Human Resource Business Partner, Banner – University Medical Center South, Tucson, AZ, p. A40
SHERWOOD, Matthew M, Chief Financial Officer, Unity Physicians Hospital, Mishawaka, IN, p. A224
SHETTLESWORTH, Amanda, Director Human Resources, Bloomington Meadows Hospital, Bloomington, IN, p. A212
SHETTY, Atul, Chief of Staff, Weirton Medical Center, Weirton, WV, p. A705
SHEW, Angel, Director Area Technology, Kaiser Permanente South San Francisco Medical Center, South San Francisco, CA, p. A96
SHEWBRIDGE, Richard K., President, Cleveland Clinic Medina Hospital, Medina, OH, p. A500
SHEYKA, Patricia, Chief Nursing Officer, Gila Regional Medical Center, Silver City, NM, p. A437
SHICKOLOVICH, William, Chief Information Officer, Tufts Medical Center, Boston, MA, p. A311
SHIELDS, Charlie
Chief Executive Officer, University Health–Lakewood Medical Center, Kansas City, MO, p. A378
President and Chief Executive Officer, University Health–Truman Medical Center, Kansas City, MO, p. A378
SHIELDS, Kristine, MSN, R.N., Chief Executive Officer, Regency Hospital of Northwest Indiana, East Chicago, IN, p. A215
SHIELDS, Todd
Vice President, Hospital Administrator, St. Charles Madras, Madras, OR, p. A529
Vice President, Hospital Administrator, St. Charles Prineville, Prineville, OR, p. A531
SHIFFERMILLER, William, M.D., Vice President Medical Affairs, Nebraska Methodist Hospital, Omaha, NE, p. A404
SHIHADY, Sharon, Director Human Resources, West Tennessee Healthcare Rehabilitation Hospital Cane Creek, A Partnership With Encompass Health, Martin, TN, p. A587
SHIKIAR, Mindy, MSN, Chief Operating Officer, Boca Raton Regional Hospital, Boca Raton, FL, p. A126
SHILKAITIS, Mary, Senior Vice President, Operations and Chief Operating Officer, Rush–Copley Medical Center, Aurora, IL, p. A186
SHILLING, Stacy, Controller, Chi St. Vincent Sherwood Rehabilitation Hospital, A Partner of Encompass Health, Sherwood, AR, p. A53
SHIM, Eunmee
R.N., MSN, President, Fort Washington and Adventist Ambulatory Networks, Adventist Healthcare Fort Washington Medical Center, Fort Washington, MD, p. A304
R.N., MSN, Vice President Operations, Adventist Healthcare Shady Grove Medical Center, Rockville, MD, p. A306
SHIMP, David, Chief Executive Officer, HCA Florida Osceola Hospital, Kissimmee, FL, p. A136
SHIMP, Rick, M.D., Chief Medical Officer, Ascension Sacred Heart Rehabilitation Hospital, Mequon, WI, p. A716
SHINAGAWA, Nate, Chief Operating Officer, Banner Ocotillo Medical Center, Chandler, AZ, p. A30
SHINAGAWA, Nathan, Chief Operating Officer, Banner Del E. Webb Medical Center, Sun City West, AZ, p. A39
SHINER, Cindy, Manager Human Resources, Lebanon Veterans Affairs Medical Center, Lebanon, PA, p. A544
SHINGLETON, Kathy J., Ed.D., Vice President, Human Resources, Virginia Mason Medical Center, Seattle, WA, p. A695
SHINICK, Mary K, Vice President Human Resources, Montefiore Nyack Hospital, Nyack, NY, p. A454
SHINWAR, Gran, Chief Executive Officer, Anchor Hospital, Atlanta, GA, p. A156
SHIPLEY, Carolyn, R.N., Chief Nursing Officer, Roane Medical Center, Harriman, TN, p. A583
SHIPLEY, Janice, M.D., Chief Medical Officer, Cibola General Hospital, Grants, NM, p. A434
SHIPLEY, Kurt, Chief Financial Officer, Holy Cross Hospital – Jordan Valley, West Jordan, UT, p. A670
SHIPP, Geraldine H, Director of Risk Management, Sampson Regional Medical Center, Clinton, NC, p. A466
SHIRAH, Anita, Director Human Resources, USA Health University Hospital, Mobile, AL, p. A22
SHIRILLA, Nicholas, Chief Executive Officer, Lovelace Regional Hospital – Roswell, Roswell, NM, p. A436

© 2025 AHA Guide Index of Health Care Professionals A971

Index of Health Care Professionals / Shirley

SHIRLEY, Christian, Director Human Resources, Geisinger Encompass Health Rehabilitation Hospital, Danville, PA, p. A538
SHIRLEY, Douglas E., Senior Executive Vice President and Chief Financial Officer, Cooper University Health Care, Camden, NJ, p. A419
SHIRLEY, Steve, Chief Information Officer, UCHealth Parkview Medical Center, Pueblo, CO, p. A113
SHIVELY, Lori, Vice President of Finance, Munson Healthcare Grayling Hospital, Grayling, MI, p. A329
SHIVERY, Toni M, Vice President Human Resources, University of Maryland Upper Chesapeake Medical Center, Bel Air, MD, p. A302
SHLOSSMAN, Amy
　Chief Operating Officer, Banner – University Medical Center Phoenix, Phoenix, AZ, p. A35
　Chief Operating Officer, Banner Thunderbird Medical Center, Glendale, AZ, p. A32
　President and Chief Operating Officer, Senior Vice President, Lifebridge Health, Sinai Hospital of Baltimore, Baltimore, MD, p. A301
SHMERLING, James E., President and Chief Executive Officer, Connecticut Children's, Hartford, CT, p. A116
SHOBE, Susan, Director Administration and Support Services, Alton Mental Health Center, Alton, IL, p. A185
SHOCK, Ernest, Chief Nursing Officer, Abbeville Area Medical Center, Abbeville, SC, p. A562
SHOCKEY, Kathryn L, Director Human Resources, Monument Health Lead–Deadwood Hospital, Deadwood, SD, p. A573
SHOEMAKER, Matt, D.O., Vice President and Chief Medical Officer, Mercy Hospital Southeast, Cap. Girardeau, MO, p. A372
SHOENER, Carl, Chief Information Officer, Lehigh Valley Hospital – Hazleton, Hazleton, PA, p. A541
SHOFNER, Connie, Chief Nursing Officer, Carlsbad Medical Center, Carlsbad, NM, p. A433
SHOLTIS, Bridget, Chief Financial Officer, Mclaren Port Huron, Port Huron, MI, p. A336
SHOMAKER, Susan, Director Information Management Systems, Dosher Memorial Hospital, Southport, NC, p. A476
SHOOK, Teressia, Chief Financial Officer, Clinch Memorial Hospital, Homerville, GA, p. A165
SHOPTAW, Michele, Director of Nursing, Chambers Memorial Hospital, Danville, AR, p. A45
SHORES, Larry, M.D., Executive Medical Director, Cedar Springs Hospital, Colorado Springs, CO, p. A104
SHORT, M Andrew, Vice President Information Services, Samaritan Medical Center, Watertown, NY, p. A461
SHORT, Penny, R.N., President, Tidalhealth Nanticoke, Seaford, DE, p. A122
SHORT, Peter H, M.D., Senior Vice President Medical Affairs, Beverly Hospital, Beverly, MA, p. A309
SHORT, Ted, Chief Financial Officer, Fairview Park Hospital, Dublin, GA, p. A163
SHORT, W L, M.D., Chief Medical Officer, Memorial Health System, Abilene, KS, p. A246
SHORTER, Beryl, Chief Operating Officer, Director Performance Improvement, Kingwood Pines Hospital, Kingwood, TX, p. A632
SHOUKAIR, Sami, M.D., Chief Medical Officer, La Palma Intercommunity Hospital, La Palma, CA, p. A69
SHOULDERS, Valerie, R.N., Chief Nursing Officer, Encompass Health Rehabilitation Hospital of Franklin, Franklin, TN, p. A583
SHOUP, Barbara
　R.N., Chief Nursing Officer, Ascension Brighton Center for Recovery, Brighton, MI, p. A323
　R.N., Hospital Administrator, Ascension Brighton Center for Recovery, Brighton, MI, p. A323
SHOUP, Emily, Director Nursing Services, Roundup Memorial Healthcare, Roundup, MT, p. A395
SHOUSE, Shellie, Chief Financial Officer, Bluegrass Community Hospital, Versailles, KY, p. A274
SHOUSE, Shellie Dube, Chief Executive Officer, Ohio County Hospital, Hartford, KY, p. A267
SHOWALTER, Shannon, Vice President and Chief Executive Officer, Norton Community Hospital, Norton, VA, p. A680
SHOWALTER, Will, Senior Vice President and Chief information Officer, Atrium Health Wake Forest Baptist Lexington Medical Center, Lexington, NC, p. A472
SHOWALTER, William, Senior Vice President and Chief Information Officer, Information Technology Services, Atrium Health Wake Forest Baptist Davie Medical Center, Bermuda Run, NC, p. A463
SHOWS, Carla
　Human Resource and Payroll Clerk, George Regional Hospital, Lucedale, MS, p. A365
　Payroll Clerk, Greene County Hospital, Leakesville, MS, p. A365

SHRESTHA, Sanjeeb, M.D., Chief Medical Staff, Medical City Weatherford, Weatherford, TX, p. A661
SHREVE, Susan, Executive Director Information Technology, Boone Memorial Hospital, Madison, WV, p. A702
SHRINER, Anne, M.D., Senior Vice President, Chief Medical Officer, UNC Health Nash, Rocky Mount, NC, p. A475
SHRIVASTAVA, Rakesh, M.D., Chief Medical Officer, Cornerstone Specialty Hospitals Shawnee, Shawnee, OK, p. A520
SHRIVER, Debra, R.N., MSN, Chief Nurse Executive, Unitypoint Health – Trinity Regional Medical Center, Fort Dodge, IA, p. A236
SHRIVER, Kren K, M.D., Clinical Director, Capital District Psychiatric Center, Albany, NY, p. A438
SHROADES, David W, Vice President Technology Services, Aultman Alliance Community Hospital, Alliance, OH, p. A484
SHROCK, Lynda J, Vice President Human Resources, Logansport Memorial Hospital, Logansport, IN, p. A223
SHROFF, Rajendra, M.D., Administrative Medical Director, SSM Health St. Mary's Hospital Centralia, Centralia, IL, p. A187
SHUART, Jeffery, M.D., Chief of Staff, Stillwater Medical Blackwell, Blackwell, OK, p. A510
SHUFFIELD, Shawn, Interim Chief Information Officer, St. Josep. Medical Center, Tacoma, WA, p. A697
SHUFFLEBARGER, Tom, President and Chief Executive Officer, Children's of Alabama, Birmingham, AL, p. A16
SHUFORD, Little, Health Information Manager, Kindred Hospital–Greensboro, Greensboro, NC, p. A469
SHUGART, Susan C., FACHE, Chief Executive Officer, Rutherford Regional Health System, Rutherfordton, NC, p. A475
SHUGHART, Deborah A, Chief Financial Officer, Fulton County Medical Center, Mc Connellsburg, PA, p. A545
SHULER, Conrad K, M.D., Chief Medical Officer, Prisma Health Oconee Memorial Hospital, Seneca, SC, p. A570
SHULL, Jennifer, R.N., Chief Nursing Officer, Adventhealth Fish Memorial, Orange City, FL, p. A143
SHULMAN, Michael, Pysician–in–Chief, Kaiser Permanente Santa Rosa Medical Center, Santa Rosa, CA, p. A95
SHULTS, Randi L., Chief Executive Officer, North Carolina Specialty Hospital, Durham, NC, p. A467
SHUMAKER, Bradley, Chief Medical Officer, HCA Florida Orange Park Hospital, Orange Park, FL, p. A144
SHUMAN, Betty, Director Human Resources, Encompass Health Rehabilitation Institute of Libertyville, Libertyville, IL, p. A200
SHUMAN, Daniel, D.O., Chief Medical Officer, Ashland Health Center, Ashland, KS, p. A246
SHUMATE, Kim, Human Resources Officer, Ohio State University Wexner Medical Center, Columbus, OH, p. A492
SHUMWAY, Barbara, Director Human Resources, North Big Horn Hospital District, Lovell, WY, p. A727
SHUMWAY, Richard, President and Chief Executive Officer, Stanford Health Care Tri–Valley, Pleasanton, CA, p. A83
SHUPERT, Charlene
　Director Staff Services, Carrus Rehabilitation Hospital, Sherman, TX, p. A653
　Director Staff Services, Carrus Specialty Hospital, Sherman, TX, p. A653
SHUPP, Susan, Chief Human Resources Officer, Nemaha County Hospital, Auburn, NE, p. A397
SHURTZ, Marc, Interim Chief Executive Officer and Chief Financial Officer, Orleans Community Health, Medina, NY, p. A446
SHUSHTARI, J. Kevin, M.D., Chief Medical Officer, Hospital for Special Care, New Britain, CT, p. A117
SHUTE, Keith M, M.D., Senior Vice President Medical Affairs and Clinical Services, Androscoggin Valley Hospital, Berlin, NH, p. A414
SHUTTS, Rebecca, R.N., Chief Nursing Officer, The University of Vermont Health Network – Alice Hyde Medical Center, Malone, NY, p. A445
SHYSHKA, Susan, Associate Director, Greater Los Angeles Hcs, Los Angeles, CA, p. A72
SIAL, Ajay, Chief Financial Officer, UC Irvine Health, UCI Health, Orange, CA, p. A82
SIBBITT, Stephen, M.D., Chief Medical Officer, Baylor Scott & White Medical Center – Temple, Temple, TX, p. A656
SIBLEY, Beth, Director of Nursing, Sage Rehabilitation Hospital, Baton Rouge, LA, p. A278
SIBLEY, Jeri, Director Revenue Cycle, VCU Health Tappahannock Hospital, Tappahannock, VA, p. A684
SICA, Vincent A., President and Chief Executive Officer, Desoto Memorial Hospital, Arcadia, FL, p. A125
SICHTS, Pam, Director Human Resources, Sycamore Springs, Lafayette, IN, p. A222
SICILIA, Bruce, M.D., Medical Director, Encompass Health Rehabilitation Hospital of York, York, PA, p. A558

SICKLES, Alan, M.D., Chief Executive Officer, Saint Michael's Medical Center, Newark, NJ, p. A425
SICKLES, Doyle R., M.D., Chief of Medical Staff, Mon Health Stonewall Jackson Memorial Hospital, Weston, WV, p. A705
SIDDIQI, Ather
　M.D., Medical Director, Nexus Specialty Hospital, Shenandoah, TX, p. A652
　M.D., Medical Director, Nexus Specialty Hospital The Woodlands, The Woodlands, TX, p. A657
SIDDIQI, Syed, M.D., President Medical Staff, Raleigh General Hospital, Beckley, WV, p. A699
SIDDIQUE, Khawar, Co–Chief Executive Officer, Docs Surgical Hospital, Los Angeles, CA, p. A72
SIDDIQUI, Joseph, Vice President Human Resources, The Aroostook Medical Center, Presque Isle, ME, p. A299
SIDER, Tod, M.D., Chief of Staff, Parkview Wabash Hospital, Wabash, IN, p. A228
SIDES, Tim, Chief Financial Officer, Valle Vista Health System, Greenwood, IN, p. A218
SIDHU, Dupinder, Chief Executive Officer and Chief Nursing Officer, Central Valley Specialty Hospital, Modesto, CA, p. A77
SIDMAN, Robert, M.D., Regional Vice President, Medical Affairs, The William W. Backus Hospital, Norwich, CT, p. A118
SIDONE, LeighAnn
　R.N., Chief Nursing Officer, Suburban Hospital, Bethesda, MD, p. A303
　R.N., President and Chief Executive Officer, Suburban Hospital, Bethesda, MD, p. A303
SIDWELL, Sherry, Chief Operating Officer, Vice President Integrated Support Services, Community Hospital Anderson, Anderson, IN, p. A212
SIEBERT, Matt, Assistant Administrator Ancillary Services, Hermann Area District Hospital, Hermann, MO, p. A376
SIEG, Greg, Support Services Executive, Healthsource Saginaw Inc., Saginaw, MI, p. A337
SIEGAN, Mitchell, M.D., Chief Medical Officer, Roper St. Francis Mount Pleasant Hospital, Mount Pleasant, SC, p. A568
SIEGEL, Fredric, M.D., Chief of Staff, Desert View Hospital, Pahrump, NV, p. A412
SIEGEL, Lesley, M.D., Medical Director, Albert J. Solnit Children's Center, Middletown, CT, p. A116
SIEGELMAN, Gary M, M.D., MSC, Senior Vice President and Chief Medical Officer, Bayhealth, Dover, DE, p. A121
SIEGFRIED, Carole A, MSN, R.N., Campus Nurse Executive, Prisma Health Richland Hospital, Columbia, SC, p. A565
SIEGLE, Lora, M.D., Chief Medical Officer, Morris County Hospital, Council Grove, KS, p. A248
SIEGLEN, Linda, M.D., Chief Medical Officer, Providence Mission Hospital Mission Viejo, Mission Viejo, CA, p. A77
SIEGMAN, Ira, M.D., Chief Medical Officer, HCA Florida Northside Hospital, Saint Petersburg, FL, p. A149
SIEGRIST, Steve, Director of Human Resources, Mesa View Regional Hospital, Mesquite, NV, p. A411
SIEMERS, Tom, Chief Executive Officer, Wilbarger General Hospital, Vernon, TX, p. A659
SIEVERT, Deana, MSN, R.N., Chief Nursing Officer, Ohio State University Wexner Medical Center, Columbus, OH, p. A492
SIEWERT, Charles
　Director Human Resources, Buffalo Psychiatric Center, Buffalo, NY, p. A440
　Director Human Resources, Western New York Children's Psychiatric Center, West Seneca, NY, p. A462
SIFERS, Carl, Director Information Technology and System Services, Centerpoint Medical Center, Independence, MO, p. A376
SIGEL, Heather
　Vice President Operations, Valley Health – Hampshire Memorial Hospital, Romney, WV, p. A704
　Vice President, Operations, Valley Health – War Memorial Hospital, Berkeley Springs, WV, p. A699
SIGNOR, Kristin, Director Finance, Sunnyview Rehabilitation Hospital, Schenectady, NY, p. A459
SIGREST, Marion, M.D., Chief of Staff, Baptist Medical Center – Yazoo, Yazoo City, MS, p. A370
SIKAND, Hardy, Chief Executive Officer, Indiana Spine Hospital, Carmel, IN, p. A214
SILARD, Kathleen A., R.N., MS, FACHE, President and Chief Executive Officer, Stamford Health, Stamford, CT, p. A119
SILAS, Maria, Manager Human Resources, Suny Downstate Health Sciences University, New York, NY, p. A453
SILBERMAN, Sam, Chief Financial Officer, San Antonio Behavioral Healthcare Hospital, San Antonio, TX, p. A650
SILJANDER, Debi, M.D., Chief Medical Officer, California Hospital Medical Center, Los Angeles, CA, p. A72
SILKEY, Julie, R.N., Vice President Patient Care, M Health Fairview Ridges Hospital, Burnsville, MN, p. A344

Index of Health Care Professionals

Index of Health Care Professionals / Singleton

SILLS, John T, Chief Information Officer, Orlando Health – Health Central Hospital, Ocoee, FL, p. A143
SILLYMAN, Bryce, Chief Operating Officer, Pottstown Hospital, Pottstown, PA, p. A553
SILVA, Ashley, Executive Director, Blueridge Vista Behavioral Health, Cincinnati, OH, p. A488
SILVA, Francisco, Financial Director, Hospital Metropolitano Dr. Susoni, Arecibo, PR, p. A731
SILVA–STEELE, Jamie A., FACHE, R.N., President and Chief Executive Officer, University of New Mexico Hospitals, Albuquerque, NM, p. A433
SILVAS, Jose, Vice President of Operations, Aspire Hospital, Conroe, TX, p. A608
SILVEIRA, Mike, Director Human Resources Business Partners, Kaiser Permanente Fresno Medical Center, Fresno, CA, p. A65
SILVER, Michael, Chief Financial Officer, Psychiatric Institute of Washington, Washington, DC, p. A124
SILVER, Timothy, M.D., Medical Director, SAH–S, Sheltering Arms Institute, Midlothian, VA, p. A679
SILVERMAN, Cole, Chief Executive Officer, SSM Select Rehabilitation Hospital, Richmond Heights, MO, p. A382
SILVERMAN, Daniel C
M.D., Chief Medical Officer, Acute Care Troy, Samaritan Hospital – Main Campus, Troy, NY, p. A460
M.D., Vice President and Chief Medical Officer, Sinai Hospital of Baltimore, Baltimore, MD, p. A301
SILVERMAN, Deven, Chief Human Resouce Officer, Broward Health Imperial Point, Fort Lauderdale, FL, p. A131
SILVERSTEIN, Joel, M.D., Chief Medical Officer, Copley Hospital, Morrisville, VT, p. A672
SILVERSTEIN, Kenneth L, M.D., Chief Clinical Officer, Christianacare, Newark, DE, p. A122
SILVERTHORNE, Samuel, Chief Information Officer, U. S. Air Force Medical Center Keesler, Keesler Afb, MS, p. A364
SILVESTRI, Scott, Vice President Finance and Chief Financial Officer, Marietta Memorial Hospital, Marietta, OH, p. A499
SILVEUS, Patrick, M.D., Medical Director, Lutheran Kosciusko Hospital, Warsaw, IN, p. A229
SILVEY, Christie, Director People Services, HSHS St. Joseph's Hospital Highland, Highland, IL, p. A197
SILVIA, Charles B, M.D., Chief Medical Officer and Vice President Medical Affairs, Tidalhealth Peninsula Regional, Salisbury, MD, p. A307
SIMARAS, Jim, Executive Vice President and Chief Financial Officer, Children's Mercy Kansas City, Kansas City, MO, p. A377
SIMARD, Genevieve, Program Administrator, Human Resources, Eleanor Slater Hospital, Cranston, RI, p. A560
SIMCHUK, Cathy J, Chief Operating Officer, Providence Holy Family Hospital, Spokane, WA, p. A696
SIMIA, Greg
Chief Financial Officer, HSHS St. Clare Memorial Hospital, Oconto Falls, WI, p. A719
Chief Financial Officer, HSHS St. Mary's Hospital Medical Center, Green Bay, WI, p. A712
Chief Financial Officer, HSHS St. Nicholas Hospital, Sheboygan, WI, p. A721
Chief Financial Officer, HSHS St. Vincent Hospital, Green Bay, WI, p. A712
SIMKINS, Palma, Chief Human Resources Management Services, Battle Creek Veterans Affairs Medical Center, Battle Creek, MI, p. A322
SIMMERMON, Eric, Chief Nursing Officer, Covenant Health Hobbs Hospital, Hobbs, NM, p. A435
SIMMONS, Angela, Chief Executive Officer, Encompass Health Rehabilitation Hospital Vision Park, Shenandoah, TX, p. A652
SIMMONS, Angela L., Chief Executive Officer, Encompass Health Rehabilitation Hospital of The Woodlands, Conroe, TX, p. A608
SIMMONS, Brad, Chief Operating Officer, Saint Luke's Hospital of Kansas City, Kansas City, MO, p. A378
SIMMONS, Daniel F, Senior Vice President and Treasurer, Penn Highlands Mon Valley, Monongahela, PA, p. A546
SIMMONS, Dorlynn, Chief Executive Officer, Mescalero Public Health Service Indian Hospital, Mescalero, NM, p. A436
SIMMONS, Dwayne, Interim Chief Information Officer, Montefiore St. Luke's Cornwall, Newburgh, NY, p. A454
SIMMONS, Jodi, Chief Nursing Officer, Hillcrest Medical Center, Tulsa, OK, p. A522
SIMMONS, Rickie, Controller, Kindred Hospital North Florida, Green Cove Springs, FL, p. A133
SIMMONS, Shelley, Chief Nursing Officer, Jackson County Memorial Hospital, Altus, OK, p. A509
SIMMONS, Taquisa, Ph.D., Executive Director, Hampton Veterans Affairs Medical Center, Hampton, VA, p. A677
SIMMONS, Vernetta, Interim Chief Executive Officer, Fairmount Behavioral Health System, Philadelphia, PA, p. A548
SIMMS, Miquel Noelani, R.N., Chief Nursing Officer, Queen's North Hawaii Community Hospital, Kamuela, HI, p. A176
SIMODEJKA, John E., Market Chief Executive Officer, Select Specialty Hospital–Camp Hill, Camp Hill, PA, p. A536
SIMON, Anha, Director Human Resources, Riceland Medical Center, Winnie, TX, p. A663
SIMON, Ashley, Chief Financial Officer, Kansas Surgery And Recovery Center, Wichita, KS, p. A262
SIMON, Kareen, Vice President of Operations, Wheeling Hospital, Wheeling, WV, p. A706
SIMON, Kenneth B, M.D., Chief of Staff, Biloxi Va Medical Center, Biloxi, MS, p. A359
SIMON, Laura
R.N., MSN, Director Quality Operations and Nursing, Baton Rouge Rehabilitation Hospital, Baton Rouge, LA, p. A277
R.N., MSN, Director, Quality Operations and Nursing, Baton Rouge Rehabilitation Hospital, Baton Rouge, LA, p. A277
SIMON, Mark, System Chief Information Officer, Benefis Health System, Great Falls, MT, p. A392
SIMON, Richard, M.D., Chief of Staff, Uconn, John Dempsey Hospital, Farmington, CT, p. A116
SIMON, Sandra, Chief Executive Officer and Nursing Home Administrator, Laguna Honda Hospital And Rehabilitation Center, San Francisco, CA, p. A91
SIMON, Stuart, M.D., Medical Director, North Central Surgical Center, Dallas, TX, p. A612
SIMON, Teresa, Director Information Systems, Nacogdoches Medical Center, Nacogdoches, TX, p. A640
SIMON, Thresa, M.D., Medical Director, Poplar Springs Hospital, Petersburg, VA, p. A681
SIMONIN, Steven J., President and Chief Executive Officer, Iowa Specialty Hospital–Clarion, Clarion, IA, p. A232
SIMONS, Christa, Chief Operating Officer, Greene County Medical Center, Jefferson, IA, p. A238
SIMONSON, John F., M.D., Medical Director, Memorial Community Hospital And Health System, Blair, NE, p. A398
SIMONSON, Paul, Vice President, Trinity Health, Minot, ND, p. A482
SIMPSON, Brenda, R.N., Chief Nursing Officer, HCA Florida Largo Hospital, Largo, FL, p. A137
SIMPSON, Chris, Chief Executive Officer, Cornerstone Specialty Hospitals West Monroe, West Monroe, LA, p. A294
SIMPSON, Greg, Chief Nursing Officer, St. Josep. Medical Center, Kansas City, MO, p. A378
SIMPSON, Joan W., Manager Human Resources, Lauderdale Community Hospital, Ripley, TN, p. A592
SIMPSON, Julie, Vice President Human Resources, University of Tennessee Medical Center, Knoxville, TN, p. A586
SIMPSON, Laura, Director Human Resources, Sabine County Hospital, Hemphill, TX, p. A624
SIMPSON, Mark, Chief Executive Officer, Welch Community Hospital, Welch, WV, p. A705
SIMPSON, Merridth, Director Human Resources, Methodist Charlton Medical Center, Dallas, TX, p. A612
SIMPSON, Micheal, Interim Chief Executive Officer, Pam Health Rehabilitation Hospital of Houston Heights, Houston, TX, p. A627
SIMPSON, Michelle, Chief Nursing Officer and Quality Leader, Lauderdale Community Hospital, Ripley, TN, p. A592
SIMPSON, Robert, Vice President Operations, Methodist Richardson Medical Center, Richardson, TX, p. A646
SIMPSON, Ryan, Chief Executive Officer, Methodist Hospital, San Antonio, TX, p. A650
SIMPSON, Shawndra, Interim Chief Executive Officer, Sutter Surgical Hospital – North Valley, Yuba City, CA, p. A102
SIMPSON, Sheila, Vice President Human Resources, Palmetto Lowcountry Behavioral Health, Charleston, SC, p. A563
SIMPSON, Steve, Chief Executive Officer, Northeastern Nevada Regional Hospital, Elko, NV, p. A408
SIMPSON, Will, Chief Financial Officer, Spring Hospital, Spring, TX, p. A654
SIMPSON–TUGGLE, Deloris, Vice President Human Resources and Organizational Development and Chief Human Resources Officer, Gbmc Healthcare, Baltimore, MD, p. A302
SIMS, Anthony, M.D., Chief of Staff, Dekalb Regional Medical Center, Fort Payne, AL, p. A19
SIMS, Brian, FACHE, Chief Executive Officer, Lucas County Health Center, Chariton, IA, p. A232
SIMS, Charles, M.D., Chief of Staff, St. Luke's Health – The Woodlands Hospital, The Woodlands, TX, p. A658
SIMS, Jason
M.D., Chief Medical Officer, Cleveland Area Hospital, Cleveland, OK, p. A511
Facility Information Security Officer, Medical City North Hills, North Richland Hills, TX, p. A641
SIMS, Joni, Chief Nursing Officer, Owensboro Health Regional Hospital, Owensboro, KY, p. A272
SIMS, Kyle
Division Vice President, Chi St. Josep. Health Burleson Hospital, Caldwell, TX, p. A606
Division Vice President, Chi St. Josep. Health Grimes Hospital, Navasota, TX, p. A641
Division Vice President, Chi St. Josep. Health Madison Hospital, Madisonville, TX, p. A637
SIMS, Mark E., Chief Executive Officer, Grand Strand Medical Center, Myrtle Beach, SC, p. A569
SIMS, Wanda
Interim Chief Executive Officer, Roosevelt Warm Springs Long Term Acute Care Hospital, Warm Springs, GA, p. A173
Interim Chief Executive Officer, Roosevelt Warm Springs Rehabilitation And Specialty Hospitals, Warm Springs, GA, p. A173
SIMZYK, Monica
Regional Chief Human Resources Officer, Ascension St. Mary – Kankakee, Kankakee, IL, p. A199
Regional Human Resource Officer, Ascension Saint Josep. – Joliet, Joliet, IL, p. A199
SINCICH, Robert, Vice President Human Resources, Trumbull Regional Medical Center, Warren, OH, p. A506
SINCLAIR, Kathy, Vice President Human Resources, Spartanburg Medical Center – Church Street Campus, Spartanburg, SC, p. A570
SINCLAIR, Kyle, Chief Executive Officer, Warm Springs Rehabilitation Hospital of San Antonio, San Antonio, TX, p. A651
SINCLAIR, Laura, Director Human Resources, Kansas City Orthopaedic Institute, Leawood, KS, p. A253
SINCLAIR, Noreen, Human Resources Administrator, Connecticut Veterans Home And Hospital, Rocky Hill, CT, p. A118
SINCLAIR–CHUNG, Opal, R.N., MS, Chief Nursing Officer, Deputy Executive Director, NYC Health + Hospitals/Kings County, New York, NY, p. A451
SINCOCK, Gregory M, Information Technology Leader, Kaiser Permanente West Los Angeles Medical Center, Los Angeles, CA, p. A73
SINDELAR, Dennis, Chief Executive Officer, UC Davis Rehabilitation Hospital, Sacramento, CA, p. A88
SINDLINGER, Julie A, Director of Human Resources, Weston County Health Services, Newcastle, WY, p. A727
SINDORF, Nicholas, Southwest Kansas City Market Vice President and Chief Information Officer, Olathe Medical Center, Olathe, KS, p. A256
SINGAL, Ankur, M.D., Chief Medical Officer, Endeavor Health Elmhurst Hospital, Elmhurst, IL, p. A194
SINGER, David, Chief Information Officer, Children's Hospital New Orleans, New Orleans, LA, p. A290
SINGER, John IV, Chief Operating Officer, Munson Healthcare Charlevoix Hospital, Charlevoix, MI, p. A323
SINGH, Amandeep. Chief Medical Officer, Monroe Hospital, Bloomington, IN, p. A213
SINGH, Gagan, Chief Information Officer, Ascension Sacred Heart Rehabilitation Hospital, Mequon, WI, p. A716
SINGH, Gagandeep. M.D., Chief Medical Officer Behavioral Health, Banner Behavioral Health Hospital – Scottsdale, Scottsdale, AZ, p. A38
SINGH, Himanshu, M.D., Associate Director, Veterans Affairs Ann Arbor Healthcare System, Ann Arbor, MI, p. A321
SINGH, Leighton, M.D., Chief of Staff, Prairie Lakes Healthcare System, Watertown, SD, p. A578
SINGH, Manish, M.D., Chief Executive Officer, Doctor's Hospital At Renaissance, Edinburg, TX, p. A615
SINGH, Matab, Chief of Staff, Good Samaritan Hospital, Bakersfield, CA, p. A57
SINGH, Mini, Chief Executive Officer, Brunswick Psych Center, Amityville, NY, p. A438
SINGH, Reeta
M.D., Chief Medical Officer, Laureate Psychiatric Clinic And Hospital, Tulsa, OK, p. A522
M.D., Chief Medical Officer, Saint Francis Hospital, Tulsa, OK, p. A523
M.D., Chief Medical Officer, Saint Francis Hospital South, Tulsa, OK, p. A523
SINGH, Rishi, President, Cleveland Clinic Martin North Hospital, Stuart, FL, p. A150
SINGH, Sabi, Executive Vice President and Chief Operating Officer, H. Lee Moffitt Cancer Center And Research Institute, Tampa, FL, p. A152
SINGH, Sam, Chief Executive Officer, Glenn Medical Center, Willows, CA, p. A101
SINGLES, James L, Chief Financial Officer, Marlette Regional Hospital, Marlette, MI, p. A333
SINGLETARY–TWYMAN, Michelle, Chief Nursing Officer, Rockford Center, Newark, DE, p. A122
SINGLETON, Al, M.D., Chief Psychiatry and Chief Medical Staff, Colorado Mental Health Institute At Pueblo, Pueblo, CO, p. A112

SINHA, Sunil K., M.D., FACHE, Chief Medical Officer, Bon Secours Memorial Regional Medical Center, Mechanicsville, VA, p. A679
SINIARD, Sandra, Vice President of Patient Care Services, Chi Memorial Hospital – Georgia, Fort Oglethorpe, GA, p. A164
SINICKAS, Robert, Director Information Services, Northwestern Medicine Marianjoy Rehabilitation Hospital, Wheaton, IL, p. A210
SINICROPE, Frank J Jr, Vice President Financial Services, Princeton Community Hospital, Princeton, WV, p. A704
SINISI, Albert, Director Information Systems, Pontiac General Hospital, Pontiac, MI, p. A335
SINNOTT, James, M.D., Chief Medical Staff, Coquille Valley Hospital, Coquille, OR, p. A526
SINNOTT, Lisa M, Director Human Resources, Select Specialty Hospital – Willingboro, Willingboro, NJ, p. A430
SINOPOLI, Angelo, M.D., Vice President Clinical Integration and Chief Medical Officer, Prisma Health Greenville Memorial Hospital, Greenville, SC, p. A567
SINOPOLI, Michele
  M.D., Chief Medical Officer, Metrowest Medical Center, Framingham, MA, p. A313
  M.D., Chief Medical Officer, Saint Vincent Hospital, Worcester, MA, p. A320
SINOTTE, Brian, Market Chief Executive officer and Interim Chief Executive Officer, Northwest Medical Center, Tucson, AZ, p. A40
SIOSON, Stephanie
  Director Human Resources, Garden Grove Hospital And Medical Center, Garden Grove, CA, p. A65
  Director Human Resources, Huntington Beach Hospital, Huntington Beach, CA, p. A67
  Director Human Resources, La Palma Intercommunity Hospital, La Palma, CA, p. A69
  Director Human Resources, West Anaheim Medical Center, Anaheim, CA, p. A55
SIOUFI, Habib, M.D., Chief Medical Officer, Umass Memorial-Marlborough Hospital, Marlborough, MA, p. A315
SIPEK, John, Supervisor Client Services, Aurora Medical Center In Washington County, Hartford, WI, p. A712
SIRATT, Mark, Director of Nursing, Richardson Medical Center, Rayville, LA, p. A291
SIRIANNI, Peter, M.D., President Medical Staff, Christus Mother Frances Hospital – Jacksonville, Jacksonville, TX, p. A630
SIRIO, Carl, M.D., Chief Medical Officer, Temple University Hospital, Philadelphia, PA, p. A550
SIRIVAR, Wendy, Chief Nurse Officer, San Ramon Regional Medical Center, San Ramon, CA, p. A93
SIRK, Donald, Director Information Systems, Medstar St. Mary's Hospital, Leonardtown, MD, p. A305
SIROTTA, Ted D.
  Chief Financial Officer, Vail Health, Vail, CO, p. A114
  Senior Vice President and Chief Financial Officer, Henry Mayo Newhall Hospital, Valencia, CA, p. A99
SISILLO, Sabato
  M.D., Chief Medical Officer, Providence Medical Center, Kansas City, KS, p. A252
  M.D., Chief Medical Officer, Saint John Hospital, Leavenworth, KS, p. A253
SISK, Glenn C., President, Coosa Valley Medical Center, Sylacauga, AL, p. A24
SISK, Jack G., President, Punxsutawney Area Hospital, Punxsutawney, PA, p. A553
SISK, Lori
  R.N., Chief Executive Officer, Sanford Canby Medical Center, Canby, MN, p. A344
  R.N., Chief Executive Officer, Sanford Clear Lake Medical Center, Clear Lake, SD, p. A572
SISLER, Debbie, Director, Human Resource, ECU Health Roanoke–Chowan Hospital, Ahoskie, NC, p. A463
SISON, Joseph, M.D., Medical Director, Heritage Oaks Hospital, Sacramento, CA, p. A86
SISSON, Travis
  Chief Executive Officer, Merit Health Biloxi, Biloxi, MS, p. A359
  Chief Executive Officer, Merit Health Wesley, Hattiesburg, MS, p. A363
SISTO, Steven A., Senior Vice President and Chief Operating Officer, USC Arcadia Hospital, Arcadia, CA, p. A56
SISTRUNK, Heather
  R.N., Chief Executive Officer, Merit Health Rankin, Brandon, MS, p. A360
  R.N., Chief Executive Officer, Merit Health Woman's Hospital, Flowood, MS, p. A362
SITLINGER, James, Chief Human Resources Management, Charles George Veterans Affairs Medical Center, Asheville, NC, p. A463
SIU, Max, Chief Information Officer, Hackensack Meridian Mountainside Medical Center, Montclair, NJ, p. A424

SIVAK, Steven, M.D., Chief Medical Officer, Einstein Physicians Philadelphia, Einstein Medical Center Philadelphia, Philadelphia, PA, p. A548
SIVLEY, Susanna S, Chief Personnel Officer, Highlands Medical Center, Scottsboro, AL, p. A24
SIX, Deborah, Coordinator Data Processing, Wayne Memorial Hospital, Jesup, GA, p. A165
SIX, Stephanie, Chief Executive Officer, Northeastern Health System Sequoyah, Sallisaw, OK, p. A520
SIY, Edmund, Chief Information Officer, Hunterdon Healthcare, Flemington, NJ, p. A421
SIZELOVE, Lyn, Director of Nursing, Beaver County Memorial Hospital, Beaver, OK, p. A510
SJOBERG, Rochelle, Chief Human Resources Officer, Ely-Bloomenson Community Hospital, Ely, MN, p. A346
SJURSETH, Karen, Chief Executive Officer, Community Memorial Hospital, Redfield, SD, p. A576
SKABELUND, Hoyt, President, Banner Payson Medical Center, Payson, AZ, p. A34
SKALA, Pat, Chief Information Officer, Laguna Honda Hospital And Rehabilitation Center, San Francisco, CA, p. A91
SKALSKI, Eileen, Chief Nursing Officer, Encompass Health Rehabilitation Hospital of Harmarville, Pittsburgh, PA, p. A551
SKARBINSKI, Elizabeth, Chief Nursing Officer, Patient Safety Officer, Central Carolina Hospital, Sanford, NC, p. A476
SKARI, Bradly, Chief of Staff, Jamestown Regional Medical Center, Jamestown, ND, p. A482
SKARKA, Kathy, MSN, R.N., Executive Vice President Patient Care Services, Nassau University Medical Center, East Meadow, NY, p. A442
SKARULIS, Patricia, Senior Vice President and Chief Information Systems Officer, Memorial Sloan Kettering Cancer Center, New York, NY, p. A449
SKEANS, John, Chief Financial Officer, Endeavor Health Northwest Community Hospital, Arlington Heights, IL, p. A185
SKEEN, Steven, R.N., Chief Nursing Officer, Mizell Memorial Hospital, Opp. AL, p. A23
SKEENS, Henrietta, CPA, Chief Financial Officer, Up Health System – Marquette, Marquette, MI, p. A333
SKEHAN, Jayme, R.N., MSN, Chief Nursing Officer, Weiser Memorial Hospital, Weiser, ID, p. A184
SKELDON, Timothy, Chief Financial Officer, Thomas Memorial Hospital, South Charleston, WV, p. A705
SKELTON, Jenny, System Integration Manager, The Women's Hospital, Newburgh, IN, p. A225
SKELTON, Katie, MSN, R.N., Vice President Nursing and Chief Nursing Officer, Providence St. Josep. Hospital Orange, Orange, CA, p. A81
SKEVINGTON, John, Interim President & Chief Executive Officer, Portsmouth Regional Hospital, Portsmouth, NH, p. A417
SKIBBA, Joshua, Chief Medical Officer, Ohio County Hospital, Hartford, KY, p. A267
SKIDMORE, Jocelyn, Director Finance, Mosaic Medical Center – Maryville, Maryville, MO, p. A380
SKIEM, Paul, Senior Vice President Human Resources, Ascension Saint Francis, Evanston, IL, p. A194
SKIFF, Jessica, Director Human Resources, Lewis County General Hospital, Lowville, NY, p. A445
SKINNER, Christopher, Chief of Staff, Corewell Health Big Rapids Hospital, Big Rapids, MI, p. A322
SKINNER, Gary, Director Information Technology, Rehabilitation Hospital of Indiana, Indianapolis, IN, p. A220
SKINNER, Kristina, Director Quality, Sanpete Valley Hospital, Mount Pleasant, UT, p. A666
SKINNER, Marjorie, Director Finance, Pershing General Hospital, Lovelock, NV, p. A411
SKINNER, Richard, Chief Information Technology Officer, UVA Health University Medical Center, Charlottesville, VA, p. A674
SKIPPER, Kymberli, Manager Human Resources, Prattville Baptist Hospital, Prattville, AL, p. A24
SKIPPER, Michelle, Director Human Resources, Kaiser Permanente Riverside Medical Center, Riverside, CA, p. A86
SKJOLDEN, Jessica, M.D., Chief of Staff, SMP Health – St. Andrew's, Bottineau, ND, p. A479
SKLAMBERG, Todd, President, Sunrise Hospital And Medical Center, Las Vegas, NV, p. A411
SKOCIK, Cindy, Chief Operating Officer, Veritas Collaborative, Durham, NC, p. A467
SKORUPA, Krista, President, East Market, Essentia Health St. Mary's Medical Center, Duluth, MN, p. A346
SKOWRON, Paul, Chief Executive Officer, Warner Hospital And Health Services, Clinton, IL, p. A192
SKRINDE, Tracie, Senior Human Resources Partner, Peacehealth United General Medical Center, Sedro-Woolley, WA, p. A695

SKULA, Erika, Chief Executive Officer, Adventhealth Ocala, Ocala, FL, p. A143
SKULA, Joe, Director Human Resources, Adventhealth Manchester, Manchester, KY, p. A271
SKURA, Sam, President, Baystate Medical Center, Springfield, MA, p. A318
SKVARENINA, Michael, Assistant Vice President Information Systems, Holy Name Medical Center, Teaneck, NJ, p. A429
SKY DICK, Brittney, Chief Executive Officer, Georgetown Behavioral Health Institute, Georgetown, TX, p. A622
SLABA, Bryan, Chief Executive Officer, Wagner Community Memorial Hospital Avera, Wagner, SD, p. A578
SLABIK, Shauna, Chief Financial Officer, Sanford Mayville Medical Center, Mayville, ND, p. A482
SLACK, Lina, Human Resources Leader, Kaiser Permanente San Jose Medical Center, San Jose, CA, p. A92
SLACK, Michael W., President and Chief Executive Officer, Kidspeace Children's Hospital, Orefield, PA, p. A547
SLACK, Randy, Chief Financial Officer, Nacogdoches Medical Center, Nacogdoches, TX, p. A640
SLADE, Rachel, Chief Executive Officer, Covenant Health Hobbs Hospital, Hobbs, NM, p. A435
SLAGLE, Julie A, R.N., MSN, Vice President Patient Care Services, Sidney Regional Medical Center, Sidney, NE, p. A406
SLATE, Sonny, Chief Operating Officer, Georgia Regional Hospital At Atlanta, Decatur, GA, p. A162
SLATER, Bill, Chief Financial Officer, Hegg Health Center Avera, Rock Valley, IA, p. A242
SLATER, Craig M, M.D., Chief Medical Officer, Atrium Health Union, Monroe, NC, p. A472
SLATER-NESUOLD, Stephanie, Director of Nursing, Landmark Hospital of Joplin, Joplin, MO, p. A377
SLATON, Brenda, Superintendent, Rusk State Hospital, Rusk, TX, p. A648
SLATTERY, Greg, Vice President Information, Community Hospitals And Wellness Centers, Bryan, OH, p. A487
SLATTERY, Robert, Vice President of Operations, Bridgton Hospital, Bridgton, ME, p. A296
SLATTERY, Susan L, Director Human Resources, Unitypoint Health – St. Luke's Hospital, Cedar Rapids, IA, p. A232
SLATTMAN, Robin, Chief Nursing Officer, Memorial Health, Marysville, OH, p. A499
SLAUGHTER, Holly D, Vice President, Human Resources, Licking Memorial Hospital, Newark, OH, p. A501
SLAWITSKY, Bruce, Vice President Human Resources, Hospital for Special Surgery, New York, NY, p. A448
SLAYMAN, Aubree, Director Patient Services, Miami County Medical Center, Paola, KS, p. A257
SLAYTON, Val, M.D., Vice President Medical Affairs, Uofl Health – Mary And Elizabeth Hospital, Louisville, KY, p. A270
SLEDGE, Cynthia Moore, M.D., Medical Director, Bryce Hospital, Tuscaloosa, AL, p. A25
SLEDGE, Tasha, Director Human Resources, Texas Health Harris Methodist Hospital Southlake, Southlake, TX, p. A653
SLEDGE, Thomas, Chief Executive Officer, North Texas Medical Center, Gainesville, TX, p. A621
SLEDGE, Tom, Chief Operating Officer, Northwest Medical Center – Springdale, Springdale, AR, p. A53
SLEE, Kim, Chief Operating Officer, Fulton County Medical Center, Mc Connellsburg, PA, p. A545
SLEEPER, Justin, Vice President Clinical Operations, Behavioral Health Network, Natchaug Hospital, Mansfield Center, CT, p. A116
SLEIME, Melanie, Director Human Resources, Memorial Hospital, North Conway, NH, p. A417
SLEITER, Michelle, Chief Executive Officer, Humboldt County Memorial Hospital, Humboldt, IA, p. A237
SLESSOR, Steve Robert., Chief Administrative Officer, Winnmed, Decorah, IA, p. A234
SLETTE, Katie, Director Human Resources, New Ulm Medical Center, New Ulm, MN, p. A352
SLICK, Lois, Director of Human Resources, Lifecare Medical Center, Roseau, MN, p. A354
SLIDER, Carol, Chief Nursing Officer, Titus Regional Medical Center, Mount Pleasant, TX, p. A640
SLIGH, Lauren, Chief Financial Officer, Tristar Horizon Medical Center, Dickson, TN, p. A582
SLITER, Elizabeth, M.D., Chairman Medical Staff, Decatur Health Systems, Oberlin, KS, p. A256
SLIVA, Paul, Chief Information Officer, Boone County Hospital, Boone, IA, p. A231
SLIWA, James, M.D., Chief Medical Officer, Shirley Ryan Abilitylab, Chicago, IL, p. A191
SLIWINSKI, Ron, Chief of Hospital Division, University Hospital, Madison, WI, p. A714
SLOAN, Brian, Chief Operating Officer, Duke Raleigh Hospital, Raleigh, NC, p. A474

SLOAN, D Christopher, Chief Operating Officer, Multicare Capital Medical Center, Olympia, WA, p. A692
SLOAN, Kirk, M.D., Senior Vice President and Chief Medical Officer, LMH Health, Lawrence, KS, p. A253
SLOAN, Patrick, Chief Financial Officer, Memorial Satilla Health, Waycross, GA, p. A174
SLOAN, Prudence, Coordinator Human Resources, Select Specialty Hospital–Pittsburgh/Upmc, Pittsburgh, PA, p. A551
SLOAN, Ronald A., FACHE, President, The Outer Banks Hospital, Nags Head, NC, p. A473
SLOAN, Steve, Chief Financial Officer, Lake Cumberland Regional Hospital, Somerset, KY, p. A274
SLOCUM, Brandon H, Senior Vice President and Chief Financial Officer, Medical West, Bessemer, AL, p. A16
SLOCUM, Gregg Y., Chief Executive Officer, Valley Forge Medical Center, Norristown, PA, p. A547
SLONIKER, Amanda, Director of Nursing, Heartland Behavioral Health Services, Nevada, MO, p. A381
SLONIM, Sheryl A, Executive Vice President and Chief Nursing Officer, Holy Name Medical Center, Teaneck, NJ, p. A429
SLONINA, Marrianne, Director Human Resources, Georgetown Community Hospital, Georgetown, KY, p. A266
SLOPER, Carol, Manager Information Technology, Cheyenne County Hospital, Saint Francis, KS, p. A259
SLUCK, Jeana, R.N., Executive Director Nursing Clinical Inpatient Departments, Allied Services Scranton Rehabilitation Hospital, Scranton, PA, p. A554
SLUSHER, Michael, FACHE, Community Chief Executive Officer, Middlesboro Arh Hospital, Middlesboro, KY, p. A271
SLUSHER, W. James (Jamie), M.D., Chief of Staff, Jackson Parish Hospital, Jonesboro, LA, p. A284
SLUTSKER, Vladimir, Medical Director, Encompass Health Rehabilitation Hospital of Gadsden, Gadsden, AL, p. A19
SLYTER, Mark F.
 FACHE, President and Chief Operating Officer, Chandler Regional Medical Center, Chandler, AZ, p. A30
 FACHE, President and Chief Operating Officer, Mercy Gilbert Medical Center, Gilbert, AZ, p. A32
SMAJSTRLA, Julie, Director Nursing, Seymour Hospital, Seymour, TX, p. A652
SMALE, Cindy, Director, Human Resources, Iredell Health System, Statesville, NC, p. A477
SMALL, Becky
 Chief Human Resources Officer, Kindred Hospital–Aurora, Aurora, CO, p. A103
 Chief Nursing Officer, North Texas Medical Center, Gainesville, TX, p. A621
SMALL, Jessica, President, Aurora Psychiatric Hospital, Wauwatosa, WI, p. A724
SMALL, Jonathan, Chief Operations Information and Technology, John D. Dingell Department of Veterans Affairs Medical Center, Detroit, MI, p. A325
SMALL, Terry L., Assistant Chief Executive Officer, William R. Sharpe, Jr. Hospital, Weston, WV, p. A706
SMALLEY, Christine, Chief Clinical Officer, Acuity Specialty Hospital–Ohio Valley At Weirton, Weirton, WV, p. A705
SMALLWOOD, Ravae, IS Coordinator, Chi Health Missouri Valley, Missouri Valley, IA, p. A240
SMARR, Susan, M.D., Physician–in–Chief, Kaiser Permanente Santa Clara Medical Center, Santa Clara, CA, p. A94
SMART, Dan, Chief Information Management Officer, Permian Regional Medical Center, Andrews, TX, p. A597
SMART, Melissa, Communication ad Public Relations Specialist, Texas Health Presbyterian Hospital Denton, Denton, TX, p. A614
SMART, Paul, CPA, Chief Financial Officer, Franklin County Medical Center, Preston, ID, p. A183
SMART, Stephanie, Chief Nursing Officer, United Hospital Center, Bridgeport, WV, p. A699
SMENDIK, Douglas, M.D., Hospital Medical Director, Corewell Health Pennock Hospital, Hastings, MI, p. A329
SMIDT, Jessica, R.N., Director of Nursing, Pipestone County Medical Center, Pipestone, MN, p. A352
SMIGA, Lance, Chief Executive Officer, Chief Financial Officer, Jackson County Hospital District, Edna, TX, p. A616
SMILEY, Amy, Chief Executive Officer, Northern Virginia Mental Health Institute, Falls Church, VA, p. A676
SMITH, Alan, Administrator, Mercy Hospital Lincoln, Troy, MO, p. A387
SMITH, Alan H
 Chief Financial Officer, Huntington Beach Hospital, Huntington Beach, CA, p. A67
 Chief Financial Officer, La Palma Intercommunity Hospital, La Palma, CA, p. A69
SMITH, Allen L., M.D., President and Chief Executive Officer, South Shore Hospital, South Weymouth, MA, p. A318
SMITH, Alyshia, R.N., Medical Center Director, Durham Va Health Care System, Durham, NC, p. A467

SMITH, Amy, Interim Chief Executive Officer, Foundations Behavioral Health, Doylestown, PA, p. A538
SMITH, Amy Christine, R.N., Chief Operating Officer, Taylor Regional Hospital, Campbellsville, KY, p. A264
SMITH, Andrew, Chief Financial Officer, HCA Florida Blake Hospital, Bradenton, FL, p. A126
SMITH, Angie B., Chief Nursing Officer, St. Bernards Medical Center, Jonesboro, AR, p. A48
SMITH, Barbara H, Senior Vice President & Chief Operating Officer, Robert Wood Johnson University Hospital At Hamilton, Hamilton, NJ, p. A422
SMITH, Bennie
 Chief Information Officer, Lady of The Sea General Hospital, Cut Off, LA, p. A281
 Director Human Resources and Risk Management, Lady of The Sea General Hospital, Cut Off, LA, p. A281
SMITH, Bernie, Chief Financial Officer, Guthrie Troy Community Hospital, Troy, PA, p. A556
SMITH, Bethany
 Controller, West Tennessee Healthcare Rehabilitation Hospital Cane Creek, A Partnership With Encompass Health, Martin, TN, p. A587
 Director of Finance, Chi Oakes Hospital, Oakes, ND, p. A483
 Vice President Finance, Chi Mercy Health, Valley City, ND, p. A483
SMITH, Betsy, Chief Nursing Officer, Effingham Health System, Springfield, GA, p. A171
SMITH, Beverly Bzdek, Chief Nursing Officer, Bon Secours – Southside Medical Center, Petersburg, VA, p. A681
SMITH, Blythe, Administrative Assistant, Faulkton Area Medical Center, Faulkton, SD, p. A573
SMITH, Bradley, President and Chief Executive Officer, Rush Memorial Hospital, Rushville, IN, p. A227
SMITH, Brandy, R.N., Chief Operations Officer, Memorial Hospital of Stilwell, Stilwell, OK, p. A521
SMITH, Brenda, Director Financial Services, Alliance Health Center, Meridian, MS, p. A366
SMITH, Brent, Chief Executive Officer, Comanche County Memorial Hospital, Lawton, OK, p. A514
SMITH, Brian
 Chief Financial Officer, Beth Israel Deaconess Hospital–Needham, Needham, MA, p. A316
 Director of Operations, Wamego Health Center, Wamego, KS, p. A261
 Vice President Human Resources, Lexington Medical Center, West Columbia, SC, p. A571
SMITH, C David, M.D., Chief Medical Officer, Jay Hospital, Jay, FL, p. A135
SMITH, Candice
 MSN, Chief Executive Officer, Hereford Regional Medical Center, Hereford, TX, p. A624
 MSN, Chief Nursing Officer, Hereford Regional Medical Center, Hereford, TX, p. A624
SMITH, Carl, Chief Information Officer, King's Daughters Medical Center, Brookhaven, MS, p. A360
SMITH, Carol
 President, Wellspan Surgery And Rehabilitation Hospital, York, PA, p. A559
 Vice President Patient Care and Chief Nursing Officer, Tift Regional Medical Center, Tifton, GA, p. A172
SMITH, Carol A, R.N., Director Operations and Nursing, Novant Health Medical Park Hospital, Winston–Salem, NC, p. A478
SMITH, Carole, Senior Human Resource Business Partner, Banner Del E. Webb Medical Center, Sun City West, AZ, p. A39
SMITH, Charles, Chief Executive Officer, Encompass Health Rehabilitation Hospital of Utah, Sandy, UT, p. A669
SMITH, Cherie L.
 Ph.D., R.N., President, Ohiohealth Dublin Methodist Hospital, Dublin, OH, p. A495
 Ph.D., R.N., President, Ohiohealth Grady Memorial Hospital, Delaware, OH, p. A494
SMITH, Cheryl, Manager Human Resources, New Braunfels Regional Rehabilitation Hospital, New Braunfels, TX, p. A641
SMITH, Chris, Chief Information Officer, Falls Community Hospital And Clinic, Marlin, TX, p. A638
SMITH, Clifford A., Ph.D., Acting Medical Center Director, Jesse Brown Va Medical Center, Chicago, IL, p. A189
SMITH, Connie, FACHE, MSN, R.N., Chief Executive Officer, The Medical Center At Bowling Green, Bowling Green, KY, p. A264
SMITH, Dan, Director Human Resources, Memorial Hospital Association, Carthage, IL, p. A187
SMITH, Daniel
 Chief Executive Officer, Memorial Hermann Surgical Hospital–First Colony, Sugar Land, TX, p. A654

 Chief Financial Officer, Palo Pinto General Hospital, Mineral Wells, TX, p. A639
 Chief Financial Officer, Top. Surgical Specialty Hospital, Houston, TX, p. A628
SMITH, Daniel B
 Chief Financial Officer, Samaritan Pacific Communities Hospital, Newport, OR, p. A529
 Vice President Finance, Good Samaritan Regional Medical Center, Corvallis, OR, p. A526
 Vice President Finance, Samaritan Albany General Hospital, Albany, OR, p. A525
 Vice President Finance, Samaritan Lebanon Community Hospital, Lebanon, OR, p. A528
SMITH, Darrin, President and Chief Executive Officer, UCHealth Parkview Medical Center, Pueblo, CO, p. A113
SMITH, David
 Chief Executive Officer, Baylor Scott & White Institute for Rehabilitation – Dallas, Dallas, TX, p. A610
 Chief Executive Officer, Hammond–Henry Hospital, Geneseo, IL, p. A196
SMITH, Debra, Chief Nursing Officer, Encompass Health Rehabilitation Hospital of Kingsport, Kingsport, TN, p. A585
SMITH, Denise, Director Health Information, Encompass Health Rehabilitation Hospital of Chattanooga, Chattanooga, TN, p. A580
SMITH, Diana B, Chief Financial Officer, KPC Promise Hospital of Dallas, Dallas, TX, p. A611
SMITH, Dianne, Director Personnel and Human Resources, WVU Medicine Potomac Valley Hospital, Keyser, WV, p. A702
SMITH, Dick, Director Human Resources, Cody Regional Health, Cody, WY, p. A726
SMITH, Donna, Ph.D., Chief Executive Officer, River Point Behavioral Health, Jacksonville, FL, p. A135
SMITH, Donna M, Chief Nursing Officer, Barstow Community Hospital, Barstow, CA, p. A57
SMITH, Donna P, R.N., Vice President Chief Operating Officer and Chief Nursing Officer, Clifton Springs Hospital And Clinic, Clifton Springs, NY, p. A441
SMITH, Donnie
 Chief Human Resources Officer, Ochsner Laird Hospital, Union, MS, p. A369
 Director Human Resources, Ochsner Rush Medical Center, Meridian, MS, p. A366
SMITH, Doug, Chief Financial Officer, Stephens Memorial Hospital, Breckenridge, TX, p. A604
SMITH, Eli
 FACHE, Chief Executive Officere, Baylor Scott & White Medical Center–Frisco, Frisco, TX, p. A621
 Chief Operating Officer, West Jefferson Medical Center, Marrero, LA, p. A288
SMITH, Ericka, Chief Operating Officer, Monterey Park Hospital, Monterey Park, CA, p. A78
SMITH, Erin, Chief Operating Officer, East Georgia Regional Medical Center, Statesboro, GA, p. A171
SMITH, Eugene, Chief Information Officer, Maniilaq Health Center, Kotzebue, AK, p. A29
SMITH, G. Todd., President, Mercy Medical Center Redding, Redding, CA, p. A85
SMITH, Gary, Chief Operating Officer, Aurelia Osborn Fox Memorial Hospital, Oneonta, NY, p. A455
SMITH, Gene, Chief Executive Officer, North Alabama Specialty Hospital, Athens, AL, p. A15
SMITH, Geoffrey, Chief Financial Officer, Lebanon Veterans Affairs Medical Center, Lebanon, PA, p. A544
SMITH, Greg, Chief Medical Officer, Lake Region Healthcare Corporation, Fergus Falls, MN, p. A347
SMITH, Gregory
 Senior Vice President and Chief Information Officer, Ascension Southeast Wisconsin Hospital – Franklin Campus, Franklin, WI, p. A711
 Senior Vice President and Chief Information Officer, Ascension St. Francis Hospital, Milwaukee, WI, p. A716
 Senior Vice President and Chief Information Officer, Midwest Orthopedic Specialty Hospital, Franklin, WI, p. A711
SMITH, Gretchen, Vice President of Operations, Risk and Compliance, and Chief Operating Officer, Rush Memorial Hospital, Rushville, IN, p. A227
SMITH, Harley, Chief Executive Officer, Izard County Medical Center, Calico Rock, AR, p. A44
SMITH, Heather, Chief Operating Officer, Welch Community Hospital, Welch, WV, p. A705
SMITH, Holt
 Chief Financial Officer, Musc Health Columbia Medical Center Downtown, Columbia, SC, p. A564
 Chief Financial Officer, Musc Health Kershaw Medical Center, Camden, SC, p. A562

Index of Health Care Professionals / Smith

Chief Financial Officer, Musc Health Lancaster Medical Center, Lancaster, SC, p. A568
SMITH, Jack, Acting Chief Information Resources Management Service, Ioannis A. Lougaris Veterans' Administration Medical Center, Reno, NV, p. A412
SMITH, Jackie, R.N., Chief Nursing Officer, Holdenville General Hospital, Holdenville, OK, p. A513
SMITH, Jameson C., FACHE, Chief Executive Officer, Kootenai Health, Coeur D'Alene, ID, p. A180
SMITH, Jamie, Supervisor Health Information Management Systems, Encompass Health Rehabilitation Hospital of Sewickley, Sewickley, PA, p. A554
SMITH, Janet, Chief Executive Officer, Wiregrass Medical Center, Geneva, AL, p. A20
SMITH, Jared, Chief Executive Officer, UT Health Quitman, Quitman, TX, p. A646
SMITH, Jared M., Chief Executive Officer, Bethesda Hospital East, Boynton Beach, FL, p. A126
SMITH, Jason
   Chief Medical Officer, Marshfield Medical Center – Beaver Dam, Beaver Dam, WI, p. A708
   Chief Operating Officer, Piedmont Athens Regional Medical Center, Athens, GA, p. A156
SMITH, Jeremy W, Director of Human Resources, Council Oak Comprehensive Healthcare, Tulsa, OK, p. A522
SMITH, Jesse, Director of Nursing, Keefe Memorial Hospital, Cheyenne Wells, CO, p. A104
SMITH, Jim, Director Information Systems, Washington County Memorial Hospital, Potosi, MO, p. A382
SMITH, Jo Beth
   Chief Operating Officer, Medical Arts Hospital, Lamesa, TX, p. A633
   Vice President Human Resources, Decatur County Hospital, Leon, IA, p. A239
SMITH, JoAnn P., R.N., Chief Nursing Officer, and Vice President Patient Care Services, UNC Health Rockingham, Eden, NC, p. A467
SMITH, Jodi, Administrative Assistant Human Resources, Eureka Springs Hospital, Eureka Springs, AR, p. A45
SMITH, Jon, Chief Financial Officer, Lost Rivers Medical Center, Arco, ID, p. A179
SMITH, Jonathan, Interim Chief Executive Officer, Blount Memorial Hospital, Maryville, TN, p. A587
SMITH, Julia
   Chief Financial Officer, Kindred Hospital-Chattanooga, Chattanooga, TN, p. A580
   Chief Financial Officer, Vibra Hospital of Charleston, Mt. Pleasant, SC, p. A569
SMITH, Julie
   R.N., MSN, Director of Nursing, Jersey Community Hospital, Jerseyville, IL, p. A199
   Chief Executive Officer, Decatur Health Systems, Oberlin, KS, p. A256
   Director Human Resources, Encompass Health Lakeshore Rehabilitation Hospital, Birmingham, AL, p. A16
   Senior Human Resources Strategic Partner, Providence Milwaukie Hospital, Milwaukie, OR, p. A529
SMITH, Justus, Chief Executive Officer, Camc Plateau Medical Center, Oak Hill, WV, p. A703
SMITH, Karen S, Director Information Services, Chilton Medical Center, Pompton Plains, NJ, p. A427
SMITH, Karla, Director Human Resources, St. Peter's Health, Helena, MT, p. A393
SMITH, Karyl, Director Human Resources, Harbor-Ucla Medical Center, Torrance, CA, p. A98
SMITH, Kelli, M.D., Chief of Staff, Magee General Hospital, Magee, MS, p. A365
SMITH, Kenneth P, Chief Medical Officer, John C. Fremont Healthcare District, Mariposa, CA, p. A76
SMITH, Kevin
   D.O., Chief of Staff, Munson Healthcare Otsego Memorial Hospital, Gaylord, MI, p. A327
   M.D., Interim Chief Medical Officer, Loyola University Medical Center, Maywood, IL, p. A201
SMITH, Kevin L, Area Finance Officer, Kaiser Permanente South Sacramento Medical Center, Sacramento, CA, p. A87
SMITH, Kris, Controller, Chi St. Josep. Health Rehabilitation Hospital, An Affiliate of Encompass Health, Bryan, TX, p. A605
SMITH, Kyle
   Administrator, Unity Psychiatric Care-Huntsville, Huntsville, AL, p. A21
   Director Information Systems, Iredell Health System, Statesville, NC, p. A477
SMITH, Lana, Human Resources Director, Ashe Memorial Hospital, Jefferson, NC, p. A471
SMITH, Larry, Senior Vice President and Chief Financial Officer, UW Medicine/Valley Medical Center, Renton, WA, p. A693

SMITH, Laura, R.N., Chief Executive Officer, Ellett Memorial Hospital, Appleton City, MO, p. A371
SMITH, Leora, Information System and Health Information Management Team Leader, Phelp. Memorial Health Center, Holdrege, NE, p. A401
SMITH, Linda T, Director Human Resources, Clay County Hospital, Ashland, AL, p. A15
SMITH, Linda V, Vice President Human Resources, HCA Florida Lake Monroe Hospital, Sanford, FL, p. A149
SMITH, Lori, Chief Financial Officer, North Big Horn Hospital District, Lovell, WY, p. A727
SMITH, Lori J., Vice President Human Resources, St. Bernards Medical Center, Jonesboro, AR, p. A48
SMITH, Lorie, Director Human Resources, Conemaugh Nason Medical Center, Roaring Spring, PA, p. A553
SMITH, Lorraine, Chief Executive Officer, Regency Hospital – Macon, Macon, GA, p. A167
SMITH, Lory Beth, Manager Human Resource, Christus Surgical Hospital, Corpus Christi, TX, p. A608
SMITH, M. Scott, President, St. Anthony's Hospital, Saint Petersburg, FL, p. A149
SMITH, Marilyn, Chief Nursing Officer, Vanderbilt Tullahoma Harton Hospital, Tullahoma, TN, p. A594
SMITH, Marisa, Director, HCA Houston Healthcare Tomball, Tomball, TX, p. A658
SMITH, Mark
   M.D., Chief Medical Officer, Methodist Richardson Medical Center, Richardson, TX, p. A646
   Director Human Resources, Providence Holy Family Hospital, Spokane, WA, p. A696
   Director Human Resources, Providence Sacred Heart Medical Center & Children's Hospital, Spokane, WA, p. A696
   Director Nursing Operations, Northern Colorado Rehabilitation Hospital, Johnstown, CO, p. A110
SMITH, Mark T., JD, CPA, President and Chief Executive Officer, Adventhealth Avista, Louisville, CO, p. A111
SMITH, Marsh, Manager Health Information, University Behavioral Health of Denton, Denton, TX, p. A614
SMITH, Martha, R.N., Chief Nursing Officer, New Orleans East Hospital, New Orleans, LA, p. A290
SMITH, Mary Clare., Director, Western State Hospital, Staunton, VA, p. A684
SMITH, Matt, Chief Executive Officer, Clark Regional Medical Center, Winchester, KY, p. A275
SMITH, Matthew, M.D., Vice President Medical Affairs and Chief Medical Officer, Carrollton Regional Medical Center, Carrollton, TX, p. A606
SMITH, Megan, M.D., Chief Medical Staff, Community Memorial Hospital, Burke, SD, p. A572
SMITH, Melinda, Chief Information Systems, Ochsner Watkins Hospital, Quitman, MS, p. A368
SMITH, Melissa
   Controller, Select Specialty Hospital–Jackson, Jackson, MS, p. A364
   Interim Vice President Human Resources, North Memorial Health Hospital, Robbinsdale, MN, p. A353
SMITH, Michael, Director of Nursing, Cypress Creek Hospital, Houston, TX, p. A625
SMITH, Michael C., President and Chief Executive Officer, Carolinaeast Health System, New Bern, NC, p. A473
SMITH, Michelle, Coordinator Human Resources, Baton Rouge Rehabilitation Hospital, Baton Rouge, LA, p. A277
SMITH, Michelle T, R.N., MSN, FACHE, Vice President Nursing Chief Nursing Officer Chief Experience Officer, Prisma Health Greenville Memorial Hospital, Greenville, SC, p. A567
SMITH, Mike
   Chief Information Officer, Cap. Coral Hospital, Cap. Coral, FL, p. A127
   Chief Information Officer, Gulf Coast Medical Center, Fort Myers, FL, p. A131
SMITH, Missy, Coordinator Human Resources, Scotland County Hospital, Memphis, MO, p. A380
SMITH, Nadine, Director Human Resources, Reeves Regional Health, Pecos, TX, p. A643
SMITH, Neil, D.O., President, Cleveland Clinic Fairview Hospital, Cleveland, OH, p. A490
SMITH, Nekeisha, Chief Executive Officer, Trinity Medical, Ferriday, LA, p. A282
SMITH, Nicole, Director Human Resources, Hi-Desert Medical Center, Joshua Tree, CA, p. A68
SMITH, Oliver, President and Chief Executive Officer, Paris Community Hospital, Paris, IL, p. A205
SMITH, Paige L, Vice President Patient Care Services and Chief Nurse Executive, Marietta Memorial Hospital, Marietta, OH, p. A499
SMITH, Pam, Chief Nursing Officer, Encompass Health Rehabilitation Hospital of Richardson, Richardson, TX, p. A646

SMITH, Patricia, Chief Nursing Officer, Prisma Health Oconee Memorial Hospital, Seneca, SC, p. A570
SMITH, Patrick
   M.D., Chief Medical Officer, Abrazo Arrowhead Campus, Glendale, AZ, p. A32
   Director Information Technology, Clay County Hospital, Ashland, AL, p. A15
SMITH, Patsy, Director Human Resources, Hereford Regional Medical Center, Hereford, TX, p. A624
SMITH, Peg, Vice President and Chief Nursing Officer, Chandler Regional Medical Center, Chandler, AZ, p. A30
SMITH, Phyllis, Vice President Human Resources, Northeastern Health System, Tahlequah, OK, p. A521
SMITH, Phyllis J., Associate Director, Birmingham Va Medical Center, Birmingham, AL, p. A16
SMITH, Randall, Executive Vice President, Jackson Park Hospital And Medical Center, Chicago, IL, p. A189
SMITH, Randy, Senior Vice President, Chief Operating Officer, South Georgia Medical Center, Valdosta, GA, p. A173
SMITH, Rhonda
   Applications Support Manager, University Hospitals Portage Medical Center, Ravenna, OH, p. A503
   Chief Nursing Officer, Benewah Community Hospital, Saint Maries, ID, p. A183
   Director Human Resources, Shriners Hospitals for Children–Portland, Portland, OR, p. A531
SMITH, Rich
   Vice President Human Resources, Kaiser Sunnyside Medical Center, Clackamas, OR, p. A526
   Vice President Human Resources, Kaiser Westside Medical Center, Hillsboro, OR, p. A527
SMITH, Richard, Chief of Staff, Carroll County Memorial Hospital, Carrollton, MO, p. A373
SMITH, Richard C.
   Chief Financial Officer, JFK Johnson Rehabilitation Institute At Hackensack Meridian Health, Edison, NJ, p. A420
   Senior Vice President and Chief Financial Officer, Hackensack Meridian Health Jfk Medical Center, Edison, NJ, p. A420
   Senior Vice President Finance, Johnson Rehabilitation Institute At Hackensack Meridian Health Ocean Medical Center, Brick, NJ, p. A418
SMITH, Rick
   Chief Executive Officer, Troy Regional Medical Center, Troy, AL, p. A25
   Chief Financial Officer, Mason Health, Shelton, WA, p. A695
   Chief Operating Officer, Orlando Health – Health Central Hospital, Ocoee, FL, p. A143
   Director Information Services, Cibola General Hospital, Grants, NM, p. A434
   Senior Vice President Human Resources and Chief Administrative Officer, Vail Health, Vail, CO, p. A114
SMITH, Robert T.
   M.D., Chief Medical Officer, Kettering Health Main Campus, Kettering, OH, p. A497
   M.D., Chief Medical Officer, Kettering Health Miamisburg, Miamisburg, OH, p. A500
SMITH, Robin C, Chief Nursing Officer, Indiana University Health White Memorial Hospital, Monticello, IN, p. A224
SMITH, Rodney
   Vice President and Administrator, Harrisburg Medical Center, Harrisburg, IL, p. A197
   Vice President and Administrator, Herrin Hospital, Herrin, IL, p. A197
SMITH, Ruth, Division Human Resources Business Partner, Banner Lassen Medical Center, Susanville, CA, p. A97
SMITH, Ryan K, Senior Vice President Information Technology, Banner – University Medical Center South, Tucson, AZ, p. A40
SMITH, Ryan K., Chief Executive Officer, South Peninsula Hospital, Homer, AK, p. A28
SMITH, Scott
   M.D., Chief Executive Officer and Chief Medical Officer, Adams Memorial Hospital, Decatur, IN, p. A215
   M.D., Chief Medical Officer, Adams Memorial Hospital, Decatur, IN, p. A215
SMITH, Scott M., Market Chief Executive Officer, Saint Francis Hospital, Memphis, TN, p. A589
SMITH, Sean, President and Chief Executive Officer, Camden Clark Medical Center, Parkersburg, WV, p. A703
SMITH, Sherry, Manager Human Resources, Dallas County Hospital, Perry, IA, p. A242
SMITH, Shirley M, Chief Financial Officer, Andalusia Health, Andalusia, AL, p. A15
SMITH, Sid, Director Information Resources, Larned State Hospital, Larned, KS, p. A252
SMITH, Skip. Vice President Finance, Iredell Health System, Statesville, NC, p. A477
SMITH, Stacey, R.N., Director of Nursing, Jefferson Hospital, Louisville, GA, p. A166

SMITH, Steve
  M.D., Chief of Staff, Providence Kodiak Island Medical Center, Kodiak, AK, p. A28
  Chief Financial Officer, Kansas Heart Hospital, Wichita, KS, p. A261
  President and Chief Executive Officer, Chi St. Gabriel's Health, Little Falls, MN, p. A349
  President and Chief Financial Officer, Chi St. Gabriel's Health, Little Falls, MN, p. A349
SMITH, Steven, Chief Information Officer, Endeavor Health Evanston Hospital, Evanston, IL, p. A195
SMITH, Suzanne E, R.N., MSN, Chief Nursing Officer, San Juan Regional Medical Center, Farmington, NM, p. A434
SMITH, Tammy
  R.N., President and Chief Executive Officer, Pratt Regional Medical Center, Pratt, KS, p. A258
  Director, Allendale County Hospital, Fairfax, SC, p. A566
SMITH, Taylor, Chief Executive Officer, Eureka Springs Hospital, Eureka Springs, AR, p. A45
SMITH, Teresa, Chief Financial Officer, Memorial Hospital Association, Carthage, IL, p. A187
SMITH, Terrance, M.D., Chairman Medical Staff, Sanford Clear Lake Medical Center, Clear Lake, SD, p. A572
SMITH, Terri, Chief Operating Officer, Ascension Sacred Heart Pensacola, Pensacola, FL, p. A146
SMITH, Thomas, M.D., Vice President Medical Affairs, Hutchinson Regional Medical Center, Hutchinson, KS, p. A251
SMITH, Tiffani, Chief Human Resources Officer, Stonesprings Hospital Center, Dulles, VA, p. A675
SMITH, Toni, Chief Nursing Officer, Kern Medical, Bakersfield, CA, p. A57
SMITH, Tonya
  Chief Financial Officer, USMD Hospital At Arlington, Arlington, TX, p. A598
  President, Valley Health – Winchester Medical Center, Winchester, VA, p. A685
SMITH, Tracy, Director Human Resources, Mercy St. Francis Hospital, Mountain View, MO, p. A381
SMITH, Trevor, Chief Management Information Services, Gunnison Valley Health, Gunnison, CO, p. A109
SMITH, Trisha, Chief Financial Officer, Mimbres Memorial Hospital, Deming, NM, p. A434
SMITH, Tyson, M.D., Chief Medical Officer, Haywood Regional Medical Center, Clyde, NC, p. A466
SMITH, Vanessa
  Chief Human Resources Officer, Community Medical Center, Toms River, NJ, p. A429
  Chief Operating Officer, Ascension Wisconsin Hospital – Menomonee Falls Campus, Menomonee Falls, WI, p. A715
  Chief Operating Officer, Dignity St. Rose – Craig Ranch, North Las Vegas, NV, p. A411
SMITH, Vincent, Chief Information Officer, NYC Health + Hospitals/Queens, New York, NY, p. A451
SMITH, W. Todd, M.D., Chief Medical Officer, Och Regional Medical Center, Starkville, MS, p. A369
SMITH, Wade, Chief Operating Officer, Baptist Health Medical Center – Drew County, Monticello, AR, p. A50
SMITH, Wendell, Chief Operating Officer, St. James Behavioral Health Hospital, Gonzales, LA, p. A282
SMITH, Wesley, M.D., FACS, Chief Medical Officer and Physician Advisor, Ascension St. Vincent's Birmingham, Birmingham, AL, p. A16
SMITH, William E., M.D., Chief Medical Officer, Cullman Regional Medical Center, Cullman, AL, p. A18
SMITH–ZUBA, Lorraina, R.N., MSN, Chief Nursing Officer, The University of Vermont Health Network Porter Medical Center, Middlebury, VT, p. A671
SMITHERS, John, Network Specialist, River Hospital, Alexandria Bay, NY, p. A438
SMITHHART, Paula, Director Human Resources, Coryell Health, Gatesville, TX, p. A622
SMITHSON, Tracey, MSN, R.N., Chief Nursing Officer, Piedmont Eastside Medical Center, Snellville, GA, p. A171
SMOKER, Bret, M.D., Clinical Director, PHS Santa Fe Indian Hospital, Santa Fe, NM, p. A436
SMORRA, Colleen, Assistant Administrator, Hackensack Meridian Health Pascack Valley Medical Center, Westwood, NJ, p. A430
SMOTHERS, Kevin, M.D., Vice President Chief Medical Officer, Adventist Healthcare Shady Grove Medical Center, Rockville, MD, p. A306
SMOTHERS, Mark, M.D., Chief Medical Officer, University of Mississipp. Medical Center Holmes County, Lexington, MS, p. A365
SMOTHERS, Stephen, Director Information Systems, Medical Center Enterprise, Enterprise, AL, p. A19

SMYTH, Thomas, President and Chief Executive Officer, University of Maryland St. Josep. Medical Center, Towson, MD, p. A307
SNAPP, Jeremy, Director Information Systems, Lindsborg Community Hospital, Lindsborg, KS, p. A253
SNAPP, William R
  III, Executive Vice President Finance and Chief Financial Officer, Ephraim Mcdowell Regional Medical Center, Danville, KY, p. A264
  III, Vice President and Chief Financial Officer, Ephraim Mcdowell Fort Logan Hospital, Stanford, KY, p. A274
SNAVELY, Gretchen, Director Human Resources, Holton Community Hospital, Holton, KS, p. A250
SNEDEGAR, Michael, Chief Financial Officer, Bourbon Community Hospital, Paris, KY, p. A273
SNEED, Farron, Chief Operating Officer, Hillcrest Medical Center, Tulsa, OK, p. A522
SNEFF, Mark, Vice President Human Resources, Good Shepherd Penn Partners, Philadelphia, PA, p. A548
SNELL, Dan, Chief Medical Officer, Portneuf Medical Center, Pocatello, ID, p. A183
SNELL, Peggy, Chief Finance Officer, Cherry County Hospital, Valentine, NE, p. A406
SNENK, Don, Chief Financial Officer, Mercy Fitzgerald Hospital, Darby, PA, p. A538
SNIDER, Charles, Vice President Human Resources, HCA Florida Oak Hill Hospital, Brooksville, FL, p. A127
SNIDER, Cheryl, Director Human Resources, St. Vincent Health, Leadville, CO, p. A111
SNIDER, Glenn R, M.D., Chief of Staff, Louis A. Johnson Veterans Affairs Medical Center, Clarksburg, WV, p. A700
SNIDER, Timothy, Manager Information Systems, Fannin Regional Hospital, Blue Ridge, GA, p. A159
SNODGRASS, Scott, Chief Executive Officer, Centennial Peaks Hospital, Louisville, CO, p. A112
SNOOK, Joel, Chief Financial Officer, Keralty Hospital Miami, Miami, FL, p. A140
SNOW, Dorothy, M.D., Chief of Staff, Veterans Affairs Maryland Health Care System–Baltimore Division, Baltimore, MD, p. A302
SNOW, Jason T, Director People Services, HSHS St. Elizabeth's Hospital, O Fallon, IL, p. A204
SNOW, John, Chief Executive Officer, Newberry County Memorial Hospital, Newberry, SC, p. A569
SNOW, Josh, Chief Executive Officer, USA Health University Hospital, Mobile, AL, p. A22
SNOW, Ryan
  Director Human Resources, Northeast Georgia Medical Center Habersham, Demorest, GA, p. A162
  Chief Executive Officer, Chatuge Regional Hospital And Nursing Home, Hiawassee, GA, p. A165
SNOWDON, Susan, Director Information Technology, Four Winds Hospital, Saratoga Springs, NY, p. A458
SNYDER, Bobby, Chief Executive Officer, Inspire Specialty Hospital, Midwest City, OK, p. A515
SNYDER, David, M.D., Chief of Staff, Emory Long–Term Acute Care, Decatur, GA, p. A162
SNYDER, Donald, M.D., Chief Medical Officer, Rush Memorial Hospital, Rushville, IN, p. A227
SNYDER, Gregg, Chief Executive Officer, Sarah D. Culbertson Memorial Hospital, Rushville, IL, p. A208
SNYDER, Kristi, Vice President Human Resources, Charleston Area Medical Center, Charleston, WV, p. A700
SNYDER, Kristine, Chief Operating Officer, Fulton County Health Center, Wauseon, OH, p. A506
SNYDER, Kyle C.
  President, Penn State Health Hampden Medical Center, Enola, PA, p. A539
  President, Penn State Health Holy Spirit Medical Center, Camp Hill, PA, p. A536
SNYDER, Leah, Director Health Information Services, Loring Hospital, Sac City, IA, p. A242
SNYDER, Mary E, Chief Operations Officer, Montrose Regional Health, Montrose, CO, p. A112
SNYDER, Matthew, R.N., Director of Nursing, Johnson County Hospital, Tecumseh, NE, p. A406
SNYDER, Norman, M.D., Medical Director, Vantage Point of Northwest Arkansas, Fayetteville, AR, p. A46
SNYDER, Phyllis, Chief Nursing Officer, Corona Regional Medical Center, Corona, CA, p. A60
SNYDER, Renae, Chief Financial Officer, Sakakawea Medical Center, Hazen, ND, p. A481
SNYDER, Sheree, Manager Human Resources, Hillcrest Hospital Henryetta, Henryetta, OK, p. A513
SNYDER, Steve, Chief Financial Officer, Ohio Hospital for Psychiatry, Columbus, OH, p. A492
SNYDER, Tammy, President and Chief Operating Officer, Rochester General Hospital, Rochester, NY, p. A457
SNYDER, Vicky, Chief Operating Officer, Cleveland Clinic Medina Hospital, Medina, OH, p. A500

SOARES, Brian, Chief Executive Officer, Encompass Health Rehabilitation Hospital of Jacksonville, Jacksonville, FL, p. A134
SOARES, Jair C., M.D., Executive Director, Uthealth Harris County Psychiatric Center, Houston, TX, p. A628
SOBERON–CASSAR, Angelica, M.D., Chief Medical Officer, Encompass Health Rehabilitation Hospital of Greenville, Greenville, SC, p. A567
SOEKEN, Charles
  Director Information Technology, Providence Medical Center, Kansas City, KS, p. A252
  Director Information Technology, Saint John Hospital, Leavenworth, KS, p. A253
SOGARD, Matt, Chief Executive Officer, Overland Park Regional Medical Center, Overland Park, KS, p. A257
SOGLIN, David, Chief Medical Officer, La Rabida Children's Hospital, Chicago, IL, p. A190
SOHN, Steven, M.D., President Medical Staff, Dallas County Hospital, Perry, IA, p. A242
SOHRAB, Sadaf, M.D., Chief Medical Officer, Mercy Hospital Springfield, Springfield, MO, p. A387
SOIFER, Gregg, M.D., Medical Director, Encompass Health Rehabilitation Hospital of Cumming, Cumming, GA, p. A162
SOILEAU, D. Kirk., FACHE, Chief Executive Officer, Natchitoches Regional Medical Center, Natchitoches, LA, p. A289
SOILEAU, Shelly
  Chief Financial Officer, Opelousas General Health System, Opelousas, LA, p. A291
  Chief Financial Officer, Savoy Medical Center, Mamou, LA, p. A287
SOIMAN, Erika, CPA, Chief Financial Officer, NYC Health + Hospitals/Woodhull, New York, NY, p. A452
SOJKA, Matthew
  M.D., Vice President Medical Affairs, Mercyone Cedar Falls Medical Center, Cedar Falls, IA, p. A231
  M.D., Vice President Medical Affairs, Mercyone Oelwein Medical Center, Oelwein, IA, p. A241
  M.D., Vice President, Medical Affairs, Mercyone Waterloo Medical Center, Waterloo, IA, p. A244
SOLA', Ivan', President Medical Staff, UPMC Carlisle, Carlisle, PA, p. A536
SOLAIMAN, Shereen, Vice President Human Resources, Ohiohealth Riverside Methodist Hospital, Columbus, OH, p. A492
SOLBERG, Don, M.D., Chief Medical Officer, Kittitas Valley Healthcare, Ellensburg, WA, p. A689
SOLCHER, Barry, M.D., Chief of Staff, The Physicians Centre Hospital, Bryan, TX, p. A605
SOLDO, Stephen, M.D., Chief Medical Officer, Saint Agnes Medical Center, Fresno, CA, p. A65
SOLE, Kelly, Chief Operating Officer, Appalachian Behavioral Healthcare, Athens, OH, p. A485
SOLEM, Terry S, Vice President of Human Resources, Endeavor Health Northwest Community Hospital, Arlington Heights, IL, p. A185
SOLER, Eddie, Chief Financial Officer, Adventhealth Orlando, Orlando, FL, p. A144
SOLES, Jason, Manager Information Systems, St. James Hospital, Hornell, NY, p. A444
SOLHEIM, Heidi, Chief Operating Officer, Waverly Health Center, Waverly, IA, p. A245
SOLIMAN, Russell, Director Information Services, Ascension St. Mary – Kankakee, Kankakee, IL, p. A199
SOLIN, Andrea
  Chief Financial Officer, Lovelace Unm Rehabilitation Hospital, Albuquerque, NM, p. A432
  Chief Financial Officer, Lovelace Westside Hospital, Albuquerque, NM, p. A432
  Interim Chief Financial Officer, Lovelace Regional Hospital – Roswell, Roswell, NM, p. A436
SOLIS, Ashley, DON Interim Administrator, Midcoast Medical Center – Crockett, Crockett, TX, p. A609
SOLIS, Gloria, R.N., MSN, Chief Nursing Officer, Saint Luke's East Hospital, Lee's Summit, MO, p. A379
SOLIVAN, Jose E
  Chief Financial Officer, Hospital Menonita De Cayey, Cayey, PR, p. A732
  Chief Financial Officer, Mennonite General Hospital, Aibonito, PR, p. A731
SOLIZ, Mindy
  Director Human Resource Strategy, Christus Spohn Hospital Kleberg, Kingsville, TX, p. A632
  Director Human Resources, Christus Spohn Hospital Alice, Alice, TX, p. A595
SOLLIS, Jeff, Chief Executive Officer, St. John's Health, Jackson, WY, p. A727
SOLOMON, John, M.D., Director, South Carolina Department of Corrections Hospital, Columbia, SC, p. A565

Index of Health Care Professionals

Index of Health Care Professionals / Solomon

SOLOMON, Oliver, M.D., Chief Medical Officer, Glendora Hospital, Glendora, CA, p. A66
SOLOMON–OWENS, Felicia, Director Human Resources, Fayette Medical Center, Fayette, AL, p. A19
SOLORIO, Roberta, Vice President, Chief Human Resource Officer, Midland Memorial Hospital, Midland, TX, p. A639
SOLORZANO, Rosa, Interim Director Human Resources, Astria Toppenish Hospital, Toppenish, WA, p. A697
SOLOW, Jodie Sartor, Director of Human Resources, UNC Health Chatham, Siler City, NC, p. A476
SOLTIS, Les, Director – Human Resources, St. Francis Hospital, Federal Way, WA, p. A690
SOLVERSON, Paul
Senior Vice President and Chief Information Officer, Cap. Cod Hospital, Hyannis, MA, p. A314
Senior Vice President and Chief Information Officer, Falmouth Hospital, Falmouth, MA, p. A313
SOMAIO, Vincent, M.D., Medical Director, Encompass Health Rehabilitation Hospital of Bluffton, Bluffton, SC, p. A562
SOMERS, Sherrie, D.O., Chief Medical Officer, HCA Florida North Florida Hospital, Gainesville, FL, p. A132
SOMERS, Susan, Chief Executive Officer, Perimeter Behavioral Hospital of Dallas, Garland, TX, p. A621
SOMERS, Tyrel, M.D., Chief Medical Officer, Russell Regional Hospital, Russell, KS, p. A258
SOMERVILLE, Jacqueline G, R.N., Ph.D., Senior Vice President and Chief Nursing Officer, Southcoast Hospitals Group. Fall River, MA, p. A313
SOMMERS, Dorene M. Associate Director Patient Care Services, Erie Veterans Affairs Medical Center, Erie, PA, p. A539
SONA, Kent, Vice President, Chief Information Officer, Methodist Fremont Health, Fremont, NE, p. A400
SONATORE, Carol, D.O., Medical Director, Encompass Health Rehabilitation Hospital of Toms River, Toms River, NJ, p. A429
SONDAG, Timothy, Senior Nursing Officer, Hopedale Medical Complex, Hopedale, IL, p. A198
SONDERMAN, Betty, Manager Human Resources, Ridgeview Institute – Smyrna, Smyrna, GA, p. A171
SONDERMAN, Thomas, M.D., Vice President and Chief Medical Officer, Columbus Regional Hospital, Columbus, IN, p. A214
SONEL, Ali, M.D., Chief of Staff, Veterans Affairs Pittsburgh Healthcare System, Pittsburgh, PA, p. A552
SONG, Daniel, Chief Financial Officer, Monterey Park Hospital, Monterey Park, CA, p. A78
SONGER, Lucille, Chief Nursing Officer, Athol Hospital, Athol, MA, p. A309
SONGER, Pat, Chief Operations Officer, Cascade Medical, Leavenworth, WA, p. A691
SONGY, O.F.M.CAP., David, President and Chief Executive Officer, Saint Luke Institute, Silver Spring, MD, p. A307
SONI, Anita, M.D., Chief Medical Officer, NYC Health + Hospitals/Lincoln, New York, NY, p. A451
SONNENBERG, Martha, M.D., Chief of Staff, Southern California Hospital At Culver City, Culver City, CA, p. A61
SONNENBERG, William, M.D., President Medical Staff, Titusville Area Hospital, Titusville, PA, p. A555
SONNENSCHEIN, Silvia, M.D., Chief of Staff, Kohala Hospital, Kohala, HI, p. A177
SONTZ, Jennifer
Director Human Resources, Evansville Psychiatric Children Center, Evansville, IN, p. A216
Director Human Resources, Evansville State Hospital, Evansville, IN, p. A216
SOOHOO, Richard, Chief Financial Officer, Sutter Medical Center, Sacramento Sacramento, CA, p. A87
SOPER, Brent, Chief Financial Officer, Adventist Health Bakersfield, Bakersfield, CA, p. A56
SOPIARZ, Edward, Chief Financial Officer, Methodist Hospital for Surgery, Addison, TX, p. A595
SOPT, Michael, M.D., Chief of Staff, Archbold Brooks, Quitman, GA, p. A169
SORBELLO, Bud, Director Management Information Systems, New York–Presbyterian/Hudson Valley Hospital, Cortlandt Manor, NY, p. A442
SORENSEN, Bonny
Chief Financial Officer, Wadley Regional Medical Center, Texarkana, TX, p. A657
Chief Financial Officer, Wadley Regional Medical Center At Hope, Hope, AR, p. A47
SORENSEN, Damon, Chief Financial Officer, Mclaren Bay Region, Bay City, MI, p. A322
SORENSEN, Lief, M.D., Chief Medical Officer, Adventhealth Avista, Louisville, CC, p. A111
SORENSEN, Vanessa, Chief Nursing Officer, Summit Medical Center, Casper, WY, p. A726
SORENSON, Chris, Chief Health Information Officer, Sheltering Arms Institute, Midlothian, VA, p. A679
SORENSON, Dennis, Supervisor Information Technology, Bronson South Haven Hospital, South Haven, MI, p. A338
SORENSON, Eric C, Chief Financial Officer, Jerry L. Pettis Memorial Veterans' Hospital, Loma Linda, CA, p. A70
SORENSON, Tawnya, Director of Nursing, Kittson Healthcare, Hallock, MN, p. A348
SORRELL, Dierdra, R.N., MSN, Chief Executive Officer, Clifton–Fine Hospital, Star Lake, NY, p. A459
SORRELL, Rachel, Chief Financial Officer, Tsehootsooi Medical Center, Fort Defiance, AZ, p. A31
SORRELL, Ralp. W Sr, Chief Financial Officer, Adena Greenfield Medical Center, Greenfield, OH, p. A497
SORRELLS, Dwane, Chief Information Officer, Choctaw Nation Health Care Center, Talihina, OK, p. A521
SORTINO, Frank, Administrator, University of Alabama Hospital, Birmingham, AL, p. A17
SOSA, Phillip. Chief Financial Officer, El Paso Behavioral Health System, El Paso, TX, p. A616
SOSEBEE, Tonya, MSN, R.N., Chief Operating and Nursing Officer, Texas Health Harris Methodist Hospital Azle, Azle, TX, p. A601
SOSKA, Christopher
President of MMC_Weston,Wisconsin Rapids and Stevens Point, Marshfield Medical Center – Weston, Weston, WI, p. A725
President, Marshfield Medical Center, Weston, Wisconsin Rapids, Stevens Point, Marshfield Medical Center – River Region, Stevens Point, WI, p. A722
SOSNOW, Peter L, Medical Director, O'Connor Hospital, Delhi, NY, p. A442
SOSNOWSKI, Karen, Director, Human Resources, Saint Clare's Denville Hospital, Denville, NJ, p. A420
SOTERAKIS, Jack, M.D., Executive Vice President Medical Affairs, St. Francis Hospital And Heart Center, Roslyn, NY, p. A458
SOTO, Ciria, Director Human Resources, Sonora Behavioral Health Hospital, Tucson, AZ, p. A41
SOTO, Itza, MSN, Chief Executive Officer, Ashford Presbyterian Community Hospital, San Juan, PR, p. A734
SOTO, Juan Carlos, Director Information Systems, Hospital San Carlos Borromeo, Moca, PR, p. A733
SOTOIZAGUIRRE, Felix, Chief Financial Officer, Wellstar North Fulton Hospital, Roswell, GA, p. A170
SOUDERS, Stuart, Chief, Human Resources, William S. Middleton Memorial Veterans' Hospital, Madison, WI, p. A715
SOUKUP, Paul, Chief Financial Officer, St. Luke Community Healthcare, Ronan, MT, p. A395
SOULAR, Dan, M.D., Vice President, Medical Affairs, Grand Itasca Clinic And Hospital, Grand Rapids, MN, p. A347
SOULE, Joyce, R.N., MSN, Chief Nursing Officer, Medical City Dallas, Dallas, TX, p. A611
SOURS, Alison, Vice President Quality & Chief Information Officer, Graham Hospital, Canton, IL, p. A187
SOUTHER, Jane, M.D., Chief Medical Officer, Blount Memorial Hospital, Maryville, TN, p. A587
SOUTHERLAND, Charles, Chief Executive Officer, Western State Hospital, Tacoma, WA, p. A697
SOUTHWICK, Mitch, Chief Operating Officer, Mclaren Bay Region, Bay City, MI, p. A322
SOUTHWICK, William, Hospital Administrator, Behavioral Health Center of Porter Village, Norman, OK, p. A515
SOUTHWORTH, Scott, M.D., Medical Director, South Davis Community Hospital, Bountiful, UT, p. A664
SOUZA, Beatrix, Chief Executive Officer, Buffalo Psychiatric Center, Buffalo, NY, p. A440
SOUZA, Darlene, Vice President, St. Josep. Health Services of Rhode Island, North Providence, RI, p. A560
SOUZA, Greg, Vice President Human Resources, Lucile Packard Children's Hospital Stanford, Palo Alto, CA, p. A82
SOUZA, Jim, Chief Medical Officer, St. Luke's Regional Medical Center, Boise, ID, p. A180
SOUZA, Liz, Coordinator Nursing Services, Atascadero State Hospital, Atascadero, CA, p. A56
SOUZA, Michael, Chief Executive Officer, Landmark Medical Center, Woonsocket, RI, p. A561
SOVETSKHY, Ed, Director Information Services, Portsmouth Regional Hospital, Portsmouth, NH, p. A417
SOWELL, Ronald G.
FACHE, Chief Financial Officer, Medical Center At Scottsville, Scottsville, KY, p. A274
FACHE, Executive Vice President, Commonwealth Regional Specialty Hospital, Bowling Green, KY, p. A263
FACHE, Executive Vice President, Medical Center At Franklin, Franklin, KY, p. A266
FACHE, Executive Vice President, The Medical Center At Bowling Green, Bowling Green, KY, p. A264
FACHE, Executive Vice President and Chief Financial Officer, The Medical Center At Caverna, Horse Cave, KY, p. A267
FACHE, Executive Vice President, Chief Financial Officer, The Medical Center At Albany, Albany, KY, p. A263
SOWELL, Vincent, Chief Nursing Officer, Otto Kaiser Memorial Hospital, Kenedy, TX, p. A632
SOWERS, Chuck, Vice President Finance and Chief Financial Officer, Mercy Gilbert Medical Center, Gilbert, AZ, p. A32
SOWIZRAL, Shirley, Chief Executive Officer, Wernersville State Hospital, Wernersville, PA, p. A557
SPACK, Paula, R.N., MSN, Vice President Nursing, Punxsutawney Area Hospital, Punxsutawney, PA, p. A553
SPACKMAN, Jared
Chief Financial Officer, Holy Cross Hospital – Davis, Layton, UT, p. A665
Chief Operating Officer, Holy Cross Hospital – Davis, Layton, UT, p. A665
SPACONE, Celia, M.D., Director Operations, Buffalo Psychiatric Center, Buffalo, NY, p. A440
SPAGNA, Lauren, Marketing Director, West Boca Medical Center, Boca Raton, FL, p. A126
SPAIN, Jeanine R.
R.N., MS, Vice President, Chief Operating Officer and Chief Nursing Officer, Carle Health Methodist Hospital, Peoria, IL, p. A205
R.N., MS, Vice President, Chief Operating Officer and Chief Nursing Officer, Carle Health Pekin Hospital, Pekin, IL, p. A205
R.N., MS, Vice President, Chief Operating Officer and Chief Nursing Officer, Carle Health Proctor Hospital, Peoria, IL, p. A206
SPAIN, Steve, Chief Operating Officer, Larned State Hospital, Larned, KS, p. A252
SPAIN, Tom, Director Operations Finance, Chi St. Alexius Health Turtle Lake Hospital, Turtle Lake, ND, p. A483
SPALDING, Cathy, Administrator, Uofl Health – Jewish Hospital, Louisville, KY, p. A270
SPANBAUER, Lisa, Financial Program Supervisor, Winnebago Mental Health Institute, Winnebago, WI, p. A725
SPANGHER, Guido, M.D., Clinical Director, Big Spring State Hospital, Big Spring, TX, p. A603
SPANGLER, Kathy, Director, Fort Belvoir Community Hospital, Fort Belvoir, VA, p. A676
SPANGLER, Mark, M.D., Chief Medical Officer, Gibson Area Hospital And Health Services, Gibson City, IL, p. A196
SPANGLER, Michael
D.O., Vice President, Medical Affairs, UPMC Memorial, York, PA, p. A559
Health Information Management Services Supervisor, Encompass Health Rehabilitation Hospital of Tallahassee, Tallahassee, FL, p. A151
SPANGLER, Wendell J, M.D., Chief of Staff, Paulding County Hospital, Paulding, OH, p. A502
SPANN, Debbie, Director Human Resources, Morehouse General Hospital, Bastrop. LA, p. A277
SPANN, Lori, Director Human Resources, Iberia Medical Center, New Iberia, LA, p. A289
SPANO, Jason, Director of Information Technology, Prowers Medical Center, Lamar, CO, p. A111
SPARE, John, Accountant, Parsons State Hospital And Training Center, Parsons, KS, p. A258
SPARER, Cynthia, Senior Vice President and Executive Director Women's & Children, Yale New Haven Hospital, New Haven, CT, p. A118
SPARKMAN, Jill, Director Human Resources, Odessa Regional Medical Center, Odessa, TX, p. A642
SPARKS, Carolyn
Chief Executive Officer, Lake Cumberland Regional Hospital, Somerset, KY, p. A274
Chief Executive Officer, Trousdale Medical Center, Hartsville, TN, p. A584
SPARKS, Dennis W.
Vice President Human Resources, Saint Michael's Medical Center, Newark, NJ, p. A425
Vice President of Human Resources, Saint Francis Hospital, Hartford, CT, p. A116
SPARKS, Gary R., Administrator, Crossridge Community Hospital, Wynne, AR, p. A54
SPARKS, Holly H., Chief Clinical Officer, South Sunflower County Hospital, Indianola, MS, p. A363
SPARKS, Jason, Director, Human Resources, Encompass Health Rehabilitation Hospital At Cincinnati, Cincinnati, OH, p. A489
SPARKS, Lisa, R.N., Chief Nursing Officer and Vice President Patient Care Services, Indiana University Health West Hospital, Avon, IN, p. A212
SPARKS, Victor, M.D., Chief of Staff, Marshall Medical Center North, Guntersville, AL, p. A20
SPARLING, Nicki, Manager Human Resources, Major Hospital, Shelbyville, IN, p. A227
SPARROW, Francis D., M.D., Medical Director, Wellspan Philhaven, Mount Gretna, PA, p. A546

A978 Index of Health Care Professionals

SPARROW, Robert T., M.D., Vice President, Chief Medical Officer, OSF Saint Francis Medical Center, Peoria, IL, p. A206
SPARTA, Mark, FACHE, President and Chief Hospital Executive, Hackensack Meridian Health Hackensack University Medical Center, Hackensack, NJ, p. A421
SPARZO, John, M.D., Chief Medical Officer, Indiana University Health Bedford Hospital, Bedford, IN, p. A212
SPATH, Deborah, R.N., MSN, Associate Director Patient and Nurses Services, Albany Stratton Veterans Affairs Medical Center, Albany, NY, p. A438
SPATZ, Patricia A, Chief Executive Officer, River Crest Hospital, San Angelo, TX, p. A648
SPEARE, Mark, Senior Associate Director Patient Relations and Human Resources, UCLA Medical Center–Santa Monica, Santa Monica, CA, p. A95
SPEARS, David, D.O., Chief of Staff, Selby General Hospital, Marietta, OH, p. A499
SPEARS, Gina, Chief Financial Officer, Thomas B. Finan Center, Cumberland, MD, p. A303
SPEARS, Kevin, Chief Executive Officer, Encompass Health Rehabilitation Hospital of Jonesboro, Jonesboro, AR, p. A48
SPEARS, LaLana, Supervisor Accounting, Claremore Indian Hospital, Claremore, OK, p. A511
SPEARS, Michael, Human Resource Leader, SSM Health St. Anthony Hospital – Shawnee, Shawnee, OK, p. A520
SPEAS, Ryan, Chief Financial Officer, Mackinac Straits Health System, Inc., Saint Ignace, MI, p. A337
SPEASE, Dorothy, Manager Business Office, Douglas County Memorial Hospital, Armour, SD, p. A572
SPECK, Michelle A
   Vice President Human Resources, UPMC Altoona, Altoona, PA, p. A534
   Vice President Human Resources, UPMC Bedford, Everett, PA, p. A540
SPECKMAN, Kelly Ann, Chief Financial Officer, Kearny County Hospital, Lakin, KS, p. A252
SPEEK, Timothy I, Director of Nursing, Glenn Medical Center, Willows, CA, p. A101
SPEELMAN, Steven, Director Information Systems, UVA Health Culpeper Medical Center, Culpeper, VA, p. A675
SPEER–SMITH, Carol, R.N., Chief Nursing Officer, Oroville Hospital, Oroville, CA, p. A82
SPEIGHT, Becky, Chief Financial Officer and Administrator, Crescent Medical Center Lancaster, Lancaster, TX, p. A634
SPEIGHT, Marianne, Vice President Information System and Chief Information Officer, Cincinnati Children's Hospital Medical Center, Cincinnati, OH, p. A488
SPELL, Kenneth R., Chief Executive Officer, Baptist Health South Florida, Homestead Hospital, Homestead, FL, p. A134
SPELL, Nicole
   Director Human Resources, ECU Health Bertie Hospital, Windsor, NC, p. A478
   Director Human Resources, ECU Health Chowan Hospital, Edenton, NC, p. A467
SPELLBERG, Brad, M.D., Chief Medical Officer, Los Angeles General Medical Center, Los Angeles, CA, p. A74
SPELLMAN, Warren K., Chief Executive Officer, Grady Memorial Hospital, Chickasha, OK, p. A511
SPELLMEIER, Rhonda, R.N., Director of Nursing, Sabetha Community Hospital, Sabetha, KS, p. A259
SPENCE, Andre, Chief Medical Staff, Sanford Bagley Medical Center, Bagley, MN, p. A343
SPENCE, Ben
   Chief Financial Officer, Cap. Coral Hospital, Cap. Coral, FL, p. A127
   Chief Financial Officer, Gulf Coast Medical Center, Fort Myers, FL, p. A131
   Chief Financial Officer, Lee Memorial Hospital, Fort Myers, FL, p. A132
SPENCE, Karie, Director Human Resources, Miller County Hospital, Colquitt, GA, p. A161
SPENCE, Karla, Director of Nursing, SMP Health – St. Andrew's, Bottineau, ND, p. A479
SPENCE, Monte
   Chief Operating Officer, Rehabilitation Hospital of Indiana, Indianapolis, IN, p. A220
   Interim Chief Executive Officer, Rehabilitation Hospital of Indiana, Indianapolis, IN, p. A220
SPENCE, Norman, President, Kettering Health Troy, Troy, OH, p. A505
SPENCE, Sheldon, Director of Revenue Cycle, IT, Memorial Hospital of Texas County Authority, Guymon, OK, p. A513
SPENCE, Steven Walter, M.D., Chief Medical Officer, Jackson Hospital, Marianna, FL, p. A138
SPENCE, Terri
   Chief Information Officer, Bon Secours Maryview Medical Center, Portsmouth, VA, p. A681
   Chief Information Officer, Bon Secours St. Mary's Hospital, Richmond, VA, p. A682
   Vice President and Regional Chief Information Officer, Bon Secours St. Francis Medical Center, Midlothian, VA, p. A679
   Vice President Information Services, Bon Secours Mary Immaculate Hospital, Newport News, VA, p. A679
SPENCER, Elizabeth, Director, Human Resources, Clark Regional Medical Center, Winchester, KY, p. A275
SPENCER, Jim, Director Information System, Mcleod Health Cheraw, Cheraw, SC, p. A563
SPENCER, Lisa
   R.N., MSN, Chief Nursing and Operating Officer, Anderson Hospital, Maryville, IL, p. A201
   R.N., MSN, President, Anderson Hospital, Maryville, IL, p. A201
SPENCER, Marie, Chief Nursing Officer and Senior Administrator, Burke Rehabilitation Hospital, White Plains, NY, p. A462
SPENCER, Mike, Chief Information Officer, Henry Community Health, New Castle, IN, p. A225
SPENCER, Misti, Director Inpatient Services, Selby General Hospital, Marietta, OH, p. A499
SPENCER, Neva, MSN, Chief Nursing Officer, HCA Florida University Hospital, Davie, FL, p. A129
SPENCER, Rachelle, Chief Executive Officer, Rehabilitation Hospital of Southern California, Rancho Mirage, CA, p. A84
SPENCER, Sarah, M.D., Chief of Staff, South Peninsula Hospital, Homer, AK, p. A28
SPENCER, Scott, Chief Financial Officer, South Shore Hospital, Chicago, IL, p. A191
SPENCER, Steven, M.D., Chief Medical Officer, Onslow Memorial Hospital, Jacksonville, NC, p. A471
SPENCER, Todd, M.D., Chief Medical Staff, Adventist Health Reedley, Reedley, CA, p. A85
SPERLING, Deanna, R.N., President and Chief Executive Officer, Rwjbarnabas Health Behavioral Health Center, Toms River, NJ, p. A429
SPERLING, Louis J, Vice President Human Resources, Rhode Island Hospital, Providence, RI, p. A561
SPERLING, Walter, M.D., Medical Director, Ellenville Regional Hospital, Ellenville, NY, p. A442
SPERRING, Jeff, M.D., Chief Executive Officer, Seattle Children's Hospital, Seattle, WA, p. A694
SPICER, Charles L.
   Jr, FACHE, President, Our Lady of The Lake Regional Medical Center, Baton Rouge, LA, p. A278
   Jr, FACHE, President, Baton Rouge Market and Northshore Market, Our Lady of The Angels Hospital, Bogalusa, LA, p. A279
   Jr, FACHE, President, Baton Rouge Market and Northshore Market, Our Lady of The Lake Regional Medical Center, Baton Rouge, LA, p. A278
SPICER, Joan G, R.N., Chief Nursing Officer, San Mateo Medical Center, San Mateo, CA, p. A93
SPICER, Michael J., President and Chief Executive Officer, Saint Joseph's Medical Center, Yonkers, NY, p. A462
SPICER, Randy, Information Technology Supervisor, Central State Hospital, Louisville, KY, p. A269
SPICER, Sam, M.D., Vice President Medical Affairs, Novant Health New Hanover Regional Medical Center, Wilmington, NC, p. A478
SPIDLE, Tara, Chief Financial Officer, Decatur County Hospital, Leon, IA, p. A239
SPIERS, Deborah, Administrator, Oceans Behavioral Hospital of Greater New Orleans, Kenner, LA, p. A284
SPIERS, Peter
   Chief Executive Officer, Southern Inyo Healthcare District, Lone Pine, CA, p. A70
   Chief Operating Officer, Southern Inyo Healthcare District, Lone Pine, CA, p. A70
SPIGEL, Michael
   Chief Executive Officer, Good Shepherd Rehabilitation Network, Allentown, PA, p. A534
   Chief Executive Officer, Good Shepherd Specialty Hospital, Bethlehem, PA, p. A535
SPIGNER, Jason, Vice President Human Resources, Advocate Good Shepherd Hospital, Barrington, IL, p. A186
SPIKE, Jennifer, Director Human Resources, St. James Hospital, Hornell, NY, p. A444
SPIKES, Christopher, M.D., President, Medical Staff, USMD Hospital At Arlington, Arlington, TX, p. A598
SPILSBURY, Lauren, R.N., MSN, Vice President for Patient Care Services, Redlands Community Hospital, Redlands, CA, p. A85
SPINA, Lori, Vice President Human Resources, Good Samaritan Hospital Medical Center, West Islip, NY, p. A461
SPINALE, Josep. W, D.O., Chief Medical Officer, St. Joseph's Hospital Health Center, Syracuse, NY, p. A460
SPIRITOS, Michael, Chief Medical Officer, Duke Raleigh Hospital, Raleigh, NC, p. A474
SPISSO, Johnese
   President, UCLA Health and Chief Executive Officer, UCLA Hospital System, UCLA Medical Center–Santa Monica, Santa Monica, CA, p. A95
   President, UCLA Health and Chief Executive Officer, UCLA Hospital System, UCLA West Valley Medical Center, Los Angeles, CA, p. A75
   President, UCLA Health/Chief Executive Officer, UCLA Hospital System, Ronald Reagan Ucla Medical Center, Los Angeles, CA, p. A75
   President, UCLA Health/Chief Executive Officer, UCLA Hospital System, Stewart & Lynda Resnick Neuropsychiatric Hospital At Ucla, Los Angeles, CA, p. A75
SPITSER, Christy
   Interim President, Chi Saint Josep. Health, Lexington, KY, p. A268
   Vice President Finance, Chi Saint Josep. Health – Saint Josep. Berea, Berea, KY, p. A263
   Vice President Finance and Business Development, Chi Saint Josep. Health – Saint Josep. London, London, KY, p. A269
SPIVEY, Amy, Chief Medical Officer, Mccullough–Hyde Memorial Hospital/Trihealth, Oxford, OH, p. A502
SPIVEY, Courtney, Chief Nursing Officer, Hardin County General Hospital, Rosiclare, IL, p. A208
SPONAUGLE, Dale, M.D., Medical Staff President, Orleans Community Health, Medina, NY, p. A446
SPONSLER, Betsy A, Chief Financial Officer, Valley Hospital Medical Center, Las Vegas, NV, p. A411
SPOON, Barry, M.D., Chief of Staff, Mercy St. Francis Hospital, Mountain View, MO, p. A381
SPOONER, Jennifer, Controller, Encompass Health Rehabilitation Hospital of Tallahassee, Tallahassee, FL, p. A151
SPOOR, David, R.N., Senior Vice President, Patient Care Services and Chief Nursing Officer, Sturdy Memorial Hospital, Attleboro, MA, p. A309
SPORE, Larry, Chief Financial Officer, Lawrence County Memorial Hospital, Lawrenceville, IL, p. A200
SPOUR, Larry, Chief Executive Officer, Community Hospital of Staunton, Staunton, IL, p. A209
SPRADLIN, John, Information Systems Director, Bayou Bend Health System, Franklin, LA, p. A282
SPRAKER, Larissa, Vice President Business Development and Chief Strategy Officer, Mercy Gilbert Medical Center, Gilbert, AZ, p. A32
SPRANGER, Lance, Chief Information Officer, St. John's Health, Jackson, WY, p. A727
SPRATT, Kelly, Vice President, Operations, Abbott Northwestern Hospital, Minneapolis, MN, p. A350
SPRECHER, Jeremy, Chief Administrative Officer, Norton Hospital, Louisville, KY, p. A270
SPREER–ALBERT, Frances, Chief Financial Officer and Executive Vice President, Albany Medical Center, Albany, NY, p. A438
SPRIGGS, Larry Floyd, CPA, Controller, Encompass Health Rehabilitation Hospital of San Antonio, San Antonio, TX, p. A649
SPRINGATE, Brian, Chief Executive Officer, Hazard Arh Regional Medical Center, Hazard, KY, p. A267
SPRINGER, Amy, Medical Director, Webster County Community Hospital, Red Cloud, NE, p. A405
SPRINGER, Ilana, Chief Executive Officer, Administrator, Safety Officer, Joyce Eisenberg–Keefer Medical Center, Reseda, CA, p. A85
SPRINGER, Madge, Director Human Resources, Adventhealth Waterman, Tavares, FL, p. A153
SPRINGER, Rebecca, MSN, R.N., Chief Nursing Officer, Hendry Regional Medical Center, Clewiston, FL, p. A128
SPRINGER, Theresa, Chief Financial Officer, OSF Holy Family Medical Center, Monmouth, IL, p. A202
SPRINGMANN, Tressa
   Vice President and Chief Information Officer, Levindale Hebrew Geriatric Center And Hospital, Baltimore, MD, p. A300
   Vice President and Chief Information Officer, Northwest Hospital, Randallstown, MD, p. A306
SPRINKLE, Patricia, Vice President, Human Resources, Bluffton Regional Medical Center, Bluffton, IN, p. A213
SPROUT, Merry, R.N., Chief Nursing Officer, Antelop. Memorial Hospital, Neligh, NE, p. A403
SPRYS, Michael, D.O., Chief of Staff, Medical Arts Hospital, Lamesa, TX, p. A633
SPUHLER, Richard, Chief Executive Officer, Brigham City Community Hospital, Brigham City, UT, p. A664

Index of Health Care Professionals

Index of Health Care Professionals / Spurlock

SPURLOCK, James, D.O., Chief of Staff, Ascension Saint Thomas Stones River, Woodbury, TN, p. A594
SPURLOCK, Steve, Director Information Systems, Buena Vista Regional Medical Center, Storm Lake, IA, p. A244
SQUIRE, Chris, Regional President, Aspirus Divine Savior Hospital & Clinics, Portage, WI, p. A720
SQUIRES, Danny
Assistant Vice President and Chief Financial Officer Network Hospital, Atrium Health Wake Forest Baptist Lexington Medical Center, Lexington, NC, p. A472
Chief Financial Officer, Atrium Health Wake Forest Baptist Davie Medical Center, Bermuda Run, NC, p. A463
SQUIRES, Elizabeth, R.N., Chief Nursing Officer, Encompass Health Rehabilitation Hospital of Tallahassee, Tallahassee, FL, p. A151
SQUIRES, Paula C, Senior Vice President, Chief Human Resources Officer and Chief Human Resources Officer, Baystate Medical Center, Springfield, MA, p. A318
SQUIRES, Teresa, R.N., Chief Nursing Officer, Lake District Hospital, Lakeview, OR, p. A528
SQUIRRELL, Sarah, Commissioner of Vermont Department of Mental Health, Vermont Psychiatric Care Hospital, Berlin, VT, p. A671
SRAON, Karandeep. FACHE, Medical Center Director, Jerry L. Pettis Memorial Veterans' Hospital, Loma Linda, CA, p. A70
SREBINSKI, Ron, Chief Financial Officer, Mclaren Caro Region, Caro, MI, p. A323
SRIKANTH, Shankaran, M.D., Chief Medical Officer, Marion Health, Marion, IN, p. A223
SRIPADA, Subra
Exec. Vice President, Chief Transformation Officer and Chief Information Officer, Corewell Health Taylor Hospital, Taylor, MI, p. A339
Executive Vice President, Chief Transformation Officer and Chief Information Officer, Corewell Health Dearborn Hospital, Dearborn, MI, p. A324
Executive Vice President, Chief Transformation Officer and Chief Information Officer, Corewell Health Wayne Hospital, Wayne, MI, p. A340
Executive Vice President, Chief Transportation Officer and Chief Information Officer, Corewell Health Beaumont Grosse Pointe Hospital, Grosse Pointe, MI, p. A329
Executive Vice President, Chief Transportation Officer and Chief Information Officer, Corewell Health Beaumont Troy Hospital, Troy, MI, p. A339
Executive Vice President, Chief Transportation Officer and Chief Information Officer, Corewell Health Farmington Hills Hospital, Farmington Hills, MI, p. A326
Executive Vice President, Chief Transportation Officer and Chief Information Officer, Corewell Health William Beaumont University Hospital, Royal Oak, MI, p. A336
SRIVASTAVA, Mohit, M.D., Chief of Staff, Bunkie General Hospital, Bunkie, LA, p. A279
ST CLAIR, Jeffery M., President and Chief Executive Officer, Springhill Medical Center, Mobile, AL, p. A22
ST. GEORGE, Scott, Chief Financial Officer, Berkshire Medical Center, Pittsfield, MA, p. A317
ST. JULIEN, Linda, Chief Executive Officer, Jefferson County Hospital, Fayette, MS, p. A361
ST. LOUIS, Charles, Director of Patient Care Services, Sutter Health Kahi Mohala, Ewa Beach, HI, p. A175
ST. PE, Laurin
Administrator – Singing River Hospital, Singing River Health System, Pascagoula, MS, p. A367
Chief Operating Officer, Singing River Health System, Pascagoula, MS, p. A367
Interim Chief Executive Officer, Singing River Health System, Pascagoula, MS, p. A367
ST. PETER, Colette, Senior Manager Human Resources, Mercy Hospital Carthage, Carthage, MO, p. A373
STAATS, Jason
Chief Executive Officer, Sun Behavioral Kentucky, Erlanger, KY, p. A265
Market Chief Executive Officer, Columbus Springs Dublin, Dublin, OH, p. A495
STACEY, Brian, Chief Financial Officer, NYC Health + Hospitals/Queens, New York, NY, p. A451
STACEY, Susan, R.N., Chief Executive, Providence Sacred Heart Medical Center & Children's Hospital, Spokane, WA, p. A696
STACHOWICZ, Peter, Interim Chief Operating Officer, Wickenburg Community Hospital, Wickenburg, AZ, p. A41
STACIE, Beverly, Director Human Resources, Clifton T. Perkins Hospital Center, Jessup, MD, p. A305
STACK, Jodi, R.N., MSN, Chief Nursing Officer and Chief Administrative Officer, Baystate Franklin Medical Center, Greenfield, MA, p. A314
STACKER, Iris, Chief Executive Officer, Delta Health–The Medical Center, Greenville, MS, p. A362
STACKHOUSE, Jenni, Chief Financial Officer, River Point Behavioral Health, Jacksonville, FL, p. A135
STACKHOUSE, Rebecca J., FACHE, Executive Director, Salem Veterans Affairs Medical Center, Salem, VA, p. A683
STACKHOUSE, Sharon, Assistant Administrator and Director Risk Management, Peachford Behavioral Health System, Atlanta, GA, p. A157
STACKLE, Mark, Commanding Officer and Chief Executive Officer, Brooke Army Medical Center, Fort Sam Houston, TX, p. A618
STACY, Roxanne, Chief Executive Officer, Community Rehabilitation Hospital North, Indianapolis, IN, p. A219
STADHEIM, Barbara, Chief Nursing Officer, West River Regional Medical Center, Hettinger, ND, p. A481
STADHEIM, Nathan, Chief Financial Officer, West River Regional Medical Center, Hettinger, ND, p. A481
STADLER, James J, M.D., Associate Administrator Medical Services, Guam Memorial Hospital Authority, Tamuning, GU, p. A730
STADLER, Matt, Information Services Site Manager, Saint Luke's North Hospital – Barry Road, Kansas City, MO, p. A378
STAFFORD, Tom, Chief Information Officer, Halifax Health Medical Center of Daytona Beach, Daytona Beach, FL, p. A130
STAFFORD, Walt, Director Information Technology, Chatuge Regional Hospital And Nursing Home, Hiawassee, GA, p. A165
STAGG, Kevin, Executive Vice President Finance and Chief Financial Officer, Christian Health, Wyckoff, NJ, p. A431
STAGGS, Nathan, Chief Executive Officer, Whidbeyhealth, Coupeville, WA, p. A688
STAHL, Anthony, FACHE, Ph.D., President, Adventist Healthcare White Oak Medical Center, Silver Spring, MD, p. A307
STAHL, Kathy, Chief Nursing Officer, Wheeling Hospital, Wheeling, WV, p. A706
STAHL, Pam, Regional Chief Human Resources Officer, Providence Holy Cross Medical Center, Los Angeles, CA, p. A75
STAHL, Steven J, Director Human Resources, Columbia County Health System, Dayton, WA, p. A689
STAHL, William D, Chief Operating Officer, Rooks County Health Center, Plainville, KS, p. A258
STAHLKUPPE, Robert F, M.D., Chief of Staff, Chatuge Regional Hospital And Nursing Home, Hiawassee, GA, p. A165
STAHULAK, Brian M, R.N., Chief Nursing Officer, Ann & Robert H. Lurie Children's Hospital of Chicago, Chicago, IL, p. A188
STAIGER, Tom, Medical Director, UW Medicine/University of Washington Medical Center, Seattle, WA, p. A695
STAIGL, Christine, Chief Nursing Officer, Tristar Skyline Medical Center, Nashville, TN, p. A591
STALCUP, Connie, Manager Information Systems, Erlanger Western Carolina Hospital, Murphy, NC, p. A473
STALKER, Neil, M.D., Chief of Staff, Dukes Memorial Hospital, Peru, IN, p. A226
STALL, Kristi, Chief Human Resources Officer, Mahnomen Health, Mahnomen, MN, p. A349
STALLINGS, Gary, Chief Nursing Officer, Pam Health Rehabilitation Hospital of Greater Indiana, Clarksville, IN, p. A214
STALLINGS, Jay, Chief Executive Officer, Washakie Medical Center, Worland, WY, p. A729
STALLINGS, Terry, M.D., Chief Medical Officer, HCA Florida West Hospital, Pensacola, FL, p. A146
STALLINGS–SICARD, Lori, R.N., Chief Nursing Officer, Dmc Huron Valley–Sinai Hospital, Commerce Township. MI, p. A324
STALLONE, Martin, M.D., President and Chief Executive Officer, Cayuga Medical Center At Ithaca, Ithaca, NY, p. A444
STALLWORTH, David, M.D., Chief of Staff, Monroe County Hospital, Monroeville, AL, p. A22
STALLWORTH, Monica, M.D., Chief of Staff, Western Maryland Hospital Center, Hagerstown, MD, p. A305
STALLWORTH, Terresa, M.D., Clinical Director, San Antonio State Hospital, San Antonio, TX, p. A650
STALNAKER, Kevin P., CPA, Chief Executive Officer, Mon Health Stonewall Jackson Memorial Hospital, Weston, WV, p. A705
STAMAS, Peter, M.D., Chief Administrative Officer, Ascension Southeast Wisconsin Hospital – St. Joseph's Campus, Milwaukee, WI, p. A716
STAMOPOULOS, Marion, Vice President Human Resources, Deborah Heart And Lung Center, Browns Mills, NJ, p. A419
STAMOS, George D., M.D., Chief Medical Officer, Overland Park Regional Medical Center, Overland Park, KS, p. A257
STAMPER, Wendy, Controller, Cameron Memorial Community Hospital, Angola, IN, p. A212
STAMPFLI, Pam, CPA, Chief Financial Officer, Weiser Memorial Hospital, Weiser, ID, p. A184
STAMPOHAR, Jeffry, President, Chi Lakewood Health, Baudette, MN, p. A343
STANBRO, Dave
Director Human Resources, Arnot Ogden Medical Center, Elmira, NY, p. A442
Director Human Resources, Ira Davenport Memorial Hospital, Bath, NY, p. A439
STANDARD, Heather, Chief Nursing Officer, Northeast Georgia Medical Center Barrow, Winder, GA, p. A174
STANDEFFER, Luke
Administrator, Dch Regional Medical Center, Tuscaloosa, AL, p. A25
Chief Executive Officer, Dch Regional Medical Center, Tuscaloosa, AL, p. A25
STANDER, Paul, M.D., Chief Medical Officer, Banner – University Medical Center Phoenix, Phoenix, AZ, p. A35
STANDLEE, Cynthia, R.N., Chief Nursing Officer, Mercy Hospital Ada, Ada, OK, p. A509
STANFIELD, Lori, Interim Chief Executive Officer, Mizell Memorial Hospital, Opp. AL, p. A23
STANFORD, Brion, Director Human Resources, New Orleans East Hospital, New Orleans, LA, p. A290
STANFORD, Tracy, Director Human Resources, Baylor Scott & White All Saints Medical Center – Fort Worth, Fort Worth, TX, p. A619
STANGE, Della G, Director Human Resources, Southwest Healthcare System, Murrieta, CA, p. A79
STANGE–KOLO, Tracey
Vice President Human Resources, UPMC Somerset, Somerset, PA, p. A555
Vice President Human Resources, UPMC St. Margaret, Pittsburgh, PA, p. A552
Vice President, Human Resources, UPMC Mercy, Pittsburgh, PA, p. A552
STANGL, Abbey, Chief Financial Officer, Cass Health, Atlantic, IA, p. A230
STANIC, Steve M, Chief Information Officer, Lake Charles Memorial Hospital, Lake Charles, LA, p. A286
STANKO, Shelley, M.D., Chief Medical Officer, Chi Saint Josep. Health – Saint Josep. London, London, KY, p. A269
STANLEY, Cassandra, Director Personnel, Eastern Shore Hospital Center, Cambridge, MD, p. A303
STANLEY, Donna K, R.N., Chief Nursing Officer, UT Health Henderson, Henderson, TX, p. A624
STANLEY, Holly
Chief Financial Officer, Mid–Valley Hospital And Clinics, Omak, WA, p. A692
Co–Chief Executive Officer, Mid–Valley Hospital And Clinics, Omak, WA, p. A692
STANLEY, Jennifer, M.D., Chief Medical Officer, Ascension St. Vincent Jennings, North Vernon, IN, p. A225
STANLEY, Kathryn, Interim Chief Executive Officer, Neuropsychiatric Hospital of Indianapolis, Indianapolis, IN, p. A220
STANLEY, Lynda, President and Chief Executive Officer, Dosher Memorial Hospital, Southport, NC, p. A476
STANLEY, Mark, Director Fiscal Services, Middle Tennessee Mental Health Institute, Nashville, TN, p. A590
STANLEY, Paul, Superintendent, Richmond State Hospital, Richmond, IN, p. A226
STANSBERY, Shawn, M.D., Chief of Staff, Wood County Hospital, Bowling Green, OH, p. A487
STANSBURY, Bill, Chief Financial Officer, Jackson Parish Hospital, Jonesboro, LA, p. A284
STANSBURY, Kevin M., Chief Executive Officer, Lincoln Health, Hugo, CO, p. A110
STANSKI, Vickie, Financial Manager, Parkview Lagrange Hospital, Lagrange, IN, p. A222
STANTON, Melanie
R.N., Chief Nursing Officer, Sycamore Shoals Hospital, Elizabethton, TN, p. A582
R.N., Chief Nursing Officer, Unicoi County Hospital, Erwin, TN, p. A583
STANTON, Melanie Steagall., Chief Executive Officer, Franklin Woods Community Hospital, Johnson City, TN, p. A584
STANTON, Mike, D.O., Medical Director, Baylor Scott & White Medical Center – Trophy Club, Trophy Club, TX, p. A658
STANUSH, Chris, Director Information Management, San Antonio State Hospital, San Antonio, TX, p. A650
STAPELFELDT, Stephanie, Director, Human Resources, Orlando Health South Lake Hospital, Clermont, FL, p. A128
STAPLES, Janet, Vice President Human Resources, South Central Regional Medical Center, Laurel, MS, p. A365
STAPLES–EVANS, Helen, MS, Chief Nursing Officer, Loma Linda University Medical Center, Loma Linda, CA, p. A70

A980 Index of Health Care Professionals

Index of Health Care Professionals / Stephens

STAPLETON, Carla J., Director Human Resources, Paintsville Arh Hospital, Paintsville, KY, p. A273
STAPLETON, Kathleen, Chief Financial Officer, Prisma Health Baptist Easley Hospital, Easley, SC, p. A565
STAPLETON, Michael, R.N., MS, FACHE, President and Chief Executive Officer, F. F. Thompson Hospital, Canandaigua, NY, p. A440
STAPLETON, Robert, Director Administration, Richard H. Hutchings Psychiatric Center, Syracuse, NY, p. A460
STARA, Jeanne, R.N., MSN, Chief Nursing Officer, Integris Health Ponca City Hospital, Ponca City, OK, p. A519
STARCK, Rebecca, M.D., Vice President, Cleveland Clinic Avon Hospital, Avon, OH, p. A485
STARK, David, Chief Financial Officer, Lancaster Rehabilitation Hospital, Lancaster, PA, p. A543
STARK, David A., FACHE, President and Chief Executive Officer, Unitypoint Health–Des Moines, Des Moines, IA, p. A235
STARK, Donna, Director Human Resources, Baylor Scott & White Medical Center – Grapevine, Grapevine, TX, p. A622
STARK, Patricia Ann, R.N., CNO, Adventhealth Deland, Deland, FL, p. A130
STARK, Sharon, R.N., Manager Clinical Information Systems, Methodist Mckinney Hospital, Mckinney, TX, p. A638
STARKEBAUM, Gordon, M.D., Chief of Staff, VA Puget Sound Healthcare System – Seattle, Seattle, WA, p. A695
STARKES, Henry, M.D., Medical Director, Orchard Hospital, Gridley, CA, p. A66
STARKEY, Michele, Director Human Resources, North Shore Health, Grand Marais, MN, p. A347
STARLING, James F, M.D., Chief Medical Officer, Sovah Health–Danville, Danville, VA, p. A675
STARLING, Terri, Director of Human Resources, Lakeside Behavioral Health System, Memphis, TN, p. A588
STARR, Erin L., Chief Nursing Officer, Jefferson Community Health And Life, Fairbury, NE, p. A399
STARR, Kay, Manager Human Resources, Vernon Memorial Healthcare, Elk Mound, WI, p. A710
STARR, Steven, Interim Chief Medical Officer, North Kansas City Hospital, North Kansas City, MO, p. A381
STASI, Josep. P, Chief Financial Officer, Saint Luke's East Hospital, Lee's Summit, MO, p. A379
STASKIN, David, Director Human Resources, Encompass Health Rehabilitation Hospital of Mechanicsburg, Mechanicsburg, PA, p. A545
STATES, Chuck, Director Information Systems, Punxsutawney Area Hospital, Punxsutawney, PA, p. A553
STATON, Donna, Chief Information Officer, Fauquier Hospital, Warrenton, VA, p. A685
STATON, Paul
Chief Financial Officer, Ronald Reagan Ucla Medical Center, Los Angeles, CA, p. A75
Chief Financial Officer, UCLA Medical Center–Santa Monica, Santa Monica, CA, p. A95
STATZ, Chris, Chief Financial Officer, Lincoln Prairie Behavioral Health Center, Springfield, IL, p. A209
STATZ, Linda Taplin, System Director, Employee Experience, SSM Health St. Mary's Hospital, Madison, WI, p. A714
STAUB, David, M.D., Chief of Staff, Coteau Des Prairies Hospital, Sisseton, SD, p. A577
STAUB, Julie, Vice President, Chief Human Resources Officer, Jackson Health System, Miami, FL, p. A140
STAUFFER, Keith, Regional Chief Information Officer, Chi St Alexius Health Carrington, Carrington, ND, p. A479
STAUSS, Laura, Director of Human Resources, Huggins Hospital, Wolfeboro, NH, p. A417
STAVELEY, Melinda, President and Chief Executive Officer, Santa Barbara Cottage Hospital, Santa Barbara, CA, p. A94
STEAD, William, Associate Vice Chancellor Health Affairs, Director Informatics Center and Chief Strategy and Information Officer, Vanderbilt University Medical Center, Nashville, TN, p. A591
STEAGALL, Susan, Vice President Information Services, VCU Medical Center, Richmond, VA, p. A683
STEARNS, Charles, Area Information Officer, Kaiser Westside Medical Center, Hillsboro, OR, p. A527
STEARNS, Tad, Chief Financial Officer, Brown County Hospital, Ainsworth, NE, p. A397
STEARNS, Zebediah, M.D., Chief of Staff, Mercy Regional Medical Center, Ville Platte, LA, p. A294
STEC, Julianne
Vice President, Patient Services, Mercy Hospital Booneville, Booneville, AR, p. A44
Vice President, Patient Services, Mercy Hospital Ozark, Ozark, AR, p. A52
Vice President, Patient Services, Mercy Hospital Paris, Paris, AR, p. A52
STECKEL, Cindy
Ph.D., R.N., Vice President Chief Nurse and Operations Executive, Scripp. Memorial Hospital–La Jolla, La Jolla, CA, p. A68
Ph.D., R.N., Vice President, Chief Operations Executive, Scripp. Memorial Hospital–La Jolla, La Jolla, CA, p. A68
STECKELBERG, James, M.D., Chief Medical Staff, Syracuse Area Health, Syracuse, NE, p. A406
STECKER, Tim, Chief Financial Officer, Kindred Hospital–Denver, Denver, CO, p. A106
STEED, Airica, Ed.D., R.N., FACHE, President and Chief Executive Officer, Metrohealth Medical Center, Cleveland, OH, p. A491
STEED, Robert A, Director Information Systems, HCA Florida Capital Hospital, Tallahassee, FL, p. A151
STEEL, Chris, Interim Chief Executive Officer, White River Health, Batesville, AR, p. A43
STEEL, Diana, Vice President Human Resources, UCLA West Valley Medical Center, Los Angeles, CA, p. A75
STEELE, Anthony, M.D., Chief Medical Officer, Witham Health Services, Lebanon, IN, p. A222
STEELE, Beth, MSN, R.N., Chief Operating Officer, Owensboro Health Regional Hospital, Owensboro, KY, p. A272
STEELE, Chrys, Director Information Systems, Musc Health Lancaster Medical Center, Lancaster, SC, p. A568
STEELE, David, Vice President Chief Information Officer, Leesburg Regional Medical Center, Leesburg, FL, p. A137
STEELE, Mark
M.D., Chief Medical Officer, University Health–Lakewood Medical Center, Kansas City, MO, p. A378
M.D., Chief Medical Officer, University Health–Truman Medical Center, Kansas City, MO, p. A378
STEELE, Michael, M.D., Chief of Staff, Mercy Hospital Perry, Perryville, MO, p. A382
STEELE, Robert, M.D., President, Mercy Hospital Springfield, Springfield, MO, p. A387
STEELE, Scott, M.D., President, Cleveland Clinic, Cleveland, OH, p. A490
STEELE, Sherri
Chief Nursing Officer, Providence Medford Medical Center, Medford, OR, p. A529
Chief Nursing Officer, Santiam Hospital, Stayton, OR, p. A532
STEELMAN, Jeffrey, Director Information Systems, Lewisgale Hospital Alleghany, Low Moor, VA, p. A678
STEELY, Jennifer, Chief Executive Officer, Patricia Neal Rehabilitation Hospital, Knoxville, TN, p. A586
STEELY, Karen, Chief Operating Officer, Adventhealth Redmond, Rome, GA, p. A170
STEEVES O'NEIL, Patricia, Interim Senior Vice President, Acting Chief Financial Officer and Treasurer, Rush University Medical Center, Chicago, IL, p. A191
STEFANIUK, Carol, Chief Nursing Officer, Vice President, Long Term Acute Care, Self Regional Healthcare, Greenwood, SC, p. A567
STEFFEN, Daniel, Vice President, Operations, Mercy Hospital, Coon Rapids, MN, p. A345
STEFFEN, Elizabeth, Director Information Technology, Seneca Healthcare District, Chester, CA, p. A59
STEFFEN, Lorri, Director of Nursing, Osage Beach Center for Behavioral Health, Llc, Osage Beach, MO, p. A381
STEFFENS, Aaron, Chief Operating Officer, Mercy Hospital Oklahoma City, Oklahoma City, OK, p. A517
STEFFIN, Renee, Chief Nursing Officer, Cuyuna Regional Medical Center, Crosby, MN, p. A345
STEGGE, Sherri, Director Human Resources, Kaiser Permanente Vallejo Medical Center, Vallejo, CA, p. A99
STEHLY, Sarah, Vice President Human Resources, Advocate Condell Medical Center, Libertyville, IL, p. A200
STEHMER, Marie F, Senior Director of Human Resources, Peacehealth Sacred Heart Medical Center At Riverbend, Springfield, OR, p. A532
STEICHEN, Barry L
Executive Vice President and Chief Operating Officer, Saint Francis Hospital South, Tulsa, OK, p. A523
Executive Vice President and Chief Operating Officer, Saint Francis Health System, Saint Francis Hospital, Tulsa, OK, p. A523
STEIGMEYER, Robert P., President and Chief Executive Officer, Concord Hospital, Concord, NH, p. A414
STEIN, Brad, Chief Financial Officer, Medical City Plano, Plano, TX, p. A645
STEIN, Cathy, Chief Inpatient Services, Sagamore Children's Psychiatric Center, Dix Hills, NY, p. A442
STEIN, Keith L
M.D., Chief Medical Officer, Baptist Medical Center Beaches, Jacksonville Beach, FL, p. A135
M.D., Senior Vice President Medical Affairs and Chief Medical Officer, Baptist Medical Center Jacksonville, Jacksonville, FL, p. A134
STEIN, Patrick, M.D., Clinical Director, Western New York Children's Psychiatric Center, West Seneca, NY, p. A462
STEIN, Paul, Chief Operating Officer, Mainegeneral Medical Center, Augusta, ME, p. A295
STEIN, Robert, M.D., Vice President Medical Management, Advocate Christ Medical Center, Oak Lawn, IL, p. A204
STEIN, Sandra, Chief Human Resources Management, VA Central California Health Care System, Fresno, CA, p. A65
STEINBERG, James P., M.D., Chief Medical Officer, Emory University Hospital Midtown, Atlanta, GA, p. A157
STEINBLOCK, Matthew, Director Information Systems, Syracuse Area Health, Syracuse, NE, p. A406
STEINES, Brian D, Chief Financial Officer, Northeast Georgia Medical Center, Gainesville, GA, p. A164
STEINES, Jeanne, D.O., Medical Director, Connecticut Mental Health Center, New Haven, CT, p. A117
STEINGALL, Patricia, MS, R.N., Vice President, Patient Care Services, Hunterdon Healthcare, Flemington, NJ, p. A421
STEINHART, Curt, M.D., Chief Medical Officer, Ou Health – University of Oklahoma Medical Center, Oklahoma City, OK, p. A518
STEINKE, Paul
D.O., President and Chief Executive Officer, Cgh Medical Center, Sterling, IL, p. A209
Chief Financial Officer, St. Bernardine Medical Center, San Bernardino, CA, p. A88
STEINMANN, Robin, Chief Human Resources Officer, Anderson Hospital, Maryville, IL, p. A201
STEINSICK, Bill, M.D., Chief Medical Staff, Asante Ashland Community Hospital, Ashland, OR, p. A525
STEITZ, David P., Chief Executive Officer, Bluegrass Community Hospital, Versailles, KY, p. A274
STELL, G Max, M.D., Medical Director, Minden Medical Center, Minden, LA, p. A288
STELLER, Wayne, Vice President Chief Nursing Officer, The Acadia Hospital, Bangor, ME, p. A295
STELLING, Jonathan, M.D., Vice President Medical Affairs, Chi Health St. Mary's, Nebraska City, NE, p. A402
STELTENPOHL, Robert, Vice President, Southern Indiana Rehabilitation Hospital, New Albany, IN, p. A225
STELZER, Jason, Director Human Resources, SSM Health St. Clare Hospital–Baraboo, Baraboo, WI, p. A707
STENCEL, Lindsay, Chief Executive Officer and Administrator, Baptist Memorial Hospital–Collierville, Collierville, TN, p. A581
STENDEL–FREELS, Robin, Coordinator Human Resources, Amg Specialty Hospital–Albuquerque, Albuquerque, NM, p. A432
STENERSON, David, Vice President and Chief Financial Officer, OSF Saint Anthony Medical Center, Rockford, IL, p. A207
STENGER, George S., D.O., Chief of Staff, Okeene Municipal Hospital, Okeene, OK, p. A516
STENGER, John D, Acting Associate Director, Charlie Norwood Veterans Affairs Medical Center, Augusta, GA, p. A158
STENGER, Sandra, Acting Chief Human Resources, Cincinnati Veterans Affairs Medical Center, Cincinnati, OH, p. A488
STENNETT, Kevin T, M.D., Chief of Staff, W. J. Mangold Memorial Hospital, Lockney, TX, p. A635
STENSON, James, Chief Information Officer, Syracuse Veterans Affairs Medical Center, Syracuse, NY, p. A460
STENSRUD, Kirk A., Chief Executive Officer, Glacial Ridge Health System, Glenwood, MN, p. A347
STENSTROM, Ella, Vice President and Chief Financial Officer, Adventhealth Hendersonville, Hendersonville, NC, p. A470
STEPHAN, Reid, Chief Information Officer, St. Luke's Regional Medical Center, Boise, ID, p. A180
STEPHANS, Bonnie, M.D., Chief Medical Officer, Community Medical Center, Missoula, MT, p. A394
STEPHENS, Brian, President and Chief Executive Officer, Door County Medical Center, Sturgeon Bay, WI, p. A722
STEPHENS, Carrie, Director Information Technology, Saunders Medical Center, Wahoo, NE, p. A406
STEPHENS, Debra, Director Personnel, Trinity Medical, Ferriday, LA, p. A282
STEPHENS, Eddy, Vice President Information Technology, Mobile Infirmary Medical Center, Mobile, AL, p. A21
STEPHENS, Ellen, Vice President Information Services, Mercy Hospital Oklahoma City, Oklahoma City, OK, p. A517
STEPHENS, Heather, Director of Information Health Technology, SSM Health St. Clare Hospital–Baraboo, Baraboo, WI, p. A707
STEPHENS, Jeremy, Vice President and Chief Human Resources Officer, Chelsea Hospital, Chelsea, MI, p. A324
STEPHENS, Kathy, Vice President of Patient Care, Decatur County Memorial Hospital, Greensburg, IN, p. A218
STEPHENS, Larry
Chief Financial Officer, Collingsworth General Hospital, Wellington, TX, p. A661

Index of Health Care Professionals

Index of Health Care Professionals

Index of Health Care Professionals / Stephens

Chief Financial Officer, Kimble Hospital, Junction, TX, p. A631
Chief Financial Officer, Sabine County Hospital, Hemphill, TX, p. A624
Chief Financial Officer, Schleicher County Medical Center, Eldorado, TX, p. A618
STEPHENS, Linda, R.N., Chief Nursing Officer, Memorial Hermann Northeast, Humble, TX, p. A629
STEPHENS, Maria, Director Human Resources, Education and Occupational Health and Wellness, VCU Health Community Memorial Hospital, South Hill, VA, p. A684
STEPHENS, Royce, Director Finance, Intermountain Medical Center, Murray, UT, p. A666
STEPHENS, Timothy, Chief Administrative Officer, Sutter Lakeside Hospital, Lakeport, CA, p. A69
STEPHENSON, Michelle, R.N., Executive Vice President & Chief Operations Officer, Ann & Robert H. Lurie Children's Hospital of Chicago, Chicago, IL, p. A188
STEPHENSON, Steve R., M.D., President and Chief Operating Officer, Unitypoint Health–Des Moines, Des Moines, IA, p. A235
STEPNEY, Precious, Executive Director, Bronx Psychiatric Center, New York, NY, p. A447
STEPP, Dana, Human Resources Officer, Mercy Health – Marcum And Wallace, Irvine, KY, p. A267
STEPP, Leonard, President and Chief Executive Officer, Ashtabula County Medical Center, Ashtabula, OH, p. A485
STERBACH, Maureen, Vice President, Human Resource Service Area, Dignity Health Arizona General Hospital Mesa, Llc, Mesa, AZ, p. A33
STERN, Barry, President and Chief Executive Officer, New York Community Hospital, New York, NY, p. A450
STERNBERG, Jan, Chief of Patient Care Services/Chief Nursing Officer, Samaritan Healthcare, Moses Lake, WA, p. A692
STERNBERG, Paul, M.D., Professor and Chairman, Vanderbilt University Medical Center, Nashville, TN, p. A591
STERNLIEB, Jonathan, M.D., Chief Medical Officer, Jefferson Lansdale Hospital, Lansdale, PA, p. A544
STERUD, Brian, Chief Information Officer, Faith Regional Health Services, Norfolk, NE, p. A403
STETTHEIMER, Timothy, Vice President and Chief Information Officer, Ascension St. Vincent's Birmingham, Birmingham, AL, p. A16
STEVEN, Eva, Chief Financial Officer, Roosevelt General Hospital, Portales, NM, p. A436
STEVENS, Dori, Chief Administrative Officer, Peacehealth Ketchikan Medical Center, Ketchikan, AK, p. A28
STEVENS, Emily, Chief Nursing Officer, Mat–Su Regional Medical Center, Palmer, AK, p. A29
STEVENS, Eric
Interim President, Adventist Health Clear Lake, Clearlake, CA, p. A59
Interim President, Adventist Health Mendocino Coast, Fort Bragg, CA, p. A63
President, Northern California Network, Adventist Health Howard Memorial, Willits, CA, p. A101
President, Northern California Network, Adventist Health Ukiah Valley, Ukiah, CA, p. A99
STEVENS, Jeffrey, Executive Vice President and Chief Human Resource Officer, Thomas Jefferson University Hospital, Philadelphia, PA, p. A550
STEVENS, Kelly, Manager Human Resources, St. Josep. Memorial Hospital, Murphysboro, IL, p. A203
STEVENS, Lori A, MSN, R.N., Interim Chief Nursing Officer, Verde Valley Medical Center, Cottonwood, AZ, p. A31
STEVENS, Mark
M.D., Chief Medical Staff, Marion General Hospital, Columbia, MS, p. A361
Director Human Resources, St. Luke's Jerome, Jerome, ID, p. A181
Senior Director Human Resources, St. Luke's Magic Valley Medical Center, Twin Falls, ID, p. A184
STEVENS, Michelle, Chief Executive Officer, Haskell Memorial Hospital, Haskell, TX, p. A624
STEVENS, Rick, FACHE, President, Christian Hospital, Saint Louis, MO, p. A385
STEVENS, Rodney, Administrator, Ascension St. Vincent Randolph, Winchester, IN, p. A229
STEVENS, Susan
Human Resources Strategic Business Partner, Transylvania Regional Hospital, Brevard, NC, p. A464
Information Technology Specialist, Fallon Medical Complex, Baker, MT, p. A389
STEVENS, Tammy, Chief Executive Officer, Madison County Memorial Hospital, Madison, FL, p. A138
STEVENSON, Angelia, Manager Finance, Tuscaloosa Va Medical Center, Tuscaloosa, AL, p. A25
STEVENSON, Brett, Controller, Kindred Hospital Northland, Kansas City, MO, p. A377
STEVENSON, John, M.D., Senior Vice President and Chief Medical Officer, South Shore Hospital, South Weymouth, MA, p. A318
STEVENSON, Linda, Chief Information Officer, Fisher–Titus Medical Center, Norwalk, OH, p. A501
STEVERSON, Denise, Director Human Resources, Dorminy Medical Center, Fitzgerald, GA, p. A164
STEVES, Sonja
Senior Vice President Human Resources, Legacy Mount Hood Medical Center, Gresham, OR, p. A527
Senior Vice President Human Resources, Legacy Salmon Creek Medical Center, Vancouver, WA, p. A698
Senior Vice President Human Resources and Marketing, Legacy Emanuel Medical Center, Portland, OR, p. A530
Vice President Human Resources and Marketing, Legacy Meridian Park Medical Center, Tualatin, OR, p. A533
Vice President Marketing, Legacy Good Samaritan Medical Center, Portland, OR, p. A530
STEWARD, Rachel, Director Human Resources, Hillcrest Hospital South, Tulsa, OK, p. A522
STEWARD, Todd E., FACHE, Chief Executive Officer, St. David's Medical Center, Austin, TX, p. A600
STEWART, Anne, Vice President and Chief Nursing Officer, Corewell Health William Beaumont University Hospital, Royal Oak, MI, p. A336
STEWART, Brandi, R.N., Vice President and Chief Nursing Officer, Integris Grove Hospital, Grove, OK, p. A513
STEWART, Candy Marie, Vice President People and Culture, Chief Human Resouces Officer, Texas Health Hospital Rockwall, Rockwall, TX, p. A647
STEWART, Caroline, Chief Nursing Officer, HCA Florida Fort Walton–Destin Hospital, Fort Walton Beach, FL, p. A132
STEWART, Cathy Joy, Vice President Patient Care Services and Chief Nursing Officer, Owensboro Health Twin Lakes Regional Medical Center, Leitchfield, KY, p. A268
STEWART, Chad, Administrative Director, Institute for Orthopaedic Surgery, Lima, OH, p. A498
STEWART, Clint
Chief Financial Officer, Blue Ridge Regional Hospital, Spruce Pine, NC, p. A476
Regional Director of Finance East, Mission Hospital Mcdowell, Marion, NC, p. A472
STEWART, Daniel, M.D., Vice President Medical Affairs, Bronson Battle Creek Hospital, Battle Creek, MI, p. A322
STEWART, David K, Senior Vice President and Chief Financial Officer, Cleveland Clinic Mercy Hospital, Canton, OH, p. A487
STEWART, Dennis W., Administrator, Noland Hospital Dothan, Dothan, AL, p. A18
STEWART, Gary, Chief Executive Officer, Henderson County Community Hospital, Lexington, TN, p. A587
STEWART, Hedda, Director Human Resources, Neshoba General, Philadelphia, MS, p. A367
STEWART, Jane, Director Information Services, HCA Florida Jfk Hospital, Atlantis, FL, p. A125
STEWART, Jessi, Director Human Resources, Rockford Center, Newark, DE, p. A122
STEWART, John, Director Finance, Burke Rehabilitation Hospital, White Plains, NY, p. A462
STEWART, Kendall, M.D., Chief Medical Officer, Southern Ohio Medical Center, Portsmouth, OH, p. A502
STEWART, Marc, M.D., Vice President and Medical Director, Fred Hutchinson Cancer Center, Seattle, WA, p. A694
STEWART, Marty, Chief Information Officer, Anmed Medical Center, Anderson, SC, p. A562
STEWART, Michael K., President, Methodist Charlton Medical Center, Dallas, TX, p. A612
STEWART, Pamela
Chief Executive Officer, Washington County Regional Medical Center, Sandersville, GA, p. A170
Director of Nursing, Washington County Regional Medical Center, Sandersville, GA, p. A170
STEWART, Paul, M.D., Medical Director, Kindred Hospital Las Vegas–Sahara, Henderson, NV, p. A409
STEWART, Ronnelle, Chief Human Resources Officer, Brookwood Baptist Medical Center, Birmingham, AL, p. A16
STEWART, Roxane, Chief Financial Officer, Magnolia Regional Medical Center, Magnolia, AR, p. A50
STEWART, Russell L, D.O., Medical Director, Braxton County Memorial Hospital, Gassaway, WV, p. A700
STEWART, Scott
M.D., Vice President Medical Management, Good Samaritan Medical Center, Brockton, MA, p. A311
Manager Information Services, Rochelle Community Hospital, Rochelle, IL, p. A207
STEWART, Sherwin, Chief Executive Officer, Saint Francis Hospital–Bartlett, Bartlett, TN, p. A579
STEWART, Stephen, M.D., Vice President Medical Affairs, SSM Health St. Mary's Hospital – Jefferson City, Jefferson City, MO, p. A376
STEWART, Stephen C., Chief Executive Officer, Holdenville General Hospital, Holdenville, OK, p. A513
STEWART, Tim, Chief Information Officer, Abbeville Area Medical Center, Abbeville, SC, p. A562
STIEKES, Robert, Chief Operating Officer, Wilkes–Barre General Hospital, Wilkes–Barre, PA, p. A558
STIFF, Patrick, Coordinator Information Technology, Madison County Memorial Hospital, Madison, FL, p. A138
STIFFARM, Kevin J., Chief Executive Officer, Indian Health Service Hospital, Rapid City, SD, p. A575
STIGGINS, Angela, Market Vice President of Operations/ Administrator, Chi Memorial Hospital – Georgia, Fort Oglethorpe, GA, p. A164
STIKELEATHER, Janie, Director Marketing and Community Relations, Davis Regional Medical Center, Statesville, NC, p. A477
STILES, Geoffrey, M.D., Chief Medical Officer, Sharp Memorial Hospital, San Diego, CA, p. A89
STILGENBAUER, Mike, Director Finance, Cleveland Clinic Marymount Hospital, Garfield Heights, OH, p. A496
STILSON, Dwain, Chief Financial Officer, Mosaic Life Care At St. Josep. – Medical Center, Saint Joseph, MO, p. A383
STILTNER, Wanda B., Director Human Resources, Buchanan General Hospital, Grundy, VA, p. A677
STIMPSON, Dan, Chief Financial Officer, Banner Del E. Webb Medical Center, Sun City West, AZ, p. A39
STIMPSON, Jared M., Chief Executive Officer, Perry County Memorial Hospital, Tell City, IN, p. A227
STIMSON, Judi
Chief Financial Officer, Desert Regional Medical Center, Palm Springs, CA, p. A82
Chief Financial Officer, Palm Beach Gardens Medical Center, Palm Beach Gardens, FL, p. A145
STIMSON, Michael, Chief Nursing Officer, Adventhealth Waterman, Tavares, FL, p. A153
STINES, Chris, Chief Executive Officer, Holy Cross Hospital – Jordan Valley, West Jordan, UT, p. A670
STINNETT, Thomas, M.D., Chief Medical Officer, Conway Behavioral Health, Conway, AR, p. A44
STINSON, Kathy, Vice President, Chief Nursing Officer and Chief Operating Officer, Honorhealth Sonoran Crossing Medical Center, Phoenix, AZ, p. A36
STINSON, Katy, Director Information Services, Alliancehealth Durant, Durant, OK, p. A512
STINSON, Martha, Director of Information Technology, HCA Florida Palms West Hospital, Loxahatchee, FL, p. A138
STINSON, Michael, Human Resources Coordinator, Select Specialty Hospital–Durham, Durham, NC, p. A467
STIPE, Chris, Chief Executive Officer, Guthrie County Hospital, Guthrie Center, IA, p. A237
STIRRUP, Jane, Vice President, Patient Care Services and Chief Nursing Officer, St. Luke's Health – Patients Medical Center, Pasadena, TX, p. A643
STITCHER, Heather, Administrator, Tanner Medical Center/ East Alabama, Wedowee, AL, p. A26
STITH, Melanie
Vice President Human Resources, Roper Hospital, Charleston, SC, p. A563
Vice President Human Resources, Roper St. Francis Mount Pleasant Hospital, Mount Pleasant, SC, p. A568
STITT, Bobby
R.N., Administrator, Mercy Hospital Watonga, Watonga, OK, p. A524
R.N., Administrator, Rural Facilities, Mercy Hospital Kingfisher, Kingfisher, OK, p. A514
R.N., Administrator, Rural Facilities, Mercy Hospital Logan County, Guthrie, OK, p. A513
STOBER, Karick
Chief Financial Officer, Pam Health Rehabilitation Hospital of Miamisburg, Miamisburg, OH, p. A500
Chief Financial Officer, Pam Specialty Hospital of Covington, Covington, LA, p. A280
STOCK, Constance, M.D., Chief Medical Officer, Monument Health Sturgis Hospital, Sturgis, SD, p. A577
STOCK, Greg K., FACHE, Chief Executive Officer, Thibodaux Regional Health System, Thibodaux, LA, p. A294
STOCK, Lesa, R.N., Chief Clinical Officer, Citizens Memorial Hospital, Bolivar, MO, p. A371
STOCK, Neil, Director Technology and Facilities, Commonspirit – Mercy Hospital, Durango, CO, p. A107
STOCKER, Trena, President, Mercy Health – Marcum And Wallace, Irvine, KY, p. A267
STOCKS, Gregory, M.D., Chief of Staff, Texas Orthopedic Hospital, Houston, TX, p. A628
STOCKTON, Linda, Chief Executive Officer, Tamp. General Hospital Crystal River, Crystal River, FL, p. A129

A982 Index of Health Care Professionals © 2025 AHA Guide

STODDARD, Mark R., Chief Executive Officer, Central Valley Medical Center, Nephi, UT, p. A666
STOEHR, Troy, Vice President and Chief Financial Officer, Good Samaritan Medical Center, Lafayette, CO, p. A110
STOFFERSON, Laura, Chief Nursing Officer, Shenandoah Medical Center, Shenandoah, IA, p. A243
STOKER, Rick, Director Management Information Systems, Tristar Horizon Medical Center, Dickson, TN, p. A582
STOKER, Vicki, Chief Nursing Officer, University Behavioral Health of Denton, Denton, TX, p. A614
STOKES, Jennifer, Chief Executive Officer, Palo Verde Behavioral Health, Tucson, AZ, p. A40
STOKES, Laura
  Director Human Resources, Roosevelt Warm Springs Long Term Acute Care Hospital, Warm Springs, GA, p. A173
  Director Human Resources, Roosevelt Warm Springs Rehabilitation And Specialty Hospitals, Warm Springs, GA, p. A173
  Human Resources Director, Upson Regional Medical Center, Thomaston, GA, p. A172
STOKES, Priscilla, MS, R.N., Vice President Patient Care and Hospital Operations, Unitypoint Health – St. Lukes's Sioux City, Sioux City, IA, p. A243
STOKES, Richard W., CPA, Chief Financial Officer, Stephens County Hospital, Toccoa, GA, p. A173
STOKES, Tina, Manager Human Resources, Regency Hospital of Florence, Florence, SC, p. A566
STOKES–LITTLE, Stephanie Central State Hospital, Milledgeville, GA, p. A168
STOKOE, Shelby
  Chief Financial Officer, Providence Holy Family Hospital, Spokane, WA, p. A696
  Senior Director Finance, Providence Sacred Heart Medical Center & Children's Hospital, Spokane, WA, p. A696
STOLDT, Garrick J, Vice President and Chief Financial Officer, Saint Peter's Healthcare System, New Brunswick, NJ, p. A425
STOLLAR, Josep. Randall, Chief Information Officer, Johnson County Hospital, Tecumseh, NE, p. A406
STOLTMAN, Erin, Administrator, Essentia Health–Ada, Ada, MN, p. A342
STOLTZ, Kim, Controller, Prohealth Rehabilitation Hospital of Wisconsin, Waukesha, WI, p. A723
STOLTZ, Kyla, Vice President Human Resources, Centerpoint Medical Center, Independence, MO, p. A376
STOLYAR, Edward B., D.O., Divisional Chief Informational Officer, New York Community Hospital, New York, NY, p. A450
STOMBERG, LeAnn, Chief Financial Officer, Minneapolis Va Health Care System, Minneapolis, MN, p. A351
STONE, D. Ryan, D.O., Chief Medical Officer, Schneck Medical Center, Seymour, IN, p. A227
STONE, Darlene
  Senior Vice President and Chief Experience Officer, Stormont Vail Health, Topeka, KS, p. A260
  Vice President Human Resources, Baptist Hospital, Pensacola, FL, p. A146
STONE, Duncan, D.D.S., Chief Medical Staff, Mississipp. State Hospital, Whitfield, MS, p. A370
STONE, Jeanette, Vice President Operations, Baptist Health South Florida, South Miami Hospital, Miami, FL, p. A139
STONE, Jill, Manager Human Resources, Lynn County Hospital District, Tahoka, TX, p. A655
STONE, Joanna, Chief Nursing Officer, Livingston Hospital And Healthcare Services, Salem, KY, p. A274
STONE, Levi Ross, R.N., Chief Nursing Officer and Chief Operating Officer, Odessa Regional Medical Center, Odessa, TX, p. A642
STONE, Loren, Chief Executive Officer, Endless Mountains Health Systems, Montrose, PA, p. A546
STONE, Patricia, R.N., MSN, Senior Vice President Operations and Chief Nursing Officer, Adventist Health White Memorial, Los Angeles, CA, p. A71
STONE, Richard, Manager, Technical Services, UHS Chenango Memorial Hospital, Norwich, NY, p. A454
STONE, Robert, JD, President/Chief Executive Officer, City of Hope's Helford Clinical Research Hospital, Duarte, CA, p. A62
STONE, Sam, Campus Administrator, Essentia Health–Virginia, Virginia, MN, p. A356
STONE, Susan, Director Human Resources, Claiborne Medical Center, Tazewell, TN, p. A594
STONE, Terry, Chief Financial Officer and Chief Information Officer, Willap. Harbor Hospital, South Bend, WA, p. A696
STONEBURNER, Marianna
  R.N., Chief Nursing Officer, UPMC Jameson, New Castle, PA, p. A547
  R.N., Vice President, Patient Care Services and Chief Nursing Officer, UPMC St. Margaret, Pittsburgh, PA, p. A552

STONER, Bill, Site Administrator, Community Behavioral Health Hospital – Annandale, Annandale, MN, p. A342
STONER, Jamey, Chief Financial Officer, Frye Regional Medical Center, Hickory, NC, p. A470
STONER, Steve, Chief Information Officer, Richard L. Roudebush Veterans Affairs Medical Center, Indianapolis, IN, p. A220
STOPPER, Jim, CPA, Chief Financial Officer, Evangelical Community Hospital, Lewisburg, PA, p. A544
STORER, Andrew, Ph.D., R.N., Chief Nursing Officer and Senior Vice President for Patient Care Services, Roswell Park Comprehensive Cancer Center, Buffalo, NY, p. A440
STOREY, Andre, President, Ascension Columbia St. Mary's Hospital Milwaukee, Milwaukee, WI, p. A716
STOREY, Kam, Director Human Resources, Sebastian River Medical Center, Sebastian, FL, p. A150
STOREY, Kevin L.
  President, Baptist Health Medical Center–Heber Springs, Heber Springs, AR, p. A47
  President, Baptist Health Medical Center–Stuttgart, Stuttgart, AR, p. A54
STORK, Elizabeth, Chief Human Resources Officer, Barton Memorial Hospital, South Lake Tahoe, CA, p. A96
STORM, Dave, Director Business Support, HSHS St. Anthony's Memorial Hospital, Effingham, IL, p. A194
STORR, Katie, Director of Human Resources, Mississipp. State Hospital, Whitfield, MS, p. A370
STORRS, Elaine, Chief Nursing Officer, Mercy Health – Springfield Regional Medical Center, Springfield, OH, p. A504
STORY, Otis L. Sr, President, Ascension St. Mary – Kankakee, Kankakee, IL, p. A199
STOTLER, Sherry, R.N., MSN, Chief Nursing Officer, Valleywise Health, Phoenix, AZ, p. A37
STOTTLEMYRE, Georgan L., Chief Human Relations Officer, Northern Inyo Hospital, Bishop, CA, p. A58
STOTTS, Vicki, Coordinator Human Resources, Flint River Hospital, Montezuma, GA, p. A168
STOUT, Amanda, Chief Nursing Officer, Minneola District Hospital, Minneola, KS, p. A255
STOUT, Bess, Director Human Resources, Tennova Healthcare–Lafollette Medical Center, La Follette, TN, p. A586
STOUT, Cindy, R.N., President and Chief Executive Officer, El Paso Children's Hospital, El Paso, TX, p. A616
STOUT, Deana
  Vice President Financial Services, Medstar Good Samaritan Hospital, Baltimore, MD, p. A300
  Vice President, Finance, Medstar Union Memorial Hospital, Baltimore, MD, p. A301
STOUT, Kimberly Dawn, Chief Nursing Officer and Chief Operating Officer, Mcalester Regional Health Center, Mcalester, OK, p. A515
STOUT, Louis, Chief Nursing Officer and Deputy Commander Health Readiness, Madigan Army Medical Center, Tacoma, WA, p. A697
STOUT, Patsy, Director Personnel, Delhi Hospital, Delhi, LA, p. A281
STOUT, Rodney, M.D., Chief Executive Officer, Holzer Medical Center, Gallipolis, OH, p. A496
STOVALL, Henry, Regional President, Ascension Sacred Heart Gulf, Port St Joe, FL, p. A147
STOVALL, Richard G, Senior Vice President Fiscal Services and Chief Financial Officer, Southern Regional Medical Center, Riverdale, GA, p. A170
STOVER, Benny, Vice President Finance, Mercy Hospital Northwest Arkansas, Rogers, AR, p. A52
STOVER, George M., Chief Executive Officer, Hospital District No 1 of Rice County, Lyons, KS, p. A254
STOVER, Nick, Director Information Systems, Camc Plateau Medical Center, Oak Hill, WV, p. A703
STOVER, Patricia A, Administrator Nursing, Doylestown Health, Doylestown, PA, p. A538
STOVER, Raymond
  Regional President, Mymichigan Medical Center Gladwin, Gladwin, MI, p. A327
  Regional President, Mymichigan Medical Center West Branch, West Branch, MI, p. A340
STOVER, Theresa, Chief Human Resource Officer, Edgefield County Healthcare, Edgefield, SC, p. A565
STOWE, Mary
  Senior Vice President and Chief Nursing Officer, Children's Medical Center Dallas, Dallas, TX, p. A611
  Senior Vice President and Chief Nursing Officer, Children's Medical Center Plano, Plano, TX, p. A644
STOWE, Rob, Chief Executive Officer, Baraga County Memorial Hospital, L'Anse, MI, p. A331
STOWELL, Dana A, Chief Information Officer, Mccurtain Memorial Hospital, Idabel, OK, p. A514

STOWMAN, Amber, Controller, Chi Lisbon Health, Lisbon, ND, p. A482
STOY, Gale, Manager Information Systems, Mid Coast Hospital, Brunswick, ME, p. A296
STOYANOFF, Pamela
  Executive Vice President and Chief Operating Officer, Methodist Dallas Medical Center, Dallas, TX, p. A612
  President and Chief Operating Officer, Methodist Charlton Medical Center, Dallas, TX, p. A612
STRABEL, Elizabeth, M.D., Chief Medical Staff, Aspirus Divine Savior Hospital & Clinics, Portage, WI, p. A720
STRACHAN, Ronald
  Chief Information Officer, Mclaren Bay Region, Bay City, MI, p. A322
  Chief Information Officer, Mclaren Flint, Flint, MI, p. A327
STRACK, Kirk, Assistant Chief Financial Officer, Uofl Health – Uofl Hospital, Louisville, KY, p. A270
STRADER, Jonathan, Chief Executive Officer, Encompass Health Rehabilitation Hospital of Humble, Humble, TX, p. A629
STRADER, Lynn, Chief Financial Officer, Cjw Medical Center, Richmond, VA, p. A683
STRADER, Yvonne M, Chief Nursing Officer, Providence St. Mary Medical Center, Walla Walla, WA, p. A698
STRADTMAN, Jackie, Director Human Resources, Chi St. Josep. Health Burleson Hospital, Caldwell, TX, p. A606
STRAIN, Donna, Director Human Resources, Ray County Hospital And Healthcare, Richmond, MO, p. A382
STRAMOWSKI, Mallary, Chief Human Resources Officer, Select Specialty Hospital–Madison, Madison, WI, p. A714
STRAND, Eric, Director Information Services, HCA Florida North Florida Hospital, Gainesville, FL, p. A132
STRANZ, Thomas, Chief Executive Officer, UH Avon Rehabilitation Hospital, Avon, OH, p. A485
STRASSER, Michael, Vice President and Chief Financial Officer, Mercy Medical Center Merced, Merced, CA, p. A77
STRASSNER III, Lawrence F, Ph.D., FACHE, R.N., MS, Senior Vice President Operations and Chief Nursing Officer, Medstar Franklin Square Medical Center, Baltimore, MD, p. A302
STRATON, Sam, Chief Nursing Officer, Ascension Saint Thomas Hospital, Nashville, TN, p. A590
STRATTON, Emilee, Chief Financial Officer, Childress Regional Medical Center, Childress, TX, p. A607
STRATTON, James, Vice President Finance, SSM Health St. Mary's Hospital – Jefferson City, Jefferson City, MO, p. A376
STRATTON, Mary, Director Human Resources, River Park Hospital, Huntington, WV, p. A701
STRATTON, Tracie, Chief Executive Officer, Los Alamos Medical Center, Los Alamos, NM, p. A435
STRAUGHAN, John, Director Information Technology, Wallowa Memorial Hospital, Enterprise, OR, p. A526
STRAUMAN, Karen S, R.N., Chief Nurse Executive, Kaiser Permanente Fresno Medical Center, Fresno, CA, p. A65
STRAUMANIS, John P., M.D., Vice President Medical Affairs and Chief Medical Officer, University of Maryland Rehabilitation & Orthopaedic Institute, Baltimore, MD, p. A302
STRAUSS, Alan
  Chief Financial Officer, Carondelet Holy Cross Hospital, Nogales, AZ, p. A34
  Chief Financial Officer, Carondelet St. Joseph's Hospital, Tucson, AZ, p. A40
STRAWN, Keith A, Vice President Human Resources, Novant Health New Hanover Regional Medical Center, Wilmington, NC, p. A478
STRAWSER, Debbie A, Director Human Resources, Lindner Center of Hope, Mason, OH, p. A499
STRAYHORN, Shelly
  R.N., Chief Nursing Officer, Wadley Regional Medical Center, Texarkana, TX, p. A657
  R.N., Chief Nursing Officer, Wadley Regional Medical Center At Hope, Hope, AR, p. A47
STRBICH, Steve, D.O., Chief of Staff, Corewell Health Ludington Hospital, Ludington, MI, p. A332
STREAR, Chris, M.D., Chief Medical Officer, Columbia Memorial Hospital, Astoria, OR, p. A525
STREATER, Vivian
  Chief Nursing Officer and Co–Acting Chief Executive Officer, Broughton Hospital, Morganton, NC, p. A473
  Co–Acting Chief Executive Officer, Broughton Hospital, Morganton, NC, p. A473
STRECKER, Robert, M.D., Chief of Staff, Colorado River Medical Center, Needles, CA, p. A80
STREDNEY, Thomas, Chief Human Resources Management Service, Aleda E. Lutz Department of Veterans Affairs Medical Center, Saginaw, MI, p. A336

Index of Health Care Professionals / Street

STREET, Rex, Senior Vice President and Chief Financial Officer, Cone Health Alamance Regional Medical Center, Burlington, NC, p. A464
STREETER, Matthew
　Chief Financial Officer, Southwest Health, Platteville, WI, p. A719
　Interim President & Chief Executive Officer, Weeks Medical Center, Lancaster, NH, p. A415
STREETER, Robert, M.D., Vice President Medical Affairs, Mercy Medical Center Merced, Merced, CA, p. A77
STREICH, Rebecca, Manager Human Resources and Education Manager, Hutchinson Health, Hutchinson, MN, p. A348
STREIER, Debbie, Regional President and Chief Executive Officer, Avera Marshall Regional Medical Center, Marshall, MN, p. A350
STREIT, Loren, Director Human Resources, Stormont Vail Health – Flint Hills Campus, Junction City, KS, p. A251
STREJC, Irene T, M.P.H., R.N., Vice President, Nursing, Methodist Richardson Medical Center, Richardson, TX, p. A646
STRICKER, Sean, President and Chief Executive Officer, Regency Hospital of Minneapolis, Golden Valley, MN, p. A347
STRICKER, Steven, M.D., Physician in Chief, Kaiser Permanente Vallejo Medical Center, Vallejo, CA, p. A99
STRICKLAND, David, Area Information Officer, Kaiser Permanente Los Angeles Medical Center, Los Angeles, CA, p. A73
STRICKLAND, Lee, Regional Director Information Technology, Adventhealth Hendersonville, Hendersonville, NC, p. A470
STRICKLAND, Morris S, Chief Financial Officer, Helen Keller Hospital, Sheffield, AL, p. A24
STRICKLER, David
　Chief Financial Officer, Nexus Specialty Hospital, Shenandoah, TX, p. A652
　Chief Financial Officer, Nexus Specialty Hospital The Woodlands, The Woodlands, TX, p. A657
STRICKLER, Jeffery C., R.N., President, UNC Health Chatham, Siler City, NC, p. A476
STRICKLER, Renae, Chief Executive Officer, Mountain View Hospital, Gadsden, AL, p. A20
STRICKLER, Stephen Todd, Clinical Nurse Manager, Sistersville General Hospital, Sistersville, WV, p. A704
STRICKLING, Keith
　Chief Accountant, Jay Hospital, Jay, FL, p. A135
　Chief Financial Officer, Atmore Community Hospital, Atmore, AL, p. A15
STRIEBICH, Shannon
　FACHE, President & Chief Executive Officer, Trinity Health Michigan Market, Trinity Health Livonia Hospital, Livonia, MI, p. A332
　FACHE, President and Chief Executive Officer of Trinity Health Michigan Market, Trinity Health Oakland Hospital, Pontiac, MI, p. A335
STRING, Sherrie
　Senior Vice President Human Resources, Hackensack Meridian Health Bayshore Community Hospital, Holmdel, NJ, p. A422
　Senior Vice President Human Resources, Hackensack Meridian Health Ocean University Medical Center, Brick Township, NJ, p. A419
　Senior Vice President Human Resources, Hackensack Meridian Health Riverview Medical Center, Red Bank, NJ, p. A428
STRINGFELLOW, Grace, M.D., Chief of Staff, Omaha Va Medical Center, Omaha, NE, p. A404
STRINGOS, Gust, M.D., Medical Staff Director, Redington–Fairview General Hospital, Skowhegan, ME, p. A299
STRINI, Rebecca, Acting Director, Columbia Va Health Care System, Columbia, SC, p. A564
STRIPLIN, Elizabeth, Chief Financial Officer, Rehabilitation Hospital of Southern New Mexico, Las Cruces, NM, p. A435
STRITTMATTER, Julie, Director Human Resources, Baylor University Medical Center, Dallas, TX, p. A610
STROBEL, Deb, R.N., Chief Nursing Officer, Russell Regional Hospital, Russell, KS, p. A258
STROBEL, Jane, Vice President and Chief Financial Officer, Commonspirit – Mercy Hospital, Durango, CO, p. A107
STROBEL, Rand
　Regional Chief Information Officer, St. Francis Hospital, Federal Way, WA, p. A690
　Regional Chief Information Officer, Information Technology Services, St. Michael Medical Center, Silverdale, WA, p. A695
STROH, Rhonda, Chief Human Resources Officer, Community Memorial Hospital, Redfield, SD, p. A576
STROHLA, Patti, R.N., Chief Nursing Officer, Concord Hospital – Franklin, Franklin, NH, p. A415

STROM, Lisa, Director Information Systems, North Big Horn Hospital District, Lovell, WY, p. A727
STROM, Sebastian, Chief Executive Officer, HCA Florida Largo Hospital, Largo, FL, p. A137
STROMBERG, Audrey, Administrator, Roosevelt Medical Center, Culbertson, MT, p. A391
STROMSTAD, Darlene, FACHE, President and Chief Executive Officer, Wynn Hospital, Utica, NY, p. A460
STRONESKI, Donna, Vice President, Human Resources, Middlesex Health, Middletown, CT, p. A117
STRONG, David, Chief Financial Officer/Vice President Finance, Cox Medical Center Branson, Branson, MO, p. A372
STRONG, Melissa D, Chief Nursing Officer, Mason Health, Shelton, WA, p. A695
STRONG, Tanya, Manager Information Technology, Harney District Hospital, Burns, OR, p. A526
STROSAKER, Robyn
　M.D., President and Chief Operating Officer, University Hospitals Beachwood Medical Center, Beachwood, OH, p. A486
　M.D., President and Chief Operating Officer, University Hospitals Lake Health, Willoughby, OH, p. A507
STROTHER, James, Site Director Information Technology Systems, Mercyone Des Moines Medical Center, Des Moines, IA, p. A235
STROTHKAMP, Brad, Chief Information Systems, Lakeland Behavioral Health System, Springfield, MO, p. A386
STROUD, Justin, Chief Financial Officer, Merit Health Central, Jackson, MS, p. A364
STROUP, Jeff, Chief Operating Officer, Oklahoma State University Medical Center, Tulsa, OK, p. A522
STROUSE, Thomas, M.D., Medical Director and Professor of Clinical Psych, Stewart & Lynda Resnick Neuropsychiatric Hospital At Ucla, Los Angeles, CA, p. A75
STRUB, Lisa, Chief Operating Officer, Centennial Peaks Hospital, Louisville, CO, p. A112
STRUYK, Douglas A., CPA, President and Chief Executive Officer, Christian Health, Wyckoff, NJ, p. A431
STRYKER, Christine Anne, Chief Nursing Officer and Chief Operating Officer, Up Health System – Marquette, Marquette, MI, p. A333
STRZELECKI, Sarah, Ed.D., R.N., Chief Nursing Officer, Phoenixville Hospital, Phoenixville, PA, p. A550
STRZEMPKO, Stanley, M.D., Vice President Medical Affairs and Chief Medical Officer, Baystate Noble Hospital, Westfield, MA, p. A319
STUART, Danna, M.D., Chief Medical Officer, Newman Memorial Hospital, Shattuck, OK, p. A520
STUART, Robin, Chief Executive Officer, Morrill County Community Hospital, Bridgeport, NE, p. A398
STUBBENDECK, Shelley, Chief Executive Officer, Milwaukee Rehabilitation Hospital At Greenfield, Milwaukee, WI, p. A717
STUBBLEFIELD, Greg, President, Baptist Health Extended Care Hospital, Little Rock, AR, p. A49
STUBBS, Don, Vice President Human Resources, Candler Hospital–Savannah, Savannah, GA, p. A170
STUBBS, Kay, Chief Nursing Officer, Northwest Medical Center, Tucson, AZ, p. A40
STUBITSCH, Brian, M.D., Chief Medical Officer, Edgerton Hospital And Health Services, Edgerton, WI, p. A710
STUCKY, Nancy, Director Human Resources and Public Relations, Kingman Community Hospital, Kingman, KS, p. A252
STUCZYNSKI, Joseph, Chief Executive Officer, Memorial Hospital West, Pembroke Pines, FL, p. A146
STUDDARD, Mark, Interim Chief Executive Officer, Encompass Health Rehabilitation Hospital, A Partner of Memorial Hospital At Gulfport, Gulfport, MS, p. A362
STUDEBAKER, Shelly, Human Resources Assistant, Clinch Memorial Hospital, Homerville, GA, p. A165
STUDER, Tim, President Medical Staff, Perham Health, Perham, MN, p. A352
STUENKEL, Kurt, FACHE, President and Chief Executive Officer, Atrium Health Floyd Medical Center, Rome, GA, p. A170
STUEVE, Debra, Administrator, Essentia Health–Graceville, Graceville, MN, p. A347
STUEVE, Jo W., Executive Vice President and Co–Chief Operating Officer, Children's Mercy Kansas City, Kansas City, MO, p. A377
STUHLMILLER, Michael, Chief Financial Officer, Mann–Grandstaff Department of Veterans Affairs Medical Center, Spokane, WA, p. A696
STULTS, Cynthia S., Executive Assistant and Human Resources Director, Rangely District Hospital, Rangely, CO, p. A113
STULTS, Kim, Director, Information Systems, Bellevue Hospital, The, Bellevue, OH, p. A486

STULTZ, Jeff, Chief Executive Officer, Bloomington Regional Rehabilitation Hospital, Bloomington, IN, p. A213
STUMBERS, Julie, Chief Executive Officer, AHS Sherman Medical Center, Sherman, TX, p. A652
STUMBO, Kathy, Chief Executive Officer, Paintsville Arh Hospital, Paintsville, KY, p. A273
STUMP, Lisa, Interim Chief Information Officer, Yale New Haven Hospital, New Haven, CT, p. A118
STUMP, Veronica, Director of Nursing, Carilion Giles Community Hospital, Pearisburg, VA, p. A681
STUMPO, Barbara J, R.N., Vice President Patient Care Services, Griffin Health, Derby, CT, p. A115
STUNKARD, Jill, R.N., MSN, Associate Chief Nurse Executive and Interim Chief Nursing Officer, Einstein Medical Center Philadelphia, Philadelphia, PA, p. A548
STURGEON, Jim, Area Director Human Resources, Kindred Hospital Las Vegas–Sahara, Henderson, NV, p. A409
STURGILL, Lori, Vice President Business Partnership. Mercy Hospital Springfield, Springfield, MO, p. A387
STURGIS, Gayle Ann, Chief Nursing Officer, Risk Management, Great Plains Regional Medical Center, Elk City, OK, p. A512
STURGIS, Jonathan, Chief Financial Officer, Houston Methodist Baytown Hospital, Baytown, TX, p. A601
STURGIS, Paul
　Chief Human Resource Officer, Sparrow Specialty Hospital, Lansing, MI, p. A331
　Director Human Resources, Dmc Rehabilitation Institute of Michigan, Detroit, MI, p. A325
　Vice President and Chief Human Resources Officer, University of Michigan Health–Sparrow Lansing, Lansing, MI, p. A332
STURMAN, Jeffrey S., Senior Vice President and Chief Information Officer, Memorial Regional Hospital, Hollywood, FL, p. A133
STURSA, Robin, Vice President, Chief Information Officer, Cleveland Clinic Mercy Hospital, Canton, OH, p. A487
STUTES, Sally
　Chief Nursing Officer, Baylor Scott & White Surgical Hospital Fort Worth, Fort Worth, TX, p. A619
　Chief Nursing Officer/Interim Chief Operating Officer, Baylor Scott & White Surgical Hospital Fort Worth, Fort Worth, TX, p. A619
　Interim Chief Operating Officer, Baylor Scott & White Surgical Hospital Fort Worth, Fort Worth, TX, p. A619
STUWE, Shannon, Director of Nursing, Faulkton Area Medical Center, Faulkton, SD, p. A573
STYER, Brent
　Chief Information Officer, Summers County Arh Hospital, Hinton, WV, p. A701
　Director Information Technology, Whitesburg Arh Hospital, Whitesburg, KY, p. A275
STYLES, Aundrea, R.N., Chief Executive Officer, Gateway Regional Medical Center, Granite City, IL, p. A196
STYRON, Stacie, Chief Nursing Officer, Lamb Healthcare Center, Littlefield, TX, p. A634
SUAREZ, Irma, Deputy Executive Director, NYC Health + Hospitals/Woodhull, New York, NY, p. A452
SUAREZ, Jose Luis, Comptroller, Multy Medical Rehabilitation Hospital San Juan, San Juan, PR, p. A735
SUAREZ, Lauren, Chief Executive Officer, Encompass Health Rehabilitation Hospital of Austin, Austin, TX, p. A600
SUAREZ, Orlando, Director Information Technology, Larkin Community Hospital–South Miami Campus, South Miami, FL, p. A150
SUBIA, Corina, Director Human Resources, Ward Memorial Hospital, Monahans, TX, p. A640
SUBLER, Jeffrey R., President and Chief Executive Officer, Wayne Healthcare, Greenville, OH, p. A497
SUBLETTE, Elizabeth, Director Finance, Providence Willamette Falls Medical Center, Oregon City, OR, p. A530
SUCATO, Daniel J, M.D., MS, Chief of Staff, Scottish Rite for Children, Dallas, TX, p. A612
SUCHER, Therese O, Senior Vice President Operations, Southern Regional Medical Center, Riverdale, GA, p. A170
SUDBURY, Russ, M.D., President Medical Staff, Aspirus Tomahawk Hospital, Tomahawk, WI, p. A723
SUDDRETH, Jerrell, Chief Nursing Officer, UNC Health Caldwell, Lenoir, NC, p. A471
SUDICKY, Mary, Chief Financial Officer, St. Mary Medical Center, Hobart, IN, p. A218
SUDOLCAN, Joseph, M.D., Medical Director, Reagan Memorial Hospital, Big Lake, TX, p. A603
SUEIRO, Edwin, Chief Executive Officer, Professional Hospital Guaynabo, Guaynabo, PR, p. A732
SUGAR, Bev, Associate Administrator and Director Human Resources, Inova Mount Vernon Hospital, Alexandria, VA, p. A673
SUGDEN, Elizabeth, M.D., Chief Medical Officer, St. Luke's Jerome, Jerome, ID, p. A181

Index of Health Care Professionals
Index of Health Care Professionals / Swartwood

SUGG, Amy, Director Human Resources, Ochsner Scott Regional, Morton, MS, p. A367
SUGGS, Heather, Manager Human Resources, Jay Hospital, Jay, FL, p. A135
SUHR, Nancy, Manager Human Resources, Pender Community Hospital, Pender, NE, p. A405
SUITTER, Marie, Chief Financial Officer, The Acadia Hospital, Bangor, ME, p. A295
SUKENIK, Richard, CPA, Vice President Finance and Chief Financial Officer, Chan Soon–Shiong Medical Center At Windber, Windber, PA, p. A558
SUKIE, Butch, Director, Information Management, Cleveland Clinic Union Hospital, Dover, OH, p. A495
SULIT, Teresa, Director of Human Resources, Seven Hills Hospital, Henderson, NV, p. A409
SULLINS, Ashley, Chief Nursing Officer, Salem Memorial District Hospital, Salem, MO, p. A386
SULLIVAN, Christopher, M.D., Chief Medical Officer, Centerpoint Medical Center, Independence, MO, p. A376
SULLIVAN, David, Director Human Resources, Ohiohealth Doctors Hospital, Columbus, OH, p. A492
SULLIVAN, Denis, Chief Human Resources Management, Black Hills Hcs, Fort Meade, SD, p. A573
SULLIVAN, Denise, Chief Executive Officer, Sycamore Springs, Lafayette, IN, p. A222
SULLIVAN, Donald, M.D., Medical Director, Encompass Health Rehabilitation Hospital of North Memphis, A Partner of Methodist Healthcare, Memphis, TN, p. A588
SULLIVAN, Gregory, Manager Human Resources, Girard Medical Center, Girard, KS, p. A249
SULLIVAN, James, M.D., Chief Medical Officer, Butler Hospital, Providence, RI, p. A560
SULLIVAN, John, M.D., Chief Medical Officer, St. Clair Health, Pittsburgh, PA, p. A551
SULLIVAN, John M., M.D., Chief of Staff, Ennis Regional Medical Center, Ennis, TX, p. A618
SULLIVAN, Katherine, Director, Human Resources, Moab Regional Hospital, Moab, UT, p. A666
SULLIVAN, Kathleen, M.D., Chief of Staff, Saddleback Medical Center, Laguna Hills, CA, p. A69
SULLIVAN, Martha
M.D., Executive Director, Creedmoor Psychiatric Center, New York, NY, p. A448
Chief Information Officer, Harrison Memorial Hospital, Cynthiana, KY, p. A264
SULLIVAN, Megan, R.N., Chief Nursing Officer, Mercy Rehabilitation Hospital Fort Smith, Fort Smith, AR, p. A47
SULLIVAN, Michael
M.D., Chief Medical Officer, Northern Maine Medical Center, Fort Kent, ME, p. A297
M.D., Medical Director Emergency Services, Peacehealth Peace Island Medical Center, Friday Harbor, WA, p. A690
SULLIVAN, Shannon, President and Chief Operating Officer, Women & Infants Hospital of Rhode Island, Providence, RI, p. A561
SULLIVAN, Staci, R.N., Chief Nursing Officer, Lane Regional Medical Center, Zachary, LA, p. A294
SULLIVAN, Theresa, Chief Executive Officer, Samaritan Healthcare, Moses Lake, WA, p. A692
SULLIVAN, William Mount Auburn Hospital, Cambridge, MA, p. A312
SULLIVAN SMITH, Mary, R.N., MS, Senior Vice President, Chief Operating Officer and Chief Nursing Officer, New England Baptist Hospital, Boston, MA, p. A311
SULLIVANT, Laura
Area Chief Information Officer, Kaiser Permanente Zion Medical Center, San Diego, CA, p. A89
Area Information Officer, Kaiser Foundation Hospital – San Marcos, San Marcos, CA, p. A93
SULSER, Jamey, Director Human Resources, South Davis Community Hospital, Bountiful, UT, p. A664
SULTA, Omer, Chief Financial Officer, University of Texas M.D. Anderson Cancer Center, Houston, TX, p. A628
SULU, Dorothy, Budget Analyst, Hop. Health Care Center, Keams Canyon, AZ, p. A32
SULZEN, Jessica, Director Human Resources, Belton Regional Medical Center, Belton, MO, p. A371
SUMMERLIN, Craig, Chief Human Resources Officer, Singing River Health System, Pascagoula, MS, p. A367
SUMMERLIN, Valerie, R.N., MS, Chief Nursing Officer, Adventist Healthcare Rehabilitation, Rockville, MD, p. A306
SUMMERS, Barbara L., Ph.D., R.N., Vice President Nursing Practice and Chief Nursing Officer, University of Texas M.D. Anderson Cancer Center, Houston, TX, p. A628
SUMMERS, Cassidi, Chief Nursing Officer, Medical City Mckinney, Mckinney, TX, p. A638
SUMMERS, Curtis, Chief Executive Officer, Summit Medical Center, Edmond, OK, p. A512
SUMMERS, Debra, Chief Nursing Officer, Calhoun Liberty Hospital, Blountstown, FL, p. A126
SUMMERS, Forrest Blue., Chief Executive Officer, Perimeter Behavioral Hospital of Jackson, Jackson, TN, p. A584
SUMMERS, Greg, Regional Director, Field Technical Services, Providence Santa Rosa Memorial Hospital, Santa Rosa, CA, p. A95
SUMMERS, Jeff, M.D., Medical Director, Select Specialty Hospital–North Knoxville, Powell, TN, p. A592
SUMMERS, Kelly, Senior Vice President, Information Technology and Chief Information Officer, Valleywise Health, Phoenix, AZ, p. A37
SUMMERSON, Tonya, Chief Clinical Officer, Dallas County Hospital, Perry, IA, p. A242
SUMMERVILLE, Wendell, Chief Financial Officer, Bryce Hospital, Tuscaloosa, AL, p. A25
SUMMITT, Dave, Chief Information Security Officer, H. Lee Moffitt Cancer Center And Research Institute, Tampa, FL, p. A152
SUMNER, Donna, Director, Human Resources and Organizational Development, St. Josep. Medical Center, Kansas City, MO, p. A378
SUMNER, Jack R, Assistant Administrator Finance, Providence Newberg Medical Center, Newberg, OR, p. A529
SUMNER, John, Chief Executive Officer, Trigg County Hospital, Cadiz, KY, p. A264
SUMRA, K S, M.D., Chief of Staff, Pembina County Memorial Hospital And Wedgewood Manor, Cavalier, ND, p. A480
SUMRALL, Josh, Chief Executive Officer, River Oaks Hospital, New Orleans, LA, p. A290
SUMRALL, Mary Ellen, R.N., Chief Nursing Officer, Baptist Memorial Hospital–Golden Triangle, Columbus, MS, p. A361
SUMTER, Rob
Executive Vice President and Chief Operating Officer, Regional One Health, Memphis, TN, p. A589
Executive Vice President and Chief Operation Officer, Regional One Health, Memphis, TN, p. A589
SUN RHODES, Neil, M.D., Chief Medical Officer, Blackfeet Community Hospital, Saint Mary, MT, p. A395
SUNDARAMOORTHY, Abirammy, M.D., Chief Medical Officer, University Hospitals Conneaut Medical Center, Conneaut, OH, p. A493
SUNDBERG, Nita, Director Human Resources, Three Rivers Behavioral Health, West Columbia, SC, p. A571
SUNDERLIN, Tammy, Director of Nursing, Auburn Community Hospital, Auburn, NY, p. A438
SUNDERMAN, Kurt, Chief Executive Officer, Rice Medical Center, Eagle Lake, TX, p. A615
SUNDHOLM, Jeffrey, Chief Information Officer, Myrtue Medical Center, Harlan, IA, p. A237
SUNDRUD, Diane
Director Human Resources, Essentia Health–Fosston, Fosston, MN, p. A347
Human Resource Service Partner, Essentia Health St. Mary's – Detroit Lakes, Detroit Lakes, MN, p. A345
SUNGA, Marcos N, M.D., Chief of Staff, Hardin County General Hospital, Rosiclare, IL, p. A208
SUNQUIST, Joanne, Chief Information Officer, Hennepin Healthcare, Minneapolis, MN, p. A350
SUNTAY, Renato, Chief Financial Officer, Meadville Medical Center, Meadville, PA, p. A545
SUNTRAPAK, Todd A., President/Chief Executive Officer, Valley Children's Healthcare, Madera, CA, p. A76
SURCOUF, Shelli, Chief Financial Officer, Georgetown Behavioral Health Institute, Georgetown, TX, p. A622
SURESH, Srinivasan, M.D., Chief Medical Information Officer, UPMC Children's Hospital of Pittsburgh, Pittsburgh, PA, p. A551
SURGUY, Jean, Vice President, Chief Nursing Officer, Mile Bluff Medical Center, Mauston, WI, p. A715
SURKALA, Karen, Chief Operating Officer, Saint Vincent Hospital, Erie, PA, p. A540
SURL, Deepak, Chief Information Officer, Eastern New Mexico Medical Center, Roswell, NM, p. A436
SURO, Marta R Mercado, Chief Operating Officer, Mennonite General Hospital, Aibonito, PR, p. A731
SURRATT, Shawn, M.D., Chief of Staff, Memorial Hospital And Manor, Bainbridge, GA, p. A159
SURROCK, Lester, Chief Financial Officer, Mission Regional Medical Center, Mission, TX, p. A640
SUSI, Jeffrey L, President and Chief Executive Officer, Cleveland Clinic Indian River Hospital, Vero Beach, FL, p. A154
SUSICK, Nancy, MSN, President, Corewell Health Beaumont Troy Hospital, Troy, MI, p. A339
SUSIE–LATTNER, Debra, M.D., Vice President Medical Management, Advocate Condell Medical Center, Libertyville, IL, p. A200
SUSSMAN, Andrew, M.D., Chief Operating Officer, Umass Memorial Medical Center, Worcester, MA, p. A320
SUSSMAN, Howard, M.D., Chief Medical Officer, St. Josep. Hospital, Bethpage, NY, p. A439
SUSTERICH, Tim, Chief Financial Officer and Chief Operating Officer, Memorial Healthcare, Owosso, MI, p. A334
SUTER, Brian, Chief Financial Officer, Mayo Clinic Health System In Fairmont, Fairmont, MN, p. A346
SUTER, Lorenzo, President and Chief Executive Officer, Mclaren Oakland, Pontiac, MI, p. A335
SUTER, Mia, Chief Administration Officer, Owensboro Health Regional Hospital, Owensboro, KY, p. A272
SUTHERLAND, Shea, Chief Financial Officer, Merit Health Madison, Canton, MS, p. A360
SUTTERFIELD, Dennis, Chief Information Officer, Suny Downstate Health Sciences University, New York, NY, p. A453
SUTTON, Andrew
Chief Human Resources Officer, Coatesville Veterans Affairs Medical Center, Coatesville, PA, p. A537
Chief, Human Resources Management Service, James A. Haley Veterans' Hospital–Tampa, Tampa, FL, p. A152
SUTTON, Angie, Chief Financial Officer, Genoa Medical Facilities, Genoa, NE, p. A400
SUTTON, Elaine, Chief Information Officer, Pershing Memorial Hospital, Brookfield, MO, p. A372
SUTTON, Janet, D.O., Medical Director, Mclaren Bay Special Care, Bay City, MI, p. A322
SUTTON, Jeffrey, Chief Information Officer, Lexington Vamc, Lexington, KY, p. A268
SUTTON, Jesse, Senior Vice President and Chief Financial Officer, Texas Health Huguley Hospital Fort Worth South, Burleson, TX, p. A606
SUTTON, Julie, Director Performance Improvement, State Hospital South, Blackfoot, ID, p. A179
SUTTON, KaSara, Director of Nursing and Clinical Services, Sanford Aberdeen Medical Center, Aberdeen, SD, p. A572
SUTTON, Michael, Chief Financial Officer, Chi Memorial, Chattanooga, TN, p. A580
SUTTON, Michele Kidd., FACHE, President and Chief Executive Officer, North Oaks Medical Center, Hammond, LA, p. A282
SUTTON, Rhonda, Director Human Resources, Richland Hospital, Richland Center, WI, p. A720
SUTTON, Richard O., FACHE, Chief Executive Officer, Southeast Alabama Medical Center, Dothan, AL, p. A18
SUTTON, Thomas, Associate Director, North Florida/South Georgia Veteran's Health System, Gainesville, FL, p. A132
SUVACAROV, Maria, Chief Clinical Officer, Kindred Hospital Chicago–Northlake, Northlake, IL, p. A204
SUVER, James A., FACHE, Chief Executive Officer, Ridgecrest Regional Hospital, Ridgecrest, CA, p. A86
SUZUKI, Daniel, M.D., Medical Director, Las Encinas Hospital, Pasadena, CA, p. A83
SVEC, David, M.D., Chief Medical Officer, Stanford Health Care Tri–Valley, Pleasanton, CA, p. A83
SVENDSEN, Mark Deyo, M.D., Medical Director, Mayo Clinic Health System – Red Cedar In Menomonie, Menomonie, WI, p. A716
SVIDERGOL–PETERMAN, Jessica
MSN, R.N., Chief Nursing Officer, Conemaugh Meyersdale Medical Center, Meyersdale, PA, p. A546
MSN, R.N., Chief Nursing Officer, Conemaugh Miners Medical Center, Hastings, PA, p. A541
SWAGERTY, Jill, Director Human Resources, Union County General Hospital, Clayton, NM, p. A434
SWAIN, Arthur D, Vice President Support Services, Grand Lake Health System, Saint Marys, OH, p. A503
SWAINE, Richard P., Chief Executive Officer, The University of Toledo Medical Center, Toledo, OH, p. A505
SWANDAL, Dianne, R.N., MSN, Vice President Patient Care, St. Josep. Hospital, Bangor, ME, p. A295
SWANGER, Cae, Chief Information Officer, Riverside Community Hospital, Riverside, CA, p. A86
SWANGER, Carol, Chief Nursing Officer, Kansas Rehabilitation Hospital, Topeka, KS, p. A260
SWANHORST, John, Interim Chief Executive Officer, Common Spirit St. Elizabeth Hospital, Fort Morgan, CO, p. A108
SWANK, Georgia, Chief Nursing Officer, Ridge Behavioral Health System, Lexington, KY, p. A269
SWANSON, Carey, Chief Executive Officer, Tidelands Health Rehabilitation Hospital, An Affiliate of Encompass Health, Murrells Inlet, SC, p. A569
SWANSON, Eric, President, Adventist Health Tillamook, Tillamook, OR, p. A533
SWANSON, Nicole, Vice President of Nursing, Aurora Medical Center – Bay Area, Marinette, WI, p. A715
SWARTOUT, Paula, Human Resources Manager, Marshfield Medical Center – Dickinson, Iron Mountain, MI, p. A330
SWARTWOOD, Peggy, Assistant Vice President, Finance and Controller, UHS Chenango Memorial Hospital, Norwich, NY, p. A454

Index of Health Care Professionals / Swartwood

SWARTWOOD, Philip. Director Information Systems, AHN Grove City, Grove City, PA, p. A541

SWARTZ, Edward, Chief Financial Officer, Spring Grove Hospital Center, Baltimore, MD, p. A302

SWARTZ, Michael J.
FACHE, Executive Director, Veterans Affairs Western New York Healthcare System, Veterans Affairs Western New York Healthcare System–Buffalo Division, Buffalo, NY, p. A440
FACHE, Interim Director, Veterans Affairs Western New York Healthcare System–Batavia Division, Batavia, NY, p. A439

SWAYNE, Angela, M.D., Chief Medical Officer, Piedmont Fayette Hospital, Fayetteville, GA, p. A164

SWEARINGEN, Angela, Chief Operating Officer, St. Mary's Medical Center, Huntington, WV, p. A701

SWEAT, Holli, Associate Administrator and Chief Nursing Officer, Memorial Satilla Health, Waycross, GA, p. A174

SWEAT, Kendra, Director Human Resources, Power County Hospital District, American Falls, ID, p. A179

SWEENEY, Brian
President, North Region, Jefferson Abington Health, Abington, PA, p. A534
President, North Region, Jefferson Einstein Montgomery Hospital, East Norriton, PA, p. A538
President, North Region, Jefferson Lansdale Hospital, Lansdale, PA, p. A544

SWEENEY, Janey, Chief Nursing Officer, Suncoast Behavioral Health Center, Bradenton, FL, p. A127

SWEENEY, Michael, Chief Information Officer, Fox Chase Cancer Center, Philadelphia, PA, p. A548

SWEENEY, Shaun, R.N., Vice President Patient Care Services, Hackensack Meridian Health Carrier Clinic, Belle Mead, NJ, p. A418

SWEET, Jeremiah, Chief Financial Officer, Oneida Healthcare, Oneida, NY, p. A455

SWEET, Renae, Chief Financial Officer, Surprise Valley Health Care District, Cedarville, CA, p. A59

SWEET, Ronda, Chief Nursing Officer, North Mississipp. Medical Center Gilmore-Amory, Amory, MS, p. A359

SWEET, Terrance J., Director Information Technology, Winnebago Mental Health Institute, Winnebago, WI, p. A725

SWEETNAM, Olivia, President & Chief Executive Officer, Grace Cottage Hospital, Townshend, VT, p. A672

SWEHA, Amir, M.D., Vice President Medical Administration, Methodist Hospital of Sacramento, Sacramento, CA, p. A87

SWEIS, Rolla, PharmD, President and Chief Executive Officer, La Rabida Children's Hospital, Chicago, IL, p. A190

SWEITZER, Gregory, Chief Medical Officer, Wright Patterson Medical Center, Wright-Patterson Afb, OH, p. A507

SWENSON, Andrea, Chief Executive Officer, Kittson Healthcare, Hallock, MN, p. A348

SWENSON, Lisa, Chief Executive Officer, Morton County Health System, Elkhart, KS, p. A248

SWENSON, Paula C., R.N., Vice President and Chief Nursing Officer, St. Catherine Hospital, East Chicago, IN, p. A215

SWENSON, Warren, Interim Executive Officer and Chief Financial Officer, United Medical Rehabilitation Hospital–Hammond, Hammond, LA, p. A283

SWICK, Michael D., President and Chief Executive Officer, Lima Memorial Health System, Lima, OH, p. A498

SWIDERSKI, Tom, Chief Financial Officer, Orthopaedic Hospital of Wisconsin, Glendale, WI, p. A711

SWIERS, Debbie, Director of Nursing, Haven Behavioral Hospital of Phoenix, Phoenix, AZ, p. A35

SWIFT, Brian M, Senior Administrator Plant Operations, Burke Rehabilitation Hospital, White Plains, NY, p. A462

SWIFT, David, Senior Vice President and Chief Human Resource Officer, Penn State Health Hampden Medical Center, Enola, PA, p. A539

SWIGER, Jared, Director Cyber Security, Ashtabula County Medical Center, Ashtabula, OH, p. A485

SWINDELL, Terry, Chief Financial Officer, West Tennessee Healthcare Camden Hospital, Camden, TN, p. A579

SWINDLE, Patrick, Chief Executive Officer, Seton Medical Center Harker Heights, Harker Heights, TX, p. A623

SWINDLER, Diana, Chief Financial Officer, Tri Valley Health System, Cambridge, NE, p. A398

SWINKO, Paul G.
Jr, Chief Finanial Officer, Aurelia Osborn Fox Memorial Hospital, Oneonta, NY, p. A455
Jr, Corporate Vice President and Chief Financial Officer, Bassett Medical Center, Cooperstown, NY, p. A441

SWINT, Ken
Adminstrative Director Finance, Promedica Memorial Hospital, Fremont, OH, p. A496
Director Finance, Promedica Defiance Regional Hospital, Defiance, OH, p. A494
Vice President Finance and Chief Financial Officer, Promedica Fostoria Community Hospital, Fostoria, OH, p. A496

SWINT, Patricia, Director Information Management Systems, Promedica Defiance Regional Hospital, Defiance, OH, p. A494

SWISHER, Kay, Chief Nursing Officer, Prisma Health Laurens County Hospital, Clinton, SC, p. A564

SWISSHELM, Patricia, Acting Chief Fiscal Service, Lexington Vamc, Lexington, KY, p. A268

SWOFFORD, William, M.D., Chief of Staff, Miller County Hospital, Colquitt, GA, p. A161

SY, Annette, Chief Nursing Officer, USC Norris Comprehensive Cancer Center And Hospital, Los Angeles, CA, p. A75

SYED, Imran, Manager Technology Information Services, Corewell Health Zeeland Hospital, Zeeland, MI, p. A341

SYED, Mamoon
Vice President Human Resources, Children's Hospital of Orange County, Orange, CA, p. A81
Vice President Human Resources, Rady Children's Hospital – San Diego, San Diego, CA, p. A89

SYKES, Angel, Director Human Resources, Memorial Hospital And Manor, Bainbridge, GA, p. A159

SYKES, Christina, Director Human Resources, Labette Health, Parsons, KS, p. A258

SYKES, Lisa
Director Information Services, Atrium Health Union, Monroe, NC, p. A472
IS/Communications Director, Atrium Health Anson, Wadesboro, NC, p. A477
Manager, Information Services, Atrium Health Cabarrus, Concord, NC, p. A466

SYKES, Rebecca S, Chief Information Officer, Mercy Health – Fairfield Hospital, Fairfield, OH, p. A495

SYLVIA, John B., President and Chief Executive Officer, Grant Memorial Hospital, Petersburg, WV, p. A703

SYLVIA-HUTCHINSON, Doreen M, Vice President Operations and Chief Nurse Executive, Fairview Hospital, Great Barrington, MA, p. A314

SYNDERGAARD, Christy, Vice President Nursing, Cherokee Regional Medical Center, Cherokee, IA, p. A232

SYNNESTVEDT, Eric, Director Information Technology, Bon Secours – Southside Medical Center, Petersburg, VA, p. A681

SYPIEN, Troy
Director Information Technology and Systems, Medical City Dallas, Dallas, TX, p. A611
Director Information Technology and Systems, Tristar Skyline Medical Center, Nashville, TN, p. A591

SZABO, Sandor, M.D., Ph.D., M.P.H., Chief of Staff, Tibor Rubin Va Medical Center, Long Beach, CA, p. A71

SZAPOR, Ann, Vice President and Chief Nursing Officer, Memorial Hermann Greater Heights Hospital, Houston, TX, p. A627

SZCZEPANSKI, Bernadette S, Senior Vice President, Human Resources, Northwestern Medicine Mchenry, Mchenry, IL, p. A201

SZCZUROWSKI, Richard, Director Human Resources, Norristown State Hospital, Norristown, PA, p. A547

SZEKELY, Lauraine, R.N., Senior Vice President, Patient Care, Northern Westchester Hospital, Mount Kisco, NY, p. A446

SZEWCZYK, Edwin, Chief Financial Officer, Wetzel County Hospital, New Martinsville, WV, p. A703

SZKOLNICKI, Michele, R.N., Senior Vice President and Chief Nursing Officer, Penn State Milton S. Hershey Medical Center, Hershey, PA, p. A542

SZOSTEK, Joshua
Chief Financial Officer, Broward Health North, Deerfield Beach, FL, p. A130
Chief Financial Officer, Pam Health Specialty Hospital of Jacksonville, Jacksonville, FL, p. A135

SZURA, Kathleen, R.N., Chief Nursing Officer, Encompass Health Rehabilitation Hospital of Bakersfield, Bakersfield, CA, p. A57

SZYMANIAK, Michael, Deputy Commander for Nursing, Bayne-Jones Army Community Hospital, Fort Polk, LA, p. A282

T

TAAFFE, Janette L., Vice President, Human Resource, St. Luke's Hospital, Chesterfield, MO, p. A373

TABIBI, Wasae S, M.D., President Medical Staff, Vibra Hospital of Houston, Houston, TX, p. A628

TABOR, Jeffrey, Director Human Resources, Jackson General Hospital, Ripley, WV, p. A704

TABOR, Tammie, Chief Executive Officer, Vibra Rehabilitation Hospital of Amarillo, Amarillo, TX, p. A596

TABOR, Theresa, Vice President of Finance and Chief Financial Officer, Family Health West, Fruita, CO, p. A108

TABORA, Knaya, Chief Operating Officer and Chief Nursing Officer, Colorado River Medical Center, Needles, CA, p. A80

TABUENCA, Arnold, M.D., Medical Director, Riverside University Health System–Medical Center, Moreno Valley, CA, p. A78

TACHIBANA, Charleen, R.N., Senior Vice President and Chief Nursing Officer, Virginia Mason Medical Center, Seattle, WA, p. A695

TACKE, Mike, Chief Executive Officer, The Vines, Ocala, FL, p. A143

TACKETT, Andrea, Chief of Staff, French Hospital Medical Center, San Luis Obispo, CA, p. A93

TACKETT, Sharon R., R.N., Chief Nursing Officer, Monroe Surgical Hospital, Monroe, LA, p. A288

TACKITT, Sue, Chief Nursing Officer, Connally Memorial Medical Center, Floresville, TX, p. A618

TADURAN, Virgilio, M.D., Chief Medical Officer, Satanta District Hospital And Long Term Care, Satanta, KS, p. A259

TAFOYA, Debbie, Vice President and Chief Information Officer, Huntington Health, Pasadena, CA, p. A83

TAFOYA, Tabatha, Director Human Resources, Newman Regional Health, Emporia, KS, p. A249

TAGGART, Christopher, M.D., Chief Medical Officer, Family Health West, Fruita, CO, p. A108

TAGGART, Travis, Director Information Technology, Rivervalley Behavioral Health Hospital, Owensboro, KY, p. A272

TAGGE, Gordon, M.D., President Medical Staff, Three Rivers Hospital, Brewster, WA, p. A687

TAHAN, Pamela S., Chief Executive Officer, Wellington Regional Medical Center, Wellington, FL, p. A154

TAHBO, Robin, Financial Management Officer, U. S. Public Health Service Indian Hospital, Parker, AZ, p. A34

TAILLEFER, Marguerite, M.D., Acting President Medical Staff, Sarah D. Culbertson Memorial Hospital, Rushville, IL, p. A208

TAIT, Matt, JD, Chief Executive Officer, Meadowbrook Rehabilitation Hospital, Gardner, KS, p. A249

TAKACS, Susan, Market Chief Operating Officer, Physicians Regional – Pine Ridge, Naples, FL, p. A142

TAKES, Kay
R.N., President, Mercyone Dubuque Medical Center, Dubuque, IA, p. A235
R.N., President, Mercyone Dyersville Medical Center, Dyersville, IA, p. A236

TAKEUCHI, Susi
Chief Human Resources and Organization Development Officer, Ronald Reagan Ucla Medical Center, Los Angeles, CA, p. A75
Chief Human Resources and Organization Development Officer, Stewart & Lynda Resnick Neuropsychiatric Hospital At Ucla, Los Angeles, CA, p. A75

TALAMANTE, Thomas, Medical Center Director, Ioannis A. Lougaris Veterans' Administration Medical Center, Reno, NV, p. A412

TALARICO, Fred, Chief Medical Officer, Wynn Hospital, Utica, NY, p. A460

TALAVERA REYES, José M.
Administrator, Wilma N. Vazquez Medical Center, Vega Baja, PR, p. A736
Executive Director, Hospital Metropolitano, San Juan, PR, p. A735

TALBERT, Bradley S., FACHE, Chief Executive Officer, Memorial Health University Medical Center, Savannah, GA, p. A171

TALBOT, Jack, Director, Human Resources, West Chester Hospital, West Chester, OH, p. A506

TALBOT, Lisa, Director Human Resources, St. David's South Austin Medical Center, Austin, TX, p. A600

TALBOTT, Drew, President, Mercy Hospital Pittsburg, Pittsburg, KS, p. A258

TALBOTT, Sarah, Chief Nursing Officer, Sanford Chamberlain Medical Center, Chamberlain, SD, p. A572

TALLEY, Cyndi, Director Information Systems, Tristar Greenview Regional Hospital, Bowling Green, KY, p. A264

TALLEY, Linda, MS, R.N., Vice President and Chief Nursing Officer, Children's National Hospital, Washington, DC, p. A123

TALLEY, Stephanie S.
Chief Human Resource Officer, The Hospitals of Providence Sierra Campus – Tenet Healthcare, El Paso, TX, p. A617
Chief Human Resource Officer, The Hospitals of Providence Transmountain Campus – Tenet Healthcare, El Paso, TX, p. A617

Index of Health Care Professionals / Taylor

Index of Health Care Professionals

Director Human Resources, Baylor Scott & White Medical Center – Centennial, Frisco, TX, p. A621
Market Chief Human Resource Officer, The Hospitals of Providence Memorial Campus – Tenet Healthcare, El Paso, TX, p. A617
TALLEY, Tracey, Chief Financial and Information Officer, Logan Health, Kalispell, MT, p. A393
TALLON, Joe, Vice President Finance, Salina Regional Health Center, Salina, KS, p. A259
TALLON, Richard, Chief Financial Officer, Jefferson County Hospital, Waurika, OK, p. A524
TALTY, Stephen, M.D., Medical Director, Encompass Health Rehabilitation Institute of Libertyville, Libertyville, IL, p. A200
TAM, David A., M.D., FACHE, President and Chief Executive Officer, Beebe Healthcare, Lewes, DE, p. A121
TAMANAHA, Nona, Vice President Human Resources, The Queen's Medical Center, Honolulu, HI, p. A176
TAMBON, Natalie
Director of Human Resources, Jenkins County Medical Center, Millen, GA, p. A168
Director of Human Resources, Optim Medical Center – Screven, Sylvania, GA, p. A172
TAMBURELLO, Leonardo, Chief Financial Officer, New York Community Hospital, New York, NY, p. A450
TAMMARO, Vincent, Chief Financial Officer and Vice President for Health Sciences, Ohio State University Wexner Medical Center, Columbus, OH, p. A492
TAMMINEN, John, M.D., President Medical Staff, Carilion Giles Community Hospital, Pearisburg, VA, p. A681
TAN, Bradford, M.D., Chief Medical Officer, City of Hop. Chicago, Zion, IL, p. A211
TANCREDO, Beth, Director Operations, South Florida Baptist Hospital, Plant City, FL, p. A147
TANDE, Brett, Chief Financial Officer, Santa Ynez Valley Cottage Hospital, Solvang, CA, p. A96
TANDON, Satwant, M.D., Director of Clinical Services, Oklahoma Forensic Center, Vinita, OK, p. A523
TANDY, Gary R, Chief Financial Officer, Pershing Memorial Hospital, Brookfield, MO, p. A372
TANDY, William C., Chief Information Officer, UPMC Hanover, Hanover, PA, p. A541
TANEBAUM, Cynthia, Director Information Services, Medstar Harbor Hospital, Baltimore, MD, p. A301
TANEJA, K. Singh, Chief Operating Officer, Saint Elizabeths Hospital, Washington, DC, p. A124
TANG, Francis, Chief Information Officer, Rancho Los Amigos National Rehabilitation Center, Downey, CA, p. A62
TANG, Shirley, R.N., Chief Nursing Officer, Monterey Park Hospital, Monterey Park, CA, p. A78
TANG, Tri, Vice President, Atrium Health Lincoln, Lincolnton, NC, p. A472
TANGEMAN, Todd
Chief Operating Officer, Nmc Health, Newton, KS, p. A255
Chief Operating Officer and Chief Human Resource Officer, Nmc Health, Newton, KS, p. A255
TANGO, Jonathan, Vice President, Operations, Monmouth Medical Center, Southern Campus, Lakewood, NJ, p. A422
TANGUAY, Denis, Chief Information Officer, Central Maine Medical Center, Lewiston, ME, p. A297
TANJUAKIO, Robert, Chief Information Resources Management, Edward Hines, Jr. Veterans Affairs Hospital, Hines, IL, p. A198
TANKEL, Nancy, R.N., Chief Nurse Executive, Kaiser Permanente Woodland Hills Medical Center, Los Angeles, CA, p. A73
TANKERSLEY, Amy, Director of Operations, Texarkana Emergency Center & Hospital, Texarkana, TX, p. A657
TANNENBAUM, Jordan, Chief Information Officer and Chief Medical Information Officer, Saint Peter's Healthcare System, New Brunswick, NJ, p. A425
TANNENBAUM, Scott, M.D., Medical Director, Encompass Health Rehabilitation Hospital of Sunrise, Sunrise, FL, p. A151
TANNER, Ashley, Director of Nursing, Wiregrass Medical Center, Geneva, AL, p. A20
TANNER, James, M.D., Chief Medical Officer, Northwest Medical Center – Springdale, Springdale, AR, p. A53
TANNOS, Paul, Chief Financial Officer, The Physicians Centre Hospital, Bryan, TX, p. A605
TANTHOREY, Geoff, Director, Information Systems, Granville Health System, Oxford, NC, p. A474
TAPIA, Hector, Manager, Information Technology, Multy Medical Rehabilitation Hospital San Juan, San Juan, PR, p. A735
TAPLETT, Dean, Controller, Quincy Valley Medical Center, Quincy, WA, p. A693
TAPLIN, Tyrrell, Chief Executive Officer, Reunion Rehabilitation Hospital Arlington, Arlington, TX, p. A598
TAPP, Gina
Director Human Resources, Samaritan North Lincoln Hospital, Lincoln City, OR, p. A528
Director Human Resources, Samaritan Pacific Communities Hospital, Newport, OR, p. A529
TARAR, Ahmad, M.D., Medical Director, Heartland Behavioral Health Services, Nevada, MO, p. A381
TARASOVICH, James, Chief Financial Officer, Mayo Clinic Health System In Saint James, Saint James, MN, p. A354
TARBAY, Amy, Director Nursing Services, Naval Hospital Pensacola, Pensacola, FL, p. A146
TARBET, Joyce, M.D., Chief Medical Officer, Murray County Medical Center, Slayton, MN, p. A355
TARDIF, Kathleen, Director of Human Resources, Central Regional Hospital, Butner, NC, p. A464
TAROLA, Robert, Chief Financial Officer, OSF Healthcare Little Company of Mary Medical Center, Evergreen Park, IL, p. A195
TARRANT, Jeffrey S., FACHE, Chief Executive Officer, Upson Regional Medical Center, Thomaston, GA, p. A172
TARRANT–FITZGERALD, Maureen, President and Chief Executive Officer, Presbyterian/St. Luke's Medical Center, Denver, CO, p. A106
TART, Chris, PharmD, President, Hoke Hospital, Raeford, NC, p. A474
TART, Michael, President, Highsmith–Rainey Specialty Hospital, Fayetteville, NC, p. A468
TARULLI, Pamela, Senior Vice President Human Resources, Good Samaritan Regional Medical Center, Suffern, NY, p. A459
TARVER, Dennis, Director Information Technology, Elkview General Hospital, Hobart, OK, p. A513
TARVER, Jeanette, Director of Finance, Sonoma Valley Hospital, Sonoma, CA, p. A96
TARVER, Rebecca, Chief Nursing Officer, Bates County Memorial Hospital, Butler, MO, p. A372
TASMAN, William, M.D., Ophthalmologist in Chief, Wills Eye Hospital, Philadelphia, PA, p. A550
TASSIN, Bruce J., Interim Chief Executive Officer, Norton Scott Hospital, Scottsburg, IN, p. A227
TATE, Charles, Director Information Technology, Lallie Kemp Medical Center, Independence, LA, p. A283
TATE, James, M.D., Chief of Staff, Patients' Hospital of Redding, Redding, CA, p. A85
TATE, Jean, Vice President Human Resources, Riverview Health, Crookston, MN, p. A345
TATE, Mary Lou, Chief Financial Officer, Morris Hospital & Healthcare Centers, Morris, IL, p. A202
TATE CURTI, Joseph, Chief Operating Officer, Elliot Hospital, Manchester, NH, p. A416
TATRO, Chad, Supervisor Information Systems, Northeast Regional Medical Center, Kirksville, MO, p. A378
TATRO, Mary Esq, Chief Nursing Officer, Millinocket Regional Hospital, Millinocket, ME, p. A298
TATU, Ryan, Chief Executive Officer, Lancaster Behavioral Health Hospital, Lancaster, PA, p. A543
TAUL, Kelly, Business Manager, Meadowbrook Rehabilitation Hospital, Gardner, KS, p. A249
TAUNTON, David, M.D., Chief of Staff, Texas Health Harris Methodist Hospital Southlake, Southlake, TX, p. A653
TAUTZ, Linda
Chief Executive Officer, Dignity Health Rehabilitation Hospital, Henderson, NV, p. A409
Market Chief Executive Officer, Dignity St. Rose – Craig Ranch, North Las Vegas, NV, p. A411
TAVARES–SILVA, Naomi, Center Director, Pocasset Mental Health Center, Pocasset, MA, p. A317
TAWNEY, Michael W, D.O., Vice President Medical Affairs, Mclaren Port Huron, Port Huron, MI, p. A336
TAYLOR, Adam, Manager Information Technology, Northern Inyo Hospital, Bishop. CA, p. A58
TAYLOR, Adrienne, Director of Health Information Management, Delta Health – Northwest Regional, Clarksdale, MS, p. A360
TAYLOR, Amy, Chief Financial Officer, Oklahoma Center for Orthopaedic And Multi–Specialty Surgery, Oklahoma City, OK, p. A518
TAYLOR, Anthony, Manager Information Technology, Cherokee Indian Hospital, Cherokee, NC, p. A466
TAYLOR, Ashley, Administrator, Medicine Lodge Memorial Hospital, Medicine Lodge, KS, p. A254
TAYLOR, Beth, Vice President, Human Resources, Newton–Wellesley Hospital, Newton Lower Falls, MA, p. A316
TAYLOR, Brenda, Director Information Systems, Texas Health Harris Methodist Hospital Cleburne, Cleburne, TX, p. A607
TAYLOR, Brett, Director Hospital Information Systems, Ohiohealth Van Wert Hospital, Van Wert, OH, p. A505
TAYLOR, Cecilia, Chief Financial Officer, City of Hop. Chicago, Zion, IL, p. A211
TAYLOR, Chase, Chief Executive Officer, San Joaquin Valley Rehabilitation Hospital, Fresno, CA, p. A65
TAYLOR, Cherie
President, Logan Health – Cut Bank, Cut Bank, MT, p. A391
President, Logan Health Chester, Chester, MT, p. A390
TAYLOR, Cheryl, R.N., Director of Nursing, Henry Ford Kingswood Hospital, Ferndale, MI, p. A326
TAYLOR, Christina, Director Human Resources, The Brook Hospital – Kmi, Louisville, KY, p. A270
TAYLOR, Clay, Chief Operating Officer, Covenant Children's Hospital, Lubbock, TX, p. A635
TAYLOR, Dana Shantel, Chief Operating Officer, Fairfield Memorial Hospital, Fairfield, IL, p. A195
TAYLOR, Danna, Interim President, South Arkansas Regional Hospital, El Dorado, AR, p. A45
TAYLOR, Deborah, Chief Information Officer, UNC Health Chatham, Siler City, NC, p. A476
TAYLOR, Debra, Chief Nursing Officer, Paris Regional Medical Center, Paris, TX, p. A642
TAYLOR, Donovan, Chief Administrative Officer, Providence Santa Rosa Memorial Hospital, Santa Rosa, CA, p. A95
TAYLOR, Dwayne, Chief Executive Officer, Southeast Market, Sycamore Shoals Hospital, Elizabethton, TN, p. A582
TAYLOR, Ernest Lee, M.D., Vice President Medical Affairs, St. Mary's Medical Center, Huntington, WV, p. A701
TAYLOR, Eulon Ross, Clinical Director, North Texas State Hospital, Wichita Falls Campus, Wichita Falls, TX, p. A662
TAYLOR, Gregory W, M.D., Vice President and Chief Operating Officer, Atrium Health Wake Foret Baptist High Point Medical Center, High Point, NC, p. A470
TAYLOR, Heather, Human Resources Manager, Tippah County Hospital, Ripley, MS, p. A368
TAYLOR, Heidi, President, Morton Hospital And Medical Center, Taunton, MA, p. A319
TAYLOR, J. Tyler., FACHE, Chief Executive Officer, Elbert Memorial Hospital, Elberton, GA, p. A163
TAYLOR, Janey, Chief Information and Technology, Overton Brooks Veterans' Administration Medical Center, Shreveport, LA, p. A292
TAYLOR, Jay, M.D., Chief of Medical Staff, Logan Health – Conrad, Conrad, MT, p. A390
TAYLOR, Jeff
Chief Executive Officer, HCA Florida Orange Park Hospital, Orange Park, FL, p. A144
Vice President Finance, St. Luke's Regional Medical Center, Boise, ID, p. A180
TAYLOR, Jim
Chief Business Office, North Florida/South Georgia Veteran's Health System, Gainesville, FL, p. A132
Computer Network Specialist II, Thomas B. Finan Center, Cumberland, MD, p. A303
TAYLOR, Joel
Chief Information Officer, Carepoint Health Bayonne Medical Center, Bayonne, NJ, p. A418
Chief Information Officer, Carepoint Health Hoboken University Medical Center, Hoboken, NJ, p. A422
TAYLOR, Joel C., Market Chief Executive Officer, Hilton Head Hospital, Hilton Head Island, SC, p. A568
TAYLOR, Julia, Area Director Human Resources, Vibra Hospital of Charleston, Mt. Pleasant, SC, p. A569
TAYLOR, Julie, Chief Executive Officer, West Tennessee Healthcare Rehabilitation Hospital Jackson, A Partnership With Encompass Health, Jackson, TN, p. A584
TAYLOR, Konnie, Chief Financial Officer, Carl Albert Community Mental Health Center, Mcalester, OK, p. A514
TAYLOR, Kristie, Chief Financial Officer, Southern Tennessee Regional Health System–Lawrenceburg, Lawrenceburg, TN, p. A586
TAYLOR, Marc, IS Director, Mountain West Medical Center, Tooele, UT, p. A670
TAYLOR, Marcia, Chief Executive Officer, Select Specialty Hospital–Memphis, Memphis, TN, p. A589
TAYLOR, Melissa, R.N., MSN, Chief Nursing Officer, Lexington Medical Center, West Columbia, SC, p. A571
TAYLOR, Meredith, Controller, South Sunflower County Hospital, Indianola, MS, p. A363
TAYLOR, Merle
President, UCHealth Highlands Ranch Hospital, Highlands Ranch, CO, p. A109
Vice President Operations, UPMC St. Margaret, Pittsburgh, PA, p. A552
TAYLOR, Michael
M.D., Chief Medical Officer, Cleveland Clinic Avon Hospital, Avon, OH, p. A485
Chief Information Officer, Bon Secours St. Francis Hospital, Charleston, SC, p. A563
Vice President Financial Services and Chief Financial Officer, St. Rose Hospital, Hayward, CA, p. A67
TAYLOR, Michael V
Senior Vice President Human Resources, Sentara Leigh Hospital, Norfolk, VA, p. A680

© 2025 AHA Guide Index of Health Care Professionals A987

Vice President Human Resources, Sentara Princess Anne Hospital, Virginia Beach, VA, p. A684
TAYLOR, Patrick, M.D., President and Chief Executive Officer, York Hospital, York, ME, p. A299
TAYLOR, Paul, Chief Executive Officer, Ozarks Community Hospital, Gravette, AR, p. A47
TAYLOR, Renae, Chief Nursing Officer, UNC Health Southeastern, Lumberton, NC, p. A472
TAYLOR, Richard, Chief Financial Officer, Western Mental Health Institute, Bolivar, TN, p. A579
TAYLOR, Robbie, Director Human Resources, North Sunflower Medical Center, Ruleville, MS, p. A368
TAYLOR, Robert
  Associate Medical Center Director, Chillicothe Veterans Affairs Medical Center, Chillicothe, OH, p. A488
  Director Information Services, St. Christopher's Hospital for Children, Philadelphia, PA, p. A550
TAYLOR, Ross, M.D., Clinical Director, Austin State Hospital, Austin, TX, p. A599
TAYLOR, Russell, Comptroller, Idaho Falls Community Hospital, Idaho Falls, ID, p. A181
TAYLOR, Sarah, Chief Human Resources, National Jewish Health, Denver, CO, p. A106
TAYLOR, Scotty, Information Technology Director, East Mississipp. State Hospital, Meridian, MS, p. A366
TAYLOR, Sharon, Human Resources Director, Allegiance Specialty Hospital of Greenville, Greenville, MS, p. A362
TAYLOR, Sheri, Director Human Resources, Union General Hospital, Farmerville, LA, p. A281
TAYLOR, Stacy, Chief Financial Officer, Nemaha County Hospital, Auburn, NE, p. A397
TAYLOR, Steve, Chief Information Officer, Baptist Anderson Regional Medical Center – South, Meridian, MS, p. A366
TAYLOR, Sue O., Vice President Nursing, ECU Health Duplin Hospital, Kenansville, NC, p. A471
TAYLOR, Todd, Chief Executive Officer, Stafford County Hospital, Stafford, KS, p. A260
TAYLOR, Tyrone, Chief Financial Officer, Veterans Affairs New Jersey Health Care System, East Orange, NJ, p. A420
TAYLOR, Venus, Director Human Resources, Bhc Alhambra Hospital, Rosemead, CA, p. A86
TEAFF, Sarah, Chief Executive Officer, Patterson Health Center, Anthony, KS, p. A246
TEAGUE, Lara Ellen, R.N., Chief Nursing Officer, Lillian M. Hudspeth Memorial Hospital, Sonora, TX, p. A653
TEAHL, Bradley, Director Human Resources, Encompass Health Rehabilitation Hospital of York, York, PA, p. A558
TEAL, Amy, Chief Executive Officer, Lancaster Rehabilitation Hospital, Lancaster, PA, p. A543
TEAL, Barbara, R.N., Associate Director Patient Care Services and Nurse Executive, Royal C. Johnson Veterans' Memorial Hospital, Sioux Falls, SD, p. A576
TEAL, Cydney, M.D., Vice President Medical Affairs, Christianacare, Union Hospital, Elkton, MD, p. A304
TEATSORTH, Neil, Vice President Human Resources, Humboldt Park Health, Chicago, IL, p. A189
TEBBE, James, M.D., Vice President Medical Affairs, Ochsner Medical Center – Kenner, Kenner, LA, p. A284
TEBRINK, Ron, Chief Information Officer, Friend Community Healthcare System, Friend, NE, p. A400
TEDDER, Cookie, Human Resources Manager, Texas Health Center for Diagnostic & Surgery, Plano, TX, p. A645
TEDESCO, Art, Interim Chief Financial Officer, Gaylord Specialty Healthcare, Wallingford, CT, p. A119
TEEL, David R., Financial Officer, Terrell State Hospital, Terrell, TX, p. A656
TEER, Chasity, Chief Nursing Officer, Ochsner Lsu Health Shreveport – St. Mary Medical Center, Llc, Shreveport, LA, p. A292
TEETER, Stephen, Business Manager, Hawaii State Hospital, Kaneohe, HI, p. A177
TEETERS, John, M.D., President and Chief Executive Officer, Nicholas H. Noyes Memorial Hospital, Dansville, NY, p. A442
TEICHMEIER, Laura, Director Human Resources, Memorial Community Health, Aurora, NE, p. A397
TEIGEN, Seth R.
  Chief Executive, Providence Mission Hospital Mission Viejo, Mission Viejo, CA, p. A77
  Chief Executive Officer, Providence Mission Hospital Mission Viejo, Mission Viejo, CA, p. A77
TEIXEIRA, Marion, Chief Executive Officer, Ascension St. Vincent Anderson, Anderson, IN, p. A212
TEJADA, Vanessa, Director Human Resources, Encompass Health Rehabilitation Hospital of San Antonio, San Antonio, TX, p. A649
TEJEDA-BLANCO, Amanda, Chief Executive Officer, Behavioral Hospital of Bellaire, Houston, TX, p. A625
TELHIARD, Nicole, Senior Vice President, Patient Care Services, Our Lady of The Lake Regional Medical Center, Baton Rouge, LA, p. A278

TELITZ, Rita, Chief Administrative Officer, Marshfield Medical Center – Ladysmith, Ladysmith, WI, p. A714
TELLOR, Tammy, Acting Director Human Resources, Choate Mental Health Center, Anna, IL, p. A185
TELTHORSTER, M.ED, Marcia M, Vice President Human Resources, Penn Medicine Princeton Medical Center, Plainsboro, NJ, p. A427
TEMPLE, Amber L, Director Human Resources, Morrison Community Hospital, Morrison, IL, p. A202
TEMPLE, Richard, Chief Information Officer, Deborah Heart And Lung Center, Browns Mills, NJ, p. A419
TEMPLETON, Gary, M.D., Medical Director, Regency Hospital of Northwest Arkansas – Springdale, Springdale, AR, p. A53
TEMPLETON, Sheryl, Chief Financial Officer, Scotland County Hospital, Memphis, MO, p. A380
TEMPLETON, William, M.D., III, Medical Director, Norton Clark Hospital, Jeffersonville, IN, p. A221
TENHOUSE, Steven, FACHE, Chief Executive Officer, Kirby Medical Center, Monticello, IL, p. A202
TENNEY, Ralph
  Chief Information Officer, Ascension Macomb–Oakland Hospital, Warren Campus, Warren, MI, p. A340
  Chief Information Officer, Ascension Providence Rochester Hospital, Rochester, MI, p. A336
  Chief Information Officer, Ascension St. John Hospital, Detroit, MI, p. A325
TENNISON, Gary, M.D., Chief of Staff, Crawford Memorial Hospital, Robinson, IL, p. A207
TENNYSON, Ruby, Director Administration, Naval Hospital Jacksonville, Jacksonville, FL, p. A135
TENREIRO, Edgardo J.
  FACHE, President and Chief Executive Officer, Baton Rouge General Medical Center, Baton Rouge, LA, p. A277
  FACHE, President and Chief Executive Officer, The General, Baton Rouge, LA, p. A278
  FACHE, President, Chief Executive Officer and Chief Operating Officer, Baton Rouge General Medical Center, Baton Rouge, LA, p. A277
TEPEDINO, Miguel, M.D., Chief Medicine, HCA Florida Lake City Hospital, Lake City, FL, p. A136
TER HORST, Thomas C, Vice President Human Resources, Aurora St. Luke's Medical Center, Milwaukee, WI, p. A717
TERAULT, Chelsey, Manager Human Resources, Pembina County Memorial Hospital And Wedgewood Manor, Cavalier, ND, p. A480
TERBUSH, Jennifer, Vice President, Patient Services, Hills & Dales Healthcare, Cass City, MI, p. A323
TERI, Anthony, Director Information Technology, Hackensack Meridian Health Pascack Valley Medical Center, Westwood, NJ, p. A430
TERPSTRA, John, M.D., Chief Medical Officer, Mercer Health, Coldwater, OH, p. A491
TERRELL, Jay, Manager Management Information Systems, Riverview Regional Medical Center, Gadsden, AL, p. A20
TERRELL-FAKOREDE, Etene, Chief Executive Officer, The Rehabilitation Institute of Ohio, Dayton, OH, p. A494
TERRINONI, Gary G., President and Chief Executive Officer, Brooklyn Hospital Center, New York, NY, p. A447
TERRY, Darrell K. Sr, M.P.H., FACHE, President and Chief Executive Officer, Newark Beth Israel Medical Center, Newark, NJ, p. A425
TERRY, Randi, Site Director Management Information Systems, Munson Healthcare Cadillac Hospital, Cadillac, MI, p. A323
TERRY, Richard, Vice President & Chief Information Officer, University of Michigan Health–Sparrow Carson, Carson City, MI, p. A323
TERRY, Shawn
  Secretary of Health, Council Oak Comprehensive Healthcare, Tulsa, OK, p. A522
  Secretary of Health, Creek Nation Community Hospital, Okemah, OK, p. A516
TERRY, Teresa, Director Human Resource, Payroll, Fisher County Hospital District, Rotan, TX, p. A647
TERRY-WILLIAMS, Teresa, R.N., Chief Nursing Officer, Pennsylvania Psychiatric Institute, Harrisburg, PA, p. A541
TERTEL, Jenifer K, Director Human Resources, Medical City Dallas, Dallas, TX, p. A611
TERWILLIGER, George, Chief Medical Officer, Grace Cottage Hospital, Townshend, VT, p. A672
TERWILLIGER, Michael, Chief Financial Officer, Friends Hospital, Philadelphia, PA, p. A548
TESKE, Mark, Chief Financial Officer, Hill Crest Behavioral Health Services, Birmingham, AL, p. A17
TESSARZIK, Connie, Business Manager, Albert J. Solnit Children's Center, Middletown, CT, p. A116
TESTA, Nick, M.D., Chief Medical Officer, Providence Saint Josep. Medical Center, Burbank, CA, p. A58

TESTER, Shawn, Chief Executive Officer, Northeastern Vermont Regional Hospital, Saint Johnsbury, VT, p. A672
TETZ, Warren
  Chief Financial Officer, Adventist Health Howard Memorial, Willits, CA, p. A101
  Chief Financial Officer, Adventist Health Mendocino Coast, Fort Bragg, CA, p. A63
  Chief Financial Officer, Adventist Health Ukiah Valley, Ukiah, CA, p. A99
TEUFEL, George, Vice President Finance, Advocate Good Shepherd Hospital, Barrington, IL, p. A186
TEUSCHER, Jill, Chief Nursing Officer, Heber Valley Hospital, Heber City, UT, p. A665
TEVES, Alicia, Coordinator Human Resources, Molokai General Hospital, Kaunakakai, HI, p. A177
TEWARI, Arun, M.D., Chief Medical Officer, Henry Community Health, New Castle, IN, p. A225
THACKER, Adam, Chief Operating Officer, Good Samaritan Hospital, Vincennes, IN, p. A228
THACKER, Kelly S., Chief Executive Officer, Old Vineyard Behavioral Health Services, Winston–Salem, NC, p. A478
THACKER, Roland, Chief Financial Officer, Piedmont Columbus Regional Northside, Columbus, GA, p. A161
THAI, Francisca, Chief Financial Officer, HCA Florida Capital Hospital, Tallahassee, FL, p. A151
THAKOR, Pratapji, M.D., Chief of Staff, SMC Regional Medical Center, Osceola, AR, p. A52
THAKUR, Abhash, M.D., Chief of Staff, Greenwood Leflore Hospital, Greenwood, MS, p. A362
THALER, Klaus, FACS, M.D., Chief Medical Officer, Houston Methodist Baytown Hospital, Baytown, TX, p. A601
THAMA, Todd, Chief Operating Officer, Fairfax Behavioral Health, Kirkland, WA, p. A691
THAMES, Stephen, Chief Financial Officer, Allen Parish Community Healthcare, Kinder, LA, p. A285
THARP, Jo, Interim Chief Executive Officer, Phillip. County Hospital, Malta, MT, p. A394
THARP, Stephen
  Medical Director, Indiana University Health Frankfort, Frankfort, IN, p. A217
  Regional Chief Medical Officer, Ascension St. Vincent Clay Hospital, Brazil, IN, p. A213
THAUNG, Htin, M.D., Chief Medical Officer, Ward Memorial Hospital, Monahans, TX, p. A640
THAYER, Charles, M.D., Chief Medical Officer, Morton Hospital And Medical Center, Taunton, MA, p. A319
THAYER, Gilbert M., M.D., Chief Medical Staff, Hardin Medical Center, Savannah, TN, p. A592
THAYER, Kendra, MSN, R.N., Chief Nursing Officer, Vice President Clinical Services, Garrett Regional Medical Center, Oakland, MD, p. A306
THEILER, Teresa
  Chief Administrative Officer, Aspirus Steven's Point Hospital & Clinics, Inc., Stevens Point, WI, p. A722
  President – North Region, Aspirus Rhinelander Hospital, Rhinelander, WI, p. A720
  President – North Region, Howard Young Medical Center, Inc., Woodruff, WI, p. A725
  President, Aspirus Eagle River Hospital, Eagle River, WI, p. A710
THEINE, Joseph, Chief Executive Officer, Southwest Health System, Cortez, CO, p. A105
THEIRING, James, Chief Executive Officer, Mission Community Hospital, Los Angeles, CA, p. A74
THEISEN, Janet
  Chief Information Officer, Sanford Tracy Medical Center, Tracy, MN, p. A356
  Chief Information Officer, Sanford Westbrook Medical Center, Westbrook, MN, p. A357
THELEN, Deann, Vice President and Chief Executive Officer, Jackson–Madison County General Hospital, Medina, TN, p. A588
THELEN, Raymond Scott, Vice President and Chief Financial Officer, Masonicare Health Center, Wallingford, CT, p. A119
THEOBALD, Terry, Chief Information Officer, Ventura County Medical Center, Ventura, CA, p. A100
THEODOROU, Andreas, Chief Medical Officer, Banner – University Medical Center Tucson, Tucson, AZ, p. A40
THERIAC, Gary, Director Information Technology, Lawrence County Memorial Hospital, Lawrenceville, IL, p. A200
THERMITUS, Manoucheka, Chief Operating Officer, Saint Francis Hospital, Memphis, TN, p. A589
THERRIEN, Charles D., President, Northern Light Mercy Hospital, Portland, ME, p. A298
THERRIEN, Tinna Marie, R.N., Chief Information Officer and Senior Director Ancillary Services, Gothenburg Health, Gothenburg, NE, p. A400
THETFORD, Carol, Chief Nursing Officer, Baptist Memorial Hospital for Women, Memphis, TN, p. A588

THEUS, Will, M.D., Chief of Staff, Adventhealth Gordon, Calhoun, GA, p. A160
THIBERT, Kimberly, R.N., MSN, Vice President Patient Care Services and Chief Nursing Officer, Samaritan Medical Center, Watertown, NY, p. A461
THIBODEAU, Helene, R.N., MSN, Vice President Patient Care Services, Northeast Rehabilitation Hospital, Salem, NH, p. A417
THIBODEAU, Jan, Director Human Resources, Encompass Health Rehabilitation Hospital of Princeton, Princeton, WV, p. A704
THIBODEAUX, Annette, Director Human Resources, Savoy Medical Center, Mamou, LA, p. A287
THIBODEAUX, Douglas, M.D., Chief Medical Officer, Oakbend Medical Center, Richmond, TX, p. A646
THIBODEAUX, Traci, Chief Executive Officer, Beauregard Health System, De Ridder, LA, p. A281
THIEL, David, M.D., Medical Director, Mayo Clinic Hospital In Florida, Jacksonville, FL, p. A135
THIEL, Stefanie
  Senior Human Resources Business Partner, Saint Alphonsus Medical Center – Nampa, Nampa, ID, p. A182
  Senior Human Resources Business Partner, Saint Alphonsus Medical Center – Ontario, Ontario, OR, p. A529
THIELEMIER, Kevin, Director Human Resources, Arkansas Methodist Medical Center, Paragould, AR, p. A52
THIELEN, Kent R., M.D., Chief Executive Officer, Mayo Clinic Hospital In Florida, Jacksonville, FL, p. A135
THIELEN, Kurt, Associate Director, Minneapolis Va Health Care System, Minneapolis, MN, p. A351
THIELS, Dustin
  Group Chief Executive Officer, Covington Behavioral Health, Covington, LA, p. A280
  Group Chief Executive Officer, River Place Behavioral Health, La Place, LA, p. A285
THIEME, Ron, Ph.D., Chief Knowledge and Information Officer, Community Hospital North, Indianapolis, IN, p. A219
THIESCHAFER, Cheryl, Interim Health Care System Director, St. Cloud Va Health Care System, Saint Cloud, MN, p. A354
THILGES, Michael, Chief Financial Officer, Clarke County Hospital, Osceola, IA, p. A241
THILL, Jennifer, Chief of Staff, Mid-Valley Hospital And Clinics, Omak, WA, p. A692
THIRUMALAREDDY, Joseph, M.D., Chief of Staff, South Central Health, Wishek, ND, p. A483
THOELE, Theresa, Director Human Resources, Coffey County Hospital, Burlington, KS, p. A247
THOENDEL, Victor, M.D., Chief Medical Officer, Butler County Health Care Center, David City, NE, p. A399
THOENY, Ben, Director Human Resources, Frances Mahon Deaconess Hospital, Glasgow, MT, p. A392
THOMAN, Dawn, Vice President Human Resources, North Central Kansas Medical Center, Concordia, KS, p. A248
THOMAN, Michele
  Chief Nursing Officer, Nch Baker Hospital, Naples, FL, p. A142
  Chief Operating Officer, Palmetto General Hospital, Hialeah, FL, p. A133
THOMAS, Abbie, Chief Financial Officer, Nemaha Valley Community Hospital, Seneca, KS, p. A260
THOMAS, Andrew, M.D., Chief Medical Officer, Ohio State University Wexner Medical Center, Columbus, OH, p. A492
THOMAS, Brian N., President and Chief Executive Officer, Jefferson Regional, Pine Bluff, AR, p. A52
THOMAS, Brook, Chief Financial Officer, West Boca Medical Center, Boca Raton, FL, p. A126
THOMAS, Chris, FACHE, President and Chief Executive Officer, Community Hospital, Grand Junction, CO, p. A108
THOMAS, Cristina, Chief Information Systems, Pella Regional Health Center, Pella, IA, p. A242
THOMAS, David, President Medical Staff, Riddle Hospital, Media, PA, p. A546
THOMAS, Dean
  FACHE, President and Chief Executive Officer, Berkeley Medical Center, Martinsburg, WV, p. A702
  FACHE, President and Chief Executive Officer, Jefferson Medical Center, Ranson, WV, p. A704
THOMAS, Deana, Vice President Finance and Chief Financial Officer, North Arkansas Regional Medical Center, Harrison, AR, p. A47
THOMAS, Debora, Chief Financial Officer, Adventhealth Daytona Beach, Daytona Beach, FL, p. A129
THOMAS, Debra A., Vice President of Patient Care Services and Chief Nursing Officer, Penn Highlands Brookville, Brookville, PA, p. A535
THOMAS, Denise, Chief Financial Officer, Spring View Hospital, Lebanon, KY, p. A268

THOMAS, Dennis, Chief Executive Officer, Hardeman County Memorial Hospital, Quanah, TX, p. A646
THOMAS, Frank D., Chief Executive Officer, Citizens Baptist Medical Center, Talladega, AL, p. A24
THOMAS, George, M.D., Chief of Staff, Palo Pinto General Hospital, Mineral Wells, TX, p. A639
THOMAS, Gina R.
  Chief Nursing Officer and Director of Patient Care Services, Carle Richland Memorial Hospital, Olney, IL, p. A204
  President, Carle Richland Memorial Hospital, Olney, IL, p. A204
THOMAS, Jayne, Chief Nursing Officer, Southwestern Medical Center, Lawton, OK, p. A514
THOMAS, Jeff, Chief Financial Officer, Deaconess Illinois Medical Center, Marion, IL, p. A200
THOMAS, Jennifer, Chief Operating Officer and Director of Public Relations, Lake Butler Hospital, Lake Butler, FL, p. A136
THOMAS, Jill, Director of Nursing, Western State Hospital, Hopkinsville, KY, p. A267
THOMAS, John, Chief Operating Officer, San Mateo Medical Center, San Mateo, CA, p. A93
THOMAS, Kathy
  MSN, R.N., Chief Operating Officer, Stone County Medical Center, Mountain View, AR, p. A51
  MSN, R.N., Vice President/Chief Operating Officer, Stone County Medical Center, Mountain View, AR, p. A51
THOMAS, Keith, M.D., Chief of Staff, Blue Mountain Hospital District, John Day, OR, p. A528
THOMAS, Laura, Chief Financial Officer, Broward Health Medical Center, Fort Lauderdale, FL, p. A131
THOMAS, Maggie, Vice President Human Resources and Practice Management, South County Hospital, Wakefield, RI, p. A561
THOMAS, Michael
  Associate Administrator, Wayne County Hospital And Clinic System, Corydon, IA, p. A233
  Chief Executive Officer, Encompass Health Rehabilitation Hospital of Altamonte Springs, Altamonte Springs, FL, p. A125
  Chief Executive Officer, Encompass Health Rehabilitation Hospital of Spring Hill, Brooksville, FL, p. A127
THOMAS, Michael S.
  President and Chief Executive Officer, John Muir Medical Center, Walnut Creek, Walnut Creek, CA, p. A100
  President and Chief Executive Officer, John Muir Health, John Muir Health, Concord Medical Center, Concord, CA, p. A60
THOMAS, Missy, Chief Nursing Officer, Medical Center Barbour, Eufaula, AL, p. A19
THOMAS, Nicky, Director Human Resources, Baptist Memorial Hospital–Union City, Union City, TN, p. A594
THOMAS, Nicole B., President, Baptist Medical Center Jacksonville, Jacksonville, FL, p. A134
THOMAS, Patricia F, Chief Nursing Officer, Sentara Halifax Regional Hospital, South Boston, VA, p. A684
THOMAS, Paula, Vice President Patient Services, UPMC Bedford, Everett, PA, p. A540
THOMAS, Phillip Jr, Director Human Resources, Jackson Parish Hospital, Jonesboro, LA, p. A284
THOMAS, Robert, M.D., Chief of Staff, Middlesboro Arh Hospital, Middlesboro, KY, p. A271
THOMAS, Ron, M.D., Chief Medical Officer, Adventhealth Palm Coast, Palm Coast, FL, p. A145
THOMAS, Russell, M.D., Chief of Staff, Rice Medical Center, Eagle Lake, TX, p. A615
THOMAS, Ruth, Chief Operating Officer, Mercy Fitzgerald Hospital, Darby, PA, p. A538
THOMAS, Sarah, Director of Human Resources, Encompass Health Rehabilitation Hospital of Littleton, Littleton, CO, p. A111
THOMAS, Scott, Administrative Director Human Resources and Communications, Granville Health System, Oxford, NC, p. A474
THOMAS, Shamieka, Administrator, Oceans Behavioral Hospital of Pasadena, Pasadena, TX, p. A643
THOMAS, Shannon, Chief Executive Officer, Eden Medical Center, Castro Valley, CA, p. A59
THOMAS, Shawn M., Director Human Resources, Banner Payson Medical Center, Payson, AZ, p. A34
THOMAS, Sue, Manager Human Resources, Beckley Arh Hospital, Beckley, WV, p. A699
THOMAS, Sylvia, Chief Nursing Officer, Jack Hughston Memorial Hospital, Phenix City, AL, p. A24
THOMAS, Tenny, M.D., Chief Medical Officer, Beth Israel Deaconess Hospital–Plymouth, Plymouth, MA, p. A317
THOMAS, Twilla, Chief Nursing Officer, Pamp. Regional Medical Center, Pampa, TX, p. A642
THOMAS, William, M.D., Jr, Medical Director Clinical and Internal Affairs, Molokai General Hospital, Kaunakakai, HI, p. A177

THOMAS EWALD, Luanne M., Chief Operating Officer, University of Michigan Medical Center, Ann Arbor, MI, p. A321
THOMAS–BOYD, Sharon, Chief Operating Officer, Oaklawn Hospital, Marshall, MI, p. A333
THOMAS–FOLDS, Lana, System Senior Director Human Resources, Jack Hughston Memorial Hospital, Phenix City, AL, p. A24
THOMAS–PHILLIP, Colleen, Chief Executive Officer, Clearvista Health And Wellness, Lorain, OH, p. A498
THOMAS–WILLIAMS, Jovita, Senior Vice President of Human Resources, Massachusetts General Hospital, Boston, MA, p. A310
THOMASON, Corey, Controller, Encompass Health Rehabilitation Hospital, A Partner of Washington Regional, Fayetteville, AR, p. A46
THOMMAN, Connie, Director of Nursing, Covenant Hospital–Levelland, Levelland, TX, p. A634
THOMPSON, Alan, M.D., President Medical Staff, Warm Springs Medical Center, Warm Springs, GA, p. A173
THOMPSON, Amy
  M.D., Chief Executive Officer, Covenant Children's Hospital, Lubbock, TX, p. A635
  M.D., Chief Executive Officer, Covenant Medical Center, Lubbock, TX, p. A636
THOMPSON, Angela, Director of Human Resources, Merit Health Biloxi, Biloxi, MS, p. A359
THOMPSON, Becki
  Administrator, Chi Lisbon Health, Lisbon, ND, p. A482
  President, Chi Oakes Hospital, Oakes, ND, p. A483
THOMPSON, Belinda, Coordinator Human Resources, Encompass Health Rehabilitation Hospital of Salisbury, Salisbury, MD, p. A307
THOMPSON, Bobby, Director Information Technology, Stephens Memorial Hospital, Breckenridge, TX, p. A604
THOMPSON, Candice M., R.N., MSN, Chief Nursing Officer, Brodstone Memorial Hospital, Superior, NE, p. A406
THOMPSON, Chad, Chief Financial Officer, Lallie Kemp Medical Center, Independence, LA, p. A283
THOMPSON, Charles, M.D., Chief Medical Officer, Nacogdoches Medical Center, Nacogdoches, TX, p. A640
THOMPSON, Cheryl
  Chief Nursing Officer, Singing River Gulfport, Gulfport, MS, p. A363
  Facility Director Human Resources, Connecticut Valley Hospital, Middletown, CT, p. A117
THOMPSON, Christopher, Human Resources Manager, Middlesboro Arh Hospital, Middlesboro, KY, p. A271
THOMPSON, Cindy, Chief Financial Officer, Northwest Surgical Hospital, Oklahoma City, OK, p. A517
THOMPSON, Craig, FACHE, Chief Executive Officer, Golden Valley Memorial Healthcare, Clinton, MO, p. A373
THOMPSON, Cynthia, Chief Financial Officer, Houlton Regional Hospital, Houlton, ME, p. A297
THOMPSON, Dale, Chief Financial Officer, Mclaren Greater Lansing, Lansing, MI, p. A331
THOMPSON, David, M.D., Chief of Staff, Richardson Medical Center, Rayville, LA, p. A291
THOMPSON, Debbie, Chief Financial Officer, Sweetwater Hospital, Sweetwater, TN, p. A594
THOMPSON, Greg, Corporate Director, Human Resources, Orlando Health Orlando Regional Medical Center, Orlando, FL, p. A144
THOMPSON, Heath, R.N., Administrator, Singing River Health System, Pascagoula, MS, p. A367
THOMPSON, Ian Jr, M.D., President, Christus Santa Rosa Health System, San Antonio, TX, p. A649
THOMPSON, Ivan, Vice President, Chief Human Resource Officer, University of Texas Southwestern Medical Center, Dallas, TX, p. A612
THOMPSON, John W, M.D., Chief of Staff, Eastern Louisiana Mental Health System, Jackson, LA, p. A283
THOMPSON, Julie
  Chief Adminstrative Officer and Chief Nursing Officer, Bluffton Regional Medical Center, Bluffton, IN, p. A213
  Chief Operating Officer and Chief Nursing Officer, Bluffton Regional Medical Center, Bluffton, IN, p. A213
  Manager Personnel and Payroll, Mayers Memorial Hospital District, Fall River Mills, CA, p. A63
THOMPSON, Kristin L., Campus Administrator, Physicians Care Surgical Hospital, Royersford, PA, p. A554
THOMPSON, Les, Chief Human Resources Officer, Promedica Toledo Hospital, Toledo, OH, p. A505
THOMPSON, Linda
  Chief Operating Officer, Rural Wellness Fairfax, Fairfax, OK, p. A512
  Senior Vice President, Human Resources and Service Excellence, New England Baptist Hospital, Boston, MA, p. A311
THOMPSON, Lisa, MSN, R.N., Director of Nursing, Amberwell Hiawatha, Hiawatha, KS, p. A250

Index of Health Care Professionals

Index of Health Care Professionals / Thompson

THOMPSON, Lori L, Manager Human Resources, Orthonebraska Hospital, Omaha, NE, p. A404
THOMPSON, Mark
M.D., President, Essentia Health Fargo, Fargo, ND, p. A480
Vice President Financial Services, Monument Health Rapid City Hospital, Rapid City, SD, p. A576
THOMPSON, Nathan, Chief Executive Officer, Story County Medical Center, Nevada, IA, p. A240
THOMPSON, Ormand P., President, Thomas Hospital, Fairhope, AL, p. A19
THOMPSON, Pamela, Chief Operations Officer, Huhukam Memorial Hospital, Sacaton, AZ, p. A37
THOMPSON, Patti, Chief Operating Officer, San Luis Valley Health, Alamosa, CO, p. A103
THOMPSON, Patty, Area Compliance Officer, Kaiser Permanente Fresno Medical Center, Fresno, CA, p. A65
THOMPSON, Ranae M, R.N., MSN, Vice President & Chief Nursing Officer, El Paso Children's Hospital, El Paso, TX, p. A616
THOMPSON, Randell, Chief Nursing Officer, Camc Plateau Medical Center, Oak Hill, WV, p. A703
THOMPSON, Randy, FACHE, Chief Executive Officer, Pam Rehabilitation Hospital of Beaumont, Beaumont, TX, p. A602
THOMPSON, Rhonda, R.N., Chief Nursing Officer and Senior Vice President, Patient Care Services, Phoenix Children's, Phoenix, AZ, p. A36
THOMPSON, Rick, M.D., FACS, FACC, President, Chi Health Nebraska Heart, Lincoln, NE, p. A401
THOMPSON, Robert, M.D., Chief Medical Officer, Pam Health Rehabilitation Hospital of Greater Indiana, Clarksville, IN, p. A214
THOMPSON, Ronnie, Chief Financial Officer, Belton Regional Medical Center, Belton, MO, p. A371
THOMPSON, Ryan, Vice President, Chief Operating Officer, Rome Health, Rome, NY, p. A458
THOMPSON, Sarah, Director Health Information Management, Hardtner Medical Center, Olla, LA, p. A291
THOMPSON, Scott, Chief Executive Officer, Russell County Hospital, Russell Springs, KY, p. A274
THOMPSON, Selva, R.N., Chief Nurse Executive, Gallup Indian Medical Center, Gallup, NM, p. A434
THOMPSON, Shawn, Manager of Information Systems, Willamette Valley Medical Center, Mcminnville, OR, p. A529
THOMPSON, Sheila, Director Human Resources, Hamilton Memorial Hospital District, Mcleansboro, IL, p. A201
THOMPSON, Stacey, Superintendent, Austin State Hospital, Austin, TX, p. A599
THOMPSON, Staci, President and Chief Executive Officer, Aurelia Osborn Fox Memorial Hospital, Oneonta, NY, p. A455
THOMPSON, Stuart, Vice President Human Resources, HCA Florida Memorial Hospital, Jacksonville, FL, p. A134
THOMPSON, Tim
Senior Vice President and Chief Informatics Officer, St. Anthony's Hospital, Saint Petersburg, FL, p. A149
Senior Vice President and Chief Information Officer, St. Joseph's Hospital, Tampa, FL, p. A152
Senior Vice President, Chief Information Officer, South Florida Baptist Hospital, Plant City, FL, p. A147
Senior Vice President, Informant Services and Chief Information Officer, Mease Countryside Hospital, Safety Harbor, FL, p. A148
Senior Vice President, Information Services and Chief Information Officer, Mease Dunedin Hospital, Dunedin, FL, p. A130
THOMPSON, Timothy
Senior Vice President and Chief Information Officer, Morton Plant Hospital, Clearwater, FL, p. A128
Senior Vice President and Chief Information Officer, Morton Plant North Bay Hospital, New Port Richey, FL, p. A142
THOMPSON, Tina H, Coordinator Human Resources, Firsthealth Montgomery Memorial Hospital, Troy, NC, p. A477
THOMPSON, Vera, Director Human Resources, Kingsboro Psychiatric Center, New York, NY, p. A448
THOMPSON, Vicki, MSN, Community Chief Nursing Officer, Middlesboro Arh Hospital, Middlesboro, KY, p. A271
THOMPSON, Wayne D., Chief Financial Officer, Northlake Behavioral Health System, Mandeville, LA, p. A287
THOMPSON, Wesley, M.D., President Medical Staff, Fairfield Memorial Hospital, Fairfield, IL, p. A195
THOMPSON, William, Chief Financial Officer, Mississippi Baptist Medical Center, Jackson, MS, p. A364
THOMPSON–COOK, Timothy, Chief Operating Officer, Contra Costa Regional Medical Center, Martinez, CA, p. A76
THOMS, Hunter, Chief Executive Officer, Rural Wellness Fairfax, Fairfax, OK, p. A512
THOMSEN, Sue, Chief Financial Officer, New Braunfels Regional Rehabilitation Hospital, New Braunfels, TX, p. A641
THOMSEN, Vicki
Director Human Resources, Aurora Behavioral Health System East, Tempe, AZ, p. A39
Director Human Resources, Aurora Behavioral Health System West, Glendale, AZ, p. A32
THOMSON, Doug, M.D., Chief Medical Officer, Commonwealth Regional Specialty Hospital, Bowling Green, KY, p. A263
THOMSON, Ken, M.D., Medical Director, Memorial Hermann Surgical Hospital–First Colony, Sugar Land, TX, p. A654
THOMSON, Steven, M.D., Medical Director, Heartland Behavioral Healthcare, Massillon, OH, p. A499
THORDARSON, Heidar, Chief Financial Officer, Adventist Health Castle, Kailua, HI, p. A176
THORE, Joe, Chief Operating Officer, Ashe Memorial Hospital, Jefferson, NC, p. A471
THORELL, Nicole, R.N., MSN, Chief Nursing Officer, Lexington Regional Health Center, Lexington, NE, p. A401
THORESON, Scott D., FACHE, Chief Executive Officer, Carroll County Memorial Hospital, Carrollton, MO, p. A373
THORESON, Shane, M.D., Chief Medical Officer, Community Memorial Healthcare, Marysville, KS, p. A254
THORN, Margaret, Interim Director of Nursing, Red Bay Hospital, Red Bay, AL, p. A24
THORN, Mark, FACHE, Executive Director, Finance, Mercy Hospital Lincoln, Troy, MO, p. A387
THORNBRUGH, Mitchell
Acting Chief Information Officer, Cherokee Nation W.W. Hastings Hospital, Tahlequah, OK, p. A521
Administrative Officer, Cherokee Nation W.W. Hastings Hospital, Tahlequah, OK, p. A521
THORNBURY, Neil
Chief Executive Officer, T. J. Samson Community Hospital, Glasgow, KY, p. A266
Chief Executive Officer, T.J. Health Columbia, Columbia, KY, p. A264
THORNE, Dana, Administrator Human Resources, Valley Hospital Medical Center, Las Vegas, NV, p. A411
THORNELL, Louise, Ph.D., R.N., Chief Nursing Officer, Christus St. Michael Health System, Texarkana, TX, p. A656
THORNELL, Timothy, FACHE, President and Chief Executive Officer, Cheyenne Regional Medical Center, Cheyenne, WY, p. A726
THORNLEY, Laura, MSN, R.N., Chief Nursing Officer, Rose Medical Center, Denver, CO, p. A107
THORNSBERRY, Michael, M.D., Chief Medical Officer, Texas Health Specialty Hospital, Fort Worth, TX, p. A620
THORNTON, Amie D., Chief Hospital Executive, Hackensack Meridian Health Jfk Medical Center, Edison, NJ, p. A420
THORNTON, Carol, Director Human Resources, Cherry Hospital, Goldsboro, NC, p. A469
THORNTON, Cayetano, Chief Information Officer, Walter Reed National Military Medical Center, Bethesda, MD, p. A303
THORNTON, Daryl W, Chief Operating Officer, Kansas Medical Center, Andover, KS, p. A246
THORNTON, Eric, President, SSM Health St. Mary's Hospital, Madison, WI, p. A714
THORNTON, Jan, Chief Nursing Officer, Ascension Sacred Heart Bay, Panama City, FL, p. A145
THORNTON, Jillisa, Director of Nursing, Coastal Harbor Treatment Center, Savannah, GA, p. A171
THORNTON, Laird, Director Information Systems, Alta Vista Regional Hospital, Las Vegas, NM, p. A435
THORNTON, Ryan, President and Chief Executive Officer, North Suburban Medical Center, Thornton, CO, p. A113
THORNTON, Thomas, M.D., Vice President of Medical Affairs, Mymichigan Medical Center Alpena, Alpena, MI, p. A321
THORPE, Judith, R.N., MSN, Vice President and Chief Nursing Officer, Umass Memorial Healthalliance–Clinton Hospital, Leominster, MA, p. A315
THORPE, Linda, Chief Executive Officer, East Morgan County Hospital, Brush, CO, p. A104
THORPE, Wendy, Area Director Information Systems, Providence St. Josep. Hospital Eureka, Eureka, CA, p. A62
THORSEN, Erik, President and Chief Executive Officer, Columbia Memorial Hospital, Astoria, OR, p. A525
THORWALD, Robert, Chief Information Officer, Washington Hospital Healthcare System, Fremont, CA, p. A64
THOTAKURA, Raj, M.D., Medical Director, Old Vineyard Behavioral Health Services, Winston–Salem, NC, p. A478
THRASH, Amanda, FACHE, President, Texas Health Presbyterian Hospital Allen, Allen, TX, p. A595
THRASHER, Amanda, Director Nursing, Ellsworth County Medical Center, Ellsworth, KS, p. A249
THRASHER, Kimberly, Controller, Encompass Health Lakeshore Rehabilitation Hospital, Birmingham, AL, p. A16
THRASHER, Sherri, Executive Human Resources Partner, Corewell Health Pennock Hospital, Hastings, MI, p. A329
THREADGILL, Christopher, M.D., Chief Executive Officer and Administrator, Baptist Memorial Hospital – Calhoun, Calhoun City, MS, p. A360
THREEWITS, Sheree, Director Human Resources, Manatee Memorial Hospital, Bradenton, FL, p. A126
THRIFT, William Kyle, Chief Nursing Officer, HCA Florida Brandon Hospital, Brandon, FL, p. A127
THULI, Karen, Information Systems Coordinator, Upland Hills Health, Dodgeville, WI, p. A709
THUN, Todd, Director Human Resources, Montana State Hospital, Warm Springs, MT, p. A396
THUN, Tracey, Director Business and Support Services, Montana State Hospital, Warm Springs, MT, p. A396
THUNELL, Adam, Chief Operating Officer and Vice President Operations, Community Memorial Hospital – Ventura, Ventura, CA, p. A100
THURBER, Joe, Director Information Technology, Central Regional Hospital, Butner, NC, p. A464
THURMER, DeAnn
President and Chief Nursing Officer, SSM Health Ripon Community Hospital, Ripon, WI, p. A721
President and Chief Nursing Officer, SSM Health St. Clare Hospital–Baraboo, Baraboo, WI, p. A707
President and Chief Nursing Officer, SSM Health Waupun Memorial Hospital, Waupun, WI, p. A724
THURSTON, Jessica, Administrator, Unity Psychiatric Care–Clarksville, Clarksville, TN, p. A581
THURSTON, Thomas, M.D., Medical Director, J. D. Mccarty Center for Children With Developmental Disabilities, Norman, OK, p. A516
THYGERSON, Scott, Chief Executive Officer, Kern Medical, Bakersfield, CA, p. A57
THYGESON, Cindy, M.D., Director Medical Affairs, Sutter Center for Psychiatry, Sacramento, CA, p. A87
THYNE, Shannon, Chief Medical Officer, Olive View–Ucla Medical Center, Los Angeles, CA, p. A74
TIBBITS, Dick, Vice President and Chief Operating Officer, Adventhealth Tampa, Tampa, FL, p. A152
TIBBITTS, Braden, Chief Financial Officer, Lone Peak Hospital, Draper, UT, p. A665
TICE, Evan, Director Information Technology and Systems, Sky Ridge Medical Center, Lone Tree, CO, p. A111
TICE, Heidi, Chief Financial Officer, Cheyenne County Hospital, Saint Francis, KS, p. A259
TICE, Kirk C., President and Chief Executive Officer, Robert Wood Johnson University Hospital Rahway, Rahway, NJ, p. A427
TICE, Linda, Director Information Systems, Sagewest Health Care, Riverton, WY, p. A728
TICHENOR, John, Chief Financial Officer, Ohio County Hospital, Hartford, KY, p. A267
TIDWELL, Jan, Chief Nursing Officer, Piedmont Cartersville, Cartersville, GA, p. A160
TIDWELL, Tim, Human Resources Director, Wiregrass Medical Center, Geneva, AL, p. A20
TIDWELL, Wesley, President, Ascension Seton Medical Center Austin, Austin, TX, p. A599
TIEDE, Brad, Director Information Systems, Memorial Community Health, Aurora, NE, p. A397
TIEDT, Douglas, M.D., Chief of Staff, Musc Health Lancaster Medical Center, Lancaster, SC, p. A568
TIEDT, Jerry, Director Information Systems, Waverly Health Center, Waverly, IA, p. A245
TIEFENTHALER, Brenda Marie., R.N., MSN, President and Chief Executive Officer, Spencer Hospital, Spencer, IA, p. A244
TIERNAN, Kelley, Interim Chief Executive Officer, River Hospital, Alexandria Bay, NY, p. A438
TIERNEY, Gregory, M.D., President, BMG and BHS Chief Medical Officer, Benefis Health System, Great Falls, MT, p. A392
TIERNEY, Mark A, Chief Financial Officer, Manatee Memorial Hospital, Bradenton, FL, p. A126
TIESI, Jeffrey
Executive Vice President and Chief Operating Officer, Excela Frick Hospital, Mount Pleasant, PA, p. A546
Executive Vice President and Chief Operating Officer, Excela Health Latrobe Hospital, Latrobe, PA, p. A544
Executive Vice President and Chief Operating Officer, Excela Health Westmoreland Hospital, Greensburg, PA, p. A541
TIETJEN, Patricia, M.D., Vice President, Medical Affairs, Danbury Hospital, Danbury, CT, p. A115
TIFF, Nikki
Human Resources Analyst, Avera Flandreau Hospital, Flandreau, SD, p. A573
Regional Manager Human Resources, Avera Dells Area Hospital, Dell Rapids, SD, p. A573

A990 Index of Health Care Professionals

Index of Health Care Professionals / Topper

Index of Health Care Professionals

TIGGELAAR, Tom, Vice President Finance, Mayo Clinic Health System In La Crosse, La Crosse, WI, p. A714
TIKKER, Chase, Chief Executive Officer, Adventhealth Orlando, Orlando, FL, p. A144
TILGHMAN, Bradley, Controller, Encompass Health Rehabilitation Hospital of Panama City, Panama City, FL, p. A146
TILLER, Jaconna Joni, Chief Nursing Officer, SSM Health St. Anthony Hospital – Midwest, Midwest City, OK, p. A515
TILLETT, Grant, Chief Information Officer, Prairie Lakes Healthcare System, Watertown, SD, p. A578
TILLMAN, Kanner, Chief Financial Officer, Encino Hospital Medical Center, Encino, CA, p. A62
TILLMAN, Pamela P., Administrator, Lifebrite Community Hospital of Stokes, Danbury, NC, p. A466
TILLMAN, Randy, M.D., Chief Medical Staff, Riverbridge Specialty Hospital, Vidalia, LA, p. A294
TILLMAN, Y. Brooke., Chief Executive Officer, Summit Oaks Hospital, Summit, NJ, p. A428
TILLMAN–TAYLOR, Susan, Manager Human Resources, Hackensack Meridian Health Southern Ocean Medical Center, Manahawkin, NJ, p. A423
TILSON, Natalie, Controller, Encompass Health Rehabilitation Hospital of Kingsport, Kingsport, TN, p. A585
TILSTRA, Michael, President and Chief Executive Officer, Iroquois Memorial Hospital And Resident Home, Watseka, IL, p. A210
TIM–YOUNG, Stephen, Director Information Technology, Adventist Healthcare Fort Washington Medical Center, Fort Washington, MD, p. A304
TIMANUS, Anthony, Chief Executive Officer, Avera Gregory Hospital, Gregory, SD, p. A574
TIMBERLAKE, Elizabeth BSN, RNC–, Chief Nursing Officer, Piedmont Newton Hospital, Covington, GA, p. A162
TIMBERS, Christopher, Vice President and Chief Information Officer, Northbay Medical Center, Fairfield, CA, p. A63
TIMBERS, Christopher T, Chief Information Officer, Sibley Memorial Hospital, Washington, DC, p. A124
TIMBERS, William, M.D., Interim Chief Medical Officer, Northern Inyo Hospital, Bishop. CA, p. A58
TIMM, Karen, R.N., MSN, Chief Nursing Officer, Grande Ronde Hospital, La Grande, OR, p. A528
TIMM, Mark, Executive Director Human Resources, Dignity Health Yavapai Regional Medical Center, Prescott, AZ, p. A37
TIMM, Matt, M.D., Chief Medical Officer, Pender Community Hospital, Pender, NE, p. A405
TIMMER, Kari, Chief Financial Officer, Sioux Center Health, Sioux Center, IA, p. A243
TIMMERMAN, Jo, Manager Accounting, Norwood Health Center, Marshfield, WI, p. A715
TIMMONS, Laurene
Chief Financial Officer, UPMC East, Monroeville, PA, p. A546
Chief Financial Officer, UPMC Mckeesport, Mckeesport, PA, p. A545
TIMMONS, Mathew, Senior Vice President and Chief Operating Officer, Children's Hospital New Orleans, New Orleans, LA, p. A290
TIMPE, James, Chief Executive Officer, Salem Township Hospital, Salem, IL, p. A208
TINAGERO, Doris, Executive Director, University of New Mexico Hospitals, Albuquerque, NM, p. A433
TINCH, Roberta, President, Inova Mount Vernon Hospital, Alexandria, VA, p. A673
TINCHER, Pat, Director Finance, Aspirus Langlade Hospital, Antigo, WI, p. A707
TINEO, Alberto, Chief Operating Officer, Halifax Health/Uf Health Medical Center of Deltona, Deltona, FL, p. A130
TINGEY, Ryan, Chief Operating Officer, Henderson Hospital, Henderson, NV, p. A409
TINGSTAD, Jonathan, Vice President and Chief Financial Officer, Fred Hutchinson Cancer Center, Seattle, WA, p. A694
TINKEL, Chad
Chief Executive Officer, Community Hospitals And Wellness Centers, Bryan, OH, p. A487
President and Chief Executive Officer, Community Hospitals And Wellness Centers–Montpelier, Montpelier, OH, p. A500
TINNERELLO, Jeremy M., R.N., MSN, Jackson Market President, St. Dominic–Jackson Memorial Hospital, Jackson, MS, p. A364
TINNEY, Sean, FACHE, Chief Executive Officer, Cedar Park Regional Medical Center, Cedar Park, TX, p. A607
TINSA, Udom, M.D., Medical Director, Ashley Medical Center, Ashley, ND, p. A479
TINSLEY, Cassie, Director, Human Resources, Powell Valley Health Care, Powell, WY, p. A728
TINSLEY, Katie, Chief Financial Officer, Neosho Memorial Regional Medical Center, Chanute, KS, p. A247
TIPNIS, Shital, Chief Executive Officer, Select Specialty Hospital–Milwaukee, Milwaukee, WI, p. A717
TIPPIN, Philip. M.D., Chief Medical Officer, Chambers Memorial Hospital, Danville, AR, p. A45
TIPPIN, Russell, President and Chief Executive Officer, Medical Center Health System, Odessa, TX, p. A642
TIPPS, Linda, Director Human Resources, Southern Tennessee Regional Health System–Winchester, Winchester, TN, p. A594
TIPTON, Gina, Hospital Administrator, Atrium Health Navicent Rehabilitation Hospital, Macon, GA, p. A167
TIPTON, Maggie, Chief Information Officer, Unicoi County Hospital, Erwin, TN, p. A583
TIPTON, Martis, Chief Information Officer, Sevier County Medical Center, De Queen, AR, p. A45
TIPTON, Melissa, Human Resource Director, HSHS St. Mary's Hospital, Decatur, IL, p. A193
TIPTON, Peggy, Chief Operating Officer and Chief Nursing Officer, Oklahoma Heart Hospital, Oklahoma City, OK, p. A518
TIRA, Cheryl, Director Information Systems, Columbus Community Hospital, Columbus, NE, p. A399
TIRADO, Norma, Vice President, Human Resources and Health Information Technology, Corewell Health Watervliet Hospital, Watervliet, MI, p. A340
TISDALE, Willis E, Director Human Resources, Shriners Hospitals for Children–Greenville, Greenville, SC, p. A567
TISDALL, Renae, Chief Financial, Compliance and Security Officer, Mobridge Regional Hospital, Mobridge, SD, p. A575
TISSIER, Becky, Chief Fiscal Service, Veterans Affairs Illiana Health Care System, Danville, IL, p. A192
TITENSOR, Greg, MSN, R.N., Vice President, Operations, Billings Clinic, Billings, MT, p. A389
TITO, David, M.D., President Medical Staff, Riverside Community Hospital, Riverside, CA, p. A86
TITUS, Monica B., R.N., Chief Executive Officer, Encompass Health Rehabilitation Hospital of Vineland, Vineland, NJ, p. A429
TIURA, Melanee, Administrator, Providence Valdez Medical Center, Valdez, AK, p. A29
TOADVINE, Stephen, M.D., Chief Medical Officer, Harrison Memorial Hospital, Cynthiana, KY, p. A264
TOALSON, Jason, Chief Executive Officer, Cottonwood Springs Hospital, Olathe, KS, p. A256
TOASTON, Tanisha, Medical Director, Reunion Rehabilitation Hospital Arlington, Arlington, TX, p. A598
TOBEY, Shelley R, R.N., MS, Chief Operating Officer, Texas Health Presbyterian Hospital Flower Mound, Flower Mound, TX, p. A618
TOBIN, Devin, Chief Operating Officer, Lewisgale Hospital Montgomery, Blacksburg, VA, p. A673
TOBIN, Hugh, Chief Financial Officer, Davis Regional Medical Center, Statesville, NC, p. A477
TOBIN, Thomas, Chief Medical Officer, Community Hospital, Grand Junction, CO, p. A108
TOBIN–PAYNE, Cindy, Director, Magee Rehabilitation, Philadelphia, PA, p. A549
TOBITT, Allyssa, Chief Executive Officer, Henrico Doctors' Hospital, Richmond, VA, p. A682
TOCCO–BRADLEY, Rosalie
Ph.D., M.D., Chief Medical Officer, Trinity Health Ann Arbor Hospital, Ypsilanti, MI, p. A341
Ph.D., M.D., Chief Medical Officer, Trinity Health Livingston Hospital, Howell, MI, p. A330
TODD, Mark, Senior Systems Administrator, Hamilton Memorial Hospital District, Mcleansboro, IL, p. A201
TODD, Nate, Chief Financial Officer, John L. Mcclellan Memorial Veterans' Hospital, Little Rock, AR, p. A50
TODD, Robbie, Director Information Technology, Horn Memorial Hospital, Ida Grove, IA, p. A237
TODD, Shawn
Interim Chief Executive Officer, Pam Health Specialty Hospital of Stoughton, Stoughton, MA, p. A319
Interim Chief Executive Officer, Warm Springs Rehabilitation Hospital of Kyle, Kyle, TX, p. A633
TODD, Steve J., Chief Executive Officer, St. Luke Community Healthcare, Ronan, MT, p. A395
TOEDT, Michael E, M.D., Director Clinical Services, Cherokee Indian Hospital, Cherokee, NC, p. A466
TOFANI, Barbara F., R.N., MSN, Senior Vice President and Chief Nursing Officer, Cincinnati Children's Hospital Medical Center, Cincinnati, OH, p. A488
TOFT, Kari, Vice President, Chief Information Officer, Regions Hospital, Saint Paul, MN, p. A354
TOJINO, Allan, Director, Information Systems, Paradise Valley Hospital, National City, CA, p. A79
TOKAR, Andrew, Chief Financial Officer, Overlake Medical Center And Clinics, Bellevue, WA, p. A687
TOLBERT, Butch, Chief Operating Officer, Richardson Medical Center, Rayville, LA, p. A291
TOLBERT, James, Director Information Systems, Saint Francis Hospital Muskogee, Muskogee, OK, p. A515
TOLEDO, Iris, Chief Nursing Officer, Hospital Pavia Arecibo, Arecibo, PR, p. A731
TOLINE, Tyler, FACHE, Chief Executive Officer, Franciscan Healthcare, West Point, NE, p. A407
TOLLE, Sonda, R.N., Vice President Patient Services, Perham Health, Perham, MN, p. A352
TOLLEFSON, Sue, Coordinator Payroll Personnel, Avera Granite Falls, Granite Falls, MN, p. A348
TOLLEY, Cherie, Chief Executive Officer, Willingway Hospital, Statesboro, GA, p. A172
TOLSON, Rick, Chief Administrative Officer and Chief Human Resources Officer, The Christ Hospital Health Network, Cincinnati, OH, p. A489
TOMAS, George, Director Information Services, Griffin Health, Derby, CT, p. A115
TOMASESKI, Gina, Chief Executive Officer, Icare Rehabilitation Hospital, Flower Mound, TX, p. A618
TOMASO, Nancy, Vice President, Patient Care Services, Milford Regional Medical Center, Milford, MA, p. A316
TOMASZEWSKI, Kelly
R.N., MSN, President and Chief Executive Officer Manistee and Paul Oliver, Munson Healthcare Manistee Hospital, Manistee, MI, p. A332
R.N., MSN, President and Chief Executive Officer Manistee and Paul Oliver, Munson Healthcare Paul Oliver Memorial Hospital, Frankfort, MI, p. A327
TOME, Michael, M.D., Medical Director, Kaiser Permanente Los Angeles Medical Center, Los Angeles, CA, p. A73
TOMLIN, Kerry W, Associate Administrator, Clay County Hospital, Ashland, AL, p. A15
TOMLIN, Teresa, R.N., Chief Nursing Officer, Patterson Health Center, Anthony, KS, p. A246
TOMLINSON, Charles M, M.D., Chief Medical Officer, Atrium Health Cleveland, Shelby, NC, p. A476
TOMLINSON, David, Executive Vice President Chief Financial Officer and Chief Information Officer, Northwestern Medicine Mchenry, Mchenry, IL, p. A201
TOMLINSON, Sallie, Manager Human Resources, Arbuckle Memorial Hospital, Sulphur, OK, p. A521
TOMLON, Eric, Chief Executive Officer, The Core Institute Specialty Hospital, Phoenix, AZ, p. A37
TOMORY, Gerald
M.D., Regional Medical Director, Kauai Veterans Memorial Hospital, Waimea, HI, p. A178
M.D., Regional Medical Director, Samuel Mahelona Memorial Hospital, Kapaa, HI, p. A177
TOMPKINS, Charles, M.D., Chief of Staff, Crenshaw Community Hospital, Luverne, AL, p. A21
TOMPKINS, Kim, Director Information Services, Detar Healthcare System, Victoria, TX, p. A660
TOMPKINS, Tommy, Vice President, Finance and Chief Financial Officer, Yukon–Kuskokwim Delta Regional Hospital, Bethel, AK, p. A27
TONER, Tina, Chief Nursing Officer, Jefferson Healthcare, Port Townsend, WA, p. A693
TONEY, Patty, R.N., MSN, Chief Nurse Executive, Christus Santa Rosa Health System, San Antonio, TX, p. A649
TONGATE, Scott A., Chief Executive Officer, Macon Community Hospital, Lafayette, TN, p. A586
TONJES, Ken, Chief Financial Officer, Peacehealth Ketchikan Medical Center, Ketchikan, AK, p. A28
TONN, Deb L, Vice President Patient Care, Campbell County Health, Gillette, WY, p. A727
TONN–KNOPF, Sheila, Chief Executive Officer, Select Specialty Hospital–Canton, Canton, OH, p. A488
TONNU, Lannie, Senior Vice President and Chief Financial Officer, Children's Hospital Los Angeles, Los Angeles, CA, p. A72
TOOKE, Ryan, Chief Executive Officer, Dahl Memorial Healthcare Association, Ekalaka, MT, p. A391
TOOLE, LaDon, Chief Executive Officer, Dodge County Hospital, Eastman, GA, p. A163
TOOLE, Patricia, President and Chief Executive Officer, Hackensack Meridian Health Carrier Clinic, Belle Mead, NJ, p. A418
TOON, William, Chief Information Officer, Baptist Hospitals of Southeast Texas, Beaumont, TX, p. A602
TOOT, Gregory P., Chief Executive Officer, Select Specialty Hospital–Camp Hill, Camp Hill, PA, p. A536
TOPPEN, Jacki, Director of Nursing, Prairie St. John's, Fargo, ND, p. A480
TOPPER, Morgan, Chief Operating Officer, Corona Regional Medical Center, Corona, CA, p. A60

© 2025 AHA Guide Index of Health Care Professionals A991

Index of Health Care Professionals

Index of Health Care Professionals / Torbett

TORBETT, Russell B, Director Human Resources, Creek Nation Community Hospital, Okemah, OK, p. A516
TORCHIA, Jude, Chief Executive Officer, Orthocolorado Hospital, Lakewood, CO, p. A110
TORGE, Andrew, Director Human Resources, Shasta Regional Medical Center, Redding, CA, p. A85
TORMANEN, John, Director Mission and Human Resources, Chi St. Joseph's Health, Park Rapids, MN, p. A352
TORO, Maribel, Chief Executive Officer, Mennonite General Hospital, Aibonito, PR, p. A731
TORO PALACIOS, Belinda L., President and Chief Executive Officer, Doctors' Center Hospital San Juan, San Juan, PR, p. A734
TOROK, Melanie, Administrator, Peterson Healthcare And Rehabilitation Hospital, Wheeling, WV, p. A706
TORONTOW, R. John, M.D., Chief Medical Staff, Cedar County Memorial Hospital, El Dorado Springs, MO, p. A374
TORREGROSSA, Tonia, Chief Nursing Officer, Horizon Medical Center, Llc, Denton, TX, p. A613
TORRES, Anthony
M.D., Chief Medical Officer, Dignity Health Yavapai Regional Medical Center, Prescott, AZ, p. A37
M.D., President and Chief Executive Officer, Dignity Health Yavapai Regional Medical Center, Prescott, AZ, p. A37
Manager Information Technology, Blue Mountain Hospital, Blanding, UT, p. A664
TORRES, Chris, Chief Financial Officer, Boone County Hospital, Boone, IA, p. A231
TORRES, Claudia, Interim Chief Executive Officer, San Antonio Rehabilitation Hospital, San Antonio, TX, p. A650
TORRES, Irene, Chief Financial Officer, Central Desert Behavioral Health Hospital, Albuquerque, NM, p. A432
TORRES, Maribel, Chief Nursing Officer, North Shore Medical Center, Miami, FL, p. A140
TORRES, Mayra, CPA, Chief Financial Officer, Ashford Presbyterian Community Hospital, San Juan, PR, p. A734
TORRES, Nicholas, Chief Executive Officer, Larkin Community Hospital–South Miami Campus, South Miami, FL, p. A150
TORRES, Paul, M.D., Medical Staff President, Excelsior Springs Hospital, Excelsior Springs, MO, p. A374
TORRES, Rodrigo, M.D., Chief Medical Officer, Adventhealth Ocala, Ocala, FL, p. A143
TORRES, Tammy, President, Lehigh Valley Hospital – Hazleton, Hazleton, PA, p. A541
TORRES, Tony, Chief Operating Officer, Poplar Bluff Regional Medical Center, Poplar Bluff, MO, p. A382
TORRES, Victor, Information Technology Specialist Administrator, El Paso Behavioral Health System, El Paso, TX, p. A616
TORRES AYALA, Eugenio, Director Information Systems, Cardiovascular Center of Puerto Rico And The Caribbean, San Juan, PR, p. A734
TORRES RIOS, Luz M., Chief Executive Officer, Hospital De Psiquiatria Forense, Ponce, PR, p. A734
TORSCH, Peter, Chief Financial Officer, St. Charles Parish Hospital, Luling, LA, p. A287
TORTELLA, Anthony, Chief Financial Officer, Fairmount Behavioral Health System, Philadelphia, PA, p. A548
TOSTEBERG, Chris, Superintendent, Cherokee Mental Health Institute, Cherokee, IA, p. A232
TOSTENSON, Brad, Chief Information Officer, Essentia Health–Graceville, Graceville, MN, p. A347
TOTAH, Sammy R.
PharmD, Senior Vice President, Area Manager Riverside & Moreno Valley, Kaiser Foundation Health Plans and Ho, Kaiser Permanente Moreno Valley Medical Center, Moreno Valley, CA, p. A78
PharmD, Senior Vice President, Area Manager Riverside & Moreno Valley, Kaiser Foundation Health Plans and Ho, Kaiser Permanente Riverside Medical Center, Riverside, CA, p. A86
TOUCHSTONE, Pat, Chief Nursing Officer, Crane Memorial Hospital, Crane, TX, p. A609
TOUPS, Sharon A, Senior Vice President and Chief Operating Officer, St. Tammany Health System, Covington, LA, p. A280
TOURE', Joahd, M.D., Chief Medical Officer, Adirondack Health, Saranac Lake, NY, p. A458
TOURIGNY, Barry
Human Resources Director, Johnson City Medical Center, Johnson City, TN, p. A585
Vice President Human Resources and Organizational Development, Cabell Huntington Hospital, Huntington, WV, p. A701
TOUROS, Krista, Chief Financial Officer, Northwest, Peacehealth St. Josep. Medical Center, Bellingham, WA, p. A687
TOUSIGNANT, Grace
R.N., MSN, Chief Nursing Officer, Aspirus Ironwood Hospital & Clinics, Inc., Ironwood, MI, p. A330
R.N., MSN, Chief Nursing Officer, Aspirus Keweenaw Hospital, Laurium, MI, p. A332
TOUSSI, Anita, M.D., Ph.D., Chief Medical Officer, St. Catherine Hospital, Garden City, KS, p. A249
TOUVELLE, Cynthia, R.N., Senior Director Care Management and Chief Nursing Officer, WVU Medicine – Barnesville Hospital, Barnesville, OH, p. A485
TOWERY, O B, M.D., Chief of Staff, John Muir Behavioral Health Center, Concord, CA, p. A60
TOWLE, Sonya, Director Human Resources, Essentia Health Moose Lake, Moose Lake, MN, p. A351
TOWN, Alex
Chief Financial Officer, Samaritan Healthcare, Moses Lake, WA, p. A692
Vice President Finance, Tri–State Memorial Hospital, Clarkston, WA, p. A688
TOWNE, Jana, Nurse Executive, U. S. Public Health Service Indian Hospital–Whiteriver, Whiteriver, AZ, p. A41
TOWNES, Tim, Director Information Systems, Grandview Medical Center, Birmingham, AL, p. A16
TOWNSEND, Cathy, Chief Nursing Officer, Banner – University Medical Center South, Tucson, AZ, p. A40
TOWNSEND, Dona E, Chief Nursing Officer, Navarro Regional Hospital, Corsicana, TX, p. A609
TOWNSEND, Gary, Chief Information Officer, Hurley Medical Center, Flint, MI, p. A326
TOWNSEND, Lori, Chief Nursing Officer, Methodist Hospital, San Antonio, TX, p. A650
TOWNSEND, Michael, Chief Information Officer, The Osuccc – James, Columbus, OH, p. A493
TOWNSEND, Mike, Interim Director Health Information Systems, Grady Memorial Hospital, Chickasha, OK, p. A511
TOWNSEND, Sammuel, LAN Administrator, University of Mississipp. Medical Center Holmes County, Lexington, MS, p. A365
TOY, Linda, Director Information Systems, Havasu Regional Medical Center, Lake Havasu City, AZ, p. A32
TOY, Stanley Jr, M.D., Chief Executive Officer, Greater El Monte Community Hospital, South El Monte, CA, p. A96
TRABAL, Milton, Chief Financial Officer, Clarinda Regional Health Center, Clarinda, IA, p. A232
TRACEY, Karen, Chief Human Resources, Select Specialty Hospital–Greensboro, Greensboro, NC, p. A469
TRACY, Allen R, Senior Vice President and Chief Financial Officer, University Hospitals St. John Medical Center, Westlake, OH, p. A507
TRACY, Karen, R.N., Chief Executive Officer, Rochelle Community Hospital, Rochelle, IL, p. A207
TRACY, Larry A. Jr, FACHE, President, Memorial Hospital of South Bend, South Bend, IN, p. A227
TRACY, Pat, Administrator, Ridgeview Behavioral Hospital, Middle Point, OH, p. A500
TRACY, Thomas Jr, Chief Medical Officer, Penn State Milton S. Hershey Medical Center, Hershey, PA, p. A542
TRACY, Timothy J., Senior Director, Sanford Vermillion Medical Center, Vermillion, SD, p. A577
TRACZ, Robert B, CPA, Senior Vice President and Chief Financial Officer, University Hospitals Lake Health, Willoughby, OH, p. A507
TRAHAN, Belinda, Chief Nursing Officer, Louisiana Extended Care Hospital of Lafayette, Lafayette, LA, p. A285
TRAHAN, Jennifer Lynch, Assistant Vice President Human Resources, Our Lady of Lourdes Regional Medical Center, Lafayette, LA, p. A286
TRAIL, Alan, Director Information Systems, Owensboro Health Muhlenberg Community Hospital, Greenville, KY, p. A266
TRAINOR, Karyn, Director Human Resources, Providence St. Patrick Hospital, Missoula, MT, p. A394
TRAINOR, Paul, Senior Vice President Finance and Chief Financial Officer, Southern New Hampshire Medical Center, Nashua, NH, p. A416
TRAISTER, Lynne, Controller, Encompass Health Rehabilitation Hospital of Tinton Falls, A Joint Venture With Monmouth Medical Center, Tinton Falls, NJ, p. A429
TRAMMELL, Patrick, Chief Executive Officer, Regional Medical Center of Central Alabama, Greenville, AL, p. A20
TRAMMELL, Sandra, Vice President, Human Resources and Support Services, Holland Hospital, Holland, MI, p. A330
TRAN, Ann, Chief Financial Officer, Pike County Memorial Hospital, Louisiana, MO, p. A379
TRAN, Huyen, Administrator, Palacios Community Medical Center, Palacios, TX, p. A642
TRAN, Khiem, M.D., Acting Chief of Staff, Veterans Affairs Illiana Health Care System, Danville, IL, p. A192
TRAN, Lac, Senior Vice President Information Services, Rush University Medical Center, Chicago, IL, p. A191
TRANSIER, Rhonda, Financial Officer, Rusk State Hospital, Rusk, TX, p. A648
TRANTALIS, Carolyn
R.N., MSN, Chief Operating Officer, East Region, Windham Hospital, Willimantic, CT, p. A120
R.N., MSN, Regional Vice President, Clinical Services and Operations, The William W. Backus Hospital, Norwich, CT, p. A118
TRANTHAM, Susan
Director Human Resources, Encompass Health Rehabilitation Hospital of Florence, Florence, SC, p. A566
Director Human Resources, Musc Health Rehabilitation Hospital, An Affiliate of Encompass Health, Charleston, SC, p. A563
TRAPNELL, Kerry A., Interim Chief Executive Officer, Monroe County Hospital, Forsyth, GA, p. A164
TRAPP, John, Vice President Medical Affairs, Bryan Medical Center, Lincoln, NE, p. A401
TRAUTMAN, Robert J., President, Chi St. Luke's Health Brazosport, Lake Jackson, TX, p. A633
TRAVIS, Calee, R.N., Chief Nursing Officer, Baylor Scott & White Medical Center – Centennial, Frisco, TX, p. A621
TRAVIS, Carol
Chief Financial Officer, Adventhealth Avista, Louisville, CO, p. A111
Chief Financial Officer, St. Anthony North Hospital, Westminster, CO, p. A114
TRAVIS, Dee Dee, Vice President Community Relations, Calais Community Hospital, Calais, ME, p. A296
TRAVIS, Paul, Regional Chair – Administration, Mayo Clinic Health System In Waseca, Waseca, MN, p. A357
TRAVIS, Sara, Chief Nursing Officer and Assistant Administrator, Palo Alto County Health System, Emmetsburg, IA, p. A236
TRAWICK, Amanda, Chief Executive Officer, Bullock County Hospital, Union Springs, AL, p. A25
TRAYLOR, Desiree, Chief Information Officer, Chickasaw Nation Medical Center, Ada, OK, p. A509
TRAYLOR, Jerri Sue, Director Human Resources, The Women's Hospital, Newburgh, IN, p. A225
TREACY, Nancy, Director Finance, Cambridge Medical Center, Cambridge, MN, p. A344
TREACY–SHIFF, Mary, Vice President Finance, Advocate Good Samaritan Hospital, Downers Grove, IL, p. A193
TREADWAY, Michael G, Controller, Christus Trinity Mother Frances Rehabilitation Hospital, A Partner of Encompass Health, Tyler, TX, p. A658
TREADWELL, Karen, Director Human Resources, Lake Martin Community Hospital, Dadeville, AL, p. A18
TREASE, Kevin, Chief Information Officer, Antelop. Memorial Hospital, Neligh, NE, p. A403
TREASURE, Angela, Chief Nursing Officer, Portneuf Medical Center, Pocatello, ID, p. A183
TREASURE, Jeffrey
Chief Financial Officer, Northern Arizona Healthcare, Flagstaff Medical Center, Flagstaff, AZ, p. A31
Chief Financial Officer, Northern Arizona Healthcare, Verde Valley Medical Center, Cottonwood, AZ, p. A31
TRECEK, Preston, Controller, Stormont Vail Health – Flint Hills Campus, Junction City, KS, p. A251
TREECE, Amy, M.D., Medical Director, Prisma Health North Greenville Hospital, Travelers Rest, SC, p. A571
TREGLOWN, Brad, Director Information Systems, Adventhealth Redmond, Rome, GA, p. A170
TREHAN, Rajeev, M.D., M.P.H., Chief of Staff, Eastern Kansas Hcs, Topeka, KS, p. A260
TREMAINE, Lisa, Manager Human Resources, Carson Valley Medical Center, Gardnerville, NV, p. A408
TREMBLE, Nakia, Chief Executive Officer, Kindred Hospital Indianapolis North, Indianapolis, IN, p. A220
TREMONTI, Carl
Chief Financial Officer, Mease Countryside Hospital, Safety Harbor, FL, p. A148
Chief Financial Officer, Mease Dunedin Hospital, Dunedin, FL, p. A130
Chief Financial Officer, Morton Plant Hospital, Clearwater, FL, p. A128
Chief Financial Officer, Morton Plant North Bay Hospital, New Port Richey, FL, p. A142
Chief Financial Officer, South Florida Baptist Hospital, Plant City, FL, p. A147
Chief Financial Officer, St. Anthony's Hospital, Saint Petersburg, FL, p. A149
TREMONTI, Yvette, Chief Financial Officer, H. Lee Moffitt Cancer Center And Research Institute, Tampa, FL, p. A152
TRENDE, Gary D, FACHE, Associate Director, Tuscaloosa Va Medical Center, Tuscaloosa, AL, p. A25
TRENSCHEL, Robert, D.O., FACHE, M.P.H., President and Chief Executive Officer, Yuma Regional Medical Center, Yuma, AZ, p. A42

A992 Index of Health Care Professionals

TRESSLER, Carrie, Vice President of Nursing and Chief Nursing Officer, Rush Memorial Hospital, Rushville, IN, p. A227
TRETINA, Mike, Senior Vice President and Chief Financial Officer, Bayhealth, Dover, DE, p. A121
TRETTER, Stan, M.D., Chief Medical Officer, Memorial Hospital And Health Care Center, Jasper, IN, p. A220
TREVATHAN, Dave, Director Information Systems, Rose Medical Center, Denver, CO, p. A107
TREVILLIAN, Michelle, President and Chief Executive Officer, Healthsource Saginaw Inc., Saginaw, MI, p. A337
TREVINO, Malissa, Director Human Resources, Pecos County Memorial Hospital, Fort Stockton, TX, p. A619
TREVINO, Paul
  Chief Executive Officer, CHRISTUS Ochsner Health Southwestern LA, Christus Ochsner Lake Area Hospital, Lake Charles, LA, p. A286
  Chief Executive Officer, CHRISTUS Ochsner Health Southwestern LA, Christus Ochsner St. Patrick, Lake Charles, LA, p. A286
  President and Chief Executive Officer, Christus Southeast Texas Hospital – St. Elizabeth, Beaumont, TX, p. A602
TRIANA, Rudy, M.D., Chief of Staff, Jackson Purchase Medical Center, Mayfield, KY, p. A271
TRICKEY, Donna, R.N., Chief Nursing Officer, Fairview Park Hospital, Dublin, GA, p. A163
TRICOU, John, M.D., Chief of Staff, Iroquois Memorial Hospital And Resident Home, Watseka, IL, p. A210
TRIGG, Terry, Director Human Resources, Merit Health Wesley, Hattiesburg, MS, p. A363
TRIGGS, Michael S., Group Chief Executive Officer and Managing Director, Poplar Springs Hospital, Petersburg, VA, p. A681
TRIMBLE, Lisa, Controller, Encompass Health Rehabilitation Hospital of Middletown, Middletown, DE, p. A121
TRIMBLE, Melody, Chief Executive Officer, St. Francis – Emory Healthcare, Columbus, GA, p. A161
TRIMMER, Matthew, Director Information Services, Holy Cross Hospital, Silver Spring, MD, p. A307
TRINH, Khiet, M.D., Chief Medical Officer, Bon Secours St. Mary's Hospital, Richmond, VA, p. A682
TRIPLETT, Daniel, Acting Chief Operating Officer, Springfield Hospital Center, Sykesville, MD, p. A307
TRIPLETT, John, D.O., President Medical Staff, Arh Our Lady of The Way, Martin, KY, p. A271
TRIPLETT, Kathryn, MSN, Chief Executive Officer, Select Specialty Hospital–Omaha, Omaha, NE, p. A404
TRIPLETT, Ruby, Chief Nursing Officer, Bailey Medical Center, Owasso, OK, p. A519
TRIPODE, Brian Frank., Senior Director Assumption Administrator, Our Lady of The Lake Assumption Community Hospital, Napoleonville, LA, p. A289
TRIPP, Gina, Director Information Systems, Tirr Memorial Hermann, Houston, TX, p. A628
TRIPPEL, Donald E, Chief Financial Officer, Hugh Chatham Health, Elkin, NC, p. A468
TRIVEDI, Harsh, M.D., President and Chief Executive Officer, Sheppard Pratt, Baltimore, MD, p. A302
TRIVETTE, Chastity, Administrator, Johnson County Community Hospital, Mountain City, TN, p. A590
TROCINO, Mark, Chief Information Officer, Emory Hillandale Hospital, Lithonia, GA, p. A166
TROGMAN, Richard, FACHE, Chief Executive Officer, Stockton Regional Rehabilitation Hospital, Stockton, CA, p. A97
TROMBATORE, Beverly, R.N., Director Managed Information Systems, Matagorda Regional Medical Center, Bay City, TX, p. A601
TROMBLEE, Julie, R.N., Chief Nursing Officer, The University of Vermont Health Network Elizabethtown Community Hospital, Elizabethtown, NY, p. A442
TROMPETER, Dawn
  President, OSF Saint Elizabeth Medical Center, Ottawa, IL, p. A204
  President, OSF Saint Paul Medical Center, Mendota, IL, p. A201
TRONCONE, Michael T, Chief Human Resources Officer, Calvary Hospital, New York, NY, p. A447
TROOSKIN, Stanley, M.D., Chief Medical Officer, Robert Wood Johnson University Hospital, New Brunswick, NJ, p. A425
TROTTER, Shaunda, R.N., Chief Nursing Officer, Anmed Medical Center, Anderson, SC, p. A562
TROTTER, Wally, Director Human Resources, Mountain View Hospital, Payson, UT, p. A667
TROUBLEFIELD, David G, Director, Human Resources, Hemphill County Hospital District, Canadian, TX, p. A606
TROUP, Bill, M.D., Chief of Staff, Stanton County Hospital, Johnson, KS, p. A251
TROUP, Matthew, FACHE, President and Chief Executive Officer, Conway Regional Health System, Conway, AR, p. A44

TROUT, Eugene, Chief Financial Officer, Weirton Medical Center, Weirton, WV, p. A705
TROUT, Joshua, Chief Executive Officer, Encompass Health Rehabilitation Hospital of Greenville, Greenville, SC, p. A567
TROUTMAN, Gary, CPA, Chief Financial Officer, Baptist Hospitals of Southeast Texas, Beaumont, TX, p. A602
TROWBRIDGE, William, President and Chief Executive Officer, Regional Mental Health Center, Merrillville, IN, p. A223
TROWHILL, Jan, Director Health Information Management Systems, West Tennessee Healthcare Rehabilitation Hospital Cane Creek, A Partnership With Encompass Health, Martin, TN, p. A587
TROXELL, Jason, President, Aspirus Medford Hospital & Clinics, Medford, WI, p. A715
TROXELL, Larry, Chief Executive Officer, Comanche County Medical Center, Comanche, TX, p. A608
TROY, Patrick J, R.N., MSN, Associate Director Patient Care Services, Veterans Affairs New Jersey Health Care System, East Orange, NJ, p. A420
TROY, Peggy N.
  President and Chief Executive Officer, Children's Hospital of Wisconsin–Fox Valley, Neenah, WI, p. A718
  President and Chief Executive Officer, Children's Wisconsin, Milwaukee, WI, p. A717
TROYER, David, Chief Information Officer, Veterans Affairs Northern Indiana Health Care System, Fort Wayne, IN, p. A217
TROYER, Devin, M.D., Medical Director, Encompass Health Rehabilitation Hospital of Columbia, Columbia, SC, p. A564
TRUE, Terry, M.D., Chief of Staff, North Alabama Shoals Hospital, Muscle Shoals, AL, p. A23
TRUESDELL, Shannon, Chief Operating Officer, Marshall Medical Center, Placerville, CA, p. A83
TRUITT, Louise
  Human Resource Director, Piedmont Macon North, Macon, GA, p. A167
  Vice President Human Resources, HCA Florida Capital Hospital, Tallahassee, FL, p. A151
TRUJILLO, Cynthia, Director Human Resources, New Mexico Rehabilitation Center, Roswell, NM, p. A436
TRUJILLO, Jesse, Chief Information Officer, St. Mark's Hospital, Salt Lake City, UT, p. A669
TRULSON, Larissa, Chief Executive Officer, Cornerstone Specialty Hospitals Shawnee, Shawnee, OK, p. A527
TRUMAN, Brant, PharmD, Chief Financial Officer, La Paz Regional Hospital, Parker, AZ, p. A34
TRUMAN, Erin, Associate Chief Nursing Officer, Metrowest Medical Center, Framingham, MA, p. A313
TRUMAN, Julia
  Chief Operating Officer, Multicare Tacoma General Hospital, Tacoma, WA, p. A697
  Vice President Human Resources, HCA Florida Fort Walton–Destin Hospital, Fort Walton Beach, FL, p. A132
TRUMAN, Lisa, Chief Nursing Officer, Sea Pines Rehabilitation Hospital, An Affiliate of Encompass Health, Melbourne, FL, p. A139
TRUMAN, Mark, Vice President of Operations, Baptist Health Floyd, New Albany, IN, p. A225
TRUMBO, Lauren, System Chief Financial Officer/Vice President of Finance, Methodist Hospitals, Gary, IN, p. A217
TRUPP, Michelle, Chief Operating Officer, Reading Hospital, West Reading, PA, p. A557
TRYON, Daniel
  President, Kettering Health Greene Memorial, Xenia, OH, p. A508
  President, Soin Medical Center, Beavercreek, OH, p. A486
TRYON, Ellen, R.N., Chief Nursing Officer, Adventist Health Portland, Portland, OR, p. A530
TRZNADEL, Marc
  Chief Executive Officer, Regency Hospital of Toledo, Sylvania, OH, p. A504
  Chief Executive Officer, Select Specialty Hospital–Madison, Madison, WI, p. A714
TSAI, James C., M.D., President, New York Eye And Ear Infirmary of Mount Sinai, New York, NY, p. A450
TSALATE, Cynthia, Human Resource Specialist, U. S. Public Health Service Indian Hospital, Zuni, NM, p. A437
TSAMBIRAS, Petros, M.D., Chief of Staff, Adventhealth Dade City, Dade City, FL, p. A129
TSAO, Sean, Director Information Technology, Blue Mountain Hospital District, John Day, OR, p. A528
TSCHABRUN, Dawn M., R.N., Chief Executive Officer, Select Specialty Hospital – Tucson, Tucson, AZ, p. A41
TSCHIDA, Jennifer, President, Centracare – Melrose, Melrose, MN, p. A350
TSE, Graham, M.D., Chief Medical Officer, Miller Children's & Women's Hospital Long Beach, Long Beach, CA, p. A71

TSENG, Allen, Chief Operations Officer, Memorial Hermann Memorial City Medical Center, Houston, TX, p. A627
TSUJI, Marian, Acting Administrator, Hawaii State Hospital, Kaneohe, HI, p. A177
TSUNEISHI, Lani, Nursing Services Manager, Hawaii State Hospital, Kaneohe, HI, p. A177
TUBBESING, Tara C., Chief Operating Officer, Northwest Missouri Psychiatric Rehabilitation Center, Saint Joseph, MO, p. A383
TUBBS, John
  M.D., Chief of Staff, Rock County Hospital, Bassett, NE, p. A397
  M.D., Chief of Staff, West Holt Medical Services, Atkinson, NE, p. A397
TUCK, Greg, Area Information Officer, Kaiser Permanente San Jose Medical Center, San Jose, CA, p. A92
TUCK, Heather N., Chief Financial Officer, Lakeside Behavioral Health System, Memphis, TN, p. A588
TUCKER, Albert, Chief Financial Officer, Miami Veterans Affairs Healthcare System, Miami, FL, p. A140
TUCKER, Amy, M.D., Chief Medical Officer, Upstate University Hospital, Syracuse, NY, p. A460
TUCKER, Andy, Chief Financial Officer, South Mississipp. State Hospital, Purvis, MS, p. A368
TUCKER, Bruce, Medical Center Director, Bath Veterans Affairs Medical Center, Bath, NY, p. A439
TUCKER, Cathy, Director Human Resources, Iraan General Hospital, Iraan, TX, p. A630
TUCKER, Denis, Chief Information Officer, Wilkes-Barre General Hospital, Wilkes-Barre, PA, p. A558
TUCKER, Heather, Administrator, Carle Hoopeston Regional Health Center, Hoopeston, IL, p. A198
TUCKER, Ian, M.D., Vice President Medical Affairs, Johnson Memorial Hospital, Stafford Springs, CT, p. A119
TUCKER, Jessie III, Ph.D., FACHE, President and Chief Executive Officer, UNC Health Wayne, Goldsboro, NC, p. A469
TUCKER, Jessie Lee III, Ph.D., Chief Executive Officer, Methodist Healthcare Memphis Hospitals, Memphis, TN, p. A589
TUCKER, John
  Chief Executive Officer, Henry County Medical Center, Paris, TN, p. A592
  Chief Nursing Executive, Center for Behavioral Medicine, Kansas City, MO, p. A377
TUCKER, Mona, Vice President Human Resources, Bsa Hospital, Llc, Amarillo, TX, p. A596
TUCKER, Rebecca, Chief Financial Officer, Memorial Hermann Northeast, Humble, TX, p. A629
TUCKER, Ron, Business Office Manager, Kiowa County Memorial Hospital, Greensburg, KS, p. A250
TUCKER, Theresa, Human Resources Officer, Sioux Center Health, Sioux Center, IA, p. A243
TUDELA, John M., M.D., Chief Medical Officer, Commonwealth Health Center, Saipan, MARIANA ISLANDS, p. A730
TUDOR, Brandon, Chief Executive Officer, Indianapolis Rehabilitation Hospital, Carmel, IN, p. A214
TULIPANA, Kevin, Executive Vice President, Arizona Market, City of Hop. Phoenix, Goodyear, AZ, p. A32
TULLIER, Debbie, Regional Vice President, Operations, Perimeter Behavioral Hospital of New Orleans, Kenner, LA, p. A284
TULLIS, Bea, Chief Financial Officer and Budget Officer, Broughton Hospital, Morganton, NC, p. A473
TUMA, Bonnie, Human Resources Team Lead, Nih Clinical Center, Bethesda, MD, p. A302
TUMA, Roman, Chief Medical Officer, St. Luke's Easton Campus, Easton, PA, p. A539
TUMMURU, Ramireddy K, M.D., Chief Medical Officer, Northwest Health – Porter, Valparaiso, IN, p. A228
TUNGATE, Rex A.
  Chief Executive Officer, Casey County Hospital, Liberty, KY, p. A269
  Chief Executive Officer, Jane Todd Crawford Hospital, Greensburg, KY, p. A266
TUNNELL, Richard, Chief Information Officer, University Hospital, Newark, NJ, p. A425
TUPPER, Malinda, Vice President and Chief Financial Officer, Kaweah Health Medical Center, Visalia, CA, p. A100
TURBAK, Shelly, R.N., Chief Nursing Officer, Prairie Lakes Healthcare System, Watertown, SD, p. A578
TUREK, Beth, Site Manager Information Systems, Advocate South Suburban Hospital, Hazel Crest, IL, p. A197
TUREK, Derrill Kent, R.N., Chief Nursing Officer, Blue Mountain Hospital, Blanding, UT, p. A664
TURK, Edward, Vice President Finance, Scripp. Mercy Hospital, San Diego, CA, p. A89
TURK, Khalid, Chief Healthcare Technology Officer, Santa Clara Valley Medical Center, San Jose, CA, p. A92

Index of Health Care Professionals

Index of Health Care Professionals / Turkal–Barrett

TURKAL–BARRETT, Kari, Flight Commander Resource Management Officer, Mike O'Callaghan Federal Hospital, Nellis Afb, NV, p. A411
TURLEY, Kenneth, Chief Executive Officer, Kessler Marlton Rehabilitation, Marlton, NJ, p. A423
TURLEY, Mary Ann, D.O., Medical Director, Honorhealth Deer Valley Medical Center, Phoenix, AZ, p. A35
TURLEY, Matt, Interim Director Information Systems, Camc Greenbrier Valley Medical Center, Ronceverte, WV, p. A704
TURMAN, Anna M., Division Vice President, Chief Information Officer, Chi Health Creighton University Medical Center – Bergan Mercy, Omaha, NE, p. A403
TURNBULL, Rosie, Director Human Resources, St. Lawrence Psychiatric Center, Ogdensburg, NY, p. A455
TURNER, Andrea, JD, Chief Executive Officer, Harbor–Ucla Medical Center, Torrance, CA, p. A98
TURNER, Arnold F., M.D., Chief Hospital Executive, Provident Hospital of Cook County, Chicago, IL, p. A190
TURNER, Barbara, Director of Nursing, Austen Riggs Center, Stockbridge, MA, p. A318
TURNER, Bill, Vice President Human Resources, Valir Rehabilitation Hospital, Oklahoma City, OK, p. A519
TURNER, Brenda C
Chief Human Resources Officer, Palomar Medical Center Escondido, Escondido, CA, p. A62
Chief Human Resources Officer, Palomar Medical Center Poway, Poway, CA, p. A84
TURNER, Chad, Chief Financial Officer, Star Valley Health, Afton, WY, p. A726
TURNER, Cindy R, Chief Executive Officer, Bacon County Hospital And Health System, Alma, GA, p. A156
TURNER, Cindy R., Chief Executive Officer, Bacon County Hospital And Health System, Alma, GA, p. A156
TURNER, Cody, M.D., Chief Medical Officer, Cleveland Clinic Union Hospital, Dover, OH, p. A495
TURNER, Dale, Chief Operating Officer, Reedsburg Area Medical Center, Reedsburg, WI, p. A720
TURNER, Jeff, FACHE, Chief Executive Officer, Moore County Hospital District, Dumas, TX, p. A615
TURNER, Justin
Chief Operating Officer, Highlands Arh Regional Medical Center, Prestonsburg, KY, p. A273
Chief Operating Officer, Rivers Health, Point Pleasant, WV, p. A704
TURNER, Karen, Chief Nursing Officer, Seneca Healthcare District, Chester, CA, p. A59
TURNER, Karissa
President and Chief Executive Officer, Wabash General Hospital, Mount Carmel, IL, p. A202
Vice President Operations, Wabash General Hospital, Mount Carmel, IL, p. A202
TURNER, Kevin, M.D., Medical Director, Pathways of Tennessee, Jackson, TN, p. A584
TURNER, Kristen, Chief Executive Officer, Encompass Health Rehabilitation Hospital of Mechanicsburg, Mechanicsburg, PA, p. A545
TURNER, Mark
Chief Executive Officer, San Bernardino Mountains Community Hospital, Lake Arrowhead, CA, p. A69
Manager Information Technology, Ojai Valley Community Hospital, Ojai, CA p. A81
TURNER, Marquita, Chief Operating Officer and Chief Nursing Officer, Atrium Medical Center, Middletown, OH, p. A500
TURNER, Maurita, Team Leader Health Information Systems Services, Chi St. Joseph. Health Madison Hospital, Madisonville, TX, p. A637
TURNER, Melissa, Senior Vice President Human Resources, Bridgeport Hospital, Bridgeport, CT, p. A115
TURNER, Michael
Chief Information Officer, Vibra Hospital of Houston, Houston, TX, p. A628
Director Human Resources, Moberly Regional Medical Center, Moberly, MO, p. A380
TURNER, Nancy, Director Communications, Sutter Roseville Medical Center, Roseville, CA, p. A86
TURNER, Peggy, Assistant Vice President and Director of Nursing, Unity Health, Searcy, AR, p. A53
TURNER, Ralph
President, Wellstar Mcg Health, Augusta, GA, p. A158
President, Wellstar Paulding Hospital, Hiram, GA, p. A165
TURNER, Randy, Chief Human Resource Management Services, Boise Va Medical Center, Boise, ID, p. A179
TURNER, Robert A, Chief Executive Officer, East Houston Hospitals & Clinics, Houston, TX, p. A625
TURNER, Sara, Director Human Resources, UC San Diego Health – East Campus, San Diego, CA, p. A90
TURNER, Saundra G, Director Human Resources, Mercy Hospital Jefferson, Festus, MO, p. A375
TURNER, Sherrilyn, Director Human Resources, Southeast Colorado Hospital District, Springfield, CO, p. A113
TURNER, Steve, Director Information Technology, Salem Township Hospital, Salem, IL, p. A208
TURNER, Teri, Chief Nursing Officer, Haskell Memorial Hospital, Haskell, TX, p. A624
TURNER, Tiffany, MSN, R.N., Vice President of Nursing and Chief Nursing Officer, Paris Community Hospital, Paris, IL, p. A205
TURNER, Will, Chief Executive Officer, Baylor Scott & White Medical Center–Waxahachie, Waxahachie, TX, p. A660
TURNEY, Amanda, Director Human Resources, Cochran Memorial Hospital, Morton, TX, p. A640
TURNEY, David, Chief Information Officer, Cochran Memorial Hospital, Morton, TX, p. A640
TURNLEY, Felicia, Chief Executive Officer, Memorial Hospital Pembroke, Pembroke Pines, FL, p. A146
TURNQUIST, Carrie, Director Human Resources, Buena Vista Regional Medical Center, Storm Lake, IA, p. A244
TURO, Albert, Vice President Human Resources, St. Mary's Healthcare, Amsterdam, NY, p. A438
TURPEN, Brad, FACHE, Chief Executive Officer, Valor Health, Emmett, ID, p. A181
TURPIN, Debra, R.N., MSN, Vice President Patient Care Services and Chief Nursing Officer, Alton Memorial Hospital, Alton, IL, p. A185
TURPIN, James
Chief Human Resource Officer, Breckinridge Memorial Hospital, Hardinsburg, KY, p. A266
Chief of Staff, Ephraim Mcdowell Fort Logan Hospital, Stanford, KY, p. A274
TURQUEZA, Sandra
Human Resources Business Partner, Chi Saint Josep. Health – Saint Josep. Berea, Berea, KY, p. A263
Senior Human Resources Business Partner, Chi Saint Josep. Health – Saint Josep. London, London, KY, p. A269
TURSO, Janet, Controller, Encompass Health Rehabilitation Hospital of Toms River, Toms River, NJ, p. A429
TURTON, Jonathan, FACHE, President, Glenwood Regional Medical Center, West Monroe, LA, p. A294
TUSCANY, Joanne E
Director Human Resources, Ascension St. John Hospital, Detroit, MI, p. A325
Senior Director Human Resources, Ascension Macomb–Oakland Hospital, Warren Campus, Warren, MI, p. A340
TUSSEY, Kathy, R.N., Chief Executive Officer, Harrison Memorial Hospital, Cynthiana, KY, p. A264
TUSTEN, Jay, President and Chief Executive Officer, Clara Barton Medical Center, Hoisington, KS, p. A250
TUSTIN, Bill, Chief Operating Officer, Piedmont Columbus Regional Midtown, Columbus, GA, p. A161
TUTT, Michael, M.D., Chief Medical Officer, Tsehootsooi Medical Center, Fort Defiance, AZ, p. A31
TUTTLE, Casey, Supervisor Information Technology, Sistersville General Hospital, Sistersville, WV, p. A704
TUTTLE, Kathryn, R.N., Director of Nursing, Tamarack Health Ashland Medical Center, Ashland, WI, p. A707
TWARDY, Cindi, Manager Human Resources, Meeker Memorial Hospital And Clinics, Litchfield, MN, p. A348
TWEED, Frances, R.N., Executive Director and Administrator, New Mexico Behavioral Health Institute At Las Vegas, Las Vegas, NM, p. A435
TWEHOUS, Debra, Medical Director, Fairlawn Rehabilitation Hospital, Worcester, MA, p. A320
TWIDWELL, Lisa, Chief Executive Officer, Madison Medical Center, Fredericktown, MO, p. A375
TWIGG, Nicole, Director Human Resources, Brook Lane, Hagerstown, MD, p. A304
TYE, Angie, Director Human Resources, Waverly Health Center, Waverly, IA, p. A245
TYLER, Holley, R.N., Chief Nursing Officer, Woman's Hospital of Texas, Houston, TX, p. A629
TYLER, Kimberly, Director of Nursing, St. Mary's Good Samaritan Hospital, Greensboro, GA, p. A164
TYLER, Philene, Chief Finance Officer, Chinle Comprehensive Health Care Facility, Chinle, AZ, p. A31
TYLER, Richard, Chief Human Resource Officer, Conway Regional Health System, Conway, AR, p. A44
TYLER, Rick, M.D., Vice President Medical Affairs, Christus Southeast Texas Hospital – St. Elizabeth, Beaumont, TX, p. A602
TYLER, Tanya, Vice President Human Resources, Chi St. Luke's Health Memorial Lufkin, Lufkin, TX, p. A636
TYO, Joanne, Chief Financial Officer, Carolinas Continuecare Hospital At Pineville, Charlotte, NC, p. A465
TYRA, Diana, Director Health Information, Kentucky River Medical Center, Jackson, KY, p. A267
TYRER, Andrew, Chief Operating Officer, Tristar Summit Medical Center, Hermitage, TN, p. A584
TYRER, Drew, Chief Executive Officer, HCA Florida Westside Hospital, Plantation, FL, p. A147
TYROL, Anne, R.N., Chief Nursing Officer, Cheshire Medical Center, Keene, NH, p. A415
TYSON, Rhoda, Chief Information Officer, Central Alabama Va Medical Center–Montgomery, Montgomery, AL, p. A22
TZANAKIS, Lisa, Chief Operating Officer, HCA Florida Fawcett Hospital, Port Charlotte, FL, p. A147

U

UBER, Charlotte M., Chief Executive Officer, Warren State Hospital, Warren, PA, p. A556
UDALL, Ben, M.D., Chief of Staff, Kimble Hospital, Junction, TX, p. A631
UDANI, Neil, M.D., Chief Medical Officer, Saint Clare's Denville Hospital, Denville, NJ, p. A420
UDOVICH, Christopher, M.D., Chief of Staff, Silver Cross Hospital, New Lenox, IL, p. A203
UGHOUWA, Ejiro, M.D., Chief of Staff, Allen Parish Community Healthcare, Kinder, LA, p. A285
UGOJI, Amanze, M.D., Chief Executive Officer, Washington Regional Medical Center, Plymouth, NC, p. A474
UGWUEKE, Michael Sr, FACHE, President and Chief Executive Officer, Methodist Healthcare Memphis Hospitals, Memphis, TN, p. A589
UHARRIET, Bart, Director Information Services, Mississipp. State Hospital, Whitfield, MS, p. A370
ULBRICHT, William G., Chief Executive Officer, Baptist Health South Florida, Baptist Hospital of Miami, Miami, FL, p. A139
ULERY, Brian, Chief Executive Officer, Saint Clare's Denville Hospital, Denville, NJ, p. A420
ULETT, John, Vice President and Chief Information Officer, Centrastate Healthcare System, Freehold, NJ, p. A421
ULFERTS, Wendy, Vice President and Chief Nursing Officer, Maple Grove Hospital, Maple Grove, MN, p. A349
ULIBARRI, Laura, M.D., Chief of Staff, Catalina Island Medical Center, Avalon, CA, p. A56
ULLRICH, John, M.D., Chief of Staff, Ivinson Memorial Hospital, Laramie, WY, p. A727
ULMER, Becky, R.N., Director of Nursing, Jasper General Hospital, Bay Springs, MS, p. A359
ULREICH, Kelly, Executive Director, Highlands Behavioral Health System, Littleton, CO, p. A111
ULREICH, Shawn, MSN, R.N., Vice President Clinical Operations and Chief Nursing Executive, Corewell Health Butterworth Hospital, Grand Rapids, MI, p. A328
ULRICH, Alan, Chief Financial Officer, Guam Memorial Hospital Authority, Tamuning, GU, p. A730
ULRICH, James P. Jr, FACHE, Chief Executive Officer, York General, York, NE, p. A407
ULRICH, Jennifer, Interim President, OSF St. Josep. Medical Center, Bloomington, IL, p. A186
ULRICH, Kari, R.N., Chief Nursing Officer, Director Operating Room, Surgical Specialty Center of Baton Rouge, Baton Rouge, LA, p. A278
ULSETH, Randy, Chief Executive Officer, Welia Health, Mora, MN, p. A351
ULVELING, Kyle, M.D., Chief of Staff, St. Anthony Regional Hospital, Carroll, IA, p. A231
UMBERGER, Lori S., Chief Nursing Officer, Boys Town National Research Hospital, Omaha, NE, p. A403
UMHAU, John, M.D., Clinical Director, U. S. Public Health Service Indian Hospital–Whiteriver, Whiteriver, AZ, p. A41
UMINA, Thomas, M.D., Executive Director, Richard H. Hutchings Psychiatric Center, Syracuse, NY, p. A460
UNDERDAHL, Steve, President and Chief Executive Officer, Northfield Hospital And Clinics, Northfield, MN, p. A352
UNDERHILL, Robert, Director of Business Services, Central State Hospital, Louisville, KY, p. A269
UNDERRINER, David T.
Executive Vice President of Oahu Operations, Chief Executive Officer, Kapiolani Medical Center for Women & Children, Honolulu, HI, p. A175
Executive Vice President of Oahu Operations, Chief Executive Officer, Pali Momi Medical Center, Aiea, HI, p. A175
Executive Vice President of Oahu Operations, Chief Executive Officer, Straub Medical Center, Honolulu, HI, p. A176
UNDERWOOD, Debbie, Manager Human Resources, Plains Memorial Hospital, Dimmitt, TX, p. A614
UNDERWOOD, Jerri C, R.N., Chief Nursing Officer, Parkridge Medical Center, Chattanooga, TN, p. A580
UNDERWOOD, Kelsey N, Director of Nursing, Gundersen Tri–County Hospital And Clinics, Whitehall, WI, p. A725

A994 Index of Health Care Professionals

Index of Health Care Professionals / Van Meter

UNDERWOOD, Phillip
Chief Executive Officer, Kindred Hospital–Dayton, Dayton, OH, p. A494
Chief Executive Officer, Regional One Health Extended Care Hospital, Memphis, TN, p. A589
UNDERWOOD, Vickie, Director Human Resources, Wyandot Memorial Hospital, Upper Sandusky, OH, p. A505
UNDERWOOD, Virgil, Chief Executive Officer, Boone Memorial Hospital, Madison, WV, p. A702
UNDLIN, Cassie, Chief Operating Officer, Navos, Seattle, WA, p. A694
UNG, David
Director, Information Technology, California Hospital Medical Center, Los Angeles, CA, p. A72
Site Director, St. Mary Medical Center Long Beach, Long Beach, CA, p. A71
UNGER, Henry D., M.D., Senior Vice President and Chief Medical Officer, Holy Redeemer Hospital, Meadowbrook, PA, p. A545
UNGER, Kevin L.
Ph.D., FACHE, President and Chief Executive Officer, UCHealth Medical Center of The Rockies, Loveland, CO, p. A112
Ph.D., FACHE, President and Chief Executive Officer, UCHealth Poudre Valley Hospital, Fort Collins, CO, p. A108
UNITAN, Carol, M.D., Chief Medical Officer, Kaiser Westside Medical Center, Hillsboro, OR, p. A527
UNRUH, Courtney, Chief Nursing Officer, Freeman Regional Health Services, Freeman, SD, p. A573
UNRUH, Dawn, R.N., Chief Executive Officer, Meade District Hospital, Meade, KS, p. A254
UPCHURCH, Jim, M.D., Chief Medical Officer, Crow/Northern Cheyenne Hospital, Crow Agency, MT, p. A391
UPCRAFT, Jeffrey, Director Information Services, Southwest Healthcare System, Murrieta, CA, p. A79
UPFIELD, Jaclyn, Chief Operating Officer, G. Werber Bryan Psychiatric Hospital, Columbia, SC, p. A564
UPHOFF, Kimberly
President and Chief Executive Officer, Sarah Bush Lincoln Health Center, Mattoon, IL, p. A201
Vice President Operations, Sarah Bush Lincoln Health Center, Mattoon, IL, p. A201
UPSHAW, Joy, Vice President and Chief Nursing Officer, TMC Health, Tucson, AZ, p. A41
UPTON, Daniel, Vice President and Chief Financial Officer, Doylestown Health, Doylestown, PA, p. A538
UPTON, LaTashia, M.D., Chief Medical Officer, Ochsner Lsu Health Shreveport – St. Mary Medical Center, Llc, Shreveport, LA, p. A292
UPTON, Matthew, M.D., Chief Medical Officer, Thomas Memorial Hospital, South Charleston, WV, p. A705
URAIZEE, Rizwan A., Chief Financial Officer, Kedren Community Health Center, Los Angeles, CA, p. A73
URBAN, Frank, Chief Financial Officer, Southwood Psychiatric Hospital, Pittsburgh, PA, p. A551
URBAN, Holly, R.N., MSN, RN, Interim Chief Nursing Officer, St. Josep. Regional Medical Center, Lewiston, ID, p. A182
URBAN, Louise, R.N., Chief Operating Officer, Select Specialty Hospital–Mckeesport, Mckeesport, PA, p. A545
URBAN, Melanie D., Administrator, Pawnee Valley Community Hospital, Larned, KS, p. A253
URBAN, Sharon, R.N., Chief Nursing Officer, Mercy Fitzgerald Hospital, Darby, PA, p. A538
URBANCSIK, Don
Director Finance, Cleveland Clinic Euclid Hospital, Euclid, OH, p. A495
Director Finance, Cleveland Clinic Lutheran Hospital, Cleveland, OH, p. A490
URBANIAK, Toyia, Chief Executive Officer, Longview Rehabilitation Hospital, Longview, TX, p. A635
URBISTONDO, Lisa, Chief Financial Officer, Atrium Health Navicent Peach, Macon, GA, p. A167
URDANETA, Alfonso, M.D., President Medical Staff, Washington County Hospital, Nashville, IL, p. A203
URISH, Abigail R., M.D., Chief of Staff, Rangely District Hospital, Rangely, CO, p. A113
URLAUB, Charles J., President, Mount St. Mary's Hospital And Health Center, Lewiston, NY, p. A445
URQUHART, Mary, R.N., Vice President Patient Care, Brattleboro Memorial Hospital, Brattleboro, VT, p. A671
URQUHART, Teresa C.
Chief Executive Officer, Palm Beach Gardens Medical Center, Palm Beach Gardens, FL, p. A145
Market Chief Executive Officer, Piedmont Medical Center, Rock Hill, SC, p. A570
URQUIA, Arianna, Chief Financial Officer, Nicklaus Children's Hospital, Miami, FL, p. A140
URSCHEL, Dorothy M., President and Chief Executive Officer, Columbia Memorial Hospital, Hudson, NY, p. A444
USELMAN, Krista, Chief Executive Officer, Encompass Health Rehabilitation Hospital The Vintage, Houston, TX, p. A625
USELMAN, Melissa, Chief Financial Officer, Gundersen Boscobel Area Hospital And Clinics, Boscobel, WI, p. A708
USHER, David, Chief Financial Officer, Ray County Hospital And Healthcare, Richmond, MO, p. A382
USRY, Ashley, Director, Human Resources, Encompass Health Rehabilitation Hospital of Cumming, Cumming, GA, p. A162
UST, Tyler, Adminstrator, Chief Executive Officer, Sanford Thief River Falls Medical Center, Thief River Falls, MN, p. A356
UTECHT, Tom
M.D., Chief Medical Officer, Community Regional Medical Center, Fresno, CA, p. A64
M.D., Corporate Chief Quality Officer, Fresno Heart And Surgical Hospital, Fresno, CA, p. A64
M.D., Senior Vice President and Chief Quality Officer, Community Behavioral Health Center, Fresno, CA, p. A64
UTLEY, Donna, Vice President Human Resources, Mercy San Juan Medical Center, Carmichael, CA, p. A58
UTLEY, Renee, Chief Financial Officer, Hamilton Center, Terre Haute, IN, p. A228
UTTENDORFSKY, Rob, Director Information Management, Lewis County General Hospital, Lowville, NY, p. A445
UTTERBACK, Julie, Chief Financial Officer, Roane Medical Center, Harriman, TN, p. A583
UYEMURA, Monte, M.D., Chief of Staff, Wray Community District Hospital, Wray, CO, p. A114
UZABEL, Samuel, M.D., Chief Medical Officer, Bonner General Health, Sandpoint, ID, p. A184
UZZO, Robert, M.D., President and Chief Executive Officer, Fox Chase Cancer Center, Philadelphia, PA, p. A548

V

VAAGENES, Carl P., Chief Executive Officer, Alomere Health, Alexandria, MN, p. A342
VAALER, Mark, M.D., Chief Medical Officer, South Florida Baptist Hospital, Plant City, FL, p. A147
VACCARO, Michael, Senior Vice President Nursing, Novant Health Ballantyne Medical Center, Charlotte, NC, p. A465
VACCARO, Stacey, Chief Operating Officer, The Children's Institute of Pittsburgh, Pittsburgh, PA, p. A551
VACHON, Scott, Director Information Technology, Littleton Regional Healthcare, Littleton, NH, p. A416
VADEN, Jim, Director Information Systems, Lauderdale Community Hospital, Ripley, TN, p. A592
VADYAK, Karen, Chief Nursing Officer, St. Luke's Easton Campus, Easton, PA, p. A539
VAEZAZIZI, Reza, M.D., Chief of Staff, Southwest Healthcare System, Murrieta, CA, p. A79
VAGUE, Jeff, Regional Manager Information Systems, Mercy Hospital Downtown, Bakersfield, CA, p. A57
VAHLBERG, Susan, Director Employee and Community Relations, Valor Health, Emmett, ID, p. A181
VAIL, Amanda, Chief Executive Officer, Cypress Creek Hospital, Houston, TX, p. A625
VAIL, B J, Director Information Systems, Morehouse General Hospital, Bastrop. LA, p. A277
VAIL, Bryan, Chief Information Officer, Clement J. Zablocki Veterans' Administration Medical Center, Milwaukee, WI, p. A717
VAIL, Ronald, M.D., Chief of Staff, Lower Umpqua Hospital District, Reedsport, OR, p. A531
VAILLANCOURT, Alex, Chief Information Officer, The Christ Hospital Health Network, Cincinnati, OH, p. A489
VAIOLETI, Stephany, President, Queen's North Hawaii Community Hospital, Kamuela, HI, p. A176
VALADEZ, Philip. Director of Nursing, Oceans Behavioral Hospital of Corpus Christi, Corpus Christi, TX, p. A609
VALDENEGRO, Maria, Chief Financial Officer, Meadow Wood Behavioral Health System, New Castle, DE, p. A122
VALDESPINO, Gustavo A., President/Chief Executive Officer, Valley Presbyterian Hospital, Los Angeles, CA, p. A75
VALDEZ, J. Alex, JD, President and Chief Executive Officer, Christus St. Vincent Regional Medical Center, Santa Fe, NM, p. A436
VALENCA, Robert, Director, Human Resources, Colleton Medical Center, Walterboro, SC, p. A571
VALENCERINA, Madeline, Chief Operating Officer, Kedren Community Health Center, Los Angeles, CA, p. A73
VALENTE, Anthony, M.D., Vice President Medical Affairs, Lehigh Valley Hospital – Hazleton, Hazleton, PA, p. A541
VALENTE, T. J., M.D., Medical Director, Lifestream Behavioral Center, Leesburg, FL, p. A137
VALENTIN, Carlos, Chief Financial Officer, St. Luke's Episcopal Hospital, Ponce, PR, p. A734
VALENTINE, Mark
President, Baylor Scott & White The Heart Hospital Denton, Denton, TX, p. A613
President, Baylor Scott & White The Heart Hospital Plano, Plano, TX, p. A644
VALENTINI, Rudolph, M.D., Chief Medical Officer, Dmc Children's Hospital of Michigan, Detroit, MI, p. A325
VALENTINO, Audra, Chief Nursing Officer, Banner Casa Grande Medical Center, Casa Grande, AZ, p. A30
VALENTO, Jessica, Director Information Systems, Fairview Range, Hibbing, MN, p. A348
VALLE, David, Chief Information Officer, Hospital Pavia Arecibo, Arecibo, PR, p. A731
VALLE, Karla, Area Chief Financial Officer, Kaiser Permanente Panorama City Medical Center, Los Angeles, CA, p. A73
VALLELY, Ian, Information Technology Site Leader, Sequoia Hospital, Redwood City, CA, p. A85
VALLIDO, Gabe, Chief Information Officer, Naval Hospital Camp Pendleton, Camp Pendleton, CA, p. A58
VALLIERE, George, Chief Executive Officer, Claremore Indian Hospital, Claremore, OK, p. A511
VALTAIRO, Fred, R.N., Chief Executive Officer, UCI Health – Placentia Linda, Placentia, CA, p. A83
VAN BRUNT, Lisa, Chief Nursing Officer, Washakie Medical Center, Worland, WY, p. A729
VAN BUSKIRK, George F, M.D., Chief of Staff, Bay Pines Veterans Affairs Healthcare System, Bay Pines, FL, p. A125
VAN BUSKIRK, Kryder III, Medical Staff President at EMRMC, Ephraim Mcdowell Regional Medical Center, Danville, KY, p. A264
VAN CAMP, Keith, Vice President Information Services, St. Dominic–Jackson Memorial Hospital, Jackson, MS, p. A364
VAN CLEAVE, Chad, Chief Financial Officer, Columbus Community Hospital, Columbus, NE, p. A399
VAN DEELEN, Nicholas, M.D., President, Aspirus St. Luke's Hospital, Duluth, MN, p. A346
VAN DEN AVYLE, Adam
Hospital Administrator, Kaiser Sunnyside Medical Center, Clackamas, OR, p. A526
Hospital Administrator, Kaiser Westside Medical Center, Hillsboro, OR, p. A527
VAN DER WEGE, Larry, Administrator, Lindsborg Community Hospital, Lindsborg, KS, p. A253
VAN DERDYS ARROYO, Giselle K., Chief Executive Officer, Hospital Buen Samaritano, Aguadilla, PR, p. A730
VAN DONSELAAR, Ryan, Chief Medical Officer, Hendricks Regional Health, Danville, IN, p. A215
VAN DRIEL, Allen E., Interim Chief Executive Officer, Hodgeman County Health Center, Jetmore, KS, p. A251
VAN DUREN, Michael, M.D., Chief Medical Officer, Bay Area Hospital, Coos Bay, OR, p. A526
VAN DYK, Holly, M.D., Interim Chief Medical Officer, Tuba City Regional Health Care Corporation, Tuba City, AZ, p. A40
VAN EPERN, Keri, Manager Human Resources, Aspirus Ironwood Hospital & Clinics, Inc., Ironwood, MI, p. A330
VAN ETTEN, Mark, M.D., Chief of Staff, Spooner Health, Spooner, WI, p. A721
VAN GENDEREN, Nathan, Executive Vice President and Chief Financial Officer, Mercy Medical Center – Cedar Rapids, Cedar Rapids, IA, p. A231
VAN GORDER, Chris D.
FACHE, President and Chief Executive Officer, Scripp. Green Hospital, La Jolla, CA, p. A68
FACHE, President and Chief Executive Officer, Scripp. Mercy Hospital, San Diego, CA, p. A89
FACHE, President, Chief Executive Officer, Scripp. Memorial Hospital–Encinitas, Encinitas, CA, p. A62
VAN HOET, Jim, Chief Financial Officer, Coffey County Hospital, Burlington, KS, p. A247
VAN HOUDEN, Charles, M.D., Chief Medical Officer, Neosho Memorial Regional Medical Center, Chanute, KS, p. A247
VAN HOUWELING, Mason, Chief Executive Officer, University Medical Center, Las Vegas, NV, p. A411
VAN KAMPEN, Cindy, Chief Nursing Officer, Trinity Health Grand Haven Hospital, Grand Haven, MI, p. A328
VAN LAUWE, Aaron, Director, Human Resources, Quad Cities Rehabilitation Institute, The, Moline, IL, p. A202
VAN MARCKE, Thibaut, President, Orlando Health Orlando Regional Medical Center, Orlando, FL, p. A144
VAN MATRE, Jennifer, Chief Financial Officer, Trinity Hospital, Weaverville, CA, p. A101
VAN MEETEREN, Robert, President and Chief Executive Officer, Reedsburg Area Medical Center, Reedsburg, WI, p. A720
VAN METER, Rex, Chief Executive Officer, St. Mary's Regional Medical Center, Enid, OK, p. A512

Index of Health Care Professionals

Index of Health Care Professionals / Van Natta

VAN NATTA, Timothy, M.D., Chief Medical Officer, Harbor–Ucla Medical Center, Torrance, CA, p. A98
VAN RANKEN, Danny, Chief Operating Officer, Kearney Regional Medical Center, Kearney, NE, p. A401
VAN RYBROEK, Greg, Chief Executive Officer, Mendota Mental Health Institute, Madison, WI, p. A714
VAN SCOYK, Mitch, Manager Information Systems, Delta Health, Delta, CO, p. A106
VAN VRANKEN, Arthur, M.D., Chief Medical Officer, Essentia Health–Graceville, Graceville, MN, p. A347
VAN VRANKEN, Ross, Executive Director, University of Utah Health, Salt Lake City, UT, p. A669
VAN WAGONER, Scott, M.D., Chief Medical Officer, American Fork Hospital, American Fork, UT, p. A664
VAN WHY, Susan, Director Human Resources, St. Luke's Hospital–Miners Campus, Coaldale, PA, p. A537
VAN WINKLE, James, M.D., Chief of Staff, Unity Medical Center, Manchester, TN, p. A587
VAN WINKLE, Melanie, Chief Financial Officer, Mammoth Hospital, Mammoth Lakes, CA, p. A76
VANBOEKEL, Tony, Director Information Systems, Shasta Regional Medical Center, Redding, CA, p. A85
VANCE, Ellen B, Chief Human Resources Officer, Sheltering Arms Institute, Midlothian, VA, p. A679
VANCE, Mark, M.D., Chief Medical Officer, Quincy Valley Medical Center, Quincy, WA, p. A693
VANCE, Ruth, Director Information Systems, Quincy Valley Medical Center, Quincy, WA, p. A693
VANCE, Stacie
Chief Nursing Officer and, Orthoindy Hospital, Indianapolis, IN, p. A220
Chief Nursing Officer and Vice President Operations, Orthoindy Hospital, Indianapolis, IN, p. A220
VANCE, Steven, Information Technology Director, Lake District Hospital, Lakeview, OR, p. A528
VANDENBARK, Heather, Human Resources Specialist, State Hospital North, Orofino, ID, p. A183
VANDENBERG, Andra, Director Human Resources, Butler County Health Care Center, David City, NE, p. A399
VANDENBOSCH, Dan, Chief Information Officer, Madison County Health Care System, Winterset, IA, p. A245
VANDENBURG, Jenene, Vice President Patient Services and Chief Nursing Officer, Methodist Jennie Edmundson Hospital, Council Bluffs, IA, p. A234
VANDERHOOFT, J Eric, M.D., President Medical Staff, St. Mark's Hospital, Salt Lake City, UT, p. A669
VANDERLINDEN, Mark A, Chief Financial Officer, Clive Behavioral Health, Clive, IA, p. A233
VANDERMARK, Jay H, Chief Financial Officer, Veterans Affairs Northern Indiana Health Care System, Fort Wayne, IN, p. A217
VANDERMEER, Nick, Director Information Systems, Banner Payson Medical Center, Payson, AZ, p. A34
VANDERPOEL, Steve, Chief Executive Officer, San Jose Behavorial Health, San Jose, CA, p. A92
VANDERPOL, Antoinette, Chief of Staff, Avera St. Benedict Health Center, Parkston, SD, p. A575
VANDERPOOL, Lee, Vice President, Dominican Hospital, Santa Cruz, CA, p. A94
VANDERSCHAAFF, Trixie
Chief Executive Officer, Commonspirit – St. Anthony Summit Medical Center, Frisco, CO, p. A108
Chief Nursing Officer, Commonspirit – St. Anthony Summit Medical Center, Frisco, CO, p. A108
VANDERSLICE, Douglas M, Senior Vice President and Chief Financial Officer, Boston Children's Hospital, Boston, MA, p. A310
VANDERSTEEG, James, Acting Chief Executive Officer, Parkwest Medical Center, Knoxville, TN, p. A586
VANDERSTOUW, Karl, Vice President, Support Services, UNC Health Lenoir, Kinston, NC, p. A471
VANDERVEER, Mark L., Chief Financial Officer, Gunnison Valley Health, Gunnison, CO, p. A109
VANDERVLIET, William, M.D., Vice President Medical Affairs, Holland Hospital, Holland, MI, p. A330
VANDERVOORT, Amanda R, Chief Operating Officer, Thayer County Health Services, Hebron, NE, p. A401
VANDEWALLE, Kathryn, JD, Chief Nurse Executive, Kaiser Sunnyside Medical Center, Clackamas, OR, p. A526
VANDEWEGE, Dana
Director Human Resources, Multicare Capital Medical Center, Olympia, WA, p. A692
Director Human Resources, Providence Centralia Hospital, Centralia, WA, p. A688
VANDONKELAAR, Rodney
Chief Financial Officer, Ascension Saint Thomas Highlands, Sparta, TN, p. A593
Chief Financial Officer, Carolina Pines Regional Medical Center, Hartsville, SC, p. A568
VANDORT, Patti J., MSN, R.N., Chief Executive Officer, Holland Hospital, Holland, MI, p. A330
VANDYKE, Jeff, Interim Chief Executive Officer, Rooks County Health Center, Plainville, KS, p. A258
VANEK, James, Chief Executive Officer, Columbus Community Hospital, Columbus, TX, p. A608
VANES, Wendell, Chief Financial Officer, Saint Mary's Regional Medical Center, Russellville, AR, p. A53
VANHAREN, James, M.D., Medical Director, Forest View Psychiatric Hospital, Grand Rapids, MI, p. A328
VANHOOZIER, Adria, President, Riverside Doctors' Hospital Williamsburg, Williamsburg, VA, p. A685
VANHOY, Michael, Director of Quality, UVA Encompass Health Rehabilitation Hospital, Charlottesville, VA, p. A674
VANHYNING, Jill, Director of Human Resources, Fairfield Memorial Hospital, Fairfield, IL, p. A195
VANKEKERIX, Emily, Director Human Resources, Osceola Regional Health Center, Sibley, IA, p. A243
VANMELKEBEKE, Alyssa, Chief Nursing Officer, Quad Cities Rehabilitation Institute, The, Moline, IL, p. A202
VANMETER, Cory, Chief Executive Officer, Mercy Rehabilitation Hospital Fort Smith, Fort Smith, AR, p. A47
VANNATTER, Janet, Chief Operating Officer, Massac Memorial Hospital, Metropolis, IL, p. A202
VANNATTER, Mistie, Chief Nursing Officer, Advanced Care Hospital of White County, Searcy, AR, p. A53
VANNOY, Charles, R.N., Vice President Patient Care Services and Chief Nursing Officer, Valley Hospital, Paramus, NJ, p. A426
VANO, Ann
Vice President Human Resources, Ascension Providence Hospital, Southfield Campus, Southfield, MI, p. A338
Vice President, Human Resources, Ascension Providence Rochester Hospital, Rochester, MI, p. A336
VANSANT, Scott, M.D., Chief Medical Officer, Central State Hospital, Milledgeville, GA, p. A168
VANSTRIEN, Amy, Director Talent Operations, City of Hop. Chicago, Zion, IL, p. A211
VANTONGEREN, Teri, Director Information Services, Corewell Health Pennock Hospital, Hastings, MI, p. A329
VANWALLAGHEN, Brenda, Interim Chief Nursing Officer, Dmc Children's Hospital of Michigan, Detroit, MI, p. A325
VANWYHE, Brenda, Senior Vice President Finance and Chief Financial Officer, Rush–Copley Medical Center, Aurora, IL, p. A186
VARELA, Nancy, Director Human Resources, Dsh Patton, Patton, CA, p. A83
VARGA, Patrick, Chief Operating Officer, Mercy Medical Center Redding, Redding, CA, p. A85
VARGAS, Bianca, Human Resources Manager, Reunion Rehabilitation Hospital Arlington, Arlington, TX, p. A598
VARGAS, Ildefonso, Executive Director, Hospital Manati Medical Center, Manati, PR, p. A733
VARGAS, Jose L, M.D., Medical Director, West Gables Rehabilitation Hospital, Miami, FL, p. A141
VARGAS, Margie, Chief Human Resources Officer, Memorial Regional Hospital, Hollywood, FL, p. A133
VARGAS, Marisol, Director Finance, Hospital Del Maestro, San Juan, PR, p. A735
VARGAS, Nancy
Chief Human Resources, St. Joseph's Behavioral Health Center, Stockton, CA, p. A97
Director Human Resources, Mark Twain Medical Center, San Andreas, CA, p. A88
Vice President Human Resources, St. Joseph's Medical Center, Stockton, CA, p. A97
VARGAS, Tim, President and Chief Executive Officer, Mclaren Lapeer Region, Lapeer, MI, p. A332
VARGAS–MAHAR, Monica, FACHE, Market Chief Executive Officer, Carondelet St. Joseph's Hospital, Tucson, AZ, p. A40
VARGHESE, Bindu, R.N., Chief Executive Officer, Encompass Health Rehabilitation Hospital of Sugar Land, Sugar Land, TX, p. A654
VARGHESE, Roy, M.D., Chief of Staff, Mary Breckinridge Arh Hospital, Hyden, KY, p. A267
VARGHESE, Shibu, Vice President Human Resources, University of Texas M.D. Anderson Cancer Center, Houston, TX, p. A628
VARIALE, Vincenzo, Chief Executive Officer, North Vista Hospital, North Las Vegas, NV, p. A412
VARIAN, Grant, M.D., Medical Director, Mary Rutan Hospital, Bellefontaine, OH, p. A486
VARJAVAND, Caitlin, Chief Human Resources Officer, Miracare Behavioral Health Care, Tinley Park, IL, p. A210
VARK, Lawrence, M.D., Chief Medical Officer, Creek Nation Community Hospital, Okemah, OK, p. A516
VARLEY, Kevin, Chief Financial Officer, Pam Health Specialty Hospital of Pittsburgh, Oakdale, PA, p. A547
VARNADO, Anjanette, M.D., Chief Medical Officer, St. Helena Parish Hospital, Greensburg, LA, p. A282
VARNADO, Darryl, Executive Vice President and Chief People Officer, Children's National Hospital, Washington, DC, p. A123
VARNADO, Kim, R.N., Chief Nursing Officer, Highland Community Hospital, Picayune, MS, p. A368
VARNADOE, Milo, Director Information Systems, Warm Springs Medical Center, Warm Springs, GA, p. A173
VARNADOE, Tiffany G., Chief Executive Officer, Ed Fraser Memorial Hospital, Macclenny, FL, p. A138
VARNADORE, Jennifer, Administrator, Christus Health Shreveport–Bossier, Shreveport, LA, p. A292
VARNAM, Jessica, Chief of Staff, Grant Regional Health Center, Lancaster, WI, p. A714
VARNELL, Misti, Chief Executive Officer, Select Specialty Hospital–Dallas, Plano, TX, p. A645
VARNER, Terry, Administrator, Yalobusha General Hospital, Water Valley, MS, p. A369
VARNEY, Tim, R.N., Chief Nursing Officer, Select Specialty Hospital – Ann Arbor, Ypsilanti, MI, p. A341
VARTANIAN, Sarkis
Chief Nursing Officer, Whittier Hospital Medical Center, Whittier, CA, p. A101
Interim Chief Executive Officer, AHMC Seton Medical Center, Daly City, CA, p. A61
VASEK, Barbara, Director Information Technology, Yoakum Community Hospital, Yoakum, TX, p. A663
VASELIADES, Aristotle A., FACHE, Commanding Officer, Bayne–Jones Army Community Hospital, Fort Polk, LA, p. A282
VASHISHTA, Ashok, M.D., Vice President Medical Affairs, Mclaren Central Michigan, Mount Pleasant, MI, p. A334
VASIL, Kathleen, Vice President Finance, St. Charles Hospital, Port Jefferson, NY, p. A456
VASILE, Ann, M.D., Medical Director, Encompass Health Rehabilitation Hospital of Tustin, Tustin, CA, p. A99
VASKO, Tom, Chief Executive Officer, Newman Memorial Hospital, Shattuck, OK, p. A520
VASQUEZ, Arthur, President, Indiana University Health Arnett Hospital, Lafayette, IN, p. A222
VASQUEZ, Barbara, Chief Nursing Officer, Kingwood Pines Hospital, Kingwood, TX, p. A632
VASQUEZ, Carlos
Chief Executive Officer, Franciscan Health Crawfordsville, Crawfordsville, IN, p. A214
Vice President and Chief Operating Officer, Franciscan Health Rensselear, Rensselaer, IN, p. A226
VASQUEZ, George
Chief Technology Officer, Clovis Community Medical Center, Clovis, CA, p. A60
Corporate Chief Information Officer, Fresno Heart And Surgical Hospital, Fresno, CA, p. A64
Vice President Information Services, Community Behavioral Health Center, Fresno, CA, p. A64
VASQUEZ, Jill
Manager Human Resources, Corewell Health Ludington Hospital, Ludington, MI, p. A332
Senior Business Partner, Corewell Health Gerber Hospital, Fremont, MI, p. A327
VASS, Paula, Vice President Clinical Operations, Walden Behavioral Care, Waltham, MA, p. A319
VASSELL, Patricia, Senior Vice President, Nursing Services and Chief Nursing Officer, Guthrie Robert Packer Hospital, Sayre, PA, p. A554
VASTOLA, David, Medical Director, Searhc Mt. Edgecumbe Hospital, Sitka, AK, p. A29
VASUNAGA, Amy, Chief Nurse Executive, Leahi Hospital, Honolulu, HI, p. A175
VAUGHAN, Alan, Director Information Technology, Share Medical Center, Alva, OK, p. A509
VAUGHAN, Amanda
Chief Financial Officer, Bob Wilson Memorial Grant County Hospital, Ulysses, KS, p. A261
Chief Financial Officer, St. Catherine Hospital, Garden City, KS, p. A249
VAUGHAN, Dee, Director Information Technology, Hermann Area District Hospital, Hermann, MO, p. A376
VAUGHAN, Paula, Chief Executive Officer, Tug Valley Arh Regional Medical Center, South Williamson, KY, p. A274
VAUGHAN, Peggy, M.D., Senior Vice President Medical Affairs, University of Maryland Upper Chesapeake Medical Center, Bel Air, MD, p. A302
VAUGHN, Barbara, R.N., Chief Nursing Officer, Carrollton Regional Medical Center, Carrollton, TX, p. A606
VAUGHN, Debbie, Chief Nursing Officer, The Medical Center of Southeast Texas, Port Arthur, TX, p. A645
VAUGHN, Joseph, FACHE, Medical Center Director, Lt. Col. Luke Weathers, Jr. Va Medical Center, Memphis, TN, p. A588
VAUGHN, Kelly, Chief Nursing Officer, Nebraska Medicine – Nebraska Medical Center, Omaha, NE, p. A404

A996 Index of Health Care Professionals

Index of Health Care Professionals / Villa

Index of Health Care Professionals

VAUGHN, Kerry, Chief Information Officer, St. Mary's Health Care System, Athens, GA, p. A156
VAUGHN, Michael, Director of Nursing, Southeast Rehabilitation Hospital, Lake Village, AR, p. A49
VAUGHN, Sandy
Director Information Services, Baylor Scott & White All Saints Medical Center – Fort Worth, Fort Worth, TX, p. A619
Director Information Systems, Baylor Scott & White Medical Center – Grapevine, Grapevine, TX, p. A622
VAUGHN, Sharma Esq, Chief Nursing Officer, Rangely District Hospital, Rangely, CO, p. A113
VAUGHN, Ted W, Director Human Resources, Unitypoint Health – Trinity Regional Medical Center, Fort Dodge, IA, p. A236
VAUGHN, Vickie, Chief Nursing Officer, Vanderbilt Bedford Hospital, Shelbyville, TN, p. A593
VAUGHT, Stacey L., MSN, President, Centra Bedford Memorial Hospital, Bedford, VA, p. A673
VAVARUTSOS, Tony, Director Information Systems, Thorek Memorial Hospital, Chicago, IL, p. A191
VAZQUEZ, Brunilda, Medical Director, Hospital De Psiquiatria, San Juan, PR, p. A735
VAZQUEZ, Emilio, M.D., Chief Medical Officer, Parkview Dekalb Hospital, Auburn, IN, p. A212
VAZQUEZ, Francisco, Director, Michael E. Debakey Department of Veterans Affairs Medical Center, Houston, TX, p. A627
VAZQUEZ, Joe, Chief Financial Officer, Methodist Hospital South, Jourdanton, TX, p. A631
VAZQUEZ CLARKE, Natalie, Director Human Resources, Chambers Health, Anahuac, TX, p. A597
VEACH, Jamie, Chief Operating Officer, Clay County Hospital, Flora, IL, p. A195
VEAL, Bonita Wells, Chief Nursing Officer, Anaheim Global Medical Center, Anaheim, CA, p. A55
VEDALA, Giridhar, M.D., Regional Chief Medical Officer, Memorial Hermann Northeast, Humble, TX, p. A629
VEERAMACHANENI, Harish, M.D., Chief of Staff, Wayne Medical Center, Waynesboro, TN, p. A594
VEESER, Tom, Chief Nursing Officer, Aspirus Steven's Point Hospital & Clinics, Inc., Stevens Point, WI, p. A722
VEGA, James, Director Information Systems, Palm Beach Gardens Medical Center, Palm Beach Gardens, FL, p. A145
VEGA, Maria, Director Human Resources, Auxilio Mutuo Hospital, San Juan, PR, p. A734
VEGA, Oscar, M.D., Chief Medical Officer, Las Palmas Medical Center, El Paso, TX, p. A616
VEGA, Zoraida, MSN, R.N., Chief Nursing Officer, St. Luke's Episcopal Hospital, Ponce, PR, p. A734
VEHIGE, Monica, Chief Executive Officer, Mcleod Health Loris, Loris, SC, p. A568
VEILLETTE, Michael D.
Senior Vice President and Chief Financial Officer, Manchester Memorial Hospital, Manchester, CT, p. A116
Senior Vice President and Chief Financial Officer, Rockville General Hospital, Vernon, CT, p. A119
VEILLEUX, Jeffrey
Executive Vice President and Chief Financial Officer, Providence Swedish First Hill, Seattle, WA, p. A694
Senior Vice President and Chief Financial Officer, Providence Swedish Cherry Hill, Seattle, WA, p. A694
VEILLON, Jarred, Chief Financial Officer, Beauregard Health System, De Ridder, LA, p. A281
VEILLON, Paul, CPA, Chief Finanial Officer, West Oaks Hospital, Houston, TX, p. A629
VELA, Javier, Director Information Technology, Baylor Scott & White Medical Center–Uptown, Dallas, TX, p. A610
VELARDI, Antonio, M.D., Chief Quality Officer, Orlando Health – Health Central Hospital, Ocoee, FL, p. A143
VELASCO, Paul, IT Manager, Kit Carson County Memorial Hospital, Burlington, CO, p. A104
VELASQUEZ, Alfred T
Area Information Officer, Kaiser Permanente Moreno Valley Medical Center, Moreno Valley, CA, p. A78
Area Information Officer, Kaiser Permanente Riverside Medical Center, Riverside, CA, p. A86
VELASQUEZ, Lin, Vice President Human Resources, St. Louise Regional Hospital, Gilroy, CA, p. A65
VELEZ, Elias, Chief Executive Officer, El Paso Ltac Hospital, El Paso, TX, p. A616
VELEZ, Emy, Director of Human Resources, Montefiore New Rochelle, New Rochelle, NY, p. A447
VELEZ, George, FACHE, Medical Center Director, Veterans Health Care System of The Ozarks, Fayetteville, AR, p. A46
VELEZ, Jonathan, President, Baptist Health Louisville, Louisville, KY, p. A269
VELEZ, Kareen, M.D., Medical Director, Pam Rehabilitation Hospital of Tavares, Tavares, FL, p. A153
VELEZ, Luz M, Director–Administration of Nursing Services, Hospital San Carlos Borromeo, Moca, PR, p. A733
VELEZ, Pablo, R.N., Ph.D., Chief Executive Officer, El Centro Regional Medical Center, El Centro, CA, p. A62
VELEZ, Raul, Information Technology Director, North Alabama Medical Center, Florence, AL, p. A19
VENA, Victor, Director of Human Resources, Atlantic Rehabilitation Institute, Madison, NJ, p. A423
VENABLE, Brett H., FACHE, Commander, William Beaumont Army Medical Center, El Paso, TX, p. A617
VENABLE, Jennifer, Chief Financial Officer, Washington County Hospital, Nashville, IL, p. A203
VENABLE, Mark
Administrator, Shriners Hospitals for Children–St. Louis, Saint Louis, MO, p. A385
Director Human Resources, Shriners Hospitals for Children–St. Louis, Saint Louis, MO, p. A385
VENABLE, Robert, M.D., Chief Medical Staff, Washington Regional Medical Center, Plymouth, NC, p. A474
VENDETTI, Marilouise, M.D., Chief Medical Officer, Atlanticare Regional Medical Center, Atlantic City Campus, Atlantic City, NJ, p. A418
VENDITTI, Angelo, R.N., Chief Nursing Executive, Co–Chair Patient Experience, Temple University Hospital, Philadelphia, PA, p. A550
VENEZIANO, Terri, Interim Chief Nursing Officer, Columbus Regional Healthcare System, Whiteville, NC, p. A477
VENGCO, Joel L., MS, Vice President, Chief Information Officer, Baystate Medical Center, Springfield, MA, p. A318
VENHUIZEN, Pamela, Chief Human Resources Officer, Dakota Regional Medical Center, Cooperstown, ND, p. A480
VENOIT, Jon–Paul
Chief Operating Officer, Masonicare Health Center, Wallingford, CT, p. A119
President and Chief Executive Officer, Masonicare Health Center, Wallingford, CT, p. A119
VENTURA, Rosemary, M.D., Chief Nursing Informatics Officer, New York–Presbyterian Hospital, New York, NY, p. A450
VENTURELLA, James
Vice President, Information Technology, Berkeley Medical Center, Martinsburg, WV, p. A702
Vice President, Information Technology, Jefferson Medical Center, Ranson, WV, p. A704
VENUTO, Frank, Chief Human Capital Officer, Nebraska Medicine – Nebraska Medical Center, Omaha, NE, p. A404
VERA, Danny, PharmD, Regional Vice President and Chief Operating Officer, Cascade Valley Hospital, Arlington, WA, p. A687
VERA, Luis F, M.D., Medical Director, Kensington Hospital, Philadelphia, PA, p. A549
VERAGIWALA, Jignesh, Chief of Staff, Mercy Hospital Logan County, Guthrie, OK, p. A513
VERCHER, Gretchen, Chief Nursing Officer, Encompass Health Rehabilitation Hospital of Montgomery, Montgomery, AL, p. A22
VERFURTH, Larry, D.O., Executive Vice President and Chief Medical Officer, Christus Good Shepherd Medical Center–Marshall, Marshall, TX, p. A638
VERGARA, Aimee, Chief Executive Officer, Hospital for Extended Recovery, Norfolk, VA, p. A680
VERGARA, Nanette, Chief Operatiang Officer, Kaiser Permanente Moreno Valley Medical Center, Moreno Valley, CA, p. A78
VERGONIO, Merlinda, Chief Information Management and Technology, U. S. Air Force Hospital, Hampton, VA, p. A677
VERGOS, Katherine
FACHE, President, SSM Health St. Agnes Hospital – Fond Du Lac, Fond Du Lac, WI, p. A711
FACHE, President and Chief Executive Officer, St. Rose Dominican Hospitals – Siena Campus, Henderson, NV, p. A409
VERINDER, David
Chief Executive Officer, Sarasota Memorial Hospital – Venice, North Venice, FL, p. A142
President & Chief Executive Officer, Sarasota Memorial Hospital – Sarasota, Sarasota, FL, p. A150
VERMA, Virendar, M.D., Medical Director, Encompass Health Rehabilitation Hospital of Jonesboro, Jonesboro, AR, p. A48
VERMILLION, Kerry, Senior Vice President Finance and Chief Financial Officer, Gulf Breeze Hospital, Gulf Breeze, FL, p. A133
VERNON, Steven, Chief Executive Officer, Cedar Creek Hospital of Michigan, Saint Johns, MI, p. A337
VERRETTE, Paul, M.D., Chief Medical Officer, St. Bernard Parish Hospital, Chalmette, LA, p. A279
VERRETTE, Paula, M.D., Senior Vice President Quality and Physician Services and Chief Medical Officer, Huntington Health, Pasadena, CA, p. A83
VERRILL, Alan, M.D., President and Chief Executive Officer, Adventhealth Shawnee Mission, Merriam, KS, p. A255
VERSALOVIC, Jim, M.D., Ph.D., Interim Physican–in–Chief, Texas Children's Hospital, Houston, TX, p. A628
VERTUNO, Ashley, Chief Executive Officer, HCA Florida Jfk Hospital, Atlantis, FL, p. A125
VERVALIN, Paul
Executive Vice President and Chief Operating Officer, Guthrie Troy Community Hospital, Troy, PA, p. A556
President, Guthrie Corning Hospital, Corning, NY, p. A441
VESS, Brett, Medical Center Director, Beckley Veterans Affairs Medical Center, Beckley, WV, p. A699
VESTRAND, Linda, Director, Human Resources, Montrose Behavioral Health Hospital, Chicago, IL, p. A190
VETTER, Norman, Chief Executive Officer, Division of Substance Abuse and Mental Health, Delaware Psychiatric Center, New Castle, DE, p. A121
VETTER, Richard, M.D., Associate Chief, Essentia Health St. Mary's – Detroit Lakes, Detroit Lakes, MN, p. A345
VIALL, John, M.D., Vice President Medical Affairs, Holzer Medical Center, Gallipolis, OH, p. A496
VIATOR, Dionne, CPA, FACHE, President and Chief Executive Officer, Iberia Medical Center, New Iberia, LA, p. A289
VIBETO, Brett, M.D., Chief of Staff, Chi St. Alexius Health Williston, Williston, ND, p. A483
VICARI, Colleen, Chief Executive Officer, Riverview Behavioral Health, Texarkana, AR, p. A54
VICE, Jeff, Chief Operating Officer, Northwest Health – Starke, Knox, IN, p. A221
VICENT, Leonardo III, Executive Director, Bronxcare Health System, New York, NY, p. A447
VICENTE, Oscar, Chief Financial Officer, Palmetto General Hospital, Hialeah, FL, p. A133
VICK, Amanda, R.N., Chief Operating Officer, Regional West Medical Center, Scottsbluff, NE, p. A406
VICKERS, Chelsea, Chief Executive Officer and Administrator, Aurora Behavioral Health System East, Tempe, AZ, p. A39
VICKERS, Cynthia, R.N., Assistant Administrator, Nursing Services, Memorial Hospital And Manor, Bainbridge, GA, p. A159
VICKERS, Dave, Chief Financial Officer, UCI Health – Los Alamitos, Los Alamitos, CA, p. A71
VICKERS, Don
Chief Executive Officer, Bmc Baytown, Baytown, TX, p. A601
Chief Executive Officer, West Chase Houston Hospital, Houston, TX, p. A629
VICKERS, Kathy, Director Human Resources, Vantage Point of Northwest Arkansas, Fayetteville, AR, p. A46
VICKERS, Selwyn, M.D., President, Memorial Sloan Kettering Cancer Center, New York, NY, p. A449
VICKERY, Ian, Director Information Technology, D. W. Mcmillan Memorial Hospital, Brewton, AL, p. A17
VICKERY, Tim, Chief Information Officer, St. Mary's Sacred Heart Hospital, Lavonia, GA, p. A166
VICKNAIR, Jennifer, R.N., Assistant Vice President, Nursing and Hospital Administration, Ochsner St. Martin Hospital, Breaux Bridge, LA, p. A279
VICKROY, Joseph, M.D., Medical Director, Encompass Health Rehabilitation Hospital of Utah, Sandy, UT, p. A669
VICKS, Ray, Senior Vice President, Finance and Chief Financial Officer, The Hsc Pediatric Center, Washington, DC, p. A124
VICTORIA, Mario, M.D., Vice President, Medical Affairs, Samaritan Medical Center, Watertown, NY, p. A461
VIEIRA, Jeanette, Chief Executive, Providence Hood River Memorial Hospital, Hood River, OR, p. A528
VIELKIND, James, Chief Financial Officer, Cobleskill Regional Hospital, Cobleskill, NY, p. A441
VIENNEAU, Marie E.
President, Northern Light Ca Dean Hospital, Greenville, ME, p. A297
President, Northern Light Mayo Hospital, Dover–Foxcroft, ME, p. A297
VIERLING, Alan, R.N., Acting Hospital Administrator, Alaska Native Medical Center, Anchorage, AK, p. A27
VIERLING, Taryn, Chief Nursing Officer, Select Specialty Hospital of Southeast Ohio, Newark, OH, p. A501
VIG, Vibha, Chief of Staff, Merit Health Madison, Canton, MS, p. A360
VIGILANTE, Sarah, Administrative Services Director, Mammoth Hospital, Mammoth Lakes, CA, p. A76
VIGNA, Greg A., M.D., Medical Director, Encompass Health Rehabilitation Hospital of Modesto, Modesto, CA, p. A77
VIGNERI, Joseph, M.D., Chief Medical Officer, Summit Medical Center, Casper, WY, p. A726
VILANOVA, Lynda, Director Patient Care Services, Shriners Hospitals for Children–Spokane, Spokane, WA, p. A696
VILLA, Jo Ellen, R.N., Chief Executive Officer, Community Hospital of Anaconda, Anaconda, MT, p. A389

© 2025 AHA Guide Index of Health Care Professionals A997

Index of Health Care Professionals

Index of Health Care Professionals / Villa

VILLA, Maria, Interim Chief Nursing Officer, HCA Florida Kendall Hospital, Miami, FL, p. A139
VILLAFUERTE, Herbert, R.N., Chief Executive Officer, Garfield Medical Center, Monterey Park, CA, p. A78
VILLALOBOS, Max, Chief Operating Officer, Kaiser Foundation Hospital – San Marcos, San Marcos, CA, p. A93
VILLANI, Travis A., FACHE, Chief Executive Officer and Senior Vice President of Operations, Rural Wellness Anadarko, Anadarko, OK, p. A509
VILLANO, Jeremi, M.D., Chief of Staff, Crook County Medical Services District, Sundance, WY, p. A728
VILLANUEVA, Jeffrey D, Chief Executive Officer, Adventhealth Orlando, Orlando, FL, p. A144
VILLANUEVA CABRERA, Sarah I., Acting Executive Director, Hospital San Carlos Borromeo, Moca, PR, p. A733
VILLARREAL, Catana, Chief Nursing Officer, Hill Regional Hospital, Hillsboro, TX, p. A624
VILLARREAL, Rick, Vice President Finance, Christus Santa Rosa Hospital – San Marcos, San Marcos, TX, p. A651
VILLARREAL, Xavier, FACHE, Chief Executive Officer, Hillcrest Medical Center, Tulsa, OK, p. A522
VILLEGAS, Lorraine, Manager Human Resources, Paradise Valley Hospital, National City, CA, p. A79
VILLEGAS, William, Vice President Finance, Kettering Health Hamilton, Hamilton, OH, p. A497
VILLIGRAN, Anthony, Chief Financial Officer, Medical City Mckinney, Mckinney, TX, p. A638
VILT, Patricia K., CPA, Senior Vice President and Chief Financial Officer, Riverside Medical Center, Kankakee, IL, p. A199
VILUMS, Karl
Chief Financial Officer, Ivinson Memorial Hospital, Laramie, WY, p. A727
Chief Financial Officer, Executive Vice President, Broadlawns Medical Center, Des Moines, IA, p. A234
VINAS, Elmo, Director Human Resources, Bayou Bend Health System, Franklin, LA, p. A282
VINCENT, Cynthia, Vice President Finance and Operations, St. Francis Regional Medical Center, Shakopee, MN, p. A355
VINCENT, David, Director Information Systems, Canonsburg Hospital, Canonsburg, PA, p. A536
VINCENT, Joan M, MSN, MS, R.N., Vice President Patient Care Services and Chief Nurse Executive, Adventist Healthcare Shady Grove Medical Center, Rockville, MD, p. A306
VINCENT, Laurence Marie, Chief Nursing Officer, Ochsner University Hospital & Clinics, Lafayette, LA, p. A286
VINCENT, Marianne, Chief Financial Officer, Cascade Medical, Leavenworth, WA, p. A691
VINCENT, Mitchell S, Vice President Organizational Support, Fairview Range, Hibbing, MN, p. A348
VINCENT, Scott, Chief Human Resource Officer, Ochsner Specialty Hospital, Meridian, MS, p. A366
VINCENT, Shawn, Chief Executive Officer, Saint Josep. Health System, Mishawaka, IN, p. A224
VINCENZ, Felix T., Ph.D., Chief Executive Officer, St. Louis Forensic Treatment Center, Saint Louis, MO, p. A384
VINCIFORA, Teresa, Chief Operating Officer, Benson Hospital, Benson, AZ, p. A30
VINCIGUERRA, Tracy, MS, Chief Executive Officer, UT Health East Texas Rehabilitation Hospital, Tyler, TX, p. A659
VINSANT, George O'Neal, M.D., Chief Medical Officer, Tennova Healthcare–Lafollette Medical Center, La Follette, TN, p. A586
VINSON, Jessica, Chief Nursing Officer, Encompass Health Rehabilitation Hospital of Pensacola, Pensacola, FL, p. A146
VIOLETTE, Brenda, M.D., Director Medical Staff, Firelands Regional Health System, Sandusky, OH, p. A503
VIRGEN, Tomas, R.N., MSN, Chief Operating Officer, El Centro Regional Medical Center, El Centro, CA, p. A62
VISCONI, Deborah D., MS, President and Chief Executive Officer, Bergen New Bridge Medical Center, Paramus, NJ, p. A426
VISH, Nancy, Ph.D., FACHE, R.N., President and Chief Nursing Officer, Baylor Scott & White Heart & Vascular Hospital–Dallas, Dallas, TX, p. A610
VISSER, Jessica, R.N. Chief Nursing Officer, Sisters of Charity Hospital of Buffalo, Buffalo, NY, p. A440
VISSER LYNCH, Amy, Chief Nursing Officer, Mt. Ascutney Hospital And Health Center, Windsor, VT, p. A672
VISSERS, Robert, M.D., President and Chief Executive Officer, Boulder Community Health, Boulder, CO, p. A104
VITALI, Joe, Director Information Technology, Parkside Psychiatric Hospital And Clinic, Tulsa, OK, p. A522
VITIELLO, Jon, Senior Vice President, Finance Operations and Analytics, Mercy Hospital Oklahoma City, Oklahoma City, OK, p. A517
VITOLAS, Victor, Acting Chief Information Technology Services, Central Texas Veterans Hcs/Temple Tx, Temple, TX, p. A656
VIVIANO, Paul S., President and Chief Executive Officer, Children's Hospital Los Angeles, Los Angeles, CA, p. A72
VIVIT, Romeo, Chief Surgeon, U. S. Public Health Service Indian Hospital, Rosebud, SD, p. A576
VIZCARRA, Edred T., M.D., Chief of Staff, St. Luke Community Healthcare, Ronan, MT, p. A395
VLAHAVAS, Beth, R.N., MSN, Vice President Patient Care Services and Chief Nursing Officer, Mercy Medical Center, Rockville Centre, NY, p. A458
VLARS, Scott, Chief Information Technology Services, Wilmington Veterans Affairs Medical Center, Wilmington, DE, p. A122
VLOSICH, Kristopher Wade., Medical Center Director, Oklahoma City Va Medical Center, Oklahoma City, OK, p. A518
VO, Tom
M.D., Chief Executive Officer, Texarkana Emergency Center & Hospital, Texarkana, TX, p. A657
M.D., Chief Executive Officer, NuTex Corporation, New Braunfels Er & Hospital, New Braunfels, TX, p. A641
VOBEJDA, William, President and Chief Executive Officer, Methodist Fremont Health, Fremont, NE, p. A400
VOBORIL, Joe, Director, Human Resources, Spring View Hospital, Lebanon, KY, p. A268
VOECKS, Barbara, Chief Information Officer, Ortonville Area Health Services, Ortonville, MN, p. A352
VOELKEL, Jonathon, Chief Executive Officer, Reagan Memorial Hospital, Big Lake, TX, p. A603
VOELKER, Justin, Chief Financial Officer, Multicare Valley Hospital, Spokane Valley, WA, p. A696
VOGEL, Clay, Administrator, Coleman County Medical Center, Coleman, TX, p. A607
VOGEL, Daniel Jr, Chief Executive Officer, Mercy Rehabilitation Hospital South, Saint Louis, MO, p. A385
VOGELSANG, Mark, Director Information Services, Providence Holy Family Hospital, Spokane, WA, p. A696
VOGENTIZ, William, M.D., Medical Director, Anmed Rehabilitation Hospital, Anderson, SC, p. A562
VOGT, Dennis, Director Information Technology, Madison Health, London, OH, p. A498
VOGT, Sam, Manager Human Resources, The Hospital At Hebrew Senior Care, West Hartford, CT, p. A120
VOHS, Lester, Manager Information Systems, Cass Regional Medical Center, Harrisonville, MO, p. A376
VOIGT, Jordan, President MercyOne Eastern Division, Genesis Medical Center – Davenport, Davenport, IA, p. A234
VOISARD, Victor
Director Human Resources, San Gabriel Valley Medical Center, San Gabriel, CA, p. A91
Senior Director Human Resources, Kaiser Foundation Hospital – San Marcos, San Marcos, CA, p. A93
VOKOUN, Cory, Chief Nursing Officer, Nevada Regional Medical Center, Nevada, MO, p. A381
VOLKERDING, Elizabeth, Director Workforce Excellence, San Juan Regional Medical Center, Farmington, NM, p. A434
VOLLER, Kristi, Director of Nursing, Mobridge Regional Hospital, Mobridge, SD, p. A575
VOLLMER, Kris, Director Patient Care Services, Avera Tyler, Tyler, MN, p. A356
VOLLSTEDT, Keith, M.D., Chief Medical Officer, Mercyone Siouxland Medical Center, Sioux City, IA, p. A243
VOLOCH, Bill, President and Chief Executive Officer, Wesley Medical Center, Wichita, KS, p. A262
VOLOVIC, Mark, Chief Information Officer, Indiana Regional Medical Center, Indiana, PA, p. A542
VOLPE, Buddy, Director Human Resources, Peterson Health, Kerrville, TX, p. A632
VOLSCH, Joyce, Chief Nursing Officer, Palomar Medical Center Poway, Poway, CA, p. A84
VON ARX, Michelle, MS, Chief Executive Officer, Encompass Health Rehabilitation Hospital of Rock Hill, Rock Hill, SC, p. A569
VON BEHREN, Rachel, Director Financial Services, Unitypoint Health – Jones Regional Medical Center, Anamosa, IA, p. A230
VON MOCK, George, Chief Executive Officer/Administrator, Hansen Family Hospital, Iowa Falls, IA, p. A238
VON NIEDA, Tij, Chief Executive Officer, Encompass Health Rehabilitation Hospital of Las Vegas, Las Vegas, NV, p. A410
VONACHEN, April, Chief Financial Officer and Vice President Financial Services, Cumberland Medical Center, Crossville, TN, p. A582
VONFELDT, Krystal, M.D., Chief of Staff, Duncan Regional Hospital, Duncan, OK, p. A512
VONK, Brandon, President, Bear River Valley Hospital, Tremonton, UT, p. A670
VOSE, Courtney, R.N., Senior Vice President, Chief Nursing Officer, Robert Wood Johnson University Hospital, New Brunswick, NJ, p. A425
VOSHELL, Shane, Director Human Resources, Adventist Health Portland, Portland, OR, p. A530
VOSKUIL, Scott, M.D., Chief Medical Officer, Aurora Medical Center – Manitowoc County, Two Rivers, WI, p. A723
VOSS, Cindy, Controlelr, Rehabilitation Institute of Southern Illinois, Llc, The, Shiloh, IL, p. A208
VOSS, Daryle, FACHE, President, Mercy Hospital Ardmore, Ardmore, OK, p. A510
VOSS, Kinsi, R.N., Chief Nursing Officer, Throckmorton County Memorial Hospital, Throckmorton, TX, p. A658
VOSS, Peter, M.D., Chief Medical Officer, Indiana University Health Ball Memorial Hospital, Muncie, IN, p. A224
VOSS, Robert, Chief Financial Officer, Laredo Specialty Hospital, Laredo, TX, p. A634
VOSS, Wayne M., Chief Executive Officer, Houston Methodist West Hospital, Houston, TX, p. A626
VOSSLER, Jeffrey W, Chief Financial Officer, Grand Lake Health System, Saint Marys, OH, p. A503
VRANA, Daniel A
Area Controller, Encompass Health Rehabilitation Hospital of Sewickley, Sewickley, PA, p. A554
Controller, Encompass Health Rehabilitation Hospital of Harmarville, Pittsburgh, PA, p. A551
VRANICAR, David, Vice Chancellor for Finance and Chief Financial Officer, The University of Kansas Hospital, Kansas City, KS, p. A252
VRANJES, Matko, Chief Operating Officer, Watsonville Community Hospital, Watsonville, CA, p. A100
VRBA, Frank, Chief Information Officer, Annie Jeffrey Memorial County Health Center, Osceola, NE, p. A405
VRBAS, Laken, R.N., Director of Nursing, Dundy County Hospital, Benkelman, NE, p. A398
VROBEL, Matthew, Vice President, Medical Operations, Cleveland Clinic Medina Hospital, Medina, OH, p. A500
VRONKO, Jeremy
Manager Information Services, Corewell Health Gerber Hospital, Fremont, MI, p. A327
Manager, Information Services, Corewell Health Ludington Hospital, Ludington, MI, p. A332
VUCETIC, Raymond, Chief Executive Officer, Summit Medical Center, Casper, WY, p. A726
VUCHAK, Jerry, Senior Vice President, Chief Information Officer, Children's Nebraska, Omaha, NE, p. A404
VUKICH, David, M.D., Senior Vice President, Chief Medical Officer and Chief Quality Officer, UF Health Jacksonville, Jacksonville, FL, p. A135
VUTRANO, Frank A, Chief Financial Officer, Wyckoff Heights Medical Center, New York, NY, p. A453
VYZOUREK, Treg, Chief Executive Officer, Brodstone Memorial Hospital, Superior, NE, p. A406

W

WAALA, Shelly, Vice President Patient Care Services and Chief Nursing Officer, Froedtert West Bend Hospital, West Bend, WI, p. A724
WACHOWIAK, Darrell
R.N., Associate Vice President Operations, Promedica Bay Park Hospital, Oregon, OH, p. A502
R.N., President, Promedica Toledo Hospital, Toledo, OH, p. A505
WACKERFUSS, Toni, Chief Executive Officer, Encompass Health Rehabilitation Hospital of Memphis, A Partner of Methodist Healthcare, Memphis, TN, p. A588
WADDELL, Joey, Chief Operating Officer, Norton Clark Hospital, Jeffersonville, IN, p. A221
WADDELL, Kathy, Administrator, Wayne General Hospital, Waynesboro, MS, p. A369
WADDELL, Lesa, Director Human Resources, Compass Memorial Healthcare, Marengo, IA, p. A239
WADDELL, Riley, Chief Executive Officer, Ochsner Lsu Health Shreveport – St. Mary Medical Center, Llc, Shreveport, LA, p. A292
WADE, Bruce, Vice President Human Resources, Indiana University Health Bedford Hospital, Bedford, IN, p. A212
WADE, Cynthia RN, BSN, President, Lincolnhealth, Damariscotta, ME, p. A296
WADE, Donna, Senior Director Human Resources, Comanche County Memorial Hospital, Lawton, OK, p. A514
WADE, Glenn, Director Information Systems, Ascension Saint Thomas Highlands, Sparta, TN, p. A593
WADE, Hong
Chief Financial Officer, Comanche County Medical Center, Comanche, TX, p. A608

A998 Index of Health Care Professionals

Index of Health Care Professionals / Walker

Index of Health Care Professionals

Chief Financial Officer, Sweeny Community Hospital, Sweeny, TX, p. A655
WADE, Hope, Chief Operating Officer, Christus St. Vincent Regional Medical Center, Santa Fe, NM, p. A436
WADE, Jon, Hospital Chief Executive Officer, Presbyterian Hospital, Albuquerque, NM, p. A433
WADEWITZ, Martin, Chief Operations Officer/Vice President, Operations, Angel Medical Center, Franklin, NC, p. A468
WADLE, Don, Interim Director Human Resources, Portneuf Medical Center, Pocatello, ID, p. A183
WADSWORTH, Barbara A, MSN, R.N., FACHE, DNP, RN, Chief Nursing Officer, Bryn Mawr Hospital, Bryn Mawr, PA, p. A536
WADSWORTH, Thadius, President, Promedica Toledo Hospital, Toledo, OH, p. A505
WAFFORD, Marty, Under Secretary of Support and Programs, Chickasaw Nation Medical Center, Ada, OK, p. A509
WAFLE, Sue, Director, Human Resources, Mile Bluff Medical Center, Mauston, WI, p. A715
WAGAR, Christina, Chief Operating Officer, Mid–Valley Hospital And Clinics, Omak, WA, p. A692
WAGERS, Rick, Senior Executive Vice President and Chief Financial Officer, Regional One Health, Memphis, TN, p. A589
WAGGENER, Yvonne, Chief Financial Officer, San Bernardino Mountains Community Hospital, Lake Arrowhead, CA, p. A69
WAGGONER, Jeff, M.D., Chief of Staff, Weisbrod Memorial County Hospital, Eads, CO, p. A107
WAGNER, Becky DNP, RN, Vice President Nursing and Patient Care Services, Iredell Health System, Statesville, NC, p. A477
WAGNER, Dale, Chief Financial Officer, Kindred Hospital–Westminster, Westminster, CA, p. A101
WAGNER, Danny J., Chief Human Resource Officer, Allegiance Behavioral Health Center of Plainview, Plainview, TX, p. A644
WAGNER, David D, Chief Information Management Service, Biloxi Va Medical Center, Biloxi, MS, p. A359
WAGNER, Elaina, Director Human Resources, Astria Sunnyside Hospital, Sunnyside, WA, p. A696
WAGNER, Fred, Chief Financial Officer, OSF St. Francis Hospital And Medical Group. Escanaba, MI, p. A326
WAGNER, Gwendolyn Dianne, R.N., MSN, Chief Nursing Officer, Mission Community Hospital, Los Angeles, CA, p. A74
WAGNER, Jefferey, Director, Information Technology, Lake Huron Medical Center, Port Huron, MI, p. A336
WAGNER, Jesse, M.D., Chief Medical Officer and Vice President, Quality and Patient Safety, Middlesex Health, Middletown, CT, p. A117
WAGNER, Kelley, Director Employee Relations, OSF St. Josep. Medical Center, Bloomington, IL, p. A186
WAGNER, Linda, Chief Financial Officer, Sanford Worthington Medical Center, Worthington, MN, p. A358
WAGNER, Melissa, Chief Financial Officer, Brookings Health System, Brookings, SD, p. A572
WAGNER, Pauletta, Manager, Human Resources, Three Rivers Health System, Inc., Three Rivers, MI, p. A339
WAGNER, Randall J, Chief Operating Officer, Trinity Health Grand Rapids Hospital, Grand Rapids, MI, p. A328
WAGNER, Renee, M.D., Chief Medical Officer, Fairfield Medical Center, Lancaster, OH, p. A498
WAGNER, Russell R, Executive Vice President and Chief Financial Officer, Holy Redeemer Hospital, Meadowbrook, PA, p. A545
WAGNER, Sarah, Human Resources Officer, Memorial Hospital of Texas County Authority, Guymon, OK, p. A513
WAGNER, Sherrie A, Manager Human Resources, The Core Institute Specialty Hospital, Phoenix, AZ, p. A37
WAGNER, Suzie, Director Human Resources, Encompass Health Rehabilitation Hospital of Alexandria, Alexandria, LA, p. A276
WAGNER, Terry, R.N., Chief Operating Officer, Pocahontas Memorial Hospital, Buckeye, WV, p. A699
WAGNER, Timothy, M.D., Chief Medical Staff, Yoakum Community Hospital, Yoakum, TX, p. A663
WAGNER, Tom, Interim Vice President Finance, Avera St. Mary's Hospital, Pierre, SD, p. A575
WAGNER, Vanessa, Chief Financial Officer, Lawrence Memorial Hospital, Walnut Ridge, AR, p. A54
WAGNON, LaNell, Director Medical Records, Comanche County Hospital, Coldwater, KS, p. A247
WAGONER, Dean, Director Human Resources, Good Samaritan Hospital, Vincennes, IN, p. A228
WAGONER, Jeremy, Chief Executive Officer, Rivendell Behavioral Health Hospital, Bowling Green, KY, p. A263
WAGONER, Renee, R.N., Director of Nursing, Gove County Medical Center, Quinter, KS, p. A258
WAHAB, Amir J., M.D., Medical Staff President, Lincoln Memorial Hospital, Lincoln, IL, p. A200
WAHKINNEY, Jennifer, Chief Nurse Executive, Lawton Indian Hospital, Lawton, OK, p. A514
WAHL, Josephine Sclafani, R.N., MS, FACHE, VP, Patient Care Services & CNO, Henry Ford Wyandotte Hospital, Wyandotte, MI, p. A341
WAHL, Tony, Chief Executive Officer, Baylor Scott & White Texas Spine & Joint Hospital–Tyler, Tyler, TX, p. A658
WAHLERS, Brenda, M.D., Chief of Staff, UPMC Cole, Coudersport, PA, p. A537
WAHLUND, Keith, Vice President Human Resources, Essentia Health Fargo, Fargo, ND, p. A480
WAIBEL, David, M.D., Medical Director, Clarks Summit State Hospital, Clarks Summit, PA, p. A537
WAIDE, Mary Beth, R.N., JD, MS, Chief Executive Officer, Deer's Head Hospital Center, Salisbury, MD, p. A307
WAIN, Matt, Chief Executive Officer, Emory University Hospital, Atlanta, GA, p. A157
WAIND, Mark, Executive Vice President, Chief Information Officer, Altru Health System, Grand Forks, ND, p. A481
WAIT, Wendy, Chief Financial Officer, Montgomery County Emergency Service, Norristown, PA, p. A547
WAITE, Douglas D
Senior Vice President and Chief Financial Officer, Ascension Seton Highland Lakes, Burnet, TX, p. A606
Senior Vice President and Chief Financial Officer, Ascension Seton Williamson, Round Rock, TX, p. A647
WAITES, Alan, Chief Financial Officer, Gove County Medical Center, Quinter, KS, p. A258
WAJDA, David, Chief Financial Officer, Nazareth Hospital, Philadelphia, PA, p. A549
WAKEFIELD, Brett
Director Human Resources, Thorek Memorial Hospital, Chicago, IL, p. A191
Vice President Human Resources, Gottlieb Memorial Hospital, Melrose Park, IL, p. A201
WAKEFIELD, Jeffrey A., CPA, Vice President and Chief Financial Officer, UNC Health Lenoir, Kinston, NC, p. A471
WAKEFIELD, Mamie
Chief Financial Officer, Miriam Hospital, Providence, RI, p. A560
Senior Vice President and Chief Financial Officer, Rhode Island Hospital, Providence, RI, p. A561
Vice President Finance and Chief Financial Officer, Emma Pendleton Bradley Hospital, East Providence, RI, p. A560
WAKEM, Jennifer, Chief Financial Officer, University Medical Center, Las Vegas, NV, p. A411
WAKIM, Tina, Vice President Information, Northside Hospital, Atlanta, GA, p. A157
WAKO, Elizabeth
M.D., Chief Executive, Providence Swedish Cherry Hill, Seattle, WA, p. A694
M.D., Chief Executive, Providence Swedish First Hill, Seattle, WA, p. A694
M.D., Chief Executive, Swedish Issaquah, Issaquah, WA, p. A690
WALCH, Tina, M.D., Medical Director, South Oaks Hospital, Amityville, NY, p. A438
WALCZYK–JOERS, Barbara, President and Chief Executive Officer, Gillette Children's Specialty Healthcare, Saint Paul, MN, p. A354
WALD, Barry, Chief Financial Officer, Atrium Health Wake Forest Baptist Wilkes Medical Center, North Wilkesboro, NC, p. A474
WALDBART, Andy, Department Manager, Heart of The Rockies Regional Medical Center, Salida, CO, p. A113
WALDBILLIG, Karla, Director Human Resources, Unitypoint Health – Finley Hospital, Dubuque, IA, p. A235
WALDBILLIG, Kurt, Chief Executive Officer, Sakakawea Medical Center, Hazen, ND, p. A481
WALDEN, Anita, Vice President and Chief Nursing Officer, Decatur Morgan Hospital, Decatur, AL, p. A18
WALDERA, John, Director Information Technology, Gundersen Tri–County Hospital And Clinics, Whitehall, WI, p. A725
WALDERS, William, Chief Information Officer, Health First Holmes Regional Medical Center, Melbourne, FL, p. A139
WALDO, Bruce, Chief Executive Officer, Aurora Behavioral Health System West, Glendale, AZ, p. A32
WALDO, Gail, Director Information Technology, Piedmont Rockdale Hospital, Conyers, GA, p. A161
WALDRON, Ray, Director Information Technology, Gordon Memorial Health Services, Gordon, NE, p. A400
WALDRON, Sheila, Finance Manager, Providence Milwaukie Hospital, Milwaukie, OR, p. A529
WALDROP, Catherine M.
Administrator, Southeast Rehabilitation Hospital, Lake Village, AR, p. A49
Administrator, Sterlington Rehabilitation Hospital, Bastrop. LA, p. A277
WALDROP, Cathy, Director, Hospital Nursing Services, North Mississipp. Medical Center–Pontotoc, Pontotoc, MS, p. A368
WALI, Jyotika, M.D., Chief of Staff, Kindred Hospital–Brea, Brea, CA, p. A58
WALIGURA, R Curtis, D.O., Vice President Medical Affairs, Chief Medical Officer, UPMC Mckeesport, Mckeesport, PA, p. A545
WALKENHORST, Debbie G
Network Vice President, SSM Health Cardinal Glennon Children's Hospital, Saint Louis, MO, p. A384
System Vice President Talent Management, SSM Health St. Josep. – St. Charles, Saint Charles, MO, p. A383
WALKER, Alene, Director Human Resources, Quincy Valley Medical Center, Quincy, WA, p. A693
WALKER, Alexander J., President and Chief Executive Officer, Catholic Medical Center, Manchester, NH, p. A416
WALKER, Amy, MSN, Chief Nursing Officer, Delta Health–The Medical Center, Greenville, MS, p. A362
WALKER, Annette
Associate Director, John D. Dingell Department of Veterans Affairs Medical Center, Detroit, MI, p. A325
Medical Center Director, Atlanta Veterans Affairs Medical Center, Decatur, GA, p. A162
WALKER, Beth
Chief Executive Officer, Ochsner Medical Center, New Orleans, LA, p. A289
Director, Information Technology, Emanuel Medical Center, Turlock, CA, p. A98
WALKER, C O, M.D., Chief of Staff, Donalsonville Hospital, Donalsonville, GA, p. A163
WALKER, Candace, Chief Financial Officer, East Central Regional Hospital, Augusta, GA, p. A158
WALKER, Carol, Chief Financial Officer, Oklahoma Heart Hospital, Oklahoma City, OK, p. A518
WALKER, Carrie, Executive Director Human Resources, Jones Memorial Hospital, Wellsville, NY, p. A461
WALKER, Cass
Vice President Administrative & Support Services, Concord Hospital – Franklin, Franklin, NH, p. A415
Vice President Administrative & Support Services, Concord Hospital – Laconia, Laconia, NH, p. A415
WALKER, Charles
Director Human Resource, Lawrence Memorial Hospital, Walnut Ridge, AR, p. A54
Director Information Technology, Kimball Health Services, Kimball, NE, p. A401
WALKER, Christine, Chief Nursing Officer, Las Palmas Medical Center, El Paso, TX, p. A616
WALKER, Christopher
Chief Nursing Officer and Operating Officer, Sharp Coronado Hospital, Coronado, CA, p. A60
Chief Operating Officer, Sharp Mesa Vista Hospital, San Diego, CA, p. A90
WALKER, Codie, Chief Financial Officer, Salem Veterans Affairs Medical Center, Salem, VA, p. A683
WALKER, Cody, President, Baptist Health Medical Center – North Little Rock, North Little Rock, AR, p. A51
WALKER, Dan, Chief Nursing Officer, Lincoln Health, Hugo, CO, p. A110
WALKER, David, Interim Chief Executive Officer, George E. Weems Memorial Hospital, Apalachicola, FL, p. A125
WALKER, Dawn, D.O., Chief of Staff, Northern Cochise Community Hospital, Willcox, AZ, p. A41
WALKER, Derrick, M.D., Chief Medical Officer, Brigham City Community Hospital, Brigham City, UT, p. A664
WALKER, Donna, Chief Nurse Executive, Weeks Medical Center, Lancaster, NH, p. A415
WALKER, Duke, Interim Chief Operating Officer, Ascension Columbia St. Mary's Hospital Milwaukee, Milwaukee, WI, p. A716
WALKER, Durwin, M.D., Chief Medical Officer, Sage Specialty Hospital (Ltac), Denham Springs, LA, p. A281
WALKER, Gerri H., President and Chief Executive Officer, Behavioral Wellness Center At Girard, The, Philadelphia, PA, p. A548
WALKER, Heather, M.D., Chief Medical Officer, Musc Health Rehabilitation Hospital, An Affiliate of Encompass Health, Charleston, SC, p. A563
WALKER, Imani, M.D., Medical Director, Gateways Hospital And Mental Health Center, Los Angeles, CA, p. A72
WALKER, Jan
Director Human Resources, Centra Lynchburg General Hospital, Lynchburg, VA, p. A678
Director Human Resources, Glenwood Regional Medical Center, West Monroe, LA, p. A294
WALKER, Jeff E., Chief Operating Officer, City of Hope's Helford Clinical Research Hospital, Duarte, CA, p. A62
WALKER, Jeremy Tyler, Vice President and Chief Financial Officer, Hendrick Medical Center, Abilene, TX, p. A595

WALKER, John, Chief Executive Officer, Medical City Lewisville, Lewisville, TX, p. A634
WALKER, Jon W., M.D., Chief Medical Officer, Medical City Decatur, Decatur, TX, p. A613
WALKER, Kristie E, M.P.H., Director Human Resources, Wythe County Community Hospital, Wytheville, VA, p. A686
WALKER, LeRoy, Vice President Human Resources, Emory Decatur Hospital, Decatur, GA, p. A162
WALKER, Lynette, R.N., Ph.D., Regional Vice President, Human Resources, Baptist Health Lexington, Lexington, KY, p. A268
WALKER, Mary, Manager Information Technology, Encompass Health Rehabilitation Hospital of Wichita Falls, Wichita Falls, TX, p. A662
WALKER, Matthew, Chief Executive Officer and Administrator, William Bee Ririe Hospital, Ely, NV, p. A408
WALKER, Melissa, CPA, Chief Financial Officer, North Texas Medical Center, Gainesville, TX, p. A621
WALKER, Pandora, Director, Human Resources, Corewell Health Beaumont Grosse Pointe Hospital, Grosse Pointe, MI, p. A329
WALKER, Randy
  Chief Nursing Officer, Hillcrest Hospital Claremore, Claremore, OK, p. A511
  Director Nursing Services, State Hospital South, Blackfoot, ID, p. A179
  Vice President, Methodist Dallas Medical Center, Dallas, TX, p. A612
WALKER, Robert, M.D., Medical Director, Encompass Health Rehabilitation Hospital of Princeton, Princeton, WV, p. A704
WALKER, Robert L., FACHE, President and Chief Executive Officer, Scottish Rite for Children, Dallas, TX, p. A612
WALKER, Robin, Chief Nursing Officer, Field Memorial Community Hospital, Centreville, MS, p. A360
WALKER, Ryan, Chief Executive Officer, Ascension Saint Thomas Hospital for Specialty Surgery, Nashville, TN, p. A590
WALKER, Samuel, Director of IT, Pocahontas Memorial Hospital, Buckeye, WV, p. A699
WALKER, Sara, Interim Superintendent, Oregon State Hospital, Salem, OR, p. A532
WALKER, Scott, Chief Human Resource Officer, American Fork Hospital, American Fork, UT, p. A664
WALKER, Taylor
  Chief Financial Officer, Marshall Medical Center North, Guntersville, AL, p. A20
  Chief Financial Officer, Marshall Medical Center South, Boaz, AL, p. A17
WALKER, Tim, Manager Information Services, Peacehealth Ketchikan Medical Center, Ketchikan, AK, p. A28
WALKER, Todd
  Chief Executive Officer, Prisma Health Greer Memorial Hospital, Greer, SC, p. A567
  Chief Executive Officer, Prisma Health Patewood Hospital, Greenville, SC, p. A567
WALKER, Troy, Director Finance, SSM Health St. Clare Hospital–Baraboo, Baraboo, WI, p. A707
WALKER, Tyree, Chief Human Resources Officer, ECU Health Medical Center, Greenville, NC, p. A470
WALKER, Virginia, Vice President Nursing Services and Chief Nursing Officer, Kuakini Medical Center, Honolulu, HI, p. A175
WALL, Debbie, Chief Nursing Officer, Cherry Hospital, Goldsboro, NC, p. A469
WALL, Doug
  M.D., Vice President Medical Affairs, UVA Health Prince William Medical Center, Manassas, VA, p. A679
  M.D., Vice President of Medical Affairs, UVA Health Haymarket Medical Center, Haymarket, VA, p. A677
WALL, Heather
  Chief Nursing Officer, Peacehealth Sacred Heart Medical Center At Riverbend, Springfield, OR, p. A532
  President, Lds Hospital, Salt Lake City, UT, p. A669
WALL, Kathryn S
  Executive Vice President Human Resources and Organizational Development, Stafford Hospital, Stafford, VA, p. A684
  Executive Vice President, Human Resources and Organizational Development, Mary Washington Hospital, Fredericksburg, VA, p. A676
WALLACE, Brad, Director Information Services, Harbor Regional Health, Aberdeen, WA, p. A687
WALLACE, Carolyn, Director Human Resources, Connecticut Mental Health Center, New Haven, CT, p. A117
WALLACE, Cyndi, R.N., MSN, Chief Nursing Officer, Cedar City Hospital, Cedar City, UT, p. A664
WALLACE, Cynthia, M.D., Medical Director, Vibra Specialty Hospital of Portland, Portland, OR, p. A531
WALLACE, David, Chief Executive Officer, Mat-Su Regional Medical Center, Palmer, AK, p. A29

WALLACE, Dianne, County Information Manager, Douglas County Community Mental Health Center, Omaha, NE, p. A404
WALLACE, Donna Geiken, Chief Operating Officer and Chief Financial Officer, Christus Mother Frances Hospital – Sulphur Springs, Sulphur Springs, TX, p. A655
WALLACE, Glenn, Chief Executive Officer, Medical City Alliance, Fort Worth, TX, p. A619
WALLACE, Mark, Chief Financial Officer, Cumberland Hall Hospital, Hopkinsville, KY, p. A267
WALLACE, Mark A.
  FACHE, Chief Executive Officer, Texas Children's Hospital, Houston, TX, p. A628
  FACHE, Chief Executive Officer, Texas Children's Hospital North Austin Campus, Austin, TX, p. A601
WALLACE, Mark T, Director Human Resources, Adventist Health Lodi Memorial, Lodi, CA, p. A70
WALLACE, Melanie, Manager Human Resources, Sutter Tracy Community Hospital, Tracy, CA, p. A98
WALLACE, Nancy
  Division Senior Vice President, Chief Human Resource Officer, Chi Health Lakeside, Omaha, NE, p. A403
  Division Senior Vice President, Chief Human Resource Officer, Chi Health Midlands, Papillion, NE, p. A405
  Senior Vice President Human Resources, Chi Health Mercy Council Bluffs, Council Bluffs, IA, p. A233
  Senior Vice President, Chief Human Resources Officer, Chi Health St Elizabeth, Lincoln, NE, p. A402
  Vice President Human Resources, Chi Health Immanuel, Omaha, NE, p. A403
  Vice President Human Resources, Chi Health Schuyler, Schuyler, NE, p. A405
  Vice President Human Resources, CHI Health, Chi Health Saint Francis, Grand Island, NE, p. A400
WALLACE, Penny, Chief Financial Officer, Guadalup. Regional Medical Center, Seguin, TX, p. A652
WALLACE, Tabatha, Director Human Resources, Adventhealth Dade City, Dade City, FL, p. A129
WALLACE, Todd, Chief Executive Officer, Encompass Health Rehabilitation Hospital of Texarkana, Texarkana, TX, p. A657
WALLACE–MOORE, Patrice, Chief Executive Officer and Executive Director, Arms Acres, Carmel, NY, p. A441
WALLACH, Perry, M.D., Chief Medical Officer, UT Health East Texas Rehabilitation Hospital, Tyler, TX, p. A659
WALLEN, Carla, Manager Human Resources, Cass Regional Medical Center, Harrisonville, MO, p. A376
WALLENTINE, Jeffrey, Chief of Staff, Mountain View Hospital, Payson, UT, p. A667
WALLER, Ernie, Director Information Technology, Ed Fraser Memorial Hospital, Macclenny, FL, p. A138
WALLER, Kenneth, Fiscal Administrator, Deer's Head Hospital Center, Salisbury, MD, p. A307
WALLER, Michelle, MSN, R.N., Chief Clinical and Operations Officer, Gateway Regional Medical Center, Granite City, IL, p. A196
WALLING, Vernon
  M.D., Chief Medical Officer, Sun Behavioral Houston, Houston, TX, p. A628
  M.D., Executive Medical Director, West Oaks Hospital, Houston, TX, p. A629
WALLINGA, Joel, Chief Financial Officer, Veterans Affairs Ann Arbor Healthcare System, Ann Arbor, MI, p. A321
WALLINGA, Melvin, M.D., Medical Director, St. Michael's Hospital Avera, Tyndall, SD, p. A577
WALLIS, Christian, Vice President Operations, Advocate Condell Medical Center, Libertyville, IL, p. A200
WALLIS, Pam B, MSN, Vice President Nursing Services, Magnolia Regional Health Center, Corinth, MS, p. A361
WALLS, Craig, M.D., Ph.D., Chief Medical Officer, Natividad, Salinas, CA, p. A88
WALLS, Martha Delaney, R.N., MSN, Chief Nursing Officer, Crestwood Medical Center, Huntsville, AL, p. A20
WALLS, Randy, Manager Information Services, Community Fairbanks Recovery Center, Indianapolis, IN, p. A219
WALLSCHLAEGER, Erich, Chief Financial Officer, Hendrick Medical Center Brownwood, Brownwood, TX, p. A605
WALLSCHLAEGER, Erich, Chief Financial Officer, Cedar Park Regional Medical Center, Cedar Park, TX, p. A607
WALRATH, Andrea, Chief Operating Officer, Forest Health Medical Center, Ypsilanti, MI, p. A341
WALRATH, Bryan, President, Ascension St. Vincent's Clay County, Middleburg, FL, p. A141
WALRAVEN, Jeff, Chief Executive Officer, Lindsay Municipal Hospital, Lindsay, OK, p. A514
WALSER, Bill, Coordinator Technology, Cameron Regional Medical Center, Cameron, MO, p. A372
WALSH, Brad, M.D., Chief of Staff, Ashley County Medical Center, Crossett, AR, p. A45

WALSH, Catherine, Interim Nursing Executive, Mercy Health – Lorain Hospital, Lorain, OH, p. A498
WALSH, Debbie, MSN, Chief Operating Officer, Maui Memorial Medical Center, Wailuku, HI, p. A177
WALSH, Gerard W., Chief Executive Officer, St. John's Episcopal Hospital, New York, NY, p. A453
WALSH, John
  FACHE, Chief Administrative Officer, Uofl Health – Jewish Hospital, Louisville, KY, p. A270
  Chief Fiscal Services, Veterans Affairs Hudson Valley Health Care System, Montrose, NY, p. A446
WALSH, Katherine, MS, R.N., Dr.PH, Vice President and Chief Nursing Officer, Houston Methodist Hospital, Houston, TX, p. A626
WALSH, Kim, Chief Nursing Officer, Signature Healthcare Brockton Hospital, Brockton, MA, p. A311
WALSH, Len, Executive Vice President and Chief Operating Officer, St. Barnabas Hospital, New York, NY, p. A452
WALSH, Linda, R.N., MSN, Vice President Chief Nursing Executive, Hackensack Meridian Health Bayshore Community Hospital, Holmdel, NJ, p. A422
WALSH, Marilyn J, Vice President Human Resources, Kent Hospital, Warwick, RI, p. A561
WALSH, Mary
  R.N., MSN, Vice President Patient Care Services and Chief Nursing Officer, Mount Sinai Beth Israel, New York, NY, p. A449
  R.N., MSN, Vice President Patient Care Services and Chief Nursing Officer, Mount Sinai Morningside, New York, NY, p. A449
WALSH, Michael
  Senior Vice President Finance and Chief Financial Officer, Jefferson Abington Health, Abington, PA, p. A534
  Senior Vice President Finance and Chief Financial Officer, Jefferson Lansdale Hospital, Lansdale, PA, p. A544
WALSH, Michele M, Chief Nursing Officer, St. Mary's Healthcare, Amsterdam, NY, p. A438
WALSTON, Emily, Chief Human Resources Officer, Incompass Healthcare, Lawrenceburg, IN, p. A222
WALSTON, John, Chief Information Officer, Tucson Va Medical Center, Tucson, AZ, p. A41
WALTER, Gayle, Director of Nursing, Thomas B. Finan Center, Cumberland, MD, p. A303
WALTER, Melissa, Director Human Resources, Clarinda Regional Health Center, Clarinda, IA, p. A232
WALTER, Stephen
  Senior Vice President and Chief Financial Officer, Community Behavioral Health Center, Fresno, CA, p. A64
  Senior Vice President and Chief Financial Officer, Community Regional Medical Center, Fresno, CA, p. A64
WALTERS, Jane, Director of Nursing, Mendota Mental Health Institute, Madison, WI, p. A714
WALTERS, Joette, Chief Executive Officer, Tuba City Regional Health Care Corporation, Tuba City, AZ, p. A40
WALTERS, Jonathan, M.D., Chief Medical Officer, Massac Memorial Hospital, Metropolis, IL, p. A202
WALTERS, Kevin, Chief Financial Officer, St. Rose Dominican Hospitals – Rose De Lima Campus, Henderson, NV, p. A409
WALTERS, Leah, R.N., Director of Nursing, Mountain Valley Regional Rehabilitation Hospital, Prescott Valley, AZ, p. A37
WALTERS, Leslie, MSN, Chief Nursing Officer, Clarion Hospital, Clarion, PA, p. A537
WALTERS, Todd, Director, Information Technology, Lane Regional Medical Center, Zachary, LA, p. A294
WALTHALL, Wayne, Vice President and Chief Financial Officer, Ascension St. John Medical Center, Tulsa, OK, p. A522
WALTHER, Diane, Controller, Henry County Hospital, Napoleon, OH, p. A501
WALTON, Amy E., M.D., Chief Medical Officer, Ascension Seton Shoal Creek, Austin, TX, p. A599
WALTON, Carlyle L E., FACHE, Chief Executive Officer, Phoebe Sumter Medical Center, Americus, GA, p. A156
WALTON, Dawn, Chief Financial Officer, Children's of Alabama, Birmingham, AL, p. A16
WALTON, Gary, M.D., Chief Medical Officer, Hill Hospital of Sumter County, York, AL, p. A26
WALTON, Georgian, Director Human Resources, Elbert Memorial Hospital, Elberton, GA, p. A163
WALTON, Lauri, Interim Chief Financial Officer, Controller, Ochsner Lsu Health Shreveport – St. Mary Medical Center, Llc, Shreveport, LA, p. A292
WALTZ, Dan, Vice President and Chief Information Officer, Mymichigan Medical Center Gladwin, Gladwin, MI, p. A327
WALZ, David Frank., Chief Executive Officer, Madelia Health, Madelia, MN, p. A349
WALZ, Rachel A, Director Patient Care, Centracare – Paynesville, Paynesville, MN, p. A352

Index of Health Care Professionals / Waters

Index of Health Care Professionals

WAMPLER, Andrew R.
Chief Financial Officer, Franklin Woods Community Hospital, Johnson City, TN, p. A584
Chief Financial Officer, UNC Health Pardee, Hendersonville, NC, p. A470
Vice President, Operational Excellence, Indian Path Community Hospital, Kingsport, TN, p. A585
WAMSLEY, Marie, Chief Financial Officer, Memorial Hospital of Lafayette County, Darlington, WI, p. A709
WANEE, Nelson Alexander., Chief Executive Officer, Red River Hospital, Llc, Wichita Falls, TX, p. A662
WANG, Richard, Chief Financial Officer, Fountain Valley Regional Hospital And Medical Center, Fountain Valley, CA, p. A64
WANG, Ted, Chief Financial Officer, UCSF Benioff Children's Hospital Oakland, Oakland, CA, p. A81
WANG, William Norberto, M.D., Chief Operating Officer, NYC Health + Hospitals/Metropolitan, New York, NY, p. A451
WANG, MD, Shu–Ming, Vice President Medical Affairs, Chi Health Saint Francis, Grand Island, NE, p. A400
WANGSMO, Gary L, Chief Financial Officer, George L. Mee Memorial Hospital, King City, CA, p. A68
WANGSNESS, Erik
Chief Executive Officer, Adventhealth Wesley Chapel, Wesley Chapel, FL, p. A154
President and Chief Executive Officer, Adventist Healthcare White Oak Medical Center, Silver Spring, MD, p. A307
WANLY, Bahaa, President, Legacy Emanuel Medical Center, Portland, OR, p. A530
WANNER, David
Chief Information Officer, Trinity Health, Minot, ND, p. A482
Director Information Technology, Trinity Kenmare Community Hospital, Kenmare, ND, p. A482
WANNER, Joe, Chief Financial Officer, Bartlett Regional Hospital, Juneau, AK, p. A28
WAPPELHORST, Andrea, Chief Nursing Officer, Top. Surgical Specialty Hospital, Houston, TX, p. A628
WAR, Melissa, Chief Executive Officer, Orthopedic Specialty Hospital of Nevada, Las Vegas, NV, p. A410
WARBURTON, Joseph, Chief Operating Officer, Cedar Park Regional Medical Center, Cedar Park, TX, p. A607
WARD, Brook, President and Chief Executive Officer, UPMC Washington, Washington, PA, p. A556
WARD, Celia F, Controller and Chief Financial Officer, Doctors Memorial Hospital, Bonifay, FL, p. A126
WARD, Charlotte, Entity Financial Officer, Texas Health Harris Methodist Hospital Southwest Fort Worth, Fort Worth, TX, p. A620
WARD, Chris, Director Management Information Systems, Dorminy Medical Center, Fitzgerald, GA, p. A164
WARD, David M, Chief Financial Officer and Chief Acquisition Officer, Cabell Huntington Hospital, Huntington, WV, p. A701
WARD, Dillon, Management Information Systems Specialist, Tennova Healthcare–Lafollette Medical Center, La Follette, TN, p. A586
WARD, Elizabeth S.
Chief Financial Officer, Tidelands Georgetown Memorial Hospital, Georgetown, SC, p. A566
Chief Financial Officer, Tidelands Waccamaw Community Hospital, Murrells Inlet, SC, p. A569
WARD, Gary, Controller, University of Iowa Health Network Rehabilitation Hospital, Coralville, IA, p. A233
WARD, Jacqueline, MSN, R.N., Chief Nursing Officer, Texas Children's Hospital, Houston, TX, p. A628
WARD, Jeffery, Director Human Resources, Cedar Park Regional Medical Center, Cedar Park, TX, p. A607
WARD, Julie
MSN, R.N., Chief Nursing Officer, St. Joseph's Hospital And Medical Center, Phoenix, AZ, p. A36
Vice President Finance, Northeastern Health System, Tahlequah, OK, p. A521
WARD, Kevin, Chief Operating Officer, San Francisco Campus for Jewish Living, San Francisco, CA, p. A91
WARD, Kevin J, Vice President and Chief Financial Officer, New York–Presbyterian Queens, New York, NY, p. A450
WARD, Kimberly J, Chief Nurse Officer, Providence St. Luke's Rehabilitation Medical Center, Spokane, WA, p. A696
WARD, Leigha, Chief Financial Officer, Pemiscot Memorial Health System, Hayti, MO, p. A376
WARD, Lesli, Vice President Human Resources, UF Health Jacksonville, Jacksonville, FL, p. A135
WARD, Lisa, Director Information Systems, Columbus Regional Healthcare System, Whiteville, NC, p. A477
WARD, Lorna J, MSN, R.N., Chief Nursing Officer, Novant Health Brunswick Medical Center, Bolivia, NC, p. A464
WARD, Louis James.
Acting Chief Executive Officer, Tahoe Forest Hospital District, Truckee, CA, p. A98
Chief Operating Officer and Administrator, Incline Village Community Hospital, Incline Village, NV, p. A409
WARD, Mark, M.D., Chief of Staff, Roundup Memorial Healthcare, Roundup. MT, p. A395
WARD, Michael, Director Information Services, Anderson Hospital, Maryville, IL, p. A201
WARD, Mike
Chief Information Officer, Morristown–Hamblen Healthcare System, Morristown, TN, p. A589
Covenant Health, Senior Vice President and Chief Information Officer, Methodist Medical Center of Oak Ridge, Oak Ridge, TN, p. A591
Senior Vice President Chief Information Officer, Roane Medical Center, Harriman, TN, p. A583
WARD, Rory, Chief Financial Officer, Pushmataha Hospital, Antlers, OK, p. A509
WARD, Silva, Director Human Resources, Center for Behavioral Medicine, Kansas City, MO, p. A377
WARD, Stormy, Chief Nurse Executive, Big Spring State Hospital, Big Spring, TX, p. A603
WARD, Virginia, Human Resources Officer, Robert E. Bush Naval Hospital, Twentynine Palms, CA, p. A99
WARD LUND, Debra, Chief Executive Officer, U. S. Public Health Service Phoenix Indian Medical Center, Phoenix, AZ, p. A37
WARDA, Paul, Chief Financial Officer, Peacehealth Sacred Heart Medical Center At Riverbend, Springfield, OR, p. A532
WARDEN, Michael S, Senior Vice President Information Technology, Banner – University Medical Center Phoenix, Phoenix, AZ, p. A35
WARDLE, Andrea, Chief Nursing Officer, Fillmore Community Hospital, Fillmore, UT, p. A665
WARDROP, Daniel, M.D., Medical Director, Heart of The Rockies Regional Medical Center, Salida, CO, p. A113
WARE, Bobbie K.
R.N., FACHE, Chief Executive Officer and Administrator, Mississipp. Baptist Medical Center, Jackson, MS, p. A364
R.N., FACHE, Vice President Patient Care and Chief Nursing Officer, Mississipp. Baptist Medical Center, Jackson, MS, p. A364
WARE, Chris, Chief Executive Officer, Russellville Hospital, Russellville, AL, p. A24
WARE, Dana, M.D., Chief of Staff, Seneca Healthcare District, Chester, CA, p. A59
WARE, Elaine LePage, R.N., Chief Nurse Executive, Kaiser Permanente San Jose Medical Center, San Jose, CA, p. A92
WARE, Jeff, Information Technology Support Technician, Stillwater Medical Perry, Perry, OK, p. A519
WARE, Judy
Chief Financial Officer, Putnam General Hospital, Eatonton, GA, p. A163
Director Human Resources, Johnson Memorial Hospital, Franklin, IN, p. A217
WARE, Judy King, Chief Financial Officer, Monroe County Hospital, Forsyth, GA, p. A164
WARE, Kathy, Director of Nursing, Daniels Memorial Healthcare Center, Scobey, MT, p. A395
WARE, Raynard, Vice President of Opeartions, HCA Florida Pasadena Hospital, Saint Petersburg, FL, p. A149
WARFIELD, William, Chief Human Resources Management, Veterans Affairs Boston Healthcare System, West Roxbury, MA, p. A319
WARING, Lance, Director Human Resources, Texas Health Harris Methodist Hospital Azle, Azle, TX, p. A601
WARLICK, Mark
Chief Information Officer, Elkhart General Hospital, Elkhart, IN, p. A215
Chief Information Officer, Memorial Hospital of South Bend, South Bend, IN, p. A227
WARLITNER, Todd, Vice President Business Operations, The Outer Banks Hospital, Nags Head, NC, p. A473
WARM, Ira, Senior Vice President Human Resources, Brooklyn Hospital Center, New York, NY, p. A447
WARMAN, Debbie, Vice President Human Resources, Metrohealth Medical Center, Cleveland, OH, p. A491
WARMBOLD, Steve, Director Information Management Service Line, VA St. Louis Health Care System, Saint Louis, MO, p. A384
WARMERDAM, David, Chief Financial Officer, Brynn Marr Hospital, Jacksonville, NC, p. A471
WARNEKE, Angela, Deputy Director and Hospital Administrator, San Diego County Psychiatric Hospital, San Diego, CA, p. A89
WARNER, Ben, R.N., Chief Nursing Officer, HCA Florida Mercy Hospital, Miami, FL, p. A140
WARNER, Cory, Chief Executive Officer, Pam Health Rehabilitation Hospital of Westminster, Westminster, CO, p. A114
WARNER, Grady, Director of Information Technology, Burgess Health Center, Onawa, IA, p. A241
WARNER, John, M.D., Chief Executive Officer, Ohio State University Wexner Medical Center, Columbus, OH, p. A492
WARNER, Petra, Chief of Staff, Shriners Children's Ohio, Dayton, OH, p. A494
WARNER LYNN, Lynne, R.N., Administrator, Ephraim Mcdowell James B. Haggin Memorial Hospital, Harrodsburg, KY, p. A266
WARNER–PACHECO, Paula, Chief Human Resources, Rio Grande Hospital, Del Norte, CO, p. A106
WARNING, Kendra, Chief Financial Officer, Davis County Hospital And Clinics, Bloomfield, IA, p. A231
WARNOCK, Dawn, Director Medical Records, Taylor Regional Hospital, Hawkinsville, GA, p. A165
WARREN, Charlene, R.N., Chief Nursing Officer, Camc Greenbrier Valley Medical Center, Ronceverte, WV, p. A704
WARREN, Denise Wilder, R.N., Executive Vice President and Chief Operating Officer, Wakemed Raleigh Campus, Raleigh, NC, p. A475
WARREN, Gidgett, Director of Nursing, T.J. Health Columbia, Columbia, KY, p. A264
WARREN, James, Interim Medical Center Director, John J. Pershing Veterans' Administration Medical Center, Poplar Bluff, MO, p. A382
WARREN, Jana, Human Resources Business Partner, Piedmont Henry Hospital, Stockbridge, GA, p. A172
WARREN, Karen, Fiscal Officer, Porterville Developmental Center, Porterville, CA, p. A84
WARREN, Linda, Director Human Resources, Cogdell Memorial Hospital, Snyder, TX, p. A653
WARREN, Sarah, Coordinator Human Resources, Hickory Trail Hospital, Desoto, TX, p. A614
WARREN, Seth, President and Chief Executive Officer, Meridian Health Services, Muncie, IN, p. A224
WARREN, Shanna, Director Human Resources, Medical City Plano, Plano, TX, p. A645
WARREN, Terri, Chief Financial Officer, Adventhealth Waterman, Tavares, FL, p. A153
WARRENER, Gerald, M.D., Chief Medical Officer, Parkview Noble Hospital, Kendallville, IN, p. A221
WARRIN, Richard, Chief Operating Officer, Musc Health Lancaster Medical Center, Lancaster, SC, p. A568
WARRINER, Ken, Market Chief Financial Officer, Physicians Regional – Pine Ridge, Naples, FL, p. A142
WARSING, Tracy, M.D., Site Leader Chief of Staff, Mayo Clinic Health System In Sparta, Sparta, WI, p. A721
WARTELLE, Scott
Chief Financial Officer, Sierra Vista Regional Medical Center, San Luis Obispo, CA, p. A93
Chief Financial Officer, Twin Cities Community Hospital, Templeton, CA, p. A97
WARWICK, Taylor, Chief Operating Officer, Mercy Hospital Springfield, Springfield, MO, p. A387
WAS, David, Chief Operating Officer, HCA Florida Aventura Hospital, Aventura, FL, p. A125
WASEK, Arthur A, Director Human Resources, Panola Medical Center, Batesville, MS, p. A359
WASHBURN, Geoff, Vice President Human Resources, Los Robles Health System, Thousand Oaks, CA, p. A97
WASHBURN, Geoffrey A., Vice President, HCA Florida Bayonet Point Hospital, Hudson, FL, p. A134
WASHBURN, Tonya, M.D., Medical Director, Valir Rehabilitation Hospital, Oklahoma City, OK, p. A519
WASHINGTON, Maurice, Chief Executive Officer, Haven Behavioral Hospital of Philadelphia, Philadelphia, PA, p. A548
WASHINGTON, Stephanie
Director Community Relations and Human Resources, Baptist Medical Center – Yazoo, Yazoo City, MS, p. A370
Human Resources Director, Baptist Medical Center – Attala, Kosciusko, MS, p. A365
WASHINGTON, Tarra, Chief Executive Officer, Encompass Health Rehabilitation Hospital of Round Rock, Round Rock, TX, p. A647
WASICEK, Corey, Chief Executive Officer, Refugio County Memorial Hospital, Refugio, TX, p. A646
WASIELEWSKI, Norine, R.N., Chief Executive Officer, Arrowhead Behavioral Health Hospital, Maumee, OH, p. A499
WASILICK, Tamara, Director Operations, Kidspeace Children's Hospital, Orefield, PA, p. A547
WASSERMANN, Joel, Chief Medical Officer, Providence St. Mary Medical Center, Walla Walla, WA, p. A698
WATERMAN, Drew, Chief Executive Officer, Grand Island Regional Medical Center, Grand Island, NE, p. A400
WATERS, Bill, M.D., Chief Medical Officer, Higgins General Hospital, Bremen, GA, p. A159
WATERS, Danny, Director, Information Services, HCA Florida Pasadena Hospital, Saint Petersburg, FL, p. A149
WATERS, Eric, Vice President Operations, Mainehealth Pen Bay Medical Center, Rockport, ME, p. A299

Index of Health Care Professionals **A1001**

Index of Health Care Professionals

Index of Health Care Professionals / Waters

WATERS, Gina, Director Human Resources, Evans Memorial Hospital, Claxton, GA, p. A160
WATERS, Jerod, Chief Nursing Officer, Chickasaw Nation Medical Center, Ada, OK, p. A509
WATERS, Karen, Chief Nursing Officer, Ascension St. Vincent Warrick, Boonville, IN, p. A213
WATERS, Kent, Administrator, Mid Coast Medical Center – Trinity, Trinity, TX, p. A658
WATERS, Laura M, Vice President Human Resources, Garrett Regional Medical Center, Oakland, MD, p. A306
WATERS, Nancy, Interim Chief Information Officer, Atrium Health Wake Foret Baptist High Point Medical Center, High Point, NC, p. A470
WATERS, Tony, Chief Information Officer, Emanuel Medical Center, Swainsboro, GA, p. A172
WATERS, William
M.D., IV, Chief Medical Officer, Tanner Medical Center–Carrollton, Carrollton, GA, p. A160
M.D., IV, Executive Vice President, Tanner Medical Center–Villa Rica, Villa Rica, GA, p. A173
WATHEN, Cheryl A, Interim Chief Financial Officer, Deaconess Midtown Hospital, Evansville, IN, p. A216
WATHEN, Susan R., Vice President Human Resources, Hannibal Regional Hospital, Hannibal, MO, p. A376
WATKINS, James, M.D., President Medical Staff, Providence Willamette Falls Medical Center, Oregon City, OR, p. A530
WATKINS, Jonathan E., President and Chief Executive Officer, City of Hop. Atlanta, Newnan, GA, p. A169
WATKINS, Michael, Chief Operating Officer, North Oaks Medical Center, Hammond, LA, p. A282
WATKINS, Michelle, Human Resources Manager, Greenwood Regional Rehabilitation Hospital, Greenwood, SC, p. A567
WATKINS, Pamela, Chief Financial Officer, Atlanta Veterans Affairs Medical Center, Decatur, GA, p. A162
WATKINS, Rolanda, Chief Human Resources Management Service, Dayton Veterans Affairs Medical Center, Dayton, OH, p. A493
WATKINS, Steve, Chief Executive Officer, Lifescape, Sioux Falls, SD, p. A576
WATRIDGE, Donna
R.N., Chief Nursing Officer, Hackettstown Medical Center, Hackettstown, NJ, p. A421
R.N., Director of Operations, Hackettstown Medical Center, Hackettstown, NJ, p. A421
WATSON, B Keith, M.D., Chief Medical Staff, North Mississipp. Medical Center–West Point, West Point, MS, p. A370
WATSON, Betty A, Chief Financial Officer, Syringa Hospital And Clinics, Grangeville, ID, p. A181
WATSON, Chad, Market Controller, Kindred Hospital Indianapolis North, Indianapolis, IN, p. A220
WATSON, Cheryl, Chief Information Officer, Howard County Medical Center, Saint Paul, NE, p. A405
WATSON, Dalph, Director of Human Resources, Corewell Health Farmington Hills Hospital, Farmington Hills, MI, p. A326
WATSON, Deagan, Chief Executive Officer, Lakeview Behavioral Health, Norcross, GA, p. A169
WATSON, Dean, M.D., Chief Medical Officer, Tallahassee Memorial Healthcare, Tallahassee, FL, p. A151
WATSON, Deborah
R.N., Chief Nursing Officer, Providence Mount Carmel Hospital, Colville, WA, p. A688
R.N., Chief Nursing Officer, Providence St. Joseph's Hospital, Chewelah, WA, p. A688
Senior Vice President and Chief Operating Officer, Bayhealth, Dover, DE, p. A121
WATSON, Deidre L, Director Human Resources, Belmont Pines Hospital, Youngstown, OH, p. A508
WATSON, Dolores, Director Health Information Management, Arms Acres, Carmel, NY, p. A441
WATSON, Heath
Controller, Encompass Health Rehabilitation Hospital of Dothan, Dothan, AL, p. A18
Controller, Encompass Health Rehabilitation Hospital of Montgomery, Montgomery, AL, p. A22
WATSON, Kathy, R.N., Administrator and Chief Nursing Officer, Ascension Saint Thomas Hospital for Specialty Surgery, Nashville, TN, p. A590
WATSON, Kelly, R.N., FACHE, Vice President and Chief Nursing Officer, Rutland Regional Medical Center, Rutland, VT, p. A672
WATSON, Kerry, Interim Chief Executive Officer, UF Health St. John's, Saint Augustine, FL, p. A148
WATSON, Kevin, Chief Operating Officer and Chief Nursing Officer, St. Luke's Jerome, Jerome, ID, p. A181
WATSON, Luke, M.D., Chief of Staff, College Medical Center, Long Beach, CA, p. A70
WATSON, Lynn, Interim Chief Nursing Officer, Ascension Saint Josep. – Joliet, Joliet, IL, p. A199
WATSON, Margie MSN, RN–B, Chief Nursing Officer, Sabine County Hospital, Hemphill, TX, p. A624
WATSON, Michael, M.D., Chief of Staff, Memorial Hospital, Seminole, TX, p. A652
WATSON, Michelle, Chief Financial Officer, Encompass Health Rehabilitation Hospital, Shreveport, LA, p. A292
WATSON, Nathan, M.D., Jr, Chief of Staff, Carrus Specialty Hospital, Sherman, TX, p. A653
WATSON, Rob, M.D., Chief Medical Officer, Baylor Scott & White Medical Center – Round Rock, Round Rock, TX, p. A647
WATSON, Susan, MSN, R.N., Vice President, Bronson Battle Creek Hospital, Battle Creek, MI, p. A322
WATSON, Teresa C., Division President, Sentara Albemarle Medical Center, Elizabeth City, NC, p. A468
WATSON, Thelma Ruth, M.D., Medical Director, Schneider Regional Medical Center, Saint Thomas, VI, p. A736
WATSON, Thomas, M.D., Chief of Staff, Mayers Memorial Hospital District, Fall River Mills, CA, p. A63
WATSON, Trey, Network Administrator, Caldwell Regional Medical Center, Caldwell, KS, p. A247
WATSON, Vicki, Manager Human Resources, Select Specialty Hospital–Jackson, Jackson, MS, p. A364
WATT, Andrew, M.D., Vice President, Information Technology & Services, Chief Information Officer, Chief Medical Information Officer, Southern New Hampshire Medical Center, Nashua, NH, p. A416
WATTENBARGER, J. Michael, M.D., Chief of Staff, Shriners Hospitals for Children–Greenville, Greenville, SC, p. A567
WATTOO, Dost, M.D., Chief of Staff, Valley Hospital Medical Center, Las Vegas, NV, p. A411
WATTS, Blake, FACHE, Chief Executive Officer, Piedmont Walton Hospital, Monroe, GA, p. A168
WATTS, Cheryl, Administrator, Prague Regional Memorial Hospital, Prague, OK, p. A520
WATTS, Dawn, Chief Executive Officer, Encompasss Health Rehabilitation Hospital of Fort Smith, Fort Smith, AR, p. A47
WATTS, Lynda, Vice President, Chief Nursing Officer, Fort Sanders Regional Medical Center, Knoxville, TN, p. A585
WATTS, Trice
Chief Financial Officer, Greeley County Health Services, Tribune, KS, p. A261
Chief Financial Officer and Chief Executive Officer, Greeley County Health Services, Tribune, KS, p. A261
WAUN, Cynthia, Chief Executive Officer, Brynn Marr Hospital, Jacksonville, NC, p. A471
WAY, Dee, Director Human Resources, Jerold Phelp. Community Hospital, Garberville, CA, p. A65
WAY, Harold, Chief Financial Officer, Montclair Hospital Medical Center, Montclair, CA, p. A78
WAYNE, Ann, Chief Executive Officer, Sun Behavioral Delaware, Georgetown, DE, p. A121
WAYNE, Denise
Chief Executive Officer, Landmark Hospital of Savannah, Savannah, GA, p. A171
Chief Executive Officer, Pioneer Specialty Hospital, Pontiac, MI, p. A335
WAYNE, Jason, Network Administrator, Suburban Community Hospital, East Norriton, PA, p. A539
WEALAND, Tanner
CPA, Chief Financial Officer and Interim Chief Executive Officer, Mcpherson Hospital, Inc., Mcpherson, KS, p. A254
CPA, President and Chief Executive Officer, Mcpherson Hospital, Inc., Mcpherson, KS, p. A254
WEATHERFORD, Dennis, Chief Executive Officer, Putnam County Hospital, Greencastle, IN, p. A218
WEATHERLY, Daniel R, Chief Operating Officer, Cap. Fear Valley Medical Center, Fayetteville, NC, p. A468
WEATHERWAX, Lisa, R.N., Chief Nursing Officer, Iowa Specialty Hospital–Belmond, Belmond, IA, p. A230
WEATHERWAX, Marlene, Vice President and Chief Financial Officer, Columbus Regional Hospital, Columbus, IN, p. A214
WEAVER, Angie L, Director Human Resources, North Mississipp. Medical Center Gilmore–Amory, Amory, MS, p. A359
WEAVER, Daryl W., Chief Executive Officer and Administrator, Baptist Medical Center – Leake, Carthage, MS, p. A360
WEAVER, Greg, Chief Executive Officer, Bates County Memorial Hospital, Butler, MO, p. A372
WEAVER, Harry, M.D., Chief of Staff, Covenant Hospital–Levelland, Levelland, TX, p. A634
WEAVER, Jason
Director Finance, Centracare – Monticello, Monticello, MN, p. A351
Director Information Systems, Southern Tennessee Regional Health System–Lawrenceburg, Lawrenceburg, TN, p. A586
WEAVER, Judy K., MS, Interim Chief Executive Officer, Kindred Hospital–Indianapolis, Indianapolis, IN, p. A220
WEAVER, Kimberli, Chief Nursing Officer, Regional Medical Center of Central Alabama, Greenville, AL, p. A20
WEAVER, Randall, M.D., Acting Chief of Staff, Central Alabama Va Medical Center–Montgomery, Montgomery, AL, p. A22
WEAVER, Rudolp. D, Vice President Human Resources, Southwestern Vermont Medical Center, Bennington, VT, p. A671
WEAVER, Sabrina, Director of Human Resources, Marshall Medical Center North, Guntersville, AL, p. A20
WEAVER, William C., Group Chief Executive Officer, Brentwood Hospital, Shreveport, LA, p. A292
WEBB, Adam, Chief Operating Officer, Emory University Hospital Midtown, Atlanta, GA, p. A157
WEBB, Casey, Chief Executive Officer, Signature Psychiatric Hospital, Kansas City, MO, p. A377
WEBB, Darrallyn, R.N., Chief Nursing Officer, Conway Regional Rehabilitation Hospital, Conway, AR, p. A44
WEBB, David, Chief Financial Officer, Baptist Memorial Hospital–Golden Triangle, Columbus, MS, p. A361
WEBB, Dee, Vice President Human Resources, St. Bernardine Medical Center, San Bernardino, CA, p. A88
WEBB, Jeffrey D, CPA, Chief Financial Officer, Franciscan Health Rensselear, Rensselaer, IN, p. A226
WEBB, Joseph, FACHE, Chief Executive Officer, Nashville General Hospital, Nashville, TN, p. A590
WEBB, Kimberly, Chief Financial Officer, Kootenai Health, Coeur D'Alene, ID, p. A180
WEBB, Kristen, Chief Nursing Officer, Duncan Regional Hospital, Duncan, OK, p. A512
WEBB, Linda, R.N., Chief Nursing Executive, Pulaski Memorial Hospital, Winamac, IN, p. A229
WEBB, Lisa
Vice President for Operational Finance, Chi Health Good Samaritan, Kearney, NE, p. A401
Vice President Operational Finance, Chi Health Saint Francis, Grand Island, NE, p. A400
WEBB, Melanie R
Vice President Human Resources, HCA Houston Healthcare Medical Center, Houston, TX, p. A625
Vice President Human Resources, HCA Houston Healthcare Northwest, Houston, TX, p. A626
WEBB, Paula G., Chief Executive Officer, Lake Butler Hospital, Lake Butler, FL, p. A136
WEBB, Renick, M.D., Chief Medical Director, Central Louisiana Surgical Hospital, Alexandria, LA, p. A276
WEBB, Rhonda
M.D., Chief Executive Officer and Chief Medical Officer, Pagosa Springs Medical Center, Pagosa Springs, CO, p. A112
M.D., Chief Executive Officer, Chief Medical Officer, Pagosa Springs Medical Center, Pagosa Springs, CO, p. A112
WEBB, William, Assistant Superintendent, Eastern Shore Hospital Center, Cambridge, MD, p. A303
WEBBER, Cathy, Director of Health Information Management, Franklin County Memorial Hospital, Franklin, NE, p. A399
WEBBER, Denise, President and Chief Executive Officer, Stillwater Medical Center, Stillwater, OK, p. A521
WEBBER, Joyce, Chief Financial Officer, Spalding Rehabilitation Hospital, Aurora, CO, p. A103
WEBER, Andrew, Vice President and Administrator, Charleston Area Medical Center, Charleston, WV, p. A700
WEBER, Barbara
Chief Operating Officer, Unitypoint Health – Trinity Bettendorf, Bettendorf, IA, p. A231
Chief Operating Officer, Unitypoint Health – Trinity Muscatine, Muscatine, IA, p. A240
Chief Operating Officer, Unitypoint Health – Trinity Rock Island, Rock Island, IL, p. A207
WEBER, Carmen, Administrator, Eureka Community Health Services Avera, Eureka, SD, p. A573
WEBER, Deborah, Chief Human Resource Officer, Northeast Georgia Medical Center, Gainesville, GA, p. A164
WEBER, Frank, Chief Executive Officer, Select Specialty Hospital–Charleston, Charleston, WV, p. A700
WEBER, Gordon, Chief Operating Officer, Clarks Summit State Hospital, Clarks Summit, PA, p. A537
WEBER, Lindsay, President and Chief Executive Officer, Avera St. Benedict Health Center, Parkston, SD, p. A575
WEBER, Mark, M.D., President Medical Staff, Mymichigan Medical Center West Branch, West Branch, MI, p. A340
WEBER, Meagan, Chief Executive Officer, Scotland County Hospital, Memphis, MO, p. A380
WEBER, Natalie, R.N., Nurse Manager, Aurora Medical Center – Manitowoc County, Two Rivers, WI, p. A723

A1002 Index of Health Care Professionals

Index of Health Care Professionals

Index of Health Care Professionals / Wellman

WEBER, Rebecca
Senior Vice President and Chief Information Officer, Hackensack Meridian Health Bayshore Community Hospital, Holmdel, NJ, p. A422
Senior Vice President and Chief Information Officer, Hackensack Meridian Health Jersey Shore University Medical Center, Neptune, NJ, p. A424
Senior Vice President and Chief Information Officer, Hackensack Meridian Health Ocean University Medical Center, Brick Township. NJ, p. A419
Senior Vice President and Chief Information Officer, Hackensack Meridian Health Southern Ocean Medical Center, Manahawkin, NJ, p. A423
Senior Vice President Information Technology, Hackensack Meridian Health Riverview Medical Center, Red Bank, NJ, p. A428
WEBER, Stephen, M.D., Senior Vice President Clinical Effectiveness and Chief Medical Officer, University of Chicago Medical Center, Chicago, IL, p. A192
WEBER, Trish, R.N., FACHE, Vice President and Chief Operating Officer, Franciscan Health Mooresville, Mooresville, IN, p. A224
WEBER, Wilson, Chief Operating Officer, Continuecare Hospital At Baptist Health Corbin, Corbin, KY, p. A264
WEBER–JOHNSON, Holly L., MSN, R.N., Chief Nursing Officer, HCA Florida Citrus Hospital, Inverness, FL, p. A134
WEBSTER, Cynthia, Vice President Financial Services, Licking Memorial Hospital, Newark, OH, p. A501
WEBSTER, Gwen, M.D., President Medical Staff, Texas Health Presbyterian Hospital Plano, Plano, TX, p. A645
WEBSTER, Janice, Director Human Resources, West Oaks Hospital, Houston, TX, p. A629
WEBSTER, Jeffrey, Administrator, Harris Health System, Bellaire, TX, p. A603
WEBSTER, Kathleen, R.N., MSN, Vice President Patient Services, New York–Presbyterian/Hudson Valley Hospital, Cortlandt Manor, NY, p. A442
WEBSTER, Mark, Vice President Finance, New York–Presbyterian/Hudson Valley Hospital, Cortlandt Manor, NY, p. A442
WEBSTER, Nancy, Administrator and Chief Operating Officer, Providence St. Luke's Rehabilitation Medical Center, Spokane, WA, p. A696
WECKESSER, Kim, Director Human Resources, Munson Healthcare Manistee Hospital, Manistee, MI, p. A332
WEDDLE, Chari, Chief Human Resource Management Service, Richard L. Roudebush Veterans Affairs Medical Center, Indianapolis, IN, p. A220
WEDGEWORTH, Joyce, Financial Clerk, Hill Hospital of Sumter County, York, AL, p. A26
WEDGWORTH, Megan, Chief Executive Officer, Vantage Point of Northwest Arkansas, Fayetteville, AR, p. A46
WEED, Warren
Director Associate Relations, Merit Health Woman's Hospital, Flowood, MS, p. A362
Director Human Resources, Merit Health River Oaks, Flowood, MS, p. A362
WEEDEN, Gerard, Chief Medical Officer, Select Specialty Hospital – Richmond, Richmond, VA, p. A682
WEEKS, Doug, FACHE, Executive Vice President and Chief Operations Officer, Baptist Health Medical Center – North Little Rock, North Little Rock, AR, p. A51
WEEKS, Ed, Manager Information Services, Paris Community Hospital, Paris, IL, p. A205
WEEKS, Matthew, Chief Medical Officer, Mcleod Health Loris, Loris, SC, p. A568
WEELDREYER, Jim, Manager Information Technology, Pershing General Hospital, Lovelock, NV, p. A411
WEEMS, Taylor, Vice President, Chief Information Officer, Midland Memorial Hospital, Midland, TX, p. A639
WEG, Jennifer, MS, R.N., Executive Director, Sanford Worthington Medical Center, Worthington, MN, p. A358
WEGLARZ, Ron, PsyD, Chief Executive Officer, Streamwood Behavioral Healthcare System, Streamwood, IL, p. A209
WEHBEH, Wehbeh, M.D., Chief Medical Officer, NYC Health + Hospitals/South Brooklyn Health, New York, NY, p. A452
WEHLING, Ed, Chief Medical Staff, Decatur County Hospital, Leon, IA, p. A239
WEHLING, Robert D, Interim Chief Financial Officer, Saint Alphonsus Medical Center – Baker City, Baker City, OR, p. A525
WEHNER, Jill, President and Chief Executive Officer, Harbor Beach Community Hospital Inc., Harbor Beach, MI, p. A329
WEHRLI, Gay, Chief Medical Officer with University Hospitals/Case Western Reserve University, University Hospitals Cleveland Medical Center, Cleveland, OH, p. A491
WEHRMEISTER, Erica, Chief Operating Officer, Ascension St. Vincent Indianapolis Hospital, Indianapolis, IN, p. A219
WEHRS, Jennifer, Market Chief Operating Officer– Greenville Market, Bon Secours St. Francis Health System, Greenville, SC, p. A566
WEIDER, Will
Chief Information Officer, Ascension Calumet Hospital, Chilton, WI, p. A709
Chief Information Officer, Ascension Northeast Wisconsin Mercy Hospital, Oshkosh, WI, p. A719
Chief Information Officer, Ascension Northeast Wisconsin St. Elizabeth Hospital, Appleton, WI, p. A707
Chief Information Officer, Aspirus Steven's Point Hospital & Clinics, Inc., Stevens Point, WI, p. A722
Chief Information Officer, Marshfield Medical Center, Marshfield, WI, p. A715
WEIDNER, Peter, Director Information Technology, St. John's Riverside Hospital, Yonkers, NY, p. A462
WEIGEL, Cherry, Director Health Information Management, Healthpartners Olivia Hospital & Clinic, Olivia, MN, p. A352
WEIL, Henry, M.D., President, Bassett Medical Center, Cooperstown, NY, p. A441
WEILAND, Brandon James., Chief Executive Officer, Select Specialty Hospital–Milwaukee, Milwaukee, WI, p. A717
WEILAND, David, M.D., Chief Medical Officer, HCA Florida Largo Hospital, Largo, FL, p. A137
WEIMER, Linn, Chief Information Officer, Adena Regional Medical Center, Chillicothe, OH, p. A488
WEINBAUM, Frederic, M.D., Interim Chief Administrative Officer, Chief Medical Officer and Chief Operating Officer, Stony Brook University Hospital, Stony Brook, NY, p. A459
WEINBERGER, April, M.D., Chief Medical Officer, Bitterroot Health – Daly Hospital, Hamilton, MT, p. A392
WEINER, Gary
Chief Information Officer, St. Catherine Hospital, East Chicago, IN, p. A215
Vice President Information Technology and Chief Information Officer, St. Mary Medical Center, Hobart, IN, p. A218
Vice President Information Technology, Chief Information Officer, Community Hospital, Munster, IN, p. A224
WEINER, Jared
Chief Financial Officer, UPMC Magee–Womens Hospital, Pittsburgh, PA, p. A551
Chief Financial Officer, UPMC Mercy, Pittsburgh, PA, p. A552
Chief Financial Officer, UPMC Presbyterian, Pittsburgh, PA, p. A552
WEINER, Jerome, M.D., Senior Vice President Medical Affairs, Good Samaritan Hospital Medical Center, West Islip. NY, p. A461
WEINFIELD, Andrew, Chief Medical Officer, Presbyterian/St. Luke's Medical Center, Denver, CO, p. A106
WEINGARTNER, Ronald, Vice President Administration, St. Charles Hospital, Port Jefferson, NY, p. A456
WEINKRANTZ, Alan, Chief Financial Officer, Finance, Rutgers University Behavioral Healthcare, Piscataway, NJ, p. A427
WEINMANN, Shannon, Director Human Resources, Community Medical Center, Inc., Falls City, NE, p. A399
WEINREIS, Brian, Vice President Operations and Finance, Abbott Northwestern Hospital, Minneapolis, MN, p. A350
WEINSTEIN, Barry S, Chief Financial Officer, Four Winds Hospital, Katonah, NY, p. A444
WEINSTEIN, Brian, M.D., Chief of Staff, HCA Florida Westside Hospital, Plantation, FL, p. A147
WEINSTEIN, Freddie, M.D., Chief Medical Officer, Dominican Hospital, Santa Cruz, CA, p. A94
WEINTRAUB, Breton, Medical Center Director, Fargo Va Medical Center, Fargo, ND, p. A480
WEIR, Elizabeth, MSN, R.N., Site Administrator and Vice President of Nursing, Ira Davenport Memorial Hospital, Bath, NY, p. A439
WEIR, Tim W., FACHE, Chief Executive Officer, Olmsted Medical Center, Rochester, MN, p. A354
WEIS, Brian, M.D., Chief Medical Officer, Northwest Texas Healthcare System, Amarillo, TX, p. A596
WEIS, Charles
Chief Financial Officer, Mount Sinai Hospital, Chicago, IL, p. A190
Chief Financial Officer, Schwab Rehabilitation Hospital, Chicago, IL, p. A191
Executive Vice President and Chief Financial Officer, Holy Cross Hospital, Chicago, IL, p. A189
WEIS, David
President and Chief Executive Officer, Adventhealth Daytona Beach, Daytona Beach, FL, p. A129
President and Chief Executive Officer, Adventhealth New Smyrna Beach, New Smyrna Beach, FL, p. A142
WEIS, Maurine, Vice President Patient Care Services and Chief Nursing Officer, Promedica Monroe Regional Hospital, Monroe, MI, p. A333
WEIS, Robert
Director Information Systems, Bingham Memorial Hospital, Blackfoot, ID, p. A179
Director Information Technology, Grove Creek Medical Center, Blackfoot, ID, p. A179
WEIS, Wade, Chief Executive Officer, Buchanan County Health Center, Independence, IA, p. A238
WEISENFREUND, Jochanan, M.D., Senior Vice President Academic and Medical Affairs, Interfaith Medical Center, New York, NY, p. A448
WEISKITTEL, Scott, Chief Operating Officer, Trident Medical Center, Charleston, SC, p. A563
WEISS, Anthony, M.D., Chief Medical Officer, Beth Israel Deaconess Medical Center, Boston, MA, p. A309
WEISS, David, M.D., Vice President, Medical Operations, Peninsula Region, St. Michael Medical Center, Silverdale, WA, p. A695
WEISS, Patrice M., M.D., Chief Medical Officer, Carilion Franklin Memorial Hospital, Rocky Mount, VA, p. A683
WEISS, Phyllis, Vice President, Human Resources, UCSF Benioff Children's Hospital Oakland, Oakland, CA, p. A81
WEISS, Terri, Chief Financial Officer, Encompass Health Rehabilitation Hospital Vision Park, Shenandoah, TX, p. A652
WEISSENBACH, Robert, Chief Information Officer, Bitterroot Health – Daly Hospital, Hamilton, MT, p. A392
WEISSENBERGER, Ralf, Director Information Systems, Adventist Health White Memorial, Los Angeles, CA, p. A71
WEISSER, Lisa, Controller, Wagner Community Memorial Hospital Avera, Wagner, SD, p. A578
WEISUL, Jonathan, M.D., Vice President Medical Affairs and Chief Medical Officer, Christus Coushatta Health Care Center, Coushatta, LA, p. A280
WEITZEL, Cassie, Director, Human Resources, Nicholas H. Noyes Memorial Hospital, Dansville, NY, p. A442
WELANDER, Jennifer
CPA, Senior Vice President Finance and Chief Financial Officer, St. Charles Bend, Bend, OR, p. A525
CPA, Senior Vice President Finance and Chief Financial Officer, St. Charles Redmond, Redmond, OR, p. A531
WELANDER, Michelle, FACHE, R.N., Chief Nursing Officer, Och Regional Medical Center, Starkville, MS, p. A369
WELCH, Abbey, Director Human Resources, Harmon Memorial Hospital, Hollis, OK, p. A513
WELCH, Bryant, Chief Human Resources, Washington Hospital Healthcare System, Fremont, CA, p. A64
WELCH, David, M.D., Medical Director, Clifton–Fine Hospital, Star Lake, NY, p. A459
WELCH, Denise, Chief Financial Officer, Arbuckle Memorial Hospital, Sulphur, OK, p. A521
WELCH, Donald E, Chief Operating Officer, Adventhealth Zephyrhills, Zephyrhills, FL, p. A155
WELCH, Nicole, Chief Human Resources Officer, Fairbanks Memorial Hospital, Fairbanks, AK, p. A28
WELCH, Robert, Chief Financial Officer, Reeves Memorial Medical Center, Bernice, LA, p. A278
WELCH, Rosemary C, R.N., Vice President and Chief Nursing Officer, Medstar National Rehabilitation Hospital, Washington, DC, p. A123
WELCH, Thomas, M.D., Chief Medical Officer, Mercy Health – St. Vincent Medical Center, Toledo, OH, p. A504
WELCH, Tony
Senior Vice President and Chief Human Resources Officer, Phoebe Putney Memorial Hospital, Albany, GA, p. A156
Vice President Human Resources, Southeast Alabama Medical Center, Dothan, AL, p. A18
WELCH, William L., FACHE, Interim Chief Executive Officer, Jefferson Community Health And Life, Fairbury, NE, p. A399
WELCOME, Andrew, Chief Operating Officer, Lewisgale Medical Center, Boones Mill, VA, p. A674
WELDAY, Doug, Chief Financial Officer, Endeavor Health Evanston Hospital, Evanston, IL, p. A195
WELDON, James, Chief Information Officer, North Mississipp. Medical Center – Tupelo, Tupelo, MS, p. A369
WELDON, Jennifer, Chief Financial Officer, Multicare Capital Medical Center, Olympia, WA, p. A692
WELDY, Alan, Vice President Human Resources, Compliance and Legal Services, Goshen Health, Goshen, IN, p. A217
WELKIE, Katy MBA, R.N., Chief Executive Officer, Primary Children's Hospital, Salt Lake City, UT, p. A669
WELLBROCK, Jenna, Chief Nursing Officer, Gateway Rehabilitation Hospital, Florence, KY, p. A265
WELLER, Samuel, Chief Executive Officer, Renown South Meadows Medical Center, Reno, NV, p. A412
WELLING, Lynn, M.D., Chief Medical Officer, Sharp Chula Vista Medical Center, Chula Vista, CA, p. A59
WELLING, Michele, M.D., Chief of Staff, Bluegrass Community Hospital, Versailles, KY, p. A274
WELLMAN, Amanda, MSN, R.N., Chief Nursing Officer, Select Specialty Hospital–Omaha, Omaha, NE, p. A404
WELLMAN, James, Senior Director Information Services, Comanche County Memorial Hospital, Lawton, OK, p. A514

Index of Health Care Professionals / Wellman

WELLMAN, Sonia I., Chief Executive Officer, HCA Florida West Tamp. Hospital, Tampa, FL, p. A152
WELLMANN, Jane, Chief Financial Officer, Baylor Scott & White Medical Center – Brenham, Brenham, TX, p. A604
WELLS, A Shane, Chief Financial Officer, Vibra Hospital of Clear Lake, Webster, TX, p. A661
WELLS, Carol, R.N., MSN, Chief Nursing Officer, Central Louisiana Surgical Hospital, Alexandria, LA, p. A276
WELLS, Craig, Chief Information Officer, George C. Grap. Community Hospital, Hamburg, IA, p. A237
WELLS, Crystal, Administrator, Archbold Grady, Cairo, GA, p. A159
WELLS, Dale W., Chief Financial and Operating Officer, Aultman Alliance Community Hospital, Alliance, OH, p. A484
WELLS, James, R.N., Chief Nursing Officer, Kingman Regional Medical Center, Kingman, AZ, p. A32
WELLS, Jason
   FACHE, President, Adventist Health Reedley, Reedley, CA, p. A85
   FACHE, President, Central California Network, Adventist Health, Adventist Health – Tulare, Tulare, CA, p. A98
   FACHE, President, Central California Network, Adventist Health, Adventist Health Bakersfield, Bakersfield, CA, p. A56
   FACHE, President, Central California Network, Adventist Health, Adventist Health Delano, Delano, CA, p. A61
   FACHE, President, Central California Network, Adventist Health, Adventist Health Hanford, Hanford, CA, p. A66
   FACHE, President, Central California Network, Adventist Health, Adventist Health Tehachap. Valley, Tehachapi, CA, p. A97
   Chief Human Resources Management Service, Fargo Va Medical Center, Fargo, ND, p. A480
WELLS, Jonathan, Supervisor Information Technology, Kansas Surgery And Recovery Center, Wichita, KS, p. A262
WELLS, Mary Ellen, FACHE, Chief Executive Officer, Meeker Memorial Hospital And Clinics, Litchfield, MN, p. A348
WELLS, Michael, President, OSF Saint Francis Medical Center, Peoria, IL, p. A206
WELLS, Pamela, R.N., MSN, Chief Nursing Officer, Sharp Memorial Hospital, San Diego, CA, p. A89
WELLS, Robert, M.D., Chief Medical Officer, Providence Portland Medical Center, Portland, OR, p. A530
WELLS, Scott E., MSN, R.N., Vice President Patient Care Services, Caromont Regional Medical Center, Gastonia, NC, p. A469
WELLS, Valerie, Manager Human Resources, Encompass Health Rehabilitation Hospital of The Woodlands, Conroe, TX, p. A608
WELSER, Jeremy, Director Information Systems, Bonner General Health, Sandpoint, ID, p. A184
WELSH, Jamie, Interim Chief Human Resources Officer, Providence Santa Rosa Memorial Hospital, Santa Rosa, CA, p. A95
WELSH, Joyce, R.N., MS, Vice President of Clinical Services and Chief Nursing Officer, Emerson Hospital, Concord, MA, p. A313
WELSON, Grant
   Chief Executive Officer, CareOne Hospital Division, Careone At Hackensack University Medical Center At Pascack Valley, Westwood, NJ, p. A430
   Chief Executive Officer, CareOne Hospital Division, Careone At Trinitas Regional Medical Center, Elizabeth, NJ, p. A420
WELTON, Brian, Chief Executive Officer and Administrator, Baptist Memorial Hospital–North Mississippi, Oxford, MS, p. A367
WELTON, Mark, M.D., Chief Medical Officer, M Health Fairview St. John's Hospital, Maplewood, MN, p. A349
WEMPE, John M, M.D., Chief of Staff, Royal C. Johnson Veterans' Memorial Hospital, Sioux Falls, SD, p. A576
WENDELL, David, Manager, Information Systems, St. Mary's Medical Center, Huntington, WV, p. A701
WENDELL, Sean
   CPA, Chief Executive Officer, Beacon Behavioral Hospital – New Orleans, New Orleans, LA, p. A290
   CPA, Chief Executive Officer, Beacon Behavioral Hospital – Northshore, Lacombe, LA, p. A285
   CPA, Chief Executive Officer, Beacon Behavioral Hospital, Bunkie, LA, p. A279
   CPA, Chief Executive Officer, Beacon Behavioral Hospital, Lutcher, LA, p. A287
WENDLER, Jake, Chief Information Officer, Dallas County Hospital, Perry, IA, p. A242
WENDT, Kelly, Director, Patient Care, Ridgeview Le Sueur Medical Center, Le Sueur, MN, p. A348
WENGER, Jill, Chief Human Resources Officer, Amberwell Health, Atchison, KS, p. A246
WENTWORTH, Cynthia, Chief Human Resource Officer, East Morgan County Hospital, Brush, CO, p. A104

WENTZ, James, Chief Financial Officer, East Jefferson General Hospital, Metairie, LA, p. A288
WENTZ, Jim, Chief Financial Officer, Chi Saint Josep. Health – Flaget Memorial Hospital, Bardstown, KY, p. A263
WENTZ, Robert J., President and Chief Executive Officer, Oroville Hospital, Oroville, CA, p. A82
WENTZEL, Chris, M.D., Interim Medical Director, Guthrie Corning Hospital, Corning, NY, p. A441
WERFT, Ronald C.
   President and Chief Executive Officer, Goleta Valley Cottage Hospital, Santa Barbara, CA, p. A94
   President and Chief Executive Officer, Santa Barbara Cottage Hospital, Santa Barbara, CA, p. A94
   President and Chief Executive Officer, Santa Ynez Valley Cottage Hospital, Solvang, CA, p. A96
WERKIN, Dave, Vice President Finance and Chief Financial Officer, Trinity Health System, Steubenville, OH, p. A504
WERNER, John, Chief Executive Officer, Pawnee County Memorial Hospital And Rural Health Clinic, Pawnee City, NE, p. A405
WERNER, Katie, Chief Financial Officer, Pembina County Memorial Hospital And Wedgewood Manor, Cavalier, ND, p. A480
WERNER, Kurt, M.D., Chief of Staff, Fort Harrison Va Medical Center, Fort Harrison, MT, p. A392
WERNER, Ted, Chief Executive Officer, Pam Rehabilitation Hospital of Dover, Dover, DE, p. A121
WERNER, Tiffany
   Senior Human Resource Business Partner, Banner Baywood Medical Center, Mesa, AZ, p. A33
   Senior Human Resource Business Partner, Banner Heart Hospital, Mesa, AZ, p. A33
WERNKE, Chris, Chief Operating Officer, Dominican Hospital, Santa Cruz, CA, p. A94
WERTH–SWEENEY, Stacey, Facility Operating Officer, Lincoln Regional Center, Lincoln, NE, p. A402
WERTHMAN, Ronald J, Senior Vice President Finance, Chief Financial Officer and Treasurer, Johns Hopkins Hospital, Baltimore, MD, p. A300
WERTZ, Jackie, Director Human Resources, George C. Grap. Community Hospital, Hamburg, IA, p. A237
WESCOATT, Sampson, Manager Information Technology, Molokai General Hospital, Kaunakakai, HI, p. A177
WESENER DIECK, Jill, Human Resources Operations Manager, Gundersen Tri–County Hospital And Clinics, Whitehall, WI, p. A725
WESLEY, Jim, Senior Vice President and Chief Information Officer, John Muir Behavioral Health Center, Concord, CA, p. A60
WESLEY, Mary Lou, R.N., Senior Vice President and Chief Nursing Officer, University of Michigan Health–Sparrow Lansing, Lansing, MI, p. A332
WESNER, Jeffrey, Chief Operating Officer, Sarasota Memorial Hospital – Venice, North Venice, FL, p. A142
WESP, Clyde, M.D., Chief Medical Officer, Valley Presbyterian Hospital, Los Angeles, CA, p. A75
WESSEL, Jason, Chief Executive Officer, Encompass Health Rehabilitation Hospital At Cincinnati, Cincinnati, OH, p. A489
WESSELS, Jana, Associate Vice President Human Resources, University of Iowa Hospitals & Clinics, Iowa City, IA, p. A238
WEST, Andrea, MS, Vice President of Human Resources, Columbus Regional Healthcare System, Whiteville, NC, p. A477
WEST, Brenda
   R.N., MSN, Chief Nursing Officer, Evergreenhealth Monroe, Monroe, WA, p. A691
   Vice President, Information Services and Interim Chief Information Officer, Einstein Medical Center Philadelphia, Philadelphia, PA, p. A548
WEST, Bridgette, Director Patient Access Services, Cobleskill Regional Hospital, Cobleskill, NY, p. A441
WEST, Charles, M.D., Chief Medical Officer, Randolp. Health, Asheboro, NC, p. A463
WEST, Cindy, Chief Executive Officer, Drumright Regional Hospital, Drumright, OK, p. A511
WEST, Darren, M.D., Interim Chief Medical Officer, Banner Ironwood Medical Center, San Tan Valley, AZ, p. A38
WEST, James R.
   President and Chief Executive Officer, PIH Health Downey Hospital, Downey, CA, p. A61
   President and Chief Executive Officer, PIH Health Good Samaritan Hospital, Los Angeles, CA, p. A74
   President/Chief Executive Officer, PIH Health Whittier Hospital, Whittier, CA, p. A101
WEST, Jennifer, R.N., Chief Nursing Officer, South Texas Spine And Surgical Hospital, San Antonio, TX, p. A651
WEST, Kenneth, Chief Executive Officer, HCA Florida Jfk Hospital, Atlantis, FL, p. A125

WEST, Melissa, Chief Financial Officer, Cedar Crest Hospital And Residential Treatment Center, Belton, TX, p. A603
WEST, Michael C, M.D., Chief of Staff, Mccurtain Memorial Hospital, Idabel, OK, p. A514
WEST, Steve, M.D., Chief Medical Officer, HCA Florida Capital Hospital, Tallahassee, FL, p. A151
WEST, Tamara, R.N., MSN, Vice President Patient Care, Nicholas H. Noyes Memorial Hospital, Dansville, NY, p. A442
WESTCOTT, Melissa
   CPA, Chief Financial Oficer, Manhattan Surgical, Manhattan, KS, p. A254
   CPA, Interim Chief Executive Officer and Chief Financial Officer, Manhattan Surgical, Manhattan, KS, p. A254
WESTENFELDER, Grant, M.D., Chief Medical Officer, Midwest Medical Center, Galena, IL, p. A195
WESTERFIELD, Jerry D., M.D., Chief of Medical Staff, Russell County Hospital, Russell Springs, KY, p. A274
WESTERHEIDE, Karen, Chief Financial Officer, VA St. Louis Health Care System, Saint Louis, MO, p. A384
WESTFALL, Gay, Senior Vice President Human Resources, Kaiser Permanente Sacramento Medical Center, Sacramento, CA, p. A86
WESTIN, Robert, M.D., Chief Medical Officer, Cuyuna Regional Medical Center, Crosby, MN, p. A345
WESTLAKE, H. Curtis, Controller, Mercy Rehabilitation Hospital Fort Smith, Fort Smith, AR, p. A47
WESTMAN, Ken, Chief Executive Officer, Riverwood Healthcare Center, Aitkin, MN, p. A342
WESTMORELAND, David, Divisional Chief Financial Officer, Eagle View Behavioral Health, Bettendorf, IA, p. A230
WESTMORELAND, Penny, Chief Financial Officer, Red Bay Hospital, Red Bay, AL, p. A24
WESTON, Betty, Chief Human Resources Officer, U. S. Public Health Service Phoenix Indian Medical Center, Phoenix, AZ, p. A37
WESTON, Lori, President, Park City Hospital, Park City, UT, p. A667
WESTON, Terry, M.D., Vice President Physician Services, Ohiohealth Mansfield Hospital, Mansfield, OH, p. A499
WESTON GRAVES, Dana, Division President, Sentara Princess Anne Hospital, Virginia Beach, VA, p. A684
WESTON–HALL, Patricia, Chief Executive Officer, Glenbeigh Hospital And Outpatient Centers, Rock Creek, OH, p. A503
WESTOVER, Teresa, Director Human Resources, North Texas Medical Center, Gainesville, TX, p. A621
WESTPHAL, Chris, Chief Information Technology Officer, Southeast Colorado Hospital District, Springfield, CO, p. A113
WESTPHAL, James, M.D., AMHD Medical Director, Hawaii State Hospital, Kaneohe, HI, p. A177
WESTPHAL, Laura R., R.N., Vice President Patient Care Services, Adventist Health Castle, Kailua, HI, p. A176
WESTPHAL, Susan, Assistant Administrator, Patient Care Services, Fairchild Medical Center, Yreka, CA, p. A102
WESTRY, Tanza, Chief Financial Officer, Hunter Holmes Mcguire Veterans Affairs Medical Center–Richmond, Richmond, VA, p. A683
WESTWOOD, Denise P, Chief Nursing Officer, Weirton Medical Center, Weirton, WV, p. A705
WETHAL, Robert, R.N., Vice President Patient Care Services and Chief Nursing Officer, Mercyone Dubuque Medical Center, Dubuque, IA, p. A235
WETMORE, Melanie, MSN, R.N., Chief Nursing Officer, HCA Florida Bayonet Point Hospital, Hudson, FL, p. A134
WETSEL, Genia, Chief Nursing Officer, Reunion Rehabilitation Hospital Arlington, Arlington, TX, p. A598
WETTLAUFER, Debbie, Chief Financial Officer, French Hospital Medical Center, San Luis Obispo, CA, p. A93
WETTON, Darlene, R.N., Group Vice President and Chief Executive Officer, Temecula Valley Hospital, Temecula, CA, p. A97
WETZ, Staci, Chief Financial Officer, Shannon Medical Center, San Angelo, TX, p. A648
WETZEL, Brian A., President, Orlando Health St. Cloud Hospital, Saint Cloud, FL, p. A148
WETZEL, Lou, M.D., Chief of Staff, The University of Kansas Hospital, Kansas City, KS, p. A252
WETZEL, Pam, M.D., Market Chief Medical Officer, Unitypoint Health Meriter, Madison, WI, p. A714
WEWEL, Beth, Chief Financial Officer, Twelve Clans Unity Hospital, Winnebago, NE, p. A407
WEYMOUTH, Deborah K.
   FACHE, Chief Executive Officer, Rockville General Hospital, Vernon, CT, p. A119
   FACHE, President and Chief Executive Officer, Manchester Memorial Hospital, Manchester, CT, p. A116
   FACHE, President and Chief Executive Officer, Waterbury Hospital, Waterbury, CT, p. A119

Index of Health Care Professionals
Index of Health Care Professionals / Whited

WEYMOUTH, Linda, Chief Financial Officer, River Oaks Hospital, New Orleans, LA, p. A290
WHALEN, Megan Joy, Vice President, Human Resources, HCA Florida Pasadena Hospital, Saint Petersburg, FL, p. A149
WHALEN, Patti, Manager Human Resources, Wichita County Health Center, Leoti, KS, p. A253
WHALEN, Thomas, Vice President Finance, Good Samaritan Medical Center, Brockton, MA, p. A311
WHALEN, Thomas V., M.D., Chief Medical Officer, Lehigh Valley Hospital–Cedar Crest, Allentown, PA, p. A534
WHALEY, Joseph, Chief, Human Resources Management Service, Fayetteville Veterans Affairs Medical Center, Fayetteville, NC, p. A468
WHALEY, Mary, Director of Acute Care, Johnson County Healthcare Center, Buffalo, WY, p. A726
WHALEY, Matthew A., Chief Executive Officer, Community Hospital of Huntington Park, Huntington Park, CA, p. A67
WHALIN, Laurie, PharmD, Chief Operating Officer, Novant Health New Hanover Regional Medical Center, Wilmington, NC, p. A478
WHARTON, Joe H, M.D., Chief of Staff, Bradley County Medical Center, Warren, AR, p. A54
WHEAT, Ken, Senior Vice President and Chief Financial Officer, Eisenhower Health, Rancho Mirage, CA, p. A84
WHEAT, Terry, R.N., M.P.H., Director of Patient Care Services, Shriners Hospitals for Children–Chicago, Chicago, IL, p. A191
WHEATLEY, Cathleen, President, Atrium Health Wake Forest Baptist Davie Medical Center, Bermuda Run, NC, p. A463
WHEATLEY, Richard, Chief Information Officer, Cooper University Hospital Cap. Regional, Cap. May Court House, NJ, p. A419
WHEATLEY, Samuel N, Chief Medical Officer, Columbus Regional Healthcare System, Whiteville, NC, p. A477
WHEATLEY, Sonya, Human Resources Manager, Central State Hospital, Louisville, KY, p. A269
WHEATON, David, Director Human Resources, Northern Light Blue Hill Hospital, Blue Hill, ME, p. A296
WHEATON, Tammy H., Interim Chief Nursing Officer, Deaconess Illinois Union County, Anna, IL, p. A185
WHEELAN, Kevin, M.D., Medical Director, Baylor Scott & White Heart & Vascular Hospital–Dallas, Dallas, TX, p. A610
WHEELER, Brent, Vice President of Operations, Mclaren Flint, Flint, MI, p. A327
WHEELER, Cambria, Communications and Marketing, Adventist Health Clear Lake, Clearlake, CA, p. A59
WHEELER, Dane, Chief Financial Officer, Adams Memorial Hospital, Decatur, IN, p. A215
WHEELER, James A, Vice President Human Relations and Community Development, Androscoggin Valley Hospital, Berlin, NH, p. A414
WHEELER, Lynette, MSN, Chief Operating Officer, University Health–Lakewood Medical Center, Kansas City, MO, p. A378
WHEELER, Newman, Chief Executive Officer, Covenant Hospital–Levelland, Levelland, TX, p. A634
WHEELER, Philip
Chief Financial Officer, Atrium Health Floyd Cherokee Medical Center, Centre, AL, p. A17
Chief Financial Officer, Atrium Health Floyd Medical Center, Rome, GA, p. A170
Chief Financial Officer, Atrium Health Floyd Polk Medical Center, Cedartown, GA, p. A160
WHEELER, Robert
Controller, Encompass Health Rehabilitation Hospital of Florence, Florence, SC, p. A566
Vice President Human Resources, South Shore Hospital, South Weymouth, MA, p. A318
WHEELER, William, M.D., Chief of Staff, Benewah Community Hospital, Saint Maries, ID, p. A183
WHEELER, Zachariah P, Senior Vice President Human Resources, John D. Archbold Memorial Hospital, Thomasville, GA, p. A172
WHEELER–MOORE, Juanita, Director Financial Services, Four Winds Hospital, Saratoga Springs, NY, p. A458
WHEELES, Locke, Information Technology Manager, Field Memorial Community Hospital, Centreville, MS, p. A360
WHEELUS, Matthew
Chief Operating Officer, Spring Valley Hospital Medical Center, Las Vegas, NV, p. A411
Vice President, Chief Operating Officer, St. Michael Medical Center, Silverdale, WA, p. A695
WHELAN, Chad, President, Miami Valley Hospital, Dayton, OH, p. A494
WHELAN, Laurie A, Senior Vice President Finance and Chief Financial Officer, Hospital for Special Care, New Britain, CT, p. A117
WHELAN, Lynn, Chief Nursing Officer, Encompass Health Rehabilitation Hospital of Cumming, Cumming, GA, p. A162
WHERRY, Robin, Risk Manager and Director Quality Assurance and Health Information Management, Encompass Health Rehabilitation Hospital of Morgantown, Morgantown, WV, p. A703
WHICHARD, Nick, Chief Information Officer, St. Luke's Hospital, Columbus, NC, p. A466
WHIDDON, Amanda, Chief Operating Officer, Union General Hospital, Farmerville, LA, p. A281
WHIDDON, William, Chief Financial Officer, Woodland Heights Medical Center, Lufkin, TX, p. A637
WHILDEN, Sean, Chief Financial Officer, Houston Medical Center, Warner Robins, GA, p. A173
WHILLOCK, Mary C, R.N., MS, Associate Nursing Officer and Chief Operating Officer, Adventhealth Carrollwood, Tampa, FL, p. A151
WHINNETT, Thomas, Chief Executive Officer, Newport News Behavioral Health Center, Newport News, VA, p. A680
WHIPKEY, Jared, Chief Financial Officer, Santa Rosa Medical Center, Milton, FL, p. A141
WHIPPLE, C Cynthia, Director of Nursing, UPMC Muncy, Muncy, PA, p. A546
WHIPPLE, Jennifer, Director Nursing, Lane County Hospital, Dighton, KS, p. A248
WHITACRE, James, Chief Executive Officer, Pam Health Specialty Hospital of Jacksonville, Jacksonville, FL, p. A135
WHITAKER, Catherine, MSN, R.N., Vice President and Chief Nursing Officer, University of Maryland Baltimore Washington Medical Center, Glen Burnie, MD, p. A304
WHITAKER, Charles, Director Information Technology, Madison Parish Hospital, Tallulah, LA, p. A293
WHITAKER, Chasity, Administrative Assistant, Madison Parish Hospital, Tallulah, LA, p. A293
WHITAKER, Doris, Vice President and Manager, Mercy Hospital Booneville, Booneville, AR, p. A44
WHITAKER, Jimmy, Director Information Systems, Central Carolina Hospital, Sanford, NC, p. A476
WHITAKER, Kelley, Chief Executive Officer, Central Desert Behavioral Health Hospital, Albuquerque, NM, p. A432
WHITAKER, Robert, Chief Executive Officer, Gila Regional Medical Center, Silver City, NM, p. A437
WHITAKER, Stacy, M.D., Medical Staff President, Grande Ronde Hospital, La Grande, OR, p. A528
WHITAKER, Stephanie C, Chief Nursing Officer, Baptist Health–Fort Smith, Fort Smith, AR, p. A46
WHITE, Alysia, Vice President, Human Resources, Legent North Houston Surgical Hospital, Tomball, TX, p. A658
WHITE, Andrea, Chief Executive Officer, Kindred Hospital–Chattanooga, Chattanooga, TN, p. A580
WHITE, Bonnie, Chief Financial Officer, University of New Mexico Hospitals, Albuquerque, NM, p. A433
WHITE, Brian
Director Strategic Operations, ECU Health Chowan Hospital, Edenton, NC, p. A467
Director Strategic Planning, ECU Health Bertie Hospital, Windsor, NC, p. A478
WHITE, Bruce D., President and Chief Executive Officer, Knox Community Hospital, Mount Vernon, OH, p. A501
WHITE, Catherine, Chief Financial Officer, Harney District Hospital, Burns, OR, p. A526
WHITE, Christina, Financial Manager, Avoyelles Hospital, Marksville, LA, p. A288
WHITE, Cindy, CPA, Vice President of Operations, Integris Canadian Valley Hospital, Yukon, OK, p. A524
WHITE, Darryl, M.D., Chief of Staff, Freestone Medical Center, Fairfield, TX, p. A618
WHITE, Deborah, Human Resource Coordinator, Faith Community Hospital, Jacksboro, TX, p. A630
WHITE, Denise
MSN, Chief Nurse Executive, Atrium Health Anson, Wadesboro, NC, p. A477
MSN, Chief Nurse Executive and Vice President Facility Executive, Atrium Health Union, Monroe, NC, p. A472
MSN, Vice President, Facility Executive, Atrium Health Union, Monroe, NC, p. A472
WHITE, Diane, Chief Clinical Officer and Chief Nursing Officer, Bridgepoint Continuing Care Hospital – National Harborside, Washington, DC, p. A123
WHITE, Gary B, M.D., Chief Medical Staff, Uintah Basin Medical Center, Roosevelt, UT, p. A668
WHITE, Harold, Vice Chancellor, Ochsner Lsu Health Shreveport – Academic Medical Center, Shreveport, LA, p. A292
WHITE, J B, Director Information Systems, Merit Health River Region, Vicksburg, MS, p. A369
WHITE, Jaime, Chief Executive Officer, Havenwyck Hospital, Inc., Auburn Hills, MI, p. A322
WHITE, Jason, M.D., Chief Medical Officer, Mclaren Bay Region, Bay City, MI, p. A322
WHITE, Jean, Vice President Finance, Avera Heart Hospital of South Dakota, Sioux Falls, SD, p. A576
WHITE, Jim, Chief Information Officer, Lompoc Valley Medical Center, Lompoc, CA, p. A70
WHITE, Joanne, Chief Information Officer, Wood County Hospital, Bowling Green, OH, p. A487
WHITE, Joe, Chief Operating Officer, Tristar Southern Hills Medical Center, Nashville, TN, p. A591
WHITE, Joel, Chief Operating Officer, Select Specialty Hospital–Omaha, Omaha, NE, p. A404
WHITE, Josh, Chief Medical Officer, Deckerville Community Hospital, Deckerville, MI, p. A324
WHITE, Karen
Chief Nursing Officer, Central Montana Medical Center, Lewistown, MT, p. A393
Interim Vice President of Human Resources, Navos, Seattle, WA, p. A694
WHITE, Kelli, Director, Human Resources, Centerpointe Hospital, Saint Charles, MO, p. A383
WHITE, Kendall, Chief Information Officer, Mount Auburn Hospital, Cambridge, MA, p. A312
WHITE, Ketrese, R.N., Senior Vice President, Texas Children's Hospital, Houston, TX, p. A628
WHITE, Kishah, Director Human Resources, Bon Secours St. Mary's Hospital, Richmond, VA, p. A682
WHITE, Knicole S, Vice–President, Human Resources, HCA Florida Kendall Hospital, Miami, FL, p. A139
WHITE, Linda E., Chief Administrative Officer, Deaconess Henderson Hospital, Henderson, KY, p. A267
WHITE, Melinda, R.N., Chief Executive Officer, Navajo Health Foundation – Sage Memorial Hospital, Ganado, AZ, p. A31
WHITE, Michael, M.D., Executive Vice President and Chief Clinical Officer, Valleywise Health, Phoenix, AZ, p. A37
WHITE, Mike, Chief Financial Officer, Hansen Family Hospital, Iowa Falls, IA, p. A238
WHITE, Nate, Executive Vice President, Sanford Medical Center Fargo, Fargo, ND, p. A481
WHITE, Nathan, Chief Information Officer, Charles A. Cannon Jr. Memorial Hospital, Newland, NC, p. A473
WHITE, Pamela, Chief Nursing Officer, North Mississipp. Medical Center–West Point, West Point, MS, p. A370
WHITE, Pamela K., R.N., MSN, Chief Nursing Officer, Mayo Clinic Health System In Eau Claire, Eau Claire, WI, p. A710
WHITE, Patricia, Vice President Human Resources, AHMC Seton Medical Center, Daly City, CA, p. A61
WHITE, Patty, R.N., Director Patient Care Services, Lecom Health Corry Memorial Hospital, Corry, PA, p. A537
WHITE, Randall, Administrator, Shriners Children's Ohio, Dayton, OH, p. A494
WHITE, Randy, Chief Nursing Officer, Baptist Memorial Hospital–Desoto, Southaven, MS, p. A369
WHITE, Sabrina, Coordinator Human Resources, Select Specialty Hospital–Charleston, Charleston, WV, p. A700
WHITE, Sam R, Chief Nursing Officer, Gateway Regional Medical Center, Granite City, IL, p. A196
WHITE, Shawna, Chief Information Officer, Magee Rehabilitation, Philadelphia, PA, p. A549
WHITE, Shelia, Director Human Resources, Bon Secours Richmond Community Hospital, Richmond, VA, p. A682
WHITE, Shirley, Director Human Resources, Ashley County Medical Center, Crossett, AR, p. A45
WHITE, Tamara, R.N., Director of Nursing, Bliant Specialty Hospital, New Orleans, LA, p. A290
WHITE, Toya
JD, MSN, Chief Nursing Officer, Texas Health Presbyterian Hospital Kaufman, Kaufman, TX, p. A631
JD, MSN, Chief Operating Officer & Chief Nursing Officer, Texas Health Presbyterian Hospital Kaufman, Kaufman, TX, p. A631
JD, MSN, Chief Operating Officer, Texas Health Presbyterian Hospital Kaufman, Kaufman, TX, p. A631
WHITE, Vicki
R.N., MS, Chief Nurse Executive, Mills–Peninsula Medical Center, Burlingame, CA, p. A58
Chief Nursing Officer, Providence Santa Rosa Memorial Hospital, Santa Rosa, CA, p. A95
WHITE, Vivian, Chief Executive Officer, UVA Encompass Health Rehabilitation Hospital, Charlottesville, VA, p. A674
WHITE, Wesley D, Chief Financial Officer, Teton Valley Health Care, Driggs, ID, p. A181
WHITE FOATE, Raven, Chief Nursing Officer, Encompass Health Rehabilitation Hospital, Shreveport, LA, p. A292
WHITE HOUSE, Judy, FACHE, Vice President Human Resources, Intermountain Health St. Mary's Regional Hospital, Grand Junction, CO, p. A109
WHITE–TREVINO, Karen, Chief Nursing Officer, HCA Florida West Hospital, Pensacola, FL, p. A146
WHITED, Brian
M.D., Physician Executive, Mayo Clinic Health System In Lake City, Lake City, MN, p. A348

Index of Health Care Professionals A1005

Index of Health Care Professionals / Whited

M.D., Physician Executive, Mayo Clinic Health System In Red Wing, Red Wing, MN, p. A353

WHITED, Steve, Chief Executive Officer, Minnie Hamilton Healthcare Center, Grantsville, WV, p. A701

WHITEHAIR, Robbie, Chief Executive Officer, Tsehootsooi Medical Center, Fort Defiance, AZ, p. A31

WHITEHEAD, Noemi, Administrative Director Human Resources, Sutter Delta Medical Center, Antioch, CA, p. A55

WHITEHOUSE, Alan, Chief Information Officer, Wellstar West Georgia Medical Center, Lagrange, GA, p. A166

WHITEHURST, Rob, Chief, Office of Information and Technology, Veterans Affairs Ann Arbor Healthcare System, Ann Arbor, MI, p. A321

WHITELOCK, Kim, Chief Executive Officer, The Horsham Clinic, Ambler, PA, p. A534

WHITEN, Myra C, Chief Nursing Officer, Pelham Medical Center, Greer, SC, p. A567

WHITESIDE, Anne, Vice President Nursing, Valley Health – Winchester Medical Center, Winchester, VA, p. A685

WHITESIDE, John, Chief Executive Officer, Sagewest Health Care, Riverton, WY, p. A728

WHITESIDE, Patrick, Manager Information Services, Corewell Health Big Rapids Hospital, Big Rapids, MI, p. A322

WHITFIELD, Brian, Chief Executive Officer, Mccurtain Memorial Hospital, Idabel, OK, p. A514

WHITFIELD, Bruce, CPA, Chief Executive Officer, Livingston Healthcare, Livingston, MT, p. A394

WHITFIELD, Howard, Chief Operating Officer, UNC Health Wayne, Goldsboro, NC, p. A469

WHITFIELD, Jay, Chief Financial Officer, Baylor University Medical Center, Dallas, TX, p. A610

WHITIS, Matt, Chief Medical Officer, Mahaska Health, Oskaloosa, IA, p. A241

WHITLEY, Carolynn, Chief Nursing Officer, Chi St. Vincent Sherwood Rehabilitation Hospital, A Partner of Encompass Health, Sherwood, AR, p. A53

WHITLEY, Darla, Manager Health Information Technology, Syringa Hospital And Clinics, Grangeville, ID, p. A181

WHITLEY, Kay L., President and Chief Executive Officer, Spanish Peaks Regional Health Center And Veterans Community Living Center, Walsenburg, CO, p. A114

WHITLEY, Myra, Vice President, Human Resources, Columbus Specialty Hospital, Columbus, GA, p. A161

WHITLEY, Pam
R.N., Chief Nursing Officer and Chief Operating Officer, Medical City Green Oaks Hospital, Dallas, TX, p. A611
R.N., Chief Operating Officer and Chief Nursing Officer, Medical City Green Oaks Hospital, Dallas, TX, p. A611

WHITLOCK, John Jr, CPA, Chief Executive Officer, Metrowest Medical Center, Framingham, MA, p. A313

WHITMAN, Timothy, Chief Operating Officer, New Hampshire Hospital, Concord, NH, p. A414

WHITMORE, Dawn Esq, Director of Nursing, Aurora Behavioral Health System East, Tempe, AZ, p. A39

WHITMORE, Stewart
Chief Financial Officer, HCA Florida North Florida Hospital, Gainesville, FL, p. A132
Chief Financial Officer, HCA Florida Putnam Hospital, Palatka, FL, p. A145

WHITNEY, Donald, Director Human Resources, Kindred Hospital–Albuquerque, Albuquerque, NM, p. A432

WHITNEY, Jennifer Anne., FACHE, FACHE, Chief Executive Officer, Palomar Health Rehabilitation Institute, Escondido, CA, p. A62

WHITNUM, Rhonda, Director Health Improvement Management, Prague Regional Memorial Hospital, Prague, OK, p. A520

WHITT, Alicia, R.N., Chief Nursing Officer, Stephens Memorial Hospital, Breckenridge, TX, p. A604

WHITT, Horace, Chief Executive Officer, Rhea Medical Center, Dayton, TN, p. A582

WHITT, Stevan, M.D., Chief Medical Officer, University Hospital, Columbia, MO, p. A374

WHITTAKER, Kelly, Vice President Nursing, Mclaren Caro Region, Caro, MI, p. A323

WHITTAKER, Shawn, Chief Nursing Officer, Miller County Hospital, Colquitt, GA, p. A161

WHITTAKER, Sheena, M.D., Chief Medical Officer, Northern Light Maine Coast Hospital, Ellsworth, ME, p. A297

WHITTEMORE, Marjorie, Director Human Resources, Rio Grande Regional Hospital, Mcallen, TX, p. A638

WHITTEMORE, Scott
Chief Financial Officer, University of Mississipp. Medical Center Grenada, Grenada, MS, p. A362
Chief Financial Officer, University of Mississipp. Medical Center Holmes County, Lexington, MS, p. A365
Chief Financial Officer and Chief of Ancillary Services, Springfield Hospital, Springfield, VT, p. A672

WHITTINGTON, Bruce, Vice President Human Resources, Pawnee Valley Community Hospital, Larned, KS, p. A253

WHITTINGTON, Dorothy, Chief Financial Officer, Ochsner Lsu Health Shreveport – Monroe Medical Center, Monroe, LA, p. A288

WHITTINGTON, Hilary, Chief Financial Officer, Jefferson Healthcare, Port Townsend, WA, p. A693

WHITTINGTON, Laurie A, Chief Operating Officer, Memorial Health, Marysville, OH, p. A499

WHITTINGTON, Michael, R.N., Chief Executive Officer, Hood Memorial Hospital, Amite, LA, p. A276

WHITTINGTON, Pam, R.N., Director of Nursing, Vermilion Behavioral Health Systems – North Campus, Lafayette, LA, p. A286

WHITTINGTON, Shane, Chief Executive Officer, Livingston Hospital And Healthcare Services, Salem, KY, p. A274

WHITTINGTON–GEPPERT, Kelley, Director Human Resources, Munson Healthcare Cadillac Hospital, Cadillac, MI, p. A323

WHITTON, Beth, Director Human Resources, Ocean Beach Hospital And Medical Clinics, Ilwaco, WA, p. A690

WHITWELL, Quentin
Chief Executive Officer, Helena Regional Medical Center, Helena, AR, p. A47
Chief Executive Officer, Irwin County Hospital, Ocilla, GA, p. A169
Interim Chief Executive Officer, Panola Medical Center, Batesville, MS, p. A359

WHITWORTH, Ben, Chief Operating Officer, Multicare Mary Bridge Children's Hospital And Health Center, Tacoma, WA, p. A697

WHOBREY, Jacquelyn, MSN, R.N., Chief Nursing Officer, Saint Francis Hospital–Bartlett, Bartlett, TN, p. A579

WHOLLEY, Diane, Director Fiscal Services, Bridgewater State Hospital, Bridgewater, MA, p. A311

WHORLEY, Chris, Chief Information Officer, Nashville General Hospital, Nashville, TN, p. A590

WIATREK, Joseph, Director Information Technology, Otto Kaiser Memorial Hospital, Kenedy, TX, p. A632

WIBBENMEYER, Christopher M., FACHE, President and Chief Executive Officer, Mercy Hospital Perry, Perryville, MO, p. A382

WIBBENS, Cheryl, M.D., Vice President Medical Staff Affairs, Memorial Hospital of South Bend, South Bend, IN, p. A227

WIBORG, Shelley
MS, R.N., Chief Nursing Officer, OSF Saint Luke Medical Center, Kewanee, IL, p. A199
MS, R.N., Director of Nursing, OSF Holy Family Medical Center, Monmouth, IL, p. A202

WICKE, Julius III, Vice President Finance and Hospital Financial Officer, Baylor Scott & White Heart & Vascular Hospital–Dallas, Dallas, TX, p. A610

WICKE, Regina, Chief Financial Officer, Columbus Community Hospital, Columbus, TX, p. A608

WICKEL, Rlynn, President and Chief Executive Officer, Inland Northwest Behavioral Health, Spokane, WA, p. A696

WICKENS, Amy Lynn, Executive Director Human Resources, Decatur County Memorial Hospital, Greensburg, IN, p. A218

WICKER, Kenneth R., FACHE, Chief Executive Officer, HCA Florida Oak Hill Hospital, Brooksville, FL, p. A127

WICKHAM, Vickie A, R.N., MSN, Senior Director of Information Services, Van Diest Medical Center, Webster City, IA, p. A245

WICKIZER, Boyd, M.D., Jr, Chief Medical Officer, Bon Secours – Southside Medical Center, Petersburg, VA, p. A681

WICKLANDER, Jeffrey
President, Aspirus Merrill Hospital & Clinics, Inc., Merrill, WI, p. A716
President, Aspirus Wausau Hospital, Inc., Wausau, WI, p. A724

WICKLINE, Melissa, Director Marketing, Camc Greenbrier Valley Medical Center, Ronceverte, WV, p. A704

WIDAWSKY, Daniel J., Chief Financial Officer, Nyu Langone Hospitals, New York, NY, p. A452

WIDEMAN, Jeff, Director Information Systems, North Mississipp. Medical Center Gilmore–Amory, Amory, MS, p. A359

WIDGEON, Belle, Chief Executive Officer, The Rehabilitation Hospital of Montana, Billings, MT, p. A390

WIDGER, Judy, M.D., Chief of Staff, Healdsburg Hospital, Healdsburg, CA, p. A67

WIDICK, Brent, Superintendent, Kansas Neurological Institute, Topeka, KS, p. A260

WIDRA, Linda S, FACHE, Ph.D., R.N., Chief Operating Officer, Lakewood Ranch Medical Center, Bradenton, FL, p. A126

WIEBE, Trevor, Business Office Manager, Information Technology, Mercy Hospital Inc., Moundridge, KS, p. A255

WIECZOREK, Pawel, Director Information Technology, Brylin Hospitals, Buffalo, NY, p. A440

WIEDEMANN, Ashleigh, Chief Administrative Officer, Roper St. Francis Mount Pleasant Hospital, Mount Pleasant, SC, p. A568

WIEMANN, Michael
M.D., Regional President & CEO, Ascension Metro West Region, Ascension Providence Hospital, Southfield Campus, Southfield, MI, p. A338
M.D., Regional President & Chief Executive Officer, Ascension Metro West Region, Ascension Providence Rochester Hospital, Rochester, MI, p. A336

WIENS, Ron, Chief Executive Officer, Big Sandy Medical Center, Big Sandy, MT, p. A389

WIENTJES, Keri, Director Human Resources, Mobridge Regional Hospital, Mobridge, SD, p. A575

WIER, Erika, Chief Financial Officer, Lourdes Health, Pasco, WA, p. A692

WIERZBICKI, Barb, Manager Human Resources, Select Specialty Hospital – Downriver, Wyandotte, MI, p. A341

WIESMAN, David H, Interim Chief Financial Officer, SBL Fayette County Hospital And Long Term Care, Vandalia, IL, p. A210

WIESMANN, Marie, Vice President of Nursing and Chief Nursing Officer, Fort Healthcare, Fort Atkinson, WI, p. A711

WIESS, Laura, Interim Chief Executive Officer, St. David's Round Rock Medical Center, Round Rock, TX, p. A648

WIETERS, David, Director of Information Systems, New Hampshire Hospital, Concord, NH, p. A414

WIGGILL, Mechelle, Chief Executive Officer, South Davis Community Hospital, Bountiful, UT, p. A664

WIGGINS, Carla, Director Human Resources, Livingston Hospital And Healthcare Services, Salem, KY, p. A274

WIGGINS, Jamie L., R.N., MS, Executive Vice President and Chief Operating Officer, Arkansas Children's Hospital, Little Rock, AR, p. A49

WIGGINS, John, Chief Financial Officer, Evans Memorial Hospital, Claxton, GA, p. A160

WIGGINS, Michael, President, Dell Children's Medical Center of Central Texas, Austin, TX, p. A600

WIGGINS, Nicole, R.N., Chief Clinical Officer, Loring Hospital, Sac City, IA, p. A242

WIGHTMAN, Lori, R.N., FACHE, Chief Executive Officer, Bothwell Regional Health Center, Sedalia, MO, p. A386

WIGLEY, Felicia, R.N., Director of Nursing, Longleaf Hospital, Alexandria, LA, p. A276

WIGMAN, Cathryn, Director Human Resources, Encompass Health Rehabilitation Hospital of Braintree, Braintree, MA, p. A311

WIIK, Jennifer, Chief Nursing Officer, Ortonville Area Health Services, Ortonville, MN, p. A352

WIJAYA, Joanne, MSN, R.N., Chief Operating Officer and Risk Manager, Hampton Behavioral Health Center, Westampton, NJ, p. A430

WILBER, Scott, President and Chief Operating Officer, Mount Carmel East Hospital, Columbus, OH, p. A491

WILBUR, Bruce, M.D., Chief Medical Officer, Good Samaritan Hospital – San Jose, San Jose, CA, p. A92

WILBUR, Shawn, Chief Executive Officer, Clearsky Rehabilitation Hospital of Rio Rancho, Rio Rancho, NM, p. A436

WILBURN, Sue, Vice President Human Resources and Organizational Development, East Tennessee Children's Hospital, Knoxville, TN, p. A585

WILCHER, Greta
Senior Vice President and Chief Financial Officer, Mercy Hospital Fort Smith, Fort Smith, AR, p. A47
Senior Vice President and Chief Financial Officer, Mercy Hospital Waldron, Waldron, AR, p. A54

WILCOX, Bill, Chief Information Technology Officer, Bristol Bay Area Health Corporation, Dillingham, AK, p. A28

WILCOX, Byron, Chief Financial Management Officer, Standing Rock Service Unit, Fort Yates Hospital, Indian Health Service, Dhhs, Fort Yates, ND, p. A481

WILCOX, David, Chief Financial Officer, Regional Medical Center of Central Alabama, Greenville, AL, p. A20

WILCOX, Jack
Chief Financial Officer, Ennis Regional Medical Center, Ennis, TX, p. A618
Chief Financial Officer, Parkview Regional Hospital, Mexia, TX, p. A639

WILCOX, Robert, Chief Financial Officer, Munson Healthcare Charlevoix Hospital, Charlevoix, MI, p. A323

WILCZEK, Vincent Scot, Controller, Pratt Regional Medical Center, Pratt, KS, p. A258

WILD, Cheryl Jean, Chief Nursing Officer, HCA Florida Palms West Hospital, Loxahatchee, FL, p. A138

WILDA, Joshua, Chief Information Officer, University of Michigan Health – West, Wyoming, MI, p. A341

WILDE, Michael, M.D., Vice President Medical Officer, Sanford Usd Medical Center, Sioux Falls, SD, p. A577

WILDER, Janet, Director Human Resources, Barbourville Arh Hospita, Barbourville, KY, p. A263

WILDER, Stephen, Director Human Resources, Parkwest Medical Center, Knoxville, TN, p. A586

Index of Health Care Professionals / Williams

Index of Health Care Professionals

WILDER, Susan
Director Financial Services, Roosevelt Warm Springs Long Term Acute Care Hospital, Warm Springs, GA, p. A173
Director Financial Services, Roosevelt Warm Springs Rehabilitation And Specialty Hospitals, Warm Springs, GA, p. A173
WILDHAGEN, Quentin, Systems Administrator, Izard County Medical Center, Calico Rock, AR, p. A44
WILDI, Lorri, Chief Executive Officer, Surgical Institute of Reading, Wyomissing, PA, p. A558
WILDS, Esther Marcia, Vice President and Chief Nursing Officer, Mcleod Health Dillon, Dillon, SC, p. A565
WILEY, Chuck, Manager Information Systems, Harrison County Hospital, Corydon, IN, p. A214
WILEY, Donald J., President and Chief Executive Officer, St. Joseph's Medical Center, Stockton, CA, p. A97
WILEY, Mark, Manager Information Systems Development, UPMC Bedford, Everett, PA, p. A540
WILEY, Rob, M.D., Chief Medical Officer, Hendrick Medical Center, Abilene, TX, p. A595
WILEY, Ronette, R.N., Executive Vice President and Chief Operating Officer, Bassett Medical Center, Cooperstown, NY, p. A441
WILFONG, Mario, Chief Financial Officer, UPMC Children's Hospital of Pittsburgh, Pittsburgh, PA, p. A551
WILHELM, Connie, Chief Financial Officer, Swisher Memorial Healthcare System, Tulia, TX, p. A658
WILHELM, Margo, Chief Financial Officer, Austin Oaks Hospital, Austin, TX, p. A599
WILHELM, Paul, M.D., Chief of Staff, Kiowa District Healthcare, Kiowa, KS, p. A252
WILHITE, James, Director Systems Information, North Mississipp. State Hospital, Tupelo, MS, p. A369
WILHITE, Jerald, Administrator Human Resources, Heartland Behavioral Healthcare, Massillon, OH, p. A499
WILK, Len, President, Ascension Resurrection, Chicago, IL, p. A188
WILKE, Kris, Manager Health Information, Avera Granite Falls, Granite Falls, MN, p. A348
WILKEN, Thomas
Senior Vice President and Chief Human Resources Officer, Christus Mother Frances Hospital – Tyler, Tyler, TX, p. A658
Vice President Human Resources, Ascension Seton Williamson, Round Rock, TX, p. A647
WILKER, Johnathan, Vice President of Finance and Chief Financial Officer, Burgess Health Center, Onawa, IA, p. A241
WILKERSON, Michelle, Chief Human Resources Officer, Abrazo West Campus, Goodyear, AZ, p. A32
WILKES, Chris, MS, Chief Human Resources, Blount Memorial Hospital, Maryville, TN, p. A587
WILKES, Margaret, Chief Fiscal Officer, Charles George Veterans Affairs Medical Center, Asheville, NC, p. A463
WILKIE, Chance, Information Technology Specialist, Quentin N. Burdick Memorial Healthcare Facility, Belcourt, ND, p. A479
WILKIE, Paula, Chief Financial Officer, SMP Health – St. Kateri, Rolla, ND, p. A483
WILKINS, Joseph, President, Bon Secours St. Francis Medical Center, Midlothian, VA, p. A679
WILKINSON, Kyle, Chief Financial Officer, Morgan Medical Center, Madison, GA, p. A167
WILKS, Angela, Finance Director, Missouri Baptist Sullivan Hospital, Sullivan, MO, p. A387
WILKS, Konita, Chief Executive Officer, Olive View–Ucla Medical Center, Los Angeles, CA, p. A74
WILL, DeDe, Director Finance, Douglas County Community Mental Health Center, Omaha, NE, p. A404
WILL, Jeoff
Chief Operating Officer, Acute Care Hospitals, M Health Fairview Southdale Hospital, Edina, MN, p. A346
Executive Vice President, Chief Operating Officer, M Health Fairview Lakes Medical Center, Wyoming, MN, p. A358
Executive Vice President, Chief Operating Officer, M Health Fairview Northland Medical Center, Princeton, MN, p. A353
Executive Vice President, Chief Operating Officer, M Health Fairview Ridges Hospital, Burnsville, MN, p. A344
Executive Vice President, Chief Operating Officer, M Health Fairview Southdale Hospital, Edina, MN, p. A346
Executive Vice President, Chief Operating Officer, M Health Fairview St. John's Hospital, Maplewood, MN, p. A349
Executive Vice President, Chief Operating Officer, M Health Fairview University of Minnesota Medical Center, Minneapolis, MN, p. A350
Executive Vice President, Chief Operating Officer, M Health Fairview Woodwinds Hospital, Woodbury, MN, p. A357
WILLAMS, Mike, Chief Information Officer, FHN Memorial Hospital, Freeport, IL, p. A195
WILLARD, Cheri, MSN, R.N., Chief Executive Officer, Evanston Regional Hospital, Evanston, WY, p. A727
WILLARD, Craig, Director Information Technology and Systems, Frankfort Regional Medical Center, Frankfort, KY, p. A266
WILLARS, Susan Lara, Senior Vice President and Chief Human Resource Officer, Valleywise Health, Phoenix, AZ, p. A37
WILLBARGER, Kathy, Chief Operating Officer, Cheshire Medical Center, Keene, NH, p. A415
WILLCUTTS, David, Chief Executive Officer, Veritas Collaborative, Dunwoody, GA, p. A163
WILLERT, Laura, Interim Chief Nursing Officer, Cherry County Hospital, Valentine, NE, p. A406
WILLET, Terry, Chief Financial Officer, Allen Parish Community Healthcare, Kinder, LA, p. A285
WILLETT, Richard D., Chief Executive Officer, Redington–Fairview General Hospital, Skowhegan, ME, p. A299
WILLETT, Simon, Director Administrative Operations, South Texas Veterans Healthcare System Audie L Murphy, San Antonio, TX, p. A651
WILLETTS, Carrie, President & Chief Executive Officer, WVU Medicine Uniontown Hospital, Uniontown, PA, p. A556
WILLEY, Randy, Business Manager, Lincoln Regional Center, Lincoln, NE, p. A402
WILLHITE, Jean, Director Human Resources, Sutter Solano Medical Center, Vallejo, CA, p. A100
WILLIAMS, Adrian, Chief Executive Officer, Serenity Springs Specialty Hospital, Ruston, LA, p. A291
WILLIAMS, Alec, Chief Information Officer, Southwest General Health Center, Middleburg Heights, OH, p. A500
WILLIAMS, Amber
Chief Executive Officer, Southwest Medical Center, Liberal, KS, p. A253
Chief Financial Officer, Vice President of Finance, Southwest Medical Center, Liberal, KS, p. A253
WILLIAMS, Angela, PharmD, MS, Medical Center Director, George E. Wahlen Department of Veterans Affairs Medical Center, Salt Lake City, UT, p. A668
WILLIAMS, Antoinette, Chief Nursing Officer, John H. Stroger Jr. Hospital of Cook County, Chicago, IL, p. A190
WILLIAMS, Arthur, M.D., Medical Director, Encompass Health Rehabilitation Hospital of Braintree, Braintree, MA, p. A311
WILLIAMS, Bernett, Interim Chief Human Resource Officer, Akron Children's Hospital, Akron, OH, p. A484
WILLIAMS, Beth, R.N., Chief Nursing Officer, Conway Behavioral Health, Conway, AR, p. A44
WILLIAMS, Beverly, R.N., Chief Nursing Officer, Washington County Memorial Hospital, Potosi, MO, p. A382
WILLIAMS, Brian
Chief Executive Officer, Winner Regional Healthcare Center, Winner, SD, p. A578
Web Services and Information Technology Manager, St. Joseph's Hospital, Buckhannon, WV, p. A699
WILLIAMS, Brian A., Chief Executive Officer, Labette Health, Parsons, KS, p. A258
WILLIAMS, Brit, M.D., President Medical Staff, Warner Hospital And Health Services, Clinton, IL, p. A192
WILLIAMS, CarolAnn, President, Massachusetts Eye And Ear, Boston, MA, p. A310
WILLIAMS, Cecille, Assistant Administrator, Shamrock General Hospital, Shamrock, TX, p. A652
WILLIAMS, Charles E., President DFW – West Region, Baylor Scott & White All Saints Medical Center – Fort Worth, Fort Worth, TX, p. A619
WILLIAMS, Chris J., FACHE, Vice President Operations, OSF Saint Clare Medical Center, Princeton, IL, p. A206
WILLIAMS, Christine, Chief Financial Officer, University Medical Center, New Orleans, LA, p. A290
WILLIAMS, Christopher, M.D., Chief of Staff, Pioneers Medical Center, Meeker, CO, p. A112
WILLIAMS, Damita, Ed.D., R.N., MSN, Chief Nursing Officer, Medical City Plano, Plano, TX, p. A645
WILLIAMS, Dan, Vice President Finance and Support, Liberty Hospital, Liberty, MO, p. A379
WILLIAMS, Dana, Chief Financial Officer, Baptist Memorial Hospital–North Mississippi, Oxford, MS, p. A367
WILLIAMS, Dana D., Chief Executive Officer, Ochsner American Legion Hospital, Jennings, LA, p. A284
WILLIAMS, Danielle H., Administrator, Caldwell Memorial Hospital, Columbia, LA, p. A280
WILLIAMS, Darek, Director Human Resources, Elgin Mental Health Center, Elgin, IL, p. A194
WILLIAMS, Darren, Chief Executive Officer, Cornerstone Specialty Hospitals Southwest Louisiana, Lake Charles, LA, p. A286
WILLIAMS, David, Director Information Technology, Franklin Hospital District, Benton, IL, p. A186
WILLIAMS, David L, M.D., Chief Medical Officer, Ascension St. Vincent Kokomo, Kokomo, IN, p. A221
WILLIAMS, Dionne, Director Human Resources, Vaughan Regional Medical Center, Selma, AL, p. A24
WILLIAMS, Douglas
President, Saint Francis Hospital, Tulsa, OK, p. A523
Vice President, Saint Francis Heart Hospital, Saint Francis Hospital, Tulsa, OK, p. A523
WILLIAMS, Eric, Senior Vice President and Area Manager Santa Clara, Kaiser Permanente Santa Clara Medical Center, Santa Clara, CA, p. A94
WILLIAMS, Frank L., Executive Vice President/Medical Director, Kedren Community Health Center, Los Angeles, CA, p. A73
WILLIAMS, Greg
Chief Financial Officer, PIH Health Downey Hospital, Downey, CA, p. A61
Chief Financial Officer, PIH Health Whittier Hospital, Whittier, CA, p. A101
WILLIAMS, Holly, Human Resources Director, Russell Medical, Alexander City, AL, p. A15
WILLIAMS, Jackie, Director Human Resources, Merit Health Madison, Canton, MS, p. A360
WILLIAMS, James
M.D., Chief of Staff, Thedacare Medical Center–Waupaca, Waupaca, WI, p. A724
Vice President and Chief Nursing Officer, Mclaren Flint, Flint, MI, p. A327
WILLIAMS, Jennifer, Vice President of Finance/Chief Financial Officer, Wayne Healthcare, Greenville, OH, p. A497
WILLIAMS, Jennifer J., Director, Human Resources, UPMC Western Maryland, Cumberland, MD, p. A304
WILLIAMS, Jeremy, Chief Financial Officer, Banner Boswell Medical Center, Sun City, AZ, p. A39
WILLIAMS, Jill, Chief Executive Officer, Samaritan Hospital, Macon, MO, p. A380
WILLIAMS, Joan, Administrative Assistant/Human Resources, Lamb Healthcare Center, Littlefield, TX, p. A634
WILLIAMS, Joanna, Chief Executive Officer, Encompass Health Rehabilitation Hospital of Alexandria, Alexandria, LA, p. A276
WILLIAMS, John
Administrator and Chief Executive Officer, Nell J. Redfield Memorial Hospital, Malad City, ID, p. A182
Chief Financial Officer, Upson Regional Medical Center, Thomaston, GA, p. A172
Chief Information Officer, Bay Pines Veterans Affairs Healthcare System, Bay Pines, FL, p. A125
WILLIAMS, John D Jr, Chief Financial Officer, Biloxi Va Medical Center, Biloxi, MS, p. A359
WILLIAMS, Joseph, Chief Executive Officer, Rehabilitation Hospital of Bowie, Bowie, MD, p. A303
WILLIAMS, Joyce, Consultant Human Resources and Organizational Development, Memorial Hermann Rehabilitation Hospital – Katy, Katy, TX, p. A631
WILLIAMS, Julie, Chief Financial Officer, Muenster Memorial Hospital, Muenster, TX, p. A640
WILLIAMS, Kathy, Chief Nursing Officer, Eastern New Mexico Medical Center, Roswell, NM, p. A436
WILLIAMS, Kenneth
M.D., Medical Director, United Medical Healthwest New Orleans, Llc, Gretna, LA, p. A282
Chief Information Officer, Fayetteville Veterans Affairs Medical Center, Fayetteville, NC, p. A468
WILLIAMS, Kevin, Vice President, Information Technology, Acuity Specialty Hospital–Ohio Valley At Weirton, Weirton, WV, p. A705
WILLIAMS, Kristie
Vice President and Hospital Administrator, Carilion Giles Community Hospital, Pearisburg, VA, p. A681
Vice President and Hospital Administrator, Carilion Tazewell Community Hospital, Tazewell, VA, p. A684
WILLIAMS, Kristin, Chief Executive Officer, Kingwood Pines Hospital, Kingwood, TX, p. A632
WILLIAMS, Kristy, Manager Finance, John J. Pershing Veterans' Administration Medical Center, Poplar Bluff, MO, p. A382
WILLIAMS, L Dale, M.D., Vice President and Chief Medical Director, Atrium Health Wake Foret Baptist High Point Medical Center, High Point, NC, p. A470
WILLIAMS, Laci, Director Human Resources, Kearny County Hospital, Lakin, KS, p. A252
WILLIAMS, Lana R, Chief Nursing Officer, Arkansas Methodist Medical Center, Paragould, AR, p. A52
WILLIAMS, Linda, Director of Nursing, Villa Feliciana Medical Complex, Jackson, LA, p. A283
WILLIAMS, Linda G., Administrator, Northeast Florida State Hospital, Macclenny, FL, p. A138
WILLIAMS, Lorie, R.N., Vice President Nursing, Samaritan Pacific Communities Hospital, Newport, OR, p. A529
WILLIAMS, Lynn
Vice President Human Resources, Commonwealth Regional Specialty Hospital, Bowling Green, KY, p. A263

Index of Health Care Professionals / Williams

Vice President Human Resources, Medical Center At Scottsville, Scottsville, KY, p. A274
Vice President Human Resources, The Medical Center At Bowling Green, Bowling Green, KY, p. A264
Vice President, Human Resources, The Medical Center At Albany, Albany, KY, p. A263
Vice President, Human Resources, The Medical Center At Caverna, Horse Cave, KY, p. A267
WILLIAMS, Margaret, Chief Financial Officer, Baptist Memorial Hospital for Women, Memphis, TN, p. A588
WILLIAMS, Margo L, R.N., Chief Nursing Officer, Anderson County Hospital, Garnett, KS, p. A249
WILLIAMS, Mary, Director Human Resources, Orleans Community Health, Medina, NY, p. A446
WILLIAMS, Michael, Vice President and Chief Information Officer, LMH Health, Lawrence, KS, p. A253
WILLIAMS, Michael D, Vice President and Administrator, Charleston Area Medical Center, Charleston, WV, p. A700
WILLIAMS, Michael F., Chief Financial Officer, Limestone Medical Center, Groesbeck, TX, p. A623
WILLIAMS, Michael L, FACHE, Vice President Human Resources, Community Howard Regional Health, Kokomo, IN, p. A221
WILLIAMS, Michelle, Administrator, Sedan City Hospital, Sedan, KS, p. A259
WILLIAMS, Mickey, Manager Information Technology, Moccasin Bend Mental Health Institute, Chattanooga, TN, p. A580
WILLIAMS, Nicole
 Chief Operating Officer, Columbia Memorial Hospital, Astoria, OR, p. A525
 Director of Human Resources Operations, Dmc Huron Valley–Sinai Hospital, Commerce Township, MI, p. A324
WILLIAMS, Pamela G, Director Human Resources, Unity Health, Searcy, AR, p. A53
WILLIAMS, Patricia, Chief Executive Officer, Fremont Hospital, Fremont, CA, p. A64
WILLIAMS, Perry E. Sr, Administrator and Chief Executive Officer, Alliance Healthcare System, Holly Springs, MS, p. A363
WILLIAMS, Qiana, Director, Human Resource Business Partner, Grant, Ohiohealth Grant Medical Center, Columbus, OH, p. A492
WILLIAMS, R.D., Chief Executive Officer, Hendry Regional Medical Center, Clewiston, FL, p. A128
WILLIAMS, Rachael, Chief Nursing Officer, Merit Health Biloxi, Biloxi, MS, p. A359
WILLIAMS, Randy, Director Management Information Systems, Maria Parham Health, Duke Lifepoint Healthcare, Henderson, NC, p. A470
WILLIAMS, Reginald, M.D., Medical Staff President, Curry General Hospital, Gold Beach, OR, p. A527
WILLIAMS, Richard, Administrator and Chief Executive Officer, Field Memorial Community Hospital, Centreville, MS, p. A360
WILLIAMS, Robert, Chief Executive Officer, Encompass Health Rehabilitation Hospital of Princeton, Princeton, WV, p. A704
WILLIAMS, Roberta A, Director of Nursing, U. S. Public Health Service Indian Hospital, Cass Lake, MN, p. A344
WILLIAMS, Roby D, Chief Executive Officer, Hardin County General Hospital, Rosiclare, IL, p. A208
WILLIAMS, Rodney W, M.D., JD, MS, Vice President Medical Affairs, Good Samaritan Regional Medical Center, Suffern, NY, p. A459
WILLIAMS, Sabrina, Interim Vice President Human Resources, Brigham And Women's Hospital, Boston, MA, p. A310
WILLIAMS, Sandra, Chief Financial Officer, Cap. Fear Valley Medical Center, Fayetteville, NC, p. A468
WILLIAMS, Scott, Chief Executive Officer, Tennova Newport Medical Center, Newport, TN, p. A591
WILLIAMS, Shane, Director Information Systems, Holy Cross Hospital – Davis, Layton, UT, p. A665
WILLIAMS, Shelton
 Chief Executive Officer, Alliancehealth Durant, Durant, OK, p. A512
 Chief Executive Officer, Alliancehealth Madill, Madill, OK, p. A514
WILLIAMS, Sheri, Chief Operating Officer, Guadalup. Regional Medical Center, Seguin, TX, p. A652
WILLIAMS, Sondra D., R.N., MSN, Chief Executive Officer, Tyler County Hospital, Woodville, TX, p. A663
WILLIAMS, Staci, PharmD, Medical Center Director, Veterans Affairs Illiana Health Care System, Danville, IL, p. A192
WILLIAMS, Stephanie, Market Director Human Resources, Lake Norman Regional Medical Center, Mooresville, NC, p. A472
WILLIAMS, Sue Ann, Chief Executive Officer, Mercy Hospital Stoddard, Dexter, MO, p. A374

WILLIAMS, Susan
 M.D., Chief Medical Officer, Conemaugh Memorial Medical Center, Johnstown, PA, p. A542
 M.D., Chief Medical Officer, Conemaugh Miners Medical Center, Hastings, PA, p. A541
WILLIAMS, Thaddeus, Controller, Encompass Health Rehabilitation Hospital of North Memphis, A Partner of Methodist Healthcare, Memphis, TN, p. A588
WILLIAMS, Todd
 Chief Financial Officer, Integris Health Woodward Hospital, Woodward, OK, p. A524
 Chief Financial Officer, Siloam Springs Regional Hospital, Siloam Springs, AR, p. A53
WILLIAMS, Tom
 Chief Executive Officer, UNC Health Johnston, Smithfield, NC, p. A476
 Vice President Human Resources, Lake Regional Health System, Osage Beach, MO, p. A381
WILLIAMS, Virginia, Chief Executive Officer, Curry General Hospital, Gold Beach, OR, p. A527
WILLIAMS, Wade, Chief Information Officer, UNC Health Rockingham, Eden, NC, p. A467
WILLIAMS, Wendell H, M.D., Jr, Medical Director, Pam Health Specialty Hospital of Jacksonville, Jacksonville, FL, p. A135
WILLIAMS–CARLSON, Laishy, Chief Information Officer, Roper St. Francis Mount Pleasant Hospital, Mount Pleasant, SC, p. A568
WILLIAMSON, Alan, M.D., Vice President, Medical Affairs and Chief Medical Officer, Eisenhower Health, Rancho Mirage, CA, p. A84
WILLIAMSON, Barry, President Medical Staff, UNC Health Southeastern, Lumberton, NC, p. A472
WILLIAMSON, Judy, R.N., President, Mckay–Dee Hospital, Ogden, UT, p. A666
WILLIAMSON, Sam, Chief Financial Officer, Tristar Northcrest Medical Center, Springfield, TN, p. A593
WILLIAMSON, Sharon, Chief Information Technology, Robert J. Dole Department of Veterans Affairs Medical And Regional Office Center, Wichita, KS, p. A262
WILLIAMSON–YOUNCE, Hop. M., Commander, Madigan Army Medical Center, Tacoma, WA, p. A697
WILLIE, David, Chief Financial Officer, Yuma Regional Medical Center, Yuma, AZ, p. A42
WILLIFORD, Sandy, Chief Health Information Management and Revenue Administration, Charlie Norwood Veterans Affairs Medical Center, Augusta, GA, p. A158
WILLINGHAM, John, Division Vice President, Carolina Center for Behavioral Health, Greer, SC, p. A567
WILLIS, Bill, Director Information Technology, River Point Behavioral Health, Jacksonville, FL, p. A135
WILLIS, Casey, Chief Executive Officer, Saint Mary's Regional Medical Center, Russellville, AR, p. A53
WILLIS, Danielle S., CPA, Interim Chief Financial Officer, Manager Finance, New Orleans East Hospital, New Orleans, LA, p. A290
WILLIS, Darrell, M.D., Chief of Staff, Dr. Dan C. Trigg Memorial Hospital, Tucumcari, NM, p. A437
WILLIS, Dawnett, Chief Executive Officer, Floyd County Medical Center, Charles City, IA, p. A232
WILLIS, James, Chief Operating Officer, VCU Medical Center, Richmond, VA, p. A683
WILLIS, Jonathon, Director Information Services, Vanderbilt Bedford Hospital, Shelbyville, TN, p. A593
WILLIS, Joy, Acting Chief Fiscal Service, G.V. (Sonny) Montgomery Department of Veterans Affairs Medical Center, Jackson, MS, p. A364
WILLIS, Kathy, M.D., Medical Director, Lallie Kemp Medical Center, Independence, LA, p. A283
WILLIS, LaDonna, Chief Operating Officer, Childress Regional Medical Center, Childress, TX, p. A607
WILLIS, Raymond, IT Manager, Choctaw Health Center, Philadelphia, MS, p. A367
WILLIS, Sandra, Director of Human Resources, Citizens Baptist Medical Center, Talladega, AL, p. A24
WILLIS, Toni, M.D., Medical Director, Encompass Health Rehabilitation Hospital of The Mid–Cities, Bedford, TX, p. A602
WILLIS, Wendy L, Vice President Human Resources, Children's Hospital New Orleans, New Orleans, LA, p. A290
WILLMANN, Adam, President and Chief Executive Officer, Goodall–Witcher Hospital, Clifton, TX, p. A607
WILLMON, Brian, M.D., Medical Director, Plains Regional Medical Center, Clovis, NM, p. A434
WILLMORE, Lois, Supervisor Health Information Management, Cedar County Memorial Hospital, El Dorado Springs, MO, p. A374
WILLOUGHBY, Kirsten, Director of Nursing, Big Horn Hospital, Hardin, MT, p. A392
WILLS, Andrea, R.N., Chief Nursing Executive, Munising Memorial Hospital, Munising, MI, p. A334

WILLS, Andy, M.D., Medical Director, Colquitt Regional Medical Center, Moultrie, GA, p. A169
WILLS, Kim, Chief Operating Officer, Southwell Medical, Adel, GA, p. A156
WILLS, Laura S.
 Administrator, Noland Hospital Birmingham, Birmingham, AL, p. A17
 Administrator, Noland Hospital Shelby, Alabaster, AL, p. A15
WILLS, Michele, Registered Health Information Administrator, Caro Center, Caro, MI, p. A323
WILLS, Robert, M.D., Chief Medical Officer, Arise Austin Medical Center, Austin, TX, p. A598
WILLS, Shannon, Director Human Resources, Delray Medical Center, Delray Beach, FL, p. A130
WILLS, Tom, R.N., Chief Operating Officer, Merit Health Central, Jackson, MS, p. A364
WILLSIE, Brett, Vice President Human Resources, Sentara Northern Virginia Medical Center, Woodbridge, VA, p. A685
WILLWERTH, Deborah J., R.N., MSN, President, UPMC Lititz, Lititz, PA, p. A544
WILLY, Randy, Chief Financial Officer, Community Medical Center, Inc., Falls City, NE, p. A399
WILMOT, Joan, Chief Finance Officer, White River Junction Veterans Affairs Medical Center, White River Junction, VT, p. A672
WILMOTH, Donna, Vice President Patient Care Services and Chief Nursing Officer, Sentara Williamsburg Regional Medical Center, Williamsburg, VA, p. A685
WILMS, Mike, Director Information Systems, HCA Florida Bayonet Point Hospital, Hudson, FL, p. A134
WILSON, Alice, FACHE, Vice President Administration, St. Luke's Hospital – Warren Campus, Phillipsburg, NJ, p. A427
WILSON, Amy, M.D., Medical Director, Baylor Scott & White Institute for Rehabilitation – Dallas, Dallas, TX, p. A610
WILSON, Andrea, Chief Executive Officer, Valley Behavioral Health System, Barling, AR, p. A43
WILSON, Andrew, Chief Executive Officer, Doctors Hospital of Laredo, Laredo, TX, p. A634
WILSON, Bill, Chief Financial Officer, North Carolina Specialty Hospital, Durham, NC, p. A467
WILSON, Bobbie, Director Human Resources, Crete Area Medical Center, Crete, NE, p. A399
WILSON, Carolyn
 R.N., Chief Operating Officer, Corewell Health Beaumont Grosse Pointe Hospital, Grosse Pointe, MI, p. A329
 R.N., Chief Operating Officer, Corewell Health Beaumont Troy Hospital, Troy, MI, p. A339
 R.N., Chief Operating Officer, Corewell Health Farmington Hills Hospital, Farmington Hills, MI, p. A326
 R.N., Chief Operating Officer, Corewell Health Taylor Hospital, Taylor, MI, p. A339
 R.N., Chief Operating Officer, Corewell Health Wayne Hospital, Wayne, MI, p. A340
 R.N., Executive Vice President, Chief Operating Officer, Corewell Health Trenton Hospital, Trenton, MI, p. A339
 Chief Operating Officer, Corewell Health Dearborn Hospital, Dearborn, MI, p. A324
WILSON, Charlene J, Vice President Human Resources, St. Francis Hospital, Wilmington, DE, p. A122
WILSON, Chase, Chief Financial Officer, Sycamore Shoals Hospital, Elizabethton, TN, p. A582
WILSON, Christopher, M.D., Inpatient Medical Director, South Texas Rehabilitation Hospital, Brownsville, TX, p. A605
WILSON, Christy, Chief Financial Officer, Merit Health Rankin, Brandon, MS, p. A360
WILSON, Clifford, Chief Executive Officer, Market President Central Kentucky, Georgetown Community Hospital, Georgetown, KY, p. A266
WILSON, Colleen, Chief Nursing Officer, Southern Inyo Healthcare District, Lone Pine, CA, p. A70
WILSON, Craig, Chief Medical Officer, Ascension St. Vincent Fishers, Fishers, IN, p. A216
WILSON, Cynthia, Director, NDI Advanced Treatment Center, Nursing and BHRA Unit Services, Neurodiagnostic Institute And Advanced Treatment Center, Indianapolis, IN, p. A220
WILSON, Daniel, R.N., Chief Operating Officer, Pennsylvania Hospital, Philadelphia, PA, p. A549
WILSON, David C., President and Chief Operation Officer, North Mississipp. Medical Center – Tupelo, Tupelo, MS, p. A369
WILSON, David R, M.D., Chief of Staff, Ascension St. Vincent's Blount, Oneonta, AL, p. A23
WILSON, Deb, Director Human Resources, Logan Health, Kalispell, MT, p. A393
WILSON, Eleanor, R.N., MSN, Vice President and Chief Operating Officer, Doylestown Health, Doylestown, PA, p. A533

Index of Health Care Professionals / Wisnoski

Index of Health Care Professionals

WILSON, Erin, Human Resource Director, Bear Valley Community Hospital, Big Bear Lake, CA, p. A58
WILSON, Fiore, Director Information Systems, Castleview Hospital, Price, UT, p. A667
WILSON, Hamlin J, Senior Vice President Human Resources, Holston Valley Medical Center, Kingsport, TN, p. A585
WILSON, Hannah, HIMS Supervisor, Quad Cities Rehabilitation Institute, The, Moline, IL, p. A202
WILSON, Jason
Administrator, Mercy Hospital Lebanon, Mercy Hospital Lebanon, Lebanon, MO, p. A379
President, American Fork Hospital, American Fork, UT, p. A664
WILSON, Jeff, Chief Executive Officer, Trident Medical Center, Charleston, SC, p. A563
WILSON, Jessica, Chief Executive Officer, Regency Hospital of Northwest Indiana, East Chicago, IN, p. A215
WILSON, John R
Chief Operating Officer, Murray–Calloway County Hospital, Murray, KY, p. A272
Vice President, Human Resources, Murray–Calloway County Hospital, Murray, KY, p. A272
WILSON, Kathleen Lerae DNP, RN, Vice President Patient Services and Chief Nursing Officer, St. Claire Regional Medical Center, Morehead, KY, p. A272
WILSON, Kenna, Vice President, Chief Nursing Officer, Integris Health Enid Hospital, Enid, OK, p. A512
WILSON, Kim, Human Resources Coordinator, Cordova Community Medical Center, Cordova, AK, p. A28
WILSON, Kimberly P, Director Human Resources, University of Kentucky Albert B. Chandler Hospital, Lexington, KY, p. A269
WILSON, Lawrence, M.D., Vice President, Chief Medical Officer, Midland Memorial Hospital, Midland, TX, p. A639
WILSON, Loretta, Chief Executive Officer/Administrator, Hill Hospital of Sumter County, York, AL, p. A26
WILSON, Mallory, Administrative Assistant and Human Resources Coordinator, Select Specialty Hospital–North Knoxville, Powell, TN, p. A592
WILSON, Marla C., Chief Executive Officer, Acute Rehabilitation Hospital of Plano., Plano, TX, p. A645
WILSON, Melissa
Administrator and Chief Executive Officer, Concho County Hospital, Eden, TX, p. A615
Chief Executive Officer, Freestone Medical Center, Fairfield, TX, p. A618
WILSON, Michael, M.D., Chief Medical Officer, Auburn Community Hospital, Auburn, NY, p. A438
WILSON, Monte A., President and Chief Executive Officer, Christus St. Frances Cabrini Hospital, Alexandria, LA, p. A276
WILSON, Morgan, Director Health Information Management, Millwood Hospital, Arlington, TX, p. A597
WILSON, Nadine, Manager, Human Resources, Sunview Medical Center, West Palm Beach, FL, p. A154
WILSON, Nancy, Chief Financial Officer, Parkview Community Hospital Medical Center, Riverside, CA, p. A86
WILSON, Nathan, R.N., Vice President and Chief Nursing Officer, Baptist Health La Grange, La Grange, KY, p. A268
WILSON, Nicole, Manager Human Resources, Bliant Specialty Hospital, New Orleans, LA, p. A290
WILSON, Patricia, Senior Vice President Human Resources, Englewood Health, Englewood, NJ, p. A421
WILSON, Preshie, Chief Financial Officer, Hillcrest Hospital South, Tulsa, OK, p. A522
WILSON, Rebecca, Chief Nursing Officer, Sebastian River Medical Center, Sebastian, FL, p. A150
WILSON, Regina, R.N., Director of Nursing, Share Medical Center, Alva, OK, p. A509
WILSON, Robert, D.O., Director Medical Services, Eagleville Hospital, Eagleville, PA, p. A538
WILSON, Robert E, Vice President and Chief Information Officer, Crozer–Chester Medical Center, Upland, PA, p. A556
WILSON, Roy, M.D., Medical Director, St. Louis Forensic Treatment Center, Saint Louis, MO, p. A384
WILSON, Sara, Director Human Resources, Cheyenne County Hospital, Saint Francis, KS, p. A259
WILSON, Shelley, R.N., Chief Nursing Officer, Henry Community Health, New Castle, IN, p. A225
WILSON, Sherry, R.N., Chief Nursing Officer, Mayers Memorial Hospital District, Fall River Mills, CA, p. A63
WILSON, Stephan A, Chief Financial Officer, Montrose Regional Health, Montrose, CO, p. A112
WILSON, Stephan A., Chief Financial Officer, Lifescape, Sioux Falls, SD, p. A576
WILSON, Tammie, R.N., MSN, Chief Nursing Officer, Adena Fayette Medical Center, Washington Court House, OH, p. A506
WILSON, Terrance E., President and Chief Executive Officer, Franciscan Health Lafayette East, Lafayette, IN, p. A221
WILSON, William, M.D., Chief Medical Officer, UCI Health, Orange, CA, p. A82
WILSON–NEIL, Carla, FACHE, Chief Operating Officer, Corewell Health Pennock Hospital, Hastings, MI, p. A329
WILSON–STUBBS, Yolande, President, Ascension Holy Family, Des Plaines, IL, p. A193
WILTERMOOD, Mike C., President and Chief Executive Officer, Enloe Health, Chico, CA, p. A59
WILTROUT, Kristy, R.N., Chief Operating Officer, Vernon Memorial Healthcare, Elk Mound, WI, p. A710
WILTROUT, Terry, President, UPMC Greene, Waynesburg, PA, p. A556
WILVER, Donald Jr, Vice President Human Resources, UPMC Williamsport, Williamsport, PA, p. A558
WIMMER, Keri, R.N., Patient Care Director, Centracare – Melrose, Melrose, MN, p. A350
WINBERY, Ben, Chief Financial Officer, Vantage Point of Northwest Arkansas, Fayetteville, AR, p. A46
WINDAS, Allison Leigh, Director of Patient Care Services–Nurse Executive, Shriners Hospitals for Children–Greenville, Greenville, SC, p. A567
WINDHAM, Joel
Vice President Human Resources, Baptist Anderson Regional Medical Center – South, Meridian, MS, p. A366
Vice President Human Resources, Baptist Anderson Regional Medical Center, Meridian, MS, p. A366
WINDHAM, Vann, Chief Financial Officer, Medical Center Barbour, Eufaula, AL, p. A19
WINDHAM, William, Chief Executive Officer, Parkridge Medical Center, Chattanooga, TN, p. A580
WINDLAND, J Michael, M.D., Chief of Staff, Southern Tennessee Regional Health System–Pulaski, Pulaski, TN, p. A592
WINDOLOVICH, Winona, Associate Chief Information Officer, Zuckerberg San Francisco General Hospital And Trauma Center, San Francisco, CA, p. A91
WINDROW, Matthew, M.D., Chief of Staff, Medina Regional Hospital, Hondo, TX, p. A624
WINDSOR, Bonnie, Senior Vice President Human Resources, Johns Hopkins Hospital, Baltimore, MD, p. A300
WINE, Lisa, Chief Financial Officer, Goshen Health, Goshen, IN, p. A217
WINEBAR, Robin Elwell, Chief Nursing Officer, Methodist Mckinney Hospital, Mckinney, TX, p. A638
WINEGEART, Steve, Chief Financial Officer, Memorial Medical Center, Las Cruces, NM, p. A435
WINEKAUF, Glen, Chief Executive Officer, Horn Memorial Hospital, Ida Grove, IA, p. A237
WINFREE, Kersey, M.D., Chief Medical Officer, SSM Health St. Anthony Hospital – Oklahoma City, Oklahoma City, OK, p. A518
WING, Lilly, Chief Nursing Officer, Three Rivers Behavioral Health, West Columbia, SC, p. A571
WING, Yakesun, Business Strategy and Finance Leader, Kaiser Permanente Walnut Creek Medical Center, Walnut Creek, CA, p. A100
WINGET, Mary, Director Human Resources, Minden Medical Center, Minden, LA, p. A288
WINGFIELD, Gena, Senior Vice President and Chief Financial Officer, Arkansas Children's Hospital, Little Rock, AR, p. A49
WINGO, Michelle, Director Human Resources, Piedmont Geriatric Hospital, Burkeville, VA, p. A674
WINIGER, Cecilia, Community Outreach and Communication Manager, Adventist Health Howard Memorial, Willits, CA, p. A101
WINK, Jeri, Director Human Resources, Grandview Medical Center, Birmingham, AL, p. A16
WINKELMAN, Dan, President and Chief Executive Officer, Yukon–Kuskokwim Delta Regional Hospital, Bethel, AK, p. A27
WINKLER, Jessica L., Chief Nursing Officer, Sonoma Valley Hospital, Sonoma, CA, p. A96
WINKS, Tyler, Chief Executive Officer, Erlanger Medical Center, Chattanooga, TN, p. A580
WINN, Ann M, M.D., R.N., FACHE, Chief Nursing Officer, Methodist Stone Oak Hospital, San Antonio, TX, p. A650
WINN, Cameron, Director Information Services, Ashley Regional Medical Center, Vernal, UT, p. A670
WINN, Holly, FACHE, Chief Operating Officer, Black River Memorial Hospital, Black River Falls, WI, p. A708
WINNER, Douglas, Chief Financial Officer, Acute Care Operations, Ascension Providence Hospital, Southfield Campus, Southfield, MI, p. A338
WINNETT, Steve, Chief Executive Officer, Townsen Memorial Hospital, Humble, TX, p. A629
WINNIK, Mitchell, FACHE, Senior Vice President, Area Manager, Downey, Kaiser Permanente Downey Medical Center, Downey, CA, p. A61
WINSLOW, Tracy, Interim Chief Nursing Officer, Desoto Memorial Hospital, Arcadia, FL, p. A125
WINSTON, Bob, M.D., Medical Director, Vermilion Behavioral Health Systems – North Campus, Lafayette, LA, p. A286
WINSTON, Patricia A, FACHE, MS, R.N., Senor Vice President, Hospital Administration, Suny Downstate Health Sciences University, New York, NY, p. A453
WINT, Jesse, Director of Nursing, Hardin Medical Center, Savannah, TN, p. A592
WINTER, Jennifer, Chief Medical Information Officer, Fort Healthcare, Fort Atkinson, WI, p. A711
WINTER, Jon R., D.O., Chief of Staff, West Tennessee Healthcare Camden Hospital, Camden, TN, p. A579
WINTER, Melissa
R.N., MSN, Chief Operating Officer and Chief Nursing Officer, Baylor Scott & White Medical Center – Grapevine, Grapevine, TX, p. A622
R.N., MSN, Chief Operating Officer and Chief Nursing Officer, Baylor Scott & White Medical Center at – Mckinney, Mckinney, TX, p. A638
R.N., MSN, Regional Chief Nursing Officer, Baylor Scott & White Medical Center – Grapevine, Grapevine, TX, p. A622
WINTERS, Heidi, Business Partner Human Resources, Chi Health Missouri Valley, Missouri Valley, IA, p. A240
WINTERS, Mary, Interim Chief Nursing Officer, SCL Health Mt – St. James Healthcare, Butte, MT, p. A390
WINTERS, Shane, Chief Information Officer, Jersey Community Hospital, Jerseyville, IL, p. A199
WIRJO, Jonathan, M.D., Medical Director, Seven Hills Hospital, Henderson, NV, p. A409
WIRTHGEN, Doug
Chief Information Officer, VA Palo Alto Heath Care System, Palo Alto, CA, p. A82
Facility Chief Information Officer, Jerry L. Pettis Memorial Veterans' Hospital, Loma Linda, CA, p. A70
WIRTZ, David
Senior LAN Administrator, Evansville State Hospital, Evansville, IN, p. A216
Supervisor Information Technology, Evansville Psychiatric Children Center, Evansville, IN, p. A216
WIRZMAN, Jillian, Cheif Nursing Officer, Fort Lauderdale Behavioral Health Center, Oakland Park, FL, p. A143
WISE, Claude, Chief Executive Officer and Managing Director, Spring Valley Hospital Medical Center, Las Vegas, NV, p. A411
WISE, Dan, Manager Information Technology, Sarah D. Culbertson Memorial Hospital, Rushville, IL, p. A208
WISE, Elizabeth, FACHE, MSN, President and Chief Executive Officer, University of Maryland Upper Chesapeake Medical Center, Bel Air, MD, p. A302
WISE, Jennifer
Chief Nursing Officer, Ochsner St. Mary, Morgan City, LA, p. A289
Hospital Administrator, Chief Nursing Officer, Ochsner St. Mary, Morgan City, LA, p. A289
WISE, Josh, Director Information Technology, Lawrence Memorial Hospital, Walnut Ridge, AR, p. A54
WISE, Kim, Director Human Resources, Bronson South Haven Hospital, South Haven, MI, p. A338
WISE, Lorina, Chief Human Resources Officer, Nationwide Children's Hospital – Toledo, Toledo, OH, p. A504
WISE, Teresa, R.N., Chief Nursing Officer, Mena Regional Health System, Mena, AR, p. A50
WISE, Timothy, Director, Information Technology, Wellstone Regional Hospital, Jeffersonville, IN, p. A221
WISEMAN, Josh, Chief Financial Officer, Portland Hcs, Portland, OR, p. A530
WISEMANN, Jacob, Chief Financial Officer, Parkland Medical Center, Derry, NH, p. A414
WISEMORE, Donna S, R.N., Vice President and Chief Nursing Officer, Parkview Dekalb Hospital, Auburn, IN, p. A212
WISER, Justin
Chief Financial Officer, Bear River Valley Hospital, Tremonton, UT, p. A670
Chief Financial Officer, Cassia Regional Hospital, Burley, ID, p. A180
Chief Financial Officer, Logan Regional Hospital, Logan, UT, p. A665
WISLER, Tam, Director Human Resources, Columbus Springs Dublin, Dublin, OH, p. A495
WISMANN, Andrea, M.D., Chief of Staff, Southeast Colorado Hospital District, Springfield, CO, p. A113
WISNER, Donna, Chief Financial Officer, Warner Hospital And Health Services, Clinton, IL, p. A192
WISNIESKI, Thomas, FACHE, Director, North Florida/South Georgia Veteran's Health System, Gainesville, FL, p. A132
WISNOSKI, Joseph, Chief Financial Officer, Mather Hospital, Port Jefferson, NY, p. A456

Index of Health Care Professionals

Index of Health Care Professionals / Wissman

WISSMAN, Sheryl, M.D., Chief Medical Officer, Ascension Providence Rochester Hospital, Rochester, MI, p. A336
WISWELL, Ashleigh, Chief Operations Officer, Moore County Hospital District, Dumas, TX, p. A615
WITENSKE, James, Chief Information Officer, Jefferson Hospital, Jefferson Hills, PA, p. A542
WITHAM, Val
Director Health Information, Avera Flandreau Hospital, Flandreau, SD, p. A573
Director of Health Information, Avera Dells Area Hospital, Dell Rapids, SD, p. A573
WITHERSPOON, Lynn, Vice President and Chief Information Officer, Ochsner Medical Center, New Orleans, LA, p. A289
WITKOP, Kimberly, M.D., Chief Medical Officer, Snoqualmie Valley Health, Snoqualmie, WA, p. A695
WITKOWICZ, Victor J, Senior Vice President and Chief Financial Officer, Madonna Rehabilitation Hospital, Lincoln, NE, p. A402
WITMER, Bruce, M.D., Medical Director, Fresno Surgical Hospital, Fresno, CA, p. A64
WITT, Cheryl M, Human Resources Director, Kaiser Permanente Moreno Valley Medical Center, Moreno Valley, CA, p. A78
WITT, David A, Vice President Finances, Houston Methodist Clear Lake Hospital, Houston, TX, p. A626
WITT, Francine, R.N., President and Chief Executive Officer, Effingham Health System, Springfield, GA, p. A171
WITT, Lacey, Director, Chi Health Good Samaritan, Kearney, NE, p. A401
WITT, Laura, Administrator Human Resources, Banner Thunderbird Medical Center, Glendale, AZ, p. A32
WITT, Lori, Site Finance Director, Mercy Health – Marcum And Wallace, Irvine, KY, p. A267
WITT, Sarah, Director Human Resources, Richmond State Hospital, Richmond, IN, p. A226
WITT, Stephen, Chief Executive Officer, College Hospital Cerritos, Cerritos, CA, p. A59
WITT, Ty, M.D., Chief Medical Officer, Lake Chelan Health, Chelan, WA, p. A683
WITTE, Kari, Director Patient Care, Windom Area Health, Windom, MN, p. A357
WITTE, Russell, Director Information Technology, Citizens Medical Center, Victoria, TX, p. A660
WITTHAUS, Patricia, Director Information Services, Valley Regional Hospital, Claremont, NH, p. A414
WITTMAN, Thomas, Chief Information Officer, Uofl Health – Jewish Hospital, Louisville, KY, p. A270
WITTMER, Rebecca, CPA, Chief Financial Officer, Greene County General Hospital, Linton, IN, p. A222
WITTWER, Julie, Chief Financial Officer, Christus Surgical Hospital, Corpus Christi, TX, p. A608
WLEKLINSKI, Maria, Chief Nursing Officer, Siloam Springs Regional Hospital, Siloam Springs, AR, p. A53
WODARZ, Christopher A., Chief, Resource Management Division, Tripler Army Medical Center, Honolulu, HI, p. A176
WODICKA, Mary Jo, Vice President Human Resources, Ascension All Saints, Racine, WI, p. A720
WOELKERS, Joe, Executive Vice President and Chief Staff, UT Health North Campus Tyler, Tyler, TX, p. A659
WOELTJEN, Bill, Chief Financial Officer, Sarasota Memorial Hospital – Sarasota, Sarasota, FL, p. A150
WOEN, Linda, Director Human Resources, Yuma Rehabilitation Hospital, An Affiliation of Encompass Health And Yuma Regional Medical Center, Yuma, AZ, p. A42
WOHLFARDT, Diana, Director Human Resources, Nashville General Hospital, Nashville, TN, p. A590
WOHLFORD, Steve, Chief Operating Officer, Johnson Memorial Hospital, Franklin, IN, p. A217
WOHLMAN, John, Manager Information Systems, Shoshone Medical Center, Kellogg, ID, p. A181
WOJNO, Kathy, R.N., MSN, Chief Executive Officer, Monrovia Memorial Hospital, Monrovia, CA, p. A78
WOJTALEWICZ, Jeanette, Chief Financial Officer, Chi Health Mercy Council Bluffs, Council Bluffs, IA, p. A233
WOLAK, Robert, Chief Information Resource Management Service, G.V. (Sonny) Montgomery Department of Veterans Affairs Medical Center, Jackson, MS, p. A364
WOLD, Lynn, Chief Executive Officer, Burgess Health Center, Onawa, IA, p. A241
WOLESKE, Chris, President and Chief Executive Officer, Bellin Hospital, Green Bay, WI, p. A712
WOLF, Chris, Director Information Technology, Clay County Medical Center, Clay Center, KS, p. A247
WOLF, Gregory A, Director Information Systems, Shriners Hospitals for Children–Honolulu, Honolulu, HI, p. A176
WOLF, Heather
Manager Human Resources, Employee Health, Information Technology, Support Services, Mercyone Newton Medical Center, Newton, IA, p. A241
Manager Human Resources, Employee Health, InformationTechnology, Support Servicess, Mercyone Newton Medical Center, Newton, IA, p. A241
WOLF, Jack, Vice President Information Systems, Montefiore Medical Center, New York, NY, p. A449
WOLF, Justin, Chief Executive Officer, Memorial Community Health, Aurora, NE, p. A397
WOLF, Marc, Assistant Vice President Human Resources, St. Barnabas Hospital, New York, NY, p. A452
WOLF, Randall, Vice President Finance, Mercy Hospital Perry, Perryville, MO, p. A382
WOLF, Robin, Chief Nursing Officer, Pam Specialty Hospital of Las Vegas, Las Vegas, NV, p. A410
WOLF, Sherry, R.N., Chief Nursing Office, RST, Mayo Clinic Hospital – Rochester, Rochester, MN, p. A353
WOLF, Stephanne, Chief Nursing Officer, Morris County Hospital, Council Grove, KS, p. A248
WOLF, Steven, D.O., Chief of Staff, Shriners Hospitals for Children, Galveston, TX, p. A621
WOLF, Tricia, Director Information Technology, Oss Health, York, PA, p. A558
WOLFE, Anita, Chief Nurse Executive, Multicare Tacoma General Hospital, Tacoma, WA, p. A697
WOLFE, Brian, Chief of Staff, Allen County Regional Hospital, Iola, KS, p. A251
WOLFE, Cathy Allyson, Vice President Patient Care and Chief Nursing Officer, Parkview Wabash Hospital, Wabash, IN, p. A228
WOLFE, Darryl
Chief Executive Officer, Olympic Medical Center, Port Angeles, WA, p. A693
Chief Operating Officer, Olympic Medical Center, Port Angeles, WA, p. A693
WOLFE, Jamie, Chief Financial Officer, Bradley County Medical Center, Warren, AR, p. A54
WOLFE, John, Chief Financial Officer, Gundersen Saint Elizabeth's Hospital & Clinics, Wabasha, MN, p. A356
WOLFE, Lisa, Chief Operating Officer, Guthrie County Hospital, Guthrie Center, IA, p. A237
WOLFE, Lois, Director Human Resources, Geisinger Community Medical Center, Scranton, PA, p. A554
WOLFE, Phillip. Vice President of Professional Operations, PIH Health Good Samaritan Hospital, Los Angeles, CA, p. A74
WOLFE, Phillip H.
Market Chief Executive Officer, Kindred Hospital–La Mirada, La Mirada, CA, p. A68
Market Chief Executive Officer, Kindred Hospital–Westminster, Westminster, CA, p. A101
WOLFE, Scott A., Chief Financial Officer, Piedmont Fayette Hospital, Fayetteville, GA, p. A164
WOLFE, Sean
Interim Chief Executive Officer, Chadron Community Hospital And Health Services, Chadron, NE, p. A398
Vice President Finance and Chief Financial Officer, Community Hospital, Mccook, NE, p. A402
WOLFE, Stephen A., President and Chief Executive Officer, Indiana Regional Medical Center, Indiana, PA, p. A542
WOLFE, Teresa E, Manager Human Resources, Kansas Heart Hospital, Wichita, KS, p. A261
WOLFF, David, Director Information Technology, Newberry County Memorial Hospital, Newberry, SC, p. A569
WOLFF, Patrice P
Director Information Services, Westfields Hospital And Clinic, New Richmond, WI, p. A718
Director Management Information Systems, Amery Hospital And Clinic, Amery, WI, p. A707
WOLFGANG, Tony, Chief Financial Officer, Coatesville Veterans Affairs Medical Center, Coatesville, PA, p. A537
WOLK, Helene, Senior Vice President Operations and Chief Operating Officer, Englewood Health, Englewood, NJ, p. A421
WOLLEN, Allison Marie, Chief Human Resources Officer, Wynn Hospital, Utica, NY, p. A460
WOLTEMATH, Kelli, D.O., Chief Medical Staff, George C. Grap. Community Hospital, Hamburg, IA, p. A237
WOLTHER, Eunice, Public Information Officer, Colorado Mental Health Institute At Pueblo, Pueblo, CO, p. A112
WOLTHUIZEN, Dianne, Director Human Resources, Sanford Sheldon Medical Center, Sheldon, IA, p. A243
WOLZ, John, M.D., Chief Medical Staff, Yuma District Hospital, Yuma, CO, p. A114
WOMACK, Heather, Chief Executive Officer, Houston Physicians Hospital, Webster, TX, p. A661
WOMACK, James, Interim Administrator, Archbold Brooks, Quitman, GA, p. A169
WOMACK, Maureen, Chief Executive Officer, Bakersfield Behavioral Healthcare Hospital, Bakersfield, CA, p. A56
WONG, Anne Marie, M.D., Chief Medical Officer, Harbor Regional Health, Aberdeen, WA, p. A687
WONG, Art, Chief Financial Officer, Heritage Oaks Hospital, Sacramento, CA, p. A86
WONG, Bryan, M.D., Medical Director, Ventura County Medical Center, Ventura, CA, p. A100
WONG, Davies, M.D., Medical Director, Kindred Hospital–San Diego, San Diego, CA, p. A89
WONG, Dionne, Vice President and Chief Human Resources Officer, Broward Health Medical Center, Fort Lauderdale, FL, p. A131
WONG, Karen, Chief Human Resources Officer, George L. Mee Memorial Hospital, King City, CA, p. A68
WONG, Lily, Director Psychiatry, JPS Health Network, Fort Worth, TX, p. A619
WONG, Philip
PsyD, Chief Executive Officer, Gateways Hospital And Mental Health Center, Los Angeles, CA, p. A72
PsyD, Chief Operating Officer, Gateways Hospital And Mental Health Center, Los Angeles, CA, p. A72
WONG, Wesley, M.D., Acting Vice President Medical and Academic Affairs, Community Hospital North, Indianapolis, IN, p. A219
WONNACOTT, Matthew, M.D., Chief Medical Officer, Barton Memorial Hospital, South Lake Tahoe, CA, p. A96
WONSER, Matt, Director, Information Services, Providence Regional Medical Center Everett, Everett, WA, p. A689
WOOD, Aaron C., President, Sanpete Valley Hospital, Mount Pleasant, UT, p. A666
WOOD, Bud, Chief Human Resources Officer, Ascension Saint Thomas Hospital, Nashville, TN, p. A590
WOOD, Clyde, Chief Executive Officer, Poplar Bluff Regional Medical Center, Poplar Bluff, MO, p. A382
WOOD, David P., FACHE, Medical Center Director, Boise Va Medical Center, Boise, ID, p. A179
WOOD, Drew, Director Information Technology, Eureka Springs Hospital, Eureka Springs, AR, p. A45
WOOD, Jim
Chief Administrative Officer, Confluence Health Hospital – Central Campus, Wenatchee, WA, p. A698
Chief Human Resources Officer, Confluence Health Hospital – Mares Campus, Wenatchee, WA, p. A698
WOOD, Joann, M.D., Chief Medical Officer, Baptist Memorial Hospital–Desoto, Southaven, MS, p. A369
WOOD, Joseph, Vice President and Chief Information Officer, Long Island Community Hospital, Patchogue, NY, p. A455
WOOD, Joyce, Vice President Organizational Improvement and Chief Nursing Officer, Riverview Health, Noblesville, IN, p. A225
WOOD, Mellissa, Chief Operating Officer, Chief Nursing Officer, Mercyone Clinton Medical Center, Clinton, IA, p. A233
WOOD, Michael, Chief Executive Officer, Mena Regional Health System, Mena, AR, p. A50
WOOD, Nicholas, Administrator, Piedmont Mcduffie, Thomson, GA, p. A172
WOOD, Phillip E. Jr, Chief Information Officer, Cap. Fear Valley Medical Center, Fayetteville, NC, p. A468
WOOD, Richard, Chief Financial Officer, AHMC Seton Medical Center, Daly City, CA, p. A61
WOOD, Sandy, MSN, R.N., Vice President Patient Services and Chief Nursing Officer, Ohiohealth O'Bleness Hospital, Athens, OH, p. A485
WOOD, Tina
Chief Operating Officer, Dmc Harper University Hospital, Detroit, MI, p. A325
Chief Operations Officer, Dmc Detroit Receiving Hospital & University Health Center, Detroit, MI, p. A325
WOOD, Troy, Chief Executive Officer, Lakeview Hospital, Bountiful, UT, p. A664
WOOD, William, M.D., Vice President Medical Affairs, St. Josep. Hospital, Bangor, ME, p. A295
WOODALL, Lois, Director Human Resources, Lighthouse Behavioral Health Hospital, Conway, SC, p. A565
WOODARD, Andy, President and Chief Executive Officer, Forrest General Hospital, Hattiesburg, MS, p. A363
WOODARD, James, Chief Nursing Officer, St. Thomas More Hospital, Canon City, CO, p. A104
WOODARD, Victor, Manager Information Technology, Dodge County Hospital, Eastman, GA, p. A163
WOODCOCK, Brenda
President, Bon Secours – Southern Virginia Medical Center, Emporia, VA, p. A675
President, Bon Secours – Southside Medical Center, Petersburg, VA, p. A681
WOODFORK, Tammy J., Corporate Director Human Resources, Adventist Healthcare Fort Washington Medical Center, Fort Washington, MD, p. A304
WOODHOUSE, Janice, Director of Nursing, Missouri River Medical Center, Fort Benton, MT, p. A392
WOODIN, Josep. L., President and Chief Executive Officer, Copley Hospital, Morrisville, VT, p. A672

A1010 Index of Health Care Professionals

Index of Health Care Professionals / Wuenschel

Index of Health Care Professionals

WOODROW, Victoria, Chief Executive Officer, Hamilton Memorial Hospital District, Mcleansboro, IL, p. A201
WOODRUFF, John, R.N., Director of Nursing, Trinity Medical, Ferriday, LA, p. A282
WOODRUFF, Kathy, R.N., MSN, Chief Nursing Officer, Marshall Medical Center North, Guntersville, AL, p. A20
WOODRUFF, Stephen, M.D., Chief Medical Officer, Nea Baptist Memorial Hospital, Jonesboro, AR, p. A48
WOODS, Bob, Chief Information Officer, Stanford Health Care Tri–Valley, Pleasanton, CA, p. A83
WOODS, Brian, Human Resources Director, Andalusia Health, Andalusia, AL, p. A15
WOODS, Cheryl, Chief Nursing Officer, Slidell Memorial Hospital East, Slidell, LA, p. A293
WOODS, Dan, Chief Executive Officer, El Camino Health, Mountain View, CA, p. A79
WOODS, Dillon, Director Human Resources, Jacksonville Memorial Hospital, Jacksonville, IL, p. A199
WOODS, Fred, Chief Financial Officer, The Bridgeway, North Little Rock, AR, p. A51
WOODS, Gina F., Chief Nursing Officer, Ohiohealth Southeastern Medical Center, Cambridge, OH, p. A487
WOODS, Josh, Director Information Systems, Camden Clark Medical Center, Parkersburg, WV, p. A703
WOODS, Julia, MSN, Vice President and Chief Nursing Officer, Saint Luke's South Hospital, Overland Park, KS, p. A257
WOODS, Marc Anthony, Chief Nursing Officer for Behavioral Health, Eastern State Hospital, Lexington, KY, p. A268
WOODS, Matthew, Vice President Finance, Winchester Hospital, Winchester, MA, p. A320
WOODS, Rashawn, Vice President Human Resources, Barlow Respiratory Hospital, Los Angeles, CA, p. A71
WOODS, Rebecca, Chief Information Officer, The University of Vermont Health Network Porter Medical Center, Middlebury, VT, p. A671
WOODS, Regetta, Chief Nursing Officer and Chief Clinical Officer, Riverbridge Specialty Hospital, Vidalia, LA, p. A294
WOODS, Trina, Administrator, Noland Hospital Anniston, Anniston, AL, p. A15
WOODSON, Leslie, Chief Nursing Officer, Mesa View Regional Hospital, Mesquite, NV, p. A411
WOODSON, Stephen, D.O., Chief of Staff, Haskell Regional Hospital, Stigler, OK, p. A521
WOODWARD, Kenyon, Chief Information Officer, Boone County Health Center, Albion, NE, p. A397
WOODWARD, Martin D, Director Acute Care Services, Larry B. Zieverink, Sr. Alcoholism Treatment Center, Raleigh, NC, p. A474
WOODWARD, Martin D., Director Acute Care Services, Larry B. Zieverink, Sr. Alcoholism Treatment Center, Raleigh, NC, p. A474
WOODWARD, Russell, M.D., Chief Medical Officer, Methodist Hospital, San Antonio, TX, p. A650
WOODWORTH, Connie, Vice President Finance, Beverly Hospital, Beverly, MA, p. A309
WOODY, Edward L., FACHE, Associate Medical Center Director, Veterans Health Care System of The Ozarks, Fayetteville, AR, p. A46
WOOLLEY, Diane, Senior Vice President, Chief Human Resources Officer, White Plains Hospital Center, White Plains, NY, p. A462
WOOLLEY, Russell, President and Chief Executive Officer, Mercy Medical Center, Roseburg, OR, p. A531
WOOLLEY, Sheila, R.N., M.P.H., Vice President, Patient Care Services, Wentworth–Douglass Hospital, Dover, NH, p. A414
WOOLSTENHULME, Daren, Chief Financial Officer, Salt Lake Behavioral Health, Salt Lake City, UT, p. A669
WOOTTON, Aaron, Vice President, Health Information Systems and Chief Information Officer, Henry Ford Jackson Hospital, Jackson, MI, p. A331
WORD, Jenni, R.N., Chief Nursing Officer, Wallowa Memorial Hospital, Enterprise, OR, p. A526
WORDEN, Connie, Chief Human Resources Officer, Fountain Valley Regional Hospital And Medical Center, Fountain Valley, CA, p. A64
WORDEN, Ian, Interim Chief Executive Officer, Bartlett Regional Hospital, Juneau, AK, p. A28
WORDEN, John, Interim Administrator, University of Kansas Health System Great Bend Campus, Great Bend, KS, p. A250
WORDEN, Kieth Anne, Director Human Resources, Mildred Mitchell–Bateman Hospital, Huntington, WV, p. A701
WORK, Michelle, Chief Executive Officer, Perimeter Behavioral Hospital of Arlington, Arlington, TX, p. A597
WORKMAN, Donovan, Director Human Capital Management, Appalachian Behavioral Healthcare, Athens, OH, p. A485
WORKMAN, Madison, Chief Operating Officer, HCA Florida University Hospital, Davie, FL, p. A129
WORRELL, James W, Chief Financial Officer, Pioneers Medical Center, Meeker, CO, p. A112
WORS, Patricia Ann., Chief Executive Officer, KPC Promise Hospital of Overland Park, Overland Park, KS, p. A257
WORSLEY, Thomas, Chief Executive Officer, Monument Health Spearfish Hospital, Spearfish, SD, p. A577
WORSOWICZ, Gregory, M.D., Medical Director, Rusk Rehabilitation Hospital, Columbia, MO, p. A374
WORTHAM, Turner, Chief Financial Officer, Grand Strand Medical Center, Myrtle Beach, SC, p. A569
WORTHINGTON, Suzanne A, President, Orlando Health Orlando Regional Medical Center, Orlando, FL, p. A144
WORTHLEY, Ronnette, Manager Human Resource, Nemaha Valley Community Hospital, Seneca, KS, p. A260
WORTHY, David, M.D., Vice President and Chief Medical Officer, Baptist Health Corbin, Corbin, KY, p. A264
WOZNIAK, Gregory, President and Chief Operating Officer, Holy Redeemer Hospital, Meadowbrook, PA, p. A545
WRAALSTAD, Kimber L., FACHE, Chief Executive Officer and Administrator, North Shore Health, Grand Marais, MN, p. A347
WRAGGE, Jean, Chief Nursing Officer, Limestone Medical Center, Groesbeck, TX, p. A623
WRATCHFORD, R. Austin, Chief Operating Officer, Parkview Regional Hospital, Mexia, TX, p. A639
WRAY, Charlotte, MSN, R.N., President, Mercy Health – St. Josep. Warren Hospital, Warren, OH, p. A506
WRAY, Dean, Vice President Finance, Southern Ohio Medical Center, Portsmouth, OH, p. A502
WRAY, Kelli, Chief Nursing Officer, UCLA West Valley Medical Center, Los Angeles, CA, p. A75
WRAY, Thomas, Director Information, Geisinger–Bloomsburg Hospital, Bloomsburg, PA, p. A535
WREN, Brian, Chief Executive Officer, Lawton Indian Hospital, Lawton, OK, p. A514
WREN, Jason
FACHE, Chief Executive Officer, Medical City Alliance, Fort Worth, TX, p. A619
FACHE, Chief Executive Officer, Medical City Decatur, Decatur, TX, p. A613
FACHE, President and Chief Executive Officer, Medical City Decatur, Decatur, TX, p. A613
FACHE, President and Chief Executive Officer, Medical City Denton, Denton, TX, p. A614
WREN, Kristine, M.D., Chief Medical Director, Community Memorial Hospital, Redfield, SD, p. A576
WREN, Kyle, Chief Executive Officer, Rangely District Hospital, Rangely, CO, p. A113
WREN, Mark A, M.D., Medical Director, Encompass Health Rehabilitation Hospital of Texarkana, Texarkana, TX, p. A657
WREN, Timothy, Chief Financial Officer, Abbeville Area Medical Center, Abbeville, SC, p. A562
WRIGHT, Ann L, R.N., MSN, Assistant Central Delivery System CNO, Presbyterian Hospital, Albuquerque, NM, p. A433
WRIGHT, April, Human Resources Officer, Collingsworth General Hospital, Wellington, TX, p. A661
WRIGHT, Birch G., Chief Operating Officer and Administrator, Washington Regional Medical System, Fayetteville, AR, p. A46
WRIGHT, Brady, Information Technology Network Administrator, Washington County Hospital, Chatom, AL, p. A17
WRIGHT, Calvin, Chief Information Officer, Hutchinson Regional Medical Center, Hutchinson, KS, p. A251
WRIGHT, Carlene, Chief Financial Officer, KPC Promise Hospital of Amarillo, Amarillo, TX, p. A596
WRIGHT, Carol, Chief Nursing Officer, Alliancehealth Madill, Madill, OK, p. A514
WRIGHT, Charles, Chief Financial Officer, Ashe Memorial Hospital, Jefferson, NC, p. A471
WRIGHT, Chris, Chief Executive Officer and Chief Nursing Officer, Purcell Municipal Hospital, Purcell, OK, p. A520
WRIGHT, Connie, Vice President Human Resources, Scottish Rite for Children, Dallas, TX, p. A612
WRIGHT, Creighton, M.D., Vice President Medical Administration, Mercy Health – West Hospital, Cincinnati, OH, p. A489
WRIGHT, Daniel, Director Information Technology, Saint Alphonsus Medical Center – Nampa, Nampa, ID, p. A182
WRIGHT, Dawn
Vice President Human Resources, UPMC Muncy, Muncy, PA, p. A546
Vice President Human Resources, UPMC Wellsboro, Wellsboro, PA, p. A557
WRIGHT, Dustin, Chief Executive Officer, Floyd Valley Healthcare, Le Mars, IA, p. A239
WRIGHT, Ellen, Chief Executive Officer, Whitesburg Arh Hospital, Whitesburg, KY, p. A275
WRIGHT, Fran, Director of Nursing, Billings Clinic Broadwater, Townsend, MT, p. A396
WRIGHT, Jeffery
Chief Executive Officer, Select Specialty Hospital–Tri Cities, Bristol, TN, p. A579
Chief Financial Officer, Dmc Sinai–Grace Hospital, Detroit, MI, p. A325
WRIGHT, Jennifer
Vice President Human Resources, Christus St. Michael Rehabilitation Hospital, Texarkana, TX, p. A656
Vice President Operations, Christus St. Michael Health System, Texarkana, TX, p. A656
WRIGHT, Jim, Interim Chief Financial Officer, St. James Hospital, Hornell, NY, p. A444
WRIGHT, Joe, Chief Executive Officer, Eastland Memorial Hospital, Eastland, TX, p. A615
WRIGHT, Julie M, Director Human Resources, Ridgeview Psychiatric Hospital And Center, Oak Ridge, TN, p. A591
WRIGHT, Kenneth Chad, Chief Financial Officer, Webster County Memorial Hospital, Webster Springs, WV, p. A705
WRIGHT, Kimberly, Executive Director, Nursing and Staff Development, Loretto Hospital, Chicago, IL, p. A190
WRIGHT, Krista, Director Human Resources, Indiana University Health Frankfort, Frankfort, IN, p. A217
WRIGHT, Kyle, Management Information System Director, Doctors' Memorial Hospital, Perry, FL, p. A147
WRIGHT, Linda, Director Information, Ottawa County Health Center, Minneapolis, KS, p. A255
WRIGHT, Mark, Vice President, Aultman Hospital, Canton, OH, p. A487
WRIGHT, Mary
Senior Vice President, Patient Services, Torrance Memorial Medical Center, Torrance, CA, p. A98
Vice President Nursing Services and Chief Nursing Officer, Guthrie Cortland Regional Medical Center, Cortland, NY, p. A441
WRIGHT, Mary Lynne, R.N., President, Huntsville Hospital, Huntsville, AL, p. A21
WRIGHT, Nancy, M.D., Chief Medical Staff, Alta Vista Regional Hospital, Las Vegas, NM, p. A435
WRIGHT, Peter J., FACHE, Chief Executive Officer, Northwestern Medical Center, Saint Albans, VT, p. A672
WRIGHT, Philoron A. II, FACHE, Chief Executive Officer, Memorial Regional Hospital, Hollywood, FL, p. A133
WRIGHT, Rory, M.D., President Medical Staff, Orthopaedic Hospital of Wisconsin, Glendale, WI, p. A711
WRIGHT, Sandrea, Chief Executive Officer, Ashland Health Center, Ashland, KS, p. A246
WRIGHT, Sharon, R.N., Vice President and Chief Nursing Officer, Baptist Health Hardin, Elizabethtown, KY, p. A265
WRIGHT, Stephanie, Director Human Resources Management, Jennifer Moreno Department of Veterans Affairs Medical Center, San Diego, CA, p. A88
WRIGHT, Stuart M., CPA, Chief Financial Officer, Upstate University Hospital, Syracuse, NY, p. A460
WRIGHT, Tom, Director Human Resources, Kindred Hospital Riverside, Perris, CA, p. A83
WRIGHT, Toni, Director Human Resources, Bridgepoint Continuing Care Hospital – Capitol Hill, Washington, DC, p. A123
WRIGHT, Trevor G.
Chief Executive Officer, Loma Linda University Children's Hospital, Loma Linda, CA, p. A70
Chief Executive Officer, Loma Linda University Medical Center, Loma Linda, CA, p. A70
Chief Executive Officer, Loma Linda University Medical Center–Murrieta, Murrieta, CA, p. A79
WRIGHT–WHITAKER, Ruth, Director Information Services, Chi Memorial Hospital – Georgia, Fort Oglethorpe, GA, p. A164
WRINN, Denise, Vice President Finance and Chief Financial Officer, Guthrie Cortland Regional Medical Center, Cortland, NY, p. A441
WROBLEWSKI, Edmund
M.D., Vice President Medical Affairs and Chief Medical Officer, Goleta Valley Cottage Hospital, Santa Barbara, CA, p. A94
M.D., Vice President Medical Affairs and Chief Medical Officer, Santa Barbara Cottage Hospital, Santa Barbara, CA, p. A94
M.D., Vice President Medical Affairs and Chief Medical Officer, Santa Ynez Valley Cottage Hospital, Solvang, CA, p. A96
WROGG, Frank, Director Information Technology, Mayo Clinic Health System – Red Cedar In Menomonie, Menomonie, WI, p. A716
WU, Kenneth, M.D., Medical Director, Kessler Marlton Rehabilitation, Marlton, NJ, p. A423
WUCHTER, Greg, Chief Executive Officer, Pam Specialty Hospital of New Braunfels, New Braunfels, TX, p. A641
WUENSCHEL, Diedra, D.O., President Medical Staff, Coryell Health, Gatesville, TX, p. A622

Index of Health Care Professionals / Wunderwald

WUNDERWALD, Wendie, R.N., Vice President Patient Care Services, Samaritan Lebanon Community Hospital, Lebanon, OR, p. A528
WURTZEL, Leann, Director Human Resources, Mayo Clinic Health System – Red Cedar In Menomonie, Menomonie, WI, p. A716
WYATT, Christy, R.N., Interim Chief Nursing Officer, Jackson Parish Hospital, Jonesboro, LA, p. A284
WYATT, Crystal, Chief Financial Officer, Brodstone Memorial Hospital, Superior, NE, p. A406
WYDICK, Sue, Director Human Resources, Ohio County Hospital, Hartford, KY, p. A267
WYER, Jolena, R.N., Chief Nursing Officer, Oklahoma Center for Orthopaedic And Multi-Specialty Surgery, Oklahoma City, OK, p. A518
WYERS, Michael, Chief Financial Officer, HCA Florida Trinity Hospital, Trinity, FL, p. A153
WYLER, Allison, Presicent, Advocate Lutheran General Hospital, Park Ridge, IL, p. A205
WYLIE, Eugene, Chief Human Resources Officer, Jerry L. Pettis Memorial Veterans' Hospital, Loma Linda, CA, p. A70
WYLIE, Patrick, Director Information Systems, Petaluma Valley Hospital, Petaluma, CA, p. A83
WYMAN, David, Presicent and Chief Executive Officer, Gracie Square Hospital, New York, NY, p. A448
WYMER, Melanie, Director Human Resources, Highland District Hospital, Hillsboro, OH, p. A497
WYNN, Katherine, Director Human Resource, Oklahoma Heart Hospital, Oklahoma City, OK, p. A518
WYNN, Leanna, Affiliate Vice President and Chief Nursing Officer, Jacksonville Memorial Hospital, Jacksonville, IL, p. A199
WYNN, Paige
  Chief Executive Officer, Dorminy Medical Center, Fitzgerald, GA, p. A164
  Chief Financial Officer, Dorminy Medical Center, Fitzgerald, GA, p. A164
WYNNE, David, President Medical Staff, Grandview Medical Center, Birmingham, AL, p. A16
WYNNE, Scott, Chief Information Officer Director, Bleckley Memorial Hospital, Cochran, GA, p. A160
WYSE, Debbie, Controller, Quillen Rehabilitation Hospital, A Joint Venture of Ballad Health And Encompass Health, Johnson City, TN, p. A585
WYSONG–HARDER, Alyson, Chief Executive Officer, Heartland Behavioral Health Services, Nevada, MO, p. A381

X

XAVIER, Geralda
  M.D., Chief Medical Officer, Hackettstown Medical Center, Hackettstown, NJ, p. A421
  M.D., Chief Medical Officer, Newton Medical Center, Newton, NJ, p. A426

Y

YAEGER, Eric
  M.D., Chief Medical Officer, Kindred Hospital–Aurora, Aurora, CO, p. A103
  M.D., Medical Director, Kindred Hospital–Denver, Denver, CO, p. A106
YAEGER, Kristy, Vice President, Patient Care Services and Chief Nursing Officer, Hudson Hospital And Clinic, Hudson, WI, p. A713
YAGGY, Lynne, MSN, R.N., Vice President, Chief Nursing Officer, Cox Medical Center Branson, Branson, MO, p. A372
YAKE, Laurie B., Vice President Finance, Aurora Medical Center Kenosha, Kenosha, WI, p. A713
YAKOVENKO, Gene, Director of Finance, Ascension Holy Family, Des Plaines, IL, p. A193
YAKULIS, Paul, MS, R.N., Senior Vice President Human Resources, Lankenau Medical Center, Wynnewood, PA, p. A558
YALLOWITZ, Joseph, M.D., Vice President and Chief Medical Officer, Valley Hospital, Paramus, NJ, p. A426
YAMADA, Jeff, Vice President, Multicare Yakima Memorial Hospital, Yakima, WA, p. A698
YAMADA, Mariko, Chief Executive Officer, Del Amo Behavioral Health System, Torrance, CA, p. A98

YANES, John C.
  President, Chi Saint Josep. Health – Saint Josep. Berea, Berea, KY, p. A263
  President, Chi Saint Josep. Health – Saint Josep. London, London, KY, p. A269
  President, Chi Saint Josep. Health – Saint Josep. Mount Sterling, Mount Sterling, KY, p. A272
YANGA, Ismael David, M.D., Chief Medical Officer, Ascension Brighton Center for Recovery, Brighton, MI, p. A323
YANKTON, Nikki, Director Human Resources, Oakleaf Surgical Hospital, Altoona, WI, p. A707
YANNI, Anthony, M.D., Vice President Medical Affairs, Regional Hospital of Scranton, Scranton, PA, p. A554
YAP, Elvy, Director of Finance, Rush Oak Park Hospital, Oak Park, IL, p. A204
YAP, Winston, M.D., Chief Medical Officer, Carroll County Memorial Hospital, Carrollton, KY, p. A264
YARBOROUGH, Dianne, Director of Information Technology, Baylor Scott & White Medical Center – Centennial, Frisco, TX, p. A621
YARLING, John, M.D., Medical Director, 4C Health, Logansport, IN, p. A222
YARMEL, Jeffrey N, Chief Operating Officer, St. Mary Medical Center, Langhorne, PA, p. A543
YARN, Jayce, Director Information Technology, Logan Health Shelby, Shelby, MT, p. A395
YAROCH, Julie, D.O., President, ProMedica Charles and Virginia Hickman Hospital, Promedica Charles And Virginia Hickman Hospital, Adrian, MI, p. A321
YARTYM, Jennifer, President, Guthrie Cortland Regional Medical Center, Cortland, NY, p. A441
YATES, Ann C, R.N., MSN, Chief Nursing Officer, Ascension St. Vincent Mercy, Elwood, IN, p. A215
YATES, Ann C., R.N., MSN, Administrator and Chief Nursing Officer, Ascension St. Vincent Mercy, Elwood, IN, p. A215
YATES, Brent, Chief Executive Officer, Mercy Rehabilitation Hospital Springfield, Springfield, MO, p. A387
YATES, Brian, Chief Executive Officer, Ashe Memorial Hospital, Jefferson, NC, p. A471
YATES, Jackie, R.N., Nurse Executive, Mississipp. State Hospital, Whitfield, MS, p. A370
YATES, Katie, Chief Financial Officer, South Sunflower County Hospital, Indianola, MS, p. A363
YATES, Ralph
  D.O., Chief Medical Officer, Salem Health West Valley, Dallas, OR, p. A526
  D.O., Chief Medical Officer, Salem Hospital, Salem, OR, p. A532
YATES, Randy, M.D., Chief Medical Officer, Straub Medical Center, Honolulu, HI, p. A176
YATES, Wendy, Chief Executive Officer, Everest Rehabilitation Hospital of Rogers, Rogers, AR, p. A52
YATSATTIE, Clyde, Administrative Officer, U. S. Public Health Service Indian Hospital, Zuni, NM, p. A437
YAWORSKY, Jason, Senior Vice President Information Systems and Chief Information Officer, Olean General Hospital, Olean, NY, p. A455
YAZAWA, Albert, M.D., Regional Medical Director, Leahi Hospital, Honolulu, HI, p. A175
YBARRA, Farra, R.N., Chief Nursing Officer, Coal County General Hospital, Coalgate, OK, p. A511
YEAGER, Angela, Director Information Technology, Palacios Community Medical Center, Palacios, TX, p. A642
YEAGER, Kerry, Director Information Technology, Berwick Hospital Center, Berwick, PA, p. A535
YEAGER, Kevin, Vice President Fiscal Services, Holzer Medical Center – Jackson, Jackson, OH, p. A497
YEATES, Alan H, Vice President Fiscal Services, Wyandot Memorial Hospital, Upper Sandusky, OH, p. A505
YEATES, Diane, FACHE, Chief Operating Officer, Terrebonne General Health System, Houma, LA, p. A283
YEATS, Melania, M.D., Chief Medical Officer, San Juan Regional Medical Center, Farmington, NM, p. A434
YEE, Martin, M.D., Medical Director, Encompass Health Rehabilitation Hospital of East Valley, Mesa, AZ, p. A33
YEHL, Warren, Chief Executive Officer, Eastern New Mexico Medical Center, Roswell, NM, p. A436
YEHLEN, Lorraine, R.N., Vice President Patient Care Services, Dch Regional Medical Center, Tuscaloosa, AL, p. A25
YEITRAKIS, Dawn, Vice President, Nursing, Medstar St. Mary's Hospital, Leonardtown, MD, p. A305
YELKEN, Kari, R.N., Director of Nursing, Franklin County Memorial Hospital, Franklin, NE, p. A399
YERRELL–GARRETT, Lori Ann, Interim Chief Nursing Executive, Saint Elizabeths Hospital, Washington, DC, p. A124
YETTER, Tad A., M.D., President Medical Staff, Mason District Hospital, Havana, IL, p. A197
YEUNG, Christopher A., M.D., Chief of Staff, The Core Institute Specialty Hospital, Phoenix, AZ, p. A37

YEZZO, Phyllis M., R.N., MS, Senior Vice President, Chief Nurse Executive, Westchester Medical Center, Valhalla, NY, p. A461
YI, Brenda, Director Medical Resource Management and Chief Financial Officer, U. S. Air Force Medical Center Keesler, Keesler Afb, MS, p. A364
YIM, Janet, Director Information Services, Trinity Health Livonia Hospital, Livonia, MI, p. A332
YIN, Khin, Medical Director, Rehabilitation Hospital of Rhode Island, North Smithfield, RI, p. A560
YINGLING, Barbara, R.N., Senior Vice President Patient Care Services and Chief Nursing Officer, Cleveland Clinic Mercy Hospital, Canton, OH, p. A487
YITBAREK, Ariam Gebrehiwot, Chief Nursing Officer, Medstar Washington Hospital Center, Washington, DC, p. A124
YITTA, Prasad, M.D., Medical Director, River Hospital, Alexandria Bay, NY, p. A438
YOCHELSON, Michael R, M.D., Vice President and Medical Director, Medstar National Rehabilitation Hospital, Washington, DC, p. A123
YOCHUM, Richard E., FACHE, President and Chief Executive Officer, Pomona Valley Hospital Medical Center, Pomona, CA, p. A84
YODER, Joseph
  President, Willamette Valley Region, Legacy Meridian Park Medical Center, Tualatin, OR, p. A533
  President, Willamette Valley Region, Legacy Silverton Medical Center, Silverton, OR, p. A532
YODER, Leslie, Executive Director, Finance, Community Hospital South, Indianapolis, IN, p. A219
YODER, Zachary, Chief Nursing Officer, HSHS St. Joseph's Hospital Breese, Breese, IL, p. A187
YOO, George, M.D., Chief Medical Officer, Karmanos Cancer Center, Detroit, MI, p. A326
YOO, Jamie, Chief Executive Officer, Cha Hollywood Presbyterian Medical Center, Los Angeles, CA, p. A72
YOON, Chris, M.D., Medical Director, Encompass Health Rehabilitation Hospital of Bakersfield, Bakersfield, CA, p. A57
YORK, Christopher, FACHE, President, Texas Health Presbyterian Hospital Dallas, Dallas, TX, p. A612
YORK, Don, Vice President and Chief Human Resource Officer, Sky Lakes Medical Center, Klamath Falls, OR, p. A528
YORK, Linda, Director Human Resource, Memorial Hospital of Converse County, Douglas, WY, p. A727
YORK, Russell W, Vice President and Chief Financial Officer, Select Specialty Hospital – Belhaven, Jackson, MS, p. A364
YORK, Scott, Chief Executive Officer, Alaska Psychiatric Institute, Anchorage, AK, p. A27
YOSHII, Brian, Vice President Information Technology and Chief Information Officer, The Queen's Medical Center, Honolulu, HI, p. A176
YOSHIOKA, Lori, Director of Human Resources, Rehabilitation Hospital of The Pacific, Honolulu, HI, p. A176
YOUNADAM, Sandro, M.D., Chief Medical Officer, Ottumwa Regional Health Center, Ottumwa, IA, p. A241
YOUNG, Abby, Chief Nursing Officer, Iowa Specialty Hospital–Clarion, Clarion, IA, p. A232
YOUNG, Anita, Chief Operating Officer, Adventhealth Waterman, Tavares, FL, p. A153
YOUNG, Anthony, Information Services Specialist, Chester Mental Health Center, Chester, IL, p. A188
YOUNG, Barry, Director Human Resources, Western Mental Health Institute, Bolivar, TN, p. A579
YOUNG, Bev, Director Human Resources, Frankfort Regional Medical Center, Frankfort, KY, p. A266
YOUNG, Brandon, Chief Executive Officer, Select Specialty Hospital – Macomb County, Mount Clemens, MI, p. A334
YOUNG, Bryce A
  Chief Operating Officer, Hays Medical Center, Hays, KS, p. A250
  Chief Operating Officer, Pawnee Valley Community Hospital, Larned, KS, p. A253
YOUNG, C. Ray, M.D., Chief Medical Officer, Bourbon Community Hospital, Paris, KY, p. A273
YOUNG, Christine, R.N., Vice President of Patient Services and Chief Nursing Officer, Akron Children's Hospital, Akron, OH, p. A484
YOUNG, Deborah, Superintendent, Big Spring State Hospital, Big Spring, TX, p. A603
YOUNG, Diane, Chief Operating Manager, Incompass Healthcare, Lawrenceburg, IN, p. A222
YOUNG, Duke, Chief Executive Officer, Mimbres Memorial Hospital, Deming, NM, p. A434
YOUNG, Eric
  M.D., Chief of Staff, Veterans Affairs Ann Arbor Healthcare System, Ann Arbor, MI, p. A321

Chief Information Officer, HCA Florida Brandon Hospital, Brandon, FL, p. A127

Chief Operating Officer, Bon Secours Memorial Regional Medical Center, Mechanicsville, VA, p. A679

YOUNG, Eric L, Chief Financial Officer, Selby General Hospital, Marietta, OH, p. A499

YOUNG, Gladys, M.D., Chief of Staff, Logan Health Chester, Chester, MT, p. A390

YOUNG, J Phillip, FACHE, Chief Executive Officer, Baptist Medical Center, San Antonio, TX, p. A648

YOUNG, James
M.D., Chief of Staff, Mcgehee Hospital, Mcgehee, AR, p. A50
Chief Executive Officer, Bolivar Medical Center, Cleveland, MS, p. A361

YOUNG, Jeffrey, Chief Human Resource Officer, South Texas Veterans Healthcare System Audie L Murphy, San Antonio, TX, p. A651

YOUNG, Jennifer, Chief Executive Officer, Lakeland Community Hospital, Haleyville, AL, p. A20

YOUNG, Lisa
CPA, Chief Financial Officer, Continuecare Hospital At Baptist Health Corbin, Corbin, KY, p. A264
CPA, Chief Financial Officer, Continuecare Hospital At Hendrick Medical Center, Abilene, TX, p. A595

YOUNG, Martha, Director Human Resources, Cumberland County Hospital, Burkesville, KY, p. A264

YOUNG, Mary, Director Human Resources, Colorado Mental Health Institute At Pueblo, Pueblo, CO, p. A112

YOUNG, Mary C., Chief Executive Officer, Moccasin Bend Mental Health Institute, Chattanooga, TN, p. A580

YOUNG, Mary Lou, Chief Nursing Officer, Continuecare Hospital At Baptist Health Paducah, Paducah, KY, p. A273

YOUNG, Matthew S., Chief Medical Officer, Texarkana Emergency Center & Hospital, Texarkana, TX, p. A657

YOUNG, Michael, Chief Financial Officer, Mad River Community Hospital, Arcata, CA, p. A56

YOUNG, Pam, Director Human Resources, Davis County Hospital And Clinics, Bloomfield, IA, p. A231

YOUNG, Patty, R.N., Chief Nursing Officer, Ashland Health Center, Ashland, KS, p. A246

YOUNG, Pete, Interim Chief Financial Officer, Community Hospital, Grand Junction, CO, p. A108

YOUNG, Rhonda, Human Resource Director, Encompass Health Rehabilitation Hospital of Gadsden, Gadsden, AL, p. A19

YOUNG, Richard T., FACHE, Director, Walter P. Reuther Psychiatric Hospital, Westland, MI, p. A340

YOUNG, Sabrina
Administrative Support Director, South Mississipp. State Hospital, Purvis, MS, p. A368
Director, South Mississipp. State Hospital, Purvis, MS, p. A368

YOUNG, Sheila, Vice President Human Resources, Mobile Infirmary Medical Center, Mobile, AL, p. A21

YOUNG, Stephanie
Associate Director, Aleda E. Lutz Department of Veterans Affairs Medical Center, Saginaw, MI, p. A336
Medical Center Director, Charles George Veterans Affairs Medical Center, Asheville, NC, p. A463

YOUNG, Stephen, Chief Executive Officer, Clay County Hospital, Ashland, AL, p. A15

YOUNG, Steve W., Chief Executive Officer, HCA Florida Blake Hospital, Bradenton, FL, p. A126

YOUNG, Terry, Chief Information Officer, Plains Memorial Hospital, Dimmitt, TX, p. A614

YOUNG, Theresa M., Senior Vice President Human Resources, Nemours Children's Hospital, Orlando, FL, p. A144

YOUNG, Tiffany, Chief Financial Officer, Acadia–St. Landry Hospital, Church Point, LA, p. A280

YOUNG, William, Chief Information Officer, Berkshire Medical Center, Pittsfield, MA, p. A317

YOUNG, William A. Jr, President and Chief Executive Officer, Southwest General Health Center, Middleburg Heights, OH, p. A500

YOUNGBLOOD, Carrie, Director of Human Resources, Kittitas Valley Healthcare, Ellensburg, WA, p. A689

YOUNGBLOOD, Erin R, Chief Human Resources Officer, Behavioral Center of Michigan, Warren, MI, p. A340

YOUNGER, Sam, Chief Operating Officer, Tristar Greenview Regional Hospital, Bowling Green, KY, p. A264

YOUNGMAN, Darrell, D.O., Chief Medical Officer, Ascension Via Christi St. Francis, Mulvane, KS, p. A255

YOUREE, Ben, Chief Executive Officer, Tennova North Knoxville Medical Center, Powell, TN, p. A592

YOURTEE, Edward, M.D., Chief Medical Officer, Parkland Medical Center, Derry, NH, p. A414

YOURZEK, Tari, Chief Nursing Officer, Boundary Community Hospital, Bonners Ferry, ID, p. A180

YOUSAITIS, Zoe, Director Human Resources, Eagleville Hospital, Eagleville, PA, p. A538

YOUSO, Michael
Chief Financial Officer, St. Croix Regional Medical Center, St Croix Falls, WI, p. A722
Interim Chief Executive Officer and Chief Financial Officer, St. Croix Regional Medical Center, St Croix Falls, WI, p. A722

YOUSSEF, Moudy, M.D., Chief Medical Officer, Fairchild Medical Center, Yreka, CA, p. A102

YU, Henry
Vice President Finance and Chief Financial Officer, California Pacific Medical Center–Mission Bernal Campus, San Francisco, CA, p. A90
Vice President Finance and Chief Financial Officer, California Pacific Medical Center–Van Ness Campus, San Francisco, CA, p. A90

YUNGMANN, Michael, President and Chief Executive Officer, Mercy Health – Lourdes Hospital, Paducah, KY, p. A273

YUNUSOV, Ed
Chief Information Officer, Creedmoor Psychiatric Center, New York, NY, p. A448
Coordinator Facility Information Center, New York City Children's Center, New York, NY, p. A450

YUST, Randall C.
Chief Financial Officer NCR, Indiana University Health Tipton Hospital, Tipton, IN, p. A228
Chief Operating Officer and Chief Financial Officer, Indiana University Health North Hospital, Carmel, IN, p. A214

Z

ZAAS, David William, M.D., Chief Executive Officer, Musc Health University Medical Center, Charleston, SC, p. A563

ZABALA, Hermelina, MSN, R.N., MSN, RN, Senior Vice President, Patient Care Services and Chief Nursing Officer, St. John's Episcopal Hospital, New York, NY, p. A453

ZABAWSKI, Denise
Chief Information Officer, Nationwide Children's Hospital – Toledo, Toledo, OH, p. A504
Vice President Information Services and Chief Information Officer, Nationwide Children's Hospital, Columbus, OH, p. A492

ZABIELSKI, Gerald C, M.D., Chief Medical Staff, Wright Memorial Hospital, Trenton, MO, p. A387

ZABROWSKI, John, Senior Vice President and Chief Financial Officer, VHC Health, Arlington, VA, p. A673

ZACHARIASEN, Keith, Chief Financial Officer, Wamego Health Center, Wamego, KS, p. A261

ZACHARY, Kevin
R.N., Chief Executive Officer, Kindred Hospital–Aurora, Aurora, CO, p. A103
R.N., Market Chief Executive Officer, Kindred Hospital–Denver, Denver, CO, p. A106

ZACIEWSKI, Gary, R.N., Chief Executive Officer, Advanced Specialty Hospital of Toledo, Toledo, OH, p. A504

ZAFEREO, Carolyn, Chief Accounting Officer, Citizens Medical Center, Victoria, TX, p. A660

ZAFONTE, Ross
D.O., President, Spaulding Hospital for Continuing Medical Care Cambridge, Cambridge, MA, p. A312
D.O., President, Spaulding Rehabilitation Hospital, Charlestown, MA, p. A312
D.O., President, Spaulding Rehabilitation Hospital Cap. Cod, East Sandwich, MA, p. A313

ZAGERMAN, Robert, Chief Financial Officer, Brooke Glen Behavioral Hospital, Fort Washington, PA, p. A540

ZAID, Ahmad, Chief Executive Officer, Atrium Medical Center, Stafford, TX, p. A654

ZAIDI, Syed A., M.D., Chief of Staff, Lauderdale Community Hospital, Ripley, TN, p. A592

ZAIOUR, Nabil, Chief Financial Officer, Dallas Behavioral Healthcare Hospital, Desoto, TX, p. A614

ZAJEC, Doris A., Director Human Resources, Cleveland Clinic South Pointe Hospital, Warrensville Heights, OH, p. A506

ZAJICEK, Tammy, Director of Nursing, Jackson County Hospital District, Edna, TX, p. A616

ZAKAI, Aminadav, M.D., Medical Director, Arbour-Fuller Hospital, Attleboro, MA, p. A309

ZALDIVAR, Rogelio, M.D., Medical Director, Keralty Hospital Miami, Miami, FL, p. A140

ZALESKI, Theodore, M.D., Vice President Clinical Effectiveness, Hackensack Meridian Health Southern Ocean Medical Center, Manahawkin, NJ, p. A423

ZALUD, Nicolette, Customer Site Manager, Mclaren Central Michigan, Mount Pleasant, MI, p. A334

ZALUSKI, Heather, M.D., President Medical Staff, Shodair Children's Hospital, Helena, MT, p. A393

ZAMBRANA, David
Ph.D., R.N., Chief Operating Officer – JHS, Jackson Health System, Miami, FL, p. A140
Ph.D., R.N., Executive Vice President Hospital Operations, Jackson Health System, Miami, FL, p. A140

ZAMBRELLO, Sally, Chief Information Officer, Carondelet St. Joseph's Hospital, Tucson, AZ, p. A40

ZAMORA, Joe, Chief Financial Officer, Riverside University Health System–Medical Center, Moreno Valley, CA, p. A78

ZAMORA DE AGUERO, Hilde, Human Resources Site Director, Baptist Health South Florida, West Kendall Baptist Hospital, Miami, FL, p. A139

ZAMPINI, Maria, Chief Operating Officer, University Medical Center of El Paso, El Paso, TX, p. A617

ZANE, Kristi, Chief Human Resources Officer, Crawford Memorial Hospital, Robinson, IL, p. A207

ZANGER, Albert, Vice President, Chief Financial Officer, University of Maryland Charles Regional Medical Center, La Plata, MD, p. A305

ZANI, Carl, Chief Technology Director, Memorial Health, Marysville, OH, p. A499

ZANIS, Tina, Director Information Systems, Lehigh Valley Hospital – Schuylkill, Pottsville, PA, p. A553

ZANNI, David M., Administrator, Adena Pike Medical Center, Waverly, OH, p. A506

ZANT, Dan, M.D., Chief of Staff, Morgan Medical Center, Madison, GA, p. A167

ZAPLIN, Michael, M.D., Physician Advisor, North Shore Medical Center, Miami, FL, p. A140

ZARAK, Tamie, Director Human Resources, Marshfield Medical Center – Neilsville, Neillsville, WI, p. A718

ZARECKY, Daniel, Chief Executive Officer, Cedar Springs Hospital, Colorado Springs, CO, p. A104

ZAREMA, Claudette A., M.D., Medical Officer, Alaska Psychiatric Institute, Anchorage, AK, p. A27

ZAREMBA, Angela
Chief Executive Officer, Quad Cities Rehabilitation Institute, The, Moline, IL, p. A202
Chief Executive Officer, University of Iowa Health Network Rehabilitation Hospital, Coralville, IA, p. A233

ZAUNER, Mike, Chief Executive Officer/Regional Vice President, Sierra Vista Hospital, Sacramento, CA, p. A87

ZAVALA, Jocelyn, Senior Information Technology Coordinator, Riveredge Hospital, Forest Park, IL, p. A195

ZAVATCHEN, Nancy, Director Information Technology, Cullman Regional Medical Center, Cullman, AL, p. A18

ZAVODNICK, Jacquelyn, M.D., Medical Director, Devereux Children's Behavioral Health Center, Malvern, PA, p. A545

ZAWACKI, Brenda, Chief Operating Manager, Providence Kodiak Island Medical Center, Kodiak, AK, p. A28

ZAWOJSKI, Paula, Regional Director, Human Resources, Ascension Resurrection, Chicago, IL, p. A188

ZDEBLICK, Mick
President/Chief Executive Officer, Community Memorial Hospital – Ventura, Ventura, CA, p. A100
President/Chief Executive Officer, Ojai Valley Community Hospital, Ojai, CA, p. A81

ZDRODOWSKI, Michael, Vice President of Operations and Ambulatory Services, Munson Healthcare Cadillac Hospital, Cadillac, MI, p. A323

ZEBIAN, Ramy, M.D., Chief Medical Officer, Musc Health Black River Medical Center, Cades, SC, p. A562

ZECH, Michelle, Chief Human Resources Officer, Blessing Hospital, Quincy, IL, p. A206

ZEHM, Laura, Vice President and Chief Financial Officer, Community Hospital of The Monterey Peninsula, Monterey, CA, p. A78

ZEIGLER, Michele
Vice President and Chief Information Officer, Wellspan Chambersburg Hospital, Chambersburg, PA, p. A536
Vice President Information Services, Wellspan Waynesboro Hospital, Waynesboro, PA, p. A556

ZEISEL, Henry
Chief Financial Officer, Northern Region, Ascension Alexian Brothers, Elk Grove Village, IL, p. A194
Chief Financial Officer, Northern Region, Ascension St. Alexius, Hoffman Estates, IL, p. A198

ZEITLER, Irvin, D.O., Vice President Medical Affairs, Shannon Medical Center, San Angelo, TX, p. A648

ZEITLER, Jenny, Network Administrator, North Okaloosa Medical Center, Crestview, FL, p. A129

ZELIN, Mira, D.O., Medical Director, Encompass Health Rehabilitation Hospital of Spring Hill, Brooksville, FL, p. A127

ZELL, John R, Chief Financial Officer, OSF St. Josep. Medical Center, Bloomington, IL, p. A186

ZELLER, Paul, Vice President Human Resources, Medstar Southern Maryland Hospital Center, Clinton, MD, p. A303
ZEMAN, Brian, Chief Human Resources, Salem Veterans Affairs Medical Center, Salem, VA, p. A683
ZEMAN, Mark, Chief Information Officer, Upstate University Hospital, Syracuse, NY, p. A460
ZENGER, Andrew, Chief Operating Officer, Medical City Mckinney, Mckinney, TX, p. A638
ZENGOTITA, Jamie, M.D., Chief Medical Staff, Mercy Hospital Cassville, Cassville, MO, p. A373
ZENNA, Rita, R.N., Vice President Patient Care Services, Deborah Heart And Lung Center, Browns Mills, NJ, p. A419
ZENNER, Diana, R.N., Chief Operating Officer, Ventura County Medical Center, Ventura, CA, p. A100
ZENONE, Michael J, Chief Financial Officer, Emerald Coast Behavioral Hospital, Panama City, FL, p. A145
ZEPHIER, Michelle, Human Resource Specialist, U. S. Public Health Service Indian Hospital, Rosebud, SD, p. A576
ZEPS, Joseph, Chief Financial Officer, Tomah Health, Tomah, WI, p. A723
ZEPS, Julie, Vice President Human Resources, Aspirus Medford Hospital & Clinics, Medford, WI, p. A715
ZERINGUE, Christopher, Chief Executive Officer, TMC Bonham Hospital, Bonham, TX, p. A604
ZERINGUE, Rhonda, R.N., Chief Nursing Officer, St. James Parish Hospital, Lutcher, LA, p. A287
ZERRER, Lana, M.D., Chief of Staff, Harry S. Truman Memorial Veterans' Hospital, Columbia, MO, p. A374
ZEVENBERGEN, Glenn, Chief Executive Officer, Hegg Health Center Avera, Rock Valley, IA, p. A242
ZEWE, Jeff S., R.N., President and Chief Executive Officer, Northern Maine Medical Center, Fort Kent, ME, p. A297
ZEYNELOGLU, Nejat, Vice President and Chief Quality Medical Officer, Long Island Community Hospital, Patchogue, NY, p. A455
ZHANG, Jian Q., MS, Chief Executive Officer, Chinese Hospital, San Francisco, CA, p. A90
ZHIRKIN, Georgii, Chief Financial Officer, Incompass Healthcare, Lawrenceburg, IN, p. A222
ZIA, Hasan A.
  President and Chief Executive Officer, Sibley Memorial Hospital, Washington, DC, p. A124
  Vice President of Medical Affairs and Chief Medical Officer, Sibley Memorial Hospital, Washington, DC, p. A124
ZIBARI, Lilit Sarah., Senior Vice President, Area Manager/West Los Angeles, Kaiser Permanente West Los Angeles Medical Center, Los Angeles, CA, p. A73
ZIEGELE, Paul, Chief Financial Officer, Chinese Hospital, San Francisco, CA, p. A90
ZIEGLER, John C, FACHE, Vice President of Operations – Support, Memorial Hospital Belleville, Belleville, IL, p. A186
ZIELINSKI, Sharon
  Chief Information Resource Officer, Veterans Affairs Maryland Health Care System–Baltimore Division, Baltimore, MD, p. A302
  Manager Health Information, Encompass Health Rehabilitation Hospital of Erie, Erie, PA, p. A539
ZIEMER, Cody, Chief Financial Officer, Banner Gateway Medical Center, Gilbert, AZ, p. A31
ZIEMER, Patrick C., Chief Executive Officer, Alvarado Parkway Institute Behavioral Health System, La Mesa, CA, p. A68
ZIEMIANSKI, Karen, R.N., MS, Senior Vice President Nursing, Erie County Medical Center, Buffalo, NY, p. A440
ZIEROLD, Bob, Senior Vice President, Chief Human Resources Officer, Christian Health, Wyckoff, NJ, p. A431
ZIGLOR, Danyale
  Vice President, Wellstar Cobb Hospital, Austell, GA, p. A159
  Vice President, Wellstar Douglas Hospital, Douglasville, GA, p. A163
ZILE, Ron, M.D., Chief of Staff, Highland District Hospital, Hillsboro, OH, p. A497
ZILKOW, Jon, Chief Financial Officer, Southwest Healthcare System, Murrieta, CA, p. A79
ZILLER, Andrew, M.D., Chief Medical Officer, Rose Medical Center, Denver, CO, p. A107
ZILLMAN, Sally E., Interim Vice President, Patient Care Services, Marshfield Medical Center – Weston, Weston, WI, p. A725
ZIMA, Cheryl F, Vice President Human Resources Ministry Health Care, Marshfield Medical Center, Marshfield, WI, p. A715

ZIMMEL, Robert, Senior Vice President Human Resources, St. Luke's University Hospital – Bethlehem Campus, Bethlehem, PA, p. A535
ZIMMER, Amy, Vice President of Patient Care Services and Chief Nursing Executive, Memorial Community Hospital And Health System, Blair, NE, p. A398
ZIMMER, Jan Leann, R.N., MSN, R.N., MS, Chief Nursing Officer, West Tennessee Healthcare Dyersburg Hospital, Dyersburg, TN, p. A582
ZIMMER, Stacey, Chief Financial Officer, Avala, Covington, LA, p. A280
ZIMMERLI, Bert, Executive Vice President and Chief Financial Officer, Sevier Valley Hospital, Richfield, UT, p. A668
ZIMMERLY, Kara, Manager Human Resources, Promedica Bay Park Hospital, Oregon, OH, p. A502
ZIMMERMAN, Aimee, R.N., Chief Executive Officer, Logan County Hospital, Oakley, KS, p. A256
ZIMMERMAN, Anne, Senior Director Patient Care Services and Chief Nursing Officer, Mercy Health – Tiffin Hospital, Tiffin, OH, p. A504
ZIMMERMAN, David, M.D., Chief of Staff, Swain Community Hospital, A Duke Lifepoint Hospital, Bryson City, NC, p. A464
ZIMMERMAN, Don, Director Human Resources, Morris County Hospital, Council Grove, KS, p. A248
ZIMMERMAN, Michael
  Human Resource Officer, OSF Heart of Mary Medical Center, Urbana, IL, p. A210
  Human Resource Officer, OSF Sacred Heart Medical Center, Danville, IL, p. A192
ZIMMERMANN, Wayne, Chief Operating Officer, NYC Health + Hospitals/Elmhurst, New York, NY, p. A451
ZINAMAN, Michael, M.D., Acting Chief Medical Officer, NYC Health + Hospitals/Jacobi, New York, NY, p. A451
ZINK, Jayne, Director of Nursing, Ohio Hospital for Psychiatry, Columbus, OH, p. A492
ZINK, Summer, Chief Financial Officer, Ellinwood District Hospital, Ellinwood, KS, p. A248
ZINKER, Dena, MSN, R.N., Vice President Patient Services, Colquitt Regional Medical Center, Moultrie, GA, p. A169
ZINKULA, Lisa, Chief Financial Officer, Grundy County Memorial Hospital, Grundy Center, IA, p. A236
ZINN, David, M.D., Vice President Medical Affairs, RMC Anniston, Anniston, AL, p. A15
ZINNANTE, David R., Commander, Womack Army Medical Center, Fort Bragg, NC, p. A468
ZINNER, Barbara, Chief Nursing Officer, Cleveland Clinic Marymount Hospital, Garfield Heights, OH, p. A496
ZINNI, Melissa, Chief Financial Officer, Hampton Behavioral Health Center, Westampton, NJ, p. A430
ZINSMEISTER, Mary Sue, Chief Nursing Officer, Rockledge Regional Medical Center, Rockledge, FL, p. A148
ZIOBRO, Ronald, Chief Operating Officer, St. Luke's Easton Campus, Easton, PA, p. A539
ZIOLKOWSKI, David, Chief Executive Officer, Carondelet St. Mary's Hospital, Tucson, AZ, p. A40
ZIRBSER, Glenn, Senior Vice President Finance and Chief Financial Officer, Jefferson Stratford Hospital, Stratford, NJ, p. A428
ZIRGER, Marion, Chief Financial Officer, Minneola District Hospital, Minneola, KS, p. A255
ZIRKELBACH, Mark
  Chief Information Officer, Loma Linda University Children's Hospital, Loma Linda, CA, p. A70
  Chief Information Officer, Loma Linda University Medical Center, Loma Linda, CA, p. A70
  Chief Information Officer, Loma Linda University Medical Center–Murrieta, Murrieta, CA, p. A79
ZIRKLE, Isaiah, Chief Operating Officer, HCA Florida Ocala Hospital, Ocala, FL, p. A143
ZIRKLE, William, Manager Information Systems, Sentara Halifax Regional Hospital, South Boston, VA, p. A684
ZISKIN, Robert, Chief Information Officer, Northport Veterans Affairs Medical Center, Northport, NY, p. A454
ZOCH, Jeremy, President and Chief Executive Officer, Northridge Hospital Medical Center, Los Angeles, CA, p. A74
ZOESCH, Jim, Information Technology Director, Prosser Memorial Health, Prosser, WA, p. A693
ZOGELMAN, Sharon, Director Human Resources, St. Luke Hospital And Living Center, Marion, KS, p. A254

ZOLKIWSKY, Walter R
  M.D., Chief Medical Officer, Reston Hospital Center, Reston, VA, p. A682
  M.D., Chief Medical Officer, Stonesprings Hospital Center, Dulles, VA, p. A675
ZOLTANSKI, Joan, Chief Medical Officer, UCSF Benioff Children's Hospital Oakland, Oakland, CA, p. A81
ZOOK, Aaron, Vice President–Operations, Hannibal Regional Hospital, Hannibal, MO, p. A376
ZORZA, Elizabeth, Assistant Administrator, OSF St. Francis Hospital And Medical Group. Escanaba, MI, p. A326
ZUANICH, Elizabeth
  Chief Financial Officer, Providence Little Company of Mary Medical Center – Torrance, Torrance, CA, p. A98
  Chief Financial Officer, Providence Little Company of Mary Medical Center San Pedro, Los Angeles, CA, p. A75
ZUBAIR, Mohammad, M.D., Chief Hospital Executive, Carepoint Health Bayonne Medical Center, Bayonne, NJ, p. A418
ZUBER, Steven, Vice President, Methodist Jennie Edmundson Hospital, Council Bluffs, IA, p. A234
ZUCCARO, Nicole, Interim Director, Avenir Behavioral Health Center, Surprise, AZ, p. A39
ZUEL, Sally, Vice President Human Resources, Union Hospital, Terre Haute, IN, p. A228
ZUHD, Dajani, M.D., President Medical Staff, Punxsutawney Area Hospital, Punxsutawney, PA, p. A553
ZUKOWSKI, Andrew, Chief Financial Officer, UNC Health Rex, Raleigh, NC, p. A475
ZULIANI, Michael E., Chief Executive Officer, Encompass Health Rehabilitation Hospital of Huntington, Huntington, WV, p. A701
ZUMALT, Ryan, Chief Executive Officer, Bridgepoint Continuing Care Hospital – Capitol Hill, Washington, DC, p. A123
ZUMPANO, Anthony, Chief Financial Officer, Penn Presbyterian Medical Center, Philadelphia, PA, p. A549
ZUMSTEIN, James F., M.D., Chief of Medicine, Jack Hughston Memorial Hospital, Phenix City, AL, p. A24
ZUPKO, Carla, R.N., Chief Nursing Officer, Riverwood Healthcare Center, Aitkin, MN, p. A342
ZUTZ–WICZEK, Sandy, Chief Operating Officer, Welia Health, Mora, MN, p. A351
ZVANUT, Michelle, Vice President Human Resources, Boone Hospital Center, Columbia, MO, p. A374
ZWALLY, Paula, Director Quality Improvement Services and Compliance, Southwest Connecticut Mental Health System, Bridgeport, CT, p. A115
ZWANZIGER, Marcia, Vice President Finance, Huron Regional Medical Center, Huron, SD, p. A574
ZWENG, Thomas
  Executive Vice President and Chief Medical Officer, Novant Health Brunswick Medical Center, Bolivia, NC, p. A464
  Executive Vice President and Chief Medical Officer, Novant Health Charlotte Orthopaedic Hospital, Charlotte, NC, p. A466
  Executive Vice President and Chief Medical Officer, Novant Health Forsyth Medical Center, Winston-Salem, NC, p. A478
  Executive Vice President and Chief Medical Officer, Novant Health Huntersville Medical Center, Huntersville, NC, p. A470
  Executive Vice President and Chief Medical Officer, Novant Health Matthews Medical Center, Matthews, NC, p. A472
  Executive Vice President and Chief Medical Officer, Novant Health Medical Park Hospital, Winston-Salem, NC, p. A478
  Executive Vice President and Chief Medical Officer, Novant Health Presbyterian Medical Center, Charlotte, NC, p. A466
  Executive Vice President and Chief Medical Officer, Novant Health Rowan Medical Center, Salisbury, NC, p. A475
  Executive Vice President and Chief Medical Officer, Novant Health Thomasville Medical Center, Thomasville, NC, p. A470
ZWIEFEL, Laura, Chief Executive officer/Chief Nursing Officer, Hancock County Health System, Britt, IA, p. A231
ZWIEG, Faye, R.N., Vice President and Chief Nursing Officer, Aurora St. Luke's Medical Center, Milwaukee, WI, p. A717
ZWINGER, Glenn, Manager Information Systems Services, VA Puget Sound Healthcare System – Seattle, Seattle, WA, p. A695
ZWOYER, Brian, R.N., Division President, Sentara Halifax Regional Hospital, South Boston, VA, p. A684
ZYCH, Anita, Director of Nursing, Arrowhead Behavioral Health Hospital, Maumee, OH, p. A499

AHA Membership Categories

The American Hospital Association is primarily an organization of hospitals and related institutions. Its object, according to its bylaws, is "to promote high-quality health care and health services for all the people through leadership in the development of public policy, leadership in the representation and advocacy of hospital and health care organization interests, and leadership in the provision of services to assist hospitals and health care organizations in meeting the health care needs of their communities."

Institutional Members

Hospitals or health services organizations or systems which provide a continuum of integrated, community health resources and which include at least one licensed hospital that is owned, leased, managed or religiously sponsored

Institutional members include hospitals, health care systems, integrated delivery systems, and physician hospital organizations (PHOs) and health maintenance organizations (HMOs) wholly or partially owned by or owning a member hospital or system. An Institutional member hospital, health care system or integrated delivery system may, at its discretion and upon approval of a membership application by the Association chief executive officer, extend membership to the health care provider organizations, other than a hospital that it owns, leases, or fully controls.

Freestanding Health Care Provider Organizations

These are health provider organizations, other than registered hospitals, that provide patient care services, including, but not limited to, ambulatory, preventive, rehabilitative, specialty, post–acute and continuing care, as well as physician groups, health insurance services, and staff and group model health maintenance organizations without a hospital component. Freestanding Health Care Provider Organizations members are not owned or controlled by an Institutional member hospital, health care system or integrated delivery system member. They may, however, be part of an organization eligible for, but not holding, Institutional membership.

Other Organizations

This category includes organizations interested in the objectives of the American Hospital Association, but not eligible for Institutional or Freestanding Health Care Provider Organization Membership. Organizations eligible for Other membership shall include, but not be limited to, associations, societies, foundations, corporations, educational and academic institutions, companies, government agencies, international health providers, and organizations having an interest in and a desire to support the objectives of the Association.

Provisional Members

Hospitals that are in the planning or construction stage and that, on completion, will be eligible for institutional membership. Provisional membership may also be granted to applicant institutions that cannot, at present, meet the requirements of Institutional or Freestanding Health Care Provider Organization membership.

Government Institution Group Members

Groups of government hospitals operated by the same unit of government may obtain institutional membership under a group plan. Membership dues are based on a special schedule set forth in the bylaws of the AHA.

Other Institutional Members

U.S. hospitals and hospitals in areas associated with the U.S. that are Institutional members of the American Hospital Association are included in the list of hospitals in section A. Canadian Institutional members of the American Hospital Association are listed below.

Other Institutional Members

Hospitals

Canada

ONTARIO

Renfrew: RENFREW VICTORIA HOSPITAL, 499 Raglan Street North, Zip K7V 1P6, tel. 613/432–4851; Julia Boudreau, President and Chief Executive Officer

Thornhill: SHOULDICE HOSPITAL, 7750 Bayview Avenue, Zip L3T 4A3; tel. 905/889–1125; John Hughes, Chief Administrative Officer

Associated University Programs in Health Administration

IOWA

Iowa City: DEPARTMENT OF HEALTH MANAGEMENT AND POLICY, UNIVERSITY OF IOWA, 105 River Street, N232A CPHB, Zip 52246; tel. 319/384-3830; Keith Mueller, Professor and Head

MARYLAND

Bethesda: NAVY MEDICINE PROFESSIONAL DEVELOPMENT CENTER, Naval Medicine, Education and Training Command, 8901 Wisconsin Avenue, Building 1, Zip 20889-5611; tel. 301/295-1251; Commander DuWayne Griepentrog, Director Administration

TEXAS

San Antonio: ARMY-BAYLOR UNIVERSITY PROGRAM IN HEALTH CARE ADMINISTRATION, 3151 Scott Road, Bldg 2841, Zip 78234-6135; tel. 210/221-6443; Lieutenant Colonel M Nicholas Coppola, Program Director

Sheppard AFB: U.S. AIR FORCE SCHOOL OF HEALTH CARE SCIENCES, Building 1900, MST/114, Academic Library, Zip 76311; tel. 817/851-2511

Hospital Schools of Nursing

PENNSYLVANIA
New Castle: JAMESON HOSPITAL School of Nursing

Other Institutional Members / Preacute and Postacute Care Facilities

Nonhospital Preacute and Postacute Care Facilities

CALIFORNIA
Winterhaven: U. S. PUBLIC HEALTH SERVICE INDIAN HOSPITAL, P O Box 1368, Zip 85366-1368; tel. 760/572-0217; Geniel Harrison, Clinic Director

DELAWARE
Newark: HEALTH CARE CENTER AT CHRISTIANA, 200 Hygeia Drive, Zip 19714; tel. 302/623-0100; Douglas P Azar, Senior Vice President, Medical Group

FLORIDA
Jacksonville: NEMOURS CHILDREN'S CLINIC, 807 Children's Way, Zip 32207; tel. 904/390-3600; William A Cover, Administrator

GEORGIA
Calhoun: ALLIANT HEALTH PLANS, INC., 401 South Wall Street, Ste 201, Zip 30701; tel. 706/629-8848; Judy Pair, Chief Executive Officer

Calhoun: GEORGIA HEALTH PLUS, 401 South Wall Street, Ste 201, Zip 30701; tel. 706/629-1833

Rome: CENTREX, 420 East Second Avenue, Zip 30161; tel. 706/235-1006; Dee B Russell, Chief Executive Officer

Rome: COMMUNITY HOSPICECARE, P O Box 233, Zip 30162-0233; tel. 706/232-0807; Kurt Stuenkel, President and Chief Executive Officer

Rome: FLOYD HOME HEALTH AGENCY, P O Box 6248, Zip 30162-6248; tel. 706/802-4600; Kurt Stuenkel, President and Chief Executive Officer

Rome: FLOYD MEDICAL OUTPATIENT SURGERY, P O Box 233, Zip 30162-0233; tel. 706/802-2070; Kurt Stuenkel, President and Chief Executive Officer

Rome: FLOYD REHABILITATION CENTER, P O Box 233, Zip 30162-0233; tel. 706/802-2091; Kurt Stuenkel, President and Chief Executive Officer

HAWAII
Honolulu: MALUHIA HOSPITAL, 1027 Hala Drive, Zip 96817; tel. 808/832-5874; Derek Akiyoshi, Chief Executive Officer

Wahiawa: THE QUEEN'S MEDICAL CENTER - WAHIAWA, 128 Lehua Street, Zip 96786-2036; tel. 808/621-8411; Robin Kalohelani, Chief Operating Officer

ILLINOIS
Oak Forest: OAK FOREST HEALTH CENTER OF COOK COUNTY, 15900 South Cicero Avenue, Zip 60452-4006; tel. 708/687-7200

MAINE
Damariscotta: COVE'S EDGE, 26 Schooner Street, Zip 4543; tel. 207/563-4645; Judy McGuire, Administrator

Damariscotta: MILES MEDICAL GROUP, INC., 35 Miles Street, Zip 4543; tel. 207/563-1234; Stacey Miller-Friant, Vice President, Physician Services

Kennebunk: SOUTHERN MAINE HEALTH AND HOME SERVICES, P O Box 739, Zip 4043; tel. 207/985-4767; Elaine Brady, Executive Director

MARYLAND
Baltimore: ST. AGNES HEALTH SERVICES, 900 Caton Avenue, Zip 21229; tel. 410/368-2945; Peter Clay, Senior Vice President Managed Care

Baltimore: ST. AGNES HOME CARE AND HOSPICE, 3421 Benson Avenue, Suite G100, Zip 21227; tel. 410/368-2825; Robin Dowell, Director

Ellicott City: ST. AGNES NURSING AND REHABILITATION CENTER, 3000 North Ridge Road, Zip 21043; tel. 410/461-7577; Barbara A Gustke, Administrator Extended Care Facility

Rockville: DEPARTMENT OF HEALTH, EDUCATION, AND WELFARE, PUBLIC HEALTH SERVICE, COMMISSIONED PERSONNEL OPERATIONS DIVISIO, 5600 Fishers Lane, Room 4-35, Zip 20852; tel. 301/443-2404

MASSACHUSETTS
Boston: JOSLIN DIABETES CENTER, 1 Joslin Place, Zip 2215; tel. 617/732-2400; John L. Brooks III, President and Chief Executive Officer

Springfield: BAY STATE VISITING NURSE ASSOCIATION AND HOSPICE, 50 Maple Street, Zip 1105; tel. 413/781-5070; Ruth Odgren, President

MICHIGAN
Big Rapids: MECOSTA HEALTH SERVICES, 650 Linden Street, Zip 49307; tel. 231/796-3200; Gail Bullard, Director

Ontonagon: ASPIRUS ONTONAGON HOSPITAL, 601 South Seventh Street, Zip 49953-1459; tel. 906/884-8000; Christine K. Harff, Regional President, Upper Peninsula

Sault Sainte Marie: SAULT SAINTE MARIE TRIBAL HEALTH AND HUMAN SERVICES CENTER, 2864 Ashmun Street, Zip 49783; tel. 906/495-5651; Russell Vizina, Division Director Health

MISSOURI
Independence: SURGI-CARE CENTER OF INDEPENDENCE, 2311 Redwood Avenue, Zip 64057; tel. 816/373-7995

NEBRASKA
North Platte: GREAT PLAINS PHO, INC., P O Box 1167, Zip 69103; tel. 308/535-7496; Todd Hlavaty, Chairman

NEW JERSEY
Jersey City: ST. FRANCIS HOSPITAL, 25 McWilliams Place, Zip 07302-1698; tel. 201/418-1000

Millburn: ATLANTIC HOME CARE AND HOSPICE, 33 Bleeker Street, Zip 7041; tel. 973/379-8400; Susan Quinn, Administrator

Morristown: ALLIANCE IMAGING CENTER, 65 Maple Street, Zip 7960; tel. 973/267-5700; Barbara Picorale, Administrator

Succasunna: DIALYSIS CENTER OF NORTHWEST NEW JERSEY, 170 Righter Road, Zip 7876; tel. 973/584-1117; Carol Cahill, Administrator

NEW MEXICO
Albuquerque: ALBUQUERQUE IHS HEALTH CENTER, 801 Vassar Drive NE, Zip 87106-2799; tel. 505/248-4000; Maria Rickert, Chief Executive Officer

NEW YORK
Tuckahoe: HOME NURSING ASSOCIATION OF WESTCHESTER, 69 Main Street, Zip 10707; tel. 919/961-2818; Mary Wehrberger, Director

NORTH CAROLINA
Jefferson: AMH SEGRAVES CARE CENTER, 200 Hospital Avenue, Zip 28640; tel. 336/246-7101

Wilson: WILMED NURSING CARE CENTER, 1705 Tarboro Street SW, Zip 27893-3428; tel. 252/399-8998; Randy Smithey, Administrator

OHIO
Cleveland: METROHEALTH CENTER FOR SKILLED NURSING CARE, 4229 Pearl Road, Zip 44109; tel. 216/957-3675; Yvette Bozman, Administrator

OKLAHOMA
Clinton: U. S. PUBLIC HEALTH SERVICE INDIAN HOSPITAL, Route 1, Box 3060, Zip 73601-9303; tel. 580/323-2884

Eufaula: EUFALA INDIAN HEALTH CENTER, 800 Forest Avenue, Zip 74432; tel. 918/689-2547; Shelly Crow, Health System Administrator

Okmulgee: OKMULGEE INDIAN HEALTH SYSTEM, 1313 East 20th, Zip 74447; tel. 918/758-1926; Kara Lee, Administrator

Sapulpa: SAPULPA INDIAN HEALTH CENTER, 1125 East Clevelend, Zip 74066; tel. 918/224-9310; Sid Daniels, Acting Administrator

PENNSYLVANIA
Warminster: ABINGTON MEMORIAL HEALTH CENTER - WARMINSTER CAMPUS, 225 Newtown Road, Zip 18974-5221; tel. 215/441-6600; Kathleen Farrell, Executive Director

TEXAS
Dallas: SURGICARE OF TRAVIS CENTER, INC., 13355 Noel Road, Suite 650, Zip 75240-6694; tel. 713/520-1782

Houston: GRAMERCY OUTPATIENT SURGERY CENTER. LTD., 2727 Gramercy, Zip 77025; tel. 713/660-6900; Hamel Patel, Administrator

Houston: WEST HOUSTON SURGICARE, 970 Campbell Road, Zip 77024; tel. 713/461-3547

Webster: BAY AREA SURGICARE CENTER, 502 Medical Center Boulevard, Zip 77598; tel. 281/332-2433; Carol Simons, Administrator

WISCONSIN
Green Bay: UNITY HOSPICE, P O Box 28345, Zip 54324-8345; tel. 920/494-0225; Donald Seibel, Executive Director

Green Bay: UNITY HOSPICE, P O Box 28345, Zip 54324-8345; tel. 920/494-0225; Donald Seibel, Executive Director

Other Institutional Members / Provisional Hospitals

Provisional Hospitals

This listing includes organizations that, as of September 16, 2015, were in the planning or construction stage and that, on completion, will be eligible for Institutional membership. Some hospitals are granted provisional membership for reasons related to other Association requirements. Hospitals classified as provisional members for reasons other than being under construction are indicated by a bullet (•).

TEXAS

Houston: BAYLOR ST. LUKE'S MEDICAL CENTER MCNAIR CAMPUS, One Baylor Plaza, BCM 100, Zip 77030–3411; tel. 713/798–4951; Paul Klotman, M.D., President

Marble Falls: WAYNE & EILEEN HURD REGIONAL MEDICAL CENTER – SCOTT & WHITE, 800 West Highway 71, Zip 78654; tel. 830/598–1204; Eric N. Looper, Chief Executive Officer

GUAM

Dededo: GUAM REGIONAL MEDICAL CITY, P.O. Box 3830, Zip 96932; tel. 671/649–4764; Gloria Long, Chief Operating Officer

Associate Members

Ambulatory Centers and Home Care Agencies

UNITED STATES

NEW YORK

MIDTOWN SURGERY CENTER, 305 East 47th Street, Zip 10017-2303; tel. 212/751-2100; Julia Ferguson, Director, Operations

PENNSYLVANIA

WILLS EYE HOSPITAL, 840 Walnut Street, Philadelphia, Zip 19107-5109; tel. 215/928-3000; Joseph P. Bilson, Executive Director

Blue Cross Plans

UNITED STATES

ARIZONA

BLUE CROSS AND BLUE SHIELD OF ARIZONA, Box 13466, Phoenix, Zip 85002-3466; tel. 602/864-4541; Vishu Jhaveri; Senior Vice President and Chief Medical Officer

Associate Members / Other

Other Members

UNITED STATES

Architecture

DEVENNEY GROUP ARCHITECTS, 201 West Indian School Road, Phoenix, Arizona Zip 85013-3203; tel: 602/943-8950, Julie Barkenbush, Chief Executive Officer; devenneygroup.com
MATTHEI AND COLIN ASSOCIATES, 332 South Michigan Avenue, Suite 614, Chicago, Illinois Zip 60604; tel: 312/939-4002, Randall Bacidore, Principal; mca-architecture.com/
MESSER CONSTRUCTION COMPANY, 643 West Court Street, Cincinnati, Ohio Zip 45203-1511; tel: 513/242-1541, Peter Bergman, Vice President; messer.com

Bank

HEALTHCARE ASSOCIATES CREDIT UNION, 1151 East Warrenville Road, Naperville, Illinois Zip 60563; tel: 630/276-5771, Jennifer Kleinhenz, Senior Vice President Strategic Initiatives; hacu.org
TD BANK, 2130 Centre Park West Drive, 2nd Floor, West Palm Beach, Florida Zip 33409-6411; tel: 561/352-2086, Colleen Mullaney, Senior Vice President; tdbank.com

Communication Systems Org

AVAILITY, LLC, 750 Old Hickory Boulevard, Building 2 Suite 270, Brentwood, Tennessee Zip 37027-4528; tel: 615/760-3361, Ashleigh Eisinger, Events and Social Media Specialist; availity.com

Construction Firm

POETTKER CONSTRUCTION COMPANY, 308 South Germantown Road, Breese, Illinois Zip 62230; tel: 618/526-7213, Curtis C. Rommerskirchen, Brand Ambassador for Healthcare Facility Services; poettkerconstruction.com

Consulting Firm

AON RISK SOLUTIONS, 5600 West 83rd Street, 8200 Tower, Minneapolis, Minnesota Zip 55402-3721; tel: 952/807-0768, James Craig Nelson, Senior Vice President; stratford360.com
ARAMARK, 10510 Twin Lakes Boulevard, Charlotte, North Carolina Zip 28269-7658; tel: 704/948-4774, Tom Elmore, Director, Industry Relations; aramark.com
AVIVA HEALTHCARE SOLUTIONS, 98 Golden Eye Lane, Port Monmouth, New Jersey Zip 07758-1647; tel: 800/530-5728, Thomas Bojko, President and Managing Partner; avivahealthsolutions.com
CARE TECH SOLUTIONS, 901 Wilshire Drive, Suite 100, Troy, Michigan Zip 48084; tel: 248/823-0950, Jody Meehan, Vice President, Marketing, Communications, and Government Affairs; caretech.com/
CARERISE|CARERISE INDEX, PO Box 880, Mandeville, Louisiana Zip 70470-0880; tel: 985/727-4740, Tim G Goux, Founder; carerise.com
CLEARWATER COMPLIANCE LLC, 106 Windward Point, Hendersonville, Tennessee Zip 37075-5108; tel: 615/800-7988, Kathy S. Ebbert, Chief Operating Officer; clearwatercompliance.com
CREATE PPO, 317 6th Avenue, Suite 1440, Des Moines, Iowa Zip 50309-4131; tel: 515/657-4888, Clayton R. Copple, President and Chief Executive Officer; createppo.com
DRAFFIN TUCKER, 5 Concourse Parkway, Suite 1250, Atlanta, Georgia Zip 30328-5350; tel: 404/220-8484, Sarah Dekutowski, Partner; https://draffin-tucker.com/
EASTER HEALTHCARE CONSULTING, 518 Neilwood Drive, Nashville, Tennessee Zip 37205-3026; tel: 615/424-3642, James G Easter (Jim), Principal and Chief Executive Officer; easterhealthcare.com
ERNST & YOUNG, 150 Fourth Avenue North, Suite 1400, Nashville, Tennessee Zip 37219-2409; tel: 615/252-8254, Chris Barber, US Health Brand, Marketing and Communications Leader; ey.com
GOLDMAN, SACHS AND COMPANY, 200 West Street, New York, New York Zip 10282-2198; tel: 212/902-1000, Cynthia Rivera, Public Sector and Infrastructure Banking
HEALTHCARE CHAPLAINCY NETWORK, INC., 65 Broadway, 12th Floor, New York, New York Zip 10010; tel: 212/644-1111, Eric J. Hall, President and Chief Executive Officer; healthcarechaplaincy.org
HEALTHCARESOURCE, 100 Sylvan Road, Suite 100, Woburn, Massachusetts Zip 01801-1851; tel: 800/691-3737, Sean Parlin, Strategic Alliances Manager; healthcaresource.com
HEALTHEQUITY, INC., 15 West Scenic Pointe Drive, Suite 100, Draper, Utah Zip 84020-6120; tel: 801/727-1000, Stephen Neeleman, Founder and Vice Chairman; healthequity.com
INTERNATIONAL CITIES MANAGEMENT ASSOCIATION-RETIREMENT CORPORATION, 777 North Capitol Street NE, Washington, District of Columbia Zip 20002-4239; tel: 866/265-5126, Kevin F. Orr, Senior Director; icmarc.org
KAUFMAN HALL, 5202 Old Orchard Road, Suite N700, Skokie, Illinois Zip 60077; tel: 847/441-8780, Jason H Sussman, Partner; kaufmanhall.com
LATHAM AND WATKINS, LLP, 633 West 5th Street, Ste 4000, Los Angeles, California Zip 90071; tel: 213/485-1234, Daniel K Settelmayer, Partner; lw.com
MCDONALD HOPKINS, LLC, 600 Superior Avenue East, Suite 2100, Cleveland, Ohio Zip 44114-2690; tel: 216/348-5400, Richard S Cooper, Member; mcdonaldhopkins.com
MCKESSON CORPORATION, 1 Post Street, 33rd Floor, San Francisco, California Zip 94104-5203; tel: 404/338-2985, Anastasia Agapoff, Assistant Manager, Library Operations; mckesson.com/
MILESTONE HEALTHCARE, LLC, 275 West Campbell Road, Suite 300, Richardson, Texas Zip 75080-3560; tel: 800/926-2388, George Thompson, General Manager; milestonehealth.com
NATIONAL CENTER FOR HEALTH STATISTICS, 3311 Toledo Road, Hyattsville, Maryland Zip 20782-2064; tel: 800/232-4636, Monica Deckers, Lead Admin Officer; cdc.gov
NATIONAL MEDICAL FUNDING SERVICES, INC., 1101 Wootton Parkway, 10th Floor, Rockville, Maryland Zip 20852-1059; tel: 301/433-7515, Sandy Waterman, Chief Executive Officer; medx.health
NAVEX GLOBAL, 6000 Meadows Road, Suite 200, Lake Oswego, Oregon Zip 97035-3172; tel: 503/924-1640, Stephen J. Molen, Vice President Strategic Solutions; navexglobal.com
NEWRISTICS, 8777 East Via de Ventura #188, Scottsdale, Arizona Zip 85258; tel: 480/947-8078, Cheryl Palay, Senior Vice President; hsmgroup.com
PROTIVITI, INC., 13727 Noel Road, Suite 800, Dallas, Texas Zip 75240-1336; tel: 214/395-1662, Richard Williams, Managing Director and Global Healthcare Industry Practice; protiviti.com
RYCAN, P O Box 306, Marshall, Minnesota Zip 56258-0306; tel: 800/201-3324, Marg Louwagie, Administrative Assistant; rycan.com
STRATA DECISION TECHNOLOGY; tel: 312/726-1227, Dan Michelson, Chief Executive Officer; stratadecision.com
STROUDWATER ASSOCIATES, 50 Sewall Street, Suite 102, Portland, Maine Zip 04102-2646; tel: 207/221-8255, Marc Voyvodich, Chief Executive Officer; stroudwater.com/
SULLIVAN COTTER & ASSOCIATES, INC, 7733 Forsyth Boulevard, Suite 1100, Clayton, Missouri Zip 63105; tel: 312/564-5883, Sean C. Butler, Director of Client Experience; sullivancotter.com
SYMPLR, 315 Capitol Street, Suite 100, Houston, Texas Zip 77002-2826; tel: 281/863-9500, Rick Pleczko, Chief Executive Officer; vcsdatabase.com
TEAMHEALTH, 265 Brookview Centre Way, Suite 400, Knoxville, Tennessee Zip 37919; tel: 865/293-5486, Leif Murphy, Chief Executive Officer; teamhealth.com
THE CHARTIS GROUP, 220 West Kinzie Street, 5th Floor, Chicago, Illinois Zip 60654-4912; tel: 312/932-3068, Celine White, Manager of Financial Operations; chartis.com
THE QUAMMEN GROUP, INC., 151 Southhall Lane, Suite 168, Maitland, Florida Zip 32751-7486; tel: 407/539-2015, Alexandra Robertson, Director of Marketing; quammengroup.com
VERRAS HEALTHCARE INTERNATIONAL; tel: 888/791-5556, Robert T. Langston, Partner; verras.com/
VIIAD SYSTEMS LLC, 1170 Wheeler Way, Suite 200, Langhorne, Pennsylvania Zip 19047-3243; tel: 866/498-4423, Tricia Bradley, Director, Sales and Marketing Support; viiad.com
WESTERN HEALTHCARE ALLIANCE, 715 Horizon Drive, Suite 401, Grand Junction, Colorado Zip 81506-8731; tel: 970/683-5223, Carolyn Bruce, Chief Executive Officer; wha1.org
XANITOS, INC., 3809 West Chester Pike, Suite 210, Newtown Square, Pennsylvania Zip 19073-2304; tel: 484/654-2300, Graeme A Crothall, Chairman and Chief Executive Officer; xanitos.com

Educational Services

NATIONAL RURAL HEALTH RESOURCE CENTER, 525 South Lake Avenue, Suite 320, Duluth, Minnesota Zip 55802; tel: 218/727-9390, Sally Buck, Chief Executive Officer; ruralcenter.org
PUBLISHING CONCEPTS INC.; tel: 800/561-4686, Gregg Jones, Education and Careers Director; pcipublishing.com

Hospice

HOSPICE OF THE VALLEY, 1510 East Flower Street, Phoenix, Arizona Zip 85014-5698; tel: 602/530-6900, Rachel Behrendt, Senior Vice President, Operations; hov.org

Information Systems

CERNER CORPORATION, 2800 Rockcreek Parkway, Kansas City, Missouri Zip 64117; tel: 816/221-1024, Laurel Vine, Program Manager, Industry Events; cerner.com
EVOLENT, 540 West Madison Street, Suite 1500, Chicago, Illinois Zip 60661; tel: 312/273-6623, Kevin Weinstein, Chief Marketing Officer; valencehealth.com
FLEMING AOD, Inc., 816 Thayer Avenue, Floor 3rd, Silver Spring, Maryland Zip 20910-4508; tel: 202/872-1033, Mary Dalrymple, Managing Director; aod.cx
IMPRIVATA, INC., 10 Maguire Road Building 4, Lexington, Massachusetts Zip 02421-3110; tel: 781/674-2700, Ed Gaudel, Chief Marketing Officer; imprivata.com
KPMG LLP, 200 East Randolph Street, Suite 5500, Chicago, Illinois Zip 60601-6607; tel: 312/665-2073, Edward J Giniat, National Line of Business Leader, Healthcare and Pharmaceuticals Practice; https://home.kpmg.com/us/en/home.html?cid=M-00002211&gclid=CKfszoeUrtACFZSFaQod82wE4g
MEDHOST, 6100 West Plano Parkway, Suite 3100, Plano, Texas Zip 75093-8342; tel: 888/218-4678, Leslie LaFon, Departmental Segment Manager; medhost.com

Associate Members / Other

REAL TIME MEDICAL SYSTEMS, LLC, 901 Elkridge Landing Road, Linthicum Heights, Maryland Zip 21090-2920; tel: 203/249-0404, Joan Neuscheler, Chief Executive Officer; realtimemed.com

Insurance Broker

BOSTON MUTUAL LIFE INSURANCE COMPANY, 120 Royall Street, Canton, Massachusetts Zip 2021; tel: 781/828-7000, Peter Tillson, Vice President; bostonmutual.com

CONSTELLATION, 7701 France Avenue South, Suite 500, Minneapolis, Minnesota Zip 55435-3201; tel: 952/838-6700, Holly Freeman, Manager; mmicgroup.com

Ironshore, 300 South Wacker Drive, Chicago, Illinois Zip 60606-6680; tel: 312/496-7535, Daniel R Nash, Senior Vice President Field Operations and Business Development; ironshore.com

LTC SOLUTIONS, 14715 North East 95th Street, Suite 200, Redmond, Washington Zip 98052; tel: 877/286-2852, Christine McCullugh, President; ltc-solutions.com

THE ALLEN J. FLOOD COMPANIES, INC., 2 Madison Avenue, Larchmont, New York Zip 10538; tel: 914/834-9326, Allen J Flood, President; ajfusa.com

Managed Care/Utilization

CENTENE CORPORATION, 111 East Capitol Street, Suite 500, Jackson, Mississippi Zip 39201; tel: 601/519-6119, K. Michael Bailey, Corporate Vice President; centene.com

Manufacturer/Supplier

3M, 3M CENTER, Building 275-4E-01, Saint Paul, Minnesota Zip 55144-1000; tel: 612/733-8183, Donald R Brewer, Director Medical-Surgical Markets; 3m.com

GE HEALTHCARE, 9900 West Innovation Drive, RP-2177, Wauwatosa, Wisconsin Zip 53226-4856; tel: 262/290-8769, Kimberly Rutherford, Business Partner and Director, Advertising & Promotion US-Canada Region; www3.gehealthcare.com

HILL-ROM, 1069 State Route 46 East, Batesville, Indiana Zip 47006-9167; tel: 812/934-7958, Thomas J Jeffers, Director Government Relations; hill-rom.com

Metro Hospital Assn

HOSPITAL ASSOCIATION OF SOUTHERN CALIFORNIA, 515 South Figueroa Street, Suite 1300, Los Angeles, California Zip 90071-3300; tel: 213/538-0700, George W Greene, President and Chief Executive Officer; hasc.org

Other Health Related

CENTER FOR MEDICAL INTEROPERABILITY, 618 Church Street Suite 220, Nashville, Tennessee Zip 37219-2453; tel: 202/617-6009, Kerry McDermott, Vice President for Public Policy and Communications; medicalinteroperability.org

Other

A3-ASHLEY ADVERTISING AGENCY, 2825 Soni Drive, Trooper, Pennsylvania Zip 19403-1275; tel: 610/631-5500, Frank Gussoni, President; ashleyadvertising.com

ACADEMIC PARTNERSHIP LLC, 600 North Pearl Street, Suite 900, Dallas, Texas Zip 75201; tel: 682/305-3063, Nimisha Savani, Vertical Chief Healthcare; aphealthcareedge.com

AMC HEALTH, INC., 39 Broadway, Suite 540, New York, New York Zip 10006; tel: 877/776-1746, Joanna Haskin, Vice President Partner Development; amchealth.com

AMERICAN ASSOCIATION FOR WOUND CARE MANAGEMENT, 4109 Glenrose Street, Kensington, Maryland Zip 20895-3718; tel: 301/933-2200, Jule Crider, Executive Director; aawcm.org

AMERICAN ASSOCIATION OF NURSE ANESTHETISTS, 222 South Prospect Avenue, Park Ridge, Illinois Zip 60068-4001; tel: 847/655-1100, Randall Moore, Chief Executive Officer; aana.com

AMERICAN BOARD OF MEDICAL SPECIALTIES, 353 North Clark Street, Suite 1400, Chicago, Illinois Zip 60654-3454; tel: 312/436-2626, Richard D Hawkins, President and Chief Executive Officer; abms.org

AMERICAN COLLEGE OF HEALTHCARE EXECUTIVES, 300 South Riverside Plaza, Suite 1900, Chicago, Illinois Zip 60606-6613; tel: 312/424-2800, Deborah Bowen, President and Chief Executive Officer; ache.org

AMERICAN HEALTH INFORMATION MANAGEMENT ASSOCIATION, 233 North Michigan Avenue, Suite 2150, Chicago, Illinois Zip 60601-5806; tel: 312/233-1100, David A Sweet, Director Library Services; ahima.org

AMERICAN SOCIETY OF ANESTHESIOLOGISTS, 1061 American Lane, Schaumburg, Illinois Zip 60173; tel: 847/268-9160, Paul Pomerantz, Chief Executive Officer; asahq.org

AMN HEALTHCARE, INC., 12400 High Bluff Drive, Suite 100, San Diego, California Zip 92130-3581; tel: 866/871-8519, Steve Wehn, Senior Vice President of Corporate Development; amnhealthcare.com

APOGEE PHYSICIANS, 15059 North Scottsdale Road, Suite 600, Scottsdale, Arizona Zip 85254-2685; tel: 602/778-3600, Michael Gregory, Chairman; apogeephysicians.com

ARENA, 502 South Sharp Street, Suite 2300, Baltimore, Maryland Zip 21201-2445; tel: 888/444-0693, Michael Finn, Vice President, Marketing; arena.io

ARIS RADIOLOGY, 5655 Hudson Drive, Suite 210, Hudson, Ohio Zip 44236; tel: 330/655-3800, Stacey Christofferson, Sales and Marketing; arisradiology.com

ASSOCIATION OF PERIOPERATIVE REGISTERED NURSES, 2170 South Parker Road, Suite 400, Denver, Colorado Zip 80231; tel: 303/755-6304, Linda Kay Groah, Executive Director and Chief Executive Officer; aorn.org

AVATAR SOLUTIONS, 25 East Washington Street, Suite 600, Chicago, Illinois Zip 60602; tel: 312/236-7170, Jeffrey Brady, Chief Executive Officer; hrsolutionsinc.com

BACTES, 8344 Clairemont Mesa Boulevard, Suite 201, San Diego, California Zip 92111-1327; tel: 858/244-1811, Rae Danell, Marketing Coordinator; bactes.com

BLUE CROSS AND BLUE SHIELD ASSOCIATION, 225 North Michigan Avenue, Chicago, Illinois Zip 60601-7680; tel: 312/297-6000, Scott P Serota, President and Chief Executive Officer; bcbs.com

BOARDVANTAGE, 4300 Bohannon Drive, Suite 110, Menlo Park, California Zip 94025; tel: 650/330-2444, Virginia Portillo, Conference and Events Coordinator; boardvantage.com

CANON SOLUTIONS AMERICA, INC., 300 Commerce Square Boulevard, Burlington, New Jersey Zip 08016-1270; tel: 847/706-3411, Paul T Murphy, Director Strategic Contract Support; solutions.canon.com

CAPROCK EMERGENCY HOSPITAL, 1630 Briarcrest Drive, Suite 100, Bryan, Texas Zip 77802-2709; tel: 979/314-2323, Lon Young, Chief Medical Officer; caprocker.com

CARECENTRIX, 20 Church Street, Floor 12th, Hartford, Connecticut Zip 06103-1246; tel: 800/808-1902, Sherl Brand, Senior Vice President Strategic Solutions; carecentrix.com

CERTIPHI SCREENING, INC., 1105 Industrial Highway, Southampton, Pennsylvania Zip 18966; tel: 888/260-1370, Tony D'Orazio, CEO; certiphi.com

CHANGE HEALTHCARE, 3535 Piedmont Road, Suite 800, Atlanta, Georgia Zip 30305-1543; tel: 404/279-5029, Kim R Williams, Chief Financial Officer; changehealthcare.com

CISCO SYSTEMS, 165 Needletree Lane, Glastonbury, Connecticut Zip 6033; tel: 860/657-8127, Michael Haymaker, Director Healthcare Industry Marketing; cisco.com

COMPREHENSIVE PHARMACY SERVICES, 6409 North Quail Hollow Road, Memphis, Tennessee Zip 38120-1414; tel: 901/748-0470, Walker Upshaw, Chief Development Officer; cpspharm.com

CROSS COUNTRY HEALTHCARE, 5201 Congress Avenue, Boca Raton, Florida Zip 33487-3629; tel: 800/347-2264, Robert Murphy, President Workforce Solutions; crosscountryhealthcare.com

CYRACOM, 5780 North Swan Road, Tucson, Arizona Zip 85718-4527; tel: 800/713-4950, Jeremy Woan, President and Chief Executive Officer; cyracom.com

DISH, PO Box 5096524, Englewood, Colorado Zip 80112-5905; tel: 720/514-6019, Steven Wilson, Manager; dish.com

FIRST AMERICAN EQUIPMENT FINANCE, 255 Woodcliff Drive, Fairport, New York Zip 14450-4219; tel: 585/643-3266, Lori Dennis, Senior Vice President; faef.com

GALLAGHER BENEFIT SERVICES, 6525 Morrison Boulevard, Suite 200, Charlotte, North Carolina Zip 28211-3532; tel: 877/332-2265, James Craig Nelson, Senior Vice President; bfbgallagher.com

GOZIO HEALTH, 75 5th Street NW, Suite 2220, Atlanta, Georgia Zip 30308-1019; tel: 772/444-6946, Barbara Kragor, Vice President Sales and Customer Experience; goziohealth.com

HEALTHCARE REVENUE SOLUTIONS, 4851 Keller Springs Road, Suite 228, Addison, Texas Zip 75001; tel: 972/546-6491, Andre Kus, Chief Executive Officer; healthcarerevenuesolutions.org

HEALTHGRID, 4203 Vineland Road, Suite K6, Orlando, Florida Zip 32811; tel: 855/624-2844, Raj Toleti, Founder and Chief Executive Officer; healthgrid.com

HEALTHWAYS, INC, 701 Cool Springs Boulevard, Franklin, Tennessee Zip 37067-2697; tel: 800/327-3822, Karen Meyer, Principal; healthways.com

HMS, 355 Quartermaster Court, Jeffersonville, Indiana Zip 47130-3670; tel: 812/704-5747, Rich Flaherty, Vice President Sales and Marketing; hms.com

HOOPER, LUNDY & BOOKMAN, INC., 1875 Century Park East, Suite 1600, Los Angeles, California Zip 90067; tel: 310/551-8111, Lloyd Bookman, Partner; health-law.com

HOSPITALRECRUITING.COM, 899 South College Mall Road, Suite 395, Bloomington, Indiana Zip 47401-6301; tel: 800/244-7236, Michael Jones, Managing Partner; hospitalrecruiting.com

HYLAND SOFTWARE, INC., 28500 Clemens Road, Westlake, Ohio Zip 44145; tel: 440/788-5814, Michael Kortan, Director Health Care Solutions; onbase.com

IMALOGIX, 1150 First Avenue, Suite 450, King Of Prussia, Pennsylvania Zip 19406-1363; tel: 855/681-9100, David Steigerwalt, Product Manager; imalogix.com

INNOVATIVE CAPITAL LLC, 1489 Baltimore Pike, Building 400, Springfield, Pennsylvania Zip 19064-3958; tel: 610/543-2490, Alan P Richman, President and Chief Executive Officer; innovativecapital.com

INTALERE; tel: 877/711-5700, Laurie McGrath, Vice President Marketing; amerinet-gpo.com

INTELLICENTRICS, INC., 1420 Lakeside Parkway, Suite 110, Flower Mound, Texas Zip 75028; tel: 972/316-6209, Nimisha Savani, Chief Marketing Officer; intellicentrics.com

INTERACTIVE HEALTH SOLUTIONS, 3800 North Wilke Road, Suite 155, Arlington Heights, Illinois Zip 60004-1278; tel: 847/754-2698, Joseph O'Brien, President; interactivesolutions.com

IP SERVICES, 2896 Crescent Avenue, Suite 201, Eugene, Oregon Zip 97408-7422; tel: 541/343-5974, Mark Allers, Vice President Business Development; ipservices.com

JEWISH GUILD HEALTHCARE, 15 West 65th Street, New York, New York Zip 10023; tel: 212/769-6200, Alan R Morse, President and Chief Executive Officer; jgb.org

LANGUAGE LINE SOLUTIONS, One Lower Ragsdale Drive, Building 2, Monterey, California Zip 93940; tel: 800/752-6096, Suzanne duMont-Perez, Government Relations and Channel Manager; languageline.com

MEDICAL INFORMATION TECHNOLOGY, INC.; tel: 781/821-3000, Lynn Robblee, Supervisor of Event Coordination and Memberships; meditech.com

MEDISOLV, INC., 10440 Little Patuexent Parkway, Suite 1000, Columbia, Maryland Zip 21044-3630; tel: 443/539-0505, Erin Heilman, Marketing Specialist; medisolv.com

MEDNAX SERVICES INC., 1301 Concord Terrace, Sunrise, Florida Zip 33323-2843; tel: 954/384-0175, Roger J Medel, President; mednax.com

MODERN HEALTHCARE, 150 North Michigan Avenue, 17th Floor, Chicago, Illinois Zip 60601-3806; tel: 312/649-5491, Fawn Lopez, Publisher; modernhealthcare.com

MUCH SHELIST, 191 North Wacker Drive, Chicago, Illinois Zip 60606-1615; tel: 312/521-2000, Ned Milenkovich, Partner; muchshelist.com

NATIONAL COUNCIL OF STATE BOARDS OF NURSING, 111 East Wacker Drive, 29th Floor, Chicago, Illinois Zip 60601-4277; tel: 312/525-3600, David Charles Benton, Chief Executive Officer; ncsbn.org

OB HOSPITALIST GROUP; tel: 800/967-2289, Guy Kohn, Director, Marketing; obhg.com

PLANON CORPORATION, 45 Braintree Hill Office Park, Suite 400, Braintree, Massachusetts Zip 02184-8730; tel: 781/356-0999, Ellen Schwier, Marketing Manager; planonsoftware.com

Associate Members / Other

PROASSURANCE, 100 Brookwood Place, Birmingham, Alabama Zip 35209–6811; tel: 205/877–4400, W Stancil Starnes, Chairman, Chief Executive Officer; proassurance.com

PROMED HEALTHCARE FINANCING, 1001 Woodward Avenue, Suite 1700, Detroit, Michigan Zip 48226–1904; tel: 631/707–4347, Dan De Chiaro, Director of Operations; promedhcf.com

QUARLES AND BRADY LLP, 300 North LaSalle Street, Suite 4000, Chicago, Illinois Zip 60654–3422; tel: 312/715–2751, Susan Stewart, Director, Client Relations; quarles.com

RRS, 416 Longshore Drive, Ann Arbor, Michigan Zip 48103; tel: 800/517–9634, Nicole Chardoul, Partner and Vice President; recycle.com

SAN-I-PAK, INC., PO Box 1183, Tracy, California Zip 95378; tel: 209/836–2310, Kristy Coleman, Project Manager; sanipak.com

SIMPLEX GRINNELL, 50 Technology Drive, Westminster, Massachusetts Zip 1441; tel: 978/731–8486, Suzanne Rahall, Marketing Manager, Healthcare Communications; simplexgrinnell.com

SUBWAY, 325 Bic Drive, Milford, Connecticut Zip 6461; tel: 800/888–4848, Joanne Kilgore, Global Account Manager; subway.com

TANDEM HOSPITAL PARTNERS, 1415 Louisiana Street, Houston, Texas Zip 77002–7360; tel: 713/999–0837, Debora Simmons, Chief Quality Officer and Chief Nursing Officer; tandemhospitalpartners.com

THE AMERICAN COLLEGE OF OBSTETRICIANS AND GYNECOLOGISTS, 409 12th Street, SW, Washington, District of Columbia Zip 20024–2188; tel: 202/638–5577, Hal Lawrence, Executive Vice President; acog.org

THE CPI GROUP, 7400 East Orchard Road, Suite 270, Englewood, Colorado Zip 80111; tel: 303/504–9999, John Van Gulik, Business Development Manager; thecpigroup.net

THE WALKER COMPANY, 31090 SW Boones Bend Road, Wilsonville, Oregon Zip 97070–6412; tel: 503/694–8539, Larry W Walker, Principal; walkercompany.com

TRACE SECURITY, 6300 Corporate Boulevard, Baton Rouge, Louisiana Zip 70809–1097; tel: 877/275–3009, Marissa Adams, Marketing Coordinator; tracesecurity.com

TRANSAMERICA RETIREMENT SOLUTIONS, 4 Manhattanville Road, Purchase, New York Zip 10577; tel: 914/697–8952, Peter Kunkel, President and Chief Executive Officer; https://www.trsretire.com

TRAPOLLO, 13900 Lincoln Park Drive, 5th Floor, Herndon, Virginia Zip 20171; tel: 866/807–5047, Lisa Majdi, Marketing Director; trapollo.com

UBS, 315 Deaderick Street, Nashville, Tennessee Zip 37238–3000; tel: 615/393–7549, Whit Mayo, Managing Director; ubs.com

UNIFORM DATA SYSTEM FOR MEDICAL REHABILITATION, 270 Northpointe Parkway, Suite 300, Amherst, New York Zip 14228; tel: 716/817–7800, Troy Hillman, Manager, Analytical Services Group; udsmr.org

USDTL, 1700 South Mount Prospect Road, Des Plaines, Illinois Zip 60018–1804; tel: 847/375–0770, Catharine Steccato, Vice President Business Development; usdtl.com

VANGUARD MODULAR BUILDING SYSTEMS, LLC, 3 Great Valley Parkway, Suite 170, Malvern, Pennsylvania Zip 19355–1417; tel: 610/240–8686, Mark Meyers, Vice President, Marketing Services; vanguardmodular.com

VERISYS CORPORATION, 1001 North Fairfax Avenue, Suite 640, Alexandria, Virginia Zip 22314–1798; tel: 703/535–1471, John Benson, Chief Operating Officer; verisys.com/

VESTAGEN TECHNICAL TEXTILES, INC., tel: 407/781–2395, Brian Crawford, Chief Business Officer; vestagen.com

VIGILANZ CORPORATION, 5775 Wayzata Boulevard, Suite 970, Minneapolis, Minnesota Zip 55416–2669; tel: 855/525–9078, David Goldsteen, Chairman and Chief Executive Officer; vigilanzcorp.com

VITAS HEALTHCARE, 201 South Biscayne Boulevard, Suite 400, Miami, Florida Zip 33131; tel: 305/374–4143, Drew Landmeier, Chief Marketing Officer; vistas.com

VIZIENT, 799 9th Street Northwest, Suite 210, Washington, District of Columbia Zip 20001–5325; tel: 202/354–2600, Shoshana Krilow, Vice President Public Policy and Government Relations; https://www.vizientinc.com/

WELLTOWER, INC., 4500 Dorr Street, Toledo, Ohio Zip 43615–4040; tel: 419/247–2800, Rachel Watson, Assistant Vice President; welltower.com

WITT/KIEFFER, 2015 Spring Rd, Ste 510, Oak Brook, Illinois Zip 60523; tel: 630/990–1370, James Gauss, Chairman of Board Services; wittkieffer.com/

YOURCARE UNIVERSE, INC, 6550 Carothers Parkway, Suite 100, Franklin, Tennessee Zip 37067; tel: 844/641–6800, Lauren Douglass, Brand Manager; yourcareuniverse.com

Recruitment Services

DOCCAFE.COM, tel: 574/453–3131, Briana Wick, Digital Marketing Director; doccafe.com

Regional Health Care Assn

TEXAS ORGANIZATION OF RURAL & COMMUNITY HOSPITALS, P O Box 203878, Austin, Texas Zip 78720–3878; tel: 512/873–0045, John Henderson, Chief Executive Officer; torchnet.org

CANADA

Provincial Hospital Assn

ONTARIO HOSPITAL ASSOCIATION, 200 Front Street West, Suite 2800, Toronto, Ontario Zip M5V 3L1; tel: 416/205–1300, Hazim Hassan, Vice President, Business Planning and Strategy; oha.com

BAHAMAS

Other

PRINCESS MARGARET HOSPITAL, P O Box N–8200, Nassau, tel: 242/322–2861, Mary Elizabeth Lightbourne-Walker, Hospital Administrator; phabahamas.org

BAHRAIN

Other

INTERNATIONAL HOSPITAL OF BAHRAIN, P O Box 1084, Manama, tel: 11/759–8222, F. S. Zeerah, President; ihb.net/

BRAZIL

Other

HOSPITAL SAMARITANO, RUA CONSELHEIRO BROTERO, 1486, Sao Paulo, Zip 01232–010; tel: 551/821–5300, Luiz Alberto Oliveira De Luca, Corporate Superintendent; samaritano.com.br

COLOMBIA

Other

ASOCIACION COLOMBIANA DE HOSPITALES Y CLINICAS, Carrera 4, No 73–15, Bogota, Juan Carlos Giraldo Valencia, Director General; achc.org.co

DOMINICAN REPUBLIC

Other

UNITED TELEMEDICINE NETWORK–HOSPITAL CHARLES DE GAULLE, Av Charles de Gaulle #43, Santo Domingo, Zip 11509; tel: 829/345–9335, Horacio Stagno, Commercial Director; hospitalunited.com

GEORGIA

Other

BOKHUA MEMORIAL CARDIOVASCULAR CENTER, Chachava 1 Street, Tbilisi, Zip 159, Giorgi Kipiani, Director

INNOVA MEDICAL CENTER, 7A Sandra Euli Street, Tbilisi, Zip 105, Giorgi Kipiani, Director; innovamedical.ge

MARITIME HOSPITAL JSC, Melikishrin 102B, Batumi, Zip 60100, Tamari Kachlishvili, Medical Director; mh.com.ge

MEDI CLUB GEORGIA, 22A, Tashkenti Street, Tbilisi, Zip 160; tel: 995/225–1991, Nugzar Abramishvili, General Director; mediclubgeorgia.ge

TBILISI CENTRAL HOSPITAL, Chachava Street 1, Tbilisi, Zip 159, Ivane Martiashuili, Co-founder; tch.ge

ZHORDANIA CLINIC, Chachava N1, Tbilisi, Zip 159, Tamar Kobiashvili, Director

JORDAN

Other

SPECIALTY HOSPITAL, P O Box 930186, Amman, Zip 11193, Fawzi Al–Hammouri, General Manager; specialty-hospital.com

LEBANON

Other

SAINT GEORGE HOSPITAL UNIVERSITY MEDICAL CENTER, P O Box 166378, Beirut, Zip 1100–2807; tel: 961/158–5700, Dimitri Haddad, Director; stgeorgehospital.org

MEXICO

Other

SHRINERS HOSPITAL FOR CHILDREN, Av Del Iman 257, Col Pedregal de Santa Ursula, Delegacion Coyoacan, Mexico City, Zip 4600; tel: 525/424–7850, Mariano Gonzalez Lugo, Administrator; shrinershospitalsforchildren.org/locations/mexicocity

MYANMAR

Other

ASIA ROYAL GENERAL HOSPITAL, 14 Baho Street, Sanchaung Township, Yangon, Zip 11162; tel: 951/153–8055, Myat Thu, Managing Director; asiaroyalmedical.com

NIGERIA

Consulting Firm

PETALICE MEDICAL CENTRE, 5/7 Marickson Hospital Way, Uyo, Akwa Ibom State, Zip 520241, Cletus Bassey, Archbishop

PANAMA

Other

CLINICA HOSPITAL SAN FERNANDO, S. A., Dept PTY 1663, P O Box 25207, Miami, Florida Zip 33102–5207; tel: 507/305–6399, Jose Manuel Teran Sitton, Medical Director; hospitalsanfernando.com

PERU

Other

BRITISH AMERICAN HOSPITAL, Avenue Alfredo Salazar 3 Era, Lima 27, tel: 511/712-3000, Gonzalo Garrido-Lecca, Director; angloamericana.com.pe

PHILIPPINES

Other

ST. LUKE'S MEDICAL CENTER, 279 East Rodriguez Sr Boulevard, Quezon City, tel: 632/723-0101, Edgardo R Cortez, President and Chief Executive Officer; stluke.com.ph/home

SAUDI ARABIA

Other

ABDUL RAHMAN AL MISHARI GENERAL HOSPITAL, OLAYA, P.O. Box 56929, Riyadh, Zip 11564; tel: 11/465-7700, Abdul Rahman Al Mishari, President; drabdulrahmanalmishari.com.sa/

MUHAMMAD SALEH BASHARAHIL HOSPITAL, P O Box 10505, Madinah Road, Omora Gadida, Makkah, tel: 9/520-4444, Turki M Basharahil, General Manager; msbasharahil.com/

NABIL AL KADI CONSULTANT ENGINEERS, Dammam, Damman, Taufik Ridani, Chief Executive Officer

SPAIN

Information Systems

SIGESA, S.A., CALLE GUATEMALA, 14, 4b, Madrid, Zip 28016; tel: 349/345-4018, Francisco Alvarez, Chief Financial Officer; sigesa.com

TURKEY

Other

ARTE CERRAHI HASTENESI, 1920 Cad. No:61 Cayyolu, Ankara, Zip 6810; tel: 903/236-1001, Oguz Engiz, Chief Executive Officer; artesaglik.com

UNITED ARAB EMIRATES

Other

AMERICAN HOSPITAL-DUBAI, Oud Metha Road, P.O. Box 5566, Dubai, tel: 11/336-7777, Saeed M Almulla, Chairman; https://www.ahdubai.com/en/

UNITED KINGDOM

Other

FINANSCO HEALTHCARE, 11A Blacka Moor Road, Sheffield, tel: 448/225-3844, Rukhsar Khan, Chief Executive Officer; finansco.com

Health Care Systems, Networks and Alliances

- **B2** Introduction
- 3 Statistics for Multihospital Health Care Systems and their Hospitals
- 4 Health Care Systems and their Hospitals
- 155 Headquarters of Health Care Systems, Geographically
- 164 Networks and their Hospitals
- 179 Alliances

Introduction

This section includes listings for networks, health care systems and alliances.

Health Care Systems
To reflect the diversity that exists among health care organizations, this publication uses the term health care system to identify both multihospital and diversified single hospital systems.

Multihospital Systems
A multihospital health care system is two or more hospitals owned, leased, sponsored, or contract managed by a central organization.

Single Hospital Systems
Single, freestanding member hospitals may be categorized as health care systems by bringing into membership three or more, and at least 25 percent, of their owned or leased non–hospital preacute and postacute health care organizations. (For purposes of definition, health care delivery is the availability of professional healthcare staff during all hours of the organization's operations). Organizations provide, or provide and finance, diagnostic, therapeutic, and/or consultative patient or client services that normally precede or follow acute, inpatient, hospitalization; or that serve to prevent or substitute for such hospitalization. These services are provided in either a freestanding facility not eligible for licensure as a hospital under state statue or through one that is a subsidiary of a hospital.

The first part of this section is an alphabetical list of health care systems which are listed under the system by state. Data for this section were compiled from the 2023 *Annual Survey* and the membership information base as published in section A of the *AHA Guide*.

One of the following codes appears after the name of each system listed to indicate the type of organizational control reported by that system:

- **CC** Catholic (Roman) church–related system, not–for–profit
- **CO** Other church–related system, not–for–profit
- **NP** Other not–for–profit system, including nonfederal, governmental systems
- **IO** Investor–owned, for profit system
- **FG** Federal Government

One of the following codes appears after the name of each hospital to indicate how that hospital is related to the system:

- **O** Owned
- **L** Leased
- **S** Sponsored
- **CM** Contract–managed

Health System Classification System
An identification system for Health Systems was developed jointly by the American Hospital Association's Health Research and Education Trust and Health Forum, and the University of California-Berkeley.[1] A health system is assigned to one of five categories based on how much they differentiate and centralized their hospital services, physician arrangements, and provider-based insurance products. Differentiation refers to the number of different products or services that the organization offers. Centralization refers to whether decision-making and service delivery emanate from the system level more so than individual hospitals.

Categories:

Centralized Health System: A delivery system in which the system centrally organizes individual hospital service delivery, physician arrangements, and insurance product development. The number of different products/services that are offered across the system is moderate.

Centralized Physician/Insurance Health System: A delivery system with highly centralized physician arrangements and insurance product development. Within this group, hospital services are relatively decentralized with individual hospitals having discretion over the array of services they offer. The number of different products/services that are offered across the system is moderate.

Moderately Centralized Health System: A delivery system that is distinguished by the presence of both centralized and decentralized activity for hospital services, physician arrangements, and insurance product development. For example, a system within this group may have centralized care of expensive, high technology services, such as open heart surgery, but allows individual hospitals to provide an array of other health services based on local needs. The number of different products/services that are offered across the system is moderate.

Decentralized Health System: A delivery system with a high degree of decentralized of hospital services, physician arrangements, and insurance product development. Within this group, systems may lack an overarching structure for coordination. Service and product differentiation is high, which may explain why centralization is hard to achieve. In this group, the system may simply service a role in sharing information and providing administrative support to highly developed local delivery systems centered around hospitals.

Independent Hospital System: A delivery system with limited differentiation in hospital services, physician arrangements, and insurance product development. These systems are largely horizontal affiliations of autonomous hospitals.

No Assignment: For some systems sufficient data from the Annual Survey were not available to determine a cluster assignment.

The second part of this section lists health care systems indexed geographically by state and city. Every effort has been made to be as inclusive and accurate as possible. However, as in all efforts of this type, there may be omissions. For further information, write to the Section for Health Care Systems, American Hospital Association, 155 N. Wacker Drive, Chicago, IL 60606.

Networks
The *AHA Guide* shows listings of networks. A network is defined as a group of hospitals, physicians, other providers, insurers and/or community agencies that work together to coordinate and deliver a broad spectrum of services to their community. Organizations listed represent the lead or hub of the network activity. Networks are listed by state, then alphabetically by name including participating partners.

The network identification process has purposely been designed to capture networks of varying organization type. Sources include but are not limited to the following: *AHA Annual Survey*, national, state and metropolitan associations, national news and periodical searches, and the networks and their health care providers themselves. Therefore, networks are included regardless of whether a hospital or healthcare system is the network lead. When an individual hospital does appear in the listing, it is indicative of the role the hospital plays as the network lead. In addition, the network listing is not mutually exclusive of the hospital, health care system or alliance listings within this publication.

Networks are very fluid in their composition as goals evolve and partners change. Therefore, some of the networks included in this listing may have dissolved, reformed, or simply been renamed as this section was being produced for publication.

The network identification process is an ongoing and responsive initiative. As more information is collected and validated, it will be made available in other venues, in addition to the *AHA Guide*. For more information concerning the network identification process, please contact The American Hospital Association Resource Center at 312/422–2050.

Alliances
An alliance is a formal organization, usually owned by shareholders/members, that works on behalf of its individual members in the provision of services and products and in the promotion of activities and ventures. The organization functions under a set of bylaws or other written rules to which each member agrees to abide.

Alliances are listed alphabetically by name. Its members are listed alphabetically by state, city, and then by member name.

---

[1] Bazzoli, CJ; Shortell, SM; Dubbs, N; Chan, C; and Kralovec, P; "A Taxonomy of Health networks and Systems: Bringing Order Out of Chaos" *Health Services Research*, February; 1999

Statistics for Health Care Systems and their Hospitals

The following tables describing health care systems refers to information in section B of the 2025 *AHA Guide*.

Table 1 shows the number of health care systems by type of control. Table 2 provides a breakdown of the number of systems that own, lease, sponsor or contract manage hospitals within each control category. Table 3 gives the number of hospitals and beds in each control category as well as total hospitals and beds. Finally, Table 4 shows the percentage of hospitals and beds in each control category.

For more information on health care systems, please write to the Section for Health Care Systems, 155 N. Wacker Drive, Chicago, Illinois 60606 or call 312/422–3000.

Table 1. Multihospital Health Care Systems, by Type of Organizaton Control

Type of Control	Code	Number of Systems
Catholic (Roman) church–related	CC	22
Other church–related	CO	10
Subtotal, church–related		32
Other not–for–profit	NP	299
Subtotal, not–for–profit		331
Investor Owned	IO	70
Federal Government	FG	7
Total		408

Table 2. Multihospital Health Care Systems, by Type of Ownership and Control

Type of Ownership	Catholic Church–Related (CC)	Other Church–Related (CO)	Total Church–Related (CC + CO)	Other Not–for–Profit (NP)	Total Not–for–Profit (CC, CO, + NP)	Investor–Owned (IO)	Federal Government (FG)	All Systems
Systems that only own, lease or sponsor	18	8	26	200	226	15	7	248
Systems that only contract–manage	0	0	0	12	12	7	0	19
Systems that manage, own, lease, or sponsor	4	2	6	87	93	48	0	141
Total	22	10	32	299	331	70	7	408

Table 3. Hospitals and Beds in Multihospital Health Care Systems, by Type of Ownership and Control

Type of Ownership	Catholic Church–Related (CC)		Other Church–Related (CO)		Total Church–Related (CC + CO)		Other Not–for–Profit (NP)		Total Not–for–Profit (CC, CO, + NP)		Investor–Owned (IO)		Federal Government (FG)		All Systems	
	H	B	H	B	H	B	H	B	H	B	H	B	H	B	H	B
Owned, leased or sponsored	563	95,987	93	21,134	656	117,121	1,775	378,213	2,431	495,334	1,298	158,583	201	29,611	3,930	683,528
Contract–managed	37	1,360	4	690	41	2,050	148	15,882	189	17,932	92	3,825	1	43	282	21,800
Total	600	97,347	97	21,824	697	119,171	3,550	394,095	4,247	513,266	1,390	162,408	202	29,654	5,839	705,328

H = hospitals; B = beds.

Table 4. Hospitals and Beds in Multihospital Health Care Systems, by Type of Ownership and Control as a Percentage of All Systems

Type of Ownership	Catholic Church–Related (CC)		Other Church–Related (CO)		Total Church–Related (CC + CO)		Other Not–for–Profit (NP)		Total Not–for–Profit (CC, CO, + NP)		Investor–Owned (IO)		Federal Government (FG)		All Systems	
	H	B	H	B	H	B	H	B	H	B	H	B	H	B	H	B
Owned, leased or sponsored	14.3	14.0	2.4	3.1	16.7	17.1	45.2	55.3	61.9	72.5	33.0	23.2	5.1	4.3	100	99.9
Contract–managed	13.1	6.2	1.4	3.2	14.5	9.4	52.5	55.3	67.0	82.3	32.6	23.2	0.4	4.3	100	92.2
Total	10.3	13.8	1.7	3.1	11.9	16.9	60.8	55.3	72.7	72.8	23.8	23.2	3.5	4.3	100.1	99.7

H = hospitals; B = beds.
*Please note that figures may not always equal the provided subtotal or total percentages due to rounding.

Health Care Systems and their Hospitals

0091: ACADIA HEALTHCARE COMPANY, INC. (IO)
6100 Tower Circle, Suite 1000, Franklin, TN Zip 37067–1509; tel. 615/861–6000, Chris Hunter, President and Chief Executive Officer
(Decentralized Health System)

ARIZONA: OASIS BEHAVIORAL HEALTH–CHANDLER (O, 146 beds) 2190 North Grace Boulevard, Chandler, AZ, Zip 85225–3416; tel. 480/917–9301, Jennifer Nunez, Chief Executive Officer
Web address: www.obhhospital.com/about/location

SIERRA TUCSON (O, 139 beds) 39580 South Lago Del Oro Parkway, Tucson, AZ, Zip 85739–1091; tel. 520/624–4000, Derek Price, Chief Executive Officer

SONORA BEHAVIORAL HEALTH HOSPITAL (O, 106 beds) 6050 North Corona Road, #3, Tucson, AZ, Zip 85704–1096; tel. 520/469–8700, Greer Foister, Chief Executive Officer

ARKANSAS: CONWAY BEHAVIORAL HEALTH (O, 80 beds) 2255 Sturgis Road, Conway, AR, Zip 72034–8029; tel. 855/808–5990, Stefanie Magalon, Interim Chief Executive Officer
Web address: www.conwaybh.com

RIVERVIEW BEHAVIORAL HEALTH (O, 62 beds) 701 Arkansas Boulevard, Texarkana, AR, Zip 71854–2105; tel. 870/772–5028, Colleen Vicari, Chief Executive Officer

VALLEY BEHAVIORAL HEALTH SYSTEM (O, 114 beds) 10301 Mayo Drive, Barling, AR, Zip 72923–1660; tel. 479/494–5700, Andrea Wilson, Chief Executive Officer
Web address: www.valleybehavioral.com

VANTAGE POINT OF NORTHWEST ARKANSAS (O, 114 beds) 4253 North Crossover Road, Fayetteville, AR, Zip 72703–4596; tel. 479/521–5731, Megan Wedgworth, Chief Executive Officer
Web address: www.vantagepointnwa.com

CALIFORNIA: PACIFIC GROVE HOSPITAL (O, 68 beds) 5900 Brockton Avenue, Riverside, CA, Zip 92506–1862; tel. 951/275–8400, Steven M. Hytry, PsyD, Chief Executive Officer
Web address: www.pacificgrovehospital.com

SAN JOSE BEHAVIORIAL HEALTH (O, 80 beds) 455 Silicon Valley Boulevard, San Jose, CA, Zip 95138–1858; tel. 888/210–2484, Steve Vanderpoel, Chief Executive Officer

DELAWARE: MEADOW WOOD BEHAVIORAL HEALTH SYSTEM (O, 53 beds) 575 South Dupont Highway, New Castle, DE, Zip 19720–4606; tel. 302/328–3330, Jennifer Shalk, Chief Executive Officer
Web address: www.meadowwoodhospital.com

FLORIDA: NORTH TAMPA BEHAVIORAL HEALTH (O, 124 beds) 29910 State Road 56, Wesley Chapel, FL, Zip 33543–8800; tel. 813/922–3300, Clint Hauger, Chief Executive Officer
Web address: www.northtampabehavioralhealth.com

PARK ROYAL HOSPITAL (O, 108 beds) 9241 Park Royal Drive, Fort Myers, FL, Zip 33908–9204; tel. 239/985–2700, Amber Hentz, Chief Executive Officer

GEORGIA: GREENLEAF BEHAVIORAL HEALTH HOSPITAL (O, 103 beds) 2209 Pineview Drive, Valdosta, GA, Zip 31602–7316; tel. 229/247–4357, Michelle Neville, Chief Executive Officer
Web address: www.greenleafcounseling.net

LAKEVIEW BEHAVIORAL HEALTH (O, 70 beds) 1 Technology Parkway South, Norcross, GA, Zip 30092–2928; tel. 678/713–2600, Deagan Watson, Chief Executive Officer

RIVERWOODS BEHAVIORAL HEALTH SYSTEM (O, 75 beds) 233 Medical Center Drive, Riverdale, GA, Zip 30274–2640; tel. 770/991–8500, Angela Harris, Chief Executive Officer
Web address: www.riverwoodsbehavioral.com

INDIANA: OPTIONS BEHAVIORAL HEALTH SYSTEM (O, 84 beds) 5602 Caito Drive, Indianapolis, IN, Zip 46226–1346; tel. 317/544–4340, Ryan Cassedy, Chief Executive Officer
Web address: www.optionsbehavioralhealthsystem.com/

LOUISIANA: COVINGTON BEHAVIORAL HEALTH (O, 84 beds) 201 Greenbrier Boulevard, Covington, LA, Zip 70433–7236; tel. 985/893–2970, Dustin Thiels, Group Chief Executive Officer

LONGLEAF HOSPITAL (O, 139 beds) 44 Versailles Boulevard, Alexandria, LA, Zip 71303–3960; tel. 318/445–5111, Jared Ferguson, Chief Executive Officer
Web address: www.longleafhospital.com/

RIVER PLACE BEHAVIORAL HEALTH (O, 48 beds) 500 Rue De Sante, La Place, LA, Zip 70068–5418; tel. 985/303–2327, Dustin Thiels, Group Chief Executive Officer
Web address: www.riverplacebh.com

VERMILION BEHAVIORAL HEALTH SYSTEMS–NORTH CAMPUS (O, 78 beds) 2520 North University Avenue, Lafayette, LA, Zip 70507–5306; tel. 337/234–5614, Amy Apperson, R.N., Chief Executive Officer

MASSACHUSETTS: SOUTHCOAST BEHAVIORAL HEALTH (O, 120 beds) 581 Faunce Corner Road, Dartmouth, MA, Zip 02747–1242; tel. 508/207–9800, Darcy Lichnerowicz, Chief Executive Officer
Web address: www.southcoastbehavioral.com

MICHIGAN: BCA STONECREST CENTER (O, 182 beds) 15000 Gratiot Avenue, Detroit, MI, Zip 48205–1973; tel. 313/245–0600, Steve Savage, Chief Executive Officer
Web address: www.stonecrestcenter.com

HARBOR OAKS HOSPITAL (O, 99 beds) 35031 23 Mile Road, New Baltimore, MI, Zip 48047–3649; tel. 586/725–5777, Anne Long, Chief Executive Officer
Web address: www.harboroaks.com

MISSOURI: LAKELAND BEHAVIORAL HEALTH SYSTEM (O, 206 beds) 440 South Market Street, Springfield, MO, Zip 65806–2026; tel. 417/865–5581, Nathan Duncan, Chief Executive Officer
Web address: https://www.lakelandbehavioralhealth.com/

NEVADA: SEVEN HILLS HOSPITAL (O, 134 beds) 3021 West Horizon Ridge Parkway, Henderson, NV, Zip 89052–3990; tel. 702/646–5000, Amanda Butler, Chief Executive Officer

NORTH CAROLINA: WILMINGTON TREATMENT CENTER (O, 44 beds) 2520 Troy Drive, Wilmington, NC, Zip 28401–7643; tel. 910/762–2727, Robert Pitts, Executive Director
Web address: www.wilmtreatment.com

OHIO: OHIO HOSPITAL FOR PSYCHIATRY (O, 130 beds) 880 Greenlawn Avenue, Columbus, OH, Zip 43223–2616; tel. 614/449–9664, Natasha Schafer, Chief Executive Officer
Web address: www.ohiohospitalforpsychiatry.com/

OKLAHOMA: ROLLING HILLS HOSPITAL (O, 112 beds) 1000 Rolling Hills Lane, Ada, OK, Zip 74820–9415; tel. 580/436–3600, Sherri Chandler, Chief Executive Officer

PENNSYLVANIA: BELMONT BEHAVIORAL HEALTH SYSTEM (O, 224 beds) 4200 Monument Road, Philadelphia, PA, Zip 19131–1625; tel. 215/877–2000, Laura Longstreet, Chief Executive Officer
Web address: https://www.belmontbehavioral.com/

SOUTHWOOD PSYCHIATRIC HOSPITAL (O, 74 beds) 2575 Boyce Plaza Road, Pittsburgh, PA, Zip 15241–3925; tel. 412/257–2290, Kim Lira, Chief Executive Officer
Web address: www.southwoodhospital.com

PUERTO RICO: SAN JUAN CAPESTRANO HOSPITAL (O, 158 beds) Rural Route 2, Box 11, San Juan, PR, Zip 926; tel. 787/625–2900, Marta Rivera. Plaza, Chief Executive Officer and Managing Director

SOUTH CAROLINA: REBOUND BEHAVIORAL HEALTH (O, 63 beds) 134 East Rebound Road, Lancaster, SC, Zip 29720–7712; tel. 855/999–9501, Alli Marion, Chief Executive Officer
Web address: www.reboundbehavioralhealth.com

TENNESSEE: CRESTWYN BEHAVIORAL HEALTH (O, 80 beds) 9485 Crestwyn Hills Cove, Memphis, TN, Zip 38125–8515; tel. 901/248–1500, Lindsey Blevins, Chief Executive Officer
Web address: www.crestwynbh.com

For explanation of codes following names, see page B2.
★ Indicates Type III membership in the American Hospital Association.

DELTA SPECIALTY HOSPITAL (O, 164 beds) 3000 Getwell Road, Memphis, TN, Zip 38118–2299; tel. 901/369–8100, Stephanie Reese, Chief Executive Officer
Web address: www.deltaspecialtyhospital.com

TRUSTPOINT HOSPITAL (O, 155 beds) 1009 North Thompson Lane, Murfreesboro, TN, Zip 37129–4351; tel. 615/867–1111, Holly Russell, Chief Executive Officer

TEXAS: CROSS CREEK HOSPITAL (O, 90 beds) 8402 Cross Park Drive, Austin, TX, Zip 78754; tel. 512/215–3900, Kay McKennery, Chief Executive Officer
Web address: www.cornerstonehealthcaregroup.com

RED RIVER HOSPITAL, LLC (O, 96 beds) 1505 Eighth Street, Wichita Falls, TX, Zip 76301–3106; tel. 940/322–3171, Nelson Alexander. Wanee, Chief Executive Officer
Web address: www.redriverhospital.com

RIO VISTA BEHAVIORAL HEALTH (O, 132 beds) 1390 Northwestern Drive, El Paso, TX, Zip 79912–8003; tel. 915/209–4513, Marie Alvarez, Chief Executive Officer

Owned, leased, sponsored:	38 hospitals	4138 beds
Contract–managed:	0 hospitals	0 beds
Totals:	38 hospitals	4138 beds

★**0895: ADENA HEALTH SYSTEM (NP)**
272 Hospital Road, Chillicothe, OH Zip 45601–9031; tel. 740/779–7500, Jeff Graham, President and Chief Executive Officer
(Independent Hospital System)

OHIO: ADENA FAYETTE MEDICAL CENTER (O, 25 beds) 1430 Columbus Avenue, Washington Court House, OH, Zip 43160–1791; tel. 740/335–1210, Josh McCoy, Senior Operations Executive Officer
Web address: www.fcmh.org

ADENA GREENFIELD MEDICAL CENTER (O, 25 beds) 550 Mirabeau Street, Greenfield, OH, Zip 45123–1617; tel. 937/981–9400, Josh McCoy, Senior Operations Executive Officer, Regional Vice President

ADENA PIKE MEDICAL CENTER (O, 25 beds) 100 Dawn Lane, Waverly, OH, Zip 45690–9138; tel. 740/947–2186, David M. Zanni, Administrator
Web address: www.adena.org

ADENA REGIONAL MEDICAL CENTER (O, 246 beds) 272 Hospital Road, Chillicothe, OH, Zip 45601–9031; tel. 740/779–7500, Jeff Graham, President and Chief Executive Officer

Owned, leased, sponsored:	4 hospitals	321 beds
Contract–managed:	0 hospitals	0 beds
Totals:	4 hospitals	321 beds

★**4165: ADVENTHEALTH (CO)**
900 Hope Way, Altamonte Springs, FL Zip 32714–1502; tel. 407/357–1000, Terry Shaw, President and Chief Executive Officer
(Decentralized Health System)

COLORADO: ADVENTHEALTH AVISTA (O, 108 beds) 100 Health Park Drive, Louisville, CO, Zip 80027–9583; tel. 303/673–1000, Mark T. Smith, JD, CPA, President and Chief Executive Officer

ADVENTHEALTH CASTLE ROCK (O, 90 beds) 2350 Meadows Boulevard, Castle Rock, CO, Zip 80109–8405; tel. 720/455–5000, Michelle Fuentes, Chief Executive Officer and President
Web address: www.castlerockhospital.org

ADVENTHEALTH LITTLETON (O, 221 beds) 7700 South Broadway Street, Littleton, CO, Zip 80122–2628; tel. 303/730–8900, Rick Dodds, Chief Executive Officer

ADVENTHEALTH PARKER (O, 162 beds) 9395 Crown Crest Boulevard, Parker, CO, Zip 80138–8573; tel. 303/269–4000, Michael Goebel, Chief Executive Officer
Web address: www.parkerhospital.org

ADVENTHEALTH PORTER (O, 227 beds) 2525 South Downing Street, Denver, CO, Zip 80210–5876; tel. 303/778–1955, Todd Folkenberg, Chief Executive Officer
Web address: www.porterhospital.org/poh/home/

FLORIDA: ADVENTHEALTH CARROLLWOOD (O, 114 beds) 7171 North Dale Mabry Highway, Tampa, FL, Zip 33614–2665; tel. 813/932–2222, Joe Johnson, FACHE, President and Chief Executive Officer
Web address: https://www.adventhealth.com/hospital/adventhealth-carrollwood

ADVENTHEALTH CONNERTON (O, 77 beds) 9441 Health Center Drive, Land O'Lakes, FL, Zip 34637–5837; tel. 813/903–3701, Michael Murrill, President and Chief Executive Officer

ADVENTHEALTH DADE CITY (O, 75 beds) 13100 Fort King Road, Dade City, FL, Zip 33525–5294; tel. 352/521–1100, Michael Murrill, President and Chief Executive Officer
Web address: www.floridahospital.com/dade-city

ADVENTHEALTH DAYTONA BEACH (O, 362 beds) 301 Memorial Medical Parkway, Daytona Beach, FL, Zip 32117–5167; tel. 386/231–6000, David Weis, President and Chief Executive Officer
Web address: https://www.adventhealth.com/hospital/adventhealth-daytona-beach

ADVENTHEALTH DELAND (O, 152 beds) 701 West Plymouth Avenue, DeLand, FL, Zip 32720–3236; tel. 386/943–4522, Eric E. Lunde, President and Chief Executive Officer

ADVENTHEALTH FISH MEMORIAL (O, 228 beds) 1055 Saxon Boulevard, Orange City, FL, Zip 32763–8468; tel. 386/917–5000, Lorenzo Brown, Chief Executive Officer West Volusia Market
Web address: www.fhfishmemorial.org

ADVENTHEALTH HEART OF FLORIDA (O, 212 beds) 40100 Highway 27, Davenport, FL, Zip 33837–5906; tel. 863/422–4971, Tim Clark, Chief Executive Officer, Acute Care Services
Web address: www.heartofflorida.com

ADVENTHEALTH LAKE WALES (O, 150 beds) 410 South 11th Street, Lake Wales, FL, Zip 33853–4256; tel. 863/676–1433, Royce Brown, Chief Executive Officer
Web address: https://www.adventhealth.com/hospital/adventhealth-lake-wales

ADVENTHEALTH NEW SMYRNA BEACH (O, 109 beds) 401 Palmetto Street, New Smyrna Beach, FL, Zip 32168–7399; tel. 386/424–5000, David Weis, President and Chief Executive Officer
Web address: https://www.floridahospital.com/new-smyrna

ADVENTHEALTH NORTH PINELLAS (O, 168 beds) 1395 South Pinellas Avenue, Tarpon Springs, FL, Zip 34689–3790; tel. 727/942–5000, Ryan Quattlebaum, President and Chief Executive Officer
Web address: www.fhnorthpinellas.com/

ADVENTHEALTH OCALA (O, 334 beds) 1500 SW 1st Avenue, Ocala, FL, Zip 34471–6504, P O Box 6000, Zip 34478–6000, tel. 352/351–7200, Erika Skula, Chief Executive Officer

ADVENTHEALTH ORLANDO (O, 2919 beds) 601 East Rollins Street, Orlando, FL, Zip 32803–1248; tel. 407/303–6611, Robert Craig. Deininger, President and Chief Executive Officer
Web address: www.floridahospital.com/orlando

ADVENTHEALTH PALM COAST PARKWAY (O, 100 beds) 1 AdventHealth Way, Palm Coast, FL, Zip 32137; tel. 386/302–1800, Walmir Wally"" De Aquino, Chief Executive Officer
Web address: https://www.adventhealth.com/hospital/adventhealth-palm-coast-parkway/adventhealth-palm-coast-parkway-leadership

ADVENTHEALTH PALM COAST (O, 99 beds) 60 Memorial Medical Parkway, Palm Coast, FL, Zip 32164–5980; tel. 386/586–2000, Denyse Bales–Chubb, Chief Executive Officer

ADVENTHEALTH SEBRING (O, 204 beds) 4200 Sun'n Lake Boulevard, Sebring, FL, Zip 33872–1986, P O Box 9400, Zip 33871–9400, tel. 863/314–4466, Jason Dunkel, Chief Executive Officer
Web address: https://www.adventhealth.com/hospital/adventhealth-sebring

ADVENTHEALTH TAMPA (O, 626 beds) 3100 East Fletcher Avenue, Tampa, FL, Zip 33613–4688; tel. 813/971–6000, Bruce Bergherm, Chief Executive Officer
Web address: www.floridahospital.com/tampa

ADVENTHEALTH WATERMAN (O, 300 beds) 1000 Waterman Way, Tavares, FL, Zip 32778–5266; tel. 352/253–3333, Abel Biri, Chief Executive Officer

Systems / Adventhealth

ADVENTHEALTH WAUCHULA (O, 25 beds) 735 South 5th Avenue, Wauchula, FL, Zip 33873-3158; tel. 863/773-3101, Jason Dunkel, Chief Executive Officer
Web address: https://www.adventhealth.com/hospital/adventhealth-wauchula

ADVENTHEALTH WESLEY CHAPEL (O, 145 beds) 2600 Bruce B Downs Bouelvard, Wesley Chapel, FL, Zip 33544-9207; tel. 813/929-5000, Erik Wangsness, Chief Executive Officer

ADVENTHEALTH ZEPHYRHILLS (O, 161 beds) 7050 Gall Boulevard, Zephyrhills, FL, Zip 33541-1399; tel. 813/788-0411, Michael Murrill, Chief Executive Officer
Web address: https://www.adventhealth.com/hospital/adventhealth-zephyrhills

GEORGIA: ADVENTHEALTH GORDON (O, 83 beds) 1035 Red Bud Road, Calhoun, GA, Zip 30701-2082, P O Box 12938, Zip 30703-7013, tel. 706/629-2895, Chris Self, Chief Executive Officer

ADVENTHEALTH MURRAY (O, 16 beds) 707 Old Dalton Ellijay Road, Chatsworth, GA, Zip 30705-2060, P O Box 1406, Zip 30705-1406, tel. 706/695-4564, Chris Self, Chief Executive Officer
Web address: https://www.adventhealth.com/hospital/adventhealth-murray

ADVENTHEALTH REDMOND (O, 230 beds) 501 Redmond Road, Rome, GA, Zip 30165-1415, P O Box 107001, Zip 30164-7001, tel. 706/291-0291, Isaac Sendros, President and Chief Executive Officer
Web address: https://www.adventhealth.com/hospital/redmond-regional-medical-center/our-location

ILLINOIS: UCHICAGO MEDICINE ADVENTHEALTH BOLINGBROOK (O, 134 beds) 500 Remington Boulevard, Bolingbrook, IL, Zip 60440-4906; tel. 630/312-5000, Kenneth Rose, President and Chief Executive Officer
Web address: https://www.adventhealth.com/hospital/adventhealth-bolingbrook

UCHICAGO MEDICINE ADVENTHEALTH GLENOAKS (O, 143 beds) 701 Winthrop Avenue, Glendale Heights, IL, Zip 60139-1403; tel. 630/545-8000, Vladimir Radivojevic, President and Chief Executive Officer
Web address: https://www.uchicagomedicineadventhealth.org/uchicago-medicine-adventhealth-glenoaks

UCHICAGO MEDICINE ADVENTHEALTH HINSDALE (O, 246 beds) 120 North Oak Street, Hinsdale, IL, Zip 60521-3890; tel. 630/856-6001, Adam Maycock, President and Chief Executive Officer
Web address: https://www.uchicagomedicineadventhealth.org/uchicago-medicine-adventhealth-hinsdale

UCHICAGO MEDICINE ADVENTHEALTH LA GRANGE (O, 177 beds) 5101 South Willow Spring Road, La Grange, IL, Zip 60525-2600; tel. 708/245-9000, Adam Maycock, President and Chief Executive Officer
Web address: https://www.uchicagomedicineadventhealth.org/uchicago-medicine-adventhealth-la-grange

KANSAS: ADVENTHEALTH OTTAWA (O, 30 beds) 1301 South Main Street, Ottawa, KS, Zip 66067-3598; tel. 785/229-8200, Shawn Perry, Chief Financial Officer
Web address: https://www.adventhealth.com/hospital/adventhealth-ottawa

ADVENTHEALTH SHAWNEE MISSION (O, 430 beds) 9100 West 74th Street, Merriam, KS, Zip 66204-4004, Box 2923, Shawnee Mission, Zip 66201-1323, tel. 913/676-2000, Alan Verrill, M.D., President and Chief Executive Officer
Web address: www.shawneemission.org

ADVENTHEALTH SOUTH OVERLAND PARK (O, 41 beds) 7820 West 165th Street, Overland Park, KS, Zip 66223-2925; tel. 913/373-1100, Dallas Purkeypile, Chief Executive Officer

KENTUCKY: ADVENTHEALTH MANCHESTER (O, 27 beds) 210 Marie Langdon Drive, Manchester, KY, Zip 40962-6388; tel. 606/598-5104, Jamie Couch, Interim Chief Executive Officer
Web address: www.manchestermemorial.org

NORTH CAROLINA: ADVENTHEALTH HENDERSONVILLE (O, 103 beds) 100 Hospital Drive, Hendersonville, NC, Zip 28792-5272; tel. 828/684-8501, Brandon M. Nudd, President and Chief Executive Officer

TEXAS: ADVENTHEALTH CENTRAL TEXAS (O, 183 beds) 2201 South Clear Creek Road, Killeen, TX, Zip 76549-4110; tel. 254/526-7523, Kevin A. Roberts, FACHE, President and Chief Executive Officer
Web address: www.mplex.org

ADVENTHEALTH ROLLINS BROOK (O, 18 beds) 608 North Key Avenue, Lampasas, TX, Zip 76550-1106, P O Box 589, Zip 76550-0032, tel. 512/556-3682, Kevin A. Roberts, FACHE, President and Chief Executive Officer
Web address: https://www.adventhealth.com/hospital/adventhealth-rollins-brook

TEXAS HEALTH HOSPITAL MANSFIELD (O, 59 beds) 2300 Lone Star Road, Mansfield, TX, Zip 76063-8744; tel. 682/341-5019, Eulanie Lashley, President and Chief Executive Officer

TEXAS HEALTH HUGULEY HOSPITAL FORT WORTH SOUTH (C, 228 beds) 11801 South Freeway, Burleson, TX, Zip 76028-7021, P O Box 6337, Fort Worth, Zip 76115-0337, tel. 817/293-9110, Penny Johnson, Chief Executive Officer
Web address: www.TexasHealthHuguley.org

WISCONSIN: ADVENTHEALTH DURAND (O, 25 beds) 1220 Third Avenue West, Durand, WI, Zip 54736-1600, P O Box 224, Zip 54736-0224, tel. 715/672-4211, Douglas R. Peterson, President and Chief Executive Officer
Web address: https://www.adventhealth.com/hospital/adventhealth-durand

Owned, leased, sponsored:	41 hospitals	9313 beds
Contract-managed:	1 hospitals	228 beds
Totals:	42 hospitals	9541 beds

★0235: ADVENTIST HEALTH (CO)

1 Adventist Health Way, Roseville, CA Zip 95661-3266, P O Box 619002, Zip 95661-9002, tel. 916/406-0000, Kerry Heinrich, JD, Chief Executive Officer
(Decentralized Health System)

CALIFORNIA: ADVENTIST HEALTH–TULARE (L, 108 beds) 869 North Cherry Street, Tulare, CA, Zip 93274-2287; tel. 559/688-0821, Jason Wells, FACHE, President, Central California Network, Adventist Health
Web address: https://www.adventisthealth.org/tulare/

ADVENTIST HEALTH BAKERSFIELD (O, 254 beds) 2615 Chester Avenue, Bakersfield, CA, Zip 93301-2014, P O Box 2615, Zip 93303-2615, tel. 661/395-3000, Jason Wells, FACHE, President, Central California Network, Adventist Health

ADVENTIST HEALTH CLEAR LAKE (O, 25 beds) 15630 18th Avenue, Clearlake, CA, Zip 95422-9336, P O Box 6710, Zip 95422, tel. 707/994-6486, Eric Stevens, Interim President
Web address: www.adventisthealth.org

ADVENTIST HEALTH DELANO (O, 100 beds) 1401 Garces Highway, Delano, CA, Zip 93215-3690, P O Box 460, Zip 93216-0460, tel. 661/725-4800, Jason Wells, FACHE, President, Central California Network, Adventist Health
Web address: www.drmc.org

ADVENTIST HEALTH GLENDALE (O, 502 beds) 1509 Wilson Terrace, Glendale, CA, Zip 91206-4007; tel. 818/409-8000, Alice H. Issai, President
Web address: https://www.adventisthealth.org/glendale/

ADVENTIST HEALTH HANFORD (O, 173 beds) 115 Mall Drive, Hanford, CA, Zip 93230-3513; tel. 559/582-9000, Jason Wells, FACHE, President, Central California Network, Adventist Health

ADVENTIST HEALTH HOWARD MEMORIAL (L, 25 beds) 1 Marcela Drive, Willits, CA, Zip 95490-5769; tel. 707/459-6801, Eric Stevens, President, Northern California Network
Web address: https://www.adventisthealth.org/howard-memorial/

ADVENTIST HEALTH LODI MEMORIAL (O, 194 beds) 975 South Fairmont Avenue, Lodi, CA, Zip 95240-5118, P O Box 3004, Zip 95241-1908, tel. 209/334-3411, Brooke McCollough, President

ADVENTIST HEALTH MENDOCINO COAST (L, 25 beds) 700 River Drive, Fort Bragg, CA, Zip 95437-5495; tel. 707/961-1234, Eric Stevens, Interim President
Web address: www.mcdh.org

ADVENTIST HEALTH REEDLEY (L, 49 beds) 372 West Cypress Avenue, Reedley, CA, Zip 93654-2199; tel. 559/638-8155, Jason Wells, FACHE, President
Web address: https://www.adventisthealth.org/reedley/

For explanation of codes following names, see page B2.
★ Indicates Type III membership in the American Hospital Association.

Systems / Advocate Aurora Health

ADVENTIST HEALTH SIMI VALLEY (O, 144 beds) 2975 North Sycamore Drive, Simi Valley, CA, Zip 93065-1277; tel. 805/955-6000, Alice H. Issai, President
Web address: www.simivalleyhospital.com

ADVENTIST HEALTH SONORA (O, 152 beds) 1000 Greenley Road, Sonora, CA, Zip 95370-4819; tel. 209/536-5000, Greg McCulloch, CPA, President
Web address: www.sonoramedicalcenter.org/

ADVENTIST HEALTH ST. HELENA (O, 82 beds) 10 Woodland Road, Saint Helena, CA, Zip 94574-9554; tel. 707/963-3611, Steven C. Herber, M.D., FACS, President

ADVENTIST HEALTH TEHACHAPI VALLEY (C, 24 beds) 115 West 'E' Street, Tehachapi, CA, Zip 93561-1607, P O Box 1900, Zip 93581-1900, tel. 661/823-3000, Jason Wells, FACHE, President, Central California Network, Adventist Health
Web address: www.tvhd.org

ADVENTIST HEALTH UKIAH VALLEY (O, 50 beds) 275 Hospital Drive, Ukiah, CA, Zip 95482-4531; tel. 707/462-3111, Eric Stevens, President, Northern California Network
Web address: www.adventisthealth.org

ADVENTIST HEALTH VALLEJO (O, 61 beds) 525 Oregon Street, Vallejo, CA, Zip 94590-3201; tel. 707/648-2200, Steven C. Herber, M.D., FACS, President
Web address: www.sthelenahospitals.org/location/center-for-behavioral-health

ADVENTIST HEALTH WHITE MEMORIAL (O, 353 beds) 1720 East Cesar E. Chavez Avenue, Los Angeles, CA, Zip 90033-2414; tel. 323/268-5000, John Raffoul, FACHE, President

ADVENTIST HEALTH AND RIDEOUT (O, 219 beds) 726 Fourth Street, Marysville, CA, Zip 95901-5600; tel. 530/749-4300, Chris Champlin, President
Web address: www.adventisthealth.org/rideout/

DAMERON HOSPITAL (C, 170 beds) 525 West Acacia Street, Stockton, CA, Zip 95203-2484; tel. 209/944-5550, Douglas Long, President
Web address: www.dameronhospital.org

SIERRA VISTA REGIONAL MEDICAL CENTER (O, 163 beds) 1010 Murray Avenue, San Luis Obispo, CA, Zip 93405-1806, P O Box 1367, Zip 93405, tel. 805/546-7600, Ryan Ashlock, President

TWIN CITIES COMMUNITY HOSPITAL (O, 49 beds) 1100 Las Tablas Road, Templeton, CA, Zip 93465-9796; tel. 805/434-3500, Eleze Armstrong, President
Web address: www.twincitieshospital.com

HAWAII: ADVENTIST HEALTH CASTLE (O, 152 beds) 640 Ulukahiki Street, Kailua, HI, Zip 96734-4454; tel. 808/263-5500, Ryan Ashlock, Interim President
Web address: www.castlemed.org

OREGON: ADVENTIST HEALTH COLUMBIA GORGE (O, 43 beds) 1700 East 19th Street, The Dalles, OR, Zip 97058-3317; tel. 541/296-1111, Kyle King, President

ADVENTIST HEALTH PORTLAND (O, 163 beds) 10123 SE Market Street, Portland, OR, Zip 97216-2599; tel. 503/257-2500, Kyle King, President
Web address: https://www.adventisthealth.org/portland/

ADVENTIST HEALTH TILLAMOOK (L, 25 beds) 1000 Third Street, Tillamook, OR, Zip 97141-3430; tel. 503/842-4444, Eric Swanson, President
Web address: https://www.adventisthealth.org/tillamook/

Owned, leased, sponsored:	23 hospitals	3111 beds
Contract-managed:	2 hospitals	194 beds
Totals:	25 hospitals	3305 beds

0214: ADVENTIST HEALTHCARE (NP)
820 West Diamond Avenue, Suite 600, Gaithersburg, MD Zip 20878-1419; tel. 301/315-3185, John Sackett, President and Chief Executive Officer
(Independent Hospital System)

DISTRICT OF COLUMBIA: HOWARD UNIVERSITY HOSPITAL (C, 239 beds) 2041 Georgia Avenue NW, Washington, DC, Zip 20060-0002; tel. 202/865-6100, Roger A. Mitchell Jr, M.D., President
Web address: www.huhealthcare.com

MARYLAND: ADVENTIST HEALTHCARE FORT WASHINGTON MEDICAL CENTER (O, 27 beds) 11711 Livingston Road, Fort Washington, MD, Zip 20744; tel. 301/292-7000, Eunmee Shim, R.N., MSN, President, Fort Washington and Adventist Ambulatory Networks

ADVENTIST HEALTHCARE REHABILITATION (O, 97 beds) 9909 Medical Center Drive, Rockville, MD, Zip 20850-6361; tel. 240/864-6000, Brent Reitz, President, Post Acute Care Services
Web address: https://www.adventisthealthcare.com/locations/profile/rehabilitation-rockville/

ADVENTIST HEALTHCARE WHITE OAK MEDICAL CENTER (O, 194 beds) 11890 Healing Way, Silver Spring, MD, Zip 20904; tel. 240/637-4000, Anthony Stahl, FACHE, Ph.D., President
Web address: https://www.adventisthealthcare.com

ADVENTIST HEALTHCARE SHADY GROVE MEDICAL CENTER (O, 339 beds) 9901 Medical Center Drive, Rockville, MD, Zip 20850-3395; tel. 240/826-6000, Daniel Cochran, President
Web address: www.adventisthealthcare.com

Owned, leased, sponsored:	4 hospitals	657 beds
Contract-managed:	1 hospitals	239 beds
Totals:	5 hospitals	896 beds

★1032: ADVOCATE AURORA HEALTH (NP)
3075 Highland Pkwy Suite 600, Downers Grove, IL Zip 60515-5563, 3075 Highland Pkwy Fl 6, Zip 60515-5563, tel. 630/929-8700, Eugene A. Woods, FACHE, Chief Executive Officer
(Decentralized Health System)

ILLINOIS: ADVOCATE CHRIST MEDICAL CENTER (O, 762 beds) 4440 West 95th Street, Oak Lawn, IL, Zip 60453-2699; tel. 708/684-8000, Mike Farrell, Interim President
Web address: https://www.advocatehealth.com/cmc/

ADVOCATE CONDELL MEDICAL CENTER (O, 275 beds) 801 South Milwaukee Avenue, Libertyville, IL, Zip 60048-3199; tel. 847/362-2900, Matthew Lee. Primack, President

ADVOCATE GOOD SAMARITAN HOSPITAL (O, 349 beds) 3815 Highland Avenue, Downers Grove, IL, Zip 60515-1590; tel. 630/275-5900, Eric Rhodes, President
Web address: www.advocatehealth.com/gsam

ADVOCATE GOOD SHEPHERD HOSPITAL (O, 176 beds) 450 West Highway 22, Barrington, IL, Zip 60010-1919; tel. 847/381-0123, Karen A. Lambert, FACHE, President

ADVOCATE ILLINOIS MASONIC MEDICAL CENTER (O, 315 beds) 836 West Wellington Avenue, Chicago, IL, Zip 60657-5147; tel. 773/975-1600, Susan Nordstrom. Lopez, President
Web address: www.advocatehealth.com/masonic

ADVOCATE LUTHERAN GENERAL HOSPITAL (O, 704 beds) 1775 Dempster Street, Park Ridge, IL, Zip 60068-1174; tel. 847/723-2210, Allison Wyler, President
Web address: www.advocatehealth.com/luth/

ADVOCATE SHERMAN HOSPITAL (O, 271 beds) 1425 North Randall Road, Elgin, IL, Zip 60123-2300; tel. 847/742-9800, Sheri De Shazo, R.N., FACHE, President
Web address: www.advocatehealth.com/sherman

ADVOCATE SOUTH SUBURBAN HOSPITAL (O, 217 beds) 17800 South Kedzie Avenue, Hazel Crest, IL, Zip 60429-0989; tel. 708/799-8000, Michelle Y. Blakely, Ph.D., FACHE, President
Web address: www.advocatehealth.com/ssub/

ADVOCATE TRINITY HOSPITAL (O, 138 beds) 2320 East 93rd Street, Chicago, IL, Zip 60617-3909; tel. 773/967-2000, Michelle Y. Blakely, Ph.D., FACHE, President

WISCONSIN: AURORA BAYCARE MEDICAL CENTER (O, 183 beds) 2845 Greenbrier Road, Green Bay, WI, Zip 54311-6519, P O Box 8900, Zip 54308-8900, tel. 920/288-8000, Thomas Miller, President
Web address: www.aurorabaycare.com

For explanation of codes following names, see page B2.
★ Indicates Type III membership in the American Hospital Association.

Systems / Advocate Aurora Health

AURORA LAKELAND MEDICAL CENTER (O, 62 beds) W3985 County Road NN, Elkhorn, WI, Zip 53121–4389; tel. 262/741–2000, Darrick Minzey, Vice President Finance
Web address: https://www.aurorahealthcare.org/locations/hospital/aurora-lakeland-medical-center/
AURORA MEDICAL CENTER–BAY AREA (O, 55 beds) 3003 University Drive, Marinette, WI, Zip 54143–4110; tel. 715/735–4200, Edward A. Harding, FACHE, President
Web address: www.bamc.org
AURORA MEDICAL CENTER–MANITOWOC COUNTY (O, 49 beds) 5000 Memorial Drive, Two Rivers, WI, Zip 54241–3900; tel. 920/794–5000, Cathie A. Kocourek, President
Web address: www.aurorahealthcare.org
AURORA MEDICAL CENTER–SHEBOYGAN COUNTY (O, 124 beds) 3400 Union Avenue, Sheboygan, WI, Zip 53081–8426; tel. 920/451–5000, Aric Kinney, President
AURORA MEDICAL CENTER BURLINGTON (O, 43 beds) 252 McHenry Street, Burlington, WI, Zip 53105–1828; tel. 262/767–6000, Darrick Minzey, Vice President Finance
Web address: https://www.aurorahealthcare.org/locations/hospital/aurora-medical-center-burlington/
AURORA MEDICAL CENTER GRAFTON (O, 132 beds) 975 Port Washington Road, Grafton, WI, Zip 53024–9201; tel. 262/329–1000, Carla Lafever, President
Web address: www.aurorahealthcare.org
AURORA MEDICAL CENTER KENOSHA (O, 193 beds) 10400 75th Street, Kenosha, WI, Zip 53142–7884; tel. 262/948–5600, Donna F. Jamieson, Ph.D., R.N., President
AURORA MEDICAL CENTER SUMMIT (O, 117 beds) 36500 Aurora Drive, Summit, WI, Zip 53066–4899; tel. 262/434–1000, Jessica Bauer, President
Web address: www.aurorahealthcare.org
AURORA MEDICAL CENTER IN WASHINGTON COUNTY (O, 35 beds) 1032 East Sumner Street, Hartford, WI, Zip 53027–1698; tel. 262/673–2300, Jessica Bauer, President
Web address: www.aurorahealthcare.org
AURORA MEDICAL CENTER OF OSHKOSH (O, 83 beds) 855 North Westhaven Drive, Oshkosh, WI, Zip 54904–7668; tel. 920/456–6000, Jeffrey Bard, President
AURORA PSYCHIATRIC HOSPITAL (O, 74 beds) 1220 Dewey Avenue, Wauwatosa, WI, Zip 53213–2598; tel. 414/454–6600, Jessica Small, President
Web address: www.aurorahealthcare.org
AURORA ST. LUKE'S MEDICAL CENTER (O, 633 beds) 2900 West Oklahoma Avenue, Milwaukee, WI, Zip 53215–4330, P O Box 2901, Zip 53201–2901, tel. 414/649–6000, Jennifer Schomburg, President
AURORA WEST ALLIS MEDICAL CENTER (O, 220 beds) 8901 West Lincoln Avenue, West Allis, WI, Zip 53227–2409, P O Box 27901, Zip 53227–0901, tel. 414/328–6000, Holly Schmidtke, FACHE, R.N., President
Web address: www.aurorahealthcare.org

Owned, leased, sponsored:	23 hospitals	5210 beds
Contract–managed:	0 hospitals	0 beds
Totals:	23 hospitals	5210 beds

★0160: ADVOCATE HEALTH (NP)
1000 Blythe Boulevard, Charlotte, NC Zip 28203–5812, Eugene A. Woods, FACHE, Chief Executive Officer

Owned, leased, sponsored:	0 hospitals	0 beds
Contract–managed:	0 hospitals	0 beds
Totals:	0 hospitals	0 beds

0312: AHMC HEALTHCARE (IO)
55 South Raymond Avenue, Suite 105, Alhambra, CA Zip 91801–7101; tel. 626/457–7400, Jonathan Wu, M.D., President and Chairman
(Independent Hospital System)

CALIFORNIA: AHMC ANAHEIM REGIONAL MEDICAL CENTER (O, 223 beds) 1111 West La Palma Avenue, Anaheim, CA, Zip 92801–2881; tel. 714/774–1450, Lisa Hahn, R.N., Chief Executive Officer
Web address: www.anaheimregionalmc.com
ALHAMBRA HOSPITAL MEDICAL CENTER (O, 144 beds) 100 South Raymond Avenue, Alhambra, CA, Zip 91801–3199, P O Box 510, Zip 91802–2510, tel. 626/570–1606, Evelyn Ku, R.N., MSN, Chief Executive Officer
GARFIELD MEDICAL CENTER (O, 210 beds) 525 North Garfield Avenue, Monterey Park, CA, Zip 91754–1205; tel. 626/573–2222, Herbert Villafuerte, R.N., Chief Executive Officer
Web address: www.garfieldmedicalcenter.com
GREATER EL MONTE COMMUNITY HOSPITAL (O, 115 beds) 1701 Santa Anita Avenue, South El Monte, CA, Zip 91733–3411; tel. 626/579–7777, Stanley Toy Jr, M.D., Chief Executive Officer
Web address: www.greaterelmonte.com
MONTEREY PARK HOSPITAL (O, 85 beds) 900 South Atlantic Boulevard, Monterey Park, CA, Zip 91754–4780; tel. 626/570–9000, Philip A. Cohen, Chief Executive Officer
PARKVIEW COMMUNITY HOSPITAL MEDICAL CENTER (O, 182 beds) 3865 Jackson Street, Riverside, CA, Zip 92503–3998; tel. 951/688–2211, David J. Batista, Chief Executive Officer, Doctors Hospital of Riverside/Executive Vice President, AHMC Healthcare, Inc
Web address: www.pchmc.org
SAN GABRIEL VALLEY MEDICAL CENTER (O, 273 beds) 438 West Las Tunas Drive, San Gabriel, CA, Zip 91776–1216, P O Box 1507, Zip 91778–1507, tel. 626/289–5454, Anthony Nguyen, Chief Executive Officer
Web address: www.sgvmc.org
WHITTIER HOSPITAL MEDICAL CENTER (O, 178 beds) 9080 Colima Road, Whittier, CA, Zip 90605–1600; tel. 562/945–3561, Mary Anne. Monje, Chief Executive Officer/Chief Financial Officer
Web address: www.whittierhospital.com

Owned, leased, sponsored:	8 hospitals	1410 beds
Contract–managed:	0 hospitals	0 beds
Totals:	8 hospitals	1410 beds

★0225: ALAMEDA HEALTH SYSTEM (NP)
15400 Foothill Boulevard, San Leandro, CA Zip 94578–1009; tel. 510/437–8500, James E.T. Jackson, M.P.H., Chief Executive Officer
(Moderately Centralized Health System)

CALIFORNIA: ALAMEDA HOSPITAL (O, 247 beds) 2070 Clinton Avenue, Alameda, CA, Zip 94501–4397; tel. 510/522–3700, James E.T. Jackson, M.P.H., Chief Executive Officer
Web address: www.alamedahealthsystem.org
HIGHLAND HOSPITAL (O, 438 beds) 1411 East 31st Street, Oakland, CA, Zip 94602–1018; tel. 510/437–4800, James E.T. Jackson, M.P.H., Chief Executive Officer
Web address: www.alamedahealthsystem.org

Owned, leased, sponsored:	2 hospitals	685 beds
Contract–managed:	0 hospitals	0 beds
Totals:	2 hospitals	685 beds

1020: ALECTO HEALTHCARE (IO)
16310 Bake Parkway, Suite 200, Irvine, CA Zip 92618–4684; tel. 949/783–3988, Lex Reddy, Chief Executive Officer
(Independent Hospital System)

CALIFORNIA: ST. ROSE HOSPITAL (C, 150 beds) 27200 Calaroga Avenue, Hayward, CA, Zip 94545–4383; tel. 510/264–4000, Lex Reddy, President and Chief Executive Officer
Web address: www.srhca.org

For explanation of codes following names, see page B2.
★ Indicates Type III membership in the American Hospital Association.

Systems / Alliant Management Services

TEXAS: AHS SHERMAN MEDICAL CENTER (O, 109 beds) 500 North Highland Avenue, Sherman, TX, Zip 75092-7354; tel. 903/870-4611, Julie Stumbers, Chief Executive Officer

Owned, leased, sponsored:	1 hospitals	109 beds
Contract-managed:	1 hospitals	150 beds
Totals:	2 hospitals	259 beds

★0199: ALLEGHENY HEALTH NETWORK (NP)

120 5th Avenue, FAPHM-294E, Pittsburgh, PA Zip 15222-3000; tel. 412/359-3131, James J. Benedict Jr, JD, CPA, FACHE, President
(Independent Hospital System)

NEW YORK: WESTFIELD MEMORIAL HOSPITAL (O, 4 beds) 189 East Main Street, Westfield, NY, Zip 14787-1195; tel. 716/326-4921, Rodney Buchanan, MSN, R.N., Interim President
Web address: https://www.ahn.org/locations/westfield-memorial-hospital

PENNSYLVANIA: AHN GROVE CITY (O, 36 beds) 631 North Broad Street Extension, Grove City, PA, Zip 16127-4603; tel. 724/450-7000, Christopher Clark, D.O., President
Web address: www.gcmcpa.org

AHN HEMPFIELD NEIGHBORHOOD HOSPITAL (O, 20 beds) 6321 State Route 30, Greensburg, PA, Zip 15601-9703; tel. 878/295-4735, Cynthia M. Dorundo, Market Chief Executive Officer

AHN WEXFORD HOSPITAL (O, 105 beds) 12351 Perry Highway, Wexford, PA, Zip 15090-8344; tel. 724/939-3673, Allan Klapper, M.D., President

ALLEGHENY GENERAL HOSPITAL (O, 350 beds) 320 East North Avenue, Pittsburgh, PA, Zip 15212-4756; tel. 412/359-3131, Imran Qadeer, President
Web address: www.wpahs.org/locations/allegheny-general-hospital

ALLEGHENY VALLEY HOSPITAL (O, 111 beds) 1301 Carlisle Street, Natrona Heights, PA, Zip 15065-1152; tel. 724/224-5100, Mark Rubino, M.D., President
Web address: www.wpahs.org

CANONSBURG HOSPITAL (O, 64 beds) 100 Medical Boulevard, Canonsburg, PA, Zip 15317-9762; tel. 724/745-6100, Chong S. Park, M.D., Chief Executive Officer

FORBES HOSPITAL (O, 314 beds) 2570 Haymaker Road, Monroeville, PA, Zip 15146-3513; tel. 412/858-2000, Mark Rubino, M.D., President
Web address: www.ahn.org

JEFFERSON HOSPITAL (O, 305 beds) 565 Coal Valley Road, Jefferson Hills, PA, Zip 15025-3703, Box 18119, Pittsburgh, Zip 15236-0119, tel. 412/469-5000, Chong S. Park, M.D., Chief Executive Officer

SAINT VINCENT HOSPITAL (O, 375 beds) 232 West 25th Street, Erie, PA, Zip 16544-0002; tel. 814/452-5000, Christopher Clark, D.O., President
Web address: www.svhs.org

WEST PENN HOSPITAL (O, 239 beds) 4800 Friendship Avenue, Pittsburgh, PA, Zip 15224-1722; tel. 412/578-5000, Brian Johnson, President and Chief Executive Officer
Web address: www.wpahs.org

Owned, leased, sponsored:	11 hospitals	1923 beds
Contract-managed:	0 hospitals	0 beds
Totals:	11 hospitals	1923 beds

0413: ALLEGIANCE HEALTH MANAGEMENT (IO)

504 Texas Street, Suite 200, Shreveport, LA Zip 71101-3526; tel. 318/226-8202, Rock Bordelon, President and Chief Executive Officer
(Independent Hospital System)

ARKANSAS: EUREKA SPRINGS HOSPITAL (O, 7 beds) 24 Norris Street, Eureka Springs, AR, Zip 72632-3541; tel. 479/253-7400, Angie Shaw, Chief Executive Officer

LOUISIANA: BIENVILLE MEDICAL CENTER (O, 21 beds) 1175 Pine Street, Suite 200, Arcadia, LA, Zip 71001-3122; tel. 318/263-4700, Kirk Lemoine, Chief Executive Officer
Web address: www.bienvillemedicalcenter.net/

BYRD REGIONAL HOSPITAL (O, 60 beds) 1020 West Fertitta Boulevard, Leesville, LA, Zip 71446-4645; tel. 337/239-9041, Kevin J. Quinn, Chief Executive Officer
Web address: www.byrdregional.com/

MERCY REGIONAL MEDICAL CENTER (O, 30 beds) 800 East Main Street, Ville Platte, LA, Zip 70586-4618; tel. 337/363-5684, Ashley Fontenot, Chief Executive Officer
Web address: www.mercyregionalmedicalcenter.com/

MINDEN MEDICAL CENTER (O, 77 beds) 1 Medical Plaza Place, Minden, LA, Zip 71055-3330, P O Box 5003, Zip 71058-5003, tel. 318/377-2321, Keith Cox, Chief Executive Officer
Web address: www.mindenmedicalcenter.com

NORTHERN LOUISIANA MEDICAL CENTER (O, 91 beds) 401 East Vaughn Avenue, Ruston, LA, Zip 71270-5950; tel. 318/254-2100, Kathy Hall, R.N., Chief Executive Officer
Web address: www.northernlouisianamedicalcenter.com

SABINE MEDICAL CENTER (O, 24 beds) 240 Highland Drive, Many, LA, Zip 71449-3718; tel. 318/256-5691, Dale Anderson, Chief Executive Officer

MISSISSIPPI: ALLEGIANCE SPECIALTY HOSPITAL OF GREENVILLE (O, 53 beds) 300 South Washington Avenue, 3rd Floor, Greenville, MS, Zip 38701-4719; tel. 662/332-7344, Vearnail Herzog, Chief Executive Officer
Web address: www.ahmgt.com

TEXAS: ALLEGIANCE BEHAVIORAL HEALTH CENTER OF PLAINVIEW (O, 20 beds) 2601 Dimmit Road, Suite 400, Suite 400, Plainview, TX, Zip 79072-1833; tel. 806/296-9191, William E. Ernst Jr, Chief Executive Officer

Owned, leased, sponsored:	9 hospitals	383 beds
Contract-managed:	0 hospitals	0 beds
Totals:	9 hospitals	383 beds

0317: ALLIANT MANAGEMENT SERVICES (IO)

2650 Eastpoint Parkway, Suite 300, Louisville, KY Zip 40223-5164; tel. 502/992-3525, Michael A. Kozar, President and Chief Executive Officer
(Moderately Centralized Health System)

FLORIDA: CALHOUN LIBERTY HOSPITAL (C, 25 beds) 20370 NE Burns Avenue, Blountstown, FL, Zip 32424-1045, P O Box 419, Zip 32424-0419, tel. 850/674-5411, Christinia Jepsen, R.N., Chief Executive Officer

NORTHWEST FLORIDA COMMUNITY HOSPITAL (C, 59 beds) 1360 Brickyard Road, Chipley, FL, Zip 32428-6303, P O Box 889, Zip 32428-0889, tel. 850/638-1610, Michael A. Kozar, Chief Executive Officer
Web address: www.nfch.org

ILLINOIS: GIBSON AREA HOSPITAL AND HEALTH SERVICES (C, 65 beds) 1120 North Melvin Street, Gibson City, IL, Zip 60936-1477, P O Box 429, Zip 60936-0429, tel. 217/784-4251, Robert C. Schmitt II, CPA, FACHE, Chief Executive Officer
Web address: www.gibsonhospital.org

PARIS COMMUNITY HOSPITAL (C, 25 beds) 721 East Court Street, Paris, IL, Zip 61944-2460; tel. 217/465-4141, Oliver Smith, President and Chief Executive Officer
Web address: https://www.myhorizonhealth.org/locations/paris-community-hospital/

SBL FAYETTE COUNTY HOSPITAL AND LONG TERM CARE (O, 110 beds) 650 West Taylor Street, Vandalia, IL, Zip 62471-1296; tel. 618/283-1231, Karen Dyer, Chief Executive Officer
Web address: https://www.sblfch.org/

WABASH GENERAL HOSPITAL (C, 25 beds) 1418 College Drive, Mount Carmel, IL, Zip 62863-2638; tel. 618/262-8621, Karissa Turner, President and Chief Executive Officer

INDIANA: PERRY COUNTY MEMORIAL HOSPITAL (C, 25 beds) 8885 State Road 237, Tell City, IN, Zip 47586-2750; tel. 812/547-7011, Jared M. Stimpson, Chief Executive Officer
Web address: www.pchospital.org

For explanation of codes following names, see page B2.
★ Indicates Type III membership in the American Hospital Association.

Systems / Alliant Management Services

KENTUCKY: BRECKINRIDGE MEMORIAL HOSPITAL (C, 43 beds) 1011 Old Highway 60, Hardinsburg, KY, Zip 40143-2597; tel. 270/756-7000, Angela Portman, Chief Executive Officer
Web address: www.breckinridgehealth.org/

CARROLL COUNTY MEMORIAL HOSPITAL (C, 25 beds) 309 11th Street, Carrollton, KY, Zip 41008-1400; tel. 502/732-4321, Kim Haverly, Chief Executive Officer

OWENSBORO HEALTH TWIN LAKES REGIONAL MEDICAL CENTER (C, 57 beds) 910 Wallace Avenue, Leitchfield, KY, Zip 42754-2414; tel. 270/259-9400, Ashley Herrington, Chief Executive Officer
Web address: https://www.owensborohealth.org/locations/profile/owensboro-health-twin-lakes-medical-center

Owned, leased, sponsored:	1 hospitals	110 beds
Contract-managed:	9 hospitals	349 beds
Totals:	10 hospitals	459 beds

★0041: ALLINA HEALTH (NP)
2925 Chicago Avenue, Minneapolis, MN Zip 55407-1321, P O Box 43, Zip 55440-0043, tel. 612/262-5000, Lisa Shannon, President and Chief Executive Officer
(Moderately Centralized Health System)

MINNESOTA: ABBOTT NORTHWESTERN HOSPITAL (O, 704 beds) 800 East 28th Street, Minneapolis, MN, Zip 55407-3799; tel. 612/863-4000, David Joos, President
Web address: www.abbottnorthwestern.com

ALLINA HEALTH FARIBAULT MEDICAL CENTER (O, 32 beds) 200 State Avenue, Faribault, MN, Zip 55021-6345; tel. 507/334-6451, Whitney Johnson, President

BUFFALO HOSPITAL (O, 39 beds) 303 Catlin Street, Buffalo, MN, Zip 55313-1947; tel. 763/682-1212, Joshua Shepherd, President
Web address: www.buffalohospital.org

CAMBRIDGE MEDICAL CENTER (O, 35 beds) 701 South Dellwood Street, Cambridge, MN, Zip 55008-1920; tel. 763/689-7700, Joshua Shepherd, President
Web address: www.allina.com/ahs/cambridge.nsf

MERCY HOSPITAL (O, 479 beds) 4050 Coon Rapids Boulevard, Coon Rapids, MN, Zip 55433-2586; tel. 763/236-6000, Michael Eric. Johnston, FACHE, President Southern Market, Mercy Hospital

NEW ULM MEDICAL CENTER (O, 34 beds) 1324 Fifth Street North, New Ulm, MN, Zip 56073-1553; tel. 507/217-5000, Toby Freier, President
Web address: www.newulmmedicalcenter.com

OWATONNA HOSPITAL (O, 40 beds) 2250 NW 26th Street, Owatonna, MN, Zip 55060-5503; tel. 507/451-3850, Whitney Johnson, President
Web address: https://www.allinahealth.org/owatonna-hospital

ST. FRANCIS REGIONAL MEDICAL CENTER (O, 89 beds) 1455 St Francis Avenue, Shakopee, MN, Zip 55379-3380; tel. 952/428-3000, Amy L. Jerdee, R.N., President
Web address: www.stfrancis-shakopee.com

UNITED HOSPITAL (O, 467 beds) 333 North Smith Avenue, Saint Paul, MN, Zip 55102-2389; tel. 651/241-8000, Jill Ostrem, President

WISCONSIN: RIVER FALLS AREA HOSPITAL (O, 18 beds) 1629 East Division Street, River Falls, WI, Zip 54022-1571; tel. 715/425-6155, Jill Ostrem, President
Web address: www.allina.com

Owned, leased, sponsored:	10 hospitals	1937 beds
Contract-managed:	0 hospitals	0 beds
Totals:	10 hospitals	1937 beds

★0877: ALTAPOINTE HEALTH SYSTEMS (IO)
5750-A Southland Drive, Mobile, AL Zip 36693-3316; tel. 251/450-2211, J. Tuerk. Schlesinger, Chief Executive Officer

ALABAMA: BAYPOINTE BEHAVIORAL HEALTH (O, 60 beds) 5800 Southland Drive, Mobile, AL, Zip 36693-3313; tel. 251/661-0153, Jarett Crum, Hospital Director
Web address: www.altapointe.org

EASTPOINTE HOSPITAL (O, 66 beds) 7400 Roper Lane, Daphne, AL, Zip 36526-5274; tel. 251/378-6500, Jarett Crum, Chief Hospital Officer
Web address: www.https://altapointe.org/eastpointe-hospital/

Owned, leased, sponsored:	2 hospitals	126 beds
Contract-managed:	0 hospitals	0 beds
Totals:	2 hospitals	126 beds

0420: AMERICAN HEALTHCARE SYSTEMS (IO)
505 North Brand Boulevard Suite 1110, Glendale, CA Zip 91203-3932; tel. 818/646-9933, Michael Sarian, Chairman and Chief Executive Officer

ILLINOIS: GATEWAY REGIONAL MEDICAL CENTER (O, 127 beds) 2100 Madison Avenue, Granite City, IL, Zip 62040-4799; tel. 618/798-3000, Aundrea Styles, R.N., Chief Executive Officer
Web address: www.gatewayregional.net

VISTA MEDICAL CENTER EAST (O, 190 beds) 1324 North Sheridan Road, Waukegan, IL, Zip 60085-2161; tel. 847/360-3000, Bianca Defilippi, Chief Executive Officer
Web address: www.https://vistahealth.com/vista-medical-center-east/

NORTH CAROLINA: RANDOLPH HEALTH (O, 70 beds) 364 White Oak Street, Asheboro, NC, Zip 27203-5400, P O Box 1048, Zip 27204-1048, tel. 336/625-5151, Tim Ford, President and Chief Executive Officer

Owned, leased, sponsored:	3 hospitals	387 beds
Contract-managed:	0 hospitals	0 beds
Totals:	3 hospitals	387 beds

2295: AMERICAN PROVINCE OF LITTLE COMPANY OF MARY SISTERS (CO)
9350 South California Avenue, Evergreen Park, IL Zip 60805-2595; tel. 708/229-5095, Sister, Carol Pacini, Region Leader
(Moderately Centralized Health System)

INDIANA: MEMORIAL HOSPITAL AND HEALTH CARE CENTER (O, 137 beds) 800 West Ninth Street, Jasper, IN, Zip 47546-2516; tel. 812/996-2345, E Kyle. Bennett, President and Chief Executive Officer
Web address: www.mhhcc.org

Owned, leased, sponsored:	1 hospitals	137 beds
Contract-managed:	0 hospitals	0 beds
Totals:	1 hospitals	137 beds

0644: AMG INTEGRATED HEALTHCARE MANAGEMENT (IO)
101 La Rue France, Suite 500, Lafayette, LA Zip 70508-3144; tel. 337/269-9828, Timothy W. Howard, Chief Executive Officer
(Independent Hospital System)

INDIANA: AMG SPECIALTY HOSPITAL NORTHWEST INDIANA (O, 40 beds) 9509 Georgia Street, Crown Point, IN, Zip 46307-6518; tel. 219/472-2200, Joe Bryant, Chief Executive Officer
Web address: www.https://amgihm.com/locations/indiana-crown-point/

LOUISIANA: AMG PHYSICAL REHABILITATION HOSPITAL (O, 24 beds) 5025 Keystone Boulevard, Suite 200, Covington, LA, Zip 70433; tel. 985/888-0301, Stephanie Dawsey, R.N., Chief Executive Officer

AMG SPECIALTY HOSPITAL-HOUMA (O, 40 beds) 629 Dunn Street, Houma, LA, Zip 70360-4707; tel. 985/274-0001, Rachelle Economides, R.N., Chief Executive Officer
Web address: www.amghouma.com/

AMG SPECIALTY HOSPITAL-LAFAYETTE (O, 18 beds) 4811 Ambassador Caffery Parkway, 4th Floor, Lafayette, LA, Zip 70508-7265; tel. 337/839-9880, April Ebeling, Chief Executive Officer

For explanation of codes following names, see page B2.
★ Indicates Type III membership in the American Hospital Association.

AMG SPECIALTY HOSPITAL–ZACHARY (O, 16 beds) 4601 McHugh Road, Building B, Zachary, LA, Zip 70791–5348; tel. 225/683–1600, John Derrick. Landreneau, R.N., Chief Executive Officer
Web address: www.amgzachary.com/

LAFAYETTE PHYSICAL REHABILITATION HOSPITAL (O, 24 beds) 307 Polly Lane, Lafayette, LA, Zip 70508–4960; tel. 337/314–1111, Kevin M. Romero, Chief Executive Officer

THE NEUROMEDICAL CENTER REHABILITATION HOSPITAL (O, 23 beds) 10101 Park Rowe Avenue, Suite 500, Baton Rouge, LA, Zip 70810–1685; tel. 225/906–2999, Bradley Pevey, Chief Executive Officer
Web address: www.theneuromedicalcenter.com

NEVADA: AMG SPECIALTY HOSPITAL–LAS VEGAS (O, 24 beds) 4015 Mcleod Drive, Las Vegas, NV, Zip 89121–4305; tel. 702/433–2200, Vicki Davis, Chief Executive Officer
Web address: www.amgihm.com/locations/#map_top

NEW MEXICO: AMG SPECIALTY HOSPITAL–ALBUQUERQUE (O, 24 beds) 5400 Gibson Boulevard SE, 3rd Floor, Albuquerque, NM, Zip 87108–4729, 5400 Gibson Boulevad SE, 3rd Floor, Zip 87108–4729, tel. 505/842–5550, Kendra Camp, R.N., Chief Executive Officer

OKLAHOMA: AMG SPECIALTY HOSPITAL–OKLAHOMA CITY (O, 30 beds) 4300 West Memorial Road, 2nd Floor, Oklahoma City, OK, Zip 73120–8304; tel. 405/936–5822, Erick Heflin, R.N., Chief Executive Officer
Web address: www.https://amgihm.com/locations/oklahoma-city/

Owned, leased, sponsored:	10 hospitals	263 beds
Contract–managed:	0 hospitals	0 beds
Totals:	10 hospitals	263 beds

★**0389: ANMED HEALTH (NP)**
800 North Fant Street, Anderson, SC Zip 29621–5793; tel. 864/512–1000, William A. Kenley, FACHE, Chief Executive Officer
(Independent Hospital System)

SOUTH CAROLINA: ANMED CANNON (O, 24 beds) 123 W G Acker Drive, Pickens, SC, Zip 29671–2739, P O Box 188, Zip 29671–0188, tel. 864/878–4791, Michael Cunningham, Vice President for Advancement

ANMED MEDICAL CENTER (O, 365 beds) 800 North Fant Street, Anderson, SC, Zip 29621–5793; tel. 864/512–1000, William A. Kenley, FACHE, Chief Executive Officer
Web address: www.anmedhealth.org

Owned, leased, sponsored:	2 hospitals	389 beds
Contract–managed:	0 hospitals	0 beds
Totals:	2 hospitals	389 beds

0145: APPALACHIAN REGIONAL HEALTHCARE, INC. (NP)
2260 Executive Drive, Lexington, KY Zip 40505–4810, P O Box 8086, Zip 40533–8086, tel. 859/226–2440, Hollie Harris Phillips, President and Chief Executive Officer
(Moderately Centralized Health System)

KENTUCKY: ARH OUR LADY OF THE WAY (O, 25 beds) 11203 Main Street, Martin, KY, Zip 41649; tel. 606/285–6400, Rocco K. Massey, Interim Chief Executive Officer
Web address: https://www.arh.org/portfolio_page/arh-our-lady-of-the-way-hospital/

HARLAN ARH HOSPITAL (O, 103 beds) 81 Ball Park Road, Harlan, KY, Zip 40831–1792; tel. 606/573–8100, Joseph Horton, Community Chief Executive Officer

HAZARD ARH REGIONAL MEDICAL CENTER (O, 358 beds) 100 Medical Center Drive, Hazard, KY, Zip 41701–9421; tel. 606/439–6600, Brian Springate, Chief Executive Officer
Web address: www.arh.org

HIGHLANDS ARH REGIONAL MEDICAL CENTER (O, 139 beds) 5000 Kentucky Route 321, Prestonsburg, KY, Zip 41653–1273, P O Box 668, Zip 41653–0668, tel. 606/886–8511, Jonathan Koonce, Chief Executive Officer
Web address: www.https://providers.arh.org/location/highlands-arh-regional-medical-center/loc0000132808

MARY BRECKINRIDGE ARH HOSPITAL (O, 25 beds) 130 Kate Ireland Drive, Hyden, KY, Zip 41749–9071, P O Box 447–A, Zip 41749–0717, tel. 606/672–2901, Mallie S. Noble, Chief Executive Officer

MCDOWELL ARH HOSPITAL (O, 25 beds) Route 122, McDowell, KY, Zip 41647, P O Box 247, Zip 41647–0247, tel. 606/377–3400, Danita Hampton, Chief Executive Officer
Web address: www.arh.org

MIDDLESBORO ARH HOSPITAL (O, 46 beds) 3600 West Cumberland Avenue, Middlesboro, KY, Zip 40965–2614, P O Box 340, Zip 40965–0340, tel. 606/242–1100, Michael Slusher, FACHE, Community Chief Executive Officer
Web address: www.arh.org/middlesboro

MORGAN COUNTY ARH HOSPITAL (L, 25 beds) 476 Liberty Road, West Liberty, KY, Zip 41472–2049, P O Box 579, Zip 41472–0579, tel. 606/743–3186, Allie Archer, Chief Executive Officer and Chief Nursing Officer
Web address: www.arh.org

PAINTSVILLE ARH HOSPITAL (O, 72 beds) 625 James S. Trimble Boulevard, Paintsville, KY, Zip 41240–0000; tel. 606/789–3511, Kathy Stumbo, Chief Executive Officer

TUG VALLEY ARH REGIONAL MEDICAL CENTER (O, 123 beds) 260 Hospital Drive, South Williamson, KY, Zip 41503–4072; tel. 606/237–1710, Paula Vaughan, Chief Executive Officer
Web address: www.arh.org/locations/tug_valley/about_us.aspx

WHITESBURG ARH HOSPITAL (O, 90 beds) 240 Hospital Road, Whitesburg, KY, Zip 41858–7627; tel. 606/633–3500, Ellen Wright, Chief Executive Officer
Web address: https://www.arh.org/portfolio_page/whitesburg-arh-hospital/

WEST VIRGINIA: BECKLEY ARH HOSPITAL (O, 109 beds) 306 Stanaford Road, Beckley, WV, Zip 25801–3142; tel. 304/255–3000, Todd Howell, Chief Executive Officer

SUMMERS COUNTY ARH HOSPITAL (L, 25 beds) 115 Summers Hospital Road, Hinton, WV, Zip 25951–5172, P.O. Box 940, Zip 25951–0940, tel. 304/466–1000, Joseph Preast, Chief Executive Officer
Web address: www.arh.org

Owned, leased, sponsored:	13 hospitals	1165 beds
Contract–managed:	0 hospitals	0 beds
Totals:	13 hospitals	1165 beds

★**0104: ARCHBOLD MEDICAL CENTER (NP)**
910 South Broad Street, Thomasville, GA Zip 31792–6113; tel. 229/228–2000, Darcy Craven, President and Chief Executive Officer
(Moderately Centralized Health System)

GEORGIA: ARCHBOLD BROOKS (L, 25 beds) 903 North Court Street, Quitman, GA, Zip 31643–1315, P O Box 5000, Zip 31643–5000, tel. 229/263–4171, James Womack, Interim Administrator

ARCHBOLD GRADY (L, 47 beds) 1155 Fifth Street SE, Cairo, GA, Zip 39828–3142, P O Box 360, Zip 39828–0360, tel. 229/377–1150, Crystal Wells, Administrator
Web address: www.archbold.org

ARCHBOLD MITCHELL (L, 181 beds) 90 East Stephens Street, Camilla, GA, Zip 31730–1836, P O Box 639, Zip 31730–0639, tel. 229/336–5284, Carla Beasley, R.N., MSN, Administrator
Web address: www.archbold.org

JOHN D. ARCHBOLD MEMORIAL HOSPITAL (O, 267 beds) 915 Gordon Avenue, Thomasville, GA, Zip 31792–6614, P O Box 1018, Zip 31799–1018, tel. 229/228–2000, Darcy Craven, President and Chief Executive Officer
Web address: www.archbold.org

Owned, leased, sponsored:	4 hospitals	520 beds
Contract–managed:	0 hospitals	0 beds
Totals:	4 hospitals	520 beds

For explanation of codes following names, see page B2.
★ Indicates Type III membership in the American Hospital Association.

Systems / Ardent Health Services

★0069: ARDENT HEALTH SERVICES (IO)
1 Burton Hills Boulevard, Suite 250, Nashville, TN Zip 37215–6195; tel. 615/296–3000, Marty J. Bonick, FACHE, President and Chief Executive Officer

(Decentralized Health System)

IDAHO: PORTNEUF MEDICAL CENTER (O, 178 beds) 777 Hospital Way, Pocatello, ID, Zip 83201–5175; tel. 208/239–1000, Nate Carter, Interim Chief Executive Officer and Chief Operating Officer
Web address: www.portmed.org

KANSAS: UNIVERSITY OF KANSAS HEALTH SYSTEM ST. FRANCIS CAMPUS (O, 131 beds) 1700 SW 7th Street, Topeka, KS, Zip 66606–1690; tel. 785/295–8000, Scott Campbell, Chief Executive Officer
Web address: www.https://kutopeka.com/

NEW JERSEY: HACKENSACK MERIDIAN HEALTH PASCACK VALLEY MEDICAL CENTER (O, 128 beds) 250 Old Hook Road, Westwood, NJ, Zip 07675–3123; tel. 201/383–1035, Michael Bell, Chief Executive Officer

HACKENSACK MERIDIAN MOUNTAINSIDE MEDICAL CENTER (O, 184 beds) 1 Bay Avenue, Montclair, NJ, Zip 07042–4898; tel. 973/429–6000, Tim O'Brien, Chief Executive Officer
Web address: www.mountainsidenow.com

NEW MEXICO: LOVELACE MEDICAL CENTER (O, 247 beds) 601 Martin Luther King Avenue NE, Albuquerque, NM, Zip 87102–3619; tel. 505/727–8000, Brian Miller, Chief Executive Officer

LOVELACE REGIONAL HOSPITAL–ROSWELL (O, 27 beds) 117 East 19th Street, Roswell, NM, Zip 88201–5151; tel. 575/627–7000, Nicholas Shirilla, Chief Executive Officer
Web address: www.lovelace.com

LOVELACE UNM REHABILITATION HOSPITAL (O, 62 beds) 505 Elm Street NE, Albuquerque, NM, Zip 87102–2500; tel. 505/727–4700, Troy Greer, Interim Chief Executive Officer
Web address: www.https://lovelace.com/location/lovelace-rehabilitation-hospital

LOVELACE WESTSIDE HOSPITAL (O, 80 beds) 10501 Golf Course Road NW, Albuquerque, NM, Zip 87114–5000; tel. 505/727–8000, Amy Blasing, R.N., MSN, Chief Executive Officer

LOVELACE WOMEN'S HOSPITAL (O, 78 beds) 4701 Montgomery Boulevard NE, Albuquerque, NM, Zip 87109–1251; tel. 505/727–7800, Amy Blasing, R.N., MSN, Chief Executive Officer
Web address: www.lovelace.com/albuquerque-hospital/lovelace-womens-hospital#.UDZ17KDhf48

OKLAHOMA: BAILEY MEDICAL CENTER (O, 46 beds) 10502 North 110th East Avenue, Owasso, OK, Zip 74055–6655; tel. 918/376–8000, Scott Lasson, Chief Executive Officer

HILLCREST HOSPITAL CLAREMORE (O, 49 beds) 1202 North Muskogee Place, Claremore, OK, Zip 74017–3036; tel. 918/341–2556, Jason L. Jones, R.N., Chief Executive Officer
Web address: www.hillcrestclaremore.com

HILLCREST HOSPITAL CUSHING (O, 27 beds) 1027 East Cherry Street, Cushing, OK, Zip 74023–4101; tel. 918/225–2915, Jonathan Schell, R.N., Chief Executive Officer
Web address: www.hillcrestcushing.com/

HILLCREST HOSPITAL HENRYETTA (O, 19 beds) 2401 West Main Street, Henryetta, OK, Zip 74437–3893, P O Box 1269, Zip 74437–1269, tel. 918/650–1100, Eric Eaton, Chief Executive Officer
Web address: www.hillcresthenryetta.com/

HILLCREST HOSPITAL PRYOR (O, 21 beds) 111 North Bailey Street, Pryor, OK, Zip 74361–4201; tel. 918/825–1600, Jason L. Jones, R.N., Chief Executive Officer
Web address: www.hillcrestpryor.com/

HILLCREST HOSPITAL SOUTH (O, 175 beds) 8801 South 101st East Avenue, Tulsa, OK, Zip 74133–5716; tel. 918/294–4000, Kevin J. Gross, FACHE, Interim Chief Executive Officer

HILLCREST MEDICAL CENTER (O, 496 beds) 1120 South Utica Avenue, Tulsa, OK, Zip 74104–4090; tel. 918/579–1000, Xavier Villarreal, FACHE, Chief Executive Officer
Web address: www.hillcrestmedicalcenter.com

TULSA SPINE AND SPECIALTY HOSPITAL (O, 38 beds) 6901 South Olympia Avenue, Tulsa, OK, Zip 74132–1843; tel. 918/388–5701, Trent Gastineau, Chief Executive Officer

TEXAS: BSA HOSPITAL, LLC (O, 379 beds) 1600 Wallace Boulevard, Amarillo, TX, Zip 79106–1799; tel. 806/212–2000, Michael Cruz, Chief Executive Officer
Web address: www.bsahs.org

PHYSICIANS SURGICAL HOSPITAL–QUAIL CREEK (O, 40 beds) 6819 Plum Creek, Amarillo, TX, Zip 79124–1602; tel. 806/354–6100, Bryan S. Bateman, Chief Executive Officer
Web address: www.physurg.com

SETON MEDICAL CENTER HARKER HEIGHTS (O, 83 beds) 850 West Central Texas Expressway, Harker Heights, TX, Zip 76548–1890; tel. 254/690–0900, Patrick Swindle, Chief Executive Officer
Web address: www.setonharkerheights.net

UT HEALTH ATHENS (O, 90 beds) 2000 South Palestine Street, Athens, TX, Zip 75751–5610; tel. 903/676–1000, Buddy Daniels, Chief Executive Officer

UT HEALTH CARTHAGE (O, 23 beds) 409 Cottage Road, Carthage, TX, Zip 75633–1466; tel. 903/693–3841, Mark Leitner, FACHE, Chief Executive Officer
Web address: www.https://uthealthcarthage.com/

UT HEALTH EAST TEXAS REHABILITATION HOSPITAL (O, 42 beds) 701 Olympic Plaza Circle, Tyler, TX, Zip 75701–1950, P O Box 7530, Zip 75711–7530, tel. 903/596–3000, Tracy Vinciguerra, MS, Chief Executive Officer

UT HEALTH HENDERSON (O, 42 beds) 300 Wilson Street, Henderson, TX, Zip 75652–5956; tel. 903/657–7541, Mark Leitner, FACHE, Administrator
Web address: www.https://uthealthhenderson.com/

UT HEALTH JACKSONVILLE (O, 38 beds) 501 South Ragsdale Street, Jacksonville, TX, Zip 75766–2413; tel. 903/541–5000, DeLeigh Haley, Chief Executive Officer
Web address: www.https://uthealthjacksonville.com/

UT HEALTH PITTSBURG (O, 25 beds) 2701 Highway 271 North, Pittsburg, TX, Zip 75686–1032; tel. 903/946–5000, Guybertho Cayo, Chief Executive Officer
Web address: www.https://uthealthpittsburg.com/

UT HEALTH QUITMAN (O, 25 beds) 117 Winnsboro Street, Quitman, TX, Zip 75783–2144, P O Box 1000, Zip 75783–1000, tel. 903/763–6300, Jared Smith, Chief Executive Officer
Web address: www.https://uthealthquitman.com/

UT HEALTH TYLER (O, 432 beds) 1000 South Beckham Street, Tyler, TX, Zip 75701–1908, Box 6400, Zip 75711–6400, tel. 903/597–0351, Zachary K. Dietze, Chief Executive Officer

Owned, leased, sponsored:	28 hospitals	3205 beds
Contract-managed:	0 hospitals	0 beds
Totals:	28 hospitals	3205 beds

0809: ARNOT HEALTH (NP)
600 Roe Avenue, Elmira, NY Zip 14905–1629; tel. 607/737–4100, Jonathan I. Lawrence, President and Chief Executive Officer

(Independent Hospital System)

NEW YORK: ARNOT OGDEN MEDICAL CENTER (O, 322 beds) 600 Roe Avenue, Elmira, NY, Zip 14905–1629; tel. 607/737–4100, Jonathan I. Lawrence, President and Chief Executive Officer
Web address: www.arnothealth.org

IRA DAVENPORT MEMORIAL HOSPITAL (O, 135 beds) 7571 State Route 54, Bath, NY, Zip 14810–9590; tel. 607/776–8500, Elizabeth Weir, MSN, R.N., Site Administrator and Vice President of Nursing

Owned, leased, sponsored:	2 hospitals	457 beds
Contract-managed:	0 hospitals	0 beds
Totals:	2 hospitals	457 beds

For explanation of codes following names, see page B2.
★ Indicates Type III membership in the American Hospital Association.

★0094: ASANTE HEALTH SYSTEM (NP)
2650 Siskiyou Boulevard, Suite 200, Medford, OR Zip 97504–8170; tel. 541/789-4100, Thomas D. Gessel, FACHE, President and Chief Executive Officer
(Centralized Health System)

OREGON: ASANTE ASHLAND COMMUNITY HOSPITAL (O, 34 beds) 280 Maple Street, Ashland, OR, Zip 97520–1593; tel. 541/201-4000, Brandon Mencini, Chief Executive Officer
Web address: https://www.asante.org/Locations/location-detail/asante-ashland-community-hospital/

ASANTE ROGUE REGIONAL MEDICAL CENTER (O, 352 beds) 2825 East Barnett Road, Medford, OR, Zip 97504–8332; tel. 541/789-7000, Brandon Mencini, Chief Executive Officer
Web address: www.asante.org

ASANTE THREE RIVERS MEDICAL CENTER (O, 123 beds) 500 SW Ramsey Avenue, Grants Pass, OR, Zip 97527–5554; tel. 541/472-7000, Patrick Sharp, Chief Executive Officer

Owned, leased, sponsored:	3 hospitals	509 beds
Contract-managed:	0 hospitals	0 beds
Totals:	3 hospitals	509 beds

★0198: ASCENSION HEALTHCARE (CC)
4600 Edmundson Road, Saint Louis, MO Zip 63134; tel. 314/733-8000, Joseph R. Impicciche, JD, Chief Executive Officer
(Decentralized Health System)

ALABAMA: ASCENSION ST. VINCENT'S BIRMINGHAM (S, 387 beds) 810 St Vincent's Drive, Birmingham, AL, Zip 35205–1695, P O Box 12407, Zip 35202–2407, tel. 205/939-7000, Tim Puthoff, President
Web address: www.https://healthcare.ascension.org/locations/alabama/albir/birmingham-ascension-st-vincents-birmingham

ASCENSION ST. VINCENT'S BLOUNT (S, 25 beds) 150 Gilbreath, Oneonta, AL, Zip 35121–2827, P O Box 1000, Zip 35121–0013, tel. 205/274-3000, Greg Brown, President
Web address: www.https://healthcare.ascension.org/locations/alabama/albir/oneonta-ascension-st-vincents-blount

ASCENSION ST. VINCENT'S CHILTON (L, 36 beds) 2030 Lay Dam Road, Clanton, AL, Zip 35045; tel. 205/258-4400, Shanon Hamilton, Administrator

ASCENSION ST. VINCENT'S EAST (S, 308 beds) 50 Medical Park East Drive, Birmingham, AL, Zip 35235–9987; tel. 205/838-3000, Suzannah Campbell, President
Web address: www.https://healthcare.ascension.org/locations/alabama/albir/birmingham-ascension-st-vincents-east

ASCENSION ST. VINCENT'S ST. CLAIR (S, 40 beds) 7063 Veterans Parkway, Pell City, AL, Zip 35125–1499; tel. 205/814-2105, Lisa Nichols, President
Web address: www.https://healthcare.ascension.org/locations/alabama/albir/pell-city-ascension-st-vincents-st-clair

FLORIDA: ASCENSION SACRED HEART BAY (O, 201 beds) 615 North Bonita Avenue, Panama City, FL, Zip 32401–3600; tel. 850/769-1511, Robin M. Godwin, MSN, Administrator

ASCENSION SACRED HEART EMERALD COAST (S, 86 beds) 7800 Highway 98 West, Miramar Beach, FL, Zip 32550; tel. 850/278-3000, Trey Abshier, Chief Executive Officer
Web address: www.https://healthcare.ascension.org/locations/florida/flpen/miramar-beach-ascension-sacred-heart-emerald-coast

ASCENSION SACRED HEART GULF (S, 19 beds) 3801 East Highway 98, Port St Joe, FL, Zip 32456–5318; tel. 850/229-5600, Henry Stovall, Regional President
Web address: www.sacred-heart.org/gulf/

ASCENSION SACRED HEART PENSACOLA (S, 465 beds) 5151 North Ninth Avenue, Pensacola, FL, Zip 32504–8795, P O Box 2700, Zip 32513–2700, tel. 850/416-7000, William Condon, President
Web address: www.https://healthcare.ascension.org/Locations/Florida/FLPEN/Pensacola-Sacred-Heart-Hospital-Pensacola

ASCENSION ST. VINCENT'S ST. JOHNS COUNTY (O, 56 beds) 205 Trinity Way, Saint Johns, FL, Zip 32259–1155; tel. 904/691-1000, Cory Darling, Chief Executive Officer

ASCENSION ST. VINCENT'S CLAY COUNTY (O, 134 beds) 1670 St. Vincent's Way, Middleburg, FL, Zip 32068–8427, 1670 St. Vincents Way, Zip 32068–8447, tel. 904/602-1000, Bryan Walrath, President
Web address: www.jaxhealth.com/

ASCENSION ST. VINCENT'S RIVERSIDE (S, 281 beds) 1 Shircliff Way, Jacksonville, FL, Zip 32204–4748, P O Box 2982, Zip 32203–2982, tel. 904/308-7300, Scott Kashman, President

ASCENSION ST. VINCENT'S SOUTHSIDE (S, 234 beds) 4201 Belfort Road, Jacksonville, FL, Zip 32216–1431; tel. 904/296-3700, Kevin Rinks, Chief Executive Officer
Web address: www.jaxhealth.com

ILLINOIS: ASCENSION ALEXIAN BROTHERS BEHAVIORAL HEALTH HOSPITAL (O, 141 beds) 1650 Moon Lake Boulevard, Hoffman Estates, IL, Zip 60169–1010; tel. 847/882-1600, Clayton Ciha, President and Chief Executive Officer
Web address: www.https://healthcare.ascension.org/locations/illinois/ilchi/hoffman-estates-ascension-alexian-brothers-behavioral-health-hospital

ASCENSION ALEXIAN BROTHERS (O, 376 beds) 800 Biesterfield Road, Elk Grove Village, IL, Zip 60007–3397; tel. 847/437-5500, Dan Doherty, Chief Executive Officer
Web address: www.https://healthcare.ascension.org/locations/illinois/ilchi/elk-grove-village-ascension-alexian-brothers

ASCENSION HOLY FAMILY (O, 178 beds) 100 North River Road, Des Plaines, IL, Zip 60016–1255; tel. 847/297-1800, Yolande Wilson-Stubbs, President

ASCENSION MERCY (O, 292 beds) 1325 North Highland Avenue, Aurora, IL, Zip 60506–1449; tel. 630/859-2222, Fernando Gruta, President
Web address: www.https://healthcare.ascension.org/locations/illinois/ilchi/aurora-ascension-mercy

ASCENSION RESURRECTION (O, 337 beds) 7435 West Talcott Avenue, Chicago, IL, Zip 60631–3746; tel. 773/774-8000, Len Wilk, President
Web address: www.https://healthcare.ascension.org/locations/illinois/ilchi/chicago-ascension-resurrection

ASCENSION SAINT FRANCIS (O, 197 beds) 355 Ridge Avenue, Evanston, IL, Zip 60202–3399; tel. 847/316-4000, Kendall Johnson, Interim Chief Executive Officer
Web address: www.https://healthcare.ascension.org/locations/illinois/ilchi/evanston-ascension-saint-francis

ASCENSION SAINT JOSEPH–CHICAGO (O, 338 beds) 2900 North Lake Shore Drive, Chicago, IL, Zip 60657–6274; tel. 773/665-3000, JOHN BAIRD, Chief Executive Officer

ASCENSION SAINT JOSEPH–ELGIN (O, 184 beds) 77 North Airlite Street, Elgin, IL, Zip 60123–4912; tel. 847/695-3200, Eva Balderrama, President
Web address: www.https://healthcare.ascension.org/locations/illinois/ilchi/elgin-ascension-saint-joseph

ASCENSION SAINT JOSEPH–JOLIET (O, 485 beds) 333 North Madison Street, Joliet, IL, Zip 60435–8200; tel. 815/725-7133, Barbara Martin, President
Web address: www.https://healthcare.ascension.org/locations/illinois/ilchi/joliet-ascension-saint-joseph

ASCENSION SAINT MARY–CHICAGO (O, 441 beds) 2233 West Division Street, Chicago, IL, Zip 60622–3086; tel. 312/770-2000, Ellis Hawkins, FACHE, President

ASCENSION ST. ALEXIUS (O, 298 beds) 1555 Barrington Road, Hoffman Estates, IL, Zip 60169–1019; tel. 847/843-2000, Roxann E. Barber, President and Chief Executive Officer
Web address: www.https://healthcare.ascension.org/locations/illinois/ilchi/hoffman-estates-ascension-saint-alexius

ASCENSION ST. MARY–KANKAKEE (O, 182 beds) 500 West Court Street, Kankakee, IL, Zip 60901–3661; tel. 815/937-2400, Otis L. Story Sr, President
Web address: www.https://healthcare.ascension.org/locations/illinois/ilchi/kankakee-ascension-saint-mary

OUR LADY OF THE RESURRECTION–LONG TERM CARE (O, 50 beds) 5645 West Addison Street, Chicago, IL, Zip 60634

RESURRECTION NURSING PAVILION (O, 295 beds) 1001 North Greenwood, Park Ridge, IL, Zip 60068, Patricia Tiernan, Administrator

For explanation of codes following names, see page B2.
★ Indicates Type III membership in the American Hospital Association.

Systems / Ascension Healthcare

INDIANA: ASCENSION ST. VINCENT ANDERSON (S, 152 beds) 2015 Jackson Street, Anderson, IN, Zip 46016-4339; tel. 765/649-2511, Marion Teixeira, Chief Executive Officer
Web address: www.https://healthcare.ascension.org/locations/indiana/ineva/anderson-ascension-st-vincent-anderson

ASCENSION ST. VINCENT CARMEL HOSPITAL (S, 121 beds) 13500 North Meridian Street, Carmel, IN, Zip 46032-1456; tel. 317/582-7000, Chad Dilley, President
Web address: https://www.stvincent.org

ASCENSION ST. VINCENT CLAY HOSPITAL (S, 25 beds) 1206 East National Avenue, Brazil, IN, Zip 47834-2797, 1206 East National Ave, Zip 47834-0489, tel. 812/442-2500, Jerry Laue, Administrator

ASCENSION ST. VINCENT EVANSVILLE (S, 384 beds) 3700 Washington Avenue, Evansville, IN, Zip 47714-0541; tel. 812/485-4000, Alex Chang, President and Chief Executive Officer
Web address: www.https://healthcare.ascension.org/locations/indiana/ineva/evansville-ascension-st-vincent-evansville

ASCENSION ST. VINCENT FISHERS (S, 46 beds) 13861 Olio Road, Fishers, IN, Zip 46037-3487; tel. 317/415-9000, Jeralene Hudson, Director
Web address: www.stvincent.org

ASCENSION ST. VINCENT HEART CENTER (S, 80 beds) 10580 North Meridian Street, Indianapolis, IN, Zip 46290-1028; tel. 317/583-5000, Lori Shannon, President

ASCENSION ST. VINCENT INDIANAPOLIS HOSPITAL (S, 787 beds) 2001 West 86th Street, Indianapolis, IN, Zip 46260-1991, P O Box 40970, Zip 46240-0970, tel. 317/338-2345, Daniel A. Parod, President Central Region
Web address: www.stvincent.org

ASCENSION ST. VINCENT JENNINGS (S, 17 beds) 301 Henry Street, North Vernon, IN, Zip 47265-1097; tel. 812/352-4200, Christina Crank, Administrator, Chief Nursing Officer
Web address: www.stvincent.org

ASCENSION ST. VINCENT KOKOMO (S, 117 beds) 1907 West Sycamore Street, Kokomo, IN, Zip 46901-4197; tel. 765/452-5611, Don Damron, Chief Executive Officer

ASCENSION ST. VINCENT MERCY (S, 18 beds) 1331 South 'A' Street, Elwood, IN, Zip 46036-1942; tel. 765/552-4600, Ann C. Yates, R.N., MSN, Administrator and Chief Nursing Officer
Web address: www.stvincent.org

ASCENSION ST. VINCENT RANDOLPH (S, 25 beds) 473 Greenville Avenue, Winchester, IN, Zip 47394-9436; tel. 765/584-0004, Rodney Stevens, Administrator
Web address: www.stvincent.org

ASCENSION ST. VINCENT SALEM (S, 25 beds) 911 North Shelby Street, Salem, IN, Zip 47167-1694; tel. 812/883-5881, Donna Cassidy, Hospital Administrator

ASCENSION ST. VINCENT SETON SPECIALTY HOSPITAL (S, 72 beds) 8050 Township Line Road, Indianapolis, IN, Zip 46260-2478; tel. 317/415-8500, Daniel A. Parod, President Central Region
Web address: www.stvincent.org/

ASCENSION ST. VINCENT WARRICK (S, 35 beds) 1116 Millis Avenue, Boonville, IN, Zip 47601-2204; tel. 812/897-4800, Marty Mattingly, Administrator
Web address: www.https://healthcare.ascension.org

ASCENSION ST. VINCENT WILLIAMSPORT (S, 16 beds) 412 North Monroe Street, Williamsport, IN, Zip 47993-1049; tel. 765/762-4000, Melanie Jane. Craigin, Chief Executive Officer and Administrator
Web address: www.stvincent.org

DAVIESS COMMUNITY HOSPITAL (C, 72 beds) 1314 East Walnut Street, Washington, IN, Zip 47501-2860, P O Box 760, Zip 47501-0760, tel. 812/254-2760, Tracy Conroy, Chief Executive Officer

KANSAS: ASCENSION VIA CHRISTI HOSPITAL ON ST. TERESA (O, 35 beds) 14800 West St. Teresa, Wichita, KS, Zip 67235-9602; tel. 316/796-7000, Laurie Labarca, President
Web address: www.via-christi.org/st-teresa

ASCENSION VIA CHRISTI HOSPITAL, MANHATTAN (O, 94 beds) 1823 College Avenue, Manhattan, KS, Zip 66502-3346; tel. 785/776-3322, Robert C. Copple, FACHE, President

ASCENSION VIA CHRISTI REHABILITATION HOSPITAL (O, 30 beds) 1151 North Rock Road, Wichita, KS, Zip 67206-1262; tel. 316/634-3400, Laurie Labarca, President
Web address: www.via-christi.org

ASCENSION VIA CHRISTI ST. FRANCIS (O, 669 beds) 211 N College Ave, Mulvane, KS, Zip 67110, 929 North St Francis Street, Wichita, Zip 67214-3882, tel. 316/268-5000, Joy Scott, Market Administrator
Web address: www.via-christi.org

WAMEGO HEALTH CENTER (O, 8 beds) 711 Genn Drive, Wamego, KS, Zip 66547-1179; tel. 785/456-2295, Brian Howells, Administrator

MARYLAND: ASCENSION SAINT AGNES (S, 367 beds) 900 South Caton Avenue, Baltimore, MD, Zip 21229-5201; tel. 667/234-6000, Beau Higginbotham, Interim Chief Executive Officer, Chief Strategy Officer and Chief Operating Officer
Web address: www.https://healthcare.ascension.org/locations/maryland/mdbal/baltimore-ascension-saint-agnes-hospital

MICHIGAN: ASCENSION BORGESS ALLEGAN HOSPITAL (O, 25 beds) 555 Linn Street, Allegan, MI, Zip 49010-1524; tel. 269/673-8424, Dean Kindler, M.D., Regional President and Chief Executive Officer
Web address: www.https://healthcare.ascension.org/locations/michigan/mikal/allegan-ascension-borgess-allegan-hospital

ASCENSION BORGESS HOSPITAL (S, 393 beds) 1521 Gull Road, Kalamazoo, MI, Zip 49048-1640; tel. 269/226-7000, Dean Kindler, M.D., Regional President and Chief Executive Officer

ASCENSION BORGESS-LEE HOSPITAL (S, 25 beds) 420 West High Street, Dowagiac, MI, Zip 49047-1943; tel. 269/782-8681, Dean Kindler, M.D., Regional President and Chief Executive Officer
Web address: www.https://healthcare.ascension.org/locations/michigan/mikal/dowagiac-ascension-borgess-lee-hospital

ASCENSION BRIGHTON CENTER FOR RECOVERY (S, 63 beds) 12851 Grand River Road, Brighton, MI, Zip 48116-8506; tel. 810/227-1211, Barbara Shoup, R.N., Hospital Administrator

ASCENSION GENESYS HOSPITAL (S, 379 beds) 1 Genesys Parkway, Grand Blanc, MI, Zip 48439-8066; tel. 810/606-5000, Douglas Apple, M.D., Chief Clinical Officer Ascension Michigan & Interim President and CEO Ascension Genesys
Web address: www.genesys.org

ASCENSION MACOMB-OAKLAND HOSPITAL, WARREN CAMPUS (S, 479 beds) 11800 East 12 Mile Road, Warren, MI, Zip 48093-3472; tel. 586/573-5000, Kevin Grady, M.D., East Region President
Web address: www.https://healthcare.ascension.org/locations/michigan/midet/warren-ascension-macomboakland-hospital-warren-campus

ASCENSION PROVIDENCE HOSPITAL, SOUTHFIELD CAMPUS (S, 628 beds) 16001 West Nine Mile Road, Southfield, MI, Zip 48075; tel. 248/849-3000, Michael Wiemann, M.D., Regional President & CEO, Ascension Metro West Region
Web address: www.https://healthcare.ascension.org/locations/michigan/midet/southfield-ascension-providence-hospital-southfield-campus

ASCENSION PROVIDENCE ROCHESTER HOSPITAL (O, 226 beds) 1101 West University Drive, Rochester, MI, Zip 48307-1831; tel. 248/652-5000, Michael Wiemann, M.D., Regional President & Chief Executive Officer, Ascension Metro West Region
Web address: www.https://healthcare.ascension.org/Locations/Michigan/MIROC/Rochester-Ascension-Providence-Rochester-Hospital

ASCENSION RIVER DISTRICT HOSPITAL (S, 12 beds) 4100 River Road, East China, MI, Zip 48054-2909; tel. 810/329-7111, Kevin Grady, M.D., East Region President
Web address: www.https://healthcare.ascension.org/Locations/Michigan/MIDET/East-China-Township-Ascension-River-District-Hospital

ASCENSION ST. JOHN HOSPITAL (S, 562 beds) 22101 Moross Road, Detroit, MI, Zip 48236-2148; tel. 313/343-4000, Kevin Grady, M.D., East Region President

OKLAHOMA: ASCENSION ST. JOHN BROKEN ARROW (O, 44 beds) 1000 West Boise Circle, Broken Arrow, OK, Zip 74012-4900; tel. 918/994-8100, Matthew Adams, President
Web address: www.stjohnbrokenarrow.com

ASCENSION ST. JOHN JANE PHILLIPS (O, 105 beds) 3500 East Frank Phillips Boulevard, Bartlesville, OK, Zip 74006-2411; tel. 918/333-7200, Bryan Cavitt, President

For explanation of codes following names, see page B2.
★ Indicates Type III membership in the American Hospital Association.

Systems / Ascension Healthcare

ASCENSION ST. JOHN MEDICAL CENTER (O, 523 beds) 1923 South Utica Avenue, Tulsa, OK, Zip 74104-6502; tel. 918/744-2345, Bo Beaudry, Chief Executive Officer
Web address: www.https://healthcare.ascension.org/Locations/Oklahoma/OKTUL/Tulsa-Ascension-St-John-Medical-Center

ASCENSION ST. JOHN NOWATA (O, 15 beds) 237 South Locust Street, Nowata, OK, Zip 74048-3660; tel. 918/273-3102, Jason McCauley, Administrator

ASCENSION ST. JOHN OWASSO (O, 36 beds) 12451 East 100th Street North, Owasso, OK, Zip 74055-4600; tel. 918/274-5000, Mark Clay, President
Web address: www.stjohnowasso.com

ASCENSION ST. JOHN SAPULPA (O, 25 beds) 1004 East Bryan Avenue, Sapulpa, OK, Zip 74066-4513, P O Box 1368, Zip 74067-1368, tel. 918/224-4280, Michael Christian, President
Web address: www.stjohnhealthsystem.com/sapulpa

TENNESSEE: ASCENSION SAINT THOMAS BEHAVIORAL HEALTH HOSPITAL (O, 76 beds) 300 Great Circle Road, Nashville, TN, Zip 37228-1752; tel. 615/813-1880, Jared Roe, Chief Executive Officer
Web address: www.saintthomasbehavioral.com

ASCENSION SAINT THOMAS DEKALB (O, 12 beds) 520 West Main Street, Smithville, TN, Zip 37166-1138, P O Box 640, Zip 37166-0640, tel. 615/215-5000, Raymond Johnson, Chief Administrative Officer
Web address: www.https://healthcare.ascension.org/Locations/Tennessee/TNNAS/Smithville-Ascension-Saint-Thomas-Dekalb

ASCENSION SAINT THOMAS HICKMAN (S, 8 beds) 135 East Swan Street, Centerville, TN, Zip 37033-1417; tel. 931/729-4271, Kevin Campbell, Chief Executive Officer

ASCENSION SAINT THOMAS HIGHLANDS (O, 26 beds) 401 Sewell Road, Sparta, TN, Zip 38583-1299; tel. 931/738-9211, Robert Peglow, Chief Administrative Officer
Web address: www.https://healthcare.ascension.org/Locations/Tennessee/TNNAS/Sparta-Ascension-Saint-Thomas-Highlands

ASCENSION SAINT THOMAS HOSPITAL FOR SPECIALTY SURGERY (S, 23 beds) 2011 Murphy Avenue, Suite 400, Nashville, TN, Zip 37203-2065; tel. 615/341-7500, Ryan Walker, Chief Executive Officer

ASCENSION SAINT THOMAS HOSPITAL (S, 864 beds) 4220 Harding Pike, Nashville, TN, Zip 37205-2095, P O Box 380, Zip 37202-0380, tel. 615/222-2111, Shubhada Jagasia, President and Chief Executive Officer
Web address: www.https://healthcare.ascension.org/Locations/Tennessee/TNNAS/Nashville-Ascension-Saint-Thomas-Hospital

ASCENSION SAINT THOMAS RIVER PARK (O, 63 beds) 1559 Sparta Street, Mc Minnville, TN, Zip 37110-1316; tel. 931/815-4000, Robert Dale. Humphrey, Chief Executive Officer

ASCENSION SAINT THOMAS RUTHERFORD (S, 368 beds) 1700 Medical Center Parkway, Murfreesboro, TN, Zip 37129-2245; tel. 615/396-4100, Gordon B. Ferguson, President and Chief Executive Officer
Web address: www.https://healthcare.ascension.org/Locations/Tennessee/TNNAS/Murfreesboro-Ascension-Saint-Thomas-Rutherford

ASCENSION SAINT THOMAS STONES RIVER (O, 36 beds) 324 Doolittle Road, Woodbury, TN, Zip 37190-1139; tel. 615/563-4001, Raymond Johnson, Chief Administrative Officer
Web address: www.https://healthcare.ascension.org/Locations/Tennessee/TNNAS/Woodbury-Ascension-Saint-Thomas-Stones-River

ASCENSION ST. THOMAS THREE RIVERS (O, 14 beds) 451 Highway 13 South, Waverly, TN, Zip 37185-2109, P O Box 437, Zip 37185-0437, tel. 931/296-4203, Freda Russell, R.N., Administrator

TEXAS: ASCENSION PROVIDENCE (S, 285 beds) 6901 Medical Parkway, Waco, TX, Zip 76712-7998, P O Box 2589, Zip 76702-2589, tel. 254/751-4000, Philip A. Patterson, President Providence Health Center/Network
Web address: www.https://healthcare.ascension.org/locations/texas/txwac/waco-ascension-providence

ASCENSION SETON BASTROP (O, 7 beds) 630 TX-71 West, Bastrop, TX, Zip 78602-4234; tel. 737/881-7400, Jace Jones, Chief Administrative Officer

ASCENSION SETON EDGAR B. DAVIS HOSPITAL (S, 15 beds) 130 Hays Street, Luling, TX, Zip 78648-3207; tel. 830/875-7000, Jace Jones, Chief Administrative Officer
Web address: www.https://healthcare.ascension.org/locations/texas/txaus/luling-ascension-seton-edgar-b-davis

ASCENSION SETON HAYS (O, 154 beds) 6001 Kyle Parkway, Kyle, TX, Zip 78640-6112; tel. 512/504-5000, Joan Ross, President

ASCENSION SETON HIGHLAND LAKES (S, 19 beds) 3201 South Water Street, Burnet, TX, Zip 78611-4510, P O Box 1219, Zip 78611-7219, tel. 512/715-3000, Karen Christine. Litterer, R.N., MSN, Chief Administrator and Chief Nursing Officer
Web address: www.https://healthcare.ascension.org/locations/texas/txaus/burnet-ascension-seton-highland-lakes

ASCENSION SETON MEDICAL CENTER AUSTIN (S, 390 beds) 1201 West 38th Street, Austin, TX, Zip 78705-1006; tel. 512/324-1000, Wesley Tidwell, President

ASCENSION SETON NORTHWEST (S, 98 beds) 11113 Research Boulevard, Austin, TX, Zip 78759-5236; tel. 512/324-6000, Steven Brockman-Weber, President Seton Southwest & Northwest
Web address: www.seton.net

ASCENSION SETON SHOAL CREEK (S, 62 beds) 3501 Mills Avenue, Austin, TX, Zip 78731-6391; tel. 512/324-2000, Sam Cunningham, Director Ascension Seton Shoal Creek

ASCENSION SETON SMITHVILLE (O, 8 beds) 1201 Hill Road, Smithville, TX, Zip 78957; tel. 512/237-3214, Jace Jones, Chief Executive Officer and Administrator
Web address: www.https://healthcare.ascension.org/Locations/Texas/TXAUS/Smithville-Ascension-Seton-Smithville

ASCENSION SETON SOUTHWEST (S, 11 beds) 7900 F M 1826, Building 1, Austin, TX, Zip 78737-1407; tel. 512/324-9000, Steven Brockman-Weber, President Seton Southwest & Northwest

ASCENSION SETON WILLIAMSON (S, 181 beds) 201 Seton Parkway, Round Rock, TX, Zip 78665-8000; tel. 512/324-4000, Andrew Gnann, President
Web address: www.https://healthcare.ascension.org/locations/texas/txaus/round-rock-ascension-seton-williamson

DELL CHILDREN'S MEDICAL CENTER OF CENTRAL TEXAS (S, 299 beds) 4900 Mueller Boulevard, Austin, TX, Zip 78723-3079; tel. 512/324-0000, Michael Wiggins, President

DELL SETON MEDICAL CENTER AT THE UNIVERSITY OF TEXAS (O, 320 beds) 1500 Red River Street, Austin, TX, Zip 78701; tel. 512/324-7000, Adam Messer, President
Web address: www.seton.net/locations/dell-seton/

WISCONSIN: ASCENSION ALL SAINTS (O, 124 beds) 3801 Spring Street, Racine, WI, Zip 53405-1690; tel. 262/687-4011, Kristin McManmon, President
Web address: www.allsaintshealth.com

ASCENSION CALUMET HOSPITAL (O, 12 beds) 614 Memorial Drive, Chilton, WI, Zip 53014-1597; tel. 920/849-2386, Michael Bergmann, President

ASCENSION COLUMBIA ST. MARY'S HOSPITAL MILWAUKEE (S, 230 beds) 2301 North Lake Drive, Milwaukee, WI, Zip 53211-4508; tel. 414/291-1000, Andre Storey, President
Web address: www.https://healthcare.ascension.org/locations/wisconsin/wimil/milwaukee-ascension-columbia-st-marys-hospital-milwaukee/

ASCENSION NORTHEAST WISCONSIN MERCY HOSPITAL (O, 41 beds) 500 South Oakwood Road, Oshkosh, WI, Zip 54904-7944; tel. 920/223-2000, Shane Carter, R.N., President
Web address: www.affinityhealth.org

ASCENSION NORTHEAST WISCONSIN ST. ELIZABETH HOSPITAL (O, 114 beds) 1506 South Oneida Street, Appleton, WI, Zip 54915-1305; tel. 920/738-2000, Michael Bergmann, President

ASCENSION SACRED HEART REHABILITATION HOSPITAL (S, 15 beds) 13111 North Port Washington Road, Mequon, WI, Zip 53097-2416; tel. 262/292-0400, Julie Jolitz, Administrator
Web address: www.https://healthcare.ascension.org/locations/wisconsin/wimil/milwaukee-ascension-sacred-heart-rehabilitation-hospital

ASCENSION SOUTHEAST WISCONSIN HOSPITAL-ELMBROOK CAMPUS (O, 46 beds) 19333 West North Avenue, Brookfield, WI, Zip 53045-4198; tel. 262/785-2000, Kurt Schley, President

ASCENSION SOUTHEAST WISCONSIN HOSPITAL-FRANKLIN CAMPUS (O, 33 beds) 10101 South 27th Street, Franklin, WI, Zip 53132-7209; tel. 414/325-4700, Jonathon Matuszewski, Hospital Administrator
Web address: www.https://healthcare.ascension.org/locations/wisconsin/wiwhe/franklin-ascension-se-wisconsin-hospital-franklin-campus?utm_campaign=gmb&utm_medium=organic&utm_source=local

For explanation of codes following names, see page B2.
★ Indicates Type III membership in the American Hospital Association.

Systems / Ascension Healthcare

ASCENSION SOUTHEAST WISCONSIN HOSPITAL–ST. JOSEPH'S CAMPUS (O, 59 beds) 5000 West Chambers Street, Milwaukee, WI, Zip 53210–1650; tel. 414/447–2000, Peter Stamas, M.D., Chief Administrative Officer

ASCENSION ST. FRANCIS HOSPITAL (O, 26 beds) 3237 South 16th Street, Milwaukee, WI, Zip 53215; tel. 414/647–5000, Jonathon Matuszewski, Hospital Administrator
Web address: www.https://healthcare.ascension.org/locations/wisconsin/wiwhe/milwaukee-ascension-st-francis-hospital

ASCENSION WISCONSIN HOSPITAL–MENOMONEE FALLS CAMPUS (O, 24 beds) N88W14275 Main Street Suite 100, Menomonee Falls, WI, Zip 53051–2315; tel. 262/415–2001, Daniel Gell, MSN, Market Chief Executive Officer
Web address: www.ascensionwisconsinhospital.org

MIDWEST ORTHOPEDIC SPECIALTY HOSPITAL (O, 16 beds) 10101 South 27th Street, 2nd Floor, Franklin, WI, Zip 53132–7209; tel. 414/817–5800

Owned, leased, sponsored:	99 hospitals	16808 beds
Contract-managed:	1 hospitals	72 beds
Totals:	100 hospitals	16880 beds

1137: ASPIRE RURAL HEALTH SYSTEM (NP)

4675 Hill Street, Cass City, MI Zip 48726–1008; tel. 989/635–4012, Angela McConnachie, MSN, R.N., Co–Chief Executive Officer

MICHIGAN: DECKERVILLE COMMUNITY HOSPITAL (O, 15 beds) 3559 Pine Street, Deckerville, MI, Zip 48427–7703, P O Box 126, Zip 48427–0126, tel. 810/376–2835, Angela McConnachie, MSN, R.N., Co–Chief Executive Officer, Aspire Rural Health System

HILLS & DALES HEALTHCARE (O, 25 beds) 4675 Hill Street, Cass City, MI, Zip 48726–1099; tel. 989/872–2121, Andy Daniels Esq, FACHE, Co–CEO, Aspire Rural Health System
Web address: www.https://hdhlth.org/

MARLETTE REGIONAL HOSPITAL (O, 74 beds) 2770 Main Street, Marlette, MI, Zip 48453–1141, P O Box 307, Zip 48453–0307, tel. 989/635–4000, Angela McConnachie, MSN, R.N., Co–CEO, Aspire Rural Health System
Web address: www.marletteregionalhospital.org

Owned, leased, sponsored:	3 hospitals	114 beds
Contract-managed:	0 hospitals	0 beds
Totals:	3 hospitals	114 beds

★0519: ASPIRUS, INC. (NP)

2200 Westwood Drive, Wausau, WI Zip 54401–7806; tel. 715/847–2118, Matthew Heywood, Chief Executive Officer
(Moderately Centralized Health System)

MICHIGAN: ASPIRUS IRON RIVER HOSPITAL (O, 7 beds) 1400 West Ice Lake Road, Iron River, MI, Zip 49935–9526; tel. 906/265–6121, Rae Kaare, Chief Administrative Officer
Web address: www.aspirus.org

ASPIRUS IRONWOOD HOSPITAL & CLINICS, INC. (O, 25 beds) N10561 Grandview Lane, Ironwood, MI, Zip 49938–9622; tel. 906/932–2525, Paula L. Chermside, Chief Administrative Officer
Web address: www.aspirus.org

ASPIRUS KEWEENAW HOSPITAL (O, 18 beds) 205 Osceola Street, Laurium, MI, Zip 49913–2134; tel. 906/337–6500, Matt Krause, Chief Administrative Officer
Web address: www.aspirus.org

MINNESOTA: ASPIRUS LAKE VIEW HOSPITAL (O, 25 beds) 325 11th Avenue, Two Harbors, MN, Zip 55616–1360; tel. 218/834–7300, Greg Ruberg, FACHE, President and Chief Executive Officer
Web address: www.lvmhospital.com

ASPIRUS ST. LUKE'S HOSPITAL (O, 267 beds) 915 East First Street, Duluth, MN, Zip 55805–2193; tel. 218/249–5555, Nicholas Van Deelen, M.D., President

WISCONSIN: ASPIRUS DIVINE SAVIOR HOSPITAL & CLINICS (O, 46 beds) 2817 New Pinery Road, Portage, WI, Zip 53901–9240, P O Box 387, Zip 53901–0387, tel. 608/742–4131, Chris Squire, Regional President
Web address: www.dshealthcare.com

ASPIRUS EAGLE RIVER HOSPITAL (O, 11 beds) 201 Hospital Road, Eagle River, WI, Zip 54521–8835; tel. 715/479–7411, Teresa Theiler, President

ASPIRUS LANGLADE HOSPITAL (O, 18 beds) 112 East Fifth Avenue, Antigo, WI, Zip 54409–2796; tel. 715/623–2331, Sherry Bunten, R.N., FACHE, President
Web address: https://www.aspirus.org/find-a-location/aspirus-langlade-hospital-283

ASPIRUS MEDFORD HOSPITAL & CLINICS (O, 54 beds) 135 South Gibson Street, Medford, WI, Zip 54451; tel. 715/748–8100, Jason Troxell, President
Web address: www.aspirus.org

ASPIRUS MERRILL HOSPITAL & CLINICS, INC. (O, 18 beds) 601 South Center Avenue, Merrill, WI, Zip 54452–3404; tel. 715/536–5511, Jeffrey Wicklander, President
Web address: https://www.aspirus.org/find-a-location/aspirus-merrill-hospital-536

ASPIRUS RHINELANDER HOSPITAL (O, 49 beds) 2251 North Shore Drive, Rhinelander, WI, Zip 54501–6710; tel. 715/361–2000, Teresa Theiler, President–North Region
Web address: https://www.aspirus.org/find-a-location/aspirus-rhinelander-hospital-535

ASPIRUS RIVERVIEW HOSPITAL AND CLINICS, INC. (O, 52 beds) 410 Dewey Street, Wisconsin Rapids, WI, Zip 54494–4715, P O Box 8080, Zip 54495–8080, tel. 715/423–6060, Brian Kief, President
Web address: www.aspirus.org

ASPIRUS STANLEY HOSPITAL & CLINICS, INC. (O, 13 beds) 1120 Pine Street, Stanley, WI, Zip 54768–1297; tel. 715/644–5571, Dale Hustedt, President

ASPIRUS STEVEN'S POINT HOSPITAL & CLINICS, INC. (O, 71 beds) 900 Illinois Avenue, Stevens Point, WI, Zip 54481–3196; tel. 715/346–5000, Teresa Theiler, Chief Administrative Officer
Web address: https://www.aspirus.org/find-a-location/aspirus-stevens-point-hospital-539

ASPIRUS TOMAHAWK HOSPITAL (O, 12 beds) 401 West Mohawk Drive, Tomahawk, WI, Zip 54487–2274; tel. 715/453–7700, Laurie Oungst, Chief Administrative Officer
Web address: https://www.aspirus.org/find-a-location/aspirus-tomahawk-hospital-537

ASPIRUS WAUSAU HOSPITAL, INC. (O, 260 beds) 333 Pine Ridge Boulevard, Wausau, WI, Zip 54401–4187, 1900 Westwood Drive, Zip 54402, tel. 715/847–2121, Jeffrey Wicklander, President
Web address: www.aspirus.org

HOWARD YOUNG MEDICAL CENTER, INC. (O, 17 beds) 240 Maple Street, Woodruff, WI, Zip 54568–9190, P O Box 470, Zip 54568–0470, tel. 715/356–8000, Teresa Theiler, President–North Region
Web address: https://www.aspirus.org/find-a-location/howard-young-medical-center-538

Owned, leased, sponsored:	17 hospitals	963 beds
Contract-managed:	0 hospitals	0 beds
Totals:	17 hospitals	963 beds

1031: ASTRIA HEALTH (NP)

1806 Yakima Valley Highway, Sunnyside, WA Zip 98944–2263; tel. 509/837–1330, Brian P. Gibbons, Interim Chief Executive Officer
(Independent Hospital System)

WASHINGTON: ASTRIA SUNNYSIDE HOSPITAL (O, 37 beds) 1016 Tacoma Avenue, Sunnyside, WA, Zip 98944–2263, P O Box 719, Zip 98944–0719, tel. 509/837–1500, Brian P. Gibbons, Chief Executive Officer
Web address: https://www.astria.health/locations/astria-sunnyside-hospital

For explanation of codes following names, see page B2.
★ Indicates Type III membership in the American Hospital Association.

Systems / Atrium Health, Inc.

ASTRIA TOPPENISH HOSPITAL (O, 48 beds) 502 West Fourth Avenue, Toppenish, WA, Zip 98948-1616, P O Box 672, Zip 98948-0672, tel. 509/865-3105, Cathy Bambrick, Administrator
Web address: https://www.astria.health/locations/astria-toppenish-hospital

Owned, leased, sponsored:	2 hospitals	85 beds
Contract-managed:	0 hospitals	0 beds
Totals:	2 hospitals	85 beds

★0865: **ATLANTIC HEALTH SYSTEM (NP)**
475 South Street, Morristown, NJ Zip 07960-6459, P O Box 1905, Zip 07962-1905, tel. 973/660-3270, Brian A. Gragnolati, FACHE, President and Chief Executive Officer
(Decentralized Health System)

NEW JERSEY: ATLANTIC REHABILITATION INSTITUTE (C, 38 beds) 4 Giralda Farms, Madison, NJ, Zip 7940; tel. 973/549-7440, Saif Salim, Chief Executive Officer
Web address: www.AtlanticRehabInstitute.com
CHILTON MEDICAL CENTER (O, 177 beds) 97 West Parkway, Pompton Plains, NJ, Zip 07444-1696; tel. 973/831-5000, Maureen Schneider, Ph.D., R.N., FACHE, President
Web address: https://www.atlantichealth.org/locations/hospitals/chilton-medical-center.html
HACKETTSTOWN MEDICAL CENTER (O, 104 beds) 651 Willow Grove Street, Hackettstown, NJ, Zip 07840-1799; tel. 908/852-5100, Robert H. Adams, President, Western Region
MORRISTOWN MEDICAL CENTER (O, 746 beds) 100 Madison Avenue, Morristown, NJ, Zip 07960-6136; tel. 973/971-5000, Trish O'Keefe, Ph.D., R.N., President
Web address: www.atlantichealth.org/Morristown/
NEWTON MEDICAL CENTER (O, 154 beds) 175 High Street, Newton, NJ, Zip 07860-1004; tel. 973/383-2121, Robert H. Adams, President, Western Region
Web address: www.atlantichealth.org/newton/
OVERLOOK MEDICAL CENTER (O, 513 beds) 99 Beauvoir Avenue, Summit, NJ, Zip 07901-3533; tel. 908/522-2000, Stephanie L. Schwartz, FACHE, President
Web address: www.atlantichealth.org/Overlook

Owned, leased, sponsored:	5 hospitals	1694 beds
Contract-managed:	1 hospitals	38 beds
Totals:	6 hospitals	1732 beds

★0293: **ATLANTICARE (NP)**
2500 English Creek Avenue, Building 500, Suite 501, Egg Harbor Township, NJ Zip 08234-5549; tel. 609/407-2309, Michael Charlton, President and Chief Executive Officer

NEW JERSEY: ATLANTICARE REGIONAL MEDICAL CENTER, ATLANTIC CITY CAMPUS (O, 593 beds) 1925 Pacific Avenue, Atlantic City, NJ, Zip 08401-6713; tel. 609/441-8994, Kevin McDonnell, Chief Hospital Executive
Web address: https://www.atlanticare.org/location/atlanticare-regional-medical-center-atlantic-city-campus

Owned, leased, sponsored:	1 hospitals	593 beds
Contract-managed:	0 hospitals	0 beds
Totals:	1 hospitals	593 beds

★9996: **ATRIUM HEALTH, INC. (NP)**
1000 Blythe Blvd, Charlotte, NC Zip 28203-5812, P.O. Box 32861, Zip 28232-2861, tel. 704/355-2000, Eugene A. Woods, FACHE, President and Chief Executive Officer

ALABAMA: ATRIUM HEALTH FLOYD CHEROKEE MEDICAL CENTER (O, 45 beds) 400 Northwood Drive, Centre, AL, Zip 35960-1023; tel. 256/927-5531, Tifani Kinard, Chief Executive Officer
Web address: www.cherokeemedicalcenter.com

GEORGIA: ATRIUM HEALTH FLOYD MEDICAL CENTER (O, 354 beds) 304 Turner McCall Boulevard, Rome, GA, Zip 30165-5621, PO Box 32861, Charlotte, NC, Zip 28232-2861, tel. 706/509-5000, Kurt Stuenkel, FACHE, President and Chief Executive Officer
ATRIUM HEALTH FLOYD POLK MEDICAL CENTER (O, 25 beds) 2360 Rockmart Highway, Cedartown, GA, Zip 30125-6029; tel. 770/748-2500, Tifani Kinard, Vice President of Rural Health in SAM
Web address: https://www.floyd.org/find-a-location/Pages/polkmedicalcenter.aspx
ATRIUM HEALTH NAVICENT BALDWIN (C, 91 beds) 821 North Cobb Street, Milledgeville, GA, Zip 31061-2351, P O Box 690, Zip 31059-0690, tel. 478/454-3505, Delvecchio Finley, FACHE, Interim Chief Executive Officer
Web address: www.navicenthealth.org/nhb/home
ATRIUM HEALTH NAVICENT PEACH (C, 25 beds) 777 Hemlock Street, Macon, GA, Zip 31201-2102; tel. 478/654-2000, Laura Gentry, Chief Executive Officer
ATRIUM HEALTH NAVICENT REHABILITATION HOSPITAL (C, 58 beds) 3351 Northside Drive, Macon, GA, Zip 31210-2587; tel. 478/201-6500, Gina Tipton, Hospital Administrator
Web address: www.navicenthealth.org/service-center/rehabilitation-hospital-navicent-health
ATRIUM HEALTH NAVICENT THE MEDICAL CENTER (C, 577 beds) 777 Hemlock Street, Macon, GA, Zip 31201-2155; tel. 478/633-1000, Delvecchio Finley, FACHE, President and Chief Executive Officer
Web address: https://www.navicenthealth.org/

NORTH CAROLINA: ATRIUM HEALTH ANSON (C, 15 beds) 2301 US Highway 74 W, Wadesboro, NC, Zip 28170-7554, 2301 U.S Highway 74 West, Zip 28170, tel. 704/994-4500, Seth Chandler. Goldwire, Interim Chief Executive Officer
ATRIUM HEALTH CABARRUS (C, 526 beds) 920 Church Street North, Concord, NC, Zip 28025-2983; tel. 704/403-3000, Asha Rodriguez, Vice President and Facility Executive
Web address: www.carolinashealthcare.org/northeast
ATRIUM HEALTH CLEVELAND (C, 244 beds) 201 East Grover Street, Shelby, NC, Zip 28150-3917; tel. 980/487-3000, Veronica Poole-Adams, R.N., Interim West Market President
Web address: www.clevelandregional.org
ATRIUM HEALTH LINCOLN (C, 101 beds) 433 McAlister Road, Lincolnton, NC, Zip 28092-4147, PO Box 677, Zip 28093-0677, tel. 980/212-2000, Tri Tang, Vice President
ATRIUM HEALTH PINEVILLE (C, 307 beds) 10628 Park Road, Charlotte, NC, Zip 28210-8407; tel. 704/667-1000, Alicia Campbell, Vice President, Facility Executive
Web address: www.carolinashealthcare.org/pineville
ATRIUM HEALTH STANLY (C, 109 beds) 301 Yadkin Street, Albemarle, NC, Zip 28001-3441, P O Box 1489, Zip 28002-1489, tel. 704/984-4000, Brian Freeman, FACHE, Senior Vice President, President West Area
ATRIUM HEALTH UNION (C, 182 beds) 600 Hospital Drive, Monroe, NC, Zip 28112-6000, P O Box 5003, Zip 28111-5003, tel. 980/993-3100, Denise White, MSN, Vice President, Facility Executive
Web address: www.https://atriumhealth.org/locations/detail/atrium-health-union
ATRIUM HEALTH UNIVERSITY CITY (C, 104 beds) 8800 North Tryon Street, Charlotte, NC, Zip 28262-3300, P O Box 560727, Zip 28256-0727, tel. 704/863-6000, William H. Leonard, President
ATRIUM HEALTH WAKE FOREST BAPTIST DAVIE MEDICAL CENTER (C, 38 beds) 329 NC Highway 801 North, Bermuda Run, NC, Zip 27006; tel. 336/998-1300, Cathleen Wheatley, President
Web address: www.wakehealth.edu/Davie-Medical-Center
ATRIUM HEALTH WAKE FOREST BAPTIST LEXINGTON MEDICAL CENTER (C, 75 beds) 250 Hospital Drive, Lexington, NC, Zip 27292-6728, P O Box 1817, Zip 27293-1817, tel. 336/248-5161, Chad J. Brown, Dr.PH, FACHE, M.P.H., President, South and West Areas
ATRIUM HEALTH WAKE FOREST BAPTIST WILKES MEDICAL CENTER (C, 80 beds) 1370 West 'D' Street, North Wilkesboro, NC, Zip 28659-3506, P O Box 609, Zip 28659-0609, tel. 336/651-8100, Chad J. Brown, Dr.PH, FACHE, M.P.H., President
Web address: www.wilkesregional.com/

For explanation of codes following names, see page B2.
★ Indicates Type III membership in the American Hospital Association.

Systems / Atrium Health, Inc.

ATRIUM HEALTH WAKE FOREST BAPTIST (C, 814 beds) Medical Center Boulevard, Winston-Salem, NC, Zip 27157-0001; tel. 336/716-2011, Julie Ann. Freischlag, M.D., FACS, Chief Executive Officer
Web address: www.wakehealth.edu

ATRIUM HEALTH WAKE FORET BAPTIST HIGH POINT MEDICAL CENTER (C, 277 beds) 601 North Elm Street, High Point, NC, Zip 27262-4398, P O Box HP-5, Zip 27261-1899, tel. 336/878-6000, James Hoekstra, M.D., President

ATRIUM HEALTH'S CAROLINAS MEDICAL CENTER (C, 1279 beds) 1000 Blythe Boulevard, Charlotte, NC, Zip 28203-5871, P O Box 32861, Zip 28232-2861, tel. 704/355-2000, D. Channing. Roush, Facility Executive
Web address: www.carolinashealthcare.org/cmc

CAROLINAS REHABILITATION (C, 150 beds) 1100 Blythe Boulevard, Charlotte, NC, Zip 28203-5864; tel. 704/355-4300, Robert G. Larrison, President
Web address: www.carolinashealthcare.org/rehabilitation

COLUMBUS REGIONAL HEALTHCARE SYSTEM (C, 85 beds) 500 Jefferson Street, Whiteville, NC, Zip 28472-3634; tel. 910/642-8011, Jason Beck, President and Chief Executive Officer
Web address: www.crhealthcare.org/

SCOTLAND HEALTH CARE SYSTEM (C, 104 beds) 500 Lauchwood Drive, Laurinburg, NC, Zip 28352-5599; tel. 910/291-7000, David L. Pope, President and Chief Executive Officer

ST. LUKE'S HOSPITAL (C, 35 beds) 101 Hospital Drive, Columbus, NC, Zip 28722-5418; tel. 828/894-3311, Alex Bell, Interim Chief Executive Officer
Web address: www.saintlukeshospital.com

Owned, leased, sponsored:	3 hospitals	424 beds
Contract-managed:	22 hospitals	5276 beds
Totals:	25 hospitals	5700 beds

0859: AULTMAN HEALTH FOUNDATION (NP)
2600 Sixth Street SW, Canton, OH Zip 44710-1702; tel. 330/363-6192, Robert Mullen, President and Chief Executive Officer

(Moderately Centralized Health System)

OHIO: AULTMAN ALLIANCE COMMUNITY HOSPITAL (O, 203 beds) 200 East State Street, Alliance, OH, Zip 44601-4936; tel. 330/596-6000, Ryan Jones, Chief Executive Officer

AULTMAN HOSPITAL (O, 482 beds) 2600 Sixth Street SW, Canton, OH, Zip 44710-1702; tel. 330/452-9911, Anne Gunther, R.N., MSN, President
Web address: www.aultman.com

AULTMAN ORRVILLE HOSPITAL (O, 25 beds) 832 South Main Street, Orrville, OH, Zip 44667-2208; tel. 330/682-3010, Ryan Jones, President
Web address: www.aultmanorrville.org

Owned, leased, sponsored:	3 hospitals	710 beds
Contract-managed:	0 hospitals	0 beds
Totals:	3 hospitals	710 beds

1010: AVEM HEALTH PARTNERS (IO)
14201 Wireless Way, Suite B-100, Oklahoma City, OK Zip 73134-2521; tel. 405/246-0218, Jeff Hill, Chief Executive Officer

OKLAHOMA: CARNEGIE TRI-COUNTY MUNICIPAL HOSPITAL (C, 17 beds) 102 North Broadway, Carnegie, OK, Zip 73015, P O Box 97, Zip 73015-0097, tel. 580/654-1050, Nathan Adam. Richmond, Administrator

RURAL WELLNESS ANADARKO (C, 25 beds) 1002 Central Boulevard East, Anadarko, OK, Zip 73005-4496; tel. 405/247-2551, Travis A. Villani, FACHE, Chief Executive Officer and Senior Vice President of Operations
Web address: www.anadarkohospital.com

Owned, leased, sponsored:	0 hospitals	0 beds
Contract-managed:	2 hospitals	42 beds
Totals:	2 hospitals	42 beds

★5255: AVERA HEALTH (CC)
3900 West Avera Drive, Suite 300, Sioux Falls, SD Zip 57108-5721; tel. 605/322-4700, James F. Dover, FACHE, President and Chief Executive Officer

(Decentralized Health System)

IOWA: AVERA HOLY FAMILY HOSPITAL (O, 22 beds) 826 North Eighth Street, Estherville, IA, Zip 51334-1598; tel. 712/362-2631, Deborah L. Herzberg, R.N., MS, FACHE, Chief Executive Officer
Web address: www.avera-holyfamily.org

AVERA MERRILL PIONEER HOSPITAL (L, 11 beds) 1100 South 10th Avenue, Rock Rapids, IA, Zip 51246-2020; tel. 712/472-5400, Craig Hohn, Chief Executive Officer
Web address: https://www.avera.org

FLOYD VALLEY HEALTHCARE (C, 25 beds) 714 Lincoln Street NE, Le Mars, IA, Zip 51031-3314; tel. 712/546-7871, Dustin Wright, Chief Executive Officer

HEGG HEALTH CENTER AVERA (C, 72 beds) 1202 21st Avenue, Rock Valley, IA, Zip 51247-1497; tel. 712/476-8000, Glenn Zevenbergen, Chief Executive Officer
Web address: www.hegghc.org

LAKES REGIONAL HEALTHCARE (C, 30 beds) 2301 Highway 71 South, Spirit Lake, IA, Zip 51360-0159; tel. 712/336-1230, Jason Harrington, FACHE, President and Chief Executive Officer
Web address: www.lakeshealth.org

OSCEOLA REGIONAL HEALTH CENTER (C, 25 beds) 600 9th Avenue North, Sibley, IA, Zip 51249-1012, P O Box 258, Zip 51249-0258, tel. 712/754-2574, Joe Heitritter, Chief Executive Officer

SIOUX CENTER HEALTH (C, 118 beds) 1101 9th Street SE, Sioux Center, IA, Zip 51250; tel. 712/722-8107, Cory D. Nelson, Administrator
Web address: www.siouxcenterhealth.org

MINNESOTA: AVERA GRANITE FALLS (L, 73 beds) 345 Tenth Avenue, Granite Falls, MN, Zip 56241-1499; tel. 320/564-3111, Thomas Kooiman, Chief Executive Officer

AVERA MARSHALL REGIONAL MEDICAL CENTER (O, 111 beds) 300 South Bruce Street, Marshall, MN, Zip 56258-3900; tel. 507/532-9661, Debbie Streier, Regional President and Chief Executive Officer
Web address: www.avera.org

AVERA TYLER (C, 50 beds) 240 Willow Street, Tyler, MN, Zip 56178-1166; tel. 507/247-5521, Thomas Kooiman, Administrator
Web address: www.avera.org

PIPESTONE COUNTY MEDICAL CENTER (C, 18 beds) 916 4th Avenue SW, Pipestone, MN, Zip 56164-1890; tel. 507/825-5811, Bradley D. Burris, Chief Executive Officer

NEBRASKA: AVERA CREIGHTON HOSPITAL (O, 70 beds) 1503 Main Street, Creighton, NE, Zip 68729-3007, P O Box 186, Zip 68729-0186, tel. 402/358-5700, Theresa L. Guenther, Chief Executive Officer
Web address: www.avera.org/creighton/

AVERA ST. ANTHONY'S HOSPITAL (O, 25 beds) 300 North Second Street, O'Neill, NE, Zip 68763-1514, P O Box 270, Oneill, Zip 68763-0270, tel. 402/336-2611, John Kozyra, Chief Executive Officer
Web address: www.avera.org/st-anthonys

SOUTH DAKOTA: AVERA DE SMET MEMORIAL HOSPITAL (L, 6 beds) 306 Prairie Avenue SW, De Smet, SD, Zip 57231-2285, P O Box 160, Zip 57231-0160, tel. 605/854-6100, Stephanie Reasy, Administrator and Chief Executive Officer

AVERA DELLS AREA HOSPITAL (L, 23 beds) 909 North Iowa Avenue, Dell Rapids, SD, Zip 57022-1231; tel. 605/428-5431, Bryan Breitling, Chief Executive Officer
Web address: https://www.avera.org/locations/profile/avera-dells-area-hospital/

AVERA FLANDREAU HOSPITAL (L, 18 beds) 214 North Prairie Street, Flandreau, SD, Zip 57028-1243; tel. 605/997-2433, Bryan Breitling, Chief Executive Officer
Web address: www.avera.org/flandreau-medical/

AVERA GREGORY HOSPITAL (O, 43 beds) 400 Park Avenue, Gregory, SD, Zip 57533-1302, P O Box 408, Zip 57533-0408, tel. 605/835-8394, Anthony Timanus, Chief Executive Officer
Web address: www.gregoryhealthcare.org

For explanation of codes following names, see page B2.
★ Indicates Type III membership in the American Hospital Association.

AVERA HAND COUNTY MEMORIAL HOSPITAL (L, 25 beds) 300 West Fifth Street, Miller, SD, Zip 57362-1238; tel. 605/853-2421, Matthew Campion, Administrator
Web address: www.avera.org

AVERA HEART HOSPITAL OF SOUTH DAKOTA (O, 53 beds) 4500 West 69th Street, Sioux Falls, SD, Zip 57108-8148; tel. 605/977-7000, Michael Gibbs, President

AVERA MCKENNAN HOSPITAL AND UNIVERSITY HEALTH CENTER (O, 705 beds) 1325 South Cliff Avenue, Sioux Falls, SD, Zip 57105-1007, P O Box 5045, Zip 57117-5045, tel. 605/322-8000, Lieutenant General, Ronald J. Place, M.D., President and Chief Executive Officer
Web address: www.averamckennan.org

AVERA MISSOURI RIVER HEALTH CENTER (O, 60 beds) 606 East Garfield Avenue, Gettysburg, SD, Zip 57442-1398; tel. 605/765-2488, Rena Robbennolt, Interim Administrator

AVERA QUEEN OF PEACE HOSPITAL (O, 109 beds) 525 North Foster, Mitchell, SD, Zip 57301-2999; tel. 605/995-2000, Douglas R. Ekeren, FACHE, Regional President and Chief Executive Officer
Web address: www.averaqueenofpeace.org

AVERA SACRED HEART HOSPITAL (O, 229 beds) 501 Summit Avenue, Yankton, SD, Zip 57078-3855; tel. 605/668-8000, Douglas R. Ekeren, FACHE, Regional President and Chief Executive Officer, Administration
Web address: www.averasacredheart.com

AVERA ST. BENEDICT HEALTH CENTER (O, 74 beds) 401 West Glynn Drive, Parkston, SD, Zip 57366-9605; tel. 605/928-3311, Lindsay Weber, President and Chief Executive Officer

AVERA ST. LUKE'S HOSPITAL (O, 197 beds) 305 South State Street, Aberdeen, SD, Zip 57401-4527; tel. 605/622-5000, Dan Bjerknes, Chief Executive Officer, Regional President
Web address: www.avera.org/st-lukes-hospital/

AVERA ST. MARY'S HOSPITAL (O, 130 beds) 801 East Sioux Avenue, Pierre, SD, Zip 57501-3323; tel. 605/224-3100, Shantel Krebs, Chief Executive Officer
Web address: www.avera.org/st-marys-pierre/

AVERA WESKOTA MEMORIAL HOSPITAL (L, 16 beds) 604 First Street NE, Wessington Springs, SD, Zip 57382-2166; tel. 605/539-1201, Stephanie Reasy, Administrator and Chief Executive Officer
Web address: www.averaweskota.org

EUREKA COMMUNITY HEALTH SERVICES AVERA (C, 4 beds) 410 Ninth Street, Eureka, SD, Zip 57437-2182, P O Box 517, Zip 57437-0517, tel. 605/284-2661, Carmen Weber, Administrator

LANDMANN-JUNGMAN MEMORIAL HOSPITAL AVERA (C, 10 beds) 600 Billars Street, Scotland, SD, Zip 57059-2026; tel. 605/583-2226, Melissa Gale, Chief Executive Officer
Web address: www.ljmh.org

MARSHALL COUNTY HEALTHCARE CENTER AVERA (C, 18 beds) 413 Ninth Street, Britton, SD, Zip 57430-2274; tel. 605/448-2253, Nick Fosness, Chief Executive Officer
Web address: www.avera.org

MILBANK AREA HOSPITAL AVERA (L, 25 beds) 301 Flynn Drive, Milbank, SD, Zip 57252-1508; tel. 605/432-4538, Natalie Gauer, Administrator

PLATTE HEALTH CENTER AVERA (C, 17 beds) 601 East Seventh, Platte, SD, Zip 57369-2123, P O Box 200, Zip 57369-0200, tel. 605/337-3364, Mark Burket, Chief Executive Officer
Web address: www.phcavera.org

ST. MICHAEL'S HOSPITAL AVERA (C, 25 beds) 410 West 16th Avenue, Tyndall, SD, Zip 57066-2318; tel. 605/589-2100, Ashli Danilko, Chief Executive Officer
Web address: www.stmichaels-bhfp.org

WAGNER COMMUNITY MEMORIAL HOSPITAL AVERA (C, 20 beds) 513 Third Street SW, Wagner, SD, Zip 57380-9675, P O Box 280, Zip 57380-0280, tel. 605/384-3611, Bryan Slaba, Chief Executive Officer
Web address: www.avera.org/wagnerhospital

Owned, leased, sponsored:	21 hospitals	2025 beds
Contract-managed:	13 hospitals	432 beds
Totals:	34 hospitals	2457 beds

★**0633: AVITA HEALTH SYSTEM (NP)**
269 Portland Way South, Galion, OH Zip 44833-2399; tel. 419/468-4841, Jerome Morasko, President and Chief Executive Officer
(Independent Hospital System)

OHIO: AVITA ONTARIO HOSPITAL (O, 26 beds) 715 Richland Mall, Ontario, OH, Zip 44906-3802; tel. 567/307-7666, Jerome Morasko, President and Chief Executive Officer
Web address: www.avitahealth.org

BUCYRUS COMMUNITY HOSPITAL (O, 25 beds) 629 North Sandusky Avenue, Bucyrus, OH, Zip 44820-1821; tel. 419/562-4677, Jerome Morasko, President and Chief Executive Officer

GALION COMMUNITY HOSPITAL (O, 35 beds) 269 Portland Way South, Galion, OH, Zip 44833-2399; tel. 419/468-4841, Jerome Morasko, President and Chief Executive Officer
Web address: www.avitahealth.org

Owned, leased, sponsored:	3 hospitals	86 beds
Contract-managed:	0 hospitals	0 beds
Totals:	3 hospitals	86 beds

1033: BALLAD HEALTH (NP)
303 Med Tech Parkway, Suite 300, Johnson City, TN Zip 37604-2391, 303 Med Tech Parkway, Zip 37604-2391, tel. 423/230-8200, Alan M. Levine, President and Chief Executive Officer
(Centralized Health System)

TENNESSEE: BRISTOL REGIONAL MEDICAL CENTER (O, 296 beds) 1 Medical Park Boulevard, Bristol, TN, Zip 37620-7430; tel. 423/844-1121, John Jeter, Chief Executive Officer
Web address: https://www.balladhealth.org/locations/hospitals/bristol-regional

FRANKLIN WOODS COMMUNITY HOSPITAL (O, 102 beds) 300 MedTech Parkway, Johnson City, TN, Zip 37604-2277; tel. 423/302-1000, Melanie Steagall. Stanton, Chief Executive Officer
Web address: www.msha.com

GREENEVILLE COMMUNITY HOSPITAL EAST (O, 121 beds) 1420 Tusculum Boulevard, Greeneville, TN, Zip 37745-5825; tel. 423/787-5000, Eric Carroll, Chief Executive Officer

HANCOCK COUNTY HOSPITAL (O, 10 beds) 1519 Main Street, Sneedville, TN, Zip 37869-3657; tel. 423/733-5000, Hunter Hamilton, Chief Executive Officer/Administrator
Web address: https://www.balladhealth.org/hospitals/hancock-county-sneedville

HAWKINS COUNTY MEMORIAL HOSPITAL (O, 16 beds) 851 Locust Street, Rogersville, TN, Zip 37857-2407, P O Box 130, Zip 37857-0130, tel. 423/921-7000, Hunter Hamilton, Chief Executive Officer
Web address: www.wellmont.org

HOLSTON VALLEY MEDICAL CENTER (O, 336 beds) 130 West Ravine Street, Kingsport, TN, Zip 37660-3837, P O Box 238, Zip 37662-0238, tel. 423/224-4000, Rebecca Beck, Chief Executive Officer

INDIAN PATH COMMUNITY HOSPITAL (O, 117 beds) 2000 Brookside Drive, Kingsport, TN, Zip 37660-4627; tel. 423/857-7000, Rebecca Beck, Chief Executive Officer
Web address: https://www.balladhealth.org/locations/hospitals/indian-path

JOHNSON CITY MEDICAL CENTER (O, 581 beds) 400 North State of Franklin Road, Johnson City, TN, Zip 37604-6094; tel. 423/431-6111, Kenny Shafer, Chief Executive Officer
Web address: https://www.balladhealth.org/hospitals/johnson-city-medical-center

JOHNSON COUNTY COMMUNITY HOSPITAL (O, 2 beds) 1901 South Shady Street, Mountain City, TN, Zip 37683-2271; tel. 423/727-1100, Chastity Trivette, Administrator

SYCAMORE SHOALS HOSPITAL (O, 74 beds) 1501 West Elk Avenue, Elizabethton, TN, Zip 37643-2874; tel. 423/542-1300, Dwayne Taylor, Chief Executive Officer, Southeast Market
Web address: www.msha.com

Systems / Ballad Health

UNICOI COUNTY HOSPITAL (O, 50 beds) 2030 Temple Hill Road, Erwin, TN, Zip 37650–8721; tel. 423/735–4700, Loveland Hobson, Chief Executive Office
Web address: https://www.balladhealth.org/hospitals/unicoi-county-hospital-erwin

VIRGINIA: DICKENSON COMMUNITY HOSPITAL (O, 11 beds) 312 Hospital Drive, Clintwood, VA, Zip 24228, P O Box 1440, Zip 24228–1440, tel. 276/926–0300, Terri Roop, Assistant Vice President and Administrator

JOHNSTON MEMORIAL HOSPITAL (O, 116 beds) 16000 Johnston Memorial Drive, Abingdon, VA, Zip 24211–7659; tel. 276/258–1000, John Jeter, Chief Executive Officer
Web address: www.jmh.org

LONESOME PINE HOSPITAL (O, 60 beds) 1990 Holton Avenue East, Big Stone Gap, VA, Zip 24219–3350; tel. 276/523–3111, Cindy Elkins, Chief Executive Officer
Web address: https://www.balladhealth.org/locations/hospitals/lonesome-pine

NORTON COMMUNITY HOSPITAL (O, 66 beds) 100 15th Street NW, Norton, VA, Zip 24273–1616; tel. 276/679–9600, Shannon Showalter, Vice President and Chief Executive Officer
Web address: www.msha.com/nch

RUSSELL COUNTY MEDICAL CENTER (O, 78 beds) 58 Carroll Street, Lebanon, VA, Zip 24266, P O Box 3600, Zip 24266–0200, tel. 276/883–8000, Greta M. Morrison, Administrator, Assistant Vice President and Chief Nursing Officer

SMYTH COUNTY COMMUNITY HOSPITAL (O, 153 beds) 245 Medical Park Drive, Marion, VA, Zip 24354, P O Box 880, Zip 24354–0880, tel. 276/378–1000, Dale M. Clark, Vice President and Chief Executive Officer
Web address: www.msha.com/scch

Owned, leased, sponsored:	17 hospitals	2189 beds
Contract-managed:	0 hospitals	0 beds
Totals:	17 hospitals	2189 beds

★0194: BANNER HEALTH (NP)

2901 North Central Avenue, Suite 160, Phoenix, AZ Zip 85012–2702; tel. 602/747–4000, Peter S. Fine, FACHE, Chief Executive Officer
(Centralized Health System)

ARIZONA: BANNER–UNIVERSITY MEDICAL CENTER PHOENIX (O, 625 beds) 1111 East McDowell Road, Phoenix, AZ, Zip 85006–2666, P O Box 2989, Zip 85062–2989, tel. 602/239–2000, Daniel Post, Chief Executive Officer
Web address: https://www.bannerhealth.com/locations/phoenix/banner-university-medical-center-phoenix

BANNER–UNIVERSITY MEDICAL CENTER SOUTH (O, 163 beds) 2800 East Ajo Way, Tucson, AZ, Zip 85713–6289; tel. 520/874–2000, Sarah Frost, Chief Executive Officer
Web address: www.bannerhealth.com

BANNER–UNIVERSITY MEDICAL CENTER TUCSON (O, 589 beds) 1501 North Campbell Avenue, Tucson, AZ, Zip 85719; tel. 520/694–0111, Sarah Frost, Chief Executive Officer
Web address: https://www.bannerhealth.com/locations/tucson/banner-university-medical-center-tucson

BANNER BAYWOOD MEDICAL CENTER (O, 337 beds) 6644 East Baywood Avenue, Mesa, AZ, Zip 85206–1797; tel. 480/321–2000, Brian Kellar, Chief Executive Officer

BANNER BEHAVIORAL HEALTH HOSPITAL–SCOTTSDALE (O, 128 beds) 7575 East Earll Drive, Scottsdale, AZ, Zip 85251–6915; tel. 480/941–7500, Debbie Flores, Chief Executive Officer
Web address: https://www.bannerhealth.com/locations/scottsdale/banner-behavioral-health-hospital

BANNER BOSWELL MEDICAL CENTER (O, 410 beds) 10401 West Thunderbird Boulevard, Sun City, AZ, Zip 85351–3004; tel. 623/832–4000, Stan Holm, FACHE, Chief Executive Officer
Web address: www.bannerhealth.com/locations/sun-city/banner-boswell-medical-center

BANNER CASA GRANDE MEDICAL CENTER (O, 141 beds) 1800 East Florence Boulevard, Casa Grande, AZ, Zip 85122–5399; tel. 520/381–6300, John Scherpf, Chief Executive Officer

BANNER DEL E. WEBB MEDICAL CENTER (O, 391 beds) 14502 West Meeker Boulevard, Sun City West, AZ, Zip 85375–5299; tel. 623/524–4000, Stan Holm, FACHE, Chief Executive Officer
Web address: www.bannerhealth.com/Locations/Arizona/Banner+Del+Webb+Medical+Center/

BANNER DESERT MEDICAL CENTER (O, 763 beds) 1400 South Dobson Road, Mesa, AZ, Zip 85202–4707; tel. 480/412–3000, Laura Robertson, R.N., Chief Executive Officer

BANNER ESTRELLA MEDICAL CENTER (O, 317 beds) 9201 West Thomas Road, Phoenix, AZ, Zip 85037–3332; tel. 623/327–4000, Courtney Ophaug, FACHE, Chief Executive Officer
Web address: https://www.bannerhealth.com/locations/phoenix/banner-estrella-medical-center

BANNER GATEWAY MEDICAL CENTER (O, 286 beds) 1900 North Higley Road, Gilbert, AZ, Zip 85234–1604; tel. 480/543–2000, Michael Herring, R.N., Chief Executive Officer
Web address: www.bannerhealth.com/Locations/Arizona/Banner+Gateway+Medical+Center/

BANNER GOLDFIELD MEDICAL CENTER (O, 20 beds) 2050 West Southern Avenue, Apache Junction, AZ, Zip 85120–7305; tel. 480/733–3300, Brian Kellar, Chief Executive Officer
Web address: www.bannerhealth.com/Locations/Arizona/Banner+Goldfield+Medical+Center/_Welcome+to+Banner+Goldfield.htm

BANNER HEART HOSPITAL (O, 111 beds) 6750 East Baywood Avenue, Mesa, AZ, Zip 85206–1749; tel. 480/854–5000, Brian Kellar, Chief Executive Officer

BANNER IRONWOOD MEDICAL CENTER (O, 89 beds) 37000 North Gantzel Road, San Tan Valley, AZ, Zip 85140–7303; tel. 480/394–4000, Brian Kellar, Chief Executive Officer
Web address: www.bannerhealth.com/Locations/Arizona/Banner+Ironwood/

BANNER OCOTILLO MEDICAL CENTER (O, 94 beds) 1405 South Alma School Road, Chandler, AZ, Zip 85286; tel. 480/256–7000, Laura Robertson, R.N., Chief Executive Officer
Web address: www.bannerhealth.com

BANNER PAYSON MEDICAL CENTER (O, 25 beds) 807 South Ponderosa Street, Payson, AZ, Zip 85541–5599; tel. 928/474–3222, Hoyt Skabelund, President

BANNER THUNDERBIRD MEDICAL CENTER (O, 595 beds) 5555 West Thunderbird Road, Glendale, AZ, Zip 85306–4696; tel. 602/865–5555, Debbie Flores, Chief Executive Officer
Web address: https://www.bannerhealth.com/locations/glendale/banner-thunderbird-medical-center

PAGE HOSPITAL (C, 25 beds) 501 North Navajo Drive, Page, AZ, Zip 86040, P O Box 1447, Zip 86040–1447, tel. 928/645–2424, Ralph Parker, Chief Executive Officer and Chief Nursing Officer
Web address: https://www.bannerhealth.com/locations/page/page-hospital?y_source=1_MTE5MDczNTQtNzE1LWxvY2F0aW9uLmdvb2dsZV93ZWJzaXRRIX292ZXJyaWRl

CALIFORNIA: BANNER LASSEN MEDICAL CENTER (O, 25 beds) 1800 Spring Ridge Drive, Susanville, CA, Zip 96130–6100; tel. 530/252–2000, Sandy Dugger, Chief Executive Officer
Web address: https://www.bannerhealth.com/locations/susanville/banner-lassen-medical-center

COLORADO: BANNER FORT COLLINS MEDICAL CENTER (O, 29 beds) 4700 Lady Moon Drive, Fort Collins, CO, Zip 80528–4426; tel. 970/821–4000, Alan Qualls, Chief Executive Officer

BANNER MCKEE MEDICAL CENTER (O, 89 beds) 2000 Boise Avenue, Loveland, CO, Zip 80538–4281; tel. 970/669–4640, Alan Qualls, Chief Executive Officer
Web address: https://www.bannerhealth.com/locations/loveland/mckee-medical-center

BANNER NORTH COLORADO MEDICAL CENTERNORTH COLORADO MEDICAL CENTER (O, 266 beds) 1801 16th Street, Greeley, CO, Zip 80631–5154; tel. 970/352–4121, Alan Qualls, Chief Executive Officer

EAST MORGAN COUNTY HOSPITAL (L, 19 beds) 2400 West Edison Street, Brush, CO, Zip 80723–1640; tel. 970/842–6200, Linda Thorpe, Chief Executive Officer
Web address: www.emchbrush.com

For explanation of codes following names, see page B2.
★ Indicates Type III membership in the American Hospital Association.

Systems / Baptist Health

STERLING REGIONAL MEDCENTER (O, 25 beds) 615 Fairhurst Street, Sterling, CO, Zip 80751-4523; tel. 970/522-0122, Ned Resch, Chief Executive Officer
Web address: https://www.bannerhealth.com/locations/sterling/sterling-regional-medcenter

NEBRASKA: OGALLALA COMMUNITY HOSPITAL (L, 18 beds) 2601 North Spruce Street, Ogallala, NE, Zip 69153-2465; tel. 308/284-4011, Timothy Gullingsrud, Chief Executive Officer
Web address: https://www.bannerhealth.com/locations/ogallala/ogallala-community-hospital

NEVADA: BANNER CHURCHILL COMMUNITY HOSPITAL (O, 25 beds) 801 East Williams Avenue, Fallon, NV, Zip 89406-3052; tel. 775/423-3151, Robert H. Carnahan II, R.N., Chief Executive Officer

WYOMING: COMMUNITY HOSPITAL (O, 25 beds) 2000 Campbell Drive, Torrington, WY, Zip 82240-1597; tel. 307/532-4181, Ingrid Long, Chief Executive Officer and Chief Nursing Officer
Web address: https://www.bannerhealth.com/locations/torrington/community-hospital

PLATTE COUNTY MEMORIAL HOSPITAL (L, 25 beds) 201 14th Street, Wheatland, WY, Zip 82201-3201, P O Box 848, Zip 82201-0848, tel. 307/322-3636, Sandy Dugger, Chief Executive Officer
Web address: https://www.bannerhealth.com/locations/wheatland/platte-county-memorial-hospital

WASHAKIE MEDICAL CENTER (L, 18 beds) 400 South 15th Street, Worland, WY, Zip 82401-3531, P O Box 700, Zip 82401-0700, tel. 307/347-3221, Jay Stallings, Chief Executive Officer
Web address: https://www.bannerhealth.com/locations/worland/washakie-medical-center

WYOMING MEDICAL CENTER (O, 249 beds) 1233 East Second Street, Casper, WY, Zip 82601-2988; tel. 307/577-7201, Lance Porter, President and Chief Executive Officer

Owned, leased, sponsored:	29 hospitals	5897 beds
Contract-managed:	1 hospitals	25 beds
Totals:	30 hospitals	5922 beds

★0005: BAPTIST HEALTH (NP)

841 Prudential Drive, Suite 1601, Jacksonville, FL Zip 32207-8202; tel. 904/202-2000, Michael A. Mayo, FACHE, President and Chief Executive Officer
(Moderately Centralized Health System)

FLORIDA: BAPTIST MEDICAL CENTER BEACHES (O, 135 beds) 1350 13th Avenue South, Jacksonville Beach, FL, Zip 32250-3205; tel. 904/627-2900, Jarret Dreicer, FACHE, President
Web address: https://www.baptistjax.com/locations/baptist-medical-center-beaches

BAPTIST MEDICAL CENTER JACKSONVILLE (O, 1147 beds) 800 Prudential Drive, Jacksonville, FL, Zip 32207-8202; tel. 904/202-2000, Nicole B. Thomas, President

BAPTIST MEDICAL CENTER NASSAU (O, 54 beds) 1250 South 18th Street, Fernandina Beach, FL, Zip 32034-3098; tel. 904/321-3500, Tara Beth Anderson, President
Web address: www.baptistjax.com/locations/baptist-medical-center-nassau

Owned, leased, sponsored:	3 hospitals	1336 beds
Contract-managed:	0 hospitals	0 beds
Totals:	3 hospitals	1336 beds

0150: BAPTIST HEALTH (NP)

301 Brown Springs Road, Montgomery, AL Zip 36117-7005; tel. 334/273-4400, W Russell. Tyner, President and Chief Executive Officer
(Independent Hospital System)

ALABAMA: BAPTIST MEDICAL CENTER EAST (O, 176 beds) 400 Taylor Road, Montgomery, AL, Zip 36117-3512, P O Box 241267, Zip 36124-1267, tel. 334/747-8330, Jeff G. Rains, Chief Executive Officer
Web address: www.baptistfirst.org

BAPTIST MEDICAL CENTER SOUTH (O, 456 beds) 2105 East South Boulevard, Montgomery, AL, Zip 36116-2409, Box 11010, Zip 36111-0010, tel. 334/288-2100, J Peter. Selman, FACHE, Chief Executive Officer

PRATTVILLE BAPTIST HOSPITAL (O, 71 beds) 124 South Memorial Drive, Prattville, AL, Zip 36067-3619, P O Box 681630, Zip 36068-1638, tel. 334/365-0651, Eric Morgan, Chief Executive Officer
Web address: www.baptistfirst.org/facilities/prattville-baptist-hospital/default.aspx

Owned, leased, sponsored:	3 hospitals	703 beds
Contract-managed:	0 hospitals	0 beds
Totals:	3 hospitals	703 beds

0315: BAPTIST HEALTH (CO)

2701 Eastpoint Parkway, Louisville, KY Zip 40223; tel. 502/896-5000, Gerard Colman, Ph.D., Chief Executive Officer
(Centralized Physician/Insurance Health System)

INDIANA: BAPTIST HEALTH FLOYD (O, 237 beds) 1850 State Street, New Albany, IN, Zip 47150-4997; tel. 812/949-5500, Mike K. Schroyer, FACHE, MSN, R.N., President
Web address: www.baptisthealth.com/floyd

KENTUCKY: BAPTIST HEALTH CORBIN (O, 273 beds) 1 Trillium Way, Corbin, KY, Zip 40701-8420; tel. 606/528-1212, Anthony Powers, Interim President and Vice President of Patient Services
Web address: www.baptisthealth.com/corbin

BAPTIST HEALTH DEACONESS MADISONVILLE, INC. (O, 165 beds) 900 Hospital Drive, Madisonville, KY, Zip 42431-1694; tel. 270/825-5100, Alisa Coleman, President
Web address: www.baptisthealthmadisonville.com

BAPTIST HEALTH HARDIN (C, 268 beds) 913 North Dixie Avenue, Elizabethtown, KY, Zip 42701-2503; tel. 270/737-1212, Robert L. Ramey, President

BAPTIST HEALTH LA GRANGE (O, 65 beds) 1025 New Moody Lane, La Grange, KY, Zip 40031-9154; tel. 502/222-5388, Clint Kaho, President
Web address: www.baptisthealthlagrange.com

BAPTIST HEALTH LEXINGTON (O, 434 beds) 1740 Nicholasville Road, Lexington, KY, Zip 40503-1499; tel. 859/260-6100, Christopher Roty, President
Web address: www.baptisthealthlexington.com

BAPTIST HEALTH LOUISVILLE (O, 473 beds) 4000 Kresge Way, Louisville, KY, Zip 40207-4676; tel. 502/897-8100, Jonathan Velez, President

BAPTIST HEALTH PADUCAH (O, 182 beds) 2501 Kentucky Avenue, Paducah, KY, Zip 42003-3200; tel. 270/575-2100, Kenneth Boyd, President
Web address: https://www.baptisthealth.com/paducah/

BAPTIST HEALTH RICHMOND (O, 58 beds) 801 Eastern Bypass, Richmond, KY, Zip 40475-2405, P O Box 1600, Zip 40476-2603, tel. 859/623-3131, Greg Donavan. Gerard, President
Web address: www.baptisthealthrichmond.com

Owned, leased, sponsored:	8 hospitals	1887 beds
Contract-managed:	1 hospitals	268 beds
Totals:	9 hospitals	2155 beds

★0355: BAPTIST HEALTH (NP)

9601 Baptist Health Drive, Little Rock, AR Zip 72205-6321; tel. 501/202-2000, Troy R. Wells, Chief Executive Officer
(Centralized Physician/Insurance Health System)

ARKANSAS: BAPTIST HEALTH-VAN BUREN (O, 74 beds) 211 Crawford Memorial Drive, Van Buren, AR, Zip 72956-5322, P O Box 409, Zip 72957-0409, tel. 479/474-3401, Jeffrey Carrier, President, Baptist Health Western Region

---

For explanation of codes following names, see page B2.
★ Indicates Type III membership in the American Hospital Association.

Systems / Baptist Health

BAPTIST HEALTH EXTENDED CARE HOSPITAL (O, 36 beds) 9601 Baptist Health Drive, Little Rock, AR, Zip 72205-7202; tel. 501/202-1070, Greg Stubblefield, President
Web address: https://www.baptist-health.com/location/baptist-health-extended-care-hospital/

BAPTIST HEALTH MEDICAL CENTER–CONWAY (O, 81 beds) 1555 Exchange Avenue, Conway, AR, Zip 72032-7824; tel. 501/585-2000, April Bennett, President
Web address: www.baptist-health.com/location/baptist-health-medical-center-conway-conway

BAPTIST HEALTH MEDICAL CENTER–DREW COUNTY (C, 60 beds) 778 Scogin Drive, Monticello, AR, Zip 71655-5729; tel. 870/367-2411, Scott G. Barrilleaux, FACHE, Chief Executive Officer

BAPTIST HEALTH MEDICAL CENTER–NORTH LITTLE ROCK (O, 255 beds) 3333 Springhill Drive, North Little Rock, AR, Zip 72117-2922; tel. 501/202-3000, Cody Walker, President
Web address: https://www.baptist-health.com/location/baptist-health-medical-center-north-little-rock-north-little-rock

BAPTIST HEALTH MEDICAL CENTER–ARKADELPHIA (L, 25 beds) 3050 Twin Rivers Drive, Arkadelphia, AR, Zip 71923-4299; tel. 870/245-2622, Jay Quebedeaux, FACHE, President

BAPTIST HEALTH MEDICAL CENTER–HEBER SPRINGS (O, 25 beds) 1800 Bypass Road, Heber Springs, AR, Zip 72543-9135; tel. 501/887-3000, Kevin L. Storey, President
Web address: www.baptist-health.com/maps-directions/bhmc-heber-springs

BAPTIST HEALTH MEDICAL CENTER–HOT SPRING COUNTY (L, 69 beds) 1001 Schneider Drive, Malvern, AR, Zip 72104-4811; tel. 501/332-1000, Jay Quebedeaux, FACHE, President
Web address: https://www.baptist-health.com/location/baptist-health-medical-center-hot-spring-county-hot-spring-county

BAPTIST HEALTH MEDICAL CENTER–LITTLE ROCK (O, 633 beds) 9601 Baptist Health Drive, Little Rock, AR, Zip 72205-7299; tel. 501/202-2000, Mike Perkins, President

BAPTIST HEALTH MEDICAL CENTER–STUTTGART (L, 49 beds) 1703 North Buerkle Road, Stuttgart, AR, Zip 72160-1905, P O Box 1905, Zip 72160-1905, tel. 870/673-3511, Kevin L. Storey, President
Web address: https://www.baptist-health.com/location/baptist-health-medical-center-stuttgart-stuttgart

BAPTIST HEALTH REHABILITATION INSTITUTE (O, 60 beds) 9501 Baptist Health Drive, Little Rock, AR, Zip 72205-6225; tel. 501/202-7000, Kourtney Matlock, President

BAPTIST HEALTH–FORT SMITH (O, 337 beds) 1001 Towson Avenue, Fort Smith, AR, Zip 72901-4921, P O Box 2406, Zip 72917-7006, tel. 479/441-4000, Jeffrey Carrier, President, Baptist Health Western Region
Web address: https://www.baptist-health.com/location/baptist-health-fort-smith/

Owned, leased, sponsored:	11 hospitals	1644 beds
Contract-managed:	1 hospitals	60 beds
Totals:	12 hospitals	1704 beds

★0185: BAPTIST HEALTH CARE CORPORATION (NP)
125 Baptist Way, Suite 6A, Pensacola, FL Zip 32503, P O Box 17500, Zip 32522-7500, tel. 850/434-4011, Mark T. Faulkner, President and Chief Executive Officer
(Centralized Physician/Insurance Health System)

FLORIDA: BAPTIST HOSPITAL (O, 340 beds) 1000 West Moreno Street, Pensacola, FL, Zip 32501-2316, 123 Baptist Way Suite 6A, Zip 32503-2254, tel. 850/434-4011, Beau Pollard, Vice President and Baptist Hospital Administrator
Web address: www.ebaptisthealthcare.org

GULF BREEZE HOSPITAL (O, 65 beds) 1110 Gulf Breeze Parkway, Gulf Breeze, FL, Zip 32561-4884; tel. 850/934-2000, Brett Aldridge, President

JAY HOSPITAL (L, 19 beds) 14114 Alabama Street, Jay, FL, Zip 32565-1219; tel. 850/675-8000, Cyd Cadena, Vice President
Web address: www.bhcpns.org/jayhospital/

Owned, leased, sponsored:	3 hospitals	424 beds
Contract-managed:	0 hospitals	0 beds
Totals:	3 hospitals	424 beds

★0122: BAPTIST HEALTH SOUTH FLORIDA (NP)
6855 Red Road, Suite 600, Coral Gables, FL Zip 33143-3632; tel. 786/662-7111, Albert Leon Boulenger, R.N., President and Chief Executive Officer
(Centralized Health System)

FLORIDA: BAPTIST HEALTH SOUTH FLORIDA, BAPTIST HOSPITAL OF MIAMI (O, 789 beds) 8900 North Kendall Drive, Miami, FL, Zip 33176-2197; tel. 786/596-1960, William G. Ulbricht, Chief Executive Officer
Web address: www.baptisthealth.net

BAPTIST HEALTH SOUTH FLORIDA, DOCTORS HOSPITAL (O, 134 beds) 5000 University Drive, Coral Gables, FL, Zip 33146-2094; tel. 786/308-3000, Javier Hernandez-Lichtl, Chief Executive Officer

BAPTIST HEALTH SOUTH FLORIDA, HOMESTEAD HOSPITAL (O, 147 beds) 975 Baptist Way, Homestead, FL, Zip 33033-7600; tel. 786/243-8000, Kenneth R. Spell, Chief Executive Officer
Web address: www.baptisthealth.net

BAPTIST HEALTH SOUTH FLORIDA, MARINERS HOSPITAL (O, 25 beds) 91500 Overseas Highway, Tavernier, FL, Zip 33070-2547; tel. 305/434-3000, Drew Grossman, Chief Executive Officer
Web address: www.baptisthealth.net/en/facilities/mariners-hospital/Pages/default.aspx

BAPTIST HEALTH SOUTH FLORIDA, SOUTH MIAMI HOSPITAL (O, 350 beds) 6200 SW 73rd Street, Miami, FL, Zip 33143-4679; tel. 786/662-4000, William M. Duquette, Chief Executive Officer
Web address: www.baptisthealth.net

BAPTIST HEALTH SOUTH FLORIDA, WEST KENDALL BAPTIST HOSPITAL (O, 186 beds) 9555 SW 162nd Avenue, Miami, FL, Zip 33196-6408; tel. 786/467-2000, Lourdes Boue, Chief Executive Officer

BETHESDA HOSPITAL EAST (O, 376 beds) 2815 South Seacrest Boulevard, Boynton Beach, FL, Zip 33435-7995; tel. 561/737-7733, Jared M. Smith, Chief Executive Officer
Web address: www.https://baptisthealth.net/locations/hospitals/bethesda-hospital-east

BOCA RATON REGIONAL HOSPITAL (O, 392 beds) 800 Meadows Road, Boca Raton, FL, Zip 33486-2368; tel. 561/955-7100, Lincoln S. Mendez, Chief Executive Officer

FISHERMEN'S HOSPITAL (O, 4 beds) 3301 Overseas Highway, Marathon, FL, Zip 33050-2329; tel. 305/743-5533, Drew Grossman, Chief Executive Officer
Web address: www.fishermenshospital.org

Owned, leased, sponsored:	9 hospitals	2403 beds
Contract-managed:	0 hospitals	0 beds
Totals:	9 hospitals	2403 beds

★1625: BAPTIST MEMORIAL HEALTH CARE CORPORATION (NP)
350 North Humphreys Boulevard, Memphis, TN Zip 38120-2177; tel. 901/227-5117, Jason Little, President and Chief Executive Officer
(Moderately Centralized Health System)

ARKANSAS: BAPTIST MEMORIAL HOSPITAL–CRITTENDEN (O, 11 beds) 2100 North 7th Street, West Memphis, AR, Zip 72301-2017; tel. 870/394-7800, Samuel Pieh, Chief Executive Officer and Administrator
Web address: www.baptistonline.org

NEA BAPTIST MEMORIAL HOSPITAL (O, 228 beds) 4800 East Johnson Avenue, Jonesboro, AR, Zip 72401-8413; tel. 870/936-1000, Samuel Lynd, Chief Executive Officer and Administrator

---

For explanation of codes following names, see page B2.
★ Indicates Type III membership in the American Hospital Association.

MISSISSIPPI: BAPTIST ANDERSON REGIONAL MEDICAL CENTER–SOUTH (O, 58 beds) 1102 Constitution Avenue, Meridian, MS, Zip 39301–4001; tel. 601/553–6000, John G. Anderson, FACHE, Chief Executive Officer and Administrator
Web address: www.andersonregional.org

BAPTIST ANDERSON REGIONAL MEDICAL CENTER (O, 170 beds) 2124 14th Street, Meridian, MS, Zip 39301–4040; tel. 601/553–6000, John G. Anderson, FACHE, Chief Executive Officer and Administrator

BAPTIST MEDICAL CENTER–ATTALA (O, 25 beds) 220 Highway 12 West, Kosciusko, MS, Zip 39090–3208, 220 Hwy 12 West, Zip 39090–0887, tel. 662/289–4311, Mac Flynt, Chief Executive Officer and Administrator
Web address: www.mbhs.org/locations/baptist-medical-center-attala/

BAPTIST MEDICAL CENTER–LEAKE (O, 25 beds) 1100 Highway 16 E, Carthage, MS, Zip 39051–3809, 1100 Hwy 16 East, Zip 39051–0909, tel. 601/267–1100, Daryl W. Weaver, Chief Executive Officer and Administrator

BAPTIST MEDICAL CENTER–YAZOO (O, 25 beds) 823 Grand Avenue, Yazoo City, MS, Zip 39194–3233; tel. 662/746–2261, Mac Flynt, Chief Executive Officer and Administrator
Web address: www.mbhs.org/locations/baptist-medical-center-yazoo/

BAPTIST MEMORIAL HOSPITAL–CALHOUN (L, 145 beds) 140 Burke–Calhoun City Road, Calhoun City, MS, Zip 38916–9690; tel. 662/628–6611, Christopher Threadgill, M.D., Chief Executive Officer and Administrator

BAPTIST MEMORIAL HOSPITAL–BOONEVILLE (L, 68 beds) 100 Hospital Street, Booneville, MS, Zip 38829–3359; tel. 662/720–5000, Ann Bishop, Chief Executive Officer and Administrator
Web address: www.bmhcc.org/booneville

BAPTIST MEMORIAL HOSPITAL–DESOTO (O, 247 beds) 7601 Southcrest Parkway, Southaven, MS, Zip 38671–4742; tel. 662/772–4000, Brian Hogan, Chief Executive Officer and Administrator
Web address: www.baptistonline.org/desoto/

BAPTIST MEMORIAL HOSPITAL–GOLDEN TRIANGLE (O, 244 beds) 2520 Fifth Street North, Columbus, MS, Zip 39705–2095, P O Box 1307, Zip 39703–1307, tel. 662/244–1000, Robert Coleman, Chief Executive Officer and Administrator

BAPTIST MEMORIAL HOSPITAL–NORTH MISSISSIPPI (O, 184 beds) 2301 South Lamar Boulevard, Oxford, MS, Zip 38655–5373, P O Box 946, Zip 38655–6002, tel. 662/232–8100, Brian Welton, Chief Executive Officer and Administrator
Web address: www.baptistonline.org/north-mississippi/

BAPTIST MEMORIAL HOSPITAL–UNION COUNTY (L, 101 beds) 200 Highway 30 West, New Albany, MS, Zip 38652–3112; tel. 662/538–7631, Ann Bishop, Chief Executive Officer and Administrator

MISSISSIPPI BAPTIST MEDICAL CENTER (O, 425 beds) 1225 North State Street, Jackson, MS, Zip 39202–2064; tel. 601/968–1000, Bobbie K. Ware, R.N., FACHE, Chief Executive Officer and Administrator
Web address: www.mbhs.org

TENNESSEE: BAPTIST MEMORIAL HOSPITAL–MEMPHIS (O, 547 beds) 6019 Walnut Grove Road, Memphis, TN, Zip 38120–2173; tel. 901/226–5000, Paul Cade, Chief Executive Officer and Administrator

BAPTIST MEMORIAL HOSPITAL FOR WOMEN (O, 140 beds) 6225 Humphreys Boulevard, Memphis, TN, Zip 38120–2373; tel. 901/227–9000, Allison Bosse, Chief Executive Officer and Administrator
Web address: www.baptistonline.org/womens/

BAPTIST MEMORIAL HOSPITAL–CARROLL COUNTY (O, 53 beds) 631 R.B. Wilson Drive, Huntingdon, TN, Zip 38344–1727; tel. 731/986–4461, Susan M. Breeden, Chief Executive Officer and Administrator
Web address: www.baptistonline.org/huntingdon/

BAPTIST MEMORIAL HOSPITAL–COLLIERVILLE (O, 81 beds) 1500 West Poplar Avenue, Collierville, TN, Zip 38017–0601; tel. 901/861–9400, Lindsay Stencel, Chief Executive Officer and Administrator

BAPTIST MEMORIAL HOSPITAL–TIPTON (O, 36 beds) 1995 Highway 51 South, Covington, TN, Zip 38019–3635; tel. 901/476–2621, Parker Harris, Chief Executive Officer and Administrator
Web address: www.baptistonline.org/tipton/

BAPTIST MEMORIAL HOSPITAL–UNION CITY (O, 63 beds) 1201 Bishop Street, Union City, TN, Zip 38261–5403, P O Box 310, Zip 38281–0310, tel. 731/885–2410, Barry Bondurant, Chief Executive Officer and Administrator
Web address: www.baptistonline.org/union-city/

BAPTIST MEMORIAL REHABILITATION HOSPITAL (O, 49 beds) 1240 South Germantown Road, Germantown, TN, Zip 38138–2226; tel. 901/275–3300, Christopher L. Bariola, Chief Executive Officer

BAPTIST MEMORIAL RESTORATIVE CARE HOSPITAL (O, 30 beds) 6019 Walnut Grove Road, Memphis, TN, Zip 38120–2113; tel. 901/226–4200, Mark Kelly, Chief Executive Officer
Web address: www.baptistonline.org/restorative-care/

Owned, leased, sponsored:	22 hospitals	2955 beds
Contract–managed:	0 hospitals	0 beds
Totals:	22 hospitals	2955 beds

★0528: BASSETT HEALTHCARE NETWORK (NP)

1 Atwell Road, Cooperstown, NY Zip 13326–1301; tel. 607/547–3456, Staci Thompson, President and Chief Executive Officer
(Independent Hospital System)

NEW YORK: AURELIA OSBORN FOX MEMORIAL HOSPITAL (O, 184 beds) 1 Norton Avenue, Oneonta, NY, Zip 13820–2629; tel. 607/432–2000, Staci Thompson, President and Chief Executive Officer
Web address: www.bassett.org/ao-fox-hospital/

BASSETT MEDICAL CENTER (O, 152 beds) 1 Atwell Road, Cooperstown, NY, Zip 13326–1394; tel. 607/547–3456, Henry Weil, M.D., President

COBLESKILL REGIONAL HOSPITAL (O, 25 beds) 178 Grandview Drive, Cobleskill, NY, Zip 12043–5144; tel. 518/254–3456, Susan Oakes Ferrucci, MS, Chief Hospital Executive
Web address: www.bassett.org

LITTLE FALLS HOSPITAL (O, 25 beds) 140 Burwell Street, Little Falls, NY, Zip 13365–1725; tel. 315/823–1000, Susan Oakes Ferrucci, MS, Chief Hospital Executive
Web address: www.bassett.org

O'CONNOR HOSPITAL (O, 23 beds) 460 Andes Road, State Route 28, Delhi, NY, Zip 13753–7407; tel. 607/746–0300, Susan Oakes Ferrucci, MS, Chief Hospital Executive

Owned, leased, sponsored:	5 hospitals	409 beds
Contract–managed:	0 hospitals	0 beds
Totals:	5 hospitals	409 beds

★1091: BAYCARE HEALTH SYSTEM (NP)

2985 Drew Street, Clearwater, FL Zip 33759–3012; tel. 727/820–8200, Stephanie Conners, R.N., President and Chief Executive Officer

FLORIDA: BARTOW REGIONAL MEDICAL CENTER (O, 72 beds) 2200 Osprey Boulevard, Bartow, FL, Zip 33830–3308; tel. 863/533–8111, Karen Kerr, R.N., President
Web address: www.bartowregional.com

BAYCARE ALLIANT HOSPITAL (O, 34 beds) 601 Main Street, MS#402, Dunedin, FL, Zip 34698–5848; tel. 727/736–9991, Maya Perez, President
Web address: www.baycare.org

BAYCARE HOSPITAL WESLEY CHAPEL (O, 86 beds) 4501 Bruce B Downs Boulevard, Wesley Chapel, FL, Zip 33544–9216; tel. 813/914–1000, Becky Schulkowski, President
Web address: www.BayCare.org

MEASE COUNTRYSIDE HOSPITAL (O, 387 beds) 3231 McMullen Booth Road, Safety Harbor, FL, Zip 34695–6607; tel. 727/725–6111, Kelly Enriquez, President, Mease Hospitals

MEASE DUNEDIN HOSPITAL (O, 120 beds) 601 Main Street, Dunedin, FL, Zip 34698–5891; tel. 727/733–1111, Kelly Enriquez, President, Mease Hospitals
Web address: www.https://baycare.org/locations/hospitals/mease-dunedin-hospital/patients-and-visitors

MORTON PLANT HOSPITAL (O, 715 beds) 300 Pinellas Street, Clearwater, FL, Zip 33756–3804; tel. 727/462–7000, Matthew Novak, President

---

For explanation of codes following names, see page B2.
★ Indicates Type III membership in the American Hospital Association.

Systems / Baycare Health System

MORTON PLANT NORTH BAY HOSPITAL (O, 222 beds) 6600 Madison Street, New Port Richey, FL, Zip 34652-1900; tel. 727/842-8468, Brandon May, President
Web address: www.https://baycare.org/locations/hospitals/morton-plant-north-bay-hospital/patients-and-visitors

SOUTH FLORIDA BAPTIST HOSPITAL (O, 141 beds) 301 North Alexander Street, Plant City, FL, Zip 33563-4303; tel. 813/757-1200, Karen Kerr, R.N., President
Web address: www.https://baycare.org/sfbh

ST. ANTHONY'S HOSPITAL (O, 448 beds) 1200 7th Ave North, Saint Petersburg, FL, Zip 33705-1388, P O Box 12588, Zip 33733-2588, tel. 727/825-1100, M. Scott Smith, President
Web address: www.stanthonys.com/

ST. JOSEPH'S HOSPITAL (O, 1367 beds) 3001 West Martin Luther King Jr. Boulevard, Tampa, FL, Zip 33607-6387, P O Box 4227, Zip 33677-4227, tel. 813/870-4000, Philip Minden, President

WINTER HAVEN HOSPITAL (O, 455 beds) 200 Avenue F NE, Winter Haven, FL, Zip 33881-4193; tel. 863/293-1121, Tom Garthwaite, President
Web address: www.https://baycare.org/hospitals/winter-haven-hospital/patients-and-visitors

Owned, leased, sponsored:	11 hospitals	4047 beds
Contract-managed:	0 hospitals	0 beds
Totals:	11 hospitals	4047 beds

★0918: **BAYLOR SCOTT & WHITE HEALTH (NP)**
301 North Washington Avenue, Dallas, TX Zip 75246; tel. 214/820-0111, Peter J. McCanna, Chief Executive Officer
(Centralized Physician/Insurance Health System)

TEXAS: BAYLOR SCOTT & WHITE ALL SAINTS MEDICAL CENTER–FORT WORTH (O, 400 beds) 1400 Eighth Avenue, Fort Worth, TX, Zip 76104-4192; tel. 817/925-2544, Charles E. Williams, President DFW–West Region
Web address: https://www.bswhealth.com/locations/fort-worth-hospital

BAYLOR SCOTT & WHITE CONTINUING CARE HOSPITAL–TEMPLE (O, 48 beds) 546 North Kegley Road, Temple, TX, Zip 76502-4069; tel. 254/215-0900, Candice Gourley, President

BAYLOR SCOTT & WHITE HOSPITAL MEDICAL CENTER–COLLEGE STATION (O, 142 beds) 700 Scott & White Drive, College Station, TX, Zip 77845; tel. 979/207-0100, Jason Jennings, FACHE, President
Web address: www.sw.org/location/college-station-hospital

BAYLOR SCOTT & WHITE MEDICAL CENTER–AUSTIN (O, 17 beds) 5245 West US Highway 290 Service Road, Austin, TX, Zip 78735, 5251 West US Highway 290, Zip 78735, tel. 512/654-2100, Jay Fox, FACHE, President
Web address: https://www.bswhealth.com/locations/austin-medical-center/pages/default.aspx

BAYLOR SCOTT & WHITE MEDICAL CENTER–BRENHAM (O, 25 beds) 700 Medical Parkway, Brenham, TX, Zip 77833-5498; tel. 979/337-5000, Jason Jennings, FACHE, President

BAYLOR SCOTT & WHITE MEDICAL CENTER–BUDA (O, 15 beds) 5330 Overpass Road, Buda, TX, Zip 78610-2300, 5330 Overpass Drive, Zip 78610-2300, tel. 737/999-6200, Jay Fox, FACHE, President
Web address: https://www.bswhealth.com/locations/buda/Pages/default.aspx

BAYLOR SCOTT & WHITE MEDICAL CENTER–CENTENNIAL (O, 106 beds) 12505 Lebanon Road, Frisco, TX, Zip 75035-8298; tel. 972/963-3333, Ryan Gebhart, FACHE, President

BAYLOR SCOTT & WHITE MEDICAL CENTER–GRAPEVINE (O, 286 beds) 1650 West College Street, Grapevine, TX, Zip 76051-3565; tel. 817/481-1588, Naman Mahajan, Chief Executive Officer
Web address: https://www.bswhealth.com/locations/grapevine/?utm_source=google-mybusiness&utm_medium=organic&utm_campaign=9488

BAYLOR SCOTT & WHITE MEDICAL CENTER–HILLCREST (O, 260 beds) 100 Hillcrest Medical Boulevard, Waco, TX, Zip 76712-8897; tel. 254/202-2000, Chris Lancaster, President
Web address: www.sw.org/hillcrest-medical-center

BAYLOR SCOTT & WHITE MEDICAL CENTER–LAKE POINTE (O, 157 beds) 6800 Scenic Drive, Rowlett, TX, Zip 75088-4552, P O Box 1550, Zip 75030-1550, tel. 972/412-2273, Donas Cole, FACHE, President

BAYLOR SCOTT & WHITE MEDICAL CENTER–MARBLE FALLS (O, 46 beds) 800 West Highway 71, Marble Falls, TX, Zip 78654; tel. 830/201-8000, Timothy A. Ols, FACHE, President
Web address: www.sw.org/location/marble-falls-hospital

BAYLOR SCOTT & WHITE MEDICAL CENTER–PFLUGERVILLE (O, 25 beds) 2600 East Pflugerville Parkway, Pflugerville, TX, Zip 78660-5998; tel. 512/654-6100, Jay Fox, FACHE, President
Web address: https://www.bswhealth.com/locations/pflugerville-mc

BAYLOR SCOTT & WHITE MEDICAL CENTER–PLANO (O, 160 beds) 4700 Alliance Boulevard, Plano, TX, Zip 75093-5323; tel. 469/814-2000, Jerri Garison, R.N., President

BAYLOR SCOTT & WHITE MEDICAL CENTER–ROUND ROCK (O, 175 beds) 300 University Boulevard, Round Rock, TX, Zip 78665-1032; tel. 512/509-0100, Jay Fox, FACHE, President
Web address: www.sw.org

BAYLOR SCOTT & WHITE MEDICAL CENTER–TAYLOR (O, 15 beds) 305 Mallard Lane, Taylor, TX, Zip 76574-1208; tel. 512/352-7611, Jay Fox, FACHE, President
Web address: https://www.bswhealth.com/locations/taylor/pages/default.aspx?utm_source=BSWHealth.com-Taylor&utm_medium=offline&utm_campaign=BSWHealth.com&utm_term=BSWHealth.com-Taylor&utm_content=redirect

BAYLOR SCOTT & WHITE MEDICAL CENTER–TEMPLE (O, 625 beds) 2401 South 31st Street, Temple, TX, Zip 76508-0002; tel. 254/724-2111, Gregory Haralson, FACHE, President
Web address: https://www.bswhealth.com/locations/temple/Pages/default.aspx

BAYLOR SCOTT & WHITE MEDICAL CENTER AT–MCKINNEY (O, 192 beds) 5252 West University Drive, McKinney, TX, Zip 75071-7822; tel. 469/764-1000, Tim Bowen, FACHE, President

BAYLOR SCOTT & WHITE MEDICAL CENTER–IRVING (L, 247 beds) 1901 North MacArthur Boulevard, Irving, TX, Zip 75061-2220; tel. 972/579-8100, Cindy K. Schamp, FACHE, President
Web address: www.bswhealth.com

BAYLOR SCOTT & WHITE MEDICAL CENTER–WAXAHACHIE (O, 128 beds) 2400 North I-35E, Waxahachie, TX, Zip 75165; tel. 469/843-4000, Will Turner, Chief Executive Officer

BAYLOR SCOTT & WHITE SURGICAL HOSPITAL–SHERMAN (O, 12 beds) 3601 North Calais Street, Sherman, TX, Zip 75090-1785; tel. 903/870-0999, Nikole Best, Chief Executive Officer
Web address: www.https://baylorsherman.com

BAYLOR SCOTT & WHITE THE HEART HOSPITAL PLANO (C, 109 beds) 1100 Allied Drive, Plano, TX, Zip 75093-5348; tel. 469/814-3278, Mark Valentine, President

BAYLOR UNIVERSITY MEDICAL CENTER (O, 812 beds) 3500 Gaston Avenue, Dallas, TX, Zip 75246-2088; tel. 214/820-0111, Kyle Armstrong, President Central Region of BSW Health
Web address: www.baylorhealth.com/PhysiciansLocations/Dallas/Pages/Default.aspx

Owned, leased, sponsored:	21 hospitals	3893 beds
Contract-managed:	1 hospitals	109 beds
Totals:	22 hospitals	4002 beds

★1095: **BAYSTATE HEALTH, INC. (NP)**
280 Chestnut Street, Springfield, MA Zip 01199-0001; tel. 413/794-0000, Peter D. Banko, FACHE, President and Chief Executive Officer
(Centralized Physician/Insurance Health System)

MASSACHUSETTS: BAYSTATE FRANKLIN MEDICAL CENTER (O, 80 beds) 164 High Street, Greenfield, MA, Zip 01301-2613; tel. 413/773-0211, Ronald Bryant, President

BAYSTATE MEDICAL CENTER (O, 746 beds) 759 Chestnut Street, Springfield, MA, Zip 01199-0001; tel. 413/794-0000, Sam Skura, President
Web address: www.baystatehealth.org/bmc

BAYSTATE NOBLE HOSPITAL (O, 85 beds) 115 West Silver Street, Westfield, MA, Zip 01085-3628; tel. 413/568-2811, Ronald Bryant, President
Web address: www.baystatehealth.org/locations/noble-hospital

For explanation of codes following names, see page B2.
★ Indicates Type III membership in the American Hospital Association.

BAYSTATE WING HOSPITAL (O, 74 beds) 40 Wright Street, Palmer, MA, Zip 01069–1138; tel. 413/283-7651, Ronald Bryant, President

Owned, leased, sponsored:	4 hospitals	985 beds
Contract-managed:	0 hospitals	0 beds
Totals:	4 hospitals	985 beds

★0940: BEACON HEALTH SYSTEM (NP)

615 North Michigan Street, South Bend, IN Zip 46601–1033; tel. 574/647-1000, Kreg Gruber, FACHE, Chief Executive Officer **(Centralized Physician/Insurance Health System)**

INDIANA: COMMUNITY HOSPITAL OF BREMEN (O, 21 beds) 1020 High Road, Bremen, IN, Zip 46506–1093, P O Box 8, Zip 46506–0008, tel. 574/546-2211, David Bailey, FACHE, President
Web address: www.bremenhospital.com

ELKHART GENERAL HOSPITAL (O, 214 beds) 600 East Boulevard, Elkhart, IN, Zip 46514–2499, P O Box 1329, Zip 46515–1329, tel. 574/294-2621, Carl W. Risk II, President
Web address: www.egh.org

MEMORIAL HOSPITAL OF SOUTH BEND (O, 426 beds) 615 North Michigan Street, South Bend, IN, Zip 46601–1033; tel. 574/647-1000, Larry A. Tracy Jr, FACHE, President
Web address: www.beaconhealthsystem.org

MICHIGAN: THREE RIVERS HEALTH SYSTEM, INC. (O, 60 beds) 701 South Health Parkway, Three Rivers, MI, Zip 49093–8352; tel. 269/278-1145, Maria Behr, President
Web address: www.threerivershealth.org

Owned, leased, sponsored:	4 hospitals	721 beds
Contract-managed:	0 hospitals	0 beds
Totals:	4 hospitals	721 beds

0538: BENEFIS HEALTH SYSTEM (NP)

1101 26th Street South, Great Falls, MT Zip 59405–5161; tel. 406/455-5000, John H. Goodnow, Chief Executive Officer **(Moderately Centralized Health System)**

MONTANA: BENEFIS HEALTH SYSTEM (O, 508 beds) 1101 26th Street South, Great Falls, MT, Zip 59405–5104; tel. 406/455-5000, John H. Goodnow, Chief Executive Officer

BENEFIS TETON MEDICAL CENTER (O, 25 beds) 915 4th Street North West, Choteau, MT, Zip 59422–9123; tel. 406/466-5763, Louie King, Chief Executive Officer
Web address: www.tetonmedicalcenter.net

MISSOURI RIVER MEDICAL CENTER (C, 25 beds) 1501 St Charles Street, Fort Benton, MT, Zip 59442–0249, P O Box 249, Zip 59442–0249, tel. 406/622-3331, Louie King, President, Harry Bold Nursing Home Administrator
Web address: www.mrmcfb.org

Owned, leased, sponsored:	2 hospitals	533 beds
Contract-managed:	1 hospitals	25 beds
Totals:	3 hospitals	558 beds

★2435: BERKSHIRE HEALTH SYSTEMS, INC. (NP)

725 North Street, Pittsfield, MA Zip 01201–4124; tel. 413/447-2750, Darlene Rodowicz, President and Chief Executive Officer **(Moderately Centralized Health System)**

MASSACHUSETTS: BERKSHIRE MEDICAL CENTER (O, 272 beds) 725 North Street, Pittsfield, MA, Zip 01201–4124; tel. 413/447-2000, Darlene Rodowicz, President and Chief Executive Officer

FAIRVIEW HOSPITAL (O, 24 beds) 29 Lewis Avenue, Great Barrington, MA, Zip 01230–1713; tel. 413/528-0790, Eugene A. Dellea, President
Web address: www.bhs1.org/body_fh.cfm?id=39

Owned, leased, sponsored:	2 hospitals	296 beds
Contract-managed:	0 hospitals	0 beds
Totals:	2 hospitals	296 beds

★0949: BETH ISRAEL LAHEY HEALTH (NP)

20 University Road, Suite 700, Cambridge, MA Zip 02138–5810; tel. 617/667-7000, Kevin Tabb, M.D., President and Chief Executive Officer

MASSACHUSETTS: ANNA JAQUES HOSPITAL (O, 123 beds) 25 Highland Avenue, Newburyport, MA, Zip 01950–3894; tel. 978/463-1000, Glenn Focht, M.D., President
Web address: www.ajh.org

BETH ISRAEL DEACONESS HOSPITAL–MILTON (O, 100 beds) 199 Reedsdale Road, Milton, MA, Zip 02186–3926; tel. 617/696-4600, Richard W. Fernandez, President and Chief Executive Officer

BETH ISRAEL DEACONESS HOSPITAL–NEEDHAM (O, 80 beds) 148 Chestnut Street, Needham, MA, Zip 2492; tel. 781/453-3000, John M. Fogarty, President and Chief Executive Officer
Web address: www.bidneedham.org/

BETH ISRAEL DEACONESS HOSPITAL–PLYMOUTH (O, 170 beds) 275 Sandwich Street, Plymouth, MA, Zip 2360, 36 Cordage Park Circle, Suite 322, Zip 2360, tel. 508/746-2000, Kevin B. Coughlin, President and Chief Executive Officer
Web address: www.bidplymouth.org

BETH ISRAEL DEACONESS MEDICAL CENTER (O, 756 beds) 330 Brookline Avenue, Boston, MA, Zip 02215–5491; tel. 617/667-7000, Peter J. Healy, Divisional President, Metro Boston and President of Beth Israel Deaconess Medical Center

BEVERLY HOSPITAL (O, 320 beds) 85 Herrick Street, Beverly, MA, Zip 01915–1777; tel. 978/922-3000, Tom Sands, FACHE, President
Web address: www.beverlyhospital.org

LAHEY HOSPITAL & MEDICAL CENTER (O, 358 beds) 41 Mall Road, Burlington, MA, Zip 01805–0001, 31 Mall Road, Zip 01805–0001, tel. 781/744-5100, Susan Moffatt-Bruce, President
Web address: www.lahey.org

MOUNT AUBURN HOSPITAL (O, 198 beds) 330 Mount Auburn Street, Cambridge, MA, Zip 02138–5597; tel. 617/492-3500, Edwin Huang, M.D., Interim President
Web address: www.mountauburnhospital.org

NEW ENGLAND BAPTIST HOSPITAL (O, 113 beds) 125 Parker Hill Avenue, Boston, MA, Zip 02120–2847; tel. 617/754-5800, David Passafaro, President

WINCHESTER HOSPITAL (O, 194 beds) 41 Highland Avenue, Winchester, MA, Zip 01890–1496; tel. 781/729-9000, Al Campbell, FACHE, R.N., President
Web address: www.winchesterhospital.org

NEW HAMPSHIRE: EXETER HOSPITAL (O, 99 beds) 5 Alumni Drive, Exeter, NH, Zip 03833–2128; tel. 603/778-7311, Debra Cresta, President

Owned, leased, sponsored:	11 hospitals	2511 beds
Contract-managed:	0 hospitals	0 beds
Totals:	11 hospitals	2511 beds

★0051: BJC HEALTH SYSTEM (NP)

4901 Forest Park Avenue, Suite 1200, Saint Louis, MO Zip 63108–1402; tel. 314/286-2000, Richard J. Liekweg, President and Chief Executive Officer **(Centralized Health System)**

ILLINOIS: ALTON MEMORIAL HOSPITAL (O, 222 beds) 1 Memorial Drive, Alton, IL, Zip 62002–6722; tel. 618/463-7311, David A. Braasch, FACHE, President
Web address: www.altonmemorialhospital.org

For explanation of codes following names, see page B2.
★ Indicates Type III membership in the American Hospital Association.

Systems / BJC Health System

MEMORIAL HOSPITAL BELLEVILLE (O, 270 beds) 4500 Memorial Drive, Belleville, IL, Zip 62226–5399; tel. 618/233–7750, Deborah Graves, R.N., President
Web address: www.memhosp.com

KANSAS: ALLEN COUNTY REGIONAL HOSPITAL (L, 10 beds) 3066 N. Kentucky St, Iola, KS Zip 66749, P O Box 540, Zip 66749–0540, tel. 620/365–1000, William Patton, Administrator
Web address: https://www.saintlukeskc.org/locations/allen-county-regional-hospital

ANDERSON COUNTY HOSPITAL (L, 40 beds) 421 South Maple, Garnett, KS, Zip 66032–1334, P O Box 309, Zip 66032–0309, tel. 785/448–3131, William Patton, Administrator

SAINT LUKE'S SOUTH HOSPITAL (O, 142 beds) 12300 Metcalf Avenue, Overland Park, KS, Zip 66213–1324; tel. 913/317–7000, Bobby Olm-Shipman, Chief Executive Officer
Web address: www.saintlukeshealthsystem.org/south

MISSOURI: BARNES–JEWISH HOSPITAL (O, 1401 beds) 1 Barnes-Jewish Hospital Plaza, Saint Louis, MO, Zip 63110–1003; tel. 314/747–3000, John Lynch, M.D., President

BARNES–JEWISH ST. PETERS HOSPITAL (O, 102 beds) 10 Hospital Drive, Saint Peters, MO, Zip 63376–1659; tel. 636/916–9000, Gregory Patterson, President
Web address: www.bjsph.org/

BARNES–JEWISH WEST COUNTY HOSPITAL (O, 100 beds) 12634 Olive Boulevard, Saint Louis, MO, Zip 63141–6337; tel. 314/996–8000, Angelleen Peters–Lewis, Ph.D., R.N., President

CHRISTIAN HOSPITAL (O, 232 beds) 11133 Dunn Road, Saint Louis, MO, Zip 63136–6119; tel. 314/653–5000, Rick Stevens, FACHE, President
Web address: www.christianhospital.org

HEDRICK MEDICAL CENTER (L, 21 beds) 2799 North Washington Street, Chillicothe, MO, Zip 64601–2902; tel. 660/646–1480, Catherine Hamilton, MSN, R.N., Administrator

MISSOURI BAPTIST MEDICAL CENTER (O, 351 beds) 3015 North Ballas Road, Saint Louis, MO, Zip 63131–2329; tel. 314/996–5000, Ann Abad, President
Web address: www.missouribaptist.org

MISSOURI BAPTIST SULLIVAN HOSPITAL (O, 35 beds) 751 Sappington Bridge Road, Sullivan, MO, Zip 63080–2354; tel. 573/468–4186, Lisa Lochner, President
Web address: www.missouribaptistsullivan.org

PARKLAND HEALTH CENTER–FARMINGTON COMMUNITY (O, 104 beds) 1101 West Liberty Street, Farmington, MO, Zip 63640–1921; tel. 573/756–6451, Annette D. Schnabel, FACHE, President, Parkland Health Center Corporation

PARKLAND HEALTH CENTER–BONNE TERRE (O, 3 beds) 7245 Raider Road, Bonne Terre, MO, Zip 63628; tel. 573/358–1400, Annette D. Schnabel, FACHE, President
Web address: www.parklandhealthcenter.org

PROGRESS WEST HOSPITAL (O, 77 beds) 2 Progress Point Parkway, O Fallon, MO, Zip 63368–2205; tel. 636/344–1000, Gregory Patterson, President
Web address: www.progresswest.org

SAINT LUKE'S EAST HOSPITAL (O, 238 beds) 100 NE Saint Luke's Boulevard, Lee's Summit, MO, Zip 64086–6000; tel. 816/347–5000, Bobby Olm-Shipman, President and Chief Executive Officer

SAINT LUKE'S HOSPITAL OF KANSAS CITY (O, 500 beds) 4401 Wornall Road, Kansas City, MO, Zip 64111–3220; tel. 816/932–3800, Jani L. Johnson, R.N., MSN, Chief Executive Officer
Web address: www.saint-lukes.org

SAINT LUKE'S NORTH HOSPITAL–BARRY ROAD (O, 125 beds) 5830 NW Barry Road, Kansas City, MO, Zip 64154–2778; tel. 816/891–6000, Darren Bass, FACHE, Chief Executive Officer, North Region

ST. LOUIS CHILDREN'S HOSPITAL (O, 355 beds) 1 Children's Place, Saint Louis, MO, Zip 63110–1002; tel. 314/454–6000, Trisha Lollo, President
Web address: www.stlouischildrens.org

WRIGHT MEMORIAL HOSPITAL (L, 10 beds) 191 Iowa Boulevard, Trenton, MO, Zip 64683–8343; tel. 660/358–5700, Catherine Hamilton, MSN, R.N., Administrator
Web address: www.saintlukeshealthsystem.org

Owned, leased, sponsored:	20 hospitals	4338 beds
Contract–managed:	0 hospitals	0 beds
Totals:	20 hospitals	4338 beds

★**0852: BLANCHARD VALLEY HEALTH SYSTEM (NP)**
1900 South Main Street, Findlay, OH Zip 45840–1214; tel. 419/423–4500, Myron D. Lewis, President and Chief Executive Officer
(Centralized Physician/Insurance Health System)

OHIO: BLANCHARD VALLEY HOSPITAL (O, 95 beds) 1900 South Main Street, Findlay, OH, Zip 45840–1214; tel. 419/423–4500, Myron D. Lewis, Chief Executive Officer
Web address: www.bvhealthsystem.org

BLUFFTON HOSPITAL (O, 25 beds) 139 Garau Street, Bluffton, OH, Zip 45817–1027; tel. 419/358–9010, Myron D. Lewis, Chief Executive Officer
Web address: www.bvhealthsystem.org/

Owned, leased, sponsored:	2 hospitals	120 beds
Contract–managed:	0 hospitals	0 beds
Totals:	2 hospitals	120 beds

★**5085: BON SECOURS MERCY HEALTH (CC)**
1701 Mercy Health Place, Cincinnati, OH Zip 45237–6147; tel. 410/442–5511, John M. Starcher Esq, President and Chief Executive Officer
(Moderately Centralized Health System)

KENTUCKY: MERCY HEALTH–LOURDES HOSPITAL (O, 281 beds) 1530 Lone Oak Road, Paducah, KY, Zip 42003–7900, P O Box 7100, Zip 42002–7100, tel. 270/444–2444, Michael Yungmann, President and Chief Executive Officer
Web address: www.lourdes-pad.org

MERCY HEALTH–MARCUM AND WALLACE (O, 25 beds) 60 Mercy Court, Irvine, KY, Zip 40336–1331; tel. 606/723–2115, Trena Stocker, President

OHIO: INSTITUTE FOR ORTHOPAEDIC SURGERY (O, 3 beds) 801 Medical Drive, Suite B, Lima, OH, Zip 45804–4030; tel. 419/224–7586, Chad Stewart, Administrative Director
Web address: www.ioshospital.com

MERCY HEALTH–ALLEN HOSPITAL (O, 25 beds) 200 West Lorain Street, Oberlin, OH, Zip 44074–1077; tel. 440/775–1211, Carrie Jankowski, President
Web address: https://www.mercy.com/locations/hospitals/lorain/mercy-allen-hospital

MERCY HEALTH–ANDERSON HOSPITAL (O, 298 beds) 7500 State Road, Cincinnati, OH, Zip 45255–2492; tel. 513/624–4500, Kathy Healy-Collier, President

MERCY HEALTH–CLERMONT HOSPITAL (O, 178 beds) 3000 Hospital Drive, Batavia, OH, Zip 45103–1921; tel. 513/732–8200, Tim Prestridge, President
Web address: https://www.mercy.com/locations/hospitals/cincinnati/mercy-health-clermont-hospital

MERCY HEALTH–DEFIANCE HOSPITAL (O, 23 beds) 1404 East Second Street, Defiance, OH, Zip 43512–2440; tel. 419/782–8444, Sonya Selhorst, R.N., President and Chief Nursing Officer

MERCY HEALTH–FAIRFIELD HOSPITAL (O, 180 beds) 3000 Mack Road, Fairfield, OH, Zip 45014–5335; tel. 513/870–7000, Justin Krueger, FACHE, President
Web address: https://www.mercy.com

MERCY HEALTH–KINGS MILLS HOSPITAL (O, 60 beds) 5440 Kings Island Drive, Mason, OH, Zip 45040–7931; tel. 513/637–9999, Jason Asic, President

---

For explanation of codes following names, see page B2.
★ Indicates Type III membership in the American Hospital Association.

Systems / Bridgepoint Healthcare

MERCY HEALTH–LORAIN HOSPITAL (O, 251 beds) 3700 Kolbe Road, Lorain, OH, Zip 44053-1697; tel. 440/960-4000, John Luellen, M.D., Market President
Web address: https://www.mercy.com/locations/hospitals/lorain/mercy-regional-medical-center

MERCY HEALTH–SPRINGFIELD REGIONAL MEDICAL CENTER (O, 259 beds) 100 Medical Center Drive, Springfield, OH, Zip 45504-2687; tel. 937/523-1000, Adam Groshans, Market President
Web address: https://www.mercy.com/locations/hospitals/springfield/springfield-medical-center

MERCY HEALTH–ST. ELIZABETH BOARDMAN HOSPITAL (O, 229 beds) 8401 Market Street, Boardman, OH, Zip 44512-6777; tel. 330/729-2929, Eugenia Aubel, President

MERCY HEALTH–ST. ELIZABETH YOUNGSTOWN HOSPITAL (O, 375 beds) 1044 Belmont Avenue, Youngstown, OH, Zip 44504-1096, P O Box 1790, Zip 44501-1790, tel. 330/746-7211, John Luellen, M.D., Market President
Web address: www.mercy.com

MERCY HEALTH–ST. JOSEPH WARREN HOSPITAL (O, 136 beds) 667 Eastland Avenue SE, Warren, OH, Zip 44484-4531, 627 Eastland Avenue, Zip 44484-4531, tel. 330/841-4000, Charlotte Wray, MSN, R.N., President

MERCY HEALTH–ST. RITA'S MEDICAL CENTER (O, 271 beds) 730 West Market Street, Lima, OH, Zip 45801-4602; tel. 419/227-3361, Ronda Lehman, PharmD, President
Web address: www.stritas.org

MERCY HEALTH–ST. VINCENT MEDICAL CENTER (O, 745 beds) 2213 Cherry Street, Toledo, OH, Zip 43608-2691; tel. 419/251-3232, Jeffrey Dempsey, President
Web address: www.mercyweb.org

MERCY HEALTH–TIFFIN HOSPITAL (O, 45 beds) 45 St Lawrence Drive, Tiffin, OH, Zip 44883-8310; tel. 419/455-7000, Andrew Morgan, President

MERCY HEALTH–URBANA HOSPITAL (O, 25 beds) 904 Scioto Street, Urbana, OH, Zip 43078-2200; tel. 937/653-5231, Jamie Houseman, President
Web address: www.health-partners.org

MERCY HEALTH–WEST HOSPITAL (O, 250 beds) 3300 Mercy Health Boulevard, Cincinnati, OH, Zip 45211-1103; tel. 513/215-5000, Bradley J. Bertke, President and Chief Operating Officer

MERCY HEALTH–WILLARD HOSPITAL (O, 25 beds) 1100 Neal Zick Road, Willard, OH, Zip 44890-9287; tel. 419/964-5000, Andrew Morgan, President
Web address: www.mercyweb.org

THE JEWISH HOSPITAL–MERCY HEALTH (O, 162 beds) 4777 East Galbraith Road, Cincinnati, OH, Zip 45236-2725; tel. 513/686-3000, Michael Kramer, President
Web address: www.jewishhospitalcincinnati.com/

SOUTH CAROLINA: BON SECOURS ST. FRANCIS HEALTH SYSTEM (O, 248 beds) 1 Saint Francis Drive, Greenville, SC, Zip 29601-3955; tel. 864/255-1000, Matthew T. Caldwell, Market President

BON SECOURS ST. FRANCIS HOSPITAL (O, 136 beds) 2095 Henry Tecklenburg Drive, Charleston, SC, Zip 29414-5733; tel. 843/402-1000, Matthew Desmond, Regional President, Bon Secours St. Francis and Mount Pleasant Hospitals & Vice President of Operations & Chief Transfor
Web address: www.rsfh.com/

ROPER HOSPITAL (O, 300 beds) 316 Calhoun Street, Charleston, SC, Zip 29401-1125; tel. 843/724-2000, Troy Powell, Regional President, Roper Hospital and Berkeley Hospital

ROPER ST. FRANCIS BERKELEY HOSPITAL (O, 50 beds) 100 Callen Boulevard, Summerville, SC, Zip 29486-2807; tel. 854/529-3100, Patrick Bosse, Chief Administrative Officer
Web address: https://www.rsfh.com/berkeley-hospital/

ROPER ST. FRANCIS MOUNT PLEASANT HOSPITAL (O, 52 beds) 3500 Highway 17 North, Mount Pleasant, SC, Zip 29466-9123, 3500 North Highway 17, Zip 29466-9123, tel. 843/606-7000, Ashleigh Wiedemann, Chief Administrative Officer

VIRGINIA: BON SECOURS–SOUTHAMPTON MEDICAL CENTER (O, 206 beds) 100 Fairview Drive, Franklin, VA, Zip 23851-1238, P O Box 817, Zip 23851-0817, tel. 757/569-6100, Kimberly W. Marks, President
Web address: https://www.bonsecours.com/locations/hospitals-medical-centers/hampton-roads/southampton-memorial-hospital

BON SECOURS–SOUTHERN VIRGINIA MEDICAL CENTER (O, 80 beds) 727 North Main Street, Emporia, VA, Zip 23847-1274; tel. 434/348-4400, Brenda Woodcock, President

BON SECOURS–SOUTHSIDE MEDICAL CENTER (O, 294 beds) 200 Medical Park Boulevard, Petersburg, VA, Zip 23805-9274; tel. 804/765-5000, Brenda Woodcock, President
Web address: www.srmconline.com

BON SECOURS MARY IMMACULATE HOSPITAL (O, 238 beds) 2 Bernardine Drive, Newport News, VA, Zip 23602-4499; tel. 757/886-6000, Alan E. George, President

BON SECOURS MARYVIEW MEDICAL CENTER (O, 466 beds) 3636 High Street, Portsmouth, VA, Zip 23707-3270; tel. 757/398-2200, Shane Knisley, President
Web address: https://www.bonsecours.com/locations/hospitals-medical-centers/hampton-roads/bon-secours-maryview-medical-center

BON SECOURS MEMORIAL REGIONAL MEDICAL CENTER (O, 251 beds) 8260 Atlee Road, Mechanicsville, VA, Zip 23116-1844; tel. 804/764-6000, John Emery, President
Web address: www.bonsecours.com

BON SECOURS RAPPAHANNOCK GENERAL HOSPITAL (O, 35 beds) 101 Harris Drive, Kilmarnock, VA, Zip 22482-3880, P O Box 1449, Zip 22482-1449, tel. 804/435-8000, John Emery, President

BON SECOURS RICHMOND COMMUNITY HOSPITAL (O, 96 beds) 1500 North 28th Street, Richmond, VA, Zip 23223-5396, P O Box 27184, Zip 23261-7184, tel. 804/225-1700, W. Bryan Lee, President
Web address: www.bonsecours.com

BON SECOURS ST. FRANCIS MEDICAL CENTER (O, 130 beds) 13710 St Francis Boulevard, Midlothian, VA, Zip 23114-3267; tel. 804/594-7300, Joseph Wilkins, President

BON SECOURS ST. MARY'S HOSPITAL (O, 391 beds) 5801 Bremo Road, Richmond, VA, Zip 23226-1907; tel. 804/285-2011, W. Bryan. Lee, President
Web address: www.bonsecours.com

Owned, leased, sponsored:	36 hospitals	6819 beds
Contract-managed:	0 hospitals	0 beds
Totals:	36 hospitals	6819 beds

2455: BRADFORD HEALTH SERVICES (IO)

2101 Magnolia Avenue South, Suite 518, Birmingham, AL Zip 35205-2853; tel. 205/251-7753, Mike Rickman, President and Chief Executive Officer

ALABAMA: BRADFORD HEALTH SERVICES AT HUNTSVILLE (O, 84 beds) 1600 Browns Ferry Road, Madison, AL, Zip 35758-9601, P O Box 1488, Zip 35758-0176, tel. 256/461-7272, Bob Hinds, Executive Director
Web address: www.bradfordhealth.com

BRADFORD HEALTH SERVICES AT WARRIOR LODGE (O, 100 beds) 1189 Allbritt Road, Warrior, AL, Zip 35180, P O Box 129, Zip 35180-0129, tel. 205/647-1945, Roy M. Ramsey, Executive Director

Owned, leased, sponsored:	2 hospitals	184 beds
Contract-managed:	0 hospitals	0 beds
Totals:	2 hospitals	184 beds

0352: BRIDGEPOINT HEALTHCARE (IO)

4601 Martin Luther King Jr Avenue Southwest Suite 244, Washington, DC Zip 20032-1131; tel. 603/570-4888, Marc C. Ferrell, President and Chief Executive Officer
(Independent Hospital System)

DISTRICT OF COLUMBIA: BRIDGEPOINT CONTINUING CARE HOSPITAL–CAPITOL HILL (O, 177 beds) 223 7th Street, NE, Washington, DC, Zip 20002-7045; tel. 202/546-5700, Ryan Zumalt, Chief Executive Officer
Web address: www.bridgepointhealthcare.com/

BRIDGEPOINT CONTINUING CARE HOSPITAL–NATIONAL HARBORSIDE (O, 177 beds) 4601 Martin Luther King Jr Avenue, SW, Washington, DC, Zip 20032-1131; tel. 202/574-5700, Reginald Lee, Chief Executive Officer
Web address: www.bridgepointhealthcare.com/

For explanation of codes following names, see page B2.
★ Indicates Type III membership in the American Hospital Association.

Systems / Bridgepoint Healthcare

LOUISIANA: BRIDGEPOINT CONTINUING CARE HOSPITAL (O, 56 beds) 1101 Medical Center Boulevard, 7th Floor, Marrero, LA, Zip 70072-3147; tel. 504/349-6836, Anthony DiGerolamo, R.N., MSN, Chief Executive Officer

Owned, leased, sponsored:	3 hospitals	410 beds
Contract-managed:	0 hospitals	0 beds
Totals:	3 hospitals	410 beds

★0595: BRONSON HEALTHCARE GROUP (NP)

301 John Street, Kalamazoo, MI Zip 49007-5295; tel. 269/341-6000, Bill Manns, President and Chief Executive Officer
(Centralized Health System)

MICHIGAN: BRONSON BATTLE CREEK HOSPITAL (O, 164 beds) 300 North Avenue, Battle Creek, MI, Zip 49017-3307; tel. 269/245-8000, Bill Manns, President and Chief Executive Officer
Web address: www.bronsonhealth.com

BRONSON LAKEVIEW HOSPITAL (O, 26 beds) 408 Hazen Street, Paw Paw, MI, Zip 49079-1019, P O Box 209, Zip 49079-0209, tel. 269/657-3141, Bill Manns, President and Chief Executive Officer, Bronson Healthcare Group
Web address: www.bronsonhealth.com/lakeview

BRONSON METHODIST HOSPITAL (O, 415 beds) 601 John Street, Kalamazoo, MI, Zip 49007-5346; tel. 269/341-6000, Bill Manns, President and Chief Executive Officer

BRONSON SOUTH HAVEN HOSPITAL (O, 8 beds) 955 South Bailey Avenue, South Haven, MI, Zip 49090-6743; tel. 269/637-5271, Bill Manns, President and Chief Executive Officer
Web address: https://www.bronsonhealth.com/locations/bronson-south-haven-hospital/

Owned, leased, sponsored:	4 hospitals	613 beds
Contract-managed:	0 hospitals	0 beds
Totals:	4 hospitals	613 beds

★3115: BROWARD HEALTH (NP)

1800 NW 49th Street, Fort Lauderdale, FL Zip 33309-3092; tel. 954/355-4400, Shane Strum, President and Chief Executive Officer

FLORIDA: BROWARD HEALTH CORAL SPRINGS (O, 250 beds) 3000 Coral Hills Drive, Cora Springs, FL, Zip 33065-4108; tel. 954/344-3000, Kristin Bowman, Chief Executive Officer
Web address: www.browardhealth.org

BROWARD HEALTH IMPERIAL POINT (O, 193 beds) 6401 North Federal Highway, Fort Lauderdale, FL, Zip 33308-1495; tel. 954/776-8500, Calvin E. Glidewell Jr, Interim Chief Executive Officer
Web address: https://www.browardhealth.org/locations/broward-health-imperial-point

BROWARD HEALTH MEDICAL CENTER (O, 622 beds) 1600 South Andrews Avenue, Fort Lauderdale, FL, Zip 33316-2510; tel. 954/355-4400, Manuel Linares, Chief Executive Officer

BROWARD HEALTH NORTH (O, 310 beds) 201 East Sample Road, Deerfield Beach, FL, Zip 33064-3502; tel. 954/941-8300, Matthew Garner, Chief Executive Officer
Web address: https://www.browardhealth.org/locations/broward-health-north

Owned, leased, sponsored:	4 hospitals	1375 beds
Contract-managed:	0 hospitals	0 beds
Totals:	4 hospitals	1375 beds

★0400: BRYAN HEALTH (NP)

1600 South 48th Street, Lincoln, NE Zip 68506-1283, 1600 S 48th ST, Zip 68506-1283, tel. 402/481-1111, Russell R. Gronewold, President and Chief Executive Officer
(Moderately Centralized Health System)

NEBRASKA: BRYAN MEDICAL CENTER (O, 557 beds) 1600 South 48th Street, Lincoln, NE, Zip 68506-1299; tel. 402/481-1111, Eric Mooss, President and Chief Executive Officer
Web address: www.bryanhealth.com

CRETE AREA MEDICAL CENTER (O, 24 beds) 2910 Betten Drive, Crete, NE, Zip 68333-3084, P O Box 220, Zip 68333-0220, tel. 402/826-2102, Stephanie Boldt, President and Chief Executive Officer
Web address: www.creteareamedicalcenter.com

GRAND ISLAND REGIONAL MEDICAL CENTER (O, 67 beds) 3533 Prairieview Street, Grand Island, NE, Zip 68803-4409; tel. 308/675-5000, Drew Waterman, Chief Executive Officer
Web address: www.giregional.org

KEARNEY REGIONAL MEDICAL CENTER (O, 92 beds) 804 22nd Avenue, Kearney, NE, Zip 68845-2206; tel. 855/404-5762, Douglas Edward. Koch, Chief Executive Officer

MERRICK MEDICAL CENTER (O, 20 beds) 1715 26th Street, Central City, NE, Zip 68826-9620; tel. 308/946-3015, Jodi Mohr, Chief Executive Officer
Web address: https://www.bryanhealth.com

SAUNDERS MEDICAL CENTER (C, 16 beds) 1760 County Road J, Wahoo, NE, Zip 68066-4152; tel. 402/443-4191, Julie A. Rezac, R.N., Chief Executive Officer
Web address: www.saundersmedicalcenter.com

Owned, leased, sponsored:	5 hospitals	760 beds
Contract-managed:	1 hospitals	16 beds
Totals:	6 hospitals	776 beds

★9655: BUREAU OF MEDICINE AND SURGERY, DEPARTMENT OF THE NAVY (FG)

7700 Arlington Boulevard, Suite 5126, Falls Church, VA Zip 22042; tel. 202/762-3701, Rear Admiral, Darin K. Via, M.D., Interim Surgeon General of the Navy and Interim Chief, Bureau of Medicine and Surgery
(Independent Hospital System)

CALIFORNIA: NAVAL HOSPITAL CAMP PENDLETON (O, 72 beds) 200 Mercy Circle, Camp Pendleton, CA, Zip 92055-5191, P O Box 555191, Zip 92055-5191, tel. 760/725-1304, Jenny S. Burkett, USN, Director
Web address: www.https://camp-pendleton.tricare.mil/

NAVAL MEDICAL CENTER SAN DIEGO (O, 285 beds) 34800 Bob Wilson Drive, San Diego, CA, Zip 92134-5000; tel. 619/532-6400, Elizabeth M. Adriano, MC, USN, Director
Web address: www.https://sandiego.tricare.mil/

ROBERT E. BUSH NAVAL HOSPITAL (O, 29 beds) 1145 Sturgis Road, Twentynine Palms, CA, Zip 92278, Box 788250, MCAGCC, Zip 92278-8250, tel. 760/830-2190
Web address: www.https://twentynine-palms.tricare.mil/

FLORIDA: NAVAL HOSPITAL JACKSONVILLE (O, 64 beds) 2080 Child Street, Jacksonville, FL, Zip 32214-5000; tel. 904/542-7300, Captain, Teresa M. Allen, Commanding Officer

NAVAL HOSPITAL PENSACOLA (O, 28 beds) 6000 West Highway 98, Pensacola, FL, Zip 32512-0003; tel. 850/505-6601, Captain, Alan Christian, Commanding Officer
Web address: https://www.med.navy.mil/sites/pcola

GUAM: U. S. NAVAL HOSPITAL GUAM (O, 55 beds) Building #50 Farenholt Avenue, Agana, GU, Zip 96910, PSC 490, Box 208, FPO, Zip 96540, tel. 671/344-9340, Captain, Daniel Cornwell, Command Officer

MARYLAND: WALTER REED NATIONAL MILITARY MEDICAL CENTER (O, 251 beds) 8901 Rockville Pike, Bethesda, MD, Zip 20889; tel. 301/295-4611, Captain, Melissa Austin, Hospital Director
Web address: www.https://walterreed.tricare.mil/

NORTH CAROLINA: NAVAL HOSPITAL CAMP LEJEUNE (O, 117 beds) 100 Brewster Boulevard, Camp Lejeune, NC, Zip 28547-2538, P O Box 10100, Zip 28547-0100, tel. 910/450-4300, Captain, Reginald S. Ewing III, Commanding Officer
Web address: www.https://camp-lejeune.tricare.mil/

For explanation of codes following names, see page B2.
★ Indicates Type III membership in the American Hospital Association.

Systems / Carilion Clinic

SOUTH CAROLINA: NAVAL HOSPITAL BEAUFORT (O, 20 beds) 1 Pinckney Boulevard, Beaufort, SC, Zip 29902–6122; tel. 843/228–5301, Captain, Raymond R. Batz, Commanding Officer
Web address: www.https://beaufort.tricare.mil/

VIRGINIA: NAVAL MEDICAL CENTER (O, 177 beds) 620 John Paul Jones Circle, Portsmouth, VA, Zip 23708–2197; tel. 757/953–1980, Captain, Brian Feldman, Commanding Officer

WASHINGTON: NAVAL HOSPITAL BREMERTON (O, 23 beds) 1 Boone Road, Bremerton, WA, Zip 98312–1898; tel. 360/475–4000, Captain, Patrick J. Fitzpatrick, Commanding Officer
Web address: www.https://bremerton.tricare.mil/

Owned, leased, sponsored:	11 hospitals	1121 beds
Contract–managed:	0 hospitals	0 beds
Totals:	11 hospitals	1121 beds

★0124: CAPE COD HEALTHCARE, INC. (NP)
88 Lewis Bay Road, Hyannis, MA Zip 02601–5210; tel. 508/862–5121, Michael K. Lauf, President and Chief Executive Officer
(Centralized Health System)

MASSACHUSETTS: CAPE COD HOSPITAL (O, 259 beds) 27 Park Street, Hyannis, MA, Zip 02601–5230; tel. 508/771–1800, Michael K. Lauf, President and Chief Executive Officer

FALMOUTH HOSPITAL (O, 81 beds) 100 Ter Heun Drive, Falmouth, MA, Zip 02540–2599; tel. 508/548–5300, Carter Hunt, Chief Executive Officer
Web address: www.capecodhealth.org

Owned, leased, sponsored:	2 hospitals	340 beds
Contract–managed:	0 hospitals	0 beds
Totals:	2 hospitals	340 beds

★0835: CAPE FEAR VALLEY HEALTH SYSTEM (NP)
1638 Owen Drive, Fayetteville, NC Zip 28304–3424, P O Box 2000, Zip 28302–2000, tel. 910/615–4000, Michael Nagowski, President and Chief Executive Officer
(Independent Hospital System)

NORTH CAROLINA: CAPE FEAR VALLEY BLADEN COUNTY HOSPITAL (O, 25 beds) 501 South Poplar Street, Elizabethtown, NC, Zip 28337–9375, P O Box 398, Zip 28337–0398, tel. 910/862–5100, Spencer Cummings, President and Chief Executive Officer

CAPE FEAR VALLEY MEDICAL CENTER (O, 634 beds) 1638 Owen Drive, Fayetteville, NC, Zip 28304–3431, P O Box 2000, Zip 28302–2000; tel. 910/615–4000, Michael Nagowski, Chief Executive Officer
Web address: www.capefearvalley.com

HARNETT HEALTH SYSTEM (C, 114 beds) 800 Tilghman Drive, Dunn, NC, Zip 28334–5599, P O Box 1706, Zip 28335–1706, tel. 910/892–1000, Cory Hess, President and Chief Executive Officer
Web address: www.myharnetthealth.org/

HIGHSMITH–RAINEY SPECIALTY HOSPITAL (O, 66 beds) 150 Robeson Street, Fayetteville, NC, Zip 28301–5570; tel. 910/615–1000, Michael Tart, President
Web address: www.capefearvalley.com

HOKE HOSPITAL (O, 29 beds) 210 Medical Pavilion Drive, Raeford, NC, Zip 28376–9111; tel. 910/904–8000, Chris Tart, PharmD, President

Owned, leased, sponsored:	4 hospitals	754 beds
Contract–managed:	1 hospitals	114 beds
Totals:	5 hospitals	868 beds

★0297: CAPITAL HEALTH (NP)
750 Brunswick Avenue, Trenton, NJ Zip 08638–4143; tel. 609/394–6000, Al Maghazehe, Ph.D., FACHE, President and Chief Executive Officer
(Independent Hospital System)

NEW JERSEY: CAPITAL HEALTH MEDICAL CENTER–HOPEWELL (O, 220 beds) 1 Capital Way, Pennington, NJ, Zip 08534–2520; tel. 609/303–4000, Al Maghazehe, Ph.D., FACHE, President and Chief Executive Officer
Web address: www.capitalhealth.org

CAPITAL HEALTH REGIONAL MEDICAL CENTER (O, 216 beds) 750 Brunswick Avenue, Trenton, NJ, Zip 08638–4143; tel. 609/394–6000, Al Maghazehe, Ph.D., FACHE, President and Chief Executive Officer
Web address: www.capitalhealth.org

Owned, leased, sponsored:	2 hospitals	436 beds
Contract–managed:	0 hospitals	0 beds
Totals:	2 hospitals	436 beds

★0099: CARE NEW ENGLAND HEALTH SYSTEM (NP)
4 Richmond Square, Providence, RI Zip 02906–5117; tel. 401/453–7900, Michael Wagner, M.D., President and Chief Executive Officer
(Moderately Centralized Health System)

RHODE ISLAND: BUTLER HOSPITAL (O, 143 beds) 345 Blackstone Boulevard, Providence, RI, Zip 02906–4829; tel. 401/455–6200, Mary Marran, MS, President and Chief Operating Officer; Interim President, The Providence Center
Web address: www.butler.org

KENT HOSPITAL (O, 309 beds) 455 Tollgate Road, Warwick, RI, Zip 02886–2770; tel. 401/737–7000, Paari Gopalakrishnan, M.D., President and Chief Operating Officer
Web address: www.kentri.org

WOMEN & INFANTS HOSPITAL OF RHODE ISLAND (O, 247 beds) 101 Dudley Street, Providence, RI, Zip 02905–2499; tel. 401/274–1100, Shannon Sullivan, President and Chief Operating Officer

Owned, leased, sponsored:	3 hospitals	699 beds
Contract–managed:	0 hospitals	0 beds
Totals:	3 hospitals	699 beds

0931: CAREPOINT HEALTH (IO)
10 Exchange Place, 15th Floor, Jersey City, NJ Zip 07302–3918; tel. 201/821–8900, Achintya Moulick, M.D., Chief Executive Officer

NEW JERSEY: CAREPOINT HEALTH BAYONNE MEDICAL CENTER (O, 178 beds) 29th Street & Avenue E, Bayonne, NJ, Zip 07002–4699, 29 East 29 Street, Zip 07002–4699, tel. 201/858–5000, Mohammad Zubair, M.D., Chief Hospital Executive

CAREPOINT HEALTH CHRIST HOSPITAL (O, 376 beds) 176 Palisade Avenue, Jersey City, NJ, Zip 07306–1196, 176 Palisades Avenue, Zip 07306–1196, tel. 201/795–8200, Marie Theresa Duffy, Chief Hospital Executive, Executive Vice President System Clinical Integration and Standards
Web address: www.carepointhealth.org

CAREPOINT HEALTH HOBOKEN UNIVERSITY MEDICAL CENTER (O, 228 beds) 308 Willow Avenue, Hoboken, NJ, Zip 07030–3889; tel. 201/418–1000, Robert P. Beauvais, Chief Hospital Executive

Owned, leased, sponsored:	3 hospitals	782 beds
Contract–managed:	0 hospitals	0 beds
Totals:	3 hospitals	782 beds

★0070: CARILION CLINIC (NP)
1 Riverside Circle, Roanoke, VA Zip 24016–4961; tel. 540/981–7000, Nancy Howell. Agee, President and Chief Executive Officer
(Moderately Centralized Health System)

VIRGINIA: CARILION FRANKLIN MEMORIAL HOSPITAL (O, 20 beds) 180 Floyd Avenue, Rocky Mount, VA, Zip 24151–1389; tel. 540/483–5277, Carl T. Cline, Vice President, Carilion Clinic and Hospital Administrator
Web address: www.carilionclinic.org/CFMH

For explanation of codes following names, see page B2.
★ Indicates Type III membership in the American Hospital Association.

Systems / Carilion Clinic

CARILION GILES COMMUNITY HOSPITAL (O, 17 beds) 159 Hartley Way, Pearisburg, VA, Zip 24134-2471; tel. 540/921-6000, Kristie Williams, Vice President and Hospital Administrator

CARILION NEW RIVER VALLEY MEDICAL CENTER (O, 95 beds) 2900 Lamb Circle, Christiansburg, VA, Zip 24073-6344, P O Box 5, Radford, Zip 24143-0005, tel. 540/731-2000, William Flattery, Vice President and Administrator Western Division
Web address: www.carilionclinic.org/Carilion/cnrv

CARILION ROANOKE MEMORIAL HOSPITAL (O, 598 beds) 1906 Belleview Avenue Southeast, Roanoke, VA, Zip 24014-1838, P O Box 13367, Zip 24033-3367, tel. 540/981-7000, Steven C. Arner, President and Chief Operating Officer, Hospital Administrator
Web address: www.carilionclinic.org

CARILION ROCKBRIDGE COMMUNITY HOSPITAL (O, 14 beds) 1 Health Circle, Lexington, VA, Zip 24450-2492; tel. 540/458-3300, Greg T. Madsen, Vice President, Hospital Administrator Carilion Rockbridge Community Hospital

CARILION TAZEWELL COMMUNITY HOSPITAL (O, 8 beds) 388 Ben Bolt Avenue, Tazewell, VA, Zip 24651-9700; tel. 276/988-8700, Kristie Williams, Vice President and Hospital Administrator
Web address: www.carilionclinic.org

Owned, leased, sponsored:	6 hospitals	752 beds
Contract-managed:	0 hospitals	0 beds
Totals:	6 hospitals	752 beds

★2575: CARLE HEALTH (NP)

611 West Park Street, Urbana, IL Zip 61801-2595; tel. 217/383-3311, James C. Leonard, M.D., President and Chief Executive Officer
(Moderately Centralized Health System)

ILLINOIS: CARLE BROMENN MEDICAL CENTER (O, 179 beds) 1304 Franklin Avenue, Normal, IL, Zip 61761-3558, P O Box 2850, Bloomington, Zip 61702-2850, tel. 309/454-1400, Colleen Kannaday, FACHE, President
Web address: www.advocatehealth.com/bromenn

CARLE EUREKA HOSPITAL (O, 18 beds) 101 South Major Street, Eureka, IL, Zip 61530-1246; tel. 309/467-2371, Anna Laible, Administrator
Web address: www.https://carle.org/locations/carle-eureka-hospital

CARLE FOUNDATION HOSPITAL (O, 458 beds) 611 West Park Street, Urbana, IL, Zip 61801-2529; tel. 217/383-3311, Elizabeth Angelo, President and Chief Nursing Officer
Web address: www.carle.org

CARLE HEALTH METHODIST HOSPITAL (O, 286 beds) 221 NE Glen Oak Avenue, Peoria, IL, Zip 61636-4310; tel. 309/672-5522, Keith Knepp, M.D., Regional President

CARLE HEALTH PEKIN HOSPITAL (O, 39 beds) 600 South 13th Street, Pekin, IL, Zip 61554-4936; tel. 309/347-1151, Keith Knepp, M.D., Regional President
Web address: www.https://carle.org/locations/carle-health-pekin-hospital

CARLE HEALTH PROCTOR HOSPITAL (O, 88 beds) 5409 North Knoxville Avenue, Peoria, IL, Zip 61614-5069; tel. 309/691-1000, Keith Knepp, M.D., Regional President
Web address: www.https://carle.org/locations/carle-health-proctor-hospital

CARLE HOOPESTON REGIONAL HEALTH CENTER (O, 13 beds) 701 East Orange Street, Hoopeston, IL, Zip 60942-1801; tel. 217/283-5531, Heather Tucker, Administrator

CARLE RICHLAND MEMORIAL HOSPITAL (O, 68 beds) 800 East Locust Street, Olney, IL, Zip 62450-2553; tel. 618/395-2131, Gina R. Thomas, President
Web address: www.carlermh.com

Owned, leased, sponsored:	8 hospitals	1149 beds
Contract-managed:	0 hospitals	0 beds
Totals:	8 hospitals	1149 beds

0656: CARRUS HEALTH (IO)

1810 West US Highway 82, Sherman, TX Zip 75092-7069; tel. 903/870-2600, Jon Michael. Rains, President and Chief Operating Officer
(Independent Hospital System)

OKLAHOMA: ATOKA COUNTY MEDICAL CENTER (C, 25 beds) 1590 West Liberty Road, Atoka, OK, Zip 74525-1621; tel. 580/364-8205, Chris Martin, Chief Operating Officer
Web address: www.atokamedicalcenter.org

TEXAS: CARRUS BEHAVIORAL HOSPITAL (O, 28 beds) 1724 West U.S. Highway 82, Suite 200, Sherman, TX, Zip 75092-7037, 1810 West U.S. Highway 82, Zip 75092-7069, tel. 903/870-1200, Anbu Nachimuthu, Chief Executive Officer and Chairman
Web address: https://www.carrushealth.com/inpatient-services/behavioral-health-coming-soon/

CARRUS REHABILITATION HOSPITAL (O, 24 beds) 1810 West US Highway 82, Suite 100, Sherman, TX, Zip 75092-7069; tel. 903/870-2600, Anbu Nachimuthu, Chief Executive Officer and Chairman

CARRUS SPECIALTY HOSPITAL (O, 33 beds) 1810 West US Highway 82, Sherman, TX, Zip 75092-7069; tel. 903/870-2600, Jon Michael. Rains, President and Chief Operating Officer
Web address: www.carrushospital.com

Owned, leased, sponsored:	3 hospitals	85 beds
Contract-managed:	1 hospitals	25 beds
Totals:	4 hospitals	110 beds

0903: CATHOLIC HEALTH SERVICES (CC)

4790 North State Road 7, Lauderdale Lakes, FL Zip 33319-5860; tel. 954/484-1515, Joseph M. Catania, President and Chief Executive Officer

FLORIDA: ST. ANTHONY'S REHABILITATION HOSPITAL (S, 26 beds) 3485 NW 30th Street, Lauderdale Lakes, FL, Zip 33311-1890; tel. 954/739-6233, Joseph M. Catania, Chief Executive Officer

ST. CATHERINE'S REHABILITATION HOSPITAL (S, 22 beds) 1050 NE 125th Street, North Miami, FL, Zip 33161-5881; tel. 305/357-1735, Jaime Gonzalez, Administrator
Web address: www.catholichealthservices.org

Owned, leased, sponsored:	2 hospitals	48 beds
Contract-managed:	0 hospitals	0 beds
Totals:	2 hospitals	48 beds

★0233: CATHOLIC HEALTH SERVICES OF LONG ISLAND (CC)

992 North Village Avenue, 1st Floor, Rockville Centre, NY Zip 11570-1002; tel. 516/705-3700, Patrick O'Shaughnessy, D.O., President and Chief Executive Officer
(Centralized Health System)

NEW YORK: GOOD SAMARITAN HOSPITAL MEDICAL CENTER (O, 409 beds) 1000 Montauk Highway, West Islip, NY, Zip 11795-4927; tel. 631/376-3000, Justin Lundbye, President
Web address: www.good-samaritan-hospital.org

MERCY MEDICAL CENTER (O, 207 beds) 1000 North Village Avenue, Rockville Centre, NY, Zip 11570-1000; tel. 516/705-2525, Joseph Manopella, President

ST. CATHERINE OF SIENA HOSPITAL (O, 522 beds) 50 Route 25-A, Smithtown, NY, Zip 11787-1348; tel. 631/862-3000, Declan Doyle, President
Web address: www.stcatherines.chsli.org/

ST. CHARLES HOSPITAL (O, 243 beds) 200 Belle Terre Road, Port Jefferson, NY, Zip 11777-1928; tel. 631/474-6000, James O'Connor, President

---

For explanation of codes following names, see page B2.
★ Indicates Type III membership in the American Hospital Association.

Systems / Centra Health, Inc.

ST. FRANCIS HOSPITAL AND HEART CENTER (O, 321 beds) 100 Port Washington Boulevard, Roslyn, NY, Zip 11576-1353; tel. 516/562-6000, Charles Lucore, M.D., President
Web address: www.stfrancisheartcenter.com/index.html

ST. JOSEPH HOSPITAL (S, 121 beds) 4295 Hempstead Turnpike, Bethpage, NY, Zip 11714-5769; tel. 516/579-6000, Christopher Nelson, President

Owned, leased, sponsored:	6 hospitals	1823 beds
Contract-managed:	0 hospitals	0 beds
Totals:	6 hospitals	1823 beds

★**0234: CATHOLIC HEALTH SYSTEM (CC)**
144 Genesee Street, Buffalo, NY Zip 14203-1560; tel. 716/862-2410, Joyce Markiewicz, President and Chief Executive Officer
(Independent Hospital System)

NEW YORK: FATHER BAKER MANOR (O, 160 beds) 6400 Powers Road, Orchard Park, NY, Zip 14127; tel. 716/667-0001, Christine Kluckhohn, President, Continuing Care

KENMORE MERCY HOSPITAL (O, 258 beds) 2950 Elmwood Avenue, Kenmore, NY, Zip 14217-1390; tel. 716/447-6100, Walter Ludwig, President
Web address: www.chsbuffalo.org

MCAULEY RESIDENCE (O, 160 beds) 1503 Military Road, Kenmore, NY, Zip 14217; tel. 716/447-6600, Christine Kluckhohn, President, Continuing Care

MERCY HOSPITAL (O, 369 beds) 565 Abbott Road, Buffalo, NY, Zip 14220-2095; tel. 716/826-7000, Martin W. Boryszak, President
Web address: www.chsbuffalo.org

MERCY NURSING FACILITY (O, 74 beds) 565 Abbott Road, Buffalo, NY, Zip 14220; tel. 716/828-2301, Christine Kluckhohn, President, Continuing Care

MOUNT ST. MARY'S HOSPITAL AND HEALTH CENTER (O, 135 beds) 5300 Military Road, Lewiston, NY, Zip 14092-1903; tel. 716/298-2017, Charles J. Urlaub, President
Web address: https://www.chsbuffalo.org/mount-st-marys-hospital/

NAZARETH HOME (O, 125 beds) 291 West North Street, Buffalo, NY, Zip 14201; tel. 716/881-2323, Christine Kluckhohn, President, Continuing Care

SISTERS OF CHARITY HOSPITAL OF BUFFALO (O, 321 beds) 2157 Main Street, Buffalo, NY, Zip 14214-2692; tel. 716/862-1000, Meghan Aldrich, President
Web address: www.chsbuffalo.org

ST. CATHERINE LABOURE (O, 80 beds) 2157 Main Street, Buffalo, NY, Zip 14214; tel. 716/862-1451, Christine Kluckhohn, President, Continuing Care

ST. ELIZABETH'S HOME (O, 117 beds) 5539 Broadway, Lancaster, NY, Zip 14086; tel. 716/683-5150, Christine Kluckhohn, President, Continuing Care

ST. FRANCIS OF BUFFALO (O, 120 beds) 34 Benwood Avenue, Buffalo, NY, Zip 14214; tel. 716/862-2500, Christine Kluckhohn, President, Continuing Care

ST. FRANCIS OF WILLIAMSVILLE (O, 142 beds) 147 Reist Street, Williamsville, NY, Zip 14221; tel. 716/633-5400, Christine Kluckhohn, President, Continuing Care

ST. JOSEPH MANOR (O, 22 beds) 2211 West State Street, Olean, NY, Zip 14760; tel. 716/372-7810, Christine Kluckhohn, President, Continuing Care

Owned, leased, sponsored:	13 hospitals	2083 beds
Contract-managed:	0 hospitals	0 beds
Totals:	13 hospitals	2083 beds

0991: CAYUGA HEALTH SYSTEM (NP)
101 Dates Drive, Ithaca, NY Zip 14850-1342; tel. 607/274-4011, Martin Stallone, M.D., President and Chief Executive Officer
(Independent Hospital System)

NEW YORK: CAYUGA MEDICAL CENTER AT ITHACA (O, 159 beds) 101 Dates Drive, Ithaca, NY, Zip 14850-1342; tel. 607/274-4011, Martin Stallone, M.D., President and Chief Executive Officer

SCHUYLER HOSPITAL (O, 145 beds) 220 Steuben Street, Montour Falls, NY, Zip 14865-9709; tel. 607/535-7121, Jasmine Canestaro, Assistant Vice President, Operations
Web address: www.schuylerhospital.org

Owned, leased, sponsored:	2 hospitals	304 beds
Contract-managed:	0 hospitals	0 beds
Totals:	2 hospitals	304 beds

★**0984: CEDARS-SINAI HEALTH SYSTEM (NP)**
8700 Beverly Boulevard, West Hollywood, CA Zip 90048-1865, Box 48750, Los Angeles, Zip 90048-0750, tel. 310/423-5000, Thomas M. Priselac, President and Chief Executive Officer
(Moderately Centralized Health System)

CALIFORNIA: CEDARS-SINAI MARINA DEL REY HOSPITAL (O, 103 beds) 4650 Lincoln Boulevard, Marina Del Rey, CA, Zip 90292-6306; tel. 310/823-8911, Bryan Croft, Executive Vice President, Hospital Operations & Chief Operating Officer
Web address: www.marinahospital.com

CEDARS-SINAI MEDICAL CENTER (O, 915 beds) 8700 Beverly Boulevard, Los Angeles, CA, Zip 90048-1865; tel. 310/423-5000, Thomas M. Priselac, President and Chief Executive Officer

HUNTINGTON HEALTH (O, 366 beds) 100 West California Boulevard, Pasadena, CA, Zip 91105-3097, P O Box 7013, Zip 91109-7013, tel. 626/397-5000, Lori J. Morgan, M.D., President/Chief Executive Officer, Huntington Health
Web address: www.huntingtonhospital.com

TORRANCE MEMORIAL MEDICAL CENTER (O, 435 beds) 3330 Lomita Boulevard, Torrance, CA, Zip 90505-5073; tel. 310/325-9110, Keith Hobbs, FACHE, President and Chief Executive Officer
Web address: www.torrancememorial.org

Owned, leased, sponsored:	4 hospitals	1819 beds
Contract-managed:	0 hospitals	0 beds
Totals:	4 hospitals	1819 beds

★**2265: CENTRA HEALTH, INC. (NP)**
1901 Tate Springs Road, Lynchburg, VA Zip 24501-1109; tel. 434/200-3000, Richard Tugman, Interim President and Chief Executive Officer
(Moderately Centralized Health System)

VIRGINIA: CENTRA BEDFORD MEMORIAL HOSPITAL (O, 33 beds) 1613 Oakwood Street, Bedford, VA, Zip 24523-1213; tel. 540/586-2441, Stacey L. Vaught, MSN, President
Web address: https://www.centrahealth.com/locations/centra-bedford-memorial-hospital

CENTRA LYNCHBURG GENERAL HOSPITAL (O, 582 beds) 1901 Tate Springs Road, Lynchburg, VA, Zip 24501-1109; tel. 434/200-4700, Tabitha Culbertson, President

CENTRA SOUTHSIDE COMMUNITY HOSPITAL (O, 86 beds) 800 Oak Street, Farmville, VA, Zip 23901-1199; tel. 434/392-8811, Thomas Angelo, Chief Executive Officer
Web address: www.sch.centrahealth.com/

CENTRA SPECIALTY HOSPITAL (O, 28 beds) 3300 Rivermont Avenue, Lynchburg, VA, Zip 24503-2030; tel. 434/200-1799, Kay Bowling, Chief Executive Officer

Owned, leased, sponsored:	4 hospitals	729 beds
Contract-managed:	0 hospitals	0 beds
Totals:	4 hospitals	729 beds

For explanation of codes following names, see page B2.
★ Indicates Type III membership in the American Hospital Association.

Systems / Centracare Health

★0184: CENTRACARE HEALTH (NP)
1406 Sixth Avenue North, Saint Cloud, MN Zip 56303–1900; tel. 320/251–2700, Kenneth D. Holmen, M.D., President and Chief Executive Officer
(Moderately Centralized Health System)

MINNESOTA: CENTRACARE–BENSON (O, 11 beds) 1815 Wisconsin Avenue, Benson, MN, Zip 56215–1653; tel. 320/843–4232, Melissa McGinty–Thompson, Administrator, Chief Nursing Officer and Clinical Officer
Web address: https://www.centracare.com/locations/centracare-benson-hospital/

CENTRACARE–LONG PRAIRIE (O, 74 beds) 50 CentraCare Drive, Long Prairie, MN, Zip 56347–2100; tel. 320/732–2141, Jose Alba, President
Web address: www.centracare.com

CENTRACARE–MELROSE (O, 155 beds) 525 Main Street West, Melrose, MN, Zip 56352–1043; tel. 320/256–4231, Jennifer Tschida, President
Web address: www.centracare.com

CENTRACARE–MONTICELLO (O, 73 beds) 1013 Hart Boulevard, Suite 1, Monticello, MN, Zip 55362–8230; tel. 763/295–2945, John Hering, M.D., President and Chief Medical Officer
Web address: https://www.centracare.com/locations/centracare-monticello/

CENTRACARE–PAYNESVILLE (O, 14 beds) 200 West 1st Street, Paynesville, MN, Zip 56362–1496; tel. 320/243–3767, Craig Henneman, President
Web address: https://www.centracare.com/locations/centracare-paynesville/

CENTRACARE–REDWOOD (O, 14 beds) 101 Caring Way, Redwood Falls, MN, Zip 56283; tel. 507/637–4500, Carnie Allex, President
Web address: https://www.centracare.com/locations/centracare-redwood-hospital/

CENTRACARE–RICE MEMORIAL HOSPITAL (L, 164 beds) 301 Becker Avenue SW, Willmar, MN, Zip 56201–3395; tel. 320/235–4543, Michael Schramm, Chief Executive Officer
Web address: https://www.centracare.com/locations/centracare-rice-memorial-hospital/

CENTRACARE–SAUK CENTRE (O, 74 beds) 425 North Elm Street, Sauk Centre, MN, Zip 56378–1010; tel. 320/352–2221, Adam Paulson, President

CENTRACARE–ST. CLOUD HOSPITAL (O, 477 beds) 1406 Sixth Avenue North, Saint Cloud, MN, Zip 56303–1901; tel. 320/251–2700, Joy Plamann, R.N., Senior Vice President Central Operations, President CentraCare–St. Cloud Hospital
Web address: www.centracare.com

MEEKER MEMORIAL HOSPITAL AND CLINICS (C, 38 beds) 612 South Sibley Avenue, Litchfield, MN, Zip 55355–3398; tel. 320/693–4500, Mary Ellen Wells, FACHE, Chief Executive Officer

Owned, leased, sponsored:	9 hospitals	1056 beds
Contract-managed:	1 hospitals	38 beds
Totals:	10 hospitals	1094 beds

1007: CENTRAL MAINE HEALTHCARE (NP)
300 Main Street, Lewiston, ME Zip 04240–7027; tel. 207/795–0111, Steven G. Littleson, FACHE, President and Chief Executive Officer
(Independent Hospital System)

MAINE: BRIDGTON HOSPITAL (O, 22 beds) 10 Hospital Drive, Bridgton, ME, Zip 04009–1148; tel. 207/647–6000, Stephany Jacques, R.N., President

CENTRAL MAINE MEDICAL CENTER (O, 190 beds) 300 Main Street, Lewiston, ME, Zip 04240–7027; tel. 207/795–0111, Steven G. Littleson, FACHE, President and Chief Executive Officer
Web address: www.cmmc.org

RUMFORD HOSPITAL (O, 25 beds) 420 Franklin Street, Rumford, ME, Zip 04276–2145; tel. 207/369–1000, Stephany Jacques, R.N., President
Web address: https://www.cmhc.org/rumford-hospital/

Owned, leased, sponsored:	3 hospitals	237 beds
Contract-managed:	0 hospitals	0 beds
Totals:	3 hospitals	237 beds

1039: CHILDREN'S HEALTH (NP)
1935 Medical District Drive, Dallas, TX Zip 75235–7701; tel. 214/456–7000, Christopher J. Durovich, President and Chief Executive Officer
(Centralized Health System)

TEXAS: CHILDREN'S MEDICAL CENTER DALLAS (O, 401 beds) 1935 Medical District Drive, Dallas, TX, Zip 75235–7701; tel. 214/456–7000, Christopher J. Durovich, President and Chief Executive Officer
Web address: www.childrens.com

CHILDREN'S MEDICAL CENTER PLANO (O, 72 beds) 7601 Preston Road, Plano, TX, Zip 75024–3214; tel. 469/303–7000, Jeremiah Radandt, Executive Vice President Northern Market / Administrator
Web address: https://www.childrens.com/location-landing/locations-and-directions/childrens-health-plano

Owned, leased, sponsored:	2 hospitals	473 beds
Contract-managed:	0 hospitals	0 beds
Totals:	2 hospitals	473 beds

1139: CHILDREN'S HOSPITAL COLORADO (NP)
13123 East 16th Avenue, Aurora, CO Zip 80045–7106; tel. 800/624–6553, Jena Hausmann, President and Chief Executive Officer

COLORADO: CHILDREN'S HOSPITAL COLORADO–COLORADO SPRINGS (O, 115 beds) 4090 Briargate Parkway, Colorado Springs, CO, Zip 80920–7815; tel. 719/305–1234, Greg Raymond, President, Southern Colorado Care System

CHILDREN'S HOSPITAL COLORADO (O, 545 beds) 13123 East 16th Avenue, Aurora, CO, Zip 80045–7106; tel. 720/777–1234, Jena Hausmann, President and Chief Executive Officer
Web address: www.thechildrenshospital.org

Owned, leased, sponsored:	2 hospitals	660 beds
Contract-managed:	0 hospitals	0 beds
Totals:	2 hospitals	660 beds

0407: CHILDREN'S WISCONSIN (NP)
9000 West Wisconsin Avenue, Milwaukee, WI Zip 53226–4810, P O Box 1997, Zip 53201–1997, tel. 414/226–2000, Peggy N. Troy, President and Chief Executive Officer
(Independent Hospital System)

WISCONSIN: CHILDREN'S HOSPITAL OF WISCONSIN–FOX VALLEY (O, 21 beds) 130 Second Street, Neenah, WI, Zip 54956–2883; tel. 920/969–7900, Peggy N. Troy, President and Chief Executive Officer
Web address: www.chw.org

CHILDREN'S WISCONSIN (O, 192 beds) 8915 West Connell Avenue, Milwaukee, WI, Zip 53226–3067, P O Box 1997, Zip 53201–1997, tel. 414/266–2000, Peggy N. Troy, President and Chief Executive Officer
Web address: www.chw.org

Owned, leased, sponsored:	2 hospitals	213 beds
Contract-managed:	0 hospitals	0 beds
Totals:	2 hospitals	213 beds

★0131: CHRISTIANACARE (NP)
501 West 14th Street, Wilmington, DE Zip 19801–1013, P O Box 1668, Zip 19899–1668, tel. 302/428–2570, Janice E. Nevin, M.D., M.P.H., President and Chief Executive Officer
(Independent Hospital System)

DELAWARE: CHRISTIANACARE (O, 1318 beds) 4755 Ogletown–Stanton Road, Newark, DE, Zip 19718–0002, P O Box 6001, Zip 19718, tel. 302/733–1000, Janice E. Nevin, M.D., M.P.H., President and Chief Executive Officer
Web address: www.christianacare.org

For explanation of codes following names, see page B2.
★ Indicates Type III membership in the American Hospital Association.

Systems / City of Hope

MARYLAND: CHRISTIANACARE, UNION HOSPITAL (O, 84 beds) 106 Bow Street, Elkton, MD, Zip 21921–5596; tel. 410/398-4000, Janice E. Nevin, M.D., M.P.H., President and Chief Executive Officer
Web address: www.uhcc.com

Owned, leased, sponsored:	2 hospitals	1402 beds
Contract-managed:	0 hospitals	0 beds
Totals:	2 hospitals	1402 beds

★0192: CHRISTUS HEALTH (CC)
919 Hidden Ridge Drive, Irving, TX Zip 75038; tel. 469/282-2000, Ernie W. Sadau, President and Chief Executive Officer
(Moderately Centralized Health System)

LOUISIANA: CHRISTUS COUSHATTA HEALTH CARE CENTER (O, 25 beds) 1635 Marvel Street, Coushatta, LA, Zip 71019–9022, P O Box 589, Zip 71019-0589, tel. 318/932-2000, Brandon Hillman, R.N., Administrator

CHRISTUS HEALTH SHREVEPORT–BOSSIER (O, 214 beds) 1453 East Bert Kouns Industrial Loop, Shreveport, LA, Zip 71105–6800; tel. 318/681–5000, Casey Robertson, President and Chief Executive Officer
Web address: www.christushealthsb.org

CHRISTUS OCHSNER LAKE AREA HOSPITAL (O, 88 beds) 4200 Nelson Road, Lake Charles, LA, Zip 70605–4118; tel. 337/474-6370, Paul Trevino, Chief Executive Officer, CHRISTUS Ochsner Health Southwestern LA
Web address: www.Lakeareamc.com

CHRISTUS OCHSNER ST. PATRICK (O, 162 beds) 524 Dr Michael Debakey Drive, Lake Charles, LA, Zip 70601–5799, P.O. Box 3401, Zip 70602–3401, tel. 337/436–2511, Paul Trevino, Chief Executive Officer, CHRISTUS Ochsner Health Southwestern LA

CHRISTUS ST. FRANCES CABRINI HOSPITAL (O, 293 beds) 3330 Masonic Drive, Alexandria, LA, Zip 71301–3899; tel. 318/487-1122, Monte A. Wilson, President and Chief Executive Officer
Web address: www.cabrini.org/

CENTRAL LOUISIANA SURGICAL HOSPITAL (O, 24 beds) 651 North Bolton Avenue, Alexandria, LA, Zip 71301–7449, P O Box 8646, Zip 71306–1646, tel. 318/443–3511, Erin Roes, R.N., MSN, Chief Executive Officer
Web address: www.clshospital.com

NATCHITOCHES REGIONAL MEDICAL CENTER (C, 91 beds) 501 Keyser Avenue, Natchitoches, LA, Zip 71457–6036, P O Box 2009, Zip 71457-2009, tel. 318/214-4200, D. Kirk. Soileau, FACHE, Chief Executive Officer

SAVOY MEDICAL CENTER (C, 60 beds) 801 Poinciana Avenue, Mamou, LA, Zip 70554–2298; tel. 337/468–5261
Web address: www.savoymedical.com/

NEW MEXICO: CHRISTUS ST. VINCENT REGIONAL MEDICAL CENTER (O, 175 beds) 455 Saint Michaels Drive, Santa Fe, NM, Zip 87505–7601, P O Box 2107, Zip 87505, tel. 505/983–3361, Lillian Montoya, President and Chief Executive Officer
Web address: www.stvin.org

GERALD CHAMPION REGIONAL MEDICAL CENTER (O, 98 beds) 2669 North Scenic Drive, Alamogordo, NM, Zip 88310–8799; tel. 575/439-6100, Robert J. Heckert Jr, Chief Executive Officer

TEXAS: CHRISTUS CHILDREN'S (O, 215 beds) 333 North Santa Rosa Street, San Antonio, TX, Zip 78207; tel. 210/704-2011, Cris Daskevich, FACHE, Senior Vice President, Maternal Services and Chief Executive Officer
Web address: www.chofsa.org

CHRISTUS GOOD SHEPHERD MEDICAL CENTER–MARSHALL (O, 574 beds) 811 South Washington Avenue, Marshall, TX, Zip 75670–5336, P O Box 1599, Zip 75671–1599, tel. 903/927–6000, Todd Hancock, Market President and Chief Executive Officer
Web address: https://www.christushealth.org/good-shepherd/marshall

CHRISTUS MOTHER FRANCES HOSPITAL–JACKSONVILLE (O, 23 beds) 2026 South Jackson, Jacksonville, TX, Zip 75766–5822; tel. 903/541–4500, Barry D. Lofquist, Chief Executive Officer

CHRISTUS MOTHER FRANCES HOSPITAL–SULPHUR SPRINGS (O, 62 beds) 115 Airport Road, Sulphur Springs, TX, Zip 75482–2105; tel. 903/885-7671, Paul Harvey, President / Chief Executive Officer
Web address: www.tmfhc.org/maps-and-locations/locations-profile/?id=72&searchId=8bcb329f-a152-e611-b37f-2c768a4e1b84&sort=11&page=1&pageSize=10

CHRISTUS MOTHER FRANCES HOSPITAL–TYLER (O, 495 beds) 800 East Dawson Street, Tyler, TX, Zip 75701–2036; tel. 903/593–8441, Jason J. Proctor, President
Web address: www.tmfhc.org

CHRISTUS MOTHER FRANCES HOSPITAL–WINNSBORO (O, 14 beds) 719 West Coke Road, Winnsboro, TX, Zip 75494–3011; tel. 903/342–5227, Paul Harvey, President and Chief Executive Officer
Web address: www.tmfhs.org

CHRISTUS SANTA ROSA HEALTH SYSTEM (O, 403 beds) 333 North Santa Rosa Street, San Antonio, TX, Zip 78207-3108, 100 NE Loop 410 Suite 800, Zip 78216–4749, tel. 210/704-2000, Cris Daskevich, FACHE, Chief Executive Officer Children's Hosp SA & SVP Maternal Svces CHRISTUS Health

CHRISTUS SANTA ROSA HOSPITAL–SAN MARCOS (O, 139 beds) 1301 Wonder World Drive, San Marcos, TX, Zip 78666–7544; tel. 512/353-8979, Robert Honeycutt, President
Web address: https://www.christushealth.org/santa-rosa/san-marcos

CHRISTUS SOUTHEAST TEXAS HOSPITAL–ST. ELIZABETH (O, 375 beds) 2830 Calder Avenue, Beaumont, TX, Zip 77702–1809, P O Box 5405, Zip 77726-5405, tel. 409/892-7171, Paul Trevino, President and Chief Executive Officer

CHRISTUS SOUTHEAST TEXAS JASPER MEMORIAL (O, 33 beds) 1275 Marvin Hancock Drive, Jasper, TX, Zip 75951–4995; tel. 409/384–5461, Crystal Goode, President / Chief Nursing Officer
Web address: https://www.christushealth.org/locations/southeast-texas-jasper

CHRISTUS SPOHN HOSPITAL ALICE (O, 42 beds) 2500 East Main Street, Alice, TX, Zip 78332–4169; tel. 361/661–8000, Richard Morin, R.N., President CHRISTUS Spohn Hospital–Alice/Kleberg

CHRISTUS SPOHN HOSPITAL BEEVILLE (O, 49 beds) 1500 East Houston Street, Beeville, TX, Zip 78102–5312; tel. 361/354–2000, Richard Morin, R.N., President CHRISTUS Spohn Hospital–Alice/Kleberg
Web address: www.christusspohn.org

CHRISTUS SPOHN HOSPITAL CORPUS CHRISTI SHORELINE (O, 368 beds) 600 Elizabeth Street, Corpus Christi, TX, Zip 78404–2235; tel. 361/881–3000, Raymond Acebo, M.D., Administrator/Chief Medical Officer
Web address: www.christusspohn.org

CHRISTUS SPOHN HOSPITAL KLEBERG (O, 50 beds) 1311 General Cavazos Boulevard, Kingsville, TX, Zip 78363–7130; tel. 361/595–1661, Richard Morin, R.N., President CHRISTUS Spohn Hospital–Alice/Kleberg
Web address: www.christusspohn.org

CHRISTUS ST. MICHAEL HEALTH SYSTEM (O, 341 beds) 2600 St Michael Drive, Texarkana, TX, Zip 75503–5220; tel. 903/614-1000, Jason Adams, President

CHRISTUS ST. MICHAEL REHABILITATION HOSPITAL (O, 50 beds) 2400 St Michael Drive, Texarkana, TX, Zip 75503–2374; tel. 903/614-4000, Kristine Bell, Administrator
Web address: www.christusstmichael.org/rehab

KATE DISHMAN REHABILITATION HOSPITAL (O, 27 beds) 2830 Calder Street, 6th Floor, Beaumont, TX, Zip 77702–1809; tel. 409/899–8380, Patrick Flannery, Chief Executive Officer and Administrator
Web address: www.https://katedishmanrehab.com/

Owned, leased, sponsored:	25 hospitals	4339 beds
Contract-managed:	2 hospitals	151 beds
Totals:	27 hospitals	4490 beds

0113: CITY OF HOPE (IO)
1336 Basswood Road, Schaumburg, IL Zip 60173–4544; tel. 847/342-7400, Pat A. Basu, M.D., President and Chief Executive Officer

ARIZONA: CITY OF HOPE PHOENIX (O, 14 beds) 14200 West Celebrate Life way, Goodyear, AZ, Zip 85338–3005; tel. 623/207–3000, Kevin Tulipana, Executive Vice President, Arizona Market

CALIFORNIA: CITY OF HOPE'S HELFORD CLINICAL RESEARCH HOSPITAL (O, 232 beds) 1500 East Duarte Road, Duarte, CA, Zip 91010–3012; tel. 626/256–4673, Robert Stone, JD, President/Chief Executive Officer
Web address: www.cityofhope.org

For explanation of codes following names, see page B2.
★ Indicates Type III membership in the American Hospital Association.

Systems / City of Hope

GEORGIA: CITY OF HOPE ATLANTA (O, 50 beds) 600 Celebrate Life Parkway, Newnan, GA, Zip 30265-8000; tel. 770/400-6000, Jonathan E. Watkins, President and Chief Executive Officer
 Web address: www.cancercenter.com/southeastern-hospital.cfm

ILLINOIS: CITY OF HOPE CHICAGO (O, 72 beds) 2520 Elisha Avenue, Zion, IL, Zip 60099-2587; tel. 847/872-4561, Pete Govorchin, President and Chief Executive Officer
 Web address: www.cancercenter.com

Owned, leased, sponsored:	4 hospitals	368 beds
Contract-managed:	0 hospitals	0 beds
Totals:	4 hospitals	368 beds

1047: CLEARSKY HEALTH (IO)

1000 Westbank Drive, Suite A, West Lake Hills, TX Zip 78746-6598; tel. 512/995-7597, Darby Brockette, Chief Executive Officer

LOUISIANA: CLEARSKY REHABILITATION HOSPITAL OF LEESVILLE (O, 16 beds) 900 South 5th Street, Leesville, LA, Zip 71446-4723; tel. 337/392-8118, Lacey Sancel, Chief Executive Officer
 Web address: https://www.clearskyhealth.com/Leesville/

CLEARSKY REHABILITATION HOSPITAL OF ROSEPINE (O, 20 beds) 8088 Hawks Road, Leesville, LA, Zip 71446-6649; tel. 337/462-8880, Robert LaFleur, Chief Executive Officer

NEW MEXICO: CLEARSKY REHABILITATION HOSPITAL OF RIO RANCHO (O, 25 beds) 2401 Westside Boulevard Southeast, Rio Rancho, NM, Zip 87124-4983; tel. 505/295-6358, Shawn Wilbur, Chief Executive Officer
 Web address: www.clearskyhealth.com/riorancho

TEXAS: CLEARSKY REHABILITATION HOSPITAL OF FLOWER MOUND (O, 29 beds) 3100 Peters Colony Road, Flower Mound, TX, Zip 75022-2949; tel. 469/933-2855, Brian Abraham, Regional Chief Executive Officer

CLEARSKY REHABILITATION HOSPITAL OF WEATHERFORD (O, 26 beds) 703 Eureka Street, Weatherford, TX, Zip 76086-6547; tel. 682/803-0100, Aaron Lee. Lopez, Chief Executive Officer
 Web address: https://www.clearskyhealth.com/Weatherford/

Owned, leased, sponsored:	5 hospitals	116 beds
Contract-managed:	0 hospitals	0 beds
Totals:	5 hospitals	116 beds

★0212: CLEVELAND CLINIC HEALTH SYSTEM (NP)

9500 Euclid, Cleveland, OH Zip 44195-5108; tel. 216/444-2200, Tomislav Mihaljevic, M.D., Chief Executive Officer and President

(Centralized Health System)

FLORIDA: CLEVELAND CLINIC FLORIDA (O, 236 beds) 2950 Cleveland Clinic Boulevard, Weston, FL, Zip 33331-3602; tel. 954/659-5000, Conor P. Delaney, M.D., Ph.D., Chief Executive Officer and President
 Web address: www.clevelandclinic.org/florida

CLEVELAND CLINIC INDIAN RIVER HOSPITAL (O, 223 beds) 1000 36th Street, Vero Beach, FL, Zip 32960-6592; tel. 772/567-4311, David J. Peter, M.D., Interim President and Chief Medical Officer
 Web address: www.https://my.clevelandclinic.org/florida/locations/indian-river-hospital

CLEVELAND CLINIC MARTIN NORTH HOSPITAL (O, 500 beds) 200 SE Hospital Avenue, Stuart, FL, Zip 34994-2346, P O Box 9010, Zip 34995-9010, tel. 772/287-5200, Rishi Singh, President

OHIO: CLEVELAND CLINIC AKRON GENERAL LODI HOSPITAL (O, 20 beds) 225 Elyria Street, Lodi, OH, Zip 44254-1096; tel. 330/948-1222, Brian J. Harte, M.D., President
 Web address: www.lodihospital.org

CLEVELAND CLINIC AKRON GENERAL (O, 485 beds) 1 Akron General Avenue, Akron, OH, Zip 44307-2433; tel. 330/344-6000, Brian J. Harte, M.D., President

CLEVELAND CLINIC AVON HOSPITAL (O, 126 beds) 33300 Cleveland Clinic Boulevard, Avon, OH, Zip 44011; tel. 440/695-5000, Rebecca Starck, M.D., Vice President
 Web address: www.my.clevelandclinic.org

CLEVELAND CLINIC CHILDREN'S HOSPITAL FOR REHABILITATION (O, 25 beds) 2801 Martin Luther King Jr Drive, Cleveland, OH, Zip 44104-3865; tel. 216/448-6400, Karen Murray, M.D., President
 Web address: www.my.clevelandclinic.org/childrens-hospital/default.aspx

CLEVELAND CLINIC EUCLID HOSPITAL (O, 146 beds) 18901 Lake Shore Boulevard, Euclid, OH, Zip 44119-1090; tel. 216/531-9000, Teresa Dews, M.D., Vice President
 Web address: www.euclidhospital.org

CLEVELAND CLINIC FAIRVIEW HOSPITAL (O, 498 beds) 18101 Lorain Avenue, Cleveland, OH, Zip 44111-5656; tel. 216/476-7000, Neil Smith, D.O., President
 Web address: www.fairviewhospital.org

CLEVELAND CLINIC HILLCREST HOSPITAL (O, 496 beds) 6780 Mayfield Road, Cleveland, OH, Zip 44124-2203; tel. 440/312-4500, Richard Parker, M.D., President
 Web address: www.hillcresthospital.org

CLEVELAND CLINIC LUTHERAN HOSPITAL (O, 194 beds) 1730 West 25th Street, Cleveland, OH, Zip 44113-3170; tel. 216/696-4300, Timothy R. Barnett, M.D., Vice President

CLEVELAND CLINIC MARYMOUNT HOSPITAL (O, 263 beds) 12300 McCracken Road, Garfield Heights, OH, Zip 44125-2975; tel. 216/581-0500, Margaret McKenzie, M.D., Vice President
 Web address: www.marymount.org

CLEVELAND CLINIC MEDINA HOSPITAL (O, 148 beds) 1000 East Washington Street, Medina, OH, Zip 44256-2170; tel. 330/725-1000, Richard K. Shewbridge, President
 Web address: www.medinahospital.org

CLEVELAND CLINIC MERCY HOSPITAL (O, 331 beds) 1320 Mercy Drive NW, Canton, OH, Zip 44708-2641; tel. 330/489-1000, Timothy Crone, M.D., Vice President

CLEVELAND CLINIC SOUTH POINTE HOSPITAL (O, 172 beds) 20000 Harvard Road, Warrensville Heights, OH, Zip 44122-6805; tel. 216/491-6000, Margaret McKenzie, M.D., Vice President
 Web address: www.southpointehospital.org

CLEVELAND CLINIC UNION HOSPITAL (O, 100 beds) 659 Boulevard Street, Dover, OH, Zip 44622-2077; tel. 330/343-3311, Thomas J. Rogers, M.D., Vice President
 Web address: www.unionhospital.org

CLEVELAND CLINIC (O, 1298 beds) 9500 Euclid Avenue, Cleveland, OH, Zip 44195-5108; tel. 216/444-2200, Scott Steele, M.D., President

Owned, leased, sponsored:	17 hospitals	5261 beds
Contract-managed:	0 hospitals	0 beds
Totals:	17 hospitals	5261 beds

0076: COLLEGE HEALTH ENTERPRISES (IO)

11627 Telegraph Road, Suite 200, Santa Fe Springs, CA Zip 90670-6814; tel. 562/923-9449, Barry J. Weiss, President

CALIFORNIA: COLLEGE HOSPITAL CERRITOS (O, 187 beds) 10802 College Place, Cerritos, CA, Zip 90703-1579; tel. 562/924-9581, Stephen Witt, Chief Executive Officer
 Web address: www.collegehospitals.com

COLLEGE HOSPITAL COSTA MESA (O, 157 beds) 301 Victoria Street, Costa Mesa, CA, Zip 92627-7131; tel. 949/642-2734, Warren Bradley, Chief Executive Officer
 Web address: www.collegehospitals.com/cosHome

Owned, leased, sponsored:	2 hospitals	344 beds
Contract-managed:	0 hospitals	0 beds
Totals:	2 hospitals	344 beds

For explanation of codes following names, see page B2.
★ Indicates Type III membership in the American Hospital Association.

★0948: **COMMONSPIRIT HEALTH (CC)**
444 West Lake Street Suite 2500, Chicago, IL Zip 60606-0097; tel. 312/741-7000, Wright L. Lassiter III, Chief Executive Officer

ARIZONA: CHANDLER REGIONAL MEDICAL CENTER (O, 429 beds) 1955 West Frye Road, Chandler, AZ, Zip 85224-6282; tel. 480/728-3000, Mark F. Slyter, FACHE, President and Chief Operating Officer
Web address: www.chandlerregional.com

DIGNITY HEALTH ARIZONA GENERAL HOSPITAL MESA, LLC (O, 50 beds) 9130 East Elliot Road, Mesa, AZ, Zip 85212-9675; tel. 480/410-4500, Jane E. Hanson, R.N., President and Chief Executive Officer
Web address: www.https://locations.dignityhealth.org/

DIGNITY HEALTH ARIZONA GENERAL HOSPITAL (O, 16 beds) 7171 South 51st Avenue, Laveen, AZ, Zip 85339-2923; tel. 623/584-5100, Jane E. Hanson, R.N., Chief Executive Officer

DIGNITY HEALTH YAVAPAI REGIONAL MEDICAL CENTER (O, 218 beds) 1003 Willow Creek Road, Prescott, AZ, Zip 86301-1668; tel. 928/445-2700, Anthony Torres, M.D., President and Chief Executive Officer
Web address: www.yrmc.org

MERCY GILBERT MEDICAL CENTER (S, 197 beds) 3555 South Val Vista Road, Gilbert, AZ, Zip 85297-7323; tel. 480/728-8000, Mark F. Slyter, FACHE, President and Chief Operating Officer

ST. JOSEPH'S HOSPITAL AND MEDICAL CENTER (S, 594 beds) 350 West Thomas Road, Phoenix, AZ, Zip 85013-4496, P O Box 2071, Zip 85001-2071, tel. 602/406-3000, Mary Ragsdale, Interim President and Chief Executive Officer
Web address: www.stjosephs-phx.org

ARKANSAS: CHI ST. VINCENT HOT SPRINGS (O, 214 beds) 300 Werner Street, Hot Springs, AR, Zip 71913-6406; tel. 501/622-1000, Douglas B. Ross, M.D., President and Chief Medical Officer

CHI ST. VINCENT INFIRMARY (S, 413 beds) 2 Saint Vincent Circle, Little Rock, AR, Zip 72205-5499; tel. 501/552-3000, William G. Jones, M.D., President and Chief Medical Officer
Web address: www.chistvincent.com/

CHI ST. VINCENT MORRILTON (S, 25 beds) 4 Hospital Drive, Morrilton, AR, Zip 72110-4510; tel. 501/977-2300
Web address: www.chistvincent.com/Hospitals/st-vincent-morrilton

CHI ST. VINCENT NORTH (S, 67 beds) 2215 Wildwood Avenue, Sherwood, AR, Zip 72120-5089; tel. 501/552-7100, Megan Bonney, President

CALIFORNIA: BAKERSFIELD MEMORIAL HOSPITAL (O, 385 beds) 420 34th Street, Bakersfield, CA, Zip 93301-2237; tel. 661/327-1792, Ken Keller, President/Chief Executive Officer
Web address: www.bakersfieldmemorial.org

CALIFORNIA HOSPITAL MEDICAL CENTER (O, 278 beds) 1401 South Grand Avenue, Los Angeles, CA, Zip 90015-3010; tel. 213/748-2411, Alina Moran, FACHE, FABC, President
Web address: www.chmcla.org

COMMUNITY HOSPITAL OF SAN BERNARDINO (O, 486 beds) 1805 Medical Center Drive, San Bernardino, CA, Zip 92411-1214; tel. 909/887-6333, June M. Collison, President
Web address: www.dignityhealth.org/san-bernardino

DOMINICAN HOSPITAL (S, 191 beds) 1555 Soquel Drive, Santa Cruz, CA, Zip 95065-1794; tel. 831/462-7700, Nanette Mickiewicz, M.D., President

FRENCH HOSPITAL MEDICAL CENTER (O, 72 beds) 1911 Johnson Avenue, San Luis Obispo, CA, Zip 93401-4197; tel. 805/543-5353, Sue Anderson, President and Chief Executive Officer
Web address: www.frenchmedicalcenter.org

GLENDALE MEMORIAL HOSPITAL AND HEALTH CENTER (O, 126 beds) 1420 South Central Avenue, Glendale, CA, Zip 91204-2594; tel. 818/502-1900, Betsy Hart, Chief Executive Officer

MARIAN REGIONAL MEDICAL CENTER (S, 339 beds) 1400 East Church Street, Santa Maria, CA, Zip 93454-5906; tel. 805/739-3000, Sue Andersen, Chief Executive Officer
Web address: www.marianmedicalcenter.org

MARK TWAIN MEDICAL CENTER (O, 25 beds) 768 Mountain Ranch Road, San Andreas, CA, Zip 95249-9998; tel. 209/754-3521, Doug Archer, President and Chief Executive Officer

MERCY GENERAL HOSPITAL (S, 313 beds) 4001 'J' Street, Sacramento, CA, Zip 95819-3600; tel. 916/453-4545, Christina Johnson, M.D., Sacramento Market President
Web address: www.mercygeneral.org

MERCY HOSPITAL DOWNTOWN (S, 229 beds) 2215 Truxtun Avenue, Bakersfield, CA, Zip 93301-3698, P O Box 119, Zip 93302-0119, tel. 661/632-5000, BJ Predum, FACHE, President/Chief Executive Officer

MERCY HOSPITAL OF FOLSOM (S, 106 beds) 1650 Creekside Drive, Folsom, CA, Zip 95630-3400; tel. 916/983-7400, Lisa Hausmann, President and Chief Executive Officer
Web address: www.mercyfolsom.org

MERCY MEDICAL CENTER MERCED (S, 186 beds) 333 Mercy Avenue, Merced, CA, Zip 95340-8319; tel. 209/564-5000, Dale Johns, FACHE, Chief Executive Officer

MERCY MEDICAL CENTER MOUNT SHASTA (S, 25 beds) 914 Pine Street, Mount Shasta, CA, Zip 96067-2143; tel. 530/926-6111, Rodger Page, President
Web address: www.mercymtshasta.org

MERCY MEDICAL CENTER REDDING (S, 266 beds) 2175 Rosaline Avenue, Redding, CA, Zip 96001-2549, P O Box 496009, Zip 96049-6009, tel. 530/225-6000, G. Todd. Smith, President
Web address: www.mercy.org

MERCY SAN JUAN MEDICAL CENTER (S, 384 beds) 6501 Coyle Avenue, Carmichael, CA, Zip 95608-0306; tel. 916/537-5000, Michael Korpiel, President

METHODIST HOSPITAL OF SACRAMENTO (O, 329 beds) 7500 Hospital Drive, Sacramento, CA, Zip 95823-5477; tel. 916/423-3000, Phyllis Baltz, Hospital President
Web address: www.methodistsacramento.org

NORTHRIDGE HOSPITAL MEDICAL CENTER (O, 394 beds) 18300 Roscoe Boulevard, Northridge, CA, Zip 91328-4167; tel. 818/885-8500, Jeremy Zoch, President and Chief Executive Officer

SEQUOIA HOSPITAL (O, 111 beds) 170 Alameda De Las Pulgas, Redwood City, CA, Zip 94062-2799; tel. 650/369-5811, Bill Graham, President
Web address: www.sequoiahospital.org

SIERRA NEVADA MEMORIAL HOSPITAL (O, 104 beds) 155 Glasson Way, Grass Valley, CA, Zip 95945-5723, P O Box 1029, Zip 95945-1029, tel. 530/274-6000, Scott Neeley, M.D., President and Chief Executive Officer

ST. BERNARDINE MEDICAL CENTER (S, 342 beds) 2101 North Waterman Avenue, San Bernardino, CA, Zip 92404-4855; tel. 909/883-8711, Douglas V. Kleam, President
Web address: www.stbernardinemedicalcenter.com

ST. ELIZABETH COMMUNITY HOSPITAL (S, 76 beds) 2550 Sister Mary Columba Drive, Red Bluff, CA, Zip 96080-4397; tel. 530/529-8000, Rodger Page, Market President, North State

ST. JOHN'S REGIONAL MEDICAL CENTER (S, 266 beds) 1600 North Rose Avenue, Oxnard, CA, Zip 93030-3723; tel. 805/988-2500, Patrick Caster, President and Chief Executive Officer
Web address: www.stjohnshealth.org

ST. JOSEPH'S BEHAVIORAL HEALTH CENTER (S, 35 beds) 2510 North California Street, Stockton, CA, Zip 95204-5568; tel. 209/461-2000, Paul Rains, R.N., MSN, President
Web address: www.stjosephscanhelp.org

ST. JOSEPH'S MEDICAL CENTER (S, 279 beds) 1800 North California Street, Stockton, CA, Zip 95204-6019, P O Box 213008, Zip 95213-9008, tel. 209/943-2000, Donald J. Wiley, President and Chief Executive Officer
Web address: www.stjosephsCARES.org

ST. MARY MEDICAL CENTER LONG BEACH (S, 307 beds) 1050 Linden Avenue, Long Beach, CA, Zip 90813-3321, P O Box 887, Zip 90801-0887, tel. 562/491-9000, Carolyn P. Caldwell, FACHE, President and Chief Executive Officer

WOODLAND MEMORIAL HOSPITAL (O, 105 beds) 1325 Cottonwood Street, Woodland, CA, Zip 95695-5199; tel. 530/662-3961, Gena Bravo, President/Chief Executive Officer
Web address: https://www.dignityhealth.org/sacramento/locations/woodland-memorial-hospital

COLORADO: COMMON SPIRIT ST. ELIZABETH HOSPITAL (O, 34 beds) 1000 Lincoln Street, Fort Morgan, CO, Zip 80701-3298; tel. 970/867-3391, John Swanhorst, Interim Chief Executive Officer

Systems / Commonspirit Health

COMMONSPIRIT–MERCY HOSPITAL (S, 82 beds) 1010 Three Springs Boulevard, Durango, CO, Zip 81301–8296; tel. 970/247–4311, Josh Neff, Chief Executive Officer
Web address: www.mercydurango.org

COMMONSPIRIT–ST. ANTHONY SUMMIT MEDICAL CENTER (S, 34 beds) 340 Peak One Drive, Frisco, CO, Zip 80443, P O Box 738, Zip 80443–0738, tel. 970/668–3300, Trixie VanderSchaaff, Chief Executive Officer
Web address: www.summitmedicalcenter.org

COMMONSPIRIT–ST. MARY–CORWIN HOSPITAL (S, 42 beds) 1008 Minnequa Avenue, Pueblo, CO, Zip 81004–3798; tel. 719/557–4000, Michael Cafasso, Chief Executive Officer
Web address: https://www.mountain.commonspirit.org/location/st-mary-corwin-hospital

LONGMONT UNITED HOSPITAL (S, 131 beds) 1950 Mountain View Avenue, Longmont, CO, Zip 80501–3162; tel. 303/651–5111, Deb Mohesky, Chief Executive Officer

ORTHOCOLORADO HOSPITAL (O, 48 beds) 11650 West 2nd Place, Lakewood, CO, Zip 80228–1527; tel. 720/321–5000, Jude Torchia, Chief Executive Officer
Web address: www.orthocolorado.org

PENROSE–ST. FRANCIS HEALTH SERVICES (S, 573 beds) 2222 North Nevada Avenue, Colorado Springs, CO, Zip 80907–6799; tel. 719/776–5000, Kristi Olson, Chief Executive Officer

ST. ANTHONY HOSPITAL (S, 237 beds) 11600 West Second Place, Lakewood, CO, Zip 80228–1527; tel. 720/321–0000, Kevin Cullinan, Chief Executive Officer
Web address: www.stanthonyhosp.org

ST. ANTHONY NORTH HOSPITAL (S, 113 beds) 14300 Orchard Parkway, Westminster, CO, Zip 80023–9206; tel. 720/627–0000, Constance Schmidt, FACHE, R.N., Chief Executive Officer
Web address: https://www.centura.org/location/st-anthony-north-hospital

ST. THOMAS MORE HOSPITAL (S, 25 beds) 1338 Phay Avenue, Canon City, CO, Zip 81212–2302; tel. 719/285–2000, Michael Cafasso, Chief Executive Officer

GEORGIA: CHI MEMORIAL HOSPITAL–GEORGIA (O, 35 beds) 100 Gross Crescent Circle, Fort Oglethorpe, GA, Zip 30742–3669; tel. 706/858–2000, Angela Stiggins, Market Vice President of Operations/Administrator
Web address: www.memorial.org/chi-memorial-hospital-georgia

IOWA: CHI HEALTH MERCY CORNING (S, 12 beds) 603 Rosary Drive, Corning, IA, Zip 50841–1683; tel. 641/322–3121, Alicia Reed, President
Web address: www.chihealth.com/en/location-search/mercy-corning.html

CHI HEALTH MERCY COUNCIL BLUFFS (S, 146 beds) 800 Mercy Drive, Council Bluffs, IA, Zip 51503–3128; tel. 712/328–5000, Derek Havens, Interim President
Web address: https://www.chihealth.com/locations/mercy-council-bluffs

CHI HEALTH MISSOURI VALLEY (S, 12 beds) 631 North Eighth Street, Missouri Valley, IA, Zip 51555–1102; tel. 712/642–2784, David J. Jones, Market President, Critical Access Hospitals (NE, IA, MN)
Web address: www.chihealth.com/chi-health-missouri-valley

KANSAS: BOB WILSON MEMORIAL GRANT COUNTY HOSPITAL (O, 26 beds) 415 North Main Street, Ulysses, KS, Zip 67880–2133; tel. 620/356–1266, Twilla Lee, Chief Executive Officer

ST. CATHERINE HOSPITAL–DODGE CITY (O, 99 beds) 3001 Avenue 'A', Dodge City, KS, Zip 67801–6508, P O Box 1478, Zip 67801–1478, tel. 620/225–8400, Twilla Lee, Chief Executive Officer
Web address: https://www.centura.org/location/st-catherine-hospital-dodge-city

ST. CATHERINE HOSPITAL (S, 100 beds) 401 East Spruce Street, Garden City, KS, Zip 67846–5679; tel. 620/272–2222, Twilla Lee, Chief Executive Officer
Web address: www.StCatherineHosp.org

KENTUCKY: CHI SAINT JOSEPH HEALTH–FLAGET MEMORIAL HOSPITAL (S, 42 beds) 4305 New Shepherdsville Road, Bardstown, KY, Zip 40004–9019; tel. 502/350–5000, Jennifer Nolan, President and Chief Executive Officer

CHI SAINT JOSEPH HEALTH–SAINT JOSEPH BEREA (S, 25 beds) 305 Estill Street, Berea, KY, Zip 40403–1909; tel. 859/986–3151, John C. Yanes, President
Web address: www.kentuckyonehealth.org/berea

CHI SAINT JOSEPH HEALTH–SAINT JOSEPH EAST (S, 150 beds) 150 North Eagle Creek Drive, Lexington, KY, Zip 40509–1805; tel. 859/967–5000, Jennifer Nolan, President
Web address: www.sjhlex.org

CHI SAINT JOSEPH HEALTH–SAINT JOSEPH LONDON (S, 116 beds) 1001 Saint Joseph Lane, London, KY, Zip 40741–8345; tel. 606/330–6000, John C. Yanes, President
Web address: www.saintjosephhealthsystem.org

CHI SAINT JOSEPH HEALTH–SAINT JOSEPH MOUNT STERLING (S, 42 beds) 225 Falcon Drive, Mount Sterling, KY, Zip 40353–1158, P O Box 7, Zip 40353–0007, tel. 859/497–5000, John C. Yanes, President
Web address: https://www.chisaintjosephhealth.org/

CHI SAINT JOSEPH HEALTH (S, 307 beds) 1 St Joseph Drive, Lexington, KY, Zip 40504–3754; tel. 859/313–1000, Christy Spitser, Interim President

CONTINUING CARE HOSPITAL (S, 23 beds) 1 Saint Joseph Drive, Lexington, KY, Zip 40504–3742; tel. 859/967–5744, Robert C. Desotelle, President and Chief Executive Officer
Web address: www.kentuckyonehealth.org

MINNESOTA: CHI LAKEWOOD HEALTH (S, 55 beds) 600 Main Avenue South, Baudette, MN, Zip 56623–2855; tel. 218/634–2120, Jeffry Stampohar, President
Web address: www.lakewoodhealthcenter.org

CHI ST. FRANCIS HEALTH (S, 105 beds) 2400 St Francis Drive, Breckenridge, MN, Zip 56520–1025; tel. 218/643–3000, David A. Nelson, President and Chief Executive Officer
Web address: www.sfcare.org

CHI ST. GABRIEL'S HEALTH (S, 25 beds) 815 Second Street SE, Little Falls, MN, Zip 56345–3596; tel. 320/632–5441, Steve Smith, President and Chief Executive Officer
Web address: www.stgabriels.com

CHI ST. JOSEPH'S HEALTH (S, 25 beds) 600 Pleasant Avenue, Park Rapids, MN, Zip 56470–1431; tel. 218/732–3311, Benjamin Koppelman, President
Web address: www.sjahs.org

NEBRASKA: CHI HEALTH CREIGHTON UNIVERSITY MEDICAL CENTER–BERGAN MERCY (S, 385 beds) 7500 Mercy Road, Omaha, NE, Zip 68124–2319; tel. 402/398–6060, Dennis Bierle, President
Web address: www.chihealth.com/chi-health-bergan-mercy

CHI HEALTH GOOD SAMARITAN (S, 252 beds) 10 East 31st Street, Kearney, NE, Zip 68847–2926, P O Box 1990, Zip 68848–1990, tel. 308/865–7100, Curt Coleman, FACHE, President

CHI HEALTH IMMANUEL (S, 276 beds) 6901 North 72nd Street, Omaha, NE, Zip 68122–1799; tel. 402/572–2121, Anthony Ashby, President
Web address: www.alegent.com/immanuel

CHI HEALTH LAKESIDE (S, 137 beds) 6901 N 72nd St, Omaha, NE, Zip 68122, 16901 Lakeside Hills Court, Zip 68130–2318, tel. 402/717–8000, Mark E. Longacre, FACHE, President

CHI HEALTH MIDLANDS (S, 58 beds) 11111 South 84th Street, Papillion, NE, Zip 68046–4122; tel. 402/593–3000, Mark E. Longacre, FACHE, President
Web address: www.CHIhealth.com

CHI HEALTH NEBRASKA HEART (S, 54 beds) 7500 South 91st Street, Lincoln, NE, Zip 68526–9437; tel. 402/327–2700, Rick Thompson, M.D., FACS, FACC, President

CHI HEALTH PLAINVIEW (S, 15 beds) 704 North Third Street, Plainview, NE, Zip 68769–2047, P O Box 489, Zip 68769–0489, tel. 402/582–4245, Connie Peters, R.N., President
Web address: www.alegentcreighton.com/plainview-hospital

CHI HEALTH SAINT FRANCIS (S, 165 beds) 2620 West Faidley Avenue, Grand Island, NE, Zip 68803–4297, P O Box 9804, Zip 68802–9804, tel. 308/384–4600, Steven M. Schieber, FACHE, President

CHI HEALTH SCHUYLER (S, 25 beds) 104 West 17th Street, Schuyler, NE, Zip 68661–1304; tel. 402/352–2441, Connie Peters, R.N., President
Web address: www.alegent.org

CHI HEALTH ST ELIZABETH (S, 235 beds) 555 South 70th Street, Lincoln, NE, Zip 68510–2494; tel. 402/219–8000, Tyler DeJong, President

CHI HEALTH ST. MARY'S (S, 18 beds) 1301 Grundman Boulevard, Nebraska City, NE, Zip 68410; tel. 402/873–3321, Daniel DeFreece, M.D., President
Web address: www.chihealthstmarys.com

For explanation of codes following names, see page B2.
★ Indicates Type III membership in the American Hospital Association.

Systems / Commonspirit Health

NEVADA: DIGNITY ST. ROSE–CRAIG RANCH (C, 8 beds) 1550 West Craig Road, Suite 100, North Las Vegas, NV, Zip 89032–0327, 8686 New Trails Drive, Suite 100, The Woodlands, TX, Zip 77381–1188, tel. 702/777–3615, Linda Tautz, Market Chief Executive Officer

ST. ROSE DOMINICAN HOSPITALS–ROSE DE LIMA CAMPUS (S, 20 beds) 102 East Lake Mead Parkway, Henderson, NV, Zip 89015–5524; tel. 702/616–5000, Tom Burns, Chief Operating Officer and Chief Nurse Executive
Web address: www.strosehospitals.org

ST. ROSE DOMINICAN HOSPITALS–SAN MARTIN CAMPUS (O, 147 beds) 8280 West Warm Springs Road, Las Vegas, NV, Zip 89113–3612; tel. 702/492–8000, Tom Burns, President and Chief Executive Officer

ST. ROSE DOMINICAN HOSPITALS–SIENA CAMPUS (S, 326 beds) 3001 St Rose Parkway, Henderson, NV, Zip 89052; tel. 702/616–5000, Katherine Vergos, FACHE, President and Chief Executive Officer
Web address: www.strosehospitals.com

NORTH DAKOTA: CHI LISBON HEALTH (S, 25 beds) 905 Main Street, Lisbon, ND, Zip 58054–4334, P O Box 353, Zip 58054–0353, tel. 701/683–6400, Becki Thompson, Administrator
Web address: www.lisbonhospital.com

CHI MERCY HEALTH (S, 19 beds) 570 Chautauqua Boulevard, Valley City, ND, Zip 58072–3199; tel. 701/845–6400, D. Ryan. Fowler, President
Web address: www.mercyhospitalvalleycity.org

CHI OAKES HOSPITAL (S, 20 beds) 1200 North Seventh Street, Oakes, ND, Zip 58474–2502; tel. 701/742–3291, Becki Thompson, President

CHI ST ALEXIUS HEALTH CARRINGTON (S, 25 beds) 800 North Fourth Street, Carrington, ND, Zip 58421–1217, P O Box 461, Zip 58421–0461, tel. 701/652–3141, Jodi Lynn. Hovdenes, R.N., President
Web address: https://www.chistalexiushealth.org/locations/carrington

CHI ST. ALEXIUS HEALTH BISMARCK (O, 237 beds) 900 East Broadway, Bismarck, ND, Zip 58501–4586, P O Box 5510, Zip 58506–5510, tel. 701/530–7000, Reed Reyman, President

CHI ST. ALEXIUS HEALTH DEVILS LAKE (S, 25 beds) 1031 Seventh Street NE, Devils Lake, ND, Zip 58301–2798; tel. 701/662–2131, Mariann Doeling, R.N., President
Web address: https://www.chistalexiushealth.org/locations/devils-lake

CHI ST. ALEXIUS HEALTH DICKINSON (S, 25 beds) 2500 Fairway Street, Dickinson, ND, Zip 58601–4399; tel. 701/456–4000, Carol Enderle, R.N., MSN, President
Web address: https://www.chistalexiushealth.org/locations/dickinson

CHI ST. ALEXIUS HEALTH GARRISON (O, 50 beds) 407 Third Avenue SE, Garrison, ND, Zip 58540–7235; tel. 701/463–2275, Adam Maus, Administrator
Web address: https://www.chistalexiushealth.org/locations/garrison

CHI ST. ALEXIUS HEALTH TURTLE LAKE HOSPITAL (O, 25 beds) 220 Fifth Avenue, Turtle Lake, ND, Zip 58575–4005, P O Box 280, Zip 58575–0280, tel. 701/448–2331, Adam Maus, Administrator
Web address: https://www.chistalexiushealth.org/turtle-lake/facilities/chi-st-alexius-health-turtle-lake-hospital

CHI ST. ALEXIUS HEALTH WILLISTON (S, 25 beds) 1301 15th Avenue West, Williston, ND, Zip 58801–3896; tel. 701/774–7400, Garrick Hyde, President
Web address: www.mercy-williston.org

OHIO: GOOD SAMARITAN HOSPITAL (S, 400 beds) 375 Dixmyth Avenue, Cincinnati, OH, Zip 45220–2489; tel. 513/862–1400, Kelvin Hanger, President and Chief Operating Officer

PROVIDENCE CARE CENTER (O, 138 beds) 2025 Hayes Avenue, Sandusky, OH, Zip 44870, Rick G. Ryan, Administrator and Chief Executive Officer

TRINITY HEALTH SYSTEM (O, 277 beds) 380 Summit Avenue, Steubenville, OH, Zip 43952–2699; tel. 740/283–7000, Matthew Grimshaw, Market Chief Executive Officer
Web address: www.trinityhealth.com

TRINITY HOSPITAL TWIN CITY (O, 12 beds) 819 North First Street, Dennison, OH, Zip 44621–1098; tel. 740/922–2800, Dwayne Richardson, President
Web address: www.trinitytwincity.org

OREGON: CHI ST. ANTHONY HOSPITAL (S, 25 beds) 2801 St Anthony Way, Pendleton, OR, Zip 97801–3800; tel. 541/276–5121, Harold S. Geller, Chief Executive Officer

MERCY MEDICAL CENTER (S, 135 beds) 2700 Northwest Stewart Parkway, Roseburg, OR, Zip 97471–1281; tel. 541/673–0611, Russell Woolley, President and Chief Executive Officer
Web address: www.mercyrose.org

TENNESSEE: CHI MEMORIAL (S, 423 beds) 2525 De Sales Avenue, Chattanooga, TN, Zip 37404–1161; tel. 423/495–2525, Janelle Reilly, Market Chief Executive Officer
Web address: www.memorial.org

TEXAS: CHI ST LUKE'S HEALTH–BAYLOR ST LUKE'S MEDICAL CENTER (O, 651 beds) 6720 Bertner Avenue, Houston, TX, Zip 77030–2697, P O Box 20269, Zip 77225–0269, tel. 832/355–1000, Bradley T. Lembcke, M.D., President

CHI ST. JOSEPH HEALTH BURLESON HOSPITAL (O, 15 beds) 1101 Woodson Drive, Caldwell, TX, Zip 77836–1052, P O Box 360, Zip 77836–0360, tel. 979/567–3245, Kyle Sims, Division Vice President
Web address: www.https://stjoseph-locations.stlukeshealth.org/location/chi-st-joseph-health-burleson-hospital

CHI ST. JOSEPH HEALTH GRIMES HOSPITAL (O, 15 beds) 210 South Judson Street, Navasota, TX, Zip 77868–3704; tel. 936/825–6585, Kyle Sims, Division Vice President
Web address: www.https://stjoseph.stlukeshealth.org/locations/chi-st-joseph-health-grimes-hospital

CHI ST. JOSEPH HEALTH MADISON HOSPITAL (O, 15 beds) 100 West Cross Street, Madisonville, TX, Zip 77864–2432, Box 698, Zip 77864–0698, tel. 936/348–2631, Kyle Sims, Division Vice President

CHI ST. JOSEPH REGIONAL HEALTH CENTER (O, 189 beds) 2801 Franciscan Drive, Bryan, TX, Zip 77802–2599; tel. 979/776–3777, Kimberly Shaw, FACHE, St. Joseph Market President
Web address: www.https://stjoseph.stlukeshealth.org/locations/chi-st-joseph-health-regional-hospital

CHI ST. LUKE'S HEALTH BRAZOSPORT (O, 93 beds) 100 Medical Drive, Lake Jackson, TX, Zip 77566–5674; tel. 979/297–4411, Robert J. Trautman, President
Web address: www.chistlukesbrazosport.org

CHI ST. LUKE'S HEALTH MEMORIAL LUFKIN (O, 159 beds) 1201 West Frank Avenue, Lufkin, TX, Zip 75904–3357, P O Box 1447, Zip 75902–1447, tel. 936/634–8111, Monte J. Bostwick, Market Chief Executive Officer
Web address: www.memorialhealth.us/centers/lufkin

CHI ST. LUKE'S HEALTH MEMORIAL SAN AUGUSTINE (O, 9 beds) 511 East Hospital Street, San Augustine, TX, Zip 75972–2121, P O Box 658, Zip 75972–0658, tel. 936/275–3446, Ashley London, R.N., Administrator
Web address: www.https://locations.stlukeshealth.org/location/memorial-san-augustine-hospital

ST. LUKE'S HEALTH–LAKESIDE HOSPITAL (O, 8 beds) 17400 St. Luke's Way, The Woodlands, TX, Zip 77384–8036; tel. 936/266–9000, James Parisi, Chief Executive Officer

ST. LUKE'S HEALTH–MEMORIAL LIVINGSTON (O, 52 beds) 1717 Highway 59 Loop North, Livingston, TX, Zip 77351–5710, P O Box 1257, Zip 77351–0022, tel. 936/329–8700, Kristi Froese, R.N., Vice President Clinical Operations
Web address: https://www.chistlukeshealthmemorial.org/centers/livingston

ST. LUKE'S HEALTH–PATIENTS MEDICAL CENTER (O, 61 beds) 4600 East Sam Houston Parkway South, Pasadena, TX, Zip 77505–3948; tel. 713/948–7000, Steven Foster, President and Chief Executive Officer

ST. LUKE'S HEALTH–SUGAR LAND HOSPITAL (O, 100 beds) 1317 Lake Pointe Parkway, Sugar Land, TX, Zip 77478–3997; tel. 281/637–7000, Steven Foster, President and Chief Executive Officer
Web address: https://www.chistlukeshealth.org/locations/sugar-land-hospital?utm_source=local-listing&utm_medium=organic&utm_campaign=website-link

ST. LUKE'S HEALTH–THE VINTAGE HOSPITAL (O, 94 beds) 20171 Chasewood Park Drive, Houston, TX, Zip 77070–1437; tel. 832/534–5000, Mario J. Garner, Ed.D., FACHE, Chief Executive Officer
Web address: www.https://locations.stlukeshealth.org/location/vintage-hospital

ST. LUKE'S HEALTH–THE WOODLANDS HOSPITAL (O, 238 beds) 17200 St. Luke's Way, The Woodlands, TX, Zip 77384–8007; tel. 936/266–2000, James Parisi, Chief Executive Officer

---

For explanation of codes following names, see page B2.
★ Indicates Type III membership in the American Hospital Association.

Systems / Commonspirit Health

UTAH: HOLY CROSS HOSPITAL–DAVIS (O, 220 beds) 1600 West Antelope Drive, Layton, UT, Zip 84041–1142; tel. 801/807–1000, Kyle J. Brostrom, Chief Executive Officer
Web address: https://www.centura.org/location/holy-cross-hospital-davis/hc
HOLY CROSS HOSPITAL–JORDAN VALLEY (O, 189 beds) 3580 West 9000 South, West Jordan, UT, Zip 84088–8812; tel. 801/561–8888, Christine McSweeney, FACHE, Chief Executive Officer
Web address: https://www.centura.org/location/holy-cross-hospital-jordan-valley/hc
HOLY CROSS HOSPITAL–SALT LAKE (O, 97 beds) 1050 East South Temple, Salt Lake City, UT, Zip 84102–1507; tel. 801/350–4111, Jeremy Bradshaw, Market President
WASHINGTON: ST. ANNE HOSPITAL (O, 115 beds) 16251 Sylvester Road SW, Burien, WA, Zip 98166–3052; tel. 206/244–9970, Deepak Devasthali, Chief Operating Officer
Web address: https://www.vmfh.org/our-hospitals/st-anne-hospital
ST. ANTHONY HOSPITAL (O, 112 beds) 11567 Canterwood Boulevard NW, Gig Harbor, WA, Zip 98332–5812; tel. 253/530–2000, Dino Johnson, R.N., Chief Operating Officer
Web address: https://www.vmfh.org/our-hospitals/st-anthony-hospital
ST. CLARE HOSPITAL (S, 104 beds) 11315 Bridgeport Way SW, Lakewood, WA, Zip 98499–3004; tel. 253/985–1711, Matthew Metsker, President
Web address: https://www.vmfh.org/our-hospitals/st-clare-hospital
ST. ELIZABETH HOSPITAL (S, 25 beds) 1455 Battersby Avenue, Enumclaw, WA, Zip 98022–3634, P O Box 218, Zip 98022–0218, tel. 360/802–8800, Danna Sharer, President
ST. FRANCIS HOSPITAL (S, 124 beds) 34515 Ninth Avenue South, Federal Way, WA, Zip 98003–6799; tel. 253/944–8100, Dino Johnson, R.N., Interim Chief Operating Officer
Web address: https://www.vmfh.org/our-hospitals/st-francis-hospital
ST. JOSEPH MEDICAL CENTER (S, 353 beds) 1717 South 'J' Street, Tacoma, WA, Zip 98405–3004, P O Box 2197, Zip 98401–2197, tel. 253/426–4101, Syd Bersante, R.N., Interim President
ST. MICHAEL MEDICAL CENTER (O, 248 beds) 1800 Northwest Myhre Road, Silverdale, WA, Zip 98383–7663; tel. 564/240–1000, Chad Melton, President
Web address: https://www.vmfh.org/our-hospitals/st-michael-medical-center.html
VIRGINIA MASON MEDICAL CENTER (O, 218 beds) 1100 Ninth Avenue, Seattle, WA, Zip 98101–2756, P O Box 900, Zip 98111–0900, tel. 206/223–6600, Monica Hilt, President
Web address: www.VirginiaMason.org
WELLFOUND BEHAVIORAL HEALTH HOSPITAL (O, 84 beds) 3402 South 19th Street, Tacoma, WA, Zip 98405–2487; tel. 253/301–5400, Angela Naylor, Interim Chief Executive Officer

Owned, leased, sponsored:	121 hospitals	18233 beds
Contract–managed:	1 hospitals	8 beds
Totals:	122 hospitals	18241 beds

★0401: COMMUNITY HEALTH NETWORK (NP)
7330 Shadeland Station, Indianapolis, IN Zip 46256–3957; tel. 317/355–1411, Bryan A. Mills, President and Chief Executive Officer
(Independent Hospital System)

INDIANA: COMMUNITY HOSPITAL ANDERSON (O, 118 beds) 1515 North Madison Avenue, Anderson, IN, Zip 46011–3453; tel. 765/298–4242, Marsha S. Meckel, R.N., Hospital Administrator
COMMUNITY HOSPITAL EAST (O, 163 beds) 1500 North Ritter Avenue, Indianapolis, IN, Zip 46219–3095; tel. 317/355–1411, Paige Dooley, R.N., MSN, Hospital Administrator, Vice President and Chief Nurse Executive
Web address: www.ecommunity.com/east/
COMMUNITY HOSPITAL NORTH (O, 352 beds) 7150 Clearvista Drive, Indianapolis, IN, Zip 46256–1695, 7250 Clearvista Drive, Suite 200, Zip 46256–1695, tel. 317/355–2469, Jennifer Hindman, Vice President, Hospital Administrator
COMMUNITY HOSPITAL SOUTH (O, 161 beds) 1402 East County Line Road South, Indianapolis, IN, Zip 46227–0963; tel. 317/887–7000, Anita Capps, R.N., Hospital Administrator and Chief Nurse Executive
Web address: www.ecommunity.com
COMMUNITY HOWARD REGIONAL HEALTH (O, 201 beds) 3500 South Lafountain Street, Kokomo, IN, Zip 46902–3803, P O Box 9011, Zip 46904–9011, tel. 765/453–0702, Derek McMichael, Administrator
Web address: https://www.ecommunity.com/locations/community-howard-regional-health
COMMUNITY REHABILITATION HOSPITAL NORTH (O, 60 beds) 7343 Clearvista Drive, Indianapolis, IN, Zip 46256–4602; tel. 317/585–5400, Roxanne Stacy, Chief Executive Officer
COMMUNITY REHABILITATION HOSPITAL SOUTH (O, 37 beds) 607 Greenwood Springs Drive, Greenwood, IN, Zip 46143–6377; tel. 317/215–3800, Michelle Russell, Chief Executive Officer
Web address: www.communityrehabhospitalsouth.com

Owned, leased, sponsored:	7 hospitals	1092 beds
Contract–managed:	0 hospitals	0 beds
Totals:	7 hospitals	1092 beds

★0080: COMMUNITY HEALTH SYSTEMS, INC. (IO)
4000 Meridian Boulevard, Franklin, TN Zip 37067–6325, P O Box 689020, Zip 37068–9020, tel. 615/465–7000, Tim Hingtgen, Chief Executive Officer
(Decentralized Health System)

ALABAMA: CRESTWOOD MEDICAL CENTER (O, 180 beds) 1 Hospital Drive, Huntsville, AL, Zip 35801–3403; tel. 256/429–4000, Matthew Banks, Chief Executive Officer
Web address: www.crestwoodmedcenter.com
FLOWERS HOSPITAL (O, 203 beds) 4370 West Main Street, Dothan, AL, Zip 36305–4000, P O Box 6907, Zip 36302–6907, tel. 334/793–5000, Jeffrey M. Brannon, Chief Executive Officer
GADSDEN REGIONAL MEDICAL CENTER (O, 272 beds) 1007 Goodyear Avenue, Gadsden, AL, Zip 35903–1195; tel. 256/494–4000, Mark Dooley, Chief Executive Officer
Web address: www.gadsdenregional.com
GRANDVIEW MEDICAL CENTER (O, 434 beds) 3690 Grandview Parkway, Birmingham, AL, Zip 35243–3326; tel. 205/971–1000, Daniel McKinney, Chief Executive Officer
MEDICAL CENTER ENTERPRISE (O, 99 beds) 400 North Edwards Street, Enterprise, AL, Zip 36330–2510; tel. 334/347–0584, Joey Hester, Chief Executive Officer
Web address: www.mcehospital.com
SOUTH BALDWIN REGIONAL MEDICAL CENTER (L, 112 beds) 1613 North McKenzie Street, Foley, AL, Zip 36535–2299; tel. 251/949–3400, Margaret Roley, Chief Executive Officer
Web address: www.southbaldwinrmc.com
ALASKA: MAT–SU REGIONAL MEDICAL CENTER (O, 125 beds) 2500 South Woodworth Loop, Palmer, AK, Zip 99645–8984, P O Box 1687, Zip 99645–1687, tel. 907/861–6000, David Wallace, Chief Executive Officer
ARIZONA: NORTHWEST MEDICAL CENTER SAHUARITA (O, 18 beds) 16260 South Rancho Sahuarita Boulevard, Sahuarita, AZ, Zip 85629–0047; tel. 520/416–7100, Brett Lee, Chief Administrative Officer
Web address: www.healthiertucson.com
NORTHWEST MEDICAL CENTER (O, 258 beds) 6200 North La Cholla Boulevard, Tucson, AZ, Zip 85741–3599; tel. 520/742–9000, Brian Sinotte, Market Chief Executive officer and Interim Chief Executive Officer
ORO VALLEY HOSPITAL (O, 146 beds) 1551 East Tangerine Road, Oro Valley, AZ, Zip 85755–6213; tel. 520/901–3500, Cody Barnhart, Chief Administrative Officer
Web address: www.orovalleyhospital.com
WESTERN ARIZONA REGIONAL MEDICAL CENTER (O, 106 beds) 2735 Silver Creek Road, Bullhead City, AZ, Zip 86442–8303; tel. 928/763–2273, Brent Parsons, Chief Executive Officer
Web address: www.warmc.com

For explanation of codes following names, see page B2.
★ Indicates Type III membership in the American Hospital Association.

Systems / Community Health Systems, Inc.

ARKANSAS: NORTHWEST HEALTH PHYSICIANS' SPECIALTY HOSPITAL (O, 20 beds) 3873 North Parkview Drive, Fayetteville, AR, Zip 72703-6286; tel. 479/571-7070, Juli McWhorter, R.N., MSN, Chief Executive Officer

NORTHWEST MEDICAL CENTER-SPRINGDALE (O, 366 beds) 609 West Maple Avenue, Springdale, AR, Zip 72764-5394, P O Box 47, Zip 72765-0047, tel. 479/751-5711, Rick R. Naegler, Market Chief Executive Officer
Web address: https://www.northwesthealth.com/nmc-springdale

SILOAM SPRINGS REGIONAL HOSPITAL (O, 46 beds) 603 North Progress Avenue, Siloam Springs, AR, Zip 72761-4352; tel. 479/215-3000, Christopher Blair, Chief Administrative Officer
Web address: www.ssrh.net

FLORIDA: LOWER KEYS MEDICAL CENTER (L, 167 beds) 5900 College Road, Key West, FL, Zip 33040-4396, P O Box 9107, Zip 33041-9107, tel. 305/294-5531, David Clay, Chief Executive Officer
Web address: www.lkmc.com

NORTH OKALOOSA MEDICAL CENTER (O, 110 beds) 151 Redstone Avenue SE, Crestview, FL, Zip 32539-6026; tel. 850/689-8100, Michael Nordness, Chief Executive Officer
Web address: www.northokaloosa.com

PHYSICIANS REGIONAL-PINE RIDGE (O, 175 beds) 6101 Pine Ridge Road, Naples, FL, Zip 34119-3900; tel. 239/348-4000, Scott Lowe, Market Chief Executive Officer

SANTA ROSA MEDICAL CENTER (L, 91 beds) 6002 Berryhill Road, Milton, FL, Zip 32570-5062; tel. 850/626-7762, Justin Serrano, Chief Executive Officer
Web address: https://www.srmcfl.com/

SHOREPOINT HEALTH PORT CHARLOTTE (O, 254 beds) 2500 Harbor Boulevard, Port Charlotte, FL, Zip 33952-5000; tel. 941/766-4122, Andrew Romine, R.N., Chief Executive Officer
Web address: https://www.shorepointhealthcharlotte.com/port-charlotte

SHOREPOINT HEALTH PUNTA GORDA (O, 133 beds) 809 East Marion Avenue, Punta Gorda, FL, Zip 33950-3819, P O Box 51-1328, Zip 33951-1328, tel. 941/639-3131, Andrew Romine, R.N., Chief Executive Officer

GEORGIA: EAST GEORGIA REGIONAL MEDICAL CENTER (O, 149 beds) 1499 Fair Road, Statesboro, GA, Zip 30458-1683, P O Box 1048, Zip 30459-1048, tel. 912/486-1000, Stephen G. Pennington, Chief Executive Officer
Web address: www.eastgeorgiaregional.com

INDIANA: BLUFFTON REGIONAL MEDICAL CENTER (O, 52 beds) 303 South Main Street, Bluffton, IN, Zip 46714-2503; tel. 260/824-3210, Julie Thompson, Chief Adminstrative Officer and Chief Nursing Officer
Web address: www.blufftonregional.com

DUKES MEMORIAL HOSPITAL (O, 28 beds) 275 West 12th Street, Peru, IN, Zip 46970-1638; tel. 765/472-8000, Debra Close, Chief Executive Officer
Web address: www.dukesmemorialhosp.com

DUPONT HOSPITAL (O, 131 beds) 2520 East Dupont Road, Fort Wayne, IN, Zip 46825-1675; tel. 260/416-3000, Brent Parsons, Chief Executive Officer

LUTHERAN DOWNTOWN HOSPITAL (O, 191 beds) 700 Broadway, Fort Wayne, IN, Zip 46802-1493; tel. 260/425-3000, Perry Gay, Chief Executive Officer
Web address: https://www.lutherandowntownhospital.com/

LUTHERAN HOSPITAL OF INDIANA (O, 407 beds) 7950 West Jefferson Boulevard, Fort Wayne, IN, Zip 46804-4140; tel. 260/435-7001, Lorie Ailor, Chief Executive Officer

LUTHERAN KOSCIUSKO HOSPITAL (O, 72 beds) 2101 East Dubois Drive, Warsaw, IN, Zip 46580-3288; tel. 574/267-3200, Lynn M. Mergen, Chief Executive Officer
Web address: https://www.lutherankosciuskohospital.com/

NORTHWEST HEALTH-LA PORTE (O, 84 beds) 1007 Lincolnway, La Porte, IN, Zip 46350-3201, P O Box 250, Zip 46352-0250, tel. 219/326-1234, Simon Ratliff, Chief Executive Officer

NORTHWEST HEALTH-PORTER (O, 446 beds) 85 East U. S. Highway 6, Valparaiso, IN, Zip 46383-8947; tel. 219/983-8300, James Leonard, M.D., Chief Executive Officer
Web address: www.porterhealth.com

NORTHWEST HEALTH-STARKE (L, 15 beds) 102 East Culver Road, Knox, IN, Zip 46534-2216, P O Box 339, Zip 46534-0339, tel. 574/772-6231, Simon Ratliff, Chief Executive Officer

ORTHOPAEDIC HOSPITAL OF LUTHERAN HEALTH NETWORK (O, 43 beds) 7952 West Jefferson Boulevard, Fort Wayne, IN, Zip 46804-4140; tel. 260/435-2999, Lorie Ailor, Chief Executive Officer, Chief Administrative Officer, Network Vice President Orthopedics and Sports Medicine
Web address: www.theorthohospital.com

MISSISSIPPI: MERIT HEALTH BILOXI (L, 124 beds) 150 Reynoir Street, Biloxi, MS, Zip 39530-4199, P O Box 128, Zip 39533-0128, tel. 228/432-1571, Travis Sisson, Chief Executive Officer
Web address: www.merithealthbiloxi.com

MERIT HEALTH CENTRAL (L, 319 beds) 1850 Chadwick Drive, Jackson, MS, Zip 39204-3479, P O Box 59001, Zip 39284-9001, tel. 601/376-1000, Vincent Brummett, Chief Administrative Officer
Web address: www.merithealthcentral.com/

MERIT HEALTH MADISON (O, 33 beds) 161 River Oaks Drive, Canton, MS, Zip 39046-5375, PO Box 1607, Zip 39046-5375, tel. 601/855-4000, David Henry, FACHE, Chief Executive Officer

MERIT HEALTH NATCHEZ (O, 81 beds) 54 Seargent 'S' Prentiss Drive, Natchez, MS, Zip 39120-4726; tel. 601/443-2100, Kevin Samrow, Chief Executive Officer
Web address: https://www.merithealthnatchez.com/

MERIT HEALTH RANKIN (L, 55 beds) 350 Crossgates Boulevard, Brandon, MS, Zip 39042-2698; tel. 601/825-2811, Heather Sistrunk, R.N., Chief Executive Officer

MERIT HEALTH RIVER OAKS (O, 118 beds) 1030 River Oaks Drive, Flowood, MS, Zip 39232-9553, P O Box 5100, Jackson, Zip 39296-5100, tel. 601/932-1030, Sam Dean, Chief Executive Officer
Web address: https://www.merithealthriveroaks.com/

MERIT HEALTH RIVER REGION (O, 361 beds) 2100 Highway 61 North, Vicksburg, MS, Zip 39183-8211, P O Box 590, Zip 39181-0590, tel. 601/883-5000, David R. Fox, FACHE, Chief Executive Officer

MERIT HEALTH WESLEY (O, 211 beds) 5001 Hardy Street, Hattiesburg, MS, Zip 39402-1308, P O Box 16509, Zip 39404-6509, tel. 601/268-8000, Travis Sisson, Chief Executive Officer
Web address: https://www.merithealthwesley.com/

MERIT HEALTH WOMAN'S HOSPITAL (O, 60 beds) 1026 North Flowood Drive, Flowood, MS, Zip 39232-9532, 1026 North Flowood Drive, Zip 39232, tel. 601/932-1000, Heather Sistrunk, R.N., Chief Executive Officer

MISSOURI: MOBERLY REGIONAL MEDICAL CENTER (O, 99 beds) 1515 Union Avenue, Moberly, MO, Zip 65270-9449; tel. 660/263-8400, Michael D. Hall, Chief Executive Officer
Web address: https://www.moberlyregionalmedicalcenter.com

NORTHEAST REGIONAL MEDICAL CENTER (L, 55 beds) 315 South Osteopathy Street, Kirksville, MO, Zip 63501-6401, P O Box C8502, Zip 63501-8599, tel. 660/785-1000, Patrick Avila, Chief Executive Officer

POPLAR BLUFF REGIONAL MEDICAL CENTER (O, 274 beds) 3100 Oak Grove Road, Poplar Bluff, MO, Zip 63901, P O Box 88, Zip 63902-0088, tel. 573/776-2000, Clyde Wood, Chief Executive Officer
Web address: www.poplarbluffregional.com

NEW MEXICO: CARLSBAD MEDICAL CENTER (O, 99 beds) 2430 West Pierce Street, Carlsbad, NM, Zip 88220-3597; tel. 575/887-4100, Nicholas Arledge, Chief Executive Officer

EASTERN NEW MEXICO MEDICAL CENTER (O, 162 beds) 405 West Country Club Road, Roswell, NM, Zip 88201-5209; tel. 575/622-8170, Warren Yehl, Chief Executive Officer
Web address: www.enmmc.com

MOUNTAINVIEW REGIONAL MEDICAL CENTER (O, 168 beds) 4311 East Lohman Avenue, Las Cruces, NM, Zip 88011-8255; tel. 575/556-7600, Matthew Conrad, Interim Chief Executive Officer and Chief Operating Officer
Web address: www.mountainviewregional.com

NORTH CAROLINA: DAVIS REGIONAL MEDICAL CENTER (O, 144 beds) 218 Old Mocksville Road, Statesville, NC, Zip 28625-1930, P O Box 1823, Zip 28687-1823, tel. 704/873-0281, Alec Grabowski, Chief Executive Officer
Web address: www.davisregional.com

LAKE NORMAN REGIONAL MEDICAL CENTER (O, 123 beds) 171 Fairview Road, Mooresville, NC, Zip 28117-9500, P O Box 3250, Zip 28117-3250, tel. 704/660-4000, Alec Grabowski, Chief Executive Officer

For explanation of codes following names, see page B2.
★ Indicates Type III membership in the American Hospital Association.

Systems / Community Health Systems, Inc.

OKLAHOMA: ALLIANCEHEALTH DURANT (O, 138 beds) 1800 University Boulevard, Durant, OK, Zip 74701-3006, P O Box 1207, Zip 74702-1207, tel. 580/924-3080, Shelton Williams, Chief Executive Officer
Web address: www.alliancehealthdurant.com/

ALLIANCEHEALTH MADILL (L, 25 beds) 901 South Fifth Avenue, Madill, OK, Zip 73446-3640, P O Box 827, Zip 73446-0827, tel. 580/795-3384, Shelton Williams, Chief Executive Officer
Web address: www.myalliancehealth.com

PENNSYLVANIA: REGIONAL HOSPITAL OF SCRANTON (O, 186 beds) 746 Jefferson Avenue, Scranton, PA, Zip 18510-1624; tel. 570/348-7100, Michael Curran, Chief Executive Officer
Web address: www.regionalhospitalofscranton.net

WILKES-BARRE GENERAL HOSPITAL (O, 160 beds) 575 North River Street, Wilkes-Barre, PA, Zip 18764-0001; tel. 570/829-8111, Christopher L. Howe, R.N., Interim Chief Executive Officer

TENNESSEE: TENNOVA HEALTHCARE-CLARKSVILLE (O, 270 beds) 651 Dunlop Lane, Clarksville, TN, Zip 37040-5015, P O Box 31629, Zip 37040-0028, tel. 931/502-1000, Andrew Emery, Chief Executive Officer
Web address: www.tennova.com/

TENNOVA HEALTHCARE-JEFFERSON MEMORIAL HOSPITAL (L, 58 beds) 110 Hospital Drive, Jefferson City, TN, Zip 37760-5281; tel. 865/471-2500, Benjamin Ridder, Chief Executive Officer
Web address: www.tennova.com/

TENNOVA HEALTHCARE-LAFOLLETTE MEDICAL CENTER (O, 164 beds) 923 East Central Avenue, La Follette, TN, Zip 37766-2768, P O Box 1301, Zip 37766-1301, tel. 423/907-1200, Mark Cain, Chief Executive Officer
Web address: www.tennova.com

TENNOVA NEWPORT MEDICAL CENTER (O, 130 beds) 435 Second Street, Newport, TN, Zip 37821-3799; tel. 423/625-2200, Scott Williams, Chief Executive Officer
Web address: www.tennova.com

TENNOVA NORTH KNOXVILLE MEDICAL CENTER (O, 116 beds) 7565 Dannaher Way, Powell, TN, Zip 37849-4029; tel. 865/859-8000, Bill Rich, Chief Executive Officer

TEXAS: CEDAR PARK REGIONAL MEDICAL CENTER (O, 126 beds) 1401 Medical Parkway, Cedar Park, TX, Zip 78613-7763; tel. 512/528-7000, Sean Tinney, FACHE, Chief Executive Officer
Web address: www.cedarparkregional.com

DETAR HEALTHCARE SYSTEM (O, 235 beds) 506 East San Antonio Street, Victoria, TX, Zip 77901-6060, P O Box 2089, Zip 77902-2089, tel. 361/575-7441, Bernard Leger, Chief Executive Officer
Web address: www.detar.com

LAKE GRANBURY MEDICAL CENTER (L, 73 beds) 1310 Paluxy Road, Granbury, TX, Zip 76048-5655; tel. 817/573-2273, Curt M. Junkins, Chief Executive Officer
Web address: www.lakegranburymedicalcenter.com

LAREDO MEDICAL CENTER (O, 326 beds) 1700 East Saunders Avenue, Laredo, TX, Zip 78041-5474, P O Box 2068, Zip 78044-2068, tel. 956/796-5000, Jorge E. Leal, FACHE, Chief Executive Officer

LONGVIEW REGIONAL MEDICAL CENTER (O, 224 beds) 2901 North Fourth Street, Longview, TX, Zip 75605-5191, P O Box 14000, Zip 75607-4000, tel. 903/758-1818, Steve Gordon, Chief Executive Officer
Web address: www.longviewregional.com

NAVARRO REGIONAL HOSPITAL (O, 49 beds) 3201 West State Highway 22, Corsicana, TX, Zip 75110-2469; tel. 903/654-6800, John Manolakis, Chief Executive Officer

WOODLAND HEIGHTS MEDICAL CENTER (O, 131 beds) 505 South John Redditt Drive, Lufkin, TX, Zip 75904-3157, P O Box 150610, Zip 75904, tel. 936/634-8311, Jose A. Echavarria, Chief Executive Officer
Web address: www.woodlandheights.net

Owned, leased, sponsored:	64 hospitals	9830 beds
Contract-managed:	0 hospitals	0 beds
Totals:	64 hospitals	9830 beds

★**0384: COMMUNITY HOSPITAL CORPORATION (NP)**
7950 Legacy Drive, Suite 1000, Plano, TX Zip 75024-0417; tel. 972/943-6400, Jim R. Kendrick, President and Chief Executive Officer
(Moderately Centralized Health System)

KENTUCKY: CONTINUECARE HOSPITAL AT BAPTIST HEALTH CORBIN (O, 32 beds) 1 Trillium Way, Lower Level, Corbin, KY, Zip 40701-8727; tel. 606/523-5150, Pam Harrison, MSN, Chief Executive Officer
Web address: www.continuecare.org

CONTINUECARE HOSPITAL AT BAPTIST HEALTH PADUCAH (O, 37 beds) 2501 Kentucky Avenue, 5th Floor, Paducah, KY, Zip 42003-3813; tel. 270/575-2598, Lee Gentry, FACHE, Chief Executive Officer
Web address: www.continuecare.org/paducah//

CONTINUECARE HOSPITAL AT MADISONVILLE (O, 35 beds) 900 Hospital Drive, 4th Floor, Madisonville, KY, Zip 42431-1644; tel. 270/825-5450, Michelle Mullen, Chief Executive Officer

NEW MEXICO: UNION COUNTY GENERAL HOSPITAL (C, 25 beds) 300 Wilson Street, Clayton, NM, Zip 88415-3304, P O Box 489, Zip 88415-0489, tel. 575/374-2585, Tammie Chavez Stump, R.N., Chief Executive Officer
Web address: www.ucgh.net/

NORTH CAROLINA: CAROLINAS CONTINUECARE HOSPITAL AT PINEVILLE (O, 40 beds) 10648 Park Road, Charlotte, NC, Zip 28210; tel. 704/667-8050, Derek Murzyn, Market Chief Executive Officer
Web address: www.continuecare.org/pineville/

SOUTH CAROLINA: CONTINUECARE HOSPITAL AT PALMETTO HEALTH BAPTIST (O, 35 beds) Taylor at Marion Street, Columbia, SC, Zip 29220, PO BOX 11069, Zip 29211-1069, tel. 803/296-3757, Holly Powell, Interim Chief Executive Officer
Web address: www.continuecare.org/palmetto//

TEXAS: BAPTIST HOSPITALS OF SOUTHEAST TEXAS (O, 315 beds) 3080 College Street, Beaumont, TX, Zip 77701-4689, P O Box 1591, Zip 77704-1591, tel. 409/212-5000, Justin Doss, Chief Executive Officer

CONTINUECARE HOSPITAL AT HENDRICK MEDICAL CENTER (O, 23 beds) 1900 Pine Street, 7th Floor, Jones Building, Abilene, TX, Zip 79601-2432; tel. 325/670-6251, Anna Rojas, Chief Executive Officer
Web address: www.https://hendrick.continuecare.org/

CONTINUECARE HOSPITAL AT MEDICAL CENTER (ODESSA) (O, 25 beds) 500 West Fourth Street, 4th Floor, Odessa, TX, Zip 79761-5001; tel. 432/640-4380, Adebola Awino, Chief Nursing Officer / Interim Chief Executive Offier
Web address: www.https://odessa.continuecare.org/

FREESTONE MEDICAL CENTER (C, 10 beds) 125 Newman Street, Fairfield, TX, Zip 75840-1499; tel. 903/389-2121, Melissa Wilson, Chief Executive Officer
Web address: www.freestonemc.com/

HUNTSVILLE MEMORIAL HOSPITAL (C, 77 beds) 110 Memorial Hospital Drive, Huntsville, TX, Zip 77340-4940, P O Box 4001, Zip 77342-4001, tel. 936/291-3411, Patrick Shannon, Chief Executive Officer
Web address: www.huntsvillememorial.com

NORTH TEXAS MEDICAL CENTER (O, 48 beds) 1900 Hospital Boulevard, Gainesville, TX, Zip 76240-2002; tel. 940/665-1751, Thomas Sledge, Chief Executive Officer

TYLER CONTINUECARE HOSPITAL (O, 51 beds) 800 East Dawson, 4th Floor, Tyler, TX, Zip 75701-2036; tel. 903/531-4080, Stephanie Hyde, R.N., MSN, Chief Executive Officer
Web address: www.continuecare.org

YOAKUM COMMUNITY HOSPITAL (O, 23 beds) 1200 Carl Ramert Drive, Yoakum, TX, Zip 77995-4868; tel. 361/293-2321, Tiffany Miller, Chief Executive Officer
Web address: www.yoakumhospital.org

Owned, leased, sponsored:	11 hospitals	664 beds
Contract-managed:	3 hospitals	112 beds
Totals:	14 hospitals	776 beds

For explanation of codes following names, see page B2.
★ Indicates Type III membership in the American Hospital Association.

1085: COMMUNITY MEDICAL CENTERS (NP)

1560 E Shaw, Fresno, CA Zip 93710, P O Box 1232, Zip 93715–1232, tel. 559/459–6000, Craig S. Castro, President and Chief Executive Officer

(Independent Hospital System)

CALIFORNIA: CLOVIS COMMUNITY MEDICAL CENTER (O, 352 beds) 2755 Herndon Avenue, Clovis, CA, Zip 93611–6801; tel. 559/324–4000, Craig S. Castro, President and Chief Executive Officer, Community Health Systems
Web address: www.communitymedical.org

COMMUNITY BEHAVIORAL HEALTH CENTER (O, 61 beds) 7171 North Cedar Avenue, Fresno, CA, Zip 93720–3311; tel. 559/449–8000, Craig S. Castro, President and Chief Executive Officer, Community Health Systems

COMMUNITY REGIONAL MEDICAL CENTER (O, 934 beds) 2823 Fresno Street, Fresno, CA, Zip 93721–1324, P O Box 1232, Zip 93715–1232, tel. 559/459–6000, Craig S. Castro, President and Chief Executive Officer, Community Health Systems
Web address: www.communitymedical.org

FRESNO HEART AND SURGICAL HOSPITAL (O, 60 beds) 15 East Audubon Drive, Fresno, CA, Zip 93720–1542; tel. 559/433–8000, Craig S. Castro, President and Chief Executive Officer, Community Health Systems

Owned, leased, sponsored:	4 hospitals	1407 beds
Contract-managed:	0 hospitals	0 beds
Totals:	4 hospitals	1407 beds

0990: COMMUNITY MEMORIAL HEALTH SYSTEM (NP)

147 North Brent Street, Ventura, CA Zip 93003–2809; tel. 805/652–5011, Mick Zdeblick, Chief Executive Officer

(Independent Hospital System)

CALIFORNIA: COMMUNITY MEMORIAL HOSPITAL–VENTURA (O, 154 beds) 147 North Brent Street, Ventura, CA, Zip 93003–2809; tel. 805/652–5011, Mick Zdeblick, President/Chief Executive Officer
Web address: www.cmhshealth.org

OJAI VALLEY COMMUNITY HOSPITAL (O, 69 beds) 1306 Maricopa Highway, Ojai, CA, Zip 93023–3163; tel. 805/646–1401, Mick Zdeblick, President/Chief Executive Officer
Web address: www.cmhshealth.org/locations/ojai-valley-community-hospital/

Owned, leased, sponsored:	2 hospitals	223 beds
Contract-managed:	0 hospitals	0 beds
Totals:	2 hospitals	223 beds

0909: COMPASS HEALTH (NP)

713 North Avenue L, Crowley, LA Zip 70526–3832; tel. 337/788–3330, Emily Hunter, Co–Chief Executive Officer

LOUISIANA: COMPASS BEHAVIORAL CENTER OF ALEXANDRIA (O, 18 beds) 6410 Masonic Drve, Alexandria, LA, Zip 71301–2319; tel. 318/442–3163, Jeremy Autin, Chief Executive Officer

COMPASS BEHAVIORAL CENTER OF HOUMA (O, 20 beds) 4701 West Park Avenue, Houma, LA, Zip 70364–4426; tel. 985/876–1715, Alaina Richards, Chief Executive Officer
Web address: https://www.compasshealthcare.com/locations/compass-behavioral-center-of-houma-2/

COMPASS BEHAVIORAL CENTER OF LAFAYETTE (O, 24 beds) 312 Youngsville Highway, Lafayette, LA, Zip 70508; tel. 337/534–4655, Andre' Robichaux, Chief Executive Officer
Web address: www.compasshealthcare.com

COMPASS BEHAVIORAL CENTER OF MARKSVILLE (O, 18 beds) 137 Dr. Childress Drive, Marksville, LA, Zip 71351; tel. 318/256–3332, Jeremy Autin, Chief Executive Officer
Web address: https://www.compasshealthcare.com/locations/

JENNINGS SENIOR CARE HOSPITAL (O, 36 beds) 1 Hospital Drive, Suite 201, Jennings, LA, Zip 70546–3641; tel. 337/824–1558, Chad Hoffpauir, Chief Executive Officer

Owned, leased, sponsored:	5 hospitals	116 beds
Contract-managed:	0 hospitals	0 beds
Totals:	5 hospitals	116 beds

1131: CONCORD HOSPITAL (NP)

250 Pleasant Street, Concord, NH Zip 03301–7559; tel. 603/225–2711

Owned, leased, sponsored:	0 hospitals	0 beds
Contract-managed:	0 hospitals	0 beds
Totals:	0 hospitals	0 beds

★0950: CONE HEALTH (NP)

1200 North Elm Street, Greensboro, NC Zip 27401–1004; tel. 336/832–7000, Mary Jo Cagle, M.D., President and Chief Executive Officer

(Independent Hospital System)

NORTH CAROLINA: CONE HEALTH ALAMANCE REGIONAL MEDICAL CENTER (O, 195 beds) 1240 Huffman Mill Road, Burlington, NC, Zip 27215–8700, P O Box 202, Zip 27216–0202, tel. 336/538–7000, Mark Gordon, President
Web address: www.armc.com

CONE HEALTH MOSES CONE HOSPITAL (O, 875 beds) 1200 North Elm Street, Greensboro, NC, Zip 27401–1020; tel. 336/832–7000, Preston W. Hammock, President

Owned, leased, sponsored:	2 hospitals	1070 beds
Contract-managed:	0 hospitals	0 beds
Totals:	2 hospitals	1070 beds

0014: CONNECTICUT DEPARTMENT OF MENTAL HEALTH AND ADDICTION SERVICES (NP)

410 Capitol Avenue, Hartford, CT Zip 06106–1367, P O Box 341431, Zip 06134–1431, tel. 860/418–7000, Nancy Navarretta, Acting Commissioner

(Independent Hospital System)

CONNECTICUT: CONNECTICUT MENTAL HEALTH CENTER (O, 32 beds) 34 Park Street, New Haven, CT, Zip 06519–1109, P O Box 1842, Zip 06508–1842, tel. 203/974–7144, Michael Sernyak, M.D., Director
Web address: www.ct.gov/dmhas/cwp/view.asp?a=2906&q=334596

CONNECTICUT VALLEY HOSPITAL (O, 361 beds) 1000 Silver Street, Middletown, CT, Zip 06457–3947; tel. 860/262–5000, Lakisha Hyatt, Chief Executive Officer

SOUTHWEST CONNECTICUT MENTAL HEALTH SYSTEM (O, 62 beds) 1635 Central Avenue, Bridgeport, CT, Zip 06610–2717; tel. 203/551–7400, Francis Giannini, Interim Chief Executive Officer
Web address: www.ct.gov/dmhas/cwp/view.asp?a=2946&q=378936

Owned, leased, sponsored:	3 hospitals	455 beds
Contract-managed:	0 hospitals	0 beds
Totals:	3 hospitals	455 beds

★0016: COOK COUNTY HEALTH AND HOSPITALS SYSTEM (NP)

1900 West Polk Street, Suite 220, Chicago, IL Zip 60612–3723; tel. 312/864–6820, Erik Mikaitis, Interim Chief Executive Officer

(Independent Hospital System)

For explanation of codes following names, see page B2.
★ Indicates Type III membership in the American Hospital Association.

Systems / Cook County Health and Hospitals System

ILLINOIS: JOHN H. STROGER JR. HOSPITAL OF COOK COUNTY (O, 414 beds) 1969 West Ogden Avenue, Chicago, IL, Zip 60612–3714; tel. 312/864–6000, Donnica Austin, Chief Executive Officer
Web address: www.https://cookcountyhealth.org/locations/john-h-stroger-jr-hospital-of-cock-county/

PROVIDENT HOSPITAL OF COOK COUNTY (O, 28 beds) 500 East 51st Street, Chicago, IL, Zip 50615–2494; tel. 312/572–2000, Arnold F. Turner, M.D., Chief Hospital Executive
Web address: www.https://cookcountyhealth.org/locations/provident-hospital-of-cook-county/

Owned, leased, sponsored:	2 hospitals	442 beds
Contract–managed:	0 hospitals	0 beds
Totals:	2 hospitals	442 beds

★1094: COREWELL HEALTH (NP)

221 Michigan Street NE, Suite 501, Grand Rapids, MI Zip 49503–2539; tel. 616/391–1774, Christina Freese Decker, FACHE, President and Chief Executive Officer

MICHIGAN: COREWELL HEALTH BEAUMONT GROSSE POINTE HOSPITAL (O, 280 beds) 458 Cadieux Road, Grosse Pointe, MI, Zip 48230–1507; tel. 313/473–1000, Derk F. Pronger, President
Web address: https://www.beaumont.org/locations/beaumont-hospital-grosse-pointe

COREWELL HEALTH BEAUMONT TROY HOSPITAL (O, 521 beds) 44201 Dequindre Road, Troy, MI, Zip 48085–1117; tel. 248/964–5000, Nancy Susick, MSN, President
Web address: https://www.beaumont.org/locations/beaumont-hospital-troy

COREWELL HEALTH BIG RAPIDS HOSPITAL (O, 49 beds) 605 Oak Street, Big Rapids, MI, Zip 49307–2099; tel. 231/796–8691, Drew H. Dostal, FACHE, Regional Market Leader

COREWELL HEALTH BUTTERWORTH HOSPITAL (O, 1599 beds) 100 Michigan Street NE, Grand Rapids, MI, Zip 49503–2560; tel. 616/391–1774, Alejandro Quiroga, M.D., President of Corewell Health West
Web address: https://www.spectrumhealth.org/locations/butterworth-hospital

COREWELL HEALTH DEARBORN HOSPITAL (O, 486 beds) 18101 Oakwood Boulevard, Dearborn, MI, Zip 48124–4089; tel. 313/593–7000, Debra Guido-Allen, R.N., FACHE, President
Web address: https://www.beaumont.org/locations/beaumont-hospital-dearborn

COREWELL HEALTH FARMINGTON HILLS HOSPITAL (O, 305 beds) 28050 Grand River Avenue, Farmington Hills, MI, Zip 48336–5933; tel. 248/471–8000, Derk F. Pronger, President
Web address: https://www.beaumont.org/locations/beaumont-hospital-farmington-hills

COREWELL HEALTH GERBER HOSPITAL (O, 25 beds) 212 South Sullivan Avenue, Fremont, MI, Zip 49412–1548; tel. 231/924–3300
Web address: www.spectrumhealth.org

COREWELL HEALTH GREENVILLE HOSPITAL (O, 119 beds) 615 South Bower Street, Greenville, MI, Zip 48838–2614; tel. 616/754–4691, Drew H. Dostal, FACHE, Regional Market Leader

COREWELL HEALTH LAKELAND HOSPITALS (O, 407 beds) 1234 Napier Avenue, Saint Joseph, MI, Zip 49085–2158; tel. 269/983–8300, Natalie Baggio, R.N., President and Chief Operating Officer
Web address: www.lakelandhealth.org

COREWELL HEALTH LUDINGTON HOSPITAL (O, 30 beds) 1 Atkinson Drive, Ludington, MI, Zip 49431–1906, 1 Atkinson Dr, Zip 49431, tel. 231/843–2591, Drew H. Dostal, FACHE, Regional Market Leader, North Region
Web address: https://www.spectrumhealth.org/locations/ludington-hospital

COREWELL HEALTH PENNOCK HOSPITAL (O, 25 beds) 1009 West Green Street, Hastings, MI, Zip 49058–1710; tel. 269/945–3451, Bill Hoefer, FACHE, Regional Market Leader

COREWELL HEALTH REED CITY HOSPITAL (O, 64 beds) 300 North Patterson Road, Reed City, MI, Zip 49677–8041; tel. 231/832–3271, Drew H. Dostal, FACHE, Regional Market Leader, North Region
Web address: www.spectrumhealth.org/reedcity

COREWELL HEALTH TAYLOR HOSPITAL (O, 148 beds) 10000 Telegraph Road, Taylor, MI, Zip 48180–3330; tel. 313/295–5000, Kristine Donahue, R.N., President
Web address: https://www.beaumont.org/locations/beaumont-hospital-taylor

COREWELL HEALTH TRENTON HOSPITAL (O, 172 beds) 5450 Fort Street, Trenton, MI, Zip 48183–4625; tel. 734/671–3800, Kristine Donahue, R.N., President
Web address: https://www.beaumont.org/locations/beaumont-hospital-trenton

COREWELL HEALTH WATERVLIET HOSPITAL (O, 44 beds) 400 Medical Park Drive, Watervliet, MI, Zip 49098–9225; tel. 269/463–3111, Christine Fox, MSN, R.N., Interim Chief Nursing Officer
Web address: https://www.spectrumhealthlakeland.org/locations/Detail/corewell-health-watervliet-hospital/f3a140ad-c230-6723-add8-ff0000ca780f

COREWELL HEALTH WAYNE HOSPITAL (O, 99 beds) 33155 Annapolis Street, Wayne, MI, Zip 48184–2405; tel. 734/467–4000, Kristine Donahue, R.N., President

COREWELL HEALTH WILLIAM BEAUMONT UNIVERSITY HOSPITAL (O, 1049 beds) 3601 West Thirteen Mile Road, Royal Oak, MI, Zip 48073–6712; tel. 248/898–5000, Daniel Carey, M.D., President
Web address: https://www.beaumont.org/locations/beaumont-hospital-royal-oak

COREWELL HEALTH ZEELAND HOSPITAL (O, 55 beds) 8333 Felch Street, Zeeland, MI, Zip 49464–2608; tel. 616/772–4644, Bill Hoefer, FACHE, President and Regional Market Leader
Web address: www.spectrumhealth.org/zeeland

Owned, leased, sponsored:	18 hospitals	5477 beds
Contract–managed:	0 hospitals	0 beds
Totals:	18 hospitals	5477 beds

0905: CORNERSTONE HEALTHCARE GROUP (IO)

2200 Ross Avenue, Suite 5400, Dallas, TX Zip 75201–7984; tel. 469/621–6700, Steve Jakubcanin, President and Chief Executive Officer

(Independent Hospital System)

Owned, leased, sponsored:	0 hospitals	0 beds
Contract–managed:	0 hospitals	0 beds
Totals:	0 hospitals	0 beds

★0103: COTTAGE HEALTH (NP)

400 West Pueblo Street, Santa Barbara Cottage Hospital, Santa Barbara, CA Zip 93105–4353, P O Box 689, Zip 93102–0689, tel. 805/569–7290, Ronald C. Werft, President and Chief Executive Officer

(Independent Hospital System)

CALIFORNIA: GOLETA VALLEY COTTAGE HOSPITAL (O, 24 beds) 351 South Patterson Avenue, Santa Barbara, CA, Zip 93111–2496, PO Box 689, Zip 93102–0689, tel. 805/967–3411, Ronald C. Werft, President and Chief Executive Officer
Web address: www.sbch.org

SANTA BARBARA COTTAGE HOSPITAL (O, 416 beds) 400 West Pueblo Street, Santa Barbara, CA, Zip 93105–4390, P O Box 689, Zip 93102–0689, tel. 805/682–7111, Ronald C. Werft, President and Chief Executive Officer

SANTA YNEZ VALLEY COTTAGE HOSPITAL (O, 11 beds) 2050 Viborg Road, Solvang, CA, Zip 93463–2295, PO Box 689, Santa Barbara, Zip 93102–0689, tel. 805/688–6431, Ronald C. Werft, President and Chief Executive Officer
Web address: www.cottagehealthsystem.org

Owned, leased, sponsored:	3 hospitals	451 beds
Contract–managed:	0 hospitals	0 beds
Totals:	3 hospitals	451 beds

For explanation of codes following names, see page B2.
★ Indicates Type III membership in the American Hospital Association.

0123: COVENANT HEALTH (NP)
1420 Centerpoint Blvd, Blvd C, Knoxville, TN Zip 37932, 244 Fort Sanders West Boulevard, Zip 37922-3353, tel. 865/531-5555, James VanderSteeg, President and Chief Executive Officer
(Centralized Health System)

TENNESSEE: CLAIBORNE MEDICAL CENTER (L, 111 beds) 1850 Old Knoxville Road, Tazewell, TN, Zip 37879-3625; tel. 423/626-4211, Patricia P. Ketterman, R.N., President and Chief Administrative Officer
Web address: www.claibornehospital.org

CUMBERLAND MEDICAL CENTER (O, 84 beds) 421 South Main Street, Crossville, TN, Zip 38555-5031; tel. 931/484-9511, Randy Davis, Chief Executive Officer

FORT LOUDOUN MEDICAL CENTER (L, 30 beds) 550 Fort Loudoun Medical Center Drive, Lenoir City, TN, Zip 37772-5673; tel. 865/271-6000, Connie Martin, President and Chief Administrative Officer
Web address: www.covenanthealth.com

FORT SANDERS REGIONAL MEDICAL CENTER (O, 365 beds) 1901 West Clinch Avenue, Knoxville, TN, Zip 37916-2307; tel. 865/541-1111, Keith Altshuler, President and Chief Administrative Officer

LECONTE MEDICAL CENTER (O, 79 beds) 742 Middle Creek Road, Sevierville, TN, Zip 37862-5019, P O Box 8005, Zip 37864-8005, tel. 865/446-7000, Aaron Burns, President and Chief Executive Officer
Web address: www.lecontemedicalcenter.com

METHODIST MEDICAL CENTER OF OAK RIDGE (O, 176 beds) 990 Oak Ridge Turnpike, Oak Ridge, TN, Zip 37830-6976, P O Box 2529, Zip 37831-2529, tel. 865/835-1000, Jeremy Biggs, President and Chief Administrative Officer

MORRISTOWN-HAMBLEN HEALTHCARE SYSTEM (O, 121 beds) 908 West Fourth North Street, Morristown, TN, Zip 37814-3894, P O Box 1178, Zip 37816-1178, tel. 423/492-9000, Gordon Lintz, President and Chief Administrative Officer
Web address: www.morristownhamblen.com

PARKWEST MEDICAL CENTER (O, 412 beds) 9352 Park West Boulevard, Knoxville, TN, Zip 37923-4325, P O Box 22993, Zip 37933-0993, tel. 865/373-1000, James VanderSteeg, Acting Chief Executive Officer

ROANE MEDICAL CENTER (O, 52 beds) 8045 Roane Medical Center Drive, Harriman, TN, Zip 37748-8333; tel. 865/316-1000, Jason B. Pilant, President and Chief Administrative Officer
Web address: www.roanemedical.com

Owned, leased, sponsored:	9 hospitals	1430 beds
Contract-managed:	0 hospitals	0 beds
Totals:	9 hospitals	1430 beds

★5885: COVENANT HEALTH (CC)
100 Ames Pond Drive, Suite 102, Tewksbury, MA Zip 01876-1240; tel. 978/654-6363, Stephen J. Grubbs, President and Chief Executive Officer
(Independent Hospital System)

MAINE: ST. JOSEPH HOSPITAL (O, 78 beds) 360 Broadway, Bangor, ME, Zip 04401-3979, P O Box 403, Zip 04402-0403, tel. 207/262-1000, Mary Prybylo, R.N., MSN, FACHE, President

ST. MARY'S REGIONAL MEDICAL CENTER (O, 350 beds) 93 Campus Avenue, Lewiston, ME, Zip 04240-6030, P O Box 291, Zip 04243-0291, tel. 207/777-8100, Cindy Segar-Miller, FACHE, R.N., President
Web address: www.stmarysmaine.com

NEW HAMPSHIRE: ST. JOSEPH HOSPITAL (O, 159 beds) 172 Kinsley Street, Nashua, NH, Zip 03060-3648; tel. 603/882-3000, John Albert. Jurczyk, FACHE, President
Web address: www.stjosephhospital.com

Owned, leased, sponsored:	3 hospitals	587 beds
Contract-managed:	0 hospitals	0 beds
Totals:	3 hospitals	587 beds

★0036: COVENANT HEALTH SYSTEM (NP)
3615 19th Street, Lubbock, TX Zip 79410-1203; tel. 806/725-0447, Walter L. Cathey, Regional Chief Executive Officer

Owned, leased, sponsored:	0 hospitals	0 beds
Contract-managed:	0 hospitals	0 beds
Totals:	0 hospitals	0 beds

0179: COXHEALTH (NP)
1423 North Jefferson Avenue, Springfield, MO Zip 65802-1988; tel. 417/269-3108, Max Buetow, President and Chief Executive Officer
(Centralized Physician/Insurance Health System)

MISSOURI: COX BARTON COUNTY MEMORIAL HOSPITAL (O, 25 beds) 29 NW First Lane, Lamar, MO, Zip 64759-8105; tel. 417/681-5100, Andrea McKay, President
Web address: www.bcmh.net

COX MEDICAL CENTER BRANSON (O, 106 beds) 525 Branson Landing Boulevard, Branson, MO, Zip 65616-2052, P O Box 650, Zip 65615-0650, tel. 417/335-7000, William K. Mahoney, FACHE, President and Senior Vice President, Community Hospital Group

COX MONETT HOSPITAL, INC (O, 25 beds) 1000 East US Highway 60, Monett, MO, Zip 65708-8258; tel. 417/235-3144, Andrea McKay, President
Web address: www.coxhealth.com

COX NORTH HOSPITAL (O, 734 beds) 1423 North Jefferson Street, Springfield, MO, Zip 65802-1988; tel. 417/269-3000, Ashley Kimberling-Casad, President of Springfield Hospitals
Web address: www.coxhealth.com

Owned, leased, sponsored:	4 hospitals	890 beds
Contract-managed:	0 hospitals	0 beds
Totals:	4 hospitals	890 beds

0960: CURAE HEALTH (NP)
121 Leinart Street, Clinton, TN Zip 37716-3632, P O Box 358, Zip 37717-0358, tel. 865/269-4074, Steve Clapp, President and Chief Executive Officer
(Moderately Centralized Health System)

ALABAMA: NORTHWEST MEDICAL CENTER (O, 56 beds) 1530 U S Highway 43, Winfield, AL, Zip 35594-5056; tel. 205/487-7000, Cathy Mitchell, Chief Eecutive Officer
Web address: www.https://northwestmedcenter.net/

RUSSELLVILLE HOSPITAL (O, 92 beds) 15155 Highway 43, Russellville, AL, Zip 35653-1975, P O Box 1089, Zip 35653-1089, tel. 256/332-1611, Chris Ware, Chief Executive Officer

Owned, leased, sponsored:	2 hospitals	148 beds
Contract-managed:	0 hospitals	0 beds
Totals:	2 hospitals	148 beds

★0090: DARTMOUTH HEALTH (NP)
1 Medical Center Drive, Lebanon, NH Zip 03756-1000, One Medical Center Drive, Zip 03756-1000, tel. 603/650-5000, Joanne M. Conroy, M.D., Chief Executive Officer and President

NEW HAMPSHIRE: ALICE PECK DAY MEMORIAL HOSPITAL (O, 23 beds) 10 Alice Peck Day Drive, Lebanon, NH, Zip 03766-2650; tel. 603/448-3121, Susan E. Mooney, M.D., MS, President and Chief Executive Officer

CHESHIRE MEDICAL CENTER (O, 94 beds) 580 Court Street, Keene, NH, Zip 03431-1718; tel. 603/354-5400, Joseph L. Perras, M.D., President and Chief Executive Officer
Web address: https://www.cheshiremed.org/

For explanation of codes following names, see page B2.
★ Indicates Type III membership in the American Hospital Association.

Systems / Dartmouth Health

DARTMOUTH–HITCHCOCK MEDICAL CENTER (O, 438 beds) 1 Medical Center Drive, Lebanon, NH, Zip 03756–1000; tel. 603/650–5000, Joanne M. Conroy, M.D., Chief Executive Officer and President
NEW LONDON HOSPITAL (O, 25 beds) 273 County Road, New London, NH, Zip 03257–5736; tel. 603/526–2911, Lauren Geddes Wirth, Interim President and Chief Executive Officer
Web address: www.newlondonhospital.org

VERMONT: MT. ASCUTNEY HOSPITAL AND HEALTH CENTER (O, 35 beds) 289 County Road, Windsor, VT, Zip 05089–9000; tel. 802/674–6711
Web address: www.mtascutneyhospital.org
SOUTHWESTERN VERMONT MEDICAL CENTER (O, 56 beds) 100 Hospital Drive, Bennington, VT, Zip 05201–5004; tel. 802/442–6361, Thomas A. Dee, President and Chief Executive Officer

Owned, leased, sponsored:	6 hospitals	671 beds
Contract-managed:	0 hospitals	0 beds
Totals:	6 hospitals	671 beds

★**0864: DAVIS HEALTH SYSTEM (NP)**
812 Gorman Avenue, Elkins, WV Zip 26241, P O Box 1697, Zip 26241–1697, tel. 304/636–3300, Mark Doak, Interim President
(Independent Hospital System)

Owned, leased, sponsored:	0 hospitals	0 beds
Contract-managed:	0 hospitals	0 beds
Totals:	0 hospitals	0 beds

1825: DCH HEALTH SYSTEM (NP)
809 University Boulevard East, Tuscaloosa, AL Zip 35401–2029; tel. 205/759–7111, Katrina Keefer, Chief Executive Officer
(Independent Hospital System)

ALABAMA: DCH REGIONAL MEDICAL CENTER (O, 577 beds) 809 University Boulevard East, Tuscaloosa, AL, Zip 35401–2029; tel. 205/759–7111, Luke Standeffer, Chief Executive Officer
Web address: https://www.dchsystem.com/locations/dch-regional-medical-center/
FAYETTE MEDICAL CENTER (L, 167 beds) 1653 Temple Avenue North, Fayette, AL, Zip 35555–1314, P O Drawer 710, Zip 35555–0710, tel. 205/932–5966, Donald J. Jones, FACHE, Administrator

Owned, leased, sponsored:	2 hospitals	744 beds
Contract-managed:	0 hospitals	0 beds
Totals:	2 hospitals	744 beds

★**0313: DEACONESS HEALTH SYSTEM (NP)**
600 Mary Street, Evansville, IN Zip 47710–1658; tel. 812/450–5000, Shawn W. McCoy, Chief Executive Officer
(Moderately Centralized Health System)

INDIANA: DEACONESS GIBSON HOSPITAL (O, 25 beds) 1808 Sherman Drive, Princeton, IN, Zip 47670–9931; tel. 812/385–3401, Lois Morgan, R.N., MSN, Chief Administrative Officer, Chief Nursing Officer
Web address: https://www.deaconess.com/Deaconess-Gibson-Hospital
DEACONESS MIDTOWN HOSPITAL (O, 654 beds) 600 Mary Street, Evansville, IN, Zip 47710–1658; tel. 812/450–5000, Shawn W. McCoy, Chief Executive Officer
THE WOMEN'S HOSPITAL (O, 74 beds) 4199 Gateway Boulevard, Newburgh, IN, Zip 47630–8940; tel. 812/842–4200, Christina M. Ryan, R.N., Chief Executive Officer
Web address: www.deaconess.com

KENTUCKY: DEACONESS HENDERSON HOSPITAL (O, 123 beds) 1305 North Elm Street, Henderson, KY, Zip 42420–2775, P O Box 48, Zip 42419–0048, tel. 270/827–7700, Linda E. White, Chief Administrative Officer
Web address: https://www.deaconess.com/Deaconess-Henderson-Hospital

DEACONESS UNION COUNTY HOSPITAL (O, 25 beds) 4604 Highway 60 West, Morganfield, KY, Zip 42437–9570; tel. 270/389–5000, Amber Powell, Chief Administrative Officer
Web address: https://www.deaconess.com/Deaconess-Union-County-Hospital

Owned, leased, sponsored:	5 hospitals	901 beds
Contract-managed:	0 hospitals	0 beds
Totals:	5 hospitals	901 beds

1092: DELTA HEALTH SYSTEM (NP)
1400 East Union Street, Greenville, MS Zip 38703–3246; tel. 662/378–3783, Iris Stacker, Chief Executive Officer

MISSISSIPPI: DELTA HEALTH–NORTHWEST REGIONAL (L, 181 beds) 1970 Hospital Drive, Clarksdale, MS, Zip 38614–7202, P O Box 1218, Zip 38614–1218, tel. 662/627–3211, Janet Benzing, Chief Administrative Officer
Web address: www.northwestmsmedicalcenter.org
DELTA HEALTH–THE MEDICAL CENTER (O, 171 beds) 1400 East Union Street, Greenville, MS, Zip 38704–5247; tel. 662/378–3783, Iris Stacker, Chief Executive Officer

Owned, leased, sponsored:	2 hospitals	352 beds
Contract-managed:	0 hospitals	0 beds
Totals:	2 hospitals	352 beds

★**0957: DEPARTMENT OF DEFENSE, HEALTH AFFAIRS (FG)**
1200 Defense Pentagon, Pentagon 3E1070, Washington, DC Zip 20301; tel. 703/697–2111, Seileen Mullen, Acting Assistant Secretary of Defense for Health Affairs

Owned, leased, sponsored:	0 hospitals	0 beds
Contract-managed:	0 hospitals	0 beds
Totals:	0 hospitals	0 beds

★**9495: DEPARTMENT OF THE AIR FORCE (FG)**
1780 Air Force Pentagon, Room 4E114, Washington, DC Zip 20330–1420; tel. 703/692–6800, Lieutenant General, Robert I. Miller, M.D., Surgeon General
(Independent Hospital System)

ALASKA: U. S. AIR FORCE REGIONAL HOSPITAL (O, 64 beds) 5955 Zeamer Avenue, Elmendorf AFB, AK, Zip 99506–3702; tel. 907/580–2778, Major, Mark Lamey, Commander
Web address: www.https://elmendorfrichardson.tricare.mil/

CALIFORNIA: DAVID GRANT USAF MEDICAL CENTER (O, 116 beds) 101 Bodin Circle, Building 777, Travis Air Force Base, CA, Zip 94535–1809; tel. 707/423–7300, Colonel, Kristin Beals, Commander

FLORIDA: U. S. AIR FORCE REGIONAL HOSPITAL (O, 57 beds) 307 Boatner Road, Suite 114, Eglin AFB, FL, Zip 32542–1282; tel. 850/883–8221, Colonel, Gregory Coleman, Commanding Officer
Web address: www.https://eglin.tricare.mil/

MISSISSIPPI: U. S. AIR FORCE MEDICAL CENTER KEESLER (O, 56 beds) 301 Fisher Street, Room 1A132, Keesler AFB, MS, Zip 39534–2519; tel. 228/376–2550, Christopher J. Estridge, Commander
Web address: www.https://keesler.tricare.mil/

NEVADA: MIKE O'CALLAGHAN FEDERAL HOSPITAL (O, 46 beds) 4700 Las Vegas Boulevard North, Suite 2419, Nellis AFB, NV, Zip 89191–6600; tel. 702/653–2000, Colonel, Brent Johnson, Commander

OHIO: WRIGHT PATTERSON MEDICAL CENTER (O, 62 beds) 4881 Sugar Maple Drive, Wright–Patterson AFB, OH, Zip 45433–5529; tel. 937/257–0837, Colonel, Dale E. Harrell, Commander, 88th Medical Group, Wright–Patterson AFB
Web address: www.wpafb.af.mil/units/wpmc/

For explanation of codes following names, see page B2.
★ Indicates Type III membership in the American Hospital Association.

Systems / Department of Veterans Affairs

VIRGINIA: U. S. AIR FORCE HOSPITAL (O, 60 beds) 77 Nealy Avenue, Hampton, VA, Zip 23665-2040; tel. 757/764-6969, Colonel, Gregory Beaulieu, Commander

Owned, leased, sponsored:	7 hospitals	461 beds
Contract-managed:	0 hospitals	0 beds
Totals:	7 hospitals	461 beds

★**9395: DEPARTMENT OF THE ARMY, OFFICE OF THE SURGEON GENERAL (FG)**
7700 Arlington Boulevard Suite 4SW112, Falls Church, VA Zip 22042-2929; tel. 703/681-3000, Lieutenant General, Mary K. Izaguirre, M.D., Surgeon General of the Army
(Moderately Centralized Health System)

ALASKA: BASSETT ARMY COMMUNITY HOSPITAL (O, 21 beds) 1060 Gaffney Road, Box 7400, Fort Wainwright, AK, Zip 99703-5001, 1060 Gaffney Road, Box 7440, Zip 99703-5001, tel. 907/361-4000, Colonel, Eli Lozano, Commander
Web address: www.https://bassett-wainwright.tricare.mil/

CALIFORNIA: WEED ARMY COMMUNITY HOSPITAL (O, 27 beds) 390 North Loop Road, Fort Irwin, CA, Zip 92310, P O Box 105109, Zip 92310-5109, tel. 760/383-5155, Colonel, F Cameron. Jackson, Hospital Commander

COLORADO: EVANS U. S. ARMY COMMUNITY HOSPITAL (O, 68 beds) 1650 Cochrane Circle, Building 7500, Fort Carson, CO, Zip 80913-4613; tel. 719/526-7200, Colonel, Kevin R. Bass, Commander
Web address: www.https://evans.tricare.mil/

GEORGIA: BENNING MARTIN ARMY COMMUNITY HOSPITAL (O, 57 beds) 6600 Van Aalst Boulevard, Fort Benning, GA, Zip 31905-2102; tel. 706/544-2516, Colonel, Kevin M. Kelly, Commander
Web address: www.https://martin.tricare.mil/

DWIGHT DAVID EISENHOWER ARMY MEDICAL CENTER (O, 107 beds) 300 West Hospital Road, Fort Gordon, GA, Zip 30905-5741; tel. 706/787-5811, Colonel, James G. Pairmore, Commander

WINN ARMY COMMUNITY HOSPITAL (O, 37 beds) 1061 Harmon Avenue, Hinesville, GA, Zip 31314-5641, 1061 Harmon Avenue, Suite 2311B, Zip 31314-5641, tel. 912/435-6965, Colonel, Julie Freeman, Commander
Web address: www.https://winn.tricare.mil/

HAWAII: TRIPLER ARMY MEDICAL CENTER (O, 143 beds) 1 Jarrett White Road, Honolulu, HI, Zip 96859-5001; tel. 808/433-6661, Colonel, Michael Ronn, Hospital Commander
Web address: www.https://tripler.tricare.mil/

KAwvNSAS: IRWIN ARMY COMMUNITY HOSPITAL (O, 44 beds) 600 Caisson Hill Road, Junction City, KS, Zip 66442-7037; tel. 785/239-7000, Colonel, Edgar Arroyo, Hospital Commander
Web address: www.https://irwin.tricare.mil

KENTUCKY: COLONEL FLORENCE A. BLANCHFIELD ARMY COMMUNITY HOSPITAL (O, 66 beds) 650 Joel Drive, Fort Campbell, KY, Zip 42223-5318; tel. 270/798-8400, Colonel, Samuel L. Preston, Commander

LOUISIANA: BAYNE-JONES ARMY COMMUNITY HOSPITAL (O, 13 beds) 1585 3rd Street, Building 283, Fort Polk, LA, Zip 71459-5102; tel. 337/531-3928, Colonel, Aristotle A. Vaseliades, FACHE, Commanding Officer
Web address: www.https://bayne-jones.tricare.mil/

MARSHALL ISLANDS: KWAJALEIN HOSPITAL (O, 14 beds) U S Army Kwajalein Atoll, Ocean Road, Kwajalein Atoll, MH, Zip 96555, Ocean Road, P.O. Box 1607, APO AP, Zip 96555-5000, tel. 805/355-2225, Elaine McMahon, Administrator

MISSOURI: GENERAL LEONARD WOOD ARMY COMMUNITY HOSPITAL (O, 46 beds) 4430 Missouri Avenue, Fort Leonard Wood, MO, Zip 65473-8952, PO Box 4430, Zip 65473-8952, tel. 573/596-0414, Colonel, Stacey S. Amos, Hospital Commander/Ozark Market Director
Web address: www.glwach.amedd.army.mil/

NEW YORK: KELLER ARMY COMMUNITY HOSPITAL (O, 12 beds) 900 Washington Road, West Point, NY, Zip 10996-1197, U S Military Academy, Building 900, Zip 10996-1197, tel. 845/938-5169, Colonel, Amy L. Jackson, Commander

NORTH CAROLINA: WOMACK ARMY MEDICAL CENTER (O, 156 beds) 2817 Reilly Road, Fort Bragg, NC, Zip 28310-7302; tel. 910/907-6000, Colonel, David R. Zinnante, Commander
Web address: www.https://womack.tricare.mil/

SOUTH CAROLINA: MONCRIEF ARMY COMMUNITY HOSPITAL (O, 60 beds) 4500 Stuart Street, Fort Jackson, SC, Zip 29207-5700; tel. 803/751-2160, Colonel, Tara Hall, Commander
Web address: www.https://moncrief.tricare.mil/

TEXAS: BROOKE ARMY MEDICAL CENTER (O, 483 beds) 3551 Roger Brooke Drive, Fort Sam Houston, TX, Zip 78234-4501; tel. 210/916-4141, Colonel, Mark Stackle, Commanding Officer and Chief Executive Officer

CARL R. DARNALL ARMY MEDICAL CENTER (O, 109 beds) 36065 Santa Fe Avenue, Fort Hood, TX, Zip 76544-5060; tel. 254/288-8000, Colonel, Daniel J. Moore, CRDAMC Commander
Web address: https://www.crdamc.amedd.army.mil/Default.aspx

WILLIAM BEAUMONT ARMY MEDICAL CENTER (O, 209 beds) 18511 Highlander Medics Street, El Paso, TX, Zip 79918; tel. 915/742-7777, Colonel, Brett H. Venable, FACHE, Commander

VIRGINIA: FORT BELVOIR COMMUNITY HOSPITAL (O, 46 beds) 9300 Dewitt Loop, Fort Belvoir, VA, Zip 22060-5285; tel. 571/231-3224, Colonel, Kathy Spangler, Director
Web address: www.https://belvoirhospital.tricare.mil/

WASHINGTON: MADIGAN ARMY MEDICAL CENTER (O, 203 beds) 9040 Jackson Avenue, Tacoma, WA, Zip 98431-1100; tel. 253/968-1110, Colonel, Hope M. Williamson-Younce, Commander
Web address: www.https://madigan.tricare.mil/

Owned, leased, sponsored:	20 hospitals	1921 beds
Contract-managed:	0 hospitals	0 beds
Totals:	20 hospitals	1921 beds

★**9295: DEPARTMENT OF VETERANS AFFAIRS (FG)**
810 Vermont Ave Northwest, Washington, DC Zip 20420-0001; tel. 202/273-5781, Honorable, Robert Wilkie, Secretary
(Decentralized Health System)

ALABAMA: BIRMINGHAM VA MEDICAL CENTER (O, 141 beds) 700 South 19th Street, Birmingham, AL, Zip 35233-1927; tel. 205/933-8101, Oladipo A. Kukoyi, M.D., Executive Director, Chief Executive Officer

CENTRAL ALABAMA VA MEDICAL CENTER-MONTGOMERY (O, 258 beds) 215 Perry Hill Road, Montgomery, AL, Zip 36109-3798; tel. 334/272-4670, Valerie Russell, Interim Medical Center Director
Web address: www.centralalabama.va.gov/

TUSCALOOSA VA MEDICAL CENTER (O, 335 beds) 3701 Loop Road East, Tuscaloosa, AL, Zip 35404-5015; tel. 205/554-2000, John F. Merkle, Medical Center Director
Web address: www.tuscaloosa.va.gov

ARIZONA: BOB STUMP DEPARTMENT OF VETERANS AFFAIRS MEDICAL CENTER (O, 220 beds) 500 Highway 89 North, Prescott, AZ, Zip 86313-5000; tel. 928/445-4860, Steven Sample, Medical Center Director

CARL T. HAYDEN VETERANS' ADMINISTRATION MEDICAL CENTER (O, 175 beds) 650 East Indian School Road, Phoenix, AZ, Zip 85012-1892; tel. 602/277-5551, Bryan C. Matthews, Medical Center Director
Web address: www.phoenix.va.gov/

TUCSON VA MEDICAL CENTER (O, 328 beds) 3601 Sout 6th Avenue, Tucson, AZ, Zip 85723-0002, 3601 South 6th Avenue, Zip 85723-0002, tel. 520/792-1450, Jennifer S. Gutowski, FACHE, Director
Web address: www.tucson.va.gov

ARKANSAS: JOHN L. MCCLELLAN MEMORIAL VETERANS' HOSPITAL (O, 505 beds) 4300 West Seventh Street, Little Rock, AR, Zip 72205-5446; tel. 501/257-1000, Margie A. Scott, M.D., Medical Center Director

VETERANS HEALTH CARE SYSTEM OF THE OZARKS (O, 81 beds) 1100 North College Avenue, Fayetteville, AR, Zip 72703-1944; tel. 479/443-4301, George Velez, FACHE, Medical Center Director
Web address: www.fayettevillear.va.gov

CALIFORNIA: GREATER LOS ANGELES HCS (O, 422 beds) 11301 Wilshire Boulevard, Los Angeles, CA, Zip 90073-1003; tel. 310/478-3711, Robert

For explanation of codes following names, see page B2.
★ Indicates Type III membership in the American Hospital Association.

Systems / Department of Veterans Affairs

Merchant, Interim Medical Center Director & Executive Director, Ambulatory Care Services
Web address: https://www.va.gov/greater-los-angeles-health-care/

JENNIFER MORENO DEPARTMENT OF VETERANS AFFAIRS MEDICAL CENTER (O, 257 beds) 3350 LaJolla Village Drive, San Diego, CA, Zip 92161-0002; tel. 858/552-8585, Frank P. Pearson, Director
Web address: www.sandiego.va.gov

JERRY L. PETTIS MEMORIAL VETERANS' HOSPITAL (O, 263 beds) 11201 Benton Street, Loma Linda, CA, Zip 92357-1000; tel. 909/825-7084, Karandeep Sraon, FACHE, Medical Center Director

SAN FRANCISCO VA HEALTH CARE SYSTEM (O, 232 beds) 4150 Clement Street, San Francisco, CA, Zip 94121-1545; tel. 415/221-4810, Jia F. Li, FACHE, Health Care System Director
Web address: www.sanfrancisco.va.gov/

TIBOR RUBIN VA MEDICAL CENTER (O, 276 beds) 5901 East 7th Street, Long Beach, CA, Zip 90822-5201; tel. 562/826-8000, Walt C. Dannenberg, FACHE, Medical Center Director

VA CENTRAL CALIFORNIA HEALTH CARE SYSTEM (O, 133 beds) 2615 East Clinton Avenue, Fresno, CA, Zip 93703-2223; tel. 559/225-6100, Maisha Moore, R.N., Interim Medical Center Director
Web address: www.fresno.va.gov/

VA PALO ALTO HEATH CARE SYSTEM (O, 768 beds) 3801 Miranda Avenue, Palo Alto, CA, Zip 94304-1207, 3801 Miranda Avenue Bldg 6, Zip 94304-1207, tel. 650/493-5000, Jean J. Gurga, Executive Medical Center Director, VA Palo Alto Health Care System

COLORADO: GRAND JUNCTION VA MEDICAL CENTER (O, 20 beds) 2121 North Avenue, Grand Junction, CO, Zip 81501-6428; tel. 970/242-0731, Richard W. Salgueiro, Medical Center Director
Web address: www.grandjunction.va.gov/

ROCKY MOUNTAIN REGIONAL VA MEDICAL CENTER (O, 271 beds) 1700 North Wheeling Street, Aurora, CO, Zip 80045; tel. 303/399-8020, Michael Moore, Interim DirectorSOUTHERN COLORADO HEALTHCARE SYSTEM (O, 299 beds)Las AnimasCO81054-0390719456-1260StuartCCollyer5139873Director

CONNECTICUT: CONNECTICUT VETERANS HOME AND HOSPITAL (O, 125 beds) 287 West Street, Rocky Hill, CT, Zip 06067-3501; tel. 860/616-3606, Thomas J. Saadi, Commissioner
Web address: www.ct.gov/ctva

VETERANS AFFAIRS CONNECTICUT HEALTHCARE SYSTEM (O, 177 beds) 950 Campbell Avenue, West Haven, CT, Zip 06516-2770; tel. 203/932-5711, Becky Rhoads, Executive Director

DELAWARE: WILMINGTON VETERANS AFFAIRS MEDICAL CENTER (O, 60 beds) 1601 Kirkwood Highway, Wilmington, DE, Zip 19805-4989; tel. 302/994-2511, Vamsee Potluri, Director
Web address: www.va.gov/wilmington

DISTRICT OF COLUMBIA: WASHINGTON DC VETERANS AFFAIRS MEDICAL CENTER (O, 291 beds) 50 Irving Street NW, Washington, DC, Zip 20422-0002; tel. 202/745-8000, Colonel, Michael S. Heimall, Medical Center Director
Web address: www.washingtondc.va.gov/

FLORIDA: BAY PINES VETERANS AFFAIRS HEALTHCARE SYSTEM (O, 168 beds) 10000 Bay Pines Boulevard, Bay Pines, FL, Zip 33744-8200, P O Box 5005, Zip 33744-5005, tel. 727/398-6661, Paul M. Russo, FACHE, Director
Web address: www.baypines.va.gov/

JAMES A. HALEY VETERANS' HOSPITAL-TAMPA (O, 493 beds) 13000 Bruce B Downs Boulevard Tampa, FL, Zip 33612-4745; tel. 813/972-2000, David K. Dunning, Medical Center Director
Web address: www.tampa.va.gov/

MIAMI VETERANS AFFAIRS HEALTHCARE SYSTEM (O, 262 beds) 1201 NW 16th Street, Miami, FL, Zip 33125-1624; tel. 305/575-7000, Kalautie JangDhari, Medical Center Director

NORTH FLORIDA/SOUTH GEORGIA VETERAN'S HEALTH SYSTEM (O, 545 beds) 1601 SW Archer Road, Gainesville, FL, Zip 32608-1135; tel. 352/376-1611, Wende Dottor, Medical Center Director
Web address: www.northflorida.va.gov

WEST PALM BEACH VETERANS AFFAIRS MEDICAL CENTER (O, 260 beds) 7305 North Military Trail, West Palm Beach, FL, Zip 33410-6400; tel. 561/422-8262, Cory P. Price, FACHE, Medical Center Director and Chief Executive Officer

GEORGIA: ATLANTA VETERANS AFFAIRS MEDICAL CENTER (O, 285 beds) 1670 Clairmont Road, Decatur, GA, Zip 30033-4004; tel. 404/321-6111, Annette Walker, Medical Center Director
Web address: www.atlanta.va.gov/

CARL VINSON VETERANS AFFAIRS MEDICAL CENTER (O, 21 beds) 1826 Veterans Boulevard, Dublin, GA, Zip 31021-3620, 1326 Veterans Boulevard, Zip 31021-3620, tel. 478/272-1210, David Reesman, Acting Director
Web address: www.dublin.va.gov/

CHARLIE NORWOOD VETERANS AFFAIRS MEDICAL CENTER (O, 133 beds) 1 Freedom Way, Augusta, GA, Zip 30904-6285; tel. 706/733-0188, Robin E. Jackson, Ph.D., Chief Executive Officer

IDAHO: BOISE VA MEDICAL CENTER (O, 92 beds) 500 West Fort Street, Boise, ID, Zip 83702-4598; tel. 208/422-1000, David P. Wood, FACHE, Medical Center Director
Web address: www.boise.va.gov/

ILLINOIS: CAPTAIN JAMES A. LOVELL FEDERAL HEALTH CARE CENTER (O, 97 beds) 3001 Green Bay Road, North Chicago, IL, Zip 60064-3049; tel. 847/688-1900, Robert G. Buckley, M.D., Medical Center Director
Web address: www.lovell.fhcc.va.gov

EDWARD HINES, JR. VETERANS AFFAIRS HOSPITAL (O, 157 beds) 5000 South Fifth Avenue, Hines, IL, Zip 60141-3030, P O Box 5000, Zip 60141-5000, tel. 708/202-8387, James Doelling, Hospital Director
Web address: www.hines.va.gov/

JESSE BROWN VA MEDICAL CENTER (O, 181 beds) 820 South Damen, Chicago, IL, Zip 60612-3776; tel. 312/569-8387, Clifford A. Smith, Ph.D., Acting Medical Center Director

MARION VETERANS AFFAIRS MEDICAL CENTER (O, 63 beds) 2401 West Main Street, Marion, IL, Zip 62959-1188; tel. 618/997-5311, Zachary Sage, Director
Web address: www.marion.va.gov

VETERANS AFFAIRS ILLIANA HEALTH CARE SYSTEM (O, 172 beds) 1900 East Main Street, Danville, IL, Zip 61832-5198; tel. 217/554-3000, Staci Williams, PharmD, Medical Center Director

INDIANA: RICHARD L. ROUDEBUSH VETERANS AFFAIRS MEDICAL CENTER (O, 159 beds) 1481 West Tenth Street, Indianapolis, IN, Zip 46202-2884; tel. 317/554-0000, Michael E. Hershman, Director
Web address: www.indianapolis.va.gov

VETERANS AFFAIRS NORTHERN INDIANA HEALTH CARE SYSTEM (O, 175 beds) 2121 Lake Avenue, Fort Wayne, IN, Zip 46805-5100; tel. 260/426-5431, Anthony Colon, Director

IOWA: IOWA CITY VA HEALTH SYSTEM (O, 66 beds) 601 Highway 6 West, Iowa City, IA, Zip 52246-2208; tel. 319/338-0581, Judith Johnson-Mekota, FACHE, Director
Web address: www.iowacity.va.gov/

VA CENTRAL IOWA HEALTH CARE SYSTEM-DES MOINES (O, 141 beds) 3600 30th Street, Des Moines, IA, Zip 50310-5753; tel. 515/699-5999, Lisa Curnes, R.N., Medical Center Director/Chief Executive Officer

KANSAS: EASTERN KANSAS HCS (O, 125 beds) 2200 South West Gage Boulevard, Topeka, KS, Zip 66622-0002, LVN-4101 4th Street Trafficway, Leavenworth, Zip 66048, tel. 785/350-3111, Anthony Rudy. Klopfer, FACHE, Director
Web address: www.topeka.va.gov/

ROBERT J. DOLE DEPARTMENT OF VETERANS AFFAIRS MEDICAL AND REGIONAL OFFICE CENTER (O, 61 beds) 5500 East Kellogg, Wichita, KS, Zip 67218-1607; tel. 316/685-2221, Michael D. Payne, Medical Center Director

KENTUCKY: LEXINGTON VAMC (O, 159 beds) 1101 Veterans Drive, Lexington, KY, Zip 40502-2235; tel. 859/281-4901, Russell Armstead, Executive Director
Web address: www.lexington.va.gov/

ROBLEY REX DEPARTMENT OF VETERANS AFFAIRS MEDICAL CENTER (O, 119 beds) 800 Zorn Avenue, Louisville, KY, Zip 40206-1499; tel. 502/287-4000, Jo-Ann M. Ginsberg, R.N., MSN, Medical Center Executive Director
Web address: www.louisville.va.gov

LOUISIANA: ALEXANDRIA VA MEDICAL CENTER (O, 119 beds) 2495 Shreveport Highway, 71 N, Pineville, LA, Zip 71360-4044, P O Box 69004,

For explanation of codes following names, see page B2.
★ *Indicates Type III membership in the American Hospital Association.*

Alexandria, Zip 71306-9004, tel. 318/473-0010, Peter C. Dancy Jr, FACHE, Medical Center Director

OVERTON BROOKS VETERANS' ADMINISTRATION MEDICAL CENTER (O, 119 beds) 510 East Stoner Avenue, Shreveport, LA, Zip 71101-4295; tel. 318/221-8411, Richard Crockett, Director
Web address: www.shreveport.va.gov

MAINE: MAINE VETERANS AFFAIRS MEDICAL CENTER (O, 109 beds) 1 VA Center, Augusta, ME, Zip 04330-6719; tel. 207/623-8411, Tracye B. Davis, FACHE, Medical Center Director
Web address: www.maine.va.gov/

MARYLAND: VETERANS AFFAIRS MARYLAND HEALTH CARE SYSTEM–BALTIMORE DIVISION (O, 394 beds) 10 North Greene Street, Baltimore, MD, Zip 21201-1524; tel. 410/605-7001, Jonathan R. Eckman, Medical Center Director
Web address: www.maryland.va.gov/

MASSACHUSETTS: BEDFORD VETERANS AFFAIRS MEDICAL CENTER, EDITH NOURSE ROGERS MEMORIAL VETERANS HOSPITAL (O, 23 beds) 200 Springs Road, Bedford, MA, Zip 01730-1198, 200 Springs Road Bldg 3, Zip 01730-1198, tel. 781/687-2000, Joan Clifford, R.N., FACHE, Medical Center Director and Chief Executive Officer

VETERANS AFFAIRS BOSTON HEALTHCARE SYSTEM BROCKTON DIVISION (O, 375 beds) 940 Belmont Street, Brockton, MA, Zip 02301-5596; tel. 508/583-4500, Vincent Ng, Director
Web address: www.boston.va.gov/

VETERANS AFFAIRS BOSTON HEALTHCARE SYSTEM (O, 491 beds) 1400 VFW Parkway, West Roxbury, MA, Zip 02132-4927; tel. 617/323-7700, Vincent Ng, Medical Center Director

VETERANS AFFAIRS CENTRAL WESTERN MASSACHUSETTS HEALTHCARE SYSTEM (O, 52 beds) 421 North Main Street, Leeds, MA, Zip 01053-9764; tel. 413/582-3000, Jonathan Kerr, Acting Director
Web address: www.centralwesternmass.va.gov/

MICHIGAN: ALEDA E. LUTZ DEPARTMENT OF VETERANS AFFAIRS MEDICAL CENTER (O, 41 beds) 1500 Weiss Street, Saginaw, MI, Zip 48602-5298; tel. 989/497-2500, Roy Samsel, Medical Center Director
Web address: www.saginaw.va.gov/

BATTLE CREEK VETERANS AFFAIRS MEDICAL CENTER (O, 208 beds) 5500 Armstrong Road, Battle Creek, MI, Zip 49037-7314; tel. 269/966-5600, Michelle Martin, Executive Medical Center Director

JOHN D. DINGELL DEPARTMENT OF VETERANS AFFAIRS MEDICAL CENTER (O, 157 beds) 4646 John 'R' Street, Detroit, MI, Zip 48201-1932; tel. 313/576-1000, Chris Cauley, FACHE, Interim Medical Center Director
Web address: www.detroit.va.gov/

OSCAR G. JOHNSON DEPARTMENT OF VETERANS AFFAIRS MEDICAL FACILITY (O, 27 beds) 325 East 'H' Street, Iron Mountain, MI, Zip 49801-4792; tel. 906/774-3300, John P. Shealey, Medical Center Director
Web address: www.ironmountain.va.gov/

VETERANS AFFAIRS ANN ARBOR HEALTHCARE SYSTEM (O, 156 beds) 2215 Fuller Road, Ann Arbor, MI, Zip 48105-2399; tel. 734/769-7100, Ginny L. Creasman, Director

MINNESOTA: MINNEAPOLIS VA HEALTH CARE SYSTEM (O, 264 beds) 1 Veterans Drive, Minneapolis, MN, Zip 55417-2399, One Veterans Drive, Zip 55417-2399, tel. 612/725-2000, Patrick J. Kelly, FACHE, Director
Web address: www.minneapolis.va.gov

ST. CLOUD VA HEALTH CARE SYSTEM (O, 240 beds) 4801 Veterans Drive, Saint Cloud, MN, Zip 56303-2099; tel. 320/252-1670, Cheryl Thieschafer, Interim Health Care System Director
Web address: https://www.va.gov/st-cloud-health-care/about-us/

MISSISSIPPI: BILOXI VA MEDICAL CENTER (O, 83 beds) 400 Veterans Avenue, Biloxi, MS, Zip 39531-2410; tel. 228/523-5000, Stephanie Repasky, PsyD, Interim Medical Center Director

G.V. (SONNY) MONTGOMERY DEPARTMENT OF VETERANS AFFAIRS MEDICAL CENTER (O, 61 beds) 1500 East Woodrow Wilson Drive, Jackson, MS, Zip 39216-5199; tel. 601/362-4471, Kai Mentzer, Interim Director
Web address: www.jackson.va.gov/

MISSOURI: HARRY S. TRUMAN MEMORIAL VETERANS' HOSPITAL (O, 130 beds) 800 Hospital Drive, Columbia, MO, Zip 65201-5275; tel. 573/814-6000, Christopher Myhaver, FACHE, Medical Center Director
Web address: www.columbiamo.va.gov

JOHN J. PERSHING VETERANS' ADMINISTRATION MEDICAL CENTER (O, 58 beds) 1500 North Westwood Boulevard, Poplar Bluff, MO, Zip 63901-3318; tel. 573/686-4151, James Warren, Interim Medical Center Director
Web address: www.poplarbluff.va.gov

KANSAS CITY VA MEDICAL CENTER (O, 97 beds) 4801 East Linwood Boulevard, Kansas City, MO, Zip 64128-2226; tel. 816/861-4700, Paul Hopkins, Director

VA ST. LOUIS HEALTH CARE SYSTEM (O, 240 beds) 915 North Grand Boulevard, Saint Louis, MO, Zip 63106-1621, 1 Jefferson Barracks Dr BLDG 57, Zip 63125, tel. 314/652-4100, Candace Ifabiyi, FACHE, Medical Center Director
Web address: www.stlouis.va.gov/

MONTANA: FORT HARRISON VA MEDICAL CENTER (O, 69 beds) 3687 Veterans Drive, Fort Harrison, MT, Zip 59636-9703, P O Box 1500, Zip 59636-1500, tel. 406/442-6410, Duane B. Gill, Acting Director

NEBRASKA: OMAHA VA MEDICAL CENTER (O, 104 beds) 4101 Woolworth Avenue, Omaha, NE, Zip 68105-1873; tel. 402/346-8800, Eileen M. Kingston, R.N., Acting Director, Chief Executive Officer
Web address: www.nebraska.va.gov/

VETERANS AFFAIRS NEBRASKA–WESTERN IOWA HEALTH CARE SYSTEM–LINCOLN (O, 132 beds) 600 South 70th Street, Lincoln, NE, Zip 68510-2493; tel. 402/489-3802, Eileen M. Kingston, R.N., Acting Director, Chief Executive Officer

NEVADA: IOANNIS A. LOUGARIS VETERANS' ADMINISTRATION MEDICAL CENTER (O, 130 beds) 975 Kirman Avenue, Reno, NV, Zip 89502-0993; tel. 775/786-7200, Thomas Talamante, Medical Center Director
Web address: www.reno.va.gov/

NORTH LAS VEGAS VA MEDICAL CENTER (O, 222 beds) 6900 North Pecos Road, North Las Vegas, NV, Zip 89086-4400; tel. 702/791-9000, William J. Caron, Medical Center Director

NEW HAMPSHIRE: MANCHESTER VETERANS AFFAIRS MEDICAL CENTER (O, 44 beds) 718 Smyth Road, Manchester, NH, Zip 03104-4098; tel. 603/624-4366, Major, Kevin Forrest, FACHE, Medical Center Director
Web address: www.manchester.va.gov

NEW JERSEY: VETERANS AFFAIRS NEW JERSEY HEALTH CARE SYSTEM (O, 343 beds) 385 Tremont Avenue, East Orange, NJ, Zip 07018-1095; tel. 973/676-1000, Patricia O'Kane, Associate Director
Web address: www.newjersey.va.gov/

NEW MEXICO: RAYMOND G. MURPHY DEPARTMENT OF VETERANS AFFAIRS MEDICAL CENTER (O, 175 beds) 1501 San Pedro SE, Albuquerque, NM, Zip 87108-5153; tel. 505/265-1711, Robert W. McKenrick, Medical Center Director

NEW YORK: ALBANY STRATTON VETERANS AFFAIRS MEDICAL CENTER (O, 110 beds) 113 Holland Avenue, Albany, NY, Zip 12208-3473; tel. 518/626-5000, Darlene DeLancey, Director
Web address: www.albany.va.gov/

BATH VETERANS AFFAIRS MEDICAL CENTER (O, 127 beds) 76 Veterans Avenue, Bath, NY, Zip 14810-0842; tel. 607/664-4000, Bruce Tucker, Medical Center Director
Web address: www.bath.va.gov

JAMES J. PETERS VETERANS AFFAIRS MEDICAL CENTER (O, 311 beds) 130 West Kingsbridge Road, Bronx, NY, Zip 10468-3904; tel. 718/584-9000, Balavenkatesh Kanna, M.D., M.P.H., FACHE, Medical Center Director
Web address: www.bronx.va.gov/

NORTHPORT VETERANS AFFAIRS MEDICAL CENTER (O, 213 beds) 79 Middleville Road, Northport, NY, Zip 11768-2200; tel. 631/261-4400, Antonio Sanchez, M.D., Executive Director
Web address: www.northport.va.gov/index.asp

SYRACUSE VETERANS AFFAIRS MEDICAL CENTER (O, 103 beds) 800 Irving Avenue, Syracuse, NY, Zip 13210-2716; tel. 315/425-4400, Michael DelDuca, Associate Medical Center Director
Web address: www.syracuse.va.gov/

VETERANS AFFAIRS HUDSON VALLEY HEALTH CARE SYSTEM (O, 166 beds) 2094 Albany Post Road, Montrose, NY, Zip 10548-1454, P O Box 100, Zip 10548-0100, tel. 914/737-4400, Dawn M. Schaal, Medical Center Director

For explanation of codes following names, see page B2.
★ Indicates Type III membership in the American Hospital Association.

Systems / Department of Veterans Affairs

VETERANS AFFAIRS NEW YORK HARBOR HEALTHCARE SYSTEM (O, 316 beds) 800 Poly Place, Brooklyn, NY, Zip 11209-7104; tel. 718/630-3500, Timothy Graham, JD, Medical Center Director
Web address: www.nyharbor.va.gov

VETERANS AFFAIRS WESTERN NEW YORK HEALTHCARE SYSTEM–BATAVIA DIVISION (O, 128 beds) 222 Richmond Avenue, Batavia, NY, Zip 14020-1288; tel. 585/297-1000, Michael J. Swartz, FACHE, Interim Director
Web address: www.buffalo.va.gov/batavia.asp

VETERANS AFFAIRS WESTERN NEW YORK HEALTHCARE SYSTEM–BUFFALO DIVISION (O, 127 beds) 3495 Bailey Avenue, Buffalo, NY, Zip 14215-1129; tel. 716/834-9200, Michael J. Swartz, FACHE, Executive Director, Veterans Affairs Western New York Healthcare System
Web address: www.buffalo.va.gov/index.asp

NORTH CAROLINA: CHARLES GEORGE VETERANS AFFAIRS MEDICAL CENTER (O, 188 beds) 1100 Tunnel Road, Asheville, NC, Zip 28805-2087; tel. 828/298-7911, Stephanie Young, Medical Center Director
Web address: www.asheville.va.gov/

DURHAM VA HEALTH CARE SYSTEM (O, 286 beds) 508 Fulton Street, Durham, NC, Zip 27705-3897; tel. 919/286-0411, Alyshia Smith, R.N., Medical Center Director

FAYETTEVILLE VETERANS AFFAIRS MEDICAL CENTER (O, 52 beds) 2300 Ramsey Street, Fayetteville, NC, Zip 28301-3899; tel. 910/488-2120, Marri Fryar, Executive Director
Web address: www.fayettevillenc.va.gov

W. G. (BILL) HEFFNER VETERANS AFFAIRS MEDICAL CENTER (O, 95 beds) 1601 Brenner Avenue, Salisbury, NC, Zip 28144-2559; tel. 704/638-9000, Kevin Amick, Executive Director
Web address: www.salisbury.va.gov

NORTH DAKOTA: FARGO VA MEDICAL CENTER (O, 38 beds) 2101 Elm Street North, Fargo, ND, Zip 58102; tel. 701/232-3241, Breton Weintraub, Medical Center Director
Web address: www.fargo.va.gov/

OHIO: CHILLICOTHE VETERANS AFFAIRS MEDICAL CENTER (O, 295 beds) 17273 State Route 104, Chillicothe, OH, Zip 45601-9718; tel. 740/773-1141, Kenneth Mortimer, Medical Center Director

CINCINNATI VETERANS AFFAIRS MEDICAL CENTER (O, 212 beds) 3200 Vine Street, Cincinnati, OH, Zip 45220-2288; tel. 513/475-6300, Jane Johnson, MSN, R.N., Executive Medical Center Director
Web address: www.cincinnati.va.gov/

DAYTON VETERANS AFFAIRS MEDICAL CENTER (O, 403 beds) 4100 West Third Street, Dayton, OH, Zip 45428-9000; tel. 937/268-6511, Jennifer A. Defrancesco, Medical Center Director
Web address: www.dayton.va.gov/

NORTHEAST OHIO VA HEALTHCARE SYSTEM (O, 617 beds) 10701 East Boulevard, Cleveland, OH, Zip 44106-1702; tel. 216/791-3800, Jill K. Dietrich Melon, JD, FACHE, Executive Director, Chief Executive Officer

OKLAHOMA: JACK C. MONTGOMERY DEPARTMENT OF VETERANS AFFAIRS MEDICAL CENTER (O, 82 beds) 1011 Honor Heights Drive, Muskogee, OK, Zip 74401-1318; tel. 918/577-3000, Kimberly Denning, R.N., Medical Director
Web address: www.muskogee.va.gov

OKLAHOMA CITY VA MEDICAL CENTER (O, 198 beds) 921 NE 13th Street, Oklahoma City, OK, Zip 73104-5028; tel. 405/456-1000, Kristopher Wade. Vlosich, Medical Center Director
Web address: www.oklahoma.va.gov

OREGON: PORTLAND HCS (O, 336 beds) 3710 SW U S Veterans Hospital Road, Portland, OR, Zip 97239-2964, 3710 SW US Veterans Hospital Road, Zip 97207-1034, tel. 503/220-8262, David Holt, Director
Web address: www.portland.va.gov/

ROSEBURG VA MEDICAL CENTER (O, 13 beds) 913 NW Garden Valley Boulevard, Roseburg, OR, Zip 97471-6513; tel. 541/440-1000, Keith M. Allen, Medical Center Director
Web address: www.roseburg.va.gov/

WHITE CITY, OR SOUTHERN OREGON REHABILITATION CENTER & CLINICS (O, 0 beds) 8495 Crater Lake Highway, White City, OR, Zip 97503; tel. 503/826-2111, David Holt, Director

PENNSYLVANIA: COATESVILLE VETERANS AFFAIRS MEDICAL CENTER (O, 302 beds) 1400 Black Horse Hill Road, Coatesville, PA, Zip 19320-2040; tel. 610/384-7711, Jennifer Harkins, Executive Director
Web address: www.coatesville.va.gov/

ERIE VETERANS AFFAIRS MEDICAL CENTER (O, 75 beds) 135 East 38th Street, Erie, PA, Zip 16504-1559; tel. 814/860-2576, John Gennaro, FACHE, Director
Web address: www.erie.va.gov/

JAMES E. VAN ZANDT VETERANS AFFAIRS MEDICAL CENTER (O, 89 beds) 2907 Pleasant Valley Boulevard, Altoona, PA, Zip 16602-4305; tel. 814/943-8164, Derek Coughenour, DPT, CLD, Medical Center Director

LEBANON VETERANS AFFAIRS MEDICAL CENTER (O, 187 beds) 1700 South Lincoln Avenue, Lebanon, PA, Zip 17042-7529; tel. 717/272-6621, Jeffrey A. Beiler II, Director
Web address: www.lebanon.va.gov

PHILADELPHIA VETERANS AFFAIRS MEDICAL CENTER (O, 279 beds) 3900 Woodland Avenue, Philadelphia, PA, Zip 19104-4594; tel. 215/823-5800, Karen Ann. Flaherty-Oxler, MSN, R.N., Medical Center Director
Web address: www.philadelphia.va.gov/

VETERANS AFFAIRS PITTSBURGH HEALTHCARE SYSTEM (O, 532 beds) University Drive C, Pittsburgh, PA, Zip 15240; tel. 866/482-7488, Donald E. Koenig, Director

WILKES-BARRE VETERANS AFFAIRS MEDICAL CENTER (O, 156 beds) 1111 East End Boulevard, Wilkes-Barre, PA, Zip 18711-0030; tel. 570/824-3521, Russell E. Lloyd, Medical Center Director
Web address: www.va.gov/vamcwb

PUERTO RICO: VETERANS AFFAIRS CARIBBEAN HEALTHCARE SYSTEM (O, 321 beds) 10 Casia Street, San Juan, PR, Zip 00921-3201; tel. 787/641-7582, Carlos R. Escobar, FACHE, Director

RHODE ISLAND: PROVIDENCE VETERANS AFFAIRS MEDICAL CENTER (O, 106 beds) 830 Chalkstone Avenue, Providence, RI, Zip 02908-4799; tel. 401/273-7100, Lawrence B. Connell, Medical Center Director
Web address: www.providence.va.gov/

SOUTH CAROLINA: COLUMBIA VA HEALTH CARE SYSTEM (O, 112 beds) 6439 Garners Ferry Road, Columbia, SC, Zip 29209-1639; tel. 803/776-4000, Rebecca Strini, Acting Director
Web address: www.columbiasc.va.gov/

RALPH H. JOHNSON VETERANS AFFAIRS MEDICAL CENTER (O, 128 beds) 109 Bee Street, Charleston, SC, Zip 29401-5799; tel. 843/577-5011, Scott R. Isaacks, FACHE, Director and Chief Executive Officer

SOUTH DAKOTA: BLACK HILLS HCS (O, 133 beds) 113 Comanche Road, Fort Meade, SD, Zip 57741-1099; tel. 605/347-2511
Web address: www.blackhills.va.gov/

ROYAL C. JOHNSON VETERANS' MEMORIAL HOSPITAL (O, 175 beds) 2501 West 22nd Street, Sioux Falls, SD, Zip 57105-1305, P O Box 5046, Zip 57117-5046, tel. 605/336-3230, Sara Ackert, Executive Director and Chief Executive Officer
Web address: www.siouxfalls.va.gov

TENNESSEE: JAMES H. QUILLEN DEPARTMENT OF VETERANS AFFAIRS MEDICAL CENTER (O, 218 beds) 809 Lamont Street, Johnson City, TN, Zip 37604-5453, P O Box 4000, Mountain Home, Zip 37684-4000, tel. 423/926-1171, Dean B. Borsos, Medical Center Director

LT. COL. LUKE WEATHERS, JR. VA MEDICAL CENTER (O, 177 beds) 1030 Jefferson Avenue, Memphis, TN, Zip 38104-2193; tel. 901/523-8990, Joseph Vaughn, FACHE, Medical Center Director
Web address: www.memphis.va.gov/

TENNESSEE VALLEY HCS–NASHVILLE AND MURFREESBORO (O, 361 beds) 1310 24th Avenue South, Nashville, TN, Zip 37212-2637; tel. 615/327-4751, Michael B. Renfrow, Medical Center Director

TEXAS: CENTRAL TEXAS VETERANS HCS / TEMPLE TX (O, 141 beds) 1901 Veterans Memorial Drive, Temple, TX, Zip 76504-7445; tel. 254/778-4811, Colonel, Michael L. Kiefer, FACHE, Medical Center Director
Web address: www.centraltexas.va.gov/

DALLAS VA NORTH TEXAS HCS (O, 467 beds) 4500 South Lancaster Road, Dallas, TX, Zip 75216-7167; tel. 214/742-8387, Jason Cave, JD, Executive Medical Center Director
Web address: www.northtexas.va.gov/

For explanation of codes following names, see page B2.
★ *Indicates Type III membership in the American Hospital Association.*

Systems / Division of Mental Health and Addiction Services, Department of Human Services, State of New Jersey

MICHAEL E. DEBAKEY DEPARTMENT OF VETERANS AFFAIRS MEDICAL CENTER (O, 357 beds) 2002 Holcombe Boulevard, Houston, TX, Zip 77030-4298; tel. 713/791-1414, Francisco Vazquez, Director
Web address: www.houston.va.gov

SOUTH TEXAS VETERANS HEALTHCARE SYSTEM AUDIE L MURPHY (O, 235 beds) 7400 Merton Minter Boulevard, San Antonio, TX, Zip 78229-4404; tel. 210/617-5300, Julianne Flynn, M.D., Executive Director

THOMAS E. CREEK DEPARTMENT OF VETERANS AFFAIRS MEDICAL CENTER (O, 38 beds) 6010 West Amarillo Boulevard, Amarillo, TX, Zip 79106-1992; tel. 806/355-9703, Rodney Gonzalez, M.D., Medical Center Director
Web address: www.amarillo.va.gov/

VA TEXAS VALLEY COASTAL HCS (O, 25 beds) 2601 Veterans Drive, Harlingen, TX, Zip 78550-8942; tel. 956/291-9000, Homero S. Martinez III, Director

WEST TEXAS VA HEALTH CARE SYSTEM (O, 149 beds) 300 Veterans Boulevard, Big Spring, TX, Zip 79720-5500, Big Springs, tel. 432/263-7361, Keith Bass, Medical Center Director
Web address: https://www.va.gov/west-texas-health-care/locations/george-h-obrien-jr-department-of-veterans-affairs-medical-center/

UTAH: GEORGE E. WAHLEN DEPARTMENT OF VETERANS AFFAIRS MEDICAL CENTER (O, 127 beds) 500 Foothill Drive, Salt Lake City, UT, Zip 84148-0002; tel. 801/582-1565, Angela Williams, PharmD, MS, Medical Center Director
Web address: www.saltlakecity.va.gov/

VERMONT: WHITE RIVER JUNCTION VETERANS AFFAIRS MEDICAL CENTER (O, 57 beds) 215 North Main Street, White River Junction, VT, Zip 05009-0001; tel. 802/295-9363, Brett Rusch, M.D., Executive Director

VIRGINIA: HAMPTON VETERANS AFFAIRS MEDICAL CENTER (O, 213 beds) 100 Emancipation Drive, Hampton, VA, Zip 23667-0001; tel. 757/722-9961, Taquisa Simmons, Ph.D., Executive Director
Web address: www.hampton.va.gov/

HUNTER HOLMES MCGUIRE VETERANS AFFAIRS MEDICAL CENTER-RICHMOND (O, 143 beds) 1201 Broad Rock Boulevard, Richmond, VA, Zip 23249-0002; tel. 804/675-5000, J. Ronald. Johnson, Medical Center Director
Web address: www.richmond.va.gov/

SALEM VETERANS AFFAIRS MEDICAL CENTER (O, 176 beds) 1970 Roanoke Boulevard, Salem, VA, Zip 24153-6478; tel. 540/982-2463, Rebecca J. Stackhouse, FACHE, Executive Director
Web address: www.salem.va.gov

WASHINGTON: MANN-GRANDSTAFF DEPARTMENT OF VETERANS AFFAIRS MEDICAL CENTER (O, 67 beds) 4815 North Assembly Street, Spokane, WA, Zip 99205-6197; tel. 509/434-7000, Robert Fischer, M.D., Medical Center Director
Web address: www.spokane.va.gov/

VA PUGET SOUND HEALTHCARE SYSTEM-SEATTLE (O, 316 beds) 1660 South Columbian Way, Seattle, WA, Zip 98108-1597; tel. 206/762-1010, Colonel, Thomas S. Bundt, Ph.D., FACHE, Executive Director

WEST VIRGINIA: BECKLEY VETERANS AFFAIRS MEDICAL CENTER (O, 23 beds) 200 Veterans Avenue, Beckley, WV, Zip 25801-6499; tel. 304/255-2121, Brett Vess, Medical Center Director
Web address: www.beckley.va.gov/

HUNTINGTON VETERANS AFFAIRS MEDICAL CENTER (O, 75 beds) 1540 Spring Valley Drive, Huntington, WV, Zip 25704-9300; tel. 304/429-6741, Brian Nimmo, Medical Center Director
Web address: www.huntington.va.gov/

LOUIS A. JOHNSON VETERANS AFFAIRS MEDICAL CENTER (O, 48 beds) 1 Medical Center Drive, Clarksburg, WV, Zip 26301-4199; tel. 304/623-3461, Barbara Forsha, Interim Medical Center Director

MARTINSBURG VETERANS AFFAIRS MEDICAL CENTER (O, 201 beds) 510 Butler Avenue, Martinsburg, WV, Zip 25405-9990; tel. 304/263-0811, Kenneth W. Allensworth, FACHE, Medical Center Director
Web address: https://www.martinsburg.va.gov/locations/directions.asp

WISCONSIN: CLEMENT J. ZABLOCKI VETERANS' ADMINISTRATION MEDICAL CENTER (O, 265 beds) 5000 West National Avenue, Milwaukee, WI, Zip 53295-0001; tel. 414/384-2000, James D. McLain, Executive Director
Web address: www.milwaukee.va.gov/

TOMAH VA MEDICAL CENTER (O, 36 beds) 500 East Veterans Street, Tomah, WI, Zip 54660-3105; tel. 608/372-3971, Karen K. Long, Medical Center Director

WILLIAM S. MIDDLETON MEMORIAL VETERANS' HOSPITAL (O, 98 beds) 2500 Overlook Terrace, Madison, WI, Zip 53705-2286; tel. 608/256-1901, Christine Kleckner, Medical Center Director
Web address: www.madison.va.gov

WYOMING: CHEYENNE VA MEDICAL CENTER (O, 32 beds) 2360 East Pershing Boulevard, Cheyenne, WY, Zip 82001-5392; tel. 307/778-7550, Paul L. Roberts, Director

SHERIDAN VA MEDICAL CENTER (O, 31 beds) 1898 Fort Road, Sheridan, WY, Zip 82801-8320; tel. 307/672-3473, Pamela Crowell, Director
Web address: www.sheridan.va.gov/

Owned, leased, sponsored:	135 hospitals	25321 beds
Contract-managed:	0 hospitals	0 beds
Totals:	135 hospitals	25321 beds

0845: DEVEREUX (NP)

444 Devereux Drive, Villanova, PA Zip 19085-1932, P O Box 638, Zip 19085-0638, tel. 610/520-3000, Robert Q. Kreider, President and Chief Executive Officer

(Independent Hospital System)

FLORIDA: DEVEREUX HOSPITAL AND CHILDREN'S CENTER OF FLORIDA (O, 100 beds) 8000 Devereux Drive, Melbourne, FL, Zip 32940-7907; tel. 321/242-9100, Michelle Llorens, Executive Director
Web address: www.devereux.org

GEORGIA: DEVEREUX ADVANCED BEHAVIORAL HEALTH GEORGIA (O, 110 beds) 1291 Stanley Road NW, Kennesaw, GA, Zip 30152-4359; tel. 770/427-0147, Kathy Goggin, Director, Finance & Support Services

PENNSYLVANIA: DEVEREUX CHILDREN'S BEHAVIORAL HEALTH CENTER (O, 48 beds) 655 Sugartown Road, Malvern, PA, Zip 19355-3303, 655 Sugartown Rd, Zip 19355-3303, tel. 800/345-1292, Patricia Hillis-Clark, Executive Director
Web address: www.devereux.org

Owned, leased, sponsored:	3 hospitals	258 beds
Contract-managed:	0 hospitals	0 beds
Totals:	3 hospitals	258 beds

0010: DIVISION OF MENTAL HEALTH AND ADDICTION SERVICES, DEPARTMENT OF HUMAN SERVICES, STATE OF NEW JERSEY (NP)

222 South Warren Street, Trenton, NJ Zip 08608-2306, P.O. Box 360, Zip 08625-0360, tel. 609/438-4351, Valerie Mielke, Assistant Commissioner

(Independent Hospital System)

NEW JERSEY: ANCORA PSYCHIATRIC HOSPITAL (O, 515 beds) 301 Spring Garden Road, Hammonton, NJ, Zip 08037-9699; tel. 609/561-1700, Christopher Morrison, Chief Executive Officer
Web address: https://www.state.nj.us/humanservices/dmhas/resources/services/treatment/aph.html

ARTHUR BRISBANE CHILDREN TREATMENT CENTER (O, 92 beds) County Road 524, Farmingdale, NJ, Zip 7727, P O Box 625, Zip 7727, Vincent Giampeitro, Chief Executive Officer

GREYSTONE PARK PSYCHIATRIC HOSPITAL (O, 468 beds) 59 Koch Avenue, Morris Plains, NJ, Zip 07950-4400; tel. 973/538-1800, Joshua Belsky, Chief Executive Officer
Web address: https://www.state.nj.us/humanservices/involved/nurses/mentalhph/greystone.html

---

For explanation of codes following names, see page B2.
★ Indicates Type III membership in the American Hospital Association.

Systems / Division of Mental Health and Addiction Services, Department of Human Services, State of New Jersey

TRENTON PSYCHIATRIC HOSPITAL (O, 431 beds) Route 29 and Sullivan Way, Trenton, NJ, Zip 08628-3425, P O Box 7500, West Trenton, Zip 08628-0500, tel. 609/633-1500, Maria Christensen, Chief Executive Officer
Web address: www.https://nj.gov/

Owned, leased, sponsored:	4 hospitals	1506 beds
Contract-managed:	0 hospitals	0 beds
Totals:	4 hospitals	1506 beds

0536: DIVISION OF MENTAL HEALTH, DEPARTMENT OF HUMAN SERVICES (NP)

319 East Madison Street, S-3B, Springfield, IL Zip 62701-1035; tel. 217/785-6023, Lorrie Rickman Jones, Ph.D., Director
(Independent Hospital System)

ILLINOIS: ALTON MENTAL HEALTH CENTER (O, 115 beds) 4500 College Avenue, Alton, IL, Zip 62002-5099; tel. 618/474-3800, Tonya Piephoff, Hospital Administrator

CHESTER MENTAL HEALTH CENTER (O, 284 beds) Chester Road, Chester, IL, Zip 62233-0031, Box 31, Zip 62233-0031, tel. 618/826-4571, Travis Nottmeier, Administrator

CHICAGO-READ MENTAL HEALTH CENTER (O, 160 beds) 4200 North Oak Park Avenue, Chicago, IL, Zip 60634-1457; tel. 773/794-4000, Ricardo Fernandez, Administrator

CHOATE MENTAL HEALTH CENTER (O, 79 beds) 1000 North Main Street, Anna, IL, Zip 62906-1699; tel. 618/833-5161, Lori Gray, Chief Executive Officer

ELGIN MENTAL HEALTH CENTER (O, 427 beds) 750 South State Street, Elgin, IL, Zip 60123-7692; tel. 847/742-1040, Michelle Evans, Administrator
Web address: www.dhs.state.il.us

ELIZABETH PARSONS WARE PACKARD MENTAL HEALTH CENTER (O, 142 beds) 901 East Southwind Road, Springfield, IL, Zip 62703-5125; tel. 217/786-6994, Lana Miller, Administrator

JOHN J. MADDEN MENTAL HEALTH CENTER (O, 125 beds) 1200 South First Avenue, Hines, IL, Zip 60141-0800; tel. 708/338-7202, Patricia Hudson, Administrator

Owned, leased, sponsored:	7 hospitals	1332 beds
Contract-managed:	0 hospitals	0 beds
Totals:	7 hospitals	1332 beds

★1027: DRH HEALTH (NP)

1407 North Whisenant Drive, Duncan, OK Zip 73533-1650; tel. 580/252-5300, Jay R. Johnson, FACHE, President and Chief Executive Officer
(Independent Hospital System)

OKLAHOMA: DUNCAN REGIONAL HOSPITAL (O, 110 beds) 1407 North Whisenant Drive, Duncan, OK, Zip 73533-1650, P O Box 2000, Zip 73534-2000, tel. 580/252-5300, Jay R. Johnson, FACHE, President and Chief Executive Officer

JEFFERSON COUNTY HOSPITAL (L, 8 beds) Highway 70 and 81, Waurika, OK, Zip 73573-3075, P O Box 90, Zip 73573-0090, tel. 580/228-2344, JP Edgar, President
Web address: https://www.duncanregional.com/jefferson-county-hospital/

Owned, leased, sponsored:	2 hospitals	118 beds
Contract-managed:	0 hospitals	0 beds
Totals:	2 hospitals	118 beds

★0190: DUKE UNIVERSITY HEALTH SYSTEM (NP)

201 Trent Drive, Durham, NC Zip 27710-3037, 324 Blackwell St Ste 800, Zip 27701-3689, tel. 919/684-2255, Craig Albanese, M.D., Chief Executive Officer
(Centralized Health System)

NORTH CAROLINA: DUKE RALEIGH HOSPITAL (O, 220 beds) 3400 Wake Forest Road, Raleigh, NC, Zip 27609-7373; tel. 919/954-3000, Barbara Griffith, M.D., President
Web address: www.dukeraleighhospital.org

DUKE REGIONAL HOSPITAL (L, 274 beds) 3643 North Roxboro Street, Durham, NC, Zip 27704-2763; tel. 919/470-4000, Devdutta Sangvai, M.D., President

DUKE UNIVERSITY HOSPITAL (O, 1041 beds) 2301 Erwin Road, DUMC Box # 3814, Durham, NC, Zip 27705-4699, P O Box 3814, Zip 27710-3708, tel. 919/684-8111, Greg Pauly, President
Web address: www.dukehealth.org

Owned, leased, sponsored:	3 hospitals	1535 beds
Contract-managed:	0 hospitals	0 beds
Totals:	3 hospitals	1535 beds

★0217: ECU HEALTH (NP)

2100 Stantonsburg Road, Greenville, NC Zip 27834-2818, P O Box 6028, Zip 27835-6028, tel. 252/847-4100, Michael Waldrum, M.D., Chief Executive Officer
(Moderately Centralized Health System)

NORTH CAROLINA: ECU HEALTH BERTIE HOSPITAL (L, 6 beds) 1403 South King Street, P O Box 40, Windsor, NC, Zip 27983-9666, P O Box 40, Zip 27983-0040, tel. 252/794-6600, Brian Harvill, President
Web address: www.https://locations.ecuhealth.org/Details/126

ECU HEALTH CHOWAN HOSPITAL (L, 19 beds) 211 Virginia Road, Edenton, NC, Zip 27932-9668, P O Box 629, Zip 27932-0629, tel. 252/482-8451, Brian Harvill, President

ECU HEALTH DUPLIN HOSPITAL (L, 81 beds) 401 North Main Street, Kenansville, NC, Zip 28349-8801, P O Box 278, Zip 28349-0278, tel. 910/296-0941, Jeffery Dial, Chief Executive Officer
Web address: www.vidanthealth.com

ECU HEALTH EDGECOMBE HOSPITAL (O, 117 beds) 111 Hospital Drive, Tarboro, NC, Zip 27886-2011; tel. 252/641-7700, Patrick Heins, President
Web address: www.https://locations.ecuhealth.org/Details/118

ECU HEALTH MEDICAL CENTER (O, 913 beds) 2100 Stantonsburg Road, Greenville, NC, Zip 27834-2818, P O Box 6028, Zip 27835-6028, tel. 252/847-4100, Jay Briley, FACHE, President

ECU HEALTH NORTH HOSPITAL (O, 204 beds) 250 Smith Church Road, Roanoke Rapids, NC, Zip 27870-4914, P O Box 1089, Zip 27870-1089, tel. 252/535-8011, Dennis Campbell II, R.N., Interim President
Web address: https://www.ecuhealth.org/

ECU HEALTH ROANOKE-CHOWAN HOSPITAL (L, 110 beds) 500 South Academy Street, Ahoskie, NC, Zip 27910-3261, P O Box 1385, Zip 27910-1385, tel. 252/209-3000, Brian Harvill, President

THE OUTER BANKS HOSPITAL (O, 21 beds) 4800 South Croatan Highway, Nags Head, NC, Zip 27959-9704; tel. 252/449-4500, Ronald A. Sloan, FACHE, President
Web address: www.https://locations.outerbankshealth.org/Details/132

Owned, leased, sponsored:	8 hospitals	1471 beds
Contract-managed:	0 hospitals	0 beds
Totals:	8 hospitals	1471 beds

★0101: EMANATE HEALTH (NP)

210 West San Bernardino Road, Covina, CA Zip 91723-1515; tel. 626/331-7331, Roger Sharma, President and Chief Executive Officer

CALIFORNIA: EMANATE HEALTH FOOTHILL PRESBYTERIAN HOSPITAL (O, 72 beds) 250 South Grand Avenue, Glendora, CA, Zip 91741-4218; tel. 626/963-8411, Roger Sharma, President and Chief Executive Officer
Web address: https://www.emanatehealth.org/locations/emanate-health-foothill-presbyterian-hospital/

For explanation of codes following names, see page B2.
★ Indicates Type III membership in the American Hospital Association.

Systems / Encompass Health Corporation

EMANATE HEALTH INTER–COMMUNITY HOSPITAL (O, 298 beds) 210 West San Bernadino Road, Covina, CA, Zip 91723-1515, P O Box 6108, Zip 91722-5108, tel. 626/331-7331, Roger Sharma, President/Chief Executive Officer

Owned, leased, sponsored:	2 hospitals	370 beds
Contract-managed:	0 hospitals	0 beds
Totals:	2 hospitals	370 beds

0879: EMERUS (IO)

8686 New Trails Drive, Suite 100, The Woodlands, TX Zip 77381-1195; tel. 281/292-2450, Victor Schmerbeck, Chief Executive Officer

OKLAHOMA: INTEGRIS HEALTH COMMUNITY HOSPITAL AT COUNCIL CROSSING (C, 64 beds) 9417 North Council Road, Oklahoma City, OK, Zip 73162-6228; tel. 405/500-3280, Christopher McAuliffe, R.N., Market Chief Executive Officer

TEXAS: BAPTIST NEIGHBORHOOD HOSPITAL AT THOUSAND OAKS (O, 41 beds) 16088 San Pedro, San Antonio, TX, Zip 78232-2249; tel. 210/402-4092, Shannon Crinion, Chief Executive Officer
Web address: www.baptistemergencyhospital.com

BAYLOR SCOTT & WHITE EMERGENCY HOSPITAL–BURLESON (O, 24 beds) 12500 South Freeway Suite 100, Burleson, TX, Zip 76028-7128; tel. 214/294-6250, Victor Schmerbeck, Chief Executive Officer
Web address: www.bayloremc.com/burleson

BAYLOR SCOTT & WHITE EMERGENCY HOSPITALS–AUBREY (O, 32 beds) 26791 Highway 380, Aubrey, TX, Zip 76227; tel. 972/347-2525, Letemia Medina, Administrator

THE HOSPITALS OF PROVIDENCE HORIZON CITY CAMPUS (O, 16 beds) 13600 Horizon Boulevard, Horizon City, TX, Zip 79928; tel. 915/407-7878, Catherine Lozano, Chief Executive Officer

Owned, leased, sponsored:	4 hospitals	113 beds
Contract-managed:	1 hospitals	64 beds
Totals:	5 hospitals	177 beds

★0256: EMORY HEALTHCARE (NP)

1440 Clifton Road NE, Suite 400, Atlanta, GA Zip 30322-1102; tel. 404/778-5000, Joon Sup. Lee, M.D., Chief Executive Officer
(Centralized Health System)

GEORGIA: EMORY DECATUR HOSPITAL (O, 415 beds) 2701 North Decatur Road, Decatur, GA, Zip 30033-5995; tel. 404/501-1000, Jennifer Schuck, Chief Executive Officer
Web address: https://www.emoryhealthcare.org/dekalbmedical/

EMORY HILLANDALE HOSPITAL (O, 99 beds) 2801 DeKalb Medical Parkway, Lithonia, GA, Zip 30058-4996; tel. 404/501-8000, Jennifer Schuck, Chief Executive Officer

EMORY JOHNS CREEK HOSPITAL (O, 154 beds) 6325 Hospital Parkway, Johns Creek, GA, Zip 30097-5775; tel. 678/474-7000, Heather Redrick, Chief Operating Officer
Web address: www.emoryjohnscreek.com

EMORY LONG–TERM ACUTE CARE (O, 50 beds) 450 North Candler Street, Decatur, GA, Zip 30030-2671; tel. 404/501-6700, Jennifer Schuck, Chief Executive Officer
Web address: https://www.emoryhealthcare.org

EMORY REHABILITATION HOSPITAL (O, 46 beds) 1441 Clifton Road NE, Atlanta, GA, Zip 30322-1004; tel. 404/712-5512, Renee Hinson, Chief Executive Officer
Web address: www.emoryhealthcare.org/rehabilitation

EMORY SAINT JOSEPH'S HOSPITAL (O, 314 beds) 5665 Peachtree Dunwoody Road NE, Atlanta, GA, Zip 30342-1701; tel. 678/843-7001, Kevin Andrews, Chief Operating Officer

EMORY UNIVERSITY HOSPITAL MIDTOWN (O, 548 beds) 550 Peachtree Street NE, Atlanta, GA, Zip 30308-2247; tel. 404/686-4411, Adam Webb, Chief Operating Officer
Web address: www.emoryhealthcare.org

EMORY UNIVERSITY HOSPITAL (O, 683 beds) 1364 Clifton Road NE, Atlanta, GA, Zip 30322; tel. 404/712-2000, Catherine Maloney, Chief Operating Officer
Web address: https://www.emoryhealthcare.org/locations/hospitals/emory-university-hospital/index.html

Owned, leased, sponsored:	8 hospitals	2309 beds
Contract-managed:	0 hospitals	0 beds
Totals:	8 hospitals	2309 beds

1128: EMPLIFY HEALTH (NP)

1900 South Avenue, La Crosse, WI Zip 54601-5467; tel. 608/782-7300, Scott W. Rathgaber, M.D., Chief Executive Officer

Owned, leased, sponsored:	0 hospitals	0 beds
Contract-managed:	0 hospitals	0 beds
Totals:	0 hospitals	0 beds

★0023: ENCOMPASS HEALTH CORPORATION (IO)

9001 Liberty Parkway, Birmingham, AL Zip 35242-7509; tel. 205/967-7116, Mark J. Tarr, President and Chief Executive Officer
(Independent Hospital System)

ALABAMA: ENCOMPASS HEALTH LAKESHORE REHABILITATION HOSPITAL (O, 100 beds) 3800 Ridgeway Drive, Birmingham, AL, Zip 35209-5599; tel. 205/868-2000, Michael Bartell, Chief Executive Officer
Web address: www.encompasshealth.com/lakeshorerehab

ENCOMPASS HEALTH REHABILITATION HOSPITAL OF DOTHAN (O, 51 beds) 1736 East Main Street, Dothan, AL, Zip 36301-3040, P O Box 6708, Zip 36302-6708, tel. 334/712-6333, Margaret A. Futch, Chief Executive Officer

ENCOMPASS HEALTH REHABILITATION HOSPITAL OF GADSDEN (O, 44 beds) 801 Goodyear Avenue, Gadsden, AL, Zip 35903-1133; tel. 256/439-5000, Al Rayburn, Chief Executive Officer
Web address: www.encompasshealth.com/gadsdenrehab

ENCOMPASS HEALTH REHABILITATION HOSPITAL OF MONTGOMERY (O, 75 beds) 4465 Narrow Lane Road, Montgomery, AL, Zip 36116-2900; tel. 334/284-7700, Erin Collier, Chief Executive Officer
Web address: www.encompasshealth.com/montgomeryrehab

ENCOMPASS HEALTH REHABILITATION HOSPITAL OF NORTH ALABAMA (O, 70 beds) 107 Governors Drive SW, Huntsville, AL, Zip 35801-4326; tel. 256/535-2300, Brent Mills, Chief Executive Officer

ENCOMPASS HEALTH REHABILITATION HOSPITAL OF SHELBY COUNTY (O, 34 beds) 900 Oak Mountain Commons Lane, Pelham, AL, Zip 35124; tel. 205/216-7600, Michael Bartell, Chief Executive Officer
Web address: www.encompasshealth.com/shelbycountyrehab

REGIONAL REHABILITATION HOSPITAL (O, 58 beds) 3715 Highway 280/431 North, Phenix City, AL, Zip 36867; tel. 334/732-2200, Lora Davis, FACHE, Chief Executive Officer

ARIZONA: ENCOMPASS HEALTH REHABILITATION HOSPITAL OF EAST VALLEY (O, 59 beds) 5652 East Baseline Road, Mesa, AZ, Zip 85206-4713; tel. 480/567-0350, Vidhya Kannan, Chief Executive Officer
Web address: https://www.encompasshealth.com/eastvalleyrehab

ENCOMPASS HEALTH REHABILITATION HOSPITAL OF NORTHWEST TUCSON (O, 60 beds) 1921 West Hospital Drive, Tucson, AZ, Zip 85704-7806; tel. 520/742-2800, Jeff Christensen, Chief Executive Officer

ENCOMPASS HEALTH REHABILITATION HOSPITAL OF SCOTTSDALE (O, 60 beds) 9630 East Shea Boulevard, Scottsdale, AZ, Zip 85260-6267; tel. 480/551-5400, Lisa Barrick, Chief Executive Officer
Web address: https://www.encompasshealth.com/locations/scottsdalerehab

ENCOMPASS HEALTH REHABILITATION INSTITUTE OF TUCSON (O, 80 beds) 2650 North Wyatt Drive, Tucson, AZ, Zip 85712-6108; tel. 520/325-1300, Jeff Christensen, Chief Executive Officer
Web address: https://www.encompasshealth.com/rehabinstituteoftucson

For explanation of codes following names, see page B2.
★ Indicates Type III membership in the American Hospital Association.

Systems / Encompass Health Corporation

ENCOMPASS HEALTH VALLEY OF THE SUN REHABILITATION HOSPITAL (O, 75 beds) 13460 North 67th Avenue, Glendale, AZ, Zip 85304-1042; tel. 623/878-8800, Mark A. Roth, Chief Executive Officer

YUMA REHABILITATION HOSPITAL, AN AFFILIATION OF ENCOMPASS HEALTH AND YUMA REGIONAL MEDICAL CENTER (O, 37 beds) 901 West 24th Street, Yuma, AZ, Zip 85364-6384; tel. 928/726-5000, Kristin Parra, Chief Executive Officer
Web address: https://www.encompasshealth.com/yumarehab

ARKANSAS: CHI ST. VINCENT HOT SPRINGS REHABILITATION HOSPITAL, A PARTNER OF ENCOMPASS HEALTH (O, 48 beds) 1636 Higdon Ferry Road, Hot Springs, AR, Zip 71913-6912; tel. 501/651-2000, Lesalee Chilcote, Chief Executive Officer

CHI ST. VINCENT SHERWOOD REHABILITATION HOSPITAL, A PARTNER OF ENCOMPASS HEALTH (O, 83 beds) 2201 Wildwood Avenue, Sherwood, AR, Zip 72120-5074; tel. 501/834-1800, Brian Cherry, Chief Executive Officer
Web address: www.stvincentrehabhospital.com/

ENCOMPASS HEALTH REHABILITATION HOSPITAL OF JONESBORO (O, 67 beds) 1201 Fleming Avenue, Jonesboro, AR, Zip 72401-4311, P O Box 1680, Zip 72403-1680, tel. 870/932-0440, Kevin Spears, Chief Executive Officer

ENCOMPASS HEALTH REHABILITATION HOSPITAL, A PARTNER OF WASHINGTON REGIONAL (O, 80 beds) 153 East Monte Painter Drive, Fayetteville, AR, Zip 72703-4002; tel. 479/444-2200, Sonja Buchanan, Chief Executive Officer
Web address: https://www.encompasshealth.com/fayettevillerehab

ENCOMPASSS HEALTH REHABILITATION HOSPITAL OF FORT SMITH (O, 65 beds) 1401 South 'J' Street, Fort Smith, AR, Zip 72901-5155; tel. 479/785-3300, Dawn Watts, Chief Executive Officer
Web address: www.healthsouthfortsmith.com

CALIFORNIA: ENCOMPASS HEALTH REHABILITATION HOSPITAL OF BAKERSFIELD (O, 70 beds) 5001 Commerce Drive, Bakersfield, CA, Zip 93309-0689; tel. 661/323-5500, Martha Samora Esq, R.N., FACHE, Chief Executive Officer
Web address: www.healthsouthbakersfield.com

ENCOMPASS HEALTH REHABILITATION HOSPITAL OF MODESTO (O, 50 beds) 1303 Mable Avenue, Modesto, CA, Zip 95355; tel. 209/857-3400, Sukhraj Dhami, Interim Chief Executive Officer
Web address: www.healthsouthmodesto.com/

ENCOMPASS HEALTH REHABILITATION HOSPITAL OF MURRIETA (O, 50 beds) 35470 Whitewood Road, Murrieta, CA, Zip 92563-2415; tel. 951/246-6500, Perry Ebeltoft, Chief Executive Officer
Web address: www.encompasshealth.com/murrietarehab

ENCOMPASS HEALTH REHABILITATION HOSPITAL OF TUSTIN (O, 48 beds) 15120 Kensington Park Drive, Tustin, CA, Zip 92782-1801; tel. 714/832-9200, Paula Redmond, Chief Executive Officer

COLORADO: ENCOMPASS HEALTH REHABILITATION HOSPITAL OF COLORADO SPRINGS (O, 62 beds) 325 Parkside Drive, Colorado Springs, CO, Zip 80910-3134; tel. 719/630-8000, Nathan Kliniske, Chief Executive Officer
Web address: www.healthsouthcoloradosprings.com

ENCOMPASS HEALTH REHABILITATION HOSPITAL OF LITTLETON (O, 48 beds) 1001 West Mineral Avenue, Littleton, CO, Zip 80120-4507; tel. 303/334-1100, Noomi Hirsch, Chief Executive Officer
Web address: www.healthsouthdenver.com

DELAWARE: ENCOMPASS HEALTH REHABILITATION HOSPITAL OF MIDDLETOWN (O, 40 beds) 250 East Hampden Road, Middletown, DE, Zip 19709-5303; tel. 302/464-3400, Dustin McFarland, Interim Chief Executive Officer
Web address: www.encompasshealth.com/middletownrehab

FLORIDA: ENCOMPASS HEALTH REHABILITATION HOSPITAL OF ALTAMONTE SPRINGS (O, 70 beds) 831 South State Road 434, Altamonte Springs, FL, Zip 32714-3502; tel. 407/587-8600, Michael Thomas, Chief Executive Officer
Web address: www.healthsouthaltamontesprings.com

ENCOMPASS HEALTH REHABILITATION HOSPITAL OF CAPE CORAL (O, 40 beds) 1730 North East Pine Island Road, Cape Coral, FL, Zip 33909-1734; tel. 239/599-3600, Michelle Fitzgerald, R.N., Chief Executive Officer
Web address: www.https://encompasshealth.com/capecoralrehab

ENCOMPASS HEALTH REHABILITATION HOSPITAL OF CLERMONT (O, 50 beds) 2901 State Road 50, Clermont, FL, Zip 34711-6037; tel. 689/946-1000, Glenda Carius, R.N., MSN, Chief Executive Officer

ENCOMPASS HEALTH REHABILITATION HOSPITAL OF JACKSONVILLE (O, 50 beds) 11595 Burnt Mill Road, Jacksonville, FL, Zip 32256-3096; tel. 904/596-5000, Brian Soares, Chief Executive Officer
Web address: www.https://encompasshealth.com/locations/jacksonvillerehab

ENCOMPASS HEALTH REHABILITATION HOSPITAL OF LAKELAND (O, 50 beds) 1201 Oakbridge Parkway, Lakeland, FL, Zip 33803-5945; tel. 863/279-1600, Sharon Hayes, Chief Executive Officer

ENCOMPASS HEALTH REHABILITATION HOSPITAL OF LARGO (O, 70 beds) 901 North Clearwater-Largo Road, Largo, FL, Zip 33770-4126; tel. 727/586-2999, Molly Arau, Chief Executive Officer
Web address: https://www.encompasshealth.com/largorehab

ENCOMPASS HEALTH REHABILITATION HOSPITAL OF MIAMI (O, 60 beds) 20601 Old Cutler Road, Cutler Bay, FL, Zip 33189-2400; tel. 305/251-3800, Zaynah Camp-Fry, Chief Executive Officer
Web address: www.https://encompasshealth.com/locations/miamirehab

ENCOMPASS HEALTH REHABILITATION HOSPITAL OF NORTH TAMPA (O, 50 beds) 3840 Atmore Grove Drive, Lutz, FL, Zip 33548-7903; tel. 813/607-3600, Tarif TC"" Chowdhury, Chief Executive Officer
Web address: www.encompasshealth.com

ENCOMPASS HEALTH REHABILITATION HOSPITAL OF OCALA (O, 80 beds) 2275 SW 22nd Lane, Ocala, FL, Zip 34471-7710; tel. 352/282-4000, Michael A. Franklin, FACHE, Chief Executive Officer
Web address: www.healthsouthocala.com

ENCOMPASS HEALTH REHABILITATION HOSPITAL OF PANAMA CITY (O, 75 beds) 1847 Florida Avenue, Panama City, FL, Zip 32405-4640; tel. 850/914-8600, Tony N. Bennett, Chief Executive Officer

ENCOMPASS HEALTH REHABILITATION HOSPITAL OF PENSACOLA (O, 40 beds) 1101 Office Woods Drive, Pensacola, FL, Zip 32504; tel. 850/805-2000, Kayla Feazell, Chief Executive Officer
Web address: www.https://encompasshealth.com/pensacolarehab

ENCOMPASS HEALTH REHABILITATION HOSPITAL OF SARASOTA (O, 96 beds) 6400 Edgelake Drive, Sarasota, FL, Zip 34240-8813; tel. 941/921-8600, Marcus Braz, Chief Executive Officer
Web address: www.healthsouthsarasota.com

ENCOMPASS HEALTH REHABILITATION HOSPITAL OF SPRING HILL (O, 80 beds) 12440 Cortez Boulevard, Brooksville, FL, Zip 34613-2628; tel. 352/592-4250, Michael Thomas, Chief Executive Officer

ENCOMPASS HEALTH REHABILITATION HOSPITAL OF ST. AUGUSTINE (O, 40 beds) 65 Silver Lane, St Augustine, FL, Zip 32084-3922; tel. 904/640-2000, Thomas Laughlin, Chief Executive Officer
Web address: www.https://encompasshealth.com/locations/staugustinerehab

ENCOMPASS HEALTH REHABILITATION HOSPITAL OF SUNRISE (O, 126 beds) 4399 North Nob Hill Road, Sunrise, FL, Zip 33351-5899; tel. 954/749-0300, Randy Gross, Chief Executive Officer

ENCOMPASS HEALTH REHABILITATION HOSPITAL OF TALLAHASSEE (O, 76 beds) 1675 Riggins Road, Tallahassee, FL, Zip 32308-5315; tel. 850/656-4800, William D. Heath, Chief Executive Officer
Web address: www.healthsouthtallahassee.com

ENCOMPASS HEALTH REHABILITATION HOSPITAL OF TREASURE COAST (O, 80 beds) 1600 37th Street, Vero Beach, FL, Zip 32960-4863; tel. 772/778-2100, Michael Morrical, Chief Executive Officer
Web address: https://www.encompasshealth.com/treasurecoastrehab

ENCOMPASS HEALTH REHABILITATION HOSPITAL, AN AFFILIATE OF MARTIN HEALTH (O, 34 beds) 5850 SE Community Drive, Stuart, FL, Zip 34997-6420; tel. 772/324-3500, Ivette Miranda, Chief Executive Officer
Web address: www.healthsouthmartin.com

REHABILITATION HOSPITAL OF NAPLES (O, 50 beds) 14305 Collier Boulevard, Naples, FL, Zip 34119-9589; tel. 239/383-6000, Enid Y. Gonzalez, Chief Executive Officer
Web address: www.https://encompasshealth.com/locations/naplesrehab

SEA PINES REHABILITATION HOSPITAL, AN AFFILIATE OF ENCOMPASS HEALTH (O, 90 beds) 101 East Florida Avenue, Melbourne, FL, Zip 32901-8301; tel. 321/984-4600, Mark Racicot, Chief Executive Officer

For explanation of codes following names, see page B2.
★ Indicates Type III membership in the American Hospital Association.

Systems / Encompass Health Corporation

GEORGIA: ENCOMPASS HEALTH REHABILITATION HOSPITAL OF CUMMING (O, 50 beds) 1165 Sanders Road, Cumming, GA, Zip 30041-5965; tel. 470/533-4200, E. Rick. Lowe, Chief Executive Officer
Web address: www.https://encompasshealth.com/cummingrehab

ENCOMPASS HEALTH REHABILITATION HOSPITAL OF NEWNAN (O, 50 beds) 2101 East Newnan Crossing Boulevard, Newnan, GA, Zip 30265-2406; tel. 678/552-6200, Stan Hickson, Chief Executive Officer

ENCOMPASS HEALTH REHABILITATION HOSPITAL OF SAVANNAH (O, 50 beds) 6510 Seawright DR, Savannah, GA, Zip 31406-2752; tel. 912/235-6000, Randal S. Hamilton, Chief Executive Officer
Web address: www.rehabilitationhospitalsavannah.com

REHABILITATION HOSPITAL OF HENRY (O, 50 beds) 2200 Patrick Henry Parkway, McDonough, GA, Zip 30253-4207; tel. 470/713-2000, Amber Hester, Area Chief Executive Officer

WALTON REHABILITATION HOSPITAL, AN AFFILIATE OF ENCOMPASS HEALTH (O, 58 beds) 1355 Independence Drive, Augusta, GA, Zip 30901-1037; tel. 706/724-7746, Eric Crossan, Chief Executive Officer
Web address: www.healthsouthwalton.com/

IDAHO: SAINT ALPHONSUS REGIONAL REHABILITATION HOSPITAL, AN AFFILIATE OF ENCOMPASS HEALTH (O, 40 beds) 711 North Curtis Road, Boise, ID, Zip 83706-1445; tel. 208/605-3000, Joe Griffin, Chief Executive Officer

ILLINOIS: ENCOMPASS HEALTH REHABILITATION INSTITUTE OF LIBERTYVILLE (O, 60 beds) 1201 American Way, Libertyville, IL, Zip 60048; tel. 847/371-6500, Gemma Fletcher, Interim Chief Executive Officer
Web address: www.https://encompasshealth.com/libertyvillerehab

QUAD CITIES REHABILITATION INSTITUTE, THE (C, 40 beds) 653 52nd Avenue, Moline, IL, Zip 61265-7058; tel. 309/581-3600, Angela Zaremba, Chief Executive Officer
Web address: www.https://encompasshealth.com/locations/quadcitiesrehab

REHABILITATION INSTITUTE OF SOUTHERN ILLINOIS, LLC, THE (O, 40 beds) 2351 Frank Scott Pkwy East, Shiloh, IL, Zip 62269-7457; tel. 618/206-7600, Cassidy Hoelscher, Chief Executive Officer

VAN MATRE ENCOMPASS HEALTH REHABILITATION HOSPITAL (O, 61 beds) 950 South Mulford Road, Rockford, IL, Zip 61108-4274; tel. 815/381-8500, Scott J. Peterson, Interim Chief Executive Officer
Web address: www.healthsouth.com

INDIANA: ENCOMPASS HEALTH DEACONESS REHABILITATION HOSPITAL (O, 98 beds) 9355 Warrick Trail, Newburgh, IN, Zip 47630-0015; tel. 812/476-9983, Blake Bunner, Chief Executive Officer

IOWA: UNIVERSITY OF IOWA HEALTH NETWORK REHABILITATION HOSPITAL (O, 40 beds) 2450 Coral Court, Coralville, IA, Zip 52241-2975; tel. 319/645-3300, Angela Zaremba, Chief Executive Officer
Web address: www.uihnrehab.com

KANSAS: KANSAS REHABILITATION HOSPITAL (O, 47 beds) 1504 SW Eighth Avenue, Topeka, KS, Zip 66606-1632; tel. 785/235-6600, Barry Muninger, Chief Executive Officer
Web address: www.kansasrehabhospital.com

MID-AMERICA REHABILITATION HOSPITAL (O, 98 beds) 5701 West 110th Street, Shawnee Mission, KS, Zip 66211-2503, Overland Park, tel. 913/491-2400, Tiffany Kiehl, Chief Executive Officer

KENTUCKY: ENCOMPASS HEALTH CARDINAL HILL REHABILITATION HOSPITAL (O, 232 beds) 2050 Versailles Road, Lexington, KY, Zip 40504-1405; tel. 859/254-5701, Susan Hart, Chief Executive Officer
Web address: www.https://encompasshealth.com/locations/cardinalhillrehab

ENCOMPASS HEALTH REHABILITATION HOSPITAL OF LAKEVIEW (O, 40 beds) 134 Heartland Drive, Elizabethtown, KY, Zip 42701-2778; tel. 270/769-3100, David Fredericks, Chief Executive Officer

ENCOMPASS HEALTH REHABILITATION HOSPITAL OF NORTHERN KENTUCKY (O, 40 beds) 201 Medical Village Drive, Edgewood, KY, Zip 41017-3407; tel. 859/341-2044, Dean Blevins, Chief Executive Officer
Web address: www.healthsouthkentucky.com

LOUISIANA: ENCOMPASS HEALTH REHABILITATION HOSPITAL OF ALEXANDRIA (O, 47 beds) 104 North Third Street, Alexandria, LA, Zip 71301-8581; tel. 318/449-1370, Joanna Williams, Chief Executive Officer

ENCOMPASS HEALTH REHABILITATION HOSPITAL (O, 40 beds) 8650 Millicent Way, Shreveport, LA, Zip 71115-2228; tel. 318/642-8100, Christopher Phillips, Chief Executive Officer
Web address: www.encompasshealth.com

MAINE: NEW ENGLAND REHABILITATION HOSPITAL OF PORTLAND (O, 90 beds) 335 Brighton Avenue, Portland, ME, Zip 04102-2363; tel. 207/775-4000, Nabarun Kundu, Chief Executive Officer
Web address: www.nerhp.org

MARYLAND: ENCOMPASS HEALTH REHABILITATION HOSPITAL OF SALISBURY (O, 54 beds) 220 Tilghman Road, Salisbury, MD, Zip 21804-1921; tel. 410/546-4600, W. Mark. Rader, Chief Executive Officer
Web address: www.healthsouthchesapeake.com

REHABILITATION HOSPITAL OF BOWIE (O, 40 beds) 17351 Melford Boulevard, Bowie, MD, Zip 20715; tel. 240/548-1300, Joseph Williams, Chief Executive Officer
Web address: www.https://encompasshealth.com/locations/bowierehab

MASSACHUSETTS: ENCOMPASS HEALTH REHABILITATION HOSPITAL OF BRAINTREE (O, 187 beds) 250 Pond Street, Braintree, MA, Zip 02184-5351; tel. 781/348-2500, Cynthia Page, FACHE, Chief Executive Officer

ENCOMPASS HEALTH REHABILITATION HOSPITAL OF NEW ENGLAND (O, 210 beds) 2 Rehabilitation Way, Woburn, MA, Zip 01801-6098; tel. 781/935-5050, David Coggins, MS, Chief Executive Officer
Web address: www.newenglandrehab.com

ENCOMPASS HEALTH REHABILITATION HOSPITAL OF WESTERN MASSACHUSETTS (O, 53 beds) 222 State Street, Ludlow, MA, Zip 01056-3437; tel. 413/308-3300, John R. Hunt, Chief Executive Officer

FAIRLAWN REHABILITATION HOSPITAL (O, 110 beds) 189 May Street, Worcester, MA, Zip 01602-4339; tel. 508/791-6351, Peter Lancette, Chief Executive Officer
Web address: www.fairlawnrehab.org

MISSISSIPPI: ENCOMPASS HEALTH REHABILITATION HOSPITAL, A PARTNER OF MEMORIAL HOSPITAL AT GULFPORT (O, 43 beds) 4500 13th Street, Suite 900, Gulfport, MS, Zip 39501-2515; tel. 228/822-6965, Mark Studdard, Interim Chief Executive Officer
Web address: www.healthsouthgulfport.com

MISSOURI: RUSK REHABILITATION HOSPITAL (O, 60 beds) 315 Business Loop 70 West, Columbia, MO, Zip 65203-3248; tel. 573/817-2703, Monica Gooch, Chief Executive Officer
Web address: https://www.encompasshealth.com/locations/ruskrehab

THE REHABILITATION INSTITUTE OF ST. LOUIS (O, 136 beds) 4455 Duncan Avenue, Saint Louis, MO, Zip 63110-1111; tel. 314/658-3800, Jeffrey Reese, Chief Executive Officer
Web address: www.rehabinstitutestl.com

NEVADA: ENCOMPASS HEALTH REHABILITATION HOSPITAL OF DESERT CANYON (O, 50 beds) 9175 West Oquendo Road, Las Vegas, NV, Zip 89148-1234; tel. 702/252-7342, Michele Butts, Chief Executive Officer

ENCOMPASS HEALTH REHABILITATION HOSPITAL OF HENDERSON (O, 90 beds) 10301 Jeffreys Street, Henderson, NV, Zip 89052-3922; tel. 702/939-9400, Varsha Chauhan, Chief Executive Officer
Web address: www.hendersonrehabhospital.com

ENCOMPASS HEALTH REHABILITATION HOSPITAL OF LAS VEGAS (O, 79 beds) 1250 South Valley View Boulevard, Las Vegas, NV, Zip 89102-1861; tel. 702/877-8898, Tij Von Nieda, Chief Executive Officer

NEW HAMPSHIRE: ENCOMPASS HEALTH REHABILITATION HOSPITAL OF CONCORD (O, 50 beds) 254 Pleasant Street, Concord, NH, Zip 03301-2508; tel. 603/226-9800, Sharon Hartl, Chief Executive Officer
Web address: www.healthsouthrehabconcordnh.com

NEW JERSEY: ENCOMPASS HEALTH REHABILITATION HOSPITAL OF TINTON FALLS, A JOINT VENTURE WITH MONMOUTH MEDICAL CENTER (O, 60 beds) 2 Centre Plaza, Tinton Falls, NJ, Zip 07724-9744; tel. 732/460-5320, Beth Sarfaty, Chief Executive Officer
Web address: www.rehabnjtintonfalls.com/

ENCOMPASS HEALTH REHABILITATION HOSPITAL OF TOMS RIVER (O, 92 beds) 14 Hospital Drive, Toms River, NJ, Zip 08755-6470; tel. 732/244-3100, Josette Meyers, Area Chief Executive Officer
Web address: www.rehabnjtomsriver.com/

For explanation of codes following names, see page B2.
★ Indicates Type III membership in the American Hospital Association.

Systems / Encompass Health Corporation

ENCOMPASS HEALTH REHABILITATION HOSPITAL OF VINELAND (O, 41 beds) 1237 West Sherman Avenue, Vineland, NJ, Zip 08360-6920; tel. 856/696-7100, Monica B. Titus, R.N., Chief Executive Officer

NEW MEXICO: ENCOMPASS HEALTH REHABILITATION HOSPITAL OF ALBUQUERQUE (O, 60 beds) 7000 Jefferson Street NE, Albuquerque, NM, Zip 87109-4313; tel. 505/344-9478, LaDessa Forrest, Chief Executive Officer
Web address: www.encompasshealth.com/albuquerehab

NORTH CAROLINA: NOVANT HEALTH REHABILITATION HOSPITAL, AN AFFILIATE OF ENCOMPASS HEALTH (O, 60 beds) 2475 Hillcrest Center Circle, Winston Salem, NC, Zip 27103-3048; tel. 336/754-3500, Christopher Fuller, Chief Executive Officer
Web address: https://www.encompasshealth.com/locations/novanthealthrehab

NORTH DAKOTA: ALTRU REHABILITATION HOSPITAL (O, 40 beds) 4500 S Washington Street, Suite B, Grand Forks, ND, Zip 58201-7217; tel. 701/732-7400, Luke Lawrimore, Chief Executive Officer
Web address: www.https://encompasshealth.com/locations/grandforksrehab

OHIO: ENCOMPASS HEALTH REHABILITATION HOSPITAL AT CINCINNATI (O, 60 beds) 151 West Galbraith Road, Cincinnati, OH, Zip 45216-1015; tel. 513/418-5600, Jason Wessel, Chief Executive Officer

ENCOMPASS HEALTH REHABILITATION HOSPITAL OF TOLEDO (O, 40 beds) 4647 Monroe Street, Toledo, OH, Zip 43623; tel. 567/290-3500
Web address: www.https://encompasshealth.com/locations/toledorehab

MOUNT CARMEL REHABILITATION HOSPITAL (O, 60 beds) 597 Executive Campus Drive, Westerville, OH, Zip 43082-8870; tel. 614/392-3400, Angela Bridges, R.N., Chief Executive Officer

THE REHABILITATION INSTITUTE OF OHIO (O, 60 beds) 835 South Main Street, Dayton, OH, Zip 45402; tel. 937/424-8200, Etene Terrell-Fakorede, Chief Executive Officer
Web address: www.https://encompasshealth.com/daytonrehab

OKLAHOMA: ASCENSION ST. JOHN REHABILITATION HOSPITAL, AN AFFILIATE OF ENCOMPASS HEALTH–OWASSO (O, 40 beds) 13402 E 86th Street North, Owasso, OK, Zip 74055-8767; tel. 918/401-3100, Harlo McCall, Chief Executive Officer

ST. JOHN REHABILITATION HOSPITAL (O, 60 beds) 1200 West Albany Drive, Broken Arrow, OK, Zip 74012-8146; tel. 918/744-2338, David Nicholas, Chief Executive Officer
Web address: www.stjohnrehab.com

PENNSYLVANIA: ENCOMPASS HEALTH REHABILITATION HOSPITAL OF ALTOONA (O, 80 beds) 2005 Valley View Boulevard, Altoona, PA, Zip 16602-4598; tel. 814/944-3535, Scott Filler, Chief Executive Officer
Web address: www.healthsouthaltoona.com

ENCOMPASS HEALTH REHABILITATION HOSPITAL OF ERIE (O, 108 beds) 143 East Second Street, Erie, PA, Zip 16507-1501; tel. 814/878-1200, Janet Hein, Chief Executive Officer

ENCOMPASS HEALTH REHABILITATION HOSPITAL OF HARMARVILLE (O, 42 beds) 320 Guys Run Road, Pittsburgh, PA, Zip 15238-0460, P O Box 11460, Zip 15238-0460, tel. 412/828-1300, Michelle P. Cunningham, Chief Executive Officer
Web address: www.https://encompasshealth.com/Harmarvillerehab

ENCOMPASS HEALTH REHABILITATION HOSPITAL OF MECHANICSBURG (O, 75 beds) 175 Lancaster Boulevard, Mechanicsburg, PA, Zip 17055-3562; tel. 717/691-3700, Kristen Turner, Chief Executive Officer
Web address: www.healthsouthpa.com

ENCOMPASS HEALTH REHABILITATION HOSPITAL OF NITTANY VALLEY (O, 73 beds) 550 West College Avenue, Pleasant Gap, PA, Zip 16823-7401; tel. 814/359-3421, Amy Lynn. Adams, Chief Executive Officer

ENCOMPASS HEALTH REHABILITATION HOSPITAL OF READING (O, 48 beds) 1623 Morgantown Road, Reading, PA, Zip 19607-9455; tel. 610/796-6000, Judy Parker, Chief Executive Officer
Web address: https://www.encompasshealth.com/readingrehab

ENCOMPASS HEALTH REHABILITATION HOSPITAL OF SEWICKLEY (O, 67 beds) 351 Camp Meeting Road, Sewickley, PA, Zip 15143-8322; tel. 412/741-9500, Leah Laffey, R.N., Chief Executive Officer

ENCOMPASS HEALTH REHABILITATION HOSPITAL OF YORK (O, 90 beds) 1850 Normandie Drive, York, PA, Zip 17408-1534; tel. 717/767-6941, Josette Meyers, Chief Executive Officer
Web address: https://www.encompasshealth.com/yorkrehab

GEISINGER ENCOMPASS HEALTH REHABILITATION HOSPITAL (O, 42 beds) 64 Rehab Lane, Danville, PA, Zip 17821-8498; tel. 570/271-6733, Lorie Dillon, Chief Executive Officer

PUERTO RICO: ENCOMPASS HEALTH REHABILITATION HOSPITAL OF MANATI (O, 40 beds) Carretera 2, Kilometro 47 7, Manati, PR, Zip 674; tel. 787/621-3800, Ruthmaris Nieves Martinez, Chief Executive Officer
Web address: www.healthsouth.com

ENCOMPASS HEALTH REHABILITATION HOSPITAL OF SAN JUAN (O, 32 beds) University Hospital, 3rd Floor, San Juan, PR, Zip 923, PMB #340 P.O. Box 70344, Zip 923, tel. 787/274-5100, Daniel Del Castillo, Chief Executive Officer

SOUTH CAROLINA: ANMED REHABILITATION HOSPITAL (O, 60 beds) 1 Spring Back Way, Anderson, SC, Zip 29621-2676; tel. 864/716-2600, Denise R. Murray, Chief Executive Officer
Web address: www.anmedrehab.com

ENCOMPASS HEALTH REHABILITATION HOSPITAL OF BLUFFTON (O, 38 beds) 107 Seagrass Station Road, Bluffton, SC, Zip 29910-9549; tel. 843/836-8200, Wayne B. Boutwell Jr, Chief Executive Officer
Web address: www.https://encompasshealth.com/blufftonrehab

ENCOMPASS HEALTH REHABILITATION HOSPITAL OF COLUMBIA (O, 96 beds) 2935 Colonial Drive, Columbia, SC, Zip 29203-6811; tel. 803/254-7777, Nicole Smith. Hendricks Woods, FACHE, Chief Executive Officer

ENCOMPASS HEALTH REHABILITATION HOSPITAL OF FLORENCE (O, 88 beds) 900 East Cheves Street, Florence, SC, Zip 29506-2704; tel. 843/679-9000, John Jones, Chief Executive Officer
Web address: www.https://encompasshealth.com/florencerehab

ENCOMPASS HEALTH REHABILITATION HOSPITAL OF GREENVILLE (O, 40 beds) 3372 Laurens Road, Greenville, SC, Zip 29607; tel. 864/537-4600, Joshua Trout, Chief Executive Officer
Web address: www.encompasshealth.com/greenvillerehab

ENCOMPASS HEALTH REHABILITATION HOSPITAL OF ROCK HILL (O, 50 beds) 1795 Dr. Frank Gaston Boulevard, Rock Hill, SC, Zip 29732-1190; tel. 803/326-3500, Michelle Von Arx, MS, Chief Executive Officer

MUSC HEALTH REHABILITATION HOSPITAL, AN AFFILIATE OF ENCOMPASS HEALTH (O, 49 beds) 9181 Medcom Street, Charleston, SC, Zip 29406-9168; tel. 843/820-7777, Richard C. Hundorfean, Chief Executive Officer
Web address: www.healthsouthcharleston.com

TIDELANDS HEALTH REHABILITATION HOSPITAL, AN AFFILIATE OF ENCOMPASS HEALTH (O, 29 beds) 4070 Highway 17 Bypass South, 4th Floor, Murrells Inlet, SC, Zip 29576-5033; tel. 843/652-1415, Carey Swanson, Chief Executive Officer
Web address: www.https://encompasshealth.com/locations/tidelandshealth-murrellsinlet

TENNESSEE: ENCOMPASS HEALTH REHABILITATION HOSPITAL OF CHATTANOOGA (O, 50 beds) 2412 McCallie Avenue, Chattanooga, TN, Zip 37404-3398; tel. 423/698-0221, Matthew Pearson, Chief Executive Officer
Web address: www.healthsouthchattanooga.com

ENCOMPASS HEALTH REHABILITATION HOSPITAL OF FRANKLIN (O, 40 beds) 1000 Physicians Way, Franklin, TN, Zip 37067-1471; tel. 615/721-4000, Scott J. Peterson, Chief Executive Officer

ENCOMPASS HEALTH REHABILITATION HOSPITAL OF KINGSPORT (O, 50 beds) 113 Cassel Drive, Kingsport, TN, Zip 37660-3775; tel. 423/246-7240, Troy Clark, Chief Executive Officer
Web address: www.healthsouthkingsport.com

ENCOMPASS HEALTH REHABILITATION HOSPITAL OF MEMPHIS, A PARTNER OF METHODIST HEALTHCARE (O, 72 beds) 1282 Union Avenue, Memphis, TN, Zip 38104-3414; tel. 901/722-2000, Toni Wackerfuss, Chief Executive Officer
Web address: www.healthsouthmemphis.com

ENCOMPASS HEALTH REHABILITATION HOSPITAL OF NORTH MEMPHIS, A PARTNER OF METHODIST HEALTHCARE (O, 50 beds) 4100 Austin Peay Highway, Memphis, TN, Zip 38128-2502; tel. 901/213-5400, Yolanda Motley, Chief Executive Officer
Web address: www.https://encompasshealth.com/

For explanation of codes following names, see page B2.
★ *Indicates Type III membership in the American Hospital Association.*

Systems / Encompass Health Corporation

PATRICIA NEAL REHABILITATION HOSPITAL (O, 51 beds) 101 Fort Sanders West Boulevard, Knoxville, TN, Zip 37922-3342; tel. 865/895-3000, Jennifer Steely, Chief Executive Officer
Web address: www.https://encompasshealth.com/knoxvillerehab

QUILLEN REHABILITATION HOSPITAL, A JOINT VENTURE OF BALLAD HEALTH AND ENCOMPASS HEALTH (O, 36 beds) 2511 Wesley Street, Johnson City, TN, Zip 37601-1723; tel. 423/952-1700, Rob Adams, Chief Executive Officer

VANDERBILT STALLWORTH REHABILITATION HOSPITAL (O, 80 beds) 2201 Childrens Way, Nashville, TN, Zip 37212-3165; tel. 615/320-7600, Jeffrey Palmucci, Chief Executive Officer
Web address: www.vanderbiltstallworthrehab.com

WEST TENNESSEE HEALTHCARE REHABILITATION HOSPITAL CANE CREEK, A PARTNERSHIP WITH ENCOMPASS HEALTH (O, 40 beds) 180 Mount Pelia Road, Martin, TN, Zip 38237-3812; tel. 731/587-4231, Jonathan McAnulty, Chief Executive Officer
Web address: https://www.encompasshealth.com/locations/canecreekrehab

WEST TENNESSEE HEALTHCARE REHABILITATION HOSPITAL JACKSON, A PARTNERSHIP WITH ENCOMPASS HEALTH (O, 48 beds) 616 West Forest Avenue, Jackson, TN, Zip 38301-3902; tel. 731/574-3000, Julie Taylor, Chief Executive Officer
Web address: www.https://encompasshealth.com/locations/jacksonrehab/

TEXAS: CHI ST. JOSEPH HEALTH REHABILITATION HOSPITAL, AN AFFILIATE OF ENCOMPASS HEALTH (O, 61 beds) 1600 Joseph Drive, Suite 2000, Bryan, TX, Zip 77802-1502; tel. 979/213-4300, Amy Gray, Chief Executive Officer

CHRISTUS TRINITY MOTHER FRANCES REHABILITATION HOSPITAL, A PARTNER OF ENCOMPASS HEALTH (O, 94 beds) 3131 Troup Highway, Tyler, TX, Zip 75701-8352; tel. 903/510-7000, Sharla Anderson, Chief Executive Officer
Web address: www.tmfrehabhospital.com

ENCOMPASS HEALTH REHABILITATION HOSPITAL THE VINTAGE (O, 60 beds) 20180 Chasewood Park Drive, Houston, TX, Zip 77070-1436; tel. 281/205-5100, Krista Uselman, Chief Executive Officer
Web address: www.reliantnwhouston.com

ENCOMPASS HEALTH REHABILITATION HOSPITAL VISION PARK (O, 60 beds) 117 Vision Park Boulevard, Shenandoah, TX, Zip 77384-3001; tel. 936/444-1700, Angela Simmons, Chief Executive Officer

ENCOMPASS HEALTH REHABILITATION HOSPITAL OF ABILENE (O, 60 beds) 6401 Directors Parkway, Abilene, TX, Zip 79606-5869; tel. 325/691-1600, Boyd Davis III, Chief Executive Officer
Web address: www.https://encompasshealth.com/locations/abilenerehab/our-programs

ENCOMPASS HEALTH REHABILITATION HOSPITAL OF ARLINGTON (O, 85 beds) 3200 Matlock Road, Arlington, TX, Zip 76015-2911; tel. 817/468-4000, Ashley Donahoe, Chief Executive Officer

ENCOMPASS HEALTH REHABILITATION HOSPITAL OF AUSTIN (O, 60 beds) 330 West Ben White Boulevard, Austin, TX, Zip 78704; tel. 512/730-4800, Lauren Suarez, Chief Executive Officer
Web address: www.healthsouthaustin.com

ENCOMPASS HEALTH REHABILITATION HOSPITAL OF CITY VIEW (O, 77 beds) 6701 Oakmont Boulevard, Fort Worth, TX, Zip 76132-2957; tel. 817/370-4700, Kyllan Cody, Chief Executive Officer

ENCOMPASS HEALTH REHABILITATION HOSPITAL OF CYPRESS (O, 60 beds) 13031 Wortham Center Drive, Houston, TX, Zip 77065-5662; tel. 832/280-2500, Katy Reed, Chief Executive Officer
Web address: www.healthsouthcypress.com

ENCOMPASS HEALTH REHABILITATION HOSPITAL OF DALLAS (O, 60 beds) 7930 Northaven Road, Dallas, TX, Zip 75230-3331; tel. 214/706-8200, Sharon Garrett, Chief Executive Officer

ENCOMPASS HEALTH REHABILITATION HOSPITAL OF HUMBLE (O, 76 beds) 19002 McKay Drive, Humble, TX, Zip 77338-5701; tel. 281/446-6148, Jonathan Strader, Chief Executive Officer
Web address: www.https://encompasshealth.com/locations/houston/humblerehab

ENCOMPASS HEALTH REHABILITATION HOSPITAL OF KATY (O, 60 beds) 23331 Grand Reserve Drive, Katy, TX, Zip 77494-4850; tel. 281/505-3500, Nicholas Hardin, FACHE, Chief Executive Officer

ENCOMPASS HEALTH REHABILITATION HOSPITAL OF MIDLAND ODESSA (O, 85 beds) 1800 Heritage Boulevard, Midland, TX, Zip 79707-9750; tel. 432/520-1600, Boyd Davis III, Interim Chief Executive Officer
Web address: www.healthsouthmidland.com

ENCOMPASS HEALTH REHABILITATION HOSPITAL OF PEARLAND (O, 60 beds) 2121 Business Center Drive, Pearland, TX, Zip 77584-2153; tel. 346/907-3000, Michael Cabiro, Chief Executive Officer
Web address: https://www.encompasshealth.com/locations/pearlandrehab

ENCOMPASS HEALTH REHABILITATION HOSPITAL OF PLANO (O, 83 beds) 2800 West 15th Street, Plano, TX, Zip 75075-7526; tel. 972/612-9000, Wray Borland, Chief Executive Officer

ENCOMPASS HEALTH REHABILITATION HOSPITAL OF RICHARDSON (O, 50 beds) 3351 Waterview Parkway, Richardson, TX, Zip 75080-1449; tel. 972/398-5700, Meagan Bailey, Chief Executive Officer
Web address: www.relianthcp.com

ENCOMPASS HEALTH REHABILITATION HOSPITAL OF ROUND ROCK (O, 75 beds) 1400 Hesters Crossing Road, Round Rock, TX, Zip 78681-8025; tel. 512/244-4400, Tarra Washington, Chief Executive Officer
Web address: https://www.encompasshealth.com/roundrockrehab

ENCOMPASS HEALTH REHABILITATION HOSPITAL OF SAN ANTONIO (O, 96 beds) 9119 Cinnamon Hill, San Antonio, TX, Zip 78240-5401; tel. 210/691-0737, Andrew Meade, Chief Executive Officer
Web address: www.hsriosa.com

ENCOMPASS HEALTH REHABILITATION HOSPITAL OF SUGAR LAND (O, 50 beds) 1325 Highway 6, Sugar Land, TX, Zip 77478-4906; tel. 281/276-7574, Bindu Varghese, R.N., Chief Executive Officer

ENCOMPASS HEALTH REHABILITATION HOSPITAL OF TEXARKANA (O, 60 beds) 515 West 12th Street, Texarkana, TX, Zip 75501-4416; tel. 903/735-5000, Todd Wallace, Chief Executive Officer
Web address: www.https://encompasshealth.com/locations/texarkanarehab

ENCOMPASS HEALTH REHABILITATION HOSPITAL OF THE WOODLANDS (O, 40 beds) 18550 'IH' 45 South, Conroe, TX, Zip 77384; tel. 281/364-2000, Angela L. Simmons, Chief Executive Officer
Web address: www.healthsouththewoodlands.com

ENCOMPASS HEALTH REHABILITATION HOSPITAL OF WACO (O, 40 beds) 3600 S Loop 340 Highway, Robinson, TX, Zip 76706-4828; tel. 254/523-2200, Donna Harris, Chief Executive Officer
Web address: www.https://encompasshealth.com/locations/wacorehab

ENCOMPASS HEALTH REHABILITATION HOSPITAL OF WICHITA FALLS (O, 63 beds) 3901 Armory Road, Wichita Falls, TX, Zip 76302-2204; tel. 940/720-5700, Jody Gregory, Chief Executive Officer

ENCOMPASS HEALTH REHABILITATION HOSPITAL OF THE MID-CITIES (O, 60 beds) 2304 State Highway 121, Bedford, TX, Zip 76021-5985; tel. 817/684-2000, Ashley Donahoe, Chief Executive Officer
Web address: www.https://encompasshealth.com/midcitiesrehab

SHANNON REHABILITATION HOSPITAL, AN AFFILIATE OF ENCOMPASS HEALTH (O, 40 beds) 6102 Appaloosa Trail, San Angelo, TX, Zip 76901; tel. 325/284-4000, Bill Perkins, Chief Executive Officer
Web address: www.https://encompasshealth.com/locations/sanangelorehab

SOUTH PLAINS REHABILITATION HOSPITAL, AN AFFILIATE OF UMC AND ENCOMPASS HEALTH (C, 66 beds) 5406 Colgate Street, Lubbock, TX, Zip 79416; tel. 806/507-3500, Beth Elder, Chief Executive Officer

UTAH: ENCOMPASS HEALTH REHABILITATION HOSPITAL OF UTAH (O, 53 beds) 8074 South 1300 East, Sandy, UT, Zip 84094-0743; tel. 801/561-3400, Charles Smith, Chief Executive Officer
Web address: https://www.encompasshealth.com/utahrehab

VIRGINIA: ENCOMPASS HEALTH REHABILITATION HOSPITAL OF FREDERICKSBURG (O, 40 beds) 300 Park Hill Drive, Fredericksburg, VA, Zip 22401-3387; tel. 540/368-7300, Anand Murthy, FACHE, Interim Chief Executive Officer

ENCOMPASS HEALTH REHABILITATION HOSPITAL OF NORTHERN VIRGINIA (O, 60 beds) 24430 Millstream Drive, Aldie, VA, Zip 20105-3098; tel. 703/957-2000, Vidhya Kannan, Chief Executive Officer
Web address: www.https://encompasshealth.com/northernvirginiarehab

ENCOMPASS HEALTH REHABILITATION HOSPITAL OF PETERSBURG (O, 53 beds) 95 Medical Park Boulevard, Petersburg, VA, Zip 23805-9233; tel. 804/504-8100, John Laurenzana, Chief Executive Officer

For explanation of codes following names, see page B2.
★ Indicates Type III membership in the American Hospital Association.

Systems / Encompass Health Corporation

ENCOMPASS HEALTH REHABILITATION HOSPITAL OF RICHMOND (O, 40 beds) 5700 Fitzhugh Avenue, Richmond, VA, Zip 23226-1800; tel. 804/288-5700, James Miller, Chief Executive Officer
Web address: https://www.encompasshealth.com
REHABILITATION HOSPITAL OF BRISTOL (O, 25 beds) 103 North Street, Bristol, VA, Zip 24201-3201; tel. 276/642-7900, Britta Milhorn, Chief Executive Officer
Web address: www.rehabilitationhospitalswvirginia.com
UVA ENCOMPASS HEALTH REHABILITATION HOSPITAL (O, 50 beds) 515 Ray C Hunt Drive, Charlottesville, VA, Zip 22903-2981; tel. 434/244-2000, Vivian White, Chief Executive Officer

WEST VIRGINIA: ENCOMPASS HEALTH REHABILITATION HOSPITAL OF HUNTINGTON (O, 60 beds) 6900 West Country Club Drive, Huntington, WV, Zip 25705-2000; tel. 304/733-1060, Michael E. Zuliani, Chief Executive Officer
Web address: https://www.encompasshealth.com/huntingtonrehab
ENCOMPASS HEALTH REHABILITATION HOSPITAL OF MORGANTOWN (O, 96 beds) 1160 Van Voorhis Road, Morgantown, WV, Zip 26505-3437; tel. 304/598-1100, Ashley Black, Chief Executive Officer
Web address: www.https://encompasshealth.com/morgantownrehab
ENCOMPASS HEALTH REHABILITATION HOSPITAL OF PARKERSBURG (O, 40 beds) 3 Western Hills Drive, Parkersburg, WV, Zip 26105-8122; tel. 304/420-1300, Nathan Ford, Chief Executive Officer
ENCOMPASS HEALTH REHABILITATION HOSPITAL OF PRINCETON (O, 45 beds) 120 Twelfth Street, Princeton, WV, Zip 24740-2352; tel. 304/487-8000, Robert Williams, Chief Executive Officer
Web address: www.healthsouthsouthernhills.com

WISCONSIN: REHABILITATION HOSPITAL OF WESTERN WISCONSIN (O, 36 beds) 900 W Clairemont Avenue, 8th Floor, Eau Claire, WI, Zip 54701-6122; tel. 715/717-2828, Anne Sadowska, Chief Executive Officer
Web address: www.https://encompasshealth.com/locations/eauclairerehab

Owned, leased, sponsored:	155 hospitals	9764 beds
Contract-managed:	2 hospitals	106 beds
Totals:	157 hospitals	9870 beds

★0470: ENDEAVOR HEALTH (NP)
1301 Central Street, Evanston, IL Zip 60201-1613; tel. 847/570-2000, J. P. Gallagher, President and Chief Executive Officer

ILLINOIS: ENDEAVOR HEALTH EDWARD HOSPITAL (O, 371 beds) 801 South Washington Street, Naperville, IL, Zip 60540-7499; tel. 630/527-3000, Yvette Saba R.N., President, Edward Hospital & South Institutes
Web address: www.eehealth.org
ENDEAVOR HEALTH ELMHURST HOSPITAL (O, 268 beds) 155 East Brush Hill Road, Elmhurst, IL, Zip 60126-5658; tel. 331/221-1000, Kimberley Darey, Chief Executive Officer
ENDEAVOR HEALTH EVANSTON HOSPITAL (O, 705 beds) 2650 Ridge Avenue, Evanston, IL, Zip 60201-1613; tel. 847/570-2000, Gabrielle Cummings, President
Web address: www.northshore.org
ENDEAVOR HEALTH LINDEN OAKS HOSPITAL (O, 108 beds) 852 South West Street, Naperville, IL, Zip 60540-6400; tel. 630/305-5500, Gina Sharp, FACHE, President
ENDEAVOR HEALTH NORTHWEST COMMUNITY HOSPITAL (O, 425 beds) 800 West Central Road, Arlington Heights, IL, Zip 60005-2392; tel. 847/618-1000, Michael Hartke, President
Web address: www.nch.org
ENDEAVOR HEALTH SWEDISH HOSPITAL (O, 255 beds) 5145 North California Avenue, Chicago, IL, Zip 60625-3661; tel. 773/878-8200, Jonathan Lind, President

Owned, leased, sponsored:	6 hospitals	2132 beds
Contract-managed:	0 hospitals	0 beds
Totals:	6 hospitals	2132 beds

0959: EPHRAIM MCDOWELL HEALTH (NP)
217 South Third Street, Danville, KY Zip 40422-1823; tel. 859/239-1000, Daniel E. McKay, Chief Executive Officer
(Independent Hospital System)

KENTUCKY: EPHRAIM MCDOWELL FORT LOGAN HOSPITAL (O, 25 beds) 110 Metker Trail, Stanford, KY, Zip 40484-1020; tel. 606/365-4600, Jason Dean, Administrator
Web address: www.fortloganhospital.org
EPHRAIM MCDOWELL JAMES B. HAGGIN MEMORIAL HOSPITAL (O, 25 beds) 464 Linden Avenue, Harrodsburg, KY, Zip 40330-1862; tel. 859/734-5441, Lynne Warner Lynn, R.N., Administrator
EPHRAIM MCDOWELL REGIONAL MEDICAL CENTER (O, 159 beds) 217 South Third Street, Danville, KY, Zip 40422-1823; tel. 859/239-1000, Daniel E. McKay, Chief Executive Officer
Web address: www.emrmc.org

Owned, leased, sponsored:	3 hospitals	209 beds
Contract-managed:	0 hospitals	0 beds
Totals:	3 hospitals	209 beds

0525: ERLANGER HEALTH SYSTEM (NP)
975 East Third Street, Chattanooga, TN Zip 37403-2147; tel. 423/778-7000, Jim Coleman Jr, President and Chief Executive Officer
(Centralized Physician/Insurance Health System)

NORTH CAROLINA: ERLANGER WESTERN CAROLINA HOSPITAL (O, 25 beds) 3990 U S Highway 64 East Alt, Murphy, NC, Zip 28906-7917; tel. 828/837-8161, Stephanie Boynton, Vice President and Chief Executive Officer
Web address: https://www.erlanger.org

TENNESSEE: ERLANGER BLEDSOE HOSPITAL (C, 25 beds) 71 Wheelertown Avenue, Pikeville, TN, Zip 37367-5246, P O Box 699, Zip 37367-0699, tel. 423/447-2112, Stephanie Boynton, Administrator
Web address: www.erlanger.org
ERLANGER MEDICAL CENTER (O, 697 beds) 975 East Third Street, Chattanooga, TN, Zip 37403-2147; tel. 423/778-7000, Jim Coleman Jr, Chief Executive Officer

Owned, leased, sponsored:	2 hospitals	722 beds
Contract-managed:	1 hospitals	25 beds
Totals:	3 hospitals	747 beds

0382: ERNEST HEALTH, INC. (IO)
7770 Jefferson Street NE, Suite 320, Albuquerque, NM Zip 87109-4386; tel. 505/856-5300, Darby Brockette, Chief Executive Officer
(Independent Hospital System)

ARIZONA: MOUNTAIN VALLEY REGIONAL REHABILITATION HOSPITAL (O, 16 beds) 3700 North Windsong Drive, Prescott Valley, AZ, Zip 86314-1253; tel. 928/759-8800, Josh Davis, R.N., Chief Executive Officer
Web address: www.https://ernesthealth.com/portfolio-item/mountain-valley-regional-rehabilitation-hospital/
REHABILITATION HOSPITAL OF NORTHERN ARIZONA (O, 40 beds) 1851 North Gemini Drive, Flagstaff, AZ, Zip 86001-1607; tel. 928/774-7070, Jon Cook, Chief Executive Officer
Web address: www.ernesthealth.com/gallery-item/rehabilitation-hospital-of-northern-arizona/

CALIFORNIA: BAKERSFIELD REHABILITATION HOSPITAL (O, 50 beds) 4400 Kirkcaldy Drive, Bakersfield, CA, Zip 93306-5542; tel. 661/374-7105, Shayne Perkovich, Chief Executive Officer
Web address: www.https://bakersfieldrehab.com/
REHABILITATION HOSPITAL OF SOUTHERN CALIFORNIA (O, 50 beds) 70077 Ramon Road, Rancho Mirage, CA, Zip 92270-5201; tel. 760/671-3425, Rachelle Spencer, Chief Executive Officer

For explanation of codes following names, see page B2.
★ Indicates Type III membership in the American Hospital Association.

Systems / Essentia Health

SACRAMENTO REHABILITATION HOSPITAL, LLC (L, 50 beds) 10 Advantage Court, Sacramento, CA, Zip 95834–2123; tel. 916/628–8301, Joseph G. Hugar, Chief Executive Officer
Web address: www.https://sacramentorehab.com/

STOCKTON REGIONAL REHABILITATION HOSPITAL (O, 50 beds) 607 East Magnolia Street, Stockton, CA, Zip 95202–1846; tel. 209/687–5490, Richard Trogman, FACHE, Chief Executive Officer
Web address: www.https://stocktonrehab.com/

COLORADO: DENVER REGIONAL REHABILITATION HOSPITAL (O, 31 beds) 8451 Pearl Street, Suite 101, Thornton, CO, Zip 80229–4803; tel. 303/301–8700, Christine Duron, Interim Chief Executive Officer

NORTHERN COLORADO LONG TERM ACUTE HOSPITAL (O, 40 beds) 4401 Union Street, Johnstown, CO, Zip 80534; tel. 970/619–3663, Christina Lea. Salas, Chief Executive Officer
Web address: www.ncltah.ernesthealth.com/

NORTHERN COLORADO REHABILITATION HOSPITAL (O, 40 beds) 4401 Union Street, Johnstown, CO, Zip 80534–2800; tel. 970/619–3400, Christina Lea. Salas, Chief Executive Officer

IDAHO: NORTHERN IDAHO ADVANCED CARE HOSPITAL (O, 40 beds) 600 North Cecil Road, Post Falls, ID, Zip 83854–6200; tel. 208/262–2800, Una Alderman, Chief Executive Officer
Web address: www.niach.ernesthealth.com

REHABILITATION HOSPITAL OF THE NORTHWEST (O, 25 beds) 3372 East Jenalan Avenue, Post Falls, ID, Zip 83854–7787; tel. 208/262–8700, David Cox, Chief Executive Officer
Web address: www.https://rhn.ernesthealth.com/

INDIANA: BLOOMINGTON REGIONAL REHABILITATION HOSPITAL (O, 50 beds) 3050 North Lintel Drive, Bloomington, IN, Zip 47404–8945; tel. 812/336–2815, Jeff Stultz, Chief Executive Officer
Web address: www.https://brrh.ernesthealth.com/

LAFAYETTE REGIONAL REHABILITATION HOSPITAL (O, 40 beds) 950 Park East Boulevard, Lafayette, IN, Zip 47905–0792; tel. 765/447–4040, Logan Savage, Chief Executive Officer

REHABILITATION HOSPITAL OF NORTHERN INDIANA (O, 50 beds) 4807 Edison Lakes Parkway, Mishawaka, IN, Zip 46545–1112; tel. 574/243–7727, Cindie McPhie, Chief Executive Officer
Web address: www.https://rhni.ernesthealth.com/

MONTANA: ADVANCED CARE HOSPITAL OF MONTANA (O, 40 beds) 3528 Gabel Road, Billings, MT, Zip 59102–7307; tel. 406/373–8000, Aubrey Peterschick, Chief Executive Officer

NEW MEXICO: ADVANCED CARE HOSPITAL OF SOUTHERN NEW MEXICO (O, 40 beds) 4451 East Lohman Avenue, Las Cruces, NM, Zip 88011–8267; tel. 575/521–6600, Sabrina Martin, Chief Executive Officer
Web address: www.https://achsnm.ernesthealth.com/

REHABILITATION HOSPITAL OF SOUTHERN NEW MEXICO (O, 40 beds) 4441 East Lohman Avenue, Las Cruces, NM, Zip 88011–8267; tel. 575/521–6400, Sabrina Martin, Chief Executive Officer

OHIO: REHABILITATION HOSPITAL OF NORTHWEST OHIO (O, 40 beds) 1455 West Medical Loop, Toledo, OH, Zip 43614; tel. 419/214–6600, Andrea Sheehy, Chief Executive Officer

SOUTH CAROLINA: GREENWOOD REGIONAL REHABILITATION HOSPITAL (O, 42 beds) 1530 Parkway, Greenwood, SC, Zip 29646–4027; tel. 864/330–1800, Kristin Manske, Chief Executive Officer
Web address: www.grrh.ernesthealth.com

MIDLANDS REGIONAL REHABILITATION HOSPITAL (O, 40 beds) 20 Pinnacle Parkway, Elgin, SC, Zip 29045–8389; tel. 803/438–8890, Rebecca Cartright, FACHE, Chief Executive Officer
Web address: www.mrrh.ernesthealth.com

SPARTANBURG REHABILITATION INSTITUTE (O, 40 beds) 160 Harold Fleming Court, Spartanburg, SC, Zip 29303–4226; tel. 864/594–9600, Richard Schulz, Chief Executive Officer
Web address: www.sri.ernesthealth.com

TEXAS: CORPUS CHRISTI REHABILITATION HOSPITAL (O, 35 beds) 5726 Esplanade Drive, Corpus Christi, TX, Zip 78414; tel. 361/906–3700, Michael L. Pierce, Chief Executive Officer

LAREDO REHABILITATION HOSPITAL (O, 21 beds) 2005a East Bustamante Street, Laredo, TX, Zip 78041; tel. 956/764–8555, Hanna Huang, Administrator and Chief Operating Officer
Web address: www.lrh.ernesthealth.com

LAREDO SPECIALTY HOSPITAL (O, 40 beds) 2005 Bustamante Street, Laredo, TX, Zip 78041–5470; tel. 956/753–5353, Hanna Huang, Administrator and Chief Operating Officer

MESQUITE REHABILITATION INSTITUTE (O, 30 beds) 1023 North Belt Line Road, Mesquite, TX, Zip 75149–1788; tel. 972/216–2400, Diana Schultz, Chief Executive Officer
Web address: www.https://mri.ernesthealth.com/

MESQUITE SPECIALTY HOSPITAL (O, 40 beds) 1024 North Galloway Avenue, Mesquite, TX, Zip 75149–2434; tel. 972/216–2300, Diana Schultz, Chief Executive Officer

NEW BRAUNFELS REGIONAL REHABILITATION HOSPITAL (O, 40 beds) 2041 Sundance Parkway, New Braunfels, TX, Zip 78130–2779; tel. 830/625–6700, Nicholas Nilest, Chief Executive Officer
Web address: www.nbrrh.ernesthealth.com

SOUTH TEXAS REHABILITATION HOSPITAL (O, 40 beds) 425 East Alton Gloor Boulevard, Brownsville, TX, Zip 78526–3361; tel. 956/554–6000, Leo Garza, Chief Executive Officer

TRUSTPOINT REHABILITATION HOSPITAL OF LUBBOCK (O, 72 beds) 4302A Princeton Street, Lubbock, TX, Zip 79415–1304; tel. 806/749–2222, Craig Bragg, Chief Executive Officer
Web address: www.trustpointhospital.com/

WESLACO REGIONAL REHABILITATION HOSPITAL (O, 32 beds) 906 South James Street, Weslaco, TX, Zip 78596–9840; tel. 956/969–2222, Diana Schultz, Chief Executive Officer

UTAH: NORTHERN UTAH REHABILITATION HOSPITAL (O, 20 beds) 5825 Harrison Boulevard, South Ogden, UT, Zip 84403–4316; tel. 801/475–5254, Reuben Jessop, Chief Executive Officer
Web address: www.ernesthealth.com/gallery-item/northern-utah-rehabilitation-hospital/

UTAH VALLEY SPECIALTY HOSPITAL (O, 40 beds) 306 River Bend Lane, Provo, UT, Zip 84604–5625; tel. 801/226–8880, Reuben Jessop, Chief Executive Officer

WYOMING: ELKHORN VALLEY REHABILITATION HOSPITAL (O, 41 beds) 5715 East 2nd Street, Casper, WY, Zip 82609–4322; tel. 307/265–0005, Connie Longwell, Chief Executive Officer
Web address: www.evrh.ernesthealth.com/

Owned, leased, sponsored:	33 hospitals	1305 beds
Contract-managed:	0 hospitals	0 beds
Totals:	33 hospitals	1305 beds

★**0396: ESSENTIA HEALTH (NP)**
502 East Second Street, Duluth, MN Zip 55805–1913; tel. 218/786–8376, David C. Herman, M.D., Chief Executive Officer

(Moderately Centralized Health System)

MINNESOTA: ESSENTIA HEALTH DULUTH (O, 154 beds) 502 East Second Street, Duluth, MN, Zip 55805–1982; tel. 218/727–8762, David C. Herman, M.D., Chief Executive Officer
Web address: www.smdcmedicalcenter.org

ESSENTIA HEALTH MOOSE LAKE (O, 25 beds) 4572 County Road 61, Moose Lake, MN, Zip 55767–9405; tel. 218/485–4481, Sam Barney, Administrator
Web address: https://www.essentiahealth.org/find-facility/profile/essentia-health-moose-lake/

ESSENTIA HEALTH NORTHERN PINES (O, 49 beds) 5211 Highway 110, Aurora, MN, Zip 55705–1599; tel. 218/229–2211, Diana Kallberg, Administrator

ESSENTIA HEALTH SANDSTONE (O, 9 beds) 705 Lundorff Drive, Sandstone, MN, Zip 55072–5009; tel. 320/245–2212, Sam Barney, Administrator
Web address: https://www.essentiahealth.org/find-facility/profile/essentia-health-sandstone/?utm_campaign=website-link&utm_medium=organic&utm_source=local-listing

---

For explanation of codes following names, see page B2.
★ Indicates Type III membership in the American Hospital Association.

Systems / Essentia Health

ESSENTIA HEALTH ST. MARY'S–DETROIT LAKES (O, 130 beds) 1027 Washington Avenue, Detroit Lakes, MN, Zip 56501–3409; tel. 218/847–5611, Tanner Goodrich, Senior Vice President, Operations–West Market

ESSENTIA HEALTH ST. MARY'S MEDICAL CENTER (O, 329 beds) 407 East Third Street, Duluth, MN, Zip 55805–1984; tel. 218/786–4000, Krista Skorupa, President, East Market
Web address: https://www.essentiahealth.org/find-facility/profile/essentia-health-st-marys-medical-center-duluth/

ESSENTIA HEALTH–ADA (O, 14 beds) 201 9th Street West, Ada, MN, Zip 56510–1279; tel. 218/784–5000, Erin Stoltman, Administrator

ESSENTIA HEALTH–DEER RIVER (O, 48 beds) 115 10th Avenue NE, Deer River, MN, Zip 56636–8795; tel. 218/246–2900, Amanda Reed, Administrator
Web address: www.essentiahealth.org

ESSENTIA HEALTH–FOSSTON (O, 68 beds) 900 Hilligoss Boulevard SE, Fosston, MN, Zip 56542–1599; tel. 218/435–1133
Web address: www.essentiahealth.org

ESSENTIA HEALTH–GRACEVILLE (O, 55 beds) 115 West Second Street, Graceville, MN, Zip 56240–4845, P O Box 157, Zip 56240–0157, tel. 320/743–7223, Debra Stueve, Administrator
Web address: www.essentiahealth.org/HolyTrinityHospital/FindaClinic/Essentia-HealthHoly-Trinity-Hospital-96.aspx

ESSENTIA HEALTH–ST. JOSEPH'S MEDICAL CENTER (O, 127 beds) 523 North Third Street, Brainerd, MN, Zip 56401–3098; tel. 218/829–2861, Todd DeFreece, Senior Vice President of Operations

ESSENTIA HEALTH–VIRGINIA (L, 124 beds) 901 Ninth Street North, Virginia, MN, Zip 55792–2398; tel. 218/741–3340, Sam Stone, Campus Administrator
Web address: www.essentiahealth.org

NORTH DAKOTA: ESSENTIA HEALTH FARGO (O, 156 beds) 3000 32nd Avenue South, Fargo, ND, Zip 58103–6132; tel. 701/364–8000, Mark Thompson, M.D., President
Web address: https://www.essentiahealth.org/find-facility/profile/essentia-health-fargo/

WISCONSIN: ESSENTIA HEALTH ST. MARY'S HOSPITAL OF SUPERIOR (O, 25 beds) 3500 Tower Avenue, Superior, WI, Zip 54880–5395; tel. 715/817–7000, Kim Renee. Pearson, Administrator

Owned, leased, sponsored:	14 hospitals	1313 beds
Contract–managed:	0 hospitals	0 beds
Totals:	14 hospitals	1313 beds

0951: EVEREST REHABILITATION HOSPITALS, LLC (IO)

5100 Belt Line Road, Suite 310, Dallas, TX Zip 75254–7559; tel. 469/713–1145, Jay Quintana, Chief Executive Officer and Co-Founder

ARKANSAS: EVEREST REHABILITATION HOSPITAL OF ROGERS (O, 36 beds) 4313 South Pleasant Crossing Boulevard, Rogers, AR, Zip 72758–1347; tel. 479/341–4003, Wendy Yates, Chief Executive Officer
Web address: www.https://everestrehab.com/hospitals/rogers-ar/

TEXAS: EVEREST REHABILITATION HOSPITAL OF EL PASO (O, 36 beds) 2230 Joe Battle Boulevard, El Paso, TX, Zip 79938; tel. 915/910–6042, Jose Huerta, Chief Executive Officer
Web address: www.https://everestrehab.com/hospitals/el-paso-tx/

LONGVIEW REHABILITATION HOSPITAL (O, 36 beds) 701 East Loop 281, Longview, TX, Zip 75605–5006; tel. 430/240–4600, Toyia Urbaniak, Chief Executive Officer

TEMPLE REHABILITATION HOSPITAL (O, 36 beds) 23621 SE H. K. Dodgen Loop, Temple, TX, Zip 76504–8664, 23621 SE H.K. Dodgen Loop, Zip 76504–8664, tel. 254/410–0555, Michael Hutka, Chief Executive Officer
Web address: www.https://everestrehab.com/hospitals/temple-tx/

Owned, leased, sponsored:	4 hospitals	144 beds
Contract–managed:	0 hospitals	0 beds
Totals:	4 hospitals	144 beds

★1325: FAIRVIEW HEALTH SERVICES (NP)

2450 Riverside Avenue, Minneapolis, MN Zip 55454–1400; tel. 612/672–6141, James Hereford, President and Chief Executive Officer
(Centralized Health System)

MINNESOTA: FAIRVIEW RANGE (O, 72 beds) 750 East 34th Street, Hibbing, MN, Zip 55746–4600; tel. 218/262–4881, Jean MacDonell, President and Chief Executive Officer
Web address: www.range.fairview.org

GRAND ITASCA CLINIC AND HOSPITAL (O, 39 beds) 1601 Golf Course Road, Grand Rapids, MN, Zip 55744–8648; tel. 218/326–5000, Jean MacDonell, President and Chief Executive Officer

M HEALTH FAIRVIEW BETHESDA HOSPITAL (O, 24 beds) 45 West 10th Street, Saint Paul, MN, Zip 55102–1053; tel. 651/232–3000, James Hereford, Executive Vice President, Chief Operating Officer
Web address: www.fairview.org

M HEALTH FAIRVIEW LAKES MEDICAL CENTER (O, 38 beds) 5200 Fairview Boulevard, Wyoming, MN, Zip 55092–8013; tel. 651/982–7000, Jeoff Will, Executive Vice President, Chief Operating Officer

M HEALTH FAIRVIEW NORTHLAND MEDICAL CENTER (O, 23 beds) 911 Northland Drive, Princeton, MN, Zip 55371–2173; tel. 763/389–1313, Jeoff Will, Executive Vice President, Chief Operating Officer
Web address: www.https://mhealthfairview.org/locations/m-health-fairview-northland-medical-center

M HEALTH FAIRVIEW RIDGES HOSPITAL (O, 173 beds) 201 East Nicollet Boulevard, Burnsville, MN, Zip 55337–5799; tel. 952/892–2000, Jeoff Will, Executive Vice President, Chief Operating Officer

M HEALTH FAIRVIEW SOUTHDALE HOSPITAL (O, 349 beds) 6401 France Avenue South, Edina, MN, Zip 55435–2199; tel. 952/924–5000, Jeoff Will, Executive Vice President, Chief Operating Officer
Web address: www.https://mhealthfairview.org/locations/m-health-fairview-southdale-hospital

M HEALTH FAIRVIEW ST. JOHN'S HOSPITAL (O, 199 beds) 1575 Beam Avenue, Maplewood, MN, Zip 55109–1126; tel. 651/232–7000, Jeoff Will, Executive Vice President, Chief Operating Officer

M HEALTH FAIRVIEW UNIVERSITY OF MINNESOTA MEDICAL CENTER (O, 903 beds) 2450 Riverside Avenue, Minneapolis, MN, Zip 55454–1400; tel. 612/624–8618, Jeoff Will, Executive Vice President, Chief Operating Officer
Web address: www.fairview.org

M HEALTH FAIRVIEW WOODWINDS HOSPITAL (O, 86 beds) 1925 Woodwinds Drive, Woodbury, MN, Zip 55125–4445; tel. 651/232–0228, Jeoff Will, Executive Vice President, Chief Operating Officer
Web address: https://www.mhealthfairview.org/locations/M-Health-Fairview-Woodwinds-Hospital–Woodbury

Owned, leased, sponsored:	10 hospitals	1906 beds
Contract–managed:	0 hospitals	0 beds
Totals:	10 hospitals	1906 beds

0814: FAITH REGIONAL HEALTH SERVICES (NP)

2700 West Norfolk Avenue, Norfolk, NE Zip 68701–4438, P O Box 869, Zip 68702–0869, tel. 402/371–4880, Kelly Driscoll, R.N., FACHE, President and Chief Executive Officer
(Independent Hospital System)

NEBRASKA: FAITH REGIONAL HEALTH SERVICES (O, 199 beds) 2700 West Norfolk Avenue, Norfolk, NE, Zip 68701–4438, P O Box 869, Zip 68702–0869, tel. 402/371–4880, Kelly Driscoll, R.N., FACHE, President and Chief Executive Officer
Web address: www.frhs.org

GENOA MEDICAL FACILITIES (C, 58 beds) 706 Ewing Avenue, Genoa, NE, Zip 68640–3035, P O Box 310, Zip 68640–0310, tel. 402/993–2283, Amanda Roebuck, Chief Executive Officer
Web address: www.genoamedical.org/

NIOBRARA VALLEY HOSPITAL (C, 20 beds) 401 South Fifth Street, Lynch, NE, Zip 68746–0118, P O Box 118, Zip 68746–0118, tel. 402/569–2451, Kelly Kalkowski, Chief Executive Officer

---

For explanation of codes following names, see page B2.
★ Indicates Type III membership in the American Hospital Association.

Systems / Franciscan Missionaries of Our Lady Health System, Inc.

WEST HOLT MEDICAL SERVICES (C, 15 beds) 406 West Neely Street, Atkinson, NE, Zip 68713-4801; tel. 402/925-2811, Jeremy Bauer, Chief Executive Officer
Web address: www.westholtmed.org

Owned, leased, sponsored:	1 hospitals	199 beds
Contract-managed:	3 hospitals	93 beds
Totals:	4 hospitals	292 beds

0397: FINGER LAKES HEALTH (NP)
196 North Street, Geneva, NY Zip 14456-1651; tel. 315/787-4000, Jose Acevedo, M.D., President and Chief Executive Officer
(Independent Hospital System)

NEW YORK: GENEVA GENERAL HOSPITAL (O, 50 beds) 196 North Street, Geneva, NY, Zip 14456-1694; tel. 315/787-4000, Jose Acevedo, M.D., President and Chief Executive Officer
Web address: www.flhealth.org

SOLDIERS AND SAILORS MEMORIAL HOSPITAL (O, 139 beds) 418 North Main Street, Penn Yan, NY, Zip 14527-1085; tel. 315/531-2000, Jose Acevedo, M.D., President and Chief Executive Officer
Web address: www.flhealth.org

Owned, leased, sponsored:	2 hospitals	189 beds
Contract-managed:	0 hospitals	0 beds
Totals:	2 hospitals	189 beds

★0243: FIRSTHEALTH OF THE CAROLINAS (NP)
155 Memorial Drive, Pinehurst, NC Zip 28374-8710, P O Box 3000, Zip 28374-3000, tel. 910/715-1000, Mickey W. Foster, Chief Executive Officer
(Centralized Physician/Insurance Health System)

NORTH CAROLINA: FIRSTHEALTH MONTGOMERY MEMORIAL HOSPITAL (O, 5 beds) 520 Allen Street, Troy, NC, Zip 27371-2802; tel. 910/571-5000, Rebecca W. Carter, MSN, R.N., FACHE, President
Web address: www.firsthealth.org

FIRSTHEALTH MOORE REGIONAL HOSPITAL (O, 362 beds) 155 Memorial Drive, Pinehurst, NC, Zip 28374-8710, P O Box 3000, Zip 28374-3000, tel. 910/715-1000, Mickey W. Foster, Chief Executive Officer

Owned, leased, sponsored:	2 hospitals	367 beds
Contract-managed:	0 hospitals	0 beds
Totals:	2 hospitals	367 beds

1016: FLOYD HEALTHCARE MANAGEMENT (NP)
304 Turner McCall Boulevard, Rome, GA Zip 30165-5621, P O Box 233, Zip 30162-0233, tel. 706/509-5000, Kurt Stuenkel, FACHE, President and Chief Executive Officer
(Moderately Centralized Health System)

Owned, leased, sponsored:	0 hospitals	0 beds
Contract-managed:	0 hospitals	0 beds
Totals:	0 hospitals	0 beds

5345: FRANCISCAN HEALTH (CC)
1515 Dragoon Trail, Mishawaka, IN Zip 46544-4710, P O Box 1290, Zip 46546-1290, tel. 574/256-3935, Kevin D. Leahy, President and Chief Executive Officer
(Independent Hospital System)

ILLINOIS: FRANCISCAN HEALTH OLYMPIA FIELDS (O, 206 beds) 20201 South Crawford Avenue, Olympia Fields, IL, Zip 60461-1010; tel. 708/747-4000, Raymond Grady, FACHE, Chief Executive Officer

INDIANA: FRANCISCAN HEALTH CARMEL (O, 6 beds) 12188B North Meridian Street, Carmel, IN, Zip 46032-4840; tel. 317/705-4500, Lori Price, R.N., President and Chief Executive Officer, Central Indiana Region
Web address: www.franciscanalliance.org/hospitals/carmel/Pages/default.aspx

FRANCISCAN HEALTH CRAWFORDSVILLE (O, 40 beds) 1710 Lafayette Road, Crawfordsville, IN, Zip 47933-1099; tel. 765/362-2800, Carlos Vasquez, Chief Executive Officer

FRANCISCAN HEALTH CROWN POINT (O, 254 beds) 1201 South Main Street, Crown Point, IN, Zip 46307-8483; tel. 219/738-2100, Daniel McCormick, M.D., President and Chief Executive Officer
Web address: www.franciscanalliance.org

FRANCISCAN HEALTH DYER (O, 341 beds) 24 Joliet Street, Dyer, IN, Zip 46311-1799; tel. 219/865-2141, Patrick J. Maloney, Chief Executive Officer

FRANCISCAN HEALTH HAMMOND (O, 406 beds) 5454 Hohman Avenue, Hammond, IN, Zip 46320-1999; tel. 219/932-2300, Patrick J. Maloney, Chief Executive Officer
Web address: https://www.franciscanhealth.org/healthcare-facilities/franciscan-health-hammond-18

FRANCISCAN HEALTH INDIANAPOLIS (O, 485 beds) 8111 South Emerson Avenue, Indianapolis, IN, Zip 46237-8601; tel. 317/528-5000, Lori Price, R.N., President and Chief Executive Officer, Central Indiana Region
Web address: https://www.franciscanhealth.org/find-a-location/franciscan-health-indianapolis-218334

FRANCISCAN HEALTH LAFAYETTE EAST (O, 203 beds) 1701 South Creasy Lane, Lafayette, IN, Zip 47905-4972; tel. 765/502-4000, Terrance E. Wilson, President and Chief Executive Officer
Web address: www.ste.org

FRANCISCAN HEALTH MICHIGAN CITY (O, 171 beds) 301 West Homer Street, Michigan City, IN, Zip 46360-4358; tel. 219/879-8511, Dean Mazzoni, President and Chief Executive Officer

FRANCISCAN HEALTH MOORESVILLE (O, 115 beds) 1201 Hadley Road, Mooresville, IN, Zip 46158-1789; tel. 317/831-1160, Lori Price, R.N., President and Chief Executive Officer, Central Indiana Region
Web address: www.franciscanalliance.org/hospitals/mooresville/Pages/default.aspx

FRANCISCAN HEALTH RENSSELEAR (O, 46 beds) 1104 East Grace Street, Rensselaer, IN, Zip 47978-3296; tel. 219/866-5141, Carlos Vasquez, Vice President and Chief Operating Officer
Web address: www.franciscanhealth.org

FRANCISCAN HEALTHCARE MUNSTER (O, 32 beds) 701 Superior Avenue, Munster, IN, Zip 46321-4037; tel. 219/924-1300, Patrick J. Maloney, Chief Executive Officer

Owned, leased, sponsored:	12 hospitals	2305 beds
Contract-managed:	0 hospitals	0 beds
Totals:	12 hospitals	2305 beds

★1475: FRANCISCAN MISSIONARIES OF OUR LADY HEALTH SYSTEM, INC. (CC)
4200 Essen Lane, Baton Rouge, LA Zip 70809-2158; tel. 225/923-2701, E.J. Kuiper, President and Chief Executive Officer
(Moderately Centralized Health System)

LOUISIANA: OUR LADY OF LOURDES REGIONAL MEDICAL CENTER (O, 393 beds) 4801 Ambassador Caffery Parkway, Lafayette, LA, Zip 70508-6917; tel. 337/470-2000, Stephanie Manson, FACHE, President, Acadiana Market
Web address: www.lourdesrmc.com

OUR LADY OF THE ANGELS HOSPITAL (O, 46 beds) 433 Plaza Street, Bogalusa, LA, Zip 70427-3793; tel. 985/730-6700, Charles L. Spicer Jr, FACHE, President, Baton Rouge Market and Northshore Market

OUR LADY OF THE LAKE ASSUMPTION COMMUNITY HOSPITAL (O, 6 beds) 135 Highway 402, Napoleonville, LA, Zip 70390-2217; tel. 985/369-3600, Brian Frank. Tripode, Senior Director Assumption Administrator
Web address: www.https://ololrmc.com/about-us/assumption-community-hospital/

For explanation of codes following names, see page B2.
★ Indicates Type III membership in the American Hospital Association.

Systems / Franciscan Missionaries of Our Lady Health System, Inc.

OUR LADY OF THE LAKE REGIONAL MEDICAL CENTER (O, 875 beds) 5000 Hennessy Boulevard, Baton Rouge, LA, Zip 70808-4375; tel. 225/765-6565, Charles L. Spicer Jr, FACHE, President, Baton Rouge Market and Northshore Market

ST. FRANCIS MEDICAL CENTER (O, 321 beds) 309 Jackson Street, Monroe, LA, Zip 71201-7407, P O Box 1901, Zip 71210-1901, tel. 318/966-4000, Thomas Gullatt, M.D., President
Web address: www.stfran.com

MISSISSIPPI: ST. DOMINIC-JACKSON MEMORIAL HOSPITAL (O, 660 beds) 969 Lakeland Drive, Jackson, MS, Zip 39216-4606; tel. 601/200-2000, Jeremy M. Tinnerello, R.N., MSN, Jackson Market President
Web address: www.stdom.com

Owned, leased, sponsored:	6 hospitals	2301 beds
Contract-managed:	0 hospitals	0 beds
Totals:	6 hospitals	2301 beds

★1455: FRANCISCAN SISTERS OF CHRISTIAN CHARITY SPONSORED MINISTRIES, INC. (CC)

2413 South Alverno Road, Manitowoc, WI Zip 54220; tel. 920/684-7071, Scott McConnaha, FACHE, President and Chief Executive Officer
(Moderately Centralized Health System)

NEBRASKA: FRANCISCAN HEALTHCARE (O, 25 beds) 430 North Monitor Street, West Point, NE, Zip 68788-1555; tel. 402/372-2404, Tyler Toline, FACHE, Chief Executive Officer
Web address: www.fcswp.org

OHIO: GENESIS HEALTHCARE SYSTEM (O, 316 beds) 2951 Maple Avenue, Zanesville, OH, Zip 43701-1406; tel. 740/454-5000, Matthew J. Perry, President and Chief Executive Officer

Owned, leased, sponsored:	2 hospitals	341 beds
Contract-managed:	0 hospitals	0 beds
Totals:	2 hospitals	341 beds

★0271: FREEMAN HEALTH SYSTEM (NP)

1102 West 32nd Street, Joplin, MO Zip 64804-3503; tel. 417/347-1111, Paula F. Baker, President and Chief Executive Officer
(Moderately Centralized Health System)

MISSOURI: FREEMAN HEALTH SYSTEM (O, 376 beds) 1102 West 32nd Street, Joplin, MO, Zip 64804-3503; tel. 417/347-1111, Paula F. Baker, President and Chief Executive Officer
Web address: www.freemanhealth.com

FREEMAN NEOSHO HOSPITAL (O, 25 beds) 113 West Hickory Street, Neosho, MO, Zip 64850-1705; tel. 417/455-4352, Renee Denton, Chief Operating Officer
Web address: www.freemanhealth.com

Owned, leased, sponsored:	2 hospitals	401 beds
Contract-managed:	0 hospitals	0 beds
Totals:	2 hospitals	401 beds

★1133: FROEDTERT THEDACARE HEALTH, INC. (NP)

9200 West Wisconsin Avenue, Milwaukee, WI Zip 53226-3522; tel. 414/805-3000, Imran A. Andrabi, M.D., President and Chief Executive Officer

WISCONSIN: FROEDTERT COMMUNITY HOSPITAL-NEW BERLIN (O, 8 beds) 4805 South Moorland Road, New Berlin, WI, Zip 53151-7401; tel. 262/796-0001, Allen Ericson, Chief Executive Officer

FROEDTERT MENOMONEE FALLS HOSPITAL (O, 202 beds) W180 N8085 Town Hall Road, Menomonee Falls, WI, Zip 53051-3518, P O Box 408, Zip 53052-0408, tel. 262/251-1000, Teresa M. Lux, President and Chief Operating Officer
Web address: https://www.froedtert.com

FROEDTERT SOUTH-KENOSHA MEDICAL CENTER (O, 95 beds) 6308 Eighth Avenue, Kenosha, WI, Zip 53143-5082; tel. 262/656-2011, Richard O. Schmidt Jr, President and Chief Executive Officer

FROEDTERT WEST BEND HOSPITAL (O, 70 beds) 3200 Pleasant Valley Road, West Bend, WI, Zip 53095-9274; tel. 262/836-5533, Allen Ericson, President
Web address: www.froedtert.com

FROEDTERT AND THE MEDICAL COLLEGE OF WISCONSIN FROEDTERT HOSPITAL (O, 717 beds) 9200 West Wisconsin Avenue, Milwaukee, WI, Zip 53226-3596, P O Box 26099, Zip 53226-0099, tel. 414/805-3000, Eric Conley, President

HOLY FAMILY MEMORIAL (O, 58 beds) 2300 Western Avenue, Manitowoc, WI, Zip 54220-3712, P O Box 1450, Zip 54221-1450, tel. 920/320-2011, Ryan T. Neville, FACHE, President Northeast Market
Web address: www.hfmhealth.org

THEDA CARE MEDICAL CENTER-WILD ROSE (O, 12 beds) 601 Grove Avenue, Wild Rose, WI, Zip 54984-6903, P O Box 243, Zip 54984-0243, tel. 920/622-3257, Tammy Bending, Vice President
Web address: https://www.thedacare.org

THEDACARE MEDICAL CENTER-BERLIN (O, 25 beds) 225 Memorial Drive, Berlin, WI, Zip 54923-1295; tel. 920/361-1313, Tammy Bending, Vice President, Critical Access Hospital

THEDACARE MEDICAL CENTER-NEW LONDON (O, 25 beds) 1405 Mill Street, New London, WI, Zip 54961-0307, P O Box 307, Zip 54961-0307, tel. 920/531-2000, Kellie Diedrick, Vice President
Web address: www.thedacare.org

THEDACARE MEDICAL CENTER-SHAWANO (O, 23 beds) 100 County Road B, Shawano, WI, Zip 54166-2127; tel. 715/526-2111, Kellie Diedrick, Interim Vice President
Web address: www.https://directory.thedacare.org/location/thedacare-medical-center-shawano

THEDACARE MEDICAL CENTER-WAUPACA (O, 25 beds) 800 Riverside Drive, Waupaca, WI, Zip 54981-1999; tel. 715/258-1000, Kellie Diedrick, Vice President
Web address: www.https://directory.thedacare.org/location/thedacare-medical-center-waupaca

THEDACARE REGIONAL MEDICAL CENTER-APPLETON (O, 143 beds) 1818 North Meade Street, Appleton, WI, Zip 54911-3496; tel. 920/731-4101, Dale Gisi, President

THEDACARE REGIONAL MEDICAL CENTER-NEENAH (O, 160 beds) 130 Second Street, Neenah, WI, Zip 54956-2883, P O Box 2021, Zip 54957-2021, tel. 920/729-3100, Lynn Detterman, Senior Vice President, President, ThedaCare South Region
Web address: www.thedacare.org

Owned, leased, sponsored:	13 hospitals	1563 beds
Contract-managed:	0 hospitals	0 beds
Totals:	13 hospitals	1563 beds

0182: FUNDAMENTAL LONG TERM CARE HOLDINGS, LLC (IO)

930 Ridgebrook Road, Sparks Glencoe, MD Zip 21152-9390; tel. 410/773-1000, Mark Fulchino, Chief Executive Officer
(Independent Hospital System)

NEVADA: HARMON MEDICAL AND REHABILITATION HOSPITAL (O, 118 beds) 2170 East Harmon Avenue, Las Vegas, NV, Zip 89119-7840; tel. 702/794-0100, Robert McClay, Chief Executive Officer

HORIZON SPECIALTY HOSPITAL (O, 79 beds) 640 Desert Lane, Las Vegas, NV, Zip 89106-4207; tel. 702/382-3155, Darrin Cook, Chief Executive Officer and Administrator
Web address: www.horizonspecialtyhosp.com/

SOUTHERN NEVADA MEDICAL AND REHABILITATION CENTER (O, 100 beds) 2945 Casa Vegas, Las Vegas, NV, Zip 89169-2248; tel. 702/735-7179, Maureen Davis, Administrator

Owned, leased, sponsored:	3 hospitals	297 beds
Contract-managed:	0 hospitals	0 beds
Totals:	3 hospitals	297 beds

For explanation of codes following names, see page B2.
★ Indicates Type III membership in the American Hospital Association.

0144: GARNET HEALTH (NP)
707 East Main Street, Middletown, NY Zip 10940-2650;
tel. 845/333-1000, Jonathan Schiller, President and Chief
Executive Officer

(Centralized Health System)

NEW YORK: GARNET HEALTH MEDICAL CENTER-CATSKILLS, CALLICOON
CAMPUS (O, 10 beds) 8881 Route 97, Callicoon, NY, Zip 12723;
tel. 845/887-5530, Jerry Dunlavey, Chief Executive Officer
GARNET HEALTH MEDICAL CENTER-CATSKILLS, HARRIS CAMPUS (O, 67
beds) 68 Harris Bushville Road, Harris, NY, Zip 12742-5030, P O Box 800,
Zip 12742-0800, tel. 845/794-3300, Jerry Dunlavey, Chief Executive Officer
Web address: https://www.garnethealth.org/locations/garnet-health-medical-center-catskills-harris-campus
GARNET HEALTH MEDICAL CENTER (O, 410 beds) 707 East Main Street,
Middletown, NY, Zip 10940-2650; tel. 845/333-1000, Jonathan Schiller,
President and Chief Executive Officer

Owned, leased, sponsored:	3 hospitals	487 beds
Contract-managed:	0 hospitals	0 beds
Totals:	3 hospitals	487 beds

★5570: GEISINGER (NP)
100 North Academy Avenue, Danville, PA Zip 17822-9800;
1000 East Mountain Drive, Wilkes Barre, Zip 18711-0027;
tel. 570/271-6211, Terry Gilliland, M.D., President and Chief
Executive Officer

(Centralized Physician/Insurance Health System)

PENNSYLVANIA: GEISINGER COMMUNITY MEDICAL CENTER (O, 318 beds)
1800 Mulberry Street, Scranton, PA, Zip 18510-2369; tel. 570/703-8000, Ronald R. Beer, FACHE, Chief Administrative Officer
GEISINGER JERSEY SHORE HOSPITAL (O, 25 beds) 1020 Thompson Street,
Jersey Shore, PA, Zip 17740-1794; tel. 570/398-0100, Tammy Anderer,
Ph.D., Vice President of Clinical Operations for the North Central Region
Web address: https://www.geisinger.org/
GEISINGER LEWISTOWN HOSPITAL (O, 133 beds) 400 Highland Avenue,
Lewistown, PA, Zip 17044-1198; tel. 717/248-5411, Tammy Anderer, Ph.D.,
Chief Administrative Officer
Web address: www.geisinger.org
GEISINGER MEDICAL CENTER MUNCY (O, 20 beds) 255 Route 220 Highway,
Muncy, PA, Zip 17756-7569; tel. 570/271-6211, Tammy Anderer, Ph.D.,
Vice President of Clinical Operations for the North Central Region
GEISINGER MEDICAL CENTER (O, 553 beds) 100 North Academy Avenue,
Danville, PA, Zip 17822-2201; tel. 570/271-6211, Megan M. Brosious, Chief
Administrative Officer, Central Region
Web address: www.geisinger.org
GEISINGER WYOMING VALLEY MEDICAL CENTER (O, 351 beds) 1000 East
Mountain Boulevard, Wilkes Barre, PA, Zip 18711-0027; tel. 570/808-7300,
Ronald R. Beer, FACHE, Chief Administrative Officer
Web address: https://www.geisinger.org/patient-care/find-a-location/geisinger-wyoming-valley-medical-center
GEISINGER-BLOOMSBURG HOSPITAL (O, 60 beds) 549 Fair Street,
Bloomsburg, PA, Zip 17815-1419; tel. 570/387-2100, Megan M. Brosious,
Chief Administrative Officer, Central Region

Owned, leased, sponsored:	7 hospitals	1460 beds
Contract-managed:	0 hospitals	0 beds
Totals:	7 hospitals	1460 beds

0993: GENERAL HEALTH SYSTEM (NP)
8585 Picardy Avenue, Baton Rouge, LA Zip 70809-3748;
tel. 225/763-4000, Edgardo J. Tenreiro, FACHE, President and
Chief Executive Officer

LOUISIANA: BATON ROUGE GENERAL MEDICAL CENTER (O, 360 beds) 8585
Picardy Avenue, Baton Rouge, LA, Zip 70809-3679; tel. 225/763-4000,
Edgardo J. Tenreiro, FACHE, President and Chief Executive Officer
THE GENERAL (O, 137 beds) 3600 Florida Street, Suite 2020, Baton Rouge,
LA, Zip 70806-3842; tel. 225/381-6393, Edgardo J. Tenreiro, FACHE,
President and Chief Executive Officer

Owned, leased, sponsored:	2 hospitals	497 beds
Contract-managed:	0 hospitals	0 beds
Totals:	2 hospitals	497 beds

0283: GILLIARD HEALTH SERVICES (IO)
101 Crestview Avenue, Evergreen, AL Zip 36401-3333;
tel. 251/578-0184, Tom McLendon, President and Chief
Executive Officer

ALABAMA: EVERGREEN MEDICAL CENTER (O, 44 beds) 101 Crestview
Avenue, Evergreen, AL, Zip 36401-3333, P O Box 706, Zip 36401-0706,
tel. 251/578-2480, Tom McLendon, President and Chief Executive Officer
Web address: www.evergreenmedical.org
JACKSON MEDICAL CENTER (O, 26 beds) 220 Hospital Drive, Jackson, AL,
Zip 36545-2459, P O Box 428, Zip 36545-0428, tel. 251/246-9021,
Jennifer M. Ryland, R.N., Chief Executive Officer
Web address: www.jacksonmedicalcenter.org

Owned, leased, sponsored:	2 hospitals	70 beds
Contract-managed:	0 hospitals	0 beds
Totals:	2 hospitals	70 beds

0648: GOOD SHEPHERD REHABILITATION NETWORK (IO)
850 South Fifth Street, Allentown, PA Zip 18103-3308;
tel. 610/776-3100, Michael Spigel, President and Chief Executive
Officer

(Independent Hospital System)

PENNSYLVANIA: GOOD SHEPHERD REHABILITATION NETWORK (O, 94 beds)
850 South 5th Street, Allentown, PA, Zip 18103-3308; tel. 610/776-3299, Michael Spigel, Chief Executive Officer
Web address: www.goodshepherdrehab.org
GOOD SHEPHERD SPECIALTY HOSPITAL (O, 32 beds) 2545 Schoenersville
Road, 4th Floor, South Tower, Bethlehem, PA, Zip 18017-7300;
tel. 484/884-5056, Michael Spigel, Chief Executive Officer

Owned, leased, sponsored:	2 hospitals	126 beds
Contract-managed:	0 hospitals	0 beds
Totals:	2 hospitals	126 beds

★1535: GREAT PLAINS HEALTH ALLIANCE, INC. (NP)
250 North Rock Road, Suite 160, Wichita, KS Zip 67206-2241;
tel. 316/685-1523, Curt Colson, Chief Executive Officer

(Decentralized Health System)

KANSAS: ASHLAND HEALTH CENTER (C, 25 beds) 709 Oak Street, Ashland,
KS, Zip 67831-0188, P O Box 188, Zip 67831-0188, tel. 620/635-2241,
Sandrea Wright, Chief Executive Officer
Web address: www.ashlandhc.org
CHEYENNE COUNTY HOSPITAL (L, 16 beds) 210 West First Street, Saint
Francis, KS, Zip 67756-3540, P O Box 547, Zip 67756-0547, tel. 785/332-2104, Jeremy Clingenpeel, Chief Executive Officer
Web address: www.cheyennecountyhospital.com
COMANCHE COUNTY HOSPITAL (C, 12 beds) 202 South Frisco Street,
Coldwater, KS, Zip 67029-9101, HC 65, Box 8A, Zip 67029-9500,
tel. 620/582-2144, Lisa Brooks, Administrator
ELLINWOOD DISTRICT HOSPITAL (L, 25 beds) 605 North Main Street,
Ellinwood, KS, Zip 67526-1440; tel. 620/564-2548, Kile Magner,
Administrator
Web address: www.ellinwooddistricthospital.org

Systems / Great Plains Health Alliance, Inc.

FREDONIA REGIONAL HOSPITAL (C, 25 beds) 1527 Madison Street, Fredonia, KS, Zip 66736-1751, P O Box 579, Zip 66736-0579, tel. 620/378-2121, Johnathan Durrett, Chief Executive Officer
Web address: www.fredoniaregionalhospital.org

GRISELL MEMORIAL HOSPITAL DISTRICT ONE (C, 25 beds) 210 South Vermont Avenue, Ransom, KS, Zip 67572-9525; tel. 785/731-2231, Frank Safrit, Ph.D., MSN, Chief Executive Officer
Web address: www.grisellmemorialhospital.org

LANE COUNTY HOSPITAL (C, 25 beds) 235 West Vine, Dighton, KS, Zip 67839-0969, P O Box 969, Zip 67839-0969, tel. 620/397-5321, Marcia Gabel, Chief Financial Officer and Co-Chief Executive Officer

MEDICINE LODGE MEMORIAL HOSPITAL (C, 25 beds) 710 North Walnut Street, Medicine Lodge, KS, Zip 67104-1019; tel. 620/886-3771, Ashley Taylor, Administrator
Web address: www.mlmh.net/

OSBORNE COUNTY MEMORIAL HOSPITAL (C, 25 beds) 424 West New Hampshire Street, Osborne, KS, Zip 67473-2314, P O Box 70, Zip 67473-0070, tel. 785/346-2121, Doris Brown, Chief Executive Officer
Web address: www.ocmh.org

OTTAWA COUNTY HEALTH CENTER (L, 25 beds) 215 East Eighth, Minneapolis, KS, Zip 67467-1902, P O Box 290, Zip 67467-0290, tel. 785/392-2122, Jody Parks, Administrator

REPUBLIC COUNTY HOSPITAL (L, 25 beds) 2420 'G' Street, Belleville, KS, Zip 66935-2400; tel. 785/527-2254, Daniel J. Kelly, Chief Executive Officer
Web address: www.rphospital.org

SABETHA COMMUNITY HOSPITAL (L, 25 beds) 14th and Oregon Streets, Sabetha, KS, Zip 66534-0229, P O Box 229, Zip 66534-0229, tel. 785/284-2121, James Longabaugh, M.D., Chief Executive Officer
Web address: www.sabethahospital.com

SATANTA DISTRICT HOSPITAL AND LONG TERM CARE (C, 59 beds) 401 South Cheyenne Street, Satanta, KS, Zip 67870-0159, P O Box 159, Zip 67870-0159, tel. 620/649-2761, Tina Pendergraft, Chief Executive Officer
Web address: www.satantahospital.org

SMITH COUNTY MEMORIAL HOSPITAL (L, 16 beds) 921 East Highway 36, Smith Center, KS, Zip 66967-9582; tel. 785/282-6845, Sarah Jane. Ragsdale, R.N., Chief Executive Officer
Web address: www.scmhks.org

TREGO COUNTY-LEMKE MEMORIAL HOSPITAL (C, 62 beds) 320 North 13th Street, Wakeeney, KS, Zip 67672-2099; tel. 785/743-2182, Jeremy Rabe, Chief Executive Officer

WICHITA COUNTY HEALTH CENTER (C, 42 beds) 211 East Earl Street, Leoti, KS, Zip 67861-9620; tel. 620/375-2233, Teresa Clark, Chief Executive Officer and Administrator
Web address: www.wichitacountyhealthcenter.com

NEBRASKA: HARLAN COUNTY HEALTH SYSTEM (C, 19 beds) 717 North Brown Street, Alma, NE, Zip 68920-2132, P O Box 836, Zip 68920-0836, tel. 308/928-2151, Stacy Neubauer, R.N., Chief Executive Officer

Owned, leased, sponsored:	6 hospitals	132 beds
Contract-managed:	11 hospitals	344 beds
Totals:	17 hospitals	476 beds

0675: GUTHRIE CLINIC (NP)

1 Guthrie Square, Sayre, PA Zip 18840-1625; tel. 570/888-5858, Edmund Sabanegh Jr, M.D., President and Chief Executive Officer
(Moderately Centralized Health System)

NEW YORK: GUTHRIE CORNING HOSPITAL (O, 65 beds) 1 Guthrie Drive, Corning, NY, Zip 14830-3696; tel. 607/937-7200, Paul VerValin, President
Web address: https://www.guthrie.org/locations/guthrie-corning-hospital

GUTHRIE LOURDES HOSPITAL (O, 197 beds) 169 Riverside Drive, Binghamton, NY, Zip 13905-4246; tel. 607/798-5111, Kathryn Connerton, President and Chief Executive Officer

PENNSYLVANIA: GUTHRIE ROBERT PACKER HOSPITAL (O, 338 beds) 1 Guthrie Square, Sayre, PA, Zip 18840-1698; tel. 570/888-6666, Joseph T. Sawyer Jr, President and Chief Operating Officer
Web address: https://www.guthrie.org/location/robert-packer-hospital

GUTHRIE TROY COMMUNITY HOSPITAL (O, 25 beds) 275 Guthrie Drive, Troy, PA, Zip 16947; tel. 570/297-2121, Paul VerValin, Executive Vice President and Chief Operating Officer

Owned, leased, sponsored:	4 hospitals	625 beds
Contract-managed:	0 hospitals	0 beds
Totals:	4 hospitals	625 beds

★1003: HACKENSACK MERIDIAN HEALTH (NP)

343 Thornall Street, 8th Floor, Edison, NJ Zip 08837-2206, 343 Thornall Street, Zip 08837-2206, tel. 844/464-9355, Robert C. Garrett, FACHE, Chief Executive Officer
(Centralized Health System)

NEW JERSEY: HACKENSACK MERIDIAN HEALTH BAYSHORE COMMUNITY HOSPITAL (O, 175 beds) 727 North Beers Street, Holmdel, NJ, Zip 07733-1598; tel. 732/739-5900, Caitlin Miller, MS, Chief Hospital Executive
Web address: https://www.bayshoremedicalcenter.org/

HACKENSACK MERIDIAN HEALTH CARRIER CLINIC (O, 363 beds) 252 County Route 601, Belle Mead, NJ, Zip 08502-0147, P O Box 147, Zip 08502-0147, tel. 908/281-1000, Patricia Toole, President and Chief Executive Officer

HACKENSACK MERIDIAN HEALTH HACKENSACK UNIVERSITY MEDICAL CENTER (O, 793 beds) loading dock A(off Essex street), 30 Prospect Avenue, Hackensack, NJ, Zip 07601-1914, 30 Prospect Avenue, Zip 07601-1914, tel. 201/996-2000, Mark Sparta, FACHE, President and Chief Hospital Executive
Web address: www.hackensackumc.org

HACKENSACK MERIDIAN HEALTH JFK MEDICAL CENTER (O, 372 beds) 65 James Street, Edison, NJ, Zip 8818; tel. 732/321-7000, Amie D. Thornton, Chief Hospital Executive

HACKENSACK MERIDIAN HEALTH JERSEY SHORE UNIVERSITY MEDICAL CENTER (O, 622 beds) 1945 Route 33, Neptune, NJ, Zip 07754-0397; tel. 732/775-5500, Vito Buccellato, Chief Hospital Executive
Web address: www.meridianhealth.com

HACKENSACK MERIDIAN HEALTH OCEAN UNIVERSITY MEDICAL CENTER (O, 313 beds) 425 Jack Martin Boulevard, Brick Township, NJ, Zip 08724-7732; tel. 732/840-2200, Frank Citara, Chief Hospital Executive
Web address: www.meridianhealth.com

HACKENSACK MERIDIAN HEALTH PALISADES MEDICAL CENTER (O, 168 beds) 7600 River Road, North Bergen, NJ, Zip 07047-6217; tel. 201/854-5000, Lisa Iachetti, President and Chief Hospital Executive

HACKENSACK MERIDIAN HEALTH RARITAN BAY MEDICAL CENTER (O, 308 beds) 530 New Brunswick Avenue, Perth Amboy, NJ, Zip 08861-3654; tel. 732/442-3700, Patricia Carroll, President and Chief Hospital Executive
Web address: www.rbmc.org

HACKENSACK MERIDIAN HEALTH RIVERVIEW MEDICAL CENTER (O, 274 beds) 1 Riverview Plaza, Red Bank, NJ, Zip 07701-1864; tel. 732/741-2700, Timothy J. Hogan, FACHE, President, Chief Hospital Executive
Web address: www.riverviewmedicalcenter.com

HACKENSACK MERIDIAN HEALTH SOUTHERN OCEAN MEDICAL CENTER (O, 156 beds) 1140 Route 72 West, Manahawkin, NJ, Zip 08050-2499; tel. 609/597-6011, Michele Morrison, R.N., M.P.H., President and Chief Hospital Executive

JFK JOHNSON REHABILITATION INSTITUTE AT HACKENSACK MERIDIAN HEALTH (O, 90 beds) 65 James Street, Edison, NJ, Zip 8818; tel. 732/321-7050, Anthony Cuzzola, Vice President, Administrator
Web address: www.njrehab.org

JOHNSON REHABILITATION INSTITUTE AT HACKENSACK MERIDIAN HEALTH OCEAN MEDICAL CENTER (O, 40 beds) 425 Jack Martin Boulevard, Brick, NJ, Zip 08724-7732; tel. 732/836-4500, Kerri Fitzgerald, Executive Director

Owned, leased, sponsored:	12 hospitals	3674 beds
Contract-managed:	0 hospitals	0 beds
Totals:	12 hospitals	3674 beds

For explanation of codes following names, see page B2.
★ Indicates Type III membership in the American Hospital Association.

Systems / Hawaii Pacific Health

★**0541: HARTFORD HEALTHCARE (NP)**
1 State Street, 19th Floor, Hartford, CT Zip 6103; tel. 860/263-4100, Jeffrey A. Flaks, President and Chief Executive Officer
(Centralized Health System)

CONNECTICUT: CHARLOTTE HUNGERFORD HOSPITAL (O, 109 beds) 540 Litchfield Street, Torrington, CT, Zip 06790-6679, P O Box 988, Zip 06790-0988, tel. 860/496-6666, Bimal Patel, President, Hartford and Northwest Regions
HARTFORD HOSPITAL (O, 906 beds) 80 Seymour Street, Hartford, CT, Zip 06102-8000, P O Box 5037, Zip 06102-5037, tel. 860/545-5000, Cheryl A. Ficara, R.N., MS, President
Web address: www.harthosp.org
MIDSTATE MEDICAL CENTER (O, 126 beds) 435 Lewis Avenue, Meriden, CT, Zip 06451-2101; tel. 203/694-8200, Gina Calder, M.P.H., FACHE, President
NATCHAUG HOSPITAL (O, 59 beds) 189 Storrs Road, Mansfield Center, CT, Zip 06250-1683; tel. 860/456-1311, James O'Dea, Chief Executive Officer
Web address: www.natchaug.org
ST. VINCENT'S MEDICAL CENTER (O, 337 beds) 2800 Main Street, Bridgeport, CT, Zip 06606-4292; tel. 203/576-6000, William Jennings, President, Fairfield Region
THE HOSPITAL OF CENTRAL CONNECTICUT (O, 231 beds) 100 Grand Street, New Britain, CT, Zip 06052-2017, P O Box 100, Zip 06052-2017, tel. 860/224-5011, Gina Calder, M.P.H., FACHE, President
Web address: www.thocc.org
THE WILLIAM W. BACKUS HOSPITAL (O, 196 beds) 326 Washington Street, Norwich, CT, Zip 06360-2740; tel. 860/889-8331, Donna Handley, President
Web address: www.backushospital.org
WINDHAM HOSPITAL (O, 58 beds) 112 Mansfield Avenue, Willimantic, CT, Zip 06226-2040; tel. 860/456-9116, Donna Handley, President
Web address: www.windhamhospital.org

Owned, leased, sponsored:	8 hospitals	2022 beds
Contract-managed:	0 hospitals	0 beds
Totals:	8 hospitals	2022 beds

0637: HAVEN BEHAVIORAL HEALTHCARE (IO)
3102 West End Avenue, Suite 1000, Nashville, TN Zip 37203-1324; tel. 615/393-8800, Kelly Gill, Chief Executive Officer

ARIZONA: HAVEN BEHAVIORAL HOSPITAL OF PHOENIX (O, 45 beds) 1201 South 7th Avenue, Suite 200, Phoenix, AZ, Zip 85007-4076; tel. 623/236-2000, Luis Gonzalez, FACHE, Chief Executive Officer
IDAHO: COTTONWOOD CREEK BEHAVIORAL HOSPITAL (O, 92 beds) 2131 South Bonito Way, Meridian, ID, Zip 83642-1659; tel. 208/202-4700, Kevan Finley, MS, Chief Executive Officer
Web address: https://www.cottonwoodcreekboise.com/
NEW MEXICO: HAVEN BEHAVIORAL SENIOR CARE OF ALBUQUERQUE (O, 48 beds) 5400 Gibson Boulevard SE, 4th Floor, Box #8, Albuquerque, NM, Zip 87108-4729; tel. 505/254-4502, Kathleen Dostalik, Chief Executive Officer
Web address: www.https://albuquerque.havenbehavioral.com/
OHIO: HAVEN BEHAVIORAL HOSPITAL OF DAYTON (O, 32 beds) One Elizabeth Place, 4th Floor Southwest Tower, Dayton, OH, Zip 45417-3445; tel. 937/234-0100, Jonathan Duckett, Chief Executive Officer
Web address: www.havenbehavioraldayton.com/
PENNSYLVANIA: HAVEN BEHAVIORAL HOSPITAL OF EASTERN PENNSYLVANIA (O, 86 beds) 145 North 6th Street, 3rd Floor, Reading, PA, Zip 19601-3096; tel. 610/406-4340, Kathryn Schane, Chief Executive Officer
HAVEN BEHAVIORAL HOSPITAL OF PHILADELPHIA (O, 36 beds) 3300 Henry Avenue, Four Falls Building, Suite 100, Philadelphia, PA, Zip 19129-1141; tel. 215/475-3400, Maurice Washington, Chief Executive Officer
Web address: www.https://philadelphia.havenbehavioral.com

TEXAS: MEDICAL CITY MENTAL HEALTH & WELLNESS CENTER–FRISCO (O, 70 beds) 5680 Frisco Square Boulevard, Suite 3000, Frisco, TX, Zip 75034-3300; tel. 469/353-2219, Jon Lasell, Chief Executive Officer

Owned, leased, sponsored:	7 hospitals	409 beds
Contract-managed:	0 hospitals	0 beds
Totals:	7 hospitals	409 beds

★**3555: HAWAII HEALTH SYSTEMS CORPORATION (NP)**
3675 Kilauea Avenue, Honolulu, HI Zip 96816-2333; tel. 808/733-4151, Edward Chu, President and Chief Executive Officer
(Independent Hospital System)

HAWAII: HALE HO'OLA HAMAKUA (O, 77 beds) 45-547 Plumeria Street, Honokaa, HI, Zip 96727-6902; tel. 808/932-4100, Denise Mackey, Administrator
Web address: www.halehoolahamakua.org
HILO MEDICAL CENTER (O, 199 beds) 1190 Waianuenue Avenue, Hilo, HI, Zip 96720-2089; tel. 808/932-3000, Dan Brinkman, R.N., Chief Executive Officer
KA'U HOSPITAL (O, 21 beds) 1 Kamani Street, Pahala, HI, Zip 96777, P O Box 40, Zip 96777-0040, tel. 808/932-4200, Denise Mackey, Administrator
Web address: https://www.kauhospital.org/
KAUAI VETERANS MEMORIAL HOSPITAL (O, 45 beds) 4643 Waimea Canyon Road, Waimea, HI, Zip 96796, P O Box 337, Zip 96796-0337, tel. 808/338-9431, Lance Segawa, Chief Executive Officer
Web address: www.kvmh.hhsc.org
KOHALA HOSPITAL (O, 28 beds) 54-383 Hospital Road, Kohala, HI, Zip 96755, P O Box 10, Kapaau, Zip 96755-0010, tel. 808/889-6211, Gino Amar, Administrator
KONA COMMUNITY HOSPITAL (O, 94 beds) 79-1019 Haukapila Street, Kealakekua, HI, Zip 96750-7920; tel. 808/322-9311, Clayton McGhan, Interim West Hawaii Regional Chief Executive Officer
Web address: www.kch.hhsc.org
LEAHI HOSPITAL (O, 126 beds) 3675 Kilauea Avenue, Honolulu, HI, Zip 96816-2398; tel. 808/733-8000, Derek Akiyoshi, Chief Executive Officer
Web address: www.hhsc.org
MALUHIA HOSPITAL (O, 146 beds) 1027 Hala Drive, Honolulu, HI, Zip 96817; tel. 808/832-5874, Derek Akiyoshi, Chief Executive Officer
SAMUEL MAHELONA MEMORIAL HOSPITAL (O, 71 beds) 4800 Kawaihau Road, Kapaa, HI, Zip 96746-1971; tel. 808/822-4961, Lance Segawa, Chief Executive Officer
Web address: www.smmh.hhsc.org

Owned, leased, sponsored:	9 hospitals	807 beds
Contract-managed:	0 hospitals	0 beds
Totals:	9 hospitals	807 beds

0266: HAWAII PACIFIC HEALTH (NP)
55 Merchant Street, Honolulu, HI Zip 96813-4306; tel. 808/949-9355, Raymond P. Vara Jr, President and Chief Executive Officer
(Centralized Health System)

HAWAII: KAPIOLANI MEDICAL CENTER FOR WOMEN & CHILDREN (O, 253 beds) 1319 Punahou Street, Honolulu, HI, Zip 96826-1001; tel. 808/983-6000, David T. Underriner, Executive Vice President of Oahu Operations, Chief Executive Officer
PALI MOMI MEDICAL CENTER (O, 118 beds) 98-1079 Moanalua Road, Aiea, HI, Zip 96701-4713; tel. 808/486-6000, David T. Underriner, Executive Vice President of Oahu Operations, Chief Executive Officer
Web address: www.palimomi.org
STRAUB MEDICAL CENTER (O, 118 beds) 888 South King Street, Honolulu, HI, Zip 96813-3097; tel. 808/522-4000, David T. Underriner, Executive Vice President of Oahu Operations, Chief Executive Officer
Web address: www.straubhealth.org

For explanation of codes following names, see page B2.
★ Indicates Type III membership in the American Hospital Association.

Systems / Hawaii Pacific Health

WILCOX MEDICAL CENTER (O, 72 beds) 3–3420 Kuhio Highway, Lihue, HI, Zip 96766–1099; tel. 808/245–1100, Jen Chahanovich, President and Chief Executive Officer

Owned, leased, sponsored:	4 hospitals	561 beds
Contract-managed:	0 hospitals	0 beds
Totals:	4 hospitals	561 beds

★0048: **HCA HEALTHCARE (IO)**
1 Park Plaza, Nashville, TN Zip 37203–1548; tel. 615/344–5248, Samuel Hazen, President and Chief Executive Officer
(Decentralized Health System)

ALASKA: ALASKA REGIONAL HOSPITAL (O, 250 beds) 2801 Debarr Road, Anchorage, AK, Zip 99508–2997; tel. 907/264–1754, Jennifer Opsut, Chief Executive Officer
Web address: www.alaskaregional.com

CALIFORNIA: GOOD SAMARITAN HOSPITAL–SAN JOSE (O, 474 beds) 2425 Samaritan Drive, San Jose, CA, Zip 95124–3997, P O Box 240002, Zip 95154–2402, tel. 408/559–2011, Patrick Rohan, FACHE, Chief Executive Officer

LOS ROBLES HEALTH SYSTEM (O, 382 beds) 215 West Janss Road, Thousand Oaks, CA, Zip 91360–1899; tel. 805/370–4421, Phil Buttell, Chief Executive Officer
Web address: www.losrobleshospital.com

REGIONAL MEDICAL CENTER OF SAN JOSE (O, 264 beds) 225 North Jackson Avenue, San Jose, CA, Zip 95116–1603; tel. 408/259–5000, Matthew Cova, Chief Executive Officer

RIVERSIDE COMMUNITY HOSPITAL (O, 478 beds) 4445 Magnolia Avenue, Riverside, CA, Zip 92501–4199; tel. 951/788–3000, Peter Hemstead, Chief Executive Officer
Web address: www.riversidecommunityhospital.com

COLORADO: MEDICAL CENTER OF AURORA (O, 432 beds) 1501 South Potomac Street, Aurora, CO, Zip 80012–5411; tel. 303/695–2600, Scott Rausch, President and Chief Executive Officer

NORTH SUBURBAN MEDICAL CENTER (O, 147 beds) 9191 Grant Street, Thornton, CO, Zip 80229–4341; tel. 303/451–7800, Ryan Thornton, President and Chief Executive Officer
Web address: www.northsuburban.com

PRESBYTERIAN/ST. LUKE'S MEDICAL CENTER (O, 381 beds) 1719 East 19th Avenue, Denver, CO, Zip 80218–1281; tel. 720/754–6000, David Donaldson, President and Chief Executive Assistant

ROSE MEDICAL CENTER (O, 247 beds) 4567 East Ninth Avenue, Denver, CO, Zip 80220–3941; tel. 303/320–2121, Casey Guber, President and Chief Executive Officer
Web address: www.rosebabies.com

SKY RIDGE MEDICAL CENTER (O, 274 beds) 10101 Ridge Gate Parkway, Lone Tree, CO, Zip 80124–5522; tel. 720/225–1000, Eric Evans, Chief Executive Officer

SPALDING REHABILITATION HOSPITAL (O, 100 beds) 900 Potomac Steet, Aurora, CO, Zip 80011–6716; tel. 303/367–1166, Scott Rausch, Chief Executive Officer
Web address: www.https://healthonecares.com/locations/spalding-rehabilitation-hospital/

SWEDISH MEDICAL CENTER (O, 371 beds) 501 East Hampden Avenue, Englewood, CO, Zip 80113–2702; tel. 303/788–5000, Scott Davis, President/Chief Executive Officer
Web address: www.swedishhospital.com

FLORIDA: HCA FLORIDA AVENTURA HOSPITAL (O, 407 beds) 20900 Biscayne Boulevard, Aventura, FL, Zip 33180–1407; tel. 305/682–7000, David LeMonte, Chief Executive Officer
Web address: https://www.hcafloridahealthcare.com/locations/aventura-hospital

HCA FLORIDA BAYONET POINT HOSPITAL (O, 392 beds) 14000 Fivay Road, Hudson, FL, Zip 34667–7199; tel. 727/869–5400, Sally Seymour, Chief Executive Officer
Web address: https://www.hcafloridahealthcare.com/locations/bayonet-point-hospital

HCA FLORIDA BLAKE HOSPITAL (O, 322 beds) 2020 59th Street West, Bradenton, FL, Zip 34209–4669; tel. 941/792–6611, Steve W. Young, Chief Executive Officer

HCA FLORIDA BRANDON HOSPITAL (O, 422 beds) 119 Oakfield Drive, Brandon, FL, Zip 33511–5779; tel. 813/681–5551, Tripp Owings, Chief Executive Officer
Web address: www.brandonhospital.com

HCA FLORIDA CAPITAL HOSPITAL (O, 270 beds) 2626 Capital Medical Boulevard, Tallahassee, FL, Zip 32308–4499; tel. 850/325–5000, J. Christopher. Mosley, Chief Executive Officer
Web address: https://www.hcafloridahealthcare.com/locations/capital-hospital

HCA FLORIDA CITRUS HOSPITAL (O, 216 beds) 502 West Highland Boulevard, Inverness, FL, Zip 34452–4754; tel. 352/726–1551, Lisa Nummi, MSN, R.N., Chief Executive Officer

HCA FLORIDA ENGLEWOOD HOSPITAL (O, 100 beds) 700 Medical Boulevard, Englewood, FL, Zip 34223–3978; tel. 941/475–6571, Joe Rudisill, Chief Executive Officer
Web address: www.englewoodcommunityhospital.com

HCA FLORIDA FAWCETT HOSPITAL (O, 253 beds) 21298 Olean Boulevard, Port Charlotte, FL, Zip 33952–6765; tel. 941/629–1181, Michael Ehrat, Chief Executive Officer

HCA FLORIDA FORT WALTON–DESTIN HOSPITAL (O, 267 beds) 1000 Mar–Walt Drive, Fort Walton Beach, FL, Zip 32547–6795; tel. 850/862–1111, Zachary McCluskey, Chief Executive Officer
Web address: https://www.hcafloridahealthcare.com/locations/fort-walton-destin-hospital

HCA FLORIDA GULF COAST HOSPITAL (O, 297 beds) 449 West 23rd Street, Panama City, FL, Zip 32405–4593, P O Box 15309, Zip 32406–5309, tel. 850/769–8341, Chase Christianson, Chief Executive Officer
Web address: https://www.hcafloridahealthcare.com/locations/gulf-coast-hospital

HCA FLORIDA HIGHLANDS HOSPITAL (O, 126 beds) 3600 South Highlands Avenue, Sebring, FL, Zip 33870–5495, Drawer 2066, Zip 33871–2066, tel. 863/385–6101, Joe Gleason, Chief Executive Officer
Web address: www.highlandsregional.com

HCA FLORIDA JFK HOSPITAL (O, 803 beds) 5301 South Congress Avenue, Atlantis, FL, Zip 33462–1197; tel. 561/965–7300, Kenneth West, Chief Executive Officer

HCA FLORIDA KENDALL HOSPITAL (O, 417 beds) 11750 Bird Road, Miami, FL, Zip 33175–3530; tel. 305/223–3000, Ben Harris, Chief Executive Officer
Web address: https://www.hcafloridahealthcare.com/locations/kendall-hospital

HCA FLORIDA LAKE CITY HOSPITAL (O, 91 beds) 340 NW Commerce Drive, Lake City, FL, Zip 32055–4709; tel. 386/719–9000, Jill B. Adams, Interim Chief Executive Officer

HCA FLORIDA LAKE MONROE HOSPITAL (O, 221 beds) 1401 West Seminole Boulevard, Sanford, FL, Zip 32771–6764; tel. 407/321–4500, John Gerhold, Chief Executive Officer
Web address: https://www.hcafloridahealthcare.com/locations/lake-monroe-hospital

HCA FLORIDA LARGO HOSPITAL (O, 455 beds) 201 14th Street SW, Largo, FL, Zip 33770–3133; tel. 727/588–5200, Sebastian Strom, Chief Executive Officer

HCA FLORIDA LAWNWOOD HOSPITAL (O, 392 beds) 1700 South 23rd Street, Fort Pierce, FL, Zip 34950–4803; tel. 772/461–4000, Eric Goldman, Chief Executive Officer
Web address: https://www.hcafloridahealthcare.com/locations/lawnwood-hospital

HCA FLORIDA MEMORIAL HOSPITAL (O, 461 beds) 3625 University Boulevard South, Jacksonville, FL, Zip 32216–4207; tel. 904/702–6111, Reed Hammond, Chief Executive Officer
Web address: https://www.hcafloridahealthcare.com/locations/memorial-hospital

HCA FLORIDA MERCY HOSPITAL (O, 473 beds) 3663 South Miami Avenue, Miami, FL, Zip 33133–4237; tel. 305/854–4400, David Donaldson, Chief Executive Officer
Web address: https://www.hcafloridahealthcare.com/locations/mercy-hospital

For explanation of codes following names, see page B2.
★ Indicates Type III membership in the American Hospital Association.

Systems / HCA Healthcare

HCA FLORIDA NORTH FLORIDA HOSPITAL (O, 548 beds) 6500 Newberry Road, Gainesville, FL, Zip 32605-4392, P O Box 147006, Zip 32614-7006, tel. 352/333-4000, Eric Lawson, Chief Executive Officer

HCA FLORIDA NORTHSIDE HOSPITAL (O, 288 beds) 6000 49th Street North, Saint Petersburg, FL, Zip 33709-2145; tel. 727/521-4411, Philip Marchesini, Chief Executive Officer
Web address: www.northsidehospital.com

HCA FLORIDA NORTHWEST HOSPITAL (O, 303 beds) 2801 North State Road 7, Margate, FL, Zip 33063-5727; tel. 954/974-0400, Kenneth Jones, Chief Executive Officer

HCA FLORIDA OAK HILL HOSPITAL (O, 361 beds) 11375 Cortez Boulevard, Brooksville, FL, Zip 34613-5409; tel. 352/596-6632, Kenneth R. Wicker, FACHE, Chief Executive Officer
Web address: www.oakhillhospital.com

HCA FLORIDA OCALA HOSPITAL (O, 430 beds) 1431 SW First Avenue, Ocala, FL, Zip 34471-6500, P O Box 2200, Zip 34478-2200, tel. 352/401-1000, Alan Keesee, Chief Executive Officer

HCA FLORIDA ORANGE PARK HOSPITAL (O, 389 beds) 2001 Kingsley Avenue, Orange Park, FL, Zip 32073-5156; tel. 904/639-8500, Jeff Taylor, Chief Executive Officer
Web address: https://www.hcafloridahealthcare.com/locations/orange-park-hospital

HCA FLORIDA OSCEOLA HOSPITAL (O, 441 beds) 700 West Oak Street, Kissimmee, FL, Zip 34741-4996; tel. 407/846-2266, David Shimp, Chief Executive Officer

HCA FLORIDA PALMS WEST HOSPITAL (O, 222 beds) 13001 Southern Boulevard, Loxahatchee, FL, Zip 33470-9203; tel. 561/798-3300, Jason L. Kimbrell, Chief Executive Officer
Web address: https://www.hcafloridahealthcare.com/locations/palms-west-hospital

HCA FLORIDA PASADENA HOSPITAL (O, 307 beds) 1501 Pasadena Avenue South, Saint Petersburg, FL, Zip 33707-3798; tel. 727/381-1000, Brent Burish, Chief Executive Officer
Web address: https://www.hcafloridahealthcare.com/locations/pasadena-hospital

HCA FLORIDA POINCIANA HOSPITAL (O, 76 beds) 325 Cypress Parkway, Kissimmee, FL, Zip 34758; tel. 407/530-2000, Cullen Brown, Chief Executive Officer

HCA FLORIDA PUTNAM HOSPITAL (O, 99 beds) 611 Zeagler Drive, Palatka, FL, Zip 32177-3810; tel. 386/328-5711, Brian Nunn, R.N., Chief Executive Officer
Web address: www.pcmcfl.com

HCA FLORIDA RAULERSON HOSPITAL (O, 100 beds) 1796 Highway 441 North, Okeechobee, FL, Zip 34972-1918, P O Box 1307, Zip 34973-1307, tel. 863/763-2151, Brian Melear, Chief Executive Officer

HCA FLORIDA SARASOTA DOCTORS HOSPITAL (O, 155 beds) 5731 Bee Ridge Road, Sarasota, FL, Zip 34233-5056; tel. 941/342-1100, Robert C. Meade, Chief Executive Officer
Web address: www.doctorsofsarasota.com

HCA FLORIDA SOUTH SHORE HOSPITAL (O, 138 beds) 4016 Sun City Center Blvd, Sun City Center, FL, Zip 33573-5298; tel. 813/634-3301, Cathy Edmisten, R.N., FACHE, Chief Executive Officer
Web address: https://www.hcafloridahealthcare.com/locations/south-shore-hospital

HCA FLORIDA ST. LUCIE HOSPITAL (O, 229 beds) 1800 SE Tiffany Avenue, Port St Lucie, FL, Zip 34952-7521; tel. 772/335-4000, Corey Lovelace, Chief Executive Officer

HCA FLORIDA ST. PETERSBURG HOSPITAL (O, 215 beds) 6500 38th Avenue North, Saint Petersburg, FL, Zip 33710-1629; tel. 727/384-1414, Brent Burish, Chief Executive Officer
Web address: www.stpetegeneral.com

HCA FLORIDA TRINITY HOSPITAL (O, 288 beds) 9330 State Road 54, Trinity, FL, Zip 34655-1808; tel. 727/834-4900, Michael Irvin, Chief Executive Officer
Web address: https://www.hcafloridahealthcare.com/locations/trinity-hospital

HCA FLORIDA TWIN CITIES HOSPITAL (O, 65 beds) 2190 Highway 85 North, Niceville, FL, Zip 32578-1045; tel. 850/678-4131, Todd Jackson, Chief Executive Officer

HCA FLORIDA UNIVERSITY HOSPITAL (O, 165 beds) 3476 South University Drive, Davie, FL, Zip 33328-2000; tel. 954/475-4311, Madeline Nava, Chief Executive Officer
Web address: https://www.hcafloridahealthcare.com/locations/university-hospital

HCA FLORIDA WEST HOSPITAL (O, 515 beds) 8383 North Davis Highway, Pensacola, FL, Zip 32514-6088; tel. 850/494-4000, Guy Bullaro, Chief Executive Officer
Web address: www.westfloridahospital.com

HCA FLORIDA WEST TAMPA HOSPITAL (O, 384 beds) 2901 Swann Avenue, Tampa, FL, Zip 33609-4057; tel. 813/873-6400, Sonia I. Wellman, Chief Executive Officer
Web address: www.memorialhospitaltampa.com

HCA FLORIDA WESTSIDE HOSPITAL (O, 250 beds) 8201 West Broward Boulevard, Plantation, FL, Zip 33324-2701; tel. 954/473-6600, Drew Tyrer, Chief Executive Officer

HCA FLORIDA WOODMONT HOSPITAL (O, 317 beds) 7201 North University Drive, Tamarac, FL, Zip 33321-2996; tel. 954/721-2200
Web address: https://www.hcafloridahealthcare.com/locations/woodmont-hospital

OVIEDO MEDICAL CENTER (O, 64 beds) 8300 Red Bug Lake Road, Oviedo, FL, Zip 32765-6801; tel. 407/890-2273, Kenneth C. Donahey, Chief Executive Officer
Web address: www.oviedomedicalcenter.com

UCF LAKE NONA MEDICAL CENTER (O, 64 beds) 6700 Lake Nona Boulevard, Orlando, FL, Zip 32827-7729; tel. 689/216-8000, Wendy H. Brandon, Chief Executive Officer
Web address: www.UCFLakeNonaMedicalCenter.com

GEORGIA: DOCTORS HOSPITAL (O, 288 beds) 3651 Wheeler Road, Augusta, GA, Zip 30909-6426; tel. 706/651-3232, Joanna J. Conley, FACHE, Chief Executive Officer

FAIRVIEW PARK HOSPITAL (O, 138 beds) 200 Industrial Boulevard, Dublin, GA, Zip 31021-2997, P O Box 1408, Zip 31040-1408, tel. 478/275-2000, Donald R. Avery, FACHE, President and Chief Executive Officer
Web address: www.fairviewparkhospital.com

MEMORIAL HEALTH MEADOWS HOSPITAL (O, 57 beds) 1 Meadows Parkway, Vidalia, GA, Zip 30474-8759, P O Box 1048, Zip 30475-1048, tel. 912/535-5555, Jared Kirby, Interim Chief Executive Officer
Web address: www.meadowsregional.org

MEMORIAL HEALTH UNIVERSITY MEDICAL CENTER (O, 564 beds) 4700 Waters Avenue, Savannah, GA, Zip 31404-6283, P O Box 23089, Zip 31403-3089, tel. 912/350-8000, Bradley S. Talbert, FACHE, Chief Executive Officer

MEMORIAL SATILLA HEALTH (O, 122 beds) 1900 Tebeau Street, Waycross, GA, Zip 31501-6357, P O Box 139, Zip 31502-0139, tel. 912/283-3030, K. Dale. Neely, FACHE, Chief Executive Officer
Web address: www.memorialsatillahealth.com/

IDAHO: EASTERN IDAHO REGIONAL MEDICAL CENTER (O, 280 beds) 3100 Channing Way, Idaho Falls, ID, Zip 83404-7533, P O Box 2077, Zip 83403-2077, tel. 208/529-6111, Elizabeth Hunsicker, Chief Executive Officer

WEST VALLEY MEDICAL CENTER (O, 105 beds) 1717 Arlington, Caldwell, ID, Zip 83605-4802; tel. 208/459-4641, Travis Leach, FACHE, Chief Executive Officer
Web address: www.westvalleymedctr.com

INDIANA: TERRE HAUTE REGIONAL HOSPITAL (O, 278 beds) 3901 South Seventh Street, Terre Haute, IN, Zip 47802-5709; tel. 812/232-0021, Mark Casanova, Chief Executive Officer
Web address: www.regionalhospital.com

KANSAS: MENORAH MEDICAL CENTER (O, 190 beds) 5721 West 119th Street, Overland Park, KS, Zip 66209-3722; tel. 913/498-6000, Kirk McCarty, R.N., MSN, Chief Executive Officer
Web address: www.menorahmedicalcenter.com

OVERLAND PARK REGIONAL MEDICAL CENTER (O, 281 beds) 10500 Quivira Road, Overland Park, KS, Zip 66215-2306, P O Box 15959, Zip 66215-5959, tel. 913/541-5000, Matt Sogard, Chief Executive Officer
Web address: www.oprmc.com

WESLEY MEDICAL CENTER (O, 573 beds) 550 North Hillside, Wichita, KS, Zip 67214-4976; tel. 316/962-2000, Bill Voloch, President and Chief Executive Officer

For explanation of codes following names, see page B2.
★ *Indicates Type III membership in the American Hospital Association.*

Systems / HCA Healthcare

KENTUCKY: FRANKFORT REGIONAL MEDICAL CENTER (O, 130 beds) 299 King's Daughters Drive, Frankfort, KY, Zip 40601-4186; tel. 502/875-5240, John Ballard, Chief Executive Officer
Web address: www.frankfortregional.com

TRISTAR GREENVIEW REGIONAL HOSPITAL (O, 211 beds) 1801 Ashley Circle, Bowling Green, KY, Zip 42104-3362; tel. 270/793-1000, Michael Sherrod, Chief Executive Officer

LOUISIANA: RAPIDES REGIONAL MEDICAL CENTER (O, 365 beds) 211 Fourth Street, Alexandria, LA, Zip 71301-8421; tel. 318/769-3000, Vernon Jones II, Chief Executive Officer
Web address: www.rapidesregional.com

MISSOURI: BELTON REGIONAL MEDICAL CENTER (O, 62 beds) 17065 South 71 Highway, Belton, MO, Zip 64012-4631; tel. 816/348-1200, Todd Krass, Chief Executive Officer
Web address: www.beltonregionalmedicalcenter.com

CENTERPOINT MEDICAL CENTER (O, 285 beds) 19600 East 39th Street, Independence, MO, Zip 64057-2301; tel. 816/698-7000, John McDonald, FACHE, Chief Executive Officer
Web address: www.centerpointmedical.com

LAFAYETTE REGIONAL HEALTH CENTER (O, 25 beds) 1500 State Street, Lexington, MO, Zip 64067-1107; tel. 660/259-2203, Darrel Box, Chief Executive Officer
Web address: www.lafayetteregionalhealthcenter.com

LEE'S SUMMIT MEDICAL CENTER (O, 88 beds) 2100 SE Blue Parkway, Lee's Summit, MO, Zip 64063-1007; tel. 816/282-5000, Gabriel Clements, Chief Executive Officer
Web address: www.leessummitmedicalcenter.com

RESEARCH MEDICAL CENTER (O, 442 beds) 2316 East Meyer Boulevard, Kansas City, MO, Zip 64132-1136; tel. 816/276-4000, Kirk McCarty, R.N., MSN, Chief Executive Officer

NEVADA: MOUNTAINVIEW HOSPITAL (O, 407 beds) 3100 North Tenaya Way, Las Vegas, NV, Zip 89128-0436; tel. 702/255-5000, Hiral Patel, M.D., Chief Executive Officer
Web address: www.mountainview-hospital.com

SOUTHERN HILLS HOSPITAL AND MEDICAL CENTER (O, 252 beds) 9300 West Sunset Road, Las Vegas, NV, Zip 89148-4844; tel. 702/880-2100, Alexis Mussi, Chief Executive Officer
Web address: www.southernhillshospital.com

SUNRISE HOSPITAL AND MEDICAL CENTER (O, 762 beds) 3186 South Maryland Parkway, Las Vegas, NV, Zip 89109-2306, P O Box 98530, Zip 89193, tel. 702/731-8000, Todd Sklamberg, President
Web address: www.sunrisehospital.com

NEW HAMPSHIRE: FRISBIE MEMORIAL HOSPITAL (O, 80 beds) 11 Whitehall Road, Rochester, NH, Zip 03867-3297; tel. 603/332-5211, Megan Gray, Interim Chief Executive Officer and Chief Nursing Officer

PARKLAND MEDICAL CENTER (O, 86 beds) 1 Parkland Drive, Derry, NH, Zip 03038-2750; tel. 603/432-1500, Jeff Scionti, Interim Chief Executive Officer
Web address: www.parklandmedicalcenter.com

PORTSMOUTH REGIONAL HOSPITAL (O, 220 beds) 333 Borthwick Avenue, Portsmouth, NH, Zip 03801-7128; tel. 603/436-5110, John Skevington, Interim President & Chief Executive Officer

NORTH CAROLINA: ANGEL MEDICAL CENTER (O, 35 beds) 124 One Center Court, Franklin, NC, Zip 28734-0192, P O Box 1209, Zip 28744-0569, tel. 828/524-8411, Clint Kendall, R.N., Chief Executive Officer and Chief Nursing Officer
Web address: www.angelmed.org

ASHEVILLE SPECIALTY HOSPITAL (O, 34 beds) 428 Biltmore Avenue, 4th Floor, Asheville, NC, Zip 28801-4502; tel. 828/213-5400, Julie A. Dikos, President and Chief Executive Officer

BLUE RIDGE REGIONAL HOSPITAL (O, 21 beds) 125 Hospital Drive, Spruce Pine, NC, Zip 28777-3035; tel. 828/765-4201, Tonia Hale, R.N., Chief Executive Officer and Chief Nursing Officer
Web address: www.https://missionhealth.org/member-hospitals/blue-ridge/

CAREPARTNERS REHABILITATION HOSPITAL (O, 80 beds) 68 Sweeten Creek Road, Asheville, NC, Zip 28803-2318, P O Box 15025, Zip 28813-0025, tel. 828/277-4800, Tracy Buchanan, Chief Executive Officer and President

HIGHLANDS–CASHIERS HOSPITAL (O, 24 beds) 190 Hospital Drive, Highlands, NC, Zip 28741-7600, P O Drawer 190, Zip 28741-0190, tel. 828/526-1200, Tom Neal, Chief Executive Officer and Chief Nursing Officer
Web address: www.hchospital.org

MISSION HOSPITAL MCDOWELL (O, 30 beds) 430 Rankin Drive, Marion, NC, Zip 28752-6568, P O Box 730, Zip 28752-0730, tel. 828/659-5000, Lee Higginbotham, Chief Executive Officer
Web address: www.https://missionhealth.org/member-hospitals/mcdowell/

MISSION HOSPITAL (O, 763 beds) 509 Biltmore Avenue, Asheville, NC, Zip 28801-4690; tel. 828/213-1111, Chad Patrick, Chief Executive Officer

TRANSYLVANIA REGIONAL HOSPITAL (O, 30 beds) 260 Hospital Drive, Brevard, NC, Zip 28712-3378; tel. 828/884-9111, Michele Pilon, President and Chief Nursing Officer
Web address: www.trhospital.org

SOUTH CAROLINA: COLLETON MEDICAL CENTER (O, 131 beds) 501 Robertson Boulevard, Walterboro, SC, Zip 29488-5714; tel. 843/782-2000, Jimmy O. Hiott III, Chief Executive Officer
Web address: www.colletonmedical.com

GRAND STRAND MEDICAL CENTER (O, 405 beds) 809 82nd Parkway, Myrtle Beach, SC, Zip 29572-4607; tel. 843/692-1000, Mark E. Sims, Chief Executive Officer

TRIDENT MEDICAL CENTER (O, 398 beds) 9330 Medical Plaza Drive, Charleston, SC, Zip 29406-9195; tel. 843/797-7000, Jeff Wilson, Chief Executive Officer
Web address: www.tridenthealthsystem.com

TENNESSEE: PARKRIDGE MEDICAL CENTER (O, 645 beds) 2333 McCallie Avenue, Chattanooga, TN, Zip 37404-3258; tel. 423/698-6061, Christopher Cosby, President and Chief Executive Officer
Web address: www.parkridgemedicalcenter.com

PINEWOOD SPRINGS (O, 60 beds) 1001 North James M. Campbell Boulevard, Columbia, TN, Zip 38401, 1001 North James M Campbell Boulevard, Zip 38401, tel. 931/777-6000, Jake Golich, Interim Chief Executive Officer
Web address: www.pinewoodsprings.com/

TRISTAR ASHLAND CITY MEDICAL CENTER (O, 12 beds) 313 North Main Street, Ashland City, TN, Zip 37015-1347; tel. 615/792-3030, Timothy McPherson, Emergency Room Director

TRISTAR CENTENNIAL MEDICAL CENTER (O, 735 beds) 2300 Patterson Street, Nashville, TN, Zip 37203-1528; tel. 615/342-1000, Thomas H. Ozburn, FACHE, President and Chief Executive Officer
Web address: www.tristarcentennial.com

TRISTAR HENDERSONVILLE MEDICAL CENTER (O, 125 beds) 355 New Shackle Island Road, Hendersonville, TN, Zip 37075-2479; tel. 615/338-1000, Justin Coury, Chief Executive Officer
Web address: www.hendersonvillemedicalcenter.com

TRISTAR HORIZON MEDICAL CENTER (O, 157 beds) 111 Highway 70 East, Dickson, TN, Zip 37055-2080; tel. 615/446-0446, Cindy Bergmeier, Chief Executive Officer

TRISTAR NORTHCREST MEDICAL CENTER (O, 90 beds) 100 Northcrest Drive, Springfield, TN, Zip 37172-3961; tel. 615/384-2411, Sean Patterson, Chief Executive Officer
Web address: https://www.tristarhealth.com/locations/tristar-northcrest-medical-center

TRISTAR SKYLINE MEDICAL CENTER (O, 407 beds) 3441 Dickerson Pike, Nashville, TN, Zip 37207-2539; tel. 615/769-2000, Mark Miller, FACHE, Chief Executive Officer

TRISTAR SOUTHERN HILLS MEDICAL CENTER (O, 87 beds) 391 Wallace Road, Nashville, TN, Zip 37211-4859; tel. 615/781-4000, Nick Howald, Chief Executive Officer
Web address: www.tristarsouthernhills.com

TRISTAR STONECREST MEDICAL CENTER (O, 101 beds) 200 StoneCrest Boulevard, Smyrna, TN, Zip 37167-6810; tel. 615/768-2000, Louis Caputo, Chief Executive Officer

TRISTAR SUMMIT MEDICAL CENTER (O, 218 beds) 5655 Frist Boulevard, Hermitage, TN, Zip 37076-2053; tel. 615/316-3000, Daphne David, Chief Executive Officer
Web address: www.summitmedctr.

TEXAS: CORPUS CHRISTI MEDICAL CENTER–DOCTORS REGIONAL (O, 424 beds) 3315 South Alameda Street, Corpus Christi, TX, Zip 78411-1883,

For explanation of codes following names, see page B2.
★ *Indicates Type III membership in the American Hospital Association.*

Systems / HCA Healthcare

P O Box 8991, Zip 78468-8991, tel. 361/761-1400, David Irizarry, Chief Executive Officer

HCA HOUSTON HEALTHCARE CLEAR LAKE (O, 596 beds) 500 W Medical Center Boulevard, Webster, TX, Zip 77598-4220, 500 West Medical Center Boulevard, Zip 77598-4220, tel. 281/332-2511, Todd Caliva, FACHE, Chief Executive Officer
Web address: www.clearlakermc.com

HCA HOUSTON HEALTHCARE CONROE (O, 304 beds) 504 Medical Boulevard, Conroe, TX, Zip 77304, P O Box 1538, Zip 77305-1538, tel. 936/539-1111, Matt Davis, FACHE, Chief Executive Officer

HCA HOUSTON HEALTHCARE KINGWOOD (O, 563 beds) 22999 U S Highway 59 North, Kingwood, TX, Zip 77339; tel. 281/348-8000, John Corbeil, Chief Executive Officer
Web address: www.kingwoodmedical.com

HCA HOUSTON HEALTHCARE MEDICAL CENTER (O, 136 beds) 1313 Hermann Drive, Houston, TX, Zip 77004-7092; tel. 713/527-5000, Chris Osentowski, Chief Executive Officer
Web address: www.https://hcahoustonhealthcare.com/locations/medical-center/

HCA HOUSTON HEALTHCARE NORTHWEST (O, 316 beds) 710 Cypress Creek Parkway, Houston, TX, Zip 77090-3402; tel. 281/440-1000, Tricia Mcgusty, Interim Chief Executive Officer

HCA HOUSTON HEALTHCARE PEARLAND (O, 48 beds) 11100 Shadow Creek Parkway, Pearland, TX, Zip 77584-7285; tel. 713/770-7000, Justin Brewer, Interim Chief Executive Officer
Web address: www.pearlandmc.com

HCA HOUSTON HEALTHCARE SOUTHEAST (O, 278 beds) 4000 Spencer Highway, Pasadena, TX, Zip 77504-1202; tel. 713/359-2000, Yasmene McDaniel, Chief Executive Officer
Web address: www.https://hcahoustonhealthcare.com/locations/southeast/

HCA HOUSTON HEALTHCARE TOMBALL (O, 261 beds) 605 Holderrieth Street, Tomball, TX, Zip 77375-6445; tel. 281/401-7500, Robert Marmerstein, Chief Executive Officer
Web address: www.tomballregionalmedicalcenter.com

HCA HOUSTON HEALTHCARE WEST (O, 251 beds) 12141 Richmond Avenue, Houston, TX, Zip 77082-2499; tel. 281/558-3444, Megan Marietta, Chief Executive Officer

LAS PALMAS MEDICAL CENTER (O, 585 beds) 1801 North Oregon Street, El Paso, TX, Zip 79902-3591; tel. 915/521-1200, Don Karl, Chief Executive Officer
Web address: www.laspalmashealth.com

MEDICAL CITY ALLIANCE (O, 123 beds) 3101 North Tarrant Parkway, Fort Worth, TX, Zip 76177; tel. 817/639-1000, Glenn Wallace, Chief Executive Officer

MEDICAL CITY ARLINGTON (O, 379 beds) 3301 Matlock Road, Arlington, TX, Zip 76015-2908; tel. 817/465-3241, LaSharndra Barbarin, Chief Executive Officer
Web address: www.medicalcenterarlington.com

MEDICAL CITY DALLAS (O, 896 beds) 7777 Forest Lane, Dallas, TX, Zip 75230-2598; tel. 972/566-7000, Jay deVenny, FACHE, Chief Executive Officer
Web address: www.https://medicalcityhealthcare.com/locations/medical-city-dallas/

MEDICAL CITY DECATUR (O, 133 beds) 609 Medical Center Drive, Decatur, TX, Zip 76234-3836; tel. 940/627-5921, Jason Wren, FACHE, President and Chief Executive Officer
Web address: https://www.wisehealthsystem.com/

MEDICAL CITY DENTON (O, 184 beds) 3535 South I-35 East, Denton, TX, Zip 76210; tel. 940/384-3535, Steven Edgar, FACHE, President and Chief Executive Officer
Web address: www.dentonregional.com

MEDICAL CITY FORT WORTH (O, 257 beds) 900 Eighth Avenue, Fort Worth, TX, Zip 76104-3902; tel. 817/336-2100, John Hoover, Chief Executive Officer
Web address: www.medicalcityfortworth.com/about/

MEDICAL CITY GREEN OAKS HOSPITAL (O, 124 beds) 7808 Clodus Fields Drive, Dallas, TX, Zip 75251-2206; tel. 972/991-9504, Krysla Karlix, Chief Executive Officer

MEDICAL CITY LAS COLINAS (O, 80 beds) 6800 North MacArthur Boulevard, Irving, TX, Zip 75039-2422; tel. 972/969-2000, Jessica O'Neal, Chief Executive Officer
Web address: www.lascolinasmedical.com

MEDICAL CITY LEWISVILLE (O, 128 beds) 500 West Main, Lewisville, TX, Zip 75057-3699; tel. 972/420-1000, John Walker, Chief Executive Officer
Web address: www.lewisvillemedical.com

MEDICAL CITY MCKINNEY (O, 306 beds) 4500 Medical Center Drive, McKinney, TX, Zip 75069-1650; tel. 972/547-8000, Mark S. Deno, FACHE, Chief Executive Officer

MEDICAL CITY NORTH HILLS (O, 142 beds) 4401 Booth Calloway Road, North Richland Hills, TX, Zip 76180-7399; tel. 817/255-1000, Mark S. Deno, FACHE, Chief Executive Officer
Web address: www.northhillshospital.com

MEDICAL CITY PLANO (O, 621 beds) 3901 West 15th Street, Plano, TX, Zip 75075-7738; tel. 972/596-6800, Ben Coogan, Chief Executive Officer
Web address: www.medicalcenterplano.com

MEDICAL CITY WEATHERFORD (O, 96 beds) 713 East Anderson Street, Weatherford, TX, Zip 76086-5705; tel. 682/582-1000, Sean Kamber, Chief Executive Officer
Web address: www.weatherfordregional.com

METHODIST HOSPITAL HILL COUNTRY (O, 58 beds) 1020 South State Highway 16, Fredericksburg, TX, Zip 78624-4471, P O Box 835, Zip 78624-0835, tel. 830/997-4353, Clint Kotal, Chief Executive Officer

METHODIST HOSPITAL SOUTH (O, 59 beds) 1905 Highway 97 East, Jourdanton, TX, Zip 78026-1504; tel. 830/769-3515, Gregory A. Seiler, Chief Executive Officer
Web address: www.https://sahealth.com/locations/methodist-hospital-atascosa/

METHODIST HOSPITAL (O, 1765 beds) 7700 Floyd Curl Drive, San Antonio, TX, Zip 78229-3993; tel. 210/575-4000, Ryan Simpson, Chief Executive Officer
Web address: www.sahealth.com

METHODIST STONE OAK HOSPITAL (O, 284 beds) 1139 E Sonterra Boulevard, San Antonio, TX, Zip 78258-4347, 1139 East Sonterra Boulevard, Zip 78258-4347, tel. 210/638-2100, Michael D. Beaver, Chief Executive Officer

RIO GRANDE REGIONAL HOSPITAL (O, 279 beds) 101 East Ridge Road, McAllen, TX, Zip 78503-1299; tel. 956/632-6000, Laura Disque, MSN, R.N., Chief Executive Officer
Web address: www.riohealth.com

ST. DAVID'S MEDICAL CENTER (O, 482 beds) 919 East 32nd Street, Austin, TX, Zip 78705-2709, P O Box 4039, Zip 78765-4039, tel. 512/476-7111, Todd E. Steward, FACHE, Chief Executive Officer

ST. DAVID'S NORTH AUSTIN MEDICAL CENTER (O, 476 beds) 12221 North MoPac Expressway, Austin, TX, Zip 78758-2496; tel. 512/901-1000, Jeremy Barclay, FACHE, Chief Executive Officer
Web address: www.northaustin.com

ST. DAVID'S ROUND ROCK MEDICAL CENTER (O, 173 beds) 2400 Round Rock Avenue, Round Rock, TX, Zip 78681-4097; tel. 512/341-1000, Laura Wiess, Interim Chief Executive Officer
Web address: www.stdavids.com

ST. DAVID'S SOUTH AUSTIN MEDICAL CENTER (O, 331 beds) 901 West Ben White Boulevard, Austin, TX, Zip 78704-6903; tel. 512/447-2211, Charles Laird, Chief Executive Officer

TEXAS ORTHOPEDIC HOSPITAL (O, 42 beds) 7401 South Main Street, Houston, TX, Zip 77030-4509; tel. 713/799-8600, Eric Becker, Chief Executive Officer
Web address: www.texasorthopedic.com

VALLEY REGIONAL MEDICAL CENTER (O, 214 beds) 100A Alton Gloor Boulevard, Brownsville, TX, Zip 78526-3354; tel. 956/350-7101, David Irizarry, Chief Executive Officer
Web address: www.valleyregionalmedicalcenter.com

WOMAN'S HOSPITAL OF TEXAS (O, 403 beds) 7600 Fannin Street, Houston, TX, Zip 77054-1906; tel. 713/790-1234, Jeanna Bamburg, FACHE, Chief Executive Officer
Web address: www.womanshospital.com

For explanation of codes following names, see page B2.
★ Indicates Type III membership in the American Hospital Association.

Systems / HCA Healthcare

UTAH: BRIGHAM CITY COMMUNITY HOSPITAL (O, 40 beds) 950 South Medical Drive, Brigham City, UT, Zip 84302–4724; tel. 435/734–9471, Richard Spuhler, Chief Executive Officer
Web address: www.brighamcityhospital.com

CACHE VALLEY HOSPITAL (O, 28 beds) 2380 North 400 East, North Logan, UT, Zip 84341–6000; tel. 435/713–9700, Blake Rose, Chief Executive Officer

LAKEVIEW HOSPITAL (O, 119 beds) 630 East Medical Drive, Bountiful, UT, Zip 84010–4908; tel. 801/299–2200, Troy Wood, Chief Executive Officer
Web address: www.lakeviewhospital.com

LONE PEAK HOSPITAL (O, 32 beds) 1925 South State Street, Draper, UT, Zip 84020; tel. 801/545–8000, Brian Lines, Chief Executive Officer
Web address: www.lonepeakhospital.com

MOUNTAIN VIEW HOSPITAL (O, 124 beds) 1000 East 100 North, Payson, UT, Zip 84651–1600; tel. 801/465–7000, Kevin Johnson, Chief Executive Officer

OGDEN REGIONAL MEDICAL CENTER (O, 232 beds) 5475 South 500 East, Ogden, UT, Zip 84405–6905; tel. 801/479–2111, Mark B. Adams, Chief Executive Officer
Web address: www.ogdenregional.com

ST. MARK'S HOSPITAL (O, 298 beds) 1200 East 3900 South, Salt Lake City, UT, Zip 84124–1390; tel. 801/268–7111, Matthew Steven. Hasbrouck, Chief Executive Officer
Web address: www.stmarkshospital.com

TIMPANOGOS REGIONAL HOSPITAL (O, 106 beds) 750 West 800 North, Orem, UT, Zip 84057–3660; tel. 801/714–6000, Austin Manning, Chief Executive Officer

VIRGINIA: CJW MEDICAL CENTER (O, 673 beds) 7101 Jahnke Road, Richmond, VA, Zip 23225–4044; tel. 804/483–0000, Lance Jones, Chief Executive Officer
Web address: www.cjwmedical.com

DOMINION HOSPITAL (O, 116 beds) 2960 Sleepy Hollow Road, Falls Church, VA, Zip 22044–2030; tel. 703/536–2000, Benjamin Brown, Chief Executive Officer
Web address: www.dominionhospital.com

HENRICO DOCTORS' HOSPITAL (O, 574 beds) 1602 Skipwith Road, Richmond, VA, Zip 23229–5205; tel. 804/289–4500, Ryan Jensen, Chief Executive Officer

LEWISGALE HOSPITAL ALLEGHANY (O, 205 beds) 1 Arh Lane, Low Moor, VA, Zip 24457, P O Box 7, Zip 24457–0007, tel. 540/862–6011, Lee Higginbotham, Chief Executive Officer
Web address: www.alleghanyregional.com

LEWISGALE HOSPITAL MONTGOMERY (O, 146 beds) 3700 South Main Street, Blacksburg, VA, Zip 24060–7081, P O Box 90004, Zip 24062–9004, tel. 540/951–1111, Lauren Dudley, Chief Executive Officer

LEWISGALE HOSPITAL PULASKI (O, 147 beds) 2400 Lee Highway, Pulaski, VA, Zip 24301–2326, P O Box 759, Zip 24301–0759, tel. 540/994–8100, Sean Pressman, Chief Executive Officer
Web address: www.lewisgale.com/

LEWISGALE MEDICAL CENTER (O, 506 beds) 8633 Grassy Hill Rd, Boones Mill, VA, Zip 24065, 1900 Electric Road, Salem, Zip 24153–7494, tel. 540/776–4000, Alan J. Fabian, Chief Executive Officer

RESTON HOSPITAL CENTER (O, 245 beds) 1850 Town Center Parkway, Reston, VA, Zip 20190–3219; tel. 703/689–9000, John A. Deardorff, President and Chief Executive, Northern Virginia Market
Web address: www.https://hcavirginia.com/locations/reston-hospital-center/

SPOTSYLVANIA REGIONAL MEDICAL CENTER (O, 137 beds) 4600 Spotsylvania Parkway, Fredericksburg, VA, Zip 22408–7762; tel. 540/498–4000, Ryan DeWeese, Chief Executive Officer

STONESPRINGS HOSPITAL CENTER (O, 71 beds) 24440 Stone Spring Boulevard, Dulles, VA, Zip 20166–2247; tel. 571/349–4000, Tammy Razmic, Chief Executive Officer
Web address: https://www.hcavirginia.com/locations/stonesprings-hospital-center

TRICITIES HOSPITAL (O, 147 beds) 411 West Randolph Road, Hopewell, VA, Zip 23860–2938; tel. 804/541–1600, Joseph Mazzo, Chief Executive Officer

Owned, leased, sponsored:	158 hospitals	43220 beds
Contract–managed:	0 hospitals	0 beds
Totals:	158 hospitals	43220 beds

0328: HEALTH FIRST, INC. (NP)
6450 US Highway 1, Rockledge, FL Zip 32955–5747; tel. 321/434–7000, Terry Forde, Chief Executive Officer
(Centralized Health System)

FLORIDA: HEALTH FIRST CAPE CANAVERAL HOSPITAL (O, 150 beds) 701 West Cocoa Beach Causeway, Cocoa Beach, FL, Zip 32931–5595, P O Box 320069, Zip 32932–0069, tel. 321/799–7111, Brett A. Esrock, President

HEALTH FIRST HOLMES REGIONAL MEDICAL CENTER (O, 539 beds) 1350 South Hickory Street, Melbourne, FL, Zip 32901–3224; tel. 321/434–7000, Brett A. Esrock, Chief Executive Officer
Web address: www.https://hf.org/healthcare-home/location-directory/holmes-regional-medical-center

HEALTH FIRST PALM BAY HOSPITAL (O, 120 beds) 1425 Malabar Road NE, Palm Bay, FL, Zip 32907–2506; tel. 321/434–8000, Brett A. Esrock, President

HEALTH FIRST VIERA HOSPITAL (O, 84 beds) 8745 North Wickham Road, Melbourne, FL, Zip 32940–5997; tel. 321/434–9164, Brett A. Esrock, President
Web address: www.https://hf.org/healthcare-home/location-directory/viera-hospital

Owned, leased, sponsored:	4 hospitals	893 beds
Contract–managed:	0 hospitals	0 beds
Totals:	4 hospitals	893 beds

0342: HEALTHPARTNERS (NP)
8170 33rd Avenue South, Bloomington, MN Zip 55425–4516; tel. 952/883–6000, Andrea Walsh, President and Chief Executive Officer
(Moderately Centralized Health System)

MINNESOTA: GLENCOE REGIONAL HEALTH (C, 133 beds) 1805 Hennepin Avenue North, Glencoe, MN, Zip 55336–1416; tel. 320/864–3121, Ben Davis, President and Chief Executive Officer
Web address: www.grhsonline.org

HEALTHPARTNERS OLIVIA HOSPITAL & CLINIC (O, 16 beds) 100 Healthy Way, Olivia, MN, Zip 56277–1117; tel. 320/523–1261, Nathan Pulscher, President
Web address: www.https://oliviahospital.com/

HUTCHINSON HEALTH (O, 36 beds) 1095 Highway 15 South, Hutchinson, MN, Zip 55350–3182; tel. 320/234–5000, Jim Lyons, President

LAKEVIEW HOSPITAL (O, 67 beds) 927 Churchill Street West, Stillwater, MN, Zip 55082–6605; tel. 651/439–5330, Brandi Lunneborg, Chief Executive Officer
Web address: www.lakeview.org

PARK NICOLLET METHODIST HOSPITAL (O, 370 beds) 6500 Excelsior Boulevard, Saint Louis Park, MN, Zip 55426–4702; tel. 952/993–5000, Jennifer Myster, President

REGIONS HOSPITAL (O, 457 beds) 640 Jackson Street, Saint Paul, MN, Zip 55101–2595; tel. 651/254–3456, Emily Blomberg, President
Web address: www.regionshospital.com

WISCONSIN: AMERY HOSPITAL AND CLINIC (O, 19 beds) 265 Griffin Street East, Amery, WI, Zip 54001–1439; tel. 715/268–8000, Debra Rudquist, FACHE, President and Chief Executive Officer

HUDSON HOSPITAL AND CLINIC (O, 24 beds) 405 Stageline Road, Hudson, WI, Zip 54016–7848; tel. 715/531–6000, Thomas Borowski, FACHE, President
Web address: www.hudsonhospital.org

WESTFIELDS HOSPITAL AND CLINIC (O, 25 beds) 535 Hospital Road, New Richmond, WI, Zip 54017–1449; tel. 715/243–2600, Steven Massey, President and Chief Executive Officer
Web address: www.westfieldshospital.com

Owned, leased, sponsored:	8 hospitals	1014 beds
Contract–managed:	1 hospitals	133 beds
Totals:	9 hospitals	1147 beds

For explanation of codes following names, see page B2.
★ Indicates Type III membership in the American Hospital Association.

Systems / Heritage Valley Health System

★**0585: HEALTHTECH MANAGEMENT SERVICES (IO)**
2745 Dallas Pkwy, Plano, TX Zip 75093–8731, 5110 Maryland Way Suite 200, Brentwood, TN, Zip 37027–2307, tel. 615/309–6053, Neil E. Todhunter, Chief Executive Officer
(Moderately Centralized Health System)

ARIZONA: COBRE VALLEY REGIONAL MEDICAL CENTER (C, 36 beds) 5880 South Hospital Drive, Globe, AZ, Zip 85501–9454; tel. 928/425–3261, Neal Jensen, Chief Executive Officer
Web address: www.cvrmc.org

GEORGIA: UPSON REGIONAL MEDICAL CENTER (C, 99 beds) 801 West Gordon Street, Thomaston, GA, Zip 30286–3426, P O Box 1059, Zip 30286–0027, tel. 706/647–8111, Jeffrey S. Tarrant, FACHE, Chief Executive Officer
Web address: www.urmc.org

ILLINOIS: CARLINVILLE AREA HOSPITAL (C, 25 beds) 20733 North Broad Street, Carlinville, IL, Zip 62626–1499; tel. 217/854–3141, Brian Burnside, FACHE, President and Chief Executive Officer
Web address: www.cahcare.com

HILLSBORO AREA HOSPITAL (C, 25 beds) 1200 East Tremont Street, Hillsboro, IL, Zip 62049–1900; tel. 217/532–6111, Michael Alexander, FACHE, Chief Executive Officer
Web address: www.hillsborohealth.org

LOUISIANA: IBERIA MEDICAL CENTER (C, 166 beds) 2315 East Main Street, New Iberia, LA, Zip 70560–4031, P O Box 13338, Zip 70562–3338, tel. 337/364–0441, Dionne Viator, CPA, FACHE, President and Chief Executive Officer

MONTANA: BARRETT HOSPITAL & HEALTHCARE (C, 18 beds) 600 Mt Highway 91 South, Dillon, MT, Zip 59725–7379; tel. 406/683–3000, Taylor Rose, Chief Executive Officer
Web address: www.barretthospital.org

NEW MEXICO: GILA REGIONAL MEDICAL CENTER (C, 25 beds) 1313 East 32nd Street, Silver City, NM, Zip 88061–7251; tel. 575/538–4000, Robert Whitaker, Chief Executive Officer
Web address: www.grmc.org

WASHINGTON: WHIDBEYHEALTH (C, 25 beds) 101 North Main Street, Coupeville, WA, Zip 98239–3413; tel. 360/678–5151, Nathan Staggs, Chief Executive Officer
Web address: www.https://whidbeyhealth.org/

WISCONSIN: SPOONER HEALTH (C, 20 beds) 1280 Chandler Drive, Spooner, WI, Zip 54801–1299; tel. 715/635–2111, Michael Schafer, Chief Executive Officer and Administrator
Web address: www.spoonerhealth.com

TOMAH HEALTH (C, 25 beds) 501 Gopher Drive, Tomah, WI, Zip 54660–4513; tel. 608/372–2181, Derek Daly, Chief Executive Officer
Web address: www.tomahhospital.org

WYOMING: HOT SPRINGS COUNTY HOSPITAL DISTRICT (C, 15 beds) 150 East Arapahoe Street, Thermopolis, WY, Zip 82443–2498; tel. 307/864–3121, Scott Alwin, Chief Executive Officer

Owned, leased, sponsored:	0 hospitals	0 beds
Contract-managed:	11 hospitals	479 beds
Totals:	11 hospitals	479 beds

★**9997: HENDRICK HEALTH SYSTEM (CO)**
1900 Pine Street, Abilene, TX Zip 79601–2432; tel. 325/670–2000, Brad D. Holland, President and Chief Executive Officer

TEXAS: HENDRICK MEDICAL CENTER BROWNWOOD (O, 68 beds) 1501 Burnet Road, Brownwood, TX, Zip 76801–8520; tel. 325/649–3302, Krista Baty, R.N., Chief Administrative & Nursing Officer

HENDRICK MEDICAL CENTER (O, 673 beds) 1900 Pine Street, Abilene, TX, Zip 79601–2432; tel. 325/670–2000, Brad D. Holland, President and Chief Executive Officer
Web address: www.ehendrick.org

Owned, leased, sponsored:	2 hospitals	741 beds
Contract-managed:	0 hospitals	0 beds
Totals:	2 hospitals	741 beds

★**9505: HENRY FORD HEALTH (NP)**
One Ford Place, Detroit, MI Zip 48202–3450, 1 Ford Place, Zip 48202–3450, tel. 313/876–8708, Robert G. Riney, President and Chief Executive Officer
(Centralized Health System)

MICHIGAN: HENRY FORD HOSPITAL (O, 769 beds) 2799 West Grand Boulevard, Detroit, MI, Zip 48202–2608; tel. 313/916–2600, Steven Kalkanis, M.D., Chief Executive Officer
Web address: www.henryfordhealth.org

HENRY FORD JACKSON HOSPITAL (O, 362 beds) 205 North East Avenue, Jackson, MI, Zip 49201–1753; tel. 517/205–4800, Emily Moorhead, FACHE, President, Henry Ford Hospital and Central Market Operations
Web address: www.allegiancehealth.org

HENRY FORD KINGSWOOD HOSPITAL (O, 98 beds) 10300 West Eight Mile Road, Ferndale, MI, Zip 48220–2100; tel. 248/398–3200, Cathrine Frank, M.D., Chairperson

HENRY FORD MACOMB HOSPITAL (O, 345 beds) 15855 19 Mile Road, Clinton Township, MI, Zip 48038–6324; tel. 586/263–2300, Shanna Johnson, FACHE, Interim President
Web address: www.henryfordmacomb.com

HENRY FORD WEST BLOOMFIELD HOSPITAL (O, 191 beds) 6777 West Maple Road, West Bloomfield, MI, Zip 48322–3013; tel. 248/325–1000, Shanna Johnson, FACHE, President

HENRY FORD WYANDOTTE HOSPITAL (O, 310 beds) 2333 Biddle Avenue, Wyandotte, MI, Zip 48192–4668; tel. 734/246–6000, Rand O'Leary, FACHE, President
Web address: https://www.henryford.com/locations/wyandotte

Owned, leased, sponsored:	6 hospitals	2075 beds
Contract-managed:	0 hospitals	0 beds
Totals:	6 hospitals	2075 beds

0309: HERITAGE VALLEY HEALTH SYSTEM (NP)
1000 Dutch Ridge Road, Beaver, PA Zip 15009–9727; tel. 724/773–2024, Norman F. Mitry, President and Chief Executive Officer
(Independent Hospital System)

PENNSYLVANIA: HERITAGE VALLEY BEAVER (O, 285 beds) 1000 Dutch Ridge Road, Beaver, PA, Zip 15009–9727; tel. 724/728–7000, Norman F. Mitry, President and Chief Executive Officer
Web address: https://www.heritagevalley.org/locations/heritage-valley-beaver/

HERITAGE VALLEY KENNEDY (O, 124 beds) 25 Heckel Road, McKees Rocks, PA, Zip 15136–1694; tel. 412/777–6161, Norman F. Mitry, President and Chief Executive Officer
Web address: www.ohiovalleyhospital.org

SEWICKLEY VALLEY HOSPITAL, (A DIVISION OF VALLEY MEDICAL FACILITIES) (O, 179 beds) 720 Blackburn Road, Sewickley, PA, Zip 15143–1459; tel. 412/741–6600, Norman F. Mitry, President and Chief Executive Officer
Web address: www.heritagevalley.org

Owned, leased, sponsored:	3 hospitals	588 beds
Contract-managed:	0 hospitals	0 beds
Totals:	3 hospitals	588 beds

For explanation of codes following names, see page B2.
★ Indicates Type III membership in the American Hospital Association.

Systems / Heywood Healthcare

★**1024: HEYWOOD HEALTHCARE (NP)**
242 Green Street, Gardner, MA Zip 01440–1336; tel. 978/632–3420, Rozanna Penney, Co–Chief Executive Officer
(Independent Hospital System)

MASSACHUSETTS: ATHOL HOSPITAL (O, 25 beds) 2033 Main Street, Athol, MA, Zip 01331–3598; tel. 978/249–3511, Rozanna Penney, Co–Chief Executive Officer

HEYWOOD HOSPITAL (O, 173 beds) 242 Green Street, Gardner, MA, Zip 01440–1373; tel. 978/632–3420, Rozanna Penney, Co–Chief Executive Officer
Web address: www.heywood.org

Owned, leased, sponsored:	2 hospitals	198 beds
Contract–managed:	0 hospitals	0 beds
Totals:	2 hospitals	198 beds

★**1014: HOLZER HEALTH SYSTEM (NP)**
500 Burlington Road, Jackson, OH Zip 45640–9360; tel. 855/446–5937, Michael R. Canady, M.D., Chief Executive Officer
(Independent Hospital System)

OHIO: HOLZER MEDICAL CENTER–JACKSON (O, 25 beds) 500 Burlington Road, Jackson, OH, Zip 45640–9360; tel. 740/288–4625, Kim Wiley. Dulaney, Vice President of Revenue Cycle
Web address: www.holzer.org

HOLZER MEDICAL CENTER (O, 100 beds) 100 Jackson Pike, Gallipolis, OH, Zip 45631–1563; tel. 740/446–5000, Rodney Stout, M.D., Chief Executive Officer
Web address: www.holzer.org

Owned, leased, sponsored:	2 hospitals	125 beds
Contract–managed:	0 hospitals	0 beds
Totals:	2 hospitals	125 beds

★**0963: HONORHEALTH (NP)**
8125 North Hayden Road, Scottsdale, AZ Zip 85258–2463; tel. 480/882–4000, Todd LaPorte, Chief Executive Officer
(Independent Hospital System)

ARIZONA: HONORHEALTH DEER VALLEY MEDICAL CENTER (O, 204 beds) 19829 North 27th Avenue, Phoenix, AZ, Zip 85027–4002; tel. 623/879–6100, Kimberly Post, R.N., Chief Operating Officer
Web address: www.jcl.com

HONORHEALTH JOHN C. LINCOLN MEDICAL CENTER (O, 239 beds) 250 East Dunlap Avenue, Phoenix, AZ, Zip 85020–2825; tel. 602/943–2381, Kimberly Post, R.N., Chief Operating Officer

HONORHEALTH SCOTTSDALE OSBORN MEDICAL CENTER (O, 303 beds) 7400 East Osborn Road, Scottsdale, AZ, Zip 85251–6403; tel. 480/882–4000, Kimberly Post, R.N., Chief Operating Officer
Web address: https://www.honorhealth.com/locations/hospitals/scottsdale-osborn-medical-center

HONORHEALTH SCOTTSDALE SHEA MEDICAL CENTER (O, 427 beds) 9003 East Shea Boulevard, Scottsdale, AZ, Zip 85260–6771; tel. 480/323–3000, Kimberly Post, R.N., Chief Operating Officer
Web address: https://www.honorhealth.com/locations/hospitals/scottsdale-shea-medical-center

HONORHEALTH SCOTTSDALE THOMPSON PEAK MEDICAL CENTER (O, 120 beds) 7400 East Thompson Peak Parkway, Scottsdale, AZ, Zip 85255–4109; tel. 480/324–7000, Kimberly Post, R.N., Chief Operating Officer

HONORHEALTH SONORAN CROSSING MEDICAL CENTER (O, 79 beds) 33400 North 32nd Avenue, Phoenix, AZ, Zip 85085–8876; tel. 623/683–5000, Kimberly Post, R.N., Chief Operating Officer
Web address: www.honorhealth.com

Owned, leased, sponsored:	6 hospitals	1372 beds
Contract–managed:	0 hospitals	0 beds
Totals:	6 hospitals	1372 beds

★**7235: HOUSTON METHODIST (CO)**
6565 Fannin Street, D–200, Houston, TX Zip 77030–2707; tel. 713/441–2221, Marc L. Boom, M.D., FACHE, President and Chief Executive Officer
(Centralized Health System)

TEXAS: HOUSTON METHODIST BAYTOWN HOSPITAL (O, 285 beds) 4401 Garth Road, Administration Department, Baytown, TX, Zip 77521–2122; tel. 281/420–8600, Adrienne Joseph, Ph.D., Chief Executive Officer
Web address: www.houstonmethodist.org

HOUSTON METHODIST CLEAR LAKE HOSPITAL (O, 134 beds) 18300 Houston Methodist Drive, Houston, TX, Zip 77058–6302; tel. 281/333–5503, Carl Little, Chief Executive Officer
Web address: https://www.houstonmethodist.org/locations/clear-lake/

HOUSTON METHODIST CONTINUING CARE HOSPITAL (O, 145 beds) 701 Fry Road, Katy, TX, Zip 77450–2255; tel. 281/599–5700, Gary L. Kempf, R.N., Chief Executive Officer

HOUSTON METHODIST HOSPITAL (O, 963 beds) 6565 Fannin Street, D200, Houston, TX, Zip 77030–2707; tel. 713/790–3311, Roberta Schwartz, Ph.D., Executive Vice President
Web address: www.methodisthealth.com

HOUSTON METHODIST SUGAR LAND HOSPITAL (O, 339 beds) 16655 SW Freeway, Sugar Land, TX, Zip 77479–2329; tel. 281/274–7000, Michael Garcia, Chief Executive Officer

HOUSTON METHODIST THE WOODLANDS HOSPITAL (O, 277 beds) 17201 Interstate 45 South, The Woodlands, TX, Zip 77385; tel. 713/790–3333, David P. Bernard, FACHE, Chief Executive Officer
Web address: www.houstonmethodist.org/locations/the-woodlands/

HOUSTON METHODIST WEST HOSPITAL (O, 271 beds) 18500 Katy Freeway, Houston, TX, Zip 77094–1110; tel. 832/522–1000, Wayne M. Voss, Chief Executive Officer

HOUSTON METHODIST WILLOWBROOK HOSPITAL (O, 358 beds) 18220 Tomball Pkwy, Houston, TX, Zip 77070–4347, 18220 Tomball Pwy, Zip 77070–4347, tel. 281/477–1000, Keith Barber, CPA, Chief Executive Officer
Web address: www.houstonmethodist.org/locations/willowbrook/

Owned, leased, sponsored:	8 hospitals	2772 beds
Contract–managed:	0 hospitals	0 beds
Totals:	8 hospitals	2772 beds

★**5355: HSHS HOSPITAL SISTERS HEALTH SYSTEM (CC)**
4936 LaVerna Road, Springfield, IL Zip 62707–9797, P O Box 19456, Zip 62794–9456, tel. 217/523–4747, Damond Boatwright, FACHE, President and Chief Executive Officer
(Decentralized Health System)

ILLINOIS: HSHS GOOD SHEPHERD HOSPITAL (O, 30 beds) 200 South Cedar Street, Shelbyville, IL, Zip 62565–1838; tel. 217/774–3961, Matthew Fry, FACHE, President and Chief Executive Officer, Central Illinois Market
Web address: https://www.hshs.org/good-shepherd

HSHS HOLY FAMILY HOSPITAL IN GREENVILLE (O, 28 beds) 200 Healthcare Drive, Greenville, IL, Zip 62246–1154; tel. 618/664–1230, Chris Klay, FACHE, President and Chief Executive Officer, Southern Illinois Market

HSHS ST. ANTHONY'S MEMORIAL HOSPITAL (O, 133 beds) 503 North Maple Street, Effingham, IL, Zip 62401–2099; tel. 217/342–2121, Matthew Fry, FACHE, President and Chief Executive Officer, Central Illinois Market
Web address: https://www.hshs.org/st-anthonys/

For explanation of codes following names, see page B2.
★ *Indicates Type III membership in the American Hospital Association.*

HSHS ST. ELIZABETH'S HOSPITAL (O, 144 beds) 1 Saint Elizabeth Boulevard, O Fallon, IL, Zip 62269-1099; tel. 618/234-2120, Chris Klay, FACHE, President and Chief Executive Officer, Southern Illinois Market and President and Chief Executive Officer

HSHS ST. FRANCIS HOSPITAL (O, 25 beds) 1215 Franciscan Drive, Litchfield, IL, Zip 62056-1799, P O Box 1215, Zip 62056-0999, tel. 217/324-2191, Matthew Fry, FACHE, President and Chief Executive Officer, Central Illinois Market
Web address: https://www.hshs.org/st-francis/

HSHS ST. JOHN'S HOSPITAL (O, 442 beds) 800 East Carpenter Street, Springfield, IL, Zip 62769-0002; tel. 217/544-6464, Matthew Fry, FACHE, President and Chief Executive Officer, Central Illinois Market and President and Chief Executive Officer
Web address: https://www.hshs.org/st-johns/

HSHS ST. JOSEPH'S HOSPITAL BREESE (O, 52 beds) 9515 Holy Cross Lane, Breese, IL, Zip 62230-3618, PO Box 99, Zip 62230-0099, tel. 618/526-4511, Chris Klay, FACHE, President and Chief Executive Officer, Southern Illinois Market

HSHS ST. JOSEPH'S HOSPITAL HIGHLAND (O, 25 beds) 12866 Troxler Avenue, Highland, IL, Zip 62249-1698; tel. 618/651-2600, Chris Klay, FACHE, President and Chief Executive Officer, Southern Illinois Market
Web address: https://www.hshs.org/st-josephs-highland

HSHS ST. MARY'S HOSPITAL (O, 102 beds) 1800 East Lake Shore Drive, Decatur, IL, Zip 62521-3883; tel. 217/464-2966, Matthew Fry, FACHE, President and Chief Executive Officer, Central Illinois Market

WISCONSIN: HSHS ST. CLARE MEMORIAL HOSPITAL (O, 22 beds) 855 South Main Street, Oconto Falls, WI, Zip 54154-1296; tel. 920/846-3444, Christopher Brabant, President and Chief Executive Officer
Web address: www.stclarememorial.org

HSHS ST. MARY'S HOSPITAL MEDICAL CENTER (O, 72 beds) 1726 Shawano Avenue, Green Bay, WI, Zip 54303-3282; tel. 920/498-4200, Robert J. Erickson, Market President and Chief Executive Officer and President and Chief Executive Officer

HSHS ST. NICHOLAS HOSPITAL (O, 49 beds) 3100 Superior Avenue, Sheboygan, WI, Zip 53081-1948; tel. 920/459-8300, Justin Selle, Chief Executive Officer
Web address: www.stnicholashospital.org

HSHS ST. VINCENT HOSPITAL (O, 224 beds) 835 South Van Buren Street, Green Bay, WI, Zip 54301-3526, P O Box 13508, Zip 54307-3508, tel. 920/433-0111, Robert J. Erickson, Market President and Chief Executive Officer and President and Chief Executive Officer

Owned, leased, sponsored:	13 hospitals	1348 beds
Contract-managed:	0 hospitals	0 beds
Totals:	13 hospitals	1348 beds

0117: HUNTSVILLE HOSPITAL HEALTH SYSTEM (NP)

101 Sivley Road SW, Huntsville, AL Zip 35801-4421; tel. 256/265-1000, Jeff Samz, Chief Executive Officer
(Independent Hospital System)

ALABAMA: ATHENS-LIMESTONE HOSPITAL (C, 71 beds) 700 West Market Street, Athens, AL, Zip 35611-2457, P O Box 999, Zip 35612-0999, tel. 256/233-9292, Traci Collins, President
Web address: www.athenslimestonehospital.com

DEKALB REGIONAL MEDICAL CENTER (O, 115 beds) 200 Medical Center Drive, Fort Payne, AL, Zip 35968-3458, P O Box 680778, Zip 35968-1608, tel. 256/845-3150, Darrell Blaylock, Chief Executive Officer
Web address: www.dekalbregional.com

DECATUR MORGAN HOSPITAL (O, 110 beds) 1201 Seventh Street SE, Decatur, AL, Zip 35601-3303, P O Box 2239, Zip 35609-2239, tel. 256/341-2000, Kelli Powers, President

HELEN KELLER HOSPITAL (C, 147 beds) 1300 South Montgomery Avenue, Sheffield, AL, Zip 35660-6334, P O Box 610, Zip 35660-0610, tel. 256/386-4196, Kyle Buchanan, President
Web address: www.helenkeller.com

HUNTSVILLE HOSPITAL (O, 942 beds) 101 Sivley Road SW, Huntsville, AL, Zip 35801-4470; tel. 256/265-1000, Jeff Samz, Chief Executive Officer

LAWRENCE MEDICAL CENTER (C, 43 beds) 202 Hospital Street, Moulton, AL, Zip 35650-1218, P O Box 39, Zip 35650-0039, tel. 256/974-2200, Kim Roberson, Interim Chief Executive Officer
Web address: www.lawrencemedicalcenter.com

RED BAY HOSPITAL (C, 22 beds) 211 Hospital Road, Red Bay, AL, Zip 35582-3858, P O Box 490, Zip 35582-0490, tel. 256/356-9532, Sherry Jolley, Administrator
Web address: www.redbayhospital.com

Owned, leased, sponsored:	3 hospitals	1167 beds
Contract-managed:	4 hospitals	283 beds
Totals:	7 hospitals	1450 beds

0422: INDEPENDENCE HEALTH SYSTEM (NP)

1 Hospital Way, Butler, PA Zip 16001-4670; tel. 724/284-4200, Kenneth DeFurio, President and Chief Executive Officer

PENNSYLVANIA: BUTLER MEMORIAL HOSPITAL (O, 261 beds) 1 Hospital Way, Butler, PA, Zip 16001-4697; tel. 724/283-6666, Karen A. Allen, R.N., President, Butler & Clarion Hospitals
Web address: www.butlerhealthsystem.org

CLARION HOSPITAL (O, 67 beds) 1 Hospital Drive, Clarion, PA, Zip 16214-8501; tel. 814/226-9500, Karen A. Allen, R.N., President
Web address: www.clarionhospital.org

EXCELA FRICK HOSPITAL (O, 33 beds) 508 South Church Street, Mount Pleasant, PA, Zip 15666-1790; tel. 724/547-1500, Brian Fritz, President

EXCELA HEALTH LATROBE HOSPITAL (O, 122 beds) 1 Mellon Way, Latrobe, PA, Zip 15650-1096; tel. 724/537-1000, Brian Fritz, President
Web address: www.excelahealth.org

EXCELA HEALTH WESTMORELAND HOSPITAL (O, 272 beds) 532 West Pittsburgh Street, Greensburg, PA, Zip 15601-2282; tel. 724/832-4000, Brian Fritz, President, Westmoreland, Latrobe, Frick Hospitals

Owned, leased, sponsored:	5 hospitals	755 beds
Contract-managed:	0 hospitals	0 beds
Totals:	5 hospitals	755 beds

★0231: INDIANA UNIVERSITY HEALTH (NP)

340 West 10th Street, Suite 6100, Indianapolis, IN Zip 46202-3082, P O Box 1367, Zip 46206-1367, tel. 317/962-2000, Dennis M. Murphy, President and Chief Executive Officer
(Moderately Centralized Health System)

INDIANA: INDIANA UNIVERSITY HEALTH ARNETT HOSPITAL (O, 199 beds) 5165 McCarty Lane, Lafayette, IN, Zip 47905-8764, P O Box 5545, Zip 47903-5545, tel. 765/448-8000, Arthur Vasquez, President

INDIANA UNIVERSITY HEALTH BALL MEMORIAL HOSPITAL (O, 325 beds) 2401 West University Avenue, Muncie, IN, Zip 47303-3499; tel. 765/747-3111, Jeffrey C. Bird, M.D., President
Web address: www.iuhealth.org

INDIANA UNIVERSITY HEALTH BEDFORD HOSPITAL (O, 25 beds) 2900 West 16th Street, Bedford, IN, Zip 47421-3583; tel. 812/275-1200, Denzil Ross, FACHE, President
Web address: www.iuhealth.org

INDIANA UNIVERSITY HEALTH BLOOMINGTON HOSPITAL (O, 201 beds) 2651 East Discovery Parkway, Bloomington, IN, Zip 47408-9059; tel. 812/336-6821, Denzil Ross, FACHE, President

INDIANA UNIVERSITY HEALTH FRANKFORT (O, 12 beds) 1300 South Jackson Street, Frankfort, IN, Zip 46041-3313; tel. 765/656-3000, Mary Minier, Chief Operating Officer
Web address: www.https://iuhealth.org/find-locations/iu-health-frankfort-hospital

INDIANA UNIVERSITY HEALTH JAY HOSPITAL (O, 21 beds) 500 West Votaw Street, Portland, IN, Zip 47371-1322; tel. 260/726-7131, Christina Marie. Schemenaur, Vice President, Chief Operating Officer and Chief Nursing Officer
Web address: www.iuhealth.org

For explanation of codes following names, see page B2.
★ Indicates Type III membership in the American Hospital Association.

Systems / Indiana University Health

INDIANA UNIVERSITY HEALTH NORTH HOSPITAL (O, 165 beds) 11700 North Meridian Street, Carmel, IN, Zip 46032-4656; tel. 317/688-2000, Soula Banich, President

INDIANA UNIVERSITY HEALTH PAOLI HOSPITAL (O, 24 beds) 642 West Hospital Road, Paoli, IN, Zip 47454-9672; tel. 812/723-2811, Denzil Ross, FACHE, Chief Operating Officer
Web address: www.iuhealth.org/paoli

INDIANA UNIVERSITY HEALTH TIPTON HOSPITAL (O, 25 beds) 1000 South Main Street, Tipton, IN, Zip 46072-9799; tel. 765/675-8500, Doug Puckett, President
Web address: www.iuhealth.org

INDIANA UNIVERSITY HEALTH UNIVERSITY HOSPITAL (O, 1329 beds) 550 University Boulevard, Indianapolis, IN, Zip 46202-5149, P O Box 1367, Zip 46206-1367, tel. 317/944-5000, Ryan Nagy, M.D., President

INDIANA UNIVERSITY HEALTH WEST HOSPITAL (O, 167 beds) 1111 North Ronald Reagan Parkway, Avon, IN, Zip 46123-7085; tel. 317/217-3000, Doug Puckett, President
Web address: www.iuhealth.org

INDIANA UNIVERSITY HEALTH WHITE MEMORIAL HOSPITAL (O, 24 beds) 720 South Sixth Street, Monticello, IN, Zip 47960-8182; tel. 574/583-7111, Mary Minier, Chief Operating Officer
Web address: www.iuhealth.org/white-memorial

REHABILITATION HOSPITAL OF INDIANA (O, 83 beds) 4141 Shore Drive, Indianapolis, IN, Zip 46254-2607; tel. 317/329-2000, Monte Spence, Interim Chief Executive Officer

Owned, leased, sponsored:	13 hospitals	2600 beds
Contract-managed:	0 hospitals	0 beds
Totals:	13 hospitals	2600 beds

2025: INFIRMARY HEALTH SYSTEM (NP)
5 Mobile Infirmary Circle, Mobile, AL Zip 36607-3513; tel. 251/435-5500, D Mark. Nix, President and Chief Executive Officer
(Independent Hospital System)

ALABAMA: INFIRMARY LONG TERM ACUTE CARE HOSPITAL (L, 38 beds) 5 Mobile Infirmary Circle, Mobile, AL, Zip 36607-3513, P O Box 2226, Zip 36652-2226, tel. 251/660-5239, Susanne Marmande, Administrator

MOBILE INFIRMARY MEDICAL CENTER (O, 538 beds) 5 Mobile Infirmary Drive North, Mobile, AL, Zip 36607-3513, P O Box 2144, Zip 36652-2144, tel. 251/435-2400, Susan E. Boudreau, President
Web address: www.infirmaryhealth.org

NORTH BALDWIN INFIRMARY (L, 113 beds) 1815 Hand Avenue, Bay Minette, AL, Zip 36507-4110, P O Box 1409, Zip 36507-1409, tel. 251/937-5521, Kenny Breal, President
Web address: https://www.infirmaryhealth.org/locations/north-baldwin-infirmary/

THOMAS HOSPITAL (L, 255 beds) 750 Morphy Avenue, Fairhope, AL, Zip 36532-1812, P O Box 929, Zip 36533-0929, tel. 251/928-2375, Ormand P. Thompson, President
Web address: www.thomashospital.com

Owned, leased, sponsored:	4 hospitals	944 beds
Contract-managed:	0 hospitals	0 beds
Totals:	4 hospitals	944 beds

★1305: INOVA HEALTH SYSTEM (NP)
8095 Innovation Park Drive, Fairfax, VA Zip 22031-4868; tel. 703/289-2069, J. Stephen. Jones, M.D., FACS, President and Chief Executive Officer
(Centralized Health System)

VIRGINIA: INOVA ALEXANDRIA HOSPITAL (O, 336 beds) 4320 Seminary Road, Alexandria, VA, Zip 22304-1535; tel. 703/504-3167, Rina Bansal, M.D., President
Web address: www.inova.org

INOVA FAIR OAKS HOSPITAL (O, 223 beds) 3600 Joseph Siewick Drive, Fairfax, VA, Zip 22033-1798; tel. 703/391-3600, Raj Chand, M.D., President
Web address: www.inova.org

INOVA FAIRFAX MEDICAL CAMPUS (O, 1036 beds) 3300 Gallows Road, Falls Church, VA, Zip 22042-3300; tel. 703/776-4001, Steve Narang, M.D., President and President, Pediatric Service Line
Web address: https://www.inova.org/locations/inova-fairfax-medical-campus

INOVA LOUDOUN HOSPITAL (O, 271 beds) 44045 Riverside Parkway, Leesburg, VA, Zip 20176-5101, P O Box 6000, Zip 20177-0600, tel. 703/858-6000, Susan T. Carroll, FACHE, President

INOVA MOUNT VERNON HOSPITAL (O, 225 beds) 2501 Parker's Lane, Alexandria, VA, Zip 22306-3209; tel. 703/664-7000, Roberta Tinch, President
Web address: www.inova.org

Owned, leased, sponsored:	5 hospitals	2091 beds
Contract-managed:	0 hospitals	0 beds
Totals:	5 hospitals	2091 beds

★0151: INSPIRA HEALTH NETWORK (NP)
165 Bridgeton Pike, Mullica Hill, NJ Zip 8062; tel. 856/641-8000, Amy B. Mansue, President and Chief Executive Officer
(Independent Hospital System)

NEW JERSEY: INSPIRA MEDICAL CENTER MULLICA HILL (O, 309 beds) 700 Mullica Hill Road, Mullica Hill, NJ, Zip 08062-4413; tel. 856/508-1000, Amy B. Mansue, President and Chief Executive Officer

INSPIRA MEDICAL CENTER-VINELAND (O, 343 beds) 1505 West Sherman Avenue, Vineland, NJ, Zip 08360-6912; tel. 856/641-8000, Amy B. Mansue, President and Chief Executive Officer
Web address: www.inspirahealthnetwork.org/?id=5280&sid=1

Owned, leased, sponsored:	2 hospitals	652 beds
Contract-managed:	0 hospitals	0 beds
Totals:	2 hospitals	652 beds

★0305: INTEGRIS HEALTH (NP)
3001 Quail Springs Parkway, Oklahoma City, OK Zip 73134; tel. 405/949-3177, Timothy T. Pehrson, President and Chief Executive Officer
(Moderately Centralized Health System)

OKLAHOMA: INTEGRIS BAPTIST MEDICAL CENTER (O, 892 beds) 3300 NW Expressway, Oklahoma City, OK, Zip 73112-4418; tel. 405/949-3011, Joshua Kemph, Chief Executive Officer

INTEGRIS CANADIAN VALLEY HOSPITAL (O, 82 beds) 1201 Health Center Parkway, Yukon, OK, Zip 73099-6381; tel. 405/717-6800, Teresa Gray, Chief Hospital Executive
Web address: www.integris-health.com

INTEGRIS GROVE HOSPITAL (O, 58 beds) 1001 East 18th Street, Grove, OK, Zip 74344-2907; tel. 918/786-2243, Jonas Rabel, Chief Hospital Executive
Web address: www.https://integrisok.com/locations/hospital/grove-hospital

INTEGRIS HEALTH EDMOND HOSPITAL (O, 99 beds) 4801 Integris Parkway, Edmond, OK, Zip 73034-8864; tel. 405/657-3000, Jonathan Rule, Chief Hospital Executive

INTEGRIS HEALTH ENID HOSPITAL (O, 155 beds) 600 South Monroe Street, Enid, OK, Zip 73701-7211, P O Box 3168, Zip 73702-3168, tel. 580/233-2300, Keaton Francis, Chief Hospital Executive
Web address: www.https://integrisok.com/locations/hospital/integris-bass-baptist-health-center

INTEGRIS HEALTH PONCA CITY HOSPITAL (O, 41 beds) 1900 North 14th Street, Ponca City, OK, Zip 74601-2099; tel. 580/765-3321, Christopher Mendoza, Chief Executive Officer
Web address: www.https://integrisok.com/locations/hospital/ponca-city-hospital

For explanation of codes following names, see page B2.
★ *Indicates Type III membership in the American Hospital Association.*

Systems / Intermountain Health

INTEGRIS HEALTH WOODWARD HOSPITAL (L, 32 beds) 900 17th Street, Woodward, OK, Zip 73801-2448; tel. 580/256-5511, Jeff Nowlin, Interim Chief Executive Officer
Web address: www.https://integrisok.com/locations/hospital/woodward-hospital
INTEGRIS MIAMI HOSPITAL (O, 44 beds) 200 Second Avenue SW, Miami, OK, Zip 74354-6830; tel. 918/542-6611, Jonas Rabel, Chief Hospital Executive
INTEGRIS SOUTHWEST MEDICAL CENTER (O, 257 beds) 4401 South Western, Oklahoma City, OK, Zip 73109-3413; tel. 405/636-7000, Phil Harrop, Chief Executive Officer
Web address: www.https://integrishealth.org/locations/hospital/integris-southwest-medical-center
LAKESIDE WOMEN'S HOSPITAL (O, 29 beds) 11200 North Portland Avenue, Oklahoma City, OK, Zip 73120-5045; tel. 405/936-1500, Leslie Buford, Chief Hospital Executive

Owned, leased, sponsored:	10 hospitals	1689 beds
Contract-managed:	0 hospitals	0 beds
Totals:	10 hospitals	1689 beds

★**1815: INTERMOUNTAIN HEALTH (NP)**
36 South State Street, 22nd Floor, Salt Lake City, UT Zip 84111-1453; tel. 801/442-2000, Rob Allen, FACHE, President and Chief Executive Officer
(Centralized Health System)

COLORADO: GOOD SAMARITAN MEDICAL CENTER (O, 185 beds) 200 Exempla Circle, Lafayette, CO, Zip 80026-3370; tel. 303/689-4000
Web address: https://www.sclhealth.org/locations/good-samaritan-medical-center/
INTERMOUNTAIN HEALTH PLATTE VALLEY HOSPITAL (O, 98 beds) 1600 Prairie Center Parkway, Brighton, CO, Zip 80601-4006; tel. 303/498-1600, Jaime Campbell, President and Chief Executive Officer
Web address: www.pvmc.org
INTERMOUNTAIN HEALTH SAINT JOSEPH HOSPITAL (O, 347 beds) 1375 East 19th Avenue, Denver, CO, Zip 80218-1126; tel. 303/837-7111, Scott Peek, Front Range Market President
Web address: www.saintjosephdenver.org/
INTERMOUNTAIN HEALTH ST. MARY'S REGIONAL HOSPITAL (O, 334 beds) 2635 North 7th Street, Grand Junction, CO, Zip 81501-8209, P O Box 1628, Zip 81502-1628, tel. 970/298-2273, Bryan L. Johnson, President
Web address: www.stmarygj.com
LUTHERAN MEDICAL CENTER (O, 336 beds) 8300 West 38th Avenue, Wheat Ridge, CO, Zip 80033-6005; tel. 303/425-4500, Andrea Burch, MS, R.N., President
IDAHO: CASSIA REGIONAL HOSPITAL (O, 25 beds) 1501 Hiland Avenue, Burley, ID, Zip 83318-2688; tel. 208/678-4444, Michael Blauer, Administrator
Web address: www.cassiaregional.org
MONTANA: HOLY ROSARY HEALTHCARE (O, 89 beds) 2600 Wilson Street, Miles City, MT, Zip 59301-5094; tel. 406/233-2600, Karen Costello, President
SCL HEALTH MT-ST. JAMES HEALTHCARE (O, 73 beds) 400 South Clark Street, Butte, MT, Zip 59701-2328; tel. 406/723-2500, Karen Costello, Chief Executive Officer
Web address: https://www.sclhealth.org/locations/st-james-healthcare/
SCL HEALTH MT-ST. VINCENT HEALTHCARE (O, 277 beds) 1233 North 30th Street, Billings, MT, Zip 59101-0165, P O Box 35200, Zip 59107-5200, tel. 406/237-7000, Lee Boyles, President, MT|WY Market and President, St. Vincent Regional Hospital
UTAH: ALTA VIEW HOSPITAL (O, 68 beds) 9660 South 1300 East, Sandy, UT, Zip 84094-3793; tel. 801/501-2600, Scott Roberson, President
Web address: www.intermountainhealthcare.org
AMERICAN FORK HOSPITAL (O, 68 beds) 170 North 1100 East, American Fork, UT, Zip 84003-2096; tel. 801/855-3300, Jason Wilson, President
BEAR RIVER VALLEY HOSPITAL (O, 16 beds) 905 North 1000 West, Tremonton, UT, Zip 84337-2497; tel. 435/207-4500, Brandon Vonk, President
Web address: www.https://intermountainhealthcare.org/locations/bear-river-valley-hospital/
CEDAR CITY HOSPITAL (O, 48 beds) 1303 North Main Street, Cedar City, UT, Zip 84721-9746; tel. 435/868-5000, Eric Packer, President
DELTA COMMUNITY MEDICAL CENTER (O, 15 beds) 126 South White Sage Avenue, Delta, UT, Zip 84624-8937; tel. 435/864-5591, Kurt Forsyth, President
Web address: www.https://intermountainhealthcare.org/locations/delta-community-hospital/
FILLMORE COMMUNITY HOSPITAL (O, 7 beds) 674 South Highway 99, Fillmore, UT, Zip 84631-5013; tel. 435/743-5591, Kurt Forsyth, President
Web address: www.ihc.com
GARFIELD MEMORIAL HOSPITAL (C, 15 beds) 200 North 400 East, Panguitch, UT, Zip 84759, P O Box 389, Zip 84759-0389, tel. 435/676-8811, DeAnn Brown, Administrator
Web address: www.https://intermountainhealthcare.org/locations/garfield-memorial-hospital/
HEBER VALLEY HOSPITAL (O, 19 beds) 1485 South Highway 40, Heber City, UT, Zip 84032-3522; tel. 435/654-2500, Si William. Hutt, President
INTERMOUNTAIN MEDICAL CENTER (O, 510 beds) 5121 South Cottonwood Street, Murray, UT, Zip 84107-5701; tel. 801/507-7000, Ralph Jean-Mary, Chief Executive Officer
Web address: www.https://intermountainhealthcare.org/locations/intermountain-medical-center/
INTERMOUNTAIN SPANISH FORK HOSPITAL (O, 33 beds) 765 East Market Place Drive, Spanish Fork, UT, Zip 84660-1396; tel. 385/344-5000, Megan Elizabeth. Johnson, President
Web address: www.https://intermountainhealthcare.org/locations/spanish-fork-hospital/
LDS HOSPITAL (O, 252 beds) Eighth Avenue and 'C' Street, Salt Lake City, UT, Zip 84143-0001; tel. 801/408-1100, Heather Wall, President
LAYTON HOSPITAL (O, 37 beds) 201 West Layton Parkway, Layton, UT, Zip 84041-3692; tel. 801/543-6000, Kelly L. Duffin, President
Web address: www.https://intermountainhealthcare.org/locations/layton-hospital/medical-services/
LOGAN REGIONAL HOSPITAL (O, 139 beds) 1400 North 500 East, Logan, UT, Zip 84341-2455; tel. 435/716-1000, Brandon McBride, President
MCKAY-DEE HOSPITAL (O, 307 beds) 4401 Harrison Boulevard, Ogden, UT, Zip 84403-3195; tel. 801/387-2800, Judy Williamson, R.N., President
Web address: www.mckay-dee.org
OREM COMMUNITY HOSPITAL (O, 24 beds) 331 North 400 West, Orem, UT, Zip 84057-1999; tel. 801/224-4080, Lenny Lyons, President
Web address: www.intermountainhealthcare.org
PARK CITY HOSPITAL (O, 37 beds) 900 Round Valley Drive, Park City, UT, Zip 84060-7552; tel. 435/658-7000, Lori Weston, President
PRIMARY CHILDREN'S HOSPITAL (O, 287 beds) 100 North Mario Capecchi Drive, Intermountain Primary Children's Hospital, Environmental Services, Salt Lake City, UT, Zip 84113-1100; tel. 801/662-1000, Katy Welkie MBA, R.N., Chief Executive Officer
Web address: www.intermountainhealthcare.org
RIVERTON HOSPITAL (O, 97 beds) 3741 West 12600 South, Riverton, UT, Zip 84065-7215; tel. 801/285-4000, Todd Neubert, President
SANPETE VALLEY HOSPITAL (O, 14 beds) 1100 South Medical Drive, Mount Pleasant, UT, Zip 84647-2222; tel. 435/462-2441, Aaron C. Wood, President
Web address: www.intermountainhealthcare.com
SEVIER VALLEY HOSPITAL (O, 24 beds) 1000 North Main Street, Richfield, UT, Zip 84701-1857; tel. 435/893-4100, Brent Schmidt, President
Web address: www.sevierhospital.org
ST. GEORGE REGIONAL HOSPITAL (O, 300 beds) 1380 East Medical Center Drive, Saint George, UT, Zip 84790-2123; tel. 435/251-1000, Natalie Ashby, President
Web address: www.https://intermountainhealthcare.org/locations/st-george-regional-hospital/
UTAH VALLEY HOSPITAL (O, 398 beds) 1034 North 500 West, Provo, UT, Zip 84604-3337; tel. 801/357-7850, Kyle A. Hansen, President

Owned, leased, sponsored:	30 hospitals	4464 beds
Contract-managed:	1 hospitals	15 beds
Totals:	31 hospitals	4479 beds

For explanation of codes following names, see page B2.
★ Indicates Type III membership in the American Hospital Association.

Systems / Iowa Specialty Hospitals & Clinics

★**0902: IOWA SPECIALTY HOSPITALS & CLINICS (NP)**
1316 South Main Street, Clarion, IA Zip 50525-2019;
tel. 515/532-2811, Steven J. Simonin, Chief Executive Officer
(Independent Hospital System)

IOWA: IOWA SPECIALTY HOSPITAL-BELMOND (C, 22 beds) 403 1st Street SE, Belmond, IA, Zip 50421-1201; tel. 641/444-3223, Amy McDaniel, Chief Executive Officer
Web address: www.iowaspecialtyhospital.com
IOWA SPECIALTY HOSPITAL-CLARION (C, 25 beds) 1316 South Main Street, Clarion, IA, Zip 50525-2019; tel. 515/532-2811, Steven J. Simonin, President and Chief Executive Officer
Web address: www.iowaspecialtyhospital.com

Owned, leased, sponsored:	0 hospitals	0 beds
Contract-managed:	2 hospitals	47 beds
Totals:	2 hospitals	47 beds

★**7775: JEFFERSON HEALTH (NP)**
1101 Market Street, 31st Floor, Philadelphia, PA Zip 19107;
tel. 610/225-6200, Joseph Cacchione, M.D., Chief Executive Officer
(Moderately Centralized Health System)

NEW JERSEY: JEFFERSON STRATFORD HOSPITAL (O, 565 beds) 18 East Laurel Road, Stratford, NJ, Zip 08084-1327; tel. 856/346-6000, Richard Galup, Chief Operating Officer
PENNSYLVANIA: EINSTEIN MEDICAL CENTER PHILADELPHIA (O, 496 beds) 5501 Old York Road, Philadelphia, PA, Zip 19141-3098; tel. 215/456-7890, Dixieanne James, President and Chief Operating Officer, Central Region
Web address: www.einstein.edu
JEFFERSON ABINGTON HEALTH (O, 574 beds) 1200 Old York Road, Abington, PA, Zip 19001-3720; tel. 215/481-2000, Brian Sweeney, President, North Region
JEFFERSON EINSTEIN MONTGOMERY HOSPITAL (O, 195 beds) 559 West Germantown Pike, East Norriton, PA, Zip 19403-4250; tel. 484/622-1000, Brian Sweeney, President, North Region
Web address: https://www.einstein.edu/einstein-medical-center-montgomery
JEFFERSON HEALTH NORTHEAST (O, 457 beds) 10800 Knights Road, Mansion House, Philadelphia, PA, Zip 19114-4200; tel. 215/612-4000, Richard Galup, President
JEFFERSON LANSDALE HOSPITAL (O, 99 beds) 100 Medical Campus Drive, Lansdale, PA, Zip 19446-1200; tel. 215/368-2100, Brian Sweeney, President, North Region
Web address: www.abingtonhealth.org/find-a-location/abington-lansdale-hospital/#.V5dyVVL9yk4
MAGEE REHABILITATION (O, 83 beds) 1513 Race Street, Philadelphia, PA, Zip 19102-1177; tel. 215/587-3000, Dixieanne James, President and Chief Operating Officer
Web address: www.mageerehab.org
THOMAS JEFFERSON UNIVERSITY HOSPITAL (O, 882 beds) 111 South 11th Street, Philadelphia, PA, Zip 19107-5084; tel. 215/955-6000, Dixieanne James, President and Chief Operating Officer

Owned, leased, sponsored:	8 hospitals	3351 beds
Contract-managed:	0 hospitals	0 beds
Totals:	8 hospitals	3351 beds

★**0324: JOHN MUIR HEALTH (NP)**
1400 Treat Boulevard, Walnut Creek, CA Zip 94597-2142;
tel. 925/941-2100, Michael S. Thomas, President and Chief Executive Officer
(Independent Hospital System)

CALIFORNIA: JOHN MUIR BEHAVIORAL HEALTH CENTER (O, 73 beds) 2740 Grant Street, Concord, CA, Zip 94520-2265; tel. 925/674-4100
Web address: www.johnmuirhealth.com
JOHN MUIR HEALTH, CONCORD MEDICAL CENTER (O, 256 beds) 2540 East Street, Concord, CA, Zip 94520-1906; tel. 925/682-8200, Michael S. Thomas, President and Chief Executive Officer, John Muir Health
Web address: www.johnmuirhealth.com
JOHN MUIR MEDICAL CENTER, WALNUT CREEK (O, 422 beds) 1601 Ygnacio Valley Road, Walnut Creek, CA, Zip 94598-3194; tel. 925/939-3000, Michael S. Thomas, President and Chief Executive Officer
Web address: https://www.johnmuirhealth.com/

Owned, leased, sponsored:	3 hospitals	751 beds
Contract-managed:	0 hospitals	0 beds
Totals:	3 hospitals	751 beds

★**1015: JOHNS HOPKINS HEALTH SYSTEM (NP)**
733 North Broadway, BRB 104, Baltimore, MD Zip 21205-1832,
733 North Broadway, MRB 104, Zip 21205-1832, tel. 410/955-5000, Kevin W. Sowers, MSN, R.N., President
(Centralized Physician/Insurance Health System)

DISTRICT OF COLUMBIA: SIBLEY MEMORIAL HOSPITAL (O, 297 beds) 5255 Loughboro Road NW, Washington, DC, Zip 20016-2633; tel. 202/537-4000, Hasan A. Zia, President and Chief Executive Officer
FLORIDA: JOHNS HOPKINS ALL CHILDREN'S HOSPITAL (O, 259 beds) 501 6th Avenue South, Saint Petersburg, FL, Zip 33701-4634; tel. 727/898-7451, K. Alicia. Schulhof, President
Web address: www.allkids.org
MARYLAND: JOHNS HOPKINS BAYVIEW MEDICAL CENTER (O, 461 beds) 4940 Eastern Avenue, Baltimore, MD, Zip 21224-2780; tel. 410/550-0100, Jennifer Nickoles, President
JOHNS HOPKINS HOSPITAL (O, 1042 beds) 1800 Orleans Street, Baltimore, MD, Zip 21287; tel. 410/955-5000, Redonda G. Miller, M.D., President
Web address: www.hopkinsmedicine.org
JOHNS HOPKINS HOWARD COUNTY MEDICAL CENTER (O, 243 beds) 5755 Cedar Lane, Columbia, MD, Zip 21044-2999; tel. 410/740-7890, Mohammed Shafeeq. Ahmed, M.D., President
Web address: www.hcgh.org
SUBURBAN HOSPITAL (O, 232 beds) 8600 Old Georgetown Road, Bethesda, MD, Zip 20814-1497; tel. 301/896-3100, LeighAnn Sidone, R.N., President and Chief Executive Officer

Owned, leased, sponsored:	6 hospitals	2534 beds
Contract-managed:	0 hospitals	0 beds
Totals:	6 hospitals	2534 beds

★**2105: KAISER FOUNDATION HOSPITALS (NP)**
1 Kaiser Plaza, 27th Floor-Office #2743, Oakland, CA
Zip 94612-3610; tel. 510/271-5910, Gregory A. Adams, Chief Executive Officer and Chairman
(Decentralized Health System)

CALIFORNIA: KAISER FOUNDATION HOSPITAL-SAN MARCOS (O, 168 beds) 360 Rush Drive, 7th Floor Regulatory Affairs, San Marcos, CA, Zip 92078-7901; tel. 442/385-7000, Elizabeth Jane. Finley, Senior Vice President and Area Manager
KAISER PERMANENTE ANTIOCH MEDICAL CENTER (O, 109 beds) 4501 Sand Creek Road, Antioch, CA, Zip 94531-8687; tel. 925/813-6500, Pamela Galley, Senior Vice President/Area Manager, Diablo Service Area
Web address: www.https://health.kaiserpermanente.org/wps/portal/facility/100382
KAISER PERMANENTE BALDWIN PARK MEDICAL CENTER (O, 271 beds) 1011 Baldwin Park Boulevard, Baldwin Park, CA, Zip 91706-5806; tel. 626/851-1011, Eugene Cho, Senior Vice President/Area Manager, Baldwin Park

For explanation of codes following names, see page B2.
★ Indicates Type III membership in the American Hospital Association.

Systems / Kaiser Foundation Hospitals

KAISER PERMANENTE DOWNEY MEDICAL CENTER (O, 424 beds) 9333 Imperial Highway, Downey, CA, Zip 90242-2812; tel. 562/657-9000, Mitchell Winnik, FACHE, Senior Vice President, Area Manager, Downey
Web address: www.kaiserpermanente.org

KAISER PERMANENTE FONTANA MEDICAL CENTER (O, 530 beds) 9961 Sierra Avenue, Fontana, CA, Zip 92335-6794; tel. 909/427-5000, Georgina R. Garcia, R.N., Senior Vice President, Area Manager for San Bernardino County
Web address: www.kaiserpermanente.org

KAISER PERMANENTE FREMONT MEDICAL CENTER (O, 100 beds) 39400 Paseo Padre Parkway, Fremont, CA, Zip 94538-2310; tel. 510/248-3000, Debra A. Flores, R.N., FACHE, Senior Vice President and Area Manager

KAISER PERMANENTE FRESNO MEDICAL CENTER (O, 169 beds) 7300 North Fresno Street, Fresno, CA, Zip 93720-2942; tel. 559/448-4500, Tyler Hedden, Senior Vice President/Area Manager
Web address: www.https://healthy.kaiserpermanente.org/northern-california/facilities/Fresno-Medical-Center-100363

KAISER PERMANENTE LOS ANGELES MEDICAL CENTER (O, 560 beds) 4867 West Sunset Boulevard, Los Angeles, CA, Zip 90027-5961; tel. 323/783-4011, Robert M. Luterbach, Interim Senior Vice President/Area Manager, Los Angeles/Chief Operating Officer

KAISER PERMANENTE MANTECA MEDICAL CENTER (O, 275 beds) 1777 West Yosemite Avenue, Manteca, CA, Zip 95337-5187; tel. 209/825-3700, Aphriekah Duhaney-West, Senior Vice President, Area Manager, Central Valley
Web address: www.kaiserpermanente.org

KAISER PERMANENTE MORENO VALLEY MEDICAL CENTER (O, 100 beds) 27300 Iris Avenue, Moreno Valley, CA, Zip 92555-4800; tel. 951/243-0811, Sammy R. Totah, PharmD, Senior Vice President, Area Manager Riverside & Moreno Valley, Kaiser Foundation Health Plans and Hospitals

KAISER PERMANENTE OAKLAND MEDICAL CENTER (O, 365 beds) 3600 Broadway, Oakland, CA, Zip 94611-5693; tel. 510/752-1000, Dante' Green, FACHE, Interim Senior Vice President & Area Manager, East Bay Area
Web address: www.kaiserpermanente.org

KAISER PERMANENTE ORANGE COUNTY ANAHEIM MEDICAL CENTER (O, 526 beds) 3440 East La Palma Avenue, Anaheim, CA, Zip 92806-2020; tel. 714/644-2000, Payman Roshan, Senior Vice President and Area Manager, Orange County
Web address: www.kp.org

KAISER PERMANENTE PANORAMA CITY MEDICAL CENTER (O, 218 beds) 13651 Willard Street, Panorama City, CA, Zip 91402; tel. 818/375-2000, Camille Applin-Jones, Senior Vice President and Area Manager

KAISER PERMANENTE REDWOOD CITY MEDICAL CENTER (O, 153 beds) 1100 Veterans Boulevard, Redwood City, CA, Zip 94063-2087; tel. 650/299-2000

KAISER PERMANENTE RIVERSIDE MEDICAL CENTER (O, 225 beds) 10800 Magnolia Avenue, Riverside, CA, Zip 92505-3000; tel. 951/353-2000, Sammy R. Totah, PharmD, Senior Vice President, Area Manager Riverside & Moreno Valley, Kaiser Foundation Health Plans and Hospitals
Web address: www.kaiserpermanente.org

KAISER PERMANENTE ROSEVILLE MEDICAL CENTER (O, 352 beds) 1600 Eureka Road, Roseville, CA, Zip 95661-3027; tel. 916/784-4000, Kimberly Menzel, Senior Vice President and Area Manager

KAISER PERMANENTE SACRAMENTO MEDICAL CENTER (O, 287 beds) 2025 Morse Avenue, Sacramento, CA, Zip 95825-2100; tel. 916/973-5000, James L. Robinson III, PsyD, Senior Vice President/Area Manager, Sacramento and South Sacramento
Web address: www.kp.org

KAISER PERMANENTE SAN FRANCISCO MEDICAL CENTER (O, 239 beds) 2425 Geary Boulevard, San Francisco, CA, Zip 94115-3358; tel. 415/833-2000, Tarek Salaway, Senior Vice President and Area Manager, Golden Gate Service Area

KAISER PERMANENTE SAN JOSE MEDICAL CENTER (O, 247 beds) 250 Hospital Parkway, San Jose, CA, Zip 95119-1199; tel. 408/972-7000, Eric Henry, Senior Vice President/Area Manager, Greater San Jose Service Area
Web address: www.https://healthy.kaiserpermanente.org/northern-california/facilities/San-Jose-Medical-Center-100322

KAISER PERMANENTE SAN LEANDRO MEDICAL CENTER (O, 216 beds) 2500 Merced Street, San Leandro, CA, Zip 94577-4201; tel. 510/454-1000, Debra A. Flores, R.N., FACHE, Senior Vice President and Area Manager

KAISER PERMANENTE SAN RAFAEL MEDICAL CENTER (O, 116 beds) 99 Montecillo Road, San Rafael, CA, Zip 94903-3397; tel. 415/444-2000, Tarek Salaway, Senior Vice President/Area Manager, Golden Gate Service Area
Web address: www.kaiserpermanente.org

KAISER PERMANENTE SANTA CLARA MEDICAL CENTER (O, 343 beds) 700 Lawrence Expressway, Santa Clara, CA, Zip 95051-5173; tel. 408/851-1000, Eric Williams, Senior Vice President and Area Manager Santa Clara
Web address: www.kaiserpermanente.org

KAISER PERMANENTE SANTA ROSA MEDICAL CENTER (O, 172 beds) 401 Bicentennial Way, Santa Rosa, CA, Zip 95403-2192; tel. 707/571-4000, Abhishek Dosi, Senior Vice President and Area Manager, Santa Rose Service Area

KAISER PERMANENTE SOUTH BAY MEDICAL CENTER (O, 257 beds) 25825 Vermont Avenue, Harbor City, CA, Zip 90710-3599; tel. 310/325-5111, Margie Harrier, MSN, R.N., Senior Vice President/Area Manager, South Bay
Web address: www.kaiserpermanente.org

KAISER PERMANENTE SOUTH SACRAMENTO MEDICAL CENTER (O, 241 beds) 6600 Bruceville Road, Sacramento, CA, Zip 95823-4691; tel. 916/688-2430, James L. Robinson III, PsyD, Senior Vice President/Area Manager, Sacramento and South Sacramento
Web address: www.kp.org

KAISER PERMANENTE SOUTH SAN FRANCISCO MEDICAL CENTER (O, 120 beds) 1200 El Camino Real, South San Francisco, CA, Zip 94080-3208; tel. 650/742-2000, Shasta Addessi, Interim Senior Vice President and Area Manager
Web address: www.kaiserpermanente.org

KAISER PERMANENTE VACAVILLE MEDICAL CENTER (O, 150 beds) 1 Quality Drive, Vacaville, CA, Zip 95688-9494; tel. 707/624-4000, Darryl B. Curry, Senior Vice President, Area Manager, Napa-Solano Area

KAISER PERMANENTE VALLEJO MEDICAL CENTER (O, 253 beds) 975 Sereno Drive, Vallejo, CA, Zip 94589-2441; tel. 707/651-1000, Darryl B. Curry, Senior Vice President, Area Manager, Napa-Solano Area
Web address: www.kaiserpermanente.org

KAISER PERMANENTE WALNUT CREEK MEDICAL CENTER (O, 196 beds) 1425 South Main Street, Walnut Creek, CA, Zip 94596-5300; tel. 925/295-4000, Pamela Galley, Senior Vice President and Area Manager, Diablo Service Area

KAISER PERMANENTE WEST LOS ANGELES MEDICAL CENTER (O, 124 beds) 6041 Cadillac Avenue, Los Angeles, CA, Zip 90034-1700; tel. 323/857-2201, Lilit Sarah. Zibari, Senior Vice President, Area Manager/West Los Angeles
Web address: www.kaiserpermanente.org

KAISER PERMANENTE WOODLAND HILLS MEDICAL CENTER (O, 204 beds) 5601 DeSoto Avenue, Woodland Hills, CA, Zip 91367-6798; tel. 818/719-2000, Murtaza Sanwari, Senior Vice President/Area Manager, Woodland Hills
Web address: www.kaiserpermanente.org

KAISER PERMANENTE ZION MEDICAL CENTER (O, 412 beds) 4647 Zion Avenue, San Diego, CA, Zip 92120-2507; tel. 619/528-5000, Elizabeth Jane. Finley, Senior Vice President and Area Manager

HAWAII: KAISER PERMANENTE MEDICAL CENTER (O, 215 beds) 3288 Moanalua Road, Honolulu, HI, Zip 96819-1469; tel. 808/432-8000, Ed Chan, FACHE, Market President, Hawaii
Web address: www.kaiserpermanente.org

KULA HOSPITAL (C, 9 beds) 100 Keokea Place, Kula, HI, Zip 96790-7450; tel. 808/878-1221, David Culbreth, Administrator

LANAI COMMUNITY HOSPITAL (C, 24 beds) 628 Seventh Street, Lanai City, HI, Zip 96763-0650; tel. 808/565-8450, David Culbreth, Administrator
Web address: https://www.mauihealthsystem.org/lanai-hospital/

MAUI MEMORIAL MEDICAL CENTER (C, 219 beds) 221 Mahalani Street, Wailuku, HI, Zip 96793-2581; tel. 808/298-2626, Lynn Fulton, Chief Executive Officer
Web address: https://www.mauihealthsystem.org/maui-memorial/

OREGON: KAISER SUNNYSIDE MEDICAL CENTER (O, 302 beds) 10180 SE Sunnyside Road, Clackamas, OR, Zip 97015-8970; tel. 503/652-2880, Adam Van Den Avyle, Hospital Administrator

For explanation of codes following names, see page B2.
★ Indicates Type III membership in the American Hospital Association.

Systems / Kaiser Foundation Hospitals

KAISER WESTSIDE MEDICAL CENTER (O, 122 beds) 2875 NE Stucki Avenue, Hillsboro, OR, Zip 97124-5806; tel. 971/310-1000, Adam Van Den Avyle, Hospital Administrator
Web address: www.kp.org

Owned, leased, sponsored:	35 hospitals	8761 beds
Contract-managed:	3 hospitals	252 beds
Totals:	38 hospitals	9013 beds

★0954: KECK MEDICINE OF USC (NP)

1510 San Pablo Street, Suite 600, Los Angeles, CA Zip 90033-5405; tel. 323/442-8500, Rodney B. Hanners, Chief Executive Officer
(Independent Hospital System)

CALIFORNIA: KECK HOSPITAL OF USC (O, 401 beds) 1500 San Pablo Street, Los Angeles, CA, Zip 90033-5313; tel. 323/442-8500, William Martin. Sargeant, Chief Executive Officer/Interim Chief, Office of Performance & Transformation
Web address: https://www.keckmedicine.org/

USC ARCADIA HOSPITAL (O, 269 beds) 300 West Huntington Drive, Arcadia, CA, Zip 91007-3473, P O Box 60016, Zip 91066-6016, tel. 626/898-8000, Ikenna Mmeje, President and Chief Executive Officer
Web address: https://www.uscarcadiahospital.org/

USC NORRIS COMPREHENSIVE CANCER CENTER AND HOSPITAL (O, 60 beds) 1441 Eastlake Avenue, Los Angeles, CA, Zip 90089-0112; tel. 323/865-3000, William Martin. Sargeant, Chief Executive Officer/Interim Chief, Office of Performance & Transformation

USC VERDUGO HILLS HOSPITAL (O, 122 beds) 1812 Verdugo Boulevard, Glendale, CA, Zip 91208-1409; tel. 818/790-7100, Armand Dorian, M.D., FACHE, Chief Executive Officer
Web address: www.uscvhh.org

Owned, leased, sponsored:	4 hospitals	852 beds
Contract-managed:	0 hospitals	0 beds
Totals:	4 hospitals	852 beds

★0258: Kettering Health (NP)

3965 Southern Boulevard, Dayton, OH Zip 45429-1229, 1 Prestige Place, Suite 905, Miamisburg, Zip 45342-3794, tel. 855/536-7543, Michael V. Gentry, Chief Executive Officer
(Independent Hospital System)

OHIO: KETTERING HEALTH DAYTON (O, 322 beds) 405 West Grand Avenue, Dayton, OH, Zip 45405-4796; tel. 937/723-3200, Michael J. Brendel, R.N., President
Web address: www.ketteringhealth.org/grandview/

KETTERING HEALTH GREENE MEMORIAL (O, 13 beds) 1141 North Monroe Drive, Xenia, OH, Zip 45385-1600; tel. 937/352-2000, Daniel Tryon, President
Web address: www.ketteringhealth.org/greene

KETTERING HEALTH HAMILTON (O, 180 beds) 630 Eaton Avenue, Hamilton, OH, Zip 45013-2770; tel. 513/867-2000, Paul Hoover, President

KETTERING HEALTH MAIN CAMPUS (O, 397 beds) 3535 Southern Boulevard, Kettering, OH, Zip 45429-1221; tel. 937/298-4331, Sharlet M. Briggs, President
Web address: www.ketteringhealth.org/kettering

KETTERING HEALTH MIAMISBURG (O, 168 beds) 4000 Miamisburg-Centerville Road, Miamisburg, OH, Zip 45342-7615; tel. 937/866-0551, Erica Schneider, President KH Miamisburg & KH Washington Township

KETTERING HEALTH TROY (O, 28 beds) 600 W Main Street, Troy, OH, Zip 45373-3384; tel. 937/980-7000, Norman Spence, President
Web address: www.https://ketteringhealth.org/troy

SOIN MEDICAL CENTER (O, 172 beds) 3535 Pentagon Boulevard, Beavercreek, OH, Zip 45431-1705; tel. 937/702-4000, Daniel Tryon, President

Owned, leased, sponsored:	7 hospitals	1280 beds
Contract-managed:	0 hospitals	0 beds
Totals:	7 hospitals	1280 beds

0333: KPC HEALTHCARE, INC. (IO)

1301 North Tustin Avenue, Santa Ana, CA Zip 92705-8619; tel. 714/953-3652, Peter R. Baronoff, Chief Executive Officer and Managing Director
(Independent Hospital System)

ARIZONA: KPC PROMISE HOSPITAL OF PHOENIX (O, 40 beds) 433 East 6th Street, Mesa, AZ, Zip 85203-7104; tel. 480/427-3000, Larry Niemann, Chief Executive Officer

CALIFORNIA: ANAHEIM GLOBAL MEDICAL CENTER (O, 188 beds) 1025 South Anaheim Boulevard, Anaheim, CA, Zip 92805-5806; tel. 714/533-6220, Kevan Metcalfe, FACHE, Chief Executive Officer
Web address: www.https://anaheimglobalmedicalcenter.com/

CHAPMAN GLOBAL MEDICAL CENTER (O, 100 beds) 2601 East Chapman Avenue, Orange, CA, Zip 92869-3296; tel. 714/633-0011, Theresa Catherine. Berton, Interim Chief Executive Officer
Web address: www.Chapmanglobalmedicalcenter.com

ORANGE COUNTY GLOBAL MEDICAL CENTER, INC. (O, 282 beds) 1001 North Tustin Avenue, Santa Ana, CA, Zip 92705-3577; tel. 714/953-3500, Derek Scott. Drake, Chief Executive Officer
Web address: https://www.orangecountyglobalmedicalcenter.com/

SOUTH COAST GLOBAL MEDICAL CENTER (O, 178 beds) 2701 South Bristol Street, Santa Ana, CA, Zip 92704-6278; tel. 714/754-5454, Kevan Metcalfe, FACHE, Chief Executive Officer

KANSAS: KPC PROMISE HOSPITAL OF OVERLAND PARK (O, 104 beds) 6509 West 103rd Street, Overland Park, KS, Zip 66212-1728; tel. 913/649-3701, Patricia Ann. Wors, Chief Executive Officer
Web address: www.overlandpark.kpcph.com

LOUISIANA: KPC PROMISE HOSPITAL OF BATON ROUGE (O, 54 beds) 5130 Mancuso Lane, Baton Rouge, LA, Zip 70809-3583; tel. 225/490-9600, LaTeka Tanette. Johnson, Chief Executive Officer

TEXAS: KPC PROMISE HOSPITAL OF DALLAS (O, 66 beds) 7955 Harry Hines Boulevard, Dallas, TX, Zip 75235-3305; tel. 214/637-0000, Rachel Bailey, Chief Executive Officer
Web address: www.dallas.kpcph.com/

KPC PROMISE HOSPITAL OF WICHITA FALLS (O, 31 beds) 1103 Grace Street, Wichita Falls, TX, Zip 76301-4414; tel. 940/720-6633, Rachel Bailey, Chief Executive Officer
Web address: www.wichitafalls.kpcph.com/

UTAH: KPC PROMISE HOSPITAL OF SALT LAKE (O, 41 beds) 8 Avenue, C Street, Salt Lake City, UT, Zip 84143; tel. 385/425-0050, Kenny Peterson, Chief Executive Officer
Web address: www.saltlake.kpcph.com/

Owned, leased, sponsored:	10 hospitals	1084 beds
Contract-managed:	0 hospitals	0 beds
Totals:	10 hospitals	1084 beds

0393: LANDMARK HOSPITALS (IO)

3255 Independence Street, Cape Girardeau, MO Zip 63701-4914; tel. 573/335-1091, William K. Kapp III, M.D., President and Chief Executive Officer
(Independent Hospital System)

FLORIDA: LANDMARK HOSPITAL OF SOUTHWEST FLORIDA (O, 50 beds) 1285 Creekside Boulevard East, Naples, FL, Zip 34108; tel. 239/529-1800, Daniel C. Dunmyer, Chief Executive Officer
Web address: https://www.landmarkhospitals.com/critical-care-hospital-system/critical-care-hospital-southwest-florida/

For explanation of codes following names, see page B2.
★ Indicates Type III membership in the American Hospital Association.

Systems / Lehigh Valley Health Network

GEORGIA: LANDMARK HOSPITAL OF ATHENS (O, 42 beds) 775 Sunset Drive, Athens, GA, Zip 30606-2211; tel. 762/356-0759, Marie Saylor, Chief Executive Officer

LANDMARK HOSPITAL OF SAVANNAH (O, 50 beds) 800 East 68th Street, Savannah, GA, Zip 31405-4710; tel. 912/298-1000, Denise Wayne, Chief Executive Officer
Web address: www.landmarkhospitals.com/savannah

MISSOURI: LANDMARK HOSPITAL OF CAPE GIRARDEAU (O, 30 beds) 3255 Independence Street, Cape Girardeau, MO, Zip 63701-4914; tel. 573/335-1091, Deborah Sabella, R.N., Chief Executive Officer
Web address: www.landmarkhospitals.com

LANDMARK HOSPITAL OF COLUMBIA (O, 23 beds) 604 Old 63 North, Columbia, MO, Zip 65201-6308; tel. 573/499-6600, Kerry Ashment, Chief Executive Officer
Web address: https://www.landmarkhospitals.com/critical-care-hospital-system/columbia-mo/

LANDMARK HOSPITAL OF JOPLIN (O, 28 beds) 2040 West 32nd Street, Joplin, MO, Zip 64804-3512; tel. 417/627-1300, Robert Samples, Chief Executive Officer

Owned, leased, sponsored:	6 hospitals	223 beds
Contract-managed:	0 hospitals	0 beds
Totals:	6 hospitals	223 beds

★0932: LCMC HEALTH (NP)
200 Henry Clay Avenue, New Orleans, LA Zip 70118-5720; tel. 504/899-9511, Greg Feirn, CPA, President and Chief Executive Officer
(Moderately Centralized Health System)

LOUISIANA: CHILDREN'S HOSPITAL NEW ORLEANS (O, 226 beds) 200 Henry Clay Avenue, New Orleans, LA, Zip 70118-5720; tel. 504/899-9511, Lucio Fragoso, President and Chief Executive Officer
Web address: www.chnola.org

EAST JEFFERSON GENERAL HOSPITAL (O, 540 beds) 4200 Houma Boulevard, Metairie, LA, Zip 70006-2996; tel. 504/503-4000, Gregory Nielsen, Chief Executive Officer

NEW ORLEANS EAST HOSPITAL (C, 34 beds) 5620 Read Boulevard, New Orleans, LA, Zip 70127-3106, 5620 Read Blvd, Zip 70127-3106, tel. 504/592-6600, Takeisha C. Davis, M.D., M.P.H., President and Chief Executive Officer
Web address: www.noehospital.org

TOURO INFIRMARY (O, 280 beds) 1401 Foucher Street, New Orleans, LA, Zip 70115-3593; tel. 504/897-7011, Christopher Lege, Chief Executive Officer

UNIVERSITY MEDICAL CENTER (O, 386 beds) 2000 Canal Street, New Orleans, LA, Zip 70112-3018; tel. 504/702-3000, John R. Nickens IV, President and Chief Executive Officer
Web address: www.umcno.org

WEST JEFFERSON MEDICAL CENTER (C, 252 beds) 1101 Medical Center Boulevard, Marrero, LA, Zip 70072-3191; tel. 504/347-5511, Rob Calhoun, President and Chief Executive Offricer
Web address: www.wjmc.org

Owned, leased, sponsored:	4 hospitals	1432 beds
Contract-managed:	2 hospitals	286 beds
Totals:	6 hospitals	1718 beds

★0369: LEE HEALTH (NP)
9800 South Healthpark Drive #405, Fort Myers, FL Zip 33908-7603, 2776 Cleveland Avenue, Zip 33901-5864, tel. 239/343-2000, Lawrence Antonucci, M.D., President and Chief Executive Officer
(Moderately Centralized Health System)

FLORIDA: CAPE CORAL HOSPITAL (O, 291 beds) 636 Del Prado Boulevard, Cape Coral, FL, Zip 33990-2695; tel. 239/424-2000, Iahn Gonsenhauser, Chief Medical Officer

GULF COAST MEDICAL CENTER (O, 624 beds) 13681 Doctor's Way, Fort Myers, FL, Zip 33912-4300; tel. 239/343-1000, Lawrence Antonucci, M.D., President/Chief Executive Officer
Web address: www.leememorial.org

LEE MEMORIAL HOSPITAL (O, 911 beds) 2776 Cleveland Avenue, Fort Myers, FL, Zip 33901-5855, P O Box 2218, Zip 33902-2218, tel. 239/343-2000, Iahn Gonsenhauser, Chief Medical Officer

Owned, leased, sponsored:	3 hospitals	1826 beds
Contract-managed:	0 hospitals	0 beds
Totals:	3 hospitals	1826 beds

★2755: LEGACY HEALTH (NP)
1919 NW Lovejoy Street, Portland, OR Zip 97209-1503; tel. 503/415-5600, Kathryn G. Correia, President and Chief Executive Officer
(Centralized Health System)

OREGON: LEGACY EMANUEL MEDICAL CENTER (O, 531 beds) 2801 North Gantenbein Avenue, Portland, OR, Zip 97227-1674; tel. 503/413-2200, Bahaa Wanly, President
Web address: www.legacyhealth.org

LEGACY GOOD SAMARITAN MEDICAL CENTER (O, 236 beds) 1015 NW 22nd Avenue, Portland, OR, Zip 97210-3099; tel. 503/413-7711, Kevin O'Boyle, President
Web address: www.legacyhealth.org

LEGACY MERIDIAN PARK MEDICAL CENTER (O, 146 beds) 19300 SW 65th Avenue, Tualatin, OR, Zip 97062-9741; tel. 503/692-1212, Joseph Yoder, President, Willamette Valley Region
Web address: www.legacyhealth.org

LEGACY MOUNT HOOD MEDICAL CENTER (O, 96 beds) 24800 SE Stark, Gresham, OR, Zip 97030-3378; tel. 503/674-1122, James Aberle, President

LEGACY SILVERTON MEDICAL CENTER (O, 47 beds) 139 Breyonna Way, Silverton, OR, Zip 97381, 342 Fairview Street, Zip 97381-1993, tel. 503/873-1500, Joseph Yoder, President, Willamette Valley Region
Web address: www.legacyhealth.org/locations/hospitals/legacy-silverton-medical-center.aspx

WASHINGTON: LEGACY SALMON CREEK MEDICAL CENTER (O, 212 beds) 2211 NE 139th Street, Vancouver, WA, Zip 98686-2742; tel. 360/487-1000, Jon Hersen, President

Owned, leased, sponsored:	6 hospitals	1268 beds
Contract-managed:	0 hospitals	0 beds
Totals:	6 hospitals	1268 beds

★0370: LEHIGH VALLEY HEALTH NETWORK (NP)
1200 South Cedar Crest Boulevard, Allentown, PA Zip 18103-6202, P O Box 689, Zip 18105-1556, tel. 610/402-8000, Brian A. Nester, D.O., President and Chief Executive Officer
(Moderately Centralized Health System)

PENNSYLVANIA: LEHIGH VALLEY HOSPITAL-HAZLETON (O, 111 beds) 700 East Broad Street, Hazleton, PA, Zip 18201-6897; tel. 570/501-4000, Tammy Torres, President
Web address: www.lvhn.org/hazleton/

LEHIGH VALLEY HOSPITAL-POCONO (O, 249 beds) 206 East Brown Street, East Stroudsburg, PA, Zip 18301-3006; tel. 570/421-4000, Cornelio R. Catena, FACHE, President

LEHIGH VALLEY HOSPITAL-SCHUYLKILL (O, 186 beds) 700 East Norwegian Street, Pottsville, PA, Zip 17901-2710; tel. 570/621-5000, Terrence J. Purcell, President
Web address: www.schuylkillhealth.com

LEHIGH VALLEY HOSPITAL-CEDAR CREST (O, 1120 beds) 1200 South Cedar Crest Boulevard, Allentown, PA, Zip 18103-6248, P O Box 689, Zip 18105-

For explanation of codes following names, see page B2.
★ Indicates Type III membership in the American Hospital Association.

Systems / Lehigh Valley Health Network

1556, tel. 610/402–8000, Robert Begliomini, President, LVH Cedar Crest and Lehigh Region

Owned, leased, sponsored:	4 hospitals	1666 beds
Contract-managed:	0 hospitals	0 beds
Totals:	4 hospitals	1666 beds

0632: LHC GROUP (IO)

901 Hugh Wallis Road South, Lafayette, LA Zip 70508–2511; tel. 337/233–1307, Keith G. Myers, Chairman and Chief Executive Officer

(Independent Hospital System)

ARKANSAS: CHRISTUS DUBUIS HOSPITAL OF FORT SMITH (O, 25 beds) 7301 Rogers Avenue, 4th Floor, Fort Smith, AR, Zip 72903–4100; tel. 479/314–4900, Nancy Owens, Administrator
Web address: www.christusdubuis.org/fortsmith

CHRISTUS DUBUIS HOSPITAL OF HOT SPRINGS (O, 25 beds) 300 Werner Street, 3rd Floor East, Hot Springs National Park, AR, Zip 71913–6406; tel. 501/609–4300, Kathy DeVore, R.N., Administrator

LOUISIANA: CHRISTUS DUBUIS HOSPITAL OF ALEXANDRIA (O, 25 beds) 3330 Masonic Drive, 4th Floor, Alexandria, LA, Zip 71301–3841; tel. 318/448–4938, George Patrick. DeRouen, Administrator
Web address: www.https://lhcgroup.com/locations/christus-dubuis-hospital-of-alexandria/

LHC GROUP–HOME HEALTHCARE (O, 25 beds) 901 Hugh Wallis Road South, Lafayette, LA, Zip 70508–2511; tel. 337/233–1307, Keith G. Myers, Chairman and Chief Executive Officer

LOUISIANA EXTENDED CARE HOSPITAL OF LAFAYETTE (O, 42 beds) 2810 Ambassador Caffery Parkway, 6th Floor, Lafayette, LA, Zip 70506–5906; tel. 337/289–8180, Chris Fox, Division President
Web address: www.https://lhcgroup.com/locations/louisiana-extended-care-hospital-of-lafayette-2/

LOUISIANA EXTENDED CARE HOSPITAL OF NATCHITOCHES (O, 21 beds) 501 Keyser Avenue, Natchitoches, LA, Zip 71457–6018; tel. 318/354–2044, TameKia Colbert, Administrator
Web address: www.https://lhcgroup.com/locations/louisiana-extended-care-hospital-of-natchitoches/

OCHSNER EXTENDED CARE HOSPITAL (O, 32 beds) 2614 Jefferson Highway, 2nd Floor, New Orleans, LA, Zip 70121–3828; tel. 504/314–4242, Len McDade, Chief Executive Officer
Web address: www.lhcgroup.com/

SPECIALTY HOSPITAL (O, 32 beds) 309 Jackson Street, 7th Floor, Monroe, LA, Zip 71201–7407, P O Box 1532, Zip 71210–1532, tel. 318/966–7045, Cleta Munholland, Administrator

TEXAS: CHRISTUS DUBUIS HOSPITAL OF BEAUMONT (O, 33 beds) 2830 Calder Avenue, 4th Floor, Beaumont, TX, Zip 77702–1809; tel. 409/899–7680, Jason Baker, Administrator
Web address: www.christusdubuis.org/BeaumontandPortArthurSystem-CHRISTUSDubuisHospitalofBeaumont

Owned, leased, sponsored:	9 hospitals	260 beds
Contract-managed:	0 hospitals	0 beds
Totals:	9 hospitals	260 beds

★0158: LIFEBRIDGE HEALTH (NP)

2401 West Belvedere Avenue, Baltimore, MD Zip 21215–5216; tel. 410/601–5134, Neil M. Meltzer, President and Chief Executive Officer

(Moderately Centralized Health System)

MARYLAND: CARROLL HOSPITAL (O, 163 beds) 200 Memorial Avenue, Westminster, MD, Zip 21157–5799; tel. 410/848–3000, Garrett W. Hoover, FACHE, President and Chief Operating Officer, Senior Vice President LifeBridge Health
Web address: www.carrollhospitalcenter.org

LEVINDALE HEBREW GERIATRIC CENTER AND HOSPITAL (O, 490 beds) 2434 West Belvedere Avenue, Baltimore, MD, Zip 21215–5267; tel. 410/601–2400, Sharon Hendricks, Chief Administrative Officer

NORTHWEST HOSPITAL (O, 210 beds) 5401 Old Court Road, Randallstown, MD, Zip 21133–5185; tel. 410/521–2200, Craig Carmichael, President and Chief Operating Officer, Senior Vice President, LifeBridge Health
Web address: https://www.lifebridgehealth.org/main/northwest-hospital

SINAI HOSPITAL OF BALTIMORE (O, 477 beds) 2401 West Belvedere Avenue, Baltimore, MD, Zip 21215–5271; tel. 410/601–9000, Amy Shlossman, President and Chief Operating Officer, Senior Vice President, Lifebridge Health

Owned, leased, sponsored:	4 hospitals	1340 beds
Contract-managed:	0 hospitals	0 beds
Totals:	4 hospitals	1340 beds

0947: LIFEBRITE HOSPITAL GROUP, LLC (IO)

3970 Five Forks Trickum Road SW Suite A, Lilburn, GA Zip 30047–2339; tel. 678/505–9657, Christian Al. Fletcher, Chief Executive Officer

GEORGIA: EARLY MEDICAL CENTER (O, 152 beds) 11740 Columbia Street, Blakely, GA, Zip 39823–2574; tel. 229/723–4241, Jeanette Filpi, Chief Executive Officer
Web address: www.pchearly.com

NORTH CAROLINA: LIFEBRITE COMMUNITY HOSPITAL OF STOKES (O, 65 beds) 1570 NC 8 & 89 Highway North, Danbury, NC, Zip 27016, P O Box 10, Zip 27016–0010, tel. 336/593–2831, Pamela P. Tillman, Administrator

Owned, leased, sponsored:	2 hospitals	217 beds
Contract-managed:	0 hospitals	0 beds
Totals:	2 hospitals	217 beds

★0180: LIFEPOINT HEALTH (IO)

330 Seven Springs Way, Brentwood, TN Zip 37027–4536; tel. 615/920–7000, David M. Dill, Chairman and Chief Executive Officer

(Decentralized Health System)

ALABAMA: NORTH ALABAMA MEDICAL CENTER (O, 239 beds) 1701 Veterans Drive, Florence, AL, Zip 35630–6033; tel. 256/629–1000, Russell Pigg, Chief Executive Officer

NORTH ALABAMA SHOALS HOSPITAL (O, 137 beds) 201 Avalon Avenue, Muscle Shoals, AL, Zip 35661–2805, P O Box 3359, Zip 35662–3359, tel. 256/386–1600, Russell Pigg, Chief Executive Officer
Web address: www.shoalshospital.com

ARIZONA: CANYON VISTA MEDICAL CENTER (O, 100 beds) 5700 East Highway 90, Sierra Vista, AZ, Zip 85635–9110; tel. 520/263–2000, Shaun Phillips, PharmD, Chief Executive Officer

HAVASU REGIONAL MEDICAL CENTER (O, 162 beds) 101 Civic Center Lane, Lake Havasu City, AZ, Zip 86403–5683; tel. 928/855–8185, Philip Fitzgerald, Chief Executive Officer
Web address: www.havasuregional.com

VALLEY VIEW MEDICAL CENTER (O, 84 beds) 5330 South Highway 95, Fort Mohave, AZ, Zip 86426–9225; tel. 928/788–2273, Jeff Bourgeois, FACHE, Interim Chief Executive Officer

ARKANSAS: NATIONAL PARK MEDICAL CENTER (O, 163 beds) 1910 Malvern Avenue, Hot Springs, AR, Zip 71901–7799; tel. 501/321–1000, Scott Bailey, Chief Executive Officer
Web address: www.nationalparkmedical.com

SAINT MARY'S REGIONAL MEDICAL CENTER (O, 129 beds) 1808 West Main Street, Russellville, AR, Zip 72801–2724; tel. 479/968–2841, Casey Willis, Chief Executive Officer
Web address: www.saintmarysregional.com

SALINE MEMORIAL HOSPITAL (O, 140 beds) 1 Medical Park Drive, Benton, AR, Zip 72015–3354; tel. 501/776–6000, Jeff Bourgeois, FACHE, Chief Executive Officer

For explanation of codes following names, see page B2.
★ Indicates Type III membership in the American Hospital Association.

Systems / Lifepoint Health

CALIFORNIA: UC DAVIS REHABILITATION HOSPITAL (O, 52 beds) 4875 Broadway, Sacramento, CA, Zip 95820–1500; tel. 279/224–6000, Dennis Sindelar, Chief Executive Officer
Web address: www.ucdavisrehabhospital.com

IOWA: OTTUMWA REGIONAL HEALTH CENTER (O, 68 beds) 1001 Pennsylvania Avenue, Ottumwa, IA, Zip 52501–2186; tel. 641/684–2300, William Kiefer, Chief Executive Officer
Web address: www.ottumwaregionalhealth.com

KENTUCKY: BLUEGRASS COMMUNITY HOSPITAL (O, 16 beds) 360 Amsden Avenue, Versailles, KY, Zip 40383–1286; tel. 859/873-3111, David P. Steitz, Chief Executive Officer

BOURBON COMMUNITY HOSPITAL (O, 58 beds) 9 Linville Drive, Paris, KY, Zip 40361–2196; tel. 859/987–3600, Tommy Haggard, Chief Executive Officer
Web address: www.bourbonhospital.com

CLARK REGIONAL MEDICAL CENTER (O, 79 beds) 175 Hospital Drive, Winchester, KY, Zip 40391–9591; tel. 859/745-3500, Matt Smith, Chief Executive Officer
Web address: www.clarkregional.org

FLEMING COUNTY HOSPITAL (O, 51 beds) 55 Foundation Drive, Flemingsburg, KY, Zip 41041–9815, P O Box 388, Zip 41041–0388, tel. 606/849-5000, Joseph G. Koch, Chief Executive Officer

GEORGETOWN COMMUNITY HOSPITAL (O, 58 beds) 1140 Lexington Road, Georgetown, KY, Zip 40324-9362; tel. 502/868–1100, Clifford Wilson, Chief Executive Officer, Market President Central Kentucky
Web address: www.georgetowncommunityhospital.com

JACKSON PURCHASE MEDICAL CENTER (O, 227 beds) 1099 Medical Center Circle, Mayfield, KY, Zip 42066–1159; tel. 270/251–4100, David Anderson, Chief Executive Officer
Web address: www.jacksonpurchase.com

LAKE CUMBERLAND REGIONAL HOSPITAL (O, 283 beds) 305 Langdon Street, Somerset, KY, Zip 42503–2750, P O Box 620, Zip 42502–0620, tel. 606/679–7441, Carolyn Sparks, Chief Executive Officer
Web address: www.lakecumberlandhospital.com

MEADOWVIEW REGIONAL MEDICAL CENTER (O, 100 beds) 989 Medical Park Drive, Maysville, KY, Zip 41056–8750; tel. 606/759-5311, Joseph G. Koch, Chief Executive Officer

SPRING VIEW HOSPITAL (O, 47 beds) 320 Loretto Road, Lebanon, KY, Zip 40033–1300; tel. 270/692-3161, Reba Celsor, Chief Executive Officer
Web address: www.springviewhospital.com

MICHIGAN: UP HEALTH SYSTEM–BELL (O, 25 beds) 901 Lakeshore Drive, Ishpeming, MI, Zip 49849–1367; tel. 906/486–4431, Mitchell D. Leckelt, FACHE, Chief Executive Officer

UP HEALTH SYSTEM–MARQUETTE (O, 211 beds) 850 West Baraga Avenue, Marquette, MI, Zip 49855–4550; tel. 906/228–9440, Tonya Darner, Chief Executive Officer
Web address: www.mgh.org

UP HEALTH SYSTEM–PORTAGE (O, 96 beds) 500 Campus Drive, Hancock, MI, Zip 49930–1569; tel. 906/483–1000, Ryan Heinonen, MSN, R.N., Chief Executive Officer

MISSOURI: MERCY REHABILITATION HOSPITAL SOUTH (O, 50 beds) 10114 Kennerly Road, Saint Louis, MO, Zip 63128–2183; tel. 314/948–2000, Daniel Vogel Jr, Chief Executive Officer
Web address: https://www.mercy.net/practice/mercy-rehabilitation-hospital-south/

MONTANA: COMMUNITY MEDICAL CENTER (O, 135 beds) 2827 Fort Missoula Road, Missoula, MT, Zip 59804–7408; tel. 406/728–4100, Robert Gomes, FACHE, Chief Executive Officer

NEVADA: NORTHEASTERN NEVADA REGIONAL HOSPITAL (O, 75 beds) 2001 Errecart Boulevard, Elko, NV, Zip 89801–8333; tel. 775/738–5151, Steve Simpson, Chief Executive Officer
Web address: www.nnrhospital.com

NEW MEXICO: LOS ALAMOS MEDICAL CENTER (O, 24 beds) 3917 West Road, Los Alamos, NM, Zip 87544–2293, PO Box 1663, Zip 87545, tel. 505/661–9500, Tracie Stratton, Chief Executive Officer

MEMORIAL MEDICAL CENTER (L, 173 beds) 2450 South Telshor Boulevard, Las Cruces, NM, Zip 88011–5076; tel. 575/522-8641, John Harris, Chief Executive Officer
Web address: www.mmclc.org

NORTH CAROLINA: CENTRAL CAROLINA HOSPITAL (O, 55 beds) 1135 Carthage Street, Sanford, NC, Zip 27330–4162; tel. 919/774-2100, Dave Santoemma, Chief Executive Officer
Web address: www.centralcarolinahosp.com

FRYE REGIONAL MEDICAL CENTER (O, 271 beds) 420 North Center Street, Hickory, NC, Zip 28601–5049, 1950 11th Street Crt. NW, Zip 28601, tel. 828/315–5000, Philip Greene, M.D., Chief Executive Officer

HARRIS REGIONAL HOSPITAL (O, 86 beds) 68 Hospital Road, Sylva, NC, Zip 28779–2722; tel. 828/586–7000, Ashley Hindman, Chief Executive Officer
Web address: https://www.myharrisregional.com/

HAYWOOD REGIONAL MEDICAL CENTER (O, 146 beds) 262 Leroy George Drive, Clyde, NC, Zip 28721–7430; tel. 828/456–7311, Chris Brown, Chief Executive Officer
Web address: www.haymed.org

MARIA PARHAM HEALTH, DUKE LIFEPOINT HEALTHCARE (O, 116 beds) 566 Ruin Creek Road, Henderson, NC, Zip 27536–2927; tel. 252/438–4143, Bert Beard, Chief Executive Officer

PERSON MEMORIAL HOSPITAL (O, 77 beds) 615 Ridge Road, Roxboro, NC, Zip 27573–4629; tel. 336/599-2121, Bert Beard, Chief Executive Officer
Web address: www.personhospital.com

RUTHERFORD REGIONAL HEALTH SYSTEM (O, 68 beds) 288 South Ridgecrest Avenue, Rutherfordton, NC, Zip 28139–2838; tel. 828/286–5000, Susan C. Shugart, FACHE, Chief Executive Officer
Web address: www.rutherfordhosp.org

SWAIN COMMUNITY HOSPITAL, A DUKE LIFEPOINT HOSPITAL (O, 25 beds) 45 Plateau Street, Bryson City, NC, Zip 28713–4200; tel. 828/488-2155, Ashley Hindman, Chief Executive Officer

WILSON MEDICAL CENTER (O, 130 beds) 1705 Tarboro Street, SW, Wilson, NC, Zip 27893–3428; tel. 252/399-8040, Christopher Munton, Chief Executive Officer
Web address: www.wilmed.org

OREGON: WILLAMETTE VALLEY MEDICAL CENTER (O, 60 beds) 2700 SE Stratus Avenue, McMinnville, OR, Zip 97128–6255; tel. 503/472–6131, Michael J. Mulkey, Chief Executive Officer

PENNSYLVANIA: CONEMAUGH MEMORIAL MEDICAL CENTER (O, 510 beds) 1086 Franklin Street, Johnstown, PA, Zip 15905–4398; tel. 814/534–9000, Rodney Reider, Chief Executive Officer
Web address: www.conemaugh.org

CONEMAUGH MEYERSDALE MEDICAL CENTER (O, 20 beds) 200 Hospital Drive, Meyersdale, PA, Zip 15552–1249; tel. 814/634–5911, Timothy Harclerode, R.N., FACHE, Chief Executive Officer
Web address: https://www.conemaugh.org/meyersdale

CONEMAUGH MINERS MEDICAL CENTER (O, 25 beds) 290 Haida Avenue, Hastings, PA, Zip 16646–5610, P O Box 689, Zip 16646–0689, tel. 814/247–3100, Timothy Harclerode, R.N., FACHE, Chief Executive Officer
Web address: www.conemaugh.org

CONEMAUGH NASON MEDICAL CENTER (O, 45 beds) 105 Nason Drive, Roaring Spring, PA, Zip 16673–1202; tel. 814/224–2141, Timothy Harclerode, R.N., FACHE, Chief Executive Officer

TENNESSEE: RIVERVIEW REGIONAL MEDICAL CENTER (O, 35 beds) 158 Hospital Drive, Carthage, TN, Zip 37030–1096; tel. 615/735–1560, Rod Harkleroad, R.N., Chief Executive Officer
Web address: www.myriverviewmedical.com/

SOUTHERN TENNESSEE REGIONAL HEALTH SYSTEM–LAWRENCEBURG (O, 80 beds) 1607 South Locust Avenue, Lawrenceburg, TN, Zip 38464–4011, P O Box 847, Zip 38464–0847, tel. 931/762–6571, Michael Howard, Chief Executive Officer
Web address: www.crocketthospital.com

SOUTHERN TENNESSEE REGIONAL HEALTH SYSTEM–PULASKI (O, 32 beds) 1265 East College Street, Pulaski, TN, Zip 38478–4541; tel. 931/363–7531, Jason Russell. Fugleberg, R.N., Chief Executive Officer
Web address: www.southerntnpulaski.com/

For explanation of codes following names, see page B2.
★ Indicates Type III membership in the American Hospital Association.

Systems / Lifepoint Health

SOUTHERN TENNESSEE REGIONAL HEALTH SYSTEM–WINCHESTER (O, 190 beds) 185 Hospital Road, Winchester, TN, Zip 37398-2404; tel. 931/967-8200, Adam Martin, Chief Executive Officer
Web address: https://www.southerntnwinchester.com/

STARR REGIONAL MEDICAL CENTER (O, 63 beds) 1114 West Madison Avenue, Athens, TN, Zip 37303-4150, P O Box 250, Zip 37371-0250, tel. 423/745-1411, John R. McLain, Chief Executive Officer

SUMNER REGIONAL MEDICAL CENTER (O, 120 beds) 555 Hartsville Pike, Gallatin, TN, Zip 37066-2400, P O Box 1558, Zip 37066-1558, tel. 615/452-4210, Rod Harkleroad, R.N., Chief Executive Officer
Web address: www.mysumnermedical.com

TROUSDALE MEDICAL CENTER (O, 25 beds) 500 Church Street, Hartsville, TN, Zip 37074-1744; tel. 615/374-2221, Carolyn Sparks, Chief Executive Officer
Web address: www.mytrousdalemedical.com

TEXAS: PARIS REGIONAL MEDICAL CENTER (O, 154 beds) 865 Deshong Drive, Paris, TX, Zip 75460-9313, P O Box 9070, Zip 75461-9070, tel. 903/785-4521, Steve Hyde, Chief Executive Officer

TEXAS REHABILITATION HOSPITAL OF FORT WORTH (O, 66 beds) 425 Alabama Avenue, Fort Worth, TX, Zip 76104-1022; tel. 817/820-3400, Jake Daggett, Market Chief Executive Officer
Web address: www.texasrehabhospital.com/

TEXAS REHABILITATION HOSPITAL OF KELLER (O, 36 beds) 791 South Main Street, Keller, TX, Zip 76248-4905; tel. 817/898-6900, Jake Daggett, Market Chief Executive Officer
Web address: www.texasrehabkeller.com

UTAH: ASHLEY REGIONAL MEDICAL CENTER (O, 39 beds) 150 West 100 North, Vernal, UT, Zip 84078-2036; tel. 435/789-3342, Alan C. Olive, Chief Executive Officer
Web address: www.ashleyregional.com

CASTLEVIEW HOSPITAL (O, 51 beds) 300 North Hospital Drive, Price, UT, Zip 84501-4200; tel. 435/637-4800, Greg Cook, Chief Executive Officer

VIRGINIA: CLINCH VALLEY MEDICAL CENTER (O, 75 beds) 6801 Governor G C Peery Highway, Richlands, VA, Zip 24641-2194; tel. 276/596-6000, Peter Mulkey, Chief Executive Officer
Web address: www.clinchvalleymedicalcenter.com

FAUQUIER HOSPITAL (O, 210 beds) 500 Hospital Drive, Warrenton, VA, Zip 20186-3099; tel. 540/316-5000, Rebecca Segal, FACHE, President and Chief Executive Officer
Web address: www.fauquierhealth.org/

SOVAH HEALTH–DANVILLE (O, 250 beds) 142 South Main Street, Danville, VA, Zip 24541-2922; tel. 434/799-2100, Steve Heatherly, Chief Executive Officer

SOVAH HEALTH–MARTINSVILLE (O, 150 beds) 320 Hospital Drive, Martinsville, VA, Zip 24112-1981, P O Box 4788, Zip 24115-4788, tel. 276/666-7200, Steve Heatherly, Chief Executive Officer
Web address: https://www.sovahhealth.com/patients-visitors/about-us/sovah-health-martinsville

TWIN COUNTY REGIONAL HEALTHCARE (O, 45 beds) 200 Hospital Drive, Galax, VA, Zip 24333-2227; tel. 276/236-8181, Sudandra Ratnasamy,FACHE, R.N., FACHE, Chief Executive Officer

WYTHE COUNTY COMMUNITY HOSPITAL (L, 70 beds) 600 West Ridge Road, Wytheville, VA, Zip 24382-1099; tel. 276/228-0200, Vicki Parks, Chief Executive Officer
Web address: www.wcchcares.com

WASHINGTON: LOURDES COUNSELING CENTER (O, 20 beds) 1175 Carondelet Drive, Richland, WA, Zip 99354-3300; tel. 509/943-9104, Mark C. Holyoak, FACHE, Chief Executive Officer
Web address: https://www.yourlourdes.com/locations/lourdes-counseling-center

LOURDES HEALTH (O, 53 beds) 520 North Fourth Avenue, Pasco, WA, Zip 99301-5257; tel. 509/547-7704, Mark C. Holyoak, FACHE, Chief Executive Officer

TRIOS HEALTH (O, 109 beds) 900 South Auburn Street, Kennewick, WA, Zip 99336-5621, P O Box 6128, Zip 99336-0128, tel. 509/221-6339, David Elgarico, Chief Executive Officer
Web address: www.trioshealth.org

WEST VIRGINIA: RALEIGH GENERAL HOSPITAL (O, 229 beds) 1710 Harper Road, Beckley, WV, Zip 25801-3397; tel. 304/256-4100, David V. Bunch, Chief Executive Officer

Owned, leased, sponsored:	63 hospitals	6718 beds
Contract-managed:	0 hospitals	0 beds
Totals:	63 hospitals	6718 beds

0060: LIFESPAN CORPORATION (NP)
167 Point Street, Providence, RI Zip 02903-4771; tel. 401/444-3500, John R. Fernandez, President and Chief Executive Officer
(Centralized Health System)

RHODE ISLAND: EMMA PENDLETON BRADLEY HOSPITAL (O, 70 beds) 1011 Veterans Memorial Parkway, East Providence, RI, Zip 02915-5099; tel. 401/432-1000, Henry T. Sachs III, M.D., President
Web address: www.lifespan.org

MIRIAM HOSPITAL (O, 247 beds) 164 Summit Avenue, Providence, RI, Zip 02906-2853; tel. 401/793-2500, Maria Ducharme, R.N., President
Web address: www.lifespan.org

NEWPORT HOSPITAL (O, 109 beds) 11 Friendship Street, Newport, RI, Zip 02840-2299; tel. 401/846-6400, Crista F. Durand, President

RHODE ISLAND HOSPITAL (O, 638 beds) 593 Eddy Street, Providence, RI, Zip 02903-4900; tel. 401/444-4000, Sarah Frost, Chief, Lifespan Hospital Operations, and President, Rhode Island Hospital and Hasbro Children's Hospital
Web address: www.rhodeislandhospital.org/

Owned, leased, sponsored:	4 hospitals	1064 beds
Contract-managed:	0 hospitals	0 beds
Totals:	4 hospitals	1064 beds

★2175: LOMA LINDA UNIVERSITY ADVENTIST HEALTH SCIENCES CENTER (NP)
11175 Campus Street, Suite 11006, Loma Linda, CA Zip 92350-1700, 11175 Campus Street, Zip 92350-1700, tel. 909/558-7572, Richard H. Hart, President and Chief Executive Officer
(Centralized Health System)

CALIFORNIA: LOMA LINDA UNIVERSITY CHILDREN'S HOSPITAL (O, 364 beds) 11234 Anderson Street, Loma Linda, CA, Zip 92354-2804; tel. 909/558-8000, Trevor G. Wright, Chief Executive Officer
Web address: www.https://lluch.org/

LOMA LINDA UNIVERSITY MEDICAL CENTER–MURRIETA (O, 136 beds) 28062 Baxter Road, Murrieta, CA, Zip 92563-1401; tel. 951/290-4000, Trevor G. Wright, Chief Executive Officer
Web address: www.https://murrieta.lluh.org/

LOMA LINDA UNIVERSITY MEDICAL CENTER (O, 482 beds) 11234 Anderson Street, Loma Linda, CA, Zip 92354-2804, P O Box 2000, Zip 92354-0200, tel. 909/558-4000, Trevor G. Wright, Chief Executive Officer

Owned, leased, sponsored:	3 hospitals	982 beds
Contract-managed:	0 hospitals	0 beds
Totals:	3 hospitals	982 beds

5755: LOS ANGELES COUNTY–DEPARTMENT OF HEALTH SERVICES (NP)
313 North Figueroa Street, Room 912, Los Angeles, CA Zip 90012-2691; tel. 213/240-8101, Christina R. Ghaly, M.D., Director
(Moderately Centralized Health System)

CALIFORNIA: HARBOR-UCLA MEDICAL CENTER (O, 373 beds) 1000 West Carson Street, Torrance, CA, Zip 90502-2059; tel. 310/222-2345, Andrea Turner, JD, Chief Executive Officer
Web address: www.harbor-ucla.org

For explanation of codes following names, see page B2.
★ Indicates Type III membership in the American Hospital Association.

Systems / Marshall Health System

LOS ANGELES GENERAL MEDICAL CENTER (O, 538 beds) 2051 Marengo Street, Los Angeles, CA, Zip 90033-1352; tel. 323/409-1000, Jorge Orozco, Chief Executive Officer

OLIVE VIEW–UCLA MEDICAL CENTER (O, 202 beds) 14445 Olive View Drive, Sylmar, CA, Zip 91342-1438; tel. 818/364-1555, Konita Wilks, Chief Executive Officer
Web address: www.dhs.lacounty.gov/wps/portal/dhs/oliveview

RANCHO LOS AMIGOS NATIONAL REHABILITATION CENTER (O, 108 beds) 7601 East Imperial Highway, Downey, CA, Zip 90242-3496; tel. 562/401-7111, Aries J. Limbaga, R.N., Chief Executive Officer, Rancho Los Amigos National Rehabilitation Center/System Chief Nursing Officer, Los Angles Count

Owned, leased, sponsored:	4 hospitals	1221 beds
Contract-managed:	0 hospitals	0 beds
Totals:	4 hospitals	1221 beds

0047: LOUISIANA STATE HOSPITALS (NP)

628 North 4th Street, Baton Rouge, LA Zip 70802-5342, P O Box 629, Zip 70821-0628, tel. 225/342-9500, Shelby Price, Chief Executive Officer
(Independent Hospital System)

LOUISIANA: CENTRAL LOUISIANA STATE HOSPITAL (O, 120 beds) 242 West Shamrock Avenue, Pineville, LA, Zip 71360-6439, P O Box 5031, Zip 71361-5031, tel. 318/484-6200, Celeste Gauthier, Mental Hospital Administrator 2

EASTERN LOUISIANA MENTAL HEALTH SYSTEM (O, 693 beds) 4502 Highway 10, Jackson, LA, Zip 70748-3507, P.O. Box 498, Zip 70748-0498, tel. 225/634-0100, Laura Lott, Chief Executive Officer
Web address: www.new.dhh.louisiana.gov/index.cfm/directory/detail/219

Owned, leased, sponsored:	2 hospitals	813 beds
Contract-managed:	0 hospitals	0 beds
Totals:	2 hospitals	813 beds

★1048: LUMINIS HEALTH (IO)

2001 Medical Parkway, Annapolis, MD Zip 21401-3773; tel. 443/481-1000, Victoria Bayless, Chief Executive Officer

MARYLAND: LUMINIS HEALTH ANNE ARUNDEL MEDICAL CENTER (O, 480 beds) 2001 Medical Parkway, Annapolis, MD, Zip 21401-3019; tel. 443/481-1000, Sherry B. Perkins, Ph.D., R.N., President
Web address: www.aahs.org

LUMINIS HEALTH DOCTORS COMMUNITY MEDICAL CENTER (O, 210 beds) 8118 Good Luck Road, Lanham, MD, Zip 20706-3574; tel. 301/552-8118, Deneen Richmond, R.N., President
Web address: www.dchweb.org

Owned, leased, sponsored:	2 hospitals	690 beds
Contract-managed:	0 hospitals	0 beds
Totals:	2 hospitals	690 beds

0614: MAINEHEALTH (NP)

110 Free Street, Portland, ME Zip 04101-3537; tel. 207/661-7001, Andrew Mueller, M.D., Chief Executive Officer
(Moderately Centralized Health System)

MAINE: FRANKLIN MEMORIAL HOSPITAL (O, 25 beds) 111 Franklin Health Commons, Farmington, ME, Zip 04938-6144; tel. 207/778-6031, Barbara Sergio, President

LINCOLNHEALTH (O, 91 beds) 35 Miles Street, Damariscotta, ME, Zip 04543-4047; tel. 207/563-1234, Cynthia Wade RN, BSN,, President
Web address: www.lchcare.org

MAINEHEALTH BEHAVIORAL HEALTH AT SPRING HARBOR (O, 95 beds) 123 Andover Road, Westbrook, ME, Zip 04092-3850; tel. 207/761-2200, Kelly Barton, President
Web address: www.springharbor.org

MAINEHEALTH MAINE MEDICAL CENTER (O, 758 beds) 22 Bramhall Street, Portland, ME, Zip 04102-3175; tel. 207/662-0111, Britt Crewse, CPA, Southern Region President

MAINEHEALTH PEN BAY MEDICAL CENTER (O, 163 beds) 6 Glen Cove Drive, Rockport, ME, Zip 04856-4240; tel. 207/921-8000, Denise Needham, PharmD, President
Web address: www.penbayhealthcare.org

MAINEHEALTH STEPHENS HOSPITAL (O, 25 beds) 181 Main Street, Norway, ME, Zip 04268-5664; tel. 207/743-5933, Jeff Noblin, FACHE, President

MID COAST HOSPITAL (O, 93 beds) 123 Medical Center Drive, Brunswick, ME, Zip 04011-2652; tel. 207/373-6000, Christopher Bowe, M.D., President
Web address: www.midcoasthealth.com

SOUTHERN MAINE HEALTH CARE–BIDDEFORD MEDICAL CENTER (O, 155 beds) 1 Medical Center Drive, Biddeford, ME, Zip 04005-9496, P O Box 626, Zip 04005-0626, tel. 207/283-7000, Britt Crewse, CPA, Southern Region President
Web address: www.smhc.org

WALDO COUNTY GENERAL HOSPITAL (O, 31 beds) 118 Northport Avenue, Belfast, ME, Zip 04915-6072, P O Box 287, Zip 04915-0287, tel. 207/338-2500, Denise Needham, PharmD, President

NEW HAMPSHIRE: MEMORIAL HOSPITAL (O, 70 beds) 3073 White Mountain Highway, North Conway, NH, Zip 03860-7101; tel. 603/356-5461, Bradley J. Chapman, President
Web address: www.memorialhospitalnh.org

Owned, leased, sponsored:	10 hospitals	1506 beds
Contract-managed:	0 hospitals	0 beds
Totals:	10 hospitals	1506 beds

★0952: MARSHALL HEALTH NETWORK (IO)

517 9th Street, Huntington, WV Zip 25701-2020; tel. 304/781-4466, Kevin Yingling, Chief Executive Officer

WEST VIRGINIA: CABELL HUNTINGTON HOSPITAL (O, 347 beds) 1340 Hal Greer Boulevard, Huntington, WV, Zip 25701-0195; tel. 304/526-2000, Tim Martin, Chief Operating Officer
Web address: www.cabellhuntington.org

RIVERS HEALTH (O, 53 beds) 2520 Valley Drive, Point Pleasant, WV, Zip 25550-2031; tel. 304/675-4340, Justin Turner, Chief Operating Officer
Web address: www.https://rivershealth.org/

ST. MARY'S MEDICAL CENTER (O, 393 beds) 2900 First Avenue, Huntington, WV, Zip 25702-1272; tel. 304/526-1234, Angela Swearingen, Chief Operating Officer

Owned, leased, sponsored:	3 hospitals	793 beds
Contract-managed:	0 hospitals	0 beds
Totals:	3 hospitals	793 beds

1975: MARSHALL HEALTH SYSTEM (NP)

227 Britany Road, Guntersville, AL Zip 35976-5766; tel. 256/894-6615, Christopher Rush, President
(Independent Hospital System)

ALABAMA: MARSHALL MEDICAL CENTER NORTH (O, 76 beds) 8000 Alabama Highway 69, Guntersville, AL, Zip 35976; tel. 256/571-8000, Christopher Rush, President
Web address: www.mmcenters.com

MARSHALL MEDICAL CENTER SOUTH (O, 107 beds) U S Highway 431 North, Boaz, AL, Zip 35957-0999, P O Box 758, Zip 35957-0758, tel. 256/593-8310, Christopher Rush, President
Web address: www.mmcenters.com//index.php/facilities/marshall_south

Owned, leased, sponsored:	2 hospitals	183 beds
Contract-managed:	0 hospitals	0 beds
Totals:	2 hospitals	183 beds

For explanation of codes following names, see page B2.
★ Indicates Type III membership in the American Hospital Association.

Systems / Marshfield Clinic Health System

★1022: **MARSHFIELD CLINIC HEALTH SYSTEM (NP)**
1000 North Oak Avenue, Marshfield, WI Zip 54449–5703; tel. 800/782–8581, Brian Hoerneman, M.D., Interim Chief Executive Officer
(Moderately Centralized Health System)

MICHIGAN: MARSHFIELD MEDICAL CENTER–DICKINSON (O, 49 beds) 1721 South Stephenson Avenue, Iron Mountain, MI, Zip 49801–3637; tel. 906/774–1313, Amanda Shelast, FACHE, President
Web address: www.dchs.org

WISCONSIN: MARSHFIELD MEDICAL CENTER–BEAVER DAM (O, 163 beds) 707 South University Avenue, Beaver Dam, WI, Zip 53916–3089; tel. 920/887–7181, Angelia Foster, Chief Administrative Officer
Web address: www.bdch.com
MARSHFIELD MEDICAL CENTER–EAU CLAIRE HOSPITAL (O, 44 beds) 2310 Craig Road, Eau Claire, WI, Zip 54701–6128; tel. 715/858–8100, Bradley D. Groseth, President–West Market
Web address: https://www.marshfieldclinic.org
MARSHFIELD MEDICAL CENTER–LADYSMITH (O, 25 beds) 900 College Avenue West, Ladysmith, WI, Zip 54848–2116; tel. 715/532–5561, Bradley D. Groseth, President
MARSHFIELD MEDICAL CENTER–MINOCQUA (O, 19 beds) 9576 State Highway 70, Minocqua, WI, Zip 54548; tel. 715/358–1710, Ty Erickson, Chief Administrative Officer
Web address: www.marshfieldclinic.org
MARSHFIELD MEDICAL CENTER–NEILSVILLE (O, 10 beds) N3708 River Avenue, Neillsville, WI, Zip 54456–7218; tel. 715/743–3101, Robert S. Chaloner, President, Central Region
Web address: www.memorialmedcenter.org
MARSHFIELD MEDICAL CENTER–PARK FALLS (O, 25 beds) 98 Sherry Avenue, Park Falls, WI, Zip 54552–1467, P O Box 310, Zip 54552–0310, tel. 715/762–2484, Ty Erickson, Chief Administrative Officer
Web address: https://www.marshfieldclinic.org/locations/centers/park%20falls%20-%20marshfield%20medical%20center
MARSHFIELD MEDICAL CENTER–RICE LAKE (O, 40 beds) 1700 West Stout Street, Rice Lake, WI, Zip 54868–5000; tel. 715/234–1515, Bradley D. Groseth, Chief Administrative Officer
Web address: www.lakeviewmedical.com
MARSHFIELD MEDICAL CENTER–RIVER REGION (O, 5 beds) 4100 State Highway 66, Stevens Point, WI, Zip 54482–8410; tel. 715/997–6000, Christopher Soska, President, Marshfield Medical Center, Weston, Wisconsin Rapids, Stevens Point
Web address: https://www.marshfieldclinic.org/locations/centers/Stevens%20Point%20-%20Marshfield%20Medical%20Center-River%20Region
MARSHFIELD MEDICAL CENTER–WESTON (O, 36 beds) 3400 Ministry Parkway, Weston, WI, Zip 54476–5220; tel. 715/393–3000, Christopher Soska, President of MMC_ Weston,Wisconsin Rapids and Stevens Point
MARSHFIELD MEDICAL CENTER (O, 205 beds) 611 St Joseph Avenue, Marshfield, WI, Zip 54449–1898; tel. 715/387–1713, Robert S. Chaloner, President, Central Region
Web address: www.stjosephs-marshfield.org

Owned, leased, sponsored:	11 hospitals	621 beds
Contract–managed:	0 hospitals	0 beds
Totals:	11 hospitals	621 beds

★0523: **MARY WASHINGTON HEALTHCARE (NP)**
1001 Sam Perry Boulevard, Suite 1005, Fredericksburg, VA Zip 22401–4453, 1001 Sam Perry Boulevard, Zip 22401–4453, tel. 540/741–3100, Michael P. McDermott, M.D., President and Chief Executive Officer
(Centralized Health System)

VIRGINIA: MARY WASHINGTON HOSPITAL (O, 471 beds) 1001 Sam Perry Boulevard, Fredericksburg, VA, Zip 22401–3354; tel. 540/741–1100, Michael P. McDermott, M.D., President and Chief Executive Officer
Web address: https://www.marywashingtonhealthcare.com/locations/mary-washington-hospital/
STAFFORD HOSPITAL (O, 100 beds) 101 Hospital Center Boulevard, Stafford, VA, Zip 22554–6200; tel. 540/741–9000, Debra Marinari, Associate Vice President Hospital Operations

Owned, leased, sponsored:	2 hospitals	571 beds
Contract–managed:	0 hospitals	0 beds
Totals:	2 hospitals	571 beds

★1785: **MASS GENERAL BRIGHAM (NP)**
800 Boylston Street, Suite 1150, Boston, MA Zip 02199–8123; tel. 617/278–1004, Anne Klibanski, M.D., President and Chief Executive Officer
(Decentralized Health System)

MASSACHUSETTS: BRIGHAM AND WOMEN'S FAULKNER HOSPITAL (O, 163 beds) 1153 Centre Street, Boston, MA, Zip 02130–3446; tel. 617/983–7000, Kevin T. Giordano, President
BRIGHAM AND WOMEN'S HOSPITAL (O, 885 beds) 75 Francis Street, Boston, MA, Zip 02115–6110; tel. 617/732–5500, Giles W. Boland, M.D., President
Web address: www.brighamandwomens.org
COOLEY DICKINSON HOSPITAL (O, 140 beds) 30 Locust Street, Northampton, MA, Zip 01060–2093, P O Box 5001, Zip 01061–5001, tel. 413/582–2000
Web address: www.cooleydickinson.org
MARTHA'S VINEYARD HOSPITAL (O, 86 beds) 1 Hospital Road, Oak Bluffs, MA, Zip 2557, P O Box 1477, Zip 02557–1477, tel. 508/693–0410, Denise Schepici, M.P.H., Chief Executive Officer and President
Web address: www.mvhospital.com/
MASSACHUSETTS EYE AND EAR (O, 41 beds) 243 Charles Street, Boston, MA, Zip 02114–3002; tel. 617/523–7900, CarolAnn Williams, President
MASSACHUSETTS GENERAL HOSPITAL (O, 1040 beds) 55 Fruit Street, Boston, MA, Zip 02114–2696, 55 Fruit Street, Bulfinch 310, Zip 02114–2696, tel. 617/726–2000, Marcela G. del Carmen, President
Web address: www.massgeneral.org
MCLEAN HOSPITAL (O, 309 beds) 115 Mill Street, Belmont, MA, Zip 02478–1064; tel. 617/855–2000, Scott L. Rauch, M.D., President and Psychiatrist in Chief
Web address: www.mcleanhospital.org
NANTUCKET COTTAGE HOSPITAL (O, 14 beds) 57 Prospect Street, Nantucket, MA, Zip 02554–2799; tel. 508/825–8100, Amy Lee, President
NEWTON–WELLESLEY HOSPITAL (O, 314 beds) 2014 Washington Street, Newton Lower Falls, MA, Zip 02462–1699; tel. 617/243–6000, Ellen Moloney, President and Chief Operating Officer
Web address: www.nwh.org
SALEM HOSPITAL (O, 367 beds) 81 Highland Avenue, Salem, MA, Zip 01970–2714; tel. 978/741–1200, Roxanne C. Ruppel, President and Chief Operating Officer
SPAULDING HOSPITAL FOR CONTINUING MEDICAL CARE CAMBRIDGE (O, 116 beds) 1575 Cambridge Street, Cambridge, MA, Zip 02138–4308; tel. 617/876–4344, Ross Zafonte, D.O., President
Web address: www.spauldingnetwork.org
SPAULDING REHABILITATION HOSPITAL CAPE COD (O, 48 beds) 311 Service Road, East Sandwich, MA, Zip 02537–1370; tel. 508/833–4000, Ross Zafonte, D.O., President
SPAULDING REHABILITATION HOSPITAL (O, 132 beds) 300 First Avenue, Charlestown, MA, Zip 02129–3109; tel. 617/952–5000, Ross Zafonte, D.O., President
Web address: www.spauldingrehab.org

NEW HAMPSHIRE: WENTWORTH–DOUGLASS HOSPITAL (O, 173 beds) 789 Central Avenue, Dover, NH, Zip 03820–2526; tel. 603/742–5252, Darin Roark, President and Chief Executive Officer

Owned, leased, sponsored:	14 hospitals	3828 beds
Contract–managed:	0 hospitals	0 beds
Totals:	14 hospitals	3828 beds

For explanation of codes following names, see page B2.
★ Indicates Type III membership in the American Hospital Association.

0013: MASSACHUSETTS DEPARTMENT OF MENTAL HEALTH (NP)

25 Staniford Street, Boston, MA Zip 02114-2575; tel. 617/626-8123, Brooke Doyle, Commissioner

MASSACHUSETTS: DR. J. CORRIGAN MENTAL HEALTH CENTER (O, 16 beds) 49 Hillside Street, Fall River, MA, Zip 02720-5266; tel. 508/235-7200, Frank O'Reilly, Director

TAUNTON STATE HOSPITAL (O, 45 beds) 60 Hodges Avenue Extension, Taunton, MA, Zip 02780-3034, PO Box 4007, Zip 02780-0997, tel. 508/977-3000, Joyce O'Connor, Chief Operating Officer
Web address: https://www.mass.gov/locations/taunton-state-hospital

WORCESTER RECOVERY CENTER AND HOSPITAL (O, 126 beds) 309 Belmont Street, Worcester, MA, Zip 01604-1695; tel. 508/368-3300, Jacqueline Ducharme, Chief Operating Officer and Interim Chief Executive Officer
Web address: https://www.mass.gov/locations/worcester-recovery-center-and-hospital-wrch

Owned, leased, sponsored:	3 hospitals	187 beds
Contract-managed:	0 hospitals	0 beds
Totals:	3 hospitals	187 beds

0280: MASSACHUSETTS DEPARTMENT OF PUBLIC HEALTH (NP)

250 Washington Street, Boston, MA Zip 02108-4619; tel. 617/624-6000, Margret R. Cooke, Acting Commissioner
(Independent Hospital System)

MASSACHUSETTS: LEMUEL SHATTUCK HOSPITAL (O, 260 beds) 170 Morton Street, Jamaica Plain, MA, Zip 02130-3735; tel. 617/522-8110, Justin Douglas, R.N., MSN, Chief Executive Officer

PAPPAS REHABILITATION HOSPITAL FOR CHILDREN (O, 80 beds) 3 Randolph Street, Canton, MA, Zip 02021-2351; tel. 781/828-2440, Brian V. Devin, Chief Executive Officer
Web address: www.prhc.us/

TEWKSBURY HOSPITAL (O, 357 beds) 365 East Street, Tewksbury, MA, Zip 01876-1998; tel. 978/851-7321, Betsy L. Schwechheimer, Chief Executive Officer
Web address: www.mass.gov

WESTERN MASSACHUSETTS HOSPITAL (O, 80 beds) 91 East Mountain Road, Westfield, MA, Zip 01085-1801; tel. 413/562-4131, Valenda M. Liptak, Chief Executive Officer
Web address: www.mass.gov/eohhs/gov/departments/dph/programs/western-massachusetts-hospital.html

Owned, leased, sponsored:	4 hospitals	777 beds
Contract-managed:	0 hospitals	0 beds
Totals:	4 hospitals	777 beds

★0882: MAURY REGIONAL HEALTH SYSTEM (NP)

1224 Trotwood Avenue, Columbia, TN Zip 38401-4802; tel. 931/381-1111, Martin Chaney, M.D., Chief Executive Officer
(Independent Hospital System)

TENNESSEE: MARSHALL MEDICAL CENTER (O, 17 beds) 1080 North Ellington Parkway, Lewisburg, TN, Zip 37091-2227, P O Box 1609, Zip 37091-1609, tel. 931/359-6241, Phyllis Brown, Chief Executive Officer
Web address: www.mauryregional.com

MAURY REGIONAL MEDICAL CENTER (O, 208 beds) 1224 Trotwood Avenue, Columbia, TN, Zip 38401-4802; tel. 931/381-1111, Martin Chaney, M.D., Chief Executive Officer

WAYNE MEDICAL CENTER (L, 18 beds) 103 J V Mangubat Drive, Waynesboro, TN, Zip 38485-2440, P O Box 580, Zip 38485-0580, tel. 931/722-5411, Phyllis Brown, Chief Executive Officer
Web address: https://www.mauryregional.com/wayne-medical-center/wayne-medical-center

Owned, leased, sponsored:	3 hospitals	243 beds
Contract-managed:	0 hospitals	0 beds
Totals:	3 hospitals	243 beds

★1875: MAYO CLINIC (NP)

200 First Street SW, Rochester, MN Zip 55905-0002, 4165 Hwy 14 W Plummer Bldg 11-37, Zip 55901, tel. 507/284-2511, Gianrico Farrugia, M.D., President
(Decentralized Health System)

ARIZONA: MAYO CLINIC HOSPITAL IN ARIZONA (O, 338 beds) 5777 East Mayo Boulevard, Phoenix, AZ, Zip 85054-4502; tel. 480/342-2000, Richard Gray, M.D., Vice President Operations
Web address: www.mayoclinic.org/arizona/

FLORIDA: MAYO CLINIC HOSPITAL IN FLORIDA (O, 307 beds) 4500 San Pablo Road South, Jacksonville, FL, Zip 32224-1865; tel. 904/953-2000, Kent R. Thielen, M.D., Chief Executive Officer
Web address: www.mayoclinic.org/jacksonville/

IOWA: WINNMED (C, 30 beds) 901 Montgomery Street, Decorah, IA, Zip 52101-2325; tel. 563/382-2911, Steve Robert. Slessor, Chief Administrative Officer
Web address: www.https://winnmed.org/

MINNESOTA: MAYO CLINIC HEALTH SYSTEM—ALBERT LEA AND AUSTIN (O, 80 beds) 404 West Fountain Street, Albert Lea, MN, Zip 56007-2473; tel. 507/373-2384, Mark Ciota, M.D., Chief Executive Officer

MAYO CLINIC HEALTH SYSTEM IN CANNON FALLS (O, 15 beds) 32021 County Road 24 Boulevard, Cannon Falls, MN, Zip 55009-1898; tel. 507/263-4221, Kenneth F. Ackerman, FACHE, Hospital Administrator
Web address: www.mayoclinichealthsystem.org/locations/cannon-falls

MAYO CLINIC HEALTH SYSTEM IN FAIRMONT (O, 25 beds) 800 Medical Center Drive, Fairmont, MN, Zip 56031-4575; tel. 507/238-8100, Amy Long, Administrator
Web address: https://www.mayoclinichealthsystem.org/locations/fairmont

MAYO CLINIC HEALTH SYSTEM IN LAKE CITY (O, 101 beds) 500 West Grant Street, Lake City, MN, Zip 55041-1143; tel. 651/345-3321, Brian Whited, M.D., Physician Executive
Web address: https://www.mayoclinichealthsystem.org/locations/lake-city

MAYO CLINIC HEALTH SYSTEM IN MANKATO (O, 156 beds) 1025 Marsh Street, Mankato, MN, Zip 56001-4752; tel. 507/625-4031, James Hebl, M.D., Regional Vice President
Web address: https://www.mayoclinichealthsystem.org/locations/mankato

MAYO CLINIC HEALTH SYSTEM IN NEW PRAGUE (O, 17 beds) 301 Second Street NE, New Prague, MN, Zip 56071-1799; tel. 952/758-4431, James Hebl, M.D., Regional Vice President
Web address: www.mayoclinichealthsystem.org/locations/new-prague

MAYO CLINIC HEALTH SYSTEM IN RED WING (O, 22 beds) 701 Hewitt Boulevard, Red Wing, MN, Zip 55066-2848, P O Box 95, Zip 55066-0095, tel. 651/267-5000, Brian Whited, M.D., Physician Executive
Web address: www.mayoclinichealthsystem.org/locations/red-wing

MAYO CLINIC HEALTH SYSTEM IN SAINT JAMES (O, 13 beds) 1101 Moulton and Parsons Drive, Saint James, MN, Zip 56081-5550; tel. 507/375-3261, James Hebl, M.D., Regional Vice President
Web address: www.mayoclinichealthsystem.org/locations/st-james

MAYO CLINIC HEALTH SYSTEM IN WASECA (O, 12 beds) 501 North State Street, Waseca, MN, Zip 56093-2811; tel. 507/835-1210, Paul Travis, Regional Chair-Administration
Web address: https://www.mayoclinichealthsystem.org/locations/waseca

MAYO CLINIC HOSPITAL—ROCHESTER (O, 1304 beds) 1216 Second Street SW, Rochester, MN, Zip 55902-1906; tel. 507/255-5123, Lindsey Lehman, Associate Administrator, Hospital Operations

For explanation of codes following names, see page B2.
★ *Indicates Type III membership in the American Hospital Association.*

Systems / Mayo Clinic

WISCONSIN: MAYO CLINIC HEALTH SYSTEM–CHIPPEWA VALLEY IN BLOOMER (O, 22 beds) 1501 Thompson Street, Bloomer, WI, Zip 54724–1299; tel. 715/568–2000, Richard Helmers, M.D., Regional Vice President
Web address: www.bloomermedicalcenter.org

MAYO CLINIC HEALTH SYSTEM–NORTHLAND IN BARRON (O, 15 beds) 1222 East Woodland Avenue, Barron, WI, Zip 54812–1798; tel. 715/537–3186, Richard Helmers, M.D., Regional Vice President

MAYO CLINIC HEALTH SYSTEM–OAKRIDGE IN OSSEO (O, 13 beds) 13025 Eighth Street, Osseo, WI, Zip 54758–7634, P O Box 70, Zip 54758–0070, tel. 715/597–3121, Richard Helmers, M.D., Regional Vice President
Web address: www.mayoclinichealthsystem.org/locations/osseo

MAYO CLINIC HEALTH SYSTEM–RED CEDAR IN MENOMONIE (O, 20 beds) 2321 Stout Road, Menomonie, WI, Zip 54751–2397; tel. 715/235–5531, Richard Helmers, M.D., Regional Vice President

MAYO CLINIC HEALTH SYSTEM IN EAU CLAIRE (O, 190 beds) 1221 Whipple Street, Eau Claire, WI, Zip 54703–5270, P O Box 4105, Zip 54702, tel. 715/838–3311, Richard Helmers, M.D., Regional Vice President
Web address: https://www.mayoclinichealthsystem.org/locations/eau-claire

MAYO CLINIC HEALTH SYSTEM IN LA CROSSE (O, 92 beds) 700 West Avenue South, La Crosse, WI, Zip 54601–4783; tel. 608/785–0940, Richard Helmers, M.D., Chief Executive Officer
Web address: https://www.mayoclinichealthsystem.org/locations/la-crosse

MAYO CLINIC HEALTH SYSTEM IN SPARTA (O, 14 beds) 310 West Main Street, Sparta, WI, Zip 54656–2171; tel. 608/269–2132, Richard Helmers, M.D., Chief Executive Officer
Web address: https://www.mayoclinichealthsystem.org/locations/sparta

Owned, leased, sponsored:	19 hospitals	2756 beds
Contract–managed:	1 hospitals	30 beds
Totals:	20 hospitals	2786 beds

0252: MCLAREN HEALTH CARE CORPORATION (NP)

3373 Regency Park Drive, Grand Blanc, MI Zip 48439, One McLaren Parkway, Zip 48439, tel. 810/342–1100, Philip A. Incarnati, President and Chief Executive Officer
(Centralized Physician/Insurance Health System)

MICHIGAN: MARWOOD MANOR NURSING HOME (O, 106 beds) 1300 Beard Street, Port Huron, MI, Zip 48060; tel. 818/982–2594, Brian Oberly, Administrator

MCLAREN BAY REGION (O, 352 beds) 1900 Columbus Avenue, Bay City, MI, Zip 48708–6831; tel. 989/894–3000, James Carter, Interim Chief Executive Officer
Web address: www.mclaren.org/bayregion

MCLAREN BAY SPECIAL CARE (O, 26 beds) 3250 East Midland Road, Suite 1, Bay City, MI, Zip 48706–2835; tel. 989/667–6851, Jeffrey Robinson, President and Chief Executive Officer

MCLAREN CARO REGION (O, 10 beds) 401 North Hooper Street, Caro, MI, Zip 48723–1476, P O Box 435, Zip 48723–0435, tel. 989/673–3141, Connie L. Koutouzos, R.N., MSN, President and Chief Executive Officer
Web address: https://www.mclaren.org/caro-region/mclaren-caro-region-home

MCLAREN CENTRAL MICHIGAN (O, 49 beds) 1221 South Drive, Mount Pleasant, MI, Zip 48858–3257; tel. 989/772–6700, Robert G. David, President and Chief Executive Officer
Web address: https://www.mclaren.org/central-michigan/mclaren-central-michigan-home

MCLAREN FLINT (O, 349 beds) 401 South Ballenger Highway, Flint, MI, Zip 48532–3685; tel. 810/342–2000, Chris Candela, President and Chief Executive Officer

MCLAREN GREATER LANSING (O, 321 beds) 2900 Collins Road, Lansing, MI, Zip 48910–8394; tel. 517/975–6000, Kirk M. Ray, President and Chief Executive Officer
Web address: www.mclaren.org

MCLAREN LAPEER REGION (O, 131 beds) 1375 North Main Street, Lapeer, MI, Zip 48446–1350; tel. 810/667–5500, Tim Vargas, President and Chief Executive Officer
Web address: https://www.mclaren.org/lapeer-region/mclaren-lapeer-region-home

MCLAREN MACOMB (O, 304 beds) 1000 Harrington Boulevard, Mount Clemens, MI, Zip 48043–2992; tel. 586/493–8000, Tracey Franovich, R.N., President and Chief Executive Officer
Web address: https://www.mclaren.org/macomb/mclaren-macomb-home

MCLAREN NORTHERN MICHIGAN (O, 200 beds) 416 Connable Avenue, Petoskey, MI, Zip 49770–2297; tel. 231/487–4000, Garfield Atchison, President and Chief Executive Officer
Web address: www.northernhealth.org

MCLAREN OAKLAND (O, 277 beds) 50 North Perry Street, Pontiac, MI, Zip 48342–2253; tel. 248/338–5000, Lorenzo Suter, President and Chief Executive Officer
Web address: www.mclaren.org/oakland

MCLAREN PORT HURON (O, 186 beds) 1221 Pine Grove Avenue, Port Huron, MI, Zip 48060–3511; tel. 810/987–5000, Eric Cecava, President and Chief Executive Officer
Web address: www.porthuronhospital.org

MCLAREN THUMB REGION (O, 16 beds) 1100 South Van Dyke Road, Bad Axe, MI, Zip 48413–9615; tel. 989/269–9521, Connie L. Koutouzos, R.N., MSN, President and Chief Executive Officer

Owned, leased, sponsored:	13 hospitals	2327 beds
Contract–managed:	0 hospitals	0 beds
Totals:	13 hospitals	2327 beds

0874: MCLEOD HEALTH (NP)

555 East Cheves Street, Florence, SC Zip 29506–2617, P O Box 100551, Zip 29502–0551, tel. 843/777–2000, Donna C. Isgett, President and Chief Executive Officer
(Centralized Health System)

SOUTH CAROLINA: MCLEOD HEALTH CHERAW (O, 31 beds) 711 Chesterfield Highway, Cheraw, SC, Zip 29520–7002; tel. 843/537–7881, Bren T. Lowe, Chief Executive Officer, Vice President, McLeod Health
Web address: https://www.mcleodhealth.org/locations/mcleod-cheraw/

MCLEOD HEALTH CLARENDON (C, 36 beds) 10 Hospital Street, Manning, SC, Zip 29102–3153, P O Box 550, Zip 29102–0550, tel. 803/433–3000, Rachel Gainey, Chief Executive Officer, Vice President McLeod Health

MCLEOD HEALTH DILLON (O, 40 beds) 301 East Jackson Street, Dillon, SC, Zip 29536–2509, P O Box 1327, Zip 29536–1327, tel. 843/774–4111, Jenny Hardee, MSN, Chief Executive Officer
Web address: https://www.mcleodhealth.org/locations/mcleod-dillon/

MCLEOD HEALTH LORIS (O, 50 beds) 3655 Mitchell Street, Loris, SC, Zip 29569–2827; tel. 843/716–7000, Michael Scott. Montgomery, Chief Executive Officer, Vice President, McLeod Health
Web address: www.mcleodhealth.org

MCLEOD REGIONAL MEDICAL CENTER (O, 551 beds) 555 East Cheves Street, Florence, SC, Zip 29506–2617, P O Box 100551, Zip 29502–0551, tel. 843/777–2000, John Will. McLeod, Chief Executive Officer

Owned, leased, sponsored:	4 hospitals	672 beds
Contract–managed:	1 hospitals	36 beds
Totals:	5 hospitals	708 beds

★1001: MEADVILLE MEDICAL CENTER (NP)

751 Liberty Street, Meadville, PA Zip 16335–2559; tel. 814/333–5000, Philip E. Pandolph, FACHE, President and Chief Executive Officer
(Independent Hospital System)

PENNSYLVANIA: MEADVILLE MEDICAL CENTER (O, 232 beds) 751 Liberty Street, Meadville, PA, Zip 16335–2559; tel. 814/333–5000, Philip E. Pandolph, FACHE, President and Chief Executive Officer

---

For explanation of codes following names, see page B2.
★ Indicates Type III membership in the American Hospital Association.

TITUSVILLE AREA HOSPITAL (O, 25 beds) 406 West Oak Street, Titusville, PA, Zip 16354-1404; tel. 814/827-1851, Lee M. Clinton, FACHE, President and Chief Executive Officer
Web address: www.titusvillehospital.org

Owned, leased, sponsored:	2 hospitals	257 beds
Contract-managed:	0 hospitals	0 beds
Totals:	2 hospitals	257 beds

0520: MED CENTER HEALTH (NP)
800 Park Street, Bowling Green, KY Zip 42101-2356; tel. 270/745-1500, Connie Smith, FACHE, MSN, R.N., President and Chief Executive Officer
(Centralized Physician/Insurance Health System)

KENTUCKY: COMMONWEALTH REGIONAL SPECIALTY HOSPITAL (O, 28 beds) 250 Park Street, 6th Floor, Bowling Green, KY, Zip 42101-1760, P O Box 90010, Zip 42102-9010, tel. 270/796-6200, Christa Atkins, Administrator
Web address: www.commonwealthregionalspecialtyhospital.org

MEDICAL CENTER AT FRANKLIN (O, 25 beds) 1100 Brookhaven Road, Franklin, KY, Zip 42134-2746; tel. 270/598-4800, Annette Runyon, Vice President and Administrator
Web address: www.themedicalcenterfranklin.org

MEDICAL CENTER AT SCOTTSVILLE (O, 135 beds) 456 Burnley Road, Scottsville, KY, Zip 42164-6355; tel. 270/622-2800, Eric Hagan, R.N., Executive Vice President and Administrator
Web address: www.themedicalcenterscottsville.org/

THE MEDICAL CENTER AT ALBANY (C, 42 beds) 723 Burkesville Road, Albany, KY, Zip 42602-1654; tel. 606/387-8000, Laura Belcher, FACHE, Administrator
Web address: www.chc.net/services/hospitals/the_medical_center_at_albany.aspx

THE MEDICAL CENTER AT BOWLING GREEN (O, 337 beds) 250 Park Street, Bowling Green, KY, Zip 42101-1795, P O Box 90010, Zip 42102-9010, tel. 270/745-1000, Connie Smith, FACHE, MSN, R.N., Chief Executive Officer

THE MEDICAL CENTER AT CAVERNA (O, 25 beds) 1501 South Dixie Street, Horse Cave, KY, Zip 42749-1477; tel. 270/786-2191, Alan B. Alexander, FACHE, Vice President and Administrator
Web address: www.TheMedicalCenterCaverna.org

THE MEDICAL CENTER AT RUSSELLVILLE (O, 46 beds) 1625 South Nashville Road, Russellville, KY, Zip 42276-8834, P O Box 10, Zip 42276-0010, tel. 270/726-4011, Andrew Bedi, Chief Executive Officer

Owned, leased, sponsored:	6 hospitals	596 beds
Contract-managed:	1 hospitals	42 beds
Totals:	7 hospitals	638 beds

★0971: MEDISYS HEALTH NETWORK (NP)
8900 Van Wyck Expressway, Jamaica, NY Zip 11418-2832; tel. 718/206-6000, Bruce J. Flanz, President and Chief Executive Officer
(Moderately Centralized Health System)

NEW YORK: FLUSHING HOSPITAL MEDICAL CENTER (C, 293 beds) 4500 Parsons Boulevard, Flushing, NY, Zip 11355-2205; tel. 718/670-5000, Bruce J. Flanz, President and Chief Executive Officer
Web address: www.flushinghospital.org

JAMAICA HOSPITAL MEDICAL CENTER (C, 612 beds) 8900 Van Wyck Expressway, Jamaica, NY, Zip 11418-2832; tel. 718/206-6000, Bruce J. Flanz, President and Chief Executive Officer
Web address: www.Jamaicahospital.org

Owned, leased, sponsored:	0 hospitals	0 beds
Contract-managed:	2 hospitals	905 beds
Totals:	2 hospitals	905 beds

★0154: MEDSTAR HEALTH (NP)
10980 Grantchester Way, Columbia, MD Zip 21044-2665; tel. 410/772-6500, Kenneth A. Samet, President and Chief Executive Officer
(Centralized Health System)

DISTRICT OF COLUMBIA: MEDSTAR GEORGETOWN UNIVERSITY HOSPITAL (O, 425 beds) 3800 Reservoir Road NW, Washington, DC, Zip 20007-2197; tel. 202/444-2000, Lisa Boyle, M.D., President

MEDSTAR NATIONAL REHABILITATION HOSPITAL (O, 137 beds) 102 Irving Street NW, Washington, DC, Zip 20010-2949; tel. 202/877-1000, John D. Rockwood, President
Web address: www.medstarnrh.org

MEDSTAR WASHINGTON HOSPITAL CENTER (O, 782 beds) 110 Irving Street NW, Washington, DC, Zip 20010-3017; tel. 202/877-7000, Gregory J. Argyros, M.D., President

MARYLAND: MEDSTAR FRANKLIN SQUARE MEDICAL CENTER (O, 392 beds) 9000 Franklin Square Drive, Baltimore, MD, Zip 21237-3901; tel. 443/777-7000, Stuart M. Levine, M.D., President
Web address: www.medstarfranklin.org

MEDSTAR GOOD SAMARITAN HOSPITAL (O, 187 beds) 5601 Loch Raven Boulevard, Baltimore, MD, Zip 21239-2995; tel. 443/444-8000, Thomas J. Senker, FACHE, President
Web address: www.goodsam-md.org

MEDSTAR HARBOR HOSPITAL (O, 123 beds) 3001 South Hanover Street, Baltimore, MD, Zip 21225-1290; tel. 410/350-3200, Jill Donaldson, President
Web address: www.harborhospital.org

MEDSTAR MONTGOMERY MEDICAL CENTER (O, 102 beds) 18101 Prince Philip Drive, Olney, MD, Zip 20832-1512; tel. 301/774-8882, Emily M. Briton, President
Web address: www.medstarmontgomery.org

MEDSTAR SOUTHERN MARYLAND HOSPITAL CENTER (O, 168 beds) 7503 Surratts Road, Clinton, MD, Zip 20735-3358; tel. 301/868-8000, Stephen T. Michaels, M.D., FACHE, President

MEDSTAR ST. MARY'S HOSPITAL (O, 92 beds) 25500 Point Lookout Road, Leonardtown, MD, Zip 20650-2015, PO Box 527, Zip 20650-0527, tel. 301/475-6001, Mimi Novello, President and Chief Medical Officer
Web address: www.medstarstmarys.org

MEDSTAR UNION MEMORIAL HOSPITAL (O, 192 beds) 201 East University Parkway, Baltimore, MD, Zip 21218-2895; tel. 410/554-2000, Thomas J. Senker, FACHE, President

Owned, leased, sponsored:	10 hospitals	2600 beds
Contract-managed:	0 hospitals	0 beds
Totals:	10 hospitals	2600 beds

★0086: MEMORIAL HEALTH (NP)
340 West Miller Street, Springfield, IL Zip 62702-4928; tel. 217/788-3000, Edgar J. Curtis, FACHE, President and Chief Executive Officer
(Centralized Health System)

ILLINOIS: DECATUR MEMORIAL HOSPITAL (O, 171 beds) 2300 North Edward Street, Decatur, IL, Zip 62526-4192; tel. 217/876-8121, Drew Early, President and Chief Executive Officer
Web address: www.dmhcares.com

JACKSONVILLE MEMORIAL HOSPITAL (O, 25 beds) 1600 West Walnut Street, Jacksonville, IL, Zip 62650-1136; tel. 217/245-9541, Michael Trevor. Huffman, Chief Executive Officer
Web address: www.https://memorial.health/jacksonville-memorial-hospital/

LINCOLN MEMORIAL HOSPITAL (O, 25 beds) 200 Stahlhut Drive, Lincoln, IL, Zip 62656-5066; tel. 217/732-2161, Dolan Dalpoas, FACHE, President and Chief Executive Officer
Web address: www.https://memorial.health/lincoln-memorial-hospital/overview

For explanation of codes following names, see page B2.
★ Indicates Type III membership in the American Hospital Association.

Systems / Memorial Health

SPRINGFIELD MEMORIAL HOSPITAL (O, 464 beds) 701 North First Street, Springfield, IL, Zip 62781–0001; tel. 217/788–3000, Jay M. Roszhart, President and Chief Executive Officer
Web address: www.https://memorial.health/springfield-memorial-hospital/

TAYLORVILLE MEMORIAL HOSPITAL (O, 25 beds) 201 East Pleasant Street, Taylorville, IL, Zip 62568–1597; tel. 217/824–3331, Kimberly L. Bourne, President and Chief Executive Officer
Web address: www.taylorvillememorial.org

Owned, leased, sponsored:	5 hospitals	710 beds
Contract-managed:	0 hospitals	0 beds
Totals:	5 hospitals	710 beds

★**0998: MEMORIAL HEALTH SYSTEM (NP)**
401 Matthew Street, Marietta, OH Zip 45750–1635; tel. 740/374–1400, J Scott. Cantley, President and Chief Executive Officer
(Independent Hospital System)

OHIO: MARIETTA MEMORIAL HOSPITAL (O, 218 beds) 401 Matthew Street, Marietta, OH, Zip 45750–1699; tel. 740/374–1400, J Scott. Cantley, President and Chief Executive Officer
Web address: www.mhsystem.org

SELBY GENERAL HOSPITAL (O, 35 beds) 1106 Colegate Drive, Marietta, OH, Zip 45750–1323; tel. 740/568–2000, Jody Bullman, President
Web address: www.https://mhsystem.org/selbygeneralhospitalcampus

Owned, leased, sponsored:	2 hospitals	253 beds
Contract-managed:	0 hospitals	0 beds
Totals:	2 hospitals	253 beds

★**0083: MEMORIAL HEALTHCARE SYSTEM (NP)**
3501 Johnson Street, Hollywood, FL Zip 33021–5421; tel. 954/987–2000, David Smith, Interim Chief Executive Officer
(Centralized Health System)

FLORIDA: MEMORIAL HOSPITAL MIRAMAR (O, 160 beds) 1901 SW 172nd Avenue, Miramar, FL, Zip 33029–5592; tel. 954/538–5000, Stephen Demers, Chief Executive Officer

MEMORIAL HOSPITAL PEMBROKE (L, 191 beds) 7800 Sheridan Street, Pembroke Pines, FL, Zip 33024–2536; tel. 954/883–8482, Felicia Turnley, Chief Executive Officer
Web address: www.memorialpembroke.com/

MEMORIAL HOSPITAL WEST (O, 486 beds) 703 North Flamingo Road, Pembroke Pines, FL, Zip 33028–1014; tel. 954/436–5000, Joseph Stuczynski, Chief Executive Officer

MEMORIAL REGIONAL HOSPITAL (O, 1079 beds) 3501 Johnson Street, Hollywood, FL, Zip 33021–5421; tel. 954/987–2000, Philoron A. Wright II, FACHE, Chief Executive Officer
Web address: www.mhs.net

Owned, leased, sponsored:	4 hospitals	1916 beds
Contract-managed:	0 hospitals	0 beds
Totals:	4 hospitals	1916 beds

★**2645: MEMORIAL HERMANN HEALTH SYSTEM (NP)**
929 Gessner, Suite 2700, Houston, TX Zip 77024–2593; tel. 713/338–5555, David L. Callender, M.D., President and Chief Executive Officer
(Centralized Health System)

TEXAS: MEMORIAL HERMANN–TEXAS MEDICAL CENTER (O, 1234 beds) 6411 Fannin Street, Houston, TX, Zip 77030–1501; tel. 713/704–4000, Jason Glover, Chief Executive Officer

MEMORIAL HERMANN GREATER HEIGHTS HOSPITAL (O, 1465 beds) 1635 North Loop West, Houston, TX, Zip 77008–1532; tel. 713/867–3380, Paul O'Sullivan, FACHE, Chief Executive Officer
Web address: www.memorialhermann.org

MEMORIAL HERMANN KATY HOSPITAL (O, 290 beds) 23900 Katy Freeway, Katy, TX, Zip 77494–1323; tel. 281/644–8453, Jerry Ashworth, Senior Vice President and Chief Executive Officer
Web address: www.memorialhermann.org/locations/katy/

MEMORIAL HERMANN MEMORIAL CITY MEDICAL CENTER (L, 444 beds) 921 Gessner Road, Houston, TX, Zip 77024–2501; tel. 713/242–3000, Paul O'Sullivan, FACHE, Chief Executive Officer

MEMORIAL HERMANN NORTHEAST (O, 227 beds) 18951 North Memorial Drive, Humble, TX, Zip 77338–4297; tel. 281/540–7700, Justin Kendrick, Senior Vice President and Chief Executive Officer
Web address: www.memorialhermann.org/locations/northeast/

MEMORIAL HERMANN REHABILITATION HOSPITAL–KATY (O, 35 beds) 21720 Kingsland Boulevard, 2nd Floor, Katy, TX, Zip 77450–2550; tel. 800/447–3422, Rhonda Abbott, Senior Vice President and Chief Executive Officer

MEMORIAL HERMANN SUGAR LAND HOSPITAL (O, 179 beds) 17500 West Grand Parkway South, Sugar Land, TX, Zip 77479–2562; tel. 281/725–5000, Malisha Patel, Senior Vice President and Chief Executive Officer
Web address: www.memorialhermann.org

MEMORIAL HERMANN SURGICAL HOSPITAL–FIRST COLONY (O, 6 beds) 16906 Southwest Freeway, Sugar Land, TX, Zip 77479–2350; tel. 281/243–1000, Daniel Smith, Chief Executive Officer

TIRR MEMORIAL HERMANN (O, 134 beds) 1333 Moursund Street, Houston, TX, Zip 77030–3405; tel. 713/799–5000, Rhonda Abbott, Senior Vice President and Chief Executive Officer
Web address: www.memorialhermann.org/locations/tirr.html

Owned, leased, sponsored:	9 hospitals	4014 beds
Contract-managed:	0 hospitals	0 beds
Totals:	9 hospitals	4014 beds

0084: MEMORIALCARE (NP)
17360 Brookhurst Street, Fountain Valley, CA Zip 92708–3720, P O Box 1428, Long Beach, Zip 90801–1428, tel. 714/377–2900, Barry S. Arbuckle, Ph.D., President and Chief Executive Officer
(Centralized Health System)

CALIFORNIA: LONG BEACH MEDICAL CENTER (O, 412 beds) 2801 Atlantic Avenue, Long Beach, CA, Zip 90806–1701, P O Box 1428, Zip 90801–1428, tel. 562/933–2000, Blair M. Kent, Executive Vice President/Chief Executive Officer, Long Beach Medical Center

MILLER CHILDREN'S & WOMEN'S HOSPITAL LONG BEACH (O, 371 beds) 2801 Atlantic Avenue, Long Beach, CA, Zip 90806–1701; tel. 562/933–5437, Blair M. Kent, Executive Vice President/Chief Executive Officer, Long Beach Medical Center
Web address: https://www.memorialcare.org/locations/miller-childrens-womens-hospital-long-beach

ORANGE COAST MEDICAL CENTER (O, 221 beds) 9920 Talbert Avenue, Fountain Valley, CA, Zip 92708–5115, 18111 Brookhurst Street, Zip 92708–5115, tel. 714/378–7000, Marcia Manker, Chief Executive Officer, Executive Vice President, Memorial Care Orange County Region
Web address: https://www.memorialcare.org/locations/orange-coast-medical-center

SADDLEBACK MEDICAL CENTER (O, 248 beds) 24451 Health Center Drive, Laguna Hills, CA, Zip 92653–3689; tel. 949/837–4500, Marcia Manker, Chief Executive Officer/Executive Vice President, MemorialCare Orange County Region

Owned, leased, sponsored:	4 hospitals	1252 beds
Contract-managed:	0 hospitals	0 beds
Totals:	4 hospitals	1252 beds

★**5185: MERCY (CC)**
14528 South Outer 40, Suite 100, Chesterfield, MO Zip 63017–5743, 14528 South Outer 40 Road, Suite 100, Zip 63017–5743, tel. 314/579–6100, Stephen Mackin, President and Chief Executive Officer
(Decentralized Health System)

For explanation of codes following names, see page B2.
★ Indicates Type III membership in the American Hospital Association.

Systems / Mercy

ARKANSAS: MERCY HOSPITAL BERRYVILLE (O, 25 beds) 214 Carter Street, Berryville, AR, Zip 72616-4303; tel. 870/423-3355, Darren Caldwell, Chief Executive Officer

MERCY HOSPITAL BOONEVILLE (O, 25 beds) 880 West Main Street, Booneville, AR, Zip 72927-3443; tel. 479/675-2800, Julianne Stec, Vice President, Patient Services
Web address: https://www.mercy.net/practice/mercy-hospital-booneville/our-locations/

MERCY HOSPITAL FORT SMITH (O, 361 beds) 7301 Rogers Avenue, Fort Smith, AR, Zip 72903-4189, P O Box 17000, Zip 72917-7000, tel. 479/314-6000, Ryan T. Gehrig, FACHE, President
Web address: www.mercy.net/fortsmithar

MERCY HOSPITAL NORTHWEST ARKANSAS (O, 262 beds) 2710 Rife Medical Lane, Rogers, AR, Zip 72758-1452; tel. 479/338-8000, Ryan T. Gehrig, FACHE, President
Web address: https://www.mercy.net/practice/mercy-hospital-northwest-arkansas/

MERCY HOSPITAL OZARK (O, 25 beds) 801 West River Street, Ozark, AR, Zip 72949-3023; tel. 479/667-4138, Julianne Stec, Vice President, Patient Services
Web address: https://www.mercy.net/practice/mercy-hospital-ozark/

MERCY HOSPITAL PARIS (O, 13 beds) 500 East Academy, Paris, AR, Zip 72855-4040; tel. 479/963-6101, Julianne Stec, Vice President, Patient Services

MERCY HOSPITAL WALDRON (O, 24 beds) 1341 West 6th Street, Waldron, AR, Zip 72958-7642; tel. 479/637-4135, Steve Gebhart, Vice President, Patient Services
Web address: https://www.mercy.net/practice/mercy-hospital-waldron/

KANSAS: MERCY HOSPITAL COLUMBUS (O, 6 beds) 220 North Pennsylvania Avenue, Columbus, KS, Zip 66725-1110; tel. 620/429-2545, Angie Saporito, Administrator
Web address: https://www.mercy.net/practice/mercy-hospital-columbus/

MERCY HOSPITAL PITTSBURG (O, 89 beds) 1 Mt. Carmel Way, Pittsburg, KS, Zip 66762-7587; tel. 620/231-6100, Drew Talbott, President
Web address: https://www.mercy.net/practice/mercy-hospital-pittsburg/

MERCY SPECIALTY HOSPITAL SOUTHEAST KANSAS (O, 25 beds) 1619 West 7th Street, Galena, KS, Zip 66739; tel. 620/783-1732, Joseph Caputo, Vice President, Operations

MISSOURI: MERCY HOSPITAL AURORA (L, 25 beds) 500 Porter Street, Aurora, MO, Zip 65605-2365; tel. 417/678-2122, Valerie Davis, Administrator
Web address: www.stjohns.com/aboutus/aurora.aspx

MERCY HOSPITAL CARTHAGE (L, 25 beds) 3125 Dr Russell Smith Way, Carthage, MO, Zip 64836-7402; tel. 417/358-8121, Jeremy Drinkwitz, President, Mercy Joplin Communities
Web address: https://www.mercy.net/practice/mercy-hospital-carthage/

MERCY HOSPITAL CASSVILLE (L, 18 beds) 94 Main Street, Cassville, MO, Zip 65625-1610; tel. 417/847-6000, Valerie Davis, Administrator
Web address: www.mercy.net/northwestarar/practice/mercy-hospital-cassville

MERCY HOSPITAL JEFFERSON (O, 209 beds) 1400 US Highway 61 South, Festus, MO, Zip 63028-4100, P O Box 350, Crystal City, Zip 63019-0350, tel. 636/933-1000, Dan Eckenfels, President, Mercy Jefferson Communities

MERCY HOSPITAL JOPLIN (O, 221 beds) 100 Mercy Way, Joplin, MO, Zip 64804-1626; tel. 417/781-2727, Jeremy Drinkwitz, President, Mercy Joplin Communities
Web address: www.mercy.net/joplinmo

MERCY HOSPITAL LEBANON (O, 58 beds) 100 Hospital Drive, Lebanon, MO, Zip 65536-9210; tel. 417/533-6100, Jason Wilson, Administrator, Mercy Hospital Lebanon
Web address: www.mercy.net/practice/mercy-hospital-lebanon

MERCY HOSPITAL LINCOLN (L, 18 beds) 1000 East Cherry Street, Troy, MO, Zip 63379-1513; tel. 636/528-8551, Alan Smith, Administrator
Web address: www.mercy.net

MERCY HOSPITAL PERRY (L, 25 beds) 434 North West Street, Perryville, MO, Zip 63775-1398; tel. 573/547-2536, Christopher M. Wibbenmeyer, FACHE, President and Chief Executive Officer

MERCY HOSPITAL SOUTH (O, 536 beds) 10010 Kennerly Road, Saint Louis, MO, Zip 63128-2106; tel. 314/525-1000, Sean Hogan, FACHE, President, Mercy South St. Louis Communities
Web address: www.stanthonysmedcenter.com

MERCY HOSPITAL SOUTHEAST (O, 130 beds) 1701 Lacey Street, Cape Girardeau, MO, Zip 63701-5230; tel. 573/334-4822, Ryan Geib, President, Mercy Southeast Communities

MERCY HOSPITAL SPRINGFIELD (O, 504 beds) 1235 East Cherokee Street, Springfield, MO, Zip 65804-2263; tel. 417/820-2000, John Myers, President, Mercy Springfield Communities
Web address: www.mercy.net/springfieldmo

MERCY HOSPITAL ST. LOUIS (O, 831 beds) 615 South New Ballas Road, Saint Louis, MO, Zip 63141-8277; tel. 314/251-6000, David Meiners, President

MERCY HOSPITAL STODDARD (O, 36 beds) 1200 North One Mile Road, Dexter, MO, Zip 63841-1000; tel. 573/624-5566, Sue Ann Williams, Chief Executive Officer
Web address: www.sehealth.org

MERCY HOSPITAL WASHINGTON (O, 97 beds) 901 East Fifth Street, Washington, MO, Zip 63090-3127; tel. 636/239-8000, Eric Eoloff, President, Mercy Washington
Web address: www.mercy.net

MERCY ST. FRANCIS HOSPITAL (O, 20 beds) 100 West Highway 60, Mountain View, MO, Zip 65548-7125; tel. 417/934-7000, Valerie Davis, Administrator, Mercy Hospital Aurora

OKLAHOMA: ARBUCKLE MEMORIAL HOSPITAL (C, 17 beds) 2011 West Broadway Street, Sulphur, OK, Zip 73086-4221, P.O. Box 1109, Zip 73086-8109, tel. 580/622-2161, Jeremy A. Jones, Administrator
Web address: www.arbucklehospital.com/

MERCY HEALTH LOVE COUNTY (C, 25 beds) 300 Wanda Street, Marietta, OK, Zip 73448-1200; tel. 580/276-3347, Wesley Scott. Callender, Administrator

MERCY HOSPITAL ADA (L, 156 beds) 430 North Monte Vista, Ada, OK, Zip 74820-4610; tel. 580/332-2323, Terence Farrell, President
Web address: https://www.mercy.net/practice/mercy-hospital-ada/

MERCY HOSPITAL ARDMORE (O, 190 beds) 1011 14th Avenue NW, Ardmore, OK, Zip 73401-1828; tel. 580/223-5400, Daryle Voss, FACHE, President
Web address: www.mercyok.net

MERCY HOSPITAL HEALDTON (L, 22 beds) 3462 Hospital Road, Healdton, OK, Zip 73438-6124, P O Box 928, Zip 73438-0928, tel. 580/229-0701, Heather Chatham, Administrator
Web address: https://www.mercy.net/practice/mercy-hospital-healdton/

MERCY HOSPITAL KINGFISHER (L, 25 beds) 1000 Hospital Cirle, Kingfisher, OK, Zip 73750-5002, P O Box 59, Zip 73750-0059, tel. 405/375-3141, Bobby Stitt, R.N., Administrator, Rural Facilities
Web address: https://www.mercy.net/practice/mercy-hospital-kingfisher/

MERCY HOSPITAL LOGAN COUNTY (O, 25 beds) 200 South Academy Road, Guthrie, OK, Zip 73044-8727, P O Box 1017, Zip 73044-1017, tel. 405/282-6700, Bobby Stitt, R.N., Administrator, Rural Facilities

MERCY HOSPITAL OKLAHOMA CITY (O, 385 beds) 4300 West Memorial Road, Oklahoma City, OK, Zip 73120-8362; tel. 405/755-1515, Bennett Geister, President, Oklahoma City Communities
Web address: www.mercyok.net

MERCY HOSPITAL TISHOMINGO (L, 12 beds) 1000 South Byrd Street, Tishomingo, OK, Zip 73460-3299; tel. 580/371-2327, Lori McMillin, Administrator
Web address: www.mercy.net/

MERCY HOSPITAL WATONGA (L, 25 beds) 500 North Clarence Nash Boulevard, Watonga, OK, Zip 73772-2845, P O Box 370, Zip 73772-0370, tel. 580/623-7211, Bobby Stitt, R.N., Administrator
Web address: www.mercy.net/watongaok/practice/mercy-hospital-watonga

Owned, leased, sponsored:	33 hospitals	4448 beds
Contract-managed:	2 hospitals	42 beds
Totals:	35 hospitals	4490 beds

For explanation of codes following names, see page B2.
★ Indicates Type III membership in the American Hospital Association.

Systems / Mercy Health System

0649: MERCY HEALTH SYSTEM (NP)
1000 Mineral Point Avenue, Janesville, WI Zip 53548–2940, P O Box 2500, Zip 53547–5003, tel. 608/756–6000, Javon R. Bea, President and Chief Executive Officer
(Centralized Physician/Insurance Health System)

ILLINOIS: MERCYHEALTH HOSPITAL AND MEDICAL CENTER–HARVARD (O, 58 beds) 901 Grant Street, Harvard, IL, Zip 60033–1898, P O Box 850, Zip 60033–0850, tel. 815/943–5431, Javon R. Bea, President and Chief Executive Officer
Web address: https://www.mercyhealthsystem.org/locations/mercyhealth-hospital-and-medical-center-harvard/
MERCYHEALTH HOSPITAL AND PHYSICIAN CLINIC–CRYSTAL LAKE (O, 13 beds) 875 South Route 31, Crystal Lake, IL, Zip 60014, 901 Grant Street, Harvard, Zip 60033–1821, tel. 608/756–6559, Javon R. Bea, President and Chief Executive Officer
MERCYHEALTH JAVON BEA HOSPITAL–RIVERSIDE CAMPUS (O, 188 beds) 8201 East Riverside Boulevard, Rockford, IL, Zip 61114–2300; tel. 815/971–7000, Javon R. Bea, President and Chief Executive Officer
Web address: https://www.mercyhealthsystem.org/locations/javon-bea-hospital-riverside/

WISCONSIN: MERCYHEALTH HOSPITAL AND MEDICAL CENTER–WALWORTH (O, 18 beds) N2950 State Road 67, Lake Geneva, WI, Zip 53147–2655; tel. 262/245–0535, Javon R. Bea, President and Chief Executive Officer
Web address: www.mercyhealthsystem.org
MERCYHEALTH HOSPITAL AND TRAUMA CENTER–JANESVILLE (O, 140 beds) 1000 Mineral Point Avenue, Janesville, WI, Zip 53548–2982; tel. 608/756–6000, Javon R. Bea, President and Chief Executive Officer

Owned, leased, sponsored:	5 hospitals	417 beds
Contract–managed:	0 hospitals	0 beds
Totals:	5 hospitals	417 beds

★0944: MERCYONE (NP)
1449 NW 128th Street, Clive, IA Zip 50325–7400; tel. 515/358–9200, Robert P. Ritz, Chief Executive Officer

IOWA: ADAIR COUNTY HEALTH SYSTEM (C, 4 beds) 609 SE Kent Street, Greenfield, IA, Zip 50849–9454; tel. 641/743–2123, Catherine Hillestad, Chief Executive Officer
Web address: www.adaircountyhealthsystem.org
DALLAS COUNTY HOSPITAL (C, 17 beds) 610 10th Street, Perry, IA, Zip 50220–2221; tel. 515/465–3547, Angela Mortoza, Chief Executive Officer
Web address: www.dallascohospital.org
DAVIS COUNTY HOSPITAL AND CLINICS (C, 13 beds) 509 North Madison Street, Bloomfield, IA, Zip 52537–1271; tel. 641/664–2145, Veronica Fuhs, Chief Executive Officer
DECATUR COUNTY HOSPITAL (C, 11 beds) 1405 NW Church Street, Leon, IA, Zip 50144–1299; tel. 641/446–4871, Mike Johnston, Chief Executive Officer
Web address: www.decaturcountyhospital.org
GUTTENBERG MUNICIPAL HOSPITAL AND CLINICS (C, 18 beds) 200 Main Street, Guttenberg, IA, Zip 52052–9108, P O Box 550, Zip 52052–0550, tel. 563/252–1121, Tim Ahlers, Chief Executive Officer
MANNING REGIONAL HEALTHCARE CENTER (C, 25 beds) 1550 6th Street, Manning, IA, Zip 51455–1093; tel. 712/655–2072, Shannon Black, Chief Executive Officer
Web address: www.mrhcia.com
MONROE COUNTY HOSPITAL AND CLINICS (C, 25 beds) 6580 165th Street, Albia, IA, Zip 52531–8793; tel. 641/932–2134, Veronica Fuhs, Chief Executive Officer
RINGGOLD COUNTY HOSPITAL (C, 16 beds) 504 North Cleveland Street, Mount Ayr, IA, Zip 50854–2201; tel. 641/464–3226, Nicholle Gilbertson, Chief Executive Officer
Web address: www.rchmtayr.org
VAN BUREN COUNTY HOSPITAL (C, 10 beds) 304 Franklin Street, Keosauqua, IA, Zip 52565–1164; tel. 319/293–3171, Garen Carpenter, Chief Executive Officer
VAN DIEST MEDICAL CENTER (C, 25 beds) 2350 Hospital Drive, Webster City, IA, Zip 50595–6600, P O Box 430, Zip 50595–0430, tel. 515/832–9400, Lisa Carolyn. Ridge, Chief Executive Officer
Web address: www.vandiestmc.org
WAYNE COUNTY HOSPITAL AND CLINIC SYSTEM (C, 25 beds) 417 South East Street, Corydon, IA, Zip 50060–1860, P O Box 305, Zip 50060–0305, tel. 641/872–2260, Daren Relph, Chief Executive Officer

Owned, leased, sponsored:	0 hospitals	0 beds
Contract–managed:	11 hospitals	189 beds
Totals:	11 hospitals	189 beds

★2735: METHODIST HEALTH SYSTEM (NP)
1441 North Beckley Avenue, Dallas, TX Zip 75203–1201, P O Box 655999, Zip 75265–5999, tel. 214/947–8181, James C. Scoggin Jr, Chief Executive Officer
(Centralized Physician/Insurance Health System)

TEXAS: METHODIST CHARLTON MEDICAL CENTER (O, 291 beds) 3500 West Wheatland Road, Dallas, TX, Zip 75237–3460, P O Box 225357, Zip 75222–5357, tel. 214/947–7777, Michael K. Stewart, President
METHODIST DALLAS MEDICAL CENTER (O, 375 beds) 1441 North Beckley Avenue, Dallas, TX, Zip 75203–1201, P O Box 655999, Zip 75265–5999, tel. 214/947–8181, John E. Phillips, FACHE, President
Web address: www.methodisthealthsystem.org/Dallas
METHODIST MANSFIELD MEDICAL CENTER (O, 262 beds) 2700 East Broad Street, Mansfield, TX, Zip 76063–5899; tel. 682/622–2000, Juan Fresquez, President
METHODIST MIDLOTHIAN MEDICAL CENTER (O, 46 beds) 1201 East US Highway 287, Midlothian, TX, Zip 76065–4107; tel. 469/846–2000, Jary M. Ganske, Chief Executive Officer and VP of Finance
Web address: www.methodisthealthsystem.org
METHODIST RICHARDSON MEDICAL CENTER (O, 312 beds) 2831 East President George Bush Highway, Richardson, TX, Zip 75082–3561; tel. 469/204–1000, E. Kenneth. Hutchenrider Jr, FACHE, President
Web address: https://www.methodisthealthsystem.org/methodist-richardson-medical-center/
METHODIST SOUTHLAKE HOSPITAL (O, 22 beds) 421 East State Highway 114, Southlake, TX, Zip 76092; tel. 817/865–4400, Benson Chacko, President

Owned, leased, sponsored:	6 hospitals	1308 beds
Contract–managed:	0 hospitals	0 beds
Totals:	6 hospitals	1308 beds

★9345: METHODIST LE BONHEUR HEALTHCARE (CO)
1211 Union Avenue, Suite 700, Memphis, TN Zip 38104–6600; tel. 901/478–0500, Michael Ugwueke Sr, FACHE, President and Chief Executive Officer
(Centralized Physician/Insurance Health System)

MISSISSIPPI: METHODIST HEALTHCARE OLIVE BRANCH HOSPITAL (O, 57 beds) 4250 Bethel Road, Olive Branch, MS, Zip 38654–8737; tel. 662/932–9000, David G. Baytos, President
Web address: www.methodisthealth.org/olivebranch

TENNESSEE: METHODIST HEALTHCARE MEMPHIS HOSPITALS (O, 1348 beds) 1265 Union Avenue, Memphis, TN, Zip 38104–3415; tel. 901/516–7000, Michael Ugwueke Sr, FACHE, President and Chief Executive Officer

Owned, leased, sponsored:	2 hospitals	1405 beds
Contract–managed:	0 hospitals	0 beds
Totals:	2 hospitals	1405 beds

0368: MINNESOTA DEPARTMENT OF HUMAN SERVICES (NP)
540 Cedar Street, Saint Paul, MN Zip 55101–2208, P O Box 64998, Zip 55164–0998, tel. 651/431–3212, Anne Barry, Deputy Commissioner
(Independent Hospital System)

For explanation of codes following names, see page B2.
★ Indicates Type III membership in the American Hospital Association.

MINNESOTA: ANOKA METRO REGIONAL TREATMENT CENTER (O, 200 beds) 3301 Seventh Avenue, Anoka, MN, Zip 55303-4516, 3301 Seventh Avenue North, Zip 55303-4516, tel. 651/431-5000, Kathryn Kallas, Interim Administrator
Web address: www.health.state.mn.us

COMMUNITY BEHAVIORAL HEALTH HOSPITAL-ALEXANDRIA (O, 16 beds) 1610 8th Avenue East, Alexandria, MN, Zip 56308-2472; tel. 320/335-6201, Kimberly Jutz, Administrator

COMMUNITY BEHAVIORAL HEALTH HOSPITAL-ANNANDALE (O, 16 beds) 400 Annandale Boulevard, Annandale, MN, Zip 55302-3141; tel. 651/259-3850, Bill Stoner, Site Administrator
Web address: www.health.state.mn.us

COMMUNITY BEHAVIORAL HEALTH HOSPITAL-BAXTER (O, 16 beds) 14241 Grand Oaks Drive, Baxter, MN, Zip 56425-8749; tel. 218/316-3101, Ryan D. Cerney, Administrator
Web address: www.business.explorebrainerdlakes.com/list/member/community-behavioral-health-hospital-baxter-8647

COMMUNITY BEHAVIORAL HEALTH HOSPITAL-BEMIDJI (O, 16 beds) 800 Bemidji Avenue North, Bemidji, MN, Zip 56601-3054; tel. 218/308-2400, Larry A. Laudon, Administrator

COMMUNITY BEHAVIORAL HEALTH HOSPITAL-FERGUS FALLS (O, 16 beds) 1801 West Alcott Avenue, Fergus Falls, MN, Zip 56537-2661, P O Box 478, Zip 56538-0478, tel. 218/332-5001, Leah Voigt. Potter, Hospital Administrator

COMMUNITY BEHAVIORAL HEALTH HOSPITAL-ROCHESTER (O, 8 beds) 251 Wood Lake Drive SE, Rochester, MN, Zip 55904-5530; tel. 507/206-2561, James Pierce, Chief Executive Officer
Web address: www.health.state.mn.us

Owned, leased, sponsored:	7 hospitals	288 beds
Contract-managed:	0 hospitals	0 beds
Totals:	7 hospitals	288 beds

★2475: MISSISSIPPI COUNTY HOSPITAL SYSTEM (NP)
1520 North Division Street, Blytheville, AR Zip 72315-1448, P O Box 108, Zip 72316-0108, tel. 870/838-7300, Bryan Hargis, CPA, FACHE, Chief Executive Officer

ARKANSAS: GREAT RIVER MEDICAL CENTER (O, 73 beds) 1520 North Division Street, Blytheville, AR, Zip 72315-1448, P O Box 108, Zip 72316-0108, tel. 870/838-7300, Bryan Hargis, CPA, FACHE, Chief Executive Officer
Web address: www.mchsys.org

Owned, leased, sponsored:	1 hospitals	73 beds
Contract-managed:	0 hospitals	0 beds
Totals:	1 hospitals	73 beds

0017: MISSISSIPPI STATE DEPARTMENT OF MENTAL HEALTH (NP)
1101 Robert E Lee Building, 239 North Lamar Street, Jackson, MS Zip 39201-1101; tel. 601/359-1288, Wendy Bailey, Executive Director
(Independent Hospital System)

MISSISSIPPI: EAST MISSISSIPPI STATE HOSPITAL (O, 250 beds) 1818 College Drive, Meridian, MS, Zip 39307, Box 4128, West Station, Zip 39304-4128, tel. 601/482-6186, Charles Carlisle, Director
Web address: www.emsh.state.ms.us

MISSISSIPPI STATE HOSPITAL (O, 259 beds) 3550 Highway 468 West, Whitfield, MS, Zip 39193-5529, P O Box 157-A, Zip 39193-0157, tel. 601/351-8000, James G. Chastain, FACHE, Director

NORTH MISSISSIPPI STATE HOSPITAL (O, 50 beds) 1937 Briar Ridge Road, Tupelo, MS, Zip 38804-5963; tel. 662/690-4200, Paul A. Callens, Ph.D., Director
Web address: www.nmsh.state.ms.us

SOUTH MISSISSIPPI STATE HOSPITAL (O, 50 beds) 823 Highway 589, Purvis, MS, Zip 39475-4194; tel. 601/794-0100, Sabrina Young, Director
Web address: www.smsh.ms.gov/

Owned, leased, sponsored:	4 hospitals	609 beds
Contract-managed:	0 hospitals	0 beds
Totals:	4 hospitals	609 beds

0343: MONTEFIORE HEALTH SYSTEM (NP)
111 East 210th Street, Bronx, NY Zip 10467-2490; tel. 718/920-4321, Philip O. Ozuah, M.D., Ph.D., President and Chief Executive Officer
(Centralized Physician/Insurance Health System)

NEW YORK: BURKE REHABILITATION HOSPITAL (O, 150 beds) 785 Mamaroneck Avenue, White Plains, NY, Zip 10605-2523; tel. 914/597-2500, Scott Edelman, Executive Director and Chief Executive Officer

MONTEFIORE MEDICAL CENTER (O, 1294 beds) 111 East 210th Street, Bronx, NY, Zip 10467-2401; tel. 718/920-4321, Philip O. Ozuah, M.D., Ph.D., Chief Executive Officer
Web address: www.montefiore.org

MONTEFIORE MOUNT VERNON (O, 33 beds) 12 North Seventh Avenue, Mount Vernon, NY, Zip 10550-2098; tel. 914/664-8000, Regginald Jordan, Executive Director

MONTEFIORE NEW ROCHELLE (O, 234 beds) 16 Guion Place, New Rochelle, NY, Zip 10801-5502; tel. 914/365-5000, Anthony Alfano, Vice President Executive Director
Web address: www.montefiorehealthsystem.org

MONTEFIORE NYACK HOSPITAL (O, 250 beds) 160 North Midland Avenue, Nyack, NY, Zip 10960-1998; tel. 845/348-2000, Mark Geller, M.D., President and Chief Executive Officer
Web address: https://www.montefiorenyack.org/

MONTEFIORE ST. LUKE'S CORNWALL (O, 201 beds) 70 Dubois Street, Newburgh, NY, Zip 12550-4851; tel. 845/561-4400, Daniel J. Maughan MSN,RN, C, President and Chief Executive Officer

WHITE PLAINS HOSPITAL CENTER (O, 292 beds) 41 East Post Road, White Plains, NY, Zip 10601-4699; tel. 914/681-0600, Susan Fox, President and Chief Executive Officer
Web address: www.wphospital.org

Owned, leased, sponsored:	7 hospitals	2454 beds
Contract-managed:	0 hospitals	0 beds
Totals:	7 hospitals	2454 beds

★8495: MONUMENT HEALTH (NP)
353 Fairmont Boulevard, Rapid City, SD Zip 57701-7375, P O Box 6000, Zip 57709-6000, tel. 605/719-1000, Paulette Davidson, FACHE, President and Chief Executive Officer
(Moderately Centralized Health System)

SOUTH DAKOTA: MONUMENT HEALTH CUSTER HOSPITAL (O, 67 beds) 1220 Montgomery Street, Custer, SD, Zip 57730-1705; tel. 605/673-2229, Barbara K. Hespen, R.N., President
Web address: www.regionalhealth.com

MONUMENT HEALTH LEAD-DEADWOOD HOSPITAL (O, 18 beds) 61 Charles Street, Deadwood, SD, Zip 57732-1303; tel. 605/717-6000, Mark C. Schmidt, President
Web address: www.regionalhealth.com

MONUMENT HEALTH RAPID CITY HOSPITAL (O, 431 beds) 353 Fairmont Boulevard, Rapid City, SD, Zip 57701-7393, P O Box 6000, Zip 57709-6000, tel. 605/755-1000, John Pierce, President

MONUMENT HEALTH SPEARFISH HOSPITAL (O, 35 beds) 1440 North Main Street, Spearfish, SD, Zip 57783-1504; tel. 605/644-4000, Thomas Worsley, Chief Executive Officer
Web address: www.regionalhealth.com/Our-Locations/Regional-Hospitals/Spearfish-Regional-Hospital.aspx

---

For explanation of codes following names, see page B2.
★ Indicates Type III membership in the American Hospital Association.

Systems / Monument Health

MONUMENT HEALTH STURGIS HOSPITAL (O, 109 beds) 2140 Junction Avenue, Sturgis, SD, Zip 57785-2452; tel. 605/720-2400, Mark C. Schmidt, President
Web address: www.https://directory.monument.health/facility/sd/sturgis/2140-junction-avenue-6671505

PHILIP HEALTH SERVICES (C, 50 beds) 503 West Pine Street, Philip, SD, Zip 57567-3300, P O Box 790, Zip 57567-0790, tel. 605/859-2511, Jeremy S. Schultes, Administrator and Chief Executive Officer

WYOMING: WESTON COUNTY HEALTH SERVICES (C, 70 beds) 1124 Washington Boulevard, Newcastle, WY, Zip 82701-2972; tel. 307/746-4491, Randy L. Lindauer, Ph.D., FACHE, Chief Executive Officer
Web address: www.wchs-wy.org

Owned, leased, sponsored:	5 hospitals	660 beds
Contract-managed:	2 hospitals	120 beds
Totals:	7 hospitals	780 beds

★0946: MOSAIC LIFE CARE (NP)
5325 Faraon Street, Saint Joseph, MO Zip 64506-3488; tel. 816/271-6000, Mike Poore, Chief Executive Officer

MISSOURI: LONG-TERM ACUTE CARE HOSPITAL, MOSAIC LIFE CARE AT ST. JOSEPH (O, 39 beds) 5325 Faraon Street, Saint Joseph, MO, Zip 64506-3488; tel. 816/271-6000, Dana Anderson, R.N., Administrator
Web address: https://www.mymosaiclifecare.org/General/Long-Term-Acute-Care-Hospital/

MOSAIC LIFE CARE AT ST. JOSEPH-MEDICAL CENTER (O, 348 beds) 5325 Faraon Street, Saint Joseph, MO, Zip 64506-3488; tel. 816/271-6000, Tony A. Claycomb, R.N., President

MOSAIC MEDICAL CENTER-ALBANY (O, 19 beds) 705 North College Street, Albany, MO, Zip 64402-1433; tel. 660/726-3941, Katie Dias, D.O., President
Web address: https://www.mymlc.com/Main/Location/albany-mo/mosaic-medical-center-albany/

MOSAIC MEDICAL CENTER-MARYVILLE (O, 50 beds) 2016 South Main Street, Maryville, MO, Zip 64468-2655; tel. 660/562-2600, Nate Blackford, President

Owned, leased, sponsored:	4 hospitals	456 beds
Contract-managed:	0 hospitals	0 beds
Totals:	4 hospitals	456 beds

★0917: MOUNT SINAI HEALTH SYSTEM (NP)
1 Gustave L. Levy Place, New York, NY Zip 10029; tel. 212/659-8888, Brendan Carr, M.D., MS, Chief Executive Officer
(Centralized Health System)

NEW YORK: MOUNT SINAI BETH ISRAEL (O, 441 beds) 281 First Avenue, New York, NY, Zip 10003-2925; tel. 212/420-2000, Elizabeth Sellman, President and Chief Operating Officer
Web address: www.bethisraelny.org

MOUNT SINAI MORNINGSIDE (O, 737 beds) 1111 Amsterdam Avenue, New York, NY, Zip 10025-1716; tel. 212/523-4000, Evan Flatow, M.D., President
Web address: https://www.mountsinai.org/locations/morningside

MOUNT SINAI SOUTH NASSAU (O, 363 beds) 1 Healthy Way, Oceanside, NY, Zip 11572-1551; tel. 516/632-3000, Adhi Sharma, M.D., President
Web address: www.southnassau.org

NEW YORK EYE AND EAR INFIRMARY OF MOUNT SINAI (O, 13 beds) 310 East 14th Street, New York, NY, Zip 10003-4201; tel. 212/979-4000, James C. Tsai, M.D., President

THE MOUNT SINAI HOSPITAL (O, 1194 beds) 1 Gustave L Levy Place, P O Box 1068, New York, NY, Zip 10029-0310; tel. 212/241-6500, David L. Reich, M.D., President and Chief Operating Officer
Web address: www.mountsinai.org

Owned, leased, sponsored:	5 hospitals	2748 beds
Contract-managed:	0 hospitals	0 beds
Totals:	5 hospitals	2748 beds

★6555: MULTICARE HEALTH SYSTEM (NP)
820 A Street, Tacoma, WA Zip 98402-5202, P O Box 5299, Zip 98415-0299, tel. 253/403-1272, William G. Robertson, Chief Executive Officer
(Centralized Physician/Insurance Health System)

WASHINGTON: MULTICARE AUBURN MEDICAL CENTER (O, 167 beds) 202 North Division, Plaza One, Auburn, WA, Zip 98001-4908; tel. 253/833-7711, June Altaras, R.N., President and Market Leader
Web address: https://www.multicare.org/auburn-medical-center/

MULTICARE DEACONESS HOSPITAL (O, 279 beds) 800 West Fifth Avenue, Spokane, WA, Zip 99204-2803, P O Box 248, Zip 99210-0248, tel. 509/458-5800, Gregory George. Repetti III, FACHE, President
Web address: https://www.multicare.org/deaconess-hospital/

MULTICARE GOOD SAMARITAN HOSPITAL (O, 333 beds) 401 15th Avenue SE, Puyallup, WA, Zip 98372-3770, P O Box 1247, Zip 98371-0192, tel. 253/697-4000, Tim Holmes, Interim President

MULTICARE MARY BRIDGE CHILDREN'S HOSPITAL AND HEALTH CENTER (O, 152 beds) 317 Martin Luther King Jr Way, Tacoma, WA, Zip 98405-4234, P O Box 5299, Zip 98415-0299, tel. 253/403-1400, Jeffrey S. Poltawsky, President and Market Leader
Web address: www.multicare.org/marybridge

MULTICARE TACOMA GENERAL HOSPITAL (O, 381 beds) 315 Martin Luther King Jr Way, Tacoma, WA, Zip 98405-4234, P O Box 5299, Zip 98415-0299, tel. 253/403-1000, Eddie Bratko, President

MULTICARE VALLEY HOSPITAL (O, 123 beds) 12606 East Mission Avenue, Spokane Valley, WA, Zip 99216-1090; tel. 509/924-6650, Gregory George. Repetti III, FACHE, President
Web address: https://www.multicare.org/location/valley-hospital/

MULTICARE YAKIMA MEMORIAL HOSPITAL (O, 259 beds) 2811 Tieton Drive, Yakima, WA, Zip 98902-3761; tel. 509/575-8000, Tammy K. Buyok, President
Web address: www.yakimamemorial.org

MULTICARE CAPITAL MEDICAL CENTER (O, 69 beds) 3900 Capital Mall Drive SW, Olympia, WA, Zip 98502-5026; tel. 360/754-5858, William Callicoat, President

MULTICARE COVINGTON MEDICAL CENTER (O, 38 beds) 17700 SE 272nd Street, Covington, WA, Zip 98042-4951; tel. 253/372-6500, June Altaras, R.N., President and Market Leader

NAVOS (O, 70 beds) 2600 SW Holden Street, Seattle, WA, Zip 98126-3505; tel. 206/933-7299, Tim Holmes, Chief Executive Officer
Web address: www.navos.org

Owned, leased, sponsored:	10 hospitals	1871 beds
Contract-managed:	0 hospitals	0 beds
Totals:	10 hospitals	1871 beds

★1465: MUNSON HEALTHCARE (NP)
1105 Sixth Street, Traverse City, MI Zip 49684-2386; tel. 231/935-5000, Edwin Ness, Munson Healthcare President and Chief Executive Officer
(Centralized Health System)

MICHIGAN: KALKASKA MEMORIAL HEALTH CENTER (C, 112 beds) 419 South Coral Street, Kalkaska, MI, Zip 49646-2503; tel. 231/258-7500, Kevin L. Rogols, FACHE, Administrator/CEO
Web address: www.munsonhealthcare.org

MUNSON HEALTHCARE CADILLAC HOSPITAL (O, 49 beds) 400 Hobart Street, Cadillac, MI, Zip 49601-2389; tel. 231/876-7200, Peter Marinoff Jr, Munson Healthcare Cadillac Hospital Community President and Munson Healthcare South Region President

MUNSON HEALTHCARE CHARLEVOIX HOSPITAL (O, 25 beds) 14700 Lake Shore Drive, Charlevoix, MI, Zip 49720-1999; tel. 231/547-4024, Joanne Schroeder, FACHE, Munson Healthcare Charlevoix Hospital President and Chief Executive Officer
Web address: www.cah.org

MUNSON HEALTHCARE GRAYLING HOSPITAL (O, 110 beds) 1100 East Michigan Avenue, Grayling, MI, Zip 49738-1312; tel. 989/348-5461,

For explanation of codes following names, see page B2.
★ Indicates Type III membership in the American Hospital Association.

Kirsten Korth–White, Munson Healthcare Grayling Hospital President and Chief Executive Officer and MHC East Region President
Web address: https://www.munsonhealthcare.org/grayling-hospital/grayling-home

MUNSON HEALTHCARE MANISTEE HOSPITAL (O, 45 beds) 1465 East Parkdale Avenue, Manistee, MI, Zip 49660–9709; tel. 231/398–1000, Kelly Tomaszewski, R.N., MSN, President and Chief Executive Officer Manistee and Paul Oliver
Web address: https://www.munsonhealthcare.org/manistee-hospital/manistee-home

MUNSON HEALTHCARE OTSEGO MEMORIAL HOSPITAL (O, 80 beds) 825 North Center Avenue, Gaylord, MI, Zip 49735–1592; tel. 989/731–2100, Robert Richardson, Interim President and Chief Executive Officer

MUNSON HEALTHCARE PAUL OLIVER MEMORIAL HOSPITAL (O, 43 beds) 224 Park Avenue, Frankfort, MI, Zip 49635–9658; tel. 231/352–2200, Kelly Tomaszewski, R.N., MSN, President and Chief Executive Officer Manistee and Paul Oliver
Web address: https://www.munsonhealthcare.org/paul-oliver-memorial-hospital/paul-oliver-home

MUNSON MEDICAL CENTER (O, 442 beds) 1105 Sixth Street, Traverse City, MI, Zip 49684–2386; tel. 231/935–5000, Joseph Hurshe, MMc President & Chief Executive Officer

Owned, leased, sponsored:	7 hospitals	794 beds
Contract–managed:	1 hospitals	112 beds
Totals:	8 hospitals	906 beds

★0976: MUSC HEALTH (NP)
22 Westedge Street, Suite 300, Charleston, SC Zip 29403–6983; tel. 843/792–0599, Patrick J. Cawley, M.D., FACHE, Chief Executive Officer

SOUTH CAROLINA: MUSC HEALTH–ORANGEBURG (O, 204 beds) 3000 St Matthews Road, Orangeburg, SC, Zip 29118–1442; tel. 803/395–2200, Walter Bennett III, FACHE, Chief Executive Officer
Web address: www.https://muschealth.org/orangeburg/

MUSC HEALTH BLACK RIVER MEDICAL CENTER (O, 25 beds) 3555 North Williamsburg County Highway, Cades, SC, Zip 29518–3008; tel. 843/210–5000, Allen Abernethy, Chief Executive Officer
Web address: www.https://muschealth.org/black-river-medical-center

MUSC HEALTH CHESTER MEDICAL CENTER (O, 43 beds) 1 Medical Park Drive, Chester, SC, Zip 29706–9769; tel. 803/581–3151, Joseph Scott. Broome, M.P.H., FACHE, Chief Executive Officer

MUSC HEALTH COLUMBIA MEDICAL CENTER DOWNTOWN (O, 199 beds) 2435 Forest Drive, Columbia, SC, Zip 29204–2098; tel. 803/865–4500, Matthew Littlejohn, FACHE, Chief Executive Officer
Web address: www.https://muschealth.org/columbia-medical-center-downtown

MUSC HEALTH FLORENCE MEDICAL CENTER (O, 183 beds) 805 Pamplico Highway, Florence, SC, Zip 29505–6050, P O Box 100550, Zip 29502–0550, tel. 843/674–5000, Jay Hinesley, FACHE, Chief Executive Officer

MUSC HEALTH KERSHAW MEDICAL CENTER (O, 72 beds) 1315 Roberts Street, Camden, SC, Zip 29020–3737, P O Box 7003, Zip 29021–7003, tel. 803/432–4311, Matthew Littlejohn, FACHE, Chief Executive Officer
Web address: www.kershawhealth.org

MUSC HEALTH LANCASTER MEDICAL CENTER (O, 93 beds) 800 West Meeting Street, Lancaster, SC, Zip 29720–2298; tel. 803/286–1214, Joseph Scott. Broome, M.P.H., FACHE, Chief Executive Officer
Web address: www.springsmemorial.com

MUSC HEALTH MARION MEDICAL CENTER (O, 56 beds) 2829 East Highway 76, Mullins, SC, Zip 29574–6035, P O Drawer 1150, Marion, Zip 29571–1150, tel. 843/431–2000, Jay Hinesley, FACHE, Chief Executive Officer

MUSC HEALTH UNIVERSITY MEDICAL CENTER (O, 843 beds) 169 Ashley Avenue, Charleston, SC, Zip 29425–8905; tel. 843/792–2300, Saju Joy, M.D., Chief Executive Officer
Web address: www.muschealth.com

Owned, leased, sponsored:	9 hospitals	1718 beds
Contract–managed:	0 hospitals	0 beds
Totals:	9 hospitals	1718 beds

Systems / National Surgical Healthcare

★0001: MYMICHIGAN HEALTH (NP)
4000 Wellness Drive, Midland, MI Zip 48670–0001; tel. 989/839–3000, Lydia Watson, M.D., President and Chief Executive Officer
(Centralized Physician/Insurance Health System)

MICHIGAN: MYMICHIGAN MEDICAL CENTER ALMA (O, 97 beds) 300 East Warwick Drive, Alma, MI, Zip 48801–1014; tel. 989/463–1101, Marita Hattem–Schiffman, FACHE, Regional President
Web address: www.midmichigan.org/gratiot

MYMICHIGAN MEDICAL CENTER ALPENA (O, 86 beds) 1501 West Chisholm Street, Alpena, MI, Zip 49707–1401; tel. 989/356–7000, Hunter Nostrant, FACHE, President
Web address: www.midmichigan.org

MYMICHIGAN MEDICAL CENTER CLARE (O, 49 beds) 703 North McEwan Street, Clare, MI, Zip 48617–1440; tel. 989/802–5000, Marita Hattem–Schiffman, FACHE, Regional President
Web address: www.midmichigan.org

MYMICHIGAN MEDICAL CENTER GLADWIN (O, 25 beds) 515 Quarter Street, Gladwin, MI, Zip 48624–1959; tel. 989/426–9286, Raymond Stover, Regional President
Web address: www.midmichigan.org

MYMICHIGAN MEDICAL CENTER MIDLAND (O, 270 beds) 4000 Wellness Drive, Midland, MI, Zip 48670–2000; tel. 989/839–3000, Chuck H. Sherwin, FACHE, President
Web address: https://www.mymichigan.org/locations/profile/medicalcenter-midland/

MYMICHIGAN MEDICAL CENTER SAGINAW (O, 210 beds) 800 South Washington Avenue, Saginaw, MI, Zip 48601–2594; tel. 989/907–8000, Michael Erickson, Northern Region President
Web address: www.https://healthcare.ascension.org/locations/michigan/misag/saginaw-ascension-st-marys-hospital?intent_source=location_title&result_position=1

MYMICHIGAN MEDICAL CENTER SAULT (O, 97 beds) 500 Osborn Boulevard, Sault Sainte Marie, MI, Zip 49783–1884; tel. 906/635–4460, Kevin Kalchik, CPA, President
Web address: www.warmemorialhospital.org

MYMICHIGAN MEDICAL CENTER STANDISH (O, 54 beds) 805 West Cedar Street, Standish, MI, Zip 48658–9526; tel. 989/846–4521, Michael Erickson, Northern Region President

MYMICHIGAN MEDICAL CENTER TAWAS (O, 47 beds) 200 Hemlock Street, Tawas City, MI, Zip 48763–9237, P O Box 659, Zip 48764–0659, tel. 989/362–3411, Michael Erickson, Northern Region President
Web address: www.https://healthcare.ascension.org/locations/michigan/mitaw/tawas-city-ascension-st-joseph-hospital

MYMICHIGAN MEDICAL CENTER WEST BRANCH (O, 86 beds) 2463 South M–30, West Branch, MI, Zip 48661–1199; tel. 989/345–3660, Raymond Stover, Regional President
Web address: https://www.mymichigan.org/locations/profile/medicalcenter-westbranch/

Owned, leased, sponsored:	10 hospitals	1021 beds
Contract–managed:	0 hospitals	0 beds
Totals:	10 hospitals	1021 beds

0261: NATIONAL SURGICAL HEALTHCARE (IO)
250 South Wacker Drive, Suite 500, Chicago, IL Zip 60606–5897; tel. 312/627–8400, David Crane, Chief Executive Officer
(Independent Hospital System)

ARIZONA: ARIZONA SPINE AND JOINT HOSPITAL (O, 23 beds) 4620 East Baseline Road, Mesa, AZ, Zip 85206–4624; tel. 480/832–4770, Elizabeth Kearney, R.N., Chief Executive Officer
Web address: www.azspineandjoint.com

GEORGIA: OPTIM MEDICAL CENTER–SCREVEN (O, 25 beds) 215 Mims Road, Sylvania, GA, Zip 30467–2097; tel. 912/564–7426, Lagina Sheffield. Evans, R.N., Chief Executive Officer
Web address: www.optimhealth.com

For explanation of codes following names, see page B2.
★ Indicates Type III membership in the American Hospital Association.

Systems / National Surgical Healthcare

OPTIM MEDICAL CENTER–TATTNALL (O, 25 beds) 247 South Main Street, Reidsville, GA, Zip 30453–4605; tel. 912/557–1000, David Flanders, Chief Executive Officer

IDAHO: NORTHWEST SPECIALTY HOSPITAL (O, 32 beds) 1593 East Polston Avenue, Post Falls, ID, Zip 83854–5326; tel. 208/262–2300, Rick Rasmussen, Chief Executive Officer
Web address: www.northwestspecialtyhospital.com

NORTH CAROLINA: NORTH CAROLINA SPECIALTY HOSPITAL (O, 18 beds) 3916 Ben Franklin Boulevard, Durham, NC, Zip 27704–2383, PO Box 15819, Zip 27704–2383, tel. 919/956–9300, Randi L. Shults, Chief Executive Officer
Web address: www.ncspecialty.com

TEXAS: CHRISTUS SURGICAL HOSPITAL (O, 20 beds) 6130 Parkway Drive, Corpus Christi, TX, Zip 78414–2455; tel. 361/993–2000, Steven Daniel, Chief Executive Officer

SOUTH TEXAS SPINE AND SURGICAL HOSPITAL (O, 32 beds) 18600 Hardy Oak Boulevard, San Antonio, TX, Zip 78258–4206; tel. 210/507–4090, Angie Kauffman, Chief Executive Officer
Web address: www.southtexassurgical.com

WISCONSIN: OAKLEAF SURGICAL HOSPITAL (O, 13 beds) 1000 OakLeaf Way, Altoona, WI, Zip 54701–3016; tel. 715/831–8130, Jim Nemeth, FACHE, Chief Executive Officer
Web address: www.oakleafmedical.com

Owned, leased, sponsored:	8 hospitals	188 beds
Contract-managed:	0 hospitals	0 beds
Totals:	8 hospitals	188 beds

★9265: NEBRASKA METHODIST HEALTH SYSTEM, INC. (CO)

825 S. 169th Street, Omaha, NE Zip 68118–9300; tel. 402/354–5411, Stephen L. Goeser, FACHE, President and Chief Executive Officer
(Centralized Physician/Insurance Health System)

IOWA: METHODIST JENNIE EDMUNDSON HOSPITAL (O, 133 beds) 933 East Pierce Street, Council Bluffs, IA, Zip 51503–4652, P O Box 2C, Zip 51502–3002, tel. 712/396–6000, David Burd, President and Chief Executive Officer
Web address: www.bestcare.org

NEBRASKA: METHODIST FREMONT HEALTH (L, 181 beds) 450 East 23rd Street, Fremont, NE, Zip 68025–2387; tel. 402/721–1610, William Vobejda, President and Chief Executive Officer
Web address: www.fremonthealth.com

NEBRASKA METHODIST HOSPITAL (O, 448 beds) 8303 Dodge Street, Omaha, NE, Zip 68114–4199; tel. 402/354–4000, Josie Abboud, R.N., FACHE, President and Chief Executive Officer
Web address: www.bestcare.org

Owned, leased, sponsored:	3 hospitals	762 beds
Contract-managed:	0 hospitals	0 beds
Totals:	3 hospitals	762 beds

★0892: NEMOURS CHILDREN HEALTH (NP)

10140 Centurion Parkway North, Jacksonville, FL Zip 32256–0532; tel. 904/697–4100, R. Lawrence. Moss, M.D., President and Chief Executive Officer
(Independent Hospital System)

DELAWARE: NEMOURS CHILDREN'S HOSPITAL, DELAWARE (O, 210 beds) 1600 Rockland Road, Wilmington, DE, Zip 19803–3616, Box 269, Zip 19899–0269, tel. 302/651–4000, Mark R. Marcantano, Enterprise Vice President, President, Chief Executive, Delaware Valley Operations

FLORIDA: NEMOURS CHILDREN'S HOSPITAL (O, 108 beds) 13535 Nemours Parkway, Orlando, FL, Zip 32827–7402; tel. 407/567–4000, Martha McGill, President, Central Florida
Web address: www.nemours.org

Owned, leased, sponsored:	2 hospitals	318 beds
Contract-managed:	0 hospitals	0 beds
Totals:	2 hospitals	318 beds

0620: NEUROPSYCHIATRIC HOSPITALS (IO)

1625 East Jefferson Boulevard, Mishawaka, IN Zip 46545–7103; tel. 574/255–1400, Cameron R. Gilbert, Ph.D., President and Chief Executive Officer

ARIZONA: MEDICAL BEHAVIORAL HOSPITAL OF NORTHERN ARIZONA (O, 24 beds) 181 Whipple Street, Prescott, AZ, Zip 86301–1705; tel. 928/227–3424, LeAnne Aragon, Chief Executive Officer

PHOENIX MEDICAL PSYCHIATRIC HOSPITAL (O, 96 beds) 1346 East McDowell Road, Phoenix, AZ, Zip 85006; tel. 623/600–2730, Steven Scott, Chief Executive Officer
Web address: https://www.neuropsychiatrichospitals.net/

INDIANA: DOCTORS NEUROPSYCHIATRIC HOSPITAL (O, 37 beds) 417 South Whitlock Street, Bremen, IN, Zip 46506–1626; tel. 574/546–0330, Victor Chatuluka, Chief Executive Officer
Web address: www.neuropsychiatrichospitals.net

MEDICAL BEHAVIORAL HOSPITAL OF MISHAWAKA (O, 30 beds) 1625 East Jefferson Boulevard, Mishawaka, IN, Zip 46545–7103; tel. 574/255–1400, Ted Paarlberg, Chief Executive Officer

NEUROBEHAVIORAL HOSPITAL OF NW INDIANA/GREATER CHICAGO (O, 70 beds) 9330 Broadway, Crown Point, IN, Zip 46307–9830; tel. 219/648–2400, Jerome Phillips, Chief Executive Officer
Web address: https://www.neuropsychiatrichospitals.net

NEUROPSYCHIATRIC HOSPITAL OF INDIANAPOLIS (O, 50 beds) 6720 Parkdale Place, Indianapolis, IN, Zip 46254–4668; tel. 317/744–9200, Kathryn Stanley, Interim Chief Executive Officer
Web address: https://www.neuropsychiatrichospitals.net

TEXAS: MEDICAL BEHAVIORAL HOSPITAL OF CLEAR LAKE (O, 92 beds) 16850 Buccaneer Lane, Houston, TX, Zip 77058; tel. 833/971–2356, Richard Remley, Chief Executive Officer

Owned, leased, sponsored:	7 hospitals	399 beds
Contract-managed:	0 hospitals	0 beds
Totals:	7 hospitals	399 beds

★0142: NEW YORK–PRESBYTERIAN (NP)

525 East 68th Street, Box 182, New York, NY Zip 10065; tel. 212/746–3745, Steven J. Corwin, M.D., President and Chief Executive Officer
(Centralized Health System)

NEW YORK: NEW YORK–PRESBYTERIAN HOSPITAL (O, 3018 beds) 525 East 68th Street, New York, NY, Zip 10065–4870; tel. 212/746–5454, Steven J. Corwin, M.D., President and Chief Executive Officer

NEW YORK–PRESBYTERIAN QUEENS (O, 512 beds) 56–45 Main Street, Flushing, NY, Zip 11355–5045; tel. 718/670–1231, Stacey Petrower, President
Web address: https://www.nyp.org/queens

NEW YORK–PRESBYTERIAN/HUDSON VALLEY HOSPITAL (O, 128 beds) 1980 Crompond Road, Cortlandt Manor, NY, Zip 10567–4182; tel. 914/737–9000, Paul Dunphey, President
Web address: www.hvhc.org

Owned, leased, sponsored:	3 hospitals	3658 beds
Contract-managed:	0 hospitals	0 beds
Totals:	3 hospitals	3658 beds

For explanation of codes following names, see page B2.
★ Indicates Type III membership in the American Hospital Association.

Systems / Nobis Rehabilitation Partners

0009: NEW YORK STATE OFFICE OF MENTAL HEALTH (NP)
44 Holland Avenue, Albany, NY Zip 12208–3411; tel. 518/474–7056, Ann Sullivan, M.D., Commissioner
(Independent Hospital System)

NEW YORK: BRONX PSYCHIATRIC CENTER (O, 156 beds) 1500 Waters Place, Bronx, NY, Zip 10461-2796; tel. 718/931-0600, Precious Stepney, Executive Director

BUFFALO PSYCHIATRIC CENTER (O, 240 beds) 400 Forest Avenue, Buffalo, NY, Zip 14213-1298; tel. 716/885-2261, Beatrix Souza, Chief Executive Officer
Web address: www.omh.ny.gov

CAPITAL DISTRICT PSYCHIATRIC CENTER (O, 100 beds) 75 New Scotland Avenue, Albany, NY, Zip 12208-3474; tel. 518/549-6000, Deborah Murray, Executive Director

CENTRAL NEW YORK PSYCHIATRIC CENTER (O, 226 beds) 9005 Old River Road, Marcy, NY, Zip 13403-3000, P O Box 300, Zip 13403-0300, tel. 315/765-3600, Danielle Dill, Executive Director
Web address: www.omh.ny.gov

CREEDMOOR PSYCHIATRIC CENTER (O, 322 beds) 79-25 Winchester Boulevard, Jamaica, NY, Zip 11427-2128; tel. 718/264-3600, Martha Sullivan, M.D., Executive Director
Web address: www.omh.ny.gov

ELMIRA PSYCHIATRIC CENTER (O, 59 beds) 100 Washington Street, Elmira, NY, Zip 14901-2898; tel. 607/737-4739, David Peppel, Executive Director

GREATER BINGHAMTON HEALTH CENTER (O, 86 beds) 425 Robinson Street, Binghamton, NY, Zip 13904-1735; tel. 607/724-1391, David Peppel, Executive Director
Web address: www.omh.ny.gov/omhweb/facilities/bipc/facility.htm

KINGSBORO PSYCHIATRIC CENTER (O, 290 beds) 681 Clarkson Avenue, Brooklyn, NY, Zip 11203-2125; tel. 718/221-7395, Deborah Parchment, Executive Director
Web address: www.omh.ny.gov/omhweb/facilities/kbpc/facility/htm

KIRBY FORENSIC PSYCHIATRIC CENTER (O, 193 beds) 600 East 125th Street, New York, NY, Zip 10035-6000; tel. 646/672-5800, Brian Belfi, M.D., Executive Director
Web address: https://www.omh.ny.gov/omhweb/facilities/krpc/

MANHATTAN PSYCHIATRIC CENTER–WARD'S ISLAND (O, 745 beds) 600 East 125th Street, New York, NY, Zip 10035-6000; tel. 646/672-6767, Brian Belfi, M.D., Executive Director
Web address: www.omh.ny.gov

MID-HUDSON FORENSIC PSYCHIATRIC CENTER (O, 285 beds) Route 17M, New Hampton, NY, Zip 10958, P O Box 158, Zip 10958-0158, tel. 845/374-8700, Kristin Orlando, Chief Executive Officer

MOHAWK VALLEY PSYCHIATRIC CENTER (O, 27 beds) 1400 Noyes Street, Utica, NY, Zip 13502-3854; tel. 315/738-3800, Anthony Gonzalez, Executive Director
Web address: www.https://omh.ny.gov/omhweb/facilities/mvpc/

NEW YORK CITY CHILDREN'S CENTER (O, 92 beds) 74-03 Commonwealth Boulevard, Jamaica, NY, Zip 11426-1890; tel. 718/264-4506, Kanika Jefferies, Executive Director

NEW YORK STATE PSYCHIATRIC INSTITUTE (O, 58 beds) 1051 Riverside Drive, New York, NY, Zip 10032-1007; tel. 646/774-5000
Web address: www.nyspi.org

PILGRIM PSYCHIATRIC CENTER (O, 569 beds) 998 Crooked Hill Road, Brentwood, NY, Zip 11717-1019; tel. 631/761-3500, Kathy O'Keefe, Executive Director

RICHARD H. HUTCHINGS PSYCHIATRIC CENTER (O, 131 beds) 620 Madison Street, Syracuse, NY, Zip 13210-2319; tel. 315/426-3632, Thomas Umina, M.D., Executive Director
Web address: www.omh.ny.gov

ROCHESTER PSYCHIATRIC CENTER (O, 180 beds) 1111 Elmwood Avenue, Rochester, NY, Zip 14620-3005; tel. 585/241-1200, Philip Griffin, Director of Operations

ROCKLAND CHILDREN'S PSYCHIATRIC CENTER (O, 54 beds) 599 Convent Road, Orangeburg, NY, Zip 10962-1162; tel. 845/359-7400, Rebecca Leland, Executive Director
Web address: www.omh.ny.gov

ROCKLAND PSYCHIATRIC CENTER (O, 337 beds) 140 Old Orangeburg Road, Orangeburg, NY, Zip 10962-1157; tel. 845/359-1000, Janet J. Monroe, R.N., Executive Director
Web address: www.omh.ny.gov/

SAGAMORE CHILDREN'S PSYCHIATRIC CENTER (O, 54 beds) 197 Half Hollow Road, Dix Hills, NY, Zip 11746-5861; tel. 631/370-1700, Kathy O'Keefe, Interim Executive Director

SOUTH BEACH PSYCHIATRIC CENTER (O, 235 beds) 777 Seaview Avenue, Staten Island, NY, Zip 10305-3409; tel. 718/667-2300, Doreen Piazza, MS, Executive Director
Web address: www.omh.ny.gov/omhweb/facilities/sbpc/facility.htm

ST. LAWRENCE PSYCHIATRIC CENTER (O, 146 beds) 1 Chimney Point Drive, Ogdensburg, NY, Zip 13669-2291; tel. 315/541-2001, Aimee Dean, Executive Director

WESTERN NEW YORK CHILDREN'S PSYCHIATRIC CENTER (O, 46 beds) 1010 East and West Road, West Seneca, NY, Zip 14224-3602; tel. 716/677-7000, David Thomas. Privett, Executive Director
Web address: www.omh.ny.gov

Owned, leased, sponsored:	23 hospitals	4631 beds
Contract-managed:	0 hospitals	0 beds
Totals:	23 hospitals	4631 beds

0353: NEXUS HEALTH SYSTEMS (IO)
One Riverway, Suite 600, Houston, TX Zip 77056–1993, 1 Riverway, Suite 600, Zip 77056–1993, tel. 713/355–6111, John W. Cassidy, M.D., President, Chief Executive Officer and Chief Medical Officer
(Independent Hospital System)

CALIFORNIA: HEALTHBRIDGE CHILDREN'S HOSPITAL (O, 27 beds) 393 South Tustin Street, Orange, CA, Zip 92866-2501; tel. 714/289-2400, Roberta Consolver, Chief Executive Officer/Chief Clinical Officer
Web address: www.HealthBridgeOrange.com

TEXAS: NEXUS CHILDREN'S HOSPITAL HOUSTON (O, 111 beds) 2929 Woodland Park Drive, Houston, TX, Zip 77082-2687; tel. 281/293-7774, Roger Caron, Chief Executive Officer

NEXUS SPECIALTY HOSPITAL (O, 55 beds) 123 Vision Park Boulevard, Shenandoah, TX, Zip 77384-3001; tel. 281/364-0317, James R. Resendez, FACHE, Chief Executive Officer
Web address: www.nexusspecialty.com

Owned, leased, sponsored:	3 hospitals	193 beds
Contract-managed:	0 hospitals	0 beds
Totals:	3 hospitals	193 beds

1127: NOBIS REHABILITATION PARTNERS (IO)
450 Century Parkway, Suite 220, Allen, TX Zip 75013–8135; tel. 469/640–6500, Chester Crouch, Founder & President

ARIZONA: REUNION REHABILITATION HOSPITAL PEORIA (C, 40 beds) 13451 North 94th Drive, Peoria, AZ, Zip 85381-5056; tel. 623/303-7101, Shawn McCallum, Chief Executive Officer
Web address: www.https://reunionrehabhospital.com/locations/peoria/

REUNION REHABILITATION HOSPITAL PHOENIX (C, 48 beds) 1675 East Villa Street, Phoenix, AZ, Zip 85006-4435; tel. 480/801-6700, Eric Mueller, Market Chief Executive Officer Phoenix Metro
Web address: www.https://reunionrehabhospital.com/locations/phoenix/

COLORADO: REUNION REHABILITATION HOSPITAL DENVER (C, 40 beds) 4650 Central Park Boulevard, Denver, CO, Zip 80238; tel. 720/734-3500, Erika Kaye, Chief Executive Officer

REUNION REHABILITATION HOSPITAL INVERNESS (C, 40 beds) 372 Inverness Drive South, Englewood, CO, Zip 80112-5899; tel. 720/741-8800, Lonnie Martinez, Chief Executive Officer
Web address: www.https://reunionrehabhospital.com/locations/inverness/

FLORIDA: ORLANDO REHABILITATION HOSPITAL (C, 60 beds) 980 Gateway Drive, Altamonte Springs, FL, Zip 32714-4807; tel. 321/989-3104
Web address: https://www.orlando-rehabhospital.com/

For explanation of codes following names, see page B2.
★ Indicates Type III membership in the American Hospital Association.

Systems / Nobis Rehabilitation Partners

INDIANA: INDIANAPOLIS REHABILITATION HOSPITAL (C, 40 beds) 1260 City Center Drive, Carmel, IN, Zip 46032–3810; tel. 463/333-9110, Brandon Tudor, Chief Executive Officer
Web address: https://www.indianapolis-rehabhospital.com/

KANSAS: JOHNSON COUNTY REHABILITATION HOSPITAL (C, 40 beds) 11325 College Boulevard, Overland Park, KS, Zip 66210; tel. 913/372-7800, Krista Jackson, Chief Executive Officer
Web address: https://www.johnsoncounty-rehab.com/

LOUISIANA: SHREVEPORT REHABILITATION HOSPITAL (C, 40 beds) 1451 Fern Circle, Shreveport, LA, Zip 71105–4177; tel. 318/232-8880, Brent Martin, Chief Executive Officer

OHIO: CINCINNATI REHABILITATION HOSPITAL (C, 40 beds) 4291 Parkview Drive, Blue Ash, OH, Zip 45242–5667; tel. 513/788-3313
Web address: https://www.cincinnati-rehabhospital.com/

OKLAHOMA: OKLAHOMA CITY REHABILITATION HOSPITAL (C, 40 beds) 10240 Broadway Extension, Oklahoma City, OK, Zip 73114–6309; tel. 405/900-8850, Stacie Goyne, Chief Executive Officer
TULSA REHABILITATION HOSPITAL (C, 40 beds) 7909 South 101st East Avenue, Tulsa, OK, Zip 74133; tel. 918/820-3499, Ian Cooper, Chief Executive Officer
Web address: https://www.tulsa-rehabhospital.com/

TEXAS: REUNION REHABILITATION HOSPITAL ARLINGTON (O, 40 beds) 4351 Centreway Place, Arlington, TX, Zip 76018; tel. 682/339-1400, Tyrrell Taplin, Chief Executive Officer
Web address: www.https://reunionrehabhospital.com/locations/arlington/
REUNION REHABILITATION HOSPITAL PLANO (C, 48 beds) 3600 Mapleshade Lane, Plano, TX, Zip 75075; tel. 469/830-2350, Ty Burgess, Chief Executive Officer
SAN ANTONIO REHABILITATION HOSPITAL (C, 48 beds) 8903 Floyd Curl Drive, San Antonio, TX, Zip 78240; tel. 726/201-5501, Claudia Torres, Interim Chief Executive Officer
Web address: https://www.sanantonio-rehabhospital.com/

WISCONSIN: MILWAUKEE REHABILITATION HOSPITAL AT GREENFIELD (C, 35 beds) 3200 South 103rd Street, Milwaukee, WI, Zip 53227–4104; tel. 414/441-0500, Shelley Stubbendeck, Chief Executive Officer
Web address: https://www.milwaukee-rehabhospital.com/

Owned, leased, sponsored:	1 hospitals	40 beds
Contract-managed:	14 hospitals	599 beds
Totals:	15 hospitals	639 beds

0349: NOLAND HEALTH SERVICES, INC. (NP)
600 Corporate Parkway, Suite 100, Birmingham, AL Zip 35242–5451; tel. 205/783-8484, Barbara Estep, Chief Executive Officer

ALABAMA: NOLAND HOSPITAL ANNISTON (O, 38 beds) 400 East 10th Street, 4th Fl, Anniston, AL, Zip 36207–4716; tel. 256/741-6141, Trina Woods, Administrator
Web address: www.nolandhealth.com
NOLAND HOSPITAL BIRMINGHAM (O, 45 beds) 50 Medical Park East Drive, 8th Floor, Birmingham, AL, Zip 35235; tel. 205/838-5100, Laura S. Wills, Administrator
NOLAND HOSPITAL DOTHAN (O, 38 beds) 1108 Ross Clark Circle, 4th Floor, Dothan, AL, Zip 36301–3022; tel. 334/699-4300, Dennis W. Stewart, Administrator
Web address: www.nolandhealth.com
NOLAND HOSPITAL MONTGOMERY (O, 65 beds) 1725 Pine Street, 5 North, Montgomery, AL, Zip 36106–1109; tel. 334/240-0532, William Elsesser, Administrator
NOLAND HOSPITAL SHELBY (O, 52 beds) 1000 First Street North, 3rd Floor, Alabaster, AL, Zip 35007–8703; tel. 205/620-8641, Laura S. Wills, Administrator
Web address: www.nolandhospitals.com

NOLAND HOSPITAL TUSCALOOSA (O, 32 beds) 809 University Blvd E, 4th Fl, Tuscaloosa, AL, Zip 35401–2029; tel. 205/759-7241, Jack Gibson, Administrator

Owned, leased, sponsored:	6 hospitals	270 beds
Contract-managed:	0 hospitals	0 beds
Totals:	6 hospitals	270 beds

★1030: NORTH COUNTRY HEALTHCARE (NP)
8 Clover Lane, Whitefield, NH Zip 03598–3343; tel. 603/444-9000, Thomas Mee, R.N., Chief Executive Officer
(Moderately Centralized Health System)

Owned, leased, sponsored:	0 hospitals	0 beds
Contract-managed:	0 hospitals	0 beds
Totals:	0 hospitals	0 beds

0887: NORTH MEMORIAL HEALTH CARE (NP)
3300 Oakdale Avenue North, Robbinsdale, MN Zip 55422–2926; tel. 763/520-5200, Trevor Sawallish, Chief Executive Officer
(Centralized Physician/Insurance Health System)

MINNESOTA: MAPLE GROVE HOSPITAL (C, 108 beds) 9875 Hospital Drive, Maple Grove, MN, Zip 55369–4648; tel. 763/581-1000, Trevor Sawallish, Chief Executive Officer
Web address: www.maplegrovehospital.org
NORTH MEMORIAL HEALTH HOSPITAL (O, 358 beds) 3300 Oakdale Avenue North, Robbinsdale, MN, Zip 55422–2926; tel. 763/520-5200, Trevor Sawallish, Chief Executive Officer
Web address: www.northmemorial.com

Owned, leased, sponsored:	1 hospitals	358 beds
Contract-managed:	1 hospitals	108 beds
Totals:	2 hospitals	466 beds

★0032: NORTH MISSISSIPPI HEALTH SERVICES, INC. (NP)
830 South Gloster Street, Tupelo, MS Zip 38801–4996; tel. 662/377-3136, M. Shane. Spees, President and Chief Executive Officer
(Centralized Physician/Insurance Health System)

ALABAMA: NORTH MISSISSIPPI MEDICAL CENTER–HAMILTON (O, 15 beds) 1256 Military Street South, Hamilton, AL, Zip 35570–5003; tel. 205/921-6200, Robin Mixon, Administrator
Web address: www.nmhs.net

MISSISSIPPI: NORTH MISSISSIPPI MEDICAL CENTER–TUPELO (O, 741 beds) 830 South Gloster Street, Tupelo, MS, Zip 38801–4934; tel. 662/377-3136, David C. Wilson, President and Chief Operation Officer
Web address: www.nmhs.net
NORTH MISSISSIPPI MEDICAL CENTER GILMORE–AMORY (O, 95 beds) 1105 Earl Frye Boulevard, Amory, MS, Zip 38821–5500, P O Box 459, Zip 38821–0459, tel. 662/256-7111, Jamie Rodgers, Administrator
NORTH MISSISSIPPI MEDICAL CENTER–EUPORA (O, 74 beds) 70 Medical Plaza, Eupora, MS, Zip 39744–4018; tel. 662/258-6221, Robin Mixon, Administrator
Web address: www.nmhs.net/eupora
NORTH MISSISSIPPI MEDICAL CENTER–IUKA (O, 48 beds) 1777 Curtis Drive, Iuka, MS, Zip 38852–1001, P O Box 860, Zip 38852–0860, tel. 662/423-6051, Barry L. Keel, Administrator
NORTH MISSISSIPPI MEDICAL CENTER–PONTOTOC (L, 69 beds) 176 South Main Street, Pontotoc, MS, Zip 38863–3311, P O Box 790, Zip 38863–0790, tel. 662/488-7640, Jamie Rodgers, Administrator
Web address: https://www.nmhs.net/locations/profile/north-mississippi-medical-center-pontotoc/

For explanation of codes following names, see page B2.
★ Indicates Type III membership in the American Hospital Association.

NORTH MISSISSIPPI MEDICAL CENTER–WEST POINT (O, 49 beds) 150 Medical Center Drive, West Point, MS, Zip 39773-0428; tel. 662/495-2300, Barry L. Keel, Administrator
Web address: www.nmhs.net/westpoint

Owned, leased, sponsored:	7 hospitals	1091 beds
Contract-managed:	0 hospitals	0 beds
Totals:	7 hospitals	1091 beds

0867: NORTH OAKS HEALTH SYSTEM (NP)

15790 Paul Vega MD Drive, Hammond, LA Zip 70403-1436, P O Box 2668, Zip 70404-2668, tel. 985/345-2700, Michele Kidd. Sutton, FACHE, President and Chief Executive Officer
(Independent Hospital System)

LOUISIANA: NORTH OAKS MEDICAL CENTER (O, 248 beds) 15790 Paul Vega, MD, Drive, Hammond, LA, Zip 70403-1436, P O Box 2668, Zip 70404-2668, tel. 985/345-2700, Michele Kidd. Sutton, FACHE, President and Chief Executive Officer

NORTH OAKS REHABILITATION HOSPITAL (O, 27 beds) 1900 South Morrison Boulevard, Hammond, LA, Zip 70403-5742; tel. 985/542-7777, Mac Barrient Jr, Administrator
Web address: www.northoaks.org

Owned, leased, sponsored:	2 hospitals	275 beds
Contract-managed:	0 hospitals	0 beds
Totals:	2 hospitals	275 beds

★1018: NORTHEAST GEORGIA HEALTH SYSTEM (NP)

743 Spring Street NE, Gainesville, GA Zip 30501-3715; tel. 770/219-9000, Carol H. Burrell, President and Chief Executive Officer
(Centralized Physician/Insurance Health System)

GEORGIA: NORTHEAST GEORGIA MEDICAL CENTER BARROW (O, 34 beds) 316 North Broad Street, Winder, GA, Zip 30680-2150, P O Box 688, Zip 30680-0688, tel. 770/867-3400, John Neidenbach, Administrator
Web address: www.barrowregional.com

NORTHEAST GEORGIA MEDICAL CENTER HABERSHAM (O, 121 beds) 541 Historic Highway 441, Demorest, GA, Zip 30535-3118, P O Box 37, Zip 30535-0037, tel. 706/754-2161, Kevin Matson, Interim Chief Executive Officer

NORTHEAST GEORGIA MEDICAL CENTER LUMPKIN (O, 23 beds) 495 Highway 400, Dahlonega, GA, Zip 30533-6823; tel. 770/219-9000, Carol H. Burrell, Chief Executive Officer
Web address: https://www.nghs.com/locations/lumpkin/

NORTHEAST GEORGIA MEDICAL CENTER (O, 937 beds) 743 Spring Street NE, Gainesville, GA, Zip 30501-3899; tel. 770/219-3553, John Kueven, President

Owned, leased, sponsored:	4 hospitals	1115 beds
Contract-managed:	0 hospitals	0 beds
Totals:	4 hospitals	1115 beds

★0281: NORTHERN ARIZONA HEALTHCARE (NP)

1200 North Beaver Street, Flagstaff, AZ Zip 86001-3118; tel. 928/779-3366, David Cheney, Chief Executive Officer
(Moderately Centralized Health System)

ARIZONA: FLAGSTAFF MEDICAL CENTER (O, 268 beds) 1200 North Beaver Street, Flagstaff, AZ, Zip 86001-3118; tel. 928/779-3366, David Cheney, President and Chief Executive Officer
Web address: www.nahealth.com

VERDE VALLEY MEDICAL CENTER (O, 87 beds) 269 South Candy Lane, Cottonwood, AZ, Zip 86326-4170; tel. 928/639-6000, Ronald Haase, Chief Administrative Officer
Web address: www.https://nahealth.com/

Owned, leased, sponsored:	2 hospitals	355 beds
Contract-managed:	0 hospitals	0 beds
Totals:	2 hospitals	355 beds

★0555: NORTHERN LIGHT HEALTH (NP)

43 Whiting Hill Road, Brewer, ME Zip 04412-1005; tel. 207/973-7045, Timothy Dentry, President and Chief Executive Officer
(Moderately Centralized Health System)

MAINE: NORTHERN LIGHT BLUE HILL HOSPITAL (O, 10 beds) 57 Water Street, Blue Hill, ME, Zip 04614-5231; tel. 207/374-3400, John Ronan, President

NORTHERN LIGHT CA DEAN HOSPITAL (O, 14 beds) 364 Pritham Avenue, Greenville, ME, Zip 04441-1395, P O Box 1129, Zip 04441-1129, tel. 207/695-5200, Marie E. Vienneau, President
Web address: www.cadean.org

NORTHERN LIGHT EASTERN MAINE MEDICAL CENTER (O, 361 beds) 489 State Street, Bangor, ME, Zip 04401-6674, P O Box 404, Zip 04402-0404, tel. 207/973-7000, Gregory LaFrancois, President

NORTHERN LIGHT INLAND HOSPITAL (O, 35 beds) 200 Kennedy Memorial Drive, Waterville, ME, Zip 04901-4595; tel. 207/861-3000, Tricia Costigan, FACHE, President
Web address: www.https://northernlighthealth.org/inland-hospital

NORTHERN LIGHT MAINE COAST HOSPITAL (O, 45 beds) 50 Union Street, Ellsworth, ME, Zip 04605-1599; tel. 207/664-5311, John Ronan, President

NORTHERN LIGHT MAYO HOSPITAL (O, 25 beds) 897 West Main Street, Dover-Foxcroft, ME, Zip 04426-1099; tel. 207/564-8401, Marie E. Vienneau, President
Web address: www.mayohospital.com

NORTHERN LIGHT MERCY HOSPITAL (O, 77 beds) 175 Fore River Parkway, Portland, ME, Zip 04102-2779; tel. 207/879-3000, Charles D. Therrien, President

NORTHERN LIGHT SEBASTICOOK VALLEY HOSPITAL (O, 25 beds) 447 North Main Street, Pittsfield, ME, Zip 04967-3707; tel. 207/487-4000, Randy Clark, President
Web address: www.sebasticookvalleyhealth.org

THE ACADIA HOSPITAL (O, 78 beds) 268 Stillwater Avenue, Bangor, ME, Zip 04401-3945, P O Box 422, Zip 04402-0422, tel. 207/973-6100, Mark Lukens, President

THE AROOSTOOK MEDICAL CENTER (O, 125 beds) 140 Academy Street, Presque Isle, ME, Zip 04769-3171, P O Box 151, Zip 04769-0151, tel. 207/768-4000, Jay Reynolds, M.D., President
Web address: www.https://northernlighthealth.org/A-R-Gould-Hospital

Owned, leased, sponsored:	10 hospitals	795 beds
Contract-managed:	0 hospitals	0 beds
Totals:	10 hospitals	795 beds

★0410: NORTHSIDE HEALTHCARE SYSTEM (NP)

1000 Johnson Ferry Road NE, Atlanta, GA Zip 30342-1611; tel. 404/851-8000, Robert Quattrocchi, President and Chief Executive Officer

GEORGIA: NORTHSIDE HOSPITAL CHEROKEE (O, 206 beds) 450 Northside Cherokee Boulevard, Canton, GA, Zip 30115-8015; tel. 770/720-5100, William M. Hayes, Chief Executive Officer

NORTHSIDE HOSPITAL FORSYTH (O, 384 beds) 1200 Northside Forsyth Drive, Cumming, GA, Zip 30041-7659; tel. 770/844-3200, Lynn Jackson, Chief Executive Officer
Web address: www.northside.com

NORTHSIDE HOSPITAL GWINNETT/DULUTH (L, 577 beds) 1000 Medical Center Boulevard, Lawrenceville, GA, Zip 30046-7694, 1000 Medical Center Blvd, Zip 30046, tel. 678/312-1000, Debbie Bilbro, Chief Executive Officer

For explanation of codes following names, see page B2.
★ Indicates Type III membership in the American Hospital Association.

Systems / Northside Healthcare System

NORTHSIDE HOSPITAL (O, 660 beds) 1000 Johnson Ferry Road Northeast, Atlanta, GA, Zip 30342-1606, 1001 Summit Blvd, Zip 30319, tel. 404/851-8000, Deidre Dixon, Chief Executive Officer
Web address: https://www.northside.com/locations/northside-hospital-atlanta

Owned, leased, sponsored:	4 hospitals	1827 beds
Contract-managed:	0 hospitals	0 beds
Totals:	4 hospitals	1827 beds

★0062: NORTHWELL HEALTH (NP)
1979 Marcus Ave Ste E 124, Lake Success, NY Zip 11042; tel. 516/321-6666, Michael J. Dowling, President and Chief Executive Officer
(Centralized Health System)

NEW YORK: GLEN COVE HOSPITAL (O, 148 beds) 101 St Andrews Lane, Glen Cove, NY, Zip 11542-2254; tel. 516/674-7300, Kerri Scanlon, R.N., Executive Director
Web address: www.northshorelij.com

HUNTINGTON HOSPITAL (O, 284 beds) 270 Park Avenue, Huntington, NY, Zip 11743-2799; tel. 631/351-2000, Nick Fitterman, M.D., Executive Director
Web address: www.https://huntington.northwell.edu

LENOX HILL HOSPITAL (O, 446 beds) 100 East 77th Street, New York, NY, Zip 10075-1850; tel. 212/434-2000, Daniel Baker, Executive Director
Web address: www.https://lenoxhill.northwell.edu/

LONG ISLAND JEWISH MEDICAL CENTER (O, 1508 beds) 270-05 76th Avenue, New Hyde Park, NY, Zip 11040-1496; tel. 718/470-7000, Michael Gitman, M.D., Executive Director

MATHER HOSPITAL (O, 248 beds) 75 North Country Road, Port Jefferson, NY, Zip 11777-2190; tel. 631/473-1320, Kevin M. McGeachy, Executive Director
Web address: www.matherhospital.com

NORTH SHORE UNIVERSITY HOSPITAL (O, 815 beds) 300 Community Drive, Manhasset, NY, Zip 11030-3816; tel. 516/562-0100, Jon Sendach, Executive Director

NORTHERN WESTCHESTER HOSPITAL (O, 199 beds) 400 East Main Street, Mount Kisco, NY, Zip 10549-3477, 400 East Main Street, G-02, Zip 10549-3477, tel. 914/666-1200, Derek Anderson, Executive Director
Web address: www.nwhc.net

PECONIC BAY MEDICAL CENTER (O, 144 beds) 1300 Roanoke Avenue, Riverhead, NY, Zip 11901-2031; tel. 631/548-6000, Amy E. Loeb, Ed.D., R.N., Executive Director
Web address: www.pbmchealth.org

PHELPS MEMORIAL HOSPITAL CENTER (O, 149 beds) 701 North Broadway, Sleepy Hollow, NY, Zip 10591-1020; tel. 914/366-3000, Beata Mastalerz, Executive Director

PLAINVIEW HOSPITAL (O, 156 beds) 888 Old Country Road, Plainview, NY, Zip 11803-4978; tel. 516/719-3000, Kerri Scanlon, R.N., Executive Director
Web address: https://www.planview.com/

SOUTH OAKS HOSPITAL (O, 202 beds) 400 Sunrise Highway, Amityville, NY, Zip 11701-2508; tel. 631/264-4000, Michael Scarpelli, Executive Director

SOUTH SHORE UNIVERSITY HOSPITAL (O, 322 beds) 301 East Main Street, Bay Shore, NY, Zip 11706-8458; tel. 631/968-3000, Irene Macyk, R.N., MS, Ph.D., Executive Director
Web address: https://www.northwell.edu/find-care/locations/southside-hospital

STATEN ISLAND UNIVERSITY HOSPITAL (O, 595 beds) 475 Seaview Avenue, Staten Island, NY, Zip 10305-3436; tel. 718/226-9000, Brahim Ardolic, M.D., Chief Executive Officer
Web address: www.siuh.edu

Owned, leased, sponsored:	13 hospitals	5216 beds
Contract-managed:	0 hospitals	0 beds
Totals:	13 hospitals	5216 beds

★0024: NORTHWESTERN MEMORIAL HEALTHCARE (NP)
251 East Huron Street, Chicago, IL Zip 60611-2908; tel. 312/926-2000, Howard Chrisman, President and Chief Executive Officer
(Centralized Health System)

ILLINOIS: NORTHWESTERN MEDICINE CENTRAL DUPAGE HOSPITAL (O, 429 beds) 25 North Winfield Road, Winfield, IL, Zip 60190; tel. 630/933-1600, Kenneth Hedley, President

NORTHWESTERN MEDICINE DELNOR HOSPITAL (O, 159 beds) 300 Randall Road, Geneva, IL, Zip 60134-4200; tel. 630/208-3000, Emily Cochran. Jakacki, President
Web address: www.nm.org

NORTHWESTERN MEDICINE KISHWAUKEE HOSPITAL (O, 98 beds) 1 Kish Hospital Drive, DeKalb, IL, Zip 60115-9602, P O Box 707, Zip 60115-0707, tel. 815/756-1521, Maura O'Toole, President

NORTHWESTERN MEDICINE LAKE FOREST HOSPITAL (O, 152 beds) 1000 North Westmoreland Road, Lake Forest, IL, Zip 60045-1696, 1000 N Westmoreland Road, Zip 60045-1658, tel. 847/234-5600, Seamus Collins, President
Web address: https://www.nm.org/locations/lake-forest-hospital

NORTHWESTERN MEDICINE MARIANJOY REHABILITATION HOSPITAL (O, 125 beds) 26 West 171 Roosevelt Road, Wheaton, IL, Zip 60187-0795, P O Box 795, Zip 60187-0795, tel. 630/909-8000, Anne Hubling, R.N., President and Chief Nurse Executive
Web address: https://www.nm.org/locations/marianjoy-rehabilitation-hospital

NORTHWESTERN MEDICINE MCHENRY (O, 327 beds) 4201 Medical Center Drive, McHenry, IL, Zip 60050-8409; tel. 815/344-5000, Catie Schmit, President

NORTHWESTERN MEDICINE PALOS HOSPITAL (O, 406 beds) 12251 South 80th Avenue, Palos Heights, IL, Zip 60463-0930; tel. 708/923-4000, Jeff Good, President
Web address: https://www.nm.org/locations/palos-hospital

NORTHWESTERN MEDICINE VALLEY WEST HOSPITAL (O, 19 beds) 1302 North Main Street, Sandwich, IL, Zip 60548-2587; tel. 815/786-8484, Maura O'Toole, President
Web address: www.nm.org

NORTHWESTERN MEMORIAL HOSPITAL (O, 943 beds) 251 East Huron Street, Chicago, IL, Zip 60611-2908; tel. 312/926-2000, Thomas J. McAfee, President

Owned, leased, sponsored:	9 hospitals	2658 beds
Contract-managed:	0 hospitals	0 beds
Totals:	9 hospitals	2658 beds

★2285: NORTON HEALTHCARE (NP)
4967 US Highway 42, Suite 100, Louisville, KY Zip 40222-6363, P O Box 35070, Zip 40232-5070, tel. 502/629-8000, Russell Cox, President and Chief Executive Officer
(Centralized Health System)

INDIANA: NORTON CLARK HOSPITAL (O, 185 beds) 1220 Missouri Avenue, Jeffersonville, IN, Zip 47130-3743, P O Box 69, Zip 47131-0600, tel. 812/282-6631, Kathleen Exline, R.N., Chief Administrative Officer
Web address: www.clarkmemorial.org

NORTON SCOTT HOSPITAL (O, 35 beds) 1451 North Gardner Street, Scottsburg, IN, Zip 47170, Box 430, Zip 47170-0430, tel. 812/752-3456, Bruce J. Tassin, Interim Chief Executive Officer
Web address: www.scottmemorial.com

KENTUCKY: NORTON CHILDREN'S HOSPITAL (O, 287 beds) 231 East Chestnut Street, Louisville, KY, Zip 40202-1821; tel. 502/629-6000, Diane M. Scardino, Chief Administrative Officer
Web address: www.https://nortonchildrens.com/location/hospitals/norton-childrens-hospital/

For explanation of codes following names, see page B2.
★ Indicates Type III membership in the American Hospital Association.

Systems / NYC Health + Hospitals

NORTON HOSPITAL (O, 1272 beds) 200 East Chestnut Street, Louisville, KY, Zip 40202-1800, P O Box 35070, Zip 40232-5070, tel. 502/629-8000, Matthew Ayers, Chief Administrative Officer

Owned, leased, sponsored:	4 hospitals	1779 beds
Contract-managed:	0 hospitals	0 beds
Totals:	4 hospitals	1779 beds

★0139: **NOVANT HEALTH (NP)**

2085 Frontis Plaza Boulevard, Winston Salem, NC Zip 27103-5614; tel. 888/976-5611, Carl S. Armato, President and Chief Executive Officer

(Independent Hospital System)

NORTH CAROLINA: ASHE MEMORIAL HOSPITAL (C, 25 beds) 200 Hospital Avenue, Jefferson, NC, Zip 28640-9244; tel. 336/846-7101, Brian Yates, Chief Executive Officer
Web address: www.ashememorial.org

NOVANT HEALTH BALLANTYNE MEDICAL CENTER (O, 36 beds) 10905 Providence Road West, Charlotte, NC, Zip 28277; tel. 980/488-4000, Joy Greear, President and Chief Operating Officer

NOVANT HEALTH BRUNSWICK MEDICAL CENTER (O, 54 beds) 240 Hospital Drive NE, Bolivia, NC, Zip 28422-8346; tel. 910/721-1000, Heather King, President and Chief Operating Officer
Web address: https://www.novanthealth.org

NOVANT HEALTH CHARLOTTE ORTHOPAEDIC HOSPITAL (O, 15 beds) 1901 Randolph Road, Charlotte, NC, Zip 28207-1195; tel. 704/316-2000, Jamie Feinour, President and Chief Operating Officer

NOVANT HEALTH FORSYTH MEDICAL CENTER (O, 915 beds) 3333 Silas Creek Parkway, Winston-Salem, NC, Zip 27103-3090; tel. 336/718-5000, Chad Setliff, Senior Vice President, President Novant Health Forsyth Medical Center and Greater Winston-Salem Market
Web address: https://www.novanthealth.org

NOVANT HEALTH HUNTERSVILLE MEDICAL CENTER (O, 91 beds) 10030 Gilead Road, Huntersville, NC, Zip 28078-7545, P O Box 3508, Zip 28070-3508, tel. 704/316-4000, Mike Riley, President and Chief Operating Officer

NOVANT HEALTH MATTHEWS MEDICAL CENTER (O, 117 beds) 1500 Matthews Township Parkway, Matthews, NC, Zip 28105-4656; tel. 704/384-6500, Jason Bernd, President and Chief Operating Officer
Web address: https://www.novanthealth.org

NOVANT HEALTH MEDICAL PARK HOSPITAL (O, 21 beds) 1950 South Hawthorne Road, Winston-Salem, NC, Zip 27103-3993; tel. 336/718-0600, Alisha C. Hutchens, President and Chief Operating Officer
Web address: https://www.novanthealth.org/medical-park-hospital.aspx

NOVANT HEALTH MINT HILL MEDICAL CENTER (O, 36 beds) 8201 Healthcare Loop, Charlotte, NC, Zip 28215-7072; tel. 980/302-1000, Joy Greear, President and Chief Operating Officer

NOVANT HEALTH NEW HANOVER REGIONAL MEDICAL CENTER (O, 697 beds) 2131 South 17th Street, Wilmington, NC, Zip 28401-7483, P O Box 9000, Zip 28402-9000, tel. 910/343-7000, Ernest L. Bovio Jr, Senior Vice President & President Novant Health New Hanover Regional Medical Center & Coastal Market
Web address: https://www.novanthealth.org/locations/medical-centers/new-hanover-regional-medical-center/

NOVANT HEALTH PENDER MEDICAL CENTER (O, 64 beds) 507 East Freemont Street, Burgaw, NC, Zip 28425-5131; tel. 910/259-5451, Ruth Glaser, President and Chief Operating Officer
Web address: www.pendermemorial.org

NOVANT HEALTH PRESBYTERIAN MEDICAL CENTER (O, 588 beds) 200 Hawthorne Lane, Charlotte, NC, Zip 28204-2528, P O Box 33549, Zip 28233-3549, tel. 704/384-4000, Saad Ehtisham, FACHE, Senior Vice President and President Novant Health Presbyterian Medical Center & Greater Charlotte Market
Web address: www.novanthealth.org

NOVANT HEALTH ROWAN MEDICAL CENTER (O, 149 beds) 612 Mocksville Avenue, Salisbury, NC, Zip 28144-2799; tel. 704/210-5000, Gary Blabon, President and Chief Operating Officer
Web address: https://www.novanthealth.org/rowan-medical-center.aspx

NOVANT HEALTH THOMASVILLE MEDICAL CENTER (O, 87 beds) 207 Old Lexington Road, Thomasville, NC, Zip 27360-3428, P O Box 789, Zip 27361-0789, tel. 336/472-2000, Jonathan D. Applebaum, President and Chief Operating Officer
Web address: www.thomasvillemedicalcenter.org

SOUTH CAROLINA: COASTAL CAROLINA HOSPITAL (O, 35 beds) 1000 Medical Center Drive, Hardeeville, SC, Zip 29927-3446; tel. 843/784-8000, Ryan D. Lee, FACHE, Chief Executive Officer
Web address: www.coastalhospital.com

EAST COOPER MEDICAL CENTER (O, 140 beds) 2000 Hospital Drive, Mount Pleasant, SC, Zip 29464-3764; tel. 843/881-0100, Tyler Sherrill, Chief Executive Officer
Web address: www.eastcoopermedctr.com

HILTON HEAD HOSPITAL (O, 93 beds) 25 Hospital Center Boulevard, Hilton Head Island, SC, Zip 29926-2738; tel. 843/681-6122, Joel C. Taylor, Market Chief Executive Officer

Owned, leased, sponsored:	16 hospitals	3138 beds
Contract-managed:	1 hospitals	25 beds
Totals:	17 hospitals	3163 beds

★1098: **NUVANCE HEALTH (NP)**

24 Hospital Avenue, Danbury, CT Zip 06810-6099; tel. 203/739-7066, John M. Murphy, M.D., President and Chief Executive Officer

CONNECTICUT: DANBURY HOSPITAL (O, 293 beds) 24 Hospital Avenue, Danbury, CT, Zip 06810-6099; tel. 203/739-7000, Sharon Adams, President
Web address: www.danburyhospital.org

NORWALK HOSPITAL (O, 139 beds) 34 Maple Street, Norwalk, CT, Zip 06850-3894; tel. 203/852-2000, Peter Cordeau, President
Web address: www.norwalkhospital.org

SHARON HOSPITAL (O, 28 beds) 50 Hospital Hill Road, Sharon, CT, Zip 06069-2096, P O Box 789, Zip 06069-0789, tel. 860/364-4000, Christina McCulloch, President
Web address: www.sharonhospital.com

NEW YORK: NORTHERN DUTCHESS HOSPITAL (O, 75 beds) 6511 Springbrook Avenue, Rhinebeck, NY, Zip 12572-3709, P O Box 5002, Zip 12572-5002, tel. 845/876-3001, Denise George, R.N., President
Web address: https://www.nuvancehealth.org/locations/northern-dutchess-hospital

PUTNAM HOSPITAL (O, 62 beds) 670 Stoneleigh Avenue, Carmel, NY, Zip 10512-3997; tel. 845/279-5711, Mark Hirko, M.D., FACS, President

VASSAR BROTHERS MEDICAL CENTER (O, 329 beds) 45 Reade Place, Poughkeepsie, NY, Zip 12601-3947; tel. 845/454-8500, Susan Browning, President
Web address: https://www.nuvancehealth.org/locations/vassar-brothers-medical-center

Owned, leased, sponsored:	6 hospitals	926 beds
Contract-managed:	0 hospitals	0 beds
Totals:	6 hospitals	926 beds

★3075: **NYC HEALTH + HOSPITALS (NP)**

50 Water Street, 17th Floor, New York, NY Zip 10004; tel. 212/788-3321, Mitchell H. Katz, M.D., Chief Executive Officer

(Decentralized Health System)

NEW YORK: NYC HEALTH + HOSPITALS / BELLEVUE (O, 853 beds) 462 First Avenue, New York, NY, Zip 10016-9198; tel. 212/562-4141, William Hicks, Chief Executive Officer
Web address: www.nyc.gov/bellevue

NYC HEALTH + HOSPITALS / ELMHURST (O, 512 beds) 79-01 Broadway, Elmhurst, NY, Zip 11373-1329; tel. 718/334-4000, Helen Arteaga. Landaverde, Chief Executive Officer
Web address: https://www.nychealthandhospitals.org/locations/elmhurst/

For explanation of codes following names, see page B2.
★ Indicates Type III membership in the American Hospital Association.

Systems / NYC Health + Hospitals

NYC HEALTH + HOSPITALS / GOUVERNEUR (O, 196 beds) 227 Madison Street, New York, NY, Zip 10002; tel. 212/238-7000, Martha Adams Sullivan, Chief Executive Officer

NYC HEALTH + HOSPITALS / HARLEM (O, 241 beds) 506 Lenox Avenue, New York, NY, Zip 10037-1802; tel. 212/939-1000, Georges Leconte, Chief Executive Officer
Web address: www.nyc.gov/html/hhc/harlem

NYC HEALTH + HOSPITALS / HENRY J CARTER SPECIALTY HOSPITAL AND MEDICAL CENTER (O, 365 beds) 1752 Park Avenue, New York, NY, Zip 10035; tel. 646/686-0000, Floyd R. Long, Executive Director

NYC HEALTH + HOSPITALS / JACOBI (O, 520 beds) 1400 Pelham Parkway South, Bronx, NY, Zip 10461-1197; tel. 718/918-5000, Christopher Mastromano, Chief Executive Officer
Web address: www.nyc.gov/html/hhc/jacobi/home.html

NYC HEALTH + HOSPITALS / KINGS COUNTY (O, 505 beds) 451 Clarkson Avenue, Brooklyn, NY, Zip 11203-2054; tel. 718/245-3131, Sheldon Mcleod, Chief Executive Officer

NYC HEALTH + HOSPITALS / LINCOLN (O, 319 beds) 234 East 149th Street, Bronx, NY, Zip 10451-5504, 234 East 149th Street, Room 2D3, Zip 10451-5504, tel. 718/579-5700, Christopher Roker, Chief Executive Officer
Web address: https://www.nychealthandhospitals.org/

NYC HEALTH + HOSPITALS / METROPOLITAN (O, 281 beds) 1901 First Avenue, New York, NY, Zip 10029-7404; tel. 212/423-6262, Cristina Contreras, Chief Executive Officer
Web address: www.nyc.gov/html/hhc/mhc/html/home/home.shtml

NYC HEALTH + HOSPITALS / QUEENS (O, 253 beds) 82-68 164th Street, Jamaica, NY, Zip 11432-1104; tel. 718/883-3000, Neil J. Moore, Chief Executive Officer

NYC HEALTH + HOSPITALS / SEA VIEW (O, 304 beds) 460 Brielle Avenue, Staten Island, NY, Zip 10314; tel. 212/390-8181, Jane M. Lyons, Executive Director

NYC HEALTH + HOSPITALS / SOUTH BROOKLYN HEALTH (O, 307 beds) 2601 Ocean Parkway, Brooklyn, NY, Zip 11235-7795; tel. 718/616-3000, Svetlana Lipyanskaya, Chief Executive Officer
Web address: https://www.nychealthandhospitals.org/Coneylsland/

NYC HEALTH + HOSPITALS / WOODHULL (O, 243 beds) 760 Broadway, Brooklyn, NY, Zip 11206-5383; tel. 718/963-8000, Gregory Calliste, Ph.D., FACHE, Chief Executive Officer
Web address: https://www.nychealthandhospitals.org/Woodhull/

Owned, leased, sponsored:	13 hospitals	4899 beds
Contract-managed:	0 hospitals	0 beds
Totals:	13 hospitals	4899 beds

0616: OCEANS HEALTHCARE (IO)

5360 Legacy Drive, Suite 101, Plano, TX Zip 75024-3130; tel. 972/464-0022, Stuart Archer, Chief Executive Officer
(Independent Hospital System)

LOUISIANA: LOUISIANA BEHAVIORAL HEALTH (O, 89 beds) 9320 Linwood Avenue, Shreveport, LA, Zip 71106-7003, 3905 Hedgcoxe Road, Unit 250249, Plano, TX, Zip 75025-0840, tel. 318/644-8830, Lee Edge, Administrator

OCEANS BEHAVIORAL HOSPITAL OF ALEXANDRIA (O, 24 beds) 2621 North Bolton Avenue, Alexandria, LA, Zip 71303-4506; tel. 318/448-8473, Justin McDaniel, R.N., Administrator
Web address: www.https://oceanshealthcare.com/ohc-location/alexandria/

OCEANS BEHAVIORAL HOSPITAL OF BATON ROUGE-SOUTH (O, 20 beds) 11135 Florida Boulevard, Baton Rouge, LA, Zip 70815-2013; tel. 225/356-7030, Valerie Dalton, R.N., Administrator
Web address: www.obhbr.info/

OCEANS BEHAVIORAL HOSPITAL OF BROUSSARD (O, 38 beds) 418 Albertson Parkway, Broussard, LA, Zip 70518-4971; tel. 337/237-6444, Amy Dysart-Credeur, Administrator

OCEANS BEHAVIORAL HOSPITAL OF DERIDDER (O, 20 beds) 1420 Blankenship Drive, Deridder, LA, Zip 70634-4604; tel. 337/460-9472, Nicholas D. Guillory, MSN, Interim Administrator, Executive Vice President, Regional Operations
Web address: www.https://oceanshealthcare.com/ohc-location/deridder/

OCEANS BEHAVIORAL HOSPITAL OF GREATER NEW ORLEANS (O, 30 beds) 716 Village Road, Kenner, LA, Zip 70065-2751; tel. 504/464-8895, Deborah Spiers, Administrator
Web address: www.obhgno.info/

OCEANS BEHAVIORAL HOSPITAL OF LAKE CHARLES (O, 40 beds) 4250 5th Avenue, Lake Charles, LA, Zip 70607-3900; tel. 337/474-7581, Misty Kelly, Chief Executive Officer and Administrator

OCEANS BEHAVIORAL HOSPITAL OF OPELOUSAS (O, 20 beds) 1310 Heather Drive, Opelousas, LA, Zip 70570-7714; tel. 337/948-8820, Cayle P. Guillory, Administrator
Web address: www.https://oceanshealthcare.com/ohc-location/opelousas/

MISSISSIPPI: OCEANS BEHAVIORAL HOSPITAL BILOXI (O, 55 beds) 180 Debuys Road, Biloxi, MS, Zip 39531-4402; tel. 228/388-0600, Cliff Hermes, Administrator
Web address: www.https://oceanshealthcare.com/biloxi

OCEANS BEHAVIORAL HOSPITAL OF TUPELO (O, 34 beds) 4579 South Eason Boulevard, Suite B, Tupelo, MS, Zip 38801-6539, 3905 Hedgcoxe Road, Unit 250249, Plano, TX, Zip 75025-0840, tel. 662/268-4418, Stuart Archer, Chief Executive Officer
Web address: www.oceanshealthcare.com

OKLAHOMA: BEHAVIORAL HEALTH CENTER OF PORTER VILLAGE (O, 48 beds) 506 Wellness Way, Norman, OK, Zip 73071, 3905 Hedgcoxe Road, Unit 250249, Plano, TX, Zip 75025, tel. 405/754-1309, William Southwick, Hospital Administrator

TEXAS: OCEANS BEHAVIORAL HEALTH CENTER PERMIAN BASIN (O, 62 beds) 3300 South FM 1788, Midland, TX, Zip 79706-2601; tel. 432/561-5915, Emileh Flitton, Administrator
Web address: www.oceanspermianbasin.com/

OCEANS BEHAVIORAL HEALTH OF WACO (O, 48 beds) 5931 Crosslake Parkway, Waco, TX, Zip 76712-6986; tel. 254/870-4874, Stuart Archer, Chief Executive Officer
Web address: www.https://oceanshealthcare.com/

OCEANS BEHAVIORAL HOSPITAL ABILENE (O, 90 beds) 4225 Woods Place, Abilene, TX, Zip 79602-7991; tel. 325/691-0030, Stacy Sanford, Administrator

OCEANS BEHAVIORAL HOSPITAL KATY (O, 48 beds) 455 Park Grove Lane, Katy, TX, Zip 77450-1572; tel. 281/492-8888, Shannon Brown, Hospital Administrator
Web address: www.memorialhermann.org/locations/katy-rehab/

OCEANS BEHAVIORAL HOSPITAL LONGVIEW (O, 24 beds) 615 Clinic Drive, Longview, TX, Zip 75605-5172; tel. 903/212-3105, Ben Kellogg, Administrator

OCEANS BEHAVIORAL HOSPITAL LUFKIN (O, 24 beds) 302 Gobblers Knob Road, Lufkin, TX, Zip 75904-5419; tel. 936/632-2276, Laci Laird, Administrator
Web address: www.oceanslufkin.com/

OCEANS BEHAVIORAL HOSPITAL OF AMARILLO (O, 28 beds) 7501 Wallace Boulevard, Suite 200, Amarillo, TX, Zip 79124-2150, 3905 Hedgcoxe Road, Unit 250249, Plano, TX, Zip 75025-0840, tel. 806/310-2205, Heather Duby, Administrator
Web address: www.oceanshealthcare.com

OCEANS BEHAVIORAL HOSPITAL OF CORPUS CHRISTI (O, 42 beds) 600 Elizabeth Street, Building B, 5th Floor, Corpus Christi, TX, Zip 78404-2235, 3905 Hedgcoxe Road Unit 250249, Plano, Zip 75025, tel. 361/371-8933, Michelle C. Lozano, Chief Executive Officer and Hospital Administrator

OCEANS BEHAVIORAL HOSPITAL OF LUBBOCK (O, 32 beds) 4202 Princeton Street, Lubbock, TX, Zip 79415, 3905 Hedgcoxe Road, Unit 250249, Plano, Zip 75025-0840, tel. 806/516-1190, Marybeth Moran Murphy, Hospital Chief Executive Officer
Web address: www.https://oceanshealthcare.com/ohc-location/lubbock/

OCEANS BEHAVIORAL HOSPITAL OF PASADENA (O, 22 beds) 4001 Preston Drive, Pasadena, TX, Zip 77505-2069; tel. 832/619-8836, Shamieka Thomas, Administrator

Owned, leased, sponsored:	21 hospitals	838 beds
Contract-managed:	0 hospitals	0 beds
Totals:	21 hospitals	838 beds

For explanation of codes following names, see page B2.
★ Indicates Type III membership in the American Hospital Association.

Systems / Oglethorpe Recovery and Behavioral Hospitals

★**0359: OCHSNER HEALTH (NP)**
1514 Jefferson Highway, New Orleans, LA Zip 70121-2429;
tel. 800/874-8984, Peter November, Chief Executive Officer
(Centralized Health System)

ALABAMA: OCHSNER CHOCTAW GENERAL (O, 25 beds) 401 Vanity Fair Avenue, Butler, AL, Zip 36904-3032; tel. 205/459-9100, Kawanda Johnson, Ph.D., MSN, Administrator
Web address: www.choctawgeneral.com/cgh/

LOUISIANA: LEONARD J. CHABERT MEDICAL CENTER (C, 45 beds) 1978 Industrial Boulevard, Houma, LA, Zip 70363-7094; tel. 985/873-2200, Fernis LeBlanc, Chief Executive Officer

OCHSNER ABROM KAPLAN MEMORIAL HOSPITAL (O, 20 beds) 1310 West Seventh Street, Kaplan, LA, Zip 70548-2910; tel. 337/643-8300, Jennifer Gerard, R.N., Assistant Vice President, Nursing and Hospital Administration
Web address: https://www.ochsner.org/locations/ochsner-abrom-kaplan-memorial-hospital

OCHSNER ACADIA GENERAL HOSPITAL (O, 30 beds) 1305 Crowley Rayne Highway, Crowley, LA, Zip 70526-8202; tel. 337/783-3222, Caroline Marceaux, MSN, R.N., Assistant Vice President, Nursing and Hospital Administration

OCHSNER AMERICAN LEGION HOSPITAL (L, 41 beds) 1634 Elton Road, Jennings, LA, Zip 70546-3614; tel. 337/616-7000, Dana D. Williams, Chief Executive Officer
Web address: www.jalh.com

OCHSNER LSU HEALTH SHREVEPORT–ACADEMIC MEDICAL CENTER (O, 251 beds) 1501 Kings Highway, Shreveport, LA, Zip 71103-4228, P O Box 33932, Zip 71130-3932, tel. 318/675-5000, Chris Mangin, Chief Executive Officer
Web address: www.lsuhscshreveport.edu

OCHSNER LSU HEALTH SHREVEPORT–MONROE MEDICAL CENTER (O, 127 beds) 4864 Jackson Street, Monroe, LA, Zip 71202-6497, P O Box 1881, Zip 71210-8005, tel. 318/330-7000, Mark A. Randolph, Chief Executive Officer

OCHSNER LSU HEALTH SHREVEPORT–ST. MARY MEDICAL CENTER, LLC (O, 133 beds) 1 Saint Mary Place, Shreveport, LA, Zip 71101-4307; tel. 318/626-0050, Riley Waddell, Chief Executive Officer
Web address: www.ochsnerlsuhs.org

OCHSNER LAFAYETTE GENERAL MEDICAL CENTER (O, 527 beds) 1214 Coolidge Boulevard, Lafayette, LA, Zip 70503-2696, P O Box 52009 OCS, Zip 70505-2009, tel. 337/289-7991, Al J. Patin, R.N., Chief Executive Officer

OCHSNER MEDICAL CENTER–BATON ROUGE (O, 169 beds) 17000 Medical Center Drive, Baton Rouge, LA, Zip 70816-3224; tel. 225/752-2470, Charles D. Daigle, Chief Executive Officer
Web address: https://www.ochsner.org/locations/ochsner-medical-center-baton-rouge

OCHSNER MEDICAL CENTER–KENNER (O, 111 beds) 180 West Esplanade Avenue, Kenner, LA, Zip 70065-6001; tel. 504/468-8600, Stephen Robinson Jr, FACHE, Chief Executive Officer
Web address: https://www.ochsner.org/locations/ochsner-medical-center-kenner/

OCHSNER MEDICAL CENTER (O, 852 beds) 1514 Jefferson Highway, New Orleans, LA, Zip 70121-2429; tel. 504/842-3000
Web address: www.ochsner.org

OCHSNER ST. ANNE GENERAL HOSPITAL (O, 28 beds) 4608 Highway 1, Raceland, LA, Zip 70394-2623; tel. 985/537-6841, Fernis LeBlanc, Chief Executive Officer, Bayou Region
Web address: https://www.ochsner.org/locations/ochsner-st-anne

OCHSNER ST. MARTIN HOSPITAL (O, 25 beds) 210 Champagne Boulevard, Breaux Bridge, LA, Zip 70517-3700, P O Box 357, Zip 70517-0357, tel. 337/332-2178, Jennifer Vicknair, R.N., Assistant Vice President, Nursing and Hospital Administration

OCHSNER ST. MARY (C, 47 beds) 1125 Marguerite Street, Morgan City, LA, Zip 70380-1855, P O Box 2308, Zip 70381-2308, tel. 985/384-2200, Jennifer Wise, Hospital Administrator, Chief Nursing Officer
Web address: https://www.ochsner.org

OCHSNER UNIVERSITY HOSPITAL & CLINICS (O, 52 beds) 2390 West Congress Street, Lafayette, LA, Zip 70506-4298; tel. 337/261-6000, Glenn Dailey, Chief Executive Officer

SLIDELL MEMORIAL HOSPITAL EAST (L, 77 beds) 100 Medical Center Drive, Slidell, LA, Zip 70461-5520; tel. 985/649-7070, Sandy Badinger, Chief Executive Officer
Web address: https://www.ochsner.org/locations/slidell-memorial-hospital-east

SLIDELL MEMORIAL HOSPITAL (C, 202 beds) 1001 Gause Boulevard, Slidell, LA, Zip 70458-2987; tel. 985/280-2200, Sandy Badinger, Chief Executive Officer
Web address: www.slidellmemorial.org

ST. BERNARD PARISH HOSPITAL (C, 24 beds) 8000 West Judge Perez Drive, Chalmette, LA, Zip 70043-1668; tel. 504/826-9500, Alanna Fast, Chief Executive Officer

ST. CHARLES PARISH HOSPITAL (C, 39 beds) 1057 Paul Maillard Road, Luling, LA, Zip 70070-4349, P O Box 87, Zip 70070-0087, tel. 985/785-6242, Keith Dacus, MSC, Chief Executive Officer
Web address: https://www.ochsner.org/locations/st-charles-parish-hospital/

MISSISSIPPI: OCHSNER LAIRD HOSPITAL (O, 25 beds) 25117 Highway 15, Union, MS, Zip 39365-9099; tel. 601/774-8214, Thomas G. Bartlett III, Administrator
Web address: www.lairdhospital.com/lh/

OCHSNER MEDICAL CENTER–HANCOCK (C, 102 beds) 149 Drinkwater Boulevard, Bay Saint Louis, MS, Zip 39520-1658, Bay St Louis, tel. 228/467-8600, Jeffery Edge, Chief Executive Officer

OCHSNER RUSH MEDICAL CENTER (O, 182 beds) 1314 19th Avenue, Meridian, MS, Zip 39301-4195; tel. 601/483-0011, Larkin Kennedy, Chief Executive Officer
Web address: www.rushhealthsystems.org/rfh/

OCHSNER SCOTT REGIONAL (O, 25 beds) 317 Highway 13 South, Morton, MS, Zip 39117-3353, P O Box 259, Zip 39117-0259, tel. 601/732-6301, Heather Davis, Administrator

OCHSNER SPECIALTY HOSPITAL (O, 30 beds) 1314 19th Avenue, Meridian, MS, Zip 39301-4116; tel. 601/703-4211, Kawanda Johnson, Ph.D., MSN, Administrator and Executive Vice President
Web address: www.specialtyhospitalofmeridian.com/shm/

OCHSNER STENNIS HOSPITAL (O, 25 beds) 14365 Highway 16 West, De Kalb, MS, Zip 39328-7974; tel. 769/486-1000, Kristin Molony, Chief Executive Officer
Web address: https://www.ochsnerrush.org/hospitals/ochsner-stennis-hospital/

OCHSNER WATKINS HOSPITAL (O, 25 beds) 605 South Archusa Avenue, Quitman, MS, Zip 39355-2331; tel. 601/776-6925, Kawanda Johnson, Ph.D., MSN, Administrator

Owned, leased, sponsored:	21 hospitals	2780 beds
Contract-managed:	6 hospitals	459 beds
Totals:	27 hospitals	3239 beds

0978: OGLETHORPE RECOVERY AND BEHAVIORAL HOSPITALS (IO)
201 North Franklin Street, Tampa, FL Zip 33602-5182;
tel. 813/978-1933, John Picciano, Chief Executive Officer

FLORIDA: PORT ST. LUCIE HOSPITAL (O, 75 beds) 2550 SE Walton Road, Port St Lucie, FL, Zip 34952-7168; tel. 772/335-0400, Julia C. Fortune, Acting Administrator/Risk Manager

SPRINGBROOK HOSPITAL (O, 66 beds) 7007 Grove Road, Brooksville, FL, Zip 34609-8610; tel. 352/596-4306, Samuel Bennett, Chief Executive Officer
Web address: www.springbrookhospital.org/

THE BLACKBERRY CENTER (O, 64 beds) 91 Beehive Circle, Saint Cloud, FL, Zip 34769-1432, St. Cloud, tel. 321/805-5090, Rick Bennett, Director
Web address: www.blackberrycenter.com

LOUISIANA: BATON ROUGE BEHAVIORAL HOSPITAL (O, 15 beds) 4040 North Boulevard, Baton Rouge, LA, Zip 70806-3829; tel. 225/300-8470, Larry Godfrey, Chief Executive Officer

For explanation of codes following names, see page B2.
★ Indicates Type III membership in the American Hospital Association.

Systems / Oglethorpe Recovery and Behavioral Hospitals

OHIO: RIDGEVIEW BEHAVIORAL HOSPITAL (O, 40 beds) 17872 Lincoln Highway, Middle Point, OH, Zip 45863–9700; tel. 419/968–2950, Pat Tracy, Administrator
Web address: www.ridgeviewhospital.net/

Owned, leased, sponsored:	5 hospitals	260 beds
Contract-managed:	0 hospitals	0 beds
Totals:	5 hospitals	260 beds

0537: OHIO DEPARTMENT OF MENTAL HEALTH (NP)
30 East Broad Street, 8th Floor, Columbus, OH Zip 43215–3430; tel. 614/466–2297, Tracy Plouck, Director
(Independent Hospital System)

OHIO: APPALACHIAN BEHAVIORAL HEALTHCARE (O, 224 beds) 100 Hospital Drive, Athens, OH, Zip 45701–2301; tel. 740/594–5000, Elaine Crnkovic, Chief Executive Officer
Web address: www.mh.state.oh.us
HEARTLAND BEHAVIORAL HEALTHCARE (O, 152 beds) 3000 Erie Stree South, Massillon, OH, Zip 44646–7993, 3000 Erie Street South, Zip 44646–7976, tel. 330/833–3135, Andrea Bucci, Chief Executive Officer
Web address: www.https://mha.ohio.gov/about-us/regional-psychiatric-hospitals/healthcare-facilities/heartland/heartland
NORTHCOAST BEHAVIORAL HEALTHCARE (O, 258 beds) 1756 Sagamore Road, Northfield, OH, Zip 44067–1086; tel. 330/467–7131, Douglas W. Kern, Chief Executive Officer
NORTHWEST OHIO PSYCHIATRIC HOSPITAL (O, 112 beds) 930 Detroit Avenue, Toledo, OH, Zip 43614–2701; tel. 419/381–1881, Charlie Hughes, Chief Executive Officer
Web address: www.https://mha.ohio.gov/about-us/regional-psychiatric-hospitals/locations/northwest-ohio-psychiatric-hospital
SUMMIT BEHAVIORAL HEALTHCARE (O, 291 beds) 1101 Summit Road, Cincinnati, OH, Zip 45237–2652; tel. 513/948–3600, Elizabeth Banks, Chief Executive Officer
Web address: www.mh.state.oh.us/
TWIN VALLEY BEHAVIORAL HEALTHCARE (O, 178 beds) 2200 West Broad Street, Columbus, OH, Zip 43223–1297; tel. 614/752–0333, Frank Beel, Chief Executive Officer
Web address: www.mh.state.oh.us/ibhs/bhos/tvbh.html

Owned, leased, sponsored:	6 hospitals	1215 beds
Contract-managed:	0 hospitals	0 beds
Totals:	6 hospitals	1215 beds

★0251: OHIO STATE UNIVERSITY HEALTH SYSTEM (NP)
370 West Ninth Avenue, Columbus, OH Zip 43210–1238; tel. 614/685–9015, John Warner, M.D., Chief Executive Officer
(Centralized Physician/Insurance Health System)

OHIO: OHIO STATE UNIVERSITY WEXNER MEDICAL CENTER (O, 1150 beds) 410 West 10th Avenue, Columbus, OH, Zip 43210–1240; tel. 614/293–8000, John Warner, M.D., Chief Executive Officer
Web address: www.https://wexnermedical.osu.edu/
THE OSUCCC–JAMES (O, 356 beds) 460 West Tenth Avenue, Columbus, OH, Zip 43210–1240; tel. 614/293–3300, David Cohn, Interim Chief Executive Officer

Owned, leased, sponsored:	2 hospitals	1506 beds
Contract-managed:	0 hospitals	0 beds
Totals:	2 hospitals	1506 beds

★0162: OHIOHEALTH (NP)
3430 Ohio Health Parkway, Columbus, OH Zip 43202–1575; tel. 614/544–4455, Stephen Markovich, M.D., President and Chief Executive Officer
(Moderately Centralized Health System)

OHIO: MORROW COUNTY HOSPITAL (C, 22 beds) 651 West Marion Road, Mount Gilead, OH, Zip 43338–1027; tel. 419/946–5015, Michael Hyek, President
OHIOHEALTH BERGER HOSPITAL (O, 56 beds) 600 North Pickaway Street, Circleville, OH, Zip 43113–1447; tel. 740/474–2126, Casey Liddy, President
Web address: https://www.ohiohealth.com/locations/hospitals/berger-hospital
OHIOHEALTH DOCTORS HOSPITAL (O, 206 beds) 5100 West Broad Street, Columbus, OH, Zip 43228–1607; tel. 614/544–1000, Lindsey Osting, President
Web address: www.ohiohealth.com
OHIOHEALTH DUBLIN METHODIST HOSPITAL (O, 113 beds) 7500 Hospital Drive, Dublin, OH, Zip 43016–8518; tel. 614/544–8000, Cherie L. Smith, Ph.D., R.N., President
OHIOHEALTH GRADY MEMORIAL HOSPITAL (O, 61 beds) 561 West Central Avenue, Delaware, OH, Zip 43015–1410; tel. 740/615–1000, Cherie L. Smith, Ph.D., R.N., President
Web address: https://www.ohiohealth.com/locations/hospitals/grady-memorial-hospital
OHIOHEALTH GRANT MEDICAL CENTER (O, 471 beds) 111 South Grant Avenue, Columbus, OH, Zip 43215–1898; tel. 614/566–9000, Michael Lawson, President
OHIOHEALTH HARDIN MEMORIAL HOSPITAL (O, 25 beds) 921 East Franklin Street, Kenton, OH, Zip 43326–2099; tel. 419/673–0761, Joy Bischoff, MSN, R.N., President
Web address: www.hardinmemorial.org
OHIOHEALTH MANSFIELD HOSPITAL (O, 259 beds) 335 Glessner Avenue, Mansfield, OH, Zip 44903–2265; tel. 419/526–8000, Curtis Gingrich, M.D., President
OHIOHEALTH MARION GENERAL HOSPITAL (O, 210 beds) 1000 McKinley Park Drive, Marion, OH, Zip 43302–6397; tel. 740/383–8400, Jim Parobek, President
Web address: https://www.ohiohealth.com/locations/hospitals/marion-general-hospital
OHIOHEALTH O'BLENESS HOSPITAL (O, 67 beds) 55 Hospital Drive, Athens, OH, Zip 45701–2302; tel. 740/593–5551, LeeAnn Helber, President
OHIOHEALTH RIVERSIDE METHODIST HOSPITAL (O, 880 beds) 3535 Olentangy River Road, Columbus, OH, Zip 43214–3998; tel. 614/566–5000, Robert J. Cercek, President
Web address: www.ohiohealth.com
OHIOHEALTH SHELBY HOSPITAL (O, 25 beds) 199 West Main Street, Shelby, OH, Zip 44875–1490, 199 West Main Street DOCK, Zip 44875–1490, tel. 419/342–5015, Curtis Gingrich, M.D., President
Web address: https://www.ohiohealth.com/locations/hospitals/shelby-hospital
OHIOHEALTH SOUTHEASTERN MEDICAL CENTER (O, 81 beds) 1341 North Clark Street, Cambridge, OH, Zip 43725–9614, 1341 Clark Street, Zip 43725–0610, tel. 740/439–8000, Wendy C. Elliott, President
OHIOHEALTH VAN WERT HOSPITAL (O, 36 beds) 1250 South Washington Street, Van Wert, OH, Zip 45891–2599; tel. 419/238–2390, Joy Bischoff, MSN, R.N., President
Web address: www.vanwerthealth.org

Owned, leased, sponsored:	13 hospitals	2490 beds
Contract-managed:	1 hospitals	22 beds
Totals:	14 hospitals	2512 beds

0018: OKLAHOMA DEPARTMENT OF MENTAL HEALTH AND SUBSTANCE ABUSE SERVICES (NP)
1200 NE 13th Street, Oklahoma City, OK Zip 73117–1022, P O Box 53277, Zip 73152–3277, tel. 405/522–3908, Carrie Slatton–Hodges, Commissioner
(Independent Hospital System)

OKLAHOMA: GRIFFIN MEMORIAL HOSPITAL (O, 120 beds) 900 East Main Street, Norman, OK, Zip 73071–5305, P O Box 151, Zip 73070–0151, tel. 405/573–6600, Henry Hartsell, Ph.D., Executive Director
NORTHWEST CENTER FOR BEHAVIORAL HEALTH (O, 24 beds) 1222 10th Street Suite 211, Woodward, OK, Zip 73801–3156, 1222 10th Street,

For explanation of codes following names, see page B2.
★ Indicates Type III membership in the American Hospital Association.

Suite 211, Zip 73801-3156, tel. 580/766-2311, Autumn Jesse. Nickelson, Executive Director
Web address: www.ncbhok.org/

OKLAHOMA FORENSIC CENTER (O, 216 beds) 24800 South 4420 Road, Vinita, OK, Zip 74301-5544, P O Box 69, Zip 74301-0069, tel. 918/256-7841, Debbie Moran, Executive Director
Web address: www.odmhsas.org

Owned, leased, sponsored:	3 hospitals	360 beds
Contract-managed:	0 hospitals	0 beds
Totals:	3 hospitals	360 beds

3355: ORLANDO HEALTH (NP)

1414 Kuhl Avenue, Orlando, FL Zip 32806-2093; tel. 321/843-7000, David W. Strong, President and Chief Executive Officer
(Moderately Centralized Health System)

FLORIDA: BAYFRONT HEALTH ST. PETERSBURG (O, 214 beds) 701 Sixth Street South, Saint Petersburg, FL, Zip 33701-4891; tel. 727/823-1234, John A. Moore, FACHE, President
Web address: www.bayfrontstpete.com

ORLANDO HEALTH–HEALTH CENTRAL HOSPITAL (O, 172 beds) 10000 West Colonial Drive, Ocoee, FL, Zip 34761-3499; tel. 407/296-1000, Philip Koovakada, President
Web address: www.orlandohealth.com/facilities/health-central-hospital

ORLANDO HEALTH ORLANDO REGIONAL MEDICAL CENTER (O, 1387 beds) 52 West Underwood Street, Orlando, FL, Zip 32806; tel. 407/841-5111, Kelly Nierstedt, President

ORLANDO HEALTH SOUTH LAKE HOSPITAL (O, 183 beds) 1900 Don Wickham Drive, Clermont, FL, Zip 34711-1979; tel. 352/394-4071, Lance Sewell, President and Chief Executive Officer
Web address: www.southlakehospital.com

ORLANDO HEALTH ST. CLOUD HOSPITAL (O, 63 beds) 2906 17th Street, Saint Cloud, FL, Zip 34769-6099; tel. 407/892-2135, Brian A. Wetzel, President
Web address: www.stcloudregional.com

Owned, leased, sponsored:	5 hospitals	2019 beds
Contract-managed:	0 hospitals	0 beds
Totals:	5 hospitals	2019 beds

★5335: OSF HEALTHCARE (CC)

800 NE Glen Oak Avenue, Peoria, IL Zip 61603-3200; tel. 309/655-2850, Robert Sehring, Chief Executive Officer
(Moderately Centralized Health System)

ILLINOIS: OSF HEALTHCARE SAINT ANTHONY'S HEALTH CENTER (O, 49 beds) 1 Saint Anthony's Way, Alton, IL, Zip 62002-4579, PO Box 340, Zip 62002-0340, tel. 618/474-6003, Jerald W. Rumph, FACHE, President

OSF HEALTHCARE LITTLE COMPANY OF MARY MEDICAL CENTER (O, 217 beds) 2800 West 95th Street, Evergreen Park, IL, Zip 60805-2795; tel. 708/229-5270, Kathleen Kinsella, President
Web address: https://www.osfhealthcare.org/little-company-of-mary/

OSF HEART OF MARY MEDICAL CENTER (O, 181 beds) 1400 West Park Street, Urbana, IL, Zip 61801-2396, P O Box 6259, Peoria, Zip 61601, tel. 217/337-2000, J. T. Barnhart, President

OSF HOLY FAMILY MEDICAL CENTER (O, 23 beds) 1000 West Harlem Avenue, Monmouth, IL, Zip 61462-1007; tel. 309/734-3141, Lisa DeKezel, R.N., President
Web address: www.osfholyfamily.org

OSF SACRED HEART MEDICAL CENTER (O, 115 beds) 812 North Logan Avenue, Danville, IL, Zip 61832-3788; tel. 217/443-5000, J. T. Barnhart, President

OSF SAINT ANTHONY MEDICAL CENTER (O, 241 beds) 5666 East State Street, Rockford, IL, Zip 61108-2425; tel. 815/226-2000, Paula A. Carynski, MS, R.N., President
Web address: www.osfhealth.com

OSF SAINT CLARE MEDICAL CENTER (O, 25 beds) 530 Park Avenue East, Princeton, IL, Zip 61356-2598; tel. 815/875-2811, Jackie Kernan, R.N., MSN, President

OSF SAINT ELIZABETH MEDICAL CENTER (O, 89 beds) 1100 East Norris Drive, Ottawa, IL, Zip 61350-1687; tel. 815/433-3100, Dawn Trompeter, President
Web address: www.osfsaintelizabeth.org

OSF SAINT FRANCIS MEDICAL CENTER (O, 642 beds) 530 NE Glen Oak Avenue, Peoria, IL, Zip 61637-0001; tel. 309/655-2000, Michael Wells, President
Web address: www.osfsaintfrancis.org

OSF SAINT JAMES–JOHN W. ALBRECHT MEDICAL CENTER (O, 38 beds) 2500 West Reynolds, Pontiac, IL, Zip 61764-9774; tel. 815/842-2828, Derrick A. Frazier, FACHE, President
Web address: www.osfsaintjames.org

OSF SAINT LUKE MEDICAL CENTER (O, 25 beds) 1051 West South Street, Kewanee, IL, Zip 61443-8354, P O Box 747, Zip 61443-0747, tel. 309/852-7500, Jackie Kernan, R.N., MSN, President

OSF SAINT PAUL MEDICAL CENTER (O, 25 beds) 1401 East 12th Street, Mendota, IL, Zip 61342-9216; tel. 815/539-7461, Dawn Trompeter, President
Web address: https://www.osfhealthcare.org/saint-paul

OSF ST. JOSEPH MEDICAL CENTER (O, 149 beds) 2200 East Washington Street, Bloomington, IL, Zip 61701-4323; tel. 309/308-6363, Jennifer Ulrich, Interim President

OSF ST. MARY MEDICAL CENTER (O, 83 beds) 3333 North Seminary Street, Galesburg, IL, Zip 61401-1299; tel. 309/344-3161, Lisa DeKezel, R.N., President
Web address: www.osfstmary.org

OSF TRANSITIONAL CARE HOSPITAL (O, 50 beds) 500 West Romeo B Garrett Avenue, Peoria, IL, Zip 61605-2301; tel. 309/680-1500, Christopher Curry, President

SAINT CLARE HOME (O, 0 beds) 5533 North Galena Road, Peoria Heights, IL, Zip 61614-4499; tel. 309/682-5428, Candy Conover, Administrator

ST. ANTHONY'S CONTINUING CARE CENTER (O, 179 beds) 767 30th Street, Rock Island, IL, Zip 61201, Sister, Mary Anthony. Mazzaferri, Administrator

MICHIGAN: OSF ST. FRANCIS HOSPITAL AND MEDICAL GROUP (O, 25 beds) 3401 Ludington Street, Escanaba, MI, Zip 49829-1377; tel. 906/399-1741, Kelly Jefferson, MSN, President
Web address: www.osfstfrancis.org

Owned, leased, sponsored:	18 hospitals	2156 beds
Contract-managed:	0 hospitals	0 beds
Totals:	18 hospitals	2156 beds

★0002: OVATION HEALTHCARE (IO)

1573 Mallory Lane, Suite 200, Brentwood, TN Zip 37027, 1573 Mallory Lane, Suite 200, Zip 37027, tel. 615/371-7979, Dwayne Gunter, President and Chief Executive Officer
(Decentralized Health System)

ARKANSAS: SMC REGIONAL MEDICAL CENTER (C, 25 beds) 611 West Lee Avenue, Osceola, AR, Zip 72370-3001, P O Box 108, Blytheville, Zip 72316-0108, tel. 870/563-7000, Bryan Hargis, CPA, FACHE, Chief Executive Officer

SOUTH ARKANSAS REGIONAL HOSPITAL (C, 65 beds) 700 West Grove Street, El Dorado, AR, Zip 71730-4416; tel. 870/863-2000, Danna Taylor, Interim President
Web address: www.https://sarhcare.org/

CALIFORNIA: BEAR VALLEY COMMUNITY HOSPITAL (C, 30 beds) 41870 Garstin Drive, Big Bear Lake, CA, Zip 92315, P O Box 1649, Zip 92315-1649, tel. 909/866-6501, Evan J. Rayner, Chief Executive Officer
Web address: www.bvchd.com

COLORADO: COMMUNITY HOSPITAL (C, 44 beds) 2351 G Road, Grand Junction, CO, Zip 81505; tel. 970/242-0920, Chris Thomas, FACHE, President and Chief Executive Officer

For explanation of codes following names, see page B2.
★ Indicates Type III membership in the American Hospital Association.

Systems / Ovation Healthcare

PIONEERS MEDICAL CENTER (C, 16 beds) 100 Pioneers Medical Center Drive, Meeker, CO, Zip 81641-3181; tel. 970/878-5047, Liz Sellers, R.N., MSN, Chief Executive Officer
Web address: www.pioneershospital.org

PROWERS MEDICAL CENTER (C, 25 beds) 401 Kendall Drive, Lamar, CO, Zip 81052-3993; tel. 719/336-4343, Karen L. Bryant, Chief Executive Officer

SOUTHEAST COLORADO HOSPITAL DISTRICT (C, 79 beds) 373 East Tenth Avenue, Springfield, CO, Zip 81073-1699; tel. 719/523-4501, Jeff Egbert, Interim Chief Executive Officer
Web address: www.sechosp.org

FLORIDA: HENDRY REGIONAL MEDICAL CENTER (C, 25 beds) 524 West Sagamore Avenue, Clewiston, FL, Zip 33440-3514; tel. 863/902-3000, R.D. Williams, Chief Executive Officer
Web address: www.hendryregional.org

JACKSON HOSPITAL (C, 68 beds) 4250 Hospital Drive, Marianna, FL, Zip 32446-1917, P O Box 1608, Zip 32447-5608, tel. 850/526-2200, Brooke G. Donaldson, Chief Executive Officer
Web address: www.jacksonhosp.com

IDAHO: GRITMAN MEDICAL CENTER (C, 25 beds) 700 South Main Street, Moscow, ID, Zip 83843-3056; tel. 208/882-4511, Kara Besst, President and Chief Executive Officer

ILLINOIS: CRAWFORD MEMORIAL HOSPITAL (C, 25 beds) 1000 North Allen Street, Robinson, IL, Zip 62454-1167; tel. 618/544-3131, Douglas Florkowski, Chief Executive Officer
Web address: www.crawfordmh.net

HAMMOND-HENRY HOSPITAL (C, 61 beds) 600 North College Avenue, Geneseo, IL, Zip 61254-1099; tel. 309/944-6431, David Smith, Chief Executive Officer

INDIANA: SULLIVAN COUNTY COMMUNITY HOSPITAL (C, 25 beds) 2200 North Section Street, Sullivan, IN, Zip 47882-7523, P O Box 10, Zip 47882-0010, tel. 812/268-4311, Michelle Franklin, Chief Executive Officer
Web address: www.schosp.com

KANSAS: NEOSHO MEMORIAL REGIONAL MEDICAL CENTER (C, 25 beds) 629 South Plummer, Chanute, KS, Zip 66720-1928, P O Box 426, Zip 66720-0426, tel. 620/431-4000, Dennis Franks, FACHE, Chief Executive Officer
Web address: www.nmrmc.com

WILSON MEDICAL CENTER (C, 15 beds) 2600 Ottawa Road, Neodesha, KS, Zip 66757-1897, P O Box 360, Zip 66757-0360, tel. 620/325-2611, Tom Hood, Chief Executive Officer
Web address: www.wilsonmedical.org

KENTUCKY: CALDWELL MEDICAL CENTER (C, 25 beds) 100 Medical Center Drive, Princeton, KY, Zip 42445-2430, P O Box 410, Zip 42445-0410, tel. 270/365-0300, Daniel Odegaard, FACHE, Chief Executive Officer

OHIO COUNTY HOSPITAL (C, 25 beds) 1211 Main Street, Hartford, KY, Zip 42347-1619; tel. 270/298-7411, Shellie Dube. Shouse, Chief Executive Officer
Web address: www.ohiocountyhospital.com

LOUISIANA: THIBODAUX REGIONAL HEALTH SYSTEM (C, 138 beds) 602 North Acadia Road, Thibodaux, LA, Zip 70301-4847, P O Box 1118, Zip 70302-1118, tel. 985/447-5500, Greg K. Stock, FACHE, Chief Executive Officer

MAINE: CARY MEDICAL CENTER (C, 47 beds) 163 Van Buren Road, Suite 1, Caribou, ME, Zip 04736-3567; tel. 207/498-3111, Kris A. Doody, Chief Executive Officer
Web address: www.carymedicalcenter.org

MINNESOTA: RIVER'S EDGE HOSPITAL AND CLINIC (C, 25 beds) 1900 North Sunrise Drive, Saint Peter, MN, Zip 56082-5376; tel. 507/931-2200, Paula Meskan, R.N., Chief Executive Officer
Web address: www.rehc.org

MISSISSIPPI: KING'S DAUGHTERS MEDICAL CENTER (C, 37 beds) 427 Highway 51 North, Brookhaven, MS, Zip 39601-2350, P O Box 948, Zip 39602-0948, tel. 601/833-6011, Scott Christensen, FACHE, Chief Executive Officer

MONTANA: CABINET PEAKS MEDICAL CENTER (C, 25 beds) 209 Health Park Drive, Libby, MT, Zip 59923-2130; tel. 406/283-7000, Tadd S. Greenfield, Chief Executive Officer
Web address: https://www.cabinetpeaks.org/

LOGAN HEALTH-CUT BANK (C, 8 beds) 802 Second Street SE, Cut Bank, MT, Zip 59427-3329; tel. 406/873-2251, Cherie Taylor, President

NEBRASKA: PHELPS MEMORIAL HEALTH CENTER (C, 25 beds) 1215 Tibbals Street, Holdrege, NE, Zip 68949-1255; tel. 308/995-2211, Mark Harrel, Chief Executive Officer
Web address: www.phelpsmemorial.com

NEW HAMPSHIRE: ANDROSCOGGIN VALLEY HOSPITAL (C, 25 beds) 59 Page Hill Road, Berlin, NH, Zip 03570-3531; tel. 603/752-2200, Michael D. Peterson, FACHE, President and Chief Executive Officer

LITTLETON REGIONAL HEALTHCARE (C, 25 beds) 600 Saint Johnsbury Road, Littleton, NH, Zip 03561-3442; tel. 603/444-9000, Robert F. Nutter, President and Chief Executive Officer
Web address: www.littletonhospital.org

UPPER CONNECTICUT VALLEY HOSPITAL (C, 16 beds) 181 Corliss Lane, Colebrook, NH, Zip 03576-3207; tel. 603/237-4971, Greg Cook, President and Chief Executive Officer

WEEKS MEDICAL CENTER (C, 25 beds) 173 Middle Street, Lancaster, NH, Zip 03584-3508; tel. 603/788-4911, Matthew Streeter, Interim President & Chief Executive Officer
Web address: www.weeksmedical.org

NEW MEXICO: CIBOLA GENERAL HOSPITAL (C, 25 beds) 1016 East Roosevelt Avenue, Grants, NM, Zip 87020-2118; tel. 505/287-4446, Maria A. Atencio, R.N., Acting Chief Executive Officer and Chief Nursing Officer
Web address: www.cibolahospital.com

HOLY CROSS HOSPITAL (C, 25 beds) 1397 Weimer Road, Taos, NM, Zip 87571-6253; tel. 575/758-8883, James Kiser, Chief Executive Officer
Web address: www.taoshospital.org

SIERRA VISTA HOSPITAL (C, 11 beds) 800 East Ninth Avenue, Truth or Consequences, NM, Zip 87901-1961; tel. 575/894-2111, Frank Corcoran, R.N., Chief Executive Officer

NEW YORK: ADIRONDACK HEALTH (C, 68 beds) 2233 State Route 86, Saranac Lake, NY, Zip 12983-5644, P O Box 471, Zip 12983-0471, tel. 518/891-4141, Aaron Kramer, Chief Executive Officer
Web address: www.adirondackhealth.org

OHIO: KNOX COMMUNITY HOSPITAL (C, 90 beds) 1330 Coshocton Road, Mount Vernon, OH, Zip 43050-1495; tel. 740/393-9000, Bruce D. White, President and Chief Executive Officer
Web address: www.kch.org

SOUTH CAROLINA: ABBEVILLE AREA MEDICAL CENTER (C, 18 beds) 420 Thomson Circle, Abbeville, SC, Zip 29620-5656, P O Box 887, Zip 29620-0887, tel. 864/366-5011, Will Gordon, Vice President and Chief Administrative Officer

NEWBERRY COUNTY MEMORIAL HOSPITAL (C, 54 beds) 2669 Kinard Street, Newberry, SC, Zip 29108-2911, P O Box 497, Zip 29108-0497, tel. 803/276-7570, John Snow, Chief Executive Officer
Web address: www.newberryhospital.org

SOUTH DAKOTA: HURON REGIONAL MEDICAL CENTER (C, 30 beds) 172 Fourth Street SE, Huron, SD, Zip 57350-2590; tel. 605/353-6200, Erick J. Larson, President and Chief Executive Officer
Web address: www.huronregional.org

TENNESSEE: MACON COMMUNITY HOSPITAL (C, 25 beds) 305 West Locust Street, Lafayette, TN, Zip 37083-1712, P O Box 378, Zip 37083-0378, tel. 615/666-2147, Scott A. Tongate, Chief Executive Officer

RHEA MEDICAL CENTER (C, 25 beds) 9400 Rhea County Highway, Dayton, TN, Zip 37321-7922; tel. 423/775-1121, Horace Whitt, Chief Executive Officer
Web address: www.rheamedical.org

TEXAS: GONZALES HEALTHCARE SYSTEMS (C, 33 beds) 1110 Sarah Dewitt Drive, Gonzales, TX, Zip 78629-3311, P O Box 587, Zip 78629-0587, tel. 830/672-7581, Brandon Anzaldua, Chief Executive Officer

MATAGORDA REGIONAL MEDICAL CENTER (C, 46 beds) 104 7th Street, Bay City, TX, Zip 77414-4853; tel. 979/245-6383, James Warren. Robicheaux, FACHE, Chief Executive Officer
Web address: www.matagordaregional.org

WILBARGER GENERAL HOSPITAL (C, 28 beds) 920 Hillcrest Drive, Vernon, TX, Zip 76384-3196; tel. 940/552-9351, Tom Siemers, Chief Executive Officer
Web address: www.wghospital.com

For explanation of codes following names, see page B2.
★ Indicates Type III membership in the American Hospital Association.

VERMONT: NORTHWESTERN MEDICAL CENTER (C, 51 beds) 133 Fairfield Street, Saint Albans, VT, Zip 05478–1726; tel. 802/524–5911, Peter J. Wright, FACHE, Chief Executive Officer

WYOMING: CODY REGIONAL HEALTH (C, 112 beds) 707 Sheridan Avenue, Cody, WY, Zip 82414–3409; tel. 307/527–7501, Douglas A. McMillan, Administrator and Chief Executive Officer
Web address: www.westparkhospital.org

MEMORIAL HOSPITAL OF CARBON COUNTY (C, 25 beds) 2221 West Elm Street, Rawlins, WY, Zip 82301–5108, P O Box 460, Zip 82301–0460, tel. 307/324–2221
Web address: www.imhcc.com

Owned, leased, sponsored:	0 hospitals	0 beds
Contract-managed:	44 hospitals	1665 beds
Totals:	44 hospitals	1665 beds

★0982: OWENSBORO HEALTH (NP)

1201 Pleasant Valley Road, Owensboro, KY Zip 42303–9811; tel. 270/417–3112, Mark A. Marsh, President and Chief Executive Officer
(Moderately Centralized Health System)

KENTUCKY: OWENSBORO HEALTH MUHLENBERG COMMUNITY HOSPITAL (O, 135 beds) 440 Hopkinsville Street, Greenville, KY, Zip 42345–1124, P O Box 387, Zip 42345–0378, tel. 270/338–8000, Ed Heath, FACHE, Chief Executive Officer
Web address: www.ww.owensborohealth.org/

OWENSBORO HEALTH REGIONAL HOSPITAL (O, 362 beds) 1201 Pleasant Valley Road, Owensboro, KY, Zip 42303; tel. 270/417–2000, Mark A. Marsh, President and Chief Executive Officer

Owned, leased, sponsored:	2 hospitals	497 beds
Contract-managed:	0 hospitals	0 beds
Totals:	2 hospitals	497 beds

★7555: PALOMAR HEALTH (NP)

2125 Citracado Pkwy Ste 300, Escondido, CA Zip 92029–4159, 2125 Citracado Parkway, Suite 300, Zip 92029–4159, tel. 760/740–6393, Diane Hansen, Chief Executive Officer
(Independent Hospital System)

CALIFORNIA: PALOMAR MEDICAL CENTER ESCONDIDO (O, 292 beds) 2185 Citracado Parkway, Escondido, CA, Zip 92029–4159; tel. 760/739–3000, Diane Hansen, President and Chief Executive Officer
Web address: www.palomarhealth.org

PALOMAR MEDICAL CENTER POWAY (O, 233 beds) 15615 Pomerado Road, Poway, CA, Zip 92064–2460; tel. 858/613–4000, Diane Hansen, President and Chief Executive Officer
Web address: https://www.palomarhealth.org/facilities/palomar-poway-outpatient/

Owned, leased, sponsored:	2 hospitals	525 beds
Contract-managed:	0 hospitals	0 beds
Totals:	2 hospitals	525 beds

★0617: PAM HEALTH (IO)

1828 Good Hope Road, Suite 102, Enola, PA Zip 17025–1233; tel. 717/731–9660, Anthony F. Misitano, Founder, Chairman and Chief Executive Officer
(Independent Hospital System)

ARIZONA: PAM HEALTH REHABILITATION HOSPITAL OF SURPRISE (O, 40 beds) 13060 West Bell Road, Surprise, AZ, Zip 85378–1200; tel. 623/499–9100, Sharon Noe, Chief Executive Officer
Web address: www.https://pamhealth.com/index.php/facilities/find-facility/rehabilitation-hospitals/pam-health-rehabilitation-hospital-surprise

COLORADO: PAM HEALTH REHABILITATION HOSPITAL OF WESTMINSTER (O, 36 beds) 6500 West 104th Avenue, Westminster, CO, Zip 80020–4189; tel. 720/653–3440, Cory Warner, Chief Executive Officer

PAM HEALTH SPECIALTY HOSPITAL OF DENVER (O, 63 beds) 1690 Meade Street, Denver, CO, Zip 80204–1552, 1690 North Meade Street, Zip 80204–1552, tel. 303/264–6900, Steph Laviolette, Chief Executive Officer
Web address: www.https://postacutemedical.com/facilities/find-facility/specialty-hospitals/PAM-Specialty-Hospital-of-Denver

DELAWARE: PAM HEALTH REHABILITATION HOSPITAL OF GEORGETOWN (O, 34 beds) 22303 Dupont Boulevard, Georgetown, DE, Zip 19947–2153; tel. 302/440–4866, George Del Farno, Chief Executive Officer
Web address: www.https://pamhealth.com/

PAM REHABILITATION HOSPITAL OF DOVER (O, 34 beds) 1240 Mckee Road, Dover, DE, Zip 19904–1381; tel. 302/672–5800, Ted Werner, Chief Executive Officer
Web address: www.https://postacutemedical.com/facilities/find-facility/rehabilitation-hospitals/pam-rehabilitation-hospital-dover

FLORIDA: PAM HEALTH SPECIALTY HOSPITAL OF JACKSONVILLE (O, 40 beds) 4901 Richard Street, Jacksonville, FL, Zip 32207–7328; tel. 904/425–0500, James Whitacre, Chief Executive Officer
Web address: www.https://pamhealth.com/index.php/facilities/find-facility/specialty-hospitals/pam-health-specialty-hospital-jacksonville

PAM REHABILITATION HOSPITAL OF JUPITER (O, 42 beds) 5075 Innovation Way, Jupiter, FL, Zip 33458–6101; tel. 561/935–3002, Nikki McCartin, Chief Executive Officer

PAM REHABILITATION HOSPITAL OF TAVARES (O, 42 beds) 1730 Mayo Drive, Tavares, FL, Zip 32778–4308; tel. 352/525–3001, Jacob McGuirt, Chief Executive Officer
Web address: www.https://pamhealth.com/facilities/find-facility/rehabilitation-hospitals/pam-health-rehabilitation-hospital-tavares

PAM SPECIALTY HOSPITAL OF SARASOTA (O, 40 beds) 6150 Edgelake Drive, Sarasota, FL, Zip 34240–8803; tel. 941/342–3000, Jacob McGuirt, Chief Executive Officer

INDIANA: PAM HEALTH REHABILITATION HOSPITAL OF GREATER INDIANA (L, 42 beds) 2101 Broadway Street, Clarksville, IN, Zip 47129–7800; tel. 812/913–6880, Waylon Maynard, Chief Executive Officer
Web address: www.https://pamhealth.com/

KANSAS: REHABILITATION HOSPITAL OF OVERLAND PARK (O, 45 beds) 5100 Indian Creek Parkway, Overland Park, KS, Zip 66207–4115; tel. 913/544–1957, Megan Hall, Chief Executive Officer
Web address: www.https://postacutemedical.com/facilities/find-facility/rehabilitation-hospitals/pam-rehabilitation-hospital-overland

LOUISIANA: PAM SPECIALTY HOSPITAL OF COVINGTON (O, 26 beds) 20050 Crestwood Boulevard, Covington, LA, Zip 70433–5207; tel. 985/875–7525, Tim Burke, Chief Executive Officer

PAM SPECIALTY HOSPITAL OF HAMMOND (O, 40 beds) 42074 Veterans Avenue, Hammond, LA, Zip 70403–1408; tel. 985/902–8148, Nicholas Paul. Mendez, Chief Executive Officer and Director of Nursing
Web address: www.postacutemedical.com/facilities/find-facility/specialty-hospitals/PAM-Specialty-Hospital-Hammond

PAM SPECIALTY HOSPITAL OF SHREVEPORT (O, 24 beds) 1541 Kings Highway, 10th Floor, Shreveport, LA, Zip 71103–4228; tel. 318/212–2200, Marc B. Pearce, Chief Executive Officer
Web address: www.postacutemedical.com

MASSACHUSETTS: PAM HEALTH SPECIALTY HOSPITAL OF STOUGHTON (O, 152 beds) 909 Sumner Street, 1st Floor, Stoughton, MA, Zip 02072–3396; tel. 781/297–8200, Shawn Todd, Interim Chief Executive Officer
Web address: www.https://pamhealth.com/index.php/facilities/find-facility/specialty-hospitals/pam-health-specialty-hospital-stoughton

MISSOURI: ST. LUKE'S REHABILITATION HOSPITAL (O, 35 beds) 14709 Olive Boulevard, Chesterfield, MO, Zip 63017–2221; tel. 314/317–5700, Bruce Eady, R.N., MSN, Chief Executive Officer
Web address: www.https://postacutemedical.com/facilities/find-facility/rehabilitation-hospitals/St-Lukes-Rehabilitation-Hospital

NEVADA: PAM REHABILITATION HOSPITAL OF CENTENNIAL HILLS (O, 44 beds) 6166 North Durango Drive, Las Vegas, NV, Zip 89149–3912; tel. 725/223–4100, Dan Kunde, Chief Executive Officer

---

For explanation of codes following names, see page B2.
★ Indicates Type III membership in the American Hospital Association.

Systems / Pam Health

PAM SPECIALTY HOSPITAL OF LAS VEGAS (O, 73 beds) 2500 North Tenaya, Las Vegas, NV, Zip 89128-0482; tel. 702/562-2021, Adrian Campos, Chief Executive Officer
Web address: www.https://pamhealth.com/facilities/find-facility/specialty-hospitals/PAM-Specialty-Hospital-of-Las-Vegas

PAM SPECIALTY HOSPITAL OF RENO (O, 24 beds) 2375 East Prater Way, Sparks, NV, Zip 89434-9641; tel. 775/355-5600, sarah castle, Chief Executive Officer

NORTH CAROLINA: PAM SPECIALTY HOSPITAL OF ROCKY MOUNT (O, 43 beds) 1051 Noell Lane, Rocky Mount, NC, Zip 27804-1761; tel. 252/451-2300, Robyn Perkerson, R.N., Administrator
Web address: www.lifecare-hospitals.com

NORTH DAKOTA: PAM REHABILITATION HOSPITAL OF FARGO (O, 42 beds) 4671 38th Avenue South, Fargo, ND, Zip 58104; tel. 701/404-5100, Jessica Franke, Chief Executive Officer
Web address: www.https://pamhealth.com/facilities/find-facility/rehabilitation-hospitals/pam-rehabilitation-hospital-fargo

OHIO: PAM HEALTH REHABILITATION HOSPITAL OF MIAMISBURG (O, 62 beds) 2310 Cross Pointe Drive, Miamisburg, OH, Zip 45342-3599; tel. 937/617-0566, Amy Broderick, Senior Division President

PAM SPECIALTY HOSPITAL OF DAYTON (O, 22 beds) 4000 Miamisburg-Centerville Road, Miamisburg, OH, Zip 45342-7615; tel. 937/384-8300, Susanna Dudley, Director of Operations
Web address: www.https://postacutemedical.com

OKLAHOMA: PAM HEALTH REHABILITATION HOSPITAL OF TULSA (O, 53 beds) 10020 East 91st Street, Tulsa, OK, Zip 74133; tel. 918/893-2400, Audra Powell, Chief Executive Officer

PAM HEALTH SPECIALTY HOSPITAL OF OKLAHOMA CITY (O, 59 beds) 1407 North Robinson Avenue, Oklahoma City, OK, Zip 73103-4823; tel. 405/232-8000, Talitha Glosemeyer-Samsel, M.P.H., FACHE, Chief Executive Officer
Web address: www.https://pamhealth.com/index.php/facilities/find-facility/specialty-hospitals/pam-health-specialty-hospital-oklahoma-city

PAM HEALTH SPECIALTY HOSPITAL OF TULSA (O, 60 beds) 3219 South 79th East Avenue, Tulsa, OK, Zip 74145-1343; tel. 918/663-8183, Karla Cody, Chief Executive Officer
Web address: www.postacutetulsa.com

PENNSYLVANIA: PAM HEALTH SPECIALTY HOSPITAL OF HERITAGE VALLEY (O, 35 beds) 1000 Dutch Ridge Road, Beaver, PA, Zip 15009-9727; tel. 724/773-8480, Emily Hensh, Chief Executive Officer
Web address: www.https://pamhealth.com/index.php/facilities/find-facility/specialty-hospitals/pam-health-specialty-hospital-heritage-valley

PAM HEALTH SPECIALTY HOSPITAL OF PITTSBURGH (O, 31 beds) 7777 Steubenville Pike, Oakdale, PA, Zip 15071-3409; tel. 412/494-5500, Carli Chakamba, Chief Executive Officer

PAM HEALTH SPECIALTY HOSPITAL OF WILKES-BARRE (O, 36 beds) 575 North River Street, 7th Floor, Wilkes Barre, PA, Zip 18702-2634; tel. 570/208-3310, David Long, Chief Executive Officer
Web address: www.https://postacutemedical.com

TEXAS: PAM HEALTH REHABILITATION HOSPITAL OF EL PASO (O, 42 beds) 1600 East Cliff Drive, El Paso, TX, Zip 79902-5130; tel. 915/975-8630, Jarrod McGee, Chief Executive Officer

PAM HEALTH REHABILITATION HOSPITAL OF HOUSTON HEIGHTS (O, 35 beds) 1917 Ashland Street, 4th Floor, Houston, TX, Zip 77008-3907; tel. 713/814-9100, Micheal Simpson, Interim Chief Executive Officer
Web address: www.https://pamhealth.com/index.php/facilities/find-facility/rehabilitation-hospitals/pam-health-rehabilitation-hospital-houston-heights

PAM REHABILITATION HOSPITAL OF ALLEN (O, 56 beds) 1001 Raintree Circle, Allen, TX, Zip 75013-4912; tel. 972/908-2015, Kyron J. Kooken, MS, Chief Executive Officer

PAM REHABILITATION HOSPITAL OF BEAUMONT (O, 31 beds) 3340 Plaza 10 Boulevard, Beaumont, TX, Zip 77707-2551; tel. 409/835-0835, Randy Thompson, FACHE, Chief Executive Officer
Web address: www.postacutemedical.com/our-facilities/outpatient-rehabilitation/rehabilitation-hospital-beaumont/

PAM REHABILITATION HOSPITAL OF CLEAR LAKE (O, 151 beds) 110 East Medical Center Boulevard, Webster, TX, Zip 77598-4301; tel. 832/224-9500, Claudia Hauser, Chief Executive Officer
Web address: www.https://postacutemedical.com

PAM REHABILITATION HOSPITAL OF CORPUS CHRISTI (O, 40 beds) 345 South Water Street, Corpus Christi, TX, Zip 78401-2819; tel. 361/500-0600, Hector Bernal, Chief Executive Officer
Web address: www.postacutemedical.com

PAM REHABILITATION HOSPITAL OF HUMBLE (O, 46 beds) 18839 McKay Drive, Humble, TX, Zip 77338-5721; tel. 281/446-3655, Ivan Besa, Chief Executive Officer

PAM REHABILITATION HOSPITAL OF ROUND ROCK (O, 40 beds) 351 Seton Parkway, Round Rock, TX, Zip 78665-8001; tel. 737/708-9800, Duke Saldivar, FACHE, Interim Chief Executive Officer
Web address: www.postacutemedical.com

PAM REHABILITATION HOSPITAL OF VICTORIA (O, 26 beds) 101 James Coleman Drive, Victoria, TX, Zip 77904-3147; tel. 361/220-7900, Tommy Beyer, Director of Operations

PAM SPECIALTY HOSPITAL OF LULING (O, 34 beds) 200 Memorial Drive, Luling, TX, Zip 78648-3213; tel. 830/875-8400, Jana Kuykendall, Chief Executive Officer
Web address: www.warmsprings.org

PAM SPECIALTY HOSPITAL OF NEW BRAUNFELS (O, 32 beds) 1445 Hanz Drive, New Braunfels, TX, Zip 78130-2567; tel. 830/627-7600, Greg Wuchter, Chief Executive Officer

PAM SPECIALTY HOSPITAL OF SAN ANTONIO CENTER (O, 62 beds) 8902 Floyd Curl Drive, San Antonio, TX, Zip 78240-1681; tel. 210/690-7000, Greg Lessard, Chief Executive Officer
Web address: www.lifecare-hospitals.com

PAM SPECIALTY HOSPITAL OF VICTORIA NORTH (O, 42 beds) 102 Medical Drive, Victoria, TX, Zip 77904-3101; tel. 361/576-6200, Jason Dan. Hudson, R.N., Chief Executive Officer

POST ACUTE MEDICAL SPECIALTY HOSPITAL OF CORPUS CHRISTI-NORTH (O, 43 beds) 600 Elizabeth Street, 3rd Floor, Corpus Christi, TX, Zip 78404-2235; tel. 361/881-3223, Hector Bernal, Chief Executive Officer
Web address: www.postacutemedical.com/our-facilities/hospitals/post-acute-medical-specialty-hospital-corpus-christi/

POST ACUTE MEDICAL SPECIALTY HOSPITAL OF TEXARKANA-NORTH (O, 30 beds) 2400 St Michael Drive, 2nd Floor, Texarkana, TX, Zip 75503-2372; tel. 903/614-7600, Greg Lessard, Chief Executive Officer

POST ACUTE/WARM SPRINGS SPECIALTY HOSPITAL OF SAN ANTONIO (O, 26 beds) 5418 N Loop 1604 W, San Antonio, TX, Zip 78247; tel. 210/921-3550, Kristen Lowe, Chief Executive Officer
Web address: www.postacutemedical.com

WARM SPRINGS REHABILITATION HOSPITAL OF KYLE (O, 40 beds) 5980 Kyle Parkway, Kyle, TX, Zip 78640-2400; tel. 512/262-0821, Shawn Todd, Interim Chief Executive Officer
Web address: www.warmsprings.org/our-facilities/outpatient-rehabilitation/warm-springs-rehabilitation-center-kyle/

WARM SPRINGS REHABILITATION HOSPITAL OF SAN ANTONIO (O, 145 beds) 5101 Medical Drive, San Antonio, TX, Zip 78229-4801; tel. 210/616-0100, Kyle Sinclair, Chief Executive Officer
Web address: www.postacutemedical.com/our-facilities/hospitals/warm-springs-rehabilitation-hospital-san-antonio/

Owned, leased, sponsored:	47 hospitals	2240 beds
Contract-managed:	0 hospitals	0 beds
Totals:	47 hospitals	2240 beds

★**0159: PARKVIEW HEALTH (NP)**
10501 Corporate Drive, Fort Wayne, IN Zip 46845-1700; tel. 260/373-7001, Rick Henvey, Chief Executive Officer
(Centralized Physician/Insurance Health System)

INDIANA: PARKVIEW DEKALB HOSPITAL (O, 57 beds) 1316 East Seventh Street, Auburn, IN, Zip 46706-2515, P O Box 542, Zip 46706-0542, tel. 260/925-4600, Natasha Eicher, President and Chief Executive Officer
Web address: www.dekalbhealth.com

PARKVIEW HUNTINGTON HOSPITAL (O, 36 beds) 2001 Stults Road, Huntington, IN, Zip 46750-1291; tel. 260/355-3000, Doug R. Selig, MSN, R.N., President
Web address: www.parkview.com

For explanation of codes following names, see page B2.
★ Indicates Type III membership in the American Hospital Association.

PARKVIEW LAGRANGE HOSPITAL (O, 25 beds) 207 North Townline Road, LaGrange, IN, Zip 46761-1325; tel. 260/463-9000, Jordi K. Disler, President
Web address: www.parkview.com

PARKVIEW NOBLE HOSPITAL (O, 31 beds) 401 Sawyer Road, Kendallville, IN, Zip 46755-2568; tel. 260/347-8700, Jordi K. Disler, Market President

PARKVIEW ORTHO HOSPITAL (O, 37 beds) 11130 Parkview Circle Drive, Fort Wayne, IN, Zip 46845-1735; tel. 260/672-5000, Marceline Rogers, Senior Vice President, Chief Operating Officer, Service Line Leader
Web address: www.parkview.com

PARKVIEW REGIONAL MEDICAL CENTER (O, 823 beds) 11109 Parkview Plaza Drive, Fort Wayne, IN, Zip 46845-1701; tel. 260/266-1000, John Bowen, President
Web address: www.parkview.com

PARKVIEW WABASH HOSPITAL (O, 18 beds) 10 John Kissinger Drive, Wabash, IN, Zip 46992-1648; tel. 260/563-3131, Debra Potempa, MSN, R.N., President

PARKVIEW WHITLEY HOSPITAL (O, 30 beds) 1260 East State Road 205, Columbia City, IN, Zip 46725-9492; tel. 260/248-9000, Scott F. Gabriel, President
Web address: www.parkview.com

Owned, leased, sponsored:	8 hospitals	1057 beds
Contract-managed:	0 hospitals	0 beds
Totals:	8 hospitals	1057 beds

★5415: PEACEHEALTH (CC)

1115 SE 164th Avenue, Vancouver, WA Zip 98683; tel. 360/729-1000, Elizabeth Dunne, President and Chief Executive Officer
(Moderately Centralized Health System)

ALASKA: PEACEHEALTH KETCHIKAN MEDICAL CENTER (L, 54 beds) 3100 Tongass Avenue, Ketchikan, AK, Zip 99901-5746; tel. 907/225-5171, Dori Stevens, Chief Administrative Officer
Web address: https://www.peacehealth.org/hospitals/ketchikan-medical-center

OREGON: PEACEHEALTH COTTAGE GROVE COMMUNITY MEDICAL CENTER (O, 14 beds) 1515 Village Drive, Cottage Grove, OR, Zip 97424-9700; tel. 541/942-0511, Jason F. Hawkins, Chief Administrative Officer

PEACEHEALTH PEACE HARBOR MEDICAL CENTER (O, 21 beds) 400 Ninth Street, Florence, OR, Zip 97439-7398; tel. 541/997-8412, Jason F. Hawkins, Chief Administrative Officer
Web address: www.peacehealth.org

PEACEHEALTH SACRED HEART MEDICAL CENTER AT RIVERBEND (O, 416 beds) 3333 Riverbend Drive, Springfield, OR, Zip 97477-8800; tel. 541/222-7300, Alicia Beymer, Chief Administrative Officer

WASHINGTON: PEACEHEALTH PEACE ISLAND MEDICAL CENTER (O, 10 beds) 1117 Spring Street, Friday Harbor, WA, Zip 98250-9782; tel. 360/378-2141, Jack Estrada, Chief Administrative Officer
Web address: www.peacehealth.org

PEACEHEALTH SOUTHWEST MEDICAL CENTER (O, 399 beds) 400 NE Mother Joseph Place, Vancouver, WA, Zip 98664-3200, P O Box 1600, Zip 98668-1600, tel. 360/256-2000, Cherelle Montanye-Ireland, Chief Hospital Executive
Web address: https://www.peacehealth.org/phmg/vancouver

PEACEHEALTH ST. JOHN MEDICAL CENTER (O, 180 beds) 1615 Delaware Street, Longview, WA, Zip 98632-2367, P O Box 3002, Zip 98632-0302, tel. 360/414-2000, Kendall Sawa, R.N., Chief Hospital Executive

PEACEHEALTH ST. JOSEPH MEDICAL CENTER (O, 274 beds) 2901 Squalicum Parkway, Bellingham, WA, Zip 98225-1851; tel. 360/734-5400, Charles Prosper, Chief Executive, PeaceHealth Northwest
Web address: www.peacehealth.org

PEACEHEALTH UNITED GENERAL MEDICAL CENTER (C, 25 beds) 2000 Hospital Drive, Sedro-Woolley, WA, Zip 98284-4327; tel. 360/856-6021, Christopher Johnston, Chief Administrative Officer
Web address: https://www.peacehealth.org/united-general

Owned, leased, sponsored:	8 hospitals	1368 beds
Contract-managed:	1 hospitals	25 beds
Totals:	9 hospitals	1393 beds

★0989: PENN STATE HEALTH (NP)

100 Crystal A Drive, Hershey, PA Zip 17033-9524; tel. 717/531-8521, Stephen M. Massini, Chief Executive Officer
(Independent Hospital System)

PENNSYLVANIA: PENN STATE HEALTH HAMPDEN MEDICAL CENTER (O, 47 beds) 2200 Good Hope Road, Enola, PA, Zip 17025-1210; tel. 787/981-9000, Kyle C. Snyder, President

PENN STATE HEALTH HOLY SPIRIT MEDICAL CENTER (O, 188 beds) 503 North 21st Street, Camp Hill, PA, Zip 17011-2204; tel. 717/763-2100, Kyle C. Snyder, President
Web address: www.pennstatehealth.org

PENN STATE HEALTH LANCASTER MEDICAL CENTER (O, 108 beds) 2160 State Road, Lancaster, PA, Zip 17601-1812; tel. 610/378-2300, Joseph Frank, Regional Hospital President, East Region
Web address: https://www.pennstatehealth.org/locations/penn-state-health-lancaster-medical-center

PENN STATE HEALTH ST. JOSEPH (O, 128 beds) 2500 Bernville Road, Reading, PA, Zip 19605-9453, P O Box 316, Zip 19603-0316, tel. 610/378-2000, Joseph Frank, Regional Hospital President, East Region

PENN STATE MILTON S. HERSHEY MEDICAL CENTER (O, 601 beds) 500 University Drive, Hershey, PA, Zip 17033-2360, P O Box 850, Zip 17033-0850, tel. 717/531-8521, Donald McKenna, President
Web address: www.pennstatehershey.org/

Owned, leased, sponsored:	5 hospitals	1072 beds
Contract-managed:	0 hospitals	0 beds
Totals:	5 hospitals	1072 beds

0973: PERIMETER HEALTHCARE (IO)

2520 Northwinds Parkway Suite 550, Alpharetta, GA Zip 30009-2236; tel. 470/554-7902, James R. Laughlin, President and Chief Executive Officer

ARKANSAS: PERIMETER BEHAVIORAL HOSPITAL OF WEST MEMPHIS (O, 24 beds) 600 North Seventh Street, West Memphis, AR, Zip 72301-3235; tel. 870/394-7100, Art Hickman, Chief Executive Officer

LOUISIANA: PERIMETER BEHAVIORAL HOSPITAL OF NEW ORLEANS (O, 36 beds) 3639 Loyola Drive, Kenner, LA, Zip 70065; tel. 504/305-2700, Gary Burns, Chief Executive Officer
Web address: https://www.perimeterhealthcare.com/new-orleans

MISSOURI: PERIMETER BEHAVIORAL HOSPITAL OF SPRINGFIELD (O, 32 beds) 2828 North National Avenue, Springfield, MO, Zip 65803-4306; tel. 417/799-7474, Alyssa Ingle, Chief Executive Officer
Web address: https://www.perimeterhealthcare.com/springfield

TENNESSEE: PERIMETER BEHAVIORAL HOSPITAL OF JACKSON (O, 45 beds) 49 Old Hickory Boulevard, Jackson, TN, Zip 38305-4551; tel. 731/668-7073, Forrest Blue. Summers, Chief Executive Officer

TEXAS: PERIMETER BEHAVIORAL HOSPITAL OF ARLINGTON (O, 116 beds) 7000 US Highway 287 South, Arlington, TX, Zip 76001; tel. 817/662-6342, Michelle Work, Chief Executive Officer
Web address: https://www.perimeterhealthcare.com/facilities/perimeter-behavioral-hospital-of-arlington/

PERIMETER BEHAVIORAL HOSPITAL OF DALLAS (O, 100 beds) 2696 West Walnut Street, Garland, TX, Zip 75042-6441; tel. 972/370-5517, Susan Somers, Chief Executive Officer
Web address: https://www.perimeterhealthcare.com/facilities/perimeter-behavioral-hospital-of-dallas/

Owned, leased, sponsored:	6 hospitals	353 beds
Contract-managed:	0 hospitals	0 beds
Totals:	6 hospitals	353 beds

For explanation of codes following names, see page B2.
★ Indicates Type III membership in the American Hospital Association.

Systems / Phoebe Putney Health System

★**0314: PHOEBE PUTNEY HEALTH SYSTEM (NP)**
417 West Third Avenue, Albany, GA Zip 31701-1943;
tel. 229/312-1000, Scott Steiner, FACHE, Chief Executive Officer
(Independent Hospital System)

GEORGIA: PHOEBE PUTNEY MEMORIAL HOSPITAL (O, 430 beds) 417 West Third Avenue, Albany, GA, Zip 31701-1943; tel. 229/312-4100, Deborah Angerami, Chief Executive Officer

PHOEBE SUMTER MEDICAL CENTER (O, 54 beds) 126 Highway, 280 West, Americus, GA, Zip 31719, 126 Highway 280 West, Zip 31719, tel. 229/924-6011, Carlyle L E. Walton, FACHE, Chief Executive Officer
Web address: www.phoebesumter.org

PHOEBE WORTH MEDICAL CENTER (O, 18 beds) 807 South Isabella Street, Sylvester, GA, Zip 31791-7554, P O Box 545, Zip 31791-0545, tel. 229/776-6961, Kim Gilman, Chief Executive Officer
Web address: www.phoebeputney.com

Owned, leased, sponsored:	3 hospitals	502 beds
Contract-managed:	0 hospitals	0 beds
Totals:	3 hospitals	502 beds

0043: PHYSICIANS FOR HEALTHY HOSPITALS (IO)
1117 East Devonshire Avenue, Hemet, CA Zip 92543-3083;
tel. 951/652-2811, Joel M. Bergenfeld, Chief Executive Officer

CALIFORNIA: HEMET GLOBAL MEDICAL CENTER (O, 454 beds) 1117 East Devonshire Avenue, Hemet, CA, Zip 92543-3083; tel. 951/652-2811, Peter R. Baranoff, Corporate Chief Executive Officer, Managing Director

MENIFEE GLOBAL MEDICAL CENTER (O, 94 beds) 28400 McCall Boulevard, Sun City, CA, Zip 92585-9537; tel. 951/679-8888, Peter R. Baranoff, Corporate Chief Executive Officer, Managing Director
Web address: https://www.menifeeglobalmedicalcenter.com/

Owned, leased, sponsored:	2 hospitals	548 beds
Contract-managed:	0 hospitals	0 beds
Totals:	2 hospitals	548 beds

0310: PIEDMONT HEALTHCARE (NP)
1800 Howell Mill Road NW, Suite 850, Roswell, GA Zip 30076, Atlanta, tel. 404/425-1314, Kevin Brown, President and Chief Executive Officer
(Moderately Centralized Health System)

GEORGIA: PIEDMONT ATHENS REGIONAL MEDICAL CENTER (O, 366 beds) 1199 Prince Avenue, Athens, GA, Zip 30606-2797; tel. 706/475-7000, Michael Burnett, Chief Executive Officer
Web address: https://www.piedmont.org/locations/piedmont-athens

PIEDMONT ATLANTA HOSPITAL (O, 534 beds) 1968 Peachtree Road NW, Atlanta, GA, Zip 30309-1281; tel. 404/605-5000, Patrick M. Battey, FACS, M.D., Chief Executive Officer
Web address: www.piedmont.org

PIEDMONT AUGUSTA (O, 474 beds) 1350 Walton Way, Augusta, GA, Zip 30901-2629; tel. 706/722-9011, Lily Henson, M.D., President and Chief Executive Officer
Web address: https://www.universityhealth.org/our-locations/university-hospital/

PIEDMONT CARTERSVILLE (O, 119 beds) 960 Joe Frank Harris Parkway, Cartersville, GA, Zip 30120-2129; tel. 470/490-1000, Lori Rakes, R.N., Chief Executive Officer
Web address: https://www.piedmont.org/locations/piedmont-cartersville/

PIEDMONT COLUMBUS REGIONAL MIDTOWN (O, 510 beds) 710 Center Street, Columbus, GA, Zip 31901-1527, P O Box 951, Zip 31902-0951, tel. 706/571-1000, M. Scott. Hill, President and Chief Executive Officer
Web address: www.columbusregional.com

PIEDMONT COLUMBUS REGIONAL NORTHSIDE (O, 100 beds) 100 Frist Court, Columbus, GA, Zip 31909-3578, P O Box 7188, Zip 31908-7188, tel. 706/494-2100, M. Scott. Hill, President and Chief Executive Officer

PIEDMONT EASTSIDE MEDICAL CENTER (O, 310 beds) 1700 Medical Way, Snellville, GA, Zip 30078-2195; tel. 770/979-0200, Larry W. Ebert Jr, Chief Executive Officer
Web address: www.eastsidemedical.com

PIEDMONT FAYETTE HOSPITAL (O, 221 beds) 1255 Highway 54 West, Fayetteville, GA, Zip 30214-4526; tel. 770/719-7000, Stephen D. Porter, Chief Executive Officer

PIEDMONT HENRY HOSPITAL (L, 254 beds) 1133 Eagle's Landing Parkway, Stockbridge, GA, Zip 30281-5099; tel. 678/604-5279, David Kent, Chief Executive Officer
Web address: www.piedmont.org

PIEDMONT MACON NORTH (O, 103 beds) 400 Charter Boulevard, Macon, GA, Zip 31210-4853, P O Box 4627, Zip 31208-4627, tel. 478/757-8200, Stephen J. Daugherty, Chief Executive Officer

PIEDMONT MACON (O, 310 beds) 350 Hospital Drive, Macon, GA, Zip 31217-3871; tel. 478/765-7000, Stephen J. Daugherty, Chief Executive Officer
Web address: www.coliseumhealthsystem.com

PIEDMONT MCDUFFIE (O, 22 beds) 2460 Washington Road, NE, Thomson, GA, Zip 30824; tel. 706/595-1411, Nicholas Wood, Administrator
Web address: www.universityhealth.org/mcduffie

PIEDMONT MOUNTAINSIDE HOSPITAL (O, 52 beds) 1266 Highway 515 South, Jasper, GA, Zip 30143-4872; tel. 706/692-2441, Denise Ray, Chief Executive Officer

PIEDMONT NEWNAN HOSPITAL (O, 146 beds) 745 Poplar Road, Newnan, GA, Zip 30265-1618; tel. 770/400-1000, Michael Robertson, Chief Executive Officer
Web address: www.piedmont.org/locations/piedmont-newnan/pnh-home

PIEDMONT NEWTON HOSPITAL (O, 103 beds) 5126 Hospital Drive, Covington, GA, Zip 30014-2567; tel. 770/786-7053, Lindsey Petrini, Chief Executive Officer
Web address: https://www.piedmont.org/locations/piedmont-newton/

PIEDMONT ROCKDALE HOSPITAL (O, 158 beds) 1412 Milstead Avenue NE, Conyers, GA, Zip 30012-3877; tel. 770/918-3000, Monica A. Hum, Chief Executive Officer
Web address: https://www.piedmont.org/locations/piedmont-rockdale

PIEDMONT WALTON HOSPITAL (O, 77 beds) 2151 West Spring Street, Monroe, GA, Zip 30655-3115, PO BOX 1346, Zip 30655-1346, tel. 770/267-8461, Blake Watts, FACHE, Chief Executive Officer

Owned, leased, sponsored:	17 hospitals	3859 beds
Contract-managed:	0 hospitals	0 beds
Totals:	17 hospitals	3859 beds

★**0958: PIH HEALTH (NP)**
12401 Washington Boulevard, Whittier, CA Zip 90602-1006;
tel. 562/698-0811, James R. West, President and Chief Executive Officer
(Moderately Centralized Health System)

CALIFORNIA: PIH HEALTH DOWNEY HOSPITAL (O, 95 beds) 11500 Brookshire Avenue, Downey, CA, Zip 90241-4917; tel. 562/904-5000, James R. West, President and Chief Executive Officer

PIH HEALTH GOOD SAMARITAN HOSPITAL (O, 346 beds) 1225 Wilshire Boulevard, Los Angeles, CA, Zip 90017-2395; tel. 213/977-2121, James R. West, President and Chief Executive Officer
Web address: www.goodsam.org

PIH HEALTH WHITTIER HOSPITAL (O, 307 beds) 12401 Washington Boulevard, Whittier, CA, Zip 90602-1099; tel. 562/698-0811, James R. West, President/Chief Executive Officer
Web address: www.PIHHealth.org

Owned, leased, sponsored:	3 hospitals	748 beds
Contract-managed:	0 hospitals	0 beds
Totals:	3 hospitals	748 beds

For explanation of codes following names, see page B2.
★ Indicates Type III membership in the American Hospital Association.

0869: PIPELINE HEALTH (IO)

898 North Pacific Coast Highway Suite 700, El Segundo, CA Zip 90245-2742; tel. 310/356-0550, Andrei Soran, MSN, Chief Executive Officer

(Independent Hospital System)

CALIFORNIA: COAST PLAZA HOSPITAL (O, 117 beds) 13100 Studebaker Road, Norwalk, CA, Zip 90650-2500; tel. 562/868-3751, Patrick W. Rafferty, Chief Operating Officer, Pipeline Los Angeles/Chief Executive Officer, Coast Plaza Hospital
Web address: https://www.coastplazahospital.com/

COMMUNITY HOSPITAL OF HUNTINGTON PARK (O, 81 beds) 2623 East Slauson Avenue, Huntington Park, CA, Zip 90255-2926; tel. 323/583-1931, Matthew A. Whaley, Chief Executive Officer

EAST LOS ANGELES DOCTORS HOSPITAL (O, 127 beds) 4060 Whittier Boulevard, Los Angeles, CA, Zip 90023-2526; tel. 323/268-5514, Rick Rufino, Chief Executive Officer
Web address: https://www.eladoctorshospital.com/

MEMORIAL HOSPITAL OF GARDENA (O, 172 beds) 1145 West Redondo Beach Boulevard, Gardena, CA, Zip 90247-3528; tel. 310/532-4200, Victor Carrasco, Chief Executive Officer

TEXAS: WHITE ROCK MEDICAL CENTER (O, 65 beds) 9440 Poppy Drive, Dallas, TX, Zip 75218-3694; tel. 214/324-6100, Mirza N. Baig, M.D., Ph.D., Chief Executive Officer
Web address: https://www.whiterockmedicalcenter.com/

Owned, leased, sponsored:	5 hospitals	562 beds
Contract-managed:	0 hospitals	0 beds
Totals:	5 hospitals	562 beds

0249: POWERS HEALTH (NP)

901 MacArthur Boulevard, Hammond, IN Zip 46321-2959; tel. 219/836-1600, Donald P. Fesko, President and Chief Executive Officer

(Independent Hospital System)

INDIANA: COMMUNITY HOSPITAL (O, 509 beds) 901 Macarthur Boulevard, Munster, IN, Zip 46321-2959; tel. 219/836-1600, Randy Neiswonger, Chief Operating Officer
Web address: www.comhs.org

ST. CATHERINE HOSPITAL (O, 138 beds) 4321 Fir Street, East Chicago, IN, Zip 46312-3097; tel. 219/392-1700, Leo Correa, Chief Executive Officer and Administrator

ST. MARY MEDICAL CENTER (O, 200 beds) 1500 South Lake Park Avenue, Hobart, IN, Zip 46342-6699; tel. 219/942-0551, Janice L. Ryba, JD, Chief Executive Officer
Web address: www.comhs.org

Owned, leased, sponsored:	3 hospitals	847 beds
Contract-managed:	0 hospitals	0 beds
Totals:	3 hospitals	847 beds

0240: PREFERRED MANAGEMENT CORPORATION (IO)

120 West MacArthur, Suite 121, Shawnee, OK Zip 74804-2005; tel. 405/878-0202, Donald Freeman, President and Chief Executive Officer

(Independent Hospital System)

TEXAS: COLEMAN COUNTY MEDICAL CENTER (L, 25 beds) 310 South Pecos Street, Coleman, TX, Zip 76834-4159; tel. 325/625-2135, Clay Vogel, Administrator

COLLINGSWORTH GENERAL HOSPITAL (L, 13 beds) 1013 15th Street, Wellington, TX, Zip 79095-3703, P O Box 1112, Zip 79095-1112, tel. 806/447-2521, Candy Powell, Administrator
Web address: www.collingsworthgeneral.net

CULBERSON HOSPITAL (L, 14 beds) Eisenhower-Farm Market Road 2185, Van Horn, TX, Zip 79855, P O Box 609, Zip 79855-0609, tel. 432/283-2760, John O'Hearn, Interim Chief Executive Officer

KIMBLE HOSPITAL (O, 15 beds) 349 Reid Road, Junction, TX, Zip 76849-3049; tel. 325/446-3321, Susan Parker, Chief Executive Officer
Web address: www.kimblehospital.org/

MULESHOE AREA MEDICAL CENTER (L, 25 beds) 708 South First Street, Muleshoe, TX, Zip 79347-3627; tel. 806/272-4524, Dennis Fleenor, R.N., Administrator
Web address: www.mahdtx.org

PARMER MEDICAL CENTER (C, 25 beds) 1307 Cleveland Street, Friona, TX, Zip 79035-1121; tel. 806/250-2754, Gayla Quillin, Administrator

SABINE COUNTY HOSPITAL (L, 25 beds) 2301 Worth Street, Hemphill, TX, Zip 75948-7216, P O Box 750, Zip 75948-0750, tel. 409/787-3300, Kaylee McDaniel, Administrator
Web address: www.sabinecountyhospital.com/

SCHLEICHER COUNTY MEDICAL CENTER (L, 14 beds) 102 North US Highway 277, Eldorado, TX, Zip 76936-4010; tel. 325/853-2507, Billie Petterson-Carter, Administrator

Owned, leased, sponsored:	7 hospitals	131 beds
Contract-managed:	1 hospitals	25 beds
Totals:	8 hospitals	156 beds

0977: PREMIER HEALTH (NP)

110 North Main Street Suite 390, Dayton, OH Zip 45402-3720; tel. 937/499-9401, Michael C. Riordan, President and Chief Executive Officer

(Centralized Physician/Insurance Health System)

OHIO: ATRIUM MEDICAL CENTER (O, 142 beds) One Medical Center Drive, Middletown, OH, Zip 45005-1066, 1 Medical Center Drive, Zip 45005-1066, tel. 513/424-2111, Kevin W. Harlan, President
Web address: www.PremierHealth.com

MIAMI VALLEY HOSPITAL (O, 824 beds) 1 Wyoming Sreet, Dayton, OH, Zip 45409-2722, 1 Wyoming Street, Zip 45409-2722, tel. 937/208-8000, Chad Whelan, President

UPPER VALLEY MEDICAL CENTER (O, 82 beds) 3130 North County Road 25A, Troy, OH, Zip 45373-1309; tel. 937/440-4000, Kevin W. Harlan, President
Web address: www.uvmc.com

Owned, leased, sponsored:	3 hospitals	1048 beds
Contract-managed:	0 hospitals	0 beds
Totals:	3 hospitals	1048 beds

★3505: PRESBYTERIAN HEALTHCARE SERVICES (NP)

9521 San Mateo Blvd. NE, Albuquerque, NM Zip 87113, P O Box 26666, Zip 87125-6666, tel. 505/841-1234, Dale Maxwell, Chief Executive Officer

(Centralized Physician/Insurance Health System)

NEW MEXICO: DR. DAN C. TRIGG MEMORIAL HOSPITAL (L, 5 beds) 301 East Miel De Luna Avenue, Tucumcari, NM, Zip 88401-3810, P O Box 608, Zip 88401-0608, tel. 575/461-7000, Vickie Gutierrez, Hospital Administrator and Chief Nursing Officer

LINCOLN COUNTY MEDICAL CENTER (L, 25 beds) 211 Sudderth Drive, Ruidoso, NM, Zip 88345-6043, P O Box 8000, Zip 88355-8000, tel. 575/257-8200, Todd Oberheu, Hospital Chief Executive
Web address: www.phs.org

PLAINS REGIONAL MEDICAL CENTER (O, 54 beds) 2100 North Doctor Martin Luther King Boulevard, Clovis, NM, Zip 88101-9412, P O Box 1688, Zip 88102-1688, tel. 575/769-2141, Bill Priest, Chief Executive Officer

PRESBYTERIAN ESPANOLA HOSPITAL (O, 48 beds) 1010 Spruce Street, Espanola, NM, Zip 87532-2746; tel. 505/753-7111, Brenda Romero, Hospital Chief
Web address: www.phs.org

For explanation of codes following names, see page B2.
★ Indicates Type III membership in the American Hospital Association.

Systems / Presbyterian Healthcare Services

PRESBYTERIAN HOSPITAL (O, 744 beds) 1100 Central Avenue SE, Albuquerque, NM, Zip 87106-4934, P O Box 26666, Zip 87125-6666, tel. 505/841-1234, Jon Wade, Hospital Chief Executive Officer

PRESBYTERIAN SANTA FE MEDICAL CENTER (O, 36 beds) 4801 Beckner Road, Santa Fe, NM, Zip 87507-3641; tel. 505/772-1234, John Adams, Hospital Chief Executive officer
Web address: www.https://santa-fe-medical-center.phs.org/Pages/default.aspx

SOCORRO GENERAL HOSPITAL (O, 24 beds) 1202 Highway 60 West, Socorro, NM, Zip 87801-3914, P O Box 1009, Zip 87801-1009, tel. 575/835-1140, Veronica Pound, R.N., Hospital Chief Executive Officer, Chief Nursing Officer and Director, Home Health Care and Hospice

Owned, leased, sponsored:	7 hospitals	936 beds
Contract-managed:	0 hospitals	0 beds
Totals:	7 hospitals	936 beds

0357: PRIME HEALTHCARE (IO)
3300 East Guasti Road, Ontario, CA Zip 91761-8655; tel. 909/235-4400, Prem Reddy, M.D., Chairman, President and Chief Executive Officer
(Moderately Centralized Health System)

ALABAMA: RIVERVIEW REGIONAL MEDICAL CENTER (O, 280 beds) 600 South Third Street, Gadsden, AL, Zip 35901-5399; tel. 256/543-5200, John Langlois, Chief Executive Officer
Web address: www.riverviewregional.com

CALIFORNIA: CENTINELA HOSPITAL MEDICAL CENTER (O, 369 beds) 555 East Hardy Street, Inglewood, CA, Zip 90301-4011; tel. 310/673-4660, Mohammad Naser, R.N., MSN, Chief Executive Officer

CHINO VALLEY MEDICAL CENTER (O, 112 beds) 5451 Walnut Avenue, Chino, CA, Zip 91710-2672; tel. 909/464-8600, Gail Aviado, MSN, R.N., Chief Executive Officer/Interim CEO of Chino Valley Medical Center
Web address: www.cvmc.com

DESERT VALLEY HOSPITAL (O, 110 beds) 16850 Bear Valley Road, Victorville, CA, Zip 92395-5795; tel. 760/241-8000, Dana Roesler, R.N., Chief Executive Officer

ENCINO HOSPITAL MEDICAL CENTER (O, 74 beds) 16237 Ventura Boulevard, Encino, CA, Zip 91436-2272; tel. 818/995-5000, EM Vitug. Garcia, Ph.D., Chief Executive Officer
Web address: www.encinomed.com

GARDEN GROVE HOSPITAL AND MEDICAL CENTER (O, 167 beds) 12601 Garden Grove Boulevard, Garden Grove, CA, Zip 92843-1959; tel. 714/537-5160, Daniel J. Brothman, Chief Executive Officer
Web address: www.gardengrovehospital.com

HUNTINGTON BEACH HOSPITAL (O, 102 beds) 17772 Beach Boulevard, Huntington Beach, CA, Zip 92647-6896; tel. 714/843-5000, Daniel J. Brothman, Chief Executive Officer
Web address: www.hbhospital.com

LA PALMA INTERCOMMUNITY HOSPITAL (O, 140 beds) 7901 Walker Street, La Palma, CA, Zip 90623-1764; tel. 714/670-7400, Ayman Mousa, R.N., Chief Executive Officer
Web address: www.lapalmaintercommunityhospital.com

MONTCLAIR HOSPITAL MEDICAL CENTER (O, 106 beds) 5000 San Bernardino Street, Montclair, CA, Zip 91763-2326; tel. 909/625-5411, Gail Aviado, MSN, R.N., Chief Executive Officer
Web address: https://www.montclair-hospital.org/

PARADISE VALLEY HOSPITAL (O, 256 beds) 2400 East Fourth Street, National City, CA, Zip 91950-2099; tel. 619/470-4321, Neerav Jadeja, Chief Executive Officer
Web address: www.paradisevalleyhospital.org

SAN DIMAS COMMUNITY HOSPITAL (O, 101 beds) 1350 West Covina Boulevard, San Dimas, CA, Zip 91773-3219; tel. 909/599-6811, Parrish Scarboro, Chief Executive Officer
Web address: www.sandimashospital.com/

SHASTA REGIONAL MEDICAL CENTER (O, 100 beds) 1100 Butte Street, Redding, CA, Zip 96001-0853, P O Box 496072, Zip 96049-6072, tel. 530/244-5400, Casey Fatch, Chief Executive Officer

SHERMAN OAKS HOSPITAL (O, 88 beds) 4929 Van Nuys Boulevard, Sherman Oaks, CA, Zip 91403-1777; tel. 818/981-7111, EM Vitug. Garcia, Ph.D., Chief Executive Officer
Web address: www.shermanoakshospital.com

ST. FRANCIS MEDICAL CENTER (O, 323 beds) 3630 East Imperial Highway, Lynwood, CA, Zip 90262-2636; tel. 310/900-8900, Clay Farell, Chief Executive Officer

WEST ANAHEIM MEDICAL CENTER (O, 219 beds) 3033 West Orange Avenue, Anaheim, CA, Zip 92804-3183; tel. 714/827-3000, Ayman Mousa, R.N., Chief Executive Officer
Web address: www.westanaheimmedctr.com

FLORIDA: LEHIGH REGIONAL MEDICAL CENTER (O, 53 beds) 1500 Lee Boulevard, Lehigh Acres, FL, Zip 33936-4835; tel. 239/369-2101, Cheryl McIntire, Chief Executive Officer and Chief Financial Officer
Web address: www.lehighregional.com

GEORGIA: SOUTHERN REGIONAL MEDICAL CENTER (O, 331 beds) 11 Upper Riverdale Road SW, Riverdale, GA, Zip 30274-2615; tel. 770/991-8000, Ela C. Lena, President and Chief Executive Officer

INDIANA: MONROE HOSPITAL (O, 32 beds) 4011 South Monroe Medical Park Boulevard, Bloomington, IN, Zip 47403-8000; tel. 812/825-1111, Nancy Bakewell, Administrator
Web address: www.monroehospital.com

KANSAS: PROVIDENCE MEDICAL CENTER (O, 161 beds) 8929 Parallel Parkway, Kansas City, KS, Zip 66112-1689; tel. 913/596-4000, Karen Orr, Administrator and Chief Nursing Officer
Web address: www.providencekc.com

SAINT JOHN HOSPITAL (O, 51 beds) 3500 South Fourth Street, Leavenworth, KS, Zip 66048-5043; tel. 913/680-6000, Billie Leonard, Chief Executive Officer
Web address: https://www.stjohnleavenworth.com/

MICHIGAN: GARDEN CITY HOSPITAL (O, 190 beds) 6245 Inkster Road, Garden City, MI, Zip 48135-4001; tel. 734/421-3300, Saju George, Regional Chief Executive Officer – Prime Healthcare Michigan Market

LAKE HURON MEDICAL CENTER (O, 68 beds) 2601 Electric Avenue, Port Huron, MI, Zip 48060-6518; tel. 810/985-1500, Jose Kottoor, Chief Executive Officer
Web address: https://www.mylakehuron.com

MISSOURI: ST. JOSEPH MEDICAL CENTER (O, 129 beds) 1000 Carondelet Drive, Kansas City, MO, Zip 64114-4673; tel. 816/942-4400, Jodi Fincher, R.N., Chief Executive Officer
Web address: www.stjosephkc.com/

ST. MARY'S MEDICAL CENTER (O, 83 beds) 201 Northwest R D Mize Road, Blue Springs, MO, Zip 64014-2518; tel. 816/228-5900, Kelly Pearce, R.N., FACHE, Chief Executive Officer

NEVADA: NORTH VISTA HOSPITAL (O, 177 beds) 1409 East Lake Mead Boulevard, North Las Vegas, NV, Zip 89030-7197; tel. 702/649-7711, Vincenzo Variale, Chief Executive Officer
Web address: www.northvistahospital.com

SAINT MARY'S REGIONAL MEDICAL CENTER (O, 305 beds) 235 West Sixth Street, Reno, NV, Zip 89503-4548; tel. 775/770-3000, Derrick Glum, Chief Executive Officer

NEW JERSEY: SAINT CLARE'S DENVILLE HOSPITAL (O, 412 beds) 25 Pocono Road, Denville, NJ, Zip 07834-2954; tel. 973/625-6000, Brian Ulery, Chief Executive Officer
Web address: www.https://saintclares.com/locations/saint-clares-denville-hospital/

SAINT MICHAEL'S MEDICAL CENTER (O, 147 beds) 111 Central Avenue, Newark, NJ, Zip 07102-1909; tel. 973/877-5000, Alan Sickles, M.D., Chief Executive Officer
Web address: https://www.smmcnj.com/

ST. MARY'S GENERAL HOSPITAL (O, 287 beds) 350 Boulevard, Passaic, NJ, Zip 07055-2840; tel. 973/365-4300, Edward Condit, President and Chief Executive Officer
Web address: www.smh-passaic.org

OHIO: COSHOCTON REGIONAL MEDICAL CENTER (O, 44 beds) 1460 Orange Street, Coshocton, OH, Zip 43812-2229, P O Box 1330, Zip 43812-6330, tel. 740/622-6411, Stephanie Conn, Chief Executive Officer
Web address: https://www.coshoctonhospital.org

For explanation of codes following names, see page B2.
★ Indicates Type III membership in the American Hospital Association.

Systems / Promedica Health System

EAST LIVERPOOL CITY HOSPITAL (O, 45 beds) 425 West Fifth Street, East Liverpool, OH, Zip 43920–2498; tel. 330/385–7200, Stephanie Conn, Chief Executive Officer
Web address: www.elch.org

PENNSYLVANIA: LOWER BUCKS HOSPITAL (O, 100 beds) 501 Bath Road, Bristol, PA, Zip 19007–3190; tel. 215/785–9200, Michael J. Motte, Chief Executive Officer

ROXBOROUGH MEMORIAL HOSPITAL (O, 72 beds) 5800 Ridge Avenue, Philadelphia, PA, Zip 19128–1737; tel. 215/483–9900, Darshan Shawn. Parekh, PharmD, FACHE, Chief Executive Officer
Web address: www.roxboroughmemorial.com

SUBURBAN COMMUNITY HOSPITAL (O, 126 beds) 2701 Dekalb Pike, East Norriton, PA, Zip 19401–1820; tel. 610/278–2000, Michael J. Motte, Chief Executive Officer

RHODE ISLAND: LANDMARK MEDICAL CENTER (O, 140 beds) 115 Cass Avenue, Woonsocket, RI, Zip 02895–4731; tel. 401/769–4100, Michael Souza, Chief Executive Officer
Web address: www.landmarkmedcenter.com

REHABILITATION HOSPITAL OF RHODE ISLAND (O, 70 beds) 116 Eddie Dowling Highway, North Smithfield, RI, Zip 02896–7327; tel. 401/766–0800, Sheri Godfrin, Chief Executive Officer

TEXAS: DALLAS MEDICAL CENTER (O, 80 beds) 7 Medical Parkway, Dallas, TX, Zip 75234–7823, P O Box 819094, Zip 75381–9094, tel. 972/247–1000, Ruben Garza, Chief Executive Officer
Web address: www.dallasmedcenter.com

DALLAS REGIONAL MEDICAL CENTER (O, 127 beds) 1011 North Galloway Avenue, Mesquite, TX, Zip 75149–2433; tel. 214/320–7000, Glenda Matchett, Chief Executive Officer

HARLINGEN MEDICAL CENTER (O, 88 beds) 5501 South Expressway 77, Harlingen, TX, Zip 78550–3213; tel. 956/365–1000, Candi Constantine-Castillo, DHA, DNP, MSN, R.N., Chief Executive Officer
Web address: www.harlingenmedicalcenter.com

KNAPP MEDICAL CENTER (O, 154 beds) 1401 East Eighth Street, Weslaco, TX, Zip 78596–6640, P O Box 1110, Zip 78599–1110, tel. 956/968–8567, Rene Lopez, Chief Executive Officer
Web address: www.knappmed.org

MISSION REGIONAL MEDICAL CENTER (O, 228 beds) 900 South Bryan Road, Mission, TX, Zip 78572–6613; tel. 956/323–9103, Kane A. Dawson, Chief Executive Officer

PAMPA REGIONAL MEDICAL CENTER (O, 25 beds) 1 Medical Plaza, Pampa, TX, Zip 79065; tel. 806/665–3721, Jonathan Gill, Chief Executive Officer
Web address: www.prmctx.com

Owned, leased, sponsored:	42 hospitals	6272 beds
Contract-managed:	0 hospitals	0 beds
Totals:	42 hospitals	6272 beds

1555: PRISMA HEALTH (NP)
701 Grove Road, Greenville, SC Zip 29605–5611; tel. 864/455–7000, Mark O'Halla, Chief Executive Officer
(Centralized Health System)

Owned, leased, sponsored:	0 hospitals	0 beds
Contract-managed:	0 hospitals	0 beds
Totals:	0 hospitals	0 beds

4155: PRISMA HEALTH–MIDLANDS (NP)
1301 Taylor Street, Suite 9-A, Columbia, SC Zip 29201–2942, P O Box 2266, Zip 29202–2266, tel. 803/296–2100, Mark O'Halla, President and Chief Executive Officer, Prisma Health
(Centralized Health System)

SOUTH CAROLINA: PRISMA HEALTH BAPTIST HOSPITAL (O, 232 beds) Taylor at Marion Street, Columbia, SC, Zip 29220–0001; tel. 803/296–5010, Michael N. Bundy, Chief Executive Officer
Web address: www.palmettohealth.org

PRISMA HEALTH BAPTIST PARKRIDGE HOSPITAL (O, 72 beds) 400 Palmetto Health Parkway, Columbia, SC, Zip 29212–1760, P.O. Box 2266, Zip 29202–2266, tel. 803/907–7000, Michael N. Bundy, Chief Executive Officer
Web address: https://www.prismahealth.org/locations/hospitals/baptist-parkridge-hospital

PRISMA HEALTH RICHLAND HOSPITAL (O, 598 beds) 5 Richland Medical Park Drive, Columbia, SC, Zip 29203–6897; tel. 803/434–7000, Michael N. Bundy, Chief Executive Officer

PRISMA HEALTH TUOMEY HOSPITAL (O, 173 beds) 129 North Washington Street, Sumter, SC, Zip 29150–4983; tel. 803/774–9000, Michael N. Bundy, Chief Executive Officer
Web address: www.https://prismahealth.org/locations/hospitals/tuomey-hospital

Owned, leased, sponsored:	4 hospitals	1075 beds
Contract-managed:	0 hospitals	0 beds
Totals:	4 hospitals	1075 beds

★0153: PROHEALTH CARE, INC. (NP)
N17 W24100 Riverwood Drive, Suite 130, Waukesha, WI Zip 53188; tel. 262/928–2242, Susan A. Edwards, President and Chief Executive Officer
(Centralized Health System)

WISCONSIN: PROHEALTH OCONOMOWOC MEMORIAL HOSPITAL (O, 63 beds) 791 Summit Avenue, Oconomowoc, WI, Zip 53066–3896; tel. 262/569–9400, Susan A. Edwards, President and Chief Executive Officer
Web address: https://www.prohealthcare.org/locations/profile/hospital-oconomowoc/

PROHEALTH WAUKESHA MEMORIAL HOSPITAL (O, 258 beds) 725 American Avenue, Waukesha, WI, Zip 53188–5099; tel. 262/928–1000, Susan A. Edwards, President and Chief Executive Officer
Web address: https://www.prohealthcare.org/locations/profile/hospital-waukesha/

Owned, leased, sponsored:	2 hospitals	321 beds
Contract-managed:	0 hospitals	0 beds
Totals:	2 hospitals	321 beds

★0197: PROMEDICA HEALTH SYSTEM (NP)
100 Madison Avenue, Toledo, OH Zip 43604–1516; tel. 567/585–9601, Arturo Polizzi, President and Chief Executive Officer
(Centralized Physician/Insurance Health System)

MICHIGAN: PROMEDICA CHARLES AND VIRGINIA HICKMAN HOSPITAL (O, 50 beds) 5640 North Adrian Hwy, Adrian, MI, Zip 49221–8318; tel. 517/577–0000, Julie Yaroch, D.O., President, ProMedica Charles and Virginia Hickman Hospital
Web address: https://www.promedica.org

PROMEDICA COLDWATER REGIONAL HOSPITAL (O, 62 beds) 274 East Chicago Street, Coldwater, MI, Zip 49036–2041; tel. 517/279–5400, Dan Schwanke, FACHE, Interim President

PROMEDICA MONROE REGIONAL HOSPITAL (O, 120 beds) 718 North Macomb Street, Monroe, MI, Zip 48162–7815; tel. 734/240–8400, Darrin Arquette, President, Regional Acute Care, Michigan and President, ProMedica Monroe Regional Hospital
Web address: www.promedica.org

OHIO: PROMEDICA BAY PARK HOSPITAL (O, 56 beds) 2801 Bay Park Drive, Oregon, OH, Zip 43616–4920; tel. 419/690–7900, Dawn M. Buskey, President, ProMedica Acute Care

PROMEDICA DEFIANCE REGIONAL HOSPITAL (O, 35 beds) 1200 Ralston Avenue, Defiance, OH, Zip 43512–1396; tel. 419/783–6955, Keith Burmeister, President
Web address: www.promedica.org

PROMEDICA FOSTORIA COMMUNITY HOSPITAL (O, 25 beds) 501 Van Buren Street, Fostoria, OH, Zip 44830–1534, P O Box 907, Zip 44830–0907,

For explanation of codes following names, see page B2.
★ Indicates Type III membership in the American Hospital Association.

Systems / Promedica Health System

tel. 419/435-7734, Jodi Rucker, MSN, R.N., President and Chief Nursing Officer, Vice President of Patient Care Services
Web address: www.promedica.org

PROMEDICA MEMORIAL HOSPITAL (O, 43 beds) 715 South Taft Avenue, Fremont, OH, Zip 43420-3237; tel. 419/332-7321, Jodi Rucker, MSN, R.N., President and Chief Nursing Officer, Vice President of Patient Care Services
Web address: https://www.promedica.org

PROMEDICA TOLEDO HOSPITAL (O, 834 beds) 2142 North Cove Boulevard, Toledo, OH, Zip 43606-3896; tel. 419/291-4000, Dawn M. Buskey, President, Acute Care
Web address: www.promedica.org

Owned, leased, sponsored:	8 hospitals	1225 beds
Contract-managed:	0 hospitals	0 beds
Totals:	8 hospitals	1225 beds

1012: PROSPECT MEDICAL HOLDINGS (IO)
10780 California Route 2 #400, Los Angeles, CA Zip 90025; tel. 714/796-5900, Mitchell Lew, M.D., President
(Independent Hospital System)

CALIFORNIA: FOOTHILL REGIONAL MEDICAL CENTER (O, 127 beds) 14662 Newport Avenue, Tustin, CA, Zip 92780-6064; tel. 714/838-9600, Araceli Lonergan, Chief Executive Officer
Web address: www.hfcis.cdph.ca.gov/longtermcare/Facility.aspx?fac=060000013

LOS ANGELES COMMUNITY HOSPITAL AT LOS ANGELES (O, 212 beds) 4081 East Olympic Boulevard, Los Angeles, CA, Zip 90023-3330; tel. 323/267-0477, Hector Hernandez, Chief Executive Officer

SOUTHERN CALIFORNIA HOSPITAL AT CULVER CITY (O, 239 beds) 3828 Delmas Terrace, Culver City, CA, Zip 90232-6806; tel. 310/836-7000, Omar Ramirez, Chief Operating Officer, California Hospitals
Web address: www.sch-culvercity.com

SOUTHERN CALIFORNIA HOSPITAL AT HOLLYWOOD (O, 45 beds) 6245 De Longpre Avenue, Los Angeles, CA, Zip 90028-9001; tel. 323/462-2271, Omar Ramirez, Chief Operating Officer, California Hospitals

CONNECTICUT: MANCHESTER MEMORIAL HOSPITAL (O, 156 beds) 71 Haynes Street, Manchester, CT, Zip 06040-4188; tel. 860/646-1222, Deborah K. Weymouth, FACHE, President and Chief Executive Officer
Web address: www.echn.org

ROCKVILLE GENERAL HOSPITAL (O, 47 beds) 31 Union Street, Vernon, CT, Zip 06066-3160; tel. 860/872-0501, Deborah K. Weymouth, FACHE, Chief Executive Officer
Web address: www.echn.org

WATERBURY HOSPITAL (O, 173 beds) 64 Robbins Street, Waterbury, CT, Zip 06708-2600; tel. 203/573-6000, Deborah K. Weymouth, FACHE, President and Chief Executive Officer
Web address: www.waterburyhospital.org

NEW JERSEY: CAREWELL HEALTH MEDICAL CENTER (O, 150 beds) 300 Central Avenue, East Orange, NJ, Zip 07018-2897; tel. 973/672-8400, Paige Dworak, FACHE, President and Chief Executive Officer
Web address: www.https://carewellhealth.org/

PENNSYLVANIA: CROZER-CHESTER MEDICAL CENTER (O, 313 beds) 1 Medical Center Boulevard, Upland, PA, Zip 19013-3995; tel. 610/447-2000, Anthony Esposito, President
Web address: www.crozer.org

RHODE ISLAND: ROGER WILLIAMS MEDICAL CENTER (O, 86 beds) 825 Chalkstone Avenue, Providence, RI, Zip 02908-4735; tel. 401/456-2000, Jeffrey H. Liebman, Chief Executive Officer

ST. JOSEPH HEALTH SERVICES OF RHODE ISLAND (O, 125 beds) 200 High Service Avenue, North Providence, RI, Zip 02904-5199; tel. 401/456-3000, Jeffrey H. Liebman, Chief Executive Officer
Web address: www.saintjosephri.com

Owned, leased, sponsored:	11 hospitals	1673 beds
Contract-managed:	0 hospitals	0 beds
Totals:	11 hospitals	1673 beds

★1006: PROVIDENCE (CC)
1801 Lind Avenue Southwest, 9016, Renton, WA Zip 98057-9016; tel. 844/510-4325, Rod Hochman, M.D., President and Chief Executive Officer
(Decentralized Health System)

ALASKA: PROVIDENCE ALASKA MEDICAL CENTER (O, 401 beds) 3200 Providence Drive, Anchorage, AK, Zip 99508-4615, P O Box 196604, Zip 99519-6604, tel. 907/562-2211, Ella M. Goss, MSN, R.N., Chief Executive Officer
Web address: www.alaska.providence.org/locations/p/pamc

PROVIDENCE KODIAK ISLAND MEDICAL CENTER (L, 21 beds) 1915 East Rezanof Drive, Kodiak, AK, Zip 99615-6602; tel. 907/486-3281, Karl Edward. Hertz, Administrator
Web address: www.providence.org

PROVIDENCE SEWARD MEDICAL CENTER (C, 46 beds) 417 First Avenue, Seward, AK, Zip 99664, P O Box 365, Zip 99664-0365, tel. 907/224-5205, Helena Maria. Jagielski, Administrator
Web address: https://www.providence.org/locations/ak/seward-medical-center

PROVIDENCE ST. ELIAS SPECIALTY HOSPITAL (O, 56 beds) 4800 Cordova Street, Anchorage, AK, Zip 99503-7218; tel. 907/561-3333, Jessica Oswald, Chief Executive Officer

PROVIDENCE VALDEZ MEDICAL CENTER (C, 21 beds) 911 Meals Avenue, Valdez, AK, Zip 99686-0550, P O Box 550, Zip 99686-0550, tel. 907/835-2249, Melanee Tiura, Administrator
Web address: https://www.providence.org/locations/ak/valdez-medical-center

CALIFORNIA: HEALDSBURG HOSPITAL (O, 43 beds) 1375 University Avenue, Healdsburg, CA, Zip 95448-3382; tel. 707/431-6500, Michelle Oxford, Chief Administrative Officer

PETALUMA VALLEY HOSPITAL (O, 80 beds) 400 North McDowell Boulevard, Petaluma, CA, Zip 94954-2366; tel. 707/778-1111, Michelle Oxford, Chief Administrative Officer
Web address: https://www.providence.org/locations/norcal/petaluma-valley-hospital

PROVIDENCE CEDARS-SINAI TARZANA MEDICAL CENTER (O, 204 beds) 18321 Clark Street, Tarzana, CA, Zip 91356-3521; tel. 818/881-0800, Nick Lymberopoulos, Chief Executive Officer
Web address: www.providence.org/tarzana.com

PROVIDENCE HOLY CROSS MEDICAL CENTER (O, 378 beds) 15031 Rinaldi Street, Mission Hills, CA, Zip 91345-1207; tel. 818/365-8051, Bernard Klein, M.D., Chief Executive

PROVIDENCE LITTLE COMPANY OF MARY MEDICAL CENTER-TORRANCE (O, 419 beds) 4101 Torrance Boulevard, Torrance, CA, Zip 90503-4664; tel. 310/540-7676, Michael Ricks, Chief Executive, Los Angeles Coastal Service Area
Web address: https://www.providence.org/locations/socal/plcm-torrance

PROVIDENCE LITTLE COMPANY OF MARY MEDICAL CENTER SAN PEDRO (O, 334 beds) 1300 West Seventh Street, San Pedro, CA, Zip 90732-3505; tel. 310/832-3311, Michael Ricks, Chief Executive, Los Angeles Coastal Service Area

PROVIDENCE MISSION HOSPITAL MISSION VIEJO (O, 269 beds) 27700 Medical Center Road, Mission Viejo, CA, Zip 92691-6474; tel. 949/364-1400, Seth R. Teigen, Chief Executive
Web address: https://www.providence.org/locations/mission-hospital-mission-viejo

PROVIDENCE QUEEN OF THE VALLEY MEDICAL CENTER (O, 136 beds) 1000 Trancas Street, Napa, CA, Zip 94558-2906, P O Box 2340, Zip 94558-0688, tel. 707/252-4411, Garry M. Olney, Chief Executive, Northern California
Web address: www.thequeen.org

PROVIDENCE REDWOOD MEMORIAL HOSPITAL (O, 25 beds) 3300 Renner Drive, Fortuna, CA, Zip 95540-3198; tel. 707/725-3361, Michael Keleman, Chief Executive Officer

PROVIDENCE SAINT JOHN'S HEALTH CENTER (O, 211 beds) 2121 Santa Monica Boulevard, Santa Monica, CA, Zip 90404-2091; tel. 310/829-5511, Michael Ricks, Chief Executive, Los Angeles Coastal Service Area
Web address: www.providence.org/saintjohns

For explanation of codes following names, see page B2.
★ Indicates Type III membership in the American Hospital Association.

Systems / Providence

PROVIDENCE SAINT JOSEPH MEDICAL CENTER (O, 385 beds) 501 South Buena Vista Street, Burbank, CA, Zip 91505-4866; tel. 818/843-5111, Karl Keeler, Chief Executive, Los Angeles Valley Service Area

PROVIDENCE SANTA ROSA MEMORIAL HOSPITAL (O, 283 beds) 1165 Montgomery Drive, Santa Rosa, CA, Zip 95405; tel. 707/522-4304, Donovan Taylor, Chief Administrative Officer
Web address: https://www.providence.org/locations/norcal/santa-rosa-memorial-hospital

PROVIDENCE ST. JOSEPH HOSPITAL EUREKA (O, 153 beds) 2700 Dolbeer Street, Eureka, CA, Zip 95501-4799; tel. 707/445-8121, Michael Keleman, Chief Executive Officer

PROVIDENCE ST. JOSEPH HOSPITAL ORANGE (O, 461 beds) 1100 West Stewart Drive, Orange, CA, Zip 92868-3849, P O Box 5600, Zip 92863-5600, tel. 714/633-9111, Brian Helleland, Chief Executive, Orange County High Desert Service Area
Web address: www.sjo.org

PROVIDENCE ST. JUDE MEDICAL CENTER (O, 290 beds) 101 East Valencia Mesa Drive, Fullerton, CA, Zip 92835-3875; tel. 714/992-3000, Laura Ramos, R.N., MSN, Chief Executive Officer

PROVIDENCE ST. MARY MEDICAL CENTER (O, 213 beds) 18300 Highway 18, Apple Valley, CA, Zip 92307-2206, P O Box 7025, Zip 92307-0725, tel. 760/242-2311, Randall Castillo, Chief Executive Officer
Web address: www.stmaryapplevalley.com/

MONTANA: PROVIDENCE ST. JOSEPH MEDICAL CENTER (O, 22 beds) 6 Thirteenth Avenue East, Polson, MT, Zip 59860-5315, P O Box 1010, Zip 59860-1010, tel. 406/883-5377, Devin Huntley, Chief Operating Officer

PROVIDENCE ST. PATRICK HOSPITAL (O, 211 beds) 500 West Broadway, Missoula, MT, Zip 59802-4096, P O Box 4587, Zip 59806-4587, tel. 406/543-7271, William Calhoun, FACHE, Chief Executive
Web address: https://www.providence.org/locations/MT/st-patrick-hospital

NEW MEXICO: COVENANT HEALTH HOBBS HOSPITAL (O, 34 beds) 5419 North Lovington Highway, Hobbs, NM, Zip 88240-9125, P O Box 3000, Zip 88241-9501, tel. 575/492-5000, Rachel Slade, Chief Executive Officer
Web address: https://www.providence.org/locations/covenant-health/hobbs-hospital

OREGON: PROVIDENCE HOOD RIVER MEMORIAL HOSPITAL (O, 25 beds) 810 12th Street, Hood River, OR, Zip 97031-1587, P O Box 149, Zip 97031-0055, tel. 541/386-3911, Jeanette Vieira, Chief Executive
Web address: www.providence.org/hoodriver

PROVIDENCE MEDFORD MEDICAL CENTER (O, 128 beds) 1111 Crater Lake Avenue, Medford, OR, Zip 97504-6241; tel. 541/732-5000, Chris Pizzi, Chief Executive Officer
Web address: www.providence.org

PROVIDENCE MILWAUKIE HOSPITAL (O, 59 beds) 10150 SE 32nd Avenue, Milwaukie, OR, Zip 97222-6516; tel. 503/513-8300, Brad Henry, Interim Chief Executive Officer
Web address: www.providence.org

PROVIDENCE NEWBERG MEDICAL CENTER (O, 40 beds) 1001 Providence Drive, Newberg, OR, Zip 97132-7485; tel. 503/537-1555, Amy Schmitt, M.D., Interim Chief Executive Officer and Chief Medical Officer
Web address: www.https://oregon.providence.org/location-directory/p/providence-newberg-medical-center/

PROVIDENCE PORTLAND MEDICAL CENTER (O, 427 beds) 4805 NE Glisan Street, Portland, OR, Zip 97213-2933; tel. 503/215-1111, Krista Farnham, Chief Executive
Web address: https://www.providence.org/locations/or/portland-medical-center

PROVIDENCE SEASIDE HOSPITAL (O, 24 beds) 725 South Wahanna Road, Seaside, OR, Zip 97138-7735; tel. 503/717-7000, Rebecca Coplin, Chief Executive Officer
Web address: www.providence.org

PROVIDENCE ST. VINCENT MEDICAL CENTER (O, 530 beds) 9205 SW Barnes Road, Portland, OR, Zip 97225-6661; tel. 503/216-1234, Jennifer Burrows, R.N., Chief Executive

PROVIDENCE WILLAMETTE FALLS MEDICAL CENTER (O, 108 beds) 1500 Division Street, Oregon City, OR, Zip 97045-1597; tel. 503/656-1631, Brad Henry, Chief Executive Officer
Web address: www.providence.org/pwfmc

TEXAS: COVENANT CHILDREN'S HOSPITAL (O, 181 beds) 4015 22nd Place, Lubbock, TX, Zip 79410; tel. 806/725-1011, Amy Thompson, M.D., Chief Executive Officer

COVENANT HOSPITAL PLAINVIEW (O, 49 beds) 2601 Dimmitt Road, Plainview, TX, Zip 79072-1833; tel. 806/296-5531, Cassie Mogg, Chief Executive Officer
Web address: www.covenantplainview.org

COVENANT HOSPITAL-LEVELLAND (L, 21 beds) 1900 College Avenue, Levelland, TX, Zip 79336-6508; tel. 806/894-4963, Newman Wheeler, Chief Executive Officer

COVENANT MEDICAL CENTER (O, 360 beds) 3615 19th Street, Lubbock, TX, Zip 79410-1203, P O Box 1201, Zip 79408-1201, tel. 806/725-0000, Amy Thompson, M.D., Chief Executive Officer
Web address: www.covenanthealth.org

COVENANT SPECIALTY HOSPITAL (O, 56 beds) 3815 20th Street, Lubbock, TX, Zip 79410-1235; tel. 806/725-9200, Ely Perea, Director & Chief Executive Officer

GRACE SURGICAL HOSPITAL (O, 32 beds) 7509 Marsha Sharp Freeway, Lubbock, TX, Zip 79407-8202; tel. 806/788-4100, Vanessa Reasoner, Chief Executive Officer
Web address: https://www.providence.org/locations/covenant-health/grace-surgical-hospital

WASHINGTON: KADLEC REGIONAL MEDICAL CENTER (O, 305 beds) 888 Swift Boulevard, Richland, WA, Zip 99352-3514; tel. 509/946-4611, Reza Kaleel, Chief Executive
Web address: https://www.kadlec.org

PROVIDENCE CENTRALIA HOSPITAL (O, 132 beds) 914 S Scheuber RD, Centralia, WA, Zip 98531-9027, 914 South Scheuber Road, Zip 98531-9027, tel. 360/736-2803, Darin Goss, FACHE, Chief Executive Officer

PROVIDENCE HOLY FAMILY HOSPITAL (O, 191 beds) 5633 North Lidgerwood Street, Spokane, WA, Zip 99208-1224; tel. 509/482-0111, Susan Scott, Chief Operating Officer
Web address: https://www.providence.org/locations/wa/holy-family-hospital

PROVIDENCE MOUNT CARMEL HOSPITAL (O, 25 beds) 982 East Columbia Avenue, Colville, WA, Zip 99114-3352; tel. 509/685-5100, Ronald G. Rehn, Chief Administrative Officer

PROVIDENCE REGIONAL MEDICAL CENTER EVERETT (O, 595 beds) 1700 13th Street, Everett, WA, Zip 98201-1689, P O Box 1147, Zip 98206-1147, tel. 425/261-2000, Kristy Carrington, R.N., Chief Executive Officer
Web address: www.providence.org

PROVIDENCE SACRED HEART MEDICAL CENTER & CHILDREN'S HOSPITAL (O, 665 beds) 101 West Eighth Avenue, Spokane, WA, Zip 99204-2364, P O Box 2555, Zip 99220-2555, tel. 509/474-3131, Susan Stacey, R.N., Chief Executive
Web address: www.shmc.org

PROVIDENCE ST. JOSEPH'S HOSPITAL (O, 15 beds) 500 East Webster Street, Chewelah, WA, Zip 99109-9523; tel. 509/935-8211, Ronald G. Rehn, Chief Executive Officer

PROVIDENCE ST. LUKE'S REHABILITATION MEDICAL CENTER (O, 72 beds) 711 South Cowley Street, Spokane, WA, Zip 99202-1388; tel. 509/473-6000, Nancy Webster, Administrator and Chief Operating Officer
Web address: www.st-lukes.org

PROVIDENCE ST. MARY MEDICAL CENTER (O, 129 beds) 401 W Poplar Street, Walla Walla, WA, Zip 99362-2846, P O Box 1477, Zip 99362-0312, tel. 509/897-3320, Reza Kaleel, Chief Executive
Web address: www.washington.providence.org/hospitals/st-mary/

PROVIDENCE ST. PETER HOSPITAL (O, 449 beds) 413 Lilly Road NE, Olympia, WA, Zip 98506-5166; tel. 360/491-9480, Darin Goss, FACHE, Chief Executive Officer

PROVIDENCE SWEDISH CHERRY HILL (O, 211 beds) 500 17th Avenue, Seattle, WA, Zip 98122-5711; tel. 206/320-2000, Elizabeth Wako, M.D., Chief Executive
Web address: https://www.swedish.org/locations/cherry-hill-campus

PROVIDENCE SWEDISH EDMONDS (O, 271 beds) 21601 76th Avenue West, Edmonds, WA, Zip 98026-7506; tel. 425/640-4000, Kristy Carrington, R.N., Chief Executive Officer
Web address: www.swedish.org

PROVIDENCE SWEDISH FIRST HILL (O, 581 beds) 747 Broadway, Seattle, WA, Zip 98122-4307; tel. 206/386-6000, Elizabeth Wako, M.D., Chief Executive

For explanation of codes following names, see page B2.
★ Indicates Type III membership in the American Hospital Association.

Systems / Providence

SWEDISH ISSAQUAH (O, 144 beds) 751 NE Blakely Drive, Issaquah, WA, Zip 98029–6201; tel. 425/313–4000, Elizabeth Wako, M.D., Chief Executive
Web address: www.swedish.org/issaquah

Owned, leased, sponsored:	50 hospitals	10454 beds
Contract-managed:	2 hospitals	67 beds
Totals:	52 hospitals	10521 beds

★0011: PUERTO RICO DEPARTMENT OF HEALTH (NP)
Building 'A'–Medical Center, San Juan, PR Zip 936, Call Box 70184, Zip 936, tel. 787/765–2929, Carlos Mellado, M.D., Secretary of Health
(Independent Hospital System)

PUERTO RICO: CARDIOVASCULAR CENTER OF PUERTO RICO AND THE CARIBBEAN (O, 164 beds) Americo Miranda Centro Medico, San Juan, PR, Zip 936, P O Box 366528, Zip 00936–6528, tel. 787/754–8500, Javier Marrero. Marrero, Executive Director

HOSPITAL CENTRO COMPRENSIVO DE CANCER, UNIVERSIDAD DE PUERTO RICO (O, 29 beds) Carr. PR–21 Int. PR–18 Bo. Monacillo Urbano, San Juan, PR, Zip 927, P.O. Box 363027, Zip 00936–3027, tel. 787/772–8300, Marcia Cruz Correa, Administrator
Web address: www.cccupr.org

HOSPITAL UNIVERSITARIO DR. RAMON RUIZ ARNAU (O, 101 beds) Avenue Laurel #100, Santa Juanita, Bayamon, PR, Zip 956; tel. 787/787–5151, Victor L. Medina Cruz, M.D., Executive Director

UNIVERSITY HOSPITAL (O, 220 beds) Nineyas 869 Rio Piedras, San Juan, PR, Zip 922, P O Box 2116, Zip 922, tel. 787/754–0101, Jorge Matta. Gonzalez, Executive Director

UNIVERSITY PEDIATRIC HOSPITAL (O, 145 beds) Barrio Monacenno, Carretera 22, Rio Piedras, PR, Zip 935, P O Box 191079, San Juan, Zip 00910–1070, tel. 787/777–3535, Victor Diaz Guzman, Executive Director
Web address: www.md.rcm.upr.edu/pediatrics/university_pediatric_hospital.php

Owned, leased, sponsored:	5 hospitals	659 beds
Contract-managed:	0 hospitals	0 beds
Totals:	5 hospitals	659 beds

★0040: QUEEN'S HEALTH SYSTEM (NP)
1301 Punchbowl Street, Honolulu, HI Zip 96813–2402; tel. 808/691–1000, Jill Hoggard Green, Ph.D., R.N., President and Chief Executive Officer
(Moderately Centralized Health System)

HAWAII: MOLOKAI GENERAL HOSPITAL (O, 15 beds) 280 Home Olu Place, Kaunakakai, HI, Zip 96748–0408, P O Box 408, Zip 96748–0408, tel. 808/553–5331, Janice Kalanihuia, President
Web address: www.queens.org

QUEEN'S NORTH HAWAII COMMUNITY HOSPITAL (O, 35 beds) 67-1125 Mamalahoa Highway, Kamuela, HI, Zip 96743–8496; tel. 808/885–4444, Stephany Vaioleti, President

THE QUEEN'S MEDICAL CENTER (O, 649 beds) 1301 Punchbowl Street, Honolulu, HI, Zip 96813–2499; tel. 808/691–1000, Jason Chang, President & Chief Executive Officer
Web address: https://www.queens.org/locations/hospitals/qmc/

Owned, leased, sponsored:	3 hospitals	699 beds
Contract-managed:	0 hospitals	0 beds
Totals:	3 hospitals	699 beds

0981: QUORUM HEALTH (IO)
1573 Mallory Lane, Suite 100, Brentwood, TN Zip 37027; tel. 615/221–1400
(Moderately Centralized Health System)

ARKANSAS: FORREST CITY MEDICAL CENTER (L, 42 beds) 1601 Newcastle Road, Forrest City, AR, Zip 72335–2218; tel. 870/261–0000, Robert Rupp, Chief Executive Officer

HELENA REGIONAL MEDICAL CENTER (L, 12 beds) 1801 Martin Luther King Drive, Helena, AR, Zip 72342, P O Box 788, Zip 72342–0788, tel. 870/338–5800, Quentin Whitwell, Chief Executive Officer
Web address: www.helenarmc.com

CALIFORNIA: BARSTOW COMMUNITY HOSPITAL (L, 34 beds) 820 East Mountain View Street, Barstow, CA, Zip 92311–3004; tel. 760/256–1761, Adam Loris, Chief Executive Officer
Web address: www.barstowhospital.com

GEORGIA: FANNIN REGIONAL HOSPITAL (O, 50 beds) 2855 Old Highway 5, Blue Ridge, GA, Zip 30513–6248; tel. 706/632–3711, William Henry, Chief Executive Officer
Web address: www.fanninregionalhospital.com

KENTUCKY: KENTUCKY RIVER MEDICAL CENTER (L, 54 beds) 540 Jett Drive, Jackson, KY, Zip 41339–9622; tel. 606/666–6000, Susie Robinette, MSN, Chief Executive Officer
Web address: www.kentuckyrivermc.com

THREE RIVERS MEDICAL CENTER (O, 90 beds) 2485 Highway 644, Louisa, KY, Zip 41230–9242, P O Box 769, Zip 41230–0769, tel. 606/638–9451, Greg Kiser, Chief Executive Officer
Web address: www.threeriversmedicalcenter.com

NEVADA: MESA VIEW REGIONAL HOSPITAL (O, 25 beds) 1299 Bertha Howe Avenue, Mesquite, NV, Zip 89027–7500; tel. 702/346–8040, Kelly Adams, Chief Executive Officer

NEW MEXICO: ALTA VISTA REGIONAL HOSPITAL (O, 54 beds) 104 Legion Drive, Las Vegas, NM, Zip 87701–4804; tel. 505/426–3500, Robert Nelson, Chief Executive Officer
Web address: www.altavistaregionalhospital.com

MIMBRES MEMORIAL HOSPITAL (O, 25 beds) 900 West Ash Street, Deming, NM, Zip 88030–4098, P O Box 710, Zip 88031–0710, tel. 575/546–5800, Duke Young, Chief Executive Officer

OREGON: MCKENZIE–WILLAMETTE MEDICAL CENTER (O, 112 beds) 1460 'G' Street, Springfield, OR, Zip 97477–4197; tel. 541/726–4400, David Butler, Chief Executive Officer
Web address: www.mckweb.com

TEXAS: BIG BEND REGIONAL MEDICAL CENTER (O, 25 beds) 2600 North State Highway 118, Alpine, TX, Zip 79830–2002; tel. 432/837–3447, Rick Flores, Chief Executive Officer

UTAH: MOUNTAIN WEST MEDICAL CENTER (O, 44 beds) 2055 North Main Street, Tooele, UT, Zip 84074–9819; tel. 435/843–3600, Philip Eaton, Chief Executive Officer
Web address: www.mountainwestmc.com

WYOMING: EVANSTON REGIONAL HOSPITAL (O, 42 beds) 190 Arrowhead Drive, Evanston, WY, Zip 82930–9266; tel. 307/789–3636, Cheri Willard, MSN, R.N., Chief Executive Officer

Owned, leased, sponsored:	13 hospitals	609 beds
Contract-managed:	0 hospitals	0 beds
Totals:	13 hospitals	609 beds

★2625: RENOWN HEALTH (NP)
1155 Mill Street (Mailstop N14), Reno, NV Zip 89502–1576; tel. 775/982–5529, Brian Erling, M.D., President and Chief Executive Officer
(Centralized Health System)

NEVADA: CARSON VALLEY MEDICAL CENTER (O, 23 beds) 1107 Hwy 395, Gardnerville, NV, Zip 89410, 1107 Highway 395, Zip 89410, tel. 775/782–1500, Jeffrey Prater, Chief Executive Officer

RENOWN REGIONAL MEDICAL CENTER (O, 616 beds) 1155 Mill Street, Reno, NV, Zip 89502–1576; tel. 775/982–4100, Chris Nicholas, Chief Executive Officer
Web address: www.renown.org

Systems / Rush University System for Health

RENOWN REHABILITATION HOSPITAL (O, 62 beds) 1495 Mill Street, Reno, NV, Zip 89502-1479; tel. 775/982-3500, Seth M. Langevin, Vice President and Administrator

RENOWN SOUTH MEADOWS MEDICAL CENTER (O, 60 beds) 10101 Double 'R' Boulevard, Reno, NV, Zip 89521-5931; tel. 775/982-7000, Samuel Weller, Chief Executive Officer
Web address: www.renown.org

Owned, leased, sponsored:	4 hospitals	761 beds
Contract-managed:	0 hospitals	0 beds
Totals:	4 hospitals	761 beds

★0964: **RIDGEVIEW MEDICAL CENTER (NP)**
500 South Maple Street, Waconia, MN Zip 55387-1752; tel. 952/442-2191, Michael Phelps, President and Chief Executive Officer
(Independent Hospital System)

MINNESOTA: RIDGEVIEW LE SUEUR MEDICAL CENTER (O, 19 beds) 621 South Fourth Street, Le Sueur, MN, Zip 56058-2298; tel. 507/665-3375, Stacey Lee, CPA, JD, Vice President and Administrator
Web address: www.mvhc.org

RIDGEVIEW MEDICAL CENTER (O, 104 beds) 500 South Maple Street, Waconia, MN, Zip 55387-1791; tel. 952/442-2191, Michael Phelps, President and Chief Executive Officer
Web address: www.ridgeviewmedical.org

RIDGEVIEW SIBLEY MEDICAL CENTER (L, 6 beds) 601 West Chandler Street, Arlington, MN, Zip 55307-2127; tel. 507/964-2271, Stacey Lee, CPA, JD, Vice President/Administrator

Owned, leased, sponsored:	3 hospitals	129 beds
Contract-managed:	0 hospitals	0 beds
Totals:	3 hospitals	129 beds

4810: **RIVERSIDE HEALTH SYSTEM (NP)**
701 Town Center Drive, Suite 1000, Newport News, VA Zip 23606-4286; tel. 757/534-7000, Michael J. Dacey, M.D., Chief Executive Officer
(Centralized Health System)

VIRGINIA: RIVERSIDE DOCTORS' HOSPITAL WILLIAMSBURG (O, 24 beds) 1500 Commonwealth Avenue, Williamsburg, VA, Zip 23185-5229; tel. 757/585-2200, Adria Vanhoozier, President

RIVERSIDE REGIONAL MEDICAL CENTER (O, 307 beds) 500 J Clyde Morris Boulevard, Newport News, VA, Zip 23601-1929; tel. 757/594-2000, Michael Oshiki, M.D., MS, FACHE, President
Web address: https://www.riversideonline.com/rrmc/index.cfm

RIVERSIDE SHORE MEMORIAL HOSPITAL (O, 20 beds) 20480 Market Street, Onancock, VA, Zip 23417-4309, P O Box 430, Zip 23417, tel. 757/302-2100, Nicolas Chuquin, President

RIVERSIDE WALTER REED HOSPITAL (O, 23 beds) 7547 Hospital Drive, Gloucester, VA, Zip 23061-4178, P O Box 1130, Zip 23061-1130, tel. 804/693-8800, Shelly Johnson, Administrator and President
Web address: www.riversideonline.com

Owned, leased, sponsored:	4 hospitals	374 beds
Contract-managed:	0 hospitals	0 beds
Totals:	4 hospitals	374 beds

★0046: **ROCHESTER REGIONAL HEALTH (NP)**
100 Kings Highway South, Rochester, NY Zip 14617-5504; tel. 585/922-4000, Richard Davis, Ph.D., Chief Executive Officer
(Centralized Health System)

NEW YORK: CANTON–POTSDAM HOSPITAL (O, 94 beds) 50 Leroy Street, Potsdam, NY, Zip 13676-1799; tel. 315/265-3300, Donna McGregor, FACHE, President

CLIFTON SPRINGS HOSPITAL AND CLINIC (O, 194 beds) 2 Coulter Road, Clifton Springs, NY, Zip 14432-1189; tel. 315/462-9561, Daniel P. Ireland, FACHE, President and Chief Operating Officer, Finger Lakes Rural Hospitals
Web address: www.cliftonspringshospital.org

GOUVERNEUR HOSPITAL (O, 25 beds) 77 West Barney Street, Gouverneur, NY, Zip 13642-1040; tel. 315/287-1000, Katherine Schleider, Interim President, Gouverneur Hospital, Senior Vice President of Operations, St. Lawrence Health
Web address: www.gvnrhospital.org

MASSENA HOSPITAL, INC. (O, 25 beds) 1 Hospital Drive, Massena, NY, Zip 13662-1097; tel. 315/764-1711, Brent Bishop, Associate Chief Operating Officer
Web address: www.massenahospital.org

NEWARK–WAYNE COMMUNITY HOSPITAL (O, 268 beds) 1200 Driving Park Avenue, Newark, NY, Zip 14513-1057, P O Box 111, Zip 14513-0111, tel. 315/332-2022, Daniel P. Ireland, FACHE, President and Chief Operating Officer, Finger Lakes Rural Hospitals
Web address: www.rochesterregional.org

ROCHESTER GENERAL HOSPITAL (O, 608 beds) 1425 Portland Avenue, Rochester, NY, Zip 14621-3099; tel. 585/922-4000, Tammy Snyder, President and Chief Operating Officer
Web address: https://www.rochesterregional.org/

UNITED MEMORIAL MEDICAL CENTER (O, 113 beds) 127 North Street, Batavia, NY, Zip 14020-1631; tel. 585/343-6030, Daniel P. Ireland, FACHE, President and Chief Operating Officer, Finger Lakes Rural Hospitals

UNITY HOSPITAL (O, 523 beds) 1555 Long Pond Road, Rochester, NY, Zip 14626-4182; tel. 585/723-7000, Jill Graziano, R.N., Senior Vice President, President and Chief Operating Officer
Web address: www.unityhealth.org

Owned, leased, sponsored:	8 hospitals	1850 beds
Contract-managed:	0 hospitals	0 beds
Totals:	8 hospitals	1850 beds

★1044: **ROPER ST. FRANCIS HEALTHCARE (NP)**
125 Doughty Street, Suite 760, Charleston, SC Zip 29403-5785; tel. 843/402-2273, Joseph DeLeon, President and Chief Executive Officer

Owned, leased, sponsored:	0 hospitals	0 beds
Contract-managed:	0 hospitals	0 beds
Totals:	0 hospitals	0 beds

★3855: **RUSH UNIVERSITY SYSTEM FOR HEALTH (NP)**
1653 West Congress Parkway, Chicago, IL Zip 60612-3864; tel. 312/942-5000, Omar Lateef, D.O., President and Chief Executive Officer
(Moderately Centralized Health System)

ILLINOIS: RUSH OAK PARK HOSPITAL (O, 87 beds) 520 South Maple Avenue, Oak Park, IL, Zip 60304-1097; tel. 708/383-9300, Dino Rumoro, D.O., M.P.H., Chief Executive Officer
Web address: www.roph.org

RUSH SPECIALTY HOSPITAL (O, 100 beds) 516 South Loomis Street, Chicago, IL, Zip 60607; tel. 872/298-9199, Michael DeLaRosa, Chief Executive Officer

RUSH UNIVERSITY MEDICAL CENTER (O, 674 beds) 1653 West Congress Parkway, Chicago, IL, Zip 60612-3833; tel. 312/942-5000, Omar Lateef, D.O., President and Chief Executive Officer
Web address: www.rush.edu

RUSH–COPLEY MEDICAL CENTER (O, 210 beds) 2000 Ogden Avenue, Aurora, IL, Zip 60504-7222; tel. 630/978-6200, John A. Diederich, FACHE, President and Chief Executive Officer

Owned, leased, sponsored:	4 hospitals	1071 beds
Contract-managed:	0 hospitals	0 beds
Totals:	4 hospitals	1071 beds

For explanation of codes following names, see page B2.
★ Indicates Type III membership in the American Hospital Association.

Systems / Rwjbarnabas Health

★0994: RWJBARNABAS HEALTH (NP)
95 Old Short Hills Road, West Orange, NJ Zip 07052–1008; tel. 973/322–4000, Mark Manigan, President
(Decentralized Health System)

NEW JERSEY: CHILDREN'S SPECIALIZED HOSPITAL (O, 158 beds) 200 Somerset Street, New Brunswick, NJ, Zip 08901–1942; tel. 732/258–7000, Matthew B. McDonald III, President and Chief Executive Officer
Web address: www.childrens-specialized.org

CLARA MAASS MEDICAL CENTER (O, 380 beds) 1 Clara Maass Drive, Belleville, NJ, Zip 07109–3557; tel. 973/450–2000, Mary Ellen Clyne, Ph.D., President and Chief Executive Officer

COMMUNITY MEDICAL CENTER (O, 353 beds) 99 Route 37 West, Toms River, NJ, Zip 08755–6423; tel. 732/557–8000, Patrick Ahearn, Chief Executive Officer
Web address: https://www.rwjbh.org/community-medical-center/

COOPERMAN BARNABAS MEDICAL CENTER (O, 565 beds) 94 Old Short Hills Rd, Livingston, NJ, Zip 07039–5672; tel. 973/322–5000, Richard Davis, President and Chief Executive Officer

JERSEY CITY MEDICAL CENTER (O, 352 beds) 355 Grand Street, Jersey City, NJ, Zip 07302–4321; tel. 201/915–2000, Michael Prilutsky, President and Chief Executive Officer
Web address: www.barnabashealth.org/Jersey-City-Medical-Center.aspx

MONMOUTH MEDICAL CENTER, LONG BRANCH CAMPUS (O, 303 beds) 300 Second Avenue, Long Branch, NJ, Zip 07740–6303; tel. 732/222–5200, Eric Carney, President and Chief Executive Officer
Web address: www.barnabashealth.org/hospitals/monmouth_medical/index.html

MONMOUTH MEDICAL CENTER, SOUTHERN CAMPUS (O, 132 beds) 600 River Avenue, Lakewood, NJ, Zip 08701–5237; tel. 732/363–1900, Eric Carney, President and Chief Executive Officer

NEWARK BETH ISRAEL MEDICAL CENTER (O, 356 beds) 201 Lyons Avenue at Osborne Terrace, Newark, NJ, Zip 07112–2027; tel. 973/926–7000, Darrell K. Terry Sr, M.P.H., FACHE, President and Chief Executive Officer
Web address: www.barnabashealth.org/hospitals/newark_beth_israel/index.html

RWJBARNABAS HEALTH BEHAVIORAL HEALTH CENTER (O, 40 beds) 1691 Highway 9, Toms River, NJ, Zip 8754; tel. 732/914–1688, Deanna Sperling, R.N., President and Chief Executive Officer

ROBERT WOOD JOHNSON UNIVERSITY HOSPITAL RAHWAY (O, 92 beds) 865 Stone Street, Rahway, NJ, Zip 07065–2797; tel. 732/381–4200, Kirk C. Tice, President and Chief Executive Officer
Web address: www.rwjuhr.com

ROBERT WOOD JOHNSON UNIVERSITY HOSPITAL SOMERSET (O, 331 beds) 110 Rehill Avenue, Somerville, NJ, Zip 08876–2598; tel. 908/685–2200, Deidre A. Blaus, Interim Chief Administrative Officer
Web address: www.rwjbh.org

ROBERT WOOD JOHNSON UNIVERSITY HOSPITAL AT HAMILTON (O, 164 beds) 1 Hamilton Health Place, Hamilton, NJ, Zip 08690–3599; tel. 609/586–7900, Lisa Breza, R.N., Chief Administrative Officer
Web address: www.rwjhamilton.org

ROBERT WOOD JOHNSON UNIVERSITY HOSPITAL (O, 660 beds) 1 Robert Wood Johnson Place, New Brunswick, NJ, Zip 08903–2601; tel. 732/828–3000, Bill Arnold, Executive Vice President, RWJBarnabas Health, President Southern Region, Chief Executive Officer, Robert Wood Johnson Un

TRINITAS REGIONAL MEDICAL CENTER (O, 449 beds) 225 Williamson Street, Elizabeth, NJ, Zip 07202–3625; tel. 908/994–5000, Nancy DiLiegro, Ph.D., FACHE, President and Chief Executive Officer
Web address: www.trinitasrmc.com

Owned, leased, sponsored:	14 hospitals	4335 beds
Contract-managed:	0 hospitals	0 beds
Totals:	14 hospitals	4335 beds

★0254: SAINT FRANCIS HEALTH SYSTEM (CC)
6161 South Yale Avenue, Tulsa, OK Zip 74136–1902; tel. 918/494–8454, Cliff Robertson, M.D., President and Chief Executive Officer
(Centralized Health System)

OKLAHOMA: LAUREATE PSYCHIATRIC CLINIC AND HOSPITAL (O, 90 beds) 6655 South Yale Avenue, Tulsa, OK, Zip 74136–3329; tel. 918/481–4000, Kenneth Moore, President

OKLAHOMA STATE UNIVERSITY MEDICAL CENTER (C, 118 beds) 744 West Ninth Street, Tulsa, OK, Zip 74127–9020; tel. 918/599–1000, Finny Mathew, President
Web address: www.osumc.com

SAINT FRANCIS HOSPITAL MUSKOGEE (O, 188 beds) 300 Rockefeller Drive, Muskogee, OK, Zip 74401–5081; tel. 918/682–5501, Michele A. Keeling, President

SAINT FRANCIS HOSPITAL SOUTH (O, 110 beds) 10501 East 91st Street, Tulsa, OK, Zip 74133–5790; tel. 918/307–6010, Todd Schuster, President
Web address: www.saintfrancis.com/south/

SAINT FRANCIS HOSPITAL VINITA (O, 27 beds) 735 North Foreman Street, Vinita, OK, Zip 74301–1418; tel. 918/256–7551, Melinda Culp, Executive Director, Administrator
Web address: https://www.saintfrancis.com/vinita/Pages/default.aspx

SAINT FRANCIS HOSPITAL (O, 910 beds) 6161 South Yale Avenue, Tulsa, OK, Zip 74136–1902; tel. 918/494–2200, Douglas Williams, President

Owned, leased, sponsored:	5 hospitals	1325 beds
Contract-managed:	1 hospitals	118 beds
Totals:	6 hospitals	1443 beds

0403: SALEM HEALTH (NP)
890 Oak Street Bldg B POB 14001, Salem, OR Zip 97309–5014; tel. 503/561–5200, Cheryl R. Nester Wolfe, R.N., President and Chief Executive Officer
(Independent Hospital System)

OREGON: SALEM HEALTH WEST VALLEY (O, 25 beds) 525 SE Washington Street, Dallas, OR, Zip 97338–2834, P O Box 378, Zip 97338–0378, tel. 503/623–8301, Cheryl R. Nester Wolfe, R.N., President and Chief Executive Officer

SALEM HOSPITAL (O, 567 beds) 890 Oak Street SE, Salem, OR, Zip 97301–3959, P O Box 14001, Zip 97309–5014, tel. 503/561–5200, Cheryl R. Nester Wolfe, R.N., President and Chief Executive Officer
Web address: www.salemhealth.org

Owned, leased, sponsored:	2 hospitals	592 beds
Contract-managed:	0 hospitals	0 beds
Totals:	2 hospitals	592 beds

★1002: SALINA REGIONAL HEALTH CENTER (NP)
400 South Santa Fe Avenue, Salina, KS Zip 67401–4198, PO Box 5080, Zip 67402–5080, tel. 785/452–7000, Joel Phelps, President and Chief Executive Officer
(Moderately Centralized Health System)

KANSAS: LINDSBORG COMMUNITY HOSPITAL (C, 12 beds) 605 West Lincoln Street, Lindsborg, KS, Zip 67456–2328; tel. 785/227–3308, Larry Van Der Wege, Administrator
Web address: www.lindsborghospital.org

MEMORIAL HEALTH SYSTEM (C, 110 beds) 511 NE Tenth Street, Abilene, KS, Zip 67410–2153; tel. 785/263–2100, Harold Courtois, Chief Executive Officer

NORTH CENTRAL KANSAS MEDICAL CENTER (C, 25 beds) 155 West College Drive, Concordia, KS, Zip 66901; tel. 785/243–1234, David Garnas, Administrator
Web address: https://www.nckmed.com/

For explanation of codes following names, see page B2.
★ Indicates Type III membership in the American Hospital Association.

Systems / Sanford Health

SALINA REGIONAL HEALTH CENTER (O, 214 beds) 400 South Santa Fe Avenue, Salina, KS, Zip 67401-4198, P O Box 5080, Zip 67402-5080, tel. 785/452-7000, Joel Phelps, President and Chief Executive Officer

Owned, leased, sponsored:	1 hospitals	214 beds
Contract-managed:	3 hospitals	147 beds
Totals:	4 hospitals	361 beds

★0186: **SAMARITAN HEALTH SERVICES (NP)**
3600 NW Samaritan Drive, Corvallis, OR Zip 97330-3737, P O Box 1068, Zip 97339-1068, tel. 541/768-5001, Doug Boysen, President and Chief Executive Officer
(Centralized Physician/Insurance Health System)

OREGON: GOOD SAMARITAN REGIONAL MEDICAL CENTER (O, 179 beds) 3600 NW Samaritan Drive, Corvallis, OR, Zip 97330-3737, P O Box 1068, Zip 97339-1068, tel. 541/768-5111
SAMARITAN ALBANY GENERAL HOSPITAL (O, 67 beds) 1046 Sixth Avenue, SW, Albany, OR, Zip 97321-1999; tel. 541/812-4000, Dan Keteri, R.N., Chief Executive Officer
Web address: www.samhealth.org
SAMARITAN LEBANON COMMUNITY HOSPITAL (O, 25 beds) 525 North Santiam Highway, Lebanon, OR, Zip 97355-4363, P O Box 739, Zip 97355-0739, tel. 541/258-2101, Dan Rackham, Chief Executive Officer
Web address: www.samhealth.org
SAMARITAN NORTH LINCOLN HOSPITAL (C, 12 beds) 3043 NE 28th Street, Lincoln City, OR, Zip 97367-4518, P O Box 767, Zip 97367-0767, tel. 541/994-3661, Lesley Ogden, M.D., Chief Executive Officer
Web address: www.samhealth.org
SAMARITAN PACIFIC COMMUNITIES HOSPITAL (C, 25 beds) 930 SW Abbey Street, Newport, OR, Zip 97365-4820, P O Box 945, Zip 97365-0072, tel. 541/265-2244, Lesley Ogden, M.D., Chief Executive Officer
Web address: www.samhealth.org

Owned, leased, sponsored:	3 hospitals	271 beds
Contract-managed:	2 hospitals	37 beds
Totals:	5 hospitals	308 beds

★0914: **SAN LUIS VALLEY HEALTH (NP)**
106 Blanca Avenue, Alamosa, CO Zip 81101-2340; tel. 719/589-2511, Konnie Martin, President and Chief Executive Officer
(Independent Hospital System)

COLORADO: SAN LUIS VALLEY HEALTH CONEJOS COUNTY HOSPITAL (O, 17 beds) 19021 U S Highway 285, La Jara, CO, Zip 81140-0639, P O Box 639, Zip 81140-0639, tel. 719/274-5121, Konnie Martin, President and Chief Executive Officer
SAN LUIS VALLEY HEALTH (O, 44 beds) 106 Blanca Avenue, Alamosa, CO, Zip 81101-2393; tel. 719/589-2511, Konnie Martin, Chief Executive Officer
Web address: www.sanluisvalleyhealth.org

Owned, leased, sponsored:	2 hospitals	61 beds
Contract-managed:	0 hospitals	0 beds
Totals:	2 hospitals	61 beds

★0530: **SANFORD HEALTH (NP)**
2301 East 60th Street North, Sioux Falls, SD Zip 57104-0569, PO Box 5039, Zip 57117-5039, tel. 605/333-1000, Bill Gassen, President and Chief Executive Officer
(Decentralized Health System)

IOWA: ORANGE CITY AREA HEALTH SYSTEM (C, 114 beds) 1000 Lincoln Circle SE, Orange City, IA, Zip 51041-1862; tel. 712/737-4984, Martin W. Guthmiller, Chief Executive Officer
Web address: www.ochealthsystem.org

SANFORD SHELDON MEDICAL CENTER (O, 93 beds) 118 North Seventh Avenue, Sheldon, IA, Zip 51201-1235, P O Box 250, Zip 51201-0250, tel. 712/324-5041, Richard E. Nordahl, Senior Director
Web address: www.sanfordsheldon.org

MINNESOTA: MAHNOMEN HEALTH (C, 50 beds) 414 West Jefferson Avenue, Mahnomen, MN, Zip 56557-4912, PO Box 396, Zip 56557-0396, tel. 218/935-2511, Dale K. Kruger, Chief Executive Officer
MURRAY COUNTY MEDICAL CENTER (C, 20 beds) 2042 Juniper Avenue, Slayton, MN, Zip 56172-1017; tel. 507/836-6111, Luke Schryvers, Chief Executive Officer
Web address: www.murraycountymed.org
ORTONVILLE AREA HEALTH SERVICES (C, 90 beds) 450 Eastvold Avenue, Ortonville, MN, Zip 56278-1133; tel. 320/839-2502, Allan Ross, Chief Exccecutive Officer
PERHAM HEALTH (C, 119 beds) 1000 Coney Street West, Perham, MN, Zip 56573-1108; tel. 218/347-4500, Chuck Hofius, FACHE, Chief Executive Officer
Web address: www.perhamhealth.org
SANFORD BAGLEY MEDICAL CENTER (O, 8 beds) 203 Fourth Street NW, Bagley, MN, Zip 56621-8307; tel. 218/694-6501, Carrie Krump, Senior Director
SANFORD BEHAVIORAL HEALTH CENTER (O, 16 beds) 120 LaBree Avenue South, Thief River Falls, MN, Zip 56701-2819, 3001 Sanford Parkway, Zip 56701-2819, tel. 218/683-4349, Heather Bregier, Administrator, Chief Executive Officer
Web address: www.sanfordhealth.org/Locations/1766896362
SANFORD BEMIDJI MEDICAL CENTER (O, 196 beds) 1300 Anne Street NW, Bemidji, MN, Zip 56601-5103; tel. 218/751-5430, Karla Eischens, Chief Executive Officer
SANFORD CANBY MEDICAL CENTER (L, 68 beds) 112 St Olaf Avenue South, Canby, MN, Zip 56220-1433; tel. 507/223-7277, Lori Sisk, R.N., Chief Executive Officer
Web address: www.sanfordcanby.org
SANFORD JACKSON MEDICAL CENTER (O, 16 beds) 1430 North Highway, Jackson, MN, Zip 56143-1093; tel. 507/847-2420, Dawn Schnell, Administrator and Chief Executive Officer
Web address: www.sanfordjackson.org
SANFORD LUVERNE MEDICAL CENTER (O, 18 beds) 1600 North Kniss Avenue, Luverne, MN, Zip 56156-1067; tel. 507/283-2321, Tammy Loosbrock, Chief Executive Officer and Administrator
Web address: https://www.sanfordhealth.org/locations/sanford-luverne-medical-center
SANFORD THIEF RIVER FALLS MEDICAL CENTER (O, 25 beds) 3001 Sanford Parkway, Thief River Falls, MN, Zip 56701-2700; tel. 218/681-4747, Tyler Ust, Adminstrator, Chief Executive Officer
Web address: www.sanfordhealth.org
SANFORD TRACY MEDICAL CENTER (O, 10 beds) 251 Fifth Street East, Tracy, MN, Zip 56175-1536; tel. 507/629-8400, Stacy Barstad, Chief Executive Officer
Web address: www.sanfordtracy.org
SANFORD WESTBROOK MEDICAL CENTER (L, 5 beds) 920 Bell Avenue, Westbrook, MN, Zip 56183-9669, P O Box 188, Zip 56183-0188, tel. 507/274-6121, Stacy Barstad, Chief Executive Officer
Web address: www.sanfordwestbrook.org
SANFORD WHEATON MEDICAL CENTER (O, 12 beds) 401 12th Street North, Wheaton, MN, Zip 56296-1099; tel. 320/563-8226, Chelsie Falk, Chief Executive Officer
Web address: www.sanfordhealth.org
SANFORD WORTHINGTON MEDICAL CENTER (O, 48 beds) 1018 Sixth Avenue, Worthington, MN, Zip 56187-2202, P O Box 997, Zip 56187-0997, tel. 507/372-2941, Jennifer Weg, MS, R.N., Executive Director
Web address: www.sanfordhealth.org
WINDOM AREA HEALTH (C, 18 beds) 2150 Hospital Drive, Windom, MN, Zip 56101-0339, P O Box 339, Zip 56101-0339, tel. 507/831-2400, Shelby Medina, Chief Executive Officer

NORTH DAKOTA: NORTHWOOD DEACONESS HEALTH CENTER (O, 57 beds) 4 North Park Street, Northwood, ND, Zip 58267-4102, P O Box 190,

For explanation of codes following names, see page B2.
★ Indicates Type III membership in the American Hospital Association.

Systems / Sanford Health

Zip 58267-0190, tel. 701/587-6060, Brock Sherva, Chief Executive Officer
Web address: www.ndhc.net

SANFORD HILLSBORO MEDICAL CENTER (O, 46 beds) 12 Third Street SE, Hillsboro, ND, Zip 58045-4840, P O Box 609, Zip 58045-0609, tel. 701/636-3200, Jac McTaggart, Chief Executive Officer

SANFORD MAYVILLE MEDICAL CENTER (O, 10 beds) 42 Sixth Avenue SE, Mayville, ND, Zip 58257-1598; tel. 701/786-3800, Jac McTaggart, Chief Executive Officer
Web address: www.unionhospital.com

SANFORD MEDICAL CENTER BISMARCK (O, 241 beds) 300 North Seventh Street, Bismarck, ND, Zip 58501-4439, P O Box 5525, Zip 58506-5525, tel. 701/323-6000, Todd Schaffer, M.D., President and Chief Executive Officer

SANFORD MEDICAL CENTER FARGO (O, 530 beds) 801 Broadway North, Fargo, ND, Zip 58122-3641; tel. 701/234-2000, Tiffany Lawrence, President and Chief Executive Officer
Web address: www.sanfordhealth.org

SOUTH DAKOTA: COMMUNITY MEMORIAL HOSPITAL (C, 16 beds) 809 Jackson Street, Burke, SD, Zip 57523-2065, P O Box 319, Zip 57523-0319, tel. 605/775-2621, Mistie Drey, Chief Executive Officer
Web address: www.sanfordhealth.org

COTEAU DES PRAIRIES HOSPITAL (C, 25 beds) 205 Orchard Drive, Sisseton, SD, Zip 57262-2398; tel. 605/698-7647, Craig A. Kantos, Chief Executive Officer
Web address: www.cdphospital.com

PIONEER MEMORIAL HOSPITAL AND HEALTH SERVICES (C, 55 beds) 315 North Washington Street, Viborg, SD, Zip 57070-2002, P O Box 368, Zip 57070-0368, tel. 605/326-5161, Isaac Gerdes, Chief Executive Officer
Web address: www.pioneermemorial.org

SANFORD ABERDEEN MEDICAL CENTER (O, 48 beds) 2905 3rd Avenue SE, Aberdeen, SD, Zip 57401-5420; tel. 605/626-4200, Kila LeGrand, Executive Director
Web address: https://www.sanfordhealth.org/locations/sanford-aberdeen-medical-center

SANFORD CANTON-INWOOD MEDICAL CENTER (O, 11 beds) 440 North Hiawatha Drive, Canton, SD, Zip 57013-5800; tel. 605/764-1400, Scott C. Larson, Chief Executive Officer

SANFORD CHAMBERLAIN MEDICAL CENTER (O, 60 beds) 300 South Byron Boulevard, Chamberlain, SD, Zip 57325-9741; tel. 605/234-5511, Erica Peterson, Chief Executive Officer
Web address: www.sanfordchamberlain.org

SANFORD CLEAR LAKE MEDICAL CENTER (L, 10 beds) 701 Third Avenue South, Clear Lake, SD, Zip 57226-2016; tel. 605/874-2141, Lori Sisk, R.N., Chief Executive Officer
Web address: www.sanforddeuelcounty.org

SANFORD USD MEDICAL CENTER (O, 410 beds) 1305 West 18th Street, Sioux Falls, SD, Zip 57105-0496, P O Box 5039, Zip 57117-5039, tel. 605/333-1000, Paul A. Hanson, FACHE, President

SANFORD VERMILLION MEDICAL CENTER (L, 88 beds) 20 South Plum Street, Vermillion, SD, Zip 57069-3346; tel. 605/677-3500, Timothy J. Tracy, Senior Director
Web address: www.sanfordvermillion.org

SANFORD WEBSTER MEDICAL CENTER (L, 20 beds) 1401 West 1st Street, Webster, SD, Zip 57274-1054, P O Box 489, Zip 57274-0489, tel. 605/345-3336, Isaac Gerdes, Chief Executive Officer
Web address: https://www.sanfordhealth.org/locations/sanford-webster-medical-center

WINNER REGIONAL HEALTHCARE CENTER (C, 104 beds) 745 East Eighth Street, Winner, SD, Zip 57580-2631; tel. 605/842-7100, Brian Williams, Chief Executive Officer

Owned, leased, sponsored:	24 hospitals	2046 beds
Contract-managed:	10 hospitals	611 beds
Totals:	34 hospitals	2657 beds

0419: SARASOTA MEMORIAL HEALTH CARE SYSTEM (NP)
1540 South Tamiami Trail, Sarasota, FL Zip 34239-2930; tel. 941/917-7322, David Verinder, Chief Executive Officer

FLORIDA: SARASOTA MEMORIAL HOSPITAL–SARASOTA (O, 901 beds) 1700 South Tamiami Trail, Sarasota, FL, Zip 34239-3555; tel. 941/917-9000, David Verinder, President & Chief Executive Officer
Web address: www.smh.com

SARASOTA MEMORIAL HOSPITAL–VENICE (O, 110 beds) 2600 Laurel Road East, North Venice, FL, Zip 34275-3226; tel. 941/261-2797, David Verinder, Chief Executive Officer
Web address: www.smh.com

Owned, leased, sponsored:	2 hospitals	1011 beds
Contract-managed:	0 hospitals	0 beds
Totals:	2 hospitals	1011 beds

★1096: SCIONHEALTH (IO)
680 South Fourth Street, Louisville, KY Zip 40202-2407; tel. 502/596-7300, Robert F. Jay, Chief Executive Officer

ALABAMA: ANDALUSIA HEALTH (O, 78 beds) 849 South Three Notch Street, Andalusia, AL, Zip 36420-5325, P O Box 760, Zip 36420-1214, tel. 334/222-8466, Vickie Demers, Chief Executive Officer
Web address: www.andalusiahealth.com

VAUGHAN REGIONAL MEDICAL CENTER (O, 149 beds) 1015 Medical Center Parkway, Selma, AL, Zip 36701-6352; tel. 334/418-4100, J. David. McCormack, Chief Executive Officer
Web address: www.vaughanregional.com

ARIZONA: CORNERSTONE SPECIALTY HOSPITALS TUCSON (O, 34 beds) 7220 East Rosewood Drive, Tucson, AZ, Zip 85710-1350; tel. 520/546-4595, Debora Bornmann, Chief Executive Officer

ARKANSAS: CORNERSTONE SPECIALTY HOSPITALS LITTLE ROCK (O, 30 beds) 2 Saint Vincent Circle, 6th Floor, Little Rock, AR, Zip 72205-5423; tel. 501/265-0600, Kiacie Andrews, Chief Executive Officer
Web address: www.chghospitals.com/littlerock/

CALIFORNIA: KINDRED HOSPITAL PARAMOUNT (O, 177 beds) 16453 South Colorado Avenue, Paramount, CA, Zip 90723-5011; tel. 562/531-3110, Mark Apodaca, Chief Executive Officer
Web address: www.promiseeastla.com

KINDRED HOSPITAL RANCHO (O, 55 beds) 10841 White Oak Avenue, Rancho Cucamonga, CA, Zip 91730-3811; tel. 909/581-6400, Julie Myers, Market Chief Executive Officer

KINDRED HOSPITAL RIVERSIDE (O, 40 beds) 2224 Medical Center Drive, Perris, CA, Zip 92571-2638; tel. 951/436-3535, Julie Myers, Market Chief Executive Officer
Web address: www.khriverside.com

KINDRED HOSPITAL SOUTH BAY (O, 84 beds) 1246 West 155th Street, Gardena, CA, Zip 90247-4062; tel. 310/323-5330, Mark Apodaca, Chief Executive Officer
Web address: www.khsouthbay.com/

KINDRED HOSPITAL–BALDWIN PARK (O, 91 beds) 14148 Francisquito Avenue, Baldwin Park, CA, Zip 91706-6120; tel. 626/388-2700, Kevin Chavez, Central District Chief Executive Officer

KINDRED HOSPITAL–BREA (O, 48 beds) 875 North Brea Boulevard, Brea, CA, Zip 92821-2699; tel. 714/529-6842, Kevin Chavez, Central District Chief Executive Officer
Web address: www.kindredhospitalbrea.com/

KINDRED HOSPITAL–LA MIRADA (O, 118 beds) 14900 East Imperial Highway, La Mirada, CA, Zip 90638-2172; tel. 562/944-1900, Phillip H. Wolfe, Market Chief Executive Officer
Web address: https://www.kindredhospitals.com/locations/ltac/kindred-hospital-la-mirada

KINDRED HOSPITAL–LOS ANGELES (O, 81 beds) 5525 West Slauson Avenue, Los Angeles, CA, Zip 90056-1067; tel. 310/642-0325, Mark Apodaca, Chief Executive Officer

KINDRED HOSPITAL–ONTARIO (O, 81 beds) 550 North Monterey Avenue, Ontario, CA, Zip 91764-3399; tel. 909/391-0333, Julie Myers, Market Chief Executive Officer
Web address: www.khontario.com/

For explanation of codes following names, see page B2.
★ Indicates Type III membership in the American Hospital Association.

Systems / Scionhealth

KINDRED HOSPITAL–SAN DIEGO (O, 58 beds) 1940 El Cajon Boulevard, San Diego, CA, Zip 92104–1096; tel. 619/543–4500, Robin Gomez, R.N., MSN, Chief Executive Officer

KINDRED HOSPITAL–SAN FRANCISCO BAY AREA (O, 99 beds) 2800 Benedict Drive, San Leandro, CA, Zip 94577–6840; tel. 510/357–8300, Larry Foster, R.N., MSN, Chief Executive Officer
Web address: www.kindredhospitalsfba.com

KINDRED HOSPITAL–WESTMINSTER (O, 109 beds) 200 Hospital Circle, Westminster, CA, Zip 92683–3910; tel. 714/893–4541, Phillip H. Wolfe, Market Chief Executive Officer
Web address: www.khwestminster.com/

COLORADO: KINDRED HOSPITAL–AURORA (O, 23 beds) 700 Potomac Street 2nd Floor, Aurora, CO, Zip 80011–6844; tel. 720/857–8333, Kevin Zachary, R.N., Chief Executive Officer

KINDRED HOSPITAL–DENVER (O, 68 beds) 1920 High Street, Denver, CO, Zip 80218–1213; tel. 303/320–5871, Kevin Zachary, R.N., Market Chief Executive Officer
Web address: www.kh-denver.com

FLORIDA: KINDRED HOSPITAL BAY AREA–TAMPA (O, 73 beds) 4555 South Manhattan Avenue, Tampa, FL, Zip 33611–2397; tel. 813/839–6341, Jeffrey Harrison, Market Chief Executive Officer
Web address: www.khtampa.com/

KINDRED HOSPITAL CENTRAL TAMPA (O, 102 beds) 4801 North Howard Avenue, Tampa, FL, Zip 33603–1411; tel. 813/874–7575, Amy Kendall, Chief Executive Officer

KINDRED HOSPITAL MELBOURNE (O, 58 beds) 765 West Nasa Boulevard, Melbourne, FL, Zip 32901–1815; tel. 321/733–5725, Pamela R. Reed, Chief Executive Officer
Web address: www.khmelbourne.com

KINDRED HOSPITAL NORTH FLORIDA (O, 80 beds) 801 Oak Street, Green Cove Springs, FL, Zip 32043–4317; tel. 904/284–9230, Robbi Hudson, Chief Executive Officer

KINDRED HOSPITAL OCALA (O, 31 beds) 1500 SW 1st Avenue, Ocala, FL, Zip 34471–6504; tel. 352/369–0513, Merlene Bhoorasingh, Administrator
Web address: www.kindredocala.com/

KINDRED HOSPITAL SOUTH FLORIDA–FORT LAUDERDALE (O, 64 beds) 1516 East Las Olas Boulevard, Fort Lauderdale, FL, Zip 33301–2399; tel. 954/764–8900, Cindy Jackson, Market Chief Executive Officer
Web address: www.khfortlauderdale.com

KINDRED HOSPITAL THE PALM BEACHES (O, 68 beds) 5555 West Blue Heron Boulevard, Riviera Beach, FL, Zip 33418–7813; tel. 561/840–0754, Elayne Honerlaw, Chief Executive Officer

GEORGIA: ST. FRANCIS–EMORY HEALTHCARE (O, 331 beds) 2122 Manchester Expressway, Columbus, GA, Zip 31904–6878, P O Box 7000, Zip 31908–7000, tel. 706/596–4000, Melody Trimble, Chief Executive Officer
Web address: www.mystfrancis.com

IDAHO: ST. JOSEPH REGIONAL MEDICAL CENTER (O, 90 beds) 415 Sixth Street, Lewiston, ID, Zip 83501–2431; tel. 208/743–2511, Edward E. Freysinger, Chief Executive Officer

ILLINOIS: KINDRED CHICAGO LAKESHORE (O, 103 beds) 6130 North Sheridan Road, Chicago, IL, Zip 60660; tel. 773/381–1222, Kathy Kelly, Market Chief Executive Officer
Web address: www.kindredhealthcare.com

KINDRED HOSPITAL CHICAGO–NORTHLAKE (O, 94 beds) 365 East North Avenue, Northlake, IL, Zip 60164–2628; tel. 708/345–8100, Kathy Kelly, Market Chief Executive Officer
Web address: https://www.kindredhospitals.com/locations/ltac/kindred-hospital-chicago-northlake-campus

KINDRED HOSPITAL–SYCAMORE (O, 69 beds) 225 Edward Street, Sycamore, IL, Zip 60178–2137; tel. 815/895–2144, Kathy Kelly, Chief Executive Officer
Web address: www.kindredhospitalsyc.com/

INDIANA: KINDRED HOSPITAL INDIANAPOLIS NORTH (O, 45 beds) 8060 Knue Road, Indianapolis, IN, Zip 46250–1976; tel. 317/813–8900, Nakia Tremble, Chief Executive Officer

KINDRED HOSPITAL–INDIANAPOLIS (O, 26 beds) 1700 West 10th Street, Indianapolis, IN, Zip 46222–3802; tel. 317/636–4400, Judy K. Weaver, MS, Interim Chief Executive Officer
Web address: www.kindredhospitalindy.com/

KENTUCKY: KINDRED HOSPITAL–LOUISVILLE (O, 117 beds) 1313 Saint Anthony Place, Louisville, KY, Zip 40204–1740; tel. 502/587–7001, Tim Phoenix, Chief Executive Officer
Web address: www.kindredlouisville.com

LOUISIANA: CORNERSTONE SPECIALTY HOSPITALS BOSSIER CITY (O, 54 beds) 4900 Medical Drive, Bossier City, LA, Zip 71112–4521; tel. 318/747–9500, Sheri Burnette, R.N., Chief Executive Officer

CORNERSTONE SPECIALTY HOSPITALS SOUTHWEST LOUISIANA (O, 28 beds) 524 Doctor Michael Debakey Drive, Lake Charles, LA, Zip 70601–5725; tel. 337/310–6000, Darren Williams, Chief Executive Officer
Web address: www.chghospitals.com/sulphur/

CORNERSTONE SPECIALTY HOSPITALS WEST MONROE (O, 40 beds) 6198 Cypress Street, West Monroe, LA, Zip 71291–9010; tel. 318/396–5600, Chris Simpson, Chief Executive Officer

MISSISSIPPI: BOLIVAR MEDICAL CENTER (O, 124 beds) 901 East Sunflower Road, Cleveland, MS, Zip 38732–2833, P O Box 1380, Zip 38732–1380, tel. 662/846–0061, James Young, Chief Executive Officer
Web address: www.bolivarmedical.com

MISSOURI: KINDRED HOSPITAL NORTHLAND (O, 42 beds) 500 Northwest 68th Street, Kansas City, MO, Zip 64118–2455; tel. 816/420–6300, Laura Inge, MSN, R.N., Chief Executive Officer
Web address: www.khnorthland.com

KINDRED HOSPITAL–ST. LOUIS (O, 98 beds) 4930 Lindell Boulevard, Saint Louis, MO, Zip 63108–1510; tel. 314/361–8700, Larry Rodgers, Market Chief Executive Officer
Web address: www.kindredstlouis.com/

NEVADA: KINDRED HOSPITAL LAS VEGAS–SAHARA (O, 238 beds) 102 East Mead Parkway, 3rd Floor, Henderson, NV, Zip 89015; tel. 702/871–1418, Robin Hager, Chief Executive Officer

NEW JERSEY: KINDRED HOSPITAL–NEW JERSEY MORRIS COUNTY (O, 45 beds) 400 West Blackwell Street, Dover, NJ, Zip 07801–2525; tel. 973/537–3818, Andrew P. Donet, Chief Executive Officer
Web address: www.khmorriscounty.com/

NEW MEXICO: KINDRED HOSPITAL–ALBUQUERQUE (O, 57 beds) 700 High Street NE, Albuquerque, NM, Zip 87102–2565; tel. 505/242–4444, Lisa Cochran, Chief Executive Officer

NORTH CAROLINA: KINDRED HOSPITAL–GREENSBORO (O, 101 beds) 2401 Southside Boulevard, Greensboro, NC, Zip 27406–3311; tel. 336/271–2800, Preston Bryant, Chief Executive Officer
Web address: https://www.kindredhospitals.com/locations/ltac/kindred-hospital-greensboro

OHIO: CMH REGIONAL HEALTH SYSTEM (O, 119 beds) 610 West Main Street, Wilmington, OH, Zip 45177–2125; tel. 937/382–6611, Tom G. Daskalakis, Chief Executive Officer
Web address: www.cmhregional.com

KINDRED HOSPITAL LIMA (O, 26 beds) 730 West Market Street, 6th Floor, Lima, OH, Zip 45801–4602; tel. 419/224–1888, Susan Krinke, Chief Executive Officer

KINDRED HOSPITAL–DAYTON (O, 67 beds) 707 South Edwin C Moses Boulevard, Dayton, OH, Zip 45417–3462; tel. 937/222–5963, Phillip Underwood, Chief Executive Officer
Web address: www.khdayton.com

OKLAHOMA: CORNERSTONE SPECIALTY HOSPITALS MUSKOGEE (O, 41 beds) 351 South 40th Street, Muskogee, OK, Zip 74401–4916; tel. 918/682–6161, Denise Benningfield. Crelia, Market Chief Executive Office & Chief Nursing Executive

CORNERSTONE SPECIALTY HOSPITALS SHAWNEE (O, 34 beds) 1900 Gordon Cooper Drive, 2nd Floor, Shawnee, OK, Zip 74801–8603, P O Box 1245, Zip 74802–1245, tel. 405/395–5800, Larissa Trulson, Chief Executive Officer
Web address: www.chghospitals.com/shawnee/

SOUTHWESTERN MEDICAL CENTER (O, 165 beds) 5602 SW Lee Boulevard, Lawton, OK, Zip 73505–9635; tel. 580/531–4700, Adam Bracks, Chief Executive Officer
Web address: www.swmconline.com

PENNSYLVANIA: KINDRED HOSPITAL PHILADELPHIA (O, 86 beds) 6129 Palmetto Street, Philadelphia, PA, Zip 19111–5729; tel. 215/722–8555, Andrew P. Donet, Market Chief Executive Officer
Web address: www.kindredphila.com/

For explanation of codes following names, see page B2.
★ Indicates Type III membership in the American Hospital Association.

Systems / Scionhealth

SOUTH CAROLINA: CAROLINA PINES REGIONAL MEDICAL CENTER (O, 116 beds) 1304 West Bobo Newsom Highway, Hartsville, SC, Zip 29550–4710; tel. 843/339–2100, William Little, Chief Executive Officer
Web address: www.cprmc.com

TENNESSEE: KINDRED HOSPITAL–CHATTANOOGA (O, 39 beds) 709 Walnut Street, Chattanooga, TN, Zip 37402–1916; tel. 423/266–7721, Andrea White, Chief Executive Officer
Web address: www.kindredchattanooga.com/

LIVINGSTON REGIONAL HOSPITAL (O, 89 beds) 315 Oak Street, Livingston, TN, Zip 38570–1728, P O Box 550, Zip 38570–0550, tel. 931/823–5611, Timothy W. McGill, Chief Executive Officer
Web address: www.MyLivingstonHospital.com

TEXAS: CORNERSTONE SPECIALTY HOSPITALS AUSTIN ROUND ROCK (O, 96 beds) 4207 Burnet Road, Austin, TX, Zip 78756–3396; tel. 512/706–1900, Curt L. Roberts, Market Chief Executive Officer

CORNERSTONE SPECIALTY HOSPITALS CONROE (O, 41 beds) 1500 Grand Lake Drive, Conroe, TX, Zip 77304–2891; tel. 936/523–1800, Suzanne Kretschmer, Chief Executive Officer
Web address: www.chghospitals.com/conroe/

ENNIS REGIONAL MEDICAL CENTER (O, 58 beds) 2201 West Lampasas Street, Ennis, TX, Zip 75119–5644; tel. 972/875–0900, Doug Holzbog, Market Chief Executive Officer

KINDRED HOSPITAL CLEAR LAKE (O, 110 beds) 350 Blossom Street, Webster, TX, Zip 77598; tel. 281/316–7800, Angel Gradney, Chief Executive Officer
Web address: www.khclearlake.com

KINDRED HOSPITAL DALLAS CENTRAL (O, 54 beds) 8050 Meadow Road, Dallas, TX, Zip 75231–3406; tel. 469/232–6500, Abiola Anyebe, Market Chief Executive Officer
Web address: www.khdallascentral.com/

KINDRED HOSPITAL EL PASO (O, 42 beds) 1740 Curie Drive, El Paso, TX, Zip 79902–2901; tel. 915/351–9044, America Jones, R.N., Chief Executive Officer

KINDRED HOSPITAL HOUSTON MEDICAL CENTER (O, 84 beds) 6441 Main Street, Houston, TX, Zip 77030–1596; tel. 713/790–0500, Laura Rodriguez, Chief Executive Officer
Web address: www.khhouston.com/

KINDRED HOSPITAL SAN ANTONIO CENTRAL (O, 44 beds) 111 Dallas Street, 4th Floor, San Antonio, TX, Zip 78205–1201; tel. 210/297–7185, Bo Bowman, Chief Executive Officer
Web address: www.kindredsanantoniocentral.com/

KINDRED HOSPITAL SUGAR LAND (O, 91 beds) 1550 First Colony Boulevard, Sugar Land, TX, Zip 77479–4000; tel. 281/275–6000, Hala Alameddine, Chief Executive Officer

KINDRED HOSPITAL TARRANT COUNTY–ARLINGTON (O, 68 beds) 1000 North Cooper Street, Arlington, TX, Zip 76011–5540; tel. 817/548–3400, Christina Richard, Chief Executive Officer
Web address: www.kindredhospitalarl.com/

KINDRED HOSPITAL–HOUSTON NORTHWEST (O, 84 beds) 11297 Fallbrook Drive, Houston, TX, Zip 77065–4292; tel. 281/897–8114, Tracy Kohler, Chief Executive Officer

KINDRED HOSPITAL–SAN ANTONIO (O, 59 beds) 3636 Medical Drive, San Antonio, TX, Zip 78229–2183; tel. 210/616–0616, Lana Bamiro, Chief Executive Officer and Chief Operating Officer
Web address: https://www.kindredhospitals.com/locations/ltac/kindred-hospital-san-antonio

PALESTINE REGIONAL MEDICAL CENTER–EAST (O, 160 beds) 2900 South Loop 256, Palestine, TX, Zip 75801–6958; tel. 903/731–1000, Doug Holzbog, Market Chief Executive Officer
Web address: www.palestineregional.com

PARKVIEW REGIONAL HOSPITAL (O, 58 beds) 600 South Bonham, Mexia, TX, Zip 76667–3603; tel. 254/562–5332, Doug Holzbog, Market Chief Executive Officer

SOLARA SPECIALTY HOSPITALS HARLINGEN–BROWNSVILLE (O, 41 beds) 333 Lorenaly Drive, Brownsville, TX, Zip 78526–4333; tel. 956/546–0808, Cynthia Issacs, Chief Executive Officer
Web address: www.chghospitals.com/brownsville

SOLARA SPECIALTY HOSPITALS MCALLEN (O, 53 beds) 301 West Expressway 83, 8th Floor, McAllen, TX, Zip 78503–3045; tel. 956/632–4880, Alberto Sanchez, Chief Executive Officer

WASHINGTON: KINDRED HOSPITAL SEATTLE–FIRST HILL (O, 10 beds) 1334 Terry Avenue, Seattle, WA, Zip 98101–2747; tel. 206/682–2661, Brian Nall, Chief Executive Officer
Web address: www.khseattlefirsthill.com

WEST VIRGINIA: CORNERSTONE SPECIALTY HOSPITALS HUNTINGTON (O, 32 beds) 2900 First Avenue, Two East, Huntington, WV, Zip 25702–1241; tel. 304/399–2600, Rodney Midkiff, Chief Executive Officer

LOGAN REGIONAL MEDICAL CENTER (O, 140 beds) 20 Hospital Drive, Logan, WV, Zip 25601–3452; tel. 304/831–1101, David L. Brash, Chief Executive Officer
Web address: www.loganregionalmedicalcenter.com

WISCONSIN: WATERTOWN REGIONAL MEDICAL CENTER (O, 64 beds) 125 Hospital Drive, Watertown, WI, Zip 53098–3303; tel. 920/261–4210, Richard Keddington, Chief Executive Officer
Web address: www.watertownregional.com/Main/Home.aspx

WYOMING: SAGEWEST HEALTH CARE (O, 145 beds) 2100 West Sunset Drive, Riverton, WY, Zip 82501–2274; tel. 307/856–4161, John Whiteside, Chief Executive Officer

Owned, leased, sponsored:	74 hospitals	5917 beds
Contract–managed:	0 hospitals	0 beds
Totals:	74 hospitals	5917 beds

★1505: SCRIPPS HEALTH (NP)
4275 Campus Point Court CP112, San Diego, CA Zip 92121–1513, 4275 Campus Point Court, Zip 92121–1513, tel. 858/678–7200, Chris D. Van Gorder, FACHE, President and Chief Executive Officer
(Centralized Health System)

CALIFORNIA: SCRIPPS GREEN HOSPITAL (O, 150 beds) 10666 North Torrey Pines Road, La Jolla, CA, Zip 92037–1093; tel. 858/455–9100, Chris D. Van Gorder, FACHE, President and Chief Executive Officer

SCRIPPS MEMORIAL HOSPITAL–ENCINITAS (O, 187 beds) 354 Santa Fe Drive, Encinitas, CA, Zip 92024–5182, P O Box 230817, Zip 92023–0817, tel. 760/633–6501, Chris D. Van Gorder, FACHE, President, Chief Executive Officer
Web address: www.scripps.org

SCRIPPS MEMORIAL HOSPITAL–LA JOLLA (O, 426 beds) 9888 Genesee Avenue, La Jolla, CA, Zip 92037–1200, P O Box 28, Zip 92038–0028, tel. 858/626–4123, Carl J. Etter, Chief Executive Officer
Web address: www.scripps.org/locations/hospitals__scripps-memorial-hospital-la-jolla

SCRIPPS MERCY HOSPITAL (O, 559 beds) 4077 Fifth Avenue, San Diego, CA, Zip 92103–2105; tel. 619/294–8111, Chris D. Van Gorder, FACHE, President and Chief Executive Officer
Web address: www.scrippshealth.org

Owned, leased, sponsored:	4 hospitals	1322 beds
Contract–managed:	0 hospitals	0 beds
Totals:	4 hospitals	1322 beds

★0181: SELECT MEDICAL CORPORATION (IO)
4714 Gettysburg Road, Mechanicsburg, PA Zip 17055–4325; tel. 717/972–1100, David S. Chernow, Chief Executive Officer
(Independent Hospital System)

ALABAMA: SELECT SPECIALTY HOSPITAL–BIRMINGHAM (O, 38 beds) 2010 Brookwood Medical Center Drive, 3rd Floor, Birmingham, AL, Zip 35209–6804; tel. 205/599–4600, Andrew Howard, Chief Executive Officer
Web address: www.birmingham.selectspecialtyhospitals.com

ARIZONA: BANNER REHABILITATION HOSPITAL PHOENIX (O, 168 beds) 775 East Willetta Street, Phoenix, AZ, Zip 85006–2723; tel. 480/581–3900, Thomas Rufrano, Chief Executive Officer

HONORHEALTH REHABILITATION HOSPITAL (O, 50 beds) 8850 East Pima Center Parkway, Scottsdale, AZ, Zip 85258–4619; tel. 480/800–3900, Ashlie Decker, Chief Executive Officer
Web address: www.scottsdale-rehab.com/

For explanation of codes following names, see page B2.
★ Indicates Type III membership in the American Hospital Association.

Systems / Select Medical Corporation

SELECT SPECIALTY HOSPITAL–TUCSON (O, 30 beds) 2025 West Orange Grove Road, Tucson, AZ, Zip 85704–1118; tel. 520/584–4500, Mark Powell, Chief Executive Officer

SELECT SPECIALTY HOSPITAL–PHOENIX DOWNTOWN (O, 32 beds) 1111 East McDowell Road, 11th Floor, Phoenix, AZ, Zip 85006–2612; tel. 602/839–6550, Raymond Ramos, FACHE, Chief Executive Officer
Web address: www.selectmedicalcorp.com

SELECT SPECIALTY HOSPITAL–PHOENIX (O, 48 beds) 350 West Thomas Road, 3rd Floor Main, Phoenix, AZ, Zip 85013–4409; tel. 602/406–6810, Karen Cawley, Chief Executive Officer

ARKANSAS: REGENCY HOSPITAL OF NORTHWEST ARKANSAS–SPRINGDALE (O, 25 beds) 609 West Maple Avenue, 6th Fl, Springdale, AR, Zip 72764; tel. 479/757–2600, Lisa Muskrat, Chief Executive Officer
Web address: www.regencyhospital.com

SELECT SPECIALTY HOSPITAL–FORT SMITH (O, 34 beds) 1001 Towson Avenue, 6 Central, Fort Smith, AR, Zip 72901–4921; tel. 479/441–3960, Shannon Grams, Chief Executive Officer

CALIFORNIA: CALIFORNIA REHABILITATION INSTITUTE (O, 138 beds) 2070 Century Park East, Los Angeles, CA, Zip 90067–1907; tel. 424/363–1000, Geoffrey Hall, Chief Executive Officer
Web address: www.californiarehabinstitute.com/

SELECT SPECIALTY HOSPITAL–SAN DIEGO (C, 80 beds) 555 Washington Street, San Diego, CA, Zip 92103–2294; tel. 619/260–8300, Tuan Le, Chief Executive Officer

DELAWARE: SELECT SPECIALTY HOSPITAL–WILMINGTON (O, 35 beds) 701 North Clayton Street, 5th Floor, Wilmington, DE, Zip 19805–3948, 501 West 14th Street, 9th Floor, Zip 19805–3948, tel. 302/421–4545, Jordan McClure, Chief Executive Officer
Web address: www.wilmington.selectspecialtyhospitals.com

FLORIDA: SELECT SPECIALTY HOSPITAL DAYTONA BEACH (O, 34 beds) 301 Memorial Medical Parkway, 11th Floor, Daytona Beach, FL, Zip 32117–5167; tel. 386/231–3436, Robert E. Mallicoat, Chief Executive Officer
Web address: www.daytonabeach.selectspecialtyhospitals.com

SELECT SPECIALTY HOSPITAL–FORT MYERS (O, 60 beds) 3050 Champion Ring Road, Fort Myers, FL, Zip 33905–5599; tel. 239/313–2900, Corey Cooper, Chief Executive Officer
Web address: www.https://fortmyers.selectspecialtyhospitals.com/

SELECT SPECIALTY HOSPITAL–GAINESVILLE (O, 44 beds) 1600 SW Archer Road, 5th Floor, Gainesville, FL, Zip 32610; tel. 352/337–3240, Rhonda Sherrod, Chief Executive Officer

SELECT SPECIALTY HOSPITAL–MIAMI LAKES (O, 60 beds) 14001 NW 82nd Avenue, Miami Lakes, FL, Zip 33016–1561; tel. 786/609–9200, Monica Madrigal, Chief Executive Officer
Web address: www.promise-miami.com

SELECT SPECIALTY HOSPITAL–MIAMI (O, 47 beds) 955 NW 3rd Street, Miami, FL, Zip 33128–1274; tel. 305/416–5700, Monica Madrigal, Interim Chief Executive Officer

SELECT SPECIALTY HOSPITAL–ORLANDO NORTH (O, 75 beds) 2250 Bedford Road, Orlando, FL, Zip 32803–1443; tel. 407/303–7869, Kelvin L. Parks, Chief Executive Officer
Web address: https://www.selectspecialtyhospitals.com/locations-and-tours/fl/orlando/orlando-north/

SELECT SPECIALTY HOSPITAL–PALM BEACH (O, 60 beds) 3060 Melaleuca Lane, Lake Worth, FL, Zip 33461–5174; tel. 561/357–7200, Larry Melby, Chief Executive Officer
Web address: www.selectspecialtyhospitals.com/company/locations/palmbeach.aspx

SELECT SPECIALTY HOSPITAL–PANAMA CITY (O, 30 beds) 615 North Bonita Avenue, 3rd Floor, Panama City, FL, Zip 32401–3623; tel. 850/767–3180, Matthew Presley, Chief Executive Officer

SELECT SPECIALTY HOSPITAL–PENSACOLA (O, 75 beds) 7000 Cobble Creek Drive, Pensacola, FL, Zip 32504–8638; tel. 850/473–4800, Randall C. Lambert, Chief Executive Officer
Web address: https://www.selectspecialtyhospitals.com/locations-and-tours/fl/pensacola/pensacola/?utm_source=gmb&utm_medium=organic

SELECT SPECIALTY HOSPITAL–TALLAHASSEE (O, 29 beds) 1554 Surgeons Drive, Tallahassee, FL, Zip 32308–4631; tel. 850/219–6950, Shawn Dilmore, Chief Executive Officer

SELECT SPECIALTY HOSPITAL–THE VILLAGES (O, 40 beds) 5050 County Road 472, Oxford, FL, Zip 34484; tel. 352/689–6400, Dennis Bencomo, JD, MSN, R.N., Chief Executive Officer
Web address: www.https://thevillages.selectspecialtyhospitals.com/

UF HEALTH REHAB HOSPITAL (O, 60 beds) 2708 Southwest Archer Road, Gainesville, FL, Zip 32608–1316; tel. 352/265–5499, Anne Roper, Chief Executive Officer

WEST GABLES REHABILITATION HOSPITAL (O, 90 beds) 2525 SW 75th Avenue, Miami, FL, Zip 33155–2800; tel. 305/262–6800, Walter Concepcion, Chief Executive Officer
Web address: www.westgablesrehabhospital.com/

GEORGIA: REGENCY HOSPITAL–MACON (O, 60 beds) 535 Coliseum Drive, Macon, GA, Zip 31217–0104; tel. 478/803–7300, Lorraine Smith, Chief Executive Officer

SELECT SPECIALTY HOSPITAL MIDTOWN ATLANTA (O, 72 beds) 705 Juniper Street NE, Atlanta, GA, Zip 30308–1307; tel. 404/873–2871, Karan Patel, Interim Chief Executive Officer
Web address: https://www.selectspecialtyhospitals.com/locations-and-tours/ga/atlanta/midtown-atlanta/

SELECT SPECIALTY HOSPITAL–AUGUSTA (O, 80 beds) 1537 Walton Way, Augusta, GA, Zip 30904–3764; tel. 706/731–1200, Cynthia Greene, Chief Executive Officer

SELECT SPECIALTY HOSPITAL–SAVANNAH (O, 40 beds) 5353 Reynolds Street, 4 South, Savannah, GA, Zip 31405–6015; tel. 912/819–7982, Stacey Craig, Chief Executive Officer
Web address: https://www.selectspecialtyhospitals.com/locations-and-tours/ga/savannah/savannah/

INDIANA: REGENCY HOSPITAL OF NORTHWEST INDIANA (O, 61 beds) 4321 Fir Street, 4th Floor, East Chicago, IN, Zip 46312–3049; tel. 219/392–7799, Kristine Shields, MSN, R.N., Chief Executive Officer
Web address: www.regencyhospital.com/company/locations/indiana-northwest-indiana.aspx

REHABILITATION HOSPITAL OF FORT WAYNE (O, 36 beds) 7970 West Jefferson Boulevard, Fort Wayne, IN, Zip 46804–4140; tel. 260/435–6100, Fabian Polo, Ph.D., Chief Executive Officer

SELECT SPECIALTY HOSPITAL–EVANSVILLE (O, 51 beds) 400 SE 4th Street, Evansville, IN, Zip 47713–1206; tel. 812/421–2500, Robyn Baehl, Interim Chief Executive Officer
Web address: www.selectspecialtyhospitals.com/company/locations/evansville.aspx

IOWA: SELECT SPECIALTY HOSPITAL–DES MOINES (O, 30 beds) 1111 6th Avenue, 4th Floor Main, Des Moines, IA, Zip 50314–2610; tel. 515/247–4400, Sam Ayres, Chief Executive Officer
Web address: www.selectspecialtyhospitals.com

SELECT SPECIALTY HOSPITAL–QUAD CITIES (O, 35 beds) 1227 East Rusholme Street, Davenport, IA, Zip 52803–2459; tel. 563/468–2000, Codie Dillie, Chief Executive Officer

KANSAS: SELECT SPECIALTY HOSPITAL–KANSAS CITY (O, 40 beds) 1731 North 90th Street, Kansas City, KS, Zip 66112–1515; tel. 913/732–5900, Brent Hanson, Chief Executive Officer
Web address: www.selectspecialtyhospitals.com

SELECT SPECIALTY HOSPITAL–WICHITA (O, 48 beds) 929 North St Francis Street, Wichita, KS, Zip 67214–3821; tel. 316/261–8303, Eric Christensen, Chief Executive Officer
Web address: www.selectspecialtyhospitals.com/company/locations/wichita.aspx

KENTUCKY: SELECT SPECIALTY HOSPITAL–CENTRAL KENTUCKY (O, 41 beds) 217 South 3rd Street, Fourth Floor, Danville, KY, Zip 40422–1823; tel. 859/712–7072, Josh Greeman, Chief Executive Officer

SELECT SPECIALTY HOSPITAL–NORTHERN KENTUCKY (O, 33 beds) 85 North Grand Avenue, Fort Thomas, KY, Zip 41075–1793; tel. 859/572–3880, Candace Moehringer, Chief Executive Officer
Web address: www.selectspecialtyhospitals.com

LOUISIANA: NORTHSHORE REHABILITATION HOSPITAL (O, 30 beds) 64030 State Highway 434, Lacombe, LA, Zip 70445; tel. 985/218–4660, Laurel DuPont, Chief Executive Officer

For explanation of codes following names, see page B2.
★ *Indicates Type III membership in the American Hospital Association.*

Systems / Select Medical Corporation

OCHSNER REHABILITATON HOSPITAL WEST CAMPUS (O, 56 beds) 2614 Jefferson Highway, Floors 4 & 5, Jefferson, LA, Zip 70121–3828; tel. 504/291–5100, Laurel DuPont, Chief Executive Officer
Web address: https://www.ochsner.org/services/rehabilitation

MICHIGAN: SELECT SPECIALTY HOSPITAL–ANN ARBOR (O, 36 beds) 5301 East Huron River Drive, 7th Floor, Ypsilanti, MI, Zip 48197–1051; tel. 734/712–6751, Michael Grace, Chief Executive Officer
Web address: www.annarbor.selectspecialtyhospitals.com/

SELECT SPECIALTY HOSPITAL–BATTLE CREEK (O, 25 beds) 300 North Avenue, 6th Floor, Battle Creek, MI, Zip 49017–3307; tel. 269/245–4675, Kenneth C. LePage, FACHE, Chief Executive Officer
Web address: www.battlecreek.selectspecialtyhospitals.com/

SELECT SPECIALTY HOSPITAL–COREWELL HEALTH GRAND RAPIDS (O, 36 beds) 1840 Wealthy Street, Southeast, Grand Rapids, MI, Zip 49506–2921; tel. 616/774–3800, Matthew J. Campbell Esq, Regional Chief Executive Officer
Web address: www.https://grandrapids.selectspecialtyhospitals.com

SELECT SPECIALTY HOSPITAL–DOWNRIVER (O, 35 beds) 2333 Biddle Avenue, 8th Floor, Wyandotte, MI, Zip 48192–4668; tel. 734/246–5500, John Ponczocha, Chief Executive Officer

SELECT SPECIALTY HOSPITAL–FLINT (O, 26 beds) 401 South Ballenger Highway, 5th Floor Central, Flint, MI, Zip 48532–3638; tel. 810/342–4545, Christina DeBlouw, R.N., Chief Executive Officer
Web address: www.selectspecialtyhospitals.com/company/locations/flint.aspx

SELECT SPECIALTY HOSPITAL–MACOMB COUNTY (O, 96 beds) 215 North Avenue, Mount Clemens, MI, Zip 48043–1700; tel. 586/307–9000, Jon P. O'Malley, Chief Executive Officer
Web address: www.macomb.selectspecialtyhospitals.com/

SELECT SPECIALTY HOSPITAL–SAGINAW (O, 25 beds) 1447 North Harrison Street, 8th Floor, Saginaw, MI, Zip 48602–4785; tel. 989/583–4235, Kelly Ann. DeBolt, R.N., Chief Executive Officer

MINNESOTA: REGENCY HOSPITAL OF MINNEAPOLIS (O, 92 beds) 1300 Hidden Lakes Parkway, Golden Valley, MN, Zip 55422–4286; tel. 763/588–2750, Sean Stricker, President and Chief Executive Officer
Web address: www.regencyhospital.com

MISSISSIPPI: REGENCY HOSPITAL OF MERIDIAN (O, 40 beds) 1102 Constitution Avenue, 2nd Floor, Meridian, MS, Zip 39301–4001; tel. 601/484–7900, Eliza Gavin, Chief Executive Officer

SELECT SPECIALTY HOSPITAL–BELHAVEN (O, 36 beds) 1225 North State Street, 5th Floor, Jackson, MS, Zip 39202–2097; tel. 601/968–1000, Cris Bourn, Chief Executive Officer
Web address: https://www.selectspecialtyhospitals.com/locations-and-tours/ms/jackson/belhaven/

SELECT SPECIALTY HOSPITAL–GULFPORT (O, 36 beds) 4500 13th Street, 3rd Floor, Gulfport, MS, Zip 39501–2515; tel. 228/575–7500, John O'Keefe, Chief Executive Officer
Web address: www.selectspecialtyhospitals.com/company/locations/gulfcoast.aspx

SELECT SPECIALTY HOSPITAL–JACKSON (O, 53 beds) 5903 Ridgewood Road, Suite 100, Jackson, MS, Zip 39211–3700; tel. 601/899–3800, Robert Shannon. Canard, Chief Executive Officer

MISSOURI: SSM SELECT REHABILITATION HOSPITAL (O, 125 beds) 1027 Bellevue Avenue, 3rd Floor, Richmond Heights, MO, Zip 63117–1851, 1027 Bellevue Avenue, Zip 63117–1851, tel. 314/768–5300, Cole Silverman, Chief Executive Officer
Web address: www.ssm-select.com

SELECT SPECIALTY HOSPITAL–SPRINGFIELD (O, 44 beds) 1630 East Primrose Street, Springfield, MO, Zip 65804–7929; tel. 417/885–4700, Elizabeth Hallam, R.N., Chief Executive Officer

SELECT SPECIALTY HOSPITAL–ST. LOUIS (O, 33 beds) 300 First Capitol Drive, Unit 1, Saint Charles, MO, Zip 63301–2844; tel. 636/947–5010, James W. McClung, Chief Executive Officer
Web address: https://www.selectspecialtyhospitals.com/locations-and-tours/mo/st-charles/st-louis/

NEBRASKA: SELECT SPECIALTY HOSPITAL–OMAHA (O, 56 beds) 1870 South 75th Street, Omaha, NE, Zip 68124–1700; tel. 402/361–5700, Kathryn Triplett, MSN, Chief Executive Officer
Web address: www.https://omaha.selectspecialtyhospitals.com

NEVADA: DIGNITY HEALTH REHABILITATION HOSPITAL (O, 60 beds) 2930 Siena Heights Drive, Henderson, NV, Zip 89052–3871; tel. 725/726–2000, Linda Tautz, Chief Executive Officer

NEW JERSEY: KESSLER INSTITUTE FOR REHABILITATION (O, 336 beds) 1199 Pleasant Valley Way, West Orange, NJ, Zip 07052–1424; tel. 973/731–3600, Michelle O'Keefe, Chief Executive Officer
Web address: www.kessler-rehab.com

KESSLER MARLTON REHABILITATION (O, 61 beds) 92 Brick Road, Marlton, NJ, Zip 08053–2177; tel. 856/988–8778, Kenneth Turley, Chief Executive Officer

SELECT SPECIALTY HOSPITAL–ATLANTIC CITY (O, 30 beds) 1925 Pacific Avenue, 7th Floor, 5 Wellness, Atlantic City, NJ, Zip 08401–6713; tel. 609/441–2122, Joanne McGovern, MSN, R.N., Chief Executive Officer
Web address: www.acuityhealthcare.net

SELECT SPECIALTY HOSPITAL–WILLINGBORO (O, 53 beds) 218 A Sunset Road, Willingboro, NJ, Zip 08046–1110, 220 Sunset Road, Zip 08046–1110, tel. 609/835–3650, Shawn Dilmore, Market Chief Executive Officer

SELECT SPECIALTY HOSPITAL–NORTHEAST NEW JERSEY (O, 62 beds) 96 Parkway, Rochelle Park, NJ, Zip 07662–4200; tel. 201/221–2352, Oleg Rivkin, Chief Executive Officer
Web address: www.northeastnewjersey.selectspecialtyhospitals.com/about/

NORTH CAROLINA: SELECT SPECIALTY HOSPITAL–DURHAM (O, 30 beds) 3643 North Roxboro Road, 6th Floor, Durham, NC, Zip 27704–2702; tel. 984/569–4040, Ian Hodge, Chief Executive Officer
Web address: www.https://durham.selectspecialtyhospitals.com/

SELECT SPECIALTY HOSPITAL–GREENSBORO (O, 30 beds) 1200 North Elm Street, 5th Floor, Greensboro, NC, Zip 27401–1004; tel. 336/832–8571, Bradley Jordan, Chief Executive Officer
Web address: www.selectspecialtyhospitals.com/company/locations/greensboro.aspx

OHIO: CLEVELAND CLINIC REHABILITATION HOSPITAL (O, 180 beds) 33355 Health Campus Boulevard, Avon, OH, Zip 44011; tel. 440/937–9099, Julie Idoine–Fries, FACHE, Chief Executive Officer
Web address: www.my.clevelandclinic.org

OHIOHEALTH REHABILITATION HOSPITAL (O, 74 beds) 1087 Dennison Avenue, 4th Floor, Columbus, OH, Zip 43201–3201; tel. 614/484–9600, Matthew Lehn, Chief Executive Officer

REGENCY HOSPITAL OF COLUMBUS (O, 66 beds) 1430 South High Street, Columbus, OH, Zip 43207–1045; tel. 614/456–0300, Ryan Hemmert, Chief Executive Officer
Web address: www.regencyhospital.com/

REGENCY HOSPITAL OF TOLEDO (O, 45 beds) 5220 Alexis Road, Sylvania, OH, Zip 43560–2504; tel. 419/318–5700, Marc Trznadel, Chief Executive Officer

REGENCY NORTH CENTRAL OHIO–CLEVELAND EAST (O, 87 beds) 4200 Interchange Corporate Center Road, Warrensville Heights, OH, Zip 44128–5631; tel. 216/910–3800, Julie Idoine–Fries, FACHE, Chief Executive Officer
Web address: www.regencyhospital.com/

SELECT SPECIALTY HOSPITAL–BOARDMAN (O, 24 beds) 8049 South Avenue, Boardman, OH, Zip 44512–6154; tel. 330/729–1750, Carl W. Nichols III, Chief Executive Officer
Web address: www.selectspecialtyhospitals.com/

SELECT SPECIALTY HOSPITAL–CLEVELAND FAIRHILL (O, 50 beds) 11900 Fairhill Road, Cleveland, OH, Zip 44120–1062; tel. 216/983–8030, Jennifer Fess, Chief Executive Officer

SELECT SPECIALTY HOSPITAL OF SOUTHEAST OHIO (O, 35 beds) 2000 Tamarack Road, Newark, OH, Zip 43055; tel. 220/564–2600, Emily Blevins, Chief Executive Officer
Web address: www.selectspecialtyhospitals.com/company/locations/zanesville.aspx

SELECT SPECIALTY HOSPITAL–AKRON (O, 60 beds) 200 East Market Street, Akron, OH, Zip 44308–2015; tel. 330/761–7500, Dawne Chaney, Chief Executive Officer
Web address: https://www.selectspecialtyhospitals.com/locations-and-tours/oh/akron/akron/

SELECT SPECIALTY HOSPITAL–CANTON (O, 30 beds) 1320 Mercy Drive NW, 6th Floor, Canton, OH, Zip 44708–2614; tel. 330/489–8189, Sheila Tonn–Knopf, Chief Executive Officer
Web address: www.selectspecialtyhospitals.com/company/locations/canton.aspx

For explanation of codes following names, see page B2.
★ Indicates Type III membership in the American Hospital Association.

Systems / Select Medical Corporation

SELECT SPECIALTY HOSPITAL–CINCINNATI (O, 71 beds) 2139 Auburn Avenue, 3rd Floor, Cincinnati, OH, Zip 45219–2906; tel. 513/572–8720

SELECT SPECIALTY HOSPITAL–COLUMBUS (O, 162 beds) 1087 Dennison Avenue, Columbus, OH, Zip 43201–3201; tel. 614/458–9000, Lisa J. Pettrey, MSN, R.N., Chief Executive Officer
Web address: https://www.selectspecialtyhospitals.com/locations-and-tours/oh/columbus/columbus-victorian-village/

SELECT SPECIALTY HOSPITAL–YOUNGSTOWN (O, 56 beds) 1044 Belmont Avenue, Youngstown, OH, Zip 44504–1006; tel. 330/480–2349, Jodi Costello, Chief Executive Officer
Web address: www.selectspecialtyhospitals.com/company/locations/youngstown.aspx

TRIHEALTH REHABILITATION HOSPITAL (O, 60 beds) 2155 Dana Avenue, Cincinnati, OH, Zip 45207; tel. 513/601–0600; Neil Fedders, Chief Executive Officer
Web address: www.trihealthrehab.com

OKLAHOMA: SELECT SPECIALTY HOSPITAL–OKLAHOMA CITY (O, 72 beds) 3524 NW 56th Street, Oklahoma City, OK, Zip 73112–4518; tel. 405/606–6700, Kelly Duke, Chief Executive Officer

SELECT SPECIALTY HOSPITAL–TULSA MIDTOWN (O, 52 beds) 744 West 9th Street, 5th Floor, Tulsa, OK, Zip 74127–9907; tel. 918/579–7300, Janette Daniels, Chief Executive Officer
Web address: www.tulsa.selectspecialtyhospitals.com/

PENNSYLVANIA: HELEN M. SIMPSON REHABILITATION HOSPITAL (C, 55 beds) 4300 Londonderry Road, Harrisburg, PA, Zip 17109–5317; tel. 717/920–4300, Brett D. McChesney, Chief Executive Officer
Web address: www.simpson-rehab.com/

PENN STATE HEALTH REHABILITATION HOSPITAL (O, 98 beds) 1135 Old West Chocolate Avenue, Hummelstown, PA, Zip 17036; tel. 717/832–2600, Mark Freeburn, Chief Executive Officer

SELECT SPECIALTY HOSPITAL–LAUREL HIGHLANDS (O, 40 beds) 1 Mellon Way, 3rd Floor, Latrobe, PA, Zip 15650–1197; tel. 724/539–3870, Stacy Carson, President
Web address: www.laurelhighlands.selectspecialtyhospitals.com/

SELECT SPECIALTY HOSPITAL–CAMP HILL (O, 92 beds) 503 North 21st Street, 5th Floor, Camp Hill, PA, Zip 17011–2204; tel. 717/972–4575, Adam Beck, Market Chief Executive Officer

SELECT SPECIALTY HOSPITAL–ERIE (O, 30 beds) 252 West 11th Street, Erie, PA, Zip 16501–1702; tel. 814/874–5300, Michael A. Post, Chief Executive Officer
Web address: www.erie.selectspecialtyhospitals.com/

SELECT SPECIALTY HOSPITAL–JOHNSTOWN (O, 39 beds) 320 Main Street, 3rd Floor, Johnstown, PA, Zip 15901–1601; tel. 814/534–7360, Kelly Blake, Chief Executive Officer
Web address: www.selectspecialtyhospitals.com/company/locations/johnstown.aspx

SELECT SPECIALTY HOSPITAL–MCKEESPORT (O, 30 beds) 1500 Fifth Avenue, 6th Floor, McKeesport, PA, Zip 15132–2422; tel. 412/664–2900, Louise Urban, R.N., Chief Operating Officer
Web address: www.mckeesport.selectspecialtyhospitals.com/

SELECT SPECIALTY HOSPITAL–PITTSBURGH/UPMC (O, 32 beds) 200 Lothrop Street, E824, Pittsburgh, PA, Zip 15213–2536, 3459 5th Avenue, MUH S872, Zip 15213, tel. 412/586–9819, John Duemmel, Chief Executive Officer

SOUTH CAROLINA: REGENCY HOSPITAL OF FLORENCE (O, 44 beds) 805 Pamplico Highway, 2nd and 3rd Floors, South Tower, Florence, SC, Zip 29505–6047, 805 Pamplico Highway 2nd and 3rd Floors, South Tower, Zip 29505–6047, tel. 843/661–3471, Amy Metz, MSN, R.N., Chief Executive Officer
Web address: www.regencyhospital.com

REGENCY HOSPITAL OF GREENVILLE (O, 32 beds) 1 Saint Francis Drive, 4th Floor, Greenville, SC, Zip 29601–3955, 1 St Francis Drive, Zip 29601–3955, tel. 864/255–1438, Tammy Ratliff, Chief Executive Officer
Web address: www.regencyhospital.com

SOUTH DAKOTA: SELECT SPECIALTY HOSPITAL–SIOUX FALLS (O, 24 beds) 1305 West 18th Street, Sioux Falls, SD, Zip 57105–0401; tel. 605/312–9500, Scott James. Hargens, Chief Executive Officer
Web address: www.selectspecialtyhospitals.com/company/locations/siouxfalls.aspx

TENNESSEE: SELECT SPECIALTY HOSPITAL–WEST TENNESSEE (O, 50 beds) 620 Skyline Drive, Floors 5 & 6, Jackson, TN, Zip 38301–3923; tel. 731/437–2500, Anupam Lahiri, Chief Executive Officer

SELECT SPECIALTY HOSPITAL NASHVILLE (O, 70 beds) 2000 Hayes Street, Suite 1502, Nashville, TN, Zip 37203–2318; tel. 615/284–4599, Jordan McClure, Chief Executive Officer
Web address: https://www.selectspecialtyhospitals.com/locations-and-tours/tn/nashville/nashville/?utm_source=gmb&utm_medium=organic

SELECT SPECIALTY HOSPITAL–MEMPHIS (O, 39 beds) 1265 Union Avenue, 10th Floor, Memphis, TN, Zip 38104–3415; tel. 901/765–1245, Marcia Taylor, Chief Executive Officer
Web address: www.selectspecialtyhospitals.com/company/locations/memphis.aspx

SELECT SPECIALTY HOSPITAL–NORTH KNOXVILLE (O, 33 beds) 7557B Dannaher Drive, Suite 145, Powell, TN, Zip 37849–3568; tel. 865/512–2450, Steve Plumlee, Chief Executive Officer

SELECT SPECIALTY HOSPITAL–TRI CITIES (O, 33 beds) 1 Medical Park Boulevard, 5th Floor, Bristol, TN, Zip 37620–8964; tel. 423/844–5900, Jeffery Wright, Chief Executive Officer
Web address: www.tricities.selectspecialtyhospitals.com/

TEXAS: BAYLOR SCOTT & WHITE INSTITUTE FOR REHABILITATION–DALLAS (O, 90 beds) 909 North Washington Avenue, Dallas, TX, Zip 75246–1520; tel. 214/820–9300, David Smith, Chief Executive Officer

BAYLOR SCOTT & WHITE INSTITUTE FOR REHABILITATION–LAKEWAY (O, 36 beds) 2000 Medical Drive, Lakeway, TX, Zip 78734–4200; tel. 512/263–4500, Sarah North, Chief Executive Officer
Web address: https://www.bswrehab.com/locations-and-tours/bswir-lakeway/

BAYLOR SCOTT & WHITE INSTITUTE FOR REHABILITATION–FORT WORTH (C, 42 beds) 6601 Harris Parkway, Fort Worth, TX, Zip 76132–6108; tel. 817/433–9600, J. Michael DeLeon, FACHE, Chief Executive Officer

BAYLOR SCOTT & WHITE INSTITUTE FOR REHABILITATION–FRISCO (O, 44 beds) 2990 Legacy Drive, Frisco, TX, Zip 75034–6066; tel. 469/888–5100, Katharine Powers, MS, Chief Executive Officer
Web address: https://www.bswrehab.com/locations-and-tours/bswir-frisco/

DENTON REHAB (O, 44 beds) 2620 Scripture Street, Denton, TX, Zip 76201–4315; tel. 940/297–6500, Andrew Carlson, Chief Executive Officer

SELECT SPECIALTY HOSPITAL–DALLAS DOWNTOWN (O, 40 beds) 2700 Walker Way, Desoto, TX, Zip 75115–2088; tel. 469/801–4500, Tremayne Myles, Chief Executive Officer
Web address: https://www.selectspecialtyhospitals.com/locations-and-tours/tx/dallas/dallas-downtown/

SELECT SPECIALTY HOSPITAL–DALLAS (O, 60 beds) 1100 Allied Drive, 4th Floor, Plano, TX, Zip 75093–5348; tel. 469/892–1400, Misti Varnell, Chief Executive Officer

VIRGINIA: COASTAL VIRGINIA REHABILITATION (C, 50 beds) 250 Josephs Drive, Yorktown, VA, Zip 23693–3405; tel. 757/928–8000, Daniel Ballin, Administrator
Web address: www.riversideonline.com/rri/index.cfm

INOVA SPECIALTY HOSPITAL (O, 32 beds) 2501 Parkers Lane, 4th Floor, Alexandria, VA, Zip 22306–3209; tel. 571/547–3600, Karan Patel, Chief Executive Officer

SELECT SPECIALTY HOSPITAL–RICHMOND (O, 50 beds) 2220 Edward Holland Drive, Richmond, VA, Zip 23230–2519; tel. 804/678–7000, Shirley Martell, Chief Executive Officer
Web address: https://www.selectspecialtyhospitals.com/locations-and-tours/va/richmond/richmond/

SELECT SPECIALTY HOSPITAL HAMPTON ROADS (O, 50 beds) 500 J. Clyde Morris Boulevard, 4 East/4 Annex, Newport News, VA, Zip 23601–1929, 500 J. Clyde Morris Boulevard, 4 East/4Annex, Zip 23601–1929, tel. 757/534–5000, Will Aycock, Chief Executive Officer
Web address: www.hamptonroadsspecialtyhospital.com

WEST VIRGINIA: ACUITY SPECIALTY HOSPITAL–OHIO VALLEY AT WEIRTON (O, 20 beds) 601 Colliers Way, Weirton, WV, Zip 26062–5014; tel. 304/919–4300, Dusty A. Bowers, Chief Executive Officer
Web address: www.https://acuityhealthcare.net

For explanation of codes following names, see page B2.
★ Indicates Type III membership in the American Hospital Association.

Systems / Select Medical Corporation

SELECT SPECIALTY HOSPITAL–MORGANTOWN (O, 25 beds) 1200 J D Anderson Drive, 4th Floor, Morgantown, WV, Zip 26505–3494; tel. 304/285–2235, Daniel C. Dunmyer, Chief Executive Officer
Web address: https://www.selectspecialtyhospitals.com/morgantown/

SELECT SPECIALTY HOSPITAL–CHARLESTON (O, 32 beds) 333 Laidley Street, 3rd Floor East, Charleston, WV, Zip 25301–1614; tel. 304/720–7234, Frank Weber, Chief Executive Officer

WISCONSIN: SELECT SPECIALTY HOSPITAL–MADISON (O, 58 beds) 801 Braxton Place, Madison, WI, Zip 53715–1415; tel. 608/260–2700, Marc Trznadel, Chief Executive Officer
Web address: www.madison.selectspecialtyhospitals.com

SELECT SPECIALTY HOSPITAL–MILWAUKEE (O, 34 beds) 8901 West Lincoln Avenue, 2nd Floor, Milwaukee, WI, Zip 53227–2409, West Allis, tel. 414/328–7700, Brandon James. Weiland, Chief Executive Officer

Owned, leased, sponsored:	107 hospitals	5896 beds
Contract-managed:	4 hospitals	227 beds
Totals:	111 hospitals	6123 beds

★**2565: SENTARA HEALTH (NP)**
1330 Sentara Park, Virginia Beach, VA Zip 23464–5884; tel. 757/455–7000, Dennis Matheis, President and Chief Executive Officer
(Centralized Physician/Insurance Health System)

NORTH CAROLINA: SENTARA ALBEMARLE MEDICAL CENTER (L, 98 beds) 1144 North Road Street, Elizabeth City, NC, Zip 27909–3473; tel. 252/335–0531, Teresa C. Watson, Division President
Web address: https://www.sentara.com/hospitalslocations/locations/new-sentara-albemarle-medical-center.aspx

VIRGINIA: SENTARA CAREPLEX HOSPITAL (O, 140 beds) 3000 Coliseum Drive, Hampton, VA, Zip 23666–5963; tel. 757/736–1000, Kirkpatrick Conley, Senior Vice President, Regional President, Central

SENTARA HALIFAX REGIONAL HOSPITAL (O, 44 beds) 2204 Wilborn Avenue, South Boston, VA, Zip 24592–1638; tel. 434/517–3100, Brian Zwoyer, R.N., Division President
Web address: https://www.sentara.com/halifax-southern-virginia/hospitalslocations/locations/sentara-halifax-regional-hospital/directions-parking.aspx

SENTARA LEIGH HOSPITAL (O, 274 beds) 830 Kempsville Road, Norfolk, VA, Zip 23502–3920; tel. 757/261–6000, Joanne Inman, Division President

SENTARA MARTHA JEFFERSON HOSPITAL (O, 135 beds) 500 Martha Jefferson Drive, Charlottesville, VA, Zip 22911–4668; tel. 434/654–7000, Rita A. Bunch, M.P.H., FACHE, Division President
Web address: www.marthajefferson.org

SENTARA NORFOLK GENERAL HOSPITAL (O, 587 beds) 600 Gresham Drive, Norfolk, VA, Zip 23507–1904; tel. 757/388–3000, Liisa Ortegon, R.N., Division President
Web address: www.sentara.com

SENTARA NORTHERN VIRGINIA MEDICAL CENTER (O, 183 beds) 2300 Opitz Boulevard, Woodbridge, VA, Zip 22191–3399; tel. 703/523–1000, Jeff Joyner, FACHE, Division President
Web address: www.sentara.com/northernvirginia

SENTARA OBICI HOSPITAL (O, 175 beds) 2800 Godwin Boulevard, Suffolk, VA, Zip 23434–8038; tel. 757/934–4000, David J. Masterson, Division President

SENTARA PRINCESS ANNE HOSPITAL (O, 174 beds) 2025 Glenn Mitchell Drive, Virginia Beach, VA, Zip 23456–0178; tel. 757/507–1000, Dana Weston Graves, Division President
Web address: www.sentara.com

SENTARA RMH MEDICAL CENTER (O, 214 beds) 2010 Health Campus Drive, Harrisonburg, VA, Zip 22801–3293; tel. 540/689–1000, Douglas J. Moyer, Division President

SENTARA VIRGINIA BEACH GENERAL HOSPITAL (O, 273 beds) 1060 First Colonial Road, Virginia Beach, VA, Zip 23454–3002; tel. 757/395–8000, Elwood Bernard. Boone III, FACHE, Division President
Web address: www.sentara.com

SENTARA WILLIAMSBURG REGIONAL MEDICAL CENTER (O, 128 beds) 100 Sentara Circle, Williamsburg, VA, Zip 23188–5713; tel. 757/984–6000, Amber Price, Division President
Web address: www.sentara.com

Owned, leased, sponsored:	12 hospitals	2425 beds
Contract-managed:	0 hospitals	0 beds
Totals:	12 hospitals	2425 beds

★**2065: SHARP HEALTHCARE (NP)**
8695 Spectrum Center Boulevard, San Diego, CA Zip 92123–1489; tel. 858/499–4000, Christopher Howard, President and Chief Executive Officer
(Centralized Health System)

CALIFORNIA: SHARP CHULA VISTA MEDICAL CENTER (O, 449 beds) 751 Medical Center Court, Chula Vista, CA, Zip 91911–6699; tel. 619/502–5800, Scott Evans, PharmD, Senior Vice President/Market Chief Executive Officer, Sharp HealthCare Regional Hospitals

SHARP CORONADO HOSPITAL (L, 155 beds) 250 Prospect Place, Coronado, CA, Zip 92118–1999; tel. 619/522–3600, Scott Evans, PharmD, Senior Vice President/Market Chief Executive Officer, Sharp HealthCare Regional Hospitals
Web address: https://www.sharp.com/hospitals/coronado/

SHARP GROSSMONT HOSPITAL (L, 514 beds) 5555 Grossmont Center Drive, La Mesa, CA, Zip 91942–3019, PO Box 158, Zip 91944–0158, tel. 619/740–6000, Scott Evans, PharmD, Senior Vice President and Market Chief Executive Officer, Sharp HealthCare Regional Hospitals
Web address: www.sharp.com

SHARP MARY BIRCH HOSPITAL FOR WOMEN AND NEWBORNS (O, 206 beds) 3003 Health Center Drive, San Diego, CA, Zip 92123–2700; tel. 858/939–3400, Trisha Khaleghi, MSN, R.N., Senior Vice President and Market Chief Executive Officer, Sharp HealthCare Metropolitan Hospitals

SHARP MEMORIAL HOSPITAL (O, 459 beds) 7901 Frost Street, San Diego, CA, Zip 92123–2701; tel. 858/939–3400, Trisha Khaleghi, MSN, R.N., Senior Vice President and Market Chief Executive Officer, Sharp HealthCare Metropolitan Hospitals
Web address: www.sharp.com

SHARP MESA VISTA HOSPITAL (O, 164 beds) 7850 Vista Hill Avenue, San Diego, CA, Zip 92123–2717; tel. 858/278–4110, Trisha Khaleghi, MSN, R.N., Senior Vice President and Market Chief Executive Officer, Sharp HealthCare Metropolitan Hospitals
Web address: www.sharp.com

Owned, leased, sponsored:	6 hospitals	1947 beds
Contract-managed:	0 hospitals	0 beds
Totals:	6 hospitals	1947 beds

4125: SHRINERS HOSPITALS FOR CHILDREN (NP)
2900 North Rocky Point Drive, Tampa, FL Zip 33607–1435, P O Box 31356, Zip 33631–3356, tel. 813/281–0300, John P. McCabe, Executive Vice President
(Independent Hospital System)

CALIFORNIA: SHRINERS CHILDREN'S–NORTHERN CALIFORNIA (O, 60 beds) 2425 Stockton Boulevard, Sacramento, CA, Zip 95817–2215; tel. 916/453–2000, Kenny Pawlek, Administrator/Chief Executive Officer
Web address: www.shrinershospitalsforchildren.org/Hospitals/Locations/NorthernCalifornia.aspx

HAWAII: SHRINERS HOSPITALS FOR CHILDREN–HONOLULU (O, 12 beds) 1310 Punahou Street, Honolulu, HI, Zip 96826–1099; tel. 808/941–4466, Andrew Graul, Administrator
Web address: www.shrinershospitalsforchildren.org/honolulu

ILLINOIS: SHRINERS HOSPITALS FOR CHILDREN–CHICAGO (O, 36 beds) 2211 North Oak Park Avenue, Chicago, IL, Zip 60707–3392; tel. 773/622–5400, Craig McGhee, FACHE, Midwest Market Administrator
Web address: www.shrinershospitalsforchildren.org/Hospitals/Locations/Chicago.aspx

---

For explanation of codes following names, see page B2.
★ Indicates Type III membership in the American Hospital Association.

Systems / Sinai Chicago

MASSACHUSETTS: SHRINERS HOSPITALS FOR CHILDREN–BOSTON (O, 9 beds) 51 Blossom Street, Boston, MA, Zip 02114–2601; tel. 617/722–3000, Frances Marthone, Ph.D., MSN, R.N., Administrator

SHRINERS HOSPITALS FOR CHILDREN–SPRINGFIELD (O, 10 beds) 516 Carew Street, Springfield, MA, Zip 01104–2396; tel. 413/787–2000, Frances Marthone, Ph.D., MSN, R.N., Administrator
Web address: www.shrinershospitalsforchildren.org/Hospitals/Locations/Springfield.aspx

MISSOURI: SHRINERS HOSPITALS FOR CHILDREN–ST. LOUIS (O, 12 beds) 4400 Clayton Avenue, Saint Louis, MO, Zip 63110–1624; tel. 314/432–3600, Mark Venable, Administrator
Web address: https://www.shrinershospitalsforchildren.org

OHIO: SHRINERS CHILDREN'S OHIO (O, 30 beds) One Childrens Plaza, 2 West, Dayton, OH, Zip 45404–1873, One Children's Plaza, Zip 45404–1873, tel. 513/872–6000, Randall White, Administrator

OREGON: SHRINERS HOSPITALS FOR CHILDREN–PORTLAND (O, 12 beds) 3101 SW Sam Jackson Park Road, Portland, OR, Zip 97239–3009; tel. 503/241–5090, Dereesa Reid, Administrator
Web address: www.shrinershospitalsforchildren.org/portland

PENNSYLVANIA: SHRINERS CHILDREN'S PHILADELPHIA (O, 39 beds) 3551 North Broad Street, Philadelphia, PA, Zip 19140–4160; tel. 215/430–4000, Gregory Passanante, Hospital Administrator

SOUTH CAROLINA: SHRINERS HOSPITALS FOR CHILDREN–GREENVILLE (O, 15 beds) 950 West Faris Road, Greenville, SC, Zip 29605–4277; tel. 864/271–3444, William Munley, Administrator
Web address: www.greenvilleshrinershospital.org

TEXAS: SHRINERS HOSPITALS FOR CHILDREN (O, 30 beds) 815 Market Street, Galveston, TX, Zip 77550–2725; tel. 409/770–6600, Mary Glendening, FACHE, Administrator

UTAH: SHRINERS HOSPITALS FOR CHILDREN–SALT LAKE CITY (O, 12 beds) 1275 East Fairfax Road, Salt Lake City, UT, Zip 84103–4399; tel. 801/536–3500, Kevin Martin, M.P.H., R.N., FACHE, Administrator
Web address: www.shrinershospitalsforchildren.org/Hospitals/Locations/SaltLakeCity.aspx

WASHINGTON: SHRINERS HOSPITALS FOR CHILDREN–SPOKANE (O, 30 beds) 911 West Fifth Avenue, Spokane, WA, Zip 99204–2901, P O Box 2472, Zip 99210–2472, tel. 509/455–7844, Peter G. Brewer, Administrator
Web address: www.shrinershospitalsforchildren.org/Hospitals/Locations/Spokane.aspx

Owned, leased, sponsored:	13 hospitals	307 beds
Contract-managed:	0 hospitals	0 beds
Totals:	13 hospitals	307 beds

0360: SIGNATURE HEALTHCARE SERVICES (IO)
4238 Green River Road, Corona, CA Zip 92880–1669; tel. 951/549–8032, Soon K. Kim, M.D., President and Chief Executive Officer
(Independent Hospital System)

ARIZONA: AURORA BEHAVIORAL HEALTH SYSTEM EAST (O, 118 beds) 6350 South Maple Street, Tempe, AZ, Zip 85283–2857; tel. 480/345–5400, Chelsea Vickers, Chief Executive Officer and Administrator
Web address: www.auroraarizona.com

AURORA BEHAVIORAL HEALTH SYSTEM WEST (O, 100 beds) 6015 West Peoria Avenue, Glendale, AZ, Zip 85302–1213; tel. 623/344–4400, Bruce Waldo, Chief Executive Officer

CALIFORNIA: AURORA BEHAVIORAL HEALTHCARE SAN DIEGO (O, 80 beds) 11878 Avenue of Industry, San Diego, CA, Zip 92128–3490; tel. 858/487–3200, Alain Azcona, Chief Executive Officer
Web address: www.sandiego.aurorabehavioral.com/

AURORA CHARTER OAK HOSPITAL (O, 146 beds) 1161 East Covina Boulevard, Covina, CA, Zip 91724–1599; tel. 626/966–1632, John Meier, Chief Executive Officer
Web address: www.charteroakhospital.com

BAKERSFIELD BEHAVIORAL HEALTHCARE HOSPITAL (O, 60 beds) 5201 White Lane, Bakersfield, CA, Zip 93309; tel. 877/755–4907, Maureen Womack, Chief Executive Officer

LAS ENCINAS HOSPITAL (O, 118 beds) 2900 East Del Mar Boulevard, Pasadena, CA, Zip 91107–4399; tel. 626/795–9901, Trevor Asmus, Chief Executive Officer
Web address: www.lasencinashospital.com

SANTA ROSA BEHAVIORAL HEALTHCARE HOSPITAL (O, 95 beds) 1287 Fulton Road, Santa Rosa, CA, Zip 95401–4923; tel. 707/800–7700, Tristan Ivy, Chief Executive Officer

VISTA DEL MAR HOSPITAL (O, 87 beds) 801 Seneca Street, Ventura, CA, Zip 93001–1411; tel. 805/653–6434, Colton Reed, Chief Executive Officer
Web address: www.vistadelmarhospital.com

MASSACHUSETTS: WESTBOROUGH BEHAVIORAL HEALTHCARE HOSPITAL (O, 120 beds) 300 Friberg Parkway, Westborough, MA, Zip 01581–3900; tel. 508/329–6112, Michelle Lynn, Chief Executive Officer

NEVADA: DESERT PARKWAY BEHAVIORAL HEALTHCARE HOSPITAL (O, 152 beds) 3247 South Maryland Parkway, Las Vegas, NV, Zip 89109–2412; tel. 702/776–3500, Jordan Peterson, Chief Executive Officer
Web address: https://www.desertparkway.com/

RENO BEHAVIORAL HEALTHCARE HOSPITAL (O, 70 beds) 6940 Sierra Center Parkway, Reno, NV, Zip 89511–2209; tel. 877/787–8518, Don Butterfield, Interim Chief Executive Officer
Web address: www.renobehavioral.com

TEXAS: DALLAS BEHAVIORAL HEALTHCARE HOSPITAL (O, 116 beds) 800 Kirnwood Drive, Desoto, TX, Zip 75115–2000; tel. 855/982–0897, Matthew Matusiak, Chief Executive Officer

GEORGETOWN BEHAVIORAL HEALTH INSTITUTE (O, 118 beds) 3101 South Austin Avenue, Georgetown, TX, Zip 78626–7541; tel. 512/819–1100, Brittney Sky Dick, Chief Executive Officer
Web address: www.georgetownbehavioral.com

HOUSTON BEHAVIORAL HEALTHCARE HOSPITAL (O, 163 beds) 2801 Gessner Road, Houston, TX, Zip 77080–2503; tel. 832/834–7710, Adrian Flores, Chief Executive Officer
Web address: www.houstonbehavioralhealth.com/

SAN ANTONIO BEHAVIORAL HEALTHCARE HOSPITAL (O, 198 beds) 8550 Huebner Road, San Antonio, TX, Zip 78240–1803; tel. 210/541–5300, Camillia McKinney, Chief Executive Officer

Owned, leased, sponsored:	15 hospitals	1741 beds
Contract-managed:	0 hospitals	0 beds
Totals:	15 hospitals	1741 beds

★0284: SINAI CHICAGO (NP)
1500 South Fairfield Avenue, Chicago, IL Zip 60608–1782; tel. 773/542–2000, Ngozi Ezike, President and Chief Executive Officer
(Centralized Health System)

ILLINOIS: HOLY CROSS HOSPITAL (O, 120 beds) 2701 West 68th Street, Chicago, IL, Zip 60629–1882; tel. 773/884–9000, Jeen-Soo Chang, M.D., MS, President and Chief Medical Officer

MOUNT SINAI HOSPITAL (O, 261 beds) 1500 South Fairfield Avenue, Chicago, IL, Zip 60608–1729; tel. 773/542–2000, Sameer Shah, PharmD, President
Web address: www.sinai.org

SCHWAB REHABILITATION HOSPITAL (O, 62 beds) 1401 South California Avenue, Chicago, IL, Zip 60608–1858; tel. 773/522–2010, Julia Libcke, R.N., President
Web address: www.schwabrehab.org

Owned, leased, sponsored:	3 hospitals	443 beds
Contract-managed:	0 hospitals	0 beds
Totals:	3 hospitals	443 beds

For explanation of codes following names, see page B2.
★ Indicates Type III membership in the American Hospital Association.

Systems / Sisters of Mary of the Presentation Health System

5805: SISTERS OF MARY OF THE PRESENTATION HEALTH SYSTEM (CC)
1202 Page Drive SW, Fargo, ND Zip 58103-2340, P O Box 10007, Zip 58106-0007, tel. 701/237-9290, Aaron K. Alton, President and Chief Executive Officer
(Moderately Centralized Health System)

NORTH DAKOTA: SMP HEALTH–ST. ALOISIUS (O, 110 beds) 325 East Brewster Street, Harvey, ND, Zip 58341-1653; tel. 701/324-4651, Ryan Mickelsen, President and Chief Executive Officer
Web address: www.https://smphealth.org/staloisius/

SMP HEALTH–ST. ANDREW'S (O, 25 beds) 316 Ohmer Street, Bottineau, ND, Zip 58318-1045; tel. 701/228-9300, Christopher Albertson, President and Chief Executive Officer

SMP HEALTH–ST. KATERI (O, 25 beds) 213 Second Avenue NE, Rolla, ND, Zip 58367-7153, P O Box 759, Zip 58367-0759, tel. 701/477-3161, Christopher Albertson, Chief Executive Officer and President
Web address: www.https://smphealth.org/stkateri/

Owned, leased, sponsored:	3 hospitals	160 beds
Contract-managed:	0 hospitals	0 beds
Totals:	3 hospitals	160 beds

0997: SKAGIT REGIONAL HEALTH (NP)
1415 E Kincaid Street, Mount Vernon, WA Zip 98274-4126; tel. 360/424-4111, Brian K. Ivie, President and Chief Executive Officer
(Independent Hospital System)

WASHINGTON: CASCADE VALLEY HOSPITAL (L, 36 beds) 330 South Stillaguamish Avenue, Arlington, WA, Zip 98223-1642; tel. 360/435-2133, Brian K. Ivie, President and Chief Executive Officer

SKAGIT VALLEY HOSPITAL (O, 137 beds) 300 Hospital Parkway, Mount Vernon, WA, Zip 98273, P O Box 1376, Zip 98273-1376, tel. 360/424-4111, Brian K. Ivie, President and Chief Executive Officer
Web address: www.skagitregionalhealth.org

Owned, leased, sponsored:	2 hospitals	173 beds
Contract-managed:	0 hospitals	0 beds
Totals:	2 hospitals	173 beds

★1042: SOLUTIONHEALTH (NP)
1 Elliot Way, Manchester, NH Zip 03103-3502; tel. 603/663-2990, Bradley Kreick, Chief Executive Officer

NEW HAMPSHIRE: ELLIOT HOSPITAL (O, 292 beds) 1 Elliot Way, Manchester, NH, Zip 03103-3502; tel. 603/669-5300, W. Gregory. Baxter, M.D., President and Chief Executive Officer

SOUTHERN NEW HAMPSHIRE MEDICAL CENTER (O, 172 beds) 8 Prospect Street, Nashua, NH, Zip 03060-3925, P O Box 2014, Zip 03061-2014, tel. 603/577-2000, Colin T. McHugh, President and Chief Executive Officer
Web address: www.snhhs.org

Owned, leased, sponsored:	2 hospitals	464 beds
Contract-managed:	0 hospitals	0 beds
Totals:	2 hospitals	464 beds

1034: SOUTH GEORGIA MEDICAL CENTER (NP)
2501 North Patterson Street, Valdosta, GA Zip 31602-1735, P O Box 1727, Zip 31603-1727, tel. 229/333-1000, Ronald Dean, President and Chief Executive Officer
(Independent Hospital System)

GEORGIA: SOUTH GEORGIA MEDICAL CENTER BERRIEN CAMPUS (O, 39 beds) 1221 East McPherson Avenue, Nashville, GA, Zip 31639-2326; tel. 229/433-8600, Kevin Moore, R.N., Hospital Administrator
Web address: www.sgmc.org/

SOUTH GEORGIA MEDICAL CENTER LANIER CAMPUS (O, 24 beds) 116 West Thigpen Avenue, Lakeland, GA, Zip 31635-1011; tel. 229/433-8440, Geoff Hardy, Administrator

SOUTH GEORGIA MEDICAL CENTER (O, 330 beds) 2501 North Patterson Street, Valdosta, GA, Zip 31602-1735, P O Box 1727, Zip 31603-1727, tel. 229/333-1000, Ronald Dean, President and Chief Executive Officer
Web address: www.sgmc.org

Owned, leased, sponsored:	3 hospitals	393 beds
Contract-managed:	0 hospitals	0 beds
Totals:	3 hospitals	393 beds

★0253: SOUTHEAST GEORGIA HEALTH SYSTEM (NP)
2415 Parkwood Drive, Brunswick, GA Zip 31520-4722, P O Box 1518, Zip 31521-1518, tel. 912/466-7000, Scott Raynes, Chief Executive Officer

GEORGIA: SOUTHEAST GEORGIA HEALTH SYSTEM BRUNSWICK CAMPUS (O, 564 beds) 2415 Parkwood Drive, Brunswick, GA, Zip 31520-4722, P O Box 1518, Zip 31521-1518, tel. 912/466-7000, Scott Raynes, President and Chief Executive Officer
Web address: www.sghs.org

SOUTHEAST GEORGIA HEALTH SYSTEM CAMDEN CAMPUS (O, 40 beds) 2000 Dan Proctor Drive, Saint Marys, GA, Zip 31558-3810; tel. 912/576-6200, Glenn Gann, Vice President and Administrator
Web address: www.sghs.org

Owned, leased, sponsored:	2 hospitals	604 beds
Contract-managed:	0 hospitals	0 beds
Totals:	2 hospitals	604 beds

4175: SOUTHERN ILLINOIS HEALTHCARE (NP)
1239 East Main Street, Carbondale, IL Zip 62901-3114, P O Box 3988, Zip 62902-3988, tel. 618/457-5200, John Antes, President and Chief Executive Officer
(Independent Hospital System)

ILLINOIS: HARRISBURG MEDICAL CENTER (O, 77 beds) 100 Dr Warren Tuttle Drive, Harrisburg, IL, Zip 62946-2718, P O Box 428, Zip 62946-0428, tel. 618/253-7671, Rodney Smith, Vice President and Administrator

HERRIN HOSPITAL (O, 114 beds) 201 South 14th Street, Herrin, IL, Zip 62948-3631; tel. 618/942-2171, Rodney Smith, Vice President and Administrator
Web address: www.sih.net

MEMORIAL HOSPITAL OF CARBONDALE (O, 175 beds) 405 West Jackson Street, Carbondale, IL, Zip 62901-1467, P O Box 10000, Zip 62902-9000, tel. 618/549-0721, Craig A. Jesiolowski, FACHE, President and Chief Executive Officer

ST. JOSEPH MEMORIAL HOSPITAL (O, 25 beds) 2 South Hospital Drive, Murphysboro, IL, Zip 62966-3333; tel. 618/684-3156, Craig A. Jesiolowski, FACHE, Vice President and Administrator
Web address: www.sih.net

Owned, leased, sponsored:	4 hospitals	391 beds
Contract-managed:	0 hospitals	0 beds
Totals:	4 hospitals	391 beds

★0652: SOUTHWEST HEALTH SYSTEMS (NP)
215 Marion Avenue, Mccomb, MS Zip 39648-2705, P O Box 1307, Zip 39649-1307, tel. 601/249-5500, Charla Rowley, Chief Executive Officer
(Independent Hospital System)

MISSISSIPPI: LAWRENCE COUNTY HOSPITAL (O, 25 beds) Highway 84 East, Monticello, MS, Zip 39654-0788, P O Box 788, Zip 39654-0788, tel. 601/587-4051, Phillip W. Langston, Administrator
Web address: www.smrmc.com

For explanation of codes following names, see page B2.
★ Indicates Type III membership in the American Hospital Association.

Systems / SSM Health

SOUTHWEST MISSISSIPPI REGIONAL MEDICAL CENTER (O, 93 beds) 215 Marion Avenue, McComb, MS, Zip 39648–2705, P O Box 1307, Zip 39649–1307, tel. 601/249–5500, Charla Rowley, Chief Executive Officer

Owned, leased, sponsored:	2 hospitals	118 beds
Contract-managed:	0 hospitals	0 beds
Totals:	2 hospitals	118 beds

★4195: SPARTANBURG REGIONAL HEALTHCARE SYSTEM (NP)
101 East Wood Street, Spartanburg, SC Zip 29303–3040; tel. 864/560–6000, Bruce Holstien, President and Chief Executive Officer
(Centralized Health System)

SOUTH CAROLINA: CHEROKEE MEDICAL CENTER (O, 31 beds) 1530 North Limestone Street, Gaffney, SC, Zip 29340–4738; tel. 864/487–4271, Cody Butts, President

PELHAM MEDICAL CENTER (O, 48 beds) 250 Westmoreland Road, Greer, SC, Zip 29651–9013; tel. 864/530–6000, Anthony Kouskolekas, FACHE, President
Web address: www.pelhammedicalcenter.com

SPARTANBURG HOSPITAL FOR RESTORATIVE CARE (O, 68 beds) 389 Serpentine Drive, Spartanburg, SC, Zip 29303–3026; tel. 864/560–3280, Jill Jolley Greene, MSN, R.N., President

SPARTANBURG MEDICAL CENTER–CHURCH STREET CAMPUS (O, 673 beds) 101 East Wood Street, Spartanburg, SC, Zip 29303–3040; tel. 864/560–6000, J Philip. Feisal, President and Chief Executive Officer
Web address: www.spartanburgregional.com

UNION MEDICAL CENTER (O, 15 beds) 322 West South Street, Union, SC, Zip 29379–2857, P O Box 789, Zip 29379–0789, tel. 864/301–2000, Paul R. Newhouse, President
Web address: https://www.spartanburgregional.com/locations/union-medical-center/

Owned, leased, sponsored:	5 hospitals	835 beds
Contract-managed:	0 hospitals	0 beds
Totals:	5 hospitals	835 beds

1037: SPRINGSTONE (IO)
101 South Fifth Street, Suite 3850, Louisville, KY Zip 40202–3127; tel. 855/595–2292, Phil Spencer, Chief Executive Officer

ARIZONA: COPPER SPRINGS HOSPITAL (O, 144 beds) 10550 West McDowell Road, Avondale, AZ, Zip 85392–4864; tel. 602/314–7800, Jessica Black, Market Chief Executive Officer

COLORADO: DENVER SPRINGS (O, 96 beds) 8835 American Way, Englewood, CO, Zip 80112–7056; tel. 720/643–4300, Scott Acus, Chief Executive Officer
Web address: www.denversprings.com/

INDIANA: BRENTWOOD SPRINGS (O, 48 beds) 4488 Roslin Road, Newburgh, IN, Zip 47630; tel. 812/858–7200, Kim Retzner, Chief Executive Officer
Web address: https://brentwoodsprings.com

SYCAMORE SPRINGS (O, 48 beds) 833 Park East Boulevard, Lafayette, IN, Zip 47905–0785; tel. 765/743–4400, Denise Sullivan, Chief Executive Officer

KANSAS: COTTONWOOD SPRINGS HOSPITAL (O, 72 beds) 13351 South Arapaho Drive, Olathe, KS, Zip 66062–1520; tel. 913/353–3000, Jason Toalson, Chief Executive Officer
Web address: www.cottonwoodsprings.com

NORTH CAROLINA: TRIANGLE SPRINGS HOSPITAL (O, 77 beds) 10901 World Trade Boulevard, Raleigh, NC, Zip 27617–4203; tel. 919/372–4408, Amanda Johanson, Chief Executive Officer
Web address: https://www.trianglesprings.com

OHIO: BECKETT SPRINGS (O, 96 beds) 8614 Shepherd Farm Drive, West Chester, OH, Zip 45069; tel. 513/942–9500, Loyal Ownes, Chief Executive Officer
Web address: www.https://beckettsprings.com/

COLUMBUS SPRINGS DUBLIN (O, 144 beds) 7625 Hospital Drive, Dublin, OH, Zip 43016–9649; tel. 614/717–1800, Anthony Guild, Chief Executive Officer

HIGHLAND SPRINGS HOSPITAL (O, 72 beds) 4199 Mill Pond Drive, Highland Hills, OH, Zip 44122–5731; tel. 602/314–7800, Brenda Bailey, Chief Executive Officer
Web address: https://www.highlandspringshealth.com

OKLAHOMA: OAKWOOD SPRINGS (O, 72 beds) 13101 Memorial Springs Court, Oklahoma City, OK, Zip 73114–2226; tel. 405/438–3000, Amir Khan, Chief Executive Officer

TEXAS: CARROLLTON SPRINGS (O, 78 beds) 2225 Parker Road, Carrollton, TX, Zip 75010–4711; tel. 972/242–4114, John Fisher, Interim Chief Executive Officer
Web address: www.carrolltonsprings.com

MESA SPRINGS (O, 72 beds) 5560 Mesa Springs Drive, Fort Worth, TX, Zip 76123; tel. 817/292–4600, Andrew Carlton, Chief Executive Officer
Web address: www.https://mesasprings.com/

ROCK SPRINGS (O, 72 beds) 700 Southeast Inner Loop, Georgetown, TX, Zip 78626; tel. 512/819–9400, Erin Basalay, PsyD, Chief Executive Officer
Web address: www.rockspringshealth.com

WESTPARK SPRINGS (O, 72 beds) 6902 South Peek Road, Richmond, TX, Zip 77407; tel. 832/532–8107, Shaun Fenton, Chief Executive Officer
Web address: www.westparksprings.com/why-westpark-springs/

WOODLAND SPRINGS HOSPITAL (O, 96 beds) 15680 Old Conroe Road, Conroe, TX, Zip 77384; tel. 936/270–7520, Dustin Davis, Chief Executive Officer
Web address: https://www.woodlandspringshealth.com/

WASHINGTON: RAINIER SPRINGS HOSPITAL (O, 72 beds) 2805 Northeast 129th Street, Vancouver, WA, Zip 98686–3324; tel. 360/356–1890, Beckie Shauinger, Interim Chief Executive Officer
Web address: https://www.rainiersprings.com

Owned, leased, sponsored:	16 hospitals	1331 beds
Contract-managed:	0 hospitals	0 beds
Totals:	16 hospitals	1331 beds

★5455: SSM HEALTH (CC)
12800 Corporate Hill Drive, Saint Louis, MO Zip 63131–1845; tel. 314/994–7800, Laura S. Kaiser, President and Chief Executive Officer
(Decentralized Health System)

ILLINOIS: CLAY COUNTY HOSPITAL (C, 20 beds) 911 Stacy Burk Drive, Flora, IL, Zip 62839–3241, P O Box 280, Zip 62839–0280, tel. 618/662–2131, Robert R. Sellers, President
Web address: www.claycountyhospital.org

SSM HEALTH GOOD SAMARITAN HOSPITAL (O, 134 beds) 1 Good Samaritan Way, Mount Vernon, IL, Zip 62864–2402; tel. 618/242–4600, Damon R. Harbison, President
Web address: https://www.ssmhealth.com/locations/southern-illinois/good-samaritan-hospital-mt-vernon

SSM HEALTH ST. MARY'S HOSPITAL CENTRALIA (O, 115 beds) 400 North Pleasant Avenue, Centralia, IL, Zip 62801–3056; tel. 618/436–8000, Damon R. Harbison, President

WASHINGTON COUNTY HOSPITAL (C, 32 beds) 705 South Grand Avenue, Nashville, IL, Zip 62263–1534; tel. 618/327–8236, Brian Monsma, President
Web address: www.washingtoncountyhospital.org

MISSOURI: SSM HEALTH CARDINAL GLENNON CHILDREN'S HOSPITAL (O, 176 beds) 1465 South Grand Boulevard, Saint Louis, MO, Zip 63104–1095; tel. 314/577–5600, Hossain Marandi, M.D., FACHE, President
Web address: www.cardinalglennon.com

SSM HEALTH DEPAUL HOSPITAL–ST. LOUIS (O, 523 beds) 12303 De Paul Drive, Bridgeton, MO, Zip 63044–2512; tel. 314/344–6000, Deborah Berini, President
Web address: https://www.ssmhealth.com/locations/st-louis/depaul-hospital-st-louis

SSM HEALTH SAINT LOUIS UNIVERSITY HOSPITAL (O, 406 beds) 1201 South Grand Boulevard, Saint Louis, MO, Zip 63104–1016, P O Box 15250,

For explanation of codes following names, see page B2.
★ Indicates Type III membership in the American Hospital Association.

Systems / SSM Health

Zip 63110–0250, tel. 314/577–8000, Steven M. Scott, M.P.H., FACHE, President
Web address: https://www.ssmhealth.com

SSM HEALTH ST. CLARE HOSPITAL–FENTON (O, 184 beds) 1015 Bowles Avenue, Fenton, MO, Zip 63026–2394; tel. 636/496–2000, Kyle Crate, President

SSM HEALTH ST. JOSEPH–ST. CHARLES (O, 212 beds) 300 First Capitol Drive, Saint Charles, MO, Zip 63301–2844; tel. 636/947–5000, Jacob Brooks, President
Web address: https://www.ssmhealth.com/locations/st-joseph-hospital-st-charles

SSM HEALTH ST. JOSEPH HOSPITAL–LAKE SAINT LOUIS (O, 213 beds) 100 Medical Plaza, Lake Saint Louis, MO, Zip 63367–1366; tel. 636/625–5200, Jerald W. Rumph, FACHE, President

SSM HEALTH ST. MARY'S HOSPITAL–JEFFERSON CITY (O, 86 beds) 2505 Mission Drive, Jefferson City, MO, Zip 65109; tel. 573/681–3000, Kenneth C. DeBoer, Regional President for Mid–Missouri
Web address: https://www.ssmhealth.com/locations/mid-missouri/st-marys-hospital-jefferson-city

SSM HEALTH ST. MARY'S HOSPITAL–ST. LOUIS (O, 394 beds) 6420 Clayton Road, Saint Louis, MO, Zip 63117–1811; tel. 314/768–8000, Steven M. Scott, M.P.H., FACHE, President
Web address: https://www.ssmhealth.com/locations/st-marys-hospital-st-louis

OKLAHOMA: SSM HEALTH ST. ANTHONY HOSPITAL–MIDWEST (L, 87 beds) 2825 Parklawn Drive, Midwest City, OK, Zip 73110–4258; tel. 405/610–4411, Stacy Coleman, MS, President

SSM HEALTH ST. ANTHONY HOSPITAL–OKLAHOMA CITY (O, 638 beds) 1000 North Lee Street, Oklahoma City, OK, Zip 73102–1080, P O Box 205, Zip 73101–0205, tel. 405/272–7000, Tammy Powell, FACHE, M.P.H., President
Web address: www.saintsok.com

SSM HEALTH ST. ANTHONY HOSPITAL–SHAWNEE (O, 70 beds) 1102 West MacArthur Street, Shawnee, OK, Zip 74804–1744; tel. 405/273–2270, Angela Mohr, R.N., MS, President

WEATHERFORD REGIONAL HOSPITAL (C, 22 beds) 3701 East Main Street, Weatherford, OK, Zip 73096–3309; tel. 580/772–5551, Darin Farrell, Chief Executive Officer
Web address: www.weatherfordhospital.com

WISCONSIN: SSM HEALTH MONROE CLINIC (O, 58 beds) 515 22nd Avenue, Monroe, WI, Zip 53566–1598; tel. 608/324–2000, Jane Curran–Meuli, President
Web address: www.monroeclinic.org

SSM HEALTH RIPON COMMUNITY HOSPITAL (O, 16 beds) 845 Parkside Street, Ripon, WI, Zip 54971–8505, P O Box 390, Zip 54971–0390, tel. 920/748–3101, DeAnn Thurmer, President and Chief Nursing Officer
Web address: https://www.ssmhealth.com/

SSM HEALTH ST. AGNES HOSPITAL–FOND DU LAC (O, 127 beds) 430 East Division Street, Fond Du Lac, WI, Zip 54935–4560, P O Box 385, Zip 54936–0385, tel. 920/929–2300, Katherine Vergos, FACHE, President

SSM HEALTH ST. CLARE HOSPITAL–BARABOO (O, 43 beds) 707 14th Street, Baraboo, WI, Zip 53913–1597; tel. 608/356–1400, DeAnn Thurmer, President and Chief Nursing Officer
Web address: www.stclare.com

SSM HEALTH ST. MARY'S HOSPITAL JANESVILLE (O, 50 beds) 3400 East Racine Street, Janesville, WI, Zip 53546–2344, 3400 East Racine Steeet, Zip 53546–2344, tel. 608/373–8000, Jane Curran–Meuli, President
Web address: www.stmarysjanesville.org

SSM HEALTH ST. MARY'S HOSPITAL (O, 374 beds) 700 South Park Street, Madison, WI, Zip 53715–1830; tel. 608/251–6100, Eric Thornton, President
Web address: https://www.ssmhealth.com/locations/st-marys-hospital-madison

SSM HEALTH WAUPUN MEMORIAL HOSPITAL (O, 25 beds) 620 West Brown Street, Waupun, WI, Zip 53963–1799; tel. 920/324–5581, DeAnn Thurmer, President and Chief Nursing Officer
Web address: https://www.ssmhealth.com/

Owned, leased, sponsored:	20 hospitals	3931 beds
Contract–managed:	3 hospitals	74 beds
Totals:	23 hospitals	4005 beds

★1046: ST. BERNARDS HEALTHCARE (CO)

225 East Washington Avenue, Jonesboro, AR Zip 72401–3111; tel. 870/207–7300, Chris B. Barber, FACHE, President and Chief Executive Officer

ARKANSAS: CROSSRIDGE COMMUNITY HOSPITAL (O, 15 beds) 310 South Falls Boulevard, Wynne, AR, Zip 72396–3013, P O Box 590, Zip 72396–0590, tel. 870/238–3300, Gary R. Sparks, Administrator

ST. BERNARDS FIVE RIVERS (O, 37 beds) 2801 Medical Center Drive, Pocahontas, AR, Zip 72455–9436; tel. 870/892–6000, Randall Barymon, Chief Executive Officer
Web address: https://www.stbernards.info/

ST. BERNARDS MEDICAL CENTER (O, 411 beds) 225 East Washington Avenue, Jonesboro, AR, Zip 72401–3111; tel. 870/207–4100, Michael K. Givens, FACHE, Administrator

Owned, leased, sponsored:	3 hospitals	463 beds
Contract–managed:	0 hospitals	0 beds
Totals:	3 hospitals	463 beds

★0250: ST. CHARLES HEALTH SYSTEM, INC. (NP)

2500 NE Neff Road, Bend, OR Zip 97701–6015; tel. 541/382–4321, Steve Gordon, M.D., President and Chief Executive Officer
(Centralized Physician/Insurance Health System)

OREGON: ST. CHARLES BEND (O, 308 beds) 2500 NE Neff Road, Bend, OR, Zip 97701–6015; tel. 541/382–4321, David Golda, Vice President, Hospital Administrator

ST. CHARLES MADRAS (O, 25 beds) 470 NE 'A' Street, Madras, OR, Zip 97741–1844; tel. 541/475–3882, Todd Shields, Vice President, Hospital Administrator
Web address: www.stcharleshealthcare.org/Our-Locations/Madras

ST. CHARLES PRINEVILLE (O, 16 beds) 384 SE Combs Flat Road, Prineville, OR, Zip 97754–1206; tel. 541/447–6254, Todd Shields, Vice President, Hospital Administrator
Web address: www.stcharleshealthcare.org

ST. CHARLES REDMOND (O, 36 beds) 1253 NW Canal Boulevard, Redmond, OR, Zip 97756–1395; tel. 541/548–8131, David Golda, Vice President Hospital and Administrator
Web address: www.stcharleshealthcare.org

Owned, leased, sponsored:	4 hospitals	385 beds
Contract–managed:	0 hospitals	0 beds
Totals:	4 hospitals	385 beds

0618: ST. ELIZABETH HEALTHCARE (CC)

1 Medical Village Drive, Edgewood, KY Zip 41017–3403; tel. 859/301–2000, Garren Colvin, Chief Executive Officer
(Centralized Physician/Insurance Health System)

INDIANA: ST. ELIZABETH DEARBORN (O, 61 beds) 600 Wilson Creek Road, Lawrenceburg, IN, Zip 47025–2751; tel. 812/537–1010, Garren Colvin, Chief Executive Officer
Web address: https://www.stelizabeth.com/location/details/st-elizabeth-dearborn

KENTUCKY: ST. ELIZABETH EDGEWOOD (O, 546 beds) 1 Medical Village Drive, Edgewood, KY, Zip 41017–3403; tel. 859/301–2000, Garren Colvin, Chief Executive Officer
Web address: www.stelizabeth.com

ST. ELIZABETH FLORENCE (O, 154 beds) 4900 Houston Road, Florence, KY, Zip 41042–4824; tel. 859/212–5200, Garren Colvin, Chief Executive Officer
Web address: www.stelizabeth.com

ST. ELIZABETH FORT THOMAS (O, 132 beds) 85 North Grand Avenue, Fort Thomas, KY, Zip 41075–1796; tel. 859/572–3100, Garren Colvin, Chief Executive Officer
Web address: www.stelizabeth.com

For explanation of codes following names, see page B2.
★ Indicates Type III membership in the American Hospital Association.

ST. ELIZABETH GRANT (O, 17 beds) 238 Barnes Road, Williamstown, KY, Zip 41097-9482; tel. 859/824-8240, Garren Colvin, Chief Executive Officer
Web address: www.stelizabeth.com

Owned, leased, sponsored:	5 hospitals	910 beds
Contract-managed:	0 hospitals	0 beds
Totals:	5 hospitals	910 beds

★0356: ST. LUKE'S HEALTH SYSTEM (NP)

190 East Bannock Street, Boise, ID Zip 83712-6241; tel. 208/381-4200, Chris Roth, President and Chief Executive Officer

(Moderately Centralized Health System)

IDAHO: ST. LUKE'S ELMORE (L, 44 beds) 895 North Sixth East Street, Mountain Home, ID, Zip 83647-2207, P O Box 1270, Zip 83647-1270, tel. 208/587-8401, Lisa Melchiorre, R.N., MS, Chief Operating Officer and Chief Nursing Officer
Web address: www.stlukesonline.org/elmore/

ST. LUKE'S JEROME (O, 25 beds) 709 North Lincoln Street, Jerome, ID, Zip 83338-1851, 709 North Lincoln Avenue, Zip 83338-1851, tel. 208/814-9500, Kevin Watson, Chief Operating Officer and Chief Nursing Officer

ST. LUKE'S MAGIC VALLEY MEDICAL CENTER (O, 224 beds) 801 Pole Line Road West, Twin Falls, ID, Zip 83301-5810, P O Box 409, Zip 83303-0409, tel. 208/814-1000, Arlen Blaylock, Chief Operating Officer and Chief Nursing Officer
Web address: www.stlukesonline.org

ST. LUKE'S MCCALL (L, 15 beds) 1000 State Street, McCall, ID, Zip 83638-3704; tel. 208/634-2221, Amber Green, R.N., Chief Operating Officer and Chief Nursing Officer

ST. LUKE'S NAMPA (O, 87 beds) 9850 West St.Luke's Drive, Nampa, ID, Zip 83687; tel. 208/505-2000, Misty Robertson, R.N., FACHE, Chief Operating Officer and Chief Nursing Officer
Web address: https://www.stlukesonline.org/communities-and-locations/facilities/hospitals-and-medical-centers/st-lukes-nampa-medical-center

ST. LUKE'S REGIONAL MEDICAL CENTER (O, 604 beds) 190 East Bannock Street, Boise, ID, Zip 83712-6241; tel. 208/381-2222, Dennis Mesaros, Vice President, Population Health / Regional Acute Care Operations

ST. LUKE'S REHABILITATION HOSPITAL (O, 30 beds) 600 North Robbins Road, Boise, ID, Zip 83702-4565, P O Box 1100, Zip 83701-1100, tel. 208/489-4444, Nolan Hoffer, Administrator Rehabilitation Services
Web address: www.idahoelksrehab.org

ST. LUKE'S WOOD RIVER MEDICAL CENTER (O, 25 beds) 100 Hospital Drive, Ketchum, ID, Zip 83340, P O Box 100, Zip 83340-0100, tel. 208/727-8800, Almita Nunnelee, R.N., Chief Operating Officer and Chief Nursing Officer

WEISER MEMORIAL HOSPITAL (C, 13 beds) 645 East Fifth Street, Weiser, ID, Zip 83672-2202; tel. 208/549-0370, Steven D. Hale, FACHE, Chief Executive Officer
Web address: www.weisermemorialhospital.org

Owned, leased, sponsored:	8 hospitals	1054 beds
Contract-managed:	1 hospitals	13 beds
Totals:	9 hospitals	1067 beds

★0140: ST. LUKE'S HOSPITAL (CO)

232 South Woods Mill Road, Chesterfield, MO Zip 63017-3406; tel. 314/434-1500, Andrew Bagnall, FACHE, President and Chief Executive Officer

MISSOURI: ST. LUKE'S DES PERES HOSPITAL (O, 55 beds) 2345 Dougherty Ferry Road, Saint Louis, MO, Zip 63122-3313; tel. 314/966-9100, Andrew Bagnall, FACHE, President and Chief Executive Officer
Web address: https://www.stlukes-stl.com/desperes/

ST. LUKE'S HOSPITAL (O, 488 beds) 232 South Woods Mill Road, Chesterfield, MO, Zip 63017-3417; tel. 314/434-1500, Andrew Bagnall, FACHE, President and Chief Executive Officer

Owned, leased, sponsored:	2 hospitals	543 beds
Contract-managed:	0 hospitals	0 beds
Totals:	2 hospitals	543 beds

0862: ST. LUKE'S UNIVERSITY HEALTH NETWORK (NP)

801 Ostrum Street, Bethlehem, PA Zip 18015-1000; tel. 610/954-4000, Richard A. Anderson, President and Chief Executive Officer

(Moderately Centralized Health System)

NEW JERSEY: ST. LUKE'S HOSPITAL-WARREN CAMPUS (O, 92 beds) 185 Roseberry Street, Phillipsburg, NJ, Zip 08865-1690; tel. 908/847-6700, Trevor Micklos, President
Web address: www.slhn.org

PENNSYLVANIA: GEISINGER ST. LUKE'S HOSPITAL (C, 40 beds) 100 Paramount Boulevard, Orwigsburg, PA, Zip 17961-2202; tel. 272/639-1000, Gabriel Kamarousky, President
Web address: https://www.geisingerstlukes.org/

ST. LUKE'S ANDERSON CAMPUS (O, 199 beds) 1872 Riverside Circle, Easton, PA, Zip 18045-5669; tel. 484/503-3000, Edward Nawrocki, President

ST. LUKE'S CARBON CAMPUS (O, 40 beds) 500 St. Luke's Drive, Lehighton, PA, Zip 18235; tel. 484/464-9000, John L. Nespoli, President
Web address: www.slhn.org/carbon

ST. LUKE'S EASTON CAMPUS (O, 23 beds) 250 South 21st Street, Easton, PA, Zip 18042-3892; tel. 610/250-4000, Linda J. Grass, President
Web address: https://www.easton-hospital.org/

ST. LUKE'S HOSPITAL-MINERS CAMPUS (O, 97 beds) 360 West Ruddle Street, Coaldale, PA, Zip 18218-1027; tel. 570/645-2131, Diane Laquintz, President

ST. LUKE'S MONROE CAMPUS (O, 98 beds) 100 St. Lukes Lane, Stroudsburg, PA, Zip 18360-6217, 100 St. Luke's Lane, Zip 18360, tel. 484/526-2116, Donald Seiple, President
Web address: www.slhn.org/Choose/choose-monroe

ST. LUKE'S QUAKERTOWN CAMPUS (O, 79 beds) 1021 Park Avenue, Quakertown, PA, Zip 18951-1573; tel. 215/538-4500, Dennis Pfleiger, President
Web address: https://www.slhn.org/quakertown

ST. LUKE'S UNIVERSITY HOSPITAL-BETHLEHEM CAMPUS (O, 959 beds) 801 Ostrum Street, Bethlehem, PA, Zip 18015-1065; tel. 484/526-4000, Carol Kuplen, R.N., MSN, President

Owned, leased, sponsored:	8 hospitals	1587 beds
Contract-managed:	1 hospitals	40 beds
Totals:	9 hospitals	1627 beds

★0156: STANFORD HEALTH CARE (NP)

300 Pasteur Drive, Palo Alto, CA Zip 94304-2299; tel. 650/723-4000, David Entwistle, President and Chief Executive Officer

(Centralized Physician/Insurance Health System)

CALIFORNIA: STANFORD HEALTH CARE TRI-VALLEY (O, 177 beds) 5555 West Las Positas Boulevard, Pleasanton, CA, Zip 94588-4000; tel. 925/847-3000, Richard Shumway, President and Chief Executive Officer
Web address: www.https://stanfordhealthcare.org/tri-valley

STANFORD HEALTH CARE (O, 649 beds) 300 Pasteur Drive, Palo Alto, CA, Zip 94305-2200; tel. 650/723-4000, David Entwistle, President and Chief Executive Officer
Web address: www.stanfordhealthcare.org

Owned, leased, sponsored:	2 hospitals	826 beds
Contract-managed:	0 hospitals	0 beds
Totals:	2 hospitals	826 beds

For explanation of codes following names, see page B2.
★ Indicates Type III membership in the American Hospital Association.

Systems / Steward Health Care System, Llc

0141: STEWARD HEALTH CARE SYSTEM, LLC (IO)
1900 North Pearl Street, Suite 2400, Dallas, TX Zip 75201; tel. 617/419–4700, Ralph de la Torre, M.D., Chairman and Chief Executive Officer
(Moderately Centralized Health System)

ARIZONA: MOUNTAIN VISTA MEDICAL CENTER (O, 178 beds) 1301 South Crismon Road, Mesa, AZ, Zip 85209–3767; tel. 480/358–6100, William J. Comer, President
Web address: https://www.mvmedicalcenter.org/

ST. LUKE'S BEHAVIORAL HEALTH CENTER (O, 85 beds) 1800 East Van Buren, Phoenix, AZ, Zip 85006–3742; tel. 602/251–8546, Gregory L. Jahn, R.N., Chief Executive Officer
Web address: https://www.stlukesbehavioralhealth.org/

TEMPE ST. LUKE'S HOSPITAL (O, 110 beds) 1500 South Mill Avenue, Tempe, AZ, Zip 85281–6699; tel. 480/784–5510, Jenifer Midgett, President and Chief Executive Officer
Web address: www.tempestlukeshospital.org

ARKANSAS: WADLEY REGIONAL MEDICAL CENTER AT HOPE (O, 48 beds) 2001 South Main Street, Hope, AR, Zip 71801–8194; tel. 870/722–3800, Thomas D. Gilbert, FACHE, Chief Executive Officer

FLORIDA: CORAL GABLES HOSPITAL (O, 256 beds) 3100 Douglas Road, Coral Gables, FL, Zip 33134–6914; tel. 305/445–8461, Jose Molliner, Interim Chief Executive Officer
Web address: www.coralgableshospital.com

HIALEAH HOSPITAL (O, 191 beds) 651 East 25th Street, Hialeah, FL, Zip 33013–3878; tel. 305/693–6100, Luis R. Allende-Ruiz, Chief Executive Officer

MELBOURNE REGIONAL MEDICAL CENTER (O, 119 beds) 250 North Wickham Road, Melbourne, FL, Zip 32935–8625; tel. 321/752–1200, Ron Gicca, Chief Executive Officer
Web address: www.wuesthoff.com/locations/wuesthoff-medical-center-melbourne

NORTH SHORE MEDICAL CENTER (O, 258 beds) 1100 NW 95th Street, Miami, FL, Zip 33150–2098; tel. 305/835–6000, Thomas Dunning, President
Web address: https://www.northshoremc.org/

PALMETTO GENERAL HOSPITAL (O, 360 beds) 2001 West 68th Street, Hialeah, FL, Zip 33016–1898; tel. 305/823–5000, Alex Contreras-Soto, President
Web address: https://www.palmettogeneral.org/

ROCKLEDGE REGIONAL MEDICAL CENTER (O, 215 beds) 110 Longwood Avenue, Rockledge, FL, Zip 32955–2887, P O Box 565002, Mail Stop 1, Zip 32956–5002, tel. 321/636–2211, Thomas Bowden, President

SEBASTIAN RIVER MEDICAL CENTER (O, 145 beds) 13695 North U S Hwy 1, Sebastian, FL, Zip 32958–3230, Box 780838, Zip 32978–0838, tel. 772/589–3186, Ronald L. Bierman, President
Web address: https://www.sebastianrivermedical.org/

LOUISIANA: GLENWOOD REGIONAL MEDICAL CENTER (O, 278 beds) 503 McMillan Road, West Monroe, LA, Zip 71291–5327; tel. 318/329–4200, Jonathan Turton, FACHE, President

MASSACHUSETTS: GOOD SAMARITAN MEDICAL CENTER (O, 190 beds) 235 North Pearl Street, Brockton, MA, Zip 02301–1794; tel. 508/427–3000, Matthew Hesketh, President
Web address: www.goodsamaritanmedical.org

HOLY FAMILY HOSPITAL (O, 329 beds) 70 East Street, Methuen, MA, Zip 01844–4597; tel. 978/687–0151
Web address: www.stewardhealth.org/Holy-Family-Hospital

MORTON HOSPITAL AND MEDICAL CENTER (O, 153 beds) 88 Washington Street, Taunton, MA, Zip 02780–2465; tel. 508/828–7000, Heidi Taylor, President
Web address: www.mortonhospital.org

SAINT ANNE'S HOSPITAL (O, 160 beds) 795 Middle Street, Fall River, MA, Zip 02721–1798; tel. 508/674–5741, Michael Bushell, President

ST. ELIZABETH'S MEDICAL CENTER (O, 338 beds) 736 Cambridge Street, Brighton, MA, Zip 02135–2997; tel. 617/789–3000, Marisela Marrero, M.D., President
Web address: www.semc.org/

OHIO: HILLSIDE REHABILITATION HOSPITAL (O, 65 beds) 8747 Squires Lane NE, Warren, OH, Zip 44484–1649; tel. 330/841–3700, Jeffrey Koontz, Chief Administrator Officer
Web address: www.https://valleycareofohio.steward.org

TRUMBULL REGIONAL MEDICAL CENTER (O, 292 beds) 1350 East Market Street, Warren, OH, Zip 44483–6628; tel. 330/841–9011, Cindy Russo, FACHE, MS, R.N., President
Web address: www.https://trumbullmemorial.org/?_ga=2.209137234.1564767671.1497292183-315051339.1497292183

PENNSYLVANIA: SHARON REGIONAL MEDICAL CENTER (O, 218 beds) 740 East State Street, Sharon, PA, Zip 16146–3395; tel. 724/983–3911, Robert Rogalski, President

TEXAS: ODESSA REGIONAL MEDICAL CENTER (O, 112 beds) 520 East Sixth Street, Odessa, TX, Zip 79761–4565, P O Box 4859, Zip 79760–4859, tel. 432/582–8000, Stacey L. Brown, Chief Executive Officer
Web address: https://www.odessaregionalmedicalcenter.org/

SCENIC MOUNTAIN MEDICAL CENTER (O, 80 beds) 1601 West 11th Place, Big Spring, TX, Zip 79720–4198; tel. 432/263–1211, Stacey L. Brown, President

ST. JOSEPH MEDICAL CENTER (O, 216 beds) 1401 St Joseph Parkway, Houston, TX, Zip 77002–8301; tel. 713/757–1000, Scott Flowers, Interim President and Chief Operating Officer
Web address: www.sjmctx.com

THE MEDICAL CENTER OF SOUTHEAST TEXAS (O, 184 beds) 2555 Jimmy Johnson Boulevard, Port Arthur, TX, Zip 77640–2007; tel. 409/724–7389, Brent A. Cope, President

WADLEY REGIONAL MEDICAL CENTER (O, 163 beds) 1000 Pine Street, Texarkana, TX, Zip 75501–5170; tel. 903/798–8000, Thomas D. Gilbert, FACHE, Chief Executive Officer
Web address: https://www.wadleyhealth.org/contact-us

Owned, leased, sponsored:	25 hospitals	4743 beds
Contract-managed:	0 hospitals	0 beds
Totals:	25 hospitals	4743 beds

0858: STRATEGIC BEHAVIORAL HEALTH, LLC (IO)
8295 Tournament Drive, Suite 201, Memphis, TN Zip 38125–8913; tel. 901/969–3100, Blair Stam, President

COLORADO: PEAK VIEW BEHAVIORAL HEALTH (O, 112 beds) 7353 Sisters Grove, Colorado Springs, CO, Zip 80923–2615; tel. 719/444–8484, Ty Meredith, Chief Executive Officer

NEW MEXICO: PEAK BEHAVIORAL HEALTH SERVICES (O, 120 beds) 5065 McNutt Road, Santa Teresa, NM, Zip 88008–9442; tel. 575/589–3000, Sandra Emanuel, Chief Executive Officer
Web address: www.peakbehavioral.com/

NORTH CAROLINA: CAROLINA DUNES BEHAVIORAL HEALTH (O, 116 beds) 2050 Mercantile Drive, Leland, NC, Zip 28451–4053; tel. 910/371–2500, Steve McCabe, Chief Executive Officer
Web address: https://www.carolinadunesbh.com/

STRATEGIC BEHAVIORAL HEALTH, LLC (O, 50 beds) 3200 Waterfield Drive, Garner, NC, Zip 27529–7727; tel. 919/800–4400, Andre Cromwell, Chief Executive Officer

WISCONSIN: WILLOW CREEK BEHAVIORAL HEALTH (O, 39 beds) 1351 Ontario Road, Green Bay, WI, Zip 54311–8302; tel. 920/328–1220, Alison Denil, Chief Executive Officer
Web address: www.willowcreekbh.com

Owned, leased, sponsored:	5 hospitals	437 beds
Contract-managed:	0 hospitals	0 beds
Totals:	5 hospitals	437 beds

★0399: SUMMA HEALTH (NP)
1077 Gorge Boulevard, Akron, OH Zip 44310; tel. 330/375–3000, T. Clifford Deveny, M.D., President and Chief Executive Officer
(Centralized Physician/Insurance Health System)

For explanation of codes following names, see page B2.
★ Indicates Type III membership in the American Hospital Association.

OHIO: SUMMA HEALTH SYSTEM–AKRON CAMPUS (O, 685 beds) 525 East Market Street, Akron, OH, Zip 44304-1619; tel. 330/375-3000, T. Clifford Deveny, M.D., Chief Executive Officer
Web address: www.summahealth.org

SUMMA REHAB HOSPITAL (O, 60 beds) 29 North Adams Street, Akron, OH, Zip 44304-1641; tel. 330/572-7300, Janet Hein, Chief Executive Officer
Web address: www.summarehabhospital.com/

Owned, leased, sponsored:	2 hospitals	745 beds
Contract-managed:	0 hospitals	0 beds
Totals:	2 hospitals	745 beds

★8795: SUTTER HEALTH (NP)
2200 River Plaza Drive, Sacramento, CA Zip 95833-4134; tel. 916/887-0000, Warner Thomas, FACHE, President and Chief Executive Officer
(Centralized Health System)

CALIFORNIA: ALTA BATES SUMMIT MEDICAL CENTER–SUMMIT CAMPUS (O, 309 beds) 350 Hawthorne Avenue, Oakland, CA, Zip 94609-3100; tel. 510/655-4000, David D. Clark, FACHE, Area Chief Executive Officer – Sutter East Bay Hospitals
Web address: www.altabatessummit.com

ALTA BATES SUMMIT MEDICAL CENTER–ALTA BATES CAMPUS (O, 403 beds) 2450 Ashby Avenue, Berkeley, CA, Zip 94705-2067; tel. 510/204-4444, David D. Clark, FACHE, Area Chief Executive Officer, Sutter East Bay Hospitals
Web address: www.altabatessummit.org/

CALIFORNIA PACIFIC MEDICAL CENTER–DAVIES CAMPUS (O, 209 beds) 45 Castro Street, San Francisco, CA, Zip 94114-1010; tel. 415/600-6000, Hamila Kownacki, R.N., Chief Executive Officer
Web address: www.cpmc.org

CALIFORNIA PACIFIC MEDICAL CENTER–MISSION BERNAL CAMPUS (O, 98 beds) 3555 Cesar Chavez Street, San Francisco, CA, Zip 94110-4403; tel. 415/600-6000, Hamila Kownacki, R.N., Chief Executive Officer
Web address: www.stlukes-sf.org

CALIFORNIA PACIFIC MEDICAL CENTER–VAN NESS CAMPUS (O, 274 beds) 1101 Van Ness Avenue, San Francisco, CA, Zip 94109-6919, P O Box 7999, Zip 94120-7999, tel. 415/600-6000, Hamila Kownacki, R.N., Chief Executive Officer

EDEN MEDICAL CENTER (O, 130 beds) 20103 Lake Chabot Road, Castro Valley, CA, Zip 94546-5305; tel. 510/537-1234, Shannon Thomas, Chief Executive Officer
Web address: www.edenmedcenter.org

MEMORIAL HOSPITAL LOS BANOS (O, 38 beds) 520 West 'I' Street, Los Banos, CA, Zip 93635-3498; tel. 209/826-0591, Kristie Lorraine. Marion, Chief Executive Officer and Chief Nurse Executive
Web address: www.memoriallosbanos.org/

MEMORIAL MEDICAL CENTER (O, 419 beds) 1700 Coffee Road, Modesto, CA, Zip 95355-2869, P O Box 942, Zip 95353-0942, tel. 209/526-4500, Tracy Roman, Chief Executive Officer
Web address: www.memorialmedicalcenter.org

MILLS–PENINSULA MEDICAL CENTER (O, 240 beds) 1501 Trousdale Drive, Burlingame, CA, Zip 94010-3282; tel. 650/696-5400, Darian Harris, Chief Executive Officer

NOVATO COMMUNITY HOSPITAL (O, 40 beds) 180 Rowland Way, Novato, CA, Zip 94945-5009; tel. 415/209-1300, Lisa Gammon, Chief Executive Officer
Web address: www.novatocommunity.sutterhealth.org

SUTTER AMADOR HOSPITAL (O, 48 beds) 200 Mission Boulevard, Jackson, CA, Zip 95642-2564; tel. 209/223-7500, Michael Cureton, FACHE, Chief Executive Officer, Sutter Amador Hospital and Sutter Davis Hospital

SUTTER AUBURN FAITH HOSPITAL (O, 64 beds) 11815 Education Street, Auburn, CA, Zip 95602-2410; tel. 530/888-4500, Shanthi Margoschis, MSN, R.N., Chief Executive Officer
Web address: www.sutterhealth.org

SUTTER CENTER FOR PSYCHIATRY (O, 73 beds) 7700 Folsom Boulevard, Sacramento, CA, Zip 95826-2608, 7919 Folsom Boulevard, Zip 95826-2608, tel. 916/386-3000, Dan Peterson, Chief Executive Officer
Web address: https://www.sutterhealth.org/find-location/facility/sutter-center-for-psychiatry

SUTTER COAST HOSPITAL (O, 49 beds) 800 East Washington Boulevard, Crescent City, CA, Zip 95531-8359; tel. 707/464-8511, Michael Lane, Chief Executive Officer

SUTTER DAVIS HOSPITAL (O, 57 beds) 2000 Sutter Place, Davis, CA, Zip 95616-6201; tel. 530/756-6440, Michael Cureton, FACHE, Chief Executive Officer, Sutter Amador Hospital and Sutter Davis Hospital
Web address: www.sutterhealth.org

SUTTER DELTA MEDICAL CENTER (O, 141 beds) 3901 Lone Tree Way, Antioch, CA, Zip 94509-6253; tel. 925/779-7200, Trevor Brand, Chief Executive Officer

SUTTER LAKESIDE HOSPITAL (O, 25 beds) 5176 Hill Road East, Lakeport, CA, Zip 95453-6300; tel. 707/262-5000, Timothy Stephens, Chief Administrative Officer
Web address: www.sutterlakeside.org

SUTTER MATERNITY AND SURGERY CENTER OF SANTA CRUZ (O, 28 beds) 2900 Chanticleer Avenue, Santa Cruz, CA, Zip 95065-1816; tel. 831/477-2200, Stephanie Connor Kent, Chief Executive Officer and Interim Chief Nursing Officer

SUTTER MEDICAL CENTER, SACRAMENTO (O, 523 beds) 2825 Capitol Avenue, Sacramento, CA, Zip 95816-6039; tel. 916/454-3333, Hollie Seeley, President and Chief Executive Officer
Web address: www.sutterhealth.org

SUTTER OAKS NURSING CENTER (O, 100 beds) 2600 L Street, Sacramento, CA, Zip 95816-5612; tel. 916/552-2200

SUTTER ROSEVILLE MEDICAL CENTER (O, 382 beds) 1 Medical Plaza Drive, Roseville, CA, Zip 95661-3037; tel. 916/781-1000, Tamara Powers, R.N., Chief Executive Officer
Web address: www.sutterroseville.org

SUTTER SANTA ROSA REGIONAL HOSPITAL (O, 124 beds) 30 Mark West Springs Road, Santa Rosa, CA, Zip 95403; tel. 707/576-4000, Megan Gillespie, R.N., FACHE, Chief Executive Officer
Web address: www.sutterhealth.org

SUTTER SOLANO MEDICAL CENTER (O, 106 beds) 300 Hospital Drive, Vallejo, CA, Zip 94589-2574; tel. 707/554-4444, Kelley Jaeger-Jackson, Chief Executive Officer
Web address: www.suttersolano.org

SUTTER SURGICAL HOSPITAL–NORTH VALLEY (O, 14 beds) 455 Plumas Boulevard, Yuba City, CA, Zip 95991-5074; tel. 530/749-5700, Shawndra Simpson, Interim Chief Executive Officer

SUTTER TRACY COMMUNITY HOSPITAL (O, 77 beds) 1420 North Tracy Boulevard, Tracy, CA, Zip 95376-3497; tel. 209/835-1500, Scott Knight, Chief Executive Officer
Web address: www.suttertracy.org

Owned, leased, sponsored:	25 hospitals	3971 beds
Contract-managed:	0 hospitals	0 beds
Totals:	25 hospitals	3971 beds

★0871: SWEDISH HEALTH SERVICES (NP)
747 Broadway, Seattle, WA Zip 98122-4379; tel. 206/386-6000, Elizabeth Wako, M.D., President and Chief Executive Officer
(Independent Hospital System)

WASHINGTON: PROVIDENCE SWEDISH CHERRY HILL (O, 211 beds) 500 17th Avenue, Seattle, WA, Zip 98122-5711; tel. 206/320-2000, Elizabeth Wako, M.D., Chief Executive
Web address: https://www.swedish.org/locations/cherry-hill-campus

PROVIDENCE SWEDISH EDMONDS (O, 271 beds) 21601 76th Avenue West, Edmonds, WA, Zip 98026-7506; tel. 425/640-4000, Kristy Carrington, R.N., Chief Executive Officer
Web address: www.swedish.org

PROVIDENCE SWEDISH FIRST HILL (O, 581 beds) 747 Broadway, Seattle, WA, Zip 98122-4307; tel. 206/386-6000, Elizabeth Wako, M.D., Chief Executive

Systems / Swedish Health Services

SWEDISH ISSAQUAH (O, 144 beds) 751 NE Blakely Drive, Issaquah, WA, Zip 98029-6201; tel. 425/313-4000, Elizabeth Wako, M.D., Chief Executive
Web address: www.swedish.org/issaquah

Owned, leased, sponsored:	4 hospitals	1207 beds
Contract-managed:	0 hospitals	0 beds
Totals:	4 hospitals	1207 beds

★0379: TAHOE FOREST HEALTH SYSTEM (NP)

10121 Pine Avenue, Truckee, CA Zip 96161-4835; tel. 530/587-6011, Louis James. Ward, Acting Chief Executive Officer

CALIFORNIA: TAHOE FOREST HOSPITAL DISTRICT (O, 66 beds) 10121 Pine Avenue, Truckee, CA, Zip 96161-4856, P O Box 759, Zip 96160-0759, tel. 530/587-6011, Louis James. Ward, Acting Chief Executive Officer
Web address: www.tfhd.com

NEVADA: INCLINE VILLAGE COMMUNITY HOSPITAL (O, 4 beds) 880 Alder Avenue, Incline Village, NV, Zip 89451-8335; tel. 775/833-4100, Louis James. Ward, Chief Operating Officer and Administrator

Owned, leased, sponsored:	2 hospitals	70 beds
Contract-managed:	0 hospitals	0 beds
Totals:	2 hospitals	70 beds

★1134: TAMARACK HEALTH (NP)

1615 Maple Lane, Ashland, WI Zip 54806-3626; tel. 715/685-5500, Luke Beirl, PharmD, Chief Executive Officer

WISCONSIN: TAMARACK HEALTH ASHLAND MEDICAL CENTER (O, 35 beds) 1615 Maple Lane, Ashland, WI, Zip 54806-3689; tel. 715/685-5500, Luke Beirl, PharmD, Interim Chief Executive Officer

TAMARACK HEALTH HAYWARD MEDICAL CENTER (O, 115 beds) 11040 North State Road 77, Hayward, WI, Zip 54843-6391; tel. 715/934-4321, Luke Beirl, PharmD, Chief Executive Officer
Web address: https://www.tamarackhealth.org/

Owned, leased, sponsored:	2 hospitals	150 beds
Contract-managed:	0 hospitals	0 beds
Totals:	2 hospitals	150 beds

★0341: TANNER HEALTH SYSTEM (NP)

705 Dixie Street, Carrollton, GA Zip 30117-3818; tel. 770/836-9580, Loy M. Howard, President and Chief Executive Officer

ALABAMA: TANNER MEDICAL CENTER/EAST ALABAMA (O, 15 beds) 1032 South Main Street, Wedowee, AL, Zip 36278-7428; tel. 256/357-2111, Heather Stitcher, Administrator
Web address: www.tanner.org/eastalabama

GEORGIA: HIGGINS GENERAL HOSPITAL (O, 23 beds) 200 Allen Memorial Drive, Bremen, GA, Zip 30110-2012; tel. 770/824-2000, Jerry Morris, Administrator

TANNER MEDICAL CENTER-CARROLLTON (O, 176 beds) 705 Dixie Street, Carrollton, GA, Zip 30117-3818; tel. 770/836-9666, Loy M. Howard, Chief Operating Officer
Web address: www.tanner.org

TANNER MEDICAL CENTER-VILLA RICA (O, 132 beds) 601 Dallas Highway, Villa Rica, GA, Zip 30180-1202; tel. 770/456-3000, Jerry Morris, Vice President and Administrator
Web address: www.tanner.org

Owned, leased, sponsored:	4 hospitals	346 beds
Contract-managed:	0 hospitals	0 beds
Totals:	4 hospitals	346 beds

★0169: TEMPLE UNIVERSITY HEALTH SYSTEM (NP)

3509 North Broad Street, 9th Floor, Philadelphia, PA Zip 19140-4105; tel. 215/707-0900, Michael A. Young, FACHE, Chief Executive Officer
(Centralized Health System)

PENNSYLVANIA: FOX CHASE CANCER CENTER (O, 60 beds) 333 Cottman Avenue, Philadelphia, PA, Zip 19111-2434; tel. 215/728-6900, Robert Uzzo, M.D., President and Chief Executive Officer
Web address: https://www.foxchase.org

TEMPLE HEALTH-CHESTNUT HILL HOSPITAL (O, 212 beds) 8835 Germantown Avenue, Philadelphia, PA, Zip 19118-2718; tel. 215/248-8200, Richard Newell, President and Chief Executive Officer
Web address: www.chhealthsystem.com

TEMPLE UNIVERSITY HOSPITAL (O, 879 beds) 3401 North Broad Street, Philadelphia, PA, Zip 19140-5103; tel. 215/707-2000, Abhinav Rastogi, President and Chief Executive Officer
Web address: www.tuh.templehealth.org/content/default.htm

Owned, leased, sponsored:	3 hospitals	1151 beds
Contract-managed:	0 hospitals	0 beds
Totals:	3 hospitals	1151 beds

★0919: TENET HEALTHCARE CORPORATION (IO)

14201 Dallas Parkway, Dallas, TX Zip 75254-2916, P O Box 1390369, Zip 75313-9036, tel. 469/893-2200, Saumya Sutaria, M.D., Chief Executive Officer
(Decentralized Health System)

ALABAMA: BROOKWOOD BAPTIST MEDICAL CENTER (O, 595 beds) 2010 Brookwood Medical Center Drive, Birmingham, AL, Zip 35209-6875; tel. 205/877-1000, Jeremy L. Clark, Chief Executive Officer
Web address: https://www.brookwoodbaptisthealth.com/

CITIZENS BAPTIST MEDICAL CENTER (O, 72 beds) 604 Stone Avenue, Talladega, AL, Zip 35160-2217, P O Box 978, Zip 35161-0978, tel. 256/362-8111, Frank D. Thomas, Chief Executive Officer
Web address: www.brookwoodbaptisthealth.org

PRINCETON BAPTIST MEDICAL CENTER (O, 315 beds) 701 Princeton Avenue SW, Birmingham, AL, Zip 35211-1303; tel. 205/783-3000, Daniel Listi, Chief Executive Officer

SHELBY BAPTIST MEDICAL CENTER (O, 231 beds) 1000 First Street North, Alabaster, AL, Zip 35007-8703; tel. 205/620-8100, Holly Dean, Chief Executive Officer
Web address: https://www.shelbybaptistmedicalcenter.com/

WALKER BAPTIST MEDICAL CENTER (O, 178 beds) 3400 Highway 78 East, Jasper, AL, Zip 35501-8907, P O Box 3547, Zip 35502-3547, tel. 205/387-4000, Sean Johnson, Chief Executive Officer
Web address: www.bhsala.com

ARIZONA: ABRAZO ARROWHEAD CAMPUS (O, 217 beds) 18701 North 67th Avenue, Glendale, AZ, Zip 85308-7100; tel. 623/561-1000, Stephen Garner, Chief Executive Officer

ABRAZO CENTRAL CAMPUS (O, 206 beds) 2000 West Bethany Home Road, Phoenix, AZ, Zip 85015-2443; tel. 602/249-0212, Gregory Pearson, Chief Executive Officer
Web address: www.abrazohealth.com

ABRAZO SCOTTSDALE CAMPUS (O, 136 beds) 3929 East Bell Road, Phoenix, AZ, Zip 85032-2196; tel. 602/923-5000, Ruben Castro, Chief Executive Officer
Web address: www.abrazoscottsdale.com

ABRAZO WEST CAMPUS (O, 188 beds) 13677 West McDowell Road, Goodyear, AZ, Zip 85395-2635; tel. 623/882-1500, Hans Driessnack, Chief Executive Officer

CARONDELET HOLY CROSS HOSPITAL (O, 25 beds) 1171 West Target Range Road, Nogales, AZ, Zip 85621-2415; tel. 520/285-3000, Dina Rojas-Sanchez, Chief Executive Officer
Web address: https://www.carondelet.org/locations/detail/holy-cross-hospital

---

For explanation of codes following names, see page B2.
★ Indicates Type III membership in the American Hospital Association.

Systems / Tennessee Health Management

CARONDELET ST. JOSEPH'S HOSPITAL (O, 486 beds) 350 North Wilmot Road, Tucson, AZ, Zip 85711-2678; tel. 520/873-3000, Monica Vargas-Mahar, FACHE, Market Chief Executive Officer
Web address: www.carondelet.org

CARONDELET ST. MARY'S HOSPITAL (O, 400 beds) 1601 West St Mary's Road, Tucson, AZ, Zip 85745-2682; tel. 520/872-3000, David Ziolkowski, Chief Executive Officer
Web address: www.carondelet.org

CALIFORNIA: DESERT REGIONAL MEDICAL CENTER (L, 337 beds) 1150 North Indian Canyon Drive, Palm Springs, CA, Zip 92262-4872; tel. 760/323-6511, Michele Finney, Chief Executive Officer, Desert Regional Medical Center
Web address: www.desertregional.com

DOCTORS HOSPITAL OF MANTECA (O, 56 beds) 1205 East North Street, Manteca, CA, Zip 95336-4900; tel. 209/823-3111, Tina Burch, Chief Executive Officer and Chief Nursing Officer

DOCTORS MEDICAL CENTER OF MODESTO (O, 461 beds) 1441 Florida Avenue, Modesto, CA, Zip 95350-4418, P O Box 4138, Zip 95352-4138, tel. 209/578-1211, Jaikumar Krishnaswamy, Chief Executive Officer
Web address: www.dmc-modesto.com

EMANUEL MEDICAL CENTER (O, 209 beds) 825 Delbon Avenue, Turlock, CA, Zip 95382-2016; tel. 209/667-4200, Murali Naidu, M.D., FACS, Chief Executive Officer
Web address: www.emanuelmedicalcenter.org

HI-DESERT MEDICAL CENTER (L, 59 beds) 6601 White Feather Road, Joshua Tree, CA, Zip 92284; tel. 760/366-3711, Karen Faulis, Chief Executive Officer

JFK MEMORIAL HOSPITAL (O, 145 beds) 47111 Monroe Street, Indio, CA, Zip 92201-6799; tel. 760/347-6191, Karen Faulis, Chief Executive Officer
Web address: www.jfkmemorialhosp.com

SAN RAMON REGIONAL MEDICAL CENTER (O, 123 beds) 6001 Norris Canyon Road, San Ramon, CA, Zip 94583-5400; tel. 925/275-9200, Beenu Chadha, Interim Chief Executive Officer and Chief Financial Officer

FLORIDA: DELRAY MEDICAL CENTER (O, 520 beds) 5352 Linton Boulevard, Delray Beach, FL, Zip 33484-6580; tel. 561/498-4440, Heather Havericak, Chief Executive Officer
Web address: www.delraymedicalctr.com

GOOD SAMARITAN MEDICAL CENTER (O, 348 beds) 1309 North Flagler Drive, West Palm Beach, FL, Zip 33401-3499; tel. 561/655-5511, Sheri Montgomery, Acting Chief Executive Officer
Web address: www.goodsamaritanmc.com

PALM BEACH GARDENS MEDICAL CENTER (L, 199 beds) 3360 Burns Road, Palm Beach Gardens, FL, Zip 33410-4323; tel. 561/622-1411, Teresa C. Urquhart, Chief Executive Officer

ST. MARY'S MEDICAL CENTER (O, 460 beds) 901 45th Street, West Palm Beach, FL, Zip 33407-2495; tel. 561/844-6300, Cynthia McCauley, Chief Executive Officer
Web address: www.stmarysmc.com

WEST BOCA MEDICAL CENTER (O, 195 beds) 21644 State Road 7, Boca Raton, FL, Zip 33428-1899; tel. 561/488-8000, Jerad Hanlon, Chief Executive Officer

MASSACHUSETTS: METROWEST MEDICAL CENTER (O, 351 beds) 115 Lincoln Street, Framingham, MA, Zip 01702-6342; tel. 508/383-1000, John Whitlock Jr, CPA, Chief Executive Officer
Web address: www.mwmc.com

SAINT VINCENT HOSPITAL (O, 288 beds) 123 Summer Street, Worcester, MA, Zip 01608-1216; tel. 508/363-5000, Carolyn Jackson, Chief Executive Officer
Web address: www.stvincenthospital.com

MICHIGAN: DMC CHILDREN'S HOSPITAL OF MICHIGAN (O, 227 beds) 3901 Beaubien Street, Detroit, MI, Zip 48201-2119; tel. 313/745-5852, Archie Drake, Chief Executive Officer
Web address: www.chmkids.org

DMC DETROIT RECEIVING HOSPITAL & UNIVERSITY HEALTH CENTER (O, 584 beds) 4201 Saint Antoine Street, Detroit, MI, Zip 48201-2153; tel. 313/745-3000, Joshua Hester, Chief Executive Officer
Web address: www.dmc.org

DMC HARPER UNIVERSITY HOSPITAL (O, 224 beds) 3990 John 'R' Street, Detroit, MI, Zip 48201-2018; tel. 313/745-8040, Joshua Hester, Chief Executive Officer

DMC HURON VALLEY-SINAI HOSPITAL (O, 156 beds) 1 William Carls Drive, Commerce Township, MI, Zip 48382-2201; tel. 248/937-3300, Lance Beus, Chief Executive Officer
Web address: www.hvsh.org

DMC REHABILITATION INSTITUTE OF MICHIGAN (O, 69 beds) 261 Mack Avenue, Detroit, MI, Zip 48201-2495; tel. 313/745-1203, Christina Michajyszyn, FACHE, Chief Executive Officer

DMC SINAI-GRACE HOSPITAL (O, 424 beds) 6071 West Outer Drive, Detroit, MI, Zip 48235-2679; tel. 313/966-3300, Gary Purushotham, Chief Executive Officer
Web address: www.sinaigrace.org

SOUTH CAROLINA: PIEDMONT MEDICAL CENTER (O, 394 beds) 222 Herlong Avenue, Rock Hill, SC, Zip 29732; tel. 803/329-1234, Teresa C. Urquhart, Market Chief Executive Officer

TENNESSEE: SAINT FRANCIS HOSPITAL-BARTLETT (O, 196 beds) 2986 Kate Bond Road, Bartlett, TN, Zip 38133-4003; tel. 901/820-7000, Sherwin Stewart, Chief Executive Officer
Web address: www.saintfrancisbartlett.com

SAINT FRANCIS HOSPITAL (O, 479 beds) 5959 Park Avenue, Memphis, TN, Zip 38119-5198; tel. 901/765-1000, Scott M. Smith, Market Chief Executive Officer
Web address: www.saintfrancishosp.com

TEXAS: BAPTIST MEDICAL CENTER (O, 1292 beds) 111 Dallas Street, San Antonio, TX, Zip 78205-1230; tel. 210/297-7000, Thomas McKinney, FACHE, Chief Executive Officer

NACOGDOCHES MEDICAL CENTER (O, 109 beds) 4920 NE Stallings Drive, Nacogdoches, TX, Zip 75965-1200; tel. 936/569-9481, Jeff Patterson, Chief Executive Officer
Web address: www.nacmedicalcenter.com

RESOLUTE HEALTH (O, 128 beds) 555 Creekside Crossing, New Braunfels, TX, Zip 78130-2594; tel. 830/500-6000, Mark L. Bernard, Chief Executive Officer

THE HOSPITALS OF PROVIDENCE EAST CAMPUS-TENET HEALTHCARE (O, 218 beds) 3280 Joe Battle Boulevard, El Paso, TX, Zip 79938-2622; tel. 915/832-2000, Tasha Hopper, MSN, R.N., FACHE, Chief Executive Officer
Web address: www.sphn.com

THE HOSPITALS OF PROVIDENCE MEMORIAL CAMPUS-TENET HEALTHCARE (O, 289 beds) 2001 North Oregon Street, El Paso, TX, Zip 79902-3368; tel. 915/577-6625, Rob J. Anderson, Chief Executive Officer
Web address: www.thehospitalsofprovidence.com

THE HOSPITALS OF PROVIDENCE SIERRA CAMPUS-TENET HEALTHCARE (O, 306 beds) 1625 Medical Center Drive, El Paso, TX, Zip 79902-5005; tel. 915/747-4000, Tasha Hopper, MSN, R.N., FACHE, Chief Executive Officer

THE HOSPITALS OF PROVIDENCE TRANSMOUNTAIN CAMPUS-TENET HEALTHCARE (O, 108 beds) 2000 Transmountain Road, El Paso, TX, Zip 79911; tel. 915/877-8300, David T. Byrd, Chief Executive Officer
Web address: https://www.thehospitalsofprovidence.com/our-locations/transmountain

VALLEY BAPTIST MEDICAL CENTER-BROWNSVILLE (O, 225 beds) 1040 West Jefferson Street, Brownsville, TX, Zip 78520-6338, P O Box 3590, Zip 78523-3590, tel. 956/698-5400, Leslie Bingham, Senior Vice President and Chief Executive Officer

VALLEY BAPTIST MEDICAL CENTER-HARLINGEN (O, 423 beds) 2101 Pease Street, Harlingen, TX, Zip 78550-8307, P O Drawer 2588, Zip 78551-2588, tel. 956/389-1100, Michael Cline, Chief Executive Officer
Web address: https://www.valleybaptist.net/locations/detail/vbmc-harlingen/

Owned, leased, sponsored:	44 hospitals	12651 beds
Contract-managed:	0 hospitals	0 beds
Totals:	44 hospitals	12651 beds

0876: TENNESSEE HEALTH MANAGEMENT (IO)
52 West Eighth Street, Parsons, TN Zip 38363-4656, PO Box 10, Zip 38363-0010, tel. 731/847-6343, Dennis Berry, Chief Executive Officer

For explanation of codes following names, see page B2.
★ Indicates Type III membership in the American Hospital Association.

Systems / Tennessee Health Management

ALABAMA: UNITY PSYCHIATRIC CARE–HUNTSVILLE (O, 20 beds) 5315 Millennium Drive NW, Huntsville, AL, Zip 35806–2458; tel. 256/964–6700, Kyle Smith, Administrator
Web address: https://www.unitypsych.com/huntsville

TENNESSEE: UNITY PSYCHIATRIC CARE–CLARKSVILLE (O, 26 beds) 930 Professional Park Drive, Clarksville, TN, Zip 37040–5136; tel. 931/538–6420, Jessica Thurston, Administrator

UNITY PSYCHIATRIC CARE–COLUMBIA (O, 16 beds) 1400 Rosewood Drive, Columbia, TN, Zip 38401–4878; tel. 931/388–6573, Morgan Reddix, Administrator
Web address: www.unitypsych.com

UNITY PSYCHIATRIC CARE–MARTIN (O, 16 beds) 458 Hannings Lane, Martin, TN, Zip 38237–3308; tel. 731/588–2830, Carrie Brawley, Administrator
Web address: www.unitypsych.com

Owned, leased, sponsored:	4 hospitals	78 beds
Contract-managed:	0 hospitals	0 beds
Totals:	4 hospitals	78 beds

0020: TEXAS DEPARTMENT OF STATE HEALTH SERVICES (NP)
1100 West 49th Street, Austin, TX Zip 78756–3199; tel. 512/458–7111, John William. Hellerstedt, M.D., Commissioner
(Independent Hospital System)

TEXAS: AUSTIN STATE HOSPITAL (O, 263 beds) 4110 Guadalupe Street, Austin, TX, Zip 78751–4296; tel. 512/452–0381, Stacey Thompson, Superintendent
Web address: www.dshs.state.tx.us/mhhospitals/austinsh/default.shtm

BIG SPRING STATE HOSPITAL (O, 144 beds) 1901 North Highway 87, Big Spring, TX, Zip 79720–0283; tel. 432/267–8216, Deborah Young, Superintendent
Web address: www.dshs.state.tx.us/mhhospitals/BigSpringSH/default.shtm

EL PASO PSYCHIATRIC CENTER (O, 74 beds) 4615 Alameda Avenue, El Paso, TX, Zip 79905–2702; tel. 915/532–2202, Zulema Carrillo, Superintendent

KERRVILLE STATE HOSPITAL (O, 290 beds) 721 Thompson Drive, Kerrville, TX, Zip 78028–5154; tel. 830/896–2211, Leigh Ann Fitzpatrick, Superintendent
Web address: www.dshs.state.tx.us/mhhospitals/KerrvilleSH/default.shtm

NORTH TEXAS STATE HOSPITAL (O, 530 beds) 4730 College Drive, Vernon, TX, Zip 76384–4009, P O Box 2231, Zip 76385–2231, tel. 940/552–9901, Albert Ragland, Superintendent

RIO GRANDE STATE CENTER/SOUTH TEXAS HEALTH CARE SYSTEM (O, 55 beds) 1401 South Rangerville Road, Harlingen, TX, Zip 78552–7638; tel. 956/364–8000, Sonia Hernandez–Keeble, Superintendent
Web address: www.dshs.state.tx.us/mhhospitals/RioGrandeSC/default.shtm

RUSK STATE HOSPITAL (O, 288 beds) 805 North Dickinson, Rusk, TX, Zip 75785–2333, P O Box 318, Zip 75785–0318, tel. 903/683–3421, Brenda Slaton, Superintendent
Web address: www.dshs.state.tx.us/mhhospitals/RuskSH/default.shtm

SAN ANTONIO STATE HOSPITAL (O, 262 beds) 6711 South New Braunfels, Suite 100, San Antonio, TX, Zip 78223–3006; tel. 210/531–7711, Robert C. Arizpe, Superintendent
Web address: www.dshs.state.tx.us/mhhospitals/SanAntonioSH/default.shtm

TERRELL STATE HOSPITAL (O, 305 beds) 1200 East Brin Street, Terrell, TX, Zip 75160–2938, P O Box 70, Zip 75160–9000, tel. 972/524–6452, Mark Messer, D.O., Interim Superintendent
Web address: www.dshs.state.tx.us/mhhospitals/terrellsh

TEXAS CENTER FOR INFECTIOUS DISEASE (O, 50 beds) 2303 SE Military Drive, San Antonio, TX, Zip 78223–3597; tel. 210/534–8857, James N. Elkins, FACHE, Director

Owned, leased, sponsored:	10 hospitals	2261 beds
Contract-managed:	0 hospitals	0 beds
Totals:	10 hospitals	2261 beds

★0129: TEXAS HEALTH RESOURCES (NP)
612 East Lamar Boulevard, Suite 900, Arlington, TX Zip 76011–4130; tel. 682/236–7900, Barclay E. Berdan, FACHE, Chief Executive Officer
(Centralized Physician/Insurance Health System)

TEXAS: TEXAS HEALTH ARLINGTON MEMORIAL HOSPITAL (O, 245 beds) 800 West Randol Mill Road, Arlington, TX, Zip 76012–2503; tel. 817/548–6100, Blake Kretz, FACHE, President
Web address: www.arlingtonmemorial.org

TEXAS HEALTH HARRIS METHODIST HOSPITAL ALLIANCE (O, 125 beds) 10864 Texas Health Trail, Fort Worth, TX, Zip 76244–4897; tel. 682/212–2000, Clint Abernathy, President
Web address: https://www.texashealth.org/alliance/Pages/default.aspx

TEXAS HEALTH HARRIS METHODIST HOSPITAL AZLE (O, 31 beds) 108 Denver Trail, Azle, TX, Zip 76020–3614; tel. 817/444–8600, Tonya Sosebee, MSN, R.N., Chief Operating and Nursing Officer

TEXAS HEALTH HARRIS METHODIST HOSPITAL CLEBURNE (O, 69 beds) 201 Walls Drive, Cleburne, TX, Zip 76033–4007; tel. 817/641–2551, Christopher Leu, President
Web address: www.texashealth.org

TEXAS HEALTH HARRIS METHODIST HOSPITAL FORT WORTH (O, 764 beds) 1301 Pennsylvania Avenue, Fort Worth, TX, Zip 76104–2122; tel. 817/250–2000, Jared Shelton, FACHE, President
Web address: www.texashealth.org

TEXAS HEALTH HARRIS METHODIST HOSPITAL HURST–EULESS–BEDFORD (O, 209 beds) 1600 Hospital Parkway, Bedford, TX, Zip 76022–6913; tel. 817/685–4000, Jared Shelton, FACHE, President

TEXAS HEALTH HARRIS METHODIST HOSPITAL SOUTHWEST FORT WORTH (O, 233 beds) 6100 Harris Parkway, Fort Worth, TX, Zip 76132–4199; tel. 817/433–5000, Ajith Pai, PharmD, FACHE, President
Web address: www.texashealth.org

TEXAS HEALTH HARRIS METHODIST HOSPITAL STEPHENVILLE (O, 47 beds) 411 North Belknap Street, Stephenville, TX, Zip 76401–3415; tel. 254/965–1500, Claudia A. Eisenmann, FACHE, President
Web address: www.texashealth.org/landing.cfm?id=108

TEXAS HEALTH HOSPITAL FRISCO (O, 77 beds) 12400 Dallas Parkway, Frisco, TX, Zip 75033–4224; tel. 469/495–2000, Brett D. Lee, President

TEXAS HEALTH PRESBYTERIAN HOSPITAL ALLEN (O, 68 beds) 1105 Central Expressway North, Suite 140, Allen, TX, Zip 75013–6103; tel. 972/747–1000, Amanda Thrash, FACHE, President
Web address: https://www.texashealth.org/Locations/Texas-Health-Allen

TEXAS HEALTH PRESBYTERIAN HOSPITAL DALLAS (O, 595 beds) 8200 Walnut Hill Lane, Dallas, TX, Zip 75231–4426; tel. 214/345–6789, Christopher York, FACHE, President
Web address: https://www.texashealth.org/Locations/Texas-Health-Dallas

TEXAS HEALTH PRESBYTERIAN HOSPITAL DENTON (O, 239 beds) 3000 North I-35, Denton, TX, Zip 76201–5119; tel. 940/898–7000, Jeff Reecer, FACHE, President
Web address: www.dentonhospital.com

TEXAS HEALTH PRESBYTERIAN HOSPITAL KAUFMAN (O, 42 beds) 850 Ed Hall Drive, Kaufman, TX, Zip 75142–1861, 850 Ed Hall Dr, Zip 75142, tel. 972/932–7200, Toya White, JD, MSN, Chief Operating Officer & Chief Nursing Officer
Web address: www.texashealth.org/Kaufman

TEXAS HEALTH PRESBYTERIAN HOSPITAL PLANO (O, 327 beds) 6200 West Parker Road, Plano, TX, Zip 75093–8185; tel. 972/981–8000, Fraser Hay, FACHE, President

TEXAS HEALTH SPECIALTY HOSPITAL (O, 10 beds) 1301 Pennsylvania Avenue, 4th Floor, Fort Worth, TX, Zip 76104–2190; tel. 817/250–5500, Pamela Duffey, R.N., Vice President/Chief Operating Office/Chief Nursing Officer
Web address: https://www.texashealth.org/texas-health-specialty-hospital/

Owned, leased, sponsored:	15 hospitals	3081 beds
Contract-managed:	0 hospitals	0 beds
Totals:	15 hospitals	3081 beds

For explanation of codes following names, see page B2.
★ Indicates Type III membership in the American Hospital Association.

1038: THE CARPENTER HEALTH NETWORK (IO)

10615 Jefferson Highway, Baton Rouge, LA Zip 70809–7230; tel. 225/769–2449, Pat Mitchell, Chief Executive Officer

LOUISIANA: SAGE REHABILITATION HOSPITAL (O, 45 beds) 8000 Summa Avenue, Baton Rouge, LA, Zip 70809–3423, P O Box 82681, Zip 70884–2681, tel. 225/819–0703, Leonard Greg. Crider, Administrator

SAGE SPECIALTY HOSPITAL (LTAC) (O, 36 beds) 8375 Florida Boulevard, Denham Springs, LA, Zip 70726–7806; tel. 225/665–2664, Sharon Faulkner, R.N., Administrator
Web address: https://www.thecarpenterhealthnetwork.com/locations/sage-specialty-hospital/

Owned, leased, sponsored:	2 hospitals	81 beds
Contract–managed:	0 hospitals	0 beds
Totals:	2 hospitals	81 beds

★1040: THE UNIVERSITY OF KANSAS HEALTH SYSTEM (NP)

4000 Cambridge Street, Kansas City, KS Zip 66160–0001; tel. 913/588–1227, Bob Page, President and Chief Executive Officer

(Moderately Centralized Health System)

KANSAS: MIAMI COUNTY MEDICAL CENTER (O, 18 beds) 2100 Baptiste Drive, Paola, KS, Zip 66071–1314, P O Box 365, Zip 66071–0365, tel. 913/294–2327, Paul W. Luce, R.N., MSN, Administrator
Web address: https://www.olathehealth.org/locations/miami-county-medical-center/

OLATHE MEDICAL CENTER (O, 268 beds) 20333 West 151st Street, Olathe, KS, Zip 66061–5350; tel. 913/791–4200, Jason Hannagan, Chief Executive Officer, Southwest Kansas City Market, and Senior Vice President, Kansas City Division

THE UNIVERSITY OF KANSAS HOSPITAL (O, 1005 beds) 4000 Cambridge Street, MS 3011, Kansas City, KS, Zip 66160–8501; tel. 913/588–5000, Bob Page, Chief Executive Officer
Web address: www.kumed.com

UNIVERSITY OF KANSAS HEALTH SYSTEM GREAT BEND CAMPUS (O, 33 beds) 514 Cleveland Street, Great Bend, KS, Zip 67530–3562; tel. 620/792–8833, John Worden, Interim Administrator

Owned, leased, sponsored:	4 hospitals	1324 beds
Contract–managed:	0 hospitals	0 beds
Totals:	4 hospitals	1324 beds

★0421: THE UNIVERSITY OF VERMONT HEALTH NETWORK (NP)

111 Colchester Avenue, Burlington, VT Zip 05401–1473; tel. 802/847–3983, Sunil Eappen, M.D., President and Chief Executive Officer

NEW YORK: THE UNIVERSITY OF VERMONT HEALTH NETWORK–ALICE HYDE MEDICAL CENTER (O, 196 beds) 133 Park Street, Malone, NY, Zip 12953–1243, P O Box 729, Zip 12953–0729, tel. 518/483–3000, Michelle LeBeau, President
Web address: www.UVMHealth.org/AHMC

THE UNIVERSITY OF VERMONT HEALTH NETWORK ELIZABETHTOWN COMMUNITY HOSPITAL (O, 25 beds) 75 Park Street, Elizabethtown, NY, Zip 12932, P O Box 277, Zip 12932–0277, tel. 518/873–6377, Robert Ortmyer, President

THE UNIVERSITY OF VERMONT HEALTH NETWORK–CHAMPLAIN VALLEY PHYSICIANS HOSPITAL (O, 254 beds) 75 Beekman Street, Plattsburgh, NY, Zip 12901–1438; tel. 518/561–2000, Michelle LeBeau, President and Chief Operating Officer
Web address: https://profiles.health.ny.gov/hospital/view/103048

VERMONT: THE UNIVERSITY OF VERMONT HEALTH NETWORK CENTRAL VERMONT MEDICAL CENTER (O, 251 beds) 130 Fisher Road, Berlin, VT, Zip 05602–9516, P O Box 547, Barre, Zip 05641–0547, tel. 802/371–4100, Anna T. Noonan, President and Chief Operating Officer

THE UNIVERSITY OF VERMONT HEALTH NETWORK PORTER MEDICAL CENTER (O, 29 beds) 115 Porter Drive, Middlebury, VT, Zip 05753–8423; tel. 802/388–4701, Robert Ortmyer, President & Chief Operating Officer
Web address: www.portermedical.org

UNIVERSITY OF VERMONT MEDICAL CENTER (O, 537 beds) 111 Colchester Avenue, Burlington, VT, Zip 05401–1473; tel. 802/847–5630, Stephen Leffler, M.D., President and Chief Operating Officer

Owned, leased, sponsored:	6 hospitals	1292 beds
Contract–managed:	0 hospitals	0 beds
Totals:	6 hospitals	1292 beds

★0992: TIDALHEALTH (IO)

100 East Carroll Street, Salisbury, MD Zip 21801–5422; tel. 410/546–6400, Steven E. Leonard, President and Chief Executive Officer

DELAWARE: TIDALHEALTH NANTICOKE (O, 99 beds) 801 Middleford Road, Seaford, DE, Zip 19973–3636; tel. 302/629–6611, Penny Short, R.N., President
Web address: www.nanticoke.org

MARYLAND: TIDALHEALTH PENINSULA REGIONAL (O, 281 beds) 100 East Carroll Street, Salisbury, MD, Zip 21801–5422; tel. 410/546–6400, Steven E. Leonard, President and Chief Executive Officer
Web address: https://www.tidalhealth.org/our-locations/tidalhealth-peninsula-regional

Owned, leased, sponsored:	2 hospitals	380 beds
Contract–managed:	0 hospitals	0 beds
Totals:	2 hospitals	380 beds

★0812: TIDELANDS HEALTH (NP)

4033 Highway 17 Suite 104, Murrells Inlet, SC Zip 29576–5032, P.O. Box 421718, Georgetown, Zip 29442–4203, tel. 843/527–7000, Bruce P. Bailey, President and Chief Executive Officer

SOUTH CAROLINA: TIDELANDS GEORGETOWN MEMORIAL HOSPITAL (O, 69 beds) 606 Black River Road, Georgetown, SC, Zip 29440–3368, P.O. Box 421718, Zip 29442–4203, tel. 843/527–7000, Bruce P. Bailey, President & Chief Executive Officer
Web address: www.tidelandshealth.org

TIDELANDS WACCAMAW COMMUNITY HOSPITAL (O, 126 beds) 4070 Highway 17 Bypass, Murrells Inlet, SC, Zip 29576–5033, P.O. Box 421718, Georgetown, Zip 29442–4203, tel. 843/652–1000, Bruce P. Bailey, President & Chief Executive Officer

Owned, leased, sponsored:	2 hospitals	195 beds
Contract–managed:	0 hospitals	0 beds
Totals:	2 hospitals	195 beds

★0910: TIFT REGIONAL HEALTH SYSTEM (NP)

901 East 18th Street, Tifton, GA Zip 31794–3648; tel. 229/353–6100, Christopher Dorman, President and Chief Executive Officer

(Independent Hospital System)

GEORGIA: SOUTHWELL MEDICAL (O, 115 beds) 260 MJ Taylor Road, Adel, GA, Zip 31620–3485; tel. 229/896–8000, Christopher Dorman, Chief Executive Officer
Web address: www.cookmedicalcenter.com

For explanation of codes following names, see page B2.
★ Indicates Type III membership in the American Hospital Association.

Systems / Tift Regional Health System

TIFT REGIONAL MEDICAL CENTER (O, 181 beds) 901 East 18th Street, Tifton, GA, Zip 31794-3648, Drawer 747, Zip 31793-0747, tel. 229/382-7120, Christopher Dorman, President and Chief Executive Officer
Web address: www.tiftregional.com

Owned, leased, sponsored:	2 hospitals	296 beds
Contract-managed:	0 hospitals	0 beds
Totals:	2 hospitals	296 beds

★1029: TOWER HEALTH (NP)

420 South Fifth Avenue, West Reading, PA Zip 19611-2143; tel. 610/988-8000, M. Sue. Perrotty, President and Chief Executive Officer
(Moderately Centralized Health System)

PENNSYLVANIA: PHOENIXVILLE HOSPITAL (O, 144 beds) 140 Nutt Road, Phoenixville, PA, Zip 19460-3900, P O Box 3001, Zip 19460-0916, tel. 610/983-1000, Richard McLaughlin, M.D., President and Chief Executive Officer
Web address: www.https://phoenixville.towerhealth.org

POTTSTOWN HOSPITAL (O, 213 beds) 1600 East High Street, Pottstown, PA, Zip 19464-5093; tel. 610/327-7000, Richard McLaughlin, M.D., President and Chief Executive Officer
Web address: www.https://pottstown.towerhealth.org/

READING HOSPITAL (O, 650 beds) 420 South Fifth Avenue, West Reading, PA, Zip 19611-2143, P O Box 16052, Zip 19612-6052, tel. 610/988-8000, Charles Barbera, M.D., President and Chief Executive Officer
Web address: www.readinghospital.org

Owned, leased, sponsored:	3 hospitals	1007 beds
Contract-managed:	0 hospitals	0 beds
Totals:	3 hospitals	1007 beds

★0906: TRINITY HEALTH (CC)

20555 Victor Parkway, Livonia, MI Zip 48152-7031; tel. 734/343-1000, Michael A. Slubowski, FACHE, President and Chief Executive Officer
(Decentralized Health System)

CALIFORNIA: SAINT AGNES MEDICAL CENTER (O, 382 beds) 1303 East Herndon Avenue, Fresno, CA, Zip 93720-3397; tel. 559/450-3000, Gurvinder Kaur, President and Market Leader

CONNECTICUT: JOHNSON MEMORIAL HOSPITAL (O, 78 beds) 201 Chestnut Hill Road, Stafford Springs, CT, Zip 06076-4005; tel. 860/684-4251, Robert Roose, M.D., Chief Executive Officer
Web address: www.jmmc.org

MOUNT SINAI REHABILITATION HOSPITAL (O, 38 beds) 490 Blue Hills Avenue, Hartford, CT, Zip 06112-1513; tel. 860/714-3500, Robert J. Krug, M.D., President and Executive Medical Director

SAINT FRANCIS HOSPITAL (O, 412 beds) 114 Woodland Street, Hartford, CT, Zip 06105-1208; tel. 860/714-4000, Valerie L. Powell-Stafford, President
Web address: https://www.trinityhealthofne.org/location/saint-francis-hospital

SAINT MARY'S HOSPITAL (O, 237 beds) 56 Franklin Street, Waterbury, CT, Zip 06706-1281; tel. 203/709-6000, Kimberly Kalajainen, FACHE, Chief Administrative Officer
Web address: www.trinityhealthofne.org

DELAWARE: ST. FRANCIS HOSPITAL (O, 127 beds) 701 North Clayton Street, Wilmington, DE, Zip 19805, P O Box 2500, Zip 19805-0500, tel. 302/421-4100, Marlow Levy, President
Web address: www.stfrancishealthcare.org

FLORIDA: HOLY CROSS HOSPITAL (O, 557 beds) 4725 North Federal Highway, Fort Lauderdale, FL, Zip 33308-4668, P O Box 23460, Zip 33307-3460, tel. 954/771-8000, Mark Doyle, President and Chief Executive Officer
Web address: www.holy-cross.com

GEORGIA: ST. MARY'S GOOD SAMARITAN HOSPITAL (O, 25 beds) 5401 Lake Oconee Parkway, Greensboro, GA, Zip 30642-4232; tel. 706/453-7331, Stonish Pierce, FACHE, President and Chief Executive Officer

ST. MARY'S HEALTH CARE SYSTEM (O, 277 beds) 1230 Baxter Street, Athens, GA, Zip 30606-3791; tel. 706/389-3000, Stonish Pierce, FACHE, President and Chief Executive Officer
Web address: www.stmarysathens.com

ST. MARY'S SACRED HEART HOSPITAL (O, 48 beds) 367 Clear Creek Parkway, Lavonia, GA, Zip 30553-4173; tel. 706/356-7800, Stonish Pierce, FACHE, President and Chief Executive Officer
Web address: www.stmaryssacredheart.org/

IDAHO: SAINT ALPHONSUS MEDICAL CENTER–NAMPA (O, 106 beds) 4300 East Flamingo Avenue, Nampa, ID, Zip 83686-6008; tel. 208/205-1000, Clint Child, R.N., President

SAINT ALPHONSUS REGIONAL MEDICAL CENTER (O, 415 beds) 1055 N Curtis Rd, Boise, ID, Zip 83706-1309, 1055 North Curtis Road, Zip 83706-1309, tel. 208/367-2121, David M. McFadyen, FACHE, President
Web address: www.saintalphonsus.org

ILLINOIS: GENESIS MEDICAL CENTER, SILVIS (O, 68 beds) 801 Illini Drive, Silvis, IL, Zip 61282-1893; tel. 309/281-4000, Theresa Main, R.N., President
Web address: www.genesishealth.com

GENESIS MEDICAL CENTER–ALEDO (O, 22 beds) 409 NW Ninth Avenue, Aledo, IL, Zip 61231-1296; tel. 309/582-9100, Ted Rogalski, Administrator

GOTTLIEB MEMORIAL HOSPITAL (O, 154 beds) 701 West North Avenue, Melrose Park, IL, Zip 60160-1612; tel. 708/681-3200, Elizabeth Early, FACHE, President
Web address: https://www.loyolamedicine.org/location/gmh

LOYOLA UNIVERSITY MEDICAL CENTER (O, 500 beds) 2160 South First Avenue, Maywood, IL, Zip 60153-3328; tel. 708/216-9000, Tad Gomez, MS, President

MACNEAL HOSPITAL (O, 300 beds) 3249 South Oak Park Avenue, Berwyn, IL, Zip 60402-0715; tel. 708/783-9100, Pierre Monice, President
Web address: www.macneal.com

INDIANA: PLYMOUTH MEDICAL CENTER (O, 48 beds) 1915 Lake Avenue, Plymouth, IN, Zip 46563-9366, P O Box 670, Zip 46563-0670, tel. 574/948-4000, Christopher J. Karam, President

SAINT JOSEPH HEALTH SYSTEM (O, 270 beds) 5215 Holy Cross Parkway, Mishawaka, IN, Zip 46545-1469; tel. 574/335-5000, Shawn Vincent, Chief Executive Officer
Web address: www.sjmed.com

IOWA: FRANKLIN GENERAL HOSPITAL (C, 77 beds) 1720 Central Avenue East, Suite A, Hampton, IA, Zip 50441-1867; tel. 641/456-5000, Kim Price, Chief Executive Officer
Web address: www.franklingeneral.com

GENESIS MEDICAL CENTER–DAVENPORT (O, 344 beds) 1227 East Rusholme Street, Davenport, IA, Zip 52803-2498; tel. 563/421-1000, Jordan Voigt, President MercyOne Eastern Division

GENESIS MEDICAL CENTER, DEWITT (O, 13 beds) 1118 11th Street, De Witt, IA, Zip 52742-1296; tel. 563/659-4200, Ted Rogalski, Administrator
Web address: www.genesishealth.com

HANCOCK COUNTY HEALTH SYSTEM (C, 25 beds) 532 First Street NW, Britt, IA, Zip 50423-1227; tel. 641/843-5000, Laura Zwiefel, Chief Executive officer/Chief Nursing Officer

HANSEN FAMILY HOSPITAL (C, 21 beds) 920 South Oak, Iowa Falls, IA, Zip 50126-9506; tel. 641/648-4631, George Von Mock, Chief Executive Officer/Administrator
Web address: www.hansenfamilyhospital.com

HAWARDEN REGIONAL HEALTHCARE (C, 14 beds) 1111 11th Street, Hawarden, IA, Zip 51023-1999; tel. 712/551-3100, Jayson Pullman, Chief Executive Officer

JACKSON COUNTY REGIONAL HEALTH CENTER (C, 12 beds) 601 Hospital Dr, Maquoketa, IA, Zip 52060; tel. 563/652-2474, Patrick Peters, Administrator/Chief Executive Officer
Web address: www.jcrhc.org

KOSSUTH REGIONAL HEALTH CENTER (C, 23 beds) 1515 South Phillips Street, Algona, IA, Zip 50511-3649; tel. 515/295-2451, Darlene M. Elbert, R.N., MS, Chief Executive Officer

---

For explanation of codes following names, see page B2.
★ Indicates Type III membership in the American Hospital Association.

Systems / Trinity Health

MERCYONE CEDAR FALLS MEDICAL CENTER (O, 35 beds) 515 College Street, Cedar Falls, IA, Zip 50613-2500; tel. 319/268-3000, Ryan Meyer, Chief Operating Officer
Web address: www.MercyOne.org

MERCYONE CENTERVILLE MEDICAL CENTER (O, 44 beds) 1 St Joseph's Drive, Centerville, IA, Zip 52544-8055; tel. 641/437-4111, Nicole Clapp, R.N., MSN, FACHE, President
Web address: www.mercycenterville.org

MERCYONE CLINTON MEDICAL CENTER (O, 73 beds) 1410 North Fourth Street, Clinton, IA, Zip 52732-2940; tel. 563/244-5555, Mellissa Wood, Chief Operating Officer, Chief Nursing Officer
Web address: www.mercyclinton.com

MERCYONE DES MOINES MEDICAL CENTER (O, 620 beds) 1111 6th Avenue, Des Moines, IA, Zip 50314-2611; tel. 515/247-3121, Kurt Andersen, M.D., President–Central Iowa Division

MERCYONE DUBUQUE MEDICAL CENTER (O, 197 beds) 250 Mercy Drive, Dubuque, IA, Zip 52001-7360; tel. 563/589-8000, Kay Takes, R.N., President
Web address: www.mercydubuque.com

MERCYONE DYERSVILLE MEDICAL CENTER (O, 8 beds) 1111 Third Street SW, Dyersville, IA, Zip 52040-1725; tel. 563/875-7101, Kay Takes, R.N., President
Web address: www.mercydubuque.com/mercy-dyersville

MERCYONE ELKADER MEDICAL CENTER (O, 15 beds) 901 Davidson Street NW, Elkader, IA, Zip 52043-9015; tel. 563/245-7000, Christopher Brady, Interim Chief Executive Officer
Web address: www.centralcommunityhospital.com

MERCYONE NEW HAMPTON MEDICAL CENTER (O, 11 beds) 308 North Maple Avenue, New Hampton, IA, Zip 50659-1142; tel. 641/394-4121, Aaron Flugum, Chief Executive Officer
Web address: www.mercynewhampton.com

MERCYONE NEWTON MEDICAL CENTER (O, 34 beds) 204 North Fourth Avenue East, Newton, IA, Zip 50208-3100; tel. 641/792-1273, Chad Kelley, Chief Operating Officer
Web address: www.skiffmed.com

MERCYONE NORTH IOWA MEDICAL CENTER (O, 238 beds) 1000 Fourth Street SW, Mason City, IA, Zip 50401-2800; tel. 641/428-7000, Chad Boore, Chief Operations Officer

MERCYONE OELWEIN MEDICAL CENTER (C, 56 beds) 201 Eighth Avenue SE, Oelwein, IA, Zip 50662-2447; tel. 319/283-6000, Ryan Meyer, Chief Operating Officer
Web address: www.wheatoniowa.org

MERCYONE PRIMGHAR MEDICAL CENTER (O, 14 beds) 255 North Welch Avenue, Primghar, IA, Zip 51245-7765, P O Box 528, Zip 51245-0528, tel. 712/957-2300, Thomas A. Clark, President, MercyOne Western Division
Web address: https://www.mercyone.org/primghar/

MERCYONE SIOUXLAND MEDICAL CENTER (O, 152 beds) 801 Fifth Street, Sioux City, IA, Zip 51101-1326, P O Box 3168, Zip 51102-3168, tel. 712/279-2010, Thomas A. Clark, President, MercyOne Western Division
Web address: www.mercysiouxcity.com

MERCYONE WATERLOO MEDICAL CENTER (O, 242 beds) 3421 West Ninth Street, Waterloo, IA, Zip 50702-5401; tel. 319/272-8000, Ryan Meyer, Chief Operating Officer
Web address: https://www.mercyone.org/location/mercyone-waterloo-medical-center-1

MITCHELL COUNTY REGIONAL HEALTH CENTER (C, 23 beds) 616 North Eighth Street, Osage, IA, Zip 50461-1498; tel. 641/732-6000, Shelly Russell, Chief Executive Officer

PALO ALTO COUNTY HEALTH SYSTEM (C, 40 beds) 3201 First Street, Emmetsburg, IA, Zip 50536-2516; tel. 712/852-5500, Jonathan Moe, Chief Executive Officer
Web address: https://www.mercyonenorthiowaaffiliates.org/pachs/

REGIONAL HEALTH SERVICES OF HOWARD COUNTY (C, 19 beds) 235 Eighth Avenue West, Cresco, IA, Zip 52136-1098; tel. 563/547-2101, Robin M. Schluter, Chief Executive Officer

MARYLAND: HOLY CROSS GERMANTOWN HOSPITAL (O, 95 beds) 19801 Observation Drive, Germantown, MD, Zip 20876-4070; tel. 301/557-6000, Louis Damiano, M.D., Chief Executive Officer
Web address: https://www.holycrosshealth.org/location/holy-cross-germantown-hospital

HOLY CROSS HOSPITAL (O, 453 beds) 1500 Forest Glen Road, Silver Spring, MD, Zip 20910-1487; tel. 301/754-7000, Louis Damiano, M.D., Chief Executive Officer
Web address: www.holycrosshealth.org

MASSACHUSETTS: FARREN CARE CENTER (O, 72 beds) 340 Montague City Road, Turners Falls, MA, Zip 01376-9983; tel. 413/774-3111, James Clifford, Administrator

MERCY MEDICAL CENTER (O, 334 beds) 271 Carew Street, Springfield, MA, Zip 01104-2398, P O Box 9012, Zip 01102-9012, tel. 413/748-9000, Deborah Bitsoli, CPA, President
Web address: www.mercycares.com

MICHIGAN: CHELSEA HOSPITAL (O, 120 beds) 775 South Main Street, Chelsea, MI, Zip 48118-1383; tel. 734/593-6000, Ben Miles, President
Web address: https://www.stjoeshealth.org/location/chelsea-hospital

TRINITY HEALTH ANN ARBOR HOSPITAL (O, 537 beds) 5301 Mcauley Drive, Ypsilanti, MI, Zip 48197-1051, P O Box 995, Ann Arbor, Zip 48106-0995, tel. 734/712-3456, Alonzo Lewis, President

TRINITY HEALTH GRAND RAPIDS HOSPITAL (O, 303 beds) 200 Jefferson Avenue Southeast, Grand Rapids, MI, Zip 49503-4598, 200 Jefferson Avenue SE, Zip 49503-4598, tel. 616/685-5000, Matt Biersack, M.D., President
Web address: https://www.mercyhealth.com/location/mercy-health-saint-marys

TRINITY HEALTH LIVINGSTON HOSPITAL (O, 42 beds) 620 Byron Road, Howell, MI, Zip 48843-1093; tel. 517/545-6000, John F. O'Malley, FACHE, President
Web address: https://www.stjoeslivingston.org/livingston

TRINITY HEALTH LIVONIA HOSPITAL (O, 304 beds) 36475 Five Mile Road, Livonia, MI, Zip 48154-1988; tel. 734/655-4800, Shannon Striebich, FACHE, President & Chief Executive Officer, Trinity Health Michigan Market
Web address: https://www.stjoeshealth.org/location/trinity-health-livonia-hospital

TRINITY HEALTH MUSKEGON HOSPITAL (O, 348 beds) 1500 East Sherman Boulevard, Muskegon, MI, Zip 49444-1849; tel. 231/672-2000, Gary Allore, President

TRINITY HEALTH OAKLAND HOSPITAL (O, 389 beds) 44405 Woodward Avenue, Pontiac, MI, Zip 48341-5023; tel. 248/858-3000, Shannon Striebich, FACHE, President and Chief Executive Officer of Trinity Health Michigan Market
Web address: https://www.stjoeshealth.org/location/trinity-health-oakland-hospital

TRINITY HEALTH SHELBY HOSPITAL (O, 24 beds) 72 South State Street, Shelby, MI, Zip 49455-1299; tel. 231/861-2156, Gary Allore, President
Web address: www.mercyhealthmuskegon.com

NEBRASKA: PENDER COMMUNITY HOSPITAL (C, 61 beds) 100 Hospital Drive, Pender, NE, Zip 68047-0100, P O Box 100, Zip 68047-0100, tel. 402/385-3083, Laura Gamble, Chief Executive Officer
Web address: www.pendercommunityhospital.com

NEW YORK: BURDETT BIRTH CENTER (O, 15 beds) 2215 Burdett Avenue, Suite 200, Troy, NY, Zip 12180-2466; tel. 518/271-3393, JoAnn Lionarons, Director

SAMARITAN HOSPITAL–MAIN CAMPUS (O, 321 beds) 2215 Burdett Avenue, Troy, NY, Zip 12180-2475; tel. 518/271-3300, Steven Hanks, M.D., President and Chief Executive Officer, St. Joseph's Health and St. Peter's Health Partners
Web address: www.sphp.com/sam

ST. JOSEPH'S HOSPITAL HEALTH CENTER (O, 451 beds) 301 Prospect Avenue, Syracuse, NY, Zip 13203-1807; tel. 315/448-5111, Meredith Price, Senior Vice President, Acute Operations

ST. PETER'S HOSPITAL (O, 482 beds) 315 South Manning Boulevard, Albany, NY, Zip 12208-1789; tel. 518/525-1550, Steven Hanks, M.D., President and Chief Executive Officer
Web address: https://www.sphp.com/location/st-peters-hospital

SUNNYVIEW REHABILITATION HOSPITAL (O, 115 beds) 1270 Belmont Avenue, Schenectady, NY, Zip 12308-2104; tel. 518/382-4500, Kim Baker, Senior Vice President, Hospital Operations
Web address: www.sunnyview.org

NORTH CAROLINA: ST. JOSEPH OF THE PINES HOSPITAL (O, 204 beds) 590 Central Drive, Southern Pines, NC, Zip 28387; tel. 910/246-1000, Ken Cormier, President and Chief Executive Officer

For explanation of codes following names, see page B2.
★ Indicates Type III membership in the American Hospital Association.

Systems / Trinity Health

OHIO: DILEY RIDGE MEDICAL CENTER (O, 10 beds) 7911 Diley Road, Canal Winchester, OH, Zip 43110–9653; tel. 614/838–7911, Stacey Collins, R.N., Site Administrator, Chief Nursing Officer
Web address: www.dileyridgemedicalcenter.com

MOUNT CARMEL EAST HOSPITAL (O, 355 beds) 6001 East Broad Street, Columbus, OH, Zip 43213; tel. 614/234–6000, Scott Wilber, President and Chief Operating Officer
Web address: https://www.mountcarmelhealth.com/location/mount-carmel-east

MOUNT CARMEL NEW ALBANY SURGICAL HOSPITAL (O, 59 beds) 7333 Smith's Mill Road, New Albany, OH, Zip 43054–9291; tel. 614/775–6600, Diane Doucette, R.N., President and Chief Operating Officer

MOUNT CARMEL ST. ANN'S (O, 304 beds) 500 South Cleveland Avenue, Westerville, OH, Zip 43081–8998; tel. 614/898–4000, Diane Doucette, R.N., President and Chief Operating Officer
Web address: www.mountcarmelhealth.com

OREGON: SAINT ALPHONSUS MEDICAL CENTER–BAKER CITY (O, 25 beds) 3325 Pocahontas Road, Baker City, OR, Zip 97814–1464; tel. 541/523–6461, Dina Ellwanger, R.N., President, Eastern Oregon

SAINT ALPHONSUS MEDICAL CENTER–ONTARIO (O, 35 beds) 351 SW Ninth Street, Ontario, OR, Zip 97914–2693; tel. 541/881–7000, Dina Ellwanger, R.N., President and Chief Nursing Officer
Web address: www.saintalphonsus.org/ontario

PENNSYLVANIA: MERCY FITZGERALD HOSPITAL (O, 104 beds) 1500 Lansdowne Avenue, Suite 100, Darby, PA, Zip 19023–1200; tel. 610/237–4000, Marlow Levy, President

NAZARETH HOSPITAL (O, 147 beds) 2601 Holme Avenue, Philadelphia, PA, Zip 19152–2096; tel. 215/335–6000, Michael Magro Jr, D.O., President
Web address: www.nazarethhospital.org

ST. MARY MEDICAL CENTER (O, 373 beds) 1201 Langhorne–Newtown Road, Langhorne, PA, Zip 19047–1201; tel. 215/710–2000, Michael Magro Jr, D.O., President

ST. MARY REHABILITATION HOSPITAL (O, 50 beds) 1208 Langhorne Newtown Road, Langhorne, PA, Zip 19047–1234; tel. 267/560–1111, Lisa Haney, Chief Executive Officer
Web address: www.stmaryhealthcare.org

Owned, leased, sponsored:	62 hospitals	12175 beds
Contract-managed:	11 hospitals	371 beds
Totals:	73 hospitals	12546 beds

1069: TRINITY HEALTH (NP)
1 Burdick Expressway West, Minot, ND Zip 58701–4406; tel. 701/857–5000, John M. Kutch, President and Chief Executive Officer

NORTH DAKOTA: TRINITY HEALTH (O, 580 beds) 1 Burdick Expressway West, Minot, ND, Zip 58701–4406, P O Box 5020, Zip 58702–5020, tel. 701/857–5766, John M. Kutch, President and Chief Executive Officer
Web address: www.trinityhealth.org

TRINITY KENMARE COMMUNITY HOSPITAL (O, 25 beds) 317 First Avenue NW, Kenmare, ND, Zip 58746–7104, P O Box 697, Zip 58746–0697, tel. 701/385–4296, Danielle Alsadon, Clinic/Hospital Manager
Web address: www.kenmarend.net/hospital.htm

Owned, leased, sponsored:	2 hospitals	605 beds
Contract-managed:	0 hospitals	0 beds
Totals:	2 hospitals	605 beds

★1071: TUFTS MEDICINE (NP)
800 District Avenue, Suite 520, Burlington, MA Zip 01803–5057; tel. 978/942–2220, Michael J. Dandorph, President and Chief Executive Officer

MASSACHUSETTS: LOWELL GENERAL HOSPITAL (C, 297 beds) 295 Varnum Avenue, Lowell, MA, Zip 01854–2134; tel. 978/937–6000, Amy J. Hoey, R.N., MS, President

MELROSEWAKEFIELD HEALTHCARE (C, 216 beds) 585 Lebanon Street, Melrose, MA, Zip 02176–3225; tel. 781/979–3000, Kelly Corbi, President and Chief Executive Officer
Web address: www.melrosewakefield.org

TUFTS MEDICAL CENTER (C, 302 beds) 800 Washington Street, Boston, MA, Zip 02111–1552; tel. 617/636–5000, Michael J. Dandorph, Chief Executive Officer
Web address: www.tuftsmedicalcenter.org

Owned, leased, sponsored:	0 hospitals	0 beds
Contract-managed:	3 hospitals	815 beds
Totals:	3 hospitals	815 beds

★9105: UAB HEALTH SYSTEM (NP)
500 22nd Street South, Suite 408, Birmingham, AL Zip 35233–3110; tel. 205/975–5362, Dawn Bulgarella, Chief Executive Officer

(Centralized Physician/Insurance Health System)

ALABAMA: MEDICAL WEST (O, 236 beds) 995 Ninth Avenue SW, Bessemer, AL, Zip 35022–4527; tel. 205/481–7000, Brian Keith. Pennington, President and Chief Executive Officer
Web address: www.medicalwesthospital.org

UNIVERSITY OF ALABAMA HOSPITAL (O, 1304 beds) 619 19th Street South, Birmingham, AL, Zip 35249–1900; tel. 205/934–4011, Brenda H. Carlisle, R.N., Chief Executive Officer
Web address: www.uabmedicine.org

WHITFIELD REGIONAL HOSPITAL (C, 47 beds) 105 U S Highway 80 East, Demopolis, AL, Zip 36732–3616, P O Box 890, Zip 36732–0890, tel. 334/289–4000, Douglas L. Brewer, Chief Executive Officer
Web address: www.bwwmh.com

Owned, leased, sponsored:	2 hospitals	1540 beds
Contract-managed:	1 hospitals	47 beds
Totals:	3 hospitals	1587 beds

0082: UC HEALTH (NP)
3200 Burnet Avenue, Cincinnati, OH Zip 45229–3019; tel. 513/585–6000, Cory D. Shaw, President and Chief Executive Officer

(Moderately Centralized Health System)

OHIO: DANIEL DRAKE CENTER FOR POST ACUTE CARE (O, 202 beds) 151 West Galbraith Road, Cincinnati, OH, Zip 45216–1015; tel. 513/418–2500, Tom Goodwin, Administrator
Web address: www.uchealth.com/danieldrakecenter/

UNIVERSITY OF CINCINNATI MEDICAL CENTER (O, 568 beds) 234 Goodman Street, Cincinnati, OH, Zip 45219–2316; tel. 513/584–1000, Teri Grau, R.N., Vice President Operations and Chief Nursing Officer

WEST CHESTER HOSPITAL (O, 175 beds) 7700 University Drive, West Chester, OH, Zip 45069–2505; tel. 513/298–3000, Jennifer Jackson, R.N., MSN, Vice President of Operations and Chief Nursing Officer
Web address: www.uchealth.com/westchesterhospital

Owned, leased, sponsored:	3 hospitals	945 beds
Contract-managed:	0 hospitals	0 beds
Totals:	3 hospitals	945 beds

★0381: UCHEALTH (NP)
12401 East 17th Avenue, Mail Stop F417, Aurora, CO Zip 80045–2548; tel. 970/495–7000, Elizabeth B. Concordia, President and Chief Executive Officer

(Moderately Centralized Health System)

COLORADO: UCHEALTH BROOMFIELD HOSPITAL (O, 38 beds) 11820 Destination Drive, Broomfield, CO, Zip 80021; tel. 303/460–6000, Ryan Rohman, MSN, R.N., President
Web address: www.uchealth.org/pages/OHAM/OrgUnitDetails.aspx?

For explanation of codes following names, see page B2.
★ Indicates Type III membership in the American Hospital Association.

Systems / Umass Memorial Health Care, Inc.

UCHEALTH GRANDVIEW HOSPITAL (O, 22 beds) 5623 Pulpit Peak View, Colorado Springs, CO, Zip 80918; tel. 719/272-3600, Ron Fitch, President/UCHealth Pikes Peak Regional Hospital/Grandview Hospital/Operations and Military Affairs/UCHealth Southern CO
Web address: https://www.uchealth.org/Pages/OHAM/OrgUnitDetails.aspx?OrganizationalUnitId=514

UCHEALTH GREELEY HOSPITAL (O, 91 beds) 6767 29th Street, Greeley, CO, Zip 80634-5474; tel. 970/652-2000, Marilyn Schock, President
Web address: https://www.uchealth.org/locations/uchealth-greeley-medical-clinic/

UCHEALTH HIGHLANDS RANCH HOSPITAL (O, 93 beds) 1500 Park Central Drive, Highlands Ranch, CO, Zip 80129-6688; tel. 720/848-0000, Merle Taylor, President
Web address: https://www.uchealth.org/locations/uchealth-highlands-ranch-hospital/

UCHEALTH LONGS PEAK HOSPITAL (O, 83 beds) 1750 East Ken Pratt Boulevard, Longmont, CO, Zip 80504-5311; tel. 970/237-7850, Ryan Rohman, MSN, R.N., President

UCHEALTH MEDICAL CENTER OF THE ROCKIES (O, 191 beds) 2500 Rocky Mountain Avenue, Loveland, CO, Zip 80538-9004; tel. 970/624-2500, Kevin L. Unger, Ph.D., FACHE, President and Chief Executive Officer
Web address: www.medctrrockies.org

UCHEALTH MEMORIAL HOSPITAL (L, 511 beds) 1400 East Boulder Street, Colorado Springs, CO, Zip 80909-5599; tel. 719/365-5000, Lonnie Cramer, President and Chief Executive Officer
Web address: www.uchealth.org/southerncolorado

UCHEALTH PARKVIEW MEDICAL CENTER (O, 292 beds) 400 West 16th Street, Pueblo, CO, Zip 81003-2781; tel. 719/584-4000, Darrin Smith, President and Chief Executive Officer
Web address: www.parkviewmc.org

UCHEALTH PIKES PEAK REGIONAL HOSPITAL (O, 13 beds) 16420 West Highway 24, Woodland Park, CO, Zip 80863; tel. 719/687-9999, Ron Fitch, President/UCHealth Pikes Peak Regional Hospital/Grandview Hospital/Operations and Military Affairs/UCHealth Southern CO

UCHEALTH POUDRE VALLEY HOSPITAL (O, 263 beds) 1024 South Lemay Avenue, Fort Collins, CO, Zip 80524-3998, 2315 East Harmony Road, Suite 200, Zip 80528, tel. 970/495-7000, Kevin L. Unger, Ph.D., FACHE, President and Chief Executive Officer
Web address: www.uchealth.org

UCHEALTH YAMPA VALLEY MEDICAL CENTER (O, 34 beds) 1024 Central Park Drive, Steamboat Springs, CO, Zip 80487-8813; tel. 970/879-1322, Soniya Fidler, MS, President
Web address: https://www.uchealth.org/locations/uchealth-yampa-valley-medical-center/

UNIVERSITY OF COLORADO HOSPITAL (O, 831 beds) 12401 East 17th Avenue, MS F417, Aurora, CO, Zip 80045-2545; tel. 720/848-0000, Thomas Gronow, President and Chief Executive Officer

Owned, leased, sponsored:	12 hospitals	2462 beds
Contract-managed:	0 hospitals	0 beds
Totals:	12 hospitals	2462 beds

★0111: UF HEALTH SHANDS (NP)
1600 SW Archer Road, Gainesville, FL Zip 32610-0326; tel. 352/733-1500, Stephen J. Motew, M.D., FACS, President and System Chief Executive Officer
(Moderately Centralized Health System)

FLORIDA: LEESBURG REGIONAL MEDICAL CENTER (O, 344 beds) 600 East Dixie Avenue, Leesburg, FL, Zip 34748-5999; tel. 352/323-5762, Heather Long, R.N., Chief Executive Officer
Web address: www.centralfloridahealth.org

UF HEALTH JACKSONVILLE (O, 644 beds) 655 West Eighth Street, Jacksonville, FL, Zip 32209-6595; tel. 904/244-0411, Patrick Green, FACHE, Chief Executive Officer
Web address: www.ufhealthjax.org/

UF HEALTH SHANDS HOSPITAL (O, 1091 beds) 1600 SW Archer Road, Gainesville, FL, Zip 32610-3003, PO Box 100326, Zip 32610-0326, tel. 352/265-0111, James J. Kelly Jr, Interim Chief Executive Officer
Web address: www.https://ufhealth.org/

UF HEALTH ST. JOHN'S (O, 204 beds) 400 Health Park Boulevard, Saint Augustine, FL, Zip 32086-5784; tel. 904/819-5155, Kerry Watson, Interim Chief Executive Officer

UF HEALTH THE VILLAGES HOSPITAL (O, 307 beds) 1451 El Camino Real, The Villages, FL, Zip 32159-0041; tel. 352/751-8000, Heather Long, R.N., Senior Vice President and Chief Operating Officer
Web address: www.cfhalliance.org

Owned, leased, sponsored:	5 hospitals	2590 beds
Contract-managed:	0 hospitals	0 beds
Totals:	5 hospitals	2590 beds

1119: UK HEALTHCARE (NP)
1000 South Limestone, Lexington, KY Zip 40506-0007; tel. 800/333-8874, Robert DiPaola, Co-Executive Vice President for Health Affairs

KENTUCKY: EASTERN STATE HOSPITAL (C, 179 beds) 1350 Bull Lea Road, Lexington, KY, Zip 40511; tel. 859/246-8000, Lindsey Jasinski, Chief Administrative Officer
Web address: www.https://ukhealthcare.uky.edu/

ST. CLAIRE REGIONAL MEDICAL CENTER (O, 149 beds) 222 Medical Circle, Morehead, KY, Zip 40351-1179; tel. 606/783-6500, Donald H. Lloyd II, President and Chief Executive Officer
Web address: www.st-claire.org

UK KING'S DAUGHTERS MEDICAL CENTER (O, 630 beds) 2201 Lexington Avenue, Ashland, KY, Zip 41101-2874, P O Box 151, Zip 41105-0151, tel. 606/408-4000, Sara Marks, President and Chief Executive Officer

UNIVERSITY OF KENTUCKY ALBERT B. CHANDLER HOSPITAL (O, 1168 beds) 800 Rose Street, Lexington, KY, Zip 40536-0293; tel. 859/323-5000, Robert DiPaola, Executive Vice President for Health Affairs
Web address: www.ukhealthcare.uky.edu

OHIO: KING'S DAUGHTERS MEDICAL CENTER OHIO (O, 12 beds) 1901 Argonne Road, Portsmouth, OH, Zip 45662-2845, 2001 Scioto Trail, Zip 45662-2845, tel. 740/991-4000, Sara Marks, President and Chief Executive Officer

Owned, leased, sponsored:	4 hospitals	1959 beds
Contract-managed:	1 hospitals	179 beds
Totals:	5 hospitals	2138 beds

★0224: UMASS MEMORIAL HEALTH CARE, INC. (NP)
365 Plantation Street, Biotech One, Worcester, MA Zip 01605-2397; tel. 508/334-0100, Eric Dickson, M.D., President and Chief Executive Officer
(Centralized Physician/Insurance Health System)

MASSACHUSETTS: UMASS MEMORIAL HEALTH-HARRINGTON (O, 119 beds) 100 South Street, Southbridge, MA, Zip 01550-4051; tel. 508/765-9771, Edward H. Moore, President

UMASS MEMORIAL HEALTHALLIANCE-CLINTON HOSPITAL (O, 152 beds) 60 Hospital Road, Leominster, MA, Zip 01453-2205; tel. 978/466-2000, Charles E. Cavagnaro III, M.D., Interim President
Web address: www.healthalliance.com

UMASS MEMORIAL MEDICAL CENTER (O, 720 beds) 119 Belmont Street, Worcester, MA, Zip 01605-2982; tel. 508/334-1000, Justin Precourt, Interim President and Chief Nursing Officer
Web address: www.umassmemorial.org

UMASS MEMORIAL-MARLBOROUGH HOSPITAL (O, 63 beds) 157 Union Street, Marlborough, MA, Zip 01752-1297; tel. 508/481-5000, Charles E. Cavagnaro III, M.D., Interim President
Web address: www.marlboroughhospital.org

Owned, leased, sponsored:	4 hospitals	1054 beds
Contract-managed:	0 hospitals	0 beds
Totals:	4 hospitals	1054 beds

For explanation of codes following names, see page B2.
★ Indicates Type III membership in the American Hospital Association.

Systems / UNC Health

★0901: UNC HEALTH (NP)
101 Manning Drive, Chapel Hill, NC Zip 27514–4220; tel. 919/966–4131, Wesley Burks, M.D., Chief Executive Officer
(Moderately Centralized Health System)

NORTH CAROLINA: APPALACHIAN REGIONAL BEHAVIORAL HEALTH (C, 27 beds) 432 Hospital Drive, Linville, NC, Zip 28646, PO Box 767, Zip 28646, tel. 828/737-7071, Stephanie Greer, President, Avery Healthcare Market
Web address: www.https://apprhs.org/appalachian-regional-behavioral-health/
CHARLES A. CANNON JR. MEMORIAL HOSPITAL (C, 31 beds) 434 Hospital Drive, Newland, NC, Zip 28646, P O Box 767, Linville, Zip 28646-0767, tel. 828/737-7000, Stephanie Greer, President, Avery Healthcare Market
ONSLOW MEMORIAL HOSPITAL (C, 149 beds) 317 Western Boulevard, Jacksonville, NC, Zip 28546-6379, P O Box 1358, Zip 28541-1358, tel. 910/577-2345, Penney Burlingame Deal, FACHE, R.N., Chief Executive Officer
Web address: www.onslow.org
UNC HEALTH BLUE RIDGE (O, 156 beds) 2201 South Sterling Street, Morganton, NC, Zip 28655-4058; tel. 828/580-5000, Gary Paxson, FACHE, President and Chief Executive Officer
UNC HEALTH CALDWELL (O, 109 beds) 321 Mulberry Street SW, Lenoir, NC, Zip 28645-5720, P O Box 1890, Zip 28645-1890, tel. 828/757-5100, David Lowry, M.D., Chief Executive Officer
Web address: www.caldwellmemorial.org
UNC HEALTH CHATHAM (O, 21 beds) 475 Progress Boulevard, Siler City, NC, Zip 27344-6787, P O Box 649, Zip 27344-0649, tel. 919/799-4000, Jeffery C. Strickler, R.N., President
Web address: https://www.chathamhospital.org/ch/
UNC HEALTH JOHNSTON (C, 153 beds) 509 North Bright Leaf Blvd, Smithfield, NC, Zip 27577-4407, P O Box 1376, Zip 27577-1376, tel. 919/934-8171, Tom Williams, Chief Executive Officer
Web address: www.johnstonhealth.org
UNC HEALTH LENOIR (C, 169 beds) 100 Airport Road, Kinston, NC, Zip 28501-1634, P O Box 1678, Zip 28503-1678, tel. 252/522-7000, Crystal Hayden, FACHE, R.N., President and Chief Executive Officer
UNC HEALTH NASH (C, 224 beds) 2460 Curtis Ellis Drive, Rocky Mount, NC, Zip 27804-2237; tel. 252/962-8000, L. Lee. Isley, FACHE, Ph.D., President and Chief Executive Officer
Web address: www.nhcs.org
UNC HEALTH PARDEE (C, 158 beds) 800 North Justice Street, Hendersonville, NC, Zip 28791-3410; tel. 828/696-1000, James M. Kirby II, President and Chief Executive Officer
UNC HEALTH REX (O, 716 beds) 4420 Lake Boone Trail, Raleigh, NC, Zip 27607-6599; tel. 919/784-3100, Kirsten Riggs, Interim President and Chief Operating Officer
Web address: www.rexhealth.com
UNC HEALTH ROCKINGHAM (O, 127 beds) 117 East King's Highway, Eden, NC, Zip 27288-5201; tel. 336/623-9711, Steven E. Eblin, Chief Executive Officer
UNC HEALTH SOUTHEASTERN (C, 335 beds) 300 West 27th Street, Lumberton, NC, Zip 28358-3075, P O Box 1408, Zip 28359-1408, tel. 910/671-5000, Christopher Ellington, President and Chief Executive Officer
Web address: www.srmc.org
UNC HEALTH WAYNE (C, 230 beds) 2700 Wayne Memorial Drive, Goldsboro, NC, Zip 27534-9494, P O Box 8001, Zip 27533-8001, tel. 919/736-1110, Jessie Tucker III, Ph.D., FACHE, President and Chief Executive Officer
UNIVERSITY OF NORTH CAROLINA HOSPITALS (O, 1001 beds) 101 Manning Drive, Chapel Hill, NC, Zip 27514-4220; tel. 984/974-1000, Janet Hadar, President
Web address: www.unchealthcare.org
WATAUGA MEDICAL CENTER (C, 99 beds) 336 Deerfield Road, Boone, NC, Zip 28607-5008, P O Box 2600, Zip 28607-2600, tel. 828/262-4100, Charles Mantooth, President and Chief Executive Officer

Owned, leased, sponsored:	6 hospitals	2130 beds
Contract–managed:	10 hospitals	1575 beds
Totals:	16 hospitals	3705 beds

★0866: UNC HEALTH APPALACHIAN (NP)
336 Deerfield Road, Boone, NC Zip 28607–5008, P O Box 2600, Zip 28607–2600, tel. 828/262-4100, Charles Mantooth, President and Chief Executive Officer
(Independent Hospital System)

Owned, leased, sponsored:	0 hospitals	0 beds
Contract–managed:	0 hospitals	0 beds
Totals:	0 hospitals	0 beds

0922: UNION GENERAL HOSPITAL, INC. (NP)
35 Hospital Road, Blairsville, GA Zip 30512–3139; tel. 706/745-2111, Kevin Bierschenk, Chief Executive Officer

GEORGIA: CHATUGE REGIONAL HOSPITAL AND NURSING HOME (O, 150 beds) 110 Main Street, Hiawassee, GA, Zip 30546-3408, P O Box 509, Zip 30546-0509, tel. 706/896-2222, Ryan Snow, Chief Executive Officer
Web address: www.chatugeregionalhospital.org
UNION GENERAL HOSPITAL (O, 195 beds) 35 Hospital Road, Blairsville, GA, Zip 30512-3139; tel. 706/745-2111, Kevin Bierschenk, Chief Executive Officer
Web address: www.uniongeneralhospital.com

Owned, leased, sponsored:	2 hospitals	345 beds
Contract–managed:	0 hospitals	0 beds
Totals:	2 hospitals	345 beds

0288: UNITED HEALTH SERVICES (NP)
10–42 Mitchell Avenue, Binghamton, NY Zip 13903–1617; tel. 607/762–2200, John M. Carrigg, President and Chief Executive Officer
(Independent Hospital System)

NEW YORK: UHS CHENANGO MEMORIAL HOSPITAL (O, 37 beds) 179 North Broad Street, Norwich, NY, Zip 13815-1097; tel. 607/337-4111, Drake M. Lamen, M.D., President and Chief Executive Officer
UHS DELAWARE VALLEY HOSPITAL (O, 21 beds) 1 Titus Place, Walton, NY, Zip 13856-1498; tel. 607/865-2100, Rolland Bojo, R.N., President and Chief Executive Officer
Web address: www.uhs.net/locations/
UNITED HEALTH SERVICES HOSPITALS–BINGHAMTON (O, 464 beds) 10–42 Mitchell Avenue, Binghamton, NY, Zip 13903-1678; tel. 607/763-6000, John M. Carrigg, President and Chief Executive Officer

Owned, leased, sponsored:	3 hospitals	522 beds
Contract–managed:	0 hospitals	0 beds
Totals:	3 hospitals	522 beds

★9605: UNITED MEDICAL CORPORATION (IO)
603 Main Street, Windermere, FL Zip 34786–3548, P O Box 1100, Zip 34786–1100, tel. 407/876-2200, Donald R. Dizney, Chairman and Chief Executive Officer

PUERTO RICO: HOSPITAL PAVIA–HATO REY (O, 180 beds) 435 Ponce De Leon Avenue, San Juan, PR, Zip 00917-3428, PO Box 190828, Zip 00917-3428, tel. 787/641-2323, Carlos Santiago Rosario, Executive Director
Web address: www.paviahealth.com
HOSPITAL PAVIA–SANTURCE (O, 155 beds) 1462 Asia Street, San Juan, PR, Zip 00909-2143, Box 11137, Santurce Station, Zip 00910-1137, tel. 787/727-6060, Domingo Cruz-Vivaldi, Executive Director
Web address: www.paviahealth.com
HOSPITAL PEREA (O, 103 beds) 15 Basora Street, Mayaguez, PR, Zip 681, P O Box 170, Zip 681, tel. 787/834-0101, Marco A. Reyes Concepcion, Executive Director

For explanation of codes following names, see page B2.
★ Indicates Type III membership in the American Hospital Association.

HOSPITAL SAN FRANCISCO (O, 133 beds) 371 Avenida De Diego, San Juan, PR, Zip 00923–1711, P O Box 29025, Zip 00929–0025, tel. 787/767–5100, Dominao Cruz Vivaldi, Executive Director
Web address: www.metropavia.com/SanFrancisco.cfm

SAN JORGE CHILDREN'S AND WOMEN HOSPITAL (O, 167 beds) 258 San Jorge Street, Santurce, Santurce, PR, Zip 00912–3310, PO Box 6308, San Juan, Zip 00912–3310, tel. 787/727–1000, Jose Luis. Rodriguez, Executive Director
Web address: www.sanjorgechildrenshospital.com

Owned, leased, sponsored:	5 hospitals	738 beds
Contract–managed:	0 hospitals	0 beds
Totals:	5 hospitals	738 beds

0937: UNITED MEDICAL REHABILITATION HOSPITALS (IO)
3201 Wall Boulevard, Suite B, Gretna, LA Zip 70056–7755; tel. 504/433–5551, John E.H. Mills, President and Chief Executive Officer

LOUISIANA: UNITED MEDICAL HEALTHWEST NEW ORLEANS, LLC (O, 26 beds) 3201 Wall Boulevard, Suite B, Gretna, LA, Zip 70056–7755; tel. 504/433–5551, Gayla Bryant, R.N., Administrator

UNITED MEDICAL REHABILITATION HOSPITAL–HAMMOND (O, 20 beds) 15717 Belle Drive, Hammond, LA, Zip 70403–1439; tel. 985/340–5998, Karen Crayton, Chief Executive Officer
Web address: www.https://umrhospital.com/locations/hammond/

Owned, leased, sponsored:	2 hospitals	46 beds
Contract–managed:	0 hospitals	0 beds
Totals:	2 hospitals	46 beds

★0968: UNITED STATES COAST GUARD (FG)
2100 Second Street SW, MS–7902, Washington, DC Zip 20024–5100; tel. 202/372–4500, Rear Admiral, Dana Thomas, M.D., Director, Health, Safety & Work–Life Chief Medical Officer

Owned, leased, sponsored:	0 hospitals	0 beds
Contract–managed:	0 hospitals	0 beds
Totals:	0 hospitals	0 beds

0322: UNITED SURGICAL PARTNERS INTERNATIONAL (IO)
15305 Dallas Parkway, Suite 1600, Addison, TX Zip 75001–6491; tel. 972/713–3500, Brett Brodnax, Chief Executive Officer
(Independent Hospital System)

ARIZONA: ARIZONA ORTHOPEDIC SURGICAL HOSPITAL (O, 24 beds) 2905 West Warner Road, Suite 1, Chandler, AZ, Zip 85224–1674; tel. 480/603–9000, Patricia K. Alice, Chief Executive Officer

OKLAHOMA: OKLAHOMA CENTER FOR ORTHOPAEDIC AND MULTI–SPECIALTY SURGERY (O, 9 beds) 8100 South Walker, Suite C, Oklahoma City, OK, Zip 73139–9402, P O Box 890609, Zip 73189–0609, tel. 405/602–6500, Landon Hise, Chief Executive Officer
Web address: www.ocomhospital.com

TEXAS: BAYLOR SCOTT & WHITE MEDICAL CENTER–SUNNYVALE (O, 70 beds) 231 South Collins Road, Sunnyvale, TX, Zip 75182–4624; tel. 972/892–3000, Jon Duckert, FACHE, Chief Executive Officer
Web address: www.BaylorScottandWhite.com/Sunnyvale

BAYLOR SCOTT & WHITE MEDICAL CENTER–FRISCO (O, 68 beds) 5601 Warren Parkway, Frisco, TX, Zip 75034–4069; tel. 214/407–5000, Eli Smith, FACHE, Chief Executive Officere

BAYLOR SCOTT & WHITE MEDICAL CENTER–UPTOWN (O, 24 beds) 2727 East Lemmon Avenue, Dallas, TX, Zip 75204–2895; tel. 214/443–3000, Kyle Armstrong, President Central Region of BSW Health
Web address: www.https://bayloruptown.com/

BAYLOR SURGICAL HOSPITAL AT LAS COLINAS (O, 12 beds) 400 West Lyndon B Johnson Freeway, Plaza 1, Suite 250, Irving, TX, Zip 75063–3718; tel. 972/868–4000, Josiah De La Garza, Chief Executive Officer

TOPS SURGICAL SPECIALTY HOSPITAL (O, 15 beds) 17080 Red Oak Drive, Houston, TX, Zip 77090–2602; tel. 281/539–2900, Grant Magness, Chief Executive Officer
Web address: www.tops-hospital.com

Owned, leased, sponsored:	7 hospitals	222 beds
Contract–managed:	0 hospitals	0 beds
Totals:	7 hospitals	222 beds

★0061: UNITYPOINT HEALTH (NP)
1776 West Lakes Parkway, Suite 400, West Des Moines, IA Zip 50266–8393; tel. 515/241–6161, Scott Kizer, President and Chief Executive Officer
(Decentralized Health System)

ILLINOIS: UNITYPOINT HEALTH–TRINITY ROCK ISLAND (O, 256 beds) 2701 17th Street, Rock Island, IL, Zip 61201–5393; tel. 309/779–5000, Shawn Morrow, FACHE, Market President
Web address: https://www.unitypoint.org

IOWA: BUENA VISTA REGIONAL MEDICAL CENTER (C, 35 beds) 1525 West Fifth Street, Storm Lake, IA, Zip 50588–3027, P O Box 309, Zip 50588–0309, tel. 712/732–4030, Steven Colerick, Chief Executive Officer
Web address: www.bvrmc.org

CHEROKEE REGIONAL MEDICAL CENTER (C, 55 beds) 300 Sioux Valley Drive, Cherokee, IA, Zip 51012–1205; tel. 712/225–5101, Gary W. Jordan, FACHE, Chief Executive Officer

CLARKE COUNTY HOSPITAL (C, 25 beds) 800 South Fillmore Street, Osceola, IA, Zip 50213–1619; tel. 641/342–2184, Brian G. Evans, FACHE, Chief Executive Officer
Web address: www.clarkehosp.org

COMMUNITY MEMORIAL HOSPITAL (O, 16 beds) 909 West First Street, Sumner, IA, Zip 50674–1203, P O Box 148, Zip 50674–0148, tel. 563/578–3275, Dawn Everding, Chief Hospital Administrator/Chief Financial Officer
Web address: www.cmhsumner.org

COMPASS MEMORIAL HEALTHCARE (C, 25 beds) 300 West May Street, Marengo, IA, Zip 52301–1261; tel. 319/642–5543, Barry Goettsch, FACHE, Chief Executive Officer

GREATER REGIONAL HEALTH (O, 25 beds) 1700 West Townline Street Suite 3, Creston, IA, Zip 50801–1099; tel. 641/782–7091, Monte Neitzel, Chief Executive Officer
Web address: www.greaterregional.org

GREENE COUNTY MEDICAL CENTER (C, 77 beds) 1000 West Lincolnway, Jefferson, IA, Zip 50129–1645; tel. 515/386–2114, Chad Butterfield, Chief Executive Officer
Web address: www.gcmchealth.com

GRUNDY COUNTY MEMORIAL HOSPITAL (C, 25 beds) 201 East 'J' Avenue, Grundy Center, IA, Zip 50638–2096; tel. 319/824–5421, Adam Scherling, President

GUTHRIE COUNTY HOSPITAL (C, 17 beds) 710 North 12th Street, Guthrie Center, IA, Zip 50115–1544; tel. 641/332–2201, Chris Stipe, Chief Executive Officer
Web address: www.guthriecountyhospital.org

HUMBOLDT COUNTY MEMORIAL HOSPITAL (C, 49 beds) 1000 North 15th Street, Humboldt, IA, Zip 50548–1008; tel. 515/332–4200, Michelle Sleiter, Chief Executive Officer
Web address: www.humboldthospital.org

LORING HOSPITAL (C, 25 beds) 211 Highland Avenue, Sac City, IA, Zip 50583–2424; tel. 712/662–7105, Matt Johnson, Chief Executive Officer
Web address: www.loringhospital.org

LUCAS COUNTY HEALTH CENTER (C, 23 beds) 1200 North Seventh Street, Chariton, IA, Zip 50049–1258; tel. 641/774–3000, Brian Sims, FACHE, Chief Executive Officer

POCAHONTAS COMMUNITY HOSPITAL (C, 20 beds) 606 NW Seventh Street, Pocahontas, IA, Zip 50574–1099; tel. 712/335–3501, James D. Roetman, President and Chief Executive Officer
Web address: www.pocahontashospital.org

STEWART MEMORIAL COMMUNITY HOSPITAL (C, 25 beds) 1301 West Main, Lake City, IA, Zip 51449–1585; tel. 712/464–3171, Linn Block, Chief Executive Officer

For explanation of codes following names, see page B2.
★ Indicates Type III membership in the American Hospital Association.

Systems / Unitypoint Health

STORY COUNTY MEDICAL CENTER (C, 17 beds) 640 South 19th Street, Nevada, IA, Zip 50201-2902; tel. 515/382-2111, Nathan Thompson, Chief Executive Officer
Web address: www.storymedical.org

UNITYPOINT HEALTH–ALLEN HOSPITAL (O, 201 beds) 1825 Logan Avenue, Waterloo, IA, Zip 50703-1916; tel. 319/235-3941, Jenni Friedly, Market President, UnityPoint Health – Waterloo
Web address: www.unitypoint.org/waterloo

UNITYPOINT HEALTH–FINLEY HOSPITAL (O, 82 beds) 350 North Grandview Avenue, Dubuque, IA, Zip 52001-6393; tel. 563/582-1881, Jennifer Havens, R.N., FACHE, Market President, UnityPoint Health – Dubuque

UNITYPOINT HEALTH–GRINNELL REGIONAL MEDICAL CENTER (O, 49 beds) 210 Fourth Avenue, Grinnell, IA, Zip 50112-1898; tel. 641/236-7511, David-Paul Cavazos, Chief Executive Officer
Web address: www.grmc.us

UNITYPOINT HEALTH–JONES REGIONAL MEDICAL CENTER (O, 22 beds) 1795 Highway 64 East, Anamosa, IA, Zip 52205-2112; tel. 319/462-6131, Eric Briesemeister, Chief Executive Officer

UNITYPOINT HEALTH–MARSHALLTOWN (O, 16 beds) 55 UnityPoint Way, Marshalltown, IA, Zip 50158-4749; tel. 641/754-5151, Jenni Friedly, Market President, UnityPoint Health – Waterloo
Web address: www.https://marshalltown.unitypoint.org

UNITYPOINT HEALTH–ST. LUKE'S HOSPITAL (O, 318 beds) 1026 'A' Avenue NE, Cedar Rapids, IA, Zip 52402-3026, P O Box 3026, Zip 52406-3026, tel. 319/369-7211, Casey Greene, Market President–UnityPoint Health Cedar Rapids

UNITYPOINT HEALTH–ST. LUKES'S SIOUX CITY (O, 188 beds) 2720 Stone Park Boulevard, Sioux City, IA, Zip 51104-3734; tel. 712/279-3500, Jane Arnold, Market President, UnityPoint Health – Sioux City
Web address: https://www.unitypoint.org/locations/unitypoint-health-st-lukes

UNITYPOINT HEALTH–TRINITY BETTENDORF (O, 90 beds) 4500 Utica Ridge Road, Bettendorf, IA, Zip 52722-1626; tel. 563/742-5000, Shawn Morrow, FACHE, Market President–UnityPoint Health Quad Cities

UNITYPOINT HEALTH–TRINITY MUSCATINE (O, 24 beds) 1518 Mulberry Avenue, Muscatine, IA, Zip 52761-3499; tel. 563/264-9100, Shawn Morrow, FACHE, Market President, UnityPoint Health – Quad Cities
Web address: www.unitypoint.org/quadcities/trinity-muscatine.aspx

UNITYPOINT HEALTH–TRINITY REGIONAL MEDICAL CENTER (O, 49 beds) 802 Kenyon Road, Fort Dodge, IA, Zip 50501-5795; tel. 515/573-3101, Leah Glasgo, R.N., Market President, UnityPoint Health – Fort Dodge

UNITYPOINT HEALTH–DES MOINES (O, 672 beds) 1200 Pleasant Street, Des Moines, IA, Zip 50309-1406; tel. 515/241-6212, Jon Rozenfeld, Market President, UnityPoint Health – Des Moines
Web address: www.unitypoint.org

VIRGINIA GAY HOSPITAL (C, 65 beds) 502 North 9th Avenue, Vinton, IA, Zip 52349-2299; tel. 319/472-6200, Barry Dietsch, Interim executive leader (Currently CFO)
Web address: www.myvgh.org

WISCONSIN: UNITYPOINT HEALTH MERITER (O, 249 beds) 202 South Park Street, Madison, WI, Zip 53715-1507; tel. 608/417-6000, James Arnett, Market President–Madison

Owned, leased, sponsored:	15 hospitals	2257 beds
Contract-managed:	14 hospitals	483 beds
Totals:	29 hospitals	2740 beds

9555: UNIVERSAL HEALTH SERVICES, INC. (IO)
367 South Gulph Road, King of Prussia, PA Zip 19406-3121, P O Box 61558, Zip 19406-0958, tel. 610/768-3300, Marc D. Miller, Chief Executive Officer
(Decentralized Health System)

ALABAMA: HILL CREST BEHAVIORAL HEALTH SERVICES (O, 170 beds) 6869 Fifth Avenue South, Birmingham, AL, Zip 35212-1866; tel. 205/833-9000, Ballard Sheppard, Ph.D., Chief Executive Officer
Web address: www.hillcrestbhs.com

LAUREL OAKS BEHAVIORAL HEALTH CENTER (O, 118 beds) 700 East Cottonwood Road, Dothan, AL, Zip 36301-3644; tel. 334/794-7373, Jeanette Jackson, Chief Executive Officer

ALASKA: NORTH STAR BEHAVIORAL HEALTH SYSTEM (O, 200 beds) 2530 DeBarr Circle, Anchorage, AK, Zip 99508-2948; tel. 907/258-7575, William Newcombe, Chief Executive Officer and Managing Director
Web address: www.northstarbehavioral.com

ARIZONA: PALO VERDE BEHAVIORAL HEALTH (O, 48 beds) 2695 North Craycroft Road, Tucson, AZ, Zip 85712-2244; tel. 520/322-2888, Jennifer Stokes, Chief Executive Officer

VALLEY HOSPITAL PHOENIX (O, 122 beds) 3550 East Pinchot Avenue, Phoenix, AZ, Zip 85018-7434; tel. 602/957-4000, Julie Miller, Chief Executive Officer
Web address: www.valleyhospital-phoenix.com

ARKANSAS: PINNACLE POINTE BEHAVIORAL HEALTHCARE SYSTEM (O, 127 beds) 11501 Financial Center Parkway, Little Rock, AR, Zip 72211-3715; tel. 501/223-3322, Courtney Bishop. Carney, Chief Executive Officer

RIVENDELL BEHAVIORAL HEALTH SERVICES (O, 80 beds) 100 Rivendell Drive, Benton, AR, Zip 72019-9100; tel. 501/316-1255, Fred Knox, Chief Executive Officer
Web address: www.rivendellofarkansas.com

SPRINGWOODS BEHAVIORAL HEALTH HOSPITAL (O, 80 beds) 1955 West Truckers Drive, Fayetteville, AR, Zip 72704-5637; tel. 479/973-6000, Jordon Babcock, Chief Executive Officer
Web address: www.springwoodsbehavioral.com

THE BRIDGEWAY (L, 127 beds) 21 Bridgeway Road, North Little Rock, AR, Zip 72113-9516; tel. 501/771-1500, Megan Miller, Chief Executive Officer
Web address: www.thebridgeway.com

CALIFORNIA: BHC ALHAMBRA HOSPITAL (O, 97 beds) 4619 North Rosemead Boulevard, Rosemead, CA, Zip 91770-1478, P O Box 369, Zip 91770-0369, tel. 626/286-1191, Peggy Minnick, R.N., Chief Executive Officer
Web address: www.bhcalhambra.com

CANYON RIDGE HOSPITAL (O, 157 beds) 5353 'G' Street, Chino, CA, Zip 91710-5250; tel. 909/590-3700, Stephanie Bernier, Chief Executive Officer

CORONA REGIONAL MEDICAL CENTER (O, 238 beds) 800 South Main Street, Corona, CA, Zip 92882-3400; tel. 951/737-4343, Alistair M. Machoka, Chief Executive Officer
Web address: www.coronaregional.com

DEL AMO BEHAVIORAL HEALTH SYSTEM (O, 70 beds) 23700 Camino Del Sol, Torrance, CA, Zip 90505-5000; tel. 310/530-1151, Mariko Yamada, Chief Executive Officer
Web address: www.delamohospital.com

FREMONT HOSPITAL (O, 148 beds) 39001 Sundale Drive, Fremont, CA, Zip 94538-2005; tel. 510/796-1100, Patricia Williams, Chief Executive Officer

HERITAGE OAKS HOSPITAL (O, 125 beds) 4250 Auburn Boulevard, Sacramento, CA, Zip 95841-4164; tel. 916/489-3336, Yannis Angouras, Chief Executive Officer
Web address: www.heritageoakshospital.com

PALMDALE REGIONAL MEDICAL CENTER (O, 184 beds) 38600 Medical Center Drive, Palmdale, CA, Zip 93551-4483; tel. 661/382-5000, Nana Deeb, Chief Executive Officer

SIERRA VISTA HOSPITAL (O, 171 beds) 8001 Bruceville Road, Sacramento, CA, Zip 95823-2329; tel. 916/288-0300, Mike Zauner, Chief Executive Officer/Regional Vice President
Web address: www.sierravistahospital.com

SOUTHWEST HEALTHCARE SYSTEM (O, 240 beds) 25500 Medical Center Drive, Murrieta, CA, Zip 92562-5965; tel. 951/696-6000, Jared Giles, FACHE, Chief Executive Officer

TEMECULA VALLEY HOSPITAL (O, 140 beds) 31700 Temecula Parkway, Temecula, CA, Zip 92592-5896; tel. 951/331-2216, Darlene Wetton, R.N., Group Vice President and Chief Executive Officer
Web address: www.temeculavalleyhospital.com

COLORADO: CEDAR SPRINGS HOSPITAL (O, 110 beds) 2135 Southgate Road, Colorado Springs, CO, Zip 80906-2693; tel. 719/633-4114, Daniel Zarecky, Chief Executive Officer

CENTENNIAL PEAKS HOSPITAL (O, 104 beds) 2255 South 88th Street, Louisville, CO, Zip 80027-9716; tel. 303/673-9990, Scott Snodgrass, Chief Executive Officer
Web address: www.centennialpeaks.com

For explanation of codes following names, see page B2.
★ Indicates Type III membership in the American Hospital Association.

Systems / Universal Health Services, Inc.

HIGHLANDS BEHAVIORAL HEALTH SYSTEM (O, 86 beds) 8565 South Poplar Way, Littleton, CO, Zip 80130-3602; tel. 720/348-2800, Kelly Ulreich, Executive Director

DELAWARE: DOVER BEHAVIORAL HEALTH SYSTEM (O, 104 beds) 725 Horsepond Road, Dover, DE, Zip 19901-7232; tel. 302/741-0140, Jean-Charles Constant, Administrator
Web address: www.doverbehavioral.com

ROCKFORD CENTER (O, 138 beds) 100 Rockford Drive, Newark, DE, Zip 19713-2121; tel. 302/996-5480, William Mason, Chief Executive Officer and Managing Director
Web address: www.rockfordcenter.com

DISTRICT OF COLUMBIA: GEORGE WASHINGTON UNIVERSITY HOSPITAL (O, 395 beds) 900 23rd Street NW, Washington, DC, Zip 20037-2342; tel. 202/715-4000, Kimberly Russo, MS, Chief Executive Officer and Managing Director
Web address: www.gwhospital.com

FLORIDA: CENTRAL FLORIDA BEHAVIORAL HOSPITAL (O, 126 beds) 6601 Central Florida Parkway, Orlando, FL, Zip 32821-8064; tel. 407/370-0111, Vickie Lewis, Chief Executive Officer
Web address: www.centralfloridabehavioral.com

EMERALD COAST BEHAVIORAL HOSPITAL (O, 86 beds) 1940 Harrison Avenue, Panama City, FL, Zip 32405-4542; tel. 850/763-0017, Tim Bedford, Chief Executive Officer
Web address: www.emeraldcoastbehavioral.com

FORT LAUDERDALE BEHAVIORAL HEALTH CENTER (L, 182 beds) 5757 North Dixie Highway, Oakland Park, FL, Zip 33301-2393; tel. 954/734-2000, Manuel R. Llano, Chief Executive Officer

LAKEWOOD RANCH MEDICAL CENTER (O, 120 beds) 8330 Lakewood Ranch Boulevard, Bradenton, FL, Zip 34202-5174; tel. 941/782-2100, Andrew Guz, Chief Executive Officer
Web address: www.lakewoodranchmedicalcenter.com

MANATEE MEMORIAL HOSPITAL (O, 319 beds) 206 Second Street East, Bradenton, FL, Zip 34208-1000; tel. 941/746-5111, Tom R. McDougal Jr, FACHE, Chief Executive Officer

RIVER POINT BEHAVIORAL HEALTH (O, 92 beds) 6300 Beach Boulevard, Jacksonville, FL, Zip 32216-2782; tel. 904/724-9202, Donna Smith, Ph.D., Chief Executive Officer
Web address: www.riverpointbehavioral.com

SUNCOAST BEHAVIORAL HEALTH CENTER (O, 60 beds) 4480 51st Street West, Bradenton, FL, Zip 34210-2855; tel. 941/251-5000, Brandy Hamilton, Chief Executive Officer

THE VINES (O, 76 beds) 3130 SW 27th Avenue, Ocala, FL, Zip 34471-4306; tel. 352/671-3130, Mike Tacke, Chief Executive Officer
Web address: www.thevineshospital.com

WEKIVA SPRINGS (O, 60 beds) 3947 Salisbury Road, Jacksonville, FL, Zip 32216-6115; tel. 904/296-3533, Sheila Carr, Chief Executive Officer
Web address: www.wekivacenter.com

WELLINGTON REGIONAL MEDICAL CENTER (L, 262 beds) 10101 Forest Hill Boulevard, Wellington, FL, Zip 33414-6199; tel. 561/798-8500, Pamela S. Tahan, Chief Executive Officer
Web address: www.wellingtonregional.com

WINDMOOR HEALTHCARE OF CLEARWATER (O, 144 beds) 11300 U S 19 North, Clearwater, FL, Zip 33764; tel. 727/541-2646, Joshua Rodriguez, Chief Executive Officer

GEORGIA: ANCHOR HOSPITAL (O, 122 beds) 5454 Yorktowne Drive, Atlanta, GA, Zip 30349-5317; tel. 770/991-6044, Gran Shinwar, Chief Executive Officer
Web address: www.anchorhospital.com

COASTAL HARBOR TREATMENT CENTER (O, 175 beds) 1150 Cornell Avenue, Savannah, GA, Zip 31406-2702; tel. 912/354-3911, Sneha Patel, Chief Executive Officer
Web address: www.coastalharbor.com

PEACHFORD BEHAVIORAL HEALTH SYSTEM (O, 246 beds) 2151 Peachford Road, Atlanta, GA, Zip 30338-6599; tel. 770/455-3200, Matthew Crouch, Chief Executive Officer and Managing Director

SAINT SIMONS BY-THE-SEA HOSPITAL (O, 101 beds) 2927 Demere Road, Saint Simons Island, GA, Zip 31522-1620; tel. 912/638-1999, Marie Renner, Chief Executive Officer
Web address: www.ssbythesea.com

TURNING POINT HOSPITAL (O, 69 beds) 3015 Veterans Parkway South, Moultrie, GA, Zip 31788-6705, P O Box 1177, Zip 31776-1177, tel. 229/985-4815, Judy H. Payne, Chief Executive Officer

IDAHO: INTERMOUNTAIN HOSPITAL (O, 151 beds) 303 North Allumbaugh Street, Boise, ID, Zip 83704-9208; tel. 208/377-8400, Todd Hurt, Chief Executive Officer
Web address: www.intermountainhospital.com

ILLINOIS: GARFIELD PARK BEHAVIORAL HOSPITAL (O, 88 beds) 520 North Ridgeway Avenue, Chicago, IL, Zip 60624-1232; tel. 773/265-3700, Steven Airhart, Group Chief Executive Officer
Web address: www.garfieldparkhospital.com

HARTGROVE BEHAVIORAL HEALTH SYSTEM (O, 160 beds) 5730 West Roosevelt Road, Chicago, IL, Zip 60644-1580, P.O. Box 61558, King of Prussia, PA, Zip 19406-0958, tel. 773/413-1700, Steven Airhart, Chief Executive Officer
Web address: www.hartgrovehospital.com

LINCOLN PRAIRIE BEHAVIORAL HEALTH CENTER (O, 97 beds) 5230 South Sixth Street, Springfield, IL, Zip 62703-5128; tel. 217/585-1180, Tom DeMarco, Interim Chief Executive Officer

RIVEREDGE HOSPITAL (O, 210 beds) 8311 West Roosevelt Road, Forest Park, IL, Zip 60130-2500; tel. 708/771-7000, Allison Davenport, Chief Executive Officer
Web address: www.riveredgehospital.com

STREAMWOOD BEHAVIORAL HEALTHCARE SYSTEM (O, 178 beds) 1400 East Irving Park Road, Streamwood, IL, Zip 60107-3203; tel. 630/837-9000, Ron Weglarz, PsyD, Chief Executive Officer

THE PAVILION (O, 110 beds) 809 West Church Street, Champaign, IL, Zip 61820-3399; tel. 217/373-1700, Shaun Doherty, Chief Executive Officer
Web address: www.pavilionhospital.com

INDIANA: BLOOMINGTON MEADOWS HOSPITAL (O, 71 beds) 3600 North Prow Road, Bloomington, IN, Zip 47404-1616; tel. 812/331-8000, Kristen Primeau, Chief Executive Officer

MICHIANA BEHAVIORAL HEALTH CENTER (O, 75 beds) 1800 North Oak Drive, Plymouth, IN, Zip 46563-3492; tel. 574/936-3784, Brian Gray, Chief Executive Officer
Web address: www.https://michianabehavioralhealth.com

VALLE VISTA HEALTH SYSTEM (O, 122 beds) 898 East Main Street, Greenwood, IN, Zip 46143-1400; tel. 317/887-1348, Kristen Primeau, Chief Executive Officer
Web address: www.vallevistahospital.com

WELLSTONE REGIONAL HOSPITAL (O, 100 beds) 2700 Vissing Park Road, Jeffersonville, IN, Zip 47130-5989; tel. 812/284-8000, Jessica Campbell, Chief Executive Officer

IOWA: CLIVE BEHAVIORAL HEALTH (C, 54 beds) 1450 NW 114th Street, Clive, IA, Zip 50325-7039; tel. 515/553-6200, Kevin Pettit, Chief Executive Officer
Web address: www.clivebehavioral.com

KENTUCKY: CUMBERLAND HALL HOSPITAL (O, 97 beds) 270 Walton Way, Hopkinsville, KY, Zip 42240-6808; tel. 270/886-1919, Jessica Estes, Chief Executive Officer

LINCOLN TRAIL BEHAVIORAL HEALTH SYSTEM (O, 140 beds) 3909 South Wilson Road, Radcliff, KY, Zip 40160-8944, P O Box 369, Zip 40159-0369, tel. 270/351-9444, Leslie Flechler, Chief Executive Officer
Web address: www.lincolnbehavioral.com

RIDGE BEHAVIORAL HEALTH SYSTEM (O, 110 beds) 3050 Rio Dosa Drive, Lexington, KY, Zip 40509-1540; tel. 859/269-2325, Keith Rankin, Chief Executive Officer and Managing Director

RIVENDELL BEHAVIORAL HEALTH HOSPITAL (O, 125 beds) 1035 Porter Pike, Bowling Green, KY, Zip 42103-9581; tel. 270/843-1199, Jeremy Wagoner, Chief Executive Officer
Web address: www.rivendellbehavioral.com

THE BROOK HOSPITAL–KMI (O, 110 beds) 8521 Old LaGrange Road, Louisville, KY, Zip 40242-3800; tel. 502/426-6380, Sherri Flood, Chief Executive Officer
Web address: www.thebrookhospitals.com

THE BROOK AT DUPONT (O, 88 beds) 1405 Browns Lane, Louisville, KY, Zip 40207-4608; tel. 502/896-0495, Shane Koch, Chief Executive Officer

For explanation of codes following names, see page B2.
★ *Indicates Type III membership in the American Hospital Association.*

Systems / Universal Health Services, Inc.

LOUISIANA: BRENTWOOD HOSPITAL (O, 238 beds) 1006 Highland Avenue, Shreveport, LA, Zip 71101-4103; tel. 318/678-7500, William C. Weaver, Group Chief Executive Officer
Web address: www.brentwoodbehavioral.com

RIVER OAKS HOSPITAL (O, 126 beds) 1525 River Oaks Road West, New Orleans, LA, Zip 70123-2162; tel. 504/734-1740, Josh Sumrall, Chief Executive Officer
Web address: www.riveroakshospital.com

MASSACHUSETTS: ARBOUR H. R. I. HOSPITAL (O, 76 beds) 227 Babcock Street, Brookline, MA, Zip 02446-6799; tel. 617/731-3200, Kurt Gunther, Chief Executive Officer
Web address: www.HRIHospital.com

ARBOUR HOSPITAL (O, 118 beds) 49 Robinwood Avenue, Boston, MA, Zip 02130-2156; tel. 617/522-4400, Stephen P. Fahey, Chief Executive Officer

ARBOUR-FULLER HOSPITAL (O, 46 beds) 200 May Street, Attleboro, MA, Zip 02703-5520; tel. 508/761-8500, Rachel Legend, Chief Executive Officer
Web address: www.arbourhealth.com

PEMBROKE HOSPITAL (O, 115 beds) 199 Oak Street, Pembroke, MA, Zip 02359-1953; tel. 781/829-7000, Steven Baroletti, Chief Executive Officer

MICHIGAN: CEDAR CREEK HOSPITAL OF MICHIGAN (O, 58 beds) 101 W Townsend Road, Saint Johns, MI, Zip 48879-9200; tel. 989/403-6022, Steven Vernon, Chief Executive Officer
Web address: www.cedarcreekhospital.com

FOREST VIEW PSYCHIATRIC HOSPITAL (O, 108 beds) 1055 Medical Park Drive SE, Grand Rapids, MI, Zip 49546-3607; tel. 616/942-9610, Michael Nanzer, FACHE, Chief Executive Officer
Web address: www.forestviewhospital.com

HAVENWYCK HOSPITAL, INC. (O, 243 beds) 1525 University Drive, Auburn Hills, MI, Zip 48326-2673; tel. 248/373-9200, Jaime White, Chief Executive Officer

MISSISSIPPI: ALLIANCE HEALTH CENTER (O, 154 beds) 5000 Highway 39 North, Meridian, MS, Zip 39301-1021; tel. 601/483-6211, Jay Shehi, Chief Executive Officer
Web address: www.alliancehealthcenter.com

BRENTWOOD BEHAVIORAL HEALTHCARE OF MISSISSIPPI (O, 105 beds) 3531 Lakeland Drive, Flowood, MS, Zip 39232-8839; tel. 601/936-2024, Alison G. Land, Chief Executive Officer

GULFPORT BEHAVIORAL HEALTH SYSTEM (O, 90 beds) 11150 Highway 49 North, Gulfport, MS, Zip 39503-4110; tel. 228/831-1700, Dean Doty, Chief Executive Officer
Web address: www.gulfportmemorial.com

PARKWOOD BEHAVIORAL HEALTH SYSTEM (O, 148 beds) 8135 Goodman Road, Olive Branch, MS, Zip 38654-2103; tel. 662/895-4900, Alicia Plunkett, Chief Executive Officer
Web address: www.parkwoodbhs.com

MISSOURI: HEARTLAND BEHAVIORAL HEALTH SERVICES (O, 69 beds) 1500 West Ashland Street, Nevada, MO, Zip 64772-1710; tel. 417/667-2666, Alyson Wysong-Harder, Chief Executive Officer
Web address: www.heartlandbehavioral.com

NEVADA: CENTENNIAL HILLS HOSPITAL MEDICAL CENTER (O, 165 beds) 6900 North Durango Drive, Las Vegas, NV, Zip 89149-4409; tel. 702/835-9700, Craig McCoy, Chief Executive Officer and Managing Director

DESERT VIEW HOSPITAL (O, 25 beds) 360 South Lola Lane, Pahrump, NV, Zip 89048-0884; tel. 775/751-7500, Susan Davila, Chief Executive Officer
Web address: www.desertviewhospital.com

HENDERSON HOSPITAL (O, 145 beds) 1050 West Galleria Drive, Henderson, NV, Zip 89011; tel. 702/963-7000, Samuel Kaufman, Chief Executive Officer
Web address: www.hendersonhospital.com/

NORTHERN NEVADA MEDICAL CENTER (O, 124 beds) 2375 East Prater Way, Sparks, NV, Zip 89434-9641; tel. 775/331-7000, Helen Lidholm, Chief Executive Officer

SPRING MOUNTAIN SAHARA (O, 30 beds) 5460 West Sahara, Las Vegas, NV, Zip 89146-3307; tel. 702/216-8900, Purcell Dye, Ph.D., Chief Executive Officer
Web address: www.springmountainsahara.com

SPRING MOUNTAIN TREATMENT CENTER (L, 110 beds) 7000 West Spring Mountain Road, Las Vegas, NV, Zip 89117-3816; tel. 702/873-2400, Purcell Dye, Ph.D., Chief Executive Officer

SPRING VALLEY HOSPITAL MEDICAL CENTER (O, 430 beds) 5400 South Rainbow Boulevard, Las Vegas, NV, Zip 89118-1859; tel. 702/853-3000, Claude Wise, Chief Executive Officer and Managing Director
Web address: www.springvalleyhospital.com

SUMMERLIN HOSPITAL MEDICAL CENTER (O, 148 beds) 657 Town Center Drive, Las Vegas, NV, Zip 89144-6367; tel. 702/233-7000, Robert S. Freymuller, Chief Executive Officer

VALLEY HOSPITAL MEDICAL CENTER (O, 306 beds) 620 Shadow Lane, Las Vegas, NV, Zip 89106-4119; tel. 702/388-4000, Collin McLaughlin, Chief Executive Officer
Web address: www.valleyhospital.net

NEW JERSEY: HAMPTON BEHAVIORAL HEALTH CENTER (O, 120 beds) 650 Rancocas Road, Westampton, NJ, Zip 08060-5613; tel. 609/267-7000, Craig Hilton, Chief Executive Officer and Managing Director

SUMMIT OAKS HOSPITAL (O, 124 beds) 19 Prospect Street, Summit, NJ, Zip 07901-2530; tel. 908/522-7000, Y. Brooke. Tillman, Chief Executive Officer
Web address: www.summitoakshospital.com/

NEW MEXICO: MESILLA VALLEY HOSPITAL (O, 115 beds) 3751 Del Rey Boulevard, Las Cruces, NM, Zip 88012-8526; tel. 575/382-3500, Anna Laliotis, Chief Executive Officer

NORTH CAROLINA: BRYNN MARR HOSPITAL (O, 99 beds) 192 Village Drive, Jacksonville, NC, Zip 28546-7299; tel. 910/577-1400, Cynthia Waun, Chief Executive Officer
Web address: www.brynnmarr.org

HOLLY HILL HOSPITAL (O, 285 beds) 3019 Falstaff Road, Raleigh, NC, Zip 27610-1812; tel. 919/250-7000, Kevin Poitinger, Chief Executive Officer and Managing Director
Web address: www.hollyhillhospital.com

OLD VINEYARD BEHAVIORAL HEALTH SERVICES (O, 158 beds) 3637 Old Vineyard Road, Winston-Salem, NC, Zip 27104-4842; tel. 336/794-3550, Kelly S. Thacker, Chief Executive Officer
Web address: www.oldvineyardbhs.com

NORTH DAKOTA: PRAIRIE ST. JOHN'S (O, 94 beds) 510 4th Street South, Fargo, ND, Zip 58103-1914; tel. 701/476-7200, Ty Hegland, Chief Executive Officer
Web address: www.prairie-stjohns.com

OHIO: ARROWHEAD BEHAVIORAL HEALTH HOSPITAL (O, 48 beds) 1725 Timber Line Road, Maumee, OH, Zip 43537-4015; tel. 419/891-9333, Norine Wasielewski, R.N., Chief Executive Officer

BELMONT PINES HOSPITAL (O, 96 beds) 615 Churchill-Hubbard Road, Youngstown, OH, Zip 44505-1379; tel. 330/759-2700, Eric Kennedy, Chief Executive Officer
Web address: www.belmontpines.com

WINDSOR-LAURELWOOD CENTER FOR BEHAVIORAL MEDICINE (O, 159 beds) 35900 Euclid Avenue, Willoughby, OH, Zip 44094-4648; tel. 440/953-3000, Douglas W. Kern, Chief Executive Officer
Web address: www.windsorlaurelwood.com

OKLAHOMA: CEDAR RIDGE (O, 172 beds) 6501 NE 50th Street, Oklahoma City, OK, Zip 73141-9118; tel. 405/605-6111, Cesiley Bouseman, Chief Executive Officer

ST. MARY'S REGIONAL MEDICAL CENTER (O, 124 beds) 305 South Fifth Street, Enid, OK, Zip 73701-5899, P O Box 232, Zip 73702-0232, tel. 580/233-6100, Rex Van Meter, Chief Executive Officer
Web address: www.stmarysregional.com

OREGON: CEDAR HILLS HOSPITAL (O, 78 beds) 10300 SW Eastridge Street, Portland, OR, Zip 97225-5004; tel. 503/944-5000, David Melear, Chief Executive Officer
Web address: www.cedarhillshospital.com

PENNSYLVANIA: BROOKE GLEN BEHAVIORAL HOSPITAL (O, 146 beds) 7170 Lafayette Avenue, Fort Washington, PA, Zip 19034-2301; tel. 215/641-5300, Neil Callahan, Chief Executive Officer

For explanation of codes following names, see page B2.
★ Indicates Type III membership in the American Hospital Association.

Systems / Universal Health Services, Inc.

CLARION PSYCHIATRIC CENTER (O, 96 beds) 2 Hospital Drive, Clarion, PA, Zip 16214-8502; tel. 814/226-9545, Jessica Hansford, Chief Executive Officer
Web address: www.clarioncenter.com

FAIRMOUNT BEHAVIORAL HEALTH SYSTEM (O, 235 beds) 561 Fairthorne Avenue, Philadelphia, PA, Zip 19128-2499; tel. 215/487-4000, Vernetta Simmons, Interim Chief Executive Officer
Web address: www.fairmountbhs.com

FOUNDATIONS BEHAVIORAL HEALTH (O, 58 beds) 833 East Butler Avenue, Doylestown, PA, Zip 18901-2280; tel. 215/345-0444, Amy Smith, Interim Chief Executive Officer
Web address: www.fbh.com

FRIENDS HOSPITAL (O, 192 beds) 4641 Roosevelt Boulevard, Philadelphia, PA, Zip 19124-2343; tel. 215/831-4600, Angela Cantwell, R.N., MSN, Chief Executive Officer

ROXBURY TREATMENT CENTER (O, 112 beds) 601 Roxbury Road, Shippensburg, PA, Zip 17257-9302; tel. 888/829-9974, Shauna Mogerman, Chief Executive Officer
Web address: www.roxburyhospital.com

THE HORSHAM CLINIC (O, 206 beds) 722 East Butler Pike, Ambler, PA, Zip 19002-2310; tel. 215/643-7800, Kim Whitelock, Chief Executive Officer

THE MEADOWS PSYCHIATRIC CENTER (O, 119 beds) 132 The Meadows Drive, Centre Hall, PA, Zip 16828-9231; tel. 814/364-2161, Rodney Kornrumpf, Chief Executive Officer
Web address: www.themeadows.net

PUERTO RICO: FIRST HOSPITAL PANAMERICANO (O, 153 beds) State Road 787 KM 1 5, Cidra, PR, Zip 739, P O Box 1400, Zip 739, tel. 787/739-5555, Astro Munoz, Executive Director

SOUTH CAROLINA: AIKEN REGIONAL MEDICAL CENTERS (O, 281 beds) 302 University Parkway, Aiken, SC, Zip 29801-6302; tel. 803/641-5000, Matthew Merrifield, Chief Executive Officer
Web address: www.aikenregional.com

CAROLINA CENTER FOR BEHAVIORAL HEALTH (O, 138 beds) 2700 East Phillips Road, Greer, SC, Zip 29650-4816; tel. 864/235-2335, John Willingham, Division Vice President
Web address: www.thecarolinacenter.com

LIGHTHOUSE BEHAVIORAL HEALTH HOSPITAL (O, 105 beds) 152 Waccamaw Medical Park Drive, Conway, SC, Zip 29526-8901; tel. 843/347-8871, Julie Parker, Chief Executive Officer

PALMETTO LOWCOUNTRY BEHAVIORAL HEALTH (O, 103 beds) 2777 Speissegger Drive, Charleston, SC, Zip 29405-8229; tel. 843/747-5830, Patrick McDaniel, Chief Executive Officer
Web address: www.palmettobehavioralhealth.com

THREE RIVERS BEHAVIORAL HEALTH (O, 129 beds) 2900 Sunset Boulevard, West Columbia, SC, Zip 29169-3422; tel. 803/796-9911, Shannon Marcus, Chief Executive Officer
Web address: www.threeriversbehavioral.org

TENNESSEE: LAKESIDE BEHAVIORAL HEALTH SYSTEM (O, 345 beds) 2911 Brunswick Road, Memphis, TN, Zip 38133-4199; tel. 901/377-4700, Joy Golden, Chief Executive Officer
Web address: www.lakesidebhs.com

ROLLING HILLS HOSPITAL (O, 130 beds) 2014 Quail Hollow Circle, Franklin, TN, Zip 37067-5967; tel. 615/628-5700, James Miller, Chief Executive Officer

TEXAS: AUSTIN OAKS HOSPITAL (O, 80 beds) 1407 West Stassney Lane, Austin, TX, Zip 78745-2947; tel. 512/440-4800, Steve Kelly, Chief Executive Officer
Web address: www.austinoakshospital.com

BEHAVIORAL HOSPITAL OF BELLAIRE (O, 122 beds) 5314 Dashwood Drive, Houston, TX, Zip 77081-4603; tel. 713/600-9500, Amanda Tejeda-Blanco, Chief Executive Officer

CANYON CREEK BEHAVIORAL HEALTH (O, 102 beds) 1201 Canyon Creek Drive, Temple, TX, Zip 76502; tel. 254/410-5100, Jennifer Card, Chief Executive Officer
Web address: www.https://canyoncreekbh.com/

CORNERSTONE REGIONAL HOSPITAL (L, 14 beds) 2302 Cornerstone Boulevard, Edinburg, TX, Zip 78539-8471; tel. 956/618-4444, Rance Ramsey, Chief Executive Officer

CYPRESS CREEK HOSPITAL (O, 128 beds) 17750 Cali Drive, Houston, TX, Zip 77090-2700; tel. 281/586-7600, Amanda Vail, Chief Executive Officer
Web address: www.cypresscreekhospital.com

DOCTORS HOSPITAL OF LAREDO (O, 183 beds) 10700 McPherson Road, Laredo, TX, Zip 78045-6268; tel. 956/523-2000, Andrew Wilson, Chief Executive Officer
Web address: www.doctorshosplaredo.com

EL PASO BEHAVIORAL HEALTH SYSTEM (O, 166 beds) 1900 Denver Avenue, El Paso, TX, Zip 79902-3008; tel. 915/544-4000, Jennifer Castaneda, Interim Chief Executive Officer

FORT DUNCAN REGIONAL MEDICAL CENTER (O, 60 beds) 3333 North Foster Maldonado Boulevard, Eagle Pass, TX, Zip 78852-5893; tel. 830/773-5321, Eladio Montalvo, Chief Executive Officer
Web address: www.fortduncanmedicalcenter.com

GLEN OAKS HOSPITAL (O, 54 beds) 301 Division Street, Greenville, TX, Zip 75401-4101; tel. 903/454-6000, Harry Lemming, Chief Executive Officer

HICKORY TRAIL HOSPITAL (O, 58 beds) 2000 Old Hickory Trail, Desoto, TX, Zip 75115-2242; tel. 972/298-7323, Jeff Baker, Chief Executive Officer
Web address: www.hickorytrail.com

KINGWOOD PINES HOSPITAL (O, 93 beds) 2001 Ladbrook Drive, Kingwood, TX, Zip 77339-3004; tel. 281/404-1001, Kristin Williams, Chief Executive Officer

LAUREL RIDGE TREATMENT CENTER (O, 288 beds) 17720 Corporate Woods Drive, San Antonio, TX, Zip 78259-3500; tel. 210/491-9400, Ashley Sacriste, Chief Executive Officer
Web address: www.laurelridgetc.com

MAYHILL HOSPITAL (O, 59 beds) 2809 South Mayhill Road, Denton, TX, Zip 76208-5910; tel. 940/239-3000, Holly Doherty, Chief Executive Officer

MILLWOOD HOSPITAL (O, 134 beds) 1011 North Cooper Street, Arlington, TX, Zip 76011-5517; tel. 817/261-3121, Loren Fouch, Chief Executive Officer
Web address: www.millwoodhospital.com

NORTHWEST TEXAS HEALTHCARE SYSTEM (O, 428 beds) 1501 South Coulter Avenue, Amarillo, TX, Zip 79106-1770, P O Box 1110, Zip 79105-1110, tel. 806/354-1000, Jason Barrett, Chief Executive Officer

RIVER CREST HOSPITAL (O, 62 beds) 1636 Hunters Glen Road, San Angelo, TX, Zip 76901-5016; tel. 325/949-5722, Patricia A Spatz, Chief Executive Officer
Web address: www.rivercresthospital.com

SOUTH TEXAS HEALTH SYSTEM (O, 919 beds) 1400 West Trenton Road, Edinburg, TX, Zip 78539-9105, 1102 West Trenton Road, Zip 78539-9105, tel. 956/388-6000, Lance Ames, Chief Executive Officer

TEXAS NEUROREHAB CENTER (O, 47 beds) 1106 West Dittmar Road, Building 9, Austin, TX, Zip 78745-6328, P O Box 150459, Zip 78715-0459, tel. 512/444-4835, Edgar E. Prettyman, PsyD, Chief Executive Officer
Web address: www.texasneurorehab.com

TEXOMA MEDICAL CENTER (O, 414 beds) 5016 South US Highway 75, Denison, TX, Zip 75020-4584, P O Box 890, Zip 75021-0890, tel. 903/416-4000, Sean T. Dardeau, FACHE, Chief Executive Officer
Web address: www.texomamedicalcenter.net

UNIVERSITY BEHAVIORAL HEALTH OF DENTON (O, 104 beds) 2026 West University Drive, Denton, TX, Zip 76201-0644; tel. 940/320-8100, Matthew Bertagnole, Chief Executive Officer

WEST OAKS HOSPITAL (O, 160 beds) 6500 Hornwood Drive, Houston, TX, Zip 77074-5095; tel. 713/995-0909, Phuong Cardoza, Chief Executive Officer
Web address: www.westoakshospital.com

UTAH: ASPEN GROVE BEHAVIORAL HOSPITAL (O, 80 beds) 1350 East 750 North, Orem, UT, Zip 84097-4345; tel. 801/852-2273, Jeremy Cottle, Ph.D., Chief Executive Officer
Web address: www.https://aspengrovehospital.com/

SALT LAKE BEHAVIORAL HEALTH (O, 118 beds) 3802 South 700 East, Salt Lake City, UT, Zip 84106-1182; tel. 801/264-6000, Kreg Gillman, Chief Executive Officer
Web address: www.saltlakebehavioralhealth.com

VIRGINIA: CUMBERLAND HOSPITAL FOR CHILDREN AND ADOLESCENTS (O, 74 beds) 9407 Cumberland Road, New Kent, VA, Zip 23124-2029; tel. 804/966-2242, Garrett Hamilton, Chief Executive Officer

For explanation of codes following names, see page B2.
★ Indicates Type III membership in the American Hospital Association.

Systems / Universal Health Services, Inc.

POPLAR SPRINGS HOSPITAL (O, 208 beds) 350 Poplar Drive, Petersburg, VA, Zip 23805–9367; tel. 804/733–6874, Michael S. Triggs, Group Chief Executive Officer and Managing Director
Web address: www.poplarsprings.com

VIRGINIA BEACH PSYCHIATRIC CENTER (O, 100 beds) 1100 First Colonial Road, Virginia Beach, VA, Zip 23454–2403; tel. 757/496–6000, Kurtis Hooks, Chief Executive Officer

WASHINGTON: FAIRFAX BEHAVIORAL HEALTH (O, 221 beds) 10200 NE 132nd Street, Kirkland, WA, Zip 98034–2899; tel. 425/821–2000, Sascha Hughes, Chief Executive Officer
Web address: www.fairfaxhospital.com

WEST VIRGINIA: RIVER PARK HOSPITAL (O, 175 beds) 1230 Sixth Avenue, Huntington, WV, Zip 25701–2312, P O Box 1875, Zip 25719–1875, tel. 304/526–9111, Steve Kuhn, Chief Executive Officer

WISCONSIN: GRANITE HILLS HOSPITAL (O, 48 beds) 1706 South 68th Street, West Allis, WI, Zip 53214–4949; tel. 414/667–4800, Angela Sanders, Chief Executive Officer
Web address: www.https://granitehillshospital.com/

WYOMING: WYOMING BEHAVIORAL INSTITUTE (O, 114 beds) 2521 East 15th Street, Casper, WY, Zip 82609–4126; tel. 307/237–7444, Mike Phillips, Chief Executive Officer

Owned, leased, sponsored:	140 hospitals	20061 beds
Contract–managed:	1 hospitals	54 beds
Totals:	141 hospitals	20115 beds

★9255: UNIVERSITY HEALTH (NP)

2301 Holmes Street, Kansas City, MO Zip 64108–2677; tel. 816/404–1000, Charlie Shields, Chief Executive Officer
(Independent Hospital System)

MISSOURI: UNIVERSITY HEALTH–LAKEWOOD MEDICAL CENTER (O, 305 beds) 7900 Lee's Summit Road, Kansas City, MO, Zip 64139–1236, 2301 Holmes Street, Zip 64108–2640, tel. 816/404–7000, Charlie Shields, Chief Executive Officer
Web address: www.trumed.org

UNIVERSITY HEALTH–TRUMAN MEDICAL CENTER (O, 258 beds) 2301 Holmes Street, Kansas City, MO, Zip 64108–2640; tel. 816/404–1000, Charlie Shields, President and Chief Executive Officer

Owned, leased, sponsored:	2 hospitals	563 beds
Contract–managed:	0 hospitals	0 beds
Totals:	2 hospitals	563 beds

★0112: UNIVERSITY HOSPITALS (NP)

11100 Euclid Avenue, Cleveland, OH Zip 44106–5000; tel. 216/844–1000, Cliff Megerian, M.D., Chief Executive Officer
(Centralized Health System)

OHIO: UNIVERSITY HOSPITALS AHUJA MEDICAL CENTER (O, 144 beds) 3999 Richmond Road, Beachwood, OH, Zip 44122–6046; tel. 216/593–5500, Alan Papa, President
Web address: https://www.uhhospitals.org/locations/uh-ahuja-medical-center

UNIVERSITY HOSPITALS BEACHWOOD MEDICAL CENTER (O, 24 beds) 25501 Chagrin Boulevard, Beachwood, OH, Zip 44122–5603; tel. 216/545–4800, Robyn Strosaker, M.D., President and Chief Operating Officer
Web address: https://www.uhhospitals.org/locations/uh-beachwood-medical-center

UNIVERSITY HOSPITALS CLEVELAND MEDICAL CENTER (O, 983 beds) 11100 Euclid Avenue, Cleveland, OH, Zip 44106–1716; tel. 216/844–1000, Stathis Antoniades, President
Web address: https://www.uhhospitals.org/locations/uh-cleveland-medical-center

UNIVERSITY HOSPITALS CONNEAUT MEDICAL CENTER (O, 25 beds) 158 West Main Road, Conneaut, OH, Zip 44030–2039; tel. 440/593–1131, M Steven. Jones, Regional President
Web address: https://www.uhhospitals.org/locations/uh-conneaut-medical-center

UNIVERSITY HOSPITALS ELYRIA MEDICAL CENTER (O, 175 beds) 630 East River Street, Elyria, OH, Zip 44035–5902; tel. 440/329–7500, Todd Harford, Chief Operating Officer
Web address: www.uhhospitals.org/elyria

UNIVERSITY HOSPITALS GEAUGA MEDICAL CENTER (O, 120 beds) 13207 Ravenna Road, Chardon, OH, Zip 44024–7032; tel. 440/269–6000, Donald DeCarlo, M.D., President

UNIVERSITY HOSPITALS GENEVA MEDICAL CENTER (O, 25 beds) 870 West Main Street, Geneva, OH, Zip 44041–1295; tel. 440/466–1141, M Steven. Jones, Regional President
Web address: https://www.uhhospitals.org/locations/uh-geneva-medical-center

UNIVERSITY HOSPITALS LAKE HEALTH (O, 308 beds) 36000 Euclid Avenue, Willoughby, OH, Zip 44094–4625; tel. 440/953–9600, Robyn Strosaker, M.D., President and Chief Operating Officer
Web address: www.lakehealth.org

UNIVERSITY HOSPITALS PARMA MEDICAL CENTER (O, 213 beds) 7007 Powers Boulevard, Parma, OH, Zip 44129–5495; tel. 440/743–3000, James Lee. Hill Sr, M.D., Chief Operating Officer

UNIVERSITY HOSPITALS PORTAGE MEDICAL CENTER (O, 97 beds) 6847 North Chestnut Street, Attn: Jeannie Fisher, Ravenna, OH, Zip 44266–3929, P O Box 1204, Zip 44266–1204, tel. 330/297–0811, William Benoit, President
Web address: www.uhportage.org

UNIVERSITY HOSPITALS RAINBOW BABIES AND CHILDREN'S (O, 244 beds) 2101 Adelbert Road, Cleveland, OH, Zip 44106–2624; tel. 216/844–3911, Patricia DePompei, President

UNIVERSITY HOSPITALS SAMARITAN MEDICAL CENTER (O, 28 beds) 1025 Center Street, Ashland, OH, Zip 44805–4011; tel. 419/289–0491, Sylvia Radziszewski, Chief Operating Officer
Web address: https://www.uhhospitals.org/locations/uh-samaritan-medical-center

UNIVERSITY HOSPITALS ST. JOHN MEDICAL CENTER (O, 124 beds) 29000 Center Ridge Road, Westlake, OH, Zip 44145–5293; tel. 440/835–8000, Jonathan Sague, Chief Operating Officer
Web address: https://www.uhhospitals.org

Owned, leased, sponsored:	13 hospitals	2510 beds
Contract–managed:	0 hospitals	0 beds
Totals:	13 hospitals	2510 beds

0915: UNIVERSITY HOSPITALS AND HEALTH SYSTEM (NP)

2500 North State Street, Jackson, MS Zip 39216–4500; tel. 601/984–1000, Alan Jones, Vice Chancellor
(Decentralized Health System)

MISSISSIPPI: UNIVERSITY OF MISSISSIPPI MEDICAL CENTER GRENADA (C, 126 beds) 960 Avent Drive, Grenada, MS, Zip 38901–5230; tel. 662/227–7000, Dodie McElmurray, FACHE, Chief Executive Officer
Web address: www.glmc.net/

UNIVERSITY OF MISSISSIPPI MEDICAL CENTER HOLMES COUNTY (O, 25 beds) 239 Bowling Green Road, Lexington, MS, Zip 39095–5167; tel. 601/496–5200, Dodie McElmurray, FACHE, Chief Executive Officer
Web address: www.ummchealth.com/holmes/

UNIVERSITY OF MISSISSIPPI MEDICAL CENTER (O, 733 beds) 2500 North State Street, Jackson, MS, Zip 39216–4505; tel. 601/984–1000, Britt Crewse, CPA, Chief Executive Officer

Owned, leased, sponsored:	2 hospitals	758 beds
Contract–managed:	1 hospitals	126 beds
Totals:	3 hospitals	884 beds

For explanation of codes following names, see page B2.
★ Indicates Type III membership in the American Hospital Association.

★6405: **UNIVERSITY OF CALIFORNIA SYSTEMWIDE ADMINISTRATION (NP)**
1111 Franklin Street, 11th Floor, Oakland, CA Zip 94607-5200; tel. 510/987-9071, Tam Ma, JD, Associate Vice President, Health Policy and Regulatory Affairs
(Decentralized Health System)

CALIFORNIA: FOUNTAIN VALLEY REGIONAL HOSPITAL AND MEDICAL CENTER (O, 380 beds) 17100 Euclid Street, Fountain Valley, CA, Zip 92708-4043; tel. 714/966-7200, Randy Rogers, FACHE, Chief Executive Officer
Web address: www.fountainvalleyhospital.com

LAKEWOOD REGIONAL MEDICAL CENTER (O, 111 beds) 3700 East South Street, Lakewood, CA, Zip 90712-1498, P O Box 6070, Zip 90712, tel. 562/531-2550, Virgis Narbutas, Chief Executive Officer

RONALD REAGAN UCLA MEDICAL CENTER (O, 445 beds) 757 Westwood Plaza, Los Angeles, CA, Zip 90095-8358; tel. 310/825-9111, Johnese Spisso, President, UCLA Health/Chief Executive Officer, UCLA Hospital System
Web address: www.uclahealth.org

STEWART & LYNDA RESNICK NEUROPSYCHIATRIC HOSPITAL AT UCLA (O, 74 beds) 150 UCLA Medical Plaza, Los Angeles, CA, Zip 90095-8353; tel. 310/825-9989, Johnese Spisso, President, UCLA Health/Chief Executive Officer, UCLA Hospital System

UC DAVIS MEDICAL CENTER (O, 632 beds) 2315 Stockton Boulevard, Sacramento, CA, Zip 95817-2282; tel. 916/734-2011, Michael Condrin, Chief Administrator/System Chief Operating Officer
Web address: www.ucdmc.ucdavis.edu

UC SAN DIEGO HEALTH–EAST CAMPUS (O, 137 beds) 6655 Alvarado Road, San Diego, CA, Zip 92120-5208; tel. 619/287-3270, Kenneth D. McFarland, Chief Executive Officer
Web address: www.alvaradohospital.com

UC SAN DIEGO MEDICAL CENTER–HILLCREST (O, 747 beds) 200 West Arbor Drive, San Diego, CA, Zip 92103-9000; tel. 619/543-6222, Patty Maysent, M.P.H., Chief Executive Officer
Web address: www.https://health.ucsd.edu

UCI HEALTH–LOS ALAMITOS (O, 120 beds) 3751 Katella Avenue, Los Alamitos, CA, Zip 90720-3164; tel. 562/598-1311, Kent G. Clayton, Chief Executive Officer

UCI HEALTH–PLACENTIA LINDA (O, 74 beds) 1301 North Rose Drive, Placentia, CA, Zip 92870-3899; tel. 714/993-2000, Fred Valtairo, R.N., Chief Executive Officer
Web address: www.placentialinda.com

UCI HEALTH (O, 459 beds) 101 The City Drive South, Orange, CA, Zip 92868-3298; tel. 714/456-6011, Chad T. Lefteris, Chief Executive Officer

UCLA MEDICAL CENTER–SANTA MONICA (O, 281 beds) 1250 16th Street, Santa Monica, CA, Zip 90404-1249; tel. 310/319-4000, Johnese Spisso, President, UCLA Health and Chief Executive Officer, UCLA Hospital System
Web address: www.healthcare.ucla.edu

UCLA WEST VALLEY MEDICAL CENTER (O, 260 beds) 7300 Medical Center Drive, West Hills, CA, Zip 91307-1900; tel. 818/676-4000, Johnese Spisso, President, UCLA Health and Chief Executive Officer, UCLA Hospital System

UCSF BENIOFF CHILDREN'S HOSPITAL OAKLAND (O, 216 beds) 747 52nd Street, Oakland, CA, Zip 94609-1859; tel. 510/428-3000, Nicholas M. Holmes, M.D., President, UCSF Benioff Children's Hospitals, SVP Children's Services UCSF Health
Web address: www.childrenshospitaloakland.org

UCSF HEALTH SAINT FRANCIS HOSPITAL (O, 239 beds) 900 Hyde Street, San Francisco, CA, Zip 94109-4899, P O Box 7726, Zip 94120-7726, tel. 415/353-6000, Daryn J. Kumar, President
Web address: www.saintfrancismemorial.org

UCSF HEALTH ST. MARY'S HOSPITAL (O, 232 beds) 450 Stanyan Street, San Francisco, CA, Zip 94117-1079; tel. 415/668-1000, Daryn J. Kumar, President
Web address: https://www.dignityhealth.org/bayarea/locations/stmarys

UCSF MEDICAL CENTER (O, 910 beds) 505 Parnassus Ave, San Francisco, CA, Zip 94143-2204, 500 Parnassus Avenue, Box 0296, Zip 94143-0296, tel. 415/476-1000, Suresh Gunasekaran, President and Chief Executive Officer

Owned, leased, sponsored:	16 hospitals	5317 beds
Contract-managed:	0 hospitals	0 beds
Totals:	16 hospitals	5317 beds

★0058: **UNIVERSITY OF CHICAGO MEDICINE (NP)**
5841 South Maryland Avenue, Chicago, IL Zip 60637-1447; tel. 773/702-6240, Thomas E. Jackiewicz, President
(Centralized Health System)

ILLINOIS: UCHICAGO MEDICINE INGALLS MEMORIAL (O, 288 beds) 1 Ingalls Drive, Harvey, IL, Zip 60426-3591; tel. 708/333-2300, Michael A. Antoniades, President
Web address: https://www.uchicagomedicine.org/find-a-location/uchicago-medicine-at-ingalls-harvey

UNIVERSITY OF CHICAGO MEDICAL CENTER (O, 758 beds) 5841 South Maryland Avenue, Chicago, IL, Zip 60637-1443; tel. 773/702-1000, Thomas E. Jackiewicz, President

Owned, leased, sponsored:	2 hospitals	1046 beds
Contract-managed:	0 hospitals	0 beds
Totals:	2 hospitals	1046 beds

1138: **UNIVERSITY OF IOWA HEALTH CARE (NP)**
200 Hawkins Drive, Iowa City, IA Zip 52242-1009; tel. 800/777-8442, Denise Jamieson, M.D., M.P.H., Vice President for Medical Affairs, Tyrone D. Artz Dean of the Roy J. and Lucille A. Carver College of Medicine

IOWA: UNIVERSITY OF IOWA HEALTH CARE MEDICAL CENTER DOWNTOWN (O, 194 beds) 500 East Market Street, Iowa City, IA, Zip 52245-2689; tel. 319/688-7525, Jennifer Miller, Chief Administrative Officer
Web address: www.mercyiowacity.org

UNIVERSITY OF IOWA HOSPITALS & CLINICS (O, 810 beds) 200 Hawkins Drive, Iowa City, IA, Zip 52242-1009; tel. 319/356-1616, Bradley Haws, Chief Executive Officer
Web address: www.uihealthcare.org

Owned, leased, sponsored:	2 hospitals	1004 beds
Contract-managed:	0 hospitals	0 beds
Totals:	2 hospitals	1004 beds

★0216: **UNIVERSITY OF MARYLAND MEDICAL SYSTEM (NP)**
250 West Pratt Street, 24th Floor, Baltimore, MD Zip 21201-1595; tel. 410/328-8667, Mohan Suntha, M.D., President and Chief Executive Officer
(Moderately Centralized Health System)

MARYLAND: MT. WASHINGTON PEDIATRIC HOSPITAL (O, 61 beds) 1708 West Rogers Avenue, Baltimore, MD, Zip 21209-4545; tel. 410/578-8600, Scott M. Klein, M.D., Chief Executive Officer

UNIVERSITY OF MARYLAND BALTIMORE WASHINGTON MEDICAL CENTER (O, 266 beds) 301 Hospital Drive, Glen Burnie, MD, Zip 21061-5899; tel. 410/787-4000, Kathleen McCollum, President and Chief Executive Officer
Web address: www.mybwmc.org

UNIVERSITY OF MARYLAND CAPITAL REGION MEDICAL CENTER (O, 245 beds) 901 Harry S Truman Drive North, Largo, MD, Zip 20774-5477; tel. 301/618-2000, Nathaniel Richardson Jr, President and Chief Executive Officer
Web address: https://www.umms.org/capital/locations/um-capital-region-medical-center

UNIVERSITY OF MARYLAND CHARLES REGIONAL MEDICAL CENTER (O, 108 beds) 5 Garrett Avenue, La Plata, MD, Zip 20646-5960, P O Box 1070, Zip 20646-1070, tel. 301/609-4000, Noel A. Cervino, President and Chief Executive Officer
Web address: https://www.umms.org/charles

For explanation of codes following names, see page B2.
★ Indicates Type III membership in the American Hospital Association.

Systems / University of Maryland Medical System

UNIVERSITY OF MARYLAND MEDICAL CENTER MIDTOWN CAMPUS (O, 125 beds) 827 Linden Avenue, Baltimore, MD, Zip 21201–4606; tel. 410/225–8000, Rebecca A. Altman, R.N., Senior Vice President and Chief Administrative Officer

UNIVERSITY OF MARYLAND MEDICAL CENTER (O, 658 beds) 22 South Greene Street, Baltimore, MD, Zip 21201–1595; tel. 410/328–9199, Bert W. O'Malley Jr, President and Chief Executive Officer
Web address: www.umm.edu

UNIVERSITY OF MARYLAND REHABILITATION & ORTHOPAEDIC INSTITUTE (O, 117 beds) 2200 Kernan Drive, Baltimore, MD, Zip 21207–6697; tel. 410/448–2500, Julie Nemens, Chief Administrative Officer

UNIVERSITY OF MARYLAND SHORE MEDICAL CENTER AT CHESTERTOWN (O, 30 beds) 100 Brown Street, Chestertown, MD, Zip 21620–1499; tel. 410/778–3300, Aaron Royston, Vice President, Rural Health Transformation and Executive Director
Web address: https://www.umms.org/shore/locations/medical-center-chestertown

UNIVERSITY OF MARYLAND SHORE MEDICAL CENTER AT EASTON (O, 132 beds) 219 South Washington Street, Easton, MD, Zip 21601–2996; tel. 410/822–1000, Kenneth D. Kozel, FACHE, President and Chief Executive Officer
Web address: www.shorehealth.org

UNIVERSITY OF MARYLAND ST. JOSEPH MEDICAL CENTER (O, 286 beds) 7601 Osler Drive, Towson, MD, Zip 21204–7582; tel. 410/337–1000, Thomas Smyth, President and Chief Executive Officer

UNIVERSITY OF MARYLAND UPPER CHESAPEAKE MEDICAL CENTER (O, 211 beds) 500 Upper Chesapeake Drive, Bel Air, MD, Zip 21014–4324; tel. 443/643–1000, Elizabeth Wise, FACHE, MSN, President and Chief Executive Officer
Web address: www.uchs.org

Owned, leased, sponsored:	11 hospitals	2239 beds
Contract-managed:	0 hospitals	0 beds
Totals:	11 hospitals	2239 beds

★**1099: UNIVERSITY OF MICHIGAN HEALTH (NP)**
1500 E Medical Center Drive, Ann Arbor, MI Zip 48109–5000; tel. 734/936–4000, David C. Miller, M.D., M.P.H., Executive Vice Dean for Clinical Affairs and President, UM Health System

MICHIGAN: SPARROW CLINTON HOSPITAL (O, 25 beds) 805 South Oakland Street, Saint Johns, MI, Zip 48879–2253; tel. 989/227–3400, Mark Brisboe, President
Web address: https://www.sparrow.org/our-hospitals-services/sparrow-hospitals/sparrow-clinton-hospital

SPARROW SPECIALTY HOSPITAL (O, 30 beds) 1215 East Michigan Avenue, 8 West Tower, Lansing, MI, Zip 48912; tel. 517/364–4840, Tina Gross, MSN, R.N., President and Chief Nursing Officer

UNIVERSITY OF MICHIGAN HEALTH–WEST (O, 208 beds) 5900 Byron Center Avenue SW, Wyoming, MI, Zip 49519–9606, P O Box 916, Zip 49509–0916, tel. 616/252–7200, Ronald Grifka, M.D., FACC, President
Web address: www.https://uofmhealthwest.org/

UNIVERSITY OF MICHIGAN HEALTH–SPARROW CARSON (O, 48 beds) 406 East Elm Street, PO Box 879, Carson City, MI, Zip 48811–9693; tel. 989/584–3131, Mark Brisboe, President

UNIVERSITY OF MICHIGAN HEALTH–SPARROW EATON (O, 25 beds) 321 East Harris Street, Charlotte, MI, Zip 48813–1629; tel. 517/543–1050, Linda Reetz, R.N., President
Web address: www.hgbhealth.com

UNIVERSITY OF MICHIGAN HEALTH–SPARROW IONIA (O, 22 beds) 3565 South State Road, Ionia, MI, Zip 48846–1870; tel. 616/523–1400, Linda Reetz, R.N., President
Web address: www.sparrow.org/sparrowionia

UNIVERSITY OF MICHIGAN HEALTH–SPARROW LANSING (O, 535 beds) 1215 East Michigan Avenue, Lansing, MI, Zip 48912–1811; tel. 517/364–1000, Denny Martin, D.O., President, University of Michigan Health–Sparrow Lansing
Web address: https://www.sparrow.org/our-hospitals-services/sparrow-hospitals/sparrow-hospital

UNIVERSITY OF MICHIGAN MEDICAL CENTER (O, 1102 beds) 1500 East Medical Center Drive, Ann Arbor, MI, Zip 48109; tel. 734/936–4000, David C. Miller, M.D., M.P.H., Executive Vice Dean for Clinical Affairs and President, UM Health System

Owned, leased, sponsored:	8 hospitals	1995 beds
Contract-managed:	0 hospitals	0 beds
Totals:	8 hospitals	1995 beds

★**0227: UNIVERSITY OF MISSOURI HEALTH CARE (NP)**
1 Hospital Drive, DC 031, Columbia, MO Zip 65212–0001, 1 Hospital Drive, DC 031, Zip 65212–0001, tel. 573/882–4141, Ric A. Ransom, Chief Executive Officer
(Moderately Centralized Health System)

MISSOURI: CAPITAL REGION MEDICAL CENTER (O, 114 beds) 1125 Madison Street, Jefferson City, MO, Zip 65101–5200, P O Box 1128, Zip 65102–1128, tel. 573/632–5000, John Dennis. Hamilton, Interim Chief Operating Officer
Web address: www.crmc.org

UNIVERSITY HOSPITAL (O, 600 beds) 1 Hospital Drive, Columbia, MO, Zip 65212–0001; tel. 573/882–4141, Ric A. Ransom, Chief Executive Officer
Web address: www.muhealth.org

Owned, leased, sponsored:	2 hospitals	714 beds
Contract-managed:	0 hospitals	0 beds
Totals:	2 hospitals	714 beds

★**0168: UNIVERSITY OF PENNSYLVANIA HEALTH SYSTEM (NP)**
3400 Civic Center Boulevard, Suite A–5, Philadelphia, PA Zip 19104–5127; tel. 215/662–2203, Kevin B. Mahoney, Chief Executive Officer
(Moderately Centralized Health System)

NEW JERSEY: PENN MEDICINE PRINCETON MEDICAL CENTER (O, 435 beds) 1 Plainsboro Road, Plainsboro, NJ, Zip 08536–1913; tel. 609/853–7100, James Demetriades, Chief Executive Officer

PENNSYLVANIA: HOSPITAL OF THE UNIVERSITY OF PENNSYLVANIA (O, 1038 beds) 3400 Spruce Street, Philadelphia, PA, Zip 19104–4206; tel. 215/662–4000, Regina Cunningham, Ph.D., R.N., Chief Executive Officer
Web address: www.pennmedicine.org

LANCASTER BEHAVIORAL HEALTH HOSPITAL (O, 126 beds) 333 Harrisburg Avenue, Lancaster, PA, Zip 17603; tel. 717/740–4100, Ryan Tatu, Chief Executive Officer

PENN MEDICINE CHESTER COUNTY HOSPITAL (O, 329 beds) 701 East Marshall Street, West Chester, PA, Zip 19380–4412; tel. 610/431–5000, Michael J. Duncan, President and Chief Executive Officer
Web address: www.chestercountyhospital.org

PENN MEDICINE LANCASTER GENERAL HEALTH (O, 620 beds) 555 North Duke Street, Lancaster, PA, Zip 17602–2250; tel. 717/544–5511, John J. Herman, FACHE, Chief Executive Officer

PENN PRESBYTERIAN MEDICAL CENTER (O, 399 beds) 51 North 39th Street, Philadelphia, PA, Zip 19104–2699; tel. 215/662–8000, Robert J. Russell, MS, FACHE, Chief Executive Officer
Web address: www.pennmedicine.org/pmc/

PENNSYLVANIA HOSPITAL (O, 503 beds) 800 Spruce Street, Philadelphia, PA, Zip 19107–6192; tel. 215/829–3000, Alicia Gresham, Chief Executive Officer

Owned, leased, sponsored:	7 hospitals	3450 beds
Contract-managed:	0 hospitals	0 beds
Totals:	7 hospitals	3450 beds

For explanation of codes following names, see page B2.
★ Indicates Type III membership in the American Hospital Association.

Systems / UPMC

★0223: **UNIVERSITY OF ROCHESTER MEDICAL CENTER (NP)**
601 Elmwood Ave Box 623, Rochester, NY Zip 14642-0002, 601 Elmwood Avenue, Zip 14642-0002, tel. 585/275-2100, Mark B. Taubman, M.D., Chief Executive Officer
(Moderately Centralized Health System)

NEW YORK: F. F. THOMPSON HOSPITAL (O, 87 beds) 350 Parrish Street, Canandaigua, NY, Zip 14424-1731; tel. 585/396-6000, Michael Stapleton, R.N., MS, FACHE, President and Chief Executive Officer

HIGHLAND HOSPITAL (O, 238 beds) 1000 South Avenue, Rochester, NY, Zip 14620-2733; tel. 585/473-2200, Steven I. Goldstein, President and Chief Executive Officer
Web address: https://www.urmc.rochester.edu/highland

JONES MEMORIAL HOSPITAL (O, 33 beds) 191 North Main Street, Wellsville, NY, Zip 14895-1150, P O Box 72, Zip 14895-0072, tel. 585/593-1100, James Helms, President and Chief Executive Officer
Web address: www.jmhny.org

NICHOLAS H. NOYES MEMORIAL HOSPITAL (O, 67 beds) 111 Clara Barton Street, Dansville, NY, Zip 14437-9503; tel. 585/335-6001, John Teeters, M.D., President and Chief Executive Officer

ST. JAMES HOSPITAL (O, 15 beds) 7329 Seneca Road North, Hornell, NY, Zip 14843; tel. 607/247-2200, Wendy Disbrow, President and Chief Executive Officer
Web address: www.stjamesmercy.org

STRONG MEMORIAL HOSPITAL OF THE UNIVERSITY OF ROCHESTER (O, 916 beds) 601 Elmwood Avenue, Rochester, NY, Zip 14642-0002, 601 Elmwood Avenue, Box 612, Zip 14642-0002, tel. 585/275-2100, Steven I. Goldstein, President and Chief Executive Officer
Web address: www.urmc.rochester.edu

Owned, leased, sponsored:	6 hospitals	1356 beds
Contract-managed:	0 hospitals	0 beds
Totals:	6 hospitals	1356 beds

★0033: **UNIVERSITY OF TEXAS SYSTEM (NP)**
210 West 7th Street, Austin, TX Zip 78701-2903; tel. 512/499-4224, John M. Zerwas, M.D., Executive Vice Chancellor for Health Affairs
(Moderately Centralized Health System)

TEXAS: UT HEALTH NORTH CAMPUS TYLER (O, 130 beds) 11937 Highway 271, Tyler, TX, Zip 75708-3154; tel. 903/877-7777, Zachary K. Dietze, Chief Executive Officer

UTHEALTH HARRIS COUNTY PSYCHIATRIC CENTER (C, 537 beds) 2800 South MacGregor Way, Houston, TX, Zip 77021-1000; tel. 713/741-7870, Jair C. Soares, M.D., Executive Director
Web address: www.https://hcpc.uth.edu/

UNIVERSITY OF TEXAS M.D. ANDERSON CANCER CENTER (O, 721 beds) 1515 Holcombe Boulevard Unit 1495, Houston, TX, Zip 77030-4000, 1515 Holcombe Boulevard, Unit 1495, Zip 77030-4000, tel. 713/792-2121, Peter Pisters, M.D., President and Chief Executive Officer

UNIVERSITY OF TEXAS MEDICAL BRANCH (O, 562 beds) 301 University Boulevard, Galveston, TX, Zip 77555-0128; tel. 409/772-1011, Jochen Reiser, President and Chief Executive Officer
Web address: www.utmb.edu

Owned, leased, sponsored:	3 hospitals	1413 beds
Contract-managed:	1 hospitals	537 beds
Totals:	4 hospitals	1950 beds

★0983: **UOFL HEALTH (NP)**
530 South Jackson Street, Louisville, KY Zip 40202-1675; tel. 502/562-3000, Thomas Miller, Chief Executive Officer

KENTUCKY: UOFL HEALTH–JEWISH HOSPITAL (O, 458 beds) 200 Abraham Flexner Way, Louisville, KY, Zip 40202-1886; tel. 502/587-4011, John Walsh, FACHE, Chief Administrative Officer
Web address: https://www.kindredhealthcare.com/locations/transitional-care-hospitals/kindred-hospital-louisville-at-jewish-hospital

UOFL HEALTH–MARY AND ELIZABETH HOSPITAL (O, 199 beds) 1850 Bluegrass Avenue, Louisville, KY, Zip 40215-1199; tel. 502/361-6000, Melisa Adkins, Chief Executive Officer
Web address: www.https://uoflhealth.org/locations/mary-elizabeth-hospital/

UOFL HEALTH–PEACE HOSPITAL (O, 261 beds) 2020 Newburg Road, Louisville, KY, Zip 40205-1879; tel. 502/479-4500, Aundrea Lewis, Interim Chief Executive Officer

UOFL HEALTH–SHELBYVILLE HOSPITAL (O, 32 beds) 727 Hospital Drive, Shelbyville, KY, Zip 40065-1699; tel. 502/647-4000, Aaron Garofola, Chief Executive Officer
Web address: www.kentuckyonehealth.org/jewish-hospital-shelbyville

UOFL HEALTH–UOFL HOSPITAL (O, 340 beds) 530 South Jackson Street, Louisville, KY, Zip 40202-3611; tel. 502/562-3000, Kenneth P. Marshall, Chief Executive Officer

Owned, leased, sponsored:	5 hospitals	1290 beds
Contract-managed:	0 hospitals	0 beds
Totals:	5 hospitals	1290 beds

★0137: **UPMC (NP)**
600 Grant Street, US Steel Tower, Suite 6262, Pittsburgh, PA Zip 15219-2702; tel. 412/647-8762, Leslie Davis, President and Chief Executive Officer
(Decentralized Health System)

MARYLAND: UPMC WESTERN MARYLAND (O, 233 beds) 12500 Willowbrook Road SE, Cumberland, MD, Zip 21502-6393, P O Box 539, Zip 21501-0539, tel. 240/964-7000, Michele R. Martz, CPA, President

NEW YORK: UPMC CHAUTAUQUA (O, 130 beds) 207 Foote Avenue, Jamestown, NY, Zip 14701-7077, P O Box 840, Zip 14702-0840, tel. 716/487-0141, Brian Durniok, President
Web address: www.wcahospital.org

PENNSYLVANIA: UPMC ALTOONA (O, 346 beds) 620 Howard Avenue, Altoona, PA, Zip 16601-4804; tel. 814/889-2011, Michael Corso, President and Chief Executive Officer, UPMC Altoona/Bedford
Web address: www.altoonaregional.org

UPMC BEDFORD (O, 24 beds) 10455 Lincoln Highway, Everett, PA, Zip 15537-7046; tel. 814/623-6161, Michael Corso, President & Chief Executive Officer
Web address: www.upmcbedfordmemorial.com

UPMC CARLISLE (O, 86 beds) 361 Alexander Spring Road, Carlisle, PA, Zip 17015-6940; tel. 717/249-1212, Jarrod G. Johnson, FACHE, President

UPMC CHILDREN'S HOSPITAL OF PITTSBURGH (O, 307 beds) 1 Childrens Hospital DR, 4401 Penn Avenue, Pittsburgh, PA, Zip 15224-1529; tel. 412/692-5325, Diane Hupp, R.N., President
Web address: www.chp.edu

UPMC COLE (O, 69 beds) 1001 East Second Street, Coudersport, PA, Zip 16915-8161; tel. 814/274-9300, Janie Marie. Hilfiger, R.N., President

UPMC EAST (O, 155 beds) 2775 Mosside Boulevard, Monroeville, PA, Zip 15146-2760; tel. 412/357-3000, Mark O'Hern, President
Web address: www.upmc.com/locations/hospitals/east/Pages/default.aspx

UPMC GREENE (O, 18 beds) 350 Bonar Avenue, Waynesburg, PA, Zip 15370-1608; tel. 724/627-3101, Terry Wiltrout, President
Web address: www.southwestregionalmedical.com/

UPMC HAMOT (O, 343 beds) 201 State Street, Erie, PA, Zip 16550-0002; tel. 814/877-6000, Brian Durniok, President

UPMC HANOVER (O, 81 beds) 300 Highland Avenue, Hanover, PA, Zip 17331-2297; tel. 717/316-3711, Michael W. Gaskins, President
Web address: www.hanoverhospital.org

UPMC HARRISBURG (O, 741 beds) 111 South Front Street, Harrisburg, PA, Zip 17101-2010, P O Box 8700, Zip 17105-8700, tel. 717/231-8900, Elizabeth Ritter, President

For explanation of codes following names, see page B2.
★ Indicates Type III membership in the American Hospital Association.

Systems / UPMC

UPMC HORIZON (O, 69 beds) 2200 Memorial Drive, Farrell, PA, Zip 16121-1357; tel. 724/588-2100, David J. Patton, President
Web address: www.upmc.com

UPMC JAMESON (O, 91 beds) 1211 Wilmington Avenue, New Castle, PA, Zip 16105-2516; tel. 724/658-9001, David J. Patton, President
Web address: www.upmcjameson.com

UPMC KANE (O, 14 beds) 4372 Route 6, Kane, PA, Zip 16735-3060; tel. 814/837-8585, Mark Papalia, President

UPMC LITITZ (O, 60 beds) 1500 Highlands Drive, Lititz, PA, Zip 17543-7694; tel. 717/625-5000, Deborah J. Willwerth, R.N., MSN, President
Web address: https://www.upmc.com/campaigns/southcentral-pa

UPMC MAGEE-WOMENS HOSPITAL (O, 339 beds) 300 Halket Street, Pittsburgh, PA, Zip 15213-3108; tel. 412/641-1000, Richard Beigi, M.D., President and Professor UPSOM

UPMC MCKEESPORT (O, 136 beds) 1500 Fifth Avenue, McKeesport, PA, Zip 15132-2422; tel. 412/664-2000, Mark O'Hern, President
Web address: www.mckeesport.upmc.com

UPMC MEMORIAL (O, 79 beds) 1701 Innovation Drive, York, PA, Zip 17408-8815, P O Box 15118, Zip 17405-7118, tel. 717/843-8623, Michelle Del Pizzo, President
Web address: www.mhyork.org

UPMC MERCY (O, 297 beds) 1400 Locust Street, Pittsburgh, PA, Zip 15219-5166; tel. 412/232-8111, Richard Beigi, M.D., President and Professor

UPMC MUNCY (O, 154 beds) 215 East Water Street, Muncy, PA, Zip 17756-8700; tel. 570/546-8282, Ronald J. Reynolds, President
Web address: www.susquehannahealth.org

UPMC NORTHWEST (O, 167 beds) 100 Fairfield Drive, Seneca, PA, Zip 16346-2130; tel. 814/676-7600, Brian Durniok, President

UPMC PASSAVANT (O, 316 beds) 9100 Babcock Boulevard, Pittsburgh, PA, Zip 15237-5815; tel. 412/748-6700, Elizabeth A. Piccione, M.D., President
Web address: https://www.upmc.com/locations/hospitals/passavant

UPMC PRESBYTERIAN (O, 1412 beds) 200 Lothrop Street, Pittsburgh, PA, Zip 15213-2536; tel. 412/647-2345, Sandra Rader, R.N., President

UPMC SOMERSET (O, 56 beds) 225 South Center Avenue, Somerset, PA, Zip 15501-2088; tel. 814/443-5000, Andrew G. Rush, President
Web address: www.somersethospital.com

UPMC ST. MARGARET (O, 181 beds) 815 Freeport Road, Pittsburgh, PA, Zip 15215-3301; tel. 412/784-4000, Andrew Ritchie, President

UPMC WASHINGTON (O, 172 beds) 155 Wilson Avenue, Washington, PA, Zip 15301-3398; tel. 724/225-7000, Brook Ward, President and Chief Executive Officer
Web address: www.https://whs.org/

UPMC WELLSBORO (O, 39 beds) 32 Central Avenue, Wellsboro, PA, Zip 16901-1899; tel. 570/723-7764, Daniel Glunk, M.D., Chief Quality Officer
Web address: www.susquehannahealth.org

UPMC WILLIAMSPORT (O, 226 beds) 700 High Street, Williamsport, PA, Zip 17701-3100; tel. 570/321-1000, Patti Jackson-Gehris, President
Web address: www.susquehannahealth.org

Owned, leased, sponsored:	29 hospitals	6341 beds
Contract-managed:	0 hospitals	0 beds
Totals:	29 hospitals	6341 beds

★9195: U. S. Indian Health Service (FG)
801 Thompson Avenue, Rockville, MD Zip 20852-1627; tel. 301/443-1083, Roselyn Tso, Director of the Indian Health Service
(Independent Hospital System)

ARIZONA: CHINLE COMPREHENSIVE HEALTH CARE FACILITY (O, 60 beds) Highway 191, Hospital Road, Chinle, AZ, Zip 86503, Highway 191 Hospital Drive, Zip 86503-8000, tel. 928/674-7001, Darlene Chee, Acting Chief Executive Officer

HOPI HEALTH CARE CENTER (O, 15 beds) Highway 264 Mile Marker 388, Keams Canyon, AZ, Zip 86042, P O Box 4000, Polacca, Zip 86042-4000, tel. 928/737-6000, Amanda Lea. Hicks, R.N., Chief Executive Officer
Web address: https://www.ihs.gov/phoenix/healthcarefacilities/hopi/

NAVAJO HEALTH FOUNDATION-SAGE MEMORIAL HOSPITAL (C, 43 beds) Highway 264, Ganado, AZ, Zip 86505, P O Box 457, Zip 86505-0457, tel. 928/755-4500, Melinda White, R.N., Chief Executive Officer

SAN CARLOS APACHE HEALTHCARE CORPORATION (O, 12 beds) 103 Medicine Way Road, Peridot, AZ, Zip 85542; tel. 928/475-1400, Victoria D. Began, R.N., MS, President and Chief Executive Officer
Web address: www.ihs.gov

U. S. PUBLIC HEALTH SERVICE INDIAN HOSPITAL-SELLS (O, 12 beds) Highway 86 & Topawa Road, Sells, AZ, Zip 85634, P O Box 548, Zip 85634-0548, tel. 520/383-7251, Veronica Geronimo, Administrator and Chief Executive Officer

U. S. PUBLIC HEALTH SERVICE INDIAN HOSPITAL-WHITERIVER (O, 35 beds) 200 West Hospital Drive, Whiteriver, AZ, Zip 85941-0860, State Route 73, Box 860, Zip 85941-0860, tel. 928/338-4911, Michelle Martinez, Chief Executive Officer
Web address: www.ihs.gov

U. S. PUBLIC HEALTH SERVICE INDIAN HOSPITAL (O, 20 beds) 12033 Agency Road, Parker, AZ, Zip 85344-7718; tel. 928/669-2137, Barbara Asher, Chief Executive Officer

U. S. PUBLIC HEALTH SERVICE PHOENIX INDIAN MEDICAL CENTER (O, 127 beds) 4212 North 16th Street, Phoenix, AZ, Zip 85016-5389; tel. 602/263-1200, Debra Ward Lund, Chief Executive Officer
Web address: www.ihs.gov

MINNESOTA: RED LAKE INDIAN HEALTH SERVICE HOSPITAL (O, 19 beds) 24760 Hospital Drive, Red Lake, MN, Zip 56671, P O Box 497, Zip 56671-0497, tel. 218/679-3912, Mary Ann. Cook, Chief Executive Officer, Red Lake Service Unit
Web address: www.rlnnredlakehospital.com/

U. S. PUBLIC HEALTH SERVICE INDIAN HOSPITAL (O, 9 beds) 425 7th Street North West, Cass Lake, MN, Zip 56633; tel. 218/335-3200, Andrew Joseph. Lankowicz, Chief Executive Officer, Cass Lake Service Unit

MONTANA: BLACKFEET COMMUNITY HOSPITAL (O, 25 beds) 760 New Hospital Circle, Saint Mary, MT, Zip 59417-0760, P O Box 760, Browning, Zip 59417-0760, tel. 406/338-6100, Lisa Racine-Wells, Interim Chief Executive Officer
Web address: www.ihs.gov

CROW/NORTHERN CHEYENNE HOSPITAL (O, 24 beds) 10110 South 7650 East, Crow Agency, MT, Zip 59022-0009, P O Box 9, Zip 59022-0009, tel. 406/638-2626, Darren Crowe, Chief Executive Officer
Web address: https://www.ihs.gov/billings/healthcarefacilities/crow/

FORT BELKNAP SERVICE UNIT (O, 6 beds) 669 Agency Main Street, Harlem, MT, Zip 59526-9455; tel. 406/353-3100, Lieutenant Commander, Matthew Frye, Acting Chies Executive Officer
Web address: www.ihs.gov

NEW MEXICO: ACOMA-CANONCITO-LAGUNA HOSPITAL (O, 6 beds) 80B Veterans Boulevard, Acoma, NM, Zip 87034, P O Box 130, San Fidel, Zip 87049-0130, tel. 505/552-5300, Delaine Alley, Chief Executive Officer
Web address: www.ihs.gov/albuquerque/index.cfm?module=dsp_abq_acoma_canoncito_laguna

GALLUP INDIAN MEDICAL CENTER (O, 57 beds) 516 East Nizhoni Boulevard, Gallup, NM, Zip 87301-5748, P O Box 1337, Zip 87301, tel. 505/722-1000, Captain, Katrina Leslie-Puhuyaoma, D.D.S., Chief Executive Officer

MESCALERO PUBLIC HEALTH SERVICE INDIAN HOSPITAL (O, 13 beds) 318 Abalone Loop, Mescalero, NM, Zip 88340, Box 210, Zip 88340-0210, tel. 505/464-3801, Dorlynn Simmons, Chief Executive Officer
Web address: www.ihs.gov

NORTHERN NAVAJO MEDICAL CENTER (O, 68 beds) Highway 491 North, Shiprock, NM, Zip 87420-0160, P O Box 160, Zip 87420-0160, tel. 505/368-6001, Captain, Katrina Leslie-Puhuyaoma, D.D.S., Chief Executive Officer
Web address: www.ihs.gov/

PHS SANTA FE INDIAN HOSPITAL (O, 4 beds) 1700 Cerrillos Road, Santa Fe, NM, Zip 87505-3554; tel. 505/988-9821, Leslie Dye, Chief Executive Officer

U. S. PUBLIC HEALTH SERVICE INDIAN HOSPITAL (O, 12 beds) Route 9 and State Road 371, Crownpoint, NM, Zip 87313, P O Box 358, Zip 87313-0358, tel. 505/786-5291, Anslem Roanhorse, Chief Executive Officer
Web address: www.ihs.gov

For explanation of codes following names, see page B2.
★ Indicates Type III membership in the American Hospital Association.

Systems / UW Health

U. S. PUBLIC HEALTH SERVICE INDIAN HOSPITAL (O, 32 beds) Route 301 North B Street, Zuni, NM, Zip 87327, P O Box 467, Zip 87327-0467, tel. 505/782-4431, Jean Othole, Chief Executive Officer
Web address: www.ihs.gov

NORTH DAKOTA: QUENTIN N. BURDICK MEMORIAL HEALTHCARE FACILITY (O, 27 beds) 1300 Hospital Loop, Belcourt, ND, Zip 58316, P O Box 160, Zip 58316-0160, tel. 701/477-6111, Shelly Harris, Chief Executive Officer
Web address: www.ihs.gov

STANDING ROCK SERVICE UNIT, FORT YATES HOSPITAL, INDIAN HEALTH SERVICE, DHHS (O, 14 beds) 10 North River Road, Fort Yates, ND, Zip 58538, P O Box 'J', Zip 58538, tel. 701/854-3831, Jana Gipp, Chief Executive Officer
Web address: www.ihs.gov

OKLAHOMA: CLAREMORE INDIAN HOSPITAL (O, 44 beds) 101 South Moore Avenue, Claremore, OK, Zip 74017-5091; tel. 918/342-6200, George Valliere, Chief Executive Officer

LAWTON INDIAN HOSPITAL (O, 26 beds) 1515 Lawrie Tatum Road, Lawton, OK, Zip 73507-3099; tel. 580/353-0350, Brian Wren, Chief Executive Officer
Web address: www.ihs.gov

SOUTH DAKOTA: INDIAN HEALTH SERVICE HOSPITAL (O, 9 beds) 3200 Canyon Lake Drive, Rapid City, SD, Zip 57702-8197; tel. 605/355-2280, Kevin J. Stiffarm, Chief Executive Officer
Web address: www.ihs.gov

U. S. PUBLIC HEALTH SERVICE INDIAN HOSPITAL (O, 8 beds) 317 Main Street, Eagle Butte, SD, Zip 57625-1012, P O Box 1012, Zip 57625-1012, tel. 605/964-7724, Charles Fisher, Chief Executive Officer

U. S. PUBLIC HEALTH SERVICE INDIAN HOSPITAL (O, 45 beds) East Highway 18, Pine Ridge, SD, Zip 57770, P O Box 1201, Zip 57770-1201, tel. 605/867-5131, Travis Scott, Service Unit Director
Web address: www.ihs.gov

U. S. PUBLIC HEALTH SERVICE INDIAN HOSPITAL (O, 35 beds) Highway 18, Soldier Creek Road, Rosebud, SD, Zip 57570; tel. 605/747-2231, Melody Price-Yonts, Chief Executive Officer
Web address: www.ihs.gov

U. S. PUBLIC HEALTH SERVICE INDIAN HOSPITAL (O, 23 beds) 111 Washington Avenue Northwest, Wagner, SD, Zip 57380-4300, Box 490, Zip 57380-4090, tel. 605/384-3621, Michael Horned Eagle, Chief Executive Officer

Owned, leased, sponsored:	28 hospitals	787 beds
Contract-managed:	1 hospitals	43 beds
Totals:	29 hospitals	830 beds

★**0057: USA HEALTH (NP)**
2451 University Hospital Drive, Mobile, AL Zip 36617-2300, 2451 University Hospital Drive, Suite 2110, Zip 36617-2238, tel. 251/471-7000, Owen Bailey, FACHE, Chief Executive Officer and Senior Associate Vice President for Medical Affairs
(Independent Hospital System)

ALABAMA: USA HEALTH CHILDREN'S & WOMEN'S HOSPITAL (O, 174 beds) 1700 Center Street, Mobile, AL, Zip 36604-3301; tel. 251/415-1000, Deborah Browning, MSN, R.N., Chief Executive Officer

USA HEALTH PROVIDENCE HOSPITAL (O, 305 beds) 6801 Airport Boulevard, Mobile, AL, Zip 36608-3785, P O Box 850429, Zip 36685-0429, tel. 251/633-1000, Richard Metzger, Interim Chief Executive Officer
Web address: www.https://healthcare.ascension.org/locations/alabama/almob/mobile-providence-hospital

USA HEALTH UNIVERSITY HOSPITAL (O, 240 beds) 2451 University Hospital Drive, Mobile, AL, Zip 36617-2293; tel. 251/471-7000, Josh Snow, Chief Executive Officer

Owned, leased, sponsored:	3 hospitals	719 beds
Contract-managed:	0 hospitals	0 beds
Totals:	3 hospitals	719 beds

0868: USMD HEALTH SYSTEM (IO)
6333 North State Highway 161 Suite 200, Irving, TX Zip 75038-2229; tel. 214/493-4000, Richard C. Johnston, M.D., Chief Executive Officer and Chief Physician Officer
(Independent Hospital System)

TEXAS: USMD HOSPITAL AT ARLINGTON (O, 34 beds) 801 West Interstate 20, Arlington, TX, Zip 76017-5851; tel. 817/472-3400, Marcia Crim, MSN, R.N., Chief Executive Officer & Chief Nursing Officer
Web address: www.usmdarlington.com

Owned, leased, sponsored:	1 hospitals	34 beds
Contract-managed:	0 hospitals	0 beds
Totals:	1 hospitals	34 beds

★**0860: UVA HEALTH (NP)**
1215 Lee Street, Charlottesville, VA Zip 22908-0816; tel. 434/924-0211, K. Craig Kent, M.D., Chief Executive Officer
(Centralized Health System)

VIRGINIA: UVA HEALTH CULPEPER MEDICAL CENTER (O, 68 beds) 501 Sunset Lane, Culpeper, VA, Zip 22701-3917, P O Box 592, Zip 22701-0500, tel. 540/829-4100, Erik Shannon, Chief Executive Officer

UVA HEALTH HAYMARKET MEDICAL CENTER (O, 18 beds) 15225 Heathcote Boulevard, Haymarket, VA, Zip 20155-4023, 14535 John Marshall Hwy, Gainesville, Zip 20155-4023, tel. 571/284-1000, Erik Shannon, Chief Executive Officer
Web address: www.novanthealth.org

UVA HEALTH PRINCE WILLIAM MEDICAL CENTER (O, 87 beds) 8700 Sudley Road, Manassas, VA, Zip 20110-4418, P O Box 2610, Zip 20108-0867, tel. 703/369-8000, Erik Shannon, Chief Executive Officer
Web address: www.https://uvahealth.com/locations/Prince-William-Medical-Center-5597282

UVA HEALTH UNIVERSITY MEDICAL CENTER IVY (O, 18 beds) 2965 Ivy Rd (250 West), Charlottesville, VA, Zip 22903-9330; tel. 434/924-8245, Wendy Michelle. Horton, PharmD, FACHE, Chief Executive Officer
Web address: www.uvahealth.com/services/transitional-care-hospital

UVA HEALTH UNIVERSITY MEDICAL CENTER (O, 659 beds) 1215 Lee Street, Charlottesville, VA, Zip 22908-0001, P O Box 800809, Zip 22908-0809, tel. 434/924-0211, Wendy Michelle. Horton, PharmD, FACHE, Chief Executive Officer

Owned, leased, sponsored:	5 hospitals	850 beds
Contract-managed:	0 hospitals	0 beds
Totals:	5 hospitals	850 beds

1009: UW HEALTH (IO)
600 Highland Avenue, Madison, WI Zip 53792-0001; tel. 608/263-6400, Alan Kaplan, M.D., Chief Executive Officer
(Moderately Centralized Health System)

ILLINOIS: UW HEALTH SWEDISHAMERICAN HOSPITAL (O, 339 beds) 1401 East State Street, Rockford, IL, Zip 61104-2315; tel. 815/968-4400, Travis Andersen, President and Chief Executive Officer
Web address: https://www.uwhealth.org/locations/swedishamerican

WISCONSIN: UW HEALTH REHABILITATION HOSPITAL (O, 50 beds) 5115 North Biltmore Lane, Madison, WI, Zip 53718-2161; tel. 608/592-8100, Kenneth Bowman, Chief Executive Officer
Web address: www.uwhealth.org

UNIVERSITY HOSPITAL (O, 675 beds) 600 Highland Avenue, Madison, WI, Zip 53792-0002; tel. 608/263-6400, Alan Kaplan, M.D., Chief Executive Officer
Web address: www.uwhealth.org

Owned, leased, sponsored:	3 hospitals	1064 beds
Contract-managed:	0 hospitals	0 beds
Totals:	3 hospitals	1064 beds

For explanation of codes following names, see page B2.
★ Indicates Type III membership in the American Hospital Association.

Systems / UW Medicine

★6415: UW MEDICINE (NP)
1959 NE Pacific Street, Seattle, WA Zip 98195–0001, P O Box 356350, Zip 98195–6350, tel. 206/543–7718, Timothy H. Dellit, M.D., Chief Executive Officer
(Independent Hospital System)

WASHINGTON: UW MEDICINE/HARBORVIEW MEDICAL CENTER (C, 463 beds) 325 Ninth Avenue, Seattle, WA, Zip 98104–2499; tel. 206/744–3000, Sommer Kleweno–Walley, Chief Executive Officer
Web address: www.uwmedicine.org/Patient-Care/Locations/HMC/Pages/default.aspx

UW MEDICINE/UNIVERSITY OF WASHINGTON MEDICAL CENTER (O, 688 beds) 1959 NE Pacific Street, Seattle, WA, Zip 98195–6151; tel. 206/598–3300, Cynthia Hecker, R.N., Chief Executive Officer
Web address: www.uwmedicine.org/uw-medical-center

UW MEDICINE/VALLEY MEDICAL CENTER (C, 325 beds) 400 South 43rd Street, Renton, WA, Zip 98055–5714, P O Box 50010, Zip 98058–5010, tel. 425/228–3450, Jeannine M. Grinnell, Interim Chief Executive Officer

Owned, leased, sponsored:	1 hospitals	688 beds
Contract–managed:	2 hospitals	788 beds
Totals:	3 hospitals	1476 beds

★0128: VALLEY HEALTH SYSTEM (NP)
220 Campus Boulevard, Suite 420, Winchester, VA Zip 22601–2889, P O Box 3340, Zip 22604–2540, tel. 540/536–8024, Mark S. Nantz, FACHE, President and Chief Executive Officer
(Moderately Centralized Health System)

VIRGINIA: VALLEY HEALTH–PAGE MEMORIAL HOSPITAL (O, 25 beds) 200 Memorial Drive, Luray, VA, Zip 22835–1005; tel. 540/743–4561, N. Travis. Clark, President
Web address: www.valleyhealthlink.com/page

VALLEY HEALTH–SHENANDOAH MEMORIAL HOSPITAL (O, 25 beds) 759 South Main Street, Woodstock, VA, Zip 22664–1127; tel. 540/459–1100, N. Travis. Clark, President
Web address: www.valleyhealthlink.com/shenandoah

VALLEY HEALTH–WARREN MEMORIAL HOSPITAL (O, 36 beds) 351 Valley Health Way, Front Royal, VA, Zip 22630; tel. 540/636–0300, Jennifer Coello, Vice President, Operations and Administrator

VALLEY HEALTH–WINCHESTER MEDICAL CENTER (O, 541 beds) 1840 Amherst Street, Winchester, VA, Zip 22601–2808, P O Box 3340, Zip 22604–2540, tel. 540/536–8000, Tonya Smith, President
Web address: www.valleyhealthlink.com/WMC

WEST VIRGINIA: VALLEY HEALTH–HAMPSHIRE MEMORIAL HOSPITAL (O, 44 beds) 363 Sunrise Boulevard, Romney, WV, Zip 26757–4607; tel. 304/822–4561, Heather Sigel, Vice President Operations
Web address: www.valleyhealthlink.com/hampshire

VALLEY HEALTH–WAR MEMORIAL HOSPITAL (O, 41 beds) 1 Healthy Way, Berkeley Springs, WV, Zip 25411–7463; tel. 304/258–1234, Heather Sigel, Vice President, Operations

Owned, leased, sponsored:	6 hospitals	712 beds
Contract–managed:	0 hospitals	0 beds
Totals:	6 hospitals	712 beds

★1122: VANDALIA HEALTH (NP)
501 Morris Street, Charleston, WV Zip 25301–1300; tel. 304/388–5432, David L. Ramsey, President and Chief Executive Officer

WEST VIRGINIA: BROADDUS HOSPITAL (O, 72 beds) 1 Healthcare Drive, Philippi, WV, Zip 26416–9405, P O Box 930, Zip 26416–0930, tel. 304/457–1760, Dana L. Gould, Chief Executive Officer
Web address: www.davishealthsystem.org/

CAMC GREENBRIER VALLEY MEDICAL CENTER (O, 78 beds) 202 Maplewood Avenue, Ronceverte, WV, Zip 24970–1334, P O Box 497, Zip 24970–0497, tel. 304/647–4411, Rebecca Harless, Chief Executive Officer
Web address: www.gvmc.com

CAMC PLATEAU MEDICAL CENTER (O, 25 beds) 430 Main Street, Oak Hill, WV, Zip 25901–3455; tel. 304/469–8600, Justus Smith, Chief Executive Officer

CHARLESTON AREA MEDICAL CENTER (O, 859 beds) 501 Morris Street, Charleston, WV, Zip 25301–1300, P O Box 1547, Zip 25326–1547, tel. 304/388–5432, Glenn Crotty Jr, M.D., President and Chief Executive Officer
Web address: www.camc.org

DAVIS MEDICAL CENTER (O, 80 beds) 812 Gorman Avenue, Elkins, WV, Zip 26241–3181, P O Box 1484, Zip 26241–1484, tel. 304/636–3300, Mark Doak, Interim President
Web address: https://www.davishealthsystem.org/index

MON HEALTH MARION NEIGHBORHOOD HOSPITAL (O, 10 beds) 140 Middletown Loop, White Hall, WV, Zip 26554–8701; tel. 304/333–1150, Carla Hamner, Hospital Administrator
Web address: https://www.monhealth.com/mhmh/mhmh-home

MON HEALTH MEDICAL CENTER (O, 160 beds) 1200 J D Anderson Drive, Morgantown, WV, Zip 26505–3486; tel. 304/598–1200, David Goldberg, President and Chief Executive Officer, Mon Health System, Executive Vice President, Vandalia Health
Web address: www.mongeneral.com

MON HEALTH PRESTON MEMORIAL HOSPITAL (O, 25 beds) 150 Memorial Drive, Kingwood, WV, Zip 26537–1495; tel. 304/329–1400, Melissa Lockwood, Chief Executive Officer

MON HEALTH STONEWALL JACKSON MEMORIAL HOSPITAL (O, 70 beds) 230 Hospital Plaza, Weston, WV, Zip 26452–8558; tel. 304/269–8000, Kevin P. Stalnaker, CPA, Chief Executive Officer
Web address: https://www.monhealth.com/main/locations/mon-health-stonewall-jackson-memorial-hospital-36

WEBSTER COUNTY MEMORIAL HOSPITAL (O, 15 beds) 324 Miller Mountain Drive, Webster Springs, WV, Zip 26288–1087, P O Box 312, Zip 26288–0312, tel. 304/847–5682, William J. Dempsey, Chief Executive Officer

Owned, leased, sponsored:	10 hospitals	1394 beds
Contract–managed:	0 hospitals	0 beds
Totals:	10 hospitals	1394 beds

★0387: VANDERBILT HEALTH (NP)
1211 22nd Avenue South, Nashville, TN Zip 37232; tel. 615/322–5000, Charles Wright. Pinson, M.D., Deputy Chief Executive Officer and Chief Health System Officer
(Moderately Centralized Health System)

TENNESSEE: VANDERBILT BEDFORD HOSPITAL (O, 32 beds) 2835 Highway 231 North, Shelbyville, TN, Zip 37160–7327; tel. 931/685–5433, Travis Capers, FACHE, Chief Executive Officer, Regional Community Hospitals
Web address: www.Tennova.com

VANDERBILT TULLAHOMA HARTON HOSPITAL (O, 91 beds) 1801 North Jackson Street, Tullahoma, TN, Zip 37388–8259; tel. 931/393–3000, Richard Ellis, President
Web address: www.hartonmedicalcenter.com

VANDERBILT UNIVERSITY MEDICAL CENTER (O, 1202 beds) 1211 Medical Center Drive, Nashville, TN, Zip 37232–2102; tel. 615/322–5000, Jeffrey R. Balser, M.D., Ph.D., President and Chief Executive Officer Vanderbilt Medical Center and Dean, Vanderbilt University School of Medicine

VANDERBILT WILSON COUNTY HOSPITAL (O, 119 beds) 1411 Baddour Parkway, Lebanon, TN, Zip 37087–2513; tel. 615/444–8262, Scott McCarver, President
Web address: https://www.vanderbiltwilsoncountyhospital.com

Owned, leased, sponsored:	4 hospitals	1444 beds
Contract–managed:	0 hospitals	0 beds
Totals:	4 hospitals	1444 beds

For explanation of codes following names, see page B2.
★ Indicates Type III membership in the American Hospital Association.

Systems / Virginia Department of Mental Health

★0939: **VCU HEALTH SYSTEM (NP)**
1200 East Marshall Street, Richmond, VA Zip 23298, P O Box 980510, Zip 23298-0510, tel. 804/828-9000, Marlon Levy, M.D., Interim Chief Executive Officer
(Moderately Centralized Health System)

VIRGINIA: CHILDREN'S HOSPITAL OF RICHMOND AT VCU (O, 36 beds) 2924 Brook Road, Richmond, VA, Zip 23220-1298, 1000 E. Broad Street, Zip 23219, tel. 804/321-7474, Elias Neujahr, President
Web address: www.chrichmond.org

VCU HEALTH COMMUNITY MEMORIAL HOSPITAL (O, 210 beds) 125 Buena Vista Circle, South Hill, VA, Zip 23970-1431, P O Box 90, Zip 23970-0090, tel. 434/447-3151, Sheldon Barr, President
Web address: www.cmh-sh.org

VCU HEALTH TAPPAHANNOCK HOSPITAL (O, 16 beds) 618 Hospital Road, Tappahannock, VA, Zip 22560-5000; tel. 804/443-3311, Elizabeth J. Martin, Hospital President
Web address: https://www.riversideonline.com

VCU MEDICAL CENTER (O, 823 beds) 1250 East Marshall Street, Richmond, VA, Zip 23298-5051, P O Box 980510, Zip 23298-0510, tel. 804/828-9000, Michael Roussos, President

Owned, leased, sponsored:	4 hospitals	1085 beds
Contract-managed:	0 hospitals	0 beds
Totals:	4 hospitals	1085 beds

1041: **VERITAS COLLABORATIVE (IO)**
4024 Stirrup Creek Drive, Durham, NC Zip 27703-9464; tel. 855/875-5812, Stacie McEntyre, Chief Executive Officer

NORTH CAROLINA: VERITAS COLLABORATIVE (L, 40 beds) 4024 Stirrup Creek Drive, Durham, NC, Zip 27703-9464; tel. 919/908-9730, Cindy Skocik, Chief Operating Officer
Web address: www.https://veritascollaborative.com

VERITAS COLLABORATIVE (L, 25 beds) 615 Douglas Street, Suite 500, Durham, NC, Zip 27705-6616; tel. 919/908-9730, Becca Eckstein, Executive Director
Web address: www.https://veritascollaborative.com

Owned, leased, sponsored:	2 hospitals	65 beds
Contract-managed:	0 hospitals	0 beds
Totals:	2 hospitals	65 beds

★0299: **VIBRA HEALTHCARE (IO)**
4600 Lena Drive, Mechanicsburg, PA Zip 17055-4904; tel. 717/591-5700, Brad Hollinger, Chairman and Chief Executive Officer
(Independent Hospital System)

CALIFORNIA: BALLARD REHABILITATION HOSPITAL (O, 60 beds) 1760 West 16th Street, San Bernardino, CA, Zip 92411-1160; tel. 909/473-1200, Natalie Merckens, Chief Executive Officer
Web address: www.ballardrehab.com

SAN JOAQUIN VALLEY REHABILITATION HOSPITAL (O, 62 beds) 7173 North Sharon Avenue, Fresno, CA, Zip 93720-3329; tel. 559/436-3600, Chase Taylor, Chief Executive Officer

VIBRA HOSPITAL OF NORTHERN CALIFORNIA (O, 56 beds) 2801 Eureka Way, Redding, CA, Zip 96001-0222; tel. 530/246-9000, Emily DeFillipo, Chief Executive Officer
Web address: www.norcalrehab.com

VIBRA HOSPITAL OF SACRAMENTO (O, 58 beds) 330 Montrose Drive, Folsom, CA, Zip 95630-2720; tel. 916/351-9151, Varun Chauhan, Chief Executive Officer

COLORADO: VIBRA HOSPITAL OF DENVER (O, 71 beds) 8451 Pearl Street, Thornton, CO, Zip 80229-4804; tel. 303/288-3000, Lamar McBride, Chief Executive Officer
Web address: www.vhdenver.com

IDAHO: VIBRA HOSPITAL OF BOISE (O, 60 beds) 6651 West Franklin Road, Boise, ID, Zip 83709-0914; tel. 877/801-2244, Tammy Pettingill, Interim Chief Executive Officer

KENTUCKY: GATEWAY REHABILITATION HOSPITAL (C, 40 beds) 5940 Merchant Street, Florence, KY, Zip 41042-1158; tel. 859/426-2400, Jennifer Jones, Chief Executive Officer
Web address: www.gatewayflorence.com/

SOUTHERN KENTUCKY REHABILITATION HOSPITAL (O, 60 beds) 1300 Campbell Lane, Bowling Green, KY, Zip 42104-4162; tel. 270/594-5980, Stuart Locke, Chief Executive Officer

MASSACHUSETTS: VIBRA HOSPITAL OF SOUTHEASTERN MASSACHUSETTS (O, 90 beds) 4499 Acushnet Avenue, New Bedford, MA, Zip 02745-4707; tel. 508/995-6900, Edward B. Leary, Chief Executive Officer
Web address: www.newbedfordrehab.com

VIBRA HOSPITAL OF WESTERN MASSACHUSETTS-CENTRAL CAMPUS (O, 10 beds) 111 Huntoon Memorial Hwy, Rochdale, MA, Zip 01542-1305, 111 Huntoon Memorial Highway, Zip 1542, tel. 508/892-6000, Edward B. Leary, Chief Executive Officer
Web address: www.https://vhwmasscentral.com/

MICHIGAN: VIBRA HOSPITALS OF SOUTHEASTERN MICHIGAN-TAYLOR CAMPUS (O, 220 beds) 26400 West Outer Drive, Lincoln Park, MI, Zip 48146-2088, 1000 Telegraph Rd 2nd Fl, Taylor, Zip 48180, tel. 313/386-2000, Brooke Saunders, Vice President of Southeastern Market
Web address: www.vhsemichigan.com/

NORTH DAKOTA: VIBRA HOSPITAL OF CENTRAL DAKOTAS (O, 41 beds) 1000 18th Street NW, Mandan, ND, Zip 58554-1612; tel. 701/667-2000, Scott Schneider, Chief Executive Officer
Web address: www.vhcentraldakotas.com

VIBRA HOSPITAL OF FARGO (O, 31 beds) 5225 23rd Avenue South, 7th Floor, Fargo, ND, Zip 58103-4940; tel. 701/241-9099, Custer Huseby, Chief Executive Officer

OREGON: VIBRA SPECIALTY HOSPITAL OF PORTLAND (O, 63 beds) 10300 NE Hancock Street, Portland, OR, Zip 97220-3831; tel. 503/257-5500, Michael Kerr, Chief Executive Officer
Web address: www.vshportland.com

SOUTH CAROLINA: VIBRA HOSPITAL OF CHARLESTON (O, 42 beds) 1200 Hospital Drive, Mt. Pleasant, SC, Zip 29464; tel. 843/375-4000, Tamra Hennis, Chief Executive Officer
Web address: www.vhcharleston.com

Owned, leased, sponsored:	14 hospitals	924 beds
Contract-managed:	1 hospitals	40 beds
Totals:	15 hospitals	964 beds

0012: **VIRGINIA DEPARTMENT OF MENTAL HEALTH (NP)**
1220 Bank Street, Richmond, VA Zip 23219-3645, P O Box 1797, Zip 23218-1797, tel. 804/786-3921, Nelson Smith, Commissioner
(Independent Hospital System)

VIRGINIA: CATAWBA HOSPITAL (O, 110 beds) 5525 Catawba Hospital Drive, Catawba, VA, Zip 24070-2115, P O Box 200, Zip 24070-0200, tel. 540/375-4200, Charles Law, Ph.D., Facility Director
Web address: www.catawba.dbhds.virginia.gov

CENTRAL STATE HOSPITAL (O, 277 beds) 26317 West Washington Street, Petersburg, VA, Zip 23803-2727, P O Box 4030, Zip 23803-0030, tel. 804/524-7000, Brandi Justice, Interim Director
Web address: www.csh.dbhds.virginia.gov

COMMONWEALTH CENTER FOR CHILDREN AND ADOLESCENTS (O, 60 beds) 1355 Richmond Road, Staunton, VA, Zip 24401-9146, Box 4000, Zip 24402-4000, tel. 540/332-2100, George Newsome, Director
Web address: www.ccca.dbhds.virginia.gov

EASTERN STATE HOSPITAL (O, 300 beds) 4601 Ironbound Road, Williamsburg, VA, Zip 23188-2652; tel. 757/253-5161, Donna Moore, PsyD, Director
Web address: www.esh.dmhmrsas.virginia.gov/

For explanation of codes following names, see page B2.
★ Indicates Type III membership in the American Hospital Association.

Systems / Virginia Department of Mental Health

HIRAM W. DAVIS MEDICAL CENTER (O, 96 beds) 26317 West Washington Street, Petersburg, VA, Zip 23803-2727, P O Box 4030, Zip 23803-0030, tel. 804/524-7420, Jarvis T. Griffin, Chief Executive Officer, Facility Director

NORTHERN VIRGINIA MENTAL HEALTH INSTITUTE (O, 134 beds) 3302 Gallows Road, Falls Church, VA, Zip 22042-3398; tel. 703/207-7100, Amy Smiley, Chief Executive Officer
Web address: www.nvmhi.dbhds.virginia.gov

PIEDMONT GERIATRIC HOSPITAL (O, 135 beds) 5001 East Patrick Henry Hwy, Burkeville, VA, Zip 23922-3460, P O Box 427, Zip 23922-0427, tel. 434/767-4401, Emma L. Lowry, M.D., Acting Facility Director, Chief Executive Officer

SOUTHERN VIRGINIA MENTAL HEALTH INSTITUTE (O, 72 beds) 382 Taylor Drive, Danville, VA, Zip 24541-4023; tel. 434/799-6220, William Cook, Director
Web address: www.svmhi.dbhds.virginia.gov

SOUTHWESTERN VIRGINIA MENTAL HEALTH INSTITUTE (O, 166 beds) 340 Bagley Circle, Marion, VA, Zip 24354-3390; tel. 276/783-1200, Cynthia McClaskey, Ph.D., Director
Web address: www.swvmhi.dmhmrsas.virginia.gov/

WESTERN STATE HOSPITAL (O, 246 beds) 103 Valley Center Drive, Staunton, VA, Zip 24401-9146, P O Box 2500, Zip 24402-2500, tel. 540/332-8000, Mary Clare. Smith, Director
Web address: www.dbhds.virginia.gov

Owned, leased, sponsored:	10 hospitals	1596 beds
Contract-managed:	0 hospitals	0 beds
Totals:	10 hospitals	1596 beds

★6725: VIRTUA HEALTH (NP)
303 Lippincott Drive, 4th Floor, Marlton, NJ Zip 08053-4160; tel. 856/355-0010, Dennis W. Pullin, FACHE, President and Chief Executive Officer
(Centralized Health System)

NEW JERSEY: VIRTUA MARLTON (O, 187 beds) 90 Brick Road, Marlton, NJ, Zip 08053-2177; tel. 856/355-6000, Dennis W. Pullin, FACHE, President and Chief Executive Officer
Web address: www.virtua.org

VIRTUA MOUNT HOLLY HOSPITAL (O, 334 beds) 175 Madison Avenue, Mount Holly, NJ, Zip 08060-2099; tel. 609/267-0700, Dennis W. Pullin, FACHE, President and Chief Executive Officer
Web address: www.virtua.org

VIRTUA OUR LADY OF LOURDES HOSPITAL (O, 325 beds) 1600 Haddon Avenue, Camden, NJ, Zip 08103-3117; tel. 856/757-3500, Mark Nessel, Executive Vice President and Chief Operating Officer

VIRTUA VOORHEES (O, 402 beds) 100 Bowman Drive, Voorhees, NJ, Zip 08043-9612; tel. 856/325-3000, Dennis W. Pullin, FACHE, President and Chief Executive Officer
Web address: www.virtua.org

VIRTUA WILLINGBORO HOSPITAL (O, 169 beds) 218-A Sunset Road, Willingboro, NJ, Zip 08046-1162; tel. 609/835-2900, John Kirby, Senior Vice President, Virtua Health and President of Virtua Mount Holly and Virtua Willingboro hospitals

Owned, leased, sponsored:	5 hospitals	1417 beds
Contract-managed:	0 hospitals	0 beds
Totals:	5 hospitals	1417 beds

★6705: WAKEMED HEALTH & HOSPITALS (NP)
3000 New Bern Avenue, Raleigh, NC Zip 27610-1231; tel. 919/350-8000, Donald R. Gintzig, President and Chief Executive Officer
(Moderately Centralized Health System)

NORTH CAROLINA: WAKEMED CARY HOSPITAL (O, 208 beds) 1900 Kildaire Farm Road, Cary, NC, Zip 27518-6616; tel. 919/350-8000, Thomas J. Gough, Executive Vice President & Chief Operating Officer
Web address: www.wakemed.org

WAKEMED RALEIGH CAMPUS (O, 714 beds) 3000 New Bern Avenue, Raleigh, NC, Zip 27610-1295; tel. 919/350-8000, Rebecca Andrews, Senior Vice President and Administrator

Owned, leased, sponsored:	2 hospitals	922 beds
Contract-managed:	0 hospitals	0 beds
Totals:	2 hospitals	922 beds

★0068: WELLSPAN HEALTH (NP)
45 Monument Road, Suite 200, York, PA Zip 17403-5071; tel. 877/232-5807, Roxanna L. Gapstur, Ph.D., R.N., President and Chief Executive Officer
(Centralized Physician/Insurance Health System)

PENNSYLVANIA: WELLSPAN CHAMBERSBURG HOSPITAL (O, 286 beds) 112 North Seventh Street, Chambersburg, PA, Zip 17201-1720; tel. 717/267-3000, John P. Massimilla, FACHE, WSH Vice President and President of Wellspan Chambersburg
Web address: https://www.wellspan.org/offices-locations/wellspan-chambersburg-hospital/

WELLSPAN EPHRATA COMMUNITY HOSPITAL (O, 141 beds) 169 Martin Avenue, Ephrata, PA, Zip 17522-1724, P O Box 1002, Zip 17522-1002, tel. 717/733-0311, Tina Citro, R.N., President and Vice President Operations
Web address: https://www.wellspan.org/locations/wellspan-ephrata-community-hospital-loc0000169489

WELLSPAN GETTYSBURG HOSPITAL (O, 76 beds) 147 Gettys Street, Gettysburg, PA, Zip 17325-2534; tel. 717/334-2121, Michael Cogliano Sr, President
Web address: www.wellspan.org

WELLSPAN GOOD SAMARITAN HOSPITAL (O, 163 beds) 252 South 4th Street, Lebanon, PA, Zip 17042-1281, 169 Martin Ave, Ephrata, Zip 17522-1724, tel. 717/270-7500, Patricia F. Donley, R.N., MSN, President

WELLSPAN PHILHAVEN (O, 140 beds) 283 Butler Road, Mount Gretna, PA, Zip 17064, P O Box 550, Zip 17064-0550, tel. 717/273-8871, Mantah Kotsalos, VP & President, WellSpan Philhaven
Web address: https://www.wellspanphilhaven.org/Locations/Lebanon-County/Mt-Gretna

WELLSPAN SURGERY AND REHABILITATION HOSPITAL (O, 73 beds) 55 Monument Road, York, PA, Zip 17403-5023; tel. 717/812-6100, Carol Smith, President

WELLSPAN YORK HOSPITAL (O, 593 beds) 1001 South George Street, York, PA, Zip 17403-3645; tel. 717/851-2345, Alyssa Moyer, President
Web address: www.wellspan.org

WELLSPAN WAYNESBORO HOSPITAL (O, 53 beds) 501 East Main Street, Waynesboro, PA, Zip 17268-2394; tel. 717/765-4000, Melissa Dubrow, Vice President Wellspan Health and President WellSpan Waynesboro Hospital

Owned, leased, sponsored:	8 hospitals	1525 beds
Contract-managed:	0 hospitals	0 beds
Totals:	8 hospitals	1525 beds

★0995: WELLSTAR HEALTH SYSTEM (NP)
793 Sawyer Road, Marietta, GA Zip 30062; tel. 770/792-5012, Candice Saunders, President and Chief Executive Officer
(Centralized Health System)

GEORGIA: WELLSTAR COBB HOSPITAL (O, 405 beds) 3950 Austell Road, Austell, GA, Zip 30106-1121; tel. 470/732-4000, Eliese Bernard, President
Web address: https://www.wellstar.org/locations/hospital/cobb-hospital

WELLSTAR DOUGLAS HOSPITAL (O, 108 beds) 8954 Hospital Drive, Douglasville, GA, Zip 30134-2282; tel. 470/644-6000, Heath King, President
Web address: https://www.wellstar.org/locations/hospital/douglas-hospital

WELLSTAR KENNESTONE HOSPITAL (O, 544 beds) 677 Church Street, Marietta, GA, Zip 30060-1148; tel. 770/793-5000, Lorrie Liang, Senior Vice President and President of WellStar Kennestone and WellStar Windy Hill
Web address: https://www.wellstar.org/locations/hospital/kennestone-regional-medical-center

---

For explanation of codes following names, see page B2.
★ Indicates Type III membership in the American Hospital Association.

WELLSTAR PAULDING HOSPITAL (O, 294 beds) 2518 Jimmy Lee Smith Parkway, Hiram, GA, Zip 30141; tel. 470/644-7000, Ralph Turner, President
WELLSTAR WINDY HILL HOSPITAL (O, 39 beds) 2540 Windy Hill Road, Marietta, GA, Zip 30067-8632; tel. 770/644-1000, Lorrie Liang, Senior Vice President and President of WellStar Kennestone and WellStar Windy Hill
Web address: www.wellstar.org
WELLSTAR MCG HEALTH (O, 486 beds) 1120 15th Street, Augusta, GA, Zip 30912-0004; tel. 706/721-0211, Ralph Turner, President
Web address: https://www.augustahealth.org/
WELLSTAR NORTH FULTON HOSPITAL (O, 155 beds) 3000 Hospital Boulevard, Roswell, GA, Zip 30076-3899; tel. 770/751-2500, Jon-Paul Croom, President
Web address: https://www.wellstar.org/locations/hospital/north-fulton-hospital
WELLSTAR SPALDING REGIONAL HOSPITAL (O, 144 beds) 601 South Eighth Street, Griffin, GA, Zip 30224-4294, P O Drawer 'V', Zip 30224-1168, tel. 770/228-2721, Tamara Ison, Senior Vice President and President
WELLSTAR SYLVAN GROVE HOSPITAL (O, 19 beds) 1050 McDonough Road, Jackson, GA, Zip 30233-1599; tel. 770/775-7861, Tamara Ison, Senior Vice President and President
Web address: www.sylvangrovehospital.com
WELLSTAR WEST GEORGIA MEDICAL CENTER (O, 386 beds) 1514 Vernon Road, Lagrange, GA, Zip 30240-4131; tel. 706/882-1411, Coleman Foss, Senior Vice President and Hospital President
Web address: https://www.wellstar.org/locations/hospital/west-georgia-medical-center

Owned, leased, sponsored:	10 hospitals	2580 beds
Contract-managed:	0 hospitals	0 beds
Totals:	10 hospitals	2580 beds

★**0004: WEST TENNESSEE HEALTHCARE (NP)**
620 Skyline Drive, Jackson, TN Zip 38301-3923; tel. 731/541-5000, James E. Ross, President and Chief Executive Officer
(Centralized Physician/Insurance Health System)

TENNESSEE: JACKSON-MADISON COUNTY GENERAL HOSPITAL (O, 580 beds) 620 Skyline Drive, 117 Colonial, Medina, TN, Zip 38355, Jackson, tel. 731/541-5000, Deann Thelen, Vice President and Chief Executive Officer
Web address: https://www.wth.org/locations/jackson-madison-co-general/
PATHWAYS OF TENNESSEE (O, 25 beds) 238 Summar Drive, Jackson, TN, Zip 38301-3906; tel. 731/541-8200, Pam Henson, Executive Director
WEST TENNESSEE HEALTHCARE BOLIVAR HOSPITAL (O, 17 beds) 650 Nuckolls Road, Bolivar, TN, Zip 38008-1532, PO Box 509, Zip 38008-0509, tel. 731/658-3100, Ruby Kirby, Chief Executive Officer
Web address: www.wth.net
WEST TENNESSEE HEALTHCARE CAMDEN HOSPITAL (O, 15 beds) 175 Hospital Drive, Camden, TN, Zip 38320-1617; tel. 731/593-6300, Ruby Kirby, Chief Executive Officer
Web address: www.wth.net
WEST TENNESSEE HEALTHCARE DYERSBURG HOSPITAL (O, 115 beds) 400 East Tickle Street, Dyersburg, TN, Zip 38024-3120; tel. 731/285-2410, Scott Barber, Chief Executive Officer
Web address: www.wth.org/locations/west-tennessee-healthcare-dyersburg-hospital
WEST TENNESSEE HEALTHCARE MILAN HOSPITAL (O, 25 beds) 4039 Highland Street, Milan, TN, Zip 38358-3483; tel. 731/686-1591, Sherry Scruggs, Chief Executive Officer
Web address: www.wth.org
WEST TENNESSEE HEALTHCARE VOLUNTEER HOSPITAL (O, 22 beds) 161 Mount Pelia Road, Martin, TN, Zip 38237-3811; tel. 731/587-4261, William (Kevin) Decker, Chief Executive Officer

Owned, leased, sponsored:	7 hospitals	799 beds
Contract-managed:	0 hospitals	0 beds
Totals:	7 hospitals	799 beds

★**0119: WEST VIRGINIA UNIVERSITY HEALTH SYSTEM (NP)**
1 Medical Center, Morgantown, WV Zip 26506-8136; tel. 304/285-7150, Albert L. Wright Jr, President and Chief Executive Officer
(Moderately Centralized Health System)

MARYLAND: GARRETT REGIONAL MEDICAL CENTER (C, 53 beds) 251 North Fourth Street, Oakland, MD, Zip 21550-1375; tel. 301/533-4000, Mark G. Boucot, FACHE, President and Chief Executive Officer
OHIO: WVU MEDICINE–BARNESVILLE HOSPITAL (C, 25 beds) 639 West Main Street, Barnesville, OH, Zip 43713-1039, P O Box 309, Zip 43713-0309, tel. 740/425-3941, Stacey Armstrong, Interim President
Web address: www.https://wvumedicine.org/barnesville/
WVU MEDICINE–HARRISON COMMUNITY HOSPITAL (O, 25 beds) 951 East Market Street, Cadiz, OH, Zip 43907-9799; tel. 740/942-4631, Stacey Armstrong, Interim President
Web address: www.harrisoncommunity.com
PENNSYLVANIA: WVU MEDICINE UNIONTOWN HOSPITAL (C, 145 beds) 500 West Berkeley Street, Uniontown, PA, Zip 15401-5596; tel. 724/430-5000, Carrie Willetts, President & Chief Executive Officer
WEST VIRGINIA: BERKELEY MEDICAL CENTER (O, 190 beds) 2500 Hospital Drive, Martinsburg, WV, Zip 25401-3402; tel. 304/264-1000, Dean Thomas, FACHE, President and Chief Executive Officer
Web address: www.https://wvumedicine.org/berkeley/
BRAXTON COUNTY MEMORIAL HOSPITAL (O, 25 beds) 100 Hoylman DR, Gassaway, WV, Zip 26624-9318, 100 Hoylman Drive, Zip 26624-9318, tel. 304/364-5156, John C. Forester, Interim President
CAMDEN CLARK MEDICAL CENTER (O, 284 beds) 800 Garfield Avenue, Parkersburg, WV, Zip 26101-5378, P O Box 718, Zip 26102-0718, tel. 304/424-2111, Sean Smith, President and Chief Executive Officer
Web address: www.https://wvumedicine.org/camden-clark/
GRANT MEMORIAL HOSPITAL (O, 25 beds) 117 Hospital Drive, Petersburg, WV, Zip 26847-9566, P O Box 1019, Zip 26847-1019, tel. 304/257-1026, John B. Sylvia, President and Chief Executive Officer
Web address: www.grantmemorial.com
JACKSON GENERAL HOSPITAL (O, 25 beds) 122 Pinnell Street, Ripley, WV, Zip 25271-9101, P O Box 720, Zip 25271-0720, tel. 304/372-2731, Candace N. Miller, President and Chief Executive Officer
Web address: www.https://wvumedicine.org/jackson-general-hospital/
JEFFERSON MEDICAL CENTER (O, 25 beds) 300 South Preston Street, Ranson, WV, Zip 25438-1631; tel. 304/728-1600, Dean Thomas, FACHE, President and Chief Executive Officer
PRINCETON COMMUNITY HOSPITAL (C, 164 beds) 122 12th Street, Princeton, WV, Zip 24740-2352, P O Box 1369, Zip 24740-1369, tel. 304/487-7000, Karen L. Bowling, MSN, R.N., President and Chief Executive Officer
Web address: www.pchonline.org
REYNOLDS MEMORIAL HOSPITAL (O, 94 beds) 800 Wheeling Avenue, Glen Dale, WV, Zip 26038-1697; tel. 304/845-3211, Tony Martinelli, PharmD, President and Chief Executive Officer
ST. JOSEPH'S HOSPITAL (O, 41 beds) 1 Amalia Drive, Buckhannon, WV, Zip 26201-2276; tel. 304/473-2000, Skip Gjolberg Jr, FACHE, President and Chief Executive Officer
Web address: www.stj.net
SUMMERSVILLE REGIONAL MEDICAL CENTER (L, 25 beds) 400 Fairview Heights Road, Summersville, WV, Zip 26651-9308; tel. 304/872-2891, John C. Forester, Interim President
Web address: https://www.summersvilleregional.org/
THOMAS MEMORIAL HOSPITAL (C, 254 beds) 4605 MacCorkle Avenue SW, South Charleston, WV, Zip 25309-1398; tel. 304/766-3600, J. Gregory. Rosencrance, M.D., President and Chief Executive Officer
UNITED HOSPITAL CENTER (O, 264 beds) 327 Medical Park Drive, Bridgeport, WV, Zip 26330-9006; tel. 681/342-1000, David F. Hess, M.D., President and Chief Executive Officer
Web address: www.https://wvumedicine.org/united-hospital-center/
WVU MEDICINE POTOMAC VALLEY HOSPITAL (O, 25 beds) 100 Pin Oak Lane, Keyser, WV, Zip 26726-5908; tel. 304/597-3500, Mark G. Boucot, FACHE, President and Chief Executive Officer
Web address: www.https://wvumedicine.org/potomac-valley-hospital/

Systems / West Virginia University Health System

WEST VIRGINIA UNIVERSITY HOSPITALS (O, 851 beds) 1 Medical Center Drive, Morgantown, WV, Zip 26506-4749; tel. 304/598-4000, Michael Grace, Ed.D., FACHE, President

WETZEL COUNTY HOSPITAL (L, 58 beds) 3 East Benjamin Drive, New Martinsville, WV, Zip 26155-2758; tel. 304/455-8000, Tony Martinelli, PharmD, President and Chief Executive Officer
Web address: www.wetzelcountyhospital.com

WHEELING HOSPITAL (C, 223 beds) 1 Medical Park, Wheeling, WV, Zip 26003-6379; tel. 304/243-3000, Douglass Harrison, Chief Executive Officer
Web address: www.wheelinghospital.org

Owned, leased, sponsored:	14 hospitals	1957 beds
Contract-managed:	6 hospitals	864 beds
Totals:	20 hospitals	2821 beds

★0468: WHITE RIVER HEALTH SYSTEM (NP)

1710 Harrison Street, Batesville, AR Zip 72501-7303; tel. 870/262-1200, Chris Steel, Interim Chief Executive Officer
(Independent Hospital System)

ARKANSAS: STONE COUNTY MEDICAL CENTER (O, 25 beds) 2106 East Main Street, Mountain View, AR, Zip 72560-6439, P O Box 510, Zip 72560-0510, tel. 870/269-4361, Kathy Thomas, MSN, R.N., Vice President/Chief Operating Officer
Web address: https://www.whiteriverhealthsystem.com/scmc

WHITE RIVER HEALTH (O, 226 beds) 1710 Harrison Street, Batesville, AR, Zip 72501-7303, P O Box 2197, Zip 72503-2197, tel. 870/262-1200, Chris Steel, Interim Chief Executive Officer

Owned, leased, sponsored:	2 hospitals	251 beds
Contract-managed:	0 hospitals	0 beds
Totals:	2 hospitals	251 beds

0646: WHITTIER HEALTH NETWORK (IO)

25 Railroad Square, Haverhill, MA Zip 01832-5721; tel. 978/556-5858, Alfred J. Arcidi, M.D., President
(Independent Hospital System)

MASSACHUSETTS: WHITTIER PAVILION (O, 65 beds) 76 Summer Street, Haverhill, MA, Zip 01830-5814; tel. 978/373-8222, Alfred J. Arcidi, M.D., Chief Executive Officer
Web address: www.whittierhealth.com

WHITTIER REHABILITATION HOSPITAL (O, 60 beds) 150 Flanders Road, Westborough, MA, Zip 01581-1017; tel. 508/871-2000, Rebecca Roman, Administrator

WHITTIER REHABILITATION HOSPITAL (O, 60 beds) 145 Ward Hill Avenue, Bradford, MA, Zip 01835-6928; tel. 978/372-8000, Robert Iannaco, Administrator
Web address: www.whittierhealth.com

Owned, leased, sponsored:	3 hospitals	185 beds
Contract-managed:	0 hospitals	0 beds
Totals:	3 hospitals	185 beds

1945: WILLIS KNIGHTON HEALTH (NP)

2600 Greenwood Road, Shreveport, LA Zip 71103-3908; tel. 318/212-4000, Jaf Fielder, President and Chief Executive Officer
(Moderately Centralized Health System)

LOUISIANA: DE SOTO REGIONAL HEALTH SYSTEM (C, 10 beds) 207 Jefferson Street, Mansfield, LA, Zip 71052-2603, P O Box 1636, Zip 71052-1636, tel. 318/872-4610, Todd Eppler, FACHE, Chief Executive Officer

SPRINGHILL MEDICAL CENTER (C, 32 beds) 2001 Doctors Drive, Springhill, LA, Zip 71075-4526, P O Box 920, Zip 71075-0920, tel. 318/539-1000, Peter B. Johnson, Chief Executive Officer
Web address: www.smccare.com

WILLIS KNIGHTON NORTH (O, 813 beds) 2600 Greenwood Road, Shreveport, LA, Zip 71103-3908, P O Box 32600, Zip 71130-2600, tel. 318/212-4000, Jaf Fielder, President and Chief Executive Officer

Owned, leased, sponsored:	1 hospitals	813 beds
Contract-managed:	2 hospitals	42 beds
Totals:	3 hospitals	855 beds

1004: WMCHEALTH (NP)

100 Woods Road, Valhalla, NY Zip 10595-1530; tel. 914/493-7000, Michael D. Israel, President and Chief Executive Officer
(Moderately Centralized Health System)

NEW YORK: BON SECOURS COMMUNITY HOSPITAL (O, 143 beds) 160 East Main Street, Port Jervis, NY, Zip 12771-2245; tel. 184/499-0381, Mary Leahy, M.D., Chief Executive Officer
Web address: www.bonsecourscommunityhosp.org

GOOD SAMARITAN REGIONAL MEDICAL CENTER (O, 308 beds) 255 Lafayette Avenue, Suffern, NY, Zip 10901-4869; tel. 845/368-5000, Mary Leahy, M.D., Chief Executive Officer
Web address: www.goodsamhosp.org

HEALTH ALLIANCE HOSPITAL-BROADWAY CAMPUS (O, 150 beds) 396 Broadway, Kingston, NY, Zip 12401-4692; tel. 845/331-3131, Michael Doyle, M.D., Executive Director and Chief Medical Officer

HEALTH ALLIANCE HOSPITAL-MARY'S AVENUE CAMPUS (O, 105 beds) 105 Marys Avenue, Kingston, NY, Zip 12401-5894; tel. 845/338-2500, Michael Doyle, M.D., Executive Director and Chief Medical Officer
Web address: www.hahv.org

MARGARETVILLE HOSPITAL (O, 15 beds) 42084 State Highway 28, Margaretville, NY, Zip 12455-2820; tel. 845/586-2631, Edward McNamara, Executive Director
Web address: www.margaretvillehospital.org

ST. ANTHONY COMMUNITY HOSPITAL (O, 60 beds) 15 Maple Avenue, Warwick, NY, Zip 10990-1028; tel. 845/986-2276, Mary Leahy, M.D., Chief Executive Officer
Web address: www.stanthonycommunityhosp.org

WESTCHESTER MEDICAL CENTER (O, 915 beds) 100 Woods Road, Valhalla, NY, Zip 10595-1530; tel. 914/493-7000, Michael D. Israel, President and Chief Executive Officer

Owned, leased, sponsored:	7 hospitals	1696 beds
Contract-managed:	0 hospitals	0 beds
Totals:	7 hospitals	1696 beds

★0157: YALE NEW HAVEN HEALTH (NP)

789 Howard Avenue, New Haven, CT Zip 06519-1304; tel. 203/688-2608, Christopher M. O'Connor, Chief Executive Officer
(Centralized Physician/Insurance Health System)

CONNECTICUT: BRIDGEPORT HOSPITAL (O, 470 beds) 267 Grant Street, Bridgeport, CT, Zip 06610-2805, P O Box 5000, Zip 06610-0120, tel. 203/384-3000, Anne Diamond, JD, President

GREENWICH HOSPITAL (O, 206 beds) 5 Perryridge Road, Greenwich, CT, Zip 06830-4697; tel. 203/863-3000, Diane P. Kelly, R.N., President
Web address: https://www.greenwichhospital.org/

LAWRENCE + MEMORIAL HOSPITAL (O, 252 beds) 365 Montauk Avenue, New London, CT, Zip 06320-4769; tel. 860/442-0711, Richard Lisitano, President
Web address: www.lmhospital.org

YALE NEW HAVEN HOSPITAL (O, 1481 beds) 20 York Street, New Haven, CT, Zip 06510-3202; tel. 203/688-4242, Katherine Heilpern, M.D., President

RHODE ISLAND: WESTERLY HOSPITAL (O, 87 beds) 25 Wells Street, Westerly, RI, Zip 02891-2934; tel. 401/596-6000, Richard Lisitano, President
Web address: www.westerlyhospital.org

Owned, leased, sponsored:	5 hospitals	2496 beds
Contract-managed:	0 hospitals	0 beds
Totals:	5 hospitals	2496 beds

For explanation of codes following names, see page B2.
★ Indicates Type III membership in the American Hospital Association.

Headquarters of Health Care Systems

Geographically

United States

ALABAMA

Birmingham: BRADFORD HEALTH SERVICES 2101 Magnolia Avenue South, Suite 518, Zip 35205-2853; tel. 205/251-7753; Mike Rickman, President and Chief Executive Officer, p. B27

★ ENCOMPASS HEALTH CORPORATION 9001 Liberty Parkway, Zip 35242-7509; tel. 205/967-7116; Mark J. Tarr, President and Chief Executive Officer, p. B51

NOLAND HEALTH SERVICES, INC. 600 Corporate Parkway, Suite 100, Zip 35242-5451; tel. 205/783-8484; Barbara Estep, Chief Executive Officer, p. B94

★ UAB HEALTH SYSTEM 500 22nd Street South, Suite 408, Zip 35233-3110; tel. 205/975-5362; Dawn Bulgarella, Chief Executive Officer, p. B136

Evergreen: GILLIARD HEALTH SERVICES 101 Crestview Avenue, Zip 36401-3333; tel. 251/578-0184; Tom McLendon, President and Chief Executive Officer, p. B61

Guntersville: MARSHALL HEALTH SYSTEM 227 Britany Road, Zip 35976-5766; tel. 256/894-6615; Christopher Rush, President, p. B81

Huntsville: HUNTSVILLE HOSPITAL HEALTH SYSTEM 101 Sivley Road SW, Zip 35801-4421; tel. 256/265-1000; Jeff Samz, Chief Executive Officer, p. B71

Mobile: ★ ALTAPOINTE HEALTH SYSTEMS 5750-A Southland Drive, Zip 36693-3316; tel. 251/450-2211; J. Tuerk. Schlesinger, Chief Executive Officer, p. B10

INFIRMARY HEALTH SYSTEM 5 Mobile Infirmary Circle, Zip 36607-3513; tel. 251/435-5500; D Mark. Nix, President and Chief Executive Officer, p. B72

★ USA HEALTH 2451 University Hospital Drive, Zip 36617-2300, 2451 University Hospital Drive, Suite 2110, 36617-2238, tel. 251/471-7000; Owen Bailey, Chief Executive Officer and Senior Associate Vice President for Medical Affairs, p. B149

Montgomery: BAPTIST HEALTH 301 Brown Springs Road, Zip 36117-7005; tel. 334/273-4400; W Russell. Tyner, President and Chief Executive Officer, p. B21

Tuscaloosa: DCH HEALTH SYSTEM 809 University Boulevard East, Zip 35401-2029; tel. 205/759-7111; Katrina Keefer, Chief Executive Officer, p. B44

ARIZONA

Flagstaff: ★ NORTHERN ARIZONA HEALTHCARE 1200 North Beaver Street, Zip 86001-3118; tel. 928/779-3366; David Cheney, Chief Executive Officer, p. B95

Phoenix: ★ BANNER HEALTH 2901 North Central Avenue, Suite 160, Zip 85012-2702; tel. 602/747-4000; Peter S. Fine, Chief Executive Officer, p. B20

Scottsdale: ★ HONORHEALTH 8125 North Hayden Road, Zip 85258-2463; tel. 480/882-4000; Todd LaPorte, Chief Executive Officer, p. B70

ARKANSAS

Batesville: ★ WHITE RIVER HEALTH SYSTEM 1710 Harrison Street, Zip 72501-7303; tel. 870/262-1200; Chris Steel, Interim Chief Executive Officer, p. B154

Blytheville: ★ MISSISSIPPI COUNTY HOSPITAL SYSTEM 1520 North Division Street, Zip 72315-1448, P O Box 108, 72316-0108, tel. 870/838-7300; Bryan Hargis, Chief Executive Officer, p. B89

Jonesboro: ★ ST. BERNARDS HEALTHCARE 225 East Washington Avenue, Zip 72401-3111; tel. 870/207-7300; Chris B. Barber, President and Chief Executive Officer, p. B126

Little Rock: ★ BAPTIST HEALTH 9601 Baptist Health Drive, Zip 72205-6321; tel. 501/202-2000; Troy R. Wells, Chief Executive Officer, p. B22

CALIFORNIA

Alhambra: AHMC HEALTHCARE 55 South Raymond Avenue, Suite 105, Zip 91801-7101; tel. 626/457-7400; Jonathan Wu, President and Chairman, p. B8

Corona: SIGNATURE HEALTHCARE SERVICES 4238 Green River Road, Zip 92880-1669; tel. 951/549-8032; Soon K. Kim, President and Chief Executive Officer, p. B123

Covina: ★ EMANATE HEALTH 210 West San Bernardino Road, Zip 91723-1515; tel. 626/331-7331; Roger Sharma, President and Chief Executive Officer, p. B50

El Segundo: PIPELINE HEALTH 898 North Pacific Coast Highway Suite 700, Zip 90245-2742; tel. 310/356-0550; Andrei Soran, Chief Executive Officer, p. B107

Escondido: ★ PALOMAR HEALTH 2125 Citracado Pkwy Ste 300, Zip 92029-4159, 2125 Citracado Parkway, Suite 300, 92029-4159, tel. 760/740-6393; Diane Hansen, Chief Executive Officer, p. B103

Fountain Valley: MEMORIALCARE 17360 Brookhurst Street, Zip 92708-3720, P O Box 1428, Long Beach, 90801-1428, tel. 714/377-2900; Barry S. Arbuckle, President and Chief Executive Officer, p. B86

Fresno: COMMUNITY MEDICAL CENTERS 1560 E Shaw, Zip 93710, P O Box 1232, 93715-1232, tel. 559/459-6000; Craig S. Castro, President and Chief Executive Officer, p. B41

Glendale: AMERICAN HEALTHCARE SYSTEMS 505 North Brand Boulevard Suite 1110, Zip 91203-3932; tel. 818/646-9933; Michael Sarian, Chairman and Chief Executive Officer, p. B10

Hemet: PHYSICIANS FOR HEALTHY HOSPITALS 1117 East Devonshire Avenue, Zip 92543-3083; tel. 951/652-2811; Joel M. Bergenfeld, Chief Executive Officer, p. B106

Irvine: ALECTO HEALTHCARE 16310 Bake Parkway, Suite 200, Zip 92618-4684; tel. 949/783-3988; Lex Reddy, Chief Executive Officer, p. B8

Loma Linda: ★ LOMA LINDA UNIVERSITY ADVENTIST HEALTH SCIENCES CENTER 11175 Campus Street, Suite 11006, Zip 92350-1700, 11175 Campus Street, 92350-1700, tel. 909/558-7572; Richard H. Hart, President and Chief Executive Officer, p. B80

Los Angeles: ★ KECK MEDICINE OF USC 1510 San Pablo Street, Suite 600, Zip 90033-5405; tel. 323/442-8500; Rodney B. Hanners, Chief Executive Officer, p. B76

LOS ANGELES COUNTY–DEPARTMENT OF HEALTH SERVICES 313 North Figueroa Street, Room 912, Zip 90012-2691; tel. 213/240-8101; Christina R. Ghaly, Director, p. B80

PROSPECT MEDICAL HOLDINGS 10780 California Route 2 #400, Zip 90025; tel. 714/796-5900; Mitchell Lew, President, p. B110

Oakland: ★ KAISER FOUNDATION HOSPITALS 1 Kaiser Plaza, 27th Floor – Office #2743, Zip 94612-3610; tel. 510/271-5910; Gregory A. Adams, Chief Executive Officer and Chairman, p. B74

★ UNIVERSITY OF CALIFORNIA SYSTEMWIDE ADMINISTRATION 1111 Franklin Street, 11th Floor, Zip 94607-5200; tel. 510/987-9071; Tam Ma, Associate Vice President, Health Policy and Regulatory Affairs, p. B145

Ontario: PRIME HEALTHCARE 3300 East Guasti Road, Zip 91761-8655; tel. 909/235-4400; Prem Reddy, Chairman, President and Chief Executive Officer, p. B108

Palo Alto: ★ STANFORD HEALTH CARE 300 Pasteur Drive, Zip 94304-2299; tel. 650/723-4000; David Entwistle, President and Chief Executive Officer, p. B127

Roseville: ★ ADVENTIST HEALTH 1 Adventist Health Way, Zip 95661-3266, P O Box 619002, 95661-9002, tel. 916/406-0000; Kerry Heinrich, Chief Executive Officer, p. B6

Sacramento: ★ SUTTER HEALTH 2200 River Plaza Drive, Zip 95833-4134; tel. 916/887-0000; Warner Thomas, President and Chief Executive Officer, p. B129

San Diego: ★ SCRIPPS HEALTH 4275 Campus Point Court CP112, Zip 92121-1513, 4275 Campus Point Court, 92121-1513, tel. 858/678-7200; Chris D. Van Gorder, President and Chief Executive Officer, p. B118

Headquarters of Health Care Systems / Geographically

★ SHARP HEALTHCARE 8695 Spectrum Center Boulevard, Zip 92123–1489; tel. 858/499–4000; Christopher Howard, President and Chief Executive Officer, p. B122

San Leandro: ★ ALAMEDA HEALTH SYSTEM 15400 Foothill Boulevard, Zip 94578–1009; tel. 510/437–8500; James E.T. Jackson, Chief Executive Officer, p. B8

Santa Ana: KPC HEALTHCARE, INC. 1301 North Tustin Avenue, Zip 92705–8619; tel. 714/953–3652; Peter R. Baronoff, Chief Executive Officer and Managing Director, p. B76

Santa Barbara: ★ COTTAGE HEALTH 400 West Pueblo Street, Santa Barbara Cottage Hospital, Zip 93105–4353, P O Box 689, 93102–0689, tel. 805/569–7290; Ronald C. Werft, President and Chief Executive Officer, p. B42

Santa Fe Springs: COLLEGE HEALTH ENTERPRISES 11627 Telegraph Road, Suite 200, Zip 90670–6814; tel. 562/923–9449; Barry J. Weiss, President, p. B34

Truckee: ★ TAHOE FOREST HEALTH SYSTEM 10121 Pine Avenue, Zip 96161–4835; tel. 530/587–6011; Louis James. Ward, Acting Chief Executive Officer, p. B130

Ventura: COMMUNITY MEMORIAL HEALTH SYSTEM 147 North Brent Street, Zip 93003–2809; tel. 805/652–5011; Mick Zdeblick, Chief Executive Officer, p. B41

Walnut Creek: ★ JOHN MUIR HEALTH 1400 Treat Boulevard, Zip 94597–2142; tel. 925/941–2100; Michael S. Thomas, President and Chief Executive Officer, p. B74

West Hollywood: ★ CEDARS–SINAI HEALTH SYSTEM 8700 Beverly Boulevard, Zip 90048–1865, Box 48750, Los Angeles, 90048–0750, tel. 310/423–5000; Thomas M. Priselac, President and Chief Executive Officer, p. B31

Whittier: ★ PIH HEALTH 12401 Washington Boulevard, Zip 90602–1006; tel. 562/698–0811; James R. West, President and Chief Executive Officer, p. B106

COLORADO

Alamosa: ★ SAN LUIS VALLEY HEALTH 106 Blanca Avenue, Zip 81101–2340; tel. 719/589–2511; Konnie Martin, President and Chief Executive Officer, p. B115

Aurora: CHILDREN'S HOSPITAL COLORADO 13123 East 16th Avenue, Zip 80045–7106; tel. 800/624–6553; Jena Hausmann, President and Chief Executive Officer, p. B32

★ UCHEALTH 12401 East 17th Avenue, Mail Stop F417, Zip 80045–2548; tel. 970/495–7000; Elizabeth B. Concordia, President and Chief Executive Officer, p. B136

CONNECTICUT

Danbury: ★ NUVANCE HEALTH 24 Hospital Avenue, Zip 06810–6099; tel. 203/739–7066; John M. Murphy, President and Chief Executive Officer, p. B97

Hartford: CONNECTICUT DEPARTMENT OF MENTAL HEALTH AND ADDICTION SERVICES 410 Capitol Avenue, Zip 06106–1367, P O Box 341431, 06134–1431, tel. 860/418–7000; Nancy Navarretta, Acting Commissioner, p. B41

★ HARTFORD HEALTHCARE 1 State Street, 19th Floor, Zip 6103; tel. 860/263–4100; Jeffrey A. Flaks, President and Chief Executive Officer, p. B63

New Haven: ★ YALE NEW HAVEN HEALTH 789 Howard Avenue, Zip 06519–1304; tel. 203/688–2608; Christopher M. O'Connor, Chief Executive Officer, p. B154

DELAWARE

Wilmington: ★ CHRISTIANACARE 501 West 14th Street, Zip 19801–1013, P O Box 1668, 19899–1668, tel. 302/428–2570; Janice E. Nevin, President and Chief Executive Officer, p. B32

DISTRICT OF COLUMBIA

Washington: BRIDGEPOINT HEALTHCARE 4601 Martin Luther King Jr Avenue Southwest Suite 244, Zip 20032–1131; tel. 603/570–4888; Marc C. Ferrell, President and Chief Executive Officer, p. B27

★ DEPARTMENT OF DEFENSE, HEALTH AFFAIRS 1200 Defense Pentagon, Pentagon 3E1070, Zip 20301; tel. 703/697–2111; Seileen Mullen, Acting Assistant Secretary of Defense for Health Affairs, p. B44

★ DEPARTMENT OF THE AIR FORCE 1780 Air Force Pentagon, Room 4E114, Zip 20330–1420; tel. 703/692–6800, Lieutenant General, Robert I. Miller, Surgeon General, p. B44

★ DEPARTMENT OF VETERANS AFFAIRS 810 Vermont Ave Northwest, Zip 20420–0001; tel. 202/273–5781, Honorable, Robert Wilkie, Secretary, p. B45

★ UNITED STATES COAST GUARD 2100 Second Street SW, MS–7902, Zip 20024–5100; tel. 202/372–4500, Rear Admiral, Dana Thomas, Director, Health, Safety & Work–Life Chief Medical Officer, p. B139

FLORIDA

Altamonte Springs: ★ ADVENTHEALTH 900 Hope Way, Zip 32714–1502; tel. 407/357–1000; Terry Shaw, President and Chief Executive Officer, p. B5

Clearwater: ★ BAYCARE HEALTH SYSTEM 2985 Drew Street, Zip 33759–3012; tel. 727/820–8200; Stephanie Conners, President and Chief Executive Officer, p. B23

Coral Gables: ★ BAPTIST HEALTH SOUTH FLORIDA 6855 Red Road, Suite 600, Zip 33143–3632; tel. 786/662–7111; Albert Leon. Boulenger, President and Chief Executive Officer, p. B22

Fort Lauderdale: ★ BROWARD HEALTH 1800 NW 49th Street, Zip 33309–3092; tel. 954/355–4400; Shane Strum, President and Chief Executive Officer, p. B28

Fort Myers: ★ LEE HEALTH 9800 South Healthpark Drive #405, Zip 33908–7603, 2776 Cleveland Avenue, 33901–5864, tel. 239/343–2000; Lawrence Antonucci, President and Chief Executive Officer, p. B77

Gainesville: ★ UF HEALTH SHANDS 1600 SW Archer Road, Zip 32610–0326; tel. 352/733–1500; Stephen J. Motew, President and System Chief Executive Officer, p. B137

Hollywood: ★ MEMORIAL HEALTHCARE SYSTEM 3501 Johnson Street, Zip 33021–5421; tel. 954/987–2000; David Smith, Interim Chief Executive Officer, p. B86

Jacksonville: ★ BAPTIST HEALTH 841 Prudential Drive, Suite 1601, Zip 32207–8202; tel. 904/202–2000; Michael A. Mayo, President and Chief Executive Officer, p. B21

★ NEMOURS CHILDREN HEALTH 10140 Centurion Parkway North, Zip 32256–0532; tel. 904/697–4100; R. Lawrence. Moss, President and Chief Executive Officer, p. B92

Lauderdale Lakes: CATHOLIC HEALTH SERVICES 4790 North State Road 7, Zip 33319–5860; tel. 954/484–1515; Joseph M. Catania, President and Chief Executive Officer, p. B30

Orlando: ORLANDO HEALTH 1414 Kuhl Avenue, Zip 32806–2093; tel. 321/843–7000; David W. Strong, President and Chief Executive Officer, p. B101

Pensacola: ★ BAPTIST HEALTH CARE CORPORATION 125 Baptist Way, Suite 6A, Zip 32503, P O Box 17500, 32522–7500, tel. 850/434–4011; Mark T. Faulkner, President and Chief Executive Officer, p. B22

Rockledge: HEALTH FIRST, INC. 6450 US Highway 1, Zip 32955–5747; tel. 321/434–7000; Terry Forde, Chief Executive Officer, p. B68

Sarasota: SARASOTA MEMORIAL HEALTH CARE SYSTEM 1540 South Tamiami Trail, Zip 34239–2930; tel. 941/917–7322; David Verinder, Chief Executive Officer, p. B116

Tampa: OGLETHORPE RECOVERY AND BEHAVIORAL HOSPITALS 201 North Franklin Street, Zip 33602–5182; tel. 813/978–1933; John Picciano, Chief Executive Officer, p. B99

SHRINERS HOSPITALS FOR CHILDREN 2900 North Rocky Point Drive, Zip 33607–1435, P O Box 31356, 33631–3356, tel. 813/281–0300; John P. McCabe, Executive Vice President, p. B122

Windermere: ★ UNITED MEDICAL CORPORATION 603 Main Street, Zip 34786–3548, P O Box 1100, 34786–1100, tel. 407/876–2200; Donald R. Dizney, Chairman and Chief Executive Officer, p. B138

GEORGIA

Albany: ★ PHOEBE PUTNEY HEALTH SYSTEM 417 West Third Avenue, Zip 31701–1943; tel. 229/312–1000; Scott Steiner, Chief Executive Officer, p. B106

Alpharetta: PERIMETER HEALTHCARE 2520 Northwinds Parkway Suite 550, Zip 30009–2236; tel. 470/554–7902; James R. Laughlin, President and Chief Executive Officer, p. B105

Atlanta: ★ EMORY HEALTHCARE 1440 Clifton Road NE, Suite 400, Zip 30322–1102; tel. 404/778–5000; Joon Sup. Lee, Chief Executive Officer, p. B51

★ NORTHSIDE HEALTHCARE SYSTEM 1000 Johnson Ferry Road NE, Zip 30342–1611; tel. 404/851–8000; Robert Quattrocchi, President and Chief Executive Officer, p. B96

Blairsville: UNION GENERAL HOSPITAL, INC. 35 Hospital Road, Zip 30512–3139; tel. 706/745–2111; Kevin Bierschenk, Chief Executive Officer, p. B138

Brunswick: ★ SOUTHEAST GEORGIA HEALTH SYSTEM 2415 Parkwood Drive, Zip 31520–4722, P O Box 1518, 31521–1518, tel. 912/466–7000; Scott Raynes, Chief Executive Officer, p. B124

Carrollton: ★ TANNER HEALTH SYSTEM 705 Dixie Street, Zip 30117–3818; tel. 770/836–9580; Loy M. Howard, President and Chief Executive Officer, p. B130

Headquarters of Health Care Systems / Geographically

Gainesville: ★ NORTHEAST GEORGIA HEALTH SYSTEM 743 Spring Street NE, Zip 30501-3715; tel. 770/219-9000; Carol H. Burrell, President and Chief Executive Officer, p. B95

Lilburn: LIFEBRITE HOSPITAL GROUP, LLC 3970 Five Forks Trickum Road SW Suite A, Zip 30047-2339; tel. 678/505-9657; Christian A. Fletcher, Chief Executive Officer, p. B78

Marietta: ★ WELLSTAR HEALTH SYSTEM 793 Sawyer Road, Zip 30062; tel. 770/792-5012; Candice Saunders, President and Chief Executive Officer, p. B152

Rome: FLOYD HEALTHCARE MANAGEMENT 304 Turner McCall Boulevard, Zip 30165-5621, P O Box 233, 30162-0233, tel. 706/509-5000; Kurt Stuenkel, President and Chief Executive Officer, p. B59

Roswell: PIEDMONT HEALTHCARE 1800 Howell Mill Road NW, Suite 850, Zip 30076, Atlanta, tel. 404/425-1314; Kevin Brown, President and Chief Executive Officer, p. B106

Thomasville: ★ ARCHBOLD MEDICAL CENTER 910 South Broad Street, Zip 31792-6113; tel. 229/228-2000; Darcy Craven, President and Chief Executive Officer, p. B11

Tifton: ★ TIFT REGIONAL HEALTH SYSTEM 901 East 18th Street, Zip 31794-3648; tel. 229/353-6100; Christopher Dorman, President and Chief Executive Officer, p. B134

Valdosta: SOUTH GEORGIA MEDICAL CENTER 2501 North Patterson Street, Zip 31602-1735, P O Box 1727, 31603-1727, tel. 229/333-1000; Ronald Dean, President and Chief Executive Officer, p. B124

HAWAII

Honolulu: ★ HAWAII HEALTH SYSTEMS CORPORATION 3675 Kilauea Avenue, Zip 96816-2333; tel. 808/733-4151; Edward Chu, President and Chief Executive Officer, p. B63

HAWAII PACIFIC HEALTH 55 Merchant Street, Zip 96813-4306; tel. 808/949-9355; Raymond P. Vara Jr, President and Chief Executive Officer, p. B63

★ QUEEN'S HEALTH SYSTEM 1301 Punchbowl Street, Zip 96813-2402; tel. 808/691-1000; Jill Hoggard Green, President and Chief Executive Officer, p. B112

IDAHO

Boise: ★ ST. LUKE'S HEALTH SYSTEM 190 East Bannock Street, Zip 83712-6241; tel. 208/381-4200; Chris Roth, President and Chief Executive Officer, p. B127

ILLINOIS

Carbondale: SOUTHERN ILLINOIS HEALTHCARE 1239 East Main Street, Zip 62901-3114, P O Box 3988, 62902-3988, tel. 618/457-5200; John Antes, President and Chief Executive Officer, p. B124

Chicago: ★ COMMONSPIRIT HEALTH 444 West Lake Street Suite 2500, Zip 60606-0097; tel. 312/741-7000; Wright L. Lassiter III, Chief Executive Officer, p. B35

★ COOK COUNTY HEALTH AND HOSPITALS SYSTEM 1900 West Polk Street, Suite 220, Zip 60612-3723; tel. 312/864-6820; Erik Mikaitis, Interim Chief Executive Officer, p. B41

NATIONAL SURGICAL HEALTHCARE 250 South Wacker Drive, Suite 500, Zip 60606-5897; tel. 312/627-8400; David Crane, Chief Executive Officer, p. B91

★ NORTHWESTERN MEMORIAL HEALTHCARE 251 East Huron Street, Zip 60611-2908; tel. 312/926-2000; Howard Chrisman, President and Chief Executive Officer, p. B96

★ RUSH UNIVERSITY SYSTEM FOR HEALTH 1653 West Congress Parkway, Zip 60612-3864; tel. 312/942-5000; Omar Lateef, President and Chief Executive Officer, p. B113

★ SINAI CHICAGO 1500 South Fairfield Avenue, Zip 60608-1782; tel. 773/542-2000; Ngozi Ezike, President and Chief Executive Officer, p. B123

★ UNIVERSITY OF CHICAGO MEDICINE 5841 South Maryland Avenue, Zip 60637-1447; tel. 773/702-6240; Thomas E. Jackiewicz, President, p. B145

Downers Grove: ★ ADVOCATE AURORA HEALTH 3075 Highland Pkwy Suite 600, Zip 60515-5563, 3075 Highland Pkwy Fl 6, 60515-5563, tel. 630/929-8700; Eugene A. Woods, Chief Executive Officer, p. B7

Evanston: ★ ENDEAVOR HEALTH 1301 Central Street, Zip 60201-1613; tel. 847/570-2000; J. P. Gallagher, President and Chief Executive Officer, p. B56

Evergreen Park: AMERICAN PROVINCE OF LITTLE COMPANY OF MARY SISTERS 9350 South California Avenue, Zip 60805-2595; tel. 708/229-5095, Sister, Carol Pacini, Region Leader, p. B10

Peoria: ★ OSF HEALTHCARE 800 NE Glen Oak Avenue, Zip 61603-3200; tel. 309/655-2850; Robert Sehring, Chief Executive Officer, p. B101

Schaumburg: CITY OF HOPE 1336 Basswood Road, Zip 60173-4544; tel. 847/342-7400; Pat A. Basu, President and Chief Executive Officer, p. B33

Springfield: DIVISION OF MENTAL HEALTH, DEPARTMENT OF HUMAN SERVICES 319 East Madison Street, S-3B, Zip 62701-1035; tel. 217/785-6023; Lorrie Rickman. Jones, Director, p. B50

HSHS HOSPITAL SISTERS HEALTH SYSTEM 4936 LaVerna Road, Zip 62707-9797, P O Box 19456, 62794-9456, tel. 217/523-4747; Damond Boatwright, President and Chief Executive Officer, p. B70

★ MEMORIAL HEALTH 340 West Miller Street, Zip 62702-4928; tel. 217/788-3000; Edgar J. Curtis, President and Chief Executive Officer, p. B85

Urbana: ★ CARLE HEALTH 611 West Park Street, Zip 61801-2595; tel. 217/383-3311; James C. Leonard, President and Chief Executive Officer, p. B30

INDIANA

Evansville: ★ DEACONESS HEALTH SYSTEM 600 Mary Street, Zip 47710-1658; tel. 812/450-5000; Shawn W. McCoy, Chief Executive Officer, p. B44

Fort Wayne: ★ PARKVIEW HEALTH 10501 Corporate Drive, Zip 46845-1700; tel. 260/373-7001; Rick Henvey, Chief Executive Officer, p. B104

Hammond: POWERS HEALTH 901 MacArthur Boulevard, Zip 46321-2959; tel. 219/836-1600; Donald P. Fesko, President and Chief Executive Officer, p. B107

Indianapolis: ★ COMMUNITY HEALTH NETWORK 7330 Shadeland Station, Zip 46256-3957; tel. 317/355-1411; Bryan A. Mills, President and Chief Executive Officer, p. B38

★ INDIANA UNIVERSITY HEALTH 340 West 10th Street, Suite 6100, Zip 46202-3082, P O Box 1367, 46206-1367, tel. 317/962-2000; Dennis M. Murphy, President and Chief Executive Officer, p. B71

Mishawaka: FRANCISCAN HEALTH 1515 Dragoon Trail, Zip 46544-4710, P O Box 1290, 46546-1290, tel. 574/256-3935; Kevin D. Leahy, President and Chief Executive Officer, p. B59

NEUROPSYCHIATRIC HOSPITALS 1625 East Jefferson Boulevard, Zip 46545-7103; tel. 574/255-1400; Cameron R. Gilbert, President and Chief Executive Officer, p. B92

South Bend: ★ BEACON HEALTH SYSTEM 615 North Michigan Street, Zip 46601-1033; tel. 574/647-1000; Kreg Gruber, Chief Executive Officer, p. B25

IOWA

Clarion: ★ IOWA SPECIALTY HOSPITALS & CLINICS 1316 South Main Street, Zip 50525-2019; tel. 515/532-2811; Steven J. Simonin, Chief Executive Officer, p. B74

Clive: ★ MERCYONE 1449 NW 128th Strret, Zip 50325-7400; tel. 515/358-9200; Robert P. Ritz, Chief Executive Officer, p. B88

Iowa City: UNIVERSITY OF IOWA HEALTH CARE 200 Hawkins Drive, Zip 52242-1009; tel. 800/777-8442; Denise Jamieson, Vice President for Medical Affairs, Tyrone D. Artz Dean of the Roy J. and Lucille A. Carver College of Medicine, p. B145

West Des Moines: ★ UNITYPOINT HEALTH 1776 West Lakes Parkway, Suite 400, Zip 50266-8393; tel. 515/241-6161; Scott Kizer, President and Chief Executive Officer, p. B139

KANSAS

Kansas City: ★ THE UNIVERSITY OF KANSAS HEALTH SYSTEM 4000 Cambridge Street, Zip 66160-0001; tel. 913/588-1227; Bob Page, President and Chief Executive Officer, p. B133

Salina: ★ SALINA REGIONAL HEALTH CENTER 400 South Santa Fe Avenue, Zip 67401-4198, PO Box 5080, 67402-5080, tel. 785/452-7000; Joel Phelps, President and Chief Executive Officer, p. B114

Wichita: ★ GREAT PLAINS HEALTH ALLIANCE, INC. 250 North Rock Road, Suite 160, Zip 67206-2241; tel. 316/685-1523; Curt Colson, Chief Executive Officer, p. B61

KENTUCKY

Bowling Green: MED CENTER HEALTH 800 Park Street, Zip 42101-2356; tel. 270/745-1500; Connie Smith, President and Chief Executive Officer, p. B85

Danville: EPHRAIM MCDOWELL HEALTH 217 South Third Street, Zip 40422-1823; tel. 859/239-1000; Daniel E. McKay, Chief Executive Officer, p. B56

Edgewood: ST. ELIZABETH HEALTHCARE 1 Medical Village Drive, Zip 41017-3403; tel. 859/301-2000; Garren Colvin, Chief Executive Officer, p. B126

© 2025 AHA Guide   Health Care Systems   B157

Headquarters of Health Care Systems / Geographically

Lexington: APPALACHIAN REGIONAL HEALTHCARE, INC. 2260 Executive Drive, Zip 40505–4810, P O Box 8086, 40533–8086, tel. 859/226–2440; Hollie Harris Phillips, President and Chief Executive Officer, p. B11

UK HEALTHCARE 1000 South Limestone, Zip 40506–0007; tel. 800/333–8874; Robert DiPaola, Co-Executive Vice President for Health Affairs, p. B137

Louisville: ALLIANT MANAGEMENT SERVICES 2650 Eastpoint Parkway, Suite 300, Zip 40223–5164; tel. 502/992–3525; Michael A. Kozar, President and Chief Executive Officer, p. B9

BAPTIST HEALTH 2701 Eastpoint Parkway, Zip 40223; tel. 502/896–5000; Gerard Colman, Chief Executive Officer, p. B21

★ NORTON HEALTHCARE 4967 US Highway 42, Suite 100, Zip 40222–6363, P O Box 35070, 40232–5070, tel. 502/629–8000; Russell Cox, President and Chief Executive Officer, p. B96

★ SCIONHEALTH 680 South Fourth Street, Zip 40202–2407; tel. 502/596–7300; Robert F. Jay, Chief Executive Officer, p. B116

SPRINGSTONE 101 South Fifth Street, Suite 3850, Zip 40202–3127; tel. 855/595–2292; Phil Spencer, Chief Executive Officer, p. B125

★ UOFL HEALTH 530 South Jackson Street, Zip 40202–1675; tel. 502/562–3000; Thomas Miller, Chief Executive Officer, p. B147

Owensboro: ★ OWENSBORO HEALTH 1201 Pleasant Valley Road, Zip 42303–9811; tel. 270/417–3112; Mark A. Marsh, President and Chief Executive Officer, p. B103

LOUISIANA

Baton Rouge: ★ FRANCISCAN MISSIONARIES OF OUR LADY HEALTH SYSTEM, INC. 4200 Essen Lane, Zip 70809–2158; tel. 225/923–2701; E.J. Kuiper, President and Chief Executive Officer, p. B59

GENERAL HEALTH SYSTEM 8585 Picardy Avenue, Zip 70809–3748; tel. 225/763–4000; Edgardo J. Tenreiro, President and Chief Executive Officer, p. B61

LOUISIANA STATE HOSPITALS 628 North 4th Street, Zip 70802–5342, P O Box 629, 70821–0628, tel. 225/342–9500; Shelby Price, Chief Executive Officer, p. B81

THE CARPENTER HEALTH NETWORK 10615 Jefferson Highway, Zip 70809–7230; tel. 225/769–2449; Pat Mitchell, Chief Executive Officer, p. B133

Crowley: COMPASS HEALTH 713 North Avenue L, Zip 70526–3832; tel. 337/788–3330; Emily Hunter, Co-Chief Executive Officer, p. B41

Gretna: UNITED MEDICAL REHABILITATION HOSPITALS 3201 Wall Boulevard, Suite B, Zip 70056–7755; tel. 504/433–5551; John E.H. Mills, President and Chief Executive Officer, p. B139

Hammond: NORTH OAKS HEALTH SYSTEM 15790 Paul Vega MD Drive, Zip 70403–1436, P O Box 2668, 70404–2668, tel. 985/345–2700; Michele Kidd. Sutton, President and Chief Executive Officer, p. B95

Lafayette: AMG INTEGRATED HEALTHCARE MANAGEMENT 101 La Rue France, Suite 500, Zip 70508–3144; tel. 337/269–9828; Timothy W. Howard, Chief Executive Officer, p. B10

LHC GROUP 901 Hugh Wallis Road South, Zip 70508–2511; tel. 337/233–1307; Keith G. Myers, Chairman and Chief Executive Officer, p. B78

New Orleans: ★ LCMC HEALTH 200 Henry Clay Avenue, Zip 70118–5720; tel. 504/899–9511; Greg Feirn, President and Chief Executive Officer, p. B77

★ OCHSNER HEALTH 1514 Jefferson Highway, Zip 70121–2429; tel. 800/874–8984; Peter November, Chief Executive Officer, p. B99

Shreveport: ALLEGIANCE HEALTH MANAGEMENT 504 Texas Street, Suite 200, Zip 71101–3526; tel. 318/226–8202; Rock Bordelon, President and Chief Executive Officer, p. B9

WILLIS KNIGHTON HEALTH 2600 Greenwood Road, Zip 71103–3908; tel. 318/212–4000; Jaf Fielder, President and Chief Executive Officer, p. B154

MAINE

Brewer: ★ NORTHERN LIGHT HEALTH 43 Whiting Hill Road, Zip 04412–1005; tel. 207/973–7045; Timothy Dentry, President and Chief Executive Officer, p. B95

Lewiston: CENTRAL MAINE HEALTHCARE 300 Main Street, Zip 04240–7027; tel. 207/795–0111; Steven G. Littleson, President and Chief Executive Officer, p. B32

Portland: MAINEHEALTH 110 Free Street, Zip 04101–3537; tel. 207/661–7001; Andrew Mueller, Chief Executive Officer, p. B81

MARYLAND

Annapolis: ★ LUMINIS HEALTH 2001 Medical Parkway, Zip 21401–3773; tel. 443/481–1000; Victoria Bayless, Chief Executive Officer, p. B81

Baltimore: ★ JOHNS HOPKINS HEALTH SYSTEM 733 North Broadway, BRB 104, Zip 21205–1832, 733 North Broadway, MRB 104, 21205–1832, tel. 410/955–5000; Kevin W. Sowers, President, p. B74

★ LIFEBRIDGE HEALTH 2401 West Belvedere Avenue, Zip 21215–5216; tel. 410/601–5134; Neil M. Meltzer, President and Chief Executive Officer, p. B78

★ UNIVERSITY OF MARYLAND MEDICAL SYSTEM 250 West Pratt Street, 24th Floor, Zip 21201–1595; tel. 410/328–8667; Mohan Suntha, President and Chief Executive Officer, p. B145

Columbia: ★ MEDSTAR HEALTH 10980 Grantchester Way, Zip 21044–2665; tel. 410/772–6500; Kenneth A. Samet, President and Chief Executive Officer, p. B85

Gaithersburg: ADVENTIST HEALTHCARE 820 West Diamond Avenue, Suite 600, Zip 20878–1419; tel. 301/315–3185; John Sackett, President and Chief Executive Officer, p. B7

Rockville: ★ U. S. INDIAN HEALTH SERVICE 801 Thompson Avenue, Zip 20852–1627; tel. 301/443–1083; Roselyn Tso, Director of the Indian Health Service, p. B148

Salisbury: ★ TIDALHEALTH 100 East Carroll Street, Zip 21801–5422; tel. 410/546–6400; Steven E. Leonard, President and Chief Executive Officer, p. B133

Sparks Glencoe: FUNDAMENTAL LONG TERM CARE HOLDINGS, LLC 930 Ridgebrook Road, Zip 21152–9390; tel. 410/773–1000; Mark Fulchino, Chief Executive Officer, p. B60

MASSACHUSETTS

Boston: ★ MASS GENERAL BRIGHAM 800 Boylston Street, Suite 1150, Zip 02199–8123; tel. 617/278–1004; Anne Klibanski, President and Chief Executive Officer, p. B82

MASSACHUSETTS DEPARTMENT OF MENTAL HEALTH 25 Staniford Street, Zip 02114–2575; tel. 617/626–8123; Brooke Doyle, Commissioner, p. B83

MASSACHUSETTS DEPARTMENT OF PUBLIC HEALTH 250 Washington Street, Zip 02108–4619; tel. 617/624–6000; Margret R. Cooke, Acting Commissioner, p. B83

Burlington: ★ TUFTS MEDICINE 800 District Avenue, Suite 520, Zip 01803–5057; tel. 978/942–2220; Michael J. Dandorph, President and Chief Executive Officer, p. B136

Cambridge: ★ BETH ISRAEL LAHEY HEALTH 20 University Road, Suite 700, Zip 02138–5810; tel. 617/667–7000; Kevin Tabb, President and Chief Executive Officer, p. B25

Gardner: ★ HEYWOOD HEALTHCARE 242 Green Street, Zip 01440–1336; tel. 978/632–3420; Rozanna Penney, Co-Chief Executive Officer, p. B70

Haverhill: WHITTIER HEALTH NETWORK 25 Railroad Square, Zip 01832–5721; tel. 978/556–5858; Alfred J. Arcidi, President, p. B154

Hyannis: ★ CAPE COD HEALTHCARE, INC. 88 Lewis Bay Road, Zip 02601–5210; tel. 508/862–5121; Michael K. Lauf, President and Chief Executive Officer, p. B29

Pittsfield: ★ BERKSHIRE HEALTH SYSTEMS, INC. 725 North Street, Zip 01201–4124; tel. 413/447–2750; Darlene Rodowicz, President and Chief Executive Officer, p. B25

Springfield: ★ BAYSTATE HEALTH, INC. 280 Chestnut Street, Zip 01199–0001; tel. 413/794–0000; Peter D. Banko, President and Chief Executive Officer, p. B24

Tewksbury: ★ COVENANT HEALTH 100 Ames Pond Drive, Suite 102, Zip 01876–1240; tel. 978/654–6363; Stephen J. Grubbs, President and Chief Executive Officer, p. B43

Worcester: ★ UMASS MEMORIAL HEALTH CARE, INC. 365 Plantation Street, Biotech One, Zip 01605–2397; tel. 508/334–0100; Eric Dickson, President and Chief Executive Officer, p. B137

MICHIGAN

Ann Arbor: ★ UNIVERSITY OF MICHIGAN HEALTH 1500 E Medical Center Drive, Zip 48109–5000; tel. 734/936–4000; David C. Miller, Executive Vice Dean for Clinical Affairs and President, UM Health System, p. B146

Cass City: ASPIRE RURAL HEALTH SYSTEM 4675 Hill Street, Zip 48726–1008; tel. 989/635–4012; Angela McConnachie, Co-Chief Executive Officer, p. B16

Detroit: ★ HENRY FORD HEALTH One Ford Place, Zip 48202–3450, 1 Ford Place, 48202–3450, tel. 313/876–8708; Robert G. Riney, President and Chief Executive Officer, p. B69

Grand Blanc: MCLAREN HEALTH CARE CORPORATION 3373 Regency Park Drive, Zip 48439, One McLaren Parkway, 48439, tel. 810/342–1100; Philip A. Incarnati, President and Chief Executive Officer, p. B84

Grand Rapids: ★ COREWELL HEALTH 221 Michigan Street NE, Suite 501, Zip 49503–2539; tel. 616/391–1774; Christina Freese Decker, President and Chief Executive Officer, p. B42

Kalamazoo: ★ BRONSON HEALTHCARE GROUP 301 John Street, Zip 49007–5295; tel. 269/341–6000; Bill Manns, President and Chief Executive Officer, p. B28

Headquarters of Health Care Systems / Geographically

Livonia: ★ TRINITY HEALTH 20555 Victor Parkway, Zip 48152-7031; tel. 734/343-1000; Michael A. Slubowski, President and Chief Executive Officer, p. B134

Midland: ★ MYMICHIGAN HEALTH 4000 Wellness Drive, Zip 48670-0001; tel. 989/839-3000; Lydia Watson, President and Chief Executive Officer, p. B91

Traverse City: ★ MUNSON HEALTHCARE 1105 Sixth Street, Zip 49684-2386; tel. 231/935-5000; Edwin Ness, Munson Healthcare President and Chief Executive Officer, p. B90

MINNESOTA

Bloomington: HEALTHPARTNERS 8170 33rd Avenue South, Zip 55425-4516; tel. 952/883-6000; Andrea Walsh, President and Chief Executive Officer, p. B68

Duluth: ★ ESSENTIA HEALTH 502 East Second Street, Zip 55805-1913; tel. 218/786-8376; David C. Herman, Chief Executive Officer, p. B57

Minneapolis: ★ ALLINA HEALTH 2925 Chicago Avenue, Zip 55407-1321, P O Box 43, 55440-0043, tel. 612/262-5000; Lisa Shannon, President and Chief Executive Officer, p. B10

★ FAIRVIEW HEALTH SERVICES 2450 Riverside Avenue, Zip 55454-1400; tel. 612/672-6141; James Hereford, President and Chief Executive Officer, p. B58

Robbinsdale: NORTH MEMORIAL HEALTH CARE 3300 Oakdale Avenue North, Zip 55422-2926; tel. 763/520-5200; Trevor Sawallish, Chief Executive Officer, p. B94

Rochester: ★ MAYO CLINIC 200 First Street SW, Zip 55905-0002, 4165 Hwy 14 W Plummer Bldg 11-37, 55901, tel. 507/284-2511; Gianrico Farrugia, President, p. B83

Saint Cloud: ★ CENTRACARE HEALTH 1406 Sixth Avenue North, Zip 56303-1900; tel. 320/251-2700; Kenneth D. Holmen, President and Chief Executive Officer, p. B32

Saint Paul: MINNESOTA DEPARTMENT OF HUMAN SERVICES 540 Cedar Street, Zip 55101-2208, P O Box 64998, 55164-0998, tel. 651/431-3212; Anne Barry, Deputy Commissioner, p. B88

Waconia: ★ RIDGEVIEW MEDICAL CENTER 500 South Maple Street, Zip 55387-1752; tel. 952/442-2191; Michael Phelps, President and Chief Executive Officer, p. B113

MISSISSIPPI

Greenville: DELTA HEALTH SYSTEM 1400 East Union Street, Zip 38703-3246; tel. 662/378-3783; Iris Stacker, Chief Executive Officer, p. B44

Jackson: MISSISSIPPI STATE DEPARTMENT OF MENTAL HEALTH 1101 Robert E Lee Building, 239 North Lamar Street, Zip 39201-1101; tel. 601/359-1288; Wendy Bailey, Executive Director, p. B89

UNIVERSITY HOSPITALS AND HEALTH SYSTEM 2500 North State Street, Zip 39216-4500; tel. 601/984-1000; Alan Jones, Vice Chancellor, p. B144

Mccomb: ★ SOUTHWEST HEALTH SYSTEMS 215 Marion Avenue, Zip 39648-2705, P O Box 1307, 39649-1307, tel. 601/249-5500; Charla Rowley, Chief Executive Officer, p. B125

Tupelo: ★ NORTH MISSISSIPPI HEALTH SERVICES, INC. 830 South Gloster Street, Zip 38801-4996; tel. 662/377-3136; M. Shane. Spees, President and Chief Executive Officer, p. B94

MISSOURI

Cape Girardeau: LANDMARK HOSPITALS 3255 Independence Street, Zip 63701-4914; tel. 573/335-1091; William K. Kapp III, President and Chief Executive Officer, p. B76

Chesterfield: ★ MERCY 14528 South Outer 40, Suite 100, Zip 63017-5743, 14528 South Outer 40 Road, Suite 100, 63017-5743, tel. 314/579-6100; Stephen Mackin, President and Chief Executive Officer, p. B86

★ ST. LUKE'S HOSPITAL 232 South Woods Mill Road, Zip 63017-3406; tel. 314/434-1500; Andrew Bagnall, President and Chief Executive Officer, p. B127

Columbia: ★ UNIVERSITY OF MISSOURI HEALTH CARE 1 Hospital Drive, DC 031, Zip 65212-0001, 1 Hospital Drive, DC 031, 65212-0001, tel. 573/882-4141; Ric A. Ransom, Chief Executive Officer, p. B146

Joplin: ★ FREEMAN HEALTH SYSTEM 1102 West 32nd Street, Zip 64804-3503; tel. 417/347-1111; Paula F. Baker, President and Chief Executive Officer, p. B60

Kansas City: ★ UNIVERSITY HEALTH 2301 Holmes Street, Zip 64108-2677; tel. 816/404-1000; Charlie Shields, Chief Executive Officer, p. B144

Saint Joseph: ★ MOSAIC LIFE CARE 5325 Faraon Street, Zip 64506-3488; tel. 816/271-6000; Mike Poore, Chief Executive Officer, p. B90

Saint Louis: ★ ASCENSION HEALTHCARE 4600 Edmundson Road, Zip 63134; tel. 314/733-8000; Joseph R. Impicciche, President and Chief Executive Officer, p. B13

★ BJC HEALTH SYSTEM 4901 Forest Park Avenue, Suite 1200, Zip 63108-1402; tel. 314/286-2000; Richard J. Liekweg, President and Chief Executive Officer, p. B25

★ SSM HEALTH 12800 Corporate Hill Drive, Zip 63131-1845; tel. 314/994-7800; Laura S. Kaiser, President and Chief Executive Officer, p. B125

Springfield: COXHEALTH 1423 North Jefferson Avenue, Zip 65802-1988; tel. 417/269-3108; Max Buetow, President and Chief Executive Officer, p. B43

MONTANA

Great Falls: BENEFIS HEALTH SYSTEM 1101 26th Street South, Zip 59405-5161; tel. 406/455-5000; John H. Goodnow, Chief Executive Officer, p. B25

NEBRASKA

Lincoln: ★ BRYAN HEALTH 1600 South 48th Street, Zip 68506-1283, 1600 S 48th ST, 68506-1283, tel. 402/481-1111; Russell R. Gronewold, President and Chief Executive Officer, p. B28

Norfolk: FAITH REGIONAL HEALTH SERVICES 2700 West Norfolk Avenue, Zip 68701-4438, P O Box 869, 68702-0869, tel. 402/371-4880; Kelly Driscoll, President and Chief Executive Officer, p. B58

Omaha: ★ NEBRASKA METHODIST HEALTH SYSTEM, INC. 825 S. 169th Street, Zip 68118-9300; tel. 402/354-5411; Stephen L. Goeser, President and Chief Executive Officer, p. B92

NEVADA

Reno: ★ RENOWN HEALTH 1155 Mill Street (Mailstop N14), Zip 89502-1576; tel. 775/982-5529; Brian Erling, President and Chief Executive Officer, p. B112

NEW HAMPSHIRE

Concord: CONCORD HOSPITAL 250 Pleasant Street, Zip 03301-7559; tel. 603/225-2711, p. B41

Lebanon: ★ DARTMOUTH HEALTH 1 Medical Center Drive, Zip 03756-1000, One Medical Center Drive, 03756-1000, tel. 603/650-5000; Joanne M. Conroy, Chief Executive Officer and President, p. B43

Manchester: ★ SOLUTIONHEALTH 1 Elliot Way, Zip 03103-3502; tel. 603/663-2990; Bradley Kreick, Chief Executive Officer, p. B124

Whitefield: ★ NORTH COUNTRY HEALTHCARE 8 Clover Lane, Zip 03598-3343; tel. 603/444-9000; Thomas Mee, Chief Executive Officer, p. B94

NEW JERSEY

Edison: ★ HACKENSACK MERIDIAN HEALTH 343 Thornall Street, 8th Floor, Zip 08837-2206, 343 Thornall Street, 08837-2206, tel. 844/464-9355; Robert C. Garrett, Chief Executive Officer, p. B62

Egg Harbor Township: ★ ATLANTICARE 2500 English Creek Avenue, Building 500, Suite 501, Zip 08234-5549; tel. 609/407-2309; Michael Charlton, President and Chief Executive Officer, p. B17

Jersey City: CAREPOINT HEALTH 10 Exchange Place, 15th Floor, Zip 07302-3918; tel. 201/821-8900; Achintya Moulick, Chief Executive Officer, p. B29

Marlton: ★ VIRTUA HEALTH 303 Lippincott Drive, 4th Floor, Zip 08053-4160; tel. 856/355-0010; Dennis W. Pullin, President and Chief Executive Officer, p. B152

Morristown: ★ ATLANTIC HEALTH SYSTEM 475 South Street, Zip 07960-6459, P O Box 1905, 07962-1905, tel. 973/660-3270; Brian A. Gragnolati, President and Chief Executive Officer, p. B17

Mullica Hill: ★ INSPIRA HEALTH NETWORK 165 Bridgeton Pike, Zip 8062; tel. 856/641-8000; Amy B. Mansue, President and Chief Executive Officer, p. B72

Trenton: ★ CAPITAL HEALTH 750 Brunswick Avenue, Zip 08638-4143; tel. 609/394-6000; Al Maghazehe, President and Chief Executive Officer, p. B29

DIVISION OF MENTAL HEALTH AND ADDICTION SERVICES, DEPARTMENT OF HUMAN SERVICES, STATE OF NEW JERSEY 222 South Warren Street, Zip 08608-2306, P.O. Box 360, 08625-0360, tel. 609/438-4351; Valerie Mielke, Assistant Commissioner, p. B49

West Orange: ★ RWJBARNABAS HEALTH 95 Old Short Hills Road, Zip 07052-1008; tel. 973/322-4000; Mark Manigan, President, p. B114

NEW MEXICO

Albuquerque: ERNEST HEALTH, INC. 7770 Jefferson Street NE, Suite 320, Zip 87109-4386; tel. 505/856-5300; Darby Brockette, Chief Executive Officer, p. B56

Headquarters of Health Care Systems / Geographically

★ PRESBYTERIAN HEALTHCARE SERVICES 9521 San Mateo Blvd. NE, Zip 87113, P O Box 26666, 87125–6666, tel. 505/841–1234; Dale Maxwell, Chief Executive Officer, p. B107

NEW YORK

Albany: NEW YORK STATE OFFICE OF MENTAL HEALTH 44 Holland Avenue, Zip 12208–3411; tel. 518/474–7056; Ann Sullivan, Commissioner, p. B93

Binghamton: UNITED HEALTH SERVICES 10–42 Mitchell Avenue, Zip 13903–1617; tel. 607/762–2200; John M. Carrigg, President and Chief Executive Officer, p. B138

Bronx: MONTEFIORE HEALTH SYSTEM 111 East 210th Street, Zip 10467–2490; tel. 718/920–4321; Philip O. Ozuah, President and Chief Executive Officer, p. B89

Buffalo: ★ CATHOLIC HEALTH SYSTEM 144 Genesee Street, Zip 14203–1560; tel. 716/862–2410; Joyce Markiewicz, President and Chief Executive Officer, p. B31

Cooperstown: ★ BASSETT HEALTHCARE NETWORK 1 Atwell Road, Zip 13326–1301; tel. 607/547–3456; Staci Thompson, President and Chief Executive Officer, p. B23

Elmira: ARNOT HEALTH 600 Roe Avenue, Zip 14905–1629; tel. 607/737–4100; Jonathan I. Lawrence, President and Chief Executive Officer, p. B12

Geneva: FINGER LAKES HEALTH 196 North Street, Zip 14456–1651; tel. 315/787–4000; Jose Acevedo, President and Chief Executive Officer, p. B59

Ithaca: CAYUGA HEALTH SYSTEM 101 Dates Drive, Zip 14850–1342; tel. 607/274–4011; Martin Stallone, President and Chief Executive Officer, p. B31

Jamaica: ★ MEDISYS HEALTH NETWORK 8900 Van Wyck Expressway, Zip 11418–2832; tel. 718/206–6000; Bruce J. Flanz, President and Chief Executive Officer, p. B85

Lake Success: ★ NORTHWELL HEALTH 1979 Marcus Ave Ste E 124, Zip 11042; tel. 516/321–6666; Michael J. Dowling, President and Chief Executive Officer, p. B96

Middletown: GARNET HEALTH 707 East Main Street, Zip 10940–2650; tel. 845/333–1000; Jonathan Schiller, President and Chief Executive Officer, p. B61

New York: ★ MOUNT SINAI HEALTH SYSTEM 1 Gustave L. Levy Place, Zip 10029; tel. 212/659–8888; Brendan Carr, Chief Executive Officer, p. B90

★ NEW YORK–PRESBYTERIAN 525 East 68th Street, Box 182, Zip 10065; tel. 212/746–3745; Steven J. Corwin, President and Chief Executive Officer, p. B92

★ NYC HEALTH + HOSPITALS 50 Water Street, 17th Floor, Zip 10004; tel. 212/788–3321; Mitchell H. Katz, Chief Executive Officer, p. B97

Rochester: ★ ROCHESTER REGIONAL HEALTH 100 Kings Highway South, Zip 14617–5504; tel. 585/922–4000; Richard Davis, Chief Executive Officer, p. B113

★ UNIVERSITY OF ROCHESTER MEDICAL CENTER 601 Elmwood Ave Box 623, Zip 14642–0002, 601 Elmwood Avenue, 14642–0002, tel. 585/275–2100; Mark B. Taubman, Chief Executive Officer, p. B147

Rockville Centre: ★ CATHOLIC HEALTH SERVICES OF LONG ISLAND 992 North Village Avenue, 1st Floor, Zip 11570–1002; tel. 516/705–3700; Patrick O'Shaughnessy, President and Chief Executive Officer, p. B30

Valhalla: WMCHEALTH 100 Woods Road, Zip 10595–1530; tel. 914/493–7000; Michael D. Israel, President and Chief Executive Officer, p. B154

NORTH CAROLINA

Boone: ★ UNC HEALTH APPALACHIAN 336 Deerfield Road, Zip 28607–5008, P O Box 2600, 28607–2600, tel. 828/262–4100; Charles Mantooth, President and Chief Executive Officer, p. B138

Chapel Hill: ★ UNC HEALTH 101 Manning Drive, Zip 27514–4220; tel. 919/966–4131; Wesley Burks, Chief Executive Officer, p. B138

Charlotte: ★ ADVOCATE HEALTH 1000 Blythe Boulevard, Zip 28203–5812, Eugene A. Woods, Chief Executive Officer, p. B8

★ ATRIUM HEALTH, INC. 1000 Blythe Blvd, Zip 28203–5812, P.O. Box 32861, 28232–2861, tel. 704/355–2000; Eugene A. Woods, President and Chief Executive Officer, p. B17

Durham: ★ DUKE UNIVERSITY HEALTH SYSTEM 201 Trent Drive, Zip 27710–3037, 324 Blackwell St Ste 800, 27701–3689, tel. 919/684–2255; Craig Albanese, Chief Executive Officer, p. B50

VERITAS COLLABORATIVE 4024 Stirrup Creek Drive, Zip 27703–9464; tel. 855/875–5812; Stacie McEntyre, Chief Executive Officer, p. B151

Fayetteville: ★ CAPE FEAR VALLEY HEALTH SYSTEM 1638 Owen Drive, Zip 28304–3424, P O Box 2000, 28302–2000, tel. 910/615–4000; Michael Nagowski, President and Chief Executive Officer, p. B29

Greensboro: ★ CONE HEALTH 1200 North Elm Street, Zip 27401–1004; tel. 336/832–7000; Mary Jo Cagle, President and Chief Executive Officer, p. B41

Greenville: ★ ECU HEALTH 2100 Stantonsburg Road, Zip 27834–2818, P O Box 6028, 27835–6028, tel. 252/847–4100; Michael Waldrum, Chief Executive Officer, p. B50

Pinehurst: ★ FIRSTHEALTH OF THE CAROLINAS 155 Memorial Drive, Zip 28374–8710, P O Box 3000, 28374–3000, tel. 910/715–1000; Mickey W. Foster, Chief Executive Officer, p. B59

Raleigh: ★ WAKEMED HEALTH & HOSPITALS 3000 New Bern Avenue, Zip 27610–1231; tel. 919/350–8000; Donald R. Gintzig, President and Chief Executive Officer, p. B152

Winston Salem: ★ NOVANT HEALTH 2085 Frontis Plaza Boulevard, Zip 27103–5614; tel. 888/976–5611; Carl S. Armato, President and Chief Executive Officer, p. B97

NORTH DAKOTA

Fargo: SISTERS OF MARY OF THE PRESENTATION HEALTH SYSTEM 1202 Page Drive SW, Zip 58103–2340, P O Box 10007, 58106–0007, tel. 701/237–9290; Aaron K. Alton, President and Chief Executive Officer, p. B124

Minot: TRINITY HEALTH 1 Burdick Expressway West, Zip 58701–4406; tel. 701/857–5000; John M. Kutch, President and Chief Executive Officer, p. B136

OHIO

Akron: ★ SUMMA HEALTH 1077 Gorge Boulevard, Zip 44310; tel. 330/375–3000; T. Clifford Deveny, President and Chief Executive Officer, p. B128

Canton: AULTMAN HEALTH FOUNDATION 2600 Sixth Street SW, Zip 44710–1702; tel. 330/363–6192; Robert Mullen, President and Chief Executive Officer, p. B18

Chillicothe: ★ ADENA HEALTH SYSTEM 272 Hospital Road, Zip 45601–9031; tel. 740/779–7500; Jeff Graham, President and Chief Executive Officer, p. B5

Cincinnati: ★ BON SECOURS MERCY HEALTH 1701 Mercy Health Place, Zip 45237–6147; tel. 410/442–5511; John M. Starcher Esq, President and Chief Executive Officer, p. B26

UC HEALTH 3200 Burnet Avenue, Zip 45229–3019; tel. 513/585–6000; Cory D. Shaw, President and Chief Executive Officer, p. B136

Cleveland: ★ CLEVELAND CLINIC HEALTH SYSTEM 9500 Euclid, Zip 44195–5108; tel. 216/444–2200; Tomislav Mihaljevic, Chief Executive Officer and President, p. B34

★ UNIVERSITY HOSPITALS 11100 Euclid Avenue, Zip 44106–5000; tel. 216/844–1000; Cliff Megerian, Chief Executive Officer, p. B144

Columbus: OHIO DEPARTMENT OF MENTAL HEALTH 30 East Broad Street, 8th Floor, Zip 43215–3430; tel. 614/466–2297; Tracy Plouck, Director, p. B100

★ OHIO STATE UNIVERSITY HEALTH SYSTEM 370 West Ninth Avenue, Zip 43210–1238; tel. 614/685–9015; John Warner, Chief Executive Officer, p. B100

★ OHIOHEALTH 3430 Ohio Health Parkway, Zip 43202–1575; tel. 614/544–4455; Stephen Markovich, President and Chief Executive Officer, p. B100

Dayton: ★ KETTERING HEALTH 3965 Southern Boulevard, Zip 45429–1229, 1 Prestige Place, Suite 905, Miamisburg, 45342–3794, tel. 855/536–7543; Michael V. Gentry, Chief Executive Officer, p. B76

PREMIER HEALTH 110 North Main Street Suite 390, Zip 45402–3720; tel. 937/499–9401; Michael C. Riordan, President and Chief Executive Officer, p. B107

Findlay: ★ BLANCHARD VALLEY HEALTH SYSTEM 1900 South Main Street, Zip 45840–1214; tel. 419/423–4500; Myron D. Lewis, President and Chief Executive Officer, p. B26

Galion: ★ AVITA HEALTH SYSTEM 269 Portland Way South, Zip 44833–2399; tel. 419/468–4841; Jerome Morasko, President and Chief Executive Officer, p. B19

Jackson: ★ HOLZER HEALTH SYSTEM 500 Burlington Road, Zip 45640–9360; tel. 855/446–5937; Michael R. Canady, Chief Executive Officer, p. B70

Marietta: ★ MEMORIAL HEALTH SYSTEM 401 Matthew Street, Zip 45750–1635; tel. 740/374–1400; J Scott. Cantley, President and Chief Executive Officer, p. B86

Toledo: ★ PROMEDICA HEALTH SYSTEM 100 Madison Avenue, Zip 43604–1516; tel. 567/585–9601; Arturo Polizzi, President and Chief Executive Officer, p. B109

Headquarters of Health Care Systems / Geographically

OKLAHOMA

Duncan: ★ DRH HEALTH 1407 North Whisenant Drive, Zip 73533–1650; tel. 580/252–5300; Jay R. Johnson, President and Chief Executive Officer, p. B50

Oklahoma City: AVEM HEALTH PARTNERS 14201 Wireless Way, Suite B-100, Zip 73134–2521; tel. 405/246–0218; Jeff Hill, Chief Executive Officer, p. B18

★ INTEGRIS HEALTH 3001 Quail Springs Parkway, Zip 73134; tel. 405/949–3177; Timothy T. Pehrson, President and Chief Executive Officer, p. B72

OKLAHOMA DEPARTMENT OF MENTAL HEALTH AND SUBSTANCE ABUSE SERVICES 1200 NE 13th Street, Zip 73117–1022, P O Box 53277, 73152–3277, tel. 405/522–3908; Carrie Slatton–Hodges, Commissioner, p. B100

Shawnee: PREFERRED MANAGEMENT CORPORATION 120 West MacArthur, Suite 121, Zip 74804–2005; tel. 405/878–0202; Donald Freeman, President and Chief Executive Officer, p. B107

Tulsa: ★ SAINT FRANCIS HEALTH SYSTEM 6161 South Yale Avenue, Zip 74136–1902; tel. 918/494–8454; Cliff Robertson, President and Chief Executive Officer, p. B114

OREGON

Bend: ★ ST. CHARLES HEALTH SYSTEM, INC. 2500 NE Neff Road, Zip 97701–6015; tel. 541/382–4321; Steve Gordon, President and Chief Executive Officer, p. B126

Corvallis: ★ SAMARITAN HEALTH SERVICES 3600 NW Samaritan Drive, Zip 97330–3737, P O Box 1068, 97339–1068, tel. 541/768–5001; Doug Boysen, President and Chief Executive Officer, p. B115

Medford: ★ ASANTE HEALTH SYSTEM 2650 Siskiyou Boulevard, Suite 200, Zip 97504–8170; tel. 541/789–4100; Thomas D. Gessel, President and Chief Executive Officer, p. B13

Portland: ★ LEGACY HEALTH 1919 NW Lovejoy Street, Zip 97209–1503; tel. 503/415–5600; Kathryn G. Correia, President and Chief Executive Officer, p. B77

Salem: SALEM HEALTH 890 Oak Street Bldg B POB 14001, Zip 97309–5014; tel. 503/561–5200; Cheryl R. Nester Wolfe, President and Chief Executive Officer, p. B114

PENNSYLVANIA

Allentown: GOOD SHEPHERD REHABILITATION NETWORK 850 South Fifth Street, Zip 18103–3308; tel. 610/776–3100; Michael Spigel, President and Chief Executive Officer, p. B61

★ LEHIGH VALLEY HEALTH NETWORK 1200 South Cedar Crest Boulevard, Zip 18103–6202, P O Box 689, 18105–1556, tel. 610/402–8000; Brian A. Nester, President and Chief Executive Officer, p. B77

Beaver: HERITAGE VALLEY HEALTH SYSTEM 1000 Dutch Ridge Road, Zip 15009–9727; tel. 724/773–2024; Norman F. Mitry, President and Chief Executive Officer, p. B69

Bethlehem: ST. LUKE'S UNIVERSITY HEALTH NETWORK 801 Ostrum Street, Zip 18015–1000; tel. 610/954–4000; Richard A. Anderson, President and Chief Executive Officer, p. B127

Butler: INDEPENDENCE HEALTH SYSTEM 1 Hospital Way, Zip 16001–4670; tel. 724/284–4200; Kenneth DeFurio, President and Chief Executive Officer, p. B71

Danville: ★ GEISINGER 100 North Academy Avenue, Zip 17822–9800, 1000 East Mountain Drive, Wilkes Barre, 18711–0027, tel. 570/271–6211; Terry Gilliland, President and Chief Executive Officer, p. B61

Enola: ★ PAM HEALTH 1828 Good Hope Road, Suite 102, Zip 17025–1233; tel. 717/731–9660; Anthony F. Misitano, Founder, Chairman and Chief Executive Officer, p. B103

Hershey: ★ PENN STATE HEALTH 100 Crystal A Drive, Zip 17033–9524; tel. 717/531–8521; Stephen M. Massini, Chief Executive Officer, p. B105

King of Prussia: UNIVERSAL HEALTH SERVICES, INC. 367 South Gulph Road, Zip 19406–3121, P O Box 61558, 19406–0958, tel. 610/768–3300; Marc D. Miller, Chief Executive Officer, p. B140

Meadville: ★ MEADVILLE MEDICAL CENTER 751 Liberty Street, Zip 16335–2559; tel. 814/333–5000; Philip E. Pandolph, President and Chief Executive Officer, p. B84

Mechanicsburg: ★ SELECT MEDICAL CORPORATION 4714 Gettysburg Road, Zip 17055–4325; tel. 717/972–1100; David S. Chernow, Chief Executive Officer, p. B118

★ VIBRA HEALTHCARE 4600 Lena Drive, Zip 17055–4904; tel. 717/591–5700; Brad Hollinger, Chairman and Chief Executive Officer, p. B151

Philadelphia: ★ JEFFERSON HEALTH 1101 Market Street, 31st Floor, Zip 19107; tel. 610/225–6200; Joseph Cacchione, Chief Executive Officer, p. B74

★ TEMPLE UNIVERSITY HEALTH SYSTEM 3509 North Broad Street, 9th Floor, Zip 19140–4105; tel. 215/707–0900; Michael A. Young, Chief Executive Officer, p. B130

★ UNIVERSITY OF PENNSYLVANIA HEALTH SYSTEM 3400 Civic Center Boulevard, Suite A–5, Zip 19104–5127; tel. 215/662–2203; Kevin B. Mahoney, Chief Executive Officer, p. B146

Pittsburgh: ★ ALLEGHENY HEALTH NETWORK 120 5th Avenue, FAPHM–294E, Zip 15222–3000; tel. 412/359–3131; James J. Benedict Jr, President, p. B9

★ UPMC 600 Grant Street, US Steel Tower, Suite 6262, Zip 15219–2702; tel. 412/647–8762; Leslie Davis, President and Chief Executive Officer, p. B147

Sayre: GUTHRIE CLINIC 1 Guthrie Square, Zip 18840–1625; tel. 570/888–5858; Edmund Sabanegh Jr, President and Chief Executive Officer, p. B62

Villanova: DEVEREUX 444 Devereux Drive, Zip 19085–1932, P O Box 638, 19085–0638, tel. 610/520–3000; Robert Q. Kreider, President and Chief Executive Officer, p. B49

West Reading: ★ TOWER HEALTH 420 South Fifth Avenue, Zip 19611–2143; tel. 610/988–8000; M. Sue. Perrotty, President and Chief Executive Officer, p. B134

York: ★ WELLSPAN HEALTH 45 Monument Road, Suite 200, Zip 17403–5071; tel. 877/232–5807; Roxanna L. Gapstur, President and Chief Executive Officer, p. B152

PUERTO RICO

San Juan: ★ PUERTO RICO DEPARTMENT OF HEALTH Building 'A' – Medical Center, Zip 936, Call Box 70184, 936, tel. 787/765–2929; Carlos Mellado, Secretary of Health, p. B112

RHODE ISLAND

Providence: ★ CARE NEW ENGLAND HEALTH SYSTEM 4 Richmond Square, Zip 02906–5117; tel. 401/453–7900; Michael Wagner, President and Chief Executive Officer, p. B29

LIFESPAN CORPORATION 167 Point Street, Zip 02903–4771; tel. 401/444–3500; John R. Fernandez, President and Chief Executive Officer, p. B80

SOUTH CAROLINA

Anderson: ★ ANMED HEALTH 800 North Fant Street, Zip 29621–5793; tel. 864/512–1000; William A. Kenley, Chief Executive Officer, p. B11

Charleston: ★ MUSC HEALTH 22 Westedge Street, Suite 300, Zip 29403–6983; tel. 843/792–0599; Patrick J. Cawley, Chief Executive Officer, p. B91

★ ROPER ST. FRANCIS HEALTHCARE 125 Doughty Street, Suite 760, Zip 29403–5785; tel. 843/402–2273; Joseph DeLeon, President and Chief Executive Officer, p. B113

Columbia: PRISMA HEALTH – MIDLANDS 1301 Taylor Street, Suite 9–A, Zip 29201–2942, P O Box 2266, 29202–2266, tel. 803/296–2100; Mark O'Halla, President and Chief Executive Officer, Prisma Health, p. B109

Florence: MCLEOD HEALTH 555 East Cheves Street, Zip 29506–2617, P O Box 100551, 29502–0551, tel. 843/777–2000; Donna C. Isgett, President and Chief Executive Officer, p. B84

Greenville: PRISMA HEALTH 701 Grove Road, Zip 29605–5611; tel. 864/455–7000; Mark O'Halla, Chief Executive Officer, p. B109

Murrells Inlet: ★ TIDELANDS HEALTH 4033 Highway 17 Suite 104, Zip 29576–5032, P.O. Box 421718, Georgetown, 29442–4203, tel. 843/527–7000; Bruce P. Bailey, President and Chief Executive Officer, p. B133

Spartanburg: ★ SPARTANBURG REGIONAL HEALTHCARE SYSTEM 101 East Wood Street, Zip 29303–3040; tel. 864/560–6000; Bruce Holstien, President and Chief Executive Officer, p. B125

SOUTH DAKOTA

Rapid City: ★ MONUMENT HEALTH 353 Fairmont Boulevard, Zip 57701–7375, P O Box 6000, 57709–6000, tel. 605/719–1000; Paulette Davidson, President and Chief Executive Officer, p. B89

Sioux Falls: ★ AVERA HEALTH 3900 West Avera Drive, Suite 300, Zip 57108–5721; tel. 605/322–4700; James F. Dover, President and Chief Executive Officer, p. B18

★ SANFORD HEALTH 2301 East 60th Street North, Zip 57104–0569, PO Box 5039, 57117–5039, tel. 605/333–1000; Bill Gassen, President and Chief Executive Officer, p. B115

TENNESSEE

Brentwood: ★ LIFEPOINT HEALTH 330 Seven Springs Way, Zip 37027–4536; tel. 615/920–7000; David M. Dill, Chairman and Chief Executive Officer, p. B78

Headquarters of Health Care Systems / Geographically

★ OVATION HEALTHCARE 1573 Mallory Lane, Suite 200, Zip 37027, 1573 Mallory Lane, Suite 200, 37027, tel. 615/371-7979; Dwayne Gunter, President and Chief Executive Officer, p. B101

QUORUM HEALTH 1573 Mallory Lane, Suite 100, Zip 37027; tel. 615/221-1400, p. B112

Chattanooga: ERLANGER HEALTH SYSTEM 975 East Third Street, Zip 37403-2147; tel. 423/778-7000; Jim Coleman Jr, President and Chief Executive Officer, p. B56

Clinton: CURAE HEALTH 121 Leinart Street, Zip 37716-3632, P O Box 358, 37717-0358, tel. 865/269-4074; Steve Clapp, President and Chief Executive Officer, p. B43

Columbia: ★ MAURY REGIONAL HEALTH SYSTEM 1224 Trotwood Avenue, Zip 38401-4802; tel. 931/381-1111; Martin Chaney, Chief Executive Officer, p. B83

Franklin: ACADIA HEALTHCARE COMPANY, INC. 6100 Tower Circle, Suite 1000, Zip 37067-1509; tel. 615/861-6000; Chris Hunter, President and Chief Executive Officer, p. B4

★ COMMUNITY HEALTH SYSTEMS, INC. 4000 Meridian Boulevard, Zip 37067-6325, P O Box 689020, 37068-9020, tel. 615/465-7000; Tim Hingtgen, Chief Executive Officer, p. B38

Jackson: ★ WEST TENNESSEE HEALTHCARE 620 Skyline Drive, Zip 38301-3923; tel. 731/541-5000; James E. Ross, President and Chief Executive Officer, p. B153

Johnson City: BALLAD HEALTH 303 Med Tech Parkway, Suite 300, Zip 37604-2391, 303 Med Tech Parkway, 37604-2391, tel. 423/230-8200; Alan M. Levine, President and Chief Executive Officer, p. B19

Knoxville: COVENANT HEALTH 1420 Centerpoint Blvd, Blvd C, Zip 37932, 244 Fort Sanders West Boulevard, 37922-3353, tel. 865/531-5555; James VanderSteeg, President and Chief Executive Officer, p. B43

Memphis: ★ BAPTIST MEMORIAL HEALTH CARE CORPORATION 350 North Humphreys Boulevard, Zip 38120-2177; tel. 901/227-5117; Jason Little, President and Chief Executive Officer, p. B22

★ METHODIST LE BONHEUR HEALTHCARE 1211 Union Avenue, Suite 700, Zip 38104-6600; tel. 901/478-0500; Michael Ugwueke Sr, President and Chief Executive Officer, p. B88

STRATEGIC BEHAVIORAL HEALTH, LLC 8295 Tournament Drive, Suite 201, Zip 38125-8913; tel. 901/969-3100; Blair Stam, President, p. B128

Nashville: ★ ARDENT HEALTH SERVICES 1 Burton Hills Boulevard, Suite 250, Zip 37215-6195; tel. 615/296-3000; Marty J. Bonick, President and Chief Executive Officer, p. B12

HAVEN BEHAVIORAL HEALTHCARE 3102 West End Avenue, Suite 1000, Zip 37203-1324; tel. 615/393-8800; Kelly Gill, Chief Executive Officer, p. B63

★ HCA HEALTHCARE 1 Park Plaza, Zip 37203-1548; tel. 615/344-5248; Samuel Hazen, President and Chief Executive Officer, p. B64

★ VANDERBILT HEALTH 1211 22nd Avenue South, Zip 37232; tel. 615/322-5000; Charles Wright. Pinson, Deputy Chief Executive Officer and Chief Health System Officer, p. B150

Parsons: TENNESSEE HEALTH MANAGEMENT 52 West Eighth Street, Zip 38363-4656, PO Box 10, 38363-0010, tel. 731/847-6343; Dennis Berry, Chief Executive Officer, p. B131

TEXAS

Abilene: ★ HENDRICK HEALTH SYSTEM 1900 Pine Street, Zip 79601-2432; tel. 325/670-2000; Brad D. Holland, President and Chief Executive Officer, p. B69

Addison: UNITED SURGICAL PARTNERS INTERNATIONAL 15305 Dallas Parkway, Suite 1600, Zip 75001-6491; tel. 972/713-3500; Brett Brodnax, Chief Executive Officer, p. B139

Allen: NOBIS REHABILITATION PARTNERS 450 Century Parkway, Suite 220, Zip 75013-8135; tel. 469/640-6500; Chester Crouch, Founder & President, p. B93

Arlington: ★ TEXAS HEALTH RESOURCES 612 East Lamar Boulevard, Suite 900, Zip 76011-4130; tel. 682/236-7900; Barclay E. Berdan, Chief Executive Officer, p. B132

Austin: TEXAS DEPARTMENT OF STATE HEALTH SERVICES 1100 West 49th Street, Zip 78756-3199; tel. 512/458-7111; John William. Hellerstedt, Commissioner, p. B132

★ UNIVERSITY OF TEXAS SYSTEM 210 West 7th Street, Zip 78701-2903; tel. 512/499-4224; John M. Zerwas, Executive Vice Chancellor for Health Affairs, p. B147

Dallas: ★ BAYLOR SCOTT & WHITE HEALTH 301 North Washington Avenue, Zip 75246; tel. 214/820-0111; Peter J. McCanna, Chief Executive Officer, p. B24

CHILDREN'S HEALTH 1935 Medical District Drive, Zip 75235-7701; tel. 214/456-7000; Christopher J. Durovich, President and Chief Executive Officer, p. B32

CORNERSTONE HEALTHCARE GROUP 2200 Ross Avenue, Suite 5400, Zip 75201-7984; tel. 469/621-6700; Steve Jakubcanin, President and Chief Executive Officer, p. B42

EVEREST REHABILITATION HOSPITALS, LLC 5100 Belt Line Road, Suite 310, Zip 75254-7559; tel. 469/713-1145; Jay Quintana, Chief Executive Officer and Co-Founder, p. B58

★ METHODIST HEALTH SYSTEM 1441 North Beckley Avenue, Zip 75203-1201, P O Box 655999, 75265-5999, tel. 214/947-8181; James C. Scoggin Jr, Chief Executive Officer, p. B88

STEWARD HEALTH CARE SYSTEM, LLC 1900 North Pearl Street, Suite 2400, Zip 75201; tel. 617/419-4700; Ralph de la Torre, Chairman and Chief Executive Officer, p. B128

★ TENET HEALTHCARE CORPORATION 14201 Dallas Parkway, Zip 75254-2916, P O Box 1390369, 75313-9036, tel. 469/893-2200; Saumya Sutaria, Chief Executive Officer, p. B130

Houston: ★ HOUSTON METHODIST 6565 Fannin Street, D-200, Zip 77030-2707; tel. 713/441-2221; Marc L. Boom, President and Chief Executive Officer, p. B70

★ MEMORIAL HERMANN HEALTH SYSTEM 929 Gessner, Suite 2700, Zip 77024-2593; tel. 713/338-5555; David L. Callender, President and Chief Executive Officer, p. B86

NEXUS HEALTH SYSTEMS One Riverway, Suite 600, Zip 77056-1993, 1 Riverway, Suite 600, 77056-1993, tel. 713/355-6111; John W. Cassidy, President, Chief Executive Officer and Chief Medical Officer, p. B93

Irving: ★ CHRISTUS HEALTH 919 Hidden Ridge Drive, Zip 75038; tel. 469/282-2000; Ernie W. Sadau, President and Chief Executive Officer, p. B33

USMD HEALTH SYSTEM 6333 North State Highway 161 Suite 200, Zip 75038-2229; tel. 214/493-4000; Richard C. Johnston, Chief Executive Officer and Chief Physician Officer, p. B149

Lubbock: ★ COVENANT HEALTH SYSTEM 3615 19th Street, Zip 79410-1203; tel. 806/725-0447; Walter L. Cathey, Regional Chief Executive Officer, p. B43

Plano: ★ COMMUNITY HOSPITAL CORPORATION 7950 Legacy Drive, Suite 1000, Zip 75024-0417; tel. 972/943-6400; Jim R. Kendrick, President and Chief Executive Officer, p. B40

★ HEALTHTECH MANAGEMENT SERVICES 2745 Dallas Pkwy, Zip 75093-8731, 5110 Maryland Way Suite 200, Brentwood, TN, 37027-2307, tel. 615/309-6053; Neil E. Todhunter, Chief Executive Officer, p. B69

OCEANS HEALTHCARE 5360 Legacy Drive, Suite 101, Zip 75024-3130; tel. 972/464-0022; Stuart Archer, Chief Executive Officer, p. B98

Sherman: CARRUS HEALTH 1810 West US Highway 82, Zip 75092-7069; tel. 903/870-2600; Jon Michael. Rains, President and Chief Operating Officer, p. B30

The Woodlands: EMERUS 8686 New Trails Drive, Suite 100, Zip 77381-1195; tel. 281/292-2450; Victor Schmerbeck, Chief Executive Officer, p. B51

West Lake Hills: CLEARSKY HEALTH 1000 Westbank Drive, Suite A, Zip 78746-6598; tel. 512/995-7597; Darby Brockette, Chief Executive Officer, p. B34

UTAH

Salt Lake City: ★ INTERMOUNTAIN HEALTH 36 South State Street, 22nd Floor, Zip 84111-1453; tel. 801/442-2000; Rob Allen, President and Chief Executive Officer, p. B73

VERMONT

Burlington: ★ THE UNIVERSITY OF VERMONT HEALTH NETWORK 111 Colchester Avenue, Zip 05401-1473; tel. 802/847-3983; Sunil Eappen, President and Chief Executive Officer, p. B133

VIRGINIA

Charlottesville: ★ UVA HEALTH 1215 Lee Street, Zip 22908-0816; tel. 434/924-0211; K. Craig Kent, Chief Executive Officer, p. B149

Fairfax: ★ INOVA HEALTH SYSTEM 8095 Innovation Park Drive, Zip 22031-4868; tel. 703/289-2069; J. Stephen. Jones, President and Chief Executive Officer, p. B72

Falls Church: ★ BUREAU OF MEDICINE AND SURGERY, DEPARTMENT OF THE NAVY 7700 Arlington Boulevard, Suite 5126, Zip 22042; tel. 202/762-3701; Rear Admiral, Darin K. Via, Interim Surgeon General of the Navy and Interim Chief, Bureau of Medicine and Surgery, p. B28

★ DEPARTMENT OF THE ARMY, OFFICE OF THE SURGEON GENERAL 7700 Arlington Boulevard Suite 4SW112, Zip 22042-2929; tel. 703/681-3000, Lieutenant General, Mary K. Izaguirre, Surgeon General of the Army, p. B45

Headquarters of Health Care Systems / Geographically

Fredericksburg: ★ MARY WASHINGTON HEALTHCARE 1001 Sam Perry Boulevard, Suite 1005, Zip 22401-4453, 1001 Sam Perry Boulevard, 22401-4453, tel. 540/741-3100; Michael P. McDermott, President and Chief Executive Officer, p. B82

Lynchburg: ★ CENTRA HEALTH, INC. 1901 Tate Springs Road, Zip 24501-1109; tel. 434/200-3000; Richard Tugman, Interim President and Chief Executive Officer, p. B31

Newport News: RIVERSIDE HEALTH SYSTEM 701 Town Center Drive, Suite 1000, Zip 23606-4286; tel. 757/534-7000; Michael J. Dacey, Chief Executive Officer, p. B113

Richmond: ★ VCU HEALTH SYSTEM 1200 East Marshall Street, Zip 23298, P O Box 980510, 23298-0510, tel. 804/828-9000; Marlon Levy, Interim Chief Executive Officer, p. B151

VIRGINIA DEPARTMENT OF MENTAL HEALTH 1220 Bank Street, Zip 23219-3645, P O Box 1797, 23218-1797, tel. 804/786-3921; Nelson Smith, Commissioner, p. B151

Roanoke: ★ CARILION CLINIC 1 Riverside Circle, Zip 24016-4961; tel. 540/981-7000; Nancy Howell. Agee, President and Chief Executive Officer, p. B29

Virginia Beach: ★ SENTARA HEALTH 1330 Sentara Park, Zip 23464-5884; tel. 757/455-7000; Dennis Matheis, President and Chief Executive Officer, p. B122

Winchester: ★ VALLEY HEALTH SYSTEM 220 Campus Boulevard, Suite 420, Zip 22601-2889, P O Box 3340, 22604-2540, tel. 540/536-8024; Mark S. Nantz, President and Chief Executive Officer, p. B150

WASHINGTON

Mount Vernon: SKAGIT REGIONAL HEALTH 1415 E Kincaid Street, Zip 98274-4126; tel. 360/424-4111; Brian K. Ivie, President and Chief Executive Officer, p. B124

Renton: ★ PROVIDENCE 1801 Lind Avenue Southwest, 9016, Zip 98057-9016; tel. 844/510-4325; Rod Hochman, President and Chief Executive Officer, p. B110

Seattle: ★ SWEDISH HEALTH SERVICES 747 Broadway, Zip 98122-4379; tel. 206/386-6000; Elizabeth Wako, President and Chief Executive Officer, p. B129

★ UW MEDICINE 1959 NE Pacific Street, Zip 98195-0001, P O Box 356350, 98195-6350, tel. 206/543-7718; Timothy H. Dellit, Chief Executive Officer, p. B150

Sunnyside: ASTRIA HEALTH 1806 Yakima Valley Highway, Zip 98944-2263; tel. 509/837-1330; Brian P. Gibbons, Interim Chief Executive Officer, p. B16

Tacoma: ★ MULTICARE HEALTH SYSTEM 820 A Street, Zip 98402-5202, P O Box 5299, 98415-0299, tel. 253/403-1272; William G. Robertson, Chief Executive Officer, p. B90

Vancouver: ★ PEACEHEALTH 1115 SE 164th Avenue, Zip 98683; tel. 360/729-1000; Elizabeth Dunne, President and Chief Executive Officer, p. B105

WEST VIRGINIA

Charleston: ★ VANDALIA HEALTH 501 Morris Street, Zip 25301-1300; tel. 304/388-5432; David L. Ramsey, President and Chief Executive Officer, p. B150

Elkins: ★ DAVIS HEALTH SYSTEM 812 Gorman Avenue, Zip 26241, P O Box 1697, 26241-1697, tel. 304/636-3300; Mark Doak, Interim President, p. B44

Huntington: ★ MARSHALL HEALTH NETWORK 517 9th Street, Zip 25701-2020; tel. 304/781-4466; Kevin Yingling, Chief Executive Officer, p. B81

Morgantown: ★ WEST VIRGINIA UNIVERSITY HEALTH SYSTEM 1 Medical Center, Zip 26506-8136; tel. 304/285-7150; Albert L. Wright Jr, President and Chief Executive Officer, p. B153

WISCONSIN

Ashland: ★ TAMARACK HEALTH 1615 Maple Lane, Zip 54806-3626; tel. 715/685-5500; Luke Beirl, Chief Executive Officer, p. B130

Janesville: MERCY HEALTH SYSTEM 1000 Mineral Point Avenue, Zip 53548-2940, P O Box 2500, 53547-5003, tel. 608/756-6000; Javon R. Bea, President and Chief Executive Officer, p. B88

La Crosse: EMPLIFY HEALTH 1900 South Avenue, Zip 54601-5467; tel. 608/782-7300; Scott W. Rathgaber, Chief Executive Officer, p. B51

Madison: UW HEALTH 600 Highland Avenue, Zip 53792-0001; tel. 608/263-6400; Alan Kaplan, Chief Executive Officer, p. B149

Manitowoc: ★ FRANCISCAN SISTERS OF CHRISTIAN CHARITY SPONSORED MINISTRIES, INC. 2413 South Alverno Road, Zip 54220; tel. 920/684-7071; Scott McConnaha, President and Chief Executive Officer, p. B60

Marshfield: ★ MARSHFIELD CLINIC HEALTH SYSTEM 1000 North Oak Avenue, Zip 54449-5703; tel. 800/782-8581; Brian Hoerneman, Interim Chief Executive Officer, p. B82

Milwaukee: CHILDREN'S WISCONSIN 9000 West Wisconsin Avenue, Zip 53226-4810, P O Box 1997, 53201-1997, tel. 414/226-2000; Peggy N. Troy, President and Chief Executive Officer, p. B32

★ FROEDTERT THEDACARE HEALTH, INC. 9200 West Wisconsin Avenue, Zip 53226-3522; tel. 414/805-3000; Imran A. Andrabi, President and Chief Executive Officer, p. B60

Waukesha: ★ PROHEALTH CARE, INC. N17 W24100 Riverwood Drive, Suite 130, Zip 53188; tel. 262/928-2242; Susan A. Edwards, President and Chief Executive Officer, p. B109

Wausau: ★ ASPIRUS, INC. 2200 Westwood Drive, Zip 54401-7806; tel. 715/847-2118; Matthew Heywood, Chief Executive Officer, p. B16

Networks and their Hospitals

ARIZONA

HONORHEALTH
8125 North Hayden Road, Scottsdale, AZ Zip 85258-2463; tel. 480/882-4000; Todd LaPorte, Chief Executive Officer

HONORHEALTH DEER VALLEY MEDICAL CENTER, 19829 North 27th Avenue, Phoenix, AZ, Zip 85027-4002; tel. 623/879-6100; Kimberly Post, R.N., Chief Operating Officer

HONORHEALTH JOHN C. LINCOLN MEDICAL CENTER, 250 East Dunlap Avenue, Phoenix, AZ, Zip 85020-2825; tel. 602/943-2381; Kimberly Post, R.N., Chief Operating Officer

HONORHEALTH REHABILITATION HOSPITAL, 8850 East Pima Center Parkway, Scottsdale, AZ, Zip 85258-4619; tel. 480/800-3900; Ashlie Decker, Chief Executive Officer

HONORHEALTH SCOTTSDALE OSBORN MEDICAL CENTER, 7400 East Osborn Road, Scottsdale, AZ, Zip 85251-6403; tel. 480/882-4000; Kimberly Post, R.N., Chief Operating Officer

HONORHEALTH SCOTTSDALE SHEA MEDICAL CENTER, 9003 East Shea Boulevard, Scottsdale, AZ, Zip 85260-6771; tel. 480/323-3000; Kimberly Post, R.N., Chief Operating Officer

HONORHEALTH SCOTTSDALE THOMPSON PEAK MEDICAL CENTER, 7400 East Thompson Peak Parkway, Scottsdale, AZ, Zip 85255-4109; tel. 480/324-7000; Kimberly Post, R.N., Chief Operating Officer

NORTHERN ARIZONA HEALTHCARE
1200 North Beaver Street, Flagstaff, AZ Zip 86001-3118; tel. 928/779-3366; Robert P. Thames, President and Chief Executive Officer

CALIFORNIA

ADVENTIST HEALTH NORTHERN CALIFORNIA NETWORK
463 Aviation Boulevard, Santa Rosa, CA Zip 95403-1079; tel. 707/571-2893; Jeff Eller, FACHE, President and Chief Executive Officer

ADVENTIST HEALTH CLEAR LAKE, 15630 18th Avenue, Clearlake, CA, Zip 95422-9336, P O Box 6710, Zip 95422, tel. 707/994-6486; Eric Stevens, Interim President

ADVENTIST HEALTH HOWARD MEMORIAL, 1 Marcela Drive, Willits, CA, Zip 95490-5769; tel. 707/459-6801; Eric Stevens, President, Northern California Network

ADVENTIST HEALTH ST. HELENA, 10 Woodland Road, Saint Helena, CA, Zip 94574-9554; tel. 707/963-3611; Steven C. Herber, M.D., FACS, President

ADVENTIST HEALTH UKIAH VALLEY, 275 Hospital Drive, Ukiah, CA, Zip 95482-4531; tel. 707/462-3111; Eric Stevens, President, Northern California Network

ADVENTIST HEALTH VALLEJO, 525 Oregon Street, Vallejo, CA, Zip 94590-3201; tel. 707/648-2200; Steven C. Herber, M.D., FACS, President

PROVIDENCE HEALTH AND SERVICES – SOUTHERN CALIFORNIA
Regional Administration, 20555 Earl Street, Torrance, CA Zip 90503-3006; tel. 714/450-5375; Erik G. Wexler, Chief Executive Officer

PROVIDENCE CEDARS–SINAI TARZANA MEDICAL CENTER, 18321 Clark Street, Tarzana, CA, Zip 91356-3521; tel. 818/881-0800; Nick Lymberopoulos, Chief Executive Officer

PROVIDENCE HOLY CROSS MEDICAL CENTER, 15031 Rinaldi Street, Mission Hills, CA, Zip 91345-1207; tel. 818/365-8051; Bernard Klein, M.D., Chief Executive

PROVIDENCE LITTLE COMPANY OF MARY MEDICAL CENTER – TORRANCE, 4101 Torrance Boulevard, Torrance, CA, Zip 90503-4664; tel. 310/540-7676; Michael Ricks, Chief Executive, Los Angeles Coastal Service Area

PROVIDENCE LITTLE COMPANY OF MARY MEDICAL CENTER SAN PEDRO, 1300 West Seventh Street, San Pedro, CA, Zip 90732-3505; tel. 310/832-3311; Michael Ricks, Chief Executive, Los Angeles Coastal Service Area

PROVIDENCE SAINT JOHN'S HEALTH CENTER, 2121 Santa Monica Boulevard, Santa Monica, CA, Zip 90404-2091; tel. 310/829-5511; Michael Ricks, Chief Executive, Los Angeles Coastal Service Area

PROVIDENCE SAINT JOSEPH MEDICAL CENTER, 501 South Buena Vista Street, Burbank, CA, Zip 91505-4866; tel. 818/843-5111; Karl Keeler, Chief Executive, Los Angeles Valley Service Area

ST. JOSEPH HOAG HEALTH
3345 Michelson Drive, Suite 100, Irvine, CA Zip 92612-0693; tel. 949/381-4019; Richard Afable, M.D., M.P.H., President and Chief Executive Officer

HOAG MEMORIAL HOSPITAL PRESBYTERIAN, 1 Hoag Drive, Newport Beach, CA, Zip 92663-4162, P O Box 6100, Zip 92658-6100, tel. 949/764-4624; Robert Braithwaite, President and Chief Executive Officer

PROVIDENCE MISSION HOSPITAL MISSION VIEJO, 27700 Medical Center Road, Mission Viejo, CA, Zip 92691-6474; tel. 949/364-1400; Seth R. Teigen, Chief Executive

PROVIDENCE ST. JOSEPH HOSPITAL ORANGE, 1100 West Stewart Drive, Orange, CA, Zip 92868-3849, P O Box 5600, Zip 92863-5600, tel. 714/633-9111; Brian Helleland, Chief Executive, Orange County High Desert Service Area

PROVIDENCE ST. MARY MEDICAL CENTER, 18300 Highway 18, Apple Valley, CA, Zip 92307-2206, P O Box 7025, Zip 92307-0725, tel. 760/242-2311; Randall Castillo, Chief Executive Officer

COLORADO

CENTURA HEALTH
188 Inverness Drive West, Suite 500, Englewood, CO Zip 80112-5204; tel. 303/290-6500

ADVENTHEALTH AVISTA, 100 Health Park Drive, Louisville, CO, Zip 80027-9583; tel. 303/673-1000; Mark T. Smith, JD, CPA, President and Chief Executive Officer

ADVENTHEALTH CASTLE ROCK, 2350 Meadows Boulevard, Castle Rock, CO, Zip 80109-8405; tel. 720/455-5000; Michelle Fuentes, Chief Executive Officer and President

ADVENTHEALTH LITTLETON, 7700 South Broadway Street, Littleton, CO, Zip 80122-2628; tel. 303/730-8900; Rick Dodds, Chief Executive Officer

ADVENTHEALTH PARKER, 9395 Crown Crest Boulevard, Parker, CO, Zip 80138-8573; tel. 303/269-4000; Michael Goebel, Chief Executive Officer

ADVENTHEALTH PORTER, 2525 South Downing Street, Denver, CO, Zip 80210-5876; tel. 303/778-1955; Todd Folkenberg, Chief Executive Officer

BOB WILSON MEMORIAL GRANT COUNTY HOSPITAL, 415 North Main Street, Ulysses, KS, Zip 67880-2133; tel. 620/356-1266; Twilla Lee, Chief Executive Officer

COMMON SPIRIT ST. ELIZABETH HOSPITAL, 1000 Lincoln Street, Fort Morgan, CO, Zip 80701-3298; tel. 970/867-3391; John Swanhorst, Interim Chief Executive Officer

COMMONSPIRIT – MERCY HOSPITAL, 1010 Three Springs Boulevard, Durango, CO, Zip 81301-8296; tel. 970/247-4311; Josh Neff, Chief Executive Officer

COMMONSPIRIT – ST. ANTHONY SUMMIT MEDICAL CENTER, 340 Peak One Drive, Frisco, CO, Zip 80443, P O Box 738, Zip 80443-0738, tel. 970/668-3300; Trixie VanderSchaaff, Chief Executive Officer

COMMONSPIRIT – ST. MARY–CORWIN HOSPITAL, 1008 Minnequa Avenue, Pueblo, CO, Zip 81004-3798; tel. 719/557-4000; Michael Cafasso, Chief Executive Officer

LONGMONT UNITED HOSPITAL, 1950 Mountain View Avenue, Longmont, CO, Zip 80501-3162; tel. 303/651-5111; Deb Mohesky, Chief Executive Officer

ORTHOCOLORADO HOSPITAL, 11650 West 2nd Place, Lakewood, CO, Zip 80228-1527; tel. 720/321-5000; Jude Torchia, Chief Executive Officer

PENROSE–ST. FRANCIS HEALTH SERVICES, 2222 North Nevada Avenue, Colorado Springs, CO, Zip 80907-6799; tel. 719/776-5000; Kristi Olson, Chief Executive Officer

ST. ANTHONY HOSPITAL, 11600 West Second Place, Lakewood, CO, Zip 80228-1527; tel. 720/321-0000; Kevin Cullinan, Chief Executive Officer

ST. ANTHONY NORTH HOSPITAL, 14300 Orchard Parkway, Westminster, CO, Zip 80023-9206; tel. 720/627-0000; Constance Schmidt, FACHE, R.N., Chief Executive Officer

ST. CATHERINE HOSPITAL – DODGE CITY, 3001 Avenue 'A', Dodge City, KS, Zip 67801-6508, P O Box 1478, Zip 67801-1478, tel. 620/225-8400; Twilla Lee, Chief Executive Officer

ST. CATHERINE HOSPITAL, 401 East Spruce Street, Garden City, KS, Zip 67846-5679; tel. 620/272-2222; Twilla Lee, Chief Executive Officer

ST. THOMAS MORE HOSPITAL, 1338 Phay Avenue, Canon City, CO, Zip 81212-2302; tel. 719/285-2000; Michael Cafasso, Chief Executive Officer

COMMUNITY HEALTH PROVIDERS ORGANIZATION
2021 North 12th Street, Grand Junction, CO Zip 81501-2980; tel. 970/256-6200; Chris Thomas, FACHE, President and Chief Executive Officer

COMMUNITY HOSPITAL, 2351 G Road, Grand Junction, CO, Zip 81505; tel. 970/242-0920; Chris Thomas, FACHE, President and Chief Executive Officer

HCA HEALTHONE, LLC (HCA HEALTHCARE CONTINENTAL DIVISION)
4900 South Monaco Street, Suite 380, Denver, CO Zip 80237-3487; tel. 303/788-2500; Chad Christianson, President

MEDICAL CENTER OF AURORA, 1501 South Potomac Street, Aurora, CO, Zip 80012-5411; tel. 303/695-2600; Scott Rausch, President and Chief Executive Officer

Networks / Lutheran Health Network

NORTH SUBURBAN MEDICAL CENTER, 9191 Grant Street, Thornton, CO, Zip 80229–4341; tel. 303/451–7800; Ryan Thornton, President and Chief Executive Officer

PRESBYTERIAN/ST. LUKE'S MEDICAL CENTER, 1719 East 19th Avenue, Denver, CO, Zip 80218–1281; tel. 720/754–6000; David Donaldson, President and Chief Executive Assistant

ROSE MEDICAL CENTER, 4567 East Ninth Avenue, Denver, CO, Zip 80220–3941; tel. 303/320–2121; Casey Guber, President and Chief Executive Officer

SKY RIDGE MEDICAL CENTER, 10101 Ridge Gate Parkway, Lone Tree, CO, Zip 80124–5522; tel. 720/225–1000; Eric Evans, Chief Executive Officer

SPALDING REHABILITATION HOSPITAL, 900 Potomac Steet, Aurora, CO, Zip 80011–6716; tel. 303/367–1166; Scott Rausch, Chief Executive Officer

SWEDISH MEDICAL CENTER, 501 East Hampden Avenue, Englewood, CO, Zip 80113–2702; tel. 303/788–5000; Scott Davis, President/Chief Executive Officer

CONNECTICUT

EASTERN CONNECTICUT HEALTH NETWORK
71 Haynes Street, Manchester, CT Zip 06040–4131; tel. 860/533–3400; Deborah K. Weymouth, FACHE, Chief Executive Officer

MANCHESTER MEMORIAL HOSPITAL, 71 Haynes Street, Manchester, CT, Zip 06040–4188; tel. 860/646–1222; Deborah K. Weymouth, FACHE, President and Chief Executive Officer

ROCKVILLE GENERAL HOSPITAL, 31 Union Street, Vernon, CT, Zip 06066–3160; tel. 860/872–0501; Deborah K. Weymouth, FACHE, Chief Executive Officer

GEORGIA

ST. JOSEPH'S/CANDLER HEALTH SYSTEM, INC.
5353 Reynolds Street, Savannah, GA Zip 31405–6015; tel. 912/819–6000; Paul P. Hinchey, President and Chief Executive Officer

APPLING HEALTHCARE SYSTEM, 163 East Tollison Street, Baxley, GA, Zip 31513–0120; tel. 912/367–9841; Andrea Pierce Graham, Chief Executive Officer

CANDLER HOSPITAL–SAVANNAH, 5353 Reynolds Street, Savannah, GA, Zip 31405–6015; tel. 912/819–6000; Paul P. Hinchey, President and Chief Executive Officer

EFFINGHAM HEALTH SYSTEM, 459 Georgia Highway 119 South, Springfield, GA, Zip 31329–3021, P O Box 386, Zip 31329–0386, tel. 912/754–6451; Francine Witt, R.N., President and Chief Executive Officer

EMORY UNIVERSITY HOSPITAL, 1364 Clifton Road NE, Atlanta, GA, Zip 30322; tel. 404/712–2000; Catherine Maloney, Chief Operating Officer

LIBERTY REGIONAL MEDICAL CENTER, 462 Elma G Miles Parkway, Hinesville, GA, Zip 31313–4000, P O Box 919, Zip 31310–0919, tel. 912/369–9400; Tammy Mims, Chief Executive Officer

MEMORIAL HEALTH MEADOWS HOSPITAL, 1 Meadows Parkway, Vidalia, GA, Zip 30474–8759, P O Box 1048, Zip 30475–1048, tel. 912/535–5555; Jared Kirby, Interim Chief Executive Officer

ST. JOSEPH'S HOSPITAL, 11705 Mercy Boulevard, Savannah, GA, Zip 31419–1791; tel. 912/819–4100; Paul P. Hinchey, President and Chief Executive Officer

IDAHO

THE HOSPITAL COOPERATIVE
500 South 11th Avenue Suite 503, Pocatello, ID Zip 83201–4881; tel. 208/239–1951; Robert Cuoio, Executive Director

BEAR LAKE MEMORIAL HOSPITAL, 164 South Fifth Street, Montpelier, ID, Zip 83254–1597; tel. 208/847–1630; Arel Hunt, Chief Executive Officer

BINGHAM MEMORIAL HOSPITAL, 98 Poplar Street, Blackfoot, ID, Zip 83221–1799; tel. 208/785–4100; Jake Erickson, Chief Executive Officer

CARIBOU MEDICAL CENTER, 300 South Third West, Soda Springs, ID, Zip 83276–1598; tel. 208/547–3341; Dillon Liechty, Interim Chief Executive Officer

CASSIA REGIONAL HOSPITAL, 1501 Hiland Avenue, Burley, ID, Zip 83318–2688; tel. 208/678–4444; Michael Blauer, Administrator

EASTERN IDAHO REGIONAL MEDICAL CENTER, 3100 Channing Way, Idaho Falls, ID, Zip 83404–7533, P O Box 2077, Zip 83403–2077, tel. 208/529–6111; Elizabeth Hunsicker, Chief Executive Officer

FRANKLIN COUNTY MEDICAL CENTER, 44 North First East Street, Preston, ID, Zip 83263–1399; tel. 208/852–0137; Darin Dransfield, Chief Executive Officer

LOST RIVERS MEDICAL CENTER, 551 Highland Drive, Arco, ID, Zip 83213–9771, P O Box 145, Zip 83213–0145, tel. 208/527–8206; Brad Huerta, Chief Executive Officer and Administrator

MADISONHEALTH, 450 East Main Street, Rexburg, ID, Zip 83440–2048, P O Box 310, Zip 83440–0310, tel. 208/359–6900; Rachel Ann. Gonzales, Chief Executive Officer

MINIDOKA MEMORIAL HOSPITAL, 1224 Eighth Street, Rupert, ID, Zip 83350–1599; tel. 208/436–0481; Tom Murphy, Chief Executive Officer

NELL J. REDFIELD MEMORIAL HOSPITAL, 150 North 200 West, Malad City, ID, Zip 83252–1239, Box 126, Zip 83252–0126, tel. 208/766–2231; John Williams, Administrator and Chief Executive Officer

NORTH CANYON MEDICAL CENTER, 267 North Canyon Drive, Gooding, ID, Zip 83330–5500; tel. 208/934–4433; J'Dee Adams, Chief Executive Officer

PORTNEUF MEDICAL CENTER, 777 Hospital Way, Pocatello, ID, Zip 83201–5175; tel. 208/239–1000; Nate Carter, Interim Chief Executive Officer and Chief Operating Officer

POWER COUNTY HOSPITAL DISTRICT, 510 Roosevelt Street, American Falls, ID, Zip 83211–1362, P O Box 420, Zip 83211–0420, tel. 208/226–3200; Dallas Clinger, Administrator

STAR VALLEY HEALTH, 901 Adams Street, Afton, WY, Zip 83110–9621, P O Box 579, Zip 83110–0579, tel. 307/885–5800; Daniel Ordyna, Chief Executive Officer

STEELE MEMORIAL MEDICAL CENTER, 203 South Daisy Street, Salmon, ID, Zip 83467–4709; tel. 208/756–5600; Preston Becker, Chief Executive Officer

TETON VALLEY HEALTH CARE, 120 E Howard Avenue, Driggs, ID, Zip 83422–5112; tel. 208/354–2383; Troy Christensen, Chief Executive Officer

ILLINOIS

AMITA HEALTH
2601 Navistar Drive, Lisle, IL Zip 60532–3661; tel. 224/273–4121

ASCENSION ALEXIAN BROTHERS BEHAVIORAL HEALTH HOSPITAL, 1650 Moon Lake Boulevard, Hoffman Estates, IL, Zip 60169–1010; tel. 847/882–1600; Clayton Ciha, President and Chief Executive Officer

UCHICAGO MEDICINE ADVENTHEALTH BOLINGBROOK, 500 Remington Boulevard, Bolingbrook, IL, Zip 60440–4906; tel. 630/312–5000; Kenneth Rose, President and Chief Executive Officer

UCHICAGO MEDICINE ADVENTHEALTH GLENOAKS, 701 Winthrop Avenue, Glendale Heights, IL, Zip 60139–1403; tel. 630/545–8000; Vladimir Radivojevic, President and Chief Executive Officer

UCHICAGO MEDICINE ADVENTHEALTH HINSDALE, 120 North Oak Street, Hinsdale, IL, Zip 60521–3890; tel. 630/856–6001; Adam Maycock, President and Chief Executive Officer

UCHICAGO MEDICINE ADVENTHEALTH LA GRANGE, 5101 South Willow Spring Road, La Grange, IL, Zip 60525–2600; tel. 708/245–9000; Adam Maycock, President and Chief Executive Officer

MERCY HEALTH CORPORATION
2400 North Rockton Avenue, Rockford, IL Zip 61103–3655; tel. 608/756–6000; Javon R. Bea, President and Chief Executive Officer

MERCYHEALTH HOSPITAL AND MEDICAL CENTER – HARVARD, 901 Grant Street, Harvard, IL, Zip 60033–1898, P O Box 850, Zip 60033–0850, tel. 815/943–5431; Javon R. Bea, President and Chief Executive Officer

MERCYHEALTH HOSPITAL AND MEDICAL CENTER – WALWORTH, N2950 State Road 67, Lake Geneva, WI, Zip 53147–2655; tel. 262/245–0535; Javon R. Bea, President and Chief Executive Officer

MERCYHEALTH HOSPITAL AND TRAUMA CENTER – JANESVILLE, 1000 Mineral Point Avenue, Janesville, WI, Zip 53548–2982; tel. 608/756–6000; Javon R. Bea, President and Chief Executive Officer

MERCYHEALTH JAVON BEA HOSPITAL – RIVERSIDE CAMPUS, 8201 East Riverside Boulevard, Rockford, IL, Zip 61114–2300; tel. 815/971–7000; Javon R. Bea, President and Chief Executive Officer

RUSH HEALTH
1645 West Jackson Boulevard Suite 501, Chicago, IL Zip 60612–2847; tel. 312/942–4061; Douglas O'Brien, Interim President and Executive Director

RIVERSIDE MEDICAL CENTER, 350 North Wall Street, Kankakee, IL, Zip 60901–2901; tel. 815/933–1671; Phillip M. Kambic, President and Chief Executive Officer

RUSH OAK PARK HOSPITAL, 520 South Maple Avenue, Oak Park, IL, Zip 60304–1097; tel. 708/383–9300; Dino Rumoro, D.O., M.P.H., Chief Executive Officer

RUSH UNIVERSITY MEDICAL CENTER, 1653 West Congress Parkway, Chicago, IL, Zip 60612–3833; tel. 312/942–5000; Omar Lateef, D.O., President and Chief Executive Officer

RUSH–COPLEY MEDICAL CENTER, 2000 Ogden Avenue, Aurora, IL, Zip 60504–7222; tel. 630/978–6200; John A. Diederich, FACHE, President and Chief Executive Officer

INDIANA

LUTHERAN HEALTH NETWORK
7950 West Jefferson Boulevard, Fort Wayne, IN Zip 46804–4140; tel. 260/435–7001; Michael Poore, Regional Vice President

Networks / Lutheran Health Network

BLUFFTON REGIONAL MEDICAL CENTER, 303 South Main Street, Bluffton, IN, Zip 46714-2503; tel. 260/824-3210; Julie Thompson, Chief Adminstrative Officer and Chief Nursing Officer

DUKES MEMORIAL HOSPITAL, 275 West 12th Street, Peru, IN, Zip 46970-1638; tel. 765/472-8000; Debra Close, Chief Executive Officer

DUPONT HOSPITAL, 2520 East Dupont Road, Fort Wayne, IN, Zip 46825-1675; tel. 260/416-3000; Brent Parsons, Chief Executive Officer

LUTHERAN DOWNTOWN HOSPITAL, 700 Broadway, Fort Wayne, IN, Zip 46802-1493; tel. 260/425-3000; Perry Gay, Chief Executive Officer

LUTHERAN HOSPITAL OF INDIANA, 7950 West Jefferson Boulevard, Fort Wayne, IN, Zip 46804-4140; tel. 260/435-7001; Lorie Ailor, Chief Executive Officer

LUTHERAN KOSCIUSKO HOSPITAL, 2101 East Dubois Drive, Warsaw, IN, Zip 46580-3288; tel. 574/267-3200; Lynn M. Mergen, Chief Executive Officer

ORTHOPAEDIC HOSPITAL OF LUTHERAN HEALTH NETWORK, 7952 West Jefferson Boulevard, Fort Wayne, IN, Zip 46804-4140; tel. 260/435-2999; Lorie Ailor, Chief Executive Officer, Chief Administrative Officer, Network Vice President Orthopedics and Sports Medicine

REHABILITATION HOSPITAL OF FORT WAYNE, 7970 West Jefferson Boulevard, Fort Wayne, IN, Zip 46804-4140; tel. 260/435-6100; Fabian Polo, Ph.D., Chief Executive Officer

ST. VINCENT HEALTH
10330 North Meridian Street, Indianapolis, IN Zip 46290; tel. 317/338-2273; Kevin Speer, JD, Senior Vice President and Ministry Market Executive, Ascension Indiana

ASCENSION ST. VINCENT ANDERSON, 2015 Jackson Street, Anderson, IN, Zip 46016-4339; tel. 765/649-2511; Marion Teixeira, Chief Executive Officer

ASCENSION ST. VINCENT CARMEL HOSPITAL, 13500 North Meridian Street, Carmel, IN, Zip 46032-1456; tel. 317/582-7000; Chad Dilley, President

ASCENSION ST. VINCENT CLAY HOSPITAL, 1206 East National Avenue, Brazil, IN, Zip 47834-2797, 1206 East National Ave, Zip 47834-0489, tel. 812/442-2500; Jerry Laue, Administrator

ASCENSION ST. VINCENT EVANSVILLE, 3700 Washington Avenue, Evansville, IN, Zip 47714-0541; tel. 812/485-4000; Alex Chang, President and Chief Executive Officer

ASCENSION ST. VINCENT FISHERS, 13861 Olio Road, Fishers, IN, Zip 46037-3487; tel. 317/415-9000; Jeralene Hudson, Director

ASCENSION ST. VINCENT HEART CENTER, 10580 North Meridian Street, Indianapolis, IN, Zip 46290-1028; tel. 317/583-5000; Lori Shannon, President

ASCENSION ST. VINCENT INDIANAPOLIS HOSPITAL, 2001 West 86th Street, Indianapolis, IN, Zip 46260-1991, P O Box 40970, Zip 46240-0970, tel. 317/338-2345; Daniel A. Parod, President Central Region

ASCENSION ST. VINCENT JENNINGS, 301 Henry Street, North Vernon, IN, Zip 47265-1097; tel. 812/352-4200; Christina Crank, Administrator, Chief Nursing Officer

ASCENSION ST. VINCENT MERCY, 1331 South 'A' Street, Elwood, IN, Zip 46036-1942; tel. 765/552-4600; Ann C. Yates, R.N., MSN, Administrator and Chief Nursing Officer

ASCENSION ST. VINCENT RANDOLPH, 473 Greenville Avenue, Winchester, IN, Zip 47394-9436; tel. 765/584-0004; Rodney Stevens, Administrator

ASCENSION ST. VINCENT SALEM, 911 North Shelby Street, Salem, IN, Zip 47167-1694; tel. 812/883-5881; Donna Cassidy, Hospital Administrator

ASCENSION ST. VINCENT SETON SPECIALTY HOSPITAL, 8050 Township Line Road, Indianapolis, IN, Zip 46260-2478; tel. 317/415-8500; Daniel A. Parod, President Central Region

ASCENSION ST. VINCENT WARRICK, 1116 Millis Avenue, Boonville, IN, Zip 47601-2204; tel. 812/897-4800; Marty Mattingly, Administrator

ASCENSION ST. VINCENT WILLIAMSPORT, 412 North Monroe Street, Williamsport, IN, Zip 47993-1049; tel. 765/762-4000; Melanie Jane. Craigin, Chief Executive Officer and Administrator

SUBURBAN HEALTH ORGANIZATION
2780 Waterfront Parkway East Drive, Suite 300, Indianapolis, IN Zip 46214; tel. 317/692-5222; Dave Lippincott, President

GOSHEN HEALTH, 200 High Park Avenue, Goshen, IN, Zip 46526-4899, P O Box 139, Zip 46527-0139, tel. 574/533-2141; Randal Christophel, President and Chief Executive Officer

HANCOCK REGIONAL HOSPITAL, 801 North State Street, Greenfield, IN, Zip 46140-1270, P O Box 827, Zip 46140-0827, tel. 317/462-5544; Steven V. Long, FACHE, President and Chief Executive Officer

HENDRICKS REGIONAL HEALTH, 1000 East Main Street, Danville, IN, Zip 46122-1948, P O Box 409, Zip 46122-0409, Michelle Fenoughty, M.D., President and Chief Executive Officer

HENRY COMMUNITY HEALTH, 1000 North 16th Street, New Castle, IN, Zip 47362-4319, P O Box 490, Zip 47362-0490, tel. 765/521-0890; Brian K. Ring, Chief Executive Officer

JOHNSON MEMORIAL HOSPITAL, 1125 West Jefferson Street, Franklin, IN, Zip 46131-2140, P O Box 549, Zip 46131-0549, tel. 317/736-3300; David Dunkle, President and Chief Executive Officer and Vice President Medical Affairs

MAJOR HOSPITAL, 150 West Washington Street, Shelbyville, IN, Zip 46176-1236, 2451 Intelliplex Drive, Zip 46176, tel. 317/392-3211; John M. Horner, President and Chief Executive Officer

MARGARET MARY HEALTH, 321 Mitchell Avenue, Batesville, IN, Zip 47006-8909, P O Box 226, Zip 47006-0226, tel. 812/934-6624; Elizabeth Leising, Interim Chief Executive Officer and President

RIVERVIEW HEALTH, 395 Westfield Road, Noblesville, IN, Zip 46060-1425, P O Box 220, Zip 46061-0220, tel. 317/773-0760; David W. Hyatt, FACHE, Chief Executive Officer

RUSH MEMORIAL HOSPITAL, 1300 North Main Street, Rushville, IN, Zip 46173-1198; tel. 765/932-4111; Bradley Smith, President and Chief Executive Officer

WITHAM HEALTH SERVICES, 2605 North Lebanon Street, Lebanon, IN, Zip 46052-1476, P O Box 1200, Zip 46052-3005, tel. 765/485-8000; Kelly Braverman, FACHE, President and Chief Executive Officer

IOWA

GENESIS HEALTH SYSTEM
1227 East Rusholme Street, Davenport, IA Zip 52803-2459; tel. 563/421-1000

GENESIS MEDICAL CENTER – DAVENPORT, 1227 East Rusholme Street, Davenport, IA, Zip 52803-2498; tel. 563/421-1000; Jordan Voigt, President MercyOne Eastern Division

GENESIS MEDICAL CENTER, DEWITT, 1118 11th Street, De Witt, IA, Zip 52742-1296; tel. 563/659-4200; Ted Rogalski, Administrator

GENESIS MEDICAL CENTER, SILVIS, 801 Illini Drive, Silvis, IL, Zip 61282-1893; tel. 309/281-4000; Theresa Main, R.N., President

GENESIS MEDICAL CENTER–ALEDO, 409 NW Ninth Avenue, Aledo, IL, Zip 61231-1296; tel. 309/582-9100; Ted Rogalski, Administrator

MERCYONE
1449 NW 128th Street, Building 5, Suite 200, Clive, IA Zip 50325; tel. 515/358-9200; Robert P. Ritz, Chief Executive Officer

ADAIR COUNTY HEALTH SYSTEM, 609 SE Kent Street, Greenfield, IA, Zip 50849-9454; tel. 641/743-2123; Catherine Hillestad, Chief Executive Officer

BOONE COUNTY HOSPITAL, 1015 Union Street, Boone, IA, Zip 50036-4821; tel. 515/432-3140; Mikaela Kienitz, Chief Executive Officer

MERCYONE PRIMGHAR MEDICAL CENTER, 255 North Welch Avenue, Primghar, IA, Zip 51245-7765, P O Box 528, Zip 51245-0528, tel. 712/957-2300; Thomas A. Clark, President, MercyOne Western Division

KANSAS

HEALTH INNOVATIONS NETWORK OF KANSAS
1500 SW 10th Avenue, Topeka, KS Zip 66604-1301; tel. 785/354-6137; Sarah Gideon, Network Director

AMBERWELL HEALTH, 800 Raven Hill Drive, Atchison, KS, Zip 66002-9204; tel. 913/367-2131; Jared Abel, Chief Executive Officer

AMBERWELL HIAWATHA, 300 Utah Street, Hiawatha, KS, Zip 66434-2314; tel. 785/742-2131; Jared Abel, Chief Executive Officer

ASCENSION VIA CHRISTI HOSPITAL, MANHATTAN, 1823 College Avenue, Manhattan, KS, Zip 66502-3346; tel. 785/776-3322; Robert C. Copple, FACHE, President

CLAY COUNTY MEDICAL CENTER, 617 Liberty Street, Clay Center, KS, Zip 67432-1564, P O Box 512, Zip 67432-0512, tel. 785/632-2144; Austin M. Gillard, FACHE, Chief Executive Officer

COFFEY COUNTY HOSPITAL, 801 North 4th Street, Burlington, KS, Zip 66839-2602; tel. 620/364-2121; Stacy Augustyn, MSN, R.N., Chief Executive Officer

COMMUNITY HEALTHCARE SYSTEM, 120 West Eighth Street, Onaga, KS, Zip 66521-9574; tel. 785/889-4272; Lorraine R. Meyer, Interim Chief Executive Officer

EASTERN KANSAS HCS, 2200 South West Gage Boulevard, Topeka, KS, Zip 66622-0002, LVN-4101 4th Street Trafficway, Leavenworth, Zip 66048, tel. 785/350-3111; Anthony Rudy. Klopfer, FACHE, Director

F. W. HUSTON MEDICAL CENTER, 408 Delaware Street, Winchester, KS, Zip 66097-4003; tel. 913/774-4340; Heidi Pickerell, Chief Executive Officer

HOLTON COMMUNITY HOSPITAL, 1110 Columbine Drive, Holton, KS, Zip 66436-8824; tel. 785/364-2116; Carrie L. Lutz, Chief Executive Officer

IRWIN ARMY COMMUNITY HOSPITAL, 600 Caisson Hill Road, Junction City, KS, Zip 66442-7037; tel. 785/239-7000; Colonel, Edgar Arroyo, Hospital Commander

KANSAS REHABILITATION HOSPITAL, 1504 SW Eighth Avenue, Topeka, KS, Zip 66606-1632; tel. 785/235-6600; Barry Muninger, Chief Executive Officer

MEMORIAL HEALTH SYSTEM, 511 NE Tenth Street, Abilene, KS, Zip 67410-2153; tel. 785/263-2100; Harold Courtois, Chief Executive Officer

MORRIS COUNTY HOSPITAL, 600 North Washington Street, Council Grove, KS, Zip 66846-1422; tel. 620/767-6811; Kevin Alan. Leeper, Chief Executive Officer

Networks / Sunflower Health Network

NEMAHA VALLEY COMMUNITY HOSPITAL, 1600 Community Drive, Seneca, KS, Zip 66538–9739; tel. 785/336–6181; Kiley Floyd, Chief Executive Officer

NEWMAN REGIONAL HEALTH, 1201 West 12th Avenue, Emporia, KS, Zip 66801–2597; tel. 620/343–6800; Cathy Pimple, MS, Chief Executive Officer

SABETHA COMMUNITY HOSPITAL, 14th and Oregon Streets, Sabetha, KS, Zip 66534–0229, P O Box 229, Zip 66534–0229, tel. 785/284–2121; James Longabaugh, M.D., Chief Executive Officer

STORMONT VAIL HEALTH – FLINT HILLS CAMPUS, 1102 St Mary's Road, Junction City, KS, Zip 66441–4196, P O Box 490, Zip 66441–0490, tel. 785/238–4131; Tracy Duran, Administrator

STORMONT VAIL HEALTH, 1500 SW Tenth Avenue, Topeka, KS, Zip 66604–1353; tel. 785/354–6000; Rob Kenagy, M.D., President and Chief Executive Officer

WAMEGO HEALTH CENTER, 711 Genn Drive, Wamego, KS, Zip 66547–1179; tel. 785/456–2295; Brian Howells, Administrator

WASHINGTON COUNTY HOSPITAL, 304 East Third Street, Washington, KS, Zip 66968–2033; tel. 785/325–2211; Roxanne Schottel, Chief Executive Officer

MED–OP, INC.
220 Canterbury Drive, Hays, KS Zip 67601; tel. 785/623–2301; Shae Veach, Executive Director

CITIZENS MEDICAL CENTER, 100 East College Drive, Colby, KS, Zip 67701–3799; tel. 785/462–7511; David McCorkle, Chief Executive Officer

CLARA BARTON MEDICAL CENTER, 250 West Ninth Street, Hoisington, KS, Zip 67544–1706; tel. 620/653–2114; Jay Tusten, President and Chief Executive Officer

GOODLAND REGIONAL MEDICAL CENTER, 220 West Second Street, Goodland, KS, Zip 67735–1602; tel. 785/890–3625; Craig Loveless, Chief Executive Officer

GOVE COUNTY MEDICAL CENTER, 520 West Fifth Street, Quinter, KS, Zip 67752–0129, P O Box 129, Zip 67752–0129, tel. 785/754–3341; Conner Mikhail. Fiscarelli, Chief Executive Officer

GRAHAM COUNTY HOSPITAL, 304 West Prout Street, Hill City, KS, Zip 67642–1435; tel. 785/421–2121; Melissa Atkins, CPA, Chief Executive Officer

HAYS MEDICAL CENTER, 2220 Canterbury Drive, Hays, KS, Zip 67601–2370; tel. 785/623–5000; Edward Herrman, R.N., FACHE, President and Chief Executive Officer

LOGAN COUNTY HOSPITAL, 211 Cherry Street, Oakley, KS, Zip 67748–1201; tel. 785/672–3211; Aimee Zimmerman, R.N., Chief Executive Officer

NESS COUNTY HOSPITAL DISTRICT NO 2, 312 Custer Street, Ness City, KS, Zip 67560–1654; tel. 785/798–2291; Aaron Kuehn, Administrator

NORTON COUNTY HOSPITAL, 102 East Holme, Norton, KS, Zip 67654–1406, P O Box 250, Zip 67654–0250, tel. 785/877–3351; Kevin Faughnder, Chief Executive Officer

PAWNEE VALLEY COMMUNITY HOSPITAL, 923 Carroll Avenue, Larned, KS, Zip 67550–2429; tel. 620/285–3161; Melanie D. Urban, Administrator

ROOKS COUNTY HEALTH CENTER, 1210 North Washington Street, Plainville, KS, Zip 67663–1632, P O Box 389, Zip 67663–0389, tel. 785/434–4553; Jeff VanDyke, Interim Chief Executive Officer

RUSH COUNTY MEMORIAL HOSPITAL, 801 Locust Street, La Crosse, KS, Zip 67548–9673, P O Box 520, Zip 67548–0520, tel. 785/222–2545; Robert Ladd, M.D., Interim Chief Executive Officer

RUSSELL REGIONAL HOSPITAL, 200 South Main Street, Russell, KS, Zip 67665–2920; tel. 785/483–3131; David Caudill, Chief Executive Officer

SCOTT COUNTY HOSPITAL, 201 East Albert Avenue, Scott City, KS, Zip 67871–1203; tel. 620/872–5811; David Mark. Burnett, President and Chief Executive Officer

SHERIDAN COUNTY HEALTH COMPLEX, 826 18th Street, Hoxie, KS, Zip 67740–0167, P O Box 167, Zip 67740–0167, tel. 785/675–3281; Chad Koster, Chief Executive Officer

PIONEER HEALTH NETWORK, INC.
310 East Walnut Street, Suite 210, Garden City, KS Zip 67846–5565; tel. 620/276–6100; Mary Adam, Executive Director

ASHLAND HEALTH CENTER, 709 Oak Street, Ashland, KS, Zip 67831–0188, P O Box 188, Zip 67831–0188, tel. 620/635–2241; Sandrea Wright, Chief Executive Officer

BOB WILSON MEMORIAL GRANT COUNTY HOSPITAL, 415 North Main Street, Ulysses, KS, Zip 67880–2133; tel. 620/356–1266; Twilla Lee, Chief Executive Officer

CITIZENS MEDICAL CENTER, 100 East College Drive, Colby, KS, Zip 67701–3799; tel. 785/462–7511; David McCorkle, Chief Executive Officer

EDWARDS COUNTY MEDICAL CENTER, 620 West Eighth Street, Kinsley, KS, Zip 67547–2329, P O Box 99, Zip 67547–0099, tel. 620/659–3621; Jimmie W. Hansel, Ph.D., Chief Executive Officer

GREELEY COUNTY HEALTH SERVICES, 506 Third Street, Tribune, KS, Zip 67879–9684, P O Box 338, Zip 67879–0338, tel. 620/376–4221; Trice Watts, Chief Financial Officer and Chief Executive Officer

HAMILTON COUNTY HOSPITAL, 700 North Huser Street, Syracuse, KS, Zip 67878–0948, P O Box 948, Zip 67878–0948, tel. 620/384–7461; Kelly Holder, Administrator

HODGEMAN COUNTY HEALTH CENTER, 809 Bramley Street, Jetmore, KS, Zip 67854–9320, P O Box 310, Zip 67854–0310, tel. 620/357–8361; Allen E. Van Driel, Interim Chief Executive Officer

KEARNY COUNTY HOSPITAL, 500 Thorpe Street, Lakin, KS, Zip 67860–9625; tel. 620/355–7111; Marley Lyn. Koons, Chief Executive Officer

LANE COUNTY HOSPITAL, 235 West Vine, Dighton, KS, Zip 67839–0969, P O Box 969, Zip 67839–0969, tel. 620/397–5321; Marcia Gabel, Chief Financial Officer and Co–Chief Executive Officer

LOGAN COUNTY HOSPITAL, 211 Cherry Street, Oakley, KS, Zip 67748–1201; tel. 785/672–3211; Aimee Zimmerman, R.N., Chief Executive Officer

MEADE DISTRICT HOSPITAL, 510 East Carthage Street, Meade, KS, Zip 67864–6401, P O Box 820, Zip 67864–0820, tel. 620/873–2141; Dawn Unruh, R.N., Chief Executive Officer

MINNEOLA DISTRICT HOSPITAL, 212 Main Street, Minneola, KS, Zip 67865–8511, P O Box 127, Zip 67865–0127, tel. 620/885–4264; Deborah Bruner, Chief Executive Officer and Administrator

MORTON COUNTY HEALTH SYSTEM, 445 Hilltop Street, Elkhart, KS, Zip 67950–0937, P O Box 937, Zip 67950–0937, tel. 620/697–2141; Lisa Swenson, Chief Executive Officer

PHILLIPS COUNTY HEALTH SYSTEMS, 1150 State Street, Phillipsburg, KS, Zip 67661–1743; tel. 785/543–5226; Tara Overmiller, Chief Executive Officer

SATANTA DISTRICT HOSPITAL AND LONG TERM CARE, 401 South Cheyenne Street, Satanta, KS, Zip 67870–0159, P O Box 159, Zip 67870–0159, tel. 620/649–2761; Tina Pendergraft, Chief Executive Officer

SCOTT COUNTY HOSPITAL, 201 East Albert Avenue, Scott City, KS, Zip 67871–1203; tel. 620/872–5811; David Mark. Burnett, President and Chief Executive Officer

SOUTHWEST MEDICAL CENTER, 315 West 15th Street, Liberal, KS, Zip 67901–2455, Box 1340, Zip 67905–1340, tel. 620/624–1651; Amber Williams, Chief Executive Officer

ST. CATHERINE HOSPITAL, 401 East Spruce Street, Garden City, KS, Zip 67846–5679; tel. 620/272–2222; Twilla Lee, Chief Executive Officer

STANTON COUNTY HOSPITAL, 404 North Chestnut Street, Johnson, KS, Zip 67855–5001, P O Box 779, Zip 67855–0779, tel. 620/492–6250; Camille Davidson, Administrator and Chief Executive Officer

STEVENS COUNTY HOSPITAL, 1006 South Jackson Street, Hugoton, KS, Zip 67951–2858, P O Box 10, Zip 67951–0010, tel. 620/544–8511; Jennifer Featherston, Chief Executive Officer

WICHITA COUNTY HEALTH CENTER, 211 East Earl Street, Leoti, KS, Zip 67861–9620; tel. 620/375–2233; Teresa Clark, Chief Executive Officer and Administrator

SUNFLOWER HEALTH NETWORK
400 South Santa Fe Avenue, Salina, KS Zip 67401–4144; tel. 785/452–6102; Heather Fuller, Executive Director

CITIZENS MEDICAL CENTER, 100 East College Drive, Colby, KS, Zip 67701–3799; tel. 785/462–7511; David McCorkle, Chief Executive Officer

CLARA BARTON MEDICAL CENTER, 250 West Ninth Street, Hoisington, KS, Zip 67544–1706; tel. 620/653–2114; Jay Tusten, President and Chief Executive Officer

CLAY COUNTY MEDICAL CENTER, 617 Liberty Street, Clay Center, KS, Zip 67432–1564, P O Box 512, Zip 67432–0512, tel. 785/632–2144; Austin M. Gillard, FACHE, Chief Executive Officer

ELLSWORTH COUNTY MEDICAL CENTER, 1604 Aylward Street, Ellsworth, KS, Zip 67439–0087, P O Box 87, Zip 67439–0087, tel. 785/472–3111; James B. Kirkbride, Chief Executive Officer

GOVE COUNTY MEDICAL CENTER, 520 West Fifth Street, Quinter, KS, Zip 67752–0129, P O Box 129, Zip 67752–0129, tel. 785/754–3341; Conner Mikhail. Fiscarelli, Chief Executive Officer

GRAHAM COUNTY HOSPITAL, 304 West Prout Street, Hill City, KS, Zip 67642–1435; tel. 785/421–2121; Melissa Atkins, CPA, Chief Executive Officer

HILLSBORO COMMUNITY HOSPITAL, 701 South Main Street, Hillsboro, KS, Zip 67063–1553; tel. 620/947–3114; Mark Rooker, Chief Executive Officer

HOSPITAL DISTRICT NO 1 OF RICE COUNTY, 619 South Clark Street, Lyons, KS, Zip 67554–3003, P O Box 828, Zip 67554–0828, tel. 620/257–5173; George M. Stover, Chief Executive Officer

JEWELL COUNTY HOSPITAL, 100 Crestvue Avenue, Mankato, KS, Zip 66956–2407, P O Box 327, Zip 66956–0327, tel. 785/378–3137; Doyle L. McKimmy, FACHE, Chief Executive Officer

LINCOLN COUNTY HOSPITAL, 624 North Second Street, Lincoln, KS, Zip 67455–1738, P O Box 406, Zip 67455–0406, tel. 785/524–4403; Tawnya Seitz, Chief Executive Officer and Chief Financial Officer

LINDSBORG COMMUNITY HOSPITAL, 605 West Lincoln Street, Lindsborg, KS, Zip 67456–2328; tel. 785/227–3308; Larry Van Der Wege, Administrator

MEMORIAL HEALTH SYSTEM, 511 NE Tenth Street, Abilene, KS, Zip 67410–2153; tel. 785/263–2100; Harold Courtois, Chief Executive Officer

MITCHELL COUNTY HOSPITAL HEALTH SYSTEMS, 400 West 8th Street, Beloit, KS, Zip 67420–1605, P O Box 399, Zip 67420–0399, tel. 785/738–2266; Janelle Kircher, MSN, R.N., Chief Executive Officer

NESS COUNTY HOSPITAL DISTRICT NO 2, 312 Custer Street, Ness City, KS, Zip 67560–1654; tel. 785/798–2291; Aaron Kuehn, Administrator

NORTH CENTRAL KANSAS MEDICAL CENTER, 155 West College Drive, Concordia, KS, Zip 66901; tel. 785/243–1234; David Garnas, Administrator

NORTON COUNTY HOSPITAL, 102 East Holme, Norton, KS, Zip 67654–1406, P O Box 250, Zip 67654–0250, tel. 785/877–3351; Kevin Faughnder, Chief Executive Officer

Networks / Sunflower Health Network

OSBORNE COUNTY MEMORIAL HOSPITAL, 424 West New Hampshire Street, Osborne, KS, Zip 67473-2314, P O Box 70, Zip 67473-0070, tel. 785/346-2121; Doris Brown, Chief Executive Officer

OTTAWA COUNTY HEALTH CENTER, 215 East Eighth, Minneapolis, KS, Zip 67467-1902, P O Box 290, Zip 67467-0290, tel. 785/392-2122; Jody Parks, Administrator

PATTERSON HEALTH CENTER, 485 N KS Hwy 2, Anthony, KS, Zip 67003-2526; tel. 620/914-1200; Sarah Teaff, Chief Executive Officer

REPUBLIC COUNTY HOSPITAL, 2420 'G' Street, Belleville, KS, Zip 66935-2400; tel. 785/527-2254; Daniel J. Kelly, Chief Executive Officer

ROOKS COUNTY HEALTH CENTER, 1210 North Washington Street, Plainville, KS, Zip 67663-1632, P O Box 389, Zip 67663-0389, tel. 785/434-4553; Jeff VanDyke, Interim Chief Executive Officer

RUSH COUNTY MEMORIAL HOSPITAL, 801 Locust Street, La Crosse, KS, Zip 67548-9673, P O Box 520, Zip 67548-0520, tel. 785/222-2545; Robert Ladd, M.D., Interim Chief Executive Officer

RUSSELL REGIONAL HOSPITAL, 200 South Main Street, Russell, KS, Zip 67665-2920; tel. 785/483-3131; David Caudill, Chief Executive Officer

SALINA REGIONAL HEALTH CENTER, 400 South Santa Fe Avenue, Salina, KS, Zip 67401-4198, P O Box 5080, Zip 67402-5080, tel. 785/452-7000; Joel Phelps, President and Chief Executive Officer

SHERIDAN COUNTY HEALTH COMPLEX, 826 18th Street, Hoxie, KS, Zip 67740-0167, P O Box 167, Zip 67740-0167, tel. 785/675-3281; Chad Koster, Chief Executive Officer

SMITH COUNTY MEMORIAL HOSPITAL, 921 East Highway 36, Smith Center, KS, Zip 66967-9582; tel. 785/282-6845; Sarah Jane. Ragsdale, R.N., Chief Executive Officer

KENTUCKY

COMMONWEALTH HEALTH CORPORATION
800 Park Street, Bowling Green, KY Zip 42101-2356; tel. 270/745-1500; Connie Smith, FACHE, MSN, R.N., Chief Executive Officer

COMMONWEALTH REGIONAL SPECIALTY HOSPITAL, 250 Park Street, 6th Floor, Bowling Green, KY, Zip 42101-1760, P O Box 90010, Zip 42102-9010, tel. 270/796-6200; Christa Atkins, Administrator

MEDICAL CENTER AT FRANKLIN, 1100 Brookhaven Road, Franklin, KY, Zip 42134-2746; tel. 270/598-4800; Annette Runyon, Vice President and Administrator

MEDICAL CENTER AT SCOTTSVILLE, 456 Burnley Road, Scottsville, KY, Zip 42164-6355; tel. 270/622-2800; Eric Hagan, R.N., Executive Vice President and Administrator

THE MEDICAL CENTER AT BOWLING GREEN, 250 Park Street, Bowling Green, KY, Zip 42101-1795, P O Box 90010, Zip 42102-9010, tel. 270/745-1000; Connie Smith, FACHE, MSN, R.N., Chief Executive Officer

COMMUNITY CARE NETWORK
110 A Second Street, Henderson, KY Zip 42420; tel. 619/278-2273; Roberta Alexander, Director

ASCENSION SAINT THOMAS HOSPITAL, 4220 Harding Pike, Nashville, TN, Zip 37205-2095, P O Box 380, Zip 37202-0380, tel. 615/222-2111; Shubhada Jagasia, President and Chief Executive Officer

ASCENSION ST. VINCENT EVANSVILLE, 3700 Washington Avenue, Evansville, IN, Zip 47714-0541; tel. 812/485-4000; Alex Chang, President and Chief Executive Officer

BAPTIST HEALTH DEACONESS MADISONVILLE, INC., 900 Hospital Drive, Madisonville, KY, Zip 42431-1694; tel. 270/825-5100; Alisa Coleman, President

BAPTIST HEALTH PADUCAH, 2501 Kentucky Avenue, Paducah, KY, Zip 42003-3200; tel. 270/575-2100; Kenneth Boyd, President

CALDWELL MEDICAL CENTER, 100 Medical Center Drive, Princeton, KY, Zip 42445-2430, P O Box 410, Zip 42445-0410, tel. 270/365-0300; Daniel Odegaard, FACHE, Chief Executive Officer

CRITTENDEN COMMUNITY HOSPITAL, 520 West Gum Street, Marion, KY, Zip 42064-1516, P O Box 386, Zip 42064-0386, tel. 270/965-5281; Shawn Bright, Chief Executive Officer

DEACONESS HENDERSON HOSPITAL, 1305 North Elm Street, Henderson, KY, Zip 42420-2775, P O Box 48, Zip 42419-0048, tel. 270/827-7700; Linda E. White, Chief Administrative Officer

DEACONESS UNION COUNTY HOSPITAL, 4604 Highway 60 West, Morganfield, KY, Zip 42437-9570; tel. 270/389-5000; Amber Powell, Chief Administrative Officer

ENCOMPASS HEALTH DEACONESS REHABILITATION HOSPITAL, 9355 Warrick Trail, Newburgh, IN, Zip 47630-0015; tel. 812/476-9983; Blake Bunner, Chief Executive Officer

JENNIE STUART MEDICAL CENTER, 320 West 18th Street, Hopkinsville, KY, Zip 42240-1965, P O Box 2400, Zip 42241-2400, tel. 270/887-0100; Eric A. Lee, President and Chief Executive Officer

LINCOLN TRAIL BEHAVIORAL HEALTH SYSTEM, 3909 South Wilson Road, Radcliff, KY, Zip 40160-8944, P O Box 369, Zip 40159-0369, tel. 270/351-9444; Leslie Flechler, Chief Executive Officer

LIVINGSTON HOSPITAL AND HEALTHCARE SERVICES, 131 Hospital Drive, Salem, KY, Zip 42078-8043; tel. 270/988-2299; Shane Whittington, Chief Executive Officer

MEDICAL CENTER AT FRANKLIN, 1100 Brookhaven Road, Franklin, KY, Zip 42134-2746; tel. 270/598-4800; Annette Runyon, Vice President and Administrator

MURRAY-CALLOWAY COUNTY HOSPITAL, 803 Poplar Street, Murray, KY, Zip 42071-2432; tel. 270/762-1100; Colonel, Jerome Penner, FACHE, Chief Executive Officer

NORTON CHILDREN'S HOSPITAL, 231 East Chestnut Street, Louisville, KY, Zip 40202-1821; tel. 502/629-6000; Diane M. Scardino, Chief Administrative Officer

NORTON HOSPITAL, 200 East Chestnut Street, Louisville, KY, Zip 40202-1800, P O Box 35070, Zip 40232-5070, tel. 502/629-8000; Matthew Ayers, Chief Administrative Officer

OHIO COUNTY HOSPITAL, 1211 Main Street, Hartford, KY, Zip 42347-1619; tel. 270/298-7411; Shellie Dube. Shouse, Chief Executive Officer

OWENSBORO HEALTH MUHLENBERG COMMUNITY HOSPITAL, 440 Hopkinsville Street, Greenville, KY, Zip 42345-1124, P O Box 387, Zip 42345-0378, tel. 270/338-8000; Ed Heath, FACHE, Chief Executive Officer

RIVERVALLEY BEHAVIORAL HEALTH HOSPITAL, 1000 Industrial Drive, Owensboro, KY, Zip 42301-8715; tel. 270/689-6500; Wanda Figueroa Peralta, President and Chief Executive Officer

TRIGG COUNTY HOSPITAL, 254 Main Street, Cadiz, KY, Zip 42211-9153, P O Box 312, Zip 42211-0312, tel. 270/522-3215; John Sumner, Chief Executive Officer

UOFL HEALTH – MARY AND ELIZABETH HOSPITAL, 1850 Bluegrass Avenue, Louisville, KY, Zip 40215-1199; tel. 502/361-6000; Melisa Adkins, Chief Executive Officer

KENTUCKYONE
200 Abraham Flexner Way, Louisville, KY Zip 40202-2877; tel. 502/587-4011; Charles W. Neumann, Interim President and Chief Executive Officer

CHI SAINT JOSEPH HEALTH – FLAGET MEMORIAL HOSPITAL, 4305 New Shepherdsville Road, Bardstown, KY, Zip 40004-9019; tel. 502/350-5000; Jennifer Nolan, President and Chief Executive Officer

CHI SAINT JOSEPH HEALTH – SAINT JOSEPH BEREA, 305 Estill Street, Berea, KY, Zip 40403-1909; tel. 859/986-3151; John C. Yanes, President

CHI SAINT JOSEPH HEALTH – SAINT JOSEPH EAST, 150 North Eagle Creek Drive, Lexington, KY, Zip 40509-1805; tel. 859/967-5000; Jennifer Nolan, President

CHI SAINT JOSEPH HEALTH – SAINT JOSEPH LONDON, 1001 Saint Joseph Lane, London, KY, Zip 40741-8345; tel. 606/330-6000; John C. Yanes, President

CHI SAINT JOSEPH HEALTH – SAINT JOSEPH MOUNT STERLING, 225 Falcon Drive, Mount Sterling, KY, Zip 40353-1158, P O Box 7, Zip 40353-0007, tel. 859/497-5000; John C. Yanes, President

CHI SAINT JOSEPH HEALTH, 1 St Joseph Drive, Lexington, KY, Zip 40504-3754; tel. 859/313-1000; Christy Spitser, Interim President

CONTINUING CARE HOSPITAL, 1 Saint Joseph Drive, Lexington, KY, Zip 40504-3742; tel. 859/967-5744; Robert C. Desotelle, President and Chief Executive Officer

UOFL HEALTH – JEWISH HOSPITAL, 200 Abraham Flexner Way, Louisville, KY, Zip 40202-1886; tel. 502/587-4011; John Walsh, FACHE, Chief Administrative Officer

UOFL HEALTH – MARY AND ELIZABETH HOSPITAL, 1850 Bluegrass Avenue, Louisville, KY, Zip 40215-1199; tel. 502/361-6000; Melisa Adkins, Chief Executive Officer

UOFL HEALTH – PEACE HOSPITAL, 2020 Newburg Road, Louisville, KY, Zip 40205-1879; tel. 502/479-4500; Aundrea Lewis, Interim Chief Executive Officer

ST. ELIZABETH HEALTHCARE
1 Medical Village Drive, Edgewood, KY Zip 41017-3403; tel. 859/301-2000; Garren Colvin, Chief Executive Officer

ST. ELIZABETH EDGEWOOD, 1 Medical Village Drive, Edgewood, KY, Zip 41017-3403; tel. 859/301-2000; Garren Colvin, Chief Executive Officer

ST. ELIZABETH FLORENCE, 4900 Houston Road, Florence, KY, Zip 41042-4824; tel. 859/212-5200; Garren Colvin, Chief Executive Officer

ST. ELIZABETH FORT THOMAS, 85 North Grand Avenue, Fort Thomas, KY, Zip 41075-1796; tel. 859/572-3100; Garren Colvin, Chief Executive Officer

ST. ELIZABETH GRANT, 238 Barnes Road, Williamstown, KY, Zip 41097-9482; tel. 859/824-8240; Garren Colvin, Chief Executive Officer

MASSACHUSETTS

LAHEY HEALTH
41 Mall Road, Burlington, MA Zip 01805-0001; tel. 781/744-7100; Howard R. Grant, M.D., President and Chief Executive Officer

BEVERLY HOSPITAL, 85 Herrick Street, Beverly, MA, Zip 01915-1777; tel. 978/922-3000; Tom Sands, FACHE, President

Networks / Montana Health Network

LAHEY HOSPITAL & MEDICAL CENTER, 41 Mall Road, Burlington, MA, Zip 01805-0001, 31 Mall Road, Zip 01805-0001, tel. 781/744-5100; Susan Moffatt-Bruce, President

WINCHESTER HOSPITAL, 41 Highland Avenue, Winchester, MA, Zip 01890-1496; tel. 781/729-9000; Al Campbell, FACHE, R.N., President

WELLFORCE
800 District Avenue, Suite 520, Burlington, MA Zip 01803-5057; tel. 978/942-2220; Michael J. Dandorph, President and Chief Executive Officer

MICHIGAN

ASCENSION GENESYS HOSPITAL
1 Genesys Parkway, Grand Blanc, MI Zip 48439-8065; tel. 810/606-5000; Elizabeth Aderholdt, Chief Executive Officer

ASCENSION MACOMB-OAKLAND HOSPITAL, WARREN CAMPUS, 11800 East 12 Mile Road, Warren, MI, Zip 48093-3472; tel. 586/573-5000; Kevin Grady, M.D., East Region President

LAKELAND REGIONAL HEALTH SYSTEM
1234 Napier Avenue, Saint Joseph, MI Zip 49085-2112; tel. 269/983-8300; Loren Hamel, M.D., President and Chief Executive Officer

COREWELL HEALTH LAKELAND HOSPITALS, 1234 Napier Avenue, Saint Joseph, MI, Zip 49085-2158; tel. 269/983-8300; Natalie Baggio, R.N., President and Chief Operating Officer

COREWELL HEALTH WATERVLIET HOSPITAL, 400 Medical Park Drive, Watervliet, MI, Zip 49098-9225; tel. 269/463-3111; Christine Fox, MSN, R.N., Interim Chief Nursing Officer

ST. JOHN PROVIDENCE HEALTH SYSTEM
28000 Dequindre Drive, Warren, MI Zip 48092; tel. 866/501-3627; Jean Meyer, President and Chief Executive Officer

ASCENSION BRIGHTON CENTER FOR RECOVERY, 12851 Grand River Road, Brighton, MI, Zip 48116-8506; tel. 810/227-1211; Barbara Shoup, R.N., Hospital Administrator

ASCENSION MACOMB-OAKLAND HOSPITAL, WARREN CAMPUS, 11800 East 12 Mile Road, Warren, MI, Zip 48093-3472; tel. 586/573-5000; Kevin Grady, M.D., East Region President

ASCENSION PROVIDENCE HOSPITAL, SOUTHFIELD CAMPUS, 16001 West Nine Mile Road, Southfield, MI, Zip 48075; tel. 248/849-3000; Michael Wiemann, M.D., Regional President & CEO, Ascension Metro West Region

ASCENSION RIVER DISTRICT HOSPITAL, 4100 River Road, East China, MI, Zip 48054-2909; tel. 810/329-7111; Kevin Grady, M.D., East Region President

ASCENSION ST. JOHN HOSPITAL, 22101 Moross Road, Detroit, MI, Zip 48236-2148; tel. 313/343-4000; Kevin Grady, M.D., East Region President

UPPER PENINSULA HEALTH CARE NETWORK (UPHCN)
228 West Washington Street, Marquette, MI Zip 49855-4330; tel. 906/225-3146; Dennis Smith, Chief Executive Officer

ASPIRUS IRON RIVER HOSPITAL, 1400 West Ice Lake Road, Iron River, MI, Zip 49935-9526; tel. 906/265-6121; Rae Kaare, Chief Administrative Officer

ASPIRUS IRONWOOD HOSPITAL & CLINICS, INC., N10561 Grandview Lane, Ironwood, MI, Zip 49938-9622; tel. 906/932-2525; Paula L. Chermside, Chief Administrative Officer

ASPIRUS KEWEENAW HOSPITAL, 205 Osceola Street, Laurium, MI, Zip 49913-2134; tel. 906/337-6500; Matt Krause, Chief Administrative Officer

BARAGA COUNTY MEMORIAL HOSPITAL, 18341 U.S. Highway 41, L'Anse, MI, Zip 49946-8024; tel. 906/524-3300; Rob Stowe, Chief Executive Officer

HELEN NEWBERRY JOY HOSPITAL & HEALTHCARE CENTER, Helen Newberry Joy Hospital Annex, 502 West Harrie Street, Newberry, MI, Zip 49868-1209; tel. 906/293-9200; Helen Johnson, Chief Executive Officer

MACKINAC STRAITS HEALTH SYSTEM, INC., 1140 North State Street, Saint Ignace, MI, Zip 49781-1048; tel. 906/643-8585; Karen Cheeseman, President and Chief Executive Officer

MARSHFIELD MEDICAL CENTER - DICKINSON, 1721 South Stephenson Avenue, Iron Mountain, MI, Zip 49801-3637; tel. 906/774-1313; Amanda Shelast, FACHE, President

MUNISING MEMORIAL HOSPITAL, 1500 Sand Point Road, Munising, MI, Zip 49862-1406; tel. 906/387-4110; Jim Parker, FACHE, Chief Executive Officer

MYMICHIGAN MEDICAL CENTER SAULT, 500 Osborn Boulevard, Sault Sainte Marie, MI, Zip 49783-1884; tel. 906/635-4460; Kevin Kalchik, CPA, President

SCHOOLCRAFT MEMORIAL HOSPITAL, 7870W US Highway 2, Manistique, MI, Zip 49854-8992; tel. 906/341-3200; Andrew Bertapelle, MSN, R.N., Chief Executive Officer

UP HEALTH SYSTEM - BELL, 901 Lakeshore Drive, Ishpeming, MI, Zip 49849-1367; tel. 906/486-4431; Mitchell D. Leckelt, FACHE, Chief Executive Officer

UP HEALTH SYSTEM - PORTAGE, 500 Campus Drive, Hancock, MI, Zip 49930-1569; tel. 906/483-1000; Ryan Heinonen, MSN, R.N., Chief Executive Officer

MINNESOTA

NORTHWEST METRO ALLIANCE
c/O Mercy Hospital, 4050 Coon Rapids Boulevard, Coon Rapids, MN Zip 55433-2586; tel. 763/236-6000

MERCY HOSPITAL, 4050 Coon Rapids Boulevard, Coon Rapids, MN, Zip 55433-2586; tel. 763/236-6000; Michael Eric. Johnston, FACHE, President Southern Market, Mercy Hospital

RIVER VALLEY HEALTH NETWORK
30 South Behl Street, Appleton, MN Zip 56208-1616; tel. 320/289-8504; Angel Molden, Marketing Manager and Public Relations Officer

APPLETON AREA HEALTH, 30 South Behl Street, Appleton, MN, Zip 56208-1699; tel. 320/289-2422; Greg Miner, Chief Executive Officer

CCM HEALTH, 824 North 11th Street, Montevideo, MN, Zip 56265-1683; tel. 320/269-8877; Brian A. Lovdahl, Chief Executive Officer

JOHNSON MEMORIAL HEALTH SERVICES, 1282 Walnut Street, Dawson, MN, Zip 56232-2333; tel. 320/769-4323; Kathy Johnson, Interim Chief Executive Officer

MADISON HEALTHCARE SERVICES, 900 Second Avenue, Madison, MN, Zip 56256-1006; tel. 320/598-7556; Erik Bjerke, Chief Executive Officer

MISSOURI

HEALTH NETWORK OF MISSOURI
One Hospital Drive, Room C1213, DC 079.00, Columbia, MO Zip 65212; tel. 573/815-8000; Marty McCormick, Chief Executive Officer

BOTHWELL REGIONAL HEALTH CENTER, 601 East 14th Street, Sedalia, MO, Zip 65301-5972, P O Box 1706, Zip 65302-1706, tel. 660/826-8833; Lori Wightman, R.N., FACHE, Chief Executive Officer

CAPITAL REGION MEDICAL CENTER, 1125 Madison Street, Jefferson City, MO, Zip 65101-5200, P O Box 1128, Zip 65102-1128, tel. 573/632-5000; John Dennis. Hamilton, Interim Chief Operating Officer

HANNIBAL REGIONAL HOSPITAL, 6000 Hospital Drive, Hannibal, MO, Zip 63401-6887, P O Box 551, Zip 63401-0551, tel. 573/248-1300; C Todd. Ahrens, FACHE, President and Chief Executive Officer

LAKE REGIONAL HEALTH SYSTEM, 54 Hospital Drive, Osage Beach, MO, Zip 65065-3050; tel. 573/348-8000; Kevin G. McRoberts, FACHE, Chief Executive Officer

SAINT FRANCIS MEDICAL CENTER, 211 St Francis Drive, Cape Girardeau, MO, Zip 63703-5049; tel. 573/331-3000; Justin Davison, President and Chief Executive Officer

UNIVERSITY HOSPITAL, 1 Hospital Drive, Columbia, MO, Zip 65212-0001; tel. 573/882-4141; Ric A. Ransom, Chief Executive Officer

MERCY HEALTH EAST
615 South New Ballas Road, Saint Louis, MO Zip 63141-8221; tel. 314/364-3000; Donn Sorensen, Regional President, West Communities

MERCY HOSPITAL JEFFERSON, 1400 US Highway 61 South, Festus, MO, Zip 63028-4100, P O Box 350, Crystal City, Zip 63019-0350, tel. 636/933-1000; Dan Eckenfels, President, Mercy Jefferson Communities

MERCY HOSPITAL ST. LOUIS, 615 South New Ballas Road, Saint Louis, MO, Zip 63141-8277; tel. 314/251-6000; David Meiners, President

MERCY HOSPITAL WASHINGTON, 901 East Fifth Street, Washington, MO, Zip 63090-3127; tel. 636/239-8000; Eric Eoloff, President, Mercy Washington

MONTANA

MONTANA HEALTH NETWORK
519 Pleasant Street, Miles City, MT Zip 59301-3030; tel. 406/234-1420; Chris Hopkins, Network Director

BILLINGS CLINIC, 2800 10th Avenue North, Attn: Angie Puckett, Billings, MT, Zip 59107, P O Box 37000, Zip 59107-7000, tel. 406/657-4000; Clint Seger, M.D., Chief Executive Officer

CENTRAL MONTANA MEDICAL CENTER, 408 Wendell Avenue, Lewistown, MT, Zip 59457-2261; tel. 406/535-7711; Cody Langbehn, Chief Executive Officer

DAHL MEMORIAL HEALTHCARE ASSOCIATION, 215 Sandy Street, Ekalaka, MT, Zip 59324, P O Box 46, Zip 59324-0046, tel. 406/775-8730; Ryan Tooke, Chief Executive Officer

DANIELS MEMORIAL HEALTHCARE CENTER, 105 Fifth Avenue East, Scobey, MT, Zip 59263, P O Box 400, Zip 59263-0400, tel. 406/487-2296; Kody Brinton, Chief Executive Officer

FALLON MEDICAL COMPLEX, 202 South 4th Street West, Baker, MT, Zip 59313-9156, P O Box 820, Zip 59313-0820, tel. 406/778-3331; David Espeland, Chief Executive Officer

FRANCES MAHON DEACONESS HOSPITAL, 621 Third Street South, Glasgow, MT, Zip 59230-2699; tel. 406/228-3500; Nick Dirkes, Chief Executive Officer

Networks / Montana Health Network

GLENDIVE MEDICAL CENTER, 202 Prospect Drive, Glendive, MT, Zip 59330-1999; tel. 406/345-3306; Parker Powell, Chief Executive Officer

HOLY ROSARY HEALTHCARE, 2600 Wilson Street, Miles City, MT, Zip 59301-5094; tel. 406/233-2600; Karen Costello, President

MCCONE COUNTY HEALTH CENTER, 605 Sullivan Avenue, Circle, MT, Zip 59215, P O Box 48, Zip 59215-0048, tel. 406/485-3381; Jacque Gardner, Chief Executive Officer

PHILLIPS COUNTY HOSPITAL, 311 South 8th Avenue East, Malta, MT, Zip 59538-0640, P O Box 640, Zip 59538-0640, tel. 406/654-1100; Jo Tharp, Interim Chief Executive Officer

POPLAR COMMUNITY HOSPITAL, 211 H Street, Poplar, MT, Zip 59255-9519, P O Box 38, Zip 59255-0038, tel. 406/768-6100; Michael Post, Chief Executive Officer

ROOSEVELT MEDICAL CENTER, 818 Second Avenue East, Culbertson, MT, Zip 59218, P O Box 419, Zip 59218-0419, tel. 406/787-6401; Audrey Stromberg, Administrator

SHERIDAN MEMORIAL HOSPITAL, 440 West Laurel Avenue, Plentywood, MT, Zip 59254-1596; tel. 406/765-3700; Kody Nelson, Chief Executive Officer

SIDNEY HEALTH CENTER, 216 14th Avenue SW, Sidney, MT, Zip 59270-3586; tel. 406/488-2100; Jennifer Doty, Chief Executive Officer

STILLWATER BILLINGS CLINIC, 44 West Fourth Avenue North, Columbus, MT, Zip 59019-0959, P O Box 959, Zip 59019-0959, tel. 406/322-5316; Luke Kobold, Chief Executive Officer

TRINITY HOSPITAL, 315 Knapp Street, Wolf Point, MT, Zip 59201-1826; tel. 406/653-6500; Michael Post, Chief Executive Officer

WHEATLAND MEMORIAL HEALTHCARE, 530 Third Street North West, Harlowton, MT, Zip 59036, P O Box 287, Zip 59036-0287, tel. 406/632-4351; Donna Neste, Chief Executive Officer

NEBRASKA

CHI HEALTH
12809 West Dodge Road, Omaha, NE Zip 68154-2155; tel. 402/343-4300

CHI HEALTH CREIGHTON UNIVERSITY MEDICAL CENTER – BERGAN MERCY, 7500 Mercy Road, Omaha, NE, Zip 68124-2319; tel. 402/398-6060; Dennis Bierle, President

CHI HEALTH GOOD SAMARITAN, 10 East 31st Street, Kearney, NE, Zip 68847-2926, P O Box 1990, Zip 68848-1990, tel. 308/865-7100; Curt Coleman, FACHE, President

CHI HEALTH IMMANUEL, 6901 North 72nd Street, Omaha, NE, Zip 68122-1799; tel. 402/572-2121; Anthony Ashby, President

CHI HEALTH LAKESIDE, 6901 N 72nd St, Omaha, NE, Zip 68122, 16901 Lakeside Hills Court, Zip 68130-2318, tel. 402/717-8000; Mark E. Longacre, FACHE, President

CHI HEALTH MERCY CORNING, 603 Rosary Drive, Corning, IA, Zip 50841-1683; tel. 641/322-3121; Alicia Reed, President

CHI HEALTH MERCY COUNCIL BLUFFS, 800 Mercy Drive, Council Bluffs, IA, Zip 51503-3128; tel. 712/328-5000; Derek Havens, Interim President

CHI HEALTH MIDLANDS, 11111 South 84th Street, Papillion, NE, Zip 68046-4122; tel. 402/593-3000; Mark E. Longacre, FACHE, President

CHI HEALTH MISSOURI VALLEY, 631 North Eighth Street, Missouri Valley, IA, Zip 51555-1102; tel. 712/642-2784; David J. Jones, Market President, Critical Access Hospitals (NE, IA, MN)

CHI HEALTH NEBRASKA HEART, 7500 South 91st Street, Lincoln, NE, Zip 68526-9437; tel. 402/327-2700; Rick Thompson, M.D., FACS, FACC, President

CHI HEALTH PLAINVIEW, 704 North Third Street, Plainview, NE, Zip 68769-2047, P O Box 489, Zip 68769-0489, tel. 402/582-4245; Connie Peters, R.N., President

CHI HEALTH SAINT FRANCIS, 2620 West Faidley Avenue, Grand Island, NE, Zip 68803-4297, P O Box 9804, Zip 68802-9804, tel. 308/384-4600; Steven M. Schieber, FACHE, President

CHI HEALTH SCHUYLER, 104 West 17th Street, Schuyler, NE, Zip 68661-1304; tel. 402/352-2441; Connie Peters, R.N., President

CHI HEALTH ST ELIZABETH, 555 South 70th Street, Lincoln, NE, Zip 68510-2494; tel. 402/219-8000; Tyler DeJong, President

CHI HEALTH ST. MARY'S, 1301 Grundman Boulevard, Nebraska City, NE, Zip 68410; tel. 402/873-3321; Daniel DeFreece, M.D., President

NEBRASKA MEDICINE
987400 Nebraska Medical Center, Omaha, NE Zip 68198-7400; tel. 877/763-0000; James Linder, M.D., Chief Executive Officer

NEBRASKA MEDICINE – BELLEVUE, 2500 Bellevue Medical Center Drive, Bellevue, NE, Zip 68123-1591; tel. 402/763-3000; Julie L. Lazure, R.N., MSN, Vice President, Nurse Executive

NEBRASKA MEDICINE – NEBRASKA MEDICAL CENTER, 987400 Nebraska Medical Center, Omaha, NE, Zip 68198-7400; tel. 402/552-2000; James Linder, M.D., Chief Executive Officer

NEW HAMPSHIRE

CARING COMMUNITY NETWORK OF THE TWIN RIVERS
c/o First Health, 841 Central Street, Franklin, NH Zip 03235-2026; tel. 603/934-0177; Rick Silverberg, Managing Director

CONCORD HOSPITAL – FRANKLIN, 15 Aiken Avenue, Franklin, NH, Zip 03235-1299; tel. 603/934-2060; Kevin L. McCarthy, Chief Administrative Officer

NEW JERSEY

QUALCARE, INC.
242 Old New Brunswick Road, Piscataway, NJ Zip 08854-3754; tel. 732/562-2800; Jerry Eisenberg, Network Contact

CAPITAL HEALTH MEDICAL CENTER–HOPEWELL, 1 Capital Way, Pennington, NJ, Zip 08534-2520; tel. 609/303-4000; Al Maghazehe, Ph.D., FACHE, President and Chief Executive Officer

CAREPOINT HEALTH CHRIST HOSPITAL, 176 Palisade Avenue, Jersey City, NJ, Zip 07306-1196, 176 Palisades Avenue, Zip 07306-1196, tel. 201/795-8200; Marie Theresa Duffy, Chief Hospital Executive, Executive Vice President System Clinical Integration and Standards

CHILTON MEDICAL CENTER, 97 West Parkway, Pompton Plains, NJ, Zip 07444-1696; tel. 973/831-5000; Maureen Schneider, Ph.D., R.N., FACHE, President

CLARA MAASS MEDICAL CENTER, 1 Clara Maass Drive, Belleville, NJ, Zip 07109-3557; tel. 973/450-2000; Mary Ellen Clyne, Ph.D., President and Chief Executive Officer

DEBORAH HEART AND LUNG CENTER, 200 Trenton Road, Browns Mills, NJ, Zip 08015-1705; tel. 609/893-6611; Jim Andrews, President and Chief Executive Officer

ENGLEWOOD HEALTH, 350 Engle Street, Englewood, NJ, Zip 07631-1898; tel. 201/894-3000; Warren Geller, President and Chief Executive Officer

HACKENSACK MERIDIAN HEALTH HACKENSACK UNIVERSITY MEDICAL CENTER, loading dock A(off Essex street), 30 Prospect Avenue, Hackensack, NJ, Zip 07601-1914, 30 Prospect Avenue, Zip 07601-1914, tel. 201/996-2000; Mark Sparta, FACHE, President and Chief Hospital Executive

HACKENSACK MERIDIAN HEALTH JFK MEDICAL CENTER, 65 James Street, Edison, NJ, Zip 8818; tel. 732/321-7000; Amie D. Thornton, Chief Hospital Executive

HACKENSACK MERIDIAN HEALTH OCEAN UNIVERSITY MEDICAL CENTER, 425 Jack Martin Boulevard, Brick Township, NJ, Zip 08724-7732; tel. 732/840-2200; Frank Citara, Chief Hospital Executive

HACKENSACK MERIDIAN HEALTH RARITAN BAY MEDICAL CENTER, 530 New Brunswick Avenue, Perth Amboy, NJ, Zip 08861-3654; tel. 732/442-3700; Patricia Carroll, President and Chief Hospital Executive

HACKENSACK MERIDIAN HEALTH RIVERVIEW MEDICAL CENTER, 1 Riverview Plaza, Red Bank, NJ, Zip 07701-1864; tel. 732/741-2700; Timothy J. Hogan, FACHE, President, Chief Hospital Executive

HACKETTSTOWN MEDICAL CENTER, 651 Willow Grove Street, Hackettstown, NJ, Zip 07840-1799; tel. 908/852-5100; Robert H. Adams, President, Western Region

INSPIRA MEDICAL CENTER–VINELAND, 1505 West Sherman Avenue, Vineland, NJ, Zip 08360-6912; tel. 856/641-8000; Amy B. Mansue, President and Chief Executive Officer

PENN MEDICINE PRINCETON MEDICAL CENTER, 1 Plainsboro Road, Plainsboro, NJ, Zip 08536-1913; tel. 609/853-7100; James Demetriades, Chief Executive Officer

PIEDMONT MOUNTAINSIDE HOSPITAL, 1266 Highway 515 South, Jasper, GA, Zip 30143-4872; tel. 706/692-2441; Denise Ray, Chief Executive Officer

ROBERT WOOD JOHNSON UNIVERSITY HOSPITAL, 1 Robert Wood Johnson Place, New Brunswick, NJ, Zip 08903-2601; tel. 732/828-3000; Bill Arnold, Executive Vice President, RWJBarnabas Health, President Southern Region, Chief Executive Officer, Robert Wood Johnson Un

SAINT MICHAEL'S MEDICAL CENTER, 111 Central Avenue, Newark, NJ, Zip 07102-1909; tel. 973/877-5000; Alan Sickles, M.D., Chief Executive Officer

ST. MARY'S GENERAL HOSPITAL, 350 Boulevard, Passaic, NJ, Zip 07055-2840; tel. 973/365-4300; Edward Condit, President and Chief Executive Officer

UNIVERSITY HOSPITAL, 150 Bergen Street, Newark, NJ, Zip 07103-2496; tel. 973/972-4300; Edward Jimenez, President and Chief Executive Officer

VIRTUA MARLTON, 90 Brick Road, Marlton, NJ, Zip 08053-2177; tel. 856/355-6000; Dennis W. Pullin, FACHE, President and Chief Executive Officer

NEW MEXICO

NEW MEXICO RURAL HOSPITAL NETWORK
7471 Pan American Freeway NE, Albuquerque, NM Zip 87109; tel. 505/346-0216; Stephen Stoddard, FACHE, Executive Director

ARTESIA GENERAL HOSPITAL, 702 North 13th Street, Artesia, NM, Zip 88210-1199; tel. 575/748-3333; Joe Salgado, M.D., Interim Chief Executive Officer

CIBOLA GENERAL HOSPITAL, 1016 East Roosevelt Avenue, Grants, NM, Zip 87020-2118; tel. 505/287-4446; Maria A. Atencio, R.N., Acting Chief Executive Officer and Chief Nursing Officer

GUADALUPE COUNTY HOSPITAL, 117 Camino de Vida, Santa Rosa, NM, Zip 88435–2267; tel. 575/472-3417

HOLY CROSS HOSPITAL, 1397 Weimer Road, Taos, NM, Zip 87571–6253; tel. 575/758-8883; James Kiser, Chief Executive Officer

MINERS' COLFAX MEDICAL CENTER, 200 Hospital Drive, Raton, NM, Zip 87740–2099; tel. 575/445-7700; Bo Beames, Chief Executive Officer

NOR–LEA HOSPITAL DISTRICT, 1600 North Main Avenue, Lovington, NM, Zip 88260–2871; tel. 575/396-6611; David B. Shaw, Chief Executive Officer and Administrator

REHOBOTH MCKINLEY CHRISTIAN HEALTH CARE SERVICES, 1901 Red Rock Drive, Gallup, NM, Zip 87301–5683; tel. 505/863-7000; William D. Patten, Jr., Interim Chief Executive Officer

ROOSEVELT GENERAL HOSPITAL, 42121 U S Highway 70, Portales, NM, Zip 88130, P O Box 868, Zip 88130–0868, tel. 575/359-1800; Kaye Green, FACHE, Chief Executive Officer

SIERRA VISTA HOSPITAL, 800 East Ninth Avenue, Truth or Consequences, NM, Zip 87901–1961; tel. 575/894-2111; Frank Corcoran, R.N., Chief Executive Officer

UNION COUNTY GENERAL HOSPITAL, 300 Wilson Street, Clayton, NM, Zip 88415–3304, P O Box 489, Zip 88415–0489, tel. 575/374-2585; Tammie Chavez Stump, R.N., Chief Executive Officer

NEW YORK

ARDENT SOLUTIONS, INC.
85 North Main Street, Suite 4, Wellsville, NY Zip 14895–1254; tel. 585/593-5223; Carrie Whitwood, Executive Director

JONES MEMORIAL HOSPITAL, 191 North Main Street, Wellsville, NY, Zip 14895–1150, P O Box 72, Zip 14895–0072, tel. 585/593-1100; James Helms, President and Chief Executive Officer

ARNOT HEALTH
600 Roe Avenue, Elmira, NY Zip 14905–1629; tel. 607/737-4100; Robert K. Lambert, M.D., FACHE, President and Chief Executive Officer

ARNOT OGDEN MEDICAL CENTER, 600 Roe Avenue, Elmira, NY, Zip 14905–1629; tel. 607/737-4100; Jonathan I. Lawrence, President and Chief Executive Officer

IRA DAVENPORT MEMORIAL HOSPITAL, 7571 State Route 54, Bath, NY, Zip 14810–9590; tel. 607/776-8500; Elizabeth Weir, MSN, R.N., Site Administrator and Vice President of Nursing

GREAT LAKES HEALTH SYSTEM OF WESTERN NEW YORK
726 Exchange Street, Suite 522, Buffalo, NY Zip 14210–1485; tel. 716/859-8820; Jody Lomeo, Interim Chief Executive Officer

ERIE COUNTY MEDICAL CENTER, 462 Grider Street, Buffalo, NY, Zip 14215–3098; tel. 716/898-3000; Thomas J. Quatroche, Jr., President and Chief Executive Officer

KALEIDA HEALTH, 100 High Street, Buffalo, NY, Zip 14203–1154; tel. 716/859-5600; Donald Boyd, President and Chief Executive Officer

LAKE ERIE REGIONAL HEALTH SYSTEM OF NEW YORK
529 Central Avenue, Dunkirk, NY Zip 14048–2514; tel. 716/366-1111; J. Gary Rhodes, FACHE, Interim Chief Executive Officer

BROOKS–TLC HOSPITAL SYSTEM, INC., 529 Central Avenue, Dunkirk, NY, Zip 14048–2599; tel. 716/366-1111; Kenneth R. Morris, President and Chief Executive Officer

MOHAWK VALLEY HEALTH SYSTEM (MVHS)
1656 Champlin Avenue, Utica, NY Zip 13502–4830; tel. 315/624-6002; Darlene Stromstad, FACHE, President and Chief Executive Officer

WYNN HOSPITAL, 111 Hospital Drive, Utica, NY, Zip 13502, P O Box 479, Zip 13503–0479, tel. 315/917-9966; Darlene Stromstad, FACHE, President and Chief Executive Officer

MOUNT SINAI NYU HEALTH NETWORK
One Gustave L. Levy Place, New York, NY Zip 10029; tel. 212/659-8888; Arthur A. Klein, M.D., President

ENGLEWOOD HEALTH, 350 Engle Street, Englewood, NJ, Zip 07631–1898; tel. 201/894-3000; Warren Geller, President and Chief Executive Officer

HUDSON REGIONAL HOSPITAL, 55 Meadowlands Parkway, Secaucus, NJ, Zip 07094–2977; tel. 201/392-3100; Nizar Kifaieh, M.D., President and Chief Executive Officer

JAMES J. PETERS VETERANS AFFAIRS MEDICAL CENTER, 130 West Kingsbridge Road, Bronx, NY, Zip 10468–3904; tel. 718/584-9000; Balavenkatesh Kanna, M.D., M.P.H., FACHE, Medical Center Director

JERSEY CITY MEDICAL CENTER, 355 Grand Street, Jersey City, NJ, Zip 07302–4321; tel. 201/915-2000; Michael Prilutsky, President and Chief Executive Officer

MONTEFIORE ST. LUKE'S CORNWALL, 70 Dubois Street, Newburgh, NY, Zip 12550–4851; tel. 845/561-4400; Daniel J. Maughan, MSN, RN, C., President and Chief Executive Officer

MORRISTOWN MEDICAL CENTER, 100 Madison Avenue, Morristown, NJ, Zip 07960–6136; tel. 973/971-5000; Trish O'Keefe, Ph.D., R.N., President

NYC HEALTH + HOSPITALS / ELMHURST, 79–01 Broadway, Elmhurst, NY, Zip 11373–1329; tel. 718/334-4000; Helen Arteaga. Landaverde, Chief Executive Officer

NYC HEALTH + HOSPITALS / QUEENS, 82–68 164th Street, Jamaica, NY, Zip 11432–1104; tel. 718/883-3000; Neil J. Moore, Chief Executive Officer

OVERLOOK MEDICAL CENTER, 99 Beauvoir Avenue, Summit, NJ, Zip 07901–3533; tel. 908/522-2000; Stephanie L. Schwartz, FACHE, President

PHELPS MEMORIAL HOSPITAL CENTER, 701 North Broadway, Sleepy Hollow, NY, Zip 10591–1020; tel. 914/366-3000; Beata Mastalerz, Executive Director

ST. JOHN'S RIVERSIDE HOSPITAL, 967 North Broadway, Yonkers, NY, Zip 10701–1399; tel. 914/964-4444; Ronald J. Corti, President and Chief Executive Officer

ST. JOSEPH'S UNIVERSITY MEDICAL CENTER, 703 Main Street, Paterson, NJ, Zip 07503–2691; tel. 973/754-2000; Dustin Riccio, M.D., President and Chief Executive Officer

THE MOUNT SINAI HOSPITAL, 1 Gustave L Levy Place, P O Box 1068, New York, NY, Zip 10029–0310; tel. 212/241-6500; David L. Reich, M.D., President and Chief Operating Officer

VASSAR BROTHERS MEDICAL CENTER, 45 Reade Place, Poughkeepsie, NY, Zip 12601–3947; tel. 845/454-8500; Susan Browning, President

NEW YORK PRESBYTERIAN REGIONAL HOSPITAL NETWORK
525 East 68th Street, Box 182, New York, NY Zip 10065–4870; tel. 212/746-3745; Steven J. Corwin, M.D., President and Chief Executive Officer

GRACIE SQUARE HOSPITAL, 420 East 76th Street, New York, NY, Zip 10021–3396; tel. 212/988-4400; David Wyman, President and Chief Executive Officer

NEW YORK COMMUNITY HOSPITAL, 2525 Kings Highway, Brooklyn, NY, Zip 11229–1705; tel. 718/692-5300; Barry Stern, President and Chief Executive Officer

ONE BROOKLYN HEALTH
1545 Atlantic Avenue, Brooklyn, NY Zip 11213–1122; tel. 718/613-7375; Sandra Scott, M.D., Interim Chief Executive Officer

BROOKDALE HOSPITAL MEDICAL CENTER, 125 Worth Street, 4th Fl Ste 418, New York, NY, Zip 10013, One Brookdale Plaza, Brooklyn, Zip 11212–3139, tel. 718/240-5000; Chris Paras, Interim Executive Director

INTERFAITH MEDICAL CENTER, 1545 Atlantic Avenue, Brooklyn, NY, Zip 11213–1122; tel. 718/613-4000; Sandra Scott, M.D., Interim Chief Executive Officer

RURAL HEALTH NETWORK OF OSWEGO COUNTY
10 George Street, Oswego, NY Zip 13126; tel. 315/592-0827; Brian Coleman, Coordinator

OSWEGO HOSPITAL, 110 West Sixth Street, Oswego, NY, Zip 13126–2507; tel. 315/349-5511; Michael Backus, President and Chief Executive Officer

STELLARIS HEALTH
135 Bedford Rd, Armonk, NY Zip 10504–1945; tel. 914/273-5454; Sharon A. Lucian, President and Chief Executive Officer

NORTHERN WESTCHESTER HOSPITAL, 400 East Main Street, Mount Kisco, NY, Zip 10549–3477, 400 East Main Street, G–02, Zip 10549–3477, tel. 914/666-1200; Derek Anderson, Executive Director

PHELPS MEMORIAL HOSPITAL CENTER, 701 North Broadway, Sleepy Hollow, NY, Zip 10591–1020; tel. 914/366-3000; Beata Mastalerz, Executive Director

WHITE PLAINS HOSPITAL CENTER, 41 East Post Road, White Plains, NY, Zip 10601–4699; tel. 914/681-0600; Susan Fox, President and Chief Executive Officer

NORTH CAROLINA

COASTAL CAROLINAS HEALTH ALLIANCE
5305–M Wrightsville Avenue, Wilmington, NC Zip 28403; tel. 910/332-8012; Yvonne Hughes, Chief Executive Officer

CAPE FEAR VALLEY BLADEN COUNTY HOSPITAL, 501 South Poplar Street, Elizabethtown, NC, Zip 28337–9375, P O Box 398, Zip 28337–0398, tel. 910/862-5100; Spencer Cummings, President and Chief Executive Officer

COLUMBUS REGIONAL HEALTHCARE SYSTEM, 500 Jefferson Street, Whiteville, NC, Zip 28472–3634; tel. 910/642-8011; Jason Beck, President and Chief Executive Officer

DOSHER MEMORIAL HOSPITAL, 924 North Howe Street, Southport, NC, Zip 28461–3099; tel. 910/457-3800; Lynda Stanley, President and Chief Executive Officer

ECU HEALTH DUPLIN HOSPITAL, 401 North Main Street, Kenansville, NC, Zip 28349–8801, P O Box 278, Zip 28349–0278, tel. 910/296-0941; Jeffery Dial, Chief Executive Officer

ECU HEALTH MEDICAL CENTER, 2100 Stantonsburg Road, Greenville, NC, Zip 27834–2818, P O Box 6028, Zip 27835–6028, tel. 252/847-4100; Jay Briley, FACHE, President

Networks / Coastal Carolinas Health Alliance

MCLEOD HEALTH LORIS, 3655 Mitchell Street, Loris, SC, Zip 29569-2827; tel. 843/716-7000; Michael Scott. Montgomery, Chief Executive Officer, Vice President, McLeod Health

MCLEOD REGIONAL MEDICAL CENTER, 555 East Cheves Street, Florence, SC, Zip 29506-2617, P O Box 100551, Zip 29502-0551, tel. 843/777-2000; John Will. McLeod, Chief Executive Officer

NOVANT HEALTH NEW HANOVER REGIONAL MEDICAL CENTER, 2131 South 17th Street, Wilmington, NC, Zip 28401-7483, P O Box 9000, Zip 28402-9000, tel. 910/343-7000; Ernest L. Bovio, Jr., Senior Vice President & President Novant Health New Hanover Regional Medical Center & Coastal Market

NOVANT HEALTH PENDER MEDICAL CENTER, 507 East Freemont Street, Burgaw, NC, Zip 28425-5131; tel. 910/259-5451; Ruth Glaser, President and Chief Operating Officer

SAMPSON REGIONAL MEDICAL CENTER, 607 Beaman Street, Clinton, NC, Zip 28328-2697, P O Box 260, Zip 28329-0260, tel. 910/592-8511; Shawn Howerton, M.D., Chief Executive Officer and President, Medical Staff

SCOTLAND HEALTH CARE SYSTEM, 500 Lauchwood Drive, Laurinburg, NC, Zip 28352-5599; tel. 910/291-7000; David L. Pope, President and Chief Executive Officer

UNC HEALTH SOUTHEASTERN, 300 West 27th Street, Lumberton, NC, Zip 28358-3075, P O Box 1408, Zip 28359-1408, tel. 910/671-5000; Christopher Ellington, President and Chief Executive Officer

MISSION HEALTH SYSTEM
509 Biltmore Avenue, Asheville, NC Zip 28801-4601; tel. 828/213-1111; Greg Lowe, President, North Carolina Division

ANGEL MEDICAL CENTER, 124 One Center Court, Franklin, NC, Zip 28734-0192, P O Box 1209, Zip 28744-0569, tel. 828/524-8411; Clint Kendall, R.N., Chief Executive Officer and Chief Nursing Officer

ASHEVILLE SPECIALTY HOSPITAL, 428 Biltmore Avenue, 4th Floor, Asheville, NC, Zip 28801-4502; tel. 828/213-5400; Julie A. Dikos, President and Chief Executive Officer

BLUE RIDGE REGIONAL HOSPITAL, 125 Hospital Drive, Spruce Pine, NC, Zip 28777-3035; tel. 828/765-4201; Tonia Hale, R.N., Chief Executive Officer and Chief Nursing Officer

CAREPARTNERS REHABILITATION HOSPITAL, 68 Sweeten Creek Road, Asheville, NC, Zip 28803-2318, P O Box 15025, Zip 28813-0025, tel. 828/277-4800; Tracy Buchanan, Chief Executive Officer and President

HIGHLANDS-CASHIERS HOSPITAL, 190 Hospital Drive, Highlands, NC, Zip 28741-7600, P O Drawer 190, Zip 28741-0190, tel. 828/526-1200; Tom Neal, Chief Executive Officer and Chief Nursing Officer

MISSION HOSPITAL MCDOWELL, 430 Rankin Drive, Marion, NC, Zip 28752-6568, P O Box 730, Zip 28752-0730, tel. 828/659-5000; Lee Higginbotham, Chief Executive Officer

MISSION HOSPITAL, 509 Biltmore Avenue, Asheville, NC, Zip 28801-4690; tel. 828/213-1111; Chad Patrick, Chief Executive Officer

TRANSYLVANIA REGIONAL HOSPITAL, 260 Hospital Drive, Brevard, NC, Zip 28712-3378; tel. 828/884-9111; Michele Pilon, President and Chief Nursing Officer

WNC HEALTH NETWORK, INC.
1200 Ridgefield Boulevard Suite 200, Asheville, NC Zip 28806-2280; tel. 828/667-8220; Heather Gates, Executive Director

ADVENTHEALTH HENDERSONVILLE, 100 Hospital Drive, Hendersonville, NC, Zip 28792-5272; tel. 828/684-8501; Brandon M. Nudd, President and Chief Executive Officer

ANGEL MEDICAL CENTER, 124 One Center Court, Franklin, NC, Zip 28734-0192, P O Box 1209, Zip 28744-0569, tel. 828/524-8411; Clint Kendall, R.N., Chief Executive Officer and Chief Nursing Officer

BLUE RIDGE REGIONAL HOSPITAL, 125 Hospital Drive, Spruce Pine, NC, Zip 28777-3035; tel. 828/765-4201; Tonia Hale, R.N., Chief Executive Officer and Chief Nursing Officer

CAREPARTNERS REHABILITATION HOSPITAL, 68 Sweeten Creek Road, Asheville, NC, Zip 28803-2318, P O Box 15025, Zip 28813-0025, tel. 828/277-4800; Tracy Buchanan, Chief Executive Officer and President

CHARLES GEORGE VETERANS AFFAIRS MEDICAL CENTER, 1100 Tunnel Road, Asheville, NC, Zip 28805-2087; tel. 828/298-7911; Stephanie Young, Medical Center Director

CHEROKEE INDIAN HOSPITAL, 1 Hospital Road, Cherokee, NC, Zip 28719; tel. 828/497-9163; Casey Cooper, Chief Executive Officer

ERLANGER WESTERN CAROLINA HOSPITAL, 3990 U S Highway 64 East Alt, Murphy, NC, Zip 28906-7917; tel. 828/837-8161; Stephanie Boynton, Vice President and Chief Executive Officer

HARRIS REGIONAL HOSPITAL, 68 Hospital Road, Sylva, NC, Zip 28779-2722; tel. 828/586-7000; Ashley Hindman, Chief Executive Officer

HAYWOOD REGIONAL MEDICAL CENTER, 262 Leroy George Drive, Clyde, NC, Zip 28721-7430; tel. 828/456-7311; Chris Brown, Chief Executive Officer

HIGHLANDS-CASHIERS HOSPITAL, 190 Hospital Drive, Highlands, NC, Zip 28741-7600, P O Drawer 190, Zip 28741-0190, tel. 828/526-1200; Tom Neal, Chief Executive Officer and Chief Nursing Officer

MISSION HOSPITAL MCDOWELL, 430 Rankin Drive, Marion, NC, Zip 28752-6568, P O Box 730, Zip 28752-0730, tel. 828/659-5000; Lee Higginbotham, Chief Executive Officer

MISSION HOSPITAL, 509 Biltmore Avenue, Asheville, NC, Zip 28801-4690; tel. 828/213-1111; Chad Patrick, Chief Executive Officer

RUTHERFORD REGIONAL HEALTH SYSTEM, 288 South Ridgecrest Avenue, Rutherfordton, NC, Zip 28139-2838; tel. 828/286-5000; Susan C. Shugart, FACHE, Chief Executive Officer

ST. LUKE'S HOSPITAL, 101 Hospital Drive, Columbus, NC, Zip 28722-6418; tel. 828/894-3311; Alex Bell, Interim Chief Executive Officer

SWAIN COMMUNITY HOSPITAL, A DUKE LIFEPOINT HOSPITAL, 45 Plateau Street, Bryson City, NC, Zip 28713-4200; tel. 828/488-2155; Ashley Hindman, Chief Executive Officer

TRANSYLVANIA REGIONAL HOSPITAL, 260 Hospital Drive, Brevard, NC, Zip 28712-3378; tel. 828/884-9111; Michele Pilon, President and Chief Nursing Officer

UNC HEALTH PARDEE, 800 North Justice Street, Hendersonville, NC, Zip 28791-3410; tel. 828/696-1000; James M. Kirby, II., President and Chief Executive Officer

NORTH DAKOTA

NORTHLAND HEALTHCARE ALLIANCE
2223 East Rosser Avenue, Bismarck, ND Zip 58501-4949; tel. 701/250-0709; Lynn Grimm, President

ASHLEY MEDICAL CENTER, 612 North Center Avenue, Ashley, ND, Zip 58413-7013, P O Box 450, Zip 58413-0450, tel. 701/288-3433; Eric Heupel, Chief Executive Officer

CHI ST. ALEXIUS HEALTH BISMARCK, 900 East Broadway, Bismarck, ND, Zip 58501-4586, P O Box 5510, Zip 58506-5510, tel. 701/530-7000; Reed Reyman, President

CHI ST. ALEXIUS HEALTH DICKINSON, 2500 Fairway Street, Dickinson, ND, Zip 58601-4399; tel. 701/456-4000; Carol Enderle, R.N., MSN, President

CHI ST. ALEXIUS HEALTH GARRISON, 407 Third Avenue SE, Garrison, ND, Zip 58540-7235; tel. 701/463-2275; Adam Maus, Administrator

CHI ST. ALEXIUS HEALTH TURTLE LAKE HOSPITAL, 220 Fifth Avenue, Turtle Lake, ND, Zip 58575-4005, P O Box 280, Zip 58575-0280, tel. 701/448-2331; Adam Maus, Administrator

LINTON REGIONAL MEDICAL CENTER, 518 North Broadway, Linton, ND, Zip 58552-7308, P O Box 850, Zip 58552-0850, tel. 701/254-4511; Lukas Fischer, R.N., Chief Executive Officer

MCKENZIE COUNTY HEALTHCARE SYSTEM, 516 North Main Street, Watford City, ND, Zip 58854-7310; tel. 701/842-3000; Peter D. Edis, Chief Executive Officer

MOBRIDGE REGIONAL HOSPITAL, 1401 Tenth Avenue West, Mobridge, SD, Zip 57601-1106, P O Box 580, Zip 57601-0580, tel. 605/845-3692; John J. Ayoub, FACHE, Chief Executive Officer

SMP HEALTH – ST. KATERI, 213 Second Avenue NE, Rolla, ND, Zip 58367-7153, P O Box 759, Zip 58367-0759, tel. 701/477-3161; Christopher Albertson, Chief Executive Officer and President

SAKAKAWEA MEDICAL CENTER, 510 Eighth Avenue NE, Hazen, ND, Zip 58545-4637; tel. 701/748-2225; Kurt Waldbillig, Chief Executive Officer

SOUTH CENTRAL HEALTH, 1007 Fourth Avenue South, Wishek, ND, Zip 58495-7527, P O Box 647, Zip 58495-0647, tel. 701/452-2326; Lukas Fischer, R.N., Chief Executive Officer

SOUTHWEST HEALTHCARE SERVICES, 802 2nd Street Northwest, Bowman, ND, Zip 58623-4483, P O Drawer 'C', Zip 58623, tel. 701/523-5265; Dennis Goebel, Chief Executive Officer

WEST RIVER REGIONAL MEDICAL CENTER, 1000 Highway 12, Hettinger, ND, Zip 58639-7530; tel. 701/567-4561; Alyson Kornele, Chief Executive Officer

SANFORD HEALTH NETWORK – FARGO MARKET
736 Broadway North, Route 1000, Fargo, ND Zip 58102-4421; tel. 701/234-6951

BOZEMAN HEALTH DEACONESS REGIONAL MEDICAL CENTER, 915 Highland Boulevard, Bozeman, MT, Zip 59715-6902; tel. 406/585-5000; Kathryn Bertany, M.D., President and Chief Executive Officer

JAMESTOWN REGIONAL MEDICAL CENTER, 2422 20th Street SW, Jamestown, ND, Zip 58401-6201; tel. 701/952-1050; Michael Delfs, President and Chief Executive Officer

KITTSON HEALTHCARE, 1010 South Birch Street, Hallock, MN, Zip 56728-4215, P O Box 700, Zip 56728-0700, tel. 218/843-3612; Andrea Swenson, Chief Executive Officer

LOGAN HEALTH CHESTER, 315 West Madison Avenue, Chester, MT, Zip 59522, P O Box 705, Zip 59522-0705, tel. 406/759-5181; Cherie Taylor, President

MAHNOMEN HEALTH, 414 West Jefferson Avenue, Mahnomen, MN, Zip 56557-4912, PO Box 396, Zip 56557-0396, tel. 218/935-2511; Dale K. Kruger, Chief Executive Officer

MCKENZIE COUNTY HEALTHCARE SYSTEM, 516 North Main Street, Watford City, ND, Zip 58854-7310; tel. 701/842-3000; Peter D. Edis, Chief Executive Officer

NORTHWOOD DEACONESS HEALTH CENTER, 4 North Park Street, Northwood, ND, Zip 58267-4102, P O Box 190, Zip 58267-0190, tel. 701/587-6060; Brock Sherva, Chief Executive Officer

PERHAM HEALTH, 1000 Coney Street West, Perham, MN, Zip 56573-1108; tel. 218/347-4500; Chuck Hofius, FACHE, Chief Executive Officer

Networks / Alliancehealth Oklahoma

RIVERVIEW HEALTH, 323 South Minnesota Street, Crookston, MN, Zip 56716-1601; tel. 218/281-9200; Carrie Michalski, President and Chief Executive Officer

SANFORD BAGLEY MEDICAL CENTER, 203 Fourth Street NW, Bagley, MN, Zip 56621-8307; tel. 218/694-6501; Carrie Krump, Senior Director

SANFORD BEHAVIORAL HEALTH CENTER, 120 LaBree Avenue South, Thief River Falls, MN, Zip 56701-2819, 3001 Sanford Parkway, Zip 56701-2819, tel. 218/683-4349; Heather Bregier, Administrator, Chief Executive Officer

SANFORD BEMIDJI MEDICAL CENTER, 1300 Anne Street NW, Bemidji, MN, Zip 56601-5103; tel. 218/751-5430; Karla Eischens, Chief Executive Officer

SANFORD MAYVILLE MEDICAL CENTER, 42 Sixth Avenue SE, Mayville, ND, Zip 58257-1598; tel. 701/786-3800; Jac McTaggart, Chief Executive Officer

SANFORD MEDICAL CENTER BISMARCK, 300 North Seventh Street, Bismarck, ND, Zip 58501-4439, P O Box 5525, Zip 58506-5525, tel. 701/323-6000; Todd Schaffer, M.D., President and Chief Executive Officer

SANFORD THIEF RIVER FALLS MEDICAL CENTER, 3001 Sanford Parkway, Thief River Falls, MN, Zip 56701-2700; tel. 218/681-4747; Tyler Ust, Adminstrator, Chief Executive Officer

SANFORD WHEATON MEDICAL CENTER, 401 12th Street North, Wheaton, MN, Zip 56296-1099; tel. 320/563-8226; Chelsie Falk, Chief Executive Officer

SIDNEY HEALTH CENTER, 216 14th Avenue SW, Sidney, MT, Zip 59270-3586; tel. 406/488-2100; Jennifer Doty, Chief Executive Officer

OHIO

CLEVELAND HEALTH NETWORK
6000 West Creek Road, Suite 20, Independence, OH Zip 44131-2139; tel. 216/986-1100; Fred M. DeGrandis, President

AKRON CHILDREN'S HOSPITAL, 1 Perkins Square, Akron, OH, Zip 44308-1063; tel. 330/543-1000; Christopher A. Gessner, President and Chief Executive Officer

ASHTABULA COUNTY MEDICAL CENTER, 2420 Lake Avenue, Ashtabula, OH, Zip 44004-4954; tel. 440/997-2262; Leonard Stepp, President and Chief Executive Officer

CLEVELAND CLINIC CHILDREN'S HOSPITAL FOR REHABILITATION, 2801 Martin Luther King Jr Drive, Cleveland, OH, Zip 44104-3865; tel. 216/448-6400; Karen Murray, M.D., President

CLEVELAND CLINIC EUCLID HOSPITAL, 18901 Lake Shore Boulevard, Euclid, OH, Zip 44119-1090; tel. 216/531-9000; Teresa Dews, M.D., Vice President

CLEVELAND CLINIC FAIRVIEW HOSPITAL, 18101 Lorain Avenue, Cleveland, OH, Zip 44111-5656; tel. 216/476-7000; Neil Smith, D.O., President

CLEVELAND CLINIC HILLCREST HOSPITAL, 6780 Mayfield Road, Cleveland, OH, Zip 44124-2203; tel. 440/312-4500; Richard Parker, M.D., President

CLEVELAND CLINIC LUTHERAN HOSPITAL, 1730 West 25th Street, Cleveland, OH, Zip 44113-3170; tel. 216/696-4300; Timothy R. Barnett, M.D., Vice President

CLEVELAND CLINIC MARYMOUNT HOSPITAL, 12300 McCracken Road, Garfield Heights, OH, Zip 44125-2975; tel. 216/581-0500; Margaret McKenzie, M.D., Vice President

CLEVELAND CLINIC MEDINA HOSPITAL, 1000 East Washington Street, Medina, OH, Zip 44256-2170; tel. 330/725-1000; Richard K. Shewbridge, President

CLEVELAND CLINIC SOUTH POINTE HOSPITAL, 20000 Harvard Road, Warrensville Heights, OH, Zip 44122-6805; tel. 216/491-6000; Margaret McKenzie, M.D., Vice President

CLEVELAND CLINIC, 9500 Euclid Avenue, Cleveland, OH, Zip 44195-5108; tel. 216/444-2200; Scott Steele, M.D., President

FIRELANDS REGIONAL HEALTH SYSTEM, 1111 Hayes Avenue, Sandusky, OH, Zip 44870-3323; tel. 419/557-7400; Jeremy Normington-Slay, FACHE, Chief Executive Officer

FISHER-TITUS MEDICAL CENTER, 272 Benedict Avenue, Norwalk, OH, Zip 44857-2374; tel. 419/668-8101; Brent Burkey, M.D., President and Chief Executive Officer

METROHEALTH MEDICAL CENTER, 2500 MetroHealth Drive, Cleveland, OH, Zip 44109-1998; tel. 216/778-7800; Airica Steed, Ed.D., R.N., FACHE, President and Chief Executive Officer

SUMMA HEALTH SYSTEM - AKRON CAMPUS, 525 East Market Street, Akron, OH, Zip 44304-1619; tel. 330/375-3000; T. Clifford Deveny, M.D., Chief Executive Officer

UNIVERSITY HOSPITALS ELYRIA MEDICAL CENTER, 630 East River Street, Elyria, OH, Zip 44035-5902; tel. 440/329-7500; Todd Harford, Chief Operating Officer

UNIVERSITY HOSPITALS PARMA MEDICAL CENTER, 7007 Powers Boulevard, Parma, OH, Zip 44129-5495; tel. 440/743-3000; James Lee. Hill, Sr., M.D., Chief Operating Officer

WESTERN RESERVE HOSPITAL, 1900 23rd Street, Cuyahoga Falls, OH, Zip 44223-1499; tel. 330/971-7000; Robert Kent, D.O., President and Chief Executive Officer

MERCY HEALTH - SOUTHWEST OHIO
4600 McAuley Place, Cincinnati, OH Zip 45242; tel. 513/981-6000; John M. Starcher Esq, President and Chief Executive Officer

MERCY HEALTH - ANDERSON HOSPITAL, 7500 State Road, Cincinnati, OH, Zip 45255-2492; tel. 513/624-4500; Kathy Healy-Collier, President

MERCY HEALTH - CLERMONT HOSPITAL, 3000 Hospital Drive, Batavia, OH, Zip 45103-1921; tel. 513/732-8200; Tim Prestridge, President

MERCY HEALTH - FAIRFIELD HOSPITAL, 3000 Mack Road, Fairfield, OH, Zip 45014-5335; tel. 513/870-7000; Justin Krueger, FACHE, President

MERCY HEALTH - WEST HOSPITAL, 3300 Mercy Health Boulevard, Cincinnati, OH, Zip 45211-1103; tel. 513/215-5000; Bradley J. Bertke, President and Chief Operating Officer

THE JEWISH HOSPITAL - MERCY HEALTH, 4777 East Galbraith Road, Cincinnati, OH, Zip 45236-2725; tel. 513/686-3000; Michael Kramer, President

THE OHIO STATE HEALTH NETWORK
660 Ackerman Road, Suite 601F, Columbus, OH Zip 43202-4500; tel. 614/293-4425; Thomas Blincoe, Executive Director

ADENA FAYETTE MEDICAL CENTER, 1430 Columbus Avenue, Washington Court House, OH, Zip 43160-1791; tel. 740/335-1210; Josh McCoy, Senior Operations Executive Officer

AVITA ONTARIO HOSPITAL, 715 Richland Mall, Ontario, OH, Zip 44906-3802; tel. 567/307-7666; Jerome Morasko, President and Chief Executive Officer

BUCYRUS COMMUNITY HOSPITAL, 629 North Sandusky Avenue, Bucyrus, OH, Zip 44820-1821; tel. 419/562-4677; Jerome Morasko, President and Chief Executive Officer

GALION COMMUNITY HOSPITAL, 269 Portland Way South, Galion, OH, Zip 44833-2399; tel. 419/468-4841; Jerome Morasko, President and Chief Executive Officer

HIGHLAND DISTRICT HOSPITAL, 1275 North High Street, Hillsboro, OH, Zip 45133-8273; tel. 937/393-6100; Timothy Parry, R.N., President and Chief Executive Officer

HOCKING VALLEY COMMUNITY HOSPITAL, 601 State Route 664 North, Logan, OH, Zip 43138-8541, P O Box 966, Zip 43138-0966, tel. 740/380-8000; Stacey Gabriel, R.N., President and Chief Executive Officer

MADISON HEALTH, 210 North Main Street, London, OH, Zip 43140-1115; tel. 740/845-7000; Dana E. Engle, Chief Executive Officer

MARY RUTAN HOSPITAL, 205 Palmer Avenue, Bellefontaine, OH, Zip 43311-2281; tel. 937/592-4015; Chad A. Ross, President and Chief Executive Officer

MERCER HEALTH, 800 West Main Street, Coldwater, OH, Zip 45828-1698; tel. 419/678-2341; Lisa R. Klenke, R.N., Chief Executive Officer

OHIO STATE UNIVERSITY WEXNER MEDICAL CENTER, 410 West 10th Avenue, Columbus, OH, Zip 43210-1240; tel. 614/293-8000; John Warner, M.D., Chief Executive Officer

WVU MEDICINE - BARNESVILLE HOSPITAL, 639 West Main Street, Barnesville, OH, Zip 43713-1039, P O Box 309, Zip 43713-0309, tel. 740/425-3941; Stacey Armstrong, Interim President

WAYNE HEALTHCARE, 835 Sweitzer Street, Greenville, OH, Zip 45331-1077; tel. 937/548-1141; Jeffrey R. Subler, President and Chief Executive Officer

WILSON MEMORIAL HOSPITAL, 915 West Michigan Street, Sidney, OH, Zip 45365-2491; tel. 937/498-2311; Mark Klosterman, FACHE, President and Chief Executive Officer

WYANDOT MEMORIAL HOSPITAL, 885 North Sandusky Avenue, Upper Sandusky, OH, Zip 43351-1098; tel. 419/294-4991; Ty Shaull, President and Chief Executive Officer

TRIHEALTH
619 Oak Street, Cincinnati, OH Zip 45206; tel. 513/569-6507; Mark C. Clement, President and Chief Executive Officer

BETHESDA NORTH HOSPITAL, 10500 Montgomery Road, Cincinnati, OH, Zip 45242-4402; tel. 513/865-1111; Clint Hutson, President and Chief Operating Officer

GOOD SAMARITAN HOSPITAL, 375 Dixmyth Avenue, Cincinnati, OH, Zip 45220-2489; tel. 513/862-1400; Kelvin Hanger, President and Chief Operating Officer

MCCULLOUGH-HYDE MEMORIAL HOSPITAL/TRIHEALTH, 110 North Poplar Street, Oxford, OH, Zip 45056-1292; tel. 513/523-2111; Jeremiah Kirkland, President and Chief Operating Officer

OKLAHOMA

ALLIANCEHEALTH OKLAHOMA
5300 North Grand Boulevard, Oklahoma City, OK Zip 73112-5647; tel. 405/815-3900

ALLIANCEHEALTH DURANT, 1800 University Boulevard, Durant, OK, Zip 74701-3006, P O Box 1207, Zip 74702-1207, tel. 580/924-3080; Shelton Williams, Chief Executive Officer

ALLIANCEHEALTH MADILL, 901 South Fifth Avenue, Madill, OK, Zip 73446-3640, P O Box 827, Zip 73446-0827, tel. 580/795-3384; Shelton Williams, Chief Executive Officer

INTEGRIS HEALTH PONCA CITY HOSPITAL, 1900 North 14th Street, Ponca City, OK, Zip 74601-2099; tel. 580/765-3321; Christopher Mendoza, Chief Executive Officer

INTEGRIS HEALTH WOODWARD HOSPITAL, 900 17th Street, Woodward, OK, Zip 73801-2448; tel. 580/256-5511; Jeff Nowlin, Interim Chief Executive Officer

SSM HEALTH ST. ANTHONY HOSPITAL - MIDWEST, 2825 Parklawn Drive, Midwest City, OK, Zip 73110-4258; tel. 405/610-4411; Stacy Coleman, MS, President

Networks / Mercy Health System of Oklahoma

MERCY HEALTH SYSTEM OF OKLAHOMA
4300 West Memorial Road, Oklahoma City, OK Zip 73120-8304;
tel. 405/752-3756; Diana Smalley, President and Chief Executive Officer

ARBUCKLE MEMORIAL HOSPITAL, 2011 West Broadway Street, Sulphur, OK, Zip 73086-4221, P.O. Box 1109, Zip 73086-8109, tel. 580/622-2161; Jeremy A. Jones, Administrator

MERCY HEALTH LOVE COUNTY, 300 Wanda Street, Marietta, OK, Zip 73448-1200; tel. 580/276-3347; Wesley Scott. Callender, Administrator

MERCY HOSPITAL ADA, 430 North Monte Vista, Ada, OK, Zip 74820-4610; tel. 580/332-2323; Terence Farrell, President

MERCY HOSPITAL ARDMORE, 1011 14th Avenue NW, Ardmore, OK, Zip 73401-1828; tel. 580/223-5400; Daryle Voss, FACHE, President

MERCY HOSPITAL HEALDTON, 3462 Hospital Road, Healdton, OK, Zip 73438-6124, P O Box 928, Zip 73438-0928, tel. 580/229-0701; Heather Chatham, Administrator

MERCY HOSPITAL KINGFISHER, 1000 Hospital Cirle, Kingfisher, OK, Zip 73750-5002, P O Box 59, Zip 73750-0059, tel. 405/375-3141; Bobby Stitt, R.N., Administrator, Rural Facilities

MERCY HOSPITAL LOGAN COUNTY, 200 South Academy Road, Guthrie, OK, Zip 73044-8727, P O Box 1017, Zip 73044-1017, tel. 405/282-6700; Bobby Stitt, R.N., Administrator, Rural Facilities

MERCY HOSPITAL OKLAHOMA CITY, 4300 West Memorial Road, Oklahoma City, OK, Zip 73120-8362; tel. 405/755-1515; Bennett Geister, President, Oklahoma City Communities

MERCY HOSPITAL TISHOMINGO, 1000 South Byrd Street, Tishomingo, OK, Zip 73460-3299; tel. 580/371-2327; Lori McMillin, Administrator

MERCY HOSPITAL WATONGA, 500 North Clarence Nash Boulevard, Watonga, OK, Zip 73772-2845, P O Box 370, Zip 73772-0370, tel. 580/623-7211; Bobby Stitt, R.N., Administrator

MERCY REHABILITATION HOSPITAL OKLAHOMA CITY, 5401 West Memorial Rd, Oklahoma City, OK, Zip 73142-2026; tel. 405/384-5211; Gina Tess Clemens, PharmD, Market Chief Executive Officer

OKLAHOMA HEART HOSPITAL SOUTH CAMPUS, 5200 East I-240 Service Road, Oklahoma City, OK, Zip 73135; tel. 405/628-6000; John Harvey, M.D., Chief Executive Officer

OKLAHOMA HEART HOSPITAL, 4050 West Memorial Road, Oklahoma City, OK, Zip 73120-8382; tel. 405/608-3200; John Harvey, M.D., Chief Executive Officer

OKLAHOMA STATE UNIVERSITY MEDICAL CENTER, 744 West Ninth Street, Tulsa, OK, Zip 74127-9020; tel. 918/599-1000; Finny Mathew, President

SEILING MUNICIPAL HOSPITAL, Highway 60 NE, Seiling, OK, Zip 73663, P O Box 720, Zip 73663-0720, tel. 580/922-7361; Rachel Farrow, Administrator

PENNSYLVANIA

BRIDGES HEALTH PARTNERS
500 Commonwealth Drive, Warrendale, PA Zip 15086-7516;
tel. 724/300-8105; Tom Boggs, President

BUTLER MEMORIAL HOSPITAL, 1 Hospital Way, Butler, PA, Zip 16001-4697; tel. 724/283-6666; Karen A. Allen, R.N., President, Butler & Clarion Hospitals

EXCELA FRICK HOSPITAL, 508 South Church Street, Mount Pleasant, PA, Zip 15666-1790; tel. 724/547-1500; Brian Fritz, President

EXCELA HEALTH LATROBE HOSPITAL, 1 Mellon Way, Latrobe, PA, Zip 15650-1096; tel. 724/537-1000; Brian Fritz, President

EXCELA HEALTH WESTMORELAND HOSPITAL, 532 West Pittsburgh Street, Greensburg, PA, Zip 15601-2282; tel. 724/832-4000; Brian Fritz, President, Westmoreland, Latrobe, Frick Hospitals

ST. CLAIR HEALTH, 1000 Bower Hill Road, Pittsburgh, PA, Zip 15243-1873; tel. 412/942-4000; Michael J. Flanagan, President and Chief Executive Officer

UPMC GREENE, 350 Bonar Avenue, Waynesburg, PA, Zip 15370-1608; tel. 724/627-3101; Terry Wiltrout, President

UPMC WASHINGTON, 155 Wilson Avenue, Washington, PA, Zip 15301-3398; tel. 724/225-7000; Brook Ward, President and Chief Executive Officer

COMMONWEALTH HEALTH
575 North River Street, Wilkes Barre, PA Zip 18764-0999; tel. 570/829-8111; Donald J. Bivacca, Chief Executive Officer

BERWICK HOSPITAL CENTER, 701 East 16th Street, Berwick, PA, Zip 18603-2397; tel. 570/759-5000; Priyam Sharma, Chief Executive Officer

REGIONAL HOSPITAL OF SCRANTON, 746 Jefferson Avenue, Scranton, PA, Zip 18510-1624; tel. 570/348-7100; Michael Curran, Chief Executive Officer

WILKES-BARRE GENERAL HOSPITAL, 575 North River Street, Wilkes-Barre, PA, Zip 18764-0001; tel. 570/829-8111; Christopher L. Howe, R.N., Interim Chief Executive Officer

PENN HIGHLANDS HEALTHCARE
204 Hospital Avenue, DuBois, PA Zip 15801-0447; tel. 814/375-6430;
Steven M. Fontaine, System Chief Executive Officer

PENN HIGHLANDS BROOKVILLE, 100 Hospital Road, Brookville, PA, Zip 15825-1367; tel. 814/849-2312; Julianne Peer, President

PENN HIGHLANDS DUBOIS, 100 Hospital Avenue, DuBois, PA, Zip 15801-1440, P O Box 447, Zip 15801-0447, tel. 814/371-2200; William A. Chinn, President

PENN HIGHLANDS ELK, 763 Johnsonburg Road, Saint Marys, PA, Zip 15857-3498; tel. 814/788-8000; Julianne Peer, President

VANTAGE HEALTHCARE NETWORK, INC.
18282 Technology Drive, Suite 202, Meadville, PA Zip 16335-8378;
tel. 814/337-0000; David Petrarca, Director Retail Operations

CLARION HOSPITAL, 1 Hospital Drive, Clarion, PA, Zip 16214-8501; tel. 814/226-9500; Karen A. Allen, R.N., President

MEADVILLE MEDICAL CENTER, 751 Liberty Street, Meadville, PA, Zip 16335-2559; tel. 814/333-5000; Philip E. Pandolph, FACHE, President and Chief Executive Officer

PENN HIGHLANDS BROOKVILLE, 100 Hospital Road, Brookville, PA, Zip 15825-1367; tel. 814/849-2312; Julianne Peer, President

PENN HIGHLANDS ELK, 763 Johnsonburg Road, Saint Marys, PA, Zip 15857-3498; tel. 814/788-8000; Julianne Peer, President

PUNXSUTAWNEY AREA HOSPITAL, 81 Hillcrest Drive, Punxsutawney, PA, Zip 15767-2616; tel. 814/938-1800; Jack G. Sisk, President

TITUSVILLE AREA HOSPITAL, 406 West Oak Street, Titusville, PA, Zip 16354-1404; tel. 814/827-1851; Lee M. Clinton, FACHE, President and Chief Executive Officer

UPMC BEDFORD, 10455 Lincoln Highway, Everett, PA, Zip 15537-7046; tel. 814/623-6161; Michael Corso, President & Chief Executive Officer

UPMC HAMOT, 201 State Street, Erie, PA, Zip 16550-0002; tel. 814/877-6000; Brian Durniok, President

UPMC JAMESON, 1211 Wilmington Avenue, New Castle, PA, Zip 16105-2516; tel. 724/658-9001; David J. Patton, President

UPMC KANE, 4372 Route 6, Kane, PA, Zip 16735-3060; tel. 814/837-8585; Mark Papalia, President

UPMC MCKEESPORT, 1500 Fifth Avenue, McKeesport, PA, Zip 15132-2422; tel. 412/664-2000; Mark O'Hern, President

UPMC NORTHWEST, 100 Fairfield Drive, Seneca, PA, Zip 16346-2130; tel. 814/676-7600; Brian Durniok, President

UPMC PASSAVANT, 9100 Babcock Boulevard, Pittsburgh, PA, Zip 15237-5815; tel. 412/748-6700; Elizabeth A. Piccione, M.D., President

UPMC ST. MARGARET, 815 Freeport Road, Pittsburgh, PA, Zip 15215-3301; tel. 412/784-4000; Andrew Ritchie, President

WARREN GENERAL HOSPITAL, 2 West Crescent Park, Warren, PA, Zip 16365-2111, P O Box 68, Zip 16365-0068, tel. 814/723-4973; Richard Allen, Chief Executive Officer

SOUTH DAKOTA

REGIONAL HEALTH
353 Fairmont Boulevard, Rapid City, SD Zip 57701-7375; tel. 605/719-1000; Brent R. Phillips, President and Chief Executive Officer

MONUMENT HEALTH CUSTER HOSPITAL, 1220 Montgomery Street, Custer, SD, Zip 57730-1705; tel. 605/673-2229; Barbara K. Hespen, R.N., President

MONUMENT HEALTH LEAD-DEADWOOD HOSPITAL, 61 Charles Street, Deadwood, SD, Zip 57732-1303; tel. 605/717-6000; Mark C. Schmidt, President

MONUMENT HEALTH RAPID CITY HOSPITAL, 353 Fairmont Boulevard, Rapid City, SD, Zip 57701-7393, P O Box 6000, Zip 57709-6000, tel. 605/755-1000; John Pierce, President

MONUMENT HEALTH SPEARFISH HOSPITAL, 1440 North Main Street, Spearfish, SD, Zip 57783-1504; tel. 605/644-4000; Thomas Worsley, Chief Executive Officer

MONUMENT HEALTH STURGIS HOSPITAL, 2140 Junction Avenue, Sturgis, SD, Zip 57785-2452; tel. 605/720-2400; Mark C. Schmidt, President

PHILIP HEALTH SERVICES, 503 West Pine Street, Philip, SD, Zip 57567-3300, P O Box 790, Zip 57567-0790, tel. 605/859-2511; Jeremy S. Schultes, Administrator and Chief Executive Officer

WESTON COUNTY HEALTH SERVICES, 1124 Washington Boulevard, Newcastle, WY, Zip 82701-2972; tel. 307/746-4491; Randy L. Lindauer, Ph.D., FACHE, Chief Executive Officer

SANFORD HEALTH NETWORK - SIOUX FALLS MARKET
1305 West 18th Street, Route 6145, Sioux Falls, SD Zip 57105-0401;
tel. 605/328-5513; Eric C. Hilmoe, Vice President Operations

COMMUNITY MEMORIAL HOSPITAL, 809 Jackson Street, Burke, SD, Zip 57523-2065, P O Box 319, Zip 57523-0319, tel. 605/775-2621; Mistie Drey, Chief Executive Officer

DOUGLAS COUNTY MEMORIAL HOSPITAL, 708 Eighth Street, Armour, SD, Zip 57313-2102; tel. 605/724-2159; Heath Brouwer, Administrator

MURRAY COUNTY MEDICAL CENTER, 2042 Juniper Avenue, Slayton, MN, Zip 56172-1017; tel. 507/836-6111; Luke Schryvers, Chief Executive Officer

ORANGE CITY AREA HEALTH SYSTEM, 1000 Lincoln Circle SE, Orange City, IA, Zip 51041-1862; tel. 712/737-4984; Martin W. Guthmiller, Chief Executive Officer

Networks / St. David's Health Network

ORTONVILLE AREA HEALTH SERVICES, 450 Eastvold Avenue, Ortonville, MN, Zip 56278-1133; tel. 320/839-2502; Allan Ross, Chief Excecutive Officer

PIONEER MEMORIAL HOSPITAL AND HEALTH SERVICES, 315 North Washington Street, Viborg, SD, Zip 57070-2002, P O Box 368, Zip 57070-0368, tel. 605/326-5161; Isaac Gerdes, Chief Executive Officer

SANFORD ABERDEEN MEDICAL CENTER, 2905 3rd Avenue SE, Aberdeen, SD, Zip 57401-5420; tel. 605/626-4200; Kila LeGrand, Executive Director

SANFORD CANBY MEDICAL CENTER, 112 St Olaf Avenue South, Canby, MN, Zip 56220-1433; tel. 507/223-7277; Lori Sisk, R.N., Chief Executive Officer

SANFORD CANTON-INWOOD MEDICAL CENTER, 440 North Hiawatha Drive, Canton, SD, Zip 57013-5800; tel. 605/764-1400; Scott C. Larson, Chief Executive Officer

SANFORD CHAMBERLAIN MEDICAL CENTER, 300 South Byron Boulevard, Chamberlain, SD, Zip 57325-9741; tel. 605/234-5511; Erica Peterson, Chief Executive Officer

SANFORD CLEAR LAKE MEDICAL CENTER, 701 Third Avenue South, Clear Lake, SD, Zip 57226-2016; tel. 605/874-2141; Lori Sisk, R.N., Chief Executive Officer

SANFORD HILLSBORO MEDICAL CENTER, 12 Third Street SE, Hillsboro, ND, Zip 58045-4840, P O Box 609, Zip 58045-0609, tel. 701/636-3200; Jac McTaggart, Chief Executive Officer

SANFORD JACKSON MEDICAL CENTER, 1430 North Highway, Jackson, MN, Zip 56143-1093; tel. 507/847-2420; Dawn Schnell, Administrator and Chief Executive Officer

SANFORD LUVERNE MEDICAL CENTER, 1600 North Kniss Avenue, Luverne, MN, Zip 56156-1067; tel. 507/283-2321; Tammy Loosbrock, Chief Executive Officer and Administrator

SANFORD SHELDON MEDICAL CENTER, 118 North Seventh Avenue, Sheldon, IA, Zip 51201-1235, P O Box 250, Zip 51201-0250, tel. 712/324-5041; Richard E. Nordahl, Senior Director

SANFORD TRACY MEDICAL CENTER, 251 Fifth Street East, Tracy, MN, Zip 56175-1536; tel. 507/629-8400; Stacy Barstad, Chief Executive Officer

SANFORD USD MEDICAL CENTER, 1305 West 18th Street, Sioux Falls, SD, Zip 57105-0496, P O Box 5039, Zip 57117-5039, tel. 605/333-1000; Paul A. Hanson, FACHE, President

SANFORD VERMILLION MEDICAL CENTER, 20 South Plum Street, Vermillion, SD, Zip 57069-3346; tel. 605/677-3500; Timothy J. Tracy, Senior Director

SANFORD WESTBROOK MEDICAL CENTER, 920 Bell Avenue, Westbrook, MN, Zip 56183-9669, P O Box 188, Zip 56183-0188, tel. 507/274-6121; Stacy Barstad, Chief Executive Officer

SANFORD WORTHINGTON MEDICAL CENTER, 1018 Sixth Avenue, Worthington, MN, Zip 56187-2202, P O Box 997, Zip 56187-0997, tel. 507/372-2941; Jennifer Weg, MS, R.N., Executive Director

WEST HOLT MEDICAL SERVICES, 406 West Neely Street, Atkinson, NE, Zip 68713-4801; tel. 402/925-2811; Jeremy Bauer, Chief Executive Officer

WINDOM AREA HEALTH, 2150 Hospital Drive, Windom, MN, Zip 56101-0339, P O Box 339, Zip 56101-0339, tel. 507/831-2400; Shelby Medina, Chief Executive Officer

WINNER REGIONAL HEALTHCARE CENTER, 745 East Eighth Street, Winner, SD, Zip 57580-2631; tel. 605/842-7100; Brian Williams, Chief Executive Officer

TENNESSEE

TRISTAR HEALTH
110 Winners Circle, First Floor, Brentwood, TN Zip 37027-5070; tel. 615/886-4900; Stephen Corbeil, President

ADVENTHEALTH REDMOND, 501 Redmond Road, Rome, GA, Zip 30165-1415, P O Box 107001, Zip 30164-7001, tel. 706/291-0291; Isaac Sendros, President and Chief Executive Officer

PARKRIDGE MEDICAL CENTER, 2333 McCallie Avenue, Chattanooga, TN, Zip 37404-3258; tel. 423/698-6061; Christopher Cosby, President and Chief Executive Officer

PIEDMONT CARTERSVILLE, 960 Joe Frank Harris Parkway, Cartersville, GA, Zip 30120-2129; tel. 470/490-1000; Lori Rakes, R.N., Chief Executive Officer

PIEDMONT EASTSIDE MEDICAL CENTER, 1700 Medical Way, Snellville, GA, Zip 30078-2195; tel. 770/979-0200; Larry W. Ebert, Jr., Chief Executive Officer

TRISTAR CENTENNIAL MEDICAL CENTER, 2300 Patterson Street, Nashville, TN, Zip 37203-1528; tel. 615/342-1000; Thomas H. Ozburn, FACHE, President and Chief Executive Officer

TRISTAR GREENVIEW REGIONAL HOSPITAL, 1801 Ashley Circle, Bowling Green, KY, Zip 42104-3362; tel. 270/793-1000; Michael Sherrod, Chief Executive Officer

TRISTAR HENDERSONVILLE MEDICAL CENTER, 355 New Shackle Island Road, Hendersonville, TN, Zip 37075-2479; tel. 615/338-1000; Justin Coury, Chief Executive Officer

TRISTAR HORIZON MEDICAL CENTER, 111 Highway 70 East, Dickson, TN, Zip 37055-2080; tel. 615/446-0446; Cindy Bergmeier, Chief Executive Officer

TRISTAR SKYLINE MEDICAL CENTER, 3441 Dickerson Pike, Nashville, TN, Zip 37207-2539; tel. 615/769-2000; Mark Miller, FACHE, Chief Executive Officer

TRISTAR SOUTHERN HILLS MEDICAL CENTER, 391 Wallace Road, Nashville, TN, Zip 37211-4859; tel. 615/781-4000; Nick Howald, Chief Executive Officer

TRISTAR STONECREST MEDICAL CENTER, 200 StoneCrest Boulevard, Smyrna, TN, Zip 37167-6810; tel. 615/768-2000; Louis Caputo, Chief Executive Officer

TRISTAR SUMMIT MEDICAL CENTER, 5655 Frist Boulevard, Hermitage, TN, Zip 37076-2053; tel. 615/316-3000; Daphne David, Chief Executive Officer

TEXAS

LITTLE RIVER HEALTHCARE
1700 Brazos Avenue, Rockdale, TX Zip 76567-2517; tel. 512/446-4500; Jeffrey Madison, FACHE, Chief Executive Officer

METHODIST HEALTHCARE SYSTEM
8109 Fredericksburg Road, San Antonio, TX Zip 78229-3311; tel. 210/575-0355

METHODIST HOSPITAL, 7700 Floyd Curl Drive, San Antonio, TX, Zip 78229-3993; tel. 210/575-4000; Ryan Simpson, Chief Executive Officer

METHODIST STONE OAK HOSPITAL, 1139 E Sonterra Boulevard, San Antonio, TX, Zip 78258-4347, 1139 East Sonterra Boulevard, Zip 78258-4347, tel. 210/638-2100; Michael D. Beaver, Chief Executive Officer

REGIONAL HEALTHCARE ALLIANCE
530 South Beckham Avenue, Tyler, TX Zip 75702-8310; tel. 903/531-4449; John Webb, President

BAYLOR UNIVERSITY MEDICAL CENTER, 3500 Gaston Avenue, Dallas, TX, Zip 75246-2088; tel. 214/820-0111; Kyle Armstrong, President Central Region of BSW Health

CHRISTUS MOTHER FRANCES HOSPITAL – JACKSONVILLE, 2026 South Jackson, Jacksonville, TX, Zip 75766-5822; tel. 903/541-4500; Barry D. Lofquist, Chief Executive Officer

CHRISTUS MOTHER FRANCES HOSPITAL – SULPHUR SPRINGS, 115 Airport Road, Sulphur Springs, TX, Zip 75482-2105; tel. 903/885-7671; Paul Harvey, President / Chief Executive Officer

CHRISTUS MOTHER FRANCES HOSPITAL – TYLER, 800 East Dawson Street, Tyler, TX, Zip 75701-2036; tel. 903/593-8441; Jason J. Proctor, President

CHRISTUS TRINITY MOTHER FRANCES REHABILITATION HOSPITAL, A PARTNER OF ENCOMPASS HEALTH, 3131 Troup Highway, Tyler, TX, Zip 75701-8352; tel. 903/510-7000; Sharla Anderson, Chief Executive Officer

CHILDREN'S MEDICAL CENTER DALLAS, 1935 Medical District Drive, Dallas, TX, Zip 75235-7701; tel. 214/456-7000; Christopher J. Durovich, President and Chief Executive Officer

NACOGDOCHES MEDICAL CENTER, 4920 NE Stallings Drive, Nacogdoches, TX, Zip 75965-1200; tel. 936/569-9481; Jeff Patterson, Chief Executive Officer

PALESTINE REGIONAL MEDICAL CENTER-EAST, 2900 South Loop 256, Palestine, TX, Zip 75801-6958; tel. 903/731-1000; Doug Holzbog, Market Chief Executive Officer

PARIS REGIONAL MEDICAL CENTER, 865 Deshong Drive, Paris, TX, Zip 75460-9313, P O Box 9070, Zip 75461-9070, tel. 903/785-4521; Steve Hyde, Chief Executive Officer

TITUS REGIONAL MEDICAL CENTER, 2001 North Jefferson Avenue, Mount Pleasant, TX, Zip 75455-2398; tel. 903/577-6000; Terry Scoggin, Chief Executive Officer

TYLER CONTINUECARE HOSPITAL, 800 East Dawson, 4th Floor, Tyler, TX, Zip 75701-2036; tel. 903/531-4080; Stephanie Hyde, R.N., MSN, Chief Executive Officer

UT HEALTH HENDERSON, 300 Wilson Street, Henderson, TX, Zip 75652-5956; tel. 903/657-7541; Mark Leitner, FACHE, Administrator

UT HEALTH NORTH CAMPUS TYLER, 11937 Highway 271, Tyler, TX, Zip 75708-3154; tel. 903/877-7777; Zachary K. Dietze, Chief Executive Officer

ST. DAVID'S HEALTH NETWORK
98 San Jacinto Boulevard, Austin, TX Zip 78701-4082; tel. 512/708-9700; David Huffstutler, President and Chief Executive Officer

ST. DAVID'S MEDICAL CENTER, 919 East 32nd Street, Austin, TX, Zip 78705-2709, P O Box 4039, Zip 78765-4039, tel. 512/476-7111; Todd E. Steward, FACHE, Chief Executive Officer

ST. DAVID'S NORTH AUSTIN MEDICAL CENTER, 12221 North MoPac Expressway, Austin, TX, Zip 78758-2496; tel. 512/901-1000; Jeremy Barclay, FACHE, Chief Executive Officer

ST. DAVID'S ROUND ROCK MEDICAL CENTER, 2400 Round Rock Avenue, Round Rock, TX, Zip 78681-4097; tel. 512/341-1000; Laura Wiess, Interim Chief Executive Officer

ST. DAVID'S SOUTH AUSTIN MEDICAL CENTER, 901 West Ben White Boulevard, Austin, TX, Zip 78704-6903; tel. 512/447-2211; Charles Laird, Chief Executive Officer

Networks / The Hospitals of Providence – Tenet Healthcare

THE HOSPITALS OF PROVIDENCE – TENET HEALTHCARE
2001 North Oregon Street, El Paso, TX Zip 79902-3320; tel. 915/577-6625; Nicholas R. Tejeda, FACHE, Market Chief Executive Officer

THE HOSPITALS OF PROVIDENCE EAST CAMPUS – TENET HEALTHCARE, 3280 Joe Battle Boulevard, El Paso, TX, Zip 79938-2622; tel. 915/832-2000; Tasha Hopper, MSN, R.N., FACHE, Chief Executive Officer

THE HOSPITALS OF PROVIDENCE MEMORIAL CAMPUS – TENET HEALTHCARE, 2001 North Oregon Street, El Paso, TX, Zip 79902-3368; tel. 915/577-6625; Rob J. Anderson, Chief Executive Officer

THE HOSPITALS OF PROVIDENCE SIERRA CAMPUS – TENET HEALTHCARE, 1625 Medical Center Drive, El Paso, TX, Zip 79902-5005; tel. 915/747-4000; Tasha Hopper, MSN, R.N., FACHE, Chief Executive Officer

THE HOSPITALS OF PROVIDENCE TRANSMOUNTAIN CAMPUS – TENET HEALTHCARE, 2000 Transmountain Road, El Paso, TX, Zip 79911; tel. 915/877-8300; David T. Byrd, Chief Executive Officer

VIRGINIA

VIRGINIA HEALTH NETWORK
7400 Beaufont Springs Drive, Suite 505, Richmond, VA Zip 23225-5521; tel. 804/320-3837; James Brittain, President

AUGUSTA HEALTH, 78 Medical Center Drive, Fishersville, VA, Zip 22939-2332, P O Box 1000, Zip 22939-1000, tel. 540/932-4000; Mary N. Mannix, FACHE, President and Chief Executive Officer

BATH COMMUNITY HOSPITAL, 106 Park Drive, Hot Springs, VA, Zip 24445-2921, P O Box Z, Zip 24445-0750, tel. 540/839-7000; Jeffrey Lingerfelt, Chief Executive Officer

BON SECOURS – SOUTHAMPTON MEDICAL CENTER, 100 Fairview Drive, Franklin, VA, Zip 23851-1238, P O Box 817, Zip 23851-0817, tel. 757/569-6100; Kimberly W. Marks, President

BON SECOURS – SOUTHERN VIRGINIA MEDICAL CENTER, 727 North Main Street, Emporia, VA, Zip 23847-1274; tel. 434/348-4400; Brenda Woodcock, President

BON SECOURS – SOUTHSIDE MEDICAL CENTER, 200 Medical Park Boulevard, Petersburg, VA, Zip 23805-9274; tel. 804/765-5000; Brenda Woodcock, President

BON SECOURS MARY IMMACULATE HOSPITAL, 2 Bernardine Drive, Newport News, VA, Zip 23602-4499; tel. 757/886-6000; Alan E. George, President

BON SECOURS MARYVIEW MEDICAL CENTER, 3636 High Street, Portsmouth, VA, Zip 23707-3270; tel. 757/398-2200; Shane Knisley, President

BON SECOURS MEMORIAL REGIONAL MEDICAL CENTER, 8260 Atlee Road, Mechanicsville, VA, Zip 23116-1844; tel. 804/764-6000; John Emery, President

BON SECOURS RAPPAHANNOCK GENERAL HOSPITAL, 101 Harris Drive, Kilmarnock, VA, Zip 22482-3880, P O Box 1449, Zip 22482-1449, tel. 804/435-8000; John Emery, President

BON SECOURS RICHMOND COMMUNITY HOSPITAL, 1500 North 28th Street, Richmond, VA, Zip 23223-5396, P O Box 27184, Zip 23261-7184, tel. 804/225-1700; W. Bryan Lee, President

BON SECOURS ST. FRANCIS MEDICAL CENTER, 13710 St Francis Boulevard, Midlothian, VA, Zip 23114-3267; tel. 804/594-7300; Joseph Wilkins, President

BON SECOURS ST. MARY'S HOSPITAL, 5801 Bremo Road, Richmond, VA, Zip 23226-1907; tel. 804/285-2011; W. Bryan. Lee, President

BUCHANAN GENERAL HOSPITAL, 1535 Slate Creek Road, Grundy, VA, Zip 24614-6974; tel. 276/935-1000; Robert D. Ruchti, Chief Executive Officer

CJW MEDICAL CENTER, 7101 Jahnke Road, Richmond, VA, Zip 23225-4044; tel. 804/483-0000; Lance Jones, Chief Executive Officer

CARILION FRANKLIN MEMORIAL HOSPITAL, 180 Floyd Avenue, Rocky Mount, VA, Zip 24151-1389; tel. 540/483-5277; Carl T. Cline, Vice President, Carilion Clinic and Hospital Administrator

CARILION GILES COMMUNITY HOSPITAL, 159 Hartley Way, Pearisburg, VA, Zip 24134-2471; tel. 540/921-6000; Kristie Williams, Vice President and Hospital Administrator

CARILION NEW RIVER VALLEY MEDICAL CENTER, 2900 Lamb Circle, Christiansburg, VA, Zip 24073-6344, P O Box 5, Radford, Zip 24143-0005, tel. 540/731-2000; William Flattery, Vice President and Administrator Western Division

CARILION ROANOKE MEMORIAL HOSPITAL, 1906 Belleview Avenue Southeast, Roanoke, VA, Zip 24014-1838, P O Box 13367, Zip 24033-3367, tel. 540/981-7000; Steven C. Arner, President and Chief Operating Officer, Hospital Administrator

CARILION ROCKBRIDGE COMMUNITY HOSPITAL, 1 Health Circle, Lexington, VA, Zip 24450-2492; tel. 540/458-3300; Greg T. Madsen, Vice President, Hospital Administrator Carilion Rockbridge Community Hospital

CARILION TAZEWELL COMMUNITY HOSPITAL, 388 Ben Bolt Avenue, Tazewell, VA, Zip 24651-9700; tel. 276/988-8700; Kristie Williams, Vice President and Hospital Administrator

CENTRA BEDFORD MEMORIAL HOSPITAL, 1613 Oakwood Street, Bedford, VA, Zip 24523-1213; tel. 540/586-2441; Stacey L. Vaught, MSN, President

CENTRA SOUTHSIDE COMMUNITY HOSPITAL, 800 Oak Street, Farmville, VA, Zip 23901-1199; tel. 434/392-8811; Thomas Angelo, Chief Executive Officer

CHESAPEAKE REGIONAL MEDICAL CENTER, 736 Battlefield Boulevard North, Chesapeake, VA, Zip 23320-4941, P O Box 2028, Zip 23327-2028, tel. 757/312-8121; Reese Jackson, President and Chief Executive Officer

CHILDREN'S HOSPITAL OF RICHMOND AT VCU, 2924 Brook Road, Richmond, VA, Zip 23220-1298, 1000 E. Broad Street, Zip 23219, tel. 804/321-7474; Elias Neujahr, President

CHILDREN'S HOSPITAL OF THE KING'S DAUGHTERS, 601 Children's Lane, Norfolk, VA, Zip 23507-1910; tel. 757/668-7000; Amy Sampson, President and Chief Executive Officer

CLINCH VALLEY MEDICAL CENTER, 6801 Governor G C Peery Highway, Richlands, VA, Zip 24641-2194; tel. 276/596-6000; Peter Mulkey, Chief Executive Officer

COASTAL VIRGINIA REHABILITATION, 250 Josephs Drive, Yorktown, VA, Zip 23693-3405; tel. 757/928-8000; Daniel Ballin, Administrator

DOMINION HOSPITAL, 2960 Sleepy Hollow Road, Falls Church, VA, Zip 22044-2030; tel. 703/536-2000; Benjamin Brown, Chief Executive Officer

ENCOMPASS HEALTH REHABILITATION HOSPITAL OF RICHMOND, 5700 Fitzhugh Avenue, Richmond, VA, Zip 23226-1800; tel. 804/288-5700; James Miller, Chief Executive Officer

FAUQUIER HOSPITAL, 500 Hospital Drive, Warrenton, VA, Zip 20186-3099; tel. 540/316-5000; Rebecca Segal, FACHE, President and Chief Executive Officer

HENRICO DOCTORS' HOSPITAL, 1602 Skipwith Road, Richmond, VA, Zip 23229-5205; tel. 804/289-4500; Ryan Jensen, Chief Executive Officer

INOVA ALEXANDRIA HOSPITAL, 4320 Seminary Road, Alexandria, VA, Zip 22304-1535; tel. 703/504-3167; Rina Bansal, M.D., President

INOVA FAIR OAKS HOSPITAL, 3600 Joseph Siewick Drive, Fairfax, VA, Zip 22033-1798; tel. 703/391-3600; Raj Chand, M.D., President

INOVA FAIRFAX MEDICAL CAMPUS, 3300 Gallows Road, Falls Church, VA, Zip 22042-3300; tel. 703/776-4001; Steve Narang, M.D., President and President, Pediatric Service Line

INOVA LOUDOUN HOSPITAL, 44045 Riverside Parkway, Leesburg, VA, Zip 20176-5101, P O Box 6000, Zip 20177-0600, tel. 703/858-6000; Susan T. Carroll, FACHE, President

INOVA MOUNT VERNON HOSPITAL, 2501 Parker's Lane, Alexandria, VA, Zip 22306-3209; tel. 703/664-7000; Roberta Tinch, President

JOHNSTON MEMORIAL HOSPITAL, 16000 Johnston Memorial Drive, Abingdon, VA, Zip 24211-7659; tel. 276/258-1000; John Jeter, Chief Executive Officer

LEWISGALE HOSPITAL ALLEGHANY, 1 Arh Lane, Low Moor, VA, Zip 24457, P O Box 7, Zip 24457-0007, tel. 540/862-6011; Lee Higginbotham, Chief Executive Officer

LEWISGALE HOSPITAL PULASKI, 2400 Lee Highway, Pulaski, VA, Zip 24301-2326, P O Box 759, Zip 24301-0759, tel. 540/994-8100; Sean Pressman, Chief Executive Officer

MARY WASHINGTON HOSPITAL, 1001 Sam Perry Boulevard, Fredericksburg, VA, Zip 22401-3354; tel. 540/741-1100; Michael P. McDermott, M.D., President and Chief Executive Officer

NORTHERN REGIONAL HOSPITAL, 830 Rockford Street, Mount Airy, NC, Zip 27030-5365, P O Box 1101, Zip 27030-1101, tel. 336/719-7000; Chris A. Lumsden, President and Chief Executive Officer

RESTON HOSPITAL CENTER, 1850 Town Center Parkway, Reston, VA, Zip 20190-3219; tel. 703/689-9000; John A. Deardorff, President and Chief Executive, Northern Virginia Market

RIVERSIDE REGIONAL MEDICAL CENTER, 500 J Clyde Morris Boulevard, Newport News, VA, Zip 23601-1929; tel. 757/594-2000; Michael Oshiki, M.D., MS, FACHE, President

RIVERSIDE SHORE MEMORIAL HOSPITAL, 20480 Market Street, Onancock, VA, Zip 23417-4309, P O Box 430, Zip 23417, tel. 757/302-2100; Nicolas Chuquin, President

RIVERSIDE WALTER REED HOSPITAL, 7547 Hospital Drive, Gloucester, VA, Zip 23061-4178, P O Box 1130, Zip 23061-1130, tel. 804/693-8800; Shelly Johnson, Administrator and President

RUSSELL COUNTY MEDICAL CENTER, 58 Carroll Street, Lebanon, VA, Zip 24266, P O Box 3600, Zip 24266-0200, tel. 276/883-8000; Greta M. Morrison, Administrator, Assistant Vice President and Chief Nursing Officer

SOVAH HEALTH–MARTINSVILLE, 320 Hospital Drive, Martinsville, VA, Zip 24112-1981, P O Box 4788, Zip 24115-4788, tel. 276/666-7200; Steve Heatherly, Chief Executive Officer

SENTARA CAREPLEX HOSPITAL, 3000 Coliseum Drive, Hampton, VA, Zip 23666-5963; tel. 757/736-1000; Kirkpatrick Conley, Senior Vice President, Regional President, Central

SENTARA LEIGH HOSPITAL, 830 Kempsville Road, Norfolk, VA, Zip 23502-3920; tel. 757/261-6000; Joanne Inman, Division President

SENTARA MARTHA JEFFERSON HOSPITAL, 500 Martha Jefferson Drive, Charlottesville, VA, Zip 22911-4668; tel. 434/654-7000; Rita A. Bunch, M.P.H., FACHE, Division President

SENTARA NORFOLK GENERAL HOSPITAL, 600 Gresham Drive, Norfolk, VA, Zip 23507-1904; tel. 757/388-3000; Liisa Ortegon, R.N., Division President

SENTARA NORTHERN VIRGINIA MEDICAL CENTER, 2300 Opitz Boulevard, Woodbridge, VA, Zip 22191-3399; tel. 703/523-1000; Jeff Joyner, FACHE, Division President

SENTARA OBICI HOSPITAL, 2800 Godwin Boulevard, Suffolk, VA, Zip 23434-8038; tel. 757/934-4000; David J. Masterson, Division President

SENTARA PRINCESS ANNE HOSPITAL, 2025 Glenn Mitchell Drive, Virginia Beach, VA, Zip 23456-0178; tel. 757/507-1000; Dana Weston Graves, Division President

SENTARA VIRGINIA BEACH GENERAL HOSPITAL, 1060 First Colonial Road, Virginia Beach, VA, Zip 23454-3002; tel. 757/395-8000; Elwood Bernard. Boone, III., FACHE, Division President

SENTARA WILLIAMSBURG REGIONAL MEDICAL CENTER, 100 Sentara Circle, Williamsburg, VA, Zip 23188-5713; tel. 757/984-6000; Amber Price, Division President

SMYTH COUNTY COMMUNITY HOSPITAL, 245 Medical Park Drive, Marion, VA, Zip 24354, P O Box 880, Zip 24354-0880, tel. 276/378-1000; Dale M. Clark, Vice President and Chief Executive Officer

TRICITIES HOSPITAL, 411 West Randolph Road, Hopewell, VA, Zip 23860-2938; tel. 804/541-1600; Joseph Mazzo, Chief Executive Officer

TWIN COUNTY REGIONAL HEALTHCARE, 200 Hospital Drive, Galax, VA, Zip 24333-2227; tel. 276/236-8181; Sudandra Ratnasamy,FACHE, R.N., FACHE, Chief Executive Officer

UVA ENCOMPASS HEALTH REHABILITATION HOSPITAL, 515 Ray C Hunt Drive, Charlottesville, VA, Zip 22903-2981; tel. 434/244-2000; Vivian White, Chief Executive Officer

UVA HEALTH CULPEPER MEDICAL CENTER, 501 Sunset Lane, Culpeper, VA, Zip 22701-3917, P O Box 592, Zip 22701-0500, tel. 540/829-4100; Erik Shannon, Chief Executive Officer

UVA HEALTH PRINCE WILLIAM MEDICAL CENTER, 8700 Sudley Road, Manassas, VA, Zip 20110-4418, P O Box 2610, Zip 20108-0867, tel. 703/369-8000; Erik Shannon, Chief Executive Officer

UVA HEALTH UNIVERSITY MEDICAL CENTER, 1215 Lee Street, Charlottesville, VA, Zip 22908-0001, P O Box 800809, Zip 22908-0809, tel. 434/924-0211; Wendy Michelle. Horton, PharmD, FACHE, Chief Executive Officer

VCU HEALTH COMMUNITY MEMORIAL HOSPITAL, 125 Buena Vista Circle, South Hill, VA, Zip 23970-1431, P O Box 90, Zip 23970-0090, tel. 434/447-3151; Sheldon Barr, President

VCU HEALTH TAPPAHANNOCK HOSPITAL, 618 Hospital Road, Tappahannock, VA, Zip 22560-5000; tel. 804/443-3311; Elizabeth J. Martin, Hospital President

VCU MEDICAL CENTER, 1250 East Marshall Street, Richmond, VA, Zip 23298-5051, P O Box 980510, Zip 23298-0510, tel. 804/828-9000; Michael Roussos, President

VHC HEALTH, 1701 North George Mason Drive, Arlington, VA, Zip 22205-3698; tel. 703/558-5000; Christopher Lane, President and Chief Executive Officer

WYTHE COUNTY COMMUNITY HOSPITAL, 600 West Ridge Road, Wytheville, VA, Zip 24382-1099; tel. 276/228-0200; Vicki Parks, Chief Executive Officer

WASHINGTON

GROUP HEALTH COOPERATIVE
320 Westlake Avenue North, Suite 100, Seattle, WA Zip 98109-5233; tel. 206/448-5083; Scott Armstrong, Chief Executive Officer

ASTRIA SUNNYSIDE HOSPITAL, 1016 Tacoma Avenue, Sunnyside, WA, Zip 98944-2263, P O Box 719, Zip 98944-0719, tel. 509/837-1500; Brian P. Gibbons, Chief Executive Officer

ASTRIA TOPPENISH HOSPITAL, 502 West Fourth Avenue, Toppenish, WA, Zip 98948-1616, P O Box 672, Zip 98948-0672, tel. 509/865-3105; Cathy Bambrick, Administrator

CASCADE VALLEY HOSPITAL, 330 South Stillaguamish Avenue, Arlington, WA, Zip 98223-1642; tel. 360/435-2133; Brian K. Ivie, President and Chief Executive Officer

COLUMBIA COUNTY HEALTH SYSTEM, 1012 South Third Street, Dayton, WA, Zip 99328-1696; tel. 509/382-2531; Shane A. McGuire, Chief Executive Officer

ISLAND HEALTH, 1211 24th Street, Anacortes, WA, Zip 98221-2562; tel. 360/299-1300; Elise Cutter, FACHE, Chief Executive Officer, Superintendent

KADLEC REGIONAL MEDICAL CENTER, 888 Swift Boulevard, Richland, WA, Zip 99352-3514; tel. 509/946-4611; Reza Kaleel, Chief Executive

KITTITAS VALLEY HEALTHCARE, 603 South Chestnut Street, Ellensburg, WA, Zip 98926-3875; tel. 509/962-7302; Julie Petersen, CPA, Chief Executive Officer

KOOTENAI HEALTH, 2003 Kootenai Health Way, Coeur D'Alene, ID, Zip 83814-2677; tel. 208/625-4000; Jameson C. Smith, FACHE, Chief Executive Officer

LOURDES HEALTH, 520 North Fourth Avenue, Pasco, WA, Zip 99301-5257; tel. 509/547-7704; Mark C. Holyoak, FACHE, Chief Executive Officer

MULTICARE DEACONESS HOSPITAL, 800 West Fifth Avenue, Spokane, WA, Zip 99204-2803, P O Box 248, Zip 99210-0248, tel. 509/458-5800; Gregory George. Repetti, III., FACHE, President

MULTICARE MARY BRIDGE CHILDREN'S HOSPITAL AND HEALTH CENTER, 317 Martin Luther King Jr Way, Tacoma, WA, Zip 98405-4234, P O Box 5299, Zip 98415-0299, tel. 253/403-1400; Jeffrey S. Poltawsky, President and Market Leader

MULTICARE VALLEY HOSPITAL, 12606 East Mission Avenue, Spokane Valley, WA, Zip 99216-1090; tel. 509/924-6650; Gregory George. Repetti, III., FACHE, President

MULTICARE YAKIMA MEMORIAL HOSPITAL, 2811 Tieton Drive, Yakima, WA, Zip 98902-3761; tel. 509/575-8000; Tammy K. Buyok, President

NORTHWEST SPECIALTY HOSPITAL, 1593 East Polston Avenue, Post Falls, ID, Zip 83854-5326; tel. 208/262-2300; Rick Rasmussen, Chief Executive Officer

OVERLAKE MEDICAL CENTER AND CLINICS, 1035 116th Avenue NE, Bellevue, WA, Zip 98004-4604; tel. 425/688-5000; J. Michael. Marsh, President and Chief Executive Officer

PEACEHEALTH ST. JOSEPH MEDICAL CENTER, 2901 Squalicum Parkway, Bellingham, WA, Zip 98225-1851; tel. 360/734-5400; Charles Prosper, Chief Executive, PeaceHealth Northwest

PEACEHEALTH UNITED GENERAL MEDICAL CENTER, 2000 Hospital Drive, Sedro-Woolley, WA, Zip 98284-4327; tel. 360/856-6021; Christopher Johnston, Chief Administrative Officer

PROSSER MEMORIAL HEALTH, 723 Memorial Street, Prosser, WA, Zip 99350-1524; tel. 509/786-2222; Craig J. Marks, FACHE, Chief Executive Officer

PROVIDENCE CENTRALIA HOSPITAL, 914 S Scheuber RD, Centralia, WA, Zip 98531-9027, 914 South Scheuber Road, Zip 98531-9027, tel. 360/736-2803; Darin Goss, FACHE, Chief Executive Officer

PROVIDENCE HOLY FAMILY HOSPITAL, 5633 North Lidgerwood Street, Spokane, WA, Zip 99208-1224; tel. 509/482-0111; Susan Scott, Chief Operating Officer

PROVIDENCE REGIONAL MEDICAL CENTER EVERETT, 1700 13th Street, Everett, WA, Zip 98201-1689, P O Box 1147, Zip 98206-1147, tel. 425/261-2000; Kristy Carrington, R.N., Chief Executive Officer

PROVIDENCE SACRED HEART MEDICAL CENTER & CHILDREN'S HOSPITAL, 101 West Eighth Avenue, Spokane, WA, Zip 99204-2364, P O Box 2555, Zip 99220-2555, tel. 509/474-3131; Susan Stacey, R.N., Chief Executive

PROVIDENCE ST. MARY MEDICAL CENTER, 401 W Poplar Street, Walla Walla, WA, Zip 99362-2846, P O Box 1477, Zip 99362-0312, tel. 509/897-3320; Reza Kaleel, Chief Executive

PULLMAN REGIONAL HOSPITAL, 835 SE Bishop Boulevard, Pullman, WA, Zip 99163-5512; tel. 509/332-2541; Matthew Forge, Chief Executive Officer

SEATTLE CHILDREN'S HOSPITAL, 4800 Sand Point Way NE, Seattle, WA, Zip 98105-3901, P O Box 5371, Zip 98145-5005, tel. 206/987-2000; Jeff Sperring, M.D., Chief Executive Officer

SKAGIT VALLEY HOSPITAL, 300 Hospital Parkway, Mount Vernon, WA, Zip 98273, P O Box 1376, Zip 98273-1376, tel. 360/424-4111; Brian K. Ivie, President and Chief Executive Officer

ST. FRANCIS HOSPITAL, 34515 Ninth Avenue South, Federal Way, WA, Zip 98003-6799; tel. 253/944-8100; Dino Johnson, R.N., Interim Chief Operating Officer

ST. JOSEPH MEDICAL CENTER, 1717 South 'J' Street, Tacoma, WA, Zip 98405-3004, P O Box 2197, Zip 98401-2197, tel. 253/426-4101; Syd Bersante, R.N., Interim President

ST. MICHAEL MEDICAL CENTER, 1800 Northwest Myhre Road, Silverdale, WA, Zip 98383-7663; tel. 564/240-1000; Chad Melton, President

TRIOS HEALTH, 900 South Auburn Street, Kennewick, WA, Zip 99336-5621, P O Box 6128, Zip 99336-0128, tel. 509/221-6339; David Elgarico, Chief Executive Officer

VIRGINIA MASON MEDICAL CENTER, 1100 Ninth Avenue, Seattle, WA, Zip 98101-2756, P O Box 900, Zip 98111-0900, tel. 206/223-6600; Monica Hilt, President

WHIDBEYHEALTH, 101 North Main Street, Coupeville, WA, Zip 98239-3413; tel. 360/678-5151; Nathan Staggs, Chief Executive Officer

WHITMAN HOSPITAL AND MEDICAL CENTER, 1200 West Fairview Street, Colfax, WA, Zip 99111-9579; tel. 509/397-3435; Hank Hanigan, FACHE, Chief Executive Officer

LINCOLN COUNTY HEALTH DEPARTMENT
90 Nichols Street, Davenport, WA Zip 99122-9729; tel. 509/725-1001; Ed Dzedzy, Public Health Administration

LINCOLN HOSPITAL, 10 Nicholls Street, Davenport, WA, Zip 99122-9729; tel. 509/725-7101; Tyson Lacy, Chief Executive Officer and Superintendent

ODESSA MEMORIAL HEALTHCARE CENTER, 502 East Amende Drive, Odessa, WA, Zip 99159-7003, P O Box 368, Zip 99159-0368, tel. 509/982-2611; Brett Antczak, Chief Executive Officer

WEST VIRGINIA

HEALTH PARTNERS NETWORK, INC.
1000 Technology Drive, Suite 2320, Fairmont, WV Zip 26554-8834; tel. 304/368-2740; William G. MacLean, Executive Director

BROADDUS HOSPITAL, 1 Healthcare Drive, Philippi, WV, Zip 26416-9405, P O Box 930, Zip 26416-0930, tel. 304/457-1760; Dana L. Gould, Chief Executive Officer

Networks / Health Partners Network, Inc.

CAMDEN CLARK MEDICAL CENTER, 800 Garfield Avenue, Parkersburg, WV, Zip 26101-5378, P O Box 718, Zip 26102-0718, tel. 304/424-2111; Sean Smith, President and Chief Executive Officer

DAVIS MEDICAL CENTER, 812 Gorman Avenue, Elkins, WV, Zip 26241-3181, P O Box 1484, Zip 26241-1484, tel. 304/636-3300; Mark Doak, Interim President

ENCOMPASS HEALTH REHABILITATION HOSPITAL OF MORGANTOWN, 1160 Van Voorhis Road, Morgantown, WV, Zip 26505-3437; tel. 304/598-1100; Ashley Black, Chief Executive Officer

GRAFTON CITY HOSPITAL, 1 Hospital Plaza, Grafton, WV, Zip 26354-1283; tel. 304/265-0400; Melissa Lockwood, Chief Administration Officer

MINNIE HAMILTON HEALTHCARE CENTER, 186 Hospital Drive, Grantsville, WV, Zip 26147-7100; tel. 304/354-9244; Steve Whited, Chief Executive Officer

MON HEALTH STONEWALL JACKSON MEMORIAL HOSPITAL, 230 Hospital Plaza, Weston, WV, Zip 26452-8558; tel. 304/269-8000; Kevin P. Stalnaker, CPA, Chief Executive Officer

ST. JOSEPH'S HOSPITAL, 1 Amalia Drive, Buckhannon, WV, Zip 26201-2276; tel. 304/473-2000; Skip Gjolberg, Jr., FACHE, President and Chief Executive Officer

UNITED HOSPITAL CENTER, 327 Medical Park Drive, Bridgeport, WV, Zip 26330-9006; tel. 681/342-1000; David F. Hess, M.D., President and Chief Executive Officer

WEBSTER COUNTY MEMORIAL HOSPITAL, 324 Miller Mountain Drive, Webster Springs, WV, Zip 26288-1087, P O Box 312, Zip 26288-0312, tel. 304/847-5682; William J. Dempsey, Chief Executive Officer

WEST VIRGINIA UNIVERSITY HOSPITALS, 1 Medical Center Drive, Morgantown, WV, Zip 26506-4749; tel. 304/598-4000; Michael Grace, Ed.D., FACHE, President

PARTNERS IN HEALTH NETWORK, INC.
405 Capitol Street, Suite 505, Charleston, WV Zip 25301-1783; tel. 304/388-7385; Terry Vaughan Cox, Executive Director

BOONE MEMORIAL HOSPITAL, 701 Madison Avenue, Madison, WV, Zip 25130-1699; tel. 304/369-1230; Virgil Underwood, Chief Executive Officer

BRAXTON COUNTY MEMORIAL HOSPITAL, 100 Hoylman DR, Gassaway, WV, Zip 26624-9318, 100 Hoylman Drive, Zip 26624-9318, tel. 304/364-5156; John C. Forester, Interim President

CHARLESTON AREA MEDICAL CENTER, 501 Morris Street, Charleston, WV, Zip 25301-1300, P O Box 1547, Zip 25326-1547, tel. 304/388-5432; Glenn Crotty, Jr., M.D., President and Chief Executive Officer

CHARLESTON SURGICAL HOSPITAL, 1306 Kanawha Boulevard East, Charleston, WV, Zip 25301-3001, P O Box 2271, Zip 25328-2271, tel. 304/343-4371; Christina Arvon, Administrator and Chief Executive Officer

HIGHLAND HOSPITAL, 300 56th Street SE, Charleston, WV, Zip 25304-2361, P O Box 4107, Zip 25364-4107, tel. 304/926-1600; Nadine Dexter, R.N., MSN, Chief Executive Officer

JACKSON GENERAL HOSPITAL, 122 Pinnell Street, Ripley, WV, Zip 25271-9101, P O Box 720, Zip 25271-0720, tel. 304/372-2731; Candace N. Miller, President and Chief Executive Officer

MINNIE HAMILTON HEALTHCARE CENTER, 186 Hospital Drive, Grantsville, WV, Zip 26147-7100; tel. 304/354-9244; Steve Whited, Chief Executive Officer

MON HEALTH STONEWALL JACKSON MEMORIAL HOSPITAL, 230 Hospital Plaza, Weston, WV, Zip 26452-8558; tel. 304/269-8000; Kevin P. Stalnaker, CPA, Chief Executive Officer

MONTGOMERY GENERAL HOSPITAL, 401 Sixth Avenue, Montgomery, WV, Zip 25136-2116, P O Box 270, Zip 25136-0270, tel. 304/442-5151; Deborah Ann. Hill, Chief Executive Officer

POCAHONTAS MEMORIAL HOSPITAL, 150 Duncan Road, Buckeye, WV, Zip 24924; tel. 304/799-7400; Michelle Deeds, Chief Executive Officer

PRINCETON COMMUNITY HOSPITAL, 122 12th Street, Princeton, WV, Zip 24740-2352, P O Box 1369, Zip 24740-1369, tel. 304/487-7000; Karen L. Bowling, MSN, R.N., President and Chief Executive Officer

ROANE GENERAL HOSPITAL, 200 Hospital Drive, Spencer, WV, Zip 25276-1050; tel. 304/927-4444; Douglas E. Bentz, Chief Executive Officer

SUMMERSVILLE REGIONAL MEDICAL CENTER, 400 Fairview Heights Road, Summersville, WV, Zip 26651-9308; tel. 304/872-2891; John C. Forester, Interim President

WEBSTER COUNTY MEMORIAL HOSPITAL, 324 Miller Mountain Drive, Webster Springs, WV, Zip 26288-1087, P O Box 312, Zip 26288-0312, tel. 304/847-5682; William J. Dempsey, Chief Executive Officer

WISCONSIN

ASPIRUS, INC.
2200 Westwood Drive, Wausau, WI Zip 54401-7806; tel. 715/847-2118; Matthew Heywood, President and Chief Executive Officer

ASPIRUS IRON RIVER HOSPITAL, 1400 West Ice Lake Road, Iron River, MI, Zip 49935-9526; tel. 906/265-6121; Rae Kaare, Chief Administrative Officer

ASPIRUS IRONWOOD HOSPITAL & CLINICS, INC., N10561 Grandview Lane, Ironwood, MI, Zip 49938-9622; tel. 906/932-2525; Paula L. Chermside, Chief Administrative Officer

ASPIRUS KEWEENAW HOSPITAL, 205 Osceola Street, Laurium, MI, Zip 49913-2134; tel. 906/337-6500; Matt Krause, Chief Administrative Officer

ASPIRUS LANGLADE HOSPITAL, 112 East Fifth Avenue, Antigo, WI, Zip 54409-2796; tel. 715/623-2331; Sherry Bunten, R.N., FACHE, President

ASPIRUS MEDFORD HOSPITAL & CLINICS, 135 South Gibson Street, Medford, WI, Zip 54451; tel. 715/748-8100; Jason Troxell, President

ASPIRUS RIVERVIEW HOSPITAL AND CLINICS, INC., 410 Dewey Street, Wisconsin Rapids, WI, Zip 54494-4715, P O Box 8080, Zip 54495-8080, tel. 715/423-6060; Brian Kief, President

ASPIRUS WAUSAU HOSPITAL, INC., 333 Pine Ridge Boulevard, Wausau, WI, Zip 54401-4187, 1900 Westwood Drive, Zip 54402, tel. 715/847-2121; Jeffrey Wicklander, President

COLUMBIA ST. MARY'S
2025 East Newport Avenue, Milwaukee, WI Zip 53211-2906; tel. 414/961-3300; Travis Andersen, President and Chief Executive Officer

ASCENSION COLUMBIA ST. MARY'S HOSPITAL MILWAUKEE, 2301 North Lake Drive, Milwaukee, WI, Zip 53211-4508; tel. 414/291-1000; Andre Storey, President

ASCENSION SACRED HEART REHABILITATION HOSPITAL, 13111 North Port Washington Road, Mequon, WI, Zip 53097-2416; tel. 262/292-0400; Julie Jolitz, Administrator

COMMUNITY HEALTH NETWORK, INC.
225 Memorial Drive, Berlin, WI Zip 54923-1243; tel. 920/361-5580

THEDA CARE MEDICAL CENTER – WILD ROSE, 601 Grove Avenue, Wild Rose, WI, Zip 54984-6903, P O Box 243, Zip 54984-0243, tel. 920/622-3257; Tammy Bending, Vice President

THEDACARE MEDICAL CENTER-BERLIN, 225 Memorial Drive, Berlin, WI, Zip 54923-1295; tel. 920/361-1313; Tammy Bending, Vice President, Critical Access Hospital

GUNDERSEN HEALTH SYSTEM
1900 South Avenue, La Crosse, WI Zip 54601-5467; tel. 608/782-7300; Scott W. Rathgaber, M.D., Chief Executive Officer

GUNDERSEN BOSCOBEL AREA HOSPITAL AND CLINICS, 205 Parker Street, Boscobel, WI, Zip 53805-1698; tel. 608/375-4112; Theresa Lynn. Braudt, Administrator

GUNDERSEN LUTHERAN MEDICAL CENTER, 1900 South Avenue, La Crosse, WI, Zip 54601-5467; tel. 608/782-7300; Scott W. Rathgaber, M.D., Chief Executive Officer

GUNDERSEN MOUNDVIEW HOSPITAL & CLINICS, 402 West Lake Street, Friendship, WI, Zip 53934-9699, P O Box 40, Zip 53934-0040, tel. 608/339-3331; Francisco Perez-Guerra, Administrator

GUNDERSEN PALMER LUTHERAN HOSPITAL AND CLINICS, 112 Jefferson Street, West Union, IA, Zip 52175-1022; tel. 563/422-3811; Patrice Kuennen, Chief Executive Officer

GUNDERSEN ST. JOSEPH'S HOSPITAL AND CLINICS, 400 Water Avenue, Hillsboro, WI, Zip 54634-9054, P O Box 527, Zip 54634-0527, tel. 608/489-8000; Kristie McCoic, Administrator

GUNDERSEN TRI-COUNTY HOSPITAL AND CLINICS, 18601 Lincoln Street, Whitehall, WI, Zip 54773-8605; tel. 715/538-4361; Joni Olson, Chief Executive Officer

Alliances

ALLIANCE OF INDEPENDENT ACADEMIC MEDICAL CENTERS
233 East Erie Street, Ste 306, Chicago, IL Zip 60611; tel. 312/836–3712; Kimberly Pierce–Boggs, Executive Director

ARIZONA
Scottsdale
Alliance
  HonorHealth

CALIFORNIA
Colton
Alliance
  Arrowhead Regional Medical Center
Los Angeles
Alliance
  Cedars–Sinai Medical Center
Oakland
Alliance
  Kaiser Permanente Oakland Medical Center

COLORADO
Aurora
Alliance
  Medical Center of Aurora
Denver
Alliance
  Intermountain Health Saint Joseph Hospital
  Presbyterian/St. Luke's Medical Center
  Rose Medical Center
Englewood
Alliance
  Swedish Medical Center
Lone Tree
Alliance
  Sky Ridge Medical Center
Thornton
Alliance
  North Suburban Medical Center

CONNECTICUT
Hartford
Alliance
  Saint Francis Hospital

DELAWARE
Newark
Alliance
  ChristianaCare

FLORIDA
Hollywood
Alliance
  Memorial Healthcare System
Orange Park
Alliance
  HCA Florida Orange Park Hospital
Orlando
Alliance
  AdventHealth Orlando
  Orlando Health Orlando Regional Medical Center

GEORGIA
Macon
Alliance
  Piedmont Macon

ILLINOIS
Chicago
Alliance
  Advocate Illinois Masonic Medical Center
Oak Lawn
Alliance
  Advocate Christ Medical Center
Park Ridge
Alliance
  Advocate Lutheran General Hospital
Peoria
Alliance
  OSF Saint Francis Medical Center

INDIANA
Indianapolis
Alliance
  Community Health Network

IOWA
West Des Moines
Alliance
  UnityPoint Health

LOUISIANA
Baton Rouge
Alliance
  Our Lady of the Lake Regional Medical Center
New Orleans
Alliance
  Ochsner Health

MAINE
Portland
Alliance
  MaineHealth Maine Medical Center

MARYLAND
Baltimore
Alliance
  Sinai Hospital of Baltimore

MASSACHUSETTS
Burlington
Alliance
  Lahey Hospital & Medical Center
Springfield
Alliance
  Baystate Medical Center

MICHIGAN
Grand Rapids
Alliance
  Trinity Health Grand Rapids Hospital
Lansing
Alliance
  University of Michigan Health–Sparrow Lansing
Rochester
Alliance
  Ascension Providence Rochester Hospital

MINNESOTA
Bloomington
Alliance
  HealthPartners

MONTANA
Billings
Alliance
  Billings Clinic

NEW JERSEY
Brick Township
Alliance
  Hackensack Meridian Health Ocean University Medical Center
Holmdel
Alliance
  Hackensack Meridian Health Bayshore Community Hospital
Livingston
Alliance
  Cooperman Barnabas Medical Center
Long Branch
Alliance
  Monmouth Medical Center, Long Branch Campus
Manahawkin
Alliance
  Hackensack Meridian Health Southern Ocean Medical Center
Neptune
Alliance
  Hackensack Meridian Health Jersey Shore University Medical Center
Newark
Alliance
  Newark Beth Israel Medical Center
Perth Amboy
Alliance
  Hackensack Meridian Health Raritan Bay Medical Center
Phillipsburg
Alliance
  St. Luke's Hospital – Warren Campus
Red Bank
Alliance
  Hackensack Meridian Health Riverview Medical Center

NEW YORK
Brooklyn
Alliance
  Maimonides Medical Center
Cooperstown
Alliance
  Bassett Medical Center

NORTH CAROLINA
Charlotte
Alliance
  Atrium Health's Carolinas Medical Center

OHIO
Akron
Alliance
  Cleveland Clinic Akron General
Cincinnati
Alliance
  The Christ Hospital Health Network
Cleveland
Alliance
  Cleveland Clinic
Columbus
Alliance
  OhioHealth Grant Medical Center
  OhioHealth Riverside Methodist Hospital

OREGON
Hood River
Alliance
  Providence Hood River Memorial Hospital
Milwaukie
Alliance
  Providence Milwaukie Hospital
Portland
Alliance
  Providence Portland Medical Center
  Providence St. Vincent Medical Center

PENNSYLVANIA
Bethlehem
Alliance
  St. Luke's University Hospital – Bethlehem Campus
Philadelphia
Alliance
  Einstein Medical Center Philadelphia
Sayre
Alliance
  Guthrie Robert Packer Hospital
Wynnewood
Alliance
  Lankenau Medical Center

Alliances

York
Alliance
  WellSpan York Hospital

SOUTH CAROLINA
Charleston
Alliance
  Trident Medical Center

Myrtle Beach
Alliance
  Grand Strand Medical Center

TEXAS
Dallas
Alliance
  Baylor Scott & White Health

Fort Worth
Alliance
  JPS Health Network

Lubbock
Alliance
  Covenant Children's Hospital
  Covenant Medical Center

WASHINGTON
Seattle
Alliance
  Providence Swedish Cherry Hill
  Providence Swedish First Hill
  Virginia Mason Medical Center

WEST VIRGINIA
Charleston
Alliance
  Charleston Area Medical Center

WISCONSIN
Marshfield
Alliance
  Marshfield Medical Center

CAPSTONE HEALTH ALLIANCE
1200 Ridgefield Boulevard, Suite 200, Asheville, NC Zip 28806; tel. 828/418–5050; Tim Bugg, President and Chief Executive Officer

ALABAMA
Butler
Alliance
  Ochsner Choctaw General

Dothan
Alliance
  Southeast Alabama Medical Center

Eufaula
Alliance
  Medical Center Barbour

Opelika
Alliance
  East Alabama Medical Center

Wedowee
Alliance
  Tanner Medical Center/East Alabama

ARKANSAS
Batesville
Alliance
  White River Health

Calico Rock
Alliance
  Izard County Medical Center

Fordyce
Alliance
  Dallas County Medical Center

Harrison
Alliance
  North Arkansas Regional Medical Center

Mountain View
Alliance
  Stone County Medical Center

Pine Bluff
Alliance
  Jefferson Regional

DELAWARE
Lewes
Alliance
  Beebe Healthcare

GEORGIA
Bremen
Alliance
  Higgins General Hospital

Carrollton
Alliance
  Tanner Medical Center–Carrollton

Jesup
Alliance
  Wayne Memorial Hospital

Lagrange
Alliance
  Wellstar West Georgia Medical Center

Savannah
Alliance
  Candler Hospital–Savannah
  St. Joseph's Hospital

Villa Rica
Alliance
  Tanner Medical Center–Villa Rica

ILLINOIS
Centreville
Alliance
  Touchette Regional Hospital

Chicago
Alliance
  Humboldt Park Health
  Loretto Hospital
  Thorek Memorial Hospital

Dixon
Alliance
  Katherine Shaw Bethea Hospital

Elmhurst
Alliance
  Endeavor Health Elmhurst Hospital

Hoopeston
Alliance
  Carle Hoopeston Regional Health Center

Kankakee
Alliance
  Riverside Medical Center

Naperville
Alliance
  Endeavor Health Edward Hospital
  Endeavor Health Linden Oaks Hospital

Urbana
Alliance
  Carle Foundation Hospital

INDIANA
Greenfield
Alliance
  Hancock Regional Hospital

Rushville
Alliance
  Rush Memorial Hospital

KANSAS
Manhattan
Alliance
  Manhattan Surgical

KENTUCKY
Albany
Alliance
  The Medical Center at Albany

Bowling Green
Alliance
  Commonwealth Regional Specialty Hospital
  The Medical Center at Bowling Green

Danville
Alliance
  Ephraim McDowell Regional Medical Center

Edgewood
Alliance
  St. Elizabeth Edgewood

Florence
Alliance
  St. Elizabeth Florence

Fort Thomas
Alliance
  St. Elizabeth Fort Thomas

Franklin
Alliance
  Medical Center at Franklin

Glasgow
Alliance
  T. J. Samson Community Hospital

Henderson
Alliance
  Deaconess Henderson Hospital

Horse Cave
Alliance
  The Medical Center at Caverna

Morganfield
Alliance
  Deaconess Union County Hospital

Murray
Alliance
  Murray–Calloway County Hospital

Scottsville
Alliance
  Medical Center at Scottsville

Stanford
Alliance
  Ephraim McDowell Fort Logan Hospital

Williamstown
Alliance
  St. Elizabeth Grant

LOUISIANA
Abbeville
Alliance
  Abbeville General Hospital

Baton Rouge
Alliance
  Baton Rouge General Medical Center
  Baton Rouge Rehabilitation Hospital
  The NeuroMedical Center Rehabilitation Hospital
  The Spine Hospital of Louisiana at The NeuroMedical Center
  Woman's Hospital

Breaux Bridge
Alliance
  Ochsner St. Martin Hospital

Bunkie
Alliance
  Bunkie General Hospital

Church Point
Alliance
  Acadia–St. Landry Hospital

Columbia
Alliance
  Citizens Medical Center

Crowley
Alliance
  Ochsner Acadia General Hospital

Delhi
Alliance
  Delhi Hospital

Hammond
Alliance
  North Oaks Medical Center
  North Oaks Rehabilitation Hospital

Houma
Alliance
  Terrebonne General Health System

Jennings
Alliance
  Ochsner American Legion Hospital

Alliances

Kaplan
Alliance
  Ochsner Abrom Kaplan Memorial Hospital
Kinder
Alliance
  Allen Parish Community Healthcare
Lafayette
Alliance
  Louisiana Extended Care Hospital of Lafayette
  Ochsner Lafayette General Medical Center
  Ochsner University Hospital & Clinics
Marrero
Alliance
  Bridgepoint Continuing Care Hospital
Monroe
Alliance
  Specialty Hospital
Natchitoches
Alliance
  Louisiana Extended Care Hospital of Natchitoches
New Iberia
Alliance
  Iberia Medical Center
New Orleans
Alliance
  Ochsner Extended Care Hospital
Rayville
Alliance
  Richardson Medical Center
Winnsboro
Alliance
  Franklin Medical Center

MARYLAND
Annapolis
Alliance
  Luminis Health Anne Arundel Medical Center
Baltimore
Alliance
  GBMC Healthcare
  Levindale Hebrew Geriatric Center and Hospital
  Mercy Medical Center
  Sinai Hospital of Baltimore
Berlin
Alliance
  Atlantic General Hospital
Cumberland
Alliance
  UPMC Western Maryland
Elkton
Alliance
  ChristianaCare, Union Hospital
Frederick
Alliance
  Frederick Health
Lanham
Alliance
  Luminis Health Doctors Community Medical Center
Randallstown
Alliance
  Northwest Hospital
Salisbury
Alliance
  TidalHealth Peninsula Regional
Westminster
Alliance
  Carroll Hospital

MICHIGAN
Ypsilanti
Alliance
  Forest Health Medical Center

MINNESOTA
Blue Earth
Alliance
  United Hospital District

MISSISSIPPI
Bay Springs
Alliance
  Jasper General Hospital
Carthage
Alliance
  Baptist Medical Center – Leake
Charleston
Alliance
  Tallahatchie General Hospital
De Kalb
Alliance
  Ochsner Stennis Hospital
Jackson
Alliance
  Mississippi Baptist Medical Center
Kosciusko
Alliance
  Baptist Medical Center – Attala
Laurel
Alliance
  South Central Regional Medical Center
Louisville
Alliance
  Winston Medical Center
Magee
Alliance
  Magee General Hospital
Mendenhall
Alliance
  Simpson General Hospital
Meridian
Alliance
  Ochsner Rush Medical Center
Morton
Alliance
  Ochsner Scott Regional
Quitman
Alliance
  Ochsner Watkins Hospital
Ruleville
Alliance
  North Sunflower Medical Center
Union
Alliance
  Ochsner Laird Hospital
Water Valley
Alliance
  Yalobusha General Hospital
Yazoo City
Alliance
  Baptist Medical Center – Yazoo

NEBRASKA
Kearney
Alliance
  Kearney Regional Medical Center

NORTH CAROLINA
Asheville
Alliance
  Asheville Specialty Hospital
  CarePartners Rehabilitation Hospital
  Mission Hospital
Boone
Alliance
  Watauga Medical Center
Brevard
Alliance
  Transylvania Regional Hospital
Bryson City
Alliance
  Swain Community Hospital, A Duke LifePoint Hospital
Cherokee
Alliance
  Cherokee Indian Hospital
Clyde
Alliance
  Haywood Regional Medical Center
Columbus
Alliance
  St. Luke's Hospital
Dunn
Alliance
  Harnett Health System
Elizabeth City
Alliance
  Sentara Albemarle Medical Center
Elizabethtown
Alliance
  Cape Fear Valley Bladen County Hospital
Fayetteville
Alliance
  Cape Fear Valley Medical Center
  Highsmith–Rainey Specialty Hospital
Franklin
Alliance
  Angel Medical Center
Gastonia
Alliance
  CaroMont Regional Medical Center
Goldsboro
Alliance
  UNC Health Wayne
Hendersonville
Alliance
  AdventHealth Hendersonville
  UNC Health Pardee
Hickory
Alliance
  Catawba Valley Medical Center
Highlands
Alliance
  Highlands–Cashiers Hospital
Marion
Alliance
  Mission Hospital McDowell
Morehead City
Alliance
  Carteret Health Care
Newland
Alliance
  Charles A. Cannon Jr. Memorial Hospital
Oxford
Alliance
  Granville Health System
Pinehurst
Alliance
  FirstHealth Moore Regional Hospital
Raeford
Alliance
  Hoke Hospital
Roanoke Rapids
Alliance
  ECU Health North Hospital
Spruce Pine
Alliance
  Blue Ridge Regional Hospital
Statesville
Alliance
  Iredell Health System
Troy
Alliance
  FirstHealth Montgomery Memorial Hospital

NORTH DAKOTA
Cavalier
Alliance
  Pembina County Memorial Hospital and Wedgewood Manor

OHIO
Amherst
Alliance
  Specialty Hospital of Lorain
Bowling Green
Alliance
  Wood County Hospital

Health Care Systems, Networks and Alliances

Alliances

Cleveland
Alliance
  Grace Hospital

Cuyahoga Falls
Alliance
  Western Reserve Hospital

Salem
Alliance
  Salem Regional Medical Center

Steubenville
Alliance
  Life Line Hospital

PENNSYLVANIA

Corry
Alliance
  LECOM Health Corry Memorial Hospital

Erie
Alliance
  LECOM Health Millcreek Community Hospital

Kittanning
Alliance
  ACMH Hospital

Meadville
Alliance
  Meadville Medical Center

State College
Alliance
  Mount Nittany Medical Center

Titusville
Alliance
  Titusville Area Hospital

Tyrone
Alliance
  Penn Highlands Tyrone

Windber
Alliance
  Chan Soon–Shiong Medical Center at Windber

SOUTH CAROLINA

Conway
Alliance
  Conway Medical Center

West Columbia
Alliance
  Lexington Medical Center

TENNESSEE

Crossville
Alliance
  Cumberland Medical Center

Elizabethton
Alliance
  Sycamore Shoals Hospital

Erwin
Alliance
  Unicoi County Hospital

Johnson City
Alliance
  Franklin Woods Community Hospital
  Johnson City Medical Center
  Quillen Rehabilitation Hospital, a joint venture of Ballad Health and Encompass Health

Kingsport
Alliance
  Indian Path Community Hospital

Knoxville
Alliance
  University of Tennessee Medical Center

Maryville
Alliance
  Blount Memorial Hospital

Mountain City
Alliance
  Johnson County Community Hospital

TEXAS

The Woodlands
Alliance
  Nexus Speciality Hospital – The Woodlands Campus

VIRGINIA

Abingdon
Alliance
  Johnston Memorial Hospital

Chesapeake
Alliance
  Chesapeake Regional Medical Center

Christiansburg
Alliance
  Carilion New River Valley Medical Center

Clintwood
Alliance
  Dickenson Community Hospital

Front Royal
Alliance
  Valley Health – Warren Memorial Hospital

Gloucester
Alliance
  Riverside Walter Reed Hospital

Grundy
Alliance
  Buchanan General Hospital

Lebanon
Alliance
  Russell County Medical Center

Lexington
Alliance
  Carilion Rockbridge Community Hospital

Luray
Alliance
  Valley Health – Page Memorial Hospital

Marion
Alliance
  Smyth County Community Hospital

Newport News
Alliance
  Riverside Regional Medical Center

Norton
Alliance
  Norton Community Hospital

Onancock
Alliance
  Riverside Shore Memorial Hospital

Pearisburg
Alliance
  Carilion Giles Community Hospital

Roanoke
Alliance
  Carilion Roanoke Memorial Hospital

Rocky Mount
Alliance
  Carilion Franklin Memorial Hospital

South Hill
Alliance
  VCU Health Community Memorial Hospital

Tappahannock
Alliance
  VCU Health Tappahannock Hospital

Tazewell
Alliance
  Carilion Tazewell Community Hospital

Williamsburg
Alliance
  Riverside Doctors' Hospital Williamsburg

Winchester
Alliance
  Valley Health – Winchester Medical Center

Woodstock
Alliance
  Valley Health – Shenandoah Memorial Hospital

WEST VIRGINIA

Berkeley Springs
Alliance
  Valley Health – War Memorial Hospital

Elkins
Alliance
  Davis Medical Center

Huntington
Alliance
  Cabell Huntington Hospital
  St. Mary's Medical Center

Kingwood
Alliance
  Mon Health Preston Memorial Hospital

Morgantown
Alliance
  Mon Health Medical Center

Point Pleasant
Alliance
  Rivers Health

Romney
Alliance
  Valley Health – Hampshire Memorial Hospital

South Charleston
Alliance
  Thomas Memorial Hospital

CATHOLIC CEO HEALTHCARE CONNECTION

50 South Main Street, Suite 200, Naperville, IL Zip 60540–5484; tel. 630/352–2220; Roger N Butler, Executive Director

ILLINOIS

Peoria
Alliance
  OSF Healthcare

Springfield
Alliance
  HSHS Hospital Sisters Health System

LOUISIANA

Baton Rouge
Alliance
  Franciscan Missionaries of Our Lady Health System, Inc.

MISSOURI

Chesterfield
Alliance
  Mercy

Saint Louis
Alliance
  Ascension Healthcare
  SSM Health

OHIO

Cincinnati
Alliance
  Bon Secours Mercy Health

SOUTH DAKOTA

Sioux Falls
Alliance
  Avera Health

TEXAS

Irving
Alliance
  CHRISTUS Health

WASHINGTON

Renton
Alliance
  Providence

Vancouver
Alliance
  PeaceHealth

WISCONSIN

Manitowoc
Alliance
  Franciscan Sisters of Christian Charity Sponsored Ministries, Inc.

Alliances

HEALTH ENTERPRISES COOPERATIVE
5825 Dry Creek Lane NE, Cedar Rapids, IA Zip 52402-1225; tel. 319/368-3619; Judy L. Sadler, President and Chief Executive Officer

IOWA
Ames
Alliance
   Mary Greeley Medical Center

Chariton
Alliance
   Lucas County Health Center

Charles City
Alliance
   Floyd County Medical Center

Cherokee
Alliance
   Cherokee Regional Medical Center

Denison
Alliance
   Crawford County Memorial Hospital

Des Moines
Alliance
   Broadlawns Medical Center

Fairfield
Alliance
   Jefferson County Health Center

Grinnell
Alliance
   UnityPoint Health – Grinnell Regional Medical Center

Guthrie Center
Alliance
   Guthrie County Hospital

Humboldt
Alliance
   Humboldt County Memorial Hospital

Ida Grove
Alliance
   Horn Memorial Hospital

Independence
Alliance
   Buchanan County Health Center

Iowa City
Alliance
   University of Iowa Health Care Medical Center Downtown

Manchester
Alliance
   Regional Medical Center

Maquoketa
Alliance
   Jackson County Regional Health Center

Marshalltown
Alliance
   UnityPoint Health – Marshalltown

Mount Pleasant
Alliance
   Henry County Health Center

Newton
Alliance
   MercyOne Newton Medical Center

Oskaloosa
Alliance
   Mahaska Health

Pella
Alliance
   Pella Regional Health Center

Pocahontas
Alliance
   Pocahontas Community Hospital

Sac City
Alliance
   Loring Hospital

Waukon
Alliance
   Veterans Memorial Hospital

Waverly
Alliance
   Waverly Health Center

West Burlington
Alliance
   Southeast Iowa Regional Medical Center, West Burlington Campus

MISSOURI
Bethany
Alliance
   Harrison County Community Hospital

Fairfax
Alliance
   Community Hospital–Fairfax

HOSPITAL ALLIANCE OF NEW JERSEY
150 West State Street, Trenton, NJ Zip 8608; tel. 609/989-8200; Suzanne Ianni, Executive Director

HOSPITAL NETWORK VENTURES, LLC
6212 American Avenue, Portage, MI Zip 49002; tel. 269/329-3200; Gregory L Hedegore, President and Chief Executive Officer

MICHIGAN
Allegan
Alliance
   Ascension Borgess Allegan Hospital

Kalamazoo
Alliance
   Bronson Healthcare Group
   Bronson Methodist Hospital

Marshall
Alliance
   Oaklawn Hospital

Sturgis
Alliance
   Sturgis Hospital

HOSPITAL SHARED SERVICES ASSOCIATION
P O Box 19741, Seattle, WA Zip 98109-6741; tel. 206/399-0865; Joe McNamee, Executive Director

OREGON
Salem
Alliance
   Oregon State Hospital

WASHINGTON
Bellevue
Alliance
   Overlake Medical Center and Clinics

Chelan
Alliance
   Lake Chelan Health

Clarkston
Alliance
   Tri-State Memorial Hospital

Davenport
Alliance
   Lincoln Hospital

Edmonds
Alliance
   Providence Swedish Edmonds

Ephrata
Alliance
   Columbia Basin Hospital

Grand Coulee
Alliance
   Coulee Medical Center

Kirkland
Alliance
   EvergreenHealth

Medical Lake
Alliance
   Eastern State Hospital

Moses Lake
Alliance
   Samaritan Healthcare

Mount Vernon
Alliance
   Skagit Valley Hospital

Newport
Alliance
   Newport Hospital and Health Services

Odessa
Alliance
   Odessa Memorial Healthcare Center

Othello
Alliance
   Othello Community Hospital

Prosser
Alliance
   Prosser Memorial Health

Pullman
Alliance
   Pullman Regional Hospital

Quincy
Alliance
   Quincy Valley Medical Center

Republic
Alliance
   Ferry County Memorial Hospital

Ritzville
Alliance
   East Adams Rural Healthcare

Tacoma
Alliance
   Western State Hospital

Tonasket
Alliance
   North Valley Hospital

KENTUCKY HEALTH COLLABORATIVE
651 Perimeter Drive, Suite 650, Lexington, KY Zip 40517-4134; tel. 859/286-3107; David Zimba, Managing Director

KENTUCKY
Bowling Green
Alliance
   The Medical Center at Bowling Green

Danville
Alliance
   Ephraim McDowell Health

Edgewood
Alliance
   St. Elizabeth Healthcare

Lexington
Alliance
   Appalachian Regional Healthcare, Inc.
   University of Kentucky Albert B. Chandler Hospital

Louisville
Alliance
   Baptist Health
   Norton Healthcare

Morehead
Alliance
   St. Claire Regional Medical Center

Owensboro
Alliance
   Owensboro Health

TENNESSEE
Brentwood
Alliance
   Lifepoint Health

Alliances

MEDI–SOTA, INC.
1280 Locust Street Suite 16, Dawson, MN Zip 56232–2375; tel. 320/769–2269; Deb Ranallo, Executive Director

MINNESOTA

Appleton
Alliance
Appleton Area Health

Arlington
Alliance
Ridgeview Sibley Medical Center

Benson
Alliance
CentraCare – Benson

Blue Earth
Alliance
United Hospital District

Canby
Alliance
Sanford Canby Medical Center

Dawson
Alliance
Johnson Memorial Health Services

Elbow Lake
Alliance
Elbow Lake Medical Center

Glencoe
Alliance
Glencoe Regional Health

Glenwood
Alliance
Glacial Ridge Health System

Graceville
Alliance
Essentia Health–Graceville

Granite Falls
Alliance
Avera Granite Falls

Hendricks
Alliance
Hendricks Community Hospital Association

Litchfield
Alliance
Meeker Memorial Hospital and Clinics

Madelia
Alliance
Madelia Health

Madison
Alliance
Madison Healthcare Services

Mahnomen
Alliance
Mahnomen Health

Marshall
Alliance
Avera Marshall Regional Medical Center

Montevideo
Alliance
CCM Health

Olivia
Alliance
HealthPartners Olivia Hospital & Clinic

Ortonville
Alliance
Ortonville Area Health Services

Paynesville
Alliance
CentraCare – Paynesville

Perham
Alliance
Perham Health

Pipestone
Alliance
Pipestone County Medical Center

Redwood Falls
Alliance
CentraCare – Redwood

Saint Peter
Alliance
River's Edge Hospital and Clinic

Slayton
Alliance
Murray County Medical Center

Sleepy Eye
Alliance
Sleepy Eye Medical Center

Staples
Alliance
Lakewood Health System

Tracy
Alliance
Sanford Tracy Medical Center

Tyler
Alliance
Avera Tyler

Wadena
Alliance
Astera Health

Willmar
Alliance
CentraCare – Rice Memorial Hospital

Windom
Alliance
Windom Area Health

NORTHWEST KANSAS HEALTH ALLIANCE
2220 Canterbury Drive, Hays, KS Zip 67601–2370; tel. 785/623–2300; Edward Herrman, President and Chief Executive Officer

KANSAS

Ashland
Alliance
Ashland Health Center

Atwood
Alliance
Rawlins County Health Center

Beloit
Alliance
Mitchell County Hospital Health Systems

Colby
Alliance
Citizens Medical Center

Dighton
Alliance
Lane County Hospital

Dodge City
Alliance
St. Catherine Hospital – Dodge City

Ellsworth
Alliance
Ellsworth County Medical Center

Garden City
Alliance
St. Catherine Hospital

Goodland
Alliance
Goodland Regional Medical Center

Great Bend
Alliance
University of Kansas Health System Great Bend Campus

Greensburg
Alliance
Kiowa County Memorial Hospital

Hill City
Alliance
Graham County Hospital

Hoisington
Alliance
Clara Barton Medical Center

Hoxie
Alliance
Sheridan County Health Complex

Hutchinson
Alliance
Hutchinson Regional Medical Center

Jetmore
Alliance
Hodgeman County Health Center

Kinsley
Alliance
Edwards County Medical Center

La Crosse
Alliance
Rush County Memorial Hospital

Larned
Alliance
Pawnee Valley Community Hospital

Lawrence
Alliance
LMH Health

Leoti
Alliance
Wichita County Health Center

Lincoln
Alliance
Lincoln County Hospital

Lyons
Alliance
Hospital District No 1 of Rice County

Minneola
Alliance
Minneola District Hospital

Ness City
Alliance
Ness County Hospital District No 2

Norton
Alliance
Norton County Hospital

Oakley
Alliance
Logan County Hospital

Oberlin
Alliance
Decatur Health Systems

Osborne
Alliance
Osborne County Memorial Hospital

Ottawa
Alliance
AdventHealth Ottawa

Phillipsburg
Alliance
Phillips County Health Systems

Plainville
Alliance
Rooks County Health Center

Quinter
Alliance
Gove County Medical Center

Ransom
Alliance
Grisell Memorial Hospital District One

Russell
Alliance
Russell Regional Hospital

Saint Francis
Alliance
Cheyenne County Hospital

Salina
Alliance
Salina Regional Health Center

Satanta
Alliance
Satanta District Hospital and Long Term Care

Scott City
Alliance
Scott County Hospital

Smith Center
Alliance
Smith County Memorial Hospital

Alliances

Stafford
Alliance
 Stafford County Hospital

Tribune
Alliance
 Greeley County Health Services

Wakeeney
Alliance
 Trego County–Lemke Memorial Hospital

OHSU PARTNERS
3303 SW Bond Avenue, Suite 6100, Mail Code: CH6P, Portland, OR Zip 97239–4501; tel. 503/494–4036; Peter F Rapp, Chief Executive Officer

OREGON

Hillsboro
Alliance
 OHSU Health Hillsboro Medical Center

Salem
Alliance
 Salem Health

PANDION OPTIMIZATION ALLIANCE
3445 Winton Place, Suite 222, Rochester, NY Zip 14623–2950; tel. 888/732–4282; Travis Heider, President and Chief Executive Officer

GEORGIA

Fort Oglethorpe
Alliance
 CHI Memorial Hospital – Georgia

NEW JERSEY

Berkeley Heights
Alliance
 Runnells Center for Rehabilitation and Healthcare

Newark
Alliance
 Silver Lake Hospital LTACH

NEW YORK

Batavia
Alliance
 United Memorial Medical Center

Bath
Alliance
 Bath Veterans Affairs Medical Center
 Ira Davenport Memorial Hospital

Buffalo
Alliance
 Erie County Medical Center
 Roswell Park Comprehensive Cancer Center
 Sisters of Charity Hospital of Buffalo

Canandaigua
Alliance
 F. F. Thompson Hospital

Clifton Springs
Alliance
 Clifton Springs Hospital and Clinic

Corning
Alliance
 Guthrie Corning Hospital

Dansville
Alliance
 Nicholas H. Noyes Memorial Hospital

Dunkirk
Alliance
 Brooks–TLC Hospital System, Inc.

Elmira
Alliance
 Arnot Ogden Medical Center

Geneva
Alliance
 Geneva General Hospital

Hornell
Alliance
 St. James Hospital

Ithaca
Alliance
 Cayuga Medical Center at Ithaca

Jamestown
Alliance
 UPMC Chautauqua

Kenmore
Alliance
 Kenmore Mercy Hospital

Lewiston
Alliance
 Mount St. Mary's Hospital and Health Center

Montour Falls
Alliance
 Schuyler Hospital

Newark
Alliance
 Newark–Wayne Community Hospital

Niagara Falls
Alliance
 Niagara Falls Memorial Medical Center

Olean
Alliance
 Olean General Hospital

Penn Yan
Alliance
 Soldiers and Sailors Memorial Hospital

Rochester
Alliance
 Highland Hospital
 Rochester General Hospital
 Strong Memorial Hospital of the University of Rochester
 Unity Hospital

Springville
Alliance
 Bertrand Chaffee Hospital

Wellsville
Alliance
 Jones Memorial Hospital

PENNANT HEALTH ALLIANCE
2122 Health Drive SW Suite 100, Wyoming, MI Zip 49519–9698; tel. 616/252–6800; Michael D. Faas, Chief Executive Officer

MICHIGAN

Ann Arbor
Alliance
 University of Michigan Medical Center

Cadillac
Alliance
 Munson Healthcare Cadillac Hospital

Grand Rapids
Alliance
 Mary Free Bed Rehabilitation Hospital
 Trinity Health Grand Rapids Hospital

Grayling
Alliance
 Munson Healthcare Grayling Hospital

Wyoming
Alliance
 University of Michigan Health – West

PREMIER, INC.
13034 Ballantyne Corporate Place, Charlotte, NC Zip 28277–1498; tel. 704/816–5353; Susan DeVore, President and Chief Executive Officer

ALABAMA

Dothan
Alliance
 Southeast Alabama Medical Center

Opelika
Alliance
 East Alabama Medical Center

ARIZONA

Phoenix
Alliance
 Banner Health

Scottsdale
Alliance
 HonorHealth

ARKANSAS

Batesville
Alliance
 White River Health

Pine Bluff
Alliance
 Jefferson Regional

CALIFORNIA

Fresno
Alliance
 Community Medical Centers

Loma Linda
Alliance
 Loma Linda University Medical Center

Mountain View
Alliance
 El Camino Health

Rancho Mirage
Alliance
 Eisenhower Health

Roseville
Alliance
 Adventist Health

CONNECTICUT

Hartford
Alliance
 Saint Francis Hospital

Waterbury
Alliance
 Saint Mary's Hospital

DELAWARE

Dover
Alliance
 Bayhealth

Lewes
Alliance
 Beebe Healthcare

FLORIDA

Altamonte Springs
Alliance
 AdventHealth

Coral Gables
Alliance
 Baptist Health South Florida

Dunedin
Alliance
 BayCare Alliant Hospital

Jacksonville
Alliance
 Baptist Health
 Nemours Children Health

Miami Beach
Alliance
 Mount Sinai Medical Center

Tampa
Alliance
 H. Lee Moffitt Cancer Center and Research Institute

Vero Beach
Alliance
 Cleveland Clinic Indian River Hospital

Winter Haven
Alliance
 Winter Haven Hospital

GEORGIA

Carrollton
Alliance
 Tanner Medical Center–Carrollton

Lagrange
Alliance
 Wellstar West Georgia Medical Center

Alliances

Savannah
Alliance
  Memorial Health University Medical Center
  St. Joseph's Hospital

HAWAII
Honolulu
Alliance
  Kuakini Medical Center

ILLINOIS
Chicago
Alliance
  Mount Sinai Hospital

Harvey
Alliance
  UChicago Medicine Ingalls Memorial

Naperville
Alliance
  Endeavor Health Edward Hospital

Peoria
Alliance
  Carle Health Methodist Hospital

Urbana
Alliance
  Carle Foundation Hospital

INDIANA
Gary
Alliance
  Methodist Hospitals

KENTUCKY
Ashland
Alliance
  UK King's Daughters Medical Center

Bowling Green
Alliance
  Commonwealth Regional Specialty Hospital

Danville
Alliance
  Ephraim McDowell Regional Medical Center

Edgewood
Alliance
  St. Elizabeth Edgewood

Glasgow
Alliance
  T. J. Samson Community Hospital

Henderson
Alliance
  Deaconess Henderson Hospital

Louisville
Alliance
  Alliant Management Services
  Baptist Health
  Norton Healthcare

Murray
Alliance
  Murray–Calloway County Hospital

LOUISIANA
Baton Rouge
Alliance
  Woman's Hospital

Hammond
Alliance
  North Oaks Health System

Houma
Alliance
  Terrebonne General Health System

Lafayette
Alliance
  Ochsner Lafayette General Medical Center

Marrero
Alliance
  West Jefferson Medical Center

MAINE
Lewiston
Alliance
  Central Maine Medical Center

MARYLAND
Annapolis
Alliance
  Luminis Health Anne Arundel Medical Center

Baltimore
Alliance
  GBMC Healthcare
  Johns Hopkins Health System
  Mercy Medical Center
  Sinai Hospital of Baltimore

Cumberland
Alliance
  UPMC Western Maryland

Elkton
Alliance
  ChristianaCare, Union Hospital

Frederick
Alliance
  Frederick Health

Gaithersburg
Alliance
  Adventist HealthCare

Hagerstown
Alliance
  Meritus Health

Lanham
Alliance
  Luminis Health Doctors Community Medical Center

Randallstown
Alliance
  Northwest Hospital

Salisbury
Alliance
  TidalHealth Peninsula Regional

Westminster
Alliance
  Carroll Hospital

MASSACHUSETTS
Boston
Alliance
  Tufts Medical Center

Fall River
Alliance
  Southcoast Hospitals Group

Springfield
Alliance
  Baystate Health, Inc.

MICHIGAN
Detroit
Alliance
  Henry Ford Health

Grand Blanc
Alliance
  McLaren Health Care Corporation

Jackson
Alliance
  Henry Ford Jackson Hospital

MINNESOTA
Minneapolis
Alliance
  Fairview Health Services

MISSISSIPPI
Laurel
Alliance
  South Central Regional Medical Center

MISSOURI
Saint Joseph
Alliance
  Mosaic Life Care at St. Joseph – Medical Center

Saint Louis
Alliance
  SSM Health

MONTANA
Billings
Alliance
  Billings Clinic

NEW MEXICO
Albuquerque
Alliance
  Presbyterian Healthcare Services

NEW YORK
Rochester
Alliance
  Rochester Regional Health

NORTH CAROLINA
Asheboro
Alliance
  Randolph Health

Boone
Alliance
  Watauga Medical Center

Fayetteville
Alliance
  Cape Fear Valley Health System

Gastonia
Alliance
  CaroMont Regional Medical Center

Goldsboro
Alliance
  UNC Health Wayne

Greensboro
Alliance
  Cone Health Moses Cone Hospital

Hendersonville
Alliance
  UNC Health Pardee

Hickory
Alliance
  Catawba Valley Medical Center

Kinston
Alliance
  UNC Health Lenoir

Lumberton
Alliance
  UNC Health Southeastern

Morehead City
Alliance
  Carteret Health Care

Pinehurst
Alliance
  FirstHealth of the Carolinas

Roanoke Rapids
Alliance
  ECU Health North Hospital

Statesville
Alliance
  Iredell Health System

OHIO
Akron
Alliance
  Summa Health System – Akron Campus

Cincinnati
Alliance
  Bon Secours Mercy Health

Cleveland
Alliance
  University Hospitals

Elyria
Alliance
  University Hospitals Elyria Medical Center

Kettering
Alliance
  Kettering Health Main Campus

Middleburg Heights
Alliance
  Southwest General Health Center

Parma
Alliance
  University Hospitals Parma Medical Center

Sandusky
Alliance
  Firelands Regional Health System

Alliances

OKLAHOMA
Tulsa
Alliance
Saint Francis Hospital

OREGON
Salem
Alliance
Salem Hospital

PENNSYLVANIA
Beaver
Alliance
Heritage Valley Health System

Bethlehem
Alliance
St. Luke's University Health Network

Danville
Alliance
Geisinger

King of Prussia
Alliance
Universal Health Services, Inc.

Washington
Alliance
UPMC Washington

SOUTH CAROLINA
Anderson
Alliance
AnMed Medical Center

Conway
Alliance
Conway Medical Center

Greenwood
Alliance
Self Regional Healthcare

West Columbia
Alliance
Lexington Medical Center

SOUTH DAKOTA
Rapid City
Alliance
Monument Health Rapid City Hospital

Sioux Falls
Alliance
Avera Health

TENNESSEE
Crossville
Alliance
Cumberland Medical Center

Knoxville
Alliance
University of Tennessee Medical Center

Maryville
Alliance
Blount Memorial Hospital

TEXAS
Arlington
Alliance
Texas Health Resources

Bellaire
Alliance
Harris Health System

Dallas
Alliance
Methodist Health System
University of Texas Southwestern Medical Center

Galveston
Alliance
University of Texas Medical Branch

Houston
Alliance
University of Texas M.D. Anderson Cancer Center

Lubbock
Alliance
University Medical Center

VIRGINIA
Abingdon
Alliance
Johnston Memorial Hospital

Chesapeake
Alliance
Chesapeake Regional Medical Center

Fairfax
Alliance
Inova Health System

Marion
Alliance
Smyth County Community Hospital

Newport News
Alliance
Riverside Health System

Roanoke
Alliance
Carilion Clinic

South Hill
Alliance
VCU Health Community Memorial Hospital

Winchester
Alliance
Valley Health System

WASHINGTON
Vancouver
Alliance
PeaceHealth

WEST VIRGINIA
Elkins
Alliance
Davis Medical Center

Huntington
Alliance
Cabell Huntington Hospital

Morgantown
Alliance
Mon Health Medical Center

Parkersburg
Alliance
Camden Clark Medical Center

Point Pleasant
Alliance
Rivers Health

South Charleston
Alliance
Thomas Memorial Hospital

Weirton
Alliance
Weirton Medical Center

THE NEW JERSEY COUNCIL OF TEACHING HOSPITALS
154 West State Street, Trenton, NJ Zip 8608; tel. 609/656-9600; Deborah S. Briggs, President

NEW JERSEY
Camden
Alliance
Cooper University Health Care

Hackensack
Alliance
Hackensack Meridian Health Hackensack University Medical Center

Marlton
Alliance
Weisman Children's Rehabilitation Hospital

Montclair
Alliance
Hackensack Meridian Mountainside Medical Center

Morristown
Alliance
Atlantic Health System
Morristown Medical Center

New Brunswick
Alliance
Children's Specialized Hospital

North Bergen
Alliance
Hackensack Meridian Health Palisades Medical Center

Paterson
Alliance
St. Joseph's University Medical Center

Summit
Alliance
Overlook Medical Center

UNITED IROQUOIS SHARED SERVICES, INC.
15 Executive Park Drive, Clifton Park, NY Zip 12065-5631; tel. 518/383-5060; Kevin M. Kerwin, Acting Chief Executive Officer

NEW YORK
Albany
Alliance
St. Peter's Hospital

Alexandria Bay
Alliance
River Hospital

Amsterdam
Alliance
St. Mary's Healthcare

Auburn
Alliance
Auburn Community Hospital

Binghamton
Alliance
Guthrie Lourdes Hospital
United Health Services Hospitals-Binghamton

Buffalo
Alliance
Roswell Park Comprehensive Cancer Center

Carthage
Alliance
Carthage Area Hospital

Cobleskill
Alliance
Cobleskill Regional Hospital

Cooperstown
Alliance
Bassett Medical Center

Cortland
Alliance
Guthrie Cortland Regional Medical Center

Cuba
Alliance
Cuba Memorial Hospital

Delhi
Alliance
O'Connor Hospital

Elizabethtown
Alliance
The University of Vermont Health Network Elizabethtown Community Hospital

Glens Falls
Alliance
Glens Falls Hospital

Glenville
Alliance
Conifer Park

Gloversville
Alliance
Nathan Littauer Hospital and Nursing Home

Hamilton
Alliance
Community Memorial Hospital

Hudson
Alliance
Columbia Memorial Hospital

Alliances

Ithaca
Alliance
  Cayuga Medical Center at Ithaca

Little Falls
Alliance
  Little Falls Hospital

Lowville
Alliance
  Lewis County General Hospital

Malone
Alliance
  The University of Vermont Health Network – Alice Hyde Medical Center

Margaretville
Alliance
  Margaretville Hospital

Massena
Alliance
  Massena Hospital, Inc.

Norwich
Alliance
  UHS Chenango Memorial Hospital

Ogdensburg
Alliance
  Claxton–Hepburn Medical Center

Olean
Alliance
  Olean General Hospital

Oneida
Alliance
  Oneida Healthcare

Oneonta
Alliance
  Aurelia Osborn Fox Memorial Hospital

Oswego
Alliance
  Oswego Hospital

Plattsburgh
Alliance
  The University of Vermont Health Network–Champlain Valley Physicians Hospital

Potsdam
Alliance
  Canton–Potsdam Hospital

Rome
Alliance
  Rome Health

Saranac Lake
Alliance
  Adirondack Health

Saratoga Springs
Alliance
  Saratoga Hospital

Schenectady
Alliance
  Ellis Medicine
  Sunnyview Rehabilitation Hospital

Springville
Alliance
  Bertrand Chaffee Hospital

Star Lake
Alliance
  Clifton–Fine Hospital

Syracuse
Alliance
  Crouse Health
  Upstate University Hospital

Troy
Alliance
  Samaritan Hospital – Main Campus

Utica
Alliance
  Wynn Hospital

Walton
Alliance
  UHS Delaware Valley Hospital

Watertown
Alliance
  Samaritan Medical Center

VANTAGE HEALTHCARE NETWORK, INC.
18282 Technology Drive, Suite 202, Meadville, PA Zip 16335; tel. 814/337-0000; David Petrarca, Director Retail Operations

PENNSYLVANIA

Corry
Alliance
  LECOM Health Corry Memorial Hospital

DuBois
Alliance
  Penn Highlands DuBois

Erie
Alliance
  LECOM Health Millcreek Community Hospital
  Saint Vincent Hospital

Farrell
Alliance
  UPMC Horizon

Kane
Alliance
  UPMC Kane

Kittanning
Alliance
  ACMH Hospital

Meadville
Alliance
  Meadville Medical Center

Saint Marys
Alliance
  Penn Highlands Elk

Seneca
Alliance
  UPMC Northwest

Titusville
Alliance
  Titusville Area Hospital

Warren
Alliance
  Warren General Hospital

VIZIENT, INC.
290 East John Carpenter Freeway, Irving, TX Zip 75062-2730; tel. 972/830-0000; Curtis W Nonomaque, President and Chief Executive Officer

ALABAMA

Alexander City
Alliance
  Russell Medical

Anniston
Alliance
  RMC Anniston

Athens
Alliance
  Athens–Limestone Hospital

Atmore
Alliance
  Atmore Community Hospital

Bay Minette
Alliance
  North Baldwin Infirmary

Bessemer
Alliance
  Medical West

Birmingham
Alliance
  University of Alabama Hospital

Boaz
Alliance
  Marshall Medical Center South

Brewton
Alliance
  D. W. McMillan Memorial Hospital

Decatur
Alliance
  Decatur Morgan Hospital

Fairhope
Alliance
  Thomas Hospital

Fayette
Alliance
  Fayette Medical Center

Guntersville
Alliance
  Marshall Health System
  Marshall Medical Center North

Huntsville
Alliance
  Huntsville Hospital

Mobile
Alliance
  Mobile Infirmary Medical Center
  USA Health Children's & Women's Hospital
  USA Health University Hospital

Montgomery
Alliance
  Baptist Medical Center East
  Baptist Medical Center South

Opp
Alliance
  Mizell Memorial Hospital

Ozark
Alliance
  Dale Medical Center

Prattville
Alliance
  Prattville Baptist Hospital

Red Bay
Alliance
  Red Bay Hospital

Scottsboro
Alliance
  Highlands Medical Center

Sheffield
Alliance
  Helen Keller Hospital

Tuscaloosa
Alliance
  DCH Health System
  DCH Regional Medical Center

Union Springs
Alliance
  Bullock County Hospital

ALASKA

Anchorage
Alliance
  Providence Alaska Medical Center
  Providence St. Elias Specialty Hospital

Cordova
Alliance
  Cordova Community Medical Center

Kodiak
Alliance
  Providence Kodiak Island Medical Center

Seward
Alliance
  Providence Seward Medical Center

Valdez
Alliance
  Providence Valdez Medical Center

Wrangell
Alliance
  Wrangell Medical Center

AMERICAN SAMOA

Pago Pago
Alliance
  Lyndon B. Johnson Tropical Medical Center

Alliances

ARIZONA
Benson
Alliance
  Benson Hospital

Bisbee
Alliance
  Copper Queen Community Hospital

Flagstaff
Alliance
  Flagstaff Medical Center

Kingman
Alliance
  Kingman Regional Medical Center

Phoenix
Alliance
  Mayo Clinic Hospital in Arizona
  Valleywise Health

Safford
Alliance
  Mt. Graham Regional Medical Center

Tucson
Alliance
  Banner – University Medical Center South
  Banner – University Medical Center Tucson
  TMC Health

Willcox
Alliance
  Northern Cochise Community Hospital

ARKANSAS
Arkadelphia
Alliance
  Baptist Health Medical Center–Arkadelphia

Booneville
Alliance
  Mercy Hospital Booneville

Clinton
Alliance
  Ozark Health Medical Center

Conway
Alliance
  Conway Regional Health System

Fayetteville
Alliance
  Washington Regional Medical System

Heber Springs
Alliance
  Baptist Health Medical Center–Heber Springs

Hot Springs
Alliance
  CHI St. Vincent Hot Springs

Jonesboro
Alliance
  NEA Baptist Memorial Hospital
  St. Bernards Medical Center

Little Rock
Alliance
  Baptist Health Extended Care Hospital
  Baptist Health Medical Center–Little Rock
  Baptist Health
  CHI St. Vincent Infirmary

Malvern
Alliance
  Baptist Health Medical Center–Hot Spring County

Morrilton
Alliance
  CHI St. Vincent Morrilton

North Little Rock
Alliance
  Baptist Health Medical Center – North Little Rock

Paragould
Alliance
  Arkansas Methodist Medical Center

Piggott
Alliance
  Piggott Health System

Stuttgart
Alliance
  Baptist Health Medical Center–Stuttgart

Walnut Ridge
Alliance
  Lawrence Memorial Hospital

Wynne
Alliance
  CrossRidge Community Hospital

CALIFORNIA
Alameda
Alliance
  Alameda Hospital

Antioch
Alliance
  Kaiser Permanente Antioch Medical Center

Arcadia
Alliance
  USC Arcadia Hospital

Auburn
Alliance
  Sutter Auburn Faith Hospital

Bakersfield
Alliance
  Kern Medical

Berkeley
Alliance
  Alta Bates Medical Center–Herrick Campus
  Alta Bates Summit Medical Center–Alta Bates Campus

Burbank
Alliance
  Providence Saint Joseph Medical Center

Burlingame
Alliance
  Mills–Peninsula Medical Center

Castro Valley
Alliance
  Eden Medical Center

Colton
Alliance
  Arrowhead Regional Medical Center

Concord
Alliance
  John Muir Health, Concord Medical Center

Covina
Alliance
  Emanate Health Inter–Community Hospital
  Emanate Health

Crescent City
Alliance
  Sutter Coast Hospital

Davis
Alliance
  Sutter Davis Hospital

Downey
Alliance
  PIH Health Downey Hospital
  Rancho Los Amigos National Rehabilitation Center

El Centro
Alliance
  El Centro Regional Medical Center

Escondido
Alliance
  Palomar Health
  Palomar Medical Center Escondido

Fairfield
Alliance
  NorthBay Medical Center

Fremont
Alliance
  Kaiser Permanente Fremont Medical Center
  Washington Hospital Healthcare System

French Camp
Alliance
  San Joaquin General Hospital

Fresno
Alliance
  Community Medical Centers
  Saint Agnes Medical Center

Glendora
Alliance
  Emanate Health Foothill Presbyterian Hospital

Jackson
Alliance
  Sutter Amador Hospital

King City
Alliance
  George L. Mee Memorial Hospital

Lakeport
Alliance
  Sutter Lakeside Hospital

Lancaster
Alliance
  Antelope Valley Medical Center

Los Angeles
Alliance
  Cedars–Sinai Medical Center
  Los Angeles General Medical Center
  MLK Community Healthcare
  Ronald Reagan UCLA Medical Center
  Stewart & Lynda Resnick Neuropsychiatric Hospital at UCLA
  USC Norris Comprehensive Cancer Center and Hospital

Los Banos
Alliance
  Memorial Hospital Los Banos

Manteca
Alliance
  Kaiser Permanente Manteca Medical Center

Marina Del Rey
Alliance
  Cedars–Sinai Marina Del Rey Hospital

Mariposa
Alliance
  John C. Fremont Healthcare District

Martinez
Alliance
  Contra Costa Regional Medical Center

Mission Hills
Alliance
  Providence Holy Cross Medical Center

Modesto
Alliance
  Memorial Medical Center

Monterey
Alliance
  Community Hospital of the Monterey Peninsula

Moreno Valley
Alliance
  Riverside University Health System–Medical Center

Mountain View
Alliance
  El Camino Health

Novato
Alliance
  Novato Community Hospital

Oakland
Alliance
  Alta Bates Summit Medical Center – Summit Campus
  Highland Hospital
  Kaiser Permanente Oakland Medical Center

Oceanside
Alliance
  Tri–City Medical Center

Ojai
Alliance
  Ojai Valley Community Hospital

Orange
Alliance
  UCI Health

Alliances

Palo Alto
Alliance
   Lucile Packard Children's Hospital Stanford
   Stanford Health Care

Pleasanton
Alliance
   Stanford Health Care Tri-Valley

Pomona
Alliance
   Pomona Valley Hospital Medical Center

Porterville
Alliance
   Sierra View Medical Center

Portola
Alliance
   Eastern Plumas Health Care

Poway
Alliance
   Palomar Medical Center Poway

Redlands
Alliance
   Redlands Community Hospital

Redwood City
Alliance
   Kaiser Permanente Redwood City Medical Center

Roseville
Alliance
   Kaiser Permanente Roseville Medical Center
   Sutter Roseville Medical Center

Sacramento
Alliance
   Kaiser Permanente Sacramento Medical Center
   Kaiser Permanente South Sacramento Medical Center
   Shriners Children's – Northern California
   Sutter Center for Psychiatry
   Sutter Health
   Sutter Medical Center, Sacramento
   UC Davis Medical Center

Salinas
Alliance
   Natividad

San Diego
Alliance
   Scripps Health
   UC San Diego Medical Center – Hillcrest

San Francisco
Alliance
   California Pacific Medical Center–Davies Campus
   California Pacific Medical Center–Mission Bernal Campus
   California Pacific Medical Center–Van Ness Campus
   Chinese Hospital
   Kaiser Permanente San Francisco Medical Center
   UCSF Medical Center
   Zuckerberg San Francisco General Hospital and Trauma Center

San Jose
Alliance
   Kaiser Permanente San Jose Medical Center
   Santa Clara Valley Medical Center

San Mateo
Alliance
   San Mateo Medical Center

San Pedro
Alliance
   Providence Little Company of Mary Medical Center San Pedro

San Rafael
Alliance
   Kaiser Permanente San Rafael Medical Center

Santa Barbara
Alliance
   Cottage Health
   Goleta Valley Cottage Hospital
   Santa Barbara Cottage Hospital

Santa Clara
Alliance
   Kaiser Permanente Santa Clara Medical Center

Santa Cruz
Alliance
   Sutter Maternity and Surgery Center of Santa Cruz

Santa Monica
Alliance
   Providence Saint John's Health Center
   UCLA Medical Center–Santa Monica

Santa Rosa
Alliance
   Kaiser Permanente Santa Rosa Medical Center
   Sutter Santa Rosa Regional Hospital

Solvang
Alliance
   Santa Ynez Valley Cottage Hospital

South San Francisco
Alliance
   Kaiser Permanente South San Francisco Medical Center

Stockton
Alliance
   Dameron Hospital

Sylmar
Alliance
   Olive View–UCLA Medical Center

Tarzana
Alliance
   Providence Cedars–Sinai Tarzana Medical Center

Torrance
Alliance
   Harbor–UCLA Medical Center
   Providence Little Company of Mary Medical Center – Torrance
   Torrance Memorial Medical Center

Tracy
Alliance
   Sutter Tracy Community Hospital

Vacaville
Alliance
   Kaiser Permanente Vacaville Medical Center

Vallejo
Alliance
   Kaiser Permanente Vallejo Medical Center
   Sutter Solano Medical Center

Ventura
Alliance
   Community Memorial Hospital – Ventura

Walnut Creek
Alliance
   John Muir Health
   John Muir Medical Center, Walnut Creek
   Kaiser Permanente Walnut Creek Medical Center

Whittier
Alliance
   PIH Health Whittier Hospital

Yuba City
Alliance
   Sutter Surgical Hospital – North Valley

COLORADO

Alamosa
Alliance
   San Luis Valley Health

Aurora
Alliance
   University of Colorado Hospital

Boulder
Alliance
   Boulder Community Health

Canon City
Alliance
   St. Thomas More Hospital

Colorado Springs
Alliance
   Penrose–St. Francis Health Services
   UCHealth Memorial Hospital

Denver
Alliance
   Denver Health
   National Jewish Health

Durango
Alliance
   CommonSpirit – Mercy Hospital

Englewood
Alliance
   Craig Hospital

Estes Park
Alliance
   Estes Park Health

Fort Collins
Alliance
   UCHealth Poudre Valley Hospital

Grand Junction
Alliance
   Intermountain Health St. Mary's Regional Hospital

Gunnison
Alliance
   Gunnison Valley Health

La Jara
Alliance
   San Luis Valley Health Conejos County Hospital

Lakewood
Alliance
   St. Anthony Hospital

Loveland
Alliance
   UCHealth Medical Center of the Rockies

Pueblo
Alliance
   CommonSpirit – St. Mary-Corwin Hospital

Steamboat Springs
Alliance
   UCHealth Yampa Valley Medical Center

Westminster
Alliance
   St. Anthony North Hospital

Yuma
Alliance
   Yuma District Hospital

CONNECTICUT

Bridgeport
Alliance
   Bridgeport Hospital

Bristol
Alliance
   Bristol Health

Danbury
Alliance
   Danbury Hospital

Farmington
Alliance
   UConn, John Dempsey Hospital

Greenwich
Alliance
   Greenwich Hospital

Hartford
Alliance
   Hartford Hospital
   Saint Francis Hospital

Manchester
Alliance
   Manchester Memorial Hospital

Middletown
Alliance
   Connecticut Valley Hospital
   Middlesex Health

New Haven
Alliance
   Connecticut Mental Health Center
   Yale New Haven Health
   Yale New Haven Hospital

Alliances

New London
Alliance
  Lawrence + Memorial Hospital

Norwalk
Alliance
  Norwalk Hospital

Putnam
Alliance
  Day Kimball Hospital

Stamford
Alliance
  Stamford Health

Torrington
Alliance
  Charlotte Hungerford Hospital

Vernon
Alliance
  Rockville General Hospital

DELAWARE

Wilmington
Alliance
  St. Francis Hospital

DISTRICT OF COLUMBIA

Washington
Alliance
  Howard University Hospital
  MedStar Georgetown University Hospital
  MedStar Washington Hospital Center
  Sibley Memorial Hospital

FLORIDA

Apalachicola
Alliance
  George E. Weems Memorial Hospital

Boca Raton
Alliance
  Boca Raton Regional Hospital

Boynton Beach
Alliance
  Bethesda Hospital East

Clermont
Alliance
  Orlando Health South Lake Hospital

Cocoa Beach
Alliance
  Health First Cape Canaveral Hospital

Coral Gables
Alliance
  Baptist Health South Florida, Doctors Hospital

Daytona Beach
Alliance
  Halifax Health Medical Center of Daytona Beach

Gainesville
Alliance
  UF Health Shands Hospital

Gulf Breeze
Alliance
  Gulf Breeze Hospital

Homestead
Alliance
  Baptist Health South Florida, Homestead Hospital

Jacksonville
Alliance
  Mayo Clinic Hospital in Florida

Jay
Alliance
  Jay Hospital

Lakeland
Alliance
  Lakeland Regional Health Medical Center

Leesburg
Alliance
  Leesburg Regional Medical Center

Melbourne
Alliance
  Health First Holmes Regional Medical Center

Miami
Alliance
  Baptist Health South Florida, Baptist Hospital of Miami
  Baptist Health South Florida, West Kendall Baptist Hospital
  Jackson Health System

Naples
Alliance
  NCH Baker Hospital

Ocoee
Alliance
  Orlando Health – Health Central Hospital

Orlando
Alliance
  Orlando Health Orlando Regional Medical Center
  Orlando Health

Palm Bay
Alliance
  Health First Palm Bay Hospital

Panama City
Alliance
  Ascension Sacred Heart Bay

Pensacola
Alliance
  Baptist Health Care Corporation
  Baptist Hospital

Perry
Alliance
  Doctors' Memorial Hospital

Rockledge
Alliance
  Health First, Inc.

Stuart
Alliance
  Cleveland Clinic Martin North Hospital

Tallahassee
Alliance
  Tallahassee Memorial HealthCare

Tampa
Alliance
  H. Lee Moffitt Cancer Center and Research Institute
  Tampa General Hospital

Tavernier
Alliance
  Baptist Health South Florida, Mariners Hospital

The Villages
Alliance
  UF Health The Villages Hospital

Titusville
Alliance
  Parrish Medical Center

Vero Beach
Alliance
  Cleveland Clinic Indian River Hospital

Weston
Alliance
  Cleveland Clinic Florida

GEORGIA

Adel
Alliance
  Southwell Medical

Albany
Alliance
  Phoebe Putney Health System
  Phoebe Putney Memorial Hospital

Americus
Alliance
  Phoebe Sumter Medical Center

Athens
Alliance
  Piedmont Athens Regional Medical Center
  St. Mary's Health Care System

Atlanta
Alliance
  Emory Saint Joseph's Hospital
  Emory University Hospital Midtown
  Emory University Hospital
  Grady Health System
  Northside Hospital

Augusta
Alliance
  Charlie Norwood Veterans Affairs Medical Center
  Piedmont Augusta
  Wellstar MCG Health

Austell
Alliance
  WellStar Cobb Hospital

Brunswick
Alliance
  Southeast Georgia Health System Brunswick Campus
  Southeast Georgia Health System

Cairo
Alliance
  Archbold Grady

Camilla
Alliance
  Archbold Mitchell

Canton
Alliance
  Northside Hospital Cherokee

Cedartown
Alliance
  Atrium Health Floyd Polk Medical Center

Claxton
Alliance
  Evans Memorial Hospital

Columbus
Alliance
  Columbus Specialty Hospital
  Piedmont Columbus Regional Midtown
  Piedmont Columbus Regional Northside

Cordele
Alliance
  Crisp Regional Hospital

Cumming
Alliance
  Northside Hospital Forsyth

Dalton
Alliance
  Hamilton Medical Center

Decatur
Alliance
  Emory Long–Term Acute Care

Douglas
Alliance
  Coffee Regional Medical Center

Douglasville
Alliance
  WellStar Douglas Hospital

Eatonton
Alliance
  Putnam General Hospital

Fitzgerald
Alliance
  Dorminy Medical Center

Gainesville
Alliance
  Northeast Georgia Medical Center

Hiram
Alliance
  WellStar Paulding Hospital

Homerville
Alliance
  Clinch Memorial Hospital

Jackson
Alliance
  Wellstar Sylvan Grove Hospital

Johns Creek
Alliance
  Emory Johns Creek Hospital

© 2025 AHA Guide Health Care Systems, Networks and Alliances

Alliances

Lakeland
Alliance
South Georgia Medical Center Lanier Campus

Lawrenceville
Alliance
Northside Hospital Gwinnett/Duluth

Lithonia
Alliance
Emory Hillandale Hospital

Macon
Alliance
Atrium Health Navicent Peach
Atrium Health Navicent Rehabilitation Hospital
Atrium Health Navicent The Medical Center

Marietta
Alliance
WellStar Health System
WellStar Kennestone Hospital
WellStar Windy Hill Hospital

Moultrie
Alliance
Colquitt Regional Medical Center

Nashville
Alliance
South Georgia Medical Center Berrien Campus

Newnan
Alliance
City of Hope Atlanta

Quitman
Alliance
Archbold Brooks

Riverdale
Alliance
Southern Regional Medical Center

Rome
Alliance
Atrium Health Floyd Medical Center

Roswell
Alliance
Wellstar North Fulton Hospital

Saint Marys
Alliance
Southeast Georgia Health System Camden Campus

Sandersville
Alliance
Washington County Regional Medical Center

Savannah
Alliance
Memorial Health University Medical Center

Swainsboro
Alliance
Emanuel Medical Center

Sylvester
Alliance
Phoebe Worth Medical Center

Thomasville
Alliance
Archbold Medical Center
John D. Archbold Memorial Hospital

Thomson
Alliance
Piedmont McDuffie

Tifton
Alliance
Tift Regional Medical Center

Valdosta
Alliance
South Georgia Medical Center

Warm Springs
Alliance
Roosevelt Warm Springs Long Term Acute Care Hospital
Roosevelt Warm Springs Rehabilitation and Specialty Hospitals

Warner Robins
Alliance
Houston Medical Center

Waycross
Alliance
Memorial Satilla Health

GUAM

Dededo
Alliance
Guam Regional Medical City

HAWAII

Aiea
Alliance
Pali Momi Medical Center

Ewa Beach
Alliance
Sutter Health Kahi Mohala

Honolulu
Alliance
Kaiser Permanente Medical Center
Queen's Health System
Shriners Hospitals for Children–Honolulu
Straub Medical Center
The Queen's Medical Center

Kamuela
Alliance
Queen's North Hawaii Community Hospital

Kaunakakai
Alliance
Molokai General Hospital

Wahiawa
Alliance
The Queen's Medical Center – Wahiawa

IDAHO

American Falls
Alliance
Power County Hospital District

Blackfoot
Alliance
Bingham Memorial Hospital

Boise
Alliance
Saint Alphonsus Regional Medical Center
St. Luke's Health System

Bonners Ferry
Alliance
Boundary Community Hospital

Cascade
Alliance
Cascade Medical Center

Coeur D'Alene
Alliance
Kootenai Health

Cottonwood
Alliance
St. Mary's Health

Emmett
Alliance
Valor Health

Orofino
Alliance
Clearwater Valley Health

Preston
Alliance
Franklin County Medical Center

Rupert
Alliance
Minidoka Memorial Hospital

Sandpoint
Alliance
Bonner General Health

Weiser
Alliance
Weiser Memorial Hospital

ILLINOIS

Alton
Alliance
Alton Memorial Hospital

Arlington Heights
Alliance
Endeavor Health Northwest Community Hospital

Aurora
Alliance
Rush–Copley Medical Center

Barrington
Alliance
Advocate Good Shepherd Hospital

Belleville
Alliance
Memorial Hospital Belleville

Bloomington
Alliance
OSF St. Joseph Medical Center

Canton
Alliance
Graham Hospital

Carbondale
Alliance
Memorial Hospital of Carbondale
Southern Illinois Healthcare

Chester
Alliance
Memorial Hospital

Chicago
Alliance
Advocate Illinois Masonic Medical Center
Advocate Trinity Hospital
Ann & Robert H. Lurie Children's Hospital of Chicago
Ascension Resurrection
Endeavor Health Swedish Hospital
Humboldt Park Health
Insight Hospital and Medical Center
John H. Stroger Jr. Hospital of Cook County
La Rabida Children's Hospital
Northwestern Memorial Hospital
Provident Hospital of Cook County
Rush University Medical Center
Shriners Hospitals for Children–Chicago
Thorek Memorial Hospital Andersonville
University of Chicago Medical Center
University of Illinois Hospital
Weiss Memorial Hospital

Decatur
Alliance
Decatur Memorial Hospital

Downers Grove
Alliance
Advocate Good Samaritan Hospital

Eldorado
Alliance
Ferrell Hospital

Elgin
Alliance
Advocate Sherman Hospital

Elmhurst
Alliance
Endeavor Health Elmhurst Hospital

Evanston
Alliance
Endeavor Health Evanston Hospital

Evergreen Park
Alliance
OSF Healthcare Little Company of Mary Medical Center

Freeport
Alliance
FHN Memorial Hospital

Galesburg
Alliance
OSF St. Mary Medical Center

Geneva
Alliance
Northwestern Medicine Delnor Hospital

Alliances

Greenville
Alliance
  HSHS Holy Family Hospital in Greenville

Harvey
Alliance
  UChicago Medicine Ingalls Memorial

Hazel Crest
Alliance
  Advocate South Suburban Hospital

Herrin
Alliance
  Herrin Hospital

Hinsdale
Alliance
  RML Specialty Hospital
  UChicago Medicine AdventHealth Hinsdale

Hoffman Estates
Alliance
  Ascension Alexian Brothers Behavioral Health Hospital

Jacksonville
Alliance
  Jacksonville Memorial Hospital

Jerseyville
Alliance
  Jersey Community Hospital

Joliet
Alliance
  Ascension Saint Joseph – Joliet

Kewanee
Alliance
  OSF Saint Luke Medical Center

Lake Forest
Alliance
  Northwestern Medicine Lake Forest Hospital

Libertyville
Alliance
  Advocate Condell Medical Center

Lincoln
Alliance
  Lincoln Memorial Hospital

Macomb
Alliance
  McDonough District Hospital

Maryville
Alliance
  Anderson Hospital

Mattoon
Alliance
  Sarah Bush Lincoln Health Center

Maywood
Alliance
  Loyola University Medical Center

McHenry
Alliance
  Northwestern Medicine McHenry

Monticello
Alliance
  Kirby Medical Center

Murphysboro
Alliance
  St. Joseph Memorial Hospital

New Lenox
Alliance
  Silver Cross Hospital

Oak Lawn
Alliance
  Advocate Christ Medical Center

Oak Park
Alliance
  Rush Oak Park Hospital

Palos Heights
Alliance
  Northwestern Medicine Palos Hospital

Park Ridge
Alliance
  Advocate Lutheran General Hospital

Peoria
Alliance
  Carle Health Methodist Hospital
  OSF Saint Francis Medical Center

Pittsfield
Alliance
  Illini Community Hospital

Pontiac
Alliance
  OSF Saint James – John W. Albrecht Medical Center

Quincy
Alliance
  Blessing Hospital

Rock Island
Alliance
  UnityPoint Health – Trinity Rock Island

Rockford
Alliance
  OSF Saint Anthony Medical Center
  UW Health SwedishAmerican Hospital

Rushville
Alliance
  Sarah D. Culbertson Memorial Hospital

Salem
Alliance
  Salem Township Hospital

Shelbyville
Alliance
  HSHS Good Shepherd Hospital

Springfield
Alliance
  Memorial Health
  Springfield Memorial Hospital

Taylorville
Alliance
  Taylorville Memorial Hospital

Urbana
Alliance
  Carle Foundation Hospital

Winfield
Alliance
  Northwestern Medicine Central DuPage Hospital

INDIANA

Anderson
Alliance
  Community Hospital Anderson

Angola
Alliance
  Cameron Memorial Community Hospital

Auburn
Alliance
  Parkview DeKalb Hospital

Avon
Alliance
  Indiana University Health West Hospital

Batesville
Alliance
  Margaret Mary Health

Bedford
Alliance
  Indiana University Health Bedford Hospital

Bloomington
Alliance
  Indiana University Health Bloomington Hospital

Carmel
Alliance
  Indiana University Health North Hospital

Clinton
Alliance
  Union Hospital Clinton

Columbia City
Alliance
  Parkview Whitley Hospital

Columbus
Alliance
  Columbus Regional Hospital

Danville
Alliance
  Hendricks Regional Health

Elkhart
Alliance
  Elkhart General Hospital

Evansville
Alliance
  Deaconess Health System
  Deaconess Midtown Hospital

Fort Wayne
Alliance
  Parkview Health
  Parkview Ortho Hospital
  Parkview Regional Medical Center

Frankfort
Alliance
  Indiana University Health Methodist Hospital

Franklin
Alliance
  Johnson Memorial Hospital

Goshen
Alliance
  Goshen Health

Huntington
Alliance
  Parkview Huntington Hospital

Indianapolis
Alliance
  Community Health Network
  Community Hospital East
  Community Hospital North
  Community Hospital South
  Eskenazi Health
  Indiana University Health University Hospital

Jasper
Alliance
  Memorial Hospital and Health Care Center

Kendallville
Alliance
  Parkview Noble Hospital

Knox
Alliance
  Northwest Health – Starke

Kokomo
Alliance
  Community Howard Regional Health

La Porte
Alliance
  Northwest Health – La Porte

LaGrange
Alliance
  Parkview LaGrange Hospital

Lafayette
Alliance
  Indiana University Health Arnett Hospital

Logansport
Alliance
  Logansport Memorial Hospital

Madison
Alliance
  Norton King's Daughters' Health

Marion
Alliance
  Marion Health

Monticello
Alliance
  Indiana University Health White Memorial Hospital

Muncie
Alliance
  Indiana University Health Ball Memorial Hospital

New Albany
Alliance
  Baptist Health Floyd
  Southern Indiana Rehabilitation Hospital

Alliances

New Castle
Alliance
　Henry Community Health

Newburgh
Alliance
　The Women's Hospital

Noblesville
Alliance
　Riverview Health

Paoli
Alliance
　Indiana University Health Paoli Hospital

Portland
Alliance
　Indiana University Health Jay Hospital

Richmond
Alliance
　Reid Health

Rochester
Alliance
　Woodlawn Hospital

Seymour
Alliance
　Schneck Medical Center

Shelbyville
Alliance
　Major Hospital

South Bend
Alliance
　Healthwin Hospital
　Memorial Hospital of South Bend

Terre Haute
Alliance
　Union Hospital

Tipton
Alliance
　Indiana University Health Tipton Hospital

Vincennes
Alliance
　Good Samaritan Hospital

Wabash
Alliance
　Parkview Wabash Hospital

IOWA

Anamosa
Alliance
　UnityPoint Health – Jones Regional Medical Center

Atlantic
Alliance
　Cass Health

Bettendorf
Alliance
　UnityPoint Health – Trinity Bettendorf

Cedar Rapids
Alliance
　UnityPoint Health – St. Luke's Hospital

Centerville
Alliance
　MercyOne Centerville Medical Center

Clarinda
Alliance
　Clarinda Regional Health Center

Clinton
Alliance
　MercyOne Clinton Medical Center

Corning
Alliance
　CHI Health Mercy Corning

Council Bluffs
Alliance
　Methodist Jennie Edmundson Hospital

Decorah
Alliance
　WinnMed

Des Moines
Alliance
　MercyOne Des Moines Medical Center

Dubuque
Alliance
　MercyOne Dubuque Medical Center
　UnityPoint Health – Finley Hospital

Fort Dodge
Alliance
　UnityPoint Health – Trinity Regional Medical Center

Grundy Center
Alliance
　Grundy County Memorial Hospital

Guttenberg
Alliance
　Guttenberg Municipal Hospital and Clinics

Hamburg
Alliance
　George C. Grape Community Hospital

Hampton
Alliance
　Franklin General Hospital

Harlan
Alliance
　Myrtue Medical Center

Iowa City
Alliance
　University of Iowa Hospitals & Clinics

Iowa Falls
Alliance
　Hansen Family Hospital

Jefferson
Alliance
　Greene County Medical Center

Keosauqua
Alliance
　Van Buren County Hospital

Lake City
Alliance
　Stewart Memorial Community Hospital

Le Mars
Alliance
　Floyd Valley Healthcare

Marengo
Alliance
　Compass Memorial Healthcare

Mason City
Alliance
　MercyOne North Iowa Medical Center

Missouri Valley
Alliance
　CHI Health Missouri Valley

Muscatine
Alliance
　UnityPoint Health – Trinity Muscatine

Nevada
Alliance
　Story County Medical Center

New Hampton
Alliance
　MercyOne New Hampton Medical Center

Orange City
Alliance
　Orange City Area Health System

Osceola
Alliance
　Clarke County Hospital

Pella
Alliance
　Pella Regional Health Center

Red Oak
Alliance
　Montgomery County Memorial Hospital

Sheldon
Alliance
　Sanford Sheldon Medical Center

Shenandoah
Alliance
　Shenandoah Medical Center

Sigourney
Alliance
　Keokuk County Hospital & Clinics

Sioux City
Alliance
　MercyOne Siouxland Medical Center
　UnityPoint Health – St. Lukes's Sioux City

Sumner
Alliance
　Community Memorial Hospital

Waverly
Alliance
　Waverly Health Center

West Des Moines
Alliance
　UnityPoint Health – Methodist West Hospital

West Union
Alliance
　Gundersen Palmer Lutheran Hospital and Clinics

KANSAS

Abilene
Alliance
　Memorial Health System

Ashland
Alliance
　Ashland Health Center

Atchison
Alliance
　Amberwell Health

Atwood
Alliance
　Rawlins County Health Center

Belleville
Alliance
　Republic County Hospital

Beloit
Alliance
　Mitchell County Hospital Health Systems

Clay Center
Alliance
　Clay County Medical Center

Colby
Alliance
　Citizens Medical Center

Coldwater
Alliance
　Comanche County Hospital

Concordia
Alliance
　North Central Kansas Medical Center

Dighton
Alliance
　Lane County Hospital

El Dorado
Alliance
　Susan B. Allen Memorial Hospital

Ellinwood
Alliance
　Ellinwood District Hospital

Ellsworth
Alliance
　Ellsworth County Medical Center

Emporia
Alliance
　Newman Regional Health

Fredonia
Alliance
　Fredonia Regional Hospital

Garden City
Alliance
　St. Catherine Hospital

Garnett
Alliance
　Anderson County Hospital

Girard
Alliance
　Girard Medical Center

Alliances

Goodland
Alliance
  Goodland Regional Medical Center

Great Bend
Alliance
  University of Kansas Health System Great Bend Campus

Greensburg
Alliance
  Kiowa County Memorial Hospital

Hays
Alliance
  Hays Medical Center

Hiawatha
Alliance
  Amberwell Hiawatha

Hill City
Alliance
  Graham County Hospital

Hoisington
Alliance
  Clara Barton Medical Center

Hoxie
Alliance
  Sheridan County Health Complex

Junction City
Alliance
  Stormont Vail Health – Flint Hills Campus

Kansas City
Alliance
  The University of Kansas Hospital

La Crosse
Alliance
  Rush County Memorial Hospital

Larned
Alliance
  Pawnee Valley Community Hospital

Lawrence
Alliance
  LMH Health

Lincoln
Alliance
  Lincoln County Hospital

Lindsborg
Alliance
  Lindsborg Community Hospital

Mankato
Alliance
  Jewell County Hospital

Medicine Lodge
Alliance
  Medicine Lodge Memorial Hospital

Minneapolis
Alliance
  Ottawa County Health Center

Minneola
Alliance
  Minneola District Hospital

Ness City
Alliance
  Ness County Hospital District No 2

Norton
Alliance
  Norton County Hospital

Oakley
Alliance
  Logan County Hospital

Overland Park
Alliance
  Menorah Medical Center
  Overland Park Regional Medical Center
  Saint Luke's South Hospital

Parsons
Alliance
  Labette Health

Phillipsburg
Alliance
  Phillips County Health Systems

Plainville
Alliance
  Rooks County Health Center

Pratt
Alliance
  Pratt Regional Medical Center

Quinter
Alliance
  Gove County Medical Center

Ransom
Alliance
  Grisell Memorial Hospital District One

Russell
Alliance
  Russell Regional Hospital

Sabetha
Alliance
  Sabetha Community Hospital

Saint Francis
Alliance
  Cheyenne County Hospital

Salina
Alliance
  Salina Regional Health Center
  Salina Surgical Hospital

Satanta
Alliance
  Satanta District Hospital and Long Term Care

Scott City
Alliance
  Scott County Hospital

Smith Center
Alliance
  Smith County Memorial Hospital

Stafford
Alliance
  Stafford County Hospital

Topeka
Alliance
  Stormont Vail Health

Wakeeney
Alliance
  Trego County–Lemke Memorial Hospital

Wichita
Alliance
  Great Plains Health Alliance, Inc.
  Kansas Spine & Specialty Hospital

KENTUCKY

Bardstown
Alliance
  CHI Saint Joseph Health – Flaget Memorial Hospital

Berea
Alliance
  CHI Saint Joseph Health – Saint Joseph Berea

Cynthiana
Alliance
  Harrison Memorial Hospital

Florence
Alliance
  St. Elizabeth Florence

Lexington
Alliance
  CHI Saint Joseph Health – Saint Joseph East
  CHI Saint Joseph Health
  Eastern State Hospital
  University of Kentucky Albert B. Chandler Hospital

London
Alliance
  CHI Saint Joseph Health – Saint Joseph London

Louisville
Alliance
  UofL Health – Jewish Hospital
  UofL Health – Peace Hospital
  UofL Health – UofL Hospital

Martin
Alliance
  ARH Our Lady of the Way

Morehead
Alliance
  St. Claire Regional Medical Center

Mount Sterling
Alliance
  CHI Saint Joseph Health – Saint Joseph Mount Sterling

Mount Vernon
Alliance
  Rockcastle Regional Hospital and Respiratory Care Center

Owensboro
Alliance
  Owensboro Health Regional Hospital

Pikeville
Alliance
  Pikeville Medical Center

Shelbyville
Alliance
  UofL Health – Shelbyville Hospital

LOUISIANA

Baton Rouge
Alliance
  Franciscan Missionaries of Our Lady Health System, Inc.
  Ochsner Medical Center – Baton Rouge
  Our Lady of the Lake Regional Medical Center

Bogalusa
Alliance
  Our Lady of the Angels Hospital

Church Point
Alliance
  Acadia–St. Landry Hospital

Covington
Alliance
  St. Tammany Health System

De Ridder
Alliance
  Beauregard Health System

Ferriday
Alliance
  Trinity Medical

Jennings
Alliance
  Ochsner American Legion Hospital

Kenner
Alliance
  Ochsner Medical Center – Kenner

Lafayette
Alliance
  Ochsner Lafayette General Medical Center
  Our Lady of Lourdes Regional Medical Center

Lake Charles
Alliance
  Lake Charles Memorial Hospital

Mansfield
Alliance
  De Soto Regional Health System

Monroe
Alliance
  Ochsner LSU Health Shreveport – Monroe Medical Center
  St. Francis Medical Center

Napoleonville
Alliance
  Our Lady of the Lake Assumption Community Hospital

Natchitoches
Alliance
  Natchitoches Regional Medical Center

New Iberia
Alliance
  Iberia Medical Center

New Orleans
Alliance
  Touro Infirmary

Raceland
Alliance
  Ochsner St. Anne General Hospital

Alliances

Shreveport
Alliance
　Ochsner LSU Health Shreveport – Academic Medical Center
　Willis Knighton Health
　Willis Knighton North

Slidell
Alliance
　Slidell Memorial Hospital East

Springhill
Alliance
　Springhill Medical Center

Sulphur
Alliance
　West Calcasieu Cameron Hospital

Vivian
Alliance
　North Caddo Medical Center

MAINE

Augusta
Alliance
　MaineGeneral Medical Center–Augusta Campus
　MaineGeneral Medical Center

Bangor
Alliance
　Northern Light Eastern Maine Medical Center
　The Acadia Hospital

Bar Harbor
Alliance
　Mount Desert Island Hospital

Belfast
Alliance
　Waldo County General Hospital

Biddeford
Alliance
　Southern Maine Health Care – Biddeford Medical Center

Blue Hill
Alliance
　Northern Light Blue Hill Hospital

Brewer
Alliance
　Northern Light Health

Brunswick
Alliance
　Mid Coast Hospital

Damariscotta
Alliance
　LincolnHealth

Dover–Foxcroft
Alliance
　Northern Light Mayo Hospital

Ellsworth
Alliance
　Northern Light Maine Coast Hospital

Farmington
Alliance
　Franklin Memorial Hospital

Fort Kent
Alliance
　Northern Maine Medical Center

Greenville
Alliance
　Northern Light CA Dean Hospital

Houlton
Alliance
　Houlton Regional Hospital

Machias
Alliance
　Down East Community Hospital

Millinocket
Alliance
　Millinocket Regional Hospital

Norway
Alliance
　MaineHealth Stephens Hospital

Pittsfield
Alliance
　Northern Light Sebasticook Valley Hospital

Portland
Alliance
　MaineHealth Maine Medical Center
　Northern Light Mercy Hospital

Presque Isle
Alliance
　The Aroostook Medical Center

Rockport
Alliance
　MaineHealth Pen Bay Medical Center

Skowhegan
Alliance
　Redington–Fairview General Hospital

Waterville
Alliance
　Northern Light Inland Hospital

Westbrook
Alliance
　MaineHealth Behavioral Health at Spring Harbor

MARYLAND

Baltimore
Alliance
　GBMC Healthcare
　Johns Hopkins Bayview Medical Center
　Johns Hopkins Hospital
　MedStar Franklin Square Medical Center
　MedStar Good Samaritan Hospital
　MedStar Harbor Hospital
　MedStar Union Memorial Hospital
　Mercy Medical Center
　Mt. Washington Pediatric Hospital
　University of Maryland Medical Center Midtown Campus
　University of Maryland Medical Center
　University of Maryland Rehabilitation & Orthopaedic Institute

Bel Air
Alliance
　University of Maryland Upper Chesapeake Medical Center

Bethesda
Alliance
　Suburban Hospital

Chestertown
Alliance
　University of Maryland Shore Medical Center at Chestertown

Clinton
Alliance
　MedStar Southern Maryland Hospital Center

Columbia
Alliance
　Johns Hopkins Howard County Medical Center
　MedStar Health

Easton
Alliance
　University of Maryland Shore Medical Center at Easton

Elkton
Alliance
　ChristianaCare, Union Hospital

Glen Burnie
Alliance
　University of Maryland Baltimore Washington Medical Center

Hagerstown
Alliance
　Meritus Health

La Plata
Alliance
　University of Maryland Charles Regional Medical Center

Largo
Alliance
　University of Maryland Capital Region Medical Center

Leonardtown
Alliance
　MedStar St. Mary's Hospital

Olney
Alliance
　MedStar Montgomery Medical Center

Prince Frederick
Alliance
　CalvertHealth Medical Center

Randallstown
Alliance
　Northwest Hospital

Rockville
Alliance
　Adventist Healthcare Shady Grove Medical Center

Silver Spring
Alliance
　Holy Cross Hospital

MASSACHUSETTS

Athol
Alliance
　Athol Hospital

Belmont
Alliance
　McLean Hospital

Beverly
Alliance
　Beverly Hospital

Boston
Alliance
　Beth Israel Deaconess Medical Center
　Boston Medical Center
　Brigham and Women's Faulkner Hospital
　Brigham and Women's Hospital
　Dana–Farber Cancer Institute
　Mass General Brigham
　Massachusetts Eye and Ear
　Massachusetts General Hospital
　Shriners Hospitals for Children–Boston
　Tufts Medical Center

Brighton
Alliance
　St. Elizabeth's Medical Center

Brockton
Alliance
　Good Samaritan Medical Center
　Signature Healthcare Brockton Hospital

Burlington
Alliance
　Lahey Hospital & Medical Center

Cambridge
Alliance
　Cambridge Health Alliance
　Mount Auburn Hospital
　Spaulding Hospital for Continuing Medical Care Cambridge

Charlestown
Alliance
　Spaulding Rehabilitation Hospital

Concord
Alliance
　Emerson Hospital

East Sandwich
Alliance
　Spaulding Rehabilitation Hospital Cape Cod

Fall River
Alliance
　Saint Anne's Hospital

Gardner
Alliance
　Heywood Hospital

Greenfield
Alliance
　Baystate Franklin Medical Center

Alliances

Holyoke
Alliance
  Holyoke Medical Center
Hyannis
Alliance
  Cape Cod Healthcare, Inc.
Leominster
Alliance
  UMass Memorial HealthAlliance–Clinton Hospital
Lowell
Alliance
  Lowell General Hospital
Marlborough
Alliance
  UMass Memorial–Marlborough Hospital
Melrose
Alliance
  Melrose–Wakefield Hospital
Methuen
Alliance
  ...

... Israel Deaconess Hospital–Plymouth
Salem
Alliance
  Salem Hospital
South Weymouth
Alliance
  South Shore Hospital
Southbridge
Alliance
  UMass Memorial Health – Harrington
Springfield
Alliance
  Baystate Medical Center
  Shriners Hospitals for Children–Springfield
Taunton
Alliance
  Morton Hospital and Medical Center
Winchester
Alliance
  Winchester Hospital
Worcester
Alliance
  UMass Memorial Medical Center

MICHIGAN

Alma
Alliance
  MyMichigan Medical Center Alma
Alpena
Alliance
  MyMichigan Medical Center Alpena
Ann Arbor
Alliance
  University of Michigan Medical Center
Battle Creek
Alliance
  Bronson Battle Creek Hospital
Bay City
Alliance
  McLaren Bay Region
  McLaren Bay Special Care
Big Rapids
Alliance
  Corewell Health Big Rapids Hospital
Cadillac
Alliance
  Munson Healthcare Cadillac Hospital
Carson City
Alliance
  University of Michigan Health–Sparrow Carson
Cass City
Alliance
  Hills & Dales Healthcare
Chelsea
Alliance
  Chelsea Hospital
Coldwater
Alliance
  ProMedica Coldwater Regional Hospital
Dearborn
Alliance
  Corewell Health Dearborn Hospital
Detroit
Alliance
  Henry Ford Hospital
Farmington Hills
Alliance
  Corewell Health Farmington Hills Hospital
Flint
Alliance
  McLaren Flint
Fremont
Alliance
  Corewell Health Gerber Hospital
Grand Haven
Alliance
  Trinity Health Grand Haven Hospital
Grand Rapids
Alliance
  Corewell Health Butterworth Hospital
  Mary Free Bed Rehabilitation Hospital
  Pine Rest Christian Mental Health Services
Grayling
Alliance
  Munson Healthcare Grayling Hospital
Greenville
Alliance
  Corewell Health Greenville Hospital
Grosse Pointe
Alliance
  Corewell Health Beaumont Grosse Pointe Hospital
Hastings
Alliance
  Corewell Health Pennock Hospital
Holland
Alliance
  Holland Hospital
Ionia
Alliance
  University of Michigan Health–Sparrow Ionia
Iron River
Alliance
  Aspirus Iron River Hospital
Ironwood
Alliance
  Aspirus Ironwood Hospital & Clinics, Inc.
Kalamazoo
Alliance
  Bronson Healthcare Group
  Bronson Methodist Hospital
Lansing
Alliance
  Sparrow Specialty Hospital
  University of Michigan Health–Sparrow Lansing
Laurium
Alliance
  Aspirus Keweenaw Hospital
Ludington
Alliance
  Corewell Health Ludington Hospital
Marlette
Alliance
  Marlette Regional Hospital
Marshall
Alliance
  Oaklawn Hospital
Midland
Alliance
  MyMichigan Medical Center Midland
Monroe
Alliance
  ProMedica Monroe Regional Hospital
Mount Clemens
Alliance
  McLaren Macomb
Mount Pleasant
Alliance
  McLaren Central Michigan
Ontonagon
Alliance
  Aspirus Ontonagon Hospital
Paw Paw
Alliance
  Bronson LakeView Hospital
Petoskey
Alliance
  McLaren Northern Michigan
Pontiac
Alliance
  McLaren Oakland
  Trinity Health Oakland Hospital
Port Huron
Alliance
  McLaren Port Huron
Reed City
Alliance
  Corewell Health Reed City Hospital
Royal Oak
Alliance
  Corewell Health William Beaumont University Hospital
Saginaw
Alliance
  Covenant HealthCare
Saint Johns
Alliance
  Sparrow Clinton Hospital
Saint Joseph
Alliance
  Corewell Health Lakeland Hospitals
Sheridan
Alliance
  Sheridan Community Hospital
South Haven
Alliance
  Bronson South Haven Hospital
Taylor
Alliance
  Corewell Health Taylor Hospital
Trenton
Alliance
  Corewell Health Trenton Hospital
Troy
Alliance
  Corewell Health Beaumont Troy Hospital
Watervliet
Alliance
  Corewell Health Watervliet Hospital
Wayne
Alliance
  Corewell Health Wayne Hospital

Alliances

West Branch
Alliance
  MyMichigan Medical Center West Branch

Wyoming
Alliance
  University of Michigan Health – West

Zeeland
Alliance
  Corewell Health Zeeland Hospital

MINNESOTA

Ada
Alliance
  Essentia Health–Ada

Albert Lea
Alliance
  Mayo Clinic Health System – Albert Lea and Austin

Arlington
Alliance
  Ridgeview Sibley Medical Center

Aurora
Alliance
  Essentia Health Northern Pines

Bagley
Alliance
  Sanford Bagley Medical Center

Baudette
Alliance
  CHI LakeWood Health

Bemidji
Alliance
  Sanford Bemidji Medical Center

Benson
Alliance
  CentraCare – Benson

Blue Earth
Alliance
  United Hospital District

Brainerd
Alliance
  Essentia Health–St. Joseph's Medical Center

Buffalo
Alliance
  Buffalo Hospital

Burnsville
Alliance
  M Health Fairview Ridges Hospital

Cambridge
Alliance
  Cambridge Medical Center

Canby
Alliance
  Sanford Canby Medical Center

Cannon Falls
Alliance
  Mayo Clinic Health System in Cannon Falls

Coon Rapids
Alliance
  Mercy Hospital

Crookston
Alliance
  RiverView Health

Deer River
Alliance
  Essentia Health–Deer River

Detroit Lakes
Alliance
  Essentia Health St. Mary's – Detroit Lakes

Duluth
Alliance
  Aspirus St. Luke's Hospital
  Essentia Health Duluth
  Essentia Health St. Mary's Medical Center
  Essentia Health

Fairmont
Alliance
  Mayo Clinic Health System in Fairmont

Faribault
Alliance
  Allina Health Faribault Medical Center

Fergus Falls
Alliance
  Lake Region Healthcare Corporation

Fosston
Alliance
  Essentia Health–Fosston

Glencoe
Alliance
  Glencoe Regional Health

Graceville
Alliance
  Essentia Health–Graceville

Grand Rapids
Alliance
  Grand Itasca Clinic and Hospital

Granite Falls
Alliance
  Avera Granite Falls

Hallock
Alliance
  Kittson Healthcare

Hutchinson
Alliance
  Hutchinson Health

Jackson
Alliance
  Sanford Jackson Medical Center

Lake City
Alliance
  Mayo Clinic Health System in Lake City

Little Falls
Alliance
  CHI St. Gabriel's Health

Long Prairie
Alliance
  CentraCare – Long Prairie

Luverne
Alliance
  Sanford Luverne Medical Center

Madelia
Alliance
  Madelia Health

Mahnomen
Alliance
  Mahnomen Health

Mankato
Alliance
  Mayo Clinic Health System in Mankato

Maple Grove
Alliance
  Maple Grove Hospital

Melrose
Alliance
  CentraCare – Melrose

Minneapolis
Alliance
  Abbott Northwestern Hospital
  Allina Health
  Hennepin Healthcare

Monticello
Alliance
  CentraCare – Monticello

New Prague
Alliance
  Mayo Clinic Health System in New Prague

New Ulm
Alliance
  New Ulm Medical Center

Ortonville
Alliance
  Ortonville Area Health Services

Owatonna
Alliance
  Owatonna Hospital

Park Rapids
Alliance
  CHI St. Joseph's Health

Paynesville
Alliance
  CentraCare – Paynesville

Perham
Alliance
  Perham Health

Princeton
Alliance
  M Health Fairview Northland Medical Center

Red Wing
Alliance
  Mayo Clinic Health

Redwood Falls
Alliance
  CentraCare – Redwood

Robbinsdale
Alliance
  North Memorial Health Hospital

Rochester
Alliance
  Mayo Clinic Hospital – Rochester
  Mayo Clinic

Roseau
Alliance
  LifeCare Medical Center

Saint Cloud
Alliance
  CentraCare – St. Cloud Hospital
  CentraCare Health

Saint James
Alliance
  Mayo Clinic Health System in Saint James

Saint Paul
Alliance
  Regions Hospital
  United Hospital

Sandstone
Alliance
  Essentia Health Sandstone

Sauk Centre
Alliance
  CentraCare – Sauk Centre

Shakopee
Alliance
  St. Francis Regional Medical Center

Slayton
Alliance
  Murray County Medical Center

Stillwater
Alliance
  Lakeview Hospital

Thief River Falls
Alliance
  Sanford Behavioral Health Center
  Sanford Thief River Falls Medical Center

Tracy
Alliance
  Sanford Tracy Medical Center

Two Harbors
Alliance
  Aspirus Lake View Hospital

Virginia
Alliance
  Essentia Health–Virginia

Waconia
Alliance
  Ridgeview Medical Center

Warren
Alliance
  North Valley Health Center

Waseca
Alliance
  Mayo Clinic Health System in Waseca

Alliances

Westbrook
Alliance
   Sanford Westbrook Medical Center

Wheaton
Alliance
   Sanford Wheaton Medical Center

Willmar
Alliance
   CentraCare – Rice Memorial Hospital

Windom
Alliance
   Windom Area Health

Worthington
Alliance
   Sanford Worthington Medical Center

Wyoming
Alliance
   M Health Fairview Lakes Medical Center

MISSISSIPPI

Booneville
Alliance
   Baptist Memorial Hospital–Booneville

Columbia
Alliance
   Marion General Hospital

Columbus
Alliance
   Baptist Memorial Hospital–Golden Triangle

Corinth
Alliance
   Magnolia Regional Health Center

Greenville
Alliance
   Delta Health–The Medical Center

Greenwood
Alliance
   Greenwood Leflore Hospital

Grenada
Alliance
   University of Mississippi Medical Center Grenada

Gulfport
Alliance
   Memorial Hospital at Gulfport

Hattiesburg
Alliance
   Forrest General Hospital

Indianola
Alliance
   South Sunflower County Hospital

Jackson
Alliance
   St. Dominic–Jackson Memorial Hospital
   University of Mississippi Medical Center

Leakesville
Alliance
   Greene County Hospital

Lexington
Alliance
   University of Mississippi Medical Center Holmes County

Lucedale
Alliance
   George Regional Hospital

Magnolia
Alliance
   Beacham Memorial Hospital

McComb
Alliance
   Southwest Mississippi Regional Medical Center

Meridian
Alliance
   Baptist Anderson Regional Medical Center – South
   Baptist Anderson Regional Medical Center

Monticello
Alliance
   Lawrence County Hospital

New Albany
Alliance
   Baptist Memorial Hospital–Union County

Olive Branch
Alliance
   Methodist Healthcare Olive Branch Hospital

Oxford
Alliance
   Baptist Memorial Hospital–North Mississippi

Pascagoula
Alliance
   Singing River Health System

Philadelphia
Alliance
   Neshoba General

Picayune
Alliance
   Highland Community Hospital

Prentiss
Alliance
   Jefferson Davis Community Hospital

Southaven
Alliance
   Baptist Memorial Hospital–Desoto

Starkville
Alliance
   OCH Regional Medical Center

Tupelo
Alliance
   North Mississippi Health Services, Inc.

Tylertown
Alliance
   Walthall General Hospital

MISSOURI

Appleton City
Alliance
   Ellett Memorial Hospital

Belton
Alliance
   Belton Regional Medical Center

Bolivar
Alliance
   Citizens Memorial Hospital

Bonne Terre
Alliance
   Parkland Health Center–Bonne Terre

Branson
Alliance
   Cox Medical Center Branson

Brookfield
Alliance
   Pershing Memorial Hospital

Cameron
Alliance
   Cameron Regional Medical Center

Cape Girardeau
Alliance
   Saint Francis Medical Center

Chillicothe
Alliance
   Hedrick Medical Center

Clinton
Alliance
   Golden Valley Memorial Healthcare

Columbia
Alliance
   Boone Hospital Center
   University Hospital

Farmington
Alliance
   Parkland Health Center – Farmington Community

Independence
Alliance
   Centerpoint Medical Center

Jefferson City
Alliance
   Capital Region Medical Center

Joplin
Alliance
   Freeman Health System
   Freeman Hospital East

Kansas City
Alliance
   Children's Mercy Kansas City
   Research Medical Center
   Saint Luke's Hospital of Kansas City
   Saint Luke's North Hospital – Barry Road
   University Health–Lakewood Medical Center
   University Health–Truman Medical Center

Lamar
Alliance
   Cox Barton County Memorial Hospital

Lee's Summit
Alliance
   Lee's Summit Medical Center
   Saint Luke's East Hospital

Lexington
Alliance
   Lafayette Regional Health Center

Liberty
Alliance
   Liberty Hospital

Macon
Alliance
   Samaritan Hospital

Marshall
Alliance
   Fitzgibbon Hospital

Milan
Alliance
   Sullivan County Memorial Hospital

Monett
Alliance
   Cox Monett Hospital, Inc

Neosho
Alliance
   Freeman Neosho Hospital

O Fallon
Alliance
   Progress West Hospital

Osage Beach
Alliance
   Lake Regional Health System

Potosi
Alliance
   Washington County Memorial Hospital

Saint Louis
Alliance
   BJC Health System
   Barnes–Jewish Hospital
   Barnes–Jewish West County Hospital
   Christian Hospital
   Missouri Baptist Medical Center
   Shriners Hospitals for Children–St. Louis
   St. Louis Children's Hospital

Saint Peters
Alliance
   Barnes–Jewish St. Peters Hospital

Salem
Alliance
   Salem Memorial District Hospital

Sikeston
Alliance
   Missouri Delta Medical Center

Springfield
Alliance
   Cox Medical Center North
   Cox North Hospital
   CoxHealth

Ste Genevieve
Alliance
   Ste. Genevieve County Memorial Hospital

Sullivan
Alliance
   Missouri Baptist Sullivan Hospital

Alliances

Trenton
Alliance
  Wright Memorial Hospital

Warrensburg
Alliance
  Western Missouri Medical Center

MONTANA

Anaconda
Alliance
  Community Hospital of Anaconda

Bozeman
Alliance
  Bozeman Health Deaconess Regional Medical Center

Columbus
Alliance
  Stillwater Billings Clinic

Conrad
Alliance
  Logan Health – Conrad

Deer Lodge
Alliance
  Deer Lodge Medical Center

Ennis
Alliance
  Madison Valley Medical Center

Hamilton
Alliance
  Bitterroot Health – Daly Hospital

Helena
Alliance
  St. Peter's Health

Kalispell
Alliance
  Logan Health

Libby
Alliance
  Cabinet Peaks Medical Center

Missoula
Alliance
  Providence St. Patrick Hospital

Philipsburg
Alliance
  Granite County Medical Center

Plains
Alliance
  Clark Fork Valley Hospital

Polson
Alliance
  Providence St. Joseph Medical Center

Ronan
Alliance
  St. Luke Community Healthcare

Sidney
Alliance
  Sidney Health Center

Townsend
Alliance
  Billings Clinic Broadwater

White Sulphur Springs
Alliance
  Mountainview Medical Center

NEBRASKA

Alliance
Alliance
  Box Butte General Hospital

Alma
Alliance
  Harlan County Health System

Atkinson
Alliance
  West Holt Medical Services

Beatrice
Alliance
  Beatrice Community Hospital and Health Center

Bellevue
Alliance
  Nebraska Medicine – Bellevue

Blair
Alliance
  Memorial Community Hospital and Health System

Bridgeport
Alliance
  Morrill County Community Hospital

Broken Bow
Alliance
  Jennie M. Melham Memorial Medical Center

Columbus
Alliance
  Columbus Community Hospital

Crete
Alliance
  Crete Area Medical Center

Falls City
Alliance
  Community Medical Center, Inc.

Franklin
Alliance
  Franklin County Memorial Hospital

Gordon
Alliance
  Gordon Memorial Health Services

Grand Island
Alliance
  CHI Health Saint Francis

Hastings
Alliance
  Mary Lanning Healthcare

Kearney
Alliance
  CHI Health Good Samaritan

Lexington
Alliance
  Lexington Regional Health Center

Lincoln
Alliance
  Bryan Health
  Bryan Medical Center
  CHI Health Nebraska Heart
  CHI Health St Elizabeth
  Madonna Rehabilitation Hospital

Lynch
Alliance
  Niobrara Valley Hospital

Minden
Alliance
  Kearney County Health Services

Nebraska City
Alliance
  CHI Health St. Mary's

Neligh
Alliance
  Antelope Memorial Hospital

Norfolk
Alliance
  Faith Regional Health Services

O'Neill
Alliance
  Avera St. Anthony's Hospital

Omaha
Alliance
  CHI Health Creighton University Medical Center – Bergan Mercy
  CHI Health Immanuel
  CHI Health Lakeside
  Nebraska Medicine – Nebraska Medical Center
  Nebraska Methodist Health System, Inc.
  Nebraska Methodist Hospital
  OrthoNebraska Hospital

Ord
Alliance
  Valley County Health System

Oshkosh
Alliance
  Regional West Garden County

Osmond
Alliance
  Osmond General Hospital

Papillion
Alliance
  CHI Health Midlands

Plainview
Alliance
  CHI Health Plainview

Schuyler
Alliance
  CHI Health Schuyler

Scottsbluff
Alliance
  Regional West Medical Center

York
Alliance
  York General

NEVADA

Las Vegas
Alliance
  Sunrise Hospital and Medical Center
  University Medical Center

NEW HAMPSHIRE

Claremont
Alliance
  Valley Regional Hospital

Colebrook
Alliance
  Upper Connecticut Valley Hospital

Dover
Alliance
  Wentworth–Douglass Hospital

Keene
Alliance
  Cheshire Medical Center

Lancaster
Alliance
  Weeks Medical Center

Lebanon
Alliance
  Alice Peck Day Memorial Hospital
  Dartmouth–Hitchcock Medical Center

Nashua
Alliance
  Southern New Hampshire Medical Center

New London
Alliance
  New London Hospital

North Conway
Alliance
  Memorial Hospital

Peterborough
Alliance
  Monadnock Community Hospital

Plymouth
Alliance
  Speare Memorial Hospital

Woodsville
Alliance
  Cottage Hospital

NEW JERSEY

Atlantic City
Alliance
  AtlantiCare Regional Medical Center, Atlantic City Campus

Camden
Alliance
  Cooper University Health Care

Cape May Court House
Alliance
  Cooper University Hospital Cape Regional

Alliances

Denville
Alliance
Saint Clare's Denville Hospital

Edison
Alliance
Hackensack Meridian Health JFK Medical Center

Egg Harbor Township
Alliance
AtlantiCare

Flemington
Alliance
Hunterdon Healthcare

Hamilton
Alliance
Robert Wood Johnson University Hospital at Hamilton

Marlton
Alliance
Virtua Marlton

Morristown
Alliance
Morristown Medical Center

Mount Holly
Alliance
Virtua Mount Holly Hospital

Mullica Hill
Alliance
Inspira Health Network

New Brunswick
Alliance
Robert Wood Johnson University Hospital

Newark
Alliance
University Hospital

Newton
Alliance
Newton Medical Center

Paramus
Alliance
Valley Hospital

Pompton Plains
Alliance
Chilton Medical Center

Rahway
Alliance
Robert Wood Johnson University Hospital Rahway

Somers Point
Alliance
Shore Medical Center

Summit
Alliance
Overlook Medical Center

Trenton
Alliance
Capital Health

Vineland
Alliance
Inspira Medical Center–Vineland

Voorhees
Alliance
Virtua Voorhees

NEW MEXICO

Albuquerque
Alliance
University of New Mexico Hospitals

Farmington
Alliance
San Juan Regional Medical Center

Gallup
Alliance
Rehoboth McKinley Christian Health Care Services

Santa Fe
Alliance
CHRISTUS St. Vincent Regional Medical Center

NEW YORK

Albany
Alliance
Albany Medical Center
St. Peter's Hospital

Alexandria Bay
Alliance
River Hospital

Binghamton
Alliance
United Health Services Hospitals–Binghamton

Bronx
Alliance
Montefiore Medical Center
NYC Health + Hospitals / Jacobi

Brooklyn
Alliance
Brooklyn Hospital Center
NYC Health + Hospitals / South Brooklyn Health
NYC Health + Hospitals / Woodhull
New York Community Hospital
SUNY Downstate Health Sciences University

Buffalo
Alliance
Erie County Medical Center
Roswell Park Comprehensive Cancer Center

Canandaigua
Alliance
F. F. Thompson Hospital

Cooperstown
Alliance
Bassett Medical Center

Corning
Alliance
Guthrie Corning Hospital

Cortlandt Manor
Alliance
New York–Presbyterian/Hudson Valley Hospital

Elizabethtown
Alliance
The University of Vermont Health Network Elizabethtown Community Hospital

Elmhurst
Alliance
NYC Health + Hospitals / Elmhurst

Flushing
Alliance
New York–Presbyterian Queens

Geneva
Alliance
Finger Lakes Health

Hamilton
Alliance
Community Memorial Hospital

Ithaca
Alliance
Cayuga Medical Center at Ithaca

Jamaica
Alliance
NYC Health + Hospitals / Queens

Jamestown
Alliance
UPMC Chautauqua

Malone
Alliance
The University of Vermont Health Network – Alice Hyde Medical Center

Montour Falls
Alliance
Schuyler Hospital

Mount Vernon
Alliance
Montefiore Mount Vernon

New Rochelle
Alliance
Montefiore New Rochelle

New York
Alliance
Gracie Square Hospital
Lenox Hill Hospital
NYC Health + Hospitals / Bellevue
NYC Health + Hospitals / Harlem
NYC Health + Hospitals / Henry J Carter Specialty Hospital and Medical Center
NYU Langone Hospitals
New York–Presbyterian Hospital
New York–Presbyterian/Columbia University Medical Center
Rockefeller University Hospital
The Mount Sinai Hospital

Norwich
Alliance
UHS Chenango Memorial Hospital

Nyack
Alliance
Montefiore Nyack Hospital

Ogdensburg
Alliance
Claxton–Hepburn Medical Center

Plattsburgh
Alliance
The University of Vermont Health Network–Champlain Valley Physicians Hospital

Riverhead
Alliance
Peconic Bay Medical Center

Rochester
Alliance
Highland Hospital
Strong Memorial Hospital of the University of Rochester
University of Rochester Medical Center

Sleepy Hollow
Alliance
Phelps Memorial Hospital Center

Staten Island
Alliance
Staten Island University Hospital

Stony Brook
Alliance
Stony Brook University Hospital

Syracuse
Alliance
Crouse Health
Upstate University Hospital

Valhalla
Alliance
Westchester Medical Center

Walton
Alliance
UHS Delaware Valley Hospital

NORTH CAROLINA

Ahoskie
Alliance
ECU Health Roanoke–Chowan Hospital

Bermuda Run
Alliance
Atrium Health Wake Forest Baptist Davie Medical Center

Bolivia
Alliance
Novant Health Brunswick Medical Center

Cary
Alliance
WakeMed Cary Hospital

Chapel Hill
Alliance
University of North Carolina Hospitals

Charlotte
Alliance
Novant Health Charlotte Orthopaedic Hospital
Novant Health Presbyterian Medical Center

Clinton
Alliance
Sampson Regional Medical Center

Dunn
Alliance
Harnett Health System

Alliances

Durham
Alliance
   Duke Regional Hospital
   Duke University Hospital

Eden
Alliance
   UNC Health Rockingham

Edenton
Alliance
   ECU Health Chowan Hospital

Elizabeth City
Alliance
   Sentara Albemarle Medical Center

Elkin
Alliance
   Hugh Chatham Health

Greenville
Alliance
   ECU Health Medical Center

Huntersville
Alliance
   Novant Health Huntersville Medical Center

Jefferson
Alliance
   Ashe Memorial Hospital

Kenansville
Alliance
   ECU Health Duplin Hospital

Lexington
Alliance
   Atrium Health Wake Forest Baptist Lexington Medical Center

Matthews
Alliance
   Novant Health Matthews Medical Center

Morehead City
Alliance
   Carteret Health Care

Nags Head
Alliance
   The Outer Banks Hospital

New Bern
Alliance
   CarolinaEast Health System

Raleigh
Alliance
   Duke Raleigh Hospital
   UNC Health Rex
   WakeMed Health & Hospitals
   WakeMed Raleigh Campus

Roanoke Rapids
Alliance
   ECU Health North Hospital

Rocky Mount
Alliance
   UNC Health Nash

Salisbury
Alliance
   Novant Health Rowan Medical Center

Siler City
Alliance
   UNC Health Chatham

Sparta
Alliance
   Alleghany Health

Tarboro
Alliance
   ECU Health Edgecombe Hospital

Thomasville
Alliance
   Novant Health Thomasville Medical Center

Wilson
Alliance
   Wilson Medical Center

Windsor
Alliance
   ECU Health Bertie Hospital

Winston Salem
Alliance
   Novant Health

Winston–Salem
Alliance
   Atrium Health Wake Forest Baptist
   Novant Health Forsyth Medical Center
   Novant Health Medical Park Hospital

NORTH DAKOTA

Bismarck
Alliance
   Sanford Medical Center Bismarck

Devils Lake
Alliance
   CHI St. Alexius Health Devils Lake

Dickinson
Alliance
   CHI St. Alexius Health Dickinson

Fargo
Alliance
   Sanford Medical Center Fargo

Grand Forks
Alliance
   Altru Health System

Hillsboro
Alliance
   Sanford Hillsboro Medical Center

Jamestown
Alliance
   Jamestown Regional Medical Center

Kenmare
Alliance
   Trinity Kenmare Community Hospital

Lisbon
Alliance
   CHI Lisbon Health

Mayville
Alliance
   Sanford Mayville Medical Center

Mcville
Alliance
   Nelson County Health System

Minot
Alliance
   Trinity Health

Northwood
Alliance
   Northwood Deaconess Health Center

Oakes
Alliance
   CHI Oakes Hospital

Valley City
Alliance
   CHI Mercy Health

OHIO

Akron
Alliance
   Akron Children's Hospital
   Cleveland Clinic Akron General

Alliance
Alliance
   Aultman Alliance Community Hospital

Ashland
Alliance
   University Hospitals Samaritan Medical Center

Ashtabula
Alliance
   Ashtabula County Medical Center

Athens
Alliance
   OhioHealth O'Bleness Hospital

Barnesville
Alliance
   WVU Medicine – Barnesville Hospital

Bellefontaine
Alliance
   Mary Rutan Hospital

Bluffton
Alliance
   Bluffton Hospital

Bucyrus
Alliance
   Bucyrus Community Hospital

Cadiz
Alliance
   WVU Medicine – Harrison Community Hospital

Cambridge
Alliance
   OhioHealth Southeastern Medical Center

Canton
Alliance
   Aultman Hospital

Chardon
Alliance
   University Hospitals Geauga Medical Center

Cincinnati
Alliance
   Cincinnati Children's Hospital Medical Center
   Good Samaritan Hospital
   The Christ Hospital Health Network
   The Jewish Hospital – Mercy Health
   UC Health
   University of Cincinnati Medical Center

Circleville
Alliance
   OhioHealth Berger Hospital

Cleveland
Alliance
   Cleveland Clinic Fairview Hospital
   Cleveland Clinic Lutheran Hospital
   Cleveland Clinic
   MetroHealth Medical Center
   University Hospitals Cleveland Medical Center

Coldwater
Alliance
   Mercer Health

Columbus
Alliance
   Ohio State University Wexner Medical Center
   OhioHealth Doctors Hospital
   OhioHealth Grant Medical Center
   OhioHealth Riverside Methodist Hospital
   OhioHealth

Conneaut
Alliance
   University Hospitals Conneaut Medical Center

Coshocton
Alliance
   Coshocton Regional Medical Center

Dayton
Alliance
   Miami Valley Hospital
   Shriners Children's Ohio

Defiance
Alliance
   ProMedica Defiance Regional Hospital

Delaware
Alliance
   OhioHealth Grady Memorial Hospital

Dover
Alliance
   Cleveland Clinic Union Hospital

Dublin
Alliance
   OhioHealth Dublin Methodist Hospital

Euclid
Alliance
   Cleveland Clinic Euclid Hospital

Findlay
Alliance
   Blanchard Valley Hospital

Alliances

Fostoria
Alliance
  ProMedica Fostoria Community Hospital

Fremont
Alliance
  ProMedica Memorial Hospital

Galion
Alliance
  Galion Community Hospital

Garfield Heights
Alliance
  Cleveland Clinic Marymount Hospital

Geneva
Alliance
  University Hospitals Geneva Medical Center

Greenville
Alliance
  Wayne HealthCare

Hamilton
Alliance
  Kettering Health Hamilton

Kenton
Alliance
  OhioHealth Hardin Memorial Hospital

Lima
Alliance
  Lima Memorial Health System

Lodi
Alliance
  Cleveland Clinic Akron General Lodi Hospital

Logan
Alliance
  Hocking Valley Community Hospital

London
Alliance
  Madison Health

Mansfield
Alliance
  OhioHealth Mansfield Hospital

Marion
Alliance
  OhioHealth Marion General Hospital

Marysville
Alliance
  Memorial Health

Mason
Alliance
  Lindner Center of HOPE

Medina
Alliance
  Cleveland Clinic Medina Hospital

Middleburg Heights
Alliance
  Southwest General Health Center

Millersburg
Alliance
  Pomerene Hospital

Mount Gilead
Alliance
  Morrow County Hospital

New Albany
Alliance
  Mount Carmel New Albany Surgical Hospital

Newark
Alliance
  Licking Memorial Hospital

Norwalk
Alliance
  Fisher-Titus Medical Center

Orrville
Alliance
  Aultman Orrville Hospital

Paulding
Alliance
  Paulding County Hospital

Portsmouth
Alliance
  Southern Ohio Medical Center

Rock Creek
Alliance
  Glenbeigh Hospital and Outpatient Centers

Shelby
Alliance
  OhioHealth Shelby Hospital

Sidney
Alliance
  Wilson Memorial Hospital

Toledo
Alliance
  ProMedica Health System
  ProMedica Toledo Hospital
  The University of Toledo Medical Center

Troy
Alliance
  Upper Valley Medical Center

Upper Sandusky
Alliance
  Wyandot Memorial Hospital

Van Wert
Alliance
  OhioHealth Van Wert Hospital

Warrensville Heights
Alliance
  Cleveland Clinic South Pointe Hospital

Washington Court House
Alliance
  Adena Fayette Medical Center

Westerville
Alliance
  Mount Carmel St. Ann's

Westlake
Alliance
  University Hospitals St. John Medical Center

Zanesville
Alliance
  Genesis HealthCare System

OKLAHOMA

Altus
Alliance
  Jackson County Memorial Hospital

Antlers
Alliance
  Pushmataha Hospital

Atoka
Alliance
  Atoka County Medical Center

Bethany
Alliance
  Bethany Children's Health Center

Carnegie
Alliance
  Carnegie Tri-County Municipal Hospital

Chickasha
Alliance
  Grady Memorial Hospital

Duncan
Alliance
  Duncan Regional Hospital

Edmond
Alliance
  INTEGRIS Health Edmond Hospital

Elk City
Alliance
  Great Plains Regional Medical Center

Enid
Alliance
  INTEGRIS Health Enid Hospital

Grove
Alliance
  INTEGRIS Grove Hospital

Hobart
Alliance
  Elkview General Hospital

Hugo
Alliance
  Choctaw Memorial Hospital

Lawton
Alliance
  Comanche County Memorial Hospital

Mcalester
Alliance
  McAlester Regional Health Center

Miami
Alliance
  INTEGRIS Miami Hospital

Norman
Alliance
  Norman Regional Health System

Oklahoma City
Alliance
  INTEGRIS Baptist Medical Center
  INTEGRIS Health
  INTEGRIS Southwest Medical Center
  Lakeside Women's Hospital

Stillwater
Alliance
  Stillwater Medical Center

Tahlequah
Alliance
  Northeastern Health System

Waurika
Alliance
  Jefferson County Hospital

Yukon
Alliance
  INTEGRIS Canadian Valley Hospital

OREGON

Forest Grove
Alliance
  Tuality Forest Grove Hospital

Grants Pass
Alliance
  Asante Three Rivers Medical Center

Hillsboro
Alliance
  OHSU Health Hillsboro Medical Center

Hood River
Alliance
  Providence Hood River Memorial Hospital

Medford
Alliance
  Asante Rogue Regional Medical Center
  Providence Medford Medical Center

Milwaukie
Alliance
  Providence Milwaukie Hospital

Newberg
Alliance
  Providence Newberg Medical Center

Ontario
Alliance
  Saint Alphonsus Medical Center – Ontario

Oregon City
Alliance
  Providence Willamette Falls Medical Center

Pendleton
Alliance
  CHI St. Anthony Hospital

Portland
Alliance
  OHSU Hospital
  Providence Portland Medical Center
  Providence St. Vincent Medical Center
  Shriners Hospitals for Children–Portland

Roseburg
Alliance
  Mercy Medical Center

Salem
Alliance
  Salem Hospital

Seaside
Alliance
  Providence Seaside Hospital

Alliances

Silverton
Alliance
　Legacy Silverton Medical Center

The Dalles
Alliance
　Adventist Health Columbia Gorge

PENNSYLVANIA
Abington
Alliance
　Jefferson Abington Health

Allentown
Alliance
　Lehigh Valley Hospital–Cedar Crest

Brookville
Alliance
　Penn Highlands Brookville

Bryn Mawr
Alliance
　Bryn Mawr Hospital

Butler
Alliance
　Butler Memorial Hospital

Chambersburg
Alliance
　WellSpan Chambersburg Hospital

Darby
Alliance
　Mercy Fitzgerald Hospital

DuBois
Alliance
　Penn Highlands DuBois

East Norriton
Alliance
　Jefferson Einstein Montgomery Hospital

East Stroudsburg
Alliance
　Lehigh Valley Hospital – Pocono

Ephrata
Alliance
　WellSpan Ephrata Community Hospital

Gettysburg
Alliance
　WellSpan Gettysburg Hospital

Greensburg
Alliance
　Excela Health Westmoreland Hospital

Hanover
Alliance
　UPMC Hanover

Harrisburg
Alliance
　UPMC Community Osteopathic
　UPMC Harrisburg

Hazleton
Alliance
　Lehigh Valley Hospital – Hazleton

Hershey
Alliance
　Penn State Milton S. Hershey Medical Center

Huntingdon
Alliance
　Penn Highlands Huntingdon

Indiana
Alliance
　Indiana Regional Medical Center

Jefferson Hills
Alliance
　Jefferson Hospital

Lancaster
Alliance
　Penn Medicine Lancaster General Health

Langhorne
Alliance
　St. Mary Medical Center

Lansdale
Alliance
　Jefferson Lansdale Hospital

Latrobe
Alliance
　Excela Health Latrobe Hospital

Lebanon
Alliance
　WellSpan Good Samaritan Hospital

Malvern
Alliance
　Bryn Mawr Rehabilitation Hospital

Meadowbrook
Alliance
　Holy Redeemer Hospital

Media
Alliance
　Riddle Hospital

Monongahela
Alliance
　Penn Highlands Mon Valley

Mount Pleasant
Alliance
　Excela Frick Hospital

Muncy
Alliance
　UPMC Muncy

New Castle
Alliance
　UPMC Jameson

Paoli
Alliance
　Paoli Hospital

Philadelphia
Alliance
　Children's Hospital of Philadelphia
　Einstein Medical Center Philadelphia
　Fox Chase Cancer Center
　Hospital of the University of Pennsylvania
　Jefferson Health Northeast
　Magee Rehabilitation
　Penn Presbyterian Medical Center
　Pennsylvania Hospital
　Temple University Hospital
　University of Pennsylvania Health System

Pittsburgh
Alliance
　St. Clair Health
　UPMC Presbyterian

Pottsville
Alliance
　Lehigh Valley Hospital – Schuylkill

Reading
Alliance
　Penn State Health St. Joseph

Saint Marys
Alliance
　Penn Highlands Elk

Sayre
Alliance
　Guthrie Clinic
　Guthrie Robert Packer Hospital

Sellersville
Alliance
　Grand View Health

Troy
Alliance
　Guthrie Troy Community Hospital

Uniontown
Alliance
　WVU Medicine Uniontown Hospital

Upland
Alliance
　Crozer–Chester Medical Center

Waynesboro
Alliance
　Wellspan Waynesboro Hospital

Wellsboro
Alliance
　UPMC Wellsboro

West Chester
Alliance
　Penn Medicine Chester County Hospital

West Reading
Alliance
　Reading Hospital

Williamsport
Alliance
　UPMC Williamsport

Wynnewood
Alliance
　Lankenau Medical Center

York
Alliance
　WellSpan Health
　WellSpan York Hospital

RHODE ISLAND
Newport
Alliance
　Newport Hospital

Providence
Alliance
　Butler Hospital
　Care New England Health System
　Lifespan Corporation
　Miriam Hospital
　Rhode Island Hospital
　Women & Infants Hospital of Rhode Island

Warwick
Alliance
　Kent Hospital

Westerly
Alliance
　Westerly Hospital

SOUTH CAROLINA
Charleston
Alliance
　MUSC Health University Medical Center

Cheraw
Alliance
　McLeod Health Cheraw

Clinton
Alliance
　Prisma Health Laurens County Hospital

Columbia
Alliance
　ContinueCARE Hospital at Palmetto Health Baptist
　MUSC Health Columbia Medical Center Downtown
　Prisma Health Baptist Hospital
　Prisma Health Baptist Parkridge Hospital
　Prisma Health Richland Hospital

Dillon
Alliance
　McLeod Health Dillon

Easley
Alliance
　Prisma Health Baptist Easley Hospital

Florence
Alliance
　McLeod Regional Medical Center

Georgetown
Alliance
　Tidelands Georgetown Memorial Hospital

Greenville
Alliance
　Prisma Health Greenville Memorial Hospital
　Prisma Health Patewood Hospital
　Shriners Hospitals for Children–Greenville

Greenwood
Alliance
　Self Regional Healthcare

Alliances

Greer
Alliance
  Prisma Health Greer Memorial Hospital

Loris
Alliance
  McLeod Health Loris

Murrells Inlet
Alliance
  Tidelands Waccamaw Community Hospital

Seneca
Alliance
  Prisma Health Oconee Memorial Hospital

Simpsonville
Alliance
  Prisma Health Hillcrest Hospital

Sumter
Alliance
  Prisma Health Tuomey Hospital

Travelers Rest
Alliance
  Prisma Health North Greenville Hospital

SOUTH DAKOTA

Aberdeen
Alliance
  Sanford Aberdeen Medical Center

Armour
Alliance
  Douglas County Memorial Hospital

Burke
Alliance
  Community Memorial Hospital

Canton
Alliance
  Sanford Canton–Inwood Medical Center

Chamberlain
Alliance
  Sanford Chamberlain Medical Center

Clear Lake
Alliance
  Sanford Clear Lake Medical Center

Sioux Falls
Alliance
  Sanford Health
  Sanford USD Medical Center

Vermillion
Alliance
  Sanford Vermillion Medical Center

Viborg
Alliance
  Pioneer Memorial Hospital and Health Services

Watertown
Alliance
  Prairie Lakes Healthcare System

Webster
Alliance
  Sanford Webster Medical Center

Winner
Alliance
  Winner Regional Healthcare Center

TENNESSEE

Chattanooga
Alliance
  Erlanger Health System
  Erlanger North Hospital

Collierville
Alliance
  Baptist Memorial Hospital–Collierville

Columbia
Alliance
  Maury Regional Medical Center

Covington
Alliance
  Baptist Memorial Hospital–Tipton

Franklin
Alliance
  Williamson Medical Center

Harriman
Alliance
  Roane Medical Center

Huntingdon
Alliance
  Baptist Memorial Hospital–Carroll County

Knoxville
Alliance
  Covenant Health
  Fort Sanders Regional Medical Center
  Parkwest Medical Center
  University of Tennessee Medical Center

Lenoir City
Alliance
  Fort Loudoun Medical Center

Lewisburg
Alliance
  Marshall Medical Center

Memphis
Alliance
  Baptist Memorial Health Care Corporation
  Baptist Memorial Hospital – Memphis
  Baptist Memorial Hospital for Women
  Methodist Healthcare Memphis Hospitals
  Regional One Health
  St. Jude Children's Research Hospital

Morristown
Alliance
  Morristown–Hamblen Healthcare System

Nashville
Alliance
  Vanderbilt University Medical Center

Oak Ridge
Alliance
  Methodist Medical Center of Oak Ridge

Sevierville
Alliance
  LeConte Medical Center

Tazewell
Alliance
  Claiborne Medical Center

Union City
Alliance
  Baptist Memorial Hospital–Union City

Waynesboro
Alliance
  Wayne Medical Center

TEXAS

Andrews
Alliance
  Permian Regional Medical Center

Baytown
Alliance
  Houston Methodist Baytown Hospital

Bellaire
Alliance
  Harris Health System

Bellville
Alliance
  MidCoast Medical Center – Bellville

Dallas
Alliance
  Baylor Scott & White Health
  Children's Medical Center Dallas
  Methodist Health System
  Parkland Health

El Paso
Alliance
  University Medical Center of El Paso

Fort Worth
Alliance
  JPS Health Network

Galveston
Alliance
  Shriners Hospitals for Children
  University of Texas Medical Branch

Houston
Alliance
  CHI St Luke's Health – Baylor St Luke's Medical Center
  Houston Methodist Hospital
  Houston Methodist West Hospital
  Houston Methodist Willowbrook Hospital
  Memorial Hermann – Texas Medical Center
  Memorial Hermann Greater Heights Hospital
  Memorial Hermann Health System
  Memorial Hermann Memorial City Medical Center
  St. Luke's Health – The Vintage Hospital
  TIRR Memorial Hermann

Humble
Alliance
  Memorial Hermann Northeast

Katy
Alliance
  Houston Methodist Continuing Care Hospital
  Memorial Hermann Katy Hospital

Livingston
Alliance
  St. Luke's Health – Memorial Livingston

Lubbock
Alliance
  Covenant Health System
  Covenant Medical Center–Lakeside

Lufkin
Alliance
  CHI St. Luke's Health Memorial Lufkin

Midland
Alliance
  Midland Memorial Hospital

Pasadena
Alliance
  St. Luke's Health – Patients Medical Center

Pearsall
Alliance
  Frio Regional Hospital

Plano
Alliance
  Community Hospital Corporation

San Antonio
Alliance
  University Health

San Augustine
Alliance
  CHI St. Luke's Health Memorial San Augustine

Sugar Land
Alliance
  Houston Methodist Sugar Land Hospital
  Memorial Hermann Sugar Land Hospital

Sweeny
Alliance
  Sweeny Community Hospital

The Woodlands
Alliance
  St. Luke's Health – Lakeside Hospital
  St. Luke's Health – The Woodlands Hospital

Tyler
Alliance
  CHRISTUS Mother Frances Hospital – Tyler
  UT Health North Campus Tyler

UTAH

Gunnison
Alliance
  Gunnison Valley Hospital

Provo
Alliance
  Utah State Hospital

Salt Lake City
Alliance
  Shriners Hospitals for Children–Salt Lake City
  University of Utah Health

Alliances

VERMONT
Bennington
Alliance
Southwestern Vermont Medical Center

Berlin
Alliance
The University of Vermont Health Network Central Vermont Medical Center

Brattleboro
Alliance
Brattleboro Memorial Hospital
Brattleboro Retreat

Burlington
Alliance
University of Vermont Medical Center

Morrisville
Alliance
Copley Hospital

Newport
Alliance
North Country Hospital and Health Center

Rutland
Alliance
Rutland Regional Medical Center

Saint Johnsbury
Alliance
Northeastern Vermont Regional Hospital

Springfield
Alliance
Springfield Hospital

Townshend
Alliance
Grace Cottage Hospital

Windsor
Alliance
Mt. Ascutney Hospital and Health Center

VIRGIN ISLANDS
Saint Thomas
Alliance
Schneider Regional Medical Center

VIRGINIA
Bedford
Alliance
Centra Bedford Memorial Hospital

Charlottesville
Alliance
Sentara Martha Jefferson Hospital
UVA Encompass Health Rehabilitation Hospital
UVA Health University Medical Center

Culpeper
Alliance
UVA Health Culpeper Medical Center

Farmville
Alliance
Centra Southside Community Hospital

Fishersville
Alliance
Augusta Health

Fredericksburg
Alliance
Mary Washington Hospital

Hampton
Alliance
Sentara CarePlex Hospital

Harrisonburg
Alliance
Sentara RMH Medical Center

Lynchburg
Alliance
Centra Lynchburg General Hospital

Manassas
Alliance
UVA Health Prince William Medical Center

Norfolk
Alliance
Hospital for Extended Recovery
Sentara Leigh Hospital
Sentara Norfolk General Hospital

Richmond
Alliance
Children's Hospital of Richmond at VCU
VCU Medical Center

South Boston
Alliance
Sentara Halifax Regional Hospital

Stafford
Alliance
Stafford Hospital

Suffolk
Alliance
Sentara Obici Hospital

Virginia Beach
Alliance
Sentara Health
Sentara Princess Anne Hospital
Sentara Virginia Beach General Hospital

Williamsburg
Alliance
Sentara Williamsburg Regional Medical Center

Woodbridge
Alliance
Sentara Northern Virginia Medical Center

WASHINGTON
Aberdeen
Alliance
Harbor Regional Health

Auburn
Alliance
MultiCare Auburn Medical Center

Bellingham
Alliance
PeaceHealth St. Joseph Medical Center

Burien
Alliance
St. Anne Hospital

Centralia
Alliance
Providence Centralia Hospital

Chewelah
Alliance
Providence St. Joseph's Hospital

Colfax
Alliance
Whitman Hospital and Medical Center

Colville
Alliance
Providence Mount Carmel Hospital

Dayton
Alliance
Columbia County Health System

Edmonds
Alliance
Providence Swedish Edmonds

Enumclaw
Alliance
St. Elizabeth Hospital

Everett
Alliance
Providence Regional Medical Center Everett

Gig Harbor
Alliance
St. Anthony Hospital

Ilwaco
Alliance
Ocean Beach Hospital and Medical Clinics

Issaquah
Alliance
Swedish Issaquah

Lakewood
Alliance
St. Clare Hospital

Morton
Alliance
Arbor Health, Morton Hospital

Olympia
Alliance
Providence St. Peter Hospital

Pomeroy
Alliance
Garfield County Public Hospital District

Port Angeles
Alliance
Olympic Medical Center

Prosser
Alliance
Prosser Memorial Health

Puyallup
Alliance
MultiCare Good Samaritan Hospital

Renton
Alliance
UW Medicine/Valley Medical Center

Richland
Alliance
Kadlec Regional Medical Center

Seattle
Alliance
Providence Swedish Cherry Hill
Providence Swedish First Hill
UW Medicine/Harborview Medical Center
UW Medicine/University of Washington Medical Center

Silverdale
Alliance
St. Michael Medical Center

Spokane
Alliance
Providence Holy Family Hospital
Providence Sacred Heart Medical Center & Children's Hospital
Providence St. Luke's Rehabilitation Medical Center
Shriners Hospitals for Children–Spokane

Tacoma
Alliance
MultiCare Health System
MultiCare Tacoma General Hospital
St. Joseph Medical Center

Walla Walla
Alliance
Providence St. Mary Medical Center

WEST VIRGINIA
Charleston
Alliance
CAMC Women and Children's Hospital
Charleston Area Medical Center

Gassaway
Alliance
Braxton County Memorial Hospital

Madison
Alliance
Boone Memorial Hospital

Martinsburg
Alliance
Berkeley Medical Center

Montgomery
Alliance
Montgomery General Hospital

Morgantown
Alliance
West Virginia University Hospitals

Princeton
Alliance
Princeton Community Hospital

Ranson
Alliance
Jefferson Medical Center

Ripley
Alliance
Jackson General Hospital

Alliances

Spencer
Alliance
 Roane General Hospital

WISCONSIN
Antigo
Alliance
 Aspirus Langlade Hospital

Barron
Alliance
 Mayo Clinic Health System – Northland in Barron

Beaver Dam
Alliance
 Marshfield Medical Center – Beaver Dam

Beloit
Alliance
 Beloit Health System

Bloomer
Alliance
 Mayo Clinic Health System – Chippewa Valley in Bloomer

Boscobel
Alliance
 Gundersen Boscobel Area Hospital and Clinics

Eau Claire
Alliance
 Mayo Clinic Health System in Eau Claire

Friendship
Alliance
 Gundersen Moundview Hospital & Clinics

Green Bay
Alliance
 Bellin Hospital
 Bellin Psychiatric Center

Hillsboro
Alliance
 Gundersen St. Joseph's Hospital and Clinics

Hudson
Alliance
 Hudson Hospital and Clinic

La Crosse
Alliance
 Gundersen Lutheran Medical Center
 Mayo Clinic Health System in La Crosse

Madison
Alliance
 UnityPoint Health Meriter
 University Hospital

Marinette
Alliance
 Aurora Medical Center – Bay Area

Medford
Alliance
 Aspirus Medford Hospital & Clinics

Menomonee Falls
Alliance
 Froedtert Menomonee Falls Hospital

Menomonie
Alliance
 Mayo Clinic Health System – Red Cedar in Menomonie

Milwaukee
Alliance
 Froedtert and the Medical College of Wisconsin Froedtert Hospital

Neenah
Alliance
 ThedaCare Regional Medical Center–Neenah

Neillsville
Alliance
 Marshfield Medical Center – Neillsville

New Richmond
Alliance
 Westfields Hospital and Clinic

Oconomowoc
Alliance
 ProHealth Oconomowoc Memorial Hospital

Oconto
Alliance
 Bellin Health Oconto Hospital

Osseo
Alliance
 Mayo Clinic Health System – Oakridge in Osseo

Portage
Alliance
 Aspirus Divine Savior Hospital & Clinics

River Falls
Alliance
 River Falls Area Hospital

Sparta
Alliance
 Mayo Clinic Health System in Sparta

Superior
Alliance
 Essentia Health St. Mary's Hospital of Superior

Waukesha
Alliance
 ProHealth Care, Inc.
 ProHealth Waukesha Memorial Hospital

Waupaca
Alliance
 ThedaCare Medical Center–Waupaca

Wausau
Alliance
 Aspirus Wausau Hospital, Inc.
 North Central Health Care

West Bend
Alliance
 Froedtert West Bend Hospital

Whitehall
Alliance
 Gundersen Tri–County Hospital and Clinics

Wild Rose
Alliance
 Theda Care Medical Center – Wild Rose

Wisconsin Rapids
Alliance
 Aspirus Riverview Hospital and Clinics, Inc.

WYOMING
Buffalo
Alliance
 Johnson County Healthcare Center

Casper
Alliance
 Wyoming Medical Center

Cheyenne
Alliance
 Cheyenne Regional Medical Center

Douglas
Alliance
 Memorial Hospital of Converse County

Laramie
Alliance
 Ivinson Memorial Hospital

Lusk
Alliance
 Niobrara Community Hospital

Sheridan
Alliance
 Sheridan Memorial Hospital

YANKEE ALLIANCE
138 River Road, Andover, MA
Zip 01810–1083; tel. 978/470–2000;
James W Oliver, President and Chief Executive Officer

CALIFORNIA
Long Beach
Alliance
 College Medical Center

Oceanside
Alliance
 Tri-City Medical Center

CONNECTICUT
Derby
Alliance
 Griffin Health

Hartford
Alliance
 Saint Francis Hospital

New London
Alliance
 Lawrence + Memorial Hospital

Stafford Springs
Alliance
 Johnson Memorial Hospital

FLORIDA
Coral Gables
Alliance
 Baptist Health South Florida, Doctors Hospital

Homestead
Alliance
 Baptist Health South Florida, Homestead Hospital

Miami Beach
Alliance
 Mount Sinai Medical Center

Miami
Alliance
 Baptist Health South Florida, Baptist Hospital of Miami
 Baptist Health South Florida, South Miami Hospital
 Baptist Health South Florida, West Kendall Baptist Hospital

Miramar
Alliance
 Memorial Hospital Miramar

Pembroke Pines
Alliance
 Memorial Hospital Pembroke
 Memorial Hospital West

South Miami
Alliance
 Larkin Community Hospital–South Miami Campus

Tavernier
Alliance
 Baptist Health South Florida, Mariners Hospital

ILLINOIS
Geneva
Alliance
 Northwestern Medicine Delnor Hospital

Winfield
Alliance
 Northwestern Medicine Central DuPage Hospital

INDIANA
Gary
Alliance
 Methodist Hospitals

Mishawaka
Alliance
 Unity Physicians Hospital

KENTUCKY
Ashland
Alliance
 UK King's Daughters Medical Center

Benton
Alliance
 Marshall County Hospital

Corbin
Alliance
 Baptist Health Corbin

Elizabethtown
Alliance
 Baptist Health Hardin

La Grange
Alliance
 Baptist Health La Grange

Lexington
Alliance
 Baptist Health Lexington

Louisville
Alliance
 Baptist Health Louisville

Madisonville
Alliance
 Baptist Health Deaconess Madisonville, Inc.

Alliances

Paducah
Alliance
  Baptist Health Paducah

Prestonsburg
Alliance
  Highlands ARH Regional Medical Center

Richmond
Alliance
  Baptist Health Richmond

MAINE

Bangor
Alliance
  St. Joseph Hospital

Lewiston
Alliance
  St. Mary's Regional Medical Center

MASSACHUSETTS

Attleboro
Alliance
  Sturdy Memorial Hospital

Boston
Alliance
  Boston Medical Center
  New England Baptist Hospital
  Tufts Medical Center

Brockton
Alliance
  Signature Healthcare Brockton Hospital

Burlington
Alliance
  Lahey Hospital & Medical Center

Fall River
Alliance
  Southcoast Hospitals Group

Great Barrington
Alliance
  Fairview Hospital

Lowell
Alliance
  Lowell General Hospital

Milford
Alliance
  Milford Regional Medical Center

Newburyport
Alliance
  Anna Jaques Hospital

Oak Bluffs
Alliance
  Martha's Vineyard Hospital

Pittsfield
Alliance
  Berkshire Medical Center

Westfield
Alliance
  Baystate Noble Hospital

Winchester
Alliance
  Winchester Hospital

NEW HAMPSHIRE

Concord
Alliance
  Concord Hospital

Exeter
Alliance
  Exeter Hospital

Franklin
Alliance
  Concord Hospital – Franklin

Laconia
Alliance
  Concord Hospital – Laconia

Manchester
Alliance
  Catholic Medical Center
  Elliot Hospital

Nashua
Alliance
  St. Joseph Hospital

North Conway
Alliance
  Memorial Hospital

Rochester
Alliance
  Frisbie Memorial Hospital

Salem
Alliance
  Northeast Rehabilitation Hospital

NEW YORK

Batavia
Alliance
  United Memorial Medical Center

Bath
Alliance
  Ira Davenport Memorial Hospital

Elizabethtown
Alliance
  The University of Vermont Health Network Elizabethtown Community Hospital

Elmira
Alliance
  Arnot Ogden Medical Center

Glens Falls
Alliance
  Glens Falls Hospital

Gloversville
Alliance
  Nathan Littauer Hospital and Nursing Home

Plattsburgh
Alliance
  The University of Vermont Health Network–Champlain Valley Physicians Hospital

Warsaw
Alliance
  Wyoming County Community Hospital

OHIO

Logan
Alliance
  Hocking Valley Community Hospital

Montpelier
Alliance
  Community Hospitals and Wellness Centers–Montpelier

Salem
Alliance
  Salem Regional Medical Center

Seaman
Alliance
  Adams County Regional Medical Center

Sidney
Alliance
  Wilson Memorial Hospital

Steubenville
Alliance
  Life Line Hospital

PENNSYLVANIA

Honesdale
Alliance
  Wayne Memorial Hospital

Washington
Alliance
  Advanced Surgical Hospital

RHODE ISLAND

Providence
Alliance
  Roger Williams Medical Center

Wakefield
Alliance
  South County Hospital

Westerly
Alliance
  Westerly Hospital

SOUTH CAROLINA

Columbia
Alliance
  MUSC Health Columbia Medical Center Downtown

Fairfax
Alliance
  Allendale County Hospital

TEXAS

Austin
Alliance
  Arise Austin Medical Center

Houston
Alliance
  Nexus Children's Hospital Houston

New Braunfels
Alliance
  PAM Specialty Hospital of New Braunfels

Plainview
Alliance
  Covenant Hospital Plainview

WEST VIRGINIA

New Martinsville
Alliance
  Wetzel County Hospital

Abbreviations Used in the AHA Guide

AB, Army Base
ACSW, Academy of Certified Social Workers
AEC, Atomic Energy Commission
AFB, Air Force Base
AHA, American Hospital Association
AK, Alaska
AL, Alabama
AODA, Alcohol and Other Drug Abuse
APO, Army Post Office
AR, Arkansas
A.R.T., Accredited Record Technician
A.S.C., Ambulatory Surgical Center
A.T.C., Alcoholism Treatment Center
Ave., Avenue
AZ, Arizona

B.A., Bachelor of Arts
B.B.A., Bachelor of Business Administration
B.C., British Columbia
Blvd., Boulevard
B.S., Bachelor of Science
B.S.Ed., Bachelor of Science in Education
B.S.H.S., Bachelor of Science in Health Studies
B.S.N., Bachelor of Science in Nursing
B.S.W., Bachelor of Science and Social Worker

CA, California; Controller of Accounts
C.A.A.D.A.C., Certified Alcohol and Drug Abuse Counselor
CAC, Certified Alcoholism Counselor
CAE, Certified Association Executive
CAP, College of American Pathologists
CAPA, Certified Ambulatory Post Anesthesia
C.A.S., Certificate of Advanced Study
CCDC, Certified Chemical Dependency Counselor
C.D., Commander of the Order of Distinction
CDR, Commander
CDS, Chemical Dependency Specialist
CFACHE, Certified Fellow American College of Healthcare Executives
CFRE, Certified Fund Raising Executive
C.G., Certified Gastroenterology
CHC, Certified Health Consultant
CHE, Certified Healthcare Executive
C.L.D., Clinical Laboratory Director
CLU, Certified Life Underwriter, Chartered Life Underwriter
CMA, Certified Medical Assistant
C.M.H.A., Certified Mental Health Administrator
CNHA, Certified Nursing Home Administrator
CNM, Certified Nurse Midwife
CNOR, Certified Operating Room Nurse
C.N.S., Clinical Nurse Specialist
CO, Colorado; Commanding Officer
COA, Certified Ophthalmic Assistant
COMT, Commandant
C.O.M.T., Certified Ophthalmic Medical Technician
Conv., Conventions
Corp., Corporation; Corporate
C.O.T., Certified Ophthalmic Technician
CPA, Certified Public Accountant
C.P.H.Q., Certified Professional in Health Care Quality
CPM, Certified Public Manager
CRNA, Certified Registered Nurse Anesthetist
CRNH, Certified Registered Nurse Hospice
C.S.J.B., Catholic Saint John the Baptist
CSW, Certified Social Worker
CT, Connecticut
CWO, Chief Warrant Officer

D.B.A., Doctor of Business Administration
DC, District of Columbia
D.D., Doctor of Divinity
D.D.S., Doctor of Dental Surgery
DE, Delaware
Diet, Dietitian; Dietary; Dietetics
D.M.D., Doctor of Dental Medicine
D.MIN., Doctor of Ministry
D.O., Doctor of Osteopathic Medicine and Surgery, Doctor of Osteopathy
DPA, Doctorate Public Administration
D.P.M., Doctor of Podiatric Medicine
Dr., Drive
Dr.P.h., Doctor of Public Health
D.Sc., Doctor of Science
D.S.W., Doctor of Social Welfare
D.V.M., Doctor of Veterinary Medicine

E., East
Ed.D., Doctor of Education
Ed.S., Specialist in Education
ENS, Ensign
Esq., Esquire
Expwy., Expressway
ext., extension

FAAN, Fellow of the American Academy of Nursing
FACATA, Fellow of the American College of Addiction Treatment Administrators
FACHE, Fellow of the American College of Healthcare Executives
FACMGA, Fellow of the American College of Medical Group Administrators
FACP, Fellow of the American College of Physicians
FACS, Fellow of the American College of Surgeons
FAX, Facsimile
FL, Florida
FPO, Fleet Post Office
FRCPSC, Fellow of the Royal College of Physicians and Surgeons of Canada
FT, Full-time

GA, Georgia
Govt., Government; Governmental

HHS, Department of Health and Human Services
HI, Hawaii
HM, Helmsman
HMO, Health Maintenance Organization
Hon., Honorable; Honorary
H.S.A., Health System Administrator
Hts., Heights
Hwy., Highway

IA, Iowa
ID, Idaho
IL, Illinois
IN, Indiana
Inc., Incorporated

J.D., Doctor of Law
J.P., Justice of the Peace
Jr., Junior

KS, Kansas
KY, Kentucky

LA, Louisiana
LCDR, Lieutenant Commander
LCSW, Licensed Certified Social Worker
L.H.D., Doctor of Humanities
L.I.S.W., Licensed Independent Social Worker
LL.D., Doctor of Laws
L.L.P., Limited Licensed Practitioner
L.M.H.C., Licensed Master of Health Care
L.M.S.W., Licensed Master of Social Work
L.N.H.A., Licensed Nursing Home Administrator
L.P.C., Licensed Professional Counselor
LPN, Licensed Practical Nurse
L.P.N., Licensed Practical Nurse
L.S.W., Licensed Social Worker
Lt., Lieutenant
LTC, Lieutenant Colonel
Ltd., Limited
LT.GEN., Lieutenant General
LTJG, Lieutenant (junior grade)

MA, Massachusetts
M.A., Master of Arts
Maj., Major
M.B., Bachelor of Medicine
M.B.A., Masters of Business Administration
MC, Medical Corps; Marine Corps
M.C., Member of Congress
MD, Maryland
M.D., Doctor of Medicine
ME, Maine
M.Ed., Master of Education
MFCC, Marriage/Family/Child Counselor
MHA, Mental Health Association
M.H.S., Masters in Health Science; Masters in Human Service
MI, Michigan
MM, Masters of Management
MN, Minnesota
M.N., Master of Nursing
MO, Missouri
M.P.A., Master of Public Administration; Master Public Affairs
M.P.H., Master of Public Health
M.P.S., Master of Professional Studies; Master of Public Science
MS, Mississippi
M.S., Master of Science
MSC, Medical Service Corps
M.S.D., Doctor of Medical Science
MSHSA, Master of Science Health Service Administration
M.S.N., Master of Science in Nursing
M.S.P.H., Master of Science in Public Health
M.S.S.W., Master of Science in Social Work
M.S.W., Master of Social Work
MT, Montana
Mt., Mount

N., North
NC, North Carolina
N.C.A.D.C., National Certification of Alcohol and Drug Counselors
ND, North Dakota
NE, Nebraska
NH, New Hampshire
NHA, National Hearing Association; Nursing Home Administrator
NJ, New Jersey
NM, New Mexico
NPA, National Perinatal Association
NV, Nevada
NY, New York

OCN, Oncology Certified Nurse
O.D., Doctor of Optometry
O.F.M., Order Franciscan Monks, Order of Friars Minor
OH, Ohio
OK, Oklahoma
OR, Oregon
O.R., Operating Room
O.R.S., Operating Room Supervisor
OSF, Order of St. Francis

PA, Pennsylvania
P.A., Professional Association
P.C., Professional Corporation
Pharm.D., Doctor of Pharmacy
Ph.B., Bachelor of Philosophy
Ph.D., Doctor of Philosophy
PHS, Public Health Service
Pkwy., Parkway
Pl., Place
PR, Puerto Rico
PS, Professional Services
PSRO, Professional Standards Review Organization

RADM, Rear Admiral
RD, Rural Delivery
Rd., Road
R.F.D., Rural Free Delivery
RI, Rhode Island
R.M., Risk Manager
R.N., Registered Nurse
RNC, Republican National Committee; Registered Nurse or Board Certified
R.Ph., Registered Pharmacist
RRA, Registered Record Administrator
R.S.M., Religious Sisters of Mercy
Rte., Route

S., South
SC, South Carolina
S.C., Surgery Center
SCAC, Senior Certified Addiction Counselor
Sc.D., Doctor of Science
Sci., Science, Scientific
SD, South Dakota
SHCC, Statewide Health Coordinating Council
Sgt., Sergeant
SNA, Surgical Nursing Assistant
SNF, Skilled Nursing Facility
Sq., Square
Sr., Senior, Sister
St., Saint, Street
Sta., Station
Ste., Saint; Suite

Tel., Telephone
Terr., Terrace
TN, Tennessee
Tpke, Turnpike
Twp., Township
TX, Texas

USA, United States Army
USAF, United States Air Force
USMC, United States Marine Corps
USN, United States Navy
USPHS, United States Public Health Service
UT, Utah

VA, Virginia
VADM, Vice Admiral
VI, Virgin Islands
Vlg., Village
VT, Vermont

W., West

WA, Washington
WI, Wisconsin
WV, West Virginia
WY, Wyoming

© 2025 AHA Guide

Index

Abbreviations Used in the AHA Guide, C1
Acknowledgements, v
AHA Offices, Officers, and Historical Data, ix
AHA Guide Hospital Listing Requirements, A2
Alliances, B179
   defined, B2
Ambulatory Centers and Home Care Agencies, A1021
Annual Survey, A6
Approval Codes, A3
Associate Members, A1021
   defined, A1015
Associated University Programs in Health Administration, A1017
Blue Cross Plans, A1021
Control and Service Classifications, A13
Explanation of Hospital Listings, A3
Facility Codes
   defined, A6
   numerically, A4
Health Care Professionals alphabetically, A783
Health Care Systems
   and their hospitals, B4
   defined, B2
   geographically, B155
   introduced, B2
   Statistics for Multihospital Health Care Systems and their Hospitals, B3
Hospital Listing Requirements, A2
Hospital Schools of Nursing, A1018
Hospitals in Areas Associated with the United States, by Area, A730
Hospitals in the United States, by state, A15
Index of Health Care Professionals, A783
Index of Hospitals, A738
Introduction, vi
   accredited Hospitals, A15
Membership Categories, A1015
Networks and their Hospitals, B164
   defined, B2
Nonhospital Preacute and Postacute Care Facilities, A1019
Nonreporting defined, A3
Other Associate Members, A1022
Other Institutional Members, A1016
   defined, A1016
Provisional Hospitals, A1020
Types of Hospitals, A2
   general, A2
   psychiatric, A2
   rehabilitation and chronic disease, A2
   special, A2
U.S. Government Hospitals Outside the United States, by Area, A737
Utilization Data, A3
   defined, A3
   expense, A3
   facilities, A4
   personnel, A3